THE

COLLEGE FOOTBALL ENCYCLOPEDIA

THE

COLLEGE FOOTBALL ENCYCLOPEDIA

A Comprehensive Modern Reference to America's Most Colorful Sport, 1953–Present

By Bob Boyles and Paul Guido

Skyhorse Publishing

Skyhorse Publishing books may be purchased in bulk at special discounts for sales promotion, corporate gifts, fund-raising, or educational purposes. Special editions can also be created to specifications. For details, contact the Special Sales Department, Skyhorse Publishing, 307 West 36th Street, 11th Floor, New York, NY 10018 or info@skyhorsepublishing.com.

Skyhorse® and Skyhorse Publishing® are registered trademarks of Skyhorse Publishing, Inc.®, a Delaware corporation.

www.skyhorsepublishing.com

10 9 8 7 6 5 4 3 2 1

Library of Congress Cataloging-in-Publication Data is available on file.

ISBN: 978-1-61608-225-3

Printed in Canada

This work is fondly dedicated to our late fathers, Houston Coleman Boyles and Robert N. Guido. Each relayed his love of college football to another generation. Also to our beautiful and loving wives, Annabelia Boyles and Ginny Somma Guido, whose patience, support, and assistance continue to mean everything to us.

TABLE OF CONTENTS

Introduction .... Page

Guide to reading this book ix

College Football Performance Formula 12

Greatest College Players Since 1953 14

1953	The Year of the Fainting Irish, King Terps in the New Basketball Conference, and Limited Substitution	18
1954	The Year of Deemphasis, No Repeat Rule, and Teams Named "Desire," "Junction Boys," and "23 Little Pigs"	20
1955	The Year of The Recocked Field Goal, Holly's Folly, and Bear's Aggie Surprise	34
1956	The Year of the Oklahoma Tornado, Iowa Wing-T, and Pacific Coast Scandal	38
1957	The Year of the End to Oklahoma's 47, the Probation Champions, and Wolfpack Road Warriors	61
1958	The Year of Chinese Bandits, Lonely End, and Two-Point Conversions	73
1959	The Year of the Orange Champion, Halloween Thriller, and Wild Card Rule	87
1960	The Year of New Career Opportunities, Oklahoma's Dethronement, and New Frontier at the Orange Bowl	100
1961	The Year of the Upside-Down Year, an Indignant Faculty, and the Wacky Horned Frogs	112
1962	The Year of a Long-Awaited No. 1 vs. No. 2 Matchup, Unrest at Ole Miss, and the Sportsman of the Year	125
1963	The Year of Significant Change, Staubach and Butkus, and Scholarly Panthers	137
1964	The Year of the Notre Dame Miracle, Ready for Primetime Thriller, and Arkansas Holiday	148
1965	The Year of Freedom of Substitution, After-Bowl Polls, and High Tide Timing	160
1966	The Year of the Game of the Century, Marketing of Gatorade, and Bad Timing for Undefeated Tide	173
1967	The Year of City of Angels Showdown, Keep the Ball Rollin', and Stallings Traps Bear	186
1968	The Year of the Greatest Sophomore Class, Unveiling of the Wishbone, and a 29-29 Win	197
1969	The Year of Beano's Crystal Ball, Nixon's Number One, and Football's Centennial	208
1970	The Year of The Year of the Quarterback, Bowl Upsets after Eleven Games, and Aeronautic Tragedy	220
1971	The Year of Nebraska's Game of the Century, Bear Learning New Tricks, and the Thunder Chickens	232
1972	The Year of Southern California Sunshine, Archie Leads Freshmen Back into Fray, and BYU's Rushing King	244
1973	The Year of Ara's Era's Big Play, Big Ten's Vengeful Vote, and Something for Joey	254
1974	The Year of Oklahoma's Half-Ignored Title, Rose Bowl Rubber Match, and Michigan's Bowl-Less Seniors	265
1975	The Year of Passing Dodo-Birds, Archie's Heisman Double, and Arizona State's Broken Hearts	275
1976	The Year of the Panthers' American Success Story, Coaching Greats into the Sunset, and Cougar SWC Debut	286
1977	The Year of the Underdogs, the Tyler Rose Blooms at Tailback, and Wearing of the Green	296
1978	The Year of the Goal-Line Admonition, Chicken Soup Comeback, and Woody's Punch Bowl	306
1979	The Year of the Tide Topping the Big Three, Mount Kush Toppled, and the Greatest Offensive Line	316
1980	The Year of "How 'Bout Dem Dawgs!?," Holiday Miracle Pass, and Controversy for the Big Ten and Pac-10	327
1981	The Year of Bear's Stagg Party, Allen's Run to Daylight, and Tigers Prowl as Last Number One	337
1982	The Year of the Ironic National Title, Herschel Leaves for "The Donald," and Elway's Strange Finale	347
1983	The Year of a Hurricane Hitting the Orange Bowl, Georgia's Senior Mission, and Auburn's Best-Ever Factor	357
1984	The Year of Flutie's Heroic Hail Mary, Television Frenzy Fed, and a Suitcase Full of Money	369
1985	The Year of Back to Basics after Aikman's Knockout, Close Heisman Shave, and Eddie Winning his 324th	381
1986	The Year of the Prime-Time Showdown in the Valley of the Sun, Steroids for Sale, and Lockbaum for Heisman	393
1987	The Year of Raising Canes, "Tie Dye," and SMU Doomed to Death	405
1988	The Year of Third-Year Magic, Mainstream Negative Stories, and Records for Nebraska, Oklahoma, and Houston	415
1989	The Year of Sal's Memorial, Double Ericksons, and Run-and-Shoot's Heisman with No Prisoners	425
1990	The Year of Helter Skelter Fifth Down and Cinderella in Atlanta, Dancing the Hokey Pokey, and Rocket's Near Glare	435
1991	The Year of Wide Right Again, Shared Title in Distant Corners, and the Struck Pose	447
1992	The Year of the First Conference Championship Game, Hurricane Andrew, and Alabama's Sugar Surprise	460
1993	The Year of the Coalition Poll, the Team that Beat the Team, and Orange Bowl Thriller	473
1994	The Year of the Only Game in Town, Slip in Bloomington occasions the Doctor's Title, and the Five-Cornered Knot	486
1995	The Year of Northwestern's Purple Dream, Bowl Alliance, and Nebraska's Repeaters	498
1996	The Year of Changing Landscape, Overtime Thrillers and Marathons, and Gators Aided by Gamesmanship	510
1997	The Year of Return to Peyton Place, Nothing Wrong with Michigan, and Another Split Decision	524
1998	The Year of the Bowl Championship Launch, Volunteer Triumph, and Bowdens in the News	537
1999	The Year of the Distracted Wire-to-Wire Win, the Magical Freshman, and November Nightmare	548
2000	The Year of Oklahoma's New Millennium, Stupid Computer Picks, and Northwest Surprises	560
2001	The Year of Helping to Heal a Nation, Cancellation in Pullman, and Return of Miami's Might	572
2002	The Year of the Twelfth Game, Irish Return to Glory, and Overtime Buckeyes	585
2003	The Year of Lack of Collegiality, Peasant's Revolt, and Three for Number One	599
2004	The Year of Finding a Quarterback, Sudden Fumble Reversal, and Auburn and AP Out of BCS	615
2005	The Year of Trojans Try for Three, Austin City Elation, and Deep South's Hurricane Devastation	631
2006	The Year of the Colossal Clash of Columbus, Monstrous Months, and Redemption for the Big East	645
2007	The Year of Utter Disbelief, Wounded Quarterbacks, and Miraculous LSU, a Two-Loss Champion	663
2008	The Year of the SEC's Triad of Titlists, Jilted Longhorns, and Hootin' Utes	682
2009	The Year of the Subcommittee Hearings, Bizarre Coaching Behavior, and Sad Farewell to Bobby	708
2010	The Year of Covetous Designs on the Big Twelve, the Un-whistled Run, and Disheartening News	733
		759

TOP 63 COLLEGE TEAM SCORES, LINEUPS, AND STATS

Alabama Crimson Tide	780	North Carolina Tar Heels	1036
Arizona Wildcats	796	North Carolina State Wolfpack	1044
Arizona State Sun Devils	788	Northwestern Wildcats	1052
Arkansas Razorbacks	804	Notre Dame Fighting Irish	1060
Auburn Tigers	812		
Baylor Bears	820	Ohio State Buckeyes	1068
Boston College Eagles	828	Oklahoma Sooners	1084
California Golden Bears	836	Oklahoma State Cowboys	1076
Clemson Tigers	844	Oregon Ducks	1092
Colorado Buffaloes	852	Oregon State Beavers	1100
Duke Blue Devils	860		
Florida Gators	868	Penn State Nittany Lions	1108
Florida State Seminoles	876	Pittsburgh Panthers	1116
Georgia Bulldogs	884	Purdue Boilermakers	1124
Georgia Tech Yellow Jackets	892	Rutgers Scarlet Knights	1132
Illinois Fighting Illini	900	South Carolina Gamecocks	1140
Indiana Hoosiers	908	Southern California Trojans	1148
Iowa Hawkeyes	924	Stanford Cardinal	1156
Iowa State Cyclones	916	Syracuse Orange	1164
Kansas Jayhawks	940	Tennessee Volunteers	1172
Kansas State Wildcats	932	Texas Longhorns	1188
Kentucky Wildcats	948	Texas A&M Aggies	1180
Louisiana State Tigers	956	Texas Christian Horned Frogs	1196
Maryland Terrapins	964	Texas Tech Red Raiders	1204
Miami Hurricanes	972	U.C.L.A. Bruins	1212
Michigan Wolverines	988	Vanderbilt Commodores	1020
Michigan State Spartans	980	Virginia Cavaliers	1228
Minnesota Golden Gophers	996	Virginia Tech Hokies	1236
Mississippi Rebels	1004	Wake Forest Demon Deacons	1244
Mississippi State Bulldogs	1012	Washington Huskies	1252
Missouri Tigers	1020	Washington State Cougars	1260
Nebraska Cornhuskers	1028	West Virginia Mountaineers	1268
		Wisconsin Badgers	1276

INTRODUCTION

The Modern Encyclopedia of College Football begins with football's 85th season, the watershed year of 1953, when a major new conference was born and the beginning of a 12-year span when athletes played both offense and defense. In writing about 55 seasons since 1953, Paul Guido and I focused on enhancing the names and numbers of the top 63 schools with the drama that took place on the field. We hope you enjoy it.

Like college football its ownself, this book was born in New Jersey. Slightly more than 120 years after Princeton and Rutgers kicked off the gridiron show, Paul, my co-author and research partner in waiting, and I sat in Castaways restaurant in Hawthorne, N.J., one winter night in 1989. Over a couple of cold beverages, we wondered aloud: With all the encyclopedias of pro football, baseball, and basketball in bookstores, why was there no book that featured game highlights, statistics, and player rosters to document the history of college football? Now we know: it is a highly daunting task to compile it all, and it took us more than 15 years.

Unlike the National Football League, Major League Baseball, or other sports encyclopedia subjects, college football records are found in no one single place, but at hundreds of schools. Over the course of several years, Paul and I traveled to nearly every major college campus. We had the chance to work with most of the sport's unsung heroes: college sports information directors (SIDs), football information specialists, secretaries, and student interns. Sports fans should know more about these people, but mainstream media rarely acknowledge them. In addition to gameday and day-to-day notes, SIDs turn out tremendously useful media guides for pre-season, bowl games, and spring drills. Paul and I depended heavily on these guides, poring over nearly 4,500 of them. Without the excellent work of SIDs, all media (from cub reporters to Brent Musberger) would appear less smart than they do. That includes us first-time authors. We offer sincere thanks to all SIDs and their staffs.

Our wonderful mothers are owed a tremendous debt of gratitude. Paul's mother Loretta, who married into the Notre Dame "Subway Alumni," stored lots of research material in her garage in New Jersey. My mother, Gretchen shivered through many wet and cold 1950s and '60s Dartmouth-Yale games wondering why Dad and I found them so vital. The chill didn't stop her from living to within four days of her 92nd birthday in 2004. She was an inspiration.

We have friends and colleagues galore who supported us in many ways, and they are, alphabetically, Fred Barnes, Donn Bernstein, the late Lee Reinke Bright, Frank "Skipper" Burns, Mario Canas, Pat Carroll, Karl Colyer, Jeff Durosko, Dave Dworsky, Darryl Early, Robert Glass, Bill Hofheimer, Dr. John D. Hogan, Rob Lynch, Neil Mack, Bill McCloskey, the late Homer "Butch" McCreary, Tim McManus, Nick Michaels, Michael Morrissey, George Pattison, Larry Suhey, Fred Strouse, Donn "Swami" Wagner, Emmett Williams, Mark Yost and Ken Zeserson. We would like to extend a special note of gratitude to Patricio Maldonado for his computer expertise.

Senior editor Mark Weinstein of Skyhorse Publishing guided this project tremendously well while helping to helm the launch of the company. Our literary representative, Farley Chase of the Scott Waxman Agency of New York, has provided terrific encouragement from the day we first spoke.

We owe very special thanks to those in the newspaper microfilm department of the Public Library of the City of New York and the Inter-Library Loan department of the Barton Barr Central Library of Phoenix.

We also received excellent assistance from the reference departments of the following libraries: Austin (Tex.) Library, Carnegie Library of Pittsburgh, Charlotte-Mecklinburg (N.C.) Public Library, Public Library of Cincinnati and Hamilton County, City of Cleveland Library, Cushing Library of Texas A&M University, Dallas Public Library, Denver Public Library, DeKalb County (Ga.) Library—Decatur Branch, Hastings-on-Hudson (N.Y.) Library, Jacksonville (Fla.) Public Library, Jefferson-Madison Regional Library (Charlottesville, Va.), Kansas City Public Library, Los Angeles Public Library, City of Miami Library, City of Orlando Library, Nashville Public Library, Free Library of Philadelphia, Ridgewood (N.J.) Library, City of Phoenix-Mericopa County Library, San Francisco Public Library, Tucson-Pima Public Library, UNC-Charlotte Library, Vanderbilt University Library, Westchester County (White Plains, N.Y.) Library, and City of Wilmington (Del.) Library.

Special thanks go to the people of three pantheons of sports research: the Joyce Sports Research Center at the University of Notre Dame Hesburgh Library, which houses a massive collection of football media, the University of Alabama's Paul W. Bryant Museum, an attraction no serious football fan should pass up, and the Amateur Athletic Foundation Library, also known as the Ziffren Library, of Los Angeles, which is a wealth of sports information and an impressive part of the legacy of the 1984 Olympic Games.

One discouraging note: College football statistics seemed less important at times than they do today. Some of the numbers are lost, perhaps never to be found. For that reason, there are small but regrettable gaps in this book.

Bob Boyles
Phoenix, Arizona
2010

Our source material was far-reaching:

Newspapers, Periodicals, News Services and Websites: Arizona Republic, Associated Press, Atlanta Journal-Constitution, Birmingham News, Boston Globe, CBSsportsline.com, Charlotte News, Charlotte Observer, Charlottesville (Va.) Daily Progress, Chicago Tribune, Chicago Sun-Times, Christian Science Monitor, Cincinnati Enquirer, Cleveland Plain-Dealer, Collegefootballnews.com, Daily Oklahoman, Dallas Morning News, Dallas Times Herald, Denver Post, Detroit Free Press, Detroit News, Florida Today, The Football News, Foxsportsnet.com, Gannett Newspapers, Houston Chronicle, Houston Post, Kansas City Times-Star, Jacksonville (Fla.) Journal, Lincoln (Neb.) Journal Star, Los Angeles Herald-Examiner, Los Angeles Times, Louisville Courier-Journal, Miami Daily News, Miami Herald, The (Nashville) Tennesseean, New Orleans Times-Picayune, New York Daily News, New York Herald-Tribune, New York Post, New York Times, Oklahoma Journal, Omaha World-Herald, Orlando Sentinel, Philadelphia Inquirer, Phoenix Gazette, Pigskinpost.com, Pittsburgh Post-Gazette, Pittsburgh Press, Richmond Times-Dispatch, Rocky Mountain News, St. Louis Post-Dispatch, San Francisco Chronicle, San Francisco Examiner, Senior Scholastic (November 3, 1955), South Bend (Ind.) Tribune, South Boston (Va.) News & Record, Sport (1950-1980), Sports Illustrated 1954-2008, The Sporting News 1953-2008, United Press International, USA Today, Washington Post, and Wilmington (Del.) News-Journal.

Annual Publications: ACC Yearbooks, Athlon Yearbooks, Jim Barnes College Football Guide, Dave Campbell's Texas Football, Lee Corso's College Football, Dell Sports Stanley Woodward's Football, Football Digest College Football Preview, Football Illustrated, Football Roundup, Football Yearbook Published by True, Game Plan College Football, Goal Post College Football, Don Heinrich's College Football, Information Please Sports Almanac, Kick-Off Football Yearbook, Lindy's Football Annuals, Official NCAA Guides (1949-2007), Petersen's College Football, Pigskin Preview, Poling's Polls, Popular Sports College Football Preview, Sports Forecast Football, Sports Illustrated 1993 Pro & College Football Almanac, Sports Illustrated Sports Almanac, Sports Review Football, Phil Steele's College Football Preview, Street & Smith College Football Yearbook, Street & Smith Pro Football Yearbook, The Sporting News College Football Yearbook, and The Sporting News Pro Football Yearbook.

Books (publishers in parenthesis):

Against All Odds: Football's Great Comebacks & Upsets by Bill Shanklin (Barclay House), The Anatomy of a Game by David M. Nelson (University of Delaware Press), The Auburn Tigers of 1957: National Champions by Paul Reeder (Brown Printing), Battle of the Blues by Bill Cromartie (Gridiron), Bear Bryant: Countdown to Glory by James A. Peterson Ph. D and Bill Cromartie (Leisure Press), Beast of the East by Tim Panaccio (Leisure Press), The Biggest Game of All: Notre Dame, Michigan State and the Fall of '66 by Mike Celizic (Simon & Schuster), The Big Bowl Football Guide by Anthony C. DiMarco (Putnam), Big Eight Football by John D. McCallum (Charles Scribner's Sons), The Big Game by John Sullivan (Leisure Press), The Big One: Michigan vs. Ohio State by Bill Cromartie (Gridiron Publishers), Big Ten Football by Mervin D. Hyman and Gordon S. White, Jr. (MacMillan), Big Ten Football Since 1895 by John D. McCallum (Chilton), The Billboard Book of Top 40 Hits by Joel Whitburn (Billboard Books), Bo by Bo Schembechler and Mitch Albom (Warner Books), Bootlegger's Boy by Barry Switzer with Bud Shrake (William Morrow), Born to Referee by Jerry Markbreit & Alan Steinberg (Morrow), Brian Piccolo: A Short Season by Jeannie Morris (Bonus Books, Inc.), Brian's Song (television screenplay) by William Blinn (Bantam Books), Buckeye by Robert Vare (Popular Library), Dave Campbell's Best of Texas Football (Host Communications), A Century of Heroes: One Hundred Years of Ole Miss Football, edited by Larry Wells (Longstreet Press), Champions of College Football by Bill Libby (Hawthorn Books), Clean Old-Fashioned Hate by Bill Cromartie (Rutledge Hill Press), College Football by Christy Walsh (House-Warven), College Football Encyclopedia—the Authoritative Guide to 124 Years of College Football by Robert Ours (Prima Publishing), College Football's Greatest Dynasties: Michigan by Melissa Larson (Smithmark), College Football's Greatest Dynasties: USC by Jack Clary (Smithmark), College Football Scorebook (Third Edition) by Kenneth N. Carlson (Rain Belt Publications), College Football U.S.A. 1869-1971 by John D. McCallum and Charles H. Pearson (Hall of Fame Publishing), The College Game by various contributors (Bobbs-Merrill), Cotton Bowl Classic: The First Fifty Years by Carlton Stowers (Host Communications), Cyclone Memories by Roger Steward (S&RS), Death Valley Days: The Glory of Clemson Football by Bob Bradley (Longstreet Press), Ditka: Monster of the Midway by Armen Keteyian (Pocket Books), A Dynasty in Blue—25 Years of Michigan Football Glory, edited by Francis J. Fitzgerald (Athlon), Even Big Guys Cry by Alex Karras (Holt, Rinehart and Winston), The Fanatic's Guide to SEC Football by Frank and Rita Cantrell Wenzel (LightSide Productions, Inc.), Field of Valor by Jack Clary (Triumph Books), The Fifty Year Seduction: How Television Manipulated College Football, from the Birth of the Modern NCAA to the Creation of the BCS by Keith Dunnavant (St. Martin's Press), Fifty Years on the Fifty: The Orange Bowl Story by Loran Smith (East Woods Press with Orange Bowl Committee), The Fighting Irish by William Gildea and Christopher Jennison (Prentice Hall), The Fighting Spirit by Lou Holtz with John Heisler (Simon & Schuster), The Fighting Tigers 1893-1993, One Hundred Years of LSU Football by Peter Finney (Louisiana State University Press), The Fireside Book of Football, edited by Jack Newcombe (Simon & Schuster), The First Hundred Years: History of South Carolina

Football by John Chandler Griffin (Longstreet Press) Focused on the Top by Jack Wilkinson (Longstreet Press), Football's Best & Brightest Stars: The Heisman Trophy Winners by Pete Alfano (Scholastic Inc.), Football Coaching, compiled by the American Football Coaches Association and edited by Dick Herbert (Charles Scribner's Sons), Football: A College History by Tom Perrin (McFarland), Football Facts, Feats, & Firsts, by the Editors of The Sporting News (Galahad Books), Football: The Greatest Moments in the Southwest Conference by Will Grimsley (Little-Brown), Football Rankings by Lowell R. Gruenke (McFarland), Forty-Seven Straight, the Wilkinson Era at Oklahoma by Harold Keith (University of Oklahoma Press), FSU One Time by James P. Jones (Sentry Press), Gators: Inside Story of Florida's First SEC Title by Steve Spurrier with Norm Carlson (Tribune), Glory Yards: Georgia vs. Florida by Derek Smith (Rutledge Hill Press), Go Gators!: An oral history of Florida's Pursuit of Gridiron Glory by Peter Golenbock (Legends Press), Great Football Rivalries by Ken Rappoport (Grosset & Dunlap), Greatest Moments in Pitt Football History, edited by Mike Bynum, Larry Eldridge Jr., and Sam Sciullo Jr. (Athlon), Greatest Moments in TCU Football History, edited by Dan Jenkins and Francis J. Fitzgerald (AdCraft Sports Marketing), Hail to the Orange and Blue by Linda Young (Sagamore), Woody Hayes: A Reflection by Paul Hornung (Sagamore), Heart Stoppers and Hail Marys: 100 of the Greatest College Football Finishes (1970-99) by Ted Mandell (Diamond Communications, Inc.), The Heisman, Great American Stories of the Men Who Won by Bill Pennington (HarperCollins Publications), The Heisman, A Symbol of Excellence by John A. Walsh (Atheneum), A High Porch Picnic with George Wine (Sports Publishing, Inc.), Howard, the Clemson Legend by Frank Howard and Friends (Howard); Horns, Hogs, and Nixon Coming: Texas vs. Arkansas in Dixie's Last Stand by Terry Frei (Simon & Schuster), I'll Tell You One Thing by Dan Jenkins (Woodford Press), Ivy League Football Since 1872 by John D. McCallum (Stein and Day), The Junction Boys by Jim Dent (St. Martin's Press), King Football: Sport & Spectacle in the Golden Age of Radio & Newsreels, Movies & Magazines, the Weekly & the Daily Press by Michael Oriard (University of North Carolina Press), The David Kopay Story by David Kopay and Perry Deane Young (Primus), The Last Coach, a Life of Paul "Bear" Bryant by Allen Barra (Norton), Lite Reading by Frank Deford (Penguin Books), LSU Football—A Golden Century Celebrations (Centennial Marketing), Many Autumns Ago: Frank Leahy Era at Boston College and Notre Dame edited by Mike Bynum (October Football Corp.), McKay: A Coach's Story by John McKay with Jim Perry (Antheneum), My Story (And I'm Sticking to It) by Alex Hawkins (Algonquin Books of Chapel Hill), NCAA Football's Finest, compiled by James M. Van Valkenburg, edited by Laura E. Bollig (National Collegiate Athletic Association), Natural Enemies: The Notre Dame-Michigan Football Feud by John Kryk (Andrews and McMeel), The New York Times Directory of the Film, 1974 (Arno Press), The Notre Dame Football Scrapbook by Richard M. Cohen, Jordan A. Deutsch and David S. Neft (Bobbs-Merrill), No. 1 Noles! by Tallahassee Democrat, Inc., Official Encyclopedia of Football (Sixth Revised Edition) by Roger Treat (South Brunswick), Oh, How They Played the Game by Allison Danzig (Macmillan), The Ohio State Football Scrapbook by Richard M. Cohen, Jordan A. Deutsch and David S. Neft (Bobbs-Merrill), Ol' Mizzou—A Century of Tiger Football by Bob Broeg (Walsworth), One Hundred Years of Alabama Football by Gene Schoor (Longstreet Press), One Hundred Years of Notre Dame Football by Gene Schoor (Avon Books), Out of Bounds: Anecdotal History of Notre Dame Football by Michael Bonifer and L.G. Weaver (Piper), Paterno by the Book by Joe Paterno with Bernard Asbell (Random House), Quotable Woody by Monte Carpenter (Towle House), The Refrigerator and the Monsters of the Midway by Brian Hewitt (Signet Book/New American Library), Rockne by Jerry Brondfield (Random House), Rose Bowl Football Since 1902 by Herb Michelson and Dave Newhouse (Stein and Day), Rough Magic: Bill Walsh's Return to Stanford Football by Lowell Cohn (Harper Collins), Seminole Seasons by Burt Reynolds & Bruce Chadwick (Taylor), Southeastern Conference Football by John D. McCallum (Charles Scribner's Sons), The Sporting News Complete Pro Football Draft Encyclopedia (Sporting News Books) compiled by Dave Sloan, The Sports Encyclopedia: Pro Football by David S. Neft and Richard M. Cohen (St. Martin's Press), The Sports Page, Quotations on Baseball, Football, Golf, and Other Sports compiled by Peter Beilenson (Peter Pauper Press), Roger Staubach: Captain America by Mike Towle (Cumberland House), The Sugar Bowl: A History 1935-1960 by various contributors (Franklin Printing), Sunshine Shootouts by Jeff Miller (Longstreet Press), Superstars of Autumn by NFL Properties (Turner Publishing), The Tailgater's Handbook by Joe Drozda (Masters Press), Third Saturday in October: Tennessee vs. Alabama by Al Browning (Cumberland House), Total Football—The Official Encyclopedia of the National Football League by Bob Carroll, Michael Gershman, David Neft, John Thorn (Harper Collins), Total Football II—The Official Encyclopedia of the National Football League by Bob Carroll, Michael Gershman, David Neft, John Thorn, Elias Sports Bureau (Harper Collins), The Trojans—Southern California Football by Don Pierson (Henry Regnery Co.), The Tumult and the Shouting by Grantland Rice (A.S. Barnes & Co.), The TV Guide TV Book by Ed Weiner & the Editors of TV Guide (Harper Perennial), The Ultimate Guide to College Football by James Quirk (University of Illinois Press), The Undefeated by Jim Dent (Thomas Dunne Books, St. Martin's Press), The University of Michigan Football Scrapbook by Richard M. Cohen, Jordan A. Deutsch and David S. Neft (Bobbs-Merrill), Upon Other Fields on Other Days, College Football's Wartime Casualties by Jim Koger (Longstreet Press), Video Hound's Golden Movie Retriever 1999, edited by Martin Connors and Jim Craddock (Visible Ink), War Stories from the Field: A "Hit & Tell" Collection of the Greatest Pro Football Stories Ever Told by Joseph Hession & Kevin Lynch (Foghorn Press), Where Tradition Began: Centennial History of Auburn Football by Wayne Hester (Seacoast), Bud Wilkinson, An Intimate Portrait of an American Legend by Jay Wilkinson and Gretchen Hirsch (Sagamore Publishing), Woody's Boys by Alan Natali (Orange Frazer Press), World Almanac and Book of Facts 1993 (Pharos Books), You Call it Sports, but I Say it's a Jungle Out There by Dan Jenkins (Fireside Book by Simon & Schuster), You Have to Pay the Price by Earl H. Blaik with Tim Cohane (Holt, Rinehart and Winston).

From the series of individual school football histories published by Strode: Between the Hedges by Jesse Outlar, The Big Orange by Russ Bebb, Bow Down to Washington by Dick Rockne, Crimson Tide by Clyde Bolton, Down on the Farm by Fred Merrick, The Fighting Illini by Lon Eubanks, The Gamecocks by Jim Hunter, Gators by Tom McEwen, The Golden Buffaloes by Fred Casotti, Hurricane Watch by Jim Martz, LSU: The Louisiana Tigers by Dan Hardesty, The Maroon Bulldogs by William W. Sorrels, Ole Miss Rebels by William W. Sorrels and Charles Cavagnaro, Ol' Mizzou by Bob Broeg, The Ramblin' Wreck by Al Thomy, The Razorbacks by Orville Henry and Jim Bailey, The Spartans by Fred W. Stabley, Tar Heel by Ken Rappoport, That Good Old Baylor Line by Denne H. Freeman, The Tigers of Princeton by Jay Dunn, Touchdown UCLA by Hendrik Van Lueven, The Twelfth Man by Wilbur Evans and H. B. McElroy, University of Iowa Football by Chuck Bright, War Eagle by Clyde Bolton, and The Wildcats by Russell Rice.

THE

COLLEGE FOOTBALL ENCYCLOPEDIA

GUIDE TO READING THIS BOOK

Abbreviation Guide
   This book contains nearly 7,500 game recaps. In the interest of saving space, we have created abbreviations most fans will quickly grasp:

GENERAL PLAYING STYLE AND TIMING:

O	offense or offensive
D	defense or defensive
Q	quarter
H	half or halftime
1st	first
2nd	second
3rd	third
4th	fourth
sec or secs	second or seconds
min or mins	minute or minutes
OT	overtime

POSITION PLAYERS AND OTHER PERSONAL TITLES:

E	end
TE	tight end
WR	wide receiver
T	tackle
G	guard
C	center
QB	quarterback
HB	halfback
FB	fullback
RB	running back
TB	tailback
IB	I-back
WB	wingback
SB	slot-back
H-B	H-back
BB	Blocking Back
K	placekicker
DL	defensive lineman
DE	defensive end
DT	defensive tackle
NG	nose guard
LB	linebacker
ILB	inside linebacker
OLB	outside linebacker
DB	defensive back
CB	cornerback
S	safety
FS	free safety
SS	strong safety
KR	kick returner
frosh	freshman
soph	sophomore
jr	junior
sr	senior
pres.	president (usually of the university)
Pres.	President of United States
Gov.	State Governor
AD	athletic director
Asst	assistant

ENTITIES AND ORGANIZATIONS

Conf	conference
AAWU	Athletic Association of Western Universities
ACC	Atlantic Coast Conference
Pac-8/Pac-10	Pacific-8/Pacific-10 Conference
SEC	Southeastern Conference
SWC	Southwest Conference
WAC	Western Athletic Conference
NFF	National Football Foundation
NFL	National Football League
JC or Juco	junior college
HS	high school

SCORING AND SPECIFIC PLAY OUTCOMES:

TD	touchdown
FG	field goal
FUM	fumble (used only as noun, spelled out as a verb)
INT	interception
RET	return (of a punt, kickoff, interception or fumble)
QK	quick kick (disguised punt)
On-side-KO	on-side kick, always on a kickoff
TO	turnover (not timeout, which always is spelled out)
OB	out of bounds
y	yards or yardage
ft	foot
YL	yard line
GL	goal line
GLS	goal line stand
EZ	end zone
KO	kick off
pt	point (plural: pts)
x-pt	extra point
3-ptr	three-pointer (as in field goal)
conv	conversion (extra point kick or two-point conversion)
kick	conversion placement kick (used always as noun)

GENERAL:

lb. or lbs.	pound or pounds (as in weight)
/	for (Always expressed with statistics. Example: 23/114y rushing, means 23 attempts for 114 yards rushing.)

Game Recap Style

Each recap starts with game score, home team in capital letters. If the game was played at a neutral site, both teams are in lower case letters, the site in parenthesis. Teams with home games at established off-campus sites (such as Alabama playing at Birmingham and Mississippi playing at Memphis) are listed in capital letters, and the site listed. W-L records as a result of the game are shown in parenthesis with the school name. The use of individual player statistics in parenthesis implies the type of statistic normally associated with the player's position, such as passing for a quarterback.

Examples of Game Recap language:

■ Florida 28 LOUISIANA STATE 7: QB Steve Spurrier (17-25/208y, 2 TDs) and HB Larry Smith (17/75y, 2 TDs) led unbeaten Florida (6-0) to 28-0 lead early in 3rd Q,...

Recap translation: Florida, playing at LSU's home stadium, won 28-7. Spurrier completed 17 of 25 passes for 208 yards and two touchdowns (interceptions are also shown in parenthesis if any occurred). Smith carried the ball 17 times and gained 75 yards, scoring twice on the ground. Any other stats such as quarterback rushing or running back pass receiving are indicated. Sometimes attempts are unavailable and thus not shown.

Mentions of a team's rank or unbeaten record are prior to the recap.

■ ARIZONA STATE 19 Nebraska 0: Top-ranked Cornhuskers (1-1) had won 26 games in row. With bevy of fans returning to Valley of Sun, site of previous year's national title Fiesta Bowl victory, mighty Nebraska looked invincible. But, improving Sun Devils (3-0) stunned Huskers early with QB Jake Plummer's scramble left for 25y TD pass to wide-open WR Keith Poole. Arizona State D rattled rookie QB Scott Frost (6-20/66y) into bad EZ pitchout that dribbled OB, inattention on Shotgun snap, and sack by DL Derrick Rodgers, all 3 of which resulted in safeties.

Recap Translation: Nebraska, which had won the national championship in the previous season's Fiesta Bowl in the Valley of the Sun returned as the seemingly invincible top-ranked team in the nation prior to its upset at the hands of Arizona State, playing at home. The Sun Devils were improving, however, and quarterback Jake Plummer threw an early touchdown pass and their defense rattled Nebraska quarterback Scott Frost into bad plays for three safeties.

■ PRINCETON 35 Dartmouth 7: Princeton (6-3), which started season by "setting back" football 100 years, closed year by surprising undefeated Dartmouth (8-1) and commandeering its own share of Ivy League title…

Recap translation: Princeton, which started the season poorly, played its last game of the season at home and beat previously unbeaten Dartmouth to tie for the championship of the Ivy League.

■ Oklahoma 12 Texas 0 (Dallas): Not in 282 games had Longhorns (4-1) been blanked, longest scoring streak in country...

Recap Translation: Oklahoma was the first team in 282 games to shut out Texas, while playing on the neutral field in Dallas' Cotton Bowl stadium.

A Game-of-the-Year is selected each season, and introduction appears in bold type. The basis for selection of one game over another is first and primarily: the importance the game played on the overall season, or at least the participating teams. Example:

■ GAME OF THE YEAR
Georgia Tech 41 VIRGINIA 38:

Virginia (7-1) QB Shawn Moore set school record with 344y passing on 18-28, and WR Herman Moore caught 9/234y, including fake-reverse 63y TD bomb in 3rd Q…(and later in recap)…Tech went 56y in 5 plays to position Sisson for game-winning FG with 7 secs left, keys being Jones-to-Bell 23y pass, Bell's 13y run on which he fell on own FUM, and Jones-to-WR Greg Lester 15y pass.

Recap Translation: No. 1 Virginia's Shawn and Herman Moore made big plays to build leads in the 1990 Game of the Year. Georgia Tech used five plays leading to Scott Sisson's winning field goal with seven seconds left.

Bowl Games

All bowls recapped in the book were played on January 1 unless otherwise noted. References to a bowl game that mention its year, such as the "1984 Rose Bowl," refer to the calendar year in which they were played. So, the 1984 Rose Bowl example refers to the game played at the end of the 1983 season. There are occasional situations where such a reference could be confusing, and this book avoids making such references. For example, Gator Bowl organizers switched their game date at the end of the 1954 season from New Year's Day to the last Saturday of December. So in effect, there were two 1954 Gator Bowls, the game following the 1953 season played on January 1, 1954, and the game following the 1954 season that was played on December 31, 1954.

We absolutely have nothing against corporate sponsorship's, except for the marking of giant player-obscuring logos on the field. This is a history book that starts long before corporate sponsorships, so we have attempted to be faithful to the original bowl names to maintain clarity of bowl locations. There are some necessary exceptions: The sly

people at John Hancock Insurance dropped Sun (their bowl's original name) for what briefly became the John Hancock Bowl. We refer to the game in El Paso as the John Hancock (Sun) Bowl during the years that Sun was dropped from the title.

Here is a sample of the 1991 recap of the Hancock-Sun Bowl:

■ John Hancock (Sun) Bowl (Dec. 31): UCLA 6 Illinois 3
It took fine D to keep alive 8-game bowl winning streak of UCLA (9-3)…

Recap Translation: UCLA won an eighth straight bowl game and played excellent defense in the John Hancock Bowl, formerly known as the Sun Bowl.

Secondly, several of the newer bowls never had a non-corporate title. We refer to the December game in Miami as the Blockbuster Bowl for its first three years starting in 1990, then pick up the Carquest name in 1993. Later, it was the Micron PC Bowl. The Copper Bowl in Tucson is now played in Tempe, Arizona, as the Insight Bowl. The Continental Tire Bowl in Charlotte has already morphed into the Meineke Car Care Bowl. This book keeps pace with the name changes.

Starting Lineups, Individual Statistics, All-America Teams, Heisman Trophy Voting, Other Major Awards, and the Pro Draft

The starting lineups and key reserve players for major schools are listed for all 55 years (1953-2008) in each school's chapter. Air Force is the one exception. Founded in 1955, the Academy did not face major teams until 1958. Thus, Air Force's scores, lineups, and stats begin in this book in 1958.

Individual passing, rushing, receiving and scoring stats are listed with each season. This is an inexact science. Players get hurt, lose their starting spots, get moved to other positions. We feel we got as many as possible. We list as many stats as we were able to collect, but we were dependent on the schools, some of which have retroactively applied bowl game stats for players in years before that practice became official in 2002.

What follows is a score-lineup-stat sample from **Colorado** in **2001**. Note that ■ indicates a bowl game and □ indicates a conference championship game:

2001 10-3

22 Fresno State	24 WR John Minardi / Cedric Cormier
41 Colorado State	14 WR Derek McCoy
51 San Jose State	15 T Justin Bates
27 Kansas	16 G Marwan Hage
16 Kansas State	6 C Wayne Lucier
31 Texas A&M	21 G Andre Gurode
7 Texas	41 T Victor Rogers
22 Oklahoma State	19 TE Daniel Graham
38 Missouri	24 QB Craig Ochs / Bobby Pesavento
40 Iowa State	27 TB Chris Brown/Bobby Purifoy/C. Johnson
62 Nebraska	36 FB Brandon Drumm
39 Texas □	37 DL Tyler Brayton
16 Oregon ■	38 DL Justin Bannan
	DL Brandon Dahdoub / DeAndre Fluellen
	DL Marques Harris
	LB Sean Tufts
	LB Joey Johnson / Jashon Sykes
	LB Drew Wahlroos / Aaron Killion
	DB Donald Strickland
	DB Roderick Sneed / Phil Jackson
	DB Robbie Robinson
	DB Michael Lewis

RUSHING: Brown 190/946y, Purifoy 157/916y, Johnson 89/567y
PASSING: Pesavento 85-139/1234y, 8TD, 61.2%
 Ochs 99-166/1220y, 7TD, 59.6%
RECEIVING: Graham 51/753y, McCoy 30/512y, Johnson 24/382y
SCORING: Brown 96pts, Jeremy Flores (K) 94pts, Graham 36pts

Also, we have listed consensus All-America selection teams, using annual NCAA Guides as our source. Prior to the split of All-America selections into offensive defensive units in the mid-1960s, all players receiving All-America mention are listed.

Each of the year's top vote getters in Heisman Trophy balloting are listed as well as the winners of the other major college awards.

The annual pro football draft is included. Because this is a college book, we attempt to list all the drafted players by their college positions. Because very few low draft picks made an impact on professional teams, only the first eight draft rounds are included in this book until it goes to seven rounds in concert with the NFL trimming its selection process to seven rounds in 1994.

If a late round selection became a star such as Johnny Unitas, Bart Starr, or Roger Staubach, we include him in his team's draft. If a late round selection became a mainstay starter for his professional team for more than five years, we include him as well. An example would be defensive back Carl "Spider" Lockhart, a 13th round choice by the New York Giants after the 1964 season out of North Texas State.

Late-round draft mentions also include people famous in other walks of sports or have achieved in other walks of life, such as coach and ESPN analyst Lee Corso, a 29th round choice of the Chicago Cardinals after the 1956 season out of Florida State, Hall of Fame NFL coach John Madden, a 21st round choice of the Philadelphia Eagles after the 1957 season out of Cal-Poly (San Luis Obispo), and Baseball Hall of Famer Dave Winfield, a 17th round choice of the Minnesota Vikings after the 1972 season out of Minnesota.

We don't date the year of each draft because only in recent decades has it firmly been established as being scheduled in April following the winter championship playoffs and Super Bowl. In the 1950s and '60s when the NFL battled the Canadian Football League and American Football League for talent, the first two rounds or so would be staged as early as mid-November.

Individual School Charts

Each of the 63 schools featured in this narrative encyclopedic approach has a comprehensive chart on the second page of the sections that focus on each school. The chart includes annual won-loss record, final AP Poll ranking (if appropriate), and conference standing (if appropriate).

The Associated Press reduced its rankings to a top 10 during much of the 1960s (1961-67 to be exact). All schools that received votes but failed to gain enough votes to crack the top 10 were listed in alphabetical order. Whenever a school earned one of these limbo spots of eleventh or better, it is noted as "11+" in the team chart.

Additionally, a team's toughest opponents (generally three to five) for each year are listed with those opponents' regular season record. Of course, many teams on a schedule have the same or similar won-loss marks. Preference for making this list went to a school's general strength. For example, Alabama with an 8-2 record received preference over Akron also with an 8-2 mark. In-conference and rivalry preference also was used in breaking ties. Bowl opponents are listed separately for each year and are not included in a team's given "toughest opponents" list unless they also met during the regular season.

In the final year of a coach's tenure his overall record at that school is listed in parenthesis. If a coach for any reason split his tenure—Johnny Majors at Pittsburgh and John Robinson at Southern California are examples—his record for the first spell of years is noted with "{see below}." After the coach's second run is concluded, his entire record at that school is displayed in parenthesis.

Interim coaches for partial seasons have that year's partial record displayed in square brackets. As an example, Frank Kush was fired at Arizona State after nearly 22 seasons midway through the 1979 season. Bob Owens finished the year as coach and made a 3-4 record. The 1979 notation for Arizona State coaches, including Kush's career record is shown as follows:

Frank Kush (176-54-1),

Bob Owens [3-4].

At the bottom of each school chart, the team's total overall record for the years 1953 to 2008 are shown in wins, losses, and ties. A winning percentage rank among the 70 schools featured in this book of is displayed next to the record. For example, the 14th best winning percentage is shown as "(14 of 70)." A similar process is used to rank the bowl records of the 70 teams.

COLLEGE FOOTBALL PERFORMANCE FORMULA

A Different Way to Compare College Teams

In this the fourth annual edition of The USA TODAY College Football Encyclopedia, the co-authors have updated their innovative College Football Performance Formula.

If readers will permit a sojourn into Major League Baseball for a moment, a simple comparison from that sport will help define the College Football Performance Formula. Think of the Formula as equivalent of the list of league batting averages: simple calculations reveal a champion and all the other players who follow. Both the football polls—Associated Press' media poll and USA TODAY's coaches poll—are akin to a league's Most Valuable Player Award. Many factors, not the least of which is the ethereal impression a given MVP candidate makes on voters, are considered in the selection of an MVP. Football polls are a lot like that.

The College Performance Formula is a specific three-leveled mathematical calculation developed to measure the achievement of every team's season since 1953 among the 70 football programs featured in this book. Additionally, any teams outside the featured top 70 that earned their way into the season-ending top 10 Associated Press Poll are factored as well. In 57 years there were only 14 such teams.

The Formula combines three measurable statistics, with two of them adjusted to the level of opposition, and adds them up to assign a decimal measurement. This figure permits readers to compare teams within a given season and to compare teams from different seasons. What follows are the three features that are totaled arithmetically to form a team's Formula:

■ Winning percentage (including bowl result) of the measured team, with wins over lower categorized teams counting as partial wins.

■ Opponents' winning percentage (including bowl results) in all other games not contested against the team being measured.

■ Adjusted scoring margin per game (x .01 so as to not assign too much numerical importance to the factor) of the measured team.

Tie games are counted as half-wins and half-losses in both winning percentage and opponents' winning percentage.

An exactly average team will score a 1.0000 Formula number. An average team would have a season record in any combination that averaged at a .5000 break-even percentage, play a group of opponents that also broke even against the teams it played other than the team being measured, and the measured team averaged a scoring margin that calculated at zero per game, that is, it scored as many points as it allowed.

The majority of top 70 teams exceed 1.0000. This is due to the relatively high percentage of easy-to-defeat, historically-unsuccessful opponents that are scheduled to pad the winning records of top 70 teams. Thus, most top teams always finish average. Interestingly, in more than 4,000 calculations, not a single team scored an exact average of 1.0000.

Understand also that a team's winning percentage and opponents' winning percentage have been adjusted downward at varying degrees to compensate for victories over three kinds of lesser opponents: those playing in FBS conferences that scheduled fewer than two games per conference member in a given year against the top 70 schools, those participating in FCS (formerly I-AA) completion, and those opponents participating at Division II or III levels. In the seasons prior to the split of the "University Division" into Divisions I-A (now known as FBS) and I-AA (now FCS) in the late 1970s, there were two adjusted opponents: those in conferences scheduled against fewer than 28 top 70 teams and College Division teams.

In this year's edition, every team's Formula number is displayed in the yearly Scores-Lineups-and-Stats "boxes" found in each team section.

The updated list of the best Formula team calculations since 1953 follows. Note:

■ Boldface indicates new entries from the 2009 season.

■ "AP" and/or "USA" indicate teams voted national champions by Associated Press media voters and/or USA TODAY (previously UPI and ESPN) coach panels.

■ "F" indicates teams that topped a season's Formula calculation.

The Top 100 Formula Teams since 1953:

1 Nebraska 1995 (AP, USA, F)	1.9434
2 Nebraska 1971 (AP, USA, F)	1.9154
3 Miami 2001 (AP, USA, F)	1.9071
4 Texas 2005 (AP, USA, F)	1.9011
5 Florida State 1993 (AP, USA, F)	1.8831
6 Syracuse 1959 (AP, USA, F)	1.8698
7 Washington 1991 (USA, F)	1.8618
8 Oklahoma 1974 (AP, F)	1.8484
9 So. California 1972 (AP, USA, F)	1.8483
10 Florida State 1999 (AP, USA, F)	1.8433
11 Miami 1988 (F)	1.8395
12 So. California 2004 (AP, USA, F)	1.8345
13 Notre Dame 1966 (AP, USA, F)	1.8314
14 Miami 1987 (AP, USA, F)	1.8290
15 Alabama 2009 (AP, USA, F)	1.8282
16 Miami 1991 (AP)	1.8189
17 Penn State 1994 (F)	1.8165
18 Nebraska 1997 (USA, F)	1.8146
19 Oklahoma 2000 (AP, USA, F)	1.8104
20 Florida 2008 (AP, USA, F)	1.8083
21 Alabama 1971	1.8025
22 Florida 1996 (AP, USA, F)	1.8018
23 Texas 2008	1.8017
24 Oklahoma 1973 (F)	1.8007
25 Auburn 2010 (AP, USA, F)	1.7989
26 Nebraska 1994 (AP, USA)	1.7935
27 Auburn 2004	1.7923
28t Notre Dame 1973 (AP)	1.7913
28t Oklahoma 1986 (F)	1.7913
30t Penn State 1969 (F)	1.7879
30t Southern California 2005	1.7879
32 Notre Dame 1988 (AP, USA)	1.7860
33 Florida State 1987	1.7828
34 Nebraska 1983 (F)	1.7712
35 Tennessee 1998 (AP, USA, F)	1.7711
36 Alabama 1992 (AP, USA, F)	1.7679
37 Oklahoma 1971	1.7667
38 Mississippi 1959	1.7660
39 Penn State 1986 (AP, USA)	1.7652
40 Florida State 1996	1.7634
41 Penn State 1973	1.7632
42 Louisiana State 1958 (AP, USA, F)	1.7608
43 Miami 2000	1.7605
44 Ohio State 2002 (AP, USA, F)	1.7588
45 Penn State 1982 (AP, USA, F)	1.7587
46 Oklahoma 1972	1.7577
47 Alabama 1973 (USA)	1.7572
48 Florida State 2000	1.7556
49 Mississippi 1960 (F)	1.7541
50 Oklahoma 1955 (AP, USA, F)	1.7521
51 Notre Dame 1977 (AP, USA, F)	1.7519
52 Florida State 1997	1.7495
53 Texas 2009	1.7483
54 Nebraska 1982	1.7474
55 Notre Dame 1989 (F)	1.7466
56 Michigan 1997 (AP)	1.7413
57 Southern California 1978 (USA, F)	1.7412
58 Arizona State 1970 (F)	1.7411
59 Oklahoma 1985 (AP, USA, F)	1.7395
60 Florida 1995	1.7391
61t Mississippi 1962 (F)	1.7390
61t TCU 2010	1.7390
63 Penn State 1977	1.7375
64 Oklahoma 1954 (F)	1.7374
65 Texas 1969 (AP, USA)	1.7357
66 Miami 1989 (AP, USA)	1.7365
67 Alabama 1966	1.7346
68 Notre Dame 1953 (F)	1.7360
69 Maryland 1953 (AP, USA)	1.7343
70 Ohio State 1996	1.7332
71 Alabama 1961 (AP, USA, F)	1.7292
72 Pittsburgh 1980 (F)	1.7291
73 Colorado 1989	1.7289
74 Ohio State 1954 (AP)	1.7278
75 Pittsburgh 1976 (AP, USA, F)	1.7271
76 Ohio State 1998	1.7269
77 Southern California 2008	1.7263
78 Oklahoma 1956 (AP, USA, F)	1.7260
79 Alabama 1979 (AP, USA, F)	1.7239
80 Auburn 1957 (AP, F)	1.7229
81 Auburn 1983	1.7225
82 Boise State 2009	1.7216
83 Florida State 1980	1.7205
84 Clemson 1981 (AP, USA, F)	1.7203
85 Penn State 1968 (F)	1.7198
86 Nebraska 1999	1.7193
87 Texas 1970 (USA)	1.7175
88 Brigham Young 1980	1.7159
89 Florida 2001	1.7191
90 Miami 1986	1.7190
91 Miami 2002	1.7189
92 Virginia Tech 2000	1.7182
93 Oklahoma 2008	1.7161
94 Ohio State 1975 (F)	1.7158
95 Alabama 1978 (AP)	1.7150
96 Arkansas 1964 (F)	1.7149
97 Ohio State 2006 (F)	1.7135
98 Florida 2009	1.7134
99 Oklahoma 2004	1.7133
100 Florida State 1992	1.7130

Teams outside the top-100 that were voted to national championships and/or were single season Performance Formula leaders:

Southern California 2003 (AP, F)	1.7025
Florida 2006 (AP, USA)	1.6968
UCLA 1954 (USA)	1.6954
Texas 1963 (AP, USA, F)	1.6942
Alabama 1964 (AP, USA)	1.6937
Southern California 1962 (AP, USA)	1.6898
Nebraska 1970 (AP)	1.6889
Miami 1990 (F)	1.6801
Oklahoma 1975 (AP, USA)	1.6786
Louisiana State 2003 (USA)	1.6784
Oklahoma 1957 (F)	1.6776
Michigan State 1965 (USA, F)	1.6773
Georgia Tech 1990 (USA)	1.6706
Brigham Young 1984 (AP, USA, F)	1.6611
Louisiana State 2007 (AP, USA, F)	1.6496
Southern California 1967 (AP, USA, F)	1.6464
Colorado 1990 (AP)	1.6452
Miami 1983 (AP, USA)	1.6396
Georgia 1980 (AP, USA)	1.6161
Southern California 1974 (USA)	1.6067
Alabama 1965 (AP)	1.5952
Ohio State 1957 (USA)	1.5818
Minnesota 1960 (AP, USA)	1.4841

In theory, a team could exceed 2.0000. But that never has happened in any season since 1953, with the 1995 Nebraska team scoring the highest at 1.9434.

To score a 2.0000, a team would have to go undefeated against an all-top-level schedule, play opponents with at least a .6000 winning percentage—a very good but not exceptional schedule—and beat their opponents by an average of 40 points per game. The latter factor is practically impossible to achieve because it represents perfection. The Formula calls for margins greater than 40 points in any single game to be adjusted down to exactly 40 points.

A 2.0000 number would most likely be achieved against a .7000 winning opponents list while beating opponents by a 30-point average margin. But only five teams since 1953 have faced a schedule with a .7000 or better percentage, and only three teams have topped .3000 in average scoring margin.

In 1995, Nebraska went undefeated against the 12th-best group of opponents of the year with a .5954 percentage. That schedule included a relatively poor out-of-conference slate but was boosted by Big 8 foes Colorado, Kansas, and Kansas State, all at 10-2, and Fiesta Bowl victim Florida, which won 12 of 13. What put Nebraska at the top was an outstanding .3450 adjusted margin in point per game differential.

The lowest Formula number was turned in at .1729 by Rutgers, which had a 0-11 record in 1997. Rutgers faced a weak .4348 opponents' percentage and lost by an average larger than 26 points per game (-.2619).

A major factor in the Formula that is often disregarded by pollsters is the winning percentage a given school's opponents achieve. The head-to-head game between the team being measured and each of its opponents is thrown out so as to not count it twice.

The Top 100 Opponents' Winning Percentage Seasons since 1953:

1 Pittsburgh 1954	.7500		32 Michigan 1956	.6757
2 UCLA 1965	.7233		33 Georgia Tech 1960	.6755
3 Notre Dame 1978	.7132		34 Miami 1993	.6743
4 Oklahoma 2005	.7077		35 Iowa 1958	.6724
5 Auburn 1983	.7016		36 Colorado 1997	.6721
6 Kentucky 1968	.6979		37 Illinois 1962	.6711
7 Notre Dame 1985	.6933		38 Auburn 1985	.6706
8 Southern California 1978	.6912		39 Florida 1991	.6705
9 Purdue 1953	.6908		40 Texas 1956	.6685
10 Florida State 1980	.6905		41 Penn State 1979	.6680
11 Penn State 1982	.6875		42t Stanford 1955	.6667
12 Miami 1962	.6863		42t Florida State 1967	.6667
13 Auburn 1998	.6860		42t Virginia Tech 1988	.6667
14 Alabama 1999	.6857		42t Michigan 1994	.6667
15 Mississippi State 1969	.6842		42t Florida 1997	.6667
16 Tennessee 1997	.6835		47 Mississippi State 2009	.6661
17 Kentucky 1959	.6828		48 Florida State 1998	.6643
18 Alabama 1971	.6825		49 Florida 1986	.6636
19 Missouri 1976	.6822		50t Mississippi State 1962	.6627
20 Texas A&M 2004	.6818		50t UCLA 1983	.6627
21 Mississippi State 1960	.6817		50t Kentucky 1969	.6615
22 Southern California 1966	.6814		50t Notre Dame 1987	.6615
23 Texas Tech 1956	.6813		54 Alabama 1985	.6614
24 Syracuse 1955	.6812		55 Mississippi State 2009	.6611
25 Notre Dame 1958	.6802		56 Florida State 1987	.6603
26 Auburn 1997	.6788		57t Auburn 1965	.6602
27 Mississippi State 1959	.6786		57t Louisiana State 1986	.6602
28 Texas A&M 2010	.6779		57t Florida 1987	.6602
29t Penn State 1981	.6774		57t UCLA 1979	.6581
29t Southern California 2002	.6774		57t Arkansas 1997	.6581
29t Alabama 2003	.6774		62 Iowa 1960	.6579
			63 Pittsburgh 1955	.6563
			64 North Carolina 2004	.6561
			65 Louisiana State 1955	.6559
			66 Rice 1957	.6553
			67 Florida 1985	.6552
			68 Florida 2000	.6545
			69 Nebraska 1973	.6545
			70 Auburn 1972	.6535
			71t Penn State 1977	.6533
			71t Florida 1993	.6533
			73 Iowa 1954	.6527
			74 Florida State 2000	.6525
			75 Florida 2006	.6518
			76t Notre Dame 1989	.6512
			76t Miami 1988	.6512
			78 Missouri 1975	.6509
			79 Alabama 1978	.6508
			80 Pittsburgh 1956	.6495
			81 Tennessee 1974	.6492
			82 Oregon 1982	.6491
			83 Florida 1972	.6486
			84 Colorado 2001	.6483
			85 Mississippi State 1966	.6474
			86t Mississippi State 1963	.6471
			86t Texas 2008	.6471
			88 Penn State 1980	.6468
			89t Florida 1954	.6467
			89t Illinois 1968	.6467
			91 Mississippi State 1971	.6466
			92t Notre Dame 1995	.6462
			92t Michigan 2005	.6462
			94 West Virginia 1963	.6461
			95 Colorado 1990	.6460
			96 Florida State 1989	.6457
			97 Florida State 1993	.6454
			98 Houston 1957	.6452
			99 Mississippi State 1977	.6447
			100 Mississippi State 1961	.6446

Pittsburgh's 1954 team scored a sizable margin to top the list of best opponents' winning percentage. It says something about this exercise. That Panther team finished with a modest 4-5 won-loss record, but would qualify for one of the five major bowl games the next two seasons. So, to survive an extremely difficult schedule sometimes is a harbinger of better records to come.

But, if readers wish to read into this Formula certain powers of game outcome predictions, we recommend against it. It takes a full season of data to sort out the best teams, and it would be difficult to evaluate a team part way into a season, based mostly on the possibility the team in question would not have played its toughest foes until the second half. That said the Formula occasionally unmasks a bowl team as overrated because of a very good record against soft opposition. The reverse is sometimes true. An undervalued bowl team sometimes has superior Formula numbers against a favored opponent.

The Top 50 Seasonal Scoring Margins

1	Oklahoma 1956	.3469
2	Nebraska 1995	.3450
3	Arizona State 1957	.3040
4	Nebraska 1971	.2969
5	Washington 1991	.2892
6	Notre Dame 1966	.2890
7	Boise State 2010	.2877
8	Houston 1989	.2845
9	Oklahoma 1986	.2833
10	Ohio State 1969	.2800
11	Nebraska 1983	.2793
12	Miami 2001	.2792
13	Oklahoma 1974	.2782
14	Texas 2005	.2770
15	UCLA 1954	.2745
16	Mississippi 1959	.2727
17	TCU 2010	.2723
18	Syracuse 1959	.2718
19	Florida 1996	.2717
20	Miami 1988	.2716
21	Arizona State 1973	.2700
22	Kansas State 2002	.2692
23	Southern California 1972	.2691
24	Florida 2001	.2675
25	Oklahoma 1955	.2673
26	Penn State 1971	.2666
27	Texas 1969	.2654
28	Louisville 2004	.2650
29	Florida State 1993	.2646
30	Nebraska 1997	.2639
31t	Nebraska 1972	.2625
31t	Michigan 1976	.2625
31t	Nebraska 1980	.2625
34	Florida State 2000	.2569
35t	Oklahoma 1987	.2567
35t	Utah 2004	.2567
37	Kansas State 1998	.2531
38	Alabama 1973	.2525
39	Oklahoma 2008	.2514
40	Ohio State 1973	.2509
41	Oklahoma 1971	.2500
42t	Nebraska 1996	.2470
42t	Southern California 2005	.2470
44	Southern California 2008	.2469
45	Penn State 1973	.2467
46	Brigham Young 1979	.2459
47	Southern California 2004	.2446
48	Brigham Young 1980	.2439
49	Ohio State 1974	.2433
50	Notre Dame 1973	.2418

A perfect scoring margin average would be .4000 because in the case of margins greater than 40 points, the winning team's point total is reduced to create a margin of 40 points.

An astounding 21 of 58 national champions crowned by Associated Press since 1953 failed to top the Formula lists in their given seasons. That fact either underscores the absurdity of "beauty pageant" polls, or it disassembles the validity of our Formula system. We believe the former, supporting the idea that way too often voters haven't properly executed their voting duties. Interestingly, nearly all discrepancies occurred before the advent of the BCS Championship era. So, while the BCS continues to receive severe criticism, at least according to the Formula, the system isn't so bad after all.

The 22 "failed" AP champions include two transparent champs that were voted no. 1 prior to losing their bowl games: Maryland in 1953, which proceeded to lose the Orange Bowl to Oklahoma, and Minnesota in 1960, which lost the Rose Bowl to Washington.

The Formula supported three champions named by the USA TODAY (or UPI) Coaches Poll when writers and coaches split their championship decisions: Michigan State (coaches' choice) over Alabama in 1965, Washington (coaches' choice) over Miami (writers' choice) in 1991 and Nebraska (coaches' choice) over Michigan (writers' choice) in 1997.

Fourteen of the 21 Formula-shunned AP titleists finished in 2nd place, four of them 3rd, in Formula calculations. But there were three national champions fell surprisingly low in Formula numbers:

■ Minnesota in 1960, which because of its uncompetitive Rose Bowl loss was perhaps the weakest-ever AP champion team, finished 6th in Formula numbers behind top-rated Mississippi.

■ Georgia's 1980 team, generally considered excellent because of the presence of all-time great Herschel Walker, played a woefully weak schedule that produced only a .4553 winning percentage. A good not great .1608 victory margin also cost the Bulldogs, who finished 5th in 1980's Formula standings. Pittsburgh topped the 1980 Formula list.

■ Miami in 1983 only came in 4th in Formula numbers. Nebraska nipped Auburn for no. 1 in Formula standings, despite losing to Miami in the Orange Bowl, mostly because the Huskers crushed their opponents by a factor of .2793. Miami's victory margin was .1475, and Auburn's was .1042 against the fifth-best opponents' percentage (.7016) since 1953. If only Tom Osborne had chosen to kick the tying extra point in that Orange Bowl, he would have won the national championship. Even ardent Miami fans likely would agree the 1983 edition of the Hurricanes was the weakest of the school's five champions that topped human polls.

The Formula affords many comparisons of teams, eras, and sections of the country. We expect that the College Football Performance Formula will receive its share of detractors. We trust readers will give it a fair shake and consider giving it a place in judging achievements of college teams. When all is said and done, there is no sport where impression counts for so much. The College Football Performance Formula is one more viable method for teams to build an impression.

The Best Won-Loss Records since 1953:

The following list comprises the won-loss percentages of the 70 featured schools over the 58 football seasons from 1953 through 2010. It captures the on-field records of each team without any adjustments. So, a win over Bucknell or Bethune-Cookman counts the same as a win over Nebraska or Notre Dame. These results include all games: regular season, conference championship, and bowl games.

Results eventually changed by forfeit are credited by the original result that took place on the field, not the forfeiture. The total number of games played appears in parenthesis.

		Wins-Losses-Ties	Percentage
1	Ohio State (652)	493-146-13	.7661
2	Oklahoma (678)	505-162-11	.7529
3	Nebraska (689)	504-178-7	.7366
4	Penn State (666)	487-174-5	.7350
5	Alabama (687)	484-185-18	.7176
6	Texas (673)	475-188-10	.7132
7	Michigan (655)	459-184-12	.7099
8	Southern California (674)	465-191-18	.7033
9	Auburn (664)	453-199-12	.6913
10	Florida (674)	449-208-17	.6788
11	Tennesee (677)	449-208-20	.6780
12	Notre Dame (656)	437-210-9	.6730
13	Florida State (677)	445-216-16	.6691
14	Georgia (670)	432-221-17	.6575
15	Miami (656)	427-224-5	.6547
16	Arizona State (651)	422-222-7	.6536
17	Louisiana State (670)	425-226-19	.6485
18	Arkansas (666)	423-233-10	.6426
19	UCLA (652)	399-236-17	.6250
20	Virginia Tech (655)	402-242-11	.6221
21	West Virginia (655)	394-250-11	.6099
22	Brigham Young (679)	409-262-8	.6082
23	Clemson (657)	393-251-13	.6081
24	Mississippi (654)	379-263-12	.5887
25	Boston College (640)	370-264-6	.5828
26	Washington (654)	374-269-11	.5803
27	Georgia Tech (663)	369-279-15	.5679
28	Texas A&M (661)	369-280-12	.5673
29	Syracuse (642)	359-275-8	.5654
30	Colorado (659)	366-282-11	.5637
31	Michigan State (642)	355-274-13	.5631
32	Texas Tech (659)	356-289-14	.5508
33	Air Force (609)	328-270-11	.5476
34	Oregon (652)	344-295-13	.5376
35	Iowa (647)	339-293-15	.5355
36	Houston (641)	335-293-13	.5328
37	North Carolina (655)	343-304-8	.5298
38	Wisconsin (643)	331-294-18	.5288
39	Arizona (644)	333-297-14	.5280
40	Pittsburgh (649)	333-300-16	.5254
41	Missouri (653)	333-303-17	.5230
42	North Carolina State (655)	333-307-15	.5198
43	Maryland (649)	333-308-8	.5193
44	Purdue (631)	315-298-18	.5135
45	Rutgers (616)	306-304-6	.5016
46	Oklahoma State (645)	316-314-15	.5015
47	South Carolina (645)	315-317-13	.4984
48	Stanford (640)	310-317-13	.4945
49	TCU (646)	304-327-15	.4822
50	Navy (640)	301-326-13	.4805
51	Minnesota (630)	287-332-11	.4643
52	Army (624)	277-333-14	.4551
53	Mississippi State (636)	281-341-14	.4528
54	California (642)	284-345-13	.4525
55	Baylor (642)	283-351-8	.4470
56	Virginia (647)	286-355-6	.4467
57	Illinois (629)	267-346-16	.4372
58	Kentucky (639)	271-355-13	.4343
58	Kansas (642)	268-357-17	.4307

60 Washington State (636)	265-358-13	.4269
61 Kansas State (646)	269-370-7	.4218
62 Southern Methodist (617)	252-352-13	.4190
63 Oregon State (640)	262-369-9	.4164
64 Iowa State (635)	250-371-14	.4047
65 Duke (633)	243-374-16	.3965
66 Indiana (624)	230-386-8	.3750
67 Wake Forest (636)	230-396-10	.3695
68 Rice (633)	225-396-12	.3649
69 Northwestern (625)	215-403-7	.3496
70 Vanderbilt (612)	194-401-17	.3309

56 Texas Tech (28)	11-16-1	.4107
57 Michigan State (20)	8-12	.4000
58 Duke (5)	2-3	.4000
59 Virginia Tech (23)	9-14	.3913
60 Minnesota (13)	5-8	.3846
61 Oregon (21)	8-13	.3810
62 West Virginia (27)	10-17	.3704
63 Illinois (14)	5-9	.3571
64 Indiana (9)	3-6	.3333
65 Rice (6)	2-4	.3333
66 Arkansas (35)	11-23-1	.3286
67 Texas A&M (25)	8-17	.3200
68 Iowa State (10)	3-7	.3000
69 South Carolina (15)	4-11	.2667
70 Northwestern (8)	0-8	.0000

The results of the 2010 produced some changes on the overall winning percentage list:

■ Penn State lost its one-year hold on third place as Nebraska's 10 wins catapulted the Cornhuskers back ahead of the Nittany Lions.

■ Alabama and Florida moved up one spot each to fifth and 10th respectively.

■ Missouri moved up three spots to 41st.

■ West Virginia, Oregon, Wisconsin, and Mississippi State each moved up two spots.

The Best Bowl Records since 1953:

The bowl marks over the last 58 years are remarkably different than the school's overall records. Because average teams play other average teams in bowls, while the top teams have to take on the best, average programs are often able to compile surprisingly good winning percentages in post-season play.

Readers need look no further than top-rated Wake Forest. The Deamon Deacons may lead in bowl percentage but rank 67th in overall record.

	Wins-Losses-Ties	Percentage
1 Wake Forest (7)	5-2	.7143
2 Mississippi (29)	20-9	.6897
3 Penn State (41)	27-13-1	.6707
4 Rutgers (6)	4-2	.6667
5 Boston College (19)	12-7	.6316
6 North Carolina State (23)	14-8-1	.6304
7 Washington State (8)	5-3	.6250
8 Vanderbilt (4)	2-1-1	.6250
9 Florida State (39)	23-14-2	.6154
10 California (13)	8-5	.6154
11 Syracuse (22)	13-8-1	.6136
12 Southern California (36)	22-14	.6111
13 Oklahoma State (18)	11-7	.6111
14 Auburn (34)	20-13-1	.6029
15 Oklahoma (39)	23-15-1	.6026
16 Arizona State (20)	12-8	.6000
17 Army (5)	3-2	.6000
18 Georgia (39)	22-15-2	.5897
19 Louisiana State (36)	21-15	.5833
20t Mississippi State (12)	7-5	.5833
20t Oregon State (12)	7-5	.5833
22 Iowa (25)	14-10-1	.5800
23 Washington (26)	15-11	.5769
24 Alabama (47)	25-20-2	.5532
25 Tennessee (40)	22-18	.5500
26 Missouri (22)	12-10	.5455
27 Kansas (11)	6-5	.5455
28 Stanford (13)	7-6	.5385
29 Miami (30)	16-14	.5333
30 Purdue (15)	8-7	.5333
31 Wisconsin (21)	11-10	.5238
32 Nebraska (46)	24-22	.5217
33 North Carolina (25)	13-12	.5200
34 UCLA (28)	14-13-1	.5179
35 Texas (41)	20-20-1	.5000
36 Florida (36)	18-18	.5000
37 Georgia Tech (30)	15-15	.5000
38 Air Force (21)	10-10-1	.5000
39 TCU (19)	9-9-1	.5000
40 Notre Dame (29)	14-15	.4828
41 Pittsburgh (23)	11-12	.4783
42 Houston (18)	8-9-1	.4722
43 Baylor (15)	7-8	.4677
44 Arizona (14)	6-7-1	.4643
45 Ohio State (39)	18-21	.4615
46 Kentucky (11)	5-6	.4545
47 Maryland (21)	9-11-1	.4524
48 Clemson (29)	13-16	.4483
49 Michigan (36)	16-20	.4444
50 Colorado (27)	12-15	.4444
51 Southern Methodist (9)	4-5	.4444
52 Navy (16)	7-9	.4375
53 Brigham Young (29)	12-16-1	.4310
54 Kansas State (14)	6-8	.4286
55 Virginia (17)	7-10	.4118

GREATEST COLLEGE PLAYERS SINCE 1953

What follows are the authors' choices for the best 250 players since 1953:

■ Offense:

Wide Receivers/Wingbacks: Fred Biletnikoff (Florida State), Tim Brown (Notre Dame), Anthony Carter (Michigan), Desmond Howard (Michigan) Larry Fitzgerald (Pittsburgh), Raghib "Rocket" Ismail (Notre Dame), John Jefferson (Arizona State), Johnny Rodgers (Nebraska), Charles Rogers (Michigan State), Ron Sellers (Florida State), J.J. Stokes (UCLA), Peter Warrick (Florida State) Roy Williams (Texas).

Tight Ends: Ron Beagle (Navy), Dave Casper (Notre Dame), Mike Ditka (Pittsburgh), Gordon Hudson (BYU), Ron Kramer (Michigan), Keith Jackson (Oklahoma), Ted Kwalick (Penn State), Ken MacAfee (Notre Dame), Pat Richter (Wisconsin), Kellen Winslow, Jr. (Miami), Dave Young (Purdue).

Tackles: Tony Boselli (Southern California), Jimbo Covert (Pittsburgh), Irv Eatman (UCLA), Jumbo Elliott (Michigan), Bill Fralic (Pittsburgh), John Hicks (Ohio State), Stan Jones (Maryland), George Kunz (Notre Dame), Tony Mandarich (Michigan State), Mark May (Pittsburgh), Chris McIntosh (Wisconsin), Jonathan Ogden (UCLA), Orlando Pace (Ohio State), Chris Samuels (Alabama), Jerry Sisemore (Texas), Ron Yary (Southern California).

Guards: Bob Brown (Nebraska), Brad Budde (Southern California), Randy Cross (UCLA), Mark Donahue (Michigan), Roy Foster (Southern California), John Hannah (Alabama), Calvin Jones (Iowa), Chip Kell (Tennessee), Randall McDaniel (Arizona State), Reggie McKenzie (Michigan), Jim Parker (Ohio State), Greg Roberts (Oklahoma), Dean Steinkuhler (Nebraska), Del Wilkes (South Carolina), Steve Wisniewski (Penn State).

Centers: Tom Brahaney (Oklahoma), Kurt Burris (Oklahoma), Greg Eslinger (Minnesota), E.J. Holub (Texas Tech), Dave Huffman (Notre Dame), Bob Johnson (Tennessee), Jay Leeuwenberg (Colorado), Jim Richter (North Carolina State), Dave Rimington (Nebraska), Dwight Stephenson (Alabama).

Quarterbacks: Troy Aikman (Oklahoma and UCLA), Ty Detmer (Brigham Young), Doug Flutie (Boston College), Tommie Frazier (Nebraska), Turner Gill (Nebraska), Bob Griese (Purdue), Mark Herrmann (Purdue), Matt Leinart (Southern California), Chuck Long (Iowa), Peyton Manning (Tennessee), Dan Marino (Pittsburgh), Jim McMahon (Brigham Young), Jim Plunkett (Stanford), Philip Rivers (North Carolina State), Roger Staubach (Navy), Tim Tebow (Florida), Michael Vick (Virginia Tech), Charlie Ward (Florida State), Vince Young (Texas).

Halfbacks/Tailbacks: Marcus Allen (Southern California), Jimmy Brown (Syracuse), Reggie Bush (Southern California), Earl Campbell (Texas), Billy Cannon (LSU), Ki-Jana Carter (Penn State), Howard Cassady (Ohio State), Ron Dayne (Wisconsin), Eric Dickerson (Southern Methodist), Tony Dorsett (Pittsburgh), Archie Griffin (Ohio State), Bo Jackson (Auburn), Rueben Mayes (Washington State), Terry Miller (Oklahoma State), Darrin Nelson (Stanford), Steve Owens (Oklahoma), Mike Rozier (Nebraska), Barry Sanders (Oklahoma State), O.J. Simpson (Southern California), Billy Sims (Oklahoma), Jim Swink (Texas Christian), Anthony Thompson (Indiana), LaDainian Tomlinson (Texas Christian), Herschel Walker (Georgia), Ricky Williams (Texas).

Fullbacks: Mike Alstott (Purdue), Alan Ameche (Wisconsin), Joe Childress (Auburn), Larry Conjar (Notre Dame), Larry Csonka (Syracuse), Sam Cunningham (Southern California), Bill Enyart (Oregon State), Bob Ferguson (Ohio State), Charlie Flowers (Mississippi), Jim Grabowski (Illinois), Brad Muster (Stanford), Tom Nowatzke (Indiana), Cory Schlesinger (Nebraska), Mosi Tatupu (Southern California), Steve Worster (Texas).

Place Kickers: Tony Franklin (Texas A&M), Martin Gramatica (Kansas State), Steve Little (Arkansas), Jason Hanson (Washington State), Sebastian Janikowski (Florida State), Nate Kaeding (Iowa), John Lee (UCLA).

■ Defense:

Ends: Peter Boulware (Florida State), Courtney Brown (Penn State), Ross Browner (Notre Dame), Leroy Cook (Alabama), Dwight Freeney (Syracuse), Hugh Green (Pittsburgh), Ted Hendricks (Miami), E.J. Junior (Alabama), Corey Moore (Virginia Tech), Julius Peppers (North Carolina), Billy Ray Smith, Jr. (Arkansas), Bubba Smith (Michigan State), Art Still (Kentucky), Terrell Suggs (Arizona State).

Tackles: Bobby Bell (Minnesota), Jerome Brown (Miami), Jack Ellena (UCLA), Steve Emtman (Washington), John Henderson (Tennessee), Chad Hennings (Air Force), Alex Karras (Iowa), Charlie Krueger (Texas A&M), Bob Lilly (Texas Christian), Lou Michaels (Kentucky), Michael Dean Perry (Clemson), Loyd Phillips (Arkansas), Mike Reid (Penn State), Tracy Rocker (Auburn), Warren Sapp (Miami), Lee Roy Selmon (Oklahoma), Kenneth Sims (Texas), Mike Stensrud (Iowa State), Ndamukong Suh (Nebraska), Randy White (Maryland).

Nose Guards: Tony Casillas (Oklahoma), Rich Glover (Nebraska), Louis Kelcher (Southern Methodist), Tim Krumrie (Wisconsin), Mike Ruth (Boston College), Ron Simmons (Florida State), Robert Stewart (Alabama), Jim Stillwagon (Ohio State), Rob Waldrop (Arizona), Chris Zorich (Notre Dame).

Linebackers: Cornelius Bennett (Alabama), Brian Bosworth (Oklahoma), Franklin Brooks (Georgia Tech), Michael Brooks (Louisiana State), Dick Butkus (Illinois), Shane Conlan (Penn State), Quentin Coryatt (Texas A&M), Pat Fitzgerald (Northwestern), Randy Gradishar (Ohio State), Wayne Harris (Arkansas), E.J. Henderson (Maryland), Dana Howard (Illinois), Ricky Hunley (Arizona), Marvin Jones (Florida State), Lee Roy Jordan (Alabama), Steve Kiner (Tennessee), Jim Lynch (Notre Dame), Larry Morris (Georgia Tech), Dat Nguyen (Texas A&M), Tommy Nobis (Texas), Dennis Onkontz (Penn State), Jack Pardee (Texas A&M), Bob Pellegrini (Maryland), Jerry Robinson (UCLA), Mike Singletary (Baylor), Gary Spani (Kansas State), Chris Spielman (Ohio State), Larry Station (Iowa), Darryl Talley (West Virginia), Jerry Tubbs (Oklahoma), George Webster (Michigan State), Richard Wood (Southern California).

Cornerbacks: Champ Bailey (Georgia), Luther Bradley (Notre Dame), Dave Brown (Michigan), John David Crow (Texas A&M), Lindon Crow (Southern California), Ernie Davis (Syracuse), Joe Haden (Florida), Michael Haynes (Arizona State), Leroy Keyes (Purdue), Terrence Newman (Kansas State), Johnny Robinson (Louisiana State), Whitey Rouviere (Miami), Deion Sanders (Florida State), Shawn Springs (Ohio State), Clendon Thomas (Oklahoma), Roger Wehrli (Missouri), Charles Woodson (Michigan), Al Worley (Washington).

Safeties: Dick Anderson (Colorado), Steve Atwater (Arkansas), Eric Berry (Tennessee), Bennie Blades (Miami), Mark Carrier (Southern California), Russell Carter (Southern Methodist), Chuck Cecil (Arizona), Tommy Casanova (LSU), Thom Darden (Michigan), Kenny Easley (UCLA), Thomas Everett (Baylor), Terry Hoage (Georgia), Johnny Johnson (Texas), Terry Kinard (Clemson), Edward Reed (Miami), Jake Scott (Georgia), Jack Tatum (Ohio State), Brad Van Pelt (Michigan State), Roy Williams (Oklahoma).

Punters: Travis Dorsch (Purdue), Russell Erxleben (Texas), Shane Lechler (Texas A&M), Jim Miller (Mississippi), Reggie Roby (Iowa), Todd Sauerbrun (West Virginia).

THE

COLLEGE FOOTBALL ENCYCLOPEDIA

1953

The Year of the Fainting Irish, King Terps in the New Basketball Conference, and Limited Substitution

A painfully controversial 14-14 tie with Iowa (5-3-1) on November 21 cost Notre Dame (9-0-1) its fifth to-date national championship and negatively placed the image-conscious Roman Catholic school on every editorial page in America. The Fighting Irish had held a spot atop the Associated Press ballot every week from the preseason until the deadlock with Iowa. Gaining lots of yards but making several errors against the determined Hawkeyes, Notre Dame found itself out of timeouts in the closing seconds of both halves. The Irish managed to score a vital touchdown each time after faking injuries to stop the clock. "Fainting" Frank Varrichione, a tackle, earned an unenviable nickname that afternoon. The ploy was perfectly legal at the time and Notre Dame was hardly the only team to use it, but the whole affair left a black eye on the countenance of the proud Fighting Irish.

The uproar in the press over the incident was seismic. In those days, voter participation in the Associated Press college football poll was somewhat arbitrary and voluntary so long as a voter carried sportswriting credentials. The next ballot after the tainted tie was scheduled for November 23. It attracted 251 sportswriting pollsters from around the nation, when only 150 ballots had been tabulated the previous week. All those indignant new voters pushed Iowa from no. 20 to no. 9. Emotional support for Iowa was so dramatic that even with their mediocre record, the Hawkeyes picked up 10 of 378 first place votes in the final AP Poll on November 30 and finished ninth, ahead of such superior-record teams as no. 10 West Virginia (8-2), no. 11 Texas Tech (11-1), and even no. 15 Wisconsin (6-2-1), which had defeated Iowa only a month earlier.

Fainting had taken on a more serious tone in South Bend earlier in the season. In his 11th and final year at Notre Dame, intense 45-year-old coach Frank Leahy collapsed of a severe pancreatic attack during a big victory over previously unbeaten Georgia Tech (9-2-1). Leahy sat out some of the Irish's closing games and ultimately retired with the second best winning percentage ever. His 13-year record was 107-13-9 (.864) at Notre Dame and Boston College. Knute Rockne's .881 percentage at Notre Dame was the only major college or pro coaching mark ever to eclipse that of Leahy's.

A new major conference bloomed in 1953. Seven of the larger schools of the 17-member Southern Conference broke away to form the Atlantic Coast Conference. Charter members were Clemson (3-5-1), Duke (7-2-1), Maryland (10-1), North Carolina (4-6), North Carolina State (1-9), South Carolina (7-3), and Wake Forest (3-6-1). Virginia (1-8), 15 years an independent, would join in 1954.

Perhaps the best-ever team at Maryland used the fresh setting of the new ACC and an undefeated run through 10 regular season foes to make a late surge to the top of the polls. Maryland, the only unbeaten and untied team in the regular season, outscored its foes 298 to 31, and only Missouri (6-4) in the season opener kept within two touchdowns of the king Terrapins. Maryland defeated Southeastern Conference champion Alabama (6-2-3) by 21-0 and SEC runner-up Mississippi (7-2-1) by 38-0 among a good slate of teams that posted a .6061 winning percentage. (Notre Dame's opponents achieved a .6080 percentage.)

No one could know at the time the fledgling ACC would become known primarily as a powerful basketball conference, so pollsters harbored no preconceptions in voting the league its first national football title. Maryland's would be the ACC's last national football title until Clemson's surprise run in 1981. Duke and North Carolina led the way as top basketball programs—ACC teams won two titles and made 17 Final Four appearances between 1953-81—it became fashionable, rightly or wrongly, to perceive the ACC as less than a great football conference. It took the 1990s arrival of powerful Florida State—a relative nobody in 1953, by the way—to enhance the idea that the ACC was sufficiently competitive on the gridiron to be capable of turning out national football champions.

Amidst the glory of taking the national crown, Maryland promptly lost 7-0 in the Orange Bowl to coach Bud Wilkinson's Oklahoma (9-1-1) team. As was the custom then, neither AP writers or UP coaches were polled after New Year's Day, so the Terrapins' national title stayed on the books, however questionable its legitimacy it might appear under history's scrutiny.

Oklahoma, ranked no. 4 before the Orange Bowl but perhaps the best team in the nation by season's end, had started poorly. The Sooners opened with a war-like loss to Notre Dame and a tie with Pittsburgh (3-5-1), which would be the last blemishes on Oklahoma's record until 1957.

The Orange Bowl game pitted two coaches who shared a strong connection from the previous decade. Jim Tatum, head man at Maryland was hired to lead Oklahoma in the post World War II era. He brought with him to Norman a bright young assistant, Bud Wilkinson. During the interview process, Wilkinson had made quite an impression, so the powers-that-be were only too happy to tap Wilkinson as Oklahoma's new coach when Tatum ran to Maryland after only one year (1946) with the Sooners.

The craziest play in bowl history, perhaps in all of football history, occurred in the Cotton Bowl. Brilliant Rice (9-2) halfback Dicky Moegle circled his right end from the Owls' five yard-line in the second quarter. Moegle burst into the clear only to be stunned by an off-the-bench tackle by Alabama's captain Tommy Lewis. Moegle was awarded a touchdown, and Lewis was profusely apologetic afterward. Such sideline misbehavior by players or coaches had and has happened occasionally but never in so conspicuous a situation as a New Year's Day bowl game. Maybe America's odd notion of celebrity was proved in the aftermath. A self-conscious and embarrassed Lewis, not Moegle, received all the attention in a mutual appearance on the next Sunday's "Ed Sullivan Show," CBS' top variety program on television.

Army (7-1-1) completed a swift return to prominence, which was launched on a 14-13 squeaker over then-no. 7 Duke and anchored on a season-ending 20-7 swamping of Navy (4-3-2). It helped that Army faced a schedule of teams that only achieved a .440 winning percentage. Coach Red Blaik's squad had been all but wiped out when 37 players were among 90 cadets dismissed in August 1951 from the academy for academic violations of West Point's honor code, that is, sharing exam information and failing to report knowledge of the exam cheating. Many of the banished cadets propped themselves up to become respected students and fine players at civilian schools, but their absence in 1951-52 greatly harmed Army's football results.

Every college team faced the difficult adjustment to a new limited substitution rule in 1953 that eliminated the use of separate offensive and defensive squads as we know them today. The new order of college football meant all players had to condition themselves for long, unrelieved spells on both offense and defense. Bobby Garrett, Stanford (6-3-1) quarterback and safety, who received All-America mention, remarkably led the nation in both completions as a passer and interceptions as a defender.

Coach Biggie Munn of Rose Bowl champion Michigan State (9-1) howled loudest, claiming imposed defensive duty would chase from the sport such light, quick attackers as Don Coleman, his 180-lb. All-America tackle of 1951. Munn was correct about small linemen fading from football, but the proliferation of 250- to 300-pounders came of better diets in future years and weight-lifting, a training method that first gained universal acceptance in the 1960s.

Auburn (7-3-1) coach Shug Jordan had his own twist on the substitution rule, using two units that each played both offense and defense. The Tigers were one of the year's surprises, reversing a 7-23 record of 1950-52. Among the regular Tiger backs were quarterback Vince Dooley, Georgia's future great coach, and halfback Fob James, future governor of Alabama. Auburn qualified for its first of three consecutive Gator Bowls.

Option running plays out of the Split-T made up the primary offensive attack of 1953. The ancient Single Wing offense lived on, despite some alumni protests. Pacific Coast champion UCLA (8-2) was highly successful with it, but other long-time purveyors of the compact, power formation like Tennessee (6-4-1), without recently retired coaching great Robert Neyland, and Princeton (5-4) slipped after several lofty seasons.

A forerunner to the Wishbone offense of the 1970s, the Split-T and its hard-to-read, quick-hitting inside handoffs and wide option pitchouts was the perfect easy-to-learn offense for players scrambling to master play on both offense and defense. Many coaches focused on defense first, and the Split-T could accommodate a back who was sharp on defense and could serve as an adequate runner or blocker. Rifle-armed throwers who also could tackle and play pass defense were in short supply. Zeke Bratkowski of Georgia (3-8) might have been the best pure passer of the season, but had several rough moments as a pass defender. The 1953 consensus All-America team was revealing; it listed no pass-oriented player in the backfield. The All-America backs included run-oriented halfbacks Johnny Lattner of Notre Dame and J.C. Caroline of Illinois. The others were Paul Giel of Minnesota and Paul Cameron of UCLA, Single Wing tailbacks who could pass but thought run first.

The single platoon approach was chipped away year by year by a variety of substitution liberalization rules, but it lasted, in effect, for 11 seasons

until 1963. Was it a success? If the objective was creating balance so that dozens of teams could compete with traditional top 10 schools, like Notre Dame, Ohio State, and Southern California, it worked very well. During that 11-year stretch there were teams that won national titles that frequently played at a medium-level otherwise. Teams like Maryland, UCLA, Auburn, and Syracuse won their first and only national titles between 1953 and 1963. Competitive during the single platoon era were Baylor, Duke, Kentucky, Mississippi, Missouri, Rice, SMU, and TCU. Each of those teams has had more downs that ups ever since.

Why did this parity occur? With only 11 regular players instead of 22, a school could develop a star or two and make its team competitive. A winning record, regardless of size of the school, influenced more top recruits to attend that school. For example, Duke, a school with high academic requirements and small enrollment, started with stars Ed Meadows and Jerry Barger, who led to Sonny Jurgensen and Wray Carlton, who led to Mike McGee and Tee Moorman, who led to Jay Wilkinson and Mike Curtis. From 1953 to '63, Duke enjoyed a 70-36-7 mark. Duke may be an isolated case, but its football record hasn't been close since.

On the other hand, college football—not far removed from top-of-the-sports-world status it shared with baseball—was challenged fiercely in the late 1950s and early 1960s for fan interest by the once-ragamuffin National Football League. College football's single platoon clearly fatigued the starting players. Tired players meant a much slower game, and the colleges were forced to react to speed up their game with free substitution by the mid-1960s.

Coach Blaik of Army complained bitterly about the ironman approach, claiming the new rule exhausted players and that it was especially tough on West Point cadets, who had the additional daily physical rigors of military academy life as well as a demanding academic cirriculum.

Without kicking specialists to call upon, wry Clemson coach Frank Howard griped that he had "never seen so many 15 and 20 yard punts. Why not (be able to) send out a boy who can kick the ball 50 yards?"

Perhaps the changes of 1953 simply were baffling to everybody. No less an accomplished coach than Bear Bryant was busy one Saturday with player substitution bookkeeping and lost track of an extra point miss by Louisiana State (5-3-3). Bryant believed for nearly two hours afterward that his Kentucky (7-2-1) team—which he chewed out for a poor performance—had lost 7-6 to the Tigers when in reality the game had ended in a 6-6 tie.

For better or worse, limited substitution created a different and interesting game. In those days, it was far easier for fans to follow the ups and downs of a whole nation of college teams because watching the exploits of only 11 regular players made it a simple pleasure to track all of college football. It certainly wasn't the golden age of the sport, but it clearly was fascinating.

Milestones

■ NCAA created new rule to limit player substitution. Once players left the field, they could return to play only in following quarter. Virtually all players were forced to compete on both offense and defense.

■ Far-flung, 17-member Southern Conference split, with seven schools forming new Atlantic Coast Conference: Clemson, Duke, Maryland, North Carolina, North Carolina State, South Carolina and Wake Forest.

■ By joining Western Conference to complete its 10-school group, Michigan State competed for its first Big Ten title. Despite its name, Big Ten Conference had embraced only nine members since University of Chicago abandoned football after 1939 season.

■ American Indian Jim Thorpe, voted in 1950 by Associated Press as greatest athlete and football player of 1st half of 20th Century, died of heart attack at age 65 on March 28. Enrolled in Carlisle (Pa.) Industrial Indian School, Thorpe twice was selected All-America halfback (1909-10) and later would play parts of 9 years of pro football after baseball career primarily with New York Giants and Cincinnati Reds. Thorpe also excelled at track and field. Because of prior semi-pro appearance in baseball, he had been stripped of Olympic gold medals in pentathlon and decathlon after 1912 Games. Jeff Cravath, former Southern California coach (1942-50), who won 4 Pacific Coast Conference titles, died at 50 as result of auto accident. Walter Koppisch, All-America halfback at Columbia (1922-24) also died. John Pappas, 21, senior guard for Boston University, died of head injury sustained in Syracuse game on October 2.

■ Longest winning streaks entering season:

Michigan State 24	Georgia Tech 17	Texas 7

■ Coaching Changes:

	Incoming	Outgoing
Arkansas	Bowden Wyatt	Otis Douglas
North Carolina	George Barclay	Carl Snavely
Southern Methodist	Woody Woodard	H.N. Russell
Tennessee	Harvey Robinson	Gen. Robert Neyland
Texas Christian	Abe Martin	Dutch Meyer
Vanderbilt	Art Guepe	Bill Edwards
Virginia	Ned McDonald	Art Guepe
Washington	John Cherberg	Howard Odell

Preseason AP Poll

1 Notre Dame (84)	1688	11 Texas	85
2 Michigan State (24)	1305	12 Rice	66
3 Georgia Tech (24)	1128	13 Navy	56
4 UCLA (12)	1065	14 California	26
5 Alabama (18)	968	15 Florida	24
6 Oklahoma (3)	672	16 West Virginia	20
7 Ohio State (3)	666	17tTennessee	18
8 Southern California	165	17tPittsburgh	18
9 Maryland (1)	143	19 Princeton	17
10 Duke (2)	86	20 Baylor	15

September 19, 1953

(Fri) Mississippi Southern 25 ALABAMA 19: Strong-armed Mississippi Southern (1-0) HB Hugh Pepper did more running (115y, including dazzling 66y TD) and catching (45y TD) than he did pitching in huge upset of no. 5 Crimson Tide (0-1). Pepper would go on to hurl one National League win for the Pittsburgh Pirates in summer of 1954, but would finish with 2-8 career pitching mark. Alabama (0-1) was able to build 19-12 lead by H on TDs by FB Tommy Lewis, HB Bill Oliver, and E Curtis Lynch. Bama regulars wilted in 4th Q, necessitating reverses taking over. Eagles proceeded to score 2 TDs against Alabama subs. Mississippi Southern, it was learned next day, had made membership application to new ACC, but never accomplished that goal.

Georgia 32 VILLANOVA 19: Don Shea, hometown Philadelphian playing G for Georgia Bulldogs (1-0), helped hold Villanova (0-1) A-A HB Gene Filipsky to 9/38y rushing as Georgia rallied from 12-0 1st Q deficit before 97,803. Wildcats FB Jack Helm (12/44y) scored at end of 81y drive, and 3 mins later, HB Ralph Cecere galloped 63y with TD pass from QB Joe McNicholas. Georgia FB Bob Clemens rushed 13/118y, including 2nd Q TD, and QB Zeke Bratkowski threw 10-18/196y, TD, and his passes of 30 and 12y to E Johnny Carson led to another 2nd Q TD for 13-12 H edge. Bulldogs put it away in 3rd Q as HB Jimmy Campagna and FB Howard Kelly scored on runs for 26-12 lead. Large crowd resulted from "Supermarket Bowl" promotion dreamed up by new Wildcats AD Bud Dudley. Acme food chain bought 60,000 tickets and distributed them at no charge to customers, many of whom saw their 1st live football action.

Duke 20 SOUTH CAROLINA 7: In 1st-ever Atlantic Coast Conf game, Duke (1-0) captain, E Howard Pitt, played key role in capturing victory. Pitt caught 29y pass from QB Worth Lutz (TD rushing) as Blue Devils charged 85y to HB Red Smith's 4y scoring run on 1st opportunity they had. Late in 2nd Q, DE Pitt dropped into secondary to pick off pass by South Carolina (0-1) QB Johnny Gramling (9-18/128y, INT) and race 25y to Gamecocks 43YL. Duke sub HB Junior McRoy converted TO into 4y TD run and 13-0 H edge. Carolina scored in 3rd on broken play: In taking low punt snap, HB-P Carl Brazell was pressured by trio of Blue defenders. Brazell stepped aside and found running room at sideline to charge 43y to score.

WILLIAM & MARY 16 Wake Forest 14 (Richmond): Wake Forest (0-1) HB John Parham dashed 15y for opening TD, only to be matched by Indians FB Bill Bowman on 71y TD charge in 1st Q. Go-ahead margin at 10-7 for William & Mary (1-0) came on 4th Q 27y FG by K L. Quinby "Hadacol" Hines, once 150-lb frosh waterboy who made himself into effective K. Tribe QB Charlie Sumner raced to 33y TD for 16-7 edge after being set up by Bowman's 42y run.

Texas A&M 7 KENTUCKY 6: Little did he know it at that time, but Kentucky (0-1) coach Paul "Bear" Bryant welcomed his soon-to-be-future team to Lexington. At season's end, Bryant would be swayed away from Kentucky by loss of top recruit Paul Hornung to Notre Dame and his footballers forever playing 2nd fiddle to coach Adolph Rupp's Wildcat basketball team. Spirited 1st Q play fell into scoreless slumber until late in 3rd Q when Texas A&M (1-0) ignited drive that carried to Cats 9YL. On 1st play of 4th Q, Aggies QB Don Ellis hit HB Connie Magouirk with pass to 1YL, and after 2 Wildcats offside PENs, Texas A&M HB-K Joe Boring booted decisive x-pt. Kentucky made it to Aggies 23YL, lost ball on downs, but eventually took it back at A&M 47YL. With 5:50 left, Wildcats FB Tom Fillion powered 9y for TD, but conv try blew up, and QB-holder Herbie Hunt unsuccessfully tried to flip pass to HB Steve Meilinger.

LOUISIANA STATE 20 Texas 7: LSU (1-0) had used players both ways in 1952, so Tigers enjoyed easy conversion to new substitution rule that forced 2-way play of all players. Bengals also played with spirit and took control early on. Although LSU HB George Brancato lost 1st Q FUM at Texas (0-1) 17YL, he came back after Tigers DE Sammy Murphy's FUM REC at Texas 10YL, to make shoestring pass catch at 8YL and then ran to 5YL.. FB Jerry Marchand scored for Tigers on next play for 7-0 lead in 1st Q. Upset of Longhorns was led by HB-turned-QB Al Doggett, who was not listed on preseason depth chart, but threw 36y pass to Marchand to set up 3rd Q TD that built 14-0 edge. In typical season opener, Longhorns were doomed by FUMs and PENs until they got on scoreboard in 4th Q on HB Doug Cameron's TD. Texas suffered only its 2nd loss in 62 season openers.

Maryland 20 MISSOURI 6: No. 9 Maryland (1-0) Ts Tom Breunich and Stan Jones carved big holes in Tigers (0-1) line, which would eventually yield 225y on ground. Sharp blocking also broke Terps HB Chet "The Jet" Hanulak for 61y TD flight in opening 2 mins of 1st Q. Maryland appeared on its way to rout until Missouri stubbornly pieced together 70y TD trip in 2nd Q after making INT. Tigers QB Tony Scardino completed 4 passes on drive to his TD sneak, but Mizzou's aerial attack would suffer 4 INTs and add only 3 more completions. Tigers missed 2 other scoring chances in 2nd Q and trailed 7-6 at H. INT late in 3rd Q produced Maryland's next TD early in 4th Q after, but not before Terps were pushed back from Tigers' 1-ft line to 5YL on 3 D surges led by Mizzou G-LB Terry Roberts. Maryland QB Bernie Faloney dropped back to pass on 4th down and dashed to TD through Mizzou's unprotected left flank. Maryland sub QB Charlie Boxold added TD pass to E Jim Kilgallen on game's last play.

Oregon 20 NEBRASKA 12: Favored Nebraska welcomed network TV cameras to Lincoln but suffered fuzzy picture. Bad punt snaps by Cornhuskers (0-1) C Tom Oliver set up Ducks for 2 early TDs. Oregon (1-0) G Jack Patera recovered QB-P Johnny Bordogna's inability to recover snap at Nebraska 36YL, and FB Cece Hughes hammered over for 6-0 lead. Ducks soon went up 13-0 when HB Dick James swept LE for 9y after Bordogna could manage only 7y punt under pressure caused by snap that sailed over his head. Soph HB Rex Fischer, 1 of long line of family members to play for Huskers, scored in 2nd Q, but Oregon HB Ted Anderson raced 57y for TD only 3 plays after following KO. So, Ducks led 20-6 at H. Fischer whipped 63y TD pass to HB Dennis Korinek in 4th Q to draw Nebraska within 20-12, but hope died when Oregon T Glenn Berry burst through to block K Korinek's x-pt try. C Oliver's odd day took another turn on 4th down pass in 4th Q. From Oregon 32YL, Bordogna's pass was deflected by Ducks defender and caught by Oliver at 18YL. It was nullified due to Nebraska's ineligible receiver downfield, which turned out to be unlucky Oliver.

RICE 20 Florida 16: Florida (0-1) welcomed back 1952 All-SEC FB Rick Casares, who until 5 days before opener had been shelved by auto accident injuries. Casares was in and out of game, his playing time limited to 5-min spurts. But, he bombed beautiful 47y FG in 3rd Q. Meanwhile, Rice (1-0) took wrappings off speedy jr HB Dicky Moegle, who had failed to earn letter in 1952. Moegle scored on 6y sweep in 1st Q, 29y pitchout in 2nd Q after C-LB Leo Rucka's INT, and, on heels of Casares' FG, took impromtu lateral from QB Leroy Fenstemaker and ran 13y to cap 68y drive for 20-3 lead in 3rd Q. Gators frosh FB-DB Joe Brodsky recovered FUM at Owls 20YL late in 3rd Q, and HB Tommy Haddock executed 19y reverse run for TD. Back in for game's closing mins, Casares plowed for 16y and caught 28y screen pass on path to QB Doug Dickey's TD sneak.

Colorado 21 WASHINGTON 20: Johnny Cherberg launched what would turn out to be unhappy and scandalous 3-year coaching career at Washington (0-1). With Colorado (1-0) regular FB Don Shelly sidelined with injury, soph subs Homer Jenkins and Emerson Wilson shared FB spot to good results. Versatile Jenkins, who occasionally switched over to TB and all-in-all served as Buffs' best runner, passed to E Gary Knafelc for 1st Q TD, and quick-kicked Buffaloes (1-0) to upset win. Not all was rosy for Jenkins: Washington (0-1) earned 7-7 deadlock in 1st Q on G Jim Noe's stunning 77y TD RET of Jenkins' mid-air FUM. FB Mike Monroe scored twice in 2nd H for Huskies, his 1st TD coming in 3rd Q for brief 13-7 lead. But, Washington K Wendell Niles missed vital x-pt. Colorado struck quickly from that moment: WB Frank Bernardi launched 49y TD pass to Knafelc, and Wilson charged 41y for 21-13 lead before 3rd Q ended.

Baylor 25 CALIFORNIA 0: Using small group dubbed "Furious 15" under new substitution rules, Baylor coach George Sauer unleashed 414y O, which was sparked by 59-min QB-S Cotton Davidson. Baylor (1-0) scored on runs in each Q as Davidson tallied twice and passed 8-15/236y, 2 INTs. HB L.G. Dupre and FB Jerry Coody tallied Bears' other TDs. Upset margin equaled worst defeat in coach Pappy Waldorf's 6 years at California (0-1). No. 14 Golden Bears stormed 71y in 3 big plays—HB Al Talley's 15y run, FB Don Marks' 30y sweep, and HB Jim Dillon's 26y burst up middle—to Baylor 8YL to open 2nd H, but threat died with failure to covert 4th down. Coody's TD was set up by DB Dupre's REC of FUM by Talley at Cal 38YL in 3rd Q.

College of Pacific 25 STANFORD 20: Stanford (0-1) launched early 7-0 lead on T Barry Smith's REC of FUM at Pacific (1-0) 33YL. From 5YL, Indians HB Ron Cook soon scored off RT standing up. COP narrowed H deficit to 13-12 as HB Art Liebscher went up middle for TD. Surprising Tigers built 25-13 edge while continuing to successfully probe midsection of Indians' D on FB Willie Richardson's 2nd TD run and QB Skip Ottoson's sneak. Slow-starting Stanford star QB Bobby Garrett (10-23/110y, TD) warmed up with 4 late completions, including TD to E Marv Tennefoss. Indians could not, however, avoid upset in 1st-ever meeting of California schools.

September 26, 1953

(Fri) MIAMI 27 Florida State 0: Hiding its bag of tricks from scouts of next week's foe, Baylor, Miami (1-0) started slowly, managing its 1st TD late in 2nd Q. Florida State (0-1) took ball away from Hurricanes at FSU 14, 25, and 24YLs in early going, but its lack of depth made it wilt in south Florida heat. Frosh QBs Lee Corso and Harry Massey could complete only 4-19/49y, 3 INTs, and FSU's aerial failure hurt it on 4 trips inside Miami 30YL. Hurricanes DE Tom Pepsin whacked Corso's arm to send pass into hands of DB Whitey Rouviere in 2nd Q. After FB Gordon Malloy rushed for 25, 10, 8, and 2y, Pepsin took pass to 4YL to set up TD run by Rouviere. Pepsin also recovered FUM to lead to later TD and made tackles for loss of 9, 8, and 14y while protecting Miami's lead.

(Fri) UCLA 19 Kansas 7: Kansas (0-2) running backs cut through powder-blue-clad no. 4 Bruins (2-0) as if they were powder puffs in 1st Q at LA Coliseum. Jayhawks owned 7-0 lead after 60y march, outgained UCLA by 110y to 10y, and earned 9 1st downs to none. Kansas climaxed its on-foot fling when HB Ralph Moody (16/69y) thumped over from 1y out. Thanks to pass interference PEN at KU 22YL, Uclans tied it in 2nd Q after finally solving Jayhawks run game and when ace TB Paul Cameron (16/52y) tore off T for 4y TD. In 3rd Q, Bruins FB Bob "Pogo" Davenport (13/65y) bounced for 1y TD leap at end of 55y trip, and BB Terry Debay blocked punt which E Myron Berliner lugged 25y to Kansas 16YL. Cameron followed with 9y TD sweep to fix final score. Although Jayhawks FB Frank Sabbatini (13/85y) was game's leading rusher, UCLA ground machine virtually had caught up at finish: Jayhawks' 190y to Bruins' 178y.

BOSTON COLLEGE 14 Clemson 14: Eagles (0-0-1) HB Dick "Zig Zag" Zotti roared 69y to TD with 1st Q punt, and BC led 14-0 at H. But, Clemson (1-0-1) E Scott Jackson turned momentum with 3rd Q blocked punt for score that pulled Tigers within TD. HB Jimmy Wells sparked Tigers' tying 4th Q 75y TD drive with 32y gain and capped it with 1y TD plunge. Starting T Frank Morze, enormously large for 1953 standards at 230 lbs., was moved all about Boston College's lineup and sparkled at E, T, and C.

Holy Cross 28 Dartmouth 6 (Lynn, Mass.): Dartmouth (0-1) home game in Hanover, N.H., was moved to Manning Bowl near Boston to accommodate TV, which, in 1953, had difficulty carting its massive equipment far from major cities. Crusaders (1-0) FB Gerry O'Leary dashed 30y only time he touched ball, but suffered compound fracture below knee in 4th Q and was never again same performer. Tall E Jack Carroll caught 26 and 40y TD passes in 1st H for Holy Cross' 14-0 H edge. HB Warren O'Donnell caught 20y TD pass from QB Bill Haley in 4th Q as Crusaders went up 28-0. QB John Reilly fired 65y TD to E Dave McLaughlin to finally to put Dartmouth on scoreboard in late going. Each school earned $60,000 share from TV appearance fund.

West Virginia 17 PITTSBURGH 7: Not in 30 years had West Virginia (1-0) won 2 in row over nearby Pittsburgh (0-1) rivals. HB-K-P Jack Stone was most dramatic contributor to Mountaineers' dominance. Stone took option pitchouts for 28 and 16y gains to set up QB Freddie Wyant's 1y sneak in 1st Q for 7-0 lead. Wyant missed 4th down pass from Pitt 37YL, and Panthers went all way to tie it in 2nd Q as QB Henry Ford (3 INTs) found HB Ray DiPasquale with his only pass completion (36y) to WVU 4YL. HB Joe Capp plunged over to tie before H. After FB-DB Tommy Allman's INT, K Stone put Mountaineers ahead 10-7 in 3rd Q with 25y FG. Panthers appeared to have golden opportunity after DT Howard Linn gobbled up FUM at WVU 19YL, but Pitt could go no farther than 11YL. In 4th Q, Stone dashed 20y to Pitt 25YL, and tacked-on roughing PEN set up WVU at 10YL for HB Joe Marconi's clinching TD run.

DUKE 19 Wake Forest 0: Heroic Demon Deacons (0-2) DT Bob Bartholomew made 16 tackles, helping maintain surprising 0-0 tie until last 20 secs of 3rd Q. Duke (2-0) then erupted for TD runs by HBs Red Smith and Lloyd Caudle and QB Jerry Barger in 11-min span over tiring Wake Forest.

FLORIDA 0 Georgia Tech 0: Yellow Jackets' 18-game winning streak blew away in hurricane conditions at Gainesville. G Joe D'Agostino and C Steve De La Torre led Gators (0-1-1) D which forced 3 lost FUMs by Georgia Tech (1-0-1) star HB Leon Hardeman. Florida FB-P Rick Casares boomed 2 key punts from his EZ, each nearly 60y against 25 mph wind.

ALABAMA 7 Louisiana State 7 (Mobile): When both teams quickly went to TDs on their opening possessions, it looked like Mobile's near-capacity crowd was in for high-scoring bout. But, as Alabama (0-1-1) charged 80y after opening KO and LSU (1-0-1) answered with tying TD on 55y trip, each D heartily settled in for stoppages. Crimson Tide QB Bart Starr (3-10/37y, 2 INTs) completed 18 and 4y passes to HB Corky Tharp to set up FB Tommy Lewis' 1st-series TD plunge. Hulking T Sid Fournet made 15y RET of short KO to start Bengals on their TD trip. LSU HB Charley Oakley's 31y reception from QB Al Doggett (6-16/64y, 2 INTs) set up HB George Brancato (10/88y, TD) for 1y TD smash. Alabama never threatened after opening TD and had to spend game defending its goal, stopping Tigers at Tide's 6YL on frosh FB Lou Deutschmann's FUM, at their 2YL on HB Chuck Johns' stumble, and FB-K Tommy Davis' missed 32y FG. Bama C-LB Ralph Carrigan was hellcat on D.

MISSISSIPPI 22 Kentucky 6: "Mr. Everything" for Kentucky (0-2), Steve Meilinger, played at E, HB, FB, and QB, but was pressured by forward-pressing Mississippi (2-0) line all game. After Ole Miss threat died at 2YL thanks to nullified 2nd Q TD, Wildcats took lead as QB Dick Shatto connected on several passes including short TD to E Al Zampino for 6-0 margin. Rebels FB Pete Mangum appeared to take QB Eagle Day's pass to long TD in 2nd Q, but was ruled OB at Kentucky 19YL. Still, soph FB Bobby "Slick" McCool ran 3 times to produce TD for 7-6 H edge. Soph star Day capped 60y drive in 3rd Q with 10y TD dash. Meilinger found himself in trouble as he ran around his own EZ in 4th Q: his impromtu incompletion was ruled intentional grounding for safety and 16-6 Ole Miss lead. Rebels QB Houston Patton climaxed 59y TD drive late in game with 10y TD run.

Michigan State 21 IOWA 7: Michigan State (1-0) made smooth transition to Big 10 membership, as defending national champion Spartans won 25th straight game. Spartans started quickly, taking 14-0 lead in 1st Q on short TD runs by HBs Billy Wells and HB Jim Ellis. Each score came after TO suffered by Iowa (0-1) QB Lou Matykiewicz: He lost FUM to Michigan State G Larry Fowler at Hawks 34YL and threw INT swiped by Spartans FB-DB Gerry Planutis at MSU 28YL. Hawkeyes FB-DB George "Binkey" Broeder recovered FUM at MSU 39YL in 3rd Q, and Broder soon hurtled over GL for 1y TD. Iowa had apparent INT in Michigan State territory in 4th Q as QB-DB Terry Moran leaped, but deflection flew back to Spartans FB Evan Slonac for 4y loss. MSU QB Tom Yewsic (9-14/109y) soon pitched over middle for 46y TD pass to Wells.

ILLINOIS 21 Nebraska 21: Fighting Illini (0-0-1) went 73y after opening KO to 7y TD pass from QB Em Lindbeck to E Cliff Waldbeser. After his 2 FUMs helped Nebraska (0-1-1) score twice for 21-7 early 4th Q lead, Illinois (0-0-1) mercurial newcomer HB J.C. Caroline traded his goat horns for hero's mantel in his varsity debut. Caroline authored swirling 73y TD run to pull Illini within 21-14 and contributed pair of important runs to set up fellow-soph HB Mickey Bates' 5y run for tying TD run with just more than 5 mins to go. Tying Illini drive came after G Jan Smid recovered FUM at Cornhuskers 39YL. In 2nd Q, Cornhuskers QB John Bordogna had sneaked over for score and thrown TD pass to HB Bob Smith for 14-7 lead. In nearly blocking Nebraska's 2nd conv kick, center of Tribe line inadvertently tipped K Bordogna's low kick over crossbar, 1st of 2 such bizarre, but effective Nebraska kicks. Cornhuskers HB Dennis Korinek gained 123y rushing, but came up just short on 4th down run toward Illini 7YL. At game's end, Illini held slight 362y (290y rushing) to 341y advantage in total O.

WISCONSIN 20 Penn State 0: Targeting Badgers FB Alan Ameche's powerful runs, Penn State (0-1) D manfully held firmly for game's opening 22 mins against injury-riddled Wisconsin (1-0). Once Badgers found themselves starting in good field position—at own 46YL—in 2nd Q, Ameche (28/115y, TD) and his rushing cohorts wore down Nittany Lions. Badgers HB Jerry Witt set up Ameche's 2nd Q TD run with 24y sprint with pitchout. Rolling in 3rd Q, Wisconsin traveled 86y, aided by pair of

passes for 35y by QB Gust Vergetis (8-12/82y, INT), to HB Clary Bratt's 9y TD sweep. Badgers went 85y in 4th Q to sub HB Bob Gingrass' 4y run. Penn State QB Tony Rados was unusually ineffective in air with 7-16/64y, 2 INTs, and It didn't help Rados' cause that Lions were limited to 50y rushing as HB Lenny Moore's 64y TD sprint was called back. LB Ameche and G-LB John Dixon helped throttle Mt Nittany runners; deepest penetration to Wisconsin 15YL early in 4th Q was earned on 2 fine catches by Lions E Jim Garrity.

Notre Dame 28 OKLAHOMA 21: Season's 1st big game in sultry Norman pitted no.1 Fighting Irish (1-0) against vengeful no. 6 Oklahoma (0-1), which had been bounced from unbeaten ranks in 1952 by Notre Dame. Irish started in hole at own 2YL after HB Johnny Lattner bobbled opening KO, and Sooners soon jumped to 7-0 lead after T Dick Bowman recovered FUM at ND 23YL by FB Neil Worden (12/78y, TD). OU HB Larry Grigg cut inside E Carl Allison's block and dashed over on 8th play of short drive. After Notre Dame recovered 1st Q FUM at Oklahoma 15YL, QB Ralph Guglielmi (5-8/88y, 2 TDs) lofted short TD pass to HB Joe Heap. Teams traded 2nd Q TDs: Sooners little HB Jack Ging tallied after QB Buddy Leake faked handoff to permit Allison to break open for 62y reception to Irish 18YL. Notre Dame countered with what Oklahoma coach Bud Wilkinson thought was game's biggest play: T Frank Varrichione blocked FB-P Max Boydston's QK and E Don Penza made REC at 9YL. Guglielmi soon scored on option run to send teams to H at 14-14. Heap's 36y catch in EZ broke 3rd Q tie after DB Guglielmi intercepted newly-appointed QB Leake (2-7/79y, INT), and Worden followed with 9y TD run for 28-14 margin. Oklahoma HB Merrill Green used great blocking to steam 60y to punt TD RET in 4th Q, but with 5 mins remaining, Irish prevailed because big play came from HB-DB Johnny Lattner, who had been limited to 13/22y rushing. From Sooners 40YL, Leake tossed screen pass to Allison who zipped 17y behind 2 blockers. But, last-tackler Lattner slipped between them to drop Allison at ND 43YL to effectively end threat. This was Oklahoma's 1st home loss in 25 games and last defeat of any sort until Notre Dame would snap Sooners' 47-game win streak on same field on November 16, 1957.

Oklahoma A&M 7 ARKANSAS 6: HB Bill Bredde (14/117y) made simple crossbuck run with less than 6 mins gone in 1st Q and was long gone for 77y TD for Cowboys (2-0) as they went ahead in regional rivalry by 11-10-1 over Arkansas (0-1). Soph QB-K Bobby Andrew made vital x-pt kick after Bredde's long score, which benefitted from blocks by T Dale Meinert, G John Payne, and FB Earl Lunsford. Razorbacks coach Bowden Wyatt saw his debut spoiled by loss of 4 FUMs by his newly-installed Single Wing O. Arkansas TB Lamar McHan passed 8-11/114y and found favored target E Floyd Sagely (6/91y) twice on 50y drive that bridged 3rd and 4th Qs to McHan's 1y plunge. K McHan missed his x-pt to left, but brought back Hogs on 35y pass to Sagely 2 mins later, only to lose FUM to E-DE Bob LaRue at Oklahoma A&M 28YL.

SOUTHERN CALIFORNIA 17 Minnesota 7: As he was wont to do, durable Golden Gophers (0-1) star TB Paul Giel (16/97y and 6-12/42y passing) accounted for 60% of his team's y. Otherwise, it was awful 1953 debut for Giel, who got little blocking help: 1952 A-A fumbled lateral at his own 14YL, which led to 1st TD by Southern California (2-0), and suffered blocked QK, which was recovered in EZ for another Troy TD. On game's opening series, USC C Dick Petty had fired high punt snap 34y back to his 21YL. But, after Minnesota marched to 3YL, Giel tossed incomplete EZ pass on 4th down. Next came USC DT Ed Fouch's REC of Giel's FUM that turned into 1-play drive: TB Aramis Dandoy's 14y TD pass to BB George Bozanic. In 2nd Q, Trojans G Irwin Spector blocked Giel's QK, and FB-LB Harold Han fell on it in EZ. G-K Sam Tsagalakis added 30y FG as Trojans trotted off leading 17-0 at H. Minnesota, twice frustrated at USC 3YL in 1st H, finally scored in 3rd Q, keyed by Giel's ramble of 67y to 12YL. Gophers FB John Baumgartner and QB Gino Cappelletti worked it to 1YL, spot from which Cappelletti wedged it over for TD.

AP Poll September 28

1 Notre Dame (71)	907	11 Mississippi State (1)	176
2 Michigan State (6)	692	12 Duke (1)	127
3 Maryland (5)	501	13 West Virginia (4)	88
4 Michigan (3)	403	14 Rice	76
5 UCLA (3)	393	15 Mississippi	68
6 Ohio State (2)	380	16 Wisconsin	54
7 Southern California (1)	346	17 Texas	53
8 Oklahoma	316	18 Georgia	49
9 Georgia Tech	242	19 Louisiana State	46
10 Baylor	188	20 Holy Cross	42

October 3, 1953

(Fri) Baylor 21 MIAMI 13: He wasn't "long gone" but HB L.G. Dupre (16/55y) did score game's opening TD: Baylor (2-0) started with 68y TD drive capped by 1y scoring dive on 4th down by Dupre. Miami (1-1) conservatively chose to punt on 1st down from own 6YL with 2:45 before H. Bears made Canes pay, beating clock with TD pass by QB Cotton Davidson (6-11/86y, TD, INT) to E Wayne Hopkins for 14-0 H lead. Bears' 2nd H hibernation allowed Miami to fashion near upset. Hurricanes QB Don James led 53y aerial TD drive, that was concluded by his own short TD run. Miami sub QB J.B. Johnston, darling of crowd all night, connected on 68y TD pass to HB Bill Smith. Hurricanes C-LB Ernest Tobey had hand in 20 tackles.

RUTGERS 20 Virginia Tech 13: Early in their season opener, Scarlet Knights (1-0) were denied 58y TD pass by QB John Fennell because officials blew whistle on great fake plunge by HB Joe Triggs. Virginia Tech (2-1) took advantge by going right to EZ: Gobblers launched 80y march capped by HB Bobby Scruggs' 2y zip around E. Tech protected 7-0 lead by twice stopping Rutgers advances inside 10YL. Gobblers jumped to 13-0 edge in 3rd Q when QB Jack Williams sneaked near midfield and found himself all alone for 52y romp to EZ. Rutgers answered right away as HB Ron Mastrolia carried 3 defenders across GL on 5y TD run. Knights launched game-breaking 91y drive that carried into 4th Q as HB Steve Johnson caught 25y pass and ran 14y to lead Rutgers to 1YL. Fennell sneaked over, and FB-K Don Duncan gave Queensmen 14-13 lead with his truly-kicked x-pt. Bad snap on 4th down set Rutgers up at Gobblers 17YL in game's last min, and FB Angelo Iannucci plunged for TD from inches away.

PENNSYLVANIA 13 Penn State 7: Nittany Lions (0-2) failed to beat in-state rival Quakers (2-0) for 1st time since 1938 tie. Before 51,000 fans, Penn State struck 1st, traveling 92y in 17 plays in 1st Q after Pennsylvania HB Walt Hynoski labeled QK for Penn State 8YL. After soph HB Lenny Moore (19/55y) gained 18y on 3 tries for 1st of 5 1st downs on drive, Lions QB Tony Rados (10-28/156y, INT) found E Jim Garrity in flat for short catch, and Garrity zipped into EZ for 30y TD. Quakers E Jim Castle's downfield block sprung HB Gary Scott for 14y TD after catch from Hynoski in 2nd Q to tie it 7-7. Penn D line, sparked by G John Cannon (sack), created 4th Q break with forced FUM by Moore recovered by T Carl Sammarco at Penn State 43YL. Hynoski's 25y TD pass to Scott won it for Quakers with 10:25 to play, but Penn had to withstand 54y drive that expired with clock at Pennsylvania 38YL.

PITTSBURGH 7 Oklahoma 7: Homestanding Panthers (0-1-1) brought about upset deadlock by owning disparity in stats: they outgained Oklahoma (0-1-1) 277y to 170y. Sooners tried only 5 passes all day, but surprised Pitt with QB Buddy Leake's 80y TD aerial to HB Larry Grigg in 2nd Q. Sooners made no 1st downs in 2nd H as Panthers D, anchored by E Dick Dietrick, overcame lost FUM at own 7YL shortly after H. Taking off from own 23YL in 3rd Q, Pitt drove all way downfield to 1st down at Sooners 1YL, but 4 plunges were stonewalled as 4th Q opened. Oklahoma punted out to its 48YL, and Panthers surged to TD sneak by QB Pete Neft, but not before Sooners front stopped 3 runs inside own 4YL. Pitt G-K Paul Blanda kicked tying pt with plenty of time remaining that neither team could use to its advantage.

Maryland 20 CLEMSON 0: Maryland (3-0) jumped to 7-0 lead on QB Bernie Faloney's 88y TD RET of opening KO. Terrapins proceeded to bobble ball on next 5 possessions, while Clemson howled about 3 interference PEN non-calls. Terps HB Dick Nolan, future NFL DB and head coach, iced it in 2nd H with pair of great plays: 64y TD catch from Faloney and 90y punt TD RET behind huge block of G Dick Shirley. Inconsistent Tigers (1-1-1) managed to gain 192y total O, but their weak passing O managed only 2-14/21y.

KENTUCKY 26 Florida 13: Sky-high Kentucky (1-2) scored in each Q as it etched long TD drives of 92, 84, 60, and 90y. Wildcats used 2 QBs, 1st-time soph starter Bob Hardy and sr Herb Hunt, and each threw pair of TD passes. In 1st H, Hardy connected with FB Ralph Paolone for 20y and HB Steve Meilinger for 60y. In 2nd H, Hunt hurled 23y to E Larry "Dude" Hennessey and 10y to HB Dick Mitchell. Kentucky passed 13-16/196y, outgaining Florida 399y to 184y in total O. Florida (0-2-1) had taken 7-6 lead on 1st Q's last play, moving 63y to FB Bill Dearing's 3y TD run through LT and QB-K Harry Speers' conv. Meilinger made brilliant, tackle-shedding run with Hardy's medium-length pass for score that provided 13-7 H edge. Florida briefly tied it 13-13 midway in 3rd Q after QB-P Dick Allen's accurate punt pinned Cats at their 5YL, and FB Joe Brodsky ran 3 times to set up Speers' 22y pass to HB Tommy Haddock, who weaved and dived for TD.

AUBURN 13 Mississippi 0: Former patsy Auburn (2-0), which entered 1953 season with 16-48-4 record since end of World War II, ruthlessly stopped no. 15 Rebels' 13-game SEC win streak. Stocking scoreboard in Tigers' favor were TD runs by QB Bobby Freeman on 1y sneak in 2nd Q and HB Fob James (11/62y) on 8y pitchout sweep of E in 3rd Q. Both scorers were members of Tigers' soph-studded back-up unit known as "Y Team." Mississippi (2-1) gained only 103y and failed to dent Auburn territory until 3rd Q. HB-DB Jimmy Patton was central figure for Rebs: Patton stopped 1st Q advance with EZ INT and çaught 49y pass from QB Lea Pasley in closing secs of 2nd Q only to be hauled down at 10YL by last-tackler, DB James. Auburn kept its shutout intact with brilliant GLS in last 4 mins of game. Tigers D sparkled as DE Vince Nardone made 9 tackles, Ole Miss ran for only 32y and passed 4-12/71y, and Rebs' flashy soph FB Bobby McCool was limited to 7/17y rushing. In many ways, Auburn would never look back, becoming consistent SEC force under coach Shug Jordan through mid-1970s and in most years beyond.

DUKE 21 Tennessee 7: Volunteers (0-2) had Duke (3-0) on its heels in 1st Q without landing knockout punch. Late in opening Q, Tennessee TB-P Jimmy Wade toed punt OB at Devils 8YL. Duke HBs Dale Boyd and Lloyd Caudle (13/89y) contributed 25 and 42y sprints to 92y TD drive, which was kept alive by roughing PEN on Vols. It reversed 4th down pass incompletion and gave Devils 1st down at 2YL as 2nd Q opened. HB Red Smith quickly scored for 7-0 lead, and Duke added 2 lightning strikes on HB Bob Pascal's 1y TD run and Caudle's 41y TD reception from QB Jerry Barger. Behind 21-0, Tennessee got its only score on ensuing drive that culminated with 1:27 left in H. WB Jerry Hyde's catch of Wade's pass was featured in march that TB Wade (23/60y) ended with 4y TD loop of LE. Vols threatened twice in 4th Q at 5 and 1YLs, but were turned back by resolute Duke tackling, led by G Bobby Burrows and T Ed "Country" Meadows.

GEORGIA TECH 6 Southern Methodist 4: Georgia Tech (2-0-1) E Dave Davis found himself smack in middle of odd game. After scoreless 1st H in which both Ds sparkled, Southern Methodist (0-1) T Jack Gunlock blocked Davis' 3rd Q punt through EZ for 2-0 lead for Mustangs. DE Davis dropped off line to make spectacular INT of Mustangs QB Duane Nutt at SMU 25YL. It set up 3-play drive to TD sneak by QB Pepper Rodgers, Georgia Tech's only score for 6-2 lead. After SMU HB-P Jerry Norton booted Engineers to their 9YL in 4th Q, P Davis dropped punt snap that turned into FUM REC by SMU C Bill Fox 1 ft short of Tech GL. But Georgia Tech's tough D, led by T Roger Frye, C-LB Larry Morris and G-LB Franklin Brooks held on 5 battering-ram tries (including PEN) by SMU. Pressed against his own GL, Rodgers next conceded game's 2nd safety to Mustangs, but Yellow Jackets punted out safely. SMU rushed for only 33y as Georgia Tech LB Brooks made 18 stops. But, Jackets only netted 33y on ground themselves and made astonishingly meager 3 1st downs.

FLORIDA STATE 59 Louisville 0: Cardinals (1-2), 2-TD favorite, were stunned by brash, young Seminoles (1-1). Florida State HB Bobby Fiveash scored 3 TDs, HB Stan Dobosz added 2 TD runs, and frosh sub QB Lee Corso was superb off bench with his Split-T magic. Corso ripped off 59y punt TD RET in 2nd Q. Louisville star QB Johnny Unitas, who had clicked on 16-22/198y and 3 TD passes in 1952 rout of FSU but was woefully without help this year, was completely throttled in his aerial attempts. Unitas was held out of 2nd H action after FSU had romped to 6-TD edge. It was Louisville's worst defeat since Vanderbilt's 68-0 shellacking of Cardinals in 1941.

NORTHWESTERN 33 Army 20: In his biography, *You Have to Pay the Price*, West Point coach Earl Blaik revealed that backfield asst Vince Lombardi, future legendary coach of Green Bay Packers, laughed aloud prior to this game as he nervously pondered his team's pass D: "I was just thinking about the first time Northwestern throws a pass. All our backs will fall down." They didn't fall down, but Cadets' weak pass D, trying to learn new system, was exposed by Northwestern (2-0) QB Dick Thomas (14-19/209y, 2 TDs, INT). Thomas frequently scanned field for former HS teammate, E Joe Collier, who caught TD and netted long catches that set up pair of Wildcats TDs. Black Knights (1-1) had scored 1st after FB-P Freddie Attaya gained field position with 77y QK. Army HB Pat Uebel blasted to Northwestern GL and fumbled, where Cadets QB Jerry Hagan was johnny-on-the-spot for TD REC and 7-0 lead. Wildcats tallied 3 times in 2nd Q for 20-14 H lead: FB Bob Lauter banged over after Collier's 38y catch, HB Dick Ranicke raced 41y to score, and Thomas beat H clock with 7y TD arrow to E Dick Peterson. Army QB Pete Vann pitched TD pass to soph E Don Holleder in 4th Q.

Notre Dame 37 PURDUE 7: Scoring pretty well as it pleased, Notre Dame (2-0) started with G-K Menil Mavraides' medium-range FG in 1st Q, enjoyed HB Johnny Lattner's explosive 86y KO TD RET in 2nd Q, and depended on workhorse FB Neil Worden for pair of 11y runs. Irish QB Ralph Guglielmi (7-9/92y) sneaked for another score. Briefly pulling within 10-7, Purdue (0-2) made its score on 65y TD play in 2nd Q: pass from QB Roy Evans to E John Kerr. But, Lattner followed immediately with his long KO RET, and Irish sub HB Dick Washington took pitchout 31y to tally late in 2nd Q. ND's 23-7 H edge rinsed away any comeback lubricant from Boilermakers.

KANSAS STATE 27 Nebraska 0: Without Big 7 conf win since 1949, Kansas State (2-1) unleashed 242y ground attack led by HBs Veryl Switzer and Corky Taylor to surprise favored Cornhuskers (0-2-1). QB Bob Whitehead tallied 1st Wildcats TD after 2nd Q FUM REC at Nebraska 1YL. Switzer capped 80y drive in 2nd Q with 9y TD romp, and Whitehead fired 40y TD to E Ed Pence in 4th Q. Huskers were held to 156y O.

Ucla 12 OREGON 0: It took until last 10 mins for no. 5 UCLA (3-0) to break 0-0 tie against Oregon's fine D, but Bruins D gave up only 174y and GL was only passably threatened. Bruins were bothered by aerial antics of Ducks QB George Shaw (10-22/104y, 3 INTs), but deepest Oregon (1-2) ever penetrated was UCLA 21YL in 3rd Q. Uclans finally mounted 90y march on 18 running calls to send TB Paul Cameron on 6y TD power sweep of RE in 4th Q. BB-LB Terry Debay later turned pass against Oregon, spearing INT off Shaw and returning it to Ducks 40YL. Bruins sub TB Primo Villanueva soon slipped down sideline for 15y TD. Both UCLA x-pts were blocked.

Ohio State 33 CALIFORNIA 19: Barrel-chested HB Bobby Watkins (145y rushing) powered for 4 Buckeyes (2-0) TDs in front of interested international fan, Crown Prince Akihito of Japan, who was visiting Berkeley. Positive-thinking Golden Bears (1-2) were outgained only 366y to 334y in seesaw shootout. California QB Paul Larson (13-25/170y, 2 INTs) gained y, and HB Al Talley tallied twice for Bears to earn 13-6 H lead. But short punt by P Larson early in 3rd Q positioned no. 6 Ohio State for 28y TD drive that tied game at 13-13. Cal's last flicker came next: Bears went 70y to reclaim lead at 19-13 on TD run by HB Don Marks. In all, Ohio created 4 TOs to help launch other short scoring drives of 28 and 33y that pressured Bears' bending D. Fading California D was pushed back for 83y TD drive in 4th Q.

AP Poll October 5

1 Notre Dame (84)	1190	11 Rice	177
2 Michigan State (15)	1022	12 West Virginia (5)	168
3 Ohio State (11)	769	13 Mississippi State (3)	164
4 Maryland (8)	733	14 Louisiana State	84
5 Michigan (4)	626	15 Texas	68
6 UCLA (2)	430	16 Oklahoma	63
7 Southern California (2)	424	17 Pittsburgh	32
8 Duke (4)	311	18 Northwestern	29
9 Baylor	288	19 Holy Cross	23
10 Georgia Tech	277	20tMississippi Southern	21
		20tPennsylvania	21

October 10, 1953

Virginia 24 GEORGE WASHINGTON 20: Eager to avenge 50-0 pasting in 1952 at Charlottesville, George Washington (2-1) wobbled on game's 1st snap to launch Virginia's 1st and only victory of 1953. Colonials QB Bob Sturm tried to handoff but ball was batted 20y backwards where it was recovered in EZ for TD by Cavaliers (1-2) FB-LB Hank Strempek. QB Rives Bailey sparkled for Virginia, hitting E Ray Quillen for 34y to set up HB Peter Potter's short TD run for 12-0 1st Q lead and lofting 51y TD pass to E Fred Moyer to overcome 1-pt deficit in 3rd Q for 18-13 edge. GW E Richie Gaskell had hauled in 79 and 21y TDs in middle Qs to provide brief 13-12 lead. Clincher came in 4th Q as GW, prone to bobbling perfect passes all night, saw E Jack Daly fumble away midfield reception to DB Bailey and send Virginia to Bailey's 13y TD keeper run around LE.

MARYLAND 40 Georgia 13: Lightning backs and carniverous line staked Maryland (4-0) to nearly unapproachable advantage. Georgia (2-2) had ball for only 3 snaps of 1st Q, and Terrapins scored twice: QB Bernie Faloney's 18y 4th down pass to E Bill Walker and Faloney's sneak from 1YL. QB Zeke Bratkowski (16-29/202y, TD, 2 INTs) fired up Bulldogs' air game in 2nd Q, guiding his mates to 2 TDs. E Johnny Carson (8/127y) caught 9y TD and made brilliant grabs on all corners of field. But, between Georgia's 2 scores, Maryland zipped to TD in 6 plays: Faloney's 24y pass to HB Dick Nolan. DB Faloney stepped in front of Bratkowski's pass at Georgia 40YL on 2nd play of 3rd Q and roared down sideline for crippling TD. Bratkowski's 2nd INT set up TD by HB Chet Hanulak (13/107y), and Georgia QB was soon knocked from game by vicious tackle.

DUKE 20 Purdue 14: QB-S Jerry Barger, 60-min performer, rallied Duke (4-0) from 14-14 tie with winning 66y drive. After his 21y scramble, Barger sprinted around RE for 7y TD run with 39 sec left. Late in 1st Q, Purdue (0-3) QB Roy Evans had whipped 38y TD pass to HB Rex Brock, but Barger quickly set up tying TD with 57y pitch to E Howard Pitt, and Blue Devils HB Bob Pascal (7/69y) swept 17y to TD. Barger's INT stopped Boilermakers early in 4th Q and led to his 49y TD pitch to HB Red Smith that made it 14-7. Purdue drove 70y, including 54y on another Evans-to-Brock pass, to tie it 14-14 on HB Karl Herkommer's TD run with 5:30 to go.

Auburn 21 MISSISSIPPI STATE 21: For 3 Qs, gifted QB-K Jackie Parker handcrafted 21-0 Mississippi State (3-0-1) lead: Parker completed 3 passes during opening 80y TD drive, pitched out to HB Zerk Wilson for 2nd Q TD, scored own TD in 3rd Q, and nailed 3 x-pts. But, Auburn (2-0-1) blew it away in jiffy: After Parker's 3rd Q TD, Tigers HB Bobby Duke followed C Jack Locklear's convoy to 100y KO TD RET, and suddenly Bulldogs were out of gas, not to earn another 1st down. Tigers G George Atkins blocked P Parker's punt for TD by E Jim Pyburn, and QB Bobby Freeman's 4th down run got Auburn to within 1 pt in closing secs. That left it to QB-K Joe Davis, whose perfect kick wrapped up Auburn's terrific comeback. On tying 65y drive, Pyburn caught passes from Freeman of 20, 23, and 31y, 64y in all.

MIAMI 39 Clemson 7: Intense bowl rivals of previous 2 New Year's Days fought to 0-0 tie in 1st H with deepest penetration coming from Clemson (1-2-1) until HB Jimmy Wells lost FUM at 12YL. After H, Hurricanes (2-1) made sudden landfall, swirling for 6 TDs in 21-min interval of 2nd H: 1st score came on QB Don James' 13y TD pass to FB Gordon Malloy and oddest on E Tom Pepsin's 44y TD run with ball snatched from passing hand of Clemson QB Tommy Williams. In between, Miami E Frank McDonald made brilliant 32y snare of pass among 2 defenders, and Tigers HB-P Joe Pagliei froze and failed to get his punt away from 13YL; each event created TD for Hurricanes. Tigers threw brief respite at Miami's 3rd string unit midway in 4th Q as QB Johnny Thompson, in for injured QB Don King, connected on 26y TD pass to E Scott Jackson, after his 40y pitch to E Dreher Gaskin. It briefly sliced Clemson's debit to 26-7.

Illinois 41 OHIO STATE 20: Illinois (2-0-1) roared into Columbus to unleash its spectacular new TD twins, Mickey Bates (23/147y, 4 TDs) and J.C. Caroline (24/192y, 2 TDs). Caroline authored mesmorizing 64y scoring sprint as he and his soph HB-mate scored all 6 TDs. Illini rushed for 443y with 4 TDs being set up by TOs. But local fans had reason for excitement at H. Ohio State DB Howard Cassady's INT early in 2nd Q set up brief flurry of sharp passing in 2nd stanza by QB John Borton, who threw 19y TD to Cassady but was intercepted 3 times among 18 passes by day's end. Still, no. 3 Buckeyes (2-1) rallied from 21-0 deficit to within 21-20 by H. Borton threw his TD and later sneaked over for score. In between, Ohio State converted Bates' FUM into HB Bobby Watkins' 12y TD burst. But, K Tad Weed missed conv after Borton's TD run to prevent Buckeyes from tying it. Still, Ohio State was primed to receive 2nd H KO. Turning point came quickly: INT 2 snaps into 3rd Q by G-LB John Bauer lit Illinois' 2nd H fireworks. It featured pair of short TD plunges by Bates and another by Caroline.

MICHIGAN 14 Iowa 13: Fired-up Iowa (1-2) turned 5 TOs into 13-0 H lead on speedy HB Earl Smith's TD runs of 27 and 6y. Hawkeyes FB-LB Roger Wiegmann got Michigan (3-0) HB Tony Branoff to lose FUM to set up 1st TD, but K Wiegmann missed conv kick. Wolverines QB Lou Baldacci hurled 26y TD pass to E Bob Topp in 3rd Q, but still Michigan attack floundered. Coach Bennie Oosterbaan found Duncan McDonald on Michigan bench, dusted off cobwebs, and sent jr QB out to rescue 4th Q win. McDonald rifled 24y pass to Topp and, on 4th down, beat pass rush to hit E Gene Knutson with 4y curl-in TD pass. K Baldacci booted winning pt with 10 mins left to play.

MICHIGAN STATE 26 Texas Christian 19: Three different Horned Frogs (1-2), QB Ray McKown, HB Ronnie Clinkscale, and sub QB Marvin Fowler, threw TD passes to press undefeated Spartans (3-0) to ropes, facing 19-7 disadvantage entering 4th Q. But, 157-lb Michigan State HB Leroy Bolden slipped over from 4YL to climax 69y drive, and soon 170-lb FB-K Evan Slonac, largest of coach Biggie Munn's "Pony Backfield," caught TD pass from QB Tom Yewcic and made conv after TD for 20-19 lead. LB Slonac grabbed INT to set up Yewcic's insurance TD pass to HB Jim Ellis. So, quickly and tidily, Michigan State scored its 27th straight win.

Oklahoma 19 Texas 14 (Dallas): Oklahoma (1-1-1) steadfitly built 19-0 edge by 4th Q, but lead nearly evaporated in closing rush by Texas. Sooners TD had come on HB Larry Grigg's TD run behind block of G J.D. Roberts at end of 1st Q drive after Texas (2-2) lost FUM at its 25YL when Sooners HB-DB Tommy Carroll tipped away pitchout. In middle of 2nd Q, Oklahoma tallied on 80y punt TD RET by HB Merrill Green, propelled by another block by Roberts. Carroll took pitchout to 48y TD run early in 4th Q. Steers soph QB Charlie Brewer (6-9/95y) immediately ignited 78y rally to TD to trim deficit to 19-7. Late in game Sooners QB Gene Calame tried to concede 4th down safety from his 1YL, but in dancing around Oklahoma's EZ to kill time he got dangerously close to GL and was smacked back out of EZ. Texas took over at Oklahoma 1YL after this odd play and scored TD on sweep by FB Ed Kelley. Sooners' edgy survival left them reeling for moment but marked launching point of historic 47-game winning streak.

Kansas 27 COLORADO 21: Feeding Colorado its own medicine, Kansas (2-2) trotted out its best rushing game. Jayhawks ran for 306y and led most of day. HB Don Hess surprised Colorado (2-2) on game's 1st scrimmage play by popping through LG on trap play for 66y TD. Jayhawks HB Ralph Moody capped 55y drive soon thereafter with 12y skirt of E and 14-0 lead in 1st Q. Buffaloes went into pursuit mode and tied it twice. Colorado WB-DB Frank Bernardi recovered FUM at Kansas 16YL, and FB

Emerson Wilson followed 15y catch from QB Don Piper with 1y TD run. Jayhawks P Moody soon blasted 57y punt to Colorado 10YL, and Buffs WB Ron Johnson roared up sideline behind great blocking for 90y TD to tie it 14-14 in 2nd Q. Moody gained 45y of Kansas' 83y TD trip after 2nd H KO for 21-14 lead, but Colorado E Gary Knafelc caught 27y TD pass for 21-21 knot. Moody scored his 2nd TD late in 4th Q for victory.

SOUTHERN METHODIST 12 Rice 7: Owls (3-1) FB Kosse Johnson took advantage of Ponies' FUM in 3rd Q to score TD, and after E-K Don Costa successfully converted x-pt, Rice owned 7-6 lead. Undefeated Rice was knocking on door of Mustangs' GL as clock dwindled down to 3 mins to play, and 50,000 dismayed fans in Cotton Bowl stadium began to file out of SWC opener. With Owls only whisker away from game's clinching TD, weary Southern Methodist (2-1) D, rose up to hold at its 2 YL. After Mustangs' top back, HB Jerry Norton, bulled away from his GL for 2y, fleet HB Frank Eidom slipped through RT, took great block from FB Dale Moore, and set sail for Rice's distant GL. Owls DE Marshall Crawford hustled to overhaul Eidom at Rice 4YL and halt Eidom's 92y gain. On 3rd down, SMU QB Duane Nutt circled LE for winning TD, his 2nd score.

BAYLOR 14 Arkansas 7: Nail-biter in Waco went to Baylor (3-0) as dependable QB Cotton Davidson clicked on TD pass to E Wayne Hopkins to crown 52y march with less than 3 mins left. Arkansas (1-2) had made 1st break of game in 2nd Q when E-DE Floyd Sagely dropped off in pass coverage to intercept Davidson's pass and return it 31y. Razorbacks TB Lamar McHan moved his troops into EZ on 18y TD pass to E Jerry Bogard. Bears snarled back to tie it on 57y voyage to HB Jerry Coody's TD run.

Texas A&M 27 TEXAS TECH 14: Inflicting season's only loss on Texas Tech (3-1), surprising Texas A&M (3-0-1) led most of way. HB Billy Pete Huddleston's 1st Q TD had Aggies ahead 7-0 after Red Raiders QB-DB Jack Kirkpatrick's pass was intercepted and returned 37y to 16YL. On 4th down, Tech HB Bobby Cavazos pitched 14y TD pass to E Paul Erwin to tie with 6:31 left in 2nd Q. Cavazos lost FUM to DB Huddleston deep in his end late in 2nd Q, and, on 4th down, A&M QB Don Ellis ran wide keeper for 3y TD. Huddleston scored again in 3rd Q for 21-7 lead for Aggies, but after FUM REC at A&M 34YL, Tech FB Rick Spinks ran 16y and soon rammed over for TD that pulled Raiders to within 21-14. Texas A&M locked it up midway in 4th Q as HB-DB Ellwood Kettler nabbed INT at Tech 36YL, and FB Johnny Salyer swept to 10y TD.

WASHINGTON 13 Southern California 13: Huskies (1-2-1) stacked pair of TDs within 2 mins of each other in 2nd Q and rolled to considerable 1st H dominance. Washington HB Jack Killingstad wrapped up 65y drive, aided by pass interference PEN call on USC DB Lindon Crow at 2YL, with TD plunge, and after Southern California (3-0-1) lost FUM, QB Sandy Lederman sneaked across for TD in short order. Washington D was so effective that Troy could make only 9y and not earn single 1st down in 1st H. Trailing 13-0, Trojans made own break in 3rd Q: TB Aramis Dandoy bobbled punt, and while downfield pursuers relaxed, he picked up ball and galloped 70y to TD to make it 13-6. At start of 4th Q, Lederman (3-12/44y, INT) was under heavy pass rush when his throw-away attempt was snared in flat by USC DB Crow, who eased down sideline on 78y INT TD RET with no Husky even close in pursuit. Huskies ran 75 plays to 45.

AP Poll October 12

1 Notre Dame (74)	1226	11 Rice	170
2 Michigan State (14)	977	12 Oklahoma (1)	152
3 Maryland (21)	961	13 Southern California	148
4 UCLA (8)	755	14 Navy	53
5 Michigan	537	15 Pittsburgh	45
6 Georgia Tech	490	16 California	44
7 Duke (3)	485	17tOhio State	42
8 Baylor	397	17tMiss. Southern (1)	42
9 Illinois	284	19 Auburn	37
10 West Virginia (9)	181	20 Mississippi State	36

October 17, 1953

Ohio State 12 PENNSYLVANIA 6: Ohio State (3-1) coach Woody Hayes claimed to have warned his troops of Penn's prowess, but it took long 4th Q drive by Buckeyes to break 6-6 tie and salt it away. Quakers (2-2) had plenty of 1st H chances, but could convert only their 1st opportunity as DE John Lavin's FUM REC occurred at Ohio 21YL. Lavin caught 10y pass between runs by TB Bob Felver (16/88y), who scored 4y TD. Penn had no speed merchant to match Buckeyes HB Howard Cassady, who tied it in 2nd Q with sudden 61y TD sprint. Before Cassady's TD, Penn squandered REC of poor punt snap at Buckeyes 11YL, 73y drive that perished on incompletions at Ohio 7YL, and midfield FUM REC. Pennsylvanians punted to Buckeyes 7YL in 4th Q, and QB Dave Leggett (6-15/76y, 2 INTs), subbing for injured superior passer John Borton, finally found his throwing eye and completed 4-4/55y on 93y TD drive. HB Bobby Watkins (22/116y, TD) made critical runs for 24y to augment Leggett's passes and blasted off RT George Jacoby's block for winning TD from 2YL.

PENN STATE 20 Syracuse 14: Never leading until final moment, Penn State (2-2) jarred Syracuse (2-1-1) with block of QB-P Eddie Albright's punt in Orange territory by T Dante DeFalco. Nittany Lions E Jim Garrity scooped up loose ball and cantered 24y to break 14-14 tie in game's last min. Syracuse had taken lead in 1st Q on 42y pass by QB Pat Stark (4-11/83y, INT) that carried to Penn State 8YL. Stark faked pass 2 plays later and scored from 6YL. It was 14-0 in 3rd Q as Orangemen HB Bob Leberman (15/139y, TD) lugged pigskin 6 straight plays at end of 83y drive to score on 12y run. Penn State finally dented scoreboard as QB Tony Rados tossed short ball to FB Charley Blockson who took it 45y to TD, and HB Lenny Moore followed with 4th Q TD to tie it.

ARMY 14 Duke 13 (New York City): TDs by HBs Tommy Bell on 9y run and Pat Uebel on 43y pass from QB Pete Vann gave determined Cadets (3-1) 14-7 H lead. Missed conv kick following Duke (4-1) QB Worth Lutz' 2nd 4y TD sneak left hopeful Army clinging to 14-13 margin in 4th Q. Late chance for Duke materialized on reverse run from Polo Grounds' baseball infield grass: Lutz handed to HB Bob Pascal running to right, who slipped it in other direction to HB Red Smith. Smith broke outside and set off toward GL in front of distant rightfield bullpen. Smith covered 73y to Army 7YL, where he was overhauled by hustling DE Bob Mischak's leaping tackle save. Coach Red Blaik later wrote, "Mischak displayed heart and a pursuit that for one single play I have never seen matched." After 3 runs and with 40 secs left, ball rested on Army 2YL. It was 4th down. Kicking tee was thrown onto field by Duke bench, but Lutz, remembering his missed x-pt, tossed it back, driving instead for Cadets GL on another sneak. When they unpiled Lutz had been halted within inch of scoring. Entire 2,400 Corps of Cadets raced onto turf to toast its heroes at final gun.

MARYLAND 26 North Carolina 0: Mistakes by flag-plagued North Carolina (3-1), with its 135y in PENs, clearly assisted 4 long TD drives by undefeated Maryland (5-0). Pair of Terrapins QBs, starter Bernie Faloney and backup Charley Boxold, each guided pair of scoring marches. Each QB notched TD on short run, while FB Ralph Felton scored on 1y vault, and E Russ Dennis on 7y pass from Boxold. Tar Heels threatened in 3rd Q while trailing 13-0, but HB Ken Keller lost FUM at Terps 1YL that was covered by Terps DT Bob Morgan. Maryland held again on its 28YL, shortly thereafter.

ALABAMA 0 Tennessee 0: Still in its infancy, TV sought many big events to beam across country. Tennessee grad Lindsey Nelson and Alabama grad Mel Allen, 1950s giants behind microphone, convinced NBC of merits of this great rivalry. Unfortunately, stumbling SEC giants wrestled without pinfall. "My goodness, a scoreless tie," said Nelson. "That was not exactly what you want on television; the folks in New York (network executives) were livid." Alabama (2-1-2) gained 287y rushing, but fumbled away many of its chances. Game's best scoring bid came in 3rd Q when Tennessee's bad punt snap allowed Crimson Tide G Charley Eckerly to slam Volunteers (1-2-1) P Bobby Brengle back into EZ. Officials ruled Brengle's forward progress had barely gotten him out of EZ and possible game-losing safety. Vols nearly pulled off their own safety on game's last play: Tide QB Bart Starr backpeddled to pass from his 11YL, and Tennessee DE Tommy Hensley nearly downed him for 2 pts.

GEORGIA TECH 36 Auburn 6: Normally-dependable Tigers HB Fob James lost pair of early FUMS to C-LB Larry Morris and DE Dave Davis, and no. 6 Georgia Tech (4-0-1) turned them into TD and FG. Little HB Leon Hardeman's 15 and 39y TD scampers helped Yellow Jackets to their 12th straight win over Auburn (2-1-1). Engineers QB Bill Brigman added 26y TD pass to E Sam Hensley. Plainsmen lost 6 FUMS, 4 leading to Georgia Tech TDs, another denying TD to Auburn HB Bobby Duke as he lost ball on dive to Tech's GL. Yellow Jackets extended nation's longest unbeaten streak (29-0-2 since November 1950) to 31 games.

Louisiana State 14 GEORGIA 6: Pass-minded Georgia (2-3) QB Zeke Bratkowski (13-23/140y) threatened Bengal Tigers (3-0-2) all game, but LSU picked off 3 of his throws to twice kill advances to Tigers 18YL. For its part, Louisiana State fumbled ball away on 4 occasions, including FB Jerry Marchand's bobble at his 18YL in 2nd Q that led to Bulldogs' TD by Bratkowski on 2y keeper. Earlier, Marchand had barreled up middle for LSU's 1st Q TD after HB Chuck Johns launched scoring probe with 17y punt RET to UGa 34YL. Ahead by 7-6, Tigers clicked to clinching score as frosh HB Lou Deutschmann and FB Tommy Davis led ground assault to Davis' 1y TD run.

Wisconsin 28 PURDUE 19: Big 10 co-champs of 1952 squared off with Rose Bowl loser Wisconsin (3-1) coming out with more decisive victory than score might indicate. Taking advantage of C-LB Gary Messner's FUM REC and INT, Badgers built 21-0 3rd Q edge. Spectacular for Badgers was soph QB Jim Miller, who stepped up as stand-in for QB Jim Haluska, lost to summer-time injury. Miller (2-6/38y, INT, and 5/88y rushing) scored twice, including weaving 50y scramble. After HB Ed Neves sparked Boilermakers with 51y punt RET, sub QB Froncie Gutman nearly rallied Purdue (0-4) by scoring twice. Aiding belated Boilers' comeback was QB-DB Roy Evans' INT RET to Wisconsin 34YL--as FB Dan Pobojewski caught 21y pass prior to his TD plunge--and DT Frank Angellotti's FUM REC at Badgers 36YL. Badgers soph HB Clary Bratt (4/113y) chipped in 76y dash to set up Miller's 1st TD in 2nd Q and 28y TD romp in 4th Q.

NOTRE DAME 23 Pittsburgh 14: Stirred-up Panthers (1-2-1) leapt to 14-0 1st H lead as Associated Press account identified no. 1 Notre Dame as "looking like sandlotters at the start of the game." FB Bobby Epps (13/55y) ended 66y drive in 1st Q with 8y TD run, which was followed in 2nd Q by pass theft by star Pitt QB-DB Henry "Model T" Ford from intended reciver, Irish E Paul Matz. Ford dashed 47y to 9YL, Pitt gained 5y by inducing offside PEN with "sucker shift," and HB Richie McCabe quickly scored on pitchout from 4y out. Irish T Frank Varrichione trapped Epps for 3rd Q safety, narrowing gap to 14-9. Then, calm Notre Dame (3-0) QB Ralph Guglielmi (7-16/98y, INT) took command, scoring on 1-ft sneak in 3rd Q to push ND ahead at 16-14. Irish failed on 74y march at beginning of 4th Q but scored clinching tally when they took over at Panthers 37YL. Guglielmi raced for 9y TD on 4th snap of series.

NEBRASKA 20 Miami 16: In 1st Q, Cornhuskers (1-3-1) HB Bob Smith made quick juke in backfield, fired through gaping hole, cut left away from Miami (2-2) DBs, and was off on 80y TD sprint. But, Hurricanes led 10-7 at H: They used short Nebraska punt to position T-K Dan Tassotti for 25y FG and QB Don James' passes set up FB Gordon Malloy's leaping TD. Huskers regained lead with 3rd Q TD, and moved to 20-10 edge early in 4th Q at end of 67y trip as HB Rex Fischer, 1st in long line of brothers playing in Lincoln, zipped around RE for TD with 13 mins left. FUM killed next Hurricanes drive, but Miami G Tom Pratt fell on FUM by QB Johnny Bordogna at Nebraska 15YL. Frosh HB Porky Oliver scored 3 plays later, but Miami could get no closer in last 5 mins.

STANFORD 21 Ucla 20: In big upset of undefeated UCLA (3-1), Stanford (3-2) QB-DB-K Bobby Garrett (18-27/196y, INT) was all over field in superb 60-min performance. Garrett recovered FUM on opening KO as Indians G Norm Manoogian cracked UCLA TB Paul Cameron. It set up 1st of Garrett's 3 right-handed TD passes. In addition to starring as defender with several tackles and INT, Garrett booted 3 left-footed conv kicks. Bruins were able to pull within 7-6 late in 1st Q as Cameron flipped 25y TD pass

to WB Bill Stits. UCLA built 20-7 lead by middle of 3rd Q as Cameron made pair of TD runs in middle Qs. But, UCLA subs were trapped in game until beginning of 4th Q, thanks to sub rules. Lead was squandered as Garrett spun his air magic against less experienced Bruins' secondary. Stanford E Sam Morley caught 10y TD late in 3rd Q, and FB Bill Wentworth charged 23y to set up Garrett's tying TD pass of 9y to HB Al Napoleon. Garrett's calm winning kick was lengthened by Stanford's offside PEN.

October 24, 1953

PENNSYLVANIA 9 Navy 6: Coming off 65-7 rout of Princeton, undefeated Navy (4-1) eyed easy match with Penn (3-2), which shunned typical Ivy slate for pres Harold Stassen's back-breaking "Victory with Honor" schedule. Quakers' 60-min DT Jack Shanafelt made 2nd Q INT and caused 3rd Q FUM that led to FB Joe Varaitis' TD at end of 36y drive. Ill-advised 4th down fling by Penn HB Bob Felver was picked off by Navy DE John Hopkins, who took it 47y to tying TD in 3rd Q. Quakers outgained Middies 229y to 150y, but needed last-min 35y FG by QB-K Ed Gramigna to break 6-6 tie.

PENN STATE 27 Texas Christian 21: With Mt Nittany shrouded in rainy mist by Homecoming afternoon's end, Penn State (3-2) had to rally late in 3rd Q after frittering away 14-0 lead in 2nd Q. Nittany Lions FB Bill Straub caught soft flat pass for TD from QB Tony Rados (13-19/166y, 2 TDs, INT), and HB Lenny Moore raced 41y for TD in 2nd Q for 14-0 lead. Unflappable Texas Christian (1-4) roared back on pair of TD passes by QB Ray McKown of 7y to E Don Sanford and 14y to HB Dave Finney for H deadlock. Rados directed 82y trip, mostly through air, to E Jim Garrity's 26y TD catch. Back came Horned Frogs after E Johnny Crouch blocked and advanced punt to Penn State 1YL for McKown to sneak across. DT Gene Danser set 70y trip to winning score for Lions with INT: key play to Rados' 2y TD keeper was E Jesse Arnelle's 21y reception.

FLORIDA 21 Louisiana State 21: Side-arming Louisiana State (3-0-3) QB Al Doggett dogged Florida (2-2-2) all game with his passes. Midway in 1st Q, Gators HB Tommy Haddock lost FUM to LSU DB Jerry Marchand at Florida 14YL, and Doggett flipped 2 passes to set up his TD sneak. Florida did what it did all afternoon, came back to tie it 7-7 as Haddock made amends with 35y catch-and-run and 33y run to set up tying TD. Doggett beat H clock with 4 passes, last to HB Charlie Oakley for 23y TD. Early in 3rd Q, LSU HB Levi Johns was surprised by ill-advised lateral by Doggett, and Johns' FUM was recovered in EZ by Haddock for TD that knotted it 14-14. Doggett found Johns for TD that gave LSU 21-14 lead, and with under 4 mins to play, Gators finally turned pass against Tigers. QB Harry Speers whipped 65y connection to HB Bob Davis to gain position for Davis' tying 2y TD run. Gators got late chance on FB-LB Mal Hammack's bobbling INT at LSU 16YL, but 15y PEN forced long missed FG.

PURDUE 6 Michigan State 0: Sub FB Dan Pobojewski, new starter in patched-up Purdue (1-4) lineup, scored early 4th Q TD to snap 28-game win streak of Spartans (4-1). Also, it was 1st shutout of Michigan State in 59 games. Following Boilermakers' TD, Michigan State HB Leroy Bolden (15/78y) raced 95y with KO but it was nullified by clipping PEN, which took starch right out of Spartans. MSU QB Tom Yewcic (2-14/30y, 5 INTs) had awful day as alert Boilermakers D stole 5 passes. Best scoring chance for Spartans came in 1st Q, but QB-DB Froncie Gutman made GL INT of Yewcic.

MINNESOTA 22 Michigan 0: Efforts of Golden Gophers' ironman turned Little Brown Jug's 50th renewal into Minnesota's 1st win over Michigan (4-1) since 1942. Gophers (2-3) TB Paul Giel set Big 10 record by handling ball remarkable 53 times and accounting for 282y O. Giel scored twice and passed 13-18/169y, TD, 4 INTs. Michigan FB Dick Balzhiser lost 2 FUMs, 1st coming at own 28YL in 1st Q to set up Giel's initial TD run. Balzhiser's 2nd bobble occurred in his own EZ and handed safety to Minnesota in 4th Q. Pinned in their own territory nearly all day, Wolverines advanced to Gophers 17YL on TB Ted Kress' dash early in 4th Q, but drive fizzled on downs.

NOTRE DAME 27 Georgia Tech 14: Ahead 7-0 at H, Fighting Irish (4-0) players "cried like babies" according to AP writer Charles Chamberlain as beloved coach Frank Leahy collapsed in locker room and was carried to hospital with what initially was feared to be heart attack. It turned out Leahy's severe pain resulted from acute pancreatitis. Notre Dame captain, E Don Penza, said afterward, "The kids were so upset that their defenses against Georgia Tech's flanker plays—something we had practiced all week and looked good on in the first half—became confused." So, Georgia Tech (4-1-1) tied it 7-7 in 3rd Q with 69y march to QB Wade Mitchell's TD run. HB Bill Teas' 12y run and E Henry Hair's 15y catch supplied key gains. QB Ralph Guglielmi's TD pass to HB Joe Heap put ND ahead 14-7 with 4:05 left in 3rd Q, which helped end Engineers' 31-game unbeaten streak. But vital TD for ND came when T Art Hunter outscrambled Georgia Tech C-P Jim Carlen to bad snap that sailed into Yellow Jackets EZ in 3rd Q. Mitchell clicked with Teas for 53y TD to start 4th Q but it wasn't enough. Irish FB Neil Worden rushed 21/101y, showing running force Tech asst coach Frank Broyles marveled over: "They have more power than any football team should have."

OKLAHOMA 27 Colorado 20: Oklahoma (3-1-1) trailed after its FUM of opening KO, which underdog Colorado (2-4) converted into HB Ron Johnson's 12y TD run. Sooners appeared to take 4th Q control on HB Bob Herndon's 33y TD run for 20-13 lead, but Buffs retaliated with 80y TD drive for 20-20 deadlock. Only :36 remained as OU HB Merrill Green cut inside E, raced 51y down sideline for stunning win.

Mississippi 28 ARKANSAS 0 (Memphis): While Arkansas (1-4) made its y at midfield, Ole Miss (5-1) D, led by G Crawford Mims and C-LB Ed Beatty, stiffened to halt Razorback probes at Rebels' 3, 17, 15, and 19YLs. Rebs went ahead 7-0 in 1st Q as HB Billy Kinard, from tall family tree of Ole Miss stars and also its future coach, went across from 1YL 5 mins into game. HB-DB Jimmy Patton recovered FUM by Arkansas WB Phil Reginelli at Hogs 32YL to poise 3rd Q TD for 14-0 Ole Miss lead. Rebs put verdict in bank in 4th Q as HB Harold Lofton charged to 86y TD run and QB Lea Paslay pitched 20y TD pass in last secs. Dangerous Arkansas TB Lamar McHan was well-contained other than 40y completion and 30y punt RET.

Rice 18 TEXAS 13: Unusual twists often framed heyday of tightly-contested Southwest Conf. This game was no different as lead changed 3 times, and Texas (3-3) sub FB-P Pat Tolar twice took intentional safties in 4th Q in desparate attempt to hold off Owls. But, Rice (4-1) E Dan Hart took 31y pass from QB Leroy Fenstemaker and slipped between pair of diving defenders to drop across GL for winning TD with 56 secs to play. HB George Robinson had given Longhorns 6-0 lead with 1y plunge in 1st Q, only to see Owls slip HB Dicky Moegle's 9y TD sweep in 19 secs before H. Texas retook lead at 13-7 on E Menan Schriewer's 27y reception in 3rd Q and had to stop Rice's 83y trip to 5YL before Tolar conceded 1st safety with less than 6 mins to play. Facing 4th down from its 5YL on its next possession, Texas had Tolar waste time by dashing around his EZ before being tackled. Down 13-11, Owls FB Kosse Johnson (111y rushing) brought free-kick back to Longhorns 45YL with 90 secs to play. Rice converted 3rd down to 31YL on double "hook-and-ladder" pass: Fenstemaker to Hart, who lateraled to Johnson, who lateraled to HB Sammy Burk. This set stage for Hart's TD tumble between Texas defenders, QB-DB Charlie Brewer and HB-DB Delano Womack. After previous week's loss to SMU, Owls' win kept them in Cotton Bowl chase.

Baylor 14 TEXAS A&M 13: Battle of undefeated teams swung on foot of Baylor (5-0) T-K Ray Smith who made both conv kicks while Bears HB Weldon Holley deflected 1st of 2 kick attempts by HB-K Ellwood Kettler for Aggies (4-1-1). When Baylor QB Cotton Davidson scored on sneak behind G Pete Erban's block with 14 sec to go in 1st H, he believed his play call had been detected by A&M D, which still couldn't stop him. Smith led Bears D that allowed only 93y rushing, but was punched for 11-19/168y passing by Aggies QB Don Ellis. A&M E Bennie Sinclair, caught 5 passes and scored on 17y throw in 4th Q.

Southern California 32 CALIFORNIA 20: Trojans (5-0-1) coach Jess Hill called it "our best game to date," earned by hard-hitting D. Ending up with -21y rushing, California (3-3) dropped 8 FUMs, losing 5 overall, 4 inside its own 10YL, and Golden Bears QB Paul Larson (8-21/179y, TD, 2 INTs) courageously stood in against fierce pass rush with Troy's D star, G-LB George Timberlake, causing much of mayhem. Southern California TB Aramis Dandoy (12/42y) pinned Cal at its 4YL and 1-ft line with QKs of 57 and 67y in 1st H. USC FB Harold Han (10/33y) scored on pair of runs that provided 7-0 lead in 1st Q and 19-0 lead in 2nd Q. Late in 3rd Q, Trojans faced 4th down at Bears 5YL and called double reverse in which LE Ron Miller ended up with ball to skirt RE for TD. Miller had nabbed 21y reception earlier on 66y drive that made it 32-14. Bears briefly had gotten back into contest in 2nd Q on TDs by HB Al Talley and big E Cliff Wright.

October 31, 1953

Syracuse 21 HOLY CROSS 0: Big day for QB Pat Stark (7-15/137y, 2 TDs, INT) translated into big day for Syracuse as Stark accounted for all 3 Orangemen TDs. Holy Cross (3-3), which suffered its 3rd straight shutout, came closest to scoring in pt-free 1st H: On last play of 2nd Q, Crusaders QB Don Jolie, making his 1st start, pitched apparent TD to E Bob Dee, but Dee was ruled to have stepped outside EZ. In 3rd Q, Holy Cross HB Pete Biocca sprinted 44y off T, but threat died at Orange 25YL. From there, Syracuse scored in 7 plays as Stark hit HB Bob Leberman with 14y pass, then faked throw and spun through open field for 49y TD run. On 1st snap of 4th Q, Crusaders relinquished ball at Orange 34YL on downs, and Stark passed 49 and 12y to HB Bruce Yancey, latter for TD. Leberman caught 48y TD pass from Stark, just 2 mins later.

West Virginia 20 PENN STATE 19: Nittany Lions (3-3) roared to 12-6 H gain on pair of TDs by QB Tony Rados: keeper run and 46y pass to HB Dick Jones. West Virginia (6-0), proud owner of nation's longest win streak, rallied in 3rd Q to earn its 12th straight victory. After Mountaineers QB Freddie Wyant sneaked over, FB-LB Tommy Allman shot through to block punt that star T Bruce Bosley gobbled up in EZ for TD. HB-K Jack Stone converted after each TD, so WVU led 20-12. Penn State HB Ron Younker slipped across GL on 20y TD catch from Rados to trim score to 20-19. DB Stone, whose kicks spelled difference in scoring, doomed Lions' fate by nesting on State FUM at his own 10YL in 4th Q and later angling punt OB at Lions 8YL.

FORDHAM 20 Miami 0: Recalling Polo Grounds glory days of 1930s when "Seven Blocks of Granite" dug in on New York home loam, Fordham (3-2) rolled over surprised Hurricanes (2-4). Rams HB Joe Yalch scored twice, including 40y punt RET, and QB Roger Franz threw 19y to E Andy Nacrelli for another score. Yalch wedged over from 1YL late in 1st Q and Nacrelli's TD catch followed in 2nd Q for 13-0 H edge. Miami, losers to no. 2 Maryland and no. 3 Baylor among its 3 prior predators, showed it had gained little from those experiences. Hurricanes' pop-gun O (134y) penetrated Rams territory only twice, and Miami lost FUMs each time. C-LB Charley Danielczuk was outstanding on D and left Fordham fans to ponder comparisons to all-time Fordham great C-LB Alex Wojchiewicz.

Dartmouth 32 YALE 0: Soph QB Bill Beagle burned Yale's nation-leading D for 4 TD passes as injury-riddled Dartmouth (1-5) reversed worst start in its long football history. Stunned Yale (3-1-2) was outgained 303y to 138y and entered Indians territory only thrice with its deepest penetration coming near end of contest. Beagle's TD passes went to Big Green HB Lou Turner (who also caught 8y TD throw from sub QB Leo McKenna in 2nd Q) for 31y in 1st Q, E Dave McLaughlin for 17 and 20y each in 3rd Q, and HB Jack Nicolette on brilliant grab in 4th Q. Indians' upset was anchored by alert D that produced 2 INTs and 6 FUM RECs. Dartmouth RECs by Turner at own 34YL, T Everett Pierson at Yale 19YL, and C-LB Paul Mackey at Elis 16YL set up each of team's 1st 3 scores.

AUBURN 16 Florida 7: Tigers (4-1-1) leapt to 13-0 lead while its rough D allowed Florida (2-3-2) only single 1st down in 1st H. Auburn's bruising attack was anchored by QB Bobby Freeman and FB Charlie Hataway's 3y TD run at end of 54y drive as Tigers rolled to 244y rushing and 141y passing. Freeman scored slippery TD in 2nd Q when he dropped back to pass on 4th down and sprinted left to avoid Gator LBs for 10y TD. Trailing 16-0, Florida powered 94y in closing mins to FB Joe Brodsky's 2y TD, with key gain coming on QB Fred Robinson's pass to HB Jackie Simpson.

Alabama 33 GEORGIA 12: Slumbering Crimson Tide (3-1-3) O came alive, sparked by HB Corky Tharp's long TD runs of 88 and 63y. Soph QB Bart Starr fired 3 TD passes for Alabama. Georgia (3-4) HB Bob "Foots" Clemens had big day on ground, scoring TD. Meanwhile, Alabama D did top job clamping down on Bulldogs aerial wizard, QB Zeke Bratkowski, who suffered 3 INTs. Leading 13-12 in 3rd Q, Tide C-LB Vince DeLaurentis swiped INT and dashed 40y to score. In odd twist of future fate, Bratkowski would understudy Starr on championship Green Bay Packers teams of 1960s.

Mississippi 27 LOUISIANA STATE 16: Bengals (3-1-3) were full of fight, taking 16-14 lead into 4th Q, but were worn down by speedy Rebels. Mississippi (6-1) had opened scoring on 1st of 3 long drives, going 68y to TD pass by QB Lea Paslay (8-14/212y, TD, INT) to E Bob Adams for 7-0 lead. Stocky FB Jerry Marchand (11/90y) brought LSU crowd to its feet with pinball-like 49y TD run to tie it in 2nd Q. At H, Ole Miss led 14-10 as last score of 2nd Q came on LSU QB-K Cliff Stringfield's 35y FG, after some good D work by Rebels G Crawford Mims and T Dennis Ott stopped Tigers at 18YL. Frosh HB-DB Lou Deutschmann made INT of Ole Miss backup QB Houston Patton (6-8/94y, INT) and authored 85y TD RET in 3rd Q. Rebs launched 82y TD trip, starting with Paslay's 43y pass to E Bob Drewry and riding mostly on inside runs by FB Bobby McCool (15/60y) late in 3rd Q and cashed McCool's go-ahead TD in early dawn of 4th Q.

Texas Tech 27 MISSISSIPPI STATE 20: Rock-ribbed Texas Tech (6-1) front wall, led by T Jerry Walker, gave outstanding Mississippi State (3-2-2) QB Jackie Parker full-fledged misery. It wasn't until late in 4th Q that harassed Parker (7-12/97y, 2 TDs) truly found his passing range. Red Raiders had scored after opening KO on 85y drive capped by TD run by HB Don Lewis. Texas Tech led 13-0 at H, and, well into 4th Q, it enjoyed 27-7 advantage as HB Bobby Cavazos contributed greatly to Raiders' 327y rushing. Tech TDs, however, were scored by 3 other backs: FB Rick Spinks, HB Tom Janes, and FB James Sides. Bulldogs HB Donald Joseph scored twice: 35y run in 3rd Q and 26y pass from Parker in 4th Q.

TULANE 0 Army 0: Rarely has ball dropped out of runners' hands as it did in 1st Q in New Orleans: Army (4-1-1) dropped 4 FUMs and Tulane (1-5-1) bobbled away 3 FUMs. Also, it was in 1st Q that Cadets lost their best chances to score. Army went 52y to Green Wave 15YL on wings of QB Pete Vann's throwing and HB Tommy Bell's running. Vann threw TD pass to E Bob Mischak, but offside PEN nullified score, and 2 plays later Tulane DE Eddie Bravo recovered Vann's FUM at 10YL. Although Army advanced its O 305y to Greenies' 210y, key to upset deadlock was sharp sideline-to-sideline tackling by Tulane C-LB Paul Rushing and G-LB Tony Sardisco. Wave's best chance came early in 4th Q when QB Pete Clement hit 2 passes to 8YL. But on 4th down, K Clement was forced to attempt FG which D-star Mischak blocked with swift charge from LE.

WISCONSIN 10 Iowa 6: Crossing midfield only twice, Iowa (3-3) still held 4th Q lead of 6-3 on HB George "Dusty" Rice's 36y TD, 4th down catch from QB Jerry Reichow late in 2nd Q. Wisconsin (4-2) considerably outgained Hawkeyes by 374y to 170y, but miscues, PENs, and fine D play of DE Frank Gilliam and QB-DB Lou Matykiewicz (INT) prevented any Badger scoring over than T-K Bill Miller's 2nd Q FG. With 8 mins left, Badgers launched 61y drive. QB Jim Miller (10-23/211y, TD, 2 INTs) fired over middle for HB Harland Carl, who spoiled apparent INT. Iowa FB-DB George "Binky" Broeder batted pass twice in full stride, only to have it pop into hands of Carl who had easy time finishing 38y TD when Broeder slipped.

Oklahoma 34 KANSAS STATE 0: Big 7 Conf titles dreams of long-suffering Kansas State (5-2) fans were dashed quickly on Homecoming in Manhattan. Unbeaten in 3 conf tests so far in 1953, Wildcats were helpless to prevent Oklahoma (4-1-1) line from tearing big holes for runners QB Gene Calame and HBs Larry Grigg and Bob Herndon. Sooners rushed for 424y and made 24 1st downs even though their passing attack tallied no completions in 4 tries. Oklahoma took opening KO and covered 79y in 19 plays to Grigg's 3y TD run. In 2nd Q, OU went 70y in 7 plays as Herndon zipped

through block of G J.D. Roberts for 15y quick-opener TD. Grigg scored again in 3rd Q after 80y march. K-State threatened only in last min of contest: QB Bob Whitehead nailed E Wilbur Stocks with 33y pass at Sooners 4YL, but vain EZ pass on next play brought final whistle.

Kentucky 19 RICE 13: Favored Owls (4-2) led 7-6 at H on HB Dicky Moegle's 5y TD sweep around LE. Up-and-down Kentucky (4-2-1) used QB Bob Hardy's 32y TD pass to HB Steve Meilinger and HB-DB Joe Platt's 45y INT TD RET with blocking procession midway in 3rd Q to take 19-7 lead. EZ interference PEN placed Rice at Wildcats 1YL, and FB Kosse Johnson slammed over for TD that got Owls close in 4th Q at 19-13. To make matters worse, Rice, playing outside its SWC, was helpless to stop Baylor's claim of undisputed conf lead with its 25-7 win over TCU.

UCLA 20 California 7: TB Paul Cameron was difference in 2nd H as no. 10 Bruins (6-1) beat big brother Golden Bears (3-4), visiting from Bay Area. P Cameron had boomed long punt to pin California deep in its end in 1st Q. UCLA D-line quickly stacked up Bears QB Paul Larson (6-16/67y, 3 INTs, 17/-15y rushing), and, as result, UCLA took punt on own 43YL. Cameron whipped 13y pass to E Myron Berliner and dashed 15y to 1YL, point from which FB Bob Davenport vaulted into EZ for 7-0 lead. In 2nd Q, Larson found his throwing rhythm and hit passes of 17y to E Joe Hibbs, 15y to HB Al Talley, and 17y to E Jim Carmichael to Uclans 10YL. Larson sneaked over on 4th down to create 7-7 deadlock 25 secs before H. Bruins took 2nd H KO and mounted 66y drive on Cameron's 12 and 8y passes and WB Bill Stits' 16y reverse run to Cameron's 3y TD run. Later in 3rd Q, DB Cameron made 22y INT RET to Bears 36YL and followed with battering 15y run up middle after fighting through fierce pass rush. Drive was capped by Cameron's 6y TD pass to Stits.

OREGON 13 Southern California 7 (Portland): Adaptable QB George Shaw (3-7/45y, 2 INTs, 8/70y rushing, 3/44y receiving), who had set NCAA INT record as DB in 1951 and Pacific Coast Conf completion record as QB in 1952, oddly switched to E for Oregon (3-3) to snare 16y TD pass at right flag in 2nd Q. Shaw contributed 2 more catches from reserve QB Barney Holland (5-9/69y, TD) on winning 4th Q drive that was capped by 3 line cracks from 12YL by HB Walt Gaffney for winning TD. To start winning drive, Webfoots gained possession on USC 48YL when punt snap went astray from Trojans TB-P Desmond Koch. Falling from unbeaten ranks, Trojans (5-1-1) lost ball on downs at Ducks 5YL after FB Addison Hawthorne led game's opening drive and got their sole TD after 2nd H KO on 4th-and-1 dive by TB Aramis Dandoy (14/45y), which earned 7-7 tie. Dandoy and HB Lindon Crow were lost to 2nd H injuries. Regardless of USC's on-field cast, C-LB Ron Pheister and G Jack Patera (FUM REC) led Oregon's D, which never again buckled. Ducks soph HB-DB Dick James put final nail in Southern Cal's coffin with INT with 2 mins to play.

November 7, 1953

ARMY 27 North Carolina State 7: Army (5-1-1) coach Earl Blaik experimented by starting his 2nd unit, and they played much of 1st Q. On upside was E Don Holleder's 59y TD bomb reception from starting QB Pete Vann; downside was revealed by poor punt coverage. North Carolina State (1-8) QB Eddie West took Army HB-P Dick Zeigler's boot, slipped 2 tacklers, and sped 68y to TD RET. Cadets FB Gerry Lodge ran 33y to set up his own short TD run in 2nd Q, so Army led 13-7 at H. West twice hit receivers inside Army 5YL but both passes were dropped, helping to keep 3rd Q scoreless. Black Knights O, which rolled up 458y, persistently plowed ahead, finally scoring 4th Q TDs on runs by Lodge and Vann.

Navy 0 Duke 0 (Norfolk): Through biting wind and slick mud, Navy (3-2-2) won O stat battle 169y to 78y, to little purpose. Duke (5-1-1) was sunk when officials erroneously allowed Devils only 3 downs from Navy 16 YL in 3rd Q. Midshipmen QB George Welsh guided game's only conserted drive in 4th Q, but Duke QB-DB Jerry Barger made game-saving INT at own 1YL. Later, Blue Devils E Howard Pitt blocked punt at Navy 32YL, but Middies HB-DB Phil Monahan quickly countered with INT at 14YL.

West Virginia 12 VIRGINIA TECH 7 (Bluefield, W. Va.): With Southern Conf repealing its ban on bowls, Sugar Bowl invitation was very much in conversation around unbeaten West Virginia (7-0). Despite being pushed up and down frozen field to tune of game-end 325y to 60y O disadvantage, Virginia Tech (5-3), enjoying 7-0 H edge and looked as though it might pull huge upset. Gobblers E-DE Roger Simmons recovered FUM by WVU HB Teddy Anderson at WVU 15YL late in 2nd Q and soon drew pass interference PEN in EZ to place ball at WVU 1YL. Mountaineers E-DE Joe Papetti knocked Tech QB Jackie Williams back to 9YL, but Williams beat H clock by pitching TD pass to HB Billy Anderson. After Mounties stopped early 3rd Q threat, QB Freddie Wyant's 44y rocket to E Bill Marker set up 1y TD blast by FB Tommy Allman (22/139y, 2 TDs). HB-K Jack Stone's conv was blocked, so Va Tech held 7-6 lead. Early in 4th Q, Allman broke loose for 40y TD run to clinch it for West Virginia.

TENNESSEE 32 Louisiana State 14: Tennessee Volunteers (4-2-1) welcomed LSU (3-2-3) to chilly Knoxville and gave up early TD, thanks to Tigers QB-P Al Doggett's expert pair of plays. Doggett (5-12/47y, INT) punted OB at Tennessee 4YL, took return punt at Vols 33YL and scooted to 5YL. HB Chuck Johns scored 2 plays later for 7-0 lead. Tennessee discovered weakness in LSU secondary, and running-passing threat

TB Jimmy Wade (15/96y, TD rushing, and 2-5/42y, 2 TDs passing) hit WB Jerry Hyde for TDs of 18y to come within 7-6 in 2nd Q and 24y for 20-7 edge in 3rd Q. Later in 3rd Q, Vols backup TB Bobby Brengle capitalized on short punt to strike quickly on 45y TD pass to E Roger Rotroff. Although Tigers T Sid Fournet made several big plays on D, Tennessee blocking was superb and rang up 266y rushing. Vols D also made 3 INTs.

Florida 21 Georgia 7 (Jacksonville): Led by FBs Joe Brodsky, Bill Dearing, and Fred Cason, Florida (3-3-2) established reliable (262y) running attack early, and cashed it on 94y TD drive in 2nd Q. It was climaxed when Gators QB and future coach Doug Dickey completed his only pass, 22y TD to E Jack O'Brien. Georgia (3-5) QB Zeke Bratkowski effectively hit 15-25/220y, TD, INT, but critical were dropped passes by E Gene White and HB Jimmy Williams deep in Gators territory in dying moments of 2nd Q. Bratkowski threw INT to Gators QB-DB Harry Spears, who returned it 27y to set up Brodsky's TD run for 14-0 lead. On next series, Bratkowski hit White for 10y, E Johnny Carson for 19y, and White for TD. Bratkowski soon was hurt in 3rd Q, and his absence took away any chance Georgia had. Florida's Dickey wedged over for TD in 4th Q to wrap up scoring.

MISSISSIPPI SOUTHERN 21 Florida State 0: With superb TB Hugh Pepper banged up, Mississippi Southern (6-1) turned to small FB Bucky McElroy for key early-game rushing y. HB Jimmie Mason scored on last play of 1st Q to put Eagles up 7-0. Pepper joined McElroy to combine for 70y TD drive in 3rd Q, and INT set up Southerners last TD, which McElroy scored from 1YL. Florida State (2-4) fashioned 2 scoring bids in 4th Q, but each was stopped on downs by Mississippi Southern's burly D.

Michigan State 28 OHIO STATE 13: TB Leroy Bolden scored 3 TDs for Michigan State (6-1), including 3y plunge in 1st Q for 7-0 lead. Buckeyes HB Bobby Watkins powered over from 15YL in 2nd Q, but E Bill Quinlan's conv block left score at 7-6 in favor of Spartans. Ohio State (5-2) QB Dave Leggett narrowed score to 14-13 with 18y TD pass to E Tom Hague. G Ferris Hallmark made key block of Buckeyes FG that preserved 14-13 lead in 4th Q and thwarted Ohio's 2nd surge to Spartans 20YL.

ILLINOIS 19 Michigan 3: Illinois (6-0-1), creators of Homecoming, drew 71,119 to its alumni weekend as Big 10 leaders smacked Michigan (5-2) for 4th year in row. Illini fumbled away ball on 1st 2 possessions at 15 and 29YLs, and once Wolverines were able to cash in for QB-K Lou Baldacci's FG. Illinois turned out to be so superior in ball control and D that superlative HB J.C. Caroline gained 30/184y on ground, adding 66y in punt RETs, and personally rushed more times than Michigan (29). Caroline ran on 8 straight plays that led to 1st of 2 TDs by Mickey Bates, Illini's other soph HB, and Caroline joined G Jan Smid in clearing blocks on Bates' TD. Tribe went 95y on 17 plays to 2nd Q score, which came when Caroline fumbled ahead into Wolverine EZ where E Steve Nosek stood far ahead of tacklers to recover for TD. Bates added his 11th TD of season on power rush in 3rd Q for 19-3 lead. Michigan was limited to 29/65y rushing.

Oklahoma 14 MISSOURI 7: Tied 7-7 in 2nd Q thanks to 12y TD catch by E Pete Corpeny on pass by Tigers QB Vic Eaton—pro rookie in 1955 who, because he could punt, would beat out Johnny Unitas for 3rd-string QB spot for Pittsburgh Steelers—Missouri (4-4) lost chance at big upset early in 4th Q. From Sooners 17YL, Missouri's Eaton fired pass to E Hal Burnine, who was open in EZ. But, Oklahoma (5-1-1) HB-DB Larry Grigg came from nowhere to knock it down. On 4th down, Missouri HB-K Ray Detring missed FG. Oklahoma (5-1-1) then gathered itself and marched 80y in 16 grueling Split-T plays called by spunky QB Gene Calame. HB Bob Burris swung around RT for 12y to launch drive that eventually earned 1st down at Tigers 3YL. Mizzou stonewalled next 3 inside runs, but Calame checked off at scrimmage line and flipped pitchout for Grigg (108y rushing) to score on wide run on 4th down, his 2nd TD of game.

TEXAS 21 Baylor 20: SWC race fell into deadlock between Baylor and Texas as Longhorns (5-3) G-K Phil Branch succeeded on all 3 of his conv kicks. Longhorns E Carlton Massey blocked Bears T-K Jim Ray Smith's 1st Q conv and it hung like London fog all day. Bears (6-1) bobbled away 4 FUMs, 2 of which led to Texas scores. HB L.G. "Long Gone" Dupre tallied thrice for Baylor, including 15y 4th Q pass from QB Cotton Davidson. But for wont of last x-pt, Baylor never could catch up.

TEXAS TECH 52 Arizona 27: Enjoying 1 of its greatest seasons, Texas Tech (7-1) struck for 568y O and 3 TDs early in each of 1st and 3rd Qs. Tech's Split-T attack sprung star HB Bobby Cavazos (13/169y) for TD runs of 5, 63, 22, and 2y. Red Raiders benefitted greatly from following 23 mph wind during their splurges, and Arizona (3-4) did same, going 80 and 90y to pair of 2nd Q TDs. Wildcats HB Kenny Cardella (11/35y), nation's 2nd-leading ground gainer, limped off after QB Barry Beasley's TD sneak in 2nd Q, but FB Don Beasley (7/73y, TD) and frosh TB Art Luppino (15/76y) contributed well. Beasley scored on 49y run in 2nd Q, and Luppino dashed 24y to set up TD in 4th Q. Leading only 20-13 at H, Raiders burst game apart in 3rd Q as QB Jack Kilpatrick (7-9/135y, TD) ran for 31y TD keeper and tossed 16y TD to HB Don Lewis. Texas Tech standout DT Buddy Lewis plugged middle, making 10 tackles.

SOUTHERN CALIFORNIA 23 Stanford 20: With thermometer reaching 106 degrees on grass surface of LA Coliseum, Stanford (5-3) QB Bobby Garrett turned hot in 3rd Q. He passed 7-7/168y and accounted for 2 TDs to earn 20-20 tie. Garrett set PCC pass y record with his game-end 324y. Earlier, Trojans (6-1-1) had scored twice for 20-7 lead: TB Aramis Dandoy caught 22y pass to set up his 3y bounce-to-outside TD run, and WB Lindon Crow raced 52y for TD pass off buck-lateral-pass from QB George Bozanic. With game tied and 1:15 to go in 4th Q, tables were turned: Garrett's last throw was picked off by USC DE Ron Miller, who charged 48y to Indians 20YL. With :13 left, Trojans little G-K Sam Tsagalakis booted winning 38y FG in late afternoon smog-enduced gloom. Afterward, "Sad Sam" talked of his Greek immigrant father attending game: "Dad was very happy (about the winning kick), but he doesn't understand football very well."

AP Poll November 9

1 Notre Dame (79)	1159	11 Mississippi (2)	127
2 Maryland (24)	1034	12 Southern California	121
3 Illinois (4)	919	13 Kentucky (1)	81
4 Michigan State (1)	741	14 Duke	68
5 Georgia Tech	650	15 Minnesota	52
6 Oklahoma (1)	591	16tRice	50
7 UCLA	467	16tStanford	50
8 West Virginia (11)	455	18 Tennessee	49
9 Baylor	402	19 Texas Tech	47
10 Texas	240	20 Auburn	23

November 14, 1953

Yale 26 PRINCETON 24: Soph TB Royce Flippin accounted for 2 TDs as Tigers (5-3) pounced on Yale (5-1-2) 17-0 by H. But, RECs of 2 KO FUMs allowed Elis amazingly to control ball for all 42 plays of 3rd Q and take 20-17 lead on TDs by QB Bob Brink, HB Pete Shears, and QB Jim Lopez. Brink tallied to cap 68y march after Yale had received 2nd H KO. Star Princeton FB and future Army head coach Homer Smith lost FUM on ensuing KO at his 37YL, and Shears ended short drive with 2y TD to lift Yale to within 17-14. Elis' best line operative, soph T Phil Tarasovic, lowered boom on Tigers BB Art Pitts to shake loose FUM at 33YL. Lopez followed with 25y dash behind fine blocking to give Yale lead at 20-17. Flippin, always clutch against Bulldogs, raced 68y in 4th Q to regain 24-20 margin for Nassau. Yale next called upon its "secret weapon," unknown trackman-turned-E Larry Reno to rejuvinate its ordinary passing attack. In last min, Reno raced into open to catch Lopez's 44y aerial and was downed on 12YL. Lopez followed with winning TD pass to HB Bob Poole who took it at GL 23 secs from end. It was Yale's 1st win over its Big 3 rivals from New Jersey in 7 seasons.

Army 21 PENNSYLVANIA 14: Trying to keep alive hopes for coach George Munger's 16th straight winning year in his last season, Pennsylvania Quakers (3-5) failed to keep up with Cadets' ironmen in nail-biter. Army (6-1-1) C-LB Norm Stephen grabbed FUM at Penn 20YL, and turned matters over to FB Gerry Lodge, who plowed over on 4th down, his 6th plunge in 7 plays. In 2nd Q, Quakers DE Jim Castle made 34y INT RET to 8YL that led to FB Joe Varaitis' 1st of 2 short TD runs, each of which would tie score. Cadets went up 14-7 when HB Tommy Bell charged 32y on option pitchout to 5YL,and HB Pat Uebel scored on same play to other side. After Varaitis tied it again early in 4th Q after 67y march, Army used QB Pete Vann's 27y pass to Bell to set up Uebel's 9y winning TD run with 10:32 to go. INTs by LB Stephen and DB Uebel clinched it.

MARYLAND 38 Mississippi 0: Exploding for 24 pts in 2nd Q, slow-starting Maryland (9-0) was led by QB Bernie Faloney, who scored 2 TDs before subs sustained stampede over no. 11 Mississippi (7-2) in 4th Q. Only scoring threat by Rebels came in 1st Q as FB Bobby McCool slammed to 2YL, but, after sack pushed Ole Miss back to 7YL, DB Faloney made great catch of EZ INT. Faloney's pick-off of Ole Miss QB Lea Paslay was 1 of 6 INTs by swift Terrapins against nation's 4th-rated statistical passing team. Maryland FB Ralph Felton charged 41y for TD behind spectacular feet-in-air wipe-out block of Rebs DE George Harris by HB Ronnie Waller. It broke open contest and came between Faloney's pair of scores: short QB sneak after C-LB John Irvine returned INT 32y to 2YL and 9y romp. Sub FB-K Dick Bielski booted FG on last play of 2nd Q for 24-0 lead and ran for TD in 4th Q. Rout by unbeaten no. 2 Terps avenged 1952's 21-14 upset loss at Ole Miss. Mississippi's swift backs were stonewalled by Maryland line, led by DT Stan Jones, and finished with only 83y rushing.

South Carolina 20 WEST VIRGINIA 14: Gamecocks (6-2) QB Johnny Gramling ran for 2 TDs and passed for another to end 13-game win streak of Mountaineers (7-1). Additionally, South Carolina gained key FUMs by employing 6-1-1-3 D to stop WVU's Split-T. Carolina's unusual D had its Gs set wide outside Ts with pair of LBs filling middle gaps. Expected to fill air with passes, Gramling threw only 8 times and instead used Carolina's 186y run game. Gamecocks HB Blackie Kincaid set up 1st Q score with 53y punt RET. Trailing 13-0, WVU went 86y late in 2nd Q mostly on passes by QB Freddie Wyant with TD coming on 47y pass to E Joe Papetti. Decisive South Carolina score came in 3rd Q, after INT by FB-DB Bill Wohrman, on 1 of only 2 completions on afternoon by Gramling: HB Gene Wilson made nifty 25y sprint with flat pass. In 3rd Q, DE Papetti dashed 40y down sideline to 5YL with INT of Gramling, and HB Joe Marconi powered over from 1y out. WVU expired in last 2 mins of 4th Q when Carolina DE Clyde Bennett picked off Wyant's pass at Cocks 8YL.

ALABAMA 13 Georgia Tech 6: Alabama (5-1-3) failed to catch its only pass attempt but picked off 2 throws by Georgia Tech (6-2-1) frosh QB Wade Mitchell in carving upset win. Outstanding Crimson Tide D was led by G Charley Eckerly and HB-DB Bobby Luna (24y INT RET). Subs HB Bill Oliver and QB Albert Elmore scored Crimson Tide TDs, Oliver's TD run came in 1st Q, and K Luna put Tide ahead 7-0. Engineers benefitted from 30y in PENs on 55y 2nd Q TD march capped by FB Glenn Turner's TD run, but QB-K Pepper Rodgers' conv try was blocked by C Ralph Carrigan, 1 of many D stars of Alabama. It looked for long time that 7-6 lead would hold up, but back-up FB-LB Rocky Stone made INT RET to Georgia Tech 48YL in 4th Q. By this time, Yellow Jackets were suffering from line injuries, and Bama pounded interior in 11 grueling plays, powered by Luna and FB Tommy Lewis, to Elmore's TD sneak from inches out.

Auburn 39 Georgia 18 (Columbus, Ga.): Tigers made big plays to tame Bulldogs for 1st time since 1942. QB Bobby Freeman went 95y for punt TD RET, HB Fob James returned INT 77y, and QB Vince Dooley hit E Vince Nardone with 13y TD after racing 65y on punt RET and threw 63y pass to E Jimmy Long to help Auburn (6-1-1) seal its most successful year since '42. With QB Zeke Bratkowski banged up, Georgia (3-6), its season crumbling, lost its 3rd straight on way to school-record to-date 8 losses. "Brat" managed brief 6-6 deadlock by connecting with his favorite target, E Johnny Carson, on long bomb that went 64y to Bulldogs TD. Georgia FB Bob Clemens roared 53y to set up his own short TD plunge that created another brief tie at 12-12. Freeman quickly took over from there with his TD sneak and long punt TD RET.

MICHIGAN STATE 14 Michigan 6: Mighty Michigan State (7-1) clinched tie atop Big 10, but question of timing remained: While Spartans now were cleared of conf probation, would sanctions be lifted in time for Rose Bowl tie-breaking vote if Illinois could win over Wisconsin to remain in 1st place deadlock with Spartans? Michigan State QB Earl Morrall flipped 5y TD pass to HB Jim Ellis in 2nd Q, and HB Bert Zagers, in for HB Billy Wells who was recovering from pneumonia, tossed his 1st collegiate pass for 4y TD to E Ellis Duckett in 3rd Q. DB Zagers contributed 2 INTs, his 2nd set up 66y drive to his TD pass for 14-0 lead in 3rd Q. Ellis lost FUM to Wolverines G Dick Beison on dangerously adventurous punt RET at own 4YL. Michigan (5-3) QB-K Lou Baldacci sneaked for TD, but his kick went wide. MSU seemed to be unraveling when it fumbled but recovered on 1st 2 plays after KO. But, Morrall tried 3rd down pass, Wolverines DE Bob Topp intercepted and lateraled to HB-DB Dan Cline for RET to Spartans 24YL with time beginning to fade. Cline's incompletion on 4th down from 14YL followed MSU DE Don Dohoney's 2nd tackle for loss, this time 3rd down sack of Baldacci, spoiled late bid.

WISCONSIN 34 Illinois 7: Wisconsin put its fate in its own hands, even though Michigan State earned at least tie for Big 10 title with win over Michigan. Meanwhile, no. 3 Illinois (6-1-1), previously undefeated in conf play fell out of Big 10 lead. Illinois got early TD from FB Ken Miller for 7-0 advantage on easy, perhaps too easy, 66y march. Wisconsin (6-2) played its strongest hand, springing 383y ground game led by FB Alan Ameche (17/145y) and HB Harland Carl (7/103y) and attempting only 3 passes. Carl sped 40y to 2nd Q TD that put Wisconsin ahead for good at 14-7. Badgers soph QB-DB Jim Miller contributed INT and tallied twice on short sneaks, including tying score at 7-7 in 1st Q. HB Mickey Bates' 39y run with screen pass late in 3rd Q gave Illini their last hope, but QB Elry Faulkenstein's 4th down pass from 33YL fell incomplete. Down by 7 pts, Illini wilted under power of Badgers' 20-pt 4th Q, that included HB Gerry Witt's 41y TD dash. Illini HB J.C. Caroline was held to 25/83y rushing, but still broke Ameche's old conf season rush y record of 774y.

COLORADO 14 Nebraska 10: With coach Bill Glassford agonizing on Nebraska (3-5-1) bench with gallstone attack, Cornhuskers were twice pained with failure within Colorado (5-4) 10YL in 4th Q, including failed stab inside Buffaloes 1YL in dying moments of game. After Buffs WB Frank Bernardi raced 30y with punt RET to set up workhorse trap-play runner, FB Emerson Wilson (22/112y, TD), for 1st Q TD dive, slumbering Huskers awoke in 2nd Q. Nebraska traveled 80y to QB Johnny Bordogna's sneak that tied it 7-7. Cornhuskers looked as though they would get another TD in 3rd Q, advancing deep into CU territory, but LB Wilson threw Huskers HB Jon McWilliams for 7y loss on 4th down to force FG by FB-K Ray Novak. Novak's 3-ptr put Nebraska ahead 10-7. Colorado retaliated immediately for what turned out to be winning pts as E Gary Knafelc nabbed 45y pass from TB Carroll Hardy (9/22y rushing) and pulled in 4y TD pass from WB Frank Bernardi on 9-play, 85y scoring threat from its 27YL. Nebraska began its fateful last, 9-play scoring threat from its 27YL. With 1st down at Bison 5YL, Huskers barely moved 2y ahead in 3 cracks. FB Novak was given 4th down TD try and appeared ready to knife over when Colorado G Dick Knowlton and C-LB Dave Hill chopped him down with 1:05 showing on clock.

Houston 37 BAYLOR 7: Missouri Valley Conf interloper Houston (3-3-1) used 382y rushing and superior line play of E Marvin Durrenburger, who blocked punt returned by E Ben Wilson for 4th Q TD, Ts Bob Choupe and Buddy Gillioz, and G Wayne Shoemaker to knock wholly-unprepared Baylor Bears (6-2) from AP Top 10. Cougars jumped to 13-0 1st Q lead on TD runs by HB Don Hargrove and FB Jack Patterson. Houston G-K Verle Cray booted 2nd Q FG, and, 2 plays later, E George Hynes' INT of Baylor QB Cotton Davidson (5-14/74y, INT) led to another TD. Choupe threw Bears backs for 25y in losses on 3 straight plays in 3rd Q. Baylor HB Jerry Coody scored belated TD in 4th Q. So thrilled was oilman Hugh Roy Cullen that he pulled out his checkbook and endowed Houston to tune of $2.25 million.

UCLA 22 Washington 6: Rare driving rainstorm in Los Angeles kept Coliseum crowd down to 13,302, but it included hearty visitors from Greece, King Paul and Queen Frederika. Washington Huskies (3-5-1) mushed most effectively in 1st Q, but UCLA (7-1) took over in 2nd Q and retained its tie atop Pacific Coast Conf with Stanford, 54-0 out-of-conf winners over San Jose State. Bruins little FB Pete Dailey raced up middle for 45y gain to Washington 28YL, and TB Paul Cameron scored on 8y run for 7-0 H lead. In 3rd Q, Cameron added another score and UCLA BB Terry Debay poured through for block Huskies punt for safety. Uclan WB Bill Stits added TD for 22-0 edge before E Jim Houston tallied Washington's only TD in 4th Q.

ARIZONA STATE 26 Brigham Young 18: By 2006, ASU had attracted largest college enrollment in U.S., but in 1953 Arizona State College of Tempe still was something of stepchild in western collegiate and football worlds. Injury-riddled ASC (4-4) leveled its season record by jumping to 14-0 H edge and staying ahead. Sun Devils HB Dick Curran, who happily finished without bruises for 1st time this season, chipped in runs of 48 and 11y before HB Danny Seivert ended 82y march with short TD plunge in 1st Q. ASC E John Allen quickly hauled in 30y TD pass from QB Dick Mackey (7-8/89y, 2 TDs), newly off injured list, and when they collaborated again on 11y jump pass TD in 4th Q, Allen had new school TD receiving record. Cougars (2-6-1) racked up 442y to 298y O edge by sticking to running game that frequently burned Sun Devils. BYU HBs Reed Stolworthy (11/163y) and Dick Felt constantly burst up middle for big gains. Felt dashed 68y to set up TD sneak by QB LaVon Satterfield (6-23/75y, 2 INTs) in 3rd Q, and Stolworthy went 12 and 48y before punching it over himself in 4th Q. Later he capped scoring with 78y explosion.

November 21, 1953

Penn State 17 PITTSBURGH 0: After its forgetable 0-2 start, Penn State (6-3) completed neat turnaround, mostly on the wing of QB Tony Rados, who passed 13-25/160y, 4 INTs. Nittany Lions E-K Jim Garrity booted 25y FG in 2nd Q after Rados and FB Bill Straub collaborated on 50y pass play that was halted from behind by speedy Pitt (3-5-1) QB-DB Henry "Model T" Ford. Moments later, lithe Lions HB Lenny Moore popped through Panthers line behind trap block and whooshed 79y to 10-0 H advantage. HB Buddy Rowell wedged across for short TD run after Rados passed for 45y of Penn State's 63y advance after 2nd H KO. Bright spot for Pittsburgh came from Ford, who nabbed 3 INTs and trotted 43y for Panthers' biggest gain that came in 3rd Q. But, Pittsburgh totaled only 119y O in face of Lions' fine D.

Harvard 13 YALE 0: Coming off big win over Princeton, Yale (5-2-2) was surprised by rival Harvard (6-2) in "The Game." Result handed unofficial Ivy League title to idle Cornell. Sturdy Crimson D clicked to attention from 2nd Q on and held Bulldogs to 148y O overall. Poor 20y punt in 2nd Q started Harvard at Yale 34YL, and sub WB Dexter Lewis dashed to 22y TD on reverse, slipping through grasp of Elis QB-DB Jim Lopez at 10YL. TB Dick Clasby and FB John Culver shared Crimson rushing duties with 5 runs each on 10-play, 85y TD drive in 3rd Q. Culver slammed 35y to end march with powerful TD. Yale went 60y to Harvard 6YL in 3rd Q, but was halted on downs.

MARYLAND 21 Alabama 0: Undefeated Terrapins (10-0) completed 6th shutout of year as HB Chet "The Jet" Hanulak improved nation's best per carry avg to 9.8y with 10/132y rushing, including 81y TD. Maryland QB Bernie Faloney hit E Bill Walker with 52y TD pass in 1st Q, but left with knee injury which would prove later to haunt Terrapins. Skidding Alabama (5-2-3) had to look ahead to Auburn game to save bowl bid. With soph QB Bart Starr having good day, Bama QBs passed 14-26/245y but were halted on every threat.

KENTUCKY 27 Tennessee 21: Legend has it that during coach Bear Bryant's victory party, after Kentucky's 1st win in 18 years over Tennessee (5-3-1), he picked up his 1st houndstooth hat, left behind by forgetful fan. Wildcats (7-2) made great use of FUM REC and 3 INTs, but especially 4th Q blocked punt. Kentucky jumped to 13-0 lead when HB Steve Meilinger powered 3y to score in 1st Q, and HB Brad Mills took clever pitchout for 5y TD in 2nd Q. Passes of TB Jimmy Wade (8-17/126y, TD, 3 INTs) set up 2 Vols TDs, and Wade hit E Dan Sekanovich for TD pass that garnered 21-20 lead on 2nd play of 4th Q. Wildcats T Harry Kirk blocked punt by Vols TB-P Bob Brengle, which was corralled by C-LB Tom Adkins at UT 25YL. On 2nd play thereafter, Kentucky QB Bob Hardy, just before being tackled, flipped lateral to FB Ralph Paolone, who charged 23y to score. LB Adkins and S Hardy came through with late INTs to secure thrilling victory for Wildcats.

GEORGIA TECH 13 Duke 10: Duke Blue Devils (6-2-1) took 3-0 lead on E-K Bernie Jack's 1st Q FG. Georgia Tech (7-2-1) QB Pepper Rodgers (7-15/89y, 2 INTs) sneaked over in 2nd Q after his passes to HB Charlie Brannon and E Henry Hair. But, Duke regained advantage at 10-6 on 3rd Q TD helped by controversial call that assisted 69y march: Blue Devils HB Lloyd Caudle flipped lateral to QB Jerry Barger, apparently after whistle, and Barger dashed 20y to Tech 22YL. FB Jack Kistler (14/61y) scored 5 plays later. Undaunted Engineers (7-2-1) E Sam Hensley, C Larry Morris, and G Orville Vereen threw key blocks—some say that included illegal clipping—to spring HB Billy Teas on brilliant 48y punt TD RET, which came with less than 4 mins left. Teas froze Duke's downfield punt coverage by faking handoff at outset of his TD RET; earlier in 4th Q he had handed off for 31y punt RET.

MICHIGAN 20 Ohio State 0: Michigan (6-3) sparred with Ohio State (6-3) early, counter-punched with 2 INTs that led to TDs, and finished by bloodying poor-tackling Buckeyes. Runs by Wolverines HB Tony Branoff (17/113y) got them started to FB Dick Balzhiser's TD plunge midway in 2nd Q and, following Balzhiser's INT, Branoff ripped up middle for another TD for 13-0 edge. In 3rd Q, Michigan DE Thad Stanford grabbed INT in flat and went 11y to Ohio State 2YL to launch game's last score. Buckeyes QBs John Borton and Dave Leggett suffered 5 INTs, and they advanced only 95y on ground with HB Bobby Watkins (19/71y) showing way. In 4th Q, Branoff's FUM, pounced upon by Watkins, plus 15y PEN placed ball at Michigna 23YL. On 4th down, Leggett hit E Tom Hague at 2YL for what seemed like sure TD, but wide open pass was dropped.

Illinois 39 NORTHWESTERN 14: While Michigan State overcame Marquette's 15-14 3rd Q lead to win 21-15 at East Lansing, Illinois (7-1-1) tied for Big 10 title as FB Ken Miller ran for TD, caught 46y TD pass from QB Elry Faulkenstein, and charged 39y to set up another score. Relinquishing 453y, cellar-dwelling Wildcats (3-6) were able to march 58y with 2nd H KO to HB Jim Troglio's TD. Initial Rose Bowl poll of conf ADs was deadlocked, but secret ballot ultimately sent Michigan State to Pasadena. Illini, winners 2 years prior, would not qualify again for Rose Bowl for another 11 seasons.

MINNESOTA 21 Wisconsin 21: Impulsive Gophers (4-4-1) knocked Wisconsin (6-2-1) from 3-way share of Big 10 crown. Minnesota scored 1st time it had ball, going 77y to TB Paul Giel's 2y TD run after his short pass to QB Gino Cappelletti was lugged 44y to 2YL. Wisconsin QB Jim Miller thrilled chilled crowd with 24y TD pass to E Norb Esser and 54y TD pass to HB Jerry Witt, latter for 14-7 Badgers' lead on last

play before H. Golden Gophers knotted it 14-14 5 mins into 3rd Q. At end of 82y trip midway through 4th Q, Badgers star FB Alan Ameche (15/88y) re-tied game at 21-21 with 3y TD blast. Minnesota then launched 73y game-threatening drive which ended in bobble at Badgers 2YL by FB Mel Holme, just as his 7y run looked to be headed for EZ. Wisconsin C-LB Bill McNamara hugged Holme's FUM to save stalemate. Earlier, Holme (24/121y, TD) had joined Giel (26/91y, TD rushing and 7-13/109y, INT passing) as Gopher heroes in their last college effort. Giel's running and passing total of 200y gave him Big 10 career total O record to date and his 1026 career runs and passes set new NCAA mark.

GAME OF THE YEAR:
NOTRE DAME 14 Iowa 14:

Notre Dame's glossy image was tarnished as it became subject of national editorials. Press held Fighting Irish to higher standard when it faked injuries to gain timeouts, even though such practice was somewhat common gamesmanship in 1953. (Iowa had used similar tactics earlier in the season.) Also, bitter deadlock with Hawkeyes (5-3-1) ended up snatching national title from Notre Dame (7-0-1), as undefeated Maryland moved atop AP Poll to stay. Twice out of timeouts, top-ranked Irish preserved TD drives in closing moments of each H by feigning injuries to stop clock. *Chicago Tribune* writers considered T Frank Varrichione to be most accomplished faker. ND HB Johnny Lattner had admiring words for Varrichione afterward, but big jr lineman remained mum on his role. For its part, up-and-down Iowa was up this week. It scored on 72y 1st Q drive after INT by DB Dusty Rice, riding runs of FB George "Pinky" Broeder (19/127y) before HB Eddie Vincent swirled around LE for uncontested 12y TD. Notre Dame controlled much of intermediate action, piling up eventual 358y to 198y O advantage. But Notre Dame E Don Penza dropped sure TD pass in EZ, and Hawkeyes gained TO on next play: C-LB Jerry Hilgenberg deflected pass to DE Bill Fenton. And so went Irish frustration until HB Lattner squirmed 41y on late 2nd Q punt RET to set up Varrichione's 1st "injury." It stopped clock after QB Ralph Guglielmi (11-27/125y, 2 TDs, 3 INTs) was sacked at Iowa 12YL by T John Hall with 2 secs left in 1st H. Guglielmi quickly flipped tying TD to E Dan Shannon. DB Broeder made INT at Hawkeyes 48YL in 4th Q and chipped in 2 good runs to bring Iowa to ND 4YL. When E Frank Gilliam made falling EZ catch, it appeared to clinch Hawkeyes' 14-7 upset with 2:06 left. But Lattner caught 3 passes as prelude to more Irish "fainting" with 6 secs on clock, and Guglielmi moved left before throwing back to right side of EZ to connect 2nd time with Shannon for TD. FB-K Don Schaefer's kick tied it before clock expired on ensuing KO.

Rice 19 TEXAS CHRISTIAN 6: Edgy Rice (7-2) blundered pair of early scoring chances and saw Texas Christian (2-7) tally on QB Ray McKown's switch to Single-Wing TB for 1y power TD run early in 2nd Q. It came after Horned Frogs DT R.C. Harris' FUM REC at Owls 39YL. Clipping PEN on punt RET soon buried TCU at its 1YL, and Rice set up at Frogs 36YL after receipt of return punt. HB Horton Nesrsta shot across from 7YL for Owls TD, and QB-K Leroy Fenstemaker's kick was true for 7-6 H lead. FB Kosse Johnson (126y rushing) had rambled 26y on pass reception to set up Nesrsta's score and made it 13-6 in 3rd Q with 5y TD run. In 4th Q, Rice HB Dicky Moegle followed HB Gordon Kellogg's 43y sweep left with 14y TD sweep in other direction to wrap up 19-6 win and 3-way tie with Baylor and Texas for SWC lead.

Ucla 13 SOUTHERN CALIFORNIA 0: Denied Rose Bowl by 2 pts in 1952, UCLA (8-1) earned its way to Pasadena after slow start in which it was held to miserly 14y in 1st H by tough Trojans (6-2-1). Southern California created its lone threat on 1st snap of 2nd Q: E-DE Leon Clarke pass-rushed Bruins TB Paul Cameron to create FUM at Bruins 40YL. TB Aramis Dandoy swept 23y on next play, but USC was halted at 8YL and missed FG attempt. Going nowhere after Uclans BB-LB Don Foster's FUM REC at USC 29YL, Bruins punted deep, and Troy was pinned at its 1YL because of clipping PEN on RET. On Troy's punt out of trouble, UCLA used WB Milt Davis' 30y RET, on which he quickly stepped aside from pair of close-in punt coverers, to set up FB Bob Davenport's 2nd Q TD on 1y dive. Bruins exploded with 236y rushing in 2nd H for game-end total of 250y, keyed by Cameron's 18/54y and Davenport's 14/56y. Southern California managed only 71y rushing for game, and its previously-stout D couldn't stop 42y march to Cameron's 6y TD run in middle of 4th Q.

STANFORD 21 California 21: Golden Bears (4-4-2), who had not lost to Stanford (6-3-1) since 1946, gleefully grabbed 5 INTs of Indians star QB Bobby Garrett (12-27/131y, TD) to power 2nd H comeback. Deadlock played before 92,500 split-school partisans kept Indians out of Rose Bowl. Garrett tied it 7-7 in 2nd Q with 4y TD pass to E Sam Morley, who threaded through pack of Bears to give Morley nation's pass receiving lead. DB Garrett made INT to set stage for his 56y TD run, which gave Stanford 21-7 lead in 3rd Q. Cal QB Paul Larson, who gained 214y to steal nation's total O crown from Garrett in this season finale, sparked Bears rally by scoring on 18y run behind block of HB Hal Norris late in 3rd Q. When C-LB Matt Hazeltine fell on FUM in 4th Q, it launched California's 54y tying drive. With 4 mins left, Bear captains combined on TD: Little HB Al Talley went 5y off block of big LT Tom Dutton.

OREGON STATE 7 Oregon 0: Sturdy Beavers (3-6) ignored strong southerly breeze and increasing rain to play ball control. Oregon State's line, led by C Joe Fulwyler, G Bill Johnson, T Howard Buettgenbach, and E Wes Ediger, pushed back Oregon (4-5-1) for Korean War veteran HB Ralph Carr to make key runs Game's only TD came on Ducks' aerial misadventure late in 1st Q. Oregon's adaptable star QB George Shaw, moved to HB as was his occasional mode of operation, and went out in flat for pass from back-up QB Barney Holland. Holland rifled throw that bounced off Shaw's chest right into arms of Oregon State FB-LB Tommy Little, who slogged 30y for unmolested TD to follow in footsteps of his father Frank Little, who scored key TD 23 years earlier to beat Oregon 15-0.

WASHINGTON STATE 25 Washington 20: Soph QB Frank Sarno, distant import from Somerville, Mass., put charge in underdog Cougars (4-6) to lead upset of Washington (3-6-1) on Huskies' soggy Homecoming. Sarno pitched TD pass to HB Wayne Berry to pull Cougars within 20-19 in 3rd Q after FB Chuck Beckel provided power runs on 60y drive. At vital moment in 4th Q, Sarno (2 FUM RECs) fell on punt blocked by Washington State T Tom Gunnari on Washington 4YL. Beckel slammed over on next play for winning score at 25-20. Berry and Sarno had tallied Wazzu's pair of TDs in opening 10 mins, but Berry went out injured for most of 2nd Q and start of 3rd Q. In spirited Berry's absence, Huskies had rallied for tying 13 pts in 2nd Q on HB Corky Bridges' 17 and 7y sweeps. In early 3rd Q, Washington went ahead 20-13 on QB Sandy Lederman pitched 17y TD to big E George Black.

AP Poll November 23

1 Maryland (154)	2347	11 West Virginia (17)	399
2 Notre Dame (47)	2009	12 Wisconsin	257
3 Michigan State (8)	1797	13 Kentucky (5)	237
4 Oklahoma (9)	1553	14 Texas Tech	219
5 UCLA (4)	140	15 South Carolina	170
6 Illinois	1111	16 Auburn (1)	164
7 Texas	671	17 Baylor	96
8 Rice	490	18 Army	70
9 Iowa (6)	453	19 Stanford	59
10 Georgia Tech	415	20 Southern California	57

November 26-28, 1953

(Th'g) PENNSYLVANIA 7 Cornell 7: Underdog Cornell (4-3-2) came from behind for deadlock which gave Big Red Ivy title with 3-0-2 slate. FB Joe Varaitis scored opening TD on 18y run for Penn (3-5-1), but Cornell earned tie in 2nd Q when sub QB Herb Bool set up his own TD with 60y strike to E Bruce Brenner. Admired Quakers coach George Munger closed 16-year career with 82-42-10 record.

(Th'g) Texas 21 TEXAS A&M 12: Texas (7-3) reeled off drives of 67, 74, 80y with FB Ed Kelley, HB Delano Womack, and QB Charlie Brewer serving as scoring aces. Womack gained 103y rushing as Texas clinched at least tie for SWC crown. Longhorns E Carlton Massey, who sparkled on both sides of ball, made leaping catch over Texas A&M (4-5-1) QB-DB Don Ellis to snag pass from Brewer at Aggies 10YL to set up Womack for 4y TD run in 2nd Q. It gave Texas 14-0 lead, which was nipped to 14-6 when Texas A&M FB Don Kachtik plunged over from 1YL later in 2nd Q. In 1951, coach Ray George's Aggies started with 4 wins and slumped; his 1953 A&M team opened 4-0-1, and similar dive this time cost him his job.

(Th'g) Utah 33 BRIGHAM YOUNG 32: National TV audience marveled at wide-open style of football that would keynote Mountain zone's WAC conf, still 9 years from formation. Big underdog BYU (2-7-1) surprised Utah (8-2) with strong aerial game that set up 3 TDs by FB Don James. Ute FB Don Peterson scored 4 TDs, and QB Don Rydalch added another score with 20y TD pitch to HB Max Pierce. After 13-13 H deadlock, game's 1st pivotal play came in 3rd Q. After scoring, Utah kicked off, and BYU was guilty of personal foul with ball aflight. Rule in force at time (amazingly) provided possession to kicking-team, Utah, and it quickly scored for 27-20 lead. After rally, BYU attempted 4th tie of afternoon in 4th Q, but QB-holder Lavon Satterfield fumbled conv snap, preventing HB-K Billy Meadows from attempting score-tying kick.

Army 20 Navy 7 (Philadelphia): In front of 100,000 witnesses, Army's return from dark days of 1951 honor code expulsions became complete on strength of soph HB Pat Uebel's 3 TDs. Uebel started early, blasting over from 5YL after Navy (4-3-2) lost FUM at its 31YL to Cadets T Howard Glock on trick opening KO. Army had purposely booted KO on unanticipated diagonal path. Cadets' 70y march in 2nd Q ended in Uebel's scoring plunge on play identical to his TD of 1st Q. Uebel's most exciting moment came with 70y punt TD RET in 3rd Q; he fielded FB-P Joe Gattuso's low punt on run and roared past all but pair of Middies, last of whom was wiped out by Glock's block. Navy never quit, gaining 239y to Army's 261y, and managed to threaten several times. Cadets (7-1-1) D, led by G Leroy Lunn and E Bob Mischak, halted Middies drives at Army 9, 31, and 6YLs. Army hardly substituted at all until late going, and its reserve players permitted Tars' 63y trip to HB Jack Garrow's last min TD run. Navy had stunningly knocked Cadets from unbeaten ranks in 1950. Last 2 years had seen pair of post-expulsions defeats, so this was Army's 1st victory over its service rival since 1949. Defeat kept Eddie Erdelatz from becoming 1st Navy coach to score 4 straight wins against West Point.

DUKE 35 North Carolina 20: Frigid temperatures greeted fans, and Blue Devils (7-2-1), already ahead 7-0 on HB Lloyd Caudle's 1y, 4th down TD smash in 1st Q, took advantage of apparent frostbite or stage fright on part of North Carolina (4-5-1) P Billy Williams. Williams failed to get off any of his punts starting in 2nd Q. From EZ near end of 1st H, Williams was knocked back over end-line for safety by Duke DE Sonny Sorrell. On opening series of 3rd Q, Williams received low snap and was forced OB. Caudle caught perfect 47y TD pass from QB Jerry Barger on next snap. Tar Heels made immediate 66y trip to QB Marshall Newman's 11y TD pass. Trailing 21-7, UNC's next punting misadventure only stalled Duke. DB Barger made INT to position Caudle's 3rd TD: 35y pitchout dash scored early in 4th Q. Heels scored again on Newman's sneak, and quickly added another when bad pitchout bounced off Caudle's helmet into hands of DB Ken Keller who raced 30y. DT Ed Meadows blocked x-pt to keep Duke ahead 28-20, but Carolina fought to 4th-and-6 setting at its 43YL. Instead of trying pass play to keep its drive alive, UNC crazily had Williams try to run out of fake punt. He was swarmed under at his 35YL to set up Duke's last TD.

GEORGIA TECH 28 Georgia 12: Ball wouldn't stay put early in game as Georgia (3-8) lost FUM, Georgia Tech (8-2-1) lost FUM, then Georgia again. Engineers G Jake Shoemaker grabbed FUM at Bulldogs 14YL, and QB Pepper "Tech's Brat" Rodgers sneaked over for 7-0 lead. Rodgers hit passes of 19y to E Henry Hair and 13y to E Jimmy Durham to position FB George Humphreys for 14y TD run up middle. After

Bulldogs HB Charley Madison scored to pull within 14-6, Georgia's "Brat," QB Zeke Bratkowski, zipped short pass to Madison who rambled loose in open field. Suddenly, Madison lost his grip and ball popped into air to trailing Georgia Tech T Ben Daugherty who happily took FUM at Tech 5YL. Yellow Jackets stormed 95y to score for 21-6 lead, just when Georgia felt certain it was close to clawing back to within 14-13.

ALABAMA 10 Auburn 7: Opposing FBs Charlie Hataway of Auburn (7-2-1) and Bill "Rocky" Stone of Alabama (6-2-3) traded 1st H TDs. QB-DB Bart Starr's 4th Q FUM REC turned game for Crimson Tide, and HB-K Bobby Luna booted winning FG with 8 mins left. When Mississippi State tied Mississippi 7-7, it gave tie-strewn SEC crown to less-than-dominant Alabama at 4-0-3.

FLORIDA STATE 23 North Carolina State 13: Wolfpack (1-9) suffered blocked punt and 3 FUMs, and each miscue was turned into Florida State (4-5) score. Seminoles E Eddie Johnson blocked NC State FB Don Langston's 1st Q punt thru EZ for safety. FSU HB Bobby Fiveash soon caught 4y TD pass from QB Harry Massey for 1st of his 2 TDs. G Jerry Jacobs bagged 2 FUMs to set up Fiveash's 2y TD run in 2nd Q and Massey's 3rd Q TD pass. HB Monte Seehorn (6/42y) scored twice for NC State.

RICE 41 Baylor 19: FB Kosse Johnson and HB Dicky Moegle each gained 137y rushing as Owls (8-2) soared past fading Baylor (7-3) into SWC title tie with Texas, each with 5-1 record. Texas AD Dana Bible graciously withdrew Longhorns from Cotton Bowl bid based on earlier 18-13 loss to Rice. Bears, losers of 3 of last 4 games, got 2nd Q TD sneak by QB Cotton Davidson, but fell behind 41-7 until 2 late scores by FB-LB Weldon Holley (35y INT RET) and E Charles Bristow (7y catch). Johnson scored 3 TDs on his way to 2nd best rushing total (944y) in SWC history. Moegle, non-letter-winner in 1952, tallied twice on his path to posting 6th-best rushing total (833y) in nation.

Notre Dame 48 SOUTHERN CALIFORNIA 14: Ailing coach Frank Leahy remained glued to radio in South Bend, listening to his 86th and next to last win as Fighting Irish coach. It turned out to be most lopsided meeting between rivals in their 25 encounters. Southern California (6-3-1) took opening KO and moved 62y to Notre Dame (8-0-1) 15YL but was halted. On next 1st Q try, Trojans faced 4th-and-1 at Irish 40YL and chose conservative punt strategy: TB-P Aramis Dandoy (11/17y, TD) punted low to HB Joe Heap, who scorched 94y on punt TD RET to truly ignite Irish. Notre Dame HB Johnny Lattner (17/157y) followed with 4 TDs, including 50y dash to ice it. Playing in front of 97,952 sun-baked fans, USC managed to trim deficit to 13-7 midway in 2nd Q as TB Desmond Koch set up his 5y TD run with 43y punt RET to ND 31YL. Irish answered right away, however, going 68y on 4 plays: FB Neil Worden (15/134y) slammed up middle and charged 55y to USC 2YL. Worden smashed over for 20-7 H edge. Troy dropped 3 of its last 4 games to stellar teams that would finish 27-9-3.

Final AP Poll November 30

1 Maryland (187)	3365	11 Texas	375
2 Notre Dame (141)	3149	12 Texas Tech	264
3 Michigan State (8)	2756	13 Alabama (1)	257
4 Oklahoma (10)	2591	14 Army	226
5 UCLA (1)	2007	15 Wisconsin	203
6 Rice (2)	1388	16 Kentucky (3)	155
7 Illinois	1248	17 Auburn	119
8 Georgia Tech	839	18 Duke	102
9 Iowa (10)	576	19 Stanford	41
10 West Virginia (14)	452	20 Michigan (1)	35

December 5, 1953

Florida State 41 TAMPA 6: Florida State (5-5) used its tricky I-formation with Split-T option plays to befuddle previously strong Tampa (6-6) D. Dashing Seminoles HB Bobby Fiveash scored twice on 68y quick opener and 5y sweep left, while HB-DB John Griner raced 85y with INT TD RET. Tampa QB Bill Minihan could complete only 8-22/56y and suffered 5 INTs, while top runner, HB Charlie Harris, was thrown for losses on his only 2 carries. Tampa could gain only 82y against Seminoles D, keyed by T Al Makowiecki, G Al Pacifico and E Jimmy Lee Taylor.

NOTRE DAME 40 Southern Methodist 14: Notre Dame (9-0-1) coach Frank Leahy was back on sideline for what would turn out to be his farewell. Recently tapped as Heisman Trophy winner, Fighting Irish HB Johnny Lattner flipped his 2nd pass of season in 1st Q: 55y to E Dan Shannon to set up FB Neil Worden's 1st of 4 TDs that launched Irish scoring avalanche. Early in 2nd Q, SMU (5-5) D held at its 5YL, but QB Duane Nutt, who later threw 44y TD pass to E Doyle Nix in 3rd Q, was dumped by ND DE Paul Matz and ball squirted loose for DT Frank Varrichione to fall on in EZ for TD. Lattner scored twice for 20-0 H lead and 27-0 edge early in 3rd Q. Mustangs passers completed 9-31/202y, including reserve QB Sam Stollenwerck's 4th Q TD to then-obscure E Raymond Berry.

HOUSTON 33 Tennessee 19: Bruising line play served Houston (4-4-1) well in upset of Tennessee (6-4-1), which continued its retreat in coach Harvey Robinson's difficult 1st year as successor to legendary Robert Neyland. Volunteers TB Jimmy Wade was superb in racking up 3 TD runs, but Tennessee trailed whole way after Cougars QB Bobby Clatterbuck opened scoring at 7-0 with 1st Q TD run. Cougars led 13-6 at H. Quartet of different backs—HB Scooter Stegall, HB Don Walker, HB Don Hargrove and FB Jack Patterson—followed Clatterbuck to Cougars' pay-dirt.

1953 Conference Standings

Ivy Group (Unofficial)

Cornell	3-0-2
Harvard	3-2
Yale	3-2-1
Princeton	3-3
Columbia	2-3
Dartmouth	2-3
Brown	0-3
Pennsylvania	0-0-1

Atlantic Coast Conference

Duke	4-0
Maryland	3-0
South Carolina	2-3
North Carolina	2-3
Wake Forest	2-3
Clemson	1-2
North Carolina State	0-3

Southern Conference

West Virginia	4-0
Furman	2-0
George Washington	4-2
William & Mary	3-2
Richmond	3-3
Virginia Tech	3-3
Virginia Military	3-3
Washington & Lee	2-4
Citadel	1-3
Davidson	0-5

Southeastern Conference

Alabama	4-0-3
Georgia Tech	4-1-1
Mississippi	4-1-1
Kentucky	4-1-1
Auburn	4-2-1
Mississippi State	3-1-3
Tennessee	3-2-1
Louisiana State	2-3-3
Florida	1-3-2
Vanderbilt	1-5
Georgia	1-5
Tulane	0-7

Big Ten

Michigan State	5-1
Illinois	5-1
Wisconsin	4-1-1
Ohio State	4-3
Michigan	3-3
Iowa	3-3
Minnesota	3-3-1
Purdue	2-4
Indiana	1-5
Northwestern	0-6

Big Seven

Oklahoma	6-0
Kansas State	4-2
Missouri	4-2
Colorado	2-4
Nebraska	2-4
Kansas	2-4
Iowa State	1-5

Missouri Valley

Oklahoma A&M	3-1
Detroit	3-1
Wichita	1-2
Houston	1-2
Tulsa	1-3

Mid-America

Ohio	5-0-1
Miami (Ohio)	3-0-1
Kent State	3-1
Toledo	2-3
Western Reserve	1-2-1
Western Michigan	0-4-1
Bowling Green	0-4

Southwest

Rice	5-1
Texas	5-1
Baylor	4-2
Southern Methodist	3-3
Arkansas	2-4
Texas A&M	1-5
Texas Christian	1-5

Border

Texas Tech	5-0
Hardin-Simmons	4-1
Texas Western	4-2
Arizona	3-2
New Mexico A&M	1-4
West Texas State	0-6

Skyline Eight

Utah	5-0
Utah State	5-2
Wyoming	4-2-1
New Mexico	3-2-1
Colorado A&M	3-4
Montana	2-4
Denver	1-5-1
Brigham Young	1-5-1

Pacific Coast

UCLA	6-1
Stanford	5-1-1
Southern California	4-2-1
California	2-2-2
Washington State	3-4
Washington	2-4-1
Oregon	2-5-1
Idaho	0-3

1953 Bowl Games
Gator Bowl: Texas Tech 35 Auburn 13

Auburn's starting "X Unit," led by QB Vince Dooley, dominated 1st H to give Tigers (7-3-1) 13-7 lead at H. On 60y drive, Dooley dealt pitchouts to HBs Bobby Duke and Fob James for 44y until Duke wedged over from inches out. After Red Raiders (11-1) tied it 7-7 on HB Bobby Cavazos' 5y run in 2nd Q, Dooley hit E Jim Pyburn for 21y, zipped 15y on keeper, and scored on 10y sweep. But Tigers' 2nd platoon, "Y Unit," couldn't cope with Texas Tech E Vic Spooner and Cavazos. After Raiders QB Jack Kirkpatrick connected with E Paul Erwin on 53y TD to take 14-13 lead, Spooner blocked punt which led to another of Cavazos' 3 TDs and 21-13 lead in 3rd Q. Cavazos (13/141y) capped Red Raiders scoring with 58y run. E Spooner scored himself by nabbing mid-air FUM out of hands of Tech HB Don Lewis to tally from 2YL.

Orange Bowl: Oklahoma 7 Maryland 0

Orange Bowl matched Terps' Jim Tatum with Bud Wilkinson, who had been brought to Oklahoma as chief asst coach in 1947 by Tatum. When Tatum left for supposed greener pastures of Maryland, Wilkinson, always favorite among OU hierarchy, was given Sooners' head coaching position. So, pride was on line in this Miami matchup. Maryland (10-1), already crowned national champion by AP, was thwarted by Oklahoma's stubborn D and absence of injured QB Bernie Faloney, who missed all but handful of hopeless plays late in 3rd Q with bad knee. Terrapins sub FB-K Dick Bielski, who had 3 FGs during regular season all longer than 41y, missed 45y 3-pt try in 1st Q.

Maryland twice gained 1st downs inside Oklahoma 10YL: Terps were stopped inches from GL on downs in 1st Q, and FB-K Ralph Felton missed FG from 13YL at start of 2nd Q. Tatum allowed that, "when we didn't score the first two times (in close), there went the ballgame." Maryland also suffered INT in OU EZ by Sooners HB-DB Larry Grigg. Oklahoma (9-1-1) scored in 2nd Q when QB Gene Calame completed 2 passes to midfield to launch 80y trip, Grigg went 11y, Calame hit HB Bob Burris for 10y, and Grigg took pitchout 26y to pay-dirt. Calame went out with separated shoulder late in 2nd Q, and his injury turned Sooners O over to less-experienced QB Jack Van Pool. Stats ended up nearly even: Oklahoma had 223y O to Maryland's 212y. Wilkinson refused to claim national title for Sooners; he called it "a helluva victory." Several Sooners felt afterward that their September conqueror, Notre Dame, no. 2 in final poll, might have been superior to Maryland.

Sugar Bowl: Georgia Tech 42 West Virginia 19

Prior to Sugar Bowl, several southern writers complained that West Virginia was a hand-picked "soft" opponent for long-time SEC powerhouse Georgia Tech (9-2-1). Regardless, Yellow Jackets were so confident that QB Pepper Rodgers admitted years later that he entered game willing to toss aside Tech's normal option run attack to try to break 1939 Sugar Bowl passing record of TCU's Davey O'Brien. Rodgers' 15-19/172y (added to Bill Brigman's 3-3/61y) helped break Sugar Bowl team record by H. Yellow Jackets Es Sam Hensley, Jimmy Durham, and Henry Hair all caught TD passes, but Rodgers' 16-26/195y, 3 TDs passing stats fell one completion short of O'Brien's mark. West Virginia (8-2) coach Art Lewis moaned, "Our defense just fell apart, but Tech never threw that much all year." Early-game 15y PEN erased FB Tommy Allman's 60y TD run, and that break helped deflate young Mountaineers. WVU outrushed Engineers 223y to 170y and got TD from HB Danny Williams that trimmed 2nd Q deficit to 14-6. Rodgers' early 3rd Q FG became cherry on his sundae and upped score to 23-6. Allman and HB Joe Marconi tacked on meaningless 4th Q TDs for WVU.

Cotton Bowl: Rice 28 Alabama 6

This edition of Cotton Bowl game became forever famous for Alabama's "12th Man Tackle." Enjoying his greatest game, Rice (9-2) HB Dicky Moegle broke free at midfield on apparent 95y TD romp in 2nd Q. But, Alabama (6-3-3) capt and FB Tommy Lewis bolted helmetless from sideline and stunned Moegle with jarring tackle. Ref Cliff Shaw immediately awarded TD to Moegle that gave Owls 14-6 lead. Moegle rushed for magnificent 11/265y of Rice's 379y ground total and also made TD runs of 79 and 34y. Apologetic Lewis, who had scored early Tide TD at end of 49y drive, could only explain: "I'm just too full of Alabama." Later, Lewis began to understand: "There's going to be a big to-do about this, huh? I know I'm going to hear about this the rest of my life." Yes, he would, as almost every Cotton Bowl telecast since that date has opened with film clip of Lewis dashing off bench to knock down Moegle.

Rose Bowl: Michigan State 28 UCLA 20

Hard-hitting Bruins (8-2) D, anchored by T Jack Ellena, banged loose 3 FUMs, and each led to TD by UCLA. Uclans TB Paul Cameron (9-22/152y, 2 TDs, INT) hit 4th down TD pass to WB Bill Stits between Michigan State (9-1) defenders HB-DB Billy Wells and C-LB Jim Neal. Cameron next plunged 2y to gave Bruins early 14-0 lead. Turning point arrived late in 2nd Q when Spartans (9-1) E Ellis Duckett blocked Cameron's punt for TD to narrow H score to 14-7. Michigan State's famed "Pony Backfield" rallied with 3rd Q TD drives of 78y in 14 plays to TB Leroy Bolden's 1y run through LG and 73y in 10 plays to HB Billy Wells' 2y plunge. Wells' score provided 21-14 lead. Early in 4th Q, Cameron threw 28y TD to E Rommie Loudd, who took pass away from QB-DB Earl Morrall to trim Spartans' lead to 21-20. WB-K Johnny Hermann missed tying conv kick after clicking on both previously. Wells (14/80y), who had been fixed up with actress Debbie Reynolds for publicity purposes during bowl week must have been inspired by his date. Wells iced verdict and his MVP Award by dashing 62y on punt RET for TD and preventing late Uclans' TD by hauling down Stits, who got loose with pass from Cameron.

1953 Top Performance Formula

1 Notre Dame	1.7360
2 Maryland	1.7343
3 Oklahoma	1.6526
4 Texas Tech	1.6445
5 Michigan State	1.5782
6 Rice	1.5538
7 Illinois	1.5064
8 UCLA	1.4981
9 Georgia Tech	1.4462
10 Wisconsin	1.4273
11 Kentucky	1.4264
12 Army	1.4155
13 Mississippi	1.3653
14 West Virginia	1.3621
15 South Carolina	1.3602
16 Mississippi State	1.3276
17 Texas	1.3411
18 Stanford	1.3222
19 Iowa	1.3143
20 Oklahoma A&M	1.2942

1953 Top Opponent Records

1	Purdue	.6908
2	Oklahoma	.6289
3	Wisconsin	.6284
4	Mississippi State	.6281
5	Alabama	.6207
6	Houston	.6190
7	Minnesota	.6081
8	Notre Dame	.6080
9	Navy	.6067
10	Maryland	.6061
11	Iowa	.5987
12	Southern Methodist	.5968
13	Texas Christian	.5944
14	Kentucky	.5914
15	Arizona	.5910
16	Stanford	.5882
17	Texas A&M	.5860
18	Clemson	.5802
19	Washington	.5795
20	Texas	.5761

1953 Out-of-Conference Records

	W-L	Percentage	Bowl W-L
Big Ten	20-7	.7241	1-0
Southeastern	28-17-1	.6196	1-2
Southwest	17-11-1	.6034	1-0
Big Seven	12-12-3	.5000	1-0
Atlantic Coast	16-18-2	.4722	0-1
Pacific Coast	11-16	.4074	0-1

1953 Individual Statistical Leaders

RUSHING YARDS	Attempts	Yards	Avg.
J.C. Caroline, Illinois	194	1256	6.5
Kosse Johnson, Rice	187	944	5.1
Ken Cardella, Arizona	148	915	6.2
Bobby Watkins, Ohio State	153	875	5.7
Neil Worden, Notre Dame	145	859	5.9
Dicky Moegle, Rice	114	833	7.3
Alan Ameche, Wisconsin	165	801	4.9
Larry Grigg, Oklahoma	130	792	6.1
Bobby Cavazos, Texas Tech	97	757	7.8
Chet Hanulak, Maryland	77	753	9.8

PASSING YARDS	Completions	Attempts	Yards	Pct.
Bobby Garrett, Stanford	118	205	1637	57.6
Zeke Bratkowski, Georgia	113	224	1461	50.4
Paul Larson, California	85	171	1431	49.7
Dick Carr, Columbia	77	191	1367	40.3
Sandy Lederman, Washington	92	187	1157	48.7
Lamar McHan, Arkansas	78	150	1107	52.0
Cotton Davidson, Baylor	74	156	1092	47.4
Pat Stark, Syracuse	73	141	1045	51.8
Johnny Grameling, South Carolina	71	141	1045	51.1
Tony Rados, Penn State	81	171	1025	47.4

RECEIVING YARDS	Catches	Yards
Johnny Carson, Georgia	45	663
Ken Buck, Pacific	45	660
Sam Morley, Stanford	45	594
Dave McLaughlin, Dartmouth	31	592
Floyd Sagely, Arkansas	30	542
John Allen, Arizona State	30	505
Gary Knafelc, Colorado	22	451
Dale Hopp, Columbia	29	437
Andy Nacrelli, Fordham	29	428
John Steinberg, Stanford	32	425

1953 Consensus All-America

End:	Don Dohoney, Michigan State
	Carlton Massey, Texas
Tackle:	Stan Jones, Maryland
	Art Hunter, Notre Dame
Guard:	J.D. Roberts, Oklahoma
	Crawford Mims, Mississippi
Center:	Larry Morris, Georgia Tech
Backs:	Johnny Lattner, Notre Dame
	Paul Giel, Minnesota
	Paul Cameron, UCLA
	J.C. Caroline, Illinois

Other All-America Choices

End:
Sam Morley, Stanford
Joe Collier, Northwestern
Steve Meilinger, Kentucky
Johnny Carson, Georgia
Ken Buck, Pacific

Tackle:
Jack Shanafelt, Pennsylvania
Jim Ray Smith, Baylor
John Hudson, Rice
Ed Meadows, Duke

Guard:
Milt Bohart, Washington
Bob Fleck, Syracuse
Ray Correll, Kentucky
Steve Eisenhauer, Navy

Center:
Jerry Hilgenberg, Iowa
Matt Hazeltine, California
Bob Orders, West Virginia

Backs:
Bobby Garrett, Stanford
Jackie Parker, Mississippi State
Kosse Johnson, Rice
Bernie Faloney, Maryland
Alan Ameche, Wisconsin

1953 Heisman Trophy Vote

Johnny Lattner, senior halfback, Notre Dame	1850
Paul Giel, senior tailback, Minnesota	1794
Paul Cameron, senior tailback, UCLA	444
Bernie Faloney, senior quarterback, Maryland	258
Bobby Garrett, senior quarterback, Stanford	231

Other Major Award Winners

Maxwell (Player)	Johnny Lattner, senior halfback, Notre Dame
Outland (Lineman)	J.D. Roberts, senior guard, Oklahoma
Walter Camp (Back)	Alan Ameche, junior fullback, Wisconsin
	Bernie Faloney, senior quarterback, Maryland
	Paul Giel, senior tailback, Minnesota
	Johnny Lattner, senior halfback, Notre Dame
Rockne (Lineman)	Stan Jones, senior tackle, Maryland
AFCA Coach of the Year	Jim Tatum, Maryland

1954

The Year of Deemphasis, No Repeat Rule, and Teams Named "Desire," "Junction Boys," and "23 Little Pigs"

Deemphasis became a buzzword in 1954 as the presidents of the ancient Ivy League, the schools that founded the sport, took control of their football. It was a takeover in the name of academics greeted with much fanfare in the Eastern press. Ivy spring drills were abolished right away, and internal, Ivy League play was scheduled to begin in 1956. Pennsylvania (0-9) was the biggest beneficiary because full-fledged Ivy play saved the Quakers from a two-year, all-losing killer schedule that included Penn State (7-2), Army (7-2), and Notre Dame (9-1).

The Ivy League was one thing, the rest of major college football was still another. Defending conference champions like Illinois (1-8), Michigan State (3-6), Oklahoma (10-0), and UCLA (9-0) certainly had no interest in banning spring practice, but even so, their respective conferences, the Big Ten, Big Seven, and Pacific Coast, had token gestures of deemphasis already in place. Each embraced the dreaded "No Repeat Rule" that prevented a conference member from playing in two consecutive bowl games. The No Repeat Rule would end up casting a dark shadow over the 1954 season.

However, the South offered a plentiful number of no-repeat dissenters, namely the bowl-happy Atlantic Coast and Southeastern Conferences. SEC members Auburn (8-3) and Georgia Tech (8-3), both bowl participants the season before, happily went bowling again. Auburn beat Baylor (7-4) in Jacksonville, Fla., playing its second of three straight Gator Bowls, and Georgia Tech defeated Arkansas (8-3) in the Cotton Bowl, a fourth straight post-season win for the Yellow Jackets.

Southern football people continued to treat deemphasis as a dirty word. When Maryland slumped in 1956, former Maryland president and football coach H.C. "Curly" Byrd snarled, "Let us deemphasize defeat!"

Among the officially deemphasized, Ivy League preseason favorite Cornell (5-4) overcame a dreadful 0-4 start to achieve an end of season tie for the unofficial conference crown with late-fading Yale (5-3-1).

Among the long-standing bowl spurners continued to be Notre Dame, led by new coach Terry Brennan, the nation's youngest at 26. Brennan faced the unenviable prospect of replacing a coaching legend, Frank Leahy, and, before the former Fighting Irish halfback finished five relatively mediocre years with a 32-18 mark in 1958, his results were criticized several times by Leahy, his one-time coach. In 1954, Brennan enjoyed the presence of Leahy's stellar veteran recruits, including quarterback Ralph Guglielmi, halfback Joe Heap, end Dan Shannon, and tackles Ray Lemek and Frank Varrichione. Twenty-three players from the 1954 team would be drafted by the NFL, but Brennan soon would be forced to recruit as if he coached Cornell or Yale. A new regime, headed by Rev. Theodore Hesburgh, had played a big role in Leahy's cloudy departure and immediately sought a higher academic image for Notre Dame. In effect, Notre Dame, everyone's image of a football powerhouse for most of the 20th Century, deemphasized itself for a time, even if it was not as extensive or as officially public as the Ivy League's approach. Notre Dame officials protested to the contrary, but Brennan's inability to recruit all he wanted of high schoolers cost him dearly. His Notre Dame career would be over before the 1959 season.

The U.S. Military Academy at West Point, another school like Notre Dame that rejected bowl bids, faced its own problems as coach Red Blaik continued to deal with the lingering realities of an honor code scandal in 1951 that had stripped his squad to the bone. Blaik admitted later that his teams never enjoyed the depth that he built during his school's glory years of the 1940s and in the 1950 season. But, Blaik's 1954 Army squad was outstanding and featured the country's most explosive offense at 448.7 yards per game. Cadets halfback Tommy Bell gained 1,020 yards rushing with an astounding 10.6 yards per try average, and Army led the nation in ground gaining with an average of 322.0 yards per game. Senior quarterback Pete Vann was brilliant in mixing in long-striking touchdown missiles, especially to All-America end Don Holleder, who averaged 29.1 yards per catch. In its only losses to South Carolina (6-4) and Navy (8-2), Blaik's depth-depleted defense couldn't overcome the absence of tackle-linebacker Bob Farris, the team captain who missed his senior season due to an eye injury sustained in the 1953 win over Navy. Farris inspired his teammates, however, by becoming a defacto assistant coach and representing his team for the weekly coin toss to start each game.

AP writers and UP coaches split their decisions for the top spot in their final polls, and the No Repeat Rule destroyed a glorious Rose Bowl match that would have pitted AP champion Ohio State (10-0) against UP champion UCLA for all the national championship marbles. Woody Hayes' first great

Ohio State team faced Southern California (7-4) in Pasadena, while Pacific Coast Conference champion UCLA, a 34-0 winner over USC, stayed home due to league rules that prevented the Bruins from following their previous year's Rose Bowl faceoff with Michigan State. The Buckeyes had been considered no better than middle-of-the-pack in the Big Ten team at season's beginning, but a superb defense and highly-skilled two-way play of All-America halfback Howard "Hopalong" Cassady and a huge newcomer at guard in sophomore Jim Parker paved the way for Buckeye greatness.

Oklahoma (10-0) enjoyed the first of three straight undefeated full seasons, but the Big Seven Conference's No Repeat Rule kept the Sooners out of the Orange Bowl. So, Big Seven runner-up Nebraska (6-5), a 55-7 loser to the Sooners, carried the conference banner to Miami. The Cornhuskers were clobbered 34-6 by Duke (8-2-1), a team that lost only to Army and Navy, but was not scheduled against defending national champion Maryland (7-2-1), the other top-notch ACC team in the conference's second season.

With two undefeated teams, no. 2 UCLA and no. 3 Oklahoma, left to sit on the sidelines, the bowl picture developed so drearily that famed singer Bing Crosby suggested a charity game be arranged to match the titanic Bruins and Sooners. The NCAA quickly scotched the crooner's plan, which, while well-meaning, still failed to satisfy the obvious hankering for a UCLA-Ohio State Rose Bowl bout, which could have settled everything.

Perhaps the national championship should have been left to a vote of the California Golden Bears (5-5), who managed to have all three major undefeated teams on their schedule. With opposition that sported a percentage of .621, it was little wonder California was a disappointment among the preseason Top 20. Prognosticators took a pounding when Texas (4-5-1), Illinois, and Michigan State, starting fourth, fifth and sixth in the AP Poll, also stumbled. Other top 20 preseason picks Iowa (5-4) and Alabama (4-5-2) also fell short of expectations.

Perhaps the year's most compelling story was authored by Navy, which as a play on words of the Tennessee Williams stage play and 1951 nominated Best Picture, "A Street Car Named Desire," was given the nickname of "A Team Named Desire." Coached by cagey Eddie Erdelatz, the Midshipmen were undersized and thin of reserves, but came up with countless clutch plays. After trouncing Stanford (4-6) and Duke away from home, Navy lost heart-breakers to Pittsburgh (4-5), 21-19, and Notre Dame, 6-0, but won its big one, a thrilling offensive battle from Army, 27-20. Navy belted Mississippi (9-2) by 21-0 as a thoroughly underappreciated Sugar Bowl underdog.

Texas A&M (1-9) had a terrible year under new coach Bear Bryant, but the young team came together at a brutally hot and task-driven preseason training camp at Junction, Texas. More than 100 players departed College Station on August 31, and only 35 stuck it out to return from Junction 10 days later. Those Aggies became winners in 1955 and conference champions in 1956. In 1999, author Jim Dent would relive the Aggie players' stories in his book, *The Junction Boys*, and ESPN would turn it into a TV movie of the same name in 2002.

Fast and deep Mississippi was criticized for a lightweight schedule, which fell one game short of the SEC's required six. Commissioner Bernie Moore designated the Rebels' game with Southwest Conference member Arkansas as official in the SEC standings, and when Bowden Wyatt's Cinderella Razorbacks pulled a 6-0 stunner, Ole Miss nearly gave away the SEC title. Almost 40 years later, Arkansas left the SWC for SEC membership, starting play in 1992. The events of 1954 provide this tricky trivia question: When did Arkansas play its first SEC game? Technically, it was the October 23, 1954, game, which developed into a win against eventual conference champion Mississippi.

After posting records of 2-8 and 3-7 in the previous two years, Arkansas (8-3) surprised the nation and even coach Wyatt by winning the SWC title after being chosen near the bottom of the standings in the preseason. Wyatt employed a primary group of 23 unassuming, but dedicated players. Led by All-America guard-linebacker Bud Brooks and speedy sophomore tailback George Walker, the Razorbacks became known as "The 23 Little Pigs."

Wisconsin fullback Alan Ameche won the Heisman Trophy, was a unanimous All-America pick, and finished his career with 3,212 yards rushing. Ameche received national notoriety as having rushed for the most yards in a college career, but his ground-gaining total turned out to be 25 yards fewer than the 3,238 of Virginia's John Papit in 1947-50. In

the two-way play necessitated of the times, Ameche also was a top drawer linebacker.

Most teams stuck to ground-oriented offenses in 1954, but passing inroads continued on the West Coast. California's highly unpredictable quarterback Paul Larson was the season's passing leader with 125 completions in 195 attempts. Larson's completion percentage of 64.1 set a new record at the time. His 1,537 passing yards helped him to second place in total offense behind Oregon (6-4) signal-caller George Shaw. As the nation's top passer, Larson extended the Far West's five-year grip on the title as recent aerial leaders had been Don Heinrich of Washington in 1950 and '52, Don Klosterman of Loyola (California) in 1951, and Bobby Garrett of Stanford in 1953.

Milestones

■ Substitution rules were somewhat liberalized to allow players to reenter games during last four minutes of second and fourth quarters, if they were on the field at the start of those quarters. In 1953, reentry of any player had been banned until new quarter began.

■ Frank Thomas, who won 115 games as coach of Alabama during 15 years starting in 1931, died of heart ailment at age 55 in early July. On July 13, legendary Grantland Rice died at 73. Rice was long-time sports reporter and columnist who called college football "our nation's finest sport." and coined famous nickname of Notre Dame's "Four Horseman" backfield in 1925. Glenn Scobey "Pop" Warner, coach at Georgia, Cornell, Carlisle, Pittsburgh, Stanford, and Temple from 1895 to 1938 (319-106-32) and innovator of Single- and Double-Wing formations, and unbalance line, died at 83 on September 7. Warner, whose name adorned youth football league, won 29 straight games at Pittsburgh, led Stanford to three Rose Bowls, and developed Carlisle's Jim Thorpe, who was voted by AP as world's greatest athlete of first half of 20th century. Two Hall of Famers also died: Charles "Gus" Dorais, famed Notre Dame quarterback who teamed with end Knute Rockne to popularize passing game in Irish's upset victory over Army in 1913, and W.W. "Pudge" Heffelfinger, thrice All-America guard at Yale from 1888-91 and believed to be first pro football player in 1892.

■ Year-old Atlantic Coast Conference added Virginia, bringing its membership to 8 schools.

■ Washington & Lee dropped football.

■ Longest winning streaks entering season:
Oklahoma 9   Cincinnati, Texas Tech 8

■ Coaching Changes:

	Incoming	Outgoing
Iowa State	Vince DiFrancesa	Abe Stuber
Kansas	Chuck Mather	J.V. Sikes
Kentucky	Blanton Collier	Paul "Bear" Bryant
Michigan State	Hugh "Duffy" Daugherty	Clarence "Biggie" Munn
Minnesota	Murray Warmath	Wes Fesler
Mississippi State	Darrell Royal	Murray Warmath
North Carolina State	Earle Edwards	Horace Hendrickson
Notre Dame	Terry Brennan	Frank Leahy
Pennsylvania	Steve Sebo	George Munger
Pittsburgh	Tom Hamilton (a)	Red Dawson
Texas A&M	Paul "Bear" Bryant	Ray George
Tulane	Andy Pilney	Raymond Wolf

(a) Hamilton (4-2) replaced ailing Dawson (0-3) in October.

Preseason AP Poll

1 Notre Dame (52)	1449	11 Iowa (1)	355
2 Oklahoma (74)	1431	12 California	241
3 Maryland (13)	910	13 Army	196
4 Texas (10)	834	14 Alabama	155
5 Illinois (2)	811	15 Duke (2)	110
6 Michigan State (7)	616	16 Rice	91
7 Georgia Tech (5)	558	17 Southern California	89
8 UCLA (1)	548	18 Oregon	39
9 Wisconsin (1)	383	19 Texas Tech	34
10 Mississippi (2)	368	20 Ohio State (1)	32

September 18, 1954

(Fri) Mississippi Southern 7 ALABAMA 2: For 2nd season in row, Mississippi Southern (1-0) stunned frustrated Alabama (0-1) in season opener, even though Crimson Tide coach Red Drew had declared it would never happen again to once-mighty Bama. In 1st Q, Alabama HB-P Bobby Luna couldn't catch bad punt snap, and Southerners took over on Tide 28YL. Eagles HB Brooks Tisdale soon scampered for 17y TD and added conv for early 7-0 lead. Bama didn't score until 4th Q when reserve T Doug Potts blocked punt by QB-P George Herring, and ball rolled through EZ for safety. Eagles won despite their poor O, earning only 3 1st downs and gaining 89y. QB Bart Starr passed 8-13/94y, but threw INT as Tide also lost 2 FUMs.

(Fri) Stanford 13 COLLEGE OF PACIFIC 12: College of Pacific Tigers (0-1) trotted out in gaudy orange and white stripes on new black helmets and jerseys. Proud Pacific led 12-6 on TD runs by HBs Ken Swearingen and Don Cornell with 8:40 left to play. But, HB Gordy Young's clutch 24y dash put Stanford (1-0) in position for FB Bill Tarr (18/84y) to charge over from 2YL for his 2nd TD. With little faith in its nervous kicking game, Stanford called upon soph QB John Brodie (9-21/83y, INT) to sweep RE for winning conv pt. Terse San Francisco Chronicle story called it "an inartistic opener" for Indians.

VIRGINIA TECH 30 North Carolina State 21: HB Howie Wright led Gobblers (1-0) to 317y rushing with 18/136y, 2 TDs, including 67y scoring run early in 2nd Q. NC State (0-1), debuting under coach Earle Edwards, lost its 8th game in row, but scored 1st on 87y drive, capped by HB John Zubaty's 4y run in last 10 secs of 1st Q. Big play came from Virginia Tech T George Preas, who nailed Wolfpack P Ed Armit in EZ for safety that built 9-7 lead in 2nd Q and set up ensuing Tech TD from QB Billy Cranwell for 16-7

H edge. Wright's 2nd TD gave Hokies 23-7 lead in 3rd Q, but NC State launched soph speedster HB George "Wagon Wheels" Marinkov to 93y KO TD RET and 2nd TD in 4th Q.

Maryland 20 KENTUCKY 0: Defending national champion Maryland (1-0) changed names but failed to protect innocent: all-new backfield of QB Charlie Boxold, HBs Ronnie Waller and Joe Horning, and FB Dick Bielski spoiled Kentucky (0-1) coach Blanton Collier's succession of Bear Bryant. Waller tallied 22y TD sweep early in 2nd Q. Boxold sneaked over late in 2nd Q and fired 30y TD pass to E Russ Dennis in 3rd Q. Wildcats QBs Bob Hardy, until he went out with sour stomach in 2nd Q, and Delmar Hughes passed for 16-28/184y, but suffered 5 INTs. Most damaging INTs were by QB-DB Frank Tamburello, who dashed 58y late in 1st Q to set up opening Terrapins' TD, and FB-DB Bielski, who turned in his pick-off at Kentucky 44YL in 2nd Q. Except for their 7 TOs, Wildcats' 310y O had similar look of Cleveland Browns, from whence Collier had come.

Georgia 14 FLORIDA STATE 0: Young Georgia (1-0) squad, looking to end 5-game losing streak, sported new look with departure of NFL-bound star pass battery of QB Zeke Bratkowski (Chicago Bears) and E Johnny Carson (Washington Redskins). Jr QB Jimmy Harper, although lacking same poise as Bratkowski, passed well, if sparingly with 6-10/100y, TD. Harper capped Bulldogs' 53y march halfway through 1st Q with 5y TD spurt after he bobbled snap. Florida State (0-1) broke in frosh QB Ted Rodrique, who completed 6 passes/109y. In 4th Q, Georgia took over on its own 44YL, lost FUM at Florida State 5YL when giant Seminoles DE Tom Feamster made terrific play. However, Bulldogs regained possession at FSU 23YL when Seminoles FB Johnny Griner lost FUM. Harper quickly pitched 21y TD pass to E Matthew Arthur to wrap up win.

Texas Christian 27 KANSAS 6: TCU's slightly more experienced 1st unit was outplayed by Kansas (0-1) under new coach Chuck Mather. But, Horned Frogs used its all-soph 2nd squad to tally 3 TDs and run away with game that was 7-6 clash at H. TCU (1-0) sophs attained 7-0 lead early in 2nd Q when HB Ken Wineburg galloped 22y with pitchout to score at end of 61y trip. Kansas came right back to pull within 7-6 as soph QB Bev Buller flipped 10y TD pass to E Don Martin. Play that turned momentum toward Purple Frogs came in 3rd Q from vet DE Johnny Crouch, who dropped into flat to pick off pass by Jayhawks' other young QB, John McFarland, and sprint 37y to TD. Quick-openers popped soph HB Jim Swink for 10 and 67y TD runs in 4th Q as TCU youngsters continued to outshine their elders.

RICE 34 Florida 14: Under powerful Rice Stadium lights, underdog Gators (0-1) held 7-6 lead in 2nd Q on HB John Burgess' clever 31y punt RET and his 1y TD run, followed by conv by QB-K Dick Allen. Rice (1-0) O was completely blunted in 2nd Q. When half of lights flickered out late in 2nd Q to cause 50-min delay including rearranged H intermission, last 3:24 of 2nd Q was contested with 2nd H KO being staged without delay. Nocturnal Owls suddenly felt right at home in darkened stadium. Rice backs, HB Morris Stone and FB Jerry Hall, both of whom spent much of 1953 on injury shelf, sparked surge of 3 TDs in 3rd Q. Stone scored his 2nd TD on 18y smash behind block of T Layton Goleman in 3rd Q. Hall it set up and subsequent TD by HB Dicky Moegle (10/52y, TD) with important gains. Moegle created another TD by HB Page Rogers with his daring 47y punt RET to Gators 42YL. Critical mistake had come after Florida FB Joe Brodsky's 49y QK was nullified in 3rd Q. It was replaced by miserable 24y punt to Gators 45YL and ignited onslaught by Owls when score still had been manageable at 13-7. Florida scored late against Rice scrubs on 15y screen pass from sub QB Fred Robinson to FB Bob Visser. Stats painted losing picture for Gators: 4 lost FUMs and INT.

TEXAS 20 Louisiana State 6: Blazing hot weather greeted fans at Austin opener, and Texas (1-0), prohibitive favorite for this season's SWC cup, went right to work avenging season-opening loss of 1953. Longhorns drove 80y in 21 exhausting plays to score early on QB Charlie Brewer's short TD dive. While checking LSU (0-1) O at only 2 1st downs in 1st H, Texas began another drive late in 1st Q which bloomed 6 secs into 2nd Q. Steers HB Billy Quinn dashed 16y and Brewer added 18y pass to E Howard Moon before sub FB Don Maroney belted over from 2YL. Tigers awoke early in 3rd Q for 81y trip to paydirt: HB Vince "Peppy" Gonzales broke clear for 44y race down sideline. But, Texas retaliated with 92y march before 3rd Q ended as HB Delano Womack scurried 37y to TD.

Texas Tech 41 TEXAS A&M 9: Texas A&M (0-1) was just days removed from brutal, drought-parched Junction, Tex., training camp that would be made famous years later by The Junction Boys book by Jim Dent and ESPN's TV movie. Aggies started with drive to QB-K Ellwood Kettler's 35y FG. But, coach Bear Bryant's thin 33-man squad couldn't cope with deeper Texas Tech (1-0) and dropped astounding 10 FUMs. Red Raiders flipped 3 Aggies FUMs into TDs and made another TD after gaining INT. Tech went ahead 14-3 by H as FUM REC led to QB Jerry Johnson's 1y TD slant off T, and HB Ronnie Herr powered 45y TD drive that overcame 15y PEN. Aggies HB Don Watson lost FUM early in 3rd Q at his 22YL, and Raiders FB Rick Spinks navigated RE for 3y TD. Spinks scored again in 3rd Q after INT. Facing 35-3 mountain, A&M HB Billy Huddleston dashed 35y and 15y PEN was tacked on. Henderson scored 3 plays later from 3YL.

Oklahoma 27 CALIFORNIA 13: Confident Golden Bears (0-1) blundered their upset opportunity with raft full of miscues, but still trailed only 7-6 at H. California QB Paul Larson converted FUM recovered at Sooners (1-0) 30YL into TD run in 2nd Q, but Bears had to trade it for 7y TD run by OU QB Gene Calame, when Bears booted poor punt OB at own 33YL. Calame, listed as doubtful because of cracked ribs, inspired his Sooner teammates because he stayed in lineup to battle for 59 mins. Decisive Oklahoma TD came early in 3rd Q as HB Buddy Leake pitched option pass from near his own GL to E Max Boydston, who took it 87y to score. Larson and E Jim Hanifan,

pass battery which would turn out to be nation's most efficient in 1954, teamed on 16y TD in 4th Q after Sooners had salted it away at 21-6 on Leake's 2y TD after C-LB Gene Mears fell on FUM at California 25YL.

September 25, 1954

(Fri) SOUTHERN CALIFORNIA 27 Pittsburgh 7: More than 50,000 fans watched Southern California (2-0) line bust frequent holes for soph TB Jon Arnett (15/118y, 3 TDs), but it took 20-pt explosion to win it in 4th Q after teams exchanged fists and several player banishments. Pitt Panthers (0-1) recovered 2 FUMs inside USC 30YL in 1st Q, but failed to cash either break. Their best chance came when FB Tom Jenkins popped 17y to Troy 8YL. Near end of 1st Q, starting TB Aramis Dandoy sparked USC with 47y punt RET to Pitt 42YL. Trojans took it in on 11 plays as sparkling sub Arnett went over from 2YL. Panthers tied it in last min before H on 49y TD pass to E Dick Scherer from HB Henry Ford, former Pitt QB. Arnett scored on 25y run early in 4th Q, and later charged 29y on punt RET to Pitt 45YL, which led to his 1y TD run after dukes-up dust had cleared. In last 1:40, Trojans WB Lindon Crow caught 67y TD pass from sub QB Ells Kissinger to wrap up scoring. During week that followed, "A Star Is Born," film starring Judy Garland, was scheduled to premier amid dazzling fanfare at Hollywood's famed Pantages Theater. *Los Angeles Times* sportswriter Jack Geyer suggested that Warner Bros. had been beaten to punch by USC with its birth of star Jon Arnett.

(Fri) Arizona State 28 BRIGHAM YOUNG 19: Rash of FUM RECs, caused in part by wet conditions, spelled whipsaw 19-0 lead going into H for BYU Cougars (0-2). Biggest 1st H play came as rumbling herd of BYU blockers convoyed G Lyle Heinz on 63y TD RET of mid-air FUM lost by Arizona State (2-0) HB Ruben Madril. Heinz's TD made it 6-0 in 1st Q, and Cougars ran off at H with 19-0 lead after FUMs also set up 2nd Q scoring runs by HBs Phil Oyler and Jim Crittenden. BYU gave it all back in 2nd H, losing 4 FUMs and also giving up INT deep in own territory. Sun Devils HB Jim Bilton (12/105y) dashed 55y off T to pull within 19-7 in 3rd Q. BYU QB Ron Bean unsuccessfully chose to run on 4th-and-2 at own 30YL late in 3rd Q, and soon thereafter ASC frosh HB Bobby Mulgado snatched pass away from Cougars DB to weave 32y for TD early in 4th Q. Mulgado added 11 and 1y TD runs in 4th Q to help Devils pull away.

South Carolina 34 ARMY 20: Starting all-new Es and LBs, Cadets (0-1) D was ill-prepared for South Carolina (1-0) Split-T, with its 2 equally-skilled backfields rambling for 446y rushing to score on devastating marches of 95, 97, and 80y. But, HB-DB Mike Zeigler raced 41y on INT RET to give Army short-lived 14-7 1st Q lead. Gamecocks HB Mike Caskey rushed 11/129y, 2 TDs, and HB Carl Brazell added 2 scores, including 4y scurry with pitchout that proved to be backbreaker at end of 97y march early in 3rd Q. Brazell's 3rd Q TD provided Carolina with 21-14 lead. Army QB Pete Vann (9-22/112y, TD) sparked 53y march that expired at Gamecocks 20YL. Carolina went 80y for sub HB Tommy Woodlee's 9y TD sprint. Cadets appeared to be back in game on Vann's TD pass to Zeigler that made it 27-20, but Caskey bolted 63y to tally soon after Army's KO. Upset was only West Point's 3rd defeat in season openers since 1890.

Florida 13 GEORGIA TECH 12: Georgia Tech (1-1), which hadn't lost at home in 4 years, was in trouble from outset. Gators (1-1) surged early, but bid was turned back at 3YL as Engineers G-LB Franklin Brooks made tackle for 6y loss and C-LB Larry Morris picked off pass. Georgia Tech stopped ensuing drives on downs at its 29 and 35YL and suffered QB Bill Brigman's INT in Florida EZ as 1st H ended in frantic 0-0 duel. Gators HB Jackie Simpson launched 3rd Q with 39y KO RET and scored on 4y sweep behind critical block of FB Mal Hammock (120y rushing). QB-K Dick Allen clicked on x-pt. Brigman scored on sneak after Allen's pass was picked off and returned to Gators 17YL, but conv snap by Morris sailed over head of HB-holder Jimmy Thompson. FUM REC by Florida HB-DB John Burgess at Tech 13YL allowed QB Bobby Lance (4-5/44y) to cut back on 5y TD keeper for 13-6 lead in 4th Q. Frisky Georgia Tech HB Billy Teas raced 26y to trim margin to 13-12 late in 4th Q, but QB-K Burton Grant's tying conv kick sailed wide. Yellow Jackets never saw possession of ball again.

TENNESSEE 19 Mississippi State 7 (Memphis): While Volunteers (1-0) wasted 2 chances in 1st Q, they still scored after E Keith Drummond blocked punt near GL by Bulldogs (1-1) QB-P Bobby Collins, future SMU coach. C-LB Bubba Howe recovered at 1YL for Tennessee, and young TB Johnny Majors blasted toward GL on 2nd down. Majors fumbled, but Drummond alertly recovered in EZ for TD and 6-0 lead. Maroons used 9 plays to travel 82y to take 7-6 lead early in 2nd Q: HB Jim Harness launched march with 16y gain and caught 34y pass from Collins to set up HB Arthur Davis' 1y TD blast. Soph Majors soon made his mark by breaking off his weakside LT and speeding away from Mississippi State DB John Morris for 80y TD dash. Starting Tennessee TB Jimmy Wade scored in 3rd Q for 19-7 edge, but 2nd H otherwise was dominated by Bulldogs. However, INTs by DB Majors and FB-DB Terry Sweeney and FUM REC by E Roger Urbano blunted Bulldogs scoring threats in Tennessee territory.

MISSISSIPPI 28 Kentucky 9 (Memphis): In nightcap of SEC doubleheader in Memphis, soph QB-K Delmar Hughes crafted sharply-angled 24y FG in 1st Q for 3-0 Kentucky (0-2) lead. QB Eagle Day soon took over and pitched passes to HBs Jimmy Patton and Billy Kinard for 70y that brought Ole Miss (2-0) to Wildcats 3YL. Kinard smashed over for TD and 7-3 lead. P Day's long, high punt sent UK HB Billy Mitchell back near

his GL in 2nd Q; Mitchell bobbled punt and had to chase it into his EZ. In trying to corral ball, Mitchell stepped past endline for Rebels safety. Mississippi's methodical 81y drive in 3rd Q netted Kinard's 2nd TD, this from 2YL. Rebels HB Red Muirhead raced 65y on punt RET in 4th Q to set up his 2y TD run for 28-3 edge. Kentucky earned late TD on E Howard Schnellenberger's 17y catch. Air attack (163y) was all Wildcats could muster since their running O was limited to meager 29/8y.

Alabama 12 LOUISIANA STATE 0: Except for trip that ended at Crimson Tide 7YL, error-prone Louisiana State (0-2) was pinned inside its 23YL by TOs for 2 Qs. Banged-up Alabama (1-1) QB Bart Starr didn't start but when he entered to hold for unsuccessful 2nd Q FG try he remained in game to spark Tide O. Starr hit 7-8/91y, TD passing, including 2nd Q 15y TD pass to HB Corky Tharp (14/66y), who frequently flanked wide to haul in 5/61y receiving. On 1st play of 4th Q, Bama FB Cecil "Hootie" Ingram raced 68y to score behind crisp block of little-known HB Jerry Chiapparelli. Bengal Tigers played well on D, led by MG Sid Fournet and G-LB Paul Ziegler, but its O could dent Tide territory only 3 times in making only 109y O. Alabama DT Sid Youngelman put considerable pressure on pass attempts by LSU QB Al Doggett (4-15/66y, 2 INTs).

NOTRE DAME 21 Texas 0: Spirited Longhorns (1-1) charged out of tunnel as HB Delano Womack raced to ND 33YL on game's 4th play, but Fighting Irish (1-0) D quickly gobbled up FUM. Sparked by QB-DB Ralph Guglielmi, who turned game around with 3 INTs in his own 22 and 2YLs with his 1st and 3rd INTs. Guglielmi's 22y TD pass to E Dan Shannon for 7-0 lead in 2nd Q was set up by Guglielmi's 42y RET of his 2nd INT. Guglielmi made 2 TD runs in 2nd H behind GL blocks of LT Sam Palumbo as retired coach Frank Leahy cast mournful glare on sharp coaching debut of young Terry Brennan. Texas reached ND 9YL late in 3rd Q, but Irish DT Ray Lemek recovered FUM by FB Don Maroney and loss became 1st time Longhorns failed to score since 1946.

IOWA 14 Michigan State 10: After 1st H in hot weather was controlled at 7-0 by Iowa (1-0), Michigan State (0-1), debuting under coach Duffy Daugherty, rebounded on TB Leroy Bolden's TD run and FB Gerry Planutis' FG for 10-7 lead in 3rd Q. With 7 mins to play, Hawkeyes run attack failed at MSU 13YL, but Spartans were stacked up by never-say-die Hawks line and were forced to punt. Unheralded Iowa HB Eldean Matheson fielded State E-P Don Kauth's 47y punt and blazed 53y to Spartans 3YL, where T Carl Nystrom briefly saved TD by knocking Matheson OB. Michigan State, seeking to hold its 3-pt lead, finally succumbed on 4th down as Hawkeyes QB Jerry Reichow wedged across from 1YL to win it. Afterward, Iowa mentor Forest Evashevski expressed his doubts about any comeback: "I thought we were finished in the third quarter when Michigan State began platooning us…and I didn't think they had the strength to pull it out."

Penn State 14 ILLINOIS 12: Vulnerable run D of highly-favored no. 6 Illinois (0-1) was exposed by lightning strikes of Penn State (1-0) for 279y on ground. Before Nittany Lions could establish run game, they permitted INT to set up Illini score in game's 1st 4 mins: QB Em Lindbeck's 20y screen pass to HB Abe Woodson. Lions followed with 2 TDs in 1st H, and after each score E-K Jim Garrity succeeded with vital x-pt kick. Penn State E-DE Jesse Arnelle captured FUM by Illini FB Mickey Bates at Illinois 28YL in 1st Q and soon caught 24y TD pass. Lions QB Don Bailey sprinted 50y in 2nd Q, then lit out again for 6y. Before Bailey could be tackled, he flipped lateral to HB Lennie Moore, who breezed remaining 12y to score for 14-6 lead. When FB-K Bob Wiman hit crossbar with kick after Woodson's 2nd TD in 3rd Q, Illinois was left to ponder its 2 missed convs. Late Illinois threats were denied by 20y sack of QB Hiles Stout by Penn State DE Jack Sherry and INT of Stout by DB Moore.

OKLAHOMA 21 Texas Christian 16: Balanced Horned Frogs attack (151y rushing and 157y passing) rendered serious damage and pushed mighty Sooners (2-0) to ropes at 16-7 in 4th Q. Soph HB Ken Wineburg's 38y TD catch in 1st H might have put game out of reach, but TCU (1-1) E Johnny Couch honorably confessed to field judge Don Rossie that ball bounced to Wineburg. Rossie, getting help from another official, reversed his call, and Purple Frogs failed to add to their lead. With QB Gene Calame on shelf, Oklahoma rallied behind sub QB Jimmy Harris' 2nd TD run that brought deficit to 16-14 in 4th Q. Sooners HB Buddy Leake's 50y punt RET set up winning TD by HB Bob Herndon that came with less than 5 mins left. Oklahoma's 47-game win streak very nearly came to abrupt end in its early stages at 10 wins prior to this match with up-and-coming TCU.

October 2, 1954

(Fri) MIAMI 19 Baylor 13: Undervalued Miami (2-0) trapped unsuspecting no. 11 Bears (2-1) in 13-13 H tie. Hurricanes whirled to early 13-0 lead, recovering Baylor soph HB Del Shofner's opening KO FUM at Bears 30YL and picking off QB Bobby Jones at 27YL 3 plays after ensuing KO. HB-DB Whitey Rouviere scored 1st TD and made INT that set up HB Gordon Malloy for runs of 23 and 3y, 2nd of which counted for Canes TD. Shofner scored on 17y sweep left, and early in 2nd H, sub FB Weldon Holley overcame his surprise at receiving spontaneous lateral from sub QB Billy Hooper to run 12y to tie it at 13-13. Midway in 4th Q, one-time Miami free-spirit-turned-captain Malloy spirited Baylor pass and returned it to Bears 32 YL. Looking to pass on rollout right,

Hurricanes QB Carl Garrigus instead swung left away from pass rushers and sprinted 18y for winning TD behind block of T Allen Rodberg, who took out 3 Bears. Late threat was ended when Rouviere made Miami's 4th INT in EZ with 5 secs to play.

(Fri) UCLA 12 Maryland 7: Bruins' outstanding FB Bob "Pogo" Davenport (23/87y) converted 1st Q Terps FUM into score when he made 1 of his patented TD leaps. Clock counting to H thwarted Maryland's thrust to UCLA (3-0) 2YL, so Terrapins (1-1) trailed 6-0 at H. Only once did Maryland sustain its O against UCLA D, led by Gs Sam Bogosian and Hardison Cureton, T Jack Ellena, E Bob Long and LB Terry Debay. Terps went 63y in waning mins of 3rd Q, and FB-K Dick Bielski's conv, following HB Howie Dare's TD reception from QB Charlie Boxold, gave Maryland 7-6 lead early in 4th Q. Maryland HB Ronnie Waller, credited with 12/70y rushing and "great game" by his coach Jim Tatum, mistakenly fielded deep UCLA punt and was dropped at his own 4YL. After PEN pushed Terps back, pressured punt disastrously went only to their 15YL. With great field position, TB Primo Villaneuva rolled left to pass on 3rd-and-6 but darted 10y to 1YL. Davenport did his pogo-stick act for winning TD on next play. Key 4th Q stop for Bruins came from Debay, who plastered Dare when 1 ft was needed for 1st down at Uclan 19YL.

Penn State 13 SYRACUSE 0: Keyed by alternating FB-LBs Charles Blockson and Bill Straub, Penn State (2-0) D held Syracuse (1-1) to mere 31y O in 1st H. Meanwhile, Nittany Lions overcame FUMs at own 18 and 35YLs on their opening 2 possessions to score after stopping Orangemen's latter thrust at their 23YL. Penn State went 77y to HB Lenny Moore's 16y TD flash around LE with pitchout. This score made it 6-0 and came in dying moments of 1st Q. Reserves dominated playing time in scoreless 2nd Q, but Lions HB Ron Younker slipped away for 50y punt RET to Syracuse 17YL in 3rd Q. Younger plunged over from 1YL for 13-0 edge. Orange, which would finish with 72y rushing, mounted its only threat early in 4th Q that carried 72y in 14 plays to Mt Nittany 17YL. Contributing to ground advance was soph HB Jimmy Brown, making name for himself for 1st time, but FB Al Vergara was halted 1y short of 1st down on 4th down run.

DUKE 7 Tennessee 6: Those fans who later enjoyed passing thrills authored by pot-bellied Washington Redskins QB Sonny Jurgensen would find it difficult to believe his exploits in his 2nd game as Duke (2-0) soph QB-DB. Jurgensen made 2 INTs in 4th Q to halt Tennessee (1-1) threats inside Blue Devils territory. Shortly after opening KO, Volunteers had gained FUM REC and moved to Duke 20YL before being stopped by superb Devils line. Duke went 88y to HB Bob Pascal's 10y TD pitchout run behind robust block by FB Worth Lutz late in 1st Q. G-K Jim Nelson, one of season's most accurate Ks, succeeded on x-pt for 7-0 lead. Tennessee took only 7 plays to traverse 91y after 2nd H KO: FB-K Tom Tracy scored on 28y run, but his kick was low and wide. Blue Devils, who had slight 279y to 221y O edge, threatened but lost HB Fred Beasley's FUM at Vols 1YL. They reached Vols 2YL late in 3rd Q, but QB Jerry Barger's pass was picked off by FB-DB Pat Oleksiak. Duke moved 36y to 17YL only to lose ball on downs in 4th Q. Tennessee soph TB Johnny Majors, in for injured Jimmy Wade, rushed 21/109y.

Virginia Tech 18 CLEMSON 7: Fast-starting Virginia Tech (3-0) had 18-0 lead by H on TD runs by QB Johnny Dean (twice) and HB Dickie Beard. Clemson (1-2) QB Don King was held out of starting lineup because of knee injury, and in his stead was soph QB Charlie Bussey, who made highly unfortunate starting debut. Bussey threw INTs on his 1st 3 pass attempts: Dean on game's 2nd play set up opening score. FUM RECs by T Bill Jamerson and sub QB Billy Cranwell sparked Gobblers' subsequent 1st H TDs. Midway in 2nd Q, Tigers O was ignited by return of King, who moved them to 3 1st downs before FB Red Whitten bobbled FUM. In 3rd Q, King completed 4th down pass to HB Joe Paglei, but big back was halted at 1YL, and Tech E-P Jim Petty bombed 57y punt out of trouble. King pitched 39y scoring pass to sub E Harry Hicks in 4th Q.

West Virginia 26 SOUTH CAROLINA 6: Coming off its big win at West Point, South Carolina (1-1) fell flat on its face against powerful West Virginia (1-0), which opened its season and sought revenge for 1953's upset loss to Gamecocks. Mountaineers scored 1st time they had possession on QB Freddy Wyant's 5y pass to E Bill Hillen after HB Bob Moss' 34y sprint up middle keyed 77y drive. Wyant sneaked over for scores at end of 52 and 73y drives in middle Qs, so WVU led 20-0 at end of 3rd Q. Birds made their only score early in 4th Q after QB Harold Lewis returned punt to WVU 49YL. QB Mackie Prickett wedged over from 1YL, but Mountaineers answered quickly. Perfectly-named sub HB Jack Rabbits gathered in KO at his 19YL and raced all way to 1YL where he was overhauled by Carolina's fastest HB, Tommy Woodlee. Rabbits scored on next play.

Florida 19 AUBURN 13: Going way back to its days in 1930s in Southern Conf, eager Gators (2-1) had never opened season with 2 straight league wins until this upset of Auburn (1-1) that followed bigger upset of Georgia Tech prior week. Enjoying 6-0 H lead, Florida QB Bobby Lance took 1st snap of 2nd H, made brilliant ball fake to FB Mal Hammack, and sped 84y through huge gap in right side of Plainsmen line. Having wasted 2 opportunities on FUMs at Florida 9 and 5YLs in 1st H, Auburn rallied to tie it at 13-13 just before mid-point of 4th Q as ace E Jim Pyburn caught 16 and 13y passes to keynote 69y TD march in 3rd Q, and, in 4th Q, Pyburn blocked Gators HB-P Don Chandler's punt to set up QB Bobby Freeman's 2nd TD run. With 8:04 to play, skinny Florida QB Dick Allen focused his team for 68y parade downfield that overcame pair of 5y PENs and resulted in his 24y TD strike to sub E Bob Burford after Allen made key run of 31y on sweep to 29YL.

Texas A&M 6 GEORGIA 0: Undermanned, tough Texas A&M (1-2) was 3-TD underdog and dressed only 31 men to take on Georgia (2-1) in blazing Athens heat. Aggies surprisingly dominated by keeping ball in Bulldogs' territory most of game even though they missed 3 FG tries. Texas A&M soph E Gene Stallings cut to center of field to catch 16y TD pass from QB Ellwood Kettler after FB-LB Don Kachtik's 2nd Q INT was returned 18y to Bulldogs 30 YL. Kachtik, as D signal-caller, had unseen advantage discovered by Aggies coaching staff: Georgia tipped its pass plays and its runs to right side of its formations. Thanks to that knowledge, relayed by Kachtik to his mates, Aggies aerial D nearly went unblemished. Bulldogs QB Jimmy Harper, who had tallied 239y passing in opening 2 wins, finally made his 1st completion in 4th Q, much too late to do any good. Georgia coach Wally Butts was puzzled: "I didn't recognize that club in red."

Wisconsin 6 MICHIGAN STATE 0: Thinking timeout was called in 2nd Q because of HB-DB Leroy Bolden's leg injury, Michigan State (0-2) had only 10 defenders on field near its own GL. Badgers (2-0) FB Alan Ameche quickly scored disputed TD, and Michigan State was headed for 1st home loss since 1949. Staunch Wisconsin D permitted only 8y rushing. Spartans' futility materialized further in E Jim Hinesly making 60y catch in open field only to stumble at Badgers 16 YL. Wisconsin stiffened at that point to end threat.

Army 26 MICHIGAN 7: Except for odd 46y pass-lateral which gave 1st Q TD to Michigan WB Ed Hickey, Army (1-1) owned stats (263y to 71y rushing) and game result, Cadets' 5th straight victory over frustrated Wolverines (1-1). Cadets struck for 1st H TD runs by HBs Mike Zeigler and Tommy Bell, and FB Pat Uebel. Volatile Bell added 46y TD run in 4th Q. After Army made FUM REC in game's 1st min, Zeigler, in for injured HB Bob Kyasky, slipped 6y around RE for TD. Uebel's TD came from 1y out at end of 58y march in 1st Q. Michigan soon got back into it as QB Duncan McDonald completed pass to E Ron Kramer, who seemed to surprise Hickey with his lateral. But, Hickey charged on to TD that pulled UM within 13-7 near end of 1st Q. Bell, nicknamed "Locomotive," rounded LE for 10y TD in 2nd Q and blasted through RT Ron Melnik's block, cut left and used his sprinter's speed to chug away to 4th Q score.

OHIO STATE 21 California 13: Buckeyes HB Howard "Hopalong" Cassady had missed previous year's match in Berkeley, so his speed and change of pace caught Golden Bears (1-2) somewhat unprepared. Ohio State (2-0) T Dick Helinski fell on FUM by California HB Sebastian Bordonaro on game's 3rd play, and Cassady whisked 26y for score practically before Cal D had buckled its chinstraps. Cassady (11/109y, 2 TDs, and 4/50y receiving) followed another FUM REC in 2nd Q by FB-LB Hubert Bobo with 8y sweep to set up 17y play-action TD pass from QB Dave Leggett (7-12/89y, TD, INT) to E Bill Michael for 14-0 lead. QB Paul Larson kept Bears in game with 68y KO RET to set up HB Hal Norris' TD plunge that sent Cal off trailing 14-7 at H. Larson (7-13/88y, 2 INTs) hit 3 straight passes in 3rd Q and raced 13y only to fumble at Ohio 5YL. But, Cal E Jim Hanifan gobbled up loose ball in EZ for TD. K Larson, however, missed tying x-pt and threw INT that DB Cassady snatched to launch his own clinching 29y TD bolt.

Purdue 27 NOTRE DAME 14: Sensational soph QB Len Dawson (7-12/213y, 4 TDs) concocted deadly dose of Purdue (2-0) passing poison for Fighting Irish (1-1). Trailing 14-0 in 1st 5 mins, reeling Notre Dame got 2 pts on bad punt snap safety on which Boilermakers HB-P Rex Brock was smothered in EZ by Irish T Ray Lemek. ND briefly regained momentum on soph QB Paul Hornung's 61y RET to 1YL of ensuing free kick, which led to HB Nick Raich's quick TD. So, Boilermakers led 14-8 at H. Irish overcame 15y holding PEN on 91y TD advance as QB Ralph Guglielmi (13-22/154y) and E Dan Shannon collaborated on 42y pass play. With score at 14-14, Dawson tossed 73y TD pass to towering, galloping E Lamar Lundy. Dawson capped 77y drive in opening 4 mins of 4th Q with 34y screen pass to FB Bill Murakowski, who turned it into clinching TD.

Arkansas 20 TEXAS CHRISTIAN 13: Amazing Arkansas (2-0) was just beginning to spin its magic as "23 Little Pigs," winning its 1st game in state of Texas since 1948. BB-DB Bobby Proctor made INT in last min of game and dramatically dashed 63y to 6YL to set up FB Henry Moore's winning 1-ft TD plunge that broke 13-13 deadlock with 28 secs to play. Earlier, Razorbacks TB George Walker had scored after TCU turned over ball at its 18YL, and Moore had rambled 48y on draw play TD that built 13-0 lead in 1st Q. Texas Christian (1-2) dominated play nearly for rest of night, holding Hogs to 19y and single 1st down in 2nd H. Horned Frogs HB Ray Taylor swept wide to 2nd Q TD, but TCU muffed 3rd Q scoring prospect and bobbled ball away at Porkers 1YL on 1st play of 4th Q. Frogs came back to tie it, however, on HB Jim Swink's 10y sweep and advanced to Arkansas 35YL until Proctor stunningly turned table with his INT.

Georgia Tech 10 SOUTHERN METHODIST 7: Georgia Tech (2-1) kept early SMU (0-1) raids at bay that reached its 3 and 24YLs. Yellow Jackets G Franklin Brooks recovered punt FUM, and K Burton Grant booted 26y FG for 3-0 lead early in 2nd Q. Mustangs overcame 15y PEN to create 13-play, 67y TD trip after ensuing 2nd Q KO. SMU QB Duane Nutt sprinkled 12, 9, and 18y passes among his receivers, and hit 12y throw to HB Don McIlhenny at 18YL. After 4 runs, Nutt wedged over from 1YL for 7-3 lead. Score stayed same as Georgia Tech could gain only 28y in 1st H, mostly because H clock ran out on Yellow Jackets at Ponies 9YL after Brooks blocked punt. As clock ticked into middle of 4th Q, SMU HB Frank Eidom lost FUM near midfield, and Rambling Wreck QB-DB Wade Mitchell recovered. On 3rd-and-10, Mitchell looped screen pass to HB George Volkert, who cut away from tacklers and sped 47y to winning TD.

Utah 7 OREGON 6: Underdog Utah (1-2) fended off vaunted air game of Oregon (1-2) and received PEN boost on its early-game 52y TD drive to score its 1st-ever win over Webfoots. Personal-foul PEN, which resulted in ejection of Oregon E Hal Reeve, moved Utes to Ducks 22YL in 1st Q. From there, HB Herb Makkem raced 17y and FB Lou Mele slammed off LG for 5y TD. K Mele booted conv, which proved to be game-winning pt. It stood until last 35 secs of 4th Q when Ducks HB Dick James slipped through T for 1y TD, but HB-K Dick Pavlet's kick flew wide. Oregon vainly outgained Utah 260y to 150y.

AP Poll October 4			
1 Oklahoma (77)	1369	11 Rice	270
2 UCLA (20)	1245	12 Penn State	244
3 Wisconsin (17)	1086	13 Maryland	145
4 Iowa (15)	1073	14 Florida (1)	140
5 Purdue (22)	1016	15 Texas	130
6 Duke (3)	622	16 West Virginia (5)	115
7 Mississippi (12)	543	17 Stanford	76
8 Notre Dame	467	18 Minnesota	72
9 Southern California	297	19tNavy	35
10 Ohio State (1)	294	19tVirginia Tech	35

October 9, 1954

(Fri) Texas Christian 20 SOUTHERN CALIFORNIA 7: Initial 2 times TCU (2-2) QB Ronnie Clinkscale ran, he made 60y TD run on blazingly-fast sneak and 58y KO RET. After Clinkscale contributed his KO RET, TCU went on to soph HB Jim Swink's 18y TD dash and led 14-7 at H. Heavily-favored, no. 9 Trojans (3-1) used 7 different passers for decidedly mixed results: 8-22/159y, but completions included 1st Q TD toss of 8y from QB Jim Contratto to E Chuck Leimbach. But, when Contratto was injured early in 2nd H, USC understudies were guilty of throwing 5 INTs, as its iffy air game bungled scoring chances when INTs were lost in Horned Frogs EZ, and at 2 and 7YLs. Clinkscale added frosting to TCU's "errorless game," according to both coaches, with 4y TD scoot around E early in 4th Q.

WAKE FOREST 13 Maryland 13: Lightly-regarded Wake Forest (2-1-1) would go on to lose remainder of its games, but against Maryland (1-1-1) Deacons surged to leads of 6-0 in 1st Q on HB John Parham's run and 13-7 in 3rd Q on QB Nick Consoles' pass. Terrapins QB Charlie Boxold tied it with TD run with 14 mins left, but normally-steady FB-K Dick Bielski missed conv. Wake hearts fluttered madly when FB Nick Maravic scored late in contest, but Deacons were called for nullifying backfield-in-motion PEN. So, potential massive upset by Deacs remained moral-victory tie instead.

Mississippi 22 VANDERBILT 7: No. 7 Mississippi (4-0) found itself in 7-7 H deadlock until HB Allen "Red" Muirhead roared around LE for 61y TD and 13-7 lead Rebs would not relinquish. Ole Miss stampeded 80y in 4th Q to 36y TD pass collaboration between unrelated Pattons: QB Houston to HB Jimmy. Rebels E Leon Harbin wrapped up scoring with late-game safety as he smothered Vanderbilt (0-3) QB Don Orr, who had fumbled into his own EZ. Scrappy Commodores had tied it 7-7 in 2nd Q on TD run by HB Charley Rolfe and x-pt kick by G-K Bobby Goodall.

GEORGIA TECH 30 Louisiana State 20: Fired-up LSU (0-4) played well enough against touted Georgia Tech (3-1) that it led 6-0 and hung close at 14-13 and 23-20. Ferocious Tigers got QB Al Doggett's 23y hit to HB Vince Gonzales to set up HB Chuck Johns' smash from 1YL that resulted in profitable EZ FUM recovered by LSU E Johnny Wood for 6-0 lead early in 2nd Q. Yellow Jackets HB Billy Teas (6/128y) had his own answer, 77y TD dash to give Tech 7-6 lead. QBs Wade Mitchell and Bill Brigman each contributed sharp passes on next Engineers drive that netted 14-6 H edge. But, LSU got lift on last play of 1st H when star G Sid Fournet stacked up Brigman on GL sneak. Doggett's 21y pass to E Joe Tuminello in 3rd Q helped bring Tigers back to 14-13 on Gonzales' TD, and although Doggett and Tuminello later teamed up for 1st TD pass allowed by Tech since 1950, in end it was speed of HB Jimmy Thompson that put game away with TD runs of 35 and 17y.

Clemson 14 FLORIDA 7 (Jacksonville): After hard-hitting 0-0 1st H that was controlled by 14-pt underdog Clemson (2-2), Gators (2-2) struck on spectacular TD in 3rd Q. Florida HB Jackie Simpson took long pass from QB Fred Robinson at Tigers 23YL and magically jitter-bugged away from 3 defenders. Sticking solely to running plays after sacks of QB Don King had ruined several 1st H chances, Clemson drove from its 20YL to inside Gators 1YL as 3rd Q died. King sneaked over for TD as 4th Q began, but Florida still led 7-6 when x-pt sailed wide. Exchange of 3 INTs left Tigers at Gators 40YL after HB-DB Crimmins Hankinson picked off Florida QB Dick Allen. Key play came at Gators 5YL: Tigers sub QB Charlie Bussey fumbled on 3rd down, but recovered his bobble in wild melee at 1YL. Bussey sneaked for 1st down, then handed to HB Jim Coleman for TD dive that made it 12-7. Clemson T Mark White made late EZ sack of Robinson.

KENTUCKY 21 Auburn 14: Kentucky (2-2) took over after opening KO and moved 76y to HB Dick Rushing's 1y TD run. Favored Auburn (1-2) tied it 7-7 on FB Joe Childress' 1y TD smash in 2nd Q that came at end of 83y march, peppered with 4 completions by QB Bobby Freeman. Wildcats T Bill Wheeler placed himself in front of Freeman's screen pass in 3rd Q for INT that put Kentucky at Tigers 17YL. On 4th down, UK QB Bob Hardy hit star E Howard Schnellenberger for 16y TD and 14-7 edge. Freeman clicked 4 times in air for 52y of 69y tying march before 3rd Q ended, as E Jim Pyburn caught Freeman's 5y throw for TD that made it 14-14. Hardy finished methodical 19-play, 71y trip for winning TD in 4th Q with 8:30 to go, and Cats stopped Tigers on 4th down at UK 42YL with 4 mins left.

MICHIGAN 14 Iowa 13: Even though it was handed 2 gift TDs before 1st Q was half over, favored Iowa (2-1) still fell victim to its enduring "Michigan Jinx" (2-13-1 all-time record). After Hawkeyes C Warren Lawson recovered FUM on opening KO at Michigan (2-1) 17YL, QB Jerry Reichow and HB Eddie Vincent alternated on runs until Reichow wedged over from 1YL. However, E Jim Freeman missed x-pt by slim margin and it would prove vital. On 2nd play after ensuing KO, Iowa G John Hall recovered FUM at 33YL that led to HB Earl Smith's 8y TD trip around RE. Early Wolverines fumblers, little WB Ed Hickey (84y rushing) and FB Dave Hill, atoned for their blunders with good runs on late 1st Q 58y TD march ended by Hill's 3y TD run. Michigan QB Jim Maddock, added spark off bench and hit E-K Ron Kramer with 29y TD in 2nd Q, and Kramer kicked conv that would hold up as winning pt. Maddock's completion was Wolverines' only successful pass in 8 tries.

Ohio State 40 ILLINOIS 7: Illinois (0-3) had launched its conf co-championship season in 1953 on back of 41-20 upset win over Ohio State, but alas 1954 was different year. HB Bobby Watkins (13/112y) scored 2 TDs as fast-improving Buckeyes (3-0) entered national picture. Double-edged Ohio State attack gained 313y on ground and 9-17/166y in air and quickly exposed Illini weakness at LB with misdirection 41y TD burst by Watkins in 1st Q. Soph FB Hubert Bobo gained 19y and followed with 3y TD for Buckeyes near end of 1st Q. Watkins scored in 2nd Q for 21-0 H lead. Ohio HB Howard Cassady mishandled 2nd H KO, but team shrugged at 98y path ahead: It went for score when Cassady pitched 42y pass to E Dean Dugger to Illinois 5YL and Cassady battered over in 2 tries. Down 33-0 in 4th Q, disappointed Illini got 42y INT TD RET from HB-DB J.C. Caroline, who was able to gain 81y rushing, but his cuffed backfield mates could add only 42y running and passing.

PURDUE 13 Duke 13: Making its 1st-ever invasion of Big 10 country, Duke (2-0-1) threw 7-man D blanket over Purdue receivers, and stellar soph QB Len Dawson was held to 6-16/47y, 2 INTs passing. Duke racked up 13-0 lead on 2nd Q TDs, but ace G-K Jim Nelson was hurt on blocking assignment during 79y drive to 1y TD sneak by QB Jerry Barger. So, with sub FB-K Bryant Aldridge in game, conv was missed after 2nd TD. Purdue (2-0-1) line, led by T Joe Krupa and G Tom Bettis, powered 2nd H ground game that was spearheaded by FB Bill Murakowski and guided by reserve QB Froncie Gutman (2-5/7y, INT passing, TD rushing). So possessive of ball were Boilermakers that Blue Devils had it for only 4 plays in 3rd Q. Purdue took 20 plays after 2nd H KO to advance to Gutman's TD sneak, but with Dawson out of game, 3rd string FB-K Jim Reichert was called upon for x-pt, which he missed. Boilers tied it early in 4th Q on Murakowski's TD run and K Dawson's kick. Game ended with Devils sub QB-DB Sonny Jurgensen making GL INT of Gutman and returning it 36y.

WISCONSIN 13 Rice 7: Rallying in game's last min, confident Wisconsin (3-0) withstood best upset effort by defending SWC champion Owls (2-1). National TV audience thrilled at 2 GLSs in 4th Q by stubbornly-strong Rice forwards and was left to ponder whether Badgers could race against clock to overtake 7-6 deficit, that was in place since 1st Q. After TV technical difficulties delayed start for 15 mins, Wisconsin FB Alan "The Horse" Ameche (21/90y, 2 TDs) lugged ball 7 times in 70y drive to TD on team's opening possession. Key gain, though, was QB Jim Miller's pass to E Jim Temp to 1YL. Owls struck right back with 69y aerial trip on which QB Pinky Nisbet clicked on 5 passes. Nisbet's last completion went for TD after he faked to ace HB Dicky Moegle, sweeping right, to find LE Lemoine Holland all alone for 28y TD pass. E-K Phil Harris made x-pt kick for Rice's 7-6 lead that was to endure to 4th Q. Badgers began their comeback late in 3rd Q as sub QB Jim Haluska hit E Dave Howard for 3 passes and E Jim Reinke for another before runs gave them 1st-and-goal at 4YL. Houstonians held at 1YL and made 3 1st downs to dig out of hole, but Wisconsin G-LB-K Paul Shwaiko, who missed x-pt in 1st Q, made INT to put Badgers at Rice 47YL. This time Owls knocked down Miller's 4th down pass from 5YL and punted out of hole with 5 mins to play. Badgers went 41y with Miller running and passing for 9y gains until Ameche projected himself into EZ for winning TD.

MINNESOTA 26 Northwestern 7: Slow-starting Golden Gophers (3-0) watched Northwestern Wildcats (1-2) dominate 1st Q and traipse to TD by HB Jim Troglio on 3y run around RE. Trailing 7-0, Minnesota got rolling in 2nd Q with powerful Split-T running attack as HB brothers Bob (12/120y, 2 TDs) and Dick McNamara joined FBs John Baumgartner (8/84y, TD) and Frank Bachman (6/55y) to take their toll. But, it was classic pitchout by sub backs, QB Dale Quist to HB Ralph Goode, that showed true stealth of option O, to score Gophers' initial 6y TD in 2nd Q for 7-6 deficit. By end of 3rd Q, Minnesota led 26-7, and whatever starch was left in Cats was drained by 2 blocked punts and loss of FUM to Gophers G Robert Hagemeister at Minny 7YL in last 4 mins.

Oklahoma 14 Texas 7 (Dallas): Longhorns (2-2), seeking to fix slow-starting season and win for 1st time in series since 1951, took strong wind at their backs to KO to start game. Strategy worked out as Texas recovered KO FUM (1 of 5 bobbles lost by Sooners) at Oklahoma (3-0) 29YL. Hustling OU sr T Don Brown stopped opening 3 Steers runs, but suffered broken ankle that would shelve him for season. At end of 1st series, QB Charley Brewer's spinning 3y TD run through T powered Texas to early 7-0 advantage. Shortly thereafter, with Sooners at own 36YL, soph QB Jimmy Harris, making his 1st career start, gambled on 4th down and sent FB Bob Herndon on 14y run to 1st down. Later on same drive, Harris' pitchout had to be fielded on bounce by HB Buddy Leake, who still ran to 1st down at Texas 1YL. Oklahoma tied it 7-7 as Leake followed straight-ahead blocks of E Carl Allison and T Cal Woodworth. On last play of 1st Q, Oklahoma sub QB Pat O'Neal pitched short pass to powerful E John Bell, who cantered 40y to Longhorns 15YL. With starters back for 2nd Q, Harris ran 1y keeper for decisive TD 5 plays later. Surprisingly, Sooners depended on effective 6-9/127y passing game for key y. Texas threatened with sustained trip to OU 10YL in closing mins, but 4th down incompletion in EZ doomed its hopes.

ARKANSAS 21 Baylor 20: Although he starred at LB, Arkansas (3-0) BB-K Preston Carpenter had already missed 2 x-pts when he was tapped by coach Bowden Wyatt to kick late, angled 22y FG that served to nip Bears (2-2). Baylor lost 4 FUMs, 3 of which were turned into Razorback scores and 4th stopped Bears drive in 4th Q. Porkers probed soft left side of Baylor line on its 1st 2 TDs as FB Henry Moore and TB George Walker scored on runs. Bears HB Allen Jones, whose FUM set up Walker's 1st Q TD, raced 46y to score against Arkansas 2nd unit early in 2nd Q, but he fumbled again when belted by Carpenter to allow Walker to throw 32y TD pass to Arkansas WB Joe Thomason. Baylor line regrouped and charged hard in 2nd H to shut down Hogs runs. Passes of QB Billy Hooper (9-16/97y, INT) clicked, and Bears went 71y to score. They took 20-18 lead after DB Hooper made INT at his 40YL, and scored on 2y keeper. But, Porkers G Wayland Roberts blocked x-pt and later recovered Bears HB Del Shofner's FUM at Baylor 11YL to make possible Carpenter's winning FG.

Colorado 40 ARIZONA 18: *Denver Post* writer Frank Haraway wrote that big Colorado (4-0) FB John Bayuk (25/183y, 4 TDs) carried Arizona (2-1) tacklers "on his broad back as though they were so many house flies." Bison backs, no. 1 in nation in rushing, ran for 421y, but lost 2 stars to minor injuries: TB Carroll Hardy, on his only carry of game, and WB Frank Bernardi. Wildcats' 3rd-largest crowd to date in Tucson booed lustily when Colorado FB-LB Emerson Wilson was tossed out of contest early in 3rd Q. Wilson was guilty of slugging back of neck of Arizona star HB Art Luppino (16/84y), who was kept well under wraps except for nifty KO RET in 1st Q. Buffs TB Homer Jenkins (14/108y) opened game with 67y KO RET before being hauled down by Wildcats G Ed Brown. Wilson scored 7 plays later. Arizona quickly tied it at 6-6 as FB Max Burnett (16/101y, TD) slammed over from 4YL after E Bill Codd caught 38y pass. Bernardi caught 23y TD pass in 1st Q to put CU ahead for good at 13-6 as Bayuk soon heated up on way to 27-6 H edge. Wildcats QB Barry Bleakley (4-6/98y, TD, 2 INTs) launched 42y TD bomb for HB Wayne Mancuso after Wilson's 15y roughing PEN and expulsion in 3rd Q.

Oregon 33 CALIFORNIA 27: Before game was 7 mins old, California (1-3) was recipient of 2 FUMs and cashed both for 13-0 1st Q gain. Ducks (2-2) QB George Shaw (9-14/160y, TD) supplimented his passing TD with go-ahead TD run at 20-13 early in 3rd Q. This prize was positioned by Oregon C-LB Ron Pheister's INT RET to Golden Bears 36YL. Oregon E Hal Reeve, whose outstanding line play enhanced that of T Keith Tucker, clutched INT thrown by California QB Paul Larson (7-11/106y, TD, 2 INTs passing and 2 TDs rushing) as part of all-out pass rush in 3rd Q. Oregon FB Jasper McGee scored at RG and it was 26-13. Cal FUM led to 3rd TD of 3rd Q for Oregon, which then held secure at 33-13. Larson wouldn't quit in 4th Q rally, passing 17y TD to E Jim Hanifan and racing 56y on punt TD RET. Oregon let big McGee's runs all but kill clock and held on for victory, making it 1st-ever Northwest-based team to beat Cal coach Pappy Waldorf on Berkeley soil.

Ucla 21 WASHINGTON 20: Despite bungling several early opportunities on drives to Huskies 10, 4, and 1YLs, Bruins (4-0) were sailing safely at 21-0 in 3rd Q, thanks to FB Bob Davenport's 2 TDs, including bullish 17y run after QB Bob Bergdahl's FUM REC of 2nd H KO. Suddenly in final 20 mins, soph QB Bobby Cox brought Washington (2-2) brimming to life by ripping 35y TD pass to HB Dean Derby after Derby had caught 26y pass that was deflected into his hands by Uclan sub FB-DB Doug Peters. Fiery Cox continued by completing 5y TD pass to uncovered E Corky Lewis on 4th-and-2 after C-LB Dell Jensen's FUM REC of UCLA TB Sam Brown's slipup at Bruins 25YL. Brown fumbled again just past midfield, and Cox drove Huskies to their final TD on pass to E Bob Green for 15y with 2:26 to go. HB-K Bobby Dunn's missed kick after 2nd TD proved fatal to Huskies rally. Reason no. 2 UCLA survived could be found in WB-K Johnny Hermann's 3 successful conv kicks.

Navy 25 STANFORD 0: Opportunistic Navy (3-0) used E Ron Beagle's EZ REC of punt block by G Len Benzi for 1st Q TD, made possible by field position gained on FB-P Dick Guest's 73y punt. Stanford (3-1) showed its only spark on O in retaliation to 6-0 deficit. Indians carved 75y out of Middies' D to advance to 3YL, but Navy QB-DB Dick Erchard made clutch break-up of 4th down pass by QB John Brodie (7-21/58y, INT) early in 2nd Q. Erchard then handed ball to FB Joe Gattuso for 65y of 93y drive to Erchard's 7y TD pass to E Jim Owen. Gattuso (14/153y, TD) blasted 37y to 3rd Q TD.

AP Poll October 11

1 Oklahoma (118)	1797	11 Minnesota (2)	347
2 Wisconsin (21)	1555	12 Arkansas (1)	326
3 UCLA (10)	1223	13 Iowa	116
4 Ohio State (14)	1180	14 West Virginia (6)	112
5 Purdue (3)	920	15 Rice	84
6 Duke (7)	889	16 Virginia Tech	70
7 Mississippi (11)	730	17 Colorado (1)	52
8 Notre Dame (2)	729	18 Army	51
9tPenn State (3)	380	19 Georgia Tech	35
9tNavy (1)	380	20 Texas Tech	30

October 16, 1954

(Fri) MIAMI 27 Mississippi State 13: Miami (4-0) line held at its 8YL early in 1st Q after Mississippi State (3-2) FB Charles "Dinky" Evans raced 51y, but it took 2nd unit to break into scoring column. Backup QB Mario Bonofiglio scooted 19 and 28y to set up 7-0 Hurricanes lead. Maroons came right back on 70y trip topped by QB Bobby Collins' 18y pass to HB Art Davis. HB Jim Harness scored from 2YL, and E-K Clovis McKissick tied it at 7-7 in most unusual way: Conv snap hopped up into McKissick's arms and he alertly swept RE for tying pt. Miami turned to power of FB Don Bosseler (15/78y, TD) and HB Gordon Malloy (16/77y) to build long, all-run drives in 2nd and 3rd Qs that netted 20-7 edge. Malloy injected clinching 71y punt TD RET early in 4th Q with block by QB Carl Garrigus, but thick HB Joe Silveri aced Miami subs for late-game 22, 18, and 13y runs before Davis made 6y TD.

Boston College 21 FORDHAM 7: Hurricane Hazel postponed Friday game to Saturday at New York's Polo Grounds. Boston College (4-0) got scare from Fordham (1-2), being held in 7-7 deadlock until 4th Q. Rams paraded 48y to BC 26 early in 4th Q only to stall, later losing possession at Eagles 34YL. Latter failure launched 66y trip by BC to deciding TD. Big play came on FB-K Dick Gagliardi's 49y romp to Fordham 8YL. Gagliardi scored on 3y run and kicked conv for 14-7 lead with 5:40 left. HB Eddie DeSilva added late TD for Eagles.

PITTSBURGH 21 Navy 19: Pitt AD and former Navy A-A back Tom Hamilton took Panthers coaching reins from ailing Red Dawson, whose heart trouble sent him permanently out of pressure-cooker of coaching. Hamilton whipped winless Panthers (1-3) into frenzy against his old team, unbeaten Midshipmen (3-1). Little-used Pitt QB-HB Corny Salvaterra was promoted to starting QB to score twice and throw 23y TD pass to HB Henry Ford, while HB-K "Bags" Bagamery's 3 convs ultimately spelled difference for Panthers. Navy scored for 6-0 lead in 1st 3 mins after profitable REC by E Ron Beagle of on-side opening KO, which led to FB Joe Gattuso's bullish 1y TD run. Quick INT by G-LB George Textor put Tars at Pitt 34YL. Hungry Navy advanced to 1st down at 10YL, but Panthers HB-DB Richie McCabe made game's key play, stopping HB Bob Craig on 4th down at 3YL. Verdict then turned as Pitt went on 97y drive that spilled over into 2nd Q. Key play leading to Salvaterra's 1y TD run was his 54y pass to tall E Fred Glatz at Navy 33YL. Middies QB Dick Echard, who although he threw 25y TD pass in 4th Q would lose his job to George Welsh in this game, soon lost FUM to Glatz on G Harold Hunter's sack at Navy 37YL. Salvaterra pitched his TD pass, and Pitt led 14-6 3 mins into 2nd Q.

West Virginia 19 PENN STATE 14: Mountaineers (3-0) coach Art Lewis tapped 7 men to play 60 min, including star T Bruce Bosley, G Gene "Beef" Lamone, and QB Freddy Wyant, future NFL referee. Nittany Lions (3-1) took 7-6 lead in 2nd Q on QB Don Bailey's 24y strike to HB Ron Younker to trump West Virginia QB Wyant's 1y push-across TD after 41y drive. On Penn State's next series that started at its 14YL, HB Lenny Moore sparkled with runs of 40 and 15y and he scored on 8y flanking dash. Mountaineers vainly had threatened thrice from inside Penn State's 11YL in 1st H and did it again when E Bill Hillen fell on Younker's 3rd Q FUM at Mount Nit 35YL. Spilling into early 4th Q, another unsuccessful march by Mounties died at 10YL. WVU would not be denied on next possession as it rallied for 68y to pull within 14-12 on Wyant's twisting 15y TD dash up middle. Wyant ran twice to open 51y drive toward upset-making TD that was scored by HB Dick Nicholson on pass from Wyant. Nicholson shook off 2 tacklers and fell across GL in arms of DB Moore.

MARYLAND 33 North Carolina 0: Having rough time defending its national title so far in 1954, Maryland (2-1-1) finally returned to home turf. Terrapins G George Palahunik set tone by nailing Tar Heels (1-2-1) HB Len Bullock at 11YL on opening KO. HB Ronnie Waller took Carolina's punt out by E-P Len Frye at UNC 40YL and skipped to 29YL. Maryland FB Dick Bielski threw terrific block, then battered line 3 times, including 11y TD. In 2nd Q, Tar Heels threatened at Terps 31YL where UNC G Jimmy Neville fell on errant pitchout, but Palahunik and C-LB John Irvine combined to take ball away from UNC QB Doug Farmer. Carolina never saw Maryland territory again. Bielski was bullwark of 3rd Q drive, and E Russ Dennis had 44y catch to set up Waller's 5y TD run. Maryland subs scored trio of TDs in 4th Q.

Army 28 DUKE 14: Hurricane Hazel ripped through North Carolina on Friday, and Army Cadets (3-1) threw 2nd punch with their 1st football successful across Mason-Dixon Line. While backfield stars HB Tommy Bell (13/150y) and FB Pat Uebel (17/89y) would fuel Army's surge to 378y rushing, opening scoring spark was lit by backups—notably HB Pete Lash who slashed for 15y TD run in 2nd Q. Cadets QB Pete Vann, who would sneak for TDs in 3rd and 4th Qs, lofted 58y pass to E Don Holleder to set up HB Mike Ziegler's 5y TD sweep. Quiet for long stretch, Duke (2-1-1) stormed back to within 21-14 on 63 and 36y marches in 3rd and 4th Qs as HBs Bernie Blaney and Bob Pascal scored for Devils. Duke's failed 4th down gamble at its 16YL led to Vann's clinching TD.

Florida State 13 NORTH CAROLINA STATE 7: Punts played big role in outcome of chilly night game in Raleigh. NC State (1-4) HB George Zubaty punted 64y to edge of Florida State (3-2) GL in 2nd Q. Seminoles FB-P Pat Versprille punted out to Wolfpack 47YL, and Wolfpack QB Eddie West capped 53y drive for 7-0 lead. Zubaty lost FUM at own 24YL in 3rd Q to FSU T Al Makowiecki. Florida State QB Harry Massey found E Jimmy Lee Taylor for 10y TD to pull within 7-6. NC State D held at its own 3YL in 4th Q, but when E-P John Lowe's punt was blocked by FSU E Ronnie Schomberger, Massey's TD pass won it.

GEORGIA TECH 14 Auburn 7: Specialty of Georgia Tech (4-1), its bevy of 150 lb HBs, scored both TDs: Jimmy Thompson on 55y dart in 1st Q and Johnny Menger on 19y sprint early in 3rd Q. Auburn (1-3) got break on G Chuck Maxime's FUM REC at Tech 40YL in 4th Q, but Tigers were stopped by EZ FUM REC by Engineers FB-LB Johnny Hunsinger. Auburn earned 231y against Georgia Tech D, led by C-LB Larry Morris and G-LB Franklin Brooks. But much of it came too late as Auburn FB Joe Childress burst over with 52 secs left to conclude 66y TD advance. Tigers lost 13th straight to Yellow Jackets.

FLORIDA 21 Kentucky 7: Opportunistic Florida (3-2) D was critical to its victory, but Wildcats (2-3) started fast with 73y spurt off opening KO, leading to short TD run by QB Bob Hardy (10-17/125y, 3 INTs). After Gators traveled 63y after ensuing KO to E Welton Lockhart's take-away TD catch from Kentucky DB Don Netoskie in EZ, Hardy's passes and runs moved Cats 83y in 2nd Q. But, Florida T Buster Hill tipped pass into hands of FB-DB Bob Visser at 9YL. Gators HB Jackie Simpson caught 2 passes on 45y TD drive that ended 1:00 into 2nd Q. UF G John Barrow fell on Hardy's FUM in 3rd Q, and Simpson's consequential 6y TD run was helped by HB Bob Davis' 17y dash and FB Joe Brodsky's 15y blast. HB-DB Bob Smith made 2 of UF's 3 INTs in 4th Q to protect its 21-7 advantage.

Alabama 27 TENNESSEE 0: QB Albert Elmore stepped in for injured Bart Starr and lifted Alabama (4-1) to its largest victory margin in Knoxville to date. Also, it was Crimson Tide's 1st win over Volunteers (2-2) since 1947. Elmore rushed for 107y and whipped 3 TD passes, caught by HBs Bobby Luna and Corky Tharp and E Nick Germanos. With Tide ahead 7-0 in 3rd Q on 11y Elmore-to-Luna 2nd Q pass, Tennessee soph TB-P Johnny Majors (3 INTs passing), filling in for injured Jimmy Wade, punted from deep in his territory, and Luna returned it to Vols 29YL. Elmore's 22y run set up his short TD pass to Tharp. In 4th Q, Tennessee scored on TB Bobby Brengle's pass, but PEN nullified it. Brengle tried again, and DB Tharp picked it off at 4YL and thrillingly raced 96y to score on INT RET.

OHIO STATE 20 Iowa 14: Ohio State (4-0) pounded out TD drives of 61, 72, and 64y to keep 1st place in Big 10, but in early going Bucks had rough time. Iowa (2-2) HB-DB Earl Smith authored fabulous 67y INT TD RET, 2nd pick-off of QB Dave Leggett in Ohio's opening 2 possessions. After Smith's long TD in 1st Q, Ohio State tied it 7-7 as HB Bobby Watkins (18/105y, TD) powered over from 1YL on 12th straight run. Watkins'

19y run and being interfered with at Hawks 5YL by QB-DB Jerry Reichow in 2nd Q contributed to 72y advance, capped by Leggett's TD sneak. So, Ohio led 14-7 at H. Smith authored another long distance call in 3rd Q: He gathered in punt and raced 75y to score. But Bucks answered with E Dick Brubaker's 13y TD catch. Trailing 20-14 in 4th Q, Hawkeyes threatened twice but were blunted at Ohio State 11YL after 76y drive as Reichow overshot HB Eddie Vincent all alone in EZ. Moments later, Iowa drive lacked inches at 5YL after 29y drive. In dominating 4th Q, Iowa permitted Buckeyes only 4 plays during 13 mins after Hawkeyes took possession 1 min into last stanza and when they relinquished ball within smelling distance of Ohio GL with 1:08 to go.

WISCONSIN 20 Purdue 6: Badly outplayed, Wisconsin (4-0) trailed 6-0 at H on Purdue (2-1-1) QB Len Dawson's short TD pass to gigantic E Lamar Lundy at end of 88y drive. Badgers rallied behind 2 long runs by QB Jim Miller, which set up pair of scores for 13-6 lead. Boilermakers threatened to tie it in 4th Q, but Badgers HB-DB Billy Lowe picked off Dawson's pass, cut back across field, and went 98y to thrilling and clinching TD RET.

Colorado 20 IOWA STATE 0: Colorado (5-0) FB John "The Beast" Bayuk rushed 18/109y for nation-leading season's to-date total of 568y. Iowa State (2-3) FB counterpart Max Burkett (16/39y) was smothered by Buffs D. Colorado overcame early lost FUM at their 42YL and launched 15-play drive from their 23YL later in 1st Q. It led to TD run by FB Emerson Wilson. Colorado's next TD by TB Homer Jenkins came after E Wally Merz fell on FUM by Cyclones HB Bruce Alexander at Iowa State 45YL. Bayuk made himself noticible on 2nd Q TD trip as he ran 10 and 20y, 2nd carry coming out of rare Colorado appearance in T-formation. Buffs led 14-0 at H, and sent TB Carroll Hardy on neat reverse for 25y TD run early in 4th Q.

UCLA 72 Stanford 0: Not since Stanford (3-2) lost 1901 Rose Bowl by 49-0 to Michigan had Indians been beaten so badly. Amazingly, pass D of no. 3 UCLA (5-0) attained more RET y—218y on 8 INTs—than y gained by Stanford's vaunted passing O (22-46/203y). Bruins TB Sam Brown added 2 TDs on electrifying punt RETs, as he set new conf game record with 3/132y. TB-DB Primo Villaneuva gave UCLA its start with 2 INTs of Indians QB John Brodie (19-35/173y, 5 INTs), each leading to TD. FB Bob Davenport bounced off Stanford LBs and churned 33y for opening TD, and WB Jim Decker ran reverse for 64y TD later in 1st Q. Villaneuva ran for 2 TDs for 27-0 H lead and passed 27y to E Rommie Loudd in 1st min of 3rd Q for 33-0 edge. It would be until 1997 that UCLA would earn victory margin so large.

AP Poll October 18

1 Oklahoma (115)	1891	11 Colorado (2)	212
2 Wisconsin (42)	1732	12 Alabama	155
3 UCLA (23)	1590	13 Purdue	134
4 Ohio State (8)	1387	14 Virginia Tech	102
5 Mississippi (9)	903	15 Georgia Tech	84
6 Notre Dame	787	16 Miami	79
7 Arkansas (4)	706	17 Southern California	68
8 Minnesota	658	18 Florida	47
9 Army	487	19 Duke	34
10 West Virginia (9)	350	20 Texas Christian	25

October 23, 1954

(Th) South Carolina 13 Clemson 8: Soph QB Mackie Prickett (125y total O) sparked Gamecocks (3-1) to fulfilling win over rival Clemson (2-3) in 52nd renewal of State Fair "Big Thursday" contest. Tigers QB Don King continued his hard-luck sr season by being knocked out in 1st H, but returned to guide 2nd H threat that nearly pulled out win. After having seen 2 scoring threats die on 4th down in South Carolina territory, Clemson led 2-0 on safety early in 2nd Q: Gamecocks HB-P Bill Tarrer dropped punt snap in EZ and had to cover it. Prickett made 3 fine runs on 40y drive, including 3y TD for 7-2 lead. Prickett threw 24y to HB Carl Brazell to set up his 3y TD for 13-2 H edge. On 3rd-and-11 in 4th Q, Tigers HB Joel Wells threw surprise option pass to HB Joe Pagliei, who sauntered 81y for sudden TD. Clemson came back later with King hitting E Walt Laraway at Carolina 10YL, but in his excitement, Laraway lateralled to ineligible G Dick DeSimone. Backed up to 39YL, King threw INT that ubiquitous DB Prickett picked off at 5YL.

(Fri) MIAMI 9 Maryland 7: Angry Miami (5-0) saw its bowl hopes blasted by NCAA probation doled out earlier in week and took its frustration out on disappointing Maryland (2-2-1). Hurricanes kept Terrapins bottled up all night with stellar D led by LB Ernest Tobey, DB John Bookman, and E Bob Nolan. Closely-covered Nolan made leaping 21y TD catch from QB Mario Bonofiglio in last 10 secs of 1st H and chipped in 3rd Q tackle, with help from DB Jack Losch, for safety on Terps HB Ronnie Waller. On 4 occasions, Miami drilled inside Maryland 15YL without scoring. FB Dick Bielski notched Maryland's late TD after roughing P PEN kept alive Terps' drive of 82y. Miami ran 76 plays to 41 for Maryland, and its 327y to 165y total O edge encouraged several Terps to claim Canes as better team than no. 3 UCLA, their early-October conqueror.

Cornell 27 PRINCETON 0: In season's 4 prior losses, Cornell (1-4) had amassed only 199y rushing, but in stunning reversal, Big Red powered for 308y on ground, on legs of FB Guy Bedrossian and HBs Art Boland, Dick Meade, and Dick Jackson. Without their injured TB Royce Flippin and his sub, Dick Frye who separated his shoulder early on D, Tigers (3-2) were lost on O and were blanked for 1st time since 1945. Princeton totaled only 195y O, meager 93y of which came on runs. Cornell got rolling to its 1st TD in 1st Q after DB Meade's midfield INT, followed by Jackson's 35y romp to 8YL. Princeton, however, threatened twice in 2nd Q at Big Red 21 and 18YLs. After FUM REC by G Charlie Sharp at 30YL, Tigers were stopped on downs at 21YL, and Cornell QB-DB Billy DeGraaf hit E John Morris with 16y TD in 3rd Q, and T Len Oniskey's 2nd FUM REC put Jackson in place for wide 16y TD run. Result was tonic to Big Red; they stormed to 5 straight wins to end season and take 11th-hour Ivy League co-championship.

Virginia Tech 6 Virginia 0 (Roanoke): Virginia Tech (5-0) played without 3 speedsters from its backfield known as "Light Brigade." But, Va Tech blanked charged-up Virginia (3-2) because Cavs twice broke pass receivers open deep, only to misconnect: E Fred Moyer was overshot in 1st Q and E Jesse Hagy dropped bomb at Gobblers 15YL in 3rd Q. Hokies scored game's only TD in 2nd Q when soph E Grover Jones slipped behind 2 defenders to nab scoring toss after replacement QB Billy Cranwell hit E Tom Petty with sideline pass. Virginia HB Henry Strempek's 3rd Q 72y punt RET was called back, so Cavs put ball in play at own 8YL instead of Gobblers 17YL. Late in game, UVa QB Rives Bailey overshot Strempek in EZ. HB Dickie Beard, only regular back to play for Tech, rushed 15/77y.

Kentucky 13 GEORGIA TECH 6: Little-known jr E Brad Mills sparked Kentucky's inspired Wildcats (3-3) with 4th down 26y TD catch from QB Bob Hardy (4-12/64y, TD, INT) after game's opening KO. Georgia Tech (4-2) waited until it received 2nd H KO to answer with TD of its own and finally looked like team that had recently gathered momentum. Yellow Jackets sped 78y to score with E Henry Hair toting QB Bill Brigman's pass 14y to pay-dirt. But, hero Mills quickly deflated Tech with his block of QB-K Wade Mitchell's conv try to maintain 7-6 edge for Wildcats. Critical moment came in 3rd Q after Tech FB-LB George Humphreys made INT of Hardy at Kentucky 20YL: Humphreys' knee touched inches short of GL on 4th down run. With score still at 7-6, Hardy clinched upset on 4th Q drive aided by Mills' 15y catch. Loss all but removed Yellow Jackets from SEC title hunt.

Mississippi State 12 ALABAMA 7: On Homecoming Saturday, Alabama (4-2), winners of 4 straight, had every reason to believe it was in SEC championship and bowl game contention. But upset by 2-TD underdog Mississippi State (4-2) signaled desertion of Bama's O as it would score only 1 more TD in last 4 games. QB Albert Elmore passed 11-17/118y, and HB Corky Tharp rushed 17/81y, but Crimson Tide could click only on Elmore's TD pass to Tharp in last 25 secs of 1st H. HB-K Bobby Luna's kick provided 7-0 lead. Bulldogs rallied in 2nd H as QB Bobby Collins fielded punt in 3rd Q and raced 59y to TD. But, Bama E Tommy Tillman blocked x-pt to keep Tide ahead 7-6. With 9 mins left in contest, Maroons DE Ron Bennett, D hero along with C-LB Harold Easterwood, recoverd FUM at Tide 30YL. On next snap, Miss State HB Joe Silveri took pitchout and charged untouched to TD. When HB-DB Jim Harness knocked down Elmore's 4th down pass at GL, Mississippi State clinched its 1st victory over Alabama since 1941.

OHIO STATE 31 Wisconsin 14: Badgers' long-suffering fate in Columbus (36 years without single win) appeared at possible end as HB Pat Levenhagen's 34y TD catch provided 7-3 H lead that carried deep into 3rd Q. Wisconsin (4-1) moved from their 48YL to Ohio 20YL and appeared ready for its 2nd TD. Game turned on HB-DB Howard "Hopalong" Cassady's clutch 88y INT TD RET in last min of 3rd Q, and, within unbelievable 9-min span, Ohio State (5-0) had 4 TDs. Badgers, unscored upon in 2nd Hs of their year's 4 wins to date, coughed up 2 FUMs and completely botched ill-advised fake-punt pass by QB Jim Miller to fuel 4th Q Buckeyes TD explosion: Cassady broke off RT for 39y and then blocked for Ohio FB Hubert Bobo's 4y TD run. After Miller's 4th down fake punt disaster, QB Dave Leggett legged it 28y on next play to bring score to 24-7 for Buckeyes. Next came T Don Schwartz's FUM REC at Wisconsin 10YL, and HB Jerry Harkrader raced for TD on 1st snap. Badgers got consolation TD against reserves cleared from Ohio bench.

MICHIGAN 34 Minnesota 0: Undefeated Golden Gophers (4-1) were brought back to earth by revived Wolverines (4-1). Michigan compiled 443y, scored at end of inspired O trips of 70, 80, 66, 69, and 37y. HB Tony Branoff, back from injury list, launched UM's scoring with 13y run and sparked its next TD drive. Wolverines TB Dan Cline dashed 22y to score and flipped 19y to E Ron Kramer for another TD. Minnesota gained but 138y and made only 5 1st downs in its demoralizing Little Brown Jug visit to Ann Arbor.

Purdue 27 MICHIGAN STATE 13: Season-long deficiency in finishing scoring threats continued to vex Spartans (1-4) until injured TB Leroy Bolden (6/30y, TD) left bench late in 3rd Q to spark O. Meanwhile, accurate Purdue (3-1-1) QB Len Dawson rifled 3 TD passes, giving him 12 for 1st half of his soph season. Between O lapses, Michigan State managed to score 1st for 6-0 lead on 68y drive in 1st Q that featured QB Earl Morrall's fast thinking before HB Bert Zagers crashed 6y up middle to score: Trapped for seemingly certain loss, Morrall wriggled away for 10y run and, as he went down, flipped lateral to FB John Matsock for extra 11y. Also, Spartans briefly gladdened record Homecoming crowd with length-of-field march to TB Leroy Bolden's 6y TD run, set up by E Jim Hinesly's 19y catch. Boilers had earned 14-6 lead at H as Dawson clicked on TD passes by E Leonard Zyzda and HB Ed Zembal. Key score came as Dawson lofted precision 73y TD pass to HB Jim Whitmer for 21-6 edge in 3rd Q.

Nebraska 20 COLORADO 6: Cornhuskers (3-2) slapped Colorado (5-1) from unbeaten ranks and showed that Buffs' earlier successes had come against less than powerful Big 7 opposition. Bison got possession on early FUM REC at Nebraska 25YL and appeared TD-bound until FB Emerson Wilson lost handle as he approached line at Huskers 3YL. Cornhuskers DE Andy Loehr gobbled up FUM at his 6YL. To open 2nd Q, Nebraska went 90y, including 3 passes which went for 47y, to HB Dennis Korinek's 2y TD sweep with pitchout. Buffs TB-DB Carroll Hardy, who made many key 1st H tackles, provided 6-6 tie with 24y TD run untouched through RT in 2nd Q after WB Frank Bernardi broke free for 39y run. Huskers soph HB Willie Greenlaw busted up H tie as he ran for 10 and 11y TDs in 2nd H. Critical to outcome was Buffaloes' inability to pass, which allowed superior D-line of Nebraska to play tight to throttle all but Colorado's 2nd Q flashes by Bernardi and Hardy. Huskers made steady march after 2nd Q KO, but appeared stopped on QB Don Brown's 4th down run at Buffs 10YL. Brown snaked his arm free to pitch out to unguarded Greenlaw for TD run. Hardy lost FUM to Nebraska DE Jack Braley, leading to Greenlaw's 4th Q 11y TD.

OKLAHOMA 21 Kansas State 0: After years of weak results, Kansas State (4-2) visited Norman to challenge high-riding, top-ranked Sooners (5-0) juggernaut. In 1st H, Oklahoma used option runs by QB Jimmy Harris (19/121y) and scored on HB Buddy Leake's 2 short TD runs and late 2nd Q plunge by soph FB Jerry Tubbs (13/88y, TD). Early in 3rd Q, Wildcats C-LB Jim Furey recovered FUM at his 44YL but drive fizzled at OU 34YL. When Sooners couldn't cross GL in 2nd H their somewhat-spoiled partisans sat in quiet boredom, expecting much more from their charges after 65-0 walloping of Kansas on previous Saturday. K-State G Tito Cordelli halted drive with FUM REC at his 20YL in 3rd Q. Oklahoma coach Bud Wilkinson gave credit elsewhere, heaping high praise on vanquished Wildcats: "With their backs to the wall they fought back wonderfully well." K-State gained only 154y as top HB Corky Taylor was cuffed with 5/-3y rushing and 3/46y receiving. OU gained 331y, taking its 14th straight win and its 42nd conf game in row without defeat.

ARKANSAS 6 Mississippi 0 (Little Rock): After posting 3-7 record in 1953, rowdy Razorbacks (5-0) embraced national attention with huge upset of undefeated Rebels (5-1). They also were gaining nickname fame with "The 23 Little Pigs," meaning that small corps of 23 players were team's driving force. Arkansas FB-LB Henry Moore stopped 4th down dive at own 5YL by Ole Miss FB Bobby McCool in 1st Q and ended Mississippi's last gasp with INT at own 20YL in 4th Q. Arkansas appeared content to accept 0-0 moral victory after receiving punt at own 17YL with 6 mins to play. But, Hogs took 3rd-and-6 gamble from own 34 YL with less than 4 mins left. TB Buddy Benson faked sweep to left, stopped and lofted long pass to BB Preston Carpenter at Rebels 35YL. Carpenter took pass over his left shoulder and fled rest of way from DB Billy Kinard for winning 66y TD. Arkansas was outgained 258y to 223y, but much of Mississippi's y was achieved near midfield. Ole Miss had more to fret about: This match with SWC foe filled its short SEC slate, so its loss counted negatively in own conf standing. TB-P George Walker, nation's leader in punting, bombed 55 and 43y boots to help pin Ole Miss in its territory. Nation's leading pass O team coming in, Rebs QBs Eagle Day and Houston Patton hit only 2-11/32y against alert Porkers D.

SOUTHERN CALIFORNIA 29 California 27: Blistering battle gave control of PCC's Rose Bowl bid to persistent Trojans (5-1). Trailing 7-0 because they lost FUM on opening KO that was turned into 3y TD run by USC WB Lindon Crow, Golden Bears (2-4) marched right down field to doorstep of Troy EZ. California HB Johnny Wilson bobbled FUM at GL, and Crow gobbled it up in EZ. Crow's 2nd TD gave USC 20-7 lead early in 3rd Q. But, resourceful Cal QB Paul Larson (14-18/167y, 2 TDs, INT) followed immediately with 84y KO RET to USC 1YL, and he sneaked for TD that pulled Bears into threatening spot at 20-14. Moments later, Larson was trapped for crucial safety by Southern California E Don McFarland and T Ed Fouch, and Trojans led 22-14. In many ways, Cal never recovered from that blow, but HB Hal Norris' 1y TD run brought Bears within 22-21 with 6:02 left. Crow, playing 60 mins in his greatest 2-way game as Trojan, scored his 3rd TD to clinch it 29-21 with 2:22 left.

AP Poll October 25

1 Ohio State (64)	1858	11 Michigan	344
2 Oklahoma (74)	1834	12 Mississippi	318
3 UCLA (45)	1800	13 Southern California	184
4 Arkansas (16)	1351	14 Virginia Tech (1)	124
5 Army (1)	974	15 Navy	78
6 Notre Dame (1)	727	16 Duke	75
7 West Virginia (6)	478	17 Texas Christian	57
8 Wisconsin	460	18 Southern Methodist	53
9 Purdue	393	19 Rice	51
10 Miami (6)	369	20 Cincinnati	39

October 30, 1954

Xavier 19 BOSTON COLLEGE 14: Winless in 12 games and without 1st down in previous week's 33-0 pasting at hands of coach Sid Gilman's powerhouse Cincinnati squad, Xavier (1-6) sloshed through Fenway Park quagmire to spring biggest surprise result of 1954. Unbeaten Boston College (5-1) tallied TDs by HB Eddie DeSilva and QB Billy Donlan for 14-0 3rd Q lead, but Muskateers HB Bob Konkoly turned game in Xavier's favor with 51y TD run. Trailing 14-13, Xavier went 70y to FB Don St. John's TD with less than 1:30 left as Eagles D, nation's leader, was helpless to stop 4th down runs at their 25 and 17YLs.

ARMY 21 Virginia 20: Go-for-broke WWII hero Gen Douglas MacArthur visited West Point on rain-drenched Saturday and must have been puzzled when losing Virginia (3-3) fans pulled down goalposts and carried their coach Ned McDonald off field on their shoulders. All this excitement for near-upset, "moral victory?" Cadets (5-1) led 7-0 early, but at own 8YL in 2nd Q they bobbled 1st of 5 FUMs they would lose, and HB Hank Strempek caught it and returned it for TD that pulled Cavs within 7-6. But, UVa HB-K Stanwood Knowles flew his kick wide. Virginia bolted ahead 13-7 early in wild 3rd Q, but Cadets quickly answered as HB Tommy Bell jetted 29y to score. Stalwart Army E Don Holleder made critical INT at Cavs 25YL, and FB Pat Uebel scored his 2nd TD. Cadets G-K Ralph Chesnauskas, who by season's end became nation's leading x-pt K, made his 3rd conv for 21-13 edge. Before end of 3rd Q, UVa lefty QB Bill Clarke arched 32y pass to E Bob Pogue, who darted away from Army DBs for TD. Ahead 21-20, Cadets threatened on passes of QB Pete Vann (11-22/157y, 2 INTs) in 4th Q, but HB Joe Cygler's midfield FUM with 1:45 left gave late hope to Virginia. Excited Commonwealth fans spilled from stands and crowded sidelines as Clarke's last-play EZ pass for Pogue was knocked down by DB Uebel.

Pittsburgh 13 WEST VIRGINIA 10: In trying to beat rival Pittsburgh for 1st time ever in Morgantown, undefeated West Virginia (4-1) scrambled to take 3-0 lead on C-K Chick Donaldson's 19y FG with 1 sec left before H. FB Joe Marconi's 4y sweep in 4th Q provided Mountaineers with 10-7 lead. Suddenly-hot Panthers (3-3) won their 3rd straight under interim coach-AD Tom Hamilton, who it earlier was announced would stay on for rest of season. Pitt rallied on newly-discovered QB Corny Salvaterra's winning TD pass to E Fred Glatz with 2:22 left. Pitt overcame 90y in PENs and called on surprisingly effective air game from run-pass threat Salvaterra and 2 other QBs to total 8-18/105y, 2 TDs, INT passing. Soph HB-K Ambrose "Bags" Bagamery had broken Panthers into scoring column by spearing 9y TD toss from Salvaterra and adding kick late in 3rd Q.

Notre Dame 6 Navy 0 (Baltimore): Notre Dame (4-1) had better of play in 1st H as it kept Navy (4-2) bottled up in its half of field and outgained Middies 186y to 20y. But, PENs squelched all Irish threats except QB Ralph Guglielmi's quicksilver 46y TD pass to HB Jim Morse. Navy (4-2) rallied in 2nd H, marching to ND 13YL only to have passes fail. Later in 3rd Q, USNA earned 1st down at Irish 1YL. Navy HB Bob Craig pounded to GL, but muddy ball squirted into EZ where DB Guglielmi fell on it for touchback that denied Middie TD. Determined more than ever, Navy drove twice, to 20YL and later to 31YL, on sharp passes of QB George Welsh (14-27/137y, 2 INTs) to E Ron Beagle, HB John Weaver, and FB Dick Guest. On each advance, Navy again was frustrated, these times by INTs, 1 of them being filched by ever-present Guglielmi.

DUKE 21 Georgia Tech 20: Engineers (4-3) played without suspended sr HB Billy Teas, who ended his career just 1y short of Georgia Tech's career rushing record at that time. Engineers built 20-0 3rd Q lead on running of swift soph HBs Jimmy Thompson and Paul Rotenberry, precise passing of QBs Wade Mitchell and Bill Brigman, and glue-fingered grabs of E Bill Sennett. Tech TDs: Rotenberry's 43y catch from Brigman, FB Dickie Mattison's short plunge after Thompson streaked 51y, and Sennett's 3 straight catches from Mitchell. Seemingly unimportant was Mitchell's conv kick miss after Sennett's 3rd Q TD. At that point, Duke (4-1-1) had made only 3 1st downs, but QB Jerry Barger completed 4 passes on 68y drive, last for TD to E Jerry Kocourek. Early in 4th Q roughing P PEN gave Duke life at Tech 22YL. FB Bryant Aldridge quickly scored to pull Blue Devils to within 20-14. Winning 82y Blue Devils drive was climaxed by HB Ed Post's TD run with :42 left and successful conv kick by G-K Jim Nelson, who remained perfect on x-pts in 1954.

ALABAMA 0 Georgia 0 (Birmingham): Favored Alabama (4-2-1) failed horribly in scoring zone as Georgia (5-1-1) D, sparked by E Joe O'Malley, G-LB Don Shea, and G Len Spadafino, made stops at its 19 and 8YLs in 1st H and 29 and 5YLs in 4th Q. Last threat was foiled when Bulldogs FB-LB Bobby Garrard stepped in front of E Nick Germanos to pick off pass from ailing Crimson Tide QB Bart Starr. Alabama outgained Bulldogs 223y to 176y, but difference was sharp Georgia tackling and timely pass D. Shea's INT in 3rd Q provided UGa with scoring chance, but G-K Joe Graff was short on 40y FG try. Crimson Tide's other QB, Albert Elmore, launched long pass in last 40 secs that Bulldogs QB-DB Jimmy Harper picked off and returned to Bama 29YL, but Harper's 4th down pass was well defended. Failure of its O continued to plague Bama for 2nd half of season.

MISSISSIPPI 21 Louisiana State 6: Speed and O flexibility of mighty Mississippi (6-1) prevailed over stubborn, but out-manned Bengal Tigers (2-5). LSU hurled back 2 threats in 1st Q and early 2nd Q on FUMs by Ole Miss FB Bobby McCool, lost to Tigers C-LB Larry Jones at 5YL, and QB Houston Patton, recovered by T Sid Fournet at 7YL. Turnaround was sudden: When LSU QB Al Doggett attempted pass, hard-charging Rebels T Billy Yelverton snatched ball from Doggett's passing stance and raced into EZ for 7-0 lead in 2nd Q. It took until late in 3rd Q for Mississippi finally to light up its O. HB Allen Muirhead dashed 26y to set up HB Jimmy Patton's 9y stand-up TD burst. DB Patton soon made INT, as he often would accomplish with NFL's New York Giants, and returned it 34y to 11YL. Rebs QB Houston Patton, no relation, soon scored on sneak. With little more than min to play, LSU QB Matt Burns rifled 16y pass to E Sammy Murphy to provide Baton Rouge Homecoming crowd with consolation TD.

Indiana 13 MICHIGAN 9: Hoosiers (2-4) knocked Michigan (4-2) from top of Big 10 standings as sr QB Florian Helinski (10-19/103y, TD) reached Big 10 record, at that time, of 118 pass attempts without INT. On other side of ball, DB Helinski picked off 3 INTs as Indiana D stymied Michigan's determined 2nd H bid to come from behind. In 1st Q, Wolverines FB Fred Baer scored on 16th play of march that went 64y. Michigan soph E-K Ron Kramer caught 3/27y and added x-pt. Later, Wolverines E Tom Maentz blocked punt for 3rd Q safety. It was not enough as Indiana notched 13 pts in 2nd Q. QB-K Helinski scored on 4th down sneak after Hoosiers T Ron Rauchmiller fell on FUM at UM 27YL, but missed his 1st conv of season. With 5 mins before H, Helinski dropped soft 20y TD pass into hands of HB Milt Campbell, speedy future 1956 Olympic decathlon gold medalist at Melbourne, Australia. Indiana FB Les Kun broke away for 46y gain in 4th Q, and although Hoosiers soon fumbled away possession, Kun's run provided needed field position. Michigan made IU 23YL on its last try, endured dropped EZ pass by HB Terry Barr, and suffered DB Helinski's INT with 1:47 left.

IOWA 13 Wisconsin 7: Nicked-up Hawkeyes (4-2) withstood running barrage of Wisconsin (4-2) FB Alan "the Horse" Ameche (26/117y, TD), who came within 39y of Ollie Matson of U of San Francisco, who was 2nd on NCAA career rushing y list. Iowa QB Jerry Reichow (16/97y rushing) completed 49y mostly-land drive with his own short TD run in 1st Q for 7-0 lead. After C-LB Gary Messner recovered Reichow's FUM at Iowa 10YL, Badgers threatened with Ameche lugging leather 3 times. But on Wisconsin 4th down at 1YL, HB Pat Levenhagen's FUM was recovered in EZ by Iowa HB-DB Bobby Stearnes. Iowa's Stearnes scored with 40 secs left in 2nd Q after 23y hook-and-ladder pass-run to 4YL from sub QB Ken Ploen to E Jim Freeman to HB Eddie Smith. Ameche keyed 65y TD drive by smashing 22y off T to Iowa 1YL near end of 3rd Q to bring about his own TD dive. Bobbled handoff between Badgers QB Jim Haluska and Ameche ruined Wisconsin's menacing move to Iowa 5YL in 4th Q.

Oklahoma 13 COLORADO 6: Formerly-injured Sooners (6-0) QB Gene Calame was hastily inserted by coach Bud Wilkinson on 4th-and-2 when Oklahoma had possession at its 43YL in 2nd Q. Ball was snapped just as Calame dashed in to try to prevent soph QB Jimmy Harris' gamble, but Colorado (5-2) held anyway and refused 12-man PEN. Golden Buffs quickly took 6-0 lead on 6 plays midway in 2nd Q when TB Carroll Hardy hit WB Frank Bernardi with 19y scoring screen pass after having clicked on 13y aerial to E Wally Merz. Oklahoma battled back with 77y drive, but FB Bob Herndon (72y

rushing) was stacked up on 4th down at Bison 1YL. Throwing late knockout punches, resilient OU logged pair of 4th Q markers. Sooners cashed in 88y drive on 14 runs for 7-6 lead, and clincher came with 4 mins left as HB Tommy McDonald's 39y option pass carried to Buffs 1YL. Coupled with Nebraska's win over Missouri, Buffaloes were all but eliminated from Orange Bowl consideration.

NEBRASKA 25 Missouri 19: Surprising Nebraska (4-2) moved to 3-1 in Big 7 Conf by knocking off its 2nd straight Orange Bowl pretender by building handsome 25-7 lead over Tigers (3-3). Cornhuskers powered for 76, 65, 63, and 73y marches with every y coming on powerful 331y rushing game, except for QB Don Brown's 23y TD pass to E Andy Loehr in 3rd Q. Missouri had brokered 7-6 edge in 2nd Q when QB-DB Tony Scardino fell on FUM at NU 41YL. FB Bob Bauman soon ripped 16y draw run, and HB Jimmy Hunter caught 14y pass to 2YL. Hunter plunged off T and HB-K Jack Fox kicked Mizzou into short-lived 1-pt lead. Brown's 2nd Q TD sneak gave Huskers 13-7 H lead. Tigers DE Jim Jennings swiped midfield FUM from Nebraska HB Don Clark (12/64y) early in 3rd Q, but DB Clark quickly atoned with REC of QB Vic Eaton's bobble on next play at Huskers 36YL. Clark and FB Bob Smith (17/91y) ripped off good y until Brown lofted rollout pass that Loehr grabbed from 2 defenders at GL for TD and 19-7 lead. Down 25-7 in middle of 4th Q, Tigers E Hal Burnine caught 15y pass from Eaton, and HB Sonny Stringer made diving 23y grab to set up Fox's 4th down reception for TD. Mizzou made INT to poise Fox for his 2nd TD grab. But, it came too late.

KANSAS STATE 28 Kansas 6: Long-suffering Kansas State (5-2) delivered another defeat to lowly Kansas (0-7), which was on its way to winless season. With win earlier in month over Nebraska, Wildcats still held out hope to capture Big 7 runnerup spot for Orange Bowl trip. FB Bill Carrington (12/78y, TD) sparked 2nd Q march of 85y with 21 and 14y bolts to his TD, and K-State soon followed with QB Jim Logsdon's 24y TD pass to HB Tony Addeo for 14-0 H ledger. After failing at 3YL late in 3rd Q, Jayhawks sub FB Tommy Webb (7/29y) narrowed count to 14-6 on 8y burrow early in 4th Q, which was all Wildcats could stand. They quickly sprung their fastest back, HB Corky Taylor, for 42 and 31y TD catches from Logsdon (3-5/97y, 3 TDs) on which he weaved all over gridiron to close chilly, but exciting afternoon in little Manhattan.

TEXAS 13 Southern Methodist 13: With 9 suspended players out, Texas (2-4-1) rallied to tie from 13-0 deficit to seriously damage SWC title hopes of SMU (3-1-1). HBs Frank Eidom and Don McIlhenny tallied in 1st H for Mustangs, but E-K Ed Bernet's 2nd conv try was blocked. Still, Methodists led 13-0 at H. Longhorns got big play in 4th Q from C-LB Johnny Tatum, who made 41y INT TD RET. Bernet played turnabout, rushing in from RE to block Texas T-K Buck Lansford's conv kick after Steers had tied it 13-13. Mustangs countered with 50y journey to Texas 11YL after ensuing KO. But Longhorns line rose up to stop McIlhenny's run on 4th-and-1 at 2YL.

Baylor 12 TEXAS CHRISTIAN 7: Soph HB Del Shofner, who would become outstanding WR in NFL, was cast out of character for key play in Baylor (5-2) triumph. Blade-thin DB Shofner moved up near scrimmage line in tightly-grouped Bears D that effectively turned its DBs into LBs. When Texas Christian (4-3) FB Harold Pollard hit middle of line in 3rd Q, ball popped in lazy arc to Shofner, who shot to his right to avoid piled-up line, stiff-armed Purple Frogs QB Chuck Curtis and outlegged HB Jim Swink for 38y TD that provided winning edge. Baylor had opened scoring early in 2nd Q as bunched TCU D was exploited on wide runs until QB Billy Hooper wedged over. Conv kick was blocked. Hooper's normally effective passing game was submerged at 2-10/59y, 3 INTs, and it was Hooper's 1st INT, by DB Pollard, that started Frogs on 61y TD drive. Swink carried several times and caught 13y pass so Curtis could sneak over. Shofner gained 42y on pass reception, but DB Swink soon made INT to launch TCU's last threat in 4th Q. It died on downs at Baylor 8YL after Bears FB-LB Rueben Saage made saving play by running down Frogs HB Ray Taylor at end of 57y catch-and-run to Bears 17YL.

Ucla 27 CALIFORNIA 6: TB Primo Villanueva was major cog in UCLA's 400y Single Wing O machine, scoring twice and tossing 8y TD pass to WB Johnny Hermann in 4th Q. Villanueva dashed 40y to set up his own 3y TD at end of 8-play, 75y march in 1st Q. His thrilling broken field run of 26y provided Bruins (7-0) with 14-0 lead in 2nd Q. Meanwhile, Californina (2-5) QB Paul Larson passed 25-38/280y, INT, his number of completions setting new Cal record. Larson led 62y scoring advance in 2nd Q which was capped by HB Sammy Williams' 7y trip around LE. Bears lost FUMs to kill promising marches at Bruins 13YL in 1st Q and 3YL in 3rd Q. Latter drive frustratingly traversed 81y. UCLA FB Bob Davenport launched himself for short TD at end of 64y march in 4th Q. Glance at Golden Bears' great 1954 schedule revealed that they now had lost to each of AP's top 3 teams.

AP Poll November 1

1 UCLA (72)	1931	11 Duke	174
2 Ohio State (69)	1903	12 Iowa	168
3 Oklahoma (42)	1666	13 Cincinnati	94
4 Arkansas (16)	1494	14 Minnesota	80
5 Notre Dame (4)	957	15 Rice	75
6 Miami	870	16 Wisconsin	67
7 Army (1)	755	17 West Virginia (1)	58
8 Purdue	685	18 Virginia Tech	55
9 Mississippi (2)	529	19 Navy	28
10 Southern California	347	20tBaylor	26
		20tNebraska	26
		20tPittsburgh	26

November 6, 1954

Army 48 YALE 7: Largest Yale Bowl crowd since 1930 watched Army (6-1) crush unbeaten Yale (5-1-1), outgaining Elis 499y to 179y. Explosive HB Tommy Bell, on his way to Army record to-date of 1020y rushing for season, bolted 61y on Cadets' 1st play of game and went on to score 3 TDs. Yale soph FB Steve Ackerman scored at end of 74y advance to briefly trim Eli's deficit to 14-7. Back after collarbone break in opener, HB Bob Kyasky added 2 TDs for Army, including 59y pass from QB Pete Vann. It was Cadets' 6th straight win.

Navy 40 Duke 7 (Norfolk): Razor-sharp Navy (5-2), perhaps season's best-schooled team in fundamentals, drowned Duke (4-2-1), frequent punching bag of military acacdemies, with 4 TDs for 26-0 lead by H. Midshipmen dominated 1st H with 260y to 13y overkill, as TDs were tallied by HB Bob Craig (24/77y) on 14y burst, QB George Welsh (8/75y rushing) on sneak, Craig on 5y sweep, and HB Bob Hepworth on 9y angled run through T. Blue Devils managed QB Jerry Barger's TD sneak at end of 59y march early in 4th Q, followed by G-K Jim Nelson's 12th x-pt kick in row. Duke was 7-20/107y passing, but suffered 7 INTs

NORTH CAROLINA 21 South Carolina 19: T Roland Perdue and HB Connie Gravitte blocked South Carolina (3-3) x-pt tries, while Tar Heels (3-3-1) HB-K Ken Keller was perfect with all 3 of his kicks to spell difference. Gamecocks went 82y on opening possession in 6 lightning plays: QB Mackie Prickett hit passes of 47y to E Joe Silas and 16y to HB Carl Brazell before sneaking over. Perdue blocked K Silas' conv try. Trailing 7-6 in 2nd Q, SC went 73y, mostly on 48y dash by HB Mike Caskey to his TD run and 13-7 H lead. UNC got terrific power running out of big, soph FB Don Klochak (12/124y) to set up QB Len Bullock's TD pass to Keller, who then kicked Heels into 14-13 lead in 3rd Q. That score lasted until last 3 mins: UNC appeared ready to put it away, but overly-fancy ballhandling allowed Birds' E Buddy Frick to intercept Heels QB Doug Farmer's pitchout and streak 75y to score. Trailing 19-14 with 2:38 left, North Carolina used Kochak's 19y KO RET and his 30y run to set up E Norman Lane's brilliant TD catch amid 2 defenders.

Georgia 14 Florida 13 (Jacksonville): Georgia (6-1-1) D-front, led by G-LB Don Shea, C-LB Billy Saye, and Es Roy Wilkins and Joe O'Malley, forced 2 FUMs in 1st H that led to TDs by QB Jimmy Harper and FB Bob "Foots" Clemens. Wilkins' 23y pass reception at 11YL set up Harper's TD sneak. When Florida (4-4) FB Joe Brodsky (11/43y) fumbled at Bulldogs 44YL, mad scramble for loose ball ensued with Gators recovering at UGa 26YL, net gain of 18y. UF HB Jackie Simpson swept 6y for TD that tied it at 7-7 late in 1st Q. HB Charlie Madison slipped through Gators line for 40y run to set up Clemens' 3y TD run in 2nd Q. When Florida HB Bob Davis scored on 3rd Q sweep to narrow it to 14-13, Wilkins broke through line to block FB-K Ed Bass' tying conv attempt. Georgia HB-P Bobby Garrard got off late punt from midfield that died at Florida 1YL. Gators fought their way to Bulldogs 22YL, where Saye made his 2nd INT.

AUBURN 14 Miami 13: Auburn (4-3) discarded its usual X and Y platoons for prime unit comprised of its best talent, but coach Shug Jordan's plan seemed futile with Miami (6-1) enjoying 13-0 lead halfway through 4th Q on TDs by E Tom Pepsin (pass reception) and QB Mario Bonofiglio (53y run). Rugged Auburn E-DE Jim Pyburn halted 4th down run at his own 32 YL., and riled-up Tigers quickly scored on QB Bobby Freeman's run. When T Frank D'Agostino fell on FUM REC with 3:56 left, it set up FB-K Joe Childress' thrilling last-min winning TD and conv.

Miami (Ohio) 6 INDIANA 0: Coach Ara Parseghian's undefeated Redskins (7-0) surprised Indiana (2-5), using 6 FUMs by Hoosiers as upset catalyst. Starring on D for Miami were 3 top-notch Es: Mel Baker, Bill Mallory, future head coach at both Miami (1969-73) and Indiana (1984-96), and Tom Mooney. DE Baker's FUM REC of bobble by Indiana HB Milt Campbell (12/70y) at Hoosiers 30 YL in 3rd Q set stage for Miami QB Dick Hunter's winning 24y TD pass to HB Bob Wallace, on which Wallace broke 3 tackles. Indiana had disastrous day throwing ball: QB Florian Helinski hit only 2-15/15y, 3 INTs as his receivers made frequent drops. Hoosiers never got inside Ohioans' 25YL, but their D, which became 1st all season to blank Redskins in any 1st H, held at their 22YL on INT by FB-LB John Bartkiewicz (11/50y) and at 21 and 7YLs on downs. HB Ed Merchant was Miami's leading rusher with 6/81y.

MISSOURI 19 Colorado 19: Tigers (3-3-1) FB Bob Bauman (10/45y, TD) tied it up by powering over from inside 1YL for TD with 1:06 to play. Colorado WB-DB Frank Bernardi quickly succeeded with "Old College Try" as he dived to block HB-K Ray Detring's potentially-winning x-pt, and ball caught Bernardi flush in face to break his nose. Tie all but eliminated both clubs from contention as Big 7 Orange Bowl representative. Missouri cashed QB Vic Eaton's 58y TD pass to E Jim Jennings after opening KO, but Buffaloes' speedy TB Carroll Hardy (9/94y, TD) tied it 17 secs later with 69y TD romp after FB Emerson Wilson hit center of line and pitched out to lonesome Hardy. Tigers led 13-7 at H, but relinquished 2 unconverted TDs to Colorado's FB John "The Beast" Bayuk in 3rd Q, who maddeningly had been stopped 6 inches from TD on 4th-and-goal in 2nd Q. That GLS was answered by Bison in middle of 4th Q when they stopped Mizzou at 1-ft line after Tigers moved from their 32YL.

ARKANSAS 28 Rice 15: Undefeated Razorbacks (7-0) were outgained for 6th time during their amazing season as Owls (4-3) had 342y to 299y margin. But, relentless Hogs perservered with late rally to take giant step toward SWC crown. Porkers' do-all soph TB George Walker scored 3 TDs including 73y punt RET, passed for 118y, rushed for 87y, and punted for 43.3y avg. Rice led 15-14 in 4th Q after FB Jerry Hall's FG, but clutch FB Henry Moore put Arkansas ahead for good at 21-15 with TD run at end of 71y drive.

BAYLOR 13 Texas 7: Inconsistent Longhorns (2-5-1) scored midway in 1st Q as FB Don Maroney capped 72y march with 2y TD run. Texas D impressively threw net over strong-armed Baylor (6-2) QB Billy Hooper's aerial game. Undaunted, Hooper changed 2nd H strategy to send his slanting backs off thunderous blocks of T Jim Ray Smith to position his own TD runs of 2 and 26y. Baylor won primarily because it managed 278y rushing.

Cincinnati 34 ARIZONA STATE 7: In 14-7 opening H, Sun Devils (5-3) hung close with powerful Bearcats (8-0), who exploded with 20 unanswered pts in 2nd H to cop their 16th straight win. Trailing 7-0 after only 4 mins, Arizona State went 78y to tie it on several smashing runs, 23y pass from QB Dick Mackey to HB Jim Bilton, and Mackey's

1y TD sneak. Cincinnati's Split-T runs racked up 287y, but long passes by QB Mike Murphy authored Bearcats' most damage, including his 30y TD to E Glen Billhoff in 1st Q. Murphy set up HB Dick Goist's 4y TD run in 3rd Q with 30y toss to Billhoff and came right back to sling 25y TD pass to E Don Presley. Knocking on door of top 10, Cincinnati, however, would drop its last 2 games to Wichita by 13-0 and Miami of Ohio by 21-9.

Texas Tech 28 ARIZONA 14: Top-notch T Jerry Walker fell on FUM at Arizona (5-3) 30YL in 1st Q and Texas Tech (4-2-1), closing in on Border Conf championship, was off and running on O. Red Raiders QB Jerry Johnson pitched 25y pass to E Claude Harland to set up early TD. Moments later, G Arlen Wesley swiped ball from Wildcats, and again Johnson fired 25y pass to poise his own TD. Playing without star HB Art Luppino who broke his nose in 1st Q as DB, Arizona looked to QB Barry Bleakley's passing. Bleakley connected 4 times in 2nd Q to set up Luppino's sub, HB Tommy Grimes, for 6y TD, and in 4th Q, Bleakley passed to HB Wayne Mancuso 3 times on 60y TD trip.

UCLA 41 Oregon 0: Top-ranked UCLA (8-0) brought its season's pt total to 333, new school record, and its fabulous D completely smothered Oregon's O-master, QB George Shaw (3-12/29y, INT and 14/3y rushing). Bruins E Rommie Loudd scored opening TD on 16y pass from TB Primo "Calexico Kid" Villanueva (9/62y rushing) and tallied another TD on EZ REC of C John Peterson's block of Shaw's punt. Ducks (4-4) probed Bruins territory only twice, their 2nd trip ending when HB Dick James was stacked up 3y short of 1st down at UCLA 9YL. Lightning-fast Bruins WB Jim Decker immediately raced 91y to score.

AP Poll November 8

1 UCLA (117)	2660	11 Miami	168
2 Ohio State (80)	2594	12 Cincinnati	155
3 Oklahoma (44)	2292	13 Minnesota	148
4 Arkansas (43)	2207	14 Wisconsin	110
5 Notre Dame (3)	1480	15 Virginia Tech	95
6 Army (4)	1452	16 West Virginia (2)	92
7 Mississippi (5)	729	17 Maryland	84
8 Southern California	672	18 Baylor	76
9 Iowa	564	19 Southern Methodist	65
10 Navy	495	20 Georgia	62

November 13, 1954

BOSTON COLLEGE 7 Boston University 6: Beantown battle matched BC's tough D vs. BU's charging O in match-up with best mutual records in many years. In 1st H, Boston U (6-2) failed at Eagles (7-1) 20, 22, and 9YLs. Key block by BC T John Miller sprung HB Eddie DeSilva's 58y dash for 7-0 lead in 4th Q. Terriers FB Sam Pino soon raced 60y to TD, but BU's chance of tie rode wide on missed kick by HB-K Bob Sylvia.

PENN STATE 37 Rutgers 14: Nittany Lions (6-2) HB Lenny Moore propelled himself to 2nd in national rushing with 171y effort against Scarlet Knights (2-6). Penn State QB-DB Don Bailey made early INT RET of 55y to Rutgers 10YL and quickly tossed 9y TD to HB Ron Younker. G-K Sam Valentine missed x-pt kick, 1st of 5 such miscues for Lions. Rutgers tallied midway in 1st Q for 7-6 lead on QB John Fennell's 4y pass to E Paul Stitik to extend nation's best 86-game team scoring streak. In 2nd Q, Penn State went 80y, 60y of which were gained by Moore, to his 1st TD run. Moore hurt his leg in 3rd Q, and upon his 4th Q return he scooted 54y to lift State's margin to 37-7. On 1st play of 4th Q, FB Jim Lockerman, making his 1st start for Lions, outlegged Knights' secondary for 64y TD run.

Princeton 21 YALE 14: Sloppy Yale (5-2-1) negated its 411y to 256y O advantage by losing 6 FUMs, 3 covered by alert Tigers sub G Art Szeglin. Princeton (4-3-1) hero was TB Royce Flippin, returning from 3 weeks inactivity to score all 3 Tigers TDs, including 70y sprint early in 4th Q. Earlier, Flippin had scored on 3y run in 1st Q after Bulldogs lost FUM at their 25YL. It would be game's only tally until Flippin's long 2nd TD made it 14-0 in 4th Q. This was especially vexing to Yale because it had gone 93y to 3YL only to lose 3rd Q FUM. Down by 2 scores in 4th Q, Yale finally clicked: QB Bob Brink connected with E Paul Lopata for 51y to set up Brink's 4th down TD sneak, and Elis soph HB Dennis McGill sparked 73y trip to his 3y TD to knot it 14-14 with 4 mins to go. But, Tigers used fake buck-lateral that turned into 36y pass by TB-turned-BB Dick Emery to position Flippin for his winning 2y TD vault with 16 secs left.

GEORGIA TECH 20 Alabama 0: Punchless Crimson Tide (4-3-2) O was blanked for 3rd straight game, and its fine 4.1 pts-per-game D was shredded by Georgia Tech (6-3). Engineers HB Jimmy Thompson scooted for 2 TDs and added 34y punt RET. Fellow soph HB Paul Rotenberry ran 45y for early TD as Georgia Tech won its 3rd straight, positioning itself for major bowl bid.

Ohio State 28 PURDUE 6: Undefeated Buckeyes (8-0) clinched tie for Big 10 title with convincing win punctuated by 407y rushing. Purdue (4-3-1) muffed 3 scoring chances on dropped passes in 1st H and could earn its only TD in 3rd Q on FB Bill Murakowski's 9y sweep. Under heavy rush, Boilermakers QB Len Dawson still completed 18-37/190y, INT, and might have provided early lead had E Lamar Lundy held on to 4th down EZ pass. Ohio State then took 93 secs to travel to its 1st score, 30y TD run by HB Bobby Watkins. Buckeyes also received 1st H TD run of 68y from HB Howard Cassady (165y rushing) for 14-0 H edge. Ohio went 80y after 2nd H KO to QB Dave Leggett's TD sneak. Ohio leapfrogged idle UCLA to no. 1 in AP Poll.

MINNESOTA 22 Iowa 20: Thrilling battle for Floyd of Rosedale trophy saw Golden Gophers (7-1) HB Bob McNamara (115y rushing) scoring in 1st Q on 36y dash. When Iowa (5-3) tied it on QB Jerry Reichow's run from 1YL, McNamara dodged his way 89y on following KO to give Minnesota 14-7 lead in 1st Q. McNamara's runs and RET y amounted to 226y by game's end, but was overtaken by Iowa's deadly pitchout sweeps, which were bread-and-butter of 321y rushing. Hawkeyes HBs Earl Smith and Eddie Vincent each scored TD. When Vincent (154y rushing) tallied from 1YL early in 3rd Q, HB Dick McNamara and E Phil McElroy blocked Iowa E-K Jim Freeman's kick. So, game stood at 20-20 in 3rd Q when clipping PEN on 81y punt RET by Smith sent Iowa back to its 3YL. Vincent then bobbled pitchout—same wide play that went unchallenged all day—and Vincent had to dive on his EZ FUM, which he covered barely ahead of Minnesota DE Jim Soltau. Safety cost Hawkeyes loss, but not before last 90 secs of contest saw ball exchanged by TOs 3 times.

Pittsburgh 21 NEBRASKA 7: Panthers (4-4) rolled up solid rushing game for 254y, but it didn't reach fruition until HB Corky Cost slipped through Nebraska (5-3) line in 3rd Q, dodged trio of tacklers, and sprinted 40y to Cornhuskers 5YL. FB Bob Grier scored from 3YL 2 plays later for 7-0 lead. Nebraska, unable to sustain running threat went to air with mixed results: Huskers completed 8-23/122y, but suffered 5 INTs. C-LB Ed Bose made 1-handed pick-off of Nebraska pass in 3rd Q and returned it 30y to Huskers 30YL. Pitt HB-K Bags Bagamery, who converted 3 times, scored on 3y run after Bose's INT. Nebraska succeeded on 57y TD pass-and-run between throwing HB Willie Greenlaw and receiving HB Ron Clark.

TEXAS 35 Texas Christian 34: In wild contest, Texas (3-5-1) tallied 3 TDs in 4th Q to overcome raft of its own FUMs and long scoring dashes by TCU (4-4) HBs Ray Taylor and Jim Swink (147y rushing). Texas gained 443y and TCU 370y as game saw 5 TDs longer than 50y, but game-winner came with 2:21 on clock by Longhorns HB Delano Womack on 4y run, followed by T-K Buck Lansford's 5th successful conv kick. Horned Frogs had hopped to 14-0 lead in 1st Q on FB Stanley Bull's short TD run after Texas FB Billy Quinn (129y rushing) lost FUM at his 20YL and Taylor's 55y TD romp on play that seemed certain to be Texas offside PEN. HB Womack got loose behind TCU secondary for 66y TD catch early in 2nd Q, but Swink countered with 68y breakaway through RT Ray Hill's block. FB-K Harold Pollard missed vital x-pt at this mid-2nd Q moment as Frogs appeared set at 27-7. HB Chester Simcik raced 62y to pull Longhorns within 27-14 at H. After scoreless 3rd Q, teams traded scores, TCU's coming on Taylor's 64y pass-and-run from QB Ronnie Clinkscale. Steers went 59y to pull to 34-28, then gobbled up Clinkscale's FUM at TCU 34YL. Next came Womack's TD, Lansford's kick for 1-pt lead, and QB-DB Pat Toler's last-sec INT of Clinkscale's pass intended for tall E O'Day Williams at Texas 29YL.

Southern Methodist 21 ARKANSAS 14: Hogs' glass slipper was shattered when SMU (5-1-1) pierced Arkansas (7-1) D for 350y rushing and built 21-0 lead after 3 Qs. Mustangs sr HB Frank Eidom had his greatest day: 22/163y, 3 TDs rushing. Comebacks had been Razorback theme all year, and furious 4th Q effort nearly pulled it off as Arkansas got TDs on TB George Walker's passes to WB Joe Thomason and E Jerry McFadden. In between, Razorbacks made failed trip to Mustangs' 4YL. Also, Porkers thieved midfield FUM, but clock ran out before they could launch last-ditch drive. SMU briefly took over SWC lead with 3-0-1 record; Arkansas' conf slate now was complete at 5-1.

SOUTHERN CALIFORNIA 41 Washington 0: Washington (2-7) showed up with 6 regulars on injured list, and it showed. When press box denizen observed that demoralized Washington was unaccustomed to California sun as HB Dean Derby bobbled punt, another wag suggested that Huskies simply weren't "used to football." Game actually was over when USC (8-1) TB Aramis Dandoy charged 95y with opening KO. It hardly stopped there as Trojans E Leon Clarke blocked punt by UW P Bill Albrecht to set up 2nd score, this by QB Jim Contratto on 2y run. Trojans, on TDs by Contratto on 2 and 29y runs and deceptive TB Jon Arnett's 15y sweep, jumped to monumental 27-0 lead after 1st Q. QB Bobby Cox had awful game for Huskies as he passed 4-14/38y, INT. USC FB Gordon Duvall, who scored on 77y run, racked up amazing 28y avg on 4/112y rushing. Washington managed to advance to Troy's 2YL in late going only to be rejected to 6YL as USC took over.

AP Poll November 15

1 Ohio State (87)	2010	11 Southern Methodist	270
2 UCLA (92)	2003	12 Michigan	244
3 Oklahoma (28)	1761	13 Maryland	151
4 Notre Dame (2)	1222	14 West Virginia	101
5 Army	1167	15 Virginia Tech	81
6 Mississippi (7)	671	16 Miami	71
7tNavy	670	17 Wisconsin	70
7tSouthern California	670	18 Auburn	51
9 Arkansas (5)	533	19 Iowa	35
10 Minnesota	271	20 Baylor	27

November 20, 1954

HARVARD 13 Yale 9: Despite half of its lineup on injury shelf, Yale (5-3-1) nursed 9-0 lead in 3rd Q. While making INT in 1st Q, Crimson (4-3-1) TB-DB Matt Botsford stumbled into his own EZ for Yale safety; rule of that time, later changed to touchback, went against any defender unable to contain momentum that carried him into EZ. Botsford later was injured on Eli TD catch by 60-min E Bryon Campbell early in 3rd Q. Yale had opened uproariously in 1st Q, but on its 4 series, Bulldogs fumbled away opportunity after Campbell's 53y catch at 20YL, lost ball on downs at 24YL, suffered Botsford's EZ INT, and lost FUM at Crimson 40YL. Harvard sub TB Jim Joslin came in for Botsford and stumbled through jittery start, fumbling on his 1st carry. But, Joslin averaged 7y per rush to set up 2 late TDs. Harvard FB Tony Gianelly powered over from 1YL on 2nd play of 4th Q, and game-winner came on WB Frank White's 38y pass to E Bob Cochran off reverse with 4:58 to play. Between Harvard TDs, Elis reached Crimson 30YL and punted frustratingly into EZ for touchback instead of trying for 1st down. By virtue of its November 6 win over Princeton, Harvard captured its 1st Big 3 title since 1941. Yale's defeat opened door to Cornell to share unofficial Ivy title with Bulldogs if Big Red cound beat Penn on Thanksgiving Day.

Syracuse 20 FORDHAM 7: Rainy day at New York's Polo Grounds ended with Syracuse (4-4) not needing single completion in its 3 pass attempts to riddle Fordham (1-8), which was nearing end of its days as major level football program. Orangemen

recovered 4 FUMs by Rams and racked up 255y rushing. After Syracuse DT Jerry Cashman recovered 1st Q FUM at Fordham 27YL, soph HB Jimmy Brown ran 10y to set up HB Ray Perkins' 10y TD run. Brown authored 39y punt RET in 2nd Q to launch 39y march to TD by FB Bill Wetzel (74y rushing) for 14-0 H lead. Orange E Tom Richardson's FUM REC sparked 33Y TD trip 3rd Q. Fordham show life in 4th Q, going 65y to HB Andy Romeo's short TD run. Rams E Bill Liptack made spectacular 1-handed, back-peddling 30y catch to keep chains moving to Fordham's score.

Penn State 13 PITTSBURGH 0: Locker room chalkboard read: "Seniors 47 Pitt 0" to signify 3-year pt total against in-state rivals as Penn State (7-2) blanked Pitt (4-5) for 3rd year in row. Panthers D kept HB Lenny Moore out of EZ for 1st time in 1954, but Moore's 68y rushing total placed him atop national rushing stat list at that moment with 1082y (8y avg), which also gave him Mt Nittany season record. DB Moore, perhaps more importantly, snuffed 2 Panthers drives inside Lions 20YL with INTs. Penn State TDs came on E Jack Sherry's 19y catch in 2nd Q from sub QB Bobby Hoffman, who came off bench to spark O, and 1st-team QB Don Bailey, who returned for TD sneak in 3rd Q after Moore made 25y run. Nittany Lions threatened twice in 1st Q after G Dick DeLuca and E Jesse Arnelle blocked punts, but State saw chances fizzle on lost FUM and missed pass to Arnelle on fake FG try. Pitt outgained Lions 252y to 219y and doubled 1st downs by 18 to 9 but was doomed by Moore's INTs.

Kentucky 14 TENNESSEE 13: In his 1st year in Lexington, Blanton Collier achieved what no other Kentucky (7-3) coach, including Bear Bryant, had accomplished in 30 years: beat Tennessee (4-5) in Knoxville. On other sideline, Harvey Robinson, 2nd-year successor to Robert Neyland, was headed for Vols' 1st losing season since 1935. Weird play: fierce EZ pressure by Vols forced Wildcats E-P Brad Mills to punt out to 30YL while using his left (non-kicking) foot. Vols took 13-7 lead in 3rd Q on TB Jimmy Wade's 39y saunter to TD. Decisive late Kentucky TD came on QB Bob Hardy's 22y pass to future coach, E Howard Schnellenberger, followed by QB-K Delmar Hughes' winning conv kick.

AUBURN 27 Clemson 6: Auburn Tigers HB Dave "Hoppy" Middleton (13/60y) spurted up middle for trio of TDs in 1st H to key Auburn (6-3) to its 5th straight victory. Middleton's scores of 11, 5, and 1y capped drives of 75, 45, and 51y by dominant Auburn. Margin would have been greater had it not been for Auburn's 100y in PENs, which included infraction that nullified 67y TD pass from QB Bobby Freeman (5-9/77y, TD, INT, and 6/56y rushing) to E Jim Pyburn (3/55y, TD). Still, outstanding SEC aerial battery connected on 20y TD late in game. Clemson (4-5) too tallied late: with 10 secs left, QB Don King found E Scott Jackson with 4y TD pass at end of 73y trip.

LOUISIANA STATE 7 Arkansas 6 (Shreveport): Injury-riddled Bengals Tigers (4-6) employed handy QB Al Doggett at all 4 backfield posts and upset reeling Razorbacks (7-2). Still, Arkansas clinched Cotton Bowl berth as Baylor knocked off SMU. After failing on 2 scoring threats, Razorbacks tallied midway in 2nd Q on TB-K Buddy Benson's pass to E Billy Lyons, but Benson missed kick. Margin of LSU win was K Doggett's 2nd Q conv after HB Chuck Johns scored. FB Lou Deutschmann sparkled at T in patched up Tigers lineup, combining with T Sid Fournet to thwart Arkansas O.

GAME OF THE YEAR
OHIO STATE 21 Michigan 7:

With Rose Bowl trip up for grabs, Michigan (6-3) opened match with 68y drive capped by TB Dan Cline's 7y intricate, Single Wing buck-lateral TD run: LE Ron Kramer pulled right as if to block as FB Fred Baer took direct snap and plunged toward middle of line, where he handed to BB Lou Baldacci, who flipped lateral to Cline, who sped left to score after having moved right on initial motion fake. Wolverines continued 1st H dominence, which they would lead in O y by 198y to 42y, but Baer lost FUM to Buckeyes E Bill Michael at Ohio 36YL and K Kramer missed 32y FG to left. Badly outplayed, Ohio State (9-0) was able to tie it 7-7 before H. Sub Wolverines QB Jim Maddock threw poor flat pass that little-used Buckeyes FB-LB Jack Gibbs picked off and returned down sideline 47y to 10YL. Gibbs' INT set up QB Dave Leggett's TD pass to E Fred Kriss for 7-7 deadlock. DE Kramer anchored Wolverines D that held Buckeyes to mere 4 1st downs through 3 Qs. To make matters worse for Ohio State, FB-P Hubert Bobo's "mine shaft" punt into stiff wind was claimed by Michigan E Tom Maentz at Bucks 14YL in closing moments of 3rd Q. Michigan then moved to 1st down at 4 YL, but FB Dave Hill's 4th down run was stopped inches from GL in disputed call. (Years later, Michigan loyalists would still gripe about officials' decision they felt robbed TD.) Determined Ohio State answered with stirring 99y drive, with clutch 52y run provided by dependable HB Howard Cassady (14/98y, TD). Leggett flipped 8y score to E Dick Brubaker to climax magnificent march. DB Cassady made important INT at his 26YL and returned it 13y. Cassady added TD plunge with :44 left to clinch Ohio's 1st spotless regular season record since 1944.

WISCONSIN 27 Minnesota 0: Wisconsin (7-2) surprisingly overpowered Golden Gophers and, in late Big 10 jockeying, ended up tied for 2nd as Minnesota (7-2) dropped to 4th place. Gophers O was diagnosed and distroyed: Minnesota advanced only 6y on ground in 1st H (69y total), and Badgers stole 7 aerials, 6 thrown by Gophers QB Don Swanson. Quick and resourceful Wisconsin HB-DB Clary Bratt (67y rushing) set conf record with 4 INTs. Badgers erupted for 20 pts in 5-min span that bridged 1st and 2nd Qs as A-A FB Alan Ameche, hobbled by bad ankle, scored twice and retired his collegiate career early in 3rd Q. Ameche finished his career with 25 TDs and NCAA record to date of 673 carries. Ameche's rushing total (3212y) was erroneously reported as new record, but he finished with 25y fewer than 3237y of Virginia's John Papit, made in 1947-50. Discrepancy came as school wrongly included Ameche's 1953 Rose Bowl rush y, which is allowed today but was not official in 1950s.

Notre Dame 34 IOWA 14: Revenge motive of fired-up Iowa (5-4) failed in "fifth quarter" remnant of 1953's controversial 14-14 tie in which Notre Dame (7-1) had faked injuries to gain timeouts to be able to score TDs near end of each H. Up-and-down Hawkeyes had spirit, but little else for superior ND in this year's rematch. In ironic twist, "Fainting" Frank Varrichione, Irish T who helped secure vital timeouts last year, was this day's fine 60-min performer. Rugged lines of each side belted each other, and, after 2 Hawkeyes needed help off field, Iowa sr T Cameron Cummins was ejected for unnecessary roughness. Even though Iowa E Frank Gilliam made great stretching grab of QB Jerry Reichow's long TD pass late in 2nd Q, Irish led 14-6 at H because HB Joe Heap raced 43y to set up TD early in 2nd Q and scored team's 2nd TD at end of 81y drive, that was slowed by 2 PENs. FB Don Schaefer and E Paul Matz, on pass from QB Ralph Guglielmi (9-14/165y, TD), scored in 3rd Q to help build ND runaway that reached 34-6. Hawkeyes managed consolation TD against Irish subs: HB Earl Smith's 76y race down sideline with pass from 3rd-string QB Don Dobrino.

OKLAHOMA 55 Nebraska 7: Barred from Orange Bowl by "No Repeat Rule," no.3 Oklahoma (9-0) exacted lesson on Big 7 bowl rep Nebraska (5-4) to tune of 577y total O. Normally land-locked, Sooners surprisingly threw for 235y with QB Gene Calame (6-8/126y) and HB Buddy Leake (3-5/50y, TD) accounting for most of aerial damage. Cornhuskers held their own in 1st Q, using 2nd-unit HBs Dennis Korinek and Don Comstock to batter into OU territory, and, after DT Pev Evans' FUM REC, they tied score at 7-7 on TD plunge by FB Bob Smith (4/23y, TD). Once 2nd Q opened, it was all Oklahoma: HB-DB Leake, who had made 1st TD happen with his pass INT and 4y TD throw to wide-open E Max Boydston (4/83y), recovered muffed punt by Comstock at 25YL. Sooners HB Tommy McDonald soon caught TD pass, and Leake later scooted 19y for 21-7 H lead. In 2nd H, Oklahoma went 74y to tally on FB Bob Herndon's blast, quickly reversed its lost FUM at Nebraska 19YL with HB Wray Littlejohn's TD run, and used E Joe Mobra's blocked punt to set up HB Bob Derrick's TD run. In all, 8 different Sooners tallied TDs.

COLORADO 38 Kansas State 14: Star Colorado (7-2-1) sr backs, TB Carroll Hardy and WB Frank Bernardi, bid farewell to Boulder with brilliant display of fleet running. Hardy, who several years later would become trivia answer as only player ever to pinch-hit for Boston Red Sox immortal Ted Williams, burst behind block of pulling T Bill Kucera and went 45y to opening TD early in 2nd Q. Hardy (10/238y, 3 TDs) dashed 79y for TD and added 46y gallop late in 4th Q to set up his 1y TD blast on last play of his Buffs career. He had scored 1st time he touched ball as frosh in 1951 game against Colorado A&M. Bernardi (9/113y, TD), on his way to NFL Chicago Cardinals, contributed 50y TD scamper in 2nd Q and 70y sprint in 4th Q that set up Buffs' 5th TD by FB John Bayuk. Starting CU FB Emerson Wilson raced 95y for TD to cap 19-pt outburst in 7 mins of 2nd Q. Kansas State (7-3), which lost flickering chance at Orange Bowl bid, actually ran 83 plays to Buffs' 38. Much of Wildcats' possession time came on 74 and 76y drives that turned into TD run by FB Bill Carrington in 3rd Q and TD catch by E Joe Moody in 4th Q.

Baylor 33 SOUTHERN METHODIST 21: On heals of big upset in Ozarks over Arkansas, Southern Methodist (5-2-1) unaccountably ran out of gas when it had chance to bury Bears and walk off with SWC title. Still, Ponies jumped to 14-0 lead in opening 9 mins: SMU went 78y after opening KO as HB Frank Eidom (9/93y, TD) rushed for 43y and caught 22y pass on way to QB Duane Nutt's 2nd-effort TD run. Nutt tried to sneak over from 1YL, but had to spin off stack for wide-run score. Eidom caught 9y TD pass from Nutt after C-LB Burleigh Arnecke caused FUM at 15YL for short scoring trip. When Baylor (7-2) rallied, Mustangs swooned. Trailing 14-6 in 2nd Q and pushed to its 21YL, Bears received critical play from soph HB-DB Del Shofner, who left his man to pick off Nutt's pass in left flat and race 87y to score. Lean Shofner, day's big star, rushed 13/90y and 2nd Q TD that gave Bears 20-14 lead, intercepted another SMU pass to set up QB Billy Hooper's TD pass to E Henry Gremminger in 3rd Q, and blocked and tackled all over field. SMU didn't score again until FB John Marshall's TD sweep came too late to deflate Baylor's 33-14 margin in 4th Q. By winning, Bears dealt themselves into conf title mix and bowl sweepstakes.

UCLA 34 Southern California 0: Season's largest crowd of 102,548 sweltered in LA heat, even though underdog Trojans (8-2) were assured Rose Bowl berth thanks to conf rules. Trojans trailed only 7-0 at H and had 3rd Q opportunity after C-LB Marv Goux's INT: USC moved from UCLA 45YL to 1st down at 8YL. But, fabulous line of Bruins (9-0), headed by E Bob Long, T Jack Ellena, and G-LBs Jim Salsbury and Hardiman Cureton, pressured USC QB Jim Contratto into underthrown flat pass for big E Leon Clarke. UCLA HB-DB Jim Decker stepped in front of Clarke and raced length of field with INT RET, only to have clipping PEN leave it at Trojans 23YL. USC held there, but its day was done. Just before end of 3rd Q, Bruins HB-DB Johnny Hermann made 44y INT RET to 22YL to set up FB Bob Davenport's patented 1y TD leap. Cureton blasted Trojans HB Jon Arnett to create FUM on following KO, and 2 plays later, Uclans enjoyed 12y TD catch by BB Terry Debay, sr captain's 1st collegiate score in his last game. UCLA's 5 INTs, which were returned 167y, paved way for 27 pts in 4th Q, including TB Primo Villanueva's deceptive 48y pass to E Bob Heydenfeldt.

CALIFORNIA 28 Stanford 20: After 57 meetings in 62 years with "Big Game" rival Stanford (4-6), California (5-5) finally took series lead at 24-23-10. Golden Bears cashed 2 FUMs and INT for 3 TDs in 2nd Q. California's spectacular QB Paul Larson, who completed 14-22/150y, TD, 2 INTs to set new NCAA season passing percentage record of 64.1, took advantage of FUM and ran for TD for 7-0 lead in 2nd Q. After Cal HB-DB Sammy Williams made INT of Indians QB John Brodie, FB Jerry Drew scored on sharp-cutting 27y run, so Bears enjoyed semmingly simple 21-0 H edge. Bears took 2nd H KO and went 70y to 28-0 lead on Larson's 8y TD pass to E Jim Hanifan, future head coach of St. Louis Cardinals. Before game became total rout, Indians fought back from middle of 3rd Q on. Stanford HB Gordy Young darted and dodged 34y for TD, but G-K Tony Mosich failed on conv kick, pt which would haunt comeback attempt. Brodie sneaked for TD in last 10 secs of 3rd Q, and when Larson threw daring pass from EZ on next series, Tribe FB-LB Bill Tarr made INT at Cal 10YL. HB Ernie Dorn pushed across TD from 2YL, but Stanford still trailed by 8 pts and couldn't punch its 2 more opportunities into Bears end.

WASHINGTON STATE 26 Washington 7: Cross-state rival WSC Cougars (4-6) leveled largest victory margin in series to date on fading Washington (2-8). Washington State QB Frank Sarno lofted 47y TD pass to HB Jim Hagerty to crack scoreless stalemate in 2nd Q, and Hagerty added 2 more scores in busy 3rd Q when Cougars jumped to 26-0 lead. Huskies avoided shutout with TD pass from QB Bobby Cox to E Corky Lewis in fading mins. Washington ended season with its worst record since turn of 20th Century.

ARIZONA 54 Arizona State 14: *Arizona Republic* quoted stunned Sun Devils (5-5) fan: "It was *so* easy." Indeed, Arizona (6-3) HB Art Luppino raced for 180y and season's total of 1205y to blow by Penn State's Lenny Moore for national rushing title. Before Luppino and other Wildcats runners could rack up 420y and score 8 TDs, recently-maligned Wildcats QB Barry Bleakley (11-21/143y, INT) opened up plenty of room on early 81y TD drive with his sharp passes. Arizona State QB Dick Mackey made decent passing effort, clicking with WB Dave Graybill for 36y TD in 1st Q, and Devils trailed only 13-7 late in 2nd Q. But pair of rapid-fire INTs by Arizona WB-DB Gove Allen and G-LB Ed Brown reaped pair of quick TDs just before H for 27-7 edge.

AP Poll November 22

1 Ohio State (115)	2259	11 Miami (2)	310
2 UCLA (85)	2162	12 West Virginia (3)	238
3 Oklahoma (31)	1953	13 Arkansas (2)	196
4 Notre Dame (4)	1569	14 Michigan	173
5 Army	1296	15 Auburn	142
6 Navy (2)	914	16 Virginia Tech	109
7 Mississippi (6)	873	17 Southern California	94
8 Wisconsin	507	18 Kentucky	55
9 Baylor	332	19 Penn State	38
10 Maryland	317	20tDuke	35
		20tMinnesota	35

November 25-27, 1954

(Th'g) BROWN 18 Colgate 14: Bruins G Bill Klaess blocked early Colgate (5-2-2) punt for TD, and Brown (6-2-1) glided to 18-0 H lead behind clever QB Pete Kohut. Brown E-P Harry Josephson had his 4th Q punt blocked by Red Raiders G Tom Miller and run in for TD by FB Ed Whitehair. QB Guy Martin's passes (15-21/159y) rallied Colgate to within 18-14 until E Josephson's INT stopped threat at his own 15YL with 2 mins left. Victory concluded Brown's best record since Joe Paterno's days at QB-DB in 1948-49.

(Th'g) Cornell 20 PENNSYLVANIA 6: Coming back from 0-4 start of season, Cornell (5-4) beat Penn (0-9) for 1st time since 1950 and earned share of Ivy title with Yale. Punt block early in 2nd Q by Big Red C Steve Miles was picked up by E John Morris, who sped 11y for 7-0 lead. Cornell QB Billy DeGraaf contributed 43y burst to set up another TD moments later by FB Guy Bedrossian. When HB Dick Jackson (14/118y, TD) dashed 61y to score for 20-0 edge in 3rd Q, Cornell's win was forgone conclusion. Quakers E Jim Castle blocked 3rd Q punt by Ithacan HB-P Art Boland, but was hauled down at 3YL after 23y RET. Penn FB Stan Chaplin (19/108y) soon scored from 1YL.

(Th'g) MARYLAND 74 Missouri 13: Fast-closing Maryland (7-2-1) made mammoth but vain effort to sway Orange Bowl selection from Duke. Game, moved from early season to oblige TV, turned into national embarassment for Missouri (4-5-1) coach Don Faurot, inventor of Split-T O. Like Monster turning on Dr. Frankenstein, Terps piled up 601y in Split-T magic of their own. Big TDs were HB Ronnie Waller's 80y sprint, QB-DB Frank Tamburello's 70y INT RET, and HB Dick Burgee's 90y dash. Tigers had to abandon Split-T, got 2 TD passes from sub QB Tony Scardino from Spread formation.

Navy 27 Army 20 (Philadelphia): As important to football fans in 1950s as any NFL "Super Bowl" would become, this was Army-Navy at its best. Middies QB George Welsh, future Navy and Virginia coach, burst into national limelight as near-perfect signal-caller. Early on, Middies HB Bob Craig slipped away for 17y run, and HB John Weaver (14/91y) made 24y gain. Welsh's screen pass to Craig soon gave Navy (7-2) early 7-0 lead, while Army (7-2) countered with 69y drive to HB Tommy Bell's 8y run to bring score to 7-6 at end of 1st Q. Trailing 14-6 after another Welsh TD pass, Army struck twice within 1-min span of 2nd Q, thanks in part to FB-DB Pat Uebel's INT. Rapid TD runs by Uebel and HB Bob Kyasky put Cadets ahead 20-14. Smelling blood at this moment, Cadets QB Pete Vann cunningly called for on-side-KO, but, in heat of battle, failed to alert his Army teammates other than G-K Ralph Chesnauskas of his tricky intention. Navy recovered on-side-KO try and sailed to 21-20 H edge on drive from midfield, fired by Weaver's 26y run and E Jim Owen's 23y catch to Welsh's TD sneak. Pitched 2nd H battle had 100,000 spectators on edge of seats, but produced only single Navy TD by E Earle Smith on pass reception, his 2nd of game from Welsh. Middies pass rush, led by A-A E Ron Beagle, pressured Vann relentlessly as Cadets were driven from their run-oriented game plan. Still, Army made it to Navy 8YL in late going, only to falter. Afterward, Naval Academy, understandably proud of 1 of its greatest teams, accepted invitation to meet Ole Miss in Sugar Bowl.

Duke 47 NORTH CAROLINA 12: Talk was in air that win by Duke (7-2-1) would send Blue Devils to Orange Bowl as ACC representative. Such patter must have inspired Duke because HB Bob Pascal scored 3 TDs, including 15y run which made it 7-0 in 1st Q. After their 1st 69y drive, Devils added 67 and 87y scoring surges before forcing North Carolina (4-5-1) into passing attack that back-fired in 4 INTs. Each Duke INT led to TD in 2nd H, and QB-DB Jerry Barger made pair of pick-offs which set up Pascal's scoring romps of 2 and 10y. Tar Heels had briefly threatened to make it interesting by pulling within 7-6 in 1st Q as Carolina went 67y to sub HB Len Bullock's TD blast, which amazingly became Tar Heels' 1st TD against Duke in any 1st Q of rivalry since 1929.

VANDERBILT 26 Tennessee 0: Poor season suddenly got whole lot better for Vanderbilt (2-7) as it completely dominated punchless Volunteers (4-6). FB Don Hunt served as chief battering-ram as Vandy outdistanced Tennessee by 247y to 75y on ground. Hunt scored Commodores' 1st pair of TDs with runs in both 1st H Qs. Before H, Vanderbilt QB Jim Looney hit E Tommy Harkins for score that made H score favor Commodores by 20-0. Vols could gain only 110y O against fired-up D and failed on its only remotely serious threat when they turned ball over on downs at Vandy 42YL in 3rd Q. HB Charlie Horton caught Looney's 4th Q pass for final TD.

Auburn 28 ALABAMA 0 (Birmingham): Losers of 3 close SEC games in row early in season, Auburn (7-3) closed regular season with 6th straight victory, most lopsided in 50 years over fierce rival Alabama (4-5-2). Tigers O stars were QB Bobby Freeman (96y, 3 TDs rushing) and FB Joe Childress (20/98y, TD), who led 354y rushing O and scored all of Auburn's pts. Crimson Tide managed only 146y O before capacity crowd, but held H deficit to 7-0 on Freeman's TD when K Childress missed FG in last 10 secs of 2nd Q. Freeman (5-7/64y) burst 41y through gaping hole to score on 3rd play of 3rd Q, and Freeman and Childress each tallied in 4th Q. It was soon on to their 2nd straight Gator Bowl for Tigers.

MISSISSIPPI 14 Mississippi State 0: When Georgia Tech triumphed over Georgia 7-3, Ole Miss' victory over Mississippi State (6-4) was essential to lock up SEC crown and Sugar Bowl date for storming Rebels (9-1). Win was secured on early TDs created by TOs: QB Houston Patton ran for score after E George Harris' INT of pitchout, and HB Earl Blair went across GL after T Billy Yelverton's FUM REC. Bulldogs (172y O) made several chances of their own on FUM RECs, but reliable Ole Miss D, led by Ts Rex Reed Boggan and Dick Weiss and G Ray James, alertly halted 4 thrusts inside its 20YL.

Miami 14 FLORIDA 0: Miami's bowl-banned Hurricanes (8-1) triumphed over pair of FUMs that wrecked 2 long 1st Q marches. In 2nd Q, Miami tallied on run by QB Mario Bonofiglio after 40y punt RET by HB Whitey Rouviere. Florida (5-5) E Jerry Bilyk caught 2 passes from QB Dick Allen on next series, his 2nd reception carrying 29y to Hurricanes 6YL. After 2 blasts by Gators FB Mal Hammack and failed pass, Hammack hammered line but was stopped on 4th down at Canes 1YL. Miami lost FUM at its 21YL, so UF had last chance before H, but QB Bobby Lance's pass was picked off in EZ on 2nd Q's last play. In middle of 3rd Q, Allen was blasted in his backfield after bobbling snap, and DB Rouviere recovered FUM at Florida 6YL. Hurricanes QB Carl Garrigus carried 3 straight plays to score for 14-0 lead. Fred Robinson, Gators' 3rd unit QB, passed well in 4th Q, but Florida lost it on downs at Miami 24YL and on FUM to ballhawk Rouviere at 18YL.

FLORIDA STATE 19 Mississippi Southern 18: Sr HB-K Billy Graham led improved Florida State (7-3) to its 4th straight win, scoring on 31y run in 3rd Q, rushing for 82y, and kicking decisive x-pt after his TD that gave Seminoles 13-12 lead in 3rd Q. Shortly thereafter, FSU QB Harry Massey hit E Tom Feamster for 22y TD pass for 19-12 edge. Mississippi Southern (6-4) had scored on its 1st possession as QB George Herring, filling in for injured Jim Davenport, tossed 17y TD pass to E Hub Waters. FSU answered right away as HB Lee Corso gathered in 20y TD pass. Eagles went 70y for 12-6 lead on Herring's sneak before end of 1st Q. Herring and Waters collaborated on another TD pass in 4th Q, but Seminoles FB-LB Joe Holt broke through to block tying kick try by HB-K Carl Bolt.

NOTRE DAME 23 Southern California 17: USC (8-3), already headed for Pasadena's Rose Bowl, pranced into soggy, chilly South Bend and nearly stole upset as Ts Ed Fouch and Mario DaRe, and G-LB Orlando Ferrante spent much of day fighting into Fighting Irish (8-1) backfield. C-LB Marv Goux jumped on FUM, 1 of 4 Troy RECs of ND bobbles, at Irish 14YL in 1st Q, and USC QB Jim Contratto soon sliced over from 1YL for 7-0 lead. With running aid from HB Joe Heap (17/110y), Irish QB Ralph Guglielmi shook off slow start and passed to soph HB Jim Morse to tie it 7-7 before H. G-K Sam Tsagalakis kicked 34y FG for 10-7 Trojans edge 4:25 into 3rd Q. After 86y march early in 4th Q put ND ahead 14-10, Trojans countered with Contratto's passes for 17-14 lead. Forced into their 3rd comeback of afternoon, Irish took lead on 72y scamper by Morse and got late safety on bad snap from USC's Single Wing setup.

Oklahoma 14 OKLAHOMA A&M 0: Mighty Sooners (10-0) vaulted to 14-0 H edge on pair of keepers by QB Gene Calame (18/54y rushing) in 2nd Q. Oklahoma's 2nd TD drive consumed 9 mins and beat H clock by 11 secs. Sooners HB Buddy Leake rushed 11/66y and was his team's top passer with 2-3/36y. Oklahoma A&M (5-4-1) had reason for "good old country pride," as described by *Daily Oklahoman*. Unable to penetrate OU territory until FB Earl Lunsford (17/66y) ran 9y to Sooners 43YL midway in 4th Q, Cowpokes were pushed to their backs but stood strong on D. On same 4th Q series, Oklahoma A&M reached 4th-and-1 at 15YL on 6y scramble by Cowboys QB Tom Pontius (1-5/7y), but Oklahoma E Carl Allison barreled through to throw Pontius for 5y loss to halt threat.

Rice 20 BAYLOR 14: Gallant GLS launched Baylor (7-3) on 99y drive and 14-13 3rd Q lead. But star E James Peters fell on FUM in 4th Q for Rice (7-3), and HB Dicky Moegle scored winning TD, just portion of his 126y rushing. Winning result for Baylor would have meant SWC crown tie with Arkansas. But, Bears saw HB Del Shofner stopped on 4th down by DB Moegle at Owls 3 YL in dying moments. A-A selection Moegle also had 91y punt TD RET. Despite rumors of Owls heading to Jacksonville, Gator Bowl skipped over Rice and invited Baylor to meet Auburn, despite Bears' defeat.

ARIZONA 42 Wyoming 40: Wild west show played Tucson as Arizona (7-3) HB Art Luppino, limping with charley horse, scored 3 TDs, his last in 4th Q to tie it 40-40. Luppino's 24 TDs and 166 pts bettered 1950 national marks set by Nebraska's Bobby Reynolds. Luppino's 1st TD, 7y run early in 1st Q, had opened scoring parade and tied Reynolds' 22-TD record. Wyoming (6-4) QB Joe "Brooklyn Cowboy" Mastrogiovanni threw 26y TD pass to HB John Watts. After Cowboys made FUM REC on KO and made quick INT, they scored twice to go ahead 19-6 until Arizona caught up 26-26 by H. TDs were traded in 3rd Q until Wyoming went up 40-33 to set stage for Luppino's 3y TD run. With 8 mins to play, Mastrogiovanni backpedaled from own 14YL, and Cats D arrived. Wildcats DT Clarence Anderson and DE Ham Vose surprised QB by flooring him for safety. Cowboys went to Arizona 7YL with 10 secs left, but K Mastrogiovanni missed sharp-angle FG try.

December 4, 1954

Notre Dame 26 SOUTHERN METHODIST 14: Fighting Irish (9-1) lined up 7 sr players to start their last game, and another, C Dick Szymanski, injured in November, would have been 8th sr starter among Frank Leahy's recruits who wrapped up 25-3-2 varsity record. Coach Terry Brennan set new Notre Dame record with 9 wins in 1st year, bettering Knute Rockne's 3 (1918), Elmer Layden's 6 (1934) and Leahy's 8 (1941). ND A-A QB Ralph Guglielmi (9-16/129y, INT) passed for 59y on PEN-plagued opening 73y drive to 4y TD run by HB Joe Heap (10/130y, 2 TDs). Indeed, Irish were flagged 15/175y. Ponies (6-3-1) went ahead 7-6 in 1st Q on QB-DB John Roach's FUM REC at his 47YL followed by his 13 and 5y passes to Es Doyle Nix and Raymond Berry and his 10y cutback run for untouched TD. Guglielmi scored on option run, and Notre Dame E Bob Scannell blocked punt for 20y TD RET in 2nd Q. Heap all but iced verdict with 89y toe-dancing TD run down sideline in 3rd Q. HB John Marshall went 66y for 4th Q TD for SMU.

1954 Conference Standings

Ivy Group (Unofficial)

Yale	4-2
Cornell	4-2
Brown	2-1-1
Harvard	3-2-1
Princeton	4-3
Dartmouth	2-3
Columbia	1-5
Pennsylvania	0-2

Atlantic Coast

Duke	4-0
Maryland	4-0-1
North Carolina	4-2
South Carolina	3-3
Clemson	1-2
Wake Forest	1-4-1
Virginia	0-2
North Carolina State	0-4

Southern

West Virginia	3-0
Furman	2-0
Virginia Tech	3-0-1
Davidson	2-1
Virginia Military	4-3
Richmond	2-3
William & Mary	1-2-2
George Washington	0-4-1
Citadel	0-4

Southeastern

Mississippi	5-1
Georgia Tech	6-2
Kentucky	5-2
Florida	5-2
Georgia	3-2-1
Auburn	3-3
Mississippi State	3-3
Alabama	3-3-2
Louisiana State	2-5
Tulane	1-6-1
Tennessee	1-5
Vanderbilt	1-5

Big Ten

Ohio State	7-0
Wisconsin	5-2
Michigan	5-2
Minnesota	4-2
Iowa	4-3
Purdue	3-3
Indiana	2-4
Michigan State	1-5
Northwestern	1-5
Illinois	0-6

Big Seven

Oklahoma	6-0
Nebraska	4-2
Colorado	3-2-1
Missouri	3-2-1
Kansas State	3-3
Iowa State	1-5
Kansas	0-6

Missouri Valley

Wichita	4-0
Houston	3-1
Oklahoma A&M	2-2
Detroit	1-3
Tulsa	0-4

Mid-American

Miami (Ohio)	4-0
Kent State	4-1
Ohio	5-2
Toledo	3-2
Western Michigan	3-4
Western Reserve	2-3
Marshall	2-5
Bowling Green	0-6

Southwest

Arkansas	5-1
Southern Methodist	4-1-1
Baylor	4-2
Rice	4-2
Texas	2-3-1
Texas Christian	2-5
Texas A&M	0-6

Border

Texas Tech	4-0
Arizona State	3-1
Texas Western	4-2
Arizona	3-2
Hardin-Simmons	2-3
West Texas State	1-5
New Mexico A&M	0-4

Skyline Eight

Denver	6-1
Wyoming	5-1
Utah State	4-3
New Mexico	3-3
Utah	3-3
Colorado A&M	3-4
Montana	1-5
Brigham Young	1-6

Pacific Coast

UCLA	6-0
Southern California	6-1
Oregon	5-3
California	4-3
Washington State	3-4
Stanford	2-4
Idaho	1-2
Oregon State	1-6
Washington	1-6

1954 Bowl Games

Gator Bowl (Dec. 31): Auburn 33 Baylor 13

Way back on 1st day of 1954, Auburn had lost Gator Bowl to Texas Tech, and Tigers (8-3) returned 365 days later to turn tables on another Lone Star State team. Baylor (7-4) FB Rueben Saage scored 1st Q TD after QB Billy Hopper's tricky T-eligible connection for 27y to standout T Jim Ray Smith, providing short-lived 7-7 tie. Then, Auburn's A-A FB Joe Childress took over, rushing 20/134y, 2 TDs, and kicking 3 conv. Tigers' 476y O set Gator Bowl mark for that time. Auburn rushed 423y, including HB Fob James' record 11.8 avg on 6/71y, TD. Auburn T M.L. Brackett received considerable credit for man-handling his Baylor counterparts and causing 2 FUMs with hard tackles. Opening KO to Baylor ended up in hands of Tigers HB Dave Middleton because Brackett walloped Bears HB Del Shofner to free up FUM at 27YL. Childress soon rammed over from 7YL. Plainsmen all but clinched verdict in 2nd Q when they scored 2 TDs for 21-7 H edge, James' 43y beauty of dash and QB Bobby Freeman's 4y TD pass to E Jim Long. Baylor HB L.G. "Long Gone" Dupre twisted magnificently for 38y TD run in 3rd Q.

Orange Bowl: Duke 34 Nebraska 7

Mediocre record and all, Nebraska Cornhuskers (6-5) represented Big 7 because no. 3, undefeated Oklahoma had gone to Miami year before, and was not permitted return trip to Orange Bowl. Duke (8-2-1) HB Bob Pascal ran for 2nd Q TD, and QB Jerry Barger hit E Jerry Kocourek in back of EZ with :35 left in H for 14-0 lead. Latter TD was set up by Blue Devils FB-LB Bryant Aldridge's INT when Cornhuskers QB Don Erway foolishly fired jump pass into crowd at Nebraska 21YL. "That intercepted pass gave us our second touchdown and put us on the ice," said Blue Devils coach Bill Murray. P Barger's dreadful 2y boot, which took bad hop and forced him to down it himself, set up Cornhuskers HB Don Comstock's 3rd Q TD run. Somehow, overmatched Nebraska briefly was back in game at 14-7, but heat of south Florida was quickly taking its toll. Barger's 15y TD pass to E Sonny Sorrell reinforced Duke's edge at 20-7. Blues HB Nick McKeithan and FB Sam Eberdt tallied 4th Q TDs against fading Huskers. Swift Duke line, led by tiny E Tracy Moon, C Johnny Palmer, Gs Jesse Birchfield and Ralph Torrance, and T Fred Campbell, provided big edge, helping to carve out 361y net O.

Sugar Bowl: Navy 21 Mississippi 0

Full house of 82,000, including Secy of Navy Charles Thomas, was stunned by dominance by Midshipmen. Making its 1st bowl appearance in 31 years, Navy (8-2), frequently called his best team by coach Eddie Erdelatz, went 70y to score on opening drive, consuming exactly half of 1st Q. Sr Navy FB Joe Gattuso, who rushed for 111y and 2 TDs, went over from 3YL. That drive quickly established difference in contest: Navy's line was far superior to that of Ole Miss (9-2). Middies launched mirror-image march to open 2nd H as HB John Weaver brilliantly snatched QB George Welsh's 15y TD pass away from 3 Rebels defenders in EZ for 14-0 lead. Mississippi QB-P Eagle Day boomed punt 72y, but it only served to lengthen Navy's last scoring march of 93y late in 3rd Q. Gattuso made runs of 21 and 20y and threw key block to spring HB John Weaver for 22y gain. Blocking of small, quick Gs Len Benzi and Alex Aronis keyed game-long Navy O edge that outgained Ole Miss 450y to 121y. Top Rebels rusher, FB Paige Cothren, managed only 24y, but as LB, Cothren made late INT RET to his 35YL. Ole Miss came to life for journey to Navy 12YL on pass receptions by E Bobby Fisher and HB Jimmy Patton, but Cothren fumbled it away at 7YL.

Cotton Bowl: Georgia Tech 14 Arkansas 6

Strong Razorbacks (8-3) D was anchored by A-A G Bud Brooks, and it made TB George Walker's 2nd Q TD plunge hold up for 6-0 lead until late in 3rd Q. Arkansas went 80y for its TD as drive was launched by FB Henry Moore's 18y slam. Nonetheless, Georgia Tech (8-3) outplayed Porkers in 1st H, 4 times entering Arkansas territory, including trips to 5 and 8YLs. FB-K Johnny Hunsinger missed FG at end of Georgia Tech's sortie to 5YL, and near end of 2nd Q, Razorbacks E Olan Burns threw Yellow Jackets sub QB Bill Brigman for 10y loss as Tech passer surveyed field for open receiver. Finally, Engineers succeeded as HB Paul Rotenberry scored on 3y sweep with 5:00 remaining in 3rd Q, and QB Wade Mitchell capped subsequent 43y TD drive with 3y run in 4th Q. Mitchell, 1 of top DBs in nation, intercepted Walker to stop Hogs' only threat of 4th Q. Georgia Tech's ground game totaled 285y, and sr FB George Humphreys gained 99y to bid farewell to his career by being named game MVP. It was coach Bobby Dodd's 6th bowl win without loss in last 10 years at Georgia Tech.

Sun Bowl: Texas Western 47 Florida State 20

On his way to eventual stardom as DB for Green Bay Packers, Texas Western (8-3) QB Jesse Whittenton earned MVP honors with 3 TD passes and 2 TD runs. Gutty, little HB Lee Corso, future coach and ESPN commentator, got Seminoles (8-4) rolling early in their bowl debut as he charged 46y with pitchout to Miners 4YL, only to be dragged down by DB Whittenton. Florida State QB Harry Massey wedged over from 2YL, 2 plays later. After 7-7 1st Q standoff, Whittenton threw his 2nd TD pass to E Rusty Rutledge, and suddenly Miners launched 27-pt 2nd Q spree. Tex-West frosh twins, FB-LB Bob and E Dick Forrest, made several good tackles, while Bob zipped 95y with KO RET to FSU 2YL in 3rd Q, and Dick caught 19y TD. FSU QBs Len Swiantic

and Massey threw TDs to E Tom Feamster and HB Billy Odom respectively in 2nd H. Miners' 47 pts remains highest total ever scored in Sun Bowl. Afterward, FSU coach Tommy Nugent expressed notion that his team arrived in bowl game "one year too early."

Rose Bowl: Ohio State 20 Southern California 7

As old song lyric goes: "It never rains in southern California, it just pours." Rare Pasadena monsoon created ankle-deep mud, slowed play, and sent Ohio State (10-0) coach Woody Hayes into uproar when both schools' bands were allowed to march on field at H. This incident became 1st example of Hayes failing to win friends among West Coast fans and sporting press. Powerful Buckeyes, AP writers' choice as national champions, embraced 14-0 2nd Q lead on TD runs by QB Dave Leggett and HB Bobby Watkins. Trojans (8-4) soon found their missing spark when TB Aramis Dandoy fielded punt on own 14YL, shook 3 tacklers, and used T Ed Fouch's crushing block to go 86y to score. USC's other standout TB, "Jaguar" Jon Arnett, later raced 70y to Ohio 26 YL, but Buckeyes D rose up to dominate as they had most of day. Ohio State A-A HB Howard Cassady sloshed to 21/94 on ground. Afterward, Hayes continued his honesty-is-best-policy stance that so infuriated Californians when he suggested there were 5 Big 10 teams capable of beating Southern California. Of course, UCLA, UP coaches' choice in split national title vote, had reason to feel it could have beaten Buckeyes. Bruins had trounced USC by 34-0 on dry and fast field, although comparative scores always have provided weak evidence throughout football history. Would Ohio State and UCLA have put on dynamic show in trying to claim both no. 1 spots? Football fans will never know, thanks to 1950s frustrating No Repeat Rule.

1954 Top Performance Formula

1	Oklahoma	1.7374
2	Ohio State	1.7278
3	UCLA	1.6954
4	Miami	1.6121
5	Notre Dame	1.5977
6	Navy	1.5723
7	Auburn	1.5266
8	Mississippi	1.5028
9	Maryland	1.4760
10	Wisconsin	1.4587
11	West Virginia	1.4731
12	Army	1.4723
13	Duke	1.4585
14	Georgia Tech	1.4194
15	Colorado	1.4094
16	Texas Tech	1.3601
17	Arizona	1.3520
18	Southern California	1.3475
19	Boston College	1.3426
20	Arkansas	1.3335

1954 Top Opponent Records

1	Pittsburgh	.7500
2	Iowa	.6527
3	Florida	.6467
4	Auburn	.6311
5	California	.6222
6	North Carolina State	.6124
7	Purdue	.6118
8	Illinois	.6096
9	Louisiana State	.6068
10	Georgia Tech	.6058
11	Kansas	.6023
12	Texas	.6022
13	Michigan State	.5946
14	Missouri	.5805
15	Texas A&M	.5769
16	Miami	.5732
17	Texas Christian	.5699
18	Virginia	.5693
19	Wisconsin	.5676
20	Stanford	.5570

1954 Out-of-Conference Records

	W-L	Percentage	Bowl W-L
Southeastern	27-14-2	.6512	2-1
Big Ten	16-9-1	.6346	1-0
Big Seven	16-11	.5926	0-1
Southwest	17-13	.5667	0-2
Atlantic Coast	17-22-2	.4390	1-0
Pacific Coast	12-17	.4138	0-1

1954 Individual Statistical Leaders

RUSHING YARDS	Attempts	Yards	Avg.
Art Luppino, Arizona	179	1359	7.6
Lenny Moore, Penn State	136	1082	8.0
Tommy Bell, Army	96	1020	10.6
Sam Pino, Boston University	154	933	6.1
Dicky Moegle, Rice	144	905	6.3
Dick Imer, Montana	111	889	8.0
Joe Childress, Auburn	148	836	5.7
John Bayuk, Colorado	145	824	5.7
Fred Mahaffey, Denver	143	813	5.7
Tom Tracy, Tennessee	116	794	6.8

PASSING YARDS	Completions	Attempts	Yards	Pct.
Paul Larson, California	125	195	1537	64.1
Len Dawson, Purdue	87	167	1464	52.1
George Shaw, Oregon	91	196	1358	46.4
Ralph Guglielmi, Notre Dame	68	127	1162	53.5
Pete Vann, Army	48	99	1102	48.5
Tommy Gastall, Boston University	58	123	1003	47.2
Kenny Ford, Hardin-Simmons	78	146	948	53.4
John Brodie, Stanford	81	163	937	49.7
Bob Hardy, Kentucky	57	108	887	52.8
Bill Beagle, Dartmouth	76	145	867	52.4

RECEIVING YARDS	Catches	Yards
John Stewart, Stanford	36	577
Jim Hanifan, California	44	569
Don Holleder, Army	17	495
Jerry Mertens, Drake	28	495
Andy Nacrelli, Fordham	25	493
Jim Pyburn, Auburn	28	460
Max Pierce, Utah	25	457
Jim Carmichael, California	33	420
Tom Feamster, Florida State	28	442
Dick James, Oregon	24	394

1954 Consensus All-America

End:	Max Boydston, Oklahoma
	Ron Beagle, Navy
Tackle:	Jack Ellena, UCLA
	Sid Fournet, Louisiana State
Guard:	Bud Brooks, Arkansas
	Calvin Jones, Iowa
Center:	Kurt Burris, Oklahoma
Backs:	Ralph Guglielmi, Notre Dame
	Dicky Moegle, Rice
	Howard Cassady, Ohio State
	Alan Ameche, Wisconsin

Other All-America Choices

End:	Don Holleder, Army
	Frank McDonald, Miami
	Dean Dugger, Ohio State
Tackle:	Art Walker, Michigan
	Rex Reed Boggan, Mississippi
	Darris McCord, Tennessee
	Frank Varrichione, Notre Dame
Guard:	Tom Bettis, Purdue
	Jim Salsbury, UCLA
	Frank Mincevich, South Carolina
	Ralph Chesnauskas, Army
Center:	Matt Hazeltine, California
	Harold Easterwood, Mississippi State
Backs:	Tommy Bell, Army
	Bob Davenport, UCLA
	Paul Larson, California
	Bob McNamara, Minnesota

1954 Heisman Trophy Vote

Alan Ameche, senior fullback, Wisconsin	1068
Kurt Burris, senior center, Oklahoma	838
Howard Cassady, junior halfback, Ohio State	810
Ralph Guglielmi, senior quarterback, Notre Dame	691
Paul Larson, senior quarterback, California	271
Dicky Moegle, senior halfback, Rice	258

Other Major Award Winners

Maxwell (Player)	Ron Beagle, junior end, Navy
Outland (Lineman)	Bud Brooks, senior guard, Arkansas
Walter Camp (Back)	Ralph Guglielmi, senior quarterback, Notre Dame
Knute Rockne (Lineman)	Max Boydston, senior end, Oklahoma
AFCA Coach-of-the-Year	Henry "Red" Sanders, UCLA

1955

The Year of The Recocked Field Goal, Holly's Folly, and Bear's Aggie Surprise

With the arrival of limited substitution to college football in 1953, no less an expert than Notre Dame head coach Frank Leahy predicted that the outstanding run of Michigan State, which owned a 26-1 record from 1950 to '52, would soon come to an end. Leahy felt it simply was too difficult for the Spartans to prepare 60 or so players to play both offense and defense and still maintain the team's complex, various-formation style of attack, known as the Multiple Offense.

For one season, coach Biggie Munn's last, Michigan State had the last laugh. It won eight of nine regular season games in 1953 and whipped UCLA in the Rose Bowl. But when the Spartans stumbled badly in 1954, many coaches knowingly nodded in agreement with Leahy's contention.

The critical whispers about coach Hugh "Duffy" Daugherty over a sour 3-6 first year at Michigan State in 1954 were exceeded only by the acclaim the witty, unassuming coach received for a 9-1 turnaround in 1955. Daugherty's peers in the American Football Coaches Association chose him as Coach of the Year by the largest margin in the first 21 years of the award.

The Spartans, 5-1 in Big Ten play that included an early loss to Michigan (7-2), needed help to earn a Rose Bowl date with UCLA (9-2). Ohio State (7-2) was bowl-ineligible, despite its eventual 6-0 Big Ten mark, because of the league's on-going edict preventing teams from going to Pasadena two years in a row. The Buckeyes, with Heisman Trophy winner Howard Cassady, beat Michigan (7-2) to capture their second straight Big Ten title. Michigan's loss put it at 5-2 and punched the Pasadena ticket for conference runner-up Michigan State.

A strange and hectic series of late fumbles and penalties in the Rose Bowl gave the Spartans a chance to break a 14-14 tie with seven seconds to play. End Dave Kaiser, a sophomore transfer from Notre Dame, lined up a 41-yard field goal. Kaiser was stunned to find the center snap arriving in the middle of a practice swing of his leg. Without stepping back or moving his plant foot, Kaiser recocked his right leg and made good on a long, flat-footed boot for a rollicking win for the Spartans.

Contributing to UCLA's Rose Bowl loss was an arcane rule that today's fans would find absurd. Michigan State earned field position for Kaiser's kick partly because prior to a Bruins punt in the dying seconds, they were pushed back to their own five yard-line by a "coaching from the sidelines" violation when an offensive assistant made a passing motion to tailback Ronnie Knox. Not only was that sin a rules infringement that no coach would have to endure today, but it was marched off as a full 15-yard foul, from the 20 yard-line. There were no half-the-distance-to-the-goal penalties in 1955. Penalties that were sufficiently long to push a team into its own end zone were marked at the one yard line, all others were walked off in their entirety.

Bucking the trend in an upset-rich 1955 season, Bud Wilkinson's Oklahoma Sooners (11-0) won the national championship by crushing 10 regular season foes that sported a weak 37-51-2 (.422) combined record in the games they played other than against Oklahoma. Only Pittsburgh (7-4) and Colorado (6-4) showed winning ledgers among Oklahoma's opponents. The Sooners built an average winning margin of 31.1 points. Jimmy Harris, an underrated option quarterback and safety who was a great punt returner in his career, had a tremendous weapon in halfback Halfback Tommy McDonald, who averaged 6.8 yards per carry on 702 yards. From Oklahoma's indispensable pass option play, McDonald completed a dazzling 17 of 24 (70.8%) for 265 yards, a spectacular 11.04 yards per attempt. Jerry Tubbs was a superb center-linebacker and Bo Bolinger an All-America guard.

Maryland (10-1) held AP's top ranking most of the year after it blanked top-ranked UCLA 7-0 in a September quagmire at College Park. Three meek late season wins demoted the undefeated Terrapins to third in the final poll before they lost to Oklahoma 20-6 in the Orange Bowl.

Pittsburgh battled its customary monstrous schedule, but enjoyed a surprise season under new coach John Michelosen. The Panthers lost 7-0 to Georgia Tech (9-1-1) in a Sugar Bowl built into a pre-game tempest by Georgia Governor Marvin Griffin, who opposed Georgia Tech facing a racially-integrated team. Georgia Tech students were more interested in football than Old South politics, and Georgia Tech president Blake Van Leer solved the confrontation by firmly stating that the school intended to honor its contract with the Sugar Bowl. It was one more episode, albeit a relatively small one, that helped desegregate southern schools during the next 10 to 15 years.

Ironically, the Sugar Bowl's only touchdown was set up when fullback-defensive back Bobby Grier, Pitt's only African-American player, committed a debatable pass interference at his own goal line early in the game. Otherwise, Grier was the game's leading rusher in the defensive battle.

During spring practice at West Point, coach Red Blaik made one of the most daring and debated personnel switches in football history. With the graduation of standout Pete Vann, Blaik was left without a single Cadet back capable of playing quarterback. So, Blaik moved All-America end Don Holleder to the field general spot and stuck with the green Holleder through some tough early losses that showed Holleder to be a highly inaccurate passer. Critics flourished as Army fans grumbled, West Pointers whispered behind Holleder's back, and newspaper columnists pointed at what they called "Holly's Folly." Vindication for both Blaik and Holleder came when run-oriented Army (6-3) upset Navy (6-2-1) and its star quarterback George Welsh 14-6 at season's end. Soldier Holleder died a hero's death in combat in Vietnam in 1967. Welsh went on to become an assistant coach at Penn State and the winningest head coach at both Navy and Virginia.

The Southwest Conference reinforced its unpredictable reputation when preseason favorite Rice (2-7-1) dropped to the bottom of the standings and anticipated tailenders finished at the top of the league. TCU (9-2), with thrilling halfback Jim Swink, and Texas A&M (7-2-1), Bear Bryant's second Aggies team, tied atop the SWC. Texas A&M beat the Horned Frogs 19-16, but TCU went to the Cotton Bowl to play one of coach Johnny Vaught's best Mississippi (10-1) teams as the Aggies were on bowl probation. Ole Miss nipped TCU 14-13 as the Frogs played the whole way without quarterback Chuck Curtis who was hurt on the opening kickoff.

Texas A&M lost its opener to UCLA in Los Angeles as the Bruins unveiled the controversial Ronnie Knox, who pitched three touchdowns in a 21-0 win. Bryant's Aggies soon proved their capability by winning their next five games, and among Texas A&M's outstanding players was a trio that would take its place in both college and pro football history as players, coaches, and administrators: halfback John David Crow, fullback Jack Pardee, and end Gene Stallings.

Vanderbilt (8-3), of all schools, became Gator Bowl champions by defeating SEC rival Auburn (8-2-1). It was the Commodores' first bowl game in 66 years of football and it would be their last until 1974. Modern fans will have a difficult time believing that Vanderbilt had an outstanding 204-80-17 record from 1900 to 1930, and it wasn't until the 1960s that the school became an annual doormat in the SEC. Vanderbilt's mainstays of 1955 get little mention today, but coach Art Guepe counted on big fullback Phil King, who would become a dependable runner for the New York Giants, versatile halfback Charley Horton, a solid pair of ends in Tommy Harkins and Joe Stephenson, an excellent middle of the line in guards Larry Hayes and Larry Frank and center Jim Cunningham, and a quarterback with good judgment but a weak passing mark in reliable Don Orr, the surprise star of the Gator Bowl.

Easily the worst walk-up ticket sales of all time in any sport occurred on a snowy day in Pullman, Wash., in November. Only one person bought a ticket for Washington State (1-7-2) hosting San Jose State, and although a handful of students and season ticket holders fought their way into Martin Stadium to see a 13-13 tie, every football fan today should pay tribute to that one hardy sole who wandered out into the cold, apparently on the spur of the moment, to take in college football.

Milestones

■ Substitution rules were slightly adjusted to allow any player starting any quarter to be withdrawn and subsequently return once in that quarter. Rules were enacted to prevent unsportsmanlike trickery: The "Hideout" or "Sleeper Play" was eliminated by requiring all offensive players to be within 15 yards of ball when play was signaled ready.

■ Harry Agganis, All-America QB at Boston University (1951) and Boston Red Sox first baseman, died of pleurisy at age 25 on June 27. Dick Hilinski, tackle on Ohio State's 1954 national title team, was killed on October 21 in auto accident in Ann Arbor, Mich. Frank Eidom, SMU's best runner of 1954, also died in auto accident.

■ Longest winning streaks entering season:

Oklahoma 19	Ohio State 10	UCLA 9

	Incoming	Outgoing
Alabama	J.B. Whitworth	Red Drew
Arizona State	Dan Devine	Clyde Smith
Arkansas	Jack Mitchell	Bowden Wyatt
Dartmouth	Bob Blackman	Tuss McLaughry
Kansas State	Bus Mertes	Bill Meek
Louisiana State	Paul Dietzel	Gaynell Tinsley
Northwestern	Lou Saban	Bob Voights
Oklahoma A&M	Cliff Speegle	J. B. Whitworth
Oregon State	Tommy Prothro	Kip Taylor
Pittsburgh	John Michelosen	Tom Hamilton (interim)
Temple	Josh Cody	Al Kawal
Tennessee	Bowden Wyatt	Harvey Robinson

Preseason AP Poll

1 UCLA (33)	1054		11 Rice		270
2 Oklahoma (32)	1001		12 Iowa (4)		234
3 Michigan (34)	870		13 Southern California (2)		152
4 Ohio State	636		14 Wisconsin		150
5 Maryland (8)	595		15 Mississippi		128
6 Notre Dame (2)	529		16 Southern Methodist		93
7 Army	333		17 Auburn		56
8 Navy (1)	329		18 Duke (1)		48
9 Miami (5)	321		19 West Virginia (1)		45
10 Georgia Tech (1)	319		20 Purdue (1)		37

September 17, 1955

(Fri) UCLA 21 Texas A&M 0: UCLA Bruins (1-0) coach Red Sanders brought controversial soph transfer Ronnie Knox (6-8/83y, 3 TDs passing and 6/41y rushing) off bench, and his young Single Wing TB threw 3 TD passes to live up to braggadocio of Knox's infamously loud stepfather, Harvey Knox. Asked afterward if he ever doubted Knox's ability, Sanders simply said, "No." UCLA rushed for 211y and passed 7-11/100y. Disappointed coach Bear Bryant said decisive loss was blessing because it toughened his young Aggies (0-1), who were held to 193y O and few scoring chances. With score at 14-0 in middle of 3rd Q, Knox lofted pass toward WB Jim Decker, who battled ace Aggies HB-DB John David Crow. Lightning-fast Decker beat Crow by eyelash for 23y TD reception. Unable to mount much of pass attack (2-9/27y, 2 INTs), Texas A&M faced tough going against run (166y) as Bruins D was sparked by E Rommie Loudd, C-LB Steve Palmer, and T Gil Moreno.

WAKE FOREST 13 Virginia Tech 0: After undefeated 1954 season, favored Virginia Tech (0-1) was highly expectant of more to come in 1955. However, completely underrated Wake Forest (1-0) gave Hokies quick slap in face. Deacons marched 66y in 14 plays after opening KO to go ahead 7-0. Keying drive with his runs (5/23y) and 3 receptions/19y, Wake HB-K Billy Ray Barnes (15/86y, TD) crashed over from 1YL and added x-pt. In 3rd Q, Deacons E Ralph Brewster recovered FUM at Va Tech 32YL. QB Nick Consoles, who was master O craftsman all day, wedged over for 1y TD. Gobblers' O was completely throttled, gaining only 68y, thanks to heavyweight tackling work of Wake Forest DT Bob Bartholomew. Swift Va Tech HB Dickie Beard was limited to 4/16y, and he coughed up FUM.

GEORGIA TECH 14 Miami 6: Except for odd early play that went Yellow Jackets' way, at-home TV audience of 1st-ever color football telecast by NBC saw Georgia Tech outgain Engineers (1-0) in 1st H, including surge to Georgia Tech 10YL. Oddity came when Georgia Tech FB Ken Owen signaled fair catch on punt, but was tackled by overeager Miami G Joe Kohut. As PEN flags flew, Tech's HB Paul Rotenberry grabbed bounding ball and went 48y to TD through baffled Hurricanes. Yellow Jackets led 7-6 after Miami FB Don Bosseler powered 13y in 3rd Q for TD. Hurricanes HB-K Ed Oliver flew his x-pt try wide. Score stood at 7-6 as Miami D halted Georgia Tech at 3YL in 4th Q, and Yellow Jackets C-LB Jimmy Morris' 25y cinching INT TD RET didn't come until game's last min.

Mississippi 26 GEORGIA 13 (Atlanta): Ole Miss (1-0) QB Eagle Day, whose so-so training camp reportedly had cost him his starting job to John Blalack, put on superb show. Day passed for 2 TDs in 1st H and ran 6y to TD in 4th Q in nightcap of Atlanta doubleheader. Additionally, Day's long punts pinned Georgia (0-1) deep in its end. Bulldogs came out of 1st Q with 7-6 lead thanks to HB Connie Manisera's 7y TD run and E-K Ken Cooper's x-pt. Bringing foot back into Ole Miss football was FB-K Paige Cothren, who booted 27 and 21y FGs in 1st H; no Rebels K had succeeded on even 1 FG since 1932. Soph SB Jimmy Orr caught 46y TD pass from QB Dick Young in 2nd Q for Georgia, which trailed 19-13 at H.

FLORIDA 20 Mississippi State 14: Except for Florida (1-0) flurry late in 2nd Q when HB Jim Rountree sparked drive near red zone, underdog Mississippi State (0-1) dictated 1st H. After short punt by Gators QB-P Dick Allen in 1st Q, Maroons sub HB Jim Tait zipped 12y and followed with 2y TD run to cap 44y trip. Miss State's next 2 threats were spoiled by roughing PENs, so it led 7-0 at H. QB-P Bobby Lance made 3rd Q INT for Florida, and Gators HB Jackie Simpson made lightning bolt dash through LG for 46y TD that pulled them within 7-6. On 4th down at UF 6YL, Tait tried option pass to left flat. Florida DB Simpson picked it off and raced 100y to score. Lance's 22y keeper TD run in 4th Q iced it at 20-7.

LOUISIANA STATE 19 Kentucky 7: Coach Paul Dietzel's LSU (1-0) debut took happy turn on opening drive when HB-turned-QB Matt Burns threw 1st of his 2 TD passes to HB Vince Gonzales. Tigers' 6-0 lead held through H. After Wildcats (0-1) went ahead 7-6 in 3rd Q by scoring on QB Bob Hardy's 16y pass to ace E Howard Schnellenberger, LSU HB Joe May responded with 95y KO RET for TD for winning pts. Kentucky's 218y rushing gave it 290y to 176y O advantage.

FLORIDA STATE 7 North Carolina State 0: Rainy afternoon was inconducive to O, and it showed in final score. Florida State (1-0) FB Pat Versprille dashed 33y in 2nd Q, but QB Vic Prinzi suffered INT. North Carolina State (0-1) countered with trip to FSU 29YL, but Seminoles HB-DB Lee Corso inflicted his own INT. Wolfpack had excellent scoring opportunity in 3rd Q: they puzzled Noles with Single Wing set up and marched to 10YL. FSU held on downs, but quickly turned over FUM at own 4YL. NC State was forced into missed FG try after Seminoles massive DE Tom Feamster threw little HB George "Wagon Wheels" Marinkov for 2y loss. FSU finally got game's only score in 4th Q by launching drive from own 14YL. Feamster caught 12y pass from QB Harry Swantic, Corso contributed 8 and 10y runs, and Feamster got open for 49y TD pass. Corso iced it with his 2nd INT with 1:30 to play.

Maryland 13 MISSOURI 12: Vengeful Missouri (0-1), 61-pt loser to Maryland in 1954, pointed all off-season to its opener and happily matched big Terrapins (1-0) with 2 TDs apiece. But, overanxious Tigers T-K Charley Mehrer kicked dribbler into Maryland line on 3rd Q conv try and was wide with 4th Q attempt. After Missouri gained 2 1st downs, Maryland scored on its 1st possession: Terps traveled 63y on option runs to HB Ed Vereb's 14y TD burst, and FB-K Bob Laughery followed with game's only successful x-pt. Terps blocked punt in 2nd Q, and QB Frank Tamburello pitched 22y to E Bill Walker for 13-0 lead that stayed intact as Maryland failed to cash C-LB Bob Pellegrini's INT RET to Tigers 33YL. Missouri was different team in 2nd H as QB Jim Hunter sparked attack with 2 TD passes, culled out of Tigers' 7-23/81y, 3 INTs air offering. In 3rd Q, FB-DB Jerry Curtright stole pass by Maryland sub QB Lynn Beightol and dashed 28y to Terps 25YL. Hunter ran 14y, then passed 7y TD to HB Sonny Stringer. Missouri went 65y to Hunter's 14y TD pass to E Hal Burnine in 4th Q.

Hawaii 6 NEBRASKA 0: Avenging 50-0 pasting in Honolulu by Nebraska in late 1954, Rainbow Warriors (1-0) turned rare mainland trip into stunning success in blazing-hot Lincoln. Although Hawaii failed on its only 1st H threat to Nebraska 17YL on E Dick Ueoka's shoestring catch, it rushed for 246y, with key runs of 40 and 30y coming from 160-lb HB Skippy Dyer. Traveling 72y after receiving 2nd H KO, frustrated Cornhuskers (0-1) lost ball on downs at Hawaii 8YL. Warriors cashed game's only score with 5 mins left to play. Hawaii HB Bill Taylor sped 37y to Nebraska 7YL, HB Ed Kanawaki drove to within inches of Huskers GL, and FB Hartwell Freitas powered over. Nebraska QB Don Erway tried desperate passes until end, but never mounted real threat.

WICHITA 20 Arizona State 20: Dan Devine made his coaching debut at Arizona State (0-0-1) and employed tricky Michigan State multiple O that relied mostly on Single Wing power to dash to 2 early TDs, by HBs Bobby Mulgado and Gene Mitcham, before Wichita (0-0-1) awoke to howls of disenchanted home fans. Wheatshockers QB Jack Conway's 35 and 22y passes were key elements in 13-13 tie midway in 3rd Q. With Shockers up 20-13 in 4th Q on HB Ray Vogl's TD run on reverse, Devils T John Jankans, standout throughout, made FUM REC on Wichita 42YL which paved way for FB Bob Sedlar's tying 1y TD blast. Win-hungry Wichita chanced loss as Conway nearly had 3 passes picked off, last near-INT came on unwise, failed 4th down from own 21YL. But, with 30 secs left, Wichita C-LB Jack O'Toole made saving INT of ASU pass.

AP Poll September 19

1 UCLA (34)	512		11 Notre Dame		118
2 Georgia Tech (3)	364		12 Texas Tech		101
3 Oklahoma (10)	319		13 Rice		80
4 Michigan (6)	284		14 Army		62
5 Maryland (1)	198		15 Miami		51
6 Ohio State	157		16 Louisiana State		47
7 Pittsburgh	142		17 Arkansas (1)		37
8 Mississippi	130		18 Baylor		31
9t Navy	124		19t Purdue (1)		20
9t Southern California (1)	124		19t Florida		20

September 24, 1955

Pittsburgh 22 SYRACUSE 12: Hopeful Syracuse (0-1) tried only 6 passes, but QB Eddie Albright clicked on 16y and 63y TDs to HBs Jim Ridlon and Billy Micho. So, Orangemen led 12-7 late in 3rd Q. In closing 20 mins of game, Pittsburgh (2-0) cashed in with 2 TDs, safety on EZ sack by DE Bob Roseborough, and fell short by 7y of another TD. Panthers' big line pushed Syracuse back to its 2YL late in 3rd Q, and punt out made it only to Orange 31YL. Pitt QB-DB Corny Salvaterra, who had been burned by Micho's deep TD reception early in 3rd Q, hit E Joe Walton with 25y jump-pass TD to go ahead 13-12. Panthers made midfield FUM REC on ensuing KO, and it brought about sub QB Pete Neff's TD plunge. DE Rosborough downed desperately-retreating Orange QB Ferd Kuczala for safety in waning moments. Syracuse star HB-K Jimmy Brown was limited to 28y rushing and missed 2 x-pt kicks.

COLGATE 21 Dartmouth 20: In complete command at 20-0 entering 4th Q, Dartmouth (0-1) had delighted new coach Bob Blackman with QB Bill Beagle's TD passes to Es Ron Fraser and Monte Pascoe. Clever Colgate (1-0) QB Guy Martin came to life by hitting 8-9 passes in 4th Q. Early in 4th Q, Martin sparked Red Raiders comeback with 4-play, 74y surge that resulted in his 37y TD pass to HB Jack Call. Call also caught comeback fever, adding 2 more TDs. With Big Green still clinging to 20-14 edge, they were pushed deep into their own territory. After P Beagle's punt from EZ only reached his 37YL, Call's last score came on 29y pass from Martin with 1:11 left. K Martin booted winning conv. Andy Kerr, former Colgate coach, said afterward, "That Dartmouth coach must feel as though he's had his pocket picked."

MARYLAND 7 Ucla 0: No. 1 Bruins (1-1) had 1st Q edge thanks to TB Ronnie Knox's 61y QK and his 3 completions to E Rommie Loudd for 37y that brought Uclans to Maryland 3YL. But at Terrapins 1YL after change of ends for 2nd Q, UCLA FB Doug Peters lost FUM, and miscue ruined scoring chance as ball was covered by Maryland (2-0) C-LB Bob Pellegrini. Later in 2nd Q, UCLA suffered disastrous 3-play sequence that lost 52y and contributed mightily to game-end deficit of -21y rushing. Bruins'

proud rushing O was stalled by slippery footing that destroyed reverse runs, and stalwart play of Pellegrini and 4 big Terrapin Ts: Mike Sandusky, Al Wharton, Ed Heuring, and Joe Lazzarino. Maryland completed 79y drive after 2nd H KO when HB Ed Vereb raced 17y to score behind FB Fred Hamilton's block on 4th down. Knox (9-13/96y, 2 INTs) hit 5-5 passing in 1st H and struggled through 2nd H after mild shoulder separation contributed to 2 costly INTs. After Terps QB-DB Lynn Beightol made late INT at UCLA 35YL, Maryland lost scoring chance when FB Hamilton was hit hard and lost FUM to BB-LB Bruce Ballard inside Bruins 5YL.

Oklahoma 13 NORTH CAROLINA 6: Juggernaut Oklahoma (0-1) opened new season with bit of scare from North Carolina (0-1). On way to 373y rushing total, Sooners penetrated to Carolina 3, 14, 18, 30, and 1YLs without breaking young UNC D, which played well. Tar Heels scored in 1st Q and held 6-0 H lead: Tar Heels E Will Frye punted to Sooners 20YL in opening 5 mins, and QB Jimmy Harris (18/117y rushing) made 25y RET, only to have clipping PEN push OU back to its 2YL. On 1st down, Harris' pitchout was bobbled, and DT John Bilich covered loose ball in EZ for Carolina TD. Early in 3rd Q, Oklahoma fired up its Split-T operation for 74y drive to HB Bob Burris' 8y TD sweep behind cracking block of FB Billy Pricer. K Harris converted for 7-6 Sooners lead. Tar Heels lost sparkling opportunity late in 3rd Q when lightning-quick Sooners HB Tommy McDonald beat Carolina HB Ed Sutton to punt FUM REC at Oklahoma 8YL. Late in 4th Q, OU HB-P Clendon Thomas knocked punt OB deep in UNC end, and Harris fair caught return punt at Heels 40YL for excellent field position. Oklahoma's McDonald raced 28y on 1st down and soon took pitchout around RE for last 2y and insurance TD.

KENTUCKY 21 Mississippi 14: Running of FB Bobby Walker and HB Don Netoskie set stage for Kentucky (1-1) QB Bob Hardy to score upset-stirring TD sneak early in 4th Q. After Kentucky traveled 67y to Hardy's 9y swing pass TD to FB Bob Dougherty after opening KO, nifty Mississippi (1-1) QB Eagle Day fired TD passes of 21y to E Bob Drewry in 1st Q and 26y to HB Billy Kinard in 3rd Q for 14-7 Rebels lead. Wildcats soph HB Woody Herzog swept around E at end of 77y march in 3rd Q for 14-14 deadlock. Game's big play was 39y punt RET to Ole Miss 27YL by Netoskie that launched winning Cats drive. Walker, who was tough-y mainstay all game, banged 14y, and Netoskie sped 12y to set up Hardy's winner.

Michigan State 20 INDIANA 13: Sr QB Earl Morrall took over as leader of Michigan State's attack and guided Spartans (1-0) to 20-7 lead that lasted until last 4 mins. However, Indiana (0-1) had surged to 7-0 lead on 22-play, 77y march early in 2nd Q ended by 2-ft sneak by QB Gene "Chick" Cichowski. Spartans answered right back, going 74y to Morrall's 6y TD pass to E Bob Jewett after same pair collaborated on 32y connection. HB Jim Wulff, 1 of Michigan State's array of soph studs, sprinted 64y on punt RET for 14-7 H edge. Indiana's O suffered as Cichowski suffered recurrence of hip injury early in 3rd Q, and Spartans TB Clarence Peaks tore off runs of 12 and 13y and caught 16y pass to set up FB Gerry Planutis' 1y TD plunge. Cichowski came back in dying moments to find E Bob Fee for 5y TD pass.

NOTRE DAME 17 Southern Methodist 0: Although he played with some regularity as QB and FB in 1954, Notre Dame (1-0) QB Paul Hornung, in effect, debuted to highly impressed nation of football fans on this sunny Saturday. Immediately showing that he was gifted alternate to graduated A-A QB Ralph Guglielmi, Hornung (2-8/28y, INT passing, 13/70y rushing) led sharp 75y drive ended by his 11y TD run. Key play of march was Hornung's 25y dash to SMU 24YL. K Hornung added 38y FG early in 2nd Q for 10-0 lead. Mustangs (0-1) moved ball 196y, but lost 4 FUMs, 3 by HB John Marshall, and had 3 INTs among their 10-26/96y passing. QB John Roach threw most of SMU's aerials and was leading rusher with 7/89y. Most of Mustangs y came near midfield. Often near-miss loser to Notre Dame in past outings, Ponies fell to 1-6 all-time record against Irish.

Miami (Ohio) 25 NORTHWESTERN 14: In assessing Ara Parseghian's coaching career, several schools applied "if you can't beat 'em, join 'em" policy. This Miami win at Evanston helped place him with Northwestern in 1956, where he often beat Notre Dame, to which he was lured with legendary success starting in 1964. Launching undefeated 1955 season, Parseghian's Redskins (1-0) were spurred by loss of ejected star C Dick Mattern and their coach's argumentative unsportsmanlike PEN that resulted from officials' decision to thumb Mattern. Effectively aroused, Miami shortly slammed across 3 TDs in 7-min span to spoil Lou Saban's Purple Wildcats coaching debut. Northwestern (0-1) had matters fairly under control at 7-6 in 3rd Q, thanks to 2 long marches in 1st H, 2nd of which netted HB Jerry Weber's 11y TD run. But, Miami QB-DB Tom Dimitroff made INT early in 3rd Q and quickly sent HB Tom Troxell on 27y wide pitchout run. Sideline clash resulted in Mattern's ejection and Parseghian's PEN. Faced with 2nd-and 42 at NW 45YL, Redskins pulled off 35y screen pass TD to E Presby Bliss. HB Tirrell Burton dashed 46y with punt to set up another TD, and Burton scored 9y TD shortly thereafter for 25-7 lead.

KANSAS 13 Washington State 0: Jayhawks (1-1) broke nation's longest existing losing streak of 17 games when HB John Francisco set up his own TD with 30y sprint early in 2nd Q. It was 1st-ever meeting between intersectional foes. Kansas HB-DB Ralph Moody made 48y INT RET for 4th Q TD after picking off throw by Cougars (0-2) QB Frank Sarno, who played most of game after starter Bob Iverson was injured. Being held to 28y in 1st H, Washington State O managed 65y voyage in 3rd Q, only to have Jayhawks QB-DB Bev Buller make EZ INT by snatching bobbler away from E Russ Quackenbush. Cougars stumbled to game total of 144y and lost 3 FUMs and 4 INTs. Kansas might have had impressive rout had it converted any of 4 trips inside Cougars 10YL, other than Francisco's TD.

OREGON STATE 10 Stanford 0 (Portland): Multnomah Stadium match saw plenty of y from sloppy Stanford (1-1)—it held 393y to 169y advantage—but Indians lost 3 FUMs and 5 INTs. Oregon State (2-0) TB Joe Francis' 1st Q 47y QK pinned Stanford deep in its territory and prompted exchange of punts. Indians soon advanced to Beavers 34YL, but lost FUM. Early in 2nd Q, Oregon State jumped to 7-0 lead on 51y TD pass from Francis to WB Sam Wesley. Pass interference PEN called on Stanford LB Joe Long at Tribe 8YL shortly after 2nd H KO permitted Oregon State BB-K Ted Searle's 20y FG. TOs ended Stanford's only 2nd H threats: lost FUM by FB Bill Tarr (25/92y) at Beavers 10YL and DB Wesley's INT at his 6YL which he returned to 33YL.

Illinois 20 CALIFORNIA 13: Powerful ground game, featuring runs of HBs Abe Woodson (8/86y), Harry Jefferson (22/127y), and Mickey Bates, allowed Illinois (1-0) to dominate throughout. Illini line showed far stronger, both blocking and tackling, after its problems during previous season. California (0-2) struck 1st, however, after Illinois squandered 2 threats and Cal sub QB Gus Gianulias (TD pass in 3rd Q) completed 2 passes so HB Ted Granger could slip across from 7YL. E Gary Francis' block paved way for Woodson to tie score at 7-7 before H on 13y run. Bates' 12y run was longest of 14 rushes right after 3rd Q KO that set up go-ahead TD pass by Illini QB Em Lindbeck to E Rod Hanson for 6y. E Norm Becker's 39y TD catch just after REC of Illinois FB Danny Wile's FUM pulled Cal within 14-13 in 3rd Q, but Lindbeck put it out of reach on 2y TD run after his 36y pass to E Bob DesEnfants.

AP Poll September 26

1 Maryland (45)	1113	11 Rice	208
2 Michigan (48)	1032	12 Pittsburgh (1)	200
3 Georgia Tech (11)	701	13 West Virginia (3)	153
4 Notre Dame (3)	671	14 Iowa (1)	141
5 Oklahoma (12)	622	15 Navy (1)	125
6 Army (10)	437	16 Duke	82
7 UCLA	358	17 Wisconsin	59
8 Ohio State (1)	299	18 Penn State (1)	53
9 Southern California (3)	269	19 Washington (1)	50
10 Texas Christian (3)	229	20 Baylor	49

October 1, 1955

(Fri) SOUTHERN CALIFORNIA 19 Texas 7: Well-balanced, no. 9 Trojans (3-0) out-fought willing Texas (1-2) in 1st-ever contest between traditional powers. USC went 76y to score on its opening possession. Sharp-passing QB Jim Contratto (5-6/73y, TD) pulled down ball and sprinted to 1st down at Texas 37YL to set up FB Gordon Duvall's 5y TD burst in 1st Q. Sub FB C.R. Roberts followed with 9y TD explosion with pitchout in 2nd Q. Longhorns QB Joe Clements was knocked woozy in 1st Q, but sub QB Dick Miller (6-11/100y, INT) threw efficiently on 3rd Q drive with 3 completions, leading to HB Walter Fondren's TD run that sliced margin to 13-7. In 4th Q, Contratto was trapped but zipped lateral to HB Don Hickman, who raced 16y to Texas 24YL. Duvall iced game with brilliant 25y, tackle-breaking TD manuever with screen pass.

ARMY 35 Penn State 6: Former A-A Army (2-0) E Don Holleder warmed to new QB duties by guiding 4 TD marches after Penn State (1-1) TOs. Holleder passed sparingly and poorly (1-7/8y), but connected for 8y TD on 4th down to E Don Satterfield in 1st Q. This opening score was made possible by field position gained through Cadets G Stan Slater's 15y sack, FB Vin Barta's 55y punt, and HB Tony Munger's 19y punt RET to Penn State 10YL. Ace Lions HB Lenny Moore was held to 65y rushing, but scored on 12y run in 3rd Q on Penn State's only trip inside Army 35YL all day. Barta tallied in 2nd and 4th Qs, and, in between, late in 2nd Q, Army HB Pat Uebel carried 3/21y with his final run going for 2y TD and 21-0 H edge.

CLEMSON 26 Georgia 7: Snarling Tigers (3-0) held Bulldogs (1-2) to -1y O in 1st H on way to 1st win over Georgia in 41 years. Clemson QB Don King hit his 1st 5 passes, finished 10-20/180y, and 31y TD to HB Joe Pagliei. Tigers FB Billy O'Dell scored twice on short plunges, his 2nd TD coming late in 3rd Q for 19-0 lead. Bulldogs recovered FUM at Clemson 30YL in 4th Q, and scored in 3 fast plays, TD coming on 9y pass from QB Dick Young to E Laneair Roberts. But shortly thereafter, Young threw again from deep in his territory, and Tigers DE Walt Laraway dropped off D-line to snare INT at Georgia 5YL and simply stepped across for final TD. Player fisticuffs soon erupted when Clemson HB Frank Griffith was pushed OB by swarm of Bulldogs tacklers. Post-game fights, that included approximately 1,000 fans who charged field, were quelled by playing of national anthem by both school bands.

Duke 21 TENNESSEE 0: Volunteers (0-2) sub TB-DB Bobby Gordon plastered Duke (2-0) QB Sonny Jurgensen in blur of bright orange as latter returned punt to Blue Devils 45YL late in scoreless 1st Q. Being belted seemed to stun Jurgensen into sharp throwing: Jurgensen clicked on 17 and 19y passes to HBs Bob Pascal and Ed Post until Pascal scored in last min of 2nd Q. Tennessee blew 2 early chances as sharp passes of TB Johnny Majors frequently were dropped. Biggest butterfingered felony came on E Roger Urbano's drop in EZ in 1st Q. Late in 3rd Q, little Duke HB Bernie Blaney slipped tackle of Vols WB-DB Bob Hibbard to race to 80y TD. Pascal scored again in 4th Q to make it 21-0.

VANDERBILT 21 Alabama 6: Commodores (1-1) spotted Crimson Tide (0-2) 6-0 lead in 1st Q as Bama QB Albert Elmore pitched 5y TD pass to HB Bill Hollis to finish off 80y drive. Vandy went up 7-6 midway in 2nd Q as HB Charlie Horton scored on 44y mad dash and E-K Earl Jalufka nailed x-pt. Amazingly, Alabama squad was late coming out for receipt of 2nd H KO, and, after delay PEN, FB-K Don Hunt pinned Tide at 3YL. Commodores took over at Tide 38YL after Bama's punt out, and QB Don Orr squeezed over for TD from 1YL. After Vandy G Larry Frank recovered FUM at Tide 27YL, HB Buddy Stack also tallied short TD run in 2nd H as Vanderbilt enjoyed 5-2-1 streak dating back to 1947 against surprisingly inept Crimson Tide.

MICHIGAN 14 Michigan State 7: In-state war would serve as Big 10 keynote until November, as 97,239 turned out on brilliant autumn afternoon. Michigan (2-0) HB-DB Tony Branoff set up 7-0 lead with 37y INT RET. Underdog Spartans slowly wrestled control, blanketing Wolverines O, and sending FB Gerry Planutis (69y rushing) and HB Clarence Peaks (68y rushing) on key gains. Michigan State (1-1) made 1st down at UM 6YL in last min of 1st H, but HB-DB Terry Barr made 2 crucial tackles: 3y loss for HB Walt Kowalczyk to 7YL on 3rd down, and cut-down of QB Earl Morrall's sweep at 3YL

on 4th down. Spartans' TD in 3rd Q resulted from linemen hurrying punt of Michigan E Ron Kramer; it shanked OB at Wolverines 39YL. Planutis soon tied it 7-7. Turning point came on Michigan sub T John Morrow's punt block, fallen on by G Ed Meads at Spartans 21YL in 4th Q. On 3rd down, Branoff burst for 13y, and QB Jim Maddock wedged over on his 2nd try for winning TD. WB-DB Ed Shannon's INT of Spartans sub QB Jim Ninowski at MSU 45YL in last min sealed win for Michigan. Wolverines completed only 1-2/15y passing, as Spartans outgained Wolverines 215y to 151y.

WISCONSIN 37 Iowa 14: Inexperienced Badgers (2-0) fell behind 7-0 on Hawkeyes HB Eddie Vincent's 5y TD run after C Don Suchy fell on FUM of opening KO. Wisconsin overcame 14-13 2nd Q deficit and pulled away with surprising ease from collapsing Iowa (1-1) for 23-14 H edge. Badgers E-DE Dave Howard grabbed 3 TD passes to tie school record, ranged far on D, and added INT, which positioned Wisconsin for another TD. QB Jim Haluska found Howard for 16 and 33y TDs among his 8-10/138y passes. Badgers QB Jim Miller delighted record crowd with 44y TD pass to Howard and 49y punt TD RET. In no way did it help Hawkeyes to lose A-A G Calvin Jones and Vincent to injuries.

Purdue 7 MINNESOTA 6: Enjoying afternoon of 302y to 194y O edge, Purdue (2-0) frittered away 3 scoring opportunities in 1st H trying to probe big line of Minnesota (0-2), its D strength, when Boilermakers probably should have utilized QB Len Dawson's hot passing hand. Dawson hit 9-12, but 2 INTs in 1st H by Gophers HB-DB Shorty Cochran at GL and in EZ hampered Purdue's assault of Minny GL. Another Boilers threat was killed by H clock at 2YL. Purdue finally scored for 7-0 lead in 3rd Q as FB Bill Murakowski scored on 1y plunge after Dawson's 23y pass and Murakowski's 13y run. Dawson kicked all-important x-pt. Long-lost Minnesota passing game peaked through as QB Don Swanson found E Tom Juhl 3 times on 4th Q drive that climaxed in FB Rich Borstad's short TD blast. Holder Dick McNamara lost handle on conv snap and was snowed under trying to run for tying pt.

OKLAHOMA 26 Pittsburgh 14: Slippery HB Tommy McDonald (11/124y, 2 TDs) spearheaded 357y ground attack that launched Oklahoma (2-0) to quick-striking TDs against Panthers (2-1). Behind pulling G Bo Bolinger, McDonald ran right and cut sharply left for 43y TD charge to climax Sooners' 77y opening drive. Oklahoma D snatched 3 of Pittsburgh QB Corny Salvaterra's passes in 1st H, and DE Don Stiller's INT RET to his 48YL halted Pitt's probe to OU 30YL and led to HB Bob Burris' short TD plunge in 2nd Q. Sub soph HB Clendon Thomas raced 31y for 19-0 H edge for Sooners. Salvaterra got Pitt moving 70y in 3rd Q, hitting E Joe Walton for 18y TD. Oklahoma lost FUM in its territory, and Panthers HB Corky Cost plunged over for short TD in 4th Q to draw within 19-14. Coach Bud Wilkinson sent in his Sooners' 1st unit, and after E John Bell wrecked Pitt run and LB Bolinger stopped 3rd down play, OU regulars charged 67y in 8 plays, cashing in McDonald's 9y gallop for insurance TD.

COLORADO 12 Kansas 0: Improved Kansas Jayhawkers (1-2) gave Colorado (2-0) all it wanted for 3 Qs, score standing at 0-0. Kansas, led by E Lynn McCarthy and C-LB Frank Black, played so well on D that Buffaloes could manage only 2 series that lasted more than 5 plays. Jayhawks QB Wally Strauch tossed pass that HB John Francisco took 43y, only to have holding PEN ruin TD pass, and clock expire in 2nd Q. Colorado overcame 15y PEN on its 4th Q 66y TD drive as FB Jack Becker smashed for TD. Kansas gambled on 4th down at its 37YL, but HB Ralph Moody was smeared for 3y loss. Sub TB Dick Harkins threaded through demoralized Jayhawks for clinching TD.

Texas Christian 26 ARKANSAS 0: Arkansas' proud defending SWC champions, fell victim to fine D of Texas Christian (3-0), which permitted only 158y O. Pair of swift TD runs by Frogs HB Jim Swink (14/72y) in 2nd and 4th Qs supplied half of TCU's scoring wattage, but DB Swink's 1st Q tackle might have been his best play. With score at 0-0, Razorbacks (2-1) FB Henry Moore (10/57y) barreled 38y and was brought down from behind by Swink at TCU 22YL. Hogs then were held on downs at 17YL, and on their next series, QB Don Christian tried screen pass. On-rushing Frogs DE Bryan Engram deflected ball squarely into arms of surprised DT Norman Hamilton who rumbled tank-like on 39y TD convoy with bevy of teammates. QB Chuck Curtis tallied TCU's 3rd Q score for 19-0 lead after DB Ken Wineburg's INT.

Maryland 20 BAYLOR 6: Terrapins (3-0) took flight for their TDs in night action in Waco. After superb DE Bill Walker made 2nd of his 2 INTs in 1st Q, Maryland QB Frank Tamburello surprised Baylor (2-1) D with 30y TD pass to E Russ Dennis. Terps followed up later in 1st Q with their pet HB-to-HB pass play: After horrible Bears punt snap gave Maryland possession at 18YL, HB Dave Nusz pitched 18y option throw to HB Howard Dare, and Terps led 13-0. Bears also enjoyed aerial game, throwing 14-25/175y. But, live as they did by pass, Baylor also died by pass, suffering 5 crippling INTs. After Bruins recovered errant pitchout by Tamburello in 2nd Q, it looked to QB Jimmy Davenport, in for injured QB Bobby Jones, to fling 20y pass to E Tony DeGrazier to 17YL. HB Charley Dupre plunged 3 times to 2YL, and HB Del Shofner swept RE for TD. Baylor trailed 13-6 at H. In 4th Q, Tamburello went back to air waves for short TD pass to Maryland HB Jack Healy, who stood alone in EZ.

TEXAS A&M 21 Houston 3: Resourceful Texas A&M (2-1), learning to win under 2nd-year coach Bear Bryant, recovered 2 FUMs to set up TDs 4 mins apart in 2nd H and added 3rd score after T Darrell Brown blocked 4th Q punt. Houston (1-1) had led 3-0 at H after QB-DB Sammy Blount made INT, and Cougars went 41y to Aggies 4YL. FB-K Donnie Caraway was hustled in with 10 secs before H to bang 21y FG. It held up until next-to-last play of 3rd Q when A&M QB Donald Grant hit 9y TD pass to E Bobby Jack Keith, 1st of his 2 TD catches. Right after KO, Aggies gained custody on another FUM REC, this by DE Bobby Marks at 21YL. C Lloyd Hale recovered EZ FUM of A&M teammate HB Loyd Taylor on 7th play. Tempers then flared as Blount followed fellow Houston QB Don Flynn to bench for flagrant PEN. Off-setting PENs forced Cougars to punt, and it was blocked to set up TD.

STANFORD 6 Ohio State 0: Surprising Stanford (2-1) scored 1st time it touched ball on 72y drive accented by passes of QB Jerry Gustafson. HB Paul Camera caught Gustafson's TD pass alone in distant corner of EZ after Gustafson and FB Bill Tarr carried out beautiful run fake. DB Camera later added INT at own 12YL to blunt 1 of several 2nd H threats by no. 8 Buckeyes (1-1). Tarr ran 20/102y, while Indians overloaded their D to hold Ohio A-A HB Howard Cassady to 37y on ground. Earlier in week, Stanford coach Chuck Taylor said he thought Cassady "could be had" and that his coaches had formulated "gambling" D to handle task. Taylor was right, despite Ohio State's slight 228y to 218y O edge, which occurred thanks to considerable, but fruitless ball control in 2nd H.

AP Poll October 3

1 Maryland (88)	1568	11 West Virginia (13)	380
2 Michigan (27)	1223	12 Navy	289
3 Oklahoma (13)	1146	13 Duke (3)	176
4 Georgia Tech (9)	1108	14 Auburn	66
5 Notre Dame (4)	1048	15 Miami	61
6 Army (8)	898	16 Clemson	55
7 UCLA	516	17 Purdue	26
8 Texas Christian (5)	514	18 Washington (1)	24
9 Wisconsin (11)	479	19 Kentucky	22
10 Southern California (3)	412	20 Stanford	16

October 8, 1955

(Fri) Notre Dame 14 MIAMI 0: This match-up under stars of Biscayne sky had south Florida in tizzy, but game's 4th down plays were more intoxicating. Pass numbers of Notre Dame (3-0) QB Paul Hornung (5-14/88y, 2 TDs, INT) looked so-so, but they supplied all of Fighting Irish's pts. Notre Dame D registered its 3rd straight shutout, but had to play tough in early mins. At end of Irish's opening possession, Miami (1-2) C Mike Hudock burst through to block Hornung's punt that was covered at ND 23YL. FB Don Bosseler (10/30y) ran 3 times to ND 16YL, and Irish D stopped HB Jack Losch on 4th down. Shortly afterward, Miami HB Whitey Rouviere was road-blocked on his 4th down slam at ND 30YL. In all, Miami failed 5 times on 4th down runs. Early in 2nd Q, Hornung followed effective running of FB Don Schaefer (11/69y) with clever bootleg TD pass to E Gene Kapish on 4th down. Hornung made boot-leg fake again in 3rd Q and his pass found HB Aubrey Lewis with in-stride TD measuring 32y. Miami's 3 QBs passed 12-13/133y as ambitious Canes were outgained only 273y to 264y.

NAVY 21 Pittsburgh 0 (Baltimore): Unscored-upon Navy (3-0) lost fumbled pitchout to Panthers DT Bob Pollock at its 35YL in early moments, but brilliant D by DE Ron Beagle, who threw HB Corky Cost for 6y loss, and C-LB Wilson Whitmire, who made 3rd down no-gain stop of QB Corky Salvaterra at 10YL, halted Pitt (2-2) on downs at Middies 4YL. Annapolis E Jim Owen caught TD pass from QB George Welsh to culminate immediate-responsive 96y drive. Welsh slipped sack attempt by Pitt DE Joe Walton to complete TD pass to Owen. Navy FB Dick Guest scored twice in 2nd H, his 2nd TD positioned by E Earle Smith's punt block. Panthers didn't get their 3rd 1st down until 4th Q and ended game with only 59y O.

AUBURN 14 Kentucky 14: G John Ilari's FUM REC boosted Wildcats (2-1-1) to 7-0 lead. Auburn (2-0-1) barged back as HB Fob James raced 67y for 14-7 H edge. FB Joe Childress (58y rushing) and James moved to 1st and 2nd on all-time, to-date Auburn career rushing list as each passed Monk Gafford's 1942 mark of 1435y. Wildcats QB Bob Hardy suffered weak passing game (4-12/49y, TD, INT) as he was chased all afternoon by Plainsmen D and was spilled for -65y while attempting to throw. Kentucky T-P Lou Michaels was nailed at own 15YL after bad punt snap with only 2 mins to play, but Cats D held, and Tigers K Childress pulled 29y FG try wide with :26 left.

Mississippi 13 Vanderbilt 0 (Memphis): Sharp play of Ole Miss (3-1) line stalwarts, C Gene Dubuisson, G Buddy Alliston, and T Dick Weiss, carved holes in Vanderbilt (1-2) line to stake Rebels to 13-0 lead by H. Mississippi FB Paige Cothren powered for 1st TD and added x-pt, followed by HB Billy Lott's 5y TD burst off block of sub LT Billy Yelverton. In 2nd H, Vandy counted on Memphis natives, E-DEs Joe Stephenson and Tommy Harkins, to exploit passing holes in Rebs' secondary and to close down Mississippi ground game. QB Don Orr (6-14/68y) hit sufficient passes as Vandy's improved effort allowed it to claim 2nd H standoff.

Georgia Tech 7 LOUISIANA STATE 0: Record crowd cheered on LSU (1-2-1), which played tough D but was incapable of mounting much O. Speedy Georgia Tech (4-0) advanced to Tigers 23 and 18YLs in early part of game, but Tigers held each time. Engineers briefly lost TD late in 2nd Q as HB Jimmy Thompson streaked 85y to score on punt RET. But, Thompson was ruled to have stepped OB at own 40YL. Tech HB Johnny Menger soon swept 12y to LSU 45YL, and stellar sub QB Toppy Vann lofted pass to HB George Volkert, who took it at Tigers 25YL and dipped away from 2 tacklers to complete 45y TD. LSU gained only 125y throughout, but made 2 chances in 2nd H: QB M.C. Reynolds completed inadequately-short 4th down pass to Tech 23YL, and later HB Chuck Johns returned QK to Yellow Jackets' 32YL.

Texas Christian 21 ALABAMA 0: Downbeaten Alabama (0-3) lost its 6th straight outing, extending its winless skein to 9 games. But, Crimson Tide played well enough on D to manage scoreless tie at H vs. undefeated Texas Christian (4-0). HB Jim Swink (18/139y, 3 TDs), nation's leading rusher, kick-started Horned Frogs with 65y TD sprint early in 3rd Q as he fired through Bama D virtually untouched. Alabama lost 4 FUMs, and costly bobble by HB Jerry McBee gave TCU possession at Tide 27YL. Swink soon plunged over from 3YL, and scored again at end of 80y drive. Crimson Tide offered anemic passing game with 1-8/9y, INT effort, but gained 149y rushing.

Virginia Tech 24 FLORIDA STATE 20: Although Virginia Tech (3-1) built 2-TD lead, game got away from Florida State (1-2) on strange KO play in 4th Q. Gobblers had gone ahead 14-0 by H thanks to 2 big plays: sub QB Leo Burke's 39y TD run up center after his brilliant fakes, and C-LB Jack Prater's 73y INT RET to FSU 17YL. Prater's

INT came very late in 2nd Q, and HB Bobby Scruggs, future NASCAR official, quickly sped 14y to set up TD plunge. Seminoles 2nd unit clicked for 69y TD drive in 4th Q with HB Billy Odom's key gain of 37y. In attempting on-side-KO, FSU T-K Bill Procter whiffed. Officials handed ball to Tech at Seminoles 40YL, rather liberal interpretation of "short free kick" rule. FB-K Frank Webster soon produced FG for 24-7 lead. Florida State's Odom countered with dazzling 89y KO TD RET with 8:40 left. On their next series, Seminoles sent HB Lee Corso for 9, 11, and 5y runs, and he caught 6y pass before crashing for 4y TD. Procter converted, but comeback was too late.

OHIO STATE 27 Illinois 12: Fighting Illini (2-1) made mistake of scoring in opening 5 mins on QB Em Lindbeck's 2y TD run, which served only to rile already-pepped-up Ohio State (2-1). Subsequent KO was returned 36y by Buckeyes HB Howard "Hopalong" Cassady (18/99y, 2 TDs), and, 3 plays later, Cassady looped right and cut back for 18y TD run that knotted it at 6-6. Illinois HB Harry Jefferson lost FUM at his own 20YL, and purportedly weak-armed Ohio State QB-DB Frank Ellwood followed his FUM REC with 15y TD pass to E Fred Kriss in right corner of EZ. Ohio took all-land sortie to Ellwood's 2nd rushing score from 3rd Q KO. Cassady's 23y run set up his own 4y TD run in 4th Q for 27-6 margin. Illinois sub QB Hiles Stout sneaked for TD following Jefferson's 25y KO RET and Stout's 2 pass completions.

Wisconsin 9 PURDUE 0: Purdue (2-1) QB Lenny Dawson's fractured thumb forced him to throw only short passes, so surprise Big 10 leader Wisconsin (3-0) was able to bunch its highly effective D near scrimmage line. Boilers, whose O-line was out-charged all day, made 1st Q scoring opportunity through D-line play. E-DE Lamar Lundy rushed Badgers QB Jim Miller and forced desperate lateral, which was collared by T-DT Dick Murley at Purdue 24YL in 1st Q. After 59y drive, Dawson suffered INT by QB-DB Jim Haluska at Wisconsin 1YL. Late in 2nd Q, P Dawson tried to punt from EZ, and Wisconsin E Jim Reinke launched himself over 700-lb wall of backfield blockers to partially deflect punt that died at Purdue 35YL. Haluska, who connected 14-18 (3 INTs), pitched 5, 13, and 5y passes to set up 6y TD run by FB Charlie Thomas (14/88y, TD). Dedicated Badgers' drive consumed 6:59 at beginning of 3rd Q; it featured Thomas' 33y wide run on 4th down from his own 30YL. Wisconsin had to settle for G-K Paul Shwaiko's 25y FG.

MICHIGAN 26 Army 2: Before capacity crowd of 97,239, Army (2-1) gained 199y on ground, but novice QB Don Holleder connected on only 1-9/27y passing, and, worse, Cadets lost astounding 8 FUMs. Game swung on superior Michigan (3-0) line, sharp tackling, and catalystic play of little-known jr HB Terry Barr. After setting up Wolverines' 1st TD with 40y catch from QB Jim Maddock, Barr blew game open at 12-0 with 82y 2nd Q punt RET for TD, on which he made nimble sidestep to avoid last tackler, Army FB-P Vin Barta. Diving tip of pass in EZ was called interference against Black Knights HB-DB Pat Uebel near end of 3rd Q, so Michigan was set for FB Ed Shannon to slam over early in 4th Q for 19-0 edge. Army appeared on its way to 4th Q TD when it lost its 8th FUM at Michigan 21YL, but gained safety when sub QB John Greenwood was tackled in EZ.

MICHIGAN STATE 38 Stanford 14: Spartans (2-1) made pass-conscious Stanford (2-2) swallow own medicine, completing 7-8/191y, including QB Earl Morrall's 49y strike to E John Lewis. Michigan State HB Clarence Peaks (15/90y) added 2 TDs in building 32-0 lead. Indians were fresh from their huge upset of Ohio State, but didn't resemble same team on distant road trip. Indeed, vaunted Tribe aerial O completely failed, hitting only 3-15/24y, TD, 3 INTs. Michigan State E Dave Kaiser caught passes of 10 and 36y from QB Earl Morrall (3-4/99y, TD) on 66y TD drive 5 mins after opening KO. Spartans made it 20-0 after G Buck Nystrom recovered FUM at Indians 39YL, and sr Morrall scored his 1st-ever TD on sneak. Stanford wedged in 2 late TDs on QB John Brodie's sneak and sub E Bob Gergan's 12y grab from QB Jack Lewis with 15 secs left.

KANSAS 7 Iowa State 7: Mostly inoffensive opening 3 Qs found Big 7 foes each failing several times in scoring position to create scoreless tie entering 4th Q. Iowa State (0-2-1) continued O frustration, stumbling at Jayhawks (1-2-1) 1YL early in 4th Q. But, Cyclones soon sprung HB Donn Lorenzen for 60y TD draw run followed by T-K Dick Callahan's feeble but good conv kick. Strangely, Cyclones chose to try 4th-and-inches QB sneak on their next possession from their 41YL. QB Jerry Finley was stacked up, and Kansas took over. FB Dick Reich caught 24y pass and burrowed up middle for TD from 1YL, and little HB-K John Handley booted tying x-pt with 1:19 left. KU HB-P Ted Rhode had bombed 84y punt in 2nd Q after Jayhawks halted Iowa State threat.

Oklahoma 20 Texas 0 (Dallas): Superb Sooners C-LB Jerry Tubbs pulled down 3 INTs among 5 timely picks of Longhorn passers. Oklahoma HB Tommy McDonald's 28 and 7y TD runs, each coming after INT by Tubbs, also helped propel Oklahoma (3-0) to its 22nd win in row. Soph QB Joe Clements passed 17-31/153y, but could move Texas (1-3) no closer than Sooners 28YL (in 3rd Q) as Longhorns were blanked for 1st time in series since 1938. Sooners clicked off 72y in 2nd H foray that ended with HB Bob Burris' 1y TD run. Depending on its mighty D, Oklahoma was content to quick-kick Texas deep 4 times in 2nd H.

BAYLOR 25 Arkansas 20: For more than 3 Qs, Baylor (3-1) used trio of QBs to concoct 25-6 lead. Then, Arkansas (2-2) got off mat for 2 late TDs and scratched to within 15y of pulling out huge 4th Q comeback. Pressured by Razorbacks O in 1st 9 mins, Bears had turned pass against Hogs in 1st Q as E-DE Tony DeGrazier spun Arkansas QB George Walker as latter attempted to pass. Baylor FB-LB Rueben Saage nabbed faltering pass and rambled 68y to Hogs 2YL. Saage finished TD job on next play, but Arkansas quickly tied it 6-6 with 66y drive to Walker's TD sneak. After passing over middle several times, Bruins QB Allan Jones launched 41y EZ corner pass to HB Dick Baker. Baylor sent soph QB Kenneth Helms into action in 3rd Q, and his passes set up TD for 19-6 lead. Helms rocketed 23y on TD keeper early in 4th Q. Hogs' comeback was sparked by 77y drive on which Bears contributed 50y in PENs: C Jay Donathan recovered teammate HB Preston Carpenter's FUM in EZ for Porkers TD. Helms threw right away, and Arkansas E-DE Teddy Souter returned INT to 10YL. FB Henry Moore took 3 dives to tally and bring score to 25-20 with 7 mins left. In last 2 mins, Hogs took over on their 20YL, and HB Joe Thomason broke away for 20y run from midfield. He flipped lateral to Moore who went another 15y to 15YL with 48 secs on clock. But, Baylor HB-DB Weldon Holley made INT at GL as game ended.

WASHINGTON 7 Southern California 0: Northwest rain swamped beach boys of USC (3-1), and 0-0 tie seemed certain with 6 mins left. But, Washington (4-0) QB Steve Roake, former E who replaced passing star Sandy Lederman at QB, hooked up with Es Jim Houston and Corky Lewis on odd, but fantastic 80y TD. Houston, 60-min performer, caught Roake's pass at own 36YL, and as he was hauled down at own 45 YL, he shoveled lateral to trailing Lewis who romped for stunning score. Huskies HB-DB Mike Monroe made INT of USC TB Ernie Zampese just 3 plays after ensuing KO. But, Washington was forced to punt, and P Roake's boot was blocked by Troy E Chuck Leimbach, but to no avail. USC had squandered 3 good chances in 1st H on FUMs at 14 and 22YLs and PEN that ruined 1st-and-goal at 4YL after TB Jon Arnett's 13y sweep and WB Don Hickman's 11y run. Trojans TB-K Bob Isaacson also missed 36y FG try.

Colorado 13 OREGON 6: Slippery Ducks (1-3) outgained Colorado (3-0) by considerable margin at 366y to 220y, but difference was 6 lost FUMs that slithered away from Oregon. Webfoots lost FUM early on, and Buffaloes TB Homer Jenkins, probing line on his team's 1st running attempt, shot away from tacklers for 29y TD and 6-0 lead. Oregon bobbled ball away 5 more times, each coming inside Colorado 35YL and including frustrating lost FUMs at Buffs 2 and 5YLs. Colorado FB Sam Maphis scored in 2nd Q, and K Jenkins made conv for 13-0 lead. HB Jim Shanley tallied for Oregon in 2nd Q on 8y TD run. P Jenkins authored several strategic QKs, including 69y boot that went OB at Ducks 11YL.

AP Poll October 10

1 Michigan (80)	1662	11 Duke (4)	316
2 Maryland (45)	1457	12 Washington (4)	307
3 Oklahoma (21)	1350	13 Michigan State	92
4 Notre Dame (7)	1286	14 Ohio State	41
5 Georgia Tech (3)	881	15 Rice	38
6 Wisconsin (11)	707	16 Southern California	29
7 Texas Christian (4)	645	17 Auburn	24
8 Navy	641	18 Army	21
9 UCLA (1)	556	19 Texas A&M	14
10 West Virginia (11)	331	20tColorado	12
		20tKentucky	12

October 15, 1955

(Fri) SOUTHERN CALIFORNIA 33 Wisconsin 21: It was thrill-a-minute in L.A. Coliseum as lead changed hands 5 times, and local hero TB-DB "Jaguar" Jon Arnett of USC (4-1) sizzled in every aspect of game. Arnett rushed 13/134y, scored 2 TDs, passed 1-1/4y, 1/14y receiving, recovered 3 FUMs, and made 87y returning 2 punts and KO. Wisconsin (3-1) QB Jim Haluska countered with brilliant passing game: 12-21/232y, TD, INT, with at least 5 dropped passes. Arnett raced 55y to TD midway in 1st Q, but Badgers came right back as HB Pat Levenhagen caught 4 passes to get to 1YL for FB Charlie Thomas' TD plunge. Wisconsin led 7-6 at H. Trojans TB Don Hickman returned 3rd Q KO 47y, and FB C.R. Roberts (2 TDs rushing) flew 30y on 4th down to score. Badgers retaliated with 80y TD drive for 14-13 edge, much of it on deflected 38y pass from Haluska to HB Billy Lowe. Back ahead 19-14 as 4th Q started, USC received short punt at own 48YL and scored again for 26-14 lead, primarily on Arnett's fleet feet. Haluska shaved margin to 26-21 with 78y TD bomb to HB John Bridgeman, but Trojans exhausted last 6 mins driving to Arnett's 2nd TD.

Maryland 25 NORTH CAROLINA 7: Maryland's marauding Terrapins (5-0) won their 10th game in row by using massive D-line to limit North Carolina (1-3) to net of 17y rushing. Terps HB Ed Vereb was scoring ace with 3 TD runs of 6, 3, and 3y, and sr HB added 9y option TD pass to HB Howard Dare in 2nd Q for 19-0 H lead. Tar Heels tallied TD on odd play: C-LB Jim Jones rushed in unblocked on Maryland pass play in 3rd Q. From blindside of Terps QB Frank Tamburello, Jones snatched ball as Tamburello cocked his arm, and Jones ran 35y to score.

FLORIDA 18 Louisiana State 14: SEC rivals met for 5th time, and Florida (3-2) claimed its 1st win over LSU (1-3-1). Wild affair saw officials reverse 2 calls and throw frequent PEN flags. Tigers marched up and down, outgaining Gators, but in Florida territory ran afoul with INT at 2YL, holding PEN at 8YL, and failed 4th down pass from 14YL. Gators HB Jim Rountree raced for 60y TD late in 1st Q for 6-0 lead. HB Don Chandler caught TD pass from QB Dick Allen after pass catch by Gators sub E Billy Ayers was ruled complete after initial wave-off. Late in 2nd Q, LSU QB M.C. Reynolds' pass to HB Vince Gonzalez was adjusted as complete but apparently quite short of spot where Gonzalez took it OB. Next pass by Reynolds was inch long in EZ for flying Tigers HB Chuck Johns. Late in 3rd Q, Rountree took punt and raced toward far sideline, whereupon, he handed to rocketing HB Jackie Simpson (6/73y), who faked sole Tiger in his path for 62y TD. Trailing 18-0, LSU rode FB O.K. Ferguson most of 75y TD drive to whittle it to 18-7 with 11:47 left. LSU E Arnold Alexander blocked punt 2 mins later, and G Paul Ziegler dug it up and dashed for TD that made it 18-14. Zany play was hardly over: Simpson ran 33y to Bengals 5YL, was hemmed in, and lunged for EZ. Ball came loose, and LSU defender batted it OB from EZ. It was ruled LSU possession on touchback with 6 mins to go. After 2 1st downs by Tigers, Reynolds' 4th down pass fell incomplete, and Gators killed clock.

Auburn 14 GEORGIA TECH 12: Auburn's 1st win over Georgia Tech (4-1) since 1940 propelled Tigers to top of SEC. Georgia Tech QB Wade Mitchell scored 2nd Q TD, but his crucial x-pt miss kept it 7-6. Engineers HB George Volkert went 59y in 3rd Q for 12-7 lead. Go-ahead TD for Tigers (3-0-1) came in 4th Q as two-way star E Jimmy Phillips caught QB Howell Tubbs' passes of 7, 12, and 20y on 80y march, and E Jerry Elliott added 32y catch. Winning margin came from FB-K Joe Childress, who kicked 2 convs.

Tennessee 20 ALABAMA 0 (Birmingham): Enroute to darkest season in its history, Alabama (0-4) lost 7th straight contest. Bama's blanking left its O with having scored only 13 pts in last 9 games, dating back to mid-1954, and not helping was its continued butter-fingered play. Crimson Tide lost 3 FUMs, 15 for season so far. Tireless Tennessee (2-2) TB Johnny Majors (30/132y, TD) overcame arm injury to pitch 8y TD pass to E Roger Urbano on 9th play of 2nd Q. Alabama had excellent chance to tie it 7-7 before H, but QB Albert Elmore lost FUM at Vols 4YL. On opening play of 4th Q, Majors swept for 2y TD after Tide lost FUM at own 19YL. Last bright moment for Bama was blocked x-pt by C-LB Knute Rockne Christian late in game after Vols FB Lon Herzbrun scored on 1y dive.

IOWA 20 Purdue 20: Hopeful Hawkeyes (2-1-1) sought to right their season's flight and found themselves in dogfight with high-wire act of Purdue (2-1-1). Boilermakers' topnotch QB Len Dawson (14-26/146y, 3 TDs, 3 INTs) made all his team's pts as he threw 3 scores, kicked 2 convs, and recovered FUM that led to score for 13-13 tie in 3rd Q. After Dawson's 14y TD pass to HB Jim Whitmer late in 1st Q, Iowa's O switched to Single Wing early in 2nd Q and powered 76y to FB Roger Weigmann's 3y TD run after HB Eddie Vincent raced 13y. Hawks quickly made it 13-7 as G Calvin Jones charged in to throw Dawson for loss and FUM at 13YL, and ancient buck-lateral pass from QB Kenny Ploen to E Jim Freeman worked for TD. Wild 4th Q opened with Iowa QB Jerry Reichow's short pass to Weigmann going all way to 6YL. Boilermakers HB-DB Erich Barnes charged in on next play to intercept pitchout, and appeared TD-bound until pursuing Reichow clipped Barnes' ankle at Iowa 44YL. Hawkeyes held at own 24YL, and Reichow hit E Jim Gibbons with pass that looked like 61y TD until Barnes flagged down Gibbons at 4YL. Reichow then swept left for TD and 20-13 edge. Iowa later lost FUM at Purdue 22YL, and Dawson cranked up passing arm for 6-10/68y on final drive. E Steve Chernicky caught Dawson's TD pass with 4 secs left, and K Dawson booted tying pt.

MICHIGAN STATE 21 Notre Dame 7: Hitherto unscored-upon Notre Dame (3-1) allowed 3 short TD plunges by Michigan State FB Gerry Planutis, QB Earl Morrall, and TB Clarence Peaks. ND had looked good early with 7-7 H tie on QB Paul Hornung's 40y TD pass to HB Jim Morse. FB-DB Planutis got game-winning TD and made FUM REC to set up clincher for Spartans (3-1), whose domination vaulted them into national limelight. "There isn't any team we feel prouder about beating than Notre Dame," admitted Michigan State coach Duffy Daugherty as he accepted ceremonial game-trophy shillelagh from ND coach Terry Brennan.

Duke 20 OHIO STATE 14: With hostile capacity crowd looking on, Duke (4-0) got into immediate trouble: HB-P Bob Pascal's punt was blocked by Ohio State (2-2) C Ken Vargo. Despite losing FUM at Devils 6YL, Buckeyes cruised to 14-0 2nd Q lead on HB Jim Roseboro's 44y TD sweep and HB Howard Cassady's 38y punt TD RET. But, Ohio never saw Blues' territory again. Pascal's 5y TD toss to HB-mate Bernie Blaney with :01 left before H swayed tide for Blue Devils. Buckeyes coach Woody Hayes claimed afterward that Blaney's knee touched before he crossed GL. In referring to official who walked away after his decision, Hayes said, "A guy who changes his mind has no guts and has no business officiating." Pascal (92y rushing) scored to tie it in 3rd Q, and QB Sonny Jurgensen (8-12/125y, INT) capped 17-play ground drive with 4th Q clinching TD. So, Duke won it by feeding Buckeyes their own ground-assault medicine.

Colorado 34 KANSAS STATE 13: Game plan of Kansas State (1-4) called for QB Bob Whitehead to pick on Bison pass D, but when Whitehead went out with groin injury on game's 1st snap, Wildcats had to adjust with QB Dick Corbin (3-7/52y, INT). They regrouped on 2nd series for 31y, 4th down TD sprint with pitchout by HB Ralph Pfeifer. That TD put K-State ahead 7-0 in 1st Q, 1st time all season Colorado (4-0) had trailed. Buffs responded with 64y TD drive to BB Sam Maphis' short scoring plunge. K-State preserved H tie with stop of Buffaloes FB John Bayuk just inches short of GL on last play of 1st H. TB Homer Jenkins, idled as ballcarrier because of leg injury, played only opening 3rd Q series for Colorado, but sparked go-ahead TD: He zoomed 41y around E and scored on 4y plunge for 14-7 lead with 5 mins played in 3rd Q. Buffs reserve players added 3 more TDs in 2nd H in a grand dispaly of superior depth.

OKLAHOMA 44 Kansas 6: On their 1st possession, Jayhawks (1-3-1) made mistake of steaming downfield 71y on 8 hard-hitting runs to FB Dick Reich's 7y TD run. Agitated Sooners HB Tommy McDonald stormed through to block x-pt kick. In winning for 23rd straight time, Oklahoma (4-0) soon made short work to 18-6 H edge. HB McDonald fueled 67y trip on 8 plays with 33y HB-pass to E John Bell and turned E for 10y TD to tie it 6-6. McDonald later raced 46y to pay-dirt. Sub HB Carl Dodd swung wide for 4y TD at end of 45y march, and OU led 12-7 at end of 1st Q. FB-LB Dennit Morris stole 2 INTs and scored on 49y RET. With OU regulars cheering from sideline, 3rd string QB Bill Sturm passed for 36y TD to HB Bob Derrick in late going.

Texas A&M 19 TEXAS CHRISTIAN 16: Texas A&M coach Bear Bryant served notice on unbeaten, no. 7 Frogs (4-1) that lowly Aggies (4-1) had completed turnaround from 1-9 ledger of 1954. Aggies HB Don Watson caught 20y TD catch from QB Jimmy Wright in 2nd Q for 6-3 H edge, and then explosively quick line, led by former Kentucky G Jim Stanley who followed Bryant to A&M, trap-blocked TCU line for 21y TD run by sub HB Bill Dendy in 3rd Q and winning 51y TD sprint by Watson in 4th Q. Purple Frogs' brightest moments came in 3rd Q when they took 16-12 lead: TCU QB Chuck Curtis pitched 7y TD pass to E Bryan Engram, and exciting HB Jim Swink popped out of pile to leg 6y to score. Ref Cliff Shaw told coaches later that it was hardest-hitting, cleanest game he had ever worked.

SOUTHERN METHODIST 20 Rice 0: Owls (2-1-1), pre-season favorites for Southwest crown, were blanked for 1st time since 1952. Rice threatened early, flying to Southern Methodist (2-2) 13YL as Owls FB-DB Jerry Hall made INT, which he returned to Mustangs 22YL. From 13YL, QB King Hill looked to EZ, but SMU DE Willard Dewveall dropped off line to make INT to end Rice's only menacing move of game. Big SMU QB John Roach broke 0-0 tie in 2nd Q with 82y punt TD RET on which nary single hand landed on him. Ahead 7-0 late in 3rd Q, Ponies went up 14-0 as Roach hit E Jim Robertson twice and passed 4y to HB Lon Slaughter for TD. SMU's 54y TD trip late in 4th Q was launched by INT by HB-DB John Marshall, and its 3rd INT, this time by HB-DB David Mitchell, wrung down curtain on Rice.

Ucla 21 STANFORD 13: Determined to avenge UCLA's 72-0 slaughter of 1954, Stanford (2-3) tapped QB John Brodie (17-28/188y) to create 2 3rd Q TDs. Earlier, Uclans (4-1) had breezed to 21-0 lead, scoring on each of their 1st Q possessions as TB Sam Brown sparked attack as stand-in for TB Ronnie Knox, out with bad shoulder. UCLA FB Bob Davenport scored from 3YL, Brown threw 59y TD pass to E John Smith, and 2nd teamers, TB Doug Bradley and BB Bruce Ballard, collaborated on 18y TD pass. Bruins nearly attained 4th TD, but Indians E-DE Gary Van Galder and DB Bill Burget halted Brown 1 foot from GL on last play of 1st H. Stanford was different team in 2nd H. Brodie threw 12y pass to HB Jerry Angove as prime play of 66y TD drive in 3rd Q. Brodie again passed Stanford into position for HB Jeri McMillin's 18y TD sweep. Game ended with Indians at UCLA 4YL. Bruins gained 303y to Stanford's 281y.

Baylor 13 WASHINGTON 7: With coach John Cherberg and QB Sandy Lederman fueding over field-general's playing time, no. 12 Washington (4-1) saw its undefeated early season begin to fall into utter collapse, rife with dissension. Cherberg suspended Lederman just 1 hour before game-time. Still, emotional Huskies forced visitors into slow start and grabbed 7-0 lead on sneak by new QB Steve Roarke, former E. But, 3rd string Baylor (4-1) QB Bobby Jones gave Bears tying TD with :04 left in H and led 15-play, 68y crunching TD march off 2nd H KO. Winning Baylor TD came when Jones flipped 6y pass to E Henry Gremminger. It was dominance of Bears line in 3rd Q which turned result permanently in their favor.

AP Poll October 17

1 Michigan (76)	1603	11 Notre Dame	242
2 Maryland (33)	1487	12 Texas A&M	137
3 Oklahoma (29)	1434	13 Georgia Tech	83
4 Navy (7)	997	14 Colorado	74
5 Duke (15)	907	15 Wisconsin	72
6 Michigan State (4)	801	16 Baylor	53
7 UCLA (3)	715	17 Boston College (1)	39
8 West Virginia (9)	583	18 Texas Christian	30
9 Auburn (5)	426	19 Yale	25
10 Southern California (1)	253	20 Holy Cross	19

October 22, 1955

(Th) Clemson 28 South Carolina 14 (Columbia, S.C.): After 6 years without win in traditional "Big Thursday" game, Clemson (4-1) reclaimed Palmetto State bragging rights. Sub QB Charlie Bussey fired 55y TD pass to E Willie Smith 3 mins into game. DB Bussey followed with INT that led to 6-play march in launching Tigers to 21-0 lead early in 3rd Q. South Carolina threatened several times in 1st H, especially when HB Carroll McClain dashed 84y with punt RET. But Bussey slipped away from 2 blockers to nail McClain at Tigers 10YL, and Clemson D held at its 5YL. Sub QB Bobby Bunch rallied Gamecocks (2-3) to within 21-14 on 73 and 75y marches that culminated early in 4th Q. McClain scored on 15y run and caught 33y pass to highlight Birds' late drives. Even though 7:00 showed on clock, Carolina tried onside-KO that backfired, and Tigers responded with sr QB Don King's 1y TD run as he enjoyed his only win over Gamecocks in his 4 years. Clemson HB Joel Wells rushed 17/116y. Afterward, Tigers mentor Frank Howard got ride on shoulders and aggravated his old sciatica complaint, but he was all smiles: "We did everything we wanted to do, except run the option."

(Fri) Texas Christian 21 MIAMI 19: Hurricanes (1-3), soon to be called greatest 3-loss team in history by Herman Hickman of *Sports Illustrated*, held 431y to 257y O edge, but lost game on foot of TCU (5-1) FB-K Harold Pollard who made all 3 of his conv kicks. Miami failed on 2 kicks, and also was stopped at TCU 1, 20, and 20YLs, even though QB Sam Scarnecchia (8-13/147y, TD) was crafty and vigorous from outset of his 1st start. Scarnecchia made daring pitchout to HB Whitey Rouviere for 17y and tossed 4th down flat pass to Rouviere for 27y to 10YL. That led to Scarnecchia's TD sneak for early 7-0 edge. TCU HB Jim Swink (18/124y) got free in EZ for 24y TD catch from QB Chuck Curtis to take 7-6 lead in 1st Q. Miami scored on FB Paul Hefti's plunge on last play of 1st Q, but missed 2 FGs in 2nd Q. Purple Frogs went up 14-12 at H as E O'Day Williams made tall TD catch at back of EZ after Swink weaved 59y to Miami 19YL. Curtis scored on sneak for 21-12 lead after T Norman "Animal" Hamilton belted Scarnecchia, who fumbled to TCU T Don Cooper at Miami 21YL. Scarnecchia's 63y TD pass to HB Jack Losch came with 90 secs left.

(Fri) UCLA 33 Iowa 13: With A-A G Calvin Jones out with bad knee, disappointing Iowa (2-2-1) was probed through Jones' spot by speedy UCLA (5-1) TB Sam Brown for 50y on opening 73y TD drive. Hawkeyes relied on option runs and QB Jerry Reichow's 26y pass to E Jim Gibbons to answer quickly with 78y TD drive and 7-6 edge. HB-DB Johnny Hermann's INT of Reichow started Bruins on 41y march that put them up for good in 2nd Q at 13-7. Brown's 67y punt TD RET started 3rd Q, and he followed with 4y TD sweep after G Jim Brown fell on Iowa HB Eddie Vincent's FUM at Iowa 18YL.

Maryland 34 SYRACUSE 13: Undefeated Terrapins (6-0) scored on their 1st possession after FUM REC by C-LB Bob Pellegrini at Syracuse (2-2) 29YL and added E Russ Dennis' 17y TD reception from HB Ed Vereb (15/132y, TD rushing) before 1st Q ended. Orangemen went 70y in 7 plays to get within 14-7 as they dusted off old-time buck-lateral pass from HB Mark Hoffman to E Don Althouse for 30y TD. Vereb scored in 2nd Q, so Maryland led 20-7 at H. Vereb got loose for 30y run after 2nd H KO, and Terps HB Jack Healy sliced through for 1st of his 2 TD runs in 3rd Q. Syracuse HB Jimmy Brown (16/74y) scored in 4th Q after toting ball 4 times on 31y drive after FUM REC.

WEST VIRGINIA 21 Penn State 7: West Virginia (5-0) defeated Penn State (2-3) for 3rd straight year, 1st time that had occurred in 46-year series history. It would be last WVU win over Penn State until 1984. Nittany Lions owned play at game's beginning and tallied only TD of 1st H after FUM REC sparked 65y march to QB Bob Hoffman's

1y TD sneak. Mountaineers' burly line, led by future NFLers T Bruce Bosley, C Chuck Howley, and T Sam Huff, caught fire in 2nd H. WVU charged 93y to HB Bob Moss' wide 9y TD run after receiving 1 of Lions QB-P Jim Hochberg's long punts that averaged 43.2y. Game stayed tied at 7-7 into 4th Q until Mountaineers HB Joe Marconi pushed across TD from 3YL. WVU and its unbeaten record were finally out of woods when Moss raced across from 12YL with less than 2 mins to play.

Virginia Tech 17 Virginia 13 (Roanoke): Virginia Tech (4-1-1) completed only 1 pass in 6 tries but it went for early 1st Q TD as QB Leo Burke threw 22y scoring arrow to HB Ray England. Cavaliers (1-4) came right back to tie it 7-7 as QB Bill Clarke connected with E Bob Gunderman on 34y TD pass. Trailing 10-7 after Virginia Tech G-K Frank Webster made 22y FG, Virginia took 13-10 lead to H as HB Herb Hartwell cruised 15y to TD. Gobblers E Grover Jones, who earlier blocked punt and made FUM REC that led to Tech FG, blocked another punt in 3rd Q. Jones recovered ball, punted by Cavs QB-P Rives Bailey, just 1 ft from GL. Burke then sneaked over for winning score.

Pittsburgh 26 DUKE 7: Powerful Pitt (4-2) line turned into TD-seeking ballhawks: T Bob Pollock and his cohorts blocked punt early in 2nd Q, and C-LB John Cenci and T Herman Canil each had FUM REC to set up TD. After punt block, QB Corny Salvaterra threw 36y TD to E Joe Walton, 1st of his 2 TD receptions. Humbled Duke (4-1) lost QB Sonny Jurgensen for most of 2nd H with bad ankle after he tossed pass which speedy HB Bernie Blaney carried to 75y TD for short-lived 7-6 H lead. Pete Neft, trying to beat out Salvaterra at QB, was Pitt's leading rusher at 5/69y, which included 43y sprint around RE in 3rd Q that set stage for HB Lou Cimarolli's decisive TD plunge for 13-7 edge.

GEORGIA TECH 34 Florida State 0: Outgunned Florida State (1-4) put up 1st Q fight. Seminoles FB-P Pat Versprille bombed 63y punt OB at Tech 3YL at end of early series. Swift HB-DB Lee Corso ran down Georgia Tech (5-1) HB George Volkert after 73y sprint to FSU 6YL, and feisty Seminoles held inches short of GL. But, Yellow Jackets QB Wade Mitchell soon fielded punt at FSU 39YL, cut back from sideline to slip into EZ for 7-0 lead. Determined Corso made 32y catch and later came up with FUM REC at own 10YL, and Seminoles QB-DB Vic Prinzi made EZ INT. Mighty effort couldn't keep Georgia Tech from spending most of 1st H in FSU end. Backup QB Toppy Vann led Tech on 49y TD march with 2 completions and TD sneak for 14-0 lead, and later Vann bootlegged around E for 20-0 H edge. Corso's FUM set up another Tech TD, E Ted Smith's 3y scoring catch. Tech reserves notched last score in 4th Q.

MISSISSIPPI 17 Arkansas 7: FB Paige Cothren, 1 of nation's leading scorers with 44 pts, and QB Eagle Day (7-15/112y, TD, INT) were prime movers in Mississippi's domination on O: Ole Miss (5-1) outgained Arkansas (3-3) 375y to 243y. Rebels scorched Hogs for 2 TDs in opening 7 mins as DB Day recovered FUM to lead to TD run by Cothren and Day threw short TD pass to E Bob Drewry. Sudden-change worked for Razorbacks in 3rd Q as QB-DB George Walker picked off Day's pass at own 45YL and dashed to Rebs 27YL. On next play, Walker arched TD pass to E Jerry Souter, who stumbled across for TD. Cothren put game away with 22y FG late in 4th Q.

Michigan 14 MINNESOTA 13: Stumbling no. 1 Michigan (5-0) regained Little Brown Jug with rally from early 13-0 Gophers' hole. Minnesota (1-4) built its edge on opportunistic play. Gophers gained field position at Wolverines 24YL after FB-P Rhody Tuszka bombed 65y punt which was bobbled back to 3YL by Michigan HB Terry Barr. Gophers HB Bob Schultz soon scored on 5y run. HB Dick McNamara (10/78y) set up FB Ken Yackel's TD run with 28y sprint and fortuitous FUM OB at UM 20YL. Michigan shrugged off doldrums in 14th min of 2nd Q. Barr made up for his early blunder with 2 big plays: 1st Q block of Minnesota G-K Mike Falls' conv kick and 5y TD run. Barr's TD was set up by 42y pass to E Mike Rotunno and lateral to speeding HB Ed Shannon. Winning margin came in 3rd Q on 9y, 4th down pass from QB Jim Van Pelt to E Tom Maentz and K Van Pelt's conv. Result failed to impress AP voters, who would drop UM to 3rd in poll.

Notre Dame 22 PURDUE 7: Fighting Irish (4-1) capitalized on 2 FUM RECs and INT for their 3 TDs that avenged their only 1954 defeat by Purdue (2-2-1). Notre Dame employed unbalanced line on O to overcome Boilermakers' bulk, and it worked for 325y rushing. Igniting march to FB Don Schaefer's 1st Q TD, Irish QB-DB Paul Hornung recovered FUM by Purdue FB Bill Murakowski (17/82y) at ND 40YL. Later in 1st Q, Hornung made INT on his 20YL that stopped hopeful probe by Boilermakers. Purdue HB Erich Barnes grabbed FUM at ND 42YL, and QB Lenny Dawson (11-21/104y, TD, 2 INTs) passed 13y to E Len Zyzda for 2nd Q 7-7 tie. Irish E-DEs Bob Scannell and Dick Prendergast put considerable 2nd H pressure on Dawson: Purdue QB lost FUM in 3rd Q at own 26YL to set up go-ahead TD by ND HB Dean Studer (15/106y) and was thrown for losses so often on 4th Q series that Boilermakers faced daunting 4th-and-50. Punt snap on next play sailed over Dawson's head for safety.

OKLAHOMA 56 Colorado 21: For 20 mins, Colorado (4-1) was fierce rattlesnake twisting and springing in hands of Oklahoma's invincible Sooners (5-0). Buffaloes led 14-0 in 2nd Q. Colorado T Sam Salerno pounced on FUM by Sooners QB Jimmy Harris at 5YL on last play of 1st Q, and FB John "The Beast" Bayuk rammed over from 3YL. Salerno created FUM REC for Buffaloes E Lamar Meyer at OU 21YL, and last 5y for TD were credited to FB Emerson Wilson, who smacked same RT hole behind Salerno that Bayuk had. Dubious pass interference call against Buffs and mistouched punt by Colorado helped Sooners to jump to 21-14 lead in 2nd Q. Sooners HB Bob Burris scored twice within 7 mins in 2nd Q to knot it at 14-14, at end of drives sparked by running and passing of HB Tommy McDonald. Weak QK by Colorado TB Homer Jenkins positioned Oklahoma for 55y go-ahead drive late in 2nd Q as McDonald ran through big hole from 2YL. Leading 21-14 in 3rd Q, Sooners enjoyed TDs from Burris and McDonald and unleashed subs on wilting Buffs for 21-pt romp in 4th Q. It was 4th straight year in which Oklahoma had to come from behind to defeat Buffaloes.

HOUSTON 7 Texas Tech 0: Teams near respective conf titles took timeout to battle as improving Cougars (4-1) gained revenge for 61-14 pasting at hands of Texas Tech (2-2-1) in 1954. Houston QB Jim Dickey passed 4y in 1st Q to HB Kenny Stegall for TD, and K Stegall added conv kick. Desperate Red Raiders took to air in late going and advanced 97y, only to be stopped at Cougars 1YL. Ended up with 4-13/71y passing, Texas Tech went nowhere in air until closing mins. Houston rushed for 232y.

October 29, 1955

Miami 21 PITTSBURGH 7: Trio of northern-born Hurricanes (2-3) felt at home in cold Pittsburgh rain as they solved tough Panthers (4-3). D. HB John Varone (Mass.), HB Jack Losch (Pa.), and QB Sam Scarnecchia (Ohio) each scored TDs. Varone, on 31y run, and Losch, on 41y reception, were able to fit their scores into 2-min span of 1st Q. Pitt hammered to Hurricanes 2YL in 2nd Q, but lost ball on downs. Panthers returned to scoring territory in 2nd Q's last min, thanks to pass interference PEN on Miami FB-DB Paul Hefti that placed ball on 1YL. FB Tom Jenkins got Pitt's TD on dive with 24 secs left before H. Scarnecchia finished clinching 61y drive in 4th Q with 3y TD keeper.

CLEMSON 19 Wake Forest 13: Clemson (5-1) FB Billy O'Dell blasted middle of Demon Deacons (3-3-1) line for 21/103y and TD runs of 2 and 1y. Wake Forest QB Nick Consoles, coming in as nation's 2nd leading passer, had miserable day with 4-17/44y, TD in air, and HB Billy Ray Barnes struggled to get 13/67y rushing. Down 7-0, Clemson G-DG Leon Kaltenbach recovered FUM on opening snap of 3rd Q, and HB Joe Pagliei quickly scored on 15y burst. Tigers soon added 82y march, but Deacs went back ahead 13-12 in 4th Q when Consoles surprised Tigers with 3rd-and-1, 9y pass to wide-open E Ralph Brewster. Clemson advanced on 11-play trip to O'Dell's winning TD.

GEORGIA TECH 27 Duke 0: Georgia Tech (6-1) line carved holes in heavier Duke front for its swift backs to scurry to 2 early TDs, including HB George Volkert's 22y run. Fatal end for Blue Devils came in 4th Q on Yellow Jackets HB Johnny Menger's 49y INT TD RET. Slumping to 2nd straight loss, Blue Devils (4-2) made but single 1st down, never moved past their own 36YL in 1st H. HB Jimmy Thompson tallied last Georgia Tech TD on 1y sweep. Duke's O managed only 133y and lost 3 TOs: 2 FUMs and Menger's INT.

Mississippi 29 LOUISIANA STATE 26: In heart of Dixie, America's home of low-scoring football, SEC rivals put on genuine, if unexpected, O slugfest. Mississippi (6-1) found tough sledding through Louisiana State (1-4-1) D-line in early going, so Rebs turned to eagle-eyed QB Eagle Day, who passed 10-15/154y with TDs to HB Earl Blair in 2nd Q and E Bob Drewry in 4th Q. HB Billy Kinard got Ole Miss moving in 1st Q with 8y TD run after Day's throws softened up Tigers. FB-K Paige Cothren also booted 1st of his 2 FGs in 1st Q for 10-0 Rebels' lead, but LSU battled back in 2nd Q for 13-10 edge. Bengals sub QB M.C. Reynolds, who would get brief fling with pro teams Chicago Cardinals and Buffalo Bills starting in 1958, made name for himself in this game by going toe-to-toe with Day in passing barrage. Soph Reynolds threw TD pass to HB Chuck Johns and scored on sneak in 2nd Q, although Rebels would come back with safety and Day's 2nd TD throw for 19-13 H edge. Behind 29-13, LSU's Reynolds completed 2 more TDs in 4th Q. As game ended, Reynolds was launching sort of crude and as-yet-unnamed "Hail Mary" passes from midfield.

TULANE 27 Auburn 13: On way to its best season since 1950, Tulane (4-3) built 21-0 lead on QB Gene Newton's TD passes to E Will Billon and HB Otis Gilmore and FB Ronnie Quillian's short TD run. Earning 2 quick TDs in 4th Q, Auburn (4-1-1) pulled to within 21-13. Reliable Tigers FB Joe Childress bulled over from 3YL with 8 mins to play, and, after Gilmore lost FUM at his own 4YL to FB-LB Jim Walsh, HB Fob James wrestled across GL on next play. Walsh wisked away another Tulane FUM just 1 min later, and Auburn moved to Green Wave 20YL with 5 mins left. Tigers QB Howell Tubbs was picked off by Tulane HB-DB Tommy Warner, who sped 87y for game's icing TD.

Michigan State 27 WISCONSIN 0: Superior line play on both sides of ball carried confident Spartans (5-1) to demolition of Wisconsin (3-3). Michigan State soph HB-DB Walt Kowalczyk (10/172y, 2 TDs) stiff-armed and sprinted 72y for 1st Q TD, and his mates turned his 8y INT RET to Badgers 39YL into another score by TB Clarence Peaks on opening play of 2nd Q. Michigan State made mess of 2nd H KO, which was followed by clipping PEN that backed it to own 1YL. Punt out of danger was carried 14y to Spartans 45YL by Wisconsin QB Jim Miller. Badgers punched it to 3YL and faced 4th down, but HB Danny Lewis slipped down on wet grass and ended Wisconsin's only threat. E-DE Dave Kaiser recovered Miller's FUM in 4th Q, and on 1st play Kowlaczyk swooped round E for 24y TD.

MINNESOTA 25 Southern California 19: In warmth of Los Angeles 2 weeks earlier, USC (5-2) spoiled Wisconsin's unbeaten record. Now on road, Trojans encountered Big 10 foe that delivered Midwestern surprise: blustery winds and driving snow. Golden Gophers (2-4) completed 0-2 passes in blowing cold, but used soph HB Rich Borstad to hammer for 2 TDs, and blocked punt to set up 3rd score. Skidding and bumbling Trojans were limited to single 1st down in 1st H, but got long special teams TDs in 3rd Q from FB Gordon Duvall on 73y KO TD RET and HB Ernie Merk on 92y

punt TD RET. In between, Minnesota QB Don Swanson trotted 65y on keeper for TD that provided 19-6 lead. Borstad applied clincher that extended lead to 25-12 with his 3y TD run early in 4th Q.

NOTRE DAME 21 Navy 7: Oldest continuous intersectional rivalry was renewed on Knute Rockne Memorial Day, which came 25 years after great coach's last season. Record crowd in Notre Dame Stadium of 59,475 enjoyed Fighting Irish (5-1) taking 10th in row from Navy (5-1), which sported nation's best D stats coming in. Probing right side of Middies D with keepers and plunges by FB Don Schaefer, QB Paul Hornung bothered passing only 3-6/18y, TD, in constructing 21-0 lead in opening 3 Qs. Hornung sneaked 1y for TD in 2nd Q and passed 15y to E Gene Kapish for TD in 3rd Q. While covering Navy A-A E Ron Beagle, DB Hornung made 2 INTs of QB George Welsh, who managed 13-25/155y in air. Navy scored on 2y TD run in 4th Q by HB Ned Oldham (15/56y). Last Middies threat was snuffed by DB Schaefer's INT at 24YL, and Navy's 9-game win streak came to end.

Missouri 20 COLORADO 12: Suffering from its familiar play-tough-against-Oklahoma-and-suffer-following-week syndrome, deflated Colorado (4-2) permitted season's only win by Missouri (1-6). Despite support from Homecoming crowd, Buffaloes watched helplessly as Tigers snarled to 20-0 H lead. Using Split-T fakes, clever Missouri QB Jimmy Hunter (7-17/84y, INT) focused on E Hal Burnine (7/87y), who consistently was open for passes that poised Tigers for their 3 TD runs: All scores came from close-range by FB Bill Rice and 2 sneaks by Hunter. Colorado finally awoke in 4th Q and scored on 2 sizable pass plays: Sub TB Bob Stransky to E Frank Clarke for 28y and TB Homer Jenkins to E Jerry Leahy for 24y. Tigers adamantly had refused to shave until winning their 1st game, so giddy coach Don Faurot greeted his traveling squad with 36 razors in post-game locker room.

ARKANSAS 7 Texas A&M 7: Pushed around for 3 Qs, hungry Razorbacks (3-3-1) still trailed only 7-0. Texas A&M (5-1-1), SWC leader but on probation and ineligible for Cotton Bowl, failed to hold 7-0 lead in 4th Q, and its tie allowed bowl organizers sigh of relief. Outgaining Arkansas 134y to 52y in 1st Q, soph-laden Aggies used HB John David Crow's runs to drive to Hogs 34 and 15YLs before being stopped on downs. Top Razorback unit reentered game for beginning of 2nd Q and marched to within 1 ft of A&M GL, but despite 3 downs to advance 6 inches for 1st down, Arkansas was pushed back by rugged Aggies D. A&M went 59y to score early in 3rd Q as QB Jimmy Wright flipped 10y TD pass to HB Loyd Taylor. Razorbacks reached Aggies 31YL in 4th Q, where on 4th down QB George Walker rifled 28y pass to HB Preston Carpenter. It required 4 line slams, but Walker finally sneaked over for tying TD. Arkansas had chance to win it from Aggies 31YL in last min, but was penalized twice while trying to get its top K into lineup. After 5 wins in row, Aggies coach Bear Bryant lamented: "We spent too much time reading our press clippings."

Oregon State 13 WASHINGTON 7: Oregon State (4-2) was dominated by Washington (4-2-1) throughout gusty 1st H as Huskies looked to stay unbeaten but once tied in PCC race. But, UW's dominance was translated only into single TD, and even that had smell of flukiness. Beavers TB Ray Westfall tried to pass under heavy pressure from deep in his own territory in 2nd Q, and his attempt at throw-away ended up in hands of charging DE Jim Houston. Houston pranced 19y to score. Early in 3rd Q, Huskies tried to add to their lead by moving to 3YL. But Oregon State DE Dwayne Fournier recovered FUM at 2YL. Washington was back on march when high pitchout bounced off Huskies FB Credell Green's hands to Beavers FB-DB Tom Berry, who raced 72y for stunning, tie-creating TD. Washington fumbled ensuing KO, and Beavers scored winning TD in 6 plays on Berry's dive.

AP Poll October 31

1 Maryland (74)	1884	11 Ohio State	161
2 Oklahoma (54)	1852	12 Texas A&M	155
3 Michigan (63)	1774	13 Miami (Ohio)	91
4 Michigan State (7)	1312	14 Auburn	79
5 UCLA (3)	1213	15 Mississippi	70
6 Notre Dame (1)	1207	16 Southern California	35
7 West Virginia (16)	869	17 Kentucky	29
8 Georgia Tech	597	18 Syracuse	27
9 Navy	305	19 Army	23
10 Texas Christian (2)	282	20 Mississippi State	20

November 5, 1955

(Fri) MIAMI 14 Boston College 7: Miami (3-3) evened its record with stout 1st H in which it gained 14-0 lead. Boston College (3-2-1) tried hard, but lost 4 FUMs and 4 INTs to frustrate its scoring threats. Penetrating Hurricanes end 10 times, Eagles gained 1st downs at Hurricanes 4YL in 2nd Q, 6YL in 3rd Q, and 5YL in 4th Q, but each thrust failed. Miami HB Jack Losch, just tapped for school's honor society earlier in week, scored both TDs: 70y sprint after taking spontaneous lateral from FB Don Bosseler in 1st Q and 44y pitchout sweep after DB Bosseler's INT in 2nd Q. After gaining 225y in 1st H, Hurricanes suddenly were limited to 31y in 2nd H. BC ran 82 plays and controlled clock, especially in 2nd H. BC HB-DB Billy Alves hit Losch hard and FUM was recovered by Eagles FB-LB Larry Plenty at Miami's 18YL with less than 6 mins to play. QB Billy Donlan then hit HB Eddie DeSilva with 14y TD pass to trim it to 14-7. Inside 2 mins, Eagles moved to Miami 46YL, where Donlan made long heave to HB Tommy Reis. DB Losch and Reis each had hands on ball, but, as they fell at 3YL, Losch ripped it away for his 2nd INT.

YALE 14 Army 12: Cadets (4-3) dominated 1st Q and took 6-0 2nd Q lead on HB Pete Lash's 21y scoring dash after FUM REC at Bulldogs (6-1) 46YL. After another FUM REC at Yale 41YL, Army soon reached Elis 29YL, and it looked as though Cadets would repeat their 48-7 triumph of 1954. Momentum clearly turned, however, when Yale QB-DB Dick Winterbauer made INT to halt Black Knights. Subsequent FUM by Cadets, 1 of 5 they lost, at their own 10YL to Bulldogs T-DT Phil Tarasovic gave Yale chance for QB Dean Loucks' 15y TD pass to E Paul Lopata and 7-6 lead on K Winterbauer's x-pt before H. Yale grabbed 14-6 lead on 56y 4th Q drive, capped by HB Al Ward's 4y TD run through LT. Army went 86y in 6 plays, 62y on 3 completions by QB Don Holleder (4-12/77y, TD, INT), his 1st aerial successes of day, to score on 8y catch by E Art Johnson with less than 3 mins left. Elis clinched 1 of most memorable upsets of 1950s by keeping ball away from Army until very last 25 secs.

Notre Dame 46 PENNSYLVANIA 14: Unknown Pennsylvania (0-7) soph HB Frank Riepl, making his 1st start, caught opening KO 8y deep in EZ. Amazingly, Riepl dashed out and picked up key blocks from HB Charley McKinney, G Bob Eichelberger, and FB Stan Chaplin to break into clear for 108y (100y in official collegiate stats) KO TD RET against exalted, no. 6 Notre Dame (6-1), favored by 40 pts. After several mins of disorganization, Irish eventually went 80y to tie it 7-7, but lost FUM in 2nd Q at own 12YL to Quakers E-DE Bob Barber. Out of Single Wing formation, TB Riepl found Barber for 9y TD. ND was hard-pressed to tie it 14-14 on QB Paul Hornung's pass before H. Fairy-tale writers would have hoped for something special in 2nd H, but talent won out. Notre Dame finished game with 513y O and added 32 pts in 2nd H, keyed by FB Don Schaefer's 2 TDs and Hornung's 20y TD pass to E Dick Prendergast.

PENN STATE 21 Syracuse 20: Dynamic HB-K Jimmy Brown (155y rushing) scored all Syracuse (3-3) pts on 2 TD runs and 6y TD catch from QB Eddie Albright as Orangemen rolled to 20-7 lead in 3rd Q. Penn State (4-3) HB-DB Lenny Moore (22/145y, TD), rekindled his star reputation by tackling well and scoring on 2y slant in 3rd Q to narrow deficit to 20-14. Syracuse marched from receipt of ensuing KO to Lions 9YL, but Orange QB Albright suffered EZ INT by QB-DB Milt Plum. Moore carried for 22 and 13y gains on winning 80y march, which was sealed by QB-K Plum's 1y sneak and clutch conv kick.

Navy 7 Duke 7 (Baltimore): Attempting respective rebounds from trying defeats, Navy (5-1-1) and Duke (4-2-1) ended up with tying result. Middies outgained Devils 330y to 199y, but had little to show for it. Navy went 84y in 16 plays in 3rd Q for TD on QB George Welsh's 13y pass to E Ron Beagle. Later, Welsh lost gamble by trying to scoop bouncing punt, and, capitalizing on his FUM, Duke went 35y to FB Bryant Aldridge's 1y TD run. Each team missed 4th Q FG try. Duke QB Sonny Jurgensen was blanked in his aerial attempts, missing all 6 passes.

TENNESSEE 7 Georgia Tech 7: Meeting of coaching proteges of Gen. Robert Neyland produced predictable low-scoring result. Tennessee (4-2-1), beginning to rev up under 1st-year coach Bowden Wyatt, took opening KO and went 58y in 8 plays to FB Tommy Bronson's 2y diving TD. Workhorse Volunteers TB Johnny Majors (25/77y) lugged pigskin on 6 plays of scoring trip, including 18y dash on game's opening snap. For much of Homecoming day, Tennessee went into D-shell, punting frequently on 3rd down as Neyland would would have approved. Yellow Jackets (6-1-1) threatened thrice in 2nd Q, but were turned back by INT by Vols C-LB Bubba Howe, 11y sack, and 4th down EZ pass batted down by C-LB Lamar Leachman. Georgia Tech QB-DB Wade Mitchell (7-15/60y, TD, 3 INTs), was superb as S, including vital, diving 4th Q INT that stopped Vols drive. Mitchell led 55y 4th Q drive that overcame 15y holding PEN with 17y catch by E Tommy Rose and ended with Mitchell's 2y bullet TD pass to E Don Ellis on 4th down. Deadlock all but ruined Jackets' chance to catch SEC leader Ole Miss.

Florida 19 Georgia 13 (Jacksonville): Favored Gators (4-3) were stunned by sometimes-starter, HB Wendell Tarleton of Georgia (4-4), who dashed 12, 30, and 1y, last run registered TD in 1st Q and 7-0 lead for Bulldogs. Georgia shrugged off bad field position from accurate punts of Florida HB-P Don Chandler, and started another long drive in 2nd Q. Bulldogs QB Jimmy Harper contributed runs of 11 and 8y, so that FB Bobby Garrard could slam over right side for 5y TD. Trailing 13-0 as 2nd H began, Gators turned on its speed: HB Jim Rountree snared skipping KO at own 15YL and took middle path, where he got clearing block from Chandler and raced 85y to score. Perhaps Chandler was winded because he missed wobbly x-pt and managed short KO only to Georgia 43YL. Moving again on ground, Bulldogs advanced to UF 29YL, but were halted on 4th down. Florida HB Jackie Simpson took punt 33y and converted 1 of 2 4th downs on tying 40y march that Rountree again converted with TD that bridged 3rd and 4th Qs. On next series, Harper's pass was deflected into hands of Gators QB-DB Dick Allen, who raced down sidelines for winning 52y INT TD RET. When UF coach Bob Woodruff was complimented afterward on what must have been stirring H speech, he said, "…if I knew anything that would do that, I'd tell them on Wednesday."

AUBURN 27 Mississippi State 26: After 6 wins in row, Mississippi State (6-2) permitted devastating play by future Gov of Alabama and missed its chance to win on 2 botched conv kicks. Auburn (5-1-1) HB-DB Fob James (10/102y), future politician, went 75y down sideline with INT in 3rd Q for TD and 13-12 lead that Tigers would not lose. Auburn QB Howell Tubbs quickly made it 20-12 with 56y bomb to E Jerry Elliott. Maroons bounced back to within 20-19 on HB-K Jim Harness' short TD plunge and kick. Tigers clinched it early in 4th Q as HB Bobby Hoppe circled E for 30y and FB Joe Childress crashed 3y to TD. Bulldogs E Ron Bennett corralled his 2nd TD pass in closing moments, but Harness' missed kick left them pt down. "We played our best ballgame of the season," said Mississippi State coach Darrell Royal as his charges surprised with 12-21/192y passing and outgained Auburn by 359y to 316y margin.

ILLINOIS 25 Michigan 6: Gathering doubts about no. 3 Michigan suddenly crystalized as Fighting Illini (4-3) outgained Wolverines (6-1) 461y to 190y. After 6-6 H tie and rib injury suffered by HB Harry Jefferson (14/60y), Illinois dusted off little-used soph HB Bobby Mitchell, who bolted 54y in 3rd Q to set up go-ahead TD that came on 24y fake-FG pass from QB-holder Em Lindbeck to HB Abe Woodson. In 4th Q, Mitchell stormed 64y for TD as he emerged as new Illini rushing star with 10/173y, TD. Michigan, outplayed and outgained throughout, briefly made it tense late in 2nd Q. Lindbeck's handoff was bobbled, and Wolverines FB-LB Lou Baldacci recovered at Illini 30 17YL. Lining up quickly, Michigan sent fleet HB Tony Branoff spurting through disorganized Illinois line for TD. Over recent 10 years, Illinois had inflicted 6 of Michigan's 13 Big 10 defeats with only Ohio State and Northwestern with as many as 2 wins over Maize-and-Blue.

November 12, 1955

PRINCETON 13 Yale 0: Dominating scoreless 1st H, Yale (6-2) lost big chance on opening drive when Elis went 67y but lost FUM to Princeton (6-2) E-DE Ben Spinelli at 1YL. Yale soon retaliated with move to Nassau 29YL, but, after TD was nullified, Bulldogs QB Dean Loucks suffered INT to Tigers WB-DB Bill Agnew. Enter Princeton TB Royce Flippin, injured all season, who came off bench for only 13 plays, but contributed his usual dramatics against Bulldogs. Flippin's 3rd Q 4y run was game's 1st TD, which he set up with 9y pass to WB Agnew. Held to 50y in 2nd H, Yale eventually was doomed by 1-handed INT by Princeton E-DE Joe DiRenzo, which he turned into 18y TD with 1:03 to go.

Penn State 34 RUTGERS 13: HB Lenny Moore (9/179y, 3 TDs) set Penn State (5-3) single-game rushing record to date, scoring on 80, 60, and 22y runs. Late in 1st Q, Moore took pitchout and zoomed around RE and up sideline for 80y, longest TD run to date in Nittany Lions history. State scored on its next series as it went 80y as FB Bill Straub dragged Rutgers (2-5) HB-DB Greg Holmes over GL. Holmes returned favor with 4y TD run at end of 52y trip that pulled Scarlet Knights within 13-6 at H. Lions QB Milt Plum keyed early 3rd Q TD drive with 19y pass on 4th down to E Jack Farls, and Plum slammed 9y to score on sneak. Moore sandwiched 2 more TDs around Knights FB Jack Laverty's 1y TD plunge that came on heels of FUM REC at Penn State 25YL.

PITTSBURGH 26 West Virginia 7: West Virginia's undefeated dream crumbled in hands of its most bitter rival. WVU (7-1) allowed Panthers (6-3) to score on 1y pass from QB Pete Neft to E Joe Walton. In 3rd Q, Pitt added quick TDs by Neft and FB Tom Jenkins off FUM RECs. Clock ran out as pass interference PEN was called against Panthers at their 5YL, and FB Joe Marconi scored on game's last play to avert Mountaineers' 1st whitewash in 43 games. With Pitt Stadium goalposts long gone to 57,996 celebrants, Pitt conceded meaningless conv kick to West Virginia.

Maryland 25 CLEMSON 12: Snarling Tigers (6-2) cornered Terrapins (9-0) with early 12-0 lead on season's 1st reception by Clemson E Dalton Rivers for 14y TD and HB Joel Wells' 50y TD burst on opening play of 2nd Q. But 15y roughness PEN called on Tigers in 2nd Q turned tide as Maryland was granted 1st down at Clemson 36YL. Terps HB Ed Vereb scored 5 plays later on 1y blast, his nation's leading 14th TD of year. Terrapins controlled 26 plays to Tigers' 5 in 3rd Q and grabbed permanent lead at 13-12 after receiving 2nd H KO. Vereb caught 14y TD pass from QB Lynn Beightol. Another Beightol TD pass in 4th Q, 16y to E Bill Walker, helped build no. 2, Orange Bowl-bound Maryland's margin.

VANDERBILT 20 Tulane 7: G Larry Frank blocked punt by Tulane (5-4) FB-P Ronnie Quillian (17/68y, TD) as early indication of Vanderbilt (6-2) line superiority as Commodores surged to their 5th win in row. From 2YL, Vandy HB Joe Scales pushed over for 7-0 lead. Vanderbilt held on its 35YL later in 1st Q and launched TD drive spiced with 10 and 17y runs by FB Phil King (16/77y). Green Wave took advantge of short punt to answer on Quillian's 13y smash to cap 26y trip to pay-dirt. HB Charley Horton registered Vandy's last TD in 3rd Q with dandy 20y gallop through RT Art Demmas' block.

MICHIGAN STATE 42 Minnesota 14: Spartans (7-1) wrapped up Big 10 season at 5-1 by trouncing Golden Gophers (2-6), but needed Rose Bowl help next Saturday from Ohio State, 20-10 winners over Iowa, against Michigan, which swamped Indiana 30-0. Minnesota put up good front early, but pair of big plays by FB Gerry Planutis launched Michigan State. Planutis blocked early punt by Gophers FB-P Kelvin Kleber, and MSU E Dave Kaiser scooped it up to score from 12y out. Gophers tied it 7-7 by going 68y in 10 runs sparked by FB Rich Borstad's 4/26y runs. Later in 1st Q, Planutis (4/67y) raced 53y to set up HB Walt Kowalczyk's TD sweep, and G Archie Matsos followed with punt block for safety. Long passes by Michigan State QB Earl Morrall (3-5/102y) and E-around TD run by sub E Tony Kodolziej helped build rout to 23-7 by H. Minnesota opened up its pass attack in 3rd Q, and Spartans came up with pair INTs by FB-DB Gary Lowe and C-LB John Matsko that led to 2 of their trio of TDs in 3rd Q.

OKLAHOMA 52 Iowa State 0: HB Bob Burris started Oklahoma (8-0) scoring rampage with 34y break behind T Cecil Morris' block. Then, when Iowa State (1-6-1) T-P Ray Tweeten boomed soaring punt toward GL, Sooners dashing HB Tommy McDonald fielded it at 9YL and sped and gyrated 91y to score. Sub HB Delbert Long took long TD pass from QB Carl Dodd, and sub HB Clendon Thomas scored another TD before H. Afterward, Cyclones HB Hank Philmon was duly impressed by no. 1 Sooners: "They're so fast you don't get much chance to see who it is that hurt you."

Texas Christian 47 TEXAS 20: Legend of TCU (7-1) HB Jim Swink mushroomed with his 235y rushing and TD runs of 1, 62, 57, and 34y. Swink's season totals reached 1086y on ground with 17 TDs and 107 pts. Horned Frogs QB Chuck Curtis clicked on 44, 36, and 41y TD passes to HB Ken Wineburg, E Bryan Engram, and E O'Day Williams respectively. TCU rolled up 523y, most to date against any Texas (4-5) team. Longhorns enjoyed short-lived 7-6 lead in 2nd Q: After Swink's 1y TD plunge, Texas

HB Delano Womack slipped off stacked-up lines and found EZ from 2YL. HB-K Walt Fondren converted for 1-pt edge, but Frogs came back for 20-7 H lead. It could have been worse, but Steers QB-DB Gene Reeves made INT and raced 83y for TD.

Texas A&M 20 RICE 12: Slumping Owls (2-5-1) threw strong D at Aggies and managed surprising 12-0 lead on 4th Q runs by QB King Hill that led to HB Paul Zipperlin's 2 TD runs. So, glorious upset by Rice seemed at hand as Owls punted ball away with 3:40 to play. In for injured HB John David Crow, Texas A&M (7-1-1) HB Loyd Taylor, from "Martian territory" of Roswell, New Mexico, took pitchout and went 58y behind blocks of Es Bobby Drake Keith and Gene Stallings, and then scored from 3YL to give his team some hope at 12-7. Stallings jumped high to take Aggies' on-side-KO REC, and Taylor got behind Owls DBs on next play for 43y TD catch from QB Jimmy Wright and sudden 14-12 Aggies lead. FB-LB Jack Pardee's 37y INT RET of Hill's long pass helped HB Don Watson's 3y run for TD, A&M's 3rd score coming within miraculous 2:18 span.

Arizona State 20 TEXAS WESTERN 13: Twice Texas Western (4-2-2) went ahead, and twice Border Conf leader Arizona State (6-1-1) came from behind. Miners HB Don Maynard swiftly went 22y to 2nd Q TD, and Sun Devils tied it 7-7 on 9y pass from QB Dave Graybill to E Charlie Mackey. In 3rd Q, Tex-West QB Jesse Whittenton threw medium-range pass to E Dick Forrest, who eluded tacklers for 90y TD. Roughing PEN on punt gave new life to Sun Devils' next drive, and Graybill sneaked over for 14-13 margin early in 4th Q. T-DT John Jankans separated Whittenton from ball at Miners 12YL, and ASU FB Bob Sedlar crashed over for insurance TD with 6:30 on clock. Sun Devils HB Bobby Mulgado rushed 18/93y.

UCLA 19 Washington 17: Washington booster R.C. "Torchy" Torrance delivered stirring pre-game speech, and previously demoralized Huskies (4-4-1) nearly upset mighty Bruins of Westwood. UCLA (8-1) lost TB Ronnie Knox early with broken fibula, and their weakened pass attack suffered 61y INT TD RET by Huskies FB-DB Jim Jones to tie it 7-7. Huskies built 17-14 lead which they nursed well into 4th Q. From deep in own end, Washington QB Steve Roake conceded safety to slice it to 17-16. UCLA took free-kick and drove to WB-K Jim Decker's winning 35y FG with :18 left.

Oregon State 16 CALIFORNIA 14: BB-K Ted Searle's 21y FG in 3rd Q topped 2 big plays in 1st Q to launch Oregon State (6-2) to undisputed 2nd place status in PCC. Beavers FB Tom Berry, substituting for injured FB Arle Wenstead, burst up middle on game's 2nd snap and raced 71y to score. After California (2-6-1) had taken 7-6 advantage on HB Ted Granger's 66y off-T scamper, Oregon State struck with 53y TD pass from TB Ray Westfall to speedy WB Sam Wesley. Still, Golden Bears enjoyed 14-13 H edge on 2nd Q TD pass by QB Hugh Maguire to FB Steve Dimeff. Wesley slipped and dodged for 32y rushing on 43y trip to Cal 4YL in 3rd Q, and when Searle made his 3-ptr, Beavers had 2-pt lead they would protect at their 22YL in 4th Q.

November 19, 1955

Syracuse 20 WEST VIRGINIA 13: Short-handed due to injuries from its bruising defeat to Pittsburgh, West Virginia (7-2) was unable to use its alternating units. It showed as Syracuse (5-3) HB Jimmy Brown wore down Mountaineers D in steady snowstorm, and Brown did it right from start, going 71y with opening KO. Orangemen failed to score on that opportunity thanks to holding PEN but stayed steady despite slipping behind 13-6 by H. West Virginia scored on HB Joe Marconi's 6y sweep early in 2nd Q after HB Bob Moss' 64y spurt, saw Orange tie it on QB Eddie Albright's short TD keeper, and went ahead late in 2nd Q on Mickey Trimarki's 24y pass to HB Ralph Anastasio. WVU made nary single 1st down in 2nd H until last 2 mins. By then it was too late as Albright launched TD passes of 47y to E Jim Ridlon and 12y to E Dick Lasse.

Pittsburgh 20 PENN STATE 0: Brawny Pittsburgh (7-3) E-DEs John Paluck and Joe Walton helped stonewall Nittany Lions (5-4) HB Lenny Moore (10/13y) in heavy snowstorm. So obscured were line markers that Panthers QB Pete Neft trusted officials only to spot his sneaks when big play was needed. Neft totaled 35y on his wedges, including 2nd Q TD after his 22y pass to Paluck. Pitt FB-DB Bob Grier hauled in INT and made 2y TD run at end of 77y drive in 3rd Q. Ahead 14-0, Pitt sub QB Corny Salvaterra clinched it by slipping through G Al Bolkovac's block and making sharp cutback on 62y TD run in 4th Q. Penn State had mounted both its threats in 1st Q: Lions were halted by INT at Panthers 18YL and went from own 30YL to Pitt 8YL before being stopped by inches on 4th down. Victory gave Pitt its best record since 1938.

DUKE 14 Wake Forest 0: HB Bob Pascal came within 5y of breaking ACC game rushing mark of Virginia FB Jim Bakhtiar by gaining 20/157y and scoring both Blue Devils (6-2-1) TDs. Pascal appeared gone for 1st Q TD when he charged 63y, only to be hauled down by Wake Forest (5-4-1) HB-DB Billy Ray Barnes at Wake 21YL. Duke QB Sonny Jurgensen made TD-saving tackle of his own in 1st Q, halting HB-DB John Parham who raced 56y with INT to Duke 36YL. Like Devils earlier, Deacons were held. Duke E-DE Bob Benson made INT at his 8YL in 2nd Q, and Blues barreled 92y to score, chiefly on Pascal's 45y run and Jurgensen's 2 passes/37y. Pascal locked it up on 1y TD blast on 4th down in 3rd Q. Myriad Wake TOs inhibited any threats.

KENTUCKY 23 Tennessee 0: Unbeaten since October, Vols (5-3-1) were stunned by Kentucky (6-3-1), which mothballed its ample air game for 246y on ground, mostly by FB Bob Dougherty. All-purpose Kentucky T-K Lou Michaels opened with 29y

FG in 1st Q. Wildcats tried only 2-3/34 passing, completing 2/34y, and E Howard Schnellenberger caught 26y TD from QB Bob Hardy. It was Kentucky's 3rd straight win over Vols and most lopsided since 1935. Wildcats advantage may have been seized week earlier when "Smoky," Tennessee's mascot hound was dognapped by Kentucky students, who promised good treatment and release in Lexington in time for game. Vols gained 229y rushing, but it was aerial game that abandoned them. They passed 3-11/32y, 5 INTs.

VANDERBILT 21 Florida 6: Vanderbilt (7-2), spying rare bowl invitation and 6th win in row, caught warm-weather Florida (4-5) in Nashville's nippy 40-degrees with 18-mph gusts. Commodores used 5:38 after opening KO to go 72y to HB Joe Scales' 19y TD run. O pass interference PEN early in 2nd Q on Gators HB Don Chandler in EZ turned ball over to Vandy at own 20YL. Smashing middle of UF line, Vandy went 74y only to be stopped at 6YL. But, QB-P Dick Allen's ensuing EZ punt was shanked to 9YL. FB Phil King scored on 1st play for 14-0 Commodores lead. Despite several threats, it took until last min of 3rd Q for Florida to score on well-blocked 39y gallop by sub FB Ed Sears. Conv kick was blocked by Vandy line, so it stood 14-6. Commodores were stopped at Gators 1YL, but Florida's resultant EZ punt gave Vandy short field for HB Charley Horton's clinching TD run.

Ohio State 17 MICHIGAN 0: Ineligible for Rose Bowl due to no repeat rule, Ohio State (7-2) spoiled Michigan's Pasadena dreams in odd game that sent Michigan State, 33-0 winner over Marquette, to Rose Bowl. Buckeyes made E-K Fred Kriss' 2nd Q carom-off-upright FG stand up for 3-0 lead into 4th Q. Early in 4th Q, Ohio A-A HB Howard Cassady fumbled at Wolverines GL, but officials ruled that Cassady scored. Michigan (7-2) howled. Moments later, Wolverines were deep in their own territory. Ricochet pass landed in hands of Michigan HB Terry Barr, who was dropped for safety by swift Ohio G Aurelius Thomas. So, Ohio State led 11-0. Late roughing PEN on Wolverines T Lionel Sigman and successive protest PENs moved Ohio inside Michigan 1YL, and Buckeyes rugged FB Don Vicic battered over. Game ended in donnybrook.

PURDUE 6 Indiana 4: Chilled crowd saw Purdue (5-3-1) lock up Old Oaken Bucket for 8th straight year. In 0-0 1st H, heroic Indiana (3-6) D, led by massive C Joe Amstutz, threw back Boilermakers bids at 4, 18, and 13YLs. Purdue O was sparked by QB Lenny Dawson (9-16/83y) and sub FB Mel Dillard (21/98y), who saw 60 mins of duty with both top FBs out with injury. Purdue HB Jim Whitmer fumbled punt deep in own end 5 mins into 3rd Q, but Dawson was Johnny-on-the-spot, swooping in to scoop up loose ball. Only trouble was that Dawson's momentum sped him in wrong direction, and he looped back into own EZ with 3 Hoosiers in pursuit. Indiana E-DE Pat Fellinger hauled him down for safety and 2-0 lead. Boilers G Bob Clasey fell on FUM at own 47YL late in 3rd Q, and Whitmer snatched pass away from 2 defenders for 1st down at Indiana 19YL. HB Ed Neves bolted over from 1YL as 4th Q began, and Purdue led 6-2. In late going, Whitmer made EZ INT, and, after PEN pushed back Boilers, Dawson ran around in EZ before conceding another safety at game's end. Afterward, Purdue coach Stu Holcomb jokingly suggested Indiana was trying to "run up the score" with its 2nd 2-pt play.

Oklahoma 41 NEBRASKA 0: Sooners (9-0) and Cornhuskers (5-5), each entering game with 5-0 conf marks, squared off for Big 7 title. Oklahoma locked up its 10th straight Big 7 crown. Hoping to provide departing gift for their colorful coach Biff Glassford, frequent wearer of battered brown derby hat, Nebraska rolled early to 8YL, but Oklahoma FB-LB Dennit Morris carried INT out to 35YL to begin drive which ignited 6-TD avalanche. Sooners QB Jimmy Harris went out early with shoulder injury, so sub QB Jay O'Neal was inserted to guide both starters and 2nd unit. O'Neal scored opening TD behind blocks of Gs Joe Oujesky and Bill Krisher and prevented Huskers speedy HB Willie Greenlaw from scoring when O'Neal was only DB in position to knock him OB. Oklahoma won stat battle 402y to 187y as HB Bob Burris scored 2 TDs and HBs Tommy McDonald and Clendon Thomas tallied 1 each.

Southern Methodist 12 BAYLOR 0: Ponies (4-5) QB John Roach (6-10/101y, INT) pitched 2 TDs to vault patched-up SMU lineup to upset win. Highly-touted Baylor (4-5) QB Doyle Traylor managed 6-9/64y passing but had to dart about in his backfield to avoid frequent pressure. Mustangs went 50y in 1st Q for TD as FB Ray Masters chipped in with 15y run and Roach hit E Tommy Gentry with 14y pass until HB Charlie Jackson slipped into EZ corner for 8y scoring pass on 4th-and-3. Bruins C-LB Lee Harrington, who was D standout, blocked x-pt. SMU traveled 69y in 10 plays in 3rd Q. Mustangs stayed on ground until 5y PEN pushed them back to 16YL, from where E Willard Dewveall beat Bears HB-DB Del Shofner for TD grab. Baylor's most menacing moment spanned 1st and 2nd Qs as E Tony DeGrazier was drilled just outside 1YL by HB-DB Don McIlhenny on 3rd down pass. Shofner then was tossed for loss by DE Gentry on 4th down sweep.

Louisiana State 13 ARKANSAS 7 (Little Rock): Grinding 0-0 conflict was spiced late in 2nd Q as Bengals (3-5-1) suddenly turned to their passing attack and achieved 3 of their game-end 4 completions to take them to 18YL. But, Arkansas QB-DB Don Christian halted that threat with GL INT. Game took abrupt switch on 1st snap of 3rd Q when LSU HB Chuck Johns shed 3 Razorbacks tacklers and bolted 65y for TD. Arkansas (5-4-1) answered immediately: WB Ronnie Underwood returned following KO 88y for 7-7 deadlock. LSU grabbed upset win on 74y 4th Q drive ended by FB O.K. Ferguson's 20y run through block of LT Earl Leggett. Johns and Ferguson starred on D as Tigers LBs who helped completely frustrate Arkansas' usually-effective wide plays, as Hogs made only 94y O.

Ucla 17 SOUTHERN CALIFORNIA 7: Opening KO sounded sour note for Trojans (5-4): TB "Jaguar" Jon Arnett went 97y, but it turned out that Troy front had lined up offside. "I always have thought that officials are supposed to help the players line up properly," complained Southern California coach Jess Hill. T Fabrian Abram lined up correctly at 50YL, but his 4 other linemates were back 5y. It was believed that loud crowd drowned out umpire Orian Landrith's attempt to aid Trojans. Sam Brown, 1 of Bruins' best Single Wing TBs in coach Red Sanders' regime, rushed 27/150y, and 4y TD in 1st Q to overtake Kenny Washington as Uclans' best to-date season rusher with 829y. USC drove deep into UCLA (9-1) territory 3 times, and perhaps most important came on Trojans' 1st series in 3rd Q. FB Gordon Duvall (12/67y) led 60y advance to Bruins 24YL, but was stopped. Only thrust that clicked for Troy went 89y in 4th Q as QB Jim Contratto's 4y bootleg run narrowed it to 10-7, but Bruins counterpunched with runs by Brown and FB Bob Davenport (22/78y, TD) for 17-7 edge with 5 mins left. Brown completed 2-2/50y on his few attempts.

OREGON 28 Oregon State 0: Surprising Beavers (6-3), in 1st year under coach Tommy Prothro, saw their 4-game win streak halted. Fired-up Ducks (6-4) staged TD drives of 71, 65, 51, and 60y. Attempting only 4 passes, Oregon depended on running of HB-duo of Jim Shanley (27/160y) and Dick James (22/114y). Frustrated Oregon State gained only 77y O.

AP Poll November 21

1 Oklahoma (114)	1889	11 Navy	219
2 Michigan State (39)	1689	12 Michigan	192
3 Maryland (35)	1683	13 Pittsburgh (1)	90
4 UCLA (6)	1374	14 Miami (2)	79
5 Notre Dame (3)	1255	15 Mississippi	73
6 Ohio State (5)	1025	16 Miami (Ohio)	46
7 Texas Christian (3)	994	17 Stanford	29
8 Texas A&M	531	18 Duke	23
9 Georgia Tech	369	19 Vanderbilt	20
10 Auburn	245	20 Syracuse	16

November 24-26, 1955

(Th'g) Texas 21 TEXAS A&M 6: One of year's great upsets was fashioned by Texas (5-5). Longhorns fumbled away 2 early chances, but fought back from 6-0 2nd Q deficit that was hatched on 80y drive during which Aggies (7-2-1) QB Jimmy Wright hit 3-4 passes and slipped across from 1YL. Texas countered right away, but it took until last 10 secs of 1st H for E Menan Schriewer to go high to snare 25y TD pass from QB Joe Clements. Longhorns HB Walt Fondren gained 98y rushing, scored TD for 14-6 lead in 4th Q. Steers HB Delano Womack gained 18/91y, while Texas A&M HB John David Crow was held to 18y on ground by fierce Texas D. Asst D coach J.T. King set plan that had DB Womack shadowing Wright on every play, but, most notably, stellar Longhorns line play kept Aggies bottled up and permitted only 30y rushing.

(Fri) West Virginia 27 NORTH CAROLINA STATE 7: Three-week slumber of mighty Mountaineers (8-2) continued through 1st H as WVU squandered scoring chances at 19, 7, 21, and 3YLs of NC State. Underdog Wolfpack (4-5-1) created 7-7 tie in 2nd Q with 79y drive that was climaxed by QB Eddie West's 7y run. Finally, West Virginia awoke: HB Bob Moss raced 25y to TD, and HB Joe Marconi added TDs of 15 and 39y in 4th Q mud.

BOSTON COLLEGE 26 Holy Cross 7: Fenway Park was site of game that saw more Holy Cross (6-4) blunders than committed by any shortstop who ever drew ire of Red Sox boobirds. Boston College (5-2-1) capitalized on staggering 6 INTs and 4 FUMs to salt away win with TD in every Q. Eagles QB Billy Donlan sneaked over twice and HB Eddie DeSilva scored on 2y run in 2nd Q and decisive 10y sweep in 3rd Q behind convoy of blockers. Crusader fans had reason to cheer late in 2nd Q when QB Tom Roberts arched perfect 46y TD to E Dick Arcand, who streaked downfield to shave deficit to 14-7. BC E-DE Emerson Dickie, dropping off scrimmage line to defend wide-open Holy Cross attack, created 2 TDs in 2nd with INTs, 2nd of which he returned 68y to 2YL.

Army 14 Navy 6 (Philadelphia): Brilliant Navy (6-2-1) QB George Welsh displayed his magic with 4 completions, including 26y strike to HB Paul Gober, on masterful 76y TD drive off opening KO. For next 26 mins, Navy sailed up and down field for 208y to Army's 39y, but could not build on its 6-0 lead. Of their 6 lost FUMs, Middies bobbled away 2 in 1st H at Black Knights 34 and 20YLs. Another drive to Army (6-3) 20YL was halted when QB-DB Don Holleder broke up 4th down pass with big hit. Shortly thereafter, Holleder recovered FB Vince Monto's FUM at 13YL after Welsh's pass to E Ron Beagle advanced to Army 20YL. Refraining from all but 1 pass, QB Don Holleder guided bloodied-but-unbowed Army 86y to Middies 1YL, but H clock frustratingly expired. In 2nd H, Army quit throwing all together, rolling 41y to 5y TD run by 60-min sr FB Pat Uebel (26/125y), his 5th TD in 3 years against Navy. Cadets HB Pete Lash dashed 23y to cap 80y march that wrapped it up with 5 mins to play in 4th Q. G Stan Slater had launched Cadets' clinching drive when he grabbed FUM by Middies A-A E Beagle, who had secured pass at end of failed 72y sortie to Army 20YL. Welsh finished with 18-29/179y passing to take season's national completion title with 94, while rarely-throwing Holleder passed 0-2, INT. Outcome ended Navy's Cotton Bowl hopes and vindicated Army coach Red Blaik for his controversial off-season switch of Holleder from A-A E to novice QB.

TENNESSEE 20 Vanderbilt 14: If Vanderbilt (7-3) could have hung on to its 14-7 lead after 3rd Q, Sugar Bowl "would have sent for the Commodores in a golden coach," according to UP game reporter. Instead, long-standing Knoxville jinx held forth over Vandy as Tennessee (6-3-1) rallied with 2 TDs in 4th Q. It appeared Commodores, who scored TD in each middle Q, would see their hopes dashed for 1st-ever bowl invitation. Coming to rescue was Gator Bowl which extended request for Vandy to meet fellow SEC member Auburn. Vanderbilt TDs were tallied by HB Charley Horton at end of 53y march in 2nd Q and powerful FB Phil King, who slammed through LG to cap 40y trip with less than 4 mins left in 3rd Q. Tennessee tied it 14-14 in 4th Q as TB Johnny Majors, SEC total O leader, passed 10y to leaping E Buddy Cruze, who caught ball at 1YL and backed over for TD. Volunteers sub TB Al Carter rifled 43y TD pass to nimble WB soph Bill Anderson for winning score.

GEORGIA TECH 21 Georgia 3: Swift Engineers (8-1-1) got surprise Sugar Bowl bid when Vanderbilt succumed to Tennessee. Georgia (4-6) opened ablaze, breaking FB Bobby Garrard on 61y run. But Garrard's right shoe flew off, allowing Tech QB-DB Wade Mitchell to haul him down and force Bulldogs to settle for E-K Ken Cooper's FG. Sub E Danny Bagwell made spectacular, but questioned TD catch for 7-3 Georgia Tech lead late in 1st Q. Georgia Tech G-LB Franklin Brooks' FUM REC led to 2nd Q score, and HB George Volkert (12/121y) raced 25y to cap 86y drive after 2nd H KO.

Auburn 26 ALABAMA 0 (Birmingham): Auburn (8-1-1) rushed for 278y and locked up 3rd straight trip to Gator Bowl by smashing its downtrodden rival. Old school of former great Dixie Howell, Alabama (0-10), lost its 13th straight game, thanks mostly to Auburn's own version of Howell. Plainsmen QB Millard Howell Tubbs, who was named in honor of Alabama's Howell and preferred to use his middle name, pitched 2 TD passes to E Jerry Elliott, ran for stand-up 2y TD at end of 85y drive in 4th Q, and piled up 146y O. Auburn A-A FB Joe Childress took control of 3rd Q drive of 20y and scored 2y TD after T Paul Terry recovered Bama FUM. Crimson Tide was able to gain 171y, and sr QB Bart Starr quietly ended college career with 6-8/54y passing.

MIAMI 7 Florida 6: Hurricanes (6-3) 3rd string QB Mario Bonofiglio, who began season as starter, resurfaced to score on 12y run in 1st Q. Miami HB-K Ed "Porky" Oliver made vital conv for 7-0 edge. Florida (4-6), 2-TD underdog, played well on D. Gators FB Joey Brodsky (10/45y, TD) lugged ball most of 78y TD drive in 2nd Q. But, unlucky Florida QB-K Dick Allen saw his conv kick blocked by Miami E-DE Don Johnson's vice-like hands. Miami D blanketed Florida's dynamic duo on ground: HBs Jim Rountree (8.9y rush avg to date in 1955) and Jackie Simpson gained 5/14y and 4/9y respectively, although Simpson proved dangerous on punt RETs. Whitey Rouviere, 1 of greatest DBs in Miami history, made important INT at his 25YL with 1:45 to play. Canes FB Don Bosseler rushed 17/64y.

MISSISSIPPI SOUTHERN 21 Florida State 6: Muddy field in Hattiesburg greeted Florida State (4-5), which entered fray with 3-game win streak. Mississippi Southern (9-1) used its fine rushing attack for 310y and scored twice in 2nd Q for 14-0 lead. Seminoles scurried inside Eagles 20YL in 3rd Q, but were halted on downs. Seminoles DBs deflected 4th Q pass but it landed in hands of Southerners E Curry Juneau for TD. Belated Florida State TD came from HB Billy Odom.

COLORADO A&M 10 Colorado 0: Skyline Conf champion Colorado A&M (8-2) knocked off its hated in-state Big 7 rivals for 1st time since 1949. Blanked for 1st time in 75 games, lethargic Colorado (6-4) held significant weight advantage in line, but swifter Rams forwards blocked crisply on 44y TD raid in 1st Q. Moving mostly with its ground attack that computed 214y by game's end, Colorado A&M sent QB Gary Glick across for 1y TD. K Glick converted for 7-0 lead. Buffaloes recovered 3 FUMs in 1st H, but without its best 2 FBs they seldom crossed midfield and never got closer than A&M's 38YL. Buffs missed their strong FBs John Bayuk, who was ejected early for unsportsmanlike conduct, and Emerson Wilson, who reinjured his leg in 1st H. K Glick missed 27y FG on last play of 2nd Q, but clicked on 28y FG in 3rd Q. Pittsburgh Steelers would stun football world 3 days later by making little-known Glick NFL's top overall pick in draft.

TEXAS CHRISTIAN 20 Southern Methodist 13: Fabulous TCU (9-1) HB Jim "The Rusk Rambler" Swink pulled his Horned Frogs out of 13-6 hole by sparking pair of scores in last 4 mins to claim TCU's 6th-ever SWC championship. After having scored on 30y tear in 1st Q, Swink capped 77y drive with tying 3y TD plunge. On Frogs' next series, Swink paced them with 48y of his game-end 131y rushing as HB Ray Taylor scored winning TD on 5y run. Southern Methodist (4-6), hungry for upset, had sent its HBs, Don McIlhenny (84y rushing) and Charlie Jackson (87y rushing) surging for TDs in middle Qs. McIlhenny plunged over in 2nd Q to knot it 6-6, and little Jackson broke away for 47y TD dash in 3rd Q.

Arizona 7 ARIZONA STATE 6: Football was like desert hot potato: 7 times possession was lost on TO, only to have original possessor regain ball moments later. Stellar Arizona (5-4-1) HB-K Art Luppino squirted over LG for 20y TD dash late in 1st Q and kicked all-important conv. Following ensuing KO, Arizona State (7-2-1) concocted 71y gain: HB Gene Mitcham carried 17y from own 28YL, was nearly trapped, cut left, and flipped lateral to E Charlie Mackey who continued to Wildcats 1YL. HB-K Bobby Mulgado dived for ASU TD, but his kick was barely wide. On Devils' long-gainer, star Arizona FB-LB Max Burnett was ejected for personal foul PEN, and FB Ed McCluskey was soon tossed out for piling on. Arizona already had 2 regulars—C Paul Hatcher and HB Pete Arrigoni—sitting out with injury, but Gs Bob Griffis and Ed Brown and T John Mellekas were stalwarts on D. Arizona WB-DB Gove Allen made 2 INTs in 4th Q to stymie Sun Devils drives. Afterward, AU coach Warren Woodson summed up his team's desire, "Things have been going right for them (Sun Devils) all year and wrong for us. We just had to have this one." ASU's conf title flew away with missed x-pt; tie would have insured Border Conf crown.

SOUTHERN CALIFORNIA 42 Notre Dame 20: Unpredictable Trojans (6-4) finished season on high note in front of 94,892 astonished fans with upset of Fighting Irish (8-2), thanks to 21-pt eruption in 4th Q. Teams swapped 1st Q TDs on 68 and 67y drives, but USC quickly added scores on wide runs by FB C.R. Roberts (15y) and TB Jon Arnett (10y) in 2nd Q. QB Paul Hornung's 78y pass to HB Jim Morse brought Notre Dame within 21-13 at H. Scoreless 3rd Q was highlighted by 2 big, but fruitless gains: Roberts broke away for 58y run, but lost FUM at ND 6YL, while Hornung maneuvered 59y to Trojans 28YL. That Irish threat died. Hornung (11-23/283y, TD, 5 INTs) pitched 60y to Morse, who carried pass to 6YL to poise Hornung for his 2nd TD. ND, now trailing 21-20 early in 4th Q, had its comeback trumped by 2 TD passes from Trojans QB Jim Contratto, who came off bench to toss short pass that superbly shifty Arnett took 64y to pay-dirt. After INT, Contratto hit E Don McFarland with 12y score, and Arnett clinched rout with 7y TD run at end of short Southern California drive.

Final AP Poll November 28

1 Oklahoma (218)	3581	11 Pittsburgh (1)	282
2 Michigan State (88)	3204	12 Michigan	217
3 Maryland (55)	3024	13 Southern California	149
4 UCLA (9)	2637	14 Miami	136
5 Ohio State (4)	1980	15 Miami (Ohio)	113
6 Texas Christian (9)	1941	16 Stanford	94
7 Georgia Tech	1301	17 Texas A&M	90
8 Auburn (6)	854	18 Navy	89
9 Notre Dame	796	19 West Virginia	88
10 Mississippi (1)	708	20 Army	66

December 3, 1955

DUKE 6 North Carolina 0: Blue Devils (7-2-1), who opened 1955 with 4 wins, now closed year with 3 victories. Duke O maneuvered length of field all day, but were halted 4 times and succeeded only on 35y TD spurt by sub HB Oliver "Skitch" Rudy, set up by HB Bob Pascal's 33y punt RET to UNC 46YL. G W.D. Fesperman (FUM REC) sprung Rudy with trap block and key block came from E Buddy Bass. North Carolina T Jack Maultsby broke through to slap G-K Jim Nelson's x-pt try back at holder-QB Sonny Jurgensen. Tar Heels (3-7) failed to venture past midfield until 3rd Q, but made it to 12YL in late going after FUM REC. Duke DB Pascal made late-game save with EZ INT. Rumors of Jim Tatum's return to coach North Carolina were heightened by curious presence in Durham of coach of Orange Bowl-bound Maryland.

HOUSTON 26 Wyoming 14: Houston (6-4) completed sweep of both of upcoming January 2's Sun Bowl combatants: Texas Tech, which lost earlier to Cougars 7-0, and Wyoming (7-3), which surrendered 19 pts in 4th Q in Houston's 80-degree heat. Cowboys opened game with 80y drive to FB Ova Stapleton's TD. On 1st play of 4th Q, Cougars G Jim Blackston blocked Wyoming punt at 8YL, and FB Curley Johnson soon plunged over to break 7-7 deadlock. Moments later, G Rod Carpenter sparked another Houston TD by HB Kennie Stegall with FUM REC at Wyoming 23YL. Stegall's 69y punt RET positioned FB Don Flynn's 16y TD catch.

1955 Conference Standings

Ivy Group

Princeton	6-1
Yale	5-1
Cornell	4-3
Dartmouth	3-3
Harvard	2-4
Brown	2-4
Columbia	1-5
Pennsylvania	0-2

Atlantic Coast

Maryland	4-0
Duke	4-0
Clemson	3-1
Wake Forest	3-3-1
North Carolina	3-3
North Carolina State	0-2-1
South Carolina	1-5
Virginia	0-4

Southern

West Virginia	4-0
Virginia Tech	2-1-1
Davidson	3-2
George Washington	3-2
Richmond	3-2-2
The Citadel	2-2
Furman	1-1
William & Mary	1-3-1
Virginia Military	1-6
Washington & Lee	0-1

Southeastern

Mississippi	5-1
Auburn	5-1-1
Georgia Tech	4-1-1
Tennessee	3-2-1
Vanderbilt	4-3
Kentucky	3-3-1
Mississippi State	4-4
Tulane	3-3-1
Louisiana State	2-3-1
Florida	3-5
Georgia	2-5
Alabama	0-7

Big Ten

Ohio State	6-0
Michigan State	5-1
Michigan	5-2
Purdue	4-2-1
Illinois	3-3-1
Wisconsin	3-4
Iowa	2-3-1
Minnesota	2-5
Indiana	1-5
Northwestern	0-6-1

Big Seven

Oklahoma	6-0
Nebraska	5-1
Colorado	3-3
Kansas State	3-3
Kansas	1-4-1
Iowa State	1-4-1
Missouri	1-5

Missouri Valley

Wichita	3-1
Detroit	3-1
Houston	2-2
Tulsa	1-3
Oklahoma A&M	1-3

Mid-American

Miami (Ohio)	5-0
Bowling Green	4-1-1
Kent State	4-1-1
Ohio	3-3
Toledo	2-4
Marshall	1-5
Western Michigan	0-5

Southwest

Texas Christian	5-1
Texas A&M	4-1-1
Texas	4-2
Arkansas	3-2-1
Baylor	2-4
Southern Methodist	2-4
Rice	0-6

Border

Texas Tech	3-0-1
Arizona State	4-1
Hardin-Simmons	3-2
Texas Western	3-2-1
Arizona	1-2-1
West Texas State	1-4-1
New Mexico A&M	0-4

Skyline Eight			Pacific Coast	
Colorado A&M	6-1		UCLA	6-0
Utah	4-1		Oregon State	5-2
Denver	5-2		Stanford	3-2-1
Wyoming	5-2		Oregon	4-3
Utah State	3-4		Washington	4-3-1
Montana	2-4		Southern California	3-3
New Mexico	1-5		California	1-5-1
Brigham Young	0-7		Washington State	1-5-1
			Idaho	0-4

1955 Major Bowl Games
Gator Bowl (Dec. 31): Vanderbilt 25 Auburn 13

It was 3rd straight trip to Jacksonville for Auburn (8-2-1). On other hand, Vanderbilt (8-3) had been reluctant to accept surprise bid because chancellor Harvey Branscomb was concerned bowl games might taint school's fine academic image. It was good thing Branscomb accepted, because Commodores rarely saw bowls thereafter. Vandy would qualify only in 1974, 1982 and 2008 thereafter. While fans sat in overcoats, 7-pt underdog Commodores won with spirit and QB Don Orr's greatest career game as he accumulated 110y of Commodores' 271y. Orr's playing status was doubtful right up to game time because of dislocated throwing elbow from season's climatic game, so he passed sparingly (4-6/67y, TD). But, Orr's throws included 7y TD pass in 1st Q to E Joe Stephenson, who got away from 2 DBs. FB Joe Childress (15/58y) was Auburn's star for 2nd bowl in row despite battling case of flu. Tigers HB Fob James caught 38y TD pass from QB Howell Tubbs in 2nd Q. Trailing 13-7 at H, Auburn's Tubbs lost his 2nd FUM to Vandy T Tommy Woodruff near midfield. Orr ran 16y and threw 20y pass to HB Joe Scales to set up his 1y sneak for 19-7 lead.

Orange Bowl (Jan. 2): Oklahoma 20 Maryland 6

Maryland (10-1) was determined to change its losing Orange Bowl outcome of 2 years earlier against Oklahoma (11-0). Game's 3rd play saw Terrapins HB Ed Vereb burst off right side for 66y to Oklahoma 10YL. Swift Sooners D held, but Terps continued to have upper hand and pressed until they gained 6-0 H lead on Vereb's 15y TD run. Energetic HB Tommy McDonald keyed Oklahoma's 2nd H reversal. McDonald's 32y punt RET started 46y go-ahead drive, which he sustained with 16y pass to HB Bob Burris and finished with 4y TD run. Sooners sub QB Jay O'Neal's 3rd Q sneak made it 14-6. Maryland threatened twice in 4th Q: Outstanding Oklahoma C-LB Jerry Tubbs halted 1st Terps threat with INT and 2nd probe was reversed by HB-DB Carl Dodd, who sprinted for 82y INT TD RET that broke back of Terrapins. Stats virtually were even: Oklahoma 254y to Maryland's 245y, but Bud Wilkinson's Sooners clearly validated their spot atop AP Poll.

Sugar Bowl (Jan. 2): Georgia Tech 7 Pittsburgh 0

Pre-game imbroglio created by Georgia Gov Marvin Griffin dwarfed game news. In political action characteristic of Deep South in 1950s, Griffin tried to bar Georgia Tech (9-1-1) from playing Pitt (7-4) because Panthers counted among their squad members Negro FB Bobby Grier. Georgia Tech pres Blake Van Leer announced he would uphold contract, so game was on. On field, play evolved into true D combat matching Pittsburgh's bulk and Georgia Tech's speed. After Panthers lost FUM on their 33YL in early moments, all eyes were on DB Grier as he was called for pass interference PEN while trying to cover Yellow Jackets E Don Ellis at Panthers GL. QB Wade Mitchell immediately scored on sneak and kicked x-pt, but later left game with injury. Afterward, teary Grier felt he had been robbed on PEN call: "He (Ellis) was pushing me all the way down the field and finally pushed me across the goal line. And they call interference on me!" Pittsburgh had clear advantage on O with its big line; Panthers outgained Tech 311y to 142y. Typical clutch play of Engineers D, led by Gs Franklin Brooks and Allen Ecker, came late in 2nd Q as QB Corny Salvaterra was stopped on 4th down sneak at Tech 1YL. Yellow Jackets mounted their only sustained drive in 4th Q behind sub QB Toppy Vann. Tech reached Pitt 7YL, but Panthers E-DEs Joe Walton and John Paluck caved in on Vann, who threw INT to Pitt HB-DB Ray DiPasquale at 5YL. Panthers 3rd string QB, Darrell Lewis, entered game for last 6 heart-stopping plays that carried to Engineers 5YL, including incomplete EZ pass. Grier was game's top rusher with 6/51y, burst for 26y run in 3rd Q, and made scintillating pass catch. Afterward, Grier added that Georgia Tech players treated him well: "They are all fine sportsmen."

Cotton Bowl (Jan. 2): Mississippi 14 Texas Christian 13

TCU (9-2) coach Abe Martin made odd, but fateful last moment pre-game comment to QB Chuck Curtis. He reminded Curtis that if he had to field short KO, Curtis should toss it back to star HB Jim Swink, because Martin didn't want his only proven passer to get injured. Sure enough, opening KO came up short. Curtis fielded it, and instinctively advanced upfield until being drilled by Ole Miss (10-1) T Dick Goehe. Curtis was lost with 2 broken ribs. Sub QB Dick Finney, who had never taken single snap with TCU's 1st unit, guided Frogs to 13-0 2nd Q lead on Swink's 2 TD runs of 1 and 39y. After Swink's 2nd score, TCU received PEN on conv try, and FB-K Harold Pollard missed longer, post-PEN kick. With little time before H, Rebels QB Eagle Day hit passes of 28 and 14y to HBs Earl Blair and Billy Kinard to poise FB Paige Cothren for TD plunge. Swink charged 41y with punt RET on last play of scoreless 3rd Q, but Horned Frogs couldn't pad their 13-7 lead. Ole Miss' winning march went 66y in last 5 mins. Facing 4th-and-5 at TCU 45 YL, Day hit 13y pass, then scrambled 25y to position HB Billy Lott's 5y TD sweep of RE and K Cothren's winning conv. Rebels G Buddy Alliston was tapped as game's top lineman.

GAME OF THE YEAR
Rose Bowl (Jan. 2): Michigan State 17 UCLA 14

As it had 2 years earlier, UCLA (9-2) jumped to Rose Bowl lead over Spartans (9-1) as FB Bob "Pogo" Davenport bounded over GL for TD early in 1st Q. Michigan State QB

Earl Morrall tied it at 7-7 in 2nd Q when he hit TB Clarence Peaks with 13y TD pass. After scoreless 3rd Q, Peaks launched 67y TD pass off pitchout to E John "Thunder" Lewis for 14-7 margin in 4th Q. But, TB Ronnie Knox, back from mid-season broken leg, guided Bruins 55y to FB Doug Peters' tying score in just 5 plays. With 5:00 left and score at 14-14, Spartans took KO and marched into UCLA territory. Top Spartans K, FB Gerry Planutis, missed 40y FG. Then, game turned rather crazy. Rules prohibited any signals from sideline, and officials caught UCLA asst coach Jim Myers making passing motion as Knox peered at bench from behind huddle. PEN of 15y moved ball back to Bruins 5YL. Knox faded into EZ to pass, but Bruins were called for ineligible receiver PEN when Knox made frantic throw to T Gil Moreno to avoid being tackled for game-losing safety. PEN pushed Bruins back to 1YL, where Knox punted out of trouble. But A-A G Hardiman Cureton mistakenly grabbed Spartans punt receiver, and UCLA was penalized 15y to its own 25YL with less than 2:00 left. Pair of quick FUMs, both anxiously recovered by Michigan State, and delay-of-game PEN served as prelude to MSU coach Duffy Daugherty's surprise move. Daugherty skipped over Planutis and tapped E-K Dave Kaiser for FG try. Stunningly, ball was snapped in middle of Kaiser's practice kick, but he adjusted to slam winner through uprights from 41y away with :07 showing on clock. It was Kaiser's 1st successful FG in college. Kaiser was near-sighted and had to turn to ref's signal to learn he made thrilling game-winning boot.

1955 Top Performance Formula

1	Oklahoma	1.7521
2	Michigan State	1.7010
3	Mississippi	1.6561
4	UCLA	1.6367
5	Maryland	1.6292
6	Georgia Tech	1.6116
7	Texas Christian	1.5459
8	Auburn	1.4705
9	West Virginia	1.4512
10	Duke	1.4372
11	Notre Dame	1.4278
12	Ohio State	1.4233
13	Texas A&M	1.3917
14	Arizona State	1.3861
15	Stanford	1.3797
16	Syracuse	1.3687
17	Michigan	1.3655
18	Texas Tech	1.3527
19	Navy	1.3492
20	Vanderbilt	1.3472

1955 Top Opponent Records

1	Syracuse	.6812
2	Stanford	.6667
3	Pittsburgh	.6563
4	Louisiana State	.6559
5	Florida	.6374
6	UCLA	.6340
7	Michigan State	.6310
8	Texas	.6290
9	Georgia Tech	.6180
10	Mississippi	.6061
11	Alabama	.5968
12	North Carolina	.5934
13	Maryland	.5928
14	Iowa	.5921
15	Duke	.5852
16	Oklahoma A&M	.5824
17	Georgia	.5798
18	Miami	.5765
19	Texas A&M	.5707
20	Texas Tech	.5700

1955 Out-of-Conference Records

	W-L	Percentage	Bowl W-L
Southeastern	26-9-1	.7361	3-1
Southwest	17-11-1	.6034	0-1
Big Ten	15-10	.6000	1-0
Pacific Coast	16-4-1	.5323	0-1
Atlantic Coast	20-19-1	.5125	0-1
Big Seven	11-17	.3929	1-0

1955 Individual Statistical Leaders

RUSHING YARDS	Attempts	Yards	Avg.
Art Luppino, Arizona	209	1313	6.3
Jim Swink, Texas Christian	157	1283	8.2
Howard Cassady, Ohio State	161	958	6.0
Fob James, Auburn	123	879	7.2
Sam Brown, UCLA	130	829	6.4
Bob Moss, West Virginia	98	807	8.2
Joel Wells, Clemson	135	782	5.8
Jim Bakhtiar, Virginia	158	733	4.6
Bob Pascal, Duke	156	750	4.8
Jim Shanley, Oregon	100	711	7.1

PASSING YARDS	Completions	Attempts	Yards	Pct.
George Welsh, Navy	94	150	1319	62.7
Dave Graybill, Arizona State	80	132	1078	60.6
Jim Haluska, Wisconsin	71	132	1036	53.8
John Brodie, Stanford	76	133	1024	57.1
Len Dawson, Purdue	87	155	1005	56.1
Claude Benham, Columbia	89	188	999	47.3
Jim Bowen, Denver	58	108	946	53.7
John Roach, Southern Methodist	64	141	907	45.4
Kenny Ford, Hardin-Simmons	73	135	854	54.1
Joe Clements, Texas	65	128	818	50.8

RECEIVING YARDS	Catches	Yards
Hal Burnine, Missouri	44	594
Gene Mitcham, Arizona State	27	552
Charlie Mackey, Arizona State	34	473
John Bredice, Boston University	35	468
Ron Beagle, Navy	30	451
Jimmy Orr, Georgia	24	443
Jim Morse, Notre Dame	17	424
Billy Kinard, Mississippi	23	371
Bill Barnes, Wake Forest	31	349
Monte Pascoe, Dartmouth	24	331

1955 Consensus All-America Team

End:	Ron Beagle, Navy
	Ron Kramer, Michigan
Tackle:	Norm Masters, Michigan State
	Bruce Bosley, West Virginia
Guard:	Bo Bolinger, Oklahoma
	Calvin Jones, Iowa
	Hardiman Cureton, UCLA
Center:	Bob Pellegrini, Maryland
Backs:	Earl Morrall, Michigan State
	Paul Hornung, Notre Dame
	Howard Cassady, Ohio State
	Jim Swink, Texas Christian

Other All-America Choices

End:	Rommie Loudd, UCLA
	Hal Burnine, Missouri
	Howard Schnellenberger, Kentucky
Tackle:	Mike Sandusky, Maryland
	Frank D'Agostino, Auburn
	Sam Huff, West Virginia
	Paul Wiggin, Stanford
	John Witte, Oregon State
	Herb Gray, Texas
Guard:	Pat Bisceglia, Notre Dame
	Jim Parker, Ohio State
	Jim Brown, UCLA
	Tony Sardisco, Tulane
	Scott Suber, Mississippi State
Center:	Hugh Pitts, Texas Christian
Backs:	Don Schaefer, Notre Dame
	Jon Arnett, Southern California
	Tommy McDonald, Oklahoma
	Art Davis, Mississippi State
	Joe Childress, Auburn
	Bob Davenport, UCLA

1955 Heisman Trophy Vote

Howard Cassady, senior halfback, Ohio State	2,219
Jim Swink, junior halfback, Texas Christian	742
George Welsh, senior quarterback, Navy	383
Earl Morrall, senior quarterback, Michigan State	323
Paul Hornung, junior quarterback, Notre Dame	321

Other Major Awards

Maxwell (Player)	Howard Cassady, senior halfback, Ohio State
Outland (Lineman)	Calvin Jones, senior guard, Iowa
Walter Camp (Back)	Howard Cassady, senior halfback, Ohio State
Knute Rockne (Lineman)	Bob Pellegrini, senior center, Maryland
AFCA Coach of the Year	Duffy Daugherty, Michigan State

1956

The Year of the Oklahoma Tornado, Iowa Wing-T, and Pacific Coast Scandal

Like a Great Plains tornado, Bud Wilkinson's Oklahoma Sooners swept across the nation, destroying 10 foes by an average margin of 41 points. The Sooners gained 481.7 yards per game, 90 yards more than any other team in the nation. Their defense yielded a low 193.8-yard average. Halfbacks Clendon Thomas and Tommy McDonald each scored more than 100 points as the team built impressive point totals: Oklahoma visited the worst-ever defeat at South Bend on Notre Dame 40-0, delivered the biggest loss in 50 years to Texas 45-0, and scored 66 and 67 points on Kansas State and Missouri. In the process, bowl-ineligible Oklahoma (10-0) finished the regular season with its 40th straight victory, eclipsing the old collegiate record of 39 in a row set by the Washington Huskies in 1908-14.

The Big Seven Conference may not have been a great collection of teams in 1956, and Oklahoma no doubt caught Texas (1-9) and Notre Dame (2-8) in down years of historical proportion, but the Sooners dominated their schedule like few teams ever had before and or since. Without argument, the 1956 Oklahoma team was an all-time great collaboration of hungry, swift players molded by exacting and demanding coaches.

Tennessee (10-1) rebounded admirably in Bowden Wyatt's second season of coaching in Knoxville. Wyatt employed the classic power-run oriented Single-Wing offense of his Volunteers mentor, Gen. Robert Neyland. The Vols used the mastery of do-all tailback Johnny Majors with the power running of fullback Tommy Bronson, surprise punting, and a swarming defense, led by end Buddy Cruze and tackle John Gordy. Tennessee beat Georgia Tech (10-1) in a conservative classic in November, but was upset by Baylor (9-2) in an ugly Sugar Bowl intensified by a violent kicking attack on Vols guard Bruce Burnham.

Iowa (9-1) surprisingly won its first Big Ten championship since 1921, thanks to the fierce line play of tackles Alex Karras and Dick Klein and end Jim Gibbons. Vital to Iowa's fine year was Forest Evashevski's conversion to the Wing-T offense, a puzzling, misdirection attack developed at little Delaware by Evashevski's former 1940 Michigan teammate, Davey Nelson. Big Ten and Rose Bowl MVP Kenny Ploen masterminded Iowa's offensive trickery and power from the quarterback slot, and remains one of the greatest one-year stars whose fame has dwindled to vague memory today.

Texas A&M (9-0-1) handed Texas Christian (8-3) its only Southwest Conference defeat, but was denied a Cotton Bowl trip when conference officials went against expectations and didn't lift sanctions late in the year. TCU, stymied all year by a slump from star runner Jim Swink, was left to contend with the great Jimmy Brown and Syracuse (7-2) in a memorable Cotton Bowl. Brown, who had scored a record 43 points against Colgate (4-5), tallied three touchowns against the Horned Frogs, but one of his conversion kicks was blocked, and TCU won a thriller 28-27. His 43 points scored in a single game was a mark that would last until 1990.

The Ivy League opened its first official, round robin schedule. Lowly Pennsylvania (4-5) beat Dartmouth (5-3-1) in early October to end the nation's longest losing streak at 19, the product of a murderous schedule the Quakers could no longer handle as the mid-1950s arrived. Yale (8-1) stumbled at mid-season against Colgate, but took the Ivy crown with a senior-laden squad, led by Paul Lopata, Mike Owseichik, Dean Loucks, Dennis McGill and Al Ward. Yale's critical victory came in a 42-20 mid-November stampede of runner-up Princeton (7-2).

Scandal ripped the Pacific Coast Conference as the conference levied sanctions against UCLA (7-3), Southern California (8-2), California (3-7), and Washington (5-5) for payment of slush funds to some players for half-baked or non-existent off-campus jobs, that were naively required by the conference to suppliment the mandatory 50-hours-per-month, on-campus job that each player maintained. The PCC was the only group in college football that required this unenforceable code, the other conferences having followed the footsteps of the Southeastern Conference and provided athletic scholarships—pretty well as we know them today—that covered tuition, room, board, and books. Washington coach John Cherberg had been fired after the 1955 season, and he vindictively blew the whistle on his school's slush fund that illegally enhanced student-athlete employment.

Be mindful that the uproar on the West Coast came in an era when there was a great deal of news coverage in favor of a "clean" brand of college pigskin. Depending upon one's perspective, this was either nobly gallant or piously hypocritical. Thus, the academicians and media found themselves cuddling together in the interest of non-professionalism or fighting at cross principles. With both local teams disassembled by PCC "do-gooders," The

Los Angeles Times ripped the college presidents and professors whose vision clearly conflicted with football-loving alumni and general sports fans.

The PCC penalties against the four schools were unusual and especially harsh, not so much on the schools, but on individual players. Seniors at the offending schools, whether they were individually guilty or not, were limited to participation in five games each, which were permitted to be arranged in consecutive blocks. USC seniors, for example, split their participation into first or second half-of-the-year segments that divided perfectly over the 10-game schedule. Defending PCC champion UCLA all but conceded a smashing loss to Michigan (7-2) on September 29 so it could align the schedules of its seniors to overlap a vengeful November 3 match with Stanford (4-6), the school that was at the core of the whistle-blowing. The Bruins crowned their year by upsetting the Indians 14-13 to help crush Stanford's Rose Bowl hopes. The big losers were the half-banned seniors, many of them innocent, but whose potential pro careers were damaged.

The scientists at Wilson Sporting Goods developed a "pebbleized" leather for a new ball with which about 40 colleges experimented. The new surface was touted as water-repellent and much easier to grip in rain and mud. The 12 teams of the National Football League also used the new ball, but college and pro ball had little else in common in 1956, especially television.

With the majority of homes in the United States furnished for the first time with (black and white) television sets, the NFL signed its first national contract with the CBS Network, which already boasted top-rated shows like "I Love Lucy," "The Jackie Gleason Show," and Ed Sullivan's "Toast of the Town." Under the direction of commissioner Bert Bell, the pros wisely delivered only road games in each of the big NFL markets and all games of regional interest to large areas of the country. For example, New York Giants games could be tuned in New York City, New England, New Jersey, and upstate New York. Los Angeles Rams contests were aired in all of southern California and in several states east of California. The occasional game of national interest went coast-to-coast over the airwaves. Meanwhile, the NCAA presented an inflexible, sometimes drab array of matches that were arranged months in advance.

Milestones

■ Eight, old northeast schools, which had pioneered college football in the 1800s, formally banded together for first time and pursued official Ivy League championship. During process, prodigal big-timer Pennsylvania was readmitted in good graces, while bowl games and spring practice were banned by members: Brown, Columbia, Cornell, Dartmouth, Harvard, Penn, Princeton, and Yale.

■ Michigan Normal, member of the Interstate Conference, changed its name to Eastern Michigan.

■ Football world mourned deaths of Hall of Famer Truxton Hare, 77, four-time All-America at Pennsylvania, and Claude "Tiny" Thornhill, 63, coach of three Rose Bowl teams at Stanford.

■ Longest winning streaks entering season:

Oklahoma 30	Miami (Ohio) 10	Mississippi 9

■ Coaching Changes:

	Incoming	Outgoing
Baylor	Sam Boyd	George Sauer
Brigham Young	Hal Kopp	Chick Atkinson
Colorado A&M	Don Mullison	Bob Davis
Maryland	Tommy Mont	Jim Tatum
Mississippi State	Wade Walker	Darrell Royal
Nebraska	Pete Elliott	Bill Glassford
New Mexico	Dick Clausen	Robert Tischenal
North Carolina	Jim Tatum	George Barclay
Northwestern	Ara Parseghian	Lou Saban
Purdue	Jack Mollenkopf	Stu Holcomb
Rutgers	John Stiegman	Harvey Harman
San Diego State	Paul Governali	Bill Schutte
South Carolina	Warren Giese	Rex Enright
Temple	Pete Stevens	Josh Cody
Virginia	Ben Martin	Ned McDonald
Wake Forest	Paul Amen	Tom Rogers
Washington	Darrell Royal	John Cherberg
Washington State	Jim Sutherland	Al Kirscher
Wisconsin	Milt Bruhn	Ivan Williamson

Preseason AP Poll

1	Oklahoma (111)	1427	11	Army	143
2	Michigan State (20)	1000	12	Tennessee (2)	122
3	Notre Dame (5)	882	13	Mississippi	101
4	Georgia Tech (3)	793	14	Stanford	92
5	Ohio State	703	15	Southern California (2)	78
6	Maryland	664	16	Duke	77
7	Texas Christian (2)	649	17	UCLA	53
8	Michigan (2)	477	18	Miami	46
9	Texas A&M	276	19	Yale	43
10	Pittsburgh (2)	217	20	Illinois	31

September 22, 1956

Pittsburgh 14 WEST VIRGINIA 13: Outplayed and outgained 239y to 96y by fired-up Mountaineers, favored Pittsburgh (1-0), touted as best in East, had to collect FUMs at 5 and 20YLs to prompt short 3rd Q TD sweeps that were scored moments apart. West Virginia (0-1) FB Larry Krutko lost handle on 1st play after Panthers FB-P Tom Jenkins accurately killed rolling punt at WVU 3YL. Sub Pitt HB Ray DiPasquale scored around LE 2 plays later for 7-6 lead. Mountaineers HB Ralph Anastasio lost FUM on next KO when he was snowed under by gang of Panthers, and another sub Pitt HB, Nick Passodelis, quickly made it 14-6, skirting LE for 5y. WVU, which had pointed to opener with its biggest rival by counting down days on locker room chalkboard, got 2nd and 4th Q TD sneaks from QB Mickey Trimarki. But, Mountaineers T-K Jim Pickett had his 2nd Q conv kick sail wide. Pickett also missed 25y FG try in 4th Q and was replaced by T-K Dick Guesman, who also missed late FG try from 41y away.

SOUTH CAROLINA 7 Duke 0: ACC favorite Duke (0-1) lost its 1st-ever conf game after 3 years, coach Bill Murray's 1st loss in 6 openers. Methodical Gamecocks (1-0) cruised 81y on 18 plays—mostly option runs—to score in 2nd Q on 1y plunge by soph HB King Dixon (14/46y, TD). Drive featured fortunate 4th down catch of deflected pass by E Julius Derrick. With 267y of O, South Carolina enjoyed 193y to 156y edge on ground, and sub G Nelson Weston and C Charlie Johnson starred on D in coach Warren Giese's debut.

North Carolina State 26 NORTH CAROLINA 6: "Like old br'er rabbit going back to the briar patch" was how coach Jim Tatum described his return to Chapel Hill where he starred as T in 1930s. Tatum and staff wore Carolina blue cowboy hats, but must have wanted to hide under them as NC State (1-0) got 1st win over Tar Heels (0-1) in 14 years. QB Tom Katich hit E John Collar for 2 of NC State's 4 TD throws. Tar Heels HB Ed Sutton swept 17y before HB Jim Varnum raced 19y to State 20YL in 2nd Q. Sutton then dragged 3 tacklers for 20y TD, but T-K Phil Blazer missed conv. UNC was back in game, trailing 7-6. But, Wolfpack answered immediately with 61y TD march, highlighted by HB Dick Christy's 17y run and capped by Kanitch's 22y TD pitch to E Bob Pepe. Afterward Christy wanted to know: "Where's Jim Tatum's All-Americans now?" referring to coach's group of stars who helped him win at Maryland.

Syracuse 26 MARYLAND 12: Winners of 15 straight regular season games, preseason no. 6 Maryland (0-1) got caught with long inactive list, including oddities such as HB Howard Dare's yellow jaundice and QB Frank Tamburello's pending call to military draft. Terps HB John McVicker raced 67y to set up opening score by QB John Fritsch for 6-0 lead in 1st Q. Fritsch and HB Bob Rusevlyan miscued on 2nd Q handoff, and Syracuse (1-0) E Dick Lasse snatched midair FUM and ran 68y to score for 13-6 edge. Orangemen HB Jimmy Brown powered to 154y rushing, scored on 1st Q pass catch and 4th Q 3y run, and inserted critical 78y 3rd Q run to Terrapins 7YL. Subsequent Syracuse 4y TD pass from QB Chuck Zimmerman (5-6 passing) to HB Jim Ridlon broke it open at 19-6.

Georgia Tech 14 KENTUCKY 6: Georgia Tech (1-0) sub QB Toppy Vann threw perfect 5y TD jump pass to E Ted Smith at end of 80y 2nd Q drive. Keys to Tech's long effort were HB George Volkert's 20y dash and Vann's 4th down 12y pass to HB Paul Rotenberry to 8YL. In 3rd Q, so T Ormand Anderson convoyed Volkert on 54y TD run for 14-0 lead. Kentucky (0-1) D, led by T Lou Michaels, allowed only 223y, but O managed but 161y and scored its only TD by QB Delmar Hughes with 26 secs left after Vann's lost FUM at Yellow Jackets 13YL.

Florida 26 MISSISSIPPI STATE 0: Soph QB Billy Stacy debuted to lead his Maroons (0-1) to overwhelming, but hollow 259y to 93y O advantage. Key to verdict was Florida (1-0) FB-LB Joe Brodsky picking off 3 INTs and supplying hidden 162y in thrilling RETs. Brodsky authored 35y TD RET and carried another 27y to set up another score. In 4th Q, Stacy drove Bulldogs downfield, only to be hit by Gators T Vel Heckman as he tossed wide pass. Brodsky stepped in front of throw and whisked his 3rd INT untouched for 100y TD RET; September's excessive heat forced him to pass out briefly while suppine in EZ.

Oregon 35 COLORADO 0: Record crowd in Boulder received early warning of what was to come from marauding Ducks (1-0). Oregon zipped 52y to score in 14 tidy plays early in 1st Q. Colorado (0-1) looked to tie it in 2nd Q when DB Boyd Dowler's INT was returned 33y to Ducks 3YL. But, Oregon D rose up and stopped 4 runs that gained only 1y. Oregon exploded for 28 pts in 2nd H as HB Jim Shanley scored on 64y pass from QB Tom Crabtree and on 2y plunge. Oregon outgained Buffs 444y to 102y.

SOUTHERN METHODIST 19 Notre Dame 13: In their 68th year of football, Fighting Irish (0-1) lost their 1st-ever game in any September as SMU (1-0) QB Charlie Arnold passed 31y to slender E Boyd Waggoner for 1st Q TD and later sneaked over for 13-0 H lead. Notre Dame had only itself to blame: each TD was promoted by variety of Irish PENs. In all, ND was flagged for 137y. But, Irish QB-P Paul Hornung passed 55y TD to HB Jim Morse in 3rd Q and gambled in 4th Q with 57y fake-punt run that knotted it 13-13. As clock ticked toward apparent tie, Arnold and HB Lon Slaughter collaborated on 31y pass to ND 14YL, and Arnold quickly dusted off Statue of Liberty run around LE for Slaughter's winning 14y TD sprint. It came with 1:40 left to play. Irish vainly went to Ponies 7YL at end, but could not score.

Southern California 44 TEXAS 20: Texas (0-1) made early-game stop at its 39YL and gained short-lived 7-0 lead when QB Joe Clements broke around LE behind brilliant blocking for 36y TD run. Then, Southern California (1-0) FB C.R. Roberts took over, rushing 12/251y, including long TDs of 73, 50, and 74y. Roberts broke USC's single game rushing record which had been on books since 1929. Trojans TB Jon Arnett propelled lead to 19-7 at H with 12 and 14y runs that followed BB-DB Wayne Kurlak's 2nd Q INT RET to Texas 26YL. Roberts clicked on his 3rd long run early in 3rd Q, and Arnett soon fired 38y TD pass to WB Don Hickman. Longhorns tallied on 17y TD pass by QB Vince Matthews to E Bob Bryant in 3rd Q and HB Walt Fondren's late 4y run up middle.

Baylor 7 CALIFORNIA 6: Intersectional battle of Bears turned into sloppy opener: Both Bruno teams suffered 100y in PENs, while Baylor (1-0) lost 4 FUMs and INT. California (0-1) E-DE Ron Wheatcroft recovered 1st Q FUM by Baylor HB Bobby Peters at Texans' 36YL. It took 11 plays to cash in on QB Gus Gianulias' 4th down 11y TD pass to E Roger Ramseier. But, x-pt snap was bobbled, and holder Gianulias got bright idea of trying to run it over GL. Bad idea: Baylor D swamped him to keep score at 6-0. Early in 2nd Q, Baylor FB Reuben Saage battered to Cal 2YL, but lost FUM to HB-DB Nat Brazill. LB Saage quickly turned tables by causing Gianulias to cough up FUM to Baylor E-DE Tony DeGrazier at California 10YL. Just 1 play later, Baylor HB Del Shofner swept wide for option pitchout, dribbled ball but kept control for TD. Baylor soph HB-K Arthur "Junior" Beall booted vital x-pt in his varsity debut. California enjoyed balanced attack with 107y rushing and 17-28/188y passing. Baylor ran for 255y, but passed only 2-7/9y.

AP Poll September 24

1 Oklahoma (91)	1150	11 Texas A&M	291
2 Georgia Tech (12)	946	12 Stanford (4)	249
3 Michigan State (9)	914	13 Michigan	241
4 Texas Christian (4)	792	14 Notre Dame	142
5 Southern Methodist (10)	627	15 Vanderbilt	94
6 Southern California (12)	591	16 Army	80
7 Syracuse (4)	469	17 South Carolina	71
8 Ohio State	458	18 Oregon	67
9 Mississippi	305	19 Florida (2)	60
10 Pittsburgh (2)	296	20 North Carolina State	53

September 29, 1956

(Fri) SOUTHERN CALIFORNIA 21 Oregon State 13: Just before KO, it was uncovered that Beavers WB-DB Sam Wesley may have attended little Lincoln University, and nation's leading intercepter of 1955 was held out of game for fear of eligibility reprisal from PCC. Swift HB "Jaguar" Jon Arnett (13/88y, 2 TDs) ran for 10y score on game's opening series and for 2y TD at end of 69y voyage just before H as Trojans (2-0) built 21-7 lead at intermission. Beavers TB Joe Francis had scored on short TD near end of 1st Q to briefly tie it 7-7. Pair of Oregon State (1-1) whippets from L.A.—TB Paul Lowe (11/74y, TD) and WB Earnell Durden (8/71y), later asst coach with L.A. Raiders—nearly ran Southern California to defeat in 2nd H. Troy was spared thanks in part to its 3 RECs of 6 Beaver bobbles, with biggest coming at end of OSC's 75y march. It was launched by C-LB Buzz Randall's INT late in 3rd Q, and Beavers then gnawed their way from their 24YL to USC 1YL. But Trojans T-DT Monte Clark stopped threat by pouncing on Francis' FUM.

PITTSBURGH 14 Syracuse 7: Revived from previous week's near loss to West Virginia, big Pitt (2-0) line practically chained itself to Syracuse (1-1) HB Jimmy Brown, holding him to somewhat modest 14/52y rushing. Yet, Orangemen gained 7-0 edge on 55y INT TD RET by FB-DB Ed Coffin. After QB Corny Salvaterra sneaked to 1y TD to tie it at end of 39y drive in 2nd Q, Pitt's decisive TD came on QB Darrell Lewis' left-handed 19y TD flip to E Joe Walton in 3rd Q. Salvaterra and Lewis were perfect alternating directorial pieces of Panthers' Split-T option O, which had probed deep into Syracuse territory twice in 1st Q. Pitt HB-K Ambrose "Bags" Bagamery, who made both his conv kicks, missed 26y FG try, and Orange stopped other threat on downs.

YALE 19 Connecticut 14: Highly-rated Yale (1-0) sprung QB Dean Loucks for 56y TD run on game's 3rd play, but fell behind 14-6 at H on Connecticut (0-2) TDs by FB Paul Whitley and HB Lenny King. Elis dominated 3rd Q with Loucks' 29y TD pass to E Mike Cavallon and 73y scoring march ended by HB Dennis McGill's TD. Overlooked UConn Huskies rallied with late 55y drive that expired on Yale 3YL as clock reached 0:00.

Tennessee 35 AUBURN 7: Except for late 98y TD drive, Auburn (0-1) was checked with 86y O by swooping Volunteers (1-0) DEs Buddy Cruze, Roger Urbano and Edd Cantrell. Tennessee TB Johnny Majors hit Cruze with pass to set up 1st Q TD. With 3 mins to play in H, Majors found elusive Cruze for 34y TD. When Tigers HB Bobby Hoppe fumbled ensuing KO to Vols T John Gordy, Majors quickly hit Cantrell for TD and comfortable 21-0 H cushion. Tennessee FB Tommy Bronson crashed over in 3rd Q after Plainsmen QB Jimmy Cook lost FUM at his 17YL. Auburn's 6th FUM set stage for UT's last TD in 4th Q, but Tigers' long march finally put them in EZ as HB Lloyd Nix banged across.

GEORGIA 3 Florida State 0: Amazingly tight game was borne out in stats: Georgia (1-1) ran 55 plays to gain 214y and Florida State (1-1) matched those figures exactly. Through scoreless 1st H, Bulldogs were buried in own end by precision punts of Seminoles HB-P Bobby Renn. Each team threatened in 3rd Q, but deadlock marched into middle of 4th Q. Using quick pitchouts and own 11y sprint, QB Lee Corso (3-8/16y, INT passing and 13/43y rushing) moved FSU from own 17YL to midfield when Georgia QB-DB Billy Hearn leaped high to steal Corso's pass from hands of E Ronnie Schomberger at UGa 38YL. With clock ticking toward 5:00 to go, Hearn keyed drive with 10y pass, and when it stalled, big E-K Ken Cooper nailed 43y FG, longest to that point in Sanford Stadium history.

FLORIDA 20 Clemson 20: Florida (1-0-1) C-LB Bill Bolton had fluctuating late-game adventures. Bolton dropped easy INT that would have ended Tigers' rallying TD drive, but came back to salvage tie with block of PEN-delayed x-pt kick. Tigers recovered Gators FUM on game's opening scrimmage and went 45y to FB Rudy Hayes' 2y TD run. After 1st Q punt, Clemson (1-0-1) drove 54y to HB Joel Wells' 2y TD slant behind block of RG John Grdijan. Trailing 14-0, little Florida QB Jimmy Dunn created short TD drive that ended on FB Joey Brodsky's TD run after HB Jackie Simpson lent 38y punt RET to Tigers 21YL. Down 14-13 in 3rd Q, Gators pounced on FUM at Clemson 14YL, and sent HB John Symank off T for his 2nd TD and 20-14 lead. With 2 min left, Symank lost handoff FUM atTigers 32YL. Tigers E-DE Willie Smith recovered, and QB Charlie Bussey engineered 68y drive, including his 11y gallop away from hard rush

on 4th-and-3 at Gators 29YL. FB Bob Spooner slashed over from 1YL, and after 5y delay PEN, QB-K Horace Turbeville's x-pt appeared to give Clemson 21-20 victory. Turbeville had to rekick when Tigers were caught holding, and Bolton blocked x-pt try.

Texas A&M 9 LOUISIANA STATE 6: With Mike II replacing recently-deceased Old Mike as roaring LSU Tigers (0-1) mascot, home team put up terrific D battle against Texas Aggies (2-0), who could brag of perhaps nation's best D group. Texas A&M scored 8 mins into 1st Q as QB Bobby Joe Conrad found sub HB Carlos Esquivel for 14y TD toss. LSU HB Olin Renfroe took ensuing KO 44y for good field position, which, along with Renfroe's later 12y run after poor Aggie punt, created Tigers threat until Renfroe lost FUM to A&M HB-DB Loyd Taylor at Aggies 17YL. QB-P Roddy Osborne pinned LSU deep in its own end in 3rd Q, and when C Dee Powell blocked punt it rolled through EZ for safety that built A&M's lead to 9-0. LSU QB Win Turner made 21y sweep that contributed to 83y drive in 4th Q that ended with 10y TD run by soph HB J.W. Brodnax.

MICHIGAN 42 Ucla 13: UCLA (1-1), required to restrict its sr players to any 5 consecutive games due to PCC probation, chose to virtually hand win to ambitious Michigan (1-0) so that full compliment of Bruins would be available for November 3 revenge game against Stanford. Youthful Bruins were no match for experienced Wolverines line. Big soph FB John Herrnstein, son and nephew of past Wolverine stars and future Philadelphia Phillies outfielder, scored twice in 1st Q, following 11y Bruins punt and Michigan HB Terry Barr's 45y RET of QK. Superb E Ron Kramer slipped behind UCLA TB-DB Don Long for 70y TD reception as Wolverines built leads of 28-0 at H and 35-7 at end of 3rd Q. FB Barry Billington and E Dick Wallen scored 2nd H TDs for UCLA.

ILLINOIS 32 California 20: HB John Stewart slanted left for 2 and 37y TD runs to provide 14-0 lead for California (0-2). C-LB Bill Cooper quickly pounced on FUM, and Bears trotted off at H with stunning 20-0 advantage after QB Joe Contestabile's 12y TD strike to E Norm Becker. "Team effort," according to Illini (1-0) coach Ray Eliot contributed to dramatic Illinois turnaround in hectic 6:36 of 3rd Q. Illinois FB Ray Nitschke lost FUM near Cal GL early in 3rd Q, and HB Abe Woodson outhustled 2 Bears for loose ball in EZ. Illini QB Hiles Stout quickly sneaked over for TD and followed with 20y TD pass to Woodson. Less than min later, FB-LB Jack Delveaux pressured Contestabile into fluttering pass, and C-LB Ken Sutter's 12y INT TD RET put Illinois ahead 26-20. Stout (9-17/153y, 2 TDs, INT) passed 11y to HB Harry Jefferson early in 4th Q to finalize reversal.

OKLAHOMA 36 North Carolina 0: Coming off narrow loss to Sooners in 1955 opener, North Carolina (0-2) hoped that last week's game under its belt would serve them well in trip to gusty Norman against no. 1 Oklahoma (1-0). Wise Sooners coach Bud Wilkinson fretted slightly over his new team: "I hope everyone tries as hard this year as last…very few people try as hard to stay good as they do to get good." Wilkinson need not have worried. Oklahoma's 1st TD didn't come until 8:31 into 2nd Q on QB Jay O'Neal's 17y run with questionable backward lateral. Next score was put into position by FB Billy Pricer's 78y QK to 7YL and it was delivered as HB Clendon Thomas ripped 12y. DB Thomas made INT and flipped lateral to HB-mate Tommy McDonald, who dashed 40y to 11YL. That big play poised Sooners' next score, McDonald's 4y TD catch from QB Jimmy Harris for 21-0 lead 44 secs before H. Scrubs contributed TD and safety in 4th Q. Carolina made 93y rushing against cat-quick Oklahomans and passed 3-12/47y. Heels' best threat was ignited by T-DT Stuart Pell's FUM REC at Sooners 40YL in 3rd Q, but QB Doug Farmer suffered INT by C-LB Bob Harrison at OU 5YL on 4th down.

COLORADO 34 Kansas State 0: Colorado (1-1) utterly turned around their fortunes after its mistake-strewn loss to Oregon. Buffs line, led by Es Jerry Leahy and Wally Merz and T Bob Salerno, soundly outhit Kansas State (0-2) forwards, and their rushing ace, FB John Bayuk (10/26y), made up for lack of run production with thunderous blocks on inside reverses for slender WB Eddie Dove (5/74y, TD). Colorado went to T-formation on 3rd-and-goal at Wildcat 5YL in 2nd Q, and TB Gene Worden took pitchout for TD. Buffaloes stampeded for 20 pts in 3rd Q as QB Boyd Dowler sparked it with 4th-and-2 gamble for 1st down from K-State 33YL. Dowler later caught 57y TD pass from sub TB Howard Cook. Wildcats managed 190y rushing, but had to punt 8 times, registered only 8 1st downs, and never penetrating Bison 20YL.

Georgia Tech 9 SOUTHERN METHODIST 7: After Yellow Jackets FB Dickie Mattison killed QK at SMU 3YL in 1st Q, Georgia Tech (2-0) held Mustangs. Tech G Don Miller then poured through to block punt for safety. Little Wingback Jimmy Thompson sparked 77y 3rd Q sortie and 9-0 lead with 32y scoot followed by his 4y TD run. SMU (1-1) G Tom Koenig's 4th Q FUM REC paved way for QB Charlie Arnold's 30y TD pass to HB Lon Slaughter, but Tech D was able to halt Mustangs at its own 8 and 17YLs in late going.

Michigan State 21 STANFORD 7: Some football historians could attribute modern "West Coast O" to Stanford's 1956 team. Indians (1-1) used their star sr QB John Brodie and sub QB Jack Douglas for ball possession via short passing. Brodie utilized 5-8/40y in air, mixed in 12 runs, and took Stanford to TD that tied it at 7-7 in 2nd Q. Scoring play came on Brodie's 2y lob netted by FB Lou Valli. Brodie was injured late in 1st H, and Michigan State (1-0) soon employed more diligent 5-man pass rush. Spartans' superior depth began to tell and splendid ball control, good for 10 min at outset of 3rd Q, resulted in FB Don Gilbert's 1y TD run. Michigan State scored again after FUM and held ball for 29 plays to Tribe's 5 in 3rd Q. Douglas' 4 incompletions spoiled Stanford's 4th Q chance, that came after it blocked punt by Spartans HB-P Clarence Peaks.

Minnesota 34 WASHINGTON 14: Home-standing Huskies (1-1) were favored, but Golden Gophers (1-0) showed typical Big 10 depth to win going away. Transfer Bobby Cox, star Huskies soph QB in 1954, returned to Seattle to haunt his old mates. Gophers Cox broke 7-7 2nd Q tie with 3y TD pass to HB Dave Lindblom after enormous Minnesota T Ed Buckingham recovered FUM at Washington 30YL. March of 75y at

outset of 3rd Q gave Gophers 21-7 lead as FB Rich Borstad scored, and Washington hope soon died as FB Jimmy Jones neared Gopher GL on 12y burst, but lost FUM to Minnesota HB-DB Dick McNamara.

October 6, 1956

(Fri) MIAMI 27 Boston College 6: Miami's forward wall spilled Boston College (0-1) QB Billy Donlan (8-18/106y, 2 INTs) 5 times while trying to pass, and Hurricanes (2-0) HB-DB John "Rebel" Bookman collared 3 INTs. Bookman picked off Donlan in 3rd Q and dashed 34y to BC 21YL to poise HB John Varone's powerful TD plunge. Bookman capped night's scoring with 82y sprint down sideline with another INT. Earlier, Miami QB Bonnie Yarborough flipped 9y TD pass to E Phil Bennett after T Gary Greaves pounced on Eagle FUM 1 play prior. BC HB-DB Alan Miller stepped in front of errant Canes flat pass in 2nd Q and returned it 55y to score. Eagles E Dick Reagan's x-pt was blocked by Varone to conserve 7-6 Miami lead with 11 mins remaining before H.

(Fri) UCLA 6 Oregon 0: Blunders by Ducks (2-1) allowed UCLA (2-1) to camp continually in Oregon territory, but without malice until Uclan E Dick Wallen's early 4th Q FUM REC at Duck 1YL became too tantalizing to pass up. Bruin TB Don Long (14/88y, TD) drove off right side for game's only score 1:28 into 4th Q, but not before UCLA off-side PEN pushed it back to 6YL. Excellent sideline-to-sideline Bruins D, led by C-LB Jim Matheny who played 60 mins, held Oregon speedsters to 128y rushing and 2.2y avg. In 1st H, Bruins lost ball on downs 3 times after gaining FUM at Oregon 19YL, getting WB Chuck Hollaway's 34y punt RET to 12YL, and driving 50y to Ducks 7YL.

PENNSYLVANIA 14 Dartmouth 7: Penn's 19-game losing streak, spawned by its unreasonable schedule, was halted by softer competition in its 1st official Ivy League game. Dartmouth (1-1) struck 1st on QB, and future Cincinnati Bengals director, Mike Brown's sneak after he hit E Monte Pascoe 48y arrow. Big Green coach Bob Blackman then sent in his weak 2nd unit, and Penn (1-1) HB John Wright bolted 56y to set up tying score by HB Neil Hyland. Solid tackling by Quakers, especially sub T Dennis Troychak, forced FUMs that twice ended Indians sorties into scoring territory. After 2nd REC, Penn went 73y to winning score on 25y TD pass from QB Rich Ross to E Dick Schafer in 2nd Q. As good news of 14-7 lead spread across campus, Franklin Field began to fill with happy students, who carried Wright off on shoulders after final whistle.

ARMY 14 Penn State 7: Cadets (2-0) struck for 1st Q TD drives of 55 and 41y, then hung on with key plays on D: QB-DB Bob Kyasky had 2nd Q INT of Nittany Lions QB Milt Plum (4-17/33y, INT) and Es Art Johnson and Dick Stephenson combined for 14y sack of Plum. Penn State (1-1) got back in game as G-LB Joe Sabal had INT of Kyasky at Army 33YL late in 3rd Q. Lions HB Bruce Gilmore's 31y sprint to 2YL set up FB Maurice Schleicher's TD plunge early in 4th Q. Kyasky saved win in late going by fending off Penn State blocker and pushing Gilmore OB at Cadets 41YL after 54y run. This bid died when Lions were called for ineligible receiver downfield PEN at Army 36YL.

Baylor 14 MARYLAND 0: For 1st time in 70 games, once-mighty, but injury-riddled Maryland (1-2) was blanked. Baylor (3-0) scored its markers in middle Qs. Bears QB Doyle Traylor converted pass on 3rd-and-9 to E Earl Miller at Terp 5YL, and HB Del Shofner slanted off RT for TD at tail end of 82y assault. Bear backups dominated 3rd Q and keyed score as HB Art Beall (9/42y) caught 11y pass at Maryland 9YL and scored 4 plays later. Slow-moving Turtles shaded Baylor 217y to 201y on O and made advances to 7 and 14YLs, only to have PENs and FUMs ruin their scoring challenges.

SOUTH CAROLINA 14 North Carolina 0: Perplexed North Carolina (0-3) coach Jim Tatum, struggling with his O in new job, finally got Tar Heels rolling in 1st H against his former Maryland asst. New mentor Warren Giese was enjoying more success to date in his debut season at South Carolina (3-1); some insiders said, "Tatum lost his brains to South Carolina." Tar Heels came up pt-less in 1st H that found them advancing to Gamecocks 14 and 1 YLs only to lose ball on downs. New QB Dave Reed (2-7 passing) also moved UNC to 4YL, but H clock expired. USC, which finished with 233y rushing, powered 96y on drive that spanned 3rd and 4th Q break as soph HB King Dixon (91/97y, TD) slipped through RT for last 3 runs and 7-0 lead. Gamecocks went 58y to QB Mackie Prickett's short TD plunge late in 4th Q. Heels, held without 1st down for 29 mins, used HB Daley Goff's 43y KO RET and 22y catch to threaten at end.

Tennessee 33 DUKE 20: TB Johnny "Drum" Majors (7/105y rushing) shined through rain-splattered afternoon to lead Tennessee (2-0) to rout of Duke (1-2). Vols led 19-13 at H, and Majors was key instrument. He punted 51y, Duke soon was pushed back to 1YL by PEN, and Vols took over on Duke 26YL after weak punt out. Majors skipped through big hole at RT and raced 17y to score, then added 28y TD run over LT at end of 5-play, 73y fling. Marching methodically on Split-T dive runs, Duke traveled on 69 and 71y TD drives, capped by short runs by QB Bob Broadhead and HB Bob Honeycutt. In between, Tennessee went 71y to FB Tommy Bronson's 1y TD leap, drive highlighted by Majors' 36y dash. Al Carter, Majors' TB understudy, ran for 2y TD and pitched 60y TD bomb to WB Bill Anderson in 3rd Q to put verdict away.

Vanderbilt 32 ALABAMA 7 (Mobile): Sleek Vanderbilt (3-0) ship sailed through eager but overmatched Alabama (0-2) for Commodores' largest win margin in 34-game series. After Tide had better of play in 1st Q, Vandy FB Jimmy Ray burst for 47y run to Bama 9YL early in 2nd Q, and QB Don Orr flipped TD pass to HB Jack Hudson. Sub QB Boyce Smith clicked on 3 passes to set up HB Danny McCall's 4y TD plunge, and Commodores enjoyed 13-0 H lead. Vandy HB Phil King dominated 52y TD march in 3rd Q with 1st of his 2 TD runs. Alabama got on scoreboard in 3rd Q on 57y move after 2nd H KO; HB Don Comstock chipped in 15 and 7y runs before diving over. Vanderbilt enjoyed 73 and 72y TD trips in 4th Q, but lost Orr to broken jaw. History rarely found Commodores condescending to Bama, but coach Art Guepe chirped about foe: "Alabama…will win some games if they play football instead of boxing."

Michigan State 9 MICHIGAN 0: After scoreless 1st H in which Michigan (1-1) used surprisingly-active pass attack (11-21/79y) to march up and down gridiron without scoring, Spartans (2-0) got 3rd Q break on G-LB Arch Matsos' INT of Michigan FB John Herrnstein. C-K John Matsko soon made good on his 1st-ever FG try of 30y, and Michigan State led 3-0. Inspired Spartans forced Herrnstein's early 4th Q FUM, and it led to 5y TD run by sub MSU HB Dennis Mendyk. Boys will be boys: wee-hour Friday night maize and blue painting party up road in East Lansing was halted by Michigan State campus police, and 4 UM students were required to relinquish tickets to next 3 games at Michigan Stadium and be confined to dormitories during those games.

MINNESOTA 21 Purdue 14: Surprising Golden Gophers (2-0), picked universally for lower middle of Big 10, stepped into possible title picture with 2nd H rally. Purdue (1-1) took 14-7 H lead on QB Len Dawson's 49y bomb to HB Erich Barnes. Dawson finished so-so day with 7-13/102y, TD, 3 INTs. Minnesota FB Rich Borstad and HB Ken Bombardier rebutted with 3rd Q TDs for 21-14 gain. Gophers beefy D played brilliantly in 4th Q, as QB-DB Dick Larson stopped Boilermakers HB Tom Fletcher on 4th down run at 3YL and C-LB Bernie Svendsen intercepted Dawson at Minny 35YL.

OHIO STATE 32 Stanford 20: Stanford (1-2) filled air with 39 passes, mostly by QB John Brodie (21-35/256y, 2 TDs, INT), to gain 20-20 3rd Q deadlock. Brodie led Stanford TD marches of 80, 83, and 52y. Big LT Troy Barbee lined up in T-eligible position and grabbed 4y TD from Brodie in 3rd Q. Indians E Joel Freis caught 24y pass in 4th Q, but coughed up FUM to Ohio HB-DB Joe Cannavino to set up winning TD, scored by HB Don Clark. FB-LB Galen Cisco made INT to set up Buckeyes' last score: HB Clark's 18y TD toss to HB Jim Roseboro. Buckeyes' meager passing stats: 1-2/18y, TD.

IOWA 14 Oregon State 13: Nobody could have foreseen this Rose Bowl preview. Iowa (2-0) spent most of day overcoming bad start as Oregon State (1-2) scored in 2 plays after opening KO FUM REC. Beavers TB Joe Francis threw 30y TD to WB Earnell Durden for early 7-0 advantage. In 3rd Q, sub TB Paul Lowe scooted 49y to give Oregon State sobering 13-0 lead. Hawkeye natives no doubt were getting restless as their team had underachieved for last 2 years. Iowa FB John Nocera ignited 4th Q rally, battering to 10YL, and then Nocera threw surprise TD pass to E Frank Gilliam. When Beavers fumbled ensuing KO, Hawkeyes happily countered with 33y TD pass by QB Randy Duncan and winning conv by E-K Bob Prescott, his 2nd x-pt.

Colorado 26 KANSAS 25: Each team scored in every Q as Big 7 tilt swung on nullified tying x-pt by Kansas (0-2-1) C-K Galen Wahlmeier, who missed longer kick in 4th Q after PEN by lineman who rocked slightly offside. Seesaw battle opened in unusual fashion: Buffaloes (2-1) E-DE Jerry Leahy burst through to swipe handoff from Jayhawkers QB Dave Preston, which Leahy took unmolested for 7y TD in 1st 5 mins. KU QB Bob Marshall came in for next series and whipped up long TD drive off option runs: HB Bobby Robinson made 21y sprint, Marshall hit E Jim Letcavits for 14y pass, and Marshall scored from 1YL. Kansas threatened in 2nd Q as HB Charley McCue (10/103y, TD) raced 30y, but Colorado held at its 27YL and powered 73y to 14-7 lead as TB Howard Cook (18/184y, 2 TDs) scored his 1st TD. TB Bob Stransky's poor QK positioned Jayhawks at Buffs 39YL for FB Homer Floyd's 24y TD catch. Floyd broke through LG Don Pfutzenreuter's block early in 3rd Q for 36y run and Kansas' 1st lead at 19-14. DB Cook made INT to set up his own TD in last 2 secs of 3rd Q, which put Bison ahead 20-19. Leahy threw key block to spring Stransky for 80y TD jaunt for 26-19 edge.

TEXAS CHRISTIAN 41 Arkansas 6: TCU (2-0) HB Ken Wineburg was so alone for 11y 1st Q TD reception from QB Chuck Curtis that he may as well have been disguised as grass. Wineburg (11/89y) also bolted to beautifully-faked, 46y counter TD run in 2nd Q. Arkansas (2-1), hopeful SWC title darkhorse, made early 3rd Q threat, but slender sub QB Don Christian, in for injured George Walker, lost FUM at TCU 27YL. Horned Frog A-A HB Jim Swink (15/71y) caught 36y pass in answering drive to set up Curtis' TD sneak and tallied himself at outset of 4th Q. Razorbacks' only score came in 4th Q on 11 plays good for 74y and TD by FB Gerald Nesbitt (10/40y).

RICE 23 Louisiana State 14: QB Frank Ryan (8-14/133y, TD, INT) came up with 2 big plays in 1st H, so speedy Rice (2-0) took 13-7 lead. After Bengals' roughing PEN negated Rice punt and allowed Owls to keep ball near midfield, Ryan arched long pass to superb soph E Buddy Dial who beat LSU (0-2) HB-DB Matt Burns for 51y TD. Tigers answered in 2nd Q when 4th-team FB Steve Thompson barreled over to tie it 7-7. Rice reached LSU 32YL in 2nd Q, and Ryan faded to pass, faked throw, and lit out for GL on scramble that brought Owls' 2nd TD. FB-K Jerry Hall made 28y FG in 3rd Q, and Houstonians' HB Howard Hoelscher broke away for spectacular 55y TD run in 4th Q. LSU's Burns got some measure of TD-revenge when he scored on 10y pass in 4th Q after HB J.W. Brodnax rambled 52y to Owls 15YL.

AP Poll October 8

1 Oklahoma (76)	1185	11 Miami (1)	137
2 Michigan State (32)	1065	12 Michigan	109
3 Georgia Tech (4)	793	13 Vanderbilt	107
4 Texas Christian (7)	740	14 Navy	83
5 Ohio State (1)	735	15 Army	82
6 Tennessee (5)	588	16 George Washington (1)	79
7 Mississippi (2)	483	17 Minnesota	75
8 Southern California	313	18 Notre Dame	55
9 Texas A&M	165	19 Southern Methodist	53
10 Baylor	150	20tSouth Carolina	21
		20tWest Virginia	21

October 13, 1956

(Fri) MIAMI 13 Maryland 6: Back home in College Park, Maryland (1-3) students hung plaintiff banner on newly opened library: "We'll swap this building for one good quarterback." Injury-devastated Terrapins, without 9 of top 22 players, lost only 2 starters this time in Orange Bowl stadium. Stunting D of Hurricanes kept Terps off balance most of stormy night. Miami (3-0) QBs Sam Scarnecchia (3-4/50y, TD) and Bonnie Yarborough (4-5/45y, TD) each threw TD pass for 13-0 lead by 3rd Q. Maryland QB-P John Fritsch punted twice for 17y each against 30 mph wind, but 88y with same zephyr. Miami sub HB Ed "Porky" Oliver dashed 50y on punt RET to set up Scarnecchia's 2nd Q 22y TD pass to HB Rebel Bookman, but with hardship as Miami overcame 20y in PENs. In last 5 mins of 4th Q, Fred Petrella, trying to become Terps' "one good QB," completed 4 passes, including 23y arrow to E Dick Porter, through driving rain to set up Petrella's 1y TD sneak on 4th down with :40 on clock.

SYRACUSE 27 West Virginia 20: HB Jimmy Brown, big Syracuse (2-1) runner, contributed 22/165y and 2 TDs on ground, and Brown was difference on O and D in otherwise even contest. West Virginia (2-2) never led, but tied it 13-13 in 2nd Q and maintained deadlock until Syracuse's 2 scores in 4th Q for 27-13 edge. Orangemen HB-DB Jim Ridlon made INT RET to WVU 18YL, and Brown raced around RE for 6-0 lead in 1st Q. Sub pass duo, QB Alex Szuch's looping throw to E John Bowles, tied it 6-6 for Mountaineers later in 1st Q. Syracuse sub QB Fred Kuczala passed to E Nick Baccile for 35y to set up Kuczala's 5y TD run on last play of 1st Q. WVU FB Larry Krutko was bullwark for answering TD and H tie. DB Brown made vital INT (Syracuse's 3rd theft of WVU QB Mickey Trimarki) in 3rd Q and rammed ball downfield for FB Ed Coffin's 1y TD.

MISSISSIPPI 16 Vanderbilt 0: Veteran Rebels (4-0) derailed blooming dreams of hopeful Vanderbilt (3-1) as FB-K Paige Cothren kicked to date SEC-record 3 FGs: 26, 27, and 35y. Vandy's meager O (35y) resulted in part from QB Don Orr's injury and mostly from Ole Miss' smothering D, led by Ts Billy Yelverton and Gene Hickerson, and G Charles Duck. Commodores penetrated only to Rebels 45 and 40YLs. In its 13th straight victory, Ole Miss marched up and down field to tune of 347y but made only single TD: QB John Blalack's 8y TD pass to HB Gayle Bowman in 4th Q.

TULANE 21 Navy 6: Fast-improving Tulane (3-1) knifed through New Orleans heat and humidity with TD drives of 74, 63 and 59y behind crunching blocks of T Dalton Truax, C Don Miller, and G Wilbur Troxclair. Led by slashing runs of HB Boo Mason, Green Wave gained 300y on ground to allow them to profit from QB Gene Newton's TD passes to E Will Billon and Mason. Mason's 4th Q TD resulted from his pair of 19y runs. Navy (2-1) reserves were in game when it scored late TD on QB Gus Prahalis' 11y toss to E John Ruth. Middies E-DE Earle Smith sparkled with blocked FG and FUM REC.

MICHIGAN 48 Army 14: While Army (2-1) was looking inept by losing 6 of 8 FUMs, Michigan (2-1) cashed 5 FUM RECs for TDs on way to 48-0 lead by end of 3rd Q. Cadet fumbleitis, mostly on C-to-QB exchanges, prompted assertion from *Newark (N.J.) Star Ledger* editor Stanley Woodward that, "Explaining Army's horrendous hosing at Michigan by failure of the center (snap) may be likened to blaming the Johnstown flood on a leaky toilet in Altoona." Seven different Wolverines scored with FB John Herrnstein streaking 60y in 3rd Q. Too late for Cadets were TDs from QB Bob Kyasky (16y run) after his 25y pass to E Dick Warner and soph HB Pete Dawkins (9y run).

Oklahoma 45 Texas 0 (Dallas): Texas (1-3) coach Ed Price projected hopeful pre-game voice: "We can upset them; they have to lose sometime." Sooners (3-0) coach Bud Wilkinson's concern was eased early by HB Tommy McDonald (16/140y, 3 TDs), who returned opening KO 54y. McDonald also caught 2/61y, including 53y TD from QB Jimmy Harris, and completed his only pass attempt for 27y. Fellow Sooners HB Clendon Thomas rushed 13/123y, 3 TDs. C Jerry Tubbs ranged far from LB spot on D (3 INTs), and Oklahoma dealt worst defeat to Texas (only 74y rushing) since 1908. In so doing, Sooners tied Pittsburgh's 33 straight wins set in 1915-19.

Baylor 14 ARKANSAS 7: Scrappy Arkansas (2-2) line played well, but watched its ball-carriers lose 6 FUMs in 1st H that it trailed 7-0. Brutish Bears (4-0) FB-LB Larry Hickman grabbed mid-air FUM at his 36YL in 2nd Q, and QB Doyle Traylor augmented runs by Hickman and HB Del Shofner with 14 and 6y passes to set up Shofner's 5y TD sweep. It might have been worse had Green-and-Gold not lost 2 of their own FUMs at Arkansas 15 and 32YLs. Hogs ate up most of 3rd Q with 69y drive to tying TD. FB Gerald Nesbitt's 3 and 5y blasts keyed march, and QB Don Christian's 12y pass to E Olan Burns contributed as well. Still, it took gambling 4th down reverse run by HB Rogers Overby to tally 2y TD for Arkansas. After Baylor T Paul Dickson recovered Porkers' only 2nd H FUM at their 38YL in 4th Q, HB Farrell Fisher used Hickman's crushing block for winning 6y TD run.

HOUSTON 14 Texas A&M 14: No. 9 Texas A&M (3-0-1) was whittled down to size by quiet Houston (1-1-1) as soph HB Billy Koons made his 1st varsity carry red-letter TD in 4th Q. HB John David Crow lost FUM on Aggies 1st snap to G Rudy Spitzenberger,

and fired-up Cougars had TD in 6 plays. HB Harold Lewis slanted last 6y for Houston TD and 7-0 lead. Determined Texas A&M march died at 6YL, but Aggies T Ken Beck blocked punt and E John Tracey fell on it in EZ for A&M TD in 1st Q. After stopping Cougar thrusts at its 1 and 17YLs in 2nd Q (latter ended by blocked FB by QB-DB Roddy Osborne), Aggies finally rekindled O deep in 3rd Q as QB Osborne ran 7/33y and hit 9y pass to HB Ken Hall before sweeping 14y to TD. Lewis hit Koons for 26y pass to set up Koons' tying 5y TD run that thrilled 67,000 Homecoming partisans with 11 mins to play. They cheered wildly as Houston halted 94y Aggies drive at 1YL in final min. Aggies coach Bear Bryant sent sub in with kicking tee for HB-K Loyd Taylor to try FG, but quickly second-guessed himself, and run failed.

October 20, 1956

Boston College 32 RUTGERS 0: Long consecutive-game scoring streak of Rutgers (1-4) ended at 99 when Boston College (2-1) blanked Queensmen for 1st time since 1944 and scored in each Q. Eagles rushed for 405y and totaled 468 O. In 1st H, BC went 62 and 65y to TDs on 12y pass to E Dick Reagan and 7y run, each by QB Billy Donlan. Rutgers came closest to scoring late in 2nd Q when it reached BC 13YL, but threat ended with INT of TB Billy Austin's pass. Rushing for only 12y, Scarlet Knights turned to air game for 8-15/168y as WB Jay Hunton caught 5/114y.

NORTH CAROLINA 34 Maryland 6: Coach Jim Tatum beat his former team for his 1st win at North Carolina (1-4). Odd play had key role: Tar Heels G Jim Jones grabbed pass by his QB Dave Reed after it was deflected by Maryland (1-4) G Paul Tonetti, taking it 17y for TD. Fast-sinking Terrapins were left to scratch their heads, feeling certain whistle had blown on Jones' TD catch. Jones soon leapt on FUM to set up 1st of HB Emil DeCantis' 2 TD runs. Early in 2nd Q, Carolina had 20-0 edge. Terrapins scored in 3rd Q as backup QB Fred Petrella clicked on 8, 2, 22, and 27y passes, last for TD to E Al Beardsley. Star T Mike Sandusky was downcast when asked if UNC was as tough as previous conquerors, saying, "When they're ahead of you, they're all tough."

Pittsburgh 27 Duke 14 (Norfolk): Oyster Bowl, which started as post-WWII tradition in Norfolk, celebrated its 10th match-up. Pittsburgh (3-1) fell behind right away as Duke (2-3) HB Bernie "Bunny" Blaney streaked up middle of field on 98y TD RET of opening KO. Resourceful Panthers came around at outset of 2nd Q when QB Corny Salvaterra ran option play for 7y TD. Within 5 mins, Pitt had 2 more TDs on 27 and 59y receptions by standout E and future New York Jets star Joe Walton. Panthers sought to widen lead in 3rd Q, but speedy Blue Devils HB-DB Eddie Rushton stepped in front of Salvaterra's pitchout, juggled it briefly, and sped 77y to bring Duke within 20-14. Southerners advanced to 26YL in 4th Q, but huge Panthers line, led by T Bob Pollack and G Harold Hunter, halted drive. Eating clock, Pitt went 74y to HB Ray DiPasquale's 1y TD buck that verified Pennsylvanians' victory.

Florida 21 VANDERBILT 7: Vanderbilt (3-2), enjoying its Homecoming game, was favored over Florida (3-1-1) for perhaps last time in history. With skilled QB Don Orr out with injury, Commodores used soph QB-P Boyce Smith. In 2nd Q, pressure from Gators FB Joe Brodsky forced Smith's 8y punt shank to Vandy 34YL, and QB Jimmy Dunn's pass to E Bob Buford earned quick UF TD. Near end of 2nd Q, Gators held on downs inside own 1YL after Smith kept long drive alive with midfield 4th down sneak. Vanderbilt HB Danny McCall lost FUM to Gators T-DT Charley Mitchell in 3rd Q, and QB Harry Speers leapt over from 1YL to finish 26y trip. Vandy completed 97y drive that spanned 3rd and 4th Q intermission and FB Jim Butler crashed for TD. Florida's subs wrapped it up with late TD, fashioned on possession that followed ensuing KO.

Tulane 10 MISSISSIPPI 3: Disagreeable Green Wave (4-1) shocked heavily-favored no. 6 Ole Miss (4-1) as driving rain limited 1st H scoring to Rebels FG by FB Paige Cothren. With moon shining over 2nd H KO, Tulane took ball at own 14YL. On 1st play, QB Gene "Mighty Mouse" Newton cut through RG, burst outside for 86y TD sprint. Clincher came on toe of T-K Emmett Zelenka, who pounded successful 31y FG through strong wind.

GEORGIA TECH 28 Auburn 7: Yellow Jackets motored 56y to early-game TD by FB Ken Owen. HB Tommy Lorino shot 11y off RG to contribute to 73y march in 1st Q as underdog Plainsmen (2-2) scored TD: Tigers QB Howell Tubbs sneaked over to knot it at 7-7 on drive's 15th play. QB-DB Wade Mitchell's clutch INT in 2nd Q halted Auburn advance to Jackets 24YL, when score could have kept Tigers in it. Versatile sr HB Johnny Menger, 3rd stringer in Georgia Tech (4-0) squadron of swift backs, broke open game in 2nd Q with superb 60y run to Auburn 1YL, as he swiveled away from 4 tacklers. Menger was soon at it again as he flashed to 87y TD on 3rd punt RET.

KENTUCKY 14 Louisiana State 0: Wildcats (2-3) fashioned 2 drives for TDs: 54y in 12 plays in 2nd Q and 60y in 12 plays in 4th Q to launch 5-game win streak. Kentucky HB Woody Herzog took pitchout around RE for 3y TD in 2nd Q, and HB Billy Mitchell rammed 4y for score behind block of LT Lou Michaels in 4th Q. Reeling LSU (0-4) made only 6-24 passes. Although QB M.C. Reynolds was most effective thrower at 5-14/60y, he missed 3 straight tosses to kill Bengals' best chance in 4th Q. When trailing 7-0, LSU moved 51y to 1st down at Kentucky 10YL. Prime gainer was 26y pass from Reynolds to E John Wood, who would have scored but for saving tackle by Wildcats QB-DB Kenny Robertson.

Michigan State 47 NOTRE DAME 14: On way to its worst record in history to date, Notre Dame (1-3) managed spirited start against no. 2 Spartans, scoring 1st as QB Paul Hornung ran 35y and passed 19y to set up HB Frank Reynolds' 5y TD run. ND allowed TD in 2nd Q when QB Pat Wilson sneaked over at end of 47y trip, but held undefeated Michigan State (4-0) to 7-7 H tie. But just as Fighting Irish hopes rose, MSU TB Dennis "The Menace" Mendyk (9/157y, 2 TDs) rampaged in 2nd H, running to 62y TD for 14-7 lead, tossing key pass to QB Mike Panitch, and adding 67y TD run for 33-14 lead by 4th Q. Key Spartans' TD came on QB Jim Ninowski's 3 passes/55y on 83y drive in 3rd Q that lifted lead to 21-7.

Penn State 7 OHIO STATE 6: Scoring was packed into game's last 4 mins as both teams squandered frequent chances. In end, big underdog Penn State (3-1) used QB-P Milt Plum's 73y punt to gain field position for HB Bruce Gilmore's TD run. Despite 333y-per-game run avg, Ohio State (3-1) took to air as E Leo Brown made 61y on 2 catches to poise HB Don Clark for 3y TD dive. Too-many-men-on-field PEN ruined QB-K Frank Kremblas' x-pt kick. Another try from 25YL, which would have tied it, missed.

Indiana 19 NEBRASKA 14: Visiting Indiana (1-4) rallied from 2-TD margin in 2nd Q with 2 scores in 4th Q to slip past surprised Nebraska (2-3). Cornhuskers FB Jerry Brown, who had volunteered in 1955 to go to G when injuries depleted squad, scored 1y TD at end of 53y march in 1st Q. Nebraska went up 14-0 on HB Willie Greenlaw's short TD run in 2nd Q before Hoosiers QB Gene Cichowski nailed 6 passes in row on 82y TD march that trimmed edge to 14-6 by H. More Cichowski passes brought Indiana to FB Bob Fee's 1st of 2 TD runs early in 4th Q. Trailing 14-13, Indiana went 48y to win it.

TEXAS A&M 7 Texas Christian 6: It became known in Texas simply as "The Hurricane Game." Texas Christian (3-1) dominated play in 90 mph winds of 0-0 1st H as ominous storm blew in from Gulf of Mexico. Horned Frogs fruitlessly got to Texas A&M (4-0-1) GL 3 times before H, including dive by HB Jim Swink that some believed crossed GL. With suddenly-clear skies in 2nd H, TCU continued to press, missing 2 FGs, but finally taking 6-0 lead on E O'Day Williams' one-handed TD grab. Purple Frogs drove early in 4th Q, but Aggies turned inspirational tide of game on HB-DB Don Watson's EZ INT. From there, A&M drove 80y, scoring on Watson's 8y TD pass to HB John David Crow. HB Loyd Taylor's conv kick served as winning pt with 9 mins remaining.

October 27, 1956

(Th) Clemson 7 South Carolina 0 (Columbia, S.C.): Resourceful Clemson (4-0-1) QB Charlie Bussey scored on 1st Q sneak after HB Jim Coleman's 39y punt RET. Late in 4th Q, South Carolina (4-2) drove 75y to Tigers 3YL, but FB Don Johnson's FUM into EZ was covered by DB Bussey to end Gamecocks' game-tying threat.

ALABAMA 13 Mississippi State 12: Proud Alabama (1-4), losers of 17 in row and 18 with 2 ties out of last 20 games, exacted satisfying, if small, revenge on Mississippi State (3-3), which had launched Crimson Tide's dark passage with 12-7 win in Denny Stadium in October 1954. Bulldogs started as if they would extend Crimson Tide's misery as HB Molly Halbert made 36y run on opening series. Miss State soon scored on FB Frank Sabbitini's short plunge and added QB Billy Stacy's 22y TD sprint, but missed both conv kicks in 1st Q. Crimson Tide QB Clay Walls pitched perfect 46y TD to HB Jim Bowdoin in 2nd Q, so Bama trailed 12-6 at H. Bama E-DE Willie Beck recovered FUM at Bulldogs 31YL in 4th Q, and steady short gains brought Alabama to 1YL where Walls dived across. Little-known E-K Pete Reeves was true with his conv kick. Homecoming crowd tore down goalposts, and players carried coach "Ears" Whitworth and Reeves off on their shoulders.

Minnesota 20 MICHIGAN 7: Michigan's bright October Homecoming date was spoiled by Minnesota (4-0-1) in Gophers' 1st win in Ann Arbor in 15 years. Familiar face of Gophers QB Bobby Cox haunted Wolverines (3-2) as he had nearly pulled off upset in 1954 opener as member of Washington Huskies. Cox scored twice in 4th Q to pull Gophers from 7-6 hole. Michigan HB Terry Barr provided 7-0 lead with 16y TD run in 2nd Q, but from that point on no. 5 Wolverines stalled. Early in 3rd Q, Minnesota drove 92y in 16 plays as Cox ran 8/36y and HB Bob Schultz roared 30y for TD. High snap ruined x-pt, so Michigan still led 7-6. HB Pinky McNamara's 37y punt RET after lateral from QB Dick Larson late in 3rd Q began winning drive as Cox went 3y to score in 4th Q.

INDIANA 19 Northwestern 13: Indiana (2-3) rode surprisingly stout passing game (15-21/176y) to beat Northwestern (1-3-1) for 4th straight time, longest such streak over 1 team in Hoosier annals to date. Wildcats continued to flounder in Big 10 since their last conf win had come in November 1954. Hoosiers HB Dave Whitsell went behind RT Bob Sobczak's block for 3y TD early in 2nd Q, but HB Bobby McKeiver's 61y scoot highlighted Northwestern's 80y answer after following KO. FB Ed Quinn powered final 2y, and NW led 7-6. After FUM REC near midfield, Wildcats QB Dale Pienta arched 51y TD pass to E Larry Van Dusen. QB Steve Filipowski beat H clock with 4 passes to tie it at 13-13 with 19 secs left in 2nd Q. Indiana E Norm Craft made INT of Pienta inside final 5 mins and returned it to NU 37YL. Hoosiers E Brad Bomba (9/105y) caught 17 and 11y passes to help bring ball to 6YL, from which point Whitsell crashed over for TD.

ILLINOIS 20 Michigan State 13: Top-ranked Michigan State (4-1) used 2 Illini FUMs to gain 13-0 H lead on short TD runs by HBs Jim Wulff and Clarence Peaks. But, Spartans lost chance for another 1st H TD when E Tony Kolodziej caught pass at 13YL but was hit hard enough to cough up FUM to Illinois (2-3) E-DE Rod Hanson. Illinois heard stirring H speech by coach Ray Eliot and thrilled its Homecoming crowd in 2nd H. Illini E Gary Francis recovered 3 FUMs, twice Michigan State HB Dennis Mendyk lost bobbles to Francis deep in Illini end at 16 and 11YLs. Illinois' Big 10 hurdles champ, HB Abe Woodson, capped 71y drive in 3rd Q with 2y TD smash and went long distance for 2 exhausting 4th Q TDs. Woodson (16/116y, 2 TDs) dashed 70y, sprung by Hanson's block, for score. Later, Woodson tallied on 82y run with screen pass from QB Bill Offenbacher, making several sharp cuts and hurdling State DB Art Johnson near midfield, to get away to break 13-13 tie in last 5 mins.

Oklahoma 40 NOTRE DAME 0: Having never beaten Notre Dame (1-4), no. 2 Oklahoma (5-0) did so in grand style, defeat being 5th worst in Fighting Irish history. While confounding ND with double flanker formation, Sooners went 68y after opening KO to QB Jimmy Harris' 14y TD pass to E John Bell. Sooners G Steve Jennings blocked Irish punt to allow sub QB Jay O'Neal to score TD from 3YL. Star Oklahoma HB-DBs Tommy McDonald and Clendon Thomas were forces on O and each scored on INT RET. Injured QB Paul Hornung brightened Notre Dame by appearing in starting lineup, but his skills could push young ND lads only to Sooners 18YL in 1st Q and 2YL in 2nd Q. It was 1st blanking of Fighting Irish in their last 48 games.

COLORADO 16 Nebraska 0: Taking another step closer to Orange Bowl bid, Colorado (5-1) D blanked Cornhuskers (2-4) with powerful 363y rushing game. Buffs switched between Single Wing and T-formation and sprung TB Bob Stransky for 15/120y and FB John Bayuk, particularly on spinner runs, for 13/108y. Bayuk whirled away for 24y and 14y TD bursts. In 2nd Q, Nebraska fell behind 9-0 as Bison FB-LB Leroy Clark added EZ tackle of Huskers HB Frank Nappi for safety when Nebraska tried surprise HB pass. Colorado went 71y in 3rd Q as Stransky raced 19 and 17y to set up Bayuk's 2nd masterful TD. Topnotch Buffaloes blocker, G John Wooten, eventually was ejected as play turned rough.

Texas A&M 19 BAYLOR 13: No. 7 Texas A&M (5-0-1) HB John David Crow threw 5y TD pass to E John Tracey, later scored decisive TD on 2y plunge in 4th Q. Using TD runs by FB Larry Hickman and HB Bobby Peters, no. 8 Baylor (4-1) led 13-12 late in 4th Q before A&M started disputable winning drive to Crow's TD. It was sustained despite Aggies FB Jack Pardee's FUM at Bears 25YL. Officials differed on FUM call, huddled to confirm A&M's retention of ball, and ref I.B. Hale later labeled it toughest decision of his career. Game was marred by 5 personal foul PENs and ejection of 2 Bears.

ARKANSAS 14 Mississippi 0 (Little Rock): Like riverboat cardsharps edgy over scoreless stalemate, Mississippi Rebels (4-2) twice gambled in 4th Q in their own territory with runs on 4th-and-ft. Outshining Ole Miss' nation-leading D, Arkansas' lean, quick, and emotional defenders stopped each try to delight of capacity crowd. Field position that resulted allowed Razorbacks to romp to TDs that broke up tight battle. Porkers QB Don Christian (122y rushing), who played 58 mins, made Rebels pay each time with 1y plunge and 30y dash to paydirt. FB Paige Cothren was Rebels' only consistent ball carrier as Ole Miss gained 171y rushing, but was blanked 0-8 in passing game. Hogs D, led by T Billy Ray Smith and FB-LB Gerald Nesbitt, allowed penetration into its end only twice with Rebs reaching no deeper than 35YL.

OREGON STATE 21 Ucla 7: Single Wing master, UCLA coach Red Sanders, was taught lesson by his former asst, coach Tommy Prothro, as improving Beavers (4-2) snapped Uclans' 19-game PCC win streak. UCLA (4-2) FB Barry Billington (13/62y) scored 1st Q TD after QB-P Don Shinnick's 68y punt gained field position, blasting through line on 11y run. Oregon State hopped right to work as WB Earnel Durden (5/76y) sprinted 51y to Uclans 24YL, and FB Tom Berry (21/66y, 3 TDs) tallied 1st of his 3 TDs, all from 1YL. After recovering Bruins FUM in 2nd Q, Beavers went 58y with TB Paul Lowe pounding for 4, 36, 2, and 7y to get Berry to his favorite 1YL spot again. Lowe and Berry blasted away at UCLA line for 73y TD drive, but it took Lowe's diving FUM REC at Bruins 1YL to allow Berry's TD. Oregonians gained 303y rushing.

STANFORD 27 Southern California 19: In his final game, sr HB "Jaguar" Jon Arnett rushed 25/117y as Trojans (4-1) got 212y on ground in 1st H and built early 13-0 lead. Gradually, Indians (4-2) coach Chuck Taylor employed "superovershift" in maneuvering his D line, led by T Paul Wiggin, Es Carl Isaacs and Ben Robinson, and G Noel Robinson, to stiffen in decisive 2nd H. Before that, Stanford QB John Brodie (10-21/144y, 2 TDs, 4 INTs) threw 30y TD pass and ran 1y for 14-13 H lead. Indians E Isaacs caught 23y Brodie TD early in 3rd Q for 21-13 advantage. USC wasn't done; it traveled 67y on 14 runs and 9y pass from Arnett to QB Frank Hall, and Arnett scored TD to pull within 21-19. Trojans had to stop Stanford drives with FUM REC at own 14YL and INTs at 1 and 46YLs, but their 4th-and-20 play near midfield was stopped with less than 4 mins left. Tribe kept ball until scoring in last 35 secs.

AP Poll October 29

1 Oklahoma (143)	1768	11 Pittsburgh	172
2 Georgia Tech (31)	1614	12 Penn State	142
3 Tennessee (8)	1302	13 Clemson	133
4 Michigan State	1029	14 George Washington	98
5 Texas A&M	957	15tBaylor	76
6 Ohio State (1)	626	15tVirginia Tech	76
7 Iowa	584	17tMichigan	69
8 Minnesota	440	17tOregon State	69
9 Miami (1)	357	17tSyracuse	69
10 Stanford	198	20 Southern California	68

November 3, 1956

COLUMBIA 25 Cornell 19: In Lou Little's last home game after 27 years, Columbia (2-4) won for its coach, described as "national symbol of fair play and sportsmanship" by Pres Dwight D. Eisenhower. After Cornell (0-6) struck for 6-0 lead on HB Bob McAniff's 1st of 2 TDs on 7y run in 1st Q, Columbia's ace 60-min QB Claude Benham began pitching TDs: E Bruce Howard for 20 and 12y and E Ron Szczypkowski for 7y. Benham (12-16/177y, 3 TDs) also wedged for TD at end of 60y air drive. Little's mark after nearly 3 decades at Columbia may not have been as grand as those of Knute Rockne or Bear Bryant, but at 110-116-10 (.487) it was far better than his school's all-time winning percentage of less than .390.

SYRACUSE 13 Penn State 9: Evenly matched pair squared off for Eastern supremacy, and difference was 6 TOs gobbled up by bowl-bound Orangemen (5-1). Surprisingly, Syracuse never completed pass in 7 tries, including INT by Mount Nit G-LB Sam Valentine in Penn State (4-2) territory. Teams traded 2nd Q TD runs by Nittany Lions HB Billy Kane after 63y march and Orangemen sub QB Dan Fogarty after HB-DB Jim Ridlon's INT. On heels of his own 33y dash, Penn State QB-K Milt Plum kicked 28y FG to break 6-6 tie just 1 sec before H. Mishandled handoff between QB Al Jacks and HB Bruce Gilmore cost Lions possession at their 19YL at end of 3rd Q. After E-DE Dick Aloise's REC and HB Jimmy Brown's 4 runs in 7 plays moved Syracuse to 1YL, QB Chuck Zimmerman pushed over for winning TD at outset of 4th Q. Penn State continued to press, but was frustrated by INTs on 3 straight series, 3 failed passes in row, and 15y PEN for illegal substitution entry by Plum.

CLEMSON 21 Virginia Tech 6: Clemson (5-0-1) held ball for nearly 10 mins to open game until giving up possession at Virginia Tech (6-2) 3YL. "That took something out of VPI," thought Tigers coach Frank Howard. Clemson's 2nd unit scored soon thereafter on strength of QB Horace Turbeville's sneak. Hokies were behind 7-0 in 3rd Q until QB Jimmy Lugar hit several effective passes to carry Tech to Tigers 12YL. Suddenly, FB-LB Rudy Hayes picked off pass at 8YL and stormed 77y until hauled down from behind. Bob Spooner, 3rd-team FB, blasted for 10y, and HB Charlie Horne, another sub, took 2 tries to push it across GL for 14-0 lead. FB Don Divers banged over from 2y to pull Gobblers to within 14-6, but Clemson subs continued their useful play. Horne took option pitchout for 20y TD in 4th Q. Starting Tigers QB Charlie Bussey, who admitted afterward he couldn't pass because of dislocated thumb, said, "Boy, it's great to be able to rest and have that second unit out there fighting for you."

Georgia Tech 7 DUKE 0: Blue Devils (3-4) HB-DB Eddie Rushton twice made INTs (1st vs Yellow Jackets all season) in 1st Q to chill Georgia Tech (6-0) ventures to Duke 13 and 29YLs. Georgia Tech FB Ken Owen boomed 66y QK in 2nd Q, but Duke soon moved from its 33YL as HB George Dutrow (8/48y) dashed 25y and made 3 bucks for 1st down at 3YL. But Tech D stalwarts, C-LB Don Stephenson, HB-DB Johnny Menger, and QB-DB Wade Mitchell, made big tackles on 4 runs that lost 2y, and 0-0 score was protected. With sheets of rain falling in 4th Q, Duke QB Sonny Jurgensen's pass caromed off Blue Devils receiver to Engineers QB-DB Toppy Vann at Tech 38YL. Owen battered line for 3/36y, but reverse run by HB Jimmy Thompson lost 15y. Mitchell then flanked out HB Paul Rotenberry and hit him twice, last pass of 13y coming on 4th-and-10 at Duke 26YL to rescue drive, to prompt FB Dickie Mattison's winning 1y TD run with 9:20 to go.

FLORIDA 20 Auburn 0: Ambitious Auburn runners twice menaced Gators territory in 1st Q, but tough Florida (5-1-1) D held each time. Gators faced daunting 3rd-and-34 after QB Harry Spears was tossed for 17y loss, but UF HB Jackie Simpson startled Tigers (3-3) with 47y TD pass to well-covered HB Jim Rountree on 2nd Q's 1st snap. Florida QB Jimmy Dunn zipped 58y on option run behind blocks of HB Bernie Parrish and E Don Fleming to another TD just 4 mins later. Auburn's best threat was concocted by 3rd-team QB Frank Riley, who entered fray in 3rd Q. Riley needed only inches for 1st down at Gators 13YL, but ball popped loose on sneak and was covered by Florida DE Dan Pelham at 10YL. After regaining possession on punt out, Plainsmen decided to punt on 4th down at Florida 44YL. There, Gators' newly-wed G Ray Midden blocked HB-P Tommy Lorino's pooch punt and scampered with it for 29y TD RET. C-LB Bill Bolton contributed 18 tackles for Florida and fell on FUM at his 41YL to launch Dunn's 2nd Q dash for pts. Win marked Gators' 1st 4-game victory streak since 1930.

Michigan 17 IOWA 14: Iowa again met its Waterloo, its oft-frustrating match with Michigan (4-2), school it had not beaten since 1924. Wolverines spotted Hawkeyes 11-pt lead and turned tables to knock Iowa (5-1) from unbeaten ranks. After E-K Ron Kramer's 22y 1st Q FG put Wolverines ahead 3-0, Hawkeyes took advantage of 2 breaks in 2nd Q: UM QB Jim Van Pelt lost handle when he was hit by E-DE Frank Gilliam while trying to pass, and sub QB Jim Maddock bobbled snap but carried through with ill-advised QK. Each time, Iowa came up with possession in Michigan territory: T Alex Karras' REC at 24YL and at 44YL after Maddock's shaky QK. QBs Randy Duncan, on 13y TD pass to HB Del Kloewer, and Kenny Ploen, on 33y scramble away from Kramer for TD, put Iowa up 14-3 by H. Michigan engineered methodical 2nd H TD drives of 74 and 80y as Hawks' O fizzled to total of 77y in last 2 Qs. HB Mike Shatusky scored both comeback TDs with help of steady plunging of FB John Herrnstein (18/66y). With 1:06 left to play, Shatusky went off RT from 2YL to crown winning Michigan drive that ate most of final 10:30.

NEBRASKA 15 Missouri 14: Nebraska (3-3) soph QB-K-P George Harshman made 2 vital plays with foot to save Cornhuskers. Missouri (3-4) lost 4 FUMs, and HB Charley James (5/65y receiving) dribbled ball away in 1st Q to set up TD run by Nebraska FB Jerry Brown (11/52y). On strength of FB George Cramer's 1st of 2 TD runs and G-K Charlie Rash's virtually-automatic conv kick, Tigers led 7-6 at H. K Harshman booted 40y FG in 3rd Q which gave Nebraska 9-7 lead. Black-and-Gold looked in great shape after Cramer scored at 3:30 of 4th Q. Punt snap sailed over P Harshman's head and bounded about at 5YL, but cool-headed Harshman booted punt safely to other side of midfield while avoiding pursuers. Defending its GL, Mizzou stopped Huskers HB Frank

Nappi for 7y loss and recovered FUM, but officials made controversial call that ruled whistle blew before FUM. Nappi then pitched winning 15y TD pass on 4th down to HB Willie Greenlaw.

Oklahoma 27 COLORADO 19: Pumped-up Colorado (5-2) jumped to 19-6 H lead as Buffs G John Wooten blocked early Sooners QK, and FB John Bayuk fell on ball in EZ. Colorado WB Eddie Dove and TB Bob Stransky scored at end of powerful 69 and 66y drives in 2nd Q. Oklahoma (6-0), admonished at H by coach Bud Wilkinson, preserved its 36-game win streak with 2nd H charge. Using his overwhelmingly successful pass-run option play, Sooners clutch HB Tommy McDonald hit HB-mate Clendon Thomas with 6y TD pass at end of 80y trip after 2nd H KO. McDonald made 11y TD run, and QB Jimmy Harris' conv gave Sooners their 1st lead at 20-19 late in 3rd Q.

UCLA 14 Stanford 13: Vengeful UCLA (5-2) lined up all its sr players to pounce on Stanford (4-3), school that blew whistle on Pacific Coast Conf rule-breakers. Bruins E-DE Hal Smith made 1st Q FUM REC at Indians 20YL after tackle by C-LB Jim Matheny on Indians FB Lou Valli (10/36y,TD), which led to TB Edison Griffin's 4y TD run. Smith also blocked punt which E Pete O'Garro took 42y to 14-0 lead midway through 1st Q. Stanford rallied for Valli's TD after 40y drive in 2nd Q. In 3rd Q, Tribe HB-K Mickey Raftery caught 21y TD pass from QB John Brodie (9-20/176y, TD, 2 INT), but Raftery's conv was blocked by FB-LB-K Don Shinnick, who incidentally toed winning pt after UCLA's 2nd TD. UCLA's pass-pressuring D rushed as many as 8 defenders to dump Brodie for -66y in sacks.

Southern California 28 WASHINGTON STATE 12: Young Cougars (2-5) D permitted USC (5-1), with several sr players out of lineup, only 55y in 1st H. Washington State led 12-7 at H, thanks to QB Bobby Newman's TD sneak at end of 66y drive and 1y TD burst by FB Eddie Stevens (14/63y) at conclusion of 72y march that mixed runs by Stevens with passes of Newman (15-28/153y, 2 TDs). Game completely turned on 2nd H KO as Trojans FB C.R. Roberts fielded ball at own 4YL and roared 96y to TD and 14-12 lead. Cougars answered with drive to USC 11YL where Trojans E-DE Hillard Hill recovered FUM by HB Chuck Morrell, and WSU never threatened again. Troy TB Ernie Zampese (18/85y), replacement for recently ineligible Jon Arnett, scored his 2nd TD on 3y run.

OREGON STATE 28 Washington 20: Oregon State (5-2), enjoying its spot atop PCC, went 83y 1st time it touched ball to FB Tom Berry's short TD run, then added WB Earnel Durden's 16y scoring catch from TB Joe Francis before 1st Q was over. Washington (3-4) trimmed Beavers' comfortable lead to 21-13 in 3rd Q as HB Mike McCluskey took QB Talbot George's pass to spectacular 65y TD. But, Durden scored his 3rd TD, breaking away for 44y run midway in 4th Q. Huskies benefitted from FUM REC at Oregon State 13YL in late going and received HB Dick Payseno's 13y run as window-dressing TD.

AP Poll November 5

1 Oklahoma (116)	1554	11 Clemson	158
2 Georgia Tech (30)	1453	12 Navy (3)	127
3 Tennessee (1)	1252	13 Florida	119
4 Michigan State (7)	1102	14 Oregon State	96
5 Texas A&M (1)	872	15 Iowa	83
6 Minnesota	680	16 Southern California	76
7 Ohio State (1)	572	17 Texas Christian	72
8 Miami (1)	453	18 Colorado	30
9 Syracuse (1)	225	19 UCLA (1)	29
10 Michigan	190	20tPittsburgh	25
		20tStanford	25

November 10, 1956

(Fri) MIAMI 20 Florida State 7: Miami's undefeated, but slightly bored Hurricanes (5-0-1) owned opening 3 Qs, then dozed as spunky Seminoles (3-3-1) cavorted in 4th Q. Florida State was kept on its side of 50YL for 1st 3 Qs with only 35y O. On passing wing of 3rd-team QB Ted Rodrique, FSU gained 120y—82y in air—in 4th Q. Earlier, Miami sub QBs Joe Plevel and Bonnie Yarbrough had grilled Seminoles D. Moved from HB to replace injured QB Sam Scarnecchia, Plevel spun away for 16y run to set up his 1y TD wedge in 1st Q and dashed off LT for 14y TD in 3rd Q. Yarbrough (9-15/82y) hit 4 passes, and FB Don Bosseler ran for 26y on 94y TD drive in 2nd Q. FSU threatened 3 times in 4th Q, but only converted HB Lee Corso's 2y slash with 2:59 left.

DUKE 7 Navy 7: Blue Devils (3-4-1) managed 3rd deadlock with Navy (5-1-1) in last 4 years as Duke E Bob Benson was interfered with at Navy 1YL by G-LB Jim Hower in key moment midway through 4th Q. QB Sonny Jurgensen (14-22 passing) pushed over for tying TD on next play. Middies had taken 7-0 lead as QB Tom Forrestal clicked on passes for 55y of 83y drive to HB Paul Gober's 1y TD run. Each team missed FGs in last 3 mins. Duke K Jim Harris was well short with FG try on game's last play, and Navy HB Chet Burchett raced it back 50y before being hauled down. Bruising affair left Navy without any of its 1st string backfield in closing stages, while Harris, who missed FG, was his team's 3rd choice due to injuries to top Ks Bernie Blaney and Buddy Bass.

GAME OF THE YEAR
Tennessee 6 GEORGIA TECH 0:

Contest has come to be considered by many as greatest Southern-style defensive battle of all time. Punts ruled game strategy as teams totaled 23 between them, often booting on 2nd or 3rd down. Vols sub TB Bobby Gordon punted 3/57.6 avg, including punt of 72y. So conservative was climate that, after HB George Volkert ran 21y into Vols territory in 1st Q, Georgia Tech (6-1) coach Bobby Dodd chose to punt on 4th-and-4 at 28YL. Engineers FB Ken Owen advanced to Vols 17YL in 2nd Q, but lost FUM when slammed by T-DT Jim Smelcher. K Sam Burklow of Tennessee (7-0) missed long FG just before H. Winning score came in 3rd Q as Vols started at own 35YL: FB Tommy Bronson made 3y and TB Johnny Majors hit E Buddy Cruze with 16y square out pass. Cruze realized coverage had loosened and asked in huddle for another throw. Cruze cut inside to beat HB-CB Paul Rotenberry for Majors' next pass, and when QB-S Wade Mitchell, Georgia Tech's star of secondary, tried to switch tackling shoulders to protect an injury to left shoulder, Cruze squirted away. He galloped 45y to Tech 1YL, pulled down finally by Owen, who came from far side of field. Bronson twisted through for TD on next play. Engineers managed late threat, ending as QB Toppy Vann suffered INT by Bronson at Vols 9YL. Total O was virtually even: Georgia Tech gained 198y, and Tennessee 177y. Vols D stars were C-LB Bubba Howe, G Bruce Burnham, E Roger Urbano, and Ts John Gordy and Charles Rader. For Georgia Tech, it was C-LB Don Stephenson, T Carl Vereen, and G Leon Askew. Afterward, Tennessee coach Bowden Wyatt, like Dodd, disciple of old-school coach Robert Neyland, was asked why Dodd didn't try for 4y on 4th down in 1st Q. Wyatt snarled: "because he wouldn't have made it."

Florida 28 Georgia 0 (Jacksonville): Hot Florida (6-1-1) won its 5th straight contest in trouncing rival Georgia (3-4-1). Part of fresh backfield that entered game well into 1st Q, Gators HB Bernie Parrish battered left side for 3y TD. It was 5th run play after QB Harry Spears opened series near midfield with 15y pass to FB Ed Sears. Trailing 7-0 early in 3rd Q, Bulldogs QB-DB Billy Hearn and G Tony Cushenberry recovered FUMs at Gators 27 and 25 YLs, but each time Florida D, led by G-LB John Barrow, halted Georgia. Gators' 2nd stop was authored by FB-DB Joe Brodsky (2 INTs), who made 64y INT RET from his GL. HB Jim Rountree gave Florida 14-0 lead with 36y cutback run on next play. Rountree added 25y TD catch from QB Jimmy Dunn in 4th Q.

KENTUCKY 7 Vanderbilt 6: For 4th time in 3 years, foot of Kentucky (5-3) QB-K Delmar Hughes delivered winning margin for Wildcats. Vanderbilt (5-3) scored early in 2nd Q when E-DE Bob Laws recovered FUM at Cats 4YL. FB Jim Butler scooted around LE on next play for 6-0 Commodores lead, but QB-K Jimmy Travis missed kick. From then on, Vandy was kept deep in own end by 7 well-placed punts by Kentucky T-P Lou Michaels. Vandy gained 157y and lost 4 INTs and 2 FUMs to Cats D, led by Michaels, T J.T. Frankenberger, and E Doug Shively. Late in 2nd Q, Shively got loose behind DBs to haul in perfect 38y TD pass from sub (by his choice) QB Hughes, who added conv kick. Hughes had begun year as starter, but offered to come off bench because he and coaches felt he was more effective in that role.

Alabama 13 TULANE 7: Suddenly-revived Alabama (2-5) won its 2nd in 3 games by rolling up 266y rushing and 113y passing. Crimson Tide scored on consecutive possessions in 1st H to lead 13-0. They went 64y in 9 plays that ended with HB Don Comstock's 2y plunge on 3rd play of 2nd Q as QB Bobby Smith sparked drive with 29y pass to E Don Owens. Tulane (5-3) threatened right after ensuing KO when QB Gene Newton burst 36y, but Bama held at its own 15YL as DE Owens, HB-DB Jim Bowdoin, and DB Smith made big plays. Tide immediately went 85y, keyed by runs of Bowdoin (8/69y), to HB George Salem's short TD dive. Newton switched to HB and caught perfect pass from QB Fred Wilcox over Alabama DBs for 71y TD in 4th Q.

Iowa 7 MINNESOTA 0: Iowa (6-1) earned only its 2nd win in last 35 years in Minneapolis by exploiting early break and withstanding 55 mins of Golden Gophers stat supremacy. Hawkeyes DE Frank Gilliam made early FUM REC at Gophers 38YL, and FB Fred Harris scored 8 plays later from 1YL. Key gain leading to Iowa TD came on QB Ken Ploen's pentultimate pass of 7y to E Jim Gibbons. Minnesota (5-1-1) HB Bob Schultz lost handle on 3 FUMs to ruin Gophers' chances. Charging Minny QB Bobby Cox rushed for 16/53y of team's 214y on ground, but Gophers air game was forced to endure Iowa HB-DB Bill Happel's 2 INTs, including critical pick-off of sub QB Dick Larson in 3rd Q at Iowa 1YL. This was Gophers' deepest probe of game, but Happel ran out of danger to Hawks 27YL. Iowa played nearly mistake-free football, enduring INT by QB Randy Duncan.

MICHIGAN STATE 12 Purdue 9: Michigan State (6-1) used 1st H TDs by Es Harold Dukes (27y pass from QB Jim Ninowski) and Tony Kolodziej (EZ FUM REC of 3rd string FB Don Arend's forward bobble), then thwarted persistent 2nd H threats by Purdue (2-3-2), which played without injured star QB Lenny Dawson. Boilermakers scored in last 47 secs of 2nd Q on 10y catch by FB Mel Dillard (21/77y) from QB Ted Krzeczowski. This made H score 12-7 for Spartans. In 3rd Q, Purdue held on downs at its 45YL and reached inside Spartans' 1YL. But, Boilers were flagged for PEN and could make it only back to 2YL where QB Bob Spoo's 4th down pass was broken up by MSU DB Ninowski. Purdue, on its way to 247y to 183y O advantage, controlled 4th Q, twice reaching 20YL without further success. On Boilers last advance with 1:31 to play, Michigan State HB-DB Blanche Martin grabbed INT but stumbled into and fumbled through EZ for safety.

MISSOURI 14 Colorado 14: Golden Buffaloes (5-2-1) all but locked up Orange Bowl bid as Big 7 Conf's runnerup, but were fortunate to waltz out of Columbia with tie. FUMs, which had bedeviled Missouri (3-4-1) 24 times so far in 1956, surfaced again to provide Colorado with short 2nd H TD marches of 37 and 34y. Tigers ran 47 plays to Buffs' 17 in 1st H, but had only 7-pt edge to show for it as sub FB Joe Wynn scored in last min of 2nd Q for 7-0 H lead. Colorado held twice at its 10YL and once at its 15YL as Mizzou rang up 361y to 161y O advantage. Tigers went 80y after 2nd H KO to HB Hank Kuhlmann's short TD run and 14-0 lead. After Missouri HB Sonny Stringer lost FUM in 3rd Q, Buffs dusted off old Single Wing buck-lateral-pass as QB Boyd Dowler found E Frank Clarke all alone for 18y TD. Tigers HB Charlie James lost FUM in 4th Q to WB-DB Eddie Dove at 37YL, and drive was enhanced by Mizzou T-DT Paul Browning's retaliatory PEN, after he apparently was bitten on arm. Dowler, under C for quick snap, passed to Clarke for another TD.

Texas Western 28 ARIZONA STATE 0: Miners (7-1) all but wrapped up their 1st Border Conf title with 5-0 loop record as they slapped Arizona State (7-1) off unbeaten pedestal. Whippet-fast Miners made 288y rushing, mostly around flanks, as HBs Jimmy Bevers (16/106y), Bob Coleman (TD runs of 35 and 14y), and Don Maynard skirted Es of Arizona State all night. ASU was dealt its share of bad breaks: opening Miners TD came on QB-P Bob Laraba's sneak after field position was gained on Laraba's punt that bounced to EZ and hopped back out to ASU 1YL. Also, Devils

gained 404y, but marches to Tex West's 25, 21, 1, 28, 15, 21, 6, and 27YLs never gained single pt. These frustrations included 3 INTs and FB Joe Belland's FUM into Miners EZ in 2nd Q.

Oregon State 20 STANFORD 19: Seeking Rose Bowl trip, Stanford (4-4) QB John Brodie (19-31/223y, TD) alternated his passes with timely running of HB Lou Valli (19/66y, TD) to build 19-7 lead, last TD coming late in 3rd Q on 4y run by HB Gordy Young. Indians' on-going x-pt issues prompted Brodie to throw for conv after Young's TD. Stanford had scored twice in 2nd Q: Valli tallied from 3YL on 1st play of 2nd Q, and Brodie hit E Gary Van Galder with 27y pass to 3YL before rolling out around RE to score standing up. Each time, however, Tribe K Doug Dick missed x-pt kick. Beavers (6-2) rallied after next KO when WB Earnell Durden (12/93y rushing) skittered all over field with 59y pass, and TB Paul Lowe reversed his direction several times on 9y TD run. Now trailing 19-14, Oregon State sent DE Norm Thiel rushing after Brodie, who tried for wide open HB Paul Camera, but threw INT instead to FB-DB Tom Berry. Durden made 13y run on 4th down, and Beavers TB Joe Francis passed 23y to E Frank Negri for game-winning TD with 8:41 left. Upset win nearly locked up Beavers' 1st-ever trip to Pasadena since their only Rose Bowl had come in 1942 and was played in Durham, N.C., because of World War II bombing threat to West Coast.

OREGON 7 Washington State 7: Sr QB Tom Crabtree pleased chilled Oregon (3-4-1) Homecoming crowd by leading 8-play, 69y march in 2nd Q to his 2y TD run. During scoring voyage, Crabtree took off on 43y dash to Washington State (2-5-1) 6 YL. Ducks amassed 223y rushing while Crabtree and his sub, QB Jack Crabtree (no relation), mixed in short passes for 10-19/93y, INT. Although Oregon had better of play, Cougars struck swiftly to tie it on 3rd snap of 4th Q. Wazzu QB Bobby Newman flipped short pass to E Bill Steiger, who spun away from tackle and outran 3 Ducks defenders for stunning 79y TD. SB-K Ron Hare toed wobbling kick that barely flopped over crossbar to earn deadlock that held up throughout quiet 4th Q.

Ucla 13 WASHINGTON 9: In Seattle's characteristic cold November rain, HB-K Dean Derby personally put Washington (3-5) into 9-0 lead by kicking 22y FG in 1st Q and adding 6y TD burst off left side 2 mins into 2nd Q. Derby's FG was placed in motion by masterful punt to 2YL by G-P Dick Day. Huskies earned 1st-and-goal at 4YL, but 5y PEN and Bruins DE Dick Wallen's pass block forced 3-pt try. HB Luther Carr caught 41y pass from QB Al Ferguson (2-8/57y, INT) to set up Derby's TD. Uclans (6-2) BB-LB Don Shinnick got them back in game at 13-7 with 1y TD smash and x-pt kick in 2nd Q after fluke "blocked" punt gained them possession at UW 2YL. TB-P Kirk Wilson had dropped 54y punt dead inches from Washington GL. When Huskies E-P Dick McVeigh tried to return punt, his punt smacked Ferguson squarely in his back, and UCLA's Shinnick recovered 2y from EZ. Later in 2nd Q, Bruins fashioned their only drive of day as they traveled 48y to TB Kirk Wilson's 11y TD to E Hal Smith, with Wallen making brilliant 32y catch along way. Amazingly, UCLA total only 6y O in 1st H. Huskies managed 4th Q drive from their 10YL, but on 4th down at Bruins 27YL, G-LB Esker Harris stopped HB Luther Carr.

November 17, 1956

(Fri) MIAMI 21 Clemson 0: Friday night fight at Orange Bowl stadium saw Miami (6-0-1) mix in passes by QB Sam Scarnecchia to enhance FB Don Bosseler's bullish 19/85y rushing, which included 4y TD. Scarnecchia scored on 8 and 4y runs, 1st coming with 1:32 left until H and 2 plays after G-LB Bob Cunio recovered FUM by Clemson (5-1-2) FB Rudy Hayes at Tigers 21YL. Hurricanes stacked 8- and 9-man lines to frustrate Clemson's rushing game. When Tigers went to air, they failed miserably, hitting on 3-15, and suffering 2 INTs. Clemson QB Charlie Bussey (3-13 passing) constructed screen pass TD to HB Jim Coleman in 2nd Q, but it was called back by PEN. Colorful coach Frank Howard groaned about that mistake: "We would have been right back in the ball game."

YALE 42 Princeton 20: Yale's unstoppable sr backfield stormed to 5 TDs in its 1st 6 possessions on way to building 35-13 H lead. Star Bulldogs (7-1) HB Dennis McGill tallied on 33 and 24y passes from QB Dean Loucks (7-11/133y, 2 TDs) and flipped 8y TD pass to E John Pendexter with 51 secs left before H. HB Al Ward (13/121y, 2 TDs) scored in 1st and 2nd Qs, and FB Steve Ackerman took blocked punt by T Charles Griffith 48y for Elis' only 2nd H tally. Princeton (7-1) TB Tom Morris (13/154y, TD) ran 71y for 1st Q TD, but even though previously-undefeated Tigers went 70y to FB Hewes Agnew's 1y TD plunge late in 2nd Q, they saw Ivy title hopes fade in face of Yale's 320y in 1st H. Tigers rushed for 256y, but its D never solved Yale's runs and pass plays that sprung McGill out of backfield.

SYRACUSE 61 Colgate 7: Syracuse (7-1) HB Jimmy Brown, year away from starting his brilliant pro career, created his most famous regular season college performance in his last home game at Archbold Stadium. Brown scored 6 TDs and booted 7 x-pts for to-date NCAA-record 43 pts in single game. Colgate (4-4), ancient upstate New York rival of Orangemen, was in way over its head this time, and long, sometimes-competitive series was ended in 1962 after Orangemen finished it with romps of 34-6, 47-0, 71-0, 46-6, and 51-8. However until this game, no Syracuse *team* had ever scored more than 43 pts against Colgate. Red Raiders' only TD came late in 1st Q on

10y pass from 60-min QB Guy Martin, who hit his opening 4 throws to E Al Jamison that briefly pared it to 14-7. Orange rushed for 511y, and Brown contributed 22/197y as he scored twice on blasts from 1YL as well as on 15, 50, 8, and 19y runs.

NAVY 34 Virginia 7 (Baltimore): Midshipmen QB Tom Forrestal clicked on 2 early passes to set ball on Virginia (3-6) 2YL, and HB Chet Burchett, who navigated muddy field for 3 TDs for Navy (6-1-1), plunged over on next play. Less than min later, Middies FB-DB Dick Dagampat plucked INT thrown by Cavs QB Nelson Yarborough and zoomed down sideline for 53y TD. Virginia advanced against Navy subs in 2nd Q as dependable FB Jim Bakhtiar wedged over from 1YL to create 14-7 H score. Burchett scored after Navy INT in 3rd Q and added his 3rd TD on 18y pitchout run early in 4th Q.

TENNESSEE 27 Mississippi 7: Eyeing upset, plotting Rebels (6-3) opened with flankers spread wide, and QB Ray Brown quickly pitched Ole Miss to 7-0 1st Q lead. With 7-7 tie in 3rd Q, game turned for Volunteers on FB-DB Tommy Bronson's 52y INT TD RET. Vols sub FB Carl Smith contributed 3 TDs in piling up late margin. But because Oklahoma pasted 67 pts on Missouri, Sooners overtook Tennessee for no. 1 in Monday's AP voting.

IOWA 6 Ohio State 0: Imposing Ohio State (6-2) brought record 17 straight conf wins to Iowa City and was seeking unprecedented 3rd straight conf crown. Instead, Iowa (7-1) cinched its 1st-ever Rose Bowl trip with 63y drive after 2nd H KO. Hawkeyes' inspiration came from locker room sign: "You have 60 minutes to beat Ohio State, and a lifetime to remember it." Pass interference call on Buckeyes HB-DB Don Clark at his own 20YL set up Iowa QB Kenny Ploen's 17y TD arrow to E Jim Gibbons at end of 63y trip. Held to 147y overall on ground, Ohio State made only 3 1st downs in 2nd H, and its last threat barely crossed midfield. Earlier, Ohio HB-K Don Sutherin was woefully short and low with 49y FG try in 2nd Q. Win locked up at least tie for Big 10 title, Iowa's 1st since 1922. Hawkeyes' robust D, led by Ts Dick Klein (FUM REC) and Alex Karras, and E Frank Gilliam (sack), stopped 29y Ohio drive at Iowa 43YL midway in 4th Q and shoved Bucks back to their 3YL in confusing last min. Hysterical fans gleefully charged field thinking game was over, and officials had to clear gridiron for 1 last play that never materialized due to PEN. Down came goalposts, and students got 2 extra days off for Pasadena trip.

MINNESOTA 14 Michigan State 13: Minnesota (6-1-1) FB-K Rich Borstad won his 3rd game of year with late-game placekick: Borstad's conv with 6:30 to go came after FB Bob Blakely's twisting 27y TD run to crown 70y march on 5 plays. Injury-riddled Michigan State (6-2) lost its chance to share Big 10 title, although it led 13-7 in 4th Q on 2nd TD sneak by QB Pat Wilson. Gophers QB-DB Bobby Cox rushed for vital 24/128y and sparkled on D with 2 INTs. Cox's initial INT came at his own 27YL and set up clock-beating trip late in 2nd Q when he ran frequent sneaks to set up his 12y TD pass to HB Dave Lindblom. Borstad's conv kick was wide, but MSU T Fran O'Brien was offside, allowing 2nd chance which Borstad turned into 7-0 H edge. Spartans tied it by going 78y after 2nd H KO to Wilson's 1st scoring sneak. Cox's 2nd pickoff thwarted late Spartans rally.

NORTHWESTERN 14 Purdue 0: Northwestern (3-4-1) won 2nd of 3 season-closing Big 10 games in revival under 1st-year coach Ara Parseghian. Wildcats failed to cash 6 Purdue (2-4-2) TOs, but stout D, led by LB Al Viola (4 FUM RECs), maintained 0-0 tie deep into 3rd Q. When Boilermakers QB-G Bob Spoo lost unwise 4th-and-1 gamble at own 16YL late in 3rd Q, Wildcats HB Bobby McKeiver quickly scored for 7-0 lead. Viola made his 4th REC when ball bounced away from Purdue QB Lenny Dawson at Dawson's 4YL. Bobble led to 4th Q insurance TD scored by Cats sub HB Frank Jeske.

ARIZONA STATE 20 Arizona 0: After 3 years of desert domination by Arizona (4-5), jubilant squad of Arizona State (9-1) enjoyed riotous fun in winning locker room. Sun Devils line was considered overmatched against Wildcats counterparts, featuring G Ed Brown and C Paul Hatcher, who was forced out by knee injury in 2nd Q. But Sun Devils forwards outcharged AU line from outset, so that Wildcats weren't comfortable trying single pass until deep into 2nd Q and had to realign D by plugging middle. That allowed ASU runners to successfully probe outside.

Wyoming 7 BRIGHAM YOUNG 6: Undefeated Wyoming (10-0) eyed Gator Bowl bid, but narrow margin over weak BYU (1-7-1) hurt perception of under-publicized Cowboys program. All-around ace TB-DB Jim Crawford raced 55y with 1st Q INT for Wyoming's only score. Cowboys mounted no other threats, relinquishing 23y 2nd Q TD pass from Cougars QB Wayne Startin to HB Burt Bullock. But, BYU missed vital kick.

November 22-24, 1956

(Th'g) OREGON STATE 14 Oregon 14: PCC champ Beavers (7-2-1) were tied when Ducks (4-4-2) struck with 1:51 left on QB Tom Crabtree's TD pass to FB Jack Morris. Oregon State had jumped to 7-0 and 14-7 leads on TDs by FB Tom Berry and WB Sterling Hammack. Hammack's TD atoned for his 3rd Q blunder when he touched punt at own 36YL, allowing Oregon REC that led to HB Jim Shanley's TD run.

Yale 42 HARVARD 14: Ivy League's 1st official championship went to veteran Yale (8-1) squad. After halting Crimson on downs at own 41YL, Yale win was launched on 59y march to HB Dennis McGill's 2y TD quick-opener midway through 1st Q. Bulldogs added 3 TDs in 2nd Q, including McGill's 78y scoring run behind E John Pendexter's perfect block. When Harvard (2-6) tallied on HB Jim Joslin's 39y run, Eli HB Al Ward answered with 77y KO RET for TD on way to 28-7 H bulge. Crimson played spirited ball in 3rd Q, holding 1st series of Elis and gaining possession at Yale 26YL on INT by FB-LB Tony Gianelly. QB John Simourian slithered into EZ on 4th down from 1 YL, and rejuvenated Harvard trailed on 28-14. Yale regained its poise and used 32y punt RET to position itself for brilliant 4th Q TD catch by E Paul Lopata. Bulldogs gained 383y on chilly day, finishing 9th nationally in total O with 355y avg and 8th in rushing O at 265y.

PITTSBURGH 7 Penn State 7: Pittsburgh's Orange Bowl hopes were spoiled by tie which saw both scores confined to 5-min stretch of 2nd Q. Penn State (6-2-1) stopped Pitt (6-2-1) on their 1YL, then launched 99y drive capped by HB Billy Kane's 3y TD run. Panthers HB Dick Bowen took following KO back 23y and added 18y run on 75y TD drive. Pitt QB Corny Salvaterra's only completion of day went for 18y TD to E Bob Rosborough. Nittany Lions QB-K Milt Plum, who didn't start game, missed 24y FG in last min.

Georgia Tech 28 FLORIDA 0: Georgia Tech (8-1) failed on all 8 of its pass attempts, but used 239y rushing and HB Paul Rotenberry's 2 TD runs to cruise to win. Florida (6-2-1) saw SEC title ambitions flicker, losing FUMs at own 25, 17, and 13YLs. In surprise coaching decision, little Jimmy Dunn, QB architect of 5 Gators wins in row, was benched as starter. Sub G Don Miller made FUM REC and blocked punt in Yellow Jackets' typically sterling D effort.

TENNESSEE 20 Kentucky 7: Opening Tennessee (9-0) score came when TB Johnny Majors lost FUM near Kentucky (6-4) GL and outstanding Vols T John Gordy alertly grabbed it to step 6y to TD. But, Wildcats played fiercely, and under direction of 60-min QB Delmar Hughes, they powered 65y in 18 plays to go ahead 7-6 on Hughes' sneak early in 3rd Q. Majors' booming 69y punt midway in 4th Q pinned Kentucky deep. Resultant field position placed Vols at own 47YL, and Majors swept RE on 7th play for winning TD. UK retaliated but HB Bobby Cravens lost FUM to Vols G Bill Johnson at Tennessee 47YL. Majors (23/143y) burst through RT and then LT on runs of 22 and 31y to score clincher.

Louisiana State 21 Arkansas 7 (Shreveport): Future star of Green Bay Packers, LSU (2-7) FB Jimmy Taylor, had his greatest game as Tiger. Taylor lugged ball 20/170y, 2 TDs, including 74y sprint, sprung by E Joe Wood's block, that launched LSU on its upset path in 2nd Q. LSU G-LB Bob Ziegler made 27y INT TD RET for 13-0 lead shortly after Taylor's burst. Arkansas (6-4) countered after next KO, moving to Tigers 39YL behind its 2nd unit. Razorbacks FB Jerry Ferguson slipped away for 14y gain, and when he was about to be hauled down, Ferguson flipped lateral to trailing HB Don Ritschel, who was free to dash remaining 25y into EZ. Bengals led 13-7 at H. T-DT Earl Leggett shook off his season-long injuries to play great game for Tigers. Leggett's FUM REC early in 3rd Q led to Taylor's short TD and 19-7 edge. LSU D held on downs at its 9 and 39YLs in 3rd Q, and QB-P M.C. Reynolds punted OB at 1YL in 4th Q to set stage for DEs Wood and Billy Smith to crash in on Porkers QB Don Christian for safety. So effective was Bengals run game, which totaled 295y, that they bothered with only 1 pass.

Michigan 19 OHIO STATE 0: Buckeyes bid for share of Big 10 crown bounded away in brace of FUMs. Ohio State won coin toss and elected to take stiff breeze from south. It backfired. Michigan (7-2) went 77y to score on opening drive as HB Terry Barr gathered in QB Jim Van Pelt's 21y TD throw. Barr soon scored his 2nd TD after Ohio State HB Jim Roseboro's 2nd FUM gave Wolverines possession at Buckeyes 9YL. Ohio may have trailed 13-0, but had best of play thereafter. Buckeyes sent FB Galen Cisco (13/66y), Roseboro (16/54y), and HB Don Clark (12/53y) slashing behind blocks of Gs Aurelius Thomas and Jim Parker. Ohio failed on 4th down at Michigan 3YL in 4th Q, then advanced as far as 26YL before finally expiring. Wolverines sent HB Jimmy Pace (16/96y) slipping through T for 46y to Bucks 24YL, and soon put game away on QB Jim Maddock's 1y TD plunge.

OKLAHOMA 54 Nebraska 6: Sooners (9-0) notched their 9th straight Big 7 crown and made it look easy with 656y total O. On game's last play, Oklahoma needed to gain but 2y to break team O record of 664y, but 4th-team QB Kenny Crossland fumbled and lost 6y. Spear-heading 506y ground attack were HBs Clendon Thomas (8/100y) and Tommy McDonald, who scored opening TD on 8y lateral and caught 3 passes/77y, including 46y TD from QB Jimmy Harris. Harris and sub HB Carl Dodd also scored twice. Nebraska (4-6) fashioned 79y TD drive early in 2nd Q as QB Gordon Englert ran option plays that used running talents of FB Jerry Brown and HB Frank Nappi. Huskers E Clarence Cook caught 5y TD pass from Englert. But, Oklahoma scored twice in 1:48 span for 34-6 H edge.

Southern California 10 UCLA 7: Men of Troy played power game to overwhelm UCLA (7-3) with their big line, led by Ts Mike Henry and Monte Clark, who was ejected in late going with C Karl Rubke and E Bob Voiles and Bruins G Esker Harris. Southern California (7-2) avoided passing all but 6 times (2-6/13y, TD, INT) but rushed for 314y. But, it was pass that earned Trojans their TD 5:39 into 3rd Q: improving QB Jim Conroy pitched out to FB C.R. Roberts (23/102y), who ran left and tossed 14y dying duck to E Hillard Hill. QB-K Ells Kissinger added victory margin with 32y FG early in 4th Q. Bruins, who gained only 23y rushing, were badly outplayed, but earned great field position on punting of TB-P Kirk Wilson (6/51.5y avg). Wilson dropped 1 punt of 59y dead on 1YL. Wilson passed 6-12/116y, INT, but didn't get going until late when his completions of 8, 13, and 17y set up FB Stu Farber for 1y TD dive in game's last min.

CALIFORNIA 20 Stanford 18: In Pappy Waldorf's last game as coach, California (3-7) upset Stanford (4-6) by striking for 2 TDs in opening 11 mins on marches of 80 and 63y. Golden Bears soph QB Joe Kapp ran 29y and 11y with each sprint ending at 1YL to position HBs Darrell Roberts and Jack Hart for Cal's 2nd and 3rd TD plunges and 14-pt lead. Indians rallied from 20-6 2nd Q deficit, but failed conv kicks beat them for 3rd time in 1956. HB-K Mike Raftery missed twice, and Bear G Don Piestrup blocked Raftery's 3rd kick try. Departing Stanford QB John Brodie (9-19/91y, TD, 2 INTs) set new PCC record with 137 completions in single season. But, Brodie had tough day: he lost FUM to E-DE Ron Wheatcroft to launch Bears' 2nd TD drive in 1st Q, made bad pitchout, while also suffering E Joel Freis' GL drop of perfect 50y pass. Waldorf closed with 67-32-4 slate, 7-1-2 in "The Big Game" against Stanford. Tribe FB Lou Valli primarily ran wide for 23/209y and 14y TD.

Washington 40 WASHINGTON STATE 26: Apple Cup O free-for-all came up glorious for Washington Huskies (5-5) as their burly line carved holes for 368y rushing. Washington bolted to 7-0 lead on game's 3rd play as HB Mike McCluskey was sprung for 58y TD dash. It was 21-0 before Washington State (3-6-1) star E-P Bill Steiger faked punt and darted 19y for 1st down in 2nd Q. Steiger soon caught sub QB Bunny Aldrich's 15y TD pass to cut Cougars' deficit to 21-6 at H. Huskies HB Dean Derby scored twice on short runs as UW built 34-6 lead at end of 3rd Q. Wazzu soph QB Bobby Newman, who earlier lost potential TD on FUM to Washington E-DE Bruce Claridge, fired trio of 4th Q TD passes: 19y to Steiger, 4y to E Don Gest, and 38y to E Stan Fanning. Newman's fabulous 4th Q gave him 3 to-date season records at Pullman: most completions (91), most tries (170), and most y (1240y).

December 1, 1956

(Th) Texas A&M 34 TEXAS 21: Wrapping up SWC crown, Aggies (9-0-1) enjoyed their 1st win in Austin's Memorial Stadium since its construction in 1924. Key elements were Texas A&M HB John David Crow's 27y TD run for early lead, QB Roddy Osborne's 2 TD runs, and FB Jack Pardee's 85y KO RET that set up another score. QB Joe Clements hit E Bob Bryant with 2 TDs, but moribund Texas (1-9) closed out its worst season ever. For Texas A&M coach Paul Bryant, it was his 1st undefeated team.

Army 7 Navy 7 (Philadelphia): Tie deflated both sides: Army (5-3-1) was unable to mine its 237y to 132y O edge for win, and Navy (6-1-2) Rear Admiral and superintendent W.R. Smedberg felt compelled to reject Cotton Bowl bid. Cotton Bowl pres Robert Cullum said, "I'm on my way to Syracuse" to present invitation to Orangemen. After scoreless 1st H in which Middies E-DE Pete Jokanovich made 4th down, drive-stopping tackle at his 20YL, Army QB-DB Dave Bourland stormed 29y on INT RET to prepare FB Bob Kyasky (18/77y, TD) for 4y TD run 3:57 into 3rd Q. Army's season-long bugaboo, butter-fingered ball handling, cropped up again midway through 4th Q, and Navy E-DE John Kanuch pounced on Bourland's poor pitchout at Army 27YL. It was 1 of 5 lost FUMs by Cadets. After 10 methodical Middies plays, little FB Dick Dagampat (11/37y, TD) plunged for 1y TD, and HB-K Ned Oldham's conv kick tied it midway in 4th Q. Black Knights' fine D effort kept Navy, which made only 5 1st downs, from advancing past its 39YL on its own power but once.

Georgia Tech 35 GEORGIA 0: Passive Bulldogs (3-6-1) entered game with only 66 points in 9 games, and coach Wally Butts said he slept downstairs all week "because I thought I might jump out the window in my sleep." Georgia's nifty assortment of D alignments made it tight game for 1st H, and aiding cause was 61y punt by E-P Ken Cooper. Starting slowly, Engineers (9-1) softened Georgia middle, then on back of FB Dickie Mattison, they staged 13-play, 86y march, without throwing pass, in 2nd Q for 7-0 lead on HB Paul Rotenberry's 8y run. Rotenberry sped 53y to Bulldogs 19YL on 1st snap of 2nd H, and QB Wade Mitchell soon scored for 14-0 lead. Three TDs in 4th Q, scored by Mattison on run and HB Stan Flowers on short buck and 12y catch, sealed coach Bobby Dodd's 100th win at Georgia Tech and Gator Bowl bid.

Auburn 34 ALABAMA 7 (Birmingham): After scoreless 1st Q, Auburn (7-3) launched its best offensive of season. Plainsmen went 54y in 2nd Q as QB Howell Tubbs lofted perfect 40y pass to E Jimmy "Red" Phillips, who was dropped at 9YL by Crimson Tide (2-7-1) DB George Salem, who had pursuit angle. Tubbs flipped 6y TD to E Jerry Elliott for 7-0 lead. Auburn went another 54y to Tubbs' 11y option TD run, and before Alabama knew what hit it, FB Don Kinderknecht bobbled FUM on ensuing KO and Tigers HB Billy Kitchens fell on EZ FUM that was lost by Auburn QB Jimmy Cook after 11y run. Tide QB Bobby Smith quickly coughed up INT by Auburn FB-LB Billy Atkins to set up Elliott's 2nd TD grab of 2nd Q. Ahead 34-0 in 3rd Q, Tigers went with D subs, but returned starters in effort to blank driving Alabama. However, Tide washed over Auburn as HB Jim Loftin powered 8y off RT Jim Cunningham's block for 3rd Q TD.

Miami 20 FLORIDA 7: Tilt was dubbed "Frustration Bowl" because each team was destined to sit out New Year's Day because of NCAA probation. Miami (8-0-1) jumped to 14-0 H lead on TD runs by QB Sam Scarnecchia and FB Don Bosseler (23/148y, 2 TDs), who, due to depletion of troops, also saw action at HB. Bosseler's 1st score came after T-DT Gary Greaves intercepted wobbly pass thrown as Florida QB Jimmy Dunn was clobbered by E-DE Phil Bennett. Gators (6-3-1) E Dan Pelham halved margin with 4th Q blocked punt by Canes E-P Jack Johnson and scooped up ball at 20YL to sprint to TD. But, Bosseler, Hurricanes' best weapon, answered within 1:07

with 72y TD bolt off LG Bob Cunio's block. Bosseler ran over Florida DB John Symank and carried DB Jim Rountree on his back from UF 5YL. It was Miami's 4th straight win in 18-game series.

MISSOURI 15 Kansas 13: Retiring Missouri (4-5-1) coach Don Faurot received odd going-away gift. Tigers QB Dave Doane hit E Larry Plumb for 14y TD with 3:21, but G-K Charley Rash's missed kick left it tied at 13-13. With less than 2 mins to go, Kansas (3-6-1) lost gutsy 4th down gamble at its own 32YL, but appeared reprieved when QB-DB Wally Strauch made EZ INT on Mizzou's subsequent series. When Jayhawks took over on their 20YL, Strauch was sacked for -16y on 1st down, then, on sweep run, Mizzou T-DT Chuck Mehrer trapped ground-giving HB Bobby Robinson in EZ for highly-rare game-winning safety. Delighted Faurot, creator of Split-T O which was nearly-universal in college ball, was carried joyfully from field with career record of 101-79-10.

Texas Christian 21 SOUTHERN METHODIST 6: Upset-minded SMU (4-6), trying to send coach Woody Woodard out as winner, took 6-0 lead made possible by G-LB Tom Koenig, who enhanced his 16 tackles with 85y INT RET to Horned Frogs' 5YL of deflected pass tossed by TCU (7-3) QB Chuck Curtis. Ponies' HB Charlie Jackson went off left side for 4y TD. TCU clinched 2nd place in SWC and Cotton Bowl bid as subs carried O on 70y drive late in 2nd Q: little HB Carlos Vacek took pitchout from QB Dick Finney and floated 10y TD pass to FB Harold Pollard to take lead for good at 7-6. David Musslewhite, SMU's 3rd string QB forced into action due to injuries to QB Charlie Arnold and Larry Glick, was working in his own territory near end of 3rd Q when he was wacked hard by Frogs T-DT Joe Robb and lost FUM. TCU went 30y to TD: Curtis hit E O'Day Williams for 15y gain, then misdirected Mustangs right and kept left for 7y TD run. Purple G Vernon Uecker sacked SMU QB Billy Dunn, and T-DT John Groom recovered at 29YL. Sloppy exchange of INT and FUM left TCU to count on 2nd stringers, QB Finney and HB Virgil Miller, to connect on 4y TD pass.

BAYLOR 46 Rice 13: Hungry Bears (8-2) tasted sugar as they clinched bid to New Orleans' Sugar Bowl. Outmanned Rice (4-6) received its worst shellacking in 124 games. Slender Baylor HB-DB Del Shofner, who scored twice, made FUM REC, broke up important Owls pass, blocked x-pt kick, and expertly covered punts and KOs to help Baylor cinch its best record since 1951. Rice stayed close to H, trailing only 20-13 as jr QBs Frank Ryan and King Hill combined for 18-33/227y passing. Owls' passing did them in, however, as Bears picked off 4 INTs. FB-DB Charlie Dupre grabbed pass by Hill and went all way for 51y and 26-13 lead in 3rd Q. Less than 3 mins later, superb Baylor G-LB Bill Glass made 1-handed INT and rumbled 44y to 3YL. Sub HB Farrell Fisher dove over and rout was underway at 33-13. Bears returned 4 INTs/160y.

SOUTHERN CALIFORNIA 28 Notre Dame 20: Notre Dame's "best effort of season" seemed to soothe spat between coach Terry Brennan and his predecessor, Frank Leahy, who had labeled Fighting Irish (2-8) "spiritless" during days prior to game. But, when had "moral victory" ever been satisfying to mighty Fighting Irish? Trojans (8-2), saying good-bye to coach Jess Hill and presenting him with his 2nd-best record in 7 years, scored 1st on 10y TD run by QB Jim Conroy, and ND spent much of day clawing to get within 1 pt. Soph QB Bob Williams (10-13, TD) sneaked 6y in 1st Q to pull within 7-6, Williams hit E Bob Wetoska for 10y TD in 2nd Q to reach 14-13 by H, and QB Paul Hornung, playing HB because of 2 dislocated thumbs, blasted 95y on KO TD RET to trim Troy lead to 21-20 late in 3rd Q. HB Ernie Zampese, clinched verdict for Trojans by slipping through RT and tearing 38y on 4th-and-1 to TD in 1st min of 4th Q. USC's formidable line allowed only 7y rushing in 2nd H. It was Troy's 2nd straight win over Fighting Irish, 1st such occurance since 1938-39.

Final AP Poll
1 Oklahoma (104)	1715	11 Baylor (1)	198
2 Tennessee (48)	1618	12 Minnesota	183
3 Iowa (15)	1270	13 Pittsburgh	175
4 Georgia Tech (4)	1211	14 Texas Christian	118
5 Texas A&M (2)	1070	15 Ohio State	60
6 Miami (12)	867	16 Navy	57
7 Michigan (1)	599	17 George Washington	51
8 Syracuse	406	18 Southern California	33
9 Michigan State	309	19 Clemson	28
10 Oregon State (3)	229	20 Colorado	25

December 8, 1956

Pittsburgh 14 MIAMI 7: Rugged Panthers (7-2-1) gained 279y, 100y more than avg permitted by nation-leading D of previously undefeated Miami (8-1-1). Hurricanes FB Don Bosseler ran sparingly (9/46y), but got TD drive sparked with 25y of power bursts late in 2nd Q. Pitt E-DE Joe Walton, who earlier caught 46y pass, pressured Canes QB Sam Scarnecchia, but impromptu lateral was flipped to HB Joe Plevel that he carried 24y behind blocks of G Tom Pratt and E Don Johnson. Pitt HB-DB Ray DiPasquale's pass interference PEN in EZ moved ball from its 11YL to 2YL. Miami QB Sam Scarnecchia sneaked over from 1YL after Panthers were whistled for offside. Pittsburgh's 2 FBs starred in 2nd H: Ralph Jelic (8/62y) burst for 9 and 23y runs during 59y TD drive that followed 2nd H KO, and Tom Jenkins' 48y sweep keynoted winning TD march that wore down Hurricanes late in game. Winning score came from sub QB Darrell Lewis' sneak with 2:45 on clock. Miami had hoped its probation would have been lifted on 2nd anniversary in October, but its bowl ban was extended by NCAA. Win in this game would have been crowning glory for Hurricanes because it would have been 3rd win over bowl-bound team, having already blanked TCU (Cotton Bowl) and Clemson (Orange Bowl).

Conference Standings

Ivy League
Yale	7-0
Princeton	5-2
Dartmouth	4-3
Pennsylvania	4-3
Brown	3-4
Columbia	2-5
Harvard	2-5
Cornell	1-6

Atlantic Coast
Clemson	4-0-1
Duke	4-1
South Carolina	5-2
Maryland	2-2-1
North Carolina	2-3-1
North Carolina State	2-4
Virginia	1-4
Wake Forest	1-5-1

Southern
West Virginia	5-0
Virginia Tech	3-0
George Washington	5-1
Furman	2-2
Davidson	2-2-1
Virginia Military	2-3-1
Richmond	2-5
The Citadel	1-3
Washington & Lee	0-1
William & Mary	0-5

Southeastern
Tennessee	6-0
Georgia Tech	7-1
Florida	5-2
Mississippi	4-2
Auburn	4-3
Kentucky	4-4
Tulane	3-3
Vanderbilt	2-5
Mississippi State	2-5
Alabama	2-5
Louisiana State	1-5
Georgia	1-6

Big Ten
Iowa	5-1
Michigan	5-2
Minnesota	4-1-2
Michigan State	4-2
Ohio State	4-2
Northwestern	3-3-1
Purdue	1-4-2
Illinois	1-4-2
Indiana	1-5
Wisconsin	0-4-3

Big Seven
Oklahoma	6-0
Colorado	4-1-1
Missouri	3-2-1
Nebraska	3-3
Kansas	2-4
Kansas State	2-4
Iowa State	0-6

Missouri Valley
Houston	4-0
Tulsa	2-1-1
Oklahoma A&M	2-1-1
Wichita	1-3
Detroit	0-4

Mid-American
Bowling Green	5-0-1
Miami (Ohio)	4-0-1
Kent State	4-2
Marshall	2-4
Ohio	2-4
Western Michigan	1-4
Toledo	1-5

Southwest
Texas A&M	6-0
Texas Christian	5-1
Baylor	4-2
Arkansas	3-3
Southern Methodist	2-4
Rice	1-5
Texas	0-6

Border
Texas Western	5-0
Arizona State	3-1
West Texas State	2-2
Hardin-Simmons	1-3
Arizona	1-3
New Mexico A&M	0-4

Skyline Eight
Wyoming	7-0
Utah	5-1
Denver	4-3
Utah State	4-3
Colorado A&M	2-4-1
New Mexico	2-4
Brigham Young	1-5-1
Montana	1-6

Pacific Coast
Oregon State	6-1-1
Southern California	5-2
UCLA	5-2
Washington	4-4
Oregon	3-3-2
Stanford	3-4
Washington State	2-5-1
California	2-5
Idaho	0-4

1956 Major Bowl Games
Gator Bowl (Dec. 29): Georgia Tech 21 Pittsburgh 14

Gator Bowl promoters liked previous year's controversial Sugar Bowl matchup so much they rekindled same North-South rivalry in Jacksonville. Pitt's northerners might have felt at home in gusty and chilly conditions. Instead, A-student and 4-year star, QB-DB Wade Mitchell, sparkled for Georgia Tech (10-1) in his last collegiate game. Mitchell was 1 of 8 Techsters who completed their careers with 4 bowl victories in row. In addition to calling excellent mix of runs and passes, Mitchell was superb as usual at S, making TD-thwarting tackle at GL and stealing pass away from Panthers A-A E Joe Walton for clinching INT at Georgia Tech 14YL in final min. FB Ken Owen, E Jerry Nabors, and HB Paul Rotenberry scored Engineers TDs in building 14-0 and 21-7 leads. Big moment came when Pittsburgh (7-3-1) answered Owen's early TD with 70y ground assault that was barred 1y short of paydirt by whole Tech line. Pitt persisted as QB Corny Salvaterra hit HB Dick Bowen with 42y TD pass in 2nd Q and ran over from 4YL in 3rd Q. Panthers outdistanced Yellow Jackets 313y to 207y in total O and became 1st team in last 17 games to score 2 TDs against Georgia Tech's D, nation's best in scoring avg at 3.3-pts per game.

Orange Bowl: Colorado 27 Clemson 21

Colorado (8-2-1), in as 2nd place Big 7 sub for non-repeatable conf champ Oklahoma, played Rocky Mountain "Ghostriders in the Sky" as Buffs exploded for 20 pts in 2nd Q

on TD runs by FB John Bayuk, QB Boyd Dowler, and TB Howard Cook. Dowler's 6y keeper came after TB-DB Bob Stransky made 36y INT RET to 10YL, and Cook's 26y sweep right followed E Frank Clarke's partially blocked punt. Buffs nearly added 4th score, but Cook lost FUM near GL. Clemson (7-2-2) coach Frank Howard became so distraught during H locker room tirade that he threatened to quit on the spot if Tigers failed to give better 2nd H effort. Flying Tigers stormed onto field for HB Joel Wells' 3rd Q TD runs of 3 and 58y. When FB Bob Spooner opened 4th Q with TD run and QB-K Charlie Bussey kicked pt, Clemson suddenly had 21-20 lead. Here K Bussey, in his enthusiasm, made devastating mistake. He tried surprise onside-KO, and Buffs G John Wooten recovered to launch Colorado's winning 53y drive to 2nd TD run by Bayuk (23/121y, 2 TDs). Howard later suggested that, with Clemson having just taken lead for 1st time in game, Bussey should have "kicked the ball into Biscayne Bay." Bison wrapped up verdict when E Jerry Leahy pressured Bussey into another INT by Stransky.

Sugar Bowl: Baylor 13 Tennessee 7

Undefeated Tennessee (10-1), nation's no. 2 team, seemed sure bet against Baylor (9-2), 3rd place finisher in SWC. Bears HB Bobby Peters provided upset keynote with 52y RET of opening KO, but potential scoring drive unraveled when delay PEN forced errant FG. Baylor launched 80y march 7 mins into 2nd Q, capped by QB Bobby Jones' 12y pitch to E Jerry Marcontell on 4th down. TB Johnny Majors carried on 8 of 10 plays to score in 3rd Q, and K Sammy Burklow booted pt for 7-6 Volunteers lead. Bruising contest was accented by flaring tempers in 3rd Q when A-A Majors, held to 15/51y rushing and picked off twice on passes, was flung down for loss. In melee that followed, Bears FB-LB Larry Hickman kicked Vols G Bruce Burnham in face. Hickman, quickly banished by officials, was highly remorseful afterward. Burnham was carried off unconscious (although his injury would prove to be minimal), and with him seemed to go Tennessee's spirit. Majors' punt FUM at his 15YL gave Bears short winning drive in 4th Q, finalized by QB Buddy Humphrey's sneak. Key to victory was Baylor D, which held Volunteers to 1-10/16y passing and forced 4 INTs, even though Vols had suffered only 6 INTs all season. Bears provided brazen moment when, with 4:45 left, tried 4th down run from their own 41YL. Tennessee stopped Baylor's 4th down try but was helpless to advance as Majors' 4th down pass fell incomplete. Of that chance, Ed Danforth, sports editor writing in *Atlanta Journal-Constitution,* lamented his pre-bowl no. 1 vote for Tennessee: "A top flight team, properly prepared, would have cashed that ticket, but the Vols looked confused and uncertain." It was 4th time in Vols history that bowl loss had ruined otherwise perfect season.

Cotton Bowl: Texas Christian 28 Syracuse 27

Magnificent Syracuse (7-2) HB Jimmy Brown swaggered through his last collegiate game, rushing 26/132y, scoring 3 TDs, completing 20y pass, and returning KOs for total of 96y. Brown succeeded on 3 of 4 conv kicks, but his 3rd conv try was blocked by Horned Frogs sub E Chico Mendoza, and it proved to be winning margin. Horned Frogs QB Chuck Curtis (12-15/174y) struck for 2 TD passes, and TCU led 14-0 early in 2nd Q. Orangemen roared back behind Brown to gain 14-14 tie. TCU collared FUMs to start 60 and 69y drives which provided 28-14 lead early in 4th Q. Last TD came on A-A HB Jim Swink's 3y run followed by FB-K Harold Pollard's 4th conv. Brown's 41y KO RET made possible his own 4y TD, but Mendoza blocked kick with his left arm, and TCU led 28-20. With 1:16 left, Syracuse QB Chuck Zimmerman hit HB Jim Ridlon with TD pass, but alas for Orangemen, Brown's x-pt could pull them only within 1 pt, and college football's 2-pt conv rule was still 2 seasons away.

Rose Bowl: Iowa 35 Oregon State 19

With UCLA and USC banned by PCC sanctions, Oregon State (7-3-1) was left to field bitter arrows of California press, which criticized Beavers' credentials and ultimately its Rose Bowl game performance. This pair of infrequent bowl visitors had met in closely-played October game won by Iowa 14-13, but this time Hawkeyes (9-1) dominated. But before Iowa's dominance, Beavers threatened twice early, each time losing FUM. QB Ken Ploen scored on 49y run after Oregon State's 1st bobble, but twisted his knee before he could help add to Iowa's eventual 14-0 1st Q lead. In 2nd H, MVP Ploen returned to display his passing skills, finishing with 9-10/83y, TD, INT in air and 8/59y, TD on ground. After initial Iowa burst, teams began traded scores, with Hawkeyes HB Collins "Mike" Hagler scoring twice. Hagler made 9y romp in 1st Q and nifty 66y reverse in 3rd Q as Ploen handed to HB Don Dobrino going right, with Hagler taking inside handoff through left side behind pulling linemen. TB Joe Francis did his best to make Beavers competitive by rushing 15/73y and passing 10-12/130y, TD, including 35y TD to WB Sterling Hammack in 4th Q. Hawks' D stars, E Frank Gilliam and T Alex Karras, each blocked x-pt kick. Iowa won stat battle 408y to 296y, and Hawkeye players dedicated their victory to 1955 A-A G Calvin Jones who perished in Canadian plane crash several weeks before Rose Bowl. Iowa coach Forest Evashevski said his team was "more explosive this game than most of the season."

1956 Top Performance Formula

1	Oklahoma	1.7260
2	Georgia Tech	1.6909
3	Tennessee	1.6891
4	Texas A&M	1.6360
5	Iowa	1.6059
6	Miami	1.5884
7	Michigan	1.5757
8	Baylor	1.4684
9	Arizona State	1.4596
10	Mississippi	1.4478
11	Minnesota	1.4472
12	Colorado	1.4345
13	Michigan State	1.3856
14	Syracuse	1.3797
15	Penn State	1.3697
16	Oregon State	1.3754
17	Pittsburgh	1.3649
18	Auburn	1.3484
19	Houston	1.3213
20	Southern California	1.3198

1956 Top Opponent Records

1	Texas Tech	.6813
2	Michigan	.6757
3	Texas	.6685
4	Pittsburgh	.6495
5	Arizona	.6418
6	Miami	.6374
7	Mississippi	.6278
8t	Kentucky	.6250
8t	Minnesota	.6250
10	Alabama	.6209
11	Notre Dame	.6207
12	Maryland	.6196
13	Louisiana State	.6154
14	Tennessee	.6100
15	Iowa	.6059
16	Florida	.6033
17	Georgia Tech	.5990
18	Auburn	.5924
19	Oregon State	.5918
20	Syracuse	.5909

1956 Out-of-Conference Records

	W-L	Percentage	Bowl W-L
Big Ten	19-5	.7917	1-0
Southeastern	23-10-2	.6857	1-1
Southwest	20-9-1	.6833	2-0
Pacific	15-10	.6000	0-1
Big Seven	12-14-1	.4630	1-0
Atlantic Coast	7-20-4	.2903	0-1

1956 Individual Statistical Leaders

RUSHING YARDS	Attempts	Yards	Avg.
Jim Crawford, Wyoming	200	1104	5.5
Bill Barnes, Wake Forest	168	1010	6.0
Jimmy Brown, Syracuse	158	986	6.2
Jack Hill, Utah State	140	920	6.6
Jim Bakhtiar, Virginia	203	879	4.3
Mel Dillard, Purdue	193	873	4.5
Tommy McDonald, Oklahoma	119	853	7.2
Clendon Thomas, Oklahoma	104	817	7.9
Don Clark, Ohio State	139	797	5.7
C.R. Roberts, Southern California	120	775	6.5

PASSING YARDS	Completions	Attempts	Yards	Pct.
John Brodie, Stanford	139	240	1633	57.9
Bobby Newman, Washington State	91	170	1240	53.5
Bob Reinhart, San Jose State	90	172	1138	52.3
Tom Flores, Pacific	73	127	1119	57.5
Guy Martin, Colgate	88	179	1100	51.8
Charlie Arnold, Southern Methodist	71	157	964	45.2
Carroll Johnston, Brigham Young	72	167	945	43.1
Bob Winters, Utah State	65	130	943	50.0
Paul Hornung, Notre Dame	59	111	917	53.2
Claude Benham, Columbia	61	129	906	47.3

RECEIVING YARDS	Catches	Yards
Bill Steiger, Washington State	39	607
Art Powell, San Jose State	40	583
Farrell Funston, Pacific	27	563
Fred Dugan, Dayton	26	481
Don Ellingsen, Washington State	27	455
Jim Morse, Notre Dame	20	442
Ernie Pitts, Denver	21	415
Brad Bomba, Indiana	31	407
Jim Phillips, Auburn	23	383

1956 Consensus All-America Team

End:	Joe Walton, Pittsburgh
	Ron Kramer, Michigan
Tackle:	John Witte, Oregon State
	Lou Michaels, Kentucky
Guard:	Jim Parker, Ohio State
	Bill Glass, Baylor
Center:	Jerry Tubbs, Oklahoma
Back:	John Brodie, Stanford
	Jimmy Brown, Syracuse
	Johnny Majors, Tennessee
	Tommy McDonald, Oklahoma

Other All-America Choices

End:	Buddy Cruze, Tennessee
	Bill Steiger, Washington State
Tackle:	Alex Karras, Iowa
	Charlie Krueger, Texas A&M
	Edmon Gray, Oklahoma
	Paul Wiggin, Stanford
	Norman Hamilton, Texas Christian
	Bob Hobert, Minnesota
Guard:	Sam Valentine, Penn State
	John Barrow, Florida
Center:	Don Stephenson, Georgia Tech
Back:	Paul Hornung, Notre Dame
	Don Bosseler, Miami
	Jim Crawford, Wyoming
	Billy Ray Barnes, Wake Forest
	Jack Pardee, Texas A&M

1956 Heisman Trophy Vote

Paul Hornung, senior quarterback, Notre Dame	1,066
Johnny Majors, senior tailback, Tennessee	994
Tommy McDonald, senior halfback, Oklahoma	973
Jerry Tubbs, senior center, Oklahoma	724
Jimmy Brown, senior halfback, Syracuse	561

Other Major Awards

Maxwell (Player)	Tommy McDonald, senior halfback, Oklahoma
Outland (Lineman)	Jim Parker, senior guard, Ohio State
Walter Camp (Back)	Paul Hornung, senior quarterback, Notre Dame
Knute Rockne (Lineman)	Jerry Tubbs, senior center, Oklahoma
AFCA Coach of the Year	Bowden Wyatt, Tennessee

1957

The Year of the End to Oklahoma's 47, the Probation Champions, and Wolfpack Road Warriors

On rode the pigskin colossus known as the Oklahoma Sooners (10-1), winning their first seven games to extend the longest winning streak in football history to 47. Oklahoma reached that point by beating Missouri (5-4-1), 39-14, on November 9. The following Saturday, Notre Dame (7-3) came to Norman for a nationally-televised game. Anticipation for the showdown had been high when the Fighting Irish reversed their losing trend of 1956 with four straight wins to open the 1957 season. Interest quickly waned, however, as Notre Dame lost two straight contests to top drawer teams—Navy (9-1-1) and Michigan State (8-1)—just prior to the Oklahoma game.

On November 16, 1957, a date that will live in Oklahoma football infamy, the Fighting Irish took early control against the Sooners, built their confidence in a nail-biting scoreless fight, and punched across a fourth quarter touchdown by halfback Dick Lynch for a 7-0 upset.

Notre Dame's win over the Sooners was one of several big upsets in 1957. Texas A&M (8-3) won eight games until Rice (7-4) sprung a 7-6 shocker to steal the Southwest Conference's spot in the Cotton Bowl. Had it not occurred on the same day as the Notre Dame upset at Norman, Rice's win might have been hailed as one of the great upsets ever, since the top-ranked Aggies seemed invincible with 14 straight wins. Instead, the Owls barely caused a blip on the radar screen of the year's upsets. Everyone interested in football in 1957 would surely remember the news of Oklahoma's upset loss. Only a precious few Owls loyalists still remember the upset authored by Rice in Houston on the same afternoon.

The upset surprises bloomed large. Purdue (5-4), so often the thorn in the side of the Spartans of Michigan State, beat them again, 20-13. North Carolina (6-4), spurting occasionally in coach Jim Tatum's second season at the Chapel Hill helm, dropped the only defeat on Cotton Bowl-bound Navy. North Carolina State (7-1-2) was a complete surprise but lost to the least likely team on its schedule, mediocre William & Mary (4-6).

With Oklahoma out of the way, Peck's Bad Boys, the Auburn Tigers (10-0), became the only team ever to win the AP national championship while cooling its heels on bowl probation. The 1957 Tigers displayed one of the greatest defenses ever, permitting opponents a mere 2.8 points per game, while pitching six shutouts. Cornerstones of the defense were nose guard Zeke Smith, linebacker Jackie Burkett, and ends Jim Phillips and Jerry Wilson. In converted halfback Lloyd Nix, the Tigers had one of the most unsung national champion quarterbacks ever. Southpaw Nix completed only 33 passes, one of the lowest totals for a passer leading a top-ranked team in the modern span of history since 1953. But, the intelligent Nix marshaled a fast-striking option attack that featured halfbacks Tommy Lorino and Bobby Hoppe and fullback Billy Atkins, who scored many key touchdowns. Starting the season with the 15th spot in AP rankings, Auburn fell out of the poll when it didn't play during the first week, and reentered at no. 7 after shutting out no. 8 Tennessee (8-3) in the season opener. The Tigers hopped to fifth after blanking Georgia Tech (4-4-2) in mid-October and even trailed one-loss, no. 1 Michigan State in the November 18 poll. Had the Associated Press staged a post-bowl poll, it is conspicuously possible that Rose Bowl champion Ohio State (9-1) could have snatched Auburn's AP title.

Michigan State coach Duffy Daugherty lauded the coaching job done by Auburn's Shug Jordan. "...It was a great accomplishment for Auburn to go undefeated when they knew all along there would be no reward in a bowl game," said Daugherty. "Jordan did a magnificent job of keeping up team morale and it's bound to be a close-knit unit that allows so few touchdowns."

Woody Hayes' Ohio State Buckeyes had stumbled late in 1956, losing their last two Big Ten games to Iowa and Michigan after a record 17 league wins in a row. The Buckeyes rebounded in 1957, sweeping seven Big Ten foes without having to play AP's eventual no. 3 Michigan State and, with Auburn on probation, the Buckeyes were picked no. 1 in the UPI coaches poll at the end of the regular season.

Led by guard Aurelius Thomas, end Jim Houston, halfback Don Clark and late-blooming fullback Bob White, the Buckeyes were heavy favorites in the Rose Bowl. Ohio State's Pasadena opponent was highly-disparaged Oregon (7-4). With UCLA, Southern California, and Washington remaining on conference probation and the PCC on its last legs, the West Coast had little to offer by way of opposition to the Big Ten, which had built a 10-1 record in Rose Bowls since 1947. Yet, Oregon outplayed Ohio State, fighting fiercely all day and losing only 10-7, truly a gigantic moral victory.

Ducks quarterback Jack Crabtree's short passes to end Ron Stover confounded Ohio State's vaunted defense, but Oregon gained most of its yardage between the 20 yard-lines.

An unheralded giant turned out to be North Carolina State (7-1-2), surprise champion of the ACC. The Wolfpack, coming off a 3-7 mark in 1956, proved to be excellent road warriors as they opened the season with five games away from Raleigh and went undefeated except for a scoreless tie against up-and-down Miami (5-4-1). Until this unusual scheduling irregularity fell out of use in the 1970s, nine University Division teams between 1953 and 1969 opened with as many as five games on the road, not counting neutral site games or alternate home sites. Only one—the 1957 North Carolina State team—ever came home without defeat. Although a nod must be give to George Washington University, which opened 5-1 in 1955, losing only at Florida.

Back at home, the Pack was tied by Duke (6-3-2), that would go to the Orange Bowl because N.C. State, like Auburn, was on probation. Halfback Dick Christy played an unbelievable game against South Carolina (5-5) on November 23 and became the first-ever Wolfpack All-America. But Christy and his teammates couldn't prevent the one-point upset loss to William & Mary, played, you guessed it, in Riddick Stadium in Raleigh.

Darrell Royal debuted at Texas (6-4-1) and produced an unexpected second place finish in the Southwest Conference and a Sugar Bowl trip. But, Mississippi (9-1-1) dominated the Longhorns by 39-7 in New Orleans behind the brilliant play of quarterback Ray Brown. It would only be the beginning of Texas greatness under coach Royal, the former quarterback tutored by Bud Wilkinson at Oklahoma in the late 1940s.

Lee Grosscup, talented Utah (6-4) passer, broke the passing percentage record (for more than 50 attempts but fewer than 150) of Alabama's Harry Gilmer, which had stood since 1945. Playing his last game against Utah State (2-7-1) on Thanksgiving Day, Grosscup finished his season having completed 94 of 137 throws for a new record percentage of 68.6. The record failed to last long. Don Meredith, slinging sophomore star of Southern Methodist (4-5-1), completed his season nine days later in early December and set another percentage mark of 69.6 on 71 completions in 102 attempts.

Still, the grandest moment of the season was Notre Dame's upset of record-setting Oklahoma. What of Oklahoma's amazing string of 47 wins in a row? Can it ever be broken?

One is inclined to offer a resounding "Yes!" given that two recent teams nearly have come within one undefeated season of catching Oklahoma's 47 in a row. Miami captured 34 straight games from September 2000 to January 2003, and Southern California also won 34 in a row from 2003 through its regular season finale of 2005. What Miami and USC had in common is precisely the biggest stumbling block to 47 wins. Each juggernaut lost in the BCS championship game, Miami in double overtime to Ohio State in the 2003 Fiesta Bowl, and Southern California to Texas in the 2006 Rose Bowl.

Remember the mid-1950s had a rule preventing teams from two straight bowl trips, so the Sooners faced a highly-ranked bowl opponent only twice (Maryland both times in the Orange Bowl) during their run. Any multi-year undefeated team in the future would be forced into a BCS championship final bowl game three or perhaps four times. Could one team win such pressure-packed games against the nation's no. 2 team four times in a row? We can count, on one historical hand, the number of teams that have won four straight bowl games of any sort, let alone bowls against the perceived second-best team. If the BCS were to die, a tiered championship might replace it, a system that would be even more difficult to scale with at least two post-season games against top-10 teams.

On the other hand, the only possibility of beating Oklahoma's mark likely would hinge on a broad increase in the number of games—perhaps as many as 20 in a year—that a future playoff system might provide to a given team. Perhaps then a great team could run off 34 or 35 wins with essentially the same personnel over a two-year period. That appears to be an unlikely scenario given the current aversion for complex playoffs among college presidents and TV networks. Even with four extra games that gigantic 16-team playoffs would offer a given champion, that future juggernaut would have to wrap at least 12 other consecutive wins around the front or back of a two-year run. With genuine parity in college football apparently here for good and superstar players leaving early for the NFL,

topnotch teams of today completely turn over their rosters in three years. Only a major overhaul in the landscape of college football—like a schedule bonus of five or six extra games—would allow Oklahoma's record to be beaten. No way! It simply can't be done.

Milestones

■ Oklahoma A&M announced name change to Oklahoma State University and was admitted to newly-named Big Eight Conference, starting play in 1960.

■ University of Detroit, in its last move before dropping football in 1964, left Missouri Valley Conference to become independent. Former independent Cincinnati replaced Detroit in Missouri Valley Conference.

■ Colorado A&M College, member of Skyline Eight, changed its name to Colorado State University.

■ Princeton head coach Charlie Caldwell, suffering from cancer, stepped aside during pre-season practice. His place was taken by assistant Dick Colman on interim basis, then full-time after Caldwell's death at age 55 on November 1. Former Fordham star and Virginia assistant coach Len Eshmont died at 39. Dying at 70 was former Yale coach Thomas "Tad" Jones (60-15-4 record in 1916-17, 1920-27), famous for his quote that playing Harvard would be most important moment in any Yale player's life.

■ Longest winning streaks entering season:

Oklahoma 40	Central Michigan 15	Wyoming 11

■ Coaching Changes

	Incoming	Outgoing
Arizona	Ed Doherty	Warren Woodson
California	Pete Elliott	Lynn Waldorf
Columbia	Aldo "Buff" Donelli	Lou Little
Harvard	John Yovicsin	Lloyd Jordan
Houston	Hal Lahar	Bill Meek
Indiana	Bob Hicks	Bernie Crimmins
Missouri	Frank Broyles	Don Faurot
Nebraska	Bill Jennings	Pete Elliott
Princeton	Dick Colman	Charlie Caldwell
Southern California	Don Clark	Jess Hill
Southern Methodist	Bill Meek	Woody Woodard
Texas	Darrell Royal	Ed Price
Texas Western	Ben Collins	Mike Brumbelow
Washington	Jim Owens	Darrell Royal
Wyoming	Bob Devaney	Phil Dickens

AP Preseason Poll

1 Oklahoma (127)	1659	11 Georgia Tech	326
2 Texas A&M (4)	996	12 Navy	301
3 Michigan State	988	13 Oregon State	208
4 Minnesota (9)	919	14 Miami (1)	202
5 Tennessee (3)	894	15 Auburn	98
6 Michigan (3)	633	16 Penn State	71
7 Baylor	517	17 Ohio State (1)	60
8 Pittsburgh	487	18 Notre Dame (2)	51
9 Iowa (4)	465	19 Southern California	40
10 Duke	331	20 Kentucky	39

September 21, 1957

(Fri) UCLA 47 Air Force 0: Flu-stricken Florida had to bow out of match-up with UCLA (1-0), so highly-inexperienced Air Force (0-1), on short notice, was offered L.A. Coliseum ambush. After poor Air Force punt went OB at its own 38YL, UCLA BB Steve Gertsman nabbed opening 11y TD pass from TB Kirk Wilson midway through 1st Q. Bruins added 19 pts in 2nd Q, highlighted by TB Chuck Kendall's 24y TD pass to E Dick Wallen, who beat tight coverage of Air Force HB-DB Phil Lane. Each of Uclans' TBs, Kendall, Wilson, and Don Long, ran in for 2nd H TDs of 9, 3, and 5y respectively. Falcons, in their 1st attempt at big time football, blocked 2 conv kicks and nearly scored twice, but UCLA E-DE Jim Steffen made INT at 20YL and Air Force was stopped on downs at Bruins 10YL.

Navy 46 BOSTON COLLEGE 6: Crowd at dedication of new, on-campus stadium at Boston College (0-1) included ex-King of Belgium, but festive atmosphere was ruined by relentless Navy O directed by QB Tom Forrestal (8-14/141y, 2 TDs, INT). Middies (1-0) gained 212y rushing and 216y passing as HB Ned Oldham scored twice. Eagles TD was delivered in 2nd Q by beautiful 94y TD bomb thrown from their from EZ by QB Don Allard to HB Tom Sullivan who caught ball at Navy 40YL and had clear sailing.

Oklahoma 26 PITTSBURGH 0: Sellout crowd at Pitt Stadium anticipated upset win because Panthers (0-1) were perceived to have best chance during 1957 to end Oklahoma's long winning streak. Instead, Sooners (1-0), with only 3 starters back from 1956 national champions, breezed to their 41st straight victory and seemed poised to sweep their schedule for 4th year in row. Oklahoma HB Jakie Sandefer and QBs Carl Dodd and David Baker all pitched TD passes. After making stands in 7-0 1st H at own 18 and 33YLs and holding on with QB-DB Bill Kaildan's INT at 10YL and DT Jim McCusker's FUM REC in own EZ, Pitt lost 2 FUMs in 3rd Q that led to demoralizing 3-TD deficit. Oklahoma HB Clendon Thomas bulled 13y through 3 tacklers to score after FB-LB Dennit Morris fell on FUM by Panthers QB Kaliden on 1st play after 2nd H KO. When Pitt HB Dick Haley lost FUM again on 1st play after ensuing KO, Dodd fired 17y score to E Don Stiller.

North Carolina State 7 NORTH CAROLINA 0: NC State's D was led by G Frank Tokar, T Darrell Dess, and E Bob Pepe to hold Tar Heels to 148y O. HB Dick Hunter charged 5y for 1st Q TD for Wolfpack (1-0), after QB Frank Cackovic set it up with odd 50y run. From his own 28YL, NC State FB Wally Prince was halted but pitched surprise lateral to Cackovic who raced down left sideline to UNC 22YL. Even after Cackovic's long

gain, TD drive seemed halted by North Carolina (0-1) HB-DB Emil DeCantis' INT, but it was nullified by D-holding PEN. NC State stopped 3 Tar Heels scoring chances with its stout D.

Duke 26 SOUTH CAROLINA 14: Gamecocks (0-1) opened scoring with 80y TD march in 2nd Q, capped by 2y run up middle by little HB King Dixon (12/46y). Duke (1-0) tied it in 2nd Q as QB Pryor Millner sneaked 1y after FUM REC at Carolina 25YL. Blue Devils turned up heat to dominate 2nd H as HB George Dutrow circled E for 7y TD, QB Bob Broadhead wedged 1y for TD, and HB Wray Carlton (12/93y) sprinted 12y to pay-dirt for 26-7 lead.

WEST VIRGINIA 6 Virginia 6: Underdog Virginia (0-0-1) threw back 2 TD dive attempts from its 1YL by West Virginia (0-0-1) FB Larry Krutko in 1st Q but was surprised by Mountaineers QB Mickey Trimarki's long TD heave to HB Ralph Anastasio that went for 62y TD just before H. Trailing 6-0, Virginia went 80y in 10 plays to tie it with 3:10 left in 4th Q. QB Nelson Yarbrough sneaked over after little HB Carl Moser raced 22y and caught 5y pass on march also paced by FB Jim Bakhtiar. Game ended with 2 failed plunges by Cavaliers after E Pat Whitaker caught pass at WVU 2YL.

Texas 26 GEORGIA 7: Tricky Split-T O arrived at Texas (1-0) as Darrell Royal's coaching era began. Longhorns FB Mike Dowdle scored twice, QB Walt Fondren once. New Georgia (0-1) QB Charlie Britt experienced hot and cold day, but was able to trim deficit to 13-7 with 5y TD pass to HB Jimmy Orr in 3rd Q. Longhorns sub QB Bobby Lackey contributed TD sneak to ice it in 4th Q.

Rice 20 LOUISIANA STATE 14: Owls (1-0) won for 1st time in Baton Rouge since 1935, but seemingly improved LSU (0-1) held 14-7 lead going into 4th Q. Tigers FB Jimmy Taylor bulled for 1y TD in 1st Q and raced 13y for score in 2nd Q. Rice used balanced O of passes by QBs Frank Ryan and King Hill blended with power runs of HB Pat Bailey and FB Ray Chilton to tally twice in 4th Q. Ryan ended 52y drive with TD sneak early in 4th Q, and, with less than 3 min to go, Owls won it on swift 51y strike. Hill passed 35y to E Buddy Dial, and Chilton roared 16y for game-winning TD.

VANDERBILT 7 Missouri 7: C-LB Tom Swaney of Missouri (0-0-1) stepped in front of flat pass by Commodores (0-0-1) QB Boyce Smith, who was under heavy pressure from FB-LB Hank Kuhlmann, and sped 51y to score in opening 90 secs. Normally-reliable Smith spoiled his Vanderbilt team's scoring threat by losing FUM at Tigers 35YL on next series, but Mizzou QB Phil Snowden gave it right back by fumbling at Vandy 31YL. Starting late in 1st Q, Commodores went 69y to tie it: HB Phil King gained 14y, FB Jim Butler swept for 13y to Tigers 33YL, and Butler battered ahead on 4 of next 6 plays/23y, including 1y TD to tie it. QKs by Mizzou HB-P Bob Haas and Vandy's King dominated 2nd H, but each team threatened once before turning it over: After Missouri DT Owen Worstell fell on FUM at Vandy 28YL late in 3rd Q, QB Ken Clemensen dropped ball as he was hit before he could handoff. Commodores drove to Mizzou 20YL, but HB Tom Moore lost FUM to DB Snowden.

Washington State 34 NEBRASKA 12: Cougars (1-0) QB Bobby Newman uncorked 74y pass to E Don Ellingsen to open game, and, even though play was called back by PEN, it was disagreeable harbinger for 1st-year Nebraska (0-1) coach Bill Jennings. Nebraska struggled on pass D throughout 1st H as Newman hit 2 TDs and his understudy, QB Bunny Aldrich, pitched 26y score to E Gail Cogdill for 20-6 lead. Cornhuskers drew to within 20-12 on QB Harry Tolly's 1y TD run in 3rd Q. Tolly's tally came as result of lost FUM by Wazzu, but Huskers soon returned favor. Next TO allowed slick Newman's 3rd TD connection to E Jack Fanning, this of 10y, giving Washington State insurmountable lead at 27-12 in 3rd Q.

TEXAS CHRISTIAN 13 Kansas 13: Driving rain pelted down on Amon Carter Stadium as visiting Kansas (0-0-1) scored with no time left, but Jayhawks K Ray Barnes failed to connect on conv kick. Texas Christian (0-0-1) simply owned 1st H, accepting gift TD, making long TD drive, and walking off at H with 207y to 4y O advantage. In opening 3 mins, punt snap had been fired over head of Kansas E-P Jim Letcavits and was recovered at 3YL for Horned Frogs G John Mitchell. FB Buddy Dike powered over on 3rd down for 7-0 lead. TCU HB Jim Shofner (12/106y; 7th) capped 78y voyage in 2nd Q, but FB-K Jack Spikes had his x-pt blocked when bad snap delayed his kicking effort. In 3rd Q, PEN pinned Purple in its province; and consequential punt was propelled only to 40YL. On ensuing 3rd down, Jayhawks QB Bob Marshall tossed short to HB Charlie McCue, who maneuvered 34y to pay-dirt. Kansas' supposed best thrower, QB Wally Strauch, connected on 30y completion to HB Don Feller to get late drive going, but Marshall (3-6/65y, 2 TDs) came off bench for last play and to find E Letcavits in corner of EZ for TD.

TEXAS A&M 21 Maryland 13 (Dallas): Texas A&M (1-0) QB-DB Roddy Osborne blocked critical Terps (0-1) x-pt kick, keeping score at 14-13 in favor of Aggies midway in 4th Q. Osborne had contributed early TD run in 1st Q and go-ahead 7y scoring toss to E John Tracey in 4th Q. On its 1st possession, Maryland reached A&M 7-7 deadlock that would hold up until H as HB-DB Howard Dare (TD run and INT) brought back KO 29y and QB Dickie Lewis slanted 3y for TD off RT Fred Cole's block. Terrapins aerial game was turned into disaster by rain and wind, producing only 1-7/3y. Bad weather hurt Terps strategy, according to coach Tommy Mont: "We kicked off with the wind to begin the second half but we suddenly found wind, rain, and Aggies staring us in the face." Texas A&M HB John David Crow wrenched his knee on last play of 1st Q when hit hard by DT Cole, and it would stymie him throughout his sr season. But, Crow would win Heisman Trophy in vote that recognized his career achievements.

HOUSTON 7 Miami 0: Excellence on D was surprise ingredient for Houston Cougars (1-0) in their debut under new coach Hal Lahar. Soph G-LB Joe Glass led Houston's D, but as Osborne had pointed out: "It was their second unit that beat us," as HB-DB Don Brown, NG Charles Caffrey, and DT John Peters so dominated Miami's backup squad that Gustafson had to employ his regulars to exhaustion. Soph HB-DB Claude King got Houston rolling to game's only TD in 2nd Q by falling on FUM at Cougars 48YL. King ran 21y in reverse to set up HB Hal Lewis'

26y TD flight up middle when King, FB Owen Mulholland, and G Burr Davis made great blocks. Miami was led by soph QB Fran Curci, who ran 11/77y on options. But, Canes' passing showed awful 2-7/0y, INT.

OREGON STATE 20 Southern California 0 (Portland): Defending loop champion Oregon State ruined coaching debut of Troy's Don Clark. Beavers (1-0) drove 71, 80, and 70y to TDs after scoreless 1st Q to capture their 1st win over Trojans (0-1) since 1946. Oregon State FB Nub Beamer (23/123y) scored on 2y plunge in 2nd Q and 31y outside-cut sprint in 4th Q. Most spectacular play came on E Dwayne Fournier's 44y double-reverse run, handed from TB Joe Francis to WB Earnel Durden (10/68y) to Fournier in 3rd Q. USC was throttled by big Beavers line, especially DTs Dave Jesmer and Ted Bates, gaining only 170y and punting 8 times.

WASHINGTON 6 Colorado 6: Visiting from Rockies, Buffaloes (0-0-1) gained mountains of y between 20YLs but couldn't cash in sufficiently to go home with win over favored Washington (0-0-1). Colorado scored in 1st Q when it successfully juggled its Single Wing power with T-formation guile to move 37y to FB Leroy Clark's unusual 11y TD run up middle. Clark lost ball as he hit hole but it dribbled right back in his hands in time to bowl over Huskies DB Carver Gayton. CU WB-CB Eddie Dove was 2 years away from good NFL career as DB but was beaten deep by Washington HB Dick Payseno for tying 58y TD pass from QB Bobby Dunn in 2nd Q. In 3rd Q, Buffs DT Jack Himelwright twice stole ball from Dunn, and each time Colorado made it to 5YL. Buffs' 1st surge died on downs, and when Dunn soon was pick-pocketed again, CU's FG try was made too long by 2 PENs and sack of QB Boyd Dowler. New Huskies coach Jim Owens predictably uttered his fraternity's favorite post-deadlock quote: "A tie is like kissing your sister!"

AP Poll September 23

1 Oklahoma (65)	720	11 Baylor	169
2 Texas A&M	460	12 Iowa (1)	127
3 Georgia Tech	374	13 Texas	60
4 Michigan State (4)	354	14 Houston	53
5 Navy (1)	297	15 Southern Methodist	35
6 Minnesota (1)	275	16tPittsburgh	26
7 Duke (2)	249	16tStanford	26
8 Tennessee	247	18 Rice	23
9 Oregon State	223	19tMississippi	21
10 Michigan	190	19tPenn State	21

September 28, 1957

(Fri) UCLA 16 Illinois 6: Even with Illinois (0-1) outgaining UCLA (2-0) 289y to 220y, well-schooled Bruins controlled play all night. Uclan FB-DB Ray Smith recovered FUM by Illini HB Dale Smith (11/56y) at Illinois 28YL midway through 1st Q. TB-K Kirk Wilson (9/64y, TD, and 3-6/33y passing), part of Bruins' TB triumverate, scored on 4th-and-2 run from 6YL, but his kick was blocked. T Bill Leeka blocked 2nd Q punt by Illini QB-P Bill Haller, and, after E Dick Wallen made brilliant 1-handed grab, UCLA FB Barry Billington launched himself over Illini D-front into EZ. When rules prohibited UCLA's best K Don Duncan from being reinserted in game, QB-K Steve Gertsman surprised by increasing Bruins' lead to 16-0 with 35y FG just before H. Illinois HB Bobby Mitchell (14/79y) lost FUM at Bruins 14YL when hit hard by WB-DB Bill Mason, but Illini followed that failed 66y drive with 91y trip to pay-dirt in 4th Q. Sub HB Don Grothe tallied.

BOSTON COLLEGE 20 Florida State 7: Far steadier than in its opener against Navy, Boston College (1-1) mastered 2 precise TD drives of 82 and 80y in 1st and 3rd Qs. Eagles' sharp QB Don Allard (12-18/145y, TD) wrapped up quick 33y march in 4th Q for 20-0 lead when he rolled out and zipped 5y TD pass to E-DE John Flanagan, who starred on both sides of ball. Outgained 381y to 113y, Florida State (1-1) finally broke from its cuffs in dying mins to create 65y march. Seminoles QB Ted Rodriquez threw 23y scoring pass to ace E Ronnie Schomberger.

ARMY 42 Nebraska 0: Black Knights soph HB Bob Anderson (13/83y,TD), future Hall of Famer, was introduced to unaware Nebraska (0-2) and admiring West Point crowd as Army (1-0) surged to overwhelming victory that featured 341y rushing. On Army's 1st series, Anderson swept 27y behind FB Vin Barta's block to set up his 6y draw run for TD. Anderson's HB partner, Pete Dawkins scored later in 1st Q after Anderson and QB Dave Bourland each completed pass. FB Harry Walters, biggest gainer of game with 21/129y, barreled 28y on 1st snap of 2nd Q to set up Barta's score for 21-0 edge, and Bourland hit E Bill Graf for 17y TD pass 8 mins later. Cornhuskers were limited to single threat late in 2nd Q: FB-LB George Cifra made FUM REC at Cadets 12YL, and scatback HB Bennie Dillard slipped around E for TD. It was called back for motion PEN, and Nebraska died on downs at 5YL.

SYRACUSE 7 Iowa State 7: Soph TB Dwight Nichols was cornerstone of Iowa State's surprising effort as he launched tying TD drive early in 4th Q. Nichols abandoned ground game and threw sharp 13 and 12y passes to E Jim Stuelke and then arched 27y TD pass to E Brian Dennis. Syracuse (0-0-1) had scored late in 3rd Q when Orangemen marched 70y to soph FB Art Baker's 7y TD gallop. Late-game Orangemen thrust, which started at Syracuse's 42YL, died at Cyclones (1-0-1) 7YL. Syracuse had stats picnic: 240y to 120y rushing advantage and 290y to 179y overall edge, but many of Orange's y came at midfield.

Columbia 23 BROWN 20: New Lions (1-0) coach Buff Donelli unwrapped new QB, and it turned out to be his son, Dick, who threw 2 TD passes. When young Dick enrolled at Columbia in 1955 his father coached Boston University, and Dick had expressed desire to skip pressure of being coached by his family member. Dick's success in coach Buff's Columbia debut was surprise. Heavily-favored Brown (0-1), 1 of several preseason Ivy title favorites, led 14-13 at H, outgained Lions 317y to 226y by game's end, and got TD runs from FBs Bob Topping and Paul Choquette, and HB Jack McTigue, but suffered 7 TOs. With game knotted 20-20, 2nd-chance, winning 4th Q FG by Lions FB-K Rudy Pegoraro came after his 1st FG try was so low from 35YL that it filtered through Columbia line, only to be recovered for extraordinarily lucky 1st down by Lions T Ed Eschenbaum.

WEST VIRGINIA 14 Virginia Tech 0: Mountaineers (1-0-1) completed no passes (0-4, INT) but their fierce D and 283y run game allowed them to dominate game. Poor Gobblers (1-1) punt set up WVU at Va Tech 34YL in 2nd Q. Bruising FB Larry Krutko scored from 1YL on 6th play. West Virginia G Bob Guenther fell on FUM at own 45YL in 4th Q, and HB Ray Peterson's runs paved way to HB Ralph Anastasio's 7y sprint to TD. Held completely in check and not crossing WVU 40YL, Virginia Tech E Carroll Dale blocked Anastasio's midfield punt. Va Tech QB-DB Billy Holsclaw scooped ball and made it to Mountaineers 12YL. Battling West Virginia D held on downs at 7YL.

Mississippi 15 KENTUCKY 0: Wildcats welcomed deep Mississippi team to Blue Grass country and popped Rebs right in mouth. Kentucky (0-2) slipped soph HB Glenn Shaw away for 49y gain on early 90y movement to 3YL, where drive died. Teams left at H, tied at no-score. It took 2nd-string QB, quick little Bobby Franklin, to launch Ole Miss' O. After sparking threat in 2nd Q, Franklin was reinserted in 3rd Q to lead 61y scoring trip to his 11y pass to E Larry Grantham. Rebels' starting QB, Ray Brown, returned to sprint 13y at end of 53y TD march for 13-0 lead. Ole Miss E Ralph Smith blocked punt in 4th Q for safety. Kentucky QB-DB Lowell Hughes earned high marks by stopping 2 drives with INTs and got Cats moving late with his passes on 88y drive stopped at 2YL.

Auburn 7 TENNESSEE 0: Auburn's Lloyd Nix, HB newly converted to QB, led upset of defending SEC champs in chilly rain. In 1st Q, Tennessee (0-1) turned back 4th down thrust of Auburn (1-0) HB Tommy Lorino inches from GL. Vol TB Bobby Gordon punted out 45y, and Vols held again at own 7YL. Tennessee G Bill Johnson blocked 1st Q punt to create 1st down at Tiger 17YL, but Auburn NG Zeke Smith threw Gordon for 3y loss and Auburn E Jim Phillips recovered FUM on next play at 18YL. Tigers' winning march of 57y was created in 2nd Q when E Jerry Wilson got paw on Tennessee TB Al Carter's punt and ball carried only 6y to Auburn 43YL. Nix completed his only pass of day to E Jerry Wilson for 10y to help position FB Billy Atkins' short TD run. Magnificent Tiger D held Vols to 84y O and stopped 4th Q advances to 23 and 29YLs.

GEORGIA TECH 0 Southern Methodist 0: Southern Methodist (1-0-1) FB-P Dave Sherer's 13 booming boots pierced wind and rain clouds to pin Georgia Tech (1-0-1) deep in its end all day. In 2nd H, workhorse Engineers FB Larry Fonts led drives of 70 and 74y which died without pts. Soph QB Don Meredith bobbled away SMU's only scoring chance at Georgia Tech 14YL.

MICHIGAN STATE 54 Indiana 0: No. 4 Michigan State (1-0) launched Big 10 season with thumping of Indiana (0-1). TDs still were being scored deep into 4th Q as 67th different Spartan was on field. MSU rushed for 441y and completed its 1st 11 passes/129y. HB Walt Kowalczyk scored opening TD, and HB Blanche Martin added 2 scores. Hoosiers, held to 80y O, managed only 1 scoring opportunity. It came in 4th Q as FB-LB Charley Kelly carried INT to Michigan State 24YL, but 16y were lost on next 2 plays.

Texas Christian 18 OHIO STATE 14: Taking page from Buckeyes coach Woody Hayes' book, TCU (1-0-1) won without completing single pass in just 3 tries, which included INT by Ohio State (0-1). Frogs gained 184y rushing, but key play came in 2nd Q on HB Jim Shofner's 90y punt RET that provided 12-7 edge. DB-P Shofner also recovered FUM and pinned Ohio State at its 6 and 7YLs with long punts. Horned Frogs came from deficits twice, 7-6 and 14-12, and smashed 2 late Ohio State bids at 5 and 20YLs. Bucks outgained TCU 262y to 184y and got TDs on 2y runs from HBs Dick LeBeau and Don Clark that provided 14-12 H edge. TCU FB Jack Spikes earned decisive TD on 16y run early in 3rd Q after DE Chico Mendoza recovered FUM at Buckeyes 31YL.

Notre Dame 12 PURDUE 0: It was hardly rousing Fighting Irish (1-0) victory in tradition of Rockne or Leahy, but after 1956's disastrous 2-8 campaign, 6-0 lead that held up all day was welcome medicine. Notre Dame drove 76y to tote 6-pt edge 2nd time it touched ball and didn't tally again until last 1:01 of 4th Q. Strong Ds on both sides and myriad of opening game blunders could be blamed for long scoreless stretch. Irish HB Dick Lynch squirmed 12y to tally in 1st Q, and new ND QB Bob Williams launched 58y toss to E Bob Wetoska to set up his 8y TD pass to HB Frank Reynolds in game's dying moments. Purdue (0-1) stopped advances at its 13YL in 2nd Q, which ended with ND HB-K Aubrey Lewis' missed FG, and at its 4YL on downs in 3rd Q. Boilermakers' best ground-gainers were its Ps, Kenny Mikes and Clyde Washington, as Purdue was forced to punt 11 times and gained 337y in field position. Best Boilermakers march was ruined by 12y loss inflicted on QB Bob Spoo at Irish 32YL.

MINNESOTA 46 Washington 7: Former Huskies QB Bobby Cox ignored ankle pain and led Big 10 co-favorite, no. 6 Minnesota (1-0), to 4 TD drives. Cox got Gophers winging early when Washington lost midfield FUM after opening KO: Cox threw 10y TD to E Jon Jelacic on 6th play of 51y trip. Gophers gained 550y and featured FB Bob Blakely's 2 TDs. Day's most dazzling play was provided by Washington (0-1-1) FB Jim Jones, who took 2nd H KO 91y to score. In front of happy record crowd at Memorial Stadium "Brick House," big Minnesota D limited Huskies to 105y O, including only 2-5/13y in air.

STANFORD 26 Northwestern 6: Typically-pass-oriented Stanford (2-0) trotted out squadron of backs who smashed for 251y on ground to complement 13-27/158y air game, led by QB Jack Douglas (12-23/142y, TD). Stanford received TDs from HB Jere McMillin (10y catch) and sub FB Gil Shea (2y run at LG) who was in for injured Lou Valli, which provided 13-0 lead late in 3rd Q. Coming off 3 wins to close 1956, favored Northwestern (0-1) was penalized whopping 140y and saw 2 drives in 1st H halted inside Indians 20YL. Wildcats created wild 36y 4th Q TD out of desperation on "hook-and-ladder" play: QB Chip Holcomb passed to E Fred Williamson, who flipped lateral to Big 10 sprint champ HB Willmer Fowler. Score vaulted NW into manageable 13-6 deficit with 10:31 left. But, Stanford answered with decisive 88y sortie that ended in 3rd-team FB Rick McMillen's 10y TD run.

1 Oklahoma (81)	1223	11 Baylor (1)	214
2 Michigan State (24)	999	12 Army	134
3 Minnesota (10)	867	13 North Carolina State	113
4 Duke (8)	629	14 Georgia Tech	110
5 Texas A&M	628	15 Mississippi	67
6 Navy (1)	472	16 Notre Dame	63
7 Auburn (6)	400	17 Stanford	59
8 Iowa (3)	378	18 Texas Christian	56
9 Oregon State	376	19 UCLA	43
10 Michigan	324	20 Texas	32

October 5, 1957

Army 27 PENN STATE 13: Hoping to demonstrate Eastern superiority, Nittany Lions (1-1) took 13-7 H lead. Penn State QB Al Jacks hit 15-32 in air, including 19y TD to E Les Walters. Lions D rose up to halt late 2nd Q drives of 60y to their 2YL and 35y to their 22YL, but such Cadet charges proved simply to be signs of what was to come after H. Army (2-0) applied rally by fashioning 3rd Q ground stampede, going 71, 66, and 40y for scores behind running of HB Pete Dawkins (17/81y, TD) and FB Vin Barta. Cadets finished with 306y total O.

NORTH CAROLINA 13 Navy 7: Suddenly-revived Tar Heels (2-1), in middle of 3-game win streak, shocked Navy (2-1) as beefy DT Leo Russavage lumbered 32y to eventual game-deciding TD for 13-0 lead in 3rd Q. North Carolina picked off 5 INTs. DE Buddy Payne keynoted UNC D by pressuring normally-reliable Middies QB Tom Forrestal (11-20/83y, 5 INTs) into Russavage's INT and picked off own INT late in contest. Quick Carolina HB-DB Emil DeCantis had pounced on punt FUM by Navy HB Ned Oldham (19/76y) at Middies 23YL in 1st Q and it led to opening score: UNC QB Dave Reed soon slipped into EZ behind LT Russavage's block from 1YL after his fine fake to FB Jim Shuler. DeCantis added his 2nd FUM REC and also picked off pass by Forrestal. Down 13-0 late in 3rd Q, Navy started methodical 73y voyage in 19 plays to 2y scoring sweep early in 4th Q by HB Harry Hurst (13/69y). C-LB Bob Reifsnyder was outstanding for Navy's D.

North Carolina State 13 CLEMSON 7: Outgained Wolfpack (3-0) used HB Dick Christy's 97y TD RET of opening KO to help surprise favored Clemson (1-2). Early in 2nd Q, NC State HB-K Jim Sciaretta missed wide on 40y FG try. Clemson immediately moved 79y primarily on HB Rabbit Chatlin's 24y run and QB Harvey White's 22y pass to E Ray Masneri, but Wolfpack held at own 1YL. Scoreless 3rd Q found teams vying at midfield without scoring. NC State FB Don Hafer and Tigers HB George Usry traded 4th Q TDs.

MIAMI 13 Baylor 7: Supposedly superior Baylor (2-1) line allowed 388y rushing, while on O it blocked for meager 17y on ground for its runners. Miami (1-1) fled 63y in 1st Q as QB Fran Curci scooted 20 and 13y on option keepers, then pitched out to HB John Varone for 10y TD romp around LE. HBs Varone and Joe Plevel keyed 59y drive in 2nd Q as Varone boomed wide to duplicate previous TD, this time from 8YL. FB Bill Sandie had 3rd Q punt partially blocked by Bears T Bobby Jack Oliver, and Baylor took over on Hurricanes 20YL. Ahead 13-7, Miami allowed Bears to pass to its 29YL, but Hurricanes DT Gary Greaves made INT, and Miami DE Doug Hildebrandt's 17y sack of Traylor ended Baylor's last threat.

Florida 14 KENTUCKY 7: In 8 tries, Florida Gators (2-0) had never beaten Wildcats (0-3) at Kentucky. This time, Gators fashioned 2 fast-striking drives of 79y in 1st Q and 63y in 3rd Q to post 14-0 lead that would hold up to break their Lexington jinx. Little Jimmy Dunn, 1 of smallest players ever to man QB post in SEC, zipped around LE, faked pitchout several times, and went 32y for TD at end of 6-play trip in 1st Q and added 27y scoring strike to HB Jim Rountree, who shook off 2 tacklers on opening possession of 3rd Q. Kentucky had probed to 17, 18, and 28YLs in 1st H with no pts, and eventually its best O became soaring punts of T-P Lou Michaels that averaged 52y. His last punt traveled 71y to 11YL to set up 49y drive to QB Lowell Hughes' dodging 6y TD scramble.

TENNESSEE 14 Mississippi State 9: Tenacious TB Bobby Gordon wouldn't quit, even though some of home crowd filed out before he turned tide in favor of Tennessee (1-1). T-K Bobby Tribble booted 25y FG for Mississippi State (1-1) early in 1st Q, and Gordon briefly delayed FB Molly Halbert's short 2nd Q TD plunge for 9-0 lead when he hauled down Bulldogs FB Willie Morgan on Vols 3YL after Morgan dashed 64y on punt RET. Tennessee's O finally awakened midway in 4th Q as Vols enjoyed 75y spree, capped by FB Neil Smith's 1y plunge. With clock ticking down, Bulldogs faced 4th down deep in own territory, and Gordon fielded HB Gil Peterson's punt at his own 45YL, darted through 1st wave of Maroons tacklers and dashed 55y to winning score.

MINNESOTA 21 Purdue 17: Minnesota (2-0) sub QB Dick Larson took 2nd Q criss-cross handoff on punt RET from HB Bob Soltis and used FB Rhody Tuszka's block for 78y TD RET, later rallied Gophers with 2 TD drives in 2nd H. QB Bob Spoo directed Purdue (0-2) to 397y O, but Boilermakers suffered 5 FUMs. Boilers earned 10-7 H lead on Spoo's 40y pitch to E Dick Brooks and HB-K Tom Fletcher's short FG. Minnesota HB-P Norman Anderson shanked punt only to his own 17YL in last min of H to set up Fletcher's FG. HB Bill Chorske caught 16y TD pass from Larson early in 3rd Q and speared Larson's 51y throw on 1st-and-28 to poise Larson for 4th down sprint for flag. Trailing 21-10, Purdue cashed TD in game's last secs when 3rd-team QB Wayne Jones threw deflected 3y TD pass to E Frank Anastasia.

MICHIGAN 26 Georgia 0: Meeting was 1st-ever between historical giants of separate regions. HB-DB Mike Shatusky scored twice for Wolverines (2-0) on 56y INT sideline sprint and 6y run behind block of T Jim Davies. Georgia (0-3) penetrated to Michigan 27YL in 1st Q and to 21YL in 2nd Q, but was ruined by 110y in PENs. QB Charlie Britt was erratic 7-19 in air, but Bulldogs trailed in total O by only 311y to 272y. Wolverines 2nd squad played well, accounting for QB Stan Noskin's 2 TD plunges.

Kansas 35 COLORADO 34: WB Eddie Dove sparked Colorado (1-1-1) with 91y TD run, and E Gary Nady followed with TD catch that provided Bison with 4th Q lead of 34-28. Left reeling by 3 quick Buffs TDs, Kansas (1-1-1) rallied in last 2 mins. Jayhawks QB Larry McKown hit HB Homer Floyd with deflected 58y pass which positioned HB Larry Carrier's TD run and HB-K Duane Morris' winning conv.

Texas A&M 28 MISSOURI 0: Missouri's stunting D gave no. 5 Aggies (3-0) some difficulty early, twice recovering FUMs. But Texas A&M used 22y run by HB Bobby Joe Conrad (13/92y) to boost 69y TD march in 2nd Q. Once Bear Bryant got good look at effectiveness of soph QB Charlie Milstead (6-9/65y, TD) on 2nd and 4th TD drives and his 6y TD pass to HB Roddy Osborne, Bryant must have taken liking to aerial attack that had been missing somewhat from his coaching repertoire since Babe Parilli departed Kentucky in 1951. When kinetic Conrad cruised 91y with 2nd H KO, verdict was about over at 21-0. However, fighting Tigers (1-1-1) battled back in late going: HB Jerry Curtright returned punt 20y and added 19y dash to HB Charley James' 4 catches to trip that ended with QB Phil Snowden's 4th down FUM at Aggies 15YL. Missouri was limited to 127y O.

ARKANSAS 20 Texas Christian 7: Arkansas (3-0) FB-K-P Gerald Nesbitt scored TD and kicked 2 convs, while his artful QKs kept TCU (1-1-1) buried in its own end. FUM REC in 1st Q gave Porkers chance for HB Donnie Stone's 2y TD sweep. Frogs tied it 7-7 in 1st Q on HB Jim Shofner's 5y run. Hogs' long drives in 2nd and 4th Q netted win.

South Carolina 27 TEXAS 21: South Carolina, whose players had vowed to beat Texas (2-1), seemed hopelessly behind at 21-7 in 4th Q but used pair of HB-option plays and pair of weak Longhorn punts to turn its ship for upset waters. Intersectional contest had begun well for Gamecocks (2-1) as HB King Dixon (11/61y) accepted block from HB Alex Hawkins at midfield to saunter 98y for TD on opening KO. That was about it for much of night for Carolina as it gained all of 9y in rest of 1st H. Texas ripped to TDs in each of 1st 3 Qs as QB Walt Fondren hit TD passes to E Richard Schulte and HB Max Alvis. Thanks to Texas' PEN for failing to heed fair-catch by Dixon, Gamecocks started at 50YL early in 4th Q and moved slowly to short TD run by Hawkins (9/36y, 2 TDs) to make it 21-13. Steers QB-P Bobby Lackey dribbled ghastly 4y punt, so Hawkins threw 36y TD pass to Dixon to pull within 21-20 with 8 mins to play. Another bad punt allowed Carolina to start at Texas 38YL, and from 18YL Hawkins faked another running pass but cut back to middle of field for TD spurt.

OREGON 21 Ucla 0 (Portland): Rain and mud, curse to California teams traveling to Pacific Northwest, greeted undefeated UCLA (2-1). Webfoots (2-1) felt right at home in sloppy conditions. "We were simply outplayed, especially from tackle to tackle," said glum Bruins coach Red Sanders. Oregon methodically drove for 70, 47, and 67y TD journeys. FB-K Jack Morris accounted for 1st score (3y plunge) late in 1st Q and converted as he did after all 3 Ducks scores. Oregon T-DT John Willener started 2nd TD trip with FUM REC at UCLA 47YL. Ducks QB Jack Crabtree (7-8/72y, TD) called on nimble target E Ron Stover (7/89y, TD) for 4y TD catch. HB Jim Shanley (20/101y, TD) scored in 3rd Q before Uclans threatened at end with passes that reached Ducks 8YL.

1 Oklahoma (65)	1047	11 Arkansas	135
2 Michigan State (21)	906	12 Notre Dame	124
3 Texas A&M (3)	698	13 North Carolina State	114
4 Minnesota (5)	557	14 Mississippi	79
5 Duke (5)	493	15 Rice	76
6 Michigan	469	16 Wisconsin	46
7 Oregon State (2)	423	17 Georgia Tech	35
8 Iowa (4)	385	18 North Carolina	28
9 Auburn (5)	351	19 Tennessee	22
10 Army	251	20 Pittsburgh	20

October 12, 1957

(Fri) North Carolina 20 MIAMI 13: Advance billing had tilt tabbed as close-to-vest D struggle. Instead, each team threw frequently and scored aerial TD. Tar Heels (3-1) pinned Miami (1-2) at 1YL on FB-P Don Coker's 42y boot and PEN in 1st Q. Hurricanes FB-P Bill Sandie's return punt went only to his 40YL, and UNC HB Jim Shuler galloped it back 14y. Coker powered 10y, and Shuler broke 16y to TD. In 2nd Q, Carolina HB Emil DeCantis fired 42y pass to HB Ron Marquette, then they switched roles as Marquette hit DeCantis for 33y TD. In 3rd Q, Miami QB Fran Curci (10-17/102y, TD, 2 INTs) fired 21y TD to HB John Varone to cut it to 14-7. Near end of 3rd Q, Varone fumbled near midfield to Carolina FB-LB Don Kemper, which launched TD trip to QB Curtis Hathaway's 1y sneak. Heels stopped drive inside their 5YL in 4th Q, only delaying Canes' TD run by Sandie. Miami pressured at UNC 20 and 23YLs before it was over.

Notre Dame 23 Army 21 (Philadelphia): Renewal of classic rivalry last played in 1947 attracted 95,000 to Memorial Stadium in Philadelphia. Army (2-1) soph HB Bob Anderson (15/186y, 2 TDs) raced 81y out of unbalanced-T for Cadets' TD on 2nd scrimmage play and added 1y TD to build seemingly safe 21-7 lead 1 min from end of 3rd Q. But, Fighting Irish (3-0) FB Nick Pietrosante (20/139y, 2 TDs), who had tied game at 7-7 in 1st Q with 1y plunge, turned momentum with 65y TD bolt to pull ND within 21-14. Notre Dame HB Jim Lynch carried on 7 of 12 snaps on 56y trip early in 4th Q, but big soph E-K Monty Stickles missed tying x-pt to keep Army ahead 21-20. Later in 4th Q, LB Pietrosante made critical INT that was tipped by DT Frank Geremia, and Stickles made winning 38y FG on his 1st career 3-pt try with slightly more than 6 mins left to play. Irish now led hard-fought series 24-7-4.

Clemson 20 VIRGINIA 6: Scoreless 1st H carried well into 3rd Q when Clemson (2-2) E Ray Masneri blocked punt by Virginia (1-2-1) HB-P Al Cash, and Tigers took over on Cavs 32YL. Soph QB Harvey White completed only 1-3 passing all day, but here he clicked on 4th-and-8 pitch to E Wyatt Cox for TD. Virginia answered with 65y TD

trip, kept alive by QB-P Nelson Yarbrough fielding high punt snap near midfield and arching 4th down pass to E Mike Riley at Tigers 33YL. Yarbrough squeezed over from 3YL for TD, but FB-K Jim Bakhtiar missed x-pt, so Cavs trailed 7-6 early in 4th Q. White launched Tigers' next move with 12y run to midfield, and FB Bob Spooner contributed 43y rushing to 72y TD march. DB White's 23y INT RET set up his own closing TD run.

North Carolina State 7 FLORIDA STATE 0: Playing mostly between 10YLs, NC State (4-0) and Florida State (1-3) slugged it out except for lightning bolt 46y TD reception that went to Wolfpack HB Dick Christy from 3rd-unit QB Ernie Driscoll in last 16 secs of 1st H. Christy's 25y burst had keyed NC State's game-opening 62y sortie that was stopped by Seminoles G Al Ulmer's FUM REC at FSU 5 YL. Wolfpack also manufactured drives to 25YL and 10YL in 2nd and 3rd Qs respectively. Florida State made it to Wolfpack 13YL, but missed FG. Seminoles HB-P Bobby Renn crafted QKs and punts for 6/46.8y avg.

LOUISIANA STATE 20 Georgia Tech 13: Legend of large and raucous crowds that would stamp Tiger Stadium as 1 of nation's most difficult venues began to grow during LSU's upset of no. 17 Georgia Tech (1-1-1). FB-K Jimmy Taylor gained 25/90y, 3 TDs rushing and scored all 20 pts for improving Louisiana State (3-1), while soph HB Billy Cannon added 17/98y rushing. QB Fred Braselton (9-13/91y, TD) passed and ran for TDs for Engineers. Braselton's 5y TD pitch to E Jerome Green came with 9:02 to play, but hope for win went away with HB-K Cal James' wide x-pt. Tigers P Cannon came up big, targeting 2 punts each to sail OB at Jackets' 7YL near end.

AUBURN 6 Kentucky 0: This seemed like preliminary bout for Auburn (3-0), and perhaps Plainsmen looked ahead to Georgia Tech showdown. Fumbled 3rd Q lateral by Kentucky (0-4) and roughing PEN called on Cats DT Lou Michaels turned game in favor of D-minded Auburn. Wildcats clawed their way to scoreless 1st H, but not without interesting developments: P Michaels gambled on 4th down punt and his run came up short when he was tackled by E Jerry Wilson at Auburn 48YL. Kentucky then stopped 4th down dash by Tigers QB Lloyd Nix. Cats' deepest penetration to 17YL came next, after FB-DB Bobby Walker fell on FUM at Auburn 21YL. Tigers E Jimmy Phillips spearheaded D, while FB-LB Billy Atkins made play of game: In 3rd Q, he swooped wide to deflect and recover Kentucky QB Lowell Hughes' pitchout at 36YL in Cats' end. Thanks in part to Michaels' 15y use-of-elbows PEN in tackling HB Tommy Lorino, Auburn advanced to Atkins' twisting lunge out of arms of Kentucky G Bob Collier to score on 6y run up middle.

OHIO STATE 21 Illinois 7: Buckeyes (2-1) coach Woody Hayes showed his most conservative strategy. Ohio State's heavy run vs. pass preponderance pointed its plunges to inside and not even wide. HB Don Clark led ground parade with 33/133y, scored 1st Q TD on 9y burst inside RG, and chipped in 24y gain to go-ahead 65y advance in 3rd Q. Illinois (1-2) gained on long passes by QB Tom Haller, future San Francisco Giants catcher. Haller launched 58y TD to E Rich Krietling for TD that knotted score at 7-7 in 3rd Q. Earlier, Illini had made 1st of pair of tremendous 2nd Q GLSs that ended at 1YL, keyed by G-LB Bill Burrell, HB-DB Doug Wallace, and DE Bob Delaney. They soon followed with Haller's 19y pass to Kreitling into Ohio territory. But, Haller soon fumbled, 1 of 4 costly TOs for Illinois. Ohio State QB Frank Kremblas powered off LT Dick Schafrath's block for 1y TD in 3rd Q for 14-7 lead and shot-putted 5y TD pass to HB Don Sutherin in 4th Q.

Wisconsin 23 PURDUE 14: Purdue's rough early season would soon turn for better but 1st it got worse on otherwise beautiful Homecoming Saturday. Unbeaten Badgers (3-0) struck for 2 key, long TD runs: Wisconsin HB Danny Lewis (8/134y) broke away for 80y dash in 2nd Q to break up 7-7 knot, and QB Sidney Williams (2-9/45y, 2 INTs) extended 17-14 edge on 73y sprint, his 2nd TD run. Boilermakers (0-3) fought back throughout: HB Kenny Mikes tied late in 1st Q as he pranced 50y on punt TD RET—helped by E John Crowl's block—and pulled them within 3 pts by plunging over on 1st snap of 4th Q. FB-LB-K Jon Hobbs (EZ INT) had gotten Badgers winging early with punt block to set up Williams' 1st Q TD sneak and tacked on 33y FG on 1st H's last play.

Michigan State 35 MICHIGAN 6: Michigan State (3-0) QB Jim Ninowski quickly found soft spot on right side of secondary and pitched 49y pass to E Dave Kaiser, and HB Walt Kowalczyk (17/143y) soon put Spartans on top 6-0 with 1st Q TD plunge. Spartans line completely dominated their counterparts in Michigan Stadium, where crowd topped 101,001 for 10th straight sellout of in-state tussle. Michigan State E Sam Williams added 2nd Q safety on block of Wolverines QB-P Jim Van Pelt's punt after UM held inside its 1YL. Michigan (2-1) clawed within 14-6 in 3rd Q when HB Jimmy Pace (15/71y, TD) raced to 10y TD. But, Spartans roared to 3 TDs in 4th Q, including sub HB Art Johnson's 62y TD burst early in 4th Q.

Oklahoma 21 Texas 7 (Dallas): HB-DB Jakie Sandefer scored late in 3rd Q to break 7-7 tie, then sealed 43rd straight Oklahoma (3-0) win with late INT. Texas (2-2) got winging early on INT RET by FB-DB Mickey Smith to Sooners 17YL to set up 7-0 lead. Oklahoma HB Clendon Thomas soon tied it behind block of G Bill Krisher, who also sparkled on D. Running and punting of Texas QB-P Walt Fondren and 4 INTs by Longhorns kept Sooners off balance most of day. Texas State Fair weekend was marred by raucous behavior of 3:00 a.m. crowd in downtown Dallas that resulted in 3 fans being knifed and many more pelted with beer bottles that were tossed from hotel windows.

Duke 7 RICE 6: Some football plays are destined to bloom to perfection, and no. 5 Duke (4-0) sprung HB Wray Carlton (16/105y) for 68y TD on game's 1st snap as Rice's entire D seemed to permit unseen corridor to open right up middle. K Carlton then added all-important conv. Blue Devils failed on 2 other 1st H drives: loss of FUM at 7YL and expiration of H clock at 2YL. Outplayed in 1st H, Owls (2-1) rallied around QBs King Hill and Frank Ryan, who took turns tossing to E Buddy Dial, who caught 5/99y. Rice scored early in 3rd Q, only to have K Hill barely miss hurried x-pt after Dial's 32y TD catch from Ryan. Owls seriously threatened twice in 4th Q, but lost TO each time. Duke HB-DB George Dutrow earned INT at his 3YL after Rice passes moved it 45y to Blue 22YL. With 8:32 to go, Owls G-LB Matt Gorges made 38y INT RET to Duke 3YL, where original passer, HB Eddie Rushton, made tackle OB. But FUM soon was created by Devils G Roy Hord's crushing tackle of Rice FB Ray Chilton (19/76y), and it bounded through EZ for touchback.

TEXAS A&M 28 Houston 6: Cougars (2-2) had marked only blemish on Aggies' 1956 record with 14-14 tie, so no. 3 Texas A&M (4-0) was ready for vengeance. Aggies QB Roddy Osborne (13/115y rushing) scored 1st of his pair of TD runs in 1st Q. It came on 9y rollout behind crushing block by HB Bobby Joe Conrad and after he had contributed 43y running to 79y TD trip. Houston, which had its share of chances at A&M's 21, 29, 16, and 39YLs without success, next saw Texas A&M DE John Tracey make INT RET to Aggies 26YL to launch drive to 14-0 lead in 2nd Q. A&M HB John David Crow (14/87y, 2 TDs) contributed 62y rushing to scoring march and big block to Osborne's 2nd TD run. T Ken Beck hustled downfield for 2 effective blocks on Osborne's 64y zig-zag that set up Crow's 1y plunge and 21-0 lead 26 secs before H. QB Sammy Blount (9-23/124y, INT) was Cougars prime passer, but QB Don McDonald came in late in 3rd Q to pitch 10, 14, and 13y arrows to create lone TD by FB Harold Lewis on 1y run.

Washington State 21 STANFORD 18: Trailing 18-7 with 4 mins left, bold Cougars (3-1) QB Bobby Newman threw short pass to E Jack Fanning, who split tackle attempts of 4th-string Indians DBs and raced 87y to TD. That was spark Wazzu needed. After HB Phil Mast followed with REC of on-side KO, Newman threw winning 18y TD to E Don Ellingsen with 44 secs left. Washington State outpassed Stanford (2-2) 328y to 136y. Indians had gotten TDs in 1st H from HB Al Harrington, who scored twice, and FB Chuck Shea. But, their convs were completely bungled: Stanford had bad snap, and Cougars G Dave Jones blocked kick and stopped conv pass short of GL.

Navy 21 CALIFORNIA 6: As he would do all year, HB-DB Ned Oldham, Navy (3-1) capt, would steady his team at just right time. California (0-4) benefitted from FUM by Tars FB Ray Wellborn at Navy 16YL, where it was fallen upon by DT Curt Iakuea. Bears HB Jack Hart zipped to 4YL and wedged over for TD on 4th down from 1y out. Behind 6-0, erratic Middies finally pulled themselves together in 3rd Q as reserves sparked 55y drive to sub QB Pat Flood's 4y TD pass to E Tom Hyde. Oldham sparkled on go-ahead 79y drive with 53y gain to QB Tom Forrestal's 3y TD drive. DB Oldham collared late INT and returned it 19y to Cal 1YL. Quickly crashing over for TD, HB-K Oldham added his 3rd conv.

AP Poll October 14

1 Michigan State (92)	1797	11 Mississippi (1)	225
2 Oklahoma (64)	1704	12 North Carolina State	200
3 Texas A&M (5)	1215	13 Wisconsin	123
4 Minnesota (6)	1184	14 North Carolina	100
5 Duke (5)	893	15 Navy	53
6 Iowa (10)	867	16 Pittsburgh	39
7 Oregon State (1)	691	17 Louisiana State	36
8 Notre Dame (3)	585	18 Michigan	30
9 Auburn (6)	548	19tWashington State	29
10 Arkansas (5)	373	19tRice	29
		19tArmy	29

October 19, 1957

(Fri) MIAMI 0 North Carolina State 0: Playing its 5th straight game on road, NC State (4-0-1) used its D line might to thwart late scoring tries by favored Miami (1-2-1). After 1st H that saw 2 Hurricanes probes reach Wolfpack's 21YL, clock rolled deep into 2nd H before either foe mounted another charge. NC State Es Bob Pepe and Don Miketa, tops on D all night, combined to block Miami punt late in 3rd Q at Hurricanes 15YL. After 3 incompletions, NC State QB-K Tom Katich tried FG that was blocked by Miami T Gary Greaves. Run on 4th down at Wolfpack 9YL with 47 sec left by 196-lb Miami FB Bill Sandie (17/55y) was halted by 163-lb State HB-DB Dick Hunter. Katich, however, nearly lost game on safety as he was spilled on 1YL when team talked coach Earle Edwards into gambling with EZ pass call. Wolfpack punted out only to its 30YL, and HB-DB Dick Christy had to slap EZ pass from hands of Hurricanes HB John Varone with 8 sec left.

ARMY 29 Pittsburgh 13: Looking good in 1st H, Pitt (3-2) line pushed Army (3-1) all over field, but its attack was halted twice at Cadets 10YL before sub QB Ivan Toncic launched 37y TD to E Dick Scherer to earn 6-6 tie at H. Black Knights' decisive score for 13-6 lead came in 3rd Q at and of 13-play, 83y march: FB Harry Walters pounded ball for 7 of 12 runs before skirting E for 2y TD. Cadets broke HB Pete Dawkins loose for 32y TD reception, and his 54y sprint soon positioned T-K Maurice Hilliard's 30y FG, those 10 pts upping Army lead to 23-6 and coming within 3-min span that carried into early 4th Q. HB Bob Anderson, Army's soph sensation, made 96y of Cadets' 273y rushing and scored 1st and last TDs on 1y plunges. In 4th Q, Toncic connected on 53y TD pass to HB Dick Haley for Pittsburgh, but DB Anderson eventually came up with his 2nd INT to set up his own late TD.

Vanderbilt 32 PENN STATE 20: Nashville invaders spoiled Homecoming at Penn State (2-2) with 2nd H rally. Nittany Lions led 20-13 at H after FUMs set up 4 of 5 TDs scored by dual combatants. Reliable HB Dave Kasperian (21/73y, 2 TDs) put Penn State on board in 1st Q after FUM was gained at Vanderbilt (2-1-2) 25YL and in 2nd Q, when his 2y TD ended 65y march. Commodores HB Phil King threw 13y TD pass to HB Tom Moore and caught 11y TD pass from QB Boyce Smith (8-13/195y, 3 TDs) after Lions bobbles in 1st H. Big play came on 2nd scrimmage of 3rd Q: Smith found Moore alone in Lions secondary for 77y TD surprise, but when FB-K Jim Travis' x-pt was missed, Vandy still trailed 20-19. E Ron Miller took 29y TD pass from Smith next time Penn State lost FUM, and it gave Vandy permanent lead at 25-20. Lions QB Al Jacks passed 13-23/184y, INT.

Navy 27 Georgia 14 (Norfolk): Sailors went digging for oysters in Norfolk's annual intersectional bowl match of same name. They nearly came up with barnacles, even though everything started well for Navy (4-1). QB Tom Forrestal completed 5-6 on

86y opening drive to his TD sneak, sub QB-DB Pat Flood quickly recovered FUM by Georgia (1-4) SB Jimmy Orr. Flood threw to FB Ray Wellborn for 5y score, and LB Wellborn raced to 31y TD with INT of Bulldogs QB Charley Britt's pass. So, Navy led 21-0 at H. Apparent new outlook in 3rd Q permitted Georgia to go 76y to FB Theron Sapp's short TD dive. Midfield FUM in 4th Q allowed UGa QB Tommy Lewis to fake out Navy D and scoot around RE standing up to make it 21-14. Reliable HB Ned Oldham ended any Academy anxiety by dashing 34y for clinching score.

MARYLAND 21 North Carolina 7: Somewhat puzzled by American football, Queen Elizabeth II of England demurely watched in crowd of 43,000 as Maryland (2-3) dealt upset loss to its former coach, Jim Tatum of North Carolina (3-2). Tar Heels took advantage of 2 FUM RECs to score in 1st Q: Terrapins HB Howard Dare lost possession to Carolina C-LB Jack Lineberger at Maryland 44YL, and, when UNC had to punt, G Fred Swearingen recovered bounding pumpkin at Maryland 35YL. Speedy HB Daley Goff skipped 11y to TD, and UNC's 7-0 lead held up until middle of 3rd Q. Big break for Terps came when P Goff couldn't field bad punt snap and was downed at his 38YL. Maryland QB Bob Rusevlyan tied it with 1y TD run, and HB Ted Kershner bolted 81y for go-ahead TD moments later. Maryland continued to dominate 2nd H and powered 67y on ground for its 3rd TD, scored by FB Jim Joyce on 13y run. At game's end, giddy Terrapins carried coach Tommy Mont across field to present him to surprised Queen. Perhaps it was best that London's tabloid newspapers hadn't yet exploded to their frenzied peak of celebrity watching.

Auburn 3 GEORGIA TECH 0: AP called Auburn (4-0) "a lumbering, punchless giant on offense, but the nation's best on defense." It took Tigers' 2nd string to move 48y to Georgia Tech (1-2-1) 16YL early in 2nd Q. Now threatened, Engineers' D posted stop sign, so FB-K Billy Atkins kicked 31y FG for 3-0 Tigers lead. Georgia Tech, underdog for 1st time since 1953 game vs. Notre Dame, also played well on D, as C-LB Don Stephenson recovered HB Tommy Lorino's FUM to blunt Auburn advance after Tech lost FUM at own 23YL. Yellow Jackets' D-line pushed back Tigers after poor Georgia Tech punt had started Auburn at Tech 34YL. Engineers threatened twice as QB Fred Braselton (10-14 passing) missed 4th down pass from Tigers 4YL just before H, and Auburn E-DE Jimmy Phillips made Braselton cough up pigskin with strong pass rush when Georgia Tech had reached 5YL on opening play of 4th Q.

Mississippi State 29 FLORIDA 20: On opening play of 2nd Q, Florida (2-1) HB Jim Rountree made great 1-handed grab away from 2 Mississippi State (3-1) DBs for 46y TD. Gators soon went 56y to 13-0 lead. Lifeless Bulldogs got jolt from little sub QB Tom Miller who raced 55y to Gators 7YL. FB Bill Schoenrock bulled over from 2YL, and after T-DT Ken Irby's FUM REC, Maroons tied it 13-13 soon thereafter. State's charge continued after 2nd H KO as it went 68y to FB Molly Halbert's TD blast and 19-13 edge. Florida responded with 77y trip after next KO for 20-19 counterpunch. Fumbling twice, Florida pinned itself deep for most of 4th Q, and Bulldogs used REC and E-K Kelly Cook's 32y FG for 22-20 lead. DB Miller made INT of Gators QB Jimmy Dunn (2-6/43y, INT), and Halbert scored after taking daring downfield lateral from Miller.

Purdue 20 MICHIGAN STATE 13: No. 1, but apparently flat Michigan State (3-1) lost 5 FUMs and relinquished 192y rushing to its oft-time 1950s nemisis Purdue (1-3). Boilermakers dug in to stop Spartans HB Dean Look's 4th down thrust inches from GL in late moments of 1st Q. Even though HB Walt Kowalczyk soon returned punt 33y to 10YL to get Spartans rolling to his 2nd Q TD run of 2y, Boilers tied it 7-7 on TD by FB Bob Jarus (17/68y). after FUM REC at Michigan State 19YL. Purdue's other FB, Mel Dillard (17/57y), twisted 4y to score 4:21 into 3rd Q. HB Ken Mikes scored clinching TD for 20-7 advantage on 34y draw play in 3rd Q, but it was masterful sub QB Ross Fichtner who transformed injury-riddled Boilermakers into Spartan-hexing "Spoilermakers." MSU QB Jim Ninowski (8-14/151y), whose passing had been ineffective most of day, nailed 3-4 on last scoring march, including 30y TD in 1st min of 4th Q to big E Sam Williams.

IOWA 21 Wisconsin 7: Experienced Hawkeyes (4-0) won tight battle as T-DTs Alex Karras and Dick Klein bottled up Badgers backs, forcing much of Wisconsin's attack to take flight: QBs Sid Williams, Dale Hackbart, and Ron Carlson combined to pitch 13-20/154y. On its 1st possession in 1st Q, Iowa went 75y as HB Mike Hagler swept far left on 7y TD sprint for 7-0 lead that held up well into 3rd Q. Wisconsin (3-1) suddenly tied it when T Jim Heineke blocked Iowa FB-P John Nocera's punt from 32YL, and FB Jon Hobbs fell on bounding ball in EZ. Hawkeyes had quick answer for Badgers' massed 8-man front: QB Randy Duncan lofted key passes during immediate TD drive as Iowa went 76y for go-ahead score at 14-7. It was tallied by FB Don Horn, who slanted through blocks of Klein and G Bob Commings and shed 3 tacklers in secondary for 35y burst. Iowa HB-DB Bill Gravel iced it with 45y INT TD RET in 4th Q.

ILLINOIS 34 Minnesota 13: Illini coach Ray Eliot had become so aggravated by performance of his 1st unit that he benched them to start game. Inspired 1st team of Illinois (2-2) entered scoreless game late in 1st Q and exploded for 21-0 H lead on way to crushing championship dream of no. 4 Golden Gophers (3-1), hot pre-season choice for Big 10 title. Illini running stars were HB Bobby Mitchell, hospital patient earlier in week, and FB Jack Delveaux, who scored twice early for Illinois. Minnesota lost pair of 1st H TOs—Illini E-DE Rod Hanson's INT and DB Mitchell's FUM REC at Gophers' 28YL—to contribute to its demise. Facing subs at 34-0 in 4th Q, Minnesota, after missing all its throws in 3 Qs, finally scored on 2 passes: QB Bobby Cox to HB Dave Lindblom and QB Jimmy Reese to E Jerry Friend. Writing in *Chicago Tribune,* Wilfrid Smith suggested, "Seldom in the history of the Western Conference (Big 10) has any team (Minnesota), near unanimous choice to win, been outplayed so completely." Gophers' once-bright prospects quickly would slide away in 1957.

Texas 17 ARKANSAS 0: Led by QB-DB Bobby Lackey and FB-LB Mike Dowdle, Texas (3-2) turned 3 Razorbacks miscues into scores to knock off unbeaten and highly-favored Arkansas (4-1). After Hogs HB Donnie Stone lost handle on punt at his 35YL in 1st Q, Longhorns' Polish refugee, K Fred Bednarski, made what was believed to be 1st-ever soccer-style FG of 40y. DB Lackey recovered FUM at his own 33YL in 2nd Q, and FB Mike Dowdle quickly burst 39y up middle to ignite 27y HB pass by Max Alvis to HB George Blanch. Arkansas drives fizzled at 9 and 13YLs until Texas iced it in 4th Q as Dowdle made INT of QB George Walker's pass and soon banged across from 1YL.

Texas A&M 7 TEXAS CHRISTIAN 0: Fidgety Frogs of TCU (2-2-1) lost FUMs on each of their 1st 2 snaps of afternoon, and Texas A&M (5-0) cashed latter of 2 bobbles as QB Roddy Osborne rolled right and turned to lob soft 10y TD pass to E Bobby Marks in EZ. It was then that Horned Frogs got down to their strategy, keeping possession and playing tough D. TCU succeeded, running 84 plays to A&M's 46, but never caught up, thanks to 4 TOs that stopped Frogs threats at Aggies 10, 5, and twice at 6YLs. FB-LB Buddy Dike was TCU's star with 24/73y rushing, and he made frequent tackles. Texas A&M star HB John David Crow (12/40y) continued to be nagged by bum knee and lost 3 FUMs. But, DB Crow came up with 2 clutch plays: he made INT inside his 10YL and caused and recovered FUM to stop Frogs' most promising drive as QB Dick Finney scrambled to 1st down at 5YL.

UCLA 26 Oregon State 7: Underdog Bruins (4-1) rallied around FB Barry Billington's opening drive TD run and used 3 TOs to bring Oregon State (4-1) crashing from its PCC tower. Bruins "were superior in every department," according to Beavers coach Tommy Prothro. UCLA TB Kirk Wilson had 51y avg on 7 punts, including 71y QK. Oregon State scored in 4th Q as sub TB Larry Sanchez threw 34y to E Jerry Doman who carried to 1YL. FB Jim Stinnette then crashed over for score that came too late.

Stanford 21 WASHINGTON 14: Indians (4-2) were thrown back on their heels in 1st Q by 18-play, 80y TD drive keyed by 24y, 3rd down run by Huskies (0-4-1) FB Jim Jones (13/52y) that resulted in 1-ft scoring dive by QB Al Ferguson. Thereafter, Stanford employed surprisingly strong running attack that piled up 235y to control balance of sunny afternoon in Seattle. Expecting Stanford to fly, Washington presented pass-oriented 4-4 D, which was carved wide open by FB Chuck Shea (29/133y, 2 TDs) and HB Al Harrington (18/86y). Tribe knotted affair in 2nd Q on 57y march to Shea's 22y TD on which he weaved through DBs to EZ. E-DE Gary Van Galder's FUM REC at Huskies 16YL prompted another TD by Indians: sneak by QB Jack Douglas (6-11/84y) for 14-7 edge. Shea's 2nd TD, tallied from 1y out with 6:42 to play, sealed fate of UW, even though Huskies went 68y to Ferguson's TD pass to HB Luther Carr in last 2 mins.

Oregon 14 WASHINGTON STATE 13: Secs and inches were difference as Rose Bowl dream of Cougars (3-2) was quieted. Meanwhile, Ducks (4-1) stayed unbeaten in PCC at 2-0, all because Washington State QB-K Bobby Newman's tying conv kick squarely struck and fell away from left upright with 1:05 remaining. Oregon was fortunate to sneak its 1st TD in before H as QB Jack Crabtree was stuffed by D-wall, then pushed across from close range as H clock showed :05. Ducks swift HB Jim Shanley caught 35y TD pass in 4th Q, and when FB-K Jack Morris clicked on his 2nd x-pt, Ducks led 14-0. Slumbering Cougars awakened and Newman hit 2 passes/29y to set up FB Eddie Stevens to go across GL from 1y out. Oregon decided to put Shanley on other end of pass strategy, and HB tossed INT taken by HB-DB Don Johnston. Wazzu charged 71y to Newman's TD sneak. Cougars coach Jim Sutherland sent in K Stevens to try x-pt, but Newman overruled him to try kick himself. Sutherland was philosophical afterward, saying, "It was his decision; he's our quarterback."

AP Poll October 21

1 Oklahoma (89)	1365	11 North Carolina State	115
2 Texas A&M (5)	1108	12 Ohio State (1)	112
3 Iowa (16)	998	13 Rice	103
4 Duke (10)	982	14 Minnesota	80
5 Auburn (11)	798	15 UCLA	58
6 Mississippi (10)	601	16tIllinois (1)	53
7 Notre Dame (4)	588	16tNavy	53
8 Michigan State (1)	547	18 Oregon	35
9 Army	196	19 Texas	34
10 Louisiana State	133	20 Michigan	33

October 26, 1957

(Th) Clemson 13 South Carolina 0: Big Thursday game at South Carolina Fairgrounds pivoted on infrequent, but effective passes of Clemson (3-2) soph QB Harvey White (3-4/96y, 2 TDs). Gamecocks (3-2) used ball control runs of HBs King Dixon and Alex Hawkins to advance to 4 1st downs and 66y to Tigers 12YL in 2nd Q. Clemson stiffened and took over on downs at own 14YL. With sudden fire, White lit out on 26y run off pass fake, flipped 28y pass to HB Bill Mathis, and found HB Sonny Quesenberry slanting across Gamecocks secondary for 15y TD pass with 1:38 before H. Clemson held ball for 7:42 on 3rd Q sortie, only to have it die at Carolina 5YL. Unattended Tigers E Whitey Jordan got behind DBs for long White pass, but lost FUM OB while nearly running in for TD. FB Rudy Hayes soon pounded over from 1YL for 13-0 edge.

Penn State 20 SYRACUSE 12: Favored Syracuse (3-1-1) lost its head in opening 2 mins: Orangemen gave Penn State (3-2) early TD, on HB Dave Kasperian's smash, when C Mike Bill's punt snap flew wildly to Orange 1YL. Nittany Lions never trailed as QB Al Jacks (3-8/75y, TD, INT), who would miss 2nd H with shoulder injury, threw 51y TD to E Les Walters in early segment of 2nd Q. But FB Ed Coffin caught 15 and 11y TD passes to bring Syracuse to within 13-12 at H. Lions' Walters grabbed 28y TD pass from back-up QB Richie Lucas to clinch it in 3rd Q. Syracuse got 4th Q chance when Penn State pass interference PEN placed it at Lions 15YL, but stout D held on downs for Penn State.

NORTH CAROLINA STATE 14 Duke 14: NC State (4-0-2) finally played home game and found that Cinderella's slipper still fit even though it produced 2nd straight tie. Duke (5-0-1) enjoyed 353y to 179y O advantage, scoring on 2 efforts by QB Bob Brodhead: short sneak and 47y pass to E Bill Thompson. Wolfpack D stopped sorties at its 15 and 1YLs, and HB Dick Christy made 2 TD catches to wipe out 14-0 deficit. Christy's 1st catch was 52y pitch from QB Tom Katich and it came in last 38 secs of 1st H. NC

State C-LB Jim "Midnight" Oddo made 53y INT RET to Devils 17YL to make way for Christy's TD grab of lobbed pass by HB Dick Hunter. Duke threatened late on runs of HB Danny Lee, including 18y zip to 3YL, but substitution rules kept HB George Dutrow, Duke's best K, on sideline and thwarted plans for last-play FG try.

Mississippi State 25 ALABAMA 13: "Win one for Whit" was Crimson Tide's Homecoming plea for coach J.B. "Ears" Whitworth, whose contract it was already announced would not be renewed at year's end. Fired-up Alabama (0-4-1) FB Jim Loftin bulled up middle on game's 2nd scrimmage and kept plowing over Bulldogs (4-1) until he broke free for 65y TD. Soon, Mississippi State QB Billy Stacy ran left, and when D came up to stop him, Stacy zipped short pass to E Charlie Weatherly, who pranced away for 57y TD and 6-6 tie in 1st Q. Bulldogs FG try was short, but Tide QB Clay Walls erred by choosing to return it from EZ to 7YL. Mississippi State took over on Bama 42YL, and on 4th down at 21YL, HB Gil Peterson used E John Benge's superb block to race for TD and 12-6 H edge. Miss State went 85y to 19-6 lead on strength of connections by 3 different passers: Stacy and HBs Bubber Trammell and Peterson. Slippery Alabama HB Marlin Dyess raced for 62y TD on late pass reception.

Georgia Tech 20 TULANE 13: Rebounding from 50-0 pasting by Mississippi, big underdog Tulane (1-5) came back from early 7-0 deficit to tie it 7-7, which stood up through H. After Georgia Tech (2-2-1) had scored in opening 3 mins on 16y TD sweep by HB Cal James following E-DE Jerry Nabors' FUM REC, Engineers turned butter-fingered. They lost 1st of 5 FUMs to Green Wave QB-DB Gene Newton on Tech's side of midfield late in 1st Q. Tulane used HB Virgil Jester's weaving 23y run to set up tying TD buck by FB Connie Andrews. Yellow Jackets soph FB Lester Simerville provided spark by taking 2nd H KO behind great blocking for 91y TD RET for 13-7 lead. Georgia Tech trumped punting match with 57y march in 4th Q: QB Fred Braselton completed pass to E Jerome Green, and HB Stan Flowers made gains of 12 and 4y to 6YL, spot from which FB Jim Benson scored with 3:08 remaining for 2-TD cushion. Pass interference PEN on Jackets, contributed to Tulane sub QB Richie Petitbon's 4y TD pass to HB Will Ellzey in dying moments.

Iowa 6 NORTHWESTERN 0: Iowa's fortunate Hawkeyes (5-0) prevented scoreless tie with lowly Northwestern (0-5) on "luckiest catch I ever made in my life," according to 4th Q TD scorer, HB Kevin Furlong. Iowa QB Randy Duncan, who hit only 4-9 passing, called his winning TD fling "the worst pass I've thrown all year." Northwestern had opened on its 1st series with its only threat, riding HB Bobby McKeiver's 13y punt RET and 25y rushing to Hawks 15YL. But, Iowa DE Don Norton perfectly detected pitchout and dumped McKeiver for 6y loss. Sack of QB John Talley pushed Wildcats back to 32YL. NW T-DT Andy Cvercko dumped Furlong for 9y loss on 4th-and-2 from Wildcats 9YL. Cold mud hampered play: In 3rd Q, DB McKeiver made INT, but Northwestern's Talley fumbled it away on next play to Iowa C-LB Bill Lapham. Cvercko recovered it right back when Hawkeyes FB Don Horn bobbled ball on next play. Wildcats HB Willmer Fowler lost FUM to Iowa T-DT Alex Karras at Cats 32YL 4 mins into 4th Q, and 2 plays later Duncan threw fateful lob to Furlong. DB Fowler seemed to have made INT, but ball slithered off Fowler's arm to Furlong, who galloped unmolested for 31y TD.

Ohio State 16 WISCONSIN 13: Badgers (3-2) HB Danny Lewis scored on 7 and 6y runs for 13-0 1st Q lead, but, in final scene near Buckeyes GL, Lewis lost FUM which killed Wisconsin's upset attempt. Trailing 13-0, Ohio State (4-1) pepped up its ground attack for TDs within 2:36 span to draw even at 13-13 before 1st Q ended. Ohio HB Don Clark used change-of-pace style to set up his blockers on beauty of 71y run, and FB Galen Cisco, future big league pitcher, plunged 5y after T-DT Jim Marshall recovered Badgers FUM on subsequent KO. It turned out that Clark's long run amounted to more than 30 percent of Bucks' 203y rushing as game fell into bend-but-don't-break D struggle after 1st Q. Wisconsin failed to score after 73y trip to 8YL in 2nd Q, and Buckeyes FUM by HB Dick LeBeau ruined DB Joe Cannavino's 41y INT RET to Badgers 7YL on last play of 3rd Q. HB-K Don Sutherin had booted winning 3rd Q chip-shot FG after Ohio State advanced 69y in 11 plays to Wisconsin 4YL. Badgers made 1st-and-goal at 5YL with 2 mins to go, but on 2nd down, Lewis busted up middle only to be hammered into FUM to FB-LB Bob White.

NOTRE DAME 13 Pittsburgh 7: Pitt G Dan Wisniewski blocked Fighting Irish's 1st Q conv, so Panthers (3-3) enjoyed 7-6 H edge after QB Bill Kaliden's 1y TD run capped 56y 2nd Q drive. When QB Bob Williams of Notre Dame (4-0) was among 3 players ejected from bitter battle, it provided opportunity for Irish sub QB George Izo to loft long, winning TD pass to streaking HB Aubrey Lewis on opening play of 4th Q. Pittsburgh was down but not done: Panthers fought to ND 10YL, but their considerable deficiency in aerial game (5-16/47y, INT) was evident in QB Ivan Toncic's 3 straight missed tosses which ended threat. Notre Dame FB Nick Pietrosante rushed 16/79y, while Pitt HB Joe Scisly provided 17/97y on ground.

OKLAHOMA 14 Colorado 13: Despite suffering blocked conv by Sooners G Bill Krisher, Buffaloes (3-2-1) briefly led 13-7 in 4th Q on TB-DB Bob Stransky's 40y INT TD RET and his 8y TD pass to BB Boyd Dowler. Indeed, fired up Colorado was able to play most of 2nd H in enemy territory. Bison finished game with 267y to 250y O edge, partly because of effective running by WB Eddie Dove (10/62y) and TB Stransky (15/54y). When Oklahoma (5-0) got 8y TD run around LE from HB Clendon Thomas (12/48y, TD) at end of 53y counter march in 4th Q, it allowed QB-K Carl Dodd's conv kick to serve as winning margin. Colorado's annual scare of Oklahoma upset AP pollsters. Texas A&M, 14-0 victors over Baylor, overtook Sooners for no. 1 spot in writers poll on Monday.

Kansas State 14 IOWA STATE 10: Kansas State (2-3-1) escaped frantic 4th Q jousting that pinned it deep in own territory by raft of PENs and sharp punting by Iowa State (2-3-1) P Ron Fontana. Wildcats had taken advantage of their only 2 trips into Cyclones end by scoring TDs in 1st and 3rd Qs. Iowa State HB Jim Lary fumbled opening KO away to K-State T Gene Meier at his 26YL, and Cats FB Tony Tiro lugged ball on last 3 tries/14y of 7-play push. K-State opened 2nd H with 79y iand march to HB George Whitney's TD run. TB Dwight Nichols had fired 27y TD pass to E Brian Dennis on 1st play of 2nd Q, but same combination lost another score when ineligible receiver was detected downfield later in 2nd Q. After Iowa State T-K Lyle Carlson made FG at end of 3rd Q, Wildcats had to count on pressure punting by P Tiro and HB-P Ray Glaze to escape late Cyclones threats.

Arkansas 12 Mississippi 6 (Memphis): Ole Miss (5-1) rolled up 291y rushing, led by FB Bill Hurst (20/92y). Rebels (5-1) QB Ray Brown returned Porkers' 3rd straight QK 15y to 50YL, and Rebs went on to score on Brown's 7y TD pass to E Larry Grantham late in 1st Q. Sub QB-P George Walker's punt to 4YL in 2nd Q gave Arkansas (5-1) field position to take return punt 54y to tie it 6-6 before H: Walker (2-3/39y) faked to FB on 3rd down at own 48YL and pitched 35y to HB Billy Kyser to set up tying 8y TD run by Kyser. Mississippi roared 80y after 2nd H KO, but on 4th-and-goal at 2YL, Brown was tossed for 13y loss by Hogs DE Bob Childress. FB Gerald Nesbitt (13/100y) took over, gaining 7y on 2 cracks until going off RT on 3rd down and sprinting along sideline. Hemmed in at Ole Miss 25YL, Nesbitt flipped lateral to omni-present Kyser, who zipped to 3YL to complete 74y gain. Kyser's 2nd TD came on 4th down pitchout that decided contest late in 3rd Q.

WASHINGTON 19 Oregon State 6: TB Larry Sanchez whipped 34y TD pass to WB Sterling Hammack, but Oregon State (4-2) never was able to build on its 6-0 advantage earned late in 1st Q. Huskies (1-4-1) QB Al Ferguson (6-8/94y, TD) offered quick answer by completing 2 long passes to lead to his run-fake 22y TD pass to HB Don Millich. Upset of Beavers was given full gas when sub HB Dick Payseno capped 65y drive with 4y plunge to lift score to 12-6. FB-LB Jimmy Jones of Washington burst for 53y TD run in closing secs of 3rd Q that upped count to 19-6 and donated 14 tackles to Huskies' D effort. Oregon State was outgained 355y to 246y as it failed to move after falling behind.

STANFORD 20 Ucla 6: Vanquished Bruins (4-2) coach Red Sanders offered that Stanford (3-2) QB Jack Douglas (10-12/128y, 2 TDs), with his rollout passing, had given his Uclans more trouble than graduated A-A passer John Brodie, who now toiled for San Francisco 49ers. In this instance, Douglas and Company delivered big win. Little-known Cards E Joel Freis, like Douglas hailing from L.A. basin, nabbed both of little QB's scoring throws: 37y in 3rd Q to increase Stanford's lead to 14-6 and 2y in 4th Q to lock it up. Not known for their D play, Indians had made big stop in early going: After UCLA TB-P Kirk Wilson stopped QK at 1YL. Stanford FB Chuck Shea (21/86y, TD) lost FUM at his 7YL. Indians permitted 2y in 3 runs and knocked down 4th down GL pass for Bruins star E Dick Wallen, who was blanked from receiving sheet. Uclans scored early in 3rd Q after DT Bill Leeka recovered another FUM by Shea, and TB Don Long flipped short pass to WB Phil Parslow.

AP Poll October 28

1 Texas A&M (59)	1457	11 Arkansas (5)	173
2 Oklahoma (51)	1418	12 Michigan	145
3 Iowa (20)	1138	13 Texas	108
4 Auburn (19)	1001	14 Mississippi	99
5 Notre Dame (4)	891	15 Oregon	77
6 Michigan State (3)	770	16 Navy (1)	72
7 Duke (3)	656	17 Tennessee	63
8 Ohio State (1)	324	18 Colorado	32
9 Army	243	19 Florida	30
10 North Carolina State	200	20 Dartmouth	18

November 2, 1957

YALE 14 Dartmouth 14: Enjoying its 1st national ranking since 1949, no. 20 Dartmouth (5-0-1) jumped to 7-0 H lead on QB Dave Bradley's deceptive, double-fake 33y TD pass to E Dave Moss. But, Yale tied it on FB Gene Coker's 3rd Q TD run and took lead with 1:50 to go in 4th Q on QB Dick Winterbauer's 19y arrow to E Pete Riddle. After ensuing KO, Yale (4-1-1) expected Big Green to fill air with passes. So, Bulldogs attempted to insert DE John Pendexter, team's best pass-rusher, but officials slapped them with misapplied illegal substitution PEN that even Dartmouth's bench records showed was erroneous. Indians took advantage of 15y jump to go 58y as Bradley hit Moss for 18 and 17y passes and then found FB Brian Hepburn in back of EZ with tying TD pass with :10 to go.

PENN STATE 27 West Virginia 6: AP reported that Nittany Lions soph QB Richie Lucas' sleight of hand had West Virginia (4-2-1) tackling wrong ball carrier time and again. Lucas (8-14/101y, 2 TDs, INT) inherited starting position when QB Al Jacks went down previous week against Syracuse. HB Andy Moconyi scored 1st of his 2 TDs to complete 78y trip on 1st play of 2nd Q for Penn State (4-2). It was followed by x-pt kick by FB-K Emil Caprara. Mountaineers soon forged their own TD on 12-play drive that was capped by 1y wedge by QB Mickey Trimarki (4-7/47y, INT). However, when HB-K Whitey Mikanik was wide with his kick, Lions led 7-6 at H. Penn State quickly put game away in 3rd Q: It went 67y from 2nd H KO to E Les Walters' 6y TD catch, and, 3 mins later, State rode Lucas' 12y pass to Walters to HB Dave Kasperian's 8y TD smash.

VANDERBILT 7 Louisiana State 0: Future LSU (4-3) stars, like HB Billy Cannon (11/46y), C-LB Max Fugler (9 tackles), and HB Johnny Robinson, were beginning to bloom, but they weren't enough to overcome fired-up and confident Vanderbilt (3-1-2). Commodores tore 77y downfield after opening KO as QB Boyce Smith (9-16/86y, TD, INT) fired 30y pass and HB Tom Moore (7/35y) ripped for 6 and 12y gains before taking 3y TD pass from Smith. DB Smith halted Tigers' trot into Vandy territory with INT, so LSU's best chance to tie game hsd to wait until 4th Q. Starting from Commodores 44YL, Bengals QB Win Turner (6-8/52y, INT) hit Cannon with 6y pass, FB Jimmy Taylor slammed for 6y, and Cannon went 7y. LSU earned 1st-and-goal at 3YL but failed primarily because G Billy Grover shot through to slam Cannon for 7y loss on 3rd down, then Turner was halted by DB Smith at 3YL.

AUBURN 13 Florida 0: Thwarted on 4th down gamble at own 26YL, confident Auburn (6-0) D regained possession after allowing only 1y to strangled Gators (3-2). Florida, led by DT Charlie Mitchell, made stand of its own in 2nd Q at 1YL, but 26y reverse run by Tigers HB Bobby Hoppe brought them right back to 5YL. FB Billy Atkins went in off LT Ben Preston's block standing up for 6-0 lead 2:07 before H. Barely more than 4 mins into 3rd Q, Auburn QB Lloyd Nix flung pass 20y downfield to E Jimmy Phillips, who set out on twisting 63y TD play in which at least 6 Gators had tackling range on him. So elusive was Phillips on his TD trip that 2 would-be tacklers bounced off each other. Phillips simply ploughed over last Florida tackler, C-LB Joel Wahlberg, at 10YL on his amazing TD.

MISSISSIPPI 20 Houston 7 (Jackson, Miss.): Cougars (2-4-1) turned out to be tougher pride than expected after Ole Miss' initial foray. Rebels (6-1) QB Ray Brown bolted 22y to Houston 6YL, and HB Billy Lott bumped across for 7-0 lead only 3:15 into game. Although Houston would never be better than 7-7 tie on 94y trip in 2nd Q capped by HB Billy Ray Dickey's TD catch, Cougars marched steadily to prove they belonged with mighty Mississippi. DE Don Williams recovered FUM near midfield late in 3rd Q, and it seemed to finally break Cougars' spirit as Rebels went 48y. They primarily rode Brown and Lott runs to Brown's TD sneak. Sub QB Bobby Franklin tacked on insurance TD in last min after UH QB Paul Sweeten lost FUM at his 6YL.

Navy 20 NOTRE DAME 6: Callow FB Ray Wellborn, buried on Navy (6-1) bench until starting FB Dick Dagampat was hurt, did what youngsters do: he lost mid-air FUM, which Irish HB Dick Lynch caught and returned for 46y TD in 1st Q. However, Midshipmen T Bob Reifsnyder broke through to block E-K Monty Stickles' x-pt try. Wellborn rebounded beautifully from his early gaffe with 10/112y, 2 TDs rushing to key Middies' 6th win over Notre Dame (4-1) in 31 tries. Wellborn scored his 3rd TD on 32y pass from QB Tom Forrestal. T-DT Reifsnyder, who threw key block to spring Wellborn on 44y screen pass to Irish 15YL, joined C-LB Milan Moncilovich to steadfastly crimp Irish O in 2nd H; Navy D allowing only 4y. Notre Dame didn't help its own momentum much in 2nd Q as 55y in PENs was paced off against it.

MICHIGAN 21 Iowa 21: TB Jim Pace's 65y punt TD RET and TD-poising INTs by FB-LB Jim Byers and HB-DB Mike Shatusky were 2nd Q events that helped maintain Michigan's long-standing hex over no. 3 Hawkeyes, winless in intermittently-played series since 1924. Earlier, Iowa (5-0-1) star DT Alex Karras fiercely rushed QB Jim Van Pelt and ripped ball from him for DE Jim Gibbons' REC at Michigan 9YL. Returning to its misdirection Wing-T O of 1956, Hawkeyes used WB-motion to quickly pull UM off-side, and FB John Nocera plunged 2y for 7-0 Iowa lead. Iowa permitted only 56y rushing (-8y in 1st H), and strong D helped overcome 21-7 H shortfall on short 2nd H TD runs by FB Don Horn and QB Randy Duncan. Hawks received 2nd H KO and traveled 68y on sweeps and Duncan's 11y pass to E Don Norton before Horn ran 17y draw play and ultimately plunged over. Wolverines (4-1-1) G-LB Marv Nyren missed tackle on Gibbons' 14y run with flat pass, and it set up Duncan's tying TD sneak in 4th Q.

Michigan State 21 WISCONSIN 7: Spartans' recent butter-fingered play continued as they lost 6 TOs to Wisconsin (3-3), losers now of 3 in row. Surprisingly, these errors barely scratched Michigan State (5-1) as it only gave up HB Danny Lewis' 1-ft plunge for 2nd Q TD and brief 7-7 deadlock. Spartans never trailed because they held Badgers to only 53y rushing, sacked QB Sidney Williams (2-6/46y, INT) 5 times/-40y, and forced 4 TOs themselves. Starting MSU backs, FB Don Gilbert, TB Blanche Martin, and WB Walt Kowalczyk, each powered for short TD run. Martin contributed game's biggest play: After Wisconsin knotted it in 2nd Q on 11y advance after FB-LB Jon Hobbs recovered FUM, Martin sped 65y with ensuing KO. Martin crashed 3y for permanent Spartans' lead at 14-7 after pass interference PEN on Badgers HB-DB Bob Altmann.

Missouri 9 COLORADO 6: Colorado (3-3-1) gained 274y rushing during game played in adverse freezing mud conditions. But, Buffaloes had only WB Eddie Dove's 6y reverse TD run just before H to show for its strong effort. Held to 123y total O, conservative Missouri (5-1-1) earned upset when FB Hank Kuhlmann barged 5y to 3rd Q TD after Colorado TB Bob Stransky lost FUM in Buffs territory. Tigers T Bob Lee added to 7-6 advantage when he blocked Bison QB-P Boyd Dowler's 4th Q punt to earn safety.

Texas A&M 7 ARKANSAS 6: America fought nationwide flu epidemic late in 1957, and Asian bug had reached Fayetteville just prior to Razorbacks' Homecoming Saturday. Happily, dozens of Arkansas Razorbacks had recovered in time. Still, no. 1 Aggies, undefeated in 16 straight games, were able to use their flu-free, but banged-up, clutch HB-DB John David Crow to power on ground for 24/116y, TD and make game-saving GL INT in dying moments. Arkansas (5-2) managed on its opening series to score 1st TD permitted by Texas A&M (7-0) in conf play so far in 1957 as Porkers 2nd unit fought 46y to QB Don Christian's 1st Q TD buck. But FB-K Gerald Nesbitt missed x-pt kick. A&M pieced together 74y drive, and at its finish Crow scored on 12y TD run in 2nd Q. HB-K Loyd Taylor nailed kick for 7-6 edge. Arkansas controlled play in 2nd H, reaching 5YL midway in 4th Q. Soph QB-K Freddy Akers was called upon for FG try that went wide left. Aggies QB Roddy Osborne was looking to kill clock in last 2 mins when he tried pass from inside Hogs 20YL. As conservative coach Bear Bryant steamed on A&M bench, Arkansas DB Don Horton picked it off and set his sail for far GL. Osborne, with help from HB Taylor caught up at A&M 27YL, which years later prompted Osborne's great line: "Horton was running for a touchdown, but I was running for my life." Hogs pushed on to 1st down at 13YL, and E Bob Childress appeared to break open at GL. DB Crow, Heisman winner in waiting, seemed to arrive out of nowhere to make INT of QB George Walker's labeled pass.

Clemson 20 RICE 7: Big Tigers line wore down Owls (3-3) in 2nd H after Rice took 7-0 lead in 2nd Q on 8y TD pass from QB King Hill (7-10/119y, INT) to E Gene Jones after Hill set up TD with 19y run. Clemson (4-2) struck back to tie it 7-7 by keeping ball for 14 plays or nearly all of remaining 8 mins of H; QB Harvey White knotted it with 20y, 4th down pass to E Whitey Jordan and x-pt kick. Clemson took 2nd H KO and rolled 72y to pay-dirt on TD pass by White, who reentered game on 4th-and-goal at 9YL. Tigers' D pushed back 2 Rice penetrations that died inside 20YL in 2nd H, including G-LB John Grdijan's leaping INT at own 5YL. Clemson wrapped it up with 85y all-land cruise that ate up 9:21 of 4th Q as FBs Mike Dukes and Doug Cline and HBs Bill Mathis and Sonny Quesenberry authored run damage.

UCLA 16 California 14: Bruins (5-2) were on verge of all but locking up game with 3-TD margin early in 3rd Q when TB Kirk Wilson (10/43y) fumbled away ball at California (1-6) 4YL. Given this reprieve, Golden Bears romped 59y to trim discrepancy to 13-7. Cal QB Joe Kapp (2-7/38y) threw 22y pass to E Mike White to help HB Jack Hart blast over from 2y out. K Wilson, who had never made FG in HS or college, booted 33y FG to extend UCLA's lead to 16-7. Earlier, Uclans E Dick Wallen had pounced on FUM at Cal 9YL in opening 5 mins of game, and soph FB Ray Smith (14/75y, TD) threw block for TB Don Long (13/59y, TD) to score. Smith, who started for injured FB Barry Billington, had scored 2nd Q TD on 6y burst up middle for 13-0 edge. Speedy Golden Bears soph FB Jack Yerman (15/82y, TD) sprinted to 5y TD halfway in 4th Q, but Cal HB Darrell Roberts lost FUM while trying to field punt on full run at his 40YL. This TO, 4th suffered by Bears, ruined their comeback bid in last 5 mins.

Oregon 27 STANFORD 26: Oregon (6-1) coach Len Casanova surprised Stanford (4-3) by opening game with 2-WR set and operating quickly without huddle, 1 of rare times it was tried in that era. Ducks went 72y on 1st series to 5y TD run by HB Jim Shanley (21/71y). What ensued was O warfare, waged without TOs, as teams traded TDs in every Q. In 1st Q, Indians received 73y TD pass from QB Jack Douglas (14-25/210y, 3 TDs) to HB Jeri McMillin, and Douglas followed at 11:23 of 2nd Q with 6y TD throw to FB Chuck Shea on 4th down. It gave Tribe its only lead at 13-7. Webfoots came right back on QB Jack Crabtree's 1st of 2 TD sneaks to retake 14-13 edge in last 5 secs of 2nd Q. Shanley caught 17y pass to Stanford 8YL after 2nd H KO so that Crabtree could call his own TD sneak again. Morris scored 2y TD early in 4th Q, but missed kick to leave it at 27-20. Less than 5 mins from end, Indians E Gary Van Galder caught Douglas' 3rd TD pass, but HB-K Al Harrington, under rush pressure from both Oregon Es, J.C. Wheeler and Ron Stover, missed wide with tying x-pt. When Indians reached 8YL in last min, Stanford coach Chuck Taylor ruled out FG try because Harrington, his only capable K, was out of lineup, ineligible to return. Douglas tried 4th down pass, but was smothered by G Bob Grottkau on game's last play.

AP Poll November 4

1 Texas A&M (65)	1777	11 Michigan	244
2 Oklahoma (48)	1562	12 Arkansas (1)	205
3 Auburn (50)	1536	13 Oregon	188
4 Michigan State (6)	1141	14 Mississippi (1)	166
5 Iowa (12)	1110	15 Notre Dame	101
6 Ohio State (10)	869	16 Duke	75
7 Navy	612	17 Mississippi State	69
8 Army	424	18 Georgia Tech	61
9 Tennessee	417	19 Missouri (1)	46
10 North Carolina State (3)	373	20 Virginia Military	18

November 9, 1957

(Fri) Miami 40 FLORIDA STATE 13: Ambitious Florida State (3-4) led Miami (4-2-1) 7-6 at H, thanks to opening 66y drive. Seminoles FB Bob Nellums bumped over from 1YL to score for 7-0 lead. After being outrushed 92y to 70y in 1st H, Hurricanes owned 2nd H as they blasted for 266y on ground. Miami's 2nd unit, led by running of HB Byron Blasko (12/76y), went 73y to Blasko's short TD run early in 3rd Q. Next time they had ball, Canes surged 56y, capped by QB Fran Curci's 6y TD pass to E Phil Gaetz. Miami HB Joe Plevel scored 2 of 3 TDs in 4th Q, giving him 3 scores in game. Soph QB Joe Majors clicked on 3 straight passes to spark FSU's only 2nd H score.

ARMY 39 Utah 33: Coach Red Blaik's ground-oriented Cadets (6-1) used HB Bob Anderson's 30/214y, 3 TDs, rushing to out-duel coach "Cactus" Jack Curtis' air-minded Utes (4-4). Utah had on exhibit strong-armed QB Lee Grosscup, whose performance influenced East Coast writers to help earn A-A mention and 1959 no. 1 draft selection by New York Giants. Teams traded 5 TDs in 4th Q, and, after dust cleared, Army had 394y on ground and Utah 316y in air. Uncomfortable with such mutually-weak D play, Blaik called this game "worst exhibition of run-sheep-run football I ever saw."

NAVY 6 Duke 6 (Baltimore): Well-matched rivals had to settle for 3rd straight dissatisfying tie. Middies (6-1-1) bogged down 5 times inside Duke 20 YL, and Blue Devils (5-1-2) bungled late 4th Q drive to Navy 2YL when PEN ruined their chance. QB Tom Forrestal threw 1st Q TD pass for Navy, which was matched by Duke HB George Dutrow's 14y TD run in 2nd Q.

William & Mary 7 NORTH CAROLINA STATE 6: "Too many mistakes," lamented NC State (5-1-2) coach Earle Edwards on his 49th birthday. Victim of INT and 4 FUMs, no. 10 Wolfpack got its only TD when alert HB Dick Christy recovered EZ FUM after FB Don Hafer barreled 69y, but lost control of ball near GL. However, HB-K Dick Hunter immediately missed fateful conv kick to ruin Wolfpack's undefeated season. William & Mary (3-5) earned big upset on HB Dave Edmunds' TD and K Bob Hardage's kick at end of 67y drive in 4th Q.

TENNESSEE 21 Georgia Tech 6: Volunteers (6-1) swept to 6th win in row as WB Bill Anderson caught 21y pass to position FB Tommy Bronson for 1y TD run, then raced 45y to sizzling TD on Tennessee's old Single-Wing staple, WB reverse play, in 3rd Q. Outplayed Georgia Tech (3-3-1) managed only QB Fred Braselton's short TD pass to E Jimmy Vickers in game's closing 30 secs. Engineers' late chance had come after DE Jack Rudolph fell on FUM at Tennessee 17YL.

Florida 22 Georgia 0 (Jacksonville): Blanked in rivalry match for 2nd straight year, Wally Butts, coach at Georgia (2-6) since 1939, became big ham on irritated alumni's hot griddle. For its dominant part, Florida (4-2) served up 3 QBs who each tossed TD pass. Starting QB Jimmy Dunn capped 1st Q drive of 47y with 9y scoring toss, his 1st

pass of day, to E Don Fleming, who eluded 2 defenders. P Dunn punted 45y to UGa 2YL in 2nd Q. Bulldogs couldn't move, and C Dave Lloyd sailed snap way over E-P Ken Cooper's head for safety that lifted Gators' lead to 9-0 before H. K Lloyd was so rattled that his 1st 2 free-kicks after safety went OB, and Florida took over on Georgia 30 YL. After exchange of FUMs near Georgia 20YL, Gators back-up QB Mickey Ellenburg hit HB Bernie Parish with 19y TD pass late in 2nd Q. Florida went to H ahead 16-0. Florida 3rd-team QB Jim Rhyne fired 4th Q TD pass.

AUBURN 15 Mississippi State 7 (Birmingham): Seeking its best record since going 7-3 in 1947, Mississippi State (5-2) scored 1st when it caught powerful Auburn (7-0) D napping late in 2nd Q. On 3rd-and-4, Bulldogs sub QB Tom Miller rolled left and targeted E Ned Brooks, who slipped deep and into clear at Tigers 25YL. Brooks romped uncontested for 57y on TD pass play that became only 3rd TD allowed by Auburn in season to date. Essentially, Miller's surprise pass was only gaffe all season for mighty Plainsmen D. Maroons HB Bubber Trammell had bolted for 16y gain on game's 1st scrimmage, but Mississippi State made no other 1st downs in 1st H other than its TD. As 2nd H opened, Auburn blazed 76y in 11 plays to FB-K Billy Atkins' 2y TD dive and tying kick. Tigers soph C-LB Jackie Burkett stormed in on Bulldogs P Bill Schoenrock, and E John Whatley followed to block punt for safety for 9-7 edge in 4th Q. Atkins added another TD after FUM REC was secured at Maroons 10YL.

VANDERBILT 12 Kentucky 7: Big Commodores (4-1-2) HBs Phil King (12/55y)—until he was injured—and Tom Moore (11/113y) were O mainstays, and DB King opened scoring with 54y INT TD RET in 1st Q. Kentucky (1-7) HB Bobby Cravens (16/93y, TD) keyed 54y drive in 3rd Q by flipping 12y pass to E Howard Ledger for 1st down at Vanderbilt 5YL. Cravens carried tough-tackling Vandy NG Billy Grover across for 4y TD 2 plays later, and 60-min T-K Lou Michaels, who had so-so punting day, booted x-pt for 7-6 lead midway in 3rd Q. Right after ensuing KO, UK QB-DB Lowell Hughes made FUM REC at Commodores 44YL, but motion PEN killed Kentucky drive inside 20YL. "That was the ball game," said Kentucky coach Blanton Collier. Still, Wildcats appeared to have sufficient D to lock up their 1st SEC win until clever Vandy QB Boyce Smith (5-14/56y, TD, INT) masterminded late 57y land drive that he capped with 9y TD pass to E Bob Laws.

Tulane 7 ALABAMA 0 (Mobile): Green Wave (2-6) washed over favored Crimson Tide (1-5-1) by using tough D that included 2 essential INTs. Game's only TD came after QB-DB Gene "Mouse" Newton picked off pass by Alabama QB Bobby Smith late in 2nd Q. Starting from Tide 33YL, Tulane inserted QB Richie Petitbon to lead 10-play march that was aided by 2 Bama offside PENs. Petitbon scored on 4th down rollout from 4YL with 1:05 remaining in 1st H. Alabama made it to Greenies 26YL on its next 2 possessions, 1st of which ended 2nd Q. Each time, heads-up DB Newton put on D clamps, knocking down Tide FB Jim Loftin to end 1st H and making another INT of Smith in 3rd Q. Tulane DT Dan Egan recovered FUM at Bama 28YL after Smith was snowed under for 24y loss trying to pass.

MISSISSIPPI 14 Louisiana State 12: Spirited Bengal Tigers (4-4) gained early momentum from 2 happenstances: Wide-open Mississippi (7-1) E Don Williams dropped 1st Q pass thrown by QB Ray Brown and Louisiana State C Max Fugler soon blocked P Brown's punt. TD sprint of 60y by FB Jimmy Taylor (15/117y) after FUM REC by DT Lynn LeBlanc and 53y TD by HB J.W. Brodnax (5/41y) on punt RET handoff from HB Billy Cannon gave LSU 12-7 H lead. Ole Miss FB-LB Bill Hurst had recovered FUM at LSU 30YL in 2nd Q that allowed Brown to score TD that briefly gave life to Rebs at 7-6. Tigers gained only 62y in 2nd H, while Rebels padded their nation's best rushing stats with 365y. Brown's lost FUM after LB Fugler's tackle at Tigers 7YL interrupted 92y Ole Miss drive in 4th Q. But, when P Cannon could punt out only to Tigers 33YL, Rebels drove to decisive score: Brown's 9y pass to Williams that allowed pass-catcher to make up for his early flub.

OHIO STATE 20 Purdue 7: Undefeated in Big 10, Ohio State (6-1) was left with Iowa and Michigan between it and Rose Bowl. Buckeyes carried 1st H as they sent HB Don Clark (4/45y), before he left with pulled leg muscle, dashing 18y for TD at end of 71y drive and HB Dick LeBeau careening 21y to close 91y march highlighted by runs of emerging soph FB Bob White. Purdue (3-4) HB-P Kenny Mikes dropped punt snap in 2nd Q to put Ohio at Boilermakers 36YL for TD on runs by QB Frank Kremblas, who scored on short keeper. Purdue threatened 6 times inside Bucks 20YL, but only in 3rd Q did it score on QB Ross Fichtner's beautiful rollout to right and throw-back left to speeding HB Tom Fletcher. Pass play covered 25y.

ILLINOIS 20 Michigan 19: Cold, stiff wind blew across Champaign's plains and it critically affected Michigan HB-P Brad Myers' dreadful 5y punt late in 3rd Q. Illinois (3-4) went 56y after Myers' short punt to 20-6 edge on HB L.T. Bonner's 5y turn of E for TD. QB Jim Van Pelt, injured previous week, came off bench in 4th Q to rally Wolverines (4-2-1) for 2 scores. Van Pelt completed 6-12/90y, including last min 9y TD to E Charles Teuscher. But, Illinois C Gene Cherney had blocked his 2nd of Van Pelt's conv kicks after FB John Herrnstein's 1y TD plunge which left score at 20-12. Earlier, in 2nd Q, Bonner (14/98y, 2 TDs) had given Illini 13-6 lead when he broke HB-DB Bob Ptacek's tackle in secondary to score on 59y run on 3rd-and-1.

IOWA 44 Minnesota 20: Many people felt this edition of Iowa Hawkeyes (6-0-1) was superior to 1956's Rose Bowl champions. But, Iowa's weakness had been producing big O, until this riotous 563y outbreak that built Hawks' highest pt total to date vs. rival Gophers (4-3). Iowa created drives of 59 and 69y 1st 2 times it owned possession, while in between Minnesota briefly was competitive with 7-7 tie on 1st of 2 TD runs by FB Bob Blakely (98y rushing). Big stars for Hawks were E Jim Gibbons, who caught pair of TD passes and set school mark with 164y receiving on 9 catches, QB Randy Duncan (11-17/180y, 2 TDs), who scored twice on short runs, and HB Bill Happel, who scored on 48y dash among his 3/88y rushing. Most important play was turned in by E-K Bob Prescott (35y FG): Minnesota P Kelvin Kleber bobbled punt snap in his EZ in 2nd Q and tried to run; Prescott took swipe at ball in Kleber's hand and fell on it in EZ for TD and 21-7 lead. Iowa led 30-7 at H, and, in unusual act of defiant confidence, sent its 15 sr players trotting, to great cheers of 58,103 fans, to locker room in single file with less than 3 mins to play.

MICHIGAN STATE 34 Notre Dame 6: Solid D of Spartans (6-1) forced flock of Irish blunders and broke open 7-0 game after H. Michigan State sub HB Art Johnson followed his 11y 2nd Q TD with 50y TD sprint to ignite 20-pt 3rd Q. Fighting Irish (4-2) dropped 2nd straight after rebuilding year's promising start. ND QB Bob Williams sparked late 81y TD drive as he hit E Monty Stickles with 20y pass and ran for 11y gain before sneaking over for TD. It was inadequate to halt 6th loss to Michigan State in last 7 meetings.

Oklahoma 39 MISSOURI 14: Another Orange Bowl berth was secured as Sooners (7-0) made Missouri (5-2-1) its 47th straight victim since 1953. Sub HB Bobby Boyd sparkled, throwing key block on HB Dick Carpenter's 19y 1st Q TD reverse run, scoring own TD on 2nd Q run, and picking up several of Oklahoma's 28 1st downs. TDs by QB Phil Snowden and FB Hank Kuhlmann were 1st scores by land allowed by Sooners all season.

KANSAS 13 Kansas State 7: With its top 2 QBs knocked out of hard-hitting game, Kansas (3-4-1) turned to 3rd-string QB Duane Morris to fire game-winning 40y TD in last 18 secs of play. It was Morris' 2nd TD pass of day, and it went to FB Homer Floyd who wriggled away from 2 tacklers enroute to score after catch at K-State's 15YL. Kansas State (2-5-1) had best of play in 1st H, while taking 7-0 lead on 2nd Q TD run by FB Tony Tiro, who soon was carried off with leg injury. Wildcats traveled 91y, but H clock foiled their voyage to Kansas 5YL. Jayhawks tied it at 7-7 in 3rd Q when Morris used 2-handed basketball-like set shot to get rid of ball to HB Don Feller, who scooted 74y to score. Little Kansas QB John Traylor, in as kick holder, bobbled snap but alertly rose up to skirt LE for tying conv.

Washington 13 OREGON 6 (Portland): Oregon (6-2) outgained Washington (2-5-1) by 305y to 230y, but Oregon HB Charley Tourville was at center of 3 miscues that helped sink Ducks. P Tourville bobbled punt snap into misadventure at his 16YL, and HB Tourville lost FUM to Washington DT Dick Day at Huskies 29YL. Oregon held on each of these situations but could not prevent Washington QB Bobby Dunn's 3y TD run in 2nd Q. It followed Tourville's passing arm being hit by onrushing Huskies DE Bruce Claridge that produced pop-up INT nabbed by UW C-LB Marv Bergmann. QB Jack Crabtree was Oregon's throwing star with 10-18/195y, including masterful 76y TD bomb to E Pete Welch at outset of 3rd Q. Washington's ace FB-LB Jim Jones stormed through to block x-pt kick. Sub QB Al Ferguson sparked clinching drive for Huskies with option runs covering 67y to his TD keeper.

AP Poll November 11

1 Texas A&M (60)	1577	11 Duke	153
2 Oklahoma (46)	1411	12 Mississippi State	88
3 Auburn (42)	1403	13 Virginia Military	76
4 Michigan State (9)	1224	14 Clemson	70
5 Iowa (19)	1112	15 Illinois	51
6 Ohio State (6)	893	16 Oregon	48
7 Tennessee (1)	859	17 Texas Christian	46
8 Mississippi (1)	347	18 Michigan	44
9 Navy	340	19 North Carolina State	35
10 Army	321	20 Rice	26

November 16, 1957

(Fri) Maryland 16 MIAMI 6: Hurricanes' Homecoming crowd was stunned by vigor shown by young Terrapins (4-5), 7-pt underdogs, as passes proved poisonous to Miami (4-3-1) D. Despite having won 3 games in row thanks to its stout D, Miami was no match for QB Bob Rusevlyan's pinpoint passes. Rusevlyan completed throws to HB Howard Dare, E Bill Turner, and HB Fred Hamilton on 1st Q charge to FB Phil Perlo's 2y TD plunge. Maryland QB-K John Fritsch soon booted FG for 10-0 lead. Pint-sized QB Fran Curci sparked Hurricanes late in 1st Q as he followed HB John Varone's 14y run with 3 straight pass connections to Maryland 15YL. Varone, back after breaking his jaw, scored in 2 runs to narrow it to 10-6. Rusevlyan flipped short TD pass to Dare in 3rd Q to extend Terps' dominance.

Yale 20 PRINCETON 13: Clever coach Jordan Oliver sprung new Yale (5-2-1) O, pro-style slot-T, on Princeton's unaware pass D. Tigers got into genuine coverage issues by assigning single DB to slot-receiver while Elis' HB-in-motion would trail uncovered into same passing lane. Still, it was single Yale receiver who truly sparkled from WR spot, catching all 3 Bulldogs' scores. Yale E Mike Cavallon caught 62y TD from QB Dick Winterbauer on game's 4th play and added 2 more TD grabs, with his winning 4th Q reception turning controversial. Cavallon's clinching catch was dropped in EZ, but officials ruled he had established possession for TD. Playing all 60 mins, DE Cavallon also made numerous stops and laid key tackle on Tigers (6-2) TB Tom Morris to end 2nd Q threat at Yale 8YL. But, Princeton continued to battle, and FB Fred Tiley's TD brought it within 14-13 in 3rd Q. Elis sr QB Winterbauer had career day, passing 14-19/207y, 2 TDs.

DUKE 7 Clemson 6: With Orange Bowl bid up for grabs, Duke (6-1-2) used x-pt kick by star HB-K Wray Carlton and last moment pass rush tackle by DE Bert Lattimore to cement narrow win and likely clinch bowl invitation to Biscayne Bay. In rolling up staggering 399y O for only 6 pts scored, Clemson (5-3) advanced close to Blue Devils' GL 5 times, only to lose 3 FUMs, be forced into incompletions on another trip, and be stopped inches short of 1st down on its 5th try. Duke scored with 2:33 to go in 2nd Q as Carlton caught 35y TD pass from QB Bob Brodhead and connected on his vital kick. FB Bob Spooner blasted through LT hole for Tigers TD with clock showing 6 mins left in 4th Q. QB-K Harvey White's kicking foot appeared to take muddy divot, and his x-pt slithered wide right. Trying to rally, White passed Clemson from own 11YL to Duke 24YL before Lattimore's sack and clock killed Tigers.

FLORIDA 14 Vanderbilt 7: Commodores (4-2-2), winners of 3 in row and losers of only single SEC game, had designs on Gator Bowl invitation. Instead, bowl-banned Florida (5-2) counted on 2-way star HB-DB Bernie Parrish (11/115y) to personally vanquish Vanderbilt. All scoring occurred within 5-min span in 2nd Q. Parrish sped 45 and 22y, each sweep around LE, for Gators TDs, and Vandy FB Phil King set up his own TD—12y catch from QB Boyce Smith—right after Parrish's 2nd tally. QB Smith's dropped C-exchange at Florida 4YL with 2 secs before H ruined Commodores' chance to tie it. Parrish made vital INT and several tackles in 2nd H as Vanderbilt vainly used potent air game to try to catch up.

Mississippi 14 Tennessee 7 (Memphis): HB Leroy Reed's sensational 41y punt RET carried Ole Miss (8-1) to Vols 2YL in 2nd Q, and FB Bill Hurst plunged over for 7-0 lead. Rebels G-LB Jackie Simpson collared FB Tommy Bronson's unfortunate FUM at Volunteers 5YL in 3rd Q, and QB Ray Brown scored on next play. Able to compile only 92y O in 3 Qs, Tennessee (6-2) turned to TB Al Carter, off injured list after 5 games, to lead 80y 4th Q march. After FB Carl Smith's 36y run, Carter hit 2 passes and quickly scored on 8y run.

OHIO STATE 17 Iowa 13: Powerful 3rd-string, but quickly-improving FB Bob White came off Ohio State (7-1) bench to clobber Hawkeyes (6-1-1) with 22/157y rushing and decisive TD in 4th Q. White powered 7/66y on 68y winning drive. Buckeyes had drawn 1st blood following opening KO when HB-K Don Sutherin knocked through 25y FG for 3-0 edge at end of march that utilized unbalanced line for 1st time since coach Woody Hayes came to Columbus. Iowa countered with rarely-used Double-Wing-T O and jumped to 6-3 lead in only 10 plays on QB Randy Duncan's 8y TD pass to E Bob Prescott. Future Hall of Famer, Ohio State DE Jim Houston, recovered FUM at Buckeyes 21YL to halt Hawkeyes threat and start long drive to QB Frank Kremblas' TD sneak. It was now 10-7 in favor of Ohio State. Hawkeyes made it to Ohio 7YL before frustratingly fumbling it away just before H. Iowa overcame Ohio State's 10-6 H bulge for 13-10 lead in 3rd Q on Duncan's QB sneak. Duncan's scoring plunge culminated trip on which E Jim Gibbons made key catches. P Kremblas booted punt to Iowa 6YL in 4th Q, and White made big play from LB spot to throw Duncan for 13y loss, break up Hawks drive, and force punt to Ohio 32YL. From that spot, FB White started his power runs.

MICHIGAN STATE 42 Minnesota 13: Spartans (7-1) rolled to game-end 436y, much of it built in 1st H which they dominated 35-0. Still, Michigan State's Rose Bowl hopes fizzled with Ohio State's win, but no. 4 Spartans jumped to no. 1 in AP Poll with both Oklahoma and Texas A&M losing their games. Golden Gophers (4-4) got early help when C Bernard Svendsen ran under opening KO and recovered FUM at 18YL. On 4th down, Minnesota tried reverse run with HB-to-HB handoff, but Michigan State DE Dave Kaiser stepped into middle of this mess and took away ball for ruinous 77y TD sprint in other direction. MSU HB Blanche Martin soon pranced 65y up sideline from his 11YL in 1st Q, and his HB-mate, Walt Kowlaczyk, followed immediately with 24y TD burst off LT Francis O'Brien's block for 13-0 lead. Spartans HB duo repeated their act in 4th Q: Martin dashed 48y from his 20YL, and Kowalczyk went untouched off LT for 32y score. Spartans' scoring included safety when G-LB Ellison Kelly and DE Sam Williams trapped FB-P Rhody Tuszka in EZ after poor snap. Disappointed Minnesota, which had started season with such high hopes, got window-dressing 2nd H TDs from QB Bobby Cox on 15y pass to HB Bob Schultz after 73y drive that Cox sparked with 28y pass, and from HB Bob Blakely on 1y plunge after Cox had made 18 and 20y runs.

GAME OF THE YEAR
Notre Dame 7 Oklahoma 0:

Seemingly invincible, 18-pt favorite Oklahoma (7-1) squandered early chances at Irish 13, 34, and 23YLs. Sooners threatened on their 1st possession to Notre Dame (5-2) 13 YL, but G-LB Al Ecuyer broke up Oklahoma QB Carl Dodd's 4th down pass. Building D confidence by holding star OU HB Clendon Thomas to 10/36y rushing and gaining stat edge (247y to 145y total O by game's end), ND had to wait until 4th Q to launch its tenacious winning drive, because it's O efforts also had been turned away in 1st H. Sooners stopped Irish twice inside 10YL. On 1st-and-goal at its 3YL, OU rose up and stopped Irish inside 1YL on effort led by DE Ross Coyle, C-LB Bob Harrison, and DB Dodd. After punt out of danger by Oklahoma, ND advanced again, including QB Bob Williams' pass to HB Jim Just to 6YL out of fake-FG formation. But, Sooners QB-DB David Baker made EZ INT of HB Frank Reynolds' pass to E Monty Stickles. During its 80y winning drive, Notre Dame bit off short gains against Sooners 2nd team, using inside bursts of FB Nick Pietrosante (17/56y) and HB Pat Doyle. Fighting Irish moved to Sooners 8YL and coach Bud Wilkinson inserted his starters who rose up to hold until 4th down at 3YL. Then, Fighting Irish's Williams (9-20/79y), who called each of 19 plays on drive without sub coming from bench, pitched wide right to HB Dick Lynch who skirted outside to score behind Pietrosante's cut-down block with 3:50 remaining. Oklahoma's record-breaking 47-game winning streak and 123-game scoring streak blew off into history.

RICE 7 Texas A&M 6: Amid rumors of coach Bear Bryant's departure, top-ranked Texas A&M (8-1) was stunned by revitalized Rice (5-3). Fine Owls QB tandem combined on difference-making 78y drive. QB Frank Ryan launched drive by Owls in 1st Q, and QB-K King Hill's 1y TD run and winning kick culminated it early in 2nd Q. Rice D, led by G Matt Gorges, T Larry Whitmore, and E Gene Jones, parried 3 Aggies drives inside its 20YL before finally yielding QB Roddy Osborne's 1y TD run on 2nd play of 4th Q. With 4 mins left, P Hill punted to Texas A&M 1YL. Determined Aggies drove to Owls 23YL only to have QB Jimmy Wright spilled for 11y loss by Gorges just before game's end.

SOUTHERN METHODIST 27 Arkansas 22: Ponies (3-3-1) stellar QB Don Meredith riddled Razorbacks (5-4) with 19-25/230y, 2 TDs passing and also scored 2 TDs while handling ball on 47 of SMU's 67 plays out of its newly-minted spread formation. Best plays for Hogs came in 1st Q from QB George Walker, who raced 66y on punt TD RET for 6-0 lead 3 mins into game, and FB Jerry Ferguson, who romped 72y to 4YL to set up QB Don Christian's TD sneak for 13-7 lead. Leading 14-13 early in 4th Q, Ponies struck for 42y TD pass to QB-turned-WR Billy Dunn, Meredith's 2nd scoring aerial. Porkers tied it 20-20, however, going 53y nearly all on runs to HB Donnie Stone's 3y score. Meredith scored winning TD on 3y smash, but it took EZ INT by all-around valuable HB-DB Charlie Jackson to put game on ice in late going. Jackson (3/23y rushing, 7/84y receiving) tumbled out of EZ to 1YL after picking off Walker's 15y pass. SMU soon conceded safety. SMU stayed in SWC debate, tied with Rice behind Texas A&M.

Oregon 16 SOUTHERN CALIFORNIA 7: For Oregon's happy followers, it was over fairly early. Swift FB-K Jack Morris ran 15/212y, notched FG and TD before 1st Q was even 6 mins old. So, Ducks (7-2) clinched Rose Bowl trip, their 1st Pasadena visit since 1920. Following his 31y FG, Morris miraculously spun out of grasp of 6 USC tacklers to speed 63y for 10-0 1st Q lead. Morris' 212y aground was most-ever against USC to date, and his day included another long burst of 58y. Trojans QB Tom Maudlin passed 12-18/141y, but Southern California (1-7) could score only once, tallying only pts of game's 2nd H: 7y burst off RT Mike Henry's block by HB Don Buford, future Baltimore Orioles outfielder. Still, coach Don Clark's young Trojans scrapped hard and ended up on short end of 334y to 333y O battle. They had gotten bad break before Oregon HB Jim Shanley's 2nd Q TD run because Troy handed out reprieve at Ducks 7YL. USC G Frank Fiorentino was called offside when he blocked punt through EZ for safety that would have pulled USC within 10-2. Oregon used its 2nd chance to roar 93y to score TD.

AP Poll November 18

1 Michigan State (87)	1851	11 Duke (1)	200
2 Auburn (88)	1842	12 Tennessee	175
3 Ohio State (23)	1573	13 Rice	146
4 Texas A&M (2)	1357	14 Mississippi State	129
5 Mississippi (5)	1074	15 Oregon	91
6 Oklahoma (4)	1062	16 Virginia Military (1)	64
7 Navy (1)	749	17 Arizona State (3)	53
8 Iowa (2)	659	18 Wisconsin	35
9 Notre Dame (2)	512	19 Michigan	29
10 Army	312	20 North Carolina State	27

November 23, 1957

PRINCETON 34 Dartmouth 14: Soph TB Danny Sachs scored 3 TDs and passed for another as Princeton Tigers (7-2) took Ivy League crown in wet snow and mud of New Jersey. After scoreless 1st Q, Sachs (3-4/62y, TD passing) took advantage of 2 pass interference PENs by pitching 20y TD pass to E Bob Shepardson. Hoping to finish its 1st unbeaten season since 1937, favored Dartmouth (7-1-1) stayed in contention when QB Dave Bradley completed 2nd Q TD passes to sub HB Don Klages, with which Klages broke clear for 63 and 59y scores. These TDs were Klages' 1st receptions all year and twice inched Indians within TD of lead at 13-7 and 20-14. Klages' 2nd scoring grab came on screen pass right at sideline's edge as he picked up 3 blockers to convoy him to TD in last min of 1st H. In between, Sachs made 40y INT TD RET in 2nd Q that prompted 5-TD parade shared by both sides in 2nd Q. Dartmouth lost FUM to T Bob Casciola at its 20YL early in 3rd Q but chilled Princeton's attack at its 27YL, then mounted counter march 49y to Nassau 24YL only to stall. Game still hung in balance barely more than 1 min into 4th Q when Sachs clinched verdict at 27-14 with 60y TD RET of low punt by Big Green QB-P Bill Gundy. Near end, Princetonians mockingly waved adieu to Big Green with their white hankies that blended into big snowflakes.

PITTSBURGH 14 Penn State 13: Nittany Lions (6-3) grabbed 13-0 lead on TD catches in 2nd and 3rd Qs by Es Ron Markiewicz and Paul North to enhance their hopes for Gator Bowl invitation. But, FB-K Emil Caprara was wide-right with x-pt after North's 9y catch from QB Al Jacks. Still being blanked early in 4th Q, Pittsburgh (4-5) rallied for 2 TDs in opening 6 mins of last Q. Panthers QB Bill Kaliden's 20y pass to E Dick Scherer helped 74y voyage to FB Fred Riddle's 2y TD run, and QB-K Ivan Toncic converted. Penn State soon punted to Pitt 22YL, and Kaliden's 45y TD pitch to Scherer tied it at 13-13. Panthers East Indian-refugee and G-K Norton Seaman booted soccer-style conv for winning pt as he became 1 of American football's 1st-ever sidewinder kickers.

WEST VIRGINIA 7 Syracuse 0: Mountaineers (7-2-1) wrapped up successful season by winning 6th of last 7 games. And West Virginia managed it by flying into face of Syracuse's strongest suit. Orangemen (5-3-1) arrived with nation's top run D, but WVU used 10 runs in 11 plays to negotiate 54y for game's only score in 2nd Q. Thrusts inside and out by FB Larry Krutko keyed scoring drive until QB Mickey Trimarki sneaked across. Syracuse was completely stymied, gaining only 49y in 1st H but took to wings of QB Chuck Zimmerman to start 3rd Q. Beginning at Orange 18YL, they took 13 plays to make it to WVU's 2YL. Hopes died when soph HB Ger Schwedes bobbled ball away to Mountaineers DB Ray Peterson as he tried to swing wide for TD run.

North Carolina 21 DUKE 13: Slender, poised QB Jack Cummings (8-16/116y, TD) pulled North Carolina (6-3) from 13-0 deficit for Heels' 1st win over Duke (6-2-2) since 1949. Earlier, though, Blue Devils had ridden HB Wray Carlton (18/117y) to 13-pt 1st H edge. Carlton lugged ball 5 of last 6 plays to end 75y TD drive after opening KO. In 2nd Q, Carlton delayed off LT, raced 20y to score, and added conv. Cummings completed 19y TD pass to E Buddy Payne and notched 2 other tosses to set up his own TD run and that of FB Giles Gaca. ACC bowl committee was left to ponder Orange Bowl vote in wake of upset of Duke, conf's leading eligible team.

North Carolina State 29 SOUTH CAROLINA 26: Apparently playing in another world and scoring all 29 Wolfpack pts, HB Dick Christy (24/79y, 4TDs) watched his game-winning 36y FG barely drop over crossbar as time expired. Just previously, HB-K Alex Hawkins of South Carolina (4-5) tossed 16y TD pass to E Julius Derrick and wobbled his conv kick through to create 26-26 tie with 1:09 to go. With :06 left, DB Hawkins made INT of long pass at own 15YL and fled all the way to NC State 17YL, where

Wolfpack C Paul Balonick made game-saving tackle. But back downfield, Gamecocks' pass interference PEN during Hawkins' INT miraculously gave life to Christy's FG try. Wondrous Wolfpack (7-1-2) took ACC title at 5-0-1, but was bowl-banned because of school's basketball violations.

KENTUCKY 20 Tennessee 6: In T Lou Michaels' greatest game, big Kentucky (3-7) A-A scored TD on 1st Q EZ FUM when Tennessee (6-3) TB Bobby Gordon bobbled Single-Wing snap that rolled off WB Bill Anderson's foot and across Volunteers' GL. K Michaels then kicked off to Gordon and clobbered him head-on at Vols 30YL. Gordon fumbled, and E Jim Urbanik fell on it at 39YL to set up 1st of 2 TD runs by Wildcats workhorse HB Bobby Cravens (26/96y, 2 TDs). K Michaels kicked conv after each TD, and he punted 10/41.1y avg. Going 70y in 2nd Q, Volunteers enjoyed their only score on Gordon's 2y plunge, but UK E Bernie Shivley blocked x-pt. Vols gained only 130y against charged-up Kentucky D, which got its spark from Michaels but also counted on G-LB Bob Collier, DE Shivley, and DT Bob Lindon. Wildcats, underachievers all season prior to today, avoided becoming 1st SEC team ever to suffer 8 losses to give coach Blanton Collier his 3rd win in 4 tries against Vols.

Auburn 29 FLORIDA STATE 7: Marching relentlessly toward bowl-less national title, Auburn Tigers (9-0) built 20-0 1st H lead, but its fabulous D showed some cracks in pass coverage. Florida State (3-6) QBs Jerry Henderson and Joe Majors combined to complete 14 passes, including TD, but they also threw 2 INTs to Tigers' ferocious defenders. Seminoles' score came in 4th Q as Majors completed 4 passes on 87y march with TD coming on 34y arrow to reserve E Bill Kimber. Plainsmen FB Billy Atkins had scored on runs of 1 and 5y and added 2 x-pts to lift his season scoring total to 66 pts, new Auburn record. Tigers D stars, Es Jimmy Phillips and Jerry Wilson, converged on Majors for window-dressing safety with 23 secs left.

ALABAMA 29 Mississippi Southern 2: In his fading days as Alabama (2-6-1) coach, Ears Whitworth enjoyed surprise bludgeoning of Tangerine-Bowl-bound Mississippi Southern (8-2), recent tormentor of once-proud Crimson Tide. Southern arrived sporting avg of 239y rushing per game, but was held to 18y net on ground by aroused Bama defenders, led by FB-LB Jim Loftin, Gs Billy Rains and Bill Hannah, father of future Alabama great John Hannah. Eagles QB-K Ollie Yates, 1-time Tide player, was short with 2nd Q FG try on Southerners' only trip into Alabama territory in 1st H. Tide answered with 80y drive keyed by HB Marlin Dyess' 28y reverse run and HB Red Stickney's 34y catch down middle to 4YL. FB Danny Wilbanks scored 1st of his 2 TDs with 1y dive for 7-0 lead. QB Bobby Skelton hit E Ralph Blaylock to set up Wilbanks' 2nd TD for 14-0 Alabama edge in 3rd Q. Mississippi Southern C Charley Ellzey fired punt snap through EZ for Bama safety. When Ellzey booted free kick, Tide HB Clay Walls charged 66y to TD to create rout at 22-0 for boisterous, win-starved Bama fans. Eagles' only score came on 4th Q safety as DL Jim Taylor wrestled Skelton to turf in EZ.

Ohio State 31 MICHIGAN 14: Coach Woody Hayes' new discovery, FB Bob White (30/165y), played enthusiastic role as Ohio battering ram in relentless 372y ground game that overcame 14-10 H disadvantage. Scoring 1st Q TD, Michigan (5-3-1) TB Jim Pace (22/164y, TD) put together 23y and 16y dashes, 2nd of which became TD on which he spun out of tacklers' arms. Pace later set up QB Jim Van Pelt's 25y TD pass to WB Brad Myers in 2nd Q by barreling 46y on reverse. Buckeyes (8-1) moved 58y to TD after 2nd H KO to take lead for good at 17-14 on HB Dick LeBeau's 8y burst, and they scored again on 68y TD trip before 3rd Q ended. QB Frank Kremblas tallied late 3rd Q score on 16y rollout behind great block on 3 Wolverines by G Herb Jones. Each scoring march was extended by 4th down fake-pass sprints by Kremblas that each made 1st down. Michigan made 377y by game's end and had chances spoiled by 2 FUMs and INT in Buckeyes territory in 2nd H.

Iowa 21 NOTRE DAME 13: There would be no 4th Q drama for Fighting Irish as there had been week earlier against Oklahoma. After falling behind 14-0, Notre Dame (5-3) made comeback bid on E Monty Stickles' 2nd Q catch and run of gorgeous 55y TD arching spiral from QB George Izo and FB Ron Toth's 15y TD sweep 1 snap after Irish DT Dick Royer belted FUM away from Iowa (7-1-1) HB Bill Gravel in 3rd Q. In between, however, Hawkeyes superb DE Don Norton blocked K Stickles' conv try after his long score. So, Iowa still led 14-13 entering 4th Q, its early TDs by FB John Nocera on 36y run in 1st Q and QB-DB Randy Duncan on 22y INT TD RET in 2nd Q firmly placed on scoreboard. Hawks HB Bill Gravel (70y rushing) was halted at ND 17YL by 4th down tackle by DE Bob Wetoska in 4th Q, but, after receiving following punt, Iowa went all way to E Norton's twice-deflected, 22y TD grab from Duncan.

KANSAS 9 Missouri 7: Soph HB-K Ray Barnes' slightly-angled, short FG with 48 secs left gave late-charging Jayhawks surprising 2nd place finish in Big 7 Conf. After coach Chuck Mather and 5 asst coaches announced their season-end resignations at mid-season, Kansas (5-4-1) closed with 4 stirring wins. Game had early fireworks: Jayhawks HB Homer Floyd's 73y TD run was more than matched by Tigers FB Hank Kuhlmann's 1y TD run and G-K Charley Rash's conv for Missouri (5-4-1) lead at 7-6 in 1st Q. Kansas was forced to withstand Kuhlmann's power rushes for balance of contest until its last min success.

ARIZONA STATE 41 College of Pacific 0: *Arizona Republic* declared Arizona State (9-0) as "West's finest football team" as undefeated Sun Devils cruised to decisive win after building 34-0 H lead. With Pacific Coast Conf suffering off season with its on-going sanctions against its top teams, newspaper pitched pretty realistic proposition. In its 1st H explosion, ASU gained 312y and its D permitted COP (5-3-2) only 36y. Sun Devils HB-K Bobby Mulgado scored 3 TDs and made 5 conv kicks. Tigers totaled only 54y rushing, so they turned to passing of QB and future NFL coach Tom Flores. Even at that, COP didn't manage its initial 1st down until past 5 min mark of 3rd Q, and had its single scoring threat perish in last mins when FB Tom Green lost FUM at Arizona State 6YL.

BRIGHAM YOUNG 26 Colorado State 9: Brigham Young (4-3-2), which had never won any conf title in its 33 years of football, stayed alive in Skyline Conf title race. Rams (2-7) opened scoring on HB-K Frank Gupton's 21y FG, but that was it until Colorado State mustered 70y TD drive to HB Bill Drake's 5y TD sweep in 4th Q. Young BYU line carried game, and its D forced 3 INTs. Biggest play came from Cougars' biggest player: DT John Kepele, 236-lb Hawaiian, swatted down Rams QB Louie Long's pass in 1st Q, caught it at CSU 30YL, and rambled 25y on truck-like RET. BYU HB Raynor Pearce soon powered for TD and 7-3 lead. Cougars NG George Kinder fell on FUM to set up FB Steve Campora's TD, and other scores were fueled by INTs by C-LB Lynn Reading and G-LB Tom Phillips.

Oregon State 10 OREGON 7: Ducks (7-3) may have been flapping their wings for Pasadena, but well-grounded Beavers (8-2) gave Oregon something to think about on Rose Bowl trip: season-ending mutual tie atop Pacific Coast Conf standings. Oregon State TB Joe Francis gained 33y on 60y trip to pay-dirt in 1st Q and notched OSC's TD with 3y run. BB-K Ted Searle gave Beavers 7-0 edge with x-pt. Oregon came right back thanks to odd change of possession brought about by Searle's intended surprise. Left-footed K Searle attempted on-side KO right after State's TD, but barely grazed ball scant 1-ft forward, possibly authoring shortest KO in history. As result, Ducks launched from take-off perch at Oregon State 40YL and tied it on HB Jim Shanley's 1y TD catch from QB Jack Crabtree. On 2nd H's opening series, Searle knocked through 27y FG for 10-7 lead. Oregon could have pulled it out in 4th Q as Shanley, Ducks' best runner, appeared headed to EZ from 1YL. But, Beavers FB-LB Nub Beamer made hard tackle and recovered FUM at 2YL.

AP Poll November 25

1 Auburn (85)	1850	11 Arizona State (11)	193
2 Ohio State (65)	1769	12 Notre Dame	141
3 Michigan State (41)	1713	13 Mississippi State	138
4 Texas A&M (2)	1370	14 Wisconsin	94
5 Oklahoma (8)	1212	15 North Carolina State	85
6 Iowa (7)	1130	16 Duke	60
7 Mississippi (6)	967	17 Virginia Military	45
8 Navy	709	18 Tennessee	38
9 Rice	384	19 Oregon State	37
10 Army	349	20 Florida	27

November 28-30, 1957

(Th'g) Virginia Military 14 Virginia Tech 6 (Roanoke): Surprising VMI (9-0-1) completed its 1st undefeated season since 1920, and then its players voted to snub all bowl invitations. Game's critical TD came in 2nd Q when HB Bobby Jordan gave Keydets 7-0 lead on 1y smash after FB Sam Horner's 9y run. Virginia Tech (4-6) was able to pull within 7-6 in 4th Q as sub QB Jimmy Lugar fired 2 passes good for 42y as prelude to HB Barry Frazee's 17y TD shot up middle. Jordan iced verdict on another smash from 4YL in game's last 4 mins.

Navy 14 Army 0 (Philadelphia): Upbeat Middies (8-1-1) credited their new light blue jerseys for their win, but viewers on black-and-white TVs, watching through veil of cold rain, wondered where Navy's gold numerals went. What really won for Navy was superb D, anchored by burly T Bob Reifsnyder, G Tony Stremic, and E Pete Jokanovich, which allowed only 55y total O in 2nd H. Army, which entered fray with nation's best 323.3y rushing avg, saw its A-A HB Bob Anderson held to 11/18y on ground. His HB-mate, Pete Dawkins, did better but made so-so 18/63y rushing as Midshipmen jitter-bugged its 8-man front to distract Cadets blocking and limit Army's total ground O to 88y. Superb sr HB Ned Oldham (11/55y, TD) scored all of Navy's pts on 6y TD run in 1st Q, 44y punt TD RET in 4th Q, and 2 kicks. DB Oldham also made 21y RET of INT and authored bundle of tackles. On its 3rd possession Navy went 72y as Oldham slipped through 3 tacklers to score at end of 1st Q. Early in 2nd Q, Army went 52y to Annapolis 10YL where lost FUM, recovered by Navy DG Rob Caldwell, spiked that opportunity. Another chance appeared early in 3rd Q as Cadets T Bill Melnik made skidding dive to recover fumbled punt by Navy HB Harry Hurst at 19YL. But, Middies QB-DB Tom Forrestal (8-18/81y, 3 INTs) made critical EZ INT in front of Cadets E Don Usry and off Army's 60-min QB Dave Bourland (5-12/44y, 3 INTs).

HOLY CROSS 14 Boston College 0: Deluge turned game into FUM derby: BC lost 8 and Crusaders 5. While Holy Cross (5-3-1) ended bowl hopes harbored by Eagles (7-2), weather thwarted Crusaders QB Tommy Greene's pursuit of national total O title. Although Greene (4-15/49y) scored on 1y plunge in 3rd Q, quagmire completely submerged Greene and he lost by 63y to Bobby Newman of Washington State. Holy Cross E Dick Berardino blocked BC QB-P Don Allard's punt for 3rd Q safety and 8-0 lead, while all along Crusaders G-LB Vince Promuto sparkled on D. Boston College's only solid spell came in 2nd Q, but sub QB Bill Brown's 4th down pass to HB Vin Hogan came up 2y short at 8YL.

Virginia 20 NORTH CAROLINA 13: North Carolina's up-and-down Tar Heels (6-4), fresh off 3 straight conf wins, laid egg vs. ACC bottom-feeder Virginia (3-6-1). Key Cavaliers were QB-DB Reese Whitley and E Dave Graham. Whitley aimed 2 TD passes at E Fred Polzer in 1st Q and made 3 INTs at critical times. Graham, giant on D all day as he jarred 2 FUMs loose from UNC QB Jack Cummings in 1st H, also rambled through Carolina tacklers on 83y pass-run from HB Sonny Randle. It set up Polzer's 1st TD reception of 4y for 7-0 lead. Carolina quickly cut it to 7-6 as Cummings (10-19/209y, TD, 2 INTs) dashed away from pass rushers and fired 39y TD to E Mac Turlington in 1st Q. Winning margin came on HB Carl Moser's 6y quick-opener TD run at LT that gave Virginia 20-6 H edge. HB Daley Goff, who blocked x-pt after 2nd Cavs TD, ended Carolina's 16-play, 66y drive in 3rd Q with 3y TD blast.

Georgia 7 GEORGIA TECH 0: Georgia FB Theron Sapp became "The Man Who Broke the Drought," scoring 4th down, 1y TD run to end 8 miserable years of UGa losses to Georgia Tech (4-4-2). Sapp carried 7/34y on 50y winning drive late in 3rd Q, possession he started with FUM REC as LB. Yellow Jackets reached Bulldogs 16YL

with just more than 5 mins left to play, but QB Fred Braselton was spilled for 11y loss by NG Cicero Lucas and DT Nat Dye, then threw incompletion in EZ on 4th down. When Georgia QB Charlie Britt immediately bobbled ball on 1st down at his 20YL, Sapp again saved day with REC. Grateful Georgia (3-7) coach Wally Butts spontaneously retired Sapp's no. 40 jersey since this rivalry victory probably saved Butts' job.

Auburn 40 ALABAMA 0 (Birmingham): Bowl-banned Auburn (10-0) wrapped up AP's national championship and its 1st-ever SEC title. With 6th shutout, magnificent Tigers D allowed mere 28 pts all year. No major school has posted so low season total since 1957. Sagging middle thanks to Tigers NG Zeke Smith helped create pair of INTs Auburn returned for long TDs: HB-DB Tommy Lorino raced 79y and C-LB Jackie Burkett for 66y. Alabama (2-7-1), with miserable 8-29-4 record since 1954, cast flirtatious eye toward alumnus coach Bear Bryant, who began reviewing his options at Texas A&M.

MISSISSIPPI STATE 7 Mississippi 7: Co-capt C-LB Jimmy Dodd led furious Bulldogs (6-2-1) D that hampered speedy Ole Miss (8-1-1). Mississippi State scored on opening 64y drive as HB Bubber Trammell tore 18y through T, but Maroons later had 2 FG tries blocked. Ole Miss HB Cowboy Woodruff countered with 16y catch from sub QB Bobby Franklin and spun through middle of line for tying 8y scoring run in 2nd Q. Mississippi sent 3 different Ks in to try FGs, but each missed, including once in 2nd Q when trio of 15y PENs pushed Rebs back from FB-LB Bill Hurst's FUM REC at Miss State 8YL. Tie cost Rebels share of SEC title, but they still were in position to accept Sugar Bowl bid to play Texas. Optimistic Mississippi State was sent into holiday season jilted at bowl alter.

Florida 14 MIAMI 0: Mighty D of Florida (6-2-1), which enjoyed its best record since 1929, never allowed Miami (4-4-1) inside its 37YL and held Hurricanes to 127y. In 1st Q, Gators DE Dan Edgington dropped into coverage to make INT of Hurricanes QB Fran Curci (3-8/19y, INT) and return to Miami 46YL. Florida's superior 2nd team executed 38y pass to 1YL: QB Wayne Williamson to HB Bill Newbern. Florida HB Jim Rountree (13/70y) led 1st unit back onto field and into EZ on 1st run try. HB-K Bernie Parrish converted for 7-0 lead. Rountree's 54y QK to 5YL pinned Miami in hole for balance of 1st H. Late in 3rd Q, Florida rushed FB-P Harry Diederich into 4y slice OB at Miami 37YL. Early in 4th Q, Gators FB Ed Sears ran for 1y TD on counter run. Hurricanes' 4-game series win streak ended partly due to abandonment of their solid run attack in favor of spread formation.

NOTRE DAME 40 Southern California 12: Trojans (1-9) from balmy L.A. froze in South Bend snow, miserably ending worst season in their glorious history. USC's tacky gold helmets, 1957's new fashion statement, never reappeared; no explanation by tradition-rich program was ever necessary. Notre Dame (6-3) enjoyed 2 TD pass connections between QB Bob Williams and E Monty Stickles, while soph HB Pat Doyle went 92y to score with 2nd H KO. It was Fighting Irish's largest victory margin since trouncing lowly Pennsylvania 46-14 in middle of 1955 season.

OKLAHOMA 53 Oklahoma A&M 6: Sports editor John Cronley's lead in *Daily Oklahoman* said it all: "Behaving as if they (Sooners) wished they were playing Notre Dame all over again…" Indeed, formerly-undefeated Oklahoma (9-1) roared past Oklahoma A&M (6-3-1) as if it hadn't single care in world and followed up its post-upset, 32-7 win over Nebraska with even larger avalanche against in-staters. Cowboys, who wouldn't score until HB Jim Wiggins (12/72y) streaked 67y in game's last 3 mins for its 1st pts vs. OU since 1953, stubbornly had hung in to trail only 6-0 with 2 mins left before H. Then, Sooners star, HB Clendon Thomas (18/162y, 2 TDs) plunged 2y for TD, and followed quickly with 24y TD pass to HB Jakie Sandefer (2 TDs). DB Sandefer launched 3-TD explosion in 3rd Q with beauty of 57y INT TD RET.

RICE 20 Baylor 0: Closing season with 4 wins, surprising Owls (7-3) flew away with SWC title and Cotton Bowl bid. Baylor (3-6-1) marched 79y from opening KO only to come up short at 1YL and, to make matters worse, it lost oft-injured star QB Doyle Traylor in 1st Q, just when it appeared star-crossed Traylor would make it through season for 1st time in his career. Still, Bears continued to threaten by making it to Rice 6YL. Owls broke up 0-0 tie when HB Larry Dueitt raced 89y with 2nd H KO to set up TD pass by QB King Hill to HB Ken Williams. Speedy Owls HB Bobby Williams soon added 80y punt TD RET. Rice back-up QB Frank Ryan provided 11y 4th Q TD pass to E Buddy Dial at finish of 72y trip. Baylor FB Larry Hickman rushed 14/57y for season total of 612y, new school record.

Texas 9 TEXAS A&M 7: Resurgent Texas (6-3-1) copped 2nd place in SWC and earning Sugar Bowl berth, handing slumping and despondent Aggies (8-2) their 2nd straight upset defeat. Longhorns QB Bobby Lackey scored 1st Q TD after QB-P Walt Fondren's 62y QK gained field position. K Lackey added FG for 9-0 Steers lead. Superb again for Texas A&M was ace HB-DB John David Crow, who contributed 57y catch to Aggies' only TD drive and batted down several Longhorns passes. After game, reluctant Aggies administration chose to release coach Bear Bryant from his contract so he could move to Alabama, his alma mater. It was heavy-hanging rumors of Bryant's departure that had created dejection among A&M players.

ARIZONA STATE 47 Arizona 7: Powerful O of Sun Devils (10-0) scored 1st 3 times it saw ball to build 20-0 lead in 2nd Q. HB Leon Burton caught 32y TD on option pass from HB Bobby Mulgado and galloped 46y with screen pass from QB John Hangartner to bring H score to 27-0. In attempt to get back in game, gambling Arizona (1-8-1) gamely tried on-side KO to start 2nd H, but ASU recovered. Burton raced to another TD and later added 19y TD catch, Hangartner's 4th TD strike. Trailing 47-0, Wildcats finally scored on last play of 3rd Q as QB Ralph Hunsaker passed 19y to reserve FB Carl Hazlett.

Final AP Poll December 2

1 Auburn (210)	3123	11 Texas	409
2 Ohio State (71)	2646	12 Arizona State (10)	324
3 Michigan State (30)	2550	13 Tennessee	232
4 Oklahoma (22)	2182	14 Mississippi State	217
5 Navy (6)	1915	15 North Carolina State	145
6 Iowa (7)	1569	16 Duke	101
7 Mississippi (3)	1316	17 Florida	94
8 Rice	1186	18 Army	89
9 Texas A&M	776	19 Wisconsin	87
10 Notre Dame	608	20 Virginia Military (1)	86

December 7, 1957

MIAMI 28 Pittsburgh 13: Disappointing seasons for Miami (5-4-1) and Pitt (4-6) came to close as Hurricanes pulled off surprise win. Pint-sized Miami QB Fran Curci set keynote with 44y run on game's 1st play, later hit HB Joe Plevel with 2 TD passes in 2nd Q for 14-0 H lead. Striving to gt back in game, Panthers got 2nd H TDs on QB Bill Kaliden's 35y pass to E Dick Scherer and HB Jim Theodore's 4y run. Whatever hope Pitt harbored, however, intermittently was dashed by Curci, who authored TD run and made clever GL pitchout to HB Byron Blasko for another TD.

Notre Dame 54 SOUTHERN METHODIST 21: Summer weather greeted Notre Dame (7-3), and Fighting Irish turned Dallas visit into day at beach. ND turned 6 TOs, including 4 INTs, into TDs for 5-score victory margin. Matchup had its ugly aspect as 9 personal fouls were called and Irish C Frank Kuchta and SMU (4-5-1) T Charley Terrell were tossed out. When star Mustangs passer, QB Don Meredith (7-15/136y, 2 TDs, 2 INTs), limped off in 4th Q it brought loud jeers at visitors, but soph QB left with to-date NCAA season's percentage record of 69.6 on 71-102/912y. Meredith's 48y TD bomb to HB Lon Slaughter had given SMU early 7-0 lead, but Notre Dame FB Charlie Lima tied it with 2y smash over RT. After Irish HB-DB Dick Lynch's INT of sub QB Charlie Arnold late in 1st Q, ND QB Bob Williams scored from 5YL. DB Williams' INT of Meredith early in 2nd Q led to Williams' 3y TD run up middle. HB Pat Doyle and sub FB Norm Odyniec each scored twice for Irish.

1957 Conference Standings

Ivy League

Princeton	6-1
Dartmouth	5-1-1
Yale	4-2-1
Brown	3-4
Pennsylvania	3-4
Cornell	3-4
Harvard	2-5
Columbia	1-6

Atlantic Coast

North Carolina State	5-0-1
Duke	5-1-1
Clemson	4-3
North Carolina	4-3
Maryland	4-3
Virginia	2-4
South Carolina	2-5
Wake Forest	0-7

Southern

Virginia Military	6-0
West Virginia	3-0
Citadel	4-2
Furman	2-4
William & Mary	2-4
Richmond	2-4
Davidson	1-3
Virginia Tech	1-3
George Washington	1-5
Washington & Lee	0-0

Southeastern

Auburn	7-0
Mississippi	5-0-1
Mississippi State	4-2-1
Florida	4-2-1
Tennessee	4-3
Vanderbilt	3-3-1
Louisiana State	4-4
Georgia Tech	3-4-1
Georgia	3-4
Alabama	1-6-1
Tulane	1-5
Kentucky	1-7

Big Ten

Ohio State	7-0
Michigan State	5-1
Iowa	4-1-1
Wisconsin	4-3
Purdue	4-3
Michigan	3-3-1
Illinois	3-4
Minnesota	3-5
Indiana	0-6
Northwestern	0-7

Big Eight

Oklahoma	6-0
Kansas	4-2
Colorado	3-3
Missouri	3-3
Iowa State	2-4
Kansas State	2-4
Nebraska	1-5
Oklahoma State *	0-2
* Ineligible	

Missouri Valley

Houston	3-0-1
North Texas State	2-2
Tulsa	2-3
Cincinnati	1-3
Wichita	1-4
Drake	1-1

Mid-American

Miami (Ohio)	5-0
Bowling Green	3-1-2
Marshall	4-2
Toledo	3-2
Western Michigan	1-4-1
Ohio	1-4-1
Kent State	1-5

Southwest

Rice	5-1
Texas	4-1-1
Texas A&M	4-2
Southern Methodist	3-3
Arkansas	2-4
Texas Christian	2-4
Baylor	0-5-1
Texas Tech *	0-3

* Ineligible

Border

Arizona State	4-0
West Texas State	3-1
Texas Western	3-2
Hardin-Simmons	3-2
New Mexico A&M	0-4
Arizona	0-4

Skyline Eight

Utah	5-1
Brigham Young	5-1-1
Denver	5-2
Wyoming	3-2-2
New Mexico	2-4
Colorado State	2-5
Montana	2-5
Utah State	1-5-1

Pacific Coast

Oregon State	6-2
Oregon	6-2
UCLA	5-2
Washington State	5-3
Stanford	4-3
Washington	3-4
California	1-6
Southern California	1-6
Idaho	0-3

1957 Bowl Games

Gator Bowl (Dec. 28) Tennessee 3 Texas A&M 0

Texas A&M's once-glorious season came crashing to a 3-loss close. After 7-6 and 9-7 defeats to complete their regular season, Aggies (8-3) watched as inspirational coach Bear Bryant announced on Thanksgiving night that he would return to Alabama to restore football program at Alabama, his alma mater. Unable to mount O, A&M D still sparkled, but got help from bumbling O of Tennessee (8-3): Volunteers provided critical clipping PEN and pair of key FUM losses. The clipping wiped out 82y TD RET by Vols TB Bobby Gordon of punt by Aggies HB-P Bobby Joe Conrad. Deep into 4th Q, game remained 0-0 until Vols mounted 50y drive. Key play was Gordon's 20y pass to WB Bill Anderson. Gordon made 11y run to A&M 6YL where he slammed head-on into Aggies Heisman-winning HB-DB John David Crow. Each star staggered to his feet, each played on. Gordon carried 3 more times to 1YL, and Tennessee coach Bowden Wyatt sent K specialist Sammy Burklow in to try FG, telling him, "It's just like an extra point." Burklow booted perfect 17y FG for Volunteers win, their 1st bowl triumph since 1951.

Orange Bowl: Oklahoma 48 Duke 21

Oklahoma QB-DB David Baker picked off early pass intended for Duke E George Atherholt by QB George Harris and bolted 94y down left sideline for TD, longest in bowl history to date. Sooners HB Clendon Thomas lined up at E, scored on reverse run. Duke (6-3-2), which surprisingly won stat battle 328y to 279y, launched 65y and 85y ground attacks behind HB Hal McElhaney and HB George Dutrow. So, mighty Oklahoma (10-1) led only 21-14 entering 4th Q. Duke QB Bob Broadhead would later say "their lowest substitute seemed to be just like the others: lean, angular and quick." Sooners proved it against tiring Devils in 4th Q. They unloaded 27 pts, including TD passes that made footnotes out of subs, QB Baker and HB Brewster Hobby. HB Hobby hit QB Baker for TD pass, and Baker returned favor to Hobby, becoming 1st pair of players to both throw and catch TDs in single game in bowl history. QB-DB Bennett Watts, Sooners 4th teamer, grabbed INT, ran 40y, and alertly tossed lateral to trailing HB-DB Dick Carpenter, who sprinted rest of way for 73y TD.

Sugar Bowl: Mississippi 39 Texas 7

Rugged Rebels linemen prevailed, blocking holes open for 304y rushing, and set stage for superlative performance by QB-DB Ray Brown in his last college game. Brown scored 1st Ole Miss (9-1-1) TD, passed to E Don Williams for 2nd score, set up 3rd with 1 of his 3 INTs, and capped his unanimous MVP selection with spectacular 4th Q run. Soon after Texas (6-4-1) HB and future Cleveland Indian third baseman Max Alvis scored Longhorns' only TD to bring tally to 26-7, P Brown fielded a high punt snap in his EZ. Pressured by in-rushing Texas E Larry Stephens, Brown sprinted away from Stephens, picked up blockers after nearly stumbling near scrimmage line, and went 92y to score. Part of blocking convoy and dreaming of glory was G Jackie Simpson, who shouted for Brown to flip him the ball. "It would have been something for Jackie to score a touchdown," said Brown, "but I was so tired I was afraid I would fumble." Any chance young Texans had of avoiding rout was punctured by 4 lost FUMS and 4 INTs.

Cotton Bowl: Navy 20 Rice 7

Strangely enough, Cotton Bowl was only game of 1957 post-season which matched pair of top 10 teams. Navy (9-1-1) coach Eddie Erdelatz pronounced this outfit to be finest in his 8 years at Annapolis, and they proved it by dominating Owls by more than score would indicate. Rice (7-4) lost FUMs which led to short Navy drives: 33y in 1st Q when sub QB Joe Tranchini scored and 20y early in 3rd Q when HB Ned Oldham carried it over. In between, QB Tom Forrestal, who passed 13-24/153y, mostly marshaled his ground troops as they posted 51y of 66y scoring march in 2nd Q. HB Harry Hurst climaxed that drive by dashing 13y for TD. Meanwhile, Owls A-A QB King Hill (1-5/13y) was having tough time and didn't complete single pass until E Buddy Dial caught, then fumbled Hill's throw on last play of 1st H. With star sub QB Frank Ryan (13-22/151y, TD, INT) going most of way in place of Hill in 2nd H, Rice still floundered. Owls had made only 2 1st downs against Navy D, led by banged up G Tony Stremic, and score stood at 20-0 4 mins deep into 3rd Q. Owls looked desperate. Then, Rice HB-DB Bob Williams' INT at Navy 36YL sparked Ryan to 4 consecutive completions, including 8y TD to HB Ken Williams. Hill returned late in game at flanker and caught

apparent TD pass from Ryan, but was ruled beyond EZ end-line. Game ended with Rice vainly having reached Navy 1YL against Tars' scrubs.

Rose Bowl: Ohio State 10 Oregon 7

Perhaps moral victories are for losers, but if ever a moral victory earned admiration, it was accomplished by highly-ridiculed Oregon (7-4). Ducks were 19-pt underdogs, and leading up to game were "derided by everybody," according to coach Len Casanova, who ended up being carried off afterward on shoulders of his team. Ohio State (9-1) opened game as if to justify its juggernaut role. Buckeyes ground out 79y after KO with land attack spiced by 37y toss from QB Frank Kremblas to E Jim Houston. Kremblas scored from 2YL for 7-0 lead. Webfoots battled back with 80y march of their own. MVP QB Jack Crabtree (10-17/135y, INT) pitched out to HB Charlie Tourville for biggest gain, added his own useful runs, and pitched out to quick HB Jim Shanley for tying 5y score. But, highly-reliable Ducks FB-K Jack Morris barely missed vital medium-range FG in 3rd Q. Deadlock wore on, but Buckeyes FB Bob White (25/104y) carried 49y of long march that reached Ducks 17YL. There, from precisely same spot as Morris' miss in previous Q, HB-K Don Sutherin booted 34y FG on 1st play of 4th Q, which held up as winning margin. Oregon E Ron Stover caught 10/144y, but his FUM after hard tackle by Buckeyes DE Leo Brown at Ohio 24YL was recovered by HB-DB Joe Cannavino, to end Ducks' last gasp at end of 56y march in 4th Q. Oregon outgained Ohio 351y to 304y with its balanced attack. Gratuitous midwestern scribes ended up lauding Oregon: Jim Schlemmer of *Akron Beacon-Journal* wrote, "Oregon won everything but the score;" and Charles Johnson of *Minneapolis Star-Tribune* noted, "...only one bad break (Stover's fumble) kept Oregon from the upset of the season."

1957 Top Performance Formula

1	Oklahoma	1.6776
2	Mississippi	1.5997
3	Arizona State	1.5840
4	Ohio State	1.5818
5	Michigan State	1.5634
6	Auburn	1.5627
7	Iowa	1.5030
8	Navy	1.4962
9	Tennessee	1.4382
10	Texas A&M	1.4038
11	Army	1.3989
12	Notre Dame	1.3904
13	North Carolina State	1.3880
14	Mississippi State	1.3710
15	Rice	1.3408
16	Wisconsin	1.3355
17	Oregon State	1.3291
18	UCLA	1.3286
19	Boston College	1.3253
20	Florida	1.3110

1957 Top Opponent Records

1	Rice	.6553
2	Houston	.6452
3	Tennessee	.6300
4	Notre Dame	.62644
5	Kentucky	.62637
6	Indiana	.6200
7	Northwestern	.6149
8	Mississippi State	.6099
9	Duke	.6078
10	Texas	.6068
11	Arkansas	.5957
12	Pittsburgh	.5787
13	Illinois	.5878
14	California	.5833
15	North Carolina	.5824
16	Texas A&M	.5784
17	Kansas State	.5778
18	Virginia	.5722
19	Kansas	.5714
20	Florida State	.5701

1957 Out-of-Conference Records

	W-L	Percentage	Bowl W-L
Big Ten	16-7	.6957	1-0
Southeastern	21-9-2	.6875	2-0
Southwest	19-10-2	.6452	0-3
Big Eight	16-11-6	.5758	1-0
Atlantic Coast	11-11-3	.5000	0-1
Pacific Coast	11-13-2	.4614	0-1

1957 Individual Statistical Leaders

RUSHING YARDS	Attempts	Yards	Avg.
Lenny Lyles, Louisville	177	1207	6.8
Leon Burton, Arizona State	117	1126	9.6
Bob Stransky, Colorado	183	1097	6.0
Bob Anderson, Army	153	983	6.4
Billy Austin, Rutgers	193	946	4.9
Chuck Shea, Stanford	163	840	5.2
Jim Bakhtiar, Virginia	194	822	4.2
Clendon Thomas, Oklahoma	130	816	6.3
Jimmy Taylor, Louisiana State	162	762	4.7
Nub Beamer, Oregons State	173	760	4.4

PASSING YARDS	Completions	Attempts	Yards	Pct.
Lee Grosscup, Utah	94	137	1398	68.6
Bobby Newman, Washington State	104	188	1391	55.3
Tommy Greene, Holy Cross	74	159	1297	46.5
Kenny Ford, Hardin-Simmons	115	205	1254	56.1
John Hangartner, Arizona State	60	100	1203	60.0
Bob Winters, Utah State	92	179	1139	51.4
Randy Duncan, Iowa	70	119	1124	58.8
Tom Forrestal, Navy	80	159	1117	50.3
Roger LaBrasca, Drake	74	145	1054	51.0
Tom Flores, Pacific	82	184	980	44.6

RECEIVING YARDS	Catches	Yards
Stuart Vaughan, Utah	53	756
Gary Kapp, Utah State	45	633
Jim Gibbons, Iowa	36	587
Don Ellingsen, Washington State	45	559
Fred Dugan, Dayton	37	546
Jerry Mertens, Drake	29	509
Buddy Dial, Rice	21	508
Stan Fanning, Washington State	24	457
Les Walters, Penn State	24	440
Al Jamison, Colgate	33	420

1957 Consensus All-America Team

End:	Jimmy Phillips, Auburn
	Dick Wallen, UCLA
Tackle:	Lou Michaels, Kentucky
	Alex Karras, Iowa
Guard:	Bill Krisher, Oklahoma
	Al Ecuyer, Notre Dame
Center:	Dan Currie, Michigan State
Back:	John David Crow, Texas A&M
	Walt Kowalczyk, Michigan State
	Bob Anderson, Army
	Clendon Thomas, Oklahoma

Other All-America Choices

End:	Jim Gibbons, Iowa
	Fred Dugan, Dayton
Tackle:	Charlie Krueger, Texas A&M
	Bob Reifsnyder, Navy
	Tom Topping, Duke
Guard:	Aurelius Thomas, Ohio State
	Bill Johnson, Tennessee
	Jackie Simpson, Mississippi
Center:	Don Stephenson, Georgia Tech
Back:	King Hill, Rice
	Bob Stransky, Colorado
	Lee Grosscup, Utah
	Dick Christy, North Carolina State
	Jimmy Pace, Michigan
	Tom Forrestal, Navy
	Jim Bakhtiar, Virginia
	Jim Taylor, Louisiana State

1957 Heisman Trophy Vote

John David Crow, senior halfback, Texas A&M	1183
Alex Karras, senior tackle, Iowa	693
Walt Kowalczyk, senior halfback, Michigan State	630
Lou Michaels, senior tackle, Kentucky	330
Tom Forrestal, senior quarterback, Navy	232

Other Major Awards

Maxwell (Player)	Bob Reifsnyder, junior tackle, Navy
Outland (Lineman)	Alex Karras, senior tackle, Iowa
Walter Camp (Back)	John David Crow, senior halfback, Texas A&M
Knute Rockne (Lineman)	Lou Michaels, senior tackle, Kentucky
AFCA Coach of the Year	Woody Hayes, Ohio State

1958

The Year of Chinese Bandits, Lonely End, and Two-Point Conversions

Innovation was the hallmark of the 1958 football season. Fourth-year Louisiana State (11-0) coach Paul Dietzel created a three-platoon system to circumvent the substitution rules, and his big band of players carried the Bayou Bengals all the way to the AP national title, despite their having started the season unranked. Dietzel's former boss, Army (8-0-1) coach Earl "Red" Blaik, bowed out after 18 years at West Point by springing The Lonely End offense on puzzled foes. And, college football saw its first change in scoring rules since 1912, the amazingly different two-point conversion opportunity available after every touchdown.

Striving to create specialized units similar to pro football's offense and defense, Dietzel took advantage of slightly liberalized substitution rules in 1958 by employing LSU in three distinct outfits: the starting White Unit that played both offense and defense and included such stars as center-linebacker Max Fugler, and halfbacks Billy Cannon and Johnny Robinson; the Gold (or Go) Unit that played only offense; and the colorful defensive unit "Chinese Bandits." The Bandits came by their name because Dietzel once read in the comic strip "Terry and the Pirates" that Chinese bandits were the most vicious people in the world. Coming off a 5-5 record in 1957, LSU broke into the top 20 after upsetting Rice (5-5) in the opener, sent coach Bear Bryant to defeat in his debut at Alabama (5-4-1), and took over no. 1 after beating Florida (6-4-1) on October 25. No. 12 Clemson (8-3) gave LSU a tough Sugar Bowl, losing by only 7-0.

Army opened its season against South Carolina (7-3), upset winner the week before against a well-regarded Duke (5-5) squad. What the Gamecocks confronted was one of the oddest, most devastating offensive schemes ever concocted. The "Lonely End" offense unveiled that September Saturday at West Point, N.Y., was a Wing-T with an unbalanced-line, simple stuff compared to space-aged offenses to come in later years, but it was a dramatic departure from Army's familiar tight-packed, infantry-like T-formation style. To force early defensive commitment and to conserve the energy of the wide-flanked strong-side end, the player never entered the huddle on offense. Lonely End Bill Carpenter got visual signals from the huddle, and his curious "lonesome" posture prompted many non-sports newspaper editorials, pontificating about a growing suburban society that was breeding aloofness. Leave it to the editorial writers to find some hidden negativity in a football strategy. Whether or not the Lonely End was symptomatic of a flawed American culture, it was a great offensive attack that helped pave the way to a more wide-open game in football's future.

In addition to being a national curiosity, the Army attack, led by scrawny quarterback Joe Caldwell and halfbacks Pete Dawkins and Bob Anderson--each a future Hal of Famer--ranking fourth overall in total offense and topped the nation in passing. The pass yardage title was a remarkable occurrence for a team coached by the conservative Blaik, because prior to 1958, Blaik had been a ground-oriented infantry man all the way.

Another service academy authored a stunning debut in big-time football in 1958. The Air Force Academy, founded in 1955, sent its first class of senior athletes, led by tackle and captain Brock Strom, to play against major opposition for the first time. The Falcons earned a 9-0-2 mark including wins over Oklahoma State (7-3), Wyoming (7-3), and ties against Rose Bowl champion Iowa (8-1-1) and Texas Christian (8-2-1) in a January 1 squareoff in the Cotton Bowl. It was likely the greatest debut to major college football of all time. The only school close to Air Force's 1958 achievement of arriving from relative obscurity is Marshall. After a devastating plane crash nearly ended Thundering Herd football completely, the school built their program gradually, starting in 1971 under the guidance of new and unknown coach Jack Lengyel. Marshall won 1-AA titles in 1992 and 1996 and splashed into 1-A with a record of 10-2 in 1997. Marshall's relaunch into 1-A included a close Motor City Bowl loss to Mississippi. Still, Air Force's undefeated debut remains the greatest, and the Falcons eventually became the most consistent football-playing service academy, winning the Commander-in-Chief Trophy many times over Army and Navy.

Adoption of the two-point conversion immersed college football in a year unlike any other with peculiar scores like 12-8, 22-16, and 32-8 becoming commonplace. Princeton coach Dick Colman was only half joking as he suggested installation of a stadium applause meter to guide his extra-point decisions. Colman's fellow coaches showed dramatic nerve, as they ordered two-point tries with surprising zeal. Collegiate teams attemped two-point tries after touchdowns an amazing 51.4 percent of the time.

The fun wouldn't last. A year later, the space between the goal posts was widened, and extra-point kicking became a much surer proposition. Kicking became much more attractive to coaches, who, by nature, tend to be conservative. The kick success rate on extra points jumped from 68.6 percent in 1958 to 75.4 in 1959. Furthermore, a "Wild Card" substitution rule in 1959 allowed, indeed, encouraged use of one-play kicking specialists, and the eventual proliferation of accurate soccer-style kickers in the 1960s and '70s further stacked the odds against a coach choosing the two-point run or pass. Nearly every team abandoned two-pointers except to break late-game ties or to bring themselves to narrower scoring margins for come-from-behind attempts. The adoption of overtime periods in the 1990s, which meant the end of tie games, were a major discouragement to late-game two-pointers that could determine a winner.

Since the 1970s, the number of two-point attempts has leveled off at 300 to 400 per year (between six and 10 percent of all tries). Successful two-pointers have not exceeded 300 since 1962, but 1970 season saw the greatest percent succeed; 47.1 percent of tries put two points on the scoreboard. Lately, two-pointers succeed about 42 percent of the time. But, in that one wonderful, wacky year of 1958, two-point conversions were successful 613 of 1,371 tries, a percentage of 44.7.

Milestones

■ NCAA Rules Committee created additional options to add excitement to conversions after touchdown. While a successful conversion kick remained as single point, teams were given option of scoring two points with run or pass over goal line. Scrimmage line for all points-after-touchdown was moved from two to three yard-line.

■ Substitution rules were liberalized to allow all players to twice enter and leave field during any quarter of play, thus opening the way for platoons to at least partially concentrate on offense or defense on exclusive basis.

■ UCLA coach Henry "Red" Sanders died on August 14 of heart attack in Hollywood hotel at age 53. His Bruins record was outstanding at 66-19-1, and it earned him nickname of "The Wizard of Westwood," a moniker later and more permanently attached to UCLA basketball coaching legend John Wooden. Evidence shows Sanders originated famous saying: "Winning isn't everything; it's the only thing," although Green Bay Packers coach Vince Lombardi is widely credited with coining phrase in 1960s. Just before beginning of season, Buzz Randall, 1957 All-PCC center-linebacker for Oregon State, succumbed to leukemia. On November 1, heavily-favored Bradley was upset 30-6 by Wabash when Little Giants used rain-splattered scouting report found near wreckage of airplane in which assistant coach Dean Stephens was killed on October 25. Stephens was returning by air to Wabash campus after scouting Bradley's game at Drake.

■ Longest Winning Streaks Entering Season:

Auburn 14	Arizona State 12	Ohio State 9

■ Coaching Changes:

	Incoming	Outgoing
Air Force	Ben Martin	Buck Shaw
Alabama	Paul "Bear" Bryant	J.B. Whitworth
Arizona State	Frank Kush	Dan Devine
Arkansas	Frank Broyles	Jack Mitchell
Indiana	Phil Dickens	Bob Hicks
Iowa State	Clay Stapleton	Jim Myers
Kansas	Jack Mitchell	Chuck Mather
Missouri	Dan Devine	Frank Broyles
Stanford	Jack Curtice	Chuck Taylor
Texas A&M	Jim Myers	Paul "Bear" Bryant
UCLA (a)	George Dickinson	Henry "Red" Sanders
UCLA (b)	Bill Barnes	George Dickinson
Utah	Ray Nagel	Jack Curtice
Virginia	Dick Voris	Ben Martin

(a) Dickinson (1-2) was named coach after Sanders' death in August.
(b) Barnes (2-4-1) replaced Dickinson, when latter was treated for mental exhaustion during season.

Preseason AP Poll

1 Ohio State (46)	859	11 Texas	121
2 Oklahoma (23)	788	12 Oregon State (2)	116
3 Notre Dame (11)	702	13 Iowa	104
4 Michigan State (4)	605	14 Wisconsin	100
5 Auburn (9)	567	15 Mississippi State (1)	94
6 Mississippi	283	16 Miami	77
7 Navy	195	17 Southern Methodist (1)	70
8 Texas Christian	185	18 Clemson	54
9 Army (1)	141	19 Pittsburgh	41
10 North Carolina (1)	140	20 Texas A&M	39

September 20, 1958

(Fri) SOUTHERN CALIFORNIA 21 Oregon State 0: Favored for its 3rd straight title in what would be last season of strife-ridden PCC, Beavers (0-1) were stunned by young squad of Trojans (1-0). Southern California HB Rex Johnston (11/56y) scored in 1st Q and added conv kick to complete 52y Trojans sojourn after they made 4th down stop of Oregon State FB Nub Beamer (7/24y, after gaining 133y vs Troy in 1957). USC QB Willie Wood passed 38y to E Hilliard Hill, and QB Tom Maudlin tossed 35y into EZ to

E Marlin McKeever to punctuate dominant 2nd Q with TD throws. Difference between new Trojans and 1-9 misadventure of 1957 seemed to be presence of 3 soph gems in line: LT Dan Ficca and McKeever twins, RG Mike and RE Marlin. Oregon State threatened after USC's opening TD, but Trojans HB-DB Tony Ortega made INT of TB Paul Lowe at own 31YL. Beavers earned much of their 204y against subs in 4th Q.

SOUTH CAROLINA 8 Duke 0: Gamecocks (1-0) C-LB Lawton Rogers recovered FUM on Duke 42YL on game's 5th play. Subsequent TD drive was fueled by HB Alex Hawkins' 4th down 12y shot-put pass to HB King Dixon which carried to Duke (0-1) 2YL. South Carolina QB Bobby Bunch tallied on TD and 2-pt conv runs. Win was upheld in 2nd Q as Gamecocks DE Jimmy Duncan and QB-DB Harvey Shiflet stopped Blue Devils HB George Dutrow's 4th down run at South Carolina 2YL. Dixon led Carolina rushers with 64y, while HB Wray Carlton rushed 11/62y for Duke.

WAKE FOREST 34 Maryland 0: Ending 12-game losing streak, Wake Forest (1-0) crafted astonishing outcome on arm of sensational soph QB Norm Snead (5-10/194y, 3 TDs). Snead engineered pair of 80y scoring drives and his 3 TD throws tied existing ACC record at that time. Maryland (0-1) was held to 154y total O and threatened only twice. After its 1st punt, Maryland fell on FUM at Wake 40YL as G Rod Breedlove rattled Snead's pass try, and later in 1st H Terrapins moved 71y on runs by FB Jim Joyce. Terps K Vince Scott missed FG at end of that march. Demon Deacons led 14-0 at H and added TD passes by Snead in 3rd Q to E Pete Manning for 22y after Manning's FUM REC and to HB Jim Dalrymple for 11y after FB-LB Neil MacLean made INT. Wake earned dandy 405y O total, its largest output in many seasons.

CLEMSON 20 Virginia 15: Thanks to bewildering variety of O formations, scrawny Virginia (0-1) QB Reece Whitley outplayed highly-rated Clemson (1-0) QB Harvey White until Tigers' ground game wore Cavs thin in 4th Q. Whitley had pitched 46 and 12y passes to bring ball near GL in 1st Q so that HB John Barger could punch through RT for 7-0 lead. Tigers came right back to within 7-6 on HB George Usry's TD run, but White was stopped on 2-pt try. Tigers' 2nd unit started 2nd H and it soon tapped FB Doug Cline and HB Bill Mathis to bull downfield until soph QB Lowndes Shingler dived over pile for 1y TD and raced wide for 2-pts. It was Clemson's 1st lead of day at 14-7. Virginia almost scored again as HB Pat Cash jumped with 2 DBs for Whitley's throw to EZ, and ball slipped away to become INT by Tigers C-LB Bill Thomas. Undaunted, Whitley whipped 22y TD pass and subsequent 2-pt pass to star HB Ulmo "Sonny" Randle early in 4th Q. Now trailing 15-14, Clemson's stellar subs drove 90y through tiring Cavs for Mathis' winning 4y TD burst.

NEBRASKA 14 Penn State 7: Dreary exchange of punts suddenly was enlivened in 4th Q. No sooner had HB Dave Kasperian finally given Penn State (0-1) 7-0 lead that soph HB Pat Fischer—last of 3 football brothers at Lincoln—raced 92y with ensuing KO for TD. Inspired Nebraska (1-0) then used 29y run by HB Larry Naviaux and 26y pass by QB George Harshman to set up FB Carroll Zaruba's winning 1y TD plunge.

Vanderbilt 12 MISSOURI 8: Mizzou Tigers (0-1) bowed in under new coach Dan Devine before national TV audience, but it was same old story: Missouri lost its 11th straight season opener. Vanderbilt (1-0) flashed brilliant blocking early as sub HB David Ray skipped 81y on punt TD RET for 6-0 lead. Tigers made vital blunder on blocked punt by soph E Danny LaRose in 1st Q when 3 of them surrounded ball when they could have run it in for TD. LaRose blocked another punt in 2nd Q for safety. Commodores went 63y, their only sustained trip of day, for 3rd Q TD and 12-2 lead. Mizzou aerials advanced it toVandy 13YL in 4th Q, spot from which HB Mel West swept left for TD that would become Tiger O staple under Devine, power sweep.

Louisiana State 26 RICE 6: Utilizing terrific speed and depth, LSU (1-0) sprung on well-regarded Owls (0-1) new 3-platoon system, innovation of its bright coach Paul Dietzel. QB Warren Rabb scored on option sweep in 1st Q out of Bengals' new wing-T attack. LSU HB Billy Cannon made 2 TDs possible: his 20y catch in 2nd Q set up FB Red Brodnax's TD run and his 3rd Q punt to 1YL and ensuing 30y punt RET set up HB Johnny Robinson's TD run. Rice FB Ray Chilton managed 4th Q TD to avoid embarrassment of whitewash.

Pittsburgh 27 UCLA 6: Conservative Pittsburgh (1-0), normally aligned in tight T, surprised Bruins by opening in pro spread and using blocks of C Don Crafton and Gs John Guzik and Ed Michaels to carve huge holes in middle of line. Panthers gained 229y by land, resulting in pass opportunities for QBs Ivan Toncic and Bill Kaliden to spoil coaching debut of George Dickinson of UCLA (0-1). Toncic sneaked across for game's 1st TD in 1st Q after his 28y pass to E Art Gob. Uclan TB Don Long (6-12/40y, INT) threw off-balance pass that DB Toncic picked off and sped 55y down left sideline on TD RET. Bruins TB Billy Kilmer, JC transfer, came off bench, arched 58y pass to WB Marv Luster and scored only 6 secs before H to shave Pitt's lead to 12-6. "It's funny but at halftime I thought we'd win," said UCLA asst coach Bill Barnes, "...it looked like they were tiring." But Pitt made all of 2nd H's scoring: G-K Norton Seaman's 24y FG, HB Dick Haley's run, and soph E Mike Ditka's 4th Q TD snare of QB Ed Sharockman's pass.

AP Poll September 22

1 Ohio State (45)	903	11 Mississippi State	144
2 Oklahoma (12)	828	12 Navy	117
3 Auburn (18)	561	13 West Virginia (2)	108
4 Michigan State	507	14 Wisconsin (2)	81
5 Notre Dame (6)	504	15tMiami	78
6 Texas Christian (12)	474	15tLouisiana State	78
7 Pittsburgh	198	17 Kentucky (2)	75
8 Army	186	18tFlorida	72
9 Mississippi	186	18tSouth Carolina	72
10 Washington State	153	20 Southern Methodist (3)	69

September 27, 1958

(Fri) GEORGIA TECH 17 Florida State 3: Seeking limelight of big-time college football, ambitious Florida State (2-1) stepped up in class and showed its might in outmaneuvering Georgia Tech (1-1) in 1st H that ended 3-3. Seminoles HB Bobby Renn dashed 51y on punt RET to stage sub HB-K John Sheppard's opening FG. Engineers came to life in 3rd Q as QB Fred Braselton keyed 60y TD push with completions to Es Tommy Rose and Jack Rudolph until soph HB Frank Nix smashed over T for 6y TD. Georgia Tech later went 41y to score on soph HB Reggie Logan's short TD run.

(Fri) Wisconsin 20 MIAMI 0: Badgers E Dave Kocourek and blitzing LB-FB Jon Hobbs wrecked havoc with Hurricane QB Fran Curci's option plays when their GL was threatened, as Miami (0-1) rushed for 123y, but failed up close. Wisconsin (1-0) QB Dale Hackbart scored on 2 sneaks after O line, led by G Jerry Stalcup and C Dick Teteak, provided time for short passes by Hackbart and back-up QB Sid Williams. Air game enhanced 225y rushing, with FB Tom Weisner dashing to 63y TD in 4th Q.

ARMY 45 South Carolina 8: Army coach Red Blaik, long-time advocate of quick-striking infantry runs from tight formations, amazed fans and revolutionized football with explosive and puzzling Wing-T for 529y O. E Bill Carpenter, soon to be labeled "The Lonely End," flanked away from Cadets' huddle to conserve his energy and force early commitment by D. Cadets HB Pete Dawkins rushed 9/113y and scored 4 times, while HB Bob Anderson passed 5-5, 2 TDs on option throws as Army (1-0) rolled to 38-0 lead before Gamecocks (1-1) crossed midfield. On Friday, confident South Carolina, with early-season win over Duke under its belt, had posed some of its cheerleaders with Confederate flag and wild cock mascot for wire service photo near New York City's Empire State Building. Carolina's self-assurance was quickly shattered on Saturday as Gamecocks gained only 132y and could score only once as HB Alex Hawkins tallied 7 mins from end of 4th Q at end of 52y march after HB-DB King Dixon's INT.

SYRACUSE 24 Boston College 14: Blocked punts were order of day in chilly Syracuse (1-0). Boston College (1-1) jumped to 14-0 lead in 1st Q as QB Don Allard scooped up partially blocked punt and dashed 55y to early TD. Allard followed with 39y TD pass to E John Flanagan. Trailing 14-6 in 3rd Q, Orangemen lit fire under its ferocious linemen: G Al Benecick blocked punt at Eagles 32YL, and QB Chuck Zimmermann tore for TD after siphoning ball off wet turf. Still, BC led 14-12 going into 4th Q, but Syracuse's pair of big DTs Ron Luciano, future MLB umpire, and Bob Yates slammed Eagles QB John Amabile and HB Jim Colclough respectively so that they relinquished FUMs deep in BC territory. Sub HB Dick Reimer reflexively scored on 6 and 7y runs for Orange.

Rutgers 28 PRINCETON 0: In 49th renewal of New Jersey rivalry that launched college football in 1869, Rutgers (1-0) pulled big surprise with its biggest victory margin and 1st-ever shutout over Princeton (0-1). Scarlet Knights TB Bill Austin (16/75y) ran for 2 TDs and threw 21 and 12y TD passes to E Bob Simms. G Bill Clark and E Dutch Wermuth joined Simms in anchoring Rutgers D that bent to tune of 208y but allowed Tigers to romp no farther than to nudge once inside 20YL. When hard hit by Clark, Princeton TB Dan Sachs (27/76y) lost FUM on punt at own 15YL in 4th Q, which led to Austin's 2nd scoring pass to Simms.

Virginia 15 DUKE 12: Unknown Virginia (1-1) stunned long-time nemesis Duke (0-2) on passing of QB Reese Whitley (12-27/169y, TD, INT) and 21y FG by E-K Bob Williams in 2nd Q for 9-6 lead. Blue Devils started well, threatening scores twice in 1st Q. Duke went 60y in 13 plays on runs by HB Wray Carlton and catches by E Bert Lattimore of 10 and 26y. But, Devils bogged down at 4YL, and, when they returned on subsequent drive to UVa's 6YL, Cavs' D stars, C-LB Bob Canavari and E Mike Scott, spilled QB Bob Broadhead back to 20YL. From there, Virginia went to work, riding aerial game and FB John Barger's plunges to Williams' FG. Devils held brief 6-3 lead after E Bob Spada recovered HB Dan Lee's FUM into EZ at end of 42y trip. Barger and Carlton traded 2nd H TD runs. Win would be Virginia's last bit of fun in 1958 as its D began to fail and Cavs were trounced in their last 6 games to finish 1-9.

CLEMSON 26 North Carolina 21: Tigers (2-0) clawed from behind 3 times to defeat North Carolina (0-2) for coach Frank Howard's 100th win in 19 years at Clemson. Teams went up and down field in even match in which Clemson's 2nd unit played key role. New 2-pt conv rule received interest as Tigers made 1 of 4: QB Harvey White's pass that afforded 8-6 lead in 1st Q. Carolina tried 2 QB sneaks, with QB Jack Cummings succeeding for 2nd Q 14-8 lead after his 4 straight completions led to his 7y TD to E Don Kemper. Clemson 2nd unit FB Doug Cline, Tigers' leading rusher with 67y, bulled over from 2YL in 3rd Q for 20-14 edge, but Tar Heels answered on FB Don Coker's 1y TD smash in 4th Q. This time Heels called on T-K Phil Blazer for conv kick and 21-20 lead. Sub unit took Clemson 59y to UNC 34YL before turning to starters, who sent FB Rudy Hayes to 18y run on 4th down and HB George Usry to winning TD.

Louisiana State 13 ALABAMA 3 (Mobile): Crimson Tide (0-1) opened their 64th season under new coach in Alabama graduate Paul "Bear" Bryant. Little would crowd realize, but Alabama football would never be same again. Spectators' thoughts were elsewhere when temporary bleachers collapsed and ambulances were needed to assist removal of 25 injured, some seriously. Scoreless deep into 2nd Q, game turned toward Tide when HB-DB Duff Morrison grabbed mid-air FUM by Tigers star HB Billy Cannon and dashed to LSU 5YL. LSU coach Paul Dietzel then inserted his new Chinese Bandits D unit, which limited Bama to 1y and forced 21y FG by T-K Fred Sington, Jr. LSU (2-0) rallied expertly in 2nd H on QB Warren Rabb's 9y TD pass to HB Johnny Robinson and Cannon's 12y TD run.

AUBURN 13 Tennessee 0: National champs of 1957, Auburn (1-0) showed it actually might have improved its potent D as Tigers amazingly held Tennessee (0-1) to –30y total O and permitted no 1st downs. Auburn D was led by T Cleve Wester, G Zeke Smith, and Es Jerry Wilson and Mike Simmons. Tiger scorers were HBs Lamar Rawson (4y) and Tommy Lorino (24y) on mirrored left and right pitchout runs. Strategic QKs of Volunteers TB Billy Majors helped keep 1st H score at 0-0.

MISSISSIPPI 27 Kentucky 6 (Memphis): Story of domination by Ole Miss (2-0) came from its D which halted 4 Kentucky (2-1) advances deep in Rebel-land. Sr HB Kent Lovelace, lost in Mississippi's long line of runners his whole career, emerged with 16y TD catch from QB Bobby Franklin and made 30y broken field run to score. That added up to 13-0 edge. Soph G Richard Price recovered FUMs to make possible Lovelace's TD run in 3rd Q and ran FUM to Wildcats 4YL later in same Q to position HB Cowboy Woodruff's TD run for 21-0 benefit. Kentucky out-gained its Dixie foes 408y to 253y, but nothing paid off until 4th Q when QB Jerry Eisaman, leader of 19-35/268y passing attack, clicked on 27y TD pass to HB Calvin Bird.

OHIO STATE 23 Southern Methodist 20: Big Buckeyes (1-0) line, led by future NFLers at T, Dick Schafrath and Jim Marshall, sent array of backs plowing for 209y rushing. Ohio coach Woody Hayes watched QB Don Meredith of SMU (0-1) complete 19-28/213y, TD, INT, but said he hoped he never would have great passer because they "never win championships." Still, trio of 2-pt conv passes would decide game result as each team tallied 3 TDs. No. 1 Ohio State converted twice on 2-pt passes as vet QB Frank Kremblas zipped throws to HB Dick LeBeau after 1st and 3rd Q TDs runs by HB Don Clark (22y) and FB Bob White (5y). When Ponies sub QB Jimmy Dunn capped 73y march with 20y TD pass to E Henry Christopher early in 2nd Q, Buckeyes broke up Dunn's 2-pt conv pass try. Meredith made 2-pt pass to HB Glyn Gregory in 2nd Q after scoring from 2YL with 2 secs left before H. That pulled Mustangs within 15-14. INTs by Buckeyes DB LeBeau (in EZ) and C-LB Dan Fronk were key to keeping them ahead at 23-14 until Meredith hit 6 straight passes in 4th Q to march SMU 73y to his TD pass to Christopher.

IOWA 17 Texas Christian 0: Opening its 70th season, frustrated Iowa (1-0) failed to cash in on its potent O in scoreless 1st H. But, Hawkeyes got lift near H when TCU (1-1) bungled its big chance when it incurred 15y PEN at Hawks 1YL. On 1st snap of 3rd Q, Iowa HB Bob Jeter broke into clear on wing-T reverse. Although Jeter dribbled ball at Horned Frogs 12YL, he cruised 61y to score. On next possession, Iowa QB Randy Duncan completed 4/46y of 72y march, and that was all she wrote for Purple Frogs. E Don Norton grabbed 6y score from Duncan to make it 14-0. E-K Bob Prescott nailed 31y FG with 6 mins remaining in 4th Q for Hawks' last score. Texas Christian, with 8 future pros in its lineup, still could manage only 215y total O, and never threatened after its 2nd Q advance to 1YL.

PURDUE 28 Nebraska 0: Using nearly twice as many players as 24 who toiled for Nebraska (1-1), Boilermakers (1-0) unleashed their foot soldiers for 354y rushing, led by HB Clyde Washington's 17/81y. After Purdue's 1st 2 drives ended fruitlessly inside Cornhuskers 10YL, little soph HB Jim Tiller registered spectacular 47y punt TD RET, but his wiggly 1st Q masterpiece was nullified by clipping PEN. So, Purdue put its head down and slammed 60y to 1-ft TD plunge by FB Bob Jarus. With shallow Huskers fading in 2nd H, Boilers added short TD runs by HB Leonard Wilson (67y rushing) and sub FB Jack Laraway. In 4th Q, QB Ross Fichtner completed Purdue's only success in 7 aerial tries for 27y TD. Nebraska, which gained only 141y, might have generated more O had 25th Husker made trip to East Lafayette: HB Pat Fischer, its best runner stayed home with flu.

NORTHWESTERN 29 Washington State 28: Despite its large final scoring tally, game was scoreless deep into 2nd Q when Northwestern (1-0) HB-DB Ron Burton made INT of Cougars QB Bobby Newman (11-17/120y, 2 TDs, 2 INTs) to set up 5y TD run by soph QB Dick Thornton. Wildcats quickly scored 2nd TD in last min of 2nd Q after DB Willmer Fowler's FUM REC at Cougars 1YL for 14-0 lead, and HB Burton built on it with 61 and 1y TD runs in 2nd H. Coming off 40-6 win over Stanford, Washington State (1-1) staged 22-pt rally in 4th Q with E Gail Cogdill getting loose for 30 and 80y TD catches. HB Keith Lincoln pitched 67y pass to Cogdill to set up FB Chuck Morrell's TD plunge and later lofted 80y TD to Cogdill, who set to-date NCAA single game receiving y record. Seemingly arbitrary use of new 2-pt conv rule by NW turned out to be margin of victory as Wildcats interrupted 4th Q Cougars rally with successful 2-pt pass from Thornton to E Elbert Kimbrough to extend 4th Q lead to 29-12 after Burton's 1y TD plunge. Back in January, Northwestern coach Ara Parseghian had called himself "apathetic" about new conv rule, but this time he happily said, "Just say I think it's a nice rule."

OKLAHOMA 47 West Virginia 14: Fast-striking Sooners (1-0) used new flanker-spread formation with unbalanced line, but bulky Mountaineers (1-1) had little trouble with OU's surprise strategy until late in 2nd Q of scoreless fight. At that point, Oklahoma E Wahoo McDaniel blocked punt at West Virginia 49YL. FB Prentice Gautt scored 6 plays later on 27y cut through T, QB David Baker ran keeper for 2 pts, and rout had begun. Baker scored less than 3 mins later on 10y run for 15-0 H edge. Sooners went 80y to HB Jakie Sandefer's 4y TD run, and sub QB Bobby Boyd found McDaniel all alone for 86y TD pass in 3rd Q. WVU G Bill Lopasky blocked attempted QK on opening play of 4th Q and recovered in EZ for TD that pulled Mountaineers within 27-6. OU answered with 3 more TDs and finished with 333y rushing and school-record 264y passing on 11-20. WVU got last min TD sneak from QB Danny Williams that ended 78y air drive in 9 plays.

October 4, 1958

(Fri) North Carolina 8 SOUTHERN CALIFORNIA 7: As Los Angeles Times writer Braven Dyer wrote in his lead: "The Trojans got their first taste of the new two-points-after-touchdown tidbit last night and it proved to be a bitter pill." Just as bitter was USC's unwilling acceptance of great North Carolina (1-2) D that squeezed Trojans (1-2) to tune of 20y O in 2nd H. Southern California scored in 1st Q when QB Tom Maudlin (9-17/83y, 3 INTs) followed his 15y pass to HB Rex Johnston with pitch toward EZ. Officials ruled that Carolina HB-DB Emil DeCantis interfered with USC E Hillard Hill. With ball at 1YL, Maudlin sneaked over for 7-0 lead. Early in 2nd Q, Maudlin, under fierce rush, threw INT to QB-DB Jack Cummings, who returned it 28y to Trojans 39YL. FB Don Coker threw key block to spring HB Wade Smith for 27y TD run, and Coker followed with 2-pt run behind block of RT Don Redding. Tar Heels D was led by Es John Schroeder and Al Goldstein and big T Earl Butler. E Marlin McKeever sparkled among Trojans defenders.

ARMY 26 Penn State 0: Huge and curious press turnout dubbed Army's adventurous new O as "The Lonely End," although "Bazooka" (which wouldn't stick) also received mention in UPI's lead paragraph. Cadets (2-0) created scorching numbers in 1st H: 93y rushing and 9-11/258y passing, while their suddenly-ignored D held Penn State (1-2) to 32y O. Army HB Pete Dawkins scored twice, including 72y pass reception from QB Joe Caldwell. Setting up HB Bob Anderson's 1y TD plunge in 1st Q with 33y pass to Lonely End Bill Carpenter, Caldwell also pitched another long TD of 55y to Carpenter. Nittany Lions coaches adjusted well at H, or Cadets simply went under wraps, as Penn State D blanked Army in 2nd H and lost 2nd H stat battle by only 150y to 120y. Lions enjoyed possession in Black Knights' territory only twice. Their best opportunity came when bad punt snap forced Army to surrender possession at its 35YL, but Cadets D, led by G-LB Bob Novogratz and E Don Usry, held on downs at their 26YL.

HOLY CROSS 14 Syracuse 13: Considering Syracuse (1-1) would sweep balance of its schedule to qualify for season-end's Orange Bowl and capture 1959 national championship, this upset by Holy Cross (1-1), football program in gradual descent to minor status, had to rank as enormous in retrospect. Play was controlled by both burly lines, but Crusaders managed 1st Q TD on FB Joe Stagnone's 4y sweep. After Orangemen tied it 6-6 in 2nd Q, they jumped ahead 13-6 as QB Chuck Zimmerman fired 35y TD strike to E Gerald Skonieczki in 3rd Q. Resourceful QB Tommy Greene relied on rushes of his HBs, Ken Hohl and Ed Hayes, to batter to Syracuse 8YL. Greene took command, scoring from 3y out and adding decisive 2-pt run in 4th Q.

South Carolina 24 GEORGIA 14: South Carolina (2-1) HB-DB Alex Hawkins opened scoring with 1st Q 45y INT RET. Hawkins rushed for 69y and added 2-pt convs thrice to lead Gamecocks in 1st renewal of rivalry broken off in 1941 when Georgia star Frank Sinkwich suffered broken jaw. Georgia (0-3) gained 301y total O in sporadic fashion, but suffered 3 damaging TOs that accounted for or led to Carolina TDs. TD that put Gamecocks up 16-0 in 2nd Q was scored by FB John Saunders; it was created by future Charlotte Motor Speedway executive, DE Jimmy Duncan, who made hard tackle and FUM REC on punt returner at Georgia 19YL. After leading 16-8 at H, Gamecocks so dominated 2nd H that UGa failed to gain any 1st down until last 3 mins of 3rd Q and moved chains only 3 times in 2nd H. With 2 mins to play, Bulldogs daringly sent QB Charlie Britt back into his EZ to throw 89y TD pass to HB George Guisler, his 2nd TD scored.

MICHIGAN STATE 12 Michigan 12: Spartans QB Mike Panitch's ill-advised 2nd Q pitchout for FB Don Arend was picked off by fast-penetrating Michigan (1-0-1) DE Gary Prahst, who raced to 45y TD. Prahst quickly induced another FUM, and HB Brad Myers scored to give Wolverines 12-0 H lead, but Myers was tackled short of GL on 2-pt pass try from QB Bob Ptacek. Michigan State (1-0-1) was revived in 3rd Q by HB Dean Look's 90y punt TD RET, behind blocks by Panitch and C Archie Matsos. Ahead 12-6, Michigan E Jon Halstead blocked P Look's punt to create scoring opportunity at 23YL. However, Ptacek's 3rd down pass was intercepted by Michigan State C-LB Jim Chastain, who returned it from EZ to his 3YL. Spartans, who had gained only 9y rushing in 1st H, immediately launched 97y ground attack for tying TD in game's final min, but suffered 2nd conv miss when E-K Sam Williams missed to right of upright with his high-booted x-pt.

INDIANA 13 West Virginia 12: Things opened badly for Indiana (1-1) as TB Tom McDonald lost FUM on game's 2nd play, and West Virginia (1-2) HB Jack Rider picked it out of air for 19y RET to 4YL. HB Ray Peterson quickly swept RE to score. Mountaineers' 6-0 lead lasted until mid-3rd Q. Little TB Teddy Smith (171y rushing) swept 53y to TD, and K McDonald's x-pt put Hoosiers in lead at 7-6. Smith dashed 55y behind block of FB Vic Jones (89y rushing) for 13-6 4th Q lead. WVU marshaled its only sustained march late in 4th Q. DE Tony Tallarico's FUM REC started 61y drive that ended with QB Dick Longfellow's 1y TD run. DB Smith knocked down WVU's attempt for tying 2-pt pass.

NORTHWESTERN 28 Stanford 0: Paying back Indians (0-3) for West Coast defeat last October, Northwestern (2-0) scored in every Q to blank Stanford. Wildcats employed 245y rushing O, led by HB Ron Burton (20/77y) who scored twice on short plunges at end of drives of 64 and 48y. Northwestern's 2nd Q TD was its exception: QB Dick Thornton (3-6/65y, TD) passed 45y to E Fred Williamson, who had slipped behind Stanford HB-DB-P Rick McMillen (QKs of 67 and 48y). Late in 2nd Q, Stanford nearly narrowed its 14-0 gap: sub QB Bob Nicolet passed to E Irv Nikolai, whose dive for GL flag came up inches short just as H ended.

IOWA 13 Air Force 13: Favored Iowa (1-0-1) was saved only by its brilliant 3rd Q GLS and 99y TD drive that followed. Air Force (1-0-1) G Howard Bronson blocked x-pt that might have won game after Iowa FB John Nocera's 3y TD blast tied it 13-13. Hawkeyes squandered 4th Q scoring chances made possible by INT by HB-DB Bob Jeter and FUM REC by DT Mac Lewis. Even at that, Hawkeyes saw E-K Bob Prescott's 31y FG try barely miss with 09 secs to go. Falcons had received TDs from

HB Mike Quinlan on 23y run that tied it 7-7 in 1st Q and QB Rich Mayo's 10y TD pass to HB George Pupich that provided 13-7 H edge. Air Force suffered its only misstep when at H their live mascot, Mach One, flew out of stadium in middle of precision-flying demonstration.

Pittsburgh 13 MINNESOTA 7: Since series began in 1933, Panthers (3-0) had suffered 8 frustrating losses to Minnesota (0-2). In scoreless 1st H, Key PENs looked as though Pitt would be frozen out again and it lost FUM on 2nd H KO to allow Gophers to glide only 33y to score. FB Roger Hagberg's 6y run gave Golden Gophers 7-0 lead in 3rd Q. Pittsburgh was stopped at Minnesota 1YL in 4th Q, but Gophers' punt out of EZ traveled only to 33YL, and personal foul PEN quickly put Panthers back at Minny 16YL. QB Bill Kaliden ran in from 1YL with 7:38 to play. Gambling for go-ahead 2 pts, Pitt tried conv run, which was stacked up by C-LB Bernard Svendsen and HB-DB Ken Schultz. Trailing 7-6, Panthers regained ball at Gophers 43YL with 5 mins left and advanced to 20YL. Kaliden next passed 6y to HB Joe Scisly and 13y to E Jim Zanos to poise his 2nd TD run for winning pts with 1:34 to go.

OKLAHOMA 6 Oregon 0: No. 1 Oklahoma's new, more wide-open O turned up so stale that capacity crowd sat on its hands most of afternoon. Oregon (1-1) out-distanced Sooners (2-0) by 261y to 156y. Ducks completely controlled 1st Q but couldn't score, then had to withstand 3 Sooner sorties inside Oregon 30YL in 2nd Q. Late in 2nd Q, Oregon sub QB Paul Grover lost FUM to Oklahoma DG Dick Corbitt at Ducks 17YL, and OU QB Bobby Boyd rolled left to zip 9y TD pass to HB Dick Carpenter for TD. Moving between 20YLs, Ducks never pierced Oklahoma 20YL, but in 3rd Q, HB Willie West broke through line and darted 53y. Sooners FB-DB Prentice Gautt swept up behind West, and after long footrace Gautt hauled down West with TD-saving tackle at 37YL.

TEXAS CHRISTIAN 12 Arkansas 7: For most of game, Arkansas (0-3) held grimly to 7-6 margin on HB Donnie Stone's 2nd Q 1y TD run and QB-K Don Horton's conv kick. Clutch TCU (2-1) FB Jack Spikes produced 39y run to Razorbacks 8YL with 5 mins left. Purple Frogs QB Hunter Enis hit E Justin Rowland with winning TD pass moments later.

Notre Dame 14 SOUTHERN METHODIST 6: Fighting Irish (2-0) took 7-0 lead in 2nd Q, using 45y run by FB Nick Pietrosante (18/94y) for half of 90y march that was climaxed when HB Red Mack cashed his only carry of game for 41y TD. Threatening often, SMU (0-2) got within 7-6 in 3rd Q as HB Tirey Wilemon went 44y to score. Ponies QB Don Meredith (9-14/105y) was knocked out of game on last play of 3rd Q, and SMU could affect only single 4y completion rest of way as sub QBs Billy Dunn and Ken Lowe also were forced to sidelines. Notre Dame's insurance TD came at end of 72y on 16 plays during 4th Q journey that was capped by QB Bob Williams' smash from 1YL. Williams keyed drive with 23y pass to FB Norm Odyniec.

CALIFORNIA 34 Washington State 14: Losers of 7 straight, California (1-2) used strong 5- or 7-man pressure against Cougars (1-2) passing star, QB Bobby Newman (22-35/195y, 2 TDs, 3 INTs), who was permitted only short passes. Bears HB-DB Jack Hart (16/58y, and 6/68y receiving) scored game's most important TD when he extended Cal's lead to 14-0 in 2nd Q by racing 55y with INT RET. This came early in 2nd Q and soon after Cal HB-DB Steve Bates had cut in front of Washington State E Don Ellingson on similar pattern to save TD with INT at Bears GL. It became 22-0 on FB Bill Patton's 1st of 3 TDs before Newman could find HB Leroy Rath with short pass which was taken 35y to TD and 22-6 H deficit. Cal QB Joe Kapp (7-10/75y, INT, and 15/52y rushing) masterminded Bears clever O that netted 316y.

AP Poll October 6

1 Auburn (43)	813	11 Louisiana State	101
2 Oklahoma (24)	714	12 Navy	94
3 Army (7)	678	13 Purdue	93
4 Notre Dame (7)	654	14 Michigan (1)	81
5 Ohio State (6)	589	15 Oregon	68
6 Wisconsin (6)	456	16 Texas	63
7 Mississippi (1)	357	17 Iowa	32
8 Clemson (4)	301	18 Southern Methodist (1)	23
9 Michigan State (1)	248	19tColorado	22
10 Pittsburgh (2)	214	19tHouston	22

October 11, 1958

(Fri) Louisiana State 41 MIAMI 0: While wide array of Louisiana State (4-0) runners and passers were credited for big romp over Miami (1-2), it was superb D, led by C-LB Max Fugler's 14 tackles, that came up with INTs and tackles for loss at vital times that was difference. Hurricanes battled hard, especially QB Fran Curci (9-17/62y, 3 INTs), who gained 62y rushing, but was thrown for 16y in losses for net of 12/46y. LSU's 2nd-team HB Don Purvis skirted E for 51y TD in 1st Q, and DG Larry Kahlden's FUM REC of punt drop at Miami 27YL in 2nd Q set up QB Warren Rabb (3-7/55y, TD, INT) for 15y TD pass to E Billy Hendrix. HB Billy Cannon boomed 46y on RET of 2nd H KO, HB Johnny Robinson nabbed 20y catch from Rabb, and FB J.W. Brodnax powered over for 21-0 lead for Tigers, who added 20 pts in 4th Q. Curci was assisted by HB Joe Plevel (14/44y, and 4/26y receiving), and Miami was outdistanced only 329y to 242y, surprising numbers considering final score.

(Fri) Florida 21 UCLA 14: Gators (2-1) had to wait year to cash in lost opportunity of 1957, when early-season flu epidemic cost them trip to L.A. that they felt would be stepping stone to greatness. This time, Gators trotted out powerful run game for 273y, while UCLA (1-3) turned in 2nd H to tremendous passing effort by TB Don Long (14-16/156y, 2 TDs). Florida sprung HB Don Deal (10/89y, TD) for wide 67y TD sprint early in 2nd Q. Even though standout Bruins E Dick Wallen (10/97y) made conf-tying single-game reception record, he couldn't hold fingertip try for TD pass near end of 1st H. It came on pass try by TB Jim Steffen (6-14/82y, 2 INTs) after C Harry Baldwin blocked Florida P Bobby Joe Green's punt and Steffen's RET to Gators 23YL nearly went for TD. Unfazed, Gators went 54y after 2nd H KO to QB Jimmy Dunn's 2y TD run and 14-0 lead. Long came off bench to twice hit Wallen for scores, 2nd of which came with 2:38 to play in 4th Q. In between, Gators FB Bob Milby (7/65y) spurted 46y up middle to set up QB Wayne Williamson, who scored on keeper for 21-6 lead at mid-point of 4th Q. UCLA WB-DB Marv Luster recovered FUM by Florida FB Jon MacBeth at Bruins 36YL with 2 mins left, but even though Long passed Uclans to UF 33YL, he was felled for losses 12 and 20y to blunt probe of Gators' territory.

Texas A&M 14 MARYLAND 10: Slightly-favored Maryland (1-3) saw 3 4th Q opportunities blow up as Texas A&M (2-2) intercepted 2 passes and recovered FUM by Terps FB Jim Joyce. Aggies C-LB Roy Northrup fell on Joyce's FUM at Texans' 21YL on 4th down slam. Terrapins had marched 65y, primarily with Joyce slamming behind G Tom Gunderman and T Fred Cole, on their 2nd possession in 1st Q to QB Bob Rusevlyan's 7y TD pass. After Aggies FB Gordon LeBoeuf crashed over behind block of BB Richard Gay from 8YL, Maryland E-K Vince Scott slipped 26y FG through uprights in last 15 secs of 1st H. Terps led 10-6 at break. Texas A&M TB Charlie Milstead (4-9/67y, INT) threw infrequently, but Terrapins pass D was again inadequate. Aggies E Don Smith went long in 3rd Q, broke left to befuddle QB-DB Dickie Lewis, and caught 37y pass from Milstead to Maryland 8YL. After another completion, Milstead slipped left around E for winning TD. On conv attempt, Milstead looked right and found WB Randy Sims cutting far left for 2-pt catch.

GEORGIA TECH 21 Tennessee 7: HB Frank Nix left injury list to give Engineers (3-1) 9-0 lead with 74y punt TD RET in 2nd Q. Tennessee (1-2) dominated 3rd Q, drawing within 9-7, as TB Billy Majors' O magic set up FB Carl Smith's short TD run. Georgia Tech HB Joe DeLany helped ice game with favored weapon of this D-minded SEC series: QK for 72y in 4th Q. When Volunteers punted back, Engineers drove 42y to HB Ronnie Lewis' TD. Georgia Tech HB Cal James' 46y punt RET set up QB Fred Braselton's closing TD run late in game.

Auburn 8 KENTUCKY 0: Led by HBs Calvin Bird, Glenn Shaw, and Bobby Cravens, Kentucky (2-2) surprised no. 1 Auburn's star-studded D-front by punching through it for 125y rushing in 1st H. But, Wildcats QB Lowell Hughes was injured in 2nd Q, and Kentucky never quite mounted true threat. Meanwhile on other side of ball, Auburn (3-0) failed on 10 straight passes against Cats' national-best pass D. But, Tigers drove 73y to Kentucky 1YL in 3rd Q only to have HB Jimmy Laster bobble ball into 11y loss and change of possession. Auburn lefty QB Lloyd Nix finally clicked on 2nd play of 4th Q when he fired pass to wide-open Laster down middle for 43y TD. In trying to get loose on punt RET in 4th Q, Bird was trapped in his EZ for safety and 8-0 lead for Plainsmen, who came within inches of Wildcats' GL in dying moments.

Clemson 12 VANDERBILT 7: Scoreless 1st H was stalemated by PENs and lost chances as dueling FBs, Rudy Hayes of Clemson (4-0) and Jim Butler of Vanderbilt (2-1-1), lost FUMs deep in the other's territory. Hayes lost 1 of his 2 bobbles at Vandy 1YL in 1st Q. Commodores scored for 7-0 lead in 3rd Q after FB-DB Pete Thompson intercepted pass to spark 66y drive to 9y TD run by HB Tom Moore (84y rushing). Daring QB Harvey White led 4th Q resurgence that took Tigers on 76y trip to within 7-6 when he scored from 1YL. Trying for go-ahead 2-pt pass, White was picked off by star Commodores G-LB George Deiderich. But, Vandy couldn't move, and Clemson took over at its 31YL. Racing clock, White stole pulsating win when he scored from 2YL with 9 secs to play.

Ohio State 19 ILLINOIS 13: Buckeyes (3-0) powered to 246y rushing, but annoying Illinois (0-3) managed 6-6 H tie. Ohio State made it 19-6 in 3rd Q with great ball control for 19-play, 71y TD drive, then followed with HB Don Clark's 42y TD run. Then, Illini pulled QB Bob Hickey off bench to fire TD pass to HB Joe Krakoski. Later, HB Dick McDade momentarily gripped Hickey bomb at Ohio 3YL, but his drop ended upset hopes.

WISCONSIN 31 Purdue 6: Hardnosed inner D provided by NG Jim Fraser, G-LB Jerry Stalcup and C-LB Dick Teteak boosted unbeaten Wisconsin (3-0). Fraser blocked Purdue HB-P Clyde Washington's punt at 2:26 of 1st Q to create TD. Boilermakers (2-1) tied it 6-6 on FB Bob Jarus' 2nd Q plunge. But, G-K Paul Shwaiko's 3rd Q FG and FB Tom Wiesner's 36y INT TD RET powered Badgers to runaway in 2nd H.

MICHIGAN STATE 22 Pittsburgh 8: Michigan State (2-0-1) required only 23 and 34y drives capped by QB Mike Panitch's sneak and HB Dean Look's 3y run to gain 16-0 lead 3 secs into 2nd Q. Meanwhile, Pittsburgh (3-1) moved 62y in 2nd Q on QB Bill Kaliden's passing, only to lose Kaliden's FUM at MSU 8YL. In 3rd Q, Panthers went 50y to 7YL where Spartans G-LB Ellison Kelly picked off QB Ivan Toncic's pass. Toncic connected for TD pass to HB Dick Haley in 4th Q to pare Michigan State lead to 16-8.

Navy 20 MICHIGAN 14: Michigan (1-1-1) led 14-12 through 3rd Q, thanks to TD runs by FB Tony Rio and HB Brad Myers and knockdown of Middies' 2-pt pass attempt on long arms of hard-rushing DE Gary Prahst. Navy (3-0) QB Joe Tranchini (8-13/171y, 2 TDs) had completed 10y TD pass to E John Kanuch in 1st Q, but was stymied by Prahst's rush, a frequent annoyance, when trying to tie game at 14-14 after HB Roland Brandquist's short TD plunge in 3rd Q. Well into 4th Q play, Midshipmen had progressed from their 15YL with key move coming when HB Joe Bellino caught 12y pass and added extra 9y with impromptu lateral to trailing FB Ray Wellborn. As its drive advanced, Navy faced critical 3rd and-11 at Wolverines 36YL. Tranchini faked several times before finding HB Ray Zembrzuski breaking open at Michigan 5YL for winning TD reception. Wolverines still had late threat in them: Michigan drove to28YL only to be penalized 15y and have QB Stan Noskin sacked for 20y loss on 4th down.

Army 14 NOTRE DAME 2: Notre Dame (2-1) lost 3 FUMs in 1st H; 2nd bobble by HB Jim Just was lost to G-LB Bob Novogratz and led to Cadets' 1st down at ND 21YL. Army (3-0) then sprung new back-in-motion play toward its Lonely End, and 16y TD ended in catch by weak-side, sub E Jack Morrison from QB Joe Caldwell for 6-0 lead. But, Fighting Irish D was able to hold off Army at its 13 and 5YLs, and trailed only 6-0 at H. G-LB Myron Pottios earned safety for ND when he tackled Black Knights punter

after bad snap in 3rd Q. Irish FB Nick Pietrosante outgained Cadets HB duo of Bob Anderson and Pete Dawkins, but Army D, led by Novogratz, built rock walls at its own 19, 19, and 30YLs in 2nd H. Dawkins capped 66y drive with 6y TD run and added 2-pt pass for 14-2 lead. But Army's TD insurance was earned despite breathtaking moment for Notre Dame: QB-DB Bob Williams nearly grabbed INT in flat with clear field ahead of him. Road victory at South Bend earned Army its 1st AP no. 1 ranking since November 1950.

GAME OF THE YEAR
Texas 15 Oklahoma 14 (Dallas):

Texas (4-0) had passed only 8-26/93y in 3 opening wins, but coach Darrell Royal, facing his mentor Bud Wilkinson, reached to his long bench for sub QB Vince Matthews, who had been throwing star of early 1956 season until suffering 2 knee injuries. Matthews shook off rust to throw 8-10/123y, including big 74y bite on late winning march. Longhorns had struck in 2nd Q score when lefty HB Rene Ramirez whipped running TD pass to HB George Blanch, and FB Don Allen slammed for 2 pts and 8-0 H lead. Meanwhile, DTs Jim Schillingburg and Dick Jones and DEs Maurice Doke and Bob Bryant pitched in to stymie mighty run attack of no. 2 Oklahoma (2-1), limiting it to 39y. Sooners, still filled with kind of pride 52-2 1-won-loss record since 1953 would muster, roared out for 2nd H. Oklahoma scored on HB Dick Carpenter's 4y TD run and G-LB Jim Davis' stunning snatch of Texas handoff. After sub C-LB Max Morris squirted through to ruin handoff to Texas FB Mike Dowdle, Davis grabbed ball off Dowdle's hip and sprinted alone for 24y TD. Sooners QB Bobby Boyd succeeded on his 2nd try for 2-pt pass for 14-8 edge. With 6:50 left, Matthews spun his air magic, taking Texas to Sooners 7YL. On nervous 4th down call, Royal inserted tall starting QB Bobby Lackey, who leapt to pitch TD jump pass to sure-handed Bryant. K-DB Lackey provided lead with orthodox x-pt kick and later clinched verdict with late INT at own 28YL.

October 18, 1958

Tulane 14 NAVY 6 (Norfolk): Record crowd for charitable Oyster Bowl received surprise effort from lowly Green Wave, especially their big line that carved holes for solid ground game. Expected to pass often, Tulane (1-4) QB Richie Petitbon tricked Navy (3-1) by sticking to running attack which totaled 214y. Petitbon rushed 18/88y and scored TDs in 2nd Q after 83y drive and in 4th Q to cap 66y trip. Greenie spirit was boosted early when its D stopped 4 plays inside its 10YL. Middies QB-DB Joe Tranchini started that threat with FUM REC at Tulane 21YL on game's 5th snap and advanced it with 11y pass to E Tom Hyde. When his Es John Kanuch and Hyde later were injured, Tranchini turned to his backs in passing 10-19/126y, including 25y TD to HB Joe Bellino (7/33y rushing) that capped Navy's 71y scoring spree in 2nd Q. Navy was held to 79y rushing, otherwise never threatened until sub QB Jim Maxfield (4-5/39y, 2 INTs) pitched pass to E Pete Van Nort in EZ with 40 secs to play. Tulane HB-DB Tommy Mason made big INT.

SYRACUSE 38 Nebraska 0: Syracuse (3-1) scored on QB Chuck Zimmerman's sneak at end of 68y march after opening KO, and its alternating units dominated Nebraska (2-3) rest of afternoon. Although Cornhuskers entered Orange territory 3 times, they could gain only 41y O all day and failed to earn their initial 1st down until early 3rd Q. Zimmerman added 2 TD passes: E Fred Mautino caught 8y lob in EZ in 2nd Q, and HB Tom Stephens took screen pass and tight-roped sideline for 52y TD in 3rd Q.

GEORGIA TECH 7 Auburn 7: During 17-game win streak, Auburn (3-0-1) won 5 games scoring 8 pts or fewer, but single TD in this trip to Atlanta could only earn tie with Georgia Tech (3-1-1). Tigers D dominated 1st H, allowing only single 1st down. Auburn HB Tommy Lorino zigzagged 26y on 1st Q's last snap to Georgia Tech 3 YL to set up FB Ed Dyas' 2y TD plunge. Engineers' big opportunity came in 4th Q when QB-DB Fred Braselton returned INT 16y to Auburn 36YL. Braselton (8-10/71y) oiled up his throwing arm to connect on passes to HB Frank Nix and E Jerome Green to 11YL. Braselton aimed for E Jack Rudolph, and Rudolph adjusted as he fell to snare ball tipped by DB Lorino. Rudolph's reception at 1YL set up Braselton's tying sneak, which took 3 tries and represented only ground TD scored against Plainsmen since end of 1956 season. As game ended, Yellow Jackets K Tommy Wells, who had tied it with conv kick, was well short with wishful 49y FG try. Although Auburn gained 236y rushing, Georgia Tech had its share of D stars in C-LB Maxie Baughan, DB Floyd Faucette (INT), and DE Rudolph.

TENNESSEE 14 Alabama 7: Using power football, Tennessee (2-2) came up with highly-improved blocking by its linemen. Volunteers sprung TB Billy Majors for 58y rushing and short TD runs in middle Qs after Majors had netted only 6y rushing in prior 3 games. Alabama (1-2-1) fashioned too-little-too-late passing flurry in 4th Q to poise QB Bobby Jackson's 1y TD run. Big play on 80y drive was Jackson's 44y pass to HB Gary O'Steen. Crimson Tide finished with formidable 7-10/129y in air, and their players left Knoxville with new-found confidence based on their belief they should have won. Victory in stats battle didn't impress coach Bear Bryant, but loss of 3 FUMs deep in Volunteers territory did so negatively.

FLORIDA 6 Vanderbilt 6: Driving rain turned Gainesville into quagmire. Game's central figure became heady Vanderbilt (2-1-2) QB Boyce Smith, who took back Florida (2-1-1) HB-P Bobby Joe Green's 3rd Q punt for 53y TD RET. But with 2:11 to play and Commodores nursing their 6-0 lead, P Smith dropped back with hope he could spiral it deep and let Vandy continue to play bending-not-breaking D. Instead, slick ball squirted off Smith's foot to Vandy 32YL. Gators took their time advancing to tying score but hustled into their huddle to maximize their number of snaps left. QB Jimmy Dunn (3-7/30y) made 2 clutch throws: 12y pass to HB Billy Booker and 6y scoring flip to E Dave Hudson, latter with 8 secs to play. With chance to win it with x-pt, Florida saw Commodores HB Tom Moore break through to block kick.

LOUISIANA STATE 32 Kentucky 7: Record crowd at expanded Tiger Stadium watched decisive win for LSU (5-0), which at no. 9 in AP Poll was threatening for national accolades. Kentucky (2-3) soph QB Jerry Eisaman (3-8/49y), in for injured QB Lowell Hughes, scored on 4y run to tie game at 7-7 in 1st Q, but LSU's 3 units began to wear down thin Wildcats. Ahead by 13-7 at H, Tigers sprung HB Billy Cannon (12/108y, 2 TDs) on 19y TD run in 3rd Q. After LSU's O specialists, Go Team, tallied on 5y TD pass by QB Durel Matherne, Cannon added 2y TD run in 4th Q. Bengals D, led by their special "Chinese Bandits" unit and starters C-LB Max Fugler, Ts Lynn Leblanc and Bo Strange, HB-DB Johnny Robinson, NG Tommy Lott, and Es Billy Hendrix and Mickey Mangham, permitted only 136y O. Indeed, Kentucky's best weapon became long punts of E-P Doug Shively (46.7y avg).

PURDUE 14 Michigan State 6: Purdue (3-1) proved once again to be irritant to Michigan State (2-1-1). Key to upset victory was Boilermakers D which limited Spartans to 103y and allowed 1st Q score only because Boilermakers HB-P Clyde Washington dropped low punt snap at his own 12YL. Purdue TD table-setters were HB Leonard Wilson, who ran 27y to MSU 4YL, and E Rich Brooks, who carried QB Ross Fichtner's 31y pass to 1YL.

NORTHWESTERN 55 Michigan 24: Chicago Tribune blared Wildcats' stunning victory with banner, front page headline. In long history of Michigan (1-2-1) football, no school, least of all lowly Northwestern, coming off 0-9 in 1957, had scored 50 pts since Cornell did it in 1891. Wildcats (4-0) nearly made 50 pts by H, surging for 4 TDs in 7 mins of 2nd Q that made 43-0 H lead. As score was disclosed in other stadia across nation, fans made double-takes and announcers often felt compelled to repeat astounding H score. HB Ron Burton scored 3 TDs for Northwestern, and QB-DB Dick Thornton (5-9/106y, TD) passed for games' 1st TD to Burton and added another on 37y INT RET. Swift NW HB-DB Willmer Fowler (14/70y, 2 TDs), tackled Michigan HB Fred Julian in EZ for safety and tallied twice. On 2 early TD moves, Thornton completed passes of 25 and 11y to E Fred Williamson and 18y to E Elbert Kimbrough. Cats' D-front, led by Ts Andy Cverko and Gene Goosage and C-LB Jim Andreotti, put considerable pressure on Michigan passers who clicked on only 3 completions and suffered 2 INTs. Wolverines may have "won" 2nd H 24-12 as DE Gary Prahst intercepted lateral and raced 33y to score in 3rd Q, but that brought deficit only to 43-8. Michigan scored after 68 and 74y marches in 4th Q against 4th stringers.

Iowa 20 WISCONSIN 9: Badgers (3-1) jumped to 9-0 lead on G-K Paul Shwaiko's FG after INT at Hawkeye 42 by D standout, G-LB Jim Fraser, and QB Dale Hackbart's 32y TD pass at end of team's only sustained march of 69y. But, Hackbart suffered 3rd Q nightmare on which upset was hinged: He lost FUM to set up 1st Iowa (3-0-1) TD and suffered INT which Hawkeyes DE Jeff Langston carried 21y to TD. As insurance, Iowa QB Randy Duncan lobbed screen pass which flying HB Bob Jeter took 68y to pay-dirt.

Oklahoma State 7 HOUSTON 0: Stiff late-game D by Oklahoma State (4-1) turned aside scoring bids by Houston (3-1) at Cowpokes 20, 37, 1, 7, and 22YLs. Earlier, it had taken heroics of 3rd string Cowboys QB Dan Wagner to chalk up contest's only score late in 2nd Q. Wagner pitched 23y pass to E Billy Dodson to 1YL, then wedged over himself for TD. Cougars seemed assured of knotting it when they received pass interference call that placed Houston on 5YL with 1st-and-goal. UH QB Lonnie Holland called his own number 4 times but came up short of GL by inches. Oklahoma State was able to run off only 13 plays from scrimmage in 2nd H and never crossed midfield until C-LB Don Hitt made clinching 26y INT RET to Houston 27YL in last 2 mins. Cowpokes were outgained 272y to 139y and ran 48 plays to Houston's 84, but Hitt, DG Jim Frazier, and DEs Jim Wood and Jorge Madamba made so many critical tackles that Oklahoma State survived.

TEXAS 24 Arkansas 6: Appropriately buttressed by its upset of Oklahoma, Texas (5-0) received quite scare from Razorbacks (0-5), whose 2nd Q TD triggered scoring flurry in last 11 mins of 2nd Q. Arkansas had early advantage, which was turned into FB Donnie Stone's 3y TD blast after C-LB Gerald Gardner's INT RET to Longhorns 24YL. Haldful of plays later, HB Rene Ramirez slipped through LT and sailed 52y to TD that pulled Longhorns ahead at 7-6. Texas quickly recovered FUM and 35y later, FB Mike Dowdle was in EZ after Ramirez gained 15y in 2 carries. T-K Jim Schillingburg booted 39y FG for 17-6 H edge for Texas. QB Vince Matthews threw 14y TD pass in 2nd H for final tally.

AIR FORCE 16 Stanford 0: Falcons (3-0-1) flew (along ground) with greatest of ease for 59y TD on their 1st series. Air Force HB Mike Quinlan (9/49y) powered for 2y TD, but it became far more difficult to fly in air or on ground against Indians until 4th Q. Early on, Stanford (1-4) lost HB Rick McMillen, previous week's ground star in upset of Washington, and looked to QB Bob Nicolet (10-21/104y) who sparked 2 drives into Falcons territory but lost FUMs each time. Air Force HB-K George Pupich, who kicked-off beyond EZ each time, nailed 20y FG, on his 3rd try, early in 2nd Q for 10-0 lead, and QB Rich Mayo opened it up in latter part of 4th Q to throw swing pass taken 16y to score by FB Mike Galios.

California 14 SOUTHERN CALIFORNIA 12: Resurgent Golden Bears (3-2) beat Trojans (1-4) for 1st time at L.A. Coliseum since their PCC championship year of 1950. Battling stifling heat and smog, California FB Bill Patton surged for 2 TDs in

1st H. Of considerable importance was Southern California jumping offside as Bears tried unsuccessfully for 2 pts after Patton's 2nd TD early in 2nd Q. Patton earned 2 pts on Cal's 2nd conv try for 14-0 lead. HB Angelo Coia (7/86y, TD) got USC back in contention with 3y TD run at end of mighty 95y trip, but 2-pt try was thwarted. QB Al Prukop tallied for Troy in last min of 3rd Q, but tying 2-pt try went haywire. Confused USC was flagged for delay when it lined up in T-formation and shifted to kick formation after Prukop's score. Coach Don Clark had wanted opposite switch into T-formation for 2-pt try. Subsequent pass was picked off by Bears QB-DB Joe Kapp. Also thwarting Trojans were 5 lost FUMs and GL INT by HB-DB Steve Bates.

Washington State 6 OREGON 0: Banged-up but sharp QB Bobby Newman, nation's leading passer, played just enough to overcome his fumbled handoff at Oregon (2-2) 2YL in 1st Q and lead Washington State (4-1) back for peek inside Rose Bowl's invitation envelope. By leading drive to game's only score in wet Eugene, Newman hit FB Chick Morrell (18/77y) with key 12y pass on 88y drive to Newman's TD sneak in 2nd Q. TD drive started when E-DB-P Bill Steiger gambled for 19y gain on 1st of his 3 successful runs out of punt formation deep in Cougars turf. Wazzu so dominated 1st H that Ducks could gain only 38y O. Oregon moved ball better in 2nd H but watched DB Steiger break up 4th down pass after C-LB Dave Fish recovered Cougars FUM at Wazzu 11YL in 3rd Q. Ducks QB Dave Grosz pitched 35y pass to HB Charlie Tourville in 4th Q but Washington State D rose up again.

Ucla 20 WASHINGTON 0: Pleased Bruins (2-3) carried off coach Bill Barnes on their shoulders to commemorate his 1st win since replacing ailing George Dickerson. Washington (2-3) was caught flatfooted as Barnes strategically spread out UCLA's traditional Single Wing with flanked Es and WB. Uclans' O leader, TB Don Long (9-20/154y, 2 TDs, 2 INTs), was among 6 sr players about to end their careers at mid-season. Although Long was wracked up for several pass attempt losses by Huskies top DT Kurt Gegner and his linemates, he led unrelenting 78y TD trip after opening KO. Bruins counted TD on 23y pass from Long to WB Marv Luster. Another UCLA TB, Kirk Wilson, produced 50y pass with E John Brown late in 1st Q to allow Long to return for 2nd Q and quick 25y TD pass to E Jim Steffen. It was 14-0 at H, and Bruins added TD pass by backup TB Chuck Kendall (3-6/26y, TD) to E Dick Wallen (5/45y, TD) in middle of 3rd Q. Washington's only 2 chances were spoiled by ill-timed PENs, and it was turned back on downs in 2nd Q.

AP Poll October 20

1 Army (90)	1446	11 Notre Dame	183
2 Ohio State (14)	1188	12 Colorado (1)	157
3 Louisiana State (22)	963	13 Wisconsin	131
4 Texas (2)	861	14 Air Force	122
5 Auburn (5)	706	15 Purdue	62
6 Mississippi (4)	693	16 Texas Christian	37
7 Iowa (13)	632	17 Georgia Tech	35
8 Northwestern (3)	618	18 Navy	31
9 Oklahoma (1)	441	19 Mississippi State	30
10 Clemson (5)	371	20 Michigan State	24

October 25, 1958

(Th) South Carolina 26 Clemson 6: Tumbling from unbeaten ranks was no. 10 Clemson (4-1) as fired-up South Carolina (3-2) shut door in 2nd H with powerful run attack and stiff D. Gamecocks DE Jim Duncan, summed it up afterward, "We really wanted this one, and last night we began to feel we could win it." Tigers scored early in 2nd Q on QB Harvey White's sneak after White's passes of 10 and 6y clicked to HB George Usry. Important Gamecocks play came on 26y improvised pass from QB Bobby Bunch to E Buddy Mayfield that set up FB John Saunders' tying TD plunge. After 2nd H KO, Carolina took muscle to Tigers on 54y trip on which HB Alex Hawkins (12/57y, TD) and Saunders battered Tiger tacklers. Hawkins' 2-pt run after Bunch's TD sneak provided 14-6 lead. Trailing 20-6 in 4th Q, White overshot wide-open HB Charlie Horne on 4th down pass to cripple Clemson comeback plans.

Syracuse 14 PENN STATE 6: Nittany Lions' 24-year jinx over Syracuse (4-1) at Beaver Stadium ended on rainy afternoon as QB Chuck Zimmerman crafted 2 TDs for Orange. Penn State (3-3) enjoyed upper hand in 1st H but left for intermission trailing 6-0. Lions went 73y in 1st Q, but lost FUM to Syracuse DE Tom Gilburg at 7YL. After Zimmerman (5-8/102y) hit passes of 35 and 29y and scored on 1y run in 2nd Q, Penn State traveled to Orange 13YL, but QB Richie Lucas (7-17/89y, INT) saw his 4th down pass slip off fingers of E John Bozick in EZ. Syracuse took 14-0 lead in 3rd Q as Zimmerman hit HB Tom Stephens (18/78y rushing) with 14y TD pass and 2-pt conv. Fumbled punt at Orange 34YL gave Lions chance for late TD, scored by HB Dave Kasperian on 4y crack.

PITTSBURGH 14 Army 14: Cadets (4-0-1) cruised to expected 14-0 2nd Q lead on TD run by HB Steve Waldrop (subbing for injured Pete Dawkins) and HB Bob Anderson's scoring pass to E Don Usry. Pitt (4-1-1) caught fire with 1:02 to go in 2nd Q: DB Dawkins unaccountably was inserted in D secondary despite his obvious limp, and his bright white jersey amid muddied brown and gray of Army-mates must have been inviting target. Panthers QB Bill Kaliden immediately found HB John Flara streaking past Dawkins' deep position for 43y TD catch. After 2nd H KO, Panthers alternating QB Ivan Toncic passed for TD to E Jim Zanos and flipped unconventional underhand pass to HB Dick Haley for tying 2-pt conv. Army was held to 165y by Panthers D, led by G-LB John Guzik. It was 276y below Black Knights' season avg. Still, Army moved to Pitt 4YL in 3rd Q, but was rebuffed on HB Ken Waldrop's 4th down smash. Pitt gained 332y on O, which helped gain position for 2 FG tries in 2nd H by injured K Norton Seaman. His 1st try of 34y was wide by less than foot. When AP Poll was revealed on Monday, Army had tumbled from its top spot and never again in football history did it return.

West Virginia 21 VIRGINIA TECH 20 (Richmond): In annual Tobacco Festival encounter, Gobblers (3-3) pushed to early advantage as QB Billy Holsclaw (13-21/154y, TD, INT) hit E Allen Whittier with 16y TD pass, found E Carroll Dale for 2-pt conv, and darted 14y for TD. Virginia Tech, seeking important win in quest of its 1st-ever Southern Conf title, broke loose HB Patrick "Give Me Liberty or Give Me Death" Henry for 74y punt TD RET and 20-8 lead in 2nd Q. But, West Virginia (2-4) HB Mel Reight speared 12y TD pass from QB Dick Longfellow in last min of 2nd Q to pull Mountaineers within 20-14 at H. WVU went back to its bruising run game for successful 12-play, 60y march in 3rd Q. Reight circled E for 5y TD run to knot it at 20-20. Using T-K Dick Guesman's quaint kick in this season of frequent 2-pointers, Mountaineers happily accepted single pt that ended up winning game.

GEORGIA 28 Kentucky 0: Furman Bisher in Atlanta Journal wrote that Georgia Homecoming took on "gay (which meant "happy" in 1958), bodacious air" after QB Fran Tarkenton ended 61y drive late in 2nd Q with 4th down, 6y TD toss to FB Theron Sapp, "that got the stopper out of the offense after 29 previous minutes of offensive frustration." Bulldogs (2-3) went 71y in 18 plays that bridged 3rd and 4th Qs to take 14-0 lead on 10y run by HB Fred Brown (10/36y). What had been tight skirmish ballooned for Bulldogs in 10-sec span as G-LB Pat Dye made INT to initiate 40y trip to 21-0 lead in 4th Q. Dye snatched Kentucky (2-4) HB Calvin Bird's FUM out of mid-air on next KO and trotted 28y for Georgia's 4th TD. Wildcats had clawed deep into UGa territory twice: After opening KO, Kentucky was stopped at Bulldogs 28YL. And, Kentucky went 63y to Georgia 24YL in 3rd Q as QB Lowell Hughes (3-9/27y, INT) hit passes of 14 and 12y, and HB Glenn Shaw (9/59y) rammed 25y. Wildcats were halted when UGa G-LB Carter Ramsey broke up Hughes' 4th down pass.

LOUISIANA STATE 10 Florida 7: Gators E Don Fleming couldn't hold QB Jimmy Dunn's pass at 4YL, so Florida (2-2-1) had to settle for early FG try which was missed by HB-K Billy Booker. Bengal Tigers (6-0) went ahead 7-0 early in 2nd Q as 59y march was sparked by HB Johnny Robinson's 11y run and QB Warren Rabb's 22y pass to E Mickey Mangham. HB-DB Billy Cannon, who starred as blocker and open field tackler, finally powered over on 4th down TD push. Using P Dunn's deft coffin-corner punting, Florida enjoyed field position advantage until it managed 7-7 tie with early 4th Q TD on sub QB Mickey Ellenburg's 2 passes, each for 14y, to E Dave Hudson and E Perry McGriff for score. After Chinese Bandits D unit forced punt from deep in Gators end, Cannon powered from Florida 43YL to 19YL where Florida's no. 3 rated D halted progress. LSU FB-K Tommy Davis then kicked winning FG with 2:59 to play.

Florida State 10 TENNESSEE 0: Little FB Freddie Pickard, who rushed for 133y, contributed 52y run in 3rd Q for upset-seeking Florida State (5-2), which scored its 1st-ever win in __ tries over any SEC foe, favored Tennessee (2-3). Pickard's charge didn't make TD but set up HB-K John Sheppard's FG for 3-0 lead, and soon therafter Vol TB George Wright was picked off by Seminole G-LB Al Ulmer, who returned INT to Tennessee 28YL. FSU E Tony Romeo took QB Vic Prinzi's pass to 1YL, and HB Bob Renn slashed over for TD and 10-0 lead. Vols had ventured to Seminole 17YL in early part of fray only to see 15y PEN spoil things. Without TB Billy Majors, who walked off in 2nd Q with banged up ribs, Tennessee could gain but 29y rushing against snarling Seminole D.

OHIO STATE 7 Wisconsin 7: Despite frustration of fruitless march to Ohio State 1YL on its opening possession, Wisconsin (3-1-1) sprung QB Dale Hackbart behind E Earl Hill's last block for 64y punt TD RET with 3rd Q punt for TD. Buckeyes (4-0-1) countered with patented, Woody Hayes-approved 20-play, 66y TD drive after reception of following KO. Ohio State kept its drive alive at Badgers 6YL when 3rd down D-holding call went against Wisconsin after HB-DB Bob Zeman spilled Bucks QB Frank Kremblas for 10y loss. FB Bob White (36/153y, TD) inched over GL with K Dave Kilgore making tying kick for Ohio State. Badgers owned 4th Q advantage, but probes to 12 and 8YLs were stopped by HB-DB Jim Herbstreit's EZ INT and DT Jim Tyrer's FUM REC at 13YL.

IOWA 26 Northwestern 20: Aerial wizardry of Iowa (4-0-1) QB Randy Duncan (14-18/174y, 3 TDs) built 20-0 margin as E Curt Merz caught 1st and 3rd Q TD passes. In between, E Don Norton grabbed another on beautifully-conceived 21y slant behind Wildcats (4-1) DB Fred Hecker, just as red-dogging LB Frank Bennett pounced on Duncan. FB-LB Don Horn's 3rd Q INT RET to NW 36YL delivered Merz's 22y TD reception for 3-TD bulge, but Northwestern QB Dick Thornton shrugged it off to rally Wildcats for 2 scores to draw within 20-12. FB Horn's 4y TD plunge built breathing room for Iowa at 26-12. Northwestern's next and last score came on impulsive 35y TD pass as Thornton found HB Ron Burton (110y rushing) on 4th-and-17 play. Hawkeyes outgained Wildcats 402y to 267y, but Cats coach Ara Parseghian was philosophical afterward: "They fought, they scrapped, and they held. You can't ask any more than that."

Purdue 29 NOTRE DAME 22: HB Jim Crotty's FUM of 2nd H KO of 7-7 game put Notre Dame (3-2) in tough spot at own 21YL. Before long, FB Bob Jarus made his 3rd scoring run as Boilermakers (4-1) erected 3 TDs in 7-min span of 3rd Q for 26-7 lead. Wild finish saw Fighting Irish QB George Izo fit most of 129y passing into 15-pt 4th Q. Izo hit E Monty Stickles with 27 and 44y TDs, but Notre Dame only could manage safety after another threatening drive deep into Boilermakers territory. Izo's FUM was recovered at 1YL by Purdue G Emory Turner, and FB-LB Nick Pietrosante immediately spilled Boilermakers FB Jack Laraway in EZ. Clock died with Irish looking for more from Purdue 27YL.

COLORADO 27 Nebraska 16: C Don Fricke's blocked punt and HB Pat Fischer's 35y punt RET paved way for 2 Cornhuskers TDs in 1st Q. Vexed by 5 lost FUMs and 79y in PENs, undefeated Colorado (5-0) climbed out of 16-13 4th Q trap set by bothersome Nebraska (2-4). Buffs finally took their 1st lead at 20-16 on TB Howard Cook's 20y TD arrow to QB Boyd Dowler in opening min of last Q.

Texas A&M 33 BAYLOR 27: With Texas A&M (3-3) fortunes slumping in 1st year after departure of coach Bear Bryant, Aggies regulars finally mastered Single Wing tactics of new coach Jim Myers. TB Charlie Milstead ran for 74y TD in 1st Q, but when FB Larry Hickman bashed for his 3rd TD late in 3rd Q, Baylor (3-3) led 27-7. Milstead spectacularly produced 4 TDs, his last score came on 63y pass to FB Luther Hall to overcome 27-26 deficit.

RICE 34 Texas 7: Previously unbeaten Longhorns (5-1) were so shackled that they penetrated only to Rice (4-2) 24YL until HB-DB Clair Branch dashed 90y with INT with 39 secs to play. Owls used sharp throws of QBs Alvin Hartman and Jon Schnable to gain 13-0 H lead, then turned Texas' FUM and INT into short 3rd Q TD runs by each QB for 27-0 edge.

Mississippi 14 ARKANSAS 12: Disappointing Porkers (0-6) gave Ole Miss (6-0) all it could handle in 2nd H as running of Arkansas HB Jim Mooty (14/120y, 2 TDs) sparked numerous threats. Rebels had started smartly at 14-0 as QB Bobby Franklin scooted across for TDs in each of opening 2 Qs. G-K Bob Khayat, future chancellor of Ole Miss, was perfect with 2 kicks. When Mooty tallied on 23y TD run in 2nd Q, game turned in Razorbacks' favor. Seeking its 3rd upset of Mississippi in 4 years, Arkansas thrice penetrated deep but only once could it dent Ole Miss' bigger line. Franklin pitched long pass for E Larry Grantham in 4th Q, but Hogs HB-DB Don Horton circled back to snatch INT and returned it to his own 44YL. Mooty slipped up middle for last 10y with less than 5 mins left, but couldn't hold QB Jim Monroe's 2-pt pass attempt in EZ. Hogs O came within 27y of matching Rebs' 311y.

November 1, 1958

Notre Dame 40 NAVY 20 (Baltimore): Fighting Irish (4-2) stormed to 522y O behind new starting QB George Izo (9-14/181y, 3 TDs). HB Red Mack caught 9y TD from Izo on 2nd possession of 1st Q, but Navy (4-2) had surprise up its sleeve. HB Dick Dagampat took ensuing KO at own 8YL, veered to right at 18YL, and slipped handoff to HB Joe Bellino, who had clear sailing down left sideline to 92y TD. Izo followed 1y TD blast by his FB Nick Pietrosante (10/60y) with TD passes of 34y to E Dick Royer and 40y to HB Pat Doyle. ND led 27-6 at H. Mack raced 64y with punt RET behind blocks of HB Jim Crotty and E Monty Stickles, and Irish built 34-6 edge. Bellino caught 54y TD pass and made 2-pt run in 3rd Q, but Notre Dame continued to have too much firepower for Middies.

MARYLAND 10 South Carolina 6: Maryland (2-5) ruggedly mounted 2 GLSs to protect leads it got on pair of bad punt snaps. Terrapins went up 3-0 in 2nd Q on QB-K Bob Rusevlyan's 29y FG after snap flew over head of South Carolina (3-3) P Doug Hatcher and allowed Terps to take over at 18YL. Nursing 6-3 lead in 4th Q, which Carolina earned after HB King Dixon spurted 23y on punt RET to Maryland 39YL, Gamecocks again fired punt snap over Hatcher's head to own 3YL. On next play, Terps HB Bob Layman bashed through GL for winning TD. Maryland stopped Carolina drives at its own 4, 1, and 15YLs, and recovered FB John Saunders' FUM at Terps 21YL with 3 mins left.

CLEMSON 14 Wake Forest 12: Thanks to masterful QB Norm Snead, Wake Forest (3-4) outpitched Clemson (5-1) 185y to 43y. But, when it came to pass plays for 2 pts, Tigers prevailed on QB Harvey White's 2-pt pass to E Wyatt Cox after 2nd Q TD. Down 14-6 with 5:14 left, Demon Deacons went 89y on Snead's arm to his 5y TD scramble on 4th down. Wake coach Paul Amen hustled sub QB Charlie Carpenter into game with 2-pt instructions, only to see Carpenter misfire on tying pass try. Snead's final-play bomb was batted down in EZ.

Auburn 6 FLORIDA 5: With QB Lloyd Nix and HB Tommy Lorino going down with injury, Auburn (5-0-1) looked cooked by Florida HB-K Billy Booker's FG which put Gators up 3-0 late in 3rd Q. But big effort was turned in on next series by Tigers E Joe Leichtnam, who bulled his way through 2 defenders at GL to carry sub QB Richard Wood's 10y pass to TD and 6-3 Auburn lead. Florida (2-3-1) E Dave Hudson appeared on his way to TD with 7 mins left, but DB Wood knocked him OB after 43y gain to Plainsmen 3YL. Tigers DE Jerry Wilson disrupted pitchout attempt to force huge TO as HB-DB Jimmy Pettus fell on Gators FUM. With P Lorino being out, Auburn was without its best punter, so it conceded safety with 5:55 to go, trimming its lead to 6-5. After receiving free-kick, Gators stormed back to 1st down Tigers 10YL in last min, but PEN and 2 plays that lost ground forced Florida into 37y FG attempt by K Joe Hergert, which he could not make. C-LB Jackie Burkett was brilliant defender for Auburn, while T-DT Vel Heckman, who went both ways, starred in Gators line.

LOUISIANA STATE 14 Mississippi 0: Bengal Tigers (7-0) built 1st win over Mississippi (6-1) since 1950 on brilliant 1st H punts of FB-P Tommy Davis and GLS keyed by C-LB Max Fugler's 4 straight tackles. In 0-0 deadlock of 2nd Q, Ole Miss took advantage of Davis' dropped punt snap and went to 1st-and-goal inside LSU 2YL. Fugler and HB-DB Billy Cannon stacked up Rebels HB Kent Lovelace's 4th down smash, Ole Miss' 4th straight run attempt. Bengals DE Gus Kinchen soon recovered FUM at Rebs 21YL, and QB Warren Rabb ran 5y for 7-0 lead. LSU's Go Team iced it with 4th Q TD run

by QB Durel Matherne after collaring partially-blocked punt at Ole Miss 33YL. Totally bound to its ground attack that gained 121y, Ole Miss failed to connect on any of its 3 pass tries.

Iowa 37 MICHIGAN 14: Iowa's "Michigan Jinx" died in its 34th year as last time Hawkeyes (5-0-1) had prevailed over their Big 10 tormentor was in 1924. It was raw speed that prevailed for Iowa after previous week's Northwestern victory foundation had been passes of QB Randy Duncan. Hawks soared long-distance to 72, 74, 24, and 62y TD dashes, but not before injury-riddled Michigan (2-3-1) played to 14-14 tie midway through 3rd Q. HBs Willie Fleming (72y punt TD RET) and Ray Jauch (74y TD jaunt around LE) given Iowa 14-0 lead in 2nd Q when Wolverines QB Bob Ptacek (13-21/147y, TD, INT) pitched way to his short TD pass to HB Darrell Harper just before H. Michigan tied it on Ptacek's sneak and HB Brad Myers' 2-pt run after 73y trip following 2nd H KO. Hawks NG Hugh Drake forced Michigan sub QB Stan Noskin to fumble at UM 3YL, and HB Bob Jeter quickly swept to go-ahead TD. Wolverines made FUM REC and pushed ahead until they died on downs at 10YL, and Iowa countered with 90y voyage to Jeter's 2nd TD (24y run) for 29-14 lead with Duncan hitting 37 and 13y passes.

NORTHWESTERN 21 Ohio State 0: In last 90 secs of 3rd Q of nervous 0-0 battle, Wildcats (5-1) QB Dick Thornton (5-10/122y, 2 TDs) threw deep pass to HB Ron Burton (16/65y rushing), who made diagonal 67y sprint for TD. It was longest scoring throw to date in Northwestern history. In effort to come back in 4th Q, Ohio State (4-1-1) gambled on 4th-and-1 at its own 44YL, and workhorse FB Bob White (17/51y) was stacked up. After 3 NW runs gained 11y, Thornton raced 32y to Ohio 1YL, and, on 5th play of drive, he plunged over to score for 13-0 edge with 6:25 left. DB Thornton picked off pass by Ohio QB Frank Kremblas and returned it 27y. QB Thornton added TD pass to E Elbert Kimbrough and 2-pt conv pass to Burton. It was Buckeyes' 1st Big 10 defeat in last 11 starts and 1st loss in last 15 games overall. Afterward, NW coach Ara Parseghian was hoisted to his players' shoulders and he lifted game ball into aerial salute. Later he said: "They (Ohio State) scored 47 points on us one year (1957's 47-6 defeat), and they can't cross our goal line the next. What do you think of that!?"

Missouri 31 NEBRASKA 0: Missouri (4-3) coach Dan Devine, said to have "imagination of a greeting-card tycoon," by Jack Rice in St. Louis Post-Dispatch, used occasional Single Wing tactics to confuse Cornhuskers (2-5) and just enough passing by QB Bob Haas to keep Nebraska from stacking its D. Haas led opening 72y drive in 6 plays with payoff coming on his 29y TD arrow to E Russ Sloan. Mizzou's next drive was stopped, but ace G-K Charley Rash nailed 23y FG, 1st of his 3-year career. Nebraska kept bobbling football in front of its distressed Homecoming crowd, and Tigers' next 2 TDs, by HB Donnie Smith and FB Jim Miles, came after FUM RECs by HB-DB Hank Kuhlmann and DE Sloan. Kuhlmann ran through RG on simple play in 4th Q and cantered untouched for 86y TD. Huskers allowed 303y rushing to Tigers, while being able to gain only 185y total O.

Oklahoma 23 COLORADO 7: Largest crowd at Folsom Field to date turned out to see Colorado (5-1), nation's O leader with 411y per-game avg, make its annual "good-try" effort to knock down Oklahoma's long conf winning streak. Instead, Sooners (5-1) cruised to 86th win in row in Big 8 as Buffs were held to paltry 87y rushing and 99y in air. Sr QB David Baker (21/67y, 2 TDs rushing) emerged from his demotion to 3rd string backfield to provide Oklahoma with best quarterbacking since Jimmy Harris left for NFL after 1956. FB Prentice Gautt rushed for 16/117y, including 48y TD dash in 1st Q. Colorado scored 1st after QB-P Boyd Dowler's 56y punt to 1YL allowed WB Eddie Dove to make punt RET of 41y deep into Sooners territory. Buffs TB Howard Cook, Big 8's leading rusher, was held to 12/18y, but rammed over from 3YL for 7-0 lead 9:59 into 1st Q. Gautt soon cut through LT to answer with his long TD run, and, from kick-holding position, Baker hopped up to pitch 2-pt pass to HB Jimmy Carpenter for 8-7 lead. That score held up to H, even though Colorado was to be so shut down that P Dowler (6/49y avg) became its best weapon. Baker added TD runs at end of 79y 3rd Q drive and 76y 4th Q trip.

Air Force 33 OKLAHOMA STATE 29: HB Jim Wiggins (9/41y, TD) got Cowpokes off toward 15-0 lead with 1st Q TD plunge, and took 2nd H KO 81y to set up HB Duane Wood to score on 4y run. Wood followed up later with 46y reception from QB Dick Soergel (4-7/61y, TD, INT) to lift Cowboys (5-2) from 18-15 H deficit to 29-18 4th Q lead. Telling moments, however, had come in 3rd Q when Oklahoma State failed to gain single pt from 2 FUM RECs and INT after Wood's early TD in 3rd Q. Air Force (5-0-1) soph QB Rich Mayo picked apart Cowboys with short and medium passes as he directed 80y aerial drive capped by HB Phil Lane's 11y catch to trim score to 29-25. Next, Mayo completed 2 throws on 4th downs to spark clutch 72y march, climaxed by E Bob Brickey's winning 13y TD catch with :09 showing on 4th Q clock. Filling air with passes, Airman Mayo made 28-48/214y, 2 TDs, while Falcons FB Steve Galios rushed 17/94y, TD.

Southern Methodist 26 TEXAS 10: Pair of long TDs encouraged Mustangs (3-3) to stampede to 4th Q romp in rugged win over no. 16 Texas (5-2), which dropped its 2nd straight. Longhorns enjoyed 10-0 lead on 1y TD run by FB Mike Dowdle (14/68y) in 1st Q and QB-K Bobby Lackey's 33y FG in 3rd Q. In command by having kept SMU out of its territory all but once, Texas seemed on brink of locking up matters when it banged QK at Mustangs 42YL just halfway of 3rd Q. QB Don Meredith (6-12/112y, TD, INT), who played sparingly in 1st H because of lingering hip pain, hit whirling HB Billy Polk who pulled away from tacklers for 35y TD. SMU trailed 10-6. Big interference PEN on Texas put Ponies at 18YL, and HB Glynn Gregory soon swept to TD and 13-10 lead in 4th Q. Steers tried HB pass by Bobby Gurwitz, but HB-DB Tirey Wilemon picked it off for 35y TD RET, and SMU HB Norman Marshall ran 75y punt TD RET after receiving spur-of-moment lateral from HB-mate Dan Bowden.

OREGON STATE 14 California 8: Oregon State (5-2) took PCC lead when it overcame early 8-0 deficit. California (4-3) QB Joe Kapp, season-long magician, pitched out on 2nd possession, but Beavers C-LB Doug Bashor picked it off and charged 33y to TD.

Beavers WB-DB John Horrillo made winning score possible when he picked off Kapp pass late in 3rd Q. Horrillo's RET went to Bears 33YL, from which point TB Paul Lowe hit 2 passes and swept E for winning 8y TD.

AP Poll November 3

1 Louisiana State (82)	1443	11 Texas Christian	209
2 Iowa (54)	1379	12 Syracuse (3)	125
3 Army (7)	1105	13 Rice	116
4 Northwestern	815	14 Notre Dame	114
5 Auburn (7)	812	15 North Carolina (1)	108
6 Oklahoma (8)	733	16 Ohio State (1)	103
7 Wisconsin	584	17 Clemson	69
8 Purdue	465	18 Rutgers (1)	45
9 Mississippi	279	19 Florida	39
10 Air Force	228	20 Southern Methodist	36

November 8, 1958

(Fri) Florida State 17 MIAMI 6: Miami (1-5) piled up 309y to 176y O advantage, but poorly-placed Hurricanes TOs and their blundered scoring chances handed mighty-mites of Florida State (7-2) its 1st victory in 6 tries against its southerly in-state rivals. Seminoles QB-DB Joe Majors sprinted 42y with INT TD RET of Hurricanes sub QB George MacIntyre in middle of 1st Q. Miami came back on HB Joe Plevel's TD run at end of 68y march late in 1st Q, but 2-pt conv failed. In 2nd Q, Miami FB Harry Deiderich fumbled away ball at own 13YL, and FSU quickly went up 14-6 on TD pass that was deflected by Hurricanes defender into arms of startled Florida State FB Freddie Pickard. Still, Miami persisted: QB Bonnie Yarbrough (7-19/91y, INT) guided his club to 21YL, had open field to run, but passed into defender's arms. Hurricanes made it to 4, 17, and 9YLs in 2nd H, but Miami lost ball each time: QB Fran Curci's FUM when slammed by FSU G Terry Moran, on Curci's INT, and on downs.

BROWN 12 Cornell 8: Tough D and robust 409y O by Brown Bruins (4-3) finally fulfilled their season-long promise. Cornell HB-DB John Webster raced 71y with INT of pitchout for TD and then followed with 2-pt catch in 1st Q, but Big Red managed only 119y O with dreadful 1-13/11y passing against Brown D, led by C-LB Don Warburton, Es Dick Judkins and Bill Traub, and HB-DB Jack McTigue. Cornell (5-2), previously 4-0 in Ivy League play, fell from conf lead as Brown QB Frank Finney passed for 18y TD to HB Ray Barry in 2nd Q to finish up 88y drive that launched on last play of 1st Q. Ithacan QB Tom Skypeck was rushed on 4th down pass from Bruins 29YL in 3rd Q. Warburton made INT of floater and Brown took over possession at Cornell 49YL. Finney finished this series with 26y TD pass to HB Bob Carlin, who was awarded custody of EZ pass when he and DB Skypeck hit ground sharing possession.

PITTSBURGH 29 Notre Dame 26: Switchboard at Pitt Stadium was swamped when late-tuning TV viewers were puzzled by Panthers' 15-14 H lead. Apparently, many casual fans were still unaware of college football's new 2-pt conv rule. (Pitt couldn't have had a safety?) Pittsburgh (5-2-1) E-P Mike Ditka booted great 52y punt OB at 2YL. Panthers' DG John Guzik fell on FUM on next play, and HB Dick Haley plowed over for 1st of his 2 TDs. QB Ivan Toncic added 2-pt pass for 8-0 lead early in 2nd Q. In addition to running for 2 scores in 2nd H, Fighting Irish (4-3) QB George Izo passed 18-26/332y, including TD throws of 11 and 8y to E Monty Stickles in 2nd Q. Izo provided 20-15 lead in 3rd Q when he squeezed over from 1YL. Pitt countered with 65y march to Toncic's 10y TD run. Izo's aerial y total for game set new Notre Dame record and his 72y pass to HB Red Mack set up his 4th Q TD run for 26-22 lead. Behind student-body-right blocks of G Guzik, HB Joe Scisly, FB Jim Cunningham and T Ernie Westwood, QB Bill Kaliden raced wide and barely squirted into EZ with 11 secs left for Pittsburgh TD. Winning sortie went 73y in 14 plays. To add injury to insult, Rev. Edmund Joyce, Notre Dame VP, required surgery at Pittsburgh's Mercy Hospital when he stepped on loose board outside stadium and it smacked him in eye.

North Carolina 42 VIRGINIA 0: Starters and reserves alike scored in easy North Carolina (6-2) victory as it sent 6 different Tar Heels across GL for scores. Carolina racked up 514y to 182 for overmatched Virginia (1-7). Heels scored on their opening possession as enormous FB Don Klochak (6/62y) sprinted to 8y TD to make up for holding PEN that had nullified his 59y dash mins earlier. QB Jack Cummings (4-6/95y, 2 TDs) hit 2-pt pass to lift Carolina lead to 8-0. Next came 27y TD catch by E Don Kemper, and Cummings and HB Emil DeCantis collaborated on 12y TD and 2-pt passes for 22-0 edge at H. Game was put away just 3 plays into 3rd Q when Cummings lofted 68y TD pass to E Al Goldstein for 30-0 benefit. Virginia added to its y total against subs in late going, but despite decent passing by soph QB Arnold Dempsey (6-14/41y), Cavs couldn't advance past UNC 18YL nor add much to ACC receiving leadership of WB Sonny Randle (1/15y).

WEST VIRGINIA 14 Penn State 14: Twice rallying from behind, West Virginia (3-4-1) used slippery paws of Nittany Lions to thwart Penn State (4-3-1) scoring opportunities. For its part, Lions secondary made 5 INTs to stop WVU's surges. Penn State soph HB Jim Kerr found his way into EZ on 13y run at end of 45y trip in 1st Q, and QB Richie Lucas (6-11/64y) delivered 2-pt run for 8-0 lead. Mountaineers tied it 8-8 in 2nd Q on QB Dick Longfellow's TD run and 2-pt pass to HB Mel Reight. Lions chose to run for 2 pts after they scored on HB Dick Hoak's 5y TD dash in 3rd Q, but failed and held 14-8 lead. When Longfellow scored again in 4th Q, T-K Dick Guesman missed potential winning x-pt.

GEORGIA TECH 13 Clemson 0: DE Gerald Burch played terrific D for Georgia Tech (5-2-1), assisting stalwart QB-DB Marvin Tibbetts (2 INTs), C-LB Maxie Baughan (INT), and DT Billy Shaw. But it was 2 great punts by P Burch that contributed greatly: his 55y boot in 1st Q helped keep Clemson (5-2) pinned deep and his soaring 77y punt in 2nd Q was key to Tech's 1st TD. Tigers HB-P Charlie Horne could answer only with sliced 6y punt to Tech 46YL. Yellow Jacket HB Floyd Faucette sprinted off T Shaw's block for 54y TD. Clemson's passing attack was off mark most of day with starting QB Harvey White limping and backup QB Lowndes Shingler on injury shelf, but 3rd-string QB Johnny Mac Goff brought Tigers back through air, only to see Tibbetts pick him off and returned to Tech 44YL. Jackets HB Joe DeLany flipped 25y pass to key 56y march to QB Fred Braselton's TD sneak before H. Clemson was stopped in 3rd Q by another INT by Tibbetts at his 8YL, but Tigers D, led by T Lou Cordileone and E Wyatt Cox, made GLS at 3YL in 4th Q.

MISSISSIPPI SOUTHERN 26 North Carolina State 14: Rated No. 1 among small colleges, ornery Mississippi Southern (7-0) displayed stone-wall D and clever play of QB George Sekul. Opening Q saw trade of TDs: Southern HB Buddy Supple burst off T to surge 68y to score, but NC State (2-5-1) used HB Ken Trowbridge's 22y run to fuel answering 69y TD drive late in 1st Q. Scoring 1st of his 2 TD catches, Wolfpack E Bob Pepe stabbed 9y TD to tie it. Ahead 13-7 at H on Sekul's 7y run, Eagles slammed Trowbridge on 2nd H KO reception and took over on FUM REC by T Charlie McCarthy at NC State 26YL. Sekul completed 21y TD pass to star E Hugh McInnis for 20-7 edge. Result remained in doubt at 20-14, however, until pass interference PEN on NC State was called as Southern HB Bob Lance attempted catch on 3rd-and-11 play at Wolfpack 39YL. Lance iced verdict with 11y TD with 3:20 on 4th Q clock.

INDIANA 6 Michigan State 0: Making his 1st game start, Indiana (4-3) 18-year-old soph E Earl Faison burst through to block 2nd Q Michigan State (2-4-1) FG try by E-K Dan Follis and sprinted length of field to tally game's only score. Spartans outgained Indiana 269y to 150y, but Hoosiers HB-DB Tom Campbell recovered 1st Q FUM at own 2YL and team D, keyed by E Ted Aucreman (14 tackles and FUM REC) held at own 11YL to set up Faison's FG block. Game put Hoosiers at 4-0 in Bloomington, making it 1st sweep of home games in any season since Indiana won its only Big 10 championship in 1945.

WISCONSIN 17 Northwestern 13: Nightmarish 17-pt 2nd Q dashed Wildcats' Big 10 title hopes. Badgers (5-1-1) FB Tom Wiesner plunged for opening score. Then HB Sam Johnson lost 1st of 4 Northwestern (5-2) FUMs, and Badgers G-LB Jerry Stalcup fell on it at Wildcats 30YL to set up FB-K Jon Hobbs' 22y FG. Wildcats HB Ron Burton bobbled away next KO at own 16YL, and HB Bob Zeman zipped 11y to TD. Wisconsin PENs helped make it close in 2nd H as Burton and QB Dick Thornton scored for Wildcats.

Iowa 28 MINNESOTA 6: With 5th straight Big 10 victory, Iowa (6-0-1) rolled to its 2nd conf title in 3 years. Losing Minnesota (0-7) coach Murray Warmath raved about Hawkeyes HBs Willie Fleming, Bob Jeter, Ray Jauch, and Kevin Furlong, who triggered 307y ground attack: "That's the finest halfback foursome I've ever see on one football team." Fleming (9/137y) was especially devastating as soph raced 46y and 63y TDs in 1st H. Trailing 21-0 after Iowa QB Randy Duncan pitched 10y TD pass to E Jeff Langston, Golden Gophers QB Larry Johnson made his team's 1st completion work for 30y TD to HB Bill Kauth. Duncan wrapped up Iowa's Rose Bowl bid in 4th Q with 10y pass to E Don Norton after 3 completions to E Curt Merz.

MISSOURI 33 Colorado 9: Pushed all over its own stadium in 1st H by Colorado (5-2), Missouri (5-3) fell behind 9-0. In 1st 5 mins of opening Q, Tigers QB Bob Haas retreated to pass and had his arm hit by Buffs DT Jack Himelwright. CU E Kirk Campbell plucked wobbling ball out of air and set sail for GL, 37y away. Colorado led 6-0, and it would hold edge until last min of 3rd Q. After TB-K Ellwin Indorf kicked FG at end of Buffs drive that faltered at 5YL, Tigers charged out for 3rd Q and turned to gimpy QB Phil Snowden for comeback. Hobbled by bad back, Snowden still found E Russ Sloan for 9y TD pass for Mizzou's only completion in 13 tries in last min of 3rd Q. Colorado sub TB Jerry Steffen fumbled 2 plays later, and, then, within 4-min span, Snowden scored on 16y keeper and 1y sneak for 20-9 lead. Tigers HB Fred Brossart added icing with 83y punt TD RET.

Army 14 RICE 7: Teams were tied 7-7 after trading 2nd Q passes in excessive Texas heat: E Buddy Dial grabbed TD pass for Rice (4-3), and E Bill Carpenter leapt high among 3 defenders for Army (6-0-1) TD. Holding Cadets to 100y rushing, Owls fought their way to victory's doorstep as HB–K Bill Bucek attempted 26y FG in closing mins. But, Cadets FB Don Bonko dramatically blocked it. Army QB Joe Caldwell soon hit clutch play: He launched long completion to HB Pete Dawkins for 64y, which Dawkins carried to TD despite DB Bucek's dire diving tackle try with 51 secs left.

CALIFORNIA 20 Ucla 17: Cal's win, coupled with Oregon State's upset loss at Pullman, Wash., allowed Golden Bears (5-3) to regain inside track to Rose Bowl. UCLA (2-6) had taken 3-0 lead on TB-K Kirk Wilson's 29y 1st Q FG. California went ahead 14-3 on FB Walt Arnold's 2nd Q TD plunge followed by HB Jack Hart's 2-pt catch, coming slightly more than 2 mins before H. P Hart set up his own 4y TD run in 3rd Q by spinning 54y punt to screeching halt at Bruins 1YL. Uclans wrestled away 3rd Q momentum when FB Ray Smith's plunge completed 72y TD foray and brought Bruins to within 14-9. Bears held UCLA at Cal 22YL early in 4th Q as Bruins TB Skip Smith barely missed E John Brown on 4th down pass. Bears in turn marched 78y to TD that provided 20-9 lead midway through 4th Q. QB Joe Kapp, fiery leader of Berkeley brigade and future Hall of Famer, was hindered by two badly bruised thighs but made Bears winner with his gutsy 13y TD toss to E Jerry Lundgren.

WASHINGTON STATE 7 Oregon State 0: Undervalued Cougars (5-3) stayed in Rose Bowl contention by knocking Oregon State (5-3) out of 1st place in PCC. Washington State mounted 2 serious threats in 2nd and 4th Qs of scoreless match, but each trip was derailed by INT by Beavers WB-DB John Horillo. Oregon State TB Dainard Paulson threw 4th Q INT, grabbed by Cougars C-LB Marv Nelson, which ended serious Beavers drive: OSC had moved 52y from its 19YL to Wazzu 29YL. Later, Paulson tried QK that sailed off his foot for short advance to his own 43YL. Washington State sent soph HB Ted Cano around LE for 11y to Beavers 14YL. Roughing PEN advanced possession to Beavers 1YL, and Cano slammed over for game-winner with 3 mins left to play.

1 Louisiana State (95)	1532	11 North Carolina (2)	218
2 Iowa (52)	1441	12 Syracuse	179
3 Army	999	13 Northwestern	166
4 Auburn (6)	976	14 Pittsburgh	152
5 Wisconsin	786	15 Southern Methodist	67
6 Oklahoma (3)	783	16 Ohio State	59
7 Mississippi (2)	535	17 Rice	43
8 Purdue	289	18 Florida	37
9 Texas Christian	287	19 Rutgers (1)	35
10 Air Force	249	20 Georgia Tech	19

November 15, 1958

Clemson 13 NORTH CAROLINA STATE 6: Clemson (6-2) wrapped up ACC title with 2 late scores against surprisingly rugged Wolfpack (2-6-1). Scoreless game turned early in 4th Q on 51y Tigers drive against wilting NC State. HB Bill Mathis' 16y run poised HB George Usry for short TD plunge. Clemson cashed short march for 13-0 lead after Wolfpack suffered awful 3y punt. Wolfpack FB Don Hafer scored late, but it wasn't enough.

Alabama 17 GEORGIA TECH 8: Coach Bear Bryant's improving Crimson Tide (4-3-1) engulfed Georgia Tech (5-3-1) with 17 pts in 1st Q as DE Baxter Booth pounced on FUM at Yellow Jackets 21YL, HB Duff Morrison galloped 37y with INT to set up E-K Pete Reeves' FG, and FB-LB Milton Frank made FUM REC at 21YL. QB Bobby Jackson scored both Alabama TDs. Engineers threatened all day, outgaining Tide 275y to 136y, but scored only when alert star T Billy Shaw grabbed teammate HB Cal James' FUM and advanced ball for short TD in 3rd Q.

TENNESSEE 18 Mississippi 16: Ole Miss (7-2) bunched 16 pts in 2nd Q on TD run and TD pass by QB Bobby Franklin. T-K Bob Khayat kicked 26y FG. Tiny soph TB Gene Etter sparked Tennessee (3-5) to upset with sizzling 4th Q 75y dash behind block of FB Carl Smith and his twist-away from ankle-tackle attempt by Rebels FB-LB Jim Anderson. Ole Miss nearly won, but usually-reliable K Khayat missed late FG after Rebels moved to Vols 4YL. Khayat, future chancellor of Mississippi, was notable for dating Ole Miss Coeds, each future Miss America, Mary Ann Mobley (1959) and Lynda Lee Mead (1960).

Auburn 21 Georgia 6 (Columbus, Ga.): Auburn (7-0-1) QBs Lloyd Nix and long Richard Wood combined for 11-19/129, INT passing and each threw TD pass that built 14-0 lead in 3rd Q. Wood lofted beautiful 44y TD in 2nd Q to HB Bobby Lauder, who rocketed past line of Georgia Bulldogs (2-6) defenders to take TD in full stride at 5YL. Nix clicked on 11y TD pass to FB Ed Dyas after Georgia HB-P Bobby Walden, nation's leading punter with 45.4y avg, squirted miserable 15y to UGa 42YL. Lauder made brilliant 20y TD run for 21-0 lead in 4th Q, but Bulldogs battled to TD as QB Charley Britt and HB Fred Brown combined on 77y pass to 11YL. Britt found HB Don Soberdash fro TD on next snap.

Louisiana State 7 MISSISSIPPI STATE 6 (Jackson, Miss.): No. 1 Tigers (9-0) had their hands full of growling Bulldogs (3-5), who scored 1st on rain-soaked field and played threatening O and masterful D game up until H. LSU stopped early threat at its 5YL as HB-DB Billy Cannon (13/57y, 2 FUMs) knocked down 4th down pass by Mississippi State QB Billy Stacy (3-10/57y) and had to defend its 13 and 16YLs before end of 1st H. After Maroons gained FUM at Bengals 23YL, Stacy scored in 2nd Q on 10y option run around LE. But, x-pt was flown wide by DT-K Bobby Tribble, who also missed pair of FGs but was outstanding on D for Miss State. Shortly after Maroons received 2nd H KO, Tigers handy FB-LB J.W. Brodnax recovered FUM by HB Gil Peterson at Bulldogs 34YL and galloped 14 and 4y to 1st down at 10YL. On 4th down, LSU QB Warren Rabb (3-6/16y, TD) threw 5y TD to E Billy Hendrix. Sr FB-K Tommy Davis, military vet who played his 1st varsity game in 1953, made good on vital 7pt.

Wisconsin 31 ILLINOIS 12: Surprisingly effective passing fueled Wisconsin (6-1-1) as QBs Dale Hackbart (8-15/127y, TD, INT) and Sidney Williams combined for 12-26/227y, TD, 2 INTs in air over Champaign. Fighting Illini (3-5) QB Johnny Easterbrook threw well too, but Illinois did so mostly in catch-up posture. Badgers sprung 50y gain on lateral-and-run by FB Jon Hobbs and HB Ron Steiner that led to Hackbart's 4y run for 7-0 lead in 1st Q. Williams' 16y pass to HB Ed Hart kept 2nd advance rolling to Williams' 5y TD run and 15-0 edge. Easterbrook (8-17/149y, TD, 3 INTs) capped 65y trip in 2nd Q to his 32y TD pass to HB Marshall Starks, but Wisconsin came back after poor Illinois punt to Hackbart's 16y TD arrow to Hart for 23-6 H edge. After 2nd H KO, Illinois pounded 67y on 14 plays to FB Jim Brown's 2y TD leap, but Badgers were right back for 66y TD trip of their own to move into 2nd place in Big 10.

Ohio State 38 IOWA 28: Each of 2 Big 10 juggernauts scored single TD in 1st Q, added pair in 2nd Q, and earned matching 7 pts in 3rd Q. But each time it was Iowa (6-1-1) that had to play nerve-wracking role of team needing to catch up. Powerful Buckeyes FB Bob White irked no. 2 Iowa for 2nd year in row, rushing 33/209y, including surprising 71y TD gallop. White carried on 11 of 14 plays on decisive 61y drive in 4th Q that broke 28-28 tie after Hawkeyes scoring power stood toe-to-toe with Bucks. K Dave Kilgore iced verdict for Ohio State (5-1-2) with 18y FG with 2:12 left after HB-DB Dick LeBeau made midfield INT. Despite fateful late INT, Iowa QB Randy Duncan passed for Big 10 record to-date 23 completions in 33 attempts for 249y, including short TD to HB Willie Fleming that tied it late in 2nd Q at 21-21. Adding to O show was Buckeyes HB Don Clark, recovered from nagging injuries and who chipped TD runs of 25 and 37y.

OKLAHOMA 39 Missouri 0: Clinching tie for their 13th straight Big 8 title (11 outright), Sooners (7-1) lit aerial skies with 10-13/160y passing. HB Brewster Hobby caught 4 passes and threw 2 TD passes, including rout-launching 74y strike to E Ross Coyle off fake sweep in 1st Q. Passing game went opposite way for Missouri (5-4) as Sooners returned 5 INTs/68y, including QB-DB Bobby Boyd's 38y TD RET. Down only 2 TDs at

H, persistent Tigers went 62y after 2nd H KO, but QB Phil Snowden was halted on 4th down sneak at Sooners 13YL by NG Dick Corbitt and brilliant C-LB Bob Harrison. OU proceeded to roll to 4 additional scores.

NEBRASKA 14 Pittsburgh 6: Three-TD underdog Nebraska (3-6) slapped another unprepared Eastern traveler: Penn State had lost 14-7 in Lincoln on September 20. HB Larry Naviaux accounted for all of Cornhuskers' pts: He completed 2 short option TD passes to E Mike Eger and HB Pat Fischer and caught 2-pt throw by Fischer. Pittsburgh (5-3-1) mined QB Bill Kaliden's TD to HB Dick Haley from its belated 4th Q passing attack. Pitt's bowl hopes were dashed because its 339y to 189y advantage in O failed to materialize on scoreboard.

TEXAS CHRISTIAN 22 Texas 8: TCU (7-1) took SWC lead, but not before Texas (6-3) line surprisingly outcharged massive Horned Frogs in 1st H. Longhorns took 8-0 lead on TD by HB George Blanch and FB-LB Mike Dowdle's EZ tackle of TCU E-P Jimmy Gilmore for safety. Texas might have added more pts in 2nd Q but Frogs G Sherrill Headrick blocked FG try, and E Bob Bryant lost FUM on end of QB Bobby Lackey's 52y pitch when he was hauled down by FB-LB Merlin Priddy at 10YL. TCU QB Hunter Enis capped 68y drive in 3rd Q with 1y TD plunge, then tossed 2-pt conv to FB Jack Spikes to tie it 8-8. C-LB Dale Walker picked off pass by Longhorns QB Larry Cooper to set up Purple Frogs score early in 4th Q. After Walker's INT, crafty Enis nailed 11y TD pass to Gilmore for 15-8 lead. Final touch came from TCU HB Marvin Lasater, who rifled 41y option pass to HB Marshall Harris for TD. Steers were crushed by Frogs D in 2nd H to extent of –5y net O.

Texas A&M 28 RICE 21: Texas A&M's 28-21 upset of Rice (4-4) knocked Owls off 1st place perch in SWC. After A&M E John Tracey (3/50y) caught 4th down TD pass in 1st Q, Owls came back for 14-7 lead in 2nd Q as FB Hart Peebles (22/63y) powered for TD. Early in 3rd Q of 14-14 deadlock, Aggies BB Gordon LeBoeuf corralled partially blocked punt by E Don Smith and sped 55y to score go-ahead TD. Texas A&M (4-5) soon added short TD run by 50-min TB Charlie Milstead (15-28/165y, TD, INT passing) to build insurmountable 28-14 lead. Rice A-A E Buddy Dial (5/50y) scored late TD on 4y reception from 3rd-unit QB Bobby Wright (6-12/76y, TD), but it was not enough for Owls, who could not keep up with Milstead, who ran for 2 TDs despite ailments that had listed him as doubtful starter.

ARKANSAS 13 Southern Methodist 6: Oft-beaten Arkansas (3-6) rose up to treat its excited Homecoming crowd to year's top performance. Since Hogs would close this season with 4 straight wins, it paved way for successful 1959 edition of Razorbacks. Arkansas D-line was so frenzied in its pass rush of Southern Methodist (4-4) ace QB Don Meredith (11-24/117y, 3 INTs) that it sometimes leapt over Mustangs linemen. Still, Meredith scored 1st H's only TD on 9y run in 2nd Q as he threatened pass on rollout from Smu's efficient spread formation. Razorbacks owned 2nd H as speedy HB Billy Kyser dashed 38y to TD and 7-6 lead in 3rd Q. Late in 3rd Q, Arkansas cashed in INT of Meredith, which was tipped by C-LB Wayne Harris to HB-DB Jim Mooty. QB Jim Monroe tagged on 10y TD pass to sub E Charlie Barnes. Ponies threatened late but Mooty came up with another INT in EZ, and later Monroe knocked down 2 EZ tosses.

1 Louisiana State (114)	1640	11 Ohio State (6)	426
2 Auburn (21)	1218	12 Florida	208
3 Army (12)	1162	13 Mississippi	197
4 Oklahoma (22)	1146	14 Vanderbilt	164
5 Wisconsin	872	15 Notre Dame	157
6 Iowa (4)	812	16 Clemson	152
7 Texas Christian	647	17 North Carolina (1)	128
8 Purdue (8)	630	18 Mississippi State	97
9 Air Force	498	19 California	85
10 Syracuse	460	20 Northwestern	76

November 22, 1958

Dartmouth 22 PRINCETON 12: Dartmouth (7-2) took its 1st Ivy League title since 1938 as fiery HB Jake Crouthamel, future Dartmouth coach and Syracuse AD, was central character. Crouthamel (13/117y, and 3/25y receiving) launched early TD with 55y dash to Tigers 3YL. After Princeton (6-3) TB Dan Sachs breezed 70y to set up his multi-deflected 9y pass to Tigers BB Gene Locks for TD and 6-6 tie, DB Crouthamel was benched for screaming about dubious pass interference call called against him. Cooled down, he soon returned for EZ INT to preserve H tie. Tigers led 12-6 on TB Hugh Scott's 3rd Q TD pass to WB John Heyd, but QB Bill Gundy (9-14/134y, TD, INT) countered with passes of 16, 20, and 23y to drive Big Green to 13-12 lead. Overcoming pair of 15y PENs, Dartmouth went 76y to clinch game on HB Bill Morton's 13y sweep, key being Gundy's gutsy 4th down 15y fake-punt pass to Crouthamel from own 41 YL. Gundy won 3 times with 4th down gambles.

RUTGERS 61 Columbia 0: Scarlet Knights (8-1), losers only to Quantico Marine Base by 1 pt, closed their best season since 1947. Despite cast on his left hand and wrist, do-everything TB Billy Austin scored 34 pts on 5 TDs and 2 conv runs of 2 pts each. Having missed previous week and only played in 8 games during 1958, Austin still had hand in 164 of Rutgers' 301 pts during season. Columbia (1-8) was blanked for 4th game in row and managed only 157y total O to Rutgers' 383y.

Duke 7 NORTH CAROLINA 6: In late 1st Q action, Tar Heels QB-DB Jack Cummings returned tipped INT 15y to Duke 7YL, making it possible for North Carolina (6-4) to lead 6-0 on FB Don Klochak's scoring plunge. But, Blue Devils standout G Mike McGee blocked T-K Phil Blazer's conv kick attempt. After Duke (5-5) DG Art Browning recovered Klochak's FUM, HB Wray Carlton carried 8 times to contribute 46y rushing to 57y march in 3rd Q. Carlton scored short TD, then put on his kicking shoe to make

conv that would turn out to be winning pt. Devils DE Jim Bartal copped 3 of North Carolina's debilitating 7 TOs, and Duke FB-DB Butch Allie's INT in last 3 mins at own 5YL snuffed UNC's flickering Sugar Bowl dreams. Heels D fashioned pair of GLSs.

CLEMSON 34 Boston College 12: Bowl scouts watched Clemson (7-2) demonstrate its best O of season in dismantling of Boston College (6-3), which dropped from bowl demand. Tigers enjoyed 353y to 242y O edge over New England visitors. Clemson E Wyatt Cox made excellent EZ catch of 2nd Q pass from QB Loundes Shingler despite Eagles HB-DB Jim Colclough draping himself all over Cox. Shingler added 2-pt pass for 8-0 H lead. FB Doug Cline bulled for 31y TD run in 3rd Q, and Tigers HB-DB Charlie Horne scored next 2 TDs, including 28y TD RET of FUM. Boston College QB John Amabile came off bench to pitch 2 cosmetic TD passes in 4th Q.

Syracuse 15 WEST VIRGINIA 12: Orange Bowl came calling for Syracuse (8-1) after Orangemen outwitted Mountaineers (4-5-1), who enjoyed 351y to 212y O edge. Key plays that set up Syracuse TDs were HB Ger Schwedes' 67y punt RET and DG Maury Youmans' 27y INT RET to WVU 23YL. Veteran Orangemen QB Chuck Zimmerman (7-10/60y, INT) followed these breaks by tossing 2 TD passes to E Dave Baker in 1st H. West Virginia matched those TDs, scoring on runs by QBs Dick Longfellow and Danny Williams. Pivotal WVU errors were failed conv run in 1st Q and T-K Dick Guesman's missed kick try in 3rd Q.

OHIO STATE 20 Michigan 14: Buckeyes (6-1-2) earned 6-6 2nd Q tie courtesy of 1 of 4 Michigan FUMs, this REC at 12YL that led to HB Dick LeBeau's 7y TD run. Michigan (2-6-1) went to air for 258y as QB Bob Ptacek's passes to E Gary Prahst, a combo that tallied all 14 pts on TDs of 7 and 31y. Wolverines outgained Buckeyes 376y to 262y. Trailing 14-6 in 2nd Q, Ohio State's little HB Jim Herbstreit fled into open and caught 25y TD pass from QB Jerry Fields. Buckeyes FB Bob White (26/78y) scored 3rd Q TD. In final min, Wolverines drove deep into Ohio territory and needed but 4y to send departing coach Bennie Oosterbaan out as winner, but Ohio DT Dick Schafrath walloped HB Brad Myers to cause FUM, recovered by QB-DB Jerry Fields at 2YL. Loss ended worst Wolverines season since 1934.

PURDUE 15 Indiana 15: Before intrastate matchup, Old Oaken Bucket, missing since September, was quietly returned to Purdue (6-1-2) by devilish Indiana (5-3-1) fraternity Sigma Pi. Deadlock, which resulted after scoreless 2nd H, delivered Hoosiers' best season since 1946, but meant Bucket would stay with Boilermakers. Purdue scored 1st when Indiana BB Tom McDonald saw his 1st Q QK blocked by E Rich Brooks and T Jerry Beabout, and Boilers FB Jack Laraway grabbed ball out of air and lit out for 27y TD. Indiana answered with 74y drive, culminated in McDonald's 15y bullet TD pass to E Ted Aucreman. E Earl Faison caught 2-pt pass for 8-7 lead. McDonald to Faison TD pass made it 15-7 in 2nd Q, but Purdue soon got rolling on HB Joe Kulbacki's 28y run. QB Bob Spoo completed Purdue's only pass of day (1-8) for 13y TD to Brooks. HB Clyde Washington pitched 2-pt pass to E Tom Franckhauser to knot game at 15-15. Boilermakers G-LB Phil Kuebbeler made EZ INT near end of 1st H, and G-K Skip Ohl missed 39y FG in 2nd H.

IOWA 31 Notre Dame 21: Big 10 champion Iowa (7-1-1) added another valued victory by dumping Notre Dame (5-4), which would finish season having faced most difficult schedule in nation. In wrapping up its regular season, Hawkeyes, interestingly, had taken on 2nd toughest slate in America. It turned into quite good O show with 878y gained combined. Iowa speed spelled difference as its fastest player, HB Willie Fleming scored on 6y run on opening play of 2nd Q and caught 36y pass from QB Randy Duncan (15-28/260y, 2 TDs, 4 INTs). Hawks secondary was caught flat-footed by Irish QB George Izo's 2nd down bomb as E Monty Stickles went 69y to TD. FB John Nocera gave Iowa breathing room at 19-7 with short TD plunge in 3rd Q after Duncan connected with E Don Norton on 4th down from ND 18YL. Izo tallied another long TD pass, this to HB Bob Scarpitto sailing past DB Duncan, early in 4th Q, but Iowa QB Duncan countered right back with 53y TD pass to Norton for 25-14 advantage.

MISSOURI 13 Kansas 13: Tigers (5-4-1) HB Mel West rushed for 102y and scored early TD. Late in 1st Q, Missouri FB Ed Mehrer pitched surprise lateral to trailing HB Jerry Curtright, and 11y gain quickly turned into 82y TD for 13-0 edge. It might have been 14-0 had Tigers G-K Charley Rash's kick not been extended too far by 2 PENs/20y on his repeated x-pt tries. Rash received another chance to kick result into W-column at 16-7 for Missouri, but in last 30 secs he missed his 3rd FG try of game from 32y out. So, Kansas put ball in play from its 20YL with little cause for hope. Amazingly, speedy HB Homer "Hot Rod" Floyd sped 80y with stunning pass catch for 13-13 tie with 18 secs left. Jayhawks, too, might have won it with kick, but Missouri E Dale Pidcock stormed in to block HB-K Duane Morris' potential winning conv.

OKLAHOMA 40 Nebraska 7: Oklahoma (8-1) wrapped up its 11th straight conf title by lambasting confident and upset-minded Nebraska (3-7). Opening Q indicated superiority of Sooners despite Cornhuskers' upset over Pittsburgh previous Saturday: Oklahoma cruised 55, 52, and 55y to TD runs by all-around HB Brewster Hobby, little sprinter HB Jakie Sandefer, and versatile QB Bobby Boyd. OU's 21-0 lead held up into 3rd Q when it was slapped with big but brief surprise. Oklahoma was headed for another TD when QB David Baker threw pass that HB-DB Larry Naviaux, future head coach at Boston University and Connecticut, intercepted and raced 93y up sideline for TD. Sooners shrugged it off and scored 3 more TDs, including Sandefer's HB pass to HB Dick Carpenter. Oklahoma outdistanced Nebraska 447y to 107y.

Texas Christian 21 RICE 10: E Buddy Dial's TD catch gave Rice (5-5) early lead in 1st Q. TCU (8-1) erased its 7-0 shortfall with HB-DB Marvin Lasater's mid-air 58y FUM TD RET on 2nd Q's 1st play. Lasater was approaching Rice ball-carrier, HB Bill Bucek from left, when Frogs C-LB Arvie Martin belted Bucek chest- and ball-high. Ball made lollypop flop into air where Lasater gathered it in stride and stormed back through dandy hole that had been created by Owls blockers. After Horned Frogs FB Jack Spikes made it 14-7 with running TD at end of 13-play, 60y journey. In questionable bit of strategy, Owls K Bucek countered with 4th Q FG with less than 7 mins to play to bring Rice's negative margin to within 14-10. With sub QB Larry Dawson flinging several completions, E Jimmy Gilmore's late 5y TD catch iced it for Cotton Bowl-bound TCU.

Arizona State 47 ARIZONA 0: HB Leon Burton (8/101y), who had derailed Arizona (3-7) previous year, was at it again for Sun Devils (6-3). Burton tallied game's opening 3 TDs: 18y screen pass reception from QB John Hangartner, and 48y and 11y TD sprints. Arizona State FB Ron Erhardt, future NFL O coordinator, slammed for 2 short TD runs. Under ASU's pass-rush pressure, Arizona QBs lost 53y net rushing. Frequent passes of Wildcats QB Ralph Hunsaker (14-25/146y) boosted SB Dave Hibbert to NCAA to-date record of 61 receptions for season. Hibbert overcame old mark of 57 set by Fordham's Ed Brown in 1952.

UCLA 15 Southern California 15: Perhaps tie failed to play well to weary cross-town combatants, but it was thriller for 58,507 partisans. After scoreless 1st H, Southern California (4-4-1) opened scoring when little HB Don Buford (14/101y) shot behind RT Ron Mix's block for 66y sprint to 1YL and QB Tom Maudlin (6-14/128y, 2 INTs) wedged across for 7-0 lead. Only 4 mins later, Trojans, again this season prone to bobbles, gave away silly, panicked backwards pitch FUM to Bruins G-LB Rod Cochran at their 6YL. UCLA (3-6-1) FB Ray Smith did high-flying leap, started years ago by Bruins FBs, for 1y TD. TB Billy Kilmer (24/92y rushing) rolled left, faked pass, and wedged past Trojans c-LB Ken Antle for 2 pts. So, UCLA led 8-7 with less than 4 mins left in 3rd Q. After missing FG, USC regained possession at its 30YL and moved to its 45YL. Here, Maudlin glided right and tossed pitchout for HB Angelo Coia, but in ball's path was Bruins DE John Brown, who scampered 45y for stunning TD and 15-7 lead 8 mins into 4th Q. Ensuing KO developed just as improbably as K Jim Steffen's short line-drive kick—purposely away from gnat HB Buford—went directly to USC E Luther Hayes who slipped past pair of tacklers and was home-free for 74y TD. Maudlin ran left and squeezed across for tying 2-pt run. USC had its late chances but INTs by DBs Kilmer and Phil Parslow and sack by NG Bob King killed Troy hopes.

CALIFORNIA 16 Stanford 15: Strawberry Canyon was populated by 81,490 fans, and, since many had to be advocates of 1958's new 2-pt rule, they must have enjoyed this dream game. Rose Bowl-bound California (7-3) twice made 2 pts to counter 2 TDs and FG by feisty Stanford (2-8). Golden Bears scored on long ground marches in 1st and 3rd Qs as HB Jack Hart scored each time and rushed for 103y. When QB Joe Kapp hit HB Wayne Crow with conv pass, Bears led 16-9 in 3rd Q. Indians seemed beaten when they took over on their own 22YL with less than 4 mins to play. Rally looked less likely after QB Dick Norman (19-35/222y, TD, INT) was trapped for 7y loss, but he proceeded to hit 4 passes. At end of 78y drive, Norman scrambled left and right before arching pass to EZ corner for 21y TD to E Joel Freis. Tribe FB Skip Face tried to sprint wide on 2-pt run for win, but was stacked up just short by FB-LB Bill Patton, G Jim Green, and Hart.

Washington State 18 WASHINGTON 14: Washington State (7-3) built early 12-0 lead, but couldn't successfully kick water-logged ball for x-pts. Huskies soph HB-K George Fleming made his 2 conv kicks—as would become his regular custom—after TDs by QB Bob Hivner and HB Mike McCluskey. So, Washington (3-7) enjoyed 14-12 H lead. Cougars rallied in 3rd Q on QB Dave Wilson's 7y TD pass to E Don Ellersick, and won their 4th of last 6 Evergreen State rivalry matches and copped 2nd place in PCC with 6-2 record.

AP Poll November 24

1 Louisiana State (115)	1445	11 Purdue	254
2 Auburn (5)	1083	12 Clemson (1)	242
3 Oklahoma (9)	1007	13 Mississippi	177
4 Iowa (16)	982	14 Florida	174
5 Army (1)	941	15 Vanderbilt	169
6 Wisconsin (3)	736	16 South Carolina	126
7 Texas Christian	722	17 California	103
8 Air Force (1)	512	18 Notre Dame	95
9 Ohio State (4)	360	19 Pittsburgh	91
10 Syracuse (1)	318	20 Rutgers	83

November 27-29, 1958

(Th'g) Penn State 25 PITTSBURGH 21: Celebrating their city's Bicentennial, Pittsburgh Panthers (5-4-1) used tenacious D to hold Nittany Lions to 12y rushing and jump to 14-0 H lead. Game turned on bad snap that forced Panthers E-P Mike Ditka to eat ball at Pitt 25YL. Penn State (6-3-1) quickly tallied TDs by FB Pat Botula and E Norm Neff to get to within 14-12. HB Chuck Reinhold raced 52y to extend Pittsburgh's lead to 21-12. In 4th Q, Lions QB Al Jacks found Neff for another TD. With 6 mins left, Penn State HB Jim Kerr made critical 43y punt RET to Pitt 28YL to launch HB Don Jonas' winning TD run.

Army 22 Navy 6 (Philadelphia): Navy (6-3), wearing blue helmets that made them look remarkably like Chicago Bears, covered opening KO FUM by Army HB Pete Dawkins in stomach of G George Fritzinger. Middies immediately sprung varied array of flankers and double-reverse runs for 6-0 lead on 3y TD run by soph HB Joe Bellino (14/45y, and 6/40y receiving). However, FB-K Ray Wellborn missed x-pt kick partly due to ripped shoe instep. Excited Middies soon set sail 74y downfield, but turnabout for Army (8-0-1) came as FB-LB Harry Walters stopped Bellino at 15YL for 2y loss on 4th-and-2 run. It took awhile but Cadets went up 7-6 just before H and 14-6 on 1st play of 4th Q as sparkling workhorse HB Bob Anderson (29/89y) scored behind block of G Bob Novogratz. G-LB star Novogratz had fallen on 2 FUM RECs to keep O possession for Army and had stopped critical series in middle of Navy-dominated 1st Q when Bellino lost FUM near midfield. Down 14-6, Midshipmen still retained chance to earn tie when it received punt at its 28YL with 2:45 to play. Clincher quickly was delivered by Army's "Gregarious" E-DE Don Usry (5/80y) who dropped into left flank on pass coverage to pick off QB Joe Tranchini's swing pass for FB Ray Wellborn and take it 38y to TD. Perfect ending to Army's storybook year saw HB Pete Dawkins hit HB-mate

Anderson with left-handed 2-pt pass. Army QB Joe Caldwell passed effectively with 10-18/145y, 2 INTs. Black Knights' Earl Blaik would bow out with 166-48-14 mark after 25 years of coaching. As parting word, he offered that his team was best in nation, saying, "When our team is functioning at 100 percent efficiency—when it is running and passing as it can—I don't think any team in the country can contain it."

GEORGIA 16 Georgia Tech 3: Underdog Bulldogs (4-6) surprised Georgia Tech (5-4-1) with stiff D that survived harrowing 3rd Q. In 1st H, Georgia built 9-0 lead as T Larry Lancaster blocked Yellow Jackets E-P Gerald Burch's punt, and E Jimmy Vickers scooped up ball at 20YL and carried it across for TD and 6-0 edge. With 10 secs left before H, Bulldogs C-K Dave Lloyd booted FG. Georgia Tech recovered 3 FUMs in 3rd Q, all in Georgia territory. All Jackets got to show for it was K Tommy Wells' late 3rd Q FG because 2 earlier stabs were halted by UGa QB-DB Charley Britt's hard tackle-for-loss on Tech HB Cal James on 4th-and-2 at 3YL and Tech QB Walter Howard being stopped inches short on 4th down scramble to 17YL. HB-P Bobby Walden got Georgia out of hole in 4th Q with 63y punt against stiff wind before HB Fred Brown (10/80y) iced verdict with 33y TD run after Britt's INT in last 4 mins.

Auburn 14 ALABAMA 8: Tigers (9-0-1) went 24th straight game without defeat as new-found passing wizard QB Richard Wood led 2 TD drives, including TD pass to HB Jimmy Pettus. With 7 mins left, Alabama (5-4-1) stoked flame with HB Marlin Dyess' TD and QB Bobby Jackson's 2-pt pass. Crimson Tide reached Auburn 28YL with 1:26 to play, but Tigers HB-DB Lamar Rawson batted away Jackson's pass at GL to help nation's best D (157.5y per game) halt rolling Tide's last surge.

Tennessee 10 VANDERBILT 6: Game ended with 2 fighting ejections and many spectators on field, like end of Chattanooga's early November upset of Volunteers, brawlingest bunch of 1958. Tennessee (4-6) soph TB Billy Majors came off bench in 2nd Q to spark its upset over Vanderbilt (5-2-3). Majors capped 91y drive with 3y TD pass to E Mike LaSorsa. Soph E-K Cotton Letner added 20y FG in 3rd Q after Vols were stalled at 3YL. Vandy, stopped thrice inside Vols 10YL during game, finally scored on 4th Q pass to E Fred Riggs.

MISSISSIPPI 21 Mississippi State 0: QB Bobby Franklin ran for 8y TD and passed for 2 others in sparking Gator Bowl-bound Ole Miss (8-2). Rebels scored all their TDs in 2nd Q, capitalizing on HB HB Cowboy Woodruff's good punt RET, FUM REC in Mississippi State territory, and long sustained march. Punchless Bulldogs (3-6) managed only 8 1st downs and completed only 2 passes/51y.

FLORIDA 12 Miami 9: Gator Bowl called Florida (6-3-1) held on to beat Hurricanes (1-8) after building 12-0 lead in 3rd Q. Top punting by HB-P Bobby Joe Green, and QBs-Ps Jimmy Dunn and Mickey Ellenburg into stiff wind provided consistent field position which eventuated FB Jon MacBeth's 1st Q TD plunge. Hot-and-cold QB Bonnie Yarborough rallied Miami on 4th Q TD pass and had Florida biting its nails with moves to Gator 19, 23, and 11YLs before FUM was lost at 7YL with 2 mins left.

Oklahoma 7 OKLAHOMA STATE 0: Each school was headed to bowl: Oklahoma (9-1) to Orange Bowl and Oklahoma State (7-3) possibly to Sugar or Cotton, but ended up in Blue Grass Bowl. As plucky, under-recruited Cowboys so often had accomplished during Oklahoma Sooners' 1950s rampage, they played extraordinary D during their alternate-year home game against OU. Despite its 3-TD underdog status, Oklahoma State outplayed its rivals most of game and at end trailed in total y only 196y to 187y. Oklahoma State covered 2nd Q FUM by OU HB Brewster Hobby on punt RET at 14YL, but Sooners FB-LB Prentice Gautt exploded this opportunity by throwing FB Vernon Sewell for 7y loss and forcing missed FG try by E-K Jim Wood. Cowpokes appeared to have earned 0-0 tie when they halted 4 cracks at their 1YL in middle of 4th Q. But, P Wood's return punt was taken to Oke State 35YL. On 3rd-and-6, 2nd-team Sooners QB Bobby Boyd checked off to option pitch to right, and after faking pitchout to trailing LHB, Boyd cut in and dashed by S for 31y TD run and 7-0 win.

Air Force 20 COLORADO 14: Miraculous Air Force (8-0-1) completed undefeated season with stirring GLS with 8 secs to go. Colorado (6-4) D halted Falcons' vaunted passing, permitting only 39y. Buffaloes held 14-6 H edge on QB Boyd Dowler's 7y TD pass and WB Eddie Dove's 31y TD run. HB Mike Quinlan raced 60y to 3rd Q TD, but otherwise Air Force needed 6 FUM RECs to help catch up to Buffs. Key bobble came in 3rd Q as Falcons HB-DB Mike Rawlins charged 20y with mid-air FUM for go-ahead score.

SOUTHERN METHODIST 20 Texas Christian 13: Even though he lost FUM at Horned Frogs 10YL, Southern Methodist (6-4) QB Don Meredith threw TD pass to each of his HBs, Tirey Wilemon and Glynn Gregory, smashed 2y for his own TD, and ran for 2-pt conv in upset of Cotton Bowl-bound TCU (8-2). TCU had scored 1st on QB Hunter Enis' 21y pass, but spent much of its 222y rushing to escape its own territory. G-LB Tommy Koenig anchored Mustangs D which forced Frogs into miserable air game: 6-23/54y.

HOUSTON 22 Texas Tech 17: Red Raiders (3-7) scored twice on short 1st Q drives after their D coerced pair of Houston (5-4) punts from Cougars 1YL. HB Floyd Dellinger plunged for 1y TD and caught 8y TD pass from QB Jerry Bell to put Texas Tech in front 14-0. Houston QB Lonnie Holland, who threw for 160y, tossed 1st of his 2 TD passes to E Bob Borah in 2nd Q. Trailing 14-6 in 3rd Q, Cougars sprung HB Harold Lewis loose for game's pivotal play: Lewis streaked 64y on punt TD RET, and Holland flipped 2-pt pass for 14-14 knot. And even though K Bell nailed 20y FG for 17-14 Tech lead, momentum belonged to Cougars, who looked to Holland, transfer from Oklahoma Sooners, to throw winning 22y TD pass to HB Billy Ray Dickey in 4th Q.

Notre Dame 20 SOUTHERN CALIFORNIA 13: Terry Brennan's weary Notre Dame (6-4) warriors, playing what turned out to be their last game for young and pressured coach, managed brilliant GLS in early 4th Q to win 30th meeting with USC (4-5-1). Trailing 6-0 after 6 mins of 1st Q, Trojans went ahead 7-6 as HB Don Buford swept right and rifled 52y TD pass to E Hilliard Hill. USC went 34y to lift its lead to 13-6 as HB

Jerry Traynham scored from 1y out. Irish traveled 70y to TD, but E-K Monty Stickles missed his 2nd x-pt kick, so Troy retained 13-12 H lead. ND went 63y to winning TD after 2nd H KO with QB Bob Williams, back in at QB for George Izo who suffered 3 INTs. Williams, who earlier in season went from sr A-A candidate to bench-warmer, pitched 21y TD to E Bob Wetoska and followed with 2-pt pass. Notre Dame's GLS started as USC HB Clark Holden made 1st down inside 1YL. Holden lost ft on 1st down, and Holden had no gains on next 2 plays. Woozy LB Bob Scholtz was replaced by LB Myron Pottios, who was key stopper on Buford's 4th down sprint off RT.

Final AP Poll December 1

1 Louisiana State (130)	1904	11 Mississippi (2)	303
2 Iowa (17)	1459	12 Clemson (1)	246
3 Army (13)	1429	13 Purdue	196
4 Auburn (9)	1396	14 Florida	134
5 Oklahoma (10)	1200	15 South Carolina	101
6 Air Force (2)	800	16 California	78
7 Wisconsin (13)	797	17 Notre Dame (1)	61
8 Ohio State (3)	571	18 Southern Methodist	52
9 Syracuse (1)	340	19 Oklahoma State	49
10 Texas Christian	311	20 Rutgers (1)	46

1958 Conference Standings

Ivy League

Dartmouth	6-1
Princeton	5-2
Cornell	5-2
Brown	4-3
Pennsylvania	4-3
Harvard	3-4
Columbia	1-6
Yale	0-7

Atlantic Coast

Clemson	5-1
South Carolina	5-2
Duke	3-2
North Carolina	4-3
Maryland	3-3
Wake Forest	2-4
North Carolina State	2-5
Virginia	1-5

Southern

West Virginia	4-0
Virginia Tech	3-1
George Washington	3-2
Virginia Military	2-2-1
Richmond	3-4
Davidson	2-3
Citadel	2-3
Furman	1-2
William & Mary	1-4-1

Southeastern

Louisiana State	6-0
Auburn	6-0-1
Mississippi	4-2
Vanderbilt	2-1-3
Tennessee	4-3
Kentucky	3-4-1
Alabama	3-4-1
Florida	2-3-1
Georgia Tech	2-3-1
Georgia	2-4
Tulane	1-5
Mississippi State	1-6

Big Ten

Iowa	5-1
Wisconsin	5-1-1
Ohio State	4-1-2
Purdue	3-1-2
Indiana	3-2-1
Illinois	4-3
Northwestern	3-4
Michigan	1-5-1
Minnesota	1-6
Michigan State	0-5-1

Big Eight

Oklahoma	6-0
Missouri	4-1-1
Colorado	4-2
Kansas	3-2-1
Kansas State	2-4
Nebraska	1-5
Iowa State	0-6
Oklahoma State *	2-1
* Ineligible	

Missouri Valley

North Texas State	2-1-1
Tulsa	2-2
Cincinnati	1-1-2
Houston	2-2
Wichita	1-2-1
Drake *	0-3
* Ineligible	

Mid-American

Miami (Ohio)	5-0
Kent State	5-1
Bowling Green	4-2
Ohio	2-4
Western Michigan	2-4
Toledo	1-4
Marshall	1-5

Southwest

Texas Christian	5-1
Southern Methodist	4-2
Rice	4-2
Texas	3-3
Arkansas	2-4
Texas A&M	2-4
Baylor	1-5
Texas Tech *	1-4
* Ineligible	

Border

Hardin-Simmons	4-0
Arizona State	4-1
Arizona	2-1
New Mexico State	1-3
Texas Western	1-4
West Texas State	1-4

Skyline Eight

Wyoming	6-1
New Mexico	5-1
Brigham Young	5-2
Colorado State	4-3
Utah	3-3
Utah State	2-5
Denver	2-5
Montana	0-7

Pacific Coast

California	6-1
Washington State	6-2
Southern California	4-2-1
Oregon State	5-3
Oregon	4-4
UCLA	2-4-1
Stanford	2-5
Washington	1-6
Idaho	0-3

1958 Major Bowl Games
Gator Bowl (Dec. 27): Mississippi 7 Florida 3

Dreadful sea of mud neutralized Ole Miss' speed advantage and also slowed small Florida (6-4) backfield in rarely-engaged intra-SEC match. As it happened, Mississippi led all-time series 6-1-1. Contest on well-worn field evolved into struggle of stout Ds, which was both teams' strength. Rebels (9-2) QB-P Bobby Franklin won MVP honors by guiding opening 70y drive and 2 well-directed punts inside 10YL. But, Franklin accidently kicked his star FB Charley Flowers in head during early going. In Flowers' place barged sub FB Jim Anderson, who scored TD from 1y out in 1st Q. Little Florida (6-4-1) QB Jimmy Dunn scooted 56y with ensuing KO, and Gators soon reached 11YL where Ole Miss D dug in to hold. So, HB-K Billy Booker kicked 27y FG to pull Gators to within 7-3. In 4th Q, Florida menaced Ole Miss GL after HB-P Bobby Joe Green's 76y QK was recovered by Gators as it was accidently touched by Rebels at their 10YL. T Bull Churchwell caused and recovered FUM by Dunn. Stiff Rebels D held again at 2YL: Florida's pint-sized backs, missing HB Bernie Parish since he had signed with baseball's Cincinnati Reds in early 1958, were no match for big Ole Miss line in heavy footing of sopped playing surface.

Orange Bowl: Oklahoma 21 Syracuse 6

Exhibiting a new fake counter, long lateral play in opening 3 mins, Oklahoma (10-1) sprung FB Prentice Gautt (6/94y, TD) on 10y run to right and 42y TD jaunt to left with E Joe Rector throwing big block. Later in 1st Q, Sooners stopped 53y drive of Syracuse (8-2) at OU 19YL. On 2nd play after lost FUM by Orangemen HB Tom Stephens, Oklahoma HB Brewster Hobby launched 79y TD pass to E Ross Coyle with Rector throwing 2 key blocks for 14-0 lead. Late in 3rd Q, Syracuse's highly-reliable G-P Tom Gilburg experienced punter's nightmare: kicking low liner from deep in his own territory. Alertly charging Hobby returned it for 40y TD faster than Sooners could expect in blocking pattern. Playing through mistake-filled, lackluster affair, Syracuse still enjoyed 239y to 152y rushing advantage, and finally cashed in with 69y TD drive in 4th Q. Orangemen HB Mark Weber doggedly pushed over TD from 15YL.

Sugar Bowl: Louisiana State 7 Clemson 0

Coming off undefeated season with its crushing 62-0 climax against rival Tulane, national champion LSU (11-0) was mildly disappointing in its effort. Feisty 17-pt underdog Clemson (8-3) played as if it had nothing to lose and made tremendous effort for moral victory. Perhaps Clemson played without nerves, thanks to coach Frank Howard's team-effacing comparison to LSU's ferocious Chinese Bandits: "My boys play like a bunch of one-armed bandits." Clemson's "One-Armed Bandits" profited when LSU QB Warren Rabb became one-armed in 1st Q, sidelined by broken passing hand. In 2nd Q, LSU managed promising drive, fueled by courageous Rabb's 26y aerial to E Mickey Mangum and Rabb's 13y sweep. But, Bayou Bengals FB Red Brodnax crashed to GL and lost FUM through EZ before he could register TD. So, score stayed 0-0. Bad punt snap by C Paul Snyder finally killed Clemson chances in 3rd Q with LSU taking over at Clemson 11YL on T Duane Leopard's REC. LSU HB-P Billy Cannon, whose game MVP award was as much for his fine punting as his O, whipped perfect 9y TD pass to Mangum in back of EZ for game's only score. Clemson's last scoring bid reached LSU 24YL on pass catches for 12y each by Es Wyatt Cox and Sam Anderson. Celebrated Chinese Bandits unit forced 2 incompletions by Clemson QB Harvey White to end threat.

Cotton Bowl: Texas Christian 0 Air Force 0

Army and Notre Dame played college football's most famous scoreless tie in their epic 1946 battle. Fordham and Pittsburgh, giants of Great Depression years, played 0-0 deadlocks in 1935, 1936, and 1937. This Cotton Bowl deadlock, last-ever scoreless matchup between Top 10 opponents, proved how worthy underappreciated Falcons (9-0-2) truly could be. They finished remarkable debut on national stage as their academy's only undefeated team in history. Pigskin deadlock in Dallas also displayed D might of TCU (8-2-1), team that would send 4 of its stars to NFL: Ts Don Floyd (Oilers), Joe Robb (Cardinals) and Bob Lilly (Cowboys) and G-LB Sherrill Headrick (Chiefs). Both sides suffered lost opportunities on O: Air Force HB-K George Pupich missed 3 FGs, and Purple Frogs FB-K Jack Spikes missed 2 FG tries. Spikes, however, was voted top back by rushing for 108y of TCU's 227y run total. Air Force threatened early with sorties to 6 and 15YLs. Horned Frogs menaced Falcons late with two deep invasions into AFA territory. Numerous FUMs piled atop missed FGs translated into scoreless draw.

Rose Bowl: Iowa 35 California 12

Hawkeyes speed piled upon more Hawkeyes speed poisoned 1st Rose Bowl trip for California (7-4) since January 1951. Iowa (8-1-1) scorched Pasadena's record books: HB Bob Jeter raced 81y in 3rd Q, longest run from scrimmage to date in Rose Bowl history. Jeter (9/194y, TD) also set records for rushing y gained at that point in time, and his 21.6y rush avg still stands today. Hawkeyes set or tied 3 team O records: 429y rushing, 516y total O, and 24 1st downs. Jeter's HB-mate out of Iowa's wicked Wing-T, Willie Fleming (9/85y), scored 2 TDs with his own impressive 9.4y rush avg. California (7-4) had gotten early break on FUM REC at Hawks 27YL, but 3rd-and-1 play went awry and 4th down pass was pressured into failure. Iowa led 20-0 at H until Golden Bears HB Jack Hart scored twice, on 1y plunge early in 3rd Q and on 17y reception from QB Joe Kapp in game's last min. Hart's 1st TD gave brief life to Bears as they drew within 20-6, but Fleming (37y) and Jeter (81y) made long TDs before 3rd Q ended. Game brought down curtain on star-crossed Pacific Coast Conf, as its teams showed pale 1-12 Rose Bowl mark against Big 10 bullies since joint-conf contract was affected in 1946. Soon-to-be-created AAWU, with many of same schools, would fare far better.

1958 Top Performance Formula

1 Louisiana State	1.7608	
2 Army	1.6969	
3 Oklahoma	1.6941	
4 Air Force	1.6634	
5 Iowa	1.6484	
6 Auburn	1.5666	
7 Syracuse	1.4904	
8 Wisconsin	1.4799	
9 Mississippi	1.4662	
10 Purdue	1.4622	
11 Ohio State	1.4600	
12 Texas Christian	1.4482	
13 Oklahoma State	1.4206	
14 Clemson	1.3481	
15 Rutgers	1.3347	
16 Notre Dame	1.3132	
17 Boston College	1.3005	
18 Penn State	1.2577	
19 Washington State	1.2539	
20 Southern Methodist	1.2412	

1958 Top Opponent Records

1 Notre Dame	.6802
2 Iowa	.6724
3 Mississippi State	.6425
4 Oklahoma State	.6324
5 Ohio State	.6267
6 Air Force	.6225
7 Rice	.6222
8 Tennessee	.6209
9 Kentucky	.6022
10 Georgia	.6196
11 Purdue	.5933
12 Nebraska	.5889
13 Miami	.5843
14 Florida	.5800
15 Houston	.5783
16 Georgia Tech	.5761
17 Louisiana State	.5735
18 Southern Methodist	.5722
19 Wake Forest	.5707
20t Indiana	.56667
20t Northwestern	.56667

1958 Out-of-Conference Records

	W-L	Percentage	Bowl W-L
Southeastern	30-9	.7692	2-1
Big Ten	18-6-1	.7400	1-0
Big Eight	20-16	.5556	2-0
Southwest	15-13-1	.5345	0-0-1
Pacific Coast	11-17	.3929	0-1
Atlantic Coast	11-19-1	.3710	0-1

1958 Individual Statistical Leaders

RUSHING YARDS	Attempts	Yards	Avg.
Dick Bass, Pacific	205	1361	6.6
Bob White, Ohio State	218	859	3.9
Dwight Nichols, Iowa State	220	815	3.7
Pete Hart, Hardin-Simmons	163	785	4.8
Billy Austin, Rutgers	145	747	5.2
Jake Crouthamel, Dartmouth	123	722	5.9
Weldon Jackson, Brigham Young	101	698	6.9
Billy Cannon, Louisiana State	115	686	6.0
Larry Hickman, Baylor	151	670	4.4
John Saunders, South Carolina	128	653	5.1

PASSING YARDS	Completions	Attempts	Yards	Pct.
Randy Duncan, Iowa	101	172	1347	58.7
Buddy Humphrey, Baylor	112	195	1316	57.4
John Hangartner, Arizona State	67	121	1210	55.4
Jack Cummings, North Carolina	68	134	1137	50.7
Charlie Milstead, Texas A&M	88	167	1135	52.7
Ralph Hunsaker, Arizona	106	191	1129	55.5
Joe Caldwell, Army	54	121	1097	44.6
George Izo, Notre Dame	60	118	1067	50.8
Rich Mayo, Air Force	98	174	1019	56.3
Billy Holsclaw, Virginia Tech	70	127	1013	55.1

RECEIVING YARDS	Catches	Yards
Rich Krietling, Illinois	23	688
Sonny Randle, Virginia	47	642
Dave Hibbert, Arizona	61	606
Chris Burford, Stanford	45	493
Bob Simms, Rutgers	33	468
John Tracey, Texas A&M	37	466
Jimmy Colclough, Boston College	24	462
Carroll Dale, Virginia Tech	25	457
Bill Carpenter, Army	22	453
Sammy Oates, Hardin-Simmons	31	402

1958 Consensus All-America Team

End:
    Buddy Dial, Rice
    Sam Williams, Michigan State
Tackle:
    Ted Bates, Oregon State
    Brock Strom, Air Force
Guard:
    John Guzik, Pittsburgh
    Zeke Smith, Auburn
    George Deiderich, Vanderbilt
Center:
    Bob Harrison, Oklahoma
Back:
    Randy Duncan, Iowa
    Pete Dawkins, Army
    Billy Cannon, Louisiana State
    Bob White, Ohio State

Other All-America Choices

End:
    Jim Houston, Ohio State
    Al Goldstein, North Carolina
    Monty Stickles, Notre Dame
    Jim Wood, Oklahoma State
    Curt Merz, Iowa
Tackle:
    Jim Marshall, Ohio State
    Ron Luciano, Syracuse
    Hogan Wharton, Houston
    Andy Cvercko, Northwestern
    Don Floyd, Texas Christian
    Vel Heckman, Florida
    Gene Selawski, Purdue
Guard:
    Al Ecuyer, Notre Dame
    John Wooten, Colorado
    Bob Novogratz, Army
Center:
    Jackie Burkett, Auburn
    Max Fugler, Louisiana State
Back:
    Don Meredith, Southern Methodist
    Joe Kapp, California
    Bob Anderson, Army
    Billy Austin, Rutgers
    Nick Pietrosante, Notre Dame

1958 Heisman Trophy Vote

Pete Dawkins, senior HB, Army	1394
Randy Duncan, senior QB, Iowa	1021
Billy Cannon, junior HB, Louisiana State	975
Bob White, junior FB, Ohio State	365
Joe Kapp, senior QB, California	227

Other Major Awards

Maxwell (Player)	Pete Dawkins, senior HB, Army
Outland (Lineman)	Zeke Smith, junior G, Auburn
Walter Camp (Back)	Randy Duncan, senior QB, Iowa
Knute Rockne (Lineman)	Bob Novogratz, senior G, Army
AFCA Coach of the Year	Paul Dietzel, Louisiana State

1959

The Year of the Orange Champion, Halloween Cannon Boom, and Wild Card Rule

The 1950s ended with its accustomed dash of unpredictability. The stories of three bowl winners—Syracuse, Washington and Mississippi—were central to the near-term future trends of the uproarious 1960s.

Syracuse (11-0) won its only national title, building one of the greatest statistical edges over its opponents of any team in any season. Syracuse outrushed its foes 3,136 to 193 yards, outscored them 390 to 59, and ranked first in the nation in both total offense and defense. In addition to sweeping both AP and UPI national championships, Syracuse also won the first MacArthur Bowl.

The Orangemen featured several African-American players, including stars in halfback Ernie Davis, fullback Art Baker, and tackle John Brown. Many schools would follow Syracuse, tapping an ever-growing black talent pool during the 1960s with the SEC, the last holdout, eventually integrating its teams in the 1970s.

Syracuse hardly was the first to put black players in important football roles. Ivy League halfback Fritz Pollard of Brown won All-American mention in 1916. Rutgers end Paul Robeson was a two-time All-America in 1917 and 1918. Iowa tackle Duke Slater was a star in the 1920s. UCLA featured three black stars in its backfield in the late 1930s and early '40s: Kenny Washington, Woody Strode, and Jackie Robinson of Brooklyn Dodger baseball fame. The greatness of Jimmy Brown, Orangemen halfback in 1954-56 and especially as fullback with the Cleveland Browns, made playing at Syracuse a great attraction for outstanding African-American athletes.

Before Syracuse could claim its national title, it won a bitter, fight-plagued January 1, 1960, Cotton Bowl over the all-white Texas Longhorns (9-2), champions of the Southwest Conference. There were on-field problems among the athletes. Texas players were accused of racial epithets that prompted animosity during a game in which Davis starred defensively and scored twice, including an 87-yard touchdown pass for the game's first score.

Employing hard-nosed Oklahoma-style football brought west by coach Jim Owens, Washington (10-1) won the inaugural Athletic Association of Western Universities (AAWU) championship in 1959. In the Rose Bowl, the Huskies stunned Wisconsin (7-3) 44-8 and turned the tide in favor of the previously-frustrated Pacific Coast schools. Even with Washington's astonishing upset, the Big Ten had won 12 of the first 14 Rose Bowls since the Big Ten started coming to Pasadena on an annual basis. When the game was over, Wisconsin found itself having suffered both Big Ten losses (1953 and 1960). In the next 27 Rose Bowl games that followed January 1, 1960, western schools won 20 times.

Mississippi (10-1) lost the year's thriller to early-season no. 1 Louisiana State (9-2), but gained vengence with a smooth 21-0 win in a rematch with the Bayou Bengals in the Sugar Bowl. The 1959 season began a magnificent five-year run of 43-2-3 for the Rebels. The only schools with comparable five-year records during the last 55 years are Oklahoma (1954-58) at 51-2, Alabama (1961-65) at 49-5-1, Penn State (1967-71) at 48-6-1, Michigan (1970-74) at 50-4-1, Oklahoma (1971-75) at 54-3-1, Miami (1987-91) at 56-4, Nebraska (1993-97) at 60-3, Florida State (1995-99) at 55-6, and Southern California (2003-07) at 58-6.

On a muggy Halloween night in Baton Rouge, LSU and Mississippi authored one of the legendary games of football history. Late in the game, Heisman Trophy winner-in-waiting Billy Cannon of the Tigers fielded a bounding punt on his own 11 yard-line, wriggled through six Ole Miss tacklers and went 89 exhausting yards to a touchdown for a 7-3 win. The fact that Tennessee (5-4-1) knocked no. 1 LSU from the unbeaten ranks a week later and that the Rebels dominated the Sugar Bowl over LSU are facts far less remembered than Cannon's storied late October boom.

Not since the turn of the century, when dropkickers such as Pat O'Dea of Wisconsin roamed the fruited plain, had the foot played so important a role in college. In 1959, the NCAA widened the goalposts to 23 feet 4 inches from 18 feet 6 inches, a more than 20 percent increase. A new rule allowed entry of one player per side whenever the clock was stopped. This "Wild Card" inspired the use of kicking specialists, and points scored by field goals nearly doubled. Karl Holzwarth of Wisconsin kicked a record seven field goals. Randy Sims of Texas A&M (3-7) made a 59-yard placekick—which exceeded the existing NFL mark of 56 yards by Bert Rechichar of the Baltimore Colts—although O'Dea had registered a 65-yard dropkick in 1898.

Another amazing boot came off the foot of John Hadl of Kansas (5-5), a 94-yard punt against Oklahoma (7-3), which won the Big 8 crown but had its worst season since 1945. The downturn started when several Sooners suffered suspicious bouts of food poisoning before an opening-game trouncing from Northwestern (6-3). The team dined at a Chicago restaurant on Thursday night. Sooner players later mentioned waitresses seemed to pinpoint players by asking what positions they played as fruit cocktail was served. On Halloween, Nebraska (4-6) tricked Oklahoma 25-21 and administered the Sooners' first defeat in 73 consecutive league games, dating back to a 16-13 loss to Kansas in 1946.

Another Big 8 team enjoyed a bit of a renaissance and coined an endearing nickname. Iowa State (7-3) had endured a 26-55-4 record in the previous nine years of the 1950s. The Cyclones were a small, close-knit group, playing the ancient Single Wing offense under second-year coach Clay Stapleton, and had only 30 players on its squad. Trainer Warren Arail shouted, "Here comes the 'Dirty Thirty'," after a 41-0 season-opening win over Drake. The next week, Iowa State went to Denver to beat the Pioneers 28-14, and sports information director Harry Burrell was stringing a post-game story to the *Des Moines Register.* Burrell picked up on the players' enjoyment of the Dirty Thirty moniker and made it famous, at least statewide, with his newspaper article.

Summer meetings among several schools nearly created a new national conference, based not on the traditional formula of regional familiarity, but on the previous year's introduction of domestic jet air service by National Airlines. The idea soon evaporated, but came close to changing the face of college football dramatically. Proposed members were Air Force, Army, Navy, Notre Dame, Penn State, Southern California, Pittsburgh, Syracuse, and UCLA.

The Ivy League, of all places, created the year's biggest coaching controversy. Steve Sebo of Pennsylvania (7-1-1) guided the Quakers to the league title in the fourth year of official Ivy competition. For his efforts, Sebo was promptly fired, despite his excellent season. Amazingly, Sebo had survived a 19-game losing streak in 1954-55 when Penn scheduled powerhouses like Notre Dame, Penn State, Army, and Navy.

Milestones

■ Rules Committee made two major changes. Goalposts were widened from 18 feet 6 inches to 23 feet 4 inches. "Wild Card" rule permitted coaches to substitute one player into lineups at any time when clock was stopped.

■ Athletic Association of Western Universities (AAWU), also known as The Big Five, was formed from ashes of Pacific Coast Conference. Charter members were California, California at Los Angeles (UCLA), Southern California, Stanford and Washington. Old PCC members Idaho, Oregon, Oregon State and Washington State became independents. Oregon and Washington State played unusual home-and-home set of games in 1959.

■ North Carolina coach Jim Tatum became ill on July 16 and died abruptly at age 45 of Rocky Mountain spotted fever. Former Yale All-America and noted collegiate referee Albie Booth died at age 51. Col. Charles Daly, 78, had been Army head coach (1913-16, 1919-22) who coached President Dwight D. Eisenhower when he was Cadet.

■ Longest winning streaks entering season:

Louisiana State 12	Mississippi Southern 9	Oklahoma 8

■ Coaching Changes

	Incoming	Outgoing
Arizona	Jim LaRue	Ed Doherty
Army	Dale Hall	Earl "Red" Blaik
Baylor	John Bridgers	Sam Boyd
Brigham Young	Tally Stevens	Hal Kopp
Brown	John McLaughery	Alva Kelley
Colorado	Sonny Grandelius	Dallas Ward
Florida State	Perry Moss	Tom Nugent
Maryland	Tom Nugent	Tommy Mont
Michigan	Bump Elliott	Bennie Oosterbaan
Navy	Wayne Hardin	Eddie Erdelatz
North Carolina	Jim Hickey	Jim Tatum
Notre Dame	Joe Kuharich	Terry Brennan

Preseason AP Poll

1 Louisiana State (60)	1440	11 Purdue (2)	394
2 Oklahoma (48)	1370	12 North Carolina (6)	388
3 Auburn (17)	1047	13 Texas Christian (2)	249
4 Southern Methodist (6)	720	14 South Carolina (4)	228
5 Army (6)	696	15 Air Force (1)	209
6 Wisconsin (10)	645	16 Notre Dame (3)	202
7 Ohio State (2)	548	17 Texas	105
8 Mississippi (5)	546	18 Clemson (1)	92
9 Iowa (4)	443	19 Michigan State (1)	51
10 Northwestern (6)	441	20 Syracuse	47

September 19, 1959

Clemson 20 NORTH CAROLINA 18: Trying to get over shock of head coach Jim Tatum's death, North Carolina (0-1) lost squeaker to Clemson (1-0). Coach Frank Howard's Tigers burst to 14-0 lead when QB Harvey White scored after Tar Heels HB Milam Wall lost FUM on opening KO and FB Doug Cline bulled over in 2nd Q. North Carolina converted FUM REC for TD as QB Jack Cummings set up score with 25y pass to E John Schroeder. HB Bill Mathis put Tigers up 20-6 after 65y drive following 2nd H KO. Wall scored twice in 4th Q, but Clemson broke up 3rd unsuccessful 2-pt pass try by Cummings with 1:20 left.

MARYLAND 27 West Virginia 7: Soph QB Dick Novak threw 3 TD passes in more wide-open Maryland (1-0) I-formation O under new coach Tom Nugent. Terps E Tony Scotti (6y) and Gary Collins (15y) and HB Jim Davidson (40y) caught Novak's TD passes. E-K Vince Scott became 1st Terrapin to succeed on 3 FGs in single game as his 3-ptrs soared 31, 41, and 48y. Scott's last FG, coming in 4th Q, broke school record of 47y held by Dick Bielski. West Virginia (0-1) stuck mostly to ground attack to trump its weight advantage in line, but used 2 completions and PEN to lead to its only score on QB Carmen Pomponio's 3y TD run. WVU was halted at Maryland's 1, 4, and 12YLs.

GEORGIA 17 Alabama 3: Flashing scrambling ability he would exhibit for 18 years in NFL, Georgia (1-0) QB Fran Tarkenton ran 19y to set up his clinching 4th Q 1y sneak. Several key catches were made by Bulldogs E Gordon Kelley, leading to FB Bill Godfrey's 40y TD dash. Alabama (0-1) fashioned steady drive with 2nd H KO, only to see it fizzle in Bulldogs territory. So, T-K Fred Sington stepped back to boot 23y FG for Bama's only pts.

Wake Forest 22 FLORIDA STATE 20: Wake Forest (1-0) scored twice in last 7 mins to visit exciting, if losing, debut to new Florida State (0-1) coach Perry Moss. Seminoles threatened early with HB-P Jack Espenship's 30y run off fake punt and HB Fred Pickard's nullified 44y TD catch and run. But Wake scored 1st on K Nick Patella's 29y FG after FB Joe Bonecutter's 17y draw run. Pass interference PEN wiped out FSU QB-DB Joe Majors' INT, so Deacons were able to score just before H on 11y pass from QB Norm Snead (8-20/127y, 2 TDs, 2 INTs) to E Bill Hull for 9-0 lead. Snead's poorly-looped pass early in 3rd Q was picked off by Pickard, who romped to 26y TD. Florida State pass D struck again early in 4th Q as HB-DB Bud Whitehead intercepted Snead and meandered 81y to for 13-9 lead. T John Spivey blocked Wake punt with 9:32 to go to set up TD pass by Majors for 20-9 Seminoles lead. But, Snead fired 37y pass to set up his 4th down 10y TD fling to E Bobby Allen, and when G Paul Martineau recovered FUM at FSU 39YL with 2:45 on clock, Snead whipped 36y pass to Allen before HB Bobby Robinson, future Clemson AD, skirted E for winning TD.

LOUISIANA STATE 26 Rice 3: Surprising Rice (0-1) took 3-0 H lead on HB-K Gordon Speer's 46y FG. But, no. 1 Bengal Tigers (1-0) rallied behind their deeper manpower afforded by 3 separate units to wear down flagging Owls in 2nd H. LSU T Lynn LeBlanc had spectacular blocking effort on 17y TD, and HB Billy Cannon faked pass and cantered away from diving tackle attempt by Rice QB-DB Jon Schnable for 7-3 lead in 3rd Q. Tigers affected 19-pt avalanche in 4th Q: After LSU HB-K Wendell Harris made 33y FG, Chinese Bandits got rare chance on O because DB Merle Schnexnaildre made quick INT of Schnable's pass and returned it 15y to Owls 20YL. Bandit-unit HB Tommy Neck scored TD from 3YL just 4 plays later.

Penn State 19 MISSOURI 8: Sr Penn State QB "Rollout" Richie Lucas rushed 7/58y and completed 10-11/154y, including 52y TD to HB Jim Kerr. Nittany Lions (1-0) held Missouri (0-1) outside their 30YL while building 19-0 lead, which included short TD runs by HB Dick Hoak and FB Pat Botula. Tigers managed 197y rushing, but took to air for late TD on tricky reverse pass from HB Donnie Smith to E Russ Sloan, and QB Phil Snowden followed with 2-pt pass to E Danny LaRose.

Washington 21 COLORADO 12: Washington (1-0) QB Bob Schloredt's 6 punts/57y avg significantly negated Colorado (0-1) O, but Buffaloes QB-DB Gale Weidner galloped 94y with INT to keep Huskies' H edge within 1 pt at 7-6. HB Carver Gayton's 6y TD run put Washington ahead 14-6 in 3rd Q. Huskies got gift on ensuing KO when Buffs HB Jerry Steffen watched it sail over head into EZ, and UW G Chuck Allen fell on it for cheap TD.

Texas Tech 20 Texas A&M 14 (Dallas): For 1st time in series history, Texas Tech (1-0) won 2 straight games from Aggies (0-1). But, game moved well into 2nd Q before Red Raiders could make their initial 1st down, while Texas A&M made several early probes into enemy territory. With only 23 secs until H, sub Texas Tech FB-DB Dick Stafford raced 54y down sideline for TD after picking off option pass by A&M soph-sensation HB Jesse McGuire. Behind 6-0, Aggies tallied 2 quick TDs for 14-6 lead in 3rd Q: QB Charlie Milstead hit E Ralph Smith with 14y pass to key 47y drive after FUM REC as McGuire (149y rushing) scored as he juggled pitchout. McGuire came right back with brilliant 64y TD run after twisting through RT and weaving through Raiders secondary. When it seemed down and out, Tech countered with immediate 75y TD bomb from QB Glen Amerson to fleet soph HB Bake Turner. Amerson tied it with 2-pt pass. Raiders went 58y next time they had ball as HB Dan Gurley raced 33y around RE for TD and 20-14 edge late in 3rd Q. A&M nearly tied it with less than 3 mins left: From Tech 3YL, McGuire took pitchout and, like earlier TD, juggled it as he crossed GL near coffin corner. McGuire couldn't control ball this time and dribbled it through EZ for Texas Tech touchback, and with his bobble went Aggies' comeback.

TEXAS CHRISTIAN 14 Kansas 7: Defending Southwest Conf champion Texas Christian (1-0) went 72y from opening KO to HB Harry Moreland's short TD run, but Horned Frogs soon found themselves in role of fumbling, frustrated 3-TD favorite over Kansas (0-1). Spell was finally shattered when TCU sprung FB Jack Spikes (15/130y) on 64y run to Jayhawks 8YL in 4th Q. Spikes was rundown by Kansas' swift HB-DB Curtis McClinton and Jayhawkers' determined pursuit nearly preserved 7-7 deadlock. On 4th down at 3YL, QB Larry Dawson faked to Spikes at RG and spun into air to fire winning jump-pass to wide-open E Jimmy Gilmore. It broke tie that had been created in 2nd Q when Dawson decided to try another of his short-range TD passes from Kansas 5YL. Jayhawks FB-LB Doyle Shick pressured Dawson and stellar Kansas soph HB-DB John Hadl stepped in front of pass at 2YL. Hadl dashed through open field until he had to swerve behind E Dale Remsberg's block on fast-closing HB Marvin Lasater at TCU 25YL. Hadl completed school-record 98y INT TD RET, on which, in his profound weariness, he accidently dribbled ball, with no harm, at Horned Frogs 5YL.

Brigham Young 18 ARIZONA 14: Under new coach Tally Stevens, Cougars (1-0) rallied from 14-0 H deficit to beat Wildcats (0-1), premiering also under new coach Jim LaRue. After HB Walt Mince's 37y RET of opening KO, Arizona used delayed, 31y draw run around right by HB Warren Livingston for 7-0 lead. Mince's turn at draw play resulted in long-gainer to BYU 6YL, and QB Jim Geist soon sneaked over and kicked conv for 14-0 edge with 6:35 left before H. After 2 failed trips inside Wildcats 20YL, Brigham Young finally scored with 3:10 left in 3rd Q. BYU started at UA 35YL after punt RET, and HB Jack Gifford blasted 9y to score. Cougars failed on 2-pt pass play. BYU QB Gary Dunn found tall E Harold Hawkins for 58y TD pass next time Cougs had ball, but failed on 2-pt run. BYU was rolling, and sub QB Ron Startin threw clutch 4th down, 35y pass to HB Howard Ringoow to 1YL in 4th Q. Cougars DE Tom Cole spoiled late bid by Arizona by making INT of deep pass by Cats QB Eddie Wilson (2-11/21y, 2 INTs).

Oregon 28 STANFORD 27: Rival QBs Dave Grosz (12-24/130y, 2 TDs) and Dick Norman (19-28/171y, 2 TDs) traded long drives all day. Often going without huddle, Ducks (1-0) placed 2 TD passes of 23 and 3y into hands of E Greg Altenhofen, and Grosz scored in between on short TD wedge early in 2nd Q. HB Mac Wylie had given Stanford (0-1) 7-0 lead on its 2nd possession in 1st Q when he went around and through Webfoots for 30y score. FB Skip Face tied it 14-14 with 2:22 to go in 2nd Q with 5y pitchout run around LE and his x-pt kick. Oregon battled back in moments before H as Altenhofen curled back from deep in EZ toward Grosz to take 3y TD pass with 6 secs on clock. Ducks paddled to H with 20-14 lead as Indians HB-DB Harold Steuber partially blocked kick. Teams traded 3rd TDs, but Grosz hit eligible T Riley Mattson for 2-pt pass after HB Harry Needham's 25y TD run, so Ducks led 28-21. Norman of Stanford (0-1) threw his 2nd TD pass, 10y toss to E Ben Robinson with 1:00 to go. Indians disdained tying kick, and Norman tried for 2 pt pass to E Chris Burford (10/91y). Speedy Oregon HB-DB Dave Grayson, future pro standout, tipped pass at last instant to save win.

AP Poll September 21

1 Louisiana State (64)	1105	11 Southern California (4)	162
2 Oklahoma (12)	506	12 Ohio State	154
3 Auburn (6)	474	13tNavy	128
4 Mississippi (6)	468	13tIowa	128
5 Clemson	370	15 Texas	112
6 Southern Methodist	262	16 Georgia Tech	106
7 Army	243	17 Georgia	88
8 Wisconsin	218	18 Penn State (2)	70
9 Texas Christian	185	19 Florida	54
10 Northwestern	164	20 South Carolina	44

September 26, 1959

SYRACUSE 35 Kansas 21: Jayhawks (0-2) led 7-0 very early in 2nd Q and 7-6 at H on 1y TD run by QB Duane Morris, who carried Syracuse (1-0) FB-LB Art Baker and 2 other defenders into EZ after bad punt snap put Kansas at 6YL. Versatile Orangeman back Ger Schwedes, alternating between QB and HB, hit E Gerry Skoniecki with 3rd Q TD pass, but Kansas HB John Hadl followed with weaving 97y KO RET for 15-12 lead. Syracuse answered with 64y drive in 15 plays to TD and 2-pt run to gain lead for good at 20-15. Schwedes scored TD from each of his 2 positions in 4th Q surge as Syracuse finished with 493y to 67y O advantage over Kansas.

WAKE FOREST 27 Virginia Tech 18: Wake Forest (2-0) QB Norm Snead (8-16/123y) collaborated with E Pete Manning on early 9y TD pass for 7-0 margin, but, from that point on, Virginia Tech (0-2) owned 1st H. Jet-propelled HB Alger Pugh (19/129y, 2 TDs) rammed over T for 4y TD, and after C-K Chuck Stephens' 23y FG, Pugh swept RE and cut back for 68y TD and 18-7 H edge for Gobblers. In 2nd H, Deacons mixed surprisingly effective runs with Snead passes for 3 TD drives. Wake mustered drive that went 70y in 3rd Q to HB Winston Futch's TD run. In 4th Q, HB-DB Bobby Robinson made GL INT and Deacs went 70y to HB Jerry Ball's 4y TD run. Trailing 20-18, Tech missed 1st down by inches near midfield and Wake used 6 plays to go 48y to sub QB Chuck Reilly's 9y TD dance through LG hole.

TENNESSEE 3 Auburn 0: Outweighed Volunteers (1-0) ended 24-game unbeaten streak of Auburn (0-1). After having missed early 28y FG try, Tennessee E-K Cotton Letner kicked 20y FG in 2nd Q after 41y drive. Vol BB-LB Ken Sadler found pitchout that glanced off Auburn FB Ed Dyas for REC at Tiger 44YL, and TB Billy Majors, rushed while looking to pass, pranced 20y to 24YL, then followed with 11y pass to E Mike LaSorsa to set up Letner's boot. DB Majors also contributed 2 crucial INTs, halting Tigers' sole penetration of Vol 20YL. Auburn T Billy Wilson stopped Tennessee's 4th Q threat with FUM REC at Tiger 32YL with 2:40 left. But, when Plainsmen QB Richard Wood tried long pass for HB James Pettus, Vol FB-DB Neyle Sollee picked it off.

LOUISIANA STATE 10 Texas Christian 0: Winning their 14th straight game, Bengal Tigers (2-0) scored their 10 pts in 2nd Q as soph HB-K Wendell Harris hammered 29y FG 4 plays into 2nd Q, and QB Warren Rabb threw 45y TD pass to HB Johnny Robinson 4 mins before H. Early in 4th Q, Texas Christian (1-1) sub FB Merlin Priddy was thrown back at LSU GL as Horned Frogs failed in 4 tries inside 6YL. LSU star HB-DB Billy Cannon (8/35y) was infrequent runner, but exploded Horned Frogs' late-game threat with INT RET to TCU 7YL.

GEORGIA TECH 16 Southern Methodist 12: SMU (0-1) QB Don Meredith (15-23/191y, 2 TDs, INT) entered new season with mountain of press clippings, but Georgia Tech (2-0) QB Fred Braselton stole day's headlines. After his early pass was dropped in EZ by HB Billy Polk, Meredith threw 2nd Q TD passes to HB Frank Jackson for 22y and HB Glynn Gregory for 37y. In between, Tech's Braselton pitched TD pass to E Jim Powell, so SMU led 12-7 at H. Braselton threw TD pass to sub E Fred Murphy for 13-12 lead. His short pass that FB Taz Anderson turned into 13y gain and 33y run to SMU 12YL contributed to decisive FG drive, ended when Tech HB-K Tommy Wells came on to make 28y FG. Trying for comeback, Meredith pitched short passes of 9 and 9y to HB Tirey Wilemon and 7y to Gregory and 5y to E Bud Jones. Engineer soph G-LB Jack Moss picked off pass at his 34YL and returned it to 41YL with 1:32 to go. Still, Jackets were required to punt, and E-P Gerald Burch's spiral went to 7YL. Mustang HB Jackson fielded it, and Georgia Tech needed T Toby Deese, last possible tackler, to knock Jackson OB on game's last play after 50y RET.

INDIANA 20 Illinois 0: Surprising Indiana (1-0) completed 5th straight Big 10 game without defeat (4-0-1 since mid-October 1958) in handing wet lesson to Illinois (0-1). Hoosiers never dropped rain-slicked ball, but Illini lost handle on 5 FUMs and 2 INTs. Indiana HB Teddy Smith used block by FB Vic Jones to take opening KO 51y to Illinois 32YL. Smith slanted for 3y TD 10 plays later. Indiana soph HB Willie Hunter (14/76y) recovered FUM at 27YL late in 1st Q, then ran 7y to cap TD drive 10 secs into 2nd Q. Illini QBs Mel Meyers and Bob Hickey, subbing for injured Johnny Easterbrook, flung 20 passes in 2nd H, but 2 were picked off. Hoosiers big DE Earl Faison stopped scoring threat inside 15YL with screen pass INT off hands of HB Marshall Starks. DE Ted Aucreman's 4th Q INT set up Faison's TD catch, Indiana's only pass completion of day.

OHIO STATE 14 Duke13: Buckeyes (1-0) opened scoring in 1st Q with 58y march to HB Bob Ferguson's 15y run off RT. It took until 4th Q for next score: Duke (0-2) HB Jack Wilson plunged over from 2YL, but 2-pt pass was incomplete. On ensuing KO, Blue Devil C Ted Royall recovered HB Tom Matte's FUM at Ohio 30YL. Twice, Duke moved within FG range, but 40y and 33y kicks fell short. But, on 2nd FG try, Duke E Bob Fetsko outhustled Ohio C Dick Anders for loose ball at 1YL. FB Jerry McGee scored for 13-7 lead with 4:47 left. Matte, OSU coach Woody Hayes' 2nd choice as replacement for QB Jerry Fields, lost to injury in 1st H, ran for 12y and passed 3-6/55y on winning 67y drive, culminated with his 22y TD pass to E Chuck Bryant. K Dave Kilgore's x-pt won it.

NORTHWESTERN 45 Oklahoma 13: Where was 1960s clairvoyant Jeanne Dixon to warn Sooners (0-1) not to order fruit cocktail? On Thursday night, 13 Oklahoma players suspiciously were striken with food poisoning after dining at Chez Paree restaurant in Chicago. Sooners reported that waitresses asked about players' positions and starting status before serving fruit appetizer to key Oklahomans. Chicago gamblers were suspected of plot, but Oklahoma complained little afterward. Saturday's game in driving rain saw early breaks for Wildcats (1-0): blocked QK by G Joe Abbatiello and 9y punt to midfield by Sooners QB-P Bob Cornell. Those breaks, with 2 good punts against wind by QB-P Dick Thornton in between, staged Northwestern's 13-0 lead. Gastronomically-impared QB Bobby Boyd lateralled to HB Dick Carpenter, who shot 7y TD pass to HB Brewster Hobby to bring Oklahoma back to within 13-7 in 2nd Q. Then roof fell in on nauseous Sooners: Wildcats HB Ron Burton (11/117y, 2 TDs) ran for 62y and 7y TDs, E Paul Yanke caught 2 TD passes, and DE Elbert Kimbrough raced 47y to score with INT of ill-timed Sooners lateral by Boyd. It was OU's worst defeat since coach Bud Wilkinson came to Norman in 1947.

Missouri 20 MICHIGAN 15: Tigers scored in 1st and 4th Qs on HB Mel West's 46y dash and QB Phil Snowden's 36y pass to E Dale Pidcock for 14-6 lead, but Michigan (0-1) appeared to lock up 15-14 win as HB Bennie McRae scored his 2nd TD on 10y run, and E-K Jon Halstead recovered late FUM to position his own 22y FG with 2:48 left. Up against clock, Missouri (1-1) was forced to go with weak-passing, D-specialist Bob Haas (2 INTs as DB) at QB, who was trapped in lineup by substitution rules in effect in 1959. Amazingly, Haas sparked 78y Tiger drive, passing 11 and 5y to E Danny LaRose, handing to West for 11y run, scrambled up middle for 13y, and hitting HB Donnie Smith for 36y before plunging over from 1YL with :02 left.

Texas A&M 9 MICHIGAN STATE 7: Afterward, forlorn Michigan State (0-1) coach Duffy Daugherty could only shake his head over 4 lost FUMs. Spartans' 1st miscue came late in 1st Q when sub QB Larry Bielat lost ball to Texas A&M (1-1) E Ralph Smith at Michigan State 35YL. In melee, MSU received 15y foul PEN to move ball to its 16YL. Aggie QB Charlie Milstead (14/56y rushing) vaulted over from 1YL on 4th down for 6-0 lead. Soon after ensuing KO, Texas A&M T Bill Godwin fell on bobble by Spartans FB Blanche Martin at 20YL, but A&M had to settle for HB-K Randy Sims' 31y FG. Before 2nd Q ended, frustrated State misfired on 4th down pass at Aggies 10YL and E-K Art Brandstatter also missed 45 and 26y FGs. After good RET of 2nd KO by Martin, Spartans HB Herb Adderley (15/78y) carried on half of 12 runs to A&M 4YL. Martin ran through LG for 1y TD, but closing 25 mins saw no more threats. Win was 1st of 3 in row for Aggies.

NOTRE DAME 28 North Carolina 8: Under new coach Joe Kuharich, Notre Dame (1-0) returned to traditional dark blue jerseys after several years in vivid Kelly green. New gold-colored plastic helmets sported Shamrock logo. Fighting Irish D held experienced North Carolina (0-2) to 160y O and no pts until game's last half-min. Even without injured O stars, QB George Izo and HB Red Mack, Notre Dame built 20-0 H lead. After HB Bob Scarpitto dove behind LG Myron Pottios' block for short TD in 1st Q and FB Jim Crotty swept left for 19y TD run, Irish scored in last min of 1st H after pressure forced short punt by UNC QB-P Jack Cummings. E Monty Stickles blocked another Cummings punt for 3rd Q safety and ND led 22-0. HB Ray Ratkowski closed Irish scoring with 43y INT TD RET until Carolina's late 67y march was capped by QB Ray Farris' TD pass.

TEXAS 26 Maryland 0: Terrapins (1-1) got off on right foot in their visit to Austin, driving to Texas (2-0) 14YL where FB Jim Joyce, who carried on every play but 1, promptly fumbled. As if to show off their speed, Longhorns sent HB Jack Collins flying for 86y TD on Texas' 1st snap. Joyce contributed pair of 1st downs as Maryland moved 59y only to expire again at Texas 8YL as H clock hit zero. Longhorns reaped 2 FUMs and INT in 3rd Q to lead to TDs by FB Clair Branch and HBs Rene Ramirez, and David Russell. When dust had cleared, vanquished Maryland held wide but superfluous advantage in O plays by 97 to 53.

ARKANSAS 13 Oklahoma State 7 (Little Rock): Young Razorbacks (2-0) sparkled as Arkansas scored on each of 1st 2 times it held ball for 13-0 lead by 2nd Q. Soph FB Curtis Cox, subbing for injured FB Joe Paul Alberty, gave Porkers 7-0 lead in 1st Q as he contributed 53y to 88y march and fulfilled it with 2y TD run. HB-K Freddy Akers, future coach of Texas and Purdue, kicked x-pt. Slippery HB Lance Alworth, another Arkansas soph, burst ahead for 44y punt RET to Oklahoma State (0-2) 35YL in 2nd Q. Soph HB Darrell Williams skirted LE for last 4y as backup unit brought Hogs their 2nd TD. Cowboys scored early in 4th Q as QB Dick Soergel whipped several short passes through Arkansas D until HB Tony Banfield vaulted to 2y TD.

Air Force 20 WYOMING 7: Erratic Cowboys (1-1) scored 1st for 7-0 lead after DE Dick Hamilton took deflected INT 44y to Falcon 4YL, and FB Jerry Hill scored on 3rd down. X-pt was added by K Tom Dempsey, who would later earn NFL fame with record 63y FG for New Orleans Saints. From that moment on, however, Airmen were in total control in blustery 40-degree weather. Balanced Air Force (1-0) attack built 12-7 lead by H as sub QB John Kuenzel lofted 13y TD pass to HB Don Baucom and HB Mike Quinlan scored from 2YL. In 3rd Q, Falcons DE Sam Hardage's hard tackle created FUM at Wyoming 17YL. On next play, QB Rich Mayo hit Hardage for game-clinching TD and followed with 2-pt pass.

Iowa 42 CALIFORNIA 12: Head-splitting New Year's hangover for Golden Bears carried over from previous January as Rose Bowl foes produced very similar repeat result. California (1-1) scored in 2 plays: QB Larry Parque's 56y pass to HB Bob Wills, followed by HB Grover Garvin's 10y TD run. But, like game of recent January 1, Hawkeyes (1-0) piled up 475y O as FB Don Horn scored twice, QB Wilburn Hollis passed and ran for TDs, and sub HB John Brown, Big 10 440y dash champ, sprinted 60y untouched for late TD. Bears scrounged up their 2nd TD on QB Wayne Crow's 36y scamper in 3rd Q but it brought score only to within 35-12. Cal enjoyed balanced 319y attack but lost 4 TOs.

AP Poll September 28

1 Louisiana State (48)	794	11 Southern California (1)	176
2 Northwestern (20)	647	12 Wisconsin	134
3 Mississippi (4)	443	13 Georgia	85
4 Army	366	14 Ohio State	81
5 Iowa (4)	359	15 Navy	64
6 Clemson (7)	336	16 South Carolina	63
7 Georgia Tech	267	17 Auburn	49
8 Notre Dama (1)	239	18 Air Force	39
9 Tennessee	229	19 Florida	36
10 Texas	178	20 Syracuse	21

October 3, 1959

(Fri) SOUTHERN CALIFORNIA 17 Ohio State 0: Buckeyes' 1st-ever night game turned exceedingly dark when Trojans (3-0) K Don Zachik's 27y 2nd Q FG was followed by QB Ben Charles' 38y TD pass to E Luther Hayes in closing secs of 1st H. Another long Charles-to-Hayes pass (33y) set up Charles' 4y rushing TD in 4th Q. FB Bob White gained 58y of Buckeye run total of 84y, but for 1st time in his career, he was tackled behind scrimmage line. White led Ohio State to 5YL (only its 2nd penetration of USC 20YL) in waning mins, but was twice thrown for losses. Afterward, frustrated Ohio State (1-1) coach Woody Hayes was accused of swinging fist at Dick Shafer, sportswriter for *Pasadena Star-News*, only to clobber back of another writer's brother. Admitting he may have at least made shove, Hayes claimed, "I barely brushed him." Shafer had different recall: "Hayes yelled at us (reporters) to get the hell out of the way, then swung and slammed me into the wall (outside Buckeyes' dressing room)."

PENNSYLVANIA 13 Dartmouth 0: Penn (2-0) HB Fred Doelling (11/89y) scored twice with clincher coming deep in 4th Q. Prior to Doelling's 2nd TD, Penn had just stopped Dartmouth (0-2) rally by sacking QB Bill Gundy thrice after penetration to Quakers 19YL, and, with 2:28 to play, Doelling used crushing blocks of FB Jack Hanlon and HB John Terpack to launch 45y TD run. Quakers D-line, led by E Barney Berlinger, G John Marchiano and C-LB Ron Champion, held Big Green (0-2) to 77y rushing in impressive blanking of defending Ivy champs. Still, sr HB Jake Crouthamel (16/55y) set new career rushing mark at Dartmouth.

SYRACUSE 29 Maryland 0: Dismal Terrapins (1-2) O could earn but 29y, worst in school history. With soph starting QB Dick Novak out injured, trio of signal-callers could muster only 2 1st downs. QB-P Dale Betty had his early punt blocked by Syracuse (2-0) G Roger Davis, which led to T-K Bob Yates' 25y FG. FB-LB John Nichols made INT late in 1st Q for Orangemen, and on next snap, HB Ger Schwedes flipped 21y TD pass to E Fred Mautino. Soph HB Ernie Davis capped Orange's only sustained drive (67y) with 26y bolt past T Maury Youmans' block for TD. Nichols powered for TD and 23-0 H edge after Syracuse recovered FUM at Maryland 15YL.

PITTSBURGH 25 Ucla 21: E Marv Luster caught 2 TD passes in 2nd Q to stake UCLA (0-1-1) to 14-0 H lead. Bruins FB Ray Smith extended lead to 21-6 with early 4th Q TD dive. But, stumbling UCLA air D finally deflated, allowing 247y by game's end. Author of Pitt (2-1) passing explosion was QB Ivan Toncic, who tossed 4 TD passes, 3 scores coming in 4th Q. Toncic hit E Mike Ditka with 45y tally to pull within 21-18, and his last TD went to E Steve Jastrzembski for game-winner in final min.

SOUTH CAROLINA 30 Georgia 14: Gamecocks (3-0) D forced 4 FUMs and blocked punt to set up new starting FB Phil Lavoie (14/77y) for 3 TD runs and 2-pt run. Carolina G Jake Bodkin blocked punt and made FUM REC, while T Ed Pitts fell on 2 FUMs. Gamecocks led 16-0 at H. Highly-skilled Georgia (2-1) air game, led by QBs Fran Tarkenton (14-20/127y, TD) and Charley Britt (3-3/68y, TD), mysteriously was held to 1y in 1st H, but came back in 2nd H, clicking for 2 TD passes: HB Bill McKenny's 6y catch from Tarkenton late in 3rd Q and HB Bobby Towns' in-stride grab of Britt's long toss that went 53y in closing moments.

VANDERBILT 7 Alabama 7: For 3rd straight season, combatants ended in deadlock, while each searched for its opening SEC win of season. Alabama (1-1-1) bungled numerous scoring opportunities. Typical Tide's scoring failure came on opening drive as HB Gary O'Steen switched to FB to power 50y drive to 9YL. But on 4th-and-1 at 9YL, O'Steen was thrown for loss by ace Commodores T Larry Wagner. After exchange of punts, Vanderbilt (0-1-1) took over on its 47YL, and soph FB Jim Burton powered for 35 of 53y needed to reach HB Tom Moore's 1y TD. QB-K Russ Morris, in for banged-up QB Jim McKee, put Vandy up 7-0 with x-pt, but Morris also missed FG tries of 38 and 44y. Crimson Tide scored early in 4th Q, primarily because Commodores were called for EZ pass interference, which placed ball on 1YL. Bama QB Pat Trammell wedged it over and T-K Dave Sington kicked pt to make 7-up theirs.

GEORGIA TECH 16 Clemson 6: With Georgia Tech (3-0) leading 7-0, Clemson (2-1) HB Bill Mathis charged up middle with 2nd H KO, cut right and raced 99y to bring Tigers to within 7-6. HB Johnny Welch's TD run and K Tommy Wells' FG vaulted Engineers to 10-pt edge. Then Yellow Jackets D halted 4th Q drives at own 3YL thanks to C Maxie Baughan and at own 5YL on INT by HB Jimmy Sides.

Northwestern 14 IOWA 10: With Iowa (1-1) coach Forest Evashevski stunning fans with Friday revelation of his retirement plans in 1963, Hawkeyes tumbled in defense of their Big 10 title. Northwestern (2-0) lost highly-valuable QB Dick Thornton to fractured ankle on opening KO, and that just was beginning of inept 1st H. Wildcats' Ara Parseghian went against coaching textbook by taking successful FG off board in scoreless 2nd Q after HB Ray Purdin's 74y pass and run from 3rd-string QB John Talley had placed NW at 6YL. Iowa PEN advanced Wildcats inside 2YL, but Northwestern failed on run as Hawkeyes DB John Brown recovered bobbled pitchout at Iowa 5YL. Another hot-potato pitchout in 3rd Q gave game's 1st score to Iowa DE Don Norton, who grabbed midair FUM by Cats HB Ron Burton, and, with open field ahead, Norton strolled 47y to TD. K Tom Moore upped Hawks' advantage to 10-0 with 23y FG, also in 3rd Q. Wildcats' 1st win over Iowa since 1936 turned before end of 3rd Q. Burton started 68y TD march with KO RET and teamed with FB Mike Stock to vault NW downfield with key runs. QB Chip Holcomb (8-16/125y, TD, INT) put Cats on board with 7y TD toss to E Elbert Kimbrough. In 4th Q, valuable DB Purdin darted in front of Iowa QB Wilburn Hollis' pass and crafted 42y TD INT RET for winning score with 5:27 to go.

ILLINOIS 20 Army 14: Surprised 20-0 by Indiana in its opener, Illinois (1-1) rose up to smite Army (1-1) as 3rd string QB Mel Meyers directed new unbalanced spread O—its version of Lonely End borrowed from Army—to 2 early TDs. Illini HB Johnny Counts caught 41y TD pass from Meyers for opening score. Cadets A-A HB Bob Anderson injured his knee, never to be same again in his career. Walloped by Illini G-LB Bill Burrell, star on both sides of ball, Anderson coughed up KO FUM that led to 2nd Q Illinois TD, by FB Jim Brown. Limited to 32y on ground by topnotch Illini D, Army took to air (17-31/187y) and tallied FB Jim Connors' short TD run and QB Joe Caldwell's 21y TD pass to E Don Usry.

PURDUE 28 Notre Dame 7: Always fired up for game with Irish, Boilermakers (1-0-1) visited 4th defeat in 6 years upon Notre Dame (1-1). Purdue FB Bob Jarus powered to 2 TDs, big part of 21-0 H lead. ND QB Don White (13-24/143y) threw 39y to E Monty Stickles and 25y to FB Jim Crotty to poise Crotty for short 3rd Q TD. Inspired Irish moved deep into Purdue end on next set of downs, but were stopped by INT by QB Bernie Allen, who relieved 1st H running star, QB Ross Fichtner, whose dashes of 25 and 16y had sparked 1st TD drive. Two plays after Allen's INT, little Boilermaker HB Jim Tiller iced final result with 74y TD sprint for 21-7 margin.

SOUTHERN METHODIST 20 Navy 7: FB Mike Hackney (57y rushing) caught 28y TD pass from QB Don Meredith on 1st possession by SMU (1-1), but Meredith was held to 56y in air rest of way. Navy (2-1) countered with 61y drive in 2nd Q capped by TD plunge of FB Joe Matalavage. Pony QB-DB Ken Lowe grabbed INT at Navy 19YL in 3rd Q to launch Meredith's short TD run and 13-7 SMU advantage. Desperate Middies failed to score from SMU 2YL, and later QB Jim Maxfield (120y passing) drove Navy to 17YL in last min. But Mustangs HB Tirey Wilemon grabbed INT and sped 95y for clinching score.

ARKANSAS 3 Texas Christian 0: Wider goalposts served as wonderful target after Arkansas (3-0) 3rd-string QB-K Freddy Akers had been required to practice his FG tries shooting at previous year's narrower width. With help from holder-QB James Monroe (2-4/22y, INT) who fielded short snap in rainy go of Fayetteville, Akers nailed 28y 3-ptr for game's only score. Texas Christian (1-2) slightly outgained Razorbacks but lost 7 TOs. With clock running down in 4th Q, desperate Frogs reached Hogs 35 and 23YLs, but lost FUM and QB Don George's pass was intercepted by Arkansas star C-LB Wayne Harris.

AP Poll October 5

1 Louisiana State (69)	1064	11 South Carolina (3)	155
2 Northwestern (30)	1041	12 Syracuse (1)	132
3 Georgia Tech	665	13 Oklahoma (2)	110
4 Texas	656	14 Auburn	88
5 Mississippi (2)	601	15 Southern Methodist	63
6 Southern California (9)	575	16 Penn State (2)	60
7 Purdue	446	17 Florida	56
8 Tennessee	429	18 Air Force	35
9 Wisconsin	233	19 Arkansas	34
10 Iowa	182	20 Illinois	33

October 10, 1959

(Fri) SOUTHERN METHODIST 23 Missouri 2: Throwing TD pass on Ponies' 1st series, QB Don Meredith (10-14/120y, 2 TDs) sparked no. 15 Southern Methodist (2-1) past frequent intersectional foe Missouri (2-2). Meredith tossed screen pass to HB Glynn Gregory for 19y gain to ste up his 4y TD pass to wide-open E Bud Jones. HB-DB Tirey Wilemon stopped Tigers march with INT of QB Phil Snowden (4-13/46y, INT) at own 4YL. Mizzou DE Russ Sloan recovered FUM and blocked punt for 2 pts in 2nd Q. Missouri HB Mel West (15/69y) made good y after 2nd H KO but was enveloped by SMU DT Jerry Mays on 4th down at Mustangs 16YL. SMU FB Jim Welch scored on short run after Gregory gained field position with 58y run. Meredith added 2-pt scramble for 15-2 lead as they headed to 4th Q. Meredith chalked up another TD pass—7y to E Henry Christopher—and scrambled for another 2-pt conv.

Penn State 17 ARMY 11: Nittany Lions (4-0) QB Richie Lucas scored twice in 1st H and starred on both sides of ball as injury-riddled Army (1-2) was leveled at home for 1st time since 1955. Cadets suffered 145y in PENs with 2 crippling flags coming late in 2nd Q. Roughness PEN on Cadets contributed to G Sam Stellatella's 20y FG, and then G Mike Casp's 64y INT TD RET was called back when Army was flagged for offside. Soon thereafter, Lucas wedged behind RG from 1YL after his 15y pass to E Henry Opperman to establish 17-3 H lead for Penn State. Cadets rallied in 3rd Q on QB Joe Caldwell's 11y TD pass to HB George Kirschenbauer and "Lonely E" Bill Carpenter's surprise 2-pt throw to make it 17-11. Army's late comeback was snuffed as Caldwell tossed INT made by DB Lucas at own 15YL with 2:20 to go.

Syracuse 32 NAVY 6 (Norfolk): Annual Oyster Bowl benefit game showcased 304y of power O from Syracuse (3-0). Despite mud, Orange QB Dave Sarette passed 7-10/119y, including 37y TD to HB Ger Schwedes. FB Art Baker scored twice—including 96y INT RET—to help construct 26-0 lead. Navy (2-2) got effective short passing from QB Joe Tranchini. But, Syracuse had 4 INTs, last of which was HB Mark Weber's 30y TD runback after yanking pass from grasp of E Tom Albershart.

AUBURN 33 Kentucky 0: HB Jimmy Pettus took opening KO and sprinted 88y to Auburn (2-1) TD. Leading Tigers to 27-0 H margin, QB Bobby Hunt scored 2 TDs and zipped 35y to set up FB-K Ed Dyas' 21y FG. Kentucky (1-3) penetrated Auburn end only 5 times while gaining 113y. Wildcats' best surge reached 16YL after blocking punt.

Georgia Tech 14 TENNESSEE 7: Redshirt HB in 1958, FB Taz Anderson earned his Ramblin' Wreck stripes, scoring both TDs for surprising Georgia Tech (4-0): catcher of 9y pass from QB Fred Braselton on opening possession of 1st Q and battering-ram of 1y up middle in 1st series of 3rd Q. Anderson had to work for 10/37y rushing, but caught 4/46y, all of them contributing to 2 scoring trips. Meanwhile, Vols (2-1) alums were discussing whether to replace Smokey, its blue tick hound mascot, with Tennessee walking horse. Smokey eventually survived in his role, but Vols were turned back on this day except for TB Gene Etter's short 2nd Q TD pass to E Marvin Phillips that tied it 7-7. Fierce Tech D relinquished only 161y total O and spotlighted C Maxie Baughan and Anderson in outstanding LB roles. Vols were tossed for –82y in losses by Tech's magnificent D. E-P Gerald Burch averaged 46.5y punting to help keep Vols at bay.

IOWA 37 Michigan State 8: TD battery of QB Olen Treadway and E Don Norton connected twice in 1st H as Iowa (2-1) cruised to easy 23-0 lead. INTs and PENs continually thwarted Spartans (1-2), and when they finally scored on QB Dean Look's 13y pass to FB Carl Charon, Hawkeyes immediately answered with HB Bob Jeter's 95y KO RET. Jeter's dash set up QB Wilburn Hollis' short TD run for formidable 29-8 edge.

PURDUE 21 Wisconsin 0: Future Minnesota Twin 2nd baseman Bernie Allen replaced injured QB Ross Fichtner and threw 3 TD passes for Purdue (2-0-1). Allen as DB also grabbed INT to set stage for his 6y TD flip to E Len Jardine. When E Dick Brooks fell on Badger FUM, Allen soon found Jardine in paydirt again. Wisconsin (2-1) gained only 111y, but remained competitive until 4th Q when Boilermakers FB Jack Laraway raced 50y to position Allen for his 3rd scoring dart.

Kansas 10 NEBRASKA 3: Jayhawks (2-2) E Dale Remsberg was knocked down in EZ, but popped up for game-winning 7y pass from HB John Hadl late in 3rd Q. After 3-3 1st H standoff developed from Kansas FB-K John Suder's 32y FG and Nebraska (2-2) QB-K Ron Meade's 30y FG, Cornhuskers HB Pat Fischer rambled 52y with 2nd H KO. Fischer and HB Carroll Zaruba led 35y trip to 11YL, but next 2 plays tossed Huskers back to 30YL. QB-P Harry Tolly punted for touchback, and KU went 80y to TD as HB Curtis McClinton made key runs. Jayhawks D held off Husker bid in 4th Q: Nebraska went to KU 6YL, but sub QB Joe Rutigliano's 4th down pass fell incomplete.

Texas 19 Oklahoma 12 (Dallas): Banged-up Sooners (1-2) surged out of locker room to 12-0 1st Q advantage. After Longhorns (4-0) QB Mike Cotten lost early FUM at his 32YL, Oklahoma QB Bob Cornell faked trap run and threw 23y TD pass to HB Jackie Holt. It wasn't long until OU HB Dick Carpenter tiptoed inches from sideline for 38y TD. HB Rene Ramirez took personal action on behalf of Texas in 2nd Q, accounting for 51y of 72y march. Ramirez ran for 15y, passed for 22y, and caught Cotton's 14y toss. It was Ramirez's running left-handed TD pass to E Larry Cooper at end of drive that jumped Steers to within 12-6. Thanks to Oklahoma injury that stopped clock, Texas squeaked in another TD with 10 secs left before H as FB Mike Dowdle rode T Larry Stephens' block in EZ, so Steers led 13-12 at H thanks to x-pt by QB-K Bobby Lackey. QB Cotten's short pass to FB swift Jack Collins quickly turned into 61y TD that settled matters in 4th Q. Sooners FB Prentice Gautt (23/135y) was effective running traps all day and his runs set up 2 late opportunities that died in hands of Texas DBs George Blanch and Cotton who made INTs.

Arkansas 23 BAYLOR 7: HBs Tommy Minter (12/54y, TD) of Baylor (1-2) and Jim Mooty of Arkansas (4-0) traded 1st H TDs for 7-7 tie, Minter's score putting Razorbacks behind for 1st time in 1959. Mooty's 50y QK rolled OB at Bears 1YL, and Mooty's RET

of P Gary Wisener's return punt set up Arkansas deep in Baylor territory. DB Mooty's 3rd Q INT, which he returned 28y to 15YL, poised his understudy and future Texas and Purdue coach, HB-K Freddy Akers, for 27y Hogs FG. Then, 4 mins later, Arkansas T Paul Henderson fell on FUM to set up 2nd unit QB George McKinney for 28y TD pass to E Les Letsinger and 17-7 lead. Another Bear FUM in 4th Q gave Mooty another TD chance on 1y run. Porkers returned 3 INTs/128y, including T Marlin Epp's 4th Q RET of 51y after LB Wayne Harris blitzed Baylor QB Ronnie Stanley into pop-up pass. Epp rambled to Bears 44YL before HB Ronnie Bull hauled him down, and Hogs failed to score on that chance.

WASHINGTON 10 Stanford 0: Rain failed to discourage air-minded Stanford (1-3), which put it up 38 times with 15 successes. But, superb pass D of Huskies (4-0) completely exasperated Tribe QB Dick Norman, nation's aerial leader. Norman had suffered only 1 INT to this point in season, but Washington secondary racked up 4 INTs as it forced miserable 4-21 result on Norman. HB-DB George Fleming picked off pass at Indians 36YL 10 mins into 1st Q, and Washington HB Don McKeta raced 30y for TD. Huskies made 268y rushing and rolled back Stanford's D all day without success until K Fleming kicked 28y FG in middle of 3rd Q. Stanford QB Rod Sears (10-16/158y) had better fortune than Norman and brought Indians within whiff of 4th Q TD after Tribe enjoyed its 1st possession inside 50YL on short Huskies punt. Pass interference and 20y strike from Sears to E Ben Robinson gave Indians 1st-and-goal at 6YL with less than 3 mins to play. On 4th down, Sears hit HB Gil Dowd, who was dropped just ft from GL by Washington soph G-LB Jim Skaggs.

October 17, 1959

(Fri) MIAMI 23 Navy 8: Underdog Miami (3-1) dominated 1st H, using FB Frank Bouffard's short TD run and K Al Dangel's 30y FG that came 4 secs before H. Dangel's FG followed T Bill Watts' FUM REC at Navy 22YL. Middies (2-3) narrowed it to 10-8 when HB Joe Bellino scored at end of 70y drive early in 3rd Q. Hurricanes blew it open with 2 long TD marches, capped by QB Fran Curci's TD pass and HB Bob Rosbaugh's TD run.

Yale 23 CORNELL 0: On its way to game-end 191y rushing, Cornell (3-1) made 8 1st downs to Bulldogs' none in 0-0 1st Q. But, Big Red's dominance quickly faded as Yale (4-0) QB-P Tom Singleton zeroed 2 punts deep into Ithacans' end, and Cornell made 2 bad punt snaps that contributed to 9-0 disadvantage at H. QB Singleton threw 2nd Q TD pass to HB Nick Kangas, and made key block on 44y punt RET by HB Lou Muller in 4th Q. Inspired Yale romped to its 5th straight shutout, week later, over Colgate 21-0. Not since Southern Cal's 1943 team had opened with 6 straight whitewash wins had any NCAA University-Division team started season that so dominated its foes on scoring D.

Auburn 7 GEORGIA TECH 6: Tight D battle turned on Tigers FB-K Ed Dyas' 3rd Q conv kick. Georgia Tech (4-1) scored in 1st Q when T Billy Shaw fell on FUM in Auburn (3-1) end, and QB Fred Braselton soon sneaked over. Tigers completed no passes, but won on 71y land march behind blocking of big T Ken Rice. Georgia Tech K Tommy Wells, who missed kick after Braselton's TD, also missed 2 FG tries in rain-soaked 4th Q.

VANDERBILT 13 Florida 6: Pre-med student and QB-DB Russ Morris (7-12/108y) had what doctor ordered in 1st H, passing Vanderbilt (1-2-1) into position for TD runs by HBs Tom Moore (18/77y, TD) and Thom Garden. Commodores led 13-0 at H even though Florida (3-1-1) threatened twice in 1st H: DB Moore's GL INT stopped Gator drive in middle of 2nd Q, and H clock killed another threat after Moore made saving tackle of reserve E Paul White at Vandy 7YL. Florida went 90y in 4th Q to score with only 35 secs left as sub QB Jack Jones pitched 27y TD pass to HB Jack Westbrook.

ALABAMA 7 Tennessee 7: TB Billy Majors scored 1st Q TD for Tennessee (2-1-1), and Alabama (2-1-2) tied it just before H when QB Pat Trammell hit E Stanley Bell with 21y scoring pass. Bruising 2nd H was punctuated by exchange of 7 punts and 2 missed FGs by Bama T-K Fred Sington.

WISCONSIN 25 Iowa 16: Hard-hitting Badgers (3-1) rocked Iowa (2-2) into 4 costly FUMs in 1st H as they took 17-0 lead. QB Jim Bakken's 49y run set up K Karl Holzwarth's FG, G Ron Perkins recovered 2 FUMs to put QB Dale Hackbart and FB Tom Wiesner in short field position for short TD runs. When Wisconsin FB Eddie Hart scored for 25-0 lead in 3rd Q, decision for home team seemed completely locked. But, Hawkeyes rallied after ensuing KO as QB Olen Treadway (26-41/304y, TD) set new Big 10 marks for completions and attempts. Treadway hit 6-8/80y passing before FB Don Horn wedged over in 3rd Q and E-DE Don Norton (9 catches and sack) nabbed 2-pt catch. After being sacked into FUM by Badgers E Henry Derleth to stop late 3rd Q threat at Wisconsin 11YL, Treadway hit his Es Norton for 21y TD and Jeff Langston for 2-pt play midway in 4th Q as Iowa outgained Wisconsin 468y to 205y, but to no avail.

OHIO STATE 15 Purdue 0: After 8 recent, scoreless Qs, Ohio State (2-2) coach Woody Hayes discarded all forms of flanker formations and returned to tried-and-true Split-T O. After K David Kilgore's 36y FG, Buckeye sub QB Tom Matte capped 80y 2nd Q TD drive with 32y run for 10-0 lead. Then, Purdue (2-1-1) HB Jim Tiller made ill-advised 16y retreat to outflank punt coverage, but was spilled for safety. Boilers

had surrendered only 212y in 3 previous games, but were defeated by 266y from Buckeyes, including FB Bob White's 111y rushing. Purdue gained 288y, but long drives failed at 1 and 11YLs.

MICHIGAN STATE 19 Notre Dame 0: Netting 420y on O, Michigan State (2-2) dominated Fighting Irish (2-2) in hard-hitting game that produced 8 lost FUMs. Spartans QB Dean Look sprinted 41y to set up HB Larry Hudas' short TD slant late in 1st Q. MSU E Fred Arbanas went high with back to Look's pass, snared it over his head, and kept his feet to dash to 52y TD. Outplayed, but trailing only 13-0 in 4th Q, ND went 40y to 1st down at Michigan State 20YL. Irish FB Frank Gargiulo swept into clear, but was drilled at 2YL by Spartans topnotch HB-DB Herb Adderley. MSU stopped 4 line smashes to end only Irish scoring threat.

KANSAS 33 Kansas State 14: Fairly quiet game, led by Kansas (3-2) 6-0 after 1st Q, exploded with 5 TDs in 2nd Q. Jayhawks' bevy of soph backs were responsible for 27-14 H lead. HB Curtis McClinton scored 3 times and added 2-pt catch from HB John Hadl. McClinton's 2nd TD, 11y run early in 2nd Q came after Hadl's 25y punt RET and his own 30y run, aided by Hadl's block. Kansas State (1-4) QB John Solmos, who wasn't supposed to play because of sore elbow, was in lineup enough to uncork 7-20/152y passing, including 64y TD bomb to E Vern Osborne that pulled State within 12-7. Kansas QB Lee Flachsbarth sneaked over after his 30y pass to E Sam Simpson set stage, but Wildcats answered with 85y drive to HB Jack Richardson's 15y TD run.

Jayhawks led 19-14 in final half-min of 1st H. Do-all Hadl then took long throw over middle for 71y TD and rolled out to toss 2-pt pass to McClinton. E John Peppercorn threw clearing block to spring McClinton for 32y TD run early in 3rd Q, and Kansas was left to defend its 33-14 lead rest of way despite K-State trips to 20 and 10YL in 4th Q.

Iowa State 27 COLORADO 0: Fame of "Dirty Thirty," began as Iowa State (4-1) won its 1st conf game under coach Clay Stapleton in 2 years. Using squad with big heart and only 30 players suited up, Cyclones ravaged surprised Buffaloes (1-4) with 327y total O. Led by TB Dwight Nichols (5-6/80y, TD passing and 21/72y, 2 TDs rushing), FB Tom Watkins (19/81y), and WB Mike Fitzgerald (6/98y, TD rushing and 2/58y, TD receiving) Iowa State stabbed Colorado with tricky single wing O, same O that had served Buffs so well for last 10 years. Alternating runs of FB Loren Schweninger and HBs Dave Rife and Don Maurer, Bisons moved nicely after opening KO, but when Cyclones realized they had Buff QB Gale Weidner (2-10/5y, INT) well-wrapped, they halted Colorado. With 14-0 lead after TDs by Nichols and Fitzgerald, Iowa State sprung Fitzgerald loose for 50y TD pass in 3rd Q after he picked off INT that bounced off shoulder pads of Colorado E Chuck McBride. LB Joe Romig was diagnostic genius for Buffs, making frequent tackles.

Indiana 23 NEBRASKA 7: Looking for 2nd win over Big 10 foe after upsetting Minnesota, Nebraska (2-3) instead became magnanimous hosts, losing 4 FUMs and INT. Husker missteps started on game's 1st scrimmage as QB Harry Tolly lost ball on own 4YL. Indiana (3-1) HB Willie Hunter quickly turned RE for 7-0 lead. After FB Don Cromer's early 2nd Q TD run, Hoosiers' illegal sub infraction and pass interference provided more than half of Nebraska's 72y needed to pull within 14-7 at H. TD came on Tolly's 18y pass to HB Carroll Zaruba after QB had dashed 25y. Key play, "the one that hurt us" according to NU coach Bill Jennings came in 3rd Q as punt snap sailed over Tolly's head and through EZ for 16-7 deficit. Indiana TB John Henry Jackson threw 36y TD pass to HB Richie Bradford in 3rd Q.

OKLAHOMA STATE 19 Houston 12: Cougars (1-4) blew 12-0 lead as HB Tony Banfield scored all 3 Oklahoma State (3-2) TDs, including 2 short plunges that pulled Cowboys from behind in 4th Q. Houston consumed more than half of 1st Q to score on 4th down pass from QB Lonnie Holland (8-12/72y, 2 TDs, INT) to E Larry Lindsey. Big Cougars E Errol "The Peril" Linden kept chains moving with 10 and 11y catches. After HB Jim Kuehne (13/83y) contributed 12y reverse run, Holland and Lindsey duplicated their 4th down TD pass for 3y in 2nd Q. Later in 2nd Q, Houston DE Robert Sanders picked off pass by Cowpokes QB Dick Soergel (12-23/179y, TD, 2 INTs), Soergel's 1st INT of season after 65 throws, and Sanders appeared gone for TD. But his own blocker inhibited Sanders at State 39YL, and when Cowboys D dug in they forced punt. After Oklahoma State went 86y to Soergel's 24y TD pass over middle to Banfield, Cowboys took command but not before having to stop HB Ken Bolin's 4th-and-goal run at their 1YL in 3rd Q. State had to overcome 1st-and-35 with 2 Soergel passes to fuel drive to Banfield's go-ahead 1y TD run in 4th Q.

Texas 13 ARKANSAS 12: With each side losing 4 FUMs, single 2nd Q conv by Texas (5-0) QB Bobby Lackey proved difference. Arkansas (4-1) opened scoring at 6-0 when T Marlin Epp fell on FUM at Texas 24YL, and QB James Monroe hit E Steve Butler with 5y TD pass. Longhorns went 60y with Lackey scoring early in 2nd Q and adding vital kick for 7-6 edge. Monroe scored for Razorbacks in 3rd Q, and HB Jack Collins caught 4th Q TD pass for Texas, but each was followed by failed 2-pt try.

Southern California 22 WASHINGTON 15: TD runs by HB Jerry Traynham (23/157y) and QB Al Prukop, latter after 85y drive, gave Southern California (4-0) 14-0 lead by midway in 2nd Q. Washington (4-1), playing before loud sellout Homecoming crowd, countered it to 14-7 by H when QB Bob Schloredt (6-15/71y, and 11/32y, 2 TDs) sped to 9y TD. On they battled in hard-hitting affair when, on last snap of 3rd Q, Troy DE Glenn Wilder recovered FUM at Washington 14YL. Although E Wilder caught TD pass, it was nullified by PEN, and USC ended up missing FG that fell short. With just more than 10 mins left in 4th Q, Huskies P Schloredt (8/44.6y avg) boomed 47y punt to Trojans 20YL, where Traynham and HB Lynn Gaskill played I'll-take-it-no-you-take-it and let ball dribble from their grasp. Sub HB Steve Millich recovered for Washington, and Schloredt soon swept for 4y TD after his 16y pass to E John Meyers. He added 2-pt run for 15-14 edge. Trojans QB Willie Wood shook off early injury and polished off powerful 8-play, 80y march with 6y TD run behind pulling G Al Bansavage and added 2-pt pass to E-DE George Van Vliet, who also was D star. Traynham chipped

in by racing 50y around RE on 3rd-and-1 to UW 29YL. Huskies weren't done as they marched to 17YL before USC C-LB Dave Morgan picked off pass in dying moments. USC finished with 309y rushing.

OREGON 20 Air Force 3 (Portland): Striking with 2nd Q thunder, Oregon (5-0) sent Air Force (3-1) to Academy's 1st defeat in last 15 games. After HB-K George Pupich's 33y FG gave Falcons 3-0 lead, Ducks countered in 2nd Q with G Dave Urell's INT, 1 of 5 TOs committed by Air Force. QB Dave Grosz hit 5'4" sub HB Cleveland Jones with startling 50y bomb, effective launching pad to 452y O and 14-3 H advantage for Oregon. QB Rich Mayo spiced 3rd Q Air Force drive with deft screen passes, but suffered GL INT by Ducks HB-DB Willie West. Oregon sub FB Harry Needham scored twice.

AP Poll October 19

1 Louisiana State (68)	1238	11 Oregon (1)	192
2 Northwestern (23)	1171	12 Wisconsin	170
3 Texas (8)	1010	13 Illinois	118
4 Mississippi (18)	989	14 Purdue	87
5 Southern Calif. (12)	769	15 Iowa	68
6 Syracuse (4)	673	16 Texas Christian	66
7 Auburn (5)	462	17 Clemson	60
8 Penn State (3)	313	18 Oklahoma	56
9 Georgia Tech	280	19 Yale (1)	52
10 Arkansas (1)	213	20 Ohio State	43

October 24, 1959

(Th) Clemson 27 SOUTH CAROLINA 0: In 57th and last "Big Thursday" encounter, which for years was played as part of S.C. State Fair, Clemson (4-1) used 186y in air to throttle South Carolina (3-2). Gamecocks were held to 118y O and failed to penetrate 20YL until late in game. Tigers QB Harvey White threw 2 TDs, while HB Bill Mathis scored twice.

PENNSYLVANIA 22 Navy 22: Penn Quakers (4-0-1), on their way to Ivy League title, jumped to H lead and, when all hopes for upset over favored Navy (2-3-1) seemed vanished, scrambled for FB-K Ed Shaw's tying 24y FG in last 1:46. After Midshipmen got off to 8-0 start on HB Bob Correll's 17y sprint, Penn began campaign that owned balance of 1st H for 19-8 H bulge. Quakers QB George Koval (8-19/128y, 2 TDs, INT) found E Barney Berlinger (3/17y, TD) for 11y TD and launched beautiful 60y bomb to HB Pete Schantz late in 1st Q. QB Joe Tranchini was banged up on 2nd H KO, so Navy had to go to sub QB Jim Maxfield, who hit only 9-25, but rallied Tars for 22-19 lead with 25y TD pass to HB Bob Correll and capped 73y drive in middle of 4th Q with 1y sneak.

North Carolina 21 WAKE FOREST 19: Blocked x-pt in 1st Q by North Carolina (3-3) line set tone for otherwise even game. Huge Tar Heels FB Don Klochak scored twice. Most importantly, G-K Bob Shupin made all 3 kicks. Wake Forest (4-2) FB-K Neil McLean scored all 3 TDs, but came away with only 1 successful x-pt kick.

Louisiana State 9 FLORIDA 0: In 18th straight win, Tigers (6-0) used sharp-fanged D to set up 2 scores in 2nd Q. Florida (3-2-1) HB-P Bobby Joe Green was pressured by LSU E Mickey Mangham and snowed under by T Bo Strange and G Emile Fournet. LSU then quickly moved 48y to TD by HB Billy Cannon (15/55y rushing). Bengals DE Gus Kinchen's INT set up HB-K Wendell Harris for FG and 9-0 lead just before H. Passes took Gators deep into LSU end twice in 4th Q, but mighty Bengals stiffened each time.

Mississippi 28 Arkansas 0 (Memphis): From outset, Mississippi (6-0) dominated game. Rebel FB Charlie Flowers iced early 80y drive with TD plunge. In 2nd Q, Arkansas (4-2) HB-P Lance Alworth's FUM of snap resulted in punt of -1y, and Rebels took it 20y to Flowers' 2nd score. DE Johnny Brewer's tipped INT of Hogs QB James Monroe led to 3rd TD. Arkansas gained 159y, but had 4 TOs and gruesome 24.8y punt avg.

Penn State 20 Illinois 9 (Cleveland): There was sparse turnout at Cleveland's cavernous Municipal Stadium, dubbed "The Mistake on the Lake," for neutral-site St. Lawrence Seaway celebration. Despite unimpressive passing numbers (4-12/71y, 4 INTs), Penn State (6-0) QB Richie Lucas accounted for 137y of Lions' 245y. Illinois (3-2) received early gift: Penn State HB Jim Kerr lost FUM at his 12YL, and Illini settled for mammoth T-K Cliff Roberts' 30y FG. Lucas ran effectively for 66y, mostly through holes at T, and scored 1st Q TD on 4y run that put Nittany Lions ahead for good at 7-3. Trailing 14-3 in 2nd Q, Illini HB-DB Ethan Blackaby picked off 1st of Lucas' poor throws, and FB Bill Brown tallied TD at end of 22y drive. Overcoming its 2nd H TOs, Penn State turned tables by gobbling up FUM at Illinois 1YL that led to HB Dick Hoak's clinching TD at 20-9. Illinois also had slippery fingers: It lost 2 FUMs and 3 INTs. Illinois gained 207y.

Northwestern 30 NOTRE DAME 24: QB John Talley launched TD aerials of 78, 54, and18y, and dashed 61y in 3rd Q for TD that provided Northwestern (5-0) with 30-14 lead in 29th renewal of rivalry, 1st since 1948. Wildcats E Irv Cross, future CBS-TV NFL anchor, caught Talley's longest bomb. Trying to play catch-up all day, Notre Dame (2-3) made profit of FUMs at Wildcats 2 and 12YLs for TDs by HB Bob Scarpitto after DB Clay Schulz recovered at 2YL and HB George Sefcik nabbed 12y catch from QB George Izo on heels of another REC by Schulz. Latter TD came early in 3rd Q after NW DB Albert Faunce broke up Izo's 4th down pass from Wildcats 12YL and brought Irish to within 18-14. Cross caught his long pass next, and, while looking for open receiver, Talley soon took off on his 61y TD. HB Scarpitto took tipped pass off fingertips of Cats DB Faunce from sub QB Don White to 52y TD. Northwestern E Elbert Kimbrough caught opening TD pass, made several tackles for losses, and his INT snuffed ND's late bid with 2 mins to play. It was Wildcats' 1st win over Notre Dame in 9 tries since 1940.

OKLAHOMA 7 Kansas 6: Interloper Kansas (3-3), tied atop Big 8 standing, was edged by kingpin Oklahoma (3-2), its 74th straight conf game without defeat. In 2nd Q, Sooners QB Bobby Boyd had 44y punt RET and gains of 13 and 11y on 36y drive. G-K Jim Davis kicked conv for 7-0 Sooner lead. Sr sub HB Dave Harris sped 60y to late 3rd Q Jayhawks TD with great fake on last tackler. But, 2-pt pass hit back of official's head, only to become Oklahoma INT. Kansas HB-P John Hadl bottled up OU all day with his booming punts and set conf mark with 4th Q 94y punt, which carried from his 4YL to distant 2YL.

MISSOURI 9 Nebraska 0: Alfred Hitchcock's film "North by Northwest" was theme for Missouri (3-3) Homecoming floats, but writer John Archibald suggested in *St. Louis Post-Dispatch* that Tigers were likely headed "south by southeast to Orange Bowl," led by "south by Mel West." HB West authored key play, 86y RET of 2nd H KO that carried all way to Huskers (2-4) 6YL before QB Harry Tolly and HB Pat Fischer rode him OB. Mizzou QB Bob Haas scored on next play for 9-0 lead. K Chuck Mehrer had booted 31y FG in 1st Q after DB Fischer knocked down 3rd down pass from Nebraska 15YL. After Nebraska stopped 4th Q move to its 7YL, Tolly hit 2 passes, including E Don Purcell's diving 39y grab at Missouri 37YL. But Tigers DE Danny LaRose bore through to smack QB Ron Meade for 10y loss to 26YL, and that ended Huskers' threat.

SOUTHERN CALIFORNIA 30 Stanford 28: Taking to advice from new backfield coach John McKay, Trojans (5-0) sr FB Clark Holden had career day, rushing 22/125y and scoring 4 TDs to tie school record. But, Stanford Indians (1-4) nearly scared gold pants off USC with 21-12 H lead. Tribe QB Dick Norman (16-32/207y, 2 TDs, INT) tossed 9 and 14y TD passes to E Chris Burford (5/46y) in 1st H in which he threw for 163y. However, in 2nd H, fired-up Trojans pressured Norman into only 5 completions, only 1 of which occurred before Holden's 21y run halfway through 4th Q iced it at 30-21. QB Willie Wood had pushed Troy 70y downfield to early 11y TD pass to HB Angelo Coia. Stanford took lead 7-6 in 1st Q after Burford made his 1st TD catch and FB-K Skip Face (5/16y, 2 TDs) made 1st of his quartet of x-pt kicks.

Oregon State 24 CALIFORNIA 20: Oregon State (2-4) snatched 13-0 H lead on 7y run by sub TB Larry Sanchez and BB-LB Marne Palmeteer's 76y INT TD RET. Trailing 13-6 after 2nd H KO, California (1-5) staged its 2nd long drive. HB Bill Patton provided power runs so that QB Wayne Crow could carry it 9y to score and follow with 2-pt pass for 14-13 edge. Beaver E Aaron Thomas kicked 1st FG of his career for 16-14 edge early in 4th Q. Completely disdaining passes, Cal went 61y to QB Larry Parque's 1y TD. Berkeley native TB Don Kasso, used sparingly in 1st 3 Qs, came off State bench to complete 4 passes on 73y march ended with less than 4 mins to play. Kasso's 31y TD pass to E Amos Marsh provided 5th and last lead change.

Washington 13 OREGON 12: Unbeaten Oregon (5-1) jumped to 1st Q lead on FB Dave Powell's 1y plunge, but conv snap was fumbled. That forced QB Dave Grosz to try futile 2-pt pass after his 2nd Q TD pass. Trailing 12-0 before H, Washington (5-1) made its 1st foray into Ducks territory on INT, and QB Bob Schloredt quickly scored. HB-K George Fleming's conv kick sailed wide, but when HB Don McKeta scored in 3rd Q, Fleming's successful kick proved to be winning margin.

AP Poll October 26

1 Louisiana State (71)	1556	11 Purdue	241
2 Northwestern (25)	1474	12 Clemson (2)	98
3 Mississippi (46)	1444	13 Yale (1)	44
4 Texas (6)	1227	14 Georgia	31
5 Syracuse (11)	994	15 Texas Christian	29
6 Southern California (6)	758	16 Oregon	25
7 Penn State (6)	715	17tArkansas	24
8 Auburn (5)	674	17tWashington	24
9 Georgia Tech (1)	344	19 Oklahoma	22
10 Wisconsin (2)	276	20 Tennessee	19

October 31, 1959

(Fri) TULANE 17 Texas Tech 7: Fog caused variety of problems, including officials accidentally marking ball 10y off its proper spot to start play in 4th Q. O balance of Tulane (3-4), which matched aerial power of Texas Tech (3-4), turned tide in 2nd H as Green Wave had HBs Terry Terrebone (18/58y) and Tommy Mason (6/30y) on whom to build effective run game. Red Raiders struck in 1st Q, going 60y on 3 completions by QB Ken Talkington, who hurtled 3 defenders to complete his TD mission of 4y run. After Tech threats were stopped by PENs and Talkington's lost FUM, Greenies countered in 2nd Q as sharing leadership on 87y march were QB Phil Nugent on quick runs and QB Bobby Cornett on passes of 23, 9, and finally 16y to E Pete Abadie for tying TD in 2nd Q. HB-K Howard Kisner booted 3rd Q FG when Tulane run attack stalled, and Mason made INT late in 3rd Q. Greenies lost ball on downs at Tech 6YL, but HB-P Bake Turner's punt out of EZ wobbled short, and Wave took over at Raiders' 26YL. Mason carried three times to score.

Dartmouth 12 YALE 8: Ivy race was thrown into hodge-podge as Dartmouth (2-3-1) broke 5-game Bulldogs' shutout string, and, in Philadelphia, Harvard toppled unbeaten Penn 12-0. Dartmouth recovered early FUMs and pressured Yale (5-1) D into making 11 tackles inside its Elis 15YL. But, it was Elis' O that mounted 1st scoring venture: 55y TD drive. FB Rich Winkler's scoring run and QB Tom Singleton's 2-pt conv run provided Yale with 8-0 H lead. Big play in Big Green's comeback in 2nd H came on 4th-and-2 near midfield: reliable HB Jake Crouthamel (25/75y) slammed for 4y to keep TD drive alive. When Dartmouth scored to finally end Bulldogs' impressive scoreless D streak at nearly 341 mins, it seemed to take some starch out of Yale. Indians owned air-lanes all day (126y to 0y), and accurate, recently-mended sr QB Bill Gundy hit HB Al Rozycki and E Seth Strickland with 2nd H TD passes.

ARMY 13 Air Force 13 (New York City): Arthur Daley wrote in *The New York Times*, "The newest of the service classics was off to a rousing start." It wasn't always artistic. Butterfingered Army (3-2-1) lost 4 FUMs which cost it opening TD by Falcons FB Monte Moorberg and later tying TD by HB Mike Quinlan. Outgained 254y to 186y, Cadets sent HB Bob Anderson slamming for TD at end of 80y march in 2nd Q. Blocked punt by Army T Dale Kuhns helped Anderson to another 2nd Q TD and 13-6 lead for

Cadets. Air Force (4-1-1) smothered Army ground game (15y) in 2nd H and used DB John Baucom's FUM REC to set up Quinlan's tying score early in 4th Q. Falcons' final drive from their own 38YL was spiced by QB Rich Mayo's 21y pass off fake FG, but ended forlornly in 31y FG try by HB-K George Pupich that sailed wide.

Syracuse 35 PITTSBURGH 0: Syracuse's growing powerhouse delivered worst defeat to beleaguered Pitt (3-4) coach John Michelosen in his 5 years at helm in Pittsburgh's Oakland section. Dominant Orangemen (6-0) D, led by G-LB Roger Davis and E Fred Mautino, squelched Panthers to tune of -6y rushing. QB Dave Sarette hit E Gerald Skonieczki with 30y pass to set up HB Ger Schwedes' 1st Q TD, and Orange's famed inside reverse "scissors" play provided 2nd Q TD. LB Dan Rackiewicz, Syracuse's 4th team FB, had day's last romp: 100y TD rumble with INT.

Penn State 28 WEST VIRGINIA 10: Despite West Virginia (3-4) D keying on QB Richie Lucas and holding him to 63y O, undefeated Penn State (7-0) charged to 20-3 H edge on outstanding line play and wizardry of its supporting backs. Lions HB-DB Jim Kerr raced 25y untouched with early INT TD RET, HB Roger Kochman turned RE for 52y TD in 1st Q, and sub QB Galen Hall found E John Bozick behind DBs for 35y TD pass in 2nd Q. Mountaineers profited by 3 inopportune FUMs by Penn State and absence of Lucas, who left early in 3rd Q after hard knock to his head. WVU FG in 1st H came after Penn State FUM, and in 4th Q, Lions repelled Mountaineers at own 17YL with FUM REC. However, Lions lost ball right back at 15YL. WVU HB Ray Peterson dented GL for TD 6 plays later.

GAME OF THE YEAR
LOUISIANA STATE 7 Mississippi 3:

Halloween brought warm, extremely muggy backdrop to one of football's legendary night venues, Tiger Stadium. A-A HB Billy Cannon's FUM, 1st of 4 by Tigers (7-0), after opening KO gave ball to Rebels at LSU 21YL. Ole Miss quickly made 1st down at 8YL. But, Tigers DE Mickey Mangum spilled QB Jake Gibbs for loss on 3rd down, and Ole Miss (6-1) was forced to accept 3-0 lead on FG by T-K Bob Khayat, Ole Miss' future chancellor. Another FUM REC provided Ole Miss with 2nd Q chance at Tigers 29YL. As 1st H clock ticked down, Rebels coach Johnny Vaught disdained FG, and QB Bobby Franklin was stopped on rollout from 7YL on last play of H. In 3rd Q, Ole Miss blocked FG try by LSU HB-K Wendell Harris and smeared Cannon's fake punt-and-run at its 35YL. With no. 1 LSU making wholesale mistakes, Vaught turned conservative to protect his 3-0 lead, ordering Gibbs to make 1st down punts, on which he nearly averaged 50y. Almost 5 mins into 4th Q, Gibbs punted again from own 42YL. Running to his right to field skidding punt, Cannon planned to let it roll, but grabbed high hop at own 11YL. He was met by Rebels G Richard Price at 19YL, but shook loose. E Jerry Daniels lost his grip on Cannon at 30YL. Last-chance tackler Gibbs made lunging try at 45YL only to slip off, and Cannon was home-free for 89y TD RET and 7-3 LSU lead with 10 mins left. Vaught made unusual choice to lead counterattack: he tapped 3rd string QB Doug Elmore. Sticking to ground game except for 9y pass to HB Cowboy Woodruff, Elmore moved Rebels to 4 1st downs against celebrated Chinese Bandits D. LSU coach Paul Dietzel reinserted his 1st team when Rebs drive reached 23YL. Min and half remained when Elmore's keeper made 1st down at 7YL. Runs by HB George Blair, Elmore, FB Jim Anderson put ball at 2YL. Ole Miss called timeout and planned Elmore to slant off left side. But, young Ole Miss lineman blocked wrong way, and Elmore was stuffed at 1YL by QB-DB Warren Rabb and Cannon with 48 sec left. Writer Fred Russell called it "fullest and finest football game I've witnessed in 31 years of sports reporting."

NEBRASKA 25 Oklahoma 21: Not since 1946, 74 games ago, had Oklahoma (3-3) tasted defeat in conf clash. After Sooners opened game with fast 72y scoring drive, Nebraska (3-4) fought back to 12-7 lead in 2nd Q lead when C-LB Jim Moore blocked QK and G Leroy Zentic carried it 36y to pay-dirt. With Oklahoma having regained lead at 14-12, Huskers DB-K Ron Meade put Nebraska back on top in 3rd Q by kicking 1st of his 2 FGs. Nebraska QB-P Harry Tolly, who authored key punts all day, scored running TD in 4th Q after HB Pat Fischer went 61y with punt RET. So, Cornhuskers led 25-14 before giving up Sooners FB Prentice Gautt's 2nd TD and ended it on Meade's EZ INT in dying secs.

KANSAS 7 Iowa State 0: Kansas (4-3) was threatened on numerous occasions by spunky Iowa State (5-2), but came up with 3 INTs to key its shutout. Jayhawks HB-DB John Hadl authored 2 INTs, snaring 1 at own 8YL and another in EZ. Heady Cyclones TB Dwight Nichols had thrown 101 passes without INT and far-ranging Kansas secondary often spoiled his aerial scoring threats. Kansas finally marshaled its O for 71y ground-oriented thrust to score in 4th Q. FB Doyle Schick, Hadl and HB Curtis McClinton probed middle of Cyclones D with McClinton galloping 15y for winning TD. On way to its best mark since 1944, loss might have cost Iowa State chance at bowl bid.

COLORADO 21 Missouri 20: Playing before jovial Homecoming crowd, Colorado (3-4) upset Missouri (3-4), its 1st win over Tigers since 1951. Missouri made struck 1st on HB Donnie Smith's 1st Q TD run and led 20-6 in 4th Q. Buffs QB Gale "The Whip" Weidner, operating out of new spread formation that faced little DL rush, was able to pass Tigers dizzy. Weidner hit E Jerry Hillebrand with TD, added 2-pt pass, and later scored himself so K Joe Dowler could kick winning x-pt.

ARIZONA STATE 35 New Mexico State 31: Soph-studded Sun Devils (5-1) lineup held off late New Mexico State (4-3) charge in desert thriller to put themselves at front of Border Conf title war. HB Bobby Gaiters was key to quick Aggies TD in 1st Q: Gaiters made runs of 15 and 12y and caught 15y TD pass from QB Charlie Johnson. QB Fran Urban pitched 2 TD passes as Arizona State's response, and Devils led 22-16 at H. HB-K Nolan Jones kicked 1st of pair of 28y FGs in 3rd Q for ASU, but Gaiters registered his 3rd TD run. So, it was Sun Devils by slim 28-23 margin in 4th Q. With 2 mins left, DB Urban made pass INT which led to ASU TD and seemingly safe 35-23 margin.

But future St. Louis Cardinal QB Johnson struck quickly on 40y TD pass to WB Pervis "Afterburner" Atkins. NMSU recovered on-side KO, but clock ran out before it could advance past Sun Devils 15YL.

Washington 23 UCLA 7: For 1st time in 19 years, on-charging Washington (6-1) beat UCLA (1-3-1) in L.A. Coliseum and took vice-grip on Rose Bowl bid. Key performer was Huskies QB Bob Schloredt (5-8/138y, 2 TDs), whose running TD for 14-7 lead in 3rd Q padded his 2-TD pass production. Bruins gained upper hand early as UW C George Pitt sailed punt snap over Schloredt's head for 33y loss to 1YL. After anxious UCLA suffered 5y PEN, TB Bobby Smith slipped 2 tacklers and scored on 6y run for 7-0 lead. It took Washington just 6 plays to tie it after KO as Schloredt whipped 44 and 15y passes to HB George Fleming. Trailing 14-7 in 3rd Q, Bruins alternated effective runs of TB Smith and FB Ray Smith for 41y to Huskies 2YL. But, Bobby Smith had ball pop into air when he was hit, and DB Fleming made REC inside 1YL. After P Schloredt's punt out from EZ, Bobby ran 17y to Huskies 25YL, but there 4 runs were stopped dead to doom wishful Uclans. K Fleming added·FG in 4th Q, and Bobby Smith again lost FUM at his 35YL after receiving KO. Schloredt instantly iced it with 35y TD fling to E Lee Folkins.

Southern California 14 CALIFORNIA 7: Brave California (1-6) mounted great GLS in 2nd Q and relinquished 385y O to undefeated no. 6 Southern California (6-0) but hung in closely enough to farm big break at end of 3rd Q for 7-6 lead. USC FB Jim Conroy had taken screen pass from QB Willie Wood (2-5/90y, TD, and 7/16y, TD rushing) 65y with 5-blocker caravan he outran. Troy led 6-0 and it held up at H because Bears D-front, led by T Frank Sally and NG Jim Piestrup, became brick wall in stopping 4 shots from its 1YL. FUM popped out of stack at Trojans 40YL late in 3rd Q, and Cal G-LB Pete Domoto took it in stride and tore off to 7YL where he was hauled down from behind. Big Bears HB Jerry Scattini bulled over from 2YL, and FB-K Bill Patton booted x-pt. With chips down now, Wood brought KO back to his 47YL and capped drive with 7y TD run with blocking convoy from McKeever brothers, G Mike and E Marlin. HB Angelo Coia made 2-pt run.

November 7, 1959

Pittsburgh 22 BOSTON COLLEGE 14: Pittsburgh (4-4) used ball control to slosh through puddles in Chestnut Hill to defeat persistent Boston College (4-3). Playing it safe in 1st H, both teams punted on early downs until Eagles got break on Panthers HB-P Fred Cox's short punt to 37YL. E Joe Sikorski made fingertip catch at 9YL to set up 3rd down, 3y TD pass by BC QB John Amabile (13-27/157y, TD, INT) to HB Bill Robinson. K Cox made 25y FG to pull Pitt within 7-3 at H. Cox broke game open with 63y reverse TD run in 3rd Q, but BC HB Vin Hogan came right back with 90y sprint right past Pitt bench with following KO. Pitt C-LB Serafino "Foge" Fazio, who was brilliant on D, recovered FUM at Eagles 30YL to provide field position for eventual 44y drive to Cox's 24y TD catch from QB Ivan Tonsic (2-8/35y, TD). Now up 15-14, Fazio made INT at own 20YL, and Jungle Cats opened 4th Q with clinching 80y drive that chewed up nearly 7 mins on way to 2y score by FB Jim Cunningham (22/106y, TD) and 22-14 edge.

Syracuse 20 PENN STATE 18: Dropped long pass kept dominant no. 7 Penn State (7-1) from building more than 6-0 1st Q lead. By time Orangemen HB Ger Schwedes scored 2nd Q TD, no. 4 Syracuse (7-0) had regained control and cruised to 20-6 margin by 4th Q. Nittany Lions soph HB Roger Kochman flew 100y on KO TD RET, and, 2 D stands later, T Andy Stynchula made punt block that positioned Penn State for 1y TD plunge by FB Sam Sobczak. Lions missed 2-pt tries after each 4th Q TD and remained behind at 20-18 as Orange killed clock with sustained power running. Despite its inspired rally, Penn State oddly gained only 2y in 2nd H against Syracuse D, led by E Fred Mautino and G-LB Roger Davis.

Georgia 21 Florida 10 (Jacksonville): HB-P Bobby Walden of Georgia (7-1) surprised Gators with early option pass for 14y to E Gordon Kelley. Trailing 14-0 in rain, Florida (3-4-1) rallied with 70y pass to 2YL from QB Dick Allen to HB Bobby Joe Green. Bulldogs held, but suffered safety on dropped EZ punt snap, making it 14-2. In 3rd Q, Allen passed Gators to 9YL, but Georgia QB-DB Charlie Britt made INT, splashed 100y for brilliant counterpoint TD. Gators HB-DB Jack Westbrook had INT TD RET too late to help.

TENNESSEE 14 Louisiana State 13: For 2nd time in 1959, Tennessee (5-1-1) ended another team's long unbeaten streak, this time 19-game skein of LSU (7-1). Vols' pair of 3rd Q TDs, including BB-DB Jim Cartwright's 54y INT RET, gave them 14-7 lead to counter 2nd Q 26y TD romp by Tigers HB Billy Cannon (122y rushing). Enjoying 334y to 112y advantage, Bayou Bengals got 4th Q break when Cannon's punt squirted away from Vols TB Billy Majors at 2YL. After quick TD made it 14-13, Cannon tried 2-pt run blast, was piled up less than ft short by DB Majors, G Wayne Grubb, and WB-LB Charles Severance.

VANDERBILT 11 Kentucky 6: QB-DB-K Russ Morris wore many Commodore hats, kicking 21y FG in 1st Q, making 4th Q INT, causing another 4th Q INT at Vanderbilt (3-3-1) 14YL, and recovering late on-side KO as his teammates bobbled it. Kentucky (2-6) O was nearly useless in 1st H that Vandy led 3-0. Burly HB Tom Moore (16/117y)

detonated up middle in 3rd Q and raced 62y to Vanderbilt score. QB Jim McKee made brief understudy appearance for Morris and flipped 2-pt pass to E Rooster Akin. In 4th Q, Wildcats came alive, reaching Commodore 20, 43, 14, and 32YLs. DB Morris made his INT at 43YL, and his hard hit on receiver allowed Vandy HB-DB Thom Garden to make another INT at 14YL. Passing on 21 of its last 22 plays, Kentucky swept to QB Jerry Eisaman's 15y TD pass to E Ronnie Cain. On-side KO with 1:36 left eluded Commodores' Akin, but Morris covered it at 32YL.

ALABAMA 19 Tulane 7 (Mobile): Coach Bear Bryant earned his 100th career victory as Crimson Tide (4-1-2) displayed improving attack as soph QB Pat Trammell supplied spark against depleted Green Wave middle, which was without 2 regular Ts and G. Trammell bothered with only 1 pass, which failed, but he scampered all over Ladd Memorial Stadium to tune of 24/143y. Trammell skirted E for 17y to sent up little HB Marlin Dyess' wide 4y TD scamper early in 2nd Q, which provided 7-0 edge. Tulane (3-5) tied it with 68y march in 2nd Q as it overcame 15y holding PEN, but also benefitted from Alabama's 15y roughing P miscue. Greenies QB Phil Nugent (3-13/29y, TD, INT) found E Pete Abadie twice on drive, including 10y TD with scant secs left before H. Trammell's sub, QB Bobby Skelton, tried only 2 passes himself, but each succeeded, including 22y scoring toss to E Tommy Brooker in 3rd Q. Bama weathered lost punt FUM at its 16YL in 4th Q.

MICHIGAN STATE 15 Purdue 0: Slim Rose Bowl chances evaporated for Purdue (3-2-2) as last year's cellar dwellers, Michigan State (4-3), "punctuated their return from the Big Ten wilderness…," according to *Chicago Tribune.* Boilermakers reached Michigan State's 11YL on early pass but illegal receiver downfield PEN spoiled throw by QB Bernie Allen (10-20 passing) and pushed them back to own 40YL. That was Purdue's frustrating day in a nutshell as they lost 5 FUMs. It also failed to solve MSU's previously porous pass D with only 156y in 33 pass tries. Fake FG pass in 1st Q by State QB Dean Look (2 TD passes) turned into 28y TD to HB Garry Ballman. Although left-footed E-K Art Brandstatter missed 2 conv kicks, he nailed 23y FG in 3rd Q for Michigan State's last pts.

INDIANA 26 Michigan 7: Hoosiers (4-3-1) capitalized on 3 TOs to score TDs and send Michigan (3-5) to decisive defeat, Indiana's 2nd straight win over Wolverines after having lost 10 of 11 from 1946 to '57. In opening 5 mins, Hoosiers C-LB Fred Lauter picked off QB Stan Noskin (14-24/164y, TD, 3 INTs) at UM 39YL, and TB Teddy Smith lashed for 22y gain before scoring from 6YL on 4th down run. Indiana WB Richie Bradford scored on 7y reverse after G Bob Battaglia's 2nd Q FUM REC. Michigan was able to retaliate with 70y trip to TD in 2nd Q, moving within 13-7 as Noskin completed 22y throw before hitting E John Halstead with 24y TD. Indiana made it 19-7 by H by answering with 85y march that was capped by FB Don Cromer's from 1y out.

Wisconsin 24 NORTHWESTERN 19: Determined Badgers (6-1) took command in 2nd Q and tied no. 2 Wildcats (6-1) atop Big 10 standings. DE Allan Schoonover recovered errant lateral at Northwestern 16YL to allow HB Ron Steiner to catch 14y TD pass in 2nd Q for Badgers' 1st lead at 10-7. Wisconsin kept at it for 17-pt 2nd Q surge, which brought visitors from behind twice and were spun on axis of QB Dale Hackbart's 2 TD passes. It was answered by 69y TD run by Northwestern HB Ron Burton (12/169y), so Badgers led 17-13 at H. With score at 24-19, Wisconsin sub QB Jim Bakken threw ill-fated INT with which fleet Wildcats DE Elbert Kimbrough appeared on his way for TD. But, Bakken was able to head off Kimbrough at 11YL. Burton fumbled ball away 3 plays later, and last-min Wildcats opportunity died on INT by superb Wisconsin G-LB Jerry Stallcup.

MISSOURI 13 Air Force 0: Stung week earlier by Colorado passes, Missouri (4-4) unleashed outstanding DEs Russ Sloan and Danny LaRose in fierce rush of Air Force (4-2-1) QB Rich Mayo (18-36/143y, INT). Meanwhile, far less heralded and far more sparing passer, Tigers QB Phil Snowden (2-5/49y, TD), came off bench in 2nd Q to fashion 58y drive for upset. Snowden passed for decisive TD, 39y arrow for which HB Norris Stevenson leaped over FB-LB Monte Moorberg to make catch and eluded Falcons HB-DB Phil Lane to run from 20YL into EZ. On Missouri's 2nd scoring drive in 3rd Q, Snowden thrice converted 4th down plays to lead to HB Donnie Smith's 11y TD reverse run behind fabulous block by Sloan that cleared last 2 defenders.

TEXAS 13 Baylor 12: Baylor (3-4) QB Ronnie Stanley passed for 13-18/120y and ran for 34y, including 3rd Q TD which gave 12-7 lead to Bears. Texas (8-0) soph HB Jack Collins twice gained 6y on critical 4th downs on winning 39y advance in 4th Q. After each Baylor score, 2-pt pass try failed, which allowed Texas QB-K Bobby Lackey's conv kick to win 1-pt SWC game for 2nd time in 1959. FB Clair Branch rushed 17/74y for Longhorns.

AP Poll November 9

1 Syracuse (111)	2325	11 Clemson (3)	362
2 Texas (85)	2313	12 Georgia (2)	263
3 Louisiana State (13)	1848	13 Washington	159
4 Southern California (14)	1576	14 Oregon (2)	101
5 Mississippi (14)	1488	15 Georgia Tech	92
6 Northwestern (2)	1311	16tIowa (1)	56
7 Wisconsin (19)	1243	16tNorth Texas State	56
8 Auburn (9)	808	18 Texas Christian	40
9 Tennessee (4)	674	19 Michigan State	33
10 Penn State	608	20 Arkansas	28

November 14, 1959

GEORGIA 14 Auburn 13: Georgia (8-1) upset Auburn (6-2) to clinch SEC title, Bulldogs' 1st crown since 1949. Tigers built on FB-K Ed Dyas' 2 long 1st H FGs for 13-7 when QB Bryant Harvard scored on sneak. Georgia's big breakthrough came with less than 3 mins to play. QB Fran Tarkenton hit FB Don Soberdash for 16 and 9y, then found E Bill Herron for TD in last 30 sec. K Durwood Pennington kicked winning pt.

Mississippi 37 Tennessee 7 (Memphis): Giant-killer Tennessee (5-2-1), architect of season's 2 biggest upsets but doomed to 3 closing losses, failed to fool another powerhouse. But, Vols TB Glenn Glass scored 2nd Q TD, providing brief 7-7 tie. Mississippi (8-1) QB Jake Gibbs passed for 2 TDs, ran for another, and FB Charley Flowers powered for 26/163y, TD on ground, perhaps A-A's greatest game for Rebels.

MICHIGAN STATE 15 Northwestern 10: Wonderful season began to unravel for previously-anointed Wildcats (6-2), and, in springing upset, Michigan State (5-3) pulled into 3-way tie for Big 10 lead with Northwestern and Wisconsin at 4-2. Wildcats led 7-3 at H, their TD coming in middle of 1st Q after surprisingly easy 61y progression led by sub QB Bob Eickhoff, who scored from 1YL. Spartans dominated 2nd H as QB Dean Look set conf single-game record for perfection passing with 7-7, including short toss that HB Herb Adderley took from scrimmage line to 28y TD. That score brought Michigan State to within 10-9 in 3rd Q, but Adderley couldn't wriggle over GL on his 2-pt reception. Spartans DE Joe Corgiat specialized in containing NW speedster HB Ron Burton and limiting him to 13/38y rushing. HB-DB Don Stewart recovered Burton's FUM at Wildcats 37YL. Michigan State FB Park Baker ran 8 and 11y to spark Look's winning TD sneak 30 secs into 4th Q

Illinois 9 WISCONSIN 6: Surprisingly strong Illinois (4-3-1) was thrice thwarted deep in Wisconsin (6-2) territory with only 1st Q safety to show for its efforts. Badgers went up 6-2 when E Henry Derleth recovered QB teammate Dale Hackbart's FUM for 1st Q TD. In dying mins of game, Illini mustered strength for 81y march, mostly with FB Bill Brown (16/106y rushing) charging behind G Bill Burrell. QB Mel Meyers hit HB Gary Kolb at 1YL with 28 secs left, and Brown's 2nd smash won it as clock showed 0:00. Illini finished with 361y to 174y O advantage. Illinois' upset win created 3-way tie atop Big 10.

OKLAHOMA 28 Army 20: Fine O effort that totaled 388y by underdog Army (4-3-1) was squandered when Cadets lost 3 FUMs in their own territory, and Sooners (5-3) turned each into TD. QB Joe Caldwell, who passed for to-date West Point record of 21-42/297y, 2 TDs, 2 INTs hit HB George Kirschenbauer with 37y TD pass on opening drive. So, Army led 6-0. HB Mike McClellan finished 17-play drive that sent OU to 7-6 lead in 1st Q, and Sooners padded lead at 14-6 in 2nd Q when DE Paul Benien fell on bounding FUM in Army EZ. Army came right back on Caldwell's 12y TD bullet to E Don Usry. Sooners QB Bobby Boyd added 2 TDs in 2nd H after FUM RECs at Army 9 and 20YLs to raise margin to 28-12 in 4th Q. Ace Army E Bill Carpenter amazingly caught 6 passes with his left arm strapped to his side to limit movement of 4-day-old dislocated shoulder.

Arkansas 17 SOUTHERN METHODIST 14: When SMU (4-3-1) QB Don Meredith (5-8/58y, TD) threw his 350th career pass he became recognized as NCAA's to-date most accurate pitcher of all-time with so many tries. California's Paul Larson (1951-54) previously held record 51.7 percent, while Meredith now stood at 218-352 for 61.9 percent. But, when Ponies needed Meredith most in 4th Q, he had to sit out 3 mins because of being leveled by hard-hitting Hogs C-LB Wayne Harris (12 tackles). Mustangs had scored in 1st Q on FB Jim Welch's 3y plunge at end of 80y land drive. Arkansas (7-2) gained 400y rushing, but 1st, HB-P Lance Alworth (131y rushing) fired 34y punt OB at 2YL to set up 36y drive that he capped by powering for 13y run to tie it 7-7 in 2nd Q. From Spread-formation just before H, Meredith found E Bud Jones alone on right side of EZ for 7y TD and 14-7 lead. Alworth and SMU C-LB Max Christian collided on Alworth's 2-pt run after Razorbacks FB Joe Paul Alberty zipped 24y for TD in 3rd Q. Alworth squirted through for 2 pts and 15-14 lead. Arkansas earned safety in dying secs as desperate Meredith tossed screen pass to Welch, who was hit so hard he lost FUM from his 4YL back through EZ for 2 pts. With Texas' loss, Arkansas clinched tie for 1st place in SWC.

Texas Christian 14 TEXAS 9: HB Harry Moreland's slanting 56y 4th Q TD run gave TCU (6-2) upset win over Texas (8-1). Texas had taken lead in 1st Q by 9-0. Longhorns gained safety by G David Kristynik on block of punt by Frogs HB-P Larry Terrell as ball bounced crazily through EZ. After TCU's free-kick, Texas steamed downfield to 2y TD run by FB Mike Dowdle. Horned Frogs' fine D gritted its teeth and allowed only single 1st down in 2nd H, and star DT Bob Lilly ended last Longhorns threat with FUM REC near midfield.

Wyoming 25 NEW MEXICO 20: Resilient Cowboys (8-1) used clever QB Jim Walden's long, crossfield fling to HB Dick Hamilton for brilliant game-winning 78y TD in last 2 mins that clinched at least tie for Wyoming's 2nd straight Skyline Conf title. Wyoming had scored on Walden's 14y pass to HB Dick Behning for 7-0 lead after game's opening KO. It wasn't until midway in 2nd Q that Lobos got break that pulled them back into contention: High snap on Cowboys' 4th down punt forced P Walden to eat ball, and New Mexico (6-3) went 46y to score. When Wyoming earned TD just moments later, New Mexico HB Don Perkins (16/72y, TD) in turn tallied after QB George Friberg (3-9/87y, INT) whipped 46y pass to E Don Black. That brought Lobos into 13-13 tie that held to H. Dynamic Perkins opened 2nd H with 90y KO TD RET, but Pokes retaliated with 66y trip that featured running of HB Jerry Hill (17/114y, TD). Hill was felled short on 2-pt run try out of single wing formation, so New Mexico led 20-19 until Walden rolled right and found Hamilton all alone after latter sneaked uncovered swinging left out of Cowboy backfield from winner.

ARIZONA STATE 27 Brigham Young 8: Dazzling performances by pair of Sun Devils (7-1) sophs sparked victory over Cougars (2-7). Arizona State HB-K Nolan Jones caught 2 TD passes, ran for another score among his 72y rushing, and tallied 21 pts, including 3 x-pts, for 92 pts for season. ASU QB Joe Zuger (10-13/142y, 3 TDs) hit 6-6/110y, 2 TDs to Jones in 21-8 1st H. Jones caught 18y TD arrow at end of 67y trip in 1st Q and cut through big Brigham Young line for 21y TD romp to cap 68y march in 2nd Q for 14-0 lead. Cougars were successful only on weak-side runs, and it was 16y reverse run by WB Jack Gifford, followed by 2-pt conversion, that netted BYU's 8 pts in 2nd Q. Jones made diving 21y TD catch of Zuger pass late in 2nd Q. BYU dominated 2nd H,

but lost ball on downs 4 times inside State 30YL and suffered Devils LB Fred Rhoades' INT deep in ASU end. Zuger added short 4th Q TD pass to E Bill Spanko with 2:32 left after LB Charley Jones made INT at Cougars 15YL.

Stanford 39 OREGON STATE 22: Stanford (3-6) QB Dick Norman was his usual stellar self in aerial game, completing 14-26/237y, 57y TD pass to E Chris Burford, and INT. Norman also found flaw in Oregon State (2-7) D that allowed faked cutbacks all afternoon with pitchouts to FB Skip Face. Using blocks of HB Mac Wylie, Face scored 3 TDs and 2-pt run. With his educated toe, Face cleared crossbar with 4 conv kicks and 31y FG for total of 27 pts. Beaver O floundered until TB Don Kasso scored 2 TDs in 4th Q, their only 1st H excitement being generated by WB Ron Miller's 2nd Q 85y KO TD RET that followed Stanford FB Rick McMillen's 19y TD that probed flaws in Oregon State's outside run D.

Oregon 7 WASHINGTON STATE 6: Soph QB Mel Melin gave Washington State (5-3) 6-0 lead in 2nd Q, but Cougars failed to get HB Perry Harper across for 2-pt run. Hopeful of Rose Bowl bid, urgent Oregon (8-1) finally broke out of own territory on QB Dave Grosz's 56y heave which HB Willie West carried to Cougar 4YL with 1:00 to play. West's TD run battered 4 would-be tacklers on 4th down from 2YL and tied it 6-6. K Roger Daniels' x-pt won it as Oregon swept only home-and-home set of games scheduled between 2 teams in 2nd half of 20th century: 14-6 on October 3 in Eugene and this 7-6 nail-biter at Pullman.

AP Poll November 16

1 Syracuse (126)	2145	11 Michigan State (1)	293
2 Mississippi (68)	1859	12 Auburn	291
3 Louisiana State (16)	1721	13 Arkansas	271
4 Southern California (16)	1627	14 Washington	240
5 Texas (1)	1090	15 Oregon (1)	119
6 Georgia (6)	1009	16 Iowa (3)	110
7 Penn State (6)	869	17 Alabama (4)	103
8 Northwestern (1)	411	18 Miami	98
9 Wisconsin	383	19 Clemson	55
10 Texas Christian	314	20 Tennessee	54

November 21, 1959

(Fri) MIAMI 18 Michigan State 13: Michigan State (5-4) became unwitting sightseer among palm trees as Miami (6-3) dealt itself into Orange Bowl picture with big upset. FG by K Al Dangel and 5y TD run by FB Frank Bouffard gave Hurricanes lead, but MSU came back by H on QB Dean Look's 9y TD pass to HB Herb Adderley to cut edge to 10-6. QB Fran Curci hit 4 passes in row for 48y on 80y TD drive to open 2nd H, and his TD and 2-pt pass proved vital at 18-6. Curci erred later as Spartans HB-DB Gary Ballman ran 51y with 4th Q INT to set up own 10y TD run.

PITTSBURGH 22 Penn State 7: Playing just their 2nd game as Pitt's starting backfield unit, Panthers' "C Boys" promoted by team publicist and future ESPN TV analyst Beano Cook and consisting of HBs Bob Clemens and Fred Cox and FB Jim Cunningham, amassed 287y rushing and scored 2 TDs. After Penn State (8-2) QB Richie Lucas was trapped for safety by future Pitt coach and NFL D coordinator, C-LB Serafino "Foge" Fazio, Panthers (6-4) scored in 9 plays on QB Ivan Toncic's sneak. Later, Clemens went 34y to score, and, this will come as a surprise for those who watched him balloon in weight as Minnesota Vikings' K, Cox twisted and spurted 86y to TD that clinched upset of no. 7, bowl-bound Lions. Penn State sub HB Dick Pae scored late in 3rd Q.

CLEMSON 33 Wake Forest 31: With ACC crown at stake, Wake Forest (5-4) rode passing arm of QB Norm Snead (9-23/196y, 2 TDs) to 17-14 lead at H and 24-14 edge in 3rd Q. Clemson (7-2) countered with 295y on ground, FB Doug Cline the chief perpetrator with 29/125y, 2 TDs. Deacons appeared to have taken game's last lead change at 31-27 midway in 4th Q, and they were pressing toward Clemson's GL. But, Tigers HB George Usry picked off Snead and made clutch 73y INT RET to 10YL. Usry fittingly bolted over for TD 2 plays later, and Clemson had its 2nd ACC title in row.

MICHIGAN 23 Ohio State 14: Worst record in coach Woody Hayes' 28 years at Ohio State (3-5-1) was sealed by spunky Michigan (4-5), led by flawless leadership of sr QB Stan Noskin. Wrapping up spotty career, Noskin hit FB Tony Rio with 1st Q TD pass, ran for 2nd Q score, and hit pair of passes to power 3rd Q TD march. FB Roger Detrick, in for injured Bob White, was workhorse in slamming 33/139y and TD for Buckeyes.

Purdue 10 INDIANA 7: Heroic Indiana (4-4-1) GLS stand in dying moments of 3rd Q seemed to project 7-7 tie, 7th deadlock between Old Oaken Bucket rivals since series began on this date in 1925. But, Purdue (5-2-2) QB-K Bernie Allen, shortstop who had beaten Indiana with 2 home runs in previous spring's baseball game, nailed 31y FG in 4th Q. In 2nd Q, Hoosiers TB Teddy Smith (13/88y) had run 40y to help overcome 15y PEN and set up 18y TD pass from TB John Henry Jackson to E Ted Aucreman. Boilers matched score for 7-7 H tie as HB Clyde Washington ended 73y drive with 4y TD run. Purdue G Fred Brandel fell on 1 of 5 IU FUMs at Hoosiers 29YL in 3rd Q, and runs advanced Boilers to 1st-and-goal at 4YL. Washington and FB Willie Jones were stopped on 4 thrusts at GL, but Smith's short QK to 37YL set stage for Allen's FG.

ILLINOIS 28 Northwestern 0: In coach Ray Eliot's last game after 18 mostly-winning autumns in Champaign-Urbana, Illinois (5-3-1) dominated drained and thinned ranks of Northwestern (6-3), which in 3 quick weeks faded from 1st place in Big 10—and no. 2 in AP Poll—to 5th place in final conf standings. Even though Illini would squander chances at Wildcats 15 and 6YLs with lost FUMS, they got rolling 12 mins into 1st Q on HB DeJustice Coleman's 37y punt RET to 9YL. HB Johnny Counts zipped 8y to set up QB John Easterbrook's TD sneak. FB Bill Brown scored 1st of his 2 TD runs in 2nd Q for 14-0 lead. Wildcats rallied slightly at outset of 2nd H as QB John Talley clicked on 3 passes for 1st downs to 18YL. But Northwestern run game made 1y in 3 tries, in fact, it gained meager 36y rushing all day as Illini G-LB Bill Burrell ranged far and wide to knock down Northwestern runners. Star Cats HB Ron Burton could make only 2y per carry.

Wisconsin 11 MINNESOTA 7: Needing and getting help from Illinois, against Northwestern, Wisconsin (7-2) earned its 1st unshared Big 10 title since 1912 and its 1st Rose Bowl date since losing conf's only to-date Pasadena trip in 1953. Early 57y lightning fueled Minnesota (2-7): QB Sandy Stephens hit HB Arlie Bomstad with long pass just 1:43 into 1st Q. Gophers, who would end up unaccountably in Big 10 cellar, played their rivals to hilt, but turning point came in 3rd Q when Badgers HB-DB Bob Altmann made 27y INT RET to Minny 8YL of pass thrown by Stephens. That set up T-K Karl Holzworth to kick his 7th FG of season, new NCAA record, and allow Badgers to pull within 7-3. QB Dale Hackbart fired up Wisconsin on winning 80y drive 6 mins into 4th Q. Hackbart (9-18/149y, and 19/74y, TD rushing) hit E Allan Schoonover with 51y pass, then scored on sneak on 10th play of drive. Hackbart added 2-pt pass to E Henry Derleth, but win would not be locked up until DB Hackbart filched pass by Gophers sub QB Larry Johnson deep in Badgers end. Johnson (5-9/94y, 2 INTs) had just connected for 34y to HB Tom King.

Notre Dame 20 IOWA 19: QB George Izo (14-25/295y, 3 TDs, 3 INTs), in and out of Notre Dame (4-5) lineup since September with bad knee, fired TD passes of 29, 45, and 56y. Iowa (5-4), bidding for 4th straight win over ND, came out of 1st Q with 7-7 tie, thanks to HB Ray Jauch. Jauch's 61y RET of INT on Izo to Irish 22YL ended Irish threat and positioned Hawkeye TD from FB Don Horn. Jerry Mauren, quick little HB, roared 80y with 2nd Q punt TD RET, and Iowa led 19-7, but was far short on QB Wilburn Hollis' 2-pt run. Izo's 44y TD to E Pat Heenan sliced it to 19-13 before H. After Iowa's GLS and HB Bernie Wyatt's INT, Izo had to wait until last 4 min to pitch winning TD to handy HB George Sefcik (11/52y, and 4/143y receiving).

OKLAHOMA 35 Iowa State 12: Iowa State's hustling "Dirty Thirty" had permitted only 2 TDs in season's previous 5 games and stood as potential roadblock to 12th straight undisputed conf crown for Sooners (6-3). But, Oklahoma's bruising ground game (348y) carried it to telling verdict. QB Bobby Boyd cut and dodged to 23y TD run at end of 59y march in 1st Q, and sub FB Ronnie Hartline quickly capped 34y drive with TD. Cyclones (7-3) narrowed gap to 14-6 on TB Dwight Nichols' 2nd Q TD pass and to 21-12 on FB Tom Watkins' 3rd Q TD run. Oklahoma's dynamic FB Prentice Gautt (14/110y) clinched it with pair of 4th Q TDs. Watkins, nation's rushing leader, was held to 68y by Sooners D.

Missouri 13 KANSAS 9: With 2nd place in Big 8 and Orange Bowl bid at stake, Kansas (5-5) became own worst enemy with 5 lost FUMs. Missouri (6-4) QB Phil Snowden keyed 58y 2nd Q TD tour with 11y rushing and 26y passing, his TD coming on 12y toss to HB Donnie Smith. Jayhawks tied it 7-7 in 3rd Q with 80y trip in 12 plays, as FB Doyle Schick gained 60y, including last 7y for score. Tigers' clincher came on FB Jim Miles' TD, which was set up by Snowden's 4th down completion to E Russ Sloan.

Ucla 10 SOUTHERN CALIFORNIA 3: It had been strange jr season for UCLA (4-3-1) TB Billy Kilmer. He started year on "fat man's training table," and, prior to USC game, he hurt ankle in phys-ed class, of all places. Behind 3-0 on Trojans (8-1) HB-K Don Zachik's early 27y FG, Bruins summoned Kilmer from bench in 2nd H. To protect himself from possible ankle twist, Kilmer shunned cleats for tennis shoes, but still drove Bruins from own 13YL to USC 15YL where WB-K Ivory Jones kicked 31y tying FG early in 4th Q. Later, Kilmer launched long bomb for E Marv Luster from USC 47YL. Trojans QB-DB Willie Wood picked it off at 1YL, but HB-DB Jerry Traynham was called for disputed pass interference PEN on play. From 7YL, Bruins FB Ray Smith shoved it over for winning TD in 3 plays.

California 20 STANFORD 17: Before 90,000 witnesses, Golden Bears (2-8) called on run-oriented QB Wayne Crow to throw 9-13/158y, and Crow used 2 rollout passes devised especially for bunched-up Stanford (3-7) D to complete TD passes for 14-0 H lead. Indians QB Dick Norman, already 16-18 passing during 1st H, continued his hot hand in 2nd H and finished with excellent 87.2% completions on 34-39/401y, TD, INT. Norman's passes set up FB Skip Face's 3y TD run in 3rd Q, followed by TD pass to E Chris Burford (12/122y). On 4th down at Cal 15YL midway in 4th Q, Stanford chose K Face's 32y FG for its 1st lead at 17-14. Bears went 64y, all on runs except HB Bill Patton's 13y catch, to twisting 2y TD by HB Jerry Scattini (12/54y). Norman brought Tribe back downfield to Bears 18YL on 14y pass to E Ben Robinson with 25 secs left, hit Burford for 8y, but couldn't get OB as he scrambled to 5YL. Game ended with Stanford trying to line up for tying 22y FG.

Oregon State 15 OREGON 7: Oregon State (3-7) suffered FUMs on each of its 1st 2 possessions with Oregon (8-2) gaining TD within 7-min mark. Littlest Duck, HB Cleveland Jones, threw 5y option pass to HB Willie West for 7-0 lead. That stoked up Rose Bowl dreams of Oregon's hopeful fans. Beavers, never getting around to completing pass all day (in 3 tries), powered 52y to TB Don Kasso's 2nd Q TD, added WB-K Amos Marsh's go-ahead FG, and wrapped up "Civil War" with FB Jim Stinnette's 4th Q TD plunge. Ducks' loss all but assured Washington of being picked over Oregon for Pasadena bowl game.

WASHINGTON 20 Washington State 0: Ferocious Washington (9-1) D, led by Ts Kurt Gegner and Bill Kinnune and G-LB Chuck Allen forced 5 Washington State (5-4) TOs, tripped up Cougars to tune of 175y O, and held star HB Keith Lincoln to 33y rushing. Meanwhile, Huskies' spectacular 1-eyed QB Bob Schloredt rolled up 209y O on 111y rushing and 98y passing. Rushing for 17y and hitting E Lee Folkins with pass, Schloredt guided 80y drive, culminated by HB Don McKeta's 4y blast into EZ on opening play of 2nd Q. Schloredt scored on short run in 3rd Q, and FB Joe Jones tallied from 2YL after Cougars committed pass interference PEN deep in their own territory.

AP Poll November 23

1 Syracuse (121)	1602	11 Auburn	202
2 Mississippi (32)	1377	12 Miami (5)	187
3 Louisiana State (1)	1216	13 Illinois	109
4 Texas	978	14 Clemson	100
5 Wisconsin (1)	753	15 Penn State	97
6 Georgia (3)	750	16 Pittsburgh	50
7 Southern California	586	17 Oklahoma	43
8 Texas Christian	467	18 Missouri (2)	40
9 Washington (4)	437	19 Alabama (1)	38
10 Arkansas (1)	257	20 UCLA	35

November 26-28, 1959

(Th'g) PENNSYLVANIA 28 Cornell 13: Sixty-sixth Turkey Day traditional saw Penn (7-1-1) wrap up Ivy League title with 2nd H reversal. Cornell (5-4) switched QB Marcy Tino to HB and used wide flankers. When Tino threw 37y TD pass at end of 71y march after 2nd H KO, Big Red was in business at 13-0. FB Jack Hanlon countered with 13y TD catch to move Penn within 13-7, but Big Red drove right back to Quakers 24YL. Penn T Jim Dunsmore fell on FUM, and with that break rest of day belonged to Penn: QB George Koval threw 3 TD passes in what was to be coach Steve Sebo's Philly finale.

(Th'g) NORTH CAROLINA 50 Duke 0: Finally surfacing was sharp Tar Heels (5-5) team for which coach Jim Tatum had predicted greatness before his untimely death in July. Carolina leapt to 28-0 H lead, and big FB Don Klochak took 2nd H KO 93y to TD and 35-0 margin. When HB George Knox scored on 32y run in 4th Q, coach Jim Hickey answered student chants of "Hickey, go for 50!" with successful 2-pt call. Despite suffering its worst-ever defeat, Duke (4-6) came out surprisingly even on O stat sheet: trailing 388y to 254y.

(Th'g) Virginia Military 37 Virginia Tech 12 (Roanoke): Underdog VMI (8-1-1), undefeated but tied by Richmond in league play, took Southern Conf title on strength of dandy QB Howard Dyer's 3 TD passes and 1y TD sneak. Unsuspecting Virginia Tech (6-4) got 2nd TD plunge from HB Pat Henry, but trailed 18-6 at H because of 3 clutch plays by VMI. Dyer hit E Dick Evans for 29y TD on 4th-and-12 and 18y on 4th-and-16 to set up FB Sam Horner's TD run, both in 1st Q. Then, HB John Traynham scored when he snatched 32y pass out of hands of VPI QB-DB Frank Eastman.

(Th'g) Texas 20 TEXAS A&M 17: Longhorns (9-1) fashioned come-from-behind win for share of SWC crown and Cotton Bowl berth. Texas A&M (3-7) rode QB Charlie Milstead—who participated in all but 1 play—as he threw 4y TD pass to HB Randy Sims late in 2nd Q. With :20 before H, Sims bombed 52y FG for 10-0 Aggie lead. Texas went 90y to TD in 3rd Q, and FB Mike Dowdle scored his 2nd TD for 14-10 lead early in 4th Q. Aggies countered with TD pass by Milstead, part of his 175y O. QB Bobby Lackey put Texas ahead for good with 2:20 left when his TD capped 75y drive, on which he made pair of 4th down conversions.

Navy 43 Army 12 (Philadelphia): Tallying highest score to date in 60th military series, Navy (5-4-1) unleashed flying HB Joe Bellino for 3 TD runs: 15, 46, and 1y. Army (4-4-1) rallied briefly in 2nd Q with TDs by its set of A-A stars: E Bill Carpenter grabbed 29y reception and gimpy HB Bob Anderson powered 12y. But, Middies led 21-12 at H break. DB Bellino's 3rd Q INT of tipped pass thrown by Black Knights QB Joe Caldwell (7-27/138y, TD) set up his 3rd score for 29-12 lead.

Wake Forest 43 South Carolina 20 (Charlotte): Wake Forest (6-4) QB Norm Snead threw 3 TD passes and set up another while breaking 5 ACC season O records. South Carolina (6-4) led 8-0, 14-6, and 20-12 on TD by FB Phil Lavoie, 2 TDs by QB Steve Satterfield. But, Gamecocks were blanked in 2nd H. Wake Forest displayed wonderfully-balanced O, gaining 246y rushing and 245y passing.

Georgia 21 GEORGIA TECH 14: Georgia Tech (6-4) FB Taz Anderson lost FUM on opening KO, and it set Tech on its heels for rest of 1st Q. After E Gerald Burch and T Billy Shaw each recovered FUM and HB-DB Billy Williamson made INT, all at own 26YL or closer, Engineers seemed to have frustrated Georgia (9-1). But, on their 4th try in Yellow Jacket territory in 1st Q, Bulldogs scored after HB Fred Brown's 38y run took ball to 2YL. Georgia jumped to 21-0 improvement as E Bill Herron made brilliant catch of QB Fran Tarkenton's 16y TD pass in 2nd Q, and QB Charley Britt connected with Brown for 40y TD 9 secs before H. Engineers owned 2nd H thanks to relief QB job by Marvin Tibbetts, who passed for TD to Burch, who made colossal effort to score on 57y play with only secs to go in 3rd Q. Bad punt snap put Yellow Jackets at Georgia 14YL on next series, but Burch dropped certain TD pass and 4th down fake FG play blew up. HB-P Bobby Walden blasted 67y punt to send Tech back to its 9YL. P Burch ran for 45y on fake punt but Engineers couldn't push it across after 1st-and-goal at Georgia 7YL. Tibbetts flew 38y TD pass to E Fred Murphy with 3:08 on clock. Master QB Tarkenton (11-15/115y, TD, INT) managed pair of 1st downs to kill clock. Bowl bids went to each team: Orange Bowl to Georgia and Gator Bowl to Georgia Tech.

ALABAMA 10 Auburn 0 (Birmingham): Crimson Tide (7-1-2) beat Auburn (7-3) for 1st time since 1953. E-K Tommy Brooker kicked 27y FG in 2nd Q, and little HB Marlin Dyess capped 75y TD drive in 3rd Q with 39y TD dash with flat pass from QB Bobby Skelton. Without single 1st down deep into 2nd H, Tigers cruised 73y on QB Bobby Hunt's 4th Q throws only to be halted by C-LB Billy Richardson's INT at Alabama 14YL.

Florida 23 Miami 14 (Jacksonville): Florida (5-4-1) QB-K Dick Allen, 26-year-old former GI, kicked 20y FG, threw TD pass in decisive 2-min span of 4th Q to spoil Orange Bowl hopes of Miami (6-4). After HB Doug Partin's 58y INT RET, Allen scored TD that gave Gators 7-0 lead. Hurricanes QB Fran Curci surmounted 5 INTs to take control of 3rd Q, Miami scoring twice for shortlived 14-13 lead. After Miami had beaten Michigan State week earlier, Orange Bowl committee promised spot to local Hurricanes. Instead, this loss and Georgia's win prompted committee to renege and tap SEC champ Bulldogs.

NOTRE DAME 16 Southern California 6: Fighting Irish (5-5) E Monty Stickles hurried USC punt by HB-P Clark Holden into short flight OB early in 1st Q, and soph FB Gerry Gray followed with 2 draw runs to cover 39y for TD. Gray scored again in 3rd Q at conclusion of 49y drive and then raced downfield to spill Trojans HB Angelo Coia for safety on ensuing KO. After pulling his reverse-of-field boner on KO, Coia got 4th Q TD on 13y pass from QB Ben Charles. It came too late to avert 2nd loss in row for late-fading Southern California (8-2).

TEXAS CHRISTIAN 19 Southern Methodist 0: TCU (8-2) used HB Marv Lasater's 2 TDs and brutish D, led by 2 future pro stars, Ts Bob Lilly and Don Floyd, to secure 3-way tie for SWC title with Texas and Arkansas. G-LB Roy Lee Rambo blitzed occasionally to help Horned Frogs sack SMU (5-4-1) QB Don Meredith so often as to submerge Mustangs' team rushing total to -1y. On his way to Dallas Cowboys and ABC Monday Night Football TV fame, Meredith (14-25/115y), extraordinary Ponies passer for 3 years, ended his career with then NCAA-record 61% completion rating.

AP Poll November 30

1 Syracuse (95)	1492	11 Alabama (6)	153
2 Mississippi (49)	1350	12 Illinois (1)	106
3 Louisiana State (6)	1128	13 Southern California	98
4 Texas	892	14 Penn State	84
5 Georgia (2)	836	15 Oklahoma	74
6 Wisconsin (15)	749	16 Wyoming	70
7 Texas Christian	562	17 UCLA	62
8 Washington (2)	428	18 Florida	40
9 Arkansas	356	19 Notre Dame	36
10 Clemson	190	20 Missouri	30

December 5, 1959

MARYLAND 33 North Carolina State 28: Terrapins (5-5) rose to 3 early TD passes by QB Dale Betty for 19-7 edge. Opportune D play, in form of T Joe Gardi's punt block and G Pete Boinis' FUM REC, gave Maryland 2 additional scores that proved decisive. Key TD was scored late in 2nd Q by Maryland FB Jim Joyce (16/82y, TD), new ACC rushing titlist, on 6y blast through RG after Gardi had blocked punt by State P Collice Moore. Trailing 26-14 at H, competitive Wolfpack (1-9) QB Roman Gabriel (23-38/279y, 2 TDs, INT) hit E Jim Tapp with 1st of 2 TD passes in 2nd H to crawl within 26-21 in 3rd Q. Betty put contest away with 5y TD run off T that especially grieved NC State coach Earle Edwards. Just before Gabriel ran wide but was forced into FUM by Boinis at 7YL, Edwards motioned his QB to punt out of danger.

Syracuse 36 UCLA 8: While completing its dominating regular season, Syracuse (10-0) left lasting impression on West Coast pollsters by gaining 456y on O and holding UCLA (5-4-1) to -13y on ground. Orangemen built 21-0 lead by 2nd Q, much of it authored by Syracuse's scintillating subs: Backup QB Dick Easterly threw 15y scoring pass to HB Mark Weber and sneaked for TD. Bruins mustered short-lived air attack that eventually totaled 160y by game's end, and scored in last min of 1st H as TB Billy Kilmer hit diving WB Jim Johnson with 20y TD pass. UCLA added 2 pts on TB Skip Smith's run. After scoreless 3rd Q which had to be chalked up as positive for Uclans, Orange HB Ger Schwedes sped to 40y gain on reverse run and then scored on 23y run for his 2nd TD and 29-8 lead. UCLA coach Bill Barnes thought his team played very well in 3rd Q but called Syracuse team "one of the greatest I've ever seen."

Final AP Poll December 7

1 Syracuse (134)	1768	11 Clemson	239
2 Mississippi (47)	1444	12 Penn State	190
3 Louisiana State (6)	1284	13 Illinois	104
4 Texas (1)	1028	14 Southern California	94
5 Georgia (3)	876	15 Wyoming	68
6 Wisconsin (5)	724	16 Wyoming	60
7 Texas Christian	580	17 Notre Dame	46
8 Washington	428	18 Missouri	40
9 Arkansas	301	19 Florida	34
10 Alabama (5)	257	20 Pittsburgh	30

1959 Conference Standings

Ivy League

Pennsylvania	6-1
Dartmouth	5-1-1
Harvard	4-3
Yale	4-3
Cornell	3-4
Princeton	3-4
Brown	1-5-1
Columbia	1-6

Atlantic Coast

Clemson	6-1
North Carolina	5-2
Maryland	4-2
Wake Forest	4-3
South Carolina	4-3
Duke	2-3
Virginia	0-5
North Carolina State	0-6

Southern

Virginia Military	5-0-1
Citadel	5-1
Virginia Tech	3-1
Furman	3-2
Richmond	4-3-1
West Virginia	2-2
William & Mary	2-5
Davidson	0-5
George Washington	0-5

Southeastern

Georgia	7-0
Louisiana State	5-1
Mississippi	5-1
Alabama	4-1-2
Vanderbilt	3-2-2
Georgia Tech	3-3
Tennessee	3-4-1
Florida	2-4
Kentucky	1-6
Tulane	0-5-1
Mississippi State	0-7

Big Ten

Wisconsin	5-2
Michigan State	4-2
Purdue	4-2-1
Illinois	4-2-1
Northwestern	4-3
Iowa	3-3
Michigan	3-4
Indiana	2-4-1
Ohio State	2-4-1
Minnesota	1-6

Big Eight

Oklahoma	5-1
Missouri	4-2
Iowa State	3-3
Kansas	3-3
Colorado	3-3
Nebraska	2-4
Kansas State	1-5
Oklahoma State	1-2 *
* ineligible: record not included	

Missouri Valley

North Texas State	3-1
Houston	3-1
Tulsa	2-2
Wichita	1-2-1
Cincinnati	0-3-1

Mid-American

Bowling Green	6-0
Ohio	4-2
Miami (Ohio)	3-2
Kent State	3-3
Western Michigan	3-3
Marshall	1-4
Toledo	0-6

Southwest

Texas	5-1
Arkansas	5-1
Texas Christian	5-1
Southern Methodist	2-3-1
Baylor	2-4
Rice	1-4-1
Texas A&M	0-6
Texas Tech	ineligible

Border

Arizona State	5-0
Arizona	2-1
New Mexico State	2-2
Hardin-Simmons	2-2
Texas Western	2-3
West Texas State	0-5

Skyline Eight

Wyoming	7-0
Colorado State	5-2
New Mexico	4-2
Utah	3-2
Utah State	2-5
Brigham Young	2-5
Denver	2-5
Montana	1-5

AAWU (Big Five)

Washington	3-1
Southern California	3-1
UCLA	3-1
California	1-3
Stanford	0-4

1959 Major Bowl Games

Liberty Bowl (Dec. 19): Penn State 7 Alabama 0

First-ever Liberty Bowl was played in frigid Philadelphia where 36,211 turned out in cavernous 100,000-seat Municipal Stadium. Icy fingers meant each side lost 4 FUMs, somewhat negating 319y to 131y O edge enjoyed by Penn State (9-2). With ace Nittany Lions QB Richie Lucas on sideline with injury, sub QB Galen Hall completed his only pass for 18y TD off fake FG to HB Roger Kochman in last min of 2nd Q. Hall's pass went to Kochman in left flat, and dandy blocks by Es Henry Oppermann and Norm Neff allowed speedster to tumble into EZ. Lions' TD was only 2nd scoring pass permitted by Crimson Tide (7-2-2) during season, and it occurred partly because Alabama HB-P Tommy White had to punt twice into biting wind. Of his Bama squad that rose up firm when pushed into its own territory, coach Bear Bryant would later say, "We weren't a real strong team, but that team would hit you." It was 1st of 24 straight Bama teams to visit bowl under Bryant.

Bluebonnet Bowl (Dec. 19): Clemson 23 Texas Christian 7

Texas Christian (8-3) arrived for inaugural Bluebonnet Bowl in Houston as tri-champ of SWC and 1 of nation's best D squads, but Frogs were burned by Tigers' surprising aerial strikes in 2nd H. TCU led 7-3 at H on 19y HB pass from sub Jack Reding to HB Harry Moreland. Frogs' TD capped 12-play, 63y trip. Neither team tallied in 3rd Q, but Clemson (9-2) went ahead for good in when QB Harvey White lofted perfect pass to E Gary Barnes, who slipped behind TCU HB-DB Marvin Lasater, for stunning 68y TD and 10-7 Tigers' lead. Sub QB Lowndes Shingler threw 23y TD pass on 4th down after Tigers G-LB-K Lon Armstrong, who had made FG in 2nd Q, returned INT of Frogs QB Don George to TCU 17YL. HB Ron Scrudato scored with 3:16 left as Clemson tallied 20 pts in 7-min duration of 4th Q. Odd about Tigers' rally was that they had completed only 1-7 passes prior to White clicking with Barnes on home run throw. Normally-efficient White had frequently overshot his receivers in 1st H.

Orange Bowl: Georgia 14 Missouri 0

Season-long pass D problems for Missouri (6-5) were exposed again as Georgia (10-1) QB Fran Tarkenton threw TD passes to HB Bill McKenny (29y) and E Aaron Box (33y). Tarkenton's 1st TD throw, which came with 14 secs remaining in 1st Q, was thing of "scrambling" beauty, a prelude to his NFL magic. Hemmed in at right sideline by bevy of Tiger rushers, Tarkenton (9-21/128y, 2 INTs) spotted McKenny tearing diagonally across field and nailed him over heads of pass defenders. Bulldogs coach Wally Butts called contest his team's worst game of season and especially was annoyed at poor open-field tackling. Missouri HB Norm Beal made punt RETs of 43, 22, and 35y that often negated great punting of Georgia HB Bobby Walden, who booted 7/46.9y avg for new Orange Bowl record. Butts briefly inspired Bulldogs, for, upon 2nd H KO, they went 71y in 8 plays. Tarkenton completed passes of 18, 13, and finally 33y for TD to Box. Missouri had 3 scoring threats. HB Mel West missed FG early in 2nd Q. Just before H, QB Phil Snowden (14-24/180y, 3 INTs) completed passes of 20, 12, and 29y to Georgia 14YL, but suffered GL INT by Bulldogs QB-DB Charley Britt. Snowden hit 4 passes on 83y advance early in 4th Q, but he ruined Tigers scoring prospects with 2 poor pitchouts. Missouri may have been vulnerable to aerial game, but its D still hit

awfully hard as evidenced on silver helmet of Britt. After being hit on keeper run, Britt's metal headgear sported dent on its upper right side about same size as Florida orange.

Sugar Bowl: Mississippi 21 Louisiana State 0

Employing strong revenge motive, Ole Miss (10-1) dominated from outset, limiting LSU (9-2), its nemesis from notorious Halloween night game, to -15y on ground and keeping all but 1 Tigers trip outside Rebs territory. Ole Miss QB Bobby Franklin (10-15/148y, 2 TDs), injured much of year, had outstanding day, and E Larry Grantham was ferocious on D. Rebel threatened early but each failed as LSU QB Warren Rabb made INT at own 5YL, Mississippi T-K Bob Khayat's missed FG, Tigers held on downs at 11YL, and LSU QB Darryl Jenkins made INT at 10YL. Rebels finally converted their domination into pts with QB Jake Gibbs' 43y TD pass to HB Cowboy Woodruff with 40 secs left in H. Franklin fired 2 TD passes in 2nd H, and Ole Miss held on downs at own 42YL after LSU sub QB Durel Matherne hit 2 4th Q passes for only penetration of Ole Miss turf.

Cotton Bowl: Syracuse 23 Texas 14

Although Syracuse (11-0) was flagged for 50y in PENs in 1st Q, it stunned fired-up Texas (9-2) with TD pass in early going and never trailed. HB Ger Schwedes flipped pass to HB Ernie Davis (8/57y, TD), who despite hamstring pain, eluded QB-DB Bobby Lackey and lugged ball for 87y score. It was longest TD pass in major bowl history to that point and underscored MVP Davis' great performance. Davis made 11y INT RET to 24YL and followed with 21y run to set up team's 3rd Q TD by Schwedes. For its part, Longhorns tackled very hard and managed to outrush Orangemen 145y to 133y. Sparking Texas, which made its best O show in 2nd H rally, were Lackey (3-9/92y, TD, INT), FB Clair Branch (11/71y) and HB Rene Ramirez (2/23y receiving), who led attack that did well to rack up 244y against nation's stingiest D (96.2y per game avg). After Orangemen had been stopped thrice on plays inside Steers 1YL at end of 80y march in 2nd Q, Davis powered over for 4th down TD and then caught 2-pt pass from QB Dave Sarette (3-5/45y, INT) for 15-0 H advantage. Late in 2nd Q, Syracuse E Ken Ericson caught 41y pass and appeared to cross GL as he was tackled, but lost ball, which rolled through EZ. Meanwhile, back at scrimmage line, fistic brouhaha broke out around Orange's African-American T John Brown. Versions differed afterward, but Texas was accused of racial slurs by white teammates of Brown, who downplayed incident himself. Syracuse was flagged for trio of 15y PENs on play, but Longhorns chose play result, touchback that they took at own 20YL. It all but ended 1st H. Lackey pitched 69y TD pass to speedy HB Jack Collins in 3rd Q, and late in 3rd Q, DG Bob Harwerth recovered FUM at Syracuse 34YL. Ramirez caught his 2 passes, but Texas could get no closer than 1YL. Texas lost opportunity with FUM at Syracuse 22YL in 4th Q, but soon cashed 54y drive as Branch dashed 36y to 1YL behind block of E Monte Lee.

Rose Bowl: Washington 44 Wisconsin 8

To astonishment of 100,000 fans and millions watching on TV, long-established Big 10 stranglehold on Rose Bowl trophy was thoroughly dashed. In apparent last year of long-term contract between Big 10 and Pacific schools, hard-hitting Washington (10-1) turned tables and possibly saved future agreement which had been wearing thin for West Coast fans. Big 10 had won 12 of 13 games prior to January 1, 1960, with 7 different members of its conf qualifying for Pasadena. Only Wisconsin was loser, including 7-0 decision to USC in 1952, failed to win of those teams that made trip west. Huskies (10-1), 6-pt underdog, got early TD from HB Don McKeta. When HB-K George Fleming added 1st Q FG for 10-0 edge after Wisconsin (7-3) HB Bill Hobbs' FUM, it "put us in control, and Wisconsin began to press," according to Huskies coach Jim Owens. Fleming soon added 53y punt TD RET, and rout was on at 17-0. FB Tom Wiesner scored Badgers' only TD on 4y run at end of well-managed 69y trip, and QB Dale Hackbart added 2-pt pass to E Allan Schoonover to pull Badgers briefly out of their hole at 17-8. But that score quickly was countered by Washington E Lee Folkins' diving EZ catch of 23y TD pass by QB Bob Schloredt (4-7/102y, TD, and 21/81y, TD rushing). Fleming had set trip in motion with 55y punt RET. Hope for Badgers was collapsed by Fleming's 28y RET of 2nd H KO. Washington soon rode FB Ray Jackson's 5/48y running to another TD.

Gator Bowl (Jan. 2): Arkansas 14 Georgia Tech 7

Arkansas (9-2) coach Frank Broyles, former Georgia Tech QB and asst coach, returned to haunt his mentor, coach Bobby Dodd of Georgia Tech (6-5). It was 1st-ever bowl loss for Dodd after 8 wins, starting with Houston's Oil Bowl on January 1, 1947. Engineers' weight advantage allowed it to dominate 1st Q, as O held ball for all but 3 plays. Georgia Tech QB Marvin Tibbetts faked handoff, looped around LE and cut back on 51y TD run on last play of 1st Q. Razorbacks were different team in 2nd Q and began exploiting their quickness advantage. FB Joe Paul Alberty (12/38y) thrice made short yardage 1st downs on 62y march in 2nd Q and tied game at 7-7 with 1y TD run. Arkansas MVP HB Jim Mooty (18/99y), who almost put out football after several head injuries in 1958, led winning 3rd Q drive and scored on 19y sweep. Engineers caused some late concern with short passes of QB Fred Braselton and finished with 8-18/64y, INT in air. Starring on D were A-A LB Maxie Baughan of Georgia Tech and less heralded, but equally sharp LBs Wayne Harris and Gerald Gardner of Arkansas.

1959 Top Performance Formula

1 Syracuse	1.8698
2 Mississippi	1.7660
3 Georgia	1.5987
4 Washington	1.5985
5 Penn State	1.5934
6 Louisiana State	1.5010
7 Texas	1.5008
8 Arkansas	1.4620
9 Arizona State	1.4294
10 Texas Christian	1.4195
11 Clemson	1.4092
12 Auburn	1.3984
13 Southern California	1.3828
14 Oregon	1.3740
15 Oklahoma	1.3667
16 Alabama	1.3343
17 Northwestern	1.2711
18 Pittsburgh	1.2519
19 Wisconsin	1.2351
20 Purdue	1.2311

1959 Top Opponent Records

1 Kentucky	.6828
2 Mississippi State	.6786
3 Penn State	.6443
4 Georgia Tech	.6359
5 Pittsburgh	.6359
6 West Virginia	.6167
7 Rice	.6105
8 Texas Christian	.6068
9 Baylor	.6011
10 California	.5989
11 Syracuse	.5980
12 Kansas	.5978
13 Tennessee	.5968
14 Houston	.5914
15 Missouri	.5900
16 Arkansas	.5874
17 Mississippi	.5842
18tAuburn	.5824175
18tFlorida State	.5824175
18tUCLA	.5824175

1959 Out-of-Conference Records

	W-L	Percentage	Bowl W-L
Southeastern	33-6-1	.8375	2-3
AAWU	20-10-1	.6833	1-0
Big Ten	14-8-1	.6304	0-1
Southwest	18-11-1	.6167	1-2
Big Eight	12-14	.4615	0-1
Atlantic Coast	11-20	.3548	1-1

1959 Individual Statistical Leaders

RUSHING YARDS	Attempts	Yards	Avg.
Pervis Atkins, New Mexico State	130	971	7.5
Tom Watkins, Iowa State	158	843	5.3
Dwight Nichols, Iowa State	207	746	3.6
Dick Bass, Pacific	139	742	5.3
Billy Brown, New Mexico	95	740	7.8
Charley Flowers, Mississippi	141	733	5.2
Abner Haynes, North Texas State	116	730	6.3
Bob Crandall, New Mexico	116	729	6.3
Fred Doelling, Pennsylvania	133	707	5.3
Nolan Jones, Arizona State	143	689	4.8

PASSING YARDS	Completions	Attempts	Yards	Pct.
Dick Norman, Stanford	152	263	1963	57.8
Pete Hall, Marquette	120	237	1589	50.6
Jackie Lee, Cincinnati	132	232	1535	56.9
Charley Johnson, New Mexico State	105	199	1449	52.8
Norm Snead, Wake Forest	82	191	1361	42.9
Joe Caldwell, Army	105	188	1343	55.9
Don Meredith, Southern Methodist	105	181	1266	58.0
Rich Mayo, Air Force	110	211	1212	52.1
John Amabile, Boston College	85	159	1200	53.5
Gale Weidner, Colorado	100	207	1200	48.3

RECEIVING YARDS	Catches	Yards
Chris Burford, Stanford	61	756
Ben Robinson, Stanford	34	595
Bill Carpenter, Army	43	591
Paul Maguire, Citadel	32	549
Gail Cogdill, Washington State	28	531
Bobby Allen, Wake Forest	25	462
Bake Turner, Texas Tech	22	444
Don Norton, Iowa	30	428
Bill Miler, Miami	33	395
Mike Quinlan, Air Force	29	373

1959 Consensus All-America Team

End:	Bill Carpenter, Army
	Monty Stickles, Notre Dame
Tackle:	Dan Lanphear, Wisconsin
	Don Floyd, Texas Christian
Guard:	Roger Davis, Syracuse
	Bill Burrell, Illinois
Center:	Maxie Baughan, Georgia Tech
Back:	Richie Lucas, Penn State
	Billy Cannon, Louisiana State
	Ron Burton, Northwestern
	Charlie Flowers, Mississippi

Other All-America Choices

End:	Marlin McKeever, Southern California
	Carroll Dale, Virginia Tech
	Fred Mautino, Syracuse
	Chris Burford, Stanford
	Don Norton, Iowa
Tackle:	Ken Rice, Auburn
	Bob Yates, Syracuse
	Mike McGee, Duke
Guard:	Zeke Smith, Auburn
	Mike McKeever, Southern California
	Maurice Doke, Texas
	Pat Dye, Georgia
	Marvin Terrell, Mississippi
Center:	E.J. Holub, Texas Tech
	Jim Andreotti, Northwestern
Back:	Bob Schloredt, Washington
	Jim Mooty, Arkansas
	Dean Look, Michigan State
	Don Meredith, Southern Methodist
	Dwight Nichols, Iowa State
	Jack Spikes, Texas Christian

1959 Heisman Trophy Vote

Billy Cannon, senior halfback, Louisiana State	1929
Richie Lucas, senior quarterback, Penn State	613
Don Meredith, senior quarterback, Southern Methodist	285
Bill Burrell, senior guard, Illinois	196

Other Major Awards

Maxwell (Player)	Richie Lucas, senior quaterback, Penn State
Outland (Lineman)	Mike McGee, senior guard, Duke
AFCA Coach of the Year	Ben Schwartzwalder, Syracuse

1960

The Year of New Career Opportunities, Oklahoma's Dethronement, and New Frontier at the Orange Bowl

College football entered a new decade of profound change brought on by strong competition from professional football. The graduating senior class of spring, 1960, which finished its eligibility during the 1959 college season, already was enjoying the new-found career prosperity offered by the American Football League, which as a competitor of the NFL, tremendously enhanced the bargaining positions of players. Until the birth of the eight-team AFL, college players interested in playing in the professional ranks rarely had options other than the well-established and thriving, by the late 1950s at least, 12-team National Football League. A college player might not like his offer from the NFL, which by NFL rule was restricted to one team. Only one team, the organization holding a player's draft rights, could bargain with him. Baseball, for example, had no such restriction, until the late 1960s, which allowed a handful of teams, notably the New York Yankees and Brooklyn/Los Angeles Dodgers, to corner big chunks of talent.

The NFL draft brought competitive balance, but by its nature, the draft ended any hope a player might harbor of a free economy. His alternative was the Canadian Football League, which for many American collegians was unattractive. The new AFL grew nicely after a few rough, but colorful moments in the first three years. It was one more step in pro football's profound growth. In only five or six years, the pros had enjoyed a spike in stadium attendance in NFL parks in the mid-1950s, a television contract with CBS that earned national exposure starting in 1956, and an exciting 1958 championship game (the first overtime contest ever) that attracted many new fans. So, big-time pro football, already having run many of the big-city collegiate programs out of business, was on the verge of becoming America's most popular sport.

While pro football created many new post-graduate jobs, it also posed a serious threat not only to live gate but also to televised college games. The pros had a brilliant TV formula created by NFL czar Bert Bell and nurtured by his successor, Pete Rozelle, in the 1960s and beyond

Plus, the expanding pro game placed teams in traditional collegiate strongholds of Boston, Dallas, Houston, and Minneapolis-St. Paul. Soon to follow were Kansas City, Miami, Cincinnati, Atlanta, and San Diego.

Defending college national title holder Syracuse (7-2) opened the 1960 season as the top-rated team, but rarely approached the domination it enjoyed in 1959. The Orangemen's 16-game win streak was ended in late October by a Pittsburgh (4-3-3) team that featured future Chicago Bears coach Mike Ditka as its firebrand captain and took on its usual juggernaut schedule. A great Pitt record was often hopeless during these days, but overconfident and unsuspecting foes were often badly mauled by the tough-as-nails Panthers.

An era ended in the Big Eight as Oklahoma (3-6-1) was dethroned, and then some, after a 14-year run as conference champion. Stepping up to command attention were Missouri (10-1), Kansas (7-2-1), Iowa State (7-3) and Colorado (6-4). Missouri, coached by Dan Devine, owned a ferocious defense, led by end Danny LaRose, that averaged 4.6 points against its first eight vanquished foes. The Tigers achieved the school's first no. 1 ranking when it beat Oklahoma 41-19 on November 12, and proud businesses and radio stations in Columbia, Mo., started answering their phones with: "We're number one!" But, an undefeated year unraveled for the Missouri team when Kansas threw a nine-man front at the Tiger running attack and easily whipped them 23-7 to close the regular season. But, the controversial Bert Coan, a transfer halfback from Texas Christian (4-4-2), played in the Missouri game in defiance of orders from the Big Eight Conference. The Jayhawks were forced to forfeit their conference title and late-season wins over Colorado and Missouri. This put Mizzou back in first place in the Big Eight, and headed to Miami for the Orange Bowl on January 2, 1961.

The Missouri Tigers righted themselves in time for the Orange Bowl where their defense thoroughly contained Heisman Trophy winner Joe Bellino of Navy (9-2) before 72,212 fans, including President-elect John F. Kennedy, a World War II Naval officer and hero who saved his crew of PT Boat 109. It was a highly upbeat atmosphere with Kennedy in attendance. Although Kennedy's election win was a narrow and controversial one over Vice President Richard Nixon, the country was in an optimistic mood, and the youthful President-elect represented every bit of the nation's spark. *Life* magazine ran a series of photos of Kennedy enjoying his time as a spectator in the Orange Bowl grandstands. A few weeks after New Year's, Kennedy launched his "New Frontier" administration, calling on Americans

in his famous inaugural speech: "Ask not what your country can do for you; ask what you can do for your country!"

Early in the 1960 football season, Navy sailed into Seattle and upset no. 3 Washington (10-1) by a single point. Washington soon lost its leader, quarterback Bob Schloredt, to a broken shoulder and struggled to several unimpressive wins before locking up its second-straight Rose Bowl appearance. The Huskies' bowl opponent was Minnesota (8-2), a huge but slow team that fashioned an improbable worst-to-first Big Ten conference turnaround. The Gophers had finished in the Big Ten cellar in 1959, but, as an unbeaten third-ranked team in 1960, they trounced no. 1 Iowa (8-1) 27-10 on November 5 to gain the regular season AP national championship despite a 23-14 surprise that came a week later, courtesy of upset-specialist Purdue (4-4-1), a Big Ten tailender.

Two highly unsung teams of 1960, Ivy League titleist Yale (9-0) and national scoring champion New Mexico State (10-0), had the season's only unblemished marks, allowing each to be posted in the AP Poll final top 20.

For the fourth time since 1950, the AP champion was beaten in a bowl game as Minnesota succumbed to Washington 17-7. The previously-unimpressive Huskies, with Schloredt back under center, dominated the first half against the Gophers and never looked back in gaining a second-straight Rose Bowl win. Minnesota became the first two-loss national champion.

Mississippi (10-0-1) quietly battered its usual soft slate, ranking fifth nationally in points scored with a per-game average of 26.6 points and fourth in points allowed with a 6.4 average. The Rebels' tie came against a so-so LSU (5-4-1) team on October 29 and dropped them from no. 2 to no. 6 in the AP Poll. As usual, Ole Miss' schedule managed to miss any confrontations with the iron of the SEC: Alabama (8-1-1), Florida (8-2), Auburn (8-2), or Georgia (6-4). Still, the Rebels edged Rice (7-4) 14-6 in the Sugar Bowl, and claimed the Football Writers Association Grantland Rice Award. The Grantland Rice Award came from the only voting panel making a post-bowl selection, and thus its committee felt comfortable in bypassing bowl-defeated Minnesota.

The Southeastern Conference, a national powerhouse for years, bagged national championships with Tennessee in 1951, Auburn in 1957, Louisiana State in 1958 and second-place voting finishes with Georgia Tech in 1952 and Ole Miss in 1959 and 1960. The league played great football for many years, and its fans continue to this day to be the most rabid of any in America. But, the SEC had one weakness until it went to two divisions in the 1990s that required full-contact, intra-division and cross-division conference schedules. Until then, it was amazing how often league champions were able to fill their slates with tail-enders and infrequently meet few of the other tough teams in the league.

A dark cloud drifted over the sport early in the season, but happily didn't stay long. Florida fullback Jon MacBeth was approached by gamblers to shave points in the Florida State (3-6-1) game in late September. MacBeth was lauded for having diligently worked to foil the bribery attempt. But, no sooner had Southeastern Conference and NCAA officials given "no credence" to assertions that fixing of college games was nationwide, somewhat low-key publicity was given to a similar bribery offer to a substitute Oregon (7-3-1) player before its game on the same day against Michigan (5-4).

With few exceptions, college football has remained remarkably clear of potential game-fixing problems, but such scandal probably remains the greatest fear of administrators and the greatest peril to the sport's integrity.

Milestones

■ Oklahoma State and Texas Tech began play as eligible members of Big Eight and Southwest Conferences respectively.

■ "Wild Card" rule was liberalized to allow a single substitute to enter game at any time, even if game clock was running.

■ Death claimed two coaches: Rex Enright, 59, who had 64-69-7 record at South Carolina (1946-55) and J.B. "Ears" Whitworth, head coach at Oklahoma A&M (1950-54) and last coach at Alabama (1955-57) prior to arrival of Bear Bryant. Also reaching death's door were Sheldon Beise, 48, All-America fullback at Minnesota (1935), Harry Hammond, 75, end and guard for Michigan (1905-08) and one-time president of Touchdown Club of New York, Ed Hunsicker, 60, end on Notre Dame's "Seven Mules" line that blocked in 1924 for famous "Four Horsemen," and Bob McWhorter, 68, Hall of Fame halfback and Georgia's first All-America player in 1913. McWhorter was Phi Beta Kappa student, for whom University of Georgia residence hall was later named.

■ Longest winning streaks entering season:
Bowling Green, Syracuse 11   Georgia, Wyoming 8

■ Coaching Changes

	Incoming	Outgoing
Boston College	Ernie Hefferle	Mike Holovak
California	Marv Levy	Pete Elliott
Florida	Ray Graves	Bob Woodruff
Florida State	Bill Peterson	Perry Moss
Illinois	Pete Elliott	Ray Eliot
Kansas State	Doug Weaver	Bus Mertes
New Mexico	Bill Weeks	Marv Levy
Pennsylvania	John Stiegman	Steve Sebo
Rutgers	John Bateman	John Stiegman
Southern California	John McKay	Don Clark
Temple	George Makris	Pete Stevens
Wake Forest	Bill Hildebrand	Paul Amen
West Virginia	Gene Coram	Art Lewis

Preseason AP Poll

1 Syracuse (26)	446	11 Texas Christian	64
2 Mississippi (21)	426	12 Auburn	51
3 Washington (1)	345	13 Georgia	48
4 Texas	257	14 Northwestern	41
5 Illinois	228	15 Iowa	33
6 Southern California	140	16 Ohio State	29
7 Pittsburgh	127	17 Notre Dame	26
8 Michigan State	126	18 Tennessee	23
9 Clemson	76	19t Penn State	20
10 Oklahoma	66	19t Arkansas	20

September 17, 1960

(Fri) Oregon State 14 SOUTHERN CALIFORNIA 0: Oregon State (1-0) coach Tommy Prothro leapt right into new wild card rule, shuttling in play calls on every down while directing entire game plan from press box. Beavers TBs Don Kasso and Terry Baker each led TD drive at outset of 1st and 2nd Hs. Kasso scored from 16YL in 1st Q, and Baker hit 3 passes/50y to set up FB Chuck Marshall's 2y TD dive in 3rd Q. Southern California (0-1), 3-TD favorite, went 65y to Beavers 7YL in 2nd Q, but QB Al Prukop lost FUM, 1 of 5 costly bobbles by Trojans.

Navy 22 BOSTON COLLEGE 7: Navy's Massachusetts hero, HB Joe Bellino, returned to home area to throw 64y TD pass to WB John Pritchard very early in game, run for 3y score that put Middies ahead to stay in 3rd Q, and catch 32y TD from new QB Hal Spooner in 4th Q. P Bellino also helped Navy (1-0) out of tough field position with QKs of 64, 50, and 51y and tacked on 2-pt run after his TD reception. Under new coach Ernie Hefferle, Boston College (0-1) earned 7-7 tie on 63y march in middle of 1st Q. BC QB John Amabile (8-17/114y) made 2 completions on drive, and Eagles scored on 3y TD run by HB Bob Perreault. Amabile was under considerable pass-rush pressure all day; C-LB Frank Visted sacked him twice and 3 other Middies nailed him on pass tries.

Maryland 31 WEST VIRGINIA 8: Coaching debut of Gene Coram of West Virginia (0-1), losers of 6 straight over 2 years, was spoiled despite opening Mountaineers' drive that carried 54y. Maryland (1-0) DE Gary Collins fell on WVU HB John Marra's FUM at Maryland 13YL to start 1st Q TD drive, and Terps clicked on their 1st 7 passes that fueled TD drives of 87 and 85y on opening 2 possessions. Sub QB Dale Betty sparked 2nd drive for 14-0 Terps lead. Midway in 2nd Q, Mountaineers QB Dale "Trigger" Evans hit 2 passes and ran 12y to Terps 8YL to position FB Bob Benke's 3y bounce-off-pile run around RE. Evans flipped 2-pt pass to HB Eli Kosanovich. Nursing 17-8 lead throughout 3rd Q, Maryland refired its O on C-LB Dave Crossna's FUM REC and scored 2 TDs in 4th Q on runs by FB Pat Drass and QB Betty.

NORTH CAROLINA STATE 29 Virginia Tech 14: Marching 46y, underdog Gobblers (0-1) used 12 methodical runs and 6y pass to NC State (1-0) 1YL before sending FB Don Vaught plunging into GL pile for TD that tied game at 14-14 halfway through 4th Q. But, QB Roman Gabriel (13-20/122y) fired up Wolfpack O for 63y advance, hitting E George Vollmar with 16 and 14y passes to set stage for winning TD run of 7y by HB Al Taylor (19/93y, 2 TDs), who had broken 7-7 deadlock with 3rd Q TD. FB-LB Jim D'Antonio soon swiped Virginia Tech pass and lumbered over 46y of open field to TD that provided insurance for NC State.

ALABAMA 21 Georgia 6: When gang-tackling wasn't obliterating Georgia (0-1) backs, who were able to gain only 34/67y, Alabama (1-0) blockers like E Tommy Brooker, G Jerry Neighbors, and T Bobby Boylston were knocking Bulldogs around Crimson Tide's backyard. Gaining 272y on ground with 168-lb FB Billy Richardson serving as leader with 102y, Crimson Tide mounted 3 scoring splurges within 9-min span of 2nd Q: They went 89, 52, and 75y to TDs that included 2 scoring runs by QB Bobby Skelton. It meant Alabama, improving swiftly in its 2nd year under coach Bear Bryant, had scored its most pts in single game in last 2 years. UGa avoided being blanked when soph DB Billy Jackson roared 78y with punt RET to Bama 3YL in final min. Bulldogs QB Fran Tarkenton (15-31/152y, TD, INT) then tossed TD pass to HB Dan Davis. Being levied 115y in PENS clearly hurt cause of Bulldogs.

GEORGIA TECH 23 Kentucky 13: Stubby soph QB Stan Gann completed 5 of his 1st 7 passes as Georgia Tech (1-0) jumped to 16-0 H edge and won its 35th straight SEC home opener. HB Chick Graning scored 3 TDs, including 11y pass from Gann. Wildcats (0-1) QB Tom Rodgers was injured early in 3rd Q and, eventually, 3rd team QB Jerry Woolum sparked Kentucky in 4th Q, leading TD drives of 81y in 10 plays and 63y in 4 plays. To analyze Woolum's effectiveness, Wildcats had 2 1st downs when soph entered game and finished with 15 more 1st downs in nearly 20 mins he played.

LOUISIANA STATE 9 Texas A&M 0: Scoreless 1st H saw each team barely budge other's D, and LSU (1-0) HB-P Jerry Stovall (11 punts/40.9y avg) begin punting duel vs. Texas A&M (0-1) HB-P George "Babe" Craig (9/38.1y avg). Aggies mounted mild peril to Tigers in 1st Q by advancing to 19YL, but DB Andy Bourgeois made INT of A&M

QB Powell Berry. Aggies HB Randy Sims made spectacular 65y punt RET in 3rd Q, but Stovall, last available tackler, fended off A&M blocker, C Larry Broaddus, to make saving stop at LSU 19YL. Berry ran for 1st down at 8YL, but 2 plays later, he suffered INT by LSU HB-DB Wendell Harris, who returned to 30YL. Bengals E Gene Sykes pressured Craig into short punt, and LSU went 28y to Harris' 1y TD. Harris added 32y FG in 4th Q.

KANSAS 21 Texas Christian 7: Jayhawks (1-0), on their 2nd possession, sent QB John Hadl on simple sneak over LG, and Hadl slipped out of grasp of Texas Christian (0-1) G Ray Pinion and raced for 52y TD. On Kansas' next possession, agile HB Bert Coan (8/69y,TD), transfer from TCU, went over RG, jumped cat-like over tackler on 26y run to 4YL to set up his own 1y TD run and 14-0 1st Q lead. Horned Frogs drew within 14-7 in 4th Q when giant, 6'7" soph QB Sonny Gibbs contributed 4/23y rushing on 12-play, 61y drive that started in 3rd Q and was capped by 3y TD run by little HB Harry Moreland. TCU may have felt it was back in game, but swift Jayhawkers D, led by DB Rodger McFarland, Ts Dick Davis and Stan Kirshman, and C-LB Fred Hageman, prevented any further penetration of its end of field. Hadl rolled left to pass in 4th Q, pulled down ball, and barreled over 3 tacklers inside 5YL on 16y TD sprint. It was Kansas' 1st win since 1952 over frequent SWC foe TCU, which still led series 12-3-3.

MISSOURI 20 Southern Methodist 0: In its 1st season-opening victory since 1947, Missouri (1-0) used its vicious D, led by Es Danny LaRose (7/44.1y punting avg) and Conrad Hitchler, to hold young Mustangs (0-1) to 39y rushing. Each Tigers TD came after their aggressive D forced SMU into error, including most vividly, HB-DB Donnie Smith's 22y 4th Q INT TD RET as LaRose's stabbing tackle on HB Doyce Walker's running pass forced poor throw. Mizzou's other scores came in 1st Q after DB Skip Snyder's INT RET to SMU 27YL and C-LB Bill McCartney's FUM REC at 12YL in 3rd Q. Tigers scorers were FB Ed Mehrer on 1y run in 1st Q and HB Mel West (15/56y, TD) on 8y dash in 3rd Q. Mustangs enjoyed late O flurry when benches were cleared of subs on both sides: Soph QB Bobby Reed's frantic passes brought SMU from its 23YL to Tigers 24YL, but Mustangs threat failed. This game marked end of intersectional series—led by SMU at 13-4-1—that had gone unbroken since 1945.

Nebraska 14 TEXAS 13: Nebraska (1-0) QB Pat Fischer, future undersized DB star in NFL, had been converted from HB since 1959 and turned out to be superbly clever QB in his new role. Cornhuskers came from behind on Fischer's long and short TDs in middle Qs to upset no. 4 Texas (0-1). Fischer used dandy blocking to sprint 76y on punt TD RET when 2nd Q was still new. Bad snap helped ruin K Ron Meade's conv kick attempt. Longhorns, 2-TD favorites coming in, got TD runs from QB Mike Cotten in 1st and 4th Qs and outgained Huskers 262y to 153y. Game swung on each team's 2-pt try in 2nd H: Fischer sprung up from his kick-holder position and clicked on 2-pt pass to FB Bill Thornton that provided 14-7 lead in 3rd Q. Texas failed on 2-pt try when Cotten was slammed back at 1YL on his running wedge at LT. Longhorns rode Cotten's 5 and 30y passes to Nebraska 17YL, but K Ray Barton's 33y FG try fell short with 30 secs left.

ARKANSAS 9 Oklahoma State 0: Big 8 Conf won 3 of 4 on this Saturday from Southwest Conf, but Arkansas (1-0) upheld SWC honor. HB-DB Lance Alworth was brilliant all-around performer for Razorbacks. Alworth's 60y punt inside Oklahoma State (0-1) 1YL was foolishly returned by HB Jim Dillard, but was swarmed over at GL for safety by horde of Hogs, led by Es James Gaston and Les Letsinger. Barely more than min later, Alworth slipped behind Cowboys DB John Maisel to haul in perfect 42y TD pass from Arkansas QB George McKinney. Alworth made saving tackle in 3rd Q as Oklahoma State DB Lonnie Buchner collared McKinney's pass at Cowboys 28YL and maneuvered into clear field. Alworth saved TD with his stop. Porkers lost another scoring chance in 3rd Q when FB Billy Joe Moody fumbled at OSU 2YL, but it offset Cowpokes QB Ron Holliday's failed 4th-and-2 sneak at Arkansas 5YL in 4th Q.

Mississippi 42 HOUSTON 0: Cougars (0-1) line, 13 lbs-per-man heavier than SEC visitor's forwards, threw up stiff run D and held no. 2 Ole Miss (1-0) to only 21y rushing in 1st H. But, resourceful Rebels QB Jake Gibbs provided 7-0 H edge late in 2nd Q with 22y TD pass to FB James Anderson. Mississippi moved 80y after 2nd H KO, and Gibbs flipped 5y score to HB George Blair. Backup QB Doug Elmore threw 28 and 9y TDs to E Woody Dabbs. When dust had cleared, Ole Miss had 6 TD passes, 3 thrown by Gibbs. Outclassed Houston O could advance no farther than Rebels 24 and 35YLs.

UCLA 8 Pittsburgh 7: Favored Panthers (0-1) took opening KO to FB Jim Cunningham's TD plunge. In 4th Q, UCLA (1-0) soph TB Ezell Singleton sparked listless Bruins, taking them from own 20YL to Pitt 22YL. DE Mike Ditka stopped Singleton on 4th down, but P Ditka could punt ball only 24y. Starting near midfield, TB Billy Kilmer passed UCLA into range, then went to bench as Singleton scored on 4y run. Kilmer reentered game as Wild Card sub to tally winning 2-pt run. Strong-legged Pitt HB-K Fred Cox was short with 48y FG try at end.

AP Poll September 19

1 Mississippi (22)	434	11 Penn State	60
2 Syracuse (22)	401	12 Nebraska	59
3 Washington (3)	378	13 Georgia Tech	53
4 Illinois	214	14 Northwestern	40
5 Alabama	182	15 Texas	37
6 Michigan State	149	16 Missouri	31
7 Kansas	132	17 Pittsburgh (1)	27
8 UCLA	78	18 Louisiana State	25
9 Clemson	65	19 Iowa	19
10 Oregon State	62	20 Ohio State	17

September 24, 1960

ARMY 20 Boston College 7: Late-afternoon lightning from Black Knights (2-0) brought down Eagles (0-2) from their early-game 7-0 perch. On pass attempt that might have provided lift to 14-0 advantage, Boston College QB John Amabile (10-24/118y, INT)

113

barely missed E Art Graham in EZ early in 3rd Q. In 11-min span that bridged end of 3rd Q and outset of 4th Q, Army struck for 3 TDs in double-time order. Matching TD passes executed by different pairs of throwers and catchers gave Army 14-7 edge by 1st min of 4th Q: Cadets QB Dick Eckert pitched to HB Paul Stanley for 29y TD late in 3rd Q, and, 4 mins later, QB Tom Blanda tossed 35y to HB George Kirschenbauer. Each time, Black Knights sent receiver in motion from backfield to area cleared out by wide-flanked Lonely E. FB Al Rushatz collected last Army TD in 4th Q. HB Bob Perreault scored BC's 1st Q TD as Eagles used nearly 10 mins to cover 78y.

PITTSBURGH 7 Michigan State 7: Big 10 co-favorite Michigan State (0-0-1) dominated stats 359y O to 173y O, but it took 66y deflected pass in last 5 secs of 1st H for Spartans to gain tie. After E Mike Ditka caught TD pass in 2nd Q for Pitt (0-1-1), Panthers DB Ed Sharockman accidently tipped pass to Spartans E Jason Harness, who broke away for long score. MSU E-K Art Brandstatter missed 2 FGs in 2nd H. Late Panthers INT at Spartans 23YL was tossed right back: Pitt QB Dave Kraus was picked off by Michigan State G-LB George Azar.

Texas 34 MARYLAND 0: Texas (1-1) foiled Maryland (1-1) QB Dale Betty with 2 EZ INTs as Terps threatened in 1st H at Texas 16 and 3YLs. Maryland pressured again at Texas 1YL, but H clock snuffed its opportunity. Steers rout was launched on Longhorns HB Jimmy Saxton's 69y 1st Q explosion with QK RET. Longhorns marched 63 and 80y to score in 2nd Q for 21-0 H margin, including 1st of 2 TD runs by HB Jack Collins. Jerry Cook, 3rd-string FB, closed scoring with 62y burst off T in 4th Q. Terps struggled to rush for 63y, while Texas stampeded for 220y on ground.

Tennessee 10 AUBURN 3 (Birmingham): Bruising contest went to Tennessee (1-0) when Volunteers cashed both their scoring chances: 14y TD run by FB Bunny Orr and 29y FG by E-K Cotton Lettner. TB Billy Majors' 46y INT RET and TB George Canale's 33y run paved way for Vols scores. Auburn (0-1) gained 246y on ground, doubled Tennessee in 1st downs, but failed on 1st Q drives that advanced to 1 and 5YLs. Tigers FB-K Ed Dyas, 1 of nation's top kickers, made 3rd Q FG.

MISSISSIPPI 21 Kentucky 6 (Memphis): Aerial magician in previous week's big win, Ole Miss (2-0) QB Jake Gibbs keyed strong ground game. But, it was Rebels' superb D that built triumph over Kentucky (0-2), Mississippi's 15th victim in last 16 games. Wildcats went halfway into 3rd Q before making their initial 1st down and had been held at that point to 16y O until QB Jerry Woolum limbered up his passing arm. Trailing 14-0 on Gibbs' 2 and 8y TD runs, Kentucky went 87y in 16 plays to score on HB Charles Sturgeon's 1y TD dive. Woolum connected on 6 passes on Kentucky's march, including 27y pitch to E Tom Hutchinson. When Mississippi failed to move on next series, Woolum passed Cats downfield. But Hutchinson dropped EZ toss, and it marked end of line for Kentucky at Rebels 31YL. QB Doug Elmore scored decisive TD on 1y plunge in 4th Q.

FLORIDA 3 Florida State 0: Honest Gators FB Jon MacBeth reported pt-shaving bribery attempt, and 2 men were arrested in Gainesville prior to game. Ironically, Florida (2-0) failed to cover 13-pt spread anyway, scoring only on soph E-K Billy Cash's angled 25y FG in 2nd Q. Using slanting runs of HB Bud Whitehead, Florida State (1-1) moved into Gators territory twice in 2nd H, but INTs halted both thrusts. Much of Seminoles' D success was attributed to use of 3 separate, thus rested, units, and FSU held off Gators' late bid for bigger win margin when it stopped Florida HB Dick Skelly for no gain on its 4YL on game's last play.

Houston 14 MISSISSIPPI STATE 10: Time and again, underdog Houston (1-1) used its big line to push downfield for scoring threats against Mississippi State (0-1). But 3 lost FUMs and 2 INTs spoiled 1 opportunity after another. Among most galling of Cougars blunders was QB Larry Lindsey's GL FUM after 80y drive inside Bulldogs 1YL early in 3rd Q. Mississippi State HB-DB Lee Welch, D star throughout, also contributed EZ INT to halt another Cougars menace. Finally, Cougars settled down, leaning on effective 313y ground game and TD bolts of HB Ken Bolin. After Bulldogs scored their 1st pts in their last 6 games, going ahead 3-0 in 1st Q, Bolin greeted their 3rd-stringers with 56y TD run off T. Bulldogs QB Tootie Hill slipped away for 34y TD run in 2nd Q for 10-6 H lead. Steady Houston continued to pound out run y until Bolin scored on 10y burst in 4th Q. Coming off bench, Mississippi State soph QB Charlie Furlow sparkled with 12-18/145y passing.

ILLINOIS 17 Indiana 6: Big 10 opener didn't count in conf standings because 1960 Indiana (0-1) results were to be eliminated due to recruiting violations. Hoosiers ate 8 mins of clock with opening 79y land drive that finished on odd play: Illinois (1-0) DB Ethan Blackaby batted away EZ pass from E Roy Pratt only to have it land in E Earl Faison's hands for 21y TD from TB Joe Maroon. Hoosiers didn't know it but they were finished despite its 6-0 lead; Indiana O would make only 2 1st downs rest of way. Illini went ahead 7-6 late in 1st Q on QB John Easterbrook's 4y run. E-K Gerald Wood's 3rd Q FG and Easterbrook's elusive 18y cutback TD run in 4th Q wrapped it up for Illinois.

MICHIGAN 21 Oregon 0: Wolverines (1-0) used 55 players to dominate wingless Ducks (1-1) and outgain them 377y to 135y. Michigan soph HB Dave Raimey raced 24y on sweep to score in 1st Q. In 2nd Q, Oregon D repulsed 2 UM advances as DE Jerry Tarr recovered Raimey's FUM at Oregon 9YL, and later Ducks D held on downs at their 6YL. UM soph QB Dave Glinka (5-11/79y) rifled TD passes in 2nd H to Es Scott Maentz and George Mans. It was later revealed that gamblers had ineffectively approached reserve Oregon HB Mickey Bruce to shave pts to insure Michigan's win margin. Coincidentally, gamblers tried to fix Florida-Florida State game on same day.

PURDUE 27 Ucla 27: Big league baseball players had experienced recent epidemic of long balls, so *Chicago Tribune* led with: "Touchdowns were as cheap in Ross-Ade Stadium Saturday as home runs in a major league ballpark." Bruins (1-0-1) TB Billy Kilmer pierced Purdue (0-0-1) pass D for 9-16/226y, 3 TDs, including 76y, on game's 1st snap, and 71y TDs to WB Gene Gaines. Moments after opening UCLA TD, Bruins T Marshall Shirk engulfed loose ball that Boilermakers failed to cover on short KO. Kilmer soon ran 11y to TD that made it 13-0 in less than 2 mins of 1st Q. Purdue never led, but scratched to tie of 13-13 in 2nd Q as QB Maury Guttman scored on sneak and took advantage of C-LB Phil Kardasz's 2nd Q REC of Bruins WB Kermit Johnson's FUM at UCLA 7YL. Boilermakers manufactured TD marches of 75, 85, and 78y. Purdue sub QB Bernie Allen gained deadlock with 3 mins left to play on 28y TD pass to E Joe Harris and 2-pt connection to tall E John Greiner.

IOWA 22 Oregon State 12: In opener, Iowa (1-0) had its O roaring on 8 cylinders, but its tackling looked rusty. Hawkeyes went 85y to 1st Q TD: 6y diving catch by E Bill Perkins. Iowa FB-K Tom Moore kicked FG in 2nd Q to make up for his early x-pt miss. Trailing 9-0 in 3rd Q, Oregon State (1-1) took advantage of 17y punt and scored on TB Don Kasso's 9y run through poor tackle by DB Bernie Wyatt. Iowa responded in 4 plays as HB Jerry Mauren slipped across for 5y counter run TD. Oregon State answered with 69y TD drive, but Hawkeyes HB Larry Ferguson excited Iowa City crowd with 85y TD gallop in 4th Q to ice verdict.

NOTRE DAME 21 California 7: Notre Dame (1-0) opened with win, but would lose its next 8 games in row. It would become bitter season that matched 1956's disaster as worst in Fighting Irish history. Still, Irish looked good in their home opener. Crushing blocks of ND soph FB Mike Lind paved way for 240y rushing and sprung HB Bob Scarpitto's 8 and 35y TD sweeps. California (0-2) earned brief 2nd Q 7-7 tie as soph QB Randy Gold hit 4 passes for 50y in 76y TD drive. Irish enhanced their 14-7 lead with odd TD: Golden Bears HB-P Jerry Scattini attempted QK from deep in own territory and ND G Nick DePola snatched ball right off surprised Scattini's foot and legged it 8y for short TD.

Northwestern 19 OKLAHOMA 3: Dominating as few Norman visitors had since before World War II, Northwestern (1-0) scored in each Q, gained 312y total O, and capitalized on host FUMs for both their TD drives. Oklahoma (0-1) was limited to 149y rushing by game's end and had to settle for G-K Karl Milstead's 35y FG after opening KO drive. Sooners' early drive went 51y on 11 patient plays but was halted. Sooners played solid D which kept decision in doubt until Wildcats QB Dick Thornton (7-13/108y, 2 TDs, 2 INTs) threw 25y scoring pass to HB Al Faunce, who went high amid 3 Oklahoma defenders to snatch TD in right corner of EZ with 4:50 to play. In 1st Q, Thornton had hit E Elbert Kimbrough at end of 65y march with 3y TD arrow in same nook of OU EZ. Mainstay Wildcats FB-K Mike Stock rushed 12/86y and missed 1st Q x-pt. But, Stock atoned with FGs of 35 and 21y in middle Qs that extended NW lead to 12-3.

Minnesota 26 NEBRASKA 14: Pair of traditional Midwestern behemoths squared off for 37th occasion, and Golden Gophers (1-0) won for 29th time by battering their way to mid-game TD drives of 49, 64, and 21y. QB Sandy Stephens accounted for 2y run and 23y pass to HB Dave Mulholland for TDs and 13-0 H edge. When Minnesota HB-DB Bill Muncey picked off Nebraska QB Pat Fischer's pass and raced 38y to score, Minnesota enjoyed comfortable 26-0 3rd Q advantage. Cornhuskers (1-1) rallied on 57y TD charge by soph FB Bill "Thunder" Thornton and stunning 28y TD RET of pitchout nabbed by fast-reacting G-LB Gary Toogood.

BAYLOR 26 Colorado 0: Bears (1-0) used brilliant HB Ronnie Bull to key their O in prestige-building win over Big 8 Buffaloes (0-1). Baylor coach John Bridgers said surprising turn around had come from Bears D, which had struggled in pre-season drills. Only once did Colorado reach Baylor 20YL when harried QB Gale Weidner (6-19/57y, 3 INTs) finally succeeded with some passes in 2nd Q. But, HB-DB Ronnie Goodwin, who earlier gave Bears 6-0 lead with 1st Q TD run, made EZ INT of tipped Weidner pass to torch that threat. Bull took punt RET handoff from Goodwin and sped down sideline for 60y TD. QB Ronnie Stanley wedged over and added 2-pt pass after Bull gored Buffs on 46y drive in 3rd Q. Colorado went back to air, but Weidner was picked off by DT John Frongillo at CU 27YL. On 3rd Q's last play, Baylor QB Bobby Ply threw 23y pass to E Bob Lane at 4YL, and FB Bob Starr slammed for TD on 1st play of 4th Q.

Wisconsin 24 STANFORD 7: Indians (0-2) controlled 1st H as they built 220y to 92y O advantage over Wisconsin (1-0). Stanford QB Dick Norman completed 5 passes on 75y trip to 1st Q TD, throwing 14y scoring strike to E Dale Ostrander for 7-0 lead. In 2nd H, Wisconsin O success was mirror image of Stanford's 1st H, outgaining losers 225y to 97y and doing it mostly in air. Difference was 3 TD passes by soph QB Ron Miller, who hit 14-16 in 20 mins that immediately followed H, as Badgers adjusted to Stanford's shutdown of their ground game in 1st H. Wisconsin E Ron Staley caught 12 and 9y TDs in 3rd Q for 14-7 lead, Miller completing 5 passes on each of 2 drives of 67 and 36y. In 4th Q, Wisconsin HB-DB Ken Montgomery made 42y INT RET to Indians 11YL of QB Rod Sears' pass, and Miller hit his 3rd TD pass for 4y TD.

AP Poll September 26

1 Mississippi (42)	426	11 Tennessee	56
2 Syracuse	414	12 Notre Dame	43
3 Washington (5)	353	13 Texas	40
4 Illinois	235	14 Arkansas	32
5 Kansas	205	15 Alabama	32
6 Northwestern (1)	188	16 UCLA	30
7 Clemson	137	17 Navy	28
8 Iowa	87	18 Minnesota	27
9 Ohio State	61	19 Missouri	24
10 Georgia Tech	59	20 Penn State	20

October 1, 1960

(Fri) MIAMI 29 North Carolina 12: Rugged running attack of Hurricanes (1-0) breezed them to 22-0 edge as 10 mins had elapsed in 2nd Q. Miami HB Jim Vollenweider scored TD on Canes' 1st possession, but it clearly was soph QB Eddie Johns (13/119y rushing) who sparked O with powerful rollouts and clever cutbacks and pitchouts. Johns pitched 13y TD to E Bill Miller, and sub QB Bobby Weaver came in to bust through GL-tackle of QB-DB John Flourney to tally 3rd score with 4:39 to go in 2nd Q.

North Carolina (0-2) battled back on E John Runco's miraculous TD steal of pass in last half-min of 2nd Q that seemed certain GL INT for Miami HB-DB Mike Harrison. Tar Heels QB Ray Farris (8-14/123y, 2 TDs, INT) tried to make game of it at 22-12 when he converted TD pass on 4th-and-goal at Miami 4YL in 4th Q. Hurricanes retaliated on 7y TD run by Johns.

Missouri 21 PENN STATE 8: Missouri (3-0) star E-DE-P Danny LaRose was all over Beaver Field, but he had to ride emotional rollercoaster: his short punts gave Penn State (1-1) 2 failed scoring chances in 1st Q; he caught 14y TD pass from QB Ron Taylor at end of 80y 1st Q drive in 2nd Q; his pass deflection on D frustratingly was caught for TD by Nittany Lions E Henry Oppermann in 3rd Q from QB Galen Hall; he picked off 1 of 3 INTs by Tigers, and his booming late punts helped seal victory. Mount Nits slightly outgained Mizzou 249y to 223y, but killed themselves with 5 costly TOs. Quick Missouri HBs, Mel West, Donnie Smith, and Norris Stevenson, sparked rushing O with frequent darts and spurts. Smith threw 28y TD pass to E Gordon Smith for 14-0 H advantage, and Stevenson iced it with 4th Q score that lifted visitors to their final victory margin with 13y dash.

Duke 20 MARYLAND 7: Surprisingly, Duke (2-0) threw no passes to E Tee Moorman, who caught 11 balls in previous week's 31-0 win over South Carolina. Instead, Duke ground out TD drives of 35, 26, and 61y. Blue Devils positioned their short-field scores with 2 of their 5 INTs captured by alert Blue D. Maryland (1-2) made FUM REC at Duke 33YL to set up for QB Dale Betty's 4th Q TD sneak, but it was too little, too late for Terrapins.

NORTH CAROLINA STATE 26 Virginia 7: NC State (3-0) QB Roman Gabriel (8-18/94y, 2 TDs) ran for 2 TDs and found TD targets in HB Claude Gibson and E George Vollmar. Trailing 7-0 on 1st Q sneak by Gabriel, Virginia (0-2) roared back on14-play, 77y sortie early in 2nd Q. Stubby HB Fred Shepherd contributed effective runs, and QB Gary Cuozzo registered 11y TD pass to HB Tony Uleha. But, Cuozzo was picked off 3 times within his 10-26/106y, TD passing, and Wolfpack turned each INT into TD.

CLEMSON 13 Virginia Tech 7: Feisty Virginia Tech (1-2) scored TD 1st time it saw ball and held lead nearly all afternoon in attempt to slay Tigers (2-0) in Clemson's "Death Valley." Gobblers got big 1st Q break as their K Aster Sizemore had 47y FG try partially blocked, but ball bounded downfield where Gobblers HB Terry Sprock fiercely wrestled away it from several Tigers at 24YL. Sprock's REC set stage for 9y TD run after pass fake by QB Warren Price. While frustrated Clemson may have enjoyed game-end O edge by 339y to 191y, it couldn't scored until late in 3rd Q: QB Lowndes Shingler sneaked 1y, but 2-pt run failed. Initially, Tigers had lined up for tying x-pt kick, but Tech jumped offside. Lured by half-distance-to-goal opportunity, Tigers FB Ron Scrudato still was stopped by NG Mike Reno. Poor Va Tech punt died at its 49YL, and Shingler went to work. On 4th-and-4 at 25YL, Shingler completed 15y pass to E Gary Barnes and soon rumbled through RT for winning 4y TD with 4:04 on clock.

FLORIDA 18 Georgia Tech 17: Early in week, Yellow Jackets coach Bobby Dodd's wife said, "I hope Bobby Jr. has a fine day, and...Tech beats the devil out of Florida." Gators (3-0) soph QB Bobby Dodd Jr. completed 33y pass to HB Don Deal (10/35y, TD) on game-winning 85y drive which ended with 3y TD pitchout run on 4th down by HB Lindy Infante, future Packer and Colt coach. Florida QB Larry Libertore (7-12/61y) followed with clutch 2-pt pass to FB Jon MacBeth with 32 secs to go. Georgia Tech (2-1) QB Stan Gann had hit E Taz Anderson with 15y TD pass to help Yellow Jackets to 10-7 H bulge. Teams rumbled through ferocious 3rd Q, spiced with bobbles and errant pitchouts, but finished with Florida E-K Billy Cash's tying FG from 33y away. Georgia Tech HB Billy Williamson broke 10-10 deadlock with 5y TD run in 3rd Q after he had set tone for 73y voyage with 40y effort with flat pass from Gann. Florida made 2 attempts to overcome 17-10 deficit with FB Don Goodman (13/66y) rushing for 50y in 4th Q. Gators failed on Cash's wide 26y FG try, but marshaled for late drive on which Dodd and Libertore alternated effectively at QB. Gators' rookie head coach Ray Graves came out winner against Georgia Tech's Bobby Dodd Sr., after serving as Dodd's asst for 14 years.

Auburn 10 KENTUCKY 7: Injured Plainsmen (1-1) FB-K Ed Dyas became hero when he came in to boot 29y FG in last 4 mins to untie 7-7 knot. Kentucky (0-3) QB Jerry Woolum (0-6/0y, INT), pass master in previous 2 games, was completely shut down because Auburn pressured him, and, as coach Blanton Collier said, "...you can't throw when you are sitting on the seat of your pants." Tigers G-LB Jimmy Putnam (INT) and C-LB Wayne Frazier were chief artisans of pass D against Woolum. Auburn scored 1st early in 2nd Q as FB John McGeever wriggled away from several defenders and raced 46y to TD. Wildcats HB Calvin Bird returned ensuing KO 66y, but Putnam made his INT 3 plays later. Former starting QB Tom Rodgers returned to guide tying UK drive of 58y. Rodgers made 18y on ground, Bird ran 12y, caught Rodgers pass for 11y, and scored on 4th down off RT from 4YL to tie it 7-7 with 3:32 to go before H. During 2nd H, Wildcats got no closer than Tigers 39YL as Tigers DT Billy Wilson halted Kentucky HB Charlie Sturgeon (9/33y) on 4th down.

ALABAMA 21 Vanderbilt 0: After 3 ties in 3 years between SEC rivals, 1st H ended at 0-0. But, Alabama (2-0-1) T Charlie Pell made big play on D on 2nd H's 1st snap: Vanderbilt (0-2) FB Jim Johnson lost FUM to Tide DB Buddy Wesley at 29YL as Pell shot through for hard hit. Alabama FB Billy Richardson erupted off T for 11y to launch 8-play drive he ended with scoring dive from 1YL. Moments later, Vandy C Cody Binkley sailed punt snap over QB-P Russ Morris for safety. Crimson Tide went 49y to score on QB Bobby Skelton's 26y pass to E Norbie Ronsonet, despite being negatively leveraged by 20y in PENs. With only 1 min left, Alabama DT Bud Moore lived lineman's dream, picking off desperate 4th down pass by Morris from punt formation, and following great blocking for 32y TD.

Baylor 7 LOUISIANA STATE 3: In 6 games against Bayou Bengals since 1907, Baylor (2-0) had never scored so much as TD against LSU (1-1). After early exchange of FUMs and Bengals T Bo Strange's block of 36y FG try, Bears' big break finally came when G Bobby Manasco made 3rd Q REC of LSU HB Hart Bourque's punt FUM at Tigers 15YL. Baylor FB Bob Starr slammed over behind block of G Everett Frazier to send Tigers to their 1st home defeat in 14 games. LSU's stout D zeroed in on Bears star HB Ronnie Bull, holding him to only 8/1y rushing and also stubbornly stacking up 4 Baylor run tries from its 1YL just before H. HB-K Wendell Harris' 25y FG in 2nd Q was LSU's only score against surprising Baylor D, which permitted only 88y rushing and 11-18/138y passing.

MICHIGAN STATE 24 Michigan 17: Old rivals presented pitched battle of long drives until both Ds made big 4th Q plays. Behind 10-7 in 2nd Q, Spartans (1-0-1) went 88y of smash-mouth runs to gain 14-10 lead on HB Gary Ballman's 4y blast over left side. Michigan (1-1) HB Dennis Fitzpatrick immediately stunned MSU with 99y KO TD RET. Spartans E-K Art Brandstatter tied it 17-17 in 3rd Q with 32y FG. C-LB Jerry Smith thwarted State's 4th Q move to 25YL with INT of QB Tom Wilson (3-9/72y, INT) at Michigan 18YL. Here, Spartans' huge DL Dave Behrman sacked Wolverines QB Dave Glinka (8-21/112y) at 3YL, and MSU HB Don Stewart returned punt to UM 30YL with 2:59 left. Spartans FB Carl Charon (14/124y) took over, rushing 4/23y, including 3y winning TD in last 2 mins of game.

Iowa 42 NORTHWESTERN 0: Hawkeyes HB Jerry Mauren scored twice in 68-sec span of 1st Q: 45y on line smash on Iowa's 1st possession, followed by his 38y INT TD RET. No. 8 Iowa (2-0) piled up 303y on ground to rout Northwestern (1-1), which played listless O football without injured QB Dick Thornton. Iowa FB-DB Larry Ferguson went 70y with INT TD RET, and sub HB Sammie Harris scored on 53y burst.

OHIO STATE 20 Southern California 0: Workhorse FB Bob Ferguson oddly never touched ball on Buckeyes' 1st 8 plays, then, on his team's 2nd possession, surged through Trojans (0-3) for scoring run of 74y against drawn-up Southern California D. Trojans E George Van Vliet blocked x-pt try, and USC moved to Ohio State (2-0) 27YL after KO on arm of QB Al Prukop (2-6/41y, INT). Ohio State sub C-LB Jim Lindner slapped back this threat with INT. Ferguson (20/157y, 3 TDs) added 2y TD run in 2nd Q, and 19y TD run in 4th Q. These were dark days for Troy, which lost 5th straight game for only 2nd time in its history. Bruising Ohio State D limited USC to 69y rushing and made 4 INTs. Trojans gained 174y overall but never got closer than Buckeyes 25YL.

Syracuse 14 KANSAS 7: On game's 3rd play, no. 5 Jayhawkers (2-1) fell on FUM at Syracuse 26YL. Moments later, HB Bert Coan ran 11y to pay-dirt, and Kansas' 7-0 lead held up through H. No. 2 Syracuse (2-0) got within 7-6 on QB Dave Sarrette's 10y pass to E Ken Ericson in 3rd Q. Disputed 4th down catch at Kansas 1YL by Orange HB Dick Reimer paved way for HB Ernie Davis' 4th Q TD, followed by his 2-pt catch. Later, illegal shift PEN frustratingly cost Kansas razzle dazzle TD scored by HB Curtis McClinton. So, Jayhawks walked out of own building thinking they had been robbed.

TEXAS 17 Texas Tech 0: Texas (2-1) opened its Southwest Conf season with dominant decision over Texas Tech (1-1-1), highlighted by marvelous passing game that struck for 194y on only 6 completions. On Longhorns' 1st scrimmage, QB Mike Cotten (3-5/123y, 2 TDs) fired long for HB Jack Collins, who bobbled pass momentarily, but righted himself for 55y TD. Late in 2nd Q, Cotten found E Larry Cooper for another 55y score. After 2nd H KO, Texas traveled 60y to Red Raiders 7YL and settled for K Dan Petty's 22y FG. Subsequent KO was returned 18y by Texas Tech HB Bake Turner, and Turner caught 10 and 16y passes to lead Raiders downfield. But, Tech, which gained only 85y all game, stalled at Steers 12YL and lost possession on downs.

Arkansas 7 TEXAS CHRISTIAN 0: Arkansas (3-0) weathered 3 1st H threats and used its persistent run game for 189y in eking out win over Texas Christian (1-2). Purple Frogs held ball for opening 8:25, but lost it on downs at Hogs 9YL. Inspired by FB Max Pierce (10/40y) who played well despite week-old forehead gash from car wreck, TCU subsequently reached 22 and 30YLs while keeping Arkansas in its own end throughout 1st H. Using HB Lance Alworth as decoy, Porkers sent FB Joe Paul Alberty (17/82y) for big chunks of 67y drive in 3rd Q. Alberty slashed over for TD from 1YL, as Arkansas owned 3rd Q with 95y to 11y O advantage. Hogs made it to 8YL in 4th Q, but K Mickey Cissell missed 25y FG try. TCU D blunted another threat with INT at its own 15YL.

Army 28 CALIFORNIA 10: Winless California (0-3) earned 10-0 H margin on 34y FG by K Jim Ferguson and FB George Pierovich's 2y TD run at end of PEN-aided 66y drive. Army (3-0) charged from locker room after H to blister Bears D in 2nd H. Cadets marched 53y in 15 plays in 3rd Q as FB Al Rushatz powered over from 3YL, after he earned 4 1st downs. Still trailing 10-6, Black Knights rode legs of Rushatz and wing of QB Tom Blanda to 2 aerial TDs in 4th Q, with HB George Kirschenbauer (14y) and HB Paul Stanley (37y) on receiving end. Army tallied its 3rd TD of 4th Q when sub FB George Pappas ran 5y. QB-K Blanda, following his footsteps of big brother George's kicking and passing in AFL, kicked 2 x-pts and added 2-pt pass. Cal gained only 135y, and practically none during Army's boisterous 2nd H.

Navy 15 WASHINGTON 14: Washington (2-1) was upset on 31y FG by Navy (3-0) E-K Greg Mather with :14 showing on clock. Middies had weathered 2 early surges they stopped at their 1YL, but still trailed 14-12 late in 4th Q thanks to their failed conv tries. Back to punt late in 4th Q, Huskies star QB-P Bob Schloredt bobbled snap at own 24YL, and 6 plays later Mather made his FG. Key play came in 1st Q as Schloredt was stopped at Middies 1YL after his 3rd down TD pass to E Pat Claridge was nullified. HB Joe Bellino scored Navy's 1st TD and launched 3rd Q TD drive with 23y KO RET after Washington FB Ray Jackson made it 14-6 with 3y TD smash. Still, Mather's missed x-pt kick and Navy's failed 2-pt run left Middies behind 14-12 until they got big break out of Schloredt's punt snap FUM.

October 8, 1960

(Fri) SOUTHERN CALIFORNIA 10 Georgia 3: By upsetting Georgia (2-2), Southern California (1-3) ended its 5-game losing streak and found talented new QB in soph Bill Nelsen. Bulldogs K Durwood Pennington tied it 3-3 with prodigious 42y FG late in 2nd Q. Although Georgia QB Fran Tarkenton (14-25/168y) was sharp with short passes, he was intercepted 4 times. USC C-LB Dave Morgan stepped in front of Tarkenton's toss in 3rd Q and returned it 19y to Bulldogs 34YL. Nelsen scored on 1y sneak, on which he climbed tall stack of players. Trojans led 10-3 with 1:13 left in 3rd Q, but Georgia soon made its 6th and 7th trips inside USC 35YL. QB-DB Jim Bates ended 1 threat with INT at USC 25. Later at Troy 12YL, DE Marlin McKeever forced Bulldog HB Fred Brown (10/16y) wide on 3rd-and-2 for loss of 4y. On 4th down, McKeever spilled Tarkenton for 15y loss.

Penn State 27 ARMY 16: Pushed about like cubs for opening 10 mins, Lions (2-1) survived opening Army (3-1) salvo, but went down 7-0 when Black Knights combined passes from QB Tom Blanda (8-15/84y, TD, INT) to E Bob Fuellhart with runs of HB Glen Adams. Then, Penn State got back on its feet as it recovered Adams' FUM. Using option runs and short passes, Penn State freed reliable HB Jim Kerr, who rushed 16/63y, caught 5 passes, and scored 3 TDs. Before Kerr could complete his heroics, Cadets earned 16-14 lead when K Blanda nailed 20y FG early in 4th Q. After receiving punt, Lions fought to Cadets 11YL where Kerr plunged to 5YL and kept going behind E Bob Mitinger's devastating block that knocked away Army tackler. So, State led for good at 20-16 with 2:35 left and added to it after FB-LB Buddy Torris made INT RET to 19YL to poise FB Dave Hayes' 1y TD run.

PITTSBURGH 17 Miami 6: With Pirates-Yankees World Series Game 3 on TV in afternoon from New York, Panthers (1-2-1) switched KO time to bleery-eyed 10 a.m. After both teams slept through quiet 0-0 1st H, Pitt capt Mike Ditka dusted off his yet-to-be-famous temper, ranting loudly at teammates in locker room. Pittsburgh's "C Boys"—HBs Bob Clemens and Fred Cox, and FB Jim Cunningham—scored all of team's 17 pts in 4th Q. With no Ditka on its roster, Miami (1-1) continued its slumber until too late, scoring only on QB Eddie Johns' 21y pass to E Bill Miller.

VIRGINIA TECH 22 Wake Forest 13: Demon Deacons (0-3) HB Bobby Robinson turned E on pitchout for 6-0 lead on opening play of 2nd Q, but it was in-and-out play by QB Norm Snead (17-38/213y, 2 INTs), in face of fierce rush, that spoiled chances of Wake Forest. However, Snead broke ACC career passing and total O records. Virginia Tech (2-2) piled up 245y rushing, 71y of it setting up QB Warren Price's 2y TD pass to HB Terry Strock that provided 7-6 lead. REC by Virginia Tech DT Don Oakes of FUM by Wake FB Jim Bonecutter set up Price's TD run and 2-pt run for 15-6 H edge. Snead's short passes led to Deacs' late TD that cut margin to 15-13 with 4:20 left to play.

Ohio State 34 ILLINOIS 7: Buckeyes (3-0) used battering runs of FB Bob Ferguson and QB Tom Matte to spoil Golden Jubilee Homecoming of Illinois (2-1), school that originated concept of alumni returning for on-campus reunions. Ohio State backup FB Roger Detrick blasted for 2y TD in 2nd Q and soon was followed by Ferguson's similar TD push behind block of T Jim Tyrer. Any hope Illinois harbored of rallying from 13-0 H deficit was shattered by Ohio HB Bill Wentz's 100y TD RET of 2nd H KO. Bucks formed pass D strategy that placed secondary in deep umbrella, so Illini went for short completions and 2 such passes by sub QB Mel Meyers allowed FB Jim Brown to score late TD.

Iowa 27 MICHIGAN STATE 15: Michigan State (1-1-1) overcame Iowa's 14-0 1st Q lead as FB Carl Charon scored 2 TDs in 2nd H. After Charon's 2nd score, Spartans QB Tommy Wilson hit E Fred Arbanas with 2-pt pass for 15-14 4th Q lead. Then, Iowa (3-0) made dramatic reversal: FB-DB Joe Williams grabbed mid-air FUM and raced 67y for 20-15 edge. Fleet and stable Hawkeyes QB Wilburn Hollis added 23y TD dash in final min.

Texas 24 Oklahoma 0 (Dallas): Pitching its 3rd straight shutout, strong Texas (3-1) D used 3 lines, backed up by G-LBs Monte Lee, Johnny Treadwell and John Seals, to keep tacklers fresh and blanket Sooners (1-2) attack. Soph Longhorns FB Ray Poage scored 2 TDs, and his second, FB-LB Pat Culpepper, clinched it with 78y INT TD RET in 4th Q. Stunned Oklahoma suffered worst loss to Texas in last 19 years.

COLORADO 35 Arizona 16: Buffs (2-1) survived 2nd H comeback by Arizona (1-2) to whip Wildcats for 11th time in 11 tries. Colorado appointed QB Gale Weidner (9-17/213y, TD) to well-timed aerial attack, and he passed Buffs into position for 4 TDs in 1st H, including his 49y scoring aerial to E Jerry Hillebrand in 2nd Q. Weidner pitched 45y to Hillebrand to open game, and soph HB Ed Coleman slipped through LG for 41y TD. Weidner's 13y pass to Hillebrand set up HB Teddy Woods' 30y scoring sprint just 5 mins later. Trailing 29-6 late in 3rd Q, Arizona reinvigorated itself on flying feet of HB Warren Livingston, who gave ground before galloping 77y on punt TD RET. Wildcats soph HB Dale West circled RE for 72y to 11YL early in 4th Q. Needing ft for 1st down just outside 1YL, Arizona chose to pass on 4th down, and sub QB Jim Faulks threw incomplete in EZ. But, Cats soon gained safety as DT Carl Runk spilled Weidner in EZ.

Baylor 28 ARKANSAS 14: Razorbacks' 8-game win streak was stopped by balanced attack of Baylor (3-0). Soph HB Ronnie Goodwin scored on 23y run in 1st Q, only to see it matched by Arkansas (3-1). Porkers DT Marlin Epp stepped between Bears QB Bobby Ply and FB Bob Starr to stunningly grab handoff at Baylor 49YL. Arkansas QB Billy Moore flipped 4th down completion to E Jimmy Collier at 16YL. FB Joe Paul Alberty plowed to GL, but lost handle. Collier made alert EZ FUM REC, TD trick he would turn for New York Giants on blocked punt in 1962 NFL championship game. Bears went ahead for good in 2nd Q when QB Ronnie Stanley hit Goodwin with 21y pass, HB Ronnie Bull with 11y screen pass, and Goodwin with 19y TD pass. Baylor ace Bull rushed 8/71y. Trailing 14-7, Razorbacks sagged noticeably as they lost HB Lance Alworth to aggravated knee injury before H. Baylor scored twice in 3rd Q on Stanley's 5y run and sub QB Bobby Ply's 3y pass.

Washington 29 STANFORD 10: Momentum rolled like tides, but in end 3 vital TOs cost combative Stanford (0-4) 3 TDs. Huskies (3-1) started afire, reaching Indians 8YL after receiving opening KO and taking HB-K George Fleming's 25y FG. Washington C Roy McKasson recovered FUM on next KO, and Huskies QB Bob Schloredt (4-8/97y, TD, INT) pitched 33y TD pass to E Lee Folkins. Stanford FB-K Skip Face kicked 24y FG late in 1st Q. Washington HB Charlie Mitchell circled punt coverage and dashed 59y for TD RET for 17-3 H edge. Stanford dominated 3rd Q, keeping ball from Huskies O for all but 6 plays, but could get no closer than 17-10 on HB Hal Steuber's 4y TD sweep because it couldn't score after DE Dale Ostrander's FUM REC at UW 11YL. Critical play came early in 4th Q: P Schloredt punted for Huskies and ball and 3 tacklers simultaneously arrived upon Stanford soph HB Gary Craig, who should have called for fair catch. FUM REC by UW produced Schloredt's 11y TD keeper up middle, followed 11 mins later by FB Ray Jackson's 35y TD catch.

CALIFORNIA 21 Washington State 21: Relying all day on all-around exploits of HB Keith "The Moose of the Palouse" Lincoln, Washington State (1-2-1) rallied for tie in last 90 secs. Lincoln rushed 22/128y, including TDs of 2 and 19y, and passed 3-5/40y. H deadlock of 7-7 was cracked when California (0-3-1) FB George Pierovich scored his 2nd TD at end of 79y Bears drive that following 2nd H KO. As 3rd Q ended, Cal was knocking on door at 2YL, but Pierovich lost 3y and QB Randy Gold (8-13/132y, TD) lost 9y trying to pass on 4th down. Lincoln gained 58y of Washington State's 86y drive, scoring on 19y run as he dragged 2 tacklers across GL. QB Mel Melin missed 2-pt pass to E Hugh Campbell, so Cougars trailed 14-13 in 4th Q. Bears HB Steve Bates barreled 45y for 21-13 lead. But, Wazzu's Melin hit E Lee Schroeder with 47y pass to 18YL and duo collaborated on 17y TD pass. Lincoln crashed around RE for tying 2-pt conv.

October 15, 1960

SYRACUSE 21 Penn State 15: With 3rd Q knotted at 7-7, Syracuse (4-0) HB-DB Mark Weber picked off Nittany Lions QB Galen Hall's pass and dashed 60y to TD. Orange seemed safe at 21-7 when they added TD late in 3rd Q, but Penn State (2-2) rallied to dominate 4th Q. First, Lions were turned back at 2YL, but used HB Don Jonas' 23y punt RET to position Hall's TD pass, followed by QB's 2-pt run. With 2 mins left, Penn State charged from own 11YL to Syracuse 4YL, but 2 Hall passes were tipped away.

MARYLAND 19 Clemson 17: Tigers D limited Terrapins to 27y, all in air, and Clemson (3-1) led 10-0 at H. Early in 3rd Q, Maryland (2-3) was stirred by DL Tom Sankovich's FUM REC at Tigers 36YL. QB Dale Betty, starting string of 8 completions in row, pitched 31y pass to E Gary Collins before FB Rex Collins' TD run brought Terps within 10-6. Clemson answered with HB Harry Pavilack's dandy 40y KO RET, and Tigers went 52y to QB Lowndes Shingler's 1y TD run for 17-6 margin. Betty (12-16/151y, 2 TDs) was just getting cranked up as he hit 44y arrow to E Vince Scott and followed with 25y TD pass to WB Tom Brown. Gaining custody of ball near midfield at start of 4th Q, Betty clicked on 12 and 11y passes before tossing to Gary Collins, who sidestepped DBs for 7y TD catch. More than 11 mins remained, but Tigers could do no more than miss 40y FG.

TENNESSEE 20 Alabama 7: Opening KO hits—among Tennessee WB Bunny Orr (KO returner) and BB Jim Cartwright, and Alabama G Buddy Wesley—were so vicious that game was held up as injured were attended to. Alabama (2-1-1) gave as good as it received, but in end, Tide was toppled by its own miscues that defined worst game it would have for long time ahead. HB Ray Abruzzese's FUM on Tide's 1st O scrimmage led, after short 18y trip, to Volunteers TB Billy Majors' 8y TD pass to WB Charles Wyrick. Later in 1st Q, Crimson Tide HB-P Tommy White's punt snap bobble popped into air and was picked off by Vols E Mike LaSorsa for 41y TD RET. Tennessee (3-0-1) padded lead on TB Glenn Glass' 2nd Q TD run. Bama 3rd team QB Laurien Stapp capped 77y 2nd Q march with TD pass to HB Leon Fuller. Alabama coach Bear Bryant saw his personal 3-school record against Tennessee slip to surprising 1-8-3 as Vols proudly took only series lead at 19-18-6 over Bama they would ever enjoy

MICHIGAN 14 Northwestern 7: E Bob Johnson, whose Michigan (3-1) practice time was limited by his dental studies, sneaked behind Northwestern (1-3) DB Ray Purdin to haul in rainy game's 1st completion 4 mins from end of 1st H: 35y TD from QB Dave Glinka. In 3rd Q, Wildcats made their 2nd move deep into UM territory on 2 passes by QB Dick Thornton (6-27/52y, 3 INTs) only to have EZ pass batted away. HB Al

Kimbrough finally put Wildcats ahead 7-6 with 19y TD run on 3rd play of 4th Q. With ball at midfield, Glinka underthrew pass and DB Kimbrough leapt high for what he expected to be his 2nd INT only to have it bounce off his chest to Johnson, who raced to 1YL. Michigan FB Bill Tunnicliff quickly plunged for winning TD.

PURDUE 24 Ohio State 21: Sr Purdue (2-1-1) FB Willie Jones (11/72y, 3 TDs) had never scored in his career, but made 2 short TD runs in 1st H. Boilermakers QB-K Bernie Allen (5-6/85y) hit 51y pass to E John Elwell and spiced upset with 3 conv kicks and tie-breaking 32y FG in 3rd Q. Down 14-0 in 2nd Q, Ohio State (3-1) had used QB Tom Matte's pass-run options to tie it by H. FB Bob Ferguson scored 1st of 2 TDs after Matte's 67y pass to E Chuck Bryant, and Matte cashed DE Sam Tidmore's FUM REC with 33y TD pass to E Tom Perdue. Bucks took 21-17 lead on 74y drive to Ferguson's 1y TD blast in 3rd Q, but Jones stunned them with winning 26y TD just before end of 3rd Q. Happily for Purdue, HB Dave Miller just had lost FUM to Ohio, but officials whistled it dead.

MINNESOTA 21 Illinois 10: Tenacious Illinois (2-2) used its 254y to 129y ground advantage and HB Joe Krakoski's 1st Q TD to cling to 10-7 edge as game entered 4th Q. Large Minnesota QB Sandy Stephens powered up middle to give surprisingly undefeated Gophers (4-0) their 1st lead of game at 14-10. Moments later, Minnesota began pulling away as Stephens fired 40y to E Bob Deegan and followed with 18y TD run, his 3rd score of day.

KANSAS 13 Oklahoma 13: Coach Jack Mitchell was adamant in forecasting victory for Kansas (3-1-1), but Oklahoma (1-2-1) silenced Jayhawks' anticipation. Sooners quickly drove 65y to score after opening KO as trip was crowned by 1st of 2 TDs by HB Mike McClellan. Jayhawks tied it at 13-13 with 9:36 to play as HB Bert Coan ended 78y drive with 9y TD sweep. Kansas drove deep into OU territory in closing moments, and when it bogged down, Mitchell tapped FB-K John Suder to try winning 26y FG try from Sooners 9YL with 22 secs left. Suder missed.

NEBRASKA 14 Army 9: Cadets (3-2) took 9-0 lead on QB-K Tom Blanda's 27y FG in 1st Q and FB Al Rushatz's 1y TD blast in 2nd Q. Army G Al Vanderbush fell on punt FUM by Nebraska (3-2) QB Pat Fischer at Huskers 9YL late in 2nd Q to position Rushatz's TD. Fischer reversed his fortunes on 2nd play after ensuing KO, making neat fake and zooming 64y to Army 14YL. He scored on 2y run to pull Nebraska within 9-7 at H. Fischer puzzled Black Knights with bootleg fake in 3rd Q, which sent fleet HB Bennie Dillard breaking for 57y TD catch. On strength of 11-22/140y passing, Army easily won stat battle, 324y to 198y, but lost war because it was halted twice at Nebraska's 5YL. Blanda's last-play pass into EZ flew long.

Arkansas 24 TEXAS 23: TD runs by FB Jerry Cook and HB Jack Collins gave Texas (3-2) 14-0 2nd Q lead. But, hot QB George McKinney fired 3 TD passes to bring Arkansas (4-1) to within 23-21 by 4th Q. After short Longhorns punt, HB Lance Alworth led charge in dying moments to Texas 25YL. In game's last min, McKinney dashed to 13YL, and K Mickey Cissell drilled low FG through uprights from 30y with 15 secs to go to put Hogs in SWC driver's seat.

Baylor 14 TEXAS TECH 7: Blow you ole blue norther' on 1st-ever SWC game in Lubbock: Driving rain and 22 mph wind pelted 1st H that confined all of game's scoring. Even so, stars were out: C-LB E.J. Holub (23 tackles, blocked pass, and FUM REC) played brilliantly for Red Raiders (1-3-1), and HB Ronnie Bull (19/69y, TD rushing and TD receiving) sparkled for Baylor (4-0). Nearly 10 mins deep into 1st Q, Bull took screen pass from 50YL behind big blocks. Bull chose to blast over tacklers on last 20y, taking smash hit from Texas Tech ace DB Dick Polson, but Bull violently spun from Polson's grip, flinging him OB, to cruise last 10y for TD. Texas Tech tied it 7-7 with wind at its back for most of 70y drive late in 1st Q as soph QB Johnny Lovelace's passes mixed with runs of soph FB Coolidge Hunt. Loveless rolled to his right early in 2nd Q for 4y TD. Bears fought 67y on 12 plays to beat H clock by 39 secs. Bull barely moved hulking Holub as he pierced for 1y TD. Holub soon countered in 3rd Q, crunching Bull to standstill on 4th-and-2 at Raiders 29YL. Raiders HB-DB Bake Turner made INT in 4th Q at his 39YL and appeared gone for TD until Bull overhauled him at Baylor 22YL. Hunt bashed to 15YL, but 15y PEN ruined Raiders' last tying opportunity.

OREGON 21 Washington State 12: Ducks (4-1) swooped for 2 TDs 42 secs apart late in 4th Q to destroy 4-year Homecoming jinx. Oregon HB Dave Grayson scored for 7-0 lead, but Washington State (1-3-1) HB Keith Lincoln flipped 4y TD pass to nation's top pass catcher, E Hugh Campbell, just when Lincoln appeared hemmed in by Ducks defenders. Lincoln's 2y TD blast gave Cougars 12-7 lead after 41y drive was started by DT Ron Green's FUM REC. P Lincoln's long punts, including 60y boot, pinned Ducks deep until, with 6 mins left, QB Dave Grosz finished 80y march with 31y TD pass to E Len Burnett for 14-12 edge. Just after ensuing KO, Ducks G Mike Rose alertly grabbed deflected INT and went 29y to TD.

WASHINGTON 10 Ucla 8: AP Wirephoto of heartbroken Washington (4-1) QB Bob Schloredt, Huskies' inspirational leader, appeared in most Sunday newspapers across country. With his college career apparently over because of broken collarbone suffered while defending UCLA's 2nd Q pass, Schloredt wept softly on sideline. QB Bob Hivner took over for Washington, leading ground marches of 54y to HB-K George Fleming's 2nd Q FG and 82y to HB Don McKeta's 3rd Q TD. UCLA (1-1-1) won stat battle 358y to 192y and traveled inside Huskies 10YL 3 times in 2nd H. Bruins converted only in game's last 5 mins on 71y drive on passes to sub E Craig Chudy for 7y TD and WB Jimmy Johnson for 2-pts from TB Billy Kilmer (10-19/150y, TD). Earlier Uclan failures could be traced to TB Bobby Smith's stumble on 4th down run from UW 6YL and pass-rush pressure put on Kilmer, who was sacked and threw incomplete on 3rd and 4th downs after having made 1st down at 8YL. Schloredt's only chance to play again would be Rose Bowl visit, and he vowed afterward that, "These Huskies will get to the Rose Bowl...They'll win without me."

October 22, 1960

Princeton 21 CORNELL 18: By beating Cornell (2-3), Princeton (4-1) gained mid-season tie for 1st place in Ivy loop with undefeated Yale, 36-14 winner over non-conf Colgate. Tigers TB John "Silky" Sullivan, nicknamed for popular Kentucky Derby entry of 1958, scored twice. HB George Telesh gained 21y on 1st Q drive that got Cornell within 7-6, but promptly tore knee ligament to end his season. Big Red QB Scott Brown's 18y TD pass to HB Dave McKinley in last 36 secs made result appear closer than it played out.

DUKE 21 Clemson 6: Early on, ACC leader Duke (4-1) used QB Don Altman's short pass to wide-set E Tee Moorman to set team's O tempo. Altman's 5 other short throws on 1st drive poised 2y TD run by HB Joel Arrington behind block of E Bob Spada. Clemson (3-2) FB Bill McGuirt carried last 7 plays for 23y of 17-play, 66y TD drive which brought Tigers to within 7-6 early in 2nd Q. Blue Devils converted 4th-and-2 at Tigers 38YL as sub QB Walt Rappold fired 6y pass to HB Dean Wright. Shortly after, Wright broke free but fumbled, and trailing Rappold scooped up FUM and dashed to 4YL to complete fluky 22y gain. Duke FB Dave Burch soon scored for 14-6 lead, but from that point forward game belonged to Clemson except for 1 big play. Blue Shirt soph HB Mark Leggett charged 70y on TD sweep in 3rd Q to cinch it, but Devils subsequently had to stop 3 threats that died at their 2, 19 and 1YLs, last on DE Dave Usher's FUM REC.

Georgia 17 KENTUCKY 13: Banged-up Georgia (4-2) HB-P Bobby Walden, restricted to punting, got off soaring 70y boot late in game that pinned Wildcats (2-4) at their 15YL and played big role in stalling Kentucky's counterpunch to Bulldogs 20YL at final gun. Early FUM by Georgia FB Bill Godfrey had allowed UK to score on 3y sweep by HB-DB Gary Steward, who had started possession with FUM REC at Bulldogs 18YL. Georgia countered immediately on 79y trip to HB Bill McKenny's 8y TD over-shoulder TD catch from QB Fran Tarkenton (6-15/67y, 2 TDs). K Durwood Pennington tied it 7-7 and soon added 34y FG for 10-7 H edge for UGa. After Tarkenton and McKenny join forces again for 3rd Q TD hook-up and 17-7 lead, Kentucky scored on 65y pass as E Dave Gash made brilliant stab and avoided would-be tacklers for TD. Coach Blanton Collier purposely sent in K Clark Mayfield as illegal substitution, so that plan could be communicated for 2-pt pass. But, 2-pt pass by UK QB Jerry Woolum (7-16/116y, TD, INT) failed, leaving score at 17-13. Walden's magnificent punt soon was made with 3 mins to play. Woolum, followed by QB Jerry Eisaman (5-13/99y, INT), pitched Wildcats into Georgia territory, only to have Bulldogs NG Wayne Williamson sack Eisaman for 10y loss, and G-LB Pat Dye force Woolum into intentional grounding PEN. Game ended as UK HB Calvin Bird took pass to 20YL where he was dropped by Dye.

Florida 13 LOUISIANA STATE 10: Al Thomy, writing in Atlanta Journal, called Louisiana State (1-4) "crossbar-jinxed Bengals" because they lost their 3rd game of year by FG margin. Gators (5-1) got winging right away, propelled by slippery QB Larry Libertore's 66y TD run on 1st play after opening KO. Soph QB Lynn Amadee, making his debut, delivered 10-7 H edge for LSU: HB-K Wendell Harris kicked 40y FG after E Gus Kinchen partially blocked punt. FB Charlie Cranford emerged from deep on LSU's depth chart to crash over for 1y TD just 9 secs before H. Amadee's passes to E Jack Gates and runs by FB Earl Gros fueled this 57y trip. Florida DE Tom Smith picked off Amadee's pass, and Gators E-K Billy Cash blasted 47y FG to knot score at 10-10 midway through 3rd Q. Less than 5 mins later, Florida DE Pat Patchen recovered FUM by Amadee at LSU 46YL. QB Bobby Dodd Jr. led Gators into position for Cash's 35y FG that decided SEC struggle.

AUBURN 20 Miami 7: Tigers spent much of 1st Q in Miami (2-2) territory, but Hurricanes stopped 4th down play at their 1YL and halted next Auburn (4-1) trip at its 10YL. Coach Shug Jordan had seen enough runs stacked up and waved in FB-K Ed Dyas for his 5th FG of season. QB Bobby Hunt passed to E Bobby Foret for 46y TD which gave Auburn 10-0 lead later in 1st Q. Miami QB Eddie Johns, who was harassed into only 3 completions, still was able to fire 43y score to E Bill Miller. When Johns went back to air game against nation's leading pass D, he suffered INT that was run back for crushing 59y TD by sub QB-DB Bryant Harvard. On strength of pass rush by outstanding DT Ken Rice, Auburn claimed its 27th straight victim at Cliff Hare Stadium.

OHIO STATE 34 Wisconsin 7: Happy grads were able to start Homecoming parties early at Ohio State (4-1) as Buckeyes opened lid on 20-pt 4th Q to win going away from persistent Wisconsin (3-2). After Wisconsin punted Buckeyes deep into hole, Buckeyes HB Bob Klein ended 90y trip by swiping 5y TD catch away from Badgers HB-DB Merritt Norvell. Ohio State FB Bob Ferguson (23/136y) scored twice, including 52y burst in 1st Q that built 14-0 edge. Wisconsin got its only score from FB Tom Wiesner, who capped 32y drive late in 2nd Q with 4y TD run after INT by HB-DB Gerald Nena. QB Ron Miller (13-27/154y, 3 INTs) saw 2 of his passes picked off in 2nd H that led to Ohio State TDs. DB Bill Hess thieved late INT, and it set up Buckeyes QB Tom Matte's 53y TD bomb to E Charles Bryant.

IOWA 21 Purdue 14: By taking 3-TD lead and despite absence of D standouts, starting T Charles Lee and G Sherwyn Thorson, Iowa (5-0) was able to minimize run game of Purdue (2-2-1). Hawkeyes built 7-0 lead in 2nd Q on QB Wilburn Hollis' whippet-quick 21y dash to 1YL, followed by his TD sneak. Critical and unusual score for

Hawkeyes came in 2nd Q when soph, 3rd string C-LB Dayton Perry grabbed mid-air FUM that popped airborne after sack of Boilermakers QB Bernie Allen. Perry rambled unmolested for 84y TD. Hollis (2-8/12y, 2 INTs) made it 21-0 in 3rd Q by running 6y for TD. Large deficit forced Allen (18-28/164y, TD) to fill airways as Purdue nearly overcame disadvantage with drives of 76 and 91y. Allen, future Minnesota Twins 2nd baseman, watched his lucky 16y pass bounce off fingertips of E Jack Elwell into welcome arms of HB Jim Tiller for 3rd Q TD. After Iowa HB-DB Bernie Wyatt was flagged for EZ pass interference, Allen sneaked across in 4th Q.

ILLINOIS 10 Penn State 8: Punting into stiff wind on game's 1st series, Penn State (2-3) C-P Charles Raisig was able only to reach midfield. With breeze in his favor, Illinois (3-2) QB John Easterbrook quickly pinpointed passes of 14, 7, and 11y to E Ed O'Bradovich, and HB Marshall Starks used FB Bill Brown's amazing block of 3 Lions tacklers to score from 3YL. Raisig's next punt went only 11y to make possible Illini E-K Gerald Wood's wobbly 24y FG for 10-0 lead, 9 mins into game. Contest turned into punting duel with P O'Bradovich whirling amazing 57y punt against wind. Lions managed late TD on short pass by QB Dick Hoak to HB Al Gursky and Hoak's 2-pt run.

Mississippi 10 ARKANSAS 7 (Little Rock): Embittered Arkansas (4-2) coach Frank Broyles always contended Mississippi (6-0) C-K Allen Green's last-play, winning 39y FG was wide of goalposts. "Everybody in the park knew it wasn't good," he said afterward. Underdog Razorbacks outplayed visitors by considerable margin and scored in 2nd Q on 3y jump pass from QB George McKinney (7-12/87y, TD, INT) to E Jim Gaston. It was matched by Ole Miss QB Jake Gibbs' 57y TD pass to E Ralph "Catfish" Smith late in 3rd Q. Gibbs (4-7/101y, TD) rallied Rebels in closing mins from own 25YL, with key gain coming on 10y pass to FB James Anderson. But, Gibbs was forced to scramble from Hogs 18YL with 25 secs left. Gibbs was thrown for loss, but managed to position ball in middle of field. Green nailed FG, but whistle was blown when it was ruled that players couldn't hear signals. Green's 2nd try was hooking left when it reached goalposts, but was called good by ref Tommy Bell.

MISSOURI 34 Iowa State 8: Registering their best start in any season since 1899, Mizzou Tigers (6-0) used 294y rushing attack, spiced with HB Donnie Smith's 88y punt TD RET, on which he was handed ball on reverse by punt-catcher, HB Norm Beal. Blanked until last 1:07, Iowa State (3-3) scored on deflected 20y TD pass by TB John Cooper, future coach of Arizona State and Ohio State. Iowa State E Larry Schreiber made GL catch after ball slipped through grasp of Cyclones' other E, Ray Horkey. Cooper then hit Horkey on 2-pt pass. Chief artisans of Missouri's powerful running attack were its maneuverable linemen who sprung HB Mel West for 20/104y, TD. West's effort made him conf's top rusher, trumping Cyclones ace TB Dave Hoppmann, who sat out this affair with injury. Missouri won its 3rd straight in Big 8 with time-eating drives of 57, 80, and 72y.

Kansas 14 OKLAHOMA STATE 7: Oklahoma State (1-4) played host to its 1st official Big 8 game, and contest stressed robust D and superb punting. Kansas (4-1-1), which sported future NFL passing great, QB John Hadl, but suffered lackluster 1-10/12y, INT passing in 1st H. So, Jayhawkers completely abandoned their air game in 2nd H. Only thrice did any ballcarrier exceed 10y on single attempt, but Cowboys QB John Maisel broke away on option run for 51y TD that tied game at 7-7 in 2nd Q. It was set up by 14y INT RET by FB-DB Rick Buck. In 3rd Q, Kansas HB Curtis McClinton went over T and sprinted 37y to Oklahoma State 17YL. Soon thereafter, KU FB Doyle Schick blasted 2y for his 2nd TD. Win was costly: Jayhawks T Stan Kirshman and HB Bert Coan were injured and would be out for weeks.

RICE 7 Texas 0: Owls (4-1) nearly ushered Texas (3-3) out of stadium with overwhelming performance in 1st H that netted, however, only 1 TD. Spark was provided by Rice's 2nd unit which marched 79y to 1YL against 3rd-team line of Texas (3-3) in 2nd Q. Although Owl subs failed to score, they provided field position for 1st-string G-LB Bobby Lively to pounce on Longhorns FUM at 24YL, soon thereafter. Rice QB Billy Cox flipped 12y pass to E Johnny Burrell and scored game's only TD on rollout run after clever fake handoff. Last-gasp Texas drive was set off by shoe-top grab and 20y gain of screen pass by HB Jimmy Saxton. Another 19y catch by Saxton, followed by QB Mike Cotten's 21y pass to FB Ray Poage, brought ball to Owls 7YL. Threat died on EZ INT 3 mins from end by HB-DB Max Webb, which preserved 3rd shutout in row for Owls' outstanding D and 1st against coach Darrell Royal since his arrival at Texas. Rice ended up with marginal 296y to 223y advantage on O, with 227y being contributed by Owls' army of runners, including Cox, HBs Butch Blume, Mike Bowen, and Jerry Candler (13/62y) and FB Roland Jackson.

Oregon 20 CALIFORNIA 0: Golden Bears' dreadful season in coach Marv Levy's debut was underscored by Oregon (5-1) dominance, except for lone, failed California (0-5-1) drive to Ducks 9YL in 1st Q. Oregon HB Cleveland Jones rushed 16/87y, accounted for TDs on both pass catch and pass thrown in 1st H. K Jones also made 2 convs. Jones' HB partner, Dave Grayson, rushed 15/121y as Ducks compiled 423y on ground. Winning pt total could have been far worse had rampaging Oregon not lost 4 FUMs in Cal territory. Bears did their best to be gallant hosts: Lost FUMs by FBs George Pierovich and Walt Arnold led to 2 of Ducks' TDs.

Washington 30 OREGON STATE 29 (Portland): While TB Terry Baker's 302y may have set another Oregon State (4-2) individual total O record in 2nd straight game; it was Washington (5-1) HB George Fleming who scored key pts in come-from-behind victory. Fleming got his team's only 1st H TD (37y run) as Baker scored twice in 1st Q to keep Huskies behind at 22-7. UW HB Charlie Mitchell scampered 36y for TD in 3rd Q, and Washington later drew within 29-23 when Fleming ended 80y march with 12y TD run. Washington QB Bob Hivner, who completed 2 vital 2-pt passes in 3rd Q, tallied 1y TD with 2:07 to play, and highly-reliable K Fleming toed Huskies into their 1st lead of day at 30-29.

AP Poll October 24

1 Iowa (34)	458	11 Tennessee	37
2 Mississippi (9)	395	12 Arkansas	15
3 Syracuse (5)	355	13 Rice	11
4 Navy	290	14 Auburn	10
5 Missouri	283	15tPurdue	8
6 Minnesota	267	15tDuke	8
7 Baylor	191	15tOregon State	8
8 Ohio State	172	18 New Mexico State	5
9 Washington	76	19 Kansas	2
10 Michigan State	41		

October 29, 1960

YALE 29 Dartmouth 0: Yale (6-0) used power runs for 209y on ground despite 8- and 9-man fronts presented by fading Dartmouth (3-3). Early on, Bulldogs QB-P Tom Singleton (2 TD passes and 2-pt run) booted 49y punt against wind to push Big Green into its end. Eli DG Paul Bursiek quickly recovered FUM by Indians QB Jack Kinderdine (15-32/171y, 2 INTs) to launch short TD trip, ended on HB Ken Wolfe's 19y catch from Singleton. T Jim King fell on Bulldogs' squib KO moments later to give Yale FB Bob Blanchard (23/78y, TD) TD and 2-pt run opportunity for 16-0 lead. It was 1st rushing score allowed by Dartmouth all season. Indians mounted their biggest threat in 3rd Q as they went from own 13YL to Yale 5YL. But, after Kinderdine hit 5 passes, he was drilled for 10y loss by Bulldogs FB-LB Ted Hard on 3rd-and-2. Win provided Elis with their best start since 1944.

Navy 14 Notre Dame 7 (Philadelphia): Unbeaten Navy (7-0) scored on HB Joe Bellino's 12y TD run at end of 81y trip after opening KO. But, from late in 1st Q, injury-riddled Fighting Irish (1-5) took command. They were halted at Middies 5YL, but quickly tied it at 7-7 when HB Angelo Dabiero skirted E after FB-DB Mike Lind's FUM REC at Navy 20YL. Navy later resisted ND drives at its 22, 5, and 14YLs before getting winning TD from Bellino at end of 64y drive in 4th Q. Stubborn Irish still reached Navy 5YL in late going before Middies C-LB Frank Visted knocked down QB George Haffner's 4th down pass.

Pittsburgh 10 SYRACUSE 0: Coming into game with 342y O avg, Syracuse (5-1) ran smack into rough Panthers D and never was able to penetrate Pitt (3-2-2) 37YL. Syracuse's masterful 16-game winning streak came to end. In early going, C-LB Andy Kuzneski's INT set up Panthers at Orangemen 15YL. Panthers QB Jim Traficant, future outspoken Ohio congressman, soon darted 14y to score. Pitt D, anchored by E Mike Ditka and NG Paul Hodge and LB Larry Vignali, held Syracuse to only 5 1st downs, 138y total O, and forced devastating 6 TOs.

MISSISSIPPI 6 Louisiana State 6: Rivals with bitter recent history each had to accept late tie created by clutch Ole Miss (6-0-1) G-K Allen Green, who booted 41y FG in last 6 secs. Rebels QB Jake Gibbs hit 4 passes on 6-play drive to move Green into tie-making position. LSU (1-4-1) had used QB Lynn Amadee's 21y sprint to set up 4th Q TD plunge by sub FB Ray Wilkins for 6-3 lead. Tigers HB-K Wendell Harris missed conv as well as short 1st H FG.

Auburn 10 FLORIDA 7: FB-K Ed Dyas' 7th FG of season tied NCAA record at that time and broke 7-7 3rd Q knot. Dyas' winning 31y 3-ptr was positioned by Tigers (5-1) QB-DB Bryant Harvard's INT of Gators (5-2) QB Larry Libertore and was aided by 15y foul PEN against Florida. HB Bob Hoover had tied it for Gators with 2nd Q TD run. Florida, never having won conf title, unhappily fell from 1st place tie in SEC.

VANDERBILT 22 Clemson 20: As Halloween approached, there was no concern over "devil's dozen" for little Vanderbilt (2-4) QB Hank Lesene, who blissfully wore jersey no. 13, practice that still was fairly rare in mid-20th century sports. Lesesne completed 17-31/215y, 2 TDs, making 7 completions in row, with 19y scoot mixed in, on decisive victory march in 4th Q. Vandy HB Thom Darden caught winning pass with 3:14 to play. Clemson (3-3) had scored 1st 2 times it touched ball. It went 70y after opening KO to FB Ron Scrudato's 1y TD plunge, and then, when Commodores couldn't move and punted, Tigers traveled 50y to QB Lowndes Shingler's 10y TD pass to E Sam Anderson. Early in 2nd Q, Vandy scored important safety: DT Bob Smith nailed Shingler as QB tried to run out of EZ. Tigers got into that predicament by their punt RET that lost y and PEN that moved them to precipice of their GL.

Ohio State 21 MICHIGAN STATE 10: Methodical Ohio State (5-1) attack, keyed on runs of QB Tom Matte and FBs Bob Ferguson and Roger Detrick, overpowered 8-man fronts of Michigan State (3-2-1). After Spartans lost early FUM at Ohio 15YL, Buckeyes turned around and sprung HB Bob Klein for 46y TD run in 2nd Q. When Ohio State E Tom Perdue, D star of day, blocked punt, Ferguson scored for 14-0 margin. Spartans E-K Art Brandstatter made late 2nd Q FG to slice H deficit to14-3. Clinching Ohio TD on Matte's pass capped 71y parade in 3rd Q that was aided by pair of 15y roughing PENs on frustrated Michigan State.

IOWA 21 Kansas 7: Dispirited by NCAA probation handed down earlier in week, Kansas (4-2-1) awoke in 2nd H, but not before 257y rushing power of no. 1 Iowa (6-0) had posted 21-0 lead. On their 2nd possession, Hawkeyes dealt out 80y TD drive and later cashed in 2 miscues by normally unflappable Jayhawks HB-QB-P John Hadl. Slick Iowa QB Wilburn Hollis logged 30y TD run in 1st Q after faking handoff and rolling around RE. Back to punt in 2nd Q, Hadl bobbled snap and was snowed under at own 4YL, and Iowa HB Larry Ferguson powered to 3y TD and 14-0 lead. In 3rd Q, Kansas finally kindled honest run attack—that would total 195y by game's end—and progressed to Iowa 21YL. But Hadl, ready to pass after double reverse, lost his footing for loss of 9y on 4th down. That surely was play he would never call in his future NFL career. Hollis immediately answered with 16-play, 67y march, twice attaining 1st-down y on 4th down runs, and went over on TD sneak. Jayhawkers gained field position on HB Curtis McClinton's 47y run late in 3rd Q and realized their only score when Hadl,

back at QB, pitched 23y pass to HB Jim Marshall and crashed over from 8YL for late TD. Kansas did not punt in 2nd H and outgained Iowa 212y to 129y, but failed at 21, 14, and 2YLs.

COLORADO 7 Oklahoma 0: In Rockies' blustery snow flurries, Buffaloes (5-1) barely dabbled in pass game (2-5/20y) and rode back of FB Chuck Weiss (22/75y, TD) on 61y march in 2nd Q for tilt's only TD. Weiss and G Joe Romig made key blocks to spring HB Jerry Steffen for 15y to launch winning drive, then Weiss lugged ball 6 times in 14 plays, including his 2nd-effort TD blast from 1y out. LB Weiss also made clutch, cross-field pursuit to prevent tying TD run by Oklahoma (2-3-1) QB Bennett Watts late in 3rd Q. Watts went over LT from his 4YL and lit out on 78y scamper until Weiss roared through E Ronnie Payne's block to bump Watts OB at Colorado 18YL. After Sooners FB Ronnie Hartline made 1st down at Buffs 6YL, LB Joe Romig took over. Romig swooped in for 3 tackles on Sooners runs that netted 1y. On 4th down, Buff DT Bill Eurich pressured HB Monte Deere into underthrown pass for Payne. Colorado ran 74 plays to Oklahoma's 34, but failed in 2 probes inside Sooners 15YL: E-K Jerry Hillebrand barely missed 30y FG in early action, and Colorado's 63y land drive died at 14YL in 3rd Q.

TEXAS CHRISTIAN 14 Baylor 6: Playing 1 of his finest games, TCU (3-2-1) T-DT Bob Lilly trapped Baylor Bears runners all day. Also, Horned Frogs secondary picked off 4 INTs to help knock off undefeated Baylor (5-1). Tall TCU QB Sonny Gibbs (7-11/55y, TD) passed and ran for TDs in upset and received "Nice game, Stinky!" salutations from coach Abe Martin. Bears had taken 6-0 lead on TD pass from QB Ronnie Stanley (9-17/106y) to glue-handed HB Ronnie Goodwin.

New Mexico State 27 ARIZONA STATE 24: Each team opened with long drives in 14-14 1st H: Sun Devils (5-2) going 92y to HB Dornal Nelson's 1y TD dive and Aggies answering with national rushing leader HB Bobby Gaiters' 4y TD run. HB-K Nolan Jones' FG gave ASU 17-14 lead in 3rd Q, and Nelson added 12y TD burst early in 4th Q for 24-14 lead for Sun Devils. New Mexico State (7-0) HB Pervis "Afterburner" Atkins, on his way to breaking single-season all-purpose y per play record of Army's Glenn Davis (Atkins finished with amazing year-end 14.7y avg on 110 runs, catches, and runbacks.) broke game in Aggies favor by dashing 98y for KO TD RET. Still leading by 24-20, Arizona State soon pounced on FUM at Aggies 15YL, but coughed it right back at 5YL. Atkins then exploded for 70y run to set up QB Charlie Johnson for winning TD pass to E Bob Kelly.

WASHINGTON 7 Oregon 6: It was 6th series victory in row for Washington (6-1) even though Ducks (5-2) vowed beforehand to stop Huskies' win string. Scoreless 1st H saw Oregon anchored in its own territory and Huskies penetrating only to Ducks 25YL. With 5 mins left in 3rd Q, Oregon went 65y to score as QB Dave Grosz's passes repeatedly found E Len Burnett until FB Bruce Snyder, future Pac-10 coach, slipped through for 5y TD run. Ducks HB-K Cleveland Jones missed his 1st conv try, but was reprieved when Washington was flagged for offside. Huskies C Ray Mansfield made clutch play by blocking Jones' 2nd kick attempt. Inside last 5 mins, UW QB-DB Bob Hivner made INT, his 3rd of game, at own 5YL. Hivner took to air, and moved Huskies into Oregon end, but faced 4th-and-6 at Ducks 47YL. Dependable HB Don McKeta wiggled free for Hivner's pass and eluded tackler for 47y TD. HB-K George Fleming kicked conv, 3rd straight tilt in which his toe won close game.

AP Poll October 31

1 Iowa (46)	476	11 Baylor	33
2 Missouri	359	12 Auburn	31
3 Minnesota (1)	350	13 Duke	29
4 Navy	324	14 Pittsburgh	19
5 Ohio State	279	15 UCLA	18
6 Mississippi	265	16 Arkansas	10
7 Washington (1)	142	17 Michigan State	9
8 Tennessee	108	18tColorado	6
9 Syracuse	91	18tUtah State	6
10 Rice	73	20 New Mexico State	5

November 5, 1960

Army 9 Syracuse 6 (New York City): Yankee Stadium throng saw Cadets (6-2) fashion upset in their 34th visit to "House That Ruth Built." Army QB-K Tom Blanda made like pro brother George and toed 29y FG for 3-0 lead in 2nd Q. Syracuse (5-2) HB Pete Brokaw followed with long run, but coughed up ball to Army DT Bob McCarthy at 20YL, 1 of 3 critical Orange FUMs. Orangemen never advanced closer than Army's 44YL in 1st H. Cadet took possession after 2nd H KO and scored on QB Dick Eckert's 2y option run for 9-0 edge. FB Al Rushatz chipped in with 46y rushing on that TD march. When QB Dick Easterly threw 15y scoring pass to E Paul Ericson midway in 4th Q, Syracuse finally dented Army's superb D, which was led by G-LB Al Vanderbush, future West Point AD.

North Carolina State 14 WAKE FOREST 12: *Charlotte Observer* writer George Cunningham pegged tight ACC contest just right:: "Roman Gabriel looked like an All-American the first half, and Norman Snead looked like an All-American the second half, but...an obscure tackle named Nick Maravich was the difference." In 1st H, Gabriel (15-25/140y, TD, INT) of NC State (6-2) ran for short TD and rolled out left to find E Jim Tapp on 8y curl-in TD pass. In 2nd H, Snead (16-27/237y, 2 TDs, INT) of Wake Forest (2-5) clicked on 2 TD passes to E Bobby Allen of 22 and 28y. But, K Snead missed kick after 1st TD and saw his 2-pt pass attempt in 4th Q batted away by Wolfpack HB-DB Tom Dellinger, thus making 1st H x-pt kicks of K Maravich, who was in for injured K Jake Shaffer, stand up for NC State win.

DUKE 19 Navy 10: Fumbleitis became contagious disease that apparently was passed from no. 13 Duke (6-1) to no. 4 Navy (7-1) during H break. Blue Devils' quintet of 1st H FUMs enabled Middies E-K Greg Mather to kick 25y FG and catch 9y TD pass in last 1:30 of 2nd Q for 10-0 lead. When Navy threatened again in 3rd Q, Duke started its rally as sub DT Art Gregory sacked QB Hal Spooner, and Spooner's resultant FUM launched drive to FB Dave Burch's TD and HB Mark Leggett's 2-pt catch. Now trailing 10-8, Devils gained 3rd Q field position on P Randy Clark's punt to Navy 3YL to set up HB Dean Wright's 7y TD and 16-10 edge. E Tee Moorman's 2 catches from QB Don Altman poised K Billy Reynolds' FG early in 4th Q to clinch upset.

GEORGIA TECH 14 Tennessee 7: Yellow Jackets (5-3) surprised their record crowd at Grant Field and unbeaten no. 8 Tennessee (5-1-1) with smothering D play of Ts Ed Nutting, Billy Shaw, and Larry Stallings, and G-LBs Dave Watson and Rufus Guthrie. Before D uprising, there was brief O outbreak which started with great punt to 1YL by Georgia Tech FB-P Don Coker. It created field position for HB Chick Graning's spinning 16y TD run that provided Tech with lead less than 6 mins into 1st Q. Next came lightning bolt KO RETs that greatly impacted final result. Vols WB Ken Waddell followed Graning's TD with 52y KO RET, then caught 7y TD pass from TB Glenn Glass on 9th play of Tennessee's drive. Jackets HB Billy Williamson (9/44y) was sprung by E Gerald Burch's block and went 93y to score with ensuing KO. With score at 14-7 still in 1st Q, long day seemed to await each team's defenders. But, Engineers D took command and permitted only 139y and 7 1st downs by end of game. Tennessee's only threat of 2nd H started with TB George Canale's 58y punt to Jackets 5YL and ended when DB Graning thwarted ensuing probe with INT of 4th down pass.

Florida 22 Georgia 14 (Jacksonville): Florida (6-2) ran 27 plays and scored on 2 short TD runs by FB Don Goodman (21/86y, 2 TDs) before Georgia (5-3) even managed play from scrimmage. UF spark was lit by little QB Larry Libertore, who rushed for 71y on tricky options and hit 2-2/38y passing. QB Bobby Dodd filled in for Libertore, who tweaked hamstring muscle, and advanced Gators 62y 1st time they touched ball in 2nd H to 22-0 lead with 1y TD wedge and 2-pt run. Throttled by tough pass D, Bulldogs finally struck for 2 scores in 4th Q. First TD came on improvised 4y run by QB Fran Tarkenton (14-28/145y, 3 INTs) after he had scrambled backwards all way back to 30YL. Unfortunately, Tarkenton was injured on his TD, and it compounded what asthma attack had already drained from him. Georgia's ace QB hung in, but in deference to his banged-up hip, he turned passing over to HB Bill Jackson, who took pitchout and lofted 26y score to HB Bobby Walden with 6:45 left. Walden dropped 2-pt pass try, so Bulldogs had little chance left at victory. Georgia regained control by stopping Dodd's 4th down sneak at midfield, but Walden's catch from Jackson fell 2y short on 4th down at Florida 31YL with 30 secs to play.

OHIO STATE 36 Indiana 7: In prepping for next week's presumed showdown with Iowa, Ohio State (6-1) raced to 27-0 H lead. Buckeyes FB Bob Ferguson and QB Tom Matte (7-9, 3 TDs passing) shared rushing duties on 56y march to Ferguson's TD in 1st Q. Matte nailed all of his 3 TDs in 2nd Q, last of which was E Chuck Bryant's 36y sensational EZ grab while covered by 2 Hoosiers. Indiana avoided shutout with late TD after G John Johnson blocked Buckeyes punt and sub E Bill Quinter caught 22y TD pass.

MINNESOTA 27 Iowa 10: Bruising Golden Gophers (7-0) won duel with undefeated no. 1 Iowa (6-1), benefitting from 3 TOs in wind and cold. Bad punt snap on which Hawkeyes P John Calhoun was pursued and swamped by E Dick Larson of Gophers gave Minnesota ball at Hawkeyes 14YL in early going, and HB Bill Munsey soon scored from 7YL. Iowa reached Gophers 6YL in 2nd Q, but Minnesota NG Tom Brown stuffed G Bill Dicindio back into Iowa QB Wilburn Hollis on 3rd down run that spilled back to 11YL. So Iowa settled for FB-K Tom Moore's 28y FG. With strong 3rd Q wind, Hawkeyes earned their only lead of day at 10-7 on FB Joe Williams' 20y burst for TD. Gophers replied with 81y voyage to QB Sandy Stephens' TD sneak which provided lead for good. Minnesota added icing TDs after Iowa HB Sammie Harris' FUM went to Gophers DT Jack Wheeler, and Iowa QB Matt Szykowny lost FUM when sacked by Gophers DE Bob Deegan. Each TO led to TD by Minnesota: FB Roger Hagberg's 42y run and QB Joe Salem's sneak.

MISSOURI 16 Colorado 6: Missouri (8-0) spotted Colorado (5-2) 6-0 1st Q lead: Buffs QB Gale Weidner threw 38y TD pass to E Gary Henson at end of 78y drive sparked by FB Chuck Weiss' 31y rushing. Backed again to own GL by Bison passing, Missouri got saving tackle from DE Tommy Carpenter. Suddenly Tigers wrested away control, getting TDs from HBs Donnie Smith on 2y run in 2nd Q and Norm Beal on 55y punt RET in 3rd Q. So Missouri led 14-6. DE Danny LaRose put game out of reach with 4th Q EZ sack of Weidner. Mizzou's mighty D showed some signs of weakness on pass D as Weidner succeeded in hitting 6 passes for 91y. But 5-game winning streak of Bison was over.

IOWA STATE 10 Oklahoma 6: Iowa State (5-3) had not beaten Oklahoma (2-4-1) since 1931, but superior line play of G Dan Celoni, T Larry Van Der Hayden, and E Don Webb keyed upset. Sooners gained 223y on ground, but never threatened after HB Mike McClellan's 2nd Q TD run was product of 71y drive that gave them 6-0 lead. Cyclones E-K Larry Schreiber kicked low, knuckling FG that was good for 38y in 3rd Q. to pull Iowa State within 3 pts. Celoni had FUM REC of ball dropped by Oklahoma HB Billy Meacham to launch Iowa State's late winning drive. Cyclones TB Dave Hoppmann (29/182y) carried on 7 of 10 plays to 1st down at Sooners 3YL. After 5y PEN against Iowa State sent it back to 8YL, it took 4 downs to accomplish FB Tom Watkins' TD run from 6 inches away. Capacity crowd at Clyde Williams Field went berserk with joy as last 3:04 counted off clock and 29 years of defeat washed away.

ARKANSAS 3 Rice 0: Fierce D battle was led by LBs: quick, little Razorbacks (6-2) C-LB Wayne Harris, future Hall of Famer, had hand in 24 tackles, while Owls (5-2) FB-LB Roland Jackson had 14 stops. Rice threatened in 3rd Q with 62y drive, built on runs of Jackson and HB Bob Wayt. But, QB Billy Cox suffered INT by omnipresent Harris at Porkers 3YL. Arkansas fashioned winning 72y drive in 4th Q, big play coming on QB Billy Moore's 36y completion to E Jimmy Collier. K Mickey Cissell booted 36y FG with 25 secs left.

Washington 34 SOUTHERN CALIFORNIA 0: Washington Huskies (7-1) felt right at home in rain in Los Angeles as they took major step for return trip to Rose Bowl. Pair of quick TDs in 1st Q put Southern California (3-4) in deep hole at very outset. Tough HB Don McKeta, covering opening KO, blasted into USC HB Nick McLean, and resultant FUM set up Huskies at 23YL. FB Ray Jackson (23/80y, 2 TDs) carried on 4 of 5 plays and slammed over from 4YL for 7-0 lead. Less than 2 mins later, Washington HB George Fleming fielded punt and slipped away from T Mike Bundra and E-P Marlin McKeever at midfield to splash 65y for TD. Trojans soph QB Bill Nelsen (17/61y rushing) sparked answering drive deep into UW territory as he was roughed on 17y keeper to 10YL. Good news was that ball was moved half distance to Huskies GL, but bad news was Nelsen, with badly cut hand, had to leave. New Troy QB Al Prukop bobbled his 1st snap, and lost FUM to Washington G-LB Chuck Allen. H clock killed USC's next trip inside 10YL late in 2nd Q. Huskies owned 2nd H as TDs were scored by Jackson and Fleming again. K Fleming made 2 FGs, and sub QB Kermit Jorgensen pushed across GL late in 4th Q. USC had arrived with desire to win for G Mike McKeever, in hospital with head injury. Coach John McKay said, "And while the score may make me sound silly, I think we would have made a good game of it if we could have closed the score to 14-7 on that drive in the first quarter."

UTAH STATE 17 Wyoming 13: Assuring tie for Skyline title honors, Utah State (8-0) set school record with 8th win in row. Aggies enjoyed 10-0 H lead but Wyoming (6-2) moved within 10-6 as QB Chuck Lamson capped 23-play, 87y drive with 14y TD pass. Utah State HB Tom Larsheid scored for 17-6 lead, and that score triggered wild ending: HB Dick Behming immediately answered with 97y KO RET for Cowboys TD that tightened Wyoming's deficit to 17-13. On-side KO succeeded for Cowboys, but Aggies D, led by once-in-lifetime T Merlin Olsen, held on for win to stay undefeated and maintain school's 1st-ever top 20 ranking.

AP Poll November 7

1 Minnesota (40)	462	11 UCLA	38
2 Missouri (4)	387	12 Pittsburgh	31
3 Ohio State (1)	335	13 Michigan State	16
4 Mississippi (1)	310	14 Tennessee	15
5 Iowa	279	15 New Mexico State	10
6 Washington (1)	241	16 Rice	9
7 Duke	156	17tYale	8
8 Navy	113	17tSyracuse	8
9 Arkansas	72	19 Utah State	7
10 Auburn	64	20 Florida	6

November 12, 1960

YALE 43 Princeton 22: Until Princeton (6-2) TB John "Silky" Sullivan was knocked out of game in 3rd Q, he rushed 19/89y with 11y TD run in 2nd Q while displaying hot passing hand with 5-6/65y. Tigers outrushed Elis 292y to 251y at game's end and stayed competitive well into 2nd Q at 14-6 deficit. Bulldogs' 2nd TD came courtesy of E Ruly Carpenter, future owner of Philadelphia Phillies, who stunningly snatched ball from Tigers punt returner, TB Hugh Scott (19/156y, TD rushing), in key 2nd Q move. That play got Yale (8-0) rolling as QB Tom Singleton (6-7/119y, 3 TDs) accounted for 3 quick scoring passes. Elis went 63y in 7 plays after 2nd H KO for 30-6 edge. HB Ken Wolfe caught his 2nd TD pass and FB Bob Blanchard added 2-pt run. Blanchard blasted for 2 more TDs as Yale cruised to 36-6 edge by early 4th Q. Scott's electifying 25y TD run was axis of Princeton's 16-pt consolation burst in 4th Q.

Maryland 22 NORTH CAROLINA 19: On their way to their 1st winning ledger since 1955, Terrapins (5-4) snatched late win and inflicted 5th straight defeat on frustrated, TO-prone North Carolina (1-7). Officials made 2 late-game decisions, which *Washington Post* called "befuddling calls." Tar Heel fans were so enraged that some exchanged fists with officials at game's end before police could hustle them to their dressing room. On strength of QB Ray Farris' 2 short TD runs and HB Moyer Smith's 26y TD gallop, Carolina built 19-7 lead early in 3rd Q, despite FB-K Bob Elliott's having missed 2 of his 3 x-pt kicks. Then, Maryland HB Dennis Condie turned tide with 90y KO TD RET to pull Terps back within 19-14 with 10 mins left in 3rd Q. Matters were quiet until HB Smith lost UNC's 5th FUM at his 37YL with 2:57 to play. From Heels 24YL, Maryland QB Dale Betty threw high GL pass to HB Tom Brown, but as Brown and Carolina DB Milam Wall mutually went up for ball, back judge called controversial pass interference PEN. On 3rd down at 1YL, Betty easily scored on wide run after fake to FB Pat Drass, but same back judge blew whistle, thinking Drass had been tackled at 3YL with ball. So, on 4th down, Betty faked and flipped winning TD pass to E Gary Collins with 1:05 left.

Mississippi 24 TENNESSEE 3: Mississippi's 14th trip to Shields-Watkins Field in Knoxville finally broke spell as Rebels won in Knoxville for 1st time ever. Wasting no time after opening KO, Ole Miss (8-0-1) QB Jake Gibbs (11-13/112y, TD) hit 3 passes to HB Bobby Crespino (8/92y, TD receiving) and rolled out for 27y to set up FB James Anderson (13/110y, 2 TDs) for 2y TD sweep. FUM REC by Volunteers (5-2-1) DG Larry Richards at Rebels 23 YL poised Tennessee for its only score: E-K Cotton Letner's 29y 2nd Q FG which pulled it to within 7-3. Mississippi added K Allen Green's 32y FG for 10-3 H edge. With 12 mins to play, Anderson dropped crusher on Vols. He went up middle on draw run, spun out of 3 tackles, and bowled over Vols' outstanding S Billy Majors to complete 43y TD romp. Tennessee's O was limited to remarkably low 24y and made only 4 1st downs.

Alabama 16 GEORGIA TECH 15: Yellow Jackets (5-4) owned 1st H, scoring on TD runs by HB Jimmy Nail and QB Stan Gann and 47y FG by K Tommy Wells. But, Wells failed on his 2 conv kicks, including 1st try when Tide HB-DB Billy Richardson shot up middle to block it. Nail's 8y TD run in 1st Q was hammered home only 1 play after Alabama (6-1-1) QB Pat Trammell was crushed into lost FUM by Tech G-LB Rufus Guthrie. Crimson Tide, that didn't earn its initial 1st down of 15-0 1st H until next-to-last play, was different team in 2nd H, scoring on HB Leon Fuller's short 4th down crash-over after 49y march, and after Trammell was injured, on sub QB Bobby Skelton's 8y TD pass to E Norbie Ronsonet. Skelton's TD pass was set up by his 28y pass to E Jerry Spruiell and 12y scramble and made score 15-13 with 8:44 to play. Fighting 4th Q clock, Skelton passed 26y to HB Butch Wilson to position Bama for E-K Richard "Digger" O'Dell's winning last play, 23y FG, which was nearly blocked by Georgia Tech T Larry Stallings.

Purdue 23 MINNESOTA 14: Minnesota (7-1) followed its emotional win over Iowa with flat 1st H effort as its vaunted D was riddled by passing of Boilermakers QB Bernie Allen and power running of FB Tom Yakubowski, who scored at end of opening 80y drive. Golden Gophers dropped half-game behind Iowa in Big 10 standings by losing its 1st conf game of season. Erratic Purdue (3-4-1) led 14-0 at H, holding Gophers to only 31y total O. Outplayed, nation's no. 1 team got off canvas to battle back on 2nd H TDs by HB Bill Munsey on 27y burst and FB Roger Hagberg, but K Allen's 3rd Q FG of 35y was wedged in between to maintain Purdue's lead at 17-14. Sub QB Larry Johnson completed 48y pass to E Bob Deegan to set up Munsey's TD that had made it 14-8 (with Munsey's 2-pt catch) after 2nd H KO. Key moment came next time Gophers got possession at their 49YL: Purdue G-LB Stan Sczurek stepped in front of short pass for INT that eventuated in Allen's FG. Boilers stopped 2 late drives and added last play TD on FUM REC. It came on unusual play as desperate Minnesota HB Tom King tried to catch punt in EZ and race length of field. In his hurry, King lost control of ball, and Purdue HB Jim Tiller recovered for TD.

IOWA 35 Ohio State 12: With Minnesota's loss, Iowa (7-1) was able to regain Big 10 top spot, clinching no worse than final tie for conf crown. Hawkeyes soph FB Joe Williams opened scoring with spectacular 49y dash for 7-0 lead late in 1st Q. Buckeyes (6-2) came within 7-6 on FB Bob Ferguson's short TD run, but K Ben Jones missed x-pt. Iowa QB Wilburn Hollis swept E for 12y TD, his understudy Matt Szykowny wedged over for score after HB Larry Ferguson's weaving 25y run, and Williams blasted over after Szykowny's 15 and 21y passes. Trailing 28-6 at H, Ohio State counted on spark of QB Tom Matte and his 22y TD run to draw within 28-12 in 3rd Q. Last Q began with Ohio nested at Iowa 6YL, but Matte's EZ pass for E Charles Bryant went incomplete, and Hawks took over. After ball was advanced out to 9YL, HB Larry Ferguson dropped clinching blow on Buckeyes by skirting E and shrugging off tackle by DB Bill Hess for long TD run. Iowa outrushed Ohio 361y to 220y, while passing was almost even.

Missouri 41 OKLAHOMA 19: Despite 70y TD sprint on game's 4th play by HB Mike McClellan, Oklahoma (2-5-1) fell behind 24-12 at H. Usually powerful run D of Tigers (9-0), which entered fray with 73y avg, allowed 323y to still-proud Sooners. So, Mizzou was left to fight back with its O and tallied 24 straight pts, including HB Donnie Smith's 2 and 30y TD runs and HB Norris Stevenson's 77y TD sweep. Sooners closed to 24-19 as QB Jimmy Carpenter's TD finished 74y drive on which FB Ronnie Hartline gained 59y. At outset of 4th Q, Oklahoma was on move until it lost pitchout to ruin drive into Missouri territory. Stevenson, who rushed for most to-date y (13/169y, 2 TDs) against any Bud Wilkinson-coached team, quickly dashed for 60y TD on Tigers' trademark power sweep. Wild Sooner pitchouts—they would lose 6 TOs including 2 INTs nabbed by Tigers HB-DB Fred Brossart—led to 10 additional Missouri pts.

KANSAS 34 Colorado 6: Tight, PEN-marred 1st H was led 7-0 by Kansas (6-2-1) on FB Jim Jarrett's 1y TD plunge that came after Colorado (5-3) HB-DB Ed Coleman was flagged for pass interference. Contest was blown open in 3rd Q by Jayhawks' double-lateral razzle-dazzle: FB Doyle Schick hit line, flipped back to QB John Hadl, who pitched out to HB Hugh Smith, much like Single Wing's old buck-lateral series. Smith slipped 2 tackles, cut left, and dashed 46y to score. On Kansas' next series, HB Bert Coan, whom Smith supplanted week earlier on starting unit, raced into open off T and churned 74y for TD behind last clearing block by HB Curtis McClinton. At 21-0, rout of Buffaloes now was in motion. Jayhawks FB Norman Mailen powered for 2 TDs after 4th Q INTs for 34-0 edge. Colorado's vaunted passing attack (7-22/116y, 2 INTs) stumbled most of day but managed QB Gale Weidner's late 34y TD pass to E Gary Henson.

BAYLOR 35 Southern California 14: Dandy HB Ronnie Bull sped to 3 TDs as Baylor (6-2) moved firmly into command at 21-0 after its drive following 2nd H KO. USC (3-5) eventually rallied to within 28-14 on QB Bill Nelsen's pair of 4th Q TD passes. Trojans lost 5 FUMs, which stifled many promising advances and set up Bull's pair of TD runs in 2nd Q. Bull enjoyed excellent game; he rushed 18/76y, caught 2/22y, and had KO RETs totaling 50y. QB Ronnie Stanley's 47y TD pass to reserve HB Jim Oldham introduced 4th Q with Bears ahead by 28-0.

ARKANSAS 26 Southern Methodist 3: Arkansas (7-2) was in high cotton as it neared its 5th Southwest Conf title. But, Southern Methodist (0-7-1), trying to avoid worst-ever season (0-8-2 in 1916), jumped to 3-0 1st Q lead on K Buddy Nichols' 34y FG that held up until last min of 1st H. Razorbacks HB-P Lance Alworth had tough 1st H: his 1st punt was partially blocked by SMU T Jerry Mays, and another punt lost 1y—setting up Nichols' FG—when it was knocked backwards to Hogs 8YL by fierce wind. QB Billy Moore (TD rushing), with excellent understudy work from QB George McKinney, was wizard on 3rd- and 4th-and-long conversions to keep alive drives of 62, 63, and 68y. McKinney's 28y rollout run tweaked 1st scoring drive that resulted in key Arkansas TD and 6-3 edge just 50 secs before H. McKinney-to-Alworth pass for 37y got Pigs to fly toward Alworth's 2y TD run in 3rd Q. HB Jim Worthington's 42y punt TD RET finished off scoring in 4th Q. Game ended on bizarre note: Mustangs HB Frank Jackson was streaking away on 20y run to Porkers 15YL when hundreds of youngsters surged from grandstands to knock down Jackson, as well as 3 pursuing Arkansas defenders and couple of officials. All this while, Hogs band played giddy, but slightly premature victory tune at midfield (See California vs. Stanford, November 20, 1982.)

1 Missouri (34)	457	11 UCLA	23
2 Iowa (7)	379	12 Michigan State	21
3 Mississippi (5)	362	13 Purdue	12
4 Minnesota (1)	328	14t Yale	9
5 Washington	268	14t Rice	9
6 Duke	205	14t New Mexico State	9
7 Arkansas	173	14t Syracuse	9
8 Navy	156	18 Alabama	8
9 Auburn (1)	104	19t Oregon	7
10 Ohio State	59	19t Florida	7

November 19, 1960

Yale 39 HARVARD 6: Yale (9-0) completed its 1st undefeated season since 1923, swamping its biggest rival. Initial possession found Elis breaking HB Ken Wolfe loose for 41y TD run behind blocks of line stars, T Mike Pyle and G Ben Balme. Yale DE John Hutcherson sped 48y with INT TD, and K Gordon Kaake kicked FG for 17-0 H lead. After Bulldogs 1st squad retired with 23-0 3rd Q edge, sub QB Bill Leckonby threw 2 TDs. Harvard (5-4) prevented shutout with late score as hobbled QB Charlie "Riverboat Gambler" Ravenel tallied on short run after throwing 56y pass to E Pete Hart.

Penn State 14 PITTSBURGH 3: HB Jim Kerr went from goat to hero as his opening KO FUM provided Pitt (4-3-3) with platform for HB-K Fred Cox's 35y FG. In 4th Q, Kerr caught 30y pass from QB Galen Hall to put Penn State (6-3) ahead for good at 6-3. For 48 mins, Panthers D, spearheaded by E Mike Ditka and G Larry Vignali, had blanketed conservative Lions O. But after Kerr's catch, Nittany Lions went 42y to another TD: E Bob Mitinger's leaping 3y catch.

NORTH CAROLINA 7 Duke 6: Scoreless 1st H saw no. 6 Duke (7-2) K Bill Reynolds miss FG from 28y out. Late in 3rd Q, HB Mark Leggett fielded punt deep in own territory and raced 55y with RET to launch favored Blue Devils' 40y TD drive. Devils FB Dave Burch surged over for TD with 11:39 left in 4th Q, but North Carolina (2-7) DL Tony Hennessey blocked x-pt kick. With 6 mins to go, G Fred Mueller gave Tar Heels field position with tackle for 12y loss that forced Duke to punt. QB Ray Farris rammed over on 4th down from 3YL, and K Bob Elliott kicked winning pt for huge upset.

OHIO STATE 7 Michigan 0: On their 4th trip of 1st H into Buckeyes territory, Wolverines (5-4) marched 68y, but E-K Bill Freehan, future Detroit Tiger catcher, missed 30y FG to right in last min of 2nd Q. Outplayed and outgained for 3 Qs, Ohio State (7-2) ended 3rd Q on HB Bob Klein's hustle: Klein alertly ran up to catch Michigan HB-P Reid Bushong's short punt at midfield and returned it to UM 42YL. Ohio proceeded finally to break scoreless tie as QB Tom Matte sneaked 5y and turned matters over to FB Bob Ferguson (16/80y), who battered 4, 2, 14 and final 17y for TD early in 4th Q. Fortunate Buckeyes INTs by G-LB Mike Ingram, who flipped lateral to HB-DB Jim Herbstreit to complete 48y RET, and QB-DB Bill Mrukowski halted late Michigan threats built on passing of QB Dave Glinka (10-17/86y, 2 INTs).

NORTHWESTERN 14 Illinois 7: Oft-injured, but highly-talented QB Dick Thornton (7-15/125y, TD, INT) was outstanding on 4 of 5 plays that straddled 3rd and 4th Qs and carried 86y to winning score for Northwestern (5-4). But initially, Thornton had gotten Wildcats rolling with 83y RET of opening KO, and he appeared gone for score when far-swifter Illinois (5-4) HB Marshall Starks leapt to haul him down. Wildcats FB-K Mike Stock scored 1st Q TD and added kick for 7-0 lead just 4 plays later. Illini drove 73y in 2nd Q to tie it after QB John Easterbrook hit E Ed O'Bradovich twice to set stage for FB Bill Brown's 3y plunge. Meanwhile, NW's O flunked as it made only single 1st down in middle 2 Qs. But, then Thornton lit his fire. He ran 3y, handed to Stock for 1y, and completed 3 in row to E Elbert Kimbrough, last of 13y for TD and 14-7 lead early in 4th Q. Still with plenty of time remaining, Illinois went to Cats 12 and 32YLs, but QB Mel Meyers was sacked 3 times, and possible Wildcats' EZ pass interference of receiver Starks was not called.

Minnesota 26 WISCONSIN 7: No. 4 Minnesota (8-1) found itself in unlikely opportunity to reclaim no. 1 national ranking, thanks to Missouri's upset to Kansas. Minnesota stormed back from its Purdue loss to tie Iowa for Big 10 title, each sporting 5-1 conf record. Wisconsin (4-5) C John Gotta lost freak FUM on C-QB exchange when QB Ron Miller backpedaled too soon and ball popped up only to find hands of Gophers fine DE Bob Deegan. Minnesota scored 7 plays later on QB Sandy Stephens' TD run. Badgers gained control of middle Qs but could manage only Miller's 15y TD pass to E Hank Derleth midway in 2nd Q to trim deficit to 12-7. Gophers repelled 2 Badgers scoring threats in 3rd Q while nursing lead, then ran away with 2 TD runs in 4th Q: HB Bill Mulholland's 4y TD run and QB Bob Johnson's 18y TD sprint with 5:36 to play.

Iowa 28 NOTRE DAME 0: Iowa (8-1) dropped record 8th straight loss on Notre Dame (1-8). It was final win for Iowa coach and future AD Forrest Evashevski against team he most wanted to defeat in his last year. After game, asst coach Jerry Burns, future Minnesota Viking coach, was named to head Hawkeyes in 1961. E-DE Bill Whisler had 2nd play FUM REC and caught 28y TD pass for Hawkeyes. Irish advanced for only 95y and managed to penetrate to Iowa 17YL no earlier than 4th Q. In Monday's AP Poll Hawkeyes attracted most 1st place votes but were leap-frogged for no. 1 by Minnesota, their conquerors from November 5.

GAME OF THE YEAR
Kansas 23 MISSOURI 7:

With whole state of Missouri in tizzy over school's first-ever no. 1 ranking, Tigers coach Dan Devine felt there were too many distractions for his tired squad. He was unable to pump up Missouri (9-1), which deflated when it couldn't benefit from 3 midfield FUM RECs. Most shocking were game-long shutdown of Tigers O and 2nd H disassembly of celebrated Mizzou D. Great rushing-D by Jayhawks prevented Tigers from gaining even single 1st down in scoreless 1st H, and at game's end Missouri had been permitted only 114y by tenacious Jayhawks. Kansas (7-2-1) launched its drive to Big 8 title with QB-K Roger Hill's 47y FG early in 2nd H. FUM REC quickly led to Jayhawks' 1st TD as QB John Hadl hit HB Bert Coan with 19y pass for 10-0 lead. Coan added 4th Q TD at end of 69y march. Only bright spot for Tigers came from QB Ron Taylor, future big league pitcher and Toronto Blue Jays team physician, who threw belated TD pass in 4th Q. Still, with Kansas on probation, Missouri received Big 8's Orange Bowl bid. Later, Kansas was forced to forfeit its wins over Missouri and Colorado (November 12) as conf belatedly declared Coan to be ineligible. Jayhawks were stripped of their conf crown, and season's most profound upset was rendered inconsequential.

RICE 23 Texas Christian 0: In worst to-date defeat for any Abe Martin-coached team at TCU (3-4-2), Rice (7-2) used 6 TOs to convert 3 of its 4 scores. TCU had solid air game in 1st H with QBs Sonny Gibbs and Don George hitting 10-14/104y, but, by game's end, Rice D had snatched 5 INTs. FB-K Max Webb gave Owls 3-0 lead in 2nd Q with 48y FG after Frogs lost FUM. Gibbs threw pair of INTs in 2nd H, and they positioned TD runs by Rice QBs Alvin Hartman (1y TD in 3rd Q) and Randall Kerbow (5y TD in 4th Q). Owls G-LB Rufus King sparkled on D, while, as always, Horned Frogs DT Bob Lilly did same in defeat.

Utah 6 UTAH STATE 0: Soph HB Bud Scalley dashed 12y to TD in 4th Q to give underdog Utah (7-2) win over previously unbeaten Utah State (9-1). Loss coupled with Wyoming's 30-6 trouncing of Brigham Young left Sun Bowl-bound Utah State in 1st place tie in Skyline Conf with Wyoming.

Southern California 17 UCLA 6: USC soph QB Bill Nelsen (7-11/87y, TD) outplayed Bruins star TB Billy Kilmer (4-17/80y, 3 INTs passing, and 10/29y, TD rushing) and stabilized upset-minded, but FUM-prone Southern California (4-5). Nelsen hit E Marlin McKeever for 21y TD pass in 1st Q. Kilmer's normally-effective run-pass option plays were often thwarted by DE McKeever, who was inspired by presence of his injured twin brother Mike, who was out of hospital and able now to sit on team bench. When Trojans HB-DB Jerry Traynham ran back INT off Kilmer for 29y, FB Hal Tobin quickly scored for 14-0 lead in 2nd Q. UCLA (5-2-1) went 75y early in 4th Q with Kilmer hammering last 2y for score. But, fine D play throughout game marked USC's upset that saw Trojans finally playing up to their capability.

OREGON STATE 14 Oregon 14: Oregon State (6-3-1) E Leon Criner set up TB Don Kasso's 2nd Q TD and 2-pt run with FUM REC at 24YL. In late game, Beavers led 8-6 and converted WB-DB Grimm Mason's INT of Oregon (7-2-1) QB Dave Grosz for Kasso's 2nd TD. But, Oregon State E-K Amos Marsh missed x-pt kick, so Beavers led 14-6. Grosz passed twice to E Kent Peterson, and pair of 15y PENs against Oregon State aided tying 72y drive. Squat Ducks HB Cleveland Jones hit E Paul Bauge for TD pass, Bauge's 1st catch of year, and then Jones tied it on reverse run for 2 pts.

Washington 8 WASHINGTON STATE 7 (Spokane): Pesky Washington State (4-5-1) nearly spoiled Washington's return trip to Rose Bowl. Cougars went ahead 7-0 as late 3rd Q INT set stage for QB Mel Melin, nation's O leader, to hit superb E Hugh Campbell with TD pass. Campbell finished season with 2 NCAA records to date: 66 receptions and 882y. Back came Huskies (9-1) with methodical 14-play, 52y drive, launched by HB Charlie Mitchell's clutch 35y KO RET. Sub QB Kermit Jorgensen scored TD, and regular QB Bob Hivner came in to hit winning 2-pt pass to reliable Marine vet HB Don McKeta.

1 Minnesota (13.5)	424.5	11 Duke	36
2 Iowa (17.5)	417.5	12 Rice	34
3 Mississippi (13)	398	13 Yale (1)	30.5
4 Washington (2)	249	14 Michigan State	19
5 Missouri	241	15t New Mexico State	9
6 Arkansas	228	15t Penn State	9
7 Navy	188	17t Syracuse	8
8 Auburn (1)	149.5	17t Alabama	8
9 Ohio State	114	19t Baylor	6
10 Kansas	48	19t Florida	6

November 24-26, 1960

Navy 17 Army 12 (Philadelphia): Orange Bowl-bound Navy (9-1) owned 1st H as over-eager Army (6-3-1) missed several tackles and lost pair of FUMs. Late in 1st Q, Having disentangled Middies from deep hole with 58y dash early in game, HB Joe Bellino (20/85y, TD) gave Navy 6-0 lead with 4y TD sweep late in 1st Q. E-K Greg Mather followed with 27y FG, and QB Hal Spooner (12-20/126y, TD, INT) and E Jim Luper collaborated on 12y TD pass late in 2nd Q. So, Middies owned tidy 17-0 lead at H. Cadets reversed their fortunes with long drives of 78y after 2nd H KO and 83y early in 4th Q to pair of TD runs by tough FB Al Rushatz (16/64y). Indeed, Army, so outclassed in 1st H, constructed 200y to -2y O advantage in 2nd H. Handoff FUM between Navy's Spooner and Bellino gave Army chance at Midshipmen 17YL with 5:30 to go. Cadets advanced to 6YL, but QB Dick Eckert's errant pitchout cost 14y. After 2 hurried passes, Black Knights lost it on downs at 15YL with 2 mins to go. Having conserved its timeouts, Army had 1 last chance, but DB Bellino, soon to be named Heisman Trophy winner, made clutch GL INT of QB Tom Blanda (9-22/112y, INT). In desperation, Blanda threw into double coverage for HB George Kirschenbauer, but Bellino cut in front of receiver and his RET sent him weaving out of danger to Navy 45YL and into arms of his happy mom moments later.

ALABAMA 3 Auburn 0 (Birmingham): Proud Auburn (8-2) lost its 1st game since opener against Tennessee, and coach Shug Jordan begrudgingly tipped his hat to Alabama (8-1-1), saying, "Alabama's line was great," but quickly added that his line hit just as hard and that his Tigers got no breaks. Crimson Tide's line tackled so well that Tigers, playing without injured FB Ed Dyas, could manage only 63y rushing. Part of Bama's D might came from its changing alignment to 4-4 instead of normal 6-2, and Plainsmen

were kept beyond Tide's 35YL all game. Auburn stars were DT Ken Rice, who had hand in 15 tackles, and QB-P Joe Dolan who averaged 41.2y on 9 soaring punts. Bama terrorized Tigers GL several times with its only success coming on 15-play drive to E-K Tommy Brooker's 22y FG with 8:31 left in 2nd Q. Brooker's 3-ptr was set up by QB Pat Trammell's 24y on runs and his 13y pass to E Bill Battle. Crimson Tide made 3 critical INTs.

MISSISSIPPI 35 Mississippi State 9: Finest to-date record for Mississippi (9-0-1) spelled Sugar Bowl bid for Rebels. Brilliant 1st H passing (9-9/90y) by Ole Miss QB Jake Gibbs included TD passes to E Johnny Brewer and HB Bobby Crespino in 2nd Q for 14-0 H advantage. After Maroons (2-6-1) QB Billy Hill narrowed it to 14-7 with 3rd Q TD pass to E David Kelley, Rebs secondary picked off 2 passes to set up TDs that hastened Egg Bowl rout. Gibbs also propelled Ole Miss' victory party with 8y TD run. Ole Miss, nation's only undefeated squad ranked in top 10, held out hope for national title. But, this drubbing of Mississippi State sparked marginal excitement in voters from outside southeast; Rebels moved up from no. 3 to no. 2, and 1-loss Minnesota walked away with AP's top spot in final balloting.

GEORGIA 7 Georgia Tech 6: Georgia (6-4) traveled 62y to Engineers 12YL on its opening series, but HB Bobby Walden, who was to later make vital 4th down run at midfield, lost FUM. From that moment of Walden's bobble, Georgia Tech (5-5) held upperhand. At end of 55y march, QB Marvin Tibbetts sneaked over to give Georgia Tech 6-0 lead in 2nd Q. HB-K Tommy Wells' kick was blocked by outstanding Bulldogs G Pat Dye, who moved to line up at RE for rush at Wells. Dye also got his paw on 38y 2nd Q FG try by Wells and helped pressure Wells' 30y FG attempt, that went wide left in last 5 mins. Georgia had remained behind by 6 pts until HB-DB Bill McKenny picked off tipped pass at Yellow Jackets 36YL but gave his UGa mates scare when his RET to 13YL late in 3rd Q had to be recovered by DB Dale Williams. Bulldogs FB Bill Godfrey plunged over on 2nd play of 4th Q, and K Durwood Pennington booted winning pt for Georgia. In his last game, sr QB Fran Tarkenton (9-14/65y, 2 INTs), playing some DB and made late INT to seal Bulldogs win. Yellow Jackets outgained their rival 254y to 170y and closed bitter break-even season in which they fell only 11 pts short of undefeated glory.

Florida 18 MIAMI 0: Florida (8-2) used effective ground game (157y) to beat Miami (5-4) and happily accepted Gator Bowl bid. Scoring in each of 1st 3 Qs, Gators tallied on runs by QBs Bobby Dodd, Jr. and Larry Libertore and FB Don Goodman. Hurricanes spent quiet 1st half between 20YLs, gaining 112y on ground and 54y in air. Miami tried to spring surprise O formation, moving effective soph QB Eddie Johns to HB to fill in for injured Jim Vollenweider and replacing Johns with sub QB Bobby Weaver. Idea failed miserably and likely contributed to Canes' fair 7-16 passing figures. Ardently-fought in-state series was now knotted at 11 wins each after Florida claimed most recent 4 games.

Air Force 16 COLORADO 6: Air Force (4-5), 2-TD underdog, limited Colorado (6-4) to 80y rushing and finally broke open 0-0 deadlock with HB Mike Quinlan's brilliant 92y punt TD RET in 3rd Q. Quinlan added 1y TD plunge, after his 56y dash, in 4th Q for 13-0 lead until Falcons C-K Mike Rawlins tacked on 29y FG. Buffaloes QB Gale Weidner suffered through weak 9-24 passing performance, but made each connection count for 195y in air, or 21.7y avg per completion. Critical GLS by Air Force early in 4th Q prevented 7-7 tie as smaller Airmen line stopped 4 smashes from inside its 5YL. Colorado could manage only late TD on FB Chuck Weiss' 1y run after Weidner's 39y pitch to E Gary Henson.

BAYLOR 12 Rice 7: Disappointed Rice (7-3) had to accept its 2nd place fate, knowing win would have given it share of SWC title with Arkansas. Still, Sugar Bowl committee surprisingly tapped Owls for New Year's Day spot against Mississippi. Bears scored in 2nd Q for 6-0 lead when T Buck McLeod fortunately fell on forward FUM into EZ by Baylor FB Jim Evans on short plunge. Thrice stopping Baylor (8-2) inside their own 10YL, desperate Owls finally crafted 80y march late in 4th Q. QB Billy Cox wedged over for TD, and HB Max Webb provided short-lived 7-6 lead with conv kick. Then, Bears turned to sub QB Bobby Ply, who launched aerial drive that carried 75y for victory. Ply hit HB Ronnie Goodwin with 9y TD pass that decided it in closing moments.

Notre Dame 17 SOUTHERN CALIFORNIA 0: Record 8-game Notre Dame (2-8) losing streak came to end in L.A. Coliseum downpour. Southern California (4-6) was held to 53y rushing, and its 2-8/21y passing prompt sarcastic rookie coach John McKay to crack, "We specialized in the dropped pass." Indeed, Trojan HB Jim Naples bobbled last-play TD pass that would have averted shutout. Fighting Irish QB Daryle Lamonica's 16y rollout set up FB-K Joe Perkowski's 31y FG on opening 71y drive. Lamonica added 1st Q TD run, and HB Bob Scarpitto went in from 9YL in 2nd Q.

Final AP Poll November 28

1 Minnesota (17.5)	433.5	11 Kansas		40
2 Mississippi (16)	411	12 Baylor		35
3 Iowa (12.5)	407.5	13 Auburn		25
4 Navy	262	14 Yale		17
5 Missouri	253	15 Michigan State		16
6 Washington (2)	250	16 Penn State		15
7 Arkansas	212	17 New Mexico State		8
8 Ohio State	138	18 Florida		6
9 Alabama	53	19t Syracuse		4
10 Duke	46	19t Purdue		4

December 3, 1960

(Fri) MIAMI 23 Air Force 14: Spirited Miami (6-4) sought to erase bad memories of recent losses to Syracuse and Florida, but Air Force (4-6) flew 78y to open game. Falcons QB Rich Mayo (8-19/147y, TD, INT) pitched 26y pass on which E Dick Brown made great catch at 1YL, and HB Mike Quinlan (16/58y) smashed over on next play.

But, FB-K Mike Rawlins missed kick. In punt setup, P Mayo saw snap sail over his head, and he retreated to his EZ to concede safety. After free-kick, Hurricanes scored early in 2nd Q on 9y TD pass on fake FG from holder George MacIntyre to E Bill Miller. Air Force regained 14-9 lead on Mayo's 18y TD pass to Brown in 3rd Q. But, smaller Flyboys began to wear down as Miami QB Eddie Johns (13/149y rushing) ate big y as Falcons LBs consistently were blocked off their feet by Canes big line, led by G Bill Diamond and T Charles Linning. Johns scored go-ahead TD on 4y run after his 66y dash went to 6YL.

SOUTH CAROLINA 26 Virginia 0: New QB-DB Buddy Bennett made 2 INTs of Virginia (0-10) QB Gary Cuozzo, once going 51y to set up TD for South Carolina (3-6-1). Bennett scored twice, including elusive 59y run. Late in game, several Gamecock sr linemen were allowed to enjoy special glory by playing skill-positions. For example: All-ACC G Jake Bodkin caught pass from E spot. Cavs perceived this fun as Carolina's way of rubbing it in, and it would remain sore spot for years to come. Loss was Virginia's 28th in row, tying NCAA record at that time held by Kansas State (1945-1948).

UCLA 27 Duke 6: Accounting directly for 2 scores, UCLA (7-2-1) TB Billy Kilmer rushed 27/147y, TD, and passed 3-8/53y, TD, to wrap up national total O title with 1889y. Kilmer opened scoring by flipping 9y TD to E Don Vena and finished matters at 27-0 early in 4th Q with 4y TD run as Bruins scored TD in every Q. His understudy, TB Bobby Smith (9/61y), turned workhorse, running on 9 straight plays from UCLA 38YL to set up FB Almose Thompson for 1y crack and Bruins TD in 3rd Q. Champions of ACC and Cotton Bowl-bound Duke (7-3) surprisingly was held to only 12 1st downs, and its run D arrived in Los Angeles having permitted avg of 125y per game. It left having relinquished 322y overland, including Kilmer's individual gains of 16, 12, 16, 13, 15, and 20y. Duke's longest run was turned in by QB Don Altman for 12y, and Big Blue failed to score until moving 61y—mostly on 2 catches by E Ed Chestnut from Altman—in 4th Q to HB Dean Wright's 2y TD run. Blue Devils had threatened once in 1st H but lost their surge at 4YL. Duke coach Bill Murray, who earlier in season faced Navy's Heisman-winning Joe Bellino, said afterward, "I'll still take Kilmer over any ballplayer I've seen this season."

Conference Standings

Ivy League

Yale	7-0
Princeton	6-1
Dartmouth	4-3
Harvard	4-3
Columbia	3-4
Pennsylvania	2-5
Brown	1-6
Cornell	1-6

Atlantic Coast

Duke	5-1
North Carolina State	4-1-1
Maryland	5-2
Clemson	4-2
South Carolina	3-3-1
North Carolina	2-5
Wake Forest	2-5
Virginia	0-6

Southern

Virginia Military	4-1
Citadel	4-2
George Washington	4-2
Virginia Tech	4-2
Furman	2-2
Richmond	3-4-1
Davidson	1-3
William & Mary	1-5
West Virginia	0-2-1

Southeastern

Mississippi	5-0-1
Florida	5-1
Alabama	5-1-1
Auburn	5-2
Tennessee	3-2-2
Georgia	4-3
Georgia Tech	4-4
Louisiana State	2-3-1
Kentucky	2-4-1
Tulane	1-4-1
Mississippi State	0-5-1
Vanderbilt	0-7

Big Ten

Minnesota	5-1
Iowa	5-1
Ohio State	4-2
Michigan State	3-2
Illinois	2-4
Michigan	2-4
Northwestern	2-4
Purdue	2-4
Wisconsin	2-5
Indiana	ineligible

NOTE: No results against ineligible, winless Indiana counted in Big Ten standings

Big Eight

Kansas (ineligible)	6-0-1
Missouri	6-1
Colorado	5-2
Iowa State	4-3
Oklahoma	2-4-1
Nebraska	2-5
Oklahoma State	2-5
Kansas State	0-7

Missouri Valley

Wichita	3-0
Tulsa	2-1
Cincinnati	1-2
North Texas State	0-3

Mid-American

Ohio	6-0
Bowling Green	5-1
Kent State	4-2
Miami (Ohio)	2-3
Western Michigan	2-4
Marshall	1-4
Toledo	0-6

Southwest

Arkansas	6-1
Baylor	5-2
Rice	5-2
Texas	5-2
Texas Christian	3-3-1
Texas Tech	1-5-1
Texas A&M	0-4-3
Southern Methodist	0-6-1

Border

New Mexico State	4-0
Arizona	3-0
Arizona State	3-2
Texas Western	2-3
West Texas State	1-4
Hardin-Simmons	0-4

Skyline Eight		AAWU	
Utah State	6-1	Washington	4-0
Wyoming	6-1	Southern California	3-1
Utah	5-1	UCLA	2-2
New Mexico	4-2	California	1-3
Montana	2-5	Stanford	0-4
Brigham Young	2-5		
Denver	1-6		
Colorado State	1-6		

1960 Bowl Games
Liberty Bowl (Dec. 17): Penn State 41 Oregon 12

Just 2 weeks earlier same stadium, Army-Navy game was played in balmy 55 degrees, but this time Philadelphia's vast, mostly empty, Municipal Stadium featured 3-foot sideline snowbanks and icy temperatures. Local favorite Penn State (7-3) mounted 2nd and 4th Q surges, each counting 3 TDs, which iced verdict. Oregon (7-3-1) QB Dave Grosz (9-15/178y, 2 INTs) had driven Ducks 88y and put them ahead 6-0 with short TD run in 1st Q. QB-DB Dick Hoak, alternating Lions signal-caller, was leading rusher on 9/61y with 2TD runs, passed 3-5/67y, TD, and grabbed 2 INTs to launch deciding 20-pt 4th Q avalanche. In all, Hoak had hand in 5 of Penn State's 6 TDs. HB Dave Grayson rushed 10/93y, and briefly encouraged Ducks by scoring in 3rd Q to bring his team within 21-12. But, Nittany Lions, who ran snappy O with little delay between many of its 87 plays, began to wear down thinner troops of Oregon. Determined Lions drove 95y to HB Ed Caye's 1y TD early in 4th Q. Hoak followed with his 2 pass pick-offs of Grosz, who was descendent of Oregon's Norm Van Brocklin, QB who was few days away in same city from helping to beat Green Bay Packers and deliver Philadelphia Eagles' last world championship. Hoak made 4th Q runbacks of 24y to set up his 11y TD run and 13y RET to put into play his 33y TD pass to HB Dick Pae.

Bluebonnet Bowl (Dec. 17): Alabama 3 Texas 3

During their careers, coaches Bear Bryant of Alabama (8-1-2) and Darrell Royal of Texas (7-3-1) met in 3 bowl games with Bryant never achieving victory. This tie was closest he ever came as Royal's Steers rolled over Crimson Tide in 1964 Orange Bowl and 1972 Cotton Bowl. Crimson Tide QB Bobby Skelton was quite sure he scored early on from 3YL after his 49y look-in pass to E Bill Rice carried to 7YL. But, officials ruled that Skelton had not crossed GL, and Longhorns D stopped FB Bobby Richardson mere inch short of GL on 4th down blast. After scoreless 1st H, Bama E-K Tommy Brooker and Texas T-K Dan Petty exchanged 2nd H FGs, Petty's coming with 3:44 to go in 4th Q. Longhorns had game's last scoring chance as Crimson Tide HB-DB Leon Fuller was called for interfering with E Bob Moses as time expired. But, Petty missed 35y FG try.

Gator Bowl (Dec. 31): Florida 13 Baylor 12

Each team scored 2 TDs: Baylor (8-3) traveled 139y for its scores, while Florida (9-2) required just 20y to earn its 13 pts. Bobbled pitchout by Bears HB Ronnie Bull was pounced upon by Gators DG Chet Collins at 20YL early in 2nd Q. FB Don Goodman scored on 5th play for 7-0 lead. Florida DT Ronnie Slack made it 13-0 before H by falling on EZ FUM by Baylor QB Ronnie Stanley. After scoreless 3rd Q, Bears got going and converted 71y drive on 4th Q's 1st play when QB Bobby Ply (12-24/162y) threw 11y TD pass to HB Ronnie Goodwin. That score made it 13-6 with Florida remaining in front. When Bull scored with 1:01 to play, Ply tried 2-pt pass, but normally-reliable Goodwin (7 catches) juggled and dropped his throw.

Orange Bowl (Jan. 2): Missouri 21 Navy 14

With Pres-elect John F. Kennedy looking on, Missouri (10-1) was cruising to opening score when HB Donnie Smith got foolishly creative. Trapped at Navy 3YL, he pitched back to QB Ron Taylor, but Middies DE Greg Mather, trailing from backside of play, stunningly intervened to steal lateral pass and rumble 96y for reversal TD. "I was sick when I saw that guy come out of nowhere," said Smith later. Mather, Navy's fine K, was winded from his long sprint in Miami's heat and humidity, so he missed conv. When HB-DB Norm Beal soon used DE Tommy Carpenter's crushing block to charge 90y with INT RET, Tigers earned lead for good at 7-6. And, Smith redeemed himself with 2nd Q TD run. Missouri's mighty D forced Navy to run awash with -8y on ground; star and Heisman Trophy winning Middies HB Joe Bellino was completely collared and could gain only 8/4y. Bellino, however, left lasting memory with brilliant over-shoulder, diving corner-of-EZ catch for 27y TD in late going.

Sugar Bowl (Jan. 2): Mississippi 14 Rice 6

No. 2 Ole Miss (10-0-1) won its 5th bowl game in row, but not before unranked Rice (7-4) threw scare into Rebels. QB Jake Gibbs launched 65y march with pass to HB George Blair after short opening KO created great field position. Key runs on 7-play drive by FB James Anderson for 13y and HB Bobby Crespino for 27y came before Gibbs went wide for 8y TD sprint. Drive was easy, so easy that perhaps Rebels went into cruise mode for awhile. Rice, which would outgain Rebs 281y to 186y, moved into Ole Miss territory 4 times in middle Qs, only to be turned back at 31, 10, 18, and 13YLs. Owls' efforts were thwarted by 2 INTs and, on their last thrust to 13YL, HB-K Max Webb's missed 30y FG try. Mississippi ganged scrimmage line with 8 or 9 defenders, daring Rice to pass. QB Billy Cox (11-20/143y, 3 INTs) hit passes of 8, 13, and 30y to lead Owls on fit-and-start 77y trip to HB Butch Blume's 1y TD run on 4th down late in 3rd Q. K Webb missed kick to trail 7-6. MVP Gibbs finally reinvigorated Rebs' O and scored on 4th down at end of 57y drive early in 4th Q. Result was less than masterpiece for Rebels, but satisfying nonetheless.

Cotton Bowl (Jan. 2): Duke 7 Arkansas 6

Duke (8-3), which had faded in late season, played superb D while its O slumbered. Blue Devils DE Dave Usher providing 2 key plays: he blocked vital x-pt and forced FUM to kill Hogs' last hope. Matchup became mighty D struggle for much of afternoon. In 3rd Q, Arkansas (8-3) HB-P Lance Alworth, who was held to 11/33y rushing, took high punt snap and was forced to kick on run to avoid 4 tacklers. Alworth still managed 38y punt that beautifully stopped dead at Duke 1YL. On Blue Devils P Randy Clark's 1st down punt out of EZ, Alworth used E Les Letsinger's block to race 49y to TD and 6-0 lead. But, Duke's Usher blocked K Mickey Cissell's conv try. In 4th Q, Duke launched 73y drive, but DB Alworth had his hands on seemingly certain INT and TD RET on pass in flat. Blue Devils A-A E Tee Moorman somehow wrestled ball away from Alworth and happily accepted 3y loss. It allowed Duke to maintain possession on its winning drive on which Moorman made 6 catches. QB Don Altman (12-15/83y, TD, INT), who hit 8-9 on march, found Moorman alone in EZ for 9y TD with 2:45 left. G-K Art Browning tacked on all-important x-pt. On following KO, Usher slammed into Alworth, whose FUM was recovered by Duke FB Jerry McGee, and victory was clinched for Blue Devils as they marched to 1YL before clock expiration ended it.

Rose Bowl (Jan. 2): Washington 17 Minnesota 7

Since AP held no post-bowl poll, Minnesota's huge Golden Gophers (8-2) had already clinched national title to which Mississippi, Missouri, and Washington all could stake realistic post-bowl claims. Effective, but under-achieving Washington (10-1) was poised for its 2nd straight surprise win in Pasadena. Biggest obstacle for Washington seemed to be how to deal with Gophers massive NG Tom Brown, fierce and mobile man in middle of D. Brown outweighed Huskies C Roy McKasson by 40 lbs, even though it was matchup of A-A linemen. Huskies devised fake sweep play that allowed McKasson to trap Brown and send QB Bob Schloredt (5/68y rushing) quickly through line on long-gaining sneaks. Huskies used this play to gain 52y in dominating 1st H as they outgained Minnesota by 158y to 61y before H. Washington HB-K George Fleming opened scoring with to-date Rose Bowl record 44y FG. Huskies made it 10-0 on run-fake pass to right flat from Schloredt to HB Brent Wooten for 4y TD. It was set up by FB Ray Jackson's 12y catch and 19y spurt through middle of line. Schloredt's sneaks made possible another TD for 17-0 Huskies lead at H. Rascals at Cal Tech infiltrated Washington's H card stunts and spelled out "Cal Tech" to amusement of 97,314 spectators. Minnesota clearly controlled 2nd H, allowed only single 1st down, and outgained foe by 192y to 35y. But, Gophers could manage only HB Bill Munsey's 18y TD sprint with option pitchout from QB Sandy Stephens 5:35 into 3rd Q. Minnesota DE Bob Deegan recovered FUM by Huskies sub QB Bob Hivner at UW 37YL early in 3rd Q to set up Munsey's score. Minnesota offered little aerial skill, and that failure kept them from cashing several chances. In 4th Q, HB-DB Don McKeta lined up at DE spot and threw Stephens for 10y loss at Washington 7YL, then made INT to halt threat.

1960 Top Performance Formula

1	Mississippi	1.7541
2	Iowa	1.6846
3	Missouri	1.6032
4	Washington	1.5806
5	Auburn	1.4959
6	Minnesota	1.4841
7	Florida	1.4727
8	Alabama	1.4633
9	Syracuse	1.4594
10	Penn State	1.4317
11	Alabama	1.4297
12	Ohio State	1.4032
13	UCLA	1.3850
14	Michigan State	1.3798
15	Navy	1.3794
16	Arkansas	1.3684
17	Duke	1.3660
18	Baylor	1.3483
19	Tennessee	1.3266
20	Rice	1.2941

1960 Top Opponent Records

1	Mississippi State	.6817
2	Georgia Tech	.6755
3	Iowa	.6579
4	Michigan	.6316
5	Southern Methodist	.6237
6	Auburn	.6209
7	Penn State	.6167
8	Mississippi	.6150
9	Nebraska	.6099
10	Purdue	.5933
11	Vanderbilt	.5924
12	Florida	.5900
13	Duke	.5850
14	Kansas	.5843
15	Indiana	.574324
16	Michigan State	.574324
17	Rice	.5714
18t	Boston College	.567416
18t	Kansas State	.567416
20	Air Force	.5604

1960 Out-of-Conference Records

	W-L	Percentage	Bowl W-L
Big Ten	19-2-2	.8696	0-1
Southeastern	30-7-1	.8026	2-0-1
Big Eight	13-11	.5417	1-0
Southwest	11-13-2	.4615	0-2-1
AAWU	13-16-2	.4516	1-0
Atlantic Coast	9-20	.3103	1-0

Other Major Awards

Maxwell (Player)	Joe Bellino, senior halfback, Navy
Outland (Lineman)	Tom Brown, senior guard, Minnesota
Walter Camp (Back)	Joe Bellino, senior halfback, Navy
Knute Rockne (Lineman)	Tom Brown, senior guard, Minnesota
AFCA Coach of the Year	Murray Warmath, Minnesota

1960 Individual Statistical Leaders

RUSHING YARDS

	Attempts	Yards	Avg.
Bobby Gaiters, New Mexico State	197	1338	6.8
Jack Larscheid, Utah State	124	1044	8.4
Ernie Davis, Syracuse	112	877	7.8
Bob Ferguson, Ohio State	160	853	5.3
Dave Hoppmann, Iowa State	161	844	5.2
Joe Bellino, Navy	168	834	5.0
Billy Kilmer, UCLA	163	803	4.9
Hugh Scott, Princeton	140	760	5.4
Bobby Thompson, Arizona	92	732	8.0
Alan Rozycki, Dartmouth	169	725	4.3

PASSING YARDS

	Completions	Attempts	Yards	Pct.
Norm Snead, Wake Forest	123	259	1676	47.4
Mel Melin, Washington State	119	221	1638	53.8
Charley Johnson, New Mexico State	109	199	1511	54.8
Ron Miller, Wisconsin	97	188	1351	51.6
Harold Stephens, Hardin-Simmons	145	256	1254	56.6
Fran Tarkenton, Georgia	108	185	1189	58.4
Roman Gabriel, North Carolina State	105	186	1176	56.5
Rich Mayo, Air Force	108	238	1168	45.4
Ronnie Stanley, Baylor	75	134	1151	56.0
Tom Blanda, Army	92	164	1119	56.1

RECEIVING YARDS

	Catches	Yards
Hugh Campbell, Washington State	66	881
Reg Carolan, Idaho	33	498
Pervis Atkins, New Mexico State	26	468
Tom Hutchinson, Kentucky	30	455
Tee Moorman, Duke	46	431
Del Williams, Texas Western	36	414
E.A. Sims, New Mexico State	30	408
Gary Collins, Maryland	30	404
Cleveland Jones, Oregon	25	402
Fred Oblak, Cincinnati	23	386

1960 Consensus All-America Team

End:	Mike Ditka, Pittsburgh
	Danny LaRose, Missouri
Tackle:	Bob Lilly, Texas Christian
	Ken Rice, Auburn
Guard:	Tom Brown, Minnesota
	Joe Romig, Colorado
Center:	E.J. Holub, Texas Tech
Backs:	Jake Gibbs, Mississippi
	Joe Bellino, Navy
	Ernie Davis, Syracuse
	Bob Ferguson, Ohio State

Other All-America Choices

End:	Tee Moorman, Duke
	Bill Miller, Miami
Tackle:	Merlin Olsen, Utah State
	Jerry Beabout, Purdue
Guard:	Mark Manders, Iowa
	Ben Balme, Yale
	Myron Pottios, Notre Dame
Center:	Roy McKasson, Washington
	Wayne Harri, Arkansas
	Jerry Smith, Michigan
Backs:	Bill Kilmer, UCLA
	Roman Gabriel, North Carolina State
	Pervis Atkins, New Mexico State
	Ed Dyas, Auburn
	John Hadl, Kansas
	Larry Ferguson, Iowa

1960 Heisman Trophy Vote

Joe Bellino, senior halfback, Navy	1793
Tom Brown, senior guard, Minnesota	731
Jake Gibbs, senior quarterback, Mississippi	453
Ed Dyas, senior fullback, Auburn	319
Billy Kilmer, senior tailback, UCLA	280

1961

The Year of the Upside-Down Year, an Indignant Faculty, and the Wacky Horned Frogs

If things were crazy in 1961, there was a reason. It was first pointed out by the cracked genius—cover boy Alfred E. Neuman—of the ever-popular, absurdist magazine of that era, *MAD*. The point was that 1961 was an "upside-down" year, meaning, that if the four digits were jotted down on paper and then spun upside-down, they still read 1961. In an upset-laden, crazy-quilt season, the faculty at Ohio State turned college football truly upside down, at least inside the bounds of the state of "O-HI-O." Think 1961 wasn't upside down? Colorado (9-2) won its first-ever Big Eight championship, Columbia (6-3) of all teams tied for the Ivy League title, and Rutgers (9-0), for Heaven's sake, went undefeated.

Woody Hayes' no. 2-ranked Ohio State Buckeyes (8-0-1), led by bulldozing All-America fullback Bob Ferguson, finished the season undefeated, with the tie coming in the opener against a wacky, upside-down Texas Christian (3-5-2) team. The Horned Frogs couldn't manage to beat mediocre Southwest Conference rivals Baylor (5-5), SMU (2-7-1), or Texas Tech (4-6). But, with its big line anchored by 240-lb tackle Bobby Plummer and 255-lb center Kent Henson, TCU sneaked by bowl-bound Kansas (7-3-1) 17-16 and inflicted the only loss on eventual no. 3 Texas (10-1), 6-0 at Austin. Plus, the Purple-clad Frogs played their surprising tie on the road against Ohio State.

The Big Ten's contract with the Rose Bowl was coming to a close, and, with little national notice, the long-frustrated Ohio State faculty already had cast the swing vote—in a long drawn-out process—to end the conference's 16-year association with the Tournament of Roses. Meanwhile on the field, the Buckeyes beat Illinois (0-9) 44-0, pre-season no. 1 Iowa (5-4) 29-13, and archrival Michigan (6-3) 50-20 to easily earn the Big Ten title. Even without the seeming foregone conclusion of a new Big Ten contract, the Tournament of Roses committee extended to Ohio State a logical and seemingly automatic bid for the trip to Pasadena. Stunningly, the faculty council voted 28 to 25 to reject the offer. Smoldering for years had been professorial indignation over the school's image as a football factory, with academics perceived as placing a distant second.

Trouble in the streets began immediately as the *Columbus Dispatch* unwisely and vindictively printed each no voter's name, address, and amount of reimbursed out-of-state travel he or she had received during the year. Hayes, perhaps the most disappointed person in all of Ohio, showed great leadership in making calming pleas that quelled potential student riots. Perhaps it was small consolation, but after the bowl season, the Buckeyes received the Grantland Rice Award, symbolic of a national championship, from the Football Writers Association.

A solid if unspectacular Minnesota (8-2) team, led by All-America quarterback Sandy Stephens, a far more gifted runner than passer, and outstanding two-way tackle Bobby Bell, went to Pasadena in Ohio State's place and redeemed itself for the previous year's embarrassing Rose Bowl loss to Washington. The Golden Gophers won easily 21-3 over a decidedly average western champion, UCLA (7-4). The Bruins had outlasted Washington (5-4-1) and Southern California (4-5-1) to win the crown of the five-team AAWU conference.

Michigan State (7-2), led by a line full of future pros—center Dave Manders, guard Ed Budde, tackles Dave Behrmann and Dave Herman, and end Lonnie Sanders—was AP's no. 1 team in mid-season and Big Ten leader, but the late-fading Spartans lost to Minnesota and Purdue (6-3) in November.

Bowl picks took some surprising turns. The major football programs of the East had no better to offer than Penn State (8-3), Syracuse (8-3), and Navy (7-3). However, the Nittany Lions and Orangemen won the Gator and Liberty Bowl games over Georgia Tech (7-4) and Miami (7-4) respectively. Meanwhile, an invitation to a bowl game was extended to neither ACC champion Duke (7-3) nor third-place Maryland (7-3).

Oklahoma (5-5) suffered its second poor year in a row under Bud Wilkinson, who had lost 11 games in the last two years after being defeated only 13 times in the 13 years from 1947 to 1959. But, in what the Associated Press chose as the sports comeback of the year, the Sooners rebounded with five straight wins after opening the year at 0-5. Talk about upside-down!

Colorado emerged as Big Eight champion behind third-year coach Sonny Grandelius but got bounced 25-7 in the Orange Bowl by Louisiana State (10-1). Soon thereafter, Grandelius got bounced himself. With NCAA investigators circling boldly around Colorado recruiting violations, school officials quickly mapped the road out of Boulder for the former Michigan State All-America halfback. Interestingly, the new coach would be William "Bud" Davis, Colorado's alumni secretary, whose appointment sent a clear message that University officials wanted to stress academics. Davis was in over his head as a coach and lasted only one season as the Buffaloes plunged to a 2-8 mark in 1962. That record represented the second worst drop-off in the last 55 years of collegiate history in a season after a major New Year's Day bowl appearance. Kansas would lose a one-point verdict to Penn State in the January 1969 Orange Bowl and plunge to 1-9 later that calendar year.

With mediocrity showing itself all around the country, it seemed that the only region of America that saw the emergence of truly outstanding teams was the Deep South. Alabama (11-0) blanked its last five regular season foes and beat Arkansas (8-3) 10-3 in the Sugar Bowl to win the AP national title for coach Bear Bryant. It was Bryant's first national championship, and he would win four more at his alma mater. When Bryant had arrived in Tuscaloosa in 1958, the once-proud Crimson Tide had a horrendous three-year record of 4-24-1. Bryant's scrappy, but undersized 1958 club managed five wins, and the 1959 and '60 editions of the Crimson Tide won seven and eight games respectively. So, entering 1961, Alabama had delivered a very good, but slightly quiet 20-6-4 ledger under Bryant.

The 1961 Crimson Tide was led by feisty quarterback Pat Trammell, a pre-medicine student with more smarts than talent, who made very few mistakes and always got the job done. With linebacker Lee Roy Jordan and All-America tackle Billy Neighbors in the middle of a fabulous defense that allowed only 25 points in 11 wins, pre-season no. 3 Alabama opened with a 32-6 trouncing of Georgia (3-7) and, except for a 9-0 win over Tulane (2-8) and 10-0 whitewash of Georgia Tech, never allowed an opponent to be close in score. Alabama averaged a 27-2 winning-score margin. However, as always seemed the custom in the SEC in the 1950s and '60s, the champion did not face either of the fiercest conference challengers, LSU or Mississippi (9-2).

For the fourth straight year, Ole Miss came to its LSU showdown with a perfect record. And for the fourth straight year, the Bengal Tigers left the Rebels with a black eye, this time a 10-7 defeat at Tiger Stadium on November 4.

Despite its stunning upset at the hands of TCU, Texas fielded one of coach Darrell Royal's finest teams, a high-scoring (sixth-best in nation 29.1 points per game average) outfit with a battalion of swift runners who averaged a nation's second-best 285.8 yards per game rushing. Texas struck from Royal's innovative flip-flop Wing-T, which always lined up the same trio of guard, tackle, and end to the strong side, with the wingback outside the end, and the other line threesome to the weak side without a flanked back. The Longhorns got winging in 1961 with a 28-3 opening victory over California (1-8-1) at Berkeley. The school didn't bring its cheerleaders all the way to the West Coast, so enterprising and well-heeled fans hired night club dancers from San Francisco to lead the Texas cheers. It must have been an inspiring season opener because it launched the Longhorns all the way to the Cotton Bowl, where Texas picked off five Ole Miss passes to turn back the Rebels 12-7, the first of five Cotton Bowl champions Royal would coach.

The New York metropolitan area was stirred up by two surprising championship interlopers. Columbia (6-3), without a winning season since 1951, and 18-62-1 over that span, went 6-1 in the Ivy League and tied Harvard (6-3) for the league title. In just six years of official play, the Ivy League had already seen six of its eight members win or share the conference crown at least once. Rutgers (9-0) whipped Columbia 32-19 to finish its first undefeated season since it had a 1-0 record in 1876. The Scarlet Knights won the little-noticed Middle Atlantic Conference crown and took its first tentative steps toward a more major schedule that would eventually land them in the Big East (with decidedly mixed results) in the 1990s. In 1961, Rutgers achieved its record on a diet of Ivy Leaguers and small Eastern schools.

Iowa (5-4) started the year as AP's pre-season no. 1 team, but seemed to leave some energy on the field after a 35-34 early-season squeaker over Southern California. The Hawkeyes opened 4-0 but fell asunder to the competitive Big Ten schedule, dropping four straight starting October 28.

Four-inch think grass sod was carted inside the Atlantic City (N.J.) Convention Center for the first indoor football game since 1939, the "Little

Army-Navy Game" won by Penn Military 35-14 over Kings Point Merchant Marine Academy.

Concern over a rash of head and neck injuries influenced the NCAA to investigate headgear and facemasks. The study was inconclusive, and, while some teams—Ohio State, Duke, Oklahoma, and Cornell (3-6)—used a padded outer-shell helmet, the padded gear eventually fell into disuse partly because the helmets muffled the robust sound of collisions that coaches so admired as a sign of a hard-hitting blocks and tackles.

Many experts steadfastly blamed facemasks for the head and neck injuries. Metal or plastic bars or cages, mounted across what had been open-faced helmets for decades, had become universal in the game by the late 1950s. Certainly, the masks diminished considerably the number of broken noses and lost teeth, but the theory went that the pre-facemask period discouraged players from hitting near the head area. Now blockers and tacklers could go for the head without concern, and so perhaps this freedom brought on the rash of head injuries. With full-head coverage, players, who once learned to tackle with a shoulder, now were taught to bull their necks and make initial tackling contact with the crown of their helmets. This was a particular trademark of national champion Alabama's defense that also was taught to "gang-tackle," that is, to arrive at the ball-carrier in swarming, multi-defender pursuit.

Milestones

Associated Press altered its voting procedure, selecting weekly top 10 lists instead of top 20. Only season's final poll, still taken before post-season bowl games, listed 20 teams.

Denver and Marquette dropped football, while Hawaii took one year off before returning in 1962.

"Quoth the Raven never more:" death took Princeton's All-America quarterback of 1889, Edgar Allen Poe, 90, nephew of famed mystery writer of same name. Coaches who died included Jesse Harper, 77, of Notre Dame (1913-17) in 1913 when Gus Dorais and Knute Rockne sprung forward pass in upset of Army, Leonard "Stub" Allison, 69, of California (1935-44), and Jim Aiken , 60, of Oregon (1947-50). Former players who died included Steve Lach, 40, All-America halfback at Duke in 1941, Stephen Dzamba, 47, who played entire Rose Bowl as Columbia guard in 1934, and George Chadwick, 81, All-America halfback at Yale in 1900 and 1902.

Longest winning streaks entering season:
Ohio University 10   Yale 9   Washington 8

Coaching Changes:

	Incoming	Outgoing
Brigham Young	Hal Mitchell	Tally Stevens
Cornell	Tom Harp	George "Lefty" James
Georgia	Johnny Griffith	Wally Butts
Iowa	Jerry Burns	Forest Evashevski
San Diego State	Don Coryell	Paul Governali
South Carolina	Marvin Bass	Warren Giese
Texas Tech	J.T. King	DeWitt Weaver
Virginia	Bill Elias	Dick Voris
Virginia Tech	Jerry Claiborne	Frank Moseley

Preseason AP Poll

1 Iowa (22)	400	6 Michigan State	168
2 Ohio State (15)	360	7 Penn State (1)	164
3 Alabama (3)	198	8 Kansas (1)	163
4 Texas (1)	196	9 Mississippi (2)	135
5 Louisiana State	195	10 Syracuse	118

Others with votes: Rice, Arkansas, UCLA, Washington, Baylor, Tennessee, Oregon State, Duke, Southern California, North Carolina State, Auburn, Purdue, Colorado, Minnesota, Maryland, Army, Notre Dame, Navy, Oregon, Missouri, Wisconsin, Clemson, Florida

September 16, 1961

Pittsburgh 10 MIAMI 7: Hurricanes (0-1) owned 1st H, played in glorious sunshine and late summer heat. Miami soph QB George Mira made his debut on national TV, hitting E Larry Wilson twice before flipping 4y TD pass to Wilson in 2nd Q. Early in 2nd H, dark gray thunderheads rolled over Orange Bowl and delivered deluge. After rain started, Pittsburgh (1-0) HB-K Fred Cox kicked 38y FG. In 4th Q, Cox splashed around LE for 20y gain to his 40YL, then tossed impromptu lateral to trailing HB Paul Martha, who raced untouched to complete spectacular, winning 80y TD.

September 23, 1961

(Fri) Georgia Tech 27 SOUTHERN CALIFORNIA 7: West Coast season kicked off under lights of L.A. Coliseum. Georgia Tech (1-0) proved its line could manage about anything, and Southern California (0-1) proved it could do little but pass (18-29/240y). Difference was Yellow Jackets' fine D-front which forced 2 FUMs that led to 2nd Q TDs. After soph back-up QB-K Billy Lothridge made 35y FG in 1st Q, DG Rufus Guthrie slammed USC FB Ernie Jones early in 2nd Q to force FUM gobbled up by G-LB Dave Watson at Trojans 10YL. Tech QB Stan Gann sneaked across for 10-0 lead. After Gann's 31y TD pass, Lothridge followed USC HB Alan Shields' FUM at Jackets 42YL with 30y TD arrow to speedy HB Joe Auer. It was 24-0 at H. While Trojans dominated 3rd Q with pair of long drives, they clicked only on sub QB Pete Beathard's 2y rollout TD after his tosses paved way for 46y drive.

PENN STATE 20 Navy 10: Midshipmen (0-1) scored from opening KO on 60y drive climaxed by short slant-in pass to HB Jim Stewart from QB Ron Klemick (6-13/55y, TD, INT). Navy E-K Greg Mather made it 10-7 with soaring 45y FG in last 5 secs of 2nd Q. It was another story in 2nd H as Penn State (1-0) controlled ball for long periods. Nittany Lions sr HB-K Don Jonas (17/71y, TD) kicked 1st 2 FGs of his career: Key find

for Lions was soph QB Don Caum who contributed clinching 4th Q, 19y TD sweep of LE at end of 3-play, 68y trip that started with his 46y pitch to HB Gary Wydman. Until that moment, Navy had snapped ball on only 16 scrimmages in 2nd H, although it would muster 1 more scoring threat on passes to Penn State 25YL before time ran out.

VIRGINIA 21 William & Mary 6: New Virginia (1-0) coach Bill Elias had auspicious debut as Cavaliers broke 28-game losing streak as they played conservatively with 67 runs and 5 passes. TD runs by FB Tommy Griggs, QB Stanford Fischer, and HB Tony Ulehla paved way for victory. William & Mary (0-1) E Dennis O'Toole spoiled shutout with 88y INT TD RET early in 4th Q. Tribe might never have scored on Virginia's newly-improved D, and their TD came when Cavs passer Fischer should have eaten ball as William & Mary FB-LB H.C. Thaxton blitzed Fischer into his bad throw. Elias had predicted end of Wahoos' streak, saying D would be much better because, "I have always been a defensive coach."

Alabama 32 GEORGIA 6: In coach Bear Bryant's 4th season at Tuscaloosa, Alabama (1-0) clearly had assembled outstanding D, which limited Georgia (0-1) to 112y total O and 5 1st downs. New Bulldogs coach Johnny Griffith's less-than-fabulous career started in hospital bed as he healed after Friday night's appendectomy. Griffith would make way for coach Vince Dooley in 3 years after posting 10-16-4 mark. Crimson Tide FB Mike Fracchia barreled to 2 TDs: Fracchia ran 12y to set up his 1y plunge that opened scoring and tallied Tide's 3rd TD on 2y run. In 3rd Q, Alabama QB Pat Trammell pitched short pass to HB Butch Wilson, and Wilson dashed 32y to score. Georgia rushed for only 48y and passed for 8-12/64y. Long after decision was final, Bulldogs TD came with subs in action: QB Dale Williams threw 13y TD to HB Carlton Guthrie.

FLORIDA 21 Clemson 17: Future NFL coach, Gators HB Lindy Infante, scored 3 times, prompting Florida (1-0) to overtake early FG by K Lon Armstrong of Clemson (0-1). Gators QB Larry Libertore (11/66y rushing), who was only 40 percent passer in 1960, but made 3-6/95y, TD. Libertore's 17y TD toss to Infante provided 7-3 lead late in 1st Q, and Florida would never again trail. Clemson's 2 FUMs in 2nd Q halted its O, and 2nd REC by UF sub C-LB Tom Kelley at Tigers 39YL paved way for Infante's catapulting 1y TD for 14-3 edge. Tigers opened 2nd H with 3 quick completions by sub QB Joe Anderson (6-9/84y), and HB Ron Scrudato scored on 9y TD run to trim deficit to 14-10. Infante iced it with another 1y run in 3rd Q. Frustrated Clemson coach Frank Howard was unimpressed, growling: "We're as good as they (Florida) are. I wouldn't mind playing 'em every Saturday."

MISSISSIPPI 16 Arkansas 0 (Jackson, Miss.): Meeting of defending conf champions was highlighted by emergence of Rebels QB Doug Elmore (142y total O), who engineered 3 scoring drives. Ole Miss went 68y in 1st Q with Elmore hitting E Woody Dabbs with 35y TD pass as Dabbs' paper-thin tear-away jersey was left in fingers of diving Porkers tackler. Rebels marched 71y to 2nd Q FG and 80y to FB Art Doty's short TD run. Arkansas (0-1) was limited to 108y, and HB Lance Alworth was held in check except for long KO RET, which would have been TD had Elmore not halted him as Rebs' last tackler.

MIAMI 14 Kentucky 7: Negative "Sun-Tan U" story with plethora of photos of bikinied coeds in *Saturday Evening Post* had city of Miami abuzz most of summer. (This was considered horrible publicity for ambitious school: it reflected poorly upon academic standing of Coral Gables campus.) Autumn arrived on winning 91y TD drive in 3rd Q as Hurricanes (1-1) QB George Mira returned from knockout tackle that sent him to sidelines in 1st Q. Mira passed 44y to HB Nick Spinelli and ran 21y on keeper to maintain drive until he found E Bill Miller on 5y TD curl-in between Kentucky (0-1) QB-DB Jerry Woolum and HB-DB Bill Ransdell. Wildcats, who would gain only 36y rushing, had driven 80y to score on FB Gary Cochran's 11y sweep on their initial possession in 1st Q. QB Woolum (17-32/166y, INT) passed for 50y on opening drive, including 2 throws to E Tom Hutchinson. Demoted and oft-ridiculed QB Bobby Weaver had been tapped by Miami after Mira went down. Although Weaver threw INT to Kentucky DT Bob Butler, he rallied by hitting 4th down pass to HB John Bahen to 2YL to key 58y TD drive in 2nd Q.

TEXAS CHRISTIAN 17 Kansas 16: Early on, Kansas C-LB Kent Staab fell on FUM at TCU 44YL, and Jayhawks (0-1) quickly converted it into HB Lee Flachsbarth's TD run. Kansas added QB John Hadl's TD run and G-K Elvin Basham's 30y FG to lead 16-7 entering 4th Q. Texas Christian (1-0) QB Sonny Gibbs, who passed only twice in 3 Qs, went to air 10 times in 4th Q. At end of 80y drive, Purple Frogs realized 24y TD pass from Gibbs to E Roy Dent, who got behind 2 Kansas defenders in EZ to pull within 16-14. Gibbs led TCU from its 44YL to Jayhawks 18YL for winning 36y FG by K Jerry Spearman.

RICE 16 Louisiana State 3: QB Billy Cox pitched TD passes to E Johnny Burrell (4y jump pass), and FB Roland Jackson (47y pass-run up middle of secondary) to spark Rice (1-0) in front of record home crowd of 73,000. Stunned no. 5 LSU (0-1) mounted early 3rd Q drive which featured QB Lynn Amadee's 11 and 15y passes to HB Jerry Stovall, but Bengal Tigers only could manage HB-K Wendell Harris' 25y FG. Owls HB-K Butch Blume made 27y FG in 4th Q.

WYOMING 15 North Carolina State 14: Wolfpack (0-1) instinctively wanted to howl in rare trip to wild-west, but instead Cowboys (2-0) lassoed NC State with 80y TD march in 4th Q. NC State jumped to 14-0 lead in 1st H as QB Roman Gabriel (10-22/115y, INT) pitched 14y TD pass after G Bill Sullivan recovered FUM at Wyoming 33YL. Wolfpack FB Jim D'Antonio roared 1y through RG for TD in last 3 mins of 2nd Q. Powerful, but wiggly Wyoming HB Chuck Lamson (19/131y, TD rushing) sparked quick drive with 25y run to his 1y TD sneak. Punt snap by NC State C Oscar Overcash in 3rd Q went way over EZ for Cowboys safety, but lead at 14-8 was retained. After NC State HB-P Dave Houtz's 56y QK, Cowboys started at 20YL in 4th Q. Lamson ran for 11 and 15y to key 80y TD drive. Wyoming FB Wayne Linton blasted for TD on 4th down to knot it at 14-14, and Lamson calmly kicked winning conv.

Syracuse 19 OREGON STATE 8: In relative obscurity of Pacific Northwest, Syracuse Orangemen (1-0) HB Ernie Davis again proved his star power. After Orangemen DG Len Slaby recovered Oregon State (0-1) FUM at Beavers 21YL in 1st Q, Davis slanted off right side, was hit hard, but knocked over would-be tackler on 16y TD run. Beavers gained 215y rushing, but lost 5 FUMs, 1 of which led to Syracuse's 2nd Q TD run by QB Dave Sarette, and other bobbles kept Oregon State bottled up in own end. But, Oregon State enjoyed fleeting 8-7 margin when QB Terry Baker turned in thrilling play: From Orangemen 36YL, Baker dropped way back to pass, was cornered at 50YL, but dodged and weaving through entire Syracuse D for astounding TD. Baker pitched 2-pt pass to HB John Thomas. Powerful line play allowed Syracuse to dominate after that, but it failed to cash in twice in 3rd Q as it was stopped by Beavers on downs at 5YL and lost FUM at 4YL. Davis scored clinching TD in 4th Q.

Purdue 13 WASHINGTON 6: Huskies (0-1) lost after winning 8 games in row because Purdue (1-0) strode into hostile Husky Stadium to dominate opening 20 mins. QB Ron DiGravio directed fast-striking Boilermakers attack which netted 2 FGs by G-K Homer "Skip" Ohl and 30y TD run by HB Dave Miller. Washington finally scored in 4th Q as sub QB Bill Siler tossed 15y TD to FB Jim Stiger.

September 30, 1961

(Fri) MIAMI 25 Penn State 8: Sore-ribbed Miami (2-1) QB George Mira overcame his frequent staggering trips to sideline and led 79y TD drive for 7-0 edge. When Mira was knocked out on last play of 1st H amid cascade of boos from partisan Orange Bowl stadium crowd, limping Bobby Weaver filled in at QB to lead 81y TD drive. After C-LB Robert Hart made FUM REC at Penn State 21YL, Miami soon had 25-0 4th Q margin. Nittany Lions (1-1) QB Pete Liske threw futile TD pass in last 10 secs.

Rutgers 16 PRINCETON 13: On strength of 2-pt convs after both its TDs, Rutgers (1-0) scored its 4th straight win over in-state rival Princeton (0-1). Opening scoring, Tigers tallied in 2nd Q on FB Bill Merlini's plunge for 7-0 lead. When Knights countered on FB Steve Simms' 2nd Q TD, QB Sam Mudie ran for 2-pt conv. Rutgers built 16-7 4th Q lead after G Bob Harrison keyed GLS, and Mudie soon slapped stunned Tigers with 87y TD pass to E Lee Curley.

Mississippi 20 KENTUCKY 6: Winning its 11th game in row and 6th straight over Kentucky (0-2), Mississippi (2-0) rode passing of QBs Doug Elmore and Glynn Griffing, who combined for 9-15/137y, 2 TDs, INT. Griffing got Ole Miss winging with 60y TD rocket to E Wes Sullivan just before end of 1st Q. Wildcats countered with K Clarkie Mayfield's 2nd FG, so game stood at 7-6 in favor of Rebs at H. Sub HB Chuck Morris put Mississippi in driver's seat with 69y INT TD RET, and Elmore later clicked on 4 straight completions to E Ralph Smith's short scoring grab. Kentucky QB Jerry Woolum (12-29/166y, 2 INTs) aimed each of his completions at E Tom Hutchinson, but Ole Miss D dug in when its GL was threatened.

FLORIDA 3 Florida State 3: Florida State (1-0-1) used its alert "Renegades" D to continually stymie Florida (1-0-1) and author 4 FUM RECs and 2 INTs. Gators attempted 4th-and-1 play near midfield on opening series, but procedure PEN forced punt, which was blocked by FSU star DB Roy Bickford (2 INTs). Advancing bounding ball to Gators 17YL, Bickford set up K Jon Harlee's FG for 3-0 Seminoles lead. In 2nd Q, Florida moved to FSU 14YL, but Bickford swiped ball off fingertips of Gators HB Lindy Infante at 7YL. Florida QB Bobby Dodd Jr. threw 34y pass to Seminoles 10YL, but E Fred Grimes spilled Gators HB Ron Stoner for 6y loss on 3rd down. So, Florida settled for K Billy Cash's 28y FG with 3:23 left before H. Second H was marked by drives stopped by TOs, including Bickford's late 4th Q INT of Dodd at FSU 14YL.

GEORGIA TECH 24 Rice 0: Solid winner previous week, confident no. 7 Rice (1-1) was completely flattened by big D-front of Georgia Tech (2-0), led by NG Rufus Guthrie, G-LB Dave Watson, and Ts Larry Stallings and Hal Ericksen. Engineers QB Stan Gann passed for 54y on opening drive and scored TD on 5y sweep. Georgia Tech presented clever O that utilized runs and blocks of FB Mike McNames, who got 2nd Q TD. HB Chick Graning also scored for 21-0 H edge. Trailing by same score, Owls advanced to Georgia Tech 23YL in 3rd Q, but QB Billy Cox's 2 passes were broken up. Behind passing of back-up QB Randall Kerbow, Rice went 63y to 7YL against Tech 3rd-stringers in 4th Q but turned it over on downs at 3YL. Yellow Jackets soph QB-P-K Billy Lothridge was ineffective on O, but he stopped punt at Rice 1YL to gain field position for McNames' TD and booted 4th Q FG, his 3rd of year.

LOUISIANA STATE 16 Texas A&M 7: Aggies (0-1-1) collared but failed to cash in 2 FUM RECs before Bayou Bengals could even run single play from scrimmage, still A&M took 7-0 lead on 1st Q TD catch by stumpy soph HB Travis Reagan as QB John Erickson scrambled to his right to throw. But, LSU's D was never threatened again. Texas A&M P Babe Craig's long punts kept his team in good field position most of night, but Louisiana State (1-1) drew within 7-2 when G-LB Roy Winston blocked his punt, and ball rolled through EZ for safety late in 2nd Q. Swift Tigers HB Wendell Harris broke up game with 62y punt TD RET in 4th Q behind block of E Gene Sykes, who flattened last-tackler Craig. That score vaulted Tigers to their 1st lead at 9-7. Momentum was rolling LSU's way now, and after Aggies HB Jim Linnstaedter's KO

RET, FB Jerry Rogers lost FUM to LSU C-LB Dennis Gaubatz at A&M 31YL. Harris gained 9y on 4th-and-3 to 15YL and FB Earl Gros' leapt 3y on 4th-and-2 to 4YL. Gros (18/64y, TD) crashed for clinching TD on next play.

Auburn 24 TENNESSEE 21: Tennessee (0-1) attacked from opening whistle to build 21-7 1st Q lead thanks to 3 FUM RECs that led to 13 and 2y scoring runs by TB Glenn Glass. Back roared Tigers (1-0) on TD passes by QBs Bobby Hunt and Mailon Kent to HB Don Machon and E Dave Edwards respectively. So, normally D-minded SEC foes found themselves in 21-21 H deadlock. K Woody Woodall gave Auburn 24-21 lead with 22y FG in 3rd Q. On following KO, Glass raced 64y to Plainsmen 29YL. Critical play came at Auburn 1YL shortly thereafter: Volunteers FB J.W. Carter, smashing for TD that would reestablish Tennessee lead, lost FUM to Auburn DE Edwards. Teams pretty well balanced out their run games as Tigers HB Jimmy Burson and FB Larry Rawson keyed 243y gained. Glass led Vols to 230y rushing. Difference came from timely aerial game that clicked for Auburn at 5-12/106y pace.

Michigan State 20 WISCONSIN 0: Michigan State (1-0) spent whole muddy day on marching toward Badgers GL, going 55, 80, and 65y to TDs. Spartans never got around to completing single pass in 4 attempts. Michigan State rushed 51/330y. Sub FB George Saimes (8/94y, 2 TDs) scored twice after FB Ron Hatcher followed HB Dewey Lincoln's 14y cruise up middle with 1y TD smash in 1st Q. QB Ron Miller (16-25/185y, 2 INTs) passed Wisconsin (1-1) to good effect and E Pat Richter caught 5/60y, but Spartans D halted Badgers at 1, 4, 15, and 23YLs. Most frustrating possession for Wisconsin came in 4th Q after DT Dale Matthews recovered FUM at MSU 17YL. Badgers had 4 cracks from 4YL, but turned it over on 4th down at Michigan State 1YL. Earlier, after Hatcher had made it 6-0 for State, Badgers answered with long drive, only to see Miller missed well-guarded Richter on 1st down when HB Jim Nettles was running free in EZ. Another time with score still 6-0 in 2nd Q, Wisconsin HB Merritt Norvell missed EZ pass from HB Lou Holland after having beaten Spartans DB Herman Johnson. QB-K Jim Bakken missed 40y FG on next play.

OHIO STATE 7 Texas Christian 7: Ohio State (0-0-1) used land power in form of FB Bob Ferguson (35/137y) to lead to short 1st Q TD pass by QB Bill Mrukowski. TCU (1-0) had QB Sonny Gibbs came through under pressure in 2nd H. Gibbs, known as "Eye-full Tower" because of his then-unusual 6'7" height, pitched 62y pass to HB Pete Hill to set up tying TD pass to E Dale Glascock in 4th Q. When Buckeyes threatened late, DB Gibbs made GL INT of Mrukowski. On game's last play, Buckeyes K Dick Van Rapphorst missed 42y FG that was fielded at 2YL by Frogs HB Larry Thomas. Retreating to his right, Thomas swept into EZ and barely escaped being tackled for game-losing safety as clock expired.

MICHIGAN 29 Ucla 6: Bus carrying Bruins to Michigan Stadium broke down, but that wasn't only thing that went wrong for pre-season West Coast favorites. Michigan (1-0), "Champions of the West," opened its 650th game with 40y land attack for TD that came after poor punt by Bruins P Keith Jensen. Top-notch Wolverines ball-carriers were FB Bill Tunnicliff and HB Dave Raimey as each scored 1st Q TD, Raimey's coming from 20y out. Trailing 23-0, UCLA threatened late in 3rd Q by advancing to UM 10YL. Uclans TB Bobby Smith tried pass that was tipped by lineman's paw, and Michigan FB-DB Ken Tureaud settled verdict by romping 92y with INT TD RET with 9 secs left in 3rd Q. That made it 29-0 for Wolverines. Held to 172y total O, UCLA (1-1) scored late on 1y plunge by FB Mitch Dimkich that followed TB-P Rob Smith's 41y sprint to 18YL on fake punt.

Missouri 6 MINNESOTA 0: Minnesota (0-1) became only 3rd team since 1936 inception of AP Poll to lose its opener in defense of national title. (Others were TCU losing to UCLA in 1939 and Ohio State losing to Iowa Seahawks military squad in 1943.) On this windy and damp day in Minneapolis, accurate punting mattered greatly. Missouri (2-0) sub QB-P Daryl Krugman booted 13 times, several after poor snaps. His most important punt went 51y to Gophers 1YL. When QB-P Sandy Stephens punted back into stiff wind Tigers were poised for 30y TD march, capped by HB Bill Tobin's 1y plunge in 2nd Q. Tigers DE Carl Crawford snuffed Minnesota's only threat with 4th Q EZ INT. Missouri ended game at Gophers 2YL as soft September snow began to fall.

NOTRE DAME 19 Oklahoma 6: Soph QB Bill Van Burkleo of Oklahoma (0-1) threw plenty of fear into Fighting Irish (1-0) when he came off bench in 1st Q. On Sooners' 2nd series, Van Burkleo hit HB Mike McClellan for 16y, sent FB Phil Lohman (11/49y) up middle for 13y, and hit McClellan for 26y to 16YL. Drive bogged down, and G-K Karl Milstead's FG try was blocked by G-LB Nick Buoniconti. That quickly sent Notre Dame HB Angelo Dabiero dashing downfield for 51y TD and 6-0 lead. Oklahoma's backup team tied it in 2nd Q on HB Jackie Cowan's 4y TD run after HB Gary Wylie roared 48y with KO. After ND QB Frank Budka threw INT and Irish held at their 26YL, FB Mike Lind romped for 16, 42, and 22y gains, last for TD that tabbed it at 13-6 at H. Dabiero and Lind, who scored last TD, collaborated on 4-play, 62y scoring voyage in 4th Q. Irish rushed for hefty 367y.

Mississippi State 10 HOUSTON 7: Houston (0-1-1) simply owned football in 1st H, running 37 plays on O to Bulldogs' 15. Cougars QB Don Sessions rifled 12y pass to E Buddy Hodges to 3YL to make possible 2y TD plunge by FB Eddie Broussard. It came at end of Houston's 54y scoring voyage. Although Mississippi State (2-0) barely made it past midfield in 1st H, it managed 35y FG by FB-K Sammy Dantone. Sparking 61y thrust that preceded Dantone's FG were 4 completions by slender sub QB Charlie Furlow. Furlow hit E Johnny Baker for 16 and 12y passes on 50y TD trip early in 3rd Q. FB Mackie Weaver powered over from 2YL for Maroons' winning pts. Mississippi State rode Furlow's timely passes to game-end team total of 10-15/115y.

AP Poll October 2

1 Iowa (24)	434	6 Michigan State (1)	203
2 Mississippi (16)	325	7 Syracuse	191
3 Georgia Tech (7)	266	8 Ohio State	128
4 Alabama (1)	259	9 Michigan	123
5 Texas (2)	218	10 Baylor	117

Others with votes: Notre Dame, Navy, Maryland, Miami, Auburn, Missouri, Northwestern, Texas Christian, Army, Stanford, Penn State, Washington, Duke, Utah State, Colorado, Memphis State, Rice, Purdue, Louisiana State, Kansas, North Carolina, South Carolina

October 7, 1961

North Carolina State 21 VIRGINIA 14: Seeking 1st ACC win since 1958, fired-up Cavaliers (1-2) outgained NC State (1-2) 129y to 100y in 1st H. But, Virginia trailed 7-6 when Wolfpack D and H clock forced UVa to turn to K Bob Rowley to make 25 and 28y FGs on his 1st career tries. NC State rallied in 2nd H, thanks to spark from stumpy Virginia-born soph HB Carson Bosher (7/73y and 3/48y receiving). Bosher, who had run over 2 tacklers to score on 37y pass from QB Roman Gabriel (10-13/81y, 2 TDs, INT) in 1st Q, raced 54y on 2nd play of 4th Q to set up HB Mike Clark's 2y TD blast for 21-6 edge. Virginia QB Gary Cuozzo pitched 8y TD pass and followed with 2-pt toss with 3 mins left. Gabriel gambled and succeeded on 4th down sneak at own 29YL to ice it in last min.

MARYLAND 22 Syracuse 21: Syracuse (2-1) took 13-7 H lead on 1st of 2 TDs by HB Ernie Davis (14/111y, 2 TDs) and E Walt Sweeney's 13y TD catch from QB Dave Sarette. Maryland (3-0) soph QB Dick Shiner accounted for all 59y of 3rd Q drive that he capped with 29y TD dash off T Walter Rock's granite block on broken pass play. After Terrapins E-P Gary Collins was forced into horribly short punt by bad snap in 4th Q, Davis dashed 43y to 1YL to catapult Orangemen to 21-14 lead. But, on next scrimmage play, Terps' day-long great run blocking (234y rushing) broke soph HB Ernie Arizzi (4/96y) for 64y sprint off RG to Orange 10YL. It took 4 plays, but Maryland HB Dennis Condie whacked over GL behind blocks of G Tom Sankovich and T Roger Shoals. Collins made fabulous reach-back catch of winning 2-pt pass from QB Dick Novak. Then 2-way Terrapins star E-DE Collins made key tackles that stopped Syracuse's next series. Maryland G Joe Kirchiro's blocks closed it on 55y trip to 6YL that took more than 5 mins.

Kentucky 14 AUBURN 12: Utterly discombobulated by fierce D of Kentucky (1-2), Auburn (1-1) had to rely on unusual D TD in 1st Q for 6-0 lead. Tiger DB John McGeever rushed FG attempt, blocked it in his midsection, and, amazingly, retained possession for 82y TD dash without hand being laid on him. Grabbing 1st of 4 FUM RECs at Tiger 26YL, Wildcats took 7-6 lead in 2nd Q on FB Perry Bryant's 1y TD dive and K Clarkie Mayfield's x-pt. Auburn HB-DB Jimmy Burson raced 46y to UK 16YL with INT in 3rd Q. QB Mailon Kent followed with 15y TD pass to wide-open E Dave Edwards, but K Woody Woodall flew his 2nd conv kick wide. Wildcat E Tom Hutchinson recovered FUM by HB Larry Rawson at Plainsmen 21YL well into 4th Q, and overcoming 15y PEN and 8y sack, Kentucky QB Jerry Woolum lofted 6y TD pass to Hutchinson, who took it over right shoulder in EZ corner. With 49 secs left, DB Woolum made INT, 2 plays after KO. Auburn was thrown for –11y rushing total while absorbing its 1st home defeat since 1955.

LOUISIANA STATE 10 Georgia Tech 0: Cheered by big crowd at Tiger Stadium, Louisiana State (2-1) D savagely stopped Georgia Tech (2-1) O, which had averaged 27 pts in 2 previous wins. Tigers D, led by G-LB Roy Winston, mounted pass rush and coverage called "best I've ever seen" by veteran Georgia Tech coach Bobby Dodd. Engineers gained 70y passing—44y on single play—and QB Stan Gann's sack losses meant he netted only 1y total O. Georgia Tech made 9 1st downs and gained 156y. Key play came in 2nd Q when Tech QB-P Billy Lothridge was swarmed upon at own 16YL after punt snap FUM. LSU FB Earl Gros blasted to 1YL in 2 tries before QB Jimmy Field wedged into EZ behind Gros' block. HB-K Wendell Harris added 22y FG in last 3 secs of 1st H after FB-LB Buddy Hamic's INT. Cincher came with LSU's 3rd Q GLS as DBs Harris and Jerry Stovall made critical stops.

Northwestern 28 ILLINOIS 7: Spunky Wildcats (2-0) overturned young and injury-riddled Illini (0-2) to take 26-25-4 advantage in unbroken intrastate series. 4 TD drives, on which NU backs averaged 7.6y per carry on 32 rushes, were led by 2 backs: Wildcats HB Bob Snider, who scored on team's 2nd possession, and FB Bill Swingle (15/64y), who scored twice including 21y TD pass from QB Fred Quinn. Illinois' shuffled backfield rushed 43/126y; FB Al Wheatland pounded for TD on 4th down in last 18 secs of 1st H. Illini sub G Frank Lollino precipitated this score with crushing tackle on punt, and E Dick Newell recovered FUM at Northwestern 18YL. Illini G Tony Parrilli played well on D, and little soph HB Mike Dundy recovered FUM in his own EZ to prevent TD.

OHIO STATE 13 Ucla 3: This contest just might have been preview of Rose Bowl match come January. Ohio State (1-0-1) took somewhat evenly played affair. (Reasons given for negative, end-of-season Ohio State faculty vote against Buckeyes making Rose Bowl trip included "likely rehash" of this result.) UCLA (1-2) scored in 1st H for 3-0 lead, thanks to runs of TB Bobby Smith (22/82y), with K Smith booting 32y FG. Hustling Uclans D held Buckeyes star FB Bob Ferguson to 13/29y rushing, so Ohio State broke loose its soph HBs Paul Warfield and Matt Snell for 4th Q TD sprints of 13y and 33y respectively.

Notre Dame 22 PURDUE 20: Irish (2-0) spotted Purdue (1-1) 14-7 lead in 2nd Q on short TD runs: Sneak by QB Ron DiGravio behind G Stan Sczurek's block and FB Roy Walker on 4y plunge. Boilermakers advanced to 20-13 H edge on 2 FGs by G-K Skip Ohl, 2nd coming 10 secs from H and traveling 40y. After scoring Irish's 2nd Q TD on 2y plunge, FB Jim Snowden sparked 3rd Q Notre Dame drive that pared margin to 20-19. QB Daryle Lamonica (5-10 passing) threw TD to E Jim Kelly, but shunned tying kick and his rollout pass for 2 pts was incomplete. Early in 4th Q, Notre Dame moved from its 42YL and FB-K Joe Perkowski redeemed himself for 2 earlier issues (blocked x-pt and missed FG try) when he hit winning 28y FG.

MICHIGAN STATE 31 Stanford 3: Not knowing that his 47-year-old father had died of heart attack in grandstand, jr QB Pete Smith sent 2 soph Michigan State (2-0) sprinters, HBs Sherman Lewis and Dewey Lincoln, blazing to key TD run each. Stanford (2-1) found Spartans D nearly impenetrable and gained only 96y. Lewis tallied Michigan State's 1st TD on 6y skirt of E early in 2nd Q. HB-K Stan Lindskog made 40y FG shortly after intermission, and Indians trailed only 7-3. Right away, Michigan State went 80y, including Smith's 33y pass to E Lonnie Sanders, to score on FB George Saimes' 3y run. Spartans weren't out of woods until Lincoln sprinted to 20y score in 4th Q.

MINNESOTA 14 Oregon 7: After scoreless 1st Q, ball was exchanged 8 times in 2nd Q. Oregon (1-2) QB Doug Post faked FG, but missed 4th down pass. But when Minnesota (1-1) QB-P Sandy Stephens punted out of EZ he managed only 6y boot. With 2:02 before H, Post overcame 15y PEN and completed 2 passes, 2nd going for 6y TD to HB Mike Gaechter. After Ducks HB-K Buck Corey missed 3rd Q FG, Gophers went on 14-play, 80y drive that appeared stopped by Oregon HB-DB Duane Cargill's EZ INT, but Cargill dropped ball. Stephens (21/92y rushing) cut back for 8y TD and pitched out to HB Jim Cairns for 2 pts and 8-7 edge. Gophers DE John Campbell fell on 4th Q FUM by HB Dennis Jackson on Oregon 18YL, and 5 plays later Stephens tallied from 3y out.

Iowa State 21 OKLAHOMA 15: Courtesy of Sooners FUMs and short wind-stalled punt, Iowa State (3-0) struck for 3 quick TDs in 1st Q. TB Dave Hoppmann rushed for 113y, and little WB Ozzie Clay scored twice for Cyclones. Oklahoma (0-2) charged back with 80y drives resulting in TDs by QB Bob Page and HB Jimmy Carpenter, but Sooners' 5th lost FUM of game doomed their last threat in Cyclones territory.

MISSOURI 14 California 14: On its way to miserable 1-win season, California (0-2-1) still couldn't have been impressed by highly-favored Missouri (2-0-1). Golden Bears weathered 98y Tigers drive to 6-0 1st Q lead, then rebounded behind passing of QB Randy Gold, who shook off month-long knee woes. Cal stopped 3 Tigers drives with INTs and led 14-6 in 3rd Q after Gold's 13y TD sweep followed 77y sprint by HB Alan Nelson. Mizzou went 53y to QB Ron Taylor's TD run midway in 4th Q, and sub QB Daryl Krugman followed with 2-pt dash around E for tying 2-pt conv.

COLORADO 20 Kansas 19: Highly-touted Kansas (0-2-1) meticulously built 13-0 H lead on TDs by HBs Rodger McFarland and Curtis McClinton. When Jayhawks lead reached 19-0 in 4th Q, contest appeared over, but heroic Colorado (2-0) QB Gale Weidner fired TD passes to E Ken Blair of 57 and 47y. Buffaloes C-LB Walt Klinker forced punt by halting Kansas QB John Hadl for no gain on 3rd down run. E Jerry Hillebrand caught 17y score from Weidner at end of 63y drive to save day for Colorado with less than 3 mins left.

Iowa 35 SOUTHERN CALIFORNIA 34: Sometimes scoring comes too easy and too early for big favorite. Top-ranked Iowa (2-0) used 2 FUM RECs and its powerful ground game to allow HB Joe Williams, shifted from FB because of injury to HB Larry Ferguson, to tally 3 TDs before game was 22 mins old. Williams earned 2 of his scores on passes by QB Wilburn Hollis (5-10/120y, 2 TDs, INT) within 7-min duration of 1st H, including neat 20y fake FG on which holder Hollis lobbed pass over on-rushing Trojans DT Frank Buncom. So, Hawkeyes comfortably led 21-0 in 2nd Q. Southern California (1-2) scrambled back with short TD runs by alternating QBs Bill Nelsen and Pete Beathard at ends of 56 and 43y drives respectively. Trojans quietly trailed only 21-14 at H. Nelsen threw 3rd Q TD pass, but K Carl Skvarna's x-pt kick never was launched. Iowa appeared to lock up game with 11 mins left in 4th Q at 35-20 as Hollis scored from 3YL after USC gave 2 offsides PEN gifts inside their 15YL. Resourceful Nelsen reinvigorated Troy by lofting perfect 40y bomb to E Hal Bedsole, who leapt with HB-DB Paul Krause to haul down pass and gallop 71y to score TD and catch 2-pt pass. Buncom recovered Hollis' FUM at Iowa 28YL with 2:25 left, and Nelson fired 5y TD pass to Bedsole. Coach John McKay said, "we didn't go out there to play a tie game," so he called a repeat of TD play for 2 pts. Nelsen's attempt to win it was tipped away by fingertips of Hawkeyes HB-DB Sammie Harris with 48 secs on clock. Narrow and exhausting victory cost Iowa its no. 1 poll spot. Ole Miss, 33-0 winners over Florida State, jumped to top of AP Poll.

AP Poll October 9

1 Mississippi (24)	384	6 Michigan (2)	240
2 Iowa (11)	341	7 Ohio State	126
3 Alabama (4)	329	8 Notre Dame (1)	103
4 Texas (3)	286	9 Baylor	98
5 Michigan State (2)	259	10 Maryland	77

Others with votes: Louisiana State, Northwestern, Washington, Duke, Colorado, Georgia Tech, Rice, Navy, Syrcause, Arkansas, Texas Christian, Penn State, Purdue, Southern California, Tennessee, Clemson, Stanford

October 14, 1961

(Fri) Colorado 9 MIAMI 7: Outplayed Colorado (3-0) used 1st Q 15y PEN and 4th Q FUM REC to its advantage in building 9-0 lead. After Miami was called for roughing PEN on punt in 1st Q, Buffs moved out of deep hole to 1st down at their own 20YL. Colorado QB Gale Weidner then hit passes of 23 and 21y before FB Loren Schweninger plunged over from 1YL for 6-0 edge. Buffs E-K Jerry Hillebrand fell on FUM in Miami (2-3) territory in 4th Q and turned it into his own 37y FG. Hurricanes scored with 4:44 left on QB John Bennett's 25y pass to E Bill Miller. Miami outgained Buffs 263y to 163y.

Army 10 PENN STATE 6: Badly beaten at Michigan previous week, Army (3-1) rebounded with surprising poise and speed to upset Penn State (2-2). Versatile QB Joe Blackgrove (40y rushing, 1/13y receiving, 2/47y on punt RETs) was shifted to HB to add speed to wide running game and sparked Cadets O with quick outside runs.

This strategy helped enable his QB sub, Dick Peterson, to tally on 2y rollout TD run in 2nd Q, score coming on previously-frustrated Army's 4th trip inside Nittany Lions' 5YL. Penn State QBs Pete Liske and Don Caum failed on all 5 of their passes in 1st H and finished with meager 5-19/66y. With Black Knights in front 7-0 in 3rd Q, Mt Nits' run game was energized and advanced from their 32YL to the Army 7YL. Knights FB-LB George Pappas made EZ INT to halt that threat, and when P Peterson booted out to his 45YL, Penn State HB Don Jonas lost FUM to Black Knights DT Bill Hawkins to launch FG drive. When Cadets K Dick Heydt made 22y 3-ptr 5 mins into 4th Q, Lions could counter only 16y TD pass by Liske to Jonas.

Columbia 11 YALE 0: Yale Bulldogs entered game with 11 straight wins. Columbia's backfield full of injuries meant promotion of obscure soph FB-DB Al Butts to 1st team. Butts responded with 2nd Q TD run at end of 85y drive, extended by HB Russ Warren's elusive run after catching QB Tom Vassel's 4th down pass. Butts enhanced his TD with 2-pt run and picked off 2 passes to halt early Yale (2-1) advances. Once Bulldogs' air game had proven inadequate (2-13/28y), Lions (2-1) D was able to mass at scrimmage line to effectively halt Yale FBs Ted Hard and Rich Niglio. In 3rd Q, Columbia stopped Yale on downs at its 25YL and on G Tony Day's FUM REC at its 9YL.

North Carolina 14 MARYLAND 8: In College Park mud bath, undefeated Maryland (3-1) was helpless to prevent North Carolina (2-1) HB Gib Carson (27/100y) from twice fumbling ball into EZ, only to have Tar Heels come up with TD RECs to clinch upset win. Rugged line play on both sides forced each team's O into multiple mistakes, as INTs (3 each side) dotted 1st H scoresheet and FUMs (again, 3 each) dominated 2nd H. UNC C-LB Joe Craver recovered FUM at Terps 19YL early in 3rd Q, and Carson carried 5 straight plays but fumbled at 1YL. HB Lenny Beck alertly pounced on it for TD. DB Beck recovered Terrapins FUM few mins later at Maryland 16YL. On 4th-and-2 at 8YL, Carson scurried to 1YL where he again was separated from ball, which wobbled on GL for moment before Heels QB Ray Farris beat Terrapins T Walter Rock to REC and 14-0 lead. Ace DE Gary Collins poised Maryland's TD with FUM REC at UNC 33YL. QB Dick Novak then passed 30y to Collins for Terps' only 1st down in 2nd H, and soph FB Bob Burton bulled over from 3YL. In scoreless 4th Q, Maryland gained only 12y and Tar Heels made 13y. Soph sensation, Terps QB Dick Shiner, failed to gain even single y.

Wake Forest 17 CLEMSON 13: Trailing 7-3 at H, Wake Forest (1-3) fashioned upset on TD drive following 2nd H KO and HB Alan White's 59y TD run in 4th Q. Clemson (1-3), losing to Demon Deacons for 1st time since 1949, scored 1st on 14y 2nd Q TD pass from QB Jim Parker to E Tommy King after Parker's 26y connection with HB Elmo Lam. Wake Forest QB Chuck Reilly hit E Bill Hull on passes of 16 and 22y to prod 3rd Q drive after KO. Reilly hit E Bill Ruby with 11y TD that put Deacs up 9-7. After White's long TD run over RT Jimmy Williams' block, Reiley got up from x-pt H position and tossed 2-pt pass. It was Deacons' 1st 2-pt success in 18 tries since rule went into effect 4 years earlier. Tigers FB Ron Scrudato closed scoring by plunging 2y for TD with 2:58 left in 4th Q. Victory ended Wake Forest's 7-game losing streak.

GEORGIA TECH 21 Duke 0: Big Georgia Tech (3-1) line turned scoreless 1st H into rollicking offensive after H intermission to shepherd Duke (3-1) from ranks of undefeated. Blue Devils advanced on ground to Engineers 36YL 1st time they had ball as Duke made 3 of its 5 1st downs it would earn during game. Tech G Dave Watson (8 tackles, FUM REC) threw HB Dean Wright (9/24y) for 4y loss to turn back Duke. Worn down by Yellow Jackets, Blue Devils permitted 75y TD drive to open 3rd Q: Tech sub HB Joe Auer caught 21y pass from QB Stan Gann (7-13/74y, INT), and Gann skirted RE for 6y TD and 7-0 lead. DB Auer intercepted pass by Duke QB Walt Rappold (0-2, INT) and scored on 25y TD RET, only to have premature whistle stop play at 18YL. Undeterred, Auer (4/36y receiving) caught 2 passes from QB Billy Lothridge before HB Chick Graning scored. Watson's FUM REC paved way for Lothridge's 4th Q TD. Duke was held to total O of 67y by Georgia Tech D led by Watson and Ts Russ Foret and Larry Stallings.

FLORIDA STATE 3 Georgia 0: Seminoles (2-1-1) tapped Georgia native, soph K Doug Messer, to knock through early 24y FG to nip discouraged Bulldogs (1-3) for Florida State's 2nd-ever victory over SEC foe. Stiff breeze blew Georgia QB-P Jake Saye's 1st Q punt into 14y popup to FSU 48YL. From there, Seminoles advanced to Bulldogs 8YL but had to settle for Messer's 3-ptr after Georgia G Wally Williamson nailed State QB Eddie Feely for –6y while Feely attempted pass. Except that HB Keith Kinderman rushed 22/101y, Florida State never much moved again, gaining only 63y in 2nd H. Georgia moved reasonably well, thanks to QB Larry Rakestraw's 15-25/144y, INT passing, but came up painfully short on sneak by Rakestraw to within inches of GL in 3rd Q. With wind at their backs in 2nd Q, Bulldogs gained 53y on exchange of punts, but K Durwood Pennington missed 50y FG try, 1st of his 2 long 3-pt misses.

Michigan State 28 MICHIGAN 0: Spartans QB Pete Smith (4-6/82y) insisted on playing despite death of his father during previous week's game. Smith passed for TD, and his runs and passes set up 2 other TDs. Michigan State (3-0) gobbled up Wolverines HB Bennie McRae's early FUM to launch HB Gary Ballman's TD run in 1st Q. FB George Saimes soon made it 14-0 with scoring run. Moments that doomed Michigan (2-1) came on nullified 23y TD run by McRae and failure to score from inside 1YL after 63y march after 2nd H KO. Other than Wolverines' opening 2nd H drive, Spartan D, led by Gs Dave Behrman and George Azer, and LB Saimes, held Michigan to 113y.

NOTRE DAME 30 Southern California 0: After wins over Oklahoma, Purdue, and USC, question on everyone's mind: Was Notre Dame (3-0) all the way back in coach Joe Kuharich's 3rd season? Irish line, led by Gs Nick Buoniconti and Norb Roy and T Joe Carollo, completely dominated Trojans. When Southern California star E Hal Bedsole went out injured late in 2nd Q, he joined HB Willie Brown and Trojans passing attack went with them. ND rushed QB Bill Nelsen (10-17/154y, 2 INTs) into 77y in losses while trying to pass. In game's opening 11 mins, QB Daryle Lamonica (8/43y, 2 TDs rushing) circled RE for 12y TD and clicked on 1 of his rare passes for 17y TD to soph E Jim Kelly on 3rd-and-3. Sparkplug ND HB Angelo Dabiero raced 43y to set up 2nd Q TD for 20-0 H lead. Lamonica sneaked for 3rd Q TD, and FB-K Joe Perkowski bombed 49y FG for ND's final pts in 4th Q after HB-DB Frank Minik's INT.

Texas 28 Oklahoma 7 (Dallas): For 1st time in Red River border series, 1 team left traditional sellout with undefeated record and other team was winless. Texas (4-0) capitalized on blocked punt at 11YL that led to HB James Saxton's 4y TD sweep in 1st Q, INT, and FUM REC to swamp beleaguered Oklahoma (0-3). Still, OU's feisty D held Steers O to 272y, far below their 504y avg. After failing to make any 1st downs in 1st Q, Texas moved 65y in 2nd Q, trip highlighted by QB Mike Cotton's completions to HB Jack Collins and E Bob Moses and Cotton's fake-pass 2y TD run. Longhorns' 1st unit played only 20 mins and continued its profile jokingly referred to as "the (starting) team that may not earn its letters." Trailing 21-0 at H, Sooners fell on Saxton's FUM of 3rd Q KO on 31YL, but failed to move, and Steers launched 73y drive to FB Ray Poage's 5y TD run. Sooners FB Phil Lohmann went 35y on trap run to set up own 1y TD run in 4th Q.

Arkansas 23 BAYLOR 13: While Arkansas (3-1) D pinched its flanks and rushed Bears passers, its O sent whippet HBs Lance Alworth and Paul Dudley wide to imprison Baylor (2-1) D for passing of QBs George McKinney and Billy Moore. Hogs built 16-0 lead in 2nd Q as each QB connected on TD pass. Back came Bears on wings of their QB tandem of Ronnie Stanley and Bobby Ply as each QB hit E Bobby Lane with scoring toss. Ahead 16-13 in 4th Q, Arkansas switched its attack to inside power for 42y TD drive ended with McKinney's 4y jump pass TD to E Jimmy Collier.

RICE 19 Florida 10: Opportunistic Owls HB-DB-K Butch Blume kicked 2 FGs and picked off 2 Gators passes. Power runs of FB Roland Jackson sent Rice (2-1) from behind for TDs in 2nd and 4th Qs. HB Lindy Infante scored Florida (2-1-1) TD in 3rd Q for brief 10-9 edge, but 3rd INT short-circuited Gators' last bid while trailing 16-10 in 4th Q.

AP Poll October 16

1 Michigan State (16)	431	6 Notre Dame (1)	268
2 Mississippi (21)	429	7 Ohio State (1)	244
3 Texas (2)	352	8 Georgia Tech	77
4 Iowa (2)	330	9 Colorado	57
5 Alabama (4)	318	10tArkansas	55
		10tLouisiana State	55

Others with votes: Missouri (1), Syracuse, Purdue, Michigan, Utah State, Memphis State, Rice, Maryland, Minnesota, Wyoming, Tennessee, Navy, Baylor, Dartmouth, Army

October 21, 1961

Columbia 26 HARVARD 14: Columbia (3-1) employed 244y run O keyed by HBs Tom Haggerty, who gained 83y, and Russ Warren, future New York Giants team physician. FB Tom O'Connor and Haggerty scored 3 mins apart in 2nd Q, latter TD having been set up at Harvard (1-3) 19YL when HB-P Bill Taylor was forced to eat ball after high snap. Trailing 12-0, Crimson HB Hank Hatch countered with 66y KO RET that positioned QB Bill Humenuk for TD pass to E Pete Hart. Warren made it 20-7 with 3y TD run and 2-pt catch on 69y trip, highlighted by only bright moments (13 and 20y completions) for QB Tom Vasell (4-13/56y, INT). Harvard ruled 3rd Q but could count only Taylor's 1y TD run.

Clemson 17 DUKE 7: Already jumbled ACC race was shaken by underdog Tigers' win over Blue Devils, previously undefeated in conf play. Clemson (2-3) coach Frank Howard copied Georgia Tech's previous success by putting double coverage on Duke's lonesome Es, and they made no receptions until deep into 4th Q. Looking elsewhere including big 3rd Q strike for 60y TD, Duke air game (14-21/204y, TD) was little affected by Tigers' strategy other than shutdown of Lonely Es. Coach Howard had his own passing fancy: emerging soph QB Jim Parker (7-14/100y, INT) set up both Tigers TDs. Duke (3-2) got 7-7 tie in 3rd Q as QB Walt Rappold hit well-covered HB Mark Leggett for 60y TD pass. Clemson waded 96y through heavy rain late in 3rd Q for decisive TD as key gains came from FB Bill McGuirt on 10y plunge and HB Harry Pavilack on 17y catch. Parker cracked left side for 1y TD that put Tigers ahead 14-7. Clemson DT Dave Hynes clawed FUM from Rappold on 4th Q pass try, and REC led to FG.

ALABAMA 34 Tennessee 3: Alabama (5-0) beat Tennessee (2-2) for 1st time since 1954 with mighty D which allowed only 61y and 5 1st downs. Volunteers enjoyed glorious moment, however, as K George Shuford made soaring 53y 1st Q FG, only 3y short of existing pro record for distance. Crimson Tide QB Pat Trammell created "Whoopee" pass—quick shotput to racing HB, and use of play helped position FB Mike Fracchia for 1st Q TD run and K Tim Davis for 2nd Q FG. Trammell scored rushing TD and passed for another. Afterward, Crimson Tide was extended bid to new National Bowl game in Washington, D.C., but Bama had bigger bowls on its mind. Slated for December 30, National Bowl never materialized.

MICHIGAN STATE 17 Notre Dame 7: Efficient Notre Dame (3-1) line and terrific tackling by LB Nick Buoniconti bottled up Spartans runners, holding them to 12y rushing in 1st H. Meanwhile, Irish raced for 170y rushing and 7-0 lead on 1st Q TD by QB Daryle Lamonica. But thanks in part to 9 PENs against them, Fighting Irish couldn't turn their dominance into pts, failing to take advantage of 3 INTs by HB-DB Angelo Dabiero. Coach Duffy Daugherty revamped Spartans (4-0) O at H by moving ace LB George Saimes to full-time FB duty and amassing huge blockers in Ts Dave Behrman and Jim Bobbitt with G Ed Budde to clear path for Saimes (14/142y) to run for 24 and 25y TDs in 3rd Q. Each TD was set up by INT; 1st pick-off turned game in MSU's favor. DB Herman Johnson grabbed Lamonica's pass after it deflected off Dabiero and Michigan State LB Wayne Fontes, returning it 38y to ND 40YL. Saimes went left on 4th-and-9 to score standing up from 24YL. FB-DB Carl Charon's INT positioned Saimes for his 2nd TD before end of 3rd Q. Trailing 14-7, Notre Dame sent 235-lb FB Jim Snowden on 4th down gamble that failed at own 36YL. Saimes chipped in 26y run before E-K Art Brandstatter made 20y FG with 9:58 to go.

INDIANA 33 Washington State 7: Indiana (1-3), outplayed by Cougars (1-4) for most of 3 Qs, still nursed 14-7 lead on 2 TD runs by HB Marv Woodson. Washington State punted to Indiana 15YL late in 3rd Q. Next 17 min turned glorious for Hoosiers, who ended 8-game losing streak that started in middle of 1960 season. Indiana cracked 85y in 10 plays to QB Woody Moore's sneak and 21-7 lead. Sub Cougars QB Dave Mathieson fumbled ball away at own 10YL. Indiana scored in 2 plays and used DB Moore's 62y INT TD RET to salt away verdict. Washington State QB Mel Melin had thrown fearlessly in early going, twice hitting E Hugh Campbell (9/115y) on TD march, his 2nd catch coming while encircled by defenders at 8YL. Wazzu HB Ken Graham completed drive with 4th down TD run.

Kansas 10 OKLAHOMA 0: Jayhawks (2-2-1) QB-HB John Hadl wore contact lenses for 1st time and produced peerless act at 2 backfield spots including 30y TD pass to E Larry Allen in 2nd Q. But, Kansas D was difference in game, holding Oklahoma (0-4) to lowest O output in coach Bud Wilkinson's 15 years: 98y, 6 1st downs, and only 2 trips across midfield. It was 1st time Big 8 Conf member had blanked any Wilkinson-coached team in Norman. Key sequence came after late 1st Q punt into strong wind: P Hadl punted to Sooners 45YL, and Oklahoma HB Paul Lea used E John Benien's crushing block to race to Kansas 14YL where last-tackler Hadl hauled him down. Determined Jayhawks dug in and held, and Sooners G-K Karl Milstead missed 25y FG in swirling breeze.

Texas 33 ARKANSAS 7: Whatever hope Razorbacks (3-2) harbored for 3rd straight SWC crown all but flickered out as Texas (5-0) took another landslide win. Longhorns QB Mike Cotten, who ran and passed for TDs, used full array of speedy backs to score in every Q. HB Tommy Ford made it 20-0 at H as he charged through Hogs on 6 straight runs, last for TD after FUM REC at 20YL. Limited to 7 1st downs and 124y total O, Arkansas turned to its passing attack in 3rd Q for its only success. Porkers scored on QB George McKinney's short toss to E Jimmy Collier. Texas' immediate answer was its longest drive of game; it went 85y in 17 plays to Cotten's 19y TD romp. Steers gained 354y rushing.

TEXAS TECH 19 Baylor 17: Red Raiders (2-3), always slightly more ornery in Lubbock, surprised Baylor (2-2) with 2 TDs in opening 6 mins: FB Calvin Coolidge Hunt, reputed to be only Texan named for quiet Vermont-born 30th U.S. President, scored from 1YL, and 2 plays later HB-DB David Rankin sped 26y on INT TD RET for 14-0 lead. Bears backup QB Bobby Ply hit 9-10/124y to spark marches of 76 and 69y. After Ply threw short pass to HB Ronnie Goodwin, who meandered to 26y TD, HB Ronnie Bull surged 6y on 4th down over RT Pete Nicklas' block to tie it 14-14 on last play of 1st H. Ahead 17-14 with secs left in 3rd Q, Baylor P Benny Corley bobbled snap, and Tech T Larry Mullins blocked punt for safety to trail 17-16. FB-K H.L. Daniels, in for Hunt who suffered late 2nd Q head injury, booted 34y FG in last 27 secs to cinch Raiders' 1st win over Bears since 1946.

ARIZONA STATE 24 Oregon State 23: Rushing attack of Oregon State (1-4) ripped through Arizona State (4-1) for 248y and leads of 16-8 at H and 23-8 in 3rd Q. Despite success of QB Terry Baker on 2-pt conv passes after Beavers TDs in 1st and 2nd Qs, coach Tommy Prothro chose to kick for 23rd pt after HB Leroy Whittle ran 8y to score in 3rd Q. Sun Devils outstanding HB Charley Taylor got loose for 64y TD reception from QB Joe Zuger in 3rd Q, and Zuger added 2-pt pass to narrow margin to 23-16 late in 3rd Q. Still, Oregon State seemed safe until it lost FUM on own 33YL with 2 mins to play. ASU took 8 plays to score on Zuger's 11y TD pass to E Herman Harrison. Sub QB John Jacobs was inserted for miraculous 2-pt play as his pass filtered through hands of Sun Devils receiver and Beavers defender before landed in grasp of E Dale Keller, who was on seat of his pants in EZ.

UCLA 20 Pittsburgh 6: Stellar UCLA (3-2) D turned 2 INTs into TDs to bail out its sagging O, which, according to coach Bill Barnes, should have run more to ram "it down their throats." Bruins TB Mike Haffner rushed 27/120y, but was 0-6 passing as UCLA missed all 7 of its throwing attempts. Haffner raced 25y to score on team's initial series of 1st Q. Bruins T Marshall Shirk pressured Pitt (1-4) QB Jim Traficant (9-25/89y, 3 INTs) into 2nd Q INT by TB-DB Bobby Smith, who used crushing block by E Chuck Hicks on Pitt DT Ernie Borghetti to romp 29y to score for 13-0 lead. Aided by fake-punt pass by Traficant to HB-P Fred Cox, Panthers drove 90y in 3rd Q to score on Cox's surprise 27y pass to HB Ed Clark. HB-DB Carmen DiPoalo returned INT 41y to Pitt 2YL in last min to set up final Bruins TD.

WASHINGTON 13 Stanford 0: Visiting Stanford (3-2) had better of play into 2nd Q, but couldn't cash any of its opportunities. Indians HB-K Stan Lindskog missed FG try early in 2nd Q, and, thereafter, Stanford lost 3 INTs to spoil all its threats. Washington (3-2) FB-DB Jim Stiger (16/94y) made INT of QB Steve Thurlow (9-24/98y, 3 INTs) in 2nd Q and returned it to Stanford 37YL. QB Pete Ohler passed 12y to HB Martin Wyatt to 2YL and sneaked over for TD and 7-0 lead. Huskies HB Bill Siler raced 44y to score in 4th Q.

AP Poll October 23

1 Michigan State (29)	444	6 Ohio State	235
2 Mississippi (11)	404	7 Louisiana State	128
3 Texas (3)	372	8 Notre Dame	118
4 Alabama (4)	331	9 Georgia Tech	108
5 Iowa (1)	327	10 Colorado	97

Others with votes: Missouri, Navy, Minnesota, Maryland, Rice, Michigan, Utah State, Southern California, Rutgers, Utah, Auburn, Army, Kansas, Clemson

October 28, 1961

(Fri) MIAMI 10 North Carolina 0: Soph QB George Mira (10-18/124y, TD, INT), back after time out with aching ribs, sparked Miami (3-3), throwing 40y TD pass to E Larry Wilson in 4th Q. E-K Bob Wilson hammered 30y FG through stiff wind in 2nd Q. North Carolina (3-2) never got started on ground, gaining only 21y, but Tar Heels managed 11-22/155y in air, mostly by QB Ray Farris. Big Miami line busted holes in North Carolina's D-front for FBs Jim Vollenweider and Sam Fernandez to combine for 160y of Hurricanes' 216y rushing.

HARVARD 21 Dartmouth 15: With HB Bill Taylor scoring twice in 1st H, Harvard (2-3) upset Dartmouth (3-2) by taking advantage of 2 INTs and FUM REC. DE Bob Boyda made 33y INT RET to Big Green 33YL at beginning of 2nd Q, and Dartmouth HB Chris Vancura lost FUM at his 35YL shortly after Taylor's 1st TD. Last Crimson TD, which provided 21-0 3rd Q lead, was aided by unusual 15y unsportsmanlike PEN when Indians D was flagged for signals sounding too similar to those barked by Harvard QB Mike Bassett. Rallying early in 4th Q, Dartmouth rode QB Bill King's passes for 80y to HB John Krumme's 9y TD run and King's 2-pt pass. King hit 3 throws after Dartmouth gained on-side KO and moved within 21-15 on King's TD sneak. Big Green kicked off with 7 mins left, but Harvard used Taylor's 3rd-and-5 and 4th-and-1 running-play conversions to run out clock and compile big piece of its 217y rushing.

PITTSBURGH 28 Navy 14: Pittsburgh (2-4) put end to its 4-game losing streak with mighty D that upset highly-favored Navy (4-2), which had won 4 in row. Midshipmen started game with on-side KO which blew up, and they added to their misfortune with 15y PEN that encouraged Pitt QB Jim Traficant's 8y TD trot up middle. Panthers limited Middies to only 24y O in 1st H, which Pitt led 7-0. However, Navy still threatened late in 1st Q as FB-LB Nick Markoff picked off Pitt HB Paul Martha's pass and returned it to Panthers 10YL. In turn, Pitt DB Glenn Lehner quickly made INT at his 1YL to snuff Middies threat. After Panthers HB-DB Ed Clark turned Navy HB John Sai's 3rd Q FUM into 13y TD run, Traficant scored to extend Panthers lead to 21-0. Leading 28-0 in 4th Q, Pitt emptied its bench, and Navy finally tallied on QB Bob Hecht's 1y sneak and his 10y pass to E Greg Mather.

GEORGIA 16 Kentucky 15: K Durwood Pennington bombed 52y FG to give Georgia (3-3) 10-7 lead in 3rd Q, even though 5y PEN had forced him to re-kick after making 47y boot. Late in game, Bulldogs drove to 3YL only to lose FUM. On ensuing 3rd down, Kentucky (2-4) QB Jerry Woolum was swarmed under in EZ, and Georgia T Bobby Green fell on FUM for TD and 16-7 lead. Woolum rallied Wildcats with TD pass to E Tommy Simpson and 2-pt pass to E Tom Hutchinson, but Kentucky's on-side KO failed.

LOUISIANA STATE 23 Florida 0: Bengal Tigers (5-1) surprisingly trounced Florida (3-2-1) while both were unbeaten in SEC. Gators inserted banged-up QB Larry Libertore midway in 1st Q, who quickly moved his team to 10YL. But, LSU C-LB Dennis Gaubatz blocked Florida K Billy Cash's FG try, and Tigers were on their way to 88y TD march capped by HB Ray Wilkins' 33y sprint off LT. LSU missed FG on next possession, which HB Hagood Clarke returned to 25YL. Libertore made unwise pitchout with 2 tacklers around his waist, and LSU DB Dwight Robinson stepped in to spear it, dashing 25y to score for 13-0 lead. Florida P Don Ringgold booted 50y punt to LSU's 14YL in 3rd Q, but Tigers HB (and future coach) Jerry Stovall got them out of hole with 38y run. QB Lynn Amadee hit 3 passes, including 17y TD to E Danny Neumann for 20-0 lead.

Mississippi State 23 MEMPHIS STATE 16: Memphis' 9-game win streak, fashioned since its 1960 loss to Mississippi State (4-2), came to end. Tigers (6-1) had outscored foes 332-44 to date in 1961. Brilliant Memphis QB James Earl Wright was hobbled, and Maroons bottled up Tigers attack, even though Wright passed for 7-0 lead in 1st Q and pitched his 2nd TD pass in 4th Q. Mississippi State HB Lee Welch caught 4y TD pass from QB John Correro, and they combined on 2-pt pass to put Bulldogs ahead 8-7 in 2nd Q. DB Welch soon raced 35y with INT TD RET that got Maroons rolling to 16 pts in 2nd Q.

PURDUE 9 Iowa 0: Heavy rain and ankle-deep mud marked 1st defeat of Big 10 front-runner Iowa (4-1) as Boilermakers (3-2) used Hawkeyes errors to gain all their pts. Without having made INT so far in 1961, Purdue snatched 2 INTs and added 3 FUM RECs to splash through downpour for huge upset over no. 5 Hawkeyes. Purdue C-LB Don Paltani intercepted Hawks QB Matt Szykowny on game's 1st series, and Boilermakers were set up at Iowa 37YL. QB Ron DiGravio clicked on 19y pass to HB Tom Bloom and FB Roy Walker converted twice on 4th down to overcome 10y in losses during TD drive that ensued. DiGravio wedged last ft for score and 6-0 edge. Early in 3rd Q, Purdue G-LB Stan Sczurek pounced on Hawkeyes HB Bernie Wyatt's FUM at Iowa 44YL. K Skip Ohl was true on 26y FG when Purdue's thrust died at Iowa 9YL. E Cloyd Webb made diving, mud-splaying catch of 31y pass from Szykowny in 4th Q but it did nothing to enhance Iowa's chances of scoring.

TEXAS 34 Rice 7: No. 3 Texas (6-0) threw its collection of whippets at Rice (3-2) and emerged with its accustomed 1-sided victory. Longhorns E-DE Bob Moses caught 5 passes, 2 for TDs, and made several key stops on D. FBs Ray Poage and Jerry Cook made 1st and last Longhorns TDs respectively. Owls harbored brief hope when QB Randall Kerbow found E Gene Raesz with 18y TD pass in 3rd Q to draw Rice to within 13-7.

SOUTHERN METHODIST 8 Texas Tech 7: Badly outgained by late 4th Q, poor SMU (2-3), non-winners in 9 straight SWC games, could boast of only 5 1st downs and single trip beyond its own 39YL in 55-and-half mins. Starting at its 27YL, Mustangs, however, reached into its past for Spread-formation that was once scourge of old Southwest. Soph QB Jerry Rhome, starting his 1st game, dropped into deep position and flipped 17y pass to HB Billy Gannon, who was loose in secondary of puzzled Texas Tech (2-4). Rhome next used his cocked-arm passing threat to set defenders on their heels for his runs for 12, 12, and 44y to Texas Tech 7YL. HB Tom Sherwin took soft swing pass left for TD, and Rhome rifled 2-pt strike to Gannon after rollout to right. T-K Jim Crowe bunted on-side KO, recovered by E Buddy Nichols, and Mustangs killed last 2 mins. Earlier, Red Raiders had marched up and down field for 337y, but were frustrated at SMU 9, 18, and 4YLs. After its strategy of QB Johnny Lovelace passing to E David

Parks had brought Tech to 4YL in 2nd Q, FB-K H.L. Daniels missed FG. Having weathered this threat with 48 secs left until H, Mustangs foolishly tried flat pass, which was picked off by assertive HB-DB David Rankin, who sailed 35y to TD.

Alabama 17 HOUSTON 0: College football's 1961 version of baseball's Eddie Stanky—he can't run, he can't pass, all he can do is beat you—Alabama (6-0) QB Pat Trammell was up to old tricks in beating Houston (2-3-1). Trammell passed for 2nd Q TD and ran for 3rd Q TD. K Tim Davis had opened scoring with 33y FG in 2nd Q when Trammell (9-17/117y, TD, 2 INTs) pitched passes for 46y of 62y TD trip capped by HB Bill Oliver's 5y scoring grab. After Bama recovered FUM at Cougars 15YL in 3rd Q, Trammell scored from 2YL after FB Mike Fracchia had fractured Houston's middle on 2 runs fro 13y. Cougars, playing their 1st year under longtime-to-be coach Bill Yeoman, built trio of threats: C-K Danny Birdwell had his 26y FG blocked by Tide HB Billy Richardson in 1st Q, H clock killed another advance, and Alabama DE Bill Battle made INT of Houston QB Don Sessions at Tide 8YL in 4th Q.

Ucla 20 STANFORD 0: Unable to move in opening 25 mins, UCLA (4-2) counted on its D to turn back several Stanford (3-3) threats, including Indians drive inside 1YL after FUM REC at Bruins 42YL. UCLA DTs Marshall Shirk and Tony Fiorentino stopped Stanford HB Stan Lindskog (11/52y) 1 ft short of GL. With 59 secs to go in 2nd Q, Bruins tendered 82y TD foray, fueled by TB Mike Haffner's 26y plummeting-quail throw to QB Jim Bergman, pass so disrespected by Stanford coach "Cactus" Jack Curtice that he said, "Man had a gun, he coulda shot it down." Bruins TD came on 1y run by Haffner (9/41y). Stanford raced clock in downfield retaliation, but bad snap discombobulated K Lindskog's 51y FG try. Bruins HB-DB Kermit Alexander returned Lindskog's low, short boot for 87y TD, running as clock expired, with assisting block by E Mel Profit. Indians gave up ball in 2nd H on FUM and 2 INTs, latter including Bruins QB-DB John Walker's 38y INT TD RET late in 3rd Q. Post-game riot between students broke out over attempted tear-down of goalposts by Uclan fans.

OREGON 7 Washington 6 (Portland): Oregon (3-3) upset Washington (3-3) by clamping down on Huskies air game (4-11/86y). Washington failed to complete single pass until late in 3rd Q when it mounted its 1st drive to catch Ducks, who had led 7-0 since 2nd Q. In 2nd Q, Oregon HB Monte Fitchett had set up TD with 32y punt RET to UW 34YL. QB Ron Veres produced 11y TD pass to E Paul Bauge 4 plays later. Early in 4th Q, Huskies went 56y to Ducks 1YL, but were turned back by Oregon's big D-line. On its next series, Washington succeeded, traveling 80y as FB Jim Stiger powered over from 2YL. Huskies attempted go-ahead 2-pt pass, but QB Pete Ohler's throw fell short of HB Charlie Mitchell.

AP Poll October 30

1 Michigan State (31)	437	6 Louisiana State	199
2 Mississippi (8)	407	7 Georgia Tech	163
3 Texas (6)	383	8 Colorado	142
4 Alabama (2)	325	9 Iowa	83
5 Ohio State	267	10 Missouri	65

Others with votes: Minnesota, Notre Dame, Purdue, Utah State, Northwestern, Kansas, Penn State, Auburn, Syracuse, Rutgers, Wyoming, Arkansas

November 4, 1961

BOSTON COLLEGE 14 Iowa State 10: Visiting Cyclones (4-3) whirled into Chestnut Hill and led almost throughout game. E-K Larry Schreiber kicked 41y FG, and Iowa State owned early 3-0 lead. When versatile TB Dave Hoppmann clicked on 44 and 35y pass connections, last for TD to WB Dick Limerick in 3rd Q, Cyclones appeared on track to 10-0 victory. At last, Boston College (3-3) applied heavy thump of FB Harry Crump. Crump sparked 4th Q reversal by setting up TD and scoring another within 4-min span. He plowed for 28y of 62y advance as QB George Van Cott chipped in 13y pass and pair of profitable 4th down runs before scoring from 1YL. On ensuing KO, Eagles E Joe Sikorski made FUM REC at Iowa State 28YL, and Crump tattered Cyclones line 5 times, scoring from 5YL. Iowa State D soon held Eagles, and Cyclones took punt near midfield, but Sikorski again played "Johnny-on-the-Spot," grabbing FUM REC at ISU 47YL.

MARYLAND 21 Penn State 17: Nobody knew it at that time, but victory by Maryland (5-2) over Penn State (4-3) would turn out to be Terrapins' only triumph over border rival in 31 meetings starting in 1960. Native Pennsylvanians, QB Dick Shiner and E-P Gary Collins, were Turtle difference-makers: Shiner (12-20/158y, 3 TDs, 2 INTs) threw for 3 early scores, last of which went to Collins (6/80y, TD receiving, and 6/46.5y punt avg) to provide 21-6 H lead. Collins' receiving y gave him new ACC career record of 1059y, topping Virginia's Sonny Randle. Nittany Lions had gotten TD in 2nd Q from HB Roger Kochman (18/89y, TD) and pulled within 21-15 on 3rd Q TD pass by QB Galen Hall (9-22/151y, TD, INT) and HB-K Don Jonas' 28y FG in 4th Q. Penn State mounted late assault that started from its 25YL after INT by DE Jim Schwab. Hall hit E Schwab for 24y and HB Junior Powell for 44y, and Hall and Kochman runs gave Lions 1st-and-goal at 4YL with barely more than 2 mins left. But 7y loss on sack by blitzing FB-LB Harry Butsko and disputed incompletion to Powell doomed Penn State's closing bid. Maryland took over and gave deliberate safety on 4th down punt snap by C Bob Hacker.

NORTH CAROLINA 22 Tennessee 21: Border foes traded TDs all game with North Carolina (4-2) breaking out on top on QB Ray Farris' 1y run in 1st Q. FUM REC set up Tennessee (3-3) for TB Glenn Glass' 60y run that led to tying 1st Q TD. Vols C-LB Mike Lucci ran 29y with 3rd Q INT to tie it at 14-14. After TB Mallon Faircloth's 4th Q TD pass put Vols in front for 1st time at 21-14, cool Farris took Tar Heels length of field in 1:06, hitting HB Ward Marslender with TD pass and HB Gib Carson with 2-pt pass with 15 secs left.

VIRGINIA 28 South Carolina 20: Virginia (3-4) HB Carl Kuhn stunningly squeezed through 4 tacklers on dandy punt RET, also caught pass to set up TD for 21-7 H lead. Cav workhorse was soph FB Doug Thomson, who rushed 18/81y, 2 TDs. Meanwhile, South Carolina (2-5) passed 11-26, 2 TDs, both caught by E Henry Crosby, who snagged 3/58y. Inspiration came from vet T Dave Graham who at H reminded Cavs of 1960 loss when Gamecocks rubbed it in by playing linemen in backfield at end of game.

LOUISIANA STATE 10 Mississippi 7: Knowing no. 1 Michigan State had been upset earlier on Saturday 6-pt favorite Ole Miss (6-1) saw nighttime chance to jump to top of polls. But several crucial plays by outgained (322y to 213y) LSU (6-1) turned momentum in Tigers' favor. On Bayou Bengals' 1st possession, HB-K Wendell Harris kicked 37y FG that Mississippi E Ralph Smith barely missed blocking. Rebels sub QB Glynn Griffing inflated his team's air attack just before H, pumping 2y TD throw to E Wes Sullivan. Midway through 3rd Q, Ole Miss failed on FG try, and 2 plays later, LSU HB Jerry Stovall raced 57y on counter run to Rebels 23YL. After 4th down catch by E Billy Truax at 12YL, Harris circled LE for winning 7y TD behind cutting block of G Monk Guillot. Tigers weathered 2 threats in 4th Q as LSU G-LB Steve Ward made INT at own 16YL and DE Gene Sykes grabbed FUM at own 34YL to end Ole Miss' last bid.

MINNESOTA 13 Michigan State 0: Powerful Spartans (5-1), who held 131-10 scoring advantage over 5 prior victims, got scorched midway in 1st Q as HB Bill Munsey took pitchout 8y for Minnesota (5-1) lead of 6-0. Michigan State proceeded to travel up and down field, but Gophers' sharp-when-it-counted D, led by FB-DB Judge Dickson, C-LB Julian Hook, Ts Carl Eller, Jim Wheeler and Bobby Bell, and Es John Campbell and Tom Hall, kept their EZ untouched. Minnesota became so occupied by defending its GL against runs by FB George Saimes and HBs Gary Ballman and Sherman Lewis of statistically-superior Spartans that it failed to log even single 1st down between its early TD and last play of 1st H. Minnesota surprisingly took upper hand at start of 2nd H, making 3 long drives to wrestle momentum and stunningly upset nation's no. 1 team. After Hall's FUM REC at Spartans 40YL, QB Sandy Stephens fired 23y pass to Munsey just inside end-line for 4th Q TD. DB Stephens locked up matters with EZ INT in last min. Victory kept Golden Gophers in 1st place tie in Big 10 with Ohio State.

OHIO STATE 29 Iowa 13: Ohio Stadium was filled with to-date record crowd of 83,795 to cheer on-rolling Buckeyes (5-0-1) powerhouse. Ohio State split open 12-7 game with 17-pt 4th Q to steamroller no. 9 slumping Iowa (4-2). Hawkeyes opened with 24 unanswered, but non-scoring, plays as E Cloyd Webb caught 6/105y. Even though Ohio State had no O snaps during that unusual 11:53 stretch, Buckeyes DE Tom Perdue dashed 55y to TD with mid-air FUM that he grabbed on failed reverse by Iowa HB Sammy Harris. Ohio State made it 12-0 by H on QB Joe Sparma's 18y TD pass after DB Dave Tingley's INT. Hawks fought back with 73y drive to narrow it to 12-7 as QB Matt Syzkowny (12-13/206y, 3 INTs) sneaked over. Buckeyes were pumped full of 4th Q inspiration by E Charles Bryant, who took short catch from Sparma and flattened 6 foes on 63y trip to EZ. Ohio FB Bob Ferguson (27/144y, TD) blasted 14y for last score after LB Gary Moeller's 53y INT RET to Iowa 20YL.

Navy 13 NOTRE DAME 10: Which way ball would bounce had capacity crowd on edge of its collective seats until end. Behind 3-0 on Fighting Irish (3-3) FB-K Joe Perkowski's 45y FG, Navy (5-2) fielded punt at own 25YL in __ Q. Sub QB Bob Hecht lofted long pass that fell among 2 Middies receivers and 2 ND defenders. Ball was tipped and came down in hands of Navy HB Jim Stewart, who raced to 3YL before HB-DB Angelo Dabiero could head him off OB. Hecht sneaked over, and E-K Greg Mather added kick and booted 42y FG before H. Notre Dame went 63y after 2nd H KO to tie it 10-10. In 4th Q, Irish QB Daryle Lamonica dropped back to pass, but under rush lost ball which was recovered at ND 9YL by Navy G-LB John Hewitt. Irish held, but Mather nailed 22y FG. In final 12 mins, Irish advanced to Navy 42, 21, and 10YLs. But in orderly failure, Lamonica had to punt, Lamonica lost 11y on FUM, and, in game's climax, E Les Traver caught 30 and 20y passes from Lamonica only to be belted at 10YL and lose flying FUM to trailing Navy DE Dave Sjuggerud at 17YL.

COLORADO 7 Missouri 6: Coming calling was nemesis Missouri, with 5-1-2 record against Colorado since 1953, so it was time for Colorado (6-0) to snatch Big 8 control. In 2nd Q, Buffaloes HB Leon Mavity sprinted past midfield on 25y with punt RET. It allowed QB Gale Weidner to hit FB Bill Harris with 21y TD pass in dying moments of 1st H, followed by x-pt kick by E-K Jerry Hillebrand, who caught 14y pass on 4-play drive. Colorado took inside track to Orange Bowl, but not before Missouri (5-1-1) finished 63y march early in 4th Q with HB Daryl Krugman taking pitchout from QB Ron Taylor (7-17/69y, 2 INTs) and tossing pass to E Don Wainright for 10y TD. But, same play in symmetrical direction failed to net 2 pts as HB Mike Hunter's throw fell harmlessly past EZ. HB-K Bill Tobin was short with 44y FG try in Tigers' desperate, late attempt to steal win.

WICHITA 25 Oklahoma State 13: Wheatshockers (7-1) rallied from 7-7 H deadlock on passing of QB Alex Zyskowski, who hit E Ron Turner with 8y go-ahead TD in 3rd Q. Wichita quickly followed with clinching 20y TD INT RET. Oklahoma State (2-5) had earned 7-7 tie in 1st Q on QB Bill Leming's 17y TD pass to E Tommy Ward.

ARKANSAS 15 Texas A&M 8: Bumbling Arkansas Razorbacks (5-2) marched up and down field to 345y to 138y O advantage but trailed Aggies (3-3-1) most of 2nd H until finally piecing together artful 90y drive to winning TD in game's last min. HB Paul Dudley had scored on 17y run in 1st Q for 7-0 Hogs lead. Less than 5 mins into 3rd Q, Texas A&M scored following Arkansas QB George McKinney's FUM at his 11YL only 1 play after A&M P Babe Craig had booted Razorbacks to their 7YL. Aggies FB Lee Roy Caffey (12/34y) blasted over from 1YL, and Aggies earned 1-pt lead as E Bobby Huntington got toe in-bounds at back of EZ on 2-pt catch. Texas A&M DB Travis Reagan made his 3rd INT and returned it 16y to Hogs 26YL inside last 8 mins of 4th Q. This TO appeared to doom Arkansas, but Hogs HB-DB Darrell Williams tipped away 4th down running pass by A&M HB Jim Linnstaedter, so Razorbacks took over on their 10YL with 4:51 left. After 2 dropped passes, Hogs used pass by HB Lance Alworth off reverse run, which Dudley hauled in for 36y gain. McKinney (3-7/26y, TD) mixed in runs with his 8 and 12y passes and looked off Alworth, cutting to middle of EZ, to loft 6y TD to E Jimmy John for winning TD. McKinney followed with 2-pt pass to Dudley.

ARIZONA 20 Wyoming 15: Enjoying its only year as independent, Arizona (5-1-1) bounced back after having its 11-game unbeaten streak squashed previous week 27-23 by West Texas State. Wildcats allowed considerable ground y near midfield but fashioned stubborn D around C-LB Bob Garis (14 tackles) and DB Ed Pollard (13 tackles) and in 1st H allowed only Cowboys HB Mike Walker to score on 2y run. After 7-7 H tie, Wyoming (5-1-2) gambled for 2 pts in 4th Q, after HB Dick Behning had blasted over for TD, and Walker caught conv pass for 15-14 lead. Arizona (5-1-1) had stopped 4 Wyoming plunges from 1-ft away from GL in 3rd Q and finally retaliated in final 1:32 of game on QB Eddie Wilson's 33y TD pass to ace HB Bobby Thompson, 2nd scoring connection of 2nd H for that sharp duo. Wilson also converted 4th-and-4 pass from Wyoming on winning drive.

AP Poll November 6

1 Texas (35)	473	6 Michigan State	202
2 Alabama (6)	410	7 Mississippi	191
3 Ohio State (7)	365	8 Colorado	173
4 Louisiana State	317	9 Georgia Tech	164
5 Minnesota	247	10 Missouri	19

Others with votes: Syracuse, Utah State, Iowa, Maryland, Purdue, UCLA, Kansas, Arkansas, Northwestern, North Carolina

November 11, 1961

COLUMBIA 35 Dartmouth 14: Columbia's rarely-ferocious Lions (5-2) took Ivy League lead as E-DE Dick Hassan scored twice in opening 6:16: Hassan fell on QK blocked by DG Tony Day and grabbed 14y pass from QB Tom Vasell after Indians' FUM. Dartmouth (4-3) struck back on 54y drive that resulted in 18y TD run by HB Tom Spangenberg and 2-pt run by QB Billy King. Lions stopped 2nd Q thrust to their 9YL as deflected 4th down EZ pass was bobbled by Big Green receiver. From that moment, Columbia took command. After leading 14-8 at H, Columbia simply owned 2nd H as HB Tom Haggerty set school record with 32 rushing tries in leading TD drives by gaining 46 and 45y respectively on scoring trips of 80 and 81y. Against Columbia reserves, Dartmouth clicked on King's 25y TD pass to E Dave Usher, but Lions HB Russ Warren burst 43y to score after Indians' failed on-side KO. With Princeton's 9-7 loss at Harvard, Columbia now surprisingly shared Ivy League lead.

Notre Dame 26 PITTSBURGH 20: Notre Dame (4-3) backup QB Frank Budka found E Les Traver for 2 big passes: 59y TD in 1st Q and 40y gain to Pitt 2YL in 3rd Q. Panthers (2-6) counted on HB-K Fred Cox, who despite bruised leg, scored TD and booted FGs of 45 and 52y, latter being 1 of college ball's longest since early 20th century dropkickers. Key Fighting Irish TD came from obscure HB Charlie O'Hara, not listed on ND depth chart, as he raced 47y in 4th Q for 26-13 lead. Pitt came back on 45y TD pass by QB Jim Traficant, who led 190y air attack. Swift-closing Pitt reached Irish 21YL in dying moments, only to have Irish D toss Traficant for 3 losses and HB Paul Martha barely miss catching Traficant's 4th down pass among 2 defenders at 5YL.

Florida 21 Georgia 14 (Jacksonville): Underdog Georgia (3-5) coughed up TOs to keep Gators (4-3-1) knocking on GL door in 1st H: Bulldogs FB Wayne Taylor lost FUM to Florida FB-LB Tommy Kelley at 16YL and HB Bill McKenny's punt FUM to DT Anton Peters at 14YL. Gators QB Tom Batten (10-18/192y, 3 TDs) pitched 15y TD to HB Lindy Infante, but UGa rose up to throw Florida back on its 2nd opportunity. Late in 2nd Q, Batton passed to HB Bob Hoover, who barely out-jumped DB Billy Knowles to gallop 48y to TD and 13-0 H edge. Lethargic Bulldogs O had made only 72y in 1st H, but got LB Dale Williams' FUM REC boost in 3rd Q. QB Larry Rakestraw threw TD, later ran in another, so suddenly awake Georgia led 14-13 in 1st min of 4th Q. With 5 mins left, Batten's 10 and 30y passes to E Sam Holland were followed by HB Ron Stoner's 16y TD catch to dot Florida's 63y winning drive. But after Rakestraw passed Bulldogs to 21YL, it took INT at Gators 11YL by HB-DB Paul White to save Florida win.

TENNESSEE 10 Georgia Tech 6: Yellow Jackets' no. 9 national ranking was ruined in upset that pivoted on only TO of contest in 1st Q. Georgia Tech (6-2) QB Stan Gann lost FUM at own 20YL to Vols DG Larry Richards. K Gary Cannon followed with 31y FG for Tennessee (4-3). Game turned in 4th Q when charging Jackets DL trapped Glenn Glass as he tried to punt from Vols 37YL. But Tech was flagged for offside, and Glass' resultant punt went all way to Jackets 3YL. Ensuing punt out left Tennessee in good position at Engineers 36YL, and TB Mallon Faircloth, big running factor all day, pitched victory-sealing 22y TD to E Mike Stratton. Gann capped 77y drive with TD run, but it was insufficient for Georgia Tech.

PURDUE 7 Michigan State 6: Purdue (5-2), which enjoyed 241y to 195y O stat edge, drove 60y to 1YL in 2nd Q, but strong D of Michigan State (5-2) dug in to hold. Late in 1st Q, G-LB Charlie Brown ignited Spartans' early 2nd Q TD with INT RET of pass bu Boilermakers QB Gary Hogan to Purdue 32YL. Michigan State FB George Saimes, outstanding also as LB, split middle of line to score from 11YL, but reliable E-K Art Brandstatter had his conv kick tipped by left hand of Boilermakers DT Don Brumm. FB Gene Donaldson (91/66y) keyed Purdue's winning drive in 3rd Q with 3 runs that earned 1st downs. Boilers QB Ron DiGravio (5-10/58y, TD) hit HB Tom Boris in flat, and Boris wriggled through 2 Michigan State tacklers to score 15y TD. G-K Skip Ohl successfully kicked winning conv. Evidence of hard-hitting action was found in combined rushing stats of 107/301y for 2.8y avg.

Minnesota 16 IOWA 9: Alert Golden Gophers (6-1) fell on 3 Iowa (4-3) FUMs and snagged 3 INTs. Grit and muscle were keystones of classic Big 10 tussle, as Minnesota turned blocked punt into TD to break open tight 3-2 contest in 4th Q. Gophers C-LB Bob Frisbee had presented inadvertent 2 pts to Iowa in 1st Q when he made INT at 1YL, momentarily lost his balance, and was tackled by Hawkeyes E Felton Rogers in EZ. Although Minnesota was stopped 3 inches from GL in 4th Q, resultant field position set stage for QB-DB Wayne Teigen's INT at Hawkeyes 44YL. Minnesota QB Sandy Stephens (5-10/66y, TD) followed with 39y TD pass to HB Bill Munsey for 10-2 lead. Quickly, Gophers C-LB Dick Enga (2 FUM RECs) blocked punt at Iowa 21YL and E John Campbell chased and covered bounding ball in EZ for 16-2

lead. Momentum had turned right after 2nd H KO: Iowa opened 3rd Q with march to Minnesota 5YL, but Hawkeyes FB Bill Perkins lost FUM to LB Enga at 3YL. Gophers DT Bobby Bell recovered Iowa HB Bernie Wyatt's bobbled punt reception at Minnesota 45YL as P Stephens punted out of EZ. Iowa was only able to score TD in last 3 secs on 33y pitch from QB Matt Szykowski (16-26/205y, TD, 3 INTs) to E Cloyd Webb.

Oklahoma 7 MISSOURI 0: Tigers (5-2-1) QB Ron Taylor arched 40y pass to E Conrad Hitchler to Oklahoma (2-5) 3YL in 1st Q, but Soonerd D-line, obviously peaked to play, rejected Missouri's 4 smacks at GL. Sooners HB Jimmy Carpenter soon reversed poor field position with 44y punt RET, and HB-DB Mike McClellan later made TD-saving tackle of Mizzou HB Norm Beal (13/92y), who made 34y dash to Oklahoma 44YL. Carpenter and McClellan teamed up in 2nd Q on HB option pass for 14y TD; ball was away just as Carpenter was leveled on pass rush by Hitchler. Game-deciding score came after Oklahoma C-LB Wayne Lee fell on FUM by Missouri HB Bill Tobin at Mizzou 43YL. OU turned 2nd H over to its D, led by Es Ronny Payne and John Benien, to remain unbeaten in Columbia since 1945. Frustrated Tigers, who failed on 4 opportunities close to Oklahoma GL, outgained their foes 262y to 168y.

Nebraska 16 IOWA STATE 13: Nation's individual leader in total O, Single-Wing TB Dave Hoppmann of Iowa State (4-4), put up 266y rushing and passing. His big play was 50y TD dash in 2nd Q that brought Cyclones to 7-7 tie. But, it was Hoppmann's only error that paved way for victory by Nebraska (3-4-1). Down by 10-7 in 4th Q, Hoppmann moved Iowa State 65y downfield, but he lost FUM at Cornhuskers 22YL. From that point, Nebraska employed heavy ground game to advance to FB Bill "Thunder" Thornton's 1y TD smash for 16-7 lead. Hoppmann completed 6y TD pass to WB Dick Limerick with 2 secs left in game. Huskers had built their early lead on QB Dennis Claridge's short TD run and K Ron Meade's pivotal 31y FG, that came against strong wind in last sec of 1st H.

Utah 21 COLORADO 12: Orange Bowl panel was left in shock after upsets of both their prime targets: Georgia Tech and Colorado (6-1). Things started well for Buffaloes as they went 73y after opening KO to E Jerry Hillebrand's 10y TD catch from QB Gale Weidner (10-24/208y, 2 TDs, INT) as HB Teddy Woods contributed 17 and 18y runs. But, many of Buffaloes regulars had played 50 mins in 4 of last 5 games, so coach Sonny Grandelius immediately brought in his 2nd unit. Against Buffs subs, surprising Utah (6-3) answered right back on sharp QB play by Gary Hertzfeldt (12-18/131y, TD), who capped counter-drive with 8y TD pass to HB Jerry Overton. Momentum now belonged to Utes, and they built 21-6 lead on 2 TDs by FB Doug Wasko. Utes E Marv Fleming caught 5/64y, while they also gained 233y rushing behind Wasko (16/57y, 2 TDs) and HBs Dennis Zito and Bud Tynes, so failing wa sin Colorado's D. Buffs HB Leon Mavity partly made up for his having bobbled 2nd Q EZ pass with late 78y TD grab. But, there was insufficient time for Colorado comeback.

WASHINGTON STATE 22 Oregon 21: Previously held back by nagging injuries, bruising FB George Reed of underdog Cougars (2-6) rushed for 108y and scored 3 TDs, including 1y game-winner in 4th Q. Reed augmented QB-K Mel Melin's 27y FG in 1st Q with 2y TD run in 2nd Q for 10-0 upper hand for Washington State. Bruising FB Jim Josephson scored 1st of his 2 TDs in 2nd Q, so Ducks (4-4) trailed 16-7 at H. Sizzling soph HB Mel Renfro provided Oregon with 21-16 lead in 3rd Q.

AP Poll November 13

1 Texas (41)	463	6 Mississippi	234
2 Alabama (3)	401	7 Purdue	101
3 Ohio State (2)	365	8 Colorado	61
4 Louisiana State (1)	336	9 Michigan State	60
5 Minnesota	307	10 Syracuse	47

Others with votes: Missouri, Georgia Tech, Maryland, Arkansas, UCLA, Kansas, Rutgers, Utah State, Duke, Wyoming, Utah, Michigan, Iowa, Notre Dame, Arizona

November 18, 1961

Oklahoma 14 ARMY 8 (New York City): Oklahoma (3-5) scouts had noted Army (6-3) was slow coming out of its D huddle. So, in 1st Q, Sooners ran short preliminary play as throw-away to set up their big surprise: Before even cameras in place for NBC's telecast were ready to focus, let along Cadets' D, Oklahoma quickly hopped into formation and delivered wide pitchout to HB Mike McClellan, who raced untouched for 74y TD. Piling-on PEN against Army helped Oklahoma's 76y TD drive in 3rd Q, and, when Cadets continued to gripe about that call, officials twice moved ball inches in amusing half-distance-to-GL PENs. QB Bob Page pushed over from well inside 1YL for 14-0 Sooners lead. Frustrated Cadets had been stopped at Oklahoma 31, 35, and 27YL in 1st H and after 2nd H KO. Army's starting QB Dick Eckert was so hurried by OU D pressure that he hit only 3-14/41y. Coach Dale Hall called 3rd team QB Cammy Lewis off bench to fire 4 completions worth 50y in leading to HB Joe Blackgrove's surprise, late 5y TD pass to E Paul Zmuida. Lewis then made 2-pt pass to Zmuida, but soon was intercepted by Sooners FB-DB Phil Lohmann to end any hopes for Black Knights.

DUKE 6 North Carolina 3: Wild finish of traditional battle for supremacy in Tar Heel State marked Duke's 5th championship in opening 9 years of ACC play. Tar Heels (4-4) struck for 3-0 lead in 2nd Q when Blue Devil (5-3) HB Jay Wilkinson lost FUM on punt at own 15YL, and UNC FB-K Bob Elliott made 22y FG. North Carolina mounted mighty GLS in 3rd Q, just 1 of Devils' 9 trips into Carolina territory. Duke finally tied it 3-3 on K Billy Reynolds' 32y boot with 6 mins left to play. Deadlock seemed inevitable when Duke failed on 4th down pass and had to turn possession over at Carolina 46YL with 33 secs to go,. But with less than 30 secs left at midfield, Tar Heels QB Ray Farris wanted no part of any tie, so he threw long down sideline for HB Ward Marslender. In angled hot pursuit, Duke HB-DB Dean Wright made outstanding over-shoulder INT and weaved his way back to UNC 37YL, where tackle by Elliott brought 15y face-masking PEN. Reynolds came running on to stunningly make winning 39y FG, longest to date in Duke's history, as clock ticked to down to 3 secs.

ALABAMA 10 Georgia Tech 0: Difference in philosophies of 2 great coaches, Bear Bryant and Bobby Dodd, was symbolized by single rough play that will mark this game forever. Much-debated incident would contribute to Georgia Tech's withdrawal from Southeastern Conf after 1963 season. Bryant taught hard-hitting, gang-tackling that was epitomized by undersized LB Darwin Holt. Dodd was more relaxed mentor, and HB Chick Graning, likeable team capt, was typical, easy-going Engineers player. Holt's tackle of Graning, simply hardnosed in view of Alabama (9-0) but dirty in eyes of Georgia Tech (6-3), created immediate rift between these schools. Graning's shattered jaw was sad byproduct of tough battle won on FB Mike Fracchia's 16y TD run in 2nd Q and K Tim Davis' 3rd Q FG. Yellow Jackets were limited to 96y total O (30y rushing) and didn't cross midfield on their own muscle until 4th Q. Bama immediately pushed Georgia Tech back across 50YL as DG Jimmy Wilson threw Engineers QB Billy Lothridge for 13y loss. Crimson Tide had hoped to gain Rose Bowl bid with victory, but students at UCLA, Pasadena's most-likely host team, made it quite clear they were against invitation to any segregated team such as those in SEC.

Mississippi 24 Tennessee 10 (Memphis): Seeking another bowl bid for 7th time in 8 years, Ole Miss (8-1) employed specific strategy. QB Doug Elmore filled air with short passes to flats, and Rebels went to long passes and runs when Tennessee (4-4) D adjusted. K Wes Sullivan booted 32y FG for Mississippi on 1st series in 1st Q, only to have it matched by Vols K Gary Cannon in 2nd Q. FB Billy Ray Adams barged over for TD just before H, and Rebs put game away at 24-3 with 2 TDs in 3rd Q: Elmore pitched 32y TD pass to HB Louis Guy, and QB Glynn Griffing weaved through entire Vols special team on 53y punt TD RET. Tennessee got its TD on 56y pass TD INT by T Ed Beard before 4th Q degenerated into fights and PENs.

MINNESOTA 10 Purdue 7: Before record crowd of 67,081 in "Brickhouse,"also known as Minneapolis' Memorial Stadium, Minnesota (7-1) stayed unbeaten in Big 10, half-game ahead of Ohio State, which went out-of-conf to beat Oregon 22-12. Joining 1953 A-A Paul Giel as only Golden Gophers to date to scale 1,000y in total O for season, QB Sandy Stephens ran 16y to set up T-K Tom Loechler's 35y FG and scored on 4y sprint, all in 2nd Q. Stephens garnered so-so 106y in total O because as often happened his passing arm betrayed him. He had poor passing game with 3-13/45y, 2 INTs. Meanwhile, Gophers' fine D prevented Purdue (5-3) from entering Minnesota territory throughout 1st H. Boilermakers went to air for more than 100y in 4th Q behind sub QB Gary Hogan, whose 53y pass to E Jack Elwell went to 3YL and set up Hogan's 1y TD run on 4th down. Purdue gained only 27y rushing against Gophers' formidable D front, led by T Bobby Bell.

NOTRE DAME 17 Syracuse 15: Early in 3rd Q after inadvertent touching of punt by Syracuse (6-3) at its 25YL, Fighting Irish (5-3) E Les Traver (6/92y) caught 2nd TD pass of QB Frank Budka (12-27/199y, 2 TDs, 3 INTs) for 14-0 lead. On 4th-and-1 later in 3rd Q, Syracuse QB Dave Sarette crossed up Notre Dame by passing to big E John Mackey, who leveled HB-DB George Sekcik with wicked stiff-arm on journey to 57y TD. Sarette quickly threw running pass to right to HB Dick Easterly for 2-pt conv. Rushing of HB Ernie Davis helped Orange control balance of 3rd Q, but early in 4th Q, Sarette was hit lustily by ND defenders at Irish 3YL and was carried off with concussion. Sub QB Bob Lelli came in and on 4th down surprised everyone with rollout to right and his left-handed pass to Easterly for 2y TD. E-K Ken Ericson booted x-pt for 15-14 Orange lead. ND suffered INTs twice in last 5 mins in efforts to drive for winning score, and took over at own 30YL with nearly hopeless 17 secs remaining. Budka scrambled 20y and completed 11y pass to allow FB-K Joe Perkowski to try 55y FG. Syracuse zealously blocked FG attempt, but was flagged for roughing K in process. Perkowski made 2nd-chance 41y FG with no time on clock. There was much post-game uproar in newspapers about Notre Dame supposedly getting undeserving 2nd try at FG.

Colorado 7 NEBRASKA 0: Thoroughly-dominant shutdown of Nebraska (3-5-1) O enhanced likelihood of Colorado receiving bid from Orange Bowl. Golden Buffaloes (7-1) amazingly held Cornhuskers to no 1st downs, only 31y rushing, and 0-12 passing. Colorado threatened 4 times but stalled thanks to sloppy post-snow footing, and were kept at bay by Nebraska QB-P Dennis Claridge's long punts. Buffaloes QB Gale Weidner came through with 1y TD run after HB-DB Claude Crabb made FUM REC at Huskers 11YL.

GAME OF THE YEAR
Texas Christian 6 TEXAS 0:

TCU's spoiler reputation, especially in Austin, had Texas (8-1) coach Darrell Royal as "nervous as a pig in a packing plant." His fears were realized early when fleet Longhorns HB James Saxton, SWC's leading rusher and known for his ability to hunt jackrabbits on foot, was knocked senseless. Like another slender HB, Tommy McDonald of Oklahoma and Philadelphia Eagles, Saxton had habit of popping to his feet after being tackled, if for no reason than to show opponents his slight frame was unhurt. Early in 1st Q, Saxton took short pass from QB Mike Cotton and zipped 45y to 10YL. He popped up but was leveled by Horned Frogs T Bobby Plummer, who trailed play and delivered accidental hip to Saxton's head. Saxton received permanent hearing loss, and, although he returned to game to rush for 85y, he spent most of it, as he described it, in "dreamland." TCU (3-4-1) gained 200y to Texas' 208y, and Frogs got their winning 50y score midway in 2nd Q when QB Sonny Gibbs fired long pass to E Buddy Iles who outraced Longhorns HB-DB Jerry Cook to EZ. Texas lost its top ranking on mistakes such as bobbled FG snaps and inability to capitalize on red-zone chances against Frogs' tough D, which was led by FB-LB Tommy Crutcher, T Bill Phillips, and E Iles. Promising drives by Longhorns died at TCU 2, 3, 8, 21, and 27YLs. Afterward, Royal likened Frogs to roaches. His quote, "It isn't what he eats or totes off, but what he falls into and messes up" was tacked on TCU bulletin boards for years to come. It didn't help much: TCU beat Royal-coached Texas teams only twice more in next 15 years.

UTAH STATE 17 Utah 6: Utah State (9-0-1) closed greatest season in school history with win over Utah (6-4). QB-K Jim Turner put Aggies on board with 36y FG in 1st Q, and Utah State would lead 11-0 in 1st H in which they permitted Utes across midfield but twice. Shifty Aggies HB Jack Larscheid iced it with 85y punt TD RET in 3rd Q. Utah rushed for 127y, but massive Utah State D, led by Ts Merlin Olsen and Clark Miller and E Lionel Aldridge, continued to lead nation with 50.8y run D avg.

Washington 17 UCLA 13: Little Billy Siler, once UCLA's waterboy and 1961's Washington (4-4-1) waterbug HB, darted 25y to winning TD in 4th Q to defeat Bruins (6-3) for whom he once dreamed of playing. After Huskies HB Charlie Mitchell had raced 90y with opening KO to score, game was defined by mistakes. Washington K Rick Smidt added 21y FG for 10-0 lead after G Dave Philips' FUM REC at Bruins 22YL. Washington's miscues were mostly confined to 2nd Q when Uclans scored 2 quick TDs for 13-10 H lead. Bruins FB-DB Mitch Dimkich returned INT to UW 47YL, and TB Mike Haffner's pass to E Tom Gutman took 34y bite out of Washington territory. Haffner circled RE for 5y TD. Right after ensuing KO, Huskies HB Dave Kopay lost FUM to UCLA E Mel Profit, and Haffner scored from1YL. Bruins sub TB-P Keith Jensen's long punt pushed Huskies near their 30YL, but foul PEN forced re-punt that was returned to UCLA 40YL by Mitchell, net gain of 26y for Washington. Siler soon darted through RT and cut back for his winning score. With nearly 13 mins left, Bruins had plenty of time, but best chance faded in agonizing EZ pass that was tipped out of hands of E Don Vena by diving Huskies HB-DB Nat Whitmyer.

AP Poll November 20

1 Alabama (39)	469	6 Mississippi (1)	266
2 Ohio State (6)	408	7 Colorado	114
3 Minnesota (2)	354	8 Michigan State	113
4 Louisiana State (1)	353	9 Arkansas	71
5 Texas	321	10 Kansas	46

Others with votes: Purdue, Michigan, Utah State, Maryland, Missouri, Duke, Syracuse, Rutgers, Notre Dame, Arizona, Georgia Tech, Wyoming, Utah

November 23-25, 1961

(Th'g) Texas 25 TEXAS A&M 0: Trying to rebound from its TCU upset, Texas (9-1) used K Eldon Moritz's pair of 1st H FGs for nervous 6-0 lead. But Longhorns came up with big play in 3rd Q: former QB James Saxton's 1st pass of year from HB spot went for 46y TD to HB Jack Collins. Another top Longhorns HB-DB Jerry Cook, burned week before on pass D, picked off QB Ronnie Brice's throw and Cook's long runback set up his own TD for 18-0 lead. Texas A&M (4-5-1) crossed midfield just 3 times, and coach Jim Myers, recently hanged in effigy at student center, was soon on his way out of College Station.

(Fri) MIAMI 10 Northwestern 6: Miami (6-3) swept to 1st Q TD as QB George Mira hit E Bill Miller for 17 and 13y completions and then found HB John Bahen loose in EZ for 27y TD. E-K Bob Wilson raised Hurricanes lead to 10-0 with 22y 3rd Q FG after Mira's 4 completions carried inside 5YL. QB Bobby Eickhoff (5-6/46y, and 11/59y rushing) entered Northwestern (4-5) backfield in 2nd H and provided spark to 3rd unit that drove 57y to Eickhoff's 11y TD sweep behind block of FB Dick Uhlir. Late in game, Wildcats advanced to 4th-and-3 at 5YL, but Eickhoff was snowed under by 3 tacklers after no gain.

RUTGERS 32 Columbia 19: Rutgers (9-0) was eyeing Lambert Trophy, but it soon would go to Penn State at 7-3 due to Nittany Lions' more prominent schedule. As Scarlet Knights daydreamed of Eastern glory, Columbia Lions (6-3), soon to be crowned Ivy League co-champs, led 19-7 in 3rd Q. Lions had turned around 7-3 H deficit with QB Tom Vasell's TD pass and HB-DB Mike Hassan's 32y INT TD RET. Vasell added 2-pt passes each time, so Columbia led 19-7. Rutgers exploded for 4 TDs in 4th Q against thin Lions, starting with QB Bill Speranza's TD pass to E Lee Curley. Speranza sneaked across GL, FB Steve Simms (20/118y) plunged for game-winning score, and HB-DB Pierce Frauenheim iced it with INT TD RET.

Penn State 47 PITTSBURGH 26: Old rivals put on show that at times was simply "implausible," according to Howard Tuckner in *The New York Times*. It turned outto be highest scoring tilt to date after 61 meetings of Keystone State rivals. C-LB Jay Huffman got Mount Nits started by blocking punt at Pitt 14YL, and QB Galen Hall scooped up ball for 6y FUM REC for 7-0 edge. Late in 2nd Q, underdog Panthers (3-7) snarled into 14-13 lead on QB Paul Martha's short TD pass and FB Rick Leeson's 5y TD run. But, Penn State (7-3) QB Hall (11-14/266y, 2 TDs), who accounted for 4 TDs, threw 23y TD pass to HB Al Gursky to regain lead for good at 19-14. Penn State scored next 3 TDs for 40-14 lead in 4th Q: Hall weaved for 11y TD in 3rd Q, his 2nd running score, followed by HB Roger Kochman's 8y TD. Pitt managed 2 superfluous TDs later in 4th Q, wrapped around Hall's 48y TD pass. Scoring for Panthers were FB Rick Leeson on elusive 49y sprint and E Steve Jastrrzembski on 6y catch from QB Jim Traficant.

Wisconsin 23 MINNESOTA 21: Miffed Badgers (6-3) used early November comment by Minnesota (7-2) QB Sandy Stephens to fire them up. Stephens launched 80y TD pass to E Tom Hall on game's opening play, but Gophers' erratic passer suffered Badgers DB Jim Nettles' 60y INT TD RET in 3rd Q. Next came reserve FB Jimmy Jones' 22y TD run and Stephens' 2-pt run for Minnesota's 15-14 lead in 3rd Q. On last play of 3rd Q, Wisconsin bounced back as QB Ron Miller (19-37/297y, 2 TDs) tossed his 2nd TD pass (21y) to E Pat Richter (6/142y, 2 TDs), who set Big 10 record with 656y receiving for season. QB-K Jim Bakken, who earlier had missed 5 FGs, made 31y 3-ptr with 3:57 left in 4th Q for 23-15 lead for Badgers. Stephens next sparked 72y drive to his TD pass, but his attempt failed at 2-pt pass that could have tied it up. Afterward, Wisconsin T Dick Grimm gleefully waved fan's sign with Stephens' regrettable omission of Badgers: "Sandy said, 'We have three tough games left—Michigan State, Iowa and Purdue.'"

Ohio State 50 MICHIGAN 20: As Minnesota fell, Ohio State (8-0-1) wrapped up Big 10 crown going away. FB Bob Ferguson rushed 30/152y, scored 2 TDs that gave Buckeyes 14-0 lead in 2nd Q. Michigan (6-3) HB Dave Raimey countered with 90y KO TD RET, but Ohio State HB Paul Warfield matched that with 69y TD run that brought it to 21-6 at H. Ohio State bolted for 29 pts in 4th Q, sparked by QB Joe Sparma's 80y TD pass to HB Bob Klein. Sore feelings resulted in last 34 secs when coach Woody Hayes called for Sparma's long pass to Warfield that set up Sparma's TD pass and 2-pt pass to E Sam Tidmore. "We were going for national recognition," said Hayes, brushing it off. "One or two more touchdowns aren't going to hurt (coach) Bump Elliott or Michigan." Hayes' remarks and late-game surge for additional pts remained sore subject in Ann Arbor for several years.

Missouri 10 KANSAS 7: Slim Jayhawkers' hope for Orange Bowl flickered out when Missouri (7-2-1) D held when it mattered most. Kansas (6-3-1) scored in 1st Q as FB Ken Coleman plowed over, and its 7-3 lead held until 1st min of 4th Q. Tigers FB Bill Tobin capped 80y scoring production with 3y TD sweep. Missouri survived late scare with lost FUM at own 25YL, but tough DTs Bucky Wegener and Ed Blaine pushed Jayhawks back to 32YL.

Ucla 10 SOUTHERN CALIFORNIA 7: Steady rain turned Coliseum into mudbath and marked 1st battle of L.A. to settle Rose Bowl berth since 1952. UCLA (7-3) TB Mike Haffner ran 61y to set up 31y FG by TB-K Bobby Smith (24/49y rushing) in 2nd Q. Trojans (4-5-1) FB-P Ernie Jones punted 60y beauty that died in mud at Bruins 4YL in 2nd Q. So, from his 8YL, Bruins sub TB Keith Jensen's QK flew to Trojans 48YL where QB-S Pete Beathard fielded it and circled to sideline to find squadron of Southern Califronia blockers and 52y free ride to TD and 7-3 H lead. USC DG Britt Williams recovered FUM at Bruins 37YL in 3rd Q, but rugged UCLA D stiffened at its 21YL, and Trojans K Carl Skvarna hit left upright with 38y FG try. Game soon turned on Bruins DE Mel Profit's deflection of Beathard's short pass for HB Willie Brown. UCLA DT Joe Bauwens lumbered 15y with tipped pass to USC 33YL. After having been thrown back on 4 scoring attempts other than its FG, UCLA finally tallied on Smith's 6y run. Smith's TD dash gave him new school season's scoring record of 85 pts. Bruins emerged from their D shell long enough to counter advantage of Jones' punt to their 2YL by sending Thompson sloshing off on 42y run through RT. Nail-biting win locked up Rose Bowl invitation for UCLA.

Oregon State 6 OREGON 2: Hot Oregon State (5-4) used tight D in frigid weather to win its 4th straight game. Bobbled pitchout tossed by Oregon (4-6) QB Doug Post for HB Larry Hill was recovered by Beavers on Ducks 20YL in 2nd Q. Oregon State QB Terry Baker passed 19y to E Roger Johnson, and FB Tom Gates plunged for TD. After being completely dominated in 1st H, Oregon turned tables in 2nd H. Beavers handed Ducks 2 pts as snap sailed over head of P Don Kasso and through EZ. After Oregon State's free-kick, Ducks' sleek HB Mel Renfro bit off big chunks of ground to 5YL, but Beavers D jelled to stop Renfro at 1YL on 4th down. Post completed 32y pass to E Paul Bauge to Beavers 34YL in 4th Q, but Oregon State HB-DB Bill Monk picked off Renfro's option pass at his 30YL.

WASHINGTON 21 Washington State 17: Spunky Cougars (3-7) scored early on QB Dave Mathieson's 34y pass to HB Jim Boylan, and Washington State led most of way, partly because of its blocked x-pt when Washington (5-4-1) made it 7-6 in 1st Q. Huskies TD came on QB Pete Ohler's 31y pass to E Gary Clark. FB George Reed lugged ball for most of 45y TD drive that gave Wazzu 14-6 lead with 1:12 left in H. But, Washington made 2 long-gainers as Ohler sprinted 50y, and QB Kermit Jorgensen flipped 28y TD pass to HB Nat Whitmyer to pull within 14-12 at H. After trade of 3rd Q FGs, Huskies had to hustle to beat clock at end: clutch HB Charlie Mitchell raced 23y to score with 1:30 left.

AP Poll November 27

1 Alabama (26)	459	6 Colorado	169
2 Ohio State (21)	452	7 Minnesota	168
3 Louisiana State (1)	366	8 Michigan State	139
4 Texas	354	9 Arkansas	131
5 Mississippi (1)	272	10 Missouri	31

Others with votes: Penn State, Rutgers, Wisconsin, UCLA, Utah State, Arizona, Purdue, Rice, Georgia Tech, Michigan, Duke, Iowa, Syracuse, Wyoming, Kansas

December 2, 1961

Navy 13 Army 7 (Philadelphia): In pre-game antics, Army D-2 Co. mocked Navy (7-3) K Greg Mather, using imposter to whiff PK. Unamused, real E-P Greg Mather punted 53y to Cadet 1YL and later as K put Middies on board with 32y FG in 2nd Q. Cadets (6-4) went 76y to TD in 3rd Q, 56y coming on pass from QB Dick Eckert to HB Tom Culver. FB Al Rushatz plunged over to give Army 7-3 lead. Navy sub QB Bob Hecht hit HB Jim Stewart with 38y pass to set up HB Bill Ulrich for 13y TD run. K Mather added 36y FG as icing for 3rd Navy win in row over Army. Soon to be gone was Cadets coach Dale Hall, who suffered unfortunate fate of many coaches: he believed he could follow his mentor who was legendary, in Army's case, Earl Blaik.

DUKE 37 Notre Dame 13: Notre Dame (5-5) simply was incapable of stopping superior 261y passing of Duke (7-3), so year that started with great hope for Fightin Irish ended in mediocrity. After ND received opening KO, HB Angelo Dabiero tight-roped left sideline on 54y TD sprint. Late in 1st Q, Blue Devils sub QB Gil Garner (6-9/88y, 2 TDs) clicked on throws of 14, 6, and 22y to poise his own 1y TD sneak. Garner followed with 21y TD pass to E Zo Potts midway in 2nd Q, and teams traded TDs with failed conv attempts: 1y plunge by Notre Dame FB Mike Lind and 16y clock-beating TD pass to E Pete Widener by Duke QB Walt Rappold (12-19/173y, 2 TDs). So, Duke led 20-13 at H. After K Billy Reynolds booted 31y FG in 3rd Q, Devils fired another pair of TD passes: Rappold linked with E Wes Crisson for 11y TD pass and Garner hit HB Jay Wilkinson for 12y TD pass.

GEORGIA TECH 22 Georgia 7: With relative ease, Georgia Tech (7-3) thrashed rival Bulldogs (3-7). HB Billy Williamson, whose 115y rushing would come within 3y of Georgia's entire O total, led ground attack on 1st possession which ended in QB Stan Gann's scoot for 8y TD. QB-K Billy Lothridge soon added FG for 10-0 lead, and Lothridge combined with Williamson for play-of-day: In 2nd Q, Lothridge ran 12y to 18YL where, when hemmed in, he lateraled to TD-bound Williamson. QB Jake Saye hit HB Billy Knowles with 30y TD pass to cap only Bulldogs drive of day: 6 plays for 67y.

ALABAMA 34 Auburn 0 (Birmingham): Awesome Alabama (10-0) D threw its 5th straight shutout at list of opponents, achieving its 1st undefeated season since 1945. In 1st 5 mins of game, ever-present Bama LB Darwin Holt grabbed FUM by Tigers FB John McGeever, and Crimson Tide FB Billy Richardson quickly scored from 11YL. QB Pat Trammell ran and passed for 2nd Q TDs. Auburn (6-4) threatened twice in 4th Q, losing ball on downs inside 1YL and on EZ INT of errant pass by QB Bobby Hunt.

Mississippi 37 MISSISSIPPI STATE 7: Rolling to big Egg Bowl win, Mississippi (9-1) gained 420y to capture national crown for this season's most prolific O with 418.5y per game avg. Rebels' win brought with it Cotton Bowl bid to play Texas, whose coach, Darrell Royal attended and lauded Mississippi. Rebs FB Billy Ray Adams scored on runs of 1 and 18y. Behind 13-0 in 2nd Q, Bulldogs (5-5) engineered their only drive, going 63y to QB Billy Hill's 9y fake-pass and run for TD. Ole Miss quickly retaliated on QB Glynn Griffing's 68y TD pass to E Ralph Smith. Rebels' D sparkled, holding Mississippi State to 134y O and forcing 5 TOs.

Miami 15 FLORIDA 6: Canes (7-3) HB John Bahen muffed fair catch at 25YL in 2nd Q, and Florida (4-5-1) scored on FB Don Goodman's run after QB Bobby Dodd hit fake-FG pass to HB Lindy Infante to 4YL. Bahen more than redeemed himself on following KO, cutting to sideline on specially-plotted RET and bolting 93y to earn 6-6 tie. Critical and fascinating play came in 3rd Q when Miami QB George Mira followed his 40y completion with left-handed TD lob to HB Nick Spinelli. Mira threw lefty because Gators DE Sam Holland, in his pass-rush charge, had draped himself on Mira's right (throwing) shoulder.

OKLAHOMA 21 Oklahoma State 13: After opening season with 5 losses, Oklahoma (5-5) completely reversed negative trend with its 5th victory in row, accomplishment that earned AP's "greatest sports comeback of 1961." Despite his mammoth success in Norman in 1950s, coach Bud Wilkinson always took pride in his 1961 team's turnaround. Oklahoma State (4-6) FB-LB Bob Adcock tackled Sooners HB Jimmy Carpenter for early safety, but subsequent free-kick FUM was recovered by Sooners E Jim McCoy. QB Bob Page soon put Oklahoma up 7-2, but Cowboys K Ted Davis' FG made it 7-5 at H. FUM RECs set up 2 Sooners TDs in 3rd Q, 2nd of which truly turned result toward OU. It came near Sooners GL as HB-DB Mike McClellan made saving tackle of Oklahoma State's runaway HB Jim Dillard, who llst critical FUM.

Colorado 29 AIR FORCE 12: Late in 2nd Q, anxious Colorado (9-1) trailed Air Force (3-7) 12-7 thanks to 2 short TD runs by Falcons QB Mike McNaughton. But, Bison went 82y to E Jerry Hillebrand's 11y TD catch from QB Gale Weidner with 42 ticks showing on H clock. When HB Teddy Woods raced 52y with 2nd H KO, Buffs were able to exercise their superior manpower for decisive score and 21-12 lead. Falcons coach Ben Martin was left to marvel: "Boy, would I love to have material like that."

Final AP Poll December 4

1 Alabama (26)	452	11 Missouri	18
2 Ohio State (20)	436	12 Purdue	15
3 Texas	348	13 Georgia Tech	12
4 Louisiana State (1)	335	14 Syracuse	11
5 Mississippi (1)	284	15 Rutgers	9
6 Minnesota	225	16 UCLA	7
7 Colorado	171	17t Rice	5
8 Michigan State	128	17t Penn State	5
9 Arkansas	105	17t Arizona	5
10 Utah State	33	20 Duke	4

1961 Conference Standings

Ivy League

Columbia	6-1
Harvard	6-1
Dartmouth	5-2
Princeton	5-2
Yale	3-4
Cornell	2-5
Pennsylvania	1-6
Brown	0-7

Atlantic Coast

Duke	5-1
North Carolina	4-3
Maryland	3-3
Clemson	3-3
North Carolina State	3-4
South Carolina	3-4
Wake Forest	3-4
Virginia	2-4

Southern

Citadel	5-1
Richmond	5-2
Virginia Military	4-2
West Virginia	2-1
Furman	2-2
George Washington	3-4
Virginia Tech	2-3
Davidson	1-4
William & Mary	1-6

Southeastern

Alabama	7-0
Louisiana State	6-0
Mississippi	5-1
Georgia Tech	4-3
Tennessee	4-3
Florida	3-3
Auburn	3-4
Kentucky	2-4
Georgia	2-5
Mississippi State	1-5
Tulane	1-5
Vanderbilt	1-6

Big Ten

Ohio State	6-0
Minnesota	6-1
Michigan State	5-2
Purdue	4-2
Wisconsin	4-3
Michigan	3-3
Iowa	2-4
Northwestern	2-4
Indiana	0-6
Illinois	0-7

Big Eight

Colorado	7-0
Missouri	5-2
Kansas	5-2
Oklahoma	4-3
Iowa State	3-4
Oklahoma State	2-5
Nebraska	2-5
Kansas State	0-7

Missouri Valley

Wichita	3-0
North Texas State	1-2
Cincinnati	1-2
Tulsa	1-2

Mid-American

Bowling Green	5-1
Western Michigan	4-1-1
Miami (Ohio)	3-2
Ohio	3-2-1
Toledo	2-4
Marshall	1-4
Kent State	1-5

Southwest

Texas	6-1
Arkansas	6-1
Rice	5-2
Texas A&M	3-4
Texas Christian	2-4-1
Baylor	2-5
Texas Tech	2-5
Southern Methodist	1-5-1

Border

Arizona State	3-0
West Texas State	3-1
New Mexico State	2-1
Texas Western	1-3
Hardin-Simmons	0-4

Skyline Eight

Utah State	5-0-1
Wyoming	5-0-1
Utah	3-3
New Mexico	3-3
Montana	2-4
Brigham Young	2-4
Colorado State	0-6

AAWU

UCLA	3-1
Washington	2-1-1
Southern California	2-1-1
Stanford	1-3
California	1-3

1961 Bowl Games

Gotham Bowl (Dec. 9): Baylor 24 Utah State 9

Soon-to-fail bowl experiment in New York City was staged before small shivering crowd in Manhattan's decaying Polo Grounds, already home of AFL's poorly attended games of New York Titans. Speaking of pro football, Utah State (9-1-1) lineup sported array of future pros in Ts Merlin Olsen and Clyde Brock, QB Bill Munson, QB-K Jim Turner, E Lionel Aldridge and HB Jack Larscheid. But, Aggies were no match for SWC's Baylor (6-5), which on this day at least played to its potential. Raft of FUMs ruined Aggies: Bears HB Ronnie Bull's TD run followed C-LB Bill Hicks' early REC at Utah State 45YL, and K Carl Choate's FG made it 10-0 after Larscheid's punt FUM at own 5YL. Utah State struck back on K Turner's 3rd Q FG, but Baylor's sharp sub QB Don Trull (11-16/116y, TD) took over to lead 20y trip after another FUM and 83y drive, all on his aerial prowess. Baylor's last TD came on 38y pass from Trull to E Tom Plumb.

Liberty Bowl (Dec. 16): Syracuse 15 Miami 14

Intriguing matchup of future Big East foes pitted HB-extraordinaire Ernie Davis of Syracuse (8-3) vs. Miami soph QB aerial artist George Mira. Bone-numbing cold prompted Miami cheerleaders to decorate seating section with plastic palms for sparse, but amused Philadelphia crowd. Hurricanes HB Nick Spinelli sped 60y with punt RET, and Mira added 2-pt pass for 14-0 lead just before H. Davis ignored whatever Heisman jinx was due him and rushed 30/140y, scored 3rd Q TD, and was tagged by QB Dave Sarette's 2-pt pass. Davis' 2-pt catch cut Miami's margin to 14-8. Davis lugged ball 4/24y on winning 51y drive. Sarette passed for 7y TD to HB Dick Easterly, and E-K Ken Ericson kicked decisive x-pt.

Bluebonnet Bowl (Dec. 16): Kansas 33 Rice 7

Jayhawks (7-3-1) rolled up 293y on ground with soph FB Ken Coleman spear-heading attack with 18/107y. Coleman's 2 TD runs provided Kansas with 12-7 H lead. Rice (7-4) QB Randall Kerbow pitched 10-16/156y and 5y TD pass to E Johnny Burrell, which had given Owls short-lived 7-6 lead in 1st Q. Kansas QB-P John Hadl (7-10/64y, 2 INTs), who denied having already signed with San Diego Chargers, ran 41y with fake punt in 1st H, directed 3 TD drives in 2nd H and called reverses that sprung HB Rodger McFarland for 9 and 12y TD runs. Jayhawks G-LB Elvin Basham sparkled on D and was voted game's top lineman. Bluebonnet would be last bowl game until 2006 season for Rice Owls.

Gator Bowl (Dec. 30): Penn State 30 Georgia Tech 15

Galen Hall, mature sr QB for Penn State (8-3) and future head coach of Florida, sparked Nittany Lions' avalanche of pts, most relinquished by Georgia Tech (7-4) since 1950. But 1st, Engineers erected 9-0 advantage. Scoring opened with safety called against Hall for intentionally grounding pass in EZ while trying to avoid Tech's pass rush. Joe Auer, Georgia Tech's free-spirited HB, soon turned in 1st of his 2 brilliant broken field runs. Auer dodged 2 DBs and raced 68y for 2nd Q TD, longest run in Gator Bowl history to date. Hall soon took charge, driving Penn State 78 and 87y via air to pair of TDs. In 3rd Q, Lions superb DE Dave Robinson recovered FUM at Georgia Tech 35YL after flattening passer. Hall quickly threw his 3rd TD pass. Auer made another

elusive TD gem to cut margin to 20-15 in 4th Q, but Engineers lost ball at own 12YL on each of their next 2 possessions. Lions tacked on FG and FB Buddy Torris' TD plunge.

Orange Bowl: Louisiana State 25 Colorado 7

Army was looking for new coach, and rumors swirled around LSU's Paul Dietzel, former West Point asst. Instead of showing up flat amid such speculation, Tigers (10-1) ferociously forced countless Colorado (9-2) errors. Perhaps LSU was fired up by bulletin board full of news clips collected by Dietzel. "Those Colorado kids talked a lot; I've never had so much ammunition...," he said. Dietzel also spotted flaw in Buffs kicking game: C tipped his punt snaps. After Tigers useful HB-K Wendell Harris kicked 30y FG in 1st Q, LSU stopped Buffs, and Bayou Bengals C Gary Kinchen pored up middle to block punt through EZ for safety. LSU's passing attack failed it early in 2nd Q as Buffs FB-DB Loren Schweninger made INT and raced 59y to TD and 7-5 lead. LSU regained lead at 11-7 after 82y march. Crowning glory came from LSU E Gene Sykes' block of another punt by E-P Chuck McBride in 3rd Q, which Sykes recovered for TD and formidable 25-7 lead. LSU D held Colorado to 24y rushing as it was spearheaded by G-LB Roy Winston. Dietzel, it turned out, was indeed headed to West Point to coach Army, but was not to be nearly as successful as he had been at LSU.

Sugar Bowl: Alabama 10 Arkansas 3

Alabama (11-0) justified its pre-bowl national championship with win over surprisingly tough Arkansas (8-3). Midway in 1st Q, Tide traveled 79y to TD. FB Mike Fracchia charged 43y to Porkers 12YL, with FB-DB Billy Joe Moody making saving tackle. Alabama QB Pat Trammell rolled out for TD run on next play. K Tim Davis made it 10-0 in 2nd Q with 32y FG. Bama D-front, led by T Billy Neighbors and C-LB Lee Roy Jordan, played decisively when it mattered most: Arkansas reached Bama 10YL in 2nd Q after HB Paul Dudley swept for 39y. On 2nd down, Jordan spilled Dudley for 4y loss, and Arkansas missed FG following poor pass on 3rd down. Razorbacks K Mickey Cissell kicked 23y FG in 3rd Q after Hogs were halted at 7YL. Arkansas made exciting late bid: HB Lance Alworth, who had slipped on soggy turf all day, broke free on long pass from Alabama 40YL, but QB George McKinney's bomb just eluded Alworth's fingertips. Moments later, Bama HB Butch Wilson made INT just inches from his own GL as he tumbled OB with ball in his arms. Trammell killed clock from shadow of his own goalpost with miniscule sneaks.

Cotton Bowl: Texas 12 Mississippi 7

Had it not been for late-season heartbreaking upsets suffered by each team, Texas (10-1) and Mississippi (9-2) might have played for clear-cut national championship as no. 1 vs. no. 2. Expected barrage of pts never materialized, even though Longhorns and Rebels finished season 4th and 1st respectively in total O with Texas tabbed as 2nd in national rushing and Ole Miss 2nd in passing. Even though they were outgained 319y to 183y, Longhorns employed solid pass D. HB-DB Jerry Cook set Cotton Bowl record with 3 pickoffs, which included vital EZ pickoff, which was tipped by G-LB Johnny Treadwell. That INT by Cook saved potential TD just before H. Earlier INT, diving effort by HB-DB Tommy Ford at Ole Miss 34YL, had set up 1st Longhorns TD in 1st Q: HB James Saxton carried it over from 1YL after FB Pat Culpepper and HB David Russell, normally D specialists, made key runs. Ace Rebels T Jim Dunaway blocked conv kick to keep it at 6-0. QB Mike Cotten accumulated all of Steers' sparkling 72y drive in 2nd Q, passing 21y, running 27y, and finally hitting HB Jack Collins with 24y TD pass for 12-0 margin. Ole Miss got its score in 3rd Q as QB Glynn Griffing similarly hogged glory by passing for 37y, running for 37y, and then hitting E Reed Davis for 20y TD. Rebels threatened in 4th Q, making it to Longhorns 23YL, but Texas DE Bob Moses, voted game's outstanding lineman, spilled Griffing for loss on 4th down.

Rose Bowl: Minnesota 21 UCLA 3

This was only year in last 16 that Big 10 was not under contract to face West Coast representative. Ultimately, 30 teams were considered as possible foe for so-so host team UCLA (7-4), including Alabama and Navy. But, AAWU stuck with tradition and looked to Midwest despite Big 10's failure to renew contract and Ohio State's turndown of Pasadena's bid. Redeeming themselves from previous year's Rose Bowl disappointment, Golden Gophers (8-2) proved to be excellent stand-in. Minnesota spotted UCLA early FG as Bruins WB Kermit Alexander added 32 and 9y reverse runs to his 31y opening KO RET. But, Gophers held at 6YL, and TB-K Bobby Smith glanced 23y FG through off left upright. Minnesota controlled ball rest of day, sending Bruins to their 5th straight defeat in Rose Bowl. Gophers A-A QB Sandy Stephens scored 1st of his 2 TD runs in 1st Q gift: Bruins FB Almose Thompson lost FUM at his own 6YL to FB-DB Judge Dickson, and Stephens scored in 3 plays for all pts Minnesota would need. With several runners sharing load, Gophers moved 75 and 84y for additional scores and piled up 297y to 107y O advantage. Minnesota, led by outstanding DE John Campbell and DTs Carl Eller and Bobby Bell, ruined Bruins with big D plays that totaled 62y in losses.

1961 Top Performance Formula

1 Alabama	1.7292
2 Louisiana State	1.6631
3 Texas	1.6440
4 Mississippi	1.6418
5 Ohio State	1.5867
6 Minnesota	1.4842
7 Colorado	1.4603
8 Michigan State	1.4555
9 Arizona	1.4223
10 Penn State	1.4138
11 Arkansas	1.3964
12 Michigan	1.3650
13 Kansas	1.3609
14 Georgia Tech	1.3557
15 Syracuse	1.3545
16 Utah State	1.3433
17 Missouri	1.3170
18 Duke	1.3143
19 Arizona State	1.3114
20 Miami	1.2995

1961 Top Opponent Records

1 Mississippi State	.6446
2 Michigan	.6438
3 Georgia Tech	.6311
4 North Carolina State	.6222
5 Texas Christian	.6211
6 Illinois	.6200
7 Rice	.6095
8 Minnesota	.6012
9 Louisiana State	.5922
10 Notre Dame	.5920
11 Arkansas	.5885
12 Mississippi	.5882
13 Oklahoma	.5860
14 Nebraska	.5826
15 Penn State	.5792
16 Pittsburgh	.5789
17 Texas Tech	.5772
18 North Carolina	.5761
19 California	.5753
20 Oregon	.5739

1961 Out-of-Conference Records

	W-L	Percentage	Bowl W-L
Big Ten	20-6-1	.7593	1-0
Southeastern	29-14-1	.6705	2-2
Southwest	14-9-2	.6000	2-2
Big Eight	12-9-3	.5625	0-1
Atlantic Coast	15-13	.5357	0-0
AAWU	12-18-1	.4032	0-1

1961 Individual Statistical Leaders

RUSHING YARDS	Attempts	Yards	Avg.
Preacher Pilot, New Mexico State	191	1278	6.7
Pete Pedro, West Texas State	137	976	7.1
Bob Ferguson, Ohio State	202	938	4.6
Dave Hoppmann, Iowa State	229	920	4.0
James Saxton, Texas	107	846	7.9
Ernie Davis, Syracuse	150	823	5.5
Jack Larscheid, Utah State	121	773	6.4
Bobby Thompson, Arizona	103	752	7.3
Earl Stoudt, Richmond	162	704	4.4
Mike Haffner, UCLA	117	696	6.0

PASSING YARDS	Completions	Attempts	Yards	Pct.
Ron Miller, Wisconsin	104	198	1487	52.5
Chon Gallegos, San Jose State	117	197	1480	59.4
Eddie Wilson, Arizona	79	154	1294	51.3
Gale Weidner, Colorado	73	162	1101	45.1
Pat McCarthy, Holy Cross	76	165	1081	46.1
Matt Szykowny, Iowa	79	139	1078	56.8
Ron Klemick, Navy	86	183	1045	47.0
Pat Trammell, Alabama	75	133	1035	56.4
John Furman, Texas Western	84	180	1026	46.7
George Mira, Miami	81	172	1000	47.1

RECEIVING YARDS	Catches	Yards
Pat Richter, Wisconsin	47	817
Hugh Campbell, Washington State	53	723
Bill Miller, Miami	43	640
Larry Vargo, Detroit	32	601
Al Snyder, Holy Cross	38	558
Tom Hutchinson, Kentucky	32	543
Hal Bedsole, Southern California	27	525
Jim Stewart, Navy	23	498
Buddy Iles, Texas Christian	31	479
Bobby Thompson, Arizona	25	468

1961 Consensus All-America Team

End:	Gary Collins, Maryland
	Bill Miller, Miami
Tackle:	Billy Neighbors, Alabama
	Merlin Olsen, Utah State
Guard:	Roy Winston, Louisiana State
	Joe Romig, Colorado
Center:	Alex Kroll, Rutgers
Backs:	Sandy Stephens, Minnesota
	Ernie Davis, Syracuse
	James Saxton, Texas
	Bob Ferguson, Ohio State

Other All-America Choices

End:	Jerry Hillebrand, Colorado
	Bob Mitinger, Penn State
	Pat Richter, Wisconsin
	Greg Mather, Navy
Tackle:	Bobby Bell, Minnesota
	Ed Blaine, Missouri
	Don Talbert, Texas
Guard:	Dave Behrmann, Michigan State
Center:	Bill Van Buren, Iowa
	Ron Hull, UCLA
Backs:	Roman Gabriel, North Carolina State
	Lance Alworth, Arkansas
	John Hadl, Kansas
	Billy Ray Adams, Mississippi

1961 Heisman Trophy Vote

Ernie Davis, senior halfback, Syracuse	824
Bob Ferguson, senior fullback, Ohio State	771
James Saxton, senior halfback, Texas	551
Sandy Stephens, senior quarterback, Minnesota	543
Pat Trammell, senior quarterback, Alabama	362

Other Major Award Winners

Maxwell (Player)	Bob Ferguson, senior fullback, Ohio State
Outland (Lineman)	Merlin Olsen, senior tackle, Utah State
Walter Camp (Back)	Ernie Davis, senior halfback, Syracuse
Knute Rockne (Lineman)	Joe Romig, senior guard, Colorado
AFCA Coach of the Year	Paul "Bear" Bryant, Alabama

The Year of a Long-Awaited No. 1 vs. No. 2 Matchup, Unrest at Ole Miss, and the Sportsman of the Year

More than 16 years had passed between November 9, 1946, when AP no. 1-ranked Army and no. 2-ranked Notre Dame tied 0-0 at New York's Yankee Stadium, and January 1, 1963, when no. 1-ranked Southern California (11-0) met no. 2-ranked Wisconsin (8-2) in the Rose Bowl to conclude the 1962 season. Since AP started its poll of sportswriters in 1936, it was by far the longest gap between meetings of the top two teams, as more than 25,000 major games were played during the long intervening stretch.

It was worth the wait. USC edged Wisconsin 42-37 in one of the greatest games ever played. The Badgers made a 23-point fourth quarter comeback from a 42-14 deficit in the gathering gloom of Pasadena, mostly on passes from quarterback Ron VanderKelen to end Pat Richter. VanderKelen more than doubled the existing Rose Bowl passing yardage record by throwing for 401 yards.

Mississippi (10-0) completed a fabulous four-year run in which the Rebels registered a 39-3-1 record including bowl games. Although their regular season opponents sported only a .449 winning percentage in 1962, Ole Miss inflicted the only defeats on good opposition presented by Memphis State (8-1) and Louisiana State (9-1-1). In the Sugar Bowl, Mississippi beat Arkansas (9-2) 17-13 after having the Razorbacks tie it twice at 3-3 and 10-10. The win gave the SEC, 25-12-6 outside its own corral in the 1962 regular season, a 4-1 record in its bowl games: LSU upset Texas (9-1-1) for new coach Charlie McClendon in the Cotton, Alabama (10-1), with sophomore quarterback Joe Namath and senior linebacker Lee Roy Jordan, blanked Oklahoma (8-3) in the Orange, and Florida (7-4), inspired by Confederate flag decals stickered to their helmet fronts, surprised Penn State (9-2) in the Gator Bowl.

Ole Miss faced disquieting international attention during the fall as federal marshals were sent to campus to insure the safety of James Meredith, the school's first black student. White fullback Buck Randall made an impassioned speech, but failed to halt student rioting. In the end, perhaps it was the excellence of Rebel football that helped calm the campus.

Three Big Ten teams were in the pre-season top 10, but each failed to capture glory as no. 1 Ohio State (6-3), no. 4 Michigan State (5-4), and no. 7 Purdue (4-4-1) suffered early disappointments. Long before the frost was on the pumpkin, the Spartans were bumped off by Stanford (5-5), the Buckeyes lost to UCLA (4-6), and the Boilermakers were tied by Washington (7-1-2) and beaten by Miami of Ohio (8-2-1).

Oregon State (9-2) clearly had the season's most spell-binding individual in quarterback Terry Baker, who not only won the Heisman Trophy as the nation's total offense leader (2,276 yards) but was named Sportsman of the Year by *Sports Illustrated* for his excellence in athletics and scholarship. Baker was the only college football player so honored until Wake Forest fullback Chip Rives was tapped in a group of eight charity-minded athletes in 1987. In an icy Liberty Bowl in Philadelphia, Baker provided the only score in a 6-0 win over Villanova (7-3), sweeping into his own end zone and racing up the left sideline for 99 yards, a bowl record that still exists more than 40 years later and can be tied, but never be broken.

Preseason no. 2 Texas and Arkansas continued their nail-biting Southwest Conference matchups with the Longhorns taking a chest-pounding, last-minute win by 7-3 and turning it into Texas' first undisputed conference title since 1952. The Longhorns-Razorbacks rivalry was fast growing into the best of the entire 1960s decade. Texas won six of 10 1960s tilts, but most were by very narrow margins, and the 1969 national title faceoff was decided by one point.

Preseason no. 3 Alabama walloped Georgia early in the season and jumped to no. 1 on September 24. Sophomore quarterback Joe Namath still had healthy knees, was an excellent runner, and made decisions on offense that pleased one of football's most demanding coaches, Bear Bryant. The Crimson Tide would finish fifth in their defense of the national title, its only loss coming by one point to emotional Georgia Tech (7-3-1).

Coaching changes brought some interesting developments. Bob Devaney resurrected Nebraska (9-2) from 3-6-1 in 1961 to third place in the Big Eight and an exciting, but frigid win over Miami (7-4) in the short-lived Gotham Bowl in New York City. In the next 35 years, the Cornhuskers, under Devaney and his successor, Tom Osborne, were in the national spotlight consistently. Osborne receives much of the credit for Nebraska's greatness because it was under his watch that the Cornhuskers revitalized its defense in the 1990s with more speed. His teams dominated the 1990s, winning two national championships and playing for a third. But football historians need

look no further than Nebraska's losing records (19-40-1) from 1956 to 1961 to understand the contribution of Devaney as a great coach. Devaney built a 101-20-2 coaching record from 1962 to 1972, including his own national championships in 1970 and '71. Also, much of Osborne's success took place under Devaney's tenure as athletic director.

Lloyd Eaton, long forgotten in the 21st century, followed Devaney at Wyoming (5-5) in 1962. Eaton enjoyed considerable success in his nine years as head coach, including a trip to the Sugar Bowl trip after a 10-0 regular season in 1967. But, Eaton, a strong disciplinarian, was swallowed by confrontation with African-American players. A 1-9 record by his demoralized team ate his reputation alive in his last season in 1970.

Paul Dietzel arrived at West Point prepared to revive the glory days of coach Red Blaik, for whom he had been an assistant. But, the West Point cupboard was bare. With the pros offering increasingly rich contracts, great high school players looked to play where no post-grad military commitment would impede their pro gridiron careers. Dietzel fled in 1966 with a so-so 21-18-1 Army record. Charlie McClendon replaced Dietzel at LSU and stayed until 1979, running up a 137-59-7 record and coaching in 13 bowl games. Charlie Bradshaw, a protégé of Alabama's dynamic Bear Bryant, brought fierce training drills to Kentucky (3-5-2), a method of "finding boys willing to pay the price for success," an approach similar to what Bryant accomplished at Texas A&M in 1954. But times were already changing in 1962, and many unwilling and disillusioned Wildcat players quit the team. The sparsely-populated squad eked out late-season wins over rivals Vanderbilt (1-9) and Tennessee (4-6), but never achieved much success under Bradshaw amid its highly-competitive Southeastern Conference rivals.

Bill Yeoman, one-time West Point cadet under coach Blaik, arrived at Houston (7-4) and had the Cougars growling by the end of the decade on the way to the school's Southwest Conference glory years of the 1970s.

Milestones

■ Western Athletic Conference was formed from two conferences with charter group of Arizona, Arizona State, Brigham Young, New Mexico, Utah and Wyoming. Former Border Conference members Hardin-Simmons, New Mexico State, Texas Western and West Texas State went independent as did former Skyline Conference members Colorado State, Denver, Montana, and Utah State.

■ Washington State entered AAWU, becoming its sixth member.

■ Rutgers left Middle Atlantic Conference to become independent.

■ Eastern Michigan left tiny Interstate Conference to become independent.

■ Mississippi Southern College changed its name to University of Southern Mississippi.

■ Gen. Robert R. Neyland, coach at Tennessee (1936-40, 46-52) died on March 28. Neyland, elected to the Hall of Fame in 1956, had a record of 173-31-12. Art "Pappy" Lewis, who had 58-38-2 coaching record at West Virginia (1950-59), died during summer.

■ Longest winning streaks entering season:

Rutgers 12	Alabama 11	Louisiana State 10

■ Coaching changes:

	Incoming	Outgoing
Army	Paul Dietzel	Dale Hall
Boston College	Jim Miller	Ernie Hefferle
Colorado	Bud Davis	Sonny Grandelius
Colorado State	Mike Lude	Don Mullison
Hawaii	Jim Asato	Hank Vasconcellos
Houston	Bill Yeoman	Hal Lahar
Kentucky	Charlie Bradshaw	Blanton Collier
Louisiana State	Charlie McClendon	Paul Dietzel
Mississippi State	Paul Davis	Wade Walker
Nebraska	Bob Devaney	Bill Jennings
Southern Methodist	Hayden Fry	Bill Meek
Texas A&M	Hank Foldberg	Jim Myers
Texas Western	O.A. "Bum" Phillips	Ben Collins
Tulane	Tommy O'Boyle	Andy Pilney
Wyoming	Lloyd Eaton	Bob Devaney

Preseason AP Poll

1 Ohio State (41)	558	6 Mississippi (2)	207
2 Texas (1)	372	7 Purdue (1)	173
3 Alabama (3)	325	8 Duke	123
4 Michigan State (2)	278	9 Penn State	111
5 Louisiana State	227	10 Washington	86

Others receiving votes: Georgia Tech, Missouri, Southern California, Arkansas, Minnesota, Pittsburgh, Syracuse, Navy, Oregon, Oklahoma, Tennessee, UCLA, Army, Notre Dame, Wisconsin, Miami, Utah State

September 15, 1962

Miami 23 PITTSBURGH 14: Miami (1-0) QB George Mira set new Hurricanes O record with 248y. Mira passed 13-25/162y, TD, but it was his dashing runs that frustrated Panthers (0-1) big D line. In 1st 3 mins, Miami E-K Bob Wilson made 25y FG that was partially blocked by Pitt G Tom Brown. Pitt FB Rick Leeson raced 45y, but was tripped up by FB-DB Nick Ryder's shoestring tackle at 3YL. Miami made GLS, defending 1st-and-goal at 3YL: 3 runs lost 1y, and Pittsburgh-native T Joe Smerdel (7 tackles) rushed hard on 4th down to spoil Panthers QB Jim Traficant's pass for HB Paul Martha. Next, Miami went 97y march in 13 plays to HB Nick Spinelli's 1y leaping TD. Martha threw 4th down 9y TD to E Al Grigallunas, but motion PEN killed Pitt's 2-pt run attempt. Ahead 10-6 at H; Miami went 73y right after 2nd H KO: Spinelli, who rushed 10/52y, caught 6/67y, and was in on 10 tackles, tallied from 8YL after Mira turned E on option for 36y run. Pitt's 2nd TD came in last min as HB Ed Clark ran 4y and Traficant (9-20/124y) tossed 2-pt pass.

September 22, 1962

PENN STATE 41 Navy 7: Penn State (1-0) HB-DBs Al Gursky and Junior Powell each scored TD on O and each had long-range INT TD RET. Gursky's INT RET went for 77y, Powell's for 52y. Navy (0-1) HB John Sai raced 35y for 2nd Q TD. Nittany Lions QBs Pete Liske, Don Caum and Ron Coates, all "rookie pitchers in the World Series" according to asst reporter Joe Paterno, combined for 16-24/234y passing.

North Carolina State 7 NORTH CAROLINA 6: Accurate Wolfpack (1-0) FB-P Dave Houtz and T-P Glenn Sasser kept North Carolina (0-1) "penned tighter than hogs in a slaughterhouse," according to reporter George Cunningham in *Charlotte Observer*. Houtz punted Tar Heels back to their 12, 16, 21, 12, and 2YLs. Soph Sasser's 1st collegiate punt took advantage of new touchback rule in 1962: his 39y boot landed in Tar Heels EZ, but bounced back to 2YL where HB Tony Koszarsky downed it. QB Jim Rossi converted 3 passes to Es Don Montgomery and Bob Faircloth on 3rd downs to soar NC State to 67y TD flight after 2nd H KO. HB Joe Scarpati slipped through LG for 5y TD, and FB-K Roger Moore nailed conv kick. Barely out of its end and unable to get beyond Wolfpack 27YL, North Carolina finally cranked up its O from 12YL midway in 4th Q. Heels QB Junior Edge completed passes of 8, 11, 8, 14, 5 and, lastly, 30y TD to E Bob Lacey. With 4:23 on clock, UNC chose to kick x-pt, but K Edge's conv was wide.

ARMY 40 Wake Forest 14: "Pepsodent" Paul Dietzel made his much-anticipated coaching debut at West Point, bringing with him his 3-unit system and colorful, D-specialists Chinese Bandits. Cadet cheering section soon donned coolie hats in recognition of Bandits. QB Joe Blackgrove, part-time HB in 1961, directed 3 TD drives. Army (1-0) E-DE John Ellerson recovered 2nd Q FUM, then caught Blackgrove's 27y TD pass. Future coach, QB John Mackovic, hurled 2 scoring passes for Wake Forest (0-1).

ALABAMA 35 Georgia 0: Game would stir up much controversy year later when Alabama (1-0) coach Bear Bryant and Georgia (0-1) AD Wally Butts were accused of exchanging vital pre-game information. Uninformed telephone eavesdropper turned out to be wrong; lawsuits were settled in coaches' favors. Stepping onto national stage for 1st time, Crimson Tide soph QB Joe Namath, already somewhat brash and called "best player I've ever seen" by Bryant, passed 10-14/179y, 3TDs. Namath (10-14/178y, 3 TDs) rolled up 215y O until he was pulled with 21-0 lead in 3rd Q. Tide HB Cotton Clark caught 2 TD passes from Namath and added 4y TD run in 4th Q. Georgia (0-1) QB Larry Rakestraw (7-19/79y, INT) was chased relentlessly by Bama D, led by C-LB Lee Roy Jordan. Bulldogs managed only 37y rushing. In sign of changing times, 2 black men sat in grandstand reserved for whites, thus integrating sporting event in Birmingham for 1st time.

GEORGIA TECH 26 Clemson 9: Incomparable Georgia Tech (1-0) QB Billy Lothridge (7-10/128y passing, 11/49y rushing) had hand in team's every pt, passing for 3 TDs and scoring another on sneak. Clemson (0-1) enjoyed early 3-0 lead on 34y FG by K Rodney Rogers, but when coach Bobby Dodd sent in reserves, Lothridge included, late in 1st Q, game turned around. Yellow Jackets went 94y to sting Tigers with Lothridge's 23y TD pass to E Billy Martin early in 2nd Q. Lothridge found HB Joe Auer alone on sideline, and using block by E Joe Chapman, Auer scored for 13-3 lead. Closing out 1st H, Lothridge pitched 34y TD to wide-open E Ted Davis, after INT by Tech G-LB Brad Yates. Clemson backup QB Joe Anderson sparked 3rd Q advance, hitting 16,12, and 13y passes until HB Jerry Taylor slanted over from 6YL. Score stayed 20-9 as Taylor's 2-pt run attempt was rebuked.

LOUISIANA STATE 21 Texas A&M 0: Largest opening night crowd in Tiger Stadium history to date enjoyed coaching debut of Charlie McClendon. LSU (1-0) QB Jimmy Field (2-6/41y) passed sparingly but his 23y connection with E Jack Gates set up 1st H's only TD of 4y by Tiger HB Bo Campbell. Field also was team's top rusher with 7/44y. HB Jerry Stovall (8/31y, TD) sparked 2nd Tiger TD as he dashed 58y with 2nd H KO and scored on 2y smash. FB Steve Ward plunged for 4th Q TD. Texas A&M (0-1), also playing before largest crowd ever to see any Aggies opener. A&M showed effective passing game (10-19/203y) at times but suffered 3 INTs, including INT by DB Field. QB Jim Keller (6-9/62y, INT) was best of 4 passers sorted through by new Aggies coach Hank Foldberg.

INDIANA 21 Kansas State 0: Ground forces of Hoosiers (1-0) set tone for 296y rushing when smaller defenders of Kansas State (0-1). HB Marv Woodson got Indiana rolling with 45y punt RET to Wildcats 40YL in 2nd Q, and HB Nate Ramsey ran 24y to set up QB Woody Moore's sneak for TD. Hoosiers went 43y before H as HB Mike Lopa circled LE for 6y TD. Last Indiana TD came in 3rd Q after Woodson's 11y INT RET of K-State QB Doug Dusenbury's pass. Sub FB-K Tom Nowatzke, who booted all 3 x-pts, contributed to running game, and Ramsey skirted

left side for 18y TD. K-State was limited to 87y rushing and 8-21/48y, 3 INTs passing. It would be typical output in woeful 0-10 season for Wildcats as they scored only 6 pts in their opening 7 games.

NORTHWESTERN 37 South Carolina 20: Legendary Otto Graham's Wildcat record of 20 completions in single game was tied by QB Tommy Myers, who passed 20-24/275y, 2 TDs. Soph Northwestern (1-0) whiz Myers also ran for TD and fell only 20y short of Graham's single-game pass y mark. Gamecocks (0-1) struck in opening 2 mins of 1st Q for 6-0 lead as DB Ed Holler fell on FUM by NW FB Bill Swingle at Wildcats 23YL. On 2nd down, Carolina HB Sammy Anderson swept 21y to score. After falling behind 22-6, South Carolina got scores from 2 future pros: HB Billy Gambrell, who raced 78y for TD, and QB Dan Reeves, who ran 4y to score and added 2-pt pass.

ARKANSAS 34 Oklahoma State 7 (Little Rock): Slippery Arkansas (1-0) QB Billy Moore ran for 2nd Q TD that provided 7-0 lead and followed it up with 8y TD pass to E Jerry Lamb. When Moore got slightly roughed up by Oklahoma State (0-1), he was replaced by even-smaller soph QB Billy Gray. Gray pitched 69y TD pass to HB Mike Parker to build 20-0 lead in 2nd Q before Cowboys managed 65y TD drive, capped by TB Don Derrick's 1y run. Gray threw 2 more TD passes in 4th Q, and Hogs ended with 431y.

Missouri 21 CALIFORNIA 10: Golden Bears (0-1) halted Tigers with flexible Monsterman D and went ahead 7-0 on QB Randy Gold's passing. HB-K Tom Blanchard gave California 20y FG just 15 secs before H, it having been set up by G John Erby's FUM REC at Missouri 4YL when HBs Vince Turner and Carl Crawford mutually misplayed punt. In his varsity debut, Missouri (1-0) soph HB Johnny Roland rushed 20/171y and scored 3 TDs, his 2nd coming in form of 58y 3rd Q sprint that overcame California's 10-7 H lead. Bears' Erby was D stalwart but was injured prior to 71y clinching march, keyed by gains by Tigers FB Paul Underhill, that made it 21-10 on Roland's 7y TD pass reception.

OREGON STATE 39 Iowa State 35: Shootout developed between Beavers QB Terry Baker, total O leader in waiting, and Cyclones TB Dave Hoppmann, defending total O champ of 1961. Iowa State (0-1) used Hoppmann TD runs of 48 and1y to build 21-13 H and 28-13 3rd Q leads. Then, Oregon State (1-0) rallied for 33-28 lead behind Baker, who had 2 TD runs and TD pass. Iowa State regained edge at 35-33 on TD catch by WB Dave Limerick. Back came Beavers as Baker hit E Jerry Neil with game-winner with 29 secs left to play.

SOUTHERN CALIFORNIA 14 Duke 7: Supposedly overmatched USC (1-0) D-line held rushing attack of no. 8 Duke (0-1) to mere 55y. Trojans D also plucked 5 INTs, 2 by LB Damon Bame. Still, Blue Devils were able to score in 1st Q as HB Jay Wilkinson eluded 2 defenders and reached high to catch 25y TD pass from QB Gil Garner. Trojans matched score at 7-7 with QB Pete Beathard's short TD pass to TB Willie Brown in 2nd Q. USC looked to its other QB, Bill Nelsen, to loft 51y TD bomb to explosive E Hal Bedsole late in 2nd Q. In 2nd H, booming punts of FB-P Ernie Jones and INTs kept Duke off balance.

WASHINGTON 7 Purdue 7: Washington (0-0-1) moved smartly after opening KO, driving 76y in 11 plays, combination of HB Charlie Mitchell sweeps and QB Bill Siler option runs, to TD plunge by FB Bob Monroe. Somewhat stunned, no. 7 Purdue (0-0-1) was in trouble until Huskies began dropping ball in 2nd Q. HB-DB Dave Miller made his 2nd FUM REC in Washington end in matter of mins. Boilermakers FB Tom Yakubowski barreled in from 2YL. Then, each team's D seized control as E Dave Ellison and T Don Brumm starred for Purdue and G-LB Rick Redman for Washington. Huskies C-K Jim Norton missed 3 FGs, including 32y try that grazed upright just 26 secs from end.

AP Poll September 24

1 Alabama (24)	342	6 Michigan State	160
2 Ohio State (19)	298	7 Mississippi (1)	123
3 Texas (3)	261	8 Georgia Tech	103
4 Penn State (3)	253	9 Southern California	102
5 Louisiana State	207	10 Missouri	42

Others with votes: Arkansas, Oklahoma, Washington, Army, Purdue, Miami, Texas Christian, Northwestern, Duke, West Virginia, Florida State, North Carolina State, Utah, Minnesota, Syracuse, New Mexico State, Notre Dame, Maryland, UCLA

September 29, 1962

West Virginia 14 VIRGINIA TECH 0 (Richmond): Tobacco Festival's 14th annual football clash went to West Virginia (2-0), thanks to QB Jerry Yost, who scored and passed for Mountaineers TDs. After teams exchanges punts in 1st Q, WVU alternated runs by its backs—FB Tom Woodeshick and HBs Jim Moss and Glenn Holton—from its 12YL to its 44YL. Yost took off around E to sprint 56y to score. In 2nd Q, Yost had his only effective aerial spurt when he beat H clock with 5-9 passing in 70y drive. His 28y TD arrow to soph E Milt Clegg came with 3 secs left in 2nd Q. Virginia Tech (1-2) mounted 2 serious threats in 2nd H, but late in 3rd Q, 61y trip was stopped at Mountaineers 5YL when Gobblers FB Tom Walker was hammered by C-LB John Skinner. Hokies drive in 4th Q died at WVU 8YL.

AUBURN 22 Tennessee 21 (Birmingham): Volunteers (0-1) turned early breaks into 14-0 1st Q lead, 1st score coming when Auburn (1-0) punt snap went into EZ, and Tennessee G Joe Foxall hustled to make TD REC. Later in 1st Q, Vols TB George Canale returned punt 17y, then tried to hit his brother, WB Whit Canale, with pass that was interfered by Tigers DB David Burson. Another Vols TB, Mallon Faircloth, then rifled 12y TD pass through tip by Auburn defender to WB Wayne Waff. After 2nd Q FG brought Auburn within 14-3, Tigers HB Jimmy Burson returned 74y to set up HB Larry Lester's 1st of 2 TDs to allow Tigers to stalk to 14-9. Soph G Steve DeLong had clogged Auburn's running game in 15-14 1st H, but Tigers soph QB Jimmy Sidle gained 52y, then went back to riddling Tennessee with his passes (11-21/118y) in 2nd

H. By game's end, Vols had gained just 86y, but their only sustained drive in 3rd Q had provided 21-15 lead as George Canale threw TD pass. Lester's 4th down plunge later in 3rd Q tied it 21-21, and K Woody Woodall overcame 15y PEN to make winning conv kick.

MISSISSIPPI 14 Kentucky 0 (Jackson): Each team felt strong degree of strain: Ole Miss (2-0) was dealing with turmoil and national spotlight focused on its campus because of arrival of 1st African-American student, James Meredith. Kentucky (0-1-1) was at minimal manpower due to 53 of 88 players quitting during intense preseason camp of coach Charlie Bradshaw. While Gov. Ross Barnett spoke at H of loving Ole Miss customs and heritage, Mississippi's onerous D-line play of E Woody Dabbs and G-LB Don Dickson had held Wildcats to 4y rushing to that point. Rebels rambled for 228y rushing as QB Glynn Griffing had wedged over from 2YL in last min of 1st H for 7-0 lead. Ole Miss traveled 67y in 13 plays after 2nd H KO as HB Chuck Holloway took pitchout to tally from 6YL. Wildcats got good mileage out of QB Jerry Woolum (13-19/128y, INT), but E Tom Hutchinson couldn't hold EZ pass amid 2 defenders in 2nd Q. Another threat late in 3rd Q was halted by Rebels FB-LB Buck Randall's INT at 34YL.

LOUISIANA STATE 6 Rice 6: Oblivious to snarling LSU (1-0-1) pass rush, far-sighted Rice (0-0-1) soph QB Walter McReynolds completed 13-23/179y, TD, INT. On 4th-and-27 play after 2 sacks of McReynolds in 2nd Q, poised soph passer flipped screen to WB Gene Fleming, who stepped past falling Tigers to 30y TD. McReynolds, who played 60 mins and started only because veteran sr signal-callers Billy Cox and Randall Kerbow were out with injuries, made only single mistake. Bengals DE Gene Sykes picked off his pass. Since Owls had missed kick after Fleming's TD, it gave LSU K Lynn Amedee chance to win it with 3rd Q conv after HB Jerry Stovall's 6y TD run. But, x-pt snap was bobbled, keeping score at 6-6. Tigers HB Danny LeBlanc frustratingly lost FUM at Owls 10YL in game's final min.

Nebraska 25 MICHIGAN 13: Seizing control in 2nd Q, surprising Nebraska (2-0) used speed of its Dennis menaces—HB Steuwe and QB Claridge (8-15/119y)—to amplify 2 powerful TD runs by FB Bill "Thunder" Thornton, who barely played in 1st H. Michigan (0-1) lost 3 FUMs and frustratingly dropped 6 on-target passes. Wolverines swift HB Dave Raimey was held to 59y rushing by immense Huskers D-line, led by T Bob Brown. Michigan trailed only 7-6 at H asa QB Dave Glinka (7-17/68y) scrambled 8y for TD in 2nd Q, but his 2-pt pass attempt went astray. It was 1st meeting of Midwest giants since Wolverines won 20-0 in 1917.

STANFORD 16 Michigan State 13: Without major win in 4 years, Stanford (2-0) spotted Spartans (0-1) 7-0 lead on FB George Saimes' 1st Q run, which came on heels of HB Dewey Lincoln's tricky 4th down reverse run. But, big Indians line took command, shutting down middle runs. Stanford QB Steve Thurlow spread Michigan State D with his passing arrows, allowing FB Anthony DeLellis to tie it 7-7 on 2nd Q TD run. Indians HB-K Stan Lindskog added 24y FG for 10-7 lead at H. Biggest play in Stanford's upset came in 3rd Q on HB John Paye's 33y run off T Chuck Buehler's block, capping 78y drive that clinched it at 16-7.

WASHINGTON 28 Illinois 7: Trip to Seattle turned into unhappy 36th birthday for Illinois (0-1) coach Pete Elliott as Washington (1-0-1) spread its TDs over all 4 Qs. Huskies launched 69y drive after opening KO; most of y came on ground as Huskies launched their rushing attack that gained 232y by game's end. HB Charlie Mitchell crashed over from 2YL for 7-0 lead. QB Bill Siler (4-6/65y, TD, INT) tossed 31y TD pass to E Lee Bernhardt in 2nd Q and set up another TD with pass. Illinois pulled within 14-7 at H on 2y TD run by FB Dave Pike. But, Washington burst out from H relaxation to tally on HB Martin Wyatt's 4y TD run within opening 5 mins of 2nd H.

October 6, 1962

(Fri) MIAMI 7 Florida State 6: Miami (3-0) QB George Mira hit HB Nick Spinelli with 1st Q passes of 32 and 39y, last for TD. Surprisingly, Florida State (2-1-1) outpassed Hurricanes 178y to 122y, but 6 FUMs prevented any scoring other than K Doug Messer's pair of FGs. Miami G-LB Jim O'Mahoney collected 2 important FUMs in 4th Q, including last min REC at his own 12 YL.

Maryland 14 NORTH CAROLINA STATE 6: Maryland (3-0) was fast proving that it had outstanding D strength, having now allowed 8 pts in 3 games so far in 1962. In fact, vital TD for Terrapins was registered by D-specialist, DB Ken Ambrusko, who romped 78y with punt RET, using terrific block by LB Joe Hrezo, to fly last 50y without company. K John Hannigan's x-pt made it 7-0. North Carolina State (1-2) pieced together 75y march in 4th Q, but otherwise could claim only 89y total O. Wolfpack ground out 20-play drive for its TD as sub QB Bill Kriger ran 9/39y, including his lean-through TD when met by brick wall on sneak from 1YL. K Glenn Sasser's kick was wide, so NC State found itself down by 14-6, but it would get another chance. WR-DB Tom Brown, who had played masterful pitch-and-catch with QB Dick Shiner (11-16/101y, INT) on O with 8 receptions, picked off NC State QB Jim Rossi's pass at 14YL on game's last play. Maryland had moved ball well, but collected only on its 62y TD drive on its 2nd try of 3rd Q. Shiner hit 4 passes, including 22y toss to Brown to set up his 4y TD bootleg run to left.

Virginia Tech 20 Virginia 15 (Roanoke): Cavaliers (1-1) dribbled ball from their grasp at most inopportune moments as Gobblers (2-2) won for 5th straight time in Commonwealth's annual game. Wahoos were impressive early on trip into hostile Roanoke as QB Gary Cuozzo whipped his team 44y to his TD sneak for 7-0 lead in 1st Q. After Virginia's 2nd FUM of 2nd Q, VPI FB Gerald Bobbitte scored 1st of his 2 TD runs in 2nd Q, but Hokies QB Lacy Edwards was tossed for loss on 2-pt run. Edwards succeeded on 2-pt pass after Bobbitte's short TD run 6 mins into 3rd Q, so Virginia Tech led 14-7. Sub FB Phil Cary zipped 8y late in 3rd Q, and Gobblers led 20-7. With 3 defenders on his heels at beginning of 78y punt TD RET, UVa HB Terry Sieg crossed GL with 20y to spare, then proved he wasn't out of breath by making 2-pt run. Cavs took possession at their 17YL with little more than 4 mins to play, and 10 plays later they had reached Tech 12YL. Cuozzo, however, lost FUM to LB Bobbitte to snuff it.

Duke 28 FLORIDA 24 (Jacksonville): In less than 6 mins of 2nd Q, upset-minded Florida (1-2) racked up 267y and 21-0 lead on 7-7 passing, including 21y TD pass, by QBs Tom Shannon and Tom Batten. Gators FB Larry Dupree stumbled with no poor effect at beginning of 70y sideline scoring dash. Equal time-share Duke (2-1) QBs Walt Rappold and Gil Garner transformed near-so-so 11-24/102y passing performance in 1st H into perfect 10-10/133y in 2nd H. Gators never found way in last 30 mins to cover alternating Blue Devils wide-flanked Es Ed Chestnutt and Stan Crisson. Duke swarmed for matching 21-pt explosion in 3rd Q as Crisson caught 30y aerial to position HB Mark Leggett's 3y TD run. Duke HB-P Hagood Clarke's failed punt after low snap started Blues on 60y drive to E Pete Widener's 33y TD catch from Garner. Blue Devils T Dick Havens soon blocked Clarke's punt and soph FB Mike Curtis scored tying TD, and, in 4th Q, winning TD.

Louisiana State 10 GEORGIA TECH 7: Rugged scoreless stalemate in 1st H was broken open on 2nd H KO by LSU (2-0-1) HB Jerry Stovall, who faked handoff to QB Jimmy Field and raced untouched 98y. Georgia Tech (2-1) QB Billy Lothridge sparked tying 72y drive, capped by his TD pass to E Billy Martin. DB Lothridge dislodged FUM from LSU FB Charles Cranford on ensuing KO, but Tigers outscrambled Engineers for loose ball to begin march to QB-K Lynn Amedee's 24y FG. Georgia Tech HB Joe Auer, racing alone in LSU secondary at 10YL, dropped Lothridge bomb with 12 secs to play.

Southern California 7 IOWA 0: Hawkeyes (1-1) HB Willie Ray Smith lost FUM to USC DB Loren Hunt at his 24YL in 1st Q, and Trojans turned new-found prize into HB Ron Heller's 19y TD dash. Playing without injured QB Matt Szykowny, who went down with bad knee early in 1st Q, Iowa missed several opportunities in 4th Q: USC HB-DB Willie Brown made INT of sub Iowa QB Bob Wallace at own 1YL to stop thrust to 29YL, Hawkeyes missed by inches on HB Paul Krause's brilliant 4th down catch at USC 14YL, and HB Larry Ferguson gave away punt RET FUM in last 2 mins of game. Trojans played listlessly themselves, missing 3 FGs by K Tom Lupo, who kicked x-pt after Heller's TD that came 11:06 into 1st Q. Iowa suffered 7 TOs and displayed dreadful 1st H punting.

MINNESOTA 21 Navy 0: After scoreless tie week earlier with Missouri, mighty Minnesota (1-0-1) D tossed up its 2nd straight blanking and did so in fearsome style. Navy (1-2) QB Ron Kelimck was chased all over "The Brickhouse," succumbing to 11 sacks that totaled 120y lost. Gophers DEs John "Soup" Campbell and Bob Prawdzik, DTs Carl Eller and Bobby Bell, and blitzing LB Paul Benson made life miserable for Middies, who ended up with −31y in net rushing. Minnesota went 72y early in 1st Q as QB Duane Blaska threw only 1 pass, but rolled out for good gains and used HBs Bill Munsey and Jim Cairns until FB Jerry Jones plowed over from 3YL. Blaska hit Cairns for 20y TD on their 1st chance of 3rd Q after Cairns' 35y punt RET of long punt by Middies P Joe Ince (10/40.2y avg). Navy's only threat came late in 2nd Q after Munsey lost FUM at his 26YL. PEN helped move ball to Minny 6YL, but Campbell and Prawdzik sacked Klemick on 1st down, and Campbell batted ball out of Klemick's raised passing hand and recovered on 2nd down.

Purdue 24 NOTRE DAME 7: Purdue (1-0-1) methodically marched to 24-0 lead over Notre Dame (1-1) until newly-found Irish QB Denis Szot (5-10/54y, TD) sparkled in 4th Q performance. Boilermakers G-K Skip Ohl booted 27y FG in 2nd Q, and sub QB Ron DiGravio (3-8/84y, TD, INT) followed with 25y TD pitch to E Forest Farmer for 10-0 upper hand at H. ND QB-P Daryle Lamonica, 3-12/33y passing, punted OB at Purdue 6YL in 3rd Q. Boilers went 94y to score on DiGravio's 1y sneak, drive keyed by his 42y pass to E Sam Longmire. Szot then relieved Lamonica, but quickly lost FUM that led to FB Gene Donaldson's 21y TD run and 24-0 edge. Szot went to work, earning 17y TD pass to E Jim Kelly and losing another score to PEN after DB Bill Pfeiffer's FUM REC.

Arkansas 42 TEXAS CHRISTIAN 14: Effective D by Arkansas (3-0), spearheaded by Ts Dave Adams and Jerry Mazzanti, allowed only 2 inconsequential TDs by TCU (1-2) HB Jim Fauver. Hogs QB Billy Moore, who would end up lead SWC in rushing, scored twice. Moore also sent fire-breathing FBs Danny Brabham and Jesse Branch crashing to 3 more TDs. Arkansas HB Ken Hatfield, future college coach, ended matters with 71y TD punt RET.

Air Force 25 SOUTHERN METHODIST 20: Mustangs (0-3) QB Don Campbell fumbled on SMU's 1st scrimmage play, and LB Dave Sicks' REC allowed Air Force (2-1) to kick 22y FG by HB-K John Gavin. SMU's Campbell (5-10/117y, 3 TDs, INT) came back with TD passes in 1st, 2nd, and 4th Qs, but never got his Ponies closer than 9-7 or 16-14 because AFA marched 89y in 11 plays to E Dick Brown's 23y TD catch and 9-0 lead later in 1st Q. Combined 161y aerial attack of QBs Terry Isaacson (9-16/108y, TD), who threw TD to Brown, and Dave "The Dealer" Backus (3-5/53y) kept Falcons undeterred. Campbell rolled out for 44y gain that led to his 1st scoring throw, 9y to HB Tommy Brennan late in 1st Q. Teams traded TDs in 2nd Q: Air Force HB Darryl Bloodworth's 1y drive at end of 64y trip was countered by Campbell's 56y TD toss to HB Bill Gannon. Falcons took 18-14 lead when Mustangs HB-P Danny Thomas had to cover bad snap in EZ in 3rd Q. Another trade of TDs in 4th Q set stage for final excitement. SMU made it to 1st-and-goal at 9YL with 1:36 on clock, but sub QB Max Derden was spilled for 6y

loss on 1st down by Air Force LB Joe Rodwell and T Gary Fausti. PEN against Ponies and 2 pass knockdowns left them with 4th-and-goal at 20YL. Derden hit E Ray Green alone at 3YL, but DB Bloodworth made smashing tackle that stopped receiver dead in tracks.

ARIZONA STATE 24 Washington State 24: Conv attempts for 2 pts, rarely better than .400 proposition, served rallying Washington State (2-0-1) well. After disastrous 1st H in which they gained only 48y, Cougars took to air to score 3 TDs and add trio of 2-pt convs to tie surprised Arizona State (2-0-1). Sun Devils had struck after opening KO as HB Charley Taylor (14/119y) skirted E for 39y to set up his duplicate 7y sweep for TD. Up 14-0 at H and possessing 259y to 48y stat edge, ASU looked totally dominant. Bad punt snap by C Steve Fedorchak allowed 3rd Q TD run by Washington State's FB George Reed. Cougars T Larry Reisbig outhustled ASU DB Larry Facchine to 2-pt REC of Reed's FUM into EZ. After T-K John Seedborg kicked FG early in 4th Q for 17-8 Devils lead, Cougars took to air as QB Dave Mathieson (13-24/223y TD, INT) hit E Gerry Shaw with 19y TD pass. Reed ran for 2 pts, so Cougars trailed 17-16. ASU QB John Jacobs and E Dale Keller combined on their 2nd TD pass for 24-16 lead, but fading Devils crumbled before 71y aerial trip by WSU. Mathieson lit fire with 13y pass to HB Herm McKee, but was benched with injury. Sub QB Dale Ford finished rally with 35y pass to Shaw. Reed, 2-pt specialist, barreled over for conv and late-game tie.

UCLA 9 Ohio State 7: Early and late, UCLA (1-0) took advantage of its only trips into Ohio State (1-1) territory. On game's 2nd play, Ohio FB Dave Francis lost FUM to Bruins DT Dave Gibbs. Bruins HB Kermit Alexander immediately raced 45y off LT Joe Bauwens' block to rousing TD for 2-TD underdogs. Early in 2nd Q, QB Joe Sparma, future Detroit Tigers pitcher, put no. 1 Buckeyes up 7-6 on 6y TD pass to E Matt Snell. Ohio QB John Mummey later crafted 78 and 65y drives, which were stopped at 3YL when Mummey fumbled C-snap, and another time as HB Paul Warfield was thrown for loss at 4YL on 4th down sweep. UCLA DG Johnny Walker keyed each GLS. QB-K Larry Zeno, UCLA's 1st T-formation QB since then-coach Red Sanders converted to Single Wing O in 1949, fired up new Bruins O for 17-play, 70y drive in last 7 mins and kicked winning 24y FG with 1:35 to go.

AP Poll October 8

1 Alabama (23)	445	6 Louisiana State	159
2 Texas (20)	422	7 Washington	141
3 Penn State (3)	321	8 Arkansas (1)	135
4 Southern California (1)	271	9 Purdue	133
5 Mississippi (1)	218	10 Ohio State	126

Others with votes: Georgia Tech, UCLA, Wisconsin, Miami, West Virginia, Nebraska, Northwestern, Oregon, Michigan State, Missouri, Minnesota, Duke, Utah State, Maryland, Pittsburgh, Kansas

October 13, 1962

ARMY 9 Penn State 6: HB-K Ron Coates gave Penn State (3-1) 6-3 lead with late 3rd Q FG, but Army (3-1) escaped in 4th Q as Lions subsequently bobbled EZ catch and later had E Bill Bowes' TD catch nullified by PEN. Cadets DT Tom Kerns fell on HB Junior Powell's 4th Q FUM at Lions 18YL, and, on 4th down, Army QB Cammy Lewis hit newly-discovered HB Dick Peterson over middle for 15y TD. Army sealed win with 2 late 4th down stops.

SYRACUSE 12 Boston College 0: Soph QB Wally Mahle had his varsity debut for Syracuse (1-2) and made most of it by scoring both TDs to beat undefeated Boston College (3-1). Outstanding work by Orangemen D held BC to meager 102y O. Only occasional pass successes by Eagles QB Jack Concannon created any threats: 2 completions in 1st Q were just about all of BC's 1st H O, and Concannon's pass from Orange 18YL was dropped in EZ to spoil 3rd Q rally. Mahle scored on 10y run at end of 74y march in 1st Q, and he capped 86y drive with 20y sprint with 7 secs to go.

West Virginia 15 PITTSBURGH 8: Pittsburgh Panthers (2-2) took 8-7 lead on HB Paul Martha's dazzling 34y TD run and 2-pt catch by E Gene Sobolewski in last min of 3rd Q. Seemingly, West Virginia (4-0) was cornered at own 9YL with 9:20 to play. But, Mountaineers HB Tom Woodeshick swept 49y up left sideline until being shoved OB by last-tackler, DB Martha, at Pitt 42YL. QB Jerry Yost then hit E Gene Heeter with 2 passes, and HB Tom Yeater crashed over for 5y winning TD for WVU. Yost and Heeter collaborated on 2-pt pass into right EZ corner. It was little consolation, but Pitt's TD broke 3-game shutout streak for undefeated Mountaineers.

Maryland 31 NORTH CAROLINA 13: Big blonde QB Dick Shiner (14-18/175y, 2 TDs) scored Maryland's 1st TD in 1st Q, threw for 2 others, and banged 9y to North Carolina (0-4) 2YL to set up Terps TD plunge by TB Len Chiaverini in 4th Q. Maryland (4-0), early-season darlings of ACC, jumped to 14-0 lead as Shiner found WB Tom Brown for 21y TD to wrap up 1st Q scoring. Fired-up Carolina inspired its Homecoming fans to their feet with 2 scores in 2nd Q: QB Junior Edge (11-14/113y, TD, INT) hit HB Ward Marslender with 9y TD pass and big FB Ken Willard tipped over top of Terps line for TD before H that ended with Maryland up 17-13. After scoreless 3rd Q standoff, Chiaverini scored his TD and Shiner added 8y scoring pass to HB Ernie Arizzi. DG Olaf Drozdov was in on action on 5 of 6 times that Terps sacked Tar Heels QBs.

GEORGIA TECH 17 Tennessee 0: Largest sports crowd (52,223) in Atlanta history to date, enjoyed hard-earned Georgia Tech (3-1) shutout over Tennessee (0-3). For 4th game in row, QB Billy Lothridge had hand in every Georgia Tech (3-1) score. Yellow Jackets scored in 6 plays after 1st taking possession in opening Q. Tech HB Tom Winingder's 14y punt RET gave it ball at own 39YL, and Lothridge (6-14/56y, TD, and 15/79y rushing) made 41y dash to 9YL to set up his 3y TD keeper. Vols failed to get 1st down until 2nd Q reached midway, but made it to Tech 20YL where FB-LB Mike McNames threw Tennessee TB Mallon Faircloth for 6y loss on 4th down. Lothridge immediately hit HS chum E Billy Martin for 23y catch and came back to Martin for 9y TD pass with 43 secs left in 1st H. K Lothridge booted 26y FG shortly after 2nd H KO. On 1st snap of 4th Q, Tennessee TB Wayne Bush hit E Buddy Fisher with TD pass on 4th down, but Fisher came down outside EZ boundary. Subsequent Vols threats were dashed by Tech DE John Wright's sack of Faircloth, FB-DB Jeff Davis' INT, long 4th down overthrow by Bush, and DE Steve Copeland's hard tackle that forced FUM. Tennessee lost its opening trio of games for 1st time ever, but not before repeatedly, but hopelessly, assaulting Georgia Tech GL during last 21 mins of game.

LOUISIANA STATE 17 Miami 3: Stellar Hurricanes (3-1) QB George Mira passed 14-33/168y, and LSU (3-0-1) was at loss to stop him except near its own GL. After teams exchanged FGs, Tigers went 80y in 10 plays with HB Jerry Stovall bursting 26y off T in 2nd Q. Soph HB Danny LeBlanc put game away in 4th Q as he bulled to 10y TD run carrying 3 Hurricanes, weighing total of 610 lbs, on his back.

MICHIGAN STATE 28 Michigan 0: Spartans (2-1) ground down bitter rival with simple, but relentless run attack for 391y. Little MSU HB Sherman Lewis caught holder Keith Smith's fake-FG pass for TD in 1st Q. Michigan (1-2) QB Bob Timberlake lost FUM on ensuing KO, and E Lonnie Sanders quickly made it 13-0 with 18y TD catch. FB-DB George Saimes made INT of Wolverines QB Dave Glinka to set up Lewis for 3rd Q TD. Michigan was held to 112y in losing for 10th time in 13 years to its perceived inferior rival, Michigan State.

Miami (Ohio) 10 PURDUE 7: Boilermakers (1-1-1) enjoyed 366y to 240y O advantage, but huge upset was hung on 5 TOs. E-K Bob Jencks put unbeaten Miami (5-0) on scoreboard in 1st Q with 31y FG at end of 65y drive. Purdue struck back on tricky 29y pass from QB Ron DiGravio to E Forest Farmer. Key play came when Jencks took QB Ernie Kellerman's soaring pass in full stride for 88y TD in 2nd Q. Victory brought Redskins record vs. Big 10 to respectable 3-4 since MAC inception in 1946. Despite its achievement, Miami would make downturn in next 2 weeks, losing to arch-rival Ohio 12-6 and being tied by Bowling Green 24-24.

WISCONSIN 17 Notre Dame 8: Sr QB Ron VanderKelen, who had played but 90 secs in his 2 previous varsity seasons, continued to show inspired generalship for unbeaten Wisconsin (3-0). Badgers dominated throughout, but were held back from larger victory margin by 8 TOs. VanderKelen provided 10-0 lead in 1st Q by firing 25y TD pass to tall E Pat Richter, who caught scoring pass in his 7th straight contest going back to 1961 season. Wisconsin D, ranked 2nd in nation in y allowed, made 4 INTs and FUM REC in 2nd H. FUM REC at Notre Dame (1-2) 5YL in 3rd Q positioned VanderKelen's 1y TD run through LG on 3rd down. Trailing 17-0, Fighting Irish finally cruised 68y in closing mins to avoid shutout. QB Denis Szot passed ND into position for FB Don Hogan's short TD run and followed with 2-pt pass to soph HB Jack Snow.

OKLAHOMA STATE 36 Colorado 16: Little HB Don Karns gave sluggish Oklahoma State (2-1) big lift in 2nd Q with zig-zagging 60y run from behind scrimmage line with short pass from QB Mike Miller. Karns' TD provided Oklags with 10-8 lead and ignited run of 5 TDs in 5 possessions. Colorado (1-3) DE Ken Blair had dropped off D-line to spear 2nd Q INT and race 41y for TD that wiped out 23y FG by Cowboys K Dave Hanna in 1st Q. Blair followed his D-oriented score with 2-pt catch for 8-3 lead. Oklahoma State HB Don Derrick rushed for 114y, much of it around Buffs flanks, and scored on 1y plunge and 32y pass from Miller in 3rd Q to up lead to 30-8. QB Frank Cesarek (8-16/103y, TD, INT) prompted 74y TD trip for Colorado in 4th Q as E John McGuire (6/64y, TD) outwrestled Cowpokes defender for 4y TD pass.

TEXAS 9 Oklahoma 6: Bad feelings bubbled to surface as Texas (4-0) beat Oklahoma (1-2) for 5th straight year. Sooners held early upper hand, but 2 key FUMs provided Longhorns with all their pts in 2nd Q: barefooted K Tony Crosby's 26y FG and C-LB Perry McWilliams' EZ REC of crazily-bouncing, ill-advised Sooners pitchout. Slender QB Ronald Fletcher used well-practiced trick passes to rally Sooners in 2nd Q: Fletcher lofted successful passes for 39y gain and 34y TD, each to HB Lance Retzel. Texas turned 2nd H over to rugged D and soph HB-P Ernie Koy's soaring punts before contest ended in free-swinging fisticuffs in closing moments. Oklahoma player piled on Texas QB Johnny Genung as he killed game-end clock, and both benches emptied in min of fury.

NEW MEXICO 14 Utah State 13: Big, rugged Utah State (4-1) nursed 13-0 lead built on 2nd Q TD runs by HBs Darrell Steele and Roger Leonard. Usually reliable K Jim Turner missed conv kick deep into 4th Q. In closing mins, New Mexico (4-1) pulled it out with 96y drive closed with HB Bobby Santiago's 22y pass—after pitchout—to E Larry Jasper, who sprinted to TD. Lobos K Ed Meadows drilled winning pt.

Washington 14 OREGON STATE 13 (Portland): As typhoon-racked city of Portland cleaned up Friday night's mess, QB Terry Baker and E Vern Burke staged Oregon State (2-2) aerial show in clear post-storm air. Burke caught 7/103y, including 2 TDs in 2nd Q that provided 13-7 lead. Washington (3-0-1) DE Lee Bernhardi recovered Beavers FUM to set up methodical 60y drive to Huskies TD. Washington HB Charlie Mitchell stretched across GL from 2YL, and C-K Jim Norton booted winning conv in last 3 mins of game.

AP Poll October 15

1 Texas (21)	458	6 Ohio State (2)	218
2 Alabama (24)	437	7 Arkansas (1)	196
3 Southern California	302	8 Northwestern (3)	165
4 Louisiana State	273	9 Washington	143
5 Mississippi	256	10 Wisconsin	128

Others with votes: Georgia Tech, Michigan State, UCLA (1), Penn State, Missouri, Oregon, West Virginia, Maryland, Duke, Army, Auburn, Nebraska, Miami (Ohio), Kansas

October 20, 1962

(Fri) MIAMI 28 Maryland 24: When Maryland (4-1) HB Tom Brown raced 98y to score with opening KO, Miami (4-1) had to play from behind. QB George Mira (21-31/288y, 3 TDs, 2 INTs) rallied Hurricanes from deficits of 6-0, 14-7, 17-14, and 24-21. QB Dick Shiner was hobbled by pulled muscle but boosted his status as nation's no. 2 passer with 15-20/176y, 3 INTs to position Maryland for his own 2y TD run. Miami HB Nick Ryder ran for TD for 14-14 tie in 2nd Q, but Terps HB Bob Chiaverini busted for 3 1st

downs on 69y drive to K John Hannigan's 26y FG late in 3rd Q. Mira passed for 61y of 71y march to WB Jack Sims' 14y TD catch early in 4th Q. Maryland reaped pass interference PEN against Canes, and Chiaverini scored from 3YL for 24-21 lead with 5:46 left. Mira took Canes on his back as he so often did: He clicked on throws of 20, 17, 14, and finally 22y TD to E Bill Sparks for 4-pt lead. Shiner wasn't done either as he passed Terrapins to Miami 17YL, but soph Hurricanes DB Mark Panther stepped in front of pass intended for Brown to make INT.

Navy 26 BOSTON COLLEGE 6: Boston College (3-2) scored on QB Jack Concannon's 2y wide option run in 1st Q. Navy (3-2) QB Roger Staubach threw 1st of his 2 TD tosses to E Jim Campbell for 6-6 H tie. Game's big play came in 3rd Q from unlikely source: 260-lb Midshipmen G Al Krekich made INT of BC sub QB Phil Carlino and chugged 39y to set up go-ahead TD by Navy FB Pat Donnelly on 6y slam up middle. FUM RECs by Navy HB-DBs Ray Snyder and Johnny Sai set up 2 TDs in 4th Q, and Middies held on downs at its 3YL and accepted HB-DB John Ounsworth's INT at 5YL.

PENN STATE 20 Syracuse 19: Penn State (4-1) had early momentum on HB Roger Kochman's 2 TDs in opening 5 min. Syracuse (1-3) wrestled lead away as improving QB Walley Mahle ran and passed for TDs around HB Don King's 35y TD sprint. After King's sprint behind right side of Syracuse line, E-K Tom Mingo barely missed 35y conv kick brought about by holding PEN called on big E Walt Sweeney. Syracuse went ahead by 5 pts in 4th Q on 86y march capped by Mahle's 11y TD pass to Sweeney. Nittany Lions E Dave Robinson then halted 2-pt run with critical tackle. Down 19-14 in 4th Q, Lions wedged FB Dave Hayes over for 20-19 lead. Penn State G Harrison Rosdahl blocked FG try on game's last play by Syracuse's Mingo.

Duke 16 CLEMSON 0: Duke (4-1) found Tigers (2-3) D concentrating on wide E, rammed through soft interior at T. Blue Devil soph FB-LB Mike Curtis made up for early FUM at Clemson 1YL with INTs in each middle Q. Curtis' picks set up 2 scores: his own 1y run and QB Walt Rappold's 4y TD rollout run. In ACC race, Duke moved within half-game of Maryland, which went outside conf and lost at Miami 28-24. Tigers suffered 5 INTs and 2 FUMs. Critical Clemson bobble came when FB Pat Crain lost FUM to Devils HB-DB Jay Wilkinson at Duke 1YL in final min of 2nd Q, time when Clemson trailed only 7-0.

Alabama 27 TENNESSEE 7: Volunteers (0-4), whose coach Bowden Wyatt heard catcalls over his allegiance to old single wing O, edged Alabama (5-0) 254y to 244y in O, but was helpless to stop soph QB Joe Namath's well-placed Crimson Tide aerials. Namath's passes positioned K Tim Davis for 2 FGs in 1st Q. Namath hit HB Benny Nelson with 35y 2nd Q score and opened 4th Q with 45y arrow to E Richard Williamson that paved way for TD by HB Cotton Clark. Meanwhile, Clark led pass D which allowed only 6-27/67y, although Tennessee got TD pass from TB Bobby Morton in 3rd Q.

AUBURN 17 Georgia Tech 14: Acting early, Auburn (4-0) sent HB Jimmy Burson scampering 57y to TD on 1st snap. Next time Burson took ball, he went 14y to set up QB Mailon Kent's TD pass to E Howard Simpson. Tigers led 17-0 at H. Georgia Tech (3-2) surged back in 2nd H behind QB Billy Lothridge, who gained nearly half of Tech's 57y march and scored from 6YL. Soph QB Gerry Bussell returned punt 75y for 4th Q TD, but Yellow Jackets could get no closer.

Northwestern 18 OHIO STATE 14: Buckeyes (2-2), intent on regaining top form, jumped to early edge: HB Bob Klein raced 90y with opening KO for TD, and FB Dave Francis barrelled 9y to close 14-play, 71y TD drive in 1st Q. Northwestern (4-0) unfurled air game in 2nd Q as E Paul Flatley (10 receptions) caught 9y TD pass from QB Tommy Myers (18-30/177y, TD, 2 INTs) after G Jack Cvercko's FUM REC. DB Roland Wahl's INT late in 2nd Q allowed FB Bill Swingle to score and bring it to 14-12 at H. Wildcats went 42y on ground for HB Steve Murphy's winner with 5 min left, then weathered 2 Ohio State trips to their 12YL.

PURDUE 37 Michigan 0: Unpredictable Purdue (2-1-1) clutched Wolverines by their throat on Boilermakers' 1st O play, and contest, in effect, was over. Michigan punted less than 2 mins into contest, and Boilermakers took over on own 46YL. Economical thrower QB Ron DiGravio (4-8/155y, 3 TDs) lofted long bomb to HB Tom Fugate, who caught it in stride for 54y TD. By 3-min mark of 2nd Q, DiGravio had 2 more TD passes, and Purdue led 23-0. Michigan (1-2) gained only 97y to Boilers' 412y, and, having already been blanked by Michigan State, was well on way to its worst record since 1936.

WISCONSIN 42 Iowa 14: Rough Big 10 encounter, in which officials make 2 ejections for fighting, turned on huge 2nd Q by undefeated Wisconsin (4-0). After Iowa (2-2) QB Matt Szykowny pitched 56y TD to swift E Cloyd Webb in 1st Q, Badgers exploded for 4 TDs in 2nd Q. Wisconsin QB Ron VanderKelen hooked up with HB Elmars Erzerins for tying 35y TD pass, and HB Ron "Pinto" Smith followed with 9y run for 1st of his 3 TDs. Szykowny wedged another TD pass, 8y to HB Larry Ferguson, among Badgers' 2nd Q scores, so it was 28-14 at H. Wisconsin went to umbrella pass D before H to significantly blunt Iowa pass game, although much of Hawks' final 16-30/259y was already on aerial stat sheets. In 3rd Q, Smith scored his 3rd TD on 4y run, and VanderKelen tossed his 3rd TD pass, this to E, and future Wisconsin AD, Pat Richter to complete rout.

Oklahoma 13 KANSAS 7: Although Kansas (3-2) soph HB Gale Sayers would finish season with 1125y and nation-leading 7.1y rush avg, this was contest controlled by D lines. Led by T Brian Schweda and C-LB Kent Converse, Jayhawks allowed no 1st downs in 1st Q, and QB Rodger McFarland converted field position advantage into 38y TD pass to speedy HB Tony Leiker. OU coach Bud Wilkinson grabbed outlandish HB Joe Don Looney at H, inspiring him to greater effort. Sooners (2-2) line, depending on blocks of C Wayne Lee and G Larry Vermillion, sprung Looney for 61y TD on trap run and QB Monte Deere for 3y sweep for winning TD at end of 56y drive in 4th Q.

TEXAS 7 Arkansas 3: Seeking leg up for 4th SWC crown in 4 years, Arkansas (4-1) took 3-0 lead in middle of 2nd Q on 41y FG from soph K Tom McKnelly, 1st FG try in his career. QB Billy Moore's direction of Hogs O, peppered with line smashes of FB Jesse Branch, kept Texas (5-0) bottled up in own territory throughout. But, Porkers blew golden 3rd Q opportunity when FB Danny Brabham smashed to 1YL, but lost FUM into EZ. QBs Duke Carlisle and Johnny Genung directed patient 20-play drive of 85y for Texas in 4th Q. It consumed nearly 7 mins, and Longhorns HB Tommy Ford powered 3y for winning TD in last min of play. After Steers DB Carlisle made INT of desperate Arkansas pass at own 44YL, tilt ended with intrusive fan exchanging punches with ref Curly Hays.

Mississippi State 9 HOUSTON 3: Mississippi State (3-1) sloshed through 2nd H deluge of rain to score late TD pass and send Cougars (2-3) to defeat. Maroons QB Charlie Furlow, who would become late pass hero, was picked off on his 1st pass to eventually provide field position for Houston K Bill McMillan's 25y FG in 1st Q. Cougars HB-DB Paul Reinhart made INT, but UH stalled at 31YL and HB-P Bobby Brezina (17/66y) pooched punt to 10YL where State HB Ronny Kirkland mistakenly touched it. Cougars G Horst Paul immediately fell on ball at 11YL, but UH had to settle for FG. P Brezina had terrible time, having 2 punts partially blocked and another slither off his foot for 7y. Punt exchanges put Cats at their own door-step, so to not risk another punt, Houston opted to down ball in EZ with 2:10 to play. But, Brezina's free-kick went only 35y, and was returned 14y by QB Mackie Weaver. Furlow soon connected with swift HB Ode Burrell on 24y TD pass to break 3-2 deficit. Fortunes for each team would quickly reverse: Houston would win its last 5 games including Tangerine Bowl, while Bulldogs went on to drop their next 5 outings for 3-6 finish.

Oregon 35 AIR FORCE 20: Air Force (3-2) dedicated new stadium before crowd of 33,343, but Oregon (4-1) soph QB Bob Berry spoiled party with 3 TD passes and scoring run at end of 4 long drives. Falcons scored in 1st H on TD runs by HB Dick Czarnota and QB Terry Isaacson. Berry's TD run tied it 14-14 at H. Ducks went 74, 86, and 73y to 2nd H TDs, and their D, thwarted in 1st H, tightened behind E Rich Schwab, G Bill Del Biaggio, and LB Bruce Snyder, future California and Arizona State coach.

Washington 14 STANFORD 0: Key to Washington (4-0-1) shutout of Stanford (2-3) was scoring early and stopping Indians threats thrice inside Huskies 5YL. With D pressing line of scrimmage to stop Huskies runs, UW QB Bill Siler flipped quick look-in pass to E Lee Bernhardt from own 45YL. Bernhardt scampered to Stanford 10YL where he was hauled down by DB Steve Purcell. Huskies HB Nat Whitmyer went wide on next play to 7-0, just 6 mins into game. Tribe QB Steve Thurlow's 2 completions sparked 60y drive in 2nd Q, but it died at UW 2YL. Stanford DB Ed Cummings had INT to stop late 2nd Q drive, but dropped it. Huskies FB Jim Stiger caught Ohler's 28y arching pass on next play to score 21 secs before H. Indians dominated 3rd Q, but 2 failed passes after HB Jack Lodata was thrown for 7y loss to Huskies 11YL doomed that scoring chance. Washington held at 1YL as QB Clark Weaver was stopped on 4th down sneak.

AP Poll October 22

1 Texas (23)	491	6 Louisiana State	232
2 Alabama (18)	465	7 Mississippi	228
3 Northwestern (8)	390	8 Washington	170
4 Southern California (1)	363	9 Arkansas	82
5 Wisconsin (1)	279	10 Michigan State	79

Others with votes: Auburn, Penn State (1), Oregon, Maryland, Ohio State, Nebraska, Duke, Miami, West Virginia, Purdue, Army, UCLA, Ohio University, Navy

October 27, 1962

CORNELL 35 Princeton 34: Cornell (2-3) jr QB Gary Wood rewrote Ivy game O records: 13-15/212y, 3 TDs, INT passing and 15/125y rushing, including 49y TD dash. Missed kick after FB Cosmo Iacavazzi's 2nd Q TD forced Princeton (3-2) into subsequent 2-pt tries. Tigers led 20-14 at H. Wood's FUM gave Iacavazzi chance for 38y TD, his 3rd, and Tigers led 34-28 4 mins into 4th Q. Moving 80y in waning time, Wood hit 5 passes, wriggled free on 4th down run, and found HB Al Aragona for 5y TD pass. Dead-eye K Pete Gogolak, pioneer of full-time soccer kicking, then made his 5th conv for upset win.

Dartmouth 24 HARVARD 6: Dartmouth (5-0) took over 1st place in Ivy League, bolting to 17-0 lead behind QB Billy King's 73y rushing that included 2 TDs in 2nd and 4th Qs. After accurate E-K Bill Wellstead closed 65y 1st Q drive with FG, key break came on 7y Harvard (3-2) punt to Crimson 34YL in 2nd Q. King quickly dashed 23y to position his TD run from 11YL. Crimson was held to 99y rushing overall, but tallied in 4th Q on perfect 82y post pattern pass from QB Mike Bassett to HB Bill Taylor, as pass barely eluded fingertips of Dartmouth DB Jack McLean. Big Green led 17-6 at that point as 2-pt pass failed. Harvard's failed onside KO led to late Indians TD drive, led by HBs Tom Spangenberg and Chris Vancura, and ended by sub QB Dana Kelly's 1y sneak.

Navy 32 Pittsburgh 9 (Norfolk): Sensational Navy (4-2) QB Roger Staubach "pitched a perfect game" according to Lincoln Werden in *New York Times*. Staubach hit 8-8/192y, including 66y TD in 1st Q to HB Jim Stewart, who lulled Pittsburgh (3-3) secondary into inattention by limping to his flanked position. Staubach also wrapped up scoring with 22y TD run in 4th Q. Panthers scored in early going when they happily gobbled up dribbled opening KO that was intended as Midshipmen surprise. FB-K Rick Leeson (55y rushing) was workhorse on 8-play drive to his 37y FG. Under substantial rush, Pitt QB Jim Traficant threw 1st Q INT that Navy G-LB Fred Marlin put into play at Panthers 36YL. HB John Sai gave Middies 12-3 lead with TD run after 7 plays, including 2 Staubach passes. After scoreless 2nd Q, Leeson answered Tars' 3rd Q TD with his own 1y blast after Traficant took late-play lateral from HB Ed Clark 36y to Navy 6YL. Pitt trailed only 18-9 at this stage, but Middies HB Bob Orlosky's 2nd TD run put it out of reach in 4th Q.

MARYLAND 13 South Carolina 11: Standout HB-DB Billy Gambrell, whose earlier 25y INT RET set up K Dean Findley's 3rd Q FG for 11-10 South Carolina (1-4-1) lead, was called for pass interference at his 10YL against Maryland (5-1) E Joe Mona with :23 left. K John Hannigan kicked winning 22y FG for Maryland 3 plays later. Terps QB Dick Shiner (17-26/174y, TD, 2 INTs) hit HB Tom Brown (8/110y, TD receiving) with 2nd Q TD pass, as Brown's catches tied school single-game mark as did his 34 receptions for season. Gambrell could manage only 15/41y rushing and lost his ACC ground-gaining leadership to Turtle TB Len Chiaverini, who battered Gamecocks' middle for 33/119y. Maryland led 10-0 late in 2nd Q when South Carolina DB Larry Gill raced 45y with pass INT to 16YL. Cocks QB Dan Reeves hit E Ken Lester with TD pass and added quick zip around LE for 2 pts. Terps led 10-8 at H. Behind 11-10 with 5:48 to play, Maryland started from its 17YL, and Shiner mixed his passes with Chiaverini runs to advance to Hannigan's winning boot.

LOUISIANA STATE 23 Florida 0: LSU's best passing attack (10-14/175y, TD, INT) of year was shared by QBs Jimmy Field and Lynn Amedee. Field hit HB Jerry Stovall for gains of 24 and 28y to lead to 1st Q FG by K Amedee. Tigers (5-1) went 80y in 16 plays in 2nd Q with sub HB Bo Campbell driving in from 5YL. Stovall scored twice in 2nd H, on 16y pass from Field right after 2nd H KO and on 8y run, to complete rout of Florida (3-3), from which Gators would turn around their season by winning next 3 games. Florida had moved 49y of smash-mouth ball after opening KO, but was halted on 4th down at Bayou Bengals 23YL. Gators took until final secs to advance again any closer than LSU 34YL as their biggest producer was QB Tom Shannon with 12-22/90y in air. Sensational soph FB Larry Dupree (10/27y) was completely stunted by Tigers D.

FLORIDA STATE 20 Virginia Tech 7: Although Virginia Tech (3-4) was outgained 326y to 134y, *Miami Herald* headline scribe wrote that "Gobblers Prove Tough Turkeys" because they kept Florida State (4-1-1) in suspense until Seminoles scored late TD for safe 13-pt edge. Virginia Tech G Vic Kreiter recovered State QB Eddie Feely's FUM in early going, and FB Sonny Utz (9/56y, TD) swept wide left for 18y TD. FSU D soon responded by forcing Hokies punt from deep in their end, and punt traveled only to 38YL. Backup Seminoles QB Steve Tensi (7-15 passing) hit E Donnie Floyd for 13y before HB Phil Spooner carried over for TD late in 1st Q. FSU went 80y in 2nd Q as HB Keith Kinderman personally accounted for 57y, including last 4y for TD and 14-7 H edge. Gobblers halted 3 FG fakes in 3rd Q, but could muster little O. Kinderman scored last min sweep from 3YL that cemented verdict.

OHIO STATE 14 Wisconsin 7: Before 85,640, Ohio State (3-2) elbowed way back into Big 10 race. Buckeyes scored 1st on QB Joe Sparma's 21y pass to HB Paul Warfield. Wisconsin (4-1) tied it in 2nd Q with surprise maneuver. After DB Jim Schenk's INT, Badgers ran plunge, then quick pass without huddle: QB Ron VanderKelen's 47y TD to HB Ron Smith. Trio of Ohio FBs combined to take advantage of personal foul on 57y 4th Q TD drive. FB Dave Francis appeared to be punched, and officials walked off PEN to Badgers 29YL. FBs Dave Katterhenrich and Bob Butts alternated driving to 1YL, and QB John Mummey sneaked over.

NORTHWESTERN 35 Notre Dame 6: Using blocked punt, INT, and FUM REC, Wildcats (5-0) jumped to 29-0 lead by 3rd Q. Northwestern QB Tommy Myers passed 11-18/118y, 2 TDs, each score caught by WR Paul Flatley. QB Daryle Lamonica (11-14/118y) was sole bright spot for Notre Dame (1-4), passing 4-5 on 4th Q 70y TD drive, ND's only trip inside Northwestern 44YL.

RICE 14 Texas 14: Owls' big soph HB Paul Piper picked peck of piercing paces through powerful D of Texas (5-0-1) in 1st Q: he scored on 48y run. Back came Longhorns as HB Tommy Ford scored in 2nd Q and raced 55y with 3rd Q punt to allow FB Jerry Cook's TD run. Down 14-7, Rice (0-3-2) QBs Randall Kerbow and Walter McReynolds alternated on 57y 4th Q TD drive. E John Sylvester caught passes from each, then QB-K Kerbow threw 18y scoring pass to HB Ronnie Graham and kicked tying pt.

Stanford 17 UCLA 7: Gift-wrapped TOs were order of day as 11 giveaways ended O possessions. Underdog Stanford (3-3) finally halted madness and scored FG and TD on "normal" drives. Each team had long TD RET of mid-air FUM: In early going, UCLA (2-2) HB Larry Zeno (3-14/36y, 5 INTs) flipped bad pitchout to HB Kermit Alexander, who bobbled ball into hands of Indians E Frank Pattitucci, who rambled 82y to score. Holding PEN spoiled Stanford drive, but HB-K Stan Lindskog made 25y FG for 10-0 margin. Zeno threw 1 of his 5 INTs to Indians DB Tim Hansel, and Tribe moved to UCLA 15YL. FB-LB Mitch Dimich hit Stanford HB Allen Curr to bang loose ball into air; Bruins DB Carl Jones rushed up to grab ball and tour 81y to score before H. Stanford marched 89y to TD as QB Steve Thurlow hit 3 passes and ran 16y to 2YL.

WASHINGTON 21 Oregon 21: After ace HBs Mel Renfro of Oregon (4-1-1) and Charlie Mitchell of Washington (4-0-2) traded 1st H TDs, Huskies marched after 2nd H KO to Mitchell's 2nd score and 14-7 lead. Renfro countered with 14y option TD pass to E Greg Willener, but Ducks missed kick and trailed 14-13. Huskies blocked punt in 4th Q and soon had 21-13 lead. But, Renfro set up HB Larry Hill's 18y TD run with 17y dash, and QB Bob Berry hit E Dick Imwaile with tying 2-pt pass.

November 3, 1962

Notre Dame 20 NAVY 12 (Philadelphia): Soph QB Roger Staubach had big game in previous week's 32-9 win vs. Pitt, but was powerless to halt QB Daryle Lamonica's leadership in Notre Dame's (2-4) upset of Navy (4-3). Lamonica scored twice, passed for another. Held to just 3y in 1st H, Middies surged to 12-7 lead on Staubach's short TD run on 1st play of 4th Q. But, onside KO failed. Lamonica hit leaping HB Denny Phillips at GL for 45y TD pass and Irish led 13-12. HB Don Hogan's 27y run, HB Frank Budka's 20y catch set stage for Lamonica's late clinching TD.

Georgia Tech 20 DUKE 9: QB-K Billy Lothridge (12-16/125y and 17/53y, TD rushing) stole show again for Georgia Tech, scoring at end of 75y drive that followed opening KO, passing to set up 2nd Q TD by FB Ray Mendheim, and kicking 2 FGs. In game that featured long, time-consuming drives by both sides, Georgia Tech scored on all 3 of its 1st H possessions for 17-3 lead. Only 1st H pts for Duke (5-2) came on K Billy Reynolds' 26y FG early in 2nd Q after 79y drive. Engineers shut down Duke ground game, limiting it to 85y, and it wasn't until 4th Q that Blue Devils QB Walt Rappold (9-17/130y, INT) began connecting on his passes. Duke E Pete Widener (5/107y) caught throws of 49 and 23y on 84y trip to set up HB Billy Futrell's 1y TD run.

FLORIDA 22 Auburn 3: Strong-jawed Florida (4-3) D bent, but didn't break as T Frank Lasky, FB-LB Tommy Kelley, and QB-DB Larry Libertore made vital plays. Gators forced 3 FUM RECs and 2 INTs. Soph FB Larry Dupree (13/69y) and HB Sam Mack made key runs on 67y Gators march in 1st Q. HB Bruce Starling recovered EZ FUM for TD and 7-0 Florida lead at end of 7y run by Mack. Ineffective on ground with 42y total, Auburn (5-1) went to air in 2nd Q, but big stops, like last-defender Libertore's tackle on HB George Rose at Gator 29YL, forced Tigers K Woody Woodall into 3 FG tries of which he made last boot of 30y. Gators recovered 2 FUMs in Auburn territory that led to 3rd Q TDs with big plays coming on QB Tom Shannon's 29y stage-setting pass to E Russ Brown and Dupree's 39y TD blast through RT.

Mississippi 15 LOUISIANA STATE 7: After 5 straight years of frustration against LSU (5-1-1), Ole Miss (6-0) gained win at Tiger Stadium in soft night rain. Mississippi had arrived at Baton Rouge each of last 4 years, starting in 1958, with undefeated record, only to have Bayou Bengals snatch away victory or tie. Rebels QB Glynn Griffing, discouraged by early INTs, guided 61y TD trip in final 2 mins of 1st H, pitching last 10y to HB A.J. Holloway for TD. Still leading 7-6 on HB Jerry Stovall's 1st Q TD, LSU permitted Ole Miss to drive 65y to Griffing's go-ahead TD pass to HB Louis Guy. Griffing finished with 15-25/142y, 2 TDs, 3 INTs passing.

Houston 7 FLORIDA STATE 0: Blanked in its last 3 Homecoming efforts, Florida State (4-2-1) tried to use nation's 6th-rated passing attack to crush Cougars (3-4). Mounting rain storm helped running game with which Houston controlled possession in scoreless 1st H. Houston fashioned biggest 1st H threat which was snuffed at Seminoles 19YL when LB Butch Gunter recovered FUM of Cougars FB Bobby Hernandez. On its opening series in 3rd Q, FSU moved across midfield on QB Eddie Feely's pass to E Jim Causey, but failed to advance inside Houston 40YL. Cougars took over on own 41YL after punt in 4th Q, and HB Bobby Brezina ran for 17 and 16y on trap plays to set up his own 1y TD slant with 4:36 to play. Seminoles got 2 more possessions, but QB Steve Tensi could connect only once as time ran out.

Illinois 14 PURDUE 10: Confident Purdue (3-2-1), 26-pt favorite, saw its Homecoming Saturday ruined by surprisingly-fierce Illinois (1-5) that won for 1st time in 15 games, cracking longest-ever losing streak for any Big 10 team to date. C-LB Dick Butkus came of age as sideline to sideline LB, and he credited strong line play, especially by G Frank Lollino, from keeping Boilermakers blockers off him. Purdue started well, advancing until Illini FB-DB Dave Pike made INT of QB Ron DiGravio at 4YL. Short punt and fair-catch interference PEN put Boilers in good spot at 15YL. But Illini D held and G-K Skip Ohl gave Purdue 3-0 lead in 1st Q. Illinois E Thurman Walker (4/90y) outmaneuvered HB-DB Charles King for 23y TD pass from QB Mike Taliaferro (10-25/199y, TD, 2 INTs) in 2nd Q, and HB Ken Zimmerman slipped through line behind T Greg Schumacher's block on 1st play of 4th Q for 30y TD run and 14-3 lead. Purdue HB Tom Bloom took short pass and raced 66y down sideline to Illini 11YL to set up DiGravio's TD pass. Purdue threatened again, but 2 sacks by Lollino and Butkus' 3rd down tackle at 12YL doomed Boilermakers bid.

Northwestern 26 Indiana 21: Northwestern (6-0) coach Ara Parseghian claimed Indiana (2-5), losers of 17 straight Big 10 games, was "just as tough" as Ohio State. Indeed, Hoosiers had no. 1 Wildcats wobbling on brink of defeat. IU scored in opening 3 plays on QB Woody Moore's sneak after shanked Northwestern punt put Indiana at 18YL, but trailed 14-7 when Wildcats QB Tommy Myers (16-26/243y, 2 TDs, 3 INTs) pitched his 2nd TD pass, 38y reception by HB Willie Stinson (4/60y, TD). As Cats pressured again, Indiana E Rudy Kuechenberg knocked down Myers for 5y loss on 4th down, then caught 13y pass to make way for HB Nate Ramsey's 29y reverse TD run that tied it 14-14 at H. NW was frustrated at Hoosier 1YL by G Don Croftcheck's 4th down tackle just before H, but took 20-14 lead after 2nd H KO. Moore threw 48y TD pass to HB Marv Woodson for 21-20 3rd Q lead. Indiana QB-P Phil Westphal made only 22y punt to own 44YL in 4th Q, and NW soon was rolling to FB Bill Swingle's winning 5y TD run off G Burt Petkus' block.

IOWA 28 Ohio State 14: Losers of 2 in row, Iowa (3-3) revamped its O formula and ended Ohio State's design on repeating as Big 10 champions. Hawkeyes QB Matt Szykowny all but disdained his air game (3-4/36y), but each of his completions figured in scoring drives. Szykowny plunged for 2 TDs in 1st H after HB Bobby Grier capped 91y 1st Q voyage with 2y TD blast, while calling variety of running plays for team's new sensation, soph FB Vic Davis. With score at 14-0, Ohio State (3-3) HB Paul Warfield,

constant but uneventful threat to catch long passes from QB Joe Sparma (3-10/20y, INT), raced 65y with KO RET. FB Bob Butts got TD on short dive early in 2nd Q to close within 14-7. Buckeye power run attack seemed to revitalize itself in 2nd H and FB Dave Katterhenrich battered 3y to trim it to 21-14. Despite Ohio sealing its fate with 4 TOs, result remained in doubt until Iowa HB Bob Sherman plunged 2y for TD with 1:32 left.

Missouri 16 NEBRASKA 7: Lost FUM by Nebraska (6-1) QB Dennis Claridge, recovered by Missouri (6-0-1) DB Daryl Krugman, allowed speedster HB Johnny Roland to race along sideline for 46y TD in 1st Q. Holding Huskers to 148y O, Tigers let down only long enough for Nebraska FB-DB Noel Martin to sprint 88y with INT for tying TD in 2nd Q. K Bill Leistritz put Missouri ahead with 45y FG in 3rd Q, and FB Paul Underhill snared punt FUM at Huskers 26YL to set up feisty QB Jim Johnson's clinching TD run early in 4th Q.

Oklahoma 62 COLORADO 0: Only shadow of its 1961 Big 8 championship form, Colorado (1-6) had dismissed several players in preseason and encouraged coach Sonny Grandelius' resignation in wake of NCAA investigation. Into mess was thrown ill-prepared administrator Bud Davis to take over as coach. Oklahoma (4-2) piled up 415y in 35-0 1st H, including 4 long TDs: QB Monte Deere's passes of 32, 83, and 41y and FB Paul Lea's 39y run. HB Joe Don Looney sparked 2nd H Sooner surge with 84y TD run. Dispirited Buffaloes saw their only threat die with FUM at 2YL after 74y drive.

TEXAS CHRISTIAN 28 Baylor 26: Horned Frogs (4-2) maintained slippery grip on SWC title hopes. TCU QB Sonny Gibbs (14-26/192y, 2 TDs, INT) vaulted for 1y TD to tie it 7-7 in 2nd Q, then added scoring tosses at end of 67 and 52y drives to HB Bobby Sanders in 2nd Q and to E Tom Magoffin (7/113y, TD) in 3rd Q. On other side of passing duel, Baylor (1-5) QB Don Trull (13-26/208y, 2 TDs) shrugged off Bears' early and mediocre run strategy, that included Trull's 7y rollout TD in 1st Q, but also his 0-5 aerial start. Even though he hadn't completed pass in opening 29 mins, Trull beat H clock with 53y bomb to HB Ronnie Goodwin and 3 other tosses, last going 5y to swift soph HB Lawrence Elkins 5 secs before H. Elkins caught 5 passes, including 27y TD in 3rd Q, but K Carl Choate missed his 1st conv in last 46 tries. Also, Elkins meandered 92y with punt TD RET to provide short-lived 26-21 4th Q lead, but 2-pt pass failed. Winning TCU trip went 69y to FB Tommy Crutcher's 4y run with barely more than 3 mins left, but not before Gibbs and HB Jim Fauver had to improvise 10y pass on 4th-and-9 from Bears 34YL.

BRIGHAM YOUNG 27 New Mexico 0: Nation's total O leader, TB Eldon "The Phantom" Fortie of BYU (3-5), gained 232y, passed for 2 TDs, and ran 5y for another in big upset that temporarily derailed New Mexico (5-2-1) charge to its 1st WAC crown. Cougars held Lobos to 107y as star Lobo HB Bobby Santiago gained 13y rushing in 1st H. Santiago was unable to play in 2nd H. Trailing 17-0 in 3rd Q, New Mexico QB Jim Cromartie pitched 68y pass to E George Heard. But on 4th down from Cougar 5YL, BYU DL John Kawaa made INT at own 2YL to kill Lobos threat.

SOUTHERN CALIFORNIA 14 Washington 0: Maturing juggernaut USC (6-0) handed 1st loss to Washington (4-1-2). Occasional starting QB Pete Beathard accounted for both Trojan scores, hitting E Hal Bedsole with 12y TD on drive after opening KO and scurrying 5y for 2nd Q TD on 4th down fake and spin. Huskies penetrated to Trojan 17, 18, and 19YLs thanks to sizable ground game led by HB Charlie Mitchell (12/91y). Fine D work by T Gary Kirner and LB Damon Bane of USC halted each Husky threat.

AP Poll November 5

1 Northwestern (24)	442	6 Arkansas	179
2 Southern California (6)	409	7 Missouri	146
3 Alabama (9)	397	8 Wisconsin	118
4 Mississippi (9)	372	9 Louisiana State	102
5 Texas (1)	278	10 Minnesota	93

Others with votes: Penn State, Oregon, Georgia Tech, Miami, Washington, Army, Dartmouth, Auburn, Oklahoma, Florida, UCLA, Kansas, Michigan State, Oregon State, Arizona State, West Virginia

November 10, 1962

BOSTON COLLEGE 42 Texas Tech 13: Sparkling play for each team came from 2 future pro Es. BC's Art Graham (3/72y, TD) caught 56y TD pass from QB Jack Concannon, then threw key block on Concannon's TD run that provided Eagles (6-2) with 14-0 H edge. Texas Tech (0-8) E David Parks set several school receiving records, completed trick pass, blocked FG try, and generally starred on D. Boston College HB-DB Jim McGowan set up 2nd Q TD with 60y INT RET and scored on 71y INT RET in 4th Q.

DUKE 10 Maryland 7: Outgained 289y to 229y, Duke (6-2) made big plays near its GL and took over ACC lead by foiling frustrated Maryland (5-3). Blue Devils twice picked off passes by QB Dick Shiner inside their own 5YL in 1st Q and took 3-0 lead on K Bill Reynolds' 2nd Q FG of 38y. Duke HB-DB Mark Leggett picked off Shiner at his 5YL to stump any questioners about Maryland trying to be 1st on scoreboard in 1st Q. Blues pieced together 57y drive in 3rd Q that featured 8, 9, and 11y runs by Leggett until FB Mike Curtis powered over for his 8th TD of season and 10-0 lead. FB Len Chiaverini (26/99y) was key to 65y drive early in 4th Q as Shiner scored on 5y rollout run to roll Terrapins off their backs. Maryland had 3 more chances to spring upset and keep its undefeated mark in ACC, but Devils came up big each time. Biggest play came from Duke LB Paul Bengel who made GL INT.

Florida 23 Georgia 15 (Jacksonville): Upswing in Florida's season took short nap as Gators (5-3) lost 2 FUMs in early going. Result was Georgia (2-3-3) TD by HB Don Porterfield. Florida came alive in 2nd Q when E Tom Gregory threw block that broke FB Larry Dupree (16/111y rushing) for 41y TD dash. Southpaw QB Tom Shannon hit HB Jack Newcomer with 2-pt pass and 8-7 lead. Dupree scored again for 15-7 H lead, and Florida got HB Bob Hoover's TD run and Shannon's 2-pt run after 2nd H KO. Ignoring stiff wind, Bulldog QB Larry Rakestraw passed 6-10 on 13-play, 73y TD drive in 3rd Q as he clicked on 7y TD toss to E Barry Wilson and hit SB Don Blackburn for 2 pts. But, UGa spent last 19 mins pinned deep in own territory as Gator T Anton Peters was D ace with several tackles for losses. Peters was aided by C-LB Roger Pettee, G Larry Travis, and E Russ Brown in clamping down Rakestraw and Bulldog O.

ALABAMA 36 Miami 3: Crimson Tide (8-0) won 19th straight game and moved to no. 1 in AP poll by trouncing Miami (6-2). Bobby Wilson's FG gave Hurricanes 3-0 edge at H as QB George Mira outgained Bama QB Joe Namath 126y to 60y in air. But, Namath sparked Tide to big 3rd Q offensive, running 38y, then passing 36y to HB Cotton Clark to set up Clark's 1st of 2 TD runs. Namath threw 12y TD to E Bill Battle for 23-3 lead before 3rd Q ended. C-LB Lee Roy Jordan starred on D as Tide speed overcame 26-lb-per-man weight disadvantage in line.

MICHIGAN 14 Illinois 10: Trying for 2nd straight Big 10 victory, Fighting Illini (1-6) owned 1st H as they scored 10 pts in 2nd Q on C-K Jim Plankenhorn's 30y FG and FB Jim Summers' 1y TD plunge at end of 27y drive. Both scores were made possible by passes of QB Mike Taliaferro (12-35/133y, 2 INTs). Taliaferro threw completions of 1, 18, and 12y to his HBs before incompletions forced FG, and E Thurman Walker's brilliant grab of Taliaferro's pass positioned Summers' TD. Michigan (2-5), which gained only 3 1st downs in 1st H, rallied in 2nd H behind better line play and more comfort of reconfigured, injury-depleted backfield. Former QB Bob Timberlake scored on 4y pass as HB from new QB Bob Chandler late in 3rd Q. Trailing 10-6 and giving up passing y to Taliaferro, Wolverines soph E Ben Farrabee made INT and dashed deep into Illini territory to 1YL. Chandler wedged over and passed for 2 pts. It was older brother Bump Elliott's 3rd straight win over Illinois' Pete in fraternal coaching rivalry.

WISCONSIN 37 Northwestern 6: Before standing room only crowd in Madison, sr HB-K Gary Kroner, without TD all season, took 2 TD passes from QB Ron VanderKelen and kicked 38y FG to give Wisconsin (6-1) 10-0 lead at H and 17-0 edge early in 3rd Q. Kroner's 3rd Q TD catch came after he raced 44y with 2nd H KO. Badgers D pressured QB Tommy Myers all day and made INT and FUM to provide HB Lou Holland with 2 TD chances and 31-0 lead before end of 3rd Q. After being turned away at 1YL in 2nd Q at point when it might have mattered, Northwestern (6-1) finally struck for 39y TD pass from Myers to HB Steve Murphy in 4th Q, when it didn't matter. TO-infected loss dropped Wildcats out of nation's top ranking and promoted Wisconsin to 4th in AP Poll.

MINNESOTA 10 Iowa 0: However meager, 78y gained on ground by Hawkeyes (3-4) was most all year against nation's best run D (25.3y avg) of Minnesota (5-1-1). But, adventurous Iowa lost early FUMs at 3YL to Golden Gophers D standout, HB-DB Jim Cairns, and at 18YL to QB-DB Paul Ramseth. Vaunted Hawkeyes air game barely succeeded (9-17/105y) as it suffered 2 INTs in Gophers territory. In 2nd Q, Minnesota T Bobby Bell threw HB Bob Sherman for 7y loss that stopped yet another Iowa drive, and QB-P Matt Szykowny's resultant punt traveled only 19y to set stage for Gopher trip to 27y FG by K Collin Versich. Minnesota QB Duane Blaska threw flat passes to his HBs to set up his own 4y TD run very early in 4th Q. Shutout was 5th in 7 games for Gophers and vaulted them into 1st place tie in Big 10 standings.

NOTRE DAME 43 Pittsburgh 22: Daryle Lamonica, finally emerging as Notre Dame (3-4) sr QB, connected on 17-27/214y, 4 TDs, including E Jim Kelly's to-date school-record 11 catches/127y, 3 TDs. Lamonica's 4 TD tosses equaled ND record held by Heisman Trophy winning QB Angelo Bertelli in 1942. Fighting Irish jumped to 22-0 1st Q lead, but Pitt (4-4) snapped back to trail 29-14 at H as QB Jim Traficant closed 60y drive with TD run, and HB Ed Clark went 56y to score on reverse run. ND got 2 TDs off blocked punt and also tackled Panther P Pete Billey for TO loss of y. Pitt soph QB Fred Mazurek dashed 93y to score with 4th Q KO after Lamonica's last TD pass.

Nebraska 40 KANSAS 16: HB Willie Ross gained 110y on ground and scored 3 TDs to lead surprisingly-unranked Nebraska (7-1) to trouncing of Kansas Jayhawks (5-3). Ross went over GL twice in 1st Q, and QB Dennis Claridge added another score on 1st snap of 2nd Q. Remarkably, Cornhuskers batted 1.000 as they succeeded on 2-pt conv plays after each of their 5 TDs; season's avg for all major schools was only .450. Jayhawks never advanced beyond own 45YL in 1st H, got TD pass from QB Rodger McFarland in 3rd Q.

Texas 27 BAYLOR 12: Longhorns (7-0-1) coach Darrell Royal, undefeated but criticized for lack of O imagination, selected new field general in QB Tommy Wade, and Texas compiled flashy 437y on O. Wade (11-23/195y, 2 TDs) had hand in 3 TDs as Texas eyed 2nd consecutive SWC title. Baylor (1-6) opened scoring in 1st Q as QB Don Trull (20-36/217y) ended 73y march with 1y TD run for 6-0 lead. Wade led 2 trips of 80y each in 2nd Q, throwing for 2 TDs, including 54y strike to E Tommy Lucas, Texas' longest play of season. Bears HB Ronnie Goodwin took pitchout and flipped 1st scoring pass of his career, 18y to E James Ingram, to draw Baylor within 21-12 in 3rd Q. But, LBs Pat Culpepper and Ben House crushed 2-pt run attempt by Bears HB Kelly Roberts, and that was that as Steers went back to building rushing y, which would peak at 242y.

Southern California 39 STANFORD 14: With news of Northwestern's loss to Wisconsin, USC (7-0) fans thought decisive win would be enough to power Trojans to top of AP Poll. Instead, Alabama leapfrogged Southern Cal. Trojans went 80y twice for HB-K Tom Lupo's 32y FG and QB Pete Beathard's 4y charge around E for TD and 10-0 H lead. On its way to 201y O, USC went for 2 TDs in 3rd Q, and LBs Damon Bame and Larry Sagouspe nailed squat Stanford (3-5) FB Ken Babajian in EZ for safety after Indians had made GLS. Trailing 25-0, Stanford QB Clark Weaver rallied his team to 72y drive that included 2 completions and 3 good QB keepers. Weaver wedged over from 2YL and passed for 2 pts. USC sub QB Bill Nelsen took to air for quick TD that put it out of reach at 33-8.

AP Poll November 12

1 Alabama (22)	455	6 Missouri	224
2 Southern California (17)	409	7 Arkansas	196
3 Mississippi (3)	375	8 Minnesota	152
4 Wisconsin (8)	328	9 Northwestern	119
5 Texas	301	10 Louisiana State	77

Others with votes: Arizona State, Auburn, Dartmouth, Georgia Tech, Nebraska, Oklahoma, Oregon, Oregon State, Penn State (1), Purdue, Washington

November 17, 1962

Pittsburgh 7 ARMY 6 (New York City): Army (6-3) negated its 209y to 151y O edge with 6 TOs. Pittsburgh (5-4) G Jim Irwin grabbed 2nd Q FUM at Cadets 15YL, and HB Bob Roeder swept to score with FB-K Rick Leeson tacking on conv kick. Midway in 3rd Q, Army's Chinese Bandits D amazingly pushed Pitt back 50y on 2 plays to its own 5YL, and HB Ken Waldrop ran back punt to Panthers 32YL. Cadets QB Joe Blackgrove followed FB Ray Paske's block into EZ, but QB Cammy Lewis' 2-pt rollout failed.

Clemson 17 MARYLAND 14: HB-DB Ernie Arizzi picked off pass by Tigers QB Jim Parker and charged 68y with INT TD RET in 2nd Q to give Maryland (5-4) 14-0 lead. Without single 1st down in opening 21 mins, Clemson (5-4) finally roared back, scoring on FB Pat Crain's 3y plunge to narrow margin to 14-7 at H. Tigers delivered 10-pt punch in 4th Q, built around 65y TD march that launched with opening play of 4th Q. HB Hal Davis sprinted 35y around E, followed by FB Charlie Dumas' 1y TD run off T to tie it 14-14 for Clemson. QB Dick Shiner appeared to put Terps ahead 21-14 with 50y TD run when he fooled everyone with skirt outside on 4th-and-2 run, but it was called back by thoroughly-unnecessary clipping PEN. Tigers went all way to Maryland 2YL with key plays coming on 18 and 16y passes from Parker to E Johnny Case and Crain's 17y sweep. Coach Frank Howard, cranky loser of 3 straight to Terps on late FGs, wanted to smash for TD on 4th down but when Clemson was assessed 5y PEN, he sent in K Rodney Rogers fittingly to boot winning 23y FG with 1:22 left to play.

NORTH CAROLINA STATE 24 Virginia 12: Long road trip of 5 games (on which it went 0-4-1) was finally at end for North Carolina State (2-6-1) and Wolfpack treated themselves to cushy lead of 24-0 through 3 Qs. Virginia (4-4) had used runs of big HB Ted Rzempoluch and HB Bobby Freeman to advance to NC State's 19YL soon after opening KO. Cavs were stopped on downs, and Wolfpack launched 81y TD drive, that featured QB Jim Rossi's 14 and 19y passes until HB Joe Scarpatti went around E from 2YL to score for 6-0 lead. Rossi hit HB Mike Clark in clear in 2nd Q, and Clark slipped around defenders for 70y TD. NC State's Scarpatti raced 27y to set up his 14y TD reception in 3rd Q. Wolfpack C-LB Walt Kudryn's FUM REC deep in Cavs end paved way for FB Pete Falzarano's 3y TD dive. In 4th Q, QB Gary Cuozzo (14-24/120y, 2 INTs) passed UVa to 10YL, spot from which Rzempoluch scored on draw run. Bad NC State punt snap to its 1YL gave Cuozzo chance to sneak for TD.

Georgia 30 AUBURN 21: It took big play on D to open O floodgates in seesaw SEC battle. Auburn (6-2) DB Bill Edge picked off pass by Georgia (3-3-3) sub QB Jake Saye in 2nd Q and raced 46y to score for 7-0 lead. Bulldogs came right back as HB Don Porterfield (4/63y, 3 TDs receiving) caught passes of 31 and 13y from QB Larry Rakestraw (12-21/167y, 3 TDs), Porterfield's last reception clicking for tying TD. Tigers answered right back on HB Larry Laster's 3y TD run and led 14-7 at H. Rakestraw and Porterfield collaborated on another TD pass, as Rakestraw ducked under 2 pass rushers, after 67y trip from 2nd H KO. Georgia K Bill McCullough made 48y FG, his 3rd of year more than 40y, for 17-14 lead early in 4th Q. Auburn retaliated, but UGa DB Joe Burson took INT on run and didn't stop until he had cantered 87y for TD and 24-14 edge. Soph QB Jimmy Sidle (10-19/120y, TD) next led Plainsmen on 68y drive to his 7y TD pass. Auburn HB Tucker Frederickson fumbled punt at his 7YL, and that TO set up Porterfield's last TD catch.

Mississippi 19 TENNESSEE 6: Tennessee (3-5), wheezing toward only its 3rd losing season since 1935, propped self up long enough to test unbeaten Ole Miss (8-0). Trailing 7-0, Volunteers marched to 4YL in 3rd Q, but Rebels salvation came in form of HB-DB Louis Guy, who stepped in front of Vols TB Mallon Faircloth's pass and raced 100y down right sideline to Ole Miss TD. Trailing 19-0, Volunteers got TB Bobby Morton's late 16y TD pass, which triggered EZ free-for-all. Rebs outgained Tennessse 280y to 220y, but what killed Vols' chances were miserable 3-13/39y passing and 111y lost in PENs.

GEORGIA TECH 7 Alabama 6: Georgia Tech (6-2-1) sprung surprise Shotgun O and used heads-up play of FB-LB Mike McNames to drop 1st loss on Alabama (8-1) in 27 games. McNames' 26y INT RET to Bama 14YL put him in position for 2nd Q 9y TD run. Engineers D, led by T Larry Stallings and NG Rufus Guthrie, bottled up Crimson Tide, which rushed for only 78y. It looked like real possibility that Georgia Tech could blank Alabama. But, Yellow Jackets QB-P Billy Lothridge accidentally touched down his knee at own 9YL while trying to punt in 4th Q. Alabama HB Cotton Clark soon made his 14th TD of season, but McNames and DT Ed Griffin stopped QB Jack Hurlbut's 2-pt run. Tide got 1 more chance, but Tech DB Don Toner intercepted deflected pass with 39 secs to play. After previous year's controversial, rough encounter, Georgia Tech coach Bobby Dodd couldn't resist commenting to Bama coach Bear Bryant: "I believe that was the cleanest game I've ever seen. What do you think, Coach?" Bryant muttered, "It certainly was. But I didn't expect anything different."

FLORIDA 20 Florida State 7: Thanks to tiny Florida State (4-3-2) QB Eddie Feely's 24y set-up pass in 2nd Q, HB Keith Kinderman ran 2y for 7-0 lead. Gators (6-3) pared it to 7-6 at H as HB-DB Bruce Starling copped FUM REC and caught TD pass from QB Tom Shannon. Gators HB Haygood Clarke broke up game with 63y punt TD RET in 3rd Q.

OKLAHOMA 13 Missouri 0: Sooners (6-2) blanked 4th foe in row by holding Missouri's national-best (290y) run game to 111y. Loss halted Mizzou's 10-game string without defeat. Oklahoma sufficiently hemmed in Tigers (7-1-1) HB Johnny Roland as to hold him to paltry 12/9y rushing. Oklahoma HB Joe Don Looney took opening KO back 40y, and QB Monte Deere flipped screen to HB Virgil Boll who went 42y to set up Looney's 3y TD run behind G Leon Cross' block. Sooners went 80y after 2nd H KO as FB Jim Grisham's 30y smash to midfield started matters, then kept hammering at Tigers' middle. Fake to Grisham (116y rushing) permitted Deere to slip behind his FB for 3y TD run.

KANSAS 33 California 21: Bothering with only 1 pass, Kansas (6-2-1) battered Golden Bears (1-8) with 347y rushing to grab its 6th win in row. Jayhawks FB Armand Baughman rushed for 32/142y and scored 3 TDs, while HB Gale Sayers gained 82y to put him over golden mark with 1,053y rushing for season. Baughman tallied at end of 55, 68, and 74y marches. Also scoring for Kansas were HB Tony Leiker and Sayers, "Kansas Comet's" TD coming on 4th Q dash of 24y. California generated little running game as its 96y total was blemished by 43y in losses as QB Craig Morton (10-19/170y, 3 TDs, INT) was swarmed by Jayhawkers pass rushers. E Bill Turner caught 2 Morton TD passes to kept Cal in game at 21-14, their 2nd collaboration coming in 3rd Q. But, Baughman soon registered his 3rd TD on way to KU-record number of carries.

Texas 14 TEXAS CHRISTIAN 0: Fleet FB Ray Poage took advantage of TCU (4-4) giveaways in Frogs' own end to score 2 TDs, and Texas (8-0-1) cruised closer to Cotton Bowl bid. Horned Frogs were held to 71y total O and 7 1st downs, but played good D themselves, led by G Robert Mangum. Twice halted inside TCU 10YL, Texas still rushed for 216y.

SOUTHERN CALIFORNIA 13 Navy 6: Trojans (8-0) clung to their no. 1 rating primarily because valiant Navy (4-5) bungled short 2nd Q FG and lost FUM into USC's EZ late in 4th Q. Southern California presented its share of sloppy play: 4 lost FUMs and INT. USC went in tank right away as HB Ken Del Conte lost FUM when hit by Navy DT Ron Testa at Troy 23YL. Middies QB Roger Staubach (11-17/106y, and 19/113y, TD rushing) began his superb game with 5 and 18y runs, latter for TD and 6-0 lead before 2 mins had elapsed. QB Pete Beathard (4-11/71y, TD) got hot hand for Trojans in 2nd Q, hitting E Hal Bedsole (4/71y) for 30, 22, and 7y passes, his 3rd catch going for TD on turn-out pattern in EZ that had Middies DB Bob Sutton in no-mans-land between Bedsole and HB Willie Brown (8/143y, TD), who later roared 56y up middle on reverse for 3rd Q TD and 13-6 Troy lead. Navy FB Pat Donnelly, who hadn't fumbled all season, lost pigskin at USC 1YL in 4th Q when leveled by DT Gary Kirner with min to play. Staubach was asked if he thought it was his best game, and he replied: "Whenever you lose, it can't be a good day."

AP Poll November 19

1 Southern California (20)	439	6 Alabama	232
2 Mississippi (15)	430	7 Arkansas	209
3 Wisconsin (7)	384	8 Oklahoma	132
4 Texas (3)	326	9 Penn State (3)	94
5 Minnesota (1)	235	10 Oklahoma	43

Others with votes: Arizona State, Dartmouth, Duke, Florida, Georgia Tech, Michigan State, Missouri, Nebraska, Northwestern, Ohio State, Washington

November 22-24, 1962

(Th'g) TEXAS 13 Texas A&M 3: It took awhile, but Texas (9-0-1) wrapped up its best season in 39 years and Cotton Bowl invitation with win over rival Aggies (3-7). Playing effectively, Texas A&M scored in 1st Q on K Mike Clark's 20y FG, but really could have run away early had it been able to convert its advance, ended on downs, at Longhorns 6YL and Clark's missed 24y FG. Although Texas easily outdistanced A&M with 292y to 170y, Longhorns struggled to reach EZ until coach Darrell Royal turned to 3rd-string QB Johnny Genung to start 4th Q. Genung sparked Texas drive to TB Jerry Cook's 10y TD run and 7-3 lead. Then QB-DB Duke Carlyle made INT at Aggies 39YL, and Genung passed to E Tommy Lucas for 28y to set up TB Tommy Ford's short TD.

(Fri) Northwestern 29 MIAMI 7: With its no. 1 ranking and Rose Bowl dreams now in ashes, Northwestern (7-2) still was able to enjoy bowl-like trip to Miami (6-3). Highly-anticipated air war never materialized between Hurricanes QB George Mira (11-25/122y, 2 INTs) and Wildcats QB Tommy Myers, who completed just 4-11 passes. Myers, however, made all his connections count for pivotal 87y as E Paul Flatley grabbed 3/81y to position 2 TDs. Northwestern powerfully rushed for 57/232y. Spotting Miami 7-0 lead on HB Nick Ryder's TD at end of opening 63y drive, NW ground out drives of 92 and 44y for short TD dives by sub FB Steve Murphy. Wildcats' short trip to Murphy's 2nd TD came when DT Joe Szczecko threw Ryder for loss on 4th down run from Miami's 46YL. DB Dick McCauley made 2 FUM RECs and snatched both of Mira's misfired missiles in 2nd H, and these TOs helped catapult Wildcats to K Pete Stamison's 22y FG and 2 more TDs.

Dartmouth 38 PRINCETON 27: Proud D of Dartmouth (9-0), led by C-LB Don McKinnon, had seen its glorious 1.29 pts-per-game scoring mark smudged by Cornell's 21 pts in 28-21 Ivy title clincher on prior Saturday, and was hard pressed in this wide-open season finale. Suddenly explosive Princeton (5-4), took 14-7 lead in 2nd Q when standout soph FB Cosmo Iacavazzi spurted 46y to score. Tigers used fabulous 83y INT TD RET by WB-DB Jim Rockenbach to lead 21-15 until Big Green QB Billy King (8-16/116y, 2 INTs and 112y, 3 TDs rushing) tied it 21-21 by H on 4th down reversed-field 7y scramble to left flank. Indians' 3 scores in 1st H came on excursions of 72, 73, and 68y. Trailing 31-21 after King scored his last TD in 3rd Q and E-K Bill Wellstead added 25y FG, Tigers got back in it on Rockenbach's 2nd INT TD (26y RET) in 4th Q. Dartmouth campaigned methodical 87y to clinch it at 38-27 as clock wound down: its slender slasher, HB Tom Spangenberg (29/208y, 2 TDs), personally contributed 10/74y to drive. Dartmouth enjoyed its 1st undefeated season since its national champions of 1925 went 8-0.

Penn State 16 PITTSBURGH 0: Nittany Lions (9-1) secured Gator Bowl bid and Eastern honors with their win. But, fired-up Panthers (5-5) had better of play with 1st of their 2 vain trips to 5YL until Nittany Lions E Bill Bowes' FUM REC in 2nd Q gave QB-K Ron Coates chance to make 36y FG for 3-0 lead. Pitt advanced to Penn State

30YL after 2nd H KO only to have HB-DB Al Gursky make EZ INT of Panthers QB Jim Traficant, future outspoken Congressman from Ohio. Nittany Lions QB Pete Liske (8-18/146y, 2 TDs) soon hit HB Roger Kochman with 56y TD pass—on which E Dick Anderson cleared away last tackler—and added another TD pass of 18y to Gursky, who wrenched possession from Pitt DB Ed Clark in 4th Q. Penn State DB Junior Powell had made meandering 48y RET of INT of Traficant (1-5/10y) to put Lions in position at 18YL.

Duke 16 NORTH CAROLINA 14: Underdog North Carolina (3-7) held 7-6 H lead on QB Junior Edge's short TD pass in 2nd Q. On 4th-and-1 at Duke (8-2) 4YL midway in 3rd Q, HB Ward Marslender was thrown for loss by Blue Devils NG Jean Berry. Duke turned tables with 92y sortie. Back came Tar Heels as Edge hit E Bob Lacey with 39y pass, and they connected again for 8y TD for 14-13 margin. After UNC made disputed, re-measured 1st down, Duke HB-DB Mark Leggett's FUM REC at UNC 27YL with 4:31 left allowed K Billy Reynolds to make winning FG with :49 showing on 4th Q clock.

Kentucky 12 TENNESSEE 10: K Clarkie Mayfield, who was 0/3 in FG tries in 1962, nailed FGs of 36 and 19y, last coming in last 16 secs as Kentucky (3-5-2) sprung upset win. Tennessee (3-6) TB George Canale scored from 1YL early in 4th Q to provide Volunteers with 10-3 lead. Wildcats HB Darrell Cox, game's rushing star with 19/111y on ground, caught thrilling 58y TD pass from QB Jerry Woolum, but when Woolum's 2-pt pass failed Vols seemed in control for 10-9 win. But, Kentucky fought back on Cox's runs and Woolum's passes, with vital pass interference PEN at Tennessee 8YL, to go 81y in 16 plays to Mayfield's winning FG. It took DB Cox's EZ pass break-up to seal it.

OHIO STATE 28 Michigan 0: Blasting between its big Ts, monotonous ground game (338y) of Ohio State (6-3) sealed unaccustomed gruesome fate of Wolverines (2-7). FB Dave Francis (31/186y, 2 TDs) led trio of battering Buckeyes FBs to 4 TDs. After scoring twice for 14-0 lead in 3rd Q, Francis streaked into open field in 4th Q on 52y run on which he would have scored had he not fallen at Wolverines 6YL. Still, FB Dave Katterhenrich, 3rd of trio of sr FBs which carried on 44 of 64 Buckeyes runs, soon tallied from 6YL. C-LB Gary Moeller, future Illinois and Michigan coach, was prime artisan of Ohio State D that limited Michigan to 36/74y rushing and forced 3-and-out series 6 times. UM's best, HB Dave Raimey barely created wisp of O with 12/31y rushing and 2/10y receiving.

WISCONSIN 14 Minnesota 9: Bitter outcome for Minnesota (6-2-1) resulted from PENs that assisted Wisconsin (8-1) on its winning 80y 4th Q drive that took 2:17 to complete and was capped by Badgers FB Ralph Kurek's 2y TD off RG with 1:37 left. On decisive march, Gophers DT Bobby Bell was called for controversial roughing PEN of Badgers QB Ron VanderKelen, even though Bell tipped VanderKelen's pass into INT by Minnesota G-LB Jack Perkovich. (In latter years, revised rules would have made for no foul and possession for Minnesota.) Another 15y PEN for unsportsmanlike conduct from irate Gophers bench moved ball to 13YL. Gophers' bid to score for late reversal was fueled by consecutive Wisconsin pass interference PENs that placed ball at its 14YL with 1:09 to play. Threat was doomed in last min by Badgers HB-DB Jim Nettles' leaping EZ INT off Minnesota QB Duane Blaska, who had thrown 2nd Q 15y TD pass to HB Jim Cairns for 6-0 advantage. Badgers had come right back as HB Lou Holland returned KO to his 35YL and they led 7-6 at H as VanderKelen rolled out to pitch 13y TD to soph E Ron Leafblad. Wisconsin clinched Big 10 title, Rose Bowl trip, and its best mark since 1912.

MISSOURI 3 Kansas 3: Knowing Missouri (7-1-2) had little passing ability, Kansas (6-3-1) stacked line with 9 defenders. Tigers were held to 137y on ground, 19y in air, and K Bill Leistritz's 20y FG early in 4th Q. Jayhawks were mirror-image of Tigers O with 191y rushing and 17y passing. Kansas received K Gary Duff's 26y FG with 2:36 to play.

OKLAHOMA 34 Nebraska 6: Sooners (8-2) wrapped up Big 8 title and Orange Bowl bid with surprise aerial tactics. "We were concerned with their running game; we should have shot the air out of the football," griped Nebraska (8-2) coach Bob Devaney as OU QB Monte Deere threw 3 TDs in leading 182y pass attack. Things started poorly for Cornhuskers as OU E John Flynn surged in to block P Jim Baffico's punt back to Nebraska 1YL. FB Jim Grisham soon powered across. Flynn also made great catch directly over his head to set up TD in 3rd Q. Afterward coach Bud Wilkinson joked, "John Flynn is the only guy I ever saw who can make the catch by rotating his head like an owl." Shut off on ground, irritated Cornhuskers got their only TD on QB Dennis Claridge's pass to E Mike Eger.

ARIZONA 20 Arizona State 17: Arizona State (7-2-1), 3-TD favorite, splurged for 17 pts in 2nd Q for 17-7 H edge. Sun Devils QB John Jacobs (11-19/123y, TD, INT) scored on sneak, T-K John Seedborg made 26y FG, and Jacobs threw school-record tying 14th TD of season, this score caught by E Herman Harrison for 16y. Arizona (5-5) fashioned its big upset over bitter rival with dramatic play in 4th Q. After Wildcats HB Lou White swept E for 3y TD to make it 17-13 with 12:55 to play, 2 punts were very important. UA E Ken Cook hurried Seedborg into 10y punt to Arizona 48YL. Wildcats failed to move, but P Bill Brechler was roughed by Sun Devils T Pat Appulese and Cats retained possession at ASU 33YL. Cook went down middle to haul in 37y pass to 6YL, and FB Ted Christy dived over from 1YL for winning TD. In last 3 mins, Jacobs converted 4th down pass to E Dale Keller at Devils 37YL, but, on attempted long HB pass, ASU's Larry Todd was forced into lost FUM by Arizona E Jim Singleton.

Southern California 14 UCLA 3: QB-K Larry Zeno had beaten no. 1 Ohio State in early October with FG. Another 3-pt boot by Zeno appeared as if it would hold up as upset catalyst for UCLA (3-5) over another no. 1 team. K Zeno made 35y FG late in 2nd Q at end of 12-play, 71y drive. Drive was aided by 15y PEN against Troy's D, but DT Marv Marinovich dropped Uclans QB Carl Jones for 5y loss at USC 18YL, and that necessitated Zeno's FG try. Trailing 3-0, Southern California (9-0) was different team after physical, D-oriented 1st H. Trojans moved to Bruins 20YL after 2nd H KO only to

lose E Hal Bedsole's FUM. Then, after UCLA QB Ezell Singleton fumbled away punt at his 21YL, USC inched to 3YL, but FB Ben Wilson was stopped inches short on 4th down by Bruins C-LB Andy Von Sonn as 4th Q began. Bruins punted out, but netted only 25y. Trojans HB Willie Brown made soaring catch at 2YL, and Wilson soon scored for 7-3 lead with less than 10 mins left. UCLA advanced to Troy 42YL, but HB Kermit Alexander tried pass that QB-DB Pete Beathard spoiled with INT at his 18YL, then launched clinching TD drive fueled by this throw to Bedsole and Wilson's 8y run to 1YL. Beathard wedged over to clinching TD.

OREGON STATE 20 Oregon 17: QB Bob Berry ran for TD and hooked up with HB Mel Renfro on 50y TD pass as Oregon (6-3-1) cruised to 17-6 H lead in Beaver State's "Civil War." QB Terry Baker rallied Oregon State (8-2) and ended his career with 4,980y in total O, just 125y off all-time mark at that time. Baker hit 2 TD passes, both coming on 4th down plays. When Beavers E Vern Burke caught Baker's 3y TD pass in opening play of 2nd Q he became all-time receiving leader with 69 in season, also 1st ever receiver with more than 1,000y receiving in season. Burke's score provided short-lived 6-0 lead for Oregon State. Soon after ensuing KO, Webfoot Berry completed 47y pass to HB H.D. Murphy and followed it with 3y TD run. K Buck Corey closed Webfoot 2nd Q surge with 38y FG that sent Oregon off with 17-6 edge. Beavers were different team in 2nd H, holding Oregon to net 36y O and getting off on right foot after 2nd H KO with 65y TD drive. Decisive score came on Baker's 13y pass to HB Dan Espalin after Ducks bobbled 4th Q punt at their 13YL.

December 1, 1962

Navy 34 Army 14 (Philadelphia): National TV audience got 1st glimpse of greatness from QB Roger Staubach (10-12/204y, 2 TDs) as Navy (5-5) beat Army (6-4) for 4th year in row. Awash in sea of errors (3 FUMs, 2 INTs) by their teammates, Cadets' Chinese Bandits unit was helpless to stop surging Staubach's 2 TD passes and 2 TD runs. Middies also won battle of gimmicks: "Beat Army" in Chinese inscribed on their helmets; Army's ploys included what was believed to be 1st full team to appear in white football shoes. Another psychological twist may have backfired on Army coach Paul Dietzel: skipping pre-game warm-up may have contributed to early safety when Black Knights punt snap sailed through EZ for 2-0 deficit. Staubach followed with 12y TD pass to E Neil Henderson, who slipped into EZ through trio of Army defenders. Staubach made it 15-0 next time Navy had possession as he authored magnificent twisting 21y run to pay-dirt. Cadets narrowed score to 15-6 in 2nd Q when QB Cammy Lewis rifled 52y pass to 2YL to set up TD run by HB Don Parcells, brother of Bill, future coach of Air Force Academy and NFL teams. That was H score when Pres. John F. Kennedy changed to Army's side of field. It only got worse for Black Knights as Staubach fired pass to FB Nick Markoff, who raced away on 65y TD connection for 22-6 edge in 3rd Q.

Virginia 41 RUTGERS 0: Football paths of Virginia (5-5) and Rutgers (5-5) hadn't crossed since 1920, and Cavs' victory wasn't as easy as it appeared. Scarlet Knights probed Virginia's 30YL 6 times, but 6 TOs and fine 2 of LBs Andy Moran and Bob Rowley and T Dave Graham ruined every Knights' chance. With even W-L mark, Virginia finished its 1st non-losing mark since it went 8-2 in 1952. Wahoos HB Bobby Freeman scored from 1YL in 1st Q, and QB Gary Cuozzo (6-9/91y, TD) threw TD pass to E Jim Hoffarth for 21-0 H edge. Freeman scored his 2nd TD and HB Johnny Greene and FB Ted Rzempoluch added TD runs as Cavaliers cruised to 401y O and sure victory.

ALABAMA 38 Auburn 0 (Birmingham): Credits to Alabama (9-1) C-LB Lee Roy Jordan in rout of archrival Auburn (6-3-1): Jordan threw block that sprung HB Butch Wilson for 92y TD RET of opening KO, blocked punt that E Bill Battle recovered for TD, and made pivotal tackles that held Tigers to 28y rushing and created 2 KO FUMs. Crimson Tide QB Joe Namath scored on 17y sprint and hit HB Cotton Clark and E Richard Williamson with TD passes. High moment for Tigers came in 4th Q as QB Jimmy Sidle hit passes of 33 and 22y to reach Bama 21YL, but suffered Battle's INT on next play.

SOUTHERN CALIFORNIA 25 Notre Dame 0: Hollywood's hip—but slow to come around—crowd abandoned 1-12-1 NFL Rams and finally discovered local-hero Trojans (10-0) as USC completed its 1st perfect season in 30 years. By trouncing rival Irish (5-5), they accelerated impending end to Joe Kuharich's coaching career. Trojans stopped ND's initial possession, then went 60y to score early TD as HB Willie Brown ran 34y with swing pass, and FB Ben Wilson (16/72y) leapt over for score. Wilson added 2nd Q TD after Brown chipped in with 21y sweep. Afterward, Capt. Wilson addressed student section, offering to fight anyone contesting USC's no. 1 ranking. He got no takers, not even AP's voters who on Monday reinforced Trojans' top spot in season's final poll.

1962 Conference Standings

Ivy League

Dartmouth	7-0
Harvard	5-2
Columbia	4-3
Princeton	4-3
Cornell	4-3
Pennsylvania	2-5
Yale	1-5-1
Brown	0-6-1

Atlantic Coast

Duke	6-0
Clemson	5-1
Maryland	5-2
South Carolina	3-4
North Carolina	3-4
North Carolina State	3-4
Virginia	1-4
Wake Forest	0-7

Southern

Virginia Military	6-0
West Virginia	4-0
Richmond	3-2
William & Mary	4-3-1
Furman	2-2
Virginia Tech	2-3
Citadel	1-4
George Washington	1-5
Davidson	0-4-1

Southeastern

Mississippi	6-0
Alabama	6-1
Louisiana State	5-1
Georgia Tech	5-2
Florida	4-2
Auburn	4-3
Georgia	2-3-1
Kentucky	2-3-1
Mississippi State	2-5
Tennessee	2-6
Vanderbilt	1-6
Tulane	0-7

Big Ten

Wisconsin	6-1
Minnesota	5-2
Northwestern	4-2
Ohio State	4-2
Michigan State	3-3
Purdue	3-3
Iowa	3-3
Illinois	2-5
Indiana	1-5
Michigan	1-6

Big Eight

Oklahoma	7-0
Missouri	5-1-1
Nebraska	5-2
Kansas	4-2-1
Iowa State	3-4
Oklahoma State	2-5
Colorado	1-6
Kansas State	0-7

Missouri Valley

Tulsa	3-0
North Texas State	2-1
Cincinnati	1-2
Wichita	0-3

Mid-American

Bowling Green	5-0-1
Ohio University	5-1
Miami (Ohio)	3-1-1
Western Michigan	3-3
Kent State	2-4
Toledo	1-5
Marshall	0-5

Southwest

Texas	6-0-1
Arkansas	6-1
Texas Christian	5-2
Baylor	3-4
Texas A&M	3-4
Rice	2-4-1
Southern Methodist	2-5
Texas Tech	0-7

Western Athletic

New Mexico	2-1-1
Arizona	2-2
Wyoming	2-2
Brigham Young	2-2
Arizona State	1-1
Utah	1-2-1

AAWU

Southern California	4-0
Washington	4-1
Stanford	2-3
UCLA	1-3
California	0-4
Washington State *	1-1

* Ineligible

1962 Bowl Games

Gotham Bowl (Dec. 15): Nebraska 36 Miami 34

It's hard to believe that Miami (7-4) turned down warm-weather, in-state Gator Bowl chance, lured instead by bright lights of New York's Broadway and legendary grounds of Yankee Stadium. But, teams found under-financed, poorly-organized bowl in its 2nd go-round. Crowd was held down significantly by New York City newspaper strike and unbearably frigid weather. Miami borrowed warmest over-capes of New York Giants. Hurricanes QB George Mira, native of Key West, Fla., who actually believed Miami weather was too cold, somehow persevered, hitting 24-46/321y, 2 TDs. But, Mira's do-or-die pass for victory to E Bill Sparks failed at GL, as Sparks slipped on icy turf and fell on face while wide open. Nebraska (9-2) had sent HB Willie Ross racing 92y to TD with KO RET, and Ross contributed 41y run that set up another score. FB Bill "Thunder" Thornton plowed for important gains behind blocks of G Bob Brown and T Lloyd Voss as cold-weather team, Nebraska, prevailed in surprisingly well-played contest made most noteworthy by thousands of frozen fingers. None of those fingers belonged to New York writers who remained on strike.

Liberty Bowl (Dec. 15): Oregon State 6 Villanova 0

Banged up with sore shoulder, QB Terry Baker of Oregon State (9-2) also felt rusty due to commitments to award banquets, including New York City ceremony at which he received Heisman Trophy. Local Philadelphia foe Villanova (7-3) was big underdog since its only major opponent, Boston College, handily had beaten Wildcats by 28-13.

With 5 mins left in 1st Q, Wildcats put Oregon State in trouble as DB Larry Glueck downed P Bill Sherlock's 52y punt just 1-ft from Beavers' EZ. Advised not to run because of his injury, Baker ran anyway. Sweeping left, Baker was nearly nailed for safety by Villanova DT Al Atkinson, but broke free of Atkinson's grasp. Baker ducked under tackle of ace DB Glueck at 9YL, picked up blockers and went 99y for longest run in bowl history. It is record, of course, that can never be broken, only duplicated. "I had both hands on him," said glum Glueck, "I don't think I'll ever forget watching him go down the sidelines." Villanova put up surprisingly good fight, making 20 1st downs and 246y rushing by effectively using its elephant backs, FB Billy Joe and HB Lou Rettino. Wildcats failed when it counted, however, losing 4 FUMs, including QB Ted Aceto's bobble to Oregon State DE Paul Seale at Beavers 8YL with 2:47 to play. Oregon State HB-DB Dan Espalin had made EZ INT in 1st H to stop another Cats threat.

Bluebonnet Bowl (Dec. 22): Missouri 14 Georgia Tech 10

Bowl visit to Houston proved to be reasonable compensation for Missouri (8-1-2), which had sagged from as high as no. 6 ranking to a season's end that was marked by loss to Oklahoma and tie with Kansas. Tigers had turned down Bluebonnet previous year, but this time took on their assignment with relish. Favored Georgia Tech (7-3-1) counted on Missouri's lack of passing talent, and Engineers D coaches proved to be correct in their scouting assessment. While Tigers completed no passes and suffered 2 INTs, they still made enough big plays to win by running with football and playing typically stout D. Teams exchanged 1st H TDs for 7-7 tie: Missouri QB Jim Johnson's bootleg run in 1st Q, and Engineers HB Joe Auer's run in 2nd Q. In 3rd Q, HB Bill Tobin used crackling block by FB Andy Russell to go 77y to Missouri TD. Even though Georgia Tech QB-K Billy Lothridge kicked 3rd Q FG to narrow deficit to 14-10, subsequent Yellow Jackets threats were squelched when Lothridge suffered 2 INTs by superb LB Russell, future star for Pittsburgh Steelers.

Gator Bowl (Dec. 29): Florida 17 Penn State 7

Penn State (9-2) was big favorite over Florida (7-4), having lost only once by 3 pts. Up-and-down Gators chose to aggravate visitors from North by adhering Confederate flag decals to front of their helmets. Fabulous Gators D, which used surprise Monster-man setup, proved pivotal, holding Penn State's most prolific to-date O to only 139y and 2 meager trips into Gators territory. Florida scored 1st on K Bobby Lyle's 43y FG. QB Tom Shannon hit HB Larry Dupree with 7y TD pass for 10-0 Gators lead in 2nd Q. Nittany Lions QB Pete Liske scored TD, leaving Gators ahead 10-7 at H. HB Haygood Clarke caught another Shannon TD pass on 1st play of 4th Q to clinch 2nd bowl win in coach Ray Graves' 1st 3 years at Florida's helm. Win also launched SEC to 4-1 bowl record for holiday season.

Orange Bowl: Alabama 17 Oklahoma 0

Pres John F. Kennedy repeated his coin toss duties from the Army-Navy game, attending his 2nd Orange Bowl in 3 years. Oklahoma (8-3) coach Bud Wilkinson was serving Kennedy Administration as youth fitness consultant, so it was natural for Kennedy to make pre-game address to Sooners team. So, Alabama (10-1) coach Bear Bryant, feeling left out, inspired his troops by telling them they had been slighted by Kennedy. In end, Wilkinson said Bama won because they were better team, 1 that gave up only 39 pts in 11 games all year. Oklahoma started with unsuccessful on-side KO, and Crimson Tide QB Joe Namath closed opening 61y drive with 25y TD pass to E Richard Williamson. Sooners struck back with 56y pass between QB Ron Fletcher, in for 1 play, and E Allen Bumgardner. But, Oklahoma FB Jim Grisham, nursing bad shoulder, coughed up FUM when belted by Tide LB Billy Piper on next play at Alabama 7YL. Sooners soon got another chance, but lost another bobble. HB Cotton Clark's 15y TD run and K Tim Davis' 19y FG wrapped up scoring for Alabama. As it turned out, Orange Bowl would end Wilkinson's career bowl record at 6-2.

Sugar Bowl: Mississippi 17 Arkansas 13

Air-minded Mississippi (10-0) completed its 1st unbeaten, untied season in 70 years behind QB Glynn Griffing's 242y passing. After Ole Miss K Billy Carl Irwin and Arkansas K Tom McKnelly missed 1st Q FG, each team's K traded 3-pters in 2nd Q. McKnelly's FG, 1st of his Suger Bowl career record to-date 2, was set up by pass connection between sub Hogs QB Billy Gray and E Jerry Lamb, battery that would later collaborate on Sugar Bowl record 68y pass. Rebels made it 10-3 at H when Griffing hit HB Louis Guy with 33y TD pass. Arkansas (9-2) countered to tie it on QB Billy Moore's 5y TD pass to TB Jesse Branch after FUM REC at Rebels 18YL. Porker hopes died on 80y Ole Miss march with following KO as Griffing hit Guy for 18 and 35y, then carried over for TD from 1YL.

Cotton Bowl: Louisiana State 13 Texas 0

Favored Texas (9-1-1) was in for surprise from LSU (9-1-1), which had completed only 40 passes all season. In unusual appearance in purple jerseys, Tigers also figuratively changed their stripes by going to air for 13-21/133y, riding passing arms of QBs Lynn Amedee and Jimmy Field. K Amedee sent LSU to locker room at H on up-note with FG with 8 secs left for 3-0 lead. Longhorns suffered 5 TOs, most critical being TB Jerry Cook's FUM of 2nd H KO at own 37YL. On 3rd-and-9, Field squirmed away from heavy rush to scramble 22y for TD for 10-0 lead. Amedee, who would become O coordinator at Texas in 1980s, had TD pass nullified, but kicked clinching FG. Steers HB-P Ernie Koy showed well with 72y punt and 46.8y avg.

GAME OF THE YEAR

Rose Bowl: Southern California 42 Wisconsin 37

Meeting was 1st square-off of no. 1- and no. 2-ranked teams since 1946, and it would become famous for its conclusion in Pasadena's gathering gloom. True O shootouts in big games were so rare during these years, even in wide open NFL, that 1963 Rose Bowl spectacular became legendary. In losing, Wisconsin (8-2) and QB Ron VanderKelen, who shattered Rose Bowl passing y record, gained more notoriety than

winning no. 1 Southern California (11-0) team, crowned in December as AP national champions. VanderKelen's 4th Q heroics took on surrealistic quality as growing gloom of Pasadena dusk descended on field, masking view for fans and clouding TV image. Trickery had opened scoring for USC as QB Pete Beathard, FG holder, stood up and pitched 13y TD to Ron Butcher on T-eligible play. Wisconsin retaliated with VanderKelen hitting A-A E Pat Richter to set up FB Ralph Kurek's short TD run. A-A LB Damon Bane picked off 1st of 3 INTs for Trojans to create TD, and HB Ron Heller swept 25y for 21-7 USC lead at H. At H, coach John McKay drew up slant pass for E Hal Bedsole, which he suggested would baffle Badgers LBs. Play went 57y for TD to open 3rd Q, and USC mounted 42-14 lead as fans headed for exits with 14 mins left. VanderKelen related later that he told his team: "...Let's at least go out and look respectable. The whole game could have been a shambles; we decided to get a touchdown or two and see what happened." VanderKelen started Wisconsin's comeback with 3 completions, and HB Lou Holland threaded through USC line for 13y TD run. It was 42-21 with 11:40 left, and McKay said, "I still didn't think we could lose unless we did something silly—which we did." FB Ben Wilson's FUM at own 29YL allowed VanderKelen to hit Richter (11/163y) at 10YL and HB Gary Kroner in EZ. USC led 42-28 with 8:32 left. Trojans refired its O, but lost ball on downs at Badgers 33YL. VanderKelen hit Richter 3 straight times to 4YL, but Troy HB-DB Willie Brown hounded Richter in EZ and made INT, critical D play as it turned out. USC was stopped, and C Larry Sagouspe fired punt snap into EZ. P Ernie Jones made good play to accept safety with 2:40 to go as it nearly became Badgers TD. After Trojans free-kick, Richter caught TD pass at end of 43y drive to make score 42-37. Another punt by Jones was forced, but curtain came down on gallant Wisconsin before it could run another play. VanderKelen finished with 33-48/401y, 2 TDs, 3 INTs.

1962 Top Performance Formula

1	Mississippi	1.7390
2	Southern California	1.6898
3	Alabama	1.6472
4	Louisiana State	1.5653
5	Wisconsin	1.5534
6	Oregon State	1.5111
7	Penn State	1.4927
8	Oklahoma	1.4892
9	Texas	1.4605
10	Missouri	1.4516
11	Arkansas	1.4487
12	Northwestern	1.4444
13	Washington	1.4407
14	Georgia Tech	1.4276
15	Arizona State	1.4005
16	Duke	1.3894
17	Minnesota	1.3789
18	Boston College	1.3598
19	West Virginia	1.3483
20	Nebraska	1.3414

1962 Top Opponent Records

1	Miami	.6863
2	Illinois	.6711
3	Mississippi State	.6627
4	Georgia Tech	.6422
5	Navy	.6378
6	Iowa	.6364
7	Notre Dame	.6307
8	California	.6277
9	Syracuse	.6196
10	Houston	.6100
11	Oklahoma	.6019
12	Oregon	.5924
13	Florida	.5874
14	Northwestern	.5844
15	Michigan	.5789
16	Minnesota	.5789
17	Iowa State	.5777
18	Wisconsin	.5774
19	Auburn	.5761
20	Louisiana State	.5735

1962 Out-of-Conference Records

	W-L	Percentage	Bowl W-L
AAWU	17-9-2	.6429	2-0
Southeastern	24-13-6	.6279	4-1
Big Ten	15-10-2	.5926	0-1
Western Athletic	19-15-1	.5571	0-0
Big Eight	13-11-1	.5400	2-1
Southwest	9-16-1	.3654	0-2
Atlantic Coast	8-18-1	.3148	0-0

1962 Individual Statistical Leaders

RUSHING YARDS	Attempts	Yards	Avg.
Preacher Pilot, New Mexico State	208	1247	6.0
Eldon Fortie, Brigham Young	199	1149	5.8
Gale Sayers, Kansas	158	1125	7.1
Gary Wood, Cornell	173	889	5.1
Joe Don Looney, Oklahoma	137	852	6.2
Pete Pedro, West Texas State	134	831	6.2
Johnny Roland, Missouri	159	830	5.2
Dave Casinelli, Memphis State	173	826	4.8
Bobby Santiago, New Mexico	151	826	4.8
Dave Hoppmann, Iowa State	198	798	4.0

PASSING YARDS	Completions	Attempts	Yards	Pct.
Terry Baker, Oregon State	112	203	1738	55.2
Don Trull, Baylor	125	229	1627	54.6
George Mira, Miami	122	260	1572	46.9
Tommy Myers, Northwestern	116	195	1537	59.5
Dave Mathieson, Washington State	104	198	1472	52.5
Jack Concannon, Boston College	97	181	1450	53.6
Dick Shiner, Maryland	121	203	1324	59.6
John Jacobs, Arizona State	77	136	1263	56.6
Junior Edge, North Carolina	103	185	1234	55.7
Joe Namath, Alabama	76	146	1192	52.1

RECEIVING YARDS	Catches	Yards
Vern Burke, Oregon State	69	1007
John Simmons, Tulsa	65	860
Hugh Campbell, Washington State	57	849
Art Graham, Boston College	41	823
Al Snyder, Holy Cross	41	703
Bob Lacey, North Carolina	44	668
Paul Flatley, Northwestern	45	632
Tom Brown, Maryland	47	557
Bill Turner, California	44	537
Jim Kelly, Notre Dame	41	523

1962 Consensus All-America

End:	Hal Bedsole, Southern California
	Pat Richter, Wisconsin
Tackle:	Bobby Bell, Minnesota
	Jim Dunaway, Mississippi
Guard:	Jack Cvercko, Northwestern
	Johnny Treadwell, Texas
Center:	Lee Roy Jordan, Alabama
Backs:	Terry Baker, Oregon State
	Mel Renfro, Oregon
	Jerry Stovall, Louisiana State
	George Saimes, Michigan State

Other All-America Choices

End:	Conrad Hitchler, Missouri
	Dave Robinson, Penn State
Tackle:	Steve Barnett, Oregon
	Don Brumm, Purdue
	Fred Miller, Louisiana State
Guard:	Damon Bane, Southern California
	Jean Berry, Duke
	Leon Cross, Oklahoma
	Rufus Guthrie, Georgia Tech
Center:	Don McKinnon, Dartmouth
Backs:	Glynn Griffing, Mississippi
	George Mira, Miami
	Billy Moore, Arkansas
	Tommy Myers, Northwestern
	Eldon Fortie, Brigham Young
	Dave Hoppman, Iowa State
	Roger Kochman, Penn State

1962 Heisman Trophy Vote

Terry Baker, senior quarterback, Oregon State	707
Jerry Stovall, senior halfback, Louisiana State	618
Bobby Bell, senior tackle, Minnesota	429
Lee Roy Jordan, senior center-linebacker Alabama	321
George Mira, junior quarterback, Miami	284

Other Major Awards

Maxwell (Player)	Terry Baker, senior QB, Oregon State
Outland (Lineman)	Bobby Bell, senior T, Minnesota
Walter Camp (Back)	Jerry Stovall, senior HB, Louisiana State
Knute Rockne (Lineman)	Pat Richter, senior E, Wisconsin
AFCA Coach of the Year	John McKay, Southern California

1963

The Year of Significant Change, Staubach and Butkus, and Scholarly Panthers

The year 1963 was one in which remarkable change took root, not only in college football, but in the lives of all Americans. On Friday afternoon, November 22, President John F. Kennedy was gunned down in a motorcade by a single shooter or multiple assassins in front of the Texas School Book Depository in Dallas. The violent death of the youngest president in U.S. history seemed to rub the last veneer of innocence from American society. Turbulent times were coming.

Kennedy was a Harvard man, and the Crimson's 80th meeting with Yale, scheduled for the next day, was one of the first public events to be postponed after the assassination. Nearly all games of November 23 were switched to the following week, some were cancelled. A handful of college games were played the Saturday after Friday's assassination in front of decidedly subdued crowds, and the NFL was robustly criticized for playing its full Sunday schedule. The rationale presented was that Kennedy "would have wanted us to play," but highly-admired NFL commissioner Pete Rozelle later admitted that it was the worst mistake he ever made. A week later, a slate of rescheduled college games provided a much-needed respite from a week of national grief.

Before his death, Kennedy sent military advisors, including 1958 Heisman Trophy winner Pete Dawkins of West Point, to the nation of Vietnam, site of a Southeast Asian civil skirmish that would soon escalate into perhaps the most politically-divisive war in American history. It was a war that would soon prompt continuous confrontation by America's youth against authority. Also in 1963, a gifted Oklahoma halfback, Joe Don Looney, punched an assistant coach and was suspended by head coach Bud Wilkinson. Vietnam would prompt a reassessment of attitudes about authority, and the Looney incident would be symptomatic of a new, rebellious order of athlete. It was interesting that 1963 would paradoxically offer the last great service academy football team until a mild renaissance for Army, Navy, and Air Force during a more conservative 1980s regime of President Ronald Reagan, whose politics may or may not have affected the academies.

Navy (9-1), led by perhaps the greatest-ever quarterback and Heisman Trophy winner Roger Staubach, lost only by four points to charged-up SMU (4-7) and slipped by equally fired-up Army (7-3) in a classic contest decided in the last seconds. The Midshipmen of coach Wayne Hardin finished the regular season ranked second in the AP Poll and accepted a Cotton Bowl showdown with top-ranked Texas. It was the second such no. 1 vs. no. 2 bowl matchup within a year, the first coming the previous January 1 when Southern California and Wisconsin met in the Rose Bowl.

Darrell Royal's Texas Longhorns (11-0) used a stout defense, led by Outland Trophy winning tackle Scott Appleton, to easily outclass Navy 28-6 and cement the national title it already had been voted. Unsung Texas quarterback Duke Carlisle, known mostly for his defensive ability, surprisingly outplayed and outpassed the heralded Staubach on offense.

Alabama (9-2) finished second in the SEC and received a Sugar Bowl bid to challenge conference champion Mississippi (7-1-2). Crimson Tide quarterback Joe Namath, who would soon become an NFL torchbearer of the 1960s generation of rebellious athlete, was caught breaking training rules and was suspended for the Sugar Bowl by no-nonsense coach Bear Bryant. Suddenly becoming a decided underdog, Alabama rose to the occasion to smite the Rebels behind a great defensive effort and the fine offensive leadership of alternate quarterback Steve Sloan.

Ole Miss coach Johnny Vaught proved with a decision in late November that most coaches still wanted regional championships and weren't ready to play for national title marbles, especially if the opportunity was slim. Vaught's undefeated no. 3 Rebels faced a fourth down at Mississippi State's three yard-line when a touchdown could have placed them in possible shape to slip past Texas for the national championship. Vaught opted for a tying field goal. "We're conference champions and (still at that point) undefeated (before losing the Sugar Bowl). If we had gambled and lost, we would not have been conference champions," he stated flatly.

Pleasant among the surprise teams were Illinois (8-1-1) and Pittsburgh (9-1). The Illini beat Washington in the Rose Bowl with a squad built around a tremendous defense led by perhaps the greatest-ever linebacker Dick Butkus and safety George Donnelly. Illinois forced a then unheard-of 41 turnovers in 10 games. Two fine offensive newcomers, fullback Jim Grabowski and quarterback Fred Custardo, helped move the pigskin for the Fighting Illini.

Illinois had dragged through some odd seasons up to this point in the 1960s. In 1960, Illinois was a popular preseason favorite for the Big Ten title, but had disappointed with a fifth place tie with three other teams and a dull overall mark of 5-4. The Illini went 0-9 in 1961, but closed with two impressive wins in 1962. Amazingly, the UPI coaches' final poll crazily voting the 2-7 Illini to no. 19 in the nation in 1962 because one coach placed Illinois no. 10 on his ballot. Could it have been Illinois' own coach, Pete Elliott, successfully trying to save his job because he suspected something special coming in 1963? Many suspected Elliott as the flipped-out voter, but no proof ever was offered of a cagey, but possibly unethical vote. Illinois clearly was a team that was defying logic in the 1960s, and the Illini surprised the experts with a Rose Bowl trip and victory after the 1963 season.

Perhaps the most important 1960s contribution to pigskin history by Illinois was the development of Butkus. It is difficult to argue that Butkus wasn't the greatest linebacker in football history. One could make the same argument about Staubach's place in the quarterbacking pantheon. Since Staubach and Butkus played the most dominant position on each of football's opposed offensive and defensive units and that 1963 was the best college season for each player, it was remarkable in retrospect for college fans to have enjoyed their brilliance in the autumn of 1963.

Pittsburgh went uninvited to any bowl game, mostly because of the delay caused by the Kennedy assassination of its season-closing game against Penn State (7-3). Still, Pitt presented a special team and plowed through its usual tough schedule—the nation's 17th-toughest slate with a .579 winning percentage—suffering only a 24-12 loss to no. 2 Navy.

The Panthers displayed a more adventurous offense at the unusual insistence of school chancellor Edward H. Litchfield, who persuaded coach John Michelosen to modify his option run attack. "He's playing for the sake of winning alone and not for the pleasure of the fans. Don't get me wrong. I consider John as valuable real estate, he just needs redevelopment," said Litchfield. Michelosen countered that he wasn't in the entertainment business and must have grumbled under his breath about meddlesome college presidents. How wrong could Michelosen have been in this year of significant change. Football was becoming more of an entertainment vehicle with each passing season in the 1960s, and college presidents would become considerably more involved in football matters. Still, imagine a veteran coach in today's environment accepting Litchfield's very frank assessment without at least firing back with both barrels.

Litchfield need not have worried about the football-playing Panthers' level of academic achievement. They proved to be true scholar-athletes as 33 entered post-graduate study programs. The team produced 30 doctors, dentists, educators or lawyers, including halfback Paul Martha, who, as San Francisco 49ers attorney in 1982, was credited with a major role in negotiating an end to that season's NFL players strike.

Milestones

■ Substitution rules were further liberalized to permit unlimited substitution when game clock became stopped, except on fourth down and on first down after an exchange of the ball. In those instances, teams were allowed to substitute two players. Also, T-formation quarterbacks became legally-eligible pass receivers.

■ Independent Louisville joined Missouri Valley Conference.

■ On March 23, *Saturday Evening Post* published article entitled "The Story of a College Fix" by Frank Graham, Jr. Article alleged Alabama coach Paul Bryant and Georgia AD Wally Butts conspired to fix Alabama's 35-0 victory over Georgia in 1962. These claims were made by insurance salesman George Burnett, who accidently was patched into long distance (and innocuous, as proven in court) telephone conversation between Bryant and Butts. Butts won his lawsuit, and when magazine was forced to settle $760,000 in damages, it soon went out of business.

■ In June, Florida A&M end Bob Hayes set a world record in 100-yard dash with time of 9.1 seconds. Hayes would win 100 meter dash gold medal at 1964 Olympic Games and play successfully with Dallas Cowboys of NFL.

■ Longest winning streaks entering season:
Dartmouth, Southern California 11   Mississippi 10

■ Coaching Changes:

	Incoming	Outgoing
Colorado	Eddie Crowder	Bud Davis
Notre Dame	Hugh Devore (interim)	Joe Kuharich
Oklahoma State	Phil Cutchin	Cliff Speegle
Stanford	John Ralston	Jack Curtice
Tennessee	Jim McDonald	Bowden Wyatt
Texas Western	Warren Harper	O.A. "Bum" Phillips
Vanderbilt	Jack Green	Art Guepe
Yale	John Pont	Jordan Olivar

Preseason AP Poll

1 Southern California (34)	484	6 Northwestern	297
2 Mississippi (9)	389	7 Wisconsin	234
3 Alabama (5)	337	8 Arkansas	148
4 Oklahoma	331	9 Navy	78
5 Texas	305	10tOhio State	53
		10tWashington	53

Others with votes: Arizona State, Army, Boston College, Clemson, Duke, Florida, Georgia Tech, Louisiana State, Miami (Fla.), Michigan State, Minnesota, Missouri, Nebraska, Notre Dame, Oregon, Penn State, Purdue, Rice, Syracuse, UCLA.

September 14, 1963

GEORGIA TECH 9 Florida 0: Georgia Tech (1-0) won its 37th home opener in row as rain pelted down. Also down was Florida (0-1) QB Tom Shannon (6-9/41y), who was thrown for 69y in losses by pass-rushing Georgia Tech DEs Ted Davis and Billy Martin. Gators finished with –5y net rushing. Also sacks combined with 2 lost FUMs and 75y in PENs had Gators paddling deep in own territory most of day. Versatile Yellow Jackets QB-K Billy Lothridge booted FG in 2nd Q after failed Gators gamble on 4th down in own territory gave possession to Georgia Tech. Florida FB Larry Dupree (11/38y) dropped FUM at own 9YL in 3rd Q, and Georgia Tech HB Joe Auer soon banged off LT for 2y TD.

September 21, 1963

(Fri) Florida State 24 MIAMI 0: Trumpeted as perhaps Miami's greatest team with QB George Mira back for sr season and coach Andy Gustafson bowing out at Coral Gables after 16 years, Hurricanes (0-1) stunningly were blanked in newly-revamped Orange Bowl stadium. Tall Florida State (1-0) QB Steve Tensi (13-20/149y, 2 TDs) outgunned Mira (18-39/182y, 2 INTs), who was under heavy pass-rush pressure all night and was unable to guide Canes inside FSU 30YL until last min of 3rd Q. Florida State WR Fred Biletnikoff (4/71y, 2 TDs) was brilliant, catching 23 and 17y TD passes from Tensi in 1st H, and when Miami reached FSU 8YL in 4th Q, DB Biletnikoff made INT, dodged tackle of HB Russ Smith, and raced 99y to TD that sent Gov. Farris Bryant and many other fans home early.

(Fri) Pittsburgh 20 UCLA 0: Panthers (1-0), perceived as ponderous on O, demonstrated dashing new attack that gained 429y. Pittsburgh FB Rick Leeson scored 14 pts on TD, 2 FGs, and 2 conv kicks, while QB Fred Mazurek passed 8-11/106y and rushed for 43y. UCLA (0-1) highlight came in 1st Q when soph DT Steve Butler picked off Mazurek pass at own 3YL and steamed 86y to Pitt 11 YL. But, Bruins lost ball on downs to practical Pitt D.

SYRACUSE 32 Boston College 21: It was Orange if by land, and Eagles by air as Eastern rivals chose different methods of attacking each other. Syracuse (1-0) scored on its 1st series and ended up gaining 334y rushing in building 26-7 lead. QB Wally Mahle ran for pair of TDs and added icing on cake at end with 6y TD pass to left flat for HB Charlie Brown. Boston College benefitted from pair of 4th FUMs and used passing of QB Jack Concannon (11-29/265y, 2 TDs, INT), especially to E Jim Whalen (6/147y, TD) to get back in game with 2 4th Q TD passes by Concannon.

Navy 51 WEST VIRGINIA 7: Record West Virginia crowd believed it might watch Mountaineers (0-1) QB Jerry Yost outpass Navy QB Roger Staubach. Instead, Yost failed to generate any pts until game's dying moments when he passed 7y to backup E Fred Hauff. Navy (1-0) had owned ball nearly all of 1st Q but had only G-K Fred Marlin's 25y FG to show for it. Enjoying plenty of time to throw, Staubach picked apart WVU in 2nd Q. His TD pass to WB Skip Orr was followed by 2 short TD dives by HB Kip Paskewich. Midshipman Orr caught 7/89, TD and, as DB, added 52y INT TD RET in 3rd Q that lifted score to 31-0. Before exiting for bench in 3rd Q, Staubach pitched 17-22/171y, as Navy gained 417y. WVU was limited to 13y rushing, but passed 12-21/104y, TD, 3 INTs.

North Carolina State 36 MARYLAND 14: Its so-called "Mafia Backfield" led North Carolina State (1-0) to 241y on ground as FB Pete Falzarano led rushers with 14/88y and his mates—QB Jim Rossi and HBs Tony Koszarsky and Joe Scarpatti—each scored TD. When Maryland (0-1) trailed 22-0 in 2nd Q, QB Dick Shiner (17-30/189y, TD) used aerial bombardment for most of 76y drive to his 13y pass to WR Andy Martin. On conv try, Terrapins lined up TE-UB Bob Burton in backfield, and he took handoff and whipped left-handed, cross-field pass behind scrimmage line to Shiner who ran for 2 pts. This play took advantage of new rule permitting QBs to accept forward passes. Terps' trickery wasn't nearly enough, however, as Scarpatti scored for Wolfpack on 6y run after 69y drive following 2nd H KO for 29-8 lead. Shiner overcame Maryland's inability to run (63y rushing) by passing it most of 63y TD trip in 2nd H. When it came time to score, Shiner faked pass and scooted 6y to TD.

Alabama 32 GEORGIA 7: Fired-up Georgia (0-1) gave Alabama (1-0) plenty of pressure in early going as C-LB Ken Davis made FUM REC of 1st of QB Joe Namath's 2 bobbles at Crimson Tide 26YL on opening series, and HB Fred Barber smacked over from 3YL for 7-0 lead. From that point on, Alabama's fabulous D throttled Bulldogs for 4th straight season. Georgia gained only 138y O, including miserable 36/34y rushing. Namath (6-14/105y, TD, INT) tied it at 7-7 in 1st Q when E Charles Stephens caught

pass and twisted away from several tacklers to complete 47y TD. Tide led only 10-7 at H, but FB Mike Fracchia (13/42y), flexing his banged up knee, rambled for 2 TDs. Bulldogs QBs Larry Rakestraw and Preston Ridlehuber combined for 10-23/104y, INT in air, but Ridlehuber was smacked for safety in 4th Q. Georgia DB Brigham Woodward made 13 tackles and made FUM REC.

KENTUCKY 33 Virginia Tech 14: Soph HB Roger Bird (157y all-purpose y) became 4th Bird brother to suit up for Kentucky (1-0) and got off to perfect career start by charging 92y to TD on opening KO. Behind powerful block of FB Ken Bocard, who himself had scored on 8y TD run behind C Clyde Richardson's block in 2nd Q, Bird tallied on 4y run in 3rd Q that broke 14-14 deadlock. Gobblers (0-1), who would come back for fine season after dropping their 5th opener in last 9 years, had gone 69y to tying TD after Bird's KO RET. Virginia Tech QB Bob Schweikert mixed in 2 completions with his 21y run to aid HB Darrell Page to short TD run in 1st Q. Schweikert guided another drive of 77y late in 2nd Q to knot it at 14-14. Schweikert completed 5 passes, last of which went for 4y TD to WB Tommy Walker.

MEMPHIS STATE 0 Mississippi 0: Rarely has one team, Memphis State, gained so much from tie result while another, Ole Miss, lost so much. Tigers (0-0-1) DT John Fred Robilio made 20-plus tackles and led GLSs that repelled Rebels (0-0-1) twice inside Memphis 2YL. Pair of top-ranked Ds of 1962, led by Mississippi's 142.2y per game avg—only 5y better than Tigers—held each other's rush O to 57y for Memphis and 87y for Rebels.

Southern California 14 COLORADO 0: Despite heavy downpour in Boulder, Colorado (0-1) officials failed to cover field beforehand. Speedy, top-ranked Trojans (1-0) sloshed aimlessly through mud, incurring 107y in PENs. These miscues wiped out QB Pete Beathard's 21y TD run and his 63y completion to E Hal Bedsole. Beathard scored both Troy TDs on identical rollouts but had off-day, passing 6-19/71y, 2 INTs. Beathard also was sacked twice by Buffaloes, led by DL Marty Harshbarger, LB Larry Ferraro and DBs Bill Symons, Noble Milton, and Bill Harris. While USC O was subpar, Troy's D, led by highly-active LB Damon Bame, throttled Colorado's run game. Opening under new coach Eddie Crowder, butterfingered Bison QBs tried only single pass all afternoon as O lost 6 FUMs and never got inside Troy 45YL.

WICHITA STATE 33 Arizona State 13: Arizona State (0-1) lost its 1st collegiate opener since 1942 even though Sun Devils jumped to 13-0 lead in 1st Q. Sun Devils HB Tony Lorick ran 9, 8, and 19y on early 71y TD drive, but soon was banished with Wheatsockers HB Miller Farr in sideline fracas. Margin was boosted to 13-0 when ASU HB Charley Taylor dodged 1st punt-coverer and raced 54y to punt TD RET. Coming off 1962 as nation's most prolific O, Sun Devils HB John Jacobs passed 5-17/83y, 3 INTs. Wichita QB Henry Schichtle (11-22/167y, and 37y rushing) came off bench to score on 3y run and pitch 72y TD pass to HB Ray Patterson (10/81y, TD rushing) to tie game at 13-13. HB Pete Mills vaulted Shockers into 19-13 lead with 5y sweep at end of 47y drive in 3rd Q. Wichita E-DE Larry Beckish, whose block had sprung Patterson's long TD gallop, recovered FUM in 4th Q to launch 53y march to Patterson's 12y TD run early in 4th Q.

Penn State 17 OREGON 7 (Portland): Unbalanced line O with flanker (known as Z-back) was sprung with moderate success by cunning Penn State (1-0). Nittany Lions HB Junior Powell caught 8y TD pass on 4th down in 1st Q. Oregon (0-1) suffered many fits and starts on O, but in 3rd Q finally found spark. Ducks HB Larry Hill opened QB Bob Berry's 6y pass and 9y run with 54y slant off LT to Penn State 11YL. HB Mel Renfro's 1y TD briefly brought Oregon back to 7-7 deadlock with 5 mins remaining in 3rd Q. QB-K Ron Coates made 32y FG to put Lions ahead 10-7 early in 4th Q. Last Ducks threat died at Penn State 30YL as DB Bud Yost diagnosed fake FG and drilled it. Don Caum, one of Z-backs used by coach Rip Engle, soon caught 40y TD pass from QB Pete Liske (11-12/113y, 2 TDs) to put Lions' long western trip on ice.

Air Force 10 WASHINGTON 7: Air Force (1-0) scored on K Bart Holiday's 25y FG in 1st Q, but moments later 145-lb Washington (0-1) HB Steve Bramwell, former AFA cadet, picked up horde of blockers and surged to 91y KO TD RET. It was 1st time Bramwell had touched ball in his varsity career. Huskies D, led by tackling and punting of LB-P Rick Redman, dominated most of game, as Washington felt it had reasonably safe 7-3 lead as it faced 4th down at Falcons 9YL with only 3:15 to play. Expecting FG try, Air Force coach Ben Martin made strategic move by inserting tall and lanky E-DE Jim Greth in hopes of Greth's blocking UW FG attempt as he had done earlier in 4th Q. Instead, Huskies tried for 1st down and were stopped. So, thanks to substitution rule, soph Greth (5/57y), completely untested on O, was stuck unexpectedly in Air Force's lineup. "All we could do was cheer him along," said Martin as Greth miraculously caught 5 of QB Terry Isaacson's 7 straight completions to Huskies 7YL. Isaacson rolled right and cut back to leaping TD run with 1:34 to go. Air Force DE Jim Puster, D star all day, soon made clinching INT.

AP Poll September 23

1 Southern Calif. (23)	361	6 Wisconsin	208
2 Alabama (16)	355	7 Northwestern (5)	197
3 Oklahoma (2)	298	8 Arkansas	152
4 Texas	237	9 Georgia Tech	84
5 Navy (3)	228	10 Pittsburgh (2)	67

Others with votes: Air Force, Army, Duke, Florida State, Louisiana State, Memphis State, Mississippi, Nebraska, North Carolina State, Notre Dame, Ohio State, Oregon, Purdue, Rice, Syracuse

September 28, 1963

PITTSBURGH 13 Washington 6: Slick QB-DB Fred Mazurek accounted for all pts scored by Panthers (2-0) and made 2 brilliant plays on D. Mazurek plunged for TD at end of 75y drive early in 2nd Q and passed 11-16/120y, INT, including 14y TD to E Joe Kuzneski, who lowered his shoulder to plow through DB into EZ in 4th Q to extend lead to 13-6. After Washington (0-2) HB Dave Kopay scored on 2y run to cap 51y drive that narrowed margin to 7-6 in 4th Q, coach Jim Owens opted for 2-pt run. DB

149

Mazurek made tackle that halted FB Charley Browning in his tracks. After Pitt went to 13-6 edge, Washington HB Steve Bramwell broke loose for 70y KO RET to Panthers 27YL. Huskies made quick 1st down at 15YL, but QB Bill Douglas (2-6/26y, INT) was intercepted when nimble Mazurek raced between 2 Washington receivers and grabbed game-saving INT. Pitt then iced verdict with 86y drive, which expired at Washington 1YL as game clock ticked to end.

GEORGIA TECH 27 Clemson 0: Ignoring continuous driving rain, star QB Billy Lothridge of Georgia Tech (2-0) used his arm to cordially spread TD passes among Es Gary Williams, Ted Davis, and Billy Martin. With his foot, K Lothridge booted 40 and 36y FGs, and made 3 conv kicks in Atlanta's muck. Clemson (0-2) managed only 102y O, prompting home-spun coach Frank Howard to moan: "We didn't do nothin' right." Indeed, Tigers bobbled ball 13 times, losing 4, and had 3 passes picked off. Yellow Jackets' Williams, 2nd unit receiver, beat Clemson DB Jimmy Bell for 27y TD in 1st Q, Davis romped alone for 22y TD when DB Mack Mathews fell down in 2nd Q, and Martin faked out Tigers DB Ellis Dantzler for 9y TD in 3rd Q. So sloppy was Clemson ball-handling that C Ted Bunton couldn't get punt snap airborne in 1st Q, and FUM gave Georgia Tech its opening TD chance at Tigers 36YL. Clemson entered foreign territory only twice all game.

Auburn 23 TENNESSEE 19: With hopes of taking win in SEC debut for coach Jim McDonald, Volunteers (1-1) took 3 of Tigers' 5 FUMs and jumped to 12-0 lead on E-K Fred Martin's 27y FG, E Al Tanara's 32y TD pass from TB Mallon Faircloth (4-6/66y, TD), and safety on EZ slip by Tigers QB Jimmy Sidle. Safety was soon traded in kind when Faircloth bobbled snap in his EZ after Plainsman P Jon Kilgore bombed punt 50y to halt at Tennessee 1YL. According to Auburn (2-0) coach Shug Jordan, masterful Sidle (8-17/85y, 2 TDs, INT and 98y rushing) played "his greatest game for us." Sidle overcame 12-2 and 19-9 deficits, starting with 8y TD pass to WB George Rose. Prevailing despite pair of 15y PENs during 77y march, Sidle clicked on passes of 12, 10, and 18y before hitting Rose for another score that pulled Auburn within 19-16 less than 2 mins into 4th Q. On winning trip that came with 3:55 showing on clock, Sidle hit E Howard Simpson with 11y pass, rolled out left for 16y gain, and sneaked 1y for game-winning TD.

Mississippi 31 KENTUCKY 7: In SEC opener for both teams, Mississippi (1-0-1) awoke from its Memphis State nightmare and unloaded on unsuspecting Kentucky (0-2). Ole Miss started somewhat slowly with 3-0 1st Q lead, but, early in 2nd Q, QB Perry Lee Dunn unleashed passing blitzkrieg. Dunn hit E Allan Brown with 12y TD, and, after DB Jimmy Heidel made 1 of Rebels' 5 INTs of Wildcats QB Rick Norton (7-21/107y, 5 INTs), Dunn found WB Larry Smith streaking for 71y TD pass. Ole Miss backup QB Jim Weatherly connected with TB Billy Sumrall for 28y TD pass and 24-0 H edge. Dunn hit Brown for another score in 3rd Q before Kentucky could make late TD on FB-LB Ken Bocard's 17y TD RET of INT of Weatherly.

NORTHWESTERN 34 Indiana 21: Tenacious Hoosiers (0-1) used inexperienced line for good pass rush and got excellent 2-way play by HB-DB Marv Woodson (15/67y, TD rushing, 2/69y KO RETs, and 2 saving tackles and tipped pass for INT on D) to earn 21-14 lead over favored Northwestern (2-0) in 3rd Q. Indiana QB Frank Stavros (7-16/69y, TD) had tossed 8y TD pass to E Bill Malinchak for its only lead of game, but Wildcats HB Willie Stinson took following KO, broke through hole right of center and went 91y to tie it 21-21. In 4th Q, Northwestern QB Tommy Myers (11-25/227y, TD, 3 INTs) clicked on 4 passes on drive to K Pete Stamison's 24y FG. Myers later ran for critical 1st down at 13YL to position FB Steve Murphy's 3 blasts that carried to TD that expanded lead to 32-21 after which Myers added 2-pt pass to E Gary Crum.

MICHIGAN 27 Southern Methodist 16: New Michigan (1-0) cast bowed in with 5 sophs in starting lineup and 15 seeing action, including QB Frosty Evashevski, 2nd-generation Wolverine, who went in early for injured QB Bob Timberlake. After recovering FUM by SMU (0-1) HB Tommy Caughran to halt 55y drive at its 2YL late in 1st Q, Michigan lit out 98y to score: HBs Jack Rindfuss and soph Jack Clancy bounced for 34 and 13y runs, Evashevski scrambled 22y and Rindfuss dipped and dodged last 19y to TD on 4th play of 2nd Q. Soon thereafter, Wolverines G-P Joe O'Donnell was back to kick on 4th down, but when soph FB Charlie Dehlin took out 3 rushers with crushing block, O'Donnell took off running for 50y score. Evashevski's 5y TD pass to E Bill Laskey, after aerial battery had collaborated on 32y pass, gave Michigan 21-0 lead at H. Trailing 27-0 in 4th Q, Ponies scored twice with 2-pt convs against UM reserves: HB Bill Gallon ran 4y and sub QB Danny Thomas wedged 1y.

MICHIGAN STATE 31 North Carolina 0: QB Steve Juday became 1st soph signal-caller to start season opener at Michigan State (1-0) since 1948, and Spartans O got going quickly. They marched 73y from opening KO to TD created by alert E Tom Krzeminski. Juday hit Krzeminski at North Carolina (1-1) 5YL, and as QB-DB Gary Black tackled big E, he flipped lateral to streaking MSU HB Sherman Lewis, who darted into EZ for 7-0 lead. Carolina entered Michigan State territory twice in 2nd Q and trailed only 10-0 at H, even though their running game was substantially stuffed. Tar Heels' only O came from occasional aerial hook-ups from QB Junior Edge (10-26/84y, 2 INTs) to E Bob Lacey (6/58y) and HB Ken Willard (4/26y). Juday dived into EZ from 1YL in 3rd Q, and Spartans burly Hawaiian FB Roger Lopes (19/157y) burst up middle for 76y TD sprint in 4th Q.

Nebraska 14 MINNESOTA 7: Long-standing, but under-appreciated corn-fed Midwestern rivalry that would go away quietly in mid-1970s, became nice homecoming for Nebraska (2-0) QB Dennis Claridge, former suburban Minneapolis HS star. Although he completed only 4 passes, Claridge managed 65y TD strike to TE Tony Jeter in 4th Q to break 7-7 deadlock. Minnesota (0-1) had scored in 1st Q after sr QB Bob Sadek (9-23/107y, INT), making his 1st start, connected with HB Jerry Pelletier for 45y to 1YL. After that, Gophers never advanced past Cornhuskers 46YL. HB Willie Ross, who rushed for 91y of Nebraska's 176y, sparked its attack. After Cornhuskers FB Bruce Smith made 3 good runs on 36y drive late in 1st Q, Claridge had rolled left as if to pass and dashed 8y to tie it 7-7. Minny HB-DB Stan Skjei made INT of Claridge on his own 1YL near end of 1st H to clip Huskers threat. After Jeter's TD catch, Gophers had only 2 more possessions, and Nebraska killed last 6:30 on methodical 82y trip to Minnesota 1YL.

IOWA 14 Washington State 14: Trying for its 10th straight season-opening win, Iowa (0-0-1) used 3y TD lob by QB Fred Riddle (8-11/112y, TD) to HB Paul Krause and Riddle's 1y TD run to claim 14-0 H edge. Hawkeyes also enjoyed 192y to 67y O upper hand in 1st H. After H, game took dramatic switch to injury-depleted Cougars. Washington State (0-1-1) rallied in 2nd H as QB Dave Mathieson and mercury-swift HB Clarence Williams (21/130y) led comeback with lots of help. E Dennis Kloke caught short TD pass from Mathieson in 3rd Q, and even with Cougars throwing option runs into their O, they didn't tie it until 6 mins remained. Wazzu got 41y burst by HB Johnny Browne, and Williams followed with 23y TD. Game featured bizarre ending as Washington State was gypped out of 4th down at Iowa 40YL. Taking over after Iowa suffered 15y PEN, Hawkeyes QB Gary Snook pitched 49y to Krause, who appeared gone for TD, but was hauled down from behind by HB-DB Willie Gaskins.

Wisconsin 14 NOTRE DAME 9: Notre Dame (0-1) used slew of slightly miscast future stars to bother Wisconsin (1-0) with jump to 9-0 start in 1st H. Next year's pass-catching star, HB Jack Snow, ran 24y for TD out of WB spot to cap Irish's 86y opening drive. Future Heisman-winning QB John Huarte was used as K, and he booted ND's conv. FB Pete Duranko, DE star in 1965-66, was ND's leading rusher with 47y. Early in 2nd Q, Notre Dame E Tom Goberville blocked punt for safety. Patient Badgers completely cuffed Irish O in 2nd H and got TD pass from QB Hal Brandt, and FB Ralph Kurek (21/68y) plunged for game-winning TD with 1:07 left to play. Winning drive went 80y in 16 plays with E Jim Jones (6/100y, TD) sustaining it with fabulous 1-handed pass catch.

KANSAS 10 Syracuse 0: Jayhawkers (1-1) HB Gale Sayers (17/122y, TD) and FB Ken Coleman combined their rushing efforts on 11-play, 78y drive after 2nd H KO to earn game's only TD on Sayers' 26y burst away from 2 tacklers on 4th down run. Sayers' dash extended Kansas' 3-0 H edge to 10-0. Syracuse (1-1) D played reasonably well (245y) as it would most of season but its temporarily pop-gun O managed only 184y, including anemic 3-13/20y, INT passing. Orangemen threatened twice after falling behind 10-0. They advanced 66y to Kansas 2YL in 3rd Q, but FB Bill Schoonover lost FUM to Jayhawks DE Jay Roberts. Late in game, Syracuse made it inside 10YL only to lose possession on downs. Sayers had caught 30y pass from Kansas QB Steve Renko, future major league baseball pitcher, to set up K Gary Duff's 28y FG in 2nd Q.

Missouri 7 ARKANSAS 6: Moving smartly on QB Billy Gray's sprint-out runs, Porkers (1-1) scored on their 1st drive on Gray's pass to HB Jim Lindsey. Quickly, Arkansas posed another threat at Missouri 27 YL. Huge Tigers (1-1) DE George Seals draped himself on Gray's anatomy for 14y loss, and Hogs were never same spirited team again. Pair of Mizzou sophs, QB Gary Lane and HB Monroe Phelps, triggered 70y march in 3rd Q on which big Missouri line overpowered smaller Arkansas D-front. Lane whipped 25y pass to E Bud Abell to Razorbacks 2YL, and FB Gus Otto slammed over for TD. K Bill Leistritz booted all-important x-pt.

RICE 21 Louisiana State 12: LSU's normally tight D gave up its most pts since 1957 as Rice Owls (1-0) QB Walter McReynolds (11-21/178y, 2 TDs) pitched TD passes to HB George Parry (10y) in 1st Q and WB Gene Fleming (65y) in 3rd Q. Another McReynolds pass of 12y to E John Sylvester carried to Tigers 4YL early in 4th Q. It set up Rice FB Paul Piper for 4y TD slam up middle, followed by K Larry Rice's 3rd conv. Trailing 21-0, Bengal Tigers (1-1) soph QB Pat Screen (12-21/103y, TD, INT) abandoned LSU's spotty running attack—which he had led with 12/52y—in 4th Q and took to airwaves. Screen hit 33 y pass to FB Don Schwab to set up HB Joe Abruzzo for 2y TD run off T midway in 4th Q. Screen hit 4 passes in final mins to E Billy Traux, last of which went for 3y TD. Score might have been larger but for McReynolds overthrowing open receivers several times in 1st H when Rice, which had 10 1st downs before LSU earned its initial 1st down in 2nd Q, moved close to Tigers GL.

Oklahoma 17 SOUTHERN CALIFORNIA 12: Oklahoma (2-0) played ball control in 110-degree on-field heat, running 100 plays to USC's 57. HB Joe Don Looney took reverse from HB Lance Rentzel and roared 19y to score in 1st Q for 7-0 lead. It was indicative of Sooners strategy as Oklahoma unknotted large bag of tricks—reverses, HB passes, and fake FG—but in end, old-school 307y rushing, mostly from FB Jim Grisham and Looney, inflicted heaviest damage on Troy D. Soph HB Mike Garrett sparked USC (1-1) comeback drive to FB Ernie Pye's 1y TD plunge late in 1st Q. Key play came when Trojans threatened to narrow 14-6 2nd Q deficit: 6-man Sooners rush spilled USC QB Pete Beathard for 21y loss and forced FUM. It led to K George Jarman's 43y FG for 17-6 OU advantage, which lasted into 4th Q. Southern California found sufficient gumption for late 93y drive that ended in HB Willie Brown's 1y TD sweep. But, it was too little.

AP Poll September 30

1 Oklahoma (36)	495	6 Navy (2)	248
2 Alabama (9)	402	7 Georgia Tech (2)	220
3 Texas (2)	365	8 Southern California	163
4tNorthwestern (1)	264	9 Pittsburgh	114
4tWisconsin (1)	264	10 Mississippi	45

Others with votes: Air Force, Arkansas, Army, Baylor, Duke, Michigan State, Missouri, Nebraska, North Carolina State, Notre Dame, Ohio State, Oregon State, Penn State, Rice, Texas Christian, Washington

October 5, 1963

PENN STATE 28 Rice 7: Protecting against wide runs, Nittany Lions (3-0) permitted only 30y rushing, but swooping Owls (1-1) fashioned 18-36/240y in air, mostly from sub QB Benny Hollingsworth. Still, Penn State D earned 5 TOs, most significant being HB-DB Don Caum's INT of Owls QB Walter McReynolds at Penn State 14YL with score tied at 7-7 in 3rd Q. Lions rushed for 257y and converted 2 FUMs and Caum's

INT into 3 TDs. Penn State G Bernie Sabol had fallen on fumbled punt at Owls 17YL in 1st Q, and FB Tom Urbanik charged up middle for TD on next play. Rice managed 80y TD drive late in 2nd Q that was capped by FB Paul Piper's 1y plunge. Nittany Lions HB Gary Klingensmith ended 60y drive with short TD plunge in 3rd Q that provided lead for good at 14-7.

Duke 30 Maryland 12 (Richmond, Va.): Leading 10-0 after 1st Q, Duke's O disappeared in middle Qs as Terps D held Devils to 10y in 2nd Q and 30y in 3rd Q. So, coach Tom Nugent must have been biting his nails as winless Maryland (0-3) clung smartly to 12-10 lead with 9:20 left. Maryland QB Dick Shiner had thrown 10y TD pass to WR Darryl Hill and scored on 2y sneak in 3rd Q after hitting Hill with 34y stop-and-go pass pattern. Shiner was lost to hip injury, and his 3 subs proved they could move Terps, but not click in red zone. Blue Devils (3-0) sprung surprise 7 mins into 4th Q: triple handoff pass which QB Scott Glacken turned into 60y TD bomb to E Stan Crisson. It proved to be elixir Duke needed. On top by 17-12, Duke next added 2 quick TDs: HB Jay Wilkinson keyed 49y drive with 4th down catch for 15y and scored on 5y cutback run. Wilkinson couldn't get on field quickly enough to replace sub HB John Gutekunst, so Gutekunst, future head coach of Minnesota, fielded Terps punt and galloped 76y to TD with barely 2 mins to play.

North Carolina 21 WAKE FOREST 0: Wake Forest (0-3) lost its 13th straight game as snoozing North Carolina (2-1) awoke from its mild 7-0 H lead and clicked on long TD pass in 3rd Q and long TD drive in 4th Q. Demon Deacons QB-P Karl Sweetan (10/41.3y avg punting) bombed cloud-skimming punts deep into UNC territory throughout 1st H, but Sweetan chose to gamble on 4th down from UNC 40YL in scoreless 2nd Q. His pass to wide-open HB George Emmons was dropped. Helped by 2 Wake Forest PENs, Carolina went 60y to score on QB Junior Edge's sneak. On 2nd play of 3rd Q, Edge found WB Ronny Jackson in clear for 72y TD pass and 14-0 lead. Frustration for Deacons was illustrated in HB-DB Wally Bridwell's 56y INT RET to Heels 14YL, only to have K Sweetan botch FG from x-pt distance. UNC sub QB Gary Black wrapped up scoring with 6y TD pass to E John Atherton in 4th Q. Carolina enjoyed 436y to 92y O advantage.

VIRGINIA TECH 10 Virginia 0 (Roanoke): Disastrous FUMs by Virginia (0-3) spoiled outstanding Cavaliers D effort, especially in 2nd H which Virginia dominated. Virginia Tech (2-1) depended on all-around play of QB Bob Schweikert, who accounted for 128y of Hokies' 135y O in 1st H. But, Schweikert finished with only 154y as Va Tech was shut down in 2nd H. Gobblers WB Tommy Hawkins recovered fumbled punt by Cavs soph HB Tommy Krebs, his 2nd bobble, at UVa 2YL in 1st Q. Hokies FB Sonny Utz quickly turned gift into game's only TD. QB-K Billy Cranwell added 41y FG late in 1st Q. Led by runs of soph HBs Krebs and John Pincavage, Virginia swarmed into Tech territory 4 times in 2nd H, but were resisted thrice and lost FUM on 4th sortie.

LOUISIANA STATE 7 Georgia Tech 6: Bengal Tigers (2-1) welcomed Yellow Jackets (2-1) to Saturday night at Tiger Stadium, putting blanket over QB Billy Lothridge (6-11/70y, INT, and 10/16y rushing) and holding Georgia Tech to 198y O. LSU scored on its 1st series: 45y drive fueled by pair of 1st down runs by QB Pat Screen (16/95y rushing) and his 7y TD sweep away from speedy DB Joe Auer. It was 1st TD scored against Georgia Tech so far this year. Tigers E-K Doug Moreau won it with conv kick to overcome Lothridge's FGs of 26 and 21y that also came in 1st H. Lothridge missed 47y FG try in 4th Q but was roughed; 15y PEN gave Georgia Tech 2nd chance at LSU 17YL. HB Auer's FUM appeared to be recovered by Tigers near sideline at 22YL, but REC was ruled OB. LB Ruffin Rodrigue threw Auer for 3y loss, and Lothridge missed another 3-pt try, this of 42y. With 1:27 to go, Jackets got last chance, but LSU DE Billy Truax tipped Lothridge's pass and spun around to make diving INT that ended it.

ILLINOIS 10 Northwestern 9: Illinois (2-0) beat no. 4 Northwestern (2-1) in upset for its 1st win over in-state rival since 1959. Wildcats had broken on top in 2nd Q at 6-0 on 29y TD pass from QB Tommy Myers (17-32/218y, TD, 2 INTs) to WR Tom O'Grady. But, high snap by NW C Joe Cerne couldn't be handled and x-pt was foiled. Wildcats FB-P Ron Rector flubbed 5y punt later in 2nd Q, and Illinois used deceptive "Flipper Dipper" play for its 32y TD. Illini QB Fred Custardo threw overhand lateral to HB Ron Fearn, former QB now playing mostly at DB. Fearn ran toward sideline and fired surprise EZ pass to HB Jim Warren. On their only possession of 3rd Q, Wildcats briefly regained 9-7 lead on K Pete Stamison's 24y FG, but C-K Jim Plankenhorn matched it with his own 3rd Q FG. Late threats by Northwestern were frustrated by Illinois D, led by C-LB Dick Butkus.

Navy 26 MICHIGAN 13: Wolverines (1-1) coach Bump Elliott called QB Roger Staubach of no. 6 Navy (3-0) "greatest quarterback I've ever seen" after watching him gain 307y running and passing. Those fat numbers broke "Roger the Dodger's" own week-old Midshipmen record set against William & Mary. Staubach ran for 5y TD and threw TDs of 54y to HB Johnny Sai and 7y to E Neil Henderson. Overrun with its own youth, Michigan called sr QB Bob Chandler off bench in 3rd Q to pass 9-10/138y, 2 TDs. Wolverines E John Henderson caught both of Chandler's scoring throws: 7y in 3rd Q and 37y in 4th Q.

Mississippi 20 HOUSTON 6: Rebels (2-0-1) QB Jim Weatherly swept 45y around his RE in 1st Q and added 2y TD run at end of 72y drive. Trying to deal with its murderous early schedule, Cougars (0-3) put pressure on no. 10 Mississippi by turning Ole Miss WB Larry Smith's FUM into hard-earned 19y TD drive. Houston QB Jack Skog passed for 1st down at Rebels 1YL. Ole Miss emerged after 3 plays with ball at its 2YL, but Skog hit TD pass to E Clem Beard on 4th down, so Houston trailed only 7-6 at H. Rebels QB Perry Lee Dunn used 11 plays on 73y drive after 2nd H KO to prompt his 23y TD pass to TB Mike Dennis and 13-6 lead. Dunn and Dennis collaborated on 30y TD pass in 4th Q.

ARKANSAS 18 Texas Christian 3: E Jerry Lamb made spectacular leaping catch off shoulder of TCU (2-1) defender and raced 56y to finish TD pass for Arkansas (2-1) midway through 1st Q. Trailing 6-0, Horned Frogs played terrific D to completely stymie Razorbacks. FB-K Jimmy McAteer pounded through 37y FG in 2nd Q, so TCU harbored plenty of hope as tight D struggle drifted into 4th Q. Arkansas' own fine D, led by C-LB Ronnie Caveness, held Frogs to 77y on ground and forced them into mildly effective passing game (12-27/137y, 2 TDs). Caveness picked off pass by TCU QB Randy Howard at Purple 28YL. Porkers QB Billy Gray flipped 11y pass to E Jim John that led to his 1y TD sneak that came after Arkansas was stopped on 3 downs. Up by 12-3, Gray scored on 7y keeper less than 2 mins later. That score came after Arkansas E Jim Finch recovered FUM on KO at TCU 26YL and Gray hit TB Jim Lindsey with 15y pass.

SOUTHERN CALIFORNIA 13 Michigan State 10: Sidewinder K Lou Bobich registered 38y FG in 1st Q, and little HB Sherman Lewis took screen pass down sideline to 88y TD from QB Steve Juday, and Spartans (1-1) enjoyed 10-0 lead through 3 Qs. Trojans (2-1) HB Mike Garrett ran trap play, breaking free for 52y TD on opening play of 4th Q. Now fired-up, Southern California came right back on its next series as HB Willie Brown zoomed 51y with pass to Michigan State 18YL. A-A E Hal Bedsole, in something of early-season catching slump, made 16y shoestring catch of QB Pete Beathard's 4th down TD pass for 13-10 win. Brown made INT in 4th Q, and USC moved to 2YL. Bedsole, however, dropped easy catch in EZ and drive expired when Beathard was stopped on run at 1YL.

AP Poll October 7

1 Oklahoma (40)	508	6 Pittsburgh (1)	228
2 Texas (5)	435	7 Southern California	157
3 Alabama (4)	430	8 Ohio State	155
4 Navy (3)	346	9 Penn State	120
5 Wisconsin (1)	279	10 Mississippi	88

Others with votes: Air Force, Arkansas, Auburn, Duke, Georgia Tech, Illinois, Louisiana State, Minnesota, Missouri, Nebraska, North Carolina State, Northwestern, Oregon, Oregon State, Purdue

October 12, 1963

(Fri) Louisiana State 3 MIAMI 0: After Ds dominated scoreless 1st H, LSU (3-1) rode runs of HB Danny LeBlanc (16/89y) to 1st-and-goal just inside Miami (2-2) 10YL in 3rd Q. Rugged Hurricanes held at their 3YL, but Tigers E-K Doug "Ducky" Moreau booted 20y FG for 1st score vs. Miami in most-recent 10 Qs. As 4th Q marched on, Hurricanes QB George Mira (12-19/138y) hit 4 straight passes for 55y but was spilled for 5y loss on 3rd down sweep by soph DT Ernest Maggiore. With 2:39 to play, Hurricanes faced 4th-and-6 at LSU 22YL. Boos rained on Canes coach Andy Gustafson as he chose to tap K Don Cifra for 39y FG try, which was missed. Miami got another chance, but E Hoyt Sparks frustratingly dropped GL pass with 1 sec showing on clock.

(Fri) SOUTHERN METHODIST 32 Navy 28: Slender SMU (2-1) soph speedster HB John Roderick scored twice and posted 13.2y rushing avg thanks to his 45, 26, and 33y dashes. QB Roger Staubach (12-22/128y, TD, INT, and 107y, TD rushing) twice returned from injuries to propel his Navy (3-1) mates. Middies sent wobbly Staubach back into fray to plunge 1y for 10-0 lead in 1st Q. But, Roderick swept 26y to set up soph QB Mac White's 22y TD dash through big hole. SMU barely beat H clock on QB Danny Thomas' 3y TD pass to E Tom Hillary and used Roderick's 2 TDs to take 26-25 advantage in 4th Q. Still, Navy earned 28-26 lead on G-K Fred Marlin's 2nd FG with 2:52 remaining. Annoyed all night by 107y in PENs, Middies committed suicidal pass interference at their own 1YL, allowing Ponies HB Billy Gannon to bash over for winning TD inside last 2 mins. Staubach engineered his Middies to 8YL with :05 on clock but his 2 passes were broken up in EZ.

Army 10 PENN STATE 7: Army (3-1) edged Penn State (3-1) 3rd straight year by 3 pts, this time on early 32y FG by K Dick Heydt. Loss had familiar look to Nittany Lions: Just as in 1961 and 1962, Penn State entered game as unbeaten, clear-cut favorite. Cadets QB Rollie Stichweh and HBs Ken Waldrop and John Seymour ran away from Lions' monster-LB all day for 220y, but game turned on play of Army D, led by E Sam Champi and G Dick Nowak, as Nittany Lions rushed for only 38y. Nation's no. 2 passer, QB Pete Liske (2-12/81y, TD, INT), had been snowed under while trying to pass on Penn State's 2nd series. Liske fumbled and Nowak recovered at Lions 34YL, which led to Heydt's 4th FG of young season. Lengthy ground assault that bridged 1st and 2nd Qs led Cadets to 4th down at 2YL, and Stichweh rolled out to flip soft TD pass to Champi. Late in 2nd Q, Liske looked left and threw long right to HB Junior Powell, who broke past Army DBs for 69y TD pass. Catch was Powell's 60th for new school career record, but was all Lions had left.

Florida 10 ALABAMA 6: In his 25 years from 1958 to 1982 at Alabama (3-1), coach Bear Bryant lost only twice in Tuscaloosa. This upset by 2-TD underdog Gators (2-1-1) was 1st such dark mark and snapped Bama's 16-game home winning streak. Florida opened game with forceful D and received short Tide punt by P Buddy French, when he juggled snap in EZ. Gators K Bob Lyle soon kicked 42y FG. Game wore on into 4th Q when Gators soph HB Dick Kirk capped 75y thrust when he breezed 41y to TD for decisive 10-0 lead. With its TO-prone O stumbling, Crimson Tide D was forced to author 2 GLSs. Alabam lost 3 FUMs, and QB Joe Namath (10-26/104y) threw 2 INTs. Namath pushed across late QB sneak TD, but Bama's 2-pt try was crushed.

FLORIDA STATE 35 Wake Forest 0: Early Florida State (2-1) 23y TD on pass from QB Steve Tensi to WR Fred Biletnikoff came because pressured Wake Forest (0-4) QB-P Karl Sweetan had to punt on run and toed it only 9y to Deacons 34YL. But, thanks to accurate passing and mostly strong punts of Sweetan (16-29/122y) and good 2-way play of E-DE Dick Cameron, Wake clung close, trailing 7-0 deficit late in 2nd Q. Tensi (18-27/236y, 4 TDs) was fairly inaccurate with his early passes, but got hot in time for 52y march on which he hit 5 in row to position FB Marion Roberts' 1y TD plunge that beat H clock for 14-0 gain. FSU's late 2nd Q surge took starch right out of Wake Forest, and Tensi continued mid-game 17-22 passing streak and threw for 2 TDs to E Max Wettstein in 2nd H.

OHIO STATE 20 Illinois 20: Record crowd at Ohio Stadium saw 52nd renewal of series provide 4th Q heroics by both Ohio State (2-0-1) and Illinois (2-0-1) and questionable conv decision by Illini coach Pete Elliott. Illinois scored 1st on HB Sam Price's plunge and led 7-3 at H. Concentrating on power ground attack (209y) that was keyed by FBs Matt Snell and Willard Sander, Buckeyes built 17-7 lead. Illini QB Mike Taliaferro (10-23/148y, TD, 2 INTs) passed 2y on 4th down TD to E Eddie Russell that trimmed deficit to 17-13, but instead of kicking conv, Taliaferro was sent on pass-run option rollout that was stopped. With Illini trailing by 4 pts, Taliaferro launched 56y pass to Price, who, although overhauled at Ohio 3YL, still set up HB Jim Warren's TD 4y run. This time, Elliott brought about 20-17 lead for Tribe by ordering x-pt kick to follow TD. But, K Dick vanRaaphorst booted to-date Big 10 record 49y FG to tie with 1:53 to go, and vanRaaphorst had another chance on 56y FG try, which he missed on game's next to last play.

MICHIGAN 7 Michigan State 7: Capacity crowd of 101,450—16th straight sellout for Michigan (1-1-1) vs. Michigan State (1-1-1)—played role of smooch voyeur as each team "kissed their sister." Rivals' 56th encounter was ruled by D strength as Wolverines led most of way after hopping to 7-0 lead in 1st Q on QB Bob Chandler's 15y TD pass to E John Henderson (4/38y). Michigan's TD had been set up by HB Jack Clancy's 42y punt RET to MSU 41YL. Although both foes scored on TD passes—Spartans countered with 84y drive in 3rd Q to HB Sherman Lewis' 7y scoring catch from QB Steve Juday—neither team would build decent passing game. With injured QB-K-P Bob Timberlake limited to kicking duties, Michigan QBs Chandler and Frosty Evashevski combined to throw 7-22/78y, INT, while Spartans QB Juday had 6-15/64y, INT aerial performance. K Timberlake, whose arm was injured in preseason, missed 43y FG near end after Michigan, which suffered weak ground attack with 36/34y, completed 3 passes to reach MSU 23YL.

NOTRE DAME 17 Southern California 14: Struggling Fighting Irish (1-2), trying to find their way under interim coach Hugh Devore, handed USC (2-2) its 2nd surprise loss in 3 weeks and its 9th straight defeat in Notre Dame Stadium. ND took lead 3 times, last coming on K Ken Ivan's 36y FG with 6:28 left to play. USC QB Pete Beathard had been picked off by Irish DB Tom MacDonald, who raced 62y to score in 1st Q thanks to FB-LB Bill Pfeiffer's thunderous block on last tackler. Beathard countered with 3y TD run and 12y TD pass to HB Mike Garrett in 2nd Q. Irish heroes were sr QB Frank Budka (18/84y rushing), who had suffered broken leg in 1962 finale against USC and returned for his 1st action of 1963 as game starter, and soph HB Bill Wolski (16/87y, TD), who enjoyed his 1st regular duty. MacDonald broke up pass that star Troy E Hal Bedsole all but locked up at Irish 3YL in 3rd Q. Ivan's winning FG came at end of march that had started on ND 17YL.

Air Force 17 NEBRASKA 13: Air Force (3-1) DG Todd Jagerson revealed after game that Falcons enjoyed silent edge because burly Nebraska (3-1) linemen tipped plays from their stances with uneven weight on hands. Still, Cornhuskers blockers got off their marks well enough to spring 2 long runs: FB Rudy Johnson stormed 76y for TD and HB Kent McCloughan dashed 44y to set up HB Bruce Smith's TD plunge for 13-10 lead in 3rd Q. QB Terry Isaacson's 38y TD pass to E Fritz Greenlee won it with 2:41 left.

Texas 28 Oklahoma 7 (Dallas): Texas (4-0) trampled Oklahoma (2-1) with dose of Sooners' own old-fashioned medicine: Split-T option runs engineered by QB Duke Carlisle, who gained 9/62y while running for TD and passing for another. Oklahoma O was held to 8 1st downs by firm Longhorns D, led by T Scott Appleton. Loss started raucous week in which Sooners HB Joe Don Looney, who carried only 4 times, was suspended by coach Bud Wilkinson for punching asst coach.

BAYLOR 14 Arkansas 10: Year's finest pass-catch duo, QB Don Trull-to-WR Lawrence Elkins, led Bears (2-1) to upset of Razorbacks (2-2). Trull passed 21-34/241y, 2 TDs, 3 INTs, with both scores going to slippery Elkins (8/110y). Coach Frank Broyles lamented that his Hogs tried hard, but said 2 men were insufficient to cover Elkins if they couldn't pressure Trull. Elkins had missed considerable practice time with leg injury and as well as he played, he still lost pass at GL that might have been 1st Q TD and 2 throws that bounced off his fingertips only to turn out as INTs for Arkansas DBs Ken Hatfield and Gary Howard. Razorbacks, still unsettled at QB, started soph QB Jon Brittenum, but he gave way to veteran QB-sometimes-DB Billy Gray (10-19/126y, INT) in 2nd Q. Gray fired apparent 2nd Q TD to WB Jim Lindsey, but it was ruled he came down on chalk line. Arkansas had to settle for K Tom McKnelly's 33y FG and trailed 7-3 at H when Trull moved Bears 84y in 6 plays. Hogs gained 10-7 lead early in 3rd Q when 31y catch and runs by Lindsey (21/71y rushing) set up FB Charles Daniel for 1y TD punch. Key play came later in 3rd Q when Baylor DT Arturo Delgado blocked Gray's pass into INT RET by Bruins DT Bobby Crenshaw at Hogs 14YL. Elkins caught 17y TD in 2 plays.

WASHINGTON 34 Oregon State 7: Beavers (3-1) became 7th team knocked from unbeaten ranks during this surprising weekend, leaving only 8 without loss or tie. Washington (1-3) overcame angry local critics of its passing game: Tall sub QB Al Libke was moved to E, and, magically, Huskies completed 9-12/2 TDs. Huskies QBs Bill Douglas and Todd Hullin each pitched scoring pass in 2nd H, and FB Charlie Browning scored twice. G-LB Rick Redman blitzed Beavers QB Gordon Queen to utter distraction, and little soph Washington HB Steve Bramwell broke open game with 92y punt TD RET in 2nd Q for 13-0 H lead. Before he was done in Seattle, Bramwell would go on to hold combined NCAA career record punt and KO TDs. In ultimate too-little-too-late action, Oregon State didn't score until last play of game on sub Phil Woodworth's 15y run.

CALIFORNIA 22 Duke 22: Golden Bears (1-2-1) E Jack Schraub went high in air among 3 Duke (3-0-1) defenders to grab QB Craig Morton's 31y TD pass in 4th Q, and Morton (14-28/205y, 2 TDs, 2 INTs) flipped tying 2-pt conv pass to HB Jerry Mosher. Morton and Schraub, aerial duo that 1st combined in grade school, had provided California with its only pts on 13y TD in 1st H. Thanks to HB Jay Wilkinson's 13y TD pass from QB Scotty Glacken (19-34/254y, TD, 2 INTs) and HB Billy Futrell's TD run, Blue Devils led 14-7 at H. Margin was advance to 16-7 in 3rd Q when Cal C Jim Phillips fired punt snap through EZ for safety. Game began to slip from Duke's grasp on next play as Futrell fumbled away free-kick that led to Morton's TD sneak. Futrell made up for his gaffe with HB pass to Wilkinson for 47y TD. When Blue Devils FB-K Mike Curtis missed conv kick score remained 22-14, so Bears were in position to tie it. With 16 secs left, K Curtis missed 45y FG try that was lengthened by 15y coaching-from-sidelines PEN for Duke coach throwing kicking tee on field.

AP Poll October 14

1 Texas (51)	546	6 Oklahoma	191
2 Wisconsin (5)	487	7 Illinois	147
3 Pittsburgh	413	8 Georgia Tech	146
4 Ohio State	238	9 Alabama	145
5 Mississippi	218	10tNavy	103
		10tNorthwestern	103

Others with votes: Air Force, Arkansas, Army, Auburn, Baylor, Duke, Florida, Iowa, Louisiana State, Mississippi State, Missouri, Nebraska, Notre Dame, North Carolina State, Oregon, Penn State, Southern California, Southern Methodist, Syracuse, Washington

October 19, 1963

(Fri) Georgia 31 MIAMI 14: Hurricanes' wonderful D run—no TDs allowed in last 3 games—came to screeching halt as 414y O contributed by Georgia (3-1-1) QB Larry Rakestraw 25-38/407y, 2 TDs, INT) personally outgained combined y of 4 previous opponents of Miami (2-3). In early going, Rakestraw led 80y drives that he capped with short run and TD passes to soph E Pat Hodgson (9/192y, 2 TDs) for 28 and 66y. Trailing 24-0 in 3rd Q, Canes QB George Mira (25-44/342y, TD, INT) moved his team 79y, hitting 4 passes in row. Mira scored on 1y sprint wide around right side. Mira quickly hit WB Nick Spinelli for 2 pts. Ready to get back into fray, Miami drove to Georgia 12YL in 3rd Q after DB John Sisk made 1-handed INT. But, Mira, who was harried all night, was sacked out of scoring range. This set up Bulldogs' last TD drive of 66y. In 4th Q, Mira hit E Ed Weisakosky (8/124y, TD) with cosmetic 6y TD.

SYRACUSE 9 Penn State 0: Failing to score against regular rival Syracuse (4-1) for 1st time since 1934, Nittany Lions (3-2) managed only 1 real scoring threat. It came late in 2nd Q when QB Pete Liske (6-19/81y) lofted 34y pass to E-WB Don Caum that was carried to Orangemen 5YL with 49 secs left before H. But, Syracuse's pointed pass rush prevented Liske from hitting any of 4 aerial tries he subsequently made before end of 2nd Q. Syracuse, tops in nation in rushing O with 272y per-game avg, created 2 great runs: Late in 2nd Q before Liske's passing circus, Orange HB Billy Hunter had rambled 53y for TD aided by blocks of T Tom Wilhelm and FB Bill Schoonover, and HB Mike Koski ran 58y early in 3rd Q, on precisely same play as what Hunter scored on, to set up K Jack Paglio's 24y FG.

NORTH CAROLINA 31 North Carolina State 10: Tar Heels (4-1) QB Junior Edge hit TE Joe Robinson twice in 2nd H with TD passes off option series fakes. Robinson's 1st score was UNC's 2nd TD in 56-sec span of 3rd Q. Wolfpack (4-1), slightly thin in troops, was worn down by alternating units employed by North Carolina coach Jim Hickey, but managed 10-10 H tie when DB Tony Kozarsky thundered 74y on zig-zag pattern with INT RET in last min of 2nd Q. Heels responded right after 2nd H KO, going 63y to TD run on 7th play by HB Ken Willard (19/91y). NC State QB Jim Rossi (11-17/80y, INT) lost FUM just 2 plays after next KO to set up Edge's 1st scoring collaboration with Robinson. Rossi was thrown for 46y in losses while trying to pass, and Pack ended with only 26y rushing.

MARYLAND 21 Air Force 14: Winless Maryland (1-4) pulled out spectacular victory on game's last play as WR Darryl Hill, Terps' 1st African-American player, took 36y pass over middle from QB Dick Shiner (17-33/210y, 2 TDs) and darted past 5 tacklers to score. Air Force (3-2) QB Terry Isaacson threw 2 TD passes of 10y each in 2nd Q for 14-0 H lead. Maryland, new team in 2nd H, scored on Shiner-to-Hill 6y TD pass in 3rd Q, but took until last 3 mins of 4th Q to tie it 14-14. Tying Terrapins drive went 67y as HB Len Chiaverini carried last 24y on 7 tries, and Shiner hit TE Bob Burton with 2-pt pass. As it had twice earlier in season, Air Force tried to fly length of field for late win, but Maryland asst coach Lee Corso had noticed passing pattern in such drives: sideline pass, rollout, and long sideline hook. Terps HB-DB Ernie Arizzi stepped in front of Falcon E Fritz Greenlee's hook route and returned INT to own 38YL. Maryland's Shiner, without timeouts and 1:10 on clock, threw several clock-stopping OB passes, but big play to set up winning TD was his 35y pitch to Hill that carried to Falcons 27YL.

Auburn 29 GEORGIA TECH 21: Auburn (5-0) installed new underhand delay pass: QB Jimmy Sidle (11-21/142y, TD, INT) hit 5-6 so-named "Selma" passes to WBs George Rose and David Rawson, 3 of which set up TDs and 2 set up FGs. Georgia Tech (3-2) had scored in 1st Q on FB Ray Mendheim's 3y run after Yellow Jackets picked off Sidle's pass. Lead was traded 3 times as teams matched TDs. Tigers had advantage of catching Jackets QB Billy Lothridge (4-12/49y, TD, INT) in EZ for 2nd Q safety, which served as difference at H as Auburn led 16-14. Georgia Tech took 21-16 lead on Lothridge's TD pass in 3rd Q, but thereafter, Plainsmen owned action, adding TD run by HB Tucker Frederickson and K Woody Woodall's 2 FGs. Jackets' last-gasp threat was ruined by DB Frederickson's INT at his 1YL.

ALABAMA 35 Tennessee 0 (Birmingham): After its upset loss previous week to Florida, Alabama (4-1) took it out on slumping Tennessee (1-4) and dropped worst defeat on Volunteers since SEC was formed in 1933. It was 4th conf loss in row for Tennessee, played drearily with only 148y O and 6 lost FUMs, including several crippling giveaways inside its 20YL. HB Benny Nelson got Crimson Tide off and winging with 36y TD run, and Bama led 14-0 at end of 1st Q. Tide QB Joe Namath passed for 141y and 3 TDs: 26y to E Jimmy Dill, 3y to E Charles Stephens, and 5y to HB Hudson Harris. Namath also notched Alabama's last TD on short run, and he added 2-pt pass to Nelson.

Purdue 23 MICHIGAN 12: Philanthropic Michigan Wolverines (1-2-1) gave away pair of FUMs in 1st Q, and they led to Boilermakers (2-2) TDs by FB Gene Donaldson on 2y run and QB Ron DiGravio on 1y plunge. At end of afternoon, however, Michigan had unbroken possession time to rally for 2 scores and had nicked-up QB Bob Timberlake pitching for receivers who were running inside Purdue 30YL. It had been in mid-game that Boilermakers sealed seams on their final product with 23-0 lead. K Gary Hogan made 31y FG, and DiGravio (14-25/198y, TD) hit HB Jim Morel with 28y TD pass 6 mins into 4th Q. It was from that moment that Michigan kept ball for pair of Timberlake TD runs with pair of successful on-side KOs to follow.

ILLINOIS 16 Minnesota 6: C-LB Dick Butkus played with banged up arm, but still made 17 tackles for undefeated Illinois (3-0-1). His sub, C-K Jim Plankenhorn, also played key role in 2nd Q flurry of plays: After making punt snap, he raced downfield to recover FUM at Golden Gophers (1-3) 9YL, and when Minnesota held, K Plankenhorn kicked 21y FG for 9-0 lead. Illini QB Fred Custardo scored clincher in 4th Q as he swept right for 9y score. Gophers drove 57y in 3rd Q as HB Jerry Pelletier zipped 6y up middle for TD. Minnesota had not allowed any pts against it by Illinois since 1960, but this season exhibited completely different Illini team.

OKLAHOMA 21 Kansas 18: Jayhawkers (2-3) HB Gale Sayers (16/110y, TD) ran brilliantly against Oklahoma (3-1), which opened defense of another Big 8 championship. Sayers stormed to 61y TD in 1st Q, and K Gary Duff made 30y FG to send Kansas off with 10-7 H lead. Midway in 3rd Q, Sooners created their own break as DE Allan Bumbardner arrived at same time as QB Steve Renko's pitchout to Sayers, and hard hit created FUM that DE John Flynn recovered at OU 47YL. Oklahoma QB Bobby Page hit 17y TD pass to E Rick McCurdy for go-ahead score on 10th play of drive. QB Norman Smith, who was surprise Sooners starter, scored his 2nd TD for 21-10 lead in 4th Q. Sayers and Renko (5-11/43y, TD, 2 INTs) combined on 8y TD connection and 2-pt pass later on.

Iowa State 19 COLORADO 7: Alert Iowa State (3-2) DG Chuck Steimle recovered 2 FUMs in 1st H to put Cyclones WB-K Dave Limerick in position for 13y TD catch and 41y FG. Iowa State led 10-7 at H, even though its D fell asleep once during 1st Q: Buffaloes (2-3) HB Bill Harris burst through RG and went for 78y TD behind E Stan Irvine's key block that tied it at 7-7 in 1st Q. Cyclones E Randy Kidd blocked Buffs QK in 3rd Q, and FB Tom Vaughn (25/99y, TD) scored on 2y dive for 17-7 lead, and Colorado QB Frank Cesarek (4-6/74y) was spilled in EZ for 4th Q safety. Effective Iowa State P Steve Balkovec continually pinned Buffs deep in their end with his 9 punts/36.9y avg.

Texas 17 ARKANSAS 13: With Arkansas (2-3) D poised for wide runs, Texas (5-0) sent FB Harold Philipp barreling up middle for 135y. By the time Hogs adjusted, Longhorns had built 17-0 lead. Next KO was returned 89y by fleet Razorbacks TB Jackie Brasuell, which allowed QB Jon Brittenum to throw 12y TD pass to WB Stan Sparks. Brittenum piloted 90y drive for another Porkers TD, but Arkansas could get no closer.

Baylor 21 TEXAS TECH 17: Big Lubbock crowd was geared up for big upset as Red Raiders (2-3) HB-DB Donny Anderson made 2 big plays. Anderson picked off pass on 1st snap of 2nd Q and returned it 26y to Baylor (3-1) 29YL. This set up E David Parks' 3y TD reception from QB James Ellis. Bears countered with FB Dalton Hoffman's 31y sprint to position FB-K Tom Davies for 38y FG, only to have Anderson catch short KO on run at his 19YL and charge 81y to TD and 14-3 lead. Trailing 17-9 and experiencing tremendous pass-rush pressure from Texas Tech DLs Bill Shaha, Bill Malone, Jimmy Walker, and Bill McLelland, Baylor ace passer, QB Don Trull (19-33/262y, 3 TDs, 2 INTs), had finally started clicking with his throws, and it showed in his 10y TD pass to HB Lawrence Elkins. Trull arched 58y TD pass to E James Ingram with 6:07 left. Bears reclaimed possession at their 17YL, and Trull moved them downfield to another Ingram TD catch with 1:51 to go.

RICE 13 Southern Methodist 7: Southern Methodist (2-2) GL D, led by G-LB John Hughes, E John Graves, T John Knee, and DBs Tommy Caughran, Billy Gannon, and John Richey, twice held off Rice (3-1) and forced FG tries in 1st H. Owls K Larry Rice made half of them: 27y 3-ptr for 3-0 H edge. Mustangs HB John Roderick (8/32y), hero of previous win over Navy, dashed KO back 56y but soon was lost with rib injury. Rice added 41y FG in 3rd Q, but SMU rallied with QB Danny Thomas' 3 straight completions in middle of 4th Q ending with sub E Jimmy Taylor's TD catch for 7-6 SMU lead. This flurry occurred after Rice HB-P Gene Fleming's shanked punt. Soon thereafter just-released-from-hospital patient Roderick came hectically charging from dressing room trying clumsily to pull his jersey over his helmeted head. Also around that time, Owls went to QB Benny Hollingsworth to rally Rice in dying moments. Hollingsworth called upon FB Paul Piper (20/128y) and HB Billy Hale to hammer ahead before hitting 4th down pass to HB George Parry and 9y game-winning TD pass to E John Sylvester.

SOUTHERN CALIFORNIA 32 Ohio State 3: Coach Woody Hayes, frequently suspicious of passing, saw his Buckeyes (2-1-1) throw more INTs (4) than completions (3-17) and growled in his post-game interview: "Our number four national ranking was a joke." Ohio State actually had gotten on scoreboard 1st as K Dick vanRaaphorst belted 44y FG in 1st Q. After Troy E Hal Bedsole downed 1st Q punt at 1YL, HB-DB Mike Garrett tackled Buckeyes HB Paul Warfield in EZ for Trojans safety that trimmed score to 3-2. QB Pete Beathard of Southern California (3-2) passed 9-13/159y, TD in barely more than H of play. Beathard also rushed 8/31y, including 1y TD in 3rd Q that provided 19-3 edge. Trojans outrushed Ohio State 215y to 119y as HB Willie Brown raced for 49y TD in 2nd Q. After losing 2 of their last 3 games, defending national champion Trojans could feel like this outcome was more like what was expected. Still, USC had right to be pleased with even break against juggernaut 4 weeks of Oklahoma, Michigan State, Notre Dame, and Ohio State. This scheduling run had prompted coach John McKay to say to former USC coach and current AD Jess Hill: "You must have realized you weren't going to be the coach."

October 26, 1963

HARVARD 17 Dartmouth 13: G-LB Ted Bracken's 1st play INT of Harvard QB Mike Bassett gave Dartmouth (4-1) ball at 26YL, and QB Dana Kelly soon rolled out to find HB John McLean for TD pass and 7-0 lead. After that setback Crimson (3-0-2) gradually began to dominate. Harvard relief QB Bill Humenuk (8-12/99y, TD) sparked O to 172y in rest of 1st H, but potential tying drive was stopped at 1YL by Indians D-line and H clock. HB Scott Harshbarger's 36y run finally knotted it in 3rd Q, and Humenuk hit E Frank Ulcickas with go-ahead TD late in 3rd Q as Dartmouth's nation-leading win streak died at 15 games. Harvard Stadium hooted EZ pass interference PEN late in 4th Q as Dartmouth E Scott Creelman went for catch, but Crimson D delayed Kelly's TD sneak long enough to all but extinguish clock.

NAVY 24 Pittsburgh 12: It was gloomy day for QBs: Rugged Pitt (4-1) line dumped Roger Staubach for 19/-33y rushing, while Navy (5-1) grabbed 2 INTs each from Panthers signal-callers Fred Mazurek and Kenny Lucas. While eluding rushers, nimble Staubach managed to pass rather well; he connected 14-19/168y, including 7/92y caught by E Jim Campbell. Each Middies INT paved way for Navy score, 1st of which was G-K Fred Marlin's 36y FG after C-LB Tom Lynch's INT. Pitt reached Navy 19YL early in 2nd Q, but illegal receiver PEN pushed Panthers back to passing distance, and Midshipman FB-DB Pat Donnelly snatched Mazurek's errant pass at 20YL. Staubach quickly hit Campbell on 18, 14, 18, and 9y passes to set up HB Johnny Sai's 1y TD slant for 10-0 edge. Staubach and Donnelly scored subsequent Navy TDs. Lucas threw pair of late, long TD passes to HB Eric Crabtree (34y) and HB Paul Martha (74y), which meant little but window-dressing for undefeated Panthers who already trailed 24-0.

NORTH CAROLINA STATE 21 Duke 7: Wolfpack (5-1) upset Duke (4-1-1) for 1st time since 1946, knocking Devils out of ACC lead. NC State HB Mike Clark ran 55y to set up HB Tony Kozarsky's 6y crack into EZ, and QB Jim Rossi positioned himself for his TD toss to HB Joe Scarpati with 55y run. Duke's TD came on QB Scotty Glacken's 37y pass to HB Jay Wilkinson, part of belated 4th Q comeback which had brought score to 14-7.

Louisiana State 14 FLORIDA 0: LSU Tigers (5-1) bottled up Florida (3-2-1) HB Larry Dupree (23/60y) and cashed pair of TOs for TDs runs by FB Don Schwab (17/59y) in 1st and 3rd Qs. G-LB Remi Prudhomme intercepted Gators QB Tom Shannon (10-22/96y, 3 INTs) to set up 40y trip to Schwab's 4th down TD dive. LSU DB Robbi Hucklebridge knocked ball from Dupree on 3rd Q's 1st snap to gain FUM at Gators 27YL. Again, Schwab made dolphin dive into EZ. Florida had gotten early taste of Tigers' stiff D when it failed after having 1st down at 12YL in 1st Q and 3rd-and-1 at 4YL in 2nd Q.

MEMPHIS STATE 17 Mississippi State 10: Brilliant Memphis State (5-0-1) QB Russell Vollmer started day with 71y KO RET and finished it directing winning TD drive over surprised Mississippi State (4-1-1). In between, Vollmer was hit late and shoved OB by 3 Bulldogs, leapt over bench, and landed hard on concrete steps. Hospital x-rays proved negative, so Vollmer rushed back to game. Tigers FB Dave Casinelli scored from 1YL after Vollmer's KO RET, but 2-pt run failed. Mississippi State had taken 10-9 H lead while Vollmer was away: G-K Justin Canale booted 36y FG and HB Price Hodges slipped around LE for 8y TD run. Cheers rang up as Vollmer returned to convert 3rd-and-5 at Bulldogs 8YL in 4th Q, and Memphis went ahead 17-10 on Casinelli's 2nd TD 2 plays later.

PURDUE 14 Iowa 0: Sweltering Lafayette Homecoming crowd left happy because Purdue (3-2) QB Ron DiGravio was able to lead his troops on 2 TD marches, while Iowa (2-2-1) QB Fred Riddle was hurried into big losses and erratic passing. Riddle was relieved in 2nd H by QB Gary Snook, who completed 60y bomb to E Cloyd Webb, but suffered 2 INTs at hands of Purdue DB Ken Eby. DiGravio sparked ground-oriented 66y drive in 1st Q as E Bob Hadrick (7/91y, TD) speared low 1y spiral from DiGravio for TD. In 3rd Q, Eby returned punt to Iowa 40YL, and DiGravio connected twice with Hadrick, HB Randy Minniear ran for 6y, and DiGravio scrambled for 11y TD.

Michigan State 15 NORTHWESTERN 7: Fast Michigan State (3-1-1) sr HB Sherman Lewis (8/104y, TD, and 4/74y, TD receiving) was as hot as Evanston's Indian-summer day for 3rd straight year against no. 9 Northwestern (4-2). Wildcats drew 1st blood on HB Willie Stinson's 6y TD run in 2nd Q, but QB Tommy Myers (8-22/110y, TD, 2 INTs) was reasonably shut down. Lewis made fortunate falling EZ catch for TD as 2 Northwestern defenders tipped QB Steve Juday's TD pass. Michigan State trailed 7-6 at H, but Lewis caught Cats napping as he broke into clear on 87y TD jaunt in 3rd Q. When K Bert Lattimore bombed 47y FG, Spartans led 15-7 in 3rd Q. Lewis was hardly done; he skated 84y on punt RET in 4th Q, and would have scored had Stinson not headed him off at NW 15YL. Spartans' strong rush spilled QB Myers for 58y in losses when he attempted to pass.

Ohio State 13 WISCONSIN 10: Buckeyes K Dick vanRaaphort's FGs of 36 and 45y overcame 25y FG by Wisconsin (4-1) K Dave Fronek, so Ohio State (3-1-1) led 6-3 at H. Invigorated D play and HB Carl Silvestri's 3rd Q TD run put Badgers (4-1) in command at 10-6. Soph QB Don Unverferth came off Buckeyes bench in 4th Q to spark their slumbering O with 4 completions in row to set up FB Matt Snell's game winning 2y run with 2:03 left.

Baylor 34 TEXAS A&M 7: Baylor (4-1) used its ace aerial tandem of QB Don Trull and WR Larry Elkins to destroy Aggies (1-4-1). Trull threw 16-31/242y with Elkins pulling in 10/149y, including 3 TDs of 22, 12, and 27y. Texas A&M managed HB-DB Mike Pitman's 2 INTs, but coach Hank Foldberg made stupefying post-game comment that, "we weren't prepared for all that passing" despite his team facing Trull, nation's no. 1 statistical passer.

STANFORD 24 Notre Dame 14: Former Stanford (2-4) QB Steve Thurlow ran from his HB post for 2 TDs, each of 5y, then unlimbered his arm to pitch wrap-up TD in 4th Q. Thurlow's decisive 7y TD throw came on 4th down and went to HB Ray Handley. Notre Dame (2-3) had exited 1st Q with 7-0 lead on graces of 53y drive which QB Frank Budka finished with 1y wedge. Indians countered with 64y drive to Thurlow's 1st TD in 2nd Q, but Irish trotted off at H with 14-10 lead. Budka threw 17y TD pass, and Stanford QB Dick Berg fumbled away late 2nd Q scoring opportunity. In 2nd H, Tribe tallied at end of 70 and 85y drives.

AP Poll October 28

1 Texas (49)	508	6 Oklahoma	246
2 Illinois (1)	358	7 Alabama	213
3 Mississippi	306	8 Wisconsin	181
4 Navy (1)	278	9 Ohio State	83
5 Auburn	266	10 Pittsburgh	76

Others with votes: Arkansas, Army, Baylor, Georgia Tech, Louisiana State, Memphis State, Michigan State, Missouri, Nebraska, North Carolina, North Carolina State, Penn State, Princeton, Purdue, Southern California, Syracuse

November 2, 1963

PITTSBURGH 35 Syracuse 27: Amid sun, snow squalls, and lightning, Syracuse (5-2) cashed its early breaks to build 21-8 H lead as sub FB Nat Duckett scored twice. Panthers briefly had led 8-7 on QB Fred Mazurek's TD run and 2-pt pass. Inspired by unusually-fiery H speech by coach John Michelosen, Pittsburgh (5-1) drove 58, 85, and 62y for 3rd Q TDs and 28-21 lead as Mazurek dashed for 41y TD, passed for TD, and totaled 255y O by game's end. Orangemen moved to within 28-27 early in 4th Q on QB Dick King's 54y TD pass to HB Mike Koski, but King came up short on 2-pt sneak. Panthers soon made pass INT to set up 45y march to powerful FB Rick Leeson's clinching TD run and conv kick.

BOSTON COLLEGE 19 Vanderbilt 6: Change of scenery to chilly Massachusetts, did nothing for woeful Vanderbilt (0-6), which lost its 7th straight over 2 seasons. Boston College (4-2) QB Jack Concannon continued to solidify his place in Eagles history by passing and running for TDs. BC scored 1st as HB Bob Budzinski zipped 35y to ignite 46y TD drive which ended with Concannon's 9y TD pass to Budzinski for 7-0 lead. Concannon's FUM, his only miscue of day, was recovered by Commodores DE Lane Wolbe at BC 30YL. It took 12 ponderous plays to cover 30y to FB Charley Trabue's 1y TD plunge. It pulled Vandy within 7-6, but x-pt kick was missed. Concannon hit 2 passes before he ran for his 4th TD of season in 2nd Q, and he dashed 26y on keeper to launch BC HB Jim McGowan's 30y TD run through T in 3rd Q.

ALABAMA 20 Mississippi State 19: Alabama (6-1) QB Joe Namath sparkled with 10-16/142y passing, but HB-DB Larry Swearengen kept boosting upset-minded Mississippi State (4-2-1). Swearengen returned INT of Namath for 45y TD that provided 12-3 2nd Q lead. HB Swearengen also added 4y TD run for 19-13 3rd Q lead. Namath's 20y rollout run spiced winning 54y 4th Q drive that took Crimson Tide off upset ropes.

AUBURN 19 Florida 0: Florida (3-3-1) hadn't been same since upsetting Alabama, and this game turned out to be 2nd straight shutout of Gators, who had all but abandoned its running attack. Record Homecoming crowd at Auburn (6-0) marveled at crashing D plays of HB-DB Tucker Frederickson (INT) and QB Jimmy Sidle's dazzling 25y TD run in 3rd Q for 12-0 lead for Plainsmen. Tigers had led 1st H 6-0 on pair of FGs by K Woody Woodall, which tied school record of 17 career 3-ptrs by Ed Dyas. LB Bill Cody capped Tigers' scoring with 42y INT RET of pass thrown by Gators lefty QB Tom Shannon (15-27/124y, 2 INTs). Florida managed only 52y rushing.

Mississippi 37 LOUISIANA STATE 3: Power running by Ole Miss (5-0-1) totaled 233y, keynoted by 3 TDs by FB Fred Roberts (13/69y). Rebels T Whaley Hall blocked punt in 1st Q to set up Roberts' 1st TD blast, and Ole Miss made 2 INTs and recovered 4 FUMs while limiting Bengals to 144y total O. Tigers' only score came on E-K Doug Moreau's 41y FG in 1st Q that pulled LSU within 7-3, but Mississippi ran off 16 pts in 2nd Q as E-K Billy Carl Irwin caught 23y TD pass and booted 22y FG. When HB Joe Labruzzo broke free for 81y RET of 3rd Q punt, it looked like LSU (5-2) might get back into game it trailed 23-3. But, big G Stan Hindman hauled down speedy Labruzzo on 1YL, and resilient Rebs dug in to hold.

MICHIGAN STATE 30 Wisconsin 13: Snarling Michigan State D held no. 8 Wisconsin (4-2) to 29y rushing and kept Spartans (4-1-1) in Rose Bowl race. Little Michigan State HB Sherman Lewis sped 87y for TD on pass from QB Steve Juday, and big FB Roger Lopes added 2 TDs in 2nd H. HB Lou Holland scored twice for Badgers, 1st TD coming on pass from QB Hal Brandt for 7-6 lead. At end of 3rd Q, Holland ran 5y for TD that pulled Wisconsin to within 20-13, but Spartans D held matters in check from there.

Army 14 Air Force 10 (Chicago): Before Soldier Field crowd of 76,660, Cadets (6-1) disdained pass most of day and used infantry for day's total of 246y rushing to dominate Air Force (4-3) in stats. However, Army squandered several 1st H chances, and despite 202y to 43y disadvantage, Falcons led 3-0 at H on HB-K Bart Holaday's 36y FG. Cadets HB Ken Waldrop sizzled 78y on punt RET in 3rd Q to set up his 1y TD run. Trailing 7-3, Falcons fashioned 4th Q reversal: QB Terry Isaacson hit E Fritz Greenlee with 47y pass to Army 7YL to set up Isaacson's 1y rollout for TD and 10-7 lead with slightly more than 6 mins left. Army answered by going 65y in 12 plays with Waldrop charging for 4, 13, and 4y runs. Drive slowed at Falcons 17YL with Black Knights facing 4th down with 1:20 left. Waldrop was sent off RT Bill Zadel's block, cut back, and romped to winning TD.

Navy 35 NOTRE DAME 14: In rare win over Notre Dame (2-4), Navy (6-1) broke 7-7 H tie which Irish had earned on QB Frank Budka's short TD run after Budka hit WB Jack Snow for 28y. Midshipmen QB Roger Staubach led 69 and 56y TD drives, and DE Gary Kellner cashed 8y INT RET for back-breaking Navy TD in 3rd Q. Staubach passed 9-15/91y, 2 TDs and set school season total O record with 3 games to go. Navy FB Pat Donnelly rushed 14/127y and scored on 41y run and 8y pass. Fighting Irish still led series, unbroken since 1927, with 27-9-1 mark over Naval Academy, and although this was Tars' 3rd win in last 4 years, it would be their last over Notre Dame with losing streak exceeding 40 games.

Nebraska 13 MISSOURI 12: In major step in quest for Big 8 title they hadn't won since 1940, Cornhuskers (6-1) improved to 4-0. Nebraska QB Dennis Claridge put his team in front 7-0 on 5y keeper in 1st Q. But, Tigers (5-2) stood within 13-12 as HB Ken Boston scored on EZ FUM in 2nd Q and 53y pass reception from QB Gary Lane in 4th Q. With 8:30 left, Mizzou chose to gamble on Lane's 2-pt pass attempt, but Nebraska HB-DB Bruce Smith broke it up. Huskers' ensuing drive padded their 299y game-end rushing total and ate 7 mins of 4th Q clock. Nebraska hadn't beaten Missouri since 1956, and huge G Bob Brown had vowed not to shave until Cornhuskers accomplished their task. Brown's beard had grown more than inch, and it took many razor swipes afterward, some by joyous teammates, to make him clean-shaven again.

WASHINGTON 22 Southern California 7: Washington (4-3) scored on game's 4th play: G Koll Hagen blocked punt by Troy FB-P Ernie Jones, and T Mike Briggs fell on it in EZ. Speedy Southern California (4-3) HB Mike Garrett (21/80y) broke free on 42y run in 1st Q, and likely would have scored with footing better than sloppy mud he had under his cleats. Huskies held at their 10YL, and, although Trojans soon tied it at 7-7 on sub QB Craig Fertig's over-middle 17y pitch to E John Thomas, Washington built 16-7 H lead. UW scored twice to earn its 9 pts: T-K Jim Norton set to-date Washington record for FG length with line-drive 45y boot and Huskies QB Bill Douglas threw 22y TD pass to E Ralph Winters, who broke into EZ when HB Dave Kopay made thunderous block. In 4th Q, Douglas collaborated with Kopay on 53y pass to set up Kopay's 4y TD run as Huskies built ample 4-0 AAWU record and took inside track to Rose Bowl.

ARIZONA STATE 30 Utah 22: Dynamic and balanced O of Arizona State (5-1) compiled 402y, but it was Sun Devils' D that pulled it through in clutch of 4th Q. Pair of 2nd H TDs and safety propelled stubborn Utah (3-4) to within 16-14 in 3rd Q and 23-22 in 4th Q. Redskins QB Gary Hertzfeldt (8-16/225y, INT) was effective all night, but Devils D came up big with 6:51 to play and leading by 1 pt. Hertzfeldt looked for receiver on 2-pt try that would put Tues ahead 24-23 but was buried by DE Alonzo Hill and DT John Seedborg. ASU S Larry Facchine made midfield INT to squelch Utah's next possession and set up Devils' TD with 5 secs left. HB Charley Taylor (9/81y, 2 TDs, and 2/66y, TD receiving) was chief weapon for Arizona State as he scored on 8y run in 2nd Q, 17y pass reception from QB John Jacobs (6-7/103y) in 2nd Q, and 33y run for 23-14 lead in 4th Q. Utes E Roy Jefferson hauled in 3 catches/109y.

AP Poll November 4

1 Texas (45)	502	6 Oklahoma	209
2 Illinois (4)	425	7 Alabama	168
3 Mississippi (1)	343	8 Pittsburgh	115
4 Navy (1)	322	9 Michigan State	109
5 Auburn (2)	310	10 Ohio State	98

Others with votes: Army, Baylor, Georgia Tech, Memphis State, Nebraska, North Carolina, North Carolina State, Princeton, Southern California, Syracuse, Washington, Wisconsin

November 9, 1963

HARVARD 21 Princeton 7: When severe blustery winds discouraged all but 3 passes and bothered Princeton's Single-wing center snaps, Harvard (4-1-2) surprised Tigers (6-1) with superior ground game, notching 226y to Princeton's 163y. Crimson HB Dave Poe and QB Mike Bassett scored to climax drives of 66 and 52y. Princeton got within 14-7 in 4th Q on FB Cosmo Iacavazzi's TD leap at end of 93y march that was keyed by WB Jim Rockenbach's big gains on reverse runs. But Tigers lost FUM to Harvard D star, G Bill Southmayd, at own 21YL and thus handed away late clinching TD run to FB Bill Grana.

Clemson 11 NORTH CAROLINA 7: North Carolina (6-2) 5-game win streak was smothered under paw of Tigers (3-4-1), which won their 3rd in row. Loss dropped Tar Heels into 3-way tie for 1st in ACC with Duke and NC State, all at 5-1. So overwhelming was Clemson's 1st H margin of play that UNC could feel glad to be trailing only 3-0 at intermission. Tar Heels directly reversed trend after 3rd Q KO as they went 82y to score in 15 plays. On drive, QB Junior Edge popped 3 quick passes to E Bob Lacey, good for 10, 9, and 9y. Bullish UNC HB Ken Willard (16/53y) rammed over from 3YL for 7-3 advance. Clemson's decisive 88y trip to winning margin came in 4th Q as QB Jim Parker whipped 1 of 4 long pass successes by Tigers, 38y completion to backup E Johnny Case to Heels 33YL. From there, Clemson hammered away with HB Mack Matthews and FB Pat Crain (19/64y) to 1y TD push by Parker. E Lou Fogle caught Parker's 2-pt pass.

NORTH CAROLINA STATE 13 Virginia Tech 7: While Wolfpack (7-1) was using dying quail TD pass, hustling FUM REC, and stout D line play to wrestle non-conf Virginia Tech (6-2) into submission, it took breather from ACC and while away they moved into 1st place tie. In opening Q, NC State QB Jim Rossi wobbled short pass to fleet scatback HB Joe Scarpati, who raced to score (his 7th TD of year) on 16y play for 6-0 lead. In 3rd Q, Gobblers HB Mike Cahill foolishly attempted over-shoulder catch of Wolfpack P Dave Houtz's 51y punt at 2YL. Ball was fumbled and with Cahill and NC State HB Tony Koszarsky making simultaneous dives, it was Koszarski, gimpy ankle and all, who came up with EZ REC for TD and 13-0 lead. Virginia Tech picked up its

O in 2nd H, but managed its solo TD when previously-corralled QB Bob Schwiekert got loose for 59y canter down sideline before Scarpati broke through 3 blockers to knock him OB. Schweikert wedged 1y for TD, 4 plays later, with 6:35 on 4th Q clock. Rossi's effective QB-keepers killed every last sec on clock.

MISSISSIPPI STATE 13 Auburn 10: Upstart Mississippi State Bulldogs (5-2-1) took lead in SEC by dominating 2nd H and scoring on QB Sonny Fisher's 22y TD to HB Ode Burrell and G-K Justin Canale's winning 36y FG with 22 secs left. In 2nd Q, unbeaten Auburn (6-1) had gone right to work after Canale had provided 3-0 lead with 25y FG: Tigers QB Jimmy Sidle (5-11/97y, INT) pitched 19y pass to E Jim Ingle and on next play raced to 47y TD. Before 2nd Q was over, Sidle passed 47y to E Howard Simpson to set up K Woody Woodall's FG for 10-3 H lead. Bulldogs only TD came in 3rd Q at end of 66y drive. HB Price Hodges' run and 15y personal foul PEN against Auburn keyed trip to Burrell's TD catch. Foes seemed headed for 10-10 deadlock late in 4th Q when Miss State DB Fisher grabbed Sidle's fateful INT and galloped 25y to Tigers 22YL. Bulldogs went nowhere against Auburn D, but Canale was true with his winning 3-ptr.

Michigan 14 ILLINOIS 8: No sooner had 2nd-ranked Illini (5-1-1), leading 8-7, stopped Wolverines' drive at midfield and forcing punt with 7 mins left in 4th Q, they seemed to start premature sniffing Pasadena's roses. Illinois suddenly lost its edge, and HB Jim Warren's pitchout FUM 2 plays later was collared by Michigan (3-3-1) HB-DB John Rowser (INT) at Tribe 11YL. Michigan soon faced 4th-and 1 at Illinois 2YL, and QB Bob Timberlake sneaked for vital 1st down. HB Mel Anthony quickly scored TD for Michigan's upset that was sealed by another Rowser FUM REC late in game. Wolverines had scored early in 2nd Q as HB Dick Rindfuss slash 3y for 7-0 lead at end of 56y drive, and rest of 1st H was D standoff. Illini outgained Wolverines 269y to 180y and had authored D-fatiguing 17-play, 92y TD march in 3rd Q. Illinois FB Al Wheatland crashed over GL for final y, and QB Mike Taliaferro ran for 2-pt conv for 1-pt edge. Elsewhere, Michigan State took sole possession of Big 10 lead at 4-0-1 with 23-0 win over Purdue.

Penn State 10 OHIO STATE 7: Penn State (6-2) lost midfield 4th down gamble in 2nd Q, and Buckeyes (4-2-1) traveled 46y in 8 plays to HB Paul Warfield's 5y TD run and 7-0 lead. Lions clever QB Pete Liske (14-24/168y, TD) tied it with 13y TD to E Bill Bowes in 3rd Q. Key to tying TD march was Liske hitting E Dick Anderson, future Rutgers coach, for 15y gain and faking handoff left to top-gainer, HB Gary Klingensmith (11/81y), before rolling right to find Bowes beyond DB Warfield in EZ. When Ohio State lost 4th down bid—1 of 3 that Penn State D stopped—at own 49 YL, Lions soon cashed HB-K Ron Coates' winning 23y FG. Buckeyes coach Woody Hayes was impressed with Lions' QB: "Liske did the best job of ball handling I have seen in the stadium since I've been here."

TEXAS 7 Baylor 0: Longhorns' ball control kept Baylor (5-2) from making single 1st down in 2nd and 3rd Qs. Threatening often, Texas (8-0) used QB Duke Carlisle's running and passing for 32y of 45y drive to finally cash in 3rd Q TD. Steers FB Tom Stockton crashed over from 1YL. Baylor QB Don Trull (19-39/204y, 2 INTs) guided Bears to 19YL with 29 secs to play. Top Baylor WR Larry Elkins (12/151y) beat Texas DB Joe Dixon in EZ, but out of nowhere came DB Carlisle for saving INT. Texas TB Tommy Ford rushed 27/101y.

AIR FORCE 48 Ucla 21: Most dismal season since World War II year of 1943 was winding down for UCLA (1-7), but Bruins managed to knot score at 7-7 early in 2nd Q when HB Mike Haffner threw 4y TD pass to sub E Gale Hickman. Then, Falcons (5-3) QB Terry Isaacson took over, passing 7-10/111y and running 5/41y, TD, before 1st H was over with Air Force enjoying 28-7 lead. Game's most spectacular play closed 1st H's scoring: Isaacson drew Uclan secondary up with clever run fake, then pitched out to HB Ken Jaggers, who threw long pass to wide-open E Fritz Greenlee to complete 67y score. Isaacson ran for 2 TDs and passed for another in 2nd H. UCLA subs managed 2 TDs in 4th Q, including blocked punt that G Dick Peterson lugged 12y to score.

NEW MEXICO 17 Wyoming 6: FUM-plagued Cowboys (5-3) were pushed from WAC lead by New Mexico (4-3) which built 17-0 lead before allowing Wyoming inside its 35YL. FB Joe Harris (24/90y) and HB Bucky Stallings (18/72y) were Lobos rushing heroes.

AP Poll November 11

1 Texas (48)	526	6 Pittsburgh	281
2 Navy (4)	446	7 Alabama	253
3 Mississippi	361	8 Illinois	133
4 Michigan State (1)	303	9 Auburn	91
5 Oklahoma	284	10 Nebraska	84

Others with votes: Army, Baylor, Georgia Tech, Memphis State, Mississippi State, North Carolina State, Ohio State, Penn State, Rice, Southern California, Syracuse, Washington, Wisconsin

November 16, 1963

PITTSBURGH 28 Army 0: Army (7-2) threatened twice early: Cadets picked up 4 1st downs after opening KO, but QB Rollie Stichweh (8-15/67y, INT), who picked up 18/46y rushing mostly out of Shotgun formation, threw pass from Pitt 35YL that was dropped. Soon, Army DB Jim Beierschmitt made FUM REC at Panthers 29YL, but K Dick Heydt missed 28y FG. Pittsburgh (7-1) HB Paul Martha (6/103y) opened scoring with 49y TD sweep around right side, and coach John Michelosen shelved his wide-open attack for effective belly series plunges and sweeps for 49/359y. Panthers QB Fred Mazurek (16/93y rushing) scored on 33y sprint in 2nd Q, and FB-K Rick Leeson kicked 29y FG in 2nd Q and scored on 5y run in 3rd Q. Getting "whipped real good in the line," according to coach Paul Dietzel, Army ended up completing 9-20/ desperate passes.

Navy 38 DUKE 25: Navy (8-1) got into 1st H shootout with Duke (5-3-1) and held nervous 31-25 margin after Blue Devils HB Jay Wilkinson, son of Oklahoma coach, smashed over with 2 secs left in H. QB Roger Staubach (7-14/122y, INT, and 72y rushing) broke George Welsh's school season records for pass completions and passing y. Staubach did much of his damage on foot, however, scoring 4y TD off RT after opening KO. Duke came right back on its 1st possession, going 65y to HB Biff Bracy's 3y TD run. Dodging and spinning, Staubach brought roar from crowd with dazzling 44y run that set up HB Johnny Sai's TD for 14-6 lead, which was end of 1st Q milestone. Wild 2nd Q, saw Duke notch 19 pts on TD run and pass by QB Scotty Glacken and Wilkinson's late TD. But Glacken also threw INT that Middies DE Dave Sjuggerud nabbed and carried 34y to TD and 31-19 bulge. Duke changed D at H and penned in Staubach to extent that he lost 23y rushing. Navy D was equally as good, and sole 2nd H TD came on Sai's 93y dash, which eclipsed Navy's 90y record set by Joe Bellino in 1960.

NORTH CAROLINA 27 Miami 16: Bowl-hungry North Carolina (7-2) came from behind twice and out-passed usually pass-happy Miami (3-4). Hurricanes QB George Mira (11-25/191y, 2 TDs) provided 7-0 lead in 1st Q with his 23y TD pass to all-alone WB Nick Spinelli, after Miami surprisingly ground out 55y of 78y trip on runs. Mira crafted dandy march from his 1YL in 3rd Q, passing 18y to HB Pete Banaszak and 47y to E Hoyt Sparks, but had to settle for K Don Cifra's 32y FG and 10-7 lead. Tar Heels line owned next drive, carving out big holes before sub QB Gary Black (7-10/70y, TD, INT) pitched go-ahead, 19y TD pass to HB Ron Tuthill. Early in 4th Q, UNC went 77y to make it 20-10 on 21y TD catch by HB Ronnie Jackson from QB Junior Edge (13-21/174y, TD, INT). Mira made last gasp 69y drive as he scrambled wide on 37y run before hitting HB John Bennett for 7y TD. Mira's 2-pt pass flunked, but Carolina added HB Ken Willard's TD run anyway. Academic to Heels' aerial attack were great hands of E Bob Lacey (8/108y).

ALABAMA 27 Georgia Tech 11: Crimson Tide (7-1) QB Joe Namath (1-3/11y) moth-balled his passing arm and managed game so well coach Bear Bryant said his asst coaches "kept phoning me (from press box)...to not call any plays." HB Ray Ogden made brilliant 44y TD run in 1st Q, and HB Benny Nelson scored twice as Alabama gained 252y rushing. Trailing 14-3 and having only QB-K Billy Lothridge's 41y FG to show for 1st H, sluggish Georgia Tech (6-3) stung Tide with impressive 3rd Q rally. Yellow Jackets drove 52y to halt at Bama 1YL, and after receiving ensuing punt, marched back 46y on 9 and 11y passes by Lothridge (10-20/99y, INT) to his TD sneak and 2-pt pass to HB Joe Auer. That shaved Crimson Tide's 3rd Q edge to 14-11. Tech soon went to Tide 24YL, but sub FB Jimmy Barber was halted inches from 1st down. Alabama answered with 76y TD drive, which was quickly followed by DB Billy Piper's INT and Namath's short TD run for 13 rapid-fire pts in closing 2:30.

Northwestern 17 OHIO STATE 8: Reversing teams' usual profiles, Wildcats (5-4) rushed for 273y, out of which sub FB Steve Murphy culled 2 TD runs of 16y on draw play and 8y run in 4th Q. Meanwhile, Ohio State (4-3-1) threw 32 mostly ineffective passes. K Pete Stamison booted 23y FG to open scoring in 2nd Q for Northwestern. Asked about Northwestern's mediocre record, Buckeye coach Woody Hayes barked, "They pass too damn much." Even so, humbled Buckeyes had to pass to avoid shutout: HB Paul Warfield caught 31y TD pass from QB Don Unverferth in game's last min. Considering that Ohio State launched so many passes, it was ironic that small plane was hired to fly above Ohio Stadium at H to trail banner that read: "Goodbye Woody!" It was reminder that Buckeyes fans had continually this season expressed their disapproval of coach Hayes' conservative play calling.

Illinois 17 WISCONSIN 7: Fighting Illini (6-1-1) kept alive their Rose Bowl hopes with bend-but-don't-break D, led by C-LB Dick Butkus, that allowed 274y and contributed DB George Donnelly's 24y INT TD RET for 14-0 2nd Q edge. Illinois' drive after opening KO had been capped by FB Jim Grabowski's 2y TD run. Wisconsin (5-3), Big 10's top statistical O despite having scored only 7 TDs in last 5 weeks, narrowed it to 14-7 on HB Lou Holland's 9y catch from QB Hal Brandt in 3rd Q. Badgers' passing game supplied weak 4.02y per attempt as they threw 16-41/165y into tough Illini secondary, led by Donnelly. Illinois C-K Jim Plankenhorn's 26y FG locked up scoring bank in last 38 secs.

Oklahoma 13 MISSOURI 3: Savage hitting marked Oklahoma's 9th victory in row over Missouri (6-3) in Columbia, but it was Bud Wilkinson's old standby, punt TD RET, that formed key moment for Sooners (7-1). Oklahoma HB Larry Shields cruised 65y on punt TD RET as his blockers knocked Tiger tacklers down like bowling pins in 1st Q. HB-K George Leistritz knocked through 43y FG in 2nd Q to keep Missouri close at 6-3. With his power run game shut down, Tigers QB Gary Lane bothered OU with 9-23/128y passing but he suffered 2 INTs at hands of wide-ranging DB Shields. Missouri E Bud Abell caught late 2nd Q pass from Lane but in so doing lost FUM at Sooners 5YL, while Oklahoma also turned over possession on pair of FUMs and INTs.

Nebraska 20 OKLAHOMA STATE 16: Nebraska (8-1) held onto 1st place in Big 8 as it awaited next week's showdown against Oklahoma. But, Cornhuskers' trip to Stillwater turned out to have grueling 4th Q. Lowly Oklahoma State (1-8), often so disproportionately tough at home, trailed 20-6 as 4th Q opened, and QB Mike Miller (19-32/165y, TD) decided to open up his aerial game. Miller pitched Cowboys downfield so that FB George Thomas could bull over form 7YL, and after forcing 2 Nebraska punts, Oklahoma State scored again in last min as Miller found HB Franklin Jeff Williams for TD that trimmed deficit to 20-16. Nebraska weathered tough road game without its injured top QB, Dennis Claridge. Soph QB Fred Duda (6-14/68y) filled in well, scoring on 8y run in 2nd Q while directing Huskers TD drives of 68, 70, and 72y in middle Qs.

TEXAS 17 Texas Christian 0: With FBs Ernie Koy and Harold Philipp out hurt, nervous 3rd-string FB Tommy Stockton gained 89y as Longhorns (9-0) clinched Cotton Bowl spot. Texas sophs Stockton and HB Phil Harris each scored from 3YL. TCU (3-4-1) managed 136y in air and made 2 deep, but failed drives into Longhorns territory.

UCLA 14 Washington 0: Big underdog UCLA (2-7) mounted 88 and 76y drives, culminating each time by TD catch by E Byron Nelson. Bruins D, pushed around so far in 1963 for 24 pts per game in team's worst year since 1943, surprisingly thwarted Washington (5-4) O at every turn. Huskies QB Bill Douglas passed 5-15/52y, while ace FB Junior Coffey managed only 11/28y rushing. *Los Angeles Times* headline explained Rose Bowl selection dilemma: "Upset Snarls Bowl Picture."

November 23, 1963

(Fri) NORTH CAROLINA STATE 42 Wake Forest 0: Wolfpack (8-2) clinched tie for ACC title with winner of upcoming Duke-North Carolina contest. Finishing his career only 70y short of Roman Gabriel's school total O record, NC State QB Jim Rossi (5-9/87y, TD) scored 2 TDs as he rushed 90y. NC State HB Mike Clark (11/129y) tallied game's 1st TD after his 48y dash to 2YL and spent most of game running wide of Deacs D. HB Joe Scarpatti made punt RETs of 50 and 26y, and each led to TD. Defeat tumbled Wake Forest (1-9) to 12th loss in its last 13 ACC games. Demon Deacons twice threatened at Wolfpack 25YL and ended game on NC State 15YL, but their biggest moment came on QB-P Karl Sweetan's 73y punt to get Wake out of deep hole in 4th Q.

Florida 27 MIAMI 21: Miami pres Henry King Stanford's 11th hour change of heart nearly cancelled game because of Friday's assassination of Pres Kennedy, but Stanford's attempt to get himself to Orange Bowl stadium announcer's booth failed to beat opening KO. So, game was on, with heartfelt pre-game ceremony for Orange Bowl stadium's largest crowd of year. Hurricanes (3-5) QB George Mira pitched 19-42/278y, 3 TDs, including 15y TD to E Hoyt Sparks out of fake-FG. That score pulled Canes to within 7-6 at H. After Miami went 76y, mostly on runs by FB Pete Banaszak, to Mira's 20y cross-field TD pass to HB Russ Smith, Gators (5-3-1) answered in kind: 76y TD march. Florida broke open game on inside-reverse handoff to HB Hagood Clarke, who sprinted 70y to 4th Q TD that broke 14-14 tie. Ill-fated Mira pitchout turned into Gators DB Alan Poe's REC at Miami 46YL, and Florida QB Tom Shannon (7-10/138y) soon scored his 2nd TD sneak.

NEBRASKA 29 Oklahoma 20: Huge Nebraska (9-1) line, led by G Bob Brown and T Lloyd Voss, held Oklahoma (8-2) to 98y rushing and sprung HB Rudy Johnson, QB Dennis Claridge, HB Kent McCloughan, and QB Fred Duda for running TDs in building safe 29-7 lead. Oklahoma was limited to 28y total O in 1st H. Sooners HB Wes Skidgel scored 2 TDs, too late to halt coach Bob Devaney's "biggest win" of his career, which earned Nebraska's 1st conf title in 23 years. Oklahoma coach Bud Wilkinson, personally close to Pres Kennedy because of his chairmanship of Counsel on Physical Fitness, was heartbroken that game went on as scheduled after Kennedy's death on Friday.

ARKANSAS 27 Texas Tech 20: Arkansas Hogs (5-5) crafted 20-0 lead using crew of dashing young backs, including future coach Ken Hatfield, who had 80y TD punt RET. QB Ben Elledge rerouted Red Raiders (5-5) to 20-20 tie, pitching TDs to Es Tommy Doyle and David Parks, and sneaking for his team's 3rd score. Arkansas went 85y in 8 plays for winning pts, TD coming on twisting 24y run by QB Billy Gray.

BRIGHAM YOUNG 24 Colorado State 20: Staunchly religious Brigham Young coach Hal Mitchell suspended 12 players, including 5 starters for "inappropriate conduct" (reported to be beer drinking) after November 9 loss to George Washington in "sin city" of Washington, D.C. (Helping to beat Cougars that day was "sleeper play" in which George Washington QB picked up ball as C and whipped wide pass for 61y TD before BYU could get out of its D huddle.) So, it was riled-up group of Cougars (2-7) who rushed for 321y out of new Straight-T formation to beat Rams (3-7). BYU broke WB Doran Merkeley on 42y TD run and HB Alan Robinson for TD runs of 38 and 73y. Colorado State closed season with dismal 5-35 record to date in 1960s.

November 28-30, 1963

(Th'g) Illinois 13 MICHIGAN STATE 0: Opening KO indicated sort of day Spartans (6-2-1) would have as HB Dewey Lincoln bobbled ball and was downed on his 3 YL. C-LB Dick Butkus' great day on D paved way for Illinois (7-1-1) win. With it came Illinois' 1st trip to Rose Bowl since beating Stanford after 1951 season. C-K Jim Plankenhorn booted FGs of 22 and 34y in 1st H, and FB Jim Grabowski made 14y TD run early in 3rd Q. It came after DG Ed Washington pounced on FUM by Michigan State QB Dick Proebstle on 2nd play of 3rd Q. HB Sherman Lewis, who scored 8 TDs during Spartans' 1st 8 games of season, was held in complete check by Illini D, which permitted only 148y rushing.

(Th'g) Texas 15 TEXAS A&M 13: No. 1 Texas (10-0) became 1st undefeated SWC championship team since TCU turned trick in its 1938 national championship season. But, Longhorns clinched nothing before Aggies (2-7-1) provided serious scare. Riled-

up Texas A&M led 13-3 going into 4th Q on 2 TD passes by QB Jim Keller. Texas sub QB Tommy Wade's sharp passing set up Longhorns' rallying TD runs by HB Tommy Ford (21/113y) and QB Duke Carlisle.

Dartmouth 22 PRINCETON 21: With Ivy League title all but wrapped up in 4th Q at 21-7, Princeton (7-2) subs allowed Dartmouth (7-2) to make TD drive, capped by gimpy Indians HB Tom Spangenberg's run and his 2-pt run which trimmed Tigers lead to 21-15. Inspired Big Green drove to Tigers 1YL on their next series, only to be halted on 4th down. Dartmouth's comeback appeared lost as Princeton fans cheered loudly. Moments later on 3rd-and-short run, however, Nassau's future Hall of Fame FB Cosmo Iacavazzi lost FUM in his backfield to Dartmouth DE Scott Creelman when Tigers lineman missed block and Iacavazzi was blasted by gap-shooting, sub DG Dave DeCalestra. "That was the hardest tackle I've seen all season," said Creelman, Dartmouth captain. Indians HB John McLean quickly scored on 2y sweep, and HB-K Gary Wilson added winning kick. Dartmouth and Princeton shared Ivy title as Harvard, which had beaten both teams, stumbled at Yale 20-6 and finished half-game back.

North Carolina 16 DUKE 14: Tar Heels (8-2) soph K Max Chapman booted 41y FG with 33 secs to play to wrap up ACC co-championship with North Carolina State and Gator Bowl bid. North Carolina enjoyed 7-0 H lead on HB Ken Willard's 14y run off left side that capped 92y march in 2nd Q. Heels added FB Eddie Kessler's 1y TD smash for 13-0 lead after 77y trip in 3rd Q. Then Duke (5-4-1) finally got rolling as QB Scotty Glacken (16-28/217y, TD, 2 INTs) lofted long pass for HB Billy Futtrell, who went high between 2 defenders to corral pass at distant 30YL and galloped in for 70y TD. Midway in 4th Q, Blue Devils HB Jay Wilkinson took screen pass 42y to set up his darting 24y TD run that tied it, and K Steve Holloway kicked Duke into 14-13 lead. UNC gained its last possession with 1:23 to play. QB Junior Edge hit passes of 17 and 15y and ran smartly OB twice on gains of 10 and 9y. Chapman's FG made it over crossbar by inches for Carolina's thrilling win.

GEORGIA TECH 14 Georgia 3: Cold helped create 9 TOs as Furman Bisher writing in *Atlanta Journal* called it "scramblesome afternoon." Yellow Jackets (7-3) used QB-P Billy Lothridge's 1st Q punt to 4YL to gain field position before Bulldogs lost FUM to C-LB Dave Simmons at 23 YL. Georgia Tech FB Ray Mendheim quickly scored short TD. After Lothridge tossed poor pitchout that Georgia (4-5-1) DE George Nowicki recovered, Bulldogs clipped edge to 7-3 on K Bill McCullough's 27yFG just 41 secs before H. Georgia threatened for last time when DE Mickey Babb recovered FUM at Engineers 37YL, and QB Larry Rakestraw fueled failed trip to Georgia Tech 11YL with 13y pass to E Pat Hodgson. Lothridge's 3y TD pass to E Frank Sexton in 4th Q iced it at end of 47y drive.

Auburn 10 ALABAMA 8: QB Mailon Kent, who had played only 6 mins all year, created both Auburn (9-1) scores as early-game reliever for injured QB Jimmy Sidle. K Woody Woodall kicked 32y FG, and Kent hit HB Tucker Frederickson with 8y TD pass in 3rd Q. Lapsing only to allow Crimson Tide (7-2) HB Benny Nelson's 80y TD run in 3rd Q, tough Tigers D was aided by P Ed Kilgore's wind-bucking punts.

MISSISSIPPI STATE 10 Mississippi 10: Sugar Bowl-bound Ole Miss (7-0-2) needed 4th Q 20y FG by big E-K Billy Carl Irwin to tie outgained—by 221y to 111y—but stubborn Mississippi State (6-2-2). Rebels, dominating 1st H, went 82y to score on 30y pass from QB Jim Weatherly (5-10/55y, TD, INT) to TB Mike Dennis late in 1st Q. Bulldogs G-K Justin Canale rammed 49y FG through goalposts in 2nd Q. Miss State D pinned Ole Miss at its 9YL and took 10-7 3rd Q lead when HB Ode Burrell completed his only pass of season for 32y TD to E Tommy Inman. Clock was ticking toward 3-mins-to-go mark when Rebels bumped stiff Maroons D to 1st-and-goal at Miss State 7YL. FB Fred Roberts (15/50y) hit brick wall at 3YL on 3rd down, and coach Johnny Vaught was faced with big decision. After Irwin made his 20y FG to tie contest and clinch SEC title, Vaught said, "If we had gambled and lost, we would not have been conference champions."

Missouri 9 KANSAS 7: In initial going, Kansas Jayhawks (5-5) moved smartly for 74y to Tigers 2YL. They immediately were stunned when FB Ken Coleman's blast-ahead run turned into FUM that squirted into arms of Missouri (7-3) FB-LB Vince Turner, who had clear sailing for 102y TD. Big-time ground-gaining HB Gale Sayers took on abnormal role to put Kansas back in game by downing HB Tony Leiker's 67y QK on 1YL. It forced Mizzou's punt from EZ that set up 44y TD drive and 7-6 lead for Jayhawkers. K Bill Leistritz won it for Mizzou with 22y FG in 4th Q. Sayers was held to 68y on ground, but became 1st Big 8 back in conf's 56-year history ever to top 2000y rushing in his 1st 2 seasons.

ARIZONA STATE 35 Arizona 6: Unbeaten in WAC, but playing insufficient number of conf games to claim title, Sun Devils (8-1) still won 8th straight game since losing their opener. Arizona State finished 3-0 in WAC by trouncing Arizona (5-4), which still retained chance at conf title in upcoming showdown with New Mexico. Keyed-up Devils nearly gave it away in swift-paced 1st Q: Wildcats HB Ricki Harris toted opening KO 95y to score, and Arizona State lost FUM on its 1st snap and also lost INT and FUM deep in own end. Sun Devils D held after each TO, and their O eventually revived itself. ASU outgained Arizona 325y to 81y, with HB Tony Lorick (115y rushing) scoring thrice, including 42y INT TD RET. Wildcats passers completed measly 3-22/37y.

STANFORD 28 California 17: West Coast's annual "Big Game" had been contested in rugby from 1906-14, and this modern football affair saw as much effective kicking as in olden days. California (4-5-1) HB-K Tom Blanchfield booted 37y FG in 1st Q, only to see it matched before H by Stanford (3-7) K Brady Beck from 36y out. Game's 3rd Q turned highly offensive with big break coming early to Indians: Golden Bears' bad snap was recovered at Cal 5YL, and QB Steve Thurlow quickly scored TD. Back came Bears as HB Jim Blakeney scored on 7y run, and Blanchfield kicked x-pt for 10-9 lead. Blanchfield soon followed with 69y punt TD RET. Trailing 17-15 in 4th Q,

Stanford called on Beck to nail 48y FG to put Tribe in front 18-17 with 12 mins left. After Thurlow's 2nd rushing TD, Bears were still within reach at 25-17, but Beck shut door with 46y FG with 4 mins to play.

WASHINGTON 16 Washington State 0: Washington (6-4) gained Rose Bowl berth behind burly runs of FB Junior Coffey, who scored twice. Cougars (3-6-1) had driven to Huskies 4YL on opening drive but were thwarted by Washington's second unit. Those players had started for coach Jim Owens, who used move as motivation for 1st unit. Game ended as Washington State QB Dave Mathieson was spilled for safety by Huskies T Chuck Bond.

OREGON 31 Oregon State 14: HB-DB H.D. Murphy made 2 INTs, each leading to 1st H Oregon (7-3) TD and also caught 29y TD pass from QB Bob Berry (18-26/249y, 2 TDs) in 3rd Q. Ducks FB Lu Bain scored twice on 4 and 13y runs. Falling behind 31-0, disappointed Beavers (5-5) earned only 4 1st downs through 3 Qs, but made show of it with 2 late TDs behind 3rd-string soph QB Marv Crowston, who tallied game's last TD.

AP Poll December 2

1 Texas (42)	485	6 Nebraska	217	
2 Navy (8)	432	7 Mississippi	168	
3 Illinois	356	8 Oklahoma	108	
4 Pittsburgh (1)	335	9 Alabama	72	
5 Auburn	226	10 Michigan State	54	

Others with votes: Arizona State, Baylor, Georgia Tech, Memphis State, Mississippi State, North Carolina, North Carolina State, Penn State, Southern California, Syracuse, Washington

December 7, 1963

GAME OF THE YEAR
Navy 21 Army 15 (Philadelphia):

Game was originally cancelled due to presidential assassination, but widow, Mrs. Jacqueline Kennedy, made special request that it be played. FB Pat Donnelly scored 3 TDs, last at end of 91y drive that gave Navy (9-1) 21-7 lead with less than 11 mins left and Tars appeared on their way to Cotton Bowl. But, unsung Army (7-3) QB Rollie Stichweh ignored his passing O and created all-infantry 52y TD march and added 2-pt run. Stichweh's TD run was shown by CBS as TV's 1st-ever instant replay. Now back to live action: Stichweh immediately fell on K Dick Heydt's perfect on-side KO at Middies 49YL and Cadets were in business. After 5 meticulous runs and 11y pass to WB Don Parcells, Army used its last timeout with ball at 7YL and 1:38 left. After 2 runs to 4YL, and with 100,000 fans in uproar, ref called time to aid Army's signal calling. Stichweh made mistake of re-huddling his team, while unaware clock was running. Cadets HB Ken Waldrop's plunge went to 2YL, but time expired with Stichweh hopelessly pleading for quiet so Army could run its 5th down play. No. 2 Navy won its 5th in row over Army, but in barely surviving Middies might have left behind some of their zest for upcoming Cotton Bowl showdown with no. 1 Texas.

PITTSBURGH 22 Penn State 21: Seesaw in-state classic was turned when Pitt (9-1) QB Fred Mazurek, shrugged off painful hip injury to limp off bench at outset of 4th Q to cap 77y drive with winning 17y TD run. Mazurek (7-15/105y, and 23/142y rushing) gained 247y total O to help overcome 2 TD passes by Nittany Lions (7-3) QB Pete Liske (11-23/173y). Mount Nit FB Ed Stuckrath blocked 1st Q punt to poise Liske for brilliant 4th down fake and counter hand-off to HB Gary Klingensmith (14/47y) who went untouched for 9y TD. Pitt trailed 7-6 early in 2nd Q and 14-12 at H because after TD runs by HB Paul Martha and FB Rick Leeson, Panthers failed on 2-pt passes. Pitt got its 1st lead at 15-14 on K Leeson's 35y FG in 3rd Q, but Penn State came right back with 75y drive, keyed by HB Chris Weber's 30y run on same scissors play that scored in 1st Q. E Don Caum (4/99y, TD) caught Liske's TD pass for Penn State. Pitt now trailed 21-15, and Mazurek became key man in winning drive in 4th Q as he made 1st downs with both pass and run, and finally flew through air at GL to complete his 17y TD scramble. Penn State HB-K Ron Coates missed potential winning 37y FG by less than foot to left of post with 1:34 left. Although there was Sun Bowl talk, every bowl promoter was either committed already or somehow was unimpressed with Panthers' record. It clearly cost Pitt to have had its last game delayed 2 weeks, and Panthers were left at home despite final AP ranking of no. 4.

AIR FORCE 17 Colorado 14: Gator Bowl bid was extended to Falcons (7-3) after they came from behind twice to defeat Colorado (2-8). Trailing 14-10 with 13 mins left, Falcon QB Terry Isaacson hit 4 passes in 80y drive, last completion for 13y TD to HB Paul Wargo. Along way, Isaacson connected with E Fritz Greenlee on 14 and 16y passes to convert 3rd downs and E Jim Greth for 14y to overcome 4th-and-7 at Buffalo 27YL. Earlier in 2nd H, Colorado FB Noble Milton played key TD role. Buffs E Stan Irvine's FUM REC of Air Force HB Dick Czarnota's bobble allowed Milton's immediate 30y TD run in 3rd Q. Early in 4th Q, Milton put Colorado ahead 14-10 with 3y run at end of 68y march that was keyed by QB Frank Cesarek's 37y pass and Milton's 25y sprint.

Final AP Poll December 9

1 Texas (34)	460	6 Nebraska	241	
2 Navy (10)	418	7 Mississippi	198	
3 Illinois	361	8 Alabama	116	
4 Pittsburgh (5)	340	9 Michigan State	109	
5 Auburn	247	10 Oklahoma	60	

Others with votes: Air Force, Arizona State, Army, Baylor, Louisiana State, Memphis State, Mississippi State, North Carolina, Southern California, Syracuse, Washington

December 14, 1963

Alabama 17 MIAMI 12: Crimson Tide (8-2) played without star QB Joe Namath, who had been suspended by coach Bear Bryant for having broken training rules. Alabama never trailed, but Tide had to sweat out its victory under hale of aerial bullets from Miami Hurricanes (3-7) QB George Mira (24-48/301y, TD, 3 INTs). Speedy HB Gary

Martin exploded 100y to score on opening KO as Bama created speedy envelope of blockers that freed Martin up left sideline. Tide DB Hudson Harris soon recovered FUM at Hurricanes 13YL, and HB Benny Nelson powered over for 1y TD and quick 14-0 lead. Another FUM REC led to K Tim Davis' 35y FG in 2nd Q, so Bama led 17-0 at H. Miami had run ball well in 1st H but turned its 2nd H O completely over to Mira's throwing in his last collegiate game. Mira riddled Bama secondary to whip up 4 drives. Tide DT Steve Wright spilled Canes HB Russell Smith for 10y loss on 4th-and-goal from 4YL, and another trip died at Alabama 21YL. But in 4th Q, Mira hit WB Nick Spinelli for 9y TD, and FB Pete Banaszak blasted over for TD. Last chance for win in retiring coach Andy Gustafson's farewell died when Tide LB Jackie Sherrill made INT at his 29YL. By leapfrogging Baylor's Don Trull, Mira ended with season's total O crown and tied to-date career completion mark (368), held by Loyola of California's Don Klosterman.

1963 Conference Standings

Ivy League
Dartmouth	5-2
Princeton	5-2
Harvard	4-2-1
Cornell	4-3
Yale	4-3
Columbia	2-4-1
Brown	2-5
Pennsylvania	1-6

Atlantic Coast
North Carolina	6-1
North Carolina State	6-1
Clemson	5-2
Duke	5-2
Maryland	2-5
South Carolina	1-5-1
Wake Forest	1-5
Virginia	0-5-1

Southern
Virginia Tech	5-0
West Virginia	3-1
Virginia Military	3-1-2
Furman	3-2
Richmond	2-2-1
William & Mary	4-4
Citadel	2-4
George Washington	1-5
Davidson	0-4-1

Southeastern
Mississippi	5-0-1
Auburn	6-1
Alabama	6-2
Mississippi State	4-1-2
Louisiana State	4-2
Georgia Tech	4-3
Florida	3-3-1
Tennessee	3-5
Georgia	2-4
Vanderbilt	0-5-2
Kentucky	0-5-1
Tulane	0-6-1

Big Ten
Illinois	5-1-1
Michigan State	4-1-1
Ohio State	4-1-1
Purdue	4-3
Northwestern	3-4
Wisconsin	3-4
Michigan	2-3-2
Iowa	2-3-1
Minnesota	2-5
Indiana	1-5

Mid-American
Ohio	5-1
Miami (Ohio)	4-1-1
Bowling Green	4-2
Marshall	3-2-1
Western Michigan	2-4
Toledo	1-5
Kent State	1-5

Big Eight
Nebraska	7-0
Oklahoma	6-1
Missouri	5-2
Kansas	3-4
Iowa State	3-4
Colorado	2-5
Kansas State	1-5
Oklahoma State	0-6

Missouri Valley
Cincinnati	3-1
Wichita	3-1
Tulsa	2-2
North Texas State	2-2
Louisville	1-3

Southwest
Texas	7-0
Baylor	6-1
Rice	4-3
Arkansas	3-4
Texas Christian	2-4-1
Texas Tech	2-5
Southern Methodist	2-5
Texas A&M	1-5-1

Western Athletic
New Mexico	3-1
Arizona	2-2
Utah	2-2
Wyoming	2-3
Brigham Young	0-4
Arizona State *	3-0
* Ineligible	

AAWU
Washington	4-1
Southern California	3-1
UCLA	2-2
Washington State	1-1
California	1-3
Stanford	1-4

1963 Bowl Games
Bluebonnet Bowl (Dec. 21): Baylor 14 Louisiana State 7

SEC's top rushing team, LSU (7-4), opened with impressive TD drive cashed in by HB Buddy Soefker. But then momentum turned toward Baylor (8-3), and even though Bears were halted at LSU 19, 26, 7, and 10 YL, they never grew frustrated. Stunningly, Baylor held Bayou Bengals' ground game to no 1st downs in game's last 55 mins. Baylor air ace, QB Don Trull, completed 26-37/255y, 2 TDs. Finally in 4th Q, undersized

Bears E James Ingram got loose for 2 TD passes from Trull, and Bears earned hard-earned win. By game's end, Baylor had built amazing 27 to 4 edge in 1st downs.

Liberty Bowl (Dec. 21): Mississippi State 16 North Carolina State 12

Mississippi State (7-2-2) overcame large number of PENs totaling 122y to edge Wolfpack (8-3) in Philadelphia, where only 8,309 spectators risked frostbite to witness game. Small crowd signaled end of late December ice bowls for awhile; Liberty Bowl was headed south to Memphis. Maroons built 16-6 H lead on TDs by E Tommy Inman on 11y punt block TD RET and QB Sonny Fisher's run after short North Carolina State punt. Outstanding Bulldog G-K Justin Canale bombed 43y FG into stiff 17 mph wind. Wolfpack had many 2nd H chances but could convert only on QB Jim Rossi's 5y TD pass to E Ray Barlow with 2:48 left. It was Barlow's 5th reception of season, but 4 went for TDs. Bulldogs' burly FB, Hoyle Granger, rushed 13/94y.

Gator Bowl (Dec. 28): North Carolina 35 Air Force 0

North Carolina's 1st-ever bowl victory projected bruising HB Ken Willard into national spotlight with MVP rushing effort for 18/94y, TD for Tar Heels (9-2). Game was rated even beforehand, but Air Force (7-4) was outclassed from outset. Willard rumbled for 51y of team's 77y voyage to his 1y run for Carolina TD in 1st Q, and 4 other Heels followed in TD procession: QB Junior Edge, E Joe Robinson, FB Eddie Kesler, and sub QB Gary Black. Heels' 2 QBs both were sharp with their passes as Edge hit 5-9/42y and Black was perfect 6-6/71y and TD throw to Robinson that made it 20-0 at H. C-LB Dave Sicks was Falcons' only bright spot, winning top lineman award with his sideline-to-sideline tackling. Air Force was forced to its aerial attack—and suffered 5 INTs—when nation's O leader, QB Terry Isaacson, was hemmed in on runs he tried from Shotgun formation.

Sun Bowl (Dec. 31): Oregon 21 Southern Methodist 14

Sun Bowl's previous 28-year history was that of springboard for smaller, but successful programs. Future major-level teams in their formative stages that won bowls in El Paso included Cincinnati (1947), Louisville (1958), New Mexico (1946), Texas Tech (1952), Tulsa (1942), Utah (1939), and West Virginia (1938 and '49). But in 1963, committee looked for 1st time to established major confs for its matchup. In this leap forward, Sun Bowl was anxious to insure presumed ticket sales security. Bypassing Pittsburgh, with its 9-1 record and no. 4 ranking, it tapped Texas-based team and opted for SMU (4-7), only 2nd team ever to enter bowl with losing record. Virginia Tech at 3-4-3 also had played in Sun Bowl and was loser to Cincinnati in 1947. To make matters worse for so-so Mustangs, several players came down with intestinal flu. Webfoots (8-3), behind HB Dennis Keller's 9y TD run and QB Bob Berry's pair of TD passes, built 21-0 H lead. SMU made nice comeback with speedy HB John Roderick's 2 4th Q TD pass reception. SMU, which outgained Oregon 377y to 319y, finally succumbed when its on-side KO rolled OB with 24 secs to play.

Orange Bowl: Nebraska 13 Auburn 7

On game's 2nd scrimmage play, Nebraska (10-1) QB Dennis Claridge (108y rushing) faked left, went right behind thunderous block of A-A G Bob Brown, and broke down right sideline for 68y TD. At that time, Claridge's run gave him new Orange Bowl distance record, exceeding by 1y run of Ole Miss' Ned Peters in 1936. E Tony Jeter began his marvelous D play for Cornhuskers on 1st series by Auburn (9-2) as he dumped QB Jimmy Sidle for 3y loss to force punt. Nebraska's 2nd possession went 47y to K Dave Theisen's 31y FG for 10-0 lead in fewer than 10 mins after opening KO. Plainsman HB George Rose fumbled P Claridge's punt on 1st play of 2nd Q, and Theisen added 36y FG, to-date distance record for Orange Bowl. Huskers were on their way to 13-0 H lead and upset win. Sidle (14-27/141y, INT) re-fired Auburn in 2nd H, scoring on 13y sweep out of Shotgun formation at end of 71y drive late in 3rd Q. Key play of drive was Sidle's 28y arrow to E Bucky Waid. Tigers were in position to win with 1:36 left after Sidle completed 5 passes. But, Sidle's toss on 4th-and-4 from 11YL for HB Doc Griffith was broken up at GL by Nebraska G-LB John Kirby and FB-DB Bruce Smith.

Sugar Bowl: Alabama 12 Mississippi 7

Sugar Bowl of 1964 is best known for most snowfall (4 inches piled on sideline) in City of New Orleans in 20th Century and Crimson Tide's big-name player who sat it out. Alabama (9-2) QB Joe Namath didn't play after having been suspended by coach Bear Bryant in mid-December. Alabama was well-guided by soph QB Steve Sloan (3-10/29y, INT) but managed only 194y total O. Coming through for to-date bowl-record 4 FGs, however, was Bama's sr K Tim Davis, who made 31, 46, 22, and 48y FGs. Davis' last 3-pt kick also set bowl record for distance at that time. Alabama's fierce D held Rebels completely without single 1st down in 1st H and forced 6 lost FUMs during game. Trailing 9-0 at H, Ole Miss (7-1-2) came to life. Rebels went 74y in 4th Q to WB Larry Smith's 5y TD catch from QB Perry Lee Dunn (8-10/125y). Game's dying moments saw apparent TD catch by Rebels E Allen Brown being ruled as beyond EZ backline. Dunn's last-play sweep was stopped at 2YL by alert Alabama D.

Cotton Bowl: Texas 28 Navy 6

Nobody in their right mind expected Texas (11-0) QB Duke Carlisle to outgain Roger Staubach of Navy (9-2) with his passes, and, contrary to history's perception, he didn't. But, clever Carlisle made his throws count: 7 completions for 213y, or 30.4y every time he connected with Longhorn receivers. On game's 6th play, Carlisle hit WB Phil Harris with 58y TD as Middies star FB-DB Pat Donnelly stumbled in his pass coverage. Harris caught another Carlisle TD of 63y, and Carlisle passed for 57y of 75y drive late in 3rd for insurmountable 28-0 lead. For his part, Staubach didn't disappoint, setting Cotton Bowl record for completions and pass y with 21-31/228y. Staubach ran for lone Middies TD, but was so harassed by dominating Steers D that Staubach's usual brilliant running ended up boxed in for net of -47y. Texas D standouts were T Scott Appleton and LB Tommy Nobis, and overall D fenced in Middies for -14y rushing. For most fans other than those inside Lone Star State, it was dissatisfying battle of top teams that quickly lost its fizz in early-game domination by Longhorns.

Rose Bowl: Illinois 17 Washington 7

Hard-hitting Illinois (8-1-1) D was hallmark of 50th Rose Bowl Classic. Washington (6-5) lost QB Bill Douglas with dislocated knee on 1st drive that died at Illini 14YL. Huskies, 1st team ever in Rose Bowl with 4 losses, managed 7-0 lead in 2nd Q. FUM REC at Illinois 27YL set up HB Dave Kopay's 7y pitchout run for score. Late 2nd Q FUM REC at Huskies 15YL got Illinois back in game as C-K Jim Plankenhorn drilled 32y FG. Inspired 2nd H D brought Illinois 2 TDs, each set up by INT from ace DB George Donnelly. HB Jim Warren and FB Jim Grabowski—voted MVP thanks to his 23/125y rushing—each scored TD run. Washington's last threat, engineered by sub QB Bill Siler, was snuffed by INT by big C-LB Dick Butkus, considered by many observers to be greatest LB in college football history.

1963 Top Performance Formula

1	Texas	1.6942
2	Pittsburgh	1.5782
3	Nebraska	1.5475
4	Arizona State	1.5329
5	Navy	1.5161
6	Auburn	1.4987
7	Oklahoma	1.4889
8	Alabama	1.4778
9	Illinois	1.4534
10	Mississippi	1.4484
11	Syracuse	1.4417
12	Michigan State	1.4219
13	Mississippi State	1.4180
14	Georgia Tech	1.3754
15	North Carolina	1.3637
16	Penn State	1.3353
17	Baylor	1.3192
18	North Carolina State	1.3091
19	Virginia Tech	1.2789
20	Missouri	1.2766

1963 Top Opponent Records

1	Mississippi State	.6471
2	West Virginia	.6461
3	Wake Forest	.6130
4	Southern Methodist	.6117
5	Auburn	.6078
6	Houston	.6075
7	Minnesota	.6067
8	Michigan State	.6053
9	Notre Dame	.6013
10	UCLA	.6000
11	Michigan	.5987
12	Oklahoma State	.5976
13	Florida State	.5934
14	Northwestern	.5933
15	Georgia Tech	.5914
16	Oklahoma	.5899
17	Penn State	.5843
18	Washington	.5765
19	Florida	.5745
20	Pittsburgh	.5722

1963 Out-of-Conference Records

	W-L	Percentage	Bowl W-L
Southeastern	25-10-1	.7083	2-3
Big Ten	16-7	.6957	1-0
Southwest	18-9	.6667	2-1
Western Athletic	16-15	.5161	0-0
Big Eight	10-13	.4348	1-0
AAWU	12-22-2	.3611	0-1
Atlantic Coast	7-17-2	.3077	1-1

1963 Individual Statistical Leaders

RUSHING YARDS	Attempts	Yards	Avg.
Dave Casinelli, Memphis State	219	1016	4.6
Jimmy Sidle, Auburn	185	1006	5.4
Gale Sayers, Kansas	132	917	7.0
Jim Grisham, Oklahoma	153	861	5.6
Bob Schweikert, Virginia Tech	155	839	5.4
Mike Garrett, Southern California	128	833	6.5
Gary Wood, Cornell	166	818	4.9
Tony Lorick, Arizona State	105	805	7.7
Terry Isaacson, Air Force	162	801	4.9
Tom Vaughn, Iowa State	190	795	4.2

PASSING YARDS	Completions	Attempts	Yards	Pct.
Don Trull, Baylor	174	308	2157	56.5
George Mira, Miami	172	335	2155	51.3
Jerry Rhome, Tulsa	150	258	1909	58.1
Bill Munson, Utah State	120	210	1699	59.7
Bob Berry, Oregon	101	171	1675	59.1
Craig Morton, California	101	207	1475	48.8
Roger Staubach, Navy	107	161	1474	66.5
Larry Rakestraw, Georgia	103	209	1297	49.3
Scotty Glacken, Duke	101	200	1265	50.5
Tom LaFramboise, Louisville	104	204	1205	51.0

RECEIVING YARDS	Catches	Yards
Larry Elkins, Baylor	70	873
Vern Burke, Oregon State	48	794
Jim Curry, Cincinnati	39	621
Stan Crisson, Duke	48	559
John Simmons, Tulsa	39	543
James Ingram, Baylor	40	537
Bob Lacey, North Carolina	48	533
Jim Whalen, Boston College	26	523
Darryl Hill, Maryland	43	516
Nick Spinelli, Miami	41	501

1963 Consensus All-America Team

End:	Vern Burke, Oregon State
	Lawrence Elkins, Baylor
Tackle:	Scott Appleton, Texas
	Carl Eller, Minnesota
Guard:	Bob Brown, Nebraska
	Rick Redman, Washington
Center:	Dick Butkus, Illinois
Backs:	Roger Staubach, Navy
	Sherman Lewis, Michigan State
	Gale Sayers, Kansas
	Paul Martha, Pittsburgh
	Jim Grisham, Oklahoma

Other All-America Choices

End:	Jim Kelly, Notre Dame
	Bob Lacey, North Carolina
	Billy Martin, Georgia Tech
	Dave Parks, Texas Tech
Tackle:	Ernie Borghetti, Pittsburgh
	Ken Kortas, Louisville
	Harry Schuh, Memphis State
Guard:	Damon Bame, Southern California
	Steve DeLong, Tennessee
	Mike Reilly, Iowa
	Herschel Turner, Kentucky
Center:	Ken Dill, Mississippi
Backs:	Billy Lothridge, Georgia Tech
	Jimmy Sidle, Auburn
	Don Trull, Baylor
	Tommy Ford, Texas
	Mel Renfro, Oregon
	Jay Wilkinson, Duke
	Tommy Crutcher, Texas Christian
	Tom Vaughn, Iowa State

1963 Heisman Trophy Vote

Roger Staubach, junior quarterback, Navy	1860
Billy Lothridge, senior quarterback, Georgia Tech	504
Sherman Lewis, senior halfback, Michigan State	369
Don Trull, senior quarterback, Baylor	253
Scott Appleton, senior tackle, Texas	194
Dick Butkus, junior center-linebacker, Illinois	172

Other Major Awards

Maxwell (Player):	Roger Staubach, junior quarterback, Navy
Outland (Lineman):	Scott Appleton, senior tackle, Texas
Walter Camp (Back):	Roger Staubach, junior quarterback, Navy
Knute Rockne (Lineman):	Dick Butkus, junior center-linebacker, Illinois
AFCA Coach of the Year:	Darrell Royal, Texas

1964

The Year of the Notre Dame Miracle, Ready for Primetime Thriller, and Arkansas Holiday

Notre Dame, which truly could be called America's Team long before such a term ever was applied to the Dallas Cowboys, had fallen on sorry times. When Terry Brennan was fired along with his so-so 32-18 record after the 1958 season, former pro coach Joe Kuharich was hired to emanicipate the slumping Irish. Luckless Kuharich managed three 5-5 seasons with a disastrous 2-8 mark in 1960 amid hefty injury lists and chants of "Joe Must Go!" One-year interim coach Hugh Devore managed no better, going 2-7 in 1963.

One of the architects of Notre Dame's demise had been Ara Parseghian, coach of Northwestern, the disadvantaged waifs of the Big Ten. In four years (1959-62), Parseghian's Wildcats, with far inferior talent, beat the Irish each time. So, in 1964, America's most famous Roman Catholic university, its teams known as the Fighting Irish, hired an Armenian Presbyterian as its new coach, and a football miracle occurred.

Parseghain retooled his personnel and found stars in halfback-turned-end Jack Snow and obscure quarterback John Huarte, Heisman winner in waiting, who was found far down Devore's depth chart. Sometimes it takes very little to completely change a team's makeup. And, oh, what a difference positive-attitude coaching made. Stunningly, Notre Dame won its first nine games, beating nemesis Purdue (6-3), Roger Staubach's crippled Navy (3-6-1) team, and Michigan State (4-5). Hidden in the Irish resurgence was that Purdue was their only victim that would end with a winning record except the season-ending foe, Southern California (7-3). A win in Los Angeles for top-ranked and favored Notre Dame on Thanksgiving Saturday was to complete a storybook national championship for Parseghian in his debut year in South Bend. But, a late touchdown catch by Trojans wide receiver Rod Sherman gave spoiler USC a huge comeback for a 20-17 upset.

The AAWU chose co-champion Oregon State (8-3) as its Rose Bowl delegate, and many in Los Angeles were outraged by the choice after the Trojans' magnificent win over Notre Dame. But, witty coach John McKay advised Trojan backers to take it easy, reminding them that "600 million Chinese couldn't care less" about indiscretions against Southern California.

The best punchline of the year came from Michigan State coach Duffy Daugherty, whose Spartans were coming off a couple of so-so years. A journalist was studying a preseason roster and seriously asked Daugherty whom he was most pleased to see return. Without batting an eye, Daugherty said, "Me!"

The AP national champion was still determined by a vote taken prior to the bowls, and Alabama (10-1) won it, only to be upset by Texas (10-1) in a stirring Orange Bowl. The landmark game was the first Orange Bowl played at night, a primetime TV thriller starring Crimson Tide quarterback Joe Namath back from a knee injury and debuting his infamous white shoes, which were not meant as a fashion gimmick, just novel-looking shoes crafted to accommodate special, safer cleats. Stacked on top of three daylight bowls, the night game created about 10 hours of TV football for the first time ever, and pushed sports deeper into mainstream entertainment. Jack Gould, TV critic of *The New York Times*, thought all-day football was overkill: "A (TV) set owner last night had visions of football...prospering to the point of extinction. The human mind does have a saturation point. NBC in conspiratorial liaison with Orange Bowl officials and the city fathers of Miami made the longest New Year's in the history of football."

Gould hadn't seen anything yet! How wrong could he be? After the schools went to court to regain their TV rights in the early 1980s there would be 10 hours of college football on video sets every Saturday. ESPN would deliver by the late 1970s an all-sports network that was hugely dependant on college sports. On its heels came the Movie Channel, the Cartoon Network, Turner Classic Movies, Comedy Central, the Food Channel, Speed Channel, Soap Network, and the Golf Channel. The human mind hasn't been saturated quite yet, Mr. Gould.

Another post-season game, New Orleans' Sugar Bowl, marked a new era. After the 1955 season, the Sugar Bowl had invited Pittsburgh to meet Georgia Tech, and the fact that the Panthers had Bobby Grier, an African-American, starting at fullback caused a major issue in the segregated South. The Sugar Bowl committee took care of that in a quiet manner. For the next eight seasons, no team other than one from the segregated Atlantic Coast, Southeastern, or Southwest Conferences was invited to play the SEC champion in New Orleans. But after the 1964 season, Syracuse (7-4), with eight blacks on its roster, was invited to meet Louisiana State (8-2-1)

in the first fully-integrated Sugar Bowl, the last such post-season game to embrace the new order.

The Football Writers Association, which polled many of the same voters as the AP ballot, made its national champion selection after the bowl games. For the sixth time in 11 years, the FWAA differed with the AP vote and this time selected Arkansas (11-0) as its titleist after Frank Broyles' Razorbacks beat Nebraska (9-2) in the Cotton Bowl. Arkansas was the only team, other than non-bowling Princeton (9-0), still standing undefeated after the postseason. The entire state of Arkansas closed down to honor its beloved Hogs on February 5, a holiday declared by Gov. Orville Faubus.

One wonders why bowl games were discounted as alien for so long. If AP writers and UPI coaches were comfortable staging a pre-season poll that clearly was based on soft data like past reputation, the previous year's results, and the ever-popular "returning lettermen" count, why not a post-season poll? Final post-season polls were still a few years away, and it took the sport's most anticipated showdown, the 1966 Michigan State-Notre Dame tussle, to really prompt full focus on reaching for the national championship.

The 1964 season had an oddity that set it aside from all others. Complete free substitution was still a season away, but the rules committee allowed free movement of players when the clock was stopped and permitted two substitutes with the clock running. The fathers of the college game had decided the pro game's better rested players, who played exclusively on offense or defense, kept NFL and AFL games moving at a sharper pace. The college coaches had preferred unlimited substitution for many years, the last straw poll in 1963 showing 516 to 169 in favor. It is interesting to note that 1964 souvenir programs printed by home collegiate teams mostly listed only 11 starters. Many players still played on both sides of the ball, but the trend was to employ specialists at quarterback, wide receiver, kicker, linebacker, and in the secondary so that when all was added up, virtually every team sported separate offensive and defensive units.

Blackie Sherrod, terrific writer of the *Dallas Morning News,* phrased it best when he wrote that "rulesmakers had been sidling up to unlimited substitution as if it were a souvenir hand grenade in the attic trunk." It was this reluctance that helped bury the college game behind the pros.

Milestones

For first time since 1952, virtual free substitution was granted by NCAA rules committee. Any number of players was permitted to be substituted when clock stopped, two players were allowed to enter games when clock was running.

Charter member Georgia Tech withdrew from Southeastern Conference after 31 seasons to become independent.

Oregon and Oregon State joined AAWU, thus, in effect, reinstituting former Pacific Coast Conference (with exclusion of Big Sky member Idaho) that had disbanded in strife after 1958 season.

Former Army quarterback Joe Caldwell (1958-59) died at age 26 in military plane crash in Vietnam, strife-stricken nation barely known to Americans in 1964. Dr. Clarence Spears, Hall of Fame coach at seven schools, 1917-44, died at age 69.

Longest winning streaks entering season:
Texas 11   Arizona State, Memphis State 8

Coaching Changes:

	Incoming	Outgoing
Brigham Young	Tom Hudspeth	Hal Mitchell
California	Ray Willsey	Marv Levy
Georgia	Vince Dooley	Johnny Griffith
Miami	Charlie Tate	Andy Gustafson
Northwestern	Alex Agase	Ara Parseghian
Notre Dame	Ara Parseghian	Hugh Devore
Oklahoma	Gomer Jones	Bud Wilkinson
Tennessee	Doug Dickey	Jim McDonald
Wake Forest	Bill Tate	Bill Hildebrand
Washington State	Bert Clark	Jim Sutherland

AP Preseason Poll

1 Mississippi (20)	425	6 Alabama (1)	196
2 Oklahoma (15)	400	7 Washington (1)	161
3 Illinois (10)	368	8 Auburn (1)	144
4 Texas	242	9 Syracuse	143
5 Ohio State	205	10 Navy	101

Others with votes: Arkansas, Army, Duke, Florida, Georgia Tech, Indiana, Louisiana State, Michigan, Missouri, Nebraska, North Carolina, Penn State, Rice, Southern California, Wisconsin

September 12, 1964

Ucla 17 PITTSBURGH 12: No West Coast team had ever won in Pitt Stadium in 10 tries, but UCLA (1-0) went 61y to QB Larry Zeno's TD pass to HB Steve Durbin early in game, were never ambushed thereafter. Zeno finished up tidy 1st H with TD pass to E Dick Witcher and 25y FG as H clock ticked to :00. Panthers (0-1) QB Freddy Mazurek scored behind G Bernie Laquinta's block in 2nd Q, but was benched with injury when QB Kenny Lucas drove Pitt to its only 2nd H score: FB Barry McKnight's short TD plunge.

September 19, 1964

BOSTON COLLEGE 21 Syracuse 14: Tall Boston College (1-0) E Bill Cronin made leaping TD catch between 2 DBs to snare QB Larry Marzetti's desperate 55y 4th down bomb with 12 secs left. Syracuse (0-1) had tied it at 14-14 on QB Wally Mahle's sneak and 2-pt run with less than 2 mins to play. It followed Orange's only pass connection of day: QB Rich King's 35y toss to soph HB Floyd Little. FB Jim Nance led Syracuse's 262y ground maneuvers, but was stymied at key times by excellent Eagles D, led by LB Ron Gentilli.

Navy 21 PENN STATE 8: Pair of ranked Eastern foes squared off with Penn State (0-1) presenting D plan that foiled Navy (1-0) QB Roger Staubach as never before. Staubach (5-13/44y and 12/–14y rushing) netted only 30y on 25 plays as he was repeatedly sacked. But, Staubach sneaked for 1st Q TD and 7-0 lead that stood up behind Midshipmen's fine D play. Lions suffered 4 TOs, most damaging being 57y INT TD RET by DB Duncan Ingraham for Middies' 14-0 lead in 3rd Q. On following drive, Lions moved within 14-8 as FB Tom Urbanik charged 43y to set up WB Tim Montgomery for 12y TD reverse. Navy soon held at its 17YL primarily because Penn State E Bill Huber dropped likely TD pass at 2YL, and Middies G-LB Fred Marlin soon grabbed critical INT to set up clinching 4th Q TD, scored by HB Tom Leiser.

Oklahoma 13 MARYLAND 3: Just 4 mins remained, and Maryland (0-1) was ready to celebrate 1 of its greatest wins: 3-0 spoiler of Gomer Jones' Oklahoma (1-0) coaching debut. Jones looked to his bench to insert strong-armed, 3rd-string QB John Hammond, who surprised by pitching perfect 90y bomb to HB Lance Retzel for 6-3 lead. Now Maryland was forced to come back, and Terrapins QB Phil Petry was soon picked off by OU DE David Voiles. It set up Sooners QB Mike Ringer for clinching TD run. Outstanding Terps D nearly made Maryland K Bernardo Bramson's early 4th Q FG stand up. Maryland defenders who sparkled included E John Kenny and Gs Jerry Fishman and Fred Joyce, and they bottled up Sooners star FB Jim Grisham and their rush O.

North Carolina State 14 NORTH CAROLINA 13: NC State (1-0) used consistently tough D and 2 critical INTs of Tar Heels soph QB Danny Talbott to upset North Carolina (0-1). DE Tony Golmont picked off Talbott's 1st collegiate pass to gave Wolfpack 7-0 H lead with 45y INT TD RET. NC State FB-LB Pete Falzarano (10/69y, TD, 9 tackles on D) grabbed INT in 4th Q at Heels 39YL and followed quickly with 38y TD run up middle as E Golmont's block in secondary erased 2 tacklers. With 1:42 left, Talbott (4-9/41y, TD, 2 INTs) rallied his UNC mates and hit soph E Billy Darnell 3 times to 18YL and found HB Ken Willard in left flat for 9y TD pass. Talbott went for win with 48 ticks left on clock, but missed 2-pt pass try when NC State QB-DB Ron Skosnik swatted it down. Wolfpack rushed for 187y as Ts Rosie Amato and Glenn Sasser opened consistent holes.

SOUTH CAROLINA 9 Duke 9: Favored Duke (0-0-1) made 2 mistakes and each led to scores by Gamecocks (0-0-1). In early going, Blue Devils E-P Rod Stewart bobbled snap and thumped punt straight up in air for 12y to Duke 46YL. South Carolina QB Dan Reeves hit 2 passes and converted 4th down run for 9y to 16YL. Carolina HB Larry Gill slashed 4y for TD 4 plays later, but Blue Shirt DB Mike Shasby blocked Cocks' x-pt try. Duke QB Scotty Glacken began hitting passes in 2nd Q for 34 and 11y that led to K Stewart's 34y FG. Bruising FB Mike Curtis carried on 7 plays and scored from 1YL on 49y Devils' TD drive in 3rd Q. Conv kick was missed, which allowed Birds K Jack McCathern to tie it with 30y FG with 1:30 to play. On last drive, Reeves hit passes of 10, 10, 6, and 9y and made 4th-and-1 rollout for 1st down at Duke 16YL. Next 3 plays went 3y, so McCathern kicked 3-ptr.

ALABAMA 31 Georgia 3: Vince Dooley began his long career as Georgia (0-1) coach, but Alabama (1-0) was superior foe on this night in Tuscaloosa. Back from year-end suspension of 1963, QB Joe Namath clicked on 16-21/167y passing and his sparkling running (11/55y) netted 3 TDs. Outgaining whole Bulldogs team (170y total O) himself, Namath racked up 222y O without trying single 2nd H pass for coach Bear Bryant, who mercifully called in reins to keep score down. Crimson Tide had gone 80y in 12 plays on its 2nd possession of 1st Q, and, despite 15y holding PEN near UGa GL, HB Hudson Harris slashed over from 5YL. Bulldogs K Bob Etter kicked 26y FG in 2nd Q after soph QB Lynn Hughes connected with HB Don Porterfield for 43y gain to 11YL. Alabama went 66y to Namath's 8y TD sprint for 14-3 H edge, and Tide earned 10 pts in 3rd Q for 24-3 lead as HB-DB-K David Ray (INT) made 27y FG and Namath wedged for TD.

FLORIDA STATE 14 Miami 0: Florida State (1-0) WR Fred Biletnkoff, his usual impeccable self vs. Miami (0-1), caught 9/165y, and tallied both Seminoles TDs. Meanwhile, Biletnikoff's nervous parents watched younger son, Hurricanes QB Bob, suffer through Miami's 5-20/79y passing night he shared with fellow unseasoned QB Rick Swan. Seminoles went 79y in 1st Q as QB Steve Tensi hit passes of 15 and 27y before rifling 15y TD to Biletnikoff in right EZ corner. FSU's 2nd TD drive of 63y came in 2nd Q, thanks mostly to 3 connections from sub QB Ed Pritchett to Biletnikoff. But, when Pritchett was dumped back to 16YL, Tensi reentered to fling TD to Biletnikoff for 14-0 lead 1:20 before H. Miami found FSU 11YL twice in 2nd H, but lost ball on downs each time. So, inexperienced Canes lost debut of coach Charlie Tate.

NORTHWESTERN 7 Oregon State 3: After Oregon State (0-1) failed by inches to make 1st down at 4YL, Wildcats FB Steve Murphy (24/94y, TD) followed exchange of punts by capping 96y drive early in 2nd Q with 1y TD plunge off LG to make happy Northwestern (1-0) debut for coach Alex Agase. Early failure of Wildcats' run attack prompted QB Tommy Myers (11-23/116y, INT) to hit 6-8 passes on Cats' long scoring assault. Oregon State (0-1) never came close to firing up its O (20y rushing, only 112y total O) as NW defenders, such as DE Pat Riley and DT Joe Szczecko, put constant pressure on Beavers QBs Paul Brothers and Marv Crowston. Oregon State DT George Carr recovered FUM by HB Woody Campbell at Northwestern 47YL in 2nd Q, and, after Wildcats DB Jim Dau made TD-saving tackle on WR Bob Grim's 26y catch, D rose up to force K Steve Clark's 32y FG. NW fashioned only threat of 2nd H: 61y trip to 5YL, but Cats came away with missed FG try.

TEXAS TECH 21 Mississippi State 7: Red Raiders (1-0) HB Donny Anderson was all-around pest to Mississippi State (0-1) as he maneuvered 68y to score with pass reception from QB Tom Wilson (7-12/127y, TD, 2 INTs) and provided powerful running to set up another TD by sr FB Jim Zanios (97y, 2 TDs rushing), who sparkled after 2 so-so seasons. Stumbling Bulldogs lost 3 FUMs and had HB Dan Bland's 89y KO TD RET nullified by needless clipping PEN perpetrated on tackler who was losing space to Bland. Texas Tech LB-K Kenneth Gill attempted his 1st collegiate FG and made it from 51y out. Red Raiders D, led by aggressive LB C.C. Willis (FUM REC), NG Doug Young, and DB Teddy Roberts (INT and FUM REC), took ball away on 4 straight Bulldogs possessions in 2nd H. Miss State's TD came after LB Pat Watson recovered FUM at Tech 14YL in 2nd Q.

ARKANSAS 14 Oklahoma State 10: Little QB Billy Gray, switched by Arkansas (1-0) to CB to start season, returned under C in 2nd Q to lead TD drives of 55 and 64y. Swift Razorbacks WB Jim Lindsey sprinted 18y to score with 3:01 to go before H, after Gray passed 23y to E Jerry Lamb. Oklahoma State (0-1) tied it 7-7 in 3rd Q as HB Larry Elliott followed solid running of FB Walt Garrison to plunge for 1y TD. Gray passed 25y, dashed for 9y and sneaked for 1st down at Cowboy 2YL in 3rd Q, just before TB Bobby Burnett sliced over for TD very late in 3rd Q. Oklahoma State K Charles Durkee, who earlier missed 2 FG tries, connected from 37y out early in 4th Q, but it would be last of 4 scoring opportunities for Cowboys.

CALIFORNIA 21 Missouri 14: New coach Ray Willsey got California (1-0) off to good start with upset of Missouri (0-1) that featured strong passing and improved D. Bears scored 1st 2 times they had ball, QB Craig Morton making 1 of his 2 TD passes. When Morton hit E Jack Schraub with 18y TD in 2nd Q, Cal led 21-0. QB Gary Lane rallied Mizzou, hitting WB Earl Denny with 80y TD pass in final secs of 1st H and added 2-pt run. Earlier in 2nd Q, Tigers HB Johnny Roland appeared headed for TD from 1YL, but Bears S Jim Hunt shoved blocker into Roland to prevent score. Lane threw another TD pass in 3rd Q and had Tigers in stride in 4th Q only to suffer pair of INTs to Hunt at Cal 16 and 22YLs. Morton's air success against Missouri convinced coach Dan Devine to move selfless Roland to DB, thus shoring up Tigers' pass D but costing Roland any chance he had as A-A RB.

Air Force 3 WASHINGTON 2: "Pitcher's duel" wrapped up oddball batch of Saturday games as Washington (0-1) became 5th team in AP poll to lose. Air Force (1-0) got FG from K Bart Holaday in 1st Q after Washington DB Tom Greenlee was flagged for interference on his brother, Falcons E Fritz Greenlee. Huskies FB Junior Coffey (26/140y) fell 6 inches short of GL on 4th down in 4th Q, and P Ken Jaggers free-kicked Falcons out of danger after Air Force took intentional safety with slightly more than 3 mins to go.

WASHINGTON STATE 29 Stanford 23 (Spokane): Single play helped switch outcome of AAWU slugfest. It came with Stanford (0-1) up 23-22 and was created by Wazzu HB-DB Clarence Williams, who stole ball after Indians HB Dick Ragsdale caught pass with 2 mins left at Washington State (1-0) 37YL. Stanford was assessed 15y PEN in FUM melee, and it launched drive to Cougars QB Tom Roth's winning TD sweep with 25 secs left. Williams and E Gerry Shaw caught 23 and 20y passes on winning march. Earlier, Washington State had taken 16-13 H lead to overcome long-range FGs of Indians K Branden Beck, who booted 3 FGs, including 52y 3-ptr. Stanford D forced Cougars' 1st punt in 3rd Q, and QB Terry DeSylvia rallied Tribe to his 8y TD run. But, Stanford missed clinching outcome when its protracted drive failed at Wazzu 1YL early in 4th Q.

September 26, 1964

SYRACUSE 38 Kansas 6: On Friday night, Kansas (1-1) coach Jack Mitchell boasted about his ace HB Gale Sayers, calling him "just about the best runner in the country." Next day, Syracuse (1-1) offered its own candidate: soph HB Floyd Little, who tallied 5 TDs, including 15 and 55y sprints among his 159y rushing. Little gained 254 all-purpose y. Orange DEs George Fair and Herb Stecker forced Jayhawks QB Steve Renko, future MLB pitcher, into keeping on option plays. Thus, Sayers carried but 4 times in 1st H. By then it was pretty well too late for Sayers to affect much as 18-0 score favored Orangemen.

HARVARD 20 Massachusetts 14: Well-documented brilliance of Harvard (1-0) scholars came into comical question as QB John McCluskey—who already had scored on 82y run in 2nd Q—dashed to EZ for apparent 4th Q TD to break 14-14 tie with pesky Massachusetts (1-1). But, embarrassed McCluskey, running in clear, dropped ball just past 5YL, thinking he had crossed GL. Redmen C-LB Bernie Dallas fell on it at 1YL. But, UMass soon was forced into short punt, and Crimson made up for gaffe by sending HB Dave Poe squirting through RT for winning 13y TD run. Redmen QB Jerry Whelchel had passed for 2 TDs in 3rd Q.

PRINCETON 10 Rutgers 7: Making little headway (only 106y total O) with its attack, Princeton (1-0) took advantage of 2 glaring miscues by Rutgers (0-1) to score all pts it needed. Tigers K Charlie Gogolak made 31y FG after Scarlet Knights lost FUM in 1st

Q, and Rutgers' bad C pass on 4th down in 3rd Q forced FB-P Bob Brendel to eat ball at his 4YL. Princeton TB Don McKay scored on next play. Scarlet Knights gained 260y, much of it on 4th Q passes by sub QB Roger Kallinger (10-16/70y, TD) who moved his team 45y to TD and 37y to Tigers 39YL before time ran out on Queensmen.

Wake Forest 38 VIRGINIA TECH 21 (Roanoke): Demon Deacons (2-0) surprised with 2nd straight upset win. Wake Forest FB Brian Piccolo dashed for 154y on ground, including 2 TDs in 2nd Q that gave Deacs lead for good at 10-7 and extend it to 17-7. Wake HB Wayne Wellborn ran for 3 TDs in 2nd H as Deacons rolled up 351y rushing. Virginia Tech (1-1) QB Bob Schweickert had wiggled his way, mostly on keepers, to TD after 46y trip to take 7-3 lead late in 1st Q. Roughing P PEN aided Wake's 72y drive to Wellborn's 3rd Q TD for 24-7 edge. Gobblers re-fired home crowd with quick-snap play early in 4th Q that found Wake napping: HB Tommy Francisco rambled 47y to 17YL, and FB Sonny Utz banged across. Wellborn raced 42y to score for 31-15 Deacs' edge. Schweikert (7-18/109y, INT) passed Tech into position for another TD by Utz.

Kentucky 27 MISSISSIPPI 21 (Jackson): Huge upset was fashioned on rugged Kentucky (2-0) D that held Ole Miss (1-1) to single 1st down in 1st H and shattering Rebels' 22-game regular season unbeaten streak. Right after opening KO, HB Rodger Bird opened Wildcats O by throwing improvised 79y TD pass which was nullified by PEN, but Cats came back with same play in 3rd Q to put them ahead 13-7. It clicked from Bird to E Rick Kestner for 32y. Badly outplayed and outgained 415y to 187y, Rebs managed to stay in game on 2 INT TD RETs: DB James Heidel's 89y RET in 1st Q and DB Tommy Luke's 65y RET in 3rd Q. After Mississippi QB Jim Weatherly hit 13y TD pass in 4th Q, Kentucky trailed 21-20 until QB Rick Norton hit sub E Kestner, for his 3rd TD catch, with 2:38 remaining to play. Verdict was clinched when Ole Miss TB Mike Dennis took Weatherly's pass to Cats 20YL, but lost FUM to Kentucky DB Talbott Todd with 30 secs left.

North Carolina 21 MICHIGAN STATE 15: With Spartans (0-1) keying heavily on huge HB Ken Willard, North Carolina (1-1) QB Danny Talbott, goat from previous week, befuddled Michigan State D with tapestry of option runs and jump passes to earn 21-0 lead by opening min of 4th Q. Talbott followed Willard's 1y TD plunge in 2nd Q with 2 of his own. Then, with 12 mins to go, Spartans rallied around their O stars: impressive soph HB Clint Jones raced 42y to TD and sr HB Dick Gordon caught 2-pt pass from HB Harry Ammons. Only 4 mins later, E Gene Washington, with Tar Heels defender draped all over him, caught 11y TD from QB Steve Juday. K Lou Bobich's soccer-style x-pt pulled MSU within 21-15. Spartans got ball back twice more late in 4th Q. Juday punched his team to midfield, and coach Duffy Daugherty argued spotting of Ammons' 4th down run. Daugherty got call to go his way but received ruinous 15y PEN for his trouble. Another major foul on Michigan State and UNC DL Frank Gallagher's sack placed Spartans in 4th-and-41, which ended in INT by Carolina DB Jimmy Eason. Last gasp pass by Juday fell into arms of Heels QB-DB Gary Black at his 18YL.

Notre Dame 31 WISCONSIN 7: Fighting Irish coaching legends Knute Rockne and Frank Leahy were 52-5-5 vs. Big 10, but Notre Dame (1-0) was feeble 4-19 during 1954-63 regimes of Terry Brennan, Joe Kuharich, and Hugh Devore. Into this history strode former Big 10 coach Ara Parseghian, making his ND debut against favored Wisconsin (1-1), which was projected for Big 10's 1st division. Surprise stars in Parseghian's new O were players he transformed: QB John Huarte (15-24/270y, 2 TDs) and E Jack Snow (9/217y, 2 TDs). Badgers clawed back into game on 45y TD pass by QB Hal Brandt to WR Jimmy Jones after 2nd H KO which brought them to within 13-7. But, Irish crushed Badgers by throwing them for -51y rushing as 9 new faces sparkled on D unit.

Nebraska 26 MINNESOTA 21: Golden Gophers (0-1) QB John Hankinson threw TD pass to TE Aaron Brown and scored on 32y run in 3rd Q. It was enough for 14-12 lead because Nebraska (2-0) botched kick and 2-pt pass after 2nd Q TDs by QB Fred Duda and HB Kent McCloughan. Minnesota seemed on its way with only 8 mins left when HB Bill Crockett steamed 80y with punt TD RET. But, Duda turned hot just secs later, hitting little FB Frank Solich, future Cornhuskers coach, with 45y TD pass. Then, after Gophers punt traveled only 19y into stiff wind, Duda found 4th down magic with pass to TE Freeman White. He followed with deflected TD throw to McCloughan.

Southern California 40 OKLAHOMA 14: QB Craig Fertig (16-28/212y, TD) completed passes totaling 79y in 2 TD marches in 1st Q as USC (2-0) finished each voyage with Fertig's short TD run. Overwhelmed Oklahoma (1-1) secondary finally changed tactics to its betterment in 2nd Q, but its pass interference PEN helped give Trojans another TD 23 secs before H on HB Ron Heller's 1y plunge. Prior to Heller's score, Sooners brightened their picture as FB Jim Grisham led 58y 2nd Q drive that narrowed count to 14-7. Oklahoma HB Lance Rentzel earned scoring honors with 10y catch nearly midway in 2nd Q. Southern California started 2nd H where it left off, scoring twice in 3rd Q for 34-7 lead. Rentzel muffed punt at his 5YL, and Trojans E Ty Salness came up with TD REC. Rentzel turned tables in 4th Q by going 48y on punt RET to poise 2y TD run by HB Larry Brown.

Florida State 10 TEXAS CHRISTIAN 0: TCU (0-2) D played heroically by making stands at its 1, 17, 16, 11, and 13YLs, but it bled just enough to allow Florida State (2-0) to take win. Seminoles' 1st series carried them to Horned Frogs 1YL, but gigantic Purple LB Ken Henson slammed down FSU FB Lee Narramore. K Les Murdock clicked on 33y FG next time Florida State marched downfield late in 1st Q. TCU depended on HB Jim Fauver (19/93y) for much of its O, and Fauver keyed 48y foray to FSU 16YL in 3rd Q with 30y rushing. But, Semimoles DE Wayne McDuffie threw Fauver for 3y loss, and Frogs had to settle for K Bruce Alford's FG try. LB Bill McDowell blocked it to launch 63y TD trip. FSU QB Steve Tensi connected on 12, 22, and 14y passes until HB Phil Spooner's 6y TD run.

ARKANSAS 31 Tulsa 22: Confident Tulsa (0-1) started season that would have its most wins since 1951 and enjoy nation's leadership in passing, scoring, and total O. Golden Hurricane QB Jerry Rhome, now eligible after transfer from SMU, connected for 20-26, 2 TDs, including score by E Howard Twilley. Tulsa jumped to 14-0 lead. Turning point was provided by Arkansas (2-0) LB Ronnie Caveness, who picked off Rhome pass and ran 12y to 2nd Q TD. Tulsa still led 14-10 at H, but Razorbacks QB BIlly Gray hit TD pass to E Jerry Lamb, scored himself, and watched WB Jim Lindsay race 41y to score.

ARIZONA 39 Brigham Young 6: Special teams of Arizona (1-0) sparkled as HB Floyd Hudlow returned 2 punts for long TDs, and HB Rickie Harris nearly replicated Hudlow's sprints by racing 41y to set up FB Rick Johnson's 2y TD plunge. Brigham Young (0-2) FUM got Wildcats started on rout early in 2nd Q as UA went 55y in 5 plays. Capper came on QB Lou White's 23y pass to Harris. Hudlow soon raced 61y for his 1st punt RET TD, and on next series, BYU was forced to punt again. But this time, Harris bobbled punt at his 27YL, and Cougars HB Kent Oborn swept right for 2y TD on dandy fake that had Arizona bunched in middle. BYU trailed only 14-6 at H. Hudlow's 2nd punt TD RET sparked Cats blast in 3rd Q. UA DT Ken Giovando made his 2nd INT to set up HB Tom Oliver's 2nd TD.

AP Poll September 28

1 Texas (14)	395	6 Navy (1)	210
2 Southern California (17)	357	7 Auburn (2)	186
3 Illinois (7)	347	8 Michigan	106
4 Alabama (4)	316	9 Notre Dame	103
5 Ohio State (2)	285	10 Washington (1)	73

Others with votes: Arkansas, Army, California, Duke, Florida, Florida State, Georgia Tech, Kentucky (1), Louisiana State, Mississippi, Nebraska, North Carolina, North Carolina State, Northwestern, Oklahoma, Oregon, Syracuse, Tampa, UCLA

October 3, 1964

NORTH CAROLINA STATE 14 Maryland 13: Young Terps (1-2) charged from locker room, sending stocky TB Tom Hickey wide left for 77y TD run on 1st play. When Maryland blocked punt in 2nd Q, HB Bobby Collins carried it 39y to TD. After his team's 2nd TD, Maryland coach Tom Nugent inexplicably gambled, and failed, on 2-pt try "to make State go for two" if it scored. NC State (3-0) did score, rallying in 2nd H on soph QB Charlie Noggle's 2 TD runs. FB-K Gus Andrews had easy time winning game with his 2 conv kicks.

VIRGINIA 20 Virginia Tech 17: It took 7 years to defeat Virginia Tech (1-2), and Cavaliers (1-2), 13-51-1 since their resounding 1957 win over Va Tech, needed late heroics from QB Tom Hodges and E Larry Molinari to turn trick. Virginia used surprise Shotgun formation in 1st H to carve 14-0 edge. Cavs HB Carroll Jarvis (9/42y, TD) ran over FB-LB Darrell Page at GL for 1st Q TD, and HB John Pincavage circled RE to score in 2nd Q. It was completely different in 3rd Q as Gobblers jumped to 17-14 lead. Va Tech DT Sandy Woody fell on FUM at UVa 36YL to set up sub QB Bobby Owens' 12y TD strike to E Bob Churchill. After missing 2 FGs in 1st H, Hokies K Billy Cranwell made 30y FG, and FB Sonny Utz bulled his way for TD and 17-14 edge. And so it stayed until Virginia coach Bill Elias alternated QBs Bob Davis and Hodges on last drive and Molinari slipped between 2 DBs with 20 secs left to catch Hodges' winning 29y pass. Afterward, UVa coach Bill Elias said, with tears welling in his eyes: "…I've never had any thrills any bigger."

KENTUCKY 20 Auburn 0: With their 2nd straight upset, red-hot Wildcats (3-0) made their 1st appearance in AP top-5 since November 20, 1950. Kentucky QB Rick Norton (8-10/83y, TD) found E Rick Kestner for 3/33y on 76y TD drive that was launched late in 1st Q and ended early in 2nd Q on HB Rodger Bird's 1y run. UK's TD was 1st allowed in 3 games so far in 1964 by no. 7 Plainsmen. Trailing 7-0 as 3rd Q was winding down, Auburn (2-1) QB Jimmy Sidle tossed to HB Tucker Frederickson for 16 and 12y gains and ran 35y sweep. But, on 4th down at 5YL, Sidle flipped pass while in grasp of charging DE Kestner. DB Bird stepped in to intercept and raced 95y for TD and 14-0 lead. Subsequent Tigers' drives of 52, 53, 47, and 65y all failed in Wildcat territory, including 4th Q threat that fizzled when Tigers sub QB Tom Bryan threw through EZ. Bird followed with 49y run to set up Kentucky's last TD. Stats couldn't tell whole story: Auburn gained 287y to Cats' 245y.

Illinois 17 NORTHWESTERN 6: Defending Big 10 champion Illinois (2-0) defended Wildcats' heralded QB Tommy Myers (9-28/166y, TD, 4 INTs) so well that only 1 play, quick TD strike in 3rd Q, even so much as ruffled Illini feathers. Indeed, game's better QB was Illinois' Fred Custardo (10-13/149y, TD) who flipped 33y TD pass to HB Sam Price in 2nd Q and added 28y FG as K to provide 4th Q breathing room. Soph E Bob Trumpy (6/106y) caught 44y aerial from Custardo in 2nd Q to allow Price to circle E for 10y TD. Northwestern HB Ron Rector made spectacular TD in 3rd Q, taking short toss over middle from Myers, cutting wide to race 78y for TD.

MICHIGAN 21 Navy 0: Unable to run because of bad ankle, Navy (2-1) QB Roger Staubach went to air for 16-30/166y, but Michigan (2-0), growing more powerful on D, had 2 INTs of Staubach and 2 FUM RECs laost by Middies receivers. Add in 3 other Navy TOs and 5 by Wolverines, and game was left to team that could sustain its drives. That team was Michigan, which pasted together 66, 80, and 72y marches amid bevy of interruptions with HB Carl Ward (18/74y) scoring twice. Staubach was sent out limping in 3rd Q after being knocked flat by swift Michigan DT Bill Yearby.

MICHIGAN STATE 17 Southern California 7: Michigan State (1-1) coach Duffy Daugherty unveiled 5-man D backfield several years before Chicago Bears defensive coach Jim Dooley "invented" nickel coverage in secondary. Novel approach made its mark as Spartans D thwarted air game of USC (2-1), holding it to 5-22/90y. Barefooted Hawaiian soph K Dick Kenney made his 1st varsity appearance and hammered 49y FG in 1st Q for Spartans record at that point. MSU added HB Clint Jones' TD run in 3rd Q for 10-0 lead. Trojans countered with short TD run by TB Mike Garrett at end of 80y drive after QB Craig Fertig hit E Dave Moton with 26y pass. Spartans iced it with QB Harry Ammon's TD pass to E Gene Washington with 5 mins to go.

IOWA 28 Washington 18: QB Gary Snook connected 19-32/215y, 2 TDs, and Iowa (2-0) riddled Washington (1-2) with 2 TDs in 1st Q. HB Karl Noonan caught 17y hook pass for 1st Hawkeyes TD and faked so well that DB tackled air at 3YL. Huskies took over in 2nd Q, zooming to 18 pts. Starting things in right direction for Washington was bad punt snap that went for safety when Huskies E Jerry Williams trapped Iowa P Mickey Moses in EZ. HB Charlie Browning scored just 7 plays after free-kick and HB-K Ron Medved scored 12y TD and added conv kick and, later, 31y FG. Trailing 18-14, Hawkeyes DB Bob Sorensen made INT of UW QB Bill Douglas in last 2 mins of 3rd Q to set up E Dick O'Hara's 6y catch in corner of EZ, Snook's 2nd TD throw. Snook iced it with short TD run after Washington G-P Rick Redman bobbled 4th down punt snap to O'Hara at own 26YL.

NOTRE DAME 34 Purdue 15: Purdue (1-1) owned 7-3 record against Fighting Irish since coach Frank Leahy retired in 1953. Boilermakers jumped to 7-0 lead on QB Bob Griese's sneak at end of 75y march late in 1st Q but didn't score again until sub QB Doug Holcomb flipped 10y TD to E Bob Hadrick in last 31 secs. In coach Ara Parseghian's home debut, Notre Dame (2-0) proved no fluke, trouncing Boilermakers. QB John Huarte sparked attack with 2 scoring passes and put Irish ahead 14-7 with 20y TD flip to E Jack Snow (6/82y). ND's immense sophs on D combined for 3rd Q TD as T Kevin Hardy blocked punt that E Alan Page picked up to streak 57y to score. That built Irish lead to 21-7.

Oklahoma State 10 MISSOURI 7: Inspired Cowboys (2-1) D prevented Missouri (1-2) from scoring except HB-DB Ken Boston's 1st Q 95y INT TD RET. Oklahoma State, universally picked for Big 8 cellar, bounced back with key EZ INT by DE Jack Jacobson and running of FB Walt Garrison. Cowboys also cashed in QB Glenn Baxter's 65y TD pass to HB Larry Elliott. With score tied at 7-7 late in 2nd Q, Tigers QB Gary Lane threw INT grabbed by DE Jack Jacobson, 1 of 4 pick-offs by OSU. K Charles Durkee followed with 49y FG, and from that moment, Oklahoma State D shut down Mizzou in 2nd H.

Kansas State 16 COLORADO 14: Wildcats (1-1) turned 2 Colorado (0-3) FUMs into 9 pts in 1st H and held on to win for 1st time in Boulder. Raft of 1st H TOs, including notable punt FUM at his 8YL by Buffs QB-DB Hale Irwin in 1st Q, allowed Kansas State HB Jerry Condit (13/61y, 2 TDs) to sweep LE for 1st Q TD. Later, K Jerry Cook made 39y FG after Wildcats DT Mike Beffa pounced on team's 4th FUM REC. Cook nearly wasn't tapped for his FG try because of wind in his face, but his success sent K-State to locker room with 9-0 lead. It took awhile for Cats FB Ron Barlow to find his stride against Colorado's D keys, but he burst 18y on 2nd H's opening series to prompt Condit's 2nd score. Bison finally expunged shutout late in 3rd Q on 36y burst by HB Estes Banks (10/64y, TD) behind T Stan Irvine's block. TD run by FB Ben Howe, who also starred as LB, capped 87y Colorado TD drive in 4th Q, but K-State used its run attack to play keep-away for last 4:38.

Wyoming 17 KANSAS 14: Cowboys (3-0) had to rally to get by Kansas (1-2). After Wyoming dominated 1st Q by keeping ball for 23 of 27 plays, magnificent Jayhawks HB Gale Sayers streaked 81y to TD behind crushing block by fireplug FB Bill Gerhards in 2nd Q. So, Kansas lead 7-3 at H. Soph QB Rick Egloff zipped 47y on punt RET early in 3rd Q to KU 21YL to break open game in which Wyoming still trailed 7-3. Wyoming QB Tom Wilkinson hit E Darryl Alleman with pass to 1YL, and Wilkinson sneaked over. FB Mike Davenport keyed 80y Cowboy drive in 4th Q and score don 9y run to lift visitors to 17-7 lead. Kansas failed to connect on single pass until last play of game when sub QB Bob Skahan threw 8y TD to E Bob Robben.

Arkansas 29 TEXAS CHRISTIAN 6: Myriad of mistakes nearly cost Arkansas (3-0): FUMs and dropped passes littered 1st H in which Hogs stopped snorting at TCU (0-3) 19, 5, 19, and 17YLs in 1st H. Porkers righted themselves long enough for DB Billy Gray, occasional QB, to come to O's aid with 9y pass to open 47y TD trip. Starting QB Fred Marshall (12-19/148y, INT) fired sideline pass to TB Jackie Brausell, who high-stepped 21y to 1YL behind T E Richard Trail's crisp block. Marshall scored on 3rd down for 7-0 lead that lasted into 4th Q. Horned Frogs coach Abe Martin inserted sore-kneed QB Kent Nix, who hit E Charles Campbell with 4/53y, including threaded 15y TD pass that brought score to 7-6. TCU DB Joe Ball quickly made INT that he returned to Porkers 34YL, but DB Gray made immediate turnaround with his own INT. Arkansas DB Harry Jones made game-breaking 24y INT TD RET for 14-6 lead, and Gray made another INT to set up TB Bobby Burnett's 5y TD smash.

TEXAS 17 Army 6: Cadets (2-1) played stunting D to smear Steers run game in 1st H. Army QB Rollie Stichweh mesmerized Texas (3-0) on 48y TD drive for early 6-0 lead after Cadets DT Bill Zadel made FUM REC. Longhorns K Dave Conway halved it to 6-3 with 38y FG. Stichweh broke away for 71y dash, but Army was flagged for clipping, part of its crippling 140y in PENs. After stern H speech by coach Darrell Royal, Longhorns D responded by allowing only 2y rushing rest of day as superb LB Tommy Nobis totaled 28 tackles. TB Ernie Koy capped 65y drive with TD run on 1st play of 4th Q for Texas' 1st lead at 10-6. P Koy's 71y QK provided field position which turned into his 2nd TD.

Oregon State 13 BAYLOR 6: Oregon State (2-1) K Steve Clark's 1st of pair of FGs put Beavers up 3-0 in 1st Q. Baylor (0-2) missed 2nd Q opportunity at Beavers 3YL after 66y drive was featured by 26 and 13y catches by HB Lawrence Elkins (6/105y). But, Bears QB Terry Southall (16-36/261y, 2 INTs) brought them right back and hit Elkins with 33y TD. Beavers QB Paul Brothers (9-12/117y, INT) rushed 16/95y and tallied Beavers' only TD on 9y trip around LE in 2nd Q. Oregon State led 10-6 at H. E Ken Hodge (6/121y) caught his share of passes from Southall, but Beavers D put plenty of pressure on Southall to clinch win.

October 10, 1964

(Fri) Georgia Tech 17 Navy 0 (Jacksonville): Brilliant Navy (2-2) QB Roger Staubach stayed back in Annapolis nursing injured ankle. So, it was Yellow Jackets (4-0) QB Bruce Fischer who showed effective aerial attack with judicious 5-7/142y, TD, INT. Midshipmen QB Bruce Bickel (7-22/73y) had tough time impersonating Staubach, although Navy's Heisman Trophy winner probably couldn't have avoided several batted-down throws by soph Georgia Tech DT Billy Schroer. Fischer's 35y peg to E George Morris took Jackets to Navy 2YL in 1st Q, and HB Johnny Gresham slammed for TD. Navy punted, and Fischer's 24y throw to HB Terry Haddock and his 30y TD to Morris made it 14-0 in 1st Q. After K Jack Clark's 20y FG built 17-0 H lead, Tech suddenly slept through 3rd Q without 1st down. Middies advanced without scoring to 6, 16, 24, and 12YLs on running of FB Pat Donnelly (10/58y). Each time, Jackets used their D speed to corral runners and break up passes.

Princeton 37 DARTMOUTH 7: G Stan Maliszewski led fierce line play that helped Tigers (3-0) stake claim as 1 of great Princeton teams by thoroughly trouncing Dartmouth (2-1), squad with which it shared 1963 Ivy crown. K Charlie Gogolak set Ivy record to that point with 3 FGs, all from long range. Tigers TB Don McKay passed for 1st Q TD and raced to 56y TD in 3rd Q to post 20-0 advantage. Indians suffered 7 TOs and didn't score until deep into 4th Q on HB Bob O'Brien's TD catch from QB Bruce Gottschall. It was coach Bob Blackman's worst defeat at Dartmouth since his arrival in 1955.

SYRACUSE 39 Ucla 0: Previously unbeaten Bruins (3-1) ran into Syracuse (3-1) D buzz-saw, unit known oddly as "The Spiders." UCLA was limited to 4-18/45y in air and its runners were tossed for game-end total of -4y rushing. Orangemen DBs Buddy Johnson and Charlie Brown had INT TD RETs of 35 and 54y respectively. Uclan QB Larry Zeno, nation's total O leader coming in, left game in 3rd Q with only 9y to his credit. Syracuse HB Floyd Little made diagonal 90y dash with punt RET with FB Jim Nance making crushing block to clear TD path. Powerful Nance scored 2 TDs himself.

FLORIDA 30 Mississippi 14: Ole Miss (2-2), heavy favorites for SEC crown, was all but ousted from title hunt by Florida (3-0) in Rebs' worst loss since 1956. Teams traded 2nd Q TDs by Gators QB Tom Shannon and Rebels HB Mike Dennis. With Florida ahead 10-7 in 3rd Q, HB Allen Trammell followed 7-man convoy into EZ on 62y punt RET. Clinching TD came from soph QB Steve Spurrier on 1st of his 2 TD passes to E Charles Casey.

LOUISIANA STATE 20 North Carolina 3: LSU (3-0) gained 319y with its new flanker O, but, as late as flickering moments of 3rd Q, remained in 3-3 tie with stubborn North Carolina (2-2). FGs by LSU's E-K Doug Moreau and Carolina's K Max Chapman had it knotted. Sub HB Gawain DiBetta broke logjam with 5y TD run, and Tigers added 10 pts in 4th Q on versatile Moreau's 2nd FG and his catch of TD pass from QB Pat Screen.

ALABAMA 21 North Carolina State 0: Bubble burst for NC State (3-1) as mighty Alabama (4-0) swatted aside Wolfpack. Also, it was game that forever changed career of Tide QB Joe Namath (7-8/52y). On rollout with 6 mins left in 0-0 2nd Q, Namath cut right and suffered knee injury that would plague his college and pro career until its end in 1977. Until this point, Namath was remarkably swift runner who could cut and sprint for y, but pro fans were denied watching those exploits. QB Steve Sloan replaced Namath, and he quickly finished drive, on which Namath had hit 3-3/27y passing, by running for 1y TD and 7-0 H lead. FB Steve Bowman tallied in 3rd Q, and Sloan added 4th Q TD pass to E Tommy Tolleson (8/81y). Tolleson's 8 catches set new Crimson Tide reception record for single game. NC State QB Ron Skosnick had pitched pass to HB Gary Rowe to Bama 9YL in 1st Q, but K Gus Andrews' 34y FG try sailed wide. Wolfpack DT Rosie Amato recovered FUM at his 34YL in 3rd Q when they trailed only 14-0. Skosnick followed with 16, 10, and 21y passes but last completion was called back, and coach Earle Edwards said, "Until that happened, we were still in the game."

FLORIDA STATE 48 Kentucky 6: Jig was up for hopeful Kentucky (3-1) as it was sent spiraling to 4-game losing streak. Building 27-0 H lead, keyed-up Seminoles (4-0) got 2 TD passes from QB Steve Tensi to WR Fred Biletnikoff and 2 TD plunges from HB Phil Spooner. Wildcats TB Rodger Bird was well-defended by FSU's nimble D-line, known as "Magnificent 7." Bird also contributed to Spooner's 1st TD in 2nd Q when he mistakenly touched punt as it bounded by him at Cats 12YL. Wildcats didn't score until last 29 secs when FB Frank Antonini plowed over, and it couldn't prevent Kentucky's worst defeat margin since 1945.

MICHIGAN 17 MICHIGAN STATE 10: Mighty Michigan (3-0) D held no. 9 Michigan State (1-2) in check, yielding just 157y O in winning its 1st victory over Spartans since 1955. Michigan State earned early 1st Q TD on 1y sneak by QB Steve Juday after Wolverines QB Bob Timberlake (9-18/122y, TD) lost errant pitchout to Spartans LB Ed Macuga at own 17YL. Wolverines O also misfired on dropped and overthrown passes. When K Larry Lukesik kicked 26y FG to give Spartans 10-3 lead in 4th Q, time for Michigan's engine to fire on all cylinders. Timberlake squirmed for key 1st down on 73y drive and connected on 5 straight passes, last of which went to HB Rick Sygar for 5y TD. Still trailing 10-9 after failed conv run was stopped by Spartans DB Charles Migyanko, Wolverines battled back as Sygar took pitchout on MSU 31YL, ran right, stopped, and threw long HB pass to E John Henderson for winning TD with less than 7 mins left to play.

Ohio State 26 ILLINOIS 0: Illinois (2-1) HB Sam Price made nice gains after opening KO, but Ohio State (3-0) turned tables as Buckeyes DB John Fill raced 48y with pass that tipped long off hands of Illini E Bob Trumpy. Fill's big play set up 24y bootleg TD run by Ohio State QB Don Unverferth (8-18/130y), and, although Illinois led at that point 4 to 0 in 1st downs, it never recovered and never penetrated Buckeyes 30YL. Twice using T-eligible passes to Jim Davidson, Ohio State gained more passing than running y for 2nd week in row. That statistical peculiarity had occurred just twice in 84 previous Ohio games under coach Woody Hayes. FB Willard Sander (19/56y) scored twice and K Bob Funk punched through 2 FGs. Bucks D warranted its design on Big 10 title by dominating defending champs, including destruction of Illini aerial game: Illinois QB Fred Custardo, who came in with 74.1% of completions, was swarmed under numerous times while passing only 10-23/79y, 2 INTs. Star Illini FB Jim Grabowski was kept to 12/32y rushing as Illinois gained only 61y on ground.

Texas 28 Oklahoma 7 (Dallas): Despite heroic effort of Sooners LB Carl McAdams who had 18 tackles, INT, and FUM REC, no. 1 Texas (4-0) won its 15th game in row, 7th straight over Oklahoma (1-2). McAdams' INT 28y RET set up HB Lance Rentzel's 1st Q TD, and Sooners managed 109y rushing in 7-7 1st H. Texas WB Phil Harris broke tie with 15y pitchout run in 3rd Q. Scoring in 4th Q for runaway Steers were FB Harold Phillip, on 1y plunge at end of 60y drive and E Pete Lammons, on 14y pass after FUM REC.

WYOMING 14 Utah 13: On its way to WAC title, Utah (2-2) hit bump in road at Wyoming (4-0), which was about to face upcoming slump. Cowboys got 2 quick scores in 2nd Q on FB Mike Davenport's plunge and QB Tom Wilkinson's 49y TD, then survived own mistakes in 2nd H. Utes WR-K Roy Jefferson, future NFL star, caught 46y 2nd Q TD pass, but missed tying conv kick in 3rd Q.

NEW MEXICO 10 Arizona 7: Power ground game presented by Lobos (3-1) was difference all night, but QB Stan Quintana's passes of 20 and 14y keyed game's 1st score in opening Q. New Mexico FB Bob Hammond plunged over from 1YL for 7-0 lead. Arizona (2-1) offered potent D, but its O could gain mere 213y, 80y of which came in single lightning bolt that lit up dull 3rd Q. Wildcats took possession on their 20YL after Lobo punt went into EZ. Arizona HB Floyd Hudlow made New Mexico D pay for bunching close to line of scrimmage. He burst through RT and was gone after barely 3 long strides. That tied it at 7-7. In 4th Q, Hudlow lost FUM after being hit hard at Arizona 28YL. Lobos made it to 4YL and 1st down, but could make only 1y more before turning game-winning chores to K Jack Abendschan, who booted 18y FG with 3:19 to play.

OREGON STATE 9 Washington 7 (Portland): Opportunistic Oregon State (3-1) D came up with 2 INTs to set up its pts, all coming in 1st H. WB-DB Dan Espalin picked off pass early in 1st Q at Huskies 39YL, and Beavers pushed across TD with FB Charlie Shaw doing honors with 1y plunge. Utterly disappointing Washington (1-3), which had envisioned 2nd straight run to Rose Bowl, managed 66y trip later in 1st Q to take 7-6 lead on 18y TD run by FB Charlie Browning. Beavers D truly turned contest in 2nd Q by pinning UW inside its own 34YL all throughout 2nd Q. Additionally, they made another INT to set up winning 21y FG by K Steve Clark.

AP Poll October 12

1 Texas (30)	387	6 Nebraska	142
2 Ohio State (7)	344	7 Syracuse	89
3 Alabama (2)	307	8 Arkansas	86
4 Notre Dame (1)	281	9 Louisiana State	59
5 Michigan	233	10 Florida State	56

Others with votes: Auburn, Duke, Florida, Georgia Tech, Illinois, Iowa, Kentucky, Michigan State, Minnesota, Mississippi, Oregon, Oregon State, Southern California, UCLA, Utah State, Wyoming

October 17, 1964

Syracuse 21 PENN STATE 14: Surprisingly woeful season for Penn State (1-4) continued, but Nittany Lions punched Syracuse (4-1) to ropes thanks to 1st H INTs. Soph-sensation HB Floyd Little contributed his now-expected long, elusive TD run—71y punt RET in 1st Q—but Penn State DBs Frank Hershey and Mike Irwin soon collected 3 INTs. P Hershey also ignited crowd with 22y pass out of punt formation to E Jerry Sandusky, which led to FB Tom Urbanik's 10y TD charge. Lions owned 14-7 H margin. Orangemen bothered with just 1 pass in 2nd H, turning attack over to FB Jim Nance (23/104y, TD), who scored on 5y run to tie it 14-14 in 3rd Q. Turning point came when Penn State had its 4th Q drive halted at Syracuse 34YL by DL Chuck Scott, who stopped Mount Nits QB Jack White inches short of 1st down. Lions probably coud have held on for tie, but QB Gary Wydman (12-25/95y, INT) was instructed to throw for victory. Wydman rolled right and threw long diagonal pass, but Orange FB-DB Roger Smith made 38y INT RET to Penn State 22YL. Syracuse QB Walley Mahle was able to break tackle of LB Bob Kane for 4y winning TD run with 37 secs left.

DUKE 35 North Carolina State 3: Wolfpack (3-2) was trounced in this game, but would win ACC crown with mediocre record as Duke (3-0-1) later would stumble down stretch with 5 losses in row. NC State opened scoring with 49y FG by star K Harold Deters, but Blue Devils dominated by sending elephant FBs Mike Curtis and Bob Matheson and HB Sonny Odom, slashing through line. After Duke had mounted 20-3 4th Q lead, DB John Gutekunst, future Minnesota Gophers coach, thrilled home fans with 83y INT TD RET.

Georgia Tech 7 AUBURN 3 (Birmingham): Old-style southern D battle unfolded at Legion Field, and for longest time it looked like Auburn (3-2) would trot off with 3-0 victory on strength of 28y FG by K Don Lewis in 2nd Q. Tigers made 3 deep probes of Georgia Tech (5-0) territory in 1st H and came away with only Lewis' FG. Yellow Jackets DB Tommy Jackson made 2 big plays to hold it at 3-0: he knocked down QB Jimmy Sidle's EZ pass in 1st Q and made critical in-bounds tackle of Auburn HB Tucker Frederickson at 1YL just before H clock ticked down its last 10 secs. Georgia Tech C-LB Bill Curry, who would leave with injury, made 10 tackles in 1st H, but Jackets had made only 24y total O to Tigers' 220y in 1st H. Although Georgia Tech showed more fire in 3rd Q, game went into 4th Q before QB Jerry Priestley started finding previously-unknown E Mike Fortier (4/52y, TD) for all of Fortier's catches for 12, 25, 10, and 5y on 80y drive. Fortier made brilliant EZ grab for winning TD with 5 mins left. Georgia Tech DB Haven Kicklicker made INT of Auburn QB Joe Campbell (5-10/52y, INT) to quiet late bid by Tigers.

Florida State 17 GEORGIA 14: Bulldogs (2-2-1) sniffed win with late lead, finally tumbling at hands of Florida State (5-0) passing combo of QB Steve Tensi (14-24/193y, TD, INT) and WR Fred Biletnikoff (8/114y, TD). Seminoles settled for 1st Q FG only because UGa S Joe Burson made 2 saving tackles: he hauled down HB Phil Spooner after 40y prance and E Don Floyd after 53y reception. FSU LB Bill McDowell recovered his 2nd FUM at Georgia 16YL in 2nd Q, and FB Lee Narramore plowed over from 1YL for 10-0 lead. Bulldogs countered with 71y ground march to QB Preston Ridlehuber's TD run. Georgia LB Leroy Dukes forced FUM at FSU 23YL in 4th Q, and HB Fred Barber scored on 7y bolt up middle for 14-10 lead. On winning 80y TD trip, Tensi and Biletnikoff combined on 3/44y, including 4th-and-5 aerial conversion, with TD coming on Biletnikoff's 20y grab and crossfield run.

Purdue 21 MICHIGAN 20: Purdue (3-1) derailed yet another unbeaten Big 10 team as it nipped Michigan (3-1) by stopping QB Bob Timberlake's 4th Q 2-pt run around E after Timberlake had raced 54y on bootleg run to TD. Purdue, which got TD passes of 66y to HB Jim Morel and 4y to HB Randy Minniear from soph QB Bob Griese in 1st and 3rd Qs, saw Minniear wedge in 2nd Q TD run of 2y for 14-14 H deadlock. Critical to Boilermakers' win were blown chances by Michigan early in 4th Q: Boilers DE Harold Wells' FUM REC at his 2YL when HB Jim Detwiler lost handle during 1st down TD-bound run, and Michigan FB Dave Fisher, fresh off bench, lost another FUM to Wells at Purdue 35YL. Wolverines twice forced 4th Q punts but ended game back at their 12YL from where 3 passes misfired, and Detwiler's catch came up 2y short of 1st down.

INDIANA 27 Michigan State 20: Indiana (1-3), without winning season in nearly 8 years and without Big 10 home triumph since 1959, took 14-13 lead in 3rd Q and kept piling it on for upset win over reeling Spartans (1-3). Michigan State QB Steve Juday (13-20/187y, 3 TDs, INT) tossed TD passes to each of his starting Es, Tom Krzemienski and Gene Washington, so MSU led 13-0 in 2nd Q. Hoosiers QB Rich Bader (13-22/215y, 2 TDs) came back with 2 scoring passes in middle Qs, pulling team within 13-12. HB John Ginter then swept RE, with block by Bader that wiped out 2 Spartans, for 2 pts and 14-13 edge. Indiana FB Tom Nowatzke (19/64y, TD) slammed across to open 4th Q, and Bader added 5y TD run for 27-13 lead after MSU bobbled away KO that followed Nowatzke's score. Juday got consolation TD pass, but Michigan State never was near victory range in 4th Q.

Illinois 14 MINNESOTA 0: Whatever opportunity Gophers (2-2) had on their Homecoming Day evaporated with 7 TOs, including 5 INTs by Fighting Illini (3-1). Minnesota QB John Hankinson missed his 1st 5 passes and was knocked cold and out of game in 1st Q. Illinois scored its 2 TDs on 1st and last plays of 2nd Q. Illini FB Jim Grabowski (23/98y, TD) followed LB Dick Butkus' 1st Q theft of ball from Minnesota FB Mike Reid at Gophers 35YL with 2y rip up middle that tore through tackle attempt of Minny LB Joe Pung. Minnesota came right back on 27y pass by sub QB Larry Peterson (9-22/133y, 5 INTs) and 28y dash by HB Fred Farthing, who would later join Hankinson on sideline with matching concussion. But, big Illini DT Archie Sutton came off bench to force and recover Reid's 2nd FUM at Illinois 4YL. Illini DE Dave Mueller made INT to position visitors with their 2nd TD chance at Gophers' 38YL. Tribe inserted Butkus at C and he blocked for QB Fred Custardo (11-17/112y, TD, INT) for 16y romp up middle to set stage for Custardo's 4y TD pass to E Bob Trumpy that beat H clock by 8 secs. Butkus-led D kept pressure on Peterson, and Illinois kept making INTs, only to lose scoring chances on FUM at Gophers' 2YL and Custardo's 19y sack in arms of Minnesota's stellar DE Aaron Brown that ruined another advance.

OHIO STATE 17 Southern California 0: Revenge was on mind of coach Woody Hayes after suffering his worst Ohio State (4-0) loss to date to USC (3-2) in 1963. Key to win was alert pass D which barged in with 3 INTs on Trojans QB Craig Fertig's 8-26/133y aerial act. FB Willard Sander (29/120y) plowed for 1st Q TD, and Bucks made it 14-0 in 2nd Q QB Don Unverferth hit immediate TD pass after TB Mike Garrett's FUM at USC 10YL. Southern California appeared to get back in game on 3rd Q TD pass by Fertig to HB Ray Cahill, but O interference in EZ, when Cahill shoved DB Don Harkins, gave Ohio touchback possession. Rule has since changed, but it sent Buckeyes rolling to K Bob Funk's clinching 4th Q FG.

NOTRE DAME 24 Ucla 0: Notre Dame (4-0) pranced to surprisingly easy verdict over suddenly-punchless UCLA Bruins (3-2). Fighting Irish scored after opening KO on HB Bill Wolski's 1y blast tp cap 90y voyage. UCLA made it across midfield only once in each H, but survived 1st H behind only 12-0. ND's 2nd score came after DB Tony Carey's 5th INT of young season set up QB John Huarte's 37y TD arrow to E Phil Sheridan. Bruins QB Larry Zeno (11-21/158y, INT) lost handoff FUM on opening scrimmage of 3rd Q, and Huarte whipped another TD pass, 16y to E Jack Snow, who attracted 3 defenders to EZ corner and wriggled away for TD grab. FB Joe Farrell notched last TD late in 3rd Q when Zeno was walloped by soph DT Alan Page and DT Paul Costa recovered at 15YL.

KANSAS 15 Oklahoma 14: HB Gale Sayers sprinted 98y with opening KO, but Kansas (3-2) fell into stupor until closing mins. Oklahoma (1-3) took control in 2nd Q as inside-outside threats, FB Jim Grisham and HB Lance Rentzel, each scored for 14-7 lead. Hopelessly trapped at own 9YL with barely more than 2 mins to play, Jayhawks threw soph QB Bob Skahan into brink. Skahan responded with 3-5/45y passing. Sooners were called for pass interference with 8 secs left, so on last play, Skahan pitched to HB Dave Crandall, who threw back to Skahan at scrimmage line. Skahan darted through bevy of OU tacklers to score. Incredibly, Kansas HB Mike Johnson then tallied on reverse, 1 of most daring 2-pt calls ever in clutch situation.

Arkansas 14 TEXAS 13: Razorbacks (5-0) stunned Texas (4-1) with gambling, blitzing D. Loss ended Longhorns' 15-game winning streak and dashed dreams of 3rd straight unbeaten season. Fleet Porkers executed perfect punt RET in 2nd Q as DB Kenny Hatfield, who was to finish his career with highest to-date 16.2y punt RET avg, streaked 81y behind flawless blocking. Steers pounded with TB Ernie Koy (26/110y), and WB Phil Harris tied it at 7-7 early in 4th Q. Hogs were called offside on K David Conway's tying x-pt for Texas, and players looked beseechingly to bench, hoping coach Darrell Royal's call would be 2-pt try from half-distance to GL. Royal decided to keep it at 7-7. Fired-up Longhorns forced 3-and-out, but were detected to have 12 men on field on Razorbacks' punt. So, Arkansas was reprieved to pounce downfield on 75y march as QB Fred Marshall (6-12/81y, TD, INT) rolled left and fired 34y TD to E Bobby Crockett. Koy retaliated by pounding away on 70y answering TD drive, scoring from 1YL with 1:27 to play. Texas gambled, and under pressure from DL James Finch, Steers QB Marv Kristynik missed TB Hix Green with 2-pt pass.

BAYLOR 28 Texas Tech 10: Baylor (1-3), which remained unbeaten at home in 9 games against Texas Tech (3-2) since 1929, rediscovered its passing game as QB Terry Southall (13-24/197y, TD, INT) and WR Lawrence Elkins (7/138y) found brotherly-like connection. Red Raiders HB Donny Anderson had to earn every bit of his 20/97y rushing as Bears D tightened as game wore on. Texas Tech answered Southall's 1st Q TD pass with 54y earthbound drive to 5y TD run off RT by HB Johnny Agan (17/75y). Teams continued to race up and down field, only to have missed FGs and INTs halt efforts. Raiders took 10-7 advantage on K Kenneth Gill's 40y FG in 2nd Q. Baylor got big break in last min-and-half of 2nd Q: bad punt snap forced P Anderson to be downed at his 3YL. In 2 run tries, Bears FB Tom Davies (16/68y) scored 1st of his 2 TDs. In 2nd H, Baylor D held Texas Tech outside its 31YL, and Davies and Southall both scored TDs.

AP Poll October 19

1 Ohio State (35)	447	6 Texas	194
2 Notre Dame (2)	380	7 Louisiana State	174
3 Alabama (5)	365	8 Syracuse	123
4 Arkansas (2)	297	9 Florida	82
5 Nebraska	230	10 Florida State	64

Others with votes: Duke, Georgia Tech, Illinois, Iowa, Michigan, Oregon, Oregon State, Purdue, Wyoming

October 24, 1964

Penn State 37 WEST VIRGINIA 8: Somber Nittany Lions (2-4) played under asst Joe Paterno because head coach Rip Engle rushed to family's side after death of his younger brother. Penn State ruined West Virginia (3-3) Homecoming by bolting to 24-0 lead, highlighted by HB Bob Riggle's 86y run, longest to-date in Lions history. WVU got 3rd Q score as QB Allen McCune topped 65y drive with TD and 2-pt passes to HB Dick Madison.

Rutgers 38 COLUMBIA 35: QB Archie Roberts (25-39/320y, 4 TDs, INT) enjoyed his greatest statistical day for Columbia (1-3-1) and lifted his career passing y to 3142y, best in Columbia Lions history that included passing greats Sid Luckman and Paul Governali. Much of Roberts' fine work was undone by Lions HB Gene Thompson's FUM at his own 18YL early in 4th Q and block of P Roberts' boot shortly thereafter by Rutgers (4-1) soph G Bob Schroeder. Punt block ended up in Scarlet Knights' hands at Columbia 4YL. Rutgers Queensmen scored TD each time to turn 27-25 deficit into 38-27 lead. Knights QB Bob Kalinger scored 2 TDs on ground and threw 44y TD pass to E Bob Stohrer.

VIRGINIA TECH 20 Florida State 11: Always tough outpost for visitors, Blacksburg proved poisonous to undefeated Florida State (5-1). Virginia Tech (3-3) QB Bob Schweikert, frequent thorn in Seminoles' side, accounted for 3 TDs, including undefended T-eligible pass to soph Erick Johnson, who had been moved from G earlier in week so that he could practice trick play. It came in 2nd Q, and put VPI in lead for 1st time at 7-3. Gobblers D strategy protected against long passes, so Seminoles QB Steve Tensi (21-39/288y, TD, 2 INTs) consistantly hit WR Fred Biletnikoff (11/182y, TD) to break FSU single-game reception mark. But, Gobblers D stiffened near its GL, allowing Seminoles duo single TD, which came with barely more than min left. Biletnikoff drew ire of crowd when he spiked ball after his TD and rifled it high in stands after his 2-pt catch. Florida State had all better of it statistically (423y to 191y), but lost 3 TOs at vital moments. Gobblers FB Sonny Utz threw several terrific blocks to free Schweikert for key runs, including 2 TD bursts in 4th Q.

Wake Forest 21 MARYLAND 17: Terrapins (2-4) jumped to 14-0 1st Q lead on TD runs out of their tricky 4-back I-formation by WB Chip Myrtle and TB Tom "Bo" Hickey (126y rushing). Myrtle scored on 13y reverse, play on which he would gain 65y in 1st H, while Hickey's 10y TD was set up by dreadful 3y punt to their 23YL by Deacs. Wake Forest (3-3) FB Brian Piccolo, nation's 2nd leading rusher, gained 27/110y and scored on 2 short TD runs, 1st coming in 2nd Q. Demon Deacons used 2 FUM RECs to position Piccolo's 1st TD run and QB John Mackovic's 40y TD pass to E Dick Cameron for 14-14 H tie. K Bernardo Bramson put Maryland ahead 17-14 with 29y FG midway in 4th Q, but Wake Forest took over with 7 mins to play. Mackovic (13-29/194y, TD, 3 INTs) started winning drive with 16y completion to HB Joe Carazo on 3rd down from his 28YL. Carazo slipped behind Terps ace DB Kenny Ambrusko for 26y grab to Maryland 18YL. Piccolo took over, running over LB Taze Proffitt for 12y gain to 3YL and scoring game-winner on 1y dive with 1:50 to play. Victory wasn't sealed until Wake DB Wayne Welborn made INT that halted Terrapin advance to Deacons 29YL.

ALABAMA 17 Florida 14: Late in 1st Q by Alabama (6-0) QB Joe Namath reinjured his knee on 3rd down rollout, and Gators (4-1) took advantage of DB Dick Kirk's FUM REC at their 47YL. Florida used 9 plays with QB Steve Spurrier rifling 15y pass to open drive and 9y scoring throw to end drive, each to E Randy Jackson. Crimson Tide tied it 7-7 late in 2nd Q when sub QB Steve Sloan (6-11/85y, INT) hit E Tommy Tolleson with 12y pass before FB Steve Bowman (14/82y, 2 TDs) crashed over from 1YL. With Florida up 14-7 in 4th Q, Bama HB John Mosley returned punt 37y to Gators 34YL. Bowman spun away for 30y TD to deadlock it at 14-14. With 3:06 left, Bama K David Ray made winning 21y FG, but Spurrier, who was perfect 7-7 passing in 2nd H, drove Florida length of field, starting with 16y pass to E Charles Casey, 19y pass to FB Larry Dupree, and 17y screen pass to 13YL by HB Don Knapp. But, Gators were out of timeouts as Spurrier was sacked and FB John Felber was dropped for loss on draw run. Florida K Jim Hall was dashed onto field only to miss heartbreaking, hurry-up 24y FG try.

MISSISSIPPI STATE 18 Houston 13: Late in 2nd Q, Houston (2-4) went ahead 7-3 with 76y TD march, sparked by HB Dickie Post who gained 21y, including 3y scoring sweep. Bulldogs (3-3) didn't offer much O (141y), depending instead on talented toe of G-K Justin Canale. Canale succeeded on FGs of 44y in 1st Q, 24y in 2nd Q, and 49y in 4th Q for 9-7 advantage. Seemingly-innocent punt deep into Cougars territory came soon: Houston HB Mike Spratt fumbled it inside his 5YL and had to scramble to cover it in EZ as Mississippi State T Bubba Hampton closed in. Safety gave Mississippi State 11-7 lead, and HB Dan Bland stunned Cougars with 73y TD RET of free-kick for quick 18-7 edge. Houston QB Bo Burris completed 2 long passes on late 60y drive that culminated in Post's 1y TD blast. After poor start to season, Mississippi State racked up its 3rd straight win.

MICHIGAN 19 Minnesota 12: In repossessing Little Brown Jug for 1st time in 5 years, Michigan (4-1) gained 19-0 lead by 3rd Q and ran twice as many plays as Minnesota (2-3). Wolverines FB Mel Anthony plunged to methodically-produced 1st Q TD, and QB-K Bob Timberlake added 29y FG and 1y TD sneak. Minnesota handed over safety on snap that sailed over P Bruce Van de Walker's head and entered Michigan zone only twice prior to late in 3rd Q when Gophers nudged to within sniffing distance of 50YL. Suddenly, they spurted 35y to UM 17YL on 3 completions by QB John Hankinson. After changeover for 4th Q, Minny E Kent Kramer nabbed Hankinson's 4th down, 11y crossing-pattern TD pass, but 2-pt pass failed. Gophers needed break, and it came as result of their D halting Wolverines' attempt to lock it up: Minnesota DB Kraig Lofquist stepped in front of short pass by Timberlake and raced 91y down sideline on thrilling INT TD RET. Gophers forced 2 more punts but never made serious threat at late victory.

NOTRE DAME 28 Stanford 6: Fighting Irish's dominance was apparent in discrepancy of 1st downs. Notre Dame (5-0) made 29 1st downs to 4 by Stanford (2-4), and while Irish O was making headlines behind record-breaking passing of QB John Huarte (21-37/300y, TD, 2 INTs), it was their magnificent D that permitted only 56y net O. Huarte became top ND single-game thrower in completions and attempts, and E Jack Snow caught 8/113y to bring his season receiving y mark to 595y, new Irish record. ND HB Bill Wolski (18/102y, 2 TDs) scored 3 times on 54y pass from Huarte in 2nd Q, 1y dive in 3rd Q, and 9y wedge behind RT Dick Leeuwenburg early in 4th Q. With bench-players on field as clock roamed toward 0:00, Indians DB Jack Lodato picked off pass by ND QB Alex Bonvechio and returned it 26y to Irish 32YL. Stanford HB Ray Handley (19/43y), previous topper of nation's rushing list, finally found room on 2 tries worth 11y and, after FB John Read made 1st down at 10YL and Irish were penalized 5y, Handley tossed TD pass to HB Dave Lewis.

Nebraska 21 COLORADO 3: Homecoming in Boulder brought out belting Buffs (1-5) as no. 5 Nebraska coughed up but recovered FUMs on its 1st 2 snaps. Early breaks continued toward Bison as DB John Marchiol picked off Huskers pass by QB Bob Churchich (9-14/154y, TD, 2 INTs) and returned it to Nebraska 17YL. Procedure PEN derailed Colorado's TD hopes but it took 3-0 lead on K Frank Rogers' 21y FG. Buffs DB Hale Irwin (late 2nd Q INT) nearly created Churchich's 2nd INT early in 2nd Q, but ball slipped through his fine future pro golf grip into mitts of Huskers HB Kent McCloughan, who dashed 53y for TD and 7-3 lead. In 3rd Q, CU HB Bernie McCall lost FUM at his 9YL, and FB Frank Solich spun across for 13-3 lead 2 plays later. Nebraska went 80y in 4th Q to clinching score finalized on Churchich's sneak after his 31y pass to HB Harry Wilson.

Texas 6 RICE 3: Facing puzzling "Houston Jinx" under which it had failed to beat Rice (2-3) on road in 12 years, no. 6 Texas (5-1) rode pair of FGs by K David Conway and spectacular punting of TB-P Ernie Koy (9/46.3y avg) to slim win. Owls flew away with extensive ball possession in final 3 Qs, gaining 227y by game's end to Texas' 89y. In fact, Rice D was so smothering that Longhorns failed to earn single 1st down and ran only 11 plays in 2nd H. What spared Texas was apply-named Rice K, Larry Rice (22y FG), who barely missed 33y and 46y FGs in 4th Q. Conway's opening FG had come at end of drive started from Texas 48YL by wobbly pass by QB Marv Kristynik (3-10/32y, INT) which was run 15y by Koy. Owls immediately countered with DB Ron Cervenka's 69y KO RET that set up Rice's tying chip-shot FG later in 1st Q.

ARIZONA 15 Wyoming 7: Preseason WAC favorite Wyoming (5-1) never got any kind of effective O rolling against fine D of Wildcats (3-2), which put wraps on Cowboy stars, QB Tom Wilkinson (4-13/50y) and FB Mike Davenport (21y rushing). In fact, it was Pokes' D that scored their team's only TD in 1st Q: after Arizona HB Ricki Harris strangely decided to fight his way out of EZ to 1YL on punt RET, Cats QB Gene Dahlquist lost snap and EZ FUM TD to Wyoming DE Darryl Alleman. Arizona took over in 2nd H, getting spark from HB Floyd Hudlow, who used T Jim Pazerski's terrific block to sprint 82y down sideline for punt TD RET. HB Jim Oliver ran for 2-pt conv, and Cats led 8-7 in 3rd Q. Arizona threatened with 75y advance to within inches of Cowboys GL late in 3rd Q, but it took next possession to cash in TD on 41y drive. Dahlquist capped it by hitting E Tim Dewan with 7y TD pass.

UTAH 16 Arizona State 3: QB Rich Groth (7-15/154y, INT) replaced Ernest "Pokey" Allen and led Utah (4-2) to upset that ended 12-game win streak of Arizona State (4-1). Sun Devils struck 1st on K Rick Davis' 28y FG at end of 62y march in 1st Q. Utes soon answered with WR-K Roy Jefferson's tying 23y FG after 65y advance. Next came decisive play: Utah P Jerry Robinson (5/44y avg) popped effective punt from Devils' 40YL to GL. ASU HB Gene Foster foolishly fielded hopping ball at 1YL and lost FUM

to Ute T John Stipech at 2YL. FB Allen Jacobs' 2y TD run gave Utah 10-3 lead. Groth scored in 2nd Q to salt away win after having set up TD with 45y pass to WB John Pease. Utah D was magnificent with scrawny DB C.D. Lowery making 3 INTs. Arizona State gained only 68y rushing, which included 57y reverse run by WB Larry Todd shortly after opening KO.

SOUTHERN CALIFORNIA 26 California 21: Effective missiles flew over L.A. Coliseum as California (3-3) QB Craig Morton passed 18-28/219y, 2 TDs, and Southern California (4-2) QB Craig Fertig fired 21-28/371y, 4 TDs, INT. Cal scored on Morton's 1st TD to HB Jerry Mosher, but QB-K Tom Blanchfield missed kick. After Fertig threw 2 TDs, Morton tied it at 14-14, clicking on 2-pt pass after his own 5y TD run. Bears led 21-14 after Morton's 2nd scoring bomb, but Fertig countered with 45y TD pass to TB Mike Garrett at end of 80y drive and 22y TD to WR Rod Sherman at end of 82y drive.

Oregon 7 WASHINGTON 0: "Casey's Commandos," D unit of undefeated Oregon (6-0), so named after active LB Tim Casey, delivered constant stream of big plays to totally frustrate sledge-hammer O of Washington (2-4), which was facing portent of its 1st losing season since 1958. Ducks defenders blanked Huskies by forcing 4 INTs, recovering 2 FUMs, twice halting run attempts at their 1YL. Game's only score came early: Oregon QB Bob Berry (6-12/183y, TD, 2 INTs) fired his troops 73y to 14y T-eligible pass to Lowell Dean. Berry, who otherwise was stymied by Huskies D, led by G-LB Rick Redman, had started scoring trip with 11y pass to E Corky Sullivan. Then HB Dennis Keller slammed 16y, and Berry found Sullivan again at Washington 26YL. UW mounted threat by going to air in 3rd Q until handing ball to FB Jeff Jordan on play at Webfoots 8YL. Jordan smashed to 1YL but ball popped into air, only to be recovered by Oregon LB Oliver McKinney. Huskies QB Jim Sartoris provided late-game glimmer of hope when he hit future Washington coach, E Jim Lambright, with pass to Ducks 27YL. Pair tried again on next down, but Webfoots DB Ron Martin picked off Sartoris' pass deep in Oregon territory.

AP Poll October 26

1 Ohio State (32)	439	6 Texas	195
2 Notre Dame (6)	387	7 Oregon	119
3 Alabama (8)	380	8 Georgia Tech	80
4 Arkansas (1)	311	9 Louisiana State	72
5 Nebraska	242	10 Florida	60

Others with votes: Colorado, Duke, Florida State, Illinois, Iowa, Michigan,Michigan State, Mississippi, North Carolina, Oregon State, Princeton, Purdue, Southern California

October 31, 1964

Notre Dame 40 Navy 0 (Philadelphia): Rolling ever onward, Fighting Irish (6-0) handed disappointing Navy (2-4-1) its worst thrashing since Notre Dame's national champs delivered same score in 1949. Even so, QB Roger Staubach was able to set Middies' record with 19 completions for 155y from Shotgun O, which helped protect his bad leg. Telling stats at game's end were ND's 6 TDs scored on 504y total O, and 54y rushing turned in by injury-riddled Navy. Irish QB John Huarte passed 10-17/274y, 3 TDs. E Jack Snow caught 2 TD passes and HB Nick Eddy went 74y to score with short 1st Q pass. It had been surprisingly long wait, but Notre Dame finally took over top spot in AP poll for 1st time since early in 1954.

Georgia Tech 21 DUKE 8: Blue Devils (4-1-1) outgained Georgia Tech (7-0) 371y to 270y as QB Scotty Glacken passed 24-38/263y, TD. But, Glacken's 3 INTs helped halt 1st H drives at Georgia Tech 27, 23, and 27YLs. Meanwhile, Engineers' Split-T option runs sprung HB Terry Haddock for 1st H TD spurts of 4 and 3y. Haddock's 55y RET of 2nd H KO positioned FB Jeff Davis for TD and 21-0 lead. Late in 3rd Q, Duke stopped Tech inches from 4th TD and, with Glacken throwing 34y from his EZ to E Jim Scott, Blue went 99y to score Q-break with Glacken firing on 4th down to E Chuck Drulis for 8y. "It's just sickening," said coach Bill Murray of Duke's inability to score. More sickening was start of Devils' 5-game slide that would cost them any shot at ACC title and send them toward only their 2nd losing season since 1946. It was trend that would sink them to regular mediocrity and worse.

LOUISIANA STATE 11 Mississippi 10: Except for early 77y FG drive led by hobbled Tigers (5-0-1) QB Pat Screen, Mississippi (3-3-1) controlled game well into 4th Q. Holding 10-3 edge primarily on QB Jim Weatherly's 3y TD run in 1st Q, Ole Miss stood to ice it with midfield possession as LSU punted from its GL with 6 mins left. Bengals G Don Ellen smartly slammed Rebels special teams blocker into HB Doug Cunningham, and Cunningham fumbled away punt at own 47YL. QB Billy Ezell, in for Screen, flipped 19y impromptu TD pass to E Billy Masters. Although tight-covering Ole Miss DB Tommy Luke tipped LSU's 2-pt pass, E Doug Moreau still caught winner from Ezell at GL flag.

Ohio State 21 IOWA 19: Miscues on both sides keyed near upset of no. 1 Ohio State (6-0). Buckeyes HB-DB Steve Dreffer picked off pass by Hawkeye (3-3) QB Gary Snook on game's 1st scrimmage play, returning it 36y to TD. Iowa came back after 2 FUM RECs to score on Snook's 2y run and his 30y pass to WR Karl Noonan. But, outstanding LB Dwight Kelley blocked conv, so Ohio State led 14-13 at H. Buckeyes QB Don Unverferth nailed HB Bo Rein with 24y TD pass in 3rd Q. Trailing 21-13 late, Iowa E Rich O'Harra made unbelievable diving catch of Snook's 4th-and-11 bomb at Ohio State 12YL. FB Craig Nourse vaulted over for 1y TD on 4th down with 2 secs left. On 2-pt conv rollout, Snook (17-33/221y, TD, 3 INTs) fooled everyone except Bucks DE Bill Spahr, and Spahr burst between blockers to halt Snook just 8 inches away from tying game.

PURDUE 26 Illinois 14: With QB Bob Griese hitting 7 passes in row, Purdue (5-1) went 60 and 55y to 1st Q scores and added 3rd TD early in 2nd Q for 20-0 lead. E Bob Hadrick caught 1 of Griese's TDs (13y), 1 of Hadrick's school-record 8 catches in game. Illinois (4-2) forged back to trail by 6 pts on QB Fred Custardo's passing (10-20/142y, 2 INTs) and FB Jim Grabowski's 2 TD runs. With hopes of repeating as Big 10 champs fading in last 2 mins, Illini gambled on 4th down pass from their EZ. Its failure was turned into Boilermakers HB Randy Minniear's 3rd TD run to wrap it up at 26-14.

NEBRASKA 9 Missouri 0: Big D plays spiced Big 8 battle and provided winning pts. Nebraska (7-0) DB Larry Wachholtz made shoestring tackle to prevent Missouri (4-3) QB Gary Lane from dashing to 1st Q TD, and it forced Tigers K Bill Bates into his 1st miss among his long-range 3-pt failures of 40, 50, and 51y. Lane also was stopped for no gain on 4th-and-inches at Nebraska 21YL in 2nd Q. Game remained scoreless early in 4th Q after Mizzou D, led by LB Rich Bernsen, stopped Cornhuskers at MU 13YL. Lane dropped back to throw surprise bomb, but was dropped inches behind his own GL by Huskers DE Langston Coleman for 2-0 tally. Nebraska moved to Tigers 37YL 7 mins later. Huskers QB Bob Churchich shook off rush attempt of Tigers DE Bud Abell and tossed pass to HB Kent McCloughan, who raced to 37y TD. Nebraska T Larry Kramer paved TD road by making miraculous block that peeled gripping tackler, DB Johnny Roland, off McCloughan.

TULSA 61 Oklahoma State 14: Magnificent Tulsa (4-2) aerial combination of QB Jerry Rhome (34-43/488y, 4 TDs, INT) and E Howard Twilley (15/217y, 2 TDs) and stern Hurricane D dropped worst drubbing on Oklahoma State (3-3) in 46-game series history. Big win also launched 6-game win streak for Tulsa. Cowboys FB Walt Garrison had stormed 74y for 1st Q TD that tied game at 7-7. Rhome scored on 2 and 7y runs when game was still in balance in 1st H and capped 2nd Q scoring with 8y TD pass to Twilley, whose 15 receptions set new Tulsa record. Hurricane led 32-7 at H as Oklahoma State could run only 14 O plays. Tulsa D intercepted 3 passes and recovered 2 FUMs, all leading to TDs and permitted only single 2nd H drive past its 40YL. Tulsa made 33 1st downs and 521y.

TEXAS CHRISTIAN 17 Baylor 14: On its Homecoming Saturday, Texas Christian (3-4) unleashed impressive run game upon Baylor (2-4) to win its 3rd game in row. Purple Frogs HB Jim Fauver ran 27/121y and FB Larry Bulaich added 22/110y as TCU played keep-away from Bears. TCU ran 87 O plays to Baylor's 37. Frogs hopped 80y on 14 plays after opening KO as Fauver gained 39y so that QB Kent Nix could loft 6y TD pass to E Joe Ball. Bears came back with 38y TD pass from QB Terry Southall (11-18/154y, 2 TDs, INT) to WR Lawrence Elkins (5/103y, TD), who had earlier on Baylor's 1st snap uncharacteristically dropped sure TD pass all alone at Frogs 30YL. Bears grabbed 8-7 lead as bad conv snap turned into improvised 2-pt catch by E Harlan Lane. TCU QB Randy Howard lost TD pass in 2nd Q to motion PEN, so Frogs settled for K Bruce Alford's 25y FG. Howard also scored on 5y rollout run in 4th Q for 17-8 lead after DB Frank Horak fell on FUM at Bears 38YL. Baylor E Ken Hodge caught 11y TD with 2:07 left.

Washington 14 SOUTHERN CALIFORNIA 13: USC (4-3) played solid football in 1st H for 2-TD lead as QB Craig Fertig (16-30/191y, TD, 4 INTs) opened scoring by zipping 8y TD pass to HB Rod Sherman just beyond fingertips of Huskies DB Mason Mitchell. Washington (3-4) made several bad judgments on 4th down, including G-P Rick Redman's 2nd Q pass incompletion out of punt formation from his own 46YL. Southern California scored in 6 plays, but Huskies DE Jim Sampson (blocked FG) pressured x-pt try into miss. USC E Fred Hill caught school-record 11/112y and TB Mike Garrett rushed for 122y as Trojans clung to 13-0 lead and Rose Bowl hopes as they entered 4th Q. Previously-injured 3rd string Huskies QB Tod Hullin (7-11/77y, TD) was pressed into action in 2nd H and fired up UW's stalled attack. Hullin found HB Charlie Browning for 3 completions on 77y TD drive, including Browning's 8y scoring catch. Washington FB Jeff Jordan powered over from 1YL after HB Steve Bramwell returned punt 10y to Trojans 47y, and HB-K Ron Medved kicked conv. "You realize," said coach Jim Owens afterward, "that this has to rank as one of the all-time great comebacks in Washington history."

Stanford 10 OREGON 8 (Portland): With AAWU race in scramble, Ducks' fall placed their bitter rival Oregon State in Rose Bowl contention. Future New York Giants coach, HB Ray Handley, put plucky Stanford (3-4) ahead 7-0 with 5y run in 3rd Q. Later in 3rd Q, HB-DB Les Palm provided Ducks (6-1) with 40y INT RET, which FB Dick Winn quickly converted with 1y TD run. Ailing QB Bob Berry quickly put Oregon ahead by 8-7 with 2-pt pass to E Ray Palm. Ducks tried to punt out of danger in late going, but short punt traveled only to their 39YL. Stanford took over and drove to 10YL to set up K Braden Beck's winning 27y FG that came with 13 secs to go.

Oregon State 24 WASHINGTON STATE 7: Halloween powers often were thrust upon schools clad in orange and black on October 31 Saturdays, but Washington State (3-4), wearing its crimson, nearly upset pumpkin cart. Oregon State (6-1) won its 6th straight since season opening loss but needed quick start to swat Cougars. Gifted Beavers QB Paul Brothers, who went most of way with bruised ribs, courageously blended effective QB keepers with his short passing game to 14-7 H advantage. Brothers threw 19y TD pass to HB Doug McDougal and scored on 12y run on Oregon State's opening 2 possessions. In between, Wazzu workhorse HB Clarence Williams scored on 2y run, which was small part of his 31/172y rushing total. Adjustments by Cougars' D completely stifled Beavers in 2nd H and kept score at 14-7 until charge in last 2 mins created Oregon State K Steve Clark's 26y FG, and HB Marv Crowston layered on late TD plunge.

AP Poll November 2

1 Notre Dame (29)	460	6 Texas	175
2 Ohio State (11)	424	7 Georgia Tech	174
3 Alabama (7)	385	8 Louisiana State	116
4 Arkansas (1)	310	9 Florida	90
5 Nebraska	259	10 Purdue	85

Others with votes: Duke, Florida State, Michigan, Michigan State, Oregon, Oregon State, Syracuse, Tulsa, Washington

November 7, 1964

Notre Dame 17 PITTSBURGH 15: Panthers (2-4-2) were unimpressed by nation's top rushing D of no. 1 Notre Dame (7-0) and were able to grind out 199y. But, Fighting Irish had opened strongly on O, going 80y in 14 plays after opening KO to FB Joe Farrell's TD. On next possession, ND QB John Huarte rifled pass to HB Nick Eddy who raced 91y to score, but it just as easily could have been 2-pt safety for Pitt as Huarte had to dance away from bevy of pass rushers. So, Fighting Irish had scored 2 opening salvos, and it looked like another romp for undefeated clan, especially after they soon recovered FUM and pressed on to Pitt 2YL. But there, Irish HB Bill Wolski fumbled it away to Panthers DB Dale Stewart. After K Joe Azzaro made 30y FG late in 2nd Q for 17-8 H edge, ND was blanked in 2nd H. Pitt rode strong back of FB Barry McKnight (93y rushing) to his 2nd TD on 1st play of 4th Q. When Panthers hopes soared on late threat, Irish swarm of defenders stopped McKnight on 4th-and-1.

WAKE FOREST 20 Duke 7: Not since 1951 had Wake Forest (4-4) beaten Duke (4-2-1). Big upset became FB Brian Piccolo's finest moment as he scored all 3 TDs, including go-ahead TD on 11y pass from QB John Mackovic (10-21/142y, TD, 3 INTs) in 3rd Q. Piccolo set ACC record with 35 rush attempts, while gaining 115y. Piccolo also caught 3/46y, TD. HB John Gutekunst got lone Blue Devils TD on 16y run in 1st Q. Wake Forest had to suffer through its own 3 pass INTs and FUM in 7-7 1st H, but its line dominated in 2nd H. Deacons G Don McMurray recovered Gutekunst's FUM at Blues 23YL to launch winning pass in 3rd Q. Duke visited Wake territory only once in 2nd H, making it to 41L.

Georgia 14 FLORIDA 7: In 1st H, Georgia (5-2-1) O managed but single 1st down while Florida (5-2) completed 83y TD drive with FB Larry Dupree's 7y run. Another Gators drive died before H with K Jim Hall's missed 25y FG. Early in 3rd Q, Bulldogs DT Ray Rissmiller dislocated his elbow, but still dislodged ball from Gators HB Allen Trammell. Nothing came of it, but Bulldogs D became enraged, creating field position that paid off in HB Fred Barber's TD early in 4th Q. Inside last 10 mins of play, Georgia reached 4th down at Florida 5YL. K Bobby Etter was sent in for FG attempt, but snap was high, and Etter made frantic dash behind blocks by holder Barry Wilson and E Frank Richter for winning TD.

ALABAMA 17 Louisiana State 9: SEC crown went to Alabama (8-0) on strength of top D play in 2nd H. Versatile E-K Doug Moreau gave LSU (5-1-1) 9-7 H lead with TD catch and 37y FG. QB Steve Sloan's pass to HB Ray Ogden keyed drive to K David Ray's FG and 10-9 lead Crimson Tide earned early in 4th Q. Bama DB Hudson Harris' 33y INT TD RET clinched it at 17-9, not before Tigers edged twice to Tide 11YL only to have Bama DT Frank McClendon bat down 4 passes. Afterward, LSU coach Charley McClendon disavowed any kinship to Alabama D hero of same name.

Tennessee 22 GEORGIA TECH 14: In 8 min span of 4th Q, Georgia Tech's dream of undefeated season went up in smoke. Despite being outgained, Engineers (7-1) enjoyed 14-3 lead in 4th Q with their prime moment coming from HB-DB Gerry Bussell's 84y INT TD RET in 3rd Q. Tennessee (4-2-1) strategically inserted sub QB Dave Leake, who hit TE Al Tanara with 23y TD. FB Jack Patterson soon scored, and Vols had their 1st lead of day at 15-14. Tennessee's spree was fulfilled by LB Doug Archibald's 69y INT TD RET.

KENTUCKY 22 Vanderbilt 21: Commodores (2-4-1), righteously claiming that "we came to win," rallied from 14-pt deficit to score in last min, only to have 2-pt pass blow up in their faces. Kentucky (3-5) held ball for nearly 11 mins to start contest, scoring on QB Rick Norton's sneak, 21st play of 83y march. Vandy went 3-and-out, and back came Cats on 33y TD pass from Norton to E Rick Kestner. Vanderbilt QB Dave Waller capped 73y drive in 2nd Q with 1y TD run, and before long Commodores enjoyed 15-14 lead that lasted into 3rd Q. Big play came from Vandy HB Steve Bevil, who used G Dave Maddux's lethal block to spring into open on 72y punt TD RET. Waller's 2-pt pass to HB Bob Sullins was made easy by Wildcats' PEN that moved conv try closer. Kentucky stopped 2 threats in 3rd Q before going ahead after DL John Andreghetti plucked blocked pass out of air and rumbled on 9y RET to Vandy 23YL. FB Frank Antonini busted over and 2-pt run made it 22-15. Waller lost FUM to Andreghetti at Kentucky 5YL, but came back with 4th down, 13y TD pass to E Bumpy Baldwin with 55 secs left. But, Waller's nemisis, Andreghetti, snowed Waller under before QB could get off his 2-pt pass for lead.

MICHIGAN 21 Illinois 6: Pair of 2nd Q Illini bobbles in 50th renewal of Big 10 rivalry sent Michigan (6-1) on its merry way to pair of TD pass receptions by HBs Carl Ward and Jim Detwiler from QB Bob Timberlake (5-8/53y 2 TDs). In between, Illinois (4-3) QB Fred Custardo (11-22/130y, TD, INT) sent soph E Bob Trumpy deep for 49y TD bomb after FB Jim Grabowski (17/62y) had softened Michigan's middle D. K Custardo was wide with his x-pt try, so Wolverines led 14-6 at H. Michigan E-P Stan Kemp earned field position by punting OB at Illini 10, 12, 13, and 3 YLs. After Illinois DB-P George Donnelly answered with his own drop-dead punt at UM 6YL, it signaled Michigan infantry to go 94y to Timberlake's TD sneak late in 3rd Q. When K Timberlake made his 3rd conv he led Big 10 scorers with 53 pts.

MICHIGAN STATE 21 Purdue 7: Dream of 1st-ever Purdue (5-2) Rose Bowl trip evaporated on blocked punt and pass interference PEN. Line domination on both sides of ball was apparent from start as Michigan State (4-3) HB Dick Gordon (24/145y and 4/31y receiving) raced 48y on Spartans' 1st snap. That drive reached 15YL but was killed by 15y PEN and 15y sack by Purdue DE Harold Wells. After FB Randy Minniear (22/80y, TD) gave Boilermakers 7-0 1st Q edge, Spartans DL Charles Thornhill blocked Purdue P Russ Pfahler's punt, and DT Harold Lucas caught high rebound and ran 3y to TD midway in 2nd Q. Michigan State threatened often in 2nd H without result until HB Clint Jones scored from 3YL. TD was set up by devastating 32y pass interference PEN on 3rd-and-long, called on Boilermakers DB Ken Erby in 3rd Q. Jones wrapped it up with 15y TD catch from QB Steve Juday in 4th Q.

NORTHWESTERN 17 Wisconsin 13: Wildcats (3-5) jumped to 17-0 H lead but capacity Homecoming crowd at Dyche Stadium nibbled its fingernails as Badgers (2-5) rode their passing attack to 2nd H rally. After spending most of season discovering he had little talent at receiver, Northwestern QB Tommy Myers (5-9/84y, INT) seldom passed, but handed off to runners who whipped up 239y rushing. FB Steve Murphy (20/70y) led Cats O, and HB Ron Rector broke away for 51y TD dash in 2nd Q for 14-0 lead. E Mike Donaldson pulled in Myers' perfectly-pitched parabola pass at Wisconsin 8YL, but NW had to settle for K Dean Dickie's short FG before H. Badgers went to Wildcats 5YL after 2nd H KO, but drive fizzled. Wisconsin HB Jimmy Jones, who caught 11/school-record 167y, tallied on 52y TD pass from backup QB Jesse Kaye in 3rd Q. Badgers C Ernest von Heimburg was at bottom of big stack of players to score TD after DB Carl Silvestri blocked punt into EZ. Critical play came next: QB Hal Brandt looked to pass, decided to run, and then zipped 2-pt pass for E Ralph Farmer who dropped it. Trailing 17-13, Wisconsin had to pass up what might have been winning FG in its late threats.

Penn State 27 OHIO STATE 0: So thorough was blanking of mighty no. 2 Ohio State (6-1), Buckeyes' 1st whitewash defeat in 46 games, that Bucks made no 1st downs and suffered through -14y total O in 1st H. Amazingly, Ohio failed to cross midfield until final min of game. "That was the soundest trouncing we ever have had," admitted Bucks coach Woody Hayes. Salvaging its flagging season, Penn State (4-4) outgained Ohio State 349y to 63y. Nittany Lions were sparked by QB Gary Wydman (12-22/148y) and FB Tom Urbanik (16/79y) and scored on efficient drives of 65, 35, 42, and 64y. HB Don Kunit tallied twice for Lions. Penn State D was so overwhelming that Buckeye fans could cheer HB Bo Rein's 6y run as its biggest gain of 1st H as Bucks couldn't advance past their 35YL in minimal 16 snaps in 1st H. It simply wasn't Ohio's day: Nittany Lions' only error didn't hurt them. Indeed, miscue turned into Penn State TD as HB Dirk Nye beat 2 Ohioans to Urbanik's FUM that went into EZ on 1st Q blast from Buckeyes 1YL.

Nebraska 14 KANSAS 7: Opportunity slipped away against undefeated Nebraska (8-0) as Jayhawks (5-3) suffered 2 exasperating misplays in 4th Q: errant 4th down pitchout stopped them at Cornhuskers 1YL, and ace HB-WR Gale Sayers (4/49y receiving), who was curtailed with only 11/27y rushing, lost handle while streaking in clear field at Nebraska 15YL. All scoring was wedged into late 1st Q and early 2nd Q. After Kansas P Wally Hingshaw's 2nd punt to Huskers' coffin corner in 1st Q left Nebraska at its 7YL, QB Bob Churchich (6-12/159y, TD) surprised D by launching 92y TD pass to tall E Freeman White (3/114y, TD). Jayhawks quickly retaliated as lefty QB Bob Skahan (9-19/136y) rolled right and pitched pass that HB Mike Johnson took 53y to set up 3y TD run by FB Ron Oelschlager. Cornhuskers explored Kansas' left side with sweeps on next possession that went 75y to TD run up middle by HB Bobby Hohn (12/84y). Kansas' Cardiac Kids seemed likely to at least tie it in late going: They went 57y as Sayers caught passes of 14 and 11y, but Skahan's wild pitchout on 4th down forced Johnson to circle back for ball and he was prevented from easy TD run. Later, Sayers grabbed pass between 2 defenders, but his high knee action, as he swirled away, knocked ball from his own grasp at Huskers 15YL.

ARKANSAS 21 Rice 0: Razorbacks (8-0) D kept Rice (2-4-1) on its side of 50YL on all but 1 of 13 Owl possessions. Ringleaders of assault on Owls were Arkansas DTs Loyd Phillips and Jim Williams, NG Jimmy Johnson, and LBs Ronnie Caveness and Ronnie Mac Smith. Hogs allowed only 102y, and HB-P Chuck Latourette (45.8y punting avg) was Owls' only useful weapon, gaining 14/64y rushing. Arkansas earned its 1st TD early in 2nd Q when TB Bobby Burnett leaped over from 1YL at end of 65y drive. Big play on march was WB Jim Lindsey's 22y option-pitch run behind crashing block of TE Jerry Lamb. Soph DB Harry Jones dashed 35y up center of field on 4th Q INT TD RET, and Burnett reprised his TD dive later on. TB Jack Brausell rushed 26/121y for Cotton Bowl-bound no. 4 Arkansas.

AP Poll November 9

1 Notre Dame (26)	380	6 Michigan	184
2 Alabama (11)	367	7 Ohio State	138
3 Arkansas (3)	334	8 Oregon State (1)	114
4 Nebraska	283	9 Louisiana State	69
5 Texas	220	10 Georgia Tech	50

Others with votes: Auburn, Bowling Green, Florida, Florida State, Georgia, Michigan State, Oregon, Penn State, Princeton, Purdue, Southern California, Syracuse, Tennessee, Tulsa

November 14, 1964

Princeton 35 YALE 14: Previously undefeated Yale Bulldogs (6-1-1) had high hopes of staging upset, and Elis gave Princeton (8-0) all it could handle in 1st H. Yale accepted opening KO and went 85y to FB Chuck Mercein's TD after QB Ed McCarthy's 61y pass to E Charlie Carter. Elis tied it at 14-14 just before H on 64y trip, capped when McCarthy threw 8y TD pass to HB Bill Henderson, who made juggling catch. In 3rd Q, Tigers FB Cosmo Iacavazzi (20/185y, 2 TDs), running as described by venerable scribe Allison Danzig in *The New York Times,* "on a one-man stampede,…shedding tacklers like a Samson," bulled 23y to set up TB Don McKay's go-ahead TD pass to BB Roy Pizzarello at 21-14. Iacavazzi, future Hall of Famer, put verdict in bank by rampaging for 39 and 47y TD runs in 4th Q and gleefully firing ball into Yale Bowl stands after each score. Victory clinched Big 3, football's oldest title, and Ivy League championship.

SYRACUSE 20 Virginia Tech 15: QB Bob Schweikert followed early 48y FG by K Billy Cranwell to put Virginia Tech (5-4) ahead 9-0 with 1st Q TD run to finish 86y march. Syracuse (7-2) countered with HB Floyd Little and FB Jim Nance, who scored from short range in 2nd and 3rd Qs respectively, each tallying his 11th TD of 1964. Little's TD turned out to be inevitable, coming after Orangemen were stopped inside Va Tech 1YL. When P Schweikert could punt only to his 36YL, it took Syracuse 7 plays to score. With Schweikert headed for hospital with eye injury he suffered late in 2nd Q, Gobblers turned to big FB Sonny Utz, who scored from 6YL in mid-4th Q after he ran 60y to

Orange 19YL. So, Virginia Tech led 15-13. With 1:26 left, Syracuse went 54y as sub QB Rich King came off bench to throw 4-5 passes, including game-winner to E Harris Elliott with 1 min to play.

VIRGINIA 31 North Carolina 27: North Carolina (4-5) boasted best pass D in ACC, but Virginia (5-4) QB Bob Davis shredded it for 13-25/196y, TD, and added 2 TDs running before hurting throwing shoulder. Sub QB Tom Hodges contributed savvy play on drive that gave Wahoos 28-21 edge. Cavs' C snap shot into air after hitting pulling G Charlie Hart, but Hodges kept his composure, snatched ball, and threw 15y pass to UNC 16YL. North Carolina HB Ken Willard rushed 28/121y, and QB Gary Black hit 3 TD passes, but neither Heels O star could produce enough for victory.

Mississippi 30 TENNESSEE 0: Translating 3 FUMs into TDs, Mississippi (5-3-1) spoiled Homecoming and bowl hopes for Tennessee (4-3-1). After scoreless 1st Q, Rebels K Billy Carl Irwin made 30y FG. When Volunteers QB Art Galiffa lost FUM at his 13YL, Ole Miss TB Mike Dennis (75y rushing and 5/50y receiving) scored on 2nd Q TD run for 10-0 H edge. Rebs E Roy Heidel pounced on his 2nd FUM REC as Vols DB Bobby Petrella lost handle at his 22YL, and Dennis scored again from 4YL. QB Jim Weatherly (11-16/126y, INT) followed another Ole Miss FUM REC at 22YL in 4th Q with 1y sneak for TD and 23-0 lead. With everything going wrong for Tennessee, Vols P Ron Widby had his punt blocked by rambunctious Rebels E Allen Brown, and T James Harvey lived lineman's dream with 20y TD runback. Volunteers were limited to 133y O on dark day in Knoxville.

Alabama 24 GEORGIA TECH 7: Outgained and twice pressed back near its own GL, Georgia Tech (7-2) was within couple mins from escaping 1st H with 0-0 tie. But, Alabama (9-0) DE Mike Hopper soon grabbed Yellow Jackets FUM at midfield, and hobbling QB Joe Namath was summoned to action: he fired 49y bomb to HB David Ray that reached 1YL. After FB Steve Bowman's TD made it 7-0, Alabama E Creed Gilmer pounced on on-side KO. Namath quickly whipped 47y pass to HB Ray Ogden and followed with 3y TD to Ray. Setting new NCAA season kick-scoring record, K Ray made 22y FG in 3rd Q for 17-0 lead. Crimson Tide sub QB Steve Sloan sparked 92y TD march with runs of 24 and 16y in 4th Q before Georgia Tech salvaged its pride on QB Johnny Priestley's TD pass in last 21 secs.

AUBURN 14 Georgia 7: With star QB Jimmy Sidle sidelined with injury, Auburn (6-3) turned to FB-DB Tucker Frederickson for 53 mins of superb play on both sides of ball. Frederickson gained 14/101y rushing, including 24y burst in 1st Q on newly-installed trap play. Tigers growled for 82y in 2nd Q as soph QB Tom Bryan (20/89y rushing) stepped around E for 5y TD. Trailing 14-0 at H and completely unfamiliar with Auburn's side of 50YL, Georgia (5-3-1) made H adjustments on D and sprung surprise play on unyielding Tigers D. On last play of 3rd Q, Bulldogs QB Lynn Hughes flipped pass to big George Patton on T-eligible play, and Patton lumbered 40y to 17YL. But, Auburn, led by D stalwarts LB Bill Cody, Ts Larry Haynie and Jack Thornton, and Frederickson at DB, held at its 2YL. But on next play after change of possession, Georgia DG Joel Darden stole ball from Auburn's Bryan. HB Preston Ridlehuber smacked stiff Plainsmen line 3 times before finally making TD. Auburn never allowed access to UGa past midfield again.

MINNESOTA 14 Purdue 7: Golden Gophers (5-3) QB John Hankinson set new school season records for completions (79) and pass gains (996y) as he hit 8-15/159y, 2 TDs. Boilermakers (5-3) saw end to their Rose Bowl hopes as soph QB Bob Griese (10-22/140y, 2 INTs) had fair performance. Purdue threatened early at 33 and 28YLs but lacked finishing knack. When Minnesota DB Jerry Newsom picked off Griese and returned INT 7y to Boilers 31YL in 2nd Q, Hankinson unlimbered his arm for TD pass to tall soph HB Kenny Last. Purdue tied it in 3rd Q because Griese hit 2 passes that got away from his receivers but were called catches. With Minneapolis crowd hooting, officials decided each pass was caught and blown dead before squirting away. Boilers' 2nd of these borderline calls put them at 1YL after E Sam Longmire spurted slippery seed into EZ from 1YL on 49y catch. FB Randy Minniear scored on next play with only 20 secs left in 3rd Q. Minnesota was 73y away from EZ when sides changed for 4th Q, and Hankinson won game in 2 plays: His 30y pitch to Last, and, when Purdue ignored TE Kent Kramer in favor of Last, Kramer was wide open for winning 43y TD arrow.

NOTRE DAME 34 Michigan State 7: For 1st time in 10 years, Notre Dame (8-0) beat Spartans (4-4), and it accomplished it in all phases of game. Fighting Irish unveiled new Double-Wing-T spread that opened hole off left side for HB Nick Eddy (2 TDs) to zoom 61y to TD in 1st Q. Conv kick failed, so Irish spent rest of day trying for 2 pts and batting 2 for 4. ND FB Joe Farrell broke open in left flank for 13y TD catch from QB John Huarte (11-17/193y, TD, 2 INTs) later in 1st Q. Michigan State was behind 20-0 in 3rd Q when it forced Irish's 1st punt. Spartans traveled 77y to score, mostly on QB Steve Juday's 51y TD pass to tall E Gene Washington. ND DB Tom Carey made INT early in 4th Q, and E Jack Snow (6/114y) caught 16y pass to set up Huarte for 21y TD keeper on 4th-and-2.

Texas 28 TEXAS CHRISTIAN 13: With Arkansas slamming SMU 44-0, Texas (8-1) was blocked from trip to Cotton Bowl, but with its win accepted Orange Bowl bid instead. FB Harold Philipp (16/106y) and QB Marv Kristynik (9/100y) led 313y ground game that reaped 2 TDs from each. TCU (3-5) exhibited good O showing up with 304y, and Purple Frogs drifted in and out of contention on QB Randy Howard's 2nd and 4th Q TD runs.

STANFORD 16 Oregon State 7: Powerful ground attack (279y), led by HB Ray Handley (141y rushing) and QB Dave Lewis, propelled Stanford (4-5) to 2nd upset over top-10 team and left 6 AAWU teams with Rose Bowl shot. Margin would have been greater had Beavers (7-2) not made 2 GLSs. Tribe scored on K Braden Beck's FG after REC of punt off foot of Oregon State WB Dan Espalin placed Indians deep, and Stanford added FB Pete Middlekauff's 3rd Q plunge. OSU edged within 9-7 in 3rd Q on QB Paul Brothers' 26y TD pass to HB Bobby Grim, but Indians HB Bob Blunt countered with 24y TD run after DB Dick Ragsdale's INT of Brothers at Stanford 25YL.

WASHINGTON 22 Ucla 20: QB Larry Zeno attempted 1-man spark of upset-minded UCLA (4-5), passing 17-31/246y, TD, 3 INTs, with his pass y setting new Bruins mark at that time. Zeno twice put Bruins ahead in 2nd Q with TD run and his pass to HB Mel Farr, who fumbled into arms of Uclans E Al Witcher in EZ. T-K Jim Norton kicked invigorating 42y FG on 1st H's last play to let Huskies (5-4) slip away with 15-14 edge at mid-game recess. Power runs FB Jeff Jordan (29/142y, 2 TDs were Washington's hallmark and his 2nd TD in 3rd Q extended Huskies' lead to 22-14. After his 4th Q TD pass to E Kurt Altenberg, Zeno's attempt at tying 2-pt pass was picked off by UW G-LB Rick Redman.

AP Poll November 16

1 Notre Dame (34)	433	6 Michigan	235
2 Alabama (9)	400	7 Ohio State	185
3 Arkansas (2)	361	8 Louisiana State	132
4 Nebraska	307	9 Syracuse	95
5 Texas	246	10 Oregon	32

Others with votes: Arizona State, Auburn, Florida, Florida State, Georgia Tech, Illinois, Minnesota, Oregon State, Penn State, Princeton, Southern California, Texas Tech, Tulsa, Utah, Washington

November 21, 1964

PENN STATE 28 Pittsburgh 0: Once dismal Penn State (6-4) prospects ended with Lions' 5th straight win, preserving school's cherished 26-year streak of winning seasons. Nittany Lions FB Tom Urbanik rushed 20/107y, 2 TDs before leaving with 3rd Q injury. Into Urbanik's shoes stepped understudy FB Dave McNaughton, who climaxed 84y 4th Q drive with his own 1y TD run. Penn State DL Glenn Ressler led D that negated Pitt (3-5-2) stars: QB Fred Mazurek made only 64y in total O and HB Eric Crabtree rushed 10/10y.

NORTH CAROLINA 21 Duke 15: With Wake Forest surprising NC State 27-13, Duke (4-5-1) was in position to sneak back into ACC title. Favored North Carolina (5-5), however, took 14-3 H control on TD run by HB Ken Willard and 9y TD pass by QB Gary Black to E Bill Axselle. Duke had gotten K Mark Caldwell's 30y FG late in 1st Q after it gained field position from P Rod Stewart's 65y punt that died inches from UNC GL. Blue Devils charged to QB Scotty Glacken's 38y TD pass to E Chuck Drulis right after 2nd H KO to pull within 14-9, but UNC rebutted with HB Eddie Kesler (19/Heels-record 172y rushing) dashing 65y to set up Willard's 2nd TD of day. Glacken's 8y TD pass, which E Dave Burdette plucked from 2 defenders at GL, closed 83y scoring trip, nearly all of it on Glacken's wing, with 6:59 left. Glacken's 2-pt pass attempt ended in pile of pale blue jerseys. Kesler and Willard pounded away until all but 25 secs had expired from 4th Q clock.

South Carolina 7 CLEMSON 3: Trailing 3-0 on Clemson (3-7) K Frank Pearce's 25y FG in 1st Q, prospects looked bleak in finale of dark season for South Carolina (3-5-2) as sr QB Dan Reeves was lost to recurring ankle injury in 3rd Q FUM scramble at Tigers 7YL. Things looked worse when Gamecocks turned ball over on Marty Rosen's 4th Q HB pass that was intercepted by Tigers DB Phil Marion. Workhorse Clemson FB Pat Crain battered to Birds 3YL, but on 4th-and-inches for TD, Crain lost FUM to Carolina DT Joe Komoroski as ball bounded back out to 7YL. With Reeves' career finished, Gamecocks tapped sub QB Jim Rogers to lead winning 93y drive in 12 plays. Big play was Rogers' 45y pass to E J.R. Wilburn that carried to Clemson 15YL. Rogers soon ducked under sack attempt at 19YL, looked 2nd time for receiver, and scrambled for winning 12y TD with 3:19 to play. Clemson could have put game away earlier, but FB Bob Baldwin twice was halted on short yardage plunges off LT at 12YL early in 2nd Q and at 17YL late in 3rd Q.

WEST VIRGINIA 28 Syracuse 27: Sugar Bowl-bound Syracuse (7-3) was upset by unpredictable West Virginia (7-3), which copped its own Liberty Bowl berth. Orangemen enjoyed 21-7 H lead as TD twins HB Floyd Little (96y rushing), FB Jim Nance (163y rushing) did their act. WVU QB Allen McCune completed 8 hook passes to E Milt Clegg, including 3rd Q TD. When FB Dick Leftridge ended 65y drive with TD run early in 4th Q, Mountaineers led 22-21. After Nance put Orangemen back ahead 27-22, McCune ignored his affinity for short passes and pitched winning 50y score to E Bob Dunlevy.

Kentucky 12 TENNESSEE 7: Besieged Kentucky (5-5) coach Charlie Bradshaw could enjoy thrilling win over rival Tennessee (4-4-1), which gave Wildcats their best SEC finish in 10 years. Cats heroes were remarkable pass battery of QB Rick Norton (16-23/236y, TD) and E Rick Kestner. Norton reached into his magic hat for 13-17/213y, TD, aerial performance in 2nd H. Kestner (7/112y), pained by broken wrist and sprained ankle, made stunning 32y TD reception for 4th Q victory. Near sideline, Kestner reached behind his head at full stride for catch as Volunteers WB-DB Jackie Cotton ran side-by-side with hands in Kestner's face. Tennessee D had crafted brilliant 1st H, allowing only 8y rushing and pair of 1st downs, as DLs Steve DeLong and Joe Graham put considerable pass-rush pressure on Norton. Sack of Norton and short, wind-halted punt by HB-P Larry Seiple gave Vols chance for 54y drive in 2nd Q. It included QB Art Galiffa's 9, 14, and 9y passes and TB Hal Wantland's brilliant catch and determined 9y TD run for 7-0 lead. Norton scored on 3y sweep to pull Cats within 7-6 after he hit 3 passes on UK's 1st series of 2nd H.

FLORIDA STATE 16 Florida 7: Extending its habit of antagonizing foes with decorations on its uniforms, Florida (5-3) trotted into enemy stadium with "Go for Seven" emblazened on jersey fronts. Reference was to Gators' desire to win 7th straight without loss in young series that had taken state government to dictate in 1958. Playing with Gator Bowl bid on line, inspired Florida State (8-1-1) struck 1st after early sparring. Seminoles QB Steve Tensi (11-22/190y, TD, INT) lofted 55y TD pass in 2nd Q to WR Fred Biletnikoff (2/78y, TD), who outmaneuvered Gators DBs Allen Trammell and Dick Kirk, tenacious defenders on nation's heretofore leading pass D, to make twisting catch over his left shoulder inside 10YL. K Les Murdock's 2 FGs of 24y—after DB Howard Ehler recovered FUM on 2nd H KO—and 34y projected FSU to 13-0 lead early in 4th Q. Gators, who had failed on 1st Q chance at 1YL, finally got on

board in 4th Q when they went 76y to score. Florida HB Jack Harper caught wobbly 35y pass from QB Steve Spurrier and then, with 9 mins left, ran over from 6YL. Gators gambled unsuccessfully with on-side KO, but it allowed Tensi to throw 26y pass to set up Murdock's 40y FG with 6:48 remaining.

Michigan 10 OHIO STATE 0: Like Beach Boys' line in their popular 1964 song "Don't Worry Baby," Michigan (8-1) knew it had "been building up inside of them for, oh, they don't know how long." Actually, Wolverines did know: frustration of not beating Ohio State (7-2) stretched back to 1959. And, Michigan had thwarted Buckeyes only twice in last 10 years. Neither team's O went anywhere in early going, and Wolverines DB Rick Volk's stellar pass breakup cancelled game's 1st break: Ohio's FUM REC at Michigan 29YL. Buckeyes had 2 chances in 2nd Q as DE Tom Kiefhuss snatched FUM, but 4 plays later K Bob Funk's FG try was woefully short and hopped back out of EZ to be downed at 1YL. UM's punt out put Buckeyes at Wolverines 33YL, but Ohio went nowhere in 4 plays. In last min of 1st H, Buckeyes HB Bo Rein's FUM of Michigan P Bob Kemp's 50y punt was encircled by Wolverines E John Henderson at Ohio 20YL. Michigan WB Jim Detwiler slipped under pass-route fakes of Henderson and TE Ben Farabee for 17y TD pass from QB Bob Timberlake. K Timberlake's 27y FG after Volk's 26y punt RET came in 3rd Q and upped score to 10-0. Volk's 2 INTs in 4th Q sealed Michigan win and its 1st trip to Rose Bowl since 1950.

PURDUE 28 Indiana 22: Old Oaken Bucket turned into ice-covered pail in Lafayette's 13-degree weather. Purdue (6-3) had to overcome 7-0 and 14-7 deficits to wrestle frigid keg from its neighbor Hoosiers (2-7). Soph E Rich Ruble, spelling injured E Bob Hadrick, caught 25y pass from Boilermakers QB Bob Griese. Purdue HB Gordon Teter (31/126y, TD) scored go-ahead TD at 21-14 in 3rd Q on 3y run to cap 74y ground transit trip. FB Randy Minniear gave Boilers 28-14 edge with 4th Q TD run, his 9th of season. But, Indiana continued to scare Purdue with late score on QB Rich Bader's 2nd TD throw, 27y peg to E Bill Malinchak. Soph Hoosiers HB John Ginter then ran for 2 pts. Bader (14-27/191y, 2 TDs, INT) had enjoyed big 1st H, hitting E Ed Kalupa for 32y before running for early TD and adding 7y TD pass to FB Tom Nowatzke later in opening Q.

OKLAHOMA 17 Nebraska 7: Disappointed Oklahoma (5-3-1) got 1st big win over Nebraska (9-1) by using Huskers' power game. Despite end of its 16-game winning streak, Nebraska clinched 2nd Big 8 title in 2 years as Missouri routed Kansas 31-14. After spotting Sooners 23y FG in 2nd Q, Huskers snapped back with 56y TD pass from QB Bob Churchich (12-24/160y, TD, 3 INTs) to E Freeman White. Oklahoma assaulted nation's top run D with 24-play, 88y 4th Q TD drive on which sub FB Jon Kennedy (19/88y) was running bellweather. OU was ahead 10-7 when Sooners DE Allen Bumgardner made midfield INT, and HB Larry Brown (12/104y) burst 48y to score upset-clinching TD.

Arkansas 17 TEXAS TECH 0: Headed toward its 1st undefeated season in 55 years, Arkansas (10-0) met 0-0 resistance in 1st H from Texas Tech (6-3-1). Razorbacks were forced twice to block FGs to maintain deadlock. Managing Hogs' FG-blocking duties were LB Charles Daniel and, on 2nd effort, it was whole DL that got collective hands up. Razorbacks TB Bobby Burnett capped 65y TD drive in 3rd Q with scoring run, and E Jerry Lamb swiped EZ pass for TD from would-be Texas Tech interceptor. Raiders HB Donny Anderson rushed 21/89y, and, when jr HB nabbed his 32nd reception of season, he also tied Dave Parks' school season receiving mark, which was set in both 1962 and '63.

OREGON STATE 7 Oregon 6: Civil War swayed toward Oregon (7-2-1) early as Beavers (8-2) stumbled and fumbled. Late in 1st H, Ducks marched 95y to HB Dennis Keller's TD plunge, with key play coming on QB Bob Berry's 53y pass to E Corky Sullivan. OSU DE Al East blocked K Herm Meister's conv try. Oregon State D took control in 2nd H behind star LB Jack "Mad Dog" O'Billovich and DL Greg Hartman. With 5:43 left, Beavers used good field position to go 41y to FB Booker Washington's TD run and K Steve Clark's winning x-pt. Next, it was on to Rose Bowl for Oregon State, its 1st Pasadena trip since January 1957.

AP Poll November 23

1 Notre Dame (36)	437	6 Louisiana State	189
2 Alabama (6)	385	7 Nebraska	158
3 Arkansas (4)	345	8 Oregon State	91
4 Michigan (1)	315	9 Ohio State	84
5 Texas	247	10 Florida State	58

Others with votes: Arizona State, Auburn, Georgia Tech, Illinois, Kentucky, Oklahoma, Oregon, Penn State, Princeton, Purdue, Southern California, Syracuse, Tulsa, Utah.

November 26-28, 1964

(Th'g) ALABAMA 21 Auburn 14 (Birmingham): Making 1 big play after another, Alabama (10-0) thwarted fired-up Auburn (6-4) despite being outgained 301y to 245y. Still, Tigers held modest 7-6 lead in 2nd Q on HB Tucker Frederickson's TD. On 2nd H KO, Crimson Tide HB Ray Ogden swept 107y (100y in official NCAA stats) with 2nd H KO for game's last lead change at 14-7. Auburn battled back but were stopped at 1YL, and later Tigers lost FUM at Bama 23YL with 8 mins left. Alabama FB Steve Bowman next dashed 52y up middle, and QB Joe Namath registered 21-7 lead with 23y TD pass to E Ray Perkins, future pro coach. Auburn narrowed it with 1:10 to go as Jimmy Sidle, switched from QB to HB in mid-year to protect his bad shoulder, caught 16y TD pass from QB Tom Bryan.

(Th'g) TEXAS 26 Texas A&M 7: Texas (9-1) won game somewhat easily, but revved-up Aggies (1-9) fans won yelling contest as described by writer Roy Edwards in *Dallas Morning News:* "Texas quarterback Marvin Kristynik stepped away from the ball a dozen times the better to appreciate the steady roar from the Aggie student section in the south portion of the east stands." Longhorns' presumably quiet but highly rambunctious D completely shut down Texas A&M to tune of 5y in 2nd H. This came on heels of Aggies having pounded their way for 88y in 18 plays in last half-min of 2nd Q.

Long drive had resulted in FB Joe Weiss' 2y TD plunge that tied it 7-7. Texas D, led by LB Tommy Nobis, Ts Olen Underwood and Frank Bedrick, and E Knox Nunnally, forced safety on bad punt snap and got quick FG by K David Conway for 12-7 edge after HB Phil Harris returned free kick to A&M 45YL. Steers sub TB Hix Green tore 24y to set up his own 2y TD sweep with 2:24 to play. Longhorns got ball back with 26 secs left, and thanks to malfunctioning clock and use of timeouts, QB Jim Hudson was allowed to throw TD pass to unknown E Garry Brown. Irritated at their rivals piling up score, Aggies started scuffle.

BOSTON COLLEGE 10 Holy Cross 8: Well-liked Holy Cross coach Dr. Eddie Anderson nearly earned his 202nd career win in his last game. His record of 201-128-15 (.6061) in 39 seasons left him behind only Pop Warner, Amos Alonzo Stagg, and Jess Neely in wins at close of 1964 season. Holy Cross (5-5) went 86y 1st time it had ball. Crusaders soph QB Jack Lentz accounted for 59y, hitting E Dick Kochansky with 21y pass and running 17y on option to set FB Pete Meehan for TD and 6-0 lead. BC got FG from K Marty DeMezza, but gave back safety on bad punt snap. Down 8-3, Eagles QB Ed Foley hit 3 quick aerials for 46y on 4th Q march which ended in E Jim Whalen's 15y TD catch. After late INT, Crusaders unsuccessfully menaced their way to BC 14YL.

ARMY 11 Navy 8: Black Knights of Hudson and Crabtown warriors each had endured injury-ruined season, although Navy (3-6-1) QB Roger Staubach was again fit, coming off his 308y O performance vs. Duke fortnight earlier. Also at peak form again was Army (4-6) QB Rollie Stichweh, ready for measure of revenge over Staubach as rival academy gladiators closed their college careers. In 1st min of game, Cadets DG Sonny Stowers threw Staubach for safety, and Stowers would key fierce, day-long pass-rush that left Staubach with -22y rushing. Army gained 215y on ground as it counted on TB John Seymour's 101y. Cadets went up 8-0 on Stichweh's 5y TD pass to E Sam Champi in 2nd Q. Despite Army's dominance of opening 20 mins, Staubach led 60y march before H which tied it 8-8 as HB Tom Leister carried ball over after FB Pat Donnelly made 4 1st downs. As 2nd H wore on, Stichweh countered with 77y drive that carried into 4th Q on which he sprinted 17y and lofted 33y pass to Champi. Cadets soph E-K Barry Nickerson booted winning 20y FG, and Cadets D took over from there.

GEORGIA 7 Georgia Tech 0: Soggy punting duel between P Mack Faircloth (9/41y avg) of Georgia (6-3-1) and P Jerry Priestley (7/39y avg) of Georgia Tech (7-3) punctuated 1st H which ended with Bulldogs E Pat Hodgson making 36y catch at Tech 6YL. Could slumping Jackets, loser of 2 straight games, be unable to accomplish more than 0-0 tie? Game's big break came late in 3rd Q: Engineers FB Jeff Davis lost FUM at own 22YL where it was collared by Bulldogs DL John Glass. UGa QB Preston Ridlehuber pitched 17y to FB Leon Armbrester at 5YL, then scored 2 plays later as he followed blocker Armbrester into hole and across GL. Amazingly, Georgia finally had its 1st lead over Georgia Tech in 4 years. In game's dying moments, Georgia Tech rose up with TD potential, but DB Faircloth made TD-saving stop at UGa 34YL of Yellow Jackets HB Jerry Jackson's 39y punt RET.

BAYLOR 27 Rice 20: Only 3rd place in Southwest Conf was at stake, but Baylor (5-5) and Rice (4-5-1) waged thrilling tussle for that honor. Bears got off to 6-0 start thanks to familiar battery of QB Terry Southall (14-28/69y, TD, INT) and WR Lawrence Elkins, good for 8y TD. Despite having gained only 37y all season, Owls FB Russell Wayt burst for 52y TD in latter part of 1st Q. Rice QB Walter McReynolds (3-11/67y, INT) wedged over for 2nd Q TD. After Baylor stopped foolish 4th down run by Owls at their 38YL, FB Tom Davies scored before H. When 2-pt run failed, Bruins still trailed 14-12. With Rice ahead 20-12 in 4th Q after McReynolds' 2nd TD, Baylor air game came alive. Big break arrived on Owls HB David Ferguson's punt FUM at Rice 37YL. Southall's pass to E Ken Hodge set up Davies' 1y TD push, and Elkins caught 2-pt pass to tie it 20-20. Bears DE Willie Walker's FUM REC positioned Hodge for 1-handed grab of Southall's 27y TD. Despite close coverage, Elkins would nab 4/28y by game's end, and it would give him new NCAA 2-year record of 120 catches.

ARIZONA 30 Arizona State 6: Fierce Wildcats D, led by LB Tom Malloy (2 INTs), upset Arizona State (8-2) and gave Arizona (6-3-1) 3-way share of WAC crown with New Mexico and idle Utah. Clutch Wildcats HB Floyd Hudlow (7/90y, 2 TDs) raced 58 and 7y for 2nd H scores as 7 TOs positioned Arizona for 4 TDs. Sun Devils QB John Torok (25-47/394y, TD) rifled 1y TD to E Jerry Smith late in 3rd Q, but suffered 6 INTs. Malloy had gotten UA rolling with 45y INT RET to set up HB Jim Oliver for short TD run and 8-0 lead in 2nd Q. Sun Devils HB Jesse Fleming fumbled screen pass late in 2nd Q, and DB Tom Phillips recovered at 18YL to launch QB Lou White to TD run and 15-0 H edge. Ahead 15-6, Arizona DB Rickie Harris made INT. It set up Hudlow for his 58y run for insurmountable 21-6 lead in 3rd Q. K Malloy ended scoring with 31y FG in 4th Q.

NEW MEXICO 9 Kansas State 7: G-K Jack Abendschan booted New Mexico (9-2) into hard fought win over Wildcats (3-7) with 3 FGs. Lobos' 1st Q drive stalled at Kansas State 7YL, and Abendschan's 24y FG provided 3-0 lead. Abendschan added 22y boot in 2nd Q when 2 runs from K-State 6YL failed and 3rd down pass by QB Stan Quintana (5-14/89y) fell harmlessly in EZ. Abendschan set new WAC distance record with 50y FG with 14 secs remaining before H. Wildcats weren't beaten yet and pulled within 9-7 on 14-play, 67y march in 3rd Q. K-State QB Ed Danieley ran beautiful option plays and used pitchouts to HBs Jerry Condit and John Christiansen on drive until he dashed 6y to score.

SOUTHERN CALIFORNIA 20 Notre Dame 17: Searching for its 1st undefeated season since 1949, no. 1 Notre Dame (9-1) smoothly erected 17-0 H lead on 25y FG by K Ken Iman, 21y TD pass to E Jack Snow from QB John Huarte (18-29/272y, TD, 2 INTs), and 5y TD run by HB Bill Wolski after Irish D smartly stopped USC at ND 15 and 28YLs. At H intermission, coach John McKay told Trojans (7-3) to "keep playing your game, you'll score." Score Troy did. After 2nd H KO, stubby TB Mike Garrett finished 11-play drive with 1y TD run. Forgotten, but critical series came in 3rd Q as Southern California halted Fighting Irish drive with DL John Lockwood's FUM REC at Troy 9YL. Soon, however, ND nearly put verdict away, but holding PEN near Trojans GL nullified

its TD early in 4th Q. Huarte missed 2 passes from 15YL to help ruin that threat. USC QB Craig Fertig (15-23/225y, 2 TDs) soon fired 23y TD to swift E Fred Hill (4/88y, TD) to trim margin to 17-13. With 2:10 to play, Trojans started drive at Irish 40YL. Fertig hit Hill for 23y to ND 17YL, but 4th down soon arrived after Hill's diving catch in EZ was ruled OB. Fertig found HB Rod Sherman cutting to post to out-leap DB Tony Carey for winning TD with 1:35 to play. Notre Dame coach Ara Parseghian, his team's dramatic turnaround to undefeated season so close at hand, hid his face behind arms he threw around his head in bitter anguish.

Final AP Poll November 30

1 Alabama (34.5)	515.5	6 Nebraska	235
2 Arkansas (11.5)	486.5	7 Louisiana State	202
3 Notre Dame (6)	442	8 Oregon State	133
4 Michigan (3)	400	9 Ohio State	97
5 Texas	322	10 Southern California	63

Others with votes: Auburn, Florida State, Georgia, Georgia Tech, Illinois, Oklahoma, Oregon, Princeton, Penn State, Syracuse, Tulsa, Utah, Washington

December 5, 1964

Florida 20 LOUISIANA STATE 6: Postponed from October 3 by Hurricane Hilda, game caught LSU (7-2-1) in pre-Sugar Bowl stumble. Florida (7-3) had not scored on Tigers since 1960, but forced 5 TOs to buoy its assault. On bitter cold night in Bayou, Gators decided to start sr QB Tom Shannon in favor of effective soph QB Steve Spurrier, who had mild ankle sprain. Gators struck 1st on methodical 80y drive, mostly on clever option runs by Shannon. March was finished by Florida FB Graham McKeel's short TD plunge, set up by Shannon's jump pass to E Charles Casey to 2YL. LSU E-K Doug Moreau booted 1st of his FGs of 25 and 32y. Next, Florida QB Spurrier came off bench to hit HB Jack Harper with TD pass in 2nd Q. Harper cinched it at 20-6 on 20y TD catch from HB Allen Trammell on fake-FG in 3rd Q. Years later, Gators HB Larry Dupree told author Peter Golenbock in *Go Gators!,* "We made the Sugar Bowl committee look very bad." Of small consolation to Bengals, who wound up 5th in SEC, were stat titles for FB Don Schwab (19/136y), who came from 4th place to overtake Kentucky's Rodger Bird for SEC rushing crown, and Moreau, whose 73 pts gave him 2 more than Alabama's David Ray.

Mississippi State 20 MISSISSIPPI 17: Chilly day saw Mississippi State (4-6) end 18 years of disappointment by beating favored Ole Miss (5-4-1). G-K Justin Canale was Bulldogs scoring ace, nailing 48y FG as 2nd Q expired for 6-3 H edge. Maroons led 13-3 well into 4th Q after swift HB Marcus Rhoden scored on 15y pass catch on last play of 3rd Q. Ole Miss QB Jim Weatherly (8-19/94y, 2 INTs), idled since H with bruised ribs, drove Rebs with 11y pass and 15y sweep until hard tackle by State C-LB Pat Watson sent him back to sideline. Sub QB Jimmy Heidel took over in time for 10y TD swing pass to TB Mike Dennis with 5:38 to go. Trailing 13-10, Ole Miss forced punt, but Heidel was stymied by MSU DT Grady Bolton's 15y sack. Banged-up Weatherly returned, but threw INT to Miss State HB-DB Dan Bland, who provided game's crucial play: 37y INT RET to Ole Miss 6YL. FB Hoyle Granger battered over for TD and 20-10 lead for Bulldogs. Slender Rebels WB Doug Cunningham gave home folks late thrill with 80y KO TD RET, however it was not enough.

1964 Conference Standings

Ivy League

Princeton	7-0
Harvard	5-2
Yale	4-2-1
Dartmouth	4-3
Cornell	3-4
Brown	3-4
Columbia	1-5-1
Pennsylvania	0-7

Atlantic Coast

North Carolina State	5-2
Duke	3-2-1
North Carolina	4-3
Wake Forest	4-3
Maryland	4-3
South Carolina	2-3-1
Clemson	2-4
Virginia	1-5

Southern

West Virginia	5-0
Virginia Tech	3-1
George Washington	3-2
William & Mary	4-3
Citadel	4-3
Richmond	2-4
Davidson	1-3
Virginia Military	1-4
Furman	1-4

Southeastern

Alabama	8-0
Florida	4-2
Kentucky	4-2
Georgia (a)	4-2
Louisiana State	4-2-1
Auburn	3-3
Mississippi	2-4-1
Mississippi State	2-5
Vanderbilt	1-4-1
Tulane (b)	1-5
Tennessee	1-5-1

(a) Win vs. Clemson counted in SEC
(b) Loss vs. Miami counted in SEC

Big Ten

Michigan	6-1
Ohio State	5-1
Purdue	5-2
Illinois	4-3
Minnesota	4-3
Michigan State	3-3
Wisconsin	2-5
Northwestern	2-5
Iowa	1-5
Indiana	1-5

Mid-American

Bowling Green	5-1
Miami (Ohio)	4-2
Marshall	4-2
Ohio University	3-2-1
Western Michigan	2-4
Kent State	1-4-1
Toledo	1-5

Big Eight

Nebraska	6-1
Oklahoma	5-1-1
Kansas	5-2
Missouri	4-2-1
Oklahoma State	3-4
Kansas State	3-4
Colorado	1-6
Iowa State	0-7

Southwest

Arkansas	7-0
Texas	6-1
Baylor	4-3
Rice	3-3-1
Texas Tech	3-3-1
Texas Christian	3-4
Texas A&M	1-6
Southern Methodist	0-7

AAWU

Oregon State	3-1
Southern California	3-1
Washington	5-2
UCLA	2-2
Stanford	3-4
Oregon	1-2-1
Washington State	1-2-1
California	0-4

Missouri Valley

Cincinnati (a)	4-0
Tulsa	3-1
Wichita State	2-2
North Texas State	1-3
Louisville (b)	0-4

(a) Win vs. North Texas State counted twice
(b) Loss vs. North Texas State counted twice

Western Athletic

Utah	3-1
New Mexico	3-1
Arizona	3-1
Wyoming	2-2
Arizona State	0-2
Brigham Young	0-4

1964 Bowl Games

Liberty Bowl (Dec. 19): Utah 32 West Virginia 6

For those who think Houston's Astrodome hosted 1st indoor bowl game, think again. Hard-packed grass field inside Atlantic City's Convention Hall served as site for Utah (9-2) romp over West Virginia (7-4), 1 of several games during college football history played in indoor temporary sites. Utes E Roy Jefferson separated his shoulder in 2nd Q, but he toughed it out and caught passes for 46y. Utah jumped to 25-0 lead on K Jefferson's 2 FGs, QB Pokey Allen's 11y TD run behind block of FB Allen Jacobs, and long distance dashes by HBs Ron Coleman and Andy Ireland. Outdistanced 466y to 228y, Mountaineers enjoyed measure of brief glory in 3rd Q when QB Allen McCune capped 67y drive with 6y TD pass to E Milt Clegg.

Bluebonnet Bowl (Dec. 19): Tulsa 14 Mississippi 7

QB Jerry Rhome, season-long aerial ace for Tulsa (9-2), was busy ball-handler, participating in 58 O plays. Mississippi (5-5-1) scored 1st, going 54y after 2nd Q punt. Key gain was QB Jim Weatherly's 30y pass to FB Frank Kinard. TB Mike Dennis then ran twice for 10y, and Weatherly sneaked over for Rebels. Not normally considered much of runner, Rhome lugged it 25y in middle of 72y 2nd Q TD march, then wedged over from 1y to tie game at 7-7. DL Willie Townes wrecked havoc in Ole Miss backfield rest of drizzly afternoon in Houston, and Tulsa softened Rebs' D with runs of TB Bob Daugherty. Winning Tulsa TD came in 4 quick surges: Rhome ran for 14y, found HB Brent Roberts for 10y, Daugherty for 35y, and E Eddie Fletcher for 35y TD.

Sun Bowl (Dec. 26): Georgia 7 Texas Tech 0

Texas Tech (6-4-1), featuring A-A HB Donny Anderson, supplied Sun Bowl with traditional Texas-based host team vs. underrated Georgia (7-3-1) which closed with 4 wins in last 5 regular season games. Story of game was Bulldogs D, spearheaded by G Joel Darden, as it limited Anderson to 7/19y rushing and prevented any 1st downs—except 1 earned on 15y PEN—until well into 4th Q. Contest's only score came as result of 52y swing pass from Georgia QB Preston Ridlehuber to HB Fred Barber, who dashed to 6YL before pulling his hamstring. FB Frank Lankewicz slammed over 3 plays later. Red Raiders drove to Georgia 17YL in 4th Q, but lost ball on downs. They immediately grabbed FUM REC, but QB Tom Wilson's pass was intercepted by Georgia DL Vance Evans.

Sugar Bowl: Louisiana State 13 Syracuse 10

Every kind of scoring was realized in odd D-oriented game. Although stomping runs of FB Jim Nance, HB Floyd Little, and QB-turned-HB Walley Mahle provided early spark for Syracuse (7-4), its secondary weakness ultimately proved fatal. Orangemen scored early on K Roger Smith's 22y FG. Moments later, LSU (8-2-1) shaved it to 3-2 as P Gerald Brown's punt was downed at 2YL, and Little was caught in EZ on sweep by Tigers fast-prowling DT George Rice. Syracuse went up 10-2 when DL Dennis Reilly slammed Bengals P Brown before latter could get his kick away: Orange DL Brad Clarke snared loose ball and ran untouched for 28y TD. Although LSU receivers were frequently open, it took until 3rd Q for QB Billy Ezell to hit WR Doug Moreau for 57y TD bomb. Ezell's 2-pt pass to HB Joe Labruzzo tied it at 10-10. Labruzzo broke away for 35y on catch of QB Pat Screen's pass in 4th Q. Syracuse D held at its 11YL, but MVP K Moreau booted game-winning 28y FG.

Cotton Bowl: Arkansas 10 Nebraska 7

Arkansas (11-0) fulfilled its greatest undefeated hope, matching its lightning-quick D strength with mammoths of Nebraska (9-2) in evenly-played contest. Hogs scored in 1st Q on K Tom McKnelly's 31y FG. Cornhuskers blended power runs of HB Harry "Little Horse" Wilson with darting draw runs of little FB Frank Solich and short passes of QB Bob Churchich. Wilson (84y rushing) set up own 1y TD run in 2nd Q with 36y catch and 10y run. Wilson dashed 45y in 4th Q, but it was then in their own territory

that Razorback D stars, LB Ronnie Caveness and Ts Jim Williams and Loyd Phillips, made their stand. So, Nebraska protected its tenuous 7-3 lead by punting into EZ. Arkansas QB Fred Marshall (11-19/131y, INT), loser of 2 earlier FUMs and pressured throughout gloomy day in Dallas, completed passes of 12, 11, 10, and 28y, and added twisting 10y scramble to Huskers 33YL. He then hit WB Jim Lindsay for 28y to 5YL, allowing TB Bobby Burnett to score game-winning TD from 3y with 4:41 left. Arkansas earned a share of the national tile.

Rose Bowl: Michigan 34 Oregon State 7

After flap over AAWU snubbing Southern California had died down, Oregon State (8-3) attempted to get down to business as 2-TD underdog against efficient Big 10 champion Michigan (9-1), losers only by single point to Purdue. Beavers struck early in 2nd Q after unusual bit of strategy. Oregon State coach Tommy Prothro, who employed usual practice of calling his plays from press box, sent E-P Len Frketich back to punt on 2nd down from his 18YL. Wolverines were tabbed with 15y PEN, so Beavers turned from conservatives to attackers, going 84y in 10 plays as QB Paul Brothers (9-17/89y, TD) completed 6 passes in row. Brothers' last completion went to E Doug McDougal for 5y TD and 7-0 lead 2:27 into 2nd Q. Midway in 2nd Q, Michigan FB Mel Anthony (13/123y, 3 TDs) swung around his RE, got key blocks from HB Carl Ward and E John Henderson, and charged unmolested for 84y TD, longest to-date in Rose Bowl history. HB Ward raced 43y to another Wolverines TD before end of 2nd Q, but Beavers managed to hold H score within reason at 12-7. Wolverines D, led by DLs Bill Yearby and Bill Laskey, completely shut down Oregon State in 2nd H. Beavers gained but 64y rushing all day. Big play of 2nd H came in middle of 3rd Q from Michigan sub G Bob Mielke, who blocked punt by OSU P Frketich (9/43.6y avg), and Anthony recovered at 15YL. Anthony drove for 1y TD 5 plays later and added 7y score later in 3rd Q for 27-7 Michigan lead.

GAME OF THE YEAR
Orange Bowl: Texas 21 Alabama 17

Extra excitement was in air as Orange Bowl launched new TV era with prime-time night game. It turned out to be true thriller. With his pen poised to sign fabulously lucrative New York Jets contract next day, Alabama (10-1) QB Joe Namath shrugged off gimpy knee and several dropped passes to stage dramatic passing display (18-37/255y, 2 TDs) which earned MVP honors in relief role of QB Steve Sloan. Despite his colossal effort, Namath's Crimson Tide fell just short of victory, and some people thought they were robbed. Throwing early haymakers, Texas (10-1) did all its damage in 1st H. TB Ernie Koy made masterful 79y TD run in 1st Q, using G Lee Hensley's midway block to set Orange Bowl long distance run record to that point in history. Crimson Tide cashed starting QB Sloan's 41y pass to HB Ray Ogden to move 64y to 7YL, but they missed short FG. Longhorns struck again as QB Jim Hudson and E George Sauer (Both would become future New York Jet teammates of Namath) connected on 69y TD pass. With score at 14-0 in favor of Texas, Namath came off bench in his unique white shoes to become "by far the most vivid figure in the stadium," according to Allison Danzig of *The New York Times*. Namath completed 6 passes/81y on 87y drive, dotting it with 7y TD to HB Wayne Trimble. Texas got its next score thanks to lucky break. Alabama blocked Longhorns FG try but turned possession right back to Texas in its frenzied desire to advance ball. Steers E Pete Lammons, another future Jet, recovered at Bama 38YL, and Texas had new set of downs. After Tide PEN moved ball to 13YL, Koy blasted for TD in 2 plays with only :27 showing on 1st H clock. Texas never crossed midfield in 2nd H, relying on P Koy's booming punts to stay out of trouble. Namath took center stage, moving Alabama 63y to E Ray Perkins' 20y TD catch. Early in 4th Q, Bama HB-K David Ray toed 26y FG to narrow deficit to 21-17. LB Jim Fuller's INT at Texas 34YL gave Tide big chance for win, and Namath quickly pitched them to 3YL. FB Steve Bowman's 2 smashes left Tide just short of EZ, and Namath tried 4th down sneak, only to be halted inches short by G Tommy Currie's submarine and LB Tommy Nobis' hole-filling tackle. "I'll go to my grave knowing I scored a touchdown on that play," Namath later said. NBC's prime time telecast attracted 40 million viewers and changed course of TV sports. It became acceptable for football to fill 8-12 hours of programming, the game becoming especially appealing to advertisers wishing to reach larger nighttime audiences. Before long, ABC would launch NFL Monday Night Football, Super Bowl would be scheduled for early evening in Eastern time zone, and Major League Baseball eventually would play all its World Series and league championship games in TV's prime-time. Yet, it took college football's prime-time thriller to start it all.

Gator Bowl (Jan. 2): Florida State 36 Oklahoma 19

In a way, game was over before it started for Oklahoma (6-4-1) as 4 key O players were ruled ineligible for having signed undated pro contracts: T Ralph Neely, HB Lance Rentzel, FB Jim Grisham, and sub E Wes Skidgel. This was symptomatic of escalating NFL-AFL bidding wars. NFL commissioner Pete Rozell promised investigation, but this early signing problem never really evaporated until common draft was instituted after pro football's two leagues agreed to merge in 1966. Sooners D was intact, but Florida State (9-1-1) QB Steve Tensi quickly tended to its dissection. Although Tensi suffered 1st of his 4 INTs on his opening attempt, tall Seminole QB passed 23-36/303y, 5 TDs. Tensi's aerial mate, WR Fred Biletnikoff, caught 13/192y, 4 TDs. Game was close in 1st Q: Seminoles DB Howard Ehler steamed 69y with INT TD RET, and Oklahoma FB Jon Kennedy plunged over to cut FSU's lead to 7-6. Despite Seminoles' aerial heroics, longest pass belonged to Sooners combination of sub QB Bernie Fletcher and E Ben Hart who collaborated on 95y TD in 4th Q. Game began with pro signings and ended same way: Biletnikoff, soon to launch terrific pro career, was inked by Al Davis of Oakland Raiders under goalposts at game's conclusion.

1964 Top Performance Formula

1	Arkansas	1.7149
2	Alabama	1.6937
3	Michigan	1.6353
4	Florida State	1.6145
5	Notre Dame	1.6100
6	Texas	1.5743
7	Nebraska	1.4123
8	Arizona State	1.3833
9	Florida	1.3777
10	Ohio State	1.3556
11	Syracuse	1.3387
12	Louisiana State	1.3376
13	Oregon	1.3241
14	Georgia	1.2967
15	Southern California	1.2770
16	Oregon State	1.2759
17	Purdue	1.2712
18	Illinois	1.2601
19	Georgia Tech	1.2529
20	Arizona	1.2265

1964 Top Opponent Records

1	Alabama	.6373
2	Auburn	.6278
3	Georgia	.6176
4	Air Force	.6167
5	Syracuse	.6050
6	California	.6011
7	Florida	.5947
8	Iowa	.5921
9	Michigan State	.5921
10	Florida State	.5909
11	Tennessee	.5891
12	Northwestern	.5855
13	Kentucky	.5851
14	Michigan	.5833
15	Mississippi State	.5815
16	Purdue	.5800
17	Oklahoma	.5784
18	UCLA	.5722
19	Stanford	.5659
20	North Carolina State	.5652

1964 Out-of-Conference Records

	W-L	Percentage	Bowl W-L
Western Athletic	30-6-4	.8000	1-0
Southeastern	25-15-1	.6220	2-2
Big Ten	15-10	.6000	1-0
AAWU	25-18	.5814	0-1
Southwest	14-12	.5385	2-1
Big Eight	8-15-1	.3642	0-2
Atlantic Coast	10-17-1	.3750	0-0

1964 Individual Statistical Leaders

RUSHING YARDS	Attempts	Yards	Avg.
Brian Piccolo, Wake Forest	252	1044	4.1
Jim Grabowski, Illinois	186	1004	5.4
Al Nelson, Cincinnati	201	973	4.8
Donny Anderson, Texas Tech	211	966	4.6
Jim Nance, Syracuse	190	951	5.0
Mike Garrett, Southern California	217	948	4.4
Ray Handley, Stanford	197	936	4.8
Cosmo Iacavazzi, Princeton	172	909	5.3
Bo Hickey, Maryland	182	894	4.9
Ken Willard, North Carolina	228	835	3.7

PASSING YARDS	Completions	Attempts	Yards	Pct.
Jerry Rhome, Tulsa	224	326	2870	68.7
John Torok, Arizona State	139	251	2356	55.4
Craig Morton, California	185	308	2121	60.1
John Huarte, Notre Dame	114	205	2062	55.6
Gary Snook, Iowa	151	311	2062	48.6
Steve Tensi, Florida State	121	204	1681	59.3
Craig Fertig, Southern California	109	209	1671	52.1
Terry Southall, Baylor	118	225	1623	52.4
Rich Badar, Indiana	121	245	1571	49.4
Rick Norton, Kentucky	106	202	1514	52.5

RECEIVING YARDS	Catches	Yards
Howard Twilley, Tulsa	95	1178
Jack Snow, Notre Dame	60	1114
Fred Biletnikoff, Florida State	57	987
Karl Noonan, Iowa	59	933
Larry Elkins, Baylor	50	851
Ben Hawkins, Arizona State	42	719
Charles Casey, Florida	47	673
Rick Kestner, Kentucky	42	639
Bill Malinchak, Indiana	46	634
Jack Schraub, California	52	633

.1964 Consensus All-America

End: Jack Snow, Notre Dame
            Fred Biletnikoff, Florida State
Tackle: Larry Kramer, Nebraska
            Ralph Neely, Oklahoma
Guard: Rick Redman, Washington=
            Glenn Ressler, Penn State
Center: Dick Butkus, Illinois
Backs: John Huarte, Notre Dame
            Gale Sayers, Kansas
            Lawrence Elkins, Baylor
            Tucker Frederickson, Auburn

Other All-America Choices

End: Harold Wells, Purdue
            Allen Brown, Mississippi
            Alphonse Dotson, Grambling
            Al Atkinson, Villanova
            Ray Rissmiller, Georgia
Tackle: Steve DeLong, Tennessee
            Jim Wilson, Georgia
            Bill Yearby, Michigan
            Dan Kearley, Alabama
            John Van Sicklen, Iowa State
            Remi Prudhomme, Louisiana State
            Stas Maliszewski, Princeton
            Jim Davidson, Ohio State
            Harry Schuh, Memphis State
Guard: Tommy Nobis, Texas
            Ronnie Caveness, Arkansas
            Bill Fisk, Southern California
            Wayne Freeman, Alabama
            Carl McAdams, Oklahoma
            Jack O'Billovich, Oregon State
            Don Croftcheck, Indiana
            Jim Carroll, Notre Dame
Center: Dwight Kelley, Ohio State
            Pat Killorin, Syracuse
            Malcolm Walker, Rice
Backs: Jerry Rhome, Tulsa
            Craig Morton, California
            Jim Grabowski, Illinois
            Clarence Williams, Washington State
            Donny Anderson, Texas Tech
            Cosmo Iacavazzi, Princeton
            Bob Berry, Oregon
            Larry Dupree, Florida
            Tom Nowatzke, Indiana
            Floyd Little, Syracuse
            Bob Schweikert, Virginia Tech
            Bob Timberlake, Michigan
            Arnold Chonko, Ohio State
            Karl Noonan, Iowa
            Mike Garrett, Southern California
            Roy Jefferson, Utah
            George Donnelly, Illinois
            Gerry Bussell, Georgia Tech

1964 Heisman Trophy Vote

John Huarte, senior quarterback, Notre Dame   1026
Jerry Rhome, senior quarterback, Tulsa   952
Dick Butkus, senior center-linebacker, Illinois   505
Bob Timberlake, senior quarterback, Michigan   361
Jack Snow, senior end, Notre Dame   187

Other Major Award Winners

Maxwell (Player)   Glenn Ressler, senior guard, Penn State
Outland (Lineman)   Steve DeLong, senior guard, Tennessee
Knute Rockne (Lineman)   Dick Butkus, senior center-linebacker, Illinois
Walter Camp (Back)   Jerry Rhome, senior quarterback, Tulsa
AFCA Coaches of the Year Frank Broyles, Arkansas
                            and Ara Parseghian, Notre Dame

1965

The Year of Freedom of Substitution, After-Bowl Polls, and High Tide Timing

Free at last, free at last, football coaches were free at last. The biggest change in college football in 1965 was the enactment of free substitution by the rules committee. In 1964, partial measures permitted offensive and defensive platoons to be employed by many coaches, but the clock had to be stopped to substitute freely. It created what Ohio State coach Woody Hayes called "the damndest burlesque I ever saw in my life."

In 1965, two substitutes were allowed with the clock running. Whole units were allowed when the clock was stopped. *And since the clock now stopped* on every change of possession, in effect, free substitution had returned for the first time since 1952. Although there were some, like NCAA Rules Committee secretary Dave Nelson of Delaware, who mourned the end of the two-way player, he expressed relief in his posthumous 1994 book, *Anatomy of a Game*, that the issue finally was settled for good: "… once the trend toward unlimited (substitution) was established, the Rules Committee should have made the 1965 change several years earlier and gotten on with the game and forgotten the annual delaying actions (that created partial and gradual liberalization)."

College football now could mirror the look of fast-paced pro football. For the sake of the continued popularity of college football, the change went a long way to freshen up the college game. One of the hallmarks of college football always has been a willingness by the game's architects to tinker to make it better. No other sport's conceptual approach retains such flexibility. College football made a bold move to improve itself and has never looked back.

In 1964, Oklahoma coach Gomer Jones had a novel way—part of Hayes' "damndest burlesque," no doubt—of preparing his defense. If a third down clock-sustaining play failed to gain ample yardage for a first down, Jones' offense went into punt formation. The poor sap playing on the receiving team's line opposite beefy All-America tackle Ralph Neely would look in for the punt snap while the Sooners center crouched motionless. Neely would blast off the ball, practically taking the opposite lineman's head off, and, strategically, draw a penalty flag to stop the clock. A new unit would trot onto the field to kick the ball away and play defense. That travesty ended in 1965, and, for better or worse, the college game now mimicked the professionals with 22 starters manning two separate units.

Another huge change in 1965 was the Associated Press' acknowledgement that its final poll needed to be staged after the results were in from New Year's Day bowl games. Along with hype attended a year later to the 1966 Michigan State-Notre Dame "Game of the Century," this move made the chase for no. 1 a far greater focus for the nation's top clubs than it ever had been before. Teams that had won previous national titles certainly were rightfully proud, but prior to this time the idea of playing under an all-or-nothing mentality had been overshadowed by strong focus on winning conference championships and being considered the best team in a given region.

Although the AP Poll process now would be identical to what today's fan knows—except that only 10 teams were ranked in 1965—the mindset of the voter followed different logic. For example, Nebraska (10-1) started as 1965 preseason no. 1 but was supplanted by Notre Dame (7-2-1) after the first week for no reason that would be apparent to today's fans. Voters made an odd decision that week. The Fighting Irish routed California (5-5), while Nebraska easily beat Texas Christian (6-4). Both Cal and TCU were considered mediocre, rated no higher than midway in their respective conferences. So, it was unusual that the Cornhuskers slipped behind the Fighting Irish when each beat common-folk.

Notre Dame was soon beaten by Purdue (7-2-1), allowing Texas (6-4) and then Arkansas (10-1) to ride the top spot until the massive Spartans of Michigan State (10-1) took over no. 1 from October 25 to the end of the regular season. When UCLA (8-2-1) stunned Michigan State 14-12 in the Rose Bowl and Alabama (9-1-1) outscored Nebraska 39-28 in the Orange Bowl, the Crimson Tide won the post-bowl AP national championship. Bear Bryant might have been the best coach in the country, but he was also one of the luckiest as his timing turned out to be impeccable. He had captured the previous season's AP title because Alabama's Orange Bowl loss to Texas came after the last poll. In 1965, his Crimson Tide team again won the national championship when bowl losses eliminated Michigan State and Arkansas, teams with better records. Regardless, Bryant joined Minnesota's Bernie Bierman (1940-41), Army's Earl Blaik (1944-45), Notre Dame's Frank Leahy (1946-47) and Oklahoma's Bud Wilkinson (1955-56)

as the only coaches, at that point in history, to win AP national titles in consecutive seasons.

Alabama showed that football truly was a team game. When star quarterback Joe Namath had signed for an enormous bonus with the New York Jets back in January 1965, he took on a mythical superstar status. So, a lot of people felt the Crimson Tide might slip badly without Namath. Instead, the Alabama defense, led by end Gilmer Creed, tackle Jim Fuller, linebacker Jackie Sherrill, and back Bobby Johns, permitted only 79 points in 10 regular season games. Quarterback Steve Sloan, a future head coach, proved to be more than an adequate replacement for Namath throwing 10 touchdown passes and running for six scores.

UCLA visited East Lansing to meet Michigan State for the season opener, and prized but nervous sophomore quarterback Gary Beban was making his first start for the Bruins. Beban noted the immense size of the Spartans during pre-game warmups even before they put on pads. Beban kept wondering: "Is this *college* football?" Michigan State won 13-3 that day, but, three and a half months later, Beban and defensive back Bob Stiles sparked the Bruins to one of the greatest upsets in Rose Bowl history over the Spartans, a team some experts felt was one of the greatest ever.

When Michigan State fell to UCLA, no. 2 Arkansas (10-1) not Alabama, was in best position to swoop in to nab a second straight national championship. Arkansas and Alabama had split the writers and coaches polls in 1964. But playing in the Cotton Bowl earlier on New Year's Day than Michigan State in the late afternoon Rose Bowl and Alabama in the nighttime Orange Bowl, the Razorbacks, the only undefeated team in the regular season besides the Spartans, bungled their chance. Arkansas fell 14-7 to previously turnover-prone Louisiana State (8-3), which ended the Razorbacks' 22-game winning streak. It didn't help Arkansas to lose star quarterback Jon Brittenum to injury for a large portion of the Cotton Bowl.

Far from the madding crowd of teams hungry for bowls and no. 1 ratings was Dartmouth (9-0), the third Ivy League champions of coach Bob Blackman in four years. The Big Green, perhaps the conference's greatest team since becoming official in 1956, overcame an early-season penchant for fumbling center-quarterback exchanges to romp undefeated. The Ivies also saw the debut in 1965 of Yale coach Carmen Cozza, who would remain as head of the Bulldogs football program through 1996.

Milestones

■ NCAA Rules Committee mandated clock stoppages for change of possession, thus liberalized substitution rules to allow virtually free movement of players in and out of games.

■ University of Detroit gave up football after 3-7 mark in its last season of 1964.

■ Death claimed grand old man of football, Amos Alonzo Stagg, on March 17 at age 102. Stagg, who was Hall of Fame end at Yale, also earned Hall of Fame honors as head coach for 57 years at Springfield (1890-91), Chicago (1892-1932) and Pacific (1933-46). Considered football's patriarch, Stagg pioneered basic concepts such as huddling before plays, T-formation, and throwing forward passes. Three young Tennessee assistant coaches died from injuries sustained in October 18 accident when their automobile was struck by train at crossing in Knoxville: Billy Majors, 26 (Tennessee 1958-60), Bobby Jones, 30 (Baylor 1954-56), and Charley Rash, 28 (Missouri 1956-58). Stanley Woodward, sports writer-editor primarily at *New York Herald Tribune*, died at age 71. Pigskin specialist Woodward was editor of Dell Football Annual, one of top preview magazines of its era.

■ Longest winning streaks entering season:

Arkansas 12	Princeton 9	Utah 7

■ Coaching Changes:

	Incoming	Outgoing
Hawaii	Clark Shaughnessy	Jim Asato
Indiana	John Pont	Phil Dickens
Navy	Bill Elias	Wayne Hardin
Oregon State	Dee Andros	Tommy Prothro
Pennsylvania	Bob Odell	John Stiegman
Texas A&M:	Gene Stallings	Hank Foldberg
Texas Western	Bobby Dobbs	Warren Harper
UCLA	Tommy Prothro	Bill Barnes
Virginia	George Blackburn	Bill Elias
Yale	Carmen Cozza	John Pont

AP Preseason Poll

1 Nebraska (11)	311	6 Arkansas (6)	252
2 Texas (7)	292	7 Southern California (4)	210
3 Notre Dame (7)	282	8 Louisiana State	147
4 Michigan (5)	277	9 Purdue (1)	118
5 Alabama (4)	267	10 Ohio State (1)	77

Others with votes: Army, Auburn, Duke, Florida, Florida State, Georgia Tech, Illinois, Iowa, Kentucky, Maryland, Miami, Michigan State, Minnesota, Mississippi, Missouri, Oregon, Oregon State, Penn State, Stanford, Syracuse, UCLA, Washington, Wyoming

September 11, 1965

Tulsa 14 HOUSTON 0: Football went indoors to major venue for 1st time, playing to disappointing crowd of 37,138 at Astrodome, which had 55,000 capacity. Grass field had long ago died inside dome because of painted roof necessitated for baseball flyballs to be seen by fielders. With creation of Astroturf still year away, teams had to run through dry dirt. Amid flying dust of rock-hard surface, ballyhooed Houston (0-1) soph HB Warren McVea skidded through miserable debut with 11/21y rushing and 4 lost FUMs. McVea nearly made colossal opening play: he headed toward wide opening near sideline on KO RET and would have been gone for TD had he not slipped at his 43YL after 35y RET. It was all downhill for McVea after that as Hurricane DT Willie Townes tackled him 5 times and caused 2 FUMs. Tulsa (1-0), defending national scoring, passing, and total O champion, featured new QB in Bill Anderson (25-47/230y, 2 TDs, INT), who completed 2nd Q TD passes of 6y and 8y to E Howard Twilley (11/111y) and WB Neal Sweeney respectively. Tulsa outgained Cougars by 321y to 220y. Houston D had its moments, forcing missed FG in 1st Q and coming up with Twilley's 4th Q FUM by DB and future major league baseball outfielder Tom Paciorek at its 5YL.

September 18, 1965

(Fri) SOUTHERN CALIFORNIA 20 Minnesota 20: "We were going to lighten the load on Garrett," said USC (0-0-1) coach John McKay, but TB Mike Garrett was only Trojan not to complain about slippery ball. So, Garrett carried 33/146y, and scored 1st TD on ground early in 2nd Q, and fireplug TB scored on TD pass from QB Troy Winslow. Trojans showed weak QB play, however, and had terrible 27.3y punting avg. While scoring 2 TDs rushing, Minnesota (0-0-1) QB John Hankinson also passed with skill as witnessed by his 17-29/203y, INT and 16y TD pass to E Kent Kramer inside last min of 2nd Q that launched Gophers to 13-7 lead. But, Trojans quickly reorganized for 77y trip to go-ahead TD at 14-13 in closing 56 secs of 1st H. Southern Cal's quick march to Winslow's 11y TD pass to Garrett was aided by questionable 36y pass interference call against Minnesota DB Stew Maples, who claimed he deflected pass before ever making contact. Strangely, Minnesota coach Murray Warmath called failed 2-pt try after its 1st TD on Hankinson's sneak 7 mins into 2nd Q, and that left Gophers behind 7-6. Home town fans were disappointed in missed x-pt by HB-K Rod Sherman after Winslow's tying 1y TD plunge midway in 4th Q. Additionally, after Gophers DB Gordon Condo tipped away potential winning pass in last half-min, USC tried 47y FG by DE-K Tim Rossovich that sailed wide.

Syracuse 14 NAVY 6: With Navy D focusing on other Syracuse (1-0) runners, QB Teddy Holman, trying to win starting job, scored twice: 6y run at end of 69y 2nd Q march and on lucky 10y run after he missed handoff to his FB in 4th Q. Trailing at H, Middies (0-1) quickly sliced it to 7-6 as soph QB John Cartwright came off bench to pass 10y to WR Calvin Huey, who made leaping EZ catch. Orangemen picked off 5 passes, 2 by DB Charley Brown, as Middies coach Bill Elias experimented with 3 QBs with little success. Elias surely daydreamed during his Annapolis debut about having Roger Staubach, now graduated, back for just 1 more year.

CLEMSON 21 North Carolina State 7: Tigers (1-0) took new approach to free sub rule: they used 4 units, 2 each on O and D, to wear down thin Wolfpack (0-1). Clemson HB Hugh Mauldin bounced off NC State DE Tony Golmont to score 2y TD in 1st Q. Officials had to huddle in 2nd Q to reverse muffed punt safety charged against Wolfpack to touchback. NC State got bigger break when DB Larry Brown caused midfield FUM which bounded back to Tigers 41YL where DE Gary Whitman recovered for NC State. Roughing PEN helped Wolfpack score to tie it on 26y march ended by HB Shelby Mansfield's 4y TD run. NC State lost pair of 3rd Q FUMs near midfield and slipped quietly away. Clemson gained 204y rushing out of its new I-formation, driving 59 and 75y for 4th Q TDs.

Michigan 31 NORTH CAROLINA 24: Michigan (1-0) struck for 3 quick TDs: QB Wally Gabler left bench and sprinted wide on 31y TD 1st time he touched ball, and HB Jim Detwiler (11/50y) scored twice after DB Dick Wells' FUM REC and DE Jeffrey Hoyne's 50y INT RET. DB Bill Darnall breathed life back into North Carolina (0-1) with 53y INT TD RET with 3:04 left before H. Precocious soph QB Jeff Beaver (8-10/87y, TD) showed maturity by guiding Tar Heels on 12-play drive from their 20YL to QB-K Danny Talbott's 21y FG just as H ended. Talbott hit E John Atherton with 12y TD pass as UNC drew within 21-16 in 3rd Q. In 4th Q, Wolverines retaliated with HB-K Rick Sygar's 33y FG and QB Jim Vidmer's 10y TD pass to E Jim Clancy. Home crowd cheered late return of Beaver, who pitched 19y TD pass to HB Max Chapman and followed with 2-pt pass to Atherton.

GEORGIA 18 Alabama 17: Georgia (1-0) jumped to 10-0 lead, highlighted by DT George Patton's 55y TD romp with INT. FUM RECs allowed favored Alabama (0-1) to tie it by 3rd Q as FB Steve Bowman had 8y TD run. Reversing his shaky start, Crimson Tide QB Steve Sloan hit 4 straight passes, then plunged for 17-10 4th Q edge. On Bulldogs' next scrimmage, QB Kirby Moore pitched short hook pass to E Pat Hodgson. Although Hodgson's knee was grounded as revealed in post-game photos, he pitched lateral to HB Bob Taylor, who raced untouched to 73y TD. When Moore made 2-pt pass to Hodgson, Georgia wrapped up stunning win with 2 mins left.

TENNESSEE 21 Army 0: In Army's 1st road opener in 76 years, Tennessee (1-0) debuted soph QB Charles Fulton, who threw 23y TD bullet to WB Hal Wantland on his 1st collegiate pass attempt. It came at end of 80y voyage that was highlighted by FB Stan Mitchell's 45y ramble that might have scored had Cadets (0-1) DB Ed Noble not hauled him down. Fulton followed in 2nd Q with 53y over-middle TD pass to E Austin Denney, and DB Jerry Smith added late 66y punt TD RET. Cadets QB Curt Cook passed 13-36/135y, but, during Cook's 8-16/82y aerial bombardment in 1st H, Army bungled several chances inside Vols 20YL, twice losing ball on downs and once on Cook's INT. Army K Barry Nickerson also was short on FG tries of 43 and 38y in 1st H led 14-0 by Tennessee. Black Knights fashioned their biggest threat in 3rd Q as workhorse HB Sonny Stowers and FB Mark Hamilton powered them to 5YL. But Cook's 3 runs could only advance 3y, and his 4th down pass fell to ground uncaught.

Baylor 14 AUBURN 8: In 4th Q of scoreless game, Auburn (0-1) P Tom Lunceford suffered partial block, and Baylor (1-0) took over on Plainsmen 45YL. Bears E Harlan Lane threw key block for HB Richard Defee's TD sweep on 7th play of subsequent drive. Tigers HB Harrison McCraw soon lost FUM at his 32YL, and Baylor QB Terry Southall threw TD pass. Auburn tallied late on QB Alex Bowden's passes for TD and 2-pts.

LOUISIANA STATE 10 Texas A&M 0: Bear Bryant coaching proteges squared off in Baton Rouge. Aggies (0-1) mentor Gene Stallings, who played under Bryant at Texas A&M, saw his coaching debut spoiled by thoroughly ineffective Q. Seeking its 6th straight season-opening win over Aggies, LSU (1-0) couldn't manage to fire up its new-look O either. So, Bengals coach Charlie McClendon relied on 2 old Tiger standbys: superb D (114y allowed) and educated kicking toe of E-K Doug Moreau. LSU DE Ernest Maggiore blocked A&M P Phil Scoggin's punt in 1st Q and scrambled after loose ball to recover it in EZ for TD. Moreau, who clicked on conv kick, made FG in 2nd Q, which was all Tigers needed. Moreau's FG was set up by FUM REC by Tigers DB Mike Robichaux at A&M 41YL. Facing LSU D, led by DLs Maggiore, George Rice, and Tommy Fussell and LB Mike Vincent, Aggies failed to muster 1st down until late spurt in 2nd Q when they got 3 1st downs to advance to Bengals 30YL. Soph QB Nelson Stokley excited home crowd, but couldn't solve LSU's passing problems as PENs and FUM killed several trips close to GL.

MICHIGAN STATE 13 Ucla 3: Humidity "dense enough to support marine life," according to Charles Maher of *Los Angeles Times,* encouraged "Hawaiian Connection" of Michigan State (1-0) to prosper. Hawaiian-punching 21y to 2nd Q TD was soph FB Bob Apisa, and barefoot K Dick Kenney from Alea boomed FGs of 34 and 23y. Picked at bottom of Pac-8, UCLA (0-1) remained tenacious throughout in debuts of coach Tommy Prothro and soph QB Gary Beban. Bruins collared 4 TOs inside their own 35YL and moved to 14 and 20YLs, but couldn't dent GL against huge Michigan State D. UCLA settled for K Kurt Zimmerman's 37y FG in 3rd Q when Beban's audible confused his team on 3rd down.

Florida 24 NORTHWESTERN 14: Gators (1-0) made rare trip to Big 10 country and cruised to 24-0 advantage by 3rd Q. Florida QB Steve Spurrier passed 3y on 4th down to E Charles Casey for 1st Q TD and sneaked over for another in 3rd Q after 76y excursion after 2nd H KO. Gators' other TD came on DB George Grandy's 14y INT TD RET behind big block of DL Brian Jetter. Florida's depth chart was getting thorough inspection by 4th Q when Northwestern (0-1) finally found scoreboard. Big Wildcats FB Bob McKelvey scored twice after 62 and 80y marches as QB Dave Milam hit several key passes.

Oregon State 12 ILLINOIS 10: QB-K Fred Custardo booted 35y FG and completed 11y TD pass to soph E Larry Jordan, allowing Illinois (0-1) to enjoy 10-0 lead in 2nd Q despite wraps held tightly on A-A FB Jim Grabowski. Oregon State (1-0) QB Paul Brothers scored on 3y run to pare Illini's lead to 10-6 at H. Illinois DE Bob Batchelder was D stalwart in holding score as is; Batchelder recovered FUM by Beavers HB Bob Grim to prevent 4th Q TD and made another REC of Grim's FUM at 11YL after Brothers whipped 20y pass to E Mike Sullivan. In end, Batchelder and 2 other Illini defenders tried to bat away Brothers pass, but 10y deflected toss ended up in hands of Oregon State HB Clayton Calhoun for TD in last 3 mins of upset.

ARKANSAS 28 Oklahoma State 14 (Little Rock): Razorbacks (1-0) dusted off brilliant jr QB Jon Brittenum (6-9/100y, TD), who had redshirted during 1964 season. Brittenum ran Arkansas O beautifully and teamed with sub WB Harry Jones (6/128y rushing, TD) on 5/65y receiving, including 3 catches on opening TD drive that ended with his 8y TD soft-toss to Jones. Interestingly, quick Jones, former DB, had battled all-but-forgotten Brittenum for open QB job in spring drills. In helping build 21-0 H, Jones scored in 2nd Q on lightning 50y pitchout run after Brittenum had lured defenders his way. Sopping with energy, Brittenum raced 40y downfield to throw last TD-clearing block for Jones. Brittenum added 8 and 15y TD runs. Oklahoma State (0-1) couldn't match Porkers' speed, but they faired well on some passes as QB Glenn Baxter hit 13-31/144y, INT. HB Larry Elliott fashioned 69y punt RET late in 4th Q to set up FB Walt Garrison's 2nd short TD run.

Washington State 7 IOWA 0: *Playboy's* preseason no. 1 Iowa (0-1) got off on wrong foot on way to Hugh Hefner's mansion. Instead, Hawkeyes took 1st tentative flight on way to horrid 1-9 final record. In rainy 1st H, Iowa failed on 5 scoring threats, twice within Cougars 5YL. Washington State (1-0) made only 1 scoring bid until last min, when QB Tom Roth zipped 20y TD pass to tall E Rich Sheron.

TEXAS TECH 26 Kansas 7: Trailing 26-7 barely into 4th Q and tornado sirens wailing in his ears, Kansas (0-1) coach Jack Mitchell asked officials to call water-logged game so that crowd could disperse. Texas Tech (1-0) had built impressive lead on air attack of QB Tom Wilson and power runs of big, fleet HB Donny Anderson. Versatile Anderson caught TD passes of 7 and 6y from Wilson. Jayhawks' brightest moment came in 1st Q as QB Bill Fenton and E Willie Smith collaborated on school-record to-date 97y TD pass.

WYOMING 31 Air Force 14: With Jack Frost dumping 10 inches of September snow, Wyoming (1-0) crafted 2 early TDs. Cowboys HB Jerry Marion gained 48y on pass from QB Tom Wilkinson and soon grabbed EZ FUM. Wyoming FB Mike Davenport scored 3 mins later after DL Bob Dinges fell on FUM at Falcons 9YL. Air Force (0-1) fought back to within 14-7 on HB Bob Barnes' 56y TD catch from QB Paul Stein in 2nd Q. Sub Cowboys QB Rick Egloff did 2nd H damage with run and pass for TDs.

Brigham Young 24 ARIZONA STATE 6: Underdog BYU (1-0) stunned Arizona State (0-1) in WAC opener that was 1st home loss for Sun Devils in last 13 contests in Tempe. It showcased talents of Cougars QB Virgil Carter (10-18/134y, TD, INT, and 10/83y, TD rushing). Late in 1st Q, Carter dived for short TD and found ace WR Phil Odle (5/92y, TD) for pass that set up K Dave Duran's 28y FG with :01 before H. BYU rubbed salt in ASU's wounds in 6-min span of 3rd Q: FB John Ogden crashed 2y for TD and Carter flipped 5y TD to Odle. Sun Devils avoided shutout midway in 4th Q as QB John Goodman (10-15/146y, TD) finally was protected—he lost 36y in sacks—and he lofted 48y TD pass to WR Ben Hawkins. BYU G Grant Wilson troubled Goodman with 3 tackles for loss that frequently interrupted Sun Devil threats.

Notre Dame 48 CALIFORNIA 6: Notre Dame (1-0) ended 5-game West Coast losing streak with dominant win. New Fighting Irish QB Bill Zloch ran for 2 TDs and passed for another. DB Nick Rassas went 65y with punt RET to build 22-0 lead in 2nd Q. Earlier, Rassas had raced 40y on INT RET of Bears QB Jim Hunt to set up opening salvo. California (0-1), suffering worst loss in 5 years, got its only score on transfer southpaw QB Dan Berry's TD pass to HB Jerry Bradley late in 2nd Q. Notre Dame totaled 449y, with 381y coming on ground, as HB Nick Eddy led South Benders' rush attack with 99y.

AP Poll September 20

1 Notre Dame (24)	472	6 Purdue	208
2 Nebraska (16)	429	7 Louisiana State	164
3 Texas (7)	376	8 Florida	95
4 Michigan (2)	289	9 Syracuse	84
5 Arkansas (4)	280	10 Kentucky	78

Others with votes: Georgia, Iowa, Michigan State, Minnesota, Mississippi, Mississippi State, Ohio State, Oregon State, Penn State, Southern California, Stanford, Tennessee, Texas Tech, West Virginia, Wyoming

September 25, 1965

PRINCETON 32 Rutgers 6: Virtually-perfect K Charlie Gogolak kicked 6 FGs, including 52y blast among his 3 in 2nd Q, in leading Tigers (1-0) to their 48th win in 56th meeting of football's 1st rivalry. Gogolak's 6 3-ptrs set new collegiate record at that time. Earlier, Princeton TB Ron Landeck provided 7-0 lead with 2y TD run in 1st Q before Gogolak stacked his 3 FGs in 2nd Q for 16-0 H edge. Scarlet Knights (0-1) managed only 216y O and avoided shutout in 3rd Q when QB Jack Callaghan wrapped up 80y voyage by hitting E Bob Brendel with 10y scoring pass. Of special note was battle of identical twin captains: DL George Paul Savidge of Princeton and C George Peter Savidge of Rutgers.

Miami 24 SYRACUSE 0: Lesser-known Biletnikoff brother, QB Bob, sparked Miami (1-1) with TD passes to E Steve Smith and FB Fred Cassidy. DL LeRoy Lewis' 2 FUM RECs and DB Larry Bodie's INT of Syracuse (1-1) QB Rick Cassata built 17-0 lead for Hurricanes by 3rd Q. Miami FB Pete Banaszak (18/104y, TD) scored 4th Q TD to build lopsided margin. Orange ground game, led by HB Floyd Little (12/60y), was well collared, totaling only 100y. Instead, Syracuse was forced into barely fruitful 11-30/149y air game.

PITTSBURGH 13 Oklahoma 9: After 6 attempts during sporadic intersectional series, Panthers (1-1) finally defeated onerous Oklahoma (0-1). Pittsburgh, trailing 3-0 in 2nd Q after Sooners K Ron Shotts nailed 24y FG, took lead for good as QB Kenny Lucas (12-23/143y, 2 TDs) passed to elusive HB Eric Crabtree for 22y score. Panthers came right back, going 72y after OU P Tom Stidham's punt was misdirected only 14y. Lucas hit E Mitch Zalnasky for 9, 12, and 8y connections, last coming on superb diving grab in EZ for TD. K Jim Jones missed x-pt after Pitt's 2nd TD of 2nd Q, but it still led 13-3. Oklahoma, which outgained their Steel City hosts 322y to 236y, could manage only 4th Q score: 8y pass from QB John Hammond to E Gordon Brown. Sooners' 2-pt pass attempt failed.

NORTH CAROLINA STATE 13 Wake Forest 11: K Harold Deters of NC State (1-1) slammed through 2 FGs of 45y each, last coming with just 35 secs remaining to beat Wake Forest (0-2). It was Wolfpack's 8th straight win at Riddick Stadium, to be abandoned at season's end. Wolfpack QB Charlie Noggle extended Deters' 1st Q FG to 10-0 lead with 15y TD keeper in 3rd Q, but Demon Deacons HB-DB Joe Carazo, who had made 1st Q INT in his EZ, caught 16y pass to set up FB Mike Kelly's 1y TD dive and followed with 2-pt catch. In 4th Q, Wake held at its 4YL and launched drive that led to K Eddie McKinney's sharp-angled 26y FG, putting Deacs up 11-10 with 4:30 to go. Noggle (13-20/120y, INT) deftly positioned NC State with his passes until Deters' toe made good.

Duke 20 South Carolina 15: Weak South Carolina (1-1) punts paved way for pair of Duke (2-0) TDs in 1st H, scored by Devils' stellar sophs, TB Jay Calabrese (15/140y, 2 TDs) and HB Jake Devonshire. After gaining safety on DB Stan Juk's EZ sack, Gamecocks unearthed talented passer, 3rd-string QB Mike Fair (12-21/116y), whose 9y TD pass to HB Bob Harris helped trim deficit to 14-9 in 4th Q. Calabrese quickly dropped hammer on South Carolina with 68y TD burst that caught USC LB out of position. Fair's pass to E Wayne Tucker set up Gamecocks' closing TD, 1y dive by HB Jule Smith.

KENTUCKY 16 Mississippi 7: Wildcats QB Rick Norton (13-24/218y, TD) pitched to HB Larry Seiple for 1st Q score after Blue Grassers went 76y after opening KO. But, Ole Miss (1-1) enjoyed 7-6 H lead on QB Jimmy Heidel's 1y sneak that capped 2nd Q drive. Kentucky (2-0) took 2-pt lead after DE-K Frank Andrighetti drilled 27y FG with 11 secs left in 3rd Q. E Bob Spanish caught 13 and 33y passes from Norton to set up FG. Ahead 9-7 with just more than 2 mins left in 4th Q, Kentucky faced 4th-and-41 at its own 30YL. While Mississippi primed itself to make vital punt RET, madcap P Seiple wonderously, but inexplicably ran with ball. Seiple's dash went for 70y TD through baffled Rebels, who were busy peeling back to eagerly deploy blocks for punt RET that never came.

Mississippi State 18 FLORIDA 13: Gators smartly dominated stats, 316y to 250y, and led most of way until final 6:29. After Mississippi State (2-0) FB Hoyle Granger had tied it at 6-6 late in 1st Q, Florida (1-1) went ahead 13-6 soon after short Maroons punt. It came on FB John Feiber's TD smash, set up by 30y pass to Gators E Charles Casey from QB Steve Spurrier (17-36/211y, INT). Mississippi State went 70y after 2nd H KO, primarily on HB Marcus Rhoden's 46y catch, but Gators DB Dick Kirk blocked x-pt kick to retain 13-12 lead. Bulldogs QB Ashby Cook capped 58y drive with 23y TD pass to HB Don Saget for 18-13 lead as 4th Q clock dwindled inside 7 mins. Miss State was able to withstand Florida drives that ended, 1st on lost FUM and later on missed T-eligible pass to Randy Jackson at GL.

North Carolina 14 OHIO STATE 3: Invaders from Dixie surprised Ohio State (0-1) with tenacious D after Tar Heels' opening TD salvo had established North Carolina (1-1) as 7-0 leaders on 6y sweep by cool QB Danny Talbott (11-16/127y, INT). Losing opener for 1st time since national title year of 1957, Buckeyes launched whopping number of passes (19-35/178y, 2 INTs in air) and had only K Bob Funk's 2nd Q FG to show for it after E Greg Lashutka dropped perfect EZ throw from QB Don Unverferth. HB Max Chapman, who set up Talbott's early TD with 27y burst, iced Carolina's cake with 48y TD dash in final min. UNC standouts included LB Jay Malobicky, DT Joe Churchill, and DBs Billy Darnell, Jack Davenport, Gene Link and Bill Edwards.

Michigan State 23 PENN STATE 0: Slight underdog Michigan State (2-0) blew open 3-0 game against Nittany Lions (0-1) with 17 pts in 2nd Q with key score provided by FB Bob Apisa's 35y TD blast through 2 tacklers. Barefoot K Dick Kenney clicked on FGs of 24 and 29y in 1st H and, after Penn State D stiffened in 2nd H, Kenney made 36y 3-ptr in 4th Q. Magnificent Spartans DE Bubba Smith began building his out-of-this-world notoriety by moving his 268-lb bulk diagonally across field to corral speedy Lions HB Mike Irwin, who appeared gone for TD. When he wasn't chasing runaway Lions, Smith seemed "permanently attached to Penn State quarterback Jack White's hide," according to Ron Smith in *Philadelphia Inquirer.* Spartans D chased White (9-19/120y, INT) all over field, prompting stunned coach Rip Engle to call Michigan State "the best football team we ever played." Whatever spirit Lions had to confront Spartans seemed to disappear in 1st Q when QB-K Tom Sherman's tying 34y FG attempt hit goalpost upright.

PURDUE 25 Notre Dame 21: Seesaw national TV show provided springboard to lasting fame for Purdue (2-0) QB-P-DB Bob Griese, who passed 19-22/283y, 3 TDs, including 28 and 14y scores to TE Jim Beirne. Griese also ran effectively, punted to 6, 7, and 26YLs, and made TD-saving tackle of Notre Dame (1-1) HB Bill Wolski on KO RET. Lead changed hands 5 times with Fighting Irish tying it—after DB Tony Carey picked off Griese—at 18-18 in 3rd Q on Wolski's 54y dash and QB Bill Zloch's 2-pt pass. Purdue threatened to break deadlock in 4th Q, but Griese was forced to run when his receivers were covered and lost FUM to ND DE Don Gmitter at Irish 39YL. After 8 plays made 54y, K Ken Ivan's likely game-winning 24y FG glanced on and over crossbar to give Notre Dame late 21-18 lead and apparently extend Irish's 1-week residence atop AP Poll. But, Griese brought back his no. 6 Boilermakers on 67y TD drive during which he hit soph WR Jim Finley for 32y before HB Gordon Teter scored on 3y run.

ARKANSAS 20 Tulsa 12: Big Tulsa (1-1) D, 40 lb-per-man heavier than sleek Arkansas (2-0), put wraps on Hogs O well into 3rd Q. E Howard Twilley's short TD catch provided Hurricane with 12-10 lead at H. Razorbacks sub QB-K Ronnie South kicked school record 45y FG in 3rd Q, and new QB discovery, Jon Brittenum, fired 10y TD pass to E Bobby Crockett at end of 77y 4th Q drive to save edgy Porkers' 14-game win streak. Arkansas D bent to tune of 223y, but did not break under pressure from Tulsa's mighty air game

Nebraska 27 AIR FORCE 17: It seemed so simple in early going: Nebraska FB (and future Huskers head coach) Frank Solich scooted to 80 and 21y TDs around HB Ron Kirkland's 6y score, and no. 2 Cornhuskers (2-0) enjoyed 21-0 lead in 1st Q. Sometimes, however, teams scored too easily and subconsciously let down. Fighting back by virtue of 2nd Q FUM REC, Air Force (0-2) got TD run from FB John Odrejka. Falcons took 2nd H KO and drove to K Dan Radtke's FG, then executed perfect on-side KO. AFA QB Paul Stein quickly made HB Bob Barnes' TD run possible with 40y connection to HB Guy Hogle. That drew Airmen to within 21-17. Solich (17/204y, 3 TDs), however was on his way to setting to-date school record for single game rush y, and he reestablished Huskers' superiority with nifty 41y TD run in 4th Q.

AP Poll September 27

1 Texas (15)	389	6 Kentucky (1)	168
2 Purdue (14)	381	7 Michigan	166
3 Nebraska (13)	363	8 Notre Dame	144
4 Arkansas (3)	264	9 Michigan State	73
5 Louisiana State	248	10 Georgia	69

Others with votes: Alabama, Arizona, Baylor, Duke, Illinois, Iowa, Maryland, Mississippi, Mississippi State, North Carolina, Ohio State, Oregon, Pittsburgh, Southern California, Washington State, West Virginia, Wyoming

October 2, 1965

Ucla 24 PENN STATE 22: Nittany Lions FB Roger Grimes battered over for 2y TD in 1st Q as coach Rip Engle went looking for his 100th win. In response, clever UCLA (1-1) soph QB Gary Beban took advantage of early Penn State (0-2) errors on D. As Lions dropped their DEs off line in anticipation of short passes, Beban (21/74y, 2 TDs rushing and 7-14/76y passing) rolled out for TD runs of 16 and 6y to vault UCLA to 17-7 lead at H. Bruins DB Bob Stiles (INT), nearby New Jersey native who was only non-Californian on squad, had slammed Penn State HB Mike Irwin in 2nd Q, and Irwin's FUM led to tie-breaking FG at 10-7 by UCLA K Kurt Zimmermann. UCLA had spent all afternoon shifting out of I-formation into variety of patterns, but, in 3rd Q, Bruins went on quick-count and ran HB Mel Farr on RT counter out of I set. Farr (11/87y) spurted for 58y TD. Now trailing 24-7 and having failed on 93y drive ruined by offside PEN,

desperate Lions were aroused too late by TD pass from QB Jack White (17-36/196y, TD, 2 INTs) to E Bill Huber, and White's 2-pt pass. White made it look close with 4y scoring run in last 9 secs.

Syracuse 24 MARYLAND 7: "Scissors Reverse," long-time staple of Syracuse (2-1) run attack under coach Ben Schwartzwalder, sprung fleet HB Floyd Little (23/152y) for 72y sprint, 1st of his 3 TD runs, in 1st Q. Terrapins (1-1), who were limited to 152y O, tied it 7-7 in 2nd Q on soph TB Ernie Torain's 14y bolt off T at end of 53y drive. Following Maryland FUM at Terps 7YL, Little quickly put Orangemen in lead for good with 2y TD blast in 3rd Q. Terrapins' hopes faded with 2 INTs deep in Syracuse territory in 4th Q.

SOUTH CAROLINA 13 North Carolina State 7: Fundamentally-sound Gamecocks (2-1) dominated NC State (1-2) by more than score would indicate. K Jimmy Poole's 42y FG on South Carolina's opening possession of 1st Q held up until middle of 3rd Q, thanks to 1st H FG misses of 52 and 21y by Wolfpack's K Harold Deters. Gamecocks soph HB Ben Garnto (5/91y) took pitchout on 3rd-and-3, zipped up sideline, and cut back for 74y TD run on team's 2nd series of 3rd Q. Poole added another FG for 13-0 edge with 3:33 to go, but Wolfpack avoided shutout as sub QB Page Ashby beat clock with 68y drive on which Ashby scored on 8y run with 33 secs left.

WAKE FOREST 7 Vanderbilt 0: Wake Forest (1-2) authored its 1st shutout in 7 years, holding Vanderbilt's skimpy O to 120y. Soph DT Robert Grant was keystone of Demon Deacons' D, twice throwing Commodores QB Bob Kerr for losses when Vandy (0-3) threatened often in game's late stages. This contest had every appearance of 0-0 deadlock as Wake Forest QB Ken Hauswald showed wildly inaccurate 5-14 passing ledger halfway into 3rd Q. But, superb 2-way Deacons HB-DB Joe Carazo, who would crush Commodores with 2 INTs in last 2 mins of game, enhanced Hauswald's suddenly-sharp throws in 3rd Q with nullified 36y broken-field TD run and 12y catch to set up his own 1y TD dive on 2nd play of 4th Q. Wake's big play, however, came on last snap of 3rd Q: Facing 3rd-and-10 at Vanderbilt 15YL, Deacons sent FB Andy Heck barreling 12y.

WEST VIRGINIA 63 Pittsburgh 48: WVU sr HB Dick Rader had never scored in his career, so naturally Rader caught 3 TD passes in this wild match that had spectators reacting in wonderment as mounting scores were read in other stadiums. West Virginia (3-0) QB Allen McCune (18-25 passing) threw 5 TD passes and ran for another. Sharp Pitt (1-2) HB Eric Crabtree scored 3 different ways: 43y catch from QB Kenny Lucas (3 TDs passing), 71y run, and 92y KO RET. McCune wrapped pair of TD passes around Crabtree's KO TD RET in 4th Q, and that held Mountaineers in lead at 49-42. Perhaps it would figure that single D play would be turning point of game that would end with 111 pts scored: WVU coach Gene Corum credited DL Bill Sullivan with key stop. Sullivan made tackle that halted Panthers' 2-pt run to conserve Mountaineers' 49-48 lead in 4th Q. HB Garrett Ford scored twice in latter half of 4th Q to advance Mountaineers to exhausting 63-48 advantage. Slugfest teams combined for 1,071y in total O in their old rivalry.

FLORIDA 14 Louisiana State 7: Gators (2-1) switched WR Alan Poe with TB Jack Harper to protect Harper's injured shoulder, but ended up successfully protecting QB Steve Spurrier (10-17/139y, TD) all but once. On that critical play, Spurrier was nearly trapped, but scrambled forward to lob 1st Q TD pass to WR Richard Trapp. LSU (2-1) tied it 7-7 just before H as QB Nelson Stokley swept in from 3YL. Florida dominated 3rd Q, taking 14-7 lead near end of Q on FB John Feiber's TD dive. Bengal Tigers threatened late, but Gators DL Lynn Matthews grabbed TB Joe Labruzzo's FUM at 2YL, LSU's 2nd frustrating FUM it lost inside Florida's 5YL.

AUBURN 23 Kentucky 18: Auburn (1-1-1) fashioned upset on balanced attack (150y rushing and 141y passing) and leadership of QB Tom Bryan, whose option runs kept Kentucky (2-1) off balance. Tigers cruised 80, 73, 45y to TDs and K Ben McDavid's FG for 23-6 lead. Wildcats' 1st TD came in 3rd Q when E Bob Windsor broke away for 76y TD after short toss from QB Rick Norton. Cats HB Larry Seiple took similar short throws, speeding away from Auburn DBs for 74 and 44y TDs.

ALABAMA 17 Mississippi 16 (Birmingham): In 1st regular season tilt since 1944 between 2 football gems of Deep South, Alabama (2-1) barely protected its mastery over Ole Miss (1-2) that now extended 55 years. Rebels earned 9-7 H advantage on K Don Keyes' 34y FG in 1st Q and QB Jerry Heidel's 9y TD pass to FB Don Street in 2nd Q. But, Keyes' conv kick failed after Street's TD. Mississippi extended its lead to 16-7 in 4th Q as Heidel wedged over after DB John Maddox's INT created good field position for Rebels. With time ticking down in 16-10 nail-biter, Crimson Tide QB Steve Sloan led 89y drive as he connected with E Ray Perkins on 35y pass to Rebels 18YL. Bama HB Leslie Kelley ran for 3 and 6y to set up 9y TD skirt off E by Sloan, his 2nd TD run. HB-K David Ray booted x-pt that won it with 1:19 left. Any last hope for Ole Miss evaporated on FUM of ensuing KO.

GEORGIA TECH 38 Clemson 6: Lightning strike delivered "snow" as Georgia Tech soph HB Lenny Snow bolted 48y on game's 1st play to set stage for soph QB Kim King's TD run. King added TD pass, and Snow later landed in EZ twice. Hopelessly behind at 38-0, Clemson (2-1) got late 23y TD run by QB Thomas Ray. It was coach Bobby Dodd's 150th career win at Georgia Tech (1-1-1).

MICHIGAN STATE 22 Illinois 12: Fighting Illini (1-2) frustrated early efforts of Michigan State (3-0), taking 10-3 and 12-9 leads on TD by masterful FB Jim Grabowski (27/125y, TD), FG by QB-K Fred Custardo, and safety in 3rd Q when Spartans DB Jess Phillips retreated on punt RET and was nailed in EZ by flying Illini HB Cyril Pinder. No. 9 Michigan State had scored 1st on barefoot K Dick Kenney's majestic 47y FG, but its fabulous and overanxious D couldn't read Illinois' backfield shifts and popped offside 6 times. Seemingly about to doze into submission late in 3rd Q, Michigan State revitalized itself by traveling 86y to FB Bob Apisa's bowling-pin 9y TD run through half-dozen Illini defenders. Spartans went for 2 pts but missed, so MSU led 15-12. Spartans D rose up to make 4th Q INT of Custardo, who passed only for 87y on 7 successes. Michigan State QB Steve Juday quickly pitched clinching 7y TD to E Gene Washington, who got away from LB Ron Acks in EZ.

WISCONSIN 16 Iowa 13: Usually, late-game conceded safety works to preserve victory, but this time it backfired on Iowa (1-2). Having played outstanding D and allowed Wisconsin (1-1-1) only 24y rushing and LB Tom Brigham's 49y punt TD RET behind wall of blockers in 1st Q, Hawkeyes clung to 13-7 lead with 4 mins to play. Badgers summoned strength for 4th Q penetration to Hawks 1YL, only to unravel on 4th down at 7YL. Iowa accepted 3rd down safety rather than punt from its own EZ. Unfortunately, Wisconsin DB Gary Bender returned free-kick to midfield, and QB Chuck Burt (10-23/124y, TD, 3 INTs) hurled 42y TD pass to E Lou Jung, which became Iowa's undoing. Earlier, Hawkeyes, favored by 2 TDs, had launched 1st Q voyage of 45y, keyed by QB Gary Snook's 30y sweep and capped by HB Jerry O'Donnell's 1y TD plunge. Iowa K Bob Anderson had hit 2 FGs in 2nd Q.

Georgia 15 MICHIGAN 7: Unbeaten and surprising Georgia (3-0) scored its 2nd major upset of season, thanks primarily to K Bob Etter's FGs of 34, 44, and 31y. Defending Big 10 champion Michigan (2-1) got its TD in 2nd Q when FB Tim Radigan scored from 1YL to finish 45y march. Etter put Bulldogs out front 3-0 in 1st Q with 34y FG and barely beat H clock with 44y FG to pull Georgia within 7-6 at end of 2nd Q. Bulldogs QB Preston Ridlehuber threw 4th Q TD pass to E Pat Hogson to earn lead at 12-7, only 4 mins from end. Georgia DB Lynn Hughes made INT, and Etter added his 3rd FG to end it.

SOUTHERN METHODIST 14 Purdue 14: Coming off disastrous 42-0 defeat by Illinois, SMU (1-1-1) surprised no. 2 Purdue (2-0-1) on QB Mac White's 2 TD passes in 2nd H. Mustangs swift WR John Roderick dropped 3 potential scoring passes, but, when he hauled in 3rd Q TD, Dallas crowd became excited in remembrance of Roderick's heroics 2 years earlier in upset of Navy. White's 2nd scoring toss came with 9:16 remaining, and it was set up by Ponies lining up with 2 QBs, soph QB Mike Livingston at HB. Livingston faked running pass and roared 27y to Purdue 22YL. White soon pitched 14y TD to E Bobby Goodrich. Boilermakers had cruised to 14-0 H lead on TD passes to E Bob Hadrick (11/136y) and HB Gordon Teter from QB Bob Griese (18-24/222y, 2 TDs, INT), but Griese got kicked in head and missed most of 3rd Q. SMU threatened as 4th Q clock ticked past halfway, but Boilermakers DB John Charles, who starred in secondary with DB Charles King, knocked down EZ pass meant for Roderick. Griese's FUM at Purdue 45YL gave Ponies last chance with 2:47 left, but Purdue DT Bob Yunaska burst through to block Mustangs K Dennis Partee's 31y FG try with 41 secs left.

Ohio State 23 WASHINGTON 21: Powerful running attacks of intersectional foes smashed at other's D units in seesaw battle on national TV. TD runs by big FBs Willard Sander and Tom Barrington gave Buckeyes (1-1) 14-7 lead in 2nd Q, but Washington (1-2) HB Don Moore blasted for 2 TDs and QB Tom Hullin flipped 2-pt pass to E Bruce Kramer for 21-14 edge in 3rd Q. QB Arnold Fontes' 3rd Q TD run moved Ohio State to within 21-20, but K Bob Funk missed conv kick. Huskies K Dave Williams had opportunity to put Washington ahead by 4 pts, but missed 23y FG try late in 4th Q. Buckeyes then powered 70y from their 20YL to Funk's late, angled 27y FG to win it.

SOUTHERN CALIFORNIA 26 Oregon State 12: With incomparable Sandy Koufax clinching National League pennant for cross-town Dodgers that afternoon, Southern California (2-0-1) still drew 52,100 to L.A. Coliseum at night to watch Troy rally behind dynamic TB Mike Garrett (31/172y, 3 TDs). Tough-minded Oregon State (1-2) jumped to 12-0 lead as it banged ahead with fireplug FB Pete Pifer's running until 6 mins remaining in 1st H. Pifer (23/126y, 2 TDs) had taken pitchout in opening 4 mins and flashed by USC DE Jim Walker for 43y TD romp. When Trojans QB Troy Winslow missed connection on 2nd Q handoff, Beavers DL Dave Ghould was there to pounce on it at USC 11YL. Pifer bulled across for 2-TD lead 6 plays later. But, neither conv try was successful. Garrett finally woke up sleepy Trojans with runs of 3, 19, 3, 14, and 10y on 82y TD march that beat H clock by 38 secs. Back in ballgame, aroused USC took 13-12 advantage after Garrett made his 2nd 10y TD sprint in 3rd Q. Game's big play came on bad 4th Q punt snap by Beavers C Al Frei, which lost 20y when it sailed over head of QB-P Paul Brothers. It set up Winslow's TD pass for HB Rod Sherman, and Garrett salted it away with late 28y TD run. Oregon State's Brothers was forced into awful passing game with 4-13/7y.

AP Poll October 4

1 Texas (25)	368	6 Purdue (1)	182
2 Nebraska (10)	355	7 Notre Dame	172
3 Arkansas (1)	285	8 Southern California	108
4 Georgia (3)	258	9 Mississippi State	47
5 Michigan State	219	10 Florida	46

Others with votes: Alabama, Auburn, Duke, Kentucky, Louisiana State, Michigan, Missouri, Ohio State, Oregon, Stanford, Syracuse, West Virginia, Wyoming

October 9, 1965

Notre Dame 17 ARMY 0 (New York City): Giants of Yankee Stadium, famous for their scoreless tie of 19 years earlier, moved to Queens to renew their rivalry at sold-out Shea Stadium, 1st such New York City rematch since their 1946 deadlock. After taking opening KO, Army (2-2) moved its infantry 52y downfield to 25YL, but Notre Dame (3-1) DB Nick Rassas made 1st of his 2 INTs. Rassas cut in front of E Sam Champi to pick off pass by QB Fred Barofsky, who otherwise was effective in his 1st H role as rollout runner. Black Knights were surprised by Fighting Irish HB-P Dan McGinn's QK on last play of 1st Q. It created field position for 2nd Q aerial attack as QB Tom Shoen, hoping to win battle for starting job with QB Bill Zloch, hit 4-7 pass attempts. From Army 48YL, Shoen lobbed 19y screen pass to FB Larry Conjar and right away hit 29y TD pass to TE Don Gmitter. Gmitter smartly broke his clear-out pattern and cut across secondary to catch pass from Shoen, who scrambled to his right. In 3rd Q, DE Tom Rhoads leaped to bat pass, then cradled INT to his chest of pass by Cadets QB

Curt Cook at Army 28YL. It set up ND HB Nick Eddy's 5y TD sweep. Rugged Conjar carried on 10 of 13 Notre Dame running plays that covering 52y in 4th Q to spot K Ken Ivan for 23y FG.

GEORGIA 23 Clemson 9: Stubborn Clemson (2-2) apparently hadn't read press clippings of undefeated Bulldogs (4-0) and gained 6-0 and 9-6 leads, which carried into 3rd Q. Tigers' biggest gainer fueled their 65y TD drive: QB Thomas Ray flipped 43y pass to E Edgar McGee. Clemson HB Hugh Maudlin ran 11 and 10y off RT, latter burst to score in 1st Q. Georgia answered quickly as QB Preston Ridlehuber launched 34y TD to E Pat Hodgson on next 1st Q series, but Bulldogs turned sleepy for rest of 1st H. Georgia G Jimmy Cooley completely turned game around in 3rd Q: Cooley blocked punt by Clemson P Don Barfield, which Bulldogs DE Larry Kohn covered in EZ for TD. Suddenly inspired, Bulldogs soon went 46y to FB Ronnie Jenkins' 3y TD run for comfortable 20-9 advantage. Victory over ACC's Tigers counted in SEC standings because Georgia needed verdict to fulfill 6 league tilts.

Louisiana State 34 MIAMI 27: QBs Bob Biletnikoff of Miami (1-3) and Nelson Stokley of LSU (3-1) traded 1st Q TD runs, but Biletnikoff was soon injured. What hurt Hurricanes worse was coughing up rash of TOs inside their own 20YL in 10-min span bridging 1st and 2nd Qs. LSU (3-1) DL Tommy Fussell scored on blocked punt by G Mike Duhon, and Tigers lead enlarged to 27-7 in 2nd Q when Hurricanes HB Russell Smith set up 2 easy LSU scores with lost FUMs. Replacing Biletnikoff for Miami was little-known soph QB Bill Miller, who excited home crowd by firing 21-39/281y, 3 TDs. Miller's 1st TD throw came just in time to beat H clock and cut deficit to 27-14. But when it counted in 2nd H, beefy LSU D stopped FB Pete Banaczak 3 times at its GL, and DB Leonard Neumann authored INT of Miller to halt opportunities when Miami drew close. Miller did, however, hit E Jim Cox with 80y TD pass-run with 2:03 left to play and found WB Jerry Daanen (11/128y, 2 TDs) for last-sec 6y TD pass.

Florida 17 MISSISSIPPI 0: Ole Miss (1-3) had not lost Homecoming game since 1949, but Florida (3-1) used QB Steve Spurrier's 18-29/223y, TD, passing and WR Charles Casey's 7/99y, TD, catching for tidy 17-0 H lead. Spurrier's 8y TD arrow to well-defended Casey drew admiration from Mississippi coach John Vaught: "Stuck it in his damn belt, by God!" Spurrier dived through DBs Bruce Newell and Tommy James on 9y, 4th down TD journey up middle in 2nd Q. For good measure, P Spurrier dropped punts OB at Rebs 5 and 10YLs in 2nd H. Unmercifully pressured by Florida's 6-1-2-2 D with LB Jack Card serving as Rover, Rebels QBs Jimmy Heidel and Harrison Walker combined to pass miserably: 5-16/15y, 2 INTs. Mississippi only ran for 85y in its 1st shutout loss since 1958.

OHIO STATE 28 Illinois 14: Sr Buckeyes (2-1) FB Tom Barrington (32/189y), who had overcome skull fracture from 1963 summertime industrial accident and 2-year search for his best O position, scored 3 TDs to crush Illinois (1-3). Before Barrington's heroics, Illini tallied on their 1st possession: HB Cyril Pinder scored from 4YL after FB Jim Grabowski (15/44y), only 125y short of immortal HB Red Grange's school career rushing mark of 2071y, carried 4 straight plays to bring Pinder into range. With scoreboard reading 7-7 in 2nd Q, Barrington burst 23y to set up his 12y TD jaunt. HB Bo Rein's 26y catch of pass by Ohio State QB Don Unverferth (4-11/92y) positioned Barrington for Bucks' 3rd TD of 2nd Q. After Barrington made it 28-7 in 3rd Q, Illinois was left to improve QB Fred Custardo's anemic-under-pressure passing of 3-15/28y. Ohio FUM at its 23YL created late Illini TD.

Purdue 17 IOWA 14: High-wire aerial showdown was expected by Iowa City Homecoming crowd, and footballs filled air with 1st Q ending in scoreless stalemate. Iowa (1-3) QB Gary Snook (13-32/180y, 2 TDs, 2 INTs) provided 7-0 lead on 42y TD pass to HB Dalton Kimble. All-around standout Purdue (3-0-1) QB Bob Griese (20-36/216y, INT) sneaked for 1y TD to knot it in 2nd Q. Vital play came with score tied at 7-7 in 3rd Q: Griese ducked into accidental facemask sack by Hawkeyes DE Dave Long on 3rd-and-6 from Purdue 21YL. Instead of having to punt, Boilermakers fashioned 16-play drive of 83y to go-ahead score at 14-7. Biggest gain on this trip came when Griese rolled out and motioned E Bob Hadrick (9/114y) to break long for 38y completion to 14YL. After pass interference was called on Iowa in EZ, FB John Kuzniewski's plunge put Purdue in lead for good. In final outcome it was K Griese's toe, which, in addition to his 2 convs, accounted for 19y 4th Q FG that serve as Boilermakers' victory margin. Purdue LB Pat Conley had prompted Griese's 3-ptr with punt block recovered at 10YL by DL Bob Yunaska. Snook suffered several dropped balls, but, in addition to his 42y TD in 2nd Q, he managed 4y TD pass for game's final tally in 4th Q. On Iowa's 72y drive, that ended with 8:53 on clock, Snook started by legging it 2 runs/28y and hitting 4 passes in row including 11y to WR Karl Noonan at 11YL.

Texas 19 Oklahoma 0 (Dallas): Winning its 8th straight Red River Rivalry game over downtrodden Oklahoma (0-3), no. 1 Texas (4-0) used its fabulous D to frustrate Sooners, who were headed to their worst record since 1924. Except for FUM REC, Oklahoma never advanced beyond own 27YL in 1st H. Texas' lost FUM quickly was negated by Steers LB Tommy Nobis' INT. Key TD came in 2nd Q to provide 9-0 Texas lead as QB Marv Kristynik (9-14/102y) ran and passed for 48y of 60y drive, including his 1y TD run. Sooners' O was limited to 84y rushing and 3-11/30y passing.

TEXAS TECH 28 Texas Christian 24: Star Texas Tech (3-1) HB Donny Anderson (18/105y) opening scoring with 54y TD jaunt through Horned Frogs (1-3). But, fellow HB Mike Leinart proved invaluable to Red Raiders. Tech trailed 17-14 after 3 Qs because TCU HB Steve Landon tallied on runs of 31 and 43y, but Leinart's 2nd TD put Texas Tech back in front at 21-17. However, Purple Frogs DB Frank Horak immediately went coast-to-coast on KO TD RET for 24-21 answer. Leinart soon pulled in QB Tom Wilson's 11y TD pass to put Raiders up for good.

Arkansas 38 BAYLOR 7: Powerful, undefeated Arkansas (4-0) claimed 6 errant passes by once-proud aeronautical Bears (2-2) and ran away with SWC verdict. Razorbacks LB Joe Black recovered early FUM in Baylor territory, and QB Jon Brittenum dashed 18y on 3rd-and-13 before pitching 14y TD to WB Harry Jones, who juggled it before blasting through 3 Bears into EZ. QB-K Ronnie South, who later would have FG try blocked by Baylor, made 41y FG in 2nd Q after Baylor DG Greg Pipes made 2 stops to halt 52y drive. In dying moments of 1st H, Hogs DB Tommy Trantham raced down sideline for 69y TD after his INT of QB Ken Stockdale, who alternated with ineffective QB Roger Mike Marshall. Arkansas TB Bobby Burnett scored twice in 2nd H, his 3rd Q 2y blast through RT coming after 73y punt RET by sub TB Jackie Brasuell. Baylor forced bad punt in 3rd Q and finally scored on 12y TD pass on 4th down from Stockdale to WR George Cheshire.

UCLA 24 Syracuse 14: Quick-revving Bruins (2-1) scored on their 1st 2 plays from scrimmage: QB Gary Beban's 27y TD run around RE after Syracuse (2-2) HB Mike Koski lost FUM to UCLA S Bob Richardson on game's 1st snap, and Beban's 79y TD bomb to E Kurt Altenberg after Orangemen punted. "We gave it away before we started to play," carped Syracuse coach Ben Schwartzwalder. Much later, Bruins CB Bob Stiles' 19y INT RET into Syracuse end set up clinching 37y TD run by HB Mel Farr (11/84y, TD) that came with 3:25 to play. Bruins D held Orange ace HB Floyd Little in check with only 16/27y rushing, but their strategy freed up Syracuse FB Larry Csonka for 27/162y rushing and 3y TD run at end of 83y march that concluded nearly halfway into 4th Q. Csonka's crashing TD trimmed debit to 17-7, but New Yorkers' next score didn't come until last 30 secs. It was Uclans' 1st victory in 5 tries to date over Syracuse, 5-pt pre-game favorite.

STANFORD 17 Oregon 14: Twin Ducks passing threats, QBs Tom Trovato and Mike Brundage, each registered scoring throw and placed Oregon (3-1) in lead at 14-10 early in 4th Q. Ducks' go-ahead TD came after pass interference PEN was called against Stanford (3-0-1) secondary. With 1:12 left, Stanford's authentic Indian (member of nearly-extinct Native American Chuckchansi Tribe) QB Dave Lewis pitched his 2nd TD, 14y fling to T-eligible Fergus Flanagan. Trick play was set up by pass interference PEN called on Oregon on 4th-and-15, which gave Stanford 1st down at 9YL.

AP Poll October 11

1 Texas (22)	438	6 Southern California	204
2 Nebraska (16)	435	7 Purdue (1)	187
3 Arkansas (4)	384	8 Notre Dame	162
4 Michigan State (3)	335	9 Florida	98
5 Georgia (2)	280	10 Mississippi State	79

Others with votes: Alabama, Duke, Kentucky, Louisiana State, Missouri, Ohio State, Stanford, Texas Western, Washington State, West Virginia

October 16, 1965

SYRACUSE 28 Penn State 21: Syracuse (3-2) ran 36 plays to 91 for Penn State (1-3), yet Orangemen had magnificent HB Floyd Little to sprint for 91, 69, and 25y scores while Lions had no such weapon. After Orangemen FB Ron Oyer had roared 17y to 2nd Q TD, Lions HB Don Kunit's FUM quickly provided Little with his 1st TD chance for 14-0 lead. Little made it 21-0 with 91y punt RET in 3rd Q before FB Mike McNaughton's 2 TDs got Penn State back in game at 21-15. Nittany Lions outgained Orange 387y to 193y.

NAVY 12 Pittsburgh 0 (Washington, DC): Fiercely-determined Midshipmen (3-1-1) blanked Pitt (1-4), holding Panthers to 24y rushing. Middies made brilliant GLS in 3rd Q that threw back 4 charges from 1YL. Navy DE Ray Hill fulfilled coach Bill Elias' prophecy by blocking Panthers' punt: Hill raced in to get hand on 1 of P Andy McGraw's 9 punts in 2nd Q, and rebound went to Pitt 2YL. Navy FB Alan Roodhouse wedged over on 1st snap for 6-0 lead, but 2-pt pass was missed. Pittsburgh QB Kenny Lucas (15-31/167y, 2 INTs) was under endless pressure and lost 73y on sacks. Middies went nowhere either, as soph QB John Cartwright threw 2 INTs and lost FUM. Navy HB Terry Murray's FUM at his 20YL appeared to give Pitt its chance in 4th Q, and Lucas threw toward EZ for HB Eric Crabtree (6/89y receiving). Officials ruled Crabtree was interfered with, and Pitt had 4 shots from 1YL for go-ahead TD. Twice FB Barry McKnight was thrust back, little HB Bob Dyer tried his hand on 3rd down, and Lucas was smashed back on 4th down sneak. Sr QB Bruce Bickel was soon at Navy's helm, and, after FB Danny Wong changed direction for 30y gain, Bickel hit E Phil Norton twice and HB Steve Shrawder for clinching TD at end of 96y drive.

NORTH CAROLINA 12 Maryland 10: Efficient North Carolina (3-2) held Maryland (2-2) to 99y rushing and built 12-3 lead midway through 4th Q, when suddenly Terrapins were resuscitated. After Maryland WB Bobby Collins had lost 1st H FUM at own 30YL, Carolina QB Danny Talbott found E Charlie Carr galloping free in EZ for 22y TD pass. Tar Heels' 6-0 lead held up through H because Collins dropped pass all alone at UNC 40YL. Chilean soccer-style K Bernardo Bramson, Maryland's so-called "Human Scoreboard" because he jumped into different jersey numbers to match his ever-changing season's pt total, made 38y FG in 3rd Q, but Heels quickly retaliated with 94y march. Talbott connected on 47y pass to WB Bud Phillips and dashed 15y on 4th down to Terps 12YL, gains that set up Talbott's 2y TD run for 12-3 edge. Turtles then came alive on 80y drive as QB Phil Petry hit Collins with 40y pass, and Petry scored from 1YL. Maryland got last chance with 1:33 left, but Bramson failed to up his gimmicky jersey number when he missed 45y FG try.

VIRGINIA 41 West Virginia 0 (Richmond): Unbeaten West Virginia (4-1) was averaging 44.5 pts in its opening victories, but received huge comeuppance from Virginia (3-2). Cavs turned pair of WVU FUMs on KO RETs into TDs and cashed in DB Jim Donley's INT for another score. Virginia's O wasn't napping itself. UVa QB Tom Hodges (16-25/185y, TD, INT) led 92 and 88y TD drives in 2nd Q to put Cavs up 21-0 at H on 7y TD pass to E Ed Carrington. When Cavaliers HB John Pincavage raced 90y with 2nd H KO, Virginia opened another 3-TD floodgate. Superb pass D by Virginia (3-2) prevented any completions by QB Allen McCune until verdict was iced in 3rd Q.

ALABAMA 7 Tennessee 7: Alabama (3-1-1) soph QB Ken Stabler went on to make few mistakes in his brilliant college and pro careers, but his critical blunder with 6 secs left cost Crimson Tide chance to win. Thanks to fine passing by Stabler, Alabama drove downfield, and it reached Tennessee (2-0-2) 4YL on Stabler's 14y dash. "The Snake" then fired pass OB to stop clock for entry of FG team. But, his incomplete pass came on 4th down. Confused Stabler thought his scramble had earned 1st down, but he had lost track of goal-to-go situation that had started with 1st down just inside 10YL. His run only had helped make up lost 10y on bad 2nd down pitchout. Earlier, rivals traded short 2nd Q TD runs: FB Stan Mitchell for Volunteers and QB Steve Sloan for Bama. Although Alabama dominated 2nd H on way to game-end 361y to 195y stat advantage, Sloan lost 2 vital FUMs. Tennessee LB Frank Emanuel pilfered pigskin at Vols 1YL in 3rd Q, and Sloan lost another at end of long drive with 4:50 to go in 4th Q. Part of coach Bear Bryant's legend was cultivated after game: Angry and frustrated, Bryant led his team to its locker room in sullen silence only to discover door was locked. "Joe, shoot the damn thing open," he demanded of Alabama state trooper Joe Smelley. Smelley demurred, claiming bullet ricochet might "kill three or four people." Bryant responded with "get your fat fanny out of my way!" and simply knocked door off its hinges. Coach Doug Dickey of Volunteers gleefully but mistakenly credited his punt game for "win." Tennessee's joy quickly ended as 3 asst coaches were killed in auto-train accident during following week.

GEORGIA TECH 23 Auburn 14: Tigers (2-2-1) had better of play in 1st H, moving into Georgia Tech (3-1-1) territory 4 times. When Tech D turned stiff, as it did each time it was threatened, Auburn settled for 2 out of 3 FG tries by K Don Lewis, including 49y boot. Soph QB Kim King (13-15/135y, TD) was O star for Yellow Jackets: Among King's opening 9 straight completions was 9y TD pass to E Corky Rogers in 2nd Q that earned 6-6 H tie, and King put Georgia Tech ahead for good early in 2nd H. When all his receivers were covered on 1st snap of 3rd Q after E Tommy Elliott's KO FUM REC, King scrambled 31y to score for 13-6 lead. Key blocks on play came from FB Ed Varner and HB Terry Haddock. Tigers' most painful wound came from DB Tommy Bleick's 57y INT TD RET to cap Tech's 17-pt 3rd Q ouburst. In late stages, Auburn QB Alex Bowden (9-20/135y, TD, INT) filled air with passes and connected with HB Joe Campbell for 37y TD in 4th Q.

LOUISIANA STATE 31 Kentucky 21: QB Nelson Stokley (15/118y rushing) and TB Joe Labruzzo (14/100y) led Louisiana State (4-1) O in vanquishing air-oriented Kentucky (3-2). Ball-hawking Bayou Bengals D stole 6 passes from SEC's top passer, Wildcats QB Rick Norton (14-31/158y, 6 INTs). On its way to 452y O, LSU scored in less than 3 mins as Stokely probed middle of line from midfield and dashed 50y to score. Tigers recovered FUM by UK HB Larry Seiple at Kentucky 34YL after exchange of punts. LSU FB Danny LeBlanc powered over for his 1st of 2 1y TD plunges. E-K Doug Moreau nailed 36y FG early in 2nd Q for 17-0 Bengals lead. Norton went to air to bring Cats 2 TDs on runs by HB Rodger Bird and Norton with successful on-side KO in between. Trailing 31-13 in 4th Q, Wildcats DB Terry Beadles made INT and ran 24y to LSU 10YL. Bird swept left for TD and Norton followed with 2-pt pass to bring score to 31-21. But, Norton suffered 2 INTs.

VANDERBILT 21 Virginia Tech 10: It wasn't Halloween yet, but it might well have been in nutty Nashville. Adventurous Gobblers (4-1) authored wacky KO RET that kept them in game in 4th Q, but in going down to defeat for 1st time in 1965 they allowed strange TD to beat them in 4th Q. Things were pretty normal in 1st H, led by Virginia Tech 3-0 on K John Utin's 32y FG. Game's oddities began in 3rd Q when Va Tech LB Clarence Culpepper made INT of Vanderbilt (1-3-1) QB Bob Kerr, but lost football when he was up-ended. Vandy T John Hammersmith made REC to set up Kerr's 4y TD pass to WR Chuck Ousley. TE Randy Humble nabbed 4y TD pass from Kerr in 4th Q, so Commordores led 14-3. On ensuing KO, sub VPI QB Tommy Stafford corralled KO on his 8YL, lateraled to starting QB Bobby Owens, who stopped after several y and fired cross-field pass to HB Dickie Longerbeam who raced 89y before being bumped OB at 1YL by Vanderbilt DB Steve Bevil. FB Claude Messamore plunged over to pull Gobblers within 14-10. But, just when Va Tech thought it could mount winning drive it was interrupted by least-likely of all Vandy interceptors: NG Sid Ransom, who rumbled 32y to score Commodores' clinching TD.

FLORIDA STATE 10 Georgia 3: Hard-hitting game turned early in 4th Q when Florida State (2-2) soph TB Bill Moreman, newly promoted from kicking team, delivered elusive 20y TD run at end of 47y march. To that point, battered Georgia (4-1) led 3-0 on K Bob Etter's 38y FG in 2nd Q and 4th down stand at own 8YL in 3rd Q. Seminoles added K Gene Roberts' late 31y FG after standout LB Bill McDowell made REC of Georgia E Pat Hodgson's fumbled reception at Bulldogs 20YL.

Purdue 17 MICHIGAN 15: Wolverines (2-3) had undefeated Purdue (4-0-1) on run in early portion of game as their D strapped Boilermakers. Michigan got game's 1st TD on HB Carl Ward's 17y run, but could have had wider margin if HB-K Rick Sygar had made 2 FGs and x-pt. WR Jim Finley had banner day for Boilers with 11/159y in receptions for school mark to-date for aerial y. Finley caught early 3rd Q pass from QB Bob Griese (22-38/273y, 2 TDs, INT) that put visitors ahead 7-6. Griese changed width of his rollouts in 2nd H and started finding his mark: E Jim Bierne caught another score for 14-6 lead. Wolverine fans forgave Sygar when he booted UM back into lead at 15-14 with short FG in 4th Q after QB Wally Gabler (9-29/137y, TD) found E Jack Clancy for 40y TD late in 3rd Q. Purdue began its winning march at its 11YL, and although Griese was surprised by coaching decision to try 35y FG, he nailed it nonetheless with 55 secs left.

MICHIGAN STATE 32 Ohio State 7: In consecutive weeks, Michigan and then Ohio State (2-2) were frustrated with minus rushing y permitted by juggernaut D of Spartans (5-0). With Buckeyes finishing at -22y, it marked 1st time in school history that Bucks ended game in negative rushing y numbers. By contrast, MSU romped for 387y rushing. Ohio State D was stung by 80y TD jaunt by HB Clinton Jones (16/132y, TD) on Michigan State's 2nd scrimmage play of 1st Q. Spartans' K Dick Kenney bare-toed 35y FG, and LB Ron Goovert trapped Ohio QB Don Unverferth for safety to give Michigan State 12-0 lead in 3rd Q. After QB Unverferth's TD pass trimmed deficit to 12-7, Spartans dropped 20-pt 4th Q avalanche on wilting Buckeyes. "It was our finest performance of the season," said coach Duffy Daugherty. "Ohio State will play ball control if it gets yardage on first down. Our game plan was to take away that first down yardage." Remarkably, Ohio was so overwhelmed in run game that it didn't try true running play in entire 2nd H as QB Don Unverferth, who hit 14-29/174y, TD, 3 INTs, was spilled 3 times on sacks and gained only 5y when flushed from pass pocket.

MISSOURI 14 Ucla 14: Growing UCLA (2-1-1) attack racked up 282y, and its improving D threw net over Missouri's tough rushing O, holding it to 116y. Bruins QB Gary Beban rifled 34y TD pass to HB Byron Nelson in 2nd Q. After Beban threw another scoring pass to E Kurt Altenberg in 4th Q, Tigers (3-1-1) DB Ray Thorpe took short KO, raced 79y to shave lead to 14-6. Moments later, Missouri HB-DB Johnny Roland fielded punt, went 65y to TD and added tying 2-pt HB pass to WB Earl Denny.

COLORADO 10 Iowa State 10: Colorado (3-0-2), on strength of INT by DB Dick Anderson, scored on HB William Harris' 3y run in 2nd Q for 7-0 edge. Buffs maintained control of Iowa State (3-1-1) by virtue of 3 INTs of Cyclones' up-and-down, but imaginative thrower-runner QB Tim Van Galder (8-20/99y, TD, INT). Score stayed 7-0 until short punt became CU's armor chink, and Iowa State finally got rolling early in 4th Q. Van Galder ran for gains of 11 and 7y, and 15y roughness PEN was tacked on to bring Cyclones to Buffs 7YL. E George Maurer jumped high to bring down Van Galder's TD pass for 7-7 knot. On following KO, Cyclones DB Ernie Kennedy recovered FUM by Buffs Anderson to position K Steve Balkovec for 34y FG and 10-7 Iowa State lead with 9:41 to play. Colorado took over at its 33YL after accepting punt and used clutch catch by former DB-turned-WR George Lewark to move to Cyclones 12YL. QB Bernie McCall's EZ toss to Lewark, who had 6 mostly spectacular receptions in his new role, looked like sure score until Iowa State DB Larry Carswell made fingertip deflection. Buffs K Frank Rogers, former WR, knocked tying 33y FG through with 21 secs left, but not before he got 2nd chance when off-setting PENs wiped away bad C snap on previous aborted FG try.

ARKANSAS 27 Texas 24: Calculated 80y drive ended on Arkansas (5-0) QB Jon Brittenum's 1y TD run with 1:32 to play. Hard-hitting Hogs D made Texas (4-1) TB Phil Harris cough up 2 1st Q FUMs which were directly converted into TDs, 2nd of which was midair number returned 77y for score by Porkers DB Tommy Trantham. Longhorns battled back to within 20-11 in 2nd Q on K David Conway's FG and QB Marv Kristynik's TD at end of 73y march. Conway (2 FGs) and Kristynik (14y TD run) repeated themselves in 2nd H as Texas took 24-20 lead and dominated stats that would end 401y to 181y in its favor. But, Brittenum rallied Razorbacks, hitting 6 passes, including falling-down grab, his 4th on drive, by E Bobby Crockett (TD catcher in 2nd Q) for 14y as key play to set up Brittenum's fateful TD plunge for win. Arkansas win streak reached 17 straight.

SOUTHERN CALIFORNIA 14 Stanford 0: Scrappy, undermanned Stanford (3-1-1) battled USC (4-0-1) to scoreless tie through game's 1st 52 mins. Led by LB Bob Rath and DL Bill Ostrander, Indians halted 4 plays by Trojans at Stanford 1YL in 3rd Q. On 3rd down play midway in 4th Q, Trojans TB Mike Garrett (31/205y) burst 76y to TD behind blocks of FB Gary Fite and HB Rod Sherman. Southern California LB Eddie King's INT off QB Dave Lewis set up Sherman for late, clinching 25y TD sweep.

CALIFORNIA 16 Washington 12: California (3-2) almost completely ignored its aerial game (1-2/3y, TD, INT) in switch from standard West Coast procedure, pounding for 249y rushing to come from behind to nip fumbling Huskies (1-4). It was Washington's 4th straight defeat before it was able to right ship for late-season surge toward even W-L mark. Big Golden Bears FB Fran Lynch, who often lined up in same backfield with fellow FB Ron Minimide, battered across from 1YL at end of 82y trip in 3rd Q for decisive TD that was icing on Lynch's 1st starting assignment. Cal K Dan Sinclair had opened scoring with 34y FG in 1st Q after QB Tod Hullin lost 1st of 3 damaging Washington FUMs in 1st H. UW failed at California 7 and 8YLs because of lost FUMs, but HB Steve Bramwell earlier had scooted 51y with KO RET to put HB Ron Medved in position for 28y TD run. Hullin pitched 45y score in 2nd Q for 12-3 lead for Huskies, but QB Dan Berry soon completed Cal's only successful pass, 3y TD to E Jerry Bradley before H.

WASHINGTON STATE 21 Arizona 3 (Spokane): Power runs by FB Larry Eilmes (21/130y) and accurate tosses by QB Tom Roth (11-17/168y, TD, INT) sparked surprising Washington State (4-1). Cougars earned game's only 1st H score as Roth pushed over from 1YL. Wildcats (2-3) DB Wally Scott blocked 2 FG tries in 2nd Q. DB Woody King nearly broke away on punt RET in 3rd Q, but Arizona had to settle for K Jan Komorowski's 31y FG when QB Phil Albert was sacked twice. Eilmes immediately fumbled at his 20YL, but Cats were pushed back so far that Komorowski missed FG. Washington State next went 80y with Roth hitting E Doug Flansburg with 33y TD pass.

AP Poll October 18

1 Arkansas (28)	468	6 Purdue	239
2 Michigan State (14)	420	7 Notre Dame	192
3 Nebraska (8)	393	8 Florida	139
4 Southern California	268	9 Louisiana State	79
5 Texas	253	10 Georgia	65

Others with votes: Alabama, Clemson, Duke, Florida State, Memphis State, Michigan, Minnesota, Mississippi State, Missouri, Oregon State, Princeton, Utah State, UCLA, Washington State

October 23, 1965

Dartmouth 14 HARVARD 0: Big Green (5-0) completely dominated 1st 25 mins. Soph Gene Ryzewicz opened at QB, sprinted 36y on 1st snap, soon moved to HB as QB Mickey Beard entered to score on 2y run. Dartmouth went 47y in 2 plays in 2nd Q as Ryzewicz threw 31y HB pass to HB Paul Klungness, who followed with 16y TD run.

Then, behind crafty 1st-time starting QB Ric Zimmerman, Harvard (3-1-1) turned game around in 3rd Q, picking off 2 passes, but losing TD on EZ FUM, and turning ball over on downs at Indians 8YL.

WAKE FOREST 12 North Carolina 10: ACC was amazingly balanced conf in 1965, and Winston-Salem fans witnessed its biggest upset of season and sole league win for tail-ender Wake Forest (2-4). Deacons coach Bill Tate turned QB reins over to jr Jon Wilson (14-26/172y, TD), whose season's experience so far had been 4 mins. Wilson played without error and pitched winning 41y TD to E Buck Henry (7/103y) with 6 mins to play. Wake Forest led 6-3 on 2 FGs by Eddie McKinney, and Deacs D had held North Carolina (3-3) completely in check. UNC was able to travel 74y to 10-6 lead on HB David Riggs' 11y sweep with 7:55 to play. Wake's answering drive was highlighted by HB Joe Carazo's 18y fingertip catch on 3rd down to set up winning bomb to Henry.

VIRGINIA TECH 22 Virginia 14: Gov. Albertis Harrison was among record crowd of Virginians to enjoy battle of Commonwealth schools at new stadium in Blacksburg. Virginia (3-3) enjoyed its success in air as QB Tom Hodges completed 14-27/182y, TD, INT, but much of Cavs' aerial charge came too late. Meanwhile, Gobblers (5-1) succeeded by running ball for 323y, even though its decisive score came on 71y TD pass in 4th Q. Virginia Tech QB Bobby Owens scored on 1y sneak and 24y burst up middle for 15-0 lead by 3rd Q. Hodges scored on 2y run in 4th and added 2-pt run to pull Cavaliers within 15-8. Just 2 plays later, Owens made long throw caught by WB Tommy Groom, who screeched on brakes to avoid Virginia DB Jim Morgan and zipped remainder of 71y TD. Hodges' 3 completions narrowed outcome as Cavs scored in last 2 mins on 32y catch by HB Ken Poates.

GEORGIA TECH 37 Navy 16: Engineers (4-1-1) QB Kim King sunk Navy (3-2-1) with 1st H 15-22/176y aerial barrage that accounted for 3 TDs and FG. Georgia Tech scored twice in 3rd Q without running single scrimmage play as DBs Bill Eastman and Sammy Burke each ran back long punt RETs for TDs. Middies QB Bruce Bickel threw 2 late TD passes to salvage some seafarers pride.

TENNESSEE 17 Houston 8: Grieving over accidental railroad-crossing deaths of 3 asst coaches, Volunteers (3-0-2) adorned their helmets with black crosses, but seemed not to have much heart in scoreless 1st H. Tennessee took 10-0 3rd Q lead as K David Leake capped 77y drive with 20y FG and LB Doug Archibald picked off pass by Cougars QB Bo Burris and retuned it for 20y TD. LB Frank Emanuel led inspired Volunteers D, which kept substandard Houston (1-5) outside 20YL until closing moments. Burris led late air attack, culminating in 6y TD pass to TE Tom Beer, then repeated same play for 2 pts.

MINNESOTA 14 Michigan 13: Minnesota (3-2-1) stayed undefeated in Big 10, but in standings trailed Michigan State, 14-10 winner over Purdue. Key to reclaiming Little Brown Jug was heavy pass-rush by DE Bob Bruggers and LB Gary Reierson that thwarted Michigan (2-4) QB Wally Gabler's 2-pt try with 1:22 left. Gophers had gone 54y in 4th Q to QB John Hankinson's sneak for 14-7 lead. Wolverines FB Dave Fisher had given 7-0 lead when he caught HB Carl Ward's toss on broken option pass play in 1st Q. Gabler brought Michigan within 14-13 on late 4y run.

NOTRE DAME 28 Southern California 7: Legendary *Los Angeles Times* columnist Jim Murray had correct sense of history and humor from his press box perch: "Outlined against the blue-grey October sky, Notre Dame kicked the bejabbers out of USC on a leaky Saturday afternoon." Sparked by LB Jim Lynch, DB Nick Rassas, and DLs Tom Rhoads and Dick Arrington, Notre Dame D put wraps on Heisman-to-be TB Mike Garrett, holding him to microscopic 9/7y rushing in 1st H and 16/43y overall. Meanwhile, Fighting Irish (4-1) FB Larry Conjar (25/116y, 4 TDs) blasted for all necessary scores to become 1st ND player to turn 4-TD trick since Johnny Lattner did it against same Trojans in 1953. Building 308y to 74y rush advantage, Irish easily crunched to leads of 21-0 at H and 28-0 in 3rd Q. Heavy rain and cold wind hampered passing attacks, but Trojans (4-1-1) finally clicked on 76y drive at beginning of 4th Q as QB Troy Winslow kept for 12 and 7y gains and threw for 21 and 8y completions as E John Thomas made special catches, latter for diving 8y TD. Trojans made it to 1st-and-goal at ND 9YL, but reverse runs failed, and USC found itself back at 38YL in 3 swift sweeps of scythe by Irish D.

NEBRASKA 38 Colorado 13: QB Fred Duda combined with E Freeman White for 2 TD passes, including new Nebraska (6-0) record play of 95y. K Frank Rogers of Colorado (3-1-2) kicked 2 FGs, but Buffaloes couldn't head off 31-6 stampede in 1st H which included 3 Duda-responsible TDs and short TD run by HB Harry Wilson. Buffs HB Larry Plantz scored on late 7y run. Huskers, nation's leading O, recorded 372y vs. country's no. 10 D.

RICE 20 Texas 17: Spirited 2nd H rally by Rice (2-3) provided intermittent win over Texas (4-2), Owls' 7th since 1946 and last until 1994. TB Robert Leach and QB Marv Kristynik produced TDs that fueled Texas' 14-3 lead. After Steers' K David Conway's FG made it 17-3 late in 3rd Q, Owls HB Chuck Latourette sped all the way to Texas 20YL with ensuing KO. Rice QB David Ferguson scored within 4 plays to end 3rd Q, and Latourette followed with 7y TD run 5 mins later to tie it 17-17. Rice DB Robert Hailey's clutch INT positioned K Richard Parker's winning 33y FG with 43 secs to play.

WYOMING 34 Brigham Young 6: Worthy Wyoming (5-1) rebounded from 42-3 thrashing by Utah to slip ahead of BYU (3-2) in WAC race. Leaping to 28-0 3rd Q lead, Cowboys displayed lots of weapons: FB Mike Davenport plunged for 2 TDs, QB Tom Wilkinson launched 68y TD pass to WB Garry McLean, and QB Rick Egloff ran 9y for score. Lone Cougars' TD came on QB Virgil Carter's 3y pass to E Phil Odle.

UCLA 56 California 3: Theoretical evenly-matched Pac-8 upstarts were close only as long as it took for K Dan Sinclair to kick 37y FG midway in 1st Q after FUM REC at UCLA (3-1-1) 36YL to keep California (3-3) within striking distance at 7-3. Dazzling QB Gary Beban (5-9/193y, TD, and 10/60y, 2 TDs rushing) placed UCLA (3-1-1) in thick of Rose Bowl race with 2 TD runs, 78y TD rocket to E Dick Witcher, and 61y pass to HB Ray Armstrong to set up another score. HB Mel Farr (12/156y, 2 TDs) contributed 21 and 45y TD runs to biggest-ever Bruins win over in-state collegiate cousins from Bay Area. Cal got another break in 2nd Q as Farr lost FUM at Uclans' 25YL. However, Bears were halted on downs at 7YL, and 3 plays later Beban launched his 78y bomb to Witcher for 28-3 lead. Bruins piled up 619y on O and scored most pts against California since USC dropped 74-0 avalanche on Bears in same L.A. Coliseum in 1930.

Washington 24 OREGON 20: Washington (2-4) gambled its way out of 4-game losing skid as it used spectacular catches of E Dave Williams and 230y passing to come from behind with big 4th Q. Oregon (3-2-1) got on board 1st on QB Tom Trovato's 8y TD pass to E Steve Bunker that climaxed 71y drive in 1st Q. Williams and sub QB Tom Sparlin connected on 70y bomb in 2nd Q to send teams off at 7-7 at H, but, as result of Ducks FUM REC, Trovato ended 28y scoring march in 3rd Q with 1y TD push. So, Washington trailed 14-7 entering decisive 4th Q, and it took only 5 plays to start its upward spiral. QB Tod Hullin and E Bruce Kramer clicked on 5y TD pass and immediately reunited for repeat of same play for 2 pts and 15-14 edge. Huskies 58y punt soon backed Ducks to their 2YL from which point, UW DT Fred Forsburg tackled Trovato for safety. Williams' 47y TD catch a few plays later clinched it at 24-14.

STANFORD 31 Army 14: Creatively speaking, Stanford (4-1-1) clinched Commander in Chief Trophy with 2nd win over service academy, plus its earlier tie with Navy. Army (3-3) struck 1st in opening Q as QB Fred Barofsky raced 24y to TD. Indians HB Ray Handley, future New York Giants coach, plowed for tying TD in 1st Q, and, after Cadets' threat was ended when their 4th down pass was batted down, QB Dave Lewis scampered 17y to extend Stanford's H lead to 17-7. Handley lost FUM to Army DB Ed Noble early in 3rd Q, and, 9 plays later, Barofsky sneaked for TD that trimmed deficit to 17-14. Indians went 68y in 3rd Q for clinching TD as soph FB Jack Root was key ground-gainer until Lewis hit E Mike Connelly for 10y TD pass. Cadets stopped threats at own 8 and 5YLs in 4th Q, but finally succumbed in game's last min as Army QB Curt Cook's FUM was pounced upon in Cadets EZ for TD by Stanford's highly-active LB Marty Brill.

AP Poll October 25

1 Michigan State (19)	473	6 Purdue	201
2 Arkansas (23)	466	7 Florida	200
3 Nebraska (9)	424	8 Southern California	93
4 Notre Dame	346	9 Texas	68
5 Louisiana State	230	10 Alabama	62

Others with votes: Clemson, Georgia, Georgia Tech, Kentucky, Minnesota, Mississippi State, Missouri, Ohio State, Penn State, Princeton, Stanford, Syracuse, Tennessee, Texas Tech, UCLA, Utah State, Washington State, Wyoming

October 30, 1965

PRINCETON 45 Brown 27: Princeton (6-0) won its 15th game in row and retained 1st place tie in Ivy League race with Dartmouth at 4-0, which was come-from-behind 20-17 winner over Yale. TB Ron Landeck threw 4 TD passes out of Tigers' ancient Single-wing O, piling up 297y on 10-13/192y passing and 22/105y rushing. Outdoing him in O-fest was Brown (1-5) QB Bob Hall, who threw 3 TD passes, dashed for 4th score in accruing 338y on 19-38/243y in air and 18/95y on ground. Important TD made it 14-0 for Princeton in 1st Q after Tigers LB Hayward Gipson blocked punt and DL Stas Maliszewski recovered at Bruins 4YL.

Georgia 47 NORTH CAROLINA 35: This was rollicking tilt that by game's end would see Carolina tote up 448y and Georgia finish with 436y. Bulldogs (5-2) discovered value of FB Ronnie Jenkins (19/81y, 2 TDs, and 4/66y, TD receiving), whose 3 scores stood as Georgia's contribution to 21-21 H deadlock. UGa nearly gave contest away by turning ball over 4 times in 3rd Q. Nifty North Carolina (3-4) QB Danny Talbott (12-24/216y, TD, 2 INTs), who accumulated 318y total O, scored with 21 secs left in 3rd Q to add to HB Dave Riggs' 7y pitchout run for TD, so Tar Heels had outcome all but under control at 35-21. Georgia QB Lynn Hughes, who was switched back from DB spot to shared duty with QB Preston Ridlehuber for this game, scored 3 TDs in 4th Q . Hughes' 2nd score moved Bulldogs to within 35-34, but Ridlehuber came off bench to try 2-pt pass, which was stopped by UNC DB Gene Link. Successful on-side KO immediately worked when Tar Heels defender apparently lost sight of high bouncing ball in bright sun of Carolina-blue sky. Bulldogs' REC of KO set up Ridlehuber to dash 31y to killing TD and 40-35 reversal.

GEORGIA TECH 35 Duke 23: Yellow Jackets (5-1-1) won 5th straight game to leap into bowl contention. Georgia Tech came from behind twice as super-soph QB Kim King (12-15/141y, 3 TDs, INT) raised nation's best completion percentage to 69.7 and threw all 3 of his scoring passes to WB Craig Baynham. Diehard Duke (4-3) went ahead for 2nd time in 3rd Q at 16-14 as QB Todd Orvald (17-27/237y, 3 TDs, 3 INTs), in for injured Scotty Glacken, tossed his 2nd TD pass. Georgia Tech took lead for good with 12:04 left in 4th Q when FB Doc Harvin capped 71y drive with 1y scrum. However, getting themselves to Duke 1YL had its anxiety for Jackets: Blue Devils DB Mike Shasby prevented TE Gary Williams from making short 4th down catch, and spinning deflection was turned into INT by Duke DB John Gutekunst. But, Shasby was flagged for interference. Shortly after Harvin's TD put Jackets up 21-16, LB Randall Edmunds clinched it by going untouched with 20y INT TD RET of Orvald.

AUBURN 28 Florida 17: Superb Florida (4-2) QB Steve Spurrier (22-41/289y, 2 TDs, 3 INTs) was pitching hard at end of agonizing defeat. In 1st H, Spurrier profited from 2 pass interference PENs to throw Gators into position for K Wayne Barfield's 26y FG and WB Jack Harper's 21y TD catch as Florida ventured into Tigers' end on 6 of 7 possessions. These scores cemented 10-0 H lead over Plainsmen (3-3-1), who had nearly non-existent O during opening 30 mins and didn't earn any 1st downs until last 2:49 of 1st H. . In 2nd H, alert Auburn LB Bill Cody twice converted Spurrier errors into TDs that vaulted Tigers into surprising SEC leadership at 2-0-1. Well into 3rd Q, Plainsmen QB Alex Bowden pitched wobbly 29y TD pass to E Scotty Long, and Cody

raced 29y on INT TD RET on 1st snap after Florida received ensuing KO. Behind for 1st time at 14-10, Gators went 80y to Spurrier's 11y TD arrow to WR Charles Casey (9/128y, TD). Bowden answered but also wobbly 69y TD bomb to E Freddie Hyatt in 4th Q. Under heavy rush, Spurrier relinquished FUM to Cody in EZ with 1:59 to play, and coach Shug Jordan clinched his 100th, victory most ever at Auburn to date.

MISSISSIPPI 23 Louisiana State 0 (Jackson, Miss.): In opener of day-night twin-bill in Jackson, Mississippi (4-3) drubbed surprised LSU (5-2) with mighty D that limited Tigers' flashy O to 52y. Rebels jumped to 17-0 lead thanks to Bengals TB Joe Labruzzo fumbling punt and 2nd H KO at own 3YL. Labruzzo's bobbles led to 10 pts even though LSU D-line did its part by stopping 3 smashes before Ole Miss K James Harvey made 20y FG in 2nd Q. After 2nd H KO FUM REC, Rebels TB Mike Dennis scored his 2nd TD. LB James Nelson nabbed 4th Q INT off Tigers QB Billy Ezell and returned it for closing TD.

Alabama 10 MISSISSIPPI STATE 7 (Jackson, Miss.): Nightcap of Jackson's Dizzy Dean Day festivities saw Alabama (5-1-1) come out throwing as QB Steve Sloan rifled 65y TD pass to WR Dennis Homan in early going. Tide LB Stan Moss' FUM REC in Mississippi State (4-3) territory in 3rd Q, and K David Ray kicked 27y FG. Trying to avoid 3rd loss in row, Bulldogs QB Ashby Cook and HB Marcus Rhoden wrapped up 79y drive with 11y TD pass collaboration in 3rd Q. Alabama blocked late FG try by Miss State K James Neill.

ILLINOIS 21 Purdue 0: Underdog Illinois (4-3) caught Purdue (4-2-1) wobbling from previous week's 14-10 loss to Michigan State and sent FB Jim Grabowski blasting for 36/163y and TD on ground. Sr Grabowski set new Big 10 career rushing record for 3-year players with 2275y, mark held by Minnesota's Paul Giel since 1953. Boilermakers had miserable day on O, gaining just 14y rushing. Blitzing Illini LB Bill Harper tossed QB Bob Griese for -74y in losses, and DL Bob Batchelder even snatched ball from Griese's hand during pass attempt.

OHIO STATE 11 Minnesota 10: On way to becoming coach Woody Hayes' 2nd 1000y passer in single season, Buckeyes (4-2) QB Don Unverferth helped dispel notion that Hayes never allowed his team to throw. Unverferth pitched 14-25/196y, including 25y TD in 2nd Q. Ohio State Sub QB Arnold Fontes followed with 2-pt run for 8-7 lead. Minnesota (3-3-1) retook 3rd Q lead in 1st meeting of teams in 15 years on K Deryl Ramey's 32y FG. Ohio State went 89y to K Bob Funk's FG with 1:17 left. Ramey missed chip-shot FG from 15YL with 14 secs to go.

Nebraska 16 MISSOURI 14: Critical Big 8 tilt found Missouri (4-2-1) bursting from locker room to build early 14-0 lead on 80y drive after opening KO and DB Johnny Roland's midfield INT. QB Gary Lane scored TD on 22y run and conferred 15, 41, and 19y pass completions to Tigers' 2 early drives. Finally getting rolling by 2nd Q, Nebraska (7-0) edged to within 14-13 on scoring marches of 57 and 89y. HB Harry "Light Horse" Wilson raced 37y to 1YL to set up FB Pete Tatman's TD plunge. On 2nd TD trip, Nebraska QB Fred Duda skirted E for 38y on 4th-and-1 to poise Tatman for another short scoring dive. Cornhuskers K Larry Wachholtz's 26y FG with 5:56 on 4th Q clock made up for his missed conv. Mizzou flubbed 2 late chances, losing it on downs and QB Lloyd Carr's INT.

Colorado 13 OKLAHOMA 0: Colorado (4-1-2) D allowed 284y O to Oklahoma (2-4) but sent Sooners to 3rd shutout in single season for only time since 1942, largely because of 3 FUM RECs and 3 INTs. Meanwhile, Buffs were aided by 27y in PENs on 48y voyage to their only TD in 1st Q. Sooners superb LB Carl McAdams (17 tackles and INT) was called for 8y pass interference and OU couldn't get its 12th defender off field in time to prevent 5y PEN to its 5YL. CU QB Bernie McCall (9-20/115y, INT) sneaked to 1YL, and HB Estes Banks blasted over for TD. K Frank Rogers made 34 and 42y FGs in middle Qs to pad Colorado's advantage to 13-0. As well as Oklahoma D played, it couldn't overcome Bison's starting possessions 7 times in OU territory, even though Colorado did all it could to stymie itself with 142y in PENs. Sooners lost battle with H clock when QB Gene Cagle was stopped at 1YL by Colorado DT Frank Bosch. Buffs' 3 late INTs, 2 by DB and future golf great Hale Irwin, completed shutout win for Colorado.

TEXAS CHRISTIAN 10 Baylor 7: Once again, Baylor's passing game, once its forte, turned against Bears (3-3) as sr Texas Christian (3-4) QB Kent Nix (11-15/94y, TD, INT) completely outshined Baylor counterpart, QB Ken Stockdale (15-36/175y, 4 INTs). Baylor got cheap, early TD when top-rate DE Donnie Laurence recovered FUM by Purple Frogs HB Kenneth Post (17/47y) at TCU 18YL. FB Billy Hayes punched it over from 4YL for 7-0 lead that lasted until Frogs' 55y TD march in 2nd Q that was aided by roughing P PEN (15y of game-end 98y flagged against Baylor) that allowed TCU to keep possession. E Joe Ball caught 3 of Nix's 5 completions, including 5y catch that tied it at 7-7 in 2nd Q. TCU went 59y in 3rd Q but was stopped at Bears 22YL, and K Bruce Alford drilled 39y FG, high and straight. TCU gambled on 4th-and-inches at own 34YL early in 4th Q, and "Good Ol' Baylor Line" buried Nix. But, on 2nd down of this big opportunity, Stockdale threw to sideline, where Frogs DB Larry Perry stepped in for INT. TCU DB Paul Smith ended it later in appropriate fashion with another INT.

Arkansas 31 TEXAS A&M 0: Arkansas (7-0) won its 19th straight, also matching Southwest Conf mark of 12, previously held by Texas A&M in 1939-40 and Texas 1962-64. Aggies (2-5) D rose up to stop each of Porkers' 1st 6 series and turned opening 22 mins into punting duel. But, Hogs TB Bobby Burnett scored 2 TDs in 2nd Q, and WB Jim Lindsay and E Bobby Crockett caught TD passes in 2nd H.

SOUTHERN METHODIST 31 Texas 14: Longhorns (4-3), so steadfast since Darrell Royal arrived as coach in 1957, completely lost their poise in 4th Q as Southern Methodist (3-2-1) exploded for 21 late pts and earned back some respect that had been missing for much of last 10 years. Mustangs jumped to 10-0 H lead as WR John Roderick went high to steal TD pass from 2 Texas DBs with 50 secs to go in 2nd Q. Steers P David Conway bounced long punt dead at SMU 5YL with Ponies nursing 10-6

lead and less than 11 mins to play. SMU FB Jim Hagle burst through and streamed 93y for longest TD run in school history, and when DB Ronnie Reel picked off pass by Longhorns QB Marv Kristynik and returned it 58y for TD, party was all but over at 24-6. All soph backfield went 80y for Texas' late TD, but SMU QB Mike Livingston lofted 45y counter-move TD bomb to Roderick. It was 3rd straight loss for surprisingly stumbling Steers.

Arizona State 28 TEXAS WESTERN 20: QB Billy Stevens (25-53/326y, TD, 3 INTs) pitched Texas Western (4-2) to 20-0 lead with more than able receiving assistance from dynamic WR Chuck Hughes (17/254y). Stevens and Hughes teamed up to position 2 TD runs by FB Dick Weeks. In between those scores in 2nd Q, Stevens hit TE Chuck Anderson with 11y TD throw. Arizona State (3-4) rallied behind aerial combination of QB John Goodman (12-20/138y) and E Dewey Forrister, who latched on to 22 and 40y passes to set up FB Jimmy Bramlet's 2y TD dive that pulled Devils to within 20-7 at H. Trailing 20-14 in 4th Q, Sun Devils HB Ben Hawkins hurdled bevy of tacklers on punt RET and raced 69y to TD and 21-20 lead. Stevens fired Miners downfield, but DB Hawkins picked off flat pass and zoomed 64y to TD.

UTAH STATE 34 Brigham Young 21: Unbeaten Utah State (7-0) mixed QB Ron Edwards' 3 TD passes with national scoring leader HB Roy Shivers' 180y, 2 TDs rushing. With BYU (3-3) in new 4-WR spread, QB Virgil Carter (22-51/365y, 3 TDs, 3 INTs) had pitched 1st of his 3 TD passes in 1st Q to provide 7-0 lead. But, resourceful Aggies D contributed 3 INTs to help regain Old Wagon Wheel trophy.

Washington State 10 OREGON STATE 8: Surprising Cougars (6-1), 4-time winners in last 2 mins of games so far in 1965, finally opened their Pac-8 schedule with script reversal. This time, Washington State scored its 10 pts in 1st H, including ponderous FB Larry Eilmes' clock-beating 1y TD run with 7 secs left in 1st H. QB Paul Brothers capped 67y Oregon State (3-4) drive with 3y TD run in 3rd Q. Cougars DB Willlie Gaskin was 4th Q hero with FUM REC and INT.

November 6, 1965

(Fri) MIAMI 27 Boston College 6: Having hot hand with scoring passes, Miami (3-4) soph QB Bill Miller (5-14/53y, 2 TDs, INT) threw his 6th and 7th TD darts since entering lineup 4 games earlier. Each Miller pitch was short shot: 6y to FB Pete Banaszak in 1st Q and 5y to sub FB Fred Cassidy in 3rd Q. Hurricanes K Don Curtright hit 2 FGs in 2nd Q: 27y and wind-aided 53y bomb. "I never kicked a ball that far in my life!," exclaimed thrilled Curtright. Boston College (4-3) was limited to miserable 33/49y rushing and middling 13-29/150y passing as Miami LB Ed Weisakosky made 12 tackles and 2 INTs. Eagles QB Ed Foley perked up his passing game in 4th Q, pitching 4 straight completions/65y, including 26y TD to E Charlie Smith (4/73y). But, Hurricanes TD-beaten DB Andy Sixkiller (8 tackles) exacted quick revenge with 50y punt TD RET.

NORTH CAROLINA 17 Clemson 13: Tigers (5-3) lost chance to wrap up ACC crown, finding all-around talents of North Carolina (3-5) QB Danny Talbott too much to handle. Clemson HB Hugh Mauldin matched UNC HB David Riggs' 67y punt TD RET with tying TD in 2nd Q. Tar Heels drove 65y to Tigers 3YL in 2nd Q, but sack of passer Talbott forced K Talbott into 26y FG and 10-7 lead. Carolina DB Jack Davenport's INT set up Talbott for 35y TD run in 4th Q. After Clemson QB Thomas Ray scored 6y TD, game ended nervously for Heels as they had their heels touching GL with ball inside their 1YL.

NORTH CAROLINA STATE 21 Duke 0: Wolfpack's surprising D-line controlled action as Duke (4-4) made only solo 1st down in 1st H and was halted at 7 and 4YLs in 2nd H. NC State (4-4) sub QB Page Ashby entered scoreless game in 2nd Q and quickly hit 2 passes/30y, then dashed 4y for 7-0 lead. After Wolfpack DB Tony Golmont made INT RET to Blue Devils 35YL, Ashby zipped 13y to allow HB Shelby Mansfield to blast over from 1YL.

WEST VIRGINIA 31 Virginia Tech 22: Mountaineers (5-3) scored 1st time they had ball and used balanced 383y O to roll over Gobblers (5-3). QB Allen McCune (16-24/144y, 2 TDs) threw his dual TD passes in 1st H that West Virginia led by 21-7. WVU FB Dick Leftridge rushed for 80y and TD to become Mountaineers' to-date career rushing leader. Virginia Tech QB Bobby Owens twice found TE Ken Barefoot for short TD passes.

Florida 14 Georgia 10 (Jacksonville): Punting duel in 1st H between QB-Ps Steve Spurrier of Florida (5-2) and Kirby Moore of Georgia (5-3) was interrupted by GL FUM by HB Jack Harper just when it appeared Gators would score. Georgia DE Larry Kohn recovered Harper's FUM in EZ. Just before H, Harper redeemed himself with 28y run with screen pass to allow FB Alan Poe to plunge for 1y TD. Late in 3rd Q, Moore completed 12 and 11y passes but stalled at 8YL, so Bulldogs K Bob Etter cut margin to 7-3. Georgia took lead at 10-7 on E Pat Hodgson's leaping, fingertip 8y TD catch from Moore on 4th-and-5 with 12 mins left. Through rain and wind of Jacksonville, Spurrier captured verdict in 2 rapier-like thrusts: with 4:02 to go, he connected with E Charles Casey for 45y to UGA 32YL and drilled Harper, who wrestled over GL with 2 Bulldogs clinging to him. Georgia S Lynn Hughes might have made INT on Harper's TD catch but slipped in sloppy conditions.

TENNESSEE 21 Georgia Tech 7: Unbeaten Tennessee (4-0-2) fashioned 7-min 3rd Q blitz to blast open scoreless affair. Georgia Tech (5-2-1) QB Kim King had accounted for 144y in 1st H, but King's INT, returned for 34y TD by Vols DB Harold Stancell, started downfall of Engineers. Tennessee's rapid FUM REC and another INT led to TD pass by QB Charlie Fulton and TD run by FB Stan Mitchell. Yellow Jackets HB Giles Smith was in for injured star HB Lenny Snow and galloped 33y for cosmetic 4th Q TD. No. 7 Georgia Tech had its victory doused at 5 in row.

Alabama 31 LOUISIANA STATE 7: No. 5 Alabama (7-0) climbed all over Bengal Tigers (5-3) as QB Steve Sloan (9-13/150y, 2 TDs) clicked for 2 aerial scores and FB Steve Bowman (13/90y, 2 TDs) powered for 2 TDs. Sloan launched rout with 1st Q 45y TD bomb to speedy E Dennis Homan and found HB David Ray with 7y score in 2nd Q. K Ray also connected on 41y FG as Crimson Tide led 24-0 at H. Bowman barreled 36y to score in 3rd Q. Meanwhile, LSU QB Nelson Stokley injured his knee in pre-game drills and had to sit out. That left signal calling to QB Pat Screen, who had reasonably good game against Bama's tough D. Screen (15-35/203y, TD, 3 INTs) accounted for all but 58y of Tigers' 275y total O, which included only 72y rushing. Screen saved LSU from whitewash with deep 4th Q TD throw of 53y to TB Joe Labruzzo (10/10y rushing) who slipped behind 2 pass defenders.

Michigan 23 ILLINOIS 3: Less than 7 mins into contest at Champaign, Fighting Illini (4-4) scored when QB-K Fred Custardo angled through 27y FG, after being sacked for 6y loss to 10YL on 3rd down. Illinois made 5 1st downs on its 67y voyage to FG. Thereafter, Illinois had only FB Jim Grabowski's well-earned 22/96y rushing to call its highlight. Michigan (4-4) used its O-line superiority to answer with 73y TD tour to HB Carl Ward's 4th down and 6y TD catch from QB Wally Gabler that overcame 5y procedure PEN that pushed Wolverines back from 1YL. On next Michigan series, Gabler, who hit 7-12 passes, flipped short aerial to E Steve Smith who turned it into 39y gain to lead to TD plunge by Ward (19/141y, TD), who reported he was finally healthy after long bout with illness that lingered from summer. HB-K Rick Sygar added 24y FG, so UM led 17-3 at H. Gabler almost ruined Michigan's drive with FUM at Illini 4YL after 2nd H KO, but he scored on 4y run off G Dennis Flanagan's block.

MINNESOTA 27 Northwestern 22: Strong ground game (212y) gave pesky Northwestern (3-5) chance for upset. Big FB Bob McKelvey, who unlike his Cats running mates was contained most of afternoon, still placed Wildcats ahead 22-21 early in 4th Q with 17y crack off LT, his 2nd TD run. Later, NW seemed to be marching for clinching score with 1st down at Minnesota 20YL, but Minnesota (4-3-1) LB Tim Wheeler fell on HB Larry Gates' FUM at 21YL. Golden Gophers QB John Hankinson (14-22/255y, TD), who had clicked for 51y score to E Kenny Last in 1st Q) crafted 8 straight short pass completions—including 11, 12, 8, and 6y to TE Aaron Brown—to position himself for winning 1y plunge in game's last 1:17.

Missouri 20 COLORADO 7: Mighty D of Missouri (5-2-1) got Tigers flying early as DB Ken Boston picked off high-thrown, tipped flat pass for Buffs FB Larry Fischer on game's 4th play. Boston returned INT 38y for TD. It was 1 of 4 INTs suffered by Colorado (4-2-2) QB Bernie McCall, total O leader of Big 8. Buffaloes answered nicely, marching to Mizzou 4YL where HB Bill Harris lost FUM. At least 3 players from each side seemed to have hands on loose ball before alert Tigers DG Don Nelson came up with possession to halt CU threat. Buffs McCall (19-32/178y, 4 INTs) threw 22y pass to WR George Lewark near conclusion of 80y drive to set up HB Estes Banks' tying TD 11 mins into 2nd Q. Tigers also went 80y before H as QB Gary Lane broke 7-7 deadlock by throwing go-ahead 2y TD pass to WB Earl Denny. Bison WR Frank Rogers was wide open for certain TD and likely 14-13 lead when he muffed HB pass by Larry Plantz just before H. Tigers DB Gary Grossnickle ended that threat with EZ INT, and same defender ruined Buffs' 3rd Q advance with another INT after Colorado had set itself up at Tigers 24YL. Lane (13/66y, TD rushing) added brilliant 15y keeper TD run for clinching score in 4th Q.

UCLA 28 Washington 24: Improving Huskies (3-5) eyed upset behind precise battery of QB Tod Hullin (17-28/354y, 3 TDs, 4 INTs) and E Dave Williams (10/257y, 3 TDs). Washington moved to 14-0 and 21-7 leads as Hullin found Williams for 50, 56, and 11y TDs in 1st H. UCLA (5-1-1) QB Gary Beban (8-13/203y, 2 TDs, INT) had pitched 58y TD to E Dick Witcher in middle of 1st Q and, with 1:28 to go in 2nd Q, capped 81y drive with TD sneak. Trailing 24-14 at H, Bruins were inspired by Beban's dazzling 60y TD run behind downfield blocks of G Barry Leventhal and E Byron Nelson on 1st snap of 2nd H. Beban hit Witcher with winning 60y bomb in 3rd Q on deceptive play: Bruins snuck Witcher out from O huddle early, positioning him as uncovered flanker as disciplined Huskies remained in D huddle with their heads down. UCLA used more pass-rush pressure in 2nd H to blank Washington, even though Huskies moved into Bruins territory 3 times. But, Hullin suffered 2 INTs and lost FUM as UW gave away 5 TOs in 2nd H. In looking at Washington's 479y of O, Uclan coach Tommy Prothro said, "We were lucky to win." Some in press box felt Witcher's 2nd H TD play was underhanded, but Washington coach Jim Owens disagreed, "I didn't think it as a sleeper…our (defensive) halfback didn't pick him up."

WASHINGTON STATE 27 Oregon 7: Power running (236y) by FB Larry Eilmes, HB Ammon McWashington, and HB Joe Lynn (15y TD run) and well-placed passes of undervalued QB Tom Roth (8-14/110y) sparked Washington State (7-1) to 5th win in row. It was Cougars' 1st such streak since 1932. With 5 members of 1916 Cougar Rose Bowl team in attendance, WSU fanned flame of Pasadena dream with 27-0 lead by 3rd Q. Oregon (4-3-1) managed just 46y rushing, while its conf-best air attack sputtered until 4th Q. That's when Ducks QB Mike Brundage flipped 11y score to E Steve Bunker.

AP Poll November 8

1 Michigan State (32)	482	6 Southern California	240
2 Arkansas (14)	459	7 UCLA	170
3 Nebraska (4)	406	8 Tennessee	96
4 Notre Dame (1)	381	9 Missouri	94
5 Alabama	288	10 Kentucky	73

Others with votes: Auburn, Dartmouth, Florida, Georgia Tech, Michigan, Minnesota, Ohio State, Princeton, Purdue, Texas, Texas Tech, Tulsa, Utah State, Washington State, Wyoming

November 13, 1965

Auburn 21 GEORGIA 19: More runner than passer, Tom Bryan switched from QB to TB for this game and dashed 41y for opening Auburn (5-3-1) score. Bryan later set up TB Richard Plagge's winning TD with runs of 25 and 24y. Georgia (5-4) countered in mid-game with SEC-record to-date 92y TD pass from QB Kirby Moore to HB Randy Wheeler. Bulldogs were forced into failed 2-pt pass after Tigers LB John Cochran blocked 1st Q kick. Still, Georgia was in position to win with 4 mins left when FB Ronnie Jenkins lost FUM to DB Robert Fulghum inside 1YL while trying for his 3rd TD.

Mississippi 14 Tennessee 13 (Memphis): With QB Charles Fulton of Volunteers (4-1-2) injured on 1st play after 13y run and QB James Heidel of Rebels (5-4) playing ineffectively, each team turned its field-general job over to soph signal-caller: QB Dewey Warren (5-11/51y) for UT and unknown QB Jody Graves, who provided spark for Ole Miss. Vols TB Walter Chadwick set up FB Stan Mitchell's 1y TD plunge in 1st Q with 55y run and put Tennessee ahead 13-7 with 2y TD run in 3rd Q. But, Vols K David Leake missed x-pt that would have provided 7-pt lead. Ole Miss moved patient 72y in 17 plays behind Graves in 4th Q. E Rocky Fleming made diving 1-handed catch on 4th down, and Graves converted 4th-and-1 with 8y scoot to within 1-ft of Tennessee GL. TB Mike Dennis went over for TD on next play, and Ole Miss K Jimmy Keyes lashed decisive x-pt as Tennessee trailed for 1st time in 1965. Chadwick lost FUM on 1st snap after ensuing KO, and Volunteers never threatened again.

LOUISIANA STATE 37 Mississippi State 20: Using 4 TOs, Bayou Bengals (6-3) sent Maroons (4-5) to 5th straight defeat as they blasted for 4 TDs in 16-min span that started in dying moments of 2nd Q. HB Marcus Rhoden sparked Mississippi State with inspired 37y punt RET in 1st Q, and HB Dan Bland followed immediately with 6y TD sweep. Bulldogs' 6-0 lead held up until LSU DE John Garlington recovered Rhoden's FUM at Miss State 16YL. Tigers QB Pat Screen (2-4/39y, TD) found OT Dave McCormick all alone on T-eligible pass for 12y TD, and LSU assumed its 1st lead at 7-6. HB Jim Dousay capped all-land 66y TD drive with 1y smash for Tigers in last 28 secs of H. HB Joe Labruzzo (15/105y) charged for 2 TDs, including nifty 46y reverse-of-field run, and Dousay blasted over again for 34-14 lead early in 4th Q. Only interruption of Bengals' gambol came when Bland ripped 44y on KO RET in 3rd Q, and Bulldogs QB Ashby Cook (12-27/115y, TD, 2 INTs) pitched 13y TD over middle to WR Don Saget and followed with 2-pt pass to TE Harland Reed.

MICHIGAN STATE 27 Indiana 13: Michigan State (9-0) claimed Big 10 title by overcoming 13-10 deficit after 3 Qs. Opening with 10-0 lead on 1st of 3 TD passes from QB Steve Juday to gazelle E Gene Washington, Spartans had to withstand air attack of Indiana (2-7) QB Frank Stavroff. Hoosiers drove 79 and 77y to TDs, primarily on Stavroff's passes to Es Bill Malinchak and Bill Couch, latter making his 1st career catches. Highlighting Michigan State's 4th Q fireworks was Juday's 43y TD arrow to Washington and LB Charles "Mad Dog" Thornhill's 37y INT RET to Hoosiers 5YL.

Nebraska 21 OKLAHOMA STATE 17: Orange Bowl-bound Nebraska (9-0) had to rally for winning TD in last 38 secs. Often tough at home, Oklahoma State (1-7) stepped to 7-0 lead on HB Larry Elliott's TD after early FUM REC. Huskers went ahead 14-7 when HB Ron Kirkland (123y rushing) scored his 2nd TD after Cowboys lost FUM on 2nd H KO. K Charles Durkee's 45y FG and QB Glenn Baxter's 3y TD run gave OSU 17-14 margin with 5:19 to go. FB Pete Tatman's 2y TD capped relentless 15-play drive that clinched win for Huskers, but not before nervous moments were sparked by tough-as-nails Cowboys FB Walt Garrison (19/121y), who dashed 18y to 5YL as time expired.

MISSOURI 30 Oklahoma 0: Strong-legged Missouri (6-2-1) QB Gary Lane (7-12/83y, TD) ran 8/72y and scored 3 TDs behind strong blocking of Ts Francis Peay and Butch Allison. Tigers DB Johnny Roland's 53y punt RET set up Lane's 3y TD run in 1st Q. Oklahoma (3-5) lost 2 FUMs to hard-hitting Mizzou D, led by T Bruce Van Dyke. Oklahoma was blanked by Mizzou for 1st time since 1941 as Sooners QB Gene Cagle was thwarted by trio of INTs manufactured by Roland, LB Rich Bernson, and DB Ken Boston.

TEXAS TECH 34 Baylor 22: Texas Tech (8-1) kept alive its SWC title hopes with rally over Baylor (3-5) and looked ahead to showdown with Arkansas. Bears led 9-0 in 1st Q on FB Billy Hayes' 5y TD run and K Charles Purvis' 47y FG. Red Raiders ace HB-P Donny Anderson, making his last home appearance, anxiously dropped pass, sliced 7y punt, and was completely corralled as runner in 1st H. But, Anderson worked loose for 43y TD on short pass from QB Tom Wilson and scored on 2y run in decisive 3rd Q as Texas Tech opened 27-9 lead. Anderson rushed 19/82y, TD, caught 5/83y, TD, and racked up 210y all-purpose. With 1 game remaining in his career, Anderson was within 25y of NCAA record of 4963y, set by Ollie Matson of San Francisco. Wilson (19-32/258y, 3 TDs, 2 INTs) added 4th Q TD pass of 2y to E Jerry Shipley (10/100y, TD). Baylor coach John Bridgers stuck with QB Roger Mike Marshall as Bears sunk but finally tapped QB Ken Stockdale (12-21/152y, TD), who made most of his less than 20 mins of play with 2y TD run and 20y TD pass to E Harlan Lane.

HOUSTON 38 Kentucky 21: Coming off 17-3 win over Ole Miss, emerging Houston (4-5) crafted 2nd straight upset of SEC team. Kentucky (6-3) QB Rick Norton threw TD passes to HB Larry Seiple (75y) and E Rick Kestner (54y) to create 21-16 H lead. Norton set 3 school records, previously held by Babe Parilli through that date, thanks to his free-wheeling 22-34/392y passing attack. But, Cougars picked off 5 of Norton's passes, and QB Bo Burris pitched 2nd H TD passes of 10 and 29y to WB Mike Spratt

and 5y to E Ken Hebert. It was P Hebert, who got his Cougars mates excited with his 61y gamble on punt-fake run on 4th-and-13 from his own 20YL. FB Mickey Don Thompson soon scored to put Houston on board for 1st time to trail 8-6 in 2nd Q. Burris' 1st TD pass to Spratt, followed by 2-pt pass to Hebert, gave Cougars their 1st lead at 24-21 in 3rd Q.

Texas Western 20 UTAH 19: E Bob Wallace put Texas Western (5-3) ahead in 2nd Q with 89y punt TD RET. Utah (3-6) leapt to 19-7 edge as TB Ben Woodson scored twice from close range and still led 19-13 in closing moments. Backed against own GL, Miners QB Billy Stevens found Wallace for miraculous 92y TD pass with 16 secs to play.

AP Poll November 15

1 Michigan State (31)	456	6 Southern California	226
2 Arkansas (15)	439	7 UCLA	180
3 Nebraska (2)	378	8 Missouri	115
4 Notre Dame	346	9 Texas Tech	86
5 Alabama	268	10 Florida	42

Others with votes: Auburn, Dartmouth, Georgia Tech, Kentucky, Louisiana State, Mississippi, Ohio State, Princeton, Purdue, Syracuse, Tennessee, Tulsa, Washington State

November 20, 1965

Dartmouth 28 PRINCETON 14: Resourceful Dartmouth (9-0) completed 3rd perfect season in its history, cutting down 17-game win string of Princeton (8-1). On scoreboard 1st were Tigers after 69y 1st Q sortie ending in TD run by virtuoso TB Ron Landeck, whose 249y allowed him to break Princeton—held by legendary Dick Kazmeier—and Ivy League season total O records. Indians bounced back in 2nd Q, scoring on TD runs by QB Mickey Beard at end of 86 and 39y marches that came within span of 2:22. HB Gene Ryzewicz went 12y to TD on 1st play of 4th Q, and Beard (12-17/229y, TD) pitched 79y TD to E Bill Calhoun for 28-7 lead. Adding comic relief to title showdown was Dartmouth's Sam Hawken, lanky DB, who, while wearing soft, ripple-soled shoes, ran up "human steps," i.e. backs of his teammates in DL, to attempt block of early FG try by Tigers ace K Charlie Gogolak. "I'm expendable," cracked Hawken of his secret but well-practiced 14-ft high vault. Tigers turned suspicious as Hawken entered game in 1st Q and delayed their C snap. Hawken, accustomed to certain timing, found himself airborne and walloped by Princeton linemen even before ball was snapped. Even though offside PEN gave Gogolak shorter attempt, he hurried it and missed. "The play was not a total loss," concluded Hawken afterward. In interest of safety, NCAA rules outlawed human steps before start of 1966 season.

SYRACUSE 21 Boston College 13: Slippery jr HB Floyd Little set several records in season finale for Syracuse (7-3). Little scored twice to set 114-pt season's scoring mark, become 1st Orangemen runner to surpass 1000y rushing (1,065y,) and tie year's receiving record with 21 catches. But, Boston College (5-4) played fine 1st H on chilly, leaden-skied afternoon. Eagles scored early after blocked punt recovered by LB Ed Lipson, who stood out on D, as BC QB Ed Foley quickly scored on 5y keeper. Moments later, Little tight-roped sideline on 62y punt TD RET to knot it at 7-7. BC led 13-7 at H when DE Dave Pesapane slammed Syracuse FB Larry Csonka early in 2nd Q and caused airborne FUM that Eagles DB Ron Gentilli carted 25y to score. Orangemen tramped 82y on 16 plays in 3rd Q as Csonka plunged for 1y TD, and Little caught pass from QB Jim Cassata to race 45y for clinching score in 4th Q.

PITTSBURGH 30 Penn State 27: QB Kenny Lucas (18-24/228y, TD), younger brother of former Nittany Lions A-A QB Richie Lucas who received little interest from Penn State, rifled 13 passes into hands of his Pittsburgh (3-7) receivers in 1st H, including E Bob Longo's 41y TD catch. So, Panthers led comfortably at 20-0. Penn State (4-5), which would lose chance to extend its 26-year streak of winning seasons, rallied to within 20-7 as QB Jack White snatched FUM at Pitt 2YL by his FB Dave McNaughton and carried it over. FB Barry McKnight's 2nd TD run gave Pitt 27-7 lead as 3rd Q ended. Nittany Lions turned game around by going back to muscle runs out of its standard I-formation with passes by White sprinkled in. McNaughton scored at end of 59y march, and when HB Don Kunit swept E for his 2nd TD of 4th Q, Penn State had tied it at 27-27 with 55 secs to play. But, normally-clutch QB-K Tom Sherman missed go-ahead kick for Lions. Pitt then went from its 40YL behind Lucas' precise sideline passes to HB Eric Crabtree once and E Longo 4 times, which Lions CB John Sladki could not stop despite his tight coverage. At 2YL, Lucas bootlegged to 1YL, and K Frank Clark made winning 18y FG with :03 on clock.

Virginia 33 MARYLAND 27: Maryland (4-5) DB Bob Sullivan, nation's leader with 10 INTs, could not cope with tall Virginia (5-5) E Ed Carrington (5/111y), whose height allowed him to haul in 4 TD passes from accurate Cavs QB Bob Davis (11-17/171y, 4 TDs, 2 INTs). Carrington snared 9, 16, 53, and 15y scores, 3 of which invaded Sullivan's province. After whirlwind 1st Q in which Terps TB Kenny Ambrusko matched Carrington's 2 TDs with 1 and 10y scoring runs, Virginia enjoyed 27-14 H lead. Davis hit 6-8/111y in 1st H, and he slapped Terps D when they were down after HB John Pincavage returned 2nd Q punt 33y. Davis immediately lofted 53y TD to Carrington on next play. Davis swept LE for 3rd Q TD that provided Virginia with 33-14 edge, which turned out to be enough when Maryland sub QB Jim Corcoran pitched 2 TD passes in 4th Q.

SOUTH CAROLINA 17 Clemson 16: South Carolina (5-5), mired in alternating win-lose pattern, batted down Clemson QB Jimmy Addison's wobbly 2-pt pass off fake conv kick with 40 secs to play to win share of ACC title and denied same to Tigers (5-5). Not fooled by fake kick, Carolina LB Bob Gunnels achieved critical pass bat-down. Gamecocks spotted Tigers 10-0 lead, tied it on K Jimmy Poole's 3rd Q FG, and took 17-10 lead on 1st play of 4th Q: QB Mike Fair swept to 7YL, then pitched out to HB Bob Harris who scampered over. Orange and Purple dominated stats, 314y to 154y, but were foiled on 2 deep penetrations in 4th Q: Carolina DB Stan Juk's FUM REC at 16YL with 11 mins on clock and DB Bobby Bryant's INT at 12YL with less than 4 mins to play. Finally, Clemson WR Phil Rogers caught 1y TD pass from QB Thomas Ray as prelude to failed conv pass.

DUKE 34 North Carolina 7: Duke (6-4) QB Todd Orvald (16-25/197y, TD) passed 9y for TD to E Dave Dunaway, and Tar Heels (4-6) counterpart Danny Talbott (9-21/117y, INT) made 4th down 7y TD run for 7-6 lead. Thanks to alert D, Blue Devils blasted open game with 22 pts in 6-min space of 2nd Q as FB Jay Calabrese scored 2 of his 3 short TDs after fumbled punt by Carolina HB Jack Davenport and short punt by UNC P Bill Edwards. Also, LB Bob Matheson raced 35y with INT for TD. Blues went 68y after 2nd KO as Calabrese scored again. With Talbott banged up and out but for handful of plays, sub QB Jeff Beaver (9-16/92y, 2 INTs) led UNC to 2 failed drives to 8YL. Stunning post-game news came from Duke coach Bill Murray, who retired with 93-51-9 slate (10-5 vs. North Carolina) and 7 ACC titles in 15 years. Duke program never came close to again enjoying same consistent quality.

TENNESSEE 19 Kentucky 3: Exchange of FGs by K David Leake of Tennessee (5-1-2) and DE-K John Andrighetti of Kentucky (6-4) took place in D-dominated 1st H. Within 4-min span that bridged 3rd and 4th Qs, Volunteers turned INTs by LBs Doug Archibald and Frank Emanuel into pair of TD sneaks by QB Dewey "Swamp Rat" Warren, who made his 1st start for Tennessee. With passing ace QB Rick Norton out with knee injury, Wildcats were forced to use DB specialist Terry Beadles at QB. It was Beadles' 2 INTs that helped break game open in 2nd H for Vols. In desperation, Beadles dropped into EZ in 4th Q in attempt to launch long bomb, but was brought down for safety.

MIAMI 16 Florida 13: With Sugar Bowl plumbs dancing in their heads, Gators (6-3) pranced to early 7-0 lead on Jack Harper's 34y HB pass to E Charles Casey. PEN on Hurricanes' punt extended new life to Miami (5-4) in 2nd Q, and FB Pete Banaszak (27/85y, TD) blasted over to shave score to 7-6. K Wayne Barfield's 2 FGs in 2nd Q gave Gators 13-6 H lead, and UF trotted off for mid-game break with 203y to 65y O advantage. Lucky hop of Miami DB-P Art Zachary's punt in 3rd Q went into hands of Hurricanes RB Doug McGee at Florida 8YL when ball accidentally grazed Gators returner Dick Kirk. Miami QB Bill Miller quickly tied it at 13-13 with 8y sweep behind Banaszak's block, and DB Zachary added to miserable night for Florida QB Steve Spurrier (8-22/79y, 2 INTs) with timely INT late in 3rd Q. Normally used exclusively as P, Zachary was in for injured S Jim Wahnee and his pick led to decisive 24y FG by Don Curtwright early in 4th Q after McGee and Banaszak hammered Gators line. Spurrier led Florida on late surge for 52y to Canes 19YL. On 2nd and 3rd downs, Spurrier was called for pass grounding PENs and was sacked by Miami DT Gene Trosch. Spurrier was rushed into high incompletion on 4th down.

Ohio State 9 MICHIGAN 7: After Buckeyes QB Don Unverferth pitched 5y TD pass to E Billy Anders midway in 1st Q, Michigan (4-6) blanked Ohio State (7-2) for next 50 mins. Ohio State coach Woody Hayes frequently stepped out of his ultra-conservative strategy in 1965 and made gambling decision just past halfway in 4th Q. Buckeyes trailed 7-6 and faced 4th-and-2 at own 17YL. Hayes ordered FB Will Sander to run up middle for 1st down, and, with 1:15 remaining, K Bob Funk was close enough to drill 27y FG for go-ahead pts. Win clinched unshared 2nd place spot in Big 10 at 6-1 for Ohio State. Wolverines had trailed 6-0 in 2nd Q as their 71y drive died at Buckeyes 6YL. But, resultant field position allowed Michigan DB Mike Bass' 10y INT RET to come to rest at Ohio 15YL. From that point, 4 plunges by Michigan FB Dave Fisher produced TD, followed by HB-K Rick Sygar's conv for 7-6 margin. Wolverines continued to stifle Ohio State and pile up its own y (335y rushing overall), but were halted on downs at 16YL and by missed FGs by Sygar after reaching 6 and 18YLs.

Michigan State 12 NOTRE DAME 3: Fighting Irish sported nation's 2nd-best run O, and never in storied history of Notre Dame (7-2) had its rushers been held to minus y until this day. Michigan State (10-0) D, tops in country in rush D, blanketed Notre Dame in throwing its runners for -12y on ground, permitting only 2-11/24y in air, and allowing only 3 1st downs and positive y on only 26 of 40 plays initiated by ND. Spartans, too, were well-checked in 1st H—leading in O y by 174y to 31y--and trailed 3-0 on Irish K Ken Ivan's FG after early FUM REC by DB Tom Longo. Irish D provided 2 more scoring chances in 1st H, but QB Bill Zloch threw INTs clutched by Michigan State LB Charles Thornhill and DB Don Japinga. Spartans HB Clinton Jones bolted 21y on trap play to set up his own 3y TD run for 6-3 edge in 3rd Q. Michigan State DB Jim Summers' 4th Q INT put HB Dwight Lee in position to slip behind ND secondary for clinching 13y TD pass from QB Steve Juday.

ARKANSAS 42 Texas Tech 24: Hopeful Texas Tech (8-2) scored 1st 3 times it had ball for 10-0 and 17-7 leads as QB Tom Wilson (26-44/320y) led attack with his aerials, and HB Donny Anderson scored twice. Confident Arkansas (10-0) shrugged off fact that it trailed 10-0 before it even ran play from scrimmage and simply stormed ahead. Razorbacks built TD drives of 68, 72, 53, 73, and 69y to complete its 2nd perfect regular season record in row. Razorbacks QB Jon Brittenum passed 14-20/245y, 2 TDs. TB Bobby Burnett rushed for 133y, his 5th game in row over 100y on ground. Burnett scored 3 TDs, including 1y dive early in 3rd Q in which he toted 83y rushing. Burnett's score provided Hogs their only TD of 3rd Q and with their 1st lead at 21-17. Brittenum started 4th Q with TD passes of 10y to E Richard Trail and 24y to E Tommy Burnett, brother of TB Bobby

UCLA 20 Southern California 16: Dominating game for 50 mins for 16-6 lead, Southern California (6-2-1) sent newly-appointed Heisman Trophy winner, TB Mike Garrett, churning for 40/210y rushing. UCLA (7-1-1) had used HB Mel Farr's 49y TD run for 6-0 lead, but Trojans countered with 1st of 2 TD passes by QB Troy Winslow (7-9/79y, 2 TDs, INT), this to WR Mickey Upton for 7-6 H edge. With Garrett fueling Trojans' 345y rushing total, USC was stymied by 2 lost FUMs in 3rd Q but appeared to ice it at 16-6 on DE-K Tim Rossovich's 20y FG in middle of 4th Q. Clock ticked under 5 mins remaining when Bruins LB Dallas Grider's hard tackle caused Winslow's FUM, Troy's 5th bobble, that LB Erwin Dutcher gobbled up at USC 34YL. Bruins QB Gary Beban (5-11/127y, 2 TDs, 2 INTs) quickly hit E Dick Witcher with TD pass. After Grider recovered

successful on-side KO, Beban lofted 52y game-winning aerial to E Kurt Altenberg. Play came on new strategy Uclans coach Tommy Prothro had designed especially for Troy, except that 1st time they tried it, Southern California DB Mike Hunter made INT. This time, Beban looked away from primary receiver Farr and arched long pass to Altenberg, who snatched it off helmet of DB Nate Shaw. Shaw, who played brilliantly all game except for winning play with 2:39 left, wept openly on his way in Trojans locker room. USC coach John McKay admitted it was his "toughest defeat by 700 miles."

STANFORD 9 California 7: Big Game's 68th renewal found, according to *Los Angeles Times*, "…tailgate parties, stylish Bay Area ladies attired in the best from Dior…It was a shame the caliber of football didn't match the pageantry." Each team squandered 1st H opportunities, especially Indians' bungling of 2nd-and-goal at California (5-5) 1YL. HB Ray Handley bobbled pitch that was covered by Bears to ruin that blooming chance and send teams to H in 0-0 knot. Scoreboard famine finally was fed by Stanford (6-3-1) HB-K Terry DeSylvia's 24y FG 9:34 into 3rd Q. Golden Bears QB Jim Hunt (6-18/99y, 2 INTs) looked upon HB Lloyd Reist for 10 and 28y receptions on 62y push to HB Tommy Relles' 4y TD slam up middle for 7-3 Cal lead early in 4th Q. Tribe immediately retaliated with winning 70y TD drive. Stanford QB Dave Lewis (8-18/100y, INT) converted 18y pass to E Bob Conrad to Bears 11YL, and Handley broke several tackles to score on next play.

November 25-27, 1965

(Th'g) NEBRASKA 21 Oklahoma 9: Cornhuskers (10-0) completed 1st perfect season in 50 years with come-from-behind win over stubborn Oklahoma (3-6), which had jumped to 9-0 lead. Sooners claimed 3 1st H FUMs which enabled LB-K Ron Shotts' FG after QB Gene Cagle's 16y pass, and HB Larry Brown's 3y TD dive. Sub QB Bob Churchich sparked Nebraska's 2nd Q rally as FB Charlie Winters blasted through 2 tacklers on 4th down and sped to 29y TD to pull within 9-7. Huskers HB Harry "Lighthorse" Wilson (19/160y, TD) broke open game in 3rd Q with 66y TD run and 38y TD catch from Churchich.

(Th'g) TULSA 48 Colorado State 20: Behind 20-15, Tulsa (8-2) QB Bill Anderson (37-57/502y, 5 TDs, INT) scored on 8y run late in 3rd Q, then pitched TD passes of 60, 63, and 51y on way to new national season total O record of 3343y. Hurricane E-K Howard Twilley (19/214y) caught 2 TDs and made 4 conv kicks to finish season with 127 pts, becoming 1st college lineman to win nation's scoring title. Colorado State (4-6) QB Bob Wolfe threw 3 TDs.

(Th'g) Texas 21 TEXAS A&M 17: Tricky Texas A&M (3-7) baffled arch-rival Texas (6-4) with SEC-record 91y TD pass and jumped to 17-0 H advantage. On deceptive play, Aggies QB Harry Ledbetter bounced long lateral that appeared to be forward pass to HB Jim Kauffman, who gestured with disgust at apparent incompletion. Kauffman then lobbed pass over relaxed Longhorns secondary to streaking E Ken McLean. Aggies held 17-pt lead deep into 3rd Q when Texas DB Gary Moore's INT RET to A&M 34YL paved way for TD drive capped by E Pete Lammons' 14y catch. Now, momentum belonged to Texas, and TB Jim Helms crashed over for 4th Q TDs at end of 80 and 55y drives.

Army 7 Navy 7 (Philadelphia): It sure looked like academy football was slipping because civilian graduates were receiving big offers from pro football, something academy players could not accept. Military academy programs came under criticism after this fairly listless game. *Sports Illustrated* wrote, "…the two teams were about as daring as a 1920 lady's bathing suit." Army (4-5-1) HB Sonny Stowers made early, barely-contested 25y TD dash because Middies were blitzing on other side of line. Amid misfires, Navy (4-4-2) QB John Cartwright found range for 3 quick 2nd H throws, last of which landed in hands of HB Terry Murray for 8y TD. Black Knights used Shotgun to good effect in 1st H, but coach Paul Dietzel was afraid to use it with his Army team buried in its own territory throughout 2nd H. *New York Times* called 2nd H "battle of utter futility" when neither team penetrated other's 30YL.

ALABAMA 30 Auburn 3: Although Auburn (5-4-1) was headed to its worst overall record since 1952, surprisingly it took this loss to Alabama (8-1-1) to knock Tigers from SEC title contention. Crimson Tide QB Steve Sloan hit TD passes of 11, 33, and 29y. Losing coach Shug Jordan lamented Auburn's horrendous 7 INTs, but fingered turning point as Bama E Ray Perkins' diving catch in 3rd Q which led to FB Leslie Kelley's TD run for Tide's 23-3 lead.

FLORIDA 30 Florida State 17: Florida State (4-5-1) DE George D'Alessandro (FUM REC) blocked punt to set up Seminoles K Pete Roberts' FG in 1st Q. Gators (7-3) built 13-3 H lead on 2 TD catches by versatile HB Jack Harper (15/78y, and 4/111y, 2 TDs receiving). Anxious Sugar Bowl officials must have been regretting their pre-game commitment to Florida when FSU QB Ed Pritchett (18-34/193y, 2 TDs, INT) drove Seminoles 85y to his 21y TD pass—his 2nd scoring throw of 2nd H—to E Jerry Jones with 2:10 to go in 4th Q. Now down 17-16, Gators QB Steve Spurrier (18-28/282y, 3 TDs) mustered his troops on 71y drive. Spurrier connected on 10, 18, and 25y passes before motioning E Charles Casey into EZ for 25y score. Florida DB Allen Trammell followed with 46y TD INT RET.

Georgia 17 GEORGIA TECH 7: Upset by Georgia (6-4) put egg on face of Gator Bowl execs. Fading late in his soph year, Georgia Tech (6-3-1) QB Kim King was pressured by gap-shooting LBs and was held to 49y passing O in 1st H. DT George Patton had

forced early FUM by King which set up TD by Bulldogs QB Kirby Moore. DB Lynn Hughes' INT poised K Bob Etter for 40y FG into wind in 2nd Q. King finally clicked in 2nd H, hitting 3 passes to E Gary Williams to allow TB Lenny Snow to pitch TD pass to Williams. Later, Snow was halted on 4th down at Georgia 11YL.

TEXAS CHRISTIAN 10 Southern Methodist 7: SMU (4-5-1) WB Larry Jernigan scored 2nd Q TD to illuminate single bright spot of Mustangs' 356y O. HB Steve Landon ties it at 7-7 for TCU (6-4) at end of 87y drive with 3y run early in 4th Q. SMU seemed headed for winning score when HB Jim Hagle lost FUM at Frogs 25YL. Alternating QBs Kent Nix and P.D. Shabay moved TCU into position for K Bruce Alford's winning 40y FG. Win earned TCU tie for 2nd place in SWC and trip to Sun Bowl.

Brigham Young 42 NEW MEXICO 8: Ace BYU (6-4) QB Virgil Carter passed 23-30/309y, 3 TDs and added 14y rushing to finish year with new WAC total O record of 2267y. Cougars E Phil Odle caught 2 scores, breaking conf record with 11 TDs via airwaves. New Mexico (3-7) earned its only score in 4th Q to make it 28-8 on FB Carl Jackson's 1y run and QB Stan Quintana's 2-pt run.

December 4, 1965

TENNESSEE 37 Ucla 34 (Memphis): December game seemed trivial for each, no. 5 UCLA (7-2-1) having beaten rival USC for Rose Bowl berth and no. 7 Tennessee (7-1-2) heading to Bluebonnet Bowl after tough SEC season in which it lost 3 asst coaches in railway-crossing accident. Instead, game became stellar O show. Volunteers bobbled opening KO which led to UCLA FB Paul Horgan's TD, but Vols bounced back for 20-7 H lead as QB Dewey Warren (19-27/274y, 2 TDs) accounted for 3 TDs. Bruins rallied with 21 pts in 3rd Q keyed by DB Tim McAteer's 35y FUM TD RET. Bundle of pass receptions by Vols E Johnny Mills (10/141y) were vital to Tennessee bounding back for 29-28 lead. UCLA QB Gary Beban scored his 3rd TD with less than 6 mins left to put Bruins in relative comfort at 34-29, but Warren drove Volunteers 65y in 9 plays, dashing over from 1YL on 4th down with 39 secs to play.

1965 Conference Standings

Ivy League

Dartmouth	7-0
Princeton	6-1
Harvard	3-2-2
Cornell	3-3-1
Yale	3-4
Pennsylvania	2-4-1
Columbia	1-6
Brown	1-6

Atlantic Coast

Duke	4-2
South Carolina	4-2
North Carolina State	4-3
Clemson	4-3
North Carolina	3-3
Maryland	3-3
Virginia	2-4
Wake Forest	1-5

Southern

West Virginia	4-0
William & Mary	5-1
East Carolina	3-1
Virginia Military	3-2
George Washington	4-3
Davidson	2-3
Furman	2-3
Citadel	2-6
Richmond	0-6

Southeastern

Alabama	6-1-1
Auburn	4-1-1
Florida	4-2
Tennessee (a)	3-1-2
Mississippi	5-3
Louisiana State	3-3
Kentucky	3-3
Georgia (b)	3-3
Vanderbilt	1-5
Tulane	1-5
Mississippi State	1-5

(a) Win vs. South Carolina counted in SEC
(b) Win vs. Clemson counted in SEC

Big Ten

Michigan State	7-0
Ohio State	6-1
Purdue	5-2
Minnesota	5-2
Illinois	4-3
Northwestern	3-4
Michigan	2-5
Wisconsin	2-5
Indiana	1-6
Iowa	0-7

Mid-American

Bowling Green	5-1
Miami (Ohio)	5-1
Western Michigan	3-2-1
Kent State	3-2-1
Toledo	2-4
Marshall	2-4
Ohio	0-6

Big Eight

Nebraska	7-0
Missouri	6-1
Colorado	4-2-1
Iowa State	3-3-1
Oklahoma	3-4
Oklahoma State	2-5
Kansas	2-5
Kansas State	0-7

Missouri Valley

Tulsa	4-0
Louisville (a)	3-1
Cincinnati (b)	2-2
North Texas State	2-2
Wichita State	0-4

(a) Win vs. Dayton counted in Mo. Valley
(b) Win vs. Dayton counted in Mo. Valley

Southwest		Western Athletic	
Arkansas	7-0	Brigham Young	4-1
Texas Tech	5-2	Arizona State	3-1
Texas Christian	5-2	Wyoming	3-2
Texas	3-4	New Mexico	2-3
Baylor	3-4	Utah	1-3
Southern Methodist	3-4	Arizona	1-4
Texas A&M	1-6		
Rice	1-6		

AAWU	
UCLA	4-0
Southern California	4-1
Washington State	2-1
Washington	4-3
Stanford	2-3
California	2-3
Oregon State	1-3
Oregon	0-5

1965 Bowl Games
Liberty Bowl (Dec. 18): Mississippi 13 Auburn 7

This post-season game was Memphis' debut as Liberty Bowl host city, but along came cold weather, same chill that traditionally dogged Liberty Bowls in Philadelphia. Surging Ole Miss (7-4) D stopped 2nd Q 4th-and-1 play near midfield and turned that effort into DL-K Jimmy Keyes' 42y FG, his 1st of 2 FGs. Auburn (5-5-1) countered in 2nd Q as game MVP TB Tom Bryan (19/111y) ripped for 42y off-T run for TD. Rebels drove 59y after receiving 2nd H KO, going ahead on QB Jody Graves' 6y TD toss to WB Doug Cunningham. With less than min to play, Tigers romped to Rebels 8YL, but QB Alex Bowden misfired on 3 passes and was sacked on 4th down by happy swarm of Rebels DLs: Jim Urbanek, Marvin McQueen, Jerry Richardson, and Keyes.

Bluebonnet Bowl (Dec. 18): Tennessee 27 Tulsa 6

Driving rain and 4 INTs by Tennessee (8-1-2) D blunted aerial scoring machine of Tulsa (8-3), but stars still sparkled: Hurricane QB Bill Anderson completed 23-47/250y and E Howard Twilley caught 8/78y. Tennessee QB Dewey Warren opened with passes of 20y to WB Hal Wantland, 13y to TB Walter Chadwick, and 4y for TD to Wantland. Then, Warren virtually abandoned Volunteers' air game. Vols converted 2 FUM RECs and DB Jerry Smith's 49y punt RET into 20-6 H edge. FB Stan Mitchell closed book on game's scoring by accounting for 34y of Tennessee's 43y on 3rd Q march, covering last 11y on his run.

Gator Bowl (Dec. 31): Georgia Tech 31 Texas Tech 21

Tireless soph TB Lenny Snow set bowl record with 35 carries, gained 136y, and scored key 3rd Q TD as Georgia Tech (7-3-1) upset Texas Tech (8-3). Red Raiders QB Tom Wilson passed 22-40/283y, 2 TDs. HB Donny Anderson was Texas Tech's go-to guy as usual, rushing for 85y, catching Wilson's passes for 138y, and finally taking pen to paper under goalposts to sign what was then NFL record-high contract with Packers. Raiders enjoyed 21-16 lead after 3 Qs, but sub Yellow Jackets QB Jerry Priestley sneaked over GL and added 2-pt run off fake pass for 24-21 edge. Soon, Georgia Tech DB Tommy Bleick picked off Wilson pass to launch Atlantans' clinching TD march.

Sun Bowl (Dec. 31): Texas Western 13 Texas Christian 12

Texas Christian (6-5) cruised to comfortable 10-0 H lead on K Bruce Alford's 35y FG and QB Kent Nix's 12y TD pass. In 2nd H, Texas Western soph QB Billy Stevens (21-34/208y, TD, 3 INTs) clicked on 35y TD pass to E Chuck Hughes. K Joe Cook's 2nd short FG provided underrated Miners (8-3) with 13-10 edge early in 4th Q. Late TCU advance died at Western 1YL as DB Curt Parsons made killing INT with 1:33 to go. After 3 perilous plunges had failed to gain, Stevens conceded safety on 4th down to narrow score to 13-12. Miners P Don Davis hit free-kick safely into Purple Frogs territory to effectively end matters.

Sugar Bowl: Missouri 20 Florida 18

Missouri (8-2-1) completely owned 1st H. "We were just dead out there," said MVP QB Steve Spurrier (27-45/352y, 2 TDs) of Florida (7-4). Keys to Tigers domination were pinching pass rush of DEs Dan Schuppan and Tom Lynn, and running of HB Charlie Brown (22/122y), who scored 10y TD and contributed scintillating 60y dash. Big play was 2nd Q FUM of punt by Gators HB Jack Harper 2 plays later on HB Johnny Roland's 11y pass to WB Earl Denny. When K Bill Bates added his 2nd FG in 3rd Q, Tigers led 20-0. Spurrier marshaled Florida forces in 4th Q, and Gators went 86y to TD. Asst coach Ed Kensler felt 20-8 would "look better" than 20-7, so Gators were ordered to try for 2 pts. When it failed, Florida couldn't use easy x-pt kicks to catch up and was forced into 2-pt tries after its closing 2 TDs. Head coach Ray Graves took heat, saying, "I thought a 2-pointer would give us a boost." E Charles Casey caught TD pass at end of 81y drive to get to 20-18, but Spurrier's 2-pt pass flew wide. Spurrier said he wished conv play call had been "a little fancier," which would form his coaching creed in years ahead.

Cotton Bowl: Louisiana State 14 Arkansas 7

Undervalued LSU (8-3), plagued by TOs at its low moments in 1965, opened calendar year 1966 with error-free O and tight D to surprise no. 2-ranked Arkansas (10-1), which would be voted no. 3 by AP writers after Michigan State lost Rose Bowl. LSU came from also-rans to take no. 8 spot in final poll. Expected to be easy fodder as 23rd straight Razorbacks' victim, Tigers took psychological cue from coach Charlie McClendon who dressed all 11 of his scout players in jerseys with symbolic no. 23 during team's pre-bowl workouts. Employing 11 plays, Hogs struck on early 87y drive.

Razorbacks QB Jon Brittenum rifled 19y TD strike to E Bobby Crockett, who went on to Cotton Bowl record 10 catches/129y. LSU retaliated with tying TD run by squat TB Joe Labruzzo to finish 87y march. Before H, Brittenum injured his shoulder, and sub QB Ronnie South, cold off bench, lost FUM on his 2nd snap at Porkers 34YL. Labruzzo (21/80y, 2 TDs) tallied what would turn out to be winning TD behind block of LT David McCormick, voted game's most outstanding lineman, with 18 secs to go before H. LSU had pounded away at same soft spot on right side of Razorbacks D-front on 16 of 18 running plays on its 2 TD drives. As much as anything, Tigers' run strategy avoided brilliant Loyd Phillips at LT. Brittenum (15-24/177y, TD, INT) returned to lead 2 long 4th Q drives that were spoiled at Tigers 20YL by DB Jerry Joseph's sideline INT and at 24YL when DT George Rice sacked Brittenum just before game clock's expiration.

GAME OF THE YEAR
Rose Bowl: UCLA 14 Michigan State 12

Looking back, 3 circumstances helped UCLA (8-2-1) create year's greatest upset. Michigan State (10-1) coach Duffy Daugherty made ill-fated decision to house his team of eclectic personalities at distant monastery. Secondly, September's 13-3 match likely made Spartans overconfident. Finally, Bruins felt Michigan State made mistake of "verbally humiliating" them during Rose Bowl pre-game drills. Ace UCLA QB Gary Beban (8-20/147y) set tone with 27y run on game's 1st play. Later in 1st Q, Bruins DB Bobby Stiles made INT of Spartans A-A QB Steve Juday and returned it 42y. Michigan State D held at that point, but DB Don Japinga bobbled ensuing punt when hit hard by Bruins E Byron Nelson. UCLA C John Erquiaga recovered Japinga's bobble at Spartans 6YL. Beban quickly scored, and K Kurt Zimmerman kicked conv. Zimmerman immediately stunned Spartans with successful on-side KO. Beban set up his 2nd TD run with 27y pass to WR Kurt Altenberg. In piling up 314y, Michigan State often threatened, but Juday, having off-day with 6-18/80y passing, suffered 3 INTs. Its leading rusher was HB Clinton Jones with 20/113y. Also, Spartans were stopped thrice on 4th down plays. With 6:13 to go and down by 2 TDs, mighty Michigan State finally erupted, going 80y in 2 plays: Juday to E Gene Washington for 42y and sub QB Jimmy Raye pitching to trailing FB Bob Apisa for 38y TD trip down sideline. MSU chose to fake kick and go for 2 pts, and Juday's pass off x-pt kick formation was batted down by UCLA DL Jerry Klein. Soon, big DE Bubba Smith partially blocked UCLA punt, and Spartans were 51y from possible tying TD. Juday knifed into EZ with 31 secs left. Apisa tried 2-pt run with pitchout, but was bumped by DE Jim Colletto and LB Dallas Grider and nailed just short of EZ by 175-lb Stiles, who was knocked unconscious. Later, Beban said, "Bobby sacrificed his life (figuratively), and we had what we thought was the biggest upset ever." Bruins victory was awfully close to biggest upset of 1960s.

Orange Bowl: Alabama 39 Nebraska 28

With Arkansas and Michigan State having fallen earlier, national title door stood open for winner of prime-time battle in Miami. No. 3 Nebraska (10-1) entered with high hopes, but host Alabama (9-1-1) struck with speed and deceit. On early plays after Huskers FUM, Bama T Jerry Duncan caught 2 T-eligible passes in row, and QB Steve Sloan fired 21y TD pass to E Ray Perkins (9/159y, 2 TDs), who later snagged 2-pt conv. Huskers countered in 2nd Q on QB Bob Churchich 33y pass to TE Tony Jeter for 7-7 tie. Sloan quickly directed Bama aerial TD marches of 89 and 93y. Then Tide's successful on-side KO allowed K David Ray to fit in FG just before H. During intermission, Crimson Tide band dispelled notion that school bands needed rehearsal when band members marched into formation of 24-7 H score to cheers of Alabama faithful. Churchich tossed 2 TD passes and scored another on run in 2nd H, but Tide never lost its edge. Due to his injured ribs, Sloan (20-28/296y, 2 TDs, 2 INTs) stuck mostly to ground game, and tough FB Steve Bowman scored twice. Alabama easily nabbed its 2nd straight AP national title.

Final AP Poll			
1 Alabama (37)	537	6 Missouri	260
2 Michigan State (18)	479	7 Tennessee	214
3 Arkansas (1)	413	8 Louisiana State	149
4 UCLA	391	9 Notre Dame	123
5 Nebraska	358	10 Southern California	80

Others receiving votes: Dartmouth, Florida, Georgia, Georgia Tech, Mississippi, Mississippi State, Ohio State, Purdue, Syracuse, Texas Tech

1965 Top Performance Formula

1 Michigan State	1.6773
2 Arkansas	1.6415
3 Alabama	1.5952
4 Nebraska	1.5946
5 Tennessee	1.5659
6 UCLA	1.5651
7 Notre Dame	1.5169
8 Southern California	1.4814
9 Missouri	1.4228
10 Purdue	1.3720
11 Louisiana State	1.3622
12 Syracuse	1.3162
13 Texas Tech	1.3076
14 Ohio State	1.2834
15 Georgia Tech	1.2801
16 Florida	1.2716
17 Kentucky	1.2473
18 Illinois	1.2429
19 Mississippi	1.2331
20 Georgia	1.1759

1965 Top Opponent Records

1	UCLA	.7233
2	Auburn	.6602
3	Tennessee	.6368
4	Wisconsin	.6333
5	Washington	.6222
6	Kentucky	.6053
7	Michigan State	.6000
8	Penn State	.5978
9	Alabama	.5962
10	Florida State	.5924
11	Texas Christian	.5922
12	Notre Dame	.5879
13t	Oklahoma State	.585106
13t	Vanderbilt	.585106
15	Southern Methodist	.5753
16	Texas A&M	.5739
17	Michigan	.5722
18	Mississippi State	.5763
19	Southern California	.5714
20	Louisiana State	.5631

1965 Out-of-Conference Records

	W-L	Percentage	Bowl W-L
AAWU	29-10-4	.7209	1-0
Southeastern	30-13-1	.6932	4-2
Southwest	15-10-1	.5962	0-3
Big Ten	14-14-2	.5000	0-1
Atlantic Coast	12-18	.4000	0-0
Big Eight	8-13-2	.3913	1-1
Western Athletic	12-19	.3871	0-0

1965 Individual Statistical Leaders

RUSHING YARDS

	Attempts	Yards	Avg.
Mike Garrett, Southern California	267	1440	5.4
Jim Grabowski, Illinois	252	1258	5.0
Jim Bohl, New Mexico State	182	1187	6.5
Pete Pifer, Oregon State	234	1095	4.7
Floyd Little, Syracuse	193	1065	5.5
Ray McDonald, Idaho	213	1000	4.7
Bobby Burnett, Arkansas	232	947	4.1
Charlie Brown, Missouri	174	937	5.4
Walt Garrison, Oklahoma State	217	924	4.3
Brendan McCarthy, Boston College	187	901	4.8

PASSING YARDS

	Completions	Attempts	Yards	Pct.
Bill Anderson, Tulsa	296	509	3464	58.2
Billy Stevens, Texas Western	196	432	3042	45.4
Tom Wilson, Texas Tech	172	283	2119	60.8
Kenny Lucas, Pittsburgh	144	268	1921	53.7
Steve Spurrier, Florida	148	287	1893	51.6
Rick Norton, Kentucky	113	214	1823	52.8
Virgil Carter, Brigham Young	120	250	1793	48.0
Benny Russell, Louisville	115	246	1791	46.7
Bob Griese, Purdue	142	238	1719	59.7
Paul Stein, Air Force	114	225	1446	50.7

RECEIVING YARDS

	Catches	Yards
Howard Twilley, Tulsa	134	1779
Chuck Hughes, Texas Western	80	1519
Neal Sweeney, Tulsa	78	883
Steve Bunker, Oregon	51	838
Dude McLean, Texas A&M	60	835
Charles Casey, Florida	58	809
Donny Anderson, Texas Tech	60	797
Dave Williams, Washington	38	795
Jack Clancy, Michigan	52	762
John Wright, Illinois	47	755

1965 Consensus All-America Team
Offense

End:	Howard Twilley, Tulsa
	Freeman White, Nebraska
Tackle:	Sam Ball, Kentucky
	Glen Ray Hines, Arkansas
Guard:	Dick Arrington, Notre Dame
	Stas Maliszewski, Princeton
Center:	Paul Crane, Alabama
Backs:	Bob Griese, Purdue
	Donny Anderson, Texas Tech
	Mike Garrett, Southern California
	Jim Grabowski, Illinois

Defense

End:	Aaron Brown, Minnesota
	Charles "Bubba" Smith, Michigan State
Tackle:	Walt Barnes, Nebraska
	Loyd Phillips, Arkansas
Guard:	Bill Yearby, Michigan
	Carl McAdams, Oklahoma
Linebacker:	Tommy Nobis, Texas
	Frank Emanuel, Tennessee
Backs:	George Webster, Michigan State
	Johnny Roland, Missouri
	Nick Rassas, Notre Dame

1965 Heisman Trophy Vote

Mike Garrett, senior tailback, Southern California	926
Howard Twilley, senior end, Tulsa	528
Jim Grabowski, senior fullback, Illinois	481
Donny Anderson, senior halfback, Texas Tech	408
Floyd Little, junior halfback, Syracuse	287

Other Major Award Winners

Maxwell (Player)	Tommy Nobis, senior linebacker, Texas
Outland (Lineman)	Tommy Nobis, senior linebacker, Texas
Knute Rockne (Lineman)	Tommy Nobis, senior linebacker, Texas
Walter Camp (Back)	Jim Grabowski, senior fullback, Illinois
AFCA Coach of the Year	Tommy Prothro, UCLA

1966

The Year of the Game of the Century, Marketing of Gatorade, and Bad Timing for Undefeated Tide

Major college teams played more than 500 games in 1966, but only one really seemed to matter. The November 19 game between no. 1 Notre Dame (9-0-1) and no. 2 Michigan State (9-0-1) game at East Lansing captured national interest for weeks, yet somehow lived up to its incredible hype to become a fitful "Game of the Century." The contest was amazingly hard-hitting with many forced turnovers, and its controversial ending created a storm of second-guessing that dogged Fighting Irish leader Ara Parseghian the rest of his career as a coach and television commentator. The undefeated titans finished in a 10-10 tie with Notre Dame safely running out the clock in its own territory at the end. The possibility of a tie had never been remotely considered, so as the game ended a lot of football fans felt terribly cheated.

At a time long before satellite video clips allowed every TV sports director in the country to show pre-game interviews and highlights, this game still took on a sense of unparalleled national anticipation. Notre Dame captain Jim Lynch, who in 1970 would play in the Super Bowl, flatly said years later that, "The Super Bowl was not as big as the Michigan State-Notre Dame game."

Coincidently, the end of the 1966 football season marked the first-ever NFL-AFL pro title matchup that would eventually be called the Super Bowl, a term coined by Kansas City Chiefs owner Lamar Hunt. The NFL-AFL Championship was staged between the Green Bay Packers and AFL Chiefs in a two-thirds full Los Angeles Coliseum and to considerably less interest than the "Game of the Century" college showdown in East Lansing.

When the big Notre Dame-Michigan State encounter ended without resolution, Parseghian was crucified for ordering substitute quarterback Coley O'Brien, a diabetic whom Parseghian felt was tiring badly, to run, not pass, the ball from the Irish 30-yard-line. Dan Jenkins wrote in *Sports Illustrated* that Notre Dame "tied one for the Gipper." As it happened, the coach sought not to blow what his injury-frayed team had attained: a road game comeback from a 10-0 deficit in one of the most bruising games ever. He based his decision on the knowledge that Notre Dame came in as no. 1 and still had a chance to win another game the following week, which it did very resoundingly, against Southern California (7-4). For his part, coach Duffy Daugherty chose to have the Spartans punt on their last possession on fourth down from his team's 36-yard-line with two minutes to play. Michigan State had an amazing defense, but it hardly was an aggressive coaching move to win the game, especially for the second-ranked team that was playing at home against an injury-depleted foe.

Still the mood on Monday was very much in favor, however briefly and insufficiently, of the Spartans. Participation in poll voting was somewhat flexible in 1966, so the AP Poll on the Monday (November 21) following the big game not surprisingly attracted 73 ballots instead of previous week's 43. Notre Dame, which walked away briefly from East Lansing with a black eye, added only two first place votes to 37, and Michigan State zoomed from six to 27 first place votes and closed a 28-point gap to three points. Alabama (11-0), now the leader among three remaining unblemished teams, stayed fairly stagnant, picking up seven first place votes to a total of eight but closing only from 93 points behind the Fighting Irish to 89 points.

Interestingly, neither Notre Dame nor Michigan State was in a position to build its reputation in a New Year's bowl game. Big Ten champion Michigan State was barred from the Rose Bowl because of the conference's arcane No Repeat Rule, and Notre Dame still shunned bowl games as school policy. In the end, Notre Dame's immense national reputation and its 51-0 win over USC a week later won it the AP and UPI titles. Considerably dismayed, Michigan State accepted as consolation the MacArthur Bowl, emblematic of the Football Writers Association's championship.

The immense criticism that engulfed Parseghian's somewhat-sensible decision (to avoid a silly mistake that could have cost everything) had a great impact on the coaching fraternity. It forced many coaches in subsequent years into radical end-game decisions. As a prime example, note the two-point pass called by Nebraska's Tom Osborne in the 1984 Orange Bowl even though a tying kick near the end of the game surely would have clinched a national title. The pass against champions-to-be Miami was tipped and fell incomplete, and Nebraska lost 31-30. To this day, it is hard to make a 1983 national championship case for Miami or any other team if Coach Osborne had felt comfortable accepting a 31-31 tie. But, the ghostly shadow of Parseghian's 1966 tie decision surely affected Osborne's choice almost 20 years later. By the mid-1990s such decisions

had evaporated because overtime made it a no-brainer to kick a point and embrace the chance for overtime victory. In recent times, a coach actually could get himself fired for not ordering a tying kick and taking his chances in overtime.

Some teams other than Notre Dame and Michigan State prospered in 1966. Coach of the Year honors went to West Point's Tom Cahill, who was elevated from freshman coach at a very late date when Paul Dietzel bailed out for South Carolina (1-9). Yet, Cahill injected a grand fighting spirit in his Army charges and shaped a won-loss record of 8-2, the best at Army since 1958. The season ended with a gratifying 20-7 win over Navy (4-6).

Vince Dooley began to make his strong presence felt at Georgia (10-1), including a Cotton Bowl win over coach Hayden Fry's Southern Methodist (8-3) team, surprise champions of the Southwest Conference. The Mustangs had a diversified offense that counted on the SWC's first black player, wingback Jerry Levias, and Mike Livingston and Mac White as interchangeable quarterbacks.

Florida (9-2) overcame losses to Georgia and Miami (8-2-1) to rise to the Orange Bowl occasion with a 27-12 win over Georgia Tech (9-2). Gators coach Ray Graves, 14 years an assistant to Bobby Dodd at Georgia Tech, called it his "sweetest victory," made possible by halfback Larry Smith's record 94-yard touchdown run. The Orange Bowl was Dodd's last game as he retired after 22 memorable seasons in Atlanta.

During the summer of 1966, a pair of University of Florida professors completed research and refinement, started the year before, on a new product to help Gator football players replenish electrolytes and stay hydrated during extremely hot and humid weather that typically—and especially in central Florida—affected players during pre-season training and early season games. The artificially-flavored lime, pale green fluid became known as Gatorade, in recognition of how it was designed to help the Florida Gators football team.

It took surprisingly little time for Gatorade to be marketed in stores all around the country. The brand later was bought by Stokely Van Camp, and today it is marketed by a Chicago-based business simply known as The Gatorade Company. Gatorade is available in many flavors and is the world's most popular in the "sports drink" category. It also has come under frequent scrutiny over the years as no more useful than water. In 1991, it was reported that Gatorade and the competitors that sprung up, such as Powerade (a Coca-Cola product), worked best in sustained, intense 60 to 90 minute workouts. So, perhaps Gatorade was better suited for Marathon runners than for the play-by-play spurts of football players for whom it was originally designed. Still, Gatorade is ingested by millions of athletes, would-be athletes, and morning-after tipplers of adult beverages. Many swear by its power of replenishment.

Whether or not Gatorade had anything to do with it, Florida quarterback Steve Spurrier won the Heisman Trophy with his prolific passing. But, it was a 40-yard field goal Spurrier kicked in the waning moments of a 30-27 victory over fired-up Auburn (4-6) that caught the public's eye. With less than three minutes to play, Spurrier and the Gators offense faced fourth down and eight yards to go at the Tigers 23-yard-line. Spurrier called timeout and pointed to his toe, a gesture to which coach Graves acknowledged affirmatively. After a molded square-toed shoe was hustled into the game, Spurrier calmly knotted it up and booted the game-winning three-pointer. Florida went on to victory in the Orange Bowl, and, to some degree, Gatorade marketers continue to claim to this day through throw-back TV commercials to have had lots to do with it.

Another highly unforgettable team in the SEC was Alabama, which finished third in the polls in quest of an unprecedented third straight national title. Thanks to the Michigan State-Notre Dame deadlock and the Crimson Tide's big Sugar Bowl win, Alabama ended up as the only major unbeaten and untied team in the nation.

Being all but ignored in the national title voting by both writers and coaches left Alabama bitter for years. The final AP Poll gave 41 first place votes to Notre Dame, eight to Michigan State, and seven to Alabama. The division in first-place votes hardly spoke of the even quality among the three great teams. Stickers were adhered to car bumpers all over the state of Alabama which read: "Notre Dame Plays Politics, 'Bama Plays Football."

Alabama had benefited from conveniently-timed blemishes on both its 1964 and 1965 records, neither of which cost the Tide a national title. In 1966, Alabama enjoyed the year's best record, maintained a winning streak

that reached 17 games by year's end, crushed Nebraska (9-2) by 34-7 in the Sugar Bowl, but suffered exquisitely bad timing. Crimson Tide fans could scream all they wanted for a third straight championship, but they forever were drowned out by the echoes of the "Game of the Century."

Milestones

Tulane withdrew from the Southeastern Conference to become an independent.

Death claimed 1957 North Carolina State All-America halfback Dick Christy at age 30. Eddie Erdelatz, coach of Navy for 10 years (1950-1959), died at age 53. Erdelatz enjoyed a 6-3-1 record against rival Army, including 5-3-1 against Hall of Fame coach Earl Blaik. He became the Oakland Raiders' first head coach in 1960.

Longest winning streaks entering season:
Dartmouth 10   East Carolina 8   Alabama 6

Coaching Changes:

	Incoming	Outgoing
Army	Tom Cahill	Paul Dietzel
Cornell	Jack Musick	Tom Harp
Duke	Tom Harp	Bill Murray
Hawaii	Phil Sarboe	Clark Shaughnessy
Iowa	Ray Nagel	Jerry Burns
Maryland	Lou Saban	Tommy Nugent
North Carolina	Bill Dooley	Jim Hickey
Oklahoma	Jim MacKenzie	Gomer Jones
Penn State	Joe Paterno	Rip Engle
Pittsburgh	Dave Hart	John Michelosen
South Carolina	Paul Dietzel	Marvin Bass
Tulane	Jim Pittman	Tommy O'Boyle
Utah	Mike Giddings	Ray Nagel
West Virginia	Jim Carlen	Gene Corum

Preseason AP Poll

1 Alabama (15)	296	6 Notre Dame	184	
2 Michigan State (12)	267	7 Syracuse	114	
3 Nebraska (2)	243	8 Purdue	78	
4 UCLA (6)	219	9 Southern California	67	
5 Arkansas	204	10 Tennessee	66	

Others with votes: Arizona, Baylor, Brigham Young, Colorado, Florida, Florida State, Georgia Tech, Illinois, Louisiana State, Miami, Michigan, Mississippi, Missouri, North Carolina, Ohio State, Texas, Texas Christian, Utah State.

September 10, 1966

BAYLOR 35 Syracuse 12: Poor pitchout to Orangemen HB Floyd Little in early moments was recovered by Baylor (1-0) DL Greg Pipes, who also contributed 18 tackles. Bears QB Terry Southall (14-28/229y, 4 TDs) was in position to throw 1st of his 4 TDs, only 1:30 into 1st Q. After reliable Little (102y rushing) scored 2nd Q TD to counter Southall's 2 TDs, Syracuse had shaved H deficit to 14-6. Bears scored upset-clinching TD in 3rd Q when sub QB Kenny Stockdale tossed short pass out of fake-FG which FB Charlie Wilson lugged 29y to score, Baylor's 5th TD pass of game.

September 17, 1966

NAVY 27 Boston College 7: Middies (1-0) gained control from outset as Boston College (0-1) bobbled away opening KO. Navy DE Bill Dow recovered KO FUM, sparkled all day on D, and helped hold Eagles touted FB Brendan McCarthy to 14/65y rushing. BC's heralded soph QB Dave Thomas threw misguided pass that DB Bernie DeGeorge picked off to score 1st Q Navy TD on 21y RET. QB John Cartwright (13-22/148y, TD, 2 INTs) scored short TD after his 40y scamper in 2nd Q and passed 18y to HB Terry Murray (20/80y, TD) for another in 3rd Q in building lead that grew to 27-0 in 4th Q. Thomas, who had taken far too long to spot BC receivers through much of game, finally came together for 97y aerial march in 4th Q. Eagles HB Dave Bennett scored on 2y flip to right corner of EZ with 9:08 to play.

PENN STATE 15 Maryland 7: New coaches bowed in: Penn State's former O coordinator Joe Paterno and Maryland's Lou Saban, fresh from triumphs with AFL Buffalo Bills. Paterno stayed at Penn State virtually forever, while Saban continued his nomadic trip through coaching ranks that still had him with whistle around his neck well into his 80s. Terrapins (0-1), who sputtered most of afternoon in gaining 169y, had HB Ernie Torain open scoring with 15y TD run, but soph Nittany Lions soph DT Mike Reid forced 1st of his 2 safeties by blocking Terps P Rich Carlson's punt through EZ in 2nd Q. Amazingly, Nittany Lions (1-0) would score trio of 2-ptrs, including downing of QB Alan Pastrana (10-18/72y, INT) in 1st min of 4th Q by Reid and DL Bob Vukmer. QB Jack White, day's best O operator with 9-17/110y, INT passing and 19/86y, TD rushing, scored 2nd Q TD for 8-7 lead that Lions would not surrender. Maryland failed to cross midfield in middle Qs, but made big threat while trailing 13-7 with 7 mins remaining in 4th Q. Torain (10/50y, TD) dashed 20y behind block of G Tom Gunderman to Penn State 8YL, but sub QB Phil Petry (3-12/53y, INT) threw incomplete over middle on 4th down from Lions 1YL.

FLORIDA 43 Northwestern 7: All-around Florida (1-0) QB-P-K Steve Spurrier passed 15-22/219y, 3 TDs, punted to Wildcats 3YL to set up safety, and kicked 1st FGs of his career: 41 and 25y. Spurrier's long FG came with only 5 secs remaining in 1st H and came on heels of TD catches by WB Richard Trapp (7/92y, 2 TDs) and WR Paul Ewaldsen. Only Northwestern (0-1) scoring drive came after 2nd H KO with HB Woody Campbell going over from 6YL after Cats cruised 72y in 13 plays. Campbell's TD pulled Wildcats within 17-7, but soon thereafter NW QB Dennis Boothe was hauled down in EZ for safety by Gators DT Red Anderson. Before end of 3rd Q, Trapp took

short pass in flat and squirmed away for 53y score. Just to pile it on, Florida topped its highest pt total in opener since 1930 with John Preston's T-eligible TD pass catch from 3rd-string QB Kay Stephenson (7-9/76y, TD).

LOUISIANA STATE 28 South Carolina 12: As luck would have it, new South Carolina (0-1) coach Paul Dietzel's first game took place at LSU (1-0), where he had bitter departure for West Point in 1962. Tigers QB Nelson Stokley directed 80 and 74y 1st H TD marches, and soph LB George Bevan blocked and recovered 3rd Q punt for TD. Gamecocks made it interesting for awhile, drawing within 7-6 while using uncharacteristic Shotgun formation, and later QB Bobby Bryant returned punt 77y for TD.

Houston 21 FLORIDA STATE 13: Typical opener was beset by PENs and TOs, but Florida State (0-1) held upper hand for much of game and nearly upset highly-touted Cougars (1-0). After Seminoles HB Bill Moreman returned opening KO all of 1y to his 9YL, FSU snapped off 10 plays to pay-dirt: QB Kim Hammond hit soph WR Ron Sellers with 43 and 13y passes before clicking with FB Jim Mankins for 8y score. Florida State D played surprisingly well with 2 sacks and 4 incompletions all in row, but when FSU K Pete Roberts missed 27y FG, Houston QB Bo Burris got his act together. Burris hit HB Warren McVea alone at midfield, and speedster zoomed 80y to TD. Future major league baseball player, Cougars DB Tom Paciorek, made INT RET to Seminoles 34YL to set up 14-7 lead that held until H as Burris rifled TD pass to E Ken Hebert to up margin to 21-13.

MICHIGAN STATE 28 North Carolina State 10: Stubborn and unheralded Wolfpack (0-1) D stuffed Spartans' short passes (7-11/36y) and surprisingly led 3-0 on K Harold Deters' soaring 49y FG in 2nd Q. But, Michigan State (1-0) HB Clinton Jones escaped 4 tacklers to race 39y to TD. Spartans FB Bob Apisa broke open game by capping 80y drive in 3rd Q with 37y run off pitchout from QB Jimmy Raye, so Spartans were on their way.

MISSOURI 24 Minnesota 0: Fighting its scorelessness, Minnesota (0-1) dominated 1st H behind running of QB Curt Wilson, but he saw his 82y bomb to E Kenny Last nullified by PEN. When Tigers QB-K William Bates kicked 42y FG with 1:14 left in H, Golden Gophers spirit seemed smashed. Missouri (1-0) struck swiftly after H as QB Gary Kombrink hit passes of 10 and 46y to poise HB Charlie Brown for 9y TD run. FB Barry Lischner later battered to Gophers 8YL where Bates threw HB pass to E Chuck Weber for 17-0 lead. Last-min INT TD RET by Tigers LB John Douglas completed scoring. P Bates had big game supported by superb Mizzou punt coverage.

Texas Tech 23 KANSAS 7: Bending but not breaking, resourceful Texas Tech (1-0) D repelled 4 Jayhawks (0-1) drives inside its 20YL, including thrust to Tech 1-ft line, when game still was in balance. QB John Scovell (11-20/150y, 2 TDs) led 3 TD drives of 73, 83, and 89y, including 2 that ended in TD passes to HB Jerry Lovelace and E Larry Gilbert (7 catches) in 1st H. After soph K Kenny Vinyard gave Red Raiders 17-0 lead in 3rd Q with 27y FG, set up by LB Mickey Merritt's FUM REC on 1st play of 3rd Q, Kansas QB Bob Skahan hit 4 passes to move Jayhawks 72y to 1st down at Tech 4YL. But, Skahan was stacked up on 3rd and 4th downs within breathing distance of GL. P Vinyard answered with booming 78y punt out of trouble. Skahan brought back Kansas to his 13y TD rollout run in 4th Q, but it became trade-off TD as Raiders scored as Scovell hit Gilbert 4 times in 89y TD drive.

Southern California 10 TEXAS 6: With former Trojans player-turned-movie-star-icon John Wayne looking on in 9-gallon hat, USC (1-0) dominated 1st H as QB Troy Winslow outplayed ballyhooed Texas (0-1) soph QB Bill Bradley. As Longhorns coach Darrell Royal said later about Southern California hogging ball for all but 15 plays of 1st H, "You don't perform much on 15 plays. He (Bradley) spent most of the afternoon with me (on the sidelines)." Winslow passed 11-22 and put 10 pts on board in 4:46 span: DE-K Tim Rossovich kicked 23y FG and Winslow scored on 9y run. In 2nd H, Bradley provoked some damage against USC, leading 2 long drives. Steers' 1st march ended in Bradley's ill-advised pitchout that became lost FUM at USC 11YL, but Texas' next voyage went 91y to Bradley's 3y TD sweep. With 8:20 left, P Bradley punted smartly to Trojans 2YL, but Southern California mightily held possession and never let go.

Wyoming 13 AIR FORCE 0: Falcons (0-1) mounted 3 serious scoring bids that were turned aside by harsh Cowboys D, which was keyed by dangerous DLs Ron "Pedro" Billingsley and Mike LaHood. Wyoming (1-0) QB Rick Egloff threw 2 TD passes: 33y to WB Hub Lindsey and 14y to HB-turned-WR Jerry Marion. Victory got Wyoming rolling toward its 1st conf championship since coach Bob Devaney wheeled off 4 in row in his last years in Laramie in 1958-61.

AP Poll September 19

1 Michigan State (12)	338	6 Arkansas (1)	140	
2 UCLA (13)	328	7 Purdue	132	
3 Alabama (10)	260	8 Notre Dame (1)	120	
4 Nebraska	202	9 Michigan (1)	106	
5 Southern California (2)	193	10 Baylor (1)	94	

Others with votes: Duke, Florida, Georgia, Georgia Tech, Louisiana State, Miami, Mississippi, Missouri, Navy, New Mexico, Ohio State, Oklahoma, Southern Methodist, Syracuse, Tennessee, Texas, Texas Christian, Tulsa, Wyoming

September 24, 1966

(Fri) HOUSTON 21 Washington State 7: Long TD that could be tied in length but never broken went into record books for Houston (2-0): QB Bo Burris (11-19/240y, 3 TDs, 2 INTs) and ferociously-quick HB Warren McVea teamed up to produce 99y pass-run TD, on which McVea rocketed away untouched from his 20YL. It broke up 7-7 tie in 3rd Q, and Houston went on to win in its 1st game played on Astrodome's new artificial surface. Washington State (0-2) was able to compile respectable 356y total O with balanced attack and scored game's opening TD. Wazzu QB Jerry Henderson

had connected on 8y TD pass to WR Doug Flansburg in 1st Q. Burris tied it 7-7 in 2nd Q with 1st of his 2 TD passes to versatile FB Dickie Post, pair of aerial plays that measured 11 and 29y.

Ucla 31 SYRACUSE 12: In rain and muck that made most runs highly treacherous, UCLA (2-0) rang up 31-0 lead as QB Gary Beban (7-10/178y, TD) and fleet E Harold Busby (5/121y, TD) formed aerial team that completely befuddled Syracuse (0-2). Rushers were less effective: Bruins HB Mel Farr was limited to 12/79y, although he contributed 38y dash that set up UCLA FG by K Kurt Zimmerman in 3rd Q, and Beban gained only 8/10y, although he opened scoring with 4y run in 2nd Q. Orangemen HB Floyd Little was effectively corralled by Bruins D, led by T John Richardson. Little gained only 9/12y, but thrilled home crowd with dazzling 65y punt TD RET in 4th Q to go with his short TD run at end of 60y 3rd Q march, sparked by soph QB Jim Del Gaizo. Game had been swept away on UCLA's 21-pt blitz in 2nd Q and WR Ray Armstrong's 62y punt TD RET in 3rd Q.

Duke 14 PITTSBURGH 7: Panthers (0-2) QB Ed James completed 15-30/205y, 2 INTs, often to his favorite receiver, E Bob Longo (9/99y), but Pitt, with 310y to 264y O edge, could score only on its opening series. Panthers went 72y from 1st Q KO to FB Mike Raklewicz's 2y dive on series' 14th play. Duke (2-0) tied it 7-7 in 2nd Q on DB Andy Beath's 49y punt TD RET. But on its 4 drives in 1st H, Blue Devils were frustrated by 2 lost FUMs, Pitt DB Joe Curtin's EZ INT, and missed FG. With starting QB Al Woodall sidelined with dislocated non-throwing elbow from 1st Q, Duke turned to backup QB Todd Orvald. In 3rd Q, Orvald completed key 3rd down pass to TE Henley Carter and rolled out for 7y to sustain winning 56y TD drive. FB Jay Calabrese shook off tackler and charged 14y to pay-dirt as Duke finally overcame its O mistakes. In 4th Q, Panthers WR Skip Orszulak got behind secondary for pass, but was stripped of ball by Beath. Blues LB Bob Matheson stopped Pitt HB Dewey Chester on 4th-and-1 at midfield.

CLEMSON 40 Virginia 35: Lead changed hands 5 times with scores coming in clumps with Cavaliers (1-1) QB Bob Davis in O spotlight, running for 3 TDs and throwing for 2 scores. Clemson (1-0) glory was shared by TB Buddy Gore (25/117y, TD) and QB Jimmy Addison (12-19/283y, 3 TDs). Tigers scored 1st on 37y TD catch by WR Phil Rogers, but Davis put Virginia up 7-6 with 4y run. DB Frank Libertore raced 44y on punt TD RET, but Clemson's 3rd missed x-pt left it with 18-7 lead in 2nd Q. Cavs quickly went ahead 21-18 by H as Davis hit 1st of 2 TD passes to HB Frank Quayle. Win rode Addison's perfect bomb to TB Jacky Jackson, who split wide and sped past Cavs DB George Stetter for 76y TD. Not yet done was Davis (26-48/312y, 2 TDs, INT), who drove Cavs downfield only to have Tigers DB Phil Marion make INT at his 10YL in last 2 mins.

Florida State 23 MIAMI 20: Sub QB Gary Pajcic of Florida State (1-1) came off bench to match 2 TD passes of QB Bill Miller of Miami (1-1). Seminoles got 2nd Q surge of 17 pts from Pajcic's 1st TD pass of 27y to WR Ron Sellers, WR T.K. Wetherell's 83y KO TD RET after lateral from HB Bill Moreman, and K Pete Roberts' FG. Pajcic's last scoring toss, 28y to E Thurston Taylor, brought FSU from behind to 23-20 edge just before midway in 4th Q. Miami FB Doug McGee (81y rushing) lost FUM at FSU 20YL on next drive and returned favor with another FUM at Seminoles 4YL after Miller completed 3 passes and raced 9y to 4YL in dying moments. DL David Braggins clutched clinching REC for Florida State.

OHIO STATE 14 Texas Christian 7: Contest started with bizarre KO RET as Buckeyes (1-0) HB Will Thomas sped 91y only to stumble at 10YL and lose FUM to Frog DB Frank Herak at TCU (0-2) 2YL. FB Paul Hudson (92y rushing) finished off 2 Ohio State drives of 47 and 78y with TD runs of 2y in 1st Q and 18y in 4th Q. Horned Frogs QB P.D. Shabay (15-24/115y, 3 INTs) climaxed 67y drive at outset of 3rd Q with 2y TD run up middle which tied it at 7-7. After sharp passes of QB Bill Long (12-14/106y) softened Purple Frogs late in 3rd Q, Hudson's winning score came early in 4th Q and behind big block of RT Dave Foley. Shabay led 3 4th Q drives that appeared capable of scoring, but 1 died on downs and Buckeyes came up with ruinous INTs by LB John Mulbach and DB Tom Portsmouth.

MICHIGAN STATE 42 Penn State 8: In rolling up 381y O, no. 1 Michigan State (2-0) starters charged to 35-0 3rd Q lead on way to biggest rout suffered by Penn State (1-1) since 1949. Spartans DE Bubba Smith's bruising tackle put Nittany Lions QB Jack White out of game early in 2nd Q. QB Jimmy Raye's TD aerials of 36 and 50y to E Gene Washington highlighted MSU's big lead. FB Bob Apisa scored twice, and his soph understudy, Regis Cavender, added another for 42-0 4th Q margin before FB Roger Grimes finally put Nittany Lions on scoreboard with 1y run.

MINNESOTA 35 Stanford 21: With future star WR Gene Washington at QB, Stanford (1-1) threw for 223y, but suffered 4 INTs. Once Minnesota (1-1) DB Tom Sakal stopped Indians opening drive with INT of Washington, Gophers started scoring spree that took them to 21-0 H lead and 35-7 edge after 3 Qs. Minnesota QB Curtis Wilson got scoring started with 5y run on which his forward FUM was recovered by E Chet Anderson in EZ for TD in 1st Q, ran for TDs in 2nd and 3rd Qs, and passed 10y to E Charles Litten for 3rd Q TD. Stanford scored early in 3rd Q to pare deficit to 21-7 when Washington passed 15y to HB Dave Lewis. Indians registered 2 late TDs to make it look artificially close as Stanford's 327y to 293y O advantage might indicate.

Oregon State 17 IOWA 3: HB Bob Grim launched visiting Beavers (1-1) to 1st series win in 6 tries against Iowa (1-1) when he raced 59y down right sideline to score on game's 4th snap. Grim spent rest of game dazzling Hawks with pitchout runs for 142y. Midway in 1st Q, Hawkeyes earned 33y FG by HB-K Bob Anderson as QB Ed Podolak (12-29/165y, 3 INTs) clicked twice to E Gary Larsen and HB Tony Williams slipped through RT Bill Smith's block for 29y dash. Oregon State went 63y to start 2nd Q as QB Paul Brothers tallied on 6y run for 14-3 edge. Beavers K Mike Haggard finished scoring with 30y FG with 3 secs left before H. Oregon State never got around to completing pass in 1st H while running for 243y, much by FB Pete Pifer who finished game with 27/119y. In 2nd H, Pifer's pounding kept Iowa at bay except when Hawkeyes made vain trip to Beavers 3YL.

NOTRE DAME 26 Purdue 14: Angry Notre Dame (1-0) D looked for redemption from 1965 disassembly by Purdue (1-1) QB Bob Griese. Irish D played well, but headlines went to soph aerial sensations making their varsity debut: QB Terry Hanratty and E Jim Seymour (13/276y). Seymour finished with 2nd-most single-game receiving y in NCAA history. However, it wasn't completely easy for Notre Dame. During 1st Q threat, HB Bob "Rocky" Bleier dribbled pitchout, briefly regained grip, but lost FUM when hit by Purdue DB John Charles and DE Robert Holmes. Boilermakers DB Leroy Keyes caught Bleier's FUM in mid-air and exploded for 94y TD RET. But, Irish HB Nick Eddy immediately countered with perfectly blocked 97y KO TD RET. After 2 long Hanratty-to-Seymour TD passes made it 20-7 early in 4th Q, Griese hit 3 passes/52y to slice Purdue's margin to 20-14. DE Alan Page forced late Griese FUM that led to Seymour's 3rd TD grab from Hanratty.

RICE 17 Louisiana State 15: LSU (1-1) took 3-0 1st Q lead on K Steve Daniel's 25y FG, then DL John Garlington keyed 15-7 H edge with 42y TD run with FUM. Owls (1-0) narrowed it to 15-10 on short 3rd Q FG. Tigers lost QB Nelson Stokley for balance of season with 4th Q shoulder separation. After LSU missed 4th Q FG, Rice went 80y for winning TD. Prime architect of Rice's upset was soph QB Robbie Shelton, who gained 50y on late drive and who was born 7 years after 1940 arrival of coach Jess Neely, who was in his 27th and last season at Rice.

Colorado 13 BAYLOR 7: Game was tied at 7-7 at H after Colorado (1-1) FB John Farler ran 23y to score and Baylor (1-1) QB Terry Southall whipped 17y TD pass to WR George Cheshire. Power-running HB Wilmer Cooks blasted 1y for 4th Q TD, but conv kick failed, so Buffs were in danger of absorbing loss during Southall's late, but vain aerial salvo.

Air Force 10 WASHINGTON 0: Air Force (1-1) continued its mastery of Washington (1-1), winning its 3rd series tilt in as many tries. Huskies' miscues—they had 5 TOs—led to each score by Airmen. Falcons got their TD late in 2nd Q after LB Dave Allen recovered FUM at Washington 44YL, and QB Sunny Litz launched 27y TD arrow to WR Carl Janssen, who made leaping grab with 1:16 clock before H. K Dick Hall wrapped up Air Force's scoring with 4th Q FG after DB Dennis Zyroll picked off pass by Washington QB Tom Sparlin, who missed most of contest with tender ankle. Sparlin involuntarily rattled Huskies' weak air game (5-20/33y) with 3 INTs, but their run game was just as inept with only 90y.

AP Poll September 26

1 Michigan State (22)	367	6 Nebraska	203
2 UCLA (11)	332	7 Arkansas (1)	201
3 Alabama (2)	266	8 Michigan (1)	122
4 Notre Dame (2)	261	9 Georgia Tech	66
5 Southern California (1)	208	10 Tennessee	64

Others with votes: Baylor, Colorado, Duke, Florida, Houston, Mississippi, Missouri, New Mexico, Ohio State, Oklahoma, Purdue, Southern Methodist, Wyoming

October 1, 1966

ARMY 11 Penn State 0: P Nick Kurilko's finely-crafted punts gained field position for FG and safety for Army (3-0). Cadets DB Henry Uberecken's INT late in 1st Q was returned 39y to Penn State (1-2) 1YL, and soph QB Steve Lindell went over on 2nd play of 2nd Q. Nittany Lions mounted 227y to 205y O advantage, built mostly during their domination of 2nd Q. But 7 TOs by Penn State O considerably helped Cadets' alert D, led by LB Townsend Clarke.

GEORGIA TECH 13 Clemson 12: Georgia Tech (3-0) TB Lenny Snow scored on 2nd H runs of 6 and 40y to pull out win. Snow's 2nd score through group of would-be Tigers (1-1) tacklers, gave him 7 TDs for young season. Clemson QB Jimmy Addison (13-22/183y, 2 TDs, 2 INTs) threw 2 TD passes to provide 6-0 lead in 1st Q and 12-7 lead in 4th Q. But, Engineers star DB Bill Eastman assured Tigers' downfall with clutch INT of pass thrown by Addison at Georgia Tech 10YL with 1:30 to play.

VIRGINIA TECH 13 West Virginia 13: TE Ken Barefoot alertly pounced on EZ FUM lost by his Virginia Tech (1-1-1) QB Tommy Stafford (7-13/80y) for 4th Q TD that rescued tie against West Virginia (1-1-1). Little British K John Utin could have won it for Gobblers but he sailed x-pt wide right. Utin had bad kicking day as he missed 2 FGs, including 39y try in last secs and had another blocked. HB John Mallory had put Mountaineers on scoreboard 1st when he galloped 57y down right sideline behind perfect blocking for punt TD RET in 1st Q. WVU HB Garrett Ford lost FUM in 1st Q, recovered by Virginia Tech DG Dave Farmer. Runs of TB Tommy Francisco (30/119y) soon brought Hokies into range for Stafford's 15y TD sweep. K Chuck Kinder booted 2 FGs to give Mountaineers 13-7 lead by 4th Q.

KENTUCKY 17 Auburn 7: HB Larry Seiple's 30 carries set Kentucky (2-1) to-date record, and Seiple gained 116y on ground and caught clinching 3rd Q TD pass from QB Terry Beadles (3-4/36y, TD). After scoreless opening Q that saw each team threaten, Seiple had followed E Dan Spanish's 20y catch with 22y sprint to set up K Chuck Arnold's 35y FG. Auburn (1-2) responded with 80y TD march after KO: TB Richard Plagge raced 54y to Wildcats 19YL before QB Tom Bryan scored from 6YL. Kentucky HB Dickie Lyons blocked Tigers K Jim Jones' 35y FG attempt late in 2nd Q as Jones had think he had found sore spot on field. He had missed from same distance in 1st Q. Cats LB Doug Van Meter scooped up blocked FG and barreled to Auburn 13YL to set up FB Al Britton's 1y TD plunge. P Seiple's 3rd Q punt grazed surprised Tiger to set up Seiple's 21y TD grab.

Alabama 17 MISSISSIPPI 7 (Jackson): Unscored-upon Mississippi (2-1) played Alabama (2-0) tough but failed to defeat Crimson Tide, something it hadn't done in 17 tries since 1910. Rebels trailed 7-0 at H after pass interference PEN called on Ole

Miss DB Tommy Luke gave Bama 1st down possession at Rebs 3YL in 2nd Q. Tide HB Les Kelley quickly powered over from 1YL. QB Ken Stabler was brilliant in leading Alabama's very sharp 16-17/144y passing attack. Stabler and E Ray Perkins (9 catches) collaborated on 28y TD pass in 3rd Q. Ole Miss rallied in 4th Q, going 92y to WB Doug Cunningham's soaring 2y TD dive. Bama DB Dicky Thompson's 3rd INT set stage for K Steve Davis' clinching 21y FG.

LOUISIANA STATE 10 Miami 8: Bengal Tigers (2-1) found O going nowhere without injured QB Nelson Stokley, but eked out typical D-dominated win at Death Valley. K Steve Daniel's FG and FB Gawain DiBetta's 1y TD run gave LSU 10-0 H lead. Miami (1-2) came back in 3rd Q with sub QB David Olivo scoring TD and starting QB Bill Miller pitching 2-pt pass. But every time Miller ignited subsequent Hurricanes charges, LSU DE Mike Robichaux would lead sack-conscious D. Play of game was LSU LB George Bevan's cross-field dash to haul down TD-bound Miami runner.

Michigan State 26 ILLINOIS 10: Big and unusual plays by Michigan State (3-0) started it toward successful defense of its Big 10 title. In 4th Q, Spartans E Al Brenner shot up middle and cut to sideline for 95y punt TD RET, longest to-date in conf history. But, 2 plays that broke open game were authored by DE Phil Hoag: Ahead 7-3 in 2nd Q on HB Dwight Lee's 10y TD run, Michigan State DE George Chatlos jarred ball loose from Illinois (0-3) QB Bob Naponic, and Hoag snatched it in mid-air. Hoag quickly lateraled to NG Pat Gallinagh who lumbered last 40y of 54y TD RET for 13-3 lead. Illini trimmed margin to 13-10 on Naponic's long TD pass to E John Wright, who scrambled away from DB Jerry Jones to complete 62y score. Spartans were frustrated at Illinois 3 and 1YLs, but, after Illini GLS, little HB Bill Huston lost FUM to Hoag at 3YL. Michigan State QB Jimmy Raye scored on next snap for comfortable 19-10 lead.

North Carolina 21 MICHIGAN 7: Wolverines (2-1) glided 58y to FB Dave Fisher's 1y TD plunge in 1st Q, and all seemed in order: big crowd would intimidate Southern invaders. But poised Tar Heels (2-1) turned 2 FUM RECs into short TD drives in middle Qs: QB Danny Talbott's 12y scoring pass to HB Tom Lampman and HB Dick Wesolowski's 5y crack up middle. E Jack Clancy hauled in Michigan's only 2nd H reception until final min. Funny thing happened to high-achieving UNC, though; fortunes would turn in other direction and Tar Heels would lose their next 7 games.

Washington 38 OHIO STATE 22: Fireplug-shaped HB Don Moore (30/221y) gave Ohio State (1-1) taste of its own medicine: large doses of power running. Washington Huskies (2-1) used Moore's blasts to position FB Jeff Jordan (12/48y) for 3 1st H TDs for 21-0 lead. So, Buckeyes were forced use their to air game, which logged 21-38/228y, 2 TDs, 2 INTs. In contrast, Ohio State gained only 34y rushing. QB Bill Long sneaked over for TD that brought Ohio State within 21-7 at H, but his 2 INTs would cost Bucks 10 pts in 2nd H. Washington DE Dean Halverson, who pressured passer all game came up with 16y INT RET to Ohio 17YL early in 3rd Q to set up TD run by Moore, and Huskies DB Dave Dillon's INT led to K Don Martin's 23y FG early in 4th Q. Buckeyes narrowed their margin to 28-15 and 31-22 in 2nd H as Long clicked for 2 short TD passes. WR Billy Anders' 2y TD catch in 4th Q got Ohio State within 9 pts before Moore's twisting 47y TD run iced upset.

Notre Dame 35 NORTHWESTERN 7: Dynamic passing duo of QB Terry Hanratty (14-23/202y, 2 INTs) and E Jim Seymour (9/141y) paced Fighting Irish (2-0) to easy win over Northwestern (0-3) as ND outgained Wildcats 425y to 159y. Early in 1st Q, Notre Dame HB Nick Eddy took pitchout and cut back off right side of line and charged 56y to score for 7-0 lead. Irish D, led by E Alan Page and LB Jim Lynch, stopped 3 Northwestern plays inside its 4YL and soon collected LB John Pergine's FUM REC at ND 46YL. Hanratty and Seymour collaborated to advance ND to 1YL where FB Larry Conjar scored for 13-0 lead. Passing combo clicked twice before Hanratty turned to his runners for 3rd Q TD and 21-0 lead. HB Rocky Bleier scored from12YL, and Hanratty added 2 pts on QB draw. Trailing 35-0, Northwestern greeted return of former coach Ara Parseghian by striking for its only score late in 4th Q: QB Bill Melzer passed 32y to E Roger Murphy.

Nebraska 12 IOWA STATE 6: Heavily-favored Nebraska (3-0) found itself in D struggle with surprising Iowa State at 6-6 late in 4th Q. In early going, K Larry Wachholtz kicked 2 medium-range FGs for Cornhuskers. Cyclones (0-3) tied it 6-6 on 16y INT TD RET by DB Don Graves. Oddly, Iowa State went for failed 2-pt try instead of x-pt kick that likely would have provided 7-6 lead. As game wound down, Nebraska found its savior in HB Harry Wilson, who burst off LT for 37y winning TD run.

TEXAS A&M 35 Texas Tech 14: Soph QB Edd Hargett (13-19/204y, 2 TDs) made memorable Kyle Field debut for Texas A&M (1-2), as Aggies stormed from behind with 3-TD explosion in 2nd Q. Favored Texas Tech (1-2) greeted beautiful evening with 72y TD drive in 1st Q that was capped by QB John Scovell's tricky fake and 3y keeper. Scovell lost FUM at his 27YL in 2nd Q, and Hargett found WB Bob Long deep in EZ for tying TD pass. Texas A&M DB Curley Hallman, future coach at LSU, returned punt 13y to launch next TD that came on FB Ronnie Lindsey's 2y TD run through T, just after E Larry Lee latched onto 34y arrow from Hargett. HB Wendell Housley (19/69y, TD) scored TD and Hargett added 2-pt pass for 21-7 lead after Hallman made INT and returned it 19y. Texas Tech HB Mike Leinart (12/118y, TD) tallied 3rd Q TD after Scovell (11-22/107y) accounted for 66y of 80y scoring trip. Hargett wrapped it up with 24y TD pass and 7y TD run in 4th Q.

UCLA 24 Missouri 15: UCLA (3-0) enjoyed casual 17-0 lead in 4th Q. Margin had been built on K Kurt Zimmerman's 25y FG in 2nd Q, FB Steve Stanley's 2y plunge at end of 15-play, 56y march in 3rd Q, and HB Mel Farr's 6y TD run after LB Dallas Grider's 28y INT RET in 4th Q. Back surged slumbering Missouri (2-1) on E Chuck Weber's diving 12y TD catch and WB Earl Denny's 2-pt grab. Enormous DL Russ Washington soon blocked Bruins punt and rumbled 20y to TD that made it 17-15. However, UCLA foiled on-side KO to spoil any comeback bid by Tigers. QB Gary Beban (11-20/204y) found Farr for 24y aerial gain, and Farr (15/87y) followed with clinching 13y TD run.

AP Poll October 3

1 Michigan State (20)	371	6 Southern California (1)	194
2 UCLA (7)	345	7 Nebraska	144
3 Notre Dame (8)	322	8 Tennessee	143
4 Alabama (3)	300	9 Georgia Tech	83
5 Arkansas (2)	206	10 Florida	69

Others with votes: Air Force, Baylor, Duke, Houston, Michigan, Missouri, Oklahoma, Purdue, Southern Methodist, Texas, Wyoming

October 8, 1966

PITTSBURGH 17 West Virginia 14: Pittsburgh (1-3) QB Ed James lost 2 FUMs in opening 18 mins, and West Virginia (1-2-1) turned each into TD. James lost ball at own 13YL, WVU HB Garrett Ford pounded 12y to GL doorstep, and HB Gary Thall dived over on next play for 7-0 lead in 1st Q. Panthers were driving in 2nd Q when James lost handle again at Mountaineers 35YL, and, 2 plays later, Ford burst through T and dashed 57y to score. James' 17y TD pass to E Bob Longo helped boost Pitt back to within 14-10 at H. Pitt's winning TD came in 4th Q on 4y run by TB Joe Jones. Like most "Backyard Brawl" games, result was unknown until end: WVU marched from own 20YL to Panthers 3YL, where Pitt DB Mickey Depp broke up Ford's HB pass to E Allen Schupbach in EZ on game's next-to-last play.

MARYLAND 21 Duke 19: QB Alan Pastrana, star of Maryland's 1st-rate lacrosse team, used his feet and arm to rally Terrapins (2-2) to upset of Duke (3-1). After Maryland FB Ralph Donofrio lost FUM on game's 1st scrimmage play, Blue Devils broke out on top with TD runs in 1st Q from WB Frank Ryan for 17y on old Statue of Liberty handoff and QB Todd Orvald's 3y romp behind FB Jay Calabrese's block. Unfortunately for Duke, FB-K Bob Matheson missed kick after 1st TD and was stopped on 2-pt plunge after 2nd score. Pastrana (11-18/151y, TD, 3 INTs) got cranked up in Terps' unexpected Slot-T, passing to SB Billy Van Heusen for 5/104y to set up 2 TDs in 2nd Q. Orvald soon went to sidelines with possible broken collarbone as *Washington Post* described him as "victim of unfriendly bearhug by Maryland LB Ron Pearson." Untried soph QB Tom Edens was no answer for suddenly bogged-down Duke O. After scoreless 3rd Q, Terps found their long-lost running game that chewed up 7:38 of 4th Q for Pastrana's 9y TD run for 21-12 lead. QB Al Woodall, already hampered by dislocated non-throwing elbow, rallied Devils to near-TD on pass knockdown in EZ by Maryland DB John Hetrick and to real TD to E Dave Dunaway with :51 on clock.

Florida 22 FLORIDA STATE 19: WR Richard Trapp grabbed 7 passes including 35y TD pass from QB Steve Spurrier (16-24/219y, 3 TD) on clock-beating 70y drive to give Florida (4-0) 14-10 H lead. Back stormed Florida State (1-2) with FB Jim Mankins scoring his 2nd TD and K Pete Roberts booting his 2nd FG for 19-14 edge. Spurrier countered with 41y TD pass to HB Larry Smith and 2-pt pass to Trapp. Lanky FSU sub WR Lane Fenner made apparent 45y catch in EZ with 17 secs to play, but officials ruled him OB. Much criticism followed when news photos revealed that Fenner's catch appeared good. Missed call was especially galling to Seminoles, who now had beaten in-state rivals only once in 9 tries.

GEORGIA 9 Mississippi 3: Georgia (4-0) D held Rebels (2-2) to K Jimmy Keyes' 39y FG after Bulldogs QB Kirby Moore lost early FUM. It started real trend for Dogs D: Ole Miss made only single 1st down in 1st H. Bulldogs workhorse FB Ronnie Jenkins carried 46y of 68y TD drive in 2nd Q. Before H, P Moore booted Rebels deep into hole. DL Bill McWhorter soon pinned Ole Miss QB Jody Graves for safety on Graves' rollout in EZ.

MICHIGAN STATE 20 Michigan 7: Usually slow-starting Spartans (4-0) got mid-1st Q 5y TD sweep from QB Jimmy Raye. Meanwhile, Michigan (2-2) filled air with QB Dick Vidmer's passes (18-48/168y, TD) and stayed within 7-0 until early in 4th Q. FB Bob Apisa's 49y dash sparked Michigan State to 80y TD drive which broke Wolverines. Raye soon added 25y TD pass to E Gene Washington for 20-0 lead before Vidmer pulled Michigan off canvas to rifle 15y TD to HB Jim Detwiler late in 4th Q.

Nebraska 31 Wisconsin 3: Growing difference between Big 8 and Big 10 football was evident as Wisconsin (2-2) in no way upheld long-time honor of Big 10. Unbeaten Nebraska (4-0) used its alert D to create miscues that led to all but 1 TD of its 31 pts. Cornhuskers K Larry Wachholtz opened scoring with 27y FG after Wisconsin lost FUM, and Huskers D continued their skullduggery with another FUM REC, blocked punt, and INT that turned into TDs. DE Langston Coleman knocked ball from Badgers QB John Ryan (10-26/149y, 3 INTs), and DT Carel Stith recovered at Wisconsin 28YL in 1st Q to set stage for Wachholtz's FG. Badgers soon tied it on K Tom Schinke's 33y 3-ptr late in 1st Q after Ryan hit Es Tom McCauley and Bill Fritz with twin 15y gains. Fritz adjusted to underthrown bomb by Ryan to put Wisconsin at Nebraska 36YL in 2nd Q. But, Coleman recovered FUM on next play, and Huskers immediately were off to 64y TD drive, capped by 9y romp by HB Ben Gregory (4/42y, TD). Early in 3rd Q, Nebraska C Wayne Meylan burst through to block and recover punt for TD and 17-3 lead. Huskers went 59y to HB Harry Wilson's TD burst, and LB Len Janik set up last TD with his INT.

NOTRE DAME 35 Army 0: Fabulous Notre Dame (3-0) soph pass battery of QB Terry Hanratty (11-20/195y, TD) and WR Jim Seymour (8/155y, TD) played only in 35-0 1st H, but still emerged from team's opening 3 wins with flashy combined total of 30/572y, 4 TDs. Fighting Irish HB Rocky Bleier had opened scoring with 3y TD run, and young aerial artists collaborated on 33y TD right after DE Pete Duranko's REC of FUM by Army (3-1) HB Carl Woessner. Hanratty was hit hard at GL, but scored on 7y run for 21-0 lead in 1st Q. Irish HB Nick Eddy tallied from 3YL after DB Jim Smithberger's 45y INT RET. Eddy scored again at tail end of 85y march for 5-TD edge before H. Notre Dame's top defenders, including E Alan Page and T Kevin Hardy, stayed until end of 3rd Q. In all, ND allowed only 158y, made 5 INTs, and recovered FUM. Cadets made FUM REC in 4th Q and advanced to Irish 22YL until INT of QB Jim O'Toole turned possession back over to ND.

OKLAHOMA STATE 11 Colorado 10: After swapping of 1st Q FGs by K Craig Kessler of Oklahoma State (1-2) and K Dave Bartelt of Colorado (2-2), FB John Farler plunged over to give Buffs 10-3 lead in 3rd Q. Farler's 1y TD came at end of 72y drive, and Bartelt kicked conv. In last 4:30, Cowboys ate up 69y on winning drive. FB Jack Reynolds went over from 1YL, and QB Ronnie Johnson calmly pitched 2-pt pass.

Oklahoma 18 Texas 9 (Dallas): Having not whipped its arch-rival since 1957, Oklahoma (3-0) suffered familiar early fate, allowing Texas to drive off opening KO to score. K David Conway gave Texas (2-2) 3-0 lead with 25y FG. Thereafter, Sooners dominated behind crisp leadership of QB Bobby Warmack (12-21/220y, and 60y rushing). But, Sooners lost 4 TOs deep in Steers territory, and Texas kept it close as it trailed 15-9 after soph QB Andy White's virtually-personal 67y TD drive midway through 4th Q. Sooners K Mike Vachon kicked his 4th FG to clinch game at 18-9 in 4th Q.

Baylor 7 ARKANSAS 0: Bears (3-1) D was perfect when pushed back into its cave, stopping Arkansas (3-1) drives at own 18, 6, 28, 15, and 36YLs. Clutch defenders were DLs Greg Pipes and Dwight Hood. Game remained scoreless until Baylor got break in 4th Q. Playing it close to vest, Arkansas chose to punt Bears into corner with boot from Baylor 19YL. But, long snap sailed over Razorbacks P Martine Bercher's head for 25y loss, and Bears took over on Arkansas 46YL. QB Terry Southall lobbed 21y winning pass to WR Bobby Green with 4:48 left. Late Arkansas TD was nullified by PEN, so Hogs lost after 24 wins in row. It was Arkansas' 1st home defeat since 1961.

Ucla 27 RICE 24: Barely escaping its 1st-ever trip to state of Texas, UCLA (4-0) tallied 11 pts in closing 2:30 to pull it out. Pesky Owls (1-2) had answer for Bruins QB Gary Beban in their QB Robby Shelton, who only was edged by Beban's 304y O by 23y. Shelton scored twice to build 24-16 3rd Q lead. Beban hit E Harold Busby with 33y TD pass, and HB Mel Farr crashed for 2 pts to create 24-24 tie late in 4th Q. Next came Shelton's costly FUM, recovered at Rice 23YL by Bruins DT Larry Agajanian. K Kurt Zimmerman kicked winning 17y FG with 7 secs to play.

WYOMING 40 Utah 7: Ace Wyoming (4-0) K Jerry Depoyster set new NCAA record with 3 FGs in excess of 50y: 54, 54, and 52y. Still, Utah (1-1), which had crushed Cowboys 42-3 in 1965, stayed within 13-7 in 3rd Q on QB Jack Gehrke's 13y TD pass. Cowboys' revenge was realized with 27-pt 4th Q, triggered by 9y TD pass and 20y TD run by QB Rick Egloff and HB Dave Hampton's 5y score.

SOUTHERN CALIFORNIA 17 Washington 14: Trojans (4-0) fashioned smooth early TD drive, but lost QB Troy Winslow who was knocked groggy on tackle by Huskies LB Cliff Coker. Washington (2-2) QB Tom Sparlin (14-33/238y, 2 TDs, 4 INTs) beat H clock with 10y TD pass to E Jim Cope (11/195y) for 7-7 tie. Same combination provided 14-7 lead midway in 3rd Q with 58y TD connection. Sub QB Toby Page (11-15/120y, TD) created USC's go-ahead 72y TD drive early in 4th Q, capping it with 5y scoring toss to E Ron Drake.

OREGON 7 Stanford 3 (Portland): It looked like same frustration this season for young Ducks of Oregon (1-3), whose sophs in vital positions mishandled ball twice in 1st Q. But, in 2nd Q, Ducks came to life, mounting 2 drives of 60y. They were unsuccessful on their 1st threat because of INT by Stanford (2-2), but 2nd trip was keyed by 7 rushes by HB Steve Jones (31/126y, TD) and QB Mike Barnes' 13y pass to E Lynn Hendrickson. Jones powered over from 1YL. Oregon sparked its 3rd march in 2nd Q that ended with E Lachland Heron's 45y catch that carried to 4YL, but H clock killed that opportunity. Indians had turned FUM REC into K Bill Shoemaker's 21y FG in 1st Q and advanced to 12, 25, and 16YLs in 2nd Q without scoring. Shoemaker's FG try was wide on 1st drive, another was blocked in 3rd Q, and Webfoots DB Jim Smith snuffed Tribe's last chance with 4th Q INT. Ducks' trip to Stanford 8YL at end of game was killed again by clock.

October 15, 1966

Alabama 11 TENNESSEE 10: Alabama (4-0) barely weathered last serious challenge to its quest for unprecedented 3rd straight national title. Volunteers (2-2) took early 10-0 lead as QB Dewey Warren flipped delay pass for 6y TD to TE Austin Denney. Tennessee P Ron Widby's 54y punt, followed by short Alabama punt, set up field position that resulted in Tennessee K Gary Wright's 40y FG. Meanwhile Bama QB Ken Stabler (7-15/72y) uncharacteristically missed on all 6 of his passing attempts in 1st H, even though he had completed 78% of his throws in Tide's opening 3 wins. Frustrated Crimson Tide finally got break at end of 3rd Q: FUM REC at Vols 64YL by DE Mike Ford. Stabler ran for short TD, then followed with 2-pt pass to E Wayne Cook. Stabler clicked on passes of 14 and 19y and sprinted 10y so that Bama K Steve Davis could provide 11-10 edge with 17y FG with 3:23 left. Out of timeouts, Vols moved to Bama 3YL, mostly on Warren's 23y pitch to WB Charles Fulton, but K Wright's 20y sharply-angled FG try missed by inches with 16y secs to play. Narrow victory hurt Bama in AP poll as it slipped from no. 3 to no. 4.

Florida 17 NORTH CAROLINA STATE 10: With its potent O sputtering in scoring range, Florida (5-0) found itself trailing 10-3 early in 4th Q. NC State (1-4) scored on QB Jim Donnan's 33y pass to WB Gary Rowe and K Harold Deters' 38y FG. Gators tied it with 9 mins left on 1y TD by HB Larry Smith (26/115y) at end of 74y march. With Wolfpack driving, Gators LB Steve Heidt made INT at own 23YL. QB Steve Spurrier (19-32/185y, TD, INT) hit 3 passes/36y, ran 10y before finding WR Richard Trapp, who took short pass, eluded 2 tacklers, went 31y to game-winning TD with 3:07 left.

Michigan State 11 OHIO STATE 8: Narrow win over sagging Ohio State (1-3) cost no. 1 Michigan State (5-0) in AP poll, but Spartans were still happy to enjoy win on road against fired-up foe. Notre Dame, 32-0 winners over North Carolina, slipped ahead of Spartans into AP Poll top spot. High winds and torrential rain forced Spartans into multiple mistakes including bad punt snap for safety. Buckeyes led 2-0 at H, never having crossed midfield. K Dick Kenney's FG gave Michigan State 3-2 lead until Ohio coach Woody Hayes called surprise 1st down pass early in 4th Q. WR Billy Anders raced to 47y TD with slant pass from QB Bill Long (11-18/144y, TD, 3 INTs) on opening snap of 4th Q, so Buckeyes led 8-3. After ensuing KO, Spartans QB Jimmy Raye (6-15/121y, INT) ignored rain and countered by nailing 4 passes on 84y drive as FB Bob Apisa finally edged over on 4th down run from 1YL. MSU K Kenney took direct snap and surprisingly passed to holder Charles Wedemeyer for tricky 2-pt play.

Purdue 22 MICHIGAN 21: Just before H, Michigan (2-3) DB Rick Volk had nabbed long pass INT in his EZ to put Wolverines at their 20YL, and, within 6 plays, Michigan had tied score at 14-14 on HB Carl Ward's 11y run with swing pass, QB Dick Vidmer's 2nd scoring throw. Wolverines took lead of 21-14 in 3rd Q on strength of sharp 80y drive to HB Jim Detwiler's 1y plunge behind LG Henry Hanna. Later in 3rd Q, Purdue (4-1) QB-P Bob Griese, with 1st Q's only score, 6y TD pass to HB Bob Hurst, already under his belt, punted toward Wolverines GL. Michigan DB Rick Sygar fielded punt at 1YL, foolishly retreated, and was belted in EZ for safety by Boilermakers DB John Charles. So, Michigan led 21-16 at end of 3rd Q. In 4th Q, Michigan P Stan Kemp punted from his EZ, but hard-charging G Frank Burke virtually took ball off Kemp's foot and caught it for spectacular, winning Purdue TD. Later, Wolverines moved 85y to 1YL but lost FUM. Home fans hooted vociferously at coaching decision to have K Sygar try 35y FG when Wolverines FB Dave Fisher (20/121y) was rolling and seemed sure of converting 4th-and-1 at Boilers 18YL. Sygar missed FG try to dismay of Michigan faithful. Purdue stayed in Big 10 contention, half-game behind undefeated Michigan State.

Arkansas 12 TEXAS 7: Each foe lost ball 5 times amid 13 bobbled, but not necessarily lost, FUMs and 4 INTs. Texas (2-3) TB Chris Gilbert provided 7-6 lead in last min of 1st H with 1y blast off LT. Decisive Razorbacks (4-1) TD came on quick 3rd Q thrust: Porkers DB Martine Bercher raced 19y with punt RET to Texas 22YL, and E Tommy Burnett took short pass and ripped through 2 would-be tacklers for what would turn out to be winning TD. Arkansas DB Gary Adams' 2 INTs—in EZ and at own 12YL—thwarted Texas' comeback tries in 4th Q.

Southern California 21 STANFORD 7: Beating Stanford (2-3) for 9th straight year, USC (5-0) scored 1st 2 times it had ball: WR Rod Sherman's leaping 7y TD catch and HB Don McCall's 1y TD dive at end of 54y trip. Sherman' score came at end of 71y voyage after opening KO. Along way, Sherman caught 32y pass from QB Troy Winslow (12-25/138y, 2 TDs, 2 INTs), and TE Bob Klein nabbed 13 and 10y aerials. Trojans LB Eddie King's INT of Indians sub QB Chuck Williams (14-26/163y, 2 INTs) was run back to 10YL in 2nd Q to prepare QB Troy Winslow's 2nd TD pass. Down 21-0 at H, Stanford still managed to score and create 7-7 stand-off during last 3 Qs. Indians tallied on FB Jack Root's TD run after S Dave Nelson pilfered Winslow's pass and returned it 24y to Troy 19YL. Stanford was outgained only 255y to 204y by game's end. Trojans McCall served as leading rusher with 22/82y, TD.

UCLA 49 Penn State 11: Its long west-bound flight behind it, Penn State (2-3) was raring to go and surprised heavy favorite UCLA (5-0) by driving to QB-K Tom Sherman's 30y FG right off opening KO. But, UCLA quickly turned tables by striking for 3 TDs in next 7 mins: HB Mel Farr ran 1 and 17y to score and QB Gary Beban dashed 5y to TD. Nittany Lions HB Bob Campbell ran 12y for TD, and TE Ted Kwalick caught 2-pt pass, so Bruins led 21-11 at H. With QB Gary Beban on bench with 3rd Q injury, Bruins turned to skilled sub QB Norman Dow, who crafted 3 TDs in 2nd H to complete rout.

California 24 WASHINGTON 20: After mortifying shutout loss to San Jose, Cal Bears (3-2) rallied from 2 TDs down to upset Washington (2-3). Huskies owned 14-0 H edge on 87 and 86y drives to TDs by FB Jeff Jordan and HB Gerald Wea, but Bears, after gaining only 32y in 1st H, were new team after 2nd H KO. Little WR Jerry Bradley (6/84y, 2 TDs) caught 5y TD pass and set up FB Frank Lynch's 1y TD with 18 and 8y catches. Bradley extended Cal lead to 24-14 with 19y E-around run and 6y TD grab from QB Barry Bronk.

October 22, 1966

ARMY 28 Pittsburgh 0: Before capacity crowd at picturesque Michie Stadium, Army (5-1) breezed to win over Pittsburgh (1-5) on outstanding performance by soph QB-K Steve Lindell. Lindell rushed for 71y, passed for 2 TDs, and kicked FGs of 34 and 29y. Black Knights D, sparked by LB Townsend Clarke and E Bud Neswiacheny, completely stifled Panthers, allowing 150y, and preventing them from entering Army territory but once in 3 Qs. Pitt HB Joe Jones executed nice 55y KO RET in 2nd Q, but that opportunity faded quickly as QB Ed James was lost to injury. Cadets led 3-0 at H, but in 3rd Q they scored on 7y TD pass to TE Gary Steele, safety when blocked punt rolled through EZ, and Lindell's 2nd FG. Leading 15-0, Lindell lofted long pass to WR Terry Young, who took it in stride, bobbled it for 10y, and traipsed into EZ unfettered for 67y TD.

HARVARD 19 Dartmouth 14: Dartmouth (3-2) overcame 2 early FUMs and 64y TD run by Harvard (5-0) HB Bobby Leo (173y rushing) to take 3rd Q lead at 14-7 as QB Mickey Beard and HB Gene Ryzewicz each ran for TD, latter after Harvard had gambled and lost on 4th down at Indians 49YL. When Crimson DB John Tyson chopped down Indians drive with FUM REC, momentum suddenly turned to Harvard. QB Ric Zimmerman ended 55y drive with 11y TD pass to E Joe Cook and later led 80y winning drive with 1:41 left. Decisive TD came on Zimmermann's sneak on heels of his completions to HB Vic Gatto for 11y, TE Carter Lord for 8y, and Cook again for 13y to Big Green 5YL. Harvard thus became East's last unbeaten squad.

Virginia Tech 24 VIRGINIA 7: Gobblers LBs Clarence Culpepper, Sal Garcia, and Ken Whitley put up fierce blitz on Virginia (2-4) QB Bob Davis (13-28/98y, 2 INTs) and threw him for 24y in losses. WB Tommy Francisco gained 91y rushing for Virginia Tech (4-1-1) and scored 3 TDs. Each team peppered its game plan with trick plays: Va Tech C Scott Dawson caught Cavaliers in their D huddle on game's 2nd snap and pitched wide to HB Eddie Bulheller, who raced 72y to score. But, Hokies were penalized due to having fewer than 7 men on line. After Virginia soph TB Frank Quayle (16/71y) tied game at 7-7 early in 2nd Q, Gobblers responded with 70y TD march to take lead for good on Francisco's 2nd TD. Trailing 24-7 early in 4th Q, Wahoos tried T-eligible pass to Bob Buchanan, but it gained only 8y when coach George Blackburn hoped big gainer might get Virginia back in it.

ALABAMA 42 Vanderbilt 6 (Birmingham): Racking up 21 pts in opening 10 mins, Crimson Tide (5-0) rolled to easy win, outgaining Vanderbilt (1-4) 413y to 114y. Alabama D got game off on right foot as DB Bobby Johns plucked afternoon's 1st pass by previously strong-armed Commodores QB Gary Davis (0-1/0y, INT) off fingertips of E Chuck Boyd and raced 40y for TD. Tide went 77y to score, capped by QB Ken Stabler faking wide run, pitching back to FB Les Kelley who lofted wobbly 29y TD pass to wide-open E Ray Perkins. Backup QB Wayne Trimble tossed TD pass for 21-0 lead before Vanderbilt earned its only tally. Vandy LB Sid Ransom fell on Kelley's FUM at Bama 30YL late in 1st Q, HB Don North burst 24y, and QB Roger May (7-16/43y, TD, INT), in for Davis, flipped 6y score to E Steve Skupas. Trimble threw his 2nd TD pass, 18y to E Dennis Homan, and dived 1y to score and wrap up Alabama's pt total in 3rd Q.

Florida 28 LOUISIANA STATE 7: Gators (6-0) LB Jack Card fell on early FUM at Tigers 14YL, and soon HB Larry Smith (17/75y, TD) caught 8y screen pass for TD from QB Steve Spurrier (17-25/209y, 2 TDs, INT). After 80y march to Smith's 2y TD run, LSU (3-2-1) HB Sammy Grezaffi lost FUM on KO. WR Richard Trapp quickly caught 2 passes, including 13y TD. Spurrier and Smith led unbeaten Florida to 28-0 lead early in 3rd Q, and then went to bench to cheer for their subs. Meanwhile, SEC's top rush attack of LSU was held without 1st down for opening 11 mins and totaled only 130y. Tigers solo TD came out of their only 2 threats and occurred after most of big, disappointed crowd had left: sub QB Trey Prather's 5y scoring pass to E Billy Masters. Gators moved into 3-way tie with Alabama and Georgia for SEC top spot.

GEORGIA TECH 35 Tulane 17: TB Lenny Snow scored twice and WR John Sias made brilliant TD catch, so Georgia Tech (6-0) was comfortably ahead 21-3 in 3rd Q. Then, Tulane (4-2) HB Warren Bankston threw surprise TD pass, moving Green Wave back into contention. Tulane's aerial attack threatened often in 4th Q, but those live by pass often die by pass. Yellow Jackets came up with big D plays: DBs Bill Eastman and Giles Smith ran back INTs for 99 and 42y TDs respectively.

MISSISSIPPI 27 Houston 6 (Memphis): Tone was set on game's 1st snap: Houston (4-1) QB Bo Burris back-peddled to attempt pass and was buried at his 2YL. Ole Miss (4-2) D picked off 7 INTs among Cougars' otherwise effective 13-31/222y passing attack. Rebels DT Jim Urbanek sacked Burris and forced FUM at Houston 19YL, spot from which WB Doug Cunningham threaded through Cougars for 11y TD run. Ole Miss DB Bruce Dillingham made INT to set up 1st of 2 FGs by DL-K Jimmy Keyes. Mississippi made it 17-0 at H on QB Bruce Newell's 46y perfect pitch to WB Rocky Fleming after DB Gerald Warfield's INT in 2nd Q. Cougars interrupted 24-pt run with their only TD: Burris' 4th Q 29y TD pass to speedy HB Warren McVea.

MICHIGAN STATE 41 Purdue 20: Spartans juggernaut marched on as 37 mph winds failed to bother Michigan State (6-0), but hampered throwing of Purdue (4-2) QB Bob Griese. In 1st H, Spartans QB Jimmy Raye's 8-16/114y passing fared better than Griese's 3-11/34y. Trailing 7-0 in 3rd Q, Boilermakers made their 2nd GLS, but P Griese's punt into wind died at his 16YL. Raye raced to TD on next play, and Michigan State led 14-0 on way to 4 unanswered TDs. After MSU DL Bubba Smith was returned to DE from his brief but havoc-wrecking stint at NG, Griese (18-30/186y) was able to revive Purdue with 3 TD drives, scoring twice himsel.

Notre Dame 38 OKLAHOMA 0: After easy wins over Northwestern, Army, and North Carolina by combined 102-7, Notre Dame (5-0) hurdled highly-regarded no. 10 Oklahoma (4-1) as if it were Great Plains tumbleweed. Sooners suffered their worst defeat since 1945. After slow start, Irish scored on 6 of 7 possessions in middle Qs, including 2 short runs by HB Nick Eddy. ND E Jim Seymour (3/47y) injured his ankle attempting 1st H EZ catch and, regrettably, was never same brilliant receiver again. Oklahoma NG Granville Liggins had superior outing until injured in 2nd Q. Thereupon, ND launched its TD parade.

Nebraska 21 COLORADO 19: Amazingly, Colorado (4-2) QB Dan Kelly's passing and rushing each exceeded unbeaten Nebraska's flimsy total O of 94y. Buffaloes led 19-7 as HB Wilmer Cooks plunged for 2 1st H TDs and Kelly added 29y TD pass to WB Larry Plantz. But, Buffs botched conv kick and subsequent 2-pt run to keep Colorado from milking all they could get on their trio of TDs. Although Kelly finished with 115y rushing and 6-17/99y, TD, 2 INTs passing, Cornhuskers (6-0) QB Bob Churchich (20-34/236y, 2 TDs) truly emerged as 2nd H star. Churchich engineered pair of 4th Q scores, including FB Pete Tatman's 2y game-winning run with 53 secs left.

Texas A&M 17 BAYLOR 13: In midst of October reversal, Texas A&M (3-2-1) took its 3rd conf win in row, upsetting Baylor (3-2). QB Edd Hargett threw TD pass to E Tommy Maxwell and ran for TD as A&M nailed down 17-0 H edge. Bears DB Jackie Allen's 2 INTs in 3rd Q set up QB Terry Southall's TD pass and HB Don Defoe's TD run. Baylor threatened at 4YL in last 5 mins, before Aggies CB Dan Westerfield made FUM REC.

Oregon State 18 ARIZONA STATE 17: Beavers (3-3) took advantage of 2 Arizona State (2-4) pass interference PENs—part of 130y in fouls by Sun Devils—to travel 79y to winning TD that was scored on 1y smash by big FB Pete Pifer (31/108y, TD). Score came at ASU DT Bob Rokita's position, and, when Sun Devils later threatened, K Rokita begged to limp in for FG try. Instead, P-K Kenny Hornbeck's boot was short from 43y out. Earlier, Arizona State had squandered 10-0 lead; Oregon State went up 12-10 as WB Bob Grim caught 10y TD pass from QB Paul Brothers (3-10/36y, TD, INT) and DB Mark Waletich tightroped 56y on punt TD RET. Devils had regained lead at 17-12 late in 3rd Q as QB John Goodman (12-18/238y, TD, INT) lofted 45y TD pass to soph WR Fair Hooker.

AP Poll October 24

1 Notre Dame (32)	397	6 Georgia Tech	186
2 Michigan State (5)	364	7 Florida	172
3 UCLA (2)	310	8 Nebraska	151
4 Alabama (1)	272	9 Arkansas	50
5 Southern California (1)	247	10 Wyoming	31

Others with votes: Baylor, Georgia, Harvard, Miami, Miami (Ohio), Mississippi, Purdue, Southern Methodist, Syracuse, Tennessee, Texas A&M

October 29, 1966

(Fri) MIAMI 10 Southern California 7: No. 5 Trojans (6-1) must have suffered jet lag on their 1st-ever trip to state of Florida. Tough Miami (4-2) D limited USC to only 81y rushing. Sole Trojans TD came in last 3 mins of 1st H as HB Rod Sherman's 6y option TD pass to E Ron Drake (10/94y) capped 59y aerial drive. Earlier in 2nd Q, Canes DB Jimmy Dye had picked off USC QB Toby Page's pass and made 21y RET to Trojans 39YL. Miami QB Bill Miller's 2 passes to WR Jerry Daanen and HB John Acuff's 10y run moved it to 6YL, but bobble forced it to accept K Ray Harris' 28y FG. So, Hurricanes trailed 7-3 at H. Late in 3rd Q, Hurricanes FB Doug McGee (13/57y), knocked woozy in 2 previous games, was key to winning 58y drive, capping it with 11y run and 4y TD blast on 1st snap of 4th Q. Trojans gained more y (250y) than Miami had allowed in any game all season, but USC failed twice in Miami territory. Initial probe died at 10YL in 2nd Q, after Troy was aided by roughing PEN suffered by its P Rich Leon. Collision with punt rushers left him with compound leg fracture. USC's next threat was stopped at 32YL after 2nd H KO.

Clemson 23 WAKE FOREST 21: Clemson (3-3) scored on each of its 1st 2 series and took 21-7 H lead on tainted 80y TD bomb in 2nd Q to TE Edgar McGee by QB Jimmy Addison (10-22/207y, 2 TDs, 2 INTs). While trying to cover McGee, Wake Forest (2-5) DB Digit Laughridge accidentally was screened by back judge. Score stood until 4th Q when underdog Wake caught fire. Demon Deacons HB Andy Heck plunged for TD, and QB Ken Erickson (13-23/187y, 2 TDs) threw his 2nd TD pass to HB Eddie Arrington with 3:12 to play. Erickson tossed 2-pt pass to FB Ken Hauswald to tie it 21-21. Tigers clawed back but were halted by last-min INT by DB Andy Harper at Wake Forest 7YL. On next play with 30 secs left, gambling Erickson dropped into EZ to pass, but was floored by Clemson DT Wilson Childers and DE James Tompkins for winning safety.

VIRGINIA TECH 23 Florida State 21: In sense, upset by Virginia Tech (6-1) pivoted on 2 pts earned on DE Dan Mooney's 1st Q tackle in EZ of Florida State (3-3) QB Kim Hammond. In late going, Gobblers D rose up grandly to stop Seminoles at Virginia Tech 1YL. In between, Virginia Tech QB Tommy Stafford threw 2 TD passes and outstanding DB Frank Loria raced 80y on punt TD RET. FSU threatened all day on arm of QB Gary Pajcic (28-53/338y, TD), while HB Bill Moreman scored all 3 TDs for Seminoles.

FLORIDA 30 Auburn 27: For all of QB Steve Spurrier's vast O contribution—he ran and passed for TDs and completed 27-40/259y—it was his clutch 40y FG with 2 mins to play that lifted unbeaten Florida (7-0). Sniffing possible upset, Auburn (3-4) played dandy catch-up all day: HB Larry Ellis raced 89y with KO for 7-7 tie in 1st Q, and LB Gusty Yearout went 91y on FUM TD RET for Tigers' 1st lead at 14-7 in 2nd Q. Gators soph HB Larry Smith rushed for 102y in 2nd H, helping to arrange Spurrier's FG to break game's 3rd tie at 27-27. Spurrier waved off Florida's usual K Wayne Barfield, who was sent in by coach Ray Graves, because crafty Spurrier felt capable at that range and believed Tigers would expect fake with Spurrier lined up to try FG. Whether Auburn believed Spurrier accepting and lacing up square-toed shoe was part of his act or not, Spurrier used shoe to nail 3-ptr. Years later, WR Richard Trapp would tell author Peter Golenbock in book *Go Gators!* that FG "caught the fancy of the nation and probably earned him (Spurrier) the Heisman award..."

GEORGIA 28 North Carolina 3: Bulldogs (6-1) gave away 3 FUMs and INT in 1st H, but survived when their D forced Tar Heels into miscues, biggest of which was LB Happy Dicks' EZ INT. Georgia cruised past slumping North Carolina (2-4) with 2nd H outburst as soph TB Kent Lawrence (10/106y) scored 2 TDs and contributed other helpful gains. Biggest play came with Tar Heels trailing 7-3, but driving behind gimpy QB Danny Talbott in 3rd Q: Georgia DE Larry Kohn grabbed pass bobbled by FB Mark Mazza for INT, broke tackle, and was escorted by his blockers 62y for TD. Plagued by 5 TOs, Carolina could manage only K Bill Dodson's 36y FG in 2nd Q. Rivalry that started in 1895 formally ended with Bulldogs, winners of 8 of last 9, leading in series by 15-12-2.

TENNESSEE 38 Army 7 (Memphis): QB Dewey Warren passed 18-25/250y, TD for Tennessee (4-2). Army (5-2) kept score within 10-0 in 2nd Q only because of FUM RECs resulting from hard hits on Vols receivers E Terry Dalton and TB Charles Fulton. Warren found WB Richmond Flowers for 17y and E Johnny Mills for 33 and 15y to position Fulton for 3y TD run and insurmountable 17-0 lead. Cadets QB Steve Lindell

(11-23/154y) countered with 3rd Q TD pass to WR Terry Young, but suffered 40y INT TD RET by Vols DE Nick Showalter, who batted ball in air before making his downfield romp.

PURDUE 25 Illinois 21: Dogged by 5 INTs, Purdue (5-2) QB Bob Griese (19-35/288y) remained relentless in comeback to surmount 21-10 deficit to Illinois (2-5) with his 2nd and 3rd TD passes in 4th Q. Winning TD came under heavy rush as Griese rolled right, heaved 32y arrow to E Jim Finley in back of EZ with 1:20 left. DB Phil Knell had been faked off balance by Purdue E Jim Beirne (9/125y, TD) on 19y TD pass in 1st Q that tied it 7-7, but Knell later earned payback with 3 INTs for Illini. Knell's last INT came in 3rd Q as he sliced cross-field to nab pass to wide-open Beirne and launch 70y scoring trip for Illinois. But most dramatic pick-off for Illinois came from DB Bruce Sullivan, who raced 93y to score on last play of 3rd Q for 21-10 lead. Griese went immediately to work, guiding Boilermakers 63y to 4y TD pitch to seldom-targeted TE Marion Griffin. Beirne quickly caught 2-pt pass to pull within 21-18. Indianans had to punt twice before launching their last opportunity from their 35YL with 3-and-half mins left. Purdue took 2nd place in conf and inside track to Rose Bowl behind undefeated but ineligible Michigan State, 22-0 winners over Northwestern.

NOTRE DAME 31 Navy 7 (Philadelphia): Series record crowd to date of 70,101 at John F. Kennedy Stadium saw no. 1 Notre Dame (6-0) be held well in check by tenacious Navy (3-4) D during 1st H. However moral as Middies' 1st H victory, they still were behind 10-0 at intermission because Irish K Joe Azzaro booted 42y FG and LB John Pergine made 1st of 3 INTs to set up FB Larry Conjar's 7y TD run. To this moment, mighty ND had all of 1 1st down, and QB Terry Hanratty had presented hideous 3-14/35y passing slate. So to begin 2nd H, Fighting Irish denounced throwing and pounded 50y to Hanratty's TD sneak, and, after Pergine's 2nd INT, they traveled 45y to sub HB Bob Gladieux's 1y TD carry. Meanwhile, Sailors themselves owned only single 1st down since 1st Q and wouldn't gain another until game's last play. However, Middies made TD in 4th Q when they rushed P Gladieux's punt and Navy E Jon Bergner bear-hugged ball at 5YL to cross over for TD.

NEBRASKA 35 Missouri 0: Rolling up 271y rushing, Nebraska (7-0) methodically beat proud Missouri (4-2-1) D after scoreless 1st Q. Early in 2nd Q, FB Pete Tatman, clutch runner all day, barreled over to score from 1YL. Cornhuskers WB Ben Gregory recovered punt FUM of Tigers HB Jim Whitaker at 16YL and soon swept to TD for 14-0 H lead. Missouri was held to 107y total O, crossed midfield just 3 times against Nebraska's formidable D, buttressed by ferocious NG Wayne Meylan and DT Carel Stitch.

Southern Methodist 13 TEXAS 12: K Dennis Partee kicked twin 4th Q FGs, his 2nd 3-ptr coming with 18 secs left to give SMU (5-1) surprise win over downcast Texas (3-4). After QB Bill Bradley's great fake, TB Chris Gilbert had raced 74y up wide-open alley to give Longhorns TD in 1st Q. But, errant, low conv kick by K David Conway started Texas' downward spiral. Mustangs WR Jerry Levias gathered in QB Mike Livingston's 10y TD strike in 2nd Q, but Conway made 31y FG to put Texas in front 9-7 at H. Conway extended edge to 12-7 in 3rd Q with 45y 3-ptr. Trailing 12-10 in 4th Q, Mustangs D was shoved to its 32YL, but DL George Wilmot fell on FUM coughed up by Steers QB Bradley. Earlier, in 3rd Q, Bradley had bungled TD opportunity at SMU 1YL. QBs Livingston and Mac White split time on Ponies' winning FG drive with White pitching key 25y pass to HB Mike Richardson. Partee's winning FG barely slipped past desperate dive of Horns DE Mike Perrin.

COLORADO STATE 12 Wyoming 10: Losers of 10 straight to Cowboys, Rams employed master trickery: Deceptive Colorado State (4-2) used double throw to score 36y TD for 9-7 lead in 3rd Q over stunned no. 10 Wyoming (6-1). Colorado State had QB Bob Wolfe pitch apparent incompletion that bounced in flat to HB Larry Jackson. After acting dismayed, Jackson retrieved ball and lofted scoring pass to wide-open E Tom Pack. K Jerry DePoyster went on to give Wyoming 10-9 lead with 4th Q FG, but Rams K Al Lavan countered with his own 3-ptr in last 2 mins after Cowboys fumbled away punt at own 44YL.

AP Poll October 31

1 Notre Dame (39)	475	6 Nebraska	246
2 Michigan State (6)	437	7 Florida	209
3 UCLA (3)	366	8 Arkansas	151
4 Alabama (1)	347	9 Southern California	66
5 Georgia Tech	261	10 Tennessee	48

Others with votes: Georgia, Harvard, Houston, Miami, Mississippi, Purdue, Southern Methodist, Syracuse, Wyoming

November 5, 1966

PRINCETON 18 Harvard 14: HB Bobby Leo gave Ivy leader Harvard (6-1) 14-3 lead in 3rd Q with 6y TD run, his 2nd score of game. Soon in possession of FUM at Princeton (5-2) 24YL, Crimson seemed poised to slay Tigers. From that point, however, Nassau DE Larry Stupsky turned momentum with consecutive tackles for –11 and -8y. Tigers LB Jim Kokoskie's INT on next play sent Princeton on 68y sortie to FB Dave Martin's 2y TD run near end of 3rd Q. TB Doug James added 2-pt pass, so Tigers trailed only 14-11. Martin capped 93y march with winning TD midway in 4th Q, and Princeton D halted Harvard's final advance on 4th down at its 16YL with 1:35 to play.

Syracuse 12 PENN STATE 10: Nittany Lions (4-4) contained Syracuse (6-2) ground game and took 10-6 H lead on QB Tom Sherman's 36y TD pass to TE Ted Kwalick and when HB Bobby Campbell raced 57y to set up K Sherman's 29y FG. In 2nd H, Orange FB Larry Csonka lugged 18/81y of his 132y game rushing total. Big play came on last play of 3rd Q: Syracuse P Don Bullard faked booting ball away and threw 4th down pass to E Dick Towne for 13y 1st down at Lions 29YL. Csonka soon plowed over for winning score.

ALABAMA 21 Louisiana State 0 (Birmingham): Blanked for 2nd week in row, LSU (3-4-1) was held to 90y total O by swarming, opportunistic Alabama (7-0) D, whose stars included DT Louis Thompson and LB Mike Hall. Bayou Bengals kept Bama out of EZ until 3rd Q. But, Crimson Tide had turned blocked punt into safety, and K Steve Davis' twin FGs had Bama ahead 8-0. DB Bobby Johns broke LSU's back late in 3rd Q with 33y INT TD RET of QB Freddie Haynes.

Georgia 27 Florida 10 (Jacksonville): Favored Florida (7-1) had never won SEC title since league's inception in 1933, and Georgia (7-1) was its last hurdle to conf glory. Gators ate more than 5 mins of clock on opening drive that ended by FB Graham McKeel's TD push. Florida led 10-3 at H. Refocusing on their run attack, Bulldogs tied it late in 3rd Q as FB Ronnie Jenkins scored from 4YL after QB Kirby Moore converted 4th down run at Gators 28YL. Under intense pressure from stalwart DT George Patton, Gators QB Steve Spurrier (16-29/133y, 3 INTs) threw INT that Bulldogs DB Lynn Hughes ran back 39y for go-ahead score at 17-10. Georgia D soon forced punt and later made 4th down stop. Each time UGa halted Blue and Orange, it led to important score: K Bob Etter's FG and Moore's TD run. Florida's O completely faded as it was limited to single 1st down in 2nd H.

Nebraska 24 KANSAS 13: Largest football crowd to date in state history gathered on Kansas Jayhawks (2-5-1) Homecoming Saturday, but no. 6 Cornhuskers (8-0) burst for 3 TDs in 2nd Q to spoil things for home folks. Nebraska HBs Ben Gregory and Harry Wilson scored on short runs, while, in between, QB Bob Churchich (11-15/101y, TD) topped 76y drive with his 27y TD sprint. Oddly, Nebraska missed all 3 kicks after TDs and led 18-0 at H. Jayhawks made it 18-7 in 3rd Q as slim QB Bill Fenton, making his 1st start, hit HB Junior Riggins with 25y TD pass. In 4th Q, Churchich found Wilson with 9y TD arrow, and Kansas managed Don Shanklin's 12y HB pass to WR Haley Kampschroeder for TD.

SOUTHERN METHODIST 21 Texas A&M 14: Dominating early, Aggies (3-4-1) turned their high hopes of knocking SMU (6-1) off SWC's top rung into 14-0 lead on QB Edd Hargett's 2 TD passes. Ponies snuck in 64y TD march just before H to trail only 14-7. SMU D was pivotal in 2nd H, making 2 of its 4 INTs in its own EZ and turning DB Wayne Rape's INT into tying 25y TD. Jet-propelled WR Jerry Levias played his role as Ponies game-breaker to perfection, exploding 83y on 4th Q punt TD RET behind magnificent block of DE George Wilmot.

BRIGHAM YOUNG 53 Texas Western 33: Cougars QB Virgil Carter won his aerial battle over Miners QB Billy Stevens, and so BYU (6-1) won war vs. Texas Western (4-3). Carter completed 29-47/513y, 5 TDs. On his way to national total O title and career total O record to date, Carter added 86y rushing for 599y O for day. Stevens passed 22-47, but suffered 3 INTs by BYU DB Bobby Roberts, including 26y INT RET for TD. Cougars built 43-15 H lead and were never in danger thereafter.

WASHINGTON 16 Ucla 3: Laying in wait at home for unbeaten UCLA (7-1) was rugged D unit of Washington (5-3). Losing for 4th straight time in Seattle, Bruins were held 33 pts below their scoring avg with chief Huskies perpetrators being DE Tom Greenlee, NG Mike Maggert, and LBs George Jugum and Cliff Coker. Huskies broke 3-3 tie in 1st Q on FB Jeff Jordan's 1y TD buck after HB Jim Satoris' 80y KO RET to Bruins 13YL. UCLA QB Gary Beban had 23y run and 30y completion to HB Ray Armstrong in 2nd H, but Bruins were frustrated at Washington's 18 and 9YLs. Upset left Southern California, 35-9 winners over California, as conf's only unbeaten team.

Washington State 14 OREGON 13: For Oregon (3-5) it was sad and frustrating farewell to 47-year-old Hayward Field, just when it looked like Ducks would pull win out of fire. Oregon moved 80y to Washington State (3-5) 2YL in dying moments, but scoreboard operators mistakenly credited 1st down to Ducks on earlier 9y run. So Ducks QB Mike Barnes threw away pass on 4th down, thinking—from his check of scoreboard—it was 3rd down. Cougars took over with 10 secs to go. Washington State DB Rick Reed (3 INTs) made INT RETs of 47 and 22y to allow HB Del Carmichael to bang across for 1 and 10y TDs in 2nd Q. Although Cougars FB-K Ted Gerela missed 3 long FG tries, he made 2 x-pts for margin of victory. E Scott Cress caught 2 long scoring passes from Barnes, but after 30y TD in 4th Q, Wazzu DG Bob Trygstad made INT of 2-pt pass to preserve 14-13 lead.

AP Poll November 7

1 Notre Dame (32)	418	6 Arkansas (1)	188
2 Michigan State (10)	393	7 Southern California	144
3 Alabama	333	8 UCLA	142
4 Nebraska	271	9 Georgia	71
5 Georgia Tech	230	10 Tennessee	68

Others with votes: Colorado, Florida, Houston, Purdue, Southern Methodist, Syracuse, Washington, Wyoming

November 12, 1966

SYRACUSE 37 Florida State 21: HB Floyd Little set new Syracuse (7-2) career rushing mark and scored 3 TDs, each of 24y, while piling up 25/193y of Orange's 337y ground attack. While Orangemen rushed at will, Florida State (4-4) succeeded in air with 242y. QBs Gary Pajcic and Kim Hammond each connected for FSU TD. Things had started terribly for Seminoles: WR T.K. Wetherell, future pres. of Florida State, slipped and fell when he was wide open on game's 1st snap, and after Pajcic was sacked for 13y loss, P John Hosack could manage only 21y punt from his 10YL. Little scored his 1st TD 3 plays later and added 2-pt run. Next, FSU tried cross-field surprise pass on KO, but HB Larry Green's toss went wild, and Noles were in hole. Little scored again after Syracuse took away FUM, and DB Tony Kyasky sprinted 44y down sideline for punt TD RET and 20-0 lead. Florida State hurried 57y to TE Thurston Taylor's TD catch just before H. Orange FB Larry Csonka barreled over from 1YL to cap 80y voyage after 2nd H KO, so Syracuse owned smart 27-7 lead. FSU went 77y to HB Green's 8y sweep that pared affair to 30-14 in 4th Q.

Clemson 14 MARYLAND 10: Tigers (5-3), undefeated at 5-0 in ACC, enjoyed coach Frank Howard's 150th career win. Led by DB Wayne Page and DE Butch Sursavage, Clemson D keynoted victory with clutch stops at 16, 9, 6 and 10YLs, but TB Buddy Gore rushed for 119y and scored Orange and Purple's 2nd TD of 1st Q on 3y run. Gore's score, which followed sub TB Jacky Jackson's TD run, provided Tigers with 14-7 lead. Maryland (4-4) QB Alan Pastrana had dived for 1y TD in 1st Q after Terrapins DB Lou Stickel made INT at Tigers 34YL. Down 14-10, Pastrana (12-30/129y, 4 INTs) created 2 threats in 4th Q, but INTs by Clemson LB Jimmy Catoe at 1YL and DB Kit Jackson at 9YL snuffed Terps' scoring efforts. Near end, Clemson QB Jimmy Addison threw INT to Maryland DB Fred Cooper, but Tigers DE Joey Branton sacked Pastrana, and DT Wilson Childers recovered FUM to end it.

Georgia 21 AUBURN 13: Shocked into reality by 2 early TDs engineered by Auburn (4-5) QB Loran Carter, Georgia (8-1) methodically reversed matters in 2nd H. Bulldogs sub FB Brad Johnson hammered for 25y gain and followed with 7y TD run in 3rd Q. QB Kirby Moore, who would be injured late in game, fired 52y TD to TB Hardy King, so Bulldogs led 14-13 after K Bobby Etter's conv. FB Ronnie Jenkins clinched it with 4th Q TD run, and Georgia wrapped up tie for SEC crown with Alabama, 24-0 victor over South Carolina.

GEORGIA TECH 21 Penn State 0: Fast-starting Georgia Tech (9-0) scored twice in 1st 3 series and continued to rack up O to tune of 359y. In for injured QB Kim King, Engineers QB Larry Good hit 5-6 passes in blistering 1st Q, ran for 4y TD, and lobbed 20y score to WB Craig Baynham. But 5 TOs prevented any more Yellow Jackets scoring except TB Lenny Snow's 12th TD of season in 4th Q. Georgia Tech's 5-DB setup baffled Penn State (4-5) QB Tom Sherman, holding him to 2-14/25y passing, with his 1st completion not coming until TE Ted Kwalick's catch in 4th Q. This loss meant Nittany Lions' 1st year coach Joe Paterno faced possible ignominy of Penn State's 1st losing season since 1938 if rival Pittsburgh could win in next week's matchup.

Purdue 16 MINNESOTA 0: Sub-freezing weather couldn't dampen high spirits of Purdue (7-2) which clinched its only trip to-date to Rose Bowl. QB-K Bob Griese booted 30y FG in 1st Q, and connected on 5 passes in row on 2nd H's opening drive. Payoff was Griese's 13y TD pitch to E Jim Bierne. Blocked 4th Q punt allowed Boilermakers to set up camp at Minnesota (4-4-1) 30YL, and they soon clinched verdict on FB Bob Baltzell's 1y TD plunge. In blanketing Gophers' most dangerous runner, QB Curt Wilson, Purdue permitted only 90y rushing.

Missouri 10 OKLAHOMA 7: Scoreless well into 3rd Q, game turned to Missouri (5-3-1) when FB Bob Powell blasted over for TD from 4YL. Later, Tigers LB Rich Bernsen grabbed INT of Oklahoma (5-3) QB Bobby Warmack's pass at Tigers 48YL. Missouri managed only 1 1st down, but it was close enough for strong-legged K William Bates to connect on 52y FG. Oklahoma bounced back, too little too late, with 68y TD drive in 4th Q as Warmack swept to 10y score.

ARKANSAS 22 Southern Methodist 0: In quest of its 3rd straight Cotton Bowl berth, Arkansas (8-1) took half-game lead over SMU (6-2), which lost its 1st SWC game of season. DB Martine Bercher provided Hogs with 9-0 H lead on his 69y punt TD RET in 2nd Q. Arkansas TB David Dickey rushed 38/133y and scored twice in 4th Q. Mustangs felt Fayetteville feeling rather overwhelmed as they managed to snap ball on only 37 plays by its O, and gained only 116y rushing.

AP Poll November 14

1 Notre Dame (35)	420	6 Arkansas (1)	206
2 Michigan State (6)	392	7 Southern California	172
3 Alabama (1)	327	8 UCLA	136
4 Nebraska	282	9 Georgia	102
5 Georgia Tech	241	10 Purdue	37

Others with votes: Colorado State, Florida, Houston, Miami, Mississippi, Oregon State, Syracuse, Wyoming

November 19, 1966

HARVARD 17 Yale 0: Except for D stand at its own 20YL, Harvard (8-1) played nearly whole game in Yale (4-5) territory. Using its rugged D to hold Bulldogs to 5 1st downs and 82y rushing, Crimson earned share of Ivy title with Dartmouth and Princeton. FUM RECs by two-way E-DE Carter Lord and LB Buzz Baker provided scoring chances in 1st H, which materialized on K Jim Babcock's 29y FG and HB Bobby Leo's 1y plunge. Leo broke over LT in 4th Q and sprinted 52y to TD. Harvard, led by Leo, soph HB Vic Gatto, and FB Tom Choquette, closed season with nation's top rushing avg of 269y per game.

Penn State 48 PITTSBURGH 24: Pressured Nittany Lions (5-5) had to win to protect their most treasured record: no losing seasons in 28 years. Penn State won by getting speedy TB Bobby Campbell (14/137y, 2 TDs, and 2/26y, TD receiving) and WB Mike Irwin wide to flanks of flimsy Pittsburgh (1-9) D. Lions pushed tally to comfortable 33-0 when Campbell accepted pitchout and raced 41y to score right after 2nd H KO. Earlier, Irwin's 34 and 22y punt RETs had set up QB Tom Sherman (10-16/146y, 3 TDs, INT) for 3y jump pass for TD to TE Ted Kwalick and Campbell's 16y reverse TD run. Blocked punt that LB Jim Flanigan took 9y to score finally put Panthers on scoreboard. Pitt QB Ed James (21-46/283y, 3 TDs, 5 INTs) kept filling air with passes and followed with 3 TD passes against Lions reserves, including 6y TD to E Bob Longo (7/147y), who set new season school marks with 46/732y.

NORTH CAROLINA STATE 32 Clemson 14: With Clemson (5-4) leading 14-7 at H on TDs by TBs Buddy Gore and Jacky Jackson, NC State (5-5) aimed ace K Harold Deters at goalposts. Deters made 2nd H FGs of 33, 41, and 33y for 21 career 3-ptrs. Deters also booted his 30th consecutive conv after ACC rushing leader HB Don DeArment dashed 53y in 4th Q. Win gave Wolfpack 5-2 conf record, but Tigers at 5-1 still had chance to cinch ACC title with win over South Carolina week hence.

TENNESSEE 28 Kentucky 19: On its way to date in Gator Bowl, Volunteers (7-3) overcame 2 long gainers in 2nd Q by Wildcats (3-6-1), which helped provide brief 13-7 edge to coach Charlie Bradshaw's downtrodden, but fierce-fighting Cats. HB Dicky Lyons tied contest at 7-7 in 2nd Q with dazzling 72y punt TD RET. Even though Kentucky earned only 2 1st downs in 1st H, it cashed 1 of them on 78y, over-middle pass from QB Terry Beadles (9-17/174y, INT) to WB Larry Seiple, who was hauled down at 2YL to set up Beadles' 1y sneak for 13-7 lead. In between, Vols LB Paul Naumoff blocked 26y FG try. Tennessee QB Dewey Warren (14-30/275y, 4 TDs, INT) whipped Vols into motion in last 1:42 of 2nd Q. They marched 61y to WB Richmond Flowers' 7y TD catch. K Gary Wright's x-pt gave Vols lead for good at 14-13. Along way, E Johnny Mills (7/225y, TD) caught Warren's 33y fling. Later, Mills hauled in 72y TD bomb from Warren on way to setting new Tennessee single game y record that would hold until Kelley Washington exceeded it in 2001.

Michigan 17 OHIO STATE 3: Capacity turnout at Ohio Stadium watched brawny ground attack of Wolverines (6-4) chop down Woody Hayes' Buckeyes (4-5) and make Ohio coach stomach only his 2nd losing ledger in 16 years in Columbus. Ks Rick Sygar of Michigan and Gary Cairns of Ohio State traded medium-range FGs through early 2nd Q. Flu-ridden and banged-up HB Jim Detwiler persevered to lead way for Michigan with 140y rushing and scored decisive TD on 7y run with 1:11 showing on 2nd Q clock. This gave Wolverines 10-3 H bulge. UM QB Dick Vidmer (6-15/110y, TD, INT) rifled 26y scoring bolt in 3rd Q to E Clayton Wilhite, who pranced into EZ by faking Ohio DB Bob Waldon off his feet. Bucks moved well between 20YLs, but had no ability to punch ball over GL. Ohio HB Bo Rein (20/82y) caught 5/59y from QB Bill Long, who passed 11-29/122y, 2 INTs.

GAME OF THE YEAR
MICHIGAN STATE 10 Notre Dame 10:

No single game in history of football ever matched level of anticipation at Notre Dame's visit to meet Michigan State on chilly, gray day in East Lansing. No. 1 Notre Dame (8-0-1) team had stepped off train to immediate disadvantage as HB Nick Eddy stumbled and reinjured his right shoulder. Early in this emotional tilt, Fighting Irish lost QB Terry Hanratty (1-4/26y) to shoulder separation and C George Goeddeke to twisted ankle. Fellow soph Coley O'Brien replaced Hanratty at QB and passed 7-19/102y, TD, INT. (Spartans later contended swift O'Brien was such an unknown they'd have rather faced Hanratty, which was odd because Hanratty was 1 of fastest Notre Damers.) In scoreless 1st Q in which no. 2 Michigan State (9-0-1) weathered FUM at own 4YL, Spartans QB Jimmy Raye (7-20/142y, 3 INTs) whipped 42y arrow to E Gene Washington that got life back in O. Pounding ND's D middle, MSU called 9 straight runs, sending FB Regis Cavender off RT for 4y TD early in 2nd Q. Raye's 30y sprint up sideline sparked next series which led to K Dick Kenney's 47y FG, but not before Irish LB Jim Lynch interrupted with INT and his immediate FUM on hit by HB Clinton Jones. O'Brien hit 3 passes in row after HB Tom Quinn's 38y KO RET, last to uncovered HB Bob Gladieux for 34y TD. With 4:30 left in 1st H, Spartans led 10-7, and game turned into clean, but brutally hard-hitting affair. Late in 3rd Q, Spartans DE Bubba Smith jumped into neutral zone and 5y PEN nullified their REC of Notre Dame FUM at MSU 25YL. On 1st play of 4th Q, Irish K Joe Azzaro cashed that break by booting 28y FG for 10-10 deadlock. O'Brien missed his last 6 passes, creating doubt about his diabetic condition with team doctors and more importantly in mind of ND coach Ara Parseghian. Notre Dame DB Tom Schoen's INT RET to MSU 18YL gave Irish chance, but missed block cost 8y loss on 2nd down tackle by DE Phil Hoag. Azzaro's 41y FG sailed slightly wide right with 4:39 left. Although it got little mention afterward, MSU tried nothing fancy from its 20YL before choosing to punt away to ND 30YL with 1:24 left. When Parseghian decided to have ND run ball instead of throwing long, daring passes, Michigan State D taunted Irish, calling them "sissies and cowards." Even though Notre Dame succeeded on risky 4th down run, clock expired on unsatisfying tie in "Game of the Century." Parseghian has been forced to defend his late-game play-calling ever since.

TEXAS TECH 21 Arkansas 16: After Razorbacks (8-2) jumped to 10-0 lead on K Bob White's 21y FG and WB Jim Whisenhunt's 9y TD sweep, Texas Tech (4-6) QB John Scovell took Cotton Bowl invitation from hands of Arkansas and virtually stuffed it in pocket of SMU, 24-22 winner over Baylor. Scovell scored on sneak at end of 61y 2nd Q drive and threw 16y TD pass to WR Larry Gilbert in 3rd Q. Vital score came on DT Gene Darr's deflected INT for 20y TD RET late in 3rd Q. Texas Tech had entered game with statistically-worst D in SWC but played tremendously.

Wyoming 47 BRIGHAM YOUNG 14: Breaking out in 2nd Q, Wyoming (9-1) grabbed WAC title with surprisingly strong air game and D which forced BYU (7-2) QB Virgil Carter into 4 INTs. Cowboys QB Rick Egloff threw 4 TD passes, and WR Jerry Marion nabbed 3 TD catches. Carter slipped 25y TD pass into 2nd Q mix to make H deficit 23-8, but his 4th Q TD run was trumped by 95y TD RET by Wyoming HB Vic Washington on ensuing KO.

UCLA 14 Southern California 7: QB Gary Beban was out with ankle injury suffered in prior week's 10-0 win over Stanford, so UCLA (9-1) turned to sub QB Norman Dow. Scoreless 1st H had 2 key plays: UCLA DT Mike Roof spilled Trojans FB Mike Hull (14/148y) for 6y loss to ruin Trojans' 73y drive, and Bruins E Harold Busby's TD catch was spoiled by his O interference PEN in EZ. Dow (112y total O) swept E for 5y TD in 3rd Q, but USC (7-2) answered when Hull's 57y sprint to 1YL set up sub FB Dan Scott's tying TD plunge. UCLA went 67y to its 4th Q winner: 21y reverse run by HB Cornell Champion. USC finished with 4-1 conf record to UCLA's 3-1, but better overall mark, as each awaited Monday's vote on Rose Bowl invitation.

OREGON STATE 20 Oregon 15: Beavers (7-3) fireplug FB Pete Pifer punched ahead for 31/130y, TD on ground to become AAWU's 1st rusher to top 1000y mark in consecutive seasons. Oregon State won its 6th straight contest while building 305y to 102y advantage in O column. Oregon State QB Paul Brothers passed for only 29y, but

boosted Beavers' margin to 10-0 with 18y sortie around E in 2nd Q. Oregon (3-7) was behind 13-0 early in 4th Q, but QB Mike Brundage connected with E Scott Cress for 25y TD. Suddenly Ducks were back in it at 13-7, but Piper's longest run, 14y burst up middle, gave OSU breathing room at 20-7 so that it could withstand late 98y FUM TD RET by Ducks S Jim Smith and Brundage's 2-pt pass.

November 24-26, 1966

(Th'g) Virginia Tech 70 VIRGINIA MILITARY 12: Bowl-bound Virginia Tech (8-1-1) finished its best season since 1954 as 2 successful on-side KOs contributed to TDs in rout of VMI (2-8). HB Tommy Francisco, who rushed 133y, scored 6 times, and TE Ken Barefoot caught 2 TDs. Keydets QB Bill Ellett was forced to throw throughout and was able to weather fierce Gobblers rush to sandwich TD passes on either side of H.

(Th'g) OKLAHOMA 10 Nebraska 9: For 2nd time in last 3 years, Oklahoma (6-3) spoiled unbeaten season of Nebraska (9-1). Sooners led 7-3 at H on QB Bobby Warmack's 48y TD to WB Eddie Hinton. FB Dick Davis crashed over in 3rd Q to give Huskers 9-7 lead, but Oklahoma DB Bob Stephenson blocked conv kick. Sooners big K Mike Vachon, who had to battle fierce wind on 33y FG try in 1st Q, missed chip-shot 23y FG early in 4th Q that would have placed OU back in lead. Nebraska threat was stopped on downs at Sooners 24YL later in 4th Q, and Oklahoma used surprise 19y run by FB Gary Harper, normally I-formation blocker, to set up Vachon's winning 21y FG with 48 secs left. Huskers DE Jerry Patton layed out and barely missed getting his fingertips on Vachon's 3-ptr. Nebraska roared back, moving into OU territory, but pass by QB Bob Churchich (7-15/76y, 3 INTs) was picked off by DB Rodney Crosswhite on game's last snap.

(Th'g) TEXAS 22 Texas A&M 14: Injury-plagued Texas (6-4) patched itself up sufficiently to earn Bluebonnet Bowl bid with win over Texas A&M (4-5-1). Steers soph QB Bill Bradley scored on 6y run in 1st Q and pitched 61y TD to E Tom Higgins in 2nd Q. K David Conway added 2 FGs in 3rd Q, and NG John Elliott swarmed over Aggies QB Charlie Riggs for 4th Q safety and 22-6 Texas edge. In late going, Riggs (12-24/145y, TD, 3 INTs) completed 17y TD to HB Lloyd Curington and added 2-pt pass.

Army 20 Navy 7 (Philadelphia): When Paul Dietzel fled West Point for South Carolina just before spring drills, Army (8-2) had little choice but to promote frosh coach Tom Cahill, who built makeshift staff of former players who were stationed at U.S. Military Academy. Win over Navy (4-6) completed 1 of greatest single season coaching jobs ever. Army FB Charlie Jarvis provided early lead by sweeping 49y to 1st Q TD. Middies tied it 7-7 in 2nd Q, taking control of game thanks to spark provided by QB John Cartwright's 7 completions in row. It took until 4th Q for Cadets to regain typical Army vs. Navy ebb-and-flow and to break deadlock. Black Knights QB Steve Lindell fired TD passes of 42y to E Terry Young and 23y to HB Carl Woessner. E Rob Taylor tied Navy reception mark with 9, including 7y TD.

Holy Cross 32 BOSTON COLLEGE 26: Spotted 19-0 1st Q lead primarily on QB Jack Lentz' TD run and pass, Holy Cross (6-3-1) was helpless to reverse 2 big breaks against it in 2nd Q. Boston College (4-6) trailed 19-7 when its alert DL Dick Kroner snatched FUM from air and went 76y to TD. On following KO, Crusaders lost FUM, and QB Joe Devito gave Eagles 20-19 advantage with 21y TD pass. TDs were traded by Lentz and Eagles HB Paul Della Villa, so BC led 26-25 early in 4th Q. Lentz hit 4 passes on winning 80y drive, including 38y TD to E Pete Kimener.

Virginia 21 NORTH CAROLINA 14: While Virginia (4-6) QB Bob Davis broke Roman Gabriel's season and career ACC total O records, soph HB Frank Quayle supplied 3 TDs. QB Danny Talbott of North Carolina (2-8) had tied game 14-14 in 3rd Q with short TD run. Wild double FUM on ensuing KO left Cavs with ball at UNC 43YL. Quayle and FB Carroll Jarvis contributed to game's rush total of 261y in advancing Virginia to 4YL. Quayle scored game-winner from there.

CLEMSON 35 South Carolina 10: Clemson (6-4) copped ACC crown and closed disappointing 1st season for coach Paul Dietzel at South Carolina (1-9). Playing with confidence, Gamecocks overcame early 7-0 deficit to take 2nd Q lead at 10-7 on QB Mike Fair's sneak and K Jimmy Poole's 20y FG. But, Tigers TB Jacky Jackson scored his 2nd TD, QB Jimmy Addison threw 2 TD passes, and G Harry Olszewski scored on 12y FUM advancement to create rout.

Miami 21 FLORIDA 16: Jumping to healthy 21-3 3rd Q lead, Miami (7-2-1) held on to win battle of bowl-bound Sunshine Staters. Hurricanes QB Bill Miller (271y total O) made 3 big plays: 46y pass to E Jim Cox that set up FB Doug McGee for 1st Q TD run, TD pass to HB Steve Smith, and his 40y TD run. Finally, Florida (8-2) got going as QB Steve Spurrier (26-49/225y) threaded 6y TD pass to WR Paul Ewaldsen and pitched Gators into position for HB Larry Smith's 30y TD draw play. Clock expired with on-charging Florida reaching Miami 30YL.

GEORGIA 23 Georgia Tech 14: Brilliance of DT George Patton of no. 7 Georgia (9-1) helped spoil perfect season of no. 5 Georgia Tech (9-1). Patton closed his great career with INT, FUM REC, and tipped pass that turned into DE Larry Kohn's INT late in 2nd Q. Bulldogs bit 1st as TB Kent Lawrence fielded early punt, swung right behind wall of blockers, and rambled past diving DB Doc Harvin at Yellow Jackets 30YL for 71y TD RET. Georgia Tech TB Lenny Snow ran 9/53y on 96y march capped by QB Kim King's 6y TD run for short-lived 7-6 edge in 2nd Q. QB Kirby Moore hit passes of 11 and 23y and ran 16y to set up Georgia FB Brad Johnson's go-ahead TD at 14-7 in 2nd Q. After

Kohn's INT RET to Georgia Tech 17YL, K Bob Etter knocked through 1st of his 3 FGs for 17-7 H edge for Cotton Bowl-bound Bulldogs. Patton and DT partner Bill Stanfill keyed Bulldogs D that shut down Jackets in 2nd H except for 4y TD sweep by QB Larry Good in last 5 secs.

MISSISSIPPI 24 Mississippi State 0: Key to Egg Bowl victory was superior play by both Ole Miss (8-2) lines, which opened gaping holes on O and held Mississippi State (2-8) to 2y rushing on D. Bulldogs gained but 42y with its attack and never threatened to score. Only Maroons bright spot was HB Marcus Rhoden's new SEC season KO RET mark of 572y. Rebels got 17 pts in 2nd Q on TDs as late-blooming QB Bruce Newell (14-24/175y, INT) enhanced TB Doug Cunningham's 13y TD run with 26y scoring pass that WB Bill Matthews took in flank and juked away from 2 Bulldogs for TD dash. Rebels NG-K Jimmy Keyes contributed 24y FG, sparkled on D, and also kicked 3 x-pts for SEC-record 35 straight conv boots. Mississippi State LB D.D. Lewis made tackles all over field and also speared INT.

Southern Methodist 21 TEXAS CHRISTIAN 0: Beating TCU (4-6) for only 3rd time in 20 years, SMU (8-2) won its 1st SWC title since 1948. Trying to brighten coach Abe Martin, who suffered heart attack in mid-November, Frogs had 3 good drives only to have tough Mustangs D halt them at 4, 8, and 10YLs. Wide-ranging Ponies secondary also filched 5 INTs. SMU QB Mac White's only 2 completions went for TDs, while TCU used 3 QBs who combined for 19-41/213y in air. Mustangs mercurial WR Jerry Levias took 68y bomb in stride in 1st Q, and TCU QB Larry Peel answered with 4 straight completions to Ponies 8YL. SMU DE George Wilmot tipped Peel's next pass into arms of LB Billy Bob Stewart for 1st of 5 pickoffs. Mustangs swiftly went 71y to White's 26y TD shot for 14-0 lead on their 1st possession of 3rd Q. Frogs frequently dusted off their once-feared Spread-O and twice advanced to SMU 4YL, but errant passes doomed them, including 4th Q misadventure that Mustangs LB Jerry Griffin stepped into for 23y INT TD RET.

Arizona State 20 ARIZONA 17: Underdog Sun Devils (5-5) rode 19y TD toss by QB John Goodman (11-20/130y, TD, INT) to WB Wes Plummer in last 1:44 to upset Arizona (3-7). Wildcats QB Mark Reed (20-38/293y, 2 TDs, 3 INTs) took national passing crown, but, more importantly, rallied Arizona from early 10-0 hole that was dug by Devils HB Travis Williams' 35y TD draw run. Reed threw 4y TD pass to WB Jim Greth (6/66y, TD) in 2nd Q, Greth's 8th TD catch of season. T-K Bob Rokita kicked his 2nd FG for ASU early in 4th Q. Reed arched 70y TD bomb to E Fritz Greenlee that earned 17-13 edge. Back came Devils for Plummer's catch, and they sealed deal with NG Curley Culp's FUM REC of Cats FB Rick Johnson after latter caught screen pass near midfield in last min.

Notre Dame 51 SOUTHERN CALIFORNIA 0: Seeking to impress pollsters, Notre Dame (9-0-1) visited largest loss margin on Southern California (7-3) in 40-year rivalry and worst in Trojan history to date. QB Coley O'Brien hit 21-31/255y, 3 TDs, and E Jim Seymour caught 11/150y, 2 TDs. Trojans gained 188y O but crossed midfield but thrice with best penetration stopping to Irish 10YL. Only moment of cheer for USC was WR Earl McCullough's block of conv kick. Vindication dominated Irish post-game mood after week of criticism over tie with Michigan State. "I would say we went out to prove we are no. 1," said coach Ara Parseghian. "And we did, didn't we?" AP writers agreed, voting Notre Dame to top spot on Monday.

December 3, 1966

ALABAMA 31 Auburn 0: Alabama (10-0) fans tried to promote their team with signs like: "Bama plays football, N. Dame plays politics," "In your heart, you know we're no. 1," and "Ara plays to tie—Bear to win." Despite nation's top scoring D, Bama was doomed to finish 3rd in AP poll with 7 of 56 1st place votes. Auburn (4-6) stayed close to Tide for scoreless 1st Q, but was done in by FUM, INT, and failed 4th down gamble at midfield. Alabama opened scoring with spectacular 63y rollout bomb from QB Ken Stabler to E Ray Perkins. Tigers QB Loran Carter (10-22/104y, 3 INT) threw INT to Tide LB Wayne Owen which allowed K Steve Davis' 23y FG for 17-0 H lead.

OKLAHOMA STATE 15 Oklahoma 14: Oklahoma State (4-5-1) DBs Charles Trimble and Willard Nahrgang buried Oklahoma (6-4) HB Ron Shotts to spoil 2-pt pass with 1:29 on clock in 4th Q. It gave Cowboys their 2nd straight win over Sooners after 19 losses in row. In 2nd Q, Cowboys QB Ronnie Johnson scored on 10y run and added 2-pt pass to HB Tommy Boone. Oklahoma tied it 8-8 in 3rd Q on 1st of Shotts' 2 TDs and QB Bobby Warmack's 2-pt pass. Early in 4th Q, Johnson scored again, and K Craig Kessler booted what proved to be winning pt.

1966 Conference Standings

Ivy League

Harvard	6-1
Dartmouth	6-1
Princeton	6-1
Cornell	4-3
Yale	3-4
Columbia	2-5
Pennsylvania	1-6
Brown	0-7

Atlantic Coast

Clemson	6-1
North Carolina State	5-2
Virginia	3-3
Maryland	3-3
Duke	2-3
Wake Forest	2-4
South Carolina	1-3
North Carolina	1-4

Southern

West Virginia	3-0
William & Mary	4-1-1
East Carolina	4-1-1
George Washington	4-3
Davidson	2-3
Citadel	3-5
Richmond	2-4
Virginia Military	1-3
Furman	1-4

Southeastern

Alabama	6-0
Georgia (a)	6-0
Florida (b)	5-1
Mississippi	5-2
Tennessee (c)	4-2
Louisiana State (d)	3-3
Kentucky	2-4
Auburn	1-5
Mississippi State	0-6
Vanderbilt (e)	0-6

(a) Win vs. No. Carolina counted in SEC
(b) Win vs. Tulane counted in SEC
(c) Win vs. So. Carolina counted in SEC
(d) Win vs. Tulane counted in SEC
(e) Loss vs. Tulane counted in SEC

Big Ten

Michigan State	7-0
Purdue	6-1
Michigan	4-3
Illinois	4-3
Minnesota	3-3-1
Ohio State	3-4
Northwestern	2-4-1
Wisconsin	2-4-1
Indiana	1-5-1
Iowa	1-6

Mid-American

Miami (Ohio)	5-1
Western Michigan	5-1
Bowling Green	4-2
Ohio	3-3
Kent State	2-4
Marshall	1-5
Toledo	1-5

Big Eight

Nebraska	6-1
Colorado	5-2
Missouri	4-2-1
Oklahoma State	4-2-1
Oklahoma	4-3
Iowa State	2-3-2
Kansas	0-6-1
Kansas State	0-6-1

Missouri Valley

North Texas State	3-1
Tulsa	3-1
Cincinnati	2-2
Louisville	1-3
Wichita State	1-3

Southwest

Southern Methodist	6-1
Arkansas	5-2
Texas	5-2
Texas A&M	4-3
Baylor	3-4
Texas Tech	2-5
Texas Christian	2-5
Rice	1-6

Western Athletic

Wyoming	5-0
Brigham Young	3-2
Utah	3-2
Arizona State	3-2
Arizona	1-4
New Mexico	0-5

AAWU

Southern California	4-1
UCLA	3-1
Oregon State	3-1
Washington	4-3
California	2-3
Washington State	1-3
Oregon	1-3
Stanford	1-4

1966 Bowl Games

Liberty Bowl (Dec. 10): Miami 14 Virginia Tech 7

Gobblers (8-2-1) proved to be rambunctious underdogs, trying occasional QKs, Statue of Liberty runs, and no-huddle plays. With A-A DB Frank Loria making tackles all over field, Virginia Tech D stonewalled Miami (8-2-1) attack with just 16y O in 1st H. HB Tony Francisco plunged to 1st Q TD after DB Jimmy Richards blocked Hurricanes punt at 21YL. That was extent of Virginia Tech O, which itself was limited to 111y during entire game. Miami O followed suit of its fine D and came to life in 2nd H, tallying on QB Bill Miller's 7y TD pass to HB Joe Mira to tie it at 7-7 in 3rd Q. FB Doug McGee scored 4th Q game-winner from 1YL, 4 plays after Miller rifled 38y pass to E Jim Cox.

Bluebonnet Bowl (Dec. 17): Texas 19 Mississippi 0

Rushing for 100y in 6th straight game, Texas (8-3) soph TB Chris Gilbert set Bluebonnet record with 156y on 26 tries. Gilbert scored in 2nd Q on 1y dive. Meanwhile, Longhorns soph QB Bill Bradley, back from injured knee, racked up 154y total O and scored on runs of 25 and 4y. Ole Miss (8-3) was blanked for 1st time in 17 games by Steers D led by LB Fred Edwards. Missing DT Dan Sartin with broken foot, favored Rebels relinquished 283y rushing despite entering game with nation's 3rd-best run D at

74.1y avg. Ole Miss' deepest penetration came in 3rd Q when sub TB Don Street was stopped on 4th down at 8YL. Texas DB Les Derrick picked off his 3rd INT in EZ to kill Rebels' last threat with 6 secs left.

Sun Bowl (Dec. 24): Wyoming 28 Florida State 20

It was Cowboys and Indians swapping blocks and tackles in West Texas as Wyoming (10-1) came from behind to beat Florida State (6-5). Leading rusher HB Jim Kiick gave Wyoming 7-0 lead in 1st Q after HB Vic Washington covered 53y with punt RET and pass reception. FSU came back in 2nd Q on arm of QB Kim Hammond. After Washington's midfield punt FUM, Hammond hit WR Ron Sellers with 49y TD. He followed that score 4 mins later with 58y TD to WR T.K. Wetherell. Wyoming QB Rick Egloff connected with WR Jerry Marion on 2 long TDs in 3rd Q to take lead for good. Cowboys D, led by DL Jerry Durling, caught up with Seminoles attack, tossing it for 21y in losses. Kiick added 14y TD run in 4th Q to build insurmountable 28-14 margin.

Gator Bowl (Dec. 31): Tennessee 18 Syracuse 12

Aerial attack of Tennessee (8-3) dominated 1st H before powerful ground game of Syracuse (8-3) turned tables. Vols lost small but feisty TB Charles Fulton to early injury, so they turned to QB Dewey Warren, who pitched 12-20/189y in 1st H before adopting more conservative plan after H. Warren passes set up 2 FGs by Gary Wright, and Warren found TE Austin Denney (off fake FG) and WB Richmond Flowers for 2nd Q TDs that provided 18-0 lead. Meanwhile, Orangemen failed to convert DB Tony Kyasky's opening KO FUM REC, but eventually launched HB Floyd Little to Gator Bowl record 216y rushing. Syracuse FB Larry Csonka (81y rushing in 2nd H, 114y overall) knocked Vols aside like bowling pins for 8y TD in 3rd Q. That shaved lead to 18-6, but Orange failed on 4th-and-3 at Tennessee 4YL on 1st play of 4th Q. So, when Little scored in last min, it wasn't enough.

Cotton Bowl (Dec. 31): Georgia 24 Southern Methodist 9

Fundamentally-sound Georgia (10-1) jumped to quick lead thanks in part to coin toss decision by Southern Methodist (8-3) coach Hayden Fry, who as native of west Texas might have known all too well about fickle gusts of his home state. Mustangs chose to kick to start game, taking what Fry called "pretty strong" wind. But, by time ball was teed up, breeze was measured at mild 7 mph. On game's 2nd play, Bulldogs TB Kent Lawrence sprung through LG for 74y TD dash on new play devised for Cotton Bowl by coach Vince Dooley. In amassing impressive game total of 284y rushing, Georgia built 17-3 lead by 2nd Q. SMU's spectacular WR Jerry Levias was double and triple covered, but managed 3/62y receiving. Levias' 2 3rd down catches propelled Ponies to their only TD late in 2nd Q. HB Mike Richardson scored it from 1YL.

Sugar Bowl (Jan. 2): Alabama 34 Nebraska 7

QB Ken Stabler (12-18/218y, TD) and E Ray Perkins (7/178y), aerial battery of no. 3 Alabama (11-0), made every effort to impress nation even though both major polls were closed, somewhat arbitrarily. Stabler whistled 45 and 42y arrows to Perkins to set up 2 early TDs en route to 24-0 H advantage. Stabler and Perkins also combined for 45y TD in 4th Q. Nebraska (9-2) went to air for 22-38/213y, but could not tally until hopelessly behind at 27-0 in 4th Q. Huskers QB Bob Churchich passed 15y to FB Dick Davis for TD. With desperate Nebraska uncharacteristically filling air with passes, it was inevitable that Alabama would steal 5 passes, including 3 by DB Bobby Johns. Coach Bear Bryant, rejoicing over his 2nd straight big bowl win over Cornhuskers, said his players "deserve to be no. 1, and if I had a vote, they would be." Alas, final ballots had been posted prior to bowl games, and Notre Dame stayed no. 1. Somewhere in Birmingham, Tide fan uttered something about collegiate championship playoff.

Rose Bowl (Jan. 2): Purdue 14 Southern California 13

Making its 1st-ever Rose Bowl appearance, Purdue (9-2) bolted from dressing room to dominate opening 17 mins of game. Boilermakers drove 68y with opening KO, only to be foiled by EZ incompletion, thanks to jarring hit by Trojans DB Bill Jaronyck. USC (7-4) could keep ball only 4 plays before punting. Purdue then went 57y on 16 methodical plays as FB Perry Williams plowed over from 1YL early in 2nd Q. Now inspired, Trojans fought back, making 9 1st downs before Boilermakers could collect another. USC used 39y connection between QB Troy Winslow (12-17/174y, TD) and WR Jim Lawrence to reach 21YL. After 2 losses to 16YL, Troy TB Don McCall (22/92y, TD) appeared to slip away with pass near sideline, but DB George Catavolos knocked ball free with tackle at 10YL that MVP DB John Charles recovered at Purdue 9YL. Back came USC with McCall ending 44y march with short dive to tying TD in last 2 mins of 1st H. USC's short punt to its 37YL turned tide back to Purdue, and Williams added his 2nd TD with 3y slant through big hole on USC's right side for 14-7 lead late in 3rd Q. Winslow arched 52y pass to WB Rod Sherman, which Catavolos saved him from being TD with tackle OB at 4YL, but Trojans hopes went fleeting because their FG try from 18YL was blocked by Boilers DE Bob Holmes. Troy fought back as clock wound down, but faced 4th down near midfield. Offside PEN against Purdue provided 1st down and allowed Winslow and Sherman to hook up on 19y TD pass with less than 3 mins left. That drew USC to within 14-13, and Trojans decided to go for victory. Beaten on Sherman's TD catch, DB Catavolos came back to etch his name in Purdue lore by saving Boilermakers' win with INT of Winslow's 2-pt crossing "pick play" pass for Lawrence.

Orange Bowl (Jan. 2): Florida 27 Georgia Tech 12

At less than his best because of sore arm, Florida (9-2) QB Steve Spurrier (14-30/160y, INT) turned to HB Larry Smith, who broke up close game with Orange Bowl record 94y TD run and totaled 187y rushing. Slight favorite Georgia Tech (9-2) got on scoreboard 1st, pressuring Spurrier into erratic throws and utilizing pass interference PEN called on Gators to position QB Kim King for 10y TD pass to WB Craig Baynham. FB Graham McKeel countered with 1st of his 2 short TD runs, and Florida led 7-6 at H. Late in 3rd Q, King launched long pass which fell into hands of Florida DB Bobby Downs at his 6YL. On 3rd-and-10, Georgia Tech blitzed DB Bill Eastman, and Smith

broke scrimmage line clean behind block of McKeel for his record run through vacated secondary. Interestingly, Smith's run became best remembered because his pants appeared to slip down for most of his long gallop. Run also enjoyed video revival in early 2000s when Gatorade (which was created at University of Florida) commercial harkened back to days of its invention and Smith's run was featured. Florida now led 14-6. McKeel's TD made it 21-6 before Yellow Jackets sent relief QB Larry Good scampering 25y to 4th Q TD. INT of Good led to window-dressing score in last 11 secs: Gators sub QB Harmon Wages, future Atlanta TV sportscaster, threw 5y TD pass. It turned out to be last game for veteran Georgia Tech coach Bobby Dodd, who later retired.

1966 Top Performance Formula

1	Notre Dame	1.8314
2	Alabama	1.7346
3	Michigan State	1.6794
4	Georgia	1.5721
5	UCLA	1.5564
6	Georgia Tech	1.5418
7	Purdue	1.5229
8	Florida	1.4886
9	Mississippi	1.4698
10	Houston	1.4554
11	Miami	1.4481
12	Brigham Young	1.4169
13	Arkansas	1.4114
14	Tennessee	1.4084
15	Nebraska	1.3986
16	Southern California	1.3923
17	Syracuse	1.3570
18	Virginia Tech	1.3254
19	Southern Methodist	1.3176
20	Army	1.2850

1966 Top Opponent Records

1	Southern California	.6814
2	Mississippi State	.6474
3	Vanderbilt	.6406
4	Mississippi	.6471
5	South Carolina	.6075
6	Pittsburgh	.5978
7	Auburn	.5947
8t	Notre Dame	.592319
8t	Penn State	.592319
10	Georgia Tech	.5882
11	Florida State	.5865
12	Miami	.5817
13	Purdue	.5792
14	Indiana	.5707
15	Rice	.5699
16	Florida	.5631
17	Kentucky	.5585
18	Illinois	.5549
19	Southern Methodist	.5539
20	Tennessee	.5529

1966 Out-of-Conference Records

	W-L	Percentage	Bowl W-L
Southeastern	29-14-2	.6667	4-1
Western Athletic	18-13	.5806	1-0
AAWU	23-19	.5476	0-1
Southwest	12-13-1	.4808	1-1
Big Eight	11-14	.4400	0-1
Big Ten	12-17-1	.4167	1-0
Atlantic Coast	7-27	.2059	0-0

1966 Individual Statistical Leaders

RUSHING YARDS	Attempts	Yards	Avg.
Ray McDonald, Idaho	259	1329	5.1
Don Fitzgerald, Kent State	296	1245	4.2
Jim Bohl, New Mexico State	218	1148	5.3
Pete Pifer, Oregon State	230	1088	4.7
Chris Gilbert, Texas	206	1080	5.2
Garrett Ford, West Virginia	236	1068	4.5
Dicky Post, Houston	185	1061	5.7
Cornelius Davis, Kansas State	210	1028	4.9
Larry Csonka, Syracuse	197	1012	5.1
Pete Larson, Cornell	206	979	4.8

PASSING YARDS	Completions	Attempts	Yards	Pct.
Mark Reed, Arizona	193	365	2368	52.9
John Eckman, Wichita State	195	458	2339	42.6
Virgil Carter, Brigham Young	141	293	2182	48.1
Billy Stevens, Texas Western	140	305	2088	45.9
Benny Russell, Louisville	142	310	2016	45.8
Steve Spurrier, Florida	179	291	2012	61.5
Terry Southall,, Baylor	173	337	1986	51.3
Danny Holman, San Jose State	160	260	1925	61.5
Bob Griese, Purdue	130	215	1749	60.5
Dewey Warren, Tennessee	136	229	1716	59.4

RECEIVING YARDS	Catches	Yards
Glenn Meltzer, Wichita State	91	1115
Jack Clancy, Michigan	76	1079
Jim Greth, Arizona	76	1003
Phil Odle, Brigham Young	58	920
Ron Sellers, Florida State	56	874
Richard Trapp, Florida	63	872
Jim Seymour, Notre Dame	48	862
John Wright, Illinois	60	831
Ken Hebert, Houston	38	800
Eppie Barney, Iowa State	56	782

1966 Consensus All-America Team

Offense

End:	Jack Clancy, Michigan
	Ray Perkins, Alabama
Tackle:	Cecil Dowdy, Alabama
	Ron Yary, Southern California
Guard:	Tom Regner, Notre Dame
	LaVerne Allers, Nebraska
Center:	Jim Breland, Georgia Tech
Back:	Steve Spurrier, Florida
	Nick Eddy, Notre Dame
	Mel Farr, UCLA
	Clinton Jones, Michigan State

Defense

End:	Alan Page, Notre Dame
	Charles "Bubba" Smith, Michigan State
Tackle:	Loyd Phillips, Arkansas
	Tom Greenlee, Washington
Guard:	Wayne Meylan, Nebraska
	John LaGrone, Southern Methodist
Linebacker:	Paul Naumoff, Tennessee
	Jim Lynch, Notre Dame
Back:	George Webster, Michigan State
	Tom Beier, Miami
	Nate Shaw, Southern California

1966 Heisman Trophy Vote

Steve Spurrier, senior quarterback, Florida	1679
Bob Griese, senior quarterback, Purdue	816
Nick Eddy, senior halfback, Notre Dame	456
Gary Beban, junior quarterback, UCLA	318
Floyd Little, senior halfback, Syracuse	296

Other Major Award Winners

Maxwell (Player):	Jim Lynch, senior linebacker, Notre Dame
Outland (Lineman):	Loyd Phillips, senior defensive tackle, Arkansas
Walter Camp (Back):	Steve Spurrier, senior quarterback, Florida
Knute Rockne (Lineman):	Jim Lynch, senior linebacker, Notre Dame
AFCA Coach of the Year:	Tom Cahill, Army

1967

The Year of City of Angels Showdown, Keep the Ball Rollin', and Stallings Traps Bear

The city of Los Angeles was the third largest in the United States in 1967 and by mid-season it was the center of the college football universe. On a collision course were crosstown rivals UCLA (7-2-1), enjoying its third season of brilliant quarterbacking by Gary "The Great One" Beban, and Southern California (10-1), which sprung on an unsuspecting football world the mercury swiftness and gliding power of junior college transfer tailback Orenthal James "O.J." Simpson. Each Los Angeles school was undefeated after the last weekend of October with USC pegged at no.1 and UCLA at no. 2. Into the picture stepped the pesky Oregon State (7-2-1) Beavers, who had already lost to average teams in Washington (5-5) and Brigham Young (6-4), but turned vicious every time they sniffed a team from the upper rungs of the AP Poll. After having already knocked off no. 2 Purdue (8-2) on October 21, the Beavers tied the Bruins 16-16, and a week later its stingy defense blanked the Trojans 3-0. But, USC and UCLA were in luck: sixth-ranked Wyoming (10-1) from the little-recognized and relatively new Western Athletic Conference stood as the nation's only undefeated team at that time, so The City of Angels showdown on November 18 remained a national title confrontation.

The UCLA-USC game was a seesaw thriller dominated early by the Bruins and Beban. But, 6'8" Trojan defensive lineman Bill Hayhoe blocked two field goals and an extra point kick by UCLA kicker Zenon Andrusyshun to keep USC within hailing distance at 20-14 in the fourth quarter. Then, the magnificent Simpson authored a 64-yard touchdown to win Los Angeles bragging rights, the Pacific-8 title, the Rose Bowl invitation, and the national title for Southern California.

The pre-season top five consisted of Notre Dame (8-2), Alabama (8-2-1), Michigan State (3-7), Texas (6-4), and Miami (7-4). Each team took an early tumble. Surprising Purdue plugged sophomore Mike Phipps right into the quarterback gap left by graduated Bob Griese and knocked off Notre Dame 28-21 in late September. Alabama saw its 17-game winning streak halted by aerial warfare from Florida State (7-2-2) in a 37-37 tie in the opener on September 23. Michigan State took a mighty fall after being depleted by graduation, disciplinary dismissals, and an injury to quarterback Jimmy Raye. Eager Houston (7-3) dropped a wholly unexpected 37-7 whipping on the Spartans in East Lansing in the year's second week. Texas lost its opener to Southern California and never got rolling. Miami was upset in its opener by Northwestern (3-7) and wilted before a tough slate of opponents that included five teams that earned at least seven wins. But, the Hurricanes only faced the 23rd toughest regular season opposition. The honor of the toughest slate went to in-state rival Florida State, which enjoyed an excellent season against teams with a .6517 winning percentage.

Wyoming had an undefeated Cinderella season going until Louisiana State (7-3-1) bested the Cowboys in a hard-fought Sugar Bowl 20-13. Wyoming boasted future Miami Dolphins star Jim Kiick at halfback, Vic Washington, a superb kick and punt returner at defensive back, receiver Gene Huey, the nation's best kicker in Jerry DePoyster, and Larry Nels at defensive tackle.

Although it couldn't have been more unlike the fierce competition of football, the "Summer of Love" was considered a major part of 1967 culture in America as hundreds of thousands of college-age youngsters, including very few football players, engaged in "peace, love and understanding" in various cities around the country. Rock 'n' Roll music was at the heart of peace, love and understanding, and a musical anthem for West Coast "hippies" was recorded by one-hit wonder Scott McKenzie in which he sang, "If you're goin' to San Francisco, be sure to wear some flowers in your hair." Also released in the summer of 1967 was the song "Keep the Ball Rollin'," by Jay and the Techniques, also a one-hit wonder. "Keep the Ball Rollin'" would become the anthem for a curious band of Indiana football players, who soon had the Hoosier state in total uproar.

The last winning season for Indiana (9-2) had been a modest 5-3-1 in 1958 and its overall record since its last Big Ten title in 1945 was a disastrous 56-130-5. Indiana came out of nowhere in 1967. Keeping with the year's theme of youthfulness, the Hoosier heroes were pretty well all sophomores, notably quarterback Harry Gonso, flanker Jade Butcher, and halfback John Isenbarger. Winning close games on last-minute heroics or opponent blunders, Indiana kept the ball rolling with victory after victory. The only exception was a bubble-bursting, late-season thrashing by Minnesota (8-2), but the Hoosiers still recovered to earn a trip to the Rose Bowl with a huge upset of Purdue in the regular season finale. Cinderella's slipper was shattered in Pasadena as Indiana was beaten by national champion USC, led by the incomparable Simpson.

Texas A&M (7-4) also fashioned a remarkable season, although it adopted no popular songs. The Aggies lost their opening four games, then rallied behind disciplinarian coach Gene Stallings for six straight to take the SWC crown. It was one of the most effective in-season turnarounds in college football history. Because of its slow start, Texas A&M wasn't taken seriously entering its Cotton Bowl game with no. 8 Alabama. After all, the Aggies had the worst record among all 16 bowl teams in the 1967 post-season. In upsetting the Crimson Tide, Texas A&M created one of the enduring memories of this and any year. Upon congratulating Stallings at midfield, a grinning Alabama coach Bear Bryant lifted his former player and assistant coach high in his arms in a gleeful bearhug that turned into a joyride halfway down the field.

Oklahoma (10-1) had bumped through eight mediocre seasons with a combined record of 46-34-1. The extraordinarily high standards set by the Sooners in the 1940s and '50s when they won three national titles, six bowl games and posted a 107-8-2 record from 1948-58, had been besmirched. A new head coach, Chuck Fairbanks, took over out of sad obligation when 37-year-old Jim MacKenzie died of a heart attack during spring practice.

Facing predictions of a second-division finish in the Big Eight, Fairbanks instead debuted with a stunning 9-1 record, plus an Orange Bowl win over Tennessee (9-2). The Sooners led the nation in scoring defense, averaging 6.8 points-per-game with a swift unit built around All-America middle guard Granville Liggins, end Jim Files, linebacker Don Pfrimmer, cornerback Bob Stephenson, and safeties Steve Barrett and Gary Harper. Powerful tailback Steve Owens never started a single game as a sophomore but was sufficiently destructive a runner to lead the conference in rushing and scoring.

Milestones

■ Twenty years after Jackie Robinson (former UCLA football player) became famous for breaking Major League Baseball's so-called color line, Southeastern Conference became America's last major sports league to integrate its ranks with Negro players. Kentucky halfback Nat Northington played in 26-13 loss to Mississippi on September 30. Another African-American player for Kentucky, sophomore Greg Page, died of spinal injury during fall practice.

■ Texas Western officially changed its name to University of Texas-El Paso.

■ Walter Camp Foundation instituted award to nation's top player in honor of Camp, considered father of American football.

■ Death claimed seven relatively young football men: Chet Gladchuk, 50, All-American center for Boston College in 1940; Maj. Don Holleder, 33, All-America Army end in 1954 and starting, selfless quarterback in 1955, died in action in Vietnam; Jim MacKenzie, 37, Oklahoma head coach died of heart attack during spring practice; Mike McKeever, 27, All-America guard at Southern California in 1959, died after 20 months in coma from head injuries suffered in auto accident; Dan Sachs, 28, tailback of 1957 Ivy League champion Princeton; Bruce Smith, 47, Minnesota halfback who won the 1941 Heisman Trophy and was subject of Hollywood film "Bruce Smith, All-America;" and Leonard Wilson, 29, two-way Purdue halfback in 1957-59. Former Ohio State and Baltimore Colts lineman and Korean War vet Joe Campanella, 36, died of heart attack on February 15 while serving as Colts general manager. Dying on September 23 was Frank Dickinson, 67, who developed his own football rating system while mathematics professor at University of Illinois. Chicago newspapers publicized Dickinson's Ratings, and presentation of Rockne Memorial Trophy to nation's top team was based on his system from 1931 to 1940. Former Louisiana State coach (83-39-6 record from 1935-47) and Hall of Famer Bernie Moore, who died on November 6 at 72, had served as Southeastern Conference commissioner from 1947-66.

■ Longest winning streaks entering season:
Alabama 17   Colgate, Georgia, Oregon State 6

■ Coaching Changes

	Incoming	Outgoing
Arizona	Darrell Mudra	Jim LaRue
Brown	Len Jardine	John McLaughry
Georgia Tech	Bud Carson	Bobby Dodd
Hawaii	Don King	Phil Sarboe
Illinois	Jim Valek	Pete Elliott
Kansas	Pepper Rodgers	Jack Mitchell
Kansas State	Vince Gibson	Doug Weaver
Maryland	Bob Ward	Lou Saban
Mississippi State	Charley Shira	Paul Davis
Oklahoma	Chuck Fairbanks	Jim MacKenzie
Oregon	Jerry Frei	Len Casanova
Rice	Bo Hagan	Jess Neely
Texas Christian	Fred Taylor	Abe Martin
Vanderbilt	Bill Pace	Jack Green
Wisconsin	John Coatta	Milt Bruhn

AP Preseason Poll

1 Notre Dame (17)	296	6 Georgia	128
2 Alabama (11)	282	7 Southern California (1)	114
3 Michigan State (1)	183	8 UCLA	113
4 Texas (2)	176	9 Tennessee	88
5 Miami	134	10 Colorado	43

Others with votes: Arkansas, Army, Clemson, Georgia Tech, Illinois, Minnesota, Mississippi, Nebraska, Ohio State, Penn State

September 16, 1967

(Fri) HOUSTON 33 Florida State 13: While minding his own business on sideline, Houston (1-0) sub QB Ken Bailey was called to relieve bruised starter Dick Woodall. Cougars already led 13-0, and Bailey passed 7-13/129y, ran for score, and called on FB Paul Gipson for 2 TDs. Behind 33-0 late in 4th Q, Florida State (0-1) finally was able to launch effective air game. Sub QB Kim Hammond threw 2 TDs after Seminoles had suffered 5 INTs, 2 by Cougars DB Gus Hollomon.

(Fri) SOUTHERN CALIFORNIA 49 Washington State 0: New Trojans (1-0) TB O.J. Simpson (17/94y, 3 TDs), JC transfer, joined fellow sprinters WR Earl McCullough (5/145y) and WR Jim Lawrence (4/54y rushing, including 26y TD) in dash to easy win. Able to stop USC early, Washington State (0-1) advanced 69y to 11YL, but K Hank Grenda's FG sailed wide. Cougars could gain only 87y in remainder of dwindling game. Troy sub FB Dan Scott scored 3 TDs, LB Sandy Durko had 43y INT TD RET, and DB Mike Battle scored on 32y punt RET, but starting QB Toby Page was lost to injury.

NORTH CAROLINA STATE 13 North Carolina 7: Tar Heels (0-1) fashioned 7-3 H lead by going 80y in 2nd Q to FB Tommy Dempsey's powerful TD plunge. But, Bill Dooley's Chapel Hill coaching debut was spoiled when North Carolina State (1-0) QB Jim Donnan (8-16/140y, TD), future coach himself, launched 4th Q 55y TD bomb to E Harry Martell off double fake. K Gerald Warren's 2 FGs kept Wolfpack within 7-6 until Donnan's blitz-beating, winning throw, which came in middle of 4th Q. North Carolina hopes died with 4th down incompletion by lefty QB Gayle Bomar at 18YL in late going. Game ball was given to NC State's 1966 All-ACC T Bill Gentry, who had been stricken by cerebral hemorrhage while coaching HS game hours earlier on Friday night.

Duke 31 Wake Forest 13 (Raleigh): Hurricane Doria's lashing winds arrived in time for 2nd game of Raleigh doubleheader. Gales kept pass percentages down, but Duke (1-0) QB Al Woodall accounted for outstanding 213y on 5-20 to position FB Jay Calabrese for 2 short TD runs that tied him for Blue Devils career record held by Ace Parker and Wray Carlton. Freddie Summers, ACC's 1st African-American QB, also had trouble with wind: 5-18/69y passing. Rushing for 69y, Summers raced for TDs of 7 and 3y, and his 1st score moved Wake Forest (0-1) to within 10-7 at H partly because Duke squandered 2 golden opportunities on INT and FUM deep in Demon Deacons territory in 1st Q.

SOUTH CAROLINA 34 Iowa State 3: Sporting new O, South Carolina (1-0) came from behind, starting late in 2nd Q, for coach Paul Dietzel's 1st win on home turf in his 2nd season in Columbia. Iowa State (0-1) got on scoreboard in 1st Q on K Vern Skripsky's 36y FG, and, although Cyclones would rush for 182y without top RB Les Webster, they never again threatened. It took until late in 2nd Q, but ISU secondary was exposed by QB Mike Fair (12-21/153y) as he passed Gamecocks to 69y TD trip that beat H clock by 7 secs. Fair scored TD on 1y outside dash. Birds FB Warren Muir (18/79y), West Point transfer who followed Dietzel, scored twice in 2nd H on short blasts up middle.

COLORADO 27 Baylor 7: Colorado (1-0) LB Kerry Mottl swiped 2 INTs deep in Baylor (0-1) territory, and composed soph QB Bob Anderson slipped into EZ thrice on runs of 7, 4, and 2y. Buffs HB Bill Harris scored decisive TD on 34y 3rd Q run with pitchout, which made amends for his twice allowing Bear DLs to steal ball from him. Baylor could only draw within 20-7 with 29y 4th Q TD pass from QB Alvin Flynn to WR Bobby Green.

Southern Methodist 20 TEXAS A&M 17: Little did SMU know it but it discovered Mighty Mouse in its opener. QB Mike Livingston suffered twisted knee while scoring to give Mustangs (1-0) 10-7 H lead. Into fray was thrown tiny QB Ines Perez, smallest SWC player at 5'4", 149 lbs, who relieved Livingston. Perez passed 10-11/107y in 2nd H and rallied SMU in last min. Perez's 6y TD pass to WR Jerry Levias at end of 4-pass, 58y drive came with 4 secs to go. Texas A&M (0-1) had taken 17-13 lead with 49 secs left on QB Edd Hargett's 29y scoring rocket to WR Bob Long.

CALIFORNIA 21 Oregon 13: New Ducks (0-1) QB Eric Olson (9-23/120y, 2 TDs, 3 INTs) came up with slippery fingers at wrong times, but managed to lay in 2 perfect passes for TDs in 2nd Q. Olson fumbled handoff at his 18YL early in 2nd Q to make possible California (1-0) FB John McGaffie's 2y TD plunge. Oregon got within 7-6 as Olson rifled 18y TD pass between 2 defenders to E Denny Schuler. On next possession, Olson lofted 36y scoring pass over Bears DB Johnny Williams to SB Roger Smith, who barely stayed in bounds at endline. Cal rallied in 4th Q when DB Bobby Smith's INT of Olson halted Duck drive and sent Bears on 63y excursion to McGaffie's 2nd TD run. With Bears ahead 14-13 with less than 3 mins to play, desperate Olson tried pass from his EZ, but it was derailed by DE Irby Augustine, who sped unmolested for 14y on INT TD RET.

OREGON STATE 13 Stanford 7 (Portland): Oregon State (1-0), which won 6 in row to wrap up 1966, extended its streak when K Mike Haggard broke 7-7 deadlock with 22 and 28y FGs in last 3 mins of 2nd Q. Stanford (0-1) moved ball reasonably well and held upper hand in 2nd H, but its only TD came on spectacular KO RET by HB Nate Kirtman in 2nd Q. Kirtman went untouched for 98y TD RET in 2nd Q answer to Beavers soph HB Billy Main's 5y TD romp at end of 54y trip. Indians couldn't overcome key rushing y lent by former LB and new Oregon State FB Bill Enyart. Beavers LB Skip Vanderbundt made key INT at his 16YL with 1:25 to play, and it snuffed last Stanford uprising.

UCLA 20 Tennessee 16: UCLA (1-0) had sour beginning: FUM on opening KO by Bruins QB Bill Bolton permitted Tennessee (0-1) QB Dewey Warren to complete 14y pass and TB Charles Fulton to ram in for 7-0 lead. Although Bruins moved ball well all night—they toted 412y in O and required only 1 punt—they botched some punt RETs and suffered bad field position. Bobbled punt left UCLA at its own 11YL in 3rd Q, and when FB Rick Purdy lost FUM on LB Steve Kiner's big hit on next play, Volunteers jumped to 13-3 lead on FB Richard Pickens' 1y TD run. Tennessee went up 16-13 in middle of 4th Q on K Karl Kremser's 35y FG. UCLA was in midst of vital drive when it faced 4th-and-2 at Vols 27YL with 4 mins left. Exhausted QB Gary Beban (9-20/107y), tagged "The Great One" by coach Tommy Prothro, summoned, as Prothro put it, "one more great play." Rolling right, Beban squirmed through T hole, burst through weary arm tackles, and cut away from last tackler, Vols DB Albert Dorsey, for winning TD run.

Nebraska 17 WASHINGTON 7: Unusual 105-degree heat greeted Cornhuskers (1-0) in Seattle, but tall soph QB Frank Patrick was up to Nebraska's ball-contol task. Husker D held Washington (0-1) to 189y and lone TD lapse. All scoring occurred in 2nd Q as Nebraska FB Dick Davis plunged for 1y TD, and Patrick capped 43y drive with TD dive. Purple and gold Huskies countered with advance to Nebraska 48YL, and QB Tom Sparlin looked to pass. With no receivers open, Sparlin maneuvered instead for broken field TD scamper. K Bill Bomberger countered with 20y FG in last 31 secs before H to make it 17-7.

AP Poll September 18

1 Notre Dame (22)	309	6 UCLA (3)	170
2 Alabama (7)	263	7 Georgia	124
3 Michigan State (1)	209	8 Miami	114
4 Southern California	184	9 Colorado	102
5 Texas (2)	175	10 Nebraska (1)	88

Others with votes: Arkansas, Army, California, Clemson, Duke, Georgia Tech, Houston, Illinois, Minnesota, Mississippi, North Carolina State, Ohio State, Pennsylvania, Penn State, Purdue, South Carolina, Southern Methodist, Tennessee, Texas A&M, Wyoming

September 23, 1967

ARMY 26 Virginia 7: Playing without its 2 top QBs—Steve Lindell and Jim O'Toole—Army (1-0) turned to soph QB Roger LeDoux (10-23/90y, and 52y running), who was shaky to begin with, but developed as game wore on. WB Van Evans, jr snatched from Cadets track team by coach Tom Cahill, raced to 41y punt TD RET and took pitchout from LeDoux to charge 24y to Army's last TD in 3rd Q. Trailing 6-0 after Black Knights HB Carl Woessner had scored on 6y run in 1st Q, Virginia (0-1) QB Gene Arnette opened 2nd Q with 34y pass to Cavaliers ace TB Frank Quayle, who followed with 3y TD run. When K Braxton Hill was true with his kick, Virginia enjoyed brief lead of 7-6.

NAVY 23 Penn State 22: Prior to game, each coach fretted about his D. When Navy (1-0) gained 489y and Penn State (0-1) made 378y, both Bill Elias and Joe Paterno proved to be correct. Lions owned 3rd Q as HB Bobby Campbell scored 7y TD after his 61y KO RET, and K Don Abbey added his 2nd FG for 14-10 Penn State lead. Dazed for much of game, Middies QB John Cartwright returned for last play of 3rd Q and immediately sparked 72y TD march for 17-14 edge. Penn State countered with 80y TD drive capped by QB Tom Sherman's pass to Campbell with 1:44 left. Campbell added 2-pt run for 22-17 lead. Cartwright came back with 78y drive as winning TD pass went to E Rob Taylor, his Navy-record 10th catch of the game. Late Middies TD represented game's 6th lead change.

ALABAMA 37 Florida State 37: Coach Bear Bryant may have had 5 starters back on his D, but he had to face fact that against O-minded Seminoles Crimson Tide (0-0-1) permitted same number of pts in 1 game it had given up in entire 1966 regular season. Stunning final score in season opener left Bryant bemoaning his pass D. Florida State (0-1-1) QB Kim Hammond threw TD pass to WR Ron Sellers, and DB Walt Sumner added 75y punt TD RET for 14-0 lead. QB Ken Stabler quickly put Tide ahead 15-14 on TD run and 51y TD pass to WR Dennis Homan. But, Seminoles built leads of 17-15, 24-22 at H, and 27-22. It was tied 30-30 in 4th Q until Alabama HB Ed Morgan carried for 3y TD after Stabler's 55y pass to Homan. Hammond (280y in air) quickly passed FSU 65y, capping it with 8y TD to HB Bill Moreman. Coach Bill Peterson opted for tying kick that ended Alabama's 17-game win streak because "I wasn't going to mess up 60 minutes of great effort by failing on a two-point try."

LOUISIANA STATE 20 Rice 14: QB Robbie Shelton (14-23/248y, TD and 23/103y rushing) had magnificent game for Rice (0-1), but it would end badly for him with shoulder separation on 4th Q TD run. Shelton's 38y TD pass to WR Larry Davis (7/150y) provided 1st H's only score, but LSU (1-0) tallied 2 TDs in 3rd Q. On 4th down at 2YL, Tigers RB Frank Matte appeared to tie score at 7-7 on wide run in 3rd Q, but QB-holder Nelson Stokley, who had made runs of 4, 15, 16, 8, and 3y on drive, couldn't control snap for kick attempt. Owls HB Lester Lehman lost FUM shortly after ensuing KO, and quick LSU HB Tommy Allen zipped 13, 4, and 11y, last run for TD and 13-7 lead. Shelton's short passes picked apart Tigers D in 4th Q, and SB Dan Van Winkle (5/113y receiving) slipped away for 56y pass play, and Shelton soon scored on his ill-fated 15y TD. Trailing 14-13 with 3:21 left in 4th Q, LSU had to go 75y to win: Stokley (4-10/64y) hurled 32y pass to WR Tommy Morel to set up HB Glenn Smith's winning 7y burst through LT with 29 secs left.

MICHIGAN 10 Duke 7: After taking opening KO, Duke (1-1) zoomed to Wolverines 1YL only to lose FUM. Blue Devils scored on their 2nd possession late in 1st Q: QB Al Woodall used HB Frank Ryan on 5 of 6 runs to travel 31y, TD coming on 4y pitchout run by Ryan around RE. Duke DB Andy Beath was 1-man gang as he stopped 3 Michigan (1-0) threats by making 2 GL INTs in 1st H and recovering FUM in 4th Q. Wolverines HB Ernie Sharpe (4/45y receiving) tied it with twisting 7y TD run in 3rd Q. In late going, Devils had to hope to maintain tie since they were pinned deep in own terrain. P Bob Baglien punted out to his 49YL in final min, and Michigan QB Dick Vidmer (13-27/174y, 2 INTs) quickly pitched passes to Sharpe and HB Ron Johnson (19/82y), latter for 23y. Vidmer carried 3 times to 10YL, and soph K Frank Titas drilled winning 27y FG with 18 secs to play.

Houston 37 MICHIGAN STATE 7: Crowd of 75,833 sat in stunned silence as blazing-fast Houston (2-0) compiled 416y against Michigan State D, now merely shadow of its spectacular 1965-66 form. Cougars went ahead on WR-K Ken Hebert's 44y FG in 1st Q, but relinquished lead in 2nd Q as Spartans HB Lamarr Thomas took pitchout and navigated E for 48y TD. Cougars HB Warren McVea (14/155y) dashed 50y to take 10-7 lead. When

rattled Spartans failed to score from 2YL at end of H, Houston was ready to explode for 27 pts in 2nd H. QB Dick Woodall threw TD bombs to WR Hebert (77y) and HB Don Bean (75y). DB Mike Simpson wrapped up scoring parade with late 59y INT TD RET.

INDIANA 12 Kentucky 10: *Chicago Tribune* called Indiana (1-0) soph QB Harry Gonso, "a bundle of energy from Findlay, O." In his debut, Gonso overcame 10-0 deficit in 2nd H to pitch 2 TD passes. Gonso contributed 272y of Indiana's 310y O total, rushing 25/115y and passing 11-15/121y, 2 TDs. Another soph, WR Jade Butcher (5/26y) caught short 3rd Q TD pass from Gonso, and TE Al Gage (3/40y) took game-winning, 4th Q throw in EZ after it was tipped off several fingertips. Earlier, Kentucky (0-1) HB Roger Gann (16/122y) burst through line in opening 4 mins of game, threw sledgehammer stiff-arm at Indiana DB Nate Cunningham, and raced 56y to score. After Hoosiers lost FUM, Wildcats tacked on K Dave Weld's 33y FG with 1:39 left before H.

NORTHWESTERN 12 Miami 7: Miffed over Miami newspaper article that called them "patsies," Wildcats (1-0) came from behind on 4th Q gift to upset Miami (0-1). Little DB Dennis White blanketed Hurricanes receivers, and Northwestern gained 130y rushing, much of it around highly-touted DE Ted Hendricks. Still, when HB Vince Opalsky rumbled over for TD and K Ray Harris converted, Miami owned 7-6 lead midway in 4th Q. With 5 mins left, Miami P Hank Collins dropped punt snap and was buried by White at 9YL. On 2nd down, Northwestern QB Bill Melzer flipped to HB Chico Kurzawski who swept right and tossed back to Melzer who raced for TD that shocked no. 8 Miami with 4:13 left.

MISSOURI 21 Southern Methodist 0: Virtually ignoring aerials, Missouri (1-0) piled up 285y rushing, but it was Tigers D that did serious damage to SMU (1-1). Little Mustangs QB Ines Perez, hero of previous week's win, was drilled by Mizzou DLs Jay Wallace and Carl Garber early on and limped off. With starting SMU QB Mike Livingston unavailable, Perez courageously returned, but Mustangs O found itself completely under control, especially in 2nd H. Missouri forced 3-and-out on 8 of Methodists' 9 2nd H possessions, and SMU gained only 31y in 2nd H. Tigers fared far poorer on O, registering only 1 TD: 6y slam in 3rd Q FB Barry Lischner (20/72y) that capped 55y drive. Missouri's other scores came on DB Butch Davis' 53y INT TD RET in 2nd Q and DB Roger Wehrli's 64y punt TD RET in 4th Q.

Purdue 24 TEXAS A&M 20: Purdue (1-0) soph QB Mike Phipps took over where Bob Griese left off, having big hand in 3 TDs and passing 17-35/269y, TD. After HB Bob Baltzell caught 35y TD and HB Leroy Keyes blasted over from 1YL for 14-3 2nd Q lead, Phipps was picked off by Texas A&M (0-2) DB Bill Hobbs who dashed 25y to score. Before H however, Boilermakers retaliated with Keyes' 14y TD pass to E Jim Bierne. QB Edd Hargett pitched 60y TD to HB Bob Long to get Aggies close.

Oklahoma State 7 ARKANSAS 6 (Little Rock): Oklahoma State (1-0-1) surprised highly-favored Arkansas (0-1) with 4th Q TD to launch Razorbacks' worst year since 1958. Porkers QB-K Ronny South clicked on FGs of 21 and 32y in 1st Q. Score of 6-0 stood until Cowboys DB Larry Kirkland recovered South's FUM at Arkansas 31YL in 4th Q. OSU HB Jack Reynolds (19/104y), playing in his native Little Rock, ripped through line for 13y TD, and when K Craig Kessler was true with his x-pt kick, Cowboys had their 1st lead. In vain attempt at victory, South was short with 49y FG try in last 10 secs.

SOUTHERN CALIFORNIA 17 Texas 13: Methodical 85y drive put Texas (0-1) on scoreboard 1st as key gains came from QB Bill Bradley on 11y scamper to USC 20YL and TB Chris Gilbert on 18y run to 2YL. Bradley found TE Deryl Comer for TD. Trojans (2-0) answered with 2y TD sweep by TB O.J. Simpson (158y rushing). With DE Tim Rossovich and DB Mike Battle taking control, USC D set stage for QB Steve Sogge's 3rd Q TD pass and K Rikki Aldridge's 4th Q FG. Bradley added late TD to make it close for Longhorns, who tumbled from no. 5 ranking.

AP Poll September 25

1 Notre Dame (31)	390	6 Colorado	118
2 Southern California (4)	340	7 Nebraska	79
3 Houston (6)	279	8 Texas	76
4 UCLA	275	9 Alabama	75
5 Georgia	260	10 Purdue	70

Others with votes: Army, Clemson, Florida, Florida State, Georgia Tech, Louisiana State, Memphis State, Miami, Michigan State, Minnesota, Missouri, Navy, Northwestern, Oklahoma, Oklahoma State, Oregon State, South Carolina, Syracuse, Tennessee, Texas Tech, West Virginia

September 30, 1967

Army 21 BOSTON COLLEGE 10: Seeking upset, Eagles (1-1) soared to TD on opening series. Boston College QB Mike Fallon (13-30/180y, 4 INTs), filling in as BC was crippled at several O positions, guided his team to 80y TD march and scoring himself from 3YL. Thereafter, Army (2-0) LBs Jim Bevans and Bud Neswiacheny sparked D that bent but was brilliant near its GL: Bevans made 2 INTs at his 5YL, and DB Henry Toczlowski picked off another Fallon pass at 10YL. Bevans blocked punt for safety in 2nd Q, and Cadets QB Roger LeDoux (7-27/133y, TD) shook off his early inaccuracies to pitch 56y TD pass to WR Terry Young, who broke West Point to-date career reception record. Army's 2nd FUM led to FG, so Eagles led 10-9 at H. Ahead 12-10 in 3rd Q, Cadets FB Charlie Jarvis swept 64y to BC 21YL. He was relieved by FB Jim Greenlee, who powered to 9y TD run and 18-10 edge.

Georgia 24 CLEMSON 17: Newly mounted stone from California's Death Valley, that was to become known as "(Coach Frank) Howard's Rock," brought no luck to Clemson (1-1) in its "Death Valley" stadium. Tenacious Georgia (2-0) D forced rash of 1st H errors to build 17-3 lead. INTs by LB Happy Dicks and DB Jake Scott prepped Bulldogs for QB Kirby Moore's 2 TD runs. Tigers turned tables in 3rd Q with dominant rally, tying game at 17-17 on infantry TD march and HB Frank Libertore's 52y punt TD RET. Bulldogs D finally stiffened, and local product TB Kent Lawrence ended 55y drive by sweeping E behind FB Ronnie Jenkins' block for 14y TD that won it for Georgia. Sub QB Charley Waters was Tigers' leading rusher with 12/87y, but he was among Clemson passers who threw 3 INTs.

North Carolina State 20 FLORIDA STATE 10: Pre-game analysis hardly mentioned accurate passing arm of NC State (3-0) QB Jim Donnan, future collegiate coach. But, Donnan contributed excellent pass y to enhance efforts of Wolfpack's fine corps of runners. Before O could take over, big D plays emphasized scoreless 1st Q: NC State DT Dennis Byrd sacked Florida State (0-2-1) QB Kim Hammond on consecutive plays, and FSU DB Walt Sumner blocked K Gerald Warren's 39y FG try. In 2nd Q, Wolfpack HB Charlie Bowers broke through line and outran 3 defenders for 49y TD. NC State FB Settle Dockery's runs to position Warren for 23y FG and 10-0 lead that held until H. Seminoles turned to QB Gary Pajcic who zipped 25y TD pass to WR Ron Sellers after poor Carolina punt to their 28YL. FUM REC by S Johnny Crowe set up FSU at NC State 16YL, but it had to settle for K Grant Guthrie's tying 33y FG. Donnan's sharp passes made possible Warren's 40y FG that barely fell over crossbar for 13-10 lead, and Wolfpack scored clinching TD on 55y drive after LB Mike Hilka picked off Pajcic.

TENNESSEE 27 Auburn 13: Tennessee (1-1) QB Dewey "Swamp Rat" Warren directed his usual early-game mayhem at Auburn (1-1) with TD pass to TE Kenny DeLong and 1y TD sneak. By H, Tigers had crept back to within 14-13 on K John Riley's 2 FGs and QB Loren Carter's short TD run. Warren was carted off in 3rd Q with knee injury, so Vols moved their always-useful QB-turned-TB Charles Fulton back to QB. Fulton sparked 2 drives in 2nd H as TB Walter Chadwick converting each with slashing TD run.

PURDUE 28 Notre Dame 21: For 3rd time since 1949, soph QB led Purdue (2-0) to upset of Notre Dame (1-1) that ended long Irish unbeaten streak. Dale Samuels sparked "Spoilermakers" to win that stopped 39-game streak in 1949. Len Dawson threw 4 TDs to end 13-game streak in 1954, and this time 12-game string was halted on hot passing hand of QB Mike Phipps (14-34/238y, 2 TDs). Phipps fired TDs to break 14-14 and 21-21 ties in 4th Q. Ably assisting was superb Purdue HB-DB Leroy Keyes, who caught 9/108y, TD, and doubled as CB to make vital INT to end late Irish comeback. Boilermakers FB Perry Williams scored twice to provide 6-0 and 14-7 leads. ND QB Terry Hanratty set 5 school records as he participate din 75 plays; he passed 29-63/366y, TD, 4 INTs, and ran for 54y. Hanratty was at his best in 1st 3 Qs that ended 14-14. Hanratty scrambled 25y and followed with 1y QB draw run for TD in 1st Q by completing 2 4th down passes to position HB Bob "Rocky" Bleier for 3rd Q score. Hanratty also found E Jim Seymour for 2 of his 8 receptions on 4th Q trip to TE Paul Snow's 31y TD catch that deadlocked score at 21-21. Irish pass rush on Phipps had been diminished by ankle injury suffered by stellar ND DT Kevin Hardy on game's 2nd play.

Southern California 21 MICHIGAN STATE 17: QB Steve Sogge was sharp with 14-16 passing that spread Spartans D for runs of TB O. J. Simpson (36/190y, 2 TDs), and USC (3-0) sauntered to 14-7 lead. Trojans' 2nd Q turned dark as Michigan State (0-2) QB Jimmy Raye arched 47y TD bomb to E Al Brenner and high snap forced USC P Rikki Aldridge into safety. Michigan State led 17-14 at H. In 3rd Q, Simpson surprised everyone with 7y TD lob to WR Jim Lawrence for winning TD. In late going, Spartans moved 70y to Trojans 5YL. But, 4th down EZ pass to Brenner was nullified, and USC held. So like that, away went Spartans' chance to turn their season around, and it headed south quickly.

Arizona 14 OHIO STATE 7: Coach Woody Hayes suffered only his 3rd setback in 17 openers as Buckeyes (0-1) faded after strong 1st Q. Ohio State went 46y to QB Gerry Ehrsam's early TD after QB Bill Long connected with E Bill Anders for 41y. Confident Arizona (1-1) received spark when sub QB Bruce Lee was inserted in 2nd Q, and he led 82y march as HB Wayne Edmonds slashed over on 14th play for 7-7 H tie. Poor Buckeyes punt to own 37YL positioned Wildcats for their winning tally in 3rd Q: Lee faked pass and dashed 9y for score. Ohio passers made only 7-26/69y, or barely more than 2-and-half y per try.

INDIANA 18 Kansas 15: Good fortune smiled on Indiana (2-0): Kansas (0-2) QB Bobby Douglass scored on TD runs in 1st and 3rd Qs, but his EZ pass in closing moments flew through fingers of would-be receiver. Hoosiers had earned 8-8 H tie as HB John Isenbarger threw 28y TD to his fellow soph, WR Jade Butcher, then caught 2-pt pass. Butcher put Indiana ahead 15-8 on 9y scoring throw from QB Harry Gonso in 3rd Q. Winning pts came on 24y FG in 4th Q by Hoosiers K Dave Kornowa, normally DB who asked to pinch-kick for regular K Dave Warner, who was suffering with arthritic toe, of all odd maladies for college kid. It was fast turning into that kind of odd and wonderful year for Cinderella Indiana.

NEBRASKA 7 Minnesota 0: Nebraska (2-0) secured its 20th straight home win by fashioning 94y TD trip in 3rd Q as QB Frank Patrick completed 11 and 9y passes. Cornhuskers HB Joe Orduna charged last 25y to score as he steamrolled 4 Golden Gophers tacklers. D battle was punctuated by Minnesota's ability to halt Cornhuskers nearly every time it mattered. Nebraska K Bill Bomberger missed 3 FGs, and Huskers coughed up FUM at Golden Gophers 7YL in 4th Q. Sole threat by Minnesota (1-1) died in 2nd Q as K Bob Stein missed 33y FG try.

Texas Tech 19 TEXAS 13: Rarely had Texas (0-2) seen running like that of QB John Scovell of Texas Tech (2-0), who broke Donny Anderson's school rushing y record for SWC game with 25/175y. After Longhorns QB Bill Bradley opened scoring with 36y pass in 1st Q, Scovell went to work with short TD run and his 21y TD pass for 16-6 lead. Texas TB Chris Gilbert's 80y TD run brought H score to 16-13. Still, it was disappointing 2nd-straight loss for Texas, which started season ranked no. 4 and lostto Texas Tech fro 1st time since 1955.

WYOMING 13 Colorado State 10: Revenge for previous year's only loss was on minds of Cowboys (3-0) who burst through "Remember '66" banner as they took field in Laramie. QB Paul Toscano riddled Colorado State (0-2) with 14-29/250y passing, including 1st Q 44y TD to WB Hub Lindsey. But, Rams held on grimly and shaved deficit to 10-7 on TB Oscar Reed's 2nd Q TD plunge. Unable to sustain attack, Wyoming counted on K Jerry DePoyster to bomb 55y FG for winning margin in 3rd Q.

October 7, 1967

Ucla 17 PENN STATE 15: Displaying grit that would typify coach Joe Paterno's top teams, underdog Penn State (1-2) crafted 79y all-land TD drive in opening 10 mins. HB Bobby Campbell went 32y on reverse and scored from 3YL. Held in own end for all of 1st Q, no. 3 UCLA (4-0) trailed 7-3 as late at midway in 3rd Q. Big break came on 9-man punt rush as Bruins DL Vic Lepisto blocked P Campbell's punt, and DL Hal Griffin fell on ball in EZ for UCLA TD. Bruins QB Gary Beban (10-16/108y, INT) kept his poise under D pressure from LBs Dennis Onkontz and Pete Johnson and DE Frank Spaziani and DT Steve Smear, as he provided key 4th Q 3y run for TD for 17-7 lead.

Louisiana State 37 FLORIDA 6: QB Nelson Stokley ran 9 and 50y for TDs, 2nd score coming in 3rd Q as backbreaker to Gators (2-1). It raised Tigers' tally to 23-0. Bengals K Roy Hurd, who had failed on 4-5 FG tries to date in 1967, righted his ship by drilling 1st H FGs of 43, 32, and 37y. Florida scored on QB Jackie Eckdahl's 29y pass to HB Larry Smith with 5 mins left.

ALABAMA 21 Mississippi 7 (Birmingham): Launched by 5 FUM RECs—3 collared by Crimson Tide DB Dickie Thompson—Alabama (2-0-1) rode QB Ken Stabler's TD pass and 8y TD run in own end for 21-0 lead. Mississippi (1-2) virtually matched Bama's O—241y to 237y—but 7 TOs thwarted each Rebels scoring attempt until 9:31 remained in 4th Q. At that point, QB Terry Collier rifled 25y TD pass to E Mac Haik.

MINNESOTA 23 Southern Methodist 3: Icy downpour greeted home-standing Golden Gophers (2-1), who bobbled ball all over "Brickhouse" gridiron in 1st H that they led 2-0 on safety: DE Bob Stein caught Southern Methodist (1-2) QB Eddie Valdez—who suffered 6 FUMs himself—in EZ while sub passer retreated to pass. After starting QB Ray Stephens fumbled 4 times in 1st H, soph QB Phil Hagen was summoned from Minnesota bench in 2nd H, and, after FUM REC by DE Del Jessen at 36YL, he got Gophers rolling to 1st of 2 short TD runs by big FB Jim Carter. Mustangs responded with 71y drive to Minny 10YL. Slick Ponies WR Jerry Levias, who gained only 97y on runbacks and receptions, slipped down while alone on 3rd down pass. So, SMU K Dennis Partee had to trim Gophers lead to 9-3 with 28y FG early in 4th Q. SMU fumbled again, and Carter scored again for 16-3 lead. Gophers went 63y in closing mins to E Chip Litten's brilliant catch of Hagen's 30y TD pass. Coaches must have wanted to shield their eyes from stat sheet: game saw 16 FUMs total.

MISSOURI 17 Arizona 3: On heels of upset of Ohio State, plucky Wildcats (1-2), "played in more rain than…they would see in a whole season back home in Tucson," according to St. Louis Post-Dispatch, which clogged both attacks and forced 11 punts per side. Playing old-fashioned, basic football, Missouri (3-0) enjoyed HB Jon Staggers' 1st Q 36y punt RET to Arizona 29YL, and it allowed QB Gary Kombrink's 5y TD pass to E Chuck Weber in corner of EZ. Tigers DB-KR John Meyer soon lost angle-bouncing punt at his own 4YL, his FUM recovered by Arizona C Tom Brennan. But D played like Tigers, throwing Wildcats for −5y on 2 runs, and soph DB Butch Davis batted down 3rd down pass. On 4th down, K Ken Sarnoski booted 24y FG for Arizona. Davis leapt to knock down 2nd Q pass in EZ to save another score against Mizzou and threw clearing block for Meyer, who turned from goat to hero, to score on 39y INT RET in 4th Q. Despite bad climate, Mizzou P Steve Kennemore punted masterful 11/40.8y avg.

North Carolina State 16 HOUSTON 6: Record Astrodome crowd saw Houston (3-1) D limit NC State (4-0) to 8y O in 1st Q. Cougars enjoyed 6-0 lead on QB Dick Woodall's TD pass, but momentum turned on avalanche of 2nd H TOs by Houston. Wolfpack WB Bobby Hall blasted over for 7-6 3rd Q edge after LB Mike Hilka's INT. NG Terry Brookshire soon recovered 1 of 7 FUMs that were murderous to Cougars cause, and K Gerald Warren booted 30y FG for 10-6 Wolfpack lead. After another INT, Hall raced 10y to score. Houston's last chance was fumbled away at North Carolina State 15YL.

WASHINGTON 13 Oregon State 6: To-date in 1960s, Washington (3-1) and Oregon State (3-1) had played 6 games settled by 7 pts or less. Undefeated Beavers gnawed their way to 6-0 1st Q lead on QB Steve Preece's 1y TD push at end of 14-play, 80y drive, and Huskies K Don Martin matched it with 2 short FGs in 2nd Q. Rugged contest featured strong D on both sides and stayed deadlocked at 6-6 until late stages. Beavers lost FUM on their own 38YL to Washington DG Rick Sharp. On 2nd play, QB Tom Manke ran 18y to set up HB Carl Wojciechowski's 18y TD run with 2 mins left. Loss ended Oregon State's victory roll at 9 games.

October 14, 1967

NAVY 27 Syracuse 14: Navy (3-1) came out throwing and jumped on Syracuse (3-1) for 14-0 lead in opening 8:23. WR Terry Murray (6/19y avg on punt RETs) caught 52y TD howitzer from QB John Cartwright (16-27/211y, 2 INT) on 1st drive. Orangemen pounced on FUM at Middies 25YL late in 1st Q, and QB Rick Cassata's TD plunge made it 14-7. But bobbled FUM into Middies hands at Navy 20YL and Cassata's ankle injury quenched any hope Syracuse harbored to overtake Midshipmen team that outgained it 310y to 220y.

TENNESSEE 24 Georgia Tech 13: Each team was without its regular QB as Tennessee (2-1) replaced QB Dewey Warren by moving handy TB Charley Fulton, and Yellow Jackets (3-1) turned to backup QB Larry Good (19-35/238y, 2 TDs, INT) for QB Kim King, who reinjured his ankle in brief 2nd Q action. Fulton didn't last long either, going out with cracked rib in 1st Q. In for Vols trotted Atlanta QB Bubba Wyche with Tennessee at Georgia Tech 5YL, and he started slowly as Volunteers had to settle for K Karl Kremser's 22y FG in 1st Q. Wyche (8-16/121y, 2 TDs, 3 INTs) soon warmed up with 7y down-and-out rifle-shot to WB Richmond Flowers (5/79y, 2 TDs receiving) in EZ in 2nd Q. On next possession, Wyche hit Flowers at Tech 30YL, and world-class speedster raced away for 50y TD play. When Vols TB Walter Chadwick (18/61y, TD) rammed over in 3rd Q at end of 60y expedition, Tennessee led 24-0. Yellow Jackets TB Lenny Snow (9/22y) was kept well in check by Vols D—led by T Dick Williams, LB Nick Showalter, and DB Jimmy Glover (INT)—and spoiled Georgia Tech scoring chance with lost FUM to Vols LB Steve Kiner inside 1YL. Pass catching of WR John Sias (7/148y, TD) and TE Steve Almond (7/53y, TD) stood out for Georgia Tech as Good authored 2 TD voyages in 4th Q.

MISSISSIPPI 29 Georgia 20 (Jackson, Miss): HB Bo Bowen scored pair of vital TDs, his 2nd TD came in 4th Q and extended lead of upset-hungry Ole Miss (2-2) to 22-14. Georgia (3-1) had opened with 66y march to QB Kirby Moore's 6y run and led 7-0 until Rebels HB Tommy James' 69y punt RET positioned Bowen's 1st TD. FUM REC by Rebs' D set up K Jimmy Keyes' 22y FG in 3rd Q which gave Ole Miss lead for good at 15-14. Remarkably, this contest was only 3rd meeting of SEC members since 1942.

AUBURN 43 Clemson 21: Three-year complaints about its mediocre O were answered as Auburn (3-1) totaled 40+ pts for 3rd time in young 1967 season. Clemson (1-3) lost 3 INTs and 2 FUMs with its 1st TO being most damaging: Auburn DB Jimmy Carter picked off pass in opening 2 mins and charged 61y to TD and 6-0 lead. Clemson QB Jimmy Addison (10-21/155y, 2 TDs, INT) overcame 9-0 deficit with 14y TD pass to WR Freddy Kelley and 28y TD pass to WR Phil Rogers (5/118y, TD). Auburn K John Riley booted 2 of his 3 FGs, and QB Loran Carter (10-18/195y, TD, INT) picked up 26y of his 208y total O with TD pass to WR Tim Christian. Plainsmen led 26-14 in late going of 1st H when Addison was injured while pitching 33y pass to Rogers. Neophyte QB Billy Ammons (6-18/56y, 2 INTs) was rushed in to hand off 4 times to TB Jacky Jackson for TD that pulled South Carolinians to within 26-21 at H. But without Addison in 2nd H, Clemson was blanked while Auburn FB Al Giffin scored his 2nd TD to open 3rd Q.

Michigan State 34 MICHIGAN 0: Michigan State (2-2) rolled up its widest margin of victory in 70-year history of intra-state histrionics. Michigan Stadium held its 2nd largest crowd to date with 103,210, but home fans and Wolverines (1-3) were stunned by Spartans' 3-TD flood late in 2nd Q that provided 27-0 lead: QB Jimmy Raye scored on 2 sneaks and added 65y TD pass to E Allen Benner and 8y to E Frank Foreman. Wolverines counted on TB Ron Johnson for 24/107y rushing, but poor pass receiving sent QB Dick Vidmer (5-15/40y, INT) to bench in 2nd H in favor of quick QB Dennis Brown (6-17/48y, INT) who thrice moved Michigan inside MSU 30YL but without mustering score.

Purdue 41 OHIO STATE 6: DB Dennis Cirbes got Purdue (4-0) off to flying start with 30y INT TD RET in opening 2 mins as Boilermakers buried Buckeyes (1-2) with 35-0 1st H. It was Ohio's 7th loss in last 11 games, and it had natives restless over coach Woody Hayes' conservative approach. Although conservatism would win handily for Hayes in future years, it would turn out to be worst defeat of his 28-year Ohio State career that would end in 1978. Boilermakers QB Mike Phipps (14-19/210y, 2 TDs), native of Columbus, saved his best game of soph season for his homecoming as he passed 5y to TE Marion Griffin and 25y to E Jim Beirne for scores. HB Leroy Keyes added 21y TD run, and FB Perry Williams chipped in with 1st of his 2 TDs on 1y plunge in Purdue's 2nd Q barrage. Buckeyes avoided shutout with 10y TD pass grabbed by E Billy Anders in 4th Q.

INDIANA 21 Iowa 17: Surprising Hoosiers (4-0) may have been America's unnoticed, undefeated team, but were not without last-min thrills. Indiana QB Harry Gonso (7-17/114y, 2 TDs, and 22/119y rushing) tossed 3y TD pass to WR Jade Butcher for 7-3 1st Q lead. Trailing 14-3 at H, Iowa (1-3) QB Ed Podolak capped 61y trip after 2nd H KO with 11y TD pass to E Paul Usinowicz. Podolak gave Hawkeyes 17-14 4th Q lead with 1y plunge, but Gonso found Butcher for 4y TD pass in last 53 secs.

Minnesota 10 ILLINOIS 7: After scoreless 1st H in which neither team went anywhere, Illinois (1-3) authored solid advance after 2nd H KO. But, Minnesota (3-1) stopped Illini at its 26YL and used several operatives to strike countering TD blow: Gopher TD-scorer FB Jim Carter (29/142y, TD) contributed 25y dash off block of RT John Williams, QB Phil Hagen (9-19/99y, 3 INTs) passed to HB George Kemp for 2/27y, and Kemp squirted 16y to 5YL behind Williams' block. Illinois came back on passing of QB Dean Volkman (12-25/163y, TD, 3 INTs), featuring 3 completions to WR John Wright (8/87y, TD), including 9y tying TD. Minnesota DB Gordon Condo made INT that set up time-consuming drive to Illini 6YL, where home team held. Minny soph QB-K Jeff Nygren booted winning 23y FG, and on his following KO, Gophers DE Del Jessen was virtually uncontested when he recovered ignored loose ball at Blue and Orange 25YL.

Southern California 24 NOTRE DAME 7: USC (4-0) LB Adrian Young, born ironically in Dublin, Ireland, ruined Fighting Irish (2-2) by grabbing 4 of 7 INTs by Trojans. Notre Dame QB Terry Hanratty, who tossed 5 INTs, provided 7-0 H lead on 3y rollout run in 2nd Q. USC all but absolved QB Steve Sogge for his 3 INTs of his own in 1st H from 2nd H passing chores as he tried just 3 throws to concentrate on USC's ground game. TB O.J. Simpson (38/150y) scored 3 TDs, including brilliant 35y dash, behind FB Dan Scott's block, which gave Trojans durable lead at 14-7 in 3rd Q. Poor punt by ND and Trojans DB Mike Battle's INT poised USC for its last 10 pts.

KANSAS 10 Nebraska 0: Suffering its 1st shutout loss in 59 games, Nebraska (3-1) penetrated Kansas (1-3) 30YL only once and not at all past midfield in 2nd H. Jayhawks went 68y in late stages of 2nd Q to QB Bobby Douglass' 4y TD run behind G Mike Reeves. Douglass gained 24y both rushing and passing on drive. Kansas DB Tommy Ball's 28y INT RET of Cornhuskers QB Frank Patrick in 4th led to clinching FG.

COLORADO 23 Missouri 9: Brothers Anderson made matters surprisingly easy for Buffaloes (4-0) to trounce unbeaten Tigers (3-1). Colorado QB Bob Anderson (7-10/71y, and 19/48y rushing) was highly deceptive in his handoffs and pitchouts to fashion 61 and 63y TD trips in 1st H. Pair of Bison runners—FB Wilmer Cooks (23/86y) and HB William Harris (23/94y)—each scored TD. Meanwhile other Anderson brother, DB Dick, recovered FUM and made pass INT to set up 3rd Q FGs by K Dave Bartelt. Missouri had taken brief 7-6 lead in 1st Q thanks Bartelt's missed kick after Cooks' 5y TD run. After ensuing KO, Tigers QB Gary Kombrink circled RE and hugged sideline for 75y TD sprint and 1-pt lead when DT-K Jay Wallace made his x-pt. Late Mizzou safety came after field position was won by Tigers P Steve Kenemore's deep punt.

Texas 9 Oklahoma 7 (Dallas): It took Oklahoma (2-1) all of 1 min to strike 78y in 5 plays for 7-0 lead on TB Ron Shotts' plunge. Sooners menaced twice more in 1st H, but QB Bobby Warmack was halted by 2 EZ INTs. Texas (2-2) found spark on D and stopped Sooners advance with 3rd Q FUM REC at Longhorns 31YL. K Rob Layne booted FG 7 plays later, 1st pts of season allowed by Oklahoma. QB Bill Bradley mixed runs with passes as Horns went 85y to Bradley's 7y option run for upset-generating TD.

Texas A&M 28 TEXAS TECH 24: Texas A&M (1-4) climbed off floor after 4 opening, but deceptive losses. Aggies' loss margin was 4.75 pts per game to teams with combined 9-4-1 record. After 5 lead changes, Texas A&M took 21-17 edge early in 4th Q on QB Edd Hargett's 13y pass to HB Larry Stegent. QB John Scovell used dual 15y PENs against Texas A*&M to dig Texas Tech (2-2) out of hole for TD and 24-21 lead with :53 on clock. Matters looked dark for visiting Aggies. They faced 4th-and-15 on Red Raiders 45YL with 11 secs left, and A&M WR Bob Long made miraculous catch for 1st down amid mob of Texas Tech DBs. Hargett rolled out from 15YL and ran for stunning victorious TD.

Brigham Young 31 OREGON STATE 13: Both teams used INTs to set up 1st Q TDs: Brigham Young (3-1) went on scoreboard 1st as FB Wally Hawkins wedged across from 1YL, and he received reply in form of Beavers (3-2) FB Bill Enyart's 1y smash. Cougars, featuring bevy of QB candidates, passed 22-40/316y, but truly didn't get rolling until late in 2nd Q when K Dennis Patera provided 10-7 lead with 39y FG late in 2nd Q. BYU got ball back, and QB John Erdhaus, JC transfer, launched 62y TD to WB Casey Boyett. Neither squad could score in 3rd Q, but Cougars launched 75y drive that culminated on 3rd play of 4th Q in QB Marc Lyons' 1y TD run. Beavers DB Mark Waletich prevented another BYU score with INT at his 2YL, and Oregon State's O responded with its only long march. HB Billy Main pulled Beavers within 24-13 with 31y TD reception, but DB Bobby Smith soon wrapped it up for BYU with 27y INT TD RET.

AP Poll October 16

1 Southern California (36)	432	6 Alabama	222
2 Purdue (7)	389	7 Tennessee	109
3 UCLA	325	8 Georgia	88
4 Colorado	280	9 Houston	87
5 No. Carolina State (1)	227	10 Wyoming	79

Others with votes: Arizona State, Army, Auburn, Brigham Young, Indiana, Louisiana State, Michigan State, Minnesota, Mississippi, Navy, Nebraska, Notre Dame, Penn State, Rice, Texas, Texas Tech, Washington

October 21, 1967

PENN STATE 21 West Virginia 14: Nittany Lions (3-2) won their 10th straight over neighboring West Virginia (4-2). Soph HB Charlie Pittman (24/137y) put minds at ease of big Homecoming crowd that might have fretted over absence of starting HB Bobby Campbell, out with injury. Mountaineers had struck in 1st Q as QB Tom Digon passed 6y to E Jim Smith for 6y TD after soph WR Oscar Patrick slipped behind Lions DB Tim Montgomery for 52y catch. Penn State, which would roll to 214y rushing, came back in 2nd Q with 2 TDs: FB Dan Lucyk's 2y run and FB Don Abbey's 6y reception from QB Tom Sherman. When WVU K Emo Schupbach lifted short KO to open 2nd H, Pittman dashed up to his 17YL, kept his momentum straight upfield, and cut to sideline past midfield to race 83y for untouched TD. Sub Mountaineers QB Garland Hudson lofted 26y TD pass in 4th Q to Patrick, but it was not enough.

William & Mary 27 NAVY 16: Navy's long-time punching bag, William & Mary (4-3) fell behind 16-0 and faced likely 13th straight loss to Middies (3-2) despite permitting only single scoring drive. Navy jumped on foes early: Indians HB Chip Young messed up opening KO RET and was felled in EZ for safety, Middies went 75y to 1st Q TD by QB John Cartwright, and DB Rick Bayer had 48y INT TD RET. In 3rd Q, Tribe QB Dan Darragh marshaled pass attack, scoring on 1y run and connecting on 2 TD throws. William & Mary WR Steve Slotnick caught winning 51y aerial with less than 4 mins left, and WB Terry Morton added late, unnecessary TD after Navy bobbled KO on own 19YL.

Clemson 13 DUKE 7: Homecoming Saturday for Duke (3-3) turned out to be rugged D battle in 1st H as teams showed nothing but 1 missed FG each. Blue Devils TB Frank Ryan (149y rushing) got his team out of hole from own 4YL with 33y run, then added 38y sweep and cutback to Clemson (2-3) 14YL so that gimpy FB Jay Calabrese (10/44y) could wedge over from 1YL for 7-0 lead. Sub TB Jacky Jackson got Tigers roaring with 40y RET of ensuing KO, and they went 54y to score, mostly on 15 and 17y passes by sore-armed QB Jimmy Addison to WR Phil Rogers. Tigers TB Buddy Gore slipped off RT for TD that tied it 7-7 with 3:04 to go in 3rd Q. Jackson raced 40y to Duke 15YL in middle of 4th Q to set up Gore for his 2nd 9y TD. Clemson stopped Devils WR Ed Hicklin 2y short of 1st down at 3YL after his 10y catch from QB Al Woodall (10-20/95y) in 4th Q.

SOUTH CAROLINA 24 Virginia 23: Coach Paul Dietzel, hobbled by recent knee surgery, inspired his Gamecocks (4-2) by arriving from hospital in plaster cast to sit in sideline golf cart. But, Dietzel's inspiration took awhile to take root. Virginia (2-3) controlled ball throughout 1st H and led 17-0 on runs by TB Frank Quayle and QB Gene Arnette. In all, Cavaliers rolled up 418y total O and added 191y in RETs, but PENs and 2 costly FUMs did them in. Wahoos' 1st TO cost them TD that could have made it 24-0 in 1st H: QB Arnette appeared to have crossed GL before officials ruled he lost FUM. UVa's 2nd FUM contributed greatly to 2 TDs allowed in 1:53-span of 3rd Q: South Carolina tallied on DB Pat Watson's 68y punt TD RET and QB Mike Fair's 11y TD pass. Fair passed only 5 times, but rushed 28/93y. Gamecocks K Jimmy Poole booted game-winning 45y FG in 4th Q, and Cavs DB-K Braxton Hill missed from same distance with 1:08 to go. Scrappy South Carolina, winners of just 1 game in 1966, found themselves in tie for ACC leadership with unbeaten NC State, whom they were not scheduled to face this season.

Tennessee 24 ALABAMA 13: Led by 3rd string QB Bubba Wyche, Volunteers (3-1) stunningly ended 25-game unbeaten string of Alabama (3-1-1). Wyche (8-14/92y, INT) took Vols 67y to TB Walter Chadwick's 1y TD after opening KO. Crimson Tide QB Ken Stabler threw 15-32/154y, but he threw 5 INTs, including 3 by Vols DB Albert Dorsey. Still, Stabler tied it at 7-7 on 8y TD run in 1st Q. P Steve Davis' booming punts for Bama briefly short-circuited in 3rd Q when his 21y punt became key lapse. Tennessee quickly scored after 2 passes from Wyche to WB Richmond Flowers. K Karl Kremser added 47y FG for 17-7 lead as 3rd Q ended. Vols nearly gave it away as Tide DB Mike Dean picked off pass to help slice margin to 17-13, but Dorsey sealed Bama's fate with 31y INT TD RET with 1:20 to play.

Indiana 27 MICHIGAN 20: Off to its best start since 1945, Indiana (5-0) secured Big 10 lead. By scoring twice in 3-min span of 1st Q, Hoosiers led 14-0 on soph HB John Isenbarger's 26y run and QB Harry Gonso's 8y TD pass to E Eric Stolberg after FUM by Michigan HB Ron Johnson at Wolverines 34YL. Isenbarger (18/101y) followed with 41y 2nd Q TD pass to WR Jade Butcher. Then, Michigan (1-4) rallied: QB Dennis Brown (18-31/211y, INT) scored from short range in 2nd and 3rd Qs to pull within 20-14. Early in 4th Q, Michigan earned 1st down at 10YL, but Hoosiers made daring stop at their 5YL. On 4th-and-2 at its 13YL, Indiana lined up to punt, but "to horror of every Hoosier within eyesight", according to *Chicago Tribune's* Roy Damer, P Isenbarger decided to run for it, and soph star would have converted 1st down had he not fumbled. So with short field presented to Michigan, Johnson tied it at 20-20 on run with 9:07 left in 4th Q. Wolverines botched go-ahead conv kick, and K Mike Hankwitz soon shanked chip-shot 22y FG with less than 5 mins to go. Despite 5y delay PEN at beginning of next Indiana series, Gonso moved Hoosiers 85y in 11 plays with Isenbarger plunging for winning TD with 1:11 left. Big plays included Isenbarger's 8 and 10y runs and TE Al Gage's 31y catch over middle. Afterward, Hoosier coach John Pont said of nearly disastrous fake-punt, "Don't look at *me*; the last thing I told Isenbarger was to kick it."

MINNESOTA 21 Michigan State 0: Switched to HB during summer, Gophers Curt Wilson returned to familiar QB spot as coach Murray Warmath sought to shore up his team's run attack. Instead, Wilson delighted Minnesota (4-1) Homecoming crowd with 14-25/262y air game and TD passes in each of 1st 3 Qs. E Chip Litten caught 19 and 23y scores in 1st H, and Wilson capped 81y surge after 2nd H KO as he whipped 33y score to WR Hubie Bryant. Michigan State (2-3) lost QB Jimmy Raye to 1st H rib injury, gained but 100y rushing, and lost 1st conf game in 17 outings since Illinois beat Spartans in 1964 finale.

Oregon State 22 PURDUE 14: Oregon State (4-2) was unimpressed by its 20-pt underdog status and 9-game win streak owned by no. 2 Purdue (4-1). Although Beavers QB Steve Preece was useful runner, he passed only 4-16/68y, 3 INT. But,, Preece hit early 18y TD to E Roger Cantlon. Boilermakers struck back on HB Leroy Keyes' 21y TD run in 1st Q but were hard pressed to finally wrest 14-10 lead late in 3rd Q as Keyes scored again on 7y run. After Oregon State trimmed it to 14-13, DL Jeff Lewis fell on his 2nd important FUM REC in 4th Q, and Beavers FB Bill "Earthquake" Enyart soon followed with go-ahead 4y TD run. K Mike Haggard kicked his 3rd FG to extend Oregon State lead to 8 pts. Purdue QB Mike Phipps threw 17-35/167y, but suffered 3 damaging INTs.

Colorado 21 NEBRASKA 16: Stampeding Buffaloes (5-0) tied Oklahoma, 46-7 winners over Kansas State, atop Big 8 standings. Upset for 2nd straight week, Cornhuskers (3-2) were pointed toward their 1st mediocre record since 3-6-1 mark of 1961. Nebraska QB Frank Patrick threw 1st Q TD pass to WB Ben Gregory, but suffered miserable fate of having 2 INTs run back for TDs. Patrick's backbreaking INT came with score at 7-7 in 2nd Q: Buffs DB Dick Anderson grabbed Patrick pass at own 38YL, was hemmed in after 17y RET when he flipped lateral to DE Mike Veeder, who charged remaining 45y to TD that put no. 4 Colorado in lead for good.

Texas 21 ARKANSAS 12 (Little Rock): Normally sharp-focused 11s of Texas (3-2) and Arkansas (1-3-1) fueled this rivalry with precision play. However, on this Saturday before national TV audience, it was comedy of errors: Razorbacks suffered 5 INTs, 4 thrown by recently-appointed starting QB John Eichler. Longhorns were clearly superior with 11 drives inside Hogs 40YL, but they all failed, mostly because of 4 FUMs and 2 INTs by Arkansas S Terry Stewart. Texas TB Chris Gilbert rushed for 162y and set new school career rushing y mark. While Gilbert scored 3 TDs, he also lost 3 FUMs. Still, Porkers coach Frank Broyles brought former starting QB Ronny South off bench with less than 7 mins to play to fire up 80y drive highlighted by his 40 and 18y passes to E Max Peacock and 7y TD pass to TB Mike Hendren. South was on verge of tying it at 14-14, but his 2-pt pass for Hendren was too well-covered by LB Corby Robertson and DB Ronnie Ehrig. Gilbert scored anyway from 12YL with 1:19 to go.

Texas A&M 20 TEXAS CHRISTIAN 0: Horned Frogs (0-4) played heady D, keeping favored Texas A&M (2-4) bottled up in its own territory for much of 3 Qs. Aggies had managed QB Edd Hargett's 28y TD pass to WR Bob Long in 2nd Q but little else. TCU mounted 3 solid threats after falling behind 7-0: DB Mike Hall fell on midfield FUM, and Frogs went 43y before giving it up at 7YL on INT by Texas A&M LB Bill Hobbs. Late in 3rd Q, TCU QB Dan Carter (13-24/144y, INT) mixed in runs of FB Kenny Post and HB Marty

Whelan and hit E Bill Ferguson with 17y pass to 7YL. But, Hobbs picked off Carter's pass just inside EZ and ambled 100y to TD and 14-0 lead on 1st play of 4th Q. Steady Texas A&M TB Larry Stegent rushed 22/94y.

RICE 14 Southern Methodist 10: Coach Hayden Fry tinkered with his Mustangs (1-4) O, moving players around like chessmen, and for most of game SMU dominated. QB Mike Livingston turned in 1 of Mustangs' greatest passing efforts with 22-44/246y, TD, 3 INTs as they went to wide-open attack. SMU led 10-0 on K Dennis Partee's 32y FG and Livingston's 4y TD pass to WB Paul Loyd. But, within 5:54 span of 2nd H, Rice (3-1) QB Robby Shelton sprinted for TDs of 2 and 42y. SMU's Cardiac Kids looked as though they would pull it out at end as Livingston passed them 53y to Owls 3YL in last 2 mins, but Rice DB Pascual Piedford went high to pull down EZ INT to preserve Owls win.

Ucla 21 STANFORD 16: While no. 1 USC overcame stubborn Washington 23-6 with 16 pts in 4th Q at Seattle, UCLA (6-0) survived 2 late upset threats by Stanford (3-3). Bruins scored TD in each of opening 3 Qs, rumbling 78, 52, and 80y. QB Gary Beban scored on runs of 11, and 3y. Meanwhile, scrappy Stanford hung around, tying it at 7-7 on QB Chuck Williams' 39y pass to HB Bill Shoemaker, taking 10-7 2nd Q lead after LB Pat Preston's INT set up K Shoemaker's 27y FG. After FB Jack Root's TD brought Indians to within 21-16 in 4th Q, they lost INT at Bruins 18YL and mis-fired on EZ pass in last 3 secs. Thanks to Oregon State's upset of no. 2 Purdue, UCLA joined cross-town rival Trojans as nation's top rated teams in Monday's AP Poll.

AP Poll October 23

1 Southern California (37)	370	6 Georgia	143
2 UCLA	303	7 Purdue	110
3 Colorado	283	8 Wyoming	91
4 Tennessee	228	9 Houston	84
5 North Carolina State	222	10 Indiana	48

Others with votes: Alabama, Arizona State, Army, Auburn, Florida State, Louisiana State, Miami, Michigan State, Minnesota, Missouri, Nebraska, Notre Dame, Oklahoma, Oregon State, Penn State, Rice, Stanford, Texas, Tulsa, Virginia Tech, Washington

October 28, 1967

ARMY 24 Stanford 20: Ball changed hands 11 times on TOs, and game ended as frustrated Stanford (3-4) soph LB Pat Preston booted ball away from its spot on scrimmage line. Preston was called for unsportsmanlike PEN for his trouble. On other hand, things ended wonderfully for Black Knights (5-1), who trailed by 3 pts but quick, little HB Van Evans broke for left sideline and dashed 36y on punt RET to Indians 13YL. HBs Lynn Moore and Hank Andrzejczak took 2 runs to put Army ahead 24-20 with less than 2 mins to play. Earlier, Tribe had taken 10-0 lead in 1st Q as FB Jack Root topped K Bill Shoemaker's 27y FG with 2y scoring bash at end of 60y march. Cadets tied it 10-10 by H, and HB Mark Woessner put them ahead 17-10 with 1y run in 3rd Q. Stanford fought hard for 92y to FB Greg Broughton's TD smash from 1 ft away. It provided 4th Q lead of 20-17.

Penn State 29 SYRACUSE 20: Seesaw 1st H saw QB Tom Sherman break 7-7 tie for Penn State (4-2) with 60y TD pass to TE Ted Kwalick in 1st Q before lead was stretched to 22-14 by H. Top Orange ground-gainer Larry Csonka switched between FB and TB to key 2nd H surge by Syracuse (4-2). Csonka scored his 2nd TD on 6y run in 3rd Q, but E Ed Nowicki dropped 2-pt pass that would have tied it. Trailing 22-20, Orangemen were forced into gambles that resulted in EZ INT by Lions DB Tim Montgomery that halted long drive and another INT that Lions LB Dennis Onkontz returned 53y for TD.

Dartmouth 23 HARVARD 21: Dartmouth (5-0) dominated well into 3rd Q as dazzling QB Gene Ryzewicz scored twice for 20-0 lead. In late moments of 3rd Q, Harvard (4-1) HB Ray Hornblower chipped away at Dartmouth D fortress, leading to his 5y TD run, which opened 4th Q. LB Bill Cobb soon blocked Indians punt, and HB Vic Gatto dove over for TD. Gatto scored again after DB Tom Wynne's INT in Crimson whirlwind, and Harvard suddenly led 21-20. Dartmouth calmed itself down and rode 16 methodical plays that consumed most of last 7 mins. Still, Big Green got lucky: K Bill Donovan missed 26y FG, but offside PEN against Harvard allowed him to try again. He drilled winning 21y FG with 57 secs left.

Virginia Tech 20 WEST VIRGINIA 7: For 1st time since 1918, Virginia Tech (7-0) had nailed down 7 straight wins. But it took 2 misadventures in West Virginia (4-3) punting game to key Hokies' victory. Boot by Mountaineers DB-P Thad Kucherawy in 2nd Q took tremendous backwards bounce to net only 9y to Gobblers 43YL. That set up 1st of 2 FGs by Virginia Tech K John Utin that became 6-0 lead. DB Ron Davidson poised Virginia Tech for TD in last 2 mins of 1st H with 73y punt RET to 3YL, where last-tackler Kucherawy brought him down. Davidson made 3rd Q INT, and FB George Constantinides scored his 2nd TD for 20-0 lead for Va Tech. WVU HB Ron Pobolish swept E for TD in 4th Q, and Davidson had to make another INT, school-record 6th of year, to snuff another WVU rally.

TENNESSEE 17 Louisiana State 14: No. 4 Tennessee (4-1) survived nail-biter as K Karl Kremser popped through winning 33y FG with 1:05 to play. But, it wasn't over: Louisiana State (4-2) FB Eddie Ray threw surprise 16y pass to spark last-moment drive that fizzled as K Roy Hurd's 36y FG flew right. Banged-up QB Dewey Warren (9-13/170y, 2 INTs) came off Volunteers bench to click on 41y and 14y passes to set up his 7y TD scramble. Vols LB Jimmy Glover made INT of Bengals QB Nelson Stokley (9-15/89y, INT) to halt LSU threat near end of 2nd Q. Tennessee went 80y to score on 6y scoring somersault by TB Walter Chadwick (21/77y), but Tigers DB Sammy Grezaffi took KO at GL and went untouched for 100y TD RET to pull LSU to within 14-7. Bengals went through 3rd Q without 1st down, but roving LB Barton Frye made EZ INT to squash Vols' menacing moves. Stokley overcame Glover's sack to lead tying 80y drive to his 14y TD scramble in 4th Q. But, LSU's 15y PEN launched winning drive for Tennessee.

MISSISSIPPI 14 Houston 13: Inhospitable Mississippi (4-2) upset upstart Houston (4-2). Little HB Don Bean flew 74y with punt RET to put Cougars ahead in 1st Q, but Ole Miss QB Bruce Newell tied it by H on 28y TD pass to E Mac Haik. Although Newell suffered 2 INTs deep in Cougars territory to DB and future MLB ballplayer Tom Paciorek, he hit TE Hank Shows with go-ahead TD pass in 3rd Q. Difference was WR-K Ken Hebert's missed conv kick after Houston QB Dick Woodall threw 42y TD pass in 4th Q.

Illinois 17 OHIO STATE 13: Overwhelmingly nicked-up Illinois (2-4) won Illi-buck Trophy for only 3rd time in last 14 meetings with Buckeyes (2-3) as HB Dave Jackson crowned team's best drive of season (77y) with 1-ft TD vault in last 34 secs. Several Illini players were in new spots due to injuries, including former WR Dean Volkman at QB. While WR John Wright drew double coverage on winning late drive, Volkman (12-20/170y) persisted in hitting him with passes of 7, 16, and 14y. Jackson (19/78y, 2 TDs) had scored on 14y run in 2nd Q to lead Illinois to 10-0 H edge, but slippery Ohio State HB Dave Brungard (28/163y, TD) swept left for 67y TD run 1:23 into 3rd Q. Ohio State ate 8 mins of 4th Q to take its only lead at 13-10 on 18-play, 65y drive to QB Bill Long's 9y TD pass to E Billy Anders, 3rd time on Buckeyes' series that passing battery succeeded on 4th down. Then, Illinois pulled out win with its clutch march.

MINNESOTA 20 Michigan 15: QB Curt Wilson (4-12/100y, TD, 3 INTs) scored 2 TDs and passed for 3rd as vengeful Minnesota (5-1) rallied to avenge previous season's 49-0 whipping in Little Brown Jug encounter and maintain its partial ownership of Big 10 lead. Michigan (1-5) used pro 4-3 D to thwart Gophers' Pro-T set-up on O, and it worked well as Wolverines jumped to 12-0 lead on long and short TD runs by HB Ron Johnson (17/108y, 2 TDs) in 1st Q. Michigan's 2nd TD was set up by DB Brian Healy's 31y INT RET to Gophers 5YL. Wolverines K Mike Hankwitz booted 21y FG late in 2nd Q for 15-0 lead, but thanks to face mask PEN that kept alive drive to Wilson's 5y TD run, Minny scored in last 49 secs of 1st H. After WR Mike Curtis' slant-in 45y TD catch from Wilson early in 4th Q, Minnesota found itself trailing 15-13 and sitting at Michigan 3YL with 4th-and-2 with 5:40 left on clock. Although coach Murray Warmath wanted to kick easy FG, his Gopher asst coaches prevailed, and Wilson faked handoff and slipped outside to score TD. Michigan wasn't done; it went 59y to Gophers 21YL behind scrambling QB Dennis Brown (9-21/94y, INT), but 4 passes fell incomplete. Wolverines' last gasp came on 54y punt RET by HB George Hoey, who might have avoided last-tackler with cut to center of field. Instead, P Dave Baldridge shoved Hoey OB at 26YL before Brown was sacked twice to end game.

NOTRE DAME 24 Michigan State 12: How different was year-after, as this matchup received dramatically less fanfare than 1966's famed 10-10 tie. Notre Dame (4-2) FB Jeff Zimmerman (20/135y, 2 TDs) was catalyst as he tallied on 7y run at end of all-running 84y drive in 1st Q and 47y sprint through LT after DB Tom O'Leary caused Michigan State (2-4) HB Lamarr Thomas to cough up ball after pass catch at ND 18YL. In between, Zimmerman put on great moves in taking short 2nd Q pass by QB Terry Hanratty (8-15/99y, TD) to score 30y TD for 17-0 H edge. Injury-riddled Spartans arrived shorthanded with additional 6 players suspended for curfew violations, but they rallied in 4th Q with 2 TDs, including 6y TD catch by WR Frank Waters (8/74y, TD) from QB Bill Feraco (12-22/124y, TD). Missed passes on 2-pt tries kept MSU in gambling mode, and it surrendered ball in late going on 4th down failure at its own 8YL.

Oklahoma 7 MISSOURI 0: Kudos were earned by respective D squads. Missouri (4-2) held Sooners' rushing attack, tops in nation at 284y avg, to 150y. Oklahoma (5-0) pitched its 3rd shutout of season, limiting Tigers to 172y total O. Sooners QB Bobby Warmack clicked on 51y pass which TE Steve Zabel carried to 7YL in 2nd Q. Warmack then scooted to 1YL, and TB Ron Shotts blasted for game's only score.

Oklahoma State 10 COLORADO 7: Cowboys (2-2-1) ended 10-game win streak by Colorado (5-1), primarily on 69y TD march after opening KO. Oklahoma State QB Ronnie Johnson mixed 2 passes to E Jerry Philpott with power sweeps before whipping wide for 7y TD. Buffs were flagged for unusual illegal procedure PEN on D that helped keep opening TD drive alive on Cowboys' 4th down. Cowboys played solid D and made it 10-0 in 3rd Q on K Craig Kessler's 26y FG. Laboring with 6 new players on O thanks to injuries, Buffaloes finally scored on sub QB Dan Kelly's sweep with less than 10 mins to play.

TEXAS 28 Rice 6: QB Bill Bradley displayed his best pass talents, completing 12-17/215y for Texas (4-2). WB Randy Peschel caught 6/126y, including plays of 43, 30y that set up TDs. Bradley scored twice, rifled 36y TD pass. Rice (3-2) earned brief 6-6 tie in 1st Q, but tumbled from conf unbeaten ranks thanks greatly to its 6 TOs.

Wyoming 15 ARIZONA STATE 13: Cowboys (7-0) opened swiftly, using QB Paul Toscano's 63y TD bomb to WR Gene Huey for 6-0 lead in 1st Q. Ace K Jerry DePoyster added 38y FG for 9-0 lead. DePoyster kicked 31y FG for 12-7 lead in 4th Q, but Arizona State (5-2) FB Max Anderson went coast-to-coast on 99y TD run. Sun Devils' try for 2-pt pass failed, but they led 13-12. DePoyster's record 30th career FG from 26y won it.

SOUTHERN CALIFORNIA 28 Oregon 6: TB Steve Grady earned Trojan trivial notoriety, subbing for TB O.J. Simpson, who limped off early in 3rd Q after rushing 23/63y. Grady gained 108y and TD in 2nd H. Southern California (7-0) presented devastating D as Ducks (1-6) managed only 25y in 1st H and failed to penetrate USC territory until 3rd Q. Trojans QB Steve Sogge threw TD pass to TE Bob Klein and set up another with his aerials. In last 2 mins, Oregon finally scored on QB Eric Olson's 9y TD pass to E Lynn Hendrickson.

AP Poll October 30

1 Southern California (43)	430	6 Purdue	206
2 UCLA	367	7 Indiana	172
3 Tennessee	305	8 Wyoming	112
4 North Carolina State	288	9 Colorado	86
5 Georgia	217	10 Notre Dame	35

Others with votes: Alabama, Army, Brigham Young, Florida State, Houston, Miami, Minnesota, Mississippi, Oklahoma, Oregon State, Penn State, Texas, Virginia Tech, Washington

November 4, 1967

YALE 56 Dartmouth 15: Yale (5-1) dropped 4 TDs on Dartmouth (5-1) in 1st 17 mins of game and tallied Elis' largest pt total in its last 319 games. Eli QB Brian Dowling, injured for better part of year and half, burst into stardom as Bulldogs savior. Dowling bootlegged

for 30y TD and pitched 67y TD to TE Bruce Weinstein. Yale FB Don Barrows crashed for 3 TDs in opening Q. Indians vainly drove for 83 and 69y TDs in 2nd H, mostly on passing of QBs Gene Ryzewicz and Bill Koenig.

WAKE FOREST 35 South Carolina 21: Previously undefeated in conf play, South Carolina (5-3) saw ACC title dreams trampled under swift feet of Wake Forest (2-6) QB Freddie Summers. HB Jack Dolbin (12/122y) ran 60y to 3YL set up Summers' opening TD run for Wake, and HB Buz Leavitt (19/103y, 2 TDs) dashed 15y to prepare FB Ron Jurewicz for 2y TD blast. Gamecocks came from behind twice to tie game, and QB Mike Fair's 2nd TD run brought Carolina to 21-21 tie in 3rd Q. K Jimmy Poole had opportunity to give Gamecocks lead with 27y FG early in 4th Q, but his boot was yanked left. Delighting Demon Deacons' Homecoming crowd, Summers dashed 17y at end of 55y trip to go-ahead TD inside last 3 mins. When Carolina gambled on last-min passes from own end, it gave ball up at own 30YL. Leavit crashed over with :14 on clock. FB Warren Muir led Cock rushers with 31/122y.

Auburn 26 FLORIDA 21: To little avail, Gators (4-2) made 378y, and 20 1st downs, to 226y for Auburn (5-2). Tigers struck for 20 pts in 3-min span of 3rd Q to overturn 7-6 H disadvantage. With help of 2 blocked punts, Auburn QB Loran Carter ran for 2 TDs and threw his 2nd TD pass, caught for 14y by E Freddie Hyatt. Florida rallied for 4th Q TDs by HB Larry Smith and QB Larry Rentz, but painful loss knocked Gators out of SEC race.

MISSISSIPPI 13 Louisiana State 13 (Jackson): Before night in Dixie was over, mercury dropped to 29 degrees, but cold couldn't chill enthusiastic Louisiana State (4-2-1), "unluckiest team in America," according to coach Charley McClendon. Ole Miss (4-2-1) D caused 8 FUMs and threw Tigers QB Nelson Stokley (10-15/126y) for 31y in losses. TB Stan Hindman (28/88y) was kept in control by Bayou Bengals D, but scored on short TD run after catching 20y pass on Rebs' 1st possession. LSU tied it on FB Jimmy Dousay's plunge. Rebels NG-K Jimmy Keyes made 2 FGs in 2nd H to tie SEC career FG record of 25 by Georgia's Bobby Etter. As 4th Q clock marched on, FB Eddie Ray kept LSU drive alive with 4th down run and made expert 15y catch at Rebs 8YL. HB Kenny Newfield (9/73y) circled LE for 8y TD, but Bengals K Steve Daniel, subbing for suspended K Roy Hurd, missed winning x-pt kick.

KENTUCKY 22 West Virginia 7: Chilly Homecoming Saturday proved to be just what was needed for winless Kentucky (1-6). Plus, Wildcats also had TB Dicky Lyons, who scored all of their pts. West Virginia (4-4) tallied 1st on 7-play, 59y drive, capped by QB Tom Digon's 10y pass to WB Ron Pobolish. Near end of 1st Q, WVU stopped Lyons on 3rd down at Mountaineers 6YL, but they wrenched his face mask, and Kentucky was awarded 1st down at 3YL. Lyons quickly scored but as K missed x-pt. WVU K Ken Juskowich tried 55y FG against wind in 2nd Q and barely was short, but his miss seemed to throw him off stride. Juskowich missed FG tries of 24, 37, and 28y in 2nd H. K Lyons, who had never attempted FG in his career, was perfect with 33y 3-ptr in 2nd Q. It looked as though Lyons' FG would have to hold up for 9-7 win until last 4:30 when Lyons bagged 2 short TD runs.

Miami 14 VIRGINIA TECH 7: Virginia Tech (7-1) had won 14 regular season games in row, but fell to mighty D of Miami (5-2), same team that beat Hokies in previous December's Liberty Bowl. Winning 5th in row, Hurricanes permitted only 57y O and allowed no 1st downs until 10 mins deep into 3rd Q. In 2nd Q, Miami QB David Olivo ran for TD, and pitched pass to E Jim Cox, who flipped lateral to speeding FB John Acuff, who scored. In between, Hokies DB Frank Loria sped 95y for TD punt RET.

INDIANA 14 Wisconsin 9: Cardiac Kids of Indiana (7-0) weathered late charge by winless Wisconsin (0-6-1) with Badgers misfiring on EZ pass as time expired. Enduring painful shoulder injury, Hoosiers QB Harry Gonso passed poorly with 2-11/57y, TD, 2 INTs, but rushed 22/127y. Gonso bit bullet and fired 15y pass to HB John Isenbarger for 1st Q TD. Badgers K Tom Schinke kicked 27y FG in 2nd Q after sub QB John Boyajian came off bench to connect twice on passes with HB Tom McCauley. After Indiana took 14-3 lead on PEN-aided 27y drive in 3rd Q, Wisconsin found something within itself to threaten throughout rest of game. Hoosiers DB Kevin Duffy had to stop Badgers' drive with INT and another sputtered at 7YL before QB Boyajian concluded 63y drive—built mostly on FB Gale Buccairelli's 4/33y rushing—with 2y TD run with 3:36 remaining. Wisconsin advanced to 10YL before time ran out on incomplete pass.

OKLAHOMA 23 Colorado 0: Energetic Oklahoma (5-1) D picked off 2 passes and recovered FUM, all in Buffaloes territory. Each TO prompted TD by Sooners as soph TB Steve Owens galloped to 2 scores and WB Eddie Hinton added another. Sooners K Mike Vachon, who had missed 7 FG tries during season's opening 5 games, finally made 21y 3-ptr to open scoring in 2nd Q. Colorado (5-2) QB Bob Anderson (4-12/43y, 3 INTs) suffered INTs returned to Bison 44 and 34YLs with DBs Bob Stephenson and Rick Goodwin making pickoffs. In losing 2nd in row, Buffs were outgained 262y to 181y. Buffs mustered only 1 threat to failed 4th down run by Anderson at OU 10YL and were incapable of moving any closer to GL than Oklahoma 43YL in 2nd H.

Texas A&M 33 ARKANSAS 21: Until this Saturday in which Texas A&M (4-4) evened its record after opening with 4 losses, Razorbacks (2-4-1) coach Frank Broyles had never lost Homecoming game in 10 seasons. Aggies went 90y to 7-0 lead after stopping opening Hogs thrust at their 10YL, and all but QB Edd Hargett's 23y pass to TE Tom Buckman came on 19 runs. A&M lost 13y on O during remainder of 1st H as Arkansas owned 2nd Q: TB David Dickey on 1y blast and WR Max Peacock on 6y pass from QB Ronny South (18-22/205y, 2 TDs, INT) scored for 14-7 H edge. Having thrown but 3 passes in 1st H, A&M's Hargett (14-26/180y, 3 TDs) unlimbered his arm to take advantage of 2nd H opportunities afforded by poor Porkers punt, FUM REC, and blocked punt. Also, Hargett moved Aggies 68y to early 4th Q, 12y TD pass to FB Wendell Housley. But when X-pt was missed, Arkansas still led 21-20. Hogs FB Glenn Hockersmith lost FUM to A&M HB-DB Tommy Maxwell at his 31YL, Hargett quickly hit Maxwell for 15y TD. Razorbacks had to punt on next possession, and Aggies T Harvey Aschenbeck blocked punt. A&M steamed 53y in 7 plays to TB Larry Stegent's 1y TD lunge with 7:04 left.

HOUSTON 15 Georgia 14: Georgia (5-2) QB Kirby Moore scored 8y TD in 2nd Q, and TB Kent Lawrence added 12y TD in 3rd Q. Tough Bulldogs D, led by LBs Happy Dicks and Tommy Lawhorne, collected 5 Houston (5-2) FUMs and appeared to have complete control at 14-0 at end of 3rd Q. Cougars trimmed it to 14-7, and when QB Dick Woodall clicked on 57y TD pass with less than 5 mins left, FB Paul Gipson (28/229y) swept for winning 2-pt run.

UCLA 16 Oregon State 16: Giant-killing Beavers (5-2-1) tied no. 2 UCLA (6-0-1) with last moment heroics. Bruins K Zenon Andrusyshun kicked 2 FGs, including school record 52y howitzer, for 13-7 H lead. Oregon State tied it 13-13 as HB Bill Main swept E for 9y TD, but K Mike Haggard had costly conv miss. Andrusyshun and Haggard traded FGs in seesaw 4th Q before QB Gary Beban (10-18/157y, INT) pitched Bruins into range for late FG try. Beavers DT Ron Boley blocked Andrusyshun's try in last 10 secs.

Stanford 14 WASHINGTON 7: Indians (4-4) lived by pass, and Huskies (5-3) died miserably by pass. QB Chuck Williams (9-20/108y, 2 TDs, INT) launched 57y TD bomb to WR Gene Washington in middle of 1st Q for 7-0 Stanford advantage. Washington QB Tom Manke, who was in spotlight of dismal 1-10/6y, 3 INTs passing effort, scored home team's only TD on run late in 1st Q: Manke caught Stanford D playing up close and slipped through RT and broke into clear for 81y TD. Winning TD came on E Jim Cross' 5y catch in 3rd Q. LB Andy Carrigan was credited with 18 tackles and pass block for Tribe and led vital stop early in 4th Q. Huskies needed only inch on 4th down at Stanford 4YL, but Indians D blasted ball-carrier for 1y loss.

AP Poll November 6

1 Southern California (39)	399	6 Indiana	160
2 Tennessee	308	7 Wyoming	130
3 North Carolina State	283	8 Oklahoma	101
4 UCLA	274	9 Notre Dame	96
5 Purdue (1)	248	10 Houston	37

Others with votes: Alabama, Army, Florida State, Georgia, Miami, Minnesota, Oregon State, Penn State, Syracuse, Texas, Yale

November 11, 1967

(Fri) MIAMI 49 Georgia Tech 7: It had been 24 years since injury-depleted Georgia Tech (4-4) had been thrashed so badly. After leading 14-7 at H, Miami (6-2) exploded with 2 TDs in 3rd Q by soph HB Vince Opalsky (7/95y, TD), including 72y burst off T. Hurricanes reserves pounded out 3 TDs in 4th Q to complete rout, Canes' 6th straight win of season. Miami QB David Olivo (6-12/84y, 2 TDs) pitched 2 TD passes, including 8y toss, which Opalsky caught for 1 of his key TDs. Only Yellow Jackets score came in 2nd Q and it sliced in half Canes' 14-0 lead: TB Bill Eastman, occasional QB in Tech's pasted-together lineup, found WR John Sias with 5y TD pass. Georgia Tech QB Kim King (8-24/125y, 2 INTs) returned from injury list, but lots of rust was revealed by 1 of nation's top Ds. Jackets were limited to 241y, while Miami romped for 440y total O.

PENN STATE 13 North Carolina State 8: Thrill of its highest-ever ranking was short-lived for no. 3 North Carolina State (8-1). Using surprise 3-WR set, Penn State (6-2) clicked on early 18y TD pass from QB Tom Sherman to TE Ted Kwalick. Nittany Lions LB Dennis Onkontz soon returned INT of Wolfpack QB Jim Donnan for 67y TD. K Gerald Warren's 2 FGs narrowed it to 13-6 in 3rd Q as Wolfpack mustered momentum. Lions DB Tim Montgomery had to make EZ INT with 7:40 to go, and LBs Onkontz and Jim Kates steadfastly halted NC State FB Settle Dockery's 4th down plunge at Lions 1YL in last min. Penn State gladly took intentional safety and resultant free-kick out of jam with 8 secs left.

Princeton 45 HARVARD 6: Tigers (6-1) fueled season-long Ivy League trend of turning anticipated cliffhangers into blowouts. Princeton FB Ellis Moore (31/138y) scored 5 times: leaping over line for 4 TDs and bursting 17y TD up middle. Harvard (5-2) might have provided stiffer competition but for 2nd Q FUM and INT lost by QB Ric Zimmerman, each time near Nassau GL. Not until it was 25-0 did Crimson tally on tricky 46y pass from HB Vic Gatto to QB Zimmerman.

Alabama 7 LOUISIANA STATE 6: Time and again, LSU (4-3-1) knocked ball loose from Crimson Tide (6-1-1) runners, only to have officials rule whistle had blown prior to Tigers REC. Early in 4th Q of 0-0 knot, LSU thought it stopped threat by jostling ball from Alabama HB Ed Morgan, but Tide FB David Chatwood kept 51y drive alive by making clutch REC at LSU 3YL. Morgan fumbled on next play but whistle killed Bengals' REC, so Morgan was able to blast over from 1YL on 3rd down. Tide K Steve Davis, who missed 3 FGs, made critical x-pt. LSU scored 4th Q TD on 4y run by HB Tommy "Trigger" Allen, but K Roy Hurd's tying x-pt missed to left when holder Freddie Haynes bobbled snap. Hurd had 43y FG try on last play, but missed. Red Elephant QB Kenny Stabler (9-16/83y, INT) was underwhelming, but he clicked on key 11 and 14y throws on winning drive.

Florida 17 Georgia 16 (Jacksonville): Favored Georgia (5-3) was able to enjoy cozy leads of 9-0 and 16-7. Bulldogs S Jake Scott's 21y 2nd Q punt RET led to 11y run by TB Kent Lawrence to short TD run by FB Ronnie Jenkins (12/46y, TD). But, tall Gators T Jim Hadley made critical block of conv kick. With H only 3:12 away, Florida (5-2) QB Larry Rentz (11-19/180y, 2 TDs, 2 INTs) rejuvenated Gators with 33y TD pass to WR Mike McCann to move within 9-7. Scott stepped in front of Rentz's pass in 3rd Q and dashed 32y for TD. Halfway into 4th Q, Florida WR Richard Trapp (9/171y, TD) took short pass, twisted and dodged 3 separate times for brilliant 52y score to draw within 16-14. UGa's tiring D came within inches of stopping Gators TB Larry Smith (23/78y) on 4th down at 14YL on late drive to K Wayne Barfield's winning 30y FG with :29 on clock.

OHIO STATE 17 Wisconsin 15: On-going Columbus jinx for woeful Badgers (0-7-1) was upheld again as Ohio State (4-3) QB Bill Long (7-21/139y) scored twice on ground and came through with ace plays. Smallest home crowd (65,470) since "Snow Bowl" of 1950 saw Wisconsin fail in Ohio Stadium where it hadn't won since 1918. Badgers QB John Boyajian (19-36/252y, 2 TDs, INT) hit E Mel Riddick with short TD pass in 1st Q, but x-pt hit upright, and miss would haunt Wisconsin. Buckeyes K Gary Cairns had made early FG, game's only pts, against 25-mph wind. Ohio went up 10-6 at H as Long hit 3 passes

before sprinting 14y only 4 secs before H. Boyajian arched 51y TD pass, and Badgers came out of its wind-aided 3rd Q with 15-10 lead. On 2nd play of 4th Q, Long's long pass to E Billy Anders gained 59y to Badgers 26YL. Long soon scored on 4y run.

PURDUE 41 Minnesota 12: Persistent Purdue (7-1) kept pace atop Big 10 standings with Indiana, while dropping Golden Gophers (6-2) out of 3-way tie. Minnesota, seeking its 1st-ever win at West Lafayette, bolted to early 10-7 lead on DE-K Bob Stein's 31y FG and WR Hubie Bryant's 57y TD sprint on reverse. Boilermakers HB Leroy Keyes (21/90y, and 6/65y receiving) negotiated slick field for 3 TDs in setting single season, to-date conf season record of 16 TDs. Running off astonishing 96 O plays, Purdue took control on Keyes' 2nd TD and QB Mike Phipps' 27y TD pass to E Jim Beirne, both coming in 2nd Q for 21-10 lead. When Keyes scored his 3rd TD in 4th Q, Boilermakers had earned 34-12 edge.

Indiana 14 MICHIGAN STATE 13: HB John Isenbarger (11/68y, TD) spent much of this hard-hitting affair banged up on Indiana (8-0) sideline but returned for decisive 69y drive on which he accounted for 59y. Keeping Hoosiers in bad field position, Spartans (2-6) led 3-0 at H on K Mitchell Pruiett's 24y FG in 2nd Q. Indiana finally broke through with 9-play, 70y TD voyage in 3rd Q as QB Harry Gonso (9-18/130y, 3 INTs) scored on run. Gonso was knocked down by Michigan State DT George Chatlos at Hoosiers 1YL and slid into EZ; officials surprisingly ruled it as safety. After free-kick, MSU barreled 51y in 5 plays to TD by HB Dwight Lee. When Spartans holder Chuck Wedemeyer jumped up from x-pt spot and threw 2-pt pass to E Al Brenner, Michigan State led 13-7 late in 3rd Q. Isenbarger returned midway in 4th Q to replace effective sub HB Mike Krivoshia (23/92y). Isenbarger ran 13y, caught pass for 15y, and added cutback run for 14y to Michigan State 24YL. FB Terry Cole gained 5y, Isenbarger 14y, and blocker Cole led Isenbarger across for winning TD with 2:50 to play. Indiana LB Ken Kaczmarek ended it right after KO with INT of Spartans QB Jimmy Raye (3-15/29y, INT).

COLORADO 12 Kansas 8: Hopeful of holding Big 8 lead, Kansas (4-4) clicked on 50y TD pass by QB Bobby Douglass in 1st Q. HB Don Shanklin immediately surprised Colorado (6-2) with 2-pt run. Buffs countered with 53y TD march in 2nd Q as QB Bob Anderson ran 10y, passed 9, 17y before HB Wilmer Cooks battered over on his 5th carry of last 6 plays. Douglass led Jayhawks' 79y drive with 44y strike to WB Junior Riggins, but advance died at Buffs 1YL as LB Kerry Mottl and DB Ike Howard led Colorado's GLS. Trailing 8-6 in 4th Q, Colorado traveled 46y in 8 plays as Cooks smashed 1y after Anderson hit E Monte Huber with 18y pass.

OREGON STATE 3 Southern California 0: Oregon State (6-2-1), grand spoiler of 1967, thrilled largest sports crowd ever assembled in Beaver State. K Mike Haggard's 30y FG in 2nd Q was all that was needed by superb Beaver D, led by DTs Ron Boley and Jess Lewis and LB Skip Vanderbundt. Top-ranked USC (8-1) sprung TB O.J. Simpson (33/188y) for 22y on its 1st snap, for 37y early in 2nd Q, but Oregon State held every time it was threatened. Contributing to win were P Gary Houser's 8/44y avg and FB Bill Enyart's 24/135y rushing, although Trojans enjoyed 200y to 196y ground edge.

AP Poll November 13

1 UCLA (19)	419	6 Wyoming	189
2 Tennessee (13)	390	7 Oklahoma	154
3 Purdue (8)	343	8 Oregon State (1)	145
4 Southern California (5)	330	9 Notre Dame	131
5 Indiana (1)	265	10 North Carolina State	84

Others with votes: Alabama, Army, Colorado, Houston, Miami, Minnesota, Nebraska, Penn State, Texas, Texas-El Paso

November 18, 1967

Yale 29 PRINCETON 7: Elis (7-1) wrapped up Ivy title, putting Tigers (6-2) in tank for 1st time since 1960. Ingenious Yale QB Brian Dowling (9-19/119y, 2 TDs, 3 INTs) threw plenty of long, wobbly passes, but still accounted for 4 scores. Early on, Dowling pitched out to HB Calvin Hill running right and slipped uncovered into Princeton secondary while Hill fired stunning 60y TD pass to Dowling for 7-0 advance. "We were ready for it," said Princeton coach Dick Colman, "but not on first down." Tigers answered with 74y TD drive capped by TB Dick Bracken's 2y run on 14th play of trip for 7-7 knot. Yale quickly responded with Dowling's 47y TD pass to TE Bruce Weinstein near end of 1st Q. Bulldogs D, led by T Steve Greenberg, son of former Detroit Tigers slugger, then took over. Elis LB Paul Tully scored 2nd Q safety by tossing back Bracken into EZ and also fell on punt blocked by DL Dick Williams at Tigers 30YL. Dowling shot 27y pass to Hill and skirted 3y to score with 14 secs to go before H. Dowling added his 2nd TD pass in 4th Q.

Army 21 PITTSBURGH 12: Gen William Westmoreland, U.S. commander in Vietnam, attended game, must have wondered about his future air D as Army (8-1) was bewitched for 3 Qs by passes of youthful Panthers. Pitt (1-8) started only 3 sr players, and 2 of them—QB Bob Bazylak (20-46/249y, 2 TDs, 4 INTs) and E Bob Longo—hooked up for TD passes in opening 5 mins and again just before H. Cadets trailed 12-7 entering 4th Q, but HB Lynn Moore handled ball for 7 of 8 plays on TD drive. QB Steve Lindell added 2-pt pass for 15-12 edge. Lindell scrambled for clinching TD in last 1:30 after DB Tom Wheelock picked off Bazylak's pass.

CLEMSON 14 North Carolina State 6: "They are in if they win," said Sugar Bowl pres Monk Simon in pre-game reference to North Carolina State (8-2). Wolfpack was encouraged by 6-0 lead in 2nd Q on K Gerald Warren's wind-aided 16th and 17th FGs of year, which broke NCAA record of Princeton's Charlie Gogolak set in 1965. While dreaming of New Orleans, NC State saw major bid blow up in 3rd Q as it chose to face 22 mph wind so it could benefit from 4th Q gusts. With 3rd Q wind, Clemson (5-4) briefly abandoned its run-block superiority for airborne TD as QB Jimmy Addison (4-8/77y, TD) hurled 28y TD pass to TB Buddy Gore, who beat stumbling Wolfpack LB Steve Diacont. Just 4 mins later, backup TB Jacky Jackson (96y rushing) ran for clinching TD from 7y out. Tigers called timeout to force NC State QB-P Jim Donnan, who earlier suffered 1y punt into wind, to face late-3rd Q gusts again. Donnan punted only 25y to Clemson 49YL, and although Tigers didn't score, they ran 6 mins off clock as workhorse Jackson lugged 10 straight plays to Wolfpack 9YL. NC State O, which made only 152y all day, was left at that point in hopeless hole.

Tennessee 20 Mississippi 7 (Memphis): Tennessee (7-1) moved closer to SEC crown with 1st success over Mississippi (4-3-1) since 1958. Waiting was Monday's Orange Bowl invitation, which Volunteers would happily pocket. Vols D, led by stellar soph LBs Jack Reynolds and Steve Kiner, kept Ole Miss running game sequestered at 52y. Tennessee TB Walter Chadwick (25/115y, TD) threw surprise, left-handed pass for 10y TD to E Terry Dalton at end of 56y 2nd Q trip, which opened door for 17-0 H lead. Tennessee DL Dick Williams pounced on 2 FUMs that led to 10 more pts in 2nd Q: Chadwick's 9y TD run and K Karl Kremser's 42y FG. After 1st H in which they made only solo 1st down, Rebels inserted soph QB Terry Collier, who generated some excitement until suffering INTs by Vols DBs Albert Dorsey and Jimmy Weatherford. Rebs went 41y to FB Bobby Wade's TD run midway in 3rd Q after DB Tommy James' INT of Vols QB Dewey Warren.

MINNESOTA 33 Indiana 7: Bubble burst on Indiana's perfect season as rampaging Minnesota (7-2) took inside track to its 3rd possible Rose Bowl in last 8 years. Trailing just 7-0 at H, but relinquishing heavy run y that would total 347y by game's end, Hoosiers (8-1) tied it 7-7 by going 76y after 2nd H KO to QB Harry Gonso's 1y TD run. Gophers answered with 68y drive as QB Curt Wilson (20/118y rushing) scored his 2nd TD in 3rd Q for 13-7 lead despite IU LB Jim Sniadecki blocking x-pt kick. Indiana's will was broken when it faltered at Gophers 26YL early in 4th Q: On 4th-and-9, Gonso ran option play, but didn't pitch to open HB John Isenbarger and gained only 5y. Then, in 20-pt spree, Wilson threw 17y TD to TE Charlie Sanders sandwiched between 2 more of his TD runs. Instrumental in Minnesota's rushing attack were RG Dick Enderle and RT John Williams who plowed over Hoosiers' left side for HB John Wintermute (23/135y) and FB Jim Carter (19/94y).

MISSOURI 10 Nebraska 7: Mizzou's 1st win in 5 years over Nebraska (6-3) officially dethroned Cornhuskers after 4 straight years as Big 8 champs. Tigers (7-2) held out chance to share conf honors as their D allowed mere 11y rushing and 161y in air. Nebraska HB Joe Orduna skyed high among 4 players for 34y TD catch to end aerial drive of 84y on which TE Dennis Richnafsky became school's all-time to-date season pass-catch leader with 33. Missouri DT-K Jay Wallace bombed 45y FG against wind in 2nd Q, so Huskers led 7-3 at H. After 2 plays of 3rd Q, Mizzou HB Jon Staggers lost FUM at his 25YL. Nebraska soon faced 4th-and-3 at 18YL, but coach Bob Devaney was misinformed that only 1 y was needed. Eschewing FG try, Huskers pushed Orduna ahead for only 1y, and that about ended their day on O. Early in 4th Q, DT Wallace partly blocked Nebraska P Dana Stephenson's punt that went 17y to Huskers 37YL. Tigers sub QB Garnett Phelps fired long pass, which Staggers hauled down for 38y TD. Missouri D, led by DE Elmer Bernhardt (6 sacks/41y), harassed QB Frank Patrick (12-20/161y, TD) without mercy.

OKLAHOMA 14 Kansas 10: Winner of 4 of its previous 5 games, expectant Kansas (4-5) charged off at H with 3-0 lead after K Bill Bell booted 23y FG. Slick Jayhawks D had held Oklahoma (7-1) to only 15y rushing in 1st H and later blocked 3rd Q punt. Kansas QB Bobby Douglass slipped into EZ behind RG on 4th down for 10-0 lead as 3rd Q drew near close. With its conf leadership in jeopardy, Sooner answered right back with TB Steve Owens' 7y TD run. Thrilling verdict was sealed on Sooners QB Bobby Warmack's 30y TD pass to TE Steve Zabel with 1:02 left. Oranges, sold in crates outside Owen Field, showered down as Oklahoma fans expressed their zeal for Orange Bowl trip.

Wyoming 21 TEXAS-EL PASO 19: Celebrating only their 2nd-ever appearance in AP Poll, Miners (5-2-1) went prospecting for upset gold against undefeated WAC champion Wyoming (10-0). UTEP led 13-3 at H on TD passes by sub QB Brooks Dawson to WR Volley Murphey and TE Ron Jones. Cowboys FB Tom Williams scored early in 4th Q, and, when Dawson soon lost FUM at own 6YL, Wyoming took 18-13 lead on QB Paul Toscano's TD pass. Cowboys lost lead at 19-18 when Murphey scored again, but counted on ace K Jerry Depoyster to win it with short FG inside in last 6 mins.

GAME OF THE YEAR
SOUTHERN CALIFORNIA 21 Ucla 20:

Before 90,772, no. 1 UCLA (7-1-1) and no. 4 Southern California (9-1) played for local, regional, and national glory. Bruins scored 1st as beneficiary of 18y punt by Troy P Rikki Aldridge that sliced OB at Trojan 47YL in 1st Q. QB Gary Beban connected on 12y pass, ran 11y to put HB Greg Jones in TD range at 12YL. Late in 1st Q, daring Beban (16-24/301y, 2 TDs, INT) erred with cross-field pass that Trojans DB Pat Cashman picked off for 55y TD RET. Bruins DB Mark Gustafson had 42y punt RET in 2nd Q, but K Zenon Andrusyshun's FG was tipped by tall USC DL Bill Hayhoe. Immediately, WR Earl McCullough put world-class speed to work for USC, racing 52y on reverse and catching 15y pass to position TB O.J. Simpson (30/177y) for 13y TD run. Hayhoe blocked another FG to maintain 14-7 H edge for USC. Beban pitched TD passes of 53y to E George Farmer and 20y to E Dave Nuttall. But after last TD, which came early in 4th Q, Hayhoe again got fingertip on Andrusyshun's conv kick to again send it wide. So, UCLA led 20-14. Within min of ensuing KO, incomparable Simpson swung wide from own 36YL and sprinted away from Bruins secondary, cut across field, and used McCullough's shielding block to author dramatic 64y TD run. Aldridge's kick made it 21-20, and Trojans D was left to harass Beban's comeback attempt in last 10 mins. He was sacked 4 times, including losses of 19y by DE Jimmy Gunn and 10y by Troy's other DE, Tim Rossovich.

California 26 STANFORD 3: While 6' 7" California (5-5) E Wayne Stewart may have been edged for Pac-8 receiving title by Indians (5-5) swift WR Gene Washington (10 catches), it was Stewart's 2 scoring grabs within 22 secs of each other in 4th Q that swung verdict to Golden Bears. Stanford led most of way since HB-K Bill Shoemaker's 33y FG in 1st Q. Mistake by Indians DB Dick Oliver created baseball-like score of 3-2 which held to H. Oliver went up near GL to pick off 2nd Q pass by Cal QB Randy Humphries, but stepped back into EZ for what he expected to be touchback. Instead, officials ruled it safety for Cal. After K Ron Miller put Bears ahead 5-3 with 24y FG in 3rd Q, Humphries and Stewart opened 4th Q with 10y pass high over Oliver's head for 10y TD. HB Nate Kirtman lost handle on ensuing KO at Tribe 21YL, and Stewart went high over Oliver again for 21y TD. It was California coach's Ray Willsey's 1st win in Big Game in 4 tries.

Oregon State 14 OREGON 10: Civil War comeback was required of Beavers (7-2-1) as Oregon (2-8) appeared poised to pull 1 of season's biggest upsets. Fresh from its tie and win over UCLA and USC respectively, Oregon State fell behind 10-0 to spiced-up Ducks. K Mark Scholl booted 27y FG for Oregon' s 3-0 H lead, and HB Claxton Welch plunged for short TD on 4th down play in 3rd Q. Fine play of Ducks LB Kent Grote, who recovered 3 FUMs, and DE Cam Molter, who blocked 2 punts, was sufficient for perhaps bigger lead, but Oregon D could not arrest Oregon State's big FB, Bill "Earthquake" Enyart (34/167y, TD), who pounded across for 4th Q TD at end of 80y trip. Drive was boosted by QB Steve Preece's 35y pass to HB Don Summers. Enyart carried load on 46y voyage to Preece's winning 4y rollout run with 2:30 to go.

ARIZONA STATE 31 Brigham Young 22: Cougars (5-4) started run-specialist Terry Sanford at QB and jumped to 9-0 lead on K Dennis Patera's 28y FG, after Monster-back Joe James' INT, and Sanford's only completion for 22y TD to WR Phil Odle. BYU went back to regular QB Marc Lyons (21-41/316y, TD, INT), who filled desert night with passes, but when he finally found TD range with 28y scoring heave in 4th Q, Arizona State (7-2) had collared 4 TDs and FG. Sun Devils sent WB J.D. Hill on 65y punt TD RET in 1st Q to ignite rally, and Hill added 33y TD pass reception. Blunt FB Max Anderson (24/151y, 2 TDs) scored on 22 and 1y runs as main cogs in ASU's 3-TD spurt in 7-min span of 2nd Q.

AP Poll November 20

1 Southern California (21)	432	6 Notre Dame	181
2 Tennessee (15)	410	7 Wyoming (1)	179
3 Purdue (9)	380	8 Oregon State	141
4 UCLA	329	9 Alabama	85
5 Oklahoma (1)	218	10 Houston	46

Others with votes: Army, Colorado, Florida, Florida State, Georgia, Indiana, Miami, Minnesota, Missouri, North Carolina State, North Texas State, Penn State, Texas A&M, Texas-El Paso, Yale

November 23-25, 1967

(Th'g) Oklahoma 21 NEBRASKA 14: Oklahoma (8-1) had been absent from Big 8 throne room for 5 years. Sooners earned 1967's conf crown with clutch TD in 4th Q and late-game INT at own 3YL. Opening KO FUM allowed Sooners K Mike Vachon to boot 1st of his 2 FGs. Trailing 13-0 in 2nd Q, Nebraska (6-4) scored both its TDs: QB Frank Patrick, who launched school-record 40 passes for 290y, carried for 1y TD, and threw 9y TD pass to WB Ben Gregory. So, Huskers led 14-13 until Oklahoma WB Eddie Hinton tallied winning TD early in 4th Q, and TE Steve Zabel caught 2-pt pass.

(Th'g) TEXAS A&M 10 Texas 7: With 6th win in row, Aggies (6-4) clinched their 1st SWC crown since 1956 and 1st Cotton Bowl berth since 1942. Texas A&M dominated 1st H but had only K Charlie Riggs' 32y FG to show for it. Texas (6-4) created 56y TD march in 4th Q on QB Bill Bradley's passing and TB Ted Koy's running. Bradley cashed it with 2y run for 7-3 lead. Aggies clutch QB Edd Hargett (10-17/203y, TD) quickly launched long pass to WR Bob Long who beat DB Ronnie Ehrig. Catching ball at Longhorn 36YL, Long dragged DB Pat Harkins into EZ to complete thrilling 80y play. Last Steers threat ended on Texas A&M LB Buster Adami's INT at his 15YL.

(Fri) Notre Dame 24 MIAMI 22: Record crowd at Orange Bowl stadium was delighted to see Notre Dame (8-2) stymied by muscular Miami (6-3) D in 1st H. In building 16-10 H lead, Canes got key contributions from DB Jimmy Dye's 49y punt RET, DL Jim Kresl's hard hit that created KO FUM, QB David Olivo's pair of TDs on pass and run. Fighting Irish rushing attack began to click in 3rd Q as FB Jeff Zimmerman ripped off good gains that led to his TD and 17-16 lead. ND DB John Pergine's INT set up HB Bob Gladieaux's 10y TD run in 4th Q. Doubt remained until Hurricanes failed on tying 2-pt pass with 3 mins to play.

YALE 24 Harvard 20: In narrow segment of 2nd Q, Yale (8-1) thrilled largest home crowd in 13 years with 17-0 jump on rival Harvard (6-3). Most spectacular score came on improvised TD pass by Eli QB Brian Dowling (5-19/153y, 2 TDs, 4 INTs), who otherwise was having poor day. Dowling scrambled deep behind line, flung pass to free-lancing HB Calvin Hill for 53y score. Crimson wrapped 2 TD drives of 80y around H break as QB Ric Zimmerman (14-29/289y, 2 TDs, INTs) provided aerial spark. Trailing 17-13, Harvard appeared to put it away at 20-17 on Zimmerman's 31y TD to E Carter Lord with 3:05 to play. Out of blue came Dowling's 66y TD pass to E Del Marting at 2:16 mark, but win was insecure until Crimson coughed up ball to LB Pat Madden at Yale 10YL in last moments.

CLEMSON 23 South Carolina 12: With its 4 losses coming vs. teams with combined 25-14-1 record, Clemson (6-4) finished undefeated in ACC and captured 6th conf crown in last 12 years. TB Buddy Gore rushed for 189y, becoming 1st Tiger to gain 1,000y in single season, and scored TD that helped build 10-0 H edge. In 3rd Q, Gore dashed 43y to set up QB Jimmy Addison's TD pass. On ensuing KO RET, South Carolina (5-5) DB Pat Watson fumbled ball away to Tiger DL Ronnie Ducworth at 24YL, and Addison's 12y TD run gave Clemson jolly 23-0 lead. Gamecocks got 2 late TDs from QB Mike Fair.

Tennessee 17 KENTUCKY 7: While its vaunted O was kept in check by spirited Kentucky (2-8), no. 2 Volunteers (8-1) used its ball-hawking secondary to gain 5 INTs, 2 of which led to short scoring drives and 10 pts. Because of LB Steve Kiner's INT, Volunteers required only 18y to move to opening 7-0 lead on 8y TD pass from QB Dewey Warren (10-16/126y, 2 TDs) to WB Bill Baker. Warren threw his 2nd TD pass at end of 68y drive later in 1st Q as sprint champion, WR Richmond Flowers, hauled screen pass to 29y TD behind ringing block of T John Boynton. Wildcats cinched up their D, led by DT Dick Palmer, in 2nd Q and dominated play by permitting no 1st downs until deep into 3rd Q. But, Kentucky drives were brought to abrupt stops by loss on downs at UT 32 and 34YLs until HB Dicky Lyons (29/165y, TD) broke away for 68y dash to 3YL and followed with TD run. K Karl Kremser made 30y FG in 4th Q when another INT of Cats QB Dave Bair (12-30/100y, 5 INTs) by Tennessee S Mike Jones set up short field at UK 27YL. Earlier, Jones lit out on 71y INT RET before being caught by Lyons at UK 19YL. "It sure is a long field they have up here, said Jones, "…the goal line kept getting farther away."

Florida State 21 FLORIDA 16: HB Larry Green provided surprise early spark for Florida State (7-2-1), which eyed Gator Bowl berth. Down 3-0 and pinned at own 4YL by Florida QB-P Harmon Wages' punt, Seminoles sprung Green for 17, 4, and 22y runs and 10y catch. That gave QB Kim Hammond room to dish 9y TD pass to HB Bill Moreman. Gators' FUM 2 min later set stage for Green runs that led to 14-3 H edge. Florida (6-3) narrowed it to 14-9 on TB Bob Christian's short TD in 3rd Q, but lost FUM at FSU 7YL in 4th Q. Hammond returned from injury to pitch 51, 38y passes to E Ron Sellers, 2nd went for clinching TD and 21-9 lead.

Ohio State 24 MICHIGAN 14: Although QB Bill Long (5-6/45y) clicked on 2 passes on early Ohio State (6-3) TD drive. Buckeyes reverted to old form by running ball on all other 1st H plays. Buckeyes gained 209y in 1st H as they built 21-0 lead as HB Rudy Hubbard (15/103y) roared for 22y TD behind T Dave Foley's block and later ran 12y. Long ripped 22y to Michigan (4-6) 3YL in 2nd Q and sneaked over. Owning only 2 1st downs, Wolverines finally powered 80y in dying moments of 2nd Q: E Jim Berline (8/89y, TD) took 6y TD pass from QB Dennis Brown (17-24/179y, 2 TDs, INT). Souped-up Michigan D held 6 inches from its GL in 3rd Q, and its O moved downfield in 4th Q until Ohio DB Tom Portsmouth was forced to make INT at own 1YL. Wolverines scored 6 plays after punt out, HB John Gabler earning TD on 13y pass. Michigan tried unsuccessful on-side KO, and Buckeyes expended 5 mins off clock on trip to K Gary Cairns' clinching 37y FG. Michigan HB Ron Johnson (20/96y) set new Big 10 season rush mark, topping 1000y.

INDIANA 19 Purdue 14: Indiana (9-1) completed storybook rags-to-riches season with stunning upset of no. 3 Purdue (8-2) to earn 3-way share of Big 10 title and trip to Rose Bowl. Minnesota joined Indiana and Purdue atop conf with 21-14 win over Wisconsin. Hoosiers sr FB Terry Cole, overshadowed much of year by his soph backfield mates, charged 42y to set up WR Jade Butcher's 7y TD catch and roared 63y in 2nd Q to provide 19-7 H lead. FB Perry Williams scored his 2nd TD for Boilermakers, and HB Leroy Keyes made 20/114y rushing before being injured in 4th Q. But, Purdue couldn't overcome 4 FUMs, especially pivotal bobble was lost at Indiana 1YL. Sparking Hoosiers D were LB Ken Kaczmarek, DB Dave Kornowa, and LB Brown Marks.

Syracuse 32 UCLA 14: Sr QB led his team to decisive victory in his last game. It was shocking that QB Rick Cassata of Syracuse (8-2) played the role of hero instead of UCLA's A-A QB Gary Beban. Cassata had hand in 4 TDs, passing 11-15/146y, 2 TDs, INT and rushing 19/119y, 2 TD. Ahead 13-0, Orangemen knocked out listless Bruins (7-2-1) and Beban early in 3rd Q. DL Dave Casmay flattened Beban for 20y loss, aggravated QB's rib injury, and created FUM REC at Bruins 17YL. Soon down 19-0, UCLA summoned sub QB BIll Bolden to mop up, and Bolden pitch 92y TD to E Ron Copeland. E Tom Coughlin, future Boston College and NFL coach, caught 4th Q 3y TD pass, made exciting by Cassata's retreat of 20y behind scrimmage line.

Final AP Poll November 27

1 Southern California (36)	474	6 Wyoming (1)	222
2 Tennessee (11)	436	7 Oregon State	154
3 Oklahoma	311	8 Alabama	152
4 Indiana	245	9 Purdue	150
5 Notre Dame (1)	243	10 Penn State	98

Others with votes: Arizona State, Army, Colorado, Florida State, Louisiana State, Miami, Minnesota, North Carolina State, Syracuse, Texas A&M, Texas-El Paso, UCLA

December 2, 1967

Navy 19 Army 14 (Philadelphia): Navy (5-4-1) sprung I-formation ball control on Army (8-2). "...We decided to take a beating (4 early losses), and keep our surprises for Army," said coach Bill Elias. Sr Middies QB John Cartwright threw enough to be able to bow out with 19-29/240y in air, while masterminding 3 scoring marches for 17-0 lead in 2nd Q. Navy sailed 59y to K John Church's FG, 45y to HB Dan Pike's short TD, and 92y to HB Jeri Balsly's 13y TD run. , Cadets seemed beaten at 19-0 in 4th Q, but turned to oft-injured QB Jim O'Toole, who sparked 51y drive to HB Lynn Moore's TD run. After Navy punt, O'Toole arched 52y TD bomb to TE Gary Steele. Poor punt gave now-excited Army its last chance at Navy 27YL with less than 7 mins on clock, but Cadets lost FUM to Middies LB Ray DeCarlo at 20YL and never saw ball again.

TENNESSEE 41 Vanderbilt 14: No. 2 Volunteers (9-1) won their 1st SEC crown since 1956 and nailed down Orange Bowl bid. QB Dewey Warren threw sparingly but smartly picked apart Vandy D for 5-6/132y in gaining 24-0 H lead and sat out 2nd H. Warren got matters off winging by clicking with WB Richmond Flowers on 64y aerial to Vandy 3YL. It was soon followed by Tennessee TB Walter Chadwick's 3y TD dive. Chadwick scored again in 2nd Q, raising his TD total to 11 for season. Trailng 24-0, tricky Commodores (2-7-1) opened 2nd H with dandy on-side KO and drove 47y to 1y TD run by HB John Valput. Vanderbilt E Bob Goodridge (13/105y) extended his to-date conf single-season receiving record to impressive 79/1114y.

SOUTHERN METHODIST 26 Texas Christian 14: Small Dallas crowd huddled together in chilly north wind and was left to ponder what might have been for SMU (3-7), had superb QB Mike Livingston (26-41/323y, 3 TDs, INT) been available during mid-season 7-game losing streak. With wind at their backs, Mustangs tallied 3 TDs in 1st Q, 2 on passes by Livingston. When Texas Christian (4-6) took over in 2nd Q with gusts helping it, Frogs QB P.D. Shabay (9-15/153y, INT) quickly fired 51y pass to E Bill Ferguson to set up TB Russ Montgomery's 1y TD run. When Montgomery scored just 4 mins later, it looked like gusty shootout. But, SMU D, led by LB Bruce Portillo's 2 INTs and FUM REC, took ball away from Frogs twice in its own end in 3rd Q. Mustangs waited to regain 4th Q wind advantage and took immediate charge with Livingston's 37y TD pass to HB Jim Hagle on 1st play.

December 9, 1967

MIAMI 20 Florida 13: LB Ken Corbin ran back INTs for 80 and 45y TDs as Hurricanes (7-3) D fulfilled its pledge to "get to" Gators QB Larry Rentz, former Miami HS hero who had enjoyed perfect 17-0 record in his games at Orange Bowl stadium. Miami went up 20-0

in 3rd Q as DB Jimmy Dye raced 79y with punt RET to set up HB Vince Opalsky's 2y TD run. QB Harmon Wages relieved Rentz late in 3rd Q and pitched 4th Q TD pass to WR Guy McTheny, and HB Larry Smith added late window-dressing TD for Gators.

1967 Conference Standings

Ivy League

Yale	7-0
Dartmouth	5-2
Cornell	4-2-1
Harvard	4-3
Princeton	4-3
Pennsylvania	2-5
Brown	1-5-1
Columbia	0-7

Atlantic Coast

Clemson	6-0
North Carolina State	5-1
South Carolina	4-2
Virginia	3-3
Wake Forest	3-4
Duke	2-4
North Carolina	2-5
Maryland	0-6

Southern

West Virginia (a)	4-0-1
East Carolina	4-1
Richmond	5-2
William & Mary	2-2-1
Virginia Military	2-3
Furman (b)	2-3
Citadel	2-4
Davidson	1-5

(a) Win vs. Villanova counted in SC
(b) Win vs. Lehigh counted in SC

Southeastern

Tennessee	6-0
Alabama	5-1
Florida	4-2
Mississippi	4-2-1
Georgia	3-2
Louisiana State	3-2-1
Auburn	3-3
Kentucky	1-6
Vanderbilt	0-5

Big Ten

Indiana	6-1
Purdue	6-1
Minnesota	6-1
Ohio State	5-2
Illinois	3-4
Michigan	3-4
Michigan State	3-4
Northwestern	2-5
Iowa	0-6-1
Wisconsin	0-6-1

Mid-American

Toledo	5-1
Miami (Ohio)	4-2
Western Michigan	4-2
Ohio	4-2
Bowling Green	2-4
Kent State	2-4
Marshall	0-6

Big Eight

Oklahoma	7-0
Colorado	5-2
Kansas	5-2
Missouri	4-3
Nebraska	3-4
Oklahoma State	3-4
Iowa State	1-6
Kansas State	0-7

Southwest

Texas A&M	6-1
Texas Tech	5-2
Texas	4-3
Texas Christian	4-3
Arkansas	3-3-1
Southern Methodist	3-4
Rice	2-5
Baylor	0-6-1

Western Athletic

Wyoming	5-0
Arizona State	4-1
Brigham Young	3-2
Utah	2-3
Arizona	1-4
New Mexico	0-5

AAWU

Southern California	6-1
UCLA	4-1-1
Oregon State	4-1-1
California	2-3
Stanford	3-4
Washington	3-4
Oregon	1-5
Washington State	1-5

1967 Major Bowl Games

Liberty Bowl (Dec. 16): North Carolina State 14 Georgia 7

In winning its 1st-ever bowl game, North Carolina State (9-2) survived 2 4th Q sorties by Georgia (7-4) to within shadow of Wolfpack goalposts. Although Bulldogs finished with 276y to 207y O advantage, their early game attack added up only to 2 missed FGs. It took Wolfpack QB Jim Donnan's 2nd Q TD pass to spur Georgia, which responded immediately with TB Kent Lawrence's 42y KO RET. Bulldogs FB Ronnie Jenkins soon tied it at 7-7. NC State earned winning TD early in 4th Q when HB Tony Barchuk polished 73y drive with TD plunge. NC State DB Bill Morrow stopped 4th down play at own 1YL, thus frustrating 98y Bulldogs march. Shortly, Georgia special teamer Gary Adams blocked punt, but QB Kirby Moore missed 4 straight passes from Wolfpack 9YL, last of which was dropped in EZ.

Bluebonnet Bowl (Dec. 23): Colorado 31 Miami 21

Hobbled by bad ankle, Colorado (9-2) QB Bob Anderson watched DB brother Dick play superbly in Buffs secondary. Miami (7-4) built 14-10 lead primarily on 77y INT TD RET by gutty DB Jimmy Dye, who played with broken jaw. QB Anderson was summoned from bench in last min of 1st H and sparked Bison attack with 2 and 38y TD runs in 2nd H. Hurricanes went to bullpen, too, inserting sub QB Bill Miller, who provided brief 21-17 lead in 4th Q when he pitched 9y TD to E Jerry Daanen. Anderson (5-10/49y, and 17/108y rushing) put Colorado ahead for good with his long TD run.

Gator Bowl (Dec. 30): Florida State 17 Penn State 17

Penn State (8-2-1) coach Joe Paterno created versatile D alignment to combat Florida State (7-2-2) air game, using occasional 5th DB. It worked magically until Penn State's unusual gamble on O backfired. Lions led 17-0 on QB-K Tom Sherman's FG and his TD passes to E Jack Curry and TE-turned-WB Ted Kwalick. Seminoles fashioned effective drive early in 3rd Q, but were stopped on downs at Lions 6YL. When Penn

State faced 4th-and-1 at their 15YL, Paterno decided to go for it, but failed. FSU overcame PEN to register 20y TD pass to WR Ron Sellers from QB Kim Hammond (37-53/362y). HB Charlie Pittman lost FUM on following KO, and Hammond's sneak made it 17-14 only 4 plays later. Starting from own 32YL with 1:30 left, FSU tied it on K Grant Guthrie's 25y FG with 15 secs left.

Sun Bowl (Dec. 30): Texas-El Paso 14 Mississippi 7

Little known Texas-El Paso (7-2-1) made rare bowl headlines just 16 months after basketball team won its only NCAA championship. Ole Miss (6-4-1) D sparkled in 1st H as DLs Dan Sartin and Mac McClure made big plays in holding UTEP to 15y rushing and Miners QB Billy Stevens to 3-9/26y passing. Key play was McClure's 2nd Q 47y INT RET of overthrown flat pass. Rebels QB Bruce Newell sneaked for 7-0 lead 2 plays later. Stevens (13-26/155y, TD, INT) got hot early in 4th Q, completing 6-7/75y on 76y march. UTEP LB Fred Carr jarred ball loose from Mississippi HB Bo Bowen at Rebels 22YL, and HB Larry McHenry lugged ball on 4 straight runs for Miners' winning TD.

Cotton Bowl: Texas A&M 20 Alabama 16

Classic matchup of student-teacher went to coach Gene Stallings of Texas A&M (7-4), 1-time player and asst coach under Bear Bryant. Aggies' victory formula, converting TOs into TDs, was precisely what Bryant had preached in 23 years as coach at Maryland, Kentucky, Texas A&M, and Alabama. Crimson Tide (8-2-1) had opened scoring with 1st of QB Ken Stabler's 2 TD runs. A&M QB Edd Hargett (11-22/143y, 2 TD) tied it 7-7 on 13y TD pass to HB Larry Stegent. HB Wendell Housley sealed Tide's fate with 20y TD sprint for 20-10 Texas A&M advantage in 3rd Q. Bryant cited missed 2-pt run after Stabler's ensuing TD run as it could have changed game as Bama moved to within 20-16 in 3rd Q. As clock wound down to end, Bryant crossed field to greet Stallings and bear-hugged his friend high off ground in admiration. Dramatic Texas Aggies joined football's all-time in-season comeback artists, sweeping their last 7 games after opening 0-4.

Sugar Bowl: Louisiana State 20 Wyoming 13

Wyoming (10-1) appeared on way to its 1st major bowl win as it rolled up 13-0 H lead on muddy field in New Orleans. Balanced Cowboys attack employed HB Jim Kiick (19/78y) and FB Tom Williams (16/64y) on ground, and QB Paul Toscano (14-23/239y) in air. Outstanding K Jerry DePoyster booted 2 FGs, including to-date Sugar-Bowl-record 49y 3-ptr. Wyoming looked for kill when it faced 3rd-and-1 decision in 3rd Q. Coach Lloyd Eaton called for unsuccessful pass, and tide turned toward deeper squad of LSU (7-3-1). Off bench came Tigers soph HB Glenn Smith to capture MVP honors with 17/74y rushing and important 39y reception. Smith scored TD at end of 80y drive late in 3rd Q, then sparked 2 TD marches in 4th Q. LSU QB Nelson Stokley threw 2 TD passes to E Tommy Morel, 2nd of which came with 4:22 left and ended Wyoming's 14-game winning streak.

Rose Bowl: Southern California 14 Indiana 3

In front of largest to-date Rose Bowl crowd, national champion Southern California (10-1) sprung TB O.J. Simpson on underdog Indiana (9-2) with expected results. Taking player-of-game award, Simpson rushed 25/128y, 2 TDs, earned plaudits from losing coach John Pont as the player who made USC nation's clear-cut best team. Yet, stunting and blitzing Hoosiers had their moments on D: their gang-tackling limited Simpson's longest run to 15y. USC created 84y TD march to Simpson's TD run in 1st Q that featured QB Steve Sogge's 3 completions for 42y. Trojans FB Dan Scott (18/85y) lost FUM into Indiana EZ while trying to cross GL. It spoiled another chance for Men of Troy, and this break recharged overmatched Hoosiers in 2nd Q. Indiana used QB Harry Gonso's 26y punt RET and his 15y pass to WR Jade Butcher to position K Dave Kornowa for 27y FG. USC led 7-3 at H. Simpson keyed 45y drive in 3rd Q, scoring behind blocks of T Ron Yary and G Dennis Born. Indiana got going in 4th Q with 53 and 50y marches. But, Gonso got banged up and had to depart briefly, and Hoosiers' initial drive of 4th Q was derailed. Trojans' strong D stopped 2nd IU advance at USC 28YL.

Orange Bowl: Oklahoma 26 Tennessee 24

Storming Sooners (10-1) dominated 1st H to tune of 19-0 as nation's top-rated D (6.8 pts per game) recovered FUM and made INT to create TDs. Lean QB Bobby Warmack accounted for 188y O in 1st H, making 7y TD run and 20y TD pass to WB Eddie Hinton. Warmack suffered 2 INTs in 2nd H, 1st resulting in LB Jimmy Glover's 36y TD RET, while his 2nd set up another Volunteers TD by TB Charles Fulton. K Karl Kremser's 26y FG brought Tennessee (9-2) to within 19-17 in 4th Q. Vols QB Dewey Warren (12-24/160y, 3 INTs), who helped spark rally, soon tossed ill-fated flat pass. OU DB Bob Stephenson stepped in front of it, dashed 25y to score killing TD for 26-17 lead. But it wasn't over. Warren narrowed it to 26-24 with late sneak. With just less than 2 mins to play, Oklahoma coach Chuck Fairbanks inexplicably called for 4th-and-1 run by TB Steve Owens from own 43YL. LB Jack Reynolds hammered Owens in backfield, and Vols earned their last chance. K Kremser was wide right with 43y FG try with :07 showing on clock.

1967 Top Performance Formula

1 Southern California	1.6464
2 Oklahoma	1.5941
3 Wyoming	1.5486
4 Purdue	1.5414
5 Notre Dame	1.5139
6 UCLA	1.4940
7 Penn State	1.4755
8 Tennessee	1.4668
9 Houston	1.4605
10 Florida State	1.4513
11 Alabama	1.4410
12 North Carolina State	1.4165
13 Arizona State	1.4015
14 Colorado	1.3887
15 Oregon State	1.3769
16 Louisiana State	1.3725
17 Syracuse	1.3441
18 Indiana	1.3278
19 Miami	1.3030
20 Minnesota	1.3027

1967 Top Opponent Records

1 Florida State	.6667
2 Mississippi State	.6330
3 UCLA	.6290
4 Michigan State	.6209
5 Kentucky	.6105
6 Purdue	.6044
7 Alabama	.6019
8 Arizona	.5978
9 Southern California	.5900
10 Mississippi	.5891
11 Pittsburgh	.5879
12 Miami	.5784
13 Brigham Young	.5778
14 Maryland	.5774
15 Oregon State	.5769
16 Louisiana State	.5762
17 Kansas	.5753
18 Penn State	.5746
19 Washington State	.5707
20 Auburn	.5691

1967 Out-of-Conference Records

	W-L	Percentage	Bowl W-L
Big Eight	16-9-1	.6346	2-0
AAWU	18-12	.6000	1-0
Western Athletic	16-14	.5333	0-1
Southeastern	22-20-2	.5227	1-4
Big Ten	12-18	.4000	0-1
Southwest	8-18	.3077	1-0
Atlantic Coast	8-20	.2857	1-0

1967 Individual Statistical Leaders

RUSHING YARDS	Attempts	Yards	Avg.
O.J. Simpson, Southern California	266	1415	5.3
Max Anderson, Arizona State	191	1188	6.2
Larry Csonka, Syracuse	261	1127	4.3
Doug Dalton, New Mexico State	177	1123	6.3
Paul Gipson, Houston	187	1100	5.9
Buddy Gore, Clemson	230	1045	4.5
Chris Gilbert, Texas	205	1019	5.0
Ron Johnson, Michigan	220	1005	4.6
Leroy Keyes, Purdue	149	986	6.6
Oscar Reed, Colorado State	213	910	4.3

PASSING YARDS	Completions	Attempts	Yards	Pct.
Sal Olivas, New Mexico State	156	321	2225	48.6
Kim Hammond, Florida State	140	241	1991	58.1
Terry Stone, New Mexico	160	336	1946	47.6
Mike Phipps, Purdue	118	243	1800	48.6
Paul Toscano, Wyoming	134	241	1791	55.6
Mike Livingston, Southern Methodist	152	250	1750	60.8
John Schneider, Toledo	127	245	1650	51.8
Tom Sherman, Penn State	104	205	1616	50.7
John Cartwright, Navy	129	241	1537	53.5
Frank Patrick, Nebraska	116	233	1449	49.8

RECEIVING YARDS	Catches	Yards
Ron Sellers, Florida State	70	1228
Rick Eber, Tulsa	78	1168
Bob Goodridge, Vanderbilt	79	1114
Ace Hendricks, New Mexico	67	1094
Phil Odle, Brigham Young	77	971
Dennis Homan, Alabama	54	820
Rob Taylor, Navy	61	818
Leroy Keyes, Purdue	45	758
Jerry Levias, Southern Methodist	57	724
Larry Davis, Rice	54	708
Richard Trapp, Florida	58	7

1967 Consensus All-America Team

Offense

End:	Dennis Homan, Alabama
	Ron Sellers, Florida State
Tackle:	Edgar Chandler, Georgia
	Ron Yary, Southern California
Guard:	Harry Olszewski, Clemson
	Rich Stotter, Houston
Center:	Bob Johnson, Tennessee
Back:	Gary Beban, UCLA
	Leroy Keyes, Purdue
	O. J. Simpson, Southern California
	Larry Csonka, Syracuse

Defense

End:	Ted Hendricks, Miami
	Tim Rossovich, Southern California
Tackle:	Dennis Byrd, North Carolina State
Guard:	Granville Liggins, Oklahoma
	Wayne Meylan, Nebraska
Linebacker:	Adrian Young, Southern California
	Don Manning, UCLA
Back:	Frank Loria, Virginia Tech
	Tom Schoen, Notre Dame
	Bobby Johns, Alabama
	Dick Anderson, Colorado

1967 Heisman Trophy Vote

Gary Beban, senior quarterback, UCLA	1968
O.J. Simpson, junior tailback, Southern California	1722
Leroy Keyes, junior halfback, Purdue	1366
Larry Csonka, senior fullback, Syracuse	136
Kim Hammond, senior quarterback, Florida State	90

Other Major Awards

Maxwell (Player):	Gary Beban, senior quarterback, UCLA
Walter Camp (Back):	O.J. Simpson, junior tailback, Southern California
Outland (Lineman):	Ron Yary, senior tackle, Southern California
Knute Rockne (Lineman):	Ron Yary, senior tackle, Southern California
AFCA Coach of the Year:	John Pont, Indiana

1968

The Year of the Greatest Sophomore Class, Unveiling of the Wishbone, and a 29-29 Win

There was never anything quiet about the coaching career of Woody Hayes, who compiled a 205-61-10 record in 28 years from 1951 to 1978 at Ohio State. Loudly opinionated, thunderously protective of his team, and always controversial, Hayes nonetheless snuck up on the Big Ten in the closing weeks of 1967. After a 1-2 start, the Buckeyes won five of their last six games, and only a late-game touchdown by Illinois prevented Ohio State from taking a four-way share of the league title. Nobody in the Big Ten, not even 1968 AP pre-season no. 1 Purdue (8-2), was prepared for the dynamic addition of almost certainly the greatest sophomore class in football history that arrived at Ohio State (10-0) in 1968. Among the stars that arrived on the Buckeye varsity that year were quarterback Rex Kern, tight end Jan White, halfbacks John Brockington, Leophus Hayden and Larry Zelina, split end Bruce Jankowski, defensive backs Jack Tatum, Tim Anderson and Mike Sensibaugh, linebacker Doug Adams, and middle guard Jim Stillwagon. Since half of them hailed from outside Ohio, much credit was owed to Lou McCullough, Hayes' recruiting coordinator.

Purdue was flying high with all-around star Leroy Keyes after beating no. 2 Notre Dame (7-2-1) in late September. But, Ohio State blanked the Boilermakers in mid-October and wrapped up an undefeated regular season with a smashing 50-14 win over rival Michigan (8-2). The win over Michigan inched the Buckeyes ahead of undefeated Southern California (9-1-1) as the top-rated team in the AP poll. A week later, on Thanksgiving Saturday, USC was tied by then-no.-9 Notre Dame, which had seen its season slip away with a loss to Michigan State (5-5).

When Ohio State beat USC in convincing fashion in the Rose Bowl, the Buckeyes were clear-cut national champions. After several years of waffling, the AP writers staged their final poll after bowl results were finished, a sensible practice that finally and forever embraced the bowl results.

During spring practice, coach Darrell Royal of Texas (9-1-1) pondered a way of getting his two outstanding fullbacks, Ted Koy and Steve Worster, sufficient playing time. The solution was provided by assistant coach Emory Bellard, who created a full-house backfield alignment with the fullback's position moved up closer to the quarterback. After an opening tie with Houston (6-2-2) and loss to Texas Tech (5-3-2), the "Y formation" or "Wishbone," as it became known, rolled to an impressive average of 37.4 points per game. Quarterback James Street became triggerman to launch a three-year, 30-game win streak, replacing "Super Bill" Bradley, who moved first to split end, then defensive back in time to pick off four passes in one game.

Perhaps no other offensive formation impacted college football so greatly during the last 55 years, both for the good and the bad. When the Wishbone was run with speed and daring, it was a magnificent show. Refer to the Oklahoma Wishbone masterminded by quarterbacks Thomas Lott, J.C. Watts, and Jamielle Holieway as an example. But, in the mid-to-late 1970s the vast majority of teams used the Wishbone offense, and when it fell into the hands of mediocre teams with backs who ran with average speed, it could be as dull as decade-old hedge clippers. Pro fans were even in a position to mock their college football friends. Ugh, the Wishbone! It permitted many people, especially those self-appointed social arbiters in the media, to look down on the college brand of football unless offenses mirrored the NFL style of attack that featured multiple receivers.

The surprise team of 1968 was Kansas (9-2), which, like Ohio State, had made quiet progress at the end of the 1967 season under new coach Pepper Rodgers. With quarterback Bobby Douglass and defensive ends Mike Zook and Vernon Vanoy leading most of the team back in 1968, Kansas charged to a 7-0 start before a narrow loss to Oklahoma (7-4). The Jayhawks locked up the Big Eight title and their best season in 60 years when defensive back Dave Morgan scored on a pass interception and recovered a fumble that led to the deciding score in a 21-19 win over Missouri (8-3).

The Orange Bowl matched Kansas with undefeated Penn State (11-0) and produced one of the oddest finishes in bowl history. Trailing 14-7, the Nittany Lions completed a desperate 48-yard pass leading to a touchdown with 15 seconds remaining. But, they failed on a two-point conversion attempt for the win. A penalty for having 12 men on the field cut short the Kansas celebration, and halfback Bobby Campbell quickly swept around end for the winning two points. A review of game films showed Penn State had run several plays and scored its touchdown against a 12-man defense.

Forlorn linebacker Rick Abernathy turned out to be the extra man on the field.

Two other Eastern teams supplied an even more exciting finish than the Orange Bowl. "The Game," the annual Harvard and Yale Ivy League encounter, saw both teams arrive undefeated and vying for the conference championship. Yale (8-0-1) built a 22-0 first half lead as wonderful quarterback Brian Dowling accounted for three touchdowns. Despite six fumbles, the Bulldogs led comfortably at 29-13 until Harvard (8-0-1) scored a touchdown with 42 seconds left. A two-point conversion and on-side kick suddenly gave the Crimson hope. Unknown back-up quarterback Frank Champi threw a scoring pass to halfback Vic Gatto on the game's last play and amazingly followed with a tying two-pointer to end Pete Varney. On Monday, *The Harvard Crimson* ran a front-page story on their team's miraculous 16 points in 42 seconds with a memorable headline: "Harvard Beats Yale, 29-29."

In some ways too, the thrilling tie was the last flickering moment for the glory days of Ivy League football. With each succeeding season until Ivy administrators demoted their brand of ball to Division 1-AA, but with disdain even for the 1-AA playoffs, Ivy Leaguers were to draw more into their ivy-covered towers and continue to preach against football as something that inhibited academic excellence. Football for Ivy Leaguers, since they pulled themselves into isolation in 1956, had come to define the symbol of athletic excess. Yet Ivy League schools continued to permit athletes from a wide variety of other unpublicized sports to participate in NCAA championships and travel far from the classroom to compete. Somehow it is permissable to allow the rowing crews, generally an Ivy sport in which the "Ancient Eight" had been and continues to be reasonably competitive on a national basis, to practice every single day of the school year. It is ironic even today that the very people who lead the chorus in singing praises of college providing a widely-expanded student horizon are the very same to have identified a Flat Earth Policy for the sport they invented.

Houston (6-2-2) dropped an unholy 100-6 drubbing on Tulsa (3-7) on November 23 as the Golden Hurricane suffered through a team-wide bout with the flu. It was the first 100-point winning total in any game involving at least one University Division team since 1949. Interestingly, after fewer than 10 100-point games in the 1800s when Ivy League teams ruled over nearly all big routs, the century scoring mark became more common in the 1900-1925 era than winning totals of today's college basketball teams. There were nearly 70 games with a team reaching 100 points during 1900-25 because it was a period of considerable shakeout. Tiny, but ambitious schools tested themselves—with mostly awful results—against reigning powerhouses. Among those blanked in 100-point loses were Marion Institute (110-0 to Alabama), Alabama Presbyterian (108-0 to Georgia), Cumberland in its famous all-time-high 222-0 disaster against Georgia Tech, Ursinus (127-0 to Navy), American Medical (142-0 to Notre Dame), Kingfisher (twice a loser to Oklahoma by 179-0 and 157-0), and Shawnee Catholic and Oklahoma Mines which lost in consecutive 1920 season-opening games by 121-0 and 151-0 to, ironically, Tulsa, football's last century-mark victim in 1968.

Milestones

■ West Virginia left ever-deemphasized Southern Conference for independence.

■ Western Athletic Conference added Colorado State and Texas-El Paso to bring its membership to eight schools.

■ Memphis State joined Missouri Valley Conference.

■ Athletic Association of Western Universities dropped its name in favor of Pacific-Eight.

■ Associated Press returned to top 20 poll after seven years of naming top 10 teams. Writers poll also established a post-bowl game final poll, a practice that has been in place ever since.

■ Rutgers' Homer Hazel, first player to be named to Walter Camp All-America teams at different positions, end in 1923 and fullback in 1924, died at age 72. Bill Hollenback, dead at 82, was 1908 All-America halfback at Pennsylvania, and later coached at Penn State, Missouri, and Syracuse (1909-16). Another Ivy League All-America in 1925, Dr. Andrew "Swede" Oberlander of Dartmouth, died at 62. Lawrence "Moon" Mullins died at age 60, having been star fullback under coach Knute Rockne at Notre Dame in 1928-30. Active NFL player Ron Rector, former Northwestern fullback, died in motorcycle accident at 24. Pat Trammell, 29, Alabama's national champion quarterback in 1961, succumbed to cancer.

■ Longest winning streaks entering season:
Oklahoma, Yale 8   Texas A&M 7

■ Coaching Changes:

	Incoming	Outgoing
Boston College	Joe Yukica	Jim Miller
Columbia	Frank Navarro	Buff Donelli
Hawaii	Dave Holmes	Don King
Iowa State	Johnny Majors	Clay Stapleton
New Mexico	Rudy Feldman	Bill Weeks
Utah	Bill Meek	Mike Giddings
Washington State	Jim Sweeney	Bert Clark

Preseason AP Poll

1 Purdue (14)	567	11 Ohio State	188
2 Southern California (10)	549	12 Texas A&M	186
3 Notre Dame (3)	542	13 Indiana	103
4 Oklahoma	331	14 Nebraska	88
5 Texas (3)	330	15 Minnesota	72
6 Oregon State (2)	271	16 Miami	50
7 Florida (1)	269	17 Arizona State	44
8 Penn State	198	18 Louisiana State	35
9 Tennessee	195	19 Syracuse	31
10 Alabama	192	20 Miami	29

September 14, 1968

North Carolina State 10 WAKE FOREST 6: Quiet 1st H marked dedication of handsome Groves Stadium before full house in Winston-Salem. North Carolina State (1-0) used K Gerald Warren's 34y 3rd Q FG for 3-0 lead, clinching win with 1:53 to play when QB Jack Klebe (3-12/20y) capped 45y drive with 1y TD run. Amazingly, Warren, previous year's leading 3-pt kicker, missed 5 FG tries to underscore Wolfpack's squandered scoring chances. Wake Forest (0-1) lost 4 FUMs and threw INT, but gave home fans late thrill with 45y drive, opened by DB Jake Whitley's 35y punt RET, on which sub FB Lee Clymer scored on game's last play. Supposedly-explosive Deacons O, fizzled as QB Freddie Summers (9-20/130y, INT) was pinched into center of field and gained only 14/2y rushing.

TENNESSEE 17 Georgia 17: Event was marked by ballyhooed introduction of Tartan Turf for 1st-ever, on-campus football game on synthetic grass. Surface was intended, in part, to reduce leg injuries, but conventional wisdom changed over time. Good D and great punting highlighted 1st H as Tennessee (0-0-1) led 7-0 on short TD run by TB Mike Jones. DB Jake Scott weaved 90y with punt TD RET, and FB Bruce Kemp barreled 80y to TD behind crushing open-field block of WB Craig Elrod, so Georgia (0-0-1) led 17-9 with 8 min left. Volunteers charged 80y in last 2:30 with QB Bubba Wyche hitting WR Gary Kreis with 21y TD on game's last play and TE Ken DeLong with tying 2-pt pass.

NEBRASKA 13 Wyoming 10: Nebraska (1-0) coach Bob Devaney started season against his old team, but he might have entertained 2nd thoughts by way Cowboys started out. Wyoming (0-1) opened with 10-0 1st Q lead on K Bob Jacobs' 35y FG and soph QB Ed Snyakowski's arched 54y TD pass to HB Gene Huey. Still trailing 10-3 in 4th Q, Devaney looked for spark from sub QB Ernie Sigler, who pitched tying 17y TD to TE Jim McFarland after his 23y scramble initiated 71y drive. Huskers moved into position for K Paul Rogers to win it with 51y FG with 21 secs on clock.

AP Poll September 16

1 Purdue (14)	584	11 Houston	136
2 Southern California (8)	536	12 Tennessee	118
3 Notre Dame (2)	488	13 Texas A&M	116
4 Texas (2)	388	14 Nebraska	106
5 Oklahoma	280	15 Indiana	100
6 Florida	266	16 Minnesota	68
7 Alabama (2)	244	16t UCLA	68
8 Oregon State	212	18 Georgia	62
9 Ohio State	162	19 Miami	42
10 Penn State	148	20 Louisiana State	32

September 21, 1968

WAKE FOREST 20 Clemson 20: After poor performance in opener, exciting QB Freddie Summers darted for 2 TDs, 2nd of which from 5YL, gave underdog Wake Forest (0-1-1) 20-13 lead with 8:51 to go in 4th Q. Clemson (0-0-1) QB Charlie Waters hunkered down and masterminded 13-play, 71y drive, contributing critical 8y run on 4th down to Demon Deacons 20YL. Tigers FB Benny Michael scored TD from 7YL, and K Mike Funderburk booted tying conv with 2 mins to go.

FLORIDA 23 Air Force 20 (Tampa): Florida (1-0) DB Steve Tannen traipsed through Air Force (0-1) for 64y punt TD RET in 2nd Q and recovered late FUM to prompt Gators win. Blazing soph TB Curtis Martin had quickly baptized Falcons' season by sprinting 98y with opening KO. Martin scored again at end of 56y advance in 3rd Q, and Air Force had proudly earned 20-16 lead. Just as summer thunderstorm struck, Martin lost 4th Q pitchout to Tannen at Falcons 22YL. Dynamic Florida FB Larry Smith (110y rushing) scored decisive TD, his 2nd, 5 plays later.

KENTUCKY 12 Missouri 6: Thanks to brilliance of DB-KR Roger Wehrli, Missouri (0-1) had nearly 3 times RET y that Wildcats (1-0) managed. But, Wehrli lost 1st Q FUM at his 46YL, and Kentucky QB Stan Forston (6-14/56y) converted pair of 3rd down passes to E Vic King and 15y pitch to HB Dicky Lyons. Lyons swept left for 2y TD and 6-0 lead for UK with 2 mins left in 1st Q. Tigers DB Butch Davis twice defended passes near GL in 2nd Q, which allowed Mizzou to take over on own 21YL. Tigers QB Terry McMillan (7-17/154y, TD, INT) quickly lofted long sideline pass to jet-propelled WR Mel Gray, who took it 79y to TD and 6-6 tie. Unfortunately for Missouri Ks, they missed x-pt and 3 fairly short FGs. With little O since 1st Q, Kentucky broke 55y pass to E Phil Thompson when Mizzou's gambling Davis missed INT. Lyons then took pitchout 26y to score winning TD.

ALABAMA 14 Virginia Tech 7 (Birmingham): Soph WR George Ranager speared 2 TD passes in 2nd Q, but Alabama (1-0) had to call bullpen for QB Scott Hunter to relieve sr starter, QB Joe Kelley, who lost FUMs on Tide's 1st 2 series. Crimson Tide DB Donnie Sutton raced 61y to 12YL on punt RET in 2nd Q. Hunter rolled out to pitch to Ranager for 8y TD on 3rd down. Ranager twisted to take shoe-top catch on Bama's next possession and whirled for 65y TD for 14-0 lead. Virginia Tech (0-1) lost QB Al Kincaid to 2nd Q injury when he was hit by whirling dervish LB Mike Hall and DT Randy Barron. That didn't keep Gobblers from scoring their only TD mins later: With 42 secs before H, Virginia Tech DL Larry Creekmore blocked punt, and DE Jud Brownell fell on ball in EZ for TD. Shut down completely by Tide D, Hokies were thrown for −17y y rushing and netted 48y.

LOUISIANA STATE 13 Texas A&M 12: Texas A&M (0-1) enjoyed 12-0 lead on bad-snap safety, QB Edd Hargett's short TD pass to WR Bob Long, and K Charlie Riggs' 31y FG. Busy Texas A&M P Steve O'Neal lofted 48, 53, 46, and 48y punts to keep Bayou Bengals caged deep in their end until latter stages of 2nd Q. LSU alternated QBs Freddie Haynes and Jimmy Gilbert to slam furious drive down Aggies' throat to FB Frank Matte's TD run. Trailing 12-6, LSU (1-0) battled in 4th Q on running of Haynes and TB Tommy "Trigger" Allen, who carried 6 times on 10-play voyage. Tigers WB Jim West scored on 3y run behind Allen's cut-down block, and K Mark Lumpkin kicked go-ahead pt. Aggies never quit and marched deep into Tigers end on QB Edd Hargett's 46y pitch to WR Jimmy Adams and rifle-shot pass to Long at 5YL. Long took pitchout wide to within inches of GL but lost FUM after being cut down by searing tackle.

California 21 MICHIGAN 7: HB Gary Fowler (18/78y) ran for 3 TDs and paced rushing attack of underdog California (1-0), which outgained Michigan (0-1) runners by 240y to 99y. Trailing 14-0 in 2nd Q, Wolverines QB Dennis Brown pitched 10 and 18y and finally for 8y TD to TE Jim Mandich (6/73y, TD), but overall Michigan air game resulted in weak 9-31/135y. Star HB Ron Johnson of Michigan was limited to 21/48y rushing, but Wolverines presented 2 gems on D. Michigan DT Tom Goss and LB Tom Stincic roamed all over field in pursuit of Bear runners. It was Wolverines' 1st opening game loss in 6 years in what would be coach Bump Elliott's last season in charge. But, 8-game winning streak was right around corner.

Southern California 29 MINNESOTA 20: USC (1-0) TB O.J. Simpson had personal best to-date rushing total of 39/236y, 4 TDs. Simpson added 6/59y receiving as Trojans rallied in 4th Q. K Ron Ayala's 29y FG broke 13-13 tie for USC early in final period. On following KO, Gophers HB George Kemp was hemmed in and pitched lateral halfway across field to lonesome HB John Wintermute, who dashed 83y to score. This gave Minnesota (0-1) lead back at 20-16. Gritty USC DB Mike Battle returned punt 13y to Gophers 45YL. Trojans adopted their best strategy, they gave ball to Simpson 6 plays in row, last of which was 7y TD run that put Trojans ahead for good at 22-20.

IOWA 21 Oregon State 20: No. 8 Oregon State (0-1) gained 309y rushing, but ended up fueling upset by youthful Iowa (1-0) with 4 lost FUMs and late-game INT. Hawkeyes TB Dennis Green, future coach of Northwestern, Stanford, and NFL's Minnesota Vikings and Arizona Cardinals, scored winning TD on 9y pitchout with 13 mins to go in 4th Q. Hawks QB Ed Podolak skipped across GL for 3y and 10y scores, each tying game in 1st H at 7-7 and 14-14. OSU scorers were its backfield mainstays: HB Billy Main who tallied on 40y run and FB Bill Enyart who powered 3y. Beavers lost QB Steve Preece to shoulder injury. His sub, Gary Barton, missed 2 handoffs and threw INT to Iowa DB Coleman Lane, thus creating 3 ruinous TOs that ruined any hope Beavers harbored for 4th Q rally. Podolak too was knocked from game, but his Iowa QB replacement, Larry Lawrence hit 4-6/62y and was prime factor on 43y trip to Green's winning TD and K Marcos Melendez's decisive x-pt.

NOTRE DAME 45 Oklahoma 21: Doing stable double duty, WB-DB Eddie Hinton (6/122y, TD receiving) gave Oklahoma (0-1) early thrills with 72y TD pass reception and 20y INT RET to position Sooners TE Steve Zabel for 1st of his 2 TD catches for 14-7 lead on last play of 1st Q. OU drove again, but was forced into errant 29y FG try. QB Terry Hanratty (18-27/202y, 2 TDs, 2 INTs) connected with E Jim Seymour (9/101y, 2 TDs) for 2 scores in 2nd Q to wrest away lead for Notre Dame (1-0). Seymour's 2nd scoring reception moved him past Leon Hart for new ND record for career TD catches. Irish allowed only single 1st down in 2nd H until game's last 5 mins. Rout was cemented as HB Bob Gladieux added 2 short TD runs in 3rd Q for 35-14 lead. Slender Oklahoma QB Bobby Warmack stood up to strong pass-rush to hit 10-26/172y, 3 TDs. Fighting Irish O was remarkably efficient against Sooners D, rolling up 571y, never punting, and clicking on impressive drives of 60, 80, 76, 54, 68, and 70y.

TEXAS 20 Houston 20: Missed scoring chances punctuated this surprise tie. Houston (0-0-1) FB Paul Gipson scored from 1, 56, and 5y out, but Cougars botched 2 late opportunities. Soph K Jerry Leiwecke missed chip-shot FG with 10:28 left, and Houston failed to score after reaching no. 4 Texas 1YL with 3:34 to play. Texas (0-0-1) TB Chris Gilbert dashed for 57 and 8y TDs, but after TB Ted Koy's 4th Q TD, potential winning kick was missed.

ARKANSAS 32 Oklahoma State 15 (Little Rock): Arkansas (1-0) snoozed for 3 Qs, trailing ambitious Oklahoma State (0-1) 15-3 at H and 15-10 after 3 Qs. Then, Razorbacks turned to their bevy of TBs to complete 4-TD avalanche in 2nd H with 3 scores in 4th Q. Cowboys had enjoyed early success, based primarily on QB Ronnie Johnson (11-14/133y, 2 TDs, 3 INTs) hitting E Jerry Philpot and WB Terry Brown with short TD passes. Johnson wedged in 2-pt run as well. Arkansas QB Bill Montgomery (16-31/157y, INT) sparked 2nd H revival: In 3rd Q, he hit WB Bruce Maxwell with 28y pass to Oklahoma State 38YL, then TB David Dickey lugged ball 7 of next 8 plays for TD. After Cowboys HB Gary Goodwin fumbled punt with 11:33 left, Dickey came back with 6y TD run. TB Bill Burnett capped 70y Hogs drive with 11y TD sweep with 4 mins to go, and DB Gary Adams' INT poised 3rd-string Porkers TB Russell Cody for icing-on-cake 4y TD run in last min.

AP Poll September 23

1 Purdue (25)	888	11 Ohio State	211
2 Notre Dame (19)	864	12 Kansas	175
3 Southern California (4)	794	13 Indiana	158
4 Penn State (1)	494	14 Louisiana State	121
5 Florida	323	15 Miami	107
6 Texas	310	16 Tennessee	102
7 Alabama	306	17 Minnesota	90
8 UCLA	284	18 Oregon State (1)	71
9 Nebraska	281	19 Arizona State	69
10 Houston	238	20 Wyoming	49

September 28, 1968

Vanderbilt 17 ARMY 13: Balance of season would send these teams to opposite ends of W-L columns, but Vanderbilt (2-0) used its passing attack (25-34/276y, TD), led by little soph sub QB John Miller, to get ahead of Army (1-1) with big 2nd Q for upset win. Cadets' 1st Q punt popped loose at Commodores 6YL when DB Doug Mathews was sandwiched by 3 Army tacklers. Big Army FB Charlie Jarvis quickly provided 7-0 lead on 2y TD run. Vandy coach Bill Pace went to his bench for Miller, who would go on to complete 23 passes, and help Commodores to keep ball for all but 11 plays of 2nd Q. WB Dave Strong caught 5y TD from Miller, and after Black Knights punt, Miller quickly hit 3 straight throws on 56y drive to TB Don North's 2y TD run. "We were actually forced into the pass attack by the early Army defense," said Pace. Down 17-7 at H, Cadets threatened 4 times in 2nd H, including TE Gary Steele's 3 catches in row to eventual demise at 5YL, but Army could earn only 2 FGs by K Arden Jensen.

Boston College 49 NAVY 15: Boston College (1-0) tallied highest pt total vs. Navy (0-2) in 43 years as QB Joe Marzetti (7-10/132y, 3 TDs) pitched 3 TD passes, and HB Dave Bennett burst through LG for 87y TD run. Middies HB Jeri Balsly scored twice, but soph QB Mike McNallen (6-22/119y, 3 INTs) was forced to run for his life under pressure from Eagles DT John Fitzgerald and DE Paul Cavanaugh.

Florida 9 FLORIDA STATE 3: Tough Gators D refused to break, even when Florida State (1-1) advanced to 1st–and-goal twice at Florida (2-0) 4YL. Seminoles managed only K Grant Guthrie's 21y FG in 2nd Q during their 2 opportunities. This had Florida coach Ray Graves nibbling his fingernails: "When FSU kept taking chances, I kept thinking we couldn't possibly hold them off all day." Meanwhile, inoffensive Gators took advantage of 26 and 24y punts by FSU P Bill Cheshire to piece together enough 2nd Q pts for win, getting 30y FG from future NFL star DT-K Jack Youngblood and sending FB Larry Smith charging on 7 powerful runs to his 3y TD. Seminoles WR Ron Sellers (6/50y) felt he was open but heavy pass-rush by Gators kept him getting passes for big gains. Afterward, he was agitated: "I beat my man (Florida CB Steve Tannen) several times but I didn't get the ball. I just want everybody to know he's not unbeatable. He thinks he's the greatest. But he isn't."

Miami 10 GEORGIA TECH 7: Seeking revenge for 49-7 pasting by Hurricanes late in 1967 season, Georgia Tech (1-1) used coach Bud Carson's masterful D plan to virtually eliminate 1st H O of Miami (2-0). Biggest threat came after DB Tony Stawarz's INT put Canes at Atlantans' 31YL. Georgia Tech held and forced missed FG. Early in 2nd Q, QB Larry Good (12-34/143y, 3 INTs) hit WR John Sias (6/101y) for 27y gain and gave Yellow Jackets 7-0 H lead with 3y TD run, while O unit gained hefty 199y. Georgia Tech failed to net even single y in 2nd H as Miami D, led by DEs Ted "The Mad Stork" Hendricks and Tony Cline and NG Jerry Pierce, stuffed every effort. Hurricanes' O was little better, gaining only 178y overall as sr Jackets S Billy Kinard made 19 tackles and FUM REC. Georgia Tech FB John Weaver lost pitchout at own 40YL in 3rd Q, and Hurricanes HB Vince Opalsky capped TD drive with 1y run. Late in 3rd Q, Hendricks swooped on FUM, and although Tech held, K Jim Huff hit winning 27y FG.

OHIO STATE 35 Southern Methodist 14: Big horseshoe stadium in Columbus had its sky filled with footballs. Soph QB Chuck Hixson launched 37-69/417y, all SMU (1-1) team passing records for completions, attempts, and y. Key to victory was clutch Ohio State (1-0) D that picked off 5 Hixson passes to halt drives at its 9, 15, 18, 2, and 10YLs. Buckeyes Rex Kern, also soph QB, ran for opening TD, passed for 18 and 20y TDs to HB Dave Brungard, who also raced to 41y TD in 2nd Q. Mustangs WR Jerry Levias was everywhere on O, catching 15/160y from Hixson.

Nebraska 17 MINNESOTA 14: Nebraska (3-0) frustrated its scoring opportunities with 5 TOs through 3 Qs as Minnesota (0-2) led 14-7. Cornhuskers reversed their mode of operation in 4th Q, using DB Dana Stephenson's INT of Golden Gophers QB Ray Stephens to lead to tying TD, which arrived on QB Ernie Sigler's 14y pass to TE Jim McFarland. Nebraska DE Sherwin Jarson picked off another pass by Stephens 5 mins later, and, with aid of personal foul PEN, Nebraska K Paul Rogers, son of former Minnesota player, kicked winning FG in last 2 mins. HB Maurice Forte, fighting for starting job in deeply-stocked Gophers' backfield, scored twice on 2y runs in 1st H.

Purdue 37 NOTRE DAME 22: Even pep rally appearance on Friday of actor Pat O'Brien, who played title role in classic film "Knute Rockne, All-American," couldn't stir 2nd-ranked Notre Dame (1-1). Purdue (2-0) became 10th no. 1 team to defeat no. 2 team in 11 such meetings to date in college history. Boilermakers HB-DB Leroy Keyes (15/90y, 2 TDs) made virtuoso performance, running for TDs of 16 and 18y, throwing 17y TD pass to WR Bob Dillingham (11/147y, 2 TDs), catching 3/33y, and being inserted at CB to blanket Irish E Jim Seymour in passing situations. QB Terry Hanratty (19-31/307y, 2 TDs, 3 INTs) pitched 1st of his 2 TDs for short-lived 7-3 ND lead early in what would become wild 2nd Q. Boilers responded with 3 TDs in next 3:30. Keyes as WR caught 3rd down pass at ND 25YL and soon followed with 16y sweep around LE for TD. DE Billy McCoy quickly deflected Hanratty's pass into INT, and Keyes wobbled his TD pass to Dillingham. Irish HB Bob Gladieux lost FUM 2 plays after KO, and Purdue QB Mike Phipps hit Dillingham for 16y score. Purdue became 1st team to beat Irish in consecutive years since arrival of Ara Parseghian as ND coach in 1964.

KANSAS 38 Indiana 20: Mantle of current season's surprise team was passed from 1967 Hoosiers to Kansas (2-0), which was on its way to nation's scoring leadership. Explosive Jayhawks HB Donnie Shanklin (8/159y, 2 TDs) showed Indiana (1-1) his vapor-trail with exciting TD runs of 59y on punt RET and 54 and 65y from scrimmage. *Chicago Tribune* writer John Husar wrote: "Move over, Gale Sayers, there's a new comet blazing trails around Kansas…" Shanklin finished with 317 all-purpose y. FB John Riggins busted ahead for 12/76y and was especially effective with 34y on opening drive to his 1y TD plunge. Indiana finally was aroused in 2nd H after precocious but injured HB John Isenbarger (17/102y, TD) entered game and scored on 4y run that took Hoosiers to within 17-6. Shanklin quickly wiped it away with his 54y TD gallop for 24-6 edge in 3rd Q. Isenbarger flipped 14y TD to WR Bob Douglas, but other Bobby Douglass, Kansas' QB, raced 71y to score later in 4th Q for overwhelming 31-12 edge.

TEXAS TECH 31 Texas 22: Red Raiders (1-0-1) surprised Texas (0-1-1) with HB Roger Freeman's 3 TDs and S Larry Alford's 84y punt TD RET. Freeman rushed 13/68y and caught 2/30y, including initial 21y TD from QB Joe Matulich. Trailing 21-0 at H, Longhorns scored all their pts in 3rd Q as TB Chris Gilbert went 6y for TD, and FB Steve Worster barreled over twice. Alford contributed another 49y punt RET that led to another TD by Tech, and K Ken Vinyard clicked on 23y FG with 7:16 to play to clinch upset win for Red Raiders.

Stanford 28 OREGON 12: Sensational Stanford (2-0) soph QB Jim Plunkett (14-26/227y, 3 TDs, 2 INTs) followed up his 4-TD debut against San Jose State by flinging TD passes in each of game's 1st 3 Qs. Indians got off to 14-0 start as Plunkett hit 18 and 6y TDs to TE Bob Moore and WR Gene Washington respectively. Ducks (0-2) used FB Greg Marshall's short TD run to pull within 14-6 at H. Less than 3 mins into 2nd H, Plunkett connected with HB Jack Lasater for 23y scoring throw after having bombed 52y pass to HB Howie Williams to Oregon 23YL. QB Alan Pitcsithley threw 4th Q TD for Ducks, but Plunkett showed he knew other part of O football by hot-footing it 7y to tally in 4th Q.

AP Poll September 30

1 Purdue (42)	894	11 Alabama	196
2 Southern California (2)	797	12 Houston	163
3 Penn State (1)	568	13 Miami	152
4 Florida	441	14 Arizona State	104
5 Notre Dame	430	15 Tennessee	100
6 Ohio State	398	16 Georgia	64
7 Nebraska	395	17 Texas A&M	49
8 Kansas	393	18 California	43
9 UCLA	342	19 Michigan State	39
10 Louisiana State	213	20 Arkansas	37

October 5, 1968

SYRACUSE 20 Ucla 7: In deep mud, Bruins (2-1) hung close to Syracuse (2-1), allowing 2 FGs by George Jakowenko and HB John Godbolt's 4y TD run. UCLA failed on 4th down at Orange 11YL when pass by QB Jim Nader (11-24/144y, 2 INTs) was batted down by Syracuse NG Gerry Beach. Midway in 4th Q, Bruins battled to within 13-7 as HB Greg Jones crowned 39y drive with 3y TD run. UCLA K Zenon Andrusyshun angled on-side KO toward right sideline, but ball bounced right up into hands of Syracuse TE Bill Maddox. It was clear sailing for 49y TD for Maddox once he broke past initial line of Bruins.

Penn State 31 WEST VIRGINIA 20: Fast-starting Mountaineers (2-1) clicked on 2 TD passes from soph QB Mike Sherwood to WR Oscar Patrick for 14-7 1st Q edge. When Penn State (3-0) FB Tom Cherry lost FUM at own 34YL, it appeared WVU was ready to make kill. Lions D held, and early in 2nd Q, ball-hawk LB Dennis Onkontz had INT RET to WVU 21YL. WR Charlie Wilson made diving snare of QB Chuck Burkhart's TD pass to tie it at 14-14. Penn State scored next 17 pts with Onkontz's 16y INT TD RET of screen pass serving to wrap it up at 31-14.

Duke 30 Maryland 28 (Norfolk): Maryland (0-3) lost its 16th straight game in painful style as Blue Devils (2-1) scored 9 pts in last 2:13 to steal verdict. Duke had opened game with 79y drive that included QB Leo Hart's 2 long completions to WR Marcel Courtillet before Hart sneaked across. After Devils went up 13-0, Terrapins recuperated with short TD runs by TBs John King and Al Thomas for 14-13 H edge. Even though Duke FB Phil Asack bolted 61y for 3rd Q TD, Maryland found itself up 28-21 when FB Billy Lovett (140y rushing) raced 33y to score with 6:33 to go. Blues QB sub QB Dave Trice scored TD but TE Jim Dearth dropped 2-pt pass to stay behind by 1 pt. Despite having already gained 268y rushing, Terps lost 3y and punted to Duke 36YL. Trice and Hart alternated in hitting Carter 3 times, but Carter appeared to trap catch at Terps 10YL. Carter dropped next throw that killed clock with 3 secs left, which allowed Duke to send in K Dave Pugh for winning 27y FG.

MISSISSIPPI 10 Alabama 8: Young Archie Manning earned his 1st headlines as sterling Ole Miss (3-0) soph QB. Rebels beat Alabama (2-1) for 1st time since 1910, but it was only 4th meeting of SEC rivals since splitting in 1934. In 2nd Q, Manning lofted perfect 49y pass to soph WB Vernon Studdard and soon hit TE Hank Shows for 6y TD. K Perry King added 44y FG in 3rd Q for 10-0 lead. Rebels D gave 254y, was on verge of dealing 1st shutout to Tide O since 1959. But, Alabama LB Mike Hall blocked 4th Q punt for TD.

Georgia 21 SOUTH CAROLINA 20: Fired-up South Carolina (1-2) bolted to 20-7 lead as DB Lynn Hodge charged 22y to INT TD RET on game's 2nd play and WR Fred Zeigler tied school reception record with 9/76y. Key to excellent Carolina D was DB Roy Don Reeves, who blocked punt, intercepted 2 passes, and set up FG with 54y INT RET. After Reeves' 1st INT on Bulldogs' 2nd series, Carolina FB Warren Muir powered 1y for 1st Q TD. Muir (50y rushing) was soon lost to hip-pointer. K Billy DuPre, Carolina's 1st soccer-stylist, nailed FGs of 42 and 23y for 20-7 H lead. Georgia (2-0-1)

rallied nicely in 2nd H: FB Brad Johnson scored his 2nd TD from 1YL in 3rd Q, and QB Mike Cavan pitched 23y to TE Dennis Hughes, ran 14y, and tossed 15y TD to TB Kent Lawrence for game-winner midway in 4th Q. Winning pt for Bulldogs was toed by K Jim McCullough.

GEORGIA TECH 24 Clemson 21: QB Larry Good (14-24/232y, 2 TDs) was cornerstone of Rambling Wrecks' 4th Q comeback from 13-10 shortfall. Clemson (0-2-1), off to slow start for 5th time in last 6 years, jumped to good start at Grant Field. Tigers D allowed only 1 1st down into 2nd Q, and O cashed FB Ray Yauger's 10y sweep for TD. Georgia Tech (2-1) K Johnny Duncan nailed 32y FG to pare edge to 6-3, and Good hit WR Tim Woodall for 39y and FB John Weaver for 43y TD for 10-6 H lead. TB Buddy Gore (28/135y, TD) scored 3rd Q TD while on his way to joining Fred Cone (1948-50) in Clemson pantheon as school's only 2000y career rushers. Leading 13-10, Tigers FB Rick Medlin lost FUM to Tech DB Tash Van Dora on opening play of 4th Q. TB Dennis James barged over for 4y TD to reclaim lead, and Good's 7y TD pass to TE Joel Stevenson provided insurance with 5:16 to play after DB Darrell Parker's INT RET to 35YL. Sub QB Billy Ammons flipped 7y TD pass to TE Jim Sursavage and followed with 2-pt pass after final whistle.

North Carolina 8 VANDERBILT 7: Alert D play made game's 2 TDs possible, but in end it was North Carolina (1-2) QB Gayle Bomar's determined option run off left side behind block of FB Ken Borries for 2 pts that won it. Exchange of FUMs, completed by Vandy LB Chip Healy at Tar Heels 36YL, got Vanderbilt (2-1) rolling in 2nd Q. Sub QB John Miller sparked lagging Commodore O with 36y TD pass to HB Allan Spear (20/93y rushing) on 2nd down. But, bad C snap to Vandy P Steve Smith turned late-game fortunes to baby blue Carolinians as DL Ron Lowry smothered Smith at Commodores 30YL. Great 3rd down catch by Heels WR Peter Davis, amid 3 defenders, gained 1st down at Vandy 3YL. HB Saulis Zemaitis ploughed over from 2YL with 4:50 to play, and set stage for 2-pt run by Bomar (21/47y rushing). Vanderbilt made late charge downfield to Heels 21YL after WB Dave Strong nearly broke away on 45y KO RET. UNC pushed 'em back, and DB Bob Hanna made 4th down INT of Miller at his 9YL to end it.

FLORIDA STATE 20 Texas A&M 14: Struggling Southwest Conf defending champ Aggies (1-2) stuck to 289y ground attack, while Florida State (2-1) flourished in air with 208y gained. Difference was 4 missed Texas A&M FGs, countered by 27 and 40y FG makes in 2nd and 4th Qs by sharp Seminoles K Grant Guthrie. Another factor that developed was bad game for Aggie passing ace, QB Edd Hargett (6-24/61y, 4 INTs), who was blitzed to distraction and frequently collared by FSU DE Ron Wallace. Texas A&M FB Dave Elmendorf (17/156y) scored TDs of 20 and 15y just 96 secs apart in 2nd Q for 14-7 lead. Elmendorf's 2nd score was set up by 46y sprint by TB Larry Stegent (21/122y). Guthrie made his 1st FG at 4:35 mark before H. Hargett soon lost pitchout to Wallace at Aggie 33YL, so Seminoles retook lead at 17-14 when QB Bill Cappleman (15-33/208y, 2 TDs, 2 INTs) found E Billy Cox for 14y TD. After scoreless 3rd Q, Guthrie connected again for 3 pts.

WYOMING 27 Arizona State 13: Sun Devils (2-1) maneuvered to 10-0 lead on FG by K Ed Gallardo after HB Larry Walton's 30y punt RET and WR J.D. Hill's 1y TD run after FUM REC at Wyoming (2-2) 10YL. K Bob Jacobs' 46y FG just 2 secs before H tied it at 10-10. WR Gene Huey scored go-ahead TD for Cowboys on 19y pass reception, and HB Jim Barrows made his 2nd long punt RET to set up QB Skip Jacobsen's TD pass.

OREGON STATE 35 Washington 21: HB Buddy Kennamer and FB Bo Cornell scored TDs and HB Carl Wojciechowski gained 106y to earn 14-7 H lead for Washington (1-1-1). Oregon State (2-1) QB Steve Preece came out throwing in 2nd H, hitting E Roger Cantlon for 17 and 11y gains and tying game on 2y TD flip to HB Billy Main. Beavers D stopped Huskies, and Main soon scored his 3rd TD. FB Bill Enyart followed with 2 TD blasts.

SOUTHERN CALIFORNIA 28 Miami 3: In 2 previous games, Miami (2-1) had allowed only total of 112y rushing and looked good early against ace Southern California (3-0) TB O.J. Simpson, who advanced only 14y on his 1st 8 tries. But Trojans eventually aimed Simpson (38/163y, 2 TDs) away from superb Hurricanes DE Ted Hendricks for fun and profit. QB Steve Sogge's 1st Q TD pass of 28y to WR Jim Lawrence came after DT Al Cowlings' FUM REC at Miami 36YL. Canes accepted poor punt at USC 30YL early in 2nd Q, but on 4th-and-goal at 5YL they spurned FG and suffered sack of QB David Olivo. Simpson scored twice, once in 2nd Q for 14-0 lead and again early in 4th Q for 21-3 edge. Miami got only K Jim Huff's 29y FG after good opportunity at Trojans 37YL midway in 3rd Q.

October 12, 1968

ARMY 10 California 7: California (3-1) had yielded only 1 TD in 3 wins so far, its best start since 1952. Bears D was pitching another shutout through H and was matched by alert Cadets (2-2), who got 3 INTs from DB Jim McCall, another from standout LB Ken Johnson. K Arden Jensen's 3rd Q FG gave Army 3-0 lead, but WR Gary Marshall lost FUM at midfield in 4th Q. California QB Randy Humphries hit 3 straight passes to

poise FB John McGaffie for TD and 7-3 lead. Army had bullet left in its gun: TE Gary Steele outjumped DB Eric Kastner and raced 62y to finish winning pass play with QB Steve Lindell with 2:48 to go.

MARYLAND 33 North Carolina 24: Terrapins (1-3) used 2 long KO RETs to rally for win over North Carolina (1-3) that broke 16-game losing streak. Heels led 17-14 at H thanks to TD run, pass by QB Gayle Bomar. Maryland TB John King's 43y KO RET set up FB Billy Lovett (39/172y) for 18y TD run in 3rd Q. FB Tom Dempsey, back from injury, scored from 1YL on his 1st carry of season, and UNC led 24-20. HB Al Thomas took ensuing KO 53y and scored 10 plays later for 26-24 Terps lead.

Virginia 50 DUKE 20: Cavaliers (3-1) stunned fans in Wallace Wade Stadium by frolicking for ACC-record 495y rushing and 603y total O. HB Frank Quayle, greatest Virginia back since Bullet Bill Dudley in early 1940s, rushed 35/182y, TD, provided keynote with runs of 44 and 62y to set up Cavs' opening TD runs by FB Jeff Anderson (24/183y, 3 TDs) and reserve TB Dave Wyncoop (2 TDs). Blue Devils (2-2) received 2 seemingly important short-yardage scores from TB Phil Asack, who put Duke ahead 7-6 in 1st Q and drew it within 21-14 in 3rd Q. But, Anderson scored on 13 and 47y runs to launch Virginia to 34-14 edge by early 4th Q. Devils earned game's last TD on 43y pass from QB Leo Hart (20-38/294y, TD, INT) to WR Wes Chesson (11/176y, TD).

GEORGIA 21 Mississippi 7: Falling behind in 1st H was becoming Georgia trademark, but Bulldogs (3-0-1) went in at H down only 7-0. Ole Miss (3-1) used dominating D and QB Archie Manning's 10y TD pass to WB Floyd Franks to build TD lead. Georgia pared it to 7-6 on K Jim McCullough's 2 FGs in 3rd Q and broke it open in 4th Q with 2-TD blast. TB Kent Lawrence scored from 7YL, and QB Mike Cavan clicked on 63y TD pass.

Tennessee 24 GEORGIA TECH 7: Football was flying all over Grant Field as 11 FUMs dribbled into enemy hands and Georgia Tech (2-2) launched unheard-of (for 1968) total of 63 passes in attempt to rally from behind. Yellow Jackets QB Larry Good (25-61/267y, TD, 2 INTs) pushed Yellow Jackets to 369y to 349y O advantage, but Tech never was really in contest despite slow start by Tennessee (3-0-1). Coming off 52y effort against Rice, Vols went 27 mins before cashing 1st score. They made 10 pts in last moments of 2nd Q: WB Lester McClain drove through several tacklers for 12y TD reception from QB Bubba Wyche (6-16/105y 2 TDs). Vols DB Nick Showalter quickly recovered FUM, and K Karl Kremser knocked through 43y with 1:06 on clock. McClain made spectacular catch for 24y TD in 3rd Q, but Good hit WR John Sias (8/79y, TD) with 10y TD at end of 83y trip.

MICHIGAN 28 Michigan State 14: Unbeaten Michigan State (3-1) earned 14-13 lead early in 4th Q when QB Charlie Wedemeyer followed FB Earl Anderson's short TD run with 2-pt pass to TE Frank Foreman off fake kick. Michigan (3-1) came right back as QB Dennis Brown's 3rd straight completion went for 53y TD to TE Jim Mandich. Spartans retaliated to Wolverines 40YL, but DB Tom Curtis' INT stopped drive. FB Garvie Craw broke 2 tackles to dash 25y for insurance TD.

OHIO STATE 13 Purdue 0: Season's biggest upset so far established youthful Ohio State (3-0) on fast track to no. 1. Top-ranked Purdue (3-1) had trouble with soph QB Rex Kern (8-16/78y, and 11/57y rushing) in scoreless 1st H, even though Kern missed 2 open receivers at GL. Drives bogged down and 5 FG tries sailed wide, 2 for each side, and Boilermakers DE Billy McKoy blocked another 3-pt try just before H. Ohio State's D, led by DB Jack Tatum's 2 sacks and 3 pass breakups, was superb all day and was catalyst in breaking into scoring column in 3rd Q: DB Ted Provost dashed 35y to INT TD when Purdue QB Mike Phipps (10-28/106y, 2 INTs) threw ill-advised cross-field pass for E Bob Dillingham. Buckeyes NG Jim Stillwagon's INT put ball at Purdue 25YL, but Kern was soon shaken up. Sub QB Bill Long found no receivers, but dashed 14y to TD and 13-0 lead. Ohio State FB Jim Otis rushed 29/144y, while Purdue HB Leroy Keyes coped with 7/19y on ground and catching 4/44y.

NOTRE DAME 27 Northwestern 7: Wildcats (0-4) DBs Dennis White and Harold Daniels did remarkable job of coverage on outstanding Notre Dame (3-1) E Jim Seymour (2/23y) while, for most of game, Northwestern frustrated air game of QB Terry Hanratty (6-16/55y, TD, 2 INTs) and his vain search for all-time ND total O record. Hanratty zipped around RE on 7y TD run in 1st Q, and Northwestern hung on behind only 7-0—helped by HB-P Chico Kurzawski's 5 effective QKs—until finally surrendering Irish HB Bob Gladieux's 1y plunge late in 3rd Q. Although Gladieux tallied again early in 4th Q, Wildcats mustered Kurzawski's short TD plunge on 61y drive that featured 21, 13, and 12y completions by QB Dave Shelbourne (10-25/142y, 2 INTs).

MISSOURI 27 Colorado 14: Even though Missouri's celebrated D allowed 3 long plays, 2 for TDs, Tigers (3-1) O came through when it counted. Colorado (2-2) QB Bob Anderson (3-11/153y, 2 TDs, 4 INTs) made his few completions count, firing 66y TD pass to SB Mike Pruett in 2nd Q and to TB Steve Engel for 80y score in 3rd Q after Engel maneuvered past LB into clear area in middle. Colorado might have scored in between, but DB Butch Davis pursued Buff FB Ward Walsh to haul him down at 2YL after 51y run before DB Roger Wehrli made EZ FUM on next play. Engel's TD pulled Buffaloes within 17-14, and it came right after Mizzou's nullified 66y punt TD RET. So, when Tigers could have been demoralized, they made vital INTs: DB Dennis Poppe picked off Anderson throw to set up FG by K Henry Brown, and Davis made 2 INTs, 2nd of which set up QB Terry McMillan for twisting 10y run that took Tigers into short TD range for FB Ron McBride (24/102y).

Kansas 23 NEBRASKA 13: No. 6 Kansas (4-0) rallied for 2 TDs late in 4th Q to beat no. 9 Nebraska (3-1) before largest crowd to date in Big 8 history. Kansas advanced to 10 and 32YLs without scoring in 1st H, while its punt team, led by strong leg of P Bill Bell, frequently cornered Cornhuskers deep in their territory. But after Jayhawks bungled punt catch, Nebraska HB Joe Orduna fell on FUM and immediately followed with 27y TD run for 6-0 H lead. Game settled into battle symptomatic of bare-knuckle, field-position showdown: 2nd down punt, QKs, and Nebraska's decision to give safety rather than punt into 3rd Q wind. HB Donnie Shanklin's short TD run gave Kansas 9-6

lead in 3rd Q. Jayhawks trailed again at 13-9 when Orduna ended 11-play, 51y drive with 1y scoot around RE. Kansas went 73y, aided by pass interference to Huskers 1YL, and QB Bobby Douglass' go-ahead TD run provided 16-13 lead with 4:09 to go. Douglass added late 10y TD sprint after Nebraska—which outgained Jayhawks 239y to 232y—failed on 4th-and-7 at its 23YL.

ARKANSAS 35 Baylor 19: Although they tired late and lost conf record-tying 10th straight SWC tilt, surprising Bears (0-4) played to their customary sharpness when visiting Ozark Mountains. Arkansas (4-0) stars were DB Gary Adams, whose INT set up 1st Hogs TD and 79y punt TD RET that provided 21-0 lead in 2nd Q. Also QB Bill Montgomery, who riddled Baylor pass D with 22-34/260y, TD, 2 INTs. Bears switched QBs—starter Alvin Flynn went out in favor of soph Steve Stuart (14-23/200y, TD)—in 2nd Q, and Stuart hit passes of 26, 17, 7, and 24y before banged-up FB Pinky Palmer (31/120y) scored from 1YL. Stuart added his own 1y TD run early in 4th Q to his 3y TD pass to WR Mark Lewis in 3rd Q. But, bad snap ruined K Terry Cozby's x-pt kick after Lewis' TD, and Stuart's 2-pt pass try was tipped away. So, Baylor trailed 21-19. Montgomery went back to passing to take Porkers 80y to score on his 4th down bootleg run with 2:51 left, and, after quick FUM, Montgomery clicked on 9y TD arrow to WR Chuck Dicus (7/99y) with 11 secs to play.

Southern Methodist 21 TEXAS CHRISTIAN 14: Feared pass-catcher, WR Jerry Levias of Southern Methodist (3-1), employed another formidable aspect of his game, punt RET, to lock up win. In 2nd Q, Horned Frogs (1-3) went 72y to WR Linzy Cole's 37y TD catch and 83y to FB Norm Bulaich's slashing 18y TD run. Trailing 14-3 in 3rd Q, Ponies had to settle for K Bicky Lesser's 2nd FG (43y), but used trickery to score TD in last 2 mins of 3rd Q: Ponies lined up TB Mike Richardson, leading conf rusher, at FB so that LB would cover him. SMU QB Chuck Hixson (24-45/309y,TD) nation's top passer, lofted 33y pass to Richardson (8 catches), who wrestled TCU DB Mike Hall off his back at 5YL to score. Hixson's 2-pt pass tied it 14-14. Levias gathered in punt at his 11YL early in 4th Q, charged upfield, spun off tackler to right sideline, and cut back to roar 89y for winning TD.

Texas 26 Oklahoma 20 (Dallas): FB Steve Worster (14/121y, 2 TDs) carried 2 Sooners tacklers over RG and across GL with 39 secs left to cap out-of-character, 85y aerial drive for Texas (2-1-1). Oklahoma (1-2) QB Bobby Warmack threw TD passes of 12 y to TE Steve Zabel and 34y to WB Eddie Hinton, but was caught for 4th Q safety by Longhorns DT Loyd Wainscott. Steers K Happy Feller personified most of early O, kicking FGs of 29y in 1st Q, 40y in 2nd Q, and 53y which bounced on and over crossbar to provide 17-14 lead in 3rd Q. Sooners trailed 19-14 until Warmack scored on 15y run with 8 mins left for 20-19 edge. Texas QB James Street battled clock, starting with 2:37 to go, and hit 3 passes to TE Deryl Comer on winning drive. TB Steve Owens gained 127y rushing for Sooners.

Southern California 27 STANFORD 24: Despite run-stop emphasis by Stanford (3-1) D, dynamic Southern California (4-0) TB O.J. Simpson (47/220y) scored on dashes of 3, 46, and 4y. Biggest play by "Juice" may have been his 15y pass to FB Dan Scott, which kept alive 4th Q drive leading to K Ron Ayala's winning FG. It was bitter defeat for ambitious Indians, who, after 10-10 H tie, jumped to 17-10 and 24-17 leads on 27y TD pass and 10y TD sweep by soph QB Jim Plunkett (14-30/246y, TD, 2 INTs).

Penn State 21 UCLA 6: Penn State (4-0) used scoring variety to slay Bruins (2-2). Mount Nittany LB Jack Ham blocked punt in 2nd Q, and LB Jim Kates carried it 36y to TD. UCLA narrowed it to 7-6 on QB Jim Nader's TD pass. In 3rd Q, Lions FB Tom Cherry slipped open as UCLA D concentrated on defending TE Ted Kwalick. Cherry took short pass from QB Chuck Burkhart and traveled 76y to score. Along way, Cherry surprisingly broke tackle of DB Mark Gustafson twice: near scrimmage line and at 3YL when Gustafson hustled in pursuit. Penn State HB Charlie Pittman's brilliant 28y TD run capped scoring in 4th Q.

AP Poll October 14

1 Southern California (23)	718	11 Syracuse	144
2 Ohio State (12)	672	12 Miami	133
3 Penn State (3)	606	13 Nebraska	122
4 Kansas (4)	540	14 Stanford	70
5 Purdue	452	15 Texas Tech	50
6 Notre Dame	348	16 Mississippi	32
7 Florida	340	17 Texas	28
8 Tennessee	319	18 Michigan	26
9 Arkansas	243	19 Indiana	22
10 Georgia	240	20tMissouri	21
		20tLouisiana State	21

October 19, 1968

NORTH CAROLINA 22 Florida 7: Plagued by 8 lost FUMs, no. 7 Florida (4-1) was stunned by North Carolina (2-3), which showed sudden reversal in its O. Tar Heels also created strong pass rush, throwing Gators QBs Jackie Eckdahl and Larry Rentz for -42y in losses. UNC K Don Hartig bombed through FGs from 47, 44, and 42y away. Pass interference, 1 of 3 called against Florida, was whistled on outstanding DB Steve Tannen to give Carolina QB Gayle Bomar chance to wedge behind G Mike Chalupka for 1st of his 2 TDs. That gave Heels 13-0 lead in 1st Q. Even saddled with their QB sacks, Gators rushed for 216y, but could manage only 8y TD run in 2nd Q by FB Larry Smith (142y rushing), who surprisingly lost 4 FUMs.

NORTH CAROLINA STATE 19 Virginia 0: Arriving with 3 wins built on 138 pts, Virginia (3-2) laid egg on waterlogged turf of NC State's Carter Stadium. Wolfpack D dominated tense contest, holding Cavaliers HB Frank Quayle, nation's 3rd leading rusher, to 18/67y rushing. NC State had scored on its 1st series, going 63y to QB Jack Klebe's 1y bang up middle. K Gerald Warren, Wolfpack's long-range ace, made it 10-0 with 2nd Q 41y FG and added 47y 3-ptr early in 4th Q. NC State scored its clinching 4th Q TD on 34y INT TD RET by CB Paul Reid in game's last 6 mins. Virginia enjoyed its only luck in late going, but were rebuffed by NC State's sacking D that completely harried Cavs QB Gene Arnette (2-10/14y, 2 INTs) after bad punt snap gave ball to Virginia at Wolfpack 17YL.

TENNESSEE 10 Alabama 9: No. 8 Volunteers (4-0-1) took advantage of short opening KO that E Terry Dalton ran 15y from his 22YL. Tennessee went 63y on 10 plays to TB Richmond Flowers' 1y TD flop, which was his 4th straight dive behind left side blocking of Vols' line. In 4th Q, K Karl Kremser gave Tennessee 10-3 lead with SEC-record, to-date, 54y FG. Alabama (3-2) motored 80y in 4th Q as QB Scott Hunter completed 7 passes, including 4th down 4y TD to WR Donnie Sutton. Tennessee stopped Tide's 2-pt run, but was incapable of halting Bama's on-side KO. Tennessee DB Jim Weatherford made big play by blocking K Mike Dean's last-play FG try from 35y out.

LOUISIANA STATE 13 Kentucky 3: Fighting Tigers (4-1) opened their SEC campaign with come-from-behind effort, their 8th straight win over Blue Wildcats (2-3). Kentucky showed well, leading 3-0 on K Bob Jones' 20y FG at H and making it inside LSU 5YL thrice. When Bengals defenders had backs to wall was when they performed best: LB Mike Anderson made 2 tackles in each of 2 anxious situations to spare Tigers' GL. Anderson also made FUM REC at his 4YL, while fellow LB, Ricki Owens, made INT at his 8YL. LSU went 71y on drive after 2nd H KO that started with TB Tommy Allen's 14y sweep and ended with his 1y TD run. K Mark Lumpkin added 42 and 29y FGs in 4th Q. Wildcats QB Stan Forston hit 10-27/148y, 3 INTs, including 5 clutch catches by E Dick King, but Kentucky could do little with its 14 plays started inside LSU 15YL.

Georgia Tech 21 AUBURN 20: Inconsistent Auburn (3-2) jumped early on up-and-down Georgia Tech (3-2) as sub TB Dwight Hurston (20/142y, TD) burst 68y for 1st Q TD, and, after immediate FUM by Georgia Tech HB Steve Harkey, Tigers QB Loran Carter added short TD pass. QB Larry Good (17-27/232y, 2 TDs) got Yellow Jackets back in game with 2 TD passes in 2nd Q, so that Tech trailed only 17-14 at H. Georgia Tech's 2nd TD was gift: Carter (10-22/95y, TD, 2 INTs) dropped FUM late in 2nd Q at his 27YL, and while Carter frantically searched for loose ball, Engineers LB Buck Shiver located it for REC. Tech HB Gene Spiotta's 27y TD catch on next play came with only 18 secs left before H. Plainsmen K John Riley's 2 FGs provided leads of 17-7 in 2nd Q and 20-14 in 3rd Q. Good found his team's long-lost running game and guided late drive to FB Kenny Bounds' 4y TD run and K Johnny Duncan's winning kick. But, Auburn wasn't done: after being pushed back to its 32YL by 57y punt, Carter threw 2 passes for 36y and Tigers pounded on ground to 22YL with 1:02 left. Riley was summoned, but his usually accurate foot produced fluttering 3-pt duck-like attempt.

PURDUE 28 Wake Forest 27: Wake Forest (0-4-1), perhaps best winless team in nation, pressed no. 5 Purdue (4-1) into 2-TD rally in 4th Q. Demon Deacons got 24y TD run from sub FB Jimmy Johnson and 4y TD run by QB Freddie Summers for 17-7 H margin. Meanwhile, Boilermakers HB Leroy Keyes (25/214y) lost 4 FUMs but scored from 19y to get within 17-14 in 3rd Q. Summers threw TD pass, and K Tom Deacon added 38y FG in 4th Q for 27-14 Wake lead. Keyes caught 27y pass to set up HB Jim Kirkpatrick's 14y TD run, and then K Jeff Jones' kick won it after Keyes' 2y TD run.

Michigan 27 INDIANA 22: Wolverines (4-1) took advantage of 2 rapid-fire errors in 3rd Q by Indiana (3-2) to take share of Big 10 lead. Hoosiers held 10-7 in 3rd Q on K Bob Warner's FG after trade of 18y TD runs by Michigan HB Ron Johnson and Indiana FB Hank Pogue. Michigan DB Jerry Hartman picked off pass by QB Harry Gonso (14-34/162y, 2 TD, 3 INT) and raced 62y to TD. Indiana HB Larry Highsmith lost FUM on following KO, and, 4 plays later, WR John Gabler made controversial EZ catch of QB Dennis Brown's 8y pass. So, Wolverines had lightning 20-10 lead it would not lose.

OHIO UNIVERSITY 24 Miami (Ohio) 7: Coming off 3 straight shutouts, Miami (4-2) boasted 98y per game D avg, best in nation. Ohio (5-0) made 359y, forced 5 TOs including 2 punt FUMs deep in Redskins territory. Bobcats D, led by MG Elmer Wanko and blitzing LB Steve Robinson, spilled Miami QB Kent Thompson 10 times for 51y in losses, but Thompson was able to tie game at 7-all with 4y TD run after DE Phil Nugent's FUM REC at Ohio 19YL. Big play came 5 min into 4th Q: E Todd Snyder turned QB Cleve Bryant's short pass into 73y TD and 21-7 Ohio advantage.

TEXAS 39 Arkansas 29: Seesaw affair tilted in 2nd Q on crushing run game of Texas (3-1-1). Longhorns trailed 15-10 after Hogs (4-1) QB Bill Montgomery hit WR Chuck Dicus with 6y TD pass. Texas fashioned next 4 TDs for insurmountable 39-15 lead: FB Steve Worster's 2 TDs, WR Cotton Speyrer's 51y TD catch, and TB Chris Gilbert's 40y TD run. Arkansas TB Bill Burnett scored his 2nd and 3rd TDs in 4th Q.

CALIFORNIA 39 Ucla 15: California (4-1), tabbed as "New Breed Bears," made up for recent torment (8 losses in last 9 games) from their L.A. cousins by rallying from 15-13 deficit at H with 23-pt earthquake in 3rd Q. In 2nd Q, UCLA (2-3) QB Bill Bolden (7-13/65y, TD, 2 INTs) passed for 12y TD to WR George Farmer at end of 80y march and ran for TD. Earlier, Bolden gambled on 4th down run out of punt formation and its failure set up Cal for 51y drive to WB Gary Fowler's TD. Bears were jolted from lethargy just before H by DT Ed White's FG block and WR Wayne Stewart's subsequent 21y TD catch. Resurgence continued early in 3rd Q as poor punt by Bruins K-P Zenon Andrusyshyn was forced by near block. Cal QB Randy Humphries (14-23/175y, 2 TDs) clicked immediately on 39y scoring arrow to TB Paul Williams. Bears DB Ken Wiedemann soon made INT to set up 1st of 2 FGs by K Ron Miller, and Wiedemann's 13y punt RET and DG Dennis Pitta's INT set up 2 more TDs in explosive 3rd Q in which California went ahead 36-15.

WASHINGTON STATE 21 Stanford 21 (Spokane): Cougars (1-3-1) QB Jerry Henderson (8-20/128y, TD, INT), Pac-8's leading passer, was outdone by Stanford (3-1-1) QB Jim Plunkett (14-30/222y, TD, 4 INTs). Henderson scored 2 running TDs in 2nd Q to keep H score in 14-14 deadlock. Indians' part in 1st H tie was authored by Plunkett and WR Gene Washington (8/110y, TD) as fleet receiver toted 39y pass to 1YL with only secs left in 1st H. Plunkett rolled out on next play for tying TD. Henderson boosted Washington State to 21-14 lead with 12y TD pass to WR Larry Thatcher in 3rd Q. With 6:18 showing on 4th Q clock, nifty Washington nabbed short

pass and banged through 2 defenders to score TD for Tribe. Stanford expected to get ball back, so it went for tying kick by K Steve Horowitz. But, Wazzu enlived matters in closing moments with 67y TD bomb from Henderson to WR Johnny Davis, but it was called back because Davis was flagged for motion as he set up.

AP Poll October 21

1 Southern California (21)	800	11 California	138
2 Ohio State (15)	784	12 Michigan	116
3 Kansas (5)	660	13 Texas	112
4 Penn State (1)	580	14 Missouri	103
5 Notre Dame	442	15 Florida	73
6 Tennessee	418	16 Arkansas	63
7 Purdue	410	17 Mississippi	60
8 Georgia	369	18 Louisiana State	43
9 Miami	194	19 Texas Tech	36
10 Syracuse	160	20 Florida State	26

October 26, 1968

Georgia 35 KENTUCKY 14: Playing their best ball of season, no. 8 silver-panted Bulldogs (5-0-1) destroyed Kentucky (2-4) with 419y on way to romp that reached 21-0 at H. While Georgia O behind clever QB Mike Cavan (12-16/123y, 3 INTs) was piling up big y, star of game was S Jake Scott, who enhanced his usually nifty punt RETs with 2 INT TD RETs. After Bulldogs K Jim McCullough missed FG try in 1st Q, Kentucky QB Doug Bair (10-28/209y, 2 TDs, 4 INTs) had UGa DL Bill Stanfill tip his pass and Scott swoop in for INT which he easily took 33y to score. Cavan hit passes of 19 and 14y on 52y TD advance that bridged 1st and 2nd Qs. Sub TB Steve Farnsworth scored 1st of his 2 TDs of 2nd Q from 3 YL. Trailing 21-0, Bair whipped 23y pass to Georgia 28YL on 1st play of 4th Q. Wildcats lost 2y, but Bair found star HB Dicky Lyons racing behind 2 defenders for 30y TD reception. Scott swiped another Bair pass and dodged and weaved and broke tackles on spectacular 35y TD RET for 28-7 lead. Bair and Lyons teamed up for short pass which Lyons broke open for 92y TD, tying SEC record for distance.

VANDERBILT 14 Florida 14: *Nashville Tennessean* writer John Bibb suggested that for Vanderbilt (2-3-1) "this tie must have been like kissing Miss America." Preseason SEC title aspirant Florida (4-1-1) scored 1st, in last min of 2nd Q, when Vandy P Steve Smith lost snap, but Florida couldn't shake tenacious Commodores. Vandy tied it 7-7 early in 3rd Q, going 57y: Runs, including 6y TD by TB John Valput, were called on 5 of 6 plays, wrapped around 30y pass by QB John Miller to WB Dave Strong. Early in 4th Q, Vandy's Smith bombed his longest punt (50y) of game, and Gators DB Steve Tannen appeared well hemmed in on his RET. But, Tannen gave ground inside his 20YL to break away for 72y punt TD RET. After taking punt on their 38YL in 4th Q, Commodores cranked up their slumbering O. QB Miller hit passes of 18 and 7y passes that led to TB Alan Spear converting 4th down run at UF 33YL. Tannen nearly spoiled Vandy TD party with INT, but WR Curt Chesley knocked pass away, and, on next play, Miller found his secondary receiver, TE Jim Cunningham, for 33y TD. Tannen's actual INT at his 19YL ruined Vandy hopes of pulling out late win.

AUBURN 31 Miami 6: Mighty effort by snarling Tigers D was key to smashing upset of no. 9 Miami (4-2). Hurricanes were battered for incredible net loss of –85y on ground as they lost y on 10 runs and 10 passes; leading way was Auburn (4-2) DT David Campbell who spectacularly scored 7 sacks/-59y. Victory got rolling midway in 1st Q when Plainsmen LB Bobby Strickland went 36y to TD with INT of harried Hurricanes QB David Olivo (8-22/191y, INT). Tigers QB Loran Carter (15-28/274y, 3 INTs) pitched 3 TD passes, including 52 and 24y to WR Tim Christian (7/151y, 2 TDs), who set new season reception mark for Auburn of 36. Only Hurricanes' score came after DB Dean Stone made INT at Auburn 49YL in 3rd Q, and Olivo made good on Miami's best play of game, 37y pitch to WR Ray Bellamy to poise HB Vince Opalsky (11/-4y, TD) for 4y TD blast up middle.

PURDUE 44 Iowa 14: Purdue (5-1), long-time purveyor of solid passing, attemptd only 3 aerials with QB Mike Phipps out with injury, and none of them succeeded. On other hand, Boilermakers rushed 92 times for new Big 10 record for attempts and gained 483y against defenseless Iowa (2-4). Hawkeyes had gone ahead 7-6 early in 2nd Q as FB Tim Sullivan caught 22y TD screen pass from QB Larry Lawrence (8-18/90y, TD, 3 INTs), which came after HB Ed Podolak's surprise 45y completion to WR Barry Crees (6/110y). HB Leroy Keyes sprinted 51y for go-ahead TD in 2nd Q and added another to start 2nd H scoring to place himself in school record book as leading career scorer. Except for Keyes' long run, all Purdue scores came on short plunges at end of drives that featured fierce but predictable power runs.

MICHIGAN 33 Minnesota 20: Little Brown Jug trophy was earned by Michigan (5-1) as it strode through Gophers' tattered D for TDs on 4 series in row and riddled Minny for 30-0 score by H. Wolverines D set up TDs with FUM REC at 10YL, HB George Hoey's 40y punt RET, and INTs by DBs Tom Curtis and Brian Healy. UM QB Dennis Brown (11-20/152y, 2 TDs) flipped 2 TD passes and HB Ron Johnson (33/84y, 2 TDs) powered over twice, while final tallies of 1st H came on K Tim Killian's 24 and 32y FGs. With Michigan reserves on field, Minnesota (3-3) made matters look more respectable with 3 TDs in 4th Q: Gophers sub QB Ray Stephens (7-19/144y, 2 TDs, 2 INTs) fired screaming 88y TD bomb to WR Chip Litten and made 12y TD pitch to E Leon Trawick, followed by his 2-pt pass to FB Jim Carter. In between, Minny FB Barry Mayer powered 5y to score after apparent Michigan INT was nullified by interference PEN.

Ohio State 31 ILLINOIS 24: Lowly Illinois (0-6) was predictably behind 24-0 at H as Ohio State (5-0) QB Rex Kern scored on runs of 11 and 16y. Then, something strange happened: Illini struck for FB Rich Johnson's TD and 2-pt run after recovering FB Jim Otis' FUM at Ohio 30YL. Still, it was Buckeyes ahead by 24-8. But, inspired Illinois went 86 and 80y to TDs by QB Bob Naponic and FB Ken Bargo, and in each case, Illini TD-scorer then responded with 2-pt run. Suddenly, it was 24-24 with 4:38 to play in 4th Q, and Champaign crowd was going completely nuts. Talent won out in end: Kern started late drive from Buckeyes 24YL, but was banged up. Sub QB Ron Maciejowski pitched 40y pass to TE Jan White and tossed 4y game-winner to Otis with 2:35 on clock.

MICHIGAN STATE 21 Notre Dame 17: Unpredictable Spartans (4-2) were annihilated on stat sheet 455y to 247y, but used on-side KO to start game and 2 GLSs to frustrate Notre Dame (4-2). Opening drive after surprise KO REC took Michigan State 42y to 1st of 2 TDs by HB Tommy Love. Behind 14-10 in 3rd Q, ND downed punt at 1YL, and DE Bob Kuechenberg recovered EZ FUM of Spartans QB Bill Triplett for TD on next play. Love's 2nd TD regained lead for Michigan State at 21-17 in 3rd Q. Last Irish surge reached MSU 3YL with 1:00 left as QB Terry Hanratty (312y passing) hit 7 passes in row. WR Al Brenner came in on D in secondary to knock down Hanratty's pass and tackle QB at 2YL to inspire dramatic GLS for Spartans.

COLORADO 41 Oklahoma 27: Rebuilding year at Colorado (4-2) took positive turn in win over disappointing Oklahoma (2-3). Dynamic CU QB Bob Anderson (8-14/70y) rushed 28/185y, 3 TDs, and crossed GL 3 times in 2nd Q, and when FBs Ward Walsh and Tom Nigbur added 3rd Q TDs, Buffs led 34-6. Meanwhile, Boulder Homecoming patrons nibbled their nails as OU compiled 508y of O, with prime perpetrator being TB Steve Owens (34/193y, 2 TDs). Abruptly, Sooners came alive early in 4th Q with Owens' 2nd TD coming on 11y ramble around left side to end 72y tour to paydirt. QB Bobby Warmack's 20y TD pass to WB Eddie Hinton concluded OU's next series, and Sooners soon went 70y to score, mostly on Warmack (14-23/217y, TD, INT) to Hinton (6/133y, TD) for 48y aerial gain. With 5 mins left, Oklahoma trailed only 34-27. Colorado then "made a heckuva drive," according to OU coach Chuck Fairbanks as Anderson carried 5/33y, including gutsy run on 4th-and-5 at 16YL. FB Nigbur scored his 2nd TD to ice it from 3y out. But, this effort would take lot out of Bison as they dropped their last 4 games to finish with their 1st losing season at 4-6 in 4 years.

Southern Methodist 39 TEXAS TECH 18: Red Raiders (3-1-2), leaders of SWC, moved to 10-0 lead as QB Joe Matulich dashed 36y to score in 1st Q. Stunningly, SMU (5-1) struck for 2 TDs within 15 secs, thanks to 2 FUM RECs: QB Chuck Hixson (29-51/296y, 2 TDs) passed 15y to E Ken Fleming and 23y to WR Jerry Levias. Mustangs added K Bicky Lesser's 2 long FGs and safety for 22-10 H lead. CB Mike Nekuza's 26y INT TD RET highlighted 2nd H as SMU built prohibitive 39-10 margin.

CALIFORNIA 43 Syracuse 0: With eye on USC showdown 2 weeks hence, Golden Bears (5-1) buried Orangemen (3-2) in Strawberry Canyon under avalanche of 9 TOs. California QB Randy Humphries ran for 10y TD after LB Jerry Woods' INT and for 8y TD after Syracuse P Art Thoms' 7y punt. TD runbacks by WB Gary Fowler (punt RET) and DB Bernie Keeles (INT RET) were shuffled among K Ron Miller's 3 FGs. Syracuse's only threat came in 4th Q when DB Tony Kyasky's 21y punt RET carried to Cal 42YL, but drive died with Bears LB Mike McCaffrey's INT at 6YL.

UCLA 20 Stanford 17: Hopeful Stanford (3-2-1) nabbed 14-0 H lead on QB Jim Plunkett's TD run and TD pass. Tribe coach John Ralston remarked later that he had never before been so sure of victory during H break. Yet, when it was over, Ralston lamented unusual official's decision in closing secs of 2nd Q. Plunkett (25-43/272y, TD, INT) misfired on EZ pass on 3rd down from 6YL, but WR Gene Washington (13/113y) was called for O pass interference and with it, Stanford turned over possession without being able to try FG for 17-0 lead. UCLA (3-3) broke out of its haze with abrupt 64y TD pass to WR Gwen Cooper at 1:03 of 3rd Q. Bruins DT Larry Agajanian quickly forced FUM by Indians HB Bubba Brown (18/114y) and another TD by Bruins pulled them to within 14-12. Stanford K Bill Shoemaker's 4th Q FG upped count to 17-12, but UCLA pounced for winning TD with 3:43 to go in 4th Q. Bruins sub QB Jim Nader was in for Bill Bolden and threw 50y pass to E Ron Copeland, who wrestled catch away from 2 defenders at Indians 3YL. UCLA TB Greg Jones dived over for TD, but DB Mark Gustafson's GL pass breakup was required.

AP Poll October 28

1 Southern California (24)	786	11 Texas	153
2 Ohio State (12)	722	12 Notre Dame	112
3 Kansas (6)	686	13 Southern Methodist	92
4 Penn State (1)	592	14 Louisiana State	74
5 Tennessee	442	15 Houston	67
6 Purdue	420	16 Michigan State	66
7 Georgia	394	17 Arkansas	63
8 California	336	18 Florida State	38
9 Michigan	260	19 Ohio University	25
10 Missouri	197	20 Florida	20

November 2, 1968

HARVARD 28 Pennsylvania 6: Unaccustomed to Ivy hierarchy as attested by its 26-50-1 record to date in 1960s, Penn (5-1) was beaten early in this showdown by equally surprising Harvard (6-0). Crimson DB Pat Conway's 2 INTs of Penn QB Bernie "Alphabet Soup" Zbrzeznj and DL John Cramer's FUM REC gave Harvard opportunity to build 14-0 1st Q lead. Before 1st Q was over, HB Vic Gatto ran back punt 70y for TD and 21-0 edge. Quakers failed to score until 4th Q when HB Ken Dunn swept RE to TD.

PENN STATE 28 Army 24: Nittany Lions' 14th straight win was littered with unexpected occurrences. Penn State (6-0) led 9-0 when it scored 1st Q safety on punt snap over head of Cadets FB-P Charlie Jarvis. Army (4-3) rallied in 2nd Q on TD pass by QB Steve Lindell (18-29/258y, 2 TD). With score 16-10 in Lions favor in 4th Q, K Bob Garthwaite's FG was held up by wind, and when Cadets DB Jim McCall accidentally kicked bounding ball, Penn State fell on it at Army 2YL. Penn State HB Bob Campbell (104y rushing) soon had his 2nd TD. Lindell hit TE Gary Steele with 58y bomb to lead to FB Jarvis' short TD run, and Army trailed 22-17. Ball squirted from frantic on-side

KO pileup, and was scooped up by Lions TE Ted Kwalick for unmolested 53y TD. Undaunted but soon out of time, Lindell connected on 4 straight passes, including 8y TD to Steele.

Clemson 24 NORTH CAROLINA STATE 19: TB Ray Yauger's 7y TD run with less than min to play gave Tigers (2-4-1) come-from-behind win. Things started well for North Carolina State (5-3), undefeated in ACC play coming in, as HB Bobby Hall raced 80y for TD on opening play of game. QB Billy Ammons went to work with TD pass and TD run, so Clemson led 17-10 in 4th Q. But, Wolfpack struck for safety and QB Jack Klebe's TD pass in less than min for 19-17 lead. Tigers went 69y in 7 plays to winning TD with HB Charlie Waters' 25y catch as key.

ALABAMA 20 Mississippi State 13: Wonderful opportunity for struggling Mississippi State (0-6-1) flew away when LG Jerry Jackson stumbled and allowed Alabama (5-2) NG Sam Gellerstedt to punch through line and deck Maroons QB Tommy Pharr at Tide 22YL as E Sammy Milner romped all alone in EZ, waiting for TD pass that could have brought tie. Earlier, Alabama TB Ed Morgan capped 62y drive with short TD run in 1st Q. Bulldogs TB Lynn Zeringue matched that TD with leap from 1YL later in 1st Q, but K Robert Culver's x-pt sailed wide. After Tide FB Pete Jilleba scored in 2nd Q, DB-K Mike Dean sent Bama off with 20-6 H edge by booting 26 and 29y FGs. Pharr, who surpassed Jackie Parker's 1953 school total O record for season with 1339y, hit Milner with TD pass in middle of 3rd Q.

Mississippi 27 LOUISIANA STATE 24: Pulling out Ole Miss (5-2) win in last min, QB Archie Manning showed brilliantly with 24-40/344y, 2 TDs passing and scored on TD run. After exchange of FGs, LSU (5-2) got 2nd Q TDs from TBs Tommy Allen and Glenn Smith on 30y catch. Yet, there was Manning to trim Tigers H lead to 17-10 with 65y TD pass to WB Floyd Franks. Rebels' FG broke 17-17 deadlock in 4th Q. Tigers countered with FB Kenny Newfield's 11y TD run to regain lead at 24-20. FB Bo Bowen started winning 75y march with 17y run, and Manning hit 4 passes in row.

TENNESSEE 42 Ucla 18: Volunteers (5-0-1), decked out in their pale orange made to match color of daisies from hills above Knoxville campus, and Bruins (3-4), wearing their powder blue and gold, renewed distant rivalry that was more heated than those pastel shades would ordinarily signify. Tennessee sputtered on 4 1st H scoring threats, twice when INTs by UCLA secondary intervened, so battle was fairly close at 14-0 for Tennessee in 1st 30 mins. Vols, who would gain 515y and 32 1st downs before carnage ended, exploded for 3 quick TDs in 3rd Q for 35-0 lead: TB Richmond Flowers on 1y dive after DB Mike Jones' INT RET to 14YL, FB Richard Pickens on 33y draw play, and 11y TD pass by QB Bobby Scott (7-15/96y, TD) to TE Terry Dalton. QB Bubba Wyche (17-24/223y, TD) had done most of his aerial damage in 1st H. HB Mickey Cureton woke up West Coasters with 99y KO TD RET, but x-pt was missed and it induced Uclans into unsuccessful 2-pt tries after QBs James Nader and Bill Bolden threw and ran for late window-dressing TDs.

Virginia Tech 40 FLORIDA STATE 22: Hokies (4-3) had recently stumbled on O, but this trip to Tallahassee found them piling up 382y rushing, while their D did pass trapping with astounding 6 INTs of Florida State (4-2). Coach Jerry Claiborne switched LB Ken Edwards to FB, and jr runner came up with 17/197y rushing with 2nd Q TDs of 14y on pass reception from QB Al Kincaid (7-15/53y, TD) and 88y dash. Each came after INT as had TB Terry Smoot's opening 3y TD run for 10-0 lead in 1st Q. With score at 24-7 in 2nd Q, Seminoles tried KO RET lateral that turned into FUM and Virginia Tech FB George Constantinides' 10y TD burst. FSU QB Bill Cappleman shrugged off his pickoffs long enough to connect with TE Jim Tyson for TD passes in 2nd and 4th Qs.

OHIO STATE 25 Michigan State 20: QBs Rex Kern (9-12/138y, TD) and Ron Maciejowski (7-14/77y, and 2y TD rushing) shared field general role for Ohio State (6-0), providing balanced attack of 214y on ground and 215y in air. E Bruce Jankowski (8/88y) caught 34y pass from Kern to spark opening 83y TD drive capped by FB Jim Otis' TD plunge. To amazement of those who typecast coach Woody Hayes, Buckeyes opened game with 3 passes in row. Kern and Jankowski hooked up on 13y TD for 13-0 lead in 2nd Q before QB Bill Triplett (9-15/137y, TD, 3 INTs) rallied Michigan State (4-3) with TD run in 2nd Q and TD pass to WR Frank Foreman. Triplett was under terrific pressure, losing 2 FUMs, while being thrown for 67y in losses while trying to pass or run option plays. Spartans lost 7 TOs to ruin any chance they had of upset and 429y to 271y O disparity helped in no way.

Nebraska 24 IOWA STATE 13: Nebraska (5-2) sent swivel-hipped HB Joe Orduna across for 2y TD run in game's opening 3:25 and followed with FB Dick Davis' picking his way through Iowa State (3-5) line for 4y TD in 2nd Q after DT Bob Liggett swallowed FUM at Cyclones 22YL. Behind 14-0, Iowa State surprised Cornhuskers with TB Jeff Allen's 35y TD run, but Nebraska struck back in 1:11 as QB Ernie Sigler (12-17/161y, TD) hit 6 passes in row, last for 8y TD to WR Tom Penney. Cyclones added late TD as QB John Warder marched his team 55y.

KANSAS 27 Colorado 14: Soph Jayhawks FB John Riggins became killer in rain, rushing 22/162y, TD and rambling 63y to set up K Bill Bell's early 20y FG. Despite twice bobbling wet ball in 1st H, Kansas (7-0) jumped to 17-0 lead as Riggins slashed through RG for 21y TD, and his brother, WB Junior Riggins, caught 6y TD pass from QB Bobby Douglass. Bell kicked another FG, this of career-long 38y. Down 27-0 in 4th Q, Colorado (4-3) sprung FB Tom Nigbur for 3y TD blast and 80y TD gallop up middle on draw play. Superb Buffs QB Bob Anderson was held to career-low 32y total O. Bowl talk, perhaps premature, sprung up in Kansas dressing room afterward, but coach Pepper Rodgers was unaffected, saying, "If we coaches tried to get them not to mention bowls or think about them, it would be just like telling 'em not to think about girls."

Arkansas 25 TEXAS A&M 22: Razorbacks (6-1) blew themselves into crowded throne room in SWC by playing stiff south wind to perfection. Of game's 7 TDs, only Arkansas TB Bill Burnett's 2y dive off RG early in 4th Q, was scored against roaring gust. Even that decisive score was positioned by Hogs' move to Texas A&M (2-5) 26YL with wind and by close of 3rd Q. Aggies got ball in 2nd Q and erased 6-0 shortfall as QB Edd Hargett (29-55/319y, 3 TDs) whipped 2 TDs passes with breeze. Arkansas chose to take wind in 3rd Q, and its 2 TD passes by QB Bill Montgomery (20-29/258y, 2 TDs) were difference as Hogs took 19-14 lead. Less than min and half remained in 3rd Q when Montgomery, who had completed his last 11 passes, went back to skies, withstanding fierce pass rush of Texas A&M DE Mike DeNiro and DT Rolf Krueger, to hit WR Max Peacock for 11y and TE Mike Sigman for 31y before having to change over for 4th Q. Hargett and WB Bob Long collaborated on their 2nd TD pass with 2:41 left.

Southern California 20 OREGON 13: Unlikely Oregon (3-4) nearly found how to succeed without really tying no. 1 USC (6-0). Ducks held Trojans TB O.J. Simpson to 67y rushing overall, staged 1-min rally in 3rd Q, and missed tying pass from 8YL with 11 secs to go. Simpson's 1y TD run, his 15th of year, gave Trojans 13-0 lead midway in 3rd Q. Suddenly, Ducks turned hot as DB Jack Gleason's INT and QB Eric Olson's 4th down pass led to 3y TD run by FB Stan Hearn. USC lost handle on next KO for REC by Ducks. Hearn dashed for EZ and his forward FUM was recovered by Olson to tie it 13-13. QB Steve Sogge's TD pass to TE Bob Klein locked win with 1:13 left, but Trojans had to weather Ducks' late goalward flight.

AP Poll November 4

1 Southern California (19)	816	11 California	192
2 Ohio State (14)	803	12 Notre Dame	183
3 Kansas (10)	758	13 Houston	140.5
4 Penn State (1)	558	14 Arkansas	124
5 Tennessee (1)	541	15 Oregon State	48
6 Purdue	415	16 Ohio University	44
7 Michigan	371	17 Michigan State	34
8 Missouri	284	18 Auburn	31
9 Georgia	277.5	19 Wyoming	29
10 Texas	263	20 Louisiana State	18

November 9, 1968

Yale 30 PENNSYLVANIA 13: Yale (7-0) won its 15th straight game and, with TD in each Q, had scored in 16 Qs in row. QB Brian Dowling (9-18/180y, 2 TDs) threw 1st H TD passes to HB Calvin Hill, who made leaping 1-handed grab for 51y, and E Del Marting for 12y. Penn (5-2) registered score for 1st time midway in 4th Q on QB Bernie Zbrzeznj's sneak at end of 40y trip. Hill (19/126y, TD) added 15y TD soon thereafter.

ARMY 58 Boston College 25: FB Charlie Jarvis gained 253y to eclipse Glenn Davis' 23-year-old Army (5-3) single-game rushing record. Boston College (3-3) had gotten off to good start as QB Frank Harris (37-57/374y, 2 TDs, 4 INTs) connected with E Barry Gallup for 48y pass, but had to settle for K Bob Gallivan's 25y FG. When Cadets exploded for 23 2nd Q pts, which included QB Steve Lindell's 2 TD passes and Jarvis reaching 200y by H, Harris had to devote much of afternoon to pitching Eagles to new school record of 374y in air. Jarvis ripped for 46y TD run and HB Lynn Moore raced 79y on punt TD RET in 3rd Q for 37-13 Army lead. BC HB Dave Bennett scored his 2nd and 3rd TDs, these on passes by Harris, to trim Cadets' edge to 44-25. But 4 Army INTs took their toll, and LB Ken Johnson's 41y INT RET set up 1 of Black Knights' 4th Q TDs.

PENN STATE 22 Miami 7: Late in 1st Q, Miami (5-3) WR Ray Bellamy slipped behind deep secondary of Penn State (7-0) for 78y TD bomb from QB David Olivo. Leading 7-0 late in 2nd Q, Hurricanes were wrecked by DE Tony Cline's knee injury: Nittany Lions were able to aim their attack at his replacement, and away from outstanding DE Ted Hendricks. Penn State HB Charlie Pittman (26/123y) rushed for 93y and all of team's 3 TDs in 2nd H. Mount Nit LB Jack Ham fell on FUM, blocked punt, and joined DLs Mike Reid, Frank Spaziani, and Lincoln Lippincott, and DB Neal Smith in limiting Miami O to 20y in 2nd H.

North Carolina State 17 DUKE 15: Wolfpack (6-3) played remarkably clutch game on D: Twice it stopped Duke (3-5) on 4th down plays inches from GL, and twice it stymied 4th Q Devil advancements with INTs. NC State DBs Jack Whitley picked off pass at his 6YL and Dick Idol made EZ INT. In 2nd Q, Duke FB Phil Asack tried power runs 4 times after 1st-and-goal at NC State 8YL, but was halted inches short by DLs Ron Carpenter and Art Hudson. After that GLS, Wolfpack responded with 99y drive to WB Bobby Hall's 2y sprint around LE. DB John Cappellano paved way for both Blue TDs in 2nd H with FUM RECs inside State territory. Duke QB Leo "Goober" Hart (18-37/189y, TD, 3 INTs) threw 17y TD pass to TE Jim Dearth in 3rd Q, but K Earl Mowry's x-pt, which sought to tie it 10-10, was blocked by Wolfpack DE Mark Capuano. With 3:50 to play, Hart rolled out to score 5y TD, but his run-pass option for tying 2-pts was buried by Carpenter and Hudson.

ALABAMA 16 Louisiana State 7 (Birmingham): QB Scott Hunter (13-22/232y, INT), latest in 1960s collection of fine Alabama (6-2) passers, threw 2 TDs, set up FG with aerial game at Birmingham. Hunter hit FB Pete Jilleba for 11y for TD in 1st Q and WR Donnie Sutton for 16y TD in 4th Q. LSU (5-3) enjoyed brief 7-6 lead in 3rd Q when QB Jimmie Gilbert gained 16, 17y on delay runs, and FB Kenny Newfield blasted for 15y TD.

AUBURN 28 Tennessee 14 (Birmingham): Conf leader Auburn (6-2) stayed undefeated in SEC with upset of unbeaten Tennessee (5-1-1) in Birmingham nightcap. QB Loran Carter threw 2 TD passes as Tigers raced to 21-0 2nd Q margin. Back came Volunteers on arm of QB Bubba Wyche (25-45/337y, 2 TDs), who tossed TD passes to WR Gary Kreis and WB George Silvey despite heavy rush pressure all night. Carter iced it on 1st play of 4th Q when he connected on 49y TD pass to E Tim Christian.

Georgia 51 Florida 0 (Jacksonville): Bulldogs (6-0-2) sloshed through tornado warnings, heavy rain that nearly drowned Gators (4-3-1). Florida gained 209y mostly in own end and lost 5 TOs in its worst defeat since 1942. Gators failed to cross

midfield until trailing 41-0 in 3rd Q. Meanwhile, QB Mike Cavan threw 2 TD passes as part of Georgia's stellar 13-16/188y air game. Bulldogs employed 7 different TD-makers.

MINNESOTA 27 Purdue 13: Flagging Rose Bowl hopes of Purdue (6-2) were dashed by Minnesota (4-4) FB Jim Carter (17/101y), who doubled in winter as rugged hockey defenseman for Gophers. Carter ran 49y to early 1st Q TD, added 2 TD plunges after D forced INT and FUM. Gophers DB Jeff Wright's INT allowed QB Ray Stephens to make it 27-0 at H on 3y rollout behind crushing block of WR Chip Litten. Ailing Boilermakers QB Mike Phipps (12-21 in air) came off bench to spark 2 TD drives in 2nd H.

Oklahoma 27 KANSAS 23: Jayhawks' joyride atop Big 8 hit significant bump as Kansas (7-1) fell full game behind Missouri, 42-7 winner over Iowa State. Oklahoma (4-3) TB Steve Owens (37/157y) and the Lead was exchanged 4 times in 2nd H as TB Donnie Shanklin and FB John Riggins scored for Jayhawks. Behind 23-20, Sooners went 81y with Owens gaining 32y and winning TD from 6YL. DB Steve Barrett wrapped it up with 1:29 left as he made EZ INT of Kansas QB Bobby Douglass, who passed 11-28/240y, including early 75y TD.

SOUTHERN CALIFORNIA 35 California 17: Cal's "Bear Minimum" D, which entered game with nation's best 5.6 per-game scoring avg, had USC (7-0) coach John McKay saying beforehand: "We're not nervous, we're scared." Instead, Trojans broke open game with 5 TDs in middle Qs. TB O.J. Simpson (31/164y) tallied on runs of 39 and 7y, then went to sideline to bask in 35-3 lead. California (5-2-1) QB Randy Humphries pitched pair of 4th Q TD passes against Trojan reserves.

AP Poll November 11

1 Southern California (32)	908		11 Tennessee	188
2 Ohio State (14)	864		12 Auburn	172
3 Penn State (1)	744		13 Oregon State	150
4 Michigan	542		14 Houston	131
5 Georgia	530		15 Purdue	111
6 Missouri	492		16 Alabama	63
7 Kansas	387		17 Ohio University	49
8 Texas	371		18 California	31
9 Notre Dame	213		19 Indiana	30
10 Arkansas	193		20 Wyoming	26

November 16, 1968

VIRGINIA 63 Tulane 47: Game was akin to new kind of scoring free-for-all that arrived in 1968 such as Iowa 68-34 over Northwestern, Arizona State 63-28 over New Mexico, West Texas State 53-36 over Western Michigan and Ohio University 60-48 over Cincinnati. Virginia's 16-year wait for winning record was delayed until it locked up frantic 1005y O battle in last 7 mins. Cavaliers (6-3) overcame 3-0 1st Q disadvantage by turning blocked punt and FUM REC into TDs. Virginia QB Gene Arnett threw 4 TD passes and HB Frank Quayle ran for 3 TDs. Tulane (2-7) sprung FB Warren Bankston for 59y TD sprint in 2nd Q and gamely fought back to within 49-47 until 2 late TDs by Quayle wrapped it up.

Virginia Tech 17 SOUTH CAROLINA 6: In downpour, Virginia Tech (6-3) all but ignored its passing game (2-4/17y, INT) but TB Terry Smoot rushed for 163y of VPI's 331y and scored game's 1st TD in 2nd Q. South Carolina (3-6), winless at home this year, saw 3 1st H threats fizzle as Gobblers LB Mike Widger sacked Gamecocks QB Tommy Suggs (20-35/239y, TD, INT) to end 2 drives. WR Fred Zeigler (8/107y) caught several passes late in 2nd Q, but clock killed Carolina drive at Va Tech 5YL. Hokies were halted after 2nd H KO, and Gamecocks rolled 70y as Suggs hit Zeigler twice and FB Warren Muir made 1st down on 4th down run. South Carolina's score came when defender deflected Suggs' pass, and Muir caught it for 19y TD. Tech answered right back on 75y drive to FB Ken Edwards' TD and led 14-6. Widger's INT set up 4th Q FG by Gobblers K Jim Simcsak.

TENNESSEE 31 Mississippi 0: Volunteers (6-1-1) rebounded handsomely from previous week's disappointment against Auburn. Tennessee launched bomb after bomb, scoring on 4 TD passes, while completely turning tables on Ole Miss (6-3) QB Archie Manning (16-40/162y, 6 INTs), who suffered through his worst game. Vols set team record with 7 INTs, including 2 each by DB Bill Young and LB Steve Kiner. Tennessee FB Richard Pickens (16/122y) barreled through Rebs on opening drive until QB Bubba Wyche (8-17/179y, 3 TDs, 2 INTs) found WR Gary Kreis for 37y TD connection. Kiner made INT on next series and returned it to 12y to Mississippi 21YL. Wyche took 1 play to whip scoring pass to WB Bill Baker and followed in 2nd Q with 37y TD strike to WB Lester McClain.

Georgia 17 AUBURN 3: Charging Auburn (6-3), winners of 6 of 7 games and standing 4-0 in SEC race, took 3-0 lead on K John Riley's 28y FG after DE Bill James' FUM REC at Bulldogs 34YL in 1st Q. From that point until deep in 4th Q, Tigers never gained another 1st down, being held to 86y O. With its D totally crimping Auburn, Georgia (7-0-2) then got down to business, securing SEC title for itself. K Jim McCullough made good on his 2nd FG try to knot it at 3-3 in 2nd Q. Bulldogs QB Mike Cavan (12-31/168y, TD, 2 INTs) connected with TB Kent Lawrence in left flat and Lawrence burst past DB Merrill Shirley for 22y TD. Just before H, Cavan connected on passes for 54y of 58y drive that ended with his TD sneak. Auburn QB Loran Carter (8-26/63y, 2 INTs), who threw 2 long passes which were picked off in 1st H by Georgia DB Jake Scott, thought things were going well early, but that "Georgia got mighty tough on defense like they always are."

MICHIGAN 34 Wisconsin 9: Michigan (8-1) advanced toward unavoidable collision with Ohio State, 33-27 road victor over Iowa. Wolverines TB Ron Johnson, brother of 1968 American League batting titleist Alex Johnson of California Angels, was overwhelming, scoring on TD runs of 35, 67, 1, 60, and 49y. Johnson's 31/346y shattered week-old

Big 10 single game rushing mark of Iowa's Ed Podolak. Trying to stare down prospect of 14th loss in row, Wisconsin (0-9) took 9-7 H lead when 2 FUM RECs led to QB John Ryan's deflected TD pass to WR Mel Reddick and K Jim Johnson's 34y FG.

NOTRE DAME 34 Georgia Tech 6: Trailing 14-0, Ramblin' Wreck were stopped on downs at Notre Dame (7-2) 17YL in 2nd Q and quickly slipped out of contention on bad play in 3rd Q. Injury-riddled Georgia Tech (4-5) compounded its lack of manpower by having 2 players—C John Collins and DB Bill Kinard (INT)—banished for personal foul PENs. It was Collins' 3rd Q ejection that hurt most: C Billy Kidd, unaccustomed to long snaps, fired midfield punt hike over P Tommy Chapman's head to 16YL. Irish FB Ron Dushney (16/87y, 2 TDs) scored his 2nd TD 5 plays later for 20-0 lead. Yellow Jackets faced their 1st shutout in 39 games, but went 73y in 4th Q as QB Jim Person (17-30/141y, TD, INT) hit 3 straight passes at end, including 16y TD to FB Steve Harkey. ND QB Joe Theismann (5-12/73y, INT) impressed in starting role for injured QB Terry Hanratty, and HB Bob Gladieux (18/77y, 2 TDs) tied Irish record at that time with his 13th TD of season.

OKLAHOMA 28 Missouri 14: Quiet winners of 7 straight, Missouri (7-2) looked to tighten its grip on Big 8 crown. Tough Tigers run D entered game with 98y per game avg, but Oklahoma (5-3) TB Steve Owens (46/177y) submerged that mark with 29/107y rushing in 1st H. Sooners led 7-6 at H break on Owens' 2y run. When Owens added 2 TD plunges and 9y TD pass to WB Eddie Hinton, Oklahoma had handsome 28-6 lead in 4th Q. HB Jon Staggers stoutheartedly made several long gains for Tigers, but moment of glory came on his 2nd Q HB pass for TD to E Chuck Webber.

Kansas 38 KANSAS STATE 29: Kansas (8-1) QB Bobby Douglass produced 4 TDs, 3 by run, as Jayhawks moved into tie for conf lead with Missouri. Kansas enjoyed 21-7 H advantage, but saw emotion switch on punt FUM at own 15YL by DB Tom Anderson. Kansas State (3-6) FB Cornelius Davis scored 4 downs later. Another FUM set up 21-21 tie earned by 1st of 2 TDs by Wildcats RB Mack Herron. K Bill Bell's 41y FG late in 3rd Q regained lead for Kansas, and Douglass' 5y TD run after FB John Riggins' 83y gain extended margin to safer 31-21.

ARKANSAS 35 Southern Methodist 29 (Little Rock): Back after week's absence, Razorbacks (8-1) TB Bill Burnett tallied 3 running TDs and QB Bill Montgomery (13-23/118y, 2 TDs) tossed short TD passes to WR Chuck Dicus and FB Bruce Maxwell. Arkansas converted 3 FUM RECs into TDs and then tacked on unrelenting TD drives of 53 and 62y. With its O stagnated in part by pass rush of Porkers DE Lynn Garner and trailing 35-0, SMU (6-3) finally got cooking in 4th Q, but by then its SWC title hopes were pretty well up in smoke, almost. QB Chuck Hixson (30-49/316y, 4 TDs, INT) fired 4 TD passes in late win bid. It actually started late in 3rd Q, crossing midfield for 1st time in 2nd H, and moving to Hixson's 8y TD to WR Jerry Levias, who had been well collared all game. SMU swarmed midfield sneak attempt on 4th down by Montgomery and struck for TD in 6 plays. Hogs led 35-14 with 11:35 to go and seemed home-free when Arkansas LB Gary Parker made INT of deflected pass at his 16YL. But, Razorbacks fumbled twice to allow 2 more TD passes by Hixson until Maxwell stopped bleeding by covering on-side KO with 56 secs left.

SOUTHERN CALIFORNIA 17 Oregon State 13: Trojans (8-0) clinched 3rd straight Rose Bowl appearance, but not before Beavers (6-3) caused anxious moments. Southern California TB O.J. Simpson was vexed by FUM and 2 dropped passes in scoreless 1st H in which he gained 84y. Oregon State FB Bill Enyart crashed over for 7-0 lead in 3rd Q, and Simpson ruined next drive with FUM at Beavers 35YL. But, "Juice" was workhorse of tying 4th Q TD drive capped by QB Steve Sogge's 22y pass to WR Terry Dekraii. USC quickly got K Ron Ayala's FG and superbly-blocked 40y TD dash by Simpson to thwart Oregon State's blitz. QB Steve Preece's 74y TD pass to HB Billy Main came too late for Beavers.

AP Poll November 18

1 Southern California (27)	704		11 Houston	120
2 Ohio State (7)	636		12 Purdue	118
3 Penn State (2)	571		13 Missouri	110
4 Michigan	545		14 Oklahoma	92
5 Georgia (1)	530		15 Alabama	65
6 Texas	359		16 Oregon State	56
7 Kansas	330		17 Ohio University	41
8 Tennessee	256		18 California	26
9 Arkansas	236		19 Auburn	23
10 Notre Dame	205		20 Wyoming	16

November 23, 1968

GAME OF THE YEAR
HARVARD 29 Yale 29:

Yale (8-0-1) ended up sharing Ivy crown with Harvard (8-0-1), but after watching its 29-13 lead evaporate in last 42 secs, Bulldogs felt final result was "the same as a defeat," according to TE Bruce Weinstein. Yale QB Brian Dowling (13-21/116y) scored on run, passed to HB Calvin Hill and E Del Marting for TDs, and Elis built comfortable 22-0 lead. Desperate Crimson coach John Yovicsin beckoned sub QB Frank Champi from bench to deliver 15y TD pass to E Bruce Freeman in last 39 secs before H. Trailing 22-6, Harvard punted early in 3rd Q, and rash of FUMs suddenly infected Yale. FB Gus Crim scored 3 plays after Harvard REC of Eli FUM of punt. Yale still led 22-13, but coughed up 2 more FUMs in 3rd Q. Dowling's 2nd running TD extended lead to 29-13, and, as 4th Q wound down, he drove Yale to Crimson 32YL. Yet another FUM, Yale's 6th, was lost on screen pass at Crimson 14YL. Harvard created 14-play, 86y drive as T Fritz Reed made big play by alertly scooping up and carrying Champi's FUM for 17y gain. Freeman caught his 2nd TD pass. Crim blasted over for 2 pts, so Harvard trailed 29-21 with 42 secs left. On-side KO was recovered by Crimson DB Bill Kelly at Yale 49YL. Champi ran for 14y, and face-mask PEN put ball at Eli 20YL. Crim's 14y draw was followed by 2 incompletions and 2y loss. Four secs remained. Champi ran in

circles looking for open receiver, finally spotting HB Vic Gatto way over in left sector of EZ for TD. With 0:00 on clock, Champi hit tying 2-pt pass to TE Pete Varney. Harvard fans ecstatically swarmed field, and memory of *The Game* would never die.

WEST VIRGINIA 23 Syracuse 6: Coach Jim Carlen's rebuilding process at West Virginia (7-3) was enhanced by stunning upset of Syracuse (6-3). Mountaineers scored 1st 3 times they possessed ball as QB Mike Sherwood started ablaze with 9 straight completions. Sherwood finished 12-19/112y, 2 TD. TB Eddie Silverio added 33/195y rushing, including 59y run to Orangemen 21YL on WVU's 1st snap. Erratic Syracuse was able to rush for 219y, but couldn't score until reserves were in action in 4th Q.

VIRGINIA 28 Maryland 23: Cavaliers (7-3) TB Frank Quayle rambled for 29/216y rushing and scored 3 TDs, including game-winner from 6YL with 4 mins left to play. Maryland (2-8) wasn't finished at that moment and moved 46y to Virginia 29YL, but 3 incompletions by QB Alan Pastrano (11-24/155y, 2 TDs, INT) killed rally. Pastrano's well-placed passes and effective running and receiving by WR Roland Merritt (4/79y, TD receiving and 3/39y rushing on reverses) kept Terps competitive all day. Quayle opened scoring with 45y run, but Maryland quickly tied as TB John King burst through hole for 92y KO TD RET in 1st Q. Quayle's 2nd TD gave Cavs 14-10 lead heading into 2nd Q, but Pastrano's short TD pass to TB Billy Lovett (111y rushing) after Merritt's juggling 43y catch gave Maryland 16-14 H edge. Teams traded TD passes until UVa consumed nearly 6 mins on winning 80y trip.

South Carolina 7 CLEMSON 3: Clemson (4-5-1) was undefeated but once tied in ACC and looked to lock up conf crown. Bitter rival South Carolina (4-6) rose up to smite Tigers with quicksilver TD in 3rd Q. Tigers had taken opening KO and marched to K Jimmy Barnette's 21y FG. But, Clemson had trouble sustaining its O, being outgained 398y to 156y by game's end. In 3rd Q, Cocks sprung DB Tyler Hellams for 73y punt TD RET. Tigers' loss handed ACC title to North Carolina State, which ended year at 6-1 in conf.

OHIO STATE 50 Michigan 14: Michigan (8-2) TB Ron Johnson (21/91y) scored 2 TDs for conf record 92 pts for season. Ohio State (9-0) got TDs from FB Jim Otis and QB Rex Kern, so titans of Big 10 found themselves even at 14-14 in 2nd Q. With 36 secs left in 1st H, Otis (34/143y, 4 TD) bounced off T Rufus Mayes' block for 2y TD to finish 86y drive called "turning point" by coach Woody Hayes. Leading 21-14, Buckeyes D completely stonewalled Michigan in 3rd Q during which HB Larry Zelina added TD for 27-14 lead. With Wolverines bucking strong 4th Q wind, they were blown away by 23-pt Buckeyes hurricane. Win sent Ohio State on its 1st Rose Bowl trip since 1958.

PURDUE 38 Indiana 35: Hoosiers (6-4) had such high hopes for 1968 season with bevy of starters back to defend their Big 10 title. But, Boilermakers (8-2) star HB Leroy Keyes punctuated his brilliant career with 4 TDs, including decision-maker on 1y run with 1:35 to play. Indiana scoffed at Purdue in early going, despite surprise appearance in locker room by previously-hospitalized Boilers coach Jack Mollenkopf. Hoosiers rode passing wing of gimpy QB Harry Gonso (11-20/132y, 4 TDs) to 28-10 lead early in 3rd Q as WR Jade Butcher (6/62y, 3 TDs) caught scoring passes of 4 and 7y. Indiana's other scores came from speedy soph HB Bob Pernell (17/115y, TD) on game-launching 64y sprint and WR Eric Stolberg's 26y reception from Gonso in 2nd Q. Purdue then set itself for reversal as QB Mike Phipps (16-33/291y, TD, 2 INTs), who suffered several dropped passes by open receivers in 1st H, hit Keyes with 46y slant-in to set up FB Perry Williams' 2y TD plunge. After Keyes scored to open 4th Q to push Purdue within 28-24, Gonso and Butcher retaliated with 29y TD connection at conclusion of 68y voyage. Keyes got loose for 56y rainbow TD throw by scrambling Phipps, and suddenly it was 35-31 in favor of Indiana. Boilers went 77y with setup coming on TE Gary Fenner's 26y romp with pass to 1YL. Remarkable Keyes scored and finished game with 28/140y, 3 TDs rushing and 6/149y, TD receiving. Football has rarely seen talent like his since.

Kansas 21 MISSOURI 19: For 17th time in 77 border meetings, result was decided by fewer than 4 pts. Kansas (9-1) prevailed partly because blocked conv kick by DB Bill Hunt in 2nd Q forced subsequent failed 2-pt try by Tigers. In 1st Q, Jayhawks leapt to 14-0 lead as DB Dave Morgan (2 INTs, FUM REC) returned INT of Tigers' 1st pass for 35y TD and QB Bobby Douglass fired 33y TD to WR George McGowan. Missouri (7-3), which held slight O edge, got 2 TD runs from HB Jon Staggers, trailed 21-12 early in 4th Q. After Tiger QB Terry McMillan's 42y completion to WR Mel Gray, he hit hit TB Greg Cook with 10y TD with 2:05 left. Kick made it 21-19, but Kansas maintained possession on TE John Mosier's 19y grab on 3rd down.

Air Force 58 COLORADO 35: Air Force (7-3) sprung HBs Jim DeOrio and Ernie Jennings for 4 TDs, and QB Gary Baxter pitched 3 TD passes. Enjoying leads of 21-7, 35-21 at H and 45-21 in 2nd H, Falcons rolled up game totals of 32 1st downs, 381y on ground, and 13-20/149y in air. Game didn't turn into rout until Colorado (4-6) lost 2 FUMs deep in own territory in 2nd H. Still, Buffs stats had appearance of winner: 381y rushing, 13-20/149y passing. QB Bob Anderson ran for 2 TDs, passed for another, and TB Steve Engel tallied twice.

Arkansas 42 TEXAS TECH 7: Arkansas (9-1) got rolling on DB Tommy Dixon's 28y INT TED RET. Hogs then used soph duo to spark 304y O. TB Bill Burnett, playing with fractured toe, ran for 2 TDs, caught 21y TD pass from QB Bill Montgomery, who also ran for TD. Texas Tech (5-3-2) managed to narrow H deficit to 14-7 when FB Jacky Stewart plunged over from 1YL in 2nd Q. Bowl-bound Arkansas waited to see Texas' Cotton Bowl fate on Thanksgiving, but had Sugar Bowl bid in back pocket.

ARIZONA 14 Wyoming 7: Before record Tucson crowd, Arizona's no.4-ranked D thoroughly corralled Cowboy (7-3) running game, shutting it down to extent of 27y. Wyoming was forced to punt 11 times, and with its loss went 16-game WAC winning streak. After exchange of 1st H TDs, Arizona (8-1) secured winning TD with 7:12 to play. Wildcats pounced on FUM at Cowboy 28YL, and FB Ed Mitchell plowed over from 1YL.

HOUSTON 100 Tulsa 6: Houston (6-1-2) piled up 100 pts for 1st time since Connecticut beat the Newport (R.I.) Naval Training School 125-0 and Wyoming trounced Northern Colorado 103-0, both in 1949. Tulsa (2-7) found itself in bad spot, giving up 49 pts in 4th Q because 15 starters began feeling puny from flu attacks. Cougars' next-to-last TD eventually gained notoriety in Country Music circles because it was scored by sub WR Larry Gatlin, who gained fame with singing Gatlin Brothers. K Terry Leiwecke booted game's 100th pt, his 13th conv kick, and said he was never so nervous as he awaited snap. Houston was on scoring binge, having beaten Idaho 77-3 in prior week.

Southern California 28 UCLA 16: Southern California (9-0) coach John McKay "implanted doubt" in minds of UCLA (3-7) D by twice sending TB O.J. Simpson in motion right while blasting FB Dan Scott ran left off blocks of T Jack O'Malley. It worked well, but Trojans' most effective weapon remained Simpson (40/200y, 3 TDs), whose season rushing totals of 334/1654y became national records at that time. For its part, UCLA gained 1st H leads of 3-0 and 10-7 on K Zenon Andrysyshun's 32y FG and HB Mickey Cureton's 1st of 2 TD runs. Trailing 21-16 in 4th Q, Bruins reached USC 1YL after 75y drive, but Trojan D braced itself: QB Jim Nader slipped down just short of GL on 3rd down run, and USC halted 4th down play. LB Jim Snow's INT of Nader halted last UCLA threat at USC 43YL. Simpson slashed for 17 and 26y and scored from 4YL to place Bruins in ruins. "Only 40 carries?," said McKay after he saw stat sheet. "O.J. can dance tonight."

OREGON STATE 41 Oregon 19: Beavers (7-3) locked up 2nd place in Pac-8 as HB Billy Main put them ahead for good with 94y KO TD RET in 2nd Q, and FB Bill Enyart rumbled for TD runs of 2, 12, and 1y. QB Eric Olson got Oregon (4-6) back in contention with a 3y TDrun early in 2nd Q that knotted it at 7-7, but Main broke away from Duck special teamers at his 30YL and raced away for his long KO RET for 13-7 lead. Oregon State followed with TDs by Enyart and Main for 27-7 bulge by H. Olson gave Duck fans something to cheer about with 30y TD peg in 4th Q that trimmed deficit to 34-19. Beavers wrested away control of in-state rivalry for 1st time at 32-31-9 since winning initial meeting in 1894.

AP Poll November 25

1 Ohio State (21.5)	935	11 Oklahoma	213
2 Southern Calif. (24.5)	925	12 Purdue	210
3 Penn State (3)	773	13 Michigan	189
4 Georgia (1)	597	14 Oregon State	96
5 Kansas	524	15 Alabama	76
6 Texas	494	16 Missouri	66
7 Tennessee	446	17 Ohio University	58
8 Arkansas	394	18 Auburn	38
9 Notre Dame	301	19 Arizona	19
10 Houston	234	20 Arizona State	17

November 28-30, 1968

(Th'g) TEXAS 35 Texas A&M 14: Longhorns (8-1-1) stampeded for 5 TDs in 1st H, clinching share of SWC and spot in Cotton Bowl. WR Cotton Speyrer followed FB Steve Worster's 1st Q TD plunge with 23y E-around TD run and added 8y TD catch. TB Chris Gilbert scored 3y TD and his 85y placed him 3rd all-time to date in career rushing with 3,231y. Texas DB Bill Bradley, recent convert from QB, tied SWC record with 4 INTs. Closing disappointing year, Aggies (3-7) didn't get rolling until DB Ross Brupbacher's 41y INT RET in 3rd Q. A&M QB Edd Hargett, who overcame strong rush to pass for 221y, followed INT with with 1st of his 2 TD passes.

Army 21 Navy 14 (Philadelphia): Army (7-3) entered 69th meeting with Navy (2-8) as prohibitive favorite. Cadets went 66y late in 1st Q mostly on sweeps to 5y TD run by FB Charlie Jarvus (21/88y). HB Hank Andrzejczak (14/94y) swept 36y to set up Jarvus' 2nd TD in 2nd Q. Things were progressing nicely for West Point until Navy TE Mike Clark fell on punt FUM at Cadet 33YL. HB Dan Pike quickly raced 21y, finished drive with 1y TD run. In 3rd Q, Middies DE Mike Lettieri tackled QB Steve Lindell during pass attempt, and ball popped right to DT Tom LaForce, who chugged 36y to tying TD. On next series, sub QB Jim O'Toole was inserted by Army and arched 64y bomb to WR Joe Albano. Jarvis exploded for winning TD 3 plays later from 10YL. Jarvis broke Glen Davis' career rushing mark at Army with 2,333y.

Tennessee 10 VANDERBILT 7: With their minds on bowl bids, Tennessee Volunteers (8-1-1) nearly got lulled into defeat by upset-minded Vanderbilt (5-4-1), that finished on winning ledger for 1st time since 1959. LB Jack "Hacksaw" Reynolds deflected pass into arms of DT Dick Williams midway in 1st Q, and Vols had only 33y to negoiate for 11y TD run by TB Richmond Flowers (18/42y, TD). Missed FGs and DB Mike Jones' EZ INT for Tennessee highlighted scoreless 2nd Q, but Commodores tied it in 3rd Q on TB Alan Spear's plunge after DE Mike Giltner forced FUM at Vols 33YL by QB Bubba Wyche (13-23/122y). Reynolds and Williams collaborated on amazingly similar deflected INT, and K Karl Kremser booted home 23y FG in last min of 3rd Q.

ALABAMA 24 Auburn 16: Versatile LB-TE Mike Hall made 2 INTs, 16 tackles and batted down 2 passes on D and changed uniform no. 54 for no. 82 to catch 5y TD for victorious Alabama (8-2). Hall's 1st INT poised TB Ed Morgan's powerful 35y TD run early in game, and his surprise TD catch from QB Scott Hunter (18-37/173y, TD, INT) provided 21-3 lead early in 3rd Q. In between, TE Hall threw key block for Morgan's 1y TD dive in 2nd Q. Auburn (6-4) had broken into its own scoring column in 1st Q with K John Riley's 22y FG after CB Don Webb blocked Bama punt at 21YL. Crimson Tide DB Tommy Wiegand's 2 INTs added to torment of Tigers' All-SEC QB Loran Carter (11-25/186y, 2 TDs, 5 INTs), but Carter got Plainsmen back in game with brilliant 4-min span starting late in 3rd Q. Auburn jumped to within 21-16 when Carter pitched late 3rd Q 70y TD to TB Mike Currier and early 4th Q 3y TD to WB Connie Frederick. Alabama was forced to punt, but Tigers S Buddy McClinton bobbled catch to set up Tide DB-K Mike Dean's 30y FG with 10:17 left.

GEORGIA 47 Georgia Tech 8: Undefeated Georgia (8-0-2) launched its most pts ever against beleaguered D of Yellow Jackets (4-6). Fighting against stellar Bulldogs D, led by S Jake Scott, LB Happy Dicks, and DLs Billy Payne, Bill Stanfill (safety in 4th Q), and Steve Greer, Georgia Tech ended up with only 30/2y net rushing. Jackets lost QB Larry Good (4-8/71y, INT) to injury during 1st Q when UGa threw 17-0 haymaker, but sub QB Jim Person (9-11/90y, INT) did his best to keep Tech in game. *Atlanta Constitution* sports editor Jesse Outlar wrote that frantic Jackets "resorted to a spread formation which put players on every site on the field except the Georgia end zone." Indeed, it was 31-0 before Georgia Tech FB Kenny Bounds scored from 1YL and added 2-pt reception in 4th Q. Bulldogs went 98y to their 1st TD, 1y bang-over by QB Mike Cavan (13-23/193y, 2 INTs). Stanfill batted Good's pass, and Dicks intercepted to set up FB Brad Johnson's 3y TD crash. Georgia DT Lee Daniel recovered FUM to spark 16y TD trip early in 3rd Q.

Oklahoma 41 OKLAHOMA STATE 7: Sooners (7-3) won 5th straight game to earn share of Big 8 title with Kansas. QB Bobby Warmack played personal game of catch with WB Eddie Hinton in 21-pt 1st Q. Warmack (12-20/189y, 2 TD, INT), who set new conf career pass y record, was 7-8 in opening Q, all caught by Hinton. TB Steve Owens rushed 34/120y and scored his 21st TD of season. Overmatched Oklahoma State (3-7) scored on 9y run by HB Bub Deerinwater after falling behind 28-0 in 3rd Q.

Arizona State 30 ARIZONA 7: Affairs were pretty dull around Tucson after Arizona State (8-2) jumped to 21-0 lead in 1st Q. Dynamic Sun Devils FB Art Malone (35/186y, 2 TDs) shot through touted Arizona D for 46y TD on game's 2nd snap. Malone added 30y scoring run, and WR J.D. Hill ran away from DBs for 42y TD. Arizona made not single y rushing, thanks to several sacks, but QBs Mark Driscoll and Buddy Lee launched 38 passes and hit only 13/178y. Blocked punt in 2nd Q by Cats LB Larry Rogge was scooped up by LB Charlie Duke for 36y TD RET. Loss left both teams with 5-1 records in WAC, costing Wildcats conf crown as Wyoming snatched it with 1 extra conf win.

SOUTHERN CALIFORNIA 21 Notre Dame 21: Notre Dame (7-2-1) soph QB Joe Theismann (10-16/152y, 4 INT) made start for injured QB Terry Hanratty. Theismann's opening was disastrous: Trojans DB Sandy Durko's 21y INT TD RET. Before 1st Q was over, Irish FB Ron Dushney and HB Bob Gladieux (57y run) made it 14-7. HB Coley O'Brien threw throw-back 13y TD pass to Theismann to extend ND lead to 21-7 in 2nd Q. With Heisman-winning TB O.J. Simpson being held to 21/55y rushing, Trojans (9-0-1) went to air in 2nd H to earn tie on Simpson's 22nd TD of year and QB Steve Sogge's 40y TD to WR Sam Dickerson. ND K Scott Hempel barely missed 33y FG with 33 secs left.

AP Poll December 2

1 Ohio State (34)	770	11 Purdue	173
2 Southern California (2)	631	12 Alabama	123
3 Penn State (3)	618	13 Michigan	115
4 Georgia	528	14 Oregon State	87
5 Texas	399	15 Ohio University	49
6 Kansas	394	16 Missouri	44
7 Notre Dame	335	17 Arizona State	26
8 Tennessee	312	18 Houston	25
9 Arkansas	285	19 Florida State	20
10 Oklahoma	228	20 Southern Methodist	14

December 7, 1968

PENN STATE 30 Syracuse 12: Penn State (10-0) locked up 1st undefeated, untied season since 1947 with its 18th regular season win in row. Oft-injured HB Bobby Campbell had his most glorious day in his last home game, rushing 24/239y, scoring on beautifully-elusive, school-record 87y dash and 19y draw play. Lions led 30-0 early in 4th Q after Campbell's 2nd TD. At that juncture, coach Joe Paterno called on reserves, and Syracuse (6-4) put across 4th Q TD runs by HB Lee Castner and QB Rich Ponczszyn. Orangemen D, ranked 2nd in nation, relinquished 422y, 205y of it coming in 14-pt 1st Q.

1968 Conference Standings

Ivy League

Harvard	6-0-1
Yale	6-0-1
Pennsylvania	5-2
Princeton	4-3
Dartmouth	3-4
Columbia	2-5
Cornell	1-6
Brown	0-7

Atlantic Coast

North Carolina State	6-1
Clemson	4-1-1
Virginia	4-2
South Carolina	4-3
Duke	3-4
Wake Forest	2-3-1
Maryland	2-5
North Carolina	1-6

Southeastern

Georgia	5-0-1
Tennessee	4-1-1
Alabama	4-2
Auburn	4-2
Louisiana State	4-2
Florida	3-2-1
Mississippi	3-2-1
Vanderbilt	2-3-1
Kentucky	0-7
Mississippi State	0-8

Big Ten

Ohio State	7-0
Michigan	6-1
Purdue	5-2
Minnesota	5-2
Indiana	4-3
Iowa	4-3
Michigan State	2-5
Illinois	1-6
Northwestern	1-6
Wisconsin	0-7

Mid-American

Ohio University	6-0
Miami (Ohio)	5-1
Bowling Green	3-2-1
Toledo	3-2-1
Western Michigan	2-4
Kent State	1-5
Marshall	0-6

Southwest

Arkansas	6-1
Texas	6-1
Southern Methodist	5-2
Texas Tech	4-3
Baylor	3-4
Texas A&M	2-5
Texas Christian	2-5
Rice	0-7

Pacific Eight

Southern California	6-0
Oregon State	5-1
Stanford	3-3-1
California	2-2-1
Oregon	2-4
UCLA	2-4
Washington State	1-3-1
Washington	1-5-1

Big Eight

Kansas	6-1
Oklahoma	6-1
Missouri	5-2
Nebraska	3-4
Oklahoma State	2-5
Kansas State	2-5
Iowa State	1-6

Western Athletic

Wyoming	6-1
Arizona	5-1
Arizona State	5-1
Texas-El Paso	4-3
Utah	2-3
Colorado State	1-4
Brigham Young	1-5
New Mexico	0-7

1968 Bowl Games

Liberty Bowl (Dec. 14): Mississippi 34 Virginia Tech 17

Going with casual no-huddle formation on game's 2nd play, Virginia Tech (7-4) QB Al Kincaid ambled over to ball, flipped pitchout to FB Ken Edwards, who raced 58y to TD past stunned Mississippi (6-4-1). When QB Archie Manning fumbled on 1st Rebels play, Gobblers HB Terry Smoot quickly made it 14-0. K Jack Simcsak's FG extended Virginia Tech lead to 17-0 near end of 1st Q. Then, Hokies tried another surprise, onside KO. When it backfired, Ole Miss needed just 7 plays for Manning (12-28/141y, 2 TDs, INT) to throw 21y TD to TE Hank Shows. Manning followed with another 2nd Q TD pass, and TB Stan Hindman (121y rushing) put Ole Miss ahead for good at 21-17 with 79y TD sprint to open 3rd Q. Able to pass only 1-7/2y, Virginia Tech saw verdict sealed by 70y INT TD RET by Rebels DB Bob Bailey in 4th Q.

Gator Bowl (Dec. 28): Missouri 35 Alabama 10

So thorough was Missouri's stunning domination of no. 12 Alabama (8-3) that it was most one-sided defeat in Bear Bryant's 11 years to date as coach of Crimson Tide. Loss also was 2nd step in puzzling bowl failure in which Bryant-coached Bama teams would lose 7 and tie 1 in post-season games, starting with January 1968 Cotton Bowl and ending with win in January 1976 Sugar Bowl, despite .841 winning percentage in those regular seasons. Missouri (8-3) QB Terry McMillan never completed single pass (0-6), but scored 3 TDs and played option run magician in attack that gained 404y. Meanwhile, Tigers DEs Elmer Benhardt and Bill Schmitt helped create 12 sacks and net of -45y rushing. Benhardt blocked crucial pass by Tide QB Scott Hunter deep in Tigers end when score was still tight at 14-7 in favor of Missouri in 3rd Q. Scoring on DB Donnie Sutton's 37y INT TD RET in 2nd Q, Tide moved within 14-10 on K Mike Dean's early 4th Q FG. But Alabama's pass O failed it as Mizzou A-A DB Roger Wehrli set up TD with 20y INT RET, and DB Dennis Poppe ran 47y to INT TD.

Sun Bowl (Dec. 28): Auburn 34 Arizona 10

Fierce west Texas wind contributed to wacky day. Auburn (7-4) picked off 8 Arizona (8-3) passes, including DB Don Webb's INT on game's opening snap. Tigers QB Loran Carter's 65y arrow to FB Mickey Zofko provided 10-0 1st Q lead, but had his troubles moving team against 40 mph winds. Wildcats came right back in 2nd Q as K Steve Hurley kicked 37y FG and QB Bruce Lee (6-24/89y, TD, 5 INTs) flipped 12y TD to WR Hal Arneson. It was knotted 10-10 at H. In 3rd Q, Auburn LB Ron Yarbrough recovered FUM at Arizona 27YL, and little sub QB Tommy Traylor sparked Tigers with 3 quick carries to Cats 9YL. Traylor then swept around LE for go-ahead TD at 17-10. Auburn was off and winging 24 secs later when MVP DB Buddy McClinton raced 31y with INT TD RET for 2-TD bulge. Carter (7-28/156y, 2 TDs, 3 INTs) returned to toss his 2nd TD pass. Day's biggest oddity, but great display of athleticism, came from Auburn WB-P Connie Frederick, who had his punt blocked at own 23YL. He retrieved ball in EZ, ran through Arizona DE Frank Jenkins and LB Larry Rogge, and re-kicked it from 9YL to his 47YL.

Peach Bowl (Dec. 30): Louisiana State 31 Florida State 27

Atlanta's addition to bowl lineup fired off quickly: Florida State (8-3) soph HB Tom Bailey (11/77y, TD) ran 36y on 1st scrimmage play to score after DB John Crowe recovered opening KO FUM. Down by 13-0, LSU (8-3) had fire lit under it by rarely-used lefty QB Mike Hillman (16-29/229y, 2 TDs, INT). Hillman came off bench to throw 2 TD passes in 3rd Q for 24-13 Tiger lead. Meanwhile, Bengals DB Gerry Kent, projected cover-man on Seminoles A-A WR Ron Sellers (8/76y, 2 TDs), was hurt in 1st Q, so LSU went to heavy pass rush, led by sub DE Bud Millican. After being held to 1 catch in 3 Qs, Sellers finally shook loose for 2 short TD catches from QB Bill Cappleman (21-41/221y, 3 TDs, INT) that put Seminoles back in charge at 27-24. With 6:15 left in 4th Q, Hillman drove LSU through cold drizzle for 61y, completing 2 big passes, including 20y toss on 3rd down to E Tommy Morel (6/103y). Hillman also zipped 14y to 3YL, and HB Maurice LeBlanc (14/97y, TD) powered over for winning TD

with 2:39 to go. FSU didn't quit, however, and Cappleman launched 4th-and-9 pass to Sellers in Tigers territory. DB Barton Frye, substituting for injured Kent, made high leap to knock it down with 1:23 to play. Despite rainy, 42-degree weather, 35,545 turned out to Grant Field and set new attendance record for 1st-year bowl, eclipsing 17,000 that witnessed 1937 Cotton Bowl.

Bluebonnet Bowl (Dec. 31): Southern Methodist 28 Oklahoma 27

With his Oklahoma (7-4) counterpart, QB Bobby Warmack (1st Q TD rushing) watching injured from sideline, SMU (8-3) QB Chuck Hixson (22-43/281y, 2 TDs, 2 INTs) tossed 4th Q TDs to WR Jerry Levias and TE Ken Fleming. So, Mustangs had earned 28-21 edge with 2:42 on clock. Sooners sub QB Mickey Ripley then shook off his poor 3rd Q by throwing his 2nd TD pass, shoestring grab by WR Johnny Barr with 1:16 left to play. OU now trailed 28-27, and went for 2-pt conv. It failed when Ripley was forced OB by SMU DE Mike Mitchell before he could find open receiver. Oklahoma had last chance after successfully recovering on-side KO, but K Bruce Derr missed 34y FG with 19 secs to go.

Cotton Bowl: Texas 36 Tennessee 13

After 16-0 Cotton Bowl loss to Texas in 1953, Tennessee team returned to Knoxville and burned white jerseys that had made rare appearance on Volunteers players that holiday afternoon. In this 1969 Cotton Bowl, Volunteers (8-2-1) again were clad in white against Texas (9-1-1), which wore its home burnt orange jerseys. Omen or not, Texas amassed 513y total O for day against Vols D that arrived with 93.3y rushing avg, built 28-0 H lead, and limited Tennessee to 31y O in 1st H. Longhorns enjoyed wide scoring array: QB James Street's 78 and 79y TD passes to WR Cotton Speyrer, FB Steve Worster's 14y TD run, WB Ted Koy's 9y TD run, and TB Chris Gilbert's 5y TD run. Tennessee, which gained only 32y O vs. Texas in 1953, finally stoked its attack in 2nd H behind sub QB Bobby Scott. Despite several dropped passes, Scott (11-30/159y, 2 TDs, 2 INTs) threw for 2 scores. Although Texas LB Tom Campbell twice took INTs out of hands of Vols WR Gary Kreis, Scott made good on 3rd Q TD to Kreis for 17y. Scott built much of his passing numbers in late 5-play, 97y trip to WR Mike Price's 3y TD catch. It would be long time before Tennessee again wore any jersey other than its traditional daisy orange.

Sugar Bowl: Arkansas 16 Georgia 2

Hitting 9 straight passes, Arkansas (10-1) QB Bill Montgomery (17-39/185y, TD, INT) ignored his team's flickering run attack (40y) and zeroed in on WR Chuck Dicus to upset Georgia (8-1-2). Dicus caught 12 passes including 27y TD early in 2nd Q when he beat A-A DB Jake Scott. Alert Razorbacks D, led by DLs Rick Kersey and Gordon McNulty, LB Cliff Powell and DB Jerry Moore, stopped 3 scoring chances, forced 5 FUMs including FB Brad Johnson's GL bobble, made 3 INTs, and allowed only 3 of 16 3rd down conversions. Bulldogs' only pts came midway in 2nd Q when DE David McKnight downed TB Bill Burnett in Razorbacks EZ for safety. Arkansas K Bob White put game away with 3 FGs. Coupled with Texas' Cotton Bowl win and SMU's Bluebonnet upset, Southwest Conf enjoyed its 1st 3-bowl sweep since 1948.

Rose Bowl: Ohio State 27 Southern California 16

Midway in 2nd Q of battle for national championship, Southern California (9-1-1) owned 3-0 lead and ball at its own 20YL. TB O.J. Simpson (28/171y) was sent off LT, broke 2 tackles on cutback, and was gone 80y down right sideline. So, no. 2 Trojans led 10-0. Then, no. 1 Ohio State (10-0) rolled up its new fishnet sleeves and rumbled 69y to score: QB Jim Otis (30/101y) dived up middle for 1y TD. Ohio K Jim Roman tied it 3 secs before H with 26y FG. With Buckeyes ahead 13-10, their hard-hitting D made big impact. DT Bill Urbanik's tackle forced Trojan QB Steve Sogge to cough up ball at USC 21YL. QB Rex Kern (9-15/101y, 2 TD, and 35y rushing) dashed 14y, then, on 1st play of 4th Q, hit HB Leo Hayden with 4y TD pass. When Simpson lost his 2nd FUM at 16YL and Buckeyes DB Mike Polaski fell on it to set up Kern's TD pass to WR Ray Gillian. Sogge's TD pass to WR Sam Dickerson in last 45 secs made score closer, but Ohio State had earned Woody Hayes' 2nd national championship, but last for any Big 10 team until 1997.

Orange Bowl: Penn State 15 Kansas 14

Orange Bowl's 35th classic became known for infamous 12th-man PEN called on Kansas Jayhawks (9-2) in closing 15 secs. Penn State (11-0) marched up and down field in 1st H, but 4 TOs highly curtailed Nittany Lions. Kansas DB Pat Hutchens' INT of QB Chuck Burkhart at Lions 45YL set up 1st Q score by FB Mike Reeves from 2YL. Penn State tied it at 7-7 as HB Charlie Pittman squirted through big hole at LT for 13y TD run. TB Donnie Shanklin, who would be prematurely selected as MVP, made fine punt RET to send Jayhawks to go-ahead TD in 4th Q. FB John Riggins (18/52y) powered over for 14-7 Jayhawks lead. Less than 2 mins remained when Kansas, close to wrapping up win, punted from own 25YL. Lions DB Neal Smith partially blocked punt, which rolled dead at Penn State 49YL. On 1st play, Burkhart (12-23/152y, INT) launched long, perfect pass to HB Bobby Campbell, who was dragged down at Kansas 3YL. After 2 failed runs, Burkhart rolled out for TD run, but his 2-pt pass was knocked down. Having appeared to prevail at 14-13 Jayhawks celebrated joyfully, but, official stepped forward from back of EZ while waving his flag above head: Kansas had been detected with having 12 men on field. On 2nd try for winning 2-pt conv, Campbell swept LE to paydirt. Joe Paterno later congratulated officials on their alertness. "Coach, we count 'em on every play," was the response, but film later revealed Kansas had stopped Penn State's 2 GL plunges with 12-man D that included LB Rick Abernathy.

1 Ohio State (44)	968	11 Oklahoma	257
2 Penn State (2)	782	12 Michigan	197
3 Texas (2)	762	13 Tennessee	165
4 Southern California	693	14 Southern Methodist	143
5 Notre Dame	482	15 Oregon State	105
6 Arkansas (1)	476	16 Auburn	36
7 Kansas	465	17 Alabama	32
8 Georgia	349	18 Houston	31
9 Missouri	297	19 Louisiana State	23
10 Purdue	263	20 Ohio University	22

1968 Top Performance Formula

1 Penn State	1.7198
2 Ohio State	1.7110
3 Georgia	1.5974
4 Arkansas	1.5920
5 Texas	1.5834
6 Southern California	1.5109
7 Kansas	1.4846
8 Purdue	1.4684
9 Houston	1.4664
10 Tennessee	1.4481
11 Army	1.4308
12 Arizona State	1.4126
13 Missouri	1.3899
14 Alabama	1.3682
15 Southern Methodist	1.3628
16 Notre Dame	1.3875
17 Michigan	1.3671
18 Oklahoma	1.3588
19 California	1.3348
20 Oregon State	1.3170

1968 Top Opponent Records

1 Kentucky	.6979
2 Illinois	.6467
3 Oklahoma State	.6368
4 Georgia	.6346
5 Navy	.6278
6 Oklahoma	.6214
7 UCLA	.6117
8 Miami	.6105
9 Mississippi	.6096
10 Southern Methodist	.6010
11 Alabama	.60000
11 Southern California	.60000
13 Army	.5979
14 Auburn	.5913
15 Houston	.5904
16 Oregon	.5870
17 Tennessee	.5817
18 California	.5802
19 Mississippi State	.5789
20 Kansas State	.5684

1968 Out-of-Conference Records

	W-L	Percentage	Bowl W-L
Southeastern	33-12-2	.7234	3-3
Pacific-8	19-11-2	.6250	0-1
Southwest	14-9-4	.5926	3-0
Big Eight	14-12	.5385	1-2
Big Ten	15-15	.5000	1-0
Western Athletic	11-23-1	.3286	0-1
Atlantic Coast	7-20	.2593	0-0

1968 Individual Statistical Leaders

RUSHING YARDS	Attempts	Yards	Avg.
O.J. Simpson, Southern California	355	1709	4.8
Paul Gipson, Houston	242	1571	6.5
Steve Owens, Oklahoma	357	1536	4.3
Art Malone, Arizona State	235	1431	6.1
Ron Johnson, Michigan	255	1391	5.5
Bill Enyart, Oregon State	293	1304	4.5
Po James, New Mexico State	225	1291	5.7
Frank Quayle, Virginia	175	1213	6.9
Bryant Mitchell, Rutgers	238	1204	5.1
Roland Moss, Toledo	267	1145	4.3

PASSING YARDS	Completions	Attempts	Yards	Pct.
Greg Cook, Cincinnati	219	411	3272	53.3
Chuck Hixson, Southern Methodist	265	468	3103	56.6
Bill Cappleman, Florida State	162	287	2410	56.4
Edd Hargett, Texas A&M	169	348	2321	48.6
Leo Hart, Duke	162	301	2238	53.8
Marty Domres, Columbia	183	344	2206	53.2
Jim Plunkett, Stanford	142	268	2156	53.0
Mike Sherwood, West Virginia	151	264	1998	57.2
Mike Stripling, Tulsa	164	347	1968	47.3
Buster O'Brien, Richmond	149	255	1961	58.4

RECEIVING YARDS	Catches	Yards
Ron Sellers, Florida State	86	1496
Elmo Wright, Houston	43	1198
Jerry Levias, Southern Methodist	80	1131
Gene Washington, Stanford	71	1117
Tom Rossley, Cincinnati	80	1072
Speedy Thomas, Utah	60	1006
Harry Wood, Tulsa	65	988
Eddie Hinton, Oklahoma	60	967
Sammy Milner, Mississippi State	64	909
John Sias, Georgia Tech	61	902

1968 Consensus All-America
Offense

End:	Jerry Levias, Southern Methodist
	Ted Kwalick, Penn State
Tackle:	Dave Foley, Ohio State
	George Kunz, Notre Dame
Guard:	Jim Barnes, Arkansas
	Mike Montler, Colorado
	Charles Rosenfelder, Tennessee
Center:	John Didion, Oregon State
Back:	Terry Hanratty, Notre Dame
	Chris Gilbert, Texas
	Leroy Keyes, Purdue
	O.J. Simpson, Southern California

Defense

End:	Ted Hendricks, Miami
	John Zook, Kansas
Tackle:	Joe Greene, North Texas State
	Bill Stanfill, Georgia
Guard:	Chuck Kyle, Purdue
	Ed White, California
Linebacker:	Steve Kiner, Tennessee
	Dennis Onkontz, Penn State
Back:	Jake Scott, Georgia
	Roger Wehrli, Missouri
	Al Worley, Washington

1968 Heisman Trophy Vote

O.J. Simpson, senior tailback, Southern California	2853
Leroy Keyes, senior halfback, Purdue	1103
Terry Hanratty, senior quarterback, Notre Dame	387
Ted Kwalick, senior tight end, Penn State	254
Ted Hendricks, senior defensive end, Miami	174

Other Major Awards

Maxwell (Player):	O.J. Simpson, senior tailback, Southern California
Outland (Lineman):	Bill Stanfill, senior defensive tackle, Georgia
Walter Camp (Player):	O.J. Simpson, senior tailback, Southern California
AFCA Coach of the Year:	Joe Paterno, Penn State

1969

The Year of Beano's Crystal Ball, Nixon's Number One, and Football's Centennial

Roone Arledge of ABC made the first college football decision of 1969, and President Richard Milhous Nixon made the last.

To some, the decisions affecting the 1969 football season didn't stop hurting until years later when Penn State coach Joe Paterno cracked, "I don't know how Richard Nixon could know so much about college football in 1969 and so little about Watergate in 1972," referring to Nixon's claim that he had little to do with the Democratic headquarters break-in scandal that forced his resignation from the nation's highest office.

Arledge, president of ABC Sports, set things in motion in the spring by asking network sports publicist Beano Cook to analyze the upcoming season. Cook foresaw three big events: preseason no. 1 Ohio State (8-1) being taken out of the national title race with a loss to Minnesota (4-5-1), Arkansas (9-2) handing Texas (11-0) its only defeat in mid-season, and Arkansas beating undefeated Penn State (11-0) in the Cotton Bowl to win the national championship.

Cook's crystal ball turned out to be surprisingly clear: Ohio State lost a Big Ten game to knock it from the no. 1 roost and Penn State went undefeated for a second straight year. Instead of Minnesota, it was surprising Michigan (8-3) that beat Ohio State at season's end as new Wolverines coach Bo Schembechler began his 10-year rivalry with mentor Woody Hayes by springing a 24-12 upset to end the Buckeyes' 22-game win streak. Prior to the Wolverines' stunning upset of Ohio State, there were murmurs of the Buckeyes perhaps being the greatest team ever to play college football.

Arledge, however, threw a curve that changed the fortunes of Arkansas, Texas, and Penn State. He induced Arkansas and Texas to postpone their Southwest Conference showdown, scheduled for October 18, until it could be nationally televised as a season-ending extravaganza on December 6.

The Arkansas-Texas matchup was a classic, with the winning Longhorns rallying from a two-touchdown deficit in probably the greatest Southwest Conference game ever played. It pitted undefeated teams ranked as the top two in the nation. President Nixon attended the contest in Fayetteville, Ark., and decreed the game a defacto battle for the national title. No matter what Penn State accomplished in its 22nd straight win, a 10-3 Orange Bowl victory over no. 6 Big Eight co-champion Missouri (9-2), it could do little to overhaul Texas, one-point winner over Arkansas, in the polls. After all, the President of the United States said so.

In theory, the Nittany Lions were in position to go to the Cotton Bowl to try to knock off no. 1 Texas. Speculation about Penn State going to Dallas cropped up in the news as November drew to its mid-point. As an independent, Penn State was unfettered to a bowl commitment and could cut nearly any deal it wanted, but bowl officials pushed for a decision and the Nittany Lions had to make known their New Year's Day choice before the outcomes of Arkansas-Texas and Michigan-Ohio State were known. Ohio State, bowl-ineligible under the Big Ten's no-repeat rule, was still no. 1 at invitation time and likely to stay there assuming, as everyone did, that it would beat Michigan. Nittany Lions coach Joe Paterno always said that he left the bowl decision to his players. They chose to visit the beaches of Miami for a second straight year even though it was normal procedure in those days to go after the highest-ranked opponent. Penn State chose to skip a chance to play the Arkansas-Texas winner, an opponent sure to be no worse than ranked second. Penn State had several black players on its roster, and their preference was to avoid Dallas, still perceived as a racially-segregated city.

Meanwhile, Notre Dame (8-2-1) suddenly and surprisingly reversed its 45-year policy of shunning bowl games. The Fighting Irish made it known to the Cotton Bowl its interest in a showdown with the winner of Arkansas-Texas, which in Texas turned out to be a top-rated team. Notre Dame vs. Texas had genuine marquee value, and the game attracted a terrific television audience.

In a rebuilding year, Ara Parseghian's Irish turned out to be very much capable of a confrontation with Texas. The Longhorns won a nail-biting 21-17 thriller. It proved the Irish were better than their rank (They actually jumped from ninth to fifth in post-bowl polls despite losing the Cotton Bowl.), and it opened the door for future post-season trips by Notre Dame. The Fighting Irish's tremendous TV drawing power changed for many years how bowl promoters managed their selection process. From January 1, 1970, forward, a bowl committee's dream focused less on two teams with deserving records and more on building an appealing TV match.

All across the nation, the centennial anniversary of the first collegiate contest was celebrated with many teams sporting 100-year helmet logos. Rutgers (6-3) and Princeton (6-3), which first met on November 6, 1869, staged a renewal at New Brunswick, N.J., on September 27. The Scarlet Knights invited their one-time quarterback and highly popular TV dad, Ozzie Nelson, to oversee the festivities. It turned out to be a happy day for Rutgers as it beat their in-state Ivy League adversary for just the tenth time in 60 tries since 1869.

Turmoil, the hallmark of the 1960s, cropped up at Wyoming (6-4) when 14 black players broke team rules, prior to the game with Brigham Young (6-4), to protest the Mormon Church's policy toward blacks. The players were dismissed from the squad by coach Lloyd Eaton. The Cowboys crushed BYU 40-7 and followed with a sixth straight win, but the incident gradually tattered team spirit. Wyoming dropped its last four games. Similar revolts by black players occurred at Indiana (4-6), Iowa (5-5), and disintegrating Washington (1-9), where coach Jim Owens' daughter was run off the road and attacked after Owens dismissed several black players.

Hard-luck Holy Cross (0-2) had to abandon its season in early autumn after a hepatitis outbreak crippled the squad. In substantial ways, the Crusaders' program that flourished in the early half of the 20th century, when urban Catholic schools enjoyed their heyday, never recovered for the Worcester, Mass., school. Holy Cross suffered mostly losing records until they found moderate success after dropping down to Division 1-AA competition in 1982.

Milestones

Middle Atlantic Conference disbanded at end of season, leaving Bucknell, Delaware, Gettysburg, Lafayette, Lehigh, Muhlenberg, and Temple to pursue various levels of independence.

Five prominent former coaches died: Harvey Harman, 69 (Sewanee, Pennsylvania, Rutgers), Bob Higgins, 75 (Penn State), Andy Kerr, 90 (Colgate), Ivan Williamson, 58 (Wisconsin), and Bowden Wyatt, 54 (Wyoming, Arkansas, Tennessee).

Longest winning streak entering season:

Ohio State 14	Penn State 11	Texas 9

Coaching Changes

	Incoming	Outgoing
Arizona	Bob Weber	Darrell Mudra
Baylor	Bill Beall	John Bridgers
Cincinnati	Ray Callahan	Homer Rice
Kentucky	John Ray	Charlie Bradshaw
Louisville	Lee Corso	Frank Camp
Maryland	Roy Lester	Bob Ward
Michigan	Glenn "Bo" Schembechler	Chalmers "Bump" Elliott
Navy	Rick Forzano	Bill Elias
Oklahoma State	Floyd Gass	Phil Cutchin
Pittsburgh	Carl dePasqua	Dave Hart

AP Preseason Poll

1 Ohio State (26)	611	11 Notre Dame	204
2 Arkansas (2)	420	12 Michigan State	148
3 Penn State (3)	390	13 Alabama	120
4 Texas (1)	343	14 Indiana	98
5 Southern California	290	15 Tennessee	67
6 Oklahoma	264	16 Stanford	53
7 Houston (1)	231	17 UCLA	52
8 Georgia	219	18 Purdue	42
9 Mississippi	211	19 Minnesota	40
10 Missouri	209	20 Auburn	37

September 13, 1969

Wake Forest 22 NORTH CAROLINA STATE 21: Demon Deacons (1-0), hoping for winning era under new coach Cal Stoll, started in right direction with late-game heroics. NC State (0-1) QB Darrell Moody led 312y ground attack with 3 TDs running to build 21-7 lead in 3rd Q. Wake Forest soph QB Larry Russell, who had thrown 31y TD pass to E Don Kobes in 1st Q, brought Deacons to within 21-14 with 17y TD run in 3rd Q. Then, Wake Forest went 40y as Russell hit 17y pass and HB Steve Bowden plunged 1y to score with 5 secs left. Gambling Deacons got winning 2 pts on Russell's pass to HB Buz Leavitt.

Air Force 26 SOUTHERN METHODIST 22: Air Force (1-0) soared to handsome 23-0 H lead as QB Gary Baxter scored on runs of 2 and 15y, and K Dennis Leuthauser kicked FGs of 44, 33, and 34y. Meanwhile, Falcons D, led by DL Harold Whelan, placed powerful pass-rush on SMU QB Chuck Hixson (34-63/356y, 2 TDs, 3 INTs) for 8/-63y. Mustangs pass blocking improved in 2nd H to allow Hixson to complete TD passes to TE Ken Fleming and WR Sam Holden and pair of 2-pt passes. As 4th Q opened, SMU (0-1) trailed 23-16. Leuthauser added another FG, and Air Force LB Glenn Leimbach made clinching INT at own 2YL with 3:14 left.

UCLA 37 Oregon State 0: Bruins (1-0) launched their new triple-option O to tune of 491y. Very early, UCLA's new QB Dennis Dummit (10-24/160y, TD) rifled short, wide pass to WR Gwen Cooper, who danced past Oregon State (0-1) DB Don Whitney and streaked 60y to score. Beavers HB Billy Main (26/115y) got loose for 52y run, but UCLA D, led all night by DLs Floyd Reese and Wes Grant and LBs Mike Ballou and Don Widmer, held on its 16YL. In no time, Bruins HB Greg Jones had scored and K Zenon Andrusyshyn had kicked 1st of his 3 FGs. Little DB Ron Carver, who ran back punts for 3/72y, set up Jones' 2nd TD with his 29y punt RET, and Uclans led 27-0 at H. Soph QB Steve Endicott (8-16/115y, 2 INTs) came off bench to build encouraging 2nd H O if not TDs for Oregon State.

September 20, 1969

SOUTH CAROLINA 27 Duke 20: Preseason ACC co-favorites were knotted 10-10 after 3 Qs. South Carolina (1-0) took 13-10 lead on K Billy DuPre's 34y FG. Next, Duke (0-1) and Gamecocks traded TDs: QB Leo Hart connected on his 2nd TD pass for Devils, but Carolina regained lead at 20-17 on QB Tommy Suggs' 48y TD run. Duke K Dave Pugh made 43y FG to tie it 20-20, 3rd time Gamecocks had lost lead. Carolina converted pair of 4th downs on winning drive as FB Warren Muir powered to decisive TD run.

Alabama 17 VIRGINIA TECH 13: Largest to-date Virginia sports crowd of 42,000 saw Hokies (0-1) take early 3-0 lead on K Jack Simcshak's 19y FG. TB Johnny Musso gave Alabama (1-0) 10-3 lead in 2nd Q, but it was matched by QB Al Kincaid's 5y TD run to knot it at 10-10 at H. DB Jerry Cash's midfield FUM REC launched Bama on winning drive in 3rd Q, which was capped by WR George Ranager's 10y TD run.

WEST VIRGINIA 31 Maryland 7: New Terrapins (0-1) coach Roy Lester saw his debut go south in jiffy. Maryland's questionable D was bruised to tune of 21 pts in 1st Q. West Virginia (2-0) FB Jim Braxton, on his way to 161y rushing, scored twice in 1st Q at Morgantown as WVU scored on its 1st 3 series. K Braxton made 4 x-pts and in 4th Q added 35y FG. Mountaineers lost FUMs twice in 2nd Q in own territory, but each time Maryland was stopped without single 1st down. Terps QB Dennis O'Hara was knocked out of game in 2nd Q when he threw adventurous, but costly block on WB Paul Fitzpatrick's 19y TD scamper. WVU QB Mike Sherwood captured 2nd H's only TD: 12y pass to WR Oscar Patrick.

FLORIDA 59 Houston 34: Highly-regarded no. 7 Houston (0-1), *Playboy* preseason choice for no. 1, fell helplessly to Florida (1-0) soph aerial battery of QB John Reaves and WR Carlos Alvarez. Reaves passed 18-30/342y, 5 TDs. Alvarez caught 6 passes with TDs of 70 and 21y. Vaunted Cougars O sputtered in 1st H, thanks to 2 FUMs and INT TD RET by another Gators' super-soph, speedy DB Jimmy Barr. Houston didn't get rolling until it trailed 38-6 in 3rd Q: QB Ken Bailey pitched 4 TDs, and 3 were grabbed by outstanding WR Elmo Wright.

LOUISIANA STATE 35 Texas A&M 6: LSU (1-0) coach Charlie McClendon, now with 8 straight wins in season openers, had such an easy time that he sent 3 QBs—Mike Hillman (13-19/139y, TD, INT), Buddy Lee (3-8/27y) and Butch Duhon—into the fray with success. Hillman and TB Art Cantrelle clicked on pass for game's opening TD early in 2nd Q. Deception gave Tigers 14-0 lead at H as WR Andy Hamilton looped around to take pitchout and scampered 15y to score. Lee led next score for Tigers, short plunge by FB Del Walker, which quickly was followed by FUM by Texas A&M QB Jimmy Sheffield (10-21/52y, and 12/139y rushing). Cantrelle added his 2nd TD, and score was 35-0 when Aggies finally dented scoresheet on QB Rocky Self's 7y aerial to TE Ross Brupbacher.

NOTRE DAME 35 Northwestern 10: Wildcats (0-1) surprised full house at Notre Dame Stadium by clawing to early 10-0 advantage on K Bill Planisek's 44y FG and, after DB Rick Telander's INT, FB Mike Hudson's 6y TD run. HB Ed Ziegler turned ND in right direction with 46y scamper off RT Gary Kos' block, and with 15y personal foul PEN tacked on, Irish soon found themselves at NW 5YL for QB Joe Theismann's 5y TD skirt of E. Notre Dame (1-0) went 96y late in 1st Q, tallying on Ziegler's 18y run, which was, according to *Chicago Tribune*, "the kind of touchdown run you see in the movies." Northwestern hung on and it wasn't until 2nd play of 4th Q that Irish DB Brian Lewallen darted and weaved 44y on punt TD RET for secure 21-10 edge. Soph DE Walt Patulski recovered FUM by Cats QB Dave Shelbourne (10-25/112y, 3 INTs) at Northwestern 38YL to launch 9 straight runs and Theismann's 8y TD pass to FB Bill Barz.

MISSOURI 19 Air Force 17: Trailing 16-7 in 3rd Q, Air Force (1-1) pulled within 6 pts on K Dennis Leuthauser's 19y FG. With only 32 secs left, Falcons QB Gary Baxter dramatically pitched 22y TD pass to E Charlie Longnecker for 17-16 lead. Air Force kicked off, and resilient Missouri (1-0) QB Terry McMillan pulled off his own drama with 24 secs left, throwing 56y pass to E John Henley at Falcons 21YL. After 2 quick runs to 12YL, Tigers K Henry Brown booted 30y FG, his Big 8 record-tying 4th 3-ptr in game.

Purdue 42 TEXAS CHRISTIAN 35: QB Mike Phipps (11-24/286y, 4 TDs, INT) was highly effective in leading Purdue (1-0) to 35-7 lead in 3rd Q. Phipps ran for TD, then aimed 4 scoring air strikes of varying length and style: longest was 67y bomb to HB Stan Brown, oddest was double deflection off FB John Bullock to TCU (0-1) DB to WR Greg Fenner. Horned Frogs got 3rd Q lift on another fluke play: As QB Steve Judy flung long pass, he was hit by on-rushing Boilermakers DL; ball popped toward sideline where surprised TCU FB Sammy Rabb caught it and ran 35y to unmolested TD. Inspired Frogs used 2nd TD catch by WR Linzy Cole (6/52y, 2 TDs) and his 70y punt TD RET to shave deficit to 42-35 with ample 4:48 to play. But, Phipps guided Purdue's ball control series to end it.

ARIZONA STATE 48 Minnesota 26: Minnesota (0-1) 2-sport star (FB in football and defenseman in hockey) Jim Carter opened scoring with 5y TD run in 1st Q, and added

7y TD run in 2nd Q. Arizona State (1-0) HB Dave Buchanan then went to work, accounting for 4 TDs. Buchanan raced 62y with punt TD RET, found his way for 10 and 9y TD runs, and pitched option TD pass to WR Calvin Demery for 29y. Demery set new ASU reception record with 11/201y as Sun Devils compiled 446y in air, another to-date school record.

Oregon 28 UTAH 17: Although net O y were about even at 378y to 347y in favor of Ducks (1-0), Oregon used 3 INTs to help fuel dynamic 2nd H as QB Tom Blanchard found his favorite target, HB Bobby Moore (nee Ahmad Rashad), for TDs of 4, 26, and 49y. Utah (0-1) had led 14-6 at H as FB Dave Smith dashed 10y for TD and QB Ray Groth pitched 40y TD pass to HB Fred Graves. K Marv Bateman tacked on Utah-record 50y FG for 17-6 3rd Q lead. With Ducks ahead 21-17 late in 3rd Q, Utah tried fake FG: QB-holder Groth pitched long pass to E Jimmy Brown, who made fingertip catch at 5YL. But, Brown was knocked cold on tackle by Oregon CB Jack Gleason and lost critical FUM.

BRIGHAM YOUNG 22 Colorado State 20: Soph K Joe Liljenquist's powerful foot delivered 5 FGs for BYU (1-0). Meanwhile, Colorado State (0-1) received 3 TDs from HB Lawrence McCutcheon. McCutcheon (16/44y) blasted over twice in 13-13 1st H. BYU took 19-13 lead, but Rams traveled 83y late in 4th Q as McCutcheon caught 3y TD pass from QB Chip Maxwell for 20-19 lead. HB Bill Glatch returned ensuing KO 26y to own 41YL to launch late Cougars' prowl. QB Marc Lyons hit FB Chris Reading twice for 39y to reach Rams 6YL. With 15 secs left, Liljenquist connected on winning 27y FG. Colorado State missed 2 terrific opportunities when it started at BYU 18 and 34YLs, but missed FG and 4th down pass.

Southern California 31 NEBRASKA 21: USC (1-0) was highly efficient behind QB Jimmy Jones (8-16/164y) as soph newcomer from Pennsylvania fired TD passes of 45y to WR Bob Chandler and 4y to FB Charles Evans. Mixed in was stellar running by another soph, TB Clarence Davis (27/114y) behind blocking of G Fred Khasigian and T John Vella, and Southern California cruised to 28-7 lead at end of 3rd Q. Only mark on Troy's visit to loud Lincoln was Jones' 2nd FUM that led to 2y TD run by Nebraska QB Van Brownson, who had otherwise up-and-down day rushing 15/13y and passing 7-11/61y. Of course, not counted among Trojans blunders was Jones' apparent crossing of scrimmage line on 2nd Q pass that set up TD for 21-7 H edge. It had Memorial Stadium crowd howling when it went uncalled. But, Trojans couldn't stand prosperity, and without much pass-rush, thanks to injury absence of DT Al Cowlings, and outbreak of pass interference fouls, USC was hit for pair of TDs in 4th Q. Leading way for Nebraska was back-up QB Jerry Tagge (8-14/76y, INT), who passed effectively and scored TD. Trailing 28-21 with 2:15 left, Huskers took over on their 32YL, but Tagge was intercepted to set up late FG by Troy DB-K Ron Ayala.

Texas 17 CALIFORNIA 0: Crushing ground game (311y) of Texas (1-0) provided 14-0 lead at H. Soph HB Jim Bertelson circled RE for 11y TD, and QB James Street rolled out for 5y TD. California (0-1) stiffened at H and stiffened in 2nd H, allowing only K Happy Feller's 32y FG after Bears QB Randy Humphries lost FUM. In last 3 mins, Golden Bears RB Bob Darby broke away for 45y run—which accounted for 35% of Cal's rushing total—before being wrestled down at Longhorns 21YL. Wave of provoked Texas defenders pushed Bears back to 34YL and took over on downs.

September 27, 1969

RUTGERS 29 Princeton 0: Celebration of 100th anniversary of college game saw re-enactment of 1869 game and host Rutgers (1-0) alumni represented by class of 1927 QB Ozzie Nelson, who starred on TV with wife Harriet and became prototype 1950s dad. There was antique car parade. Black student protesters were booed. When attention finally turned to modern game, Scarlet Knights QB Rich Policastro dazzled in 21-0 1st H with 14-19/164y, TD passing, and he scored on keeper sweep. Utilizing Pro-set O after 23 years of single wing O alignment, Princeton (0-1) was held to 35y in 1st H. Brightest spot in Tigers' feeble O was virtual statistical flyspeck: FB Ellis Moore's 42y rushing. Press box wag suggested Princeton's new attack "had set *back* football 100 years."

PENN STATE 27 Colorado 3: Unbeaten in 21 straight games, Penn State (2-0) lost HB Charlie Pittman to injury in scoreless 1st Q, but picked off 3 passes (2 by DB Neal Smith). FB Don Abbey burst 40y to score in opening moments of 2nd Q, and Mount Nits were on their way. Before H, Lions added K Mike Reitz's FG and FB Franco Harris' 5y TD run. Colorado (1-1) QB Bob Anderson, who had rushed for 163y prior week vs. Tulsa, was held to 4y on ground in 2nd H. After K Dave Haney gave Buffs 27y FG in 3rd Q, Penn State DB Paul Johnson answered with 91y KO TD RET for insurmountable 24-3 lead.

North Carolina State 24 MARYLAND 7: NC State Wolfpack (2-1) O stumbled in trip to College Park but were handed 16 pts on avalanche of TOs by bumbling Maryland (0-2). Terrapins cruised to 7-0 lead in 1st Q on 10y TD pass to WR Sonny Demczuk by QB Dennis O'Hara (8-17/87y, TD, 3 INTs). O'Hara proceeded to give away INTs on next 2 series: DB Jack Whitley snared O'Hara's pass at Terps 42YL and returned it for NC State TD, and DB Jim Smith nabbed another INT to set up Wolfpack K Mike Charron for 33y FG and 10-7 lead. Maryland trailed by 3 pts at H despite its 142y to

76y O advantage. O'Hara's FUM in 3rd Q at his 31YL cleared path for NC State HB Charlie Bowers to crash for 3y TD and 16-7 edge. Wolfpack finally scored on its own steam as WB Leon Mason cracked through several tackles for 74y TD sprint in 4th Q.

TENNESSEE 45 Auburn 19: Tennessee (2-0) turned 3 Auburn (1-1) TOs into 21-3 lead by 2nd Q. Trailing 24-3 at H, Tigers edged back into game as stellar soph QB Pat Sullivan (12-24/190y, 2 TDs, 5 INTs) learned some bitter lessons before he authored 70 and 34y TD passes to TB Tim Currier. When K John Riley added his 2nd FG, Auburn moved back into contention at 24-19 in 4th Q. However with 4:35 to go, Volunteers QB Bobby Scott pitched 33y TD to WR Gary Kries. Moments later, Vols DB Benny Dalton returned his 2nd INT to 1YL to set up FB Curt Watson's TD, and DB Ken Priest went 38y for INT TD RET.

KENTUCKY 10 Mississippi 9: Ole Miss (1-1) moved smoothly to 9-0 lead in 2nd Q as K Jim Poole kicked 24y FG and QB Archie Manning breezed 64y on TD romp. But, Wildcats S Dave Hunter blocked K Poole's conv try after Manning's score. Kentucky (1-1) narrowed it to 9-3 on K Bobby Jones' 36y FG as H clock expired. Wildcats went 63y to winning TD in 3rd Q with HB Roger Gann carrying for 13y and catching 14y pass to get close. Kentucky QB Bernie Scruggs raced over from 6YL, and after Jones successfully converted kick, Cats owned 1-pt lead. Rebels blew 4th Q chances with FUM and INT. Capacity crowd at Stoll Field cheered new coach Johnny Ray's victory in his SEC debut.

GEORGIA TECH 17 Baylor 10: Georgia Tech's flimsy O turned ball over 6 times via 3 FUMs and 3 INTs, but magnificent Yellow Jackets (2-0) D stonewalled 2 thrusts near its GL and effectively fended off Baylor (0-2). In game's opening 2 mins, Tech LB John Riggle jarred loose FUM to poise K Jack Moore for 28y FG. Bears didn't catch up until late in 3rd Q when K Terry Cozby knotted it 3-3 with short FG after Jackets DT Rock Perdoni and LB Buck Shiver sparked D into holding at its 2YL. Earlier, Engineers had built dam at their 4YL. Without TD for more than 45 mins, each team grabbed 7 pts within initial 2 mins of 4th Q. Georgia Tech DB Jeff Ford (2 INTs) scooted 16y with INT on 1st play of 4th Q, and 3 plays after KO, Baylor WR Lanny Cook took long pass from QB Si Southall (4-11/105y, TD, 2 INTs), juggled it, and made 1-handed grab before dashing on for 69y TD. Jackets DB Dave Polk made INT of Southall at Georgia Tech 46YL, and, with help of 18y pass interference PEN, Jackets QB Charlie Dudish (6-13/57y, TD, INT) flipped winning 21y TD down middle of field to HB Steve Harkey with 44 secs to play.

PURDUE 28 Notre Dame 14: Underrated Purdue (2-0) coach Jack Mollenkopf won his 10th game in 14 career tries against Notre Dame (1-1), and QB Mike Phipps (12-20/213y, TD) became 1st QB ever to lead his team to 3 straight victories over Fighting Irish. After Boilermakers DB Tim Foley returned punt into Irish territory in 1st Q, Phipps connected with HB Randy Cooper for TD pass of 37y. Phipps also ran for short TD and completed 6 important passes in 3rd down situations. Boilermakers HB Stan Brown tallied on runs of 3 and 2y. Notre Dame felt it had gotten back into it at 14-7 in 2nd Q after TB Dennis Allan (7/63y) contributed 28y dash to 78y scoring trip to HB Ed Ziegler's 10y TD catch. Midway in 3rd Q, ND, still trailing 14-7, reached 3rd-and-1 at Purdue 26YL but were pushed back by PEN and 17y loss perpetrated by Boilermakers DE Bill McKoy on tackle of Irish QB Joe Theismann (14-26/153y, 2 TDs, INT) on run attempt. Purdue immediately went 9 plays to Phipps' TD sneak for insurmountable 21-7 lead.

California 17 INDIANA 14: High-powered Indiana (1-1), coming off 58-pt performance against Kentucky, looked as though it would enjoy another O explosion as Hoosiers jumped to 14-0 lead on its 1st 2 series. Irrepressible HB John Isenbarger (26/96y) whipped 45y TD pass to WR Jade Butcher, and, after S Jay Mathias made 17y INT RET with 15y PEN tacked on, Butcher caught 6y TD pass from QB Harry Gonso (12-34/102y, TD, 2 INTs). Butcher's score gave him 23 for his career to tie him with former Indiana and Philadelphia Eagles star Pete Pihos. But, something happened to Hoosiers, according to Gonso: "We got fat after we had that 14-point lead." Before 1st Q was over, California (1-1) S Ken Weidemann came up with 1st of his 2 INTs and stepped in 18y for TD that brought Bears to within 14-7. Indiana was back on move to15YL in 2nd Q when Weidemann struck again by taking INT in his EZ. Meanwhile, Cal was going nowhere, and game had advanced to beginning of 4th Q when Bears K Ray Wersching nailed 29y FG after Gonso had lost FUM. Cal won on single big play: sub QB Steve Curtis (5-13/84y, TD) was in for nicked up QB Randy Humphries and rolled out to find sub WR Ken Adams behind secondary for 61y TD with just less than 10 mins left. Indiana had no answer.

Ucla 34 WISCONSIN 23: High-powered UCLA (3-0) stormed to 21-9 H edge and 27-9 3rd Q lead as QB Dennis Dummit totaled 209y in air and ran for 2 TDs. Bruins TB Greg Jones rushed 26/145y and scored 3 TDs. Losing for 17th time in row, Wisconsin (0-2) still looked at this defeat as something to build on. Badgers managed K Roger Jaeger's 3 FGs in 1st H and soph FB Alan Thompson's 2 TD runs in 2nd H. When Jones drove into EZ early in 4th Q it put Bruins ahead 34-15 and seemed to end game try by Wisconsin, which had only tie to show in its last 22 games. Badgers made neat, land-bound 49y drive to "A-Train" Thompson's 9y TD romp, keyed by soph TB Greg "Grape Juice" Johnson's 17y sweep. UCLA WB George Farmer nabbed 9/125y from Dummit.

MICHIGAN STATE 23 Southern Methodist 15: QB Chuck Hixson (17-30/244y, TD, INT) broke Doak Walker's SMU total O record as Walker looked on as enthused spectator. Mustangs (0-3) built 15-7 lead by end of 3rd Q on Hixson's 2nd Q TD run, K Bicky Lesser's 48y FG, and Hixson's 41y TD bomb to WR Gordon Gilder. Michigan State (2-0) bounced back in 4th Q as DB Harold Phillips' INT set up K Gary Boyce's 36y FG, and DT Ron Joseph's FUM REC launched 65y TD drive. Joseph fell on another FUM to set up QB Bill Triplett's 5y TD pass to TE Bruce Kulesza as Spartans won going away.

Wyoming 27 AIR FORCE 25: Air Force (1-2) enjoyed 12-0 and 15-3 leads in 2nd Q, but 2 failed x-pts would come back to haunt Falcons. QB Gary Baxter fired 3 TD passes for Air Force, but active Wyoming (2-0) DLs Larry Nels and Tony McGee threw him for frequent losses. Cowboys QB Gary Fox ran and passed for TDs, and K Bob Jacobs' 2nd FG gave Wyoming its lead for good at 20-18 in 3rd Q.

October 4, 1969

Boston University 13 HARVARD 10: Never in Boston University (3-0) history had it beaten Harvard (1-1), its Charles River neighbor. Crimson, sporting 10-game unbeaten string, led 10-7 at H on 1y TD smash by HB Gus Crim's and 22y FG by K Rich Szaro, who had been recruited by Sen. Robert F. Kennedy before latter's death at assassin's hand. Haughty Harvard band derided "inferior" foe during H by playing Mickey Mouse theme sufficiently loud to be heard in visitors' locker room. Angry Terriers snapped back to score on QB Pete Yetten to WB Gary Capehart pass early in 4th Q. Then, BU counted on its fierce D, which allowed only 100y in 2nd H to pave upset win. Crimson was 8-16/32y in air thanks to snappingly tight coverage by Terriers ace CBs Bruce Taylor, future NFL D rookie-of-year, and Fred Barry.

BOSTON COLLEGE 28 Tulane 24: Behind 14-0 in opening 5 mins because Boston College (2-0) sprung HB Fred Willis (26/97y, 3 TDs) for TD runs of 19 and 3y, Tulane (0-3) clawed back into it as sub QB Rusty Lachaussee (12-32/184y, TD, 2 INTs) rallied his team with 200y total O to 17-14 lead near end of 3rd Q. Green Wave soph HB Jim Batey rushed for 80y, including 5y TD just before H and another score after BC FUM in 3rd Q. BC DB Gary Dancewicz made his 2nd of 3 INTs at GL and returned it 35y early in 4th Q to turn tide. Eagles QB Red Harris (15-36/175y) hit 3 passes, and HBs Jim Catone and Willis hammered it across for 21-17 lead. Catone soon bolted for clinching 66y TD.

NORTH CAROLINA 38 Vanderbilt 22: Even though Tar Heels (1-2) scored their most pts under coach Bill Dooley and amassed 497y, it was their D that kept Vanderbilt (0-3) bottled up inside its 28YL while North Carolina built 17-0 lead. HB Don McCauley (21/132y) scored 1st Heels TD, and QB John Swofford (8-12/139y, 3 TDs) came of age in amping up UNC O. Vanderbilt climbed within 17-6 as converted C Denny Painter was sent in at QB to throw ball: Painter lofted 49y TD to swift HB Doug Matthews, isolated on LB John Bunting. Early in 2nd H, Vandy had 2 TDs on 1 possession retrieved by officials calling clipping PENs. Finally, WB Dave Strong scored from 3YL and 2-pt conv was added to pull Commodores within 17-14. Swofford, future ACC commissioner, then took control with TD passes to McCauley and WB Lewis Jolley on next 2 of North Carolina's series.

ALABAMA 33 Mississippi 32 (Birmingham): QB Scott Hunter outdueled QB Archie Manning, but difference between Alabama (3-0) and Mississippi (1-2) came down to missed conv by Rebels K Perry King. Manning's fine hand was evident in each Rebs score: he ran for 1, 2, and 17y TDs and threw 2 TD passes. Ole Miss enjoyed lead of 32-27 with 7:15 left. Having already scored once himself and passed to set up TDs by HBs Johnny Musso and Bubba Sawyer, Hunter sparked winning 80y TD drive. Hunter hit 3 passes, but faced 4th down at 15YL. He found WR George Ranager open for catch, and Ranager broke free of tackle at 3YL to score winning TD with 3:42 to go.

GEORGIA 41 South Carolina 16: Mighty D of no. 7 Georgia (3-0) swarmed pressure all over South Carolina (2-1) QB Tommy Suggs (4-15/49y, 3 INTs). Still, within 51-sec span late in 2nd Q came 1y TD plunge by FB Warren Muir (21/136y, TD) and K Billy DuPre's 46y FG to bring Gamecocks to within 14-10 at H. "I am glad to see this Georgia team not let the game get out of control when it looked like the other team had some momentum going," said UGa coach Vince Dooley. Score stayed at 14-10 through 3rd Q until Georgia QB Mike Cavan opened 4th Q at Carolina 9YL and, on 3rd-and-goal, rolled left, then right before being stopped at 1YL. From that moment on, powerful running by FBs Bruce Kemp (31/142y, TD), who scored on next snap on 4th down, and Julian Smiley (16/80y, 2 TDs) sparked Bulldogs' 27-pt explosion in 4th Q.

Clemson 21 GEORGIA TECH 10: For 24 years under coach Frank Howard, Clemson (2-1) had visited Atlanta without win against Georgia Tech. TB Ray Yauger (23/146y, TD) ran like tiger and his 10 and 5y TD catches from QB Tommy Kendrick (10-21/141y, 2 TDs, 2 INTs) helped overcome 10-0 H deficit. K Johnny Duncan had walloped 54y FG in 1st Q to set Yellow Jackets distance record, and DB Jeff Ford made 47y INT RET to launch beat-the-clock TD drive to enormous TE Steve Foster's 5y reception from QB Charlie Dudish (5-10/33y, TD). But Dudish was hurt early in 3rd Q, and Georgia Tech committed foolish roughing PEN on punt that put ball at its 38YL. Yauger powered 28y and then beat LB-coverage for 10y TD catch. Clemson went 77y to Yauger's 2nd TD catch early in 4th Q after WR Charlie Waters (7/101y) made dazzling 19y grab at 3YL. Downed punt at Tech 2YL, followed by FUM at 6YL set up Yauger's clinching score with 7 mins to play.

Missouri 40 MICHIGAN 17: Wolverines (2-1), winners of last 10 of 11 games, took 3-0 lead in 1st Q on K Tim Killian's 41y FG, then suffered through amazing 2nd Q, described by coach Bo Schembechler as "a nightmare and I wouldn't have believed it unless I was there." DB Dennis Poppe grabbed 2 of 4 TOs forced by Missouri (3-0) in 2nd Q. Twice Michigan D was drawn offside with back-in-motion near its GL to help Mizzou

FB Ron McBride and HB Jon Staggers slash for TDs. Tigers QB Terry McMillan (7-12/120y, INT) beat H clock by 13 secs with passes of 19, 19, and 18y, last of which WR Mel Gray took OB at 1YL. McBride scored for 24-3 H edge. After T Dan Dierdorf downed punt at 1YL in 3rd Q, Michigan DB Barry Pierson returned Mizzou's answering punt 50y to 10YL. Quickly, Wolverines trimmed it to 24-17 on FB Garvie Craw's 2 TD runs and brought crowd back to life. But in opening min of 4th Q, Missouri DE Mike Bennett blocked Wolverines P Mark Werner's punt at 12YL to set up FG, and HB Joe Moore (19/117y) sprinted 62y on draw-play TD. Coach Dan Devine upped his record to 9-1-1 against Big 10 since his arrival at Mizzou in 1958.

PURDUE 36 Stanford 35: QBs Mike Phipps (28-39/429y, 5 TDs) of Purdue (3-0) and Jim Plunkett (23-46/355y, 4 TDs, 2 INTs) of Stanford (2-1) put on spectacular passing show in 1st-ever meeting of schools that each boasted traditional QB greatness. Of 10 TDs on scoreboard at day's end, only Indians FB Howie Williams' opening 2y plunge was scored on ground. Stanford held 35-21 lead entering 4th Q after Plunkett connected with TE Bob Moore and TE-LB Ron Kadziel for 3rd Q tallies. Phipps retaliated in 4th Q with TD arrows to FB John Bullock and HB Stan Brown, and, with 3:03 left, he hit WR Greg Fenner with pressure-packed 2-pt pass. Last Tribe hope died when Plunkett's pass was intercepted by Boilermakers DB Mike Renie with 2:04 to play.

Nebraska 42 MINNESOTA 14: Cornhuskers (2-1) destroyed porous Minnesota (0-2-1) D with 591y total O as QB Jerry Tagge (15-23/219y, 2 TDs, 2 INTs) and IB Jeff Kinney (13/49y, 2 TDs) combined for 4 TDs. Kinney even tossed TD passes for both sides: He threw 12y pass to Nebraska WR Guy Ingles for tying TD at 7-7 in 2nd Q, and Golden Gophers DB Gary Hohman sprung surprise when he stepped in front of Tagge on Kinney's foolish impromptu pass out of jam near Minny GL. Hohman's 99y INT TD RET in 2nd Q provided short-lived 14-7 lead. Deadlocked at 14-14 at H, Huskers exploded on Kinney's TD run and rode with Tagge, who hit 43y TD pass to HB Larry Frost, their 2nd scoring connection. Frost would father future Nebraska QB Scott Frost, star of 1997 co-national champions. Soph LB Bob Bailey recovered FUM and made INT for Minnesota.

NOTRE DAME 42 Michigan State 28: Converting 7 passes on 3rd down for 1st downs, Notre Dame QB Joe Theismann (20-33/294y, 3 TDs, 2 INTs) pitched 3 TD passes and zipped to 7y TD early in 3rd Q. Key play likely was Theismann's 29y TD pass to HB Ed Ziegler for 21-14 lead with 49 secs left before H. Michigan State (2-1) had earned 7-7 and 14-14 ties on scores by HBs Tommy Love and Don Highsmith before Ziegler's catch. Spartans QB Bill Triplett was stymied on triple option, but hit 9-25/178y passing, including 35y 4th Q TD pass to WR Gordon Bowdell.

Penn State 17 KANSAS STATE 14: Suddenly-forceful Kansas State (2-1) made numerous early threats, but was turned back by 2 FUMs, 2 INTs, and 4th down failure. Penn State (3-0) HB Lydell Mitchell broke away for 58y TD run in 2nd Q. When FB Franco Harris capped 60y aerial drive with 3y TD run in 3rd Q, Lions had 17-0 edge. Wildcats stormed back too late in 4th Q as HB Mack Herron plunged across, and QB Lynn Dickey (18-31/219y, TD, 2 INTs) launched 63y TD bomb to E Mike Creed.

COLORADO 30 Indiana 7: Amid early season snow, Colorado (2-1) coach Eddie Crowder switched QB Bob Anderson to TB, and Anderson (29/161y) plowed for 3 TDs. Buffs' 4th TD was tallied by new QB Paul Arendt on 3y run in 4th Q. Unpredictable Indiana (1-2) had enjoyed 7-3 lead in 1st Q after QB Harry Gonso pitched 17y TD pass to WR Jade Butcher. It was rare visit to Boulder by Big 10 team since Colorado showed only tie with Wisconsin in its previous home encounters with Big 10.

ARKANSAS 24 Texas Christian 6 (Little Rock): Even though Texas Christian (0-3) had 3 key O players out or limping, QB Steve Judy (20-38/245y, INT) smartly maneuvered Frogs on 2 long, early drives as he converted several 3rd down passes. But, sub TB Marty Whelan, in for banged-up Norm Bulaich, lost FUM while sweeping from Arkansas (3-0) 4YL, and on 2nd march, TCU had to settle for K Wayne Merritt's 21y FG. Down 3-0 and soon after KO, Hogs QB Bill Montgomery (13-26/208y, 2 TDs) fooled D on 3rd-and-2, faking run and launching long, crossing-pattern bomb to WR Chuck Dicus, who rambled 73y for TD. In last min of 2nd Q, Merritt made FG at end of 73y TCU drive from its 22YL, kept alive by Judy's 14y pass on 4th down. So, Frogs trailed 10-6 at H. Key score came right after 2nd H KO as Montgomery and Dicus reconnected on 23y TD at end of 80y trip. Hogs TB Bill Burnett scored 4th Q TD after drive was sustained by 15y PEN on Frogs.

Ohio State 41 WASHINGTON 14: Huskies (0-3) brightened home fans by making 2 early stops of mighty Buckeyes (2-0), but fleet Ohio State QB Rex Kern (13-20/120y, INT) burst for 64y TD run off RT Chuck Hutchison's block. Buckeyes FB Jim Otis (20/111y, 3 TDs) soon started wearing his path to EZ with TDs in 1st and 2nd Qs and another after H. Ohio State scored on its 1st 2 possessions of 3rd Q for 35-7 avalanche. Washington QB-P Gene Willis (1-3/6y, INT) had created his own short TD run by punting OB at Bucks 3YL in 2nd Q and, after Ohio's punt out, capping 54y TD trip with 1y sneak.

Oregon 25 WASHINGTON STATE 24: Star HB Bobby Moore scored twice for Oregon (2-1) to compliment passing of QB Tom Blanchard (8-16/170y, TD, INT). Blanchard rifled 38y TD pass to WR Bob Newland in 2nd Q as Ducks glided to 19-6 lead at H. Washington State (1-2) fell behind 25-6 in 3rd Q, and Cougars' inability to convert after their 1st 2 TDs later forced them into failed 2-pt tries. Late in 3rd Q, Wazzu TB Chuck Hawthorne broke away for 65y TD run. QB Jack Wigmore sliced for 1y TD midway in 4th Q to pull Cougars within 25-18, and he raced around LE in game's last min to score. Washington State's 2-pt run attempt by TB Richard Lee Smith was crushed at line of scrimmage.

October 11, 1969

(Fri) Louisiana State 20 MIAMI 0: Knocked out of AP Top 10 in each of last 2 years by Miami (1-2), LSU (4-0) exacted revenge but not without battle displayed by stubborn Hurricanes D. Tops in nation in scoring so far in 1969, Tigers failed to tally on any of their 1st 10 possessions until they went 80y to FB Eddie Ray's leaping 1y TD with 3:54 left in 3rd Q. Unable to generate O while using 3 QBs in 54 mins, Miami reinserted starting QB Lew Pytel (4-10/41y, INT), who promptly threw 26y completion to WR Ray Bellamy. But, Pytel was blindsided on next play and lost FUM at UM 33YL to LSU DE Buddy Mullican. On 5th Tigers play, Ray (13/81y) dragged tacklers to 1YL, and HB Tommy Casanova scored for 13-0 lead with 3:43 left. Pytel tried swing pass after KO, and Bayou Bengals DB Don Addison picked it off and zipped by to TD.

Notre Dame 45 ARMY 0 (New York City): Notre Dame (3-1) marched onto hallowed turf of Yankee Stadium to hand Army (2-2) coach Tom Cahill unpleasant 50th birthday gift: 617y O, most to date ever permitted by proud Cadets. Army stopped ND's 1st 2 series on INT and forced punt, so there was hope this ancient rivalry might still have spark. But, Irish K Scott Hempel soon opened scoring with 20y FG. QB Joe Theismann whipped 55y TD pass to E Tom Gatewood (9/164y) before end of 1st Q and Irish scorers soon paraded into EZ like it was St. Patrick's Day on New York's Fifth Avenue. Theismann (15-24/215y, 2 TDs, 2 INTs) ran for 4y TD, and followed with repeat TD throw to Gatewood. Overmatched Black Knights put up continuous effort but were limited to 48y rushing because they couldn't penetrate Notre Dame D-line led by Ts Mike McCoy and Jim Reilly, latter from nearby Yonkers, N.Y.

PENN STATE 20 West Virginia 0: As usual, Penn State (4-0) D held fort while Lions got their O act together. National team rushing leader West Virginia (4-1) threw runners FB Jim Braxton (23/96y) and HB Bob Gresham at Nittany Lions D on early 73y drive. But, bad pitchout and PEN halted WVU's march. FB Franco Harris put Penn State on board at 7-0 with pass mid-way in 2nd Q after QB Chuck Burkhart's 67y pass to HB Lydell Mitchell. HBs Mitchell and Charlie Pittman, back from injury, scored in 2nd H. In their 23rd game in row without loss, Lions' snarling D picked off 4 INTs to stifle Mountaineers attack.

Syracuse 20 MARYLAND 9: Terrapins (1-3) and favored Orangemen (3-1) reached H in surprising 3-3 deadlock, but that occurred primarily on 3 FUMs that offered scoring chances to Maryland. Syracuse held Maryland to 80y rushing overall, and its pass-rush trapped Terps QB Dennis O'Hara for -27y and forced him into ineffective 2-5/24y passing effort in 2nd H. Orange, who had wedged their FG into closing moments of 2nd Q thanks to QB Randy Zur's 19 and 15y dashes and his 13y pass to HB Greg Allen, went ahead for good on K George Jakowenko's 32y FG in 3rd Q. Syracuse went 80y to TE Tony Gabriel's 15y TD catch from QB Rich Panczyszyn. Out of nowhere, Terps struck in 4th Q when fleet WR Roland Merritt took pass for 90y TD to pull within 13-9. Orangemen retaliated right away with another Panczyszyn-to-Gabriel TD of 22y.

VANDERBILT 14 Alabama 10: Future college coach, soph QB Watson Brown, came off bench for Vanderbilt (1-3) to end winning 92y drive in 4th Q with 11y TD pass to TE Jim Cunningham in left corner of EZ. Brown shared laurels on winning drive with fellow Vandy soph QB Denny Painter, who masterminded most of vital charge downfield. Actually, upset was keyed on Commodores limiting Alabama (3-1) O to 201y while it stunningly cruised to 473y. Batch of Vanderbilt PENs and brilliant GLS by Bama prevented earlier clinching by Commodores. Crimson Tide earned 10-7 advantage on early 3rd Q 19y TD sweep by WR George Ranager after Vandy fumbled possession away to Bama LB Wayne Rhoads shortly after 2nd H KO. Alabama appeared on schedule to take 17-7 advantage when Dores DB Christie Hauck swiped pass by Tide QB Scott Hunter and dashed 8y out of EZ to launch critical TD march. Painter followed with 5, 18, 19, and 17y completions and 4 and 11y runs before coach Bill Pace inserted Brown for clutch TD pitch.

MISSISSIPPI 25 Georgia 17 (Jackson, Miss.): QB Archie Manning (16-28/195y, 2 TDs, INT), who had walked off Birmingham's Legion Field in tears of frustration on previous Saturday, this time majestically led his never-say-die Rebels (2-2) to victory over no. 6 Georgia (3-1). Things started poorly for Manning: Bulldogs DE David McKnight picked off 2nd pass of game and loped 34y to score. Ole Miss TE Jim Poole (8/81y, TD) capped 17-play drive with TD catch after Manning had launched 88y trip by retreating inside his 5YL before finding WR Floyd Franks for 29y completion. INT by Mississippi S Glenn Cannon pitched K Perry Lee King into position for 29y FG, and long-range soph bomber, K Cloyce Hinton, later nailed 59y FG. However, Georgia came to life for FB Bruce Kemp's 4y TD blast late in 2nd Q. With Manning off hurt, UGa DL Phillip Russell knocked ball loose from QB Shug Chumbler, Manning's replacement, and K Jim McCullough's 31y FG upped Bulldogs margin to 17-13. Manning returned to hit 2 passes before TB Leon Felts (10/42y, TD) ripped 17y for TD and 19-17 lead. Manning's 4th Q TD bomb to WR Riley Myers drilled home final result. Led by WB-TB Dennis Hughes (9/62y rushing and 6/54y receiving) Georgia won ground war (176y to 96y), but Ole Miss passed for 233y.

223

OHIO STATE 54 Michigan State 21: Ohio State (3-0) coach Woody Hayes may have fretted about Big 10's archaic no-repeat rule that created, in his words, "lack of Rose Bowl incentive," but Buckeyes QB Rex Kern cheered record crowd by accounting for 5 TDs, 3 by air. HB Larry Zelina added 73y punt TD RET as Ohio upped its season scoring avg to 52 pts. What started Buckeyes to 20-0 lead in opening 8:20 was DE Mark Debevc's INT of Michigan State (2-2) QB Bill Triplett's pass on Spartans 14YL. Debevc trotted for TD and 7-0 lead and made REC 22 secs later of MSU HB Tommy Love's FUM at 26YL. Spartans were able only to enjoy QB Bill Triplett's 2 stunning TD passes of 76 and 40y to WR Frank Foreman in 1st H. Despite Spartans having made 218y passing, Hayes said difference was "the quickness of our defense." It was Ohio State's 16th win in row, 12th straight in Big 10.

MICHIGAN 31 Purdue 20: Surprisingly, Wolverines QB Don Moorhead (15-25/247y, TD, INT) more than matched Boilermakers counterpart, QB Mike Phipps (22-44/250y, TD, 4 INTs). Michigan (3-1) marched to TB Glenn Doughty's opening 6y TD run as TE Jim Mandich (10/156y) caught 3 of his 7 1st Q receptions on this drive. Phipps went over for short TD and rolled out to hit TE Ashley Bell with 6y TD as Boilermakers (3-1) earned 14-14 tie 19 secs before H. DB Tom Curtis picked off Phipps' pass to set up C-K Tim Killian's 3rd Q FG, which gave Michigan lead for good at 17-14. Then, just 2 plays after KO, Phipps pulled away from C too quickly, and ball ended up in hands of Michigan DE Al Carpenter. TB Billy Taylor popped up middle for 26y, and Moorhead sneaked over for TD. Margin grew to 31-14 on Mandich's diving 5y TD catch in 4th Q.

Toledo 27 BOWLING GREEN 26: K Ken Crots started 17-pt 1st H spree for Toledo (4-0) when he booted 34y FG. Bowling Green (2-2) QB Vern Wireman got Falcons rolling in 2nd H, and, as clock ticked down, Falcons still had opportunity. Wireman launched BGSU for 70y in 3 magical plays to score on 5y pass to TE Steve Lanning with 1:31 left. Even though important conv kick was missed, Falcons still led 26-24. After ensuing KO, Rockets went 31y in 4 plays, and Crots bombed winning 37y FG against 25 mph wind with 2 secs left.

MISSOURI 17 Nebraska 7: Nebraska (2-2) chose rather early in game that it wouldn't be able to run much (38/36y) against great Missouri (4-0) D, so its passing numbers made it look more like 2004 than 1969: 19-42/232y, TD, 2 INTs. Huskers' only TD came in 3rd Q as TB Jeff Kinney took short pass from QB Jerry Tagge, and Tigers DBs George Fountain (9 tackles, INT) and Dennis Poppe simultaneously bounced off Kinney, "like black-helmeted billy goats," according to St. Louis Post-Dispatch. So, Nebraska's Kinney took off for 77y TD to bring Big Red's deficit to 14-7. In 1st H, Missouri, which wouldn't succeed often with its passing (5-21/110y, 2 INTs), still had enjoyed QB Terry McMillan's fortuitous pair of TD connections: 69y bomb to speedster WR Mel Gray on game's 2nd play and 8y rifle-shot to TE Tom Shryock with 7 secs left before H. Fountain made up for his tackling booboo by coming from nowhere to tip away sure TD pass from hands of Huskers HB Larry Frost. Pass was thrown by sub QB Van Brownson early in 4th Q when Nebraska TD could have jumped it back into contention at 17-14.

Texas 27 Oklahoma 17 (Dallas): TB Steve Owens (30/123y) keyed early 14-0 Sooners uprising by scoring on 7y run in 1st Q. With Texas' option run attack shut down, Texas' dormant pass O was unlimbered in 4th straight win over Oklahoma (2-1). Although INTs led to 10 Sooner pts, Longhorn QB James Street and WR Cotton Speyrer collaborated on 8 passes. Speyrer caught 24y TD to halve 2-TD deficit in 1st Q and his reception set up Happy Feller's 3rd Q go-ahead FG at 20-17. Texas (4-0) star OT Bob McKay recovered punt FUM by DB Glenn King at Sooner 23YL with 6:25 to play. Steer FB Steve Worster scored 5 plays later to ice it.

UTAH 24 Arizona State 23: Suddenly vulnerable Arizona State (2-2) had its dynamic O shut down by Utah (3-1) from middle of 2nd Q on. Before then, Sun Devils had jumped to 15-0 lead on safety on DL Junior Ah You's blocked punt and 2 TD runs by quick, little HB Dave Buchanan. Ah You had roared in block Utah P Craig Smith's punt, but it was Smith who hustled back into EZ for REC that saved TD. Trio of major PENs against ASU significantly aided Utes' 92y TD drive just before H. When FB Dave Smith opened Utah's 1st series of 2nd H with 10y TD run it brought Redskins to within 15-13. In 4th Q, Utes QB Ray Groth (11-22/152y) sped 7y to tally, then added 2-pt pass to HB Billy Hunter (19/89y, and 2/28y, TD receiving) for 21-15 lead. Utah DB Norm Thompson soon intercepted pass by Arizona State QB Joe Spagnola (11-23/95y, TD, 2 INTs) before K Marv Bateman's decisive 23y FG in 4th Q built margin to 24-15. ASU WR Calvin Demery (5/57y) caught 4 passes including 5y TD in 4th Q, and while Sun Devils made 2-pt conv on run by FB Art Malone (23/104y) to stand 1 pt behind, they got only 1 other possession rest of way.

SOUTHERN CALIFORNIA 26 Stanford 24: QB Jim Plunkett (25-37/296y, 2 INTs) whipped 2 TD passes to give Stanford (2-2) 12-0 advantage in 2nd Q, although x-pt failure of kick and 2-pt pass would linger like smog over Indians. Southern California (4-0) DB Tyrone Hudson sped 57y to INT TD RET that created 14-12 H edge. No. 4 Trojans led again 20-15 at end of 3rd Q after TE Gerry Mullins caught 19y TD pass from QB Jimmy Jones (12-24/180y, TD, 3 INTs). Indians regained margin at 21-20 as RB Bubba Brown crashed over for TD after 30y pass interference PEN was called on USC LB John Young. Ks Ron Ayala and Steve Horowitz traded FGs with Horowitz' giving Stanford 24-23 lead with 1:02 to play. Trojans moved swiftly for 70y from own 15YL to Ayala's winning 34y FG (7th lead change in game) on game's dramatic last play. With no timeouts left, USC FG team had to smartly race on field as Mullins was unable to get OB with 14y catch at Stanford 15YL.

October 18, 1969

Penn State 15 SYRACUSE 14: Not since 21-0 loss late in 1966 season had no. 5 Penn State (5-0) trailed by as much as 14 pts, but swift-striking Syracuse (3-2) jumped ahead 14-0 by 1st min of 2nd Q. Orange S Gary Bletsch's 20y INT RET prompted FB Al Newton's short TD plunge, and HB Greg Allen's 2nd of 3 long punt RETs poised QB Randy Zur's 6y TD sweep. After his 61y and 65y punt RETs, pesky Allen went 46y to Penn State 29YL late in 2nd Q. But, Allen was tripped up by fast-closing DB Neal Smith on failed 4th-and-2 run from 3YL. Meanwhile, Syracuse D was completely dominating play as it held mighty Lions to 64y net O and 3 1st downs in 1st H. Early in 4th Q, Nittany Lions DT Steve Smear caused 2nd of 2 FUMs he jolted free, and LB Jack Ham recovered at Syracuse 32YL. After pass interference against Syracuse LB Richard Kokosky on 4th down from 15YL, HB Lydell Mitchell ran 4y to score. Penn State 1st failed on 2-pt pass, but holding PEN against Orangemen allowed FB Franco Harris to plunge for 2-pts that narrowed it to 14-8. Lions took over after short Syracuse punt, and Harris rambled for 36y TD on counter-run block by G Bob Holuba. K Jack Reitz's go-ahead x-pt came at 7:01 mark of 4th Q, only 3:17 after 1st Penn State TD, and turnaround completely punctured spirit of Orangemen.

Tennessee 41 ALABAMA 14 (Birmingham): Early surge by volatile Volunteers (5-0) sent Alabama (3-2) reeling to its worst defeat to date under coach Bear Bryant. Tennessee's victory also marked 1st time any school had won 3 straight games against Bear Bryant-coached Crimson Tide team. After Tennessee QB Bobby Scott threw TD pass to WR Gary Kreis, DB Bobby Majors raced 71y to punt TD RET. Going from bad to worse, Tide QB Neb Hayden saw his pitchout swiped by Tennessee LB Jackie Walker for 27y TD RET. Scott ran for TD and Vols built 34-0 lead early in 4th Q before HB Johnny Musso gave Bama 2 late TDs for Crimson window-dressing. Tennessee star LB Steve Kiner was all over field, blitzing passers for 5 sacks/-43y and pulling down INT. Just before Vols' 1st-team D finished man-handling of Tide and left contest for good in 4th Q, Kiner screamed at Alabama players: "Look over there at that poor old man (coach Bryant). He looks pitiful…You sorry sons-of-bitches have let him down. You should be ashamed of yourselves!"

Auburn 17 GEORGIA TECH 14: Auburn (4-1) saw its explosive O stymied by wide-ranging Georgia Tech (2-3) D, but Tigers turned tables with LB Bobby Strickland's INT at Tech 36YL in game's last 5 mins to set up K John Riley for winning 18y FG with 1:01 on clock. Earlier, Yellow Jackets had blocked pair of 3-pt attempts by Riley. FB Wallace Clark, who rambled for 122y rushing, had put Tigers ahead with 2y TD run in 2nd Q, but it was matched by Georgia Tech HB Gene Spiotta's similar TD run for 7-7 H knot. Engineers DB Jeff Ford blocked Riley's 37 and 51y FG tries in 2nd Q. Auburn's dynamic passing duo of QB Pat Sullivan and E Terry Beasley hooked up on 20y TD in 3rd Q, but again Tech tied it, this time on FB Steve Harkey's 4y run. After Strickland's INT, TB Mickey Zofko gained 23y to put Tigers at 1YL and in position that Riley could quickly hit game-winning chip-shot FG. LB Bill Flowers was credited with 18 tackles for Jackets.

MICHIGAN STATE 23 Michigan 12: After 6-pt underdog Spartans (3-2) spotted Michigan (3-2) 3-0 lead early in 2nd Q on big K Tim Killian's 29y FG, MSU's upset win was fashioned on superb option-play runs of QB Bill Triplett (18/142y, TD) and HB Don Highsmith (30/129y, 2 TDs). Michigan State amassed 348y ground game, scored 16 pts in 2nd Q, and jumped to 23-3 lead in 3rd Q as Highsmith capped 80y drive with 2y run, Triplett made nifty 10y TD sweep, and Highsmith scored his 2nd TD on 4y burst at close of 60y trip. Wolverines piled up 340y themselves, but it took until 4th Q for QB Don Moorhead (60 play: 13-35/164y, and 25/57y rushing) to finally spark O to TD on TB Glenn Doughty's 7y run after DB Frank Gusich had recovered FUM at MSU 21YL. Doughty had accidentally handed Spartans 2nd Q safety when he fielded KO at his 1YL and retreated into EZ to touch knee for what he thought was touchback.

OHIO STATE 34 Minnesota 7: Ohio State (4-0) won its 18th game in row as keyed-up Golden Gophers (0-4-1) were buried by their own TOs, even though they were able to burrow inside Buckeyes 20YL on 5 occasions. Ohio State FB Jim Otis powered to dual 1st Q TDs after weak Minnesota punts twice opened door to its GL. QB Phil Hagen's wild pitchout spoiled promising Gophers trip to Ohio 1YL, and Buckeyes responded with 87y TD drive for 20-0 H edge. Gophers LB Rich Crawford went 51y with FUM RET to set up FB Jim Carter's 6y TD run in 3rd Q.

NOTRE DAME 14 Southern California 14: After both stellar Ds dominated in scoreless 1st H, Irish (3-1-1) opened 2nd H with 74y march to FB Bill Barz's 1y TD blast. USC (4-0-1) QB Jimmy Jones matched it with 18y TD pass at end of 74y trip. Trojans DB Tyrone Hudson stepped in front of ND QB Joe Theismann for INT that positioned Jones' 2nd TD pass. Irish DL Mike McCoy, who helped frustrate USC TB Clarence Davis to tune of 30/75y rushing, split 2 blockers to block punt which was recovered at USC 7YL by DE Walt Patulski. It set up HB Denny Allan's tying 1y TD. ND coach Ara Parseghian, no stranger to controversial tie games, adamantly defended his going for tying kick with 6-and-half mins to play. Deadlock was assured when Notre Dame K Scott Hempel's 48y FG try bounced off crossbar in final 2 mins.

OKLAHOMA 42 Colorado 30: Sooners TB Steve Owens (28/112y, 4 TDs) eclipsed 100y rushing barrier for 14th straight game, but Oklahoma (3-1) had to survive Colorado (3-2) comeback bid. Sooners used speed to construct 28-9 lead in 2nd Q as TE Steve Zabel got open for TD pass from QB Jack Mildren (7-17/114y, TD, INT) and FB Roy Bell (12/130y, TD) dashed to 53y TD in 2nd Q for 21-9 lead. Buffs QB Paul Arendt (4-8/34y, INT) had his problems when he had fumbled deep in Sooners territory on game's opening bid and thrown INT to OU LB Steve Casteel that set up Mildren's TD pass for 14-3 lead in 2nd Q. Arendt was yanked in favor of little QB Jimmy Bratten (6-17/79y, TD) who provided some spark and 35y TD to E Monte Huber (5/70y, TD) in 2nd Q. Led by TB Bob Anderson's 26/123y, Buffaloes outrushed Sooners 319y to 289y. Anderson's 3rd TD at end of 80y drive trimmed deficit to 35-30 with 2:37 to play, but Oklahoma recovered Colorado's on-side KO just before wave of Buffs arrived. Sooners then went 70y to late score as TD-maker Owens bulldozed on 6 of 9 plays to surpass that era's record-holder, Alan Ameche of Wisconsin, for most career rushing attempts with 683.

WYOMING 40 Brigham Young 7: Wyoming (5-0) sent 5 different players into EZ while its D delivered overwhelming effort that limited BYU (2-3) to 129y O. Cowboys' big win, 4th straight in WAC, was achieved without 14 black players, who were dismissed from squad for their threat to not play because of perceived negative racial policies of BYU and Mormon Church. QB Marc Lyons contributed sole Cougars TD with 4y run in 2nd Q.

UCLA 32 California 0: UCLA QB Dennis Dummit (9-13/202y) pitched 8 and 65y TDs to WR Gwen Cooper in 1st H, and previous year's Bruins QB, Bill Bolden, raced 65 and 41y to 4th Q TDs from reserve TB spot. No. 6 Bruins (6-0) didn't allow initial 1st down by California (3-2) until midway in 2nd Q as Bears traveled no deeper than UCLA 35YL in 1st H. California gained but 197y and was forced into 8 punts. Golden Bears coach Ray Willsey, his team outgained 570y to 197y, raved about Bruins, whose coach, Tommy Prothro, went out of his way to introduce his superb front-7 to media afterward: DEs Bob Geddes and Wesley Grant, DTs Floyd Reese and Bruce Jorgensen, and LBs Mike Ballou, Don Widmer, and Jim Ford.

AP Poll October 20

1 Ohio State (27)	666	11 Oklahoma	152
2 Texas (5)	612	12 Notre Dame	126
3 Tennessee (1)	435	13 Georgia	102
4 Arkansas	417	14 Auburn	67
5 Missouri	355	15 Purdue	47
6 UCLA	341	16 Wyoming	46
7 Southern California	297	17 Mississippi	31
8 Penn State (1)	294	18 Kansas State	29
9 Louisiana State	226	19 Stanford	23
10 Florida	222	20 Air Force	4

October 25, 1969

LOUISIANA STATE 21 Auburn 20: Hard-charging D of undefeated LSU (6-0) blocked FG and conv in trumping nation's leading D of Auburn (4-2). On game's 1st scrimmage play, LSU struck for 62y TD pass from TB Jimmy Gilbert to WR Andy Hamilton, but Auburn countered with 74y TD drive. Plainsmen D soon made 2 mistakes that cost it dearly. Trade of 2nd Q TDs left 14-14 H deadlock, but Bengals' 2y TD pass by sub QB Mike Hillman had resulted from roughing K PEN on K Mark Lumpkin's wide-left 44y FG try. Auburn's 2nd D miscue came on 3rd-and-15 at its 36YL: pass interference was called on DB Merrill Shirley, which provided 1st down at Auburn 26YL. LSU TB Allen Shorey soon plunged for TD in middle of 3rd Q, and Lumpkin converted for 7-pt lead. Auburn QB Pat Sullivan (19-34/224y, 2TDs, INT) tossed his 2nd TD pass, 14y to TB Mickey Zofko, at end of 95y march with 12:52 to play. But, LSU LB Bill Thomason, with assist from DT George Bevan, blocked K John Riley's conv kick. Thomason had blocked Riley's FG try earlier.

Michigan 35 MINNESOTA 9: Excitable Michigan Wolverines (4-2) coach Bo Schembechler was hot under his collar as 1st H ended. Minnesota (0-5-1) K Mel Anderson had just kicked Gophers' 3rd FG (37y) of 1st H for 9-7 lead even though it was apparent that Minnesota WR George Kemp was still fighting for y at Michigan 19YL when Gophers were granted timeout. Schembechler growled afterward: "I think that one should belong to the Minnesota timer." But, contest's 2nd H was whole new ballgame as Wolverines stormed for 4 TDs to win going away. TB Billy Taylor (151y rushing), who started his 1st game for injured TB Glenn Doughty, scored 2 of his 3 TDs in 3rd Q at end of 75 and 66y sorties by Wolverines. Another pair of scores came in 4th Q. Gophers coach Murray Warmath shook up his lineup by moving his starting C Ron King to LB where he had hand in 24 tackles. Shakeup had delayed effect as Minnesota started 4-game win streak following week.

KANSAS STATE 59 Oklahoma 21: Kansas State (5-1) authored what could be considered greatest victory in school history. Wildcats QB Lynn Dickey passed 28-42/380y, 3 TDs, 2 INTs in their 1st win over Oklahoma (3-2) since 1934, while Sooners relinquished most pts in their history to date. Dickey's completions bested his own Big 8 mark and his pass y broke 18-year-old set by Missouri's Tony Scardino. FB Jerry Lawson, in for injured FB Mike Montgomery, rushed for 77y and caught 6/37y. K-State built 49-14 lead in 3rd Q then enjoyed its reserves playing out most of 4th Q. Oklahoma's only 1st H bright spots came on 77 and 66y TD bombs by QB Jack Mildren (7-21/193y, 2 TDs, 2 INTs). Sooners still harbored hope, trailing 28-14 at H, especially since they had gifted 2 scores by losing FUMs at their 15 and 17YLs. Midway in 3rd Q, K-State DB Henry Hawthorne took punt 37y to set up Dickey's 26y TD arrow to E Bob Long, and rout began. OU ventured into Wildcats end only once in 2nd H, to TD by TB Steve Owens (29/105y, TD).

COLORADO 31 Missouri 24: Buffs TB Bob Anderson (34/132y, 2 TDs) became school's career rushing and scoring leader to that point in history and outdueled Tigers TB Joe Moore (19/68y), nation's no. 4 rusher, who was limited to 11y in 1st H. Colorado

led 24-10 at H. No. 5 Missouri (5-1) had struck in 2nd Q for 75y TD from QB Terry McMillan to WR Mel Gray, but it soon was matched by Colorado (4-2) sub QB Paul Arendt (2-2/137y, TD), who made most of his 10 plays when new starting QB Jimmy Bratten got banged up. Arendt pitched 79y TD bomb to E Monte Huber and scored from 6YL, all in 2nd Q. Tigers were forced into uncharacteristic passing game in 2nd H as McMillan (15-35/273y, 2 TDs, 2 INTs) made TD on sneak and found E John Henley for 13y TD in 4th Q. But, Bison LB Phil Irwin (brother of golfer, Hale) and DB Eric Harris preserved 7-pt lead with 4th Q INTs.

HOUSTON 25 Mississippi 11: Short, near-sighted QB Gary Mullins affected yester-year "Revenge of the Nerds" as he ran and passed for critical TDs for rebounding Houston (3-2). Cool QB Archie Manning, "Big Man on Campus" for Mississippi (3-3), could manage only 11-29/137y, TD in air. Big difference, however, was blooming ground game of Cougars which outflanked Ole Miss 351y to 83y.

STANFORD 20 Ucla 20: Undefeated UCLA (6-0-1) needed LB Mike Ballou's game-ending FG block to save tie. Stanford (3-2-1) QB Jim Plunkett (26-44/263y, 2INT) pitched 2 TD passes to WR Randy Vataha as Indians built 17-6 H edge. QB Dennis Dummit's 3rd short TD run boosted Bruins to 20-17 lead in 4th Q. K Steve Horowitz's 30y FG tied it before Uclans reached Stanford 5YL on HB Mickey Cureton's run. Holding PEN forced missed Bruins FG, which was followed by Ballou's block of 32y FG try by Horowitz.

SOUTHERN CALIFORNIA 29 Georgia Tech 18: Yellow Jackets (2-4), 3-TD underdog, had no. 7 USC (5-0-1) shaking in its boots at 18-15 with 3 mins to play. Georgia Tech had bounced to 10-0 lead in 2nd Q on K Jack Moore's 32y FG after DB Jeff Ford made 44y INT RET and QB Charlie Dudish's 4th down 23y TD pass to RB Brent Cunningham. Trojans earned quick 15 pts as TB Clarence Davis (23/93y, 2 TDs) and QB Jimmy Jones (8-19/165y, 2 TDs, 2 INTs) starred. Jackets D, led by T Rock Perdoni, LBs John Riggle and Bill Flowers, and DBs Ford and Mike Wysong, held its own through 3rd Q until USC sub QB Jim Fassel, future head coach of Utah and New York Giants, was picked off by Tech DT Wayne Laircey at Troy 13YL. Dudish soon scored and added 2-pt pass for 18-15 4th Q lead with 5:22 to play. Jones, who had already been flattened for −46y while trying to pass, appeared hemmed in, but escaped to spiral long pass to WR Sam Dickerson (6/138y, 2 TDs), who dramatically wriggled away for 55y score. Georgia Tech tried multi-laterals on KO but it blew up. Trojans recovered bobble at Jackets 9YL, and Davis scored on next snap.

Utah 7 OREGON STATE 3 (Portland): Surprising Utes (5-1) won their 5th straight game on late 81y rallying drive to TD. Utah FB Dave Smith made 39y run, and QB Clint Harden clicked on 21y pass to E Jim Brown to bring Utes inside Oregon State (3-3) 10YL late in 4th Q. Smith shot through right side of his line 3 plays later for 11y TD. Beavers had taken 1st lead in D struggle on K Mike Nehl's 33y FG in 3rd Q. It was only 2nd time Oregon State had lost to Utah in 10-game series to date.

AP Poll October 27

1 Ohio State (35)	772	11 Georgia	164
2 Texas (2)	692	12 Kansas State	146
3 Tennessee (1)	570	13 Purdue	104
4 Arkansas	547	14 Missouri	91
5 Penn State (1)	453	15 Wyoming	67
6 Southern California	396	16 Stanford	60
7 Florida	353	17 Auburn	37
8 Louisiana State	344	18 Colorado	17
9 UCLA	292	19 Air Force	14
10 Notre Dame	174	20 Michigan	13

November 1, 1969

Dartmouth 42 YALE 21: Balanced attack of Elis (4-2) totaled 349y, so undefeated Big Green (6-0) allowed nearly double its D avg of 176y. Yale QB Joe Massey threw 19-40/176y, including 3rd Q 40y TD to WB Bob Milligan. But, Massey was afflicted by 4 INTs, 1st leading to Dartmouth HB Bob Mlakar's game-tying 3y TD run in 1st Q. Elis HB Don Martin raced to 72y TD to provide 14-7 edge before 1st Q was over. Another INT set up Dartmouth for its 1st lead at 21-14 late in 2nd Q when QB Jim Chasey dashed over. Game came crashing down on Bulldogs when they fouled up reception of 2nd H KO, and Dartmouth quickly cashed HB John Short's tackle-breaking 16y TD run for 2-TD lead. Big Green HB Tommy Quinn iced it 42-21 with 54y punt TD RET in 4th Q.

PITTSBURGH 21 Syracuse 20: Long-buried Pittsburgh (3-4) won its 3rd game for 1st time in any season since 1965. Panthers TB Dennis Ferris rushed 20/107y, caught 4/84y, and scored 2 1st H TDs to boost Pitt to 21-14 H margin. Syracuse (3-3) had started game with QB Randy Zur's 37y pass to TE Tony Gabriel and scored on Zur's 8y option run. Trade of quick-succession TDs, including Ferris' cordoned-off 60y sideline number, left 15-14 in favor of Pitt. Ferris' 2nd score on short pass from QB Jim Friedl (19-29/186y, 2 TDs, 2 INTs) beat H clock by 19 secs. Punting difficulties that vexed Pitt P Joe Spicko gave Syracuse (3-3) 2 chances in 3rd Q: Orangemen DL Joe Ehrmann blocked Spicko's punt at Pitt 37YL, and Spicko's 15y wobbler gave ball to Syracuse only 35y from Pitt GL. Each time, Panthers D rose up to force FGs by K George Jakowenko (28 and 48y), so they maintained lead of 21-20. With 4:36 remaining, Jakowenko's 25y FG try sailed wide.

North Carolina 12 VIRGINIA 0: Tar Heels (3-4) TB Don McCauley (27/145y, TD) epitomized elephant-back so popular in this era. McCauley shed tacklers like fleas and rumbled for 36y score in 3rd Q that put game beyond reach of offensively-inept Virginia (3-4), which was blanked for 3rd straight outing. WB Lew Jolley had taken reverse 40y to Carolina's 1st TD in 2nd Q. All Cavaliers fans had to cheer was 2 blocked FGs and 3 INTs, including pair by UVa S Bob Rannigan. Virginia was thwarted at Heels' 17, 17, and 13YLs, but got good results from young QB Mike Cubbage. Cavs had started Cubbage, future major league baseball infielder, at QB, and soph responded with 10-

19/141y passing and 13/41y rushing. However, Cubbage was shelved early in 4th Q when he dislocated his left elbow. Cubbage said, "I was more let down with myself…I just wanted to keep on playing."

AUBURN 38 Florida 12: Young Florida (6-1) team was sky-high with its play so far this season, but it had never won at Cliff Hare Stadium at Auburn (5-2). Gators QB John Reaves (33-66/369y, 2 TDs, 9 INTs) fired SEC-record 66 passes, but Auburn's QB counterpart Pat Sullivan (22-39/218y) was more efficient with 2 TD passes and 2 TD runs. Tigers led 25-0 at H and Florida scored on Reaves' TD passes HB Tommy Durrance in 3rd Q and TE Bill Dowdy in 4th Q. Season's TD total of 22 passes brought Reaves within 2 TDs of 1950 record of Kentucky's Babe Parilli. Reaves' 379y passing pushed his total (2133y) past Florida's Steve Spurrier's SEC mark for season pass y, but his 9 INTs also set NCAA single-game record that still stands in pass-happy play of 2000s. Reaves said, "I didn't think they made any spectacular plays really, just played well all day, particularly their linebackers. And I was bad." Auburn LBs Sonny Ferguson (3 INTs) and Bobby Strickland (2 INTs) were main culprits, but S Buddy McClinton and CB Larry Willingham also contributed 2 pickoffs each. Tigers got off to 6-0 lead in 1st Q as K John Riley tapped 22y FG through, and followed shortly with 52y 3-pt bomb after Ferguson made Auburn's 1st INT. Next came Strickland's 1st INT, which led to Sullivan's 16y TD pass to WB Connie Frederick in opening min of 2nd Q. Ferguson galloped 39y with INT on next series, and Sullivan skirted RE for 3y TD on next play. Ferguson picked off another pass, this of desperation by Reaves from EZ, and went 11y to score in 3rd Q.

Tennessee 17 GEORGIA 3: Proud Georgia (5-2) D, which had pitched 3 shutouts and held foes to 86y rush avg, died in steady Athens rain. Tennessee (6-0) bolted for 386y rushing with G Chip Kell carving big holes in Bulldogs front. Vols lost 4 FUMs, 1st leading to K Jim McCullough's 21y FG in 1st Q, but Tennessee countered with 2nd Q TD runs from TB Don McLeary and FB Curt Watson (19/197y). Vols' D shut down Georgia in 2nd H, allowing no advances beyond its 33YL.

MISSISSIPPI 26 Louisiana State 23 (Jackson, Miss.): Schizophrenic Ole Miss (4-3) devoured Tigers (6-1) as QB Archie Manning's quick feet accounted for 3 TDs and his golden arm registered 22-36/210y, TD, INT. DB Tommy Casanova's INT launched LSU to TB Jimmy Gilbert's 1st Q TD. Manning hit TE Jim Poole 4 times in row to draw Rebels within 7-6. K Mark Lumpkin's 1st of 3 FGs gave LSU 10-6 2nd Q lead, but Manning rallied Rebels from 23-12 3rd Q disadvantage with 77y TD march and 22y TD thrust after Tigers QB Mike Hillman lost FUM.

West Virginia 7 KENTUCKY 6: WVU's 6 INTs was story of narrow win over Kentucky (2-5) as CB Mike Slater led way with 4 INTs himself. West Virginia (6-1) got on board 1st as FB Jim Braxton capitalized on Wildcats P Dave Hardt's bobble off good snap at his 19YL in 2nd Q. Mountaineers QB Mike Sherwood (10-18/114y) found E Jim Smith alone for 15y pass to 4YL to send Braxton on his merry way up middle for score, followed by K Braxton's x-pt. Kentucky drove 60y to its TD as QB Bernie Scruggs (12-33/149y, 6 INTs) kept ball in hands of his receivers for 42y, with 15y Mountaineers PEN mixed in, until FB Roger Gann slugged over GL. Cats went for 2 pts even though much of 2nd H remained, and they were called for O interference that ruined crossing pattern that freed Gann in corner of EZ. Kentucky threatened again, but WVU DB Ron Pobolish picked off Scruggs' throw 2y deep in EZ and steamed out of danger to his 41YL.

FLORIDA STATE 34 South Carolina 9: Once-beaten South Carolina (5-2) was focused on ACC championship, so this sojourn to Tallahassee might have caught coach Paul Dietzel's troops bit flat. Not at beginning, however, as Gamecocks enjoyed 3-0 lead through middle of 2nd Q on K Billy DuPre's 32y FG. Florida State (5-1) DE Ronnie Wallace, his unit's inspirational holler-guy, led charge that threw South Carolina QB Tommy Suggs for losses to his 10YL and ignited 20-pt surge. Short Cocks punt from danger put Seminoles in position for FSU FB Paul Magalski, who rushed for 111y and scored 2 TDs, to quickly tally his 1st TD on 33y charge. Florida State K Grant Guthrie added FGs of 42 and 40y, and HB Tom Bailey flipped 16y TD pass to FB Mike Gray, Gray's 2nd such HB to FB scoring pass in as many games. Soph DB John Montgomery upped Seminoles' margin to 27-3 with 27y 3rd Q TD RET of INT of Suggs. Backup Gamecocks QB Randy Yoakum fired 20y TD pass to TE Doug Hamrick in 3rd Q to draw Carolina to within 27-9. Florida State QB Bill Cappleman passed 17-29/203y, INT.

MICHIGAN 35 Wisconsin 7: Wolverines (5-2) packed all their punch in 35-0 1st H, then watched Wisconsin (2-5) squander all but 1 of several 2nd H chances. After Michigan P Mark Werner's punt rolled dead, Badgers could punt out of 1YL hole only to their 38YL. UM soph TB Billy Taylor (15/142y, 2 TDs) quickly sauntered 37y to score on power run and followed with similar 51y TD burst, also in 1st Q. FB Garvie Craw completed 80y march with 1y TD dive in 2nd Q. DB Barry Pierson's 51y punt TD RET and TE Jim Mandich's 12y, clock-beating TD grab wrapped up Michigan's 1st H onslaught. Wisconsin QB Neil Graff did his best, hitting 20-34/195y, INT, but miscues kept spoiling Badgers' comeback bids, even though HB Danny Crooks galloped 30y for 3rd Q TD.

Ohio State 35 NORTHWESTERN 6: QB Maurie Daigneau (22-36/294y, 2 INTs) made auspicious debut for Northwestern (2-5), breaking school mark for completions and coming within single y of passing Otto Graham's record of 295y in 1942. No. 1 Ohio State (6-0) kept its win streak in good hands: Its punishing D, led by LB Doug Adams, NG Jim Stillwagon, and S Jack Tatum, knocked Daigneau flat on 11 occasions for -100y. Wildcats' only good running play among -29y net was FB Mike Hudson's 10y burst up middle for TD in late going. Meanwhile, Bucks QB Rex Kern (10-17/117y, TD, INT) rushed for 94y and hit E Jan White for key TD, 21y score on 4th down at end of 93y trip in 2nd Q that launched Ohio to 14-0 lead. FB Jim Otis rushed 25/127y and scored 3 times, including 12y TD catch in 4th Q.

Toledo 14 MIAMI (OHIO) 10: Rockets (7-0) won their 7th straight game as their D consistently thwarted Miami of Ohio (5-2) in scoreless 2nd H to clinch Mid-American crown. It also meant Toledo was bound for Orlando's Tangerine Bowl in late

December. Toledo scored twice in 2nd Q, with QB Chuck Ealey's 52y pass to E Don Fair giving it 14-10 edge. HB Cleve Dickerson (100y rushing) had staked Redskins to 7-0 1st Q lead on 2y TD plunge. Darkness and rain threatened to roll in during in scoreless 2nd H as Rockets defenders frequently were pinned down in their own territory. But, Toledo stopped 4 trips inside its 20YL, and DB Kent Thompson intercepted pass at his 13YL to kill another menacing Miami move. Rockets D coordinator Jack Murphy felt his unit inspired itself at H: "They got together…and said they were going to shut Miami out in the second half. They just knew it." Toledo clinched its 1st undisputed conf title since 1927.

MISSOURI 41 Kansas State 38: HB Jon Staggers was key ingredient in Missouri (6-1) winning big game to join K-State in 3-way tie for Big 8 lead with Nebraska, 20-7 winner over Colorado. Staggers threw TD pass to WR Mel Gray, scored 3 TDs including breathtaking 99y KO RET for 28-12 lead midway in 3rd Q. HB Mack Herron scored 4 TDs for Wildcats (5-2) including 4th Q 26y pass from QB Lynn Dickey, whose 411y O set conf record. K-State squandered 2 late chances with TOs and began tumble to season-ending 4 losses.

ARIZONA STATE 30 Wyoming 14: Arizona State (4-2), on early end of what would become 6-game win streak, started downward spiral of demoralized Wyoming (6-1), which was fast losing its spirit thanks to suspension of its black players. Cowboys gained only 14y rushing, so QBs Gary Fox and Ed Synakowski combined for 26-45/276y passing, but suffered 5 INTs and 9 sacks. Sun Devils also concentrated on aerial game as QB Joe Spagnola (17-33/278y, TD, 3 INTs) looked for WR Calvin Demery (9/165y), who was healthy for change. ASU HB David Buchanan tossed 4y TD pass on 4th down to TE Ron Carothers, and FB Art Malone battered for 6y TD among his 69y that broke WAC career rushing record. DE George Kellerman, who had tallied 2nd Q safety, also blocked punt and fell on it for TD to lift Cowboys within 27-14 in 4th Q.

November 8, 1969

DUKE 34 Clemson 27: It was as if opponents swapped game-plans: Duke (2-5-1) passing star, QB Leo Hart (17-27/212y), ran for 3 TDs for 21-9 lead in 3rd Q, and Clemson (4-4), considered 1 of league's better running threats, scored twice on pass receptions by TE John McMakin and once when QB Jimmy Kendrick (12-26/239y, TD, INT) arched 50y bomb to TE Jim Sursavage. Tigers, looking to stay unbeaten in ACC play, had prowled for 9-0 lead as WR Charlie Waters turned passer to find McMakin for 32y score early in 2nd Q. TOs got Blue Devils back into it as LB Lanny Murdock fell on FUM and S Rich Searle picked off Tigers pass to set up TD runs by Hart. K Jimmy Barnette booted 27y FG late in 3rd Q to pull Clemson within 21-19, but Duke turned right around for 79y voyage to TB John Cappellano's 1y TD dive.

Florida 13 Georgia 13 (Jacksonville): Record Gator Bowl stadium crowd walked out scratching its collective heads over 2nd-try Florida (6-1-1) FG late in 2nd Q that provided Gators with 10-0 H lead. After Bulldogs (5-2-1) had 8y TD run nullified in 1st Q, revved-up Florida held at its 1YL. FB Mike Rich smashed for 12y for Florida TD, and Gators moved deep into UGa territory late in 2nd Q. Florida called fake FG with 1:34 left before H, only to have HB John Schnebly's run soundly flattened by alert Bulldogs D. But, official apparently had blown his whistle before snap because photographers and fans had crowded into back of EZ. Reprieved from its disaster, Gators chose to take K Richard Franco's 36y FG for 10-0 H lead. Georgia bounced back with 13-pt 3rd Q as starting QB Mike Cavan (8-14/76y) left bench to spark drive to HB Steve Farnsworth's TD run and HB Trav Paine raced 46y to score on draw play. Franco tied it with 21y FG in 4th Q after TB Tommy Durrance (21/97y) burst for 34 and 16y runs, but Franco missed from 22y out because of bad snap in last 15 secs of game.

LOUISIANA STATE 20 Alabama 15: TB Allen Shorey (26/129y) broke 3-3 H tie with 3rd Q TD plunge and ran 3y in 4th Q to put LSU (7-1) out of reach at 20-9. Alabama (5-3) QB Scott Hunter passed 18-38/284y, including TDs to TE Hunter Husband and WR David Bailey. Tigers earned 1st win over Tide since 1958 in part because of early 4th Q FUM REC at LSU 5YL by alert DB Tommy Casanova.

TENNESSEE 29 South Carolina 14: Leaders of ACC, Gamecocks (5-3) proved to be troublesome foe to undefeated Tennessee (7-0) of SEC. South Carolina outgained Volunteers 347y to 315y, stymied Vol ground game (101y), and used sound strategy for FB Warren Muir (31/159y, TD) to power for good y up middle and romp on reverses from Double-Wing-T setup. Despite Carolina's dominance in 1st H, Vols DB Bill Young stepped in for INT late in 2nd Q that provided chance for TB Don McLeary to leave Gamecocks LB Greg Crabb in dust on 20y TD catch for 10-7 H bulge. South Carolina edged within 16-14 in 4th Q when Gamecocks QB Randy Yoakum left bench for injured QB Tommy Suggs (10-21/101y, 2 INTs) to fire 22y TD pass to TB Rudy Holloman. Tennessee put it away with his 2nd and 3rd TD passes to WR Gary Kries for 40y and TE Ken DeLong for 7y.

Iowa 28 INDIANA 17: Its manpower considerably depleted—not to mention its spirit— Indiana (4-4) forged on without 10 of 14 black players who walked out on their team by listing 8 social grievances against program. Thinking afterward that his Hoosiers had tried too hard, highly-stressed coach John Pont watched his troops stand toe-to-toe

with Hawkeyes (4-4), each scoring 2 TDs until big plays went Iowa's way late in 3rd Q. Iowa QB Larry Lawrence (13-20/168y, TD) legged it 40y after breaking through tacklers on TD scramble in 2nd Q. E John Andrews, Indiana's only African-American on O grabbed pass at 4YL to set up HB John Isenbarger (21/140y, and 2/27y receiving) for TD run that tied it 7-7 before H. Big 10 foes swapped 3rd Q TDs with Indiana enjoying its only lead at 14-13 because Hawks missed x-pt. Critical moment came when Iowa G Jerry Nelson blocked P Isenbarger's punt to set up HB Dennis Green for his 1st of 2 TD runs and 21-14 lead. Trailing 21-17 4 mins left, Indiana had pass by QB Harry Gonso (10-16/136y, INT) picked off by DB Dave Brooks, who returned it 23y to 5YL. Green scored again to ice it.

MISSOURI 44 Oklahoma 10: With weak secondary of Oklahoma (4-3) already revealed in losses to Texas and Kansas State, run-favoring Missouri (7-1) chose pass-oriented game plan with prodigious results. Tigers QB Terry McMillan passed 17-37/312y, 3 TDs, 2 INTs, most single-game aerial y total in 12 years under coach Dan Devine. It led to largest to-date win margin over Mizzou's hated Norman conquerors. Missouri WR Mel Gray's blazing speed was impossible to cover, as he caught 6/171y, 2 TDs. But 1st, Sooners jumped to 10-0 lead early in 2nd Q as TB Steve Owens (29/109y) swept to 5y TD, tying collegiate career TD mark. K Henry Brown put Mizzou on scoreboard with 21y FG 5:30 into 2nd Q to light 37-pt fire that erupted over next 21 mins. McMillan hit Gray with 24y TD, and HB Joe Moore (23/110y, TD) scored on 22y draw run to create 17-10 Tigers beat at H. After 2 more Mizzou TDs in 3rd Q, Owens' FUM of KO slithered into EZ for TD REC by Missouri DE Dan Borgard, which lifted margin to 37-10. McMillan and Gray set school single-game marks for pass y.

NEBRASKA 17 Iowa State 3: Coach Bob Devaney scored his 100th career win, and his sound decision of calling QB Jerry Tagge off bench in 2nd H paved way to Nebraska (6-2) victory. After scoreless 1st Q, lethargic Husker attack managed QB Van Brownson's short TD run, but Iowa State (3-4) came back with K Vern Skripsky's 30y FG to stay close at H at 7-3. Tagge's throws in 3rd Q helped deliver 10 pts, including his 9y TD pass with FB Mike Green. Cyclones were limited to 28y rushing and 147y total O.

TEXAS 56 Baylor 14: Despite having had 27 players stricken by virus, Texas (7-0) rolled to school-record to-date 16th win in row. With starters retired in 2nd Q with 28-0 lead, even some of ill Longhorns followed into scoring act, including sub HB Bobby Callison who tallied on runs of 1, 1, and 37y. Backup Texas QB Eddie Phillips added 2 TD runs. Hapless Baylor (0-7) was on way to winless season, but got 2 TDs from RB Gordon Utgard.

TEXAS CHRISTIAN 35 Texas Tech 26: Fighting to keep its vague Cotton Bowl hopes alive, Texas Tech (4-4) found itself in 7-7 tie in 1st Q and 16-14 lead at H. Red Raiders DE Richard Campbell blocked and recovered punt for TD in 1st Q, and K Jerry Don Sanders' 8th FG of season provided 2-pt edge at H. Texas Christian (3-5) had countered with clutch play of WR Linzy Cole. Cole raced 66y with game-opening KO, which led to his 12y scoring catch from QB Steve Judy. In 2nd Q, Cole charged 81y on punt TD RET. Judy ran and threw for TDs in 3rd Q, but Tech came back to within 28-26 as it was forced into taking Sanders' 31y FG when its drive faltered at Frogs 14YL. TCU ate 6:09 of final 8:22 to go 65y to FB Norm Bulaich's 1y scoring blast off RG.

Arkansas 30 RICE 6: For awhile, hopeful Rice (1-6) hung close to undefeated Arkansas (7-0), tying game at 3-3 in 2nd Q on K Tim Davis' 33y FG. Leading only 10-6 at H, Razorbacks burst from locker room for TDs on their 1st 2 possessions of 3rd Q: QB Bill Montgomery connected with WR John Rees for 14y TD, and TB Bill Burnett dashed 23y to his 2nd score. Arkansas won its 13th game in row.

SOUTHERN CALIFORNIA 28 Washington State 7: Rash of O offside PENs against Southern California (7-0-1) had coach John McKay furious. Lowly Cougars (1-7) used "Now!" as barked signal to jump their D into different format, and since USC preferred signaling its O snap with "Go!" Trojans kept jumping offside. McKay cracked, "If we can't distinguish between 'Go' and 'Now,' then we're all in trouble." Still, Trojans won easily, sending Wazzu to its 7th straight defeat and USC soph TB Clarence Davis, successor to O.J. Simpson, past 1000y rushing mark. Davis (34/196y, TD) led way to opening TD but stepped aside for bigger sub TB Mike Berry to blast across from 1YL and scored on later in 1st Q on 7y run after DE Jimmy Gunn fell on Cougars FUM. But, USC played just as well as it needed to, and allowed strong rush to disrupt P Ron Ayala's 2nd Q punt. It went 28y to set up 52y TD march for Washington State. Cougars scored in 10 plays as FB Bob Ewan (12/30y) went 5y to make it 14-7. Fleet QB Jimmy Jones (5-16/47y, INT) scored twice in 2nd H for Troy.

AP Poll November 10

1 Ohio State (25)	618	11 Auburn	148
2 Texas (4)	570	12 Louisiana State	144
3 Tennessee (2)	509	13 Stanford	76
4 Arkansas	403	14 Michigan	61
5 Penn State (1)	361	15 Florida	50
6 Southern California	294	16 Georgia	28
7 UCLA	275	17 Nebraska	26
8 Missouri	225	18tMississippi	16
9 Notre Dame	216	18tHouston	16
10 Purdue	206	20 Air Force	15

November 15, 1969

Yale 17 PRINCETON 14: Yale (6-2) knocked Princeton (5-3) out of tie for 1st place in Ivy League and thus handed Dartmouth, 24-7 winner over Cornell, clinching possession of title tie. Amid flurry of their 8 TOs, Tigers gained 290y, 95y more than Bulldogs, and still managed scoring drives of 56y in 2nd Q and 41y in 4th Q, each ending with FB Ellis Moore's scoring run. Elis QB Joe Massey (9-21/166y, INT) hit WB Bob Milligan with 34 and 36y passes to lead to FB Bill Primps' TD run that created 7-7 tie at H and Massey's 6y dash for 14-7 lead at end of 3rd Q. Yale reached 1YL late in 4th Q but had to settle for K Harry Klebanoff's FG. Back came Princeton, charging 52y to 11YL as QB Scott McBean (10-23/104y, 4 INTs) mixed passes with draw runs. But, when Yale DL John Biancamano stopped Moore on 3rd down at 11YL, Tigers' K Arnold Holtberg missed tying FG from 29y away with 1:53 remaining. "I had to go against my individual tendencies," said Princeton coach Jake McCandless of his decision to try tying 3-ptr, "A tie (this week) and a win next week (against Dartmouth) would have given us all the (Ivy League title) marbles."

South Carolina 24 WAKE FOREST 6: Rollicking Gamecocks (6-3) improved its ACC record to 5-0 and clinched their 1st-ever conf title when Clemson lost. Wake Forest (3-6) managed to hand 9 TOs to South Carolina, leading to all 3 Gamecocks' TDs. QB Tommy Suggs (8-15/96y) passed modestly but set new school career aerial y mark as he hit 3 TD passes. In 4th Q, Carolina S Andy Chavous made FUM REC at his 3YL—after Wake HB Tom Gavin rolled 14y—and made INT moments later. Deacons HB Steve Bowden had lost FUM at his 10YL only secs into game to set up Suggs' TD pass to E Fred Zeigler, but Bowden came back to score TD in 2nd Q and send teams to H with Carolina ahead 14-6.

NORTH CAROLINA 32 Clemson 15: Revitalized Tar Heels (5-4) won their 4th straight game with 22-pt flurry in 2nd Q. With starting QB John Swofford on bench with arm injury and Carolina trailing 15-14 with 3:46 left in 2nd Q, E-converted-to-QB Ricky Lanier (3-4/44y, and 25/91y, TD rushing) hit 2 passes and dashed 27y to set up his 3y TD run and 2-pt pass. North Carolina DE Bill Brafford soon recovered FUM by Clemson (4-5) QB Tommy Kendrick, and HB Don McCauley (112y rushing) turned RE for TD and 29-15 lead 32 secs before H. In 2nd H, Heels D put on clamps and it picked off 4 passes, including 2 each for DBs Ricky Packard and Ken Price. Hendrick had made 2 big plays for Tigers in 1st Q: Trailing 7-0 on Swofford's early 3y TD slice behind UNC RG Ed Chalupka's block, Clemson encouraged Kendrick as he sparked 69y TD trip for 8-7 lead for Tigers. He found TE John McMakin for 17y TD, and when x-pt snap got away, he brightly scrambled until TE Charlie Tolley broke free for 2-pt lob.

Auburn 16 GEORGIA 3: Auburn (7-2) Auburn D was so forceful that Furman Bischer reported in *Atlanta Journal-Constitution* "the home team's best weapon was the penalty." Indeed, Georgia (5-2-1) netted only 101y O while Tigers were flagged for 112y. Auburn QB Pat Sullivan (10-34/137y, TD, 2 INTs) avoided rush of DG Tim Callaway to whip 24y TD pass to WB Connie Frederick in 1st Q, but after early success his receivers developed case of "drops" in 30-degree temps. In odd turn, Plainsmen couldn't stop themselves from roughing UGa P Spike Jones (12/44y avg), ending game with 4 such PENs/60y. Bulldogs got within 7-3 at H when DB Buck Swindle made INT at Tigers 26YL near end of 1st Q and K Jim McCullough followed with 31y FG. Auburn burst from locker room for 3rd Q and clicked on 41y pass from Sullivan to WR Terry Beasley to 15YL. TB Mickey Zofko soon scored, but x-pt block by Georgia left score at 13-3. K John Riley added FG on next 3rd Q series, and Tigers D kept Bulldogs totally in check rest of way.

MISSISSIPPI 38 Tennessee 0 (Jackson): Just as whispers of no. 3 Tennessee's greatness grew louder, Mississippi (6-3) delivered worst defeat Volunteers (7-1) had suffered in 46 years. Fueling fire was Tennessee LB Steve Kiner's preseason remark that termed Reb stars as "mules, not horses." Bowl picture was severely scrambled as result, but Ole Miss was beginning to look like genuine Sugar Bowl candidate. Rebels registered 3 TDs in 1st Q, including scoring run and pass by QB Archie Manning, who tabbed it "team effort." In between, Manning fumbled at Tennessee 1YL, and lucky Rebs profited on TB Randy Reed's hustling EZ REC for TD. Vols threatened thrice, losing ball twice at Ole Miss 1YL and throwing INT at Rebs 5YL. Decisive moments came late in 2nd Q: Vols QB Bobby Scott's 4th down EZ pass for TE Ken DeLong mistakenly was speared by Tennessee WB Richard Callaway who couldn't avoid tumbling OB at 1YL. Rebs took over and went to 42y FG by K Cloyce Hinton, 3-ptr that hit on crossbar and toppled over for 24-0 H edge.

Notre Dame 38 GEORGIA TECH 20: Smacking their lips in anticipation for 1st possible bowl game since 1924, Fighting Irish (7-1-1) threw 21-pt 1st Q punch at hard-luck Georgia Tech (3-6), which was mindlessly handing over 4 INTs and 3 FUMs in 1st H. Notre Dame QB Joe Theismann passed and ran for TDs in 1st Q, and DB Clarence Ellis cruised 70y with INT thrown by Yellow Jackets QB Jack Williams, who also lost 2 FUMs to Notre Dame LB John Raterman. Theismann was looking for TD pass to extend Irish's 31-0 lead, but Georgia Tech DB Jeff Ford picked off pass in his EZ and scurried 100y for TD. Theismann accounted for his 3rd TD with 8y run in 3rd Q. Scrubs scored Georgia Tech's 2 late TDs.

OHIO STATE 42 Purdue 14: In Columbus' icy breeze, Ohio State (8-0) steamed to 22nd straight win, trying to prove growing media projections as greatest college team of all time. QB Rex Kern scored from 6YL after bad Purdue FG snap gave Buckeyes good field position. Kern added another TD after DB Mike Sensibaugh's INT RET to 6YL, and later rifled 38y TD pass to E Bruce Jankowski. Lone Purdue (7-2) flurry came next: HB Stan Brown went down sideline for 98y KO TD RET, and, just 26 secs later, INT of Kern put ball at Ohio 34YL. But Sensibaugh stepped in front of TE Ashley Bell for 1 of 5 INTs taken off passes by Boilermakers QB Mike Phipps (19-45/203y, TD).

Nebraska 10 KANSAS STATE 7: Relentless pass-rush on Kansas State (5-4) QB Lynn Dickey was key to Nebraska (7-2) maintaining tie atop Big 8 with Missouri, 40-13 winners over Iowa State. Dickey completed 3 passes on early 80y TD drive, but was sacked 5 times. K Paul Rogers missed 2 FGs but brought Huskers within 7-3 with 39y boot in 3rd Q. Nebraska sub FB Dan Schneiss dashed 34y around E early in 4th Q to position winning TD by QB Van Brownson. Dickey (19-35/216y, INT) hurriedly moved Wildcats to Huskers 7YL but to no avail as clock expired.

Arkansas 28 SOUTHERN METHODIST 15: Undefeated Arkansas (8-0) and Texas inched closer to their made-for-TV season-ending showdown. Fading Mustangs (2-7) hung with Hogs, leading 3-0 after 1st Q and trailing only 14-12 at H as QB Chuck

Hixson fired 19y TD to TE Ken Fleming. Arkansas' fabulous TD-maker, TB Bill Burnett, caught QB Bill Montgomery's 2nd TD pass in 2nd Q, then charged to 2nd H TD runs of 4 and 9y.

TEXAS 69 Texas Christian 7: Sam Blair, writing in the *Dallas Morning News,* presented it best: "(No. 2) Texas played (no. 1) Ohio State for national collegiate football supremacy in Memorial Stadium Saturday and poor TCU happened to get caught in the middle." Ohio State had whipped Texas Christian (3-6) by 62 pts in September, and Longhorns (8-0) subs scored 4 times in 4th Q to match Buckeyes' margin against Frogs. Revenge for perceived hex Horned Frogs held over Steers in Austin also fueled fire; TCU had won 5 of 7 since 1955 at Memorial Stadium. Texas paraded for 651y O, 517y on ground, as 3 starting backs, HB Jim Bertelsen, FB Steve Worster, and QB James Street, all scored in 21-0 1st Q. Frogs HB-WR Linzy Cole broke away for 65y punt TD RET in 2nd Q, and TCU followed with drive that died at Texas 28YL. But that was all she wrote. Worster scored again for Longhorns in 2nd Q, followed by Street's 18y TD pass to WR Cotton Speyrer. When HB Billy Dale flew 51y to score in 3rd Q it was 41-7, and Texas coach Darrell Royal began emptying his bench.

STANFORD 47 Air Force 34: Stanford (6-2-1) QB Jim Plunkett (22-38/278y) threw 2 TD passes to eclipse existing conf record with 18 for season. Plunkett also bested own Pac-8 total O mark for year. Fast WR Randy Vataha added TD catch from RB Bubba Brown and 62y punt TD RET. For its part of scoring parade, Air Force (6-3) tallied on TD runs by TBs Curtis Martin and Brian Bream, and QB Gary Baxter's TD run and pass.

Ucla 13 OREGON 10: Nervous Bruins (8-0-1) faced extinction on Ducks' likely TD late in game, but little Uclans CB Ron "Mighty Mouse" Carver took ball away in his EZ from Oregon (4-4-1) HB Bobby Moore, who had 5-inch, 60-lb size advantage. With 1:39 left, Ducks sub QB John Harrington (16-38/166y, 2 INTs) suffered another Carver steal. Earlier, UCLA TB Greg Jones (21/103y, TD) had provided 2nd Q TD for 7-0 lead that stayed put nearly 6 mins into 3rd Q. But, Bruins C Dave Dalby fired punt snap through wickets of P Zenon Andrusyshyn for Oregon safety. Harrington lofted 45y pass to WR Bob Newland to set up Harrington's TD sneak and 2-pt pass. Behind 10-7 early in 4th Q, UCLA went 49y on 19y pass by QB Dennis Dummit (10-22/157y, TD, INT) to his 3y TD to WR Gwen Cooper.

AP Poll November 17

1 Ohio State (31)	736	11 Auburn	214
2 Texas (7)	688	12 Michigan	119
3 Arkansas	556	13 Mississippi	110
4 Penn State (1)	554	14 Stanford	88
5 Southern California	416	15 Florida	67
6 UCLA	360	16 Nebraska	43
7 Missouri	352	17 Purdue	37
8 Notre Dame	294	18 West Virginia	29
9 Tennessee	249	19 Houston	20
10 Louisiana State	240	20 Toledo	6

November 22, 1969

PRINCETON 35 Dartmouth 7: Princeton (6-3), which started season by "setting back" football 100 years, closed centennial year by surprising undefeated Dartmouth (8-1) and commandeering its own share of Ivy League title. Indians made 3 miscues: HB Bob Mlakar's poor QK, QB Jim Chasey's underthrown INT, and Chasey's FUM at his own 13YL. Each error positioned Tigers for TDs that all but salted away result at 21-0 by H. Starting only his 2nd game of season, soph HB Hank Bjorklund rushed 30/132y and scored 3 times for Princeton.

Penn State 27 PITTSBURGH 7: Inspired Pittsburgh (4-6), enjoying mild renaissance under new coach Carl dePasqua, identified Penn State (9-0) game as glorious opportunity. Panthers D, sparked by LBs Ralph Cindrich and George Brown and DTs Lloyd Weston and John Stevens, held Lions ground game well in check during 7-7 deadlock in 1st H. Only exception was Nittany Lions FB Franco Harris' 24y TD run. FB Tony Esposito tied it in 2nd Q after Pitt got benefit of 4th down roughing P foul. Despite throwing his shoe, Penn State LB Dennis Onkontz returned Pitt punt 71y to 5YL in 3rd Q, and it led to 1st of 2 TD runs by HB Charlie Pittman. Lions D allowed no 1st downs in 2nd H and set up team's last TD with DB Paul Johnson's INT.

West Virginia 13 SYRACUSE 10: Syracuse (5-4), hard-luck losers of 2 games by 1 pt each, seemed headed for spoiler role against Peach Bowl-bound West Virginia (9-1). Mountaineers bobbled ball 6 times, losing 3, and these miscues aided Orangemen's 10-0 H lead. FB Al Newton followed K George Jakowenko's 47y FG with 1y TD run in 2nd Q for Syracuse. After losing FUM at Syracuse 5YL, WVU came back with 51y march as QB Mike Sherwood (8-13/98y, TD, INT) pitched 4y TD pass on 4th down. Less than 2 mins later, Sherwood flipped tricky lateral to FB Jim Braxton, who went 65y to winning TD.

Maryland 17 VIRGINIA 14: Maryland (3-7) coach Roy Lester welcomed end of tough 1st season as fumbleitis reared its head once again to infect Virginia (3-7) and send Cavs to 6th straight loss. Terrapins led 7-6 at H as FB Tom Miller (77y rushing) scored in 1st Q, and UVa WR-K Jim Carrington booted 2 FGs. Terps went up 14-6 in 3rd Q when WB Larry Marshall scored on 4y run after Maryland ran wild double-reverse pass that was tipped three times before landing in arms of WR Roland Merritt. Virginia QB Danny Fassio converted 3rd-and-39 later in 3rd Q with 36y pass to Carrington and 10y throw to WR Bob Bischoff. This miraculous trick led to TD run by TB Dave Wyncoop and Fassio's tying 2-pt sweep. But in game's last min, Fassio was hammered by LB Mike Brant and lost FUM at 11YL. K Greg Fries nailed 27y FG with 20 secs left.

SOUTH CAROLINA 27 Clemson 13: Gamecocks (7-3), who already had clinched their 1st and only ACC crown, put icing on cake with pull-away win over archrival Clemson (4-6) to complete undefeated conf schedule. Hard running by FB Warren Muir led to HB Rudy Holloman's 2 TDs, including pass from QB Tommy Suggs (16-24/230y, TD, INT). Playing their last game under beloved coach Frank Howard, tense Tigers failed to make 1st down until 2nd Q but had quick burst to nudge within 17-13 at H: TB Ray Yauger scored 6:38 before H, then caught 15y TD pass from QB Tommy Kendrick after LB Bill Depew blocked South Carolina's punt.

MICHIGAN 24 Ohio State 12: Seemingly invincible no. 1 Buckeyes (8-1) saw their 22-game win string come to stunning halt. Michigan (8-2) claimed Rose Bowl bid confident coach Bo Schembechler said it would have rejected had it lost. Ohio State scored 1st on 1y plunge by FB Jim Otis (144y rushing), but missed kick. When FB Garvie Craw scored 1st of his 2 TDs, Wolverines led 7-6, 1st time all season Ohio State had trailed. QB Rex Kern,

who later would be yanked with 4 INTs, threaded 22y TD to TE Jan White for 12-7 Ohio lead early in 2nd Q. Michigan answered with 67y drive for 14-12 lead. Key play came next: Wolverines DB Barry Pierson (3 INTs) returned punt 60y to lead to QB Don Moorhead's TD run. Neither team scored in 2nd H as Michigan executed "great plays on defense" according to Schembechler. Ohio coach Woody Hayes called his 2nd H O "miserable" as it failed to penetrate UM 44YL until late going.

Nebraska 44 OKLAHOMA 14: Nebraska (8-2) headed to Sun Bowl after gaining share of Big 8 title with Missouri, which trounced Kansas 69-21. TB Jeff Kinney sparked Cornhuskers with boatload of O gems: 35/127y rushing including 3 and 11y TD runs, 6y TD catch from WB Van Brownson, and surprise TD pass to WB Guy Ingles. But, it was Nebraska's magnificent D that limited Sooners' Big 8-best rushing attack to 121y. Oklahoma (5-4) TB Steve Owens (21/71y) saw end to his record 17-game 100y+ rushing streak that had started after Notre Dame had stopped him way back in 1968 season opener. Owens also failed to score TD for 1st time in 16 games. Oklahoma QB Jack Mildren had provided brief 7-0 lead with 18y run and added late 16y TD pass to WB Geoffrey Nordgren. In between, Huskers tied it on Brownson's 1y run in 1st Q, took 14-7 lead on Kinney's 1st score in 1st Q, and blew it open in 3rd Q when Kinney scored and threw TDs for 30-7 advantage.

COLORADO 45 Kansas State 32: Never trailing in their regular season finale, Buffaloes (7-3) earned their 2nd bowl trip in 3 years but never could rest under onslaught of Kansas State (5-5) O stars, QB Lynn Dickey (28-61/439y, 3 TDs, INT) and WB Mack Herron (12/171y receiving, and 8/21y, TD rushing). Wildcats fought from behind to 28-24 and 38-32 2nd H deficits. Colorado had scored on its 2nd snap as HB Bobby Anderson (18/54y, 2 TDs) hauled in 44y TD pass from QB Jimmy Bratten (11-21/251y, 2 TDs). K-State did it better: Dickey launched 70y TD pass to E Charlie Collins on Cats' 1st play. So, game was tied 7-7 after only 28 secs. Bratten threw another TD pass in 2nd Q, and following Herron's sensational 70y KO RET, squat WB scored for K-State to tie it 14-14 on 1y run. Colorado scored after long passes by Bratten fueled 51 and 83y TD marches for 28-14 H edge. Scoring action in 3rd Q belonged to K-State as it tallied FG and Dickey's 15y TD pass to TE Forrest Wells. Anderson ended Buffs' next drive with 1y TD plunge—his 19th of season—early in 4th Q, and with it he copped Big 8 career total O record previously held by Oklahoma's Bobby Warmack. Buffs CB Jim Cooch nabbed INT that led to FG, but K-State scored in 6 quick plays on Dickey's TD and 2-pt passes to trail 38-32. Roughing P PEN on next series dearly cost Cats as Colorado was able to kill clock down to 3:02. K-State still threatened until CU DE Herb Orvis spilled Dickey for 12y loss and Herron couldn't hold tall pass on 4th down.

Utah 16 BRIGHAM YOUNG 6: K Marv Bateman nailed 3 FGs as Utah (8-2) took temporary tie for 1st place in WAC. Loss ended 4-game winning streak for BYU (6-4). Bateman's successful boots came week after his critical missed x-pt cost tie in 17-16 loss to Arizona. If Utes had been able to close with wins over Arizona and BYU, it would have walked away with undefeated WAC title. Cougars had enjoyed 6-3 lead in 1st Q on QB Marc Lyons' 17y TD pass to WB Wes Homolik, but students of football since mid-1970s would be stunned at BYU's utter passing inefficiency: 5-16/67y, TD, 2 INTs. Utes stuck to ground, making 335y, tying it 6-6 by H, and taking 9-6 lead on Bateman's 34y 3-ptr in 4th Q. Utah locked it up with 14-play, 88y march late in 4th Q. Sub QB Clint Harden led Utes downfield, pitching out to HB Fred Graves for 3y TD run that iced it.

SOUTHERN CALIFORNIA 14 Ucla 12: Trojans (9-0-1) marched to their 4th straight Rose Bowl berth, nipping rival UCLA (8-1-1) in 1st match since 1952 that pitted unbeaten cross-town rivals. Bruins had opened with growl as QB Dennis Dummit (21-43/253y, TD, 5 INTs) hit 3 passes before TB Greg Jones lofted surprise 41y TD pass to WB George Farmer. But, Bruins' 2-pt pass failed when Dummit's throw was tipped by on-rushing Troy DE Charlie Weaver. USC continued to launch its "Wild Bunch" D in Dummit's direction, sacking him 9 times and forcing 5 INTs. Still, Dummit managed 80y drive with just over 3 mins left to play, mostly on his passes, topping it with 7y TD pass to WR Gwen Cooper for 12-7 lead, after soph WB Brad Lyman caught 57y pass. Trojans QB Jimmy Jones (5-21/58y, TD, INT), who had posted miserable passing day with only 1 completion in 1st 57 mins, suddenly came alive with 3 straight connections. Jones missed his next 4 throws, but UCLA DB Danny Graham committed interference on WR Sam Dickerson as receiver broke to sideline for short pass on 4th-and-10 from UCLA 43YL. Jones' pass sailed high, and, in another era, PEN against Graham would have been overruled as "uncatchable pass." But, no such rule existed in 1969. Jones launched 32y winning score to Dickerson on next play as speedy WR beat DB Doug Huff with surge to deep left corner of EZ with 1:32 to go. Afterward, Graham summed it up for broken-hearted Bruins: "It seems like my whole life just went down the drain." This result was 12th time in last 20 games that USC had rallied in 4th Q to win or tie.

STANFORD 29 California 28: As expected, passes of Stanford (7-2-1) QB Jim Plunkett (22-42/381y, 2 TDs, 3 INTs) got Indians rolling early. Plunkett connected with HB Howie Williams for 47y TD and WR Jack Lasater for 72y TD on Tribe's 1st 2 possessions. Golden Bears (5-5) trailed 17-0, but little-known QB Dave Penhall (23-38/321y, TD, INT) rallied them to within 20-14 at H. Striking for Penhall's 4y TD run

and 37y TD pass in 2-min span of 4th Q, Cal suddenly enjoyed 28-23 edge. Stanford retaliated with 80y ground march, capped by Williams' winning 4y TD burst up middle with 4 mins left.

November 27-29, 1969

(Th'g) Mississippi 48 MISSISSIPPI STATE 22: Sugar Bowl-bound Ole Miss (7-3) exploded for 27 pts in 4th Q to ice close game with Mississippi State (3-7). Rivals were knotted 14-14 until Rebels FB Bo Bowen ended 76y march late in 3rd Q with 17y TD burst up middle. In runaway 4th Q, Mississippi QB Archie Manning threw 2 TD passes to WR Vernon Studdard and scored TD himself. Bulldogs QB Tommy Pharr, out most of year, outgained Manning in air and threw 2 TD passes, but on desperation pass he suffered 12y INT TD runback by CB Bill Jones during Ole Miss' late spree.

(Th'g) Texas 49 TEXAS A&M 12: Dynamic Texas (9-0) built 39-0 lead, scoring on 6 of its 8 1st H possessions. Highlights included HB Jim Bertelsen's 63y TD run up middle and WR Cotton Speyrer's 37y TD pass to TE Randy Peschel off E-around run-fake. Texas A&M (3-7-1) scored 2 TDs long after Longhorn starters had departed in 4th Q: TE Ross Brupbacher's short TD catch and DE Jim Piper's TD RET of blocked punt.

(Th'g) ARKANSAS 33 Texas Tech 0 (Little Rock): Coach Frank Broyles earned his 100th career win on strength of 3 TDs by Arkansas (9-0) ace TB Bill Burnett. Burnett, now possessed 19 TDs in 1969, broke school scoring record set by his brother Bobby in 1965. Facing tough Arkansas' D, Texas Tech (5-5) failed to make single 1st down until 2nd Q, but penetrated to Hogs 6, 16, and 19YLs only to come away empty. Red Raiders QBs passed 17-43/216y, but suffered 5 INTs, 2 by Razorbacks DB Bobby Field.

BOSTON COLLEGE 35 Syracuse 10: Each team had been scheduled to play dry-docked Holy Cross, so this season-closing appointment was struck in mid-season. Dark sky and chilly air finally woke up Boston College (5-4) in middle of 2nd Q as Eagles won its 3rd game in row. Syracuse (5-5), suffering its worst season since 1962, held 10-0 lead on strength of easy 80y drive wrapped up by QB Randy Zur's sneak. Without 1st down for opening 22 mins, BC got injection of pep from HB Ed Rideout's 32y RET of punt by P-K George Jakowenko, who earlier made school-record 49y FG for Ornagemen. Eagles QB Red Harris found TE John Bonistalli scurrying along entire EZ's backline for TD that pulled Eagles to within 10-7 at H. Harris (23-41/250y, 4 TDs, INT) filled air with passes and picked apart nation's 1st-ranked D in 2nd H as HB Fred Willis snared 2 TD catches and TE George Gill hauling in 21y TD.

Army 27 Navy 0 (Philadelphia): Having rushed for but 5y against Navy in 1968, Army (4-5-1) workhorse HB Lynn Moore charged to 40/206y, 2 TDs on ground this time. Moore, who originally had wanted to attend Naval Academy, broke Bob Anderson's 12-year-old record for rush y in service academy classic. Cadets tallied 438y on 83 rushes out of new power-I, clicking on TD drives of 74, 52, and 67y. Afterward, Army coach Tom Cahill said with smile: "We don't have too extensive a game plan—Moore right and Moore left." Middies (1-9) made it to Black Knights 23YL late in 2nd Q, but when QB Mike McNallen rolled out and lofted ball into EZ, Army DB John Brenner stepped in for his 7th INT of year. Navy reached Cadets 1YL in last 5 mins only to have runs by WB Ron Marchetti and QB McNallen thrown back by shutout-focused Black Knights D. It was widest Army margin over Navy in 20 years.

Auburn 49 ALABAMA 26 (Birmingham): With traditionally-tough Ds apparently tossed aside, bitter rivals compiled 1074y of O. Difference in outcome was 4 lost FUMs among 6 TOs by Alabama (6-4) as Crimson Tide was left with its worst record since 1958. Bama QB Scott Hunter (30-55/484y, 2 TDs, 2 INTs) outpassed Tigers QB Pat Sullivan (13-26/192y, 2 INTs), but 349y rushing, led by FB Wallace Clark's 117y and HB-P Tommie Frederick's 85y TD run out of punt setup, served as heady elixir for Auburn (8-2). Tigers simply owned 2nd H after leading 14-10 at H. Only WR George Ranager's 100y KO TD RET in 3rd Q and last moment TD pass interrupted Auburn's dominance.

TENNESSEE 40 Vanderbilt 27: Cruising to SEC title, Tennessee (9-1) methodically built 26-7 H margin as QB Bobby Scott threw 23y TD pass and ran 2y for another score. Even though he was knocked from game for spell, Vanderbilt (4-6) QB Watson Brown was formidable with 34y TD run, 6y TD pass, and 9y TD catch from TB Doug Mathews (128y rushing) as Commodores tallied 20 pts in 4th Q. Volunteers FB Curt Watson rushed for 115y and scored twice.

Florida 35 MIAMI 16: Outstanding Gators (8-1-1) O threw their trio of flying sophs at Hurricanes (4-6). Gators HB Tommy Durrance scored 3 TDs, including important 62y sprint after Miami had trimmed score to 22-16 midway in 4th Q. Florida QB John Reaves (30-43/346y, 3 INTs) threw 2 TDs to WR Carlos Alvarez (15/237y), who broke 3 SEC receiving marks for season. Miami QB Kelly Cochrane threw for 223y, including 25y TD in 4th Q to bounce back from early safety on tackle by Gators LB Dave Ghesquiere.

Oklahoma 28 OKLAHOMA STATE 27: Heisman-winning Oklahoma (6-4) TB Steve Owens saved his best for his last college game. Owens rushed 55 times for to-date NCAA record, gained 261y, and scored twice for then-record 56 TDs in 3-year career.

Sooners enjoyed 14-0 1st Q lead, but Oklahoma State (5-5) scored 3 unanswered TDs for 21-14 H edge. When QB Jack Mildren went 34y to score, Sooners owned 28-21 4th Q lead. Accounting for team's 4th TD, Cowboys QB Bob Cutburth threw 6y strike to E Herman Eban with 1:33 left. After delay-of-game PEN, Cutburth was sacked attempting 2-pt pass. With that failure went any chance at victory for underdog Cowpokes.

HOUSTON 41 Florida State 13: TB Jim Strong rushed 22/200y, scored 39y TD that provided Houston with 13-13 deadlock in 2nd Q. Cougars QB Gary Mullins pitched go-ahead 23y TD to WR Elmo Wright (8/68y) before H. Strong added TD runs of 16, 37y in runaway 4th Q. Florida State (6-3-1) QB Bill Cappleman passed 18-37/265y, 2 TDs in 1st H, but his 2nd INT with 1:30 left in 4th Q was run back for TD by TE L.D. Rowden. Houston (8-2) D helped seal its 8th win in row by sacking Cappleman 9 times.

December 6, 1969

GAME OF THE YEAR
Texas 15 ARKANSAS 14:

National title was up for grabs on gray, chilly day in Fayetteville. With Pres Richard M. Nixon attending in person and millions watching on TV, Texas (10-0) cashed pair of 4th Q gambles to register comeback over Arkansas (9-1) for national championship. Anti-Vietnam War demonstrators were outside stadium, but Razorbacks put on better early show for Nixon, self-professed biggest football fan in country. Porkers had turned 2 FUMs into 14-0 lead, prompting their screaming partisans to wave "We're No. 1" placards. Just 2 plays into game, Longhorns bobble at their 22YL paved way for Hogs TB Bill Burnett to smash over from 1YL. Early in 3rd Q, Arkansas went 53y to score after another FUM REC. QB Bill Montgomery (14-22/205y, 2 INTs) pitched perfect 29y TD to WR Chuck Dicus (9/146y). So, no. 1 Texas found itself outhustled and pushed to brink as 4th Q opened. On 1st play of 4th Q, QB James Street dropped to pass, but scrambled magnificently to 42y TD run. Street followed with slanting 2-pt option run to complete Longhorns' 1st big gamble and earn 14-8 deficit. Facing 4th-and-2 at their own 43YL at 4:47 left, Steers coach Darrell Royal decided "every now and then you have to suck it up and pick a number." Number Royal called was long crossing pattern for TE Randy Peschel, whom Street found behind 2 defenders for 44y gain. HB Jim Bertelsen slanted off LG for tying TD less than min later, and K Happy Feller kicked conv for 15-14 lead. Result remained in doubt as Montgomery moved Razorbacks from own 20YL to Texas 39YL, but, with 1:13 to go, Longhorns DB Tom Campbell angled in front of Dicus for clinching INT. Afterward, Nixon declared Texas as national champions despite Longhorns having to line up on New Year's Day against Notre Dame in Cotton Bowl.

1969 Conference Standings

Ivy League

Dartmouth	6-1
Yale	6-1
Princeton	6-1
Cornell	4-3
Harvard	2-5
Pennsylvania	2-5
Brown	1-6
Columbia	1-6

Atlantic Coast

South Carolina	6-0
North Carolina State	3-2-1
Clemson	3-3
Duke	3-3-1
North Carolina	3-3
Maryland	3-3
Wake Forest	2-5
Virginia	1-5

Southeastern

Tennessee	5-1
Louisiana State	4-1
Auburn	5-2
Florida	3-1-1
Mississippi	4-2
Georgia	2-3-1
Vanderbilt	2-3
Alabama	2-4
Kentucky	1-6
Mississippi State	0-5

Big Ten

Ohio State	6-1
Michigan	6-1
Purdue	5-2
Minnesota	4-3
Iowa	3-4
Indiana	3-4
Wisconsin	3-4
Northwestern	3-4
Michigan State	2-5
Illinois	0-7

Mid-American

Toledo	5-0
Bowling Green	4-1
Miami (Ohio)	2-3
Ohio	2-3
Kent State	1-4
Western Michigan	1-4

Big Eight

Missouri	6-1
Nebraska	6-1
Colorado	5-2
Oklahoma	4-3
Kansas State	3-4
Oklahoma State	3-4
Iowa State	1-6
Kansas	0-7

Southwest

Texas	7-0
Arkansas	6-1
Texas Tech	4-3
Texas Christian	4-3
Southern Methodist	3-4
Rice	2-5
Texas A&M	2-5
Baylor	0-7

Western Athletic

Arizona State	6-1
Utah	5-1
Brigham Young	4-3
Wyoming	4-3
Arizona	3-3
Texas-El Paso	2-5
New Mexico	1-5
Colorado State	0-4

Pacific Eight

Southern California	6-0
UCLA	5-1-1
Stanford	5-1-1
Oregon State	4-3
Oregon	2-3
California	2-4
Washington	1-6
Washington State	0-7

1969 Bowl Games

Liberty Bowl (Dec. 13): Colorado 47 Alabama 33

Wild scoring fluctuations marked Liberty Bowl as Colorado (8-3) built big early edge, then saw Alabama (6-5) rally behind sub QB Neb Hayden for 2-pt lead at 33-31, and finally score 16 unchallenged pts in 4th Q. TB Bob Anderson (35/254y) scored his 1st TD as Buffs dominated pts for 17-0 lead early in 2nd Q. TB Johnny Musso's TD brought Tide within 24-19, but Buffs answered with tricky handoff on KO which sprung TB Steve Engel for 91y TD RET just 46 secs before H. Hayden hit 2 TD passes in 3rd Q to put Bama ahead 33-31. Anderson scored twice in 4th Q to enhance Colorado's pressure D which nailed Hayden 4 times for losses, including safety.

Sun Bowl (Dec. 20): Nebraska 45 Georgia 6

Using 1st Q tailwind, K Paul Rogers made 4 FGs, and TB Jeff Kinney blasted for 11y TD as budding juggernaut Nebraska (9-2) stampeded Georgia (5-5-1) with 18-0 jump-start. Another spree in 3rd Q put game out of reach as Cornhuskers QB Van Brownson hit FB Mike Green for 11y TD and plunged for TD moments later. Injury-riddled Bulldogs O crossed midfield only 3 times but got late-game TD from QB Paul Gilbert.

Gator Bowl (Dec. 27): Florida 14 Tennessee 13

Gator Bowl became only 8th bowl game to date which matched same-conf rivals. Everyone expected O explosion, but each team's D turned up very sharp. Tennessee (9-2) moved smartly but failed to convert 3 1st downs at Gators 10YL or closer. Florida (9-1-1) DB Steve Tannen blocked 1st Q punt, and LB Mike Kelley scooped it up for 8y TD RET for 7-0 advantage. Heads-up Kelley also collected INT and FUM. Volunteers tallied 10 pts in 2nd Q including QB Bobby Scott's 12y TD pass to WR Lester McClain. Gators in turn took 14-10 lead in 3rd Q on QB John Reaves' TD pass to WR Carlos Alvarez. From that point on, Gators built D fortress and also executed GLS. Week-long rumors that coach Doug Dickey was headed to Florida, his alma mater, probably helped to distract Volunteers. Rumors turned out to be true, and fact that Florida had won this game made for Dickey's rocky early relationship with his new players in Gainesville.

Peach Bowl (Dec. 30): West Virginia 14 South Carolina 3

West Virginia (10-1) coach Jim Carlen pulled neat trick for Peach Bowl. He installed run-oriented Wishbone O, and weather played right into his hands as downpour created quagmire on playing surface. Little-used Mountaineers FB Eddie Williams was surprise starter and carried 35/208y after running only 53 times during regular season for WVU. Mountaineers dominated with 365y rushing against Gamecocks defenders, but could score only on HB Bob Gresham's 10y TD run early in 1st Q and FB Jim Braxton's 1y plunge in game's last min. Atrocious conditions hampered air game of South Carolina (7-4), which still connected 11-23/126y. West Virginia D, led by disruptive NG Carl Crennel (FUM REC), forced 2 INTs. Gamecocks tallied on K Billy Dupre's 37y FG with 3:49 to go before H that brought them within 7-3.

Astro-Bluebonnet Bowl (Dec. 31): Houston 36 Auburn 7

WR Terry Beasley's FUM of opening KO got favored Auburn (8-3) off on wrong foot, and Tigers never were able to regroup. TB Jim Strong (32/184y) of home-standing Houston (9-2) quickly gained 22y to put QB Gary Mullins in position to sneak for opening TD. K Carlos Lopez kicked 27y FG, and Strong added 1st of his 2 TDs after cantering 74y on set-up run. Trailing 16-0, Auburn drew within 9 pts by making its only TD: Mickey Zofko's 36y HB pass to WB Connie Frederick. Cougars rolled up 376y rushing, more than 200y more than Auburn's no. 3-ranked D had allowed in any game in 1969. On other side of ledger, Houston D, led by DE Jerry Drones and LB Charlie Hall, tossed QB Pat Sullivan for losses of 50y to drop Tigers' net rush total to self-conscious 1y.

Sugar Bowl: Mississippi 27 Arkansas 22

Early in Sugar Bowl, deflated Arkansas (9-2) found it troublesome rebounding from its defining late-season Texas loss. Underdog Mississippi (8-3) jumped to 14-0 lead in 1st Q as FB Bo Bowen put quick punctuation on 80y drive with 69y TD sprint behind blocks of G Skip Jernigan and T Worthy McClure. Usually-reliable Porkers K Bill McClard missed FGs after 2 Arkansas drives, and Rebels QB Archie Manning (21-35/273y, TD, 2 INTs) zipped around E on 4th-and-1 for 18y TD and 14-0 lead. TB Bill Burnett got Razorbacks back in game at 14-6 with 12y TD run, and QB Bill Montgomery, who outpassed MVP Manning with 17-32/340y, 2 TDs, 2 INTs, trimmed Ole Miss lead to 24-12 with 47y TD pass to WR Chuck Dicus just 35 secs before H. Teams traded 3rd Q FGs, and Montgomery added another TD pass in 4th Q, so Ole Miss led 27-22. Porkers set up shop at Rebs 38YL with 5 mins to play, and it seemed as though Arkansas would finally gain control. Instead, Ole Miss came up with some big D plays as S Glenn Cannon. Cannon broke up 3 passes by Montgomery to halt threat. Arkansas again surged goalward in last 2 mins, and Dicus broke open for pass he carried to Ole Miss 25YL. Cannon knocked Dicus flat and recovered his FUM to explode Hogs' comeback hopes.

Cotton Bowl: Texas 21 Notre Dame 17

Eyes of nation were upon no. 1 Texas (11-0) and no. 9 Notre Dame (8-2-1) as Fighting Irish made their 1st psot-season appearance since their 1925 Rose Bowl win over Stanford. Longhorns dedicated game to courageous, little DB Freddie Steinmark, who stood with crutches on sidelines, his leg having been amputated on Dec 12 because of cancerous tumor. Mighty Texas Wishbone O churned forward for 331y on ground. Irish never got much of ground game going, but QB Joe Theismann (17-27/231y, 2 TDs, 2 INTs) expertly scrambled about his backfield to free himself for clutch passing. Theismann found E Tom Gatewood (6/112y) for 54y TD pass in 2nd Q for 10-0 lead. After Texas HB Jim Bertelsen (18/81y) scored TD later in 2nd Q, Longhorns advanced again toward ND's EZ. Twice Notre Dame LB Bob Olson, voted game's top defender, stuffed HB Billy Dale with 1y to go at Irish 7YL as 4th down try fell less than inch short. So, ND led 10-7 at H. Texas HB Ted Koy traded 4th Q TD with Theismann, who got away from pass-rush pressure to wing 24y TD to wide-open E Jim Yoder. From their own 24YL and trailing 17-14, Longhorns began fateful drive, which would prove to be 1 of most dramatic in bowl history. Texas' march ate 5:48 of clock as FB Steve Worster (20/155) continually battered ND. Texas faced 4th-and-2 at Irish 20YL, and Koy rammed for necessary 2y. Coach Darrell Royal called surprise on next 4th down gamble, when Steers needed 2y from 10YL. QB James Street (6-11/107y, INT) passed to left sideline to E Cotton Speyrer (4/70y), who made brilliant shoestring catch at 2YL. It took 3 tries, but Dale took Street's pitchout for winning 1y TD with 1:08 to play. Game ball from Texas' 20th straight victory was presented to Steinmark, who tragically would live to see only 1 more football season.

Rose Bowl: Southern California 10 Michigan 3

Michigan (8-3) coach Bo Schembechler missed coaching in his 1st Rose Bowl when mild heart attack sent him to hospital night before game. Filling in was Wolverines D coach Jim Young, future Hall of Famer who would make his mark coaching at Arizona, Purdue, and Army, who said, "All of us were playing under difficult circumstances." Southern California (10-0-1) coach John McKay revised his D into 5-man front when LB Greg Sough played little because of injury. Troy also looked to ball-control O, which netted 323y to Wolverines' 289y. Ks Ron Ayala of USC and Jim Killian of Michigan swapped short 1st H FGs after each team's long, methodical drive bogged down. Playing in their 4th straight Rose Bowl, Trojans displayed what McKay called his "best-ever" D. In 3rd Q, DB Sandy Durko made diving INT near midfield, and Trojans QB Jimmy Jones soon whipped crossing-pattern pass to WR Bob Chandler, who broke tackle of Wolverines DB Brian Healy for 33y TD. QB Don Moorhead pitched Michigan into Southern California end 3 times in 4th Q, reaching 13, 9, and 34YLs. But, USC's "Wild Bunch" D sparkled when it counted, stopping each advance. In end, Trojans DB Tyrone Hudson helped defuse 3 game-ending bombs by Moorhead. McKay felt vindicated after season full of narrow wins: "We are the most criticized 10-game winning team in football history, without question." His team would end up 3rd in final poll.

Orange Bowl: Penn State 10 Missouri 3

Undefeated no. 2 Penn State (11-0) must have wondered what might have been if foresight had prompted it to have accepted Cotton Bowl opportunity against Texas. Nittany Lions needed to impress pollsters who harbored notion that they had played weak schedule, although of AP's Top 10 teams prior to bowl games, Penn State's opponents' winning percentage at .5393 was bettered only by no. 5 USC's .5778. (No. 1 Texas had faced teams with a .4340 percentage.) Underrated QB Chuck Burkhart, who remained undefeated for 22nd straight game as Nittany QB (plus 20 wins in row in HS), completed 3 passes to set up K Mike Reitz's 29y 1st Q FG. Moments later, Tigers ace HB Joe Moore lost FUM to Penn State DB Mike Smith, and Burkhart sprinted out to find HB Lydell Mitchell for 28y TD pass. Missouri D tightened thereafter, but 10-0 deficit forced Tigers QBs Terry McMillan and Chuck Roper to air game, not team's strong suit. Result, under pass-rush pressure from DTs Mike Reid and Steve Smear, was 7 INTs clutched by Lions. Still, Missouri outgained Penn State 306y to 244y, and threatening 4 times with only K Henry Brown's late 2nd Q 33y FG to show for it. Lions DE John Ebersole contributed big play, colliding with WR Mel Gray to separate ball and receiver at Penn State 7YL in 2nd Q. Biggest D play came inside last min of 4th Q when DB George Landis picked off Roper at own 2YL and made 55y RET to ice Penn State's win.

1 Texas (36)	910	11 Nebraska	207	
2 Penn State (7)	822	12 Houston	204	
3 Southern California	695	13 UCLA	203	
4 Ohio State (2)	659	14 Florida	183	
5 Notre Dame	457	15 Tennessee	88	
6 Missouri	336	16 Colorado	70	
7 Arkansas	335	17 West Virginia	62	
8 Mississippi	317	18 Purdue	46	
9 Michigan	301	19 Stanford	25	
10 Louisiana State	285	20 Auburn	23	

1969 Top Performance Formula

1 Penn State	1.7879
2 Texas	1.7357
3 Southern California	1.6716
4 Ohio State	1.5896
5 Tennessee	1.5632
6 UCLA	1.5621
7 Missouri	1.5516
8 Louisiana State	1.5474
9 West Virginia	1.5408
10 Florida	1.5337
11 Houston	1.5259
12 Notre Dame	1.5167
13 Nebraska	1.5046
14 Mississippi	1.5030
15 Arizona State	1.4776
16 Auburn	1.4722
17 Stanford	1.4703
18 Michigan	1.4583
19 Arkansas	1.4576
20 Purdue	1.4395

1969 Top Opponent Records

1 Mississippi State	.6842
2 Kentucky	.6615
3 Mississippi	.6394
4 Oklahoma State	.6105
5 Tennessee	.6095
6 Oregon State	.6087
7 Southern California	.5980
8 Washington	.5978
9 Alabama	.5971
10 Auburn	.5922
11 Pittsburgh	.5914
12 Georgia	.5905
13 Penn State	.5842
14 Missouri	.5825
15tArizona	.582418
15tNavy	.582418
17 Miami	.5753
18 Oklahoma	.5745
19 Minnesota	.5719
20 Northwestern	.5714

1969 Out-of-Conference Records

	W-L	Percentage	Bowl W-L
Southeastern	34-12	.7391	2-4
Big Eight	18-9	.6667	2-1
Pacific-8	18-10-2	.6333	1-0
Western Athletic	17-12	.5862	0-0
Big Ten	12-17-1	.4167	0-1
Southwest	10-16	.3846	1-1
Atlantic Coast	7-24	.2258	0-1

1969 Individual Statistical Leaders

RUSHING YARDS	Attempts	Yards	Avg.
Steve Owens, Oklahoma	358	1523	4.3
Ed Marinaro, Cornell	277	1409	5.1
Joe Moore, Missouri	260	1312	5.0
Jim Strong, Houston	190	1293	6.8
Clarence Davis, Southern California	282	1275	4.5
John Isenbarger, Indiana	233	1217	5.2
Po James, New Mexico State	258	1181	4.6
Don McCauley, North Carolina	204	1092	5.4
Bob Gresham, West Virginia	190	1057	5.6
Jim Otis, Ohio State	225	1027	4.6

PASSING YARDS	Completions	Attempts	Yards	Pct.
Dennis Shaw, San Diego State	199	335	3185	59.4
John Reaves, Florida	222	396	2896	56.1
Jim Plunkett, Stanford	197	336	2673	58.6
Mike Phipps, Purdue	169	321	2527	52.6
Lynn Dickey, Kansas State	196	372	2476	52.7
Bill Cappleman, Florida State	183	344	2467	53.2
Chuck Hixson, Southern Methodist	217	362	2313	59.9
Scott Hunter, Alabama	157	266	2188	59.0
Gary Baxter, Air Force	127	273	1783	46.5
Archie Manning, Mississippi	154	265	1762	58.1

RECEIVING YARDS	Catches	Yards
Carlos Alvarez, Florida	88	1329
Elmo Wright, Houston	63	1275
Tim Delaney, San Diego State	85	1259
Walker Gillette, Richmond	57	1090
Todd Snyder, Ohio University	62	835
Calvin Demery, Arizona State	45	816
Bobby Moore, Oregon	54	786
David Bailey, Alabama	56	781
Sammy Milner, Mississippi State	64	745
Tom Gatewood, Notre Dame	47	743

1969 Consensus All-America Team
Offense:

End:	Walker Gillette, Richmond
	Carlos Alvarez, Florida
	Jim Mandich, Michigan
Tackle:	Bob McKay, Texas
	John Ward, Oklahoma State
Guard:	Chip Kell, Tennessee
	Bill Bridges, Houston
Center:	Rodney Brand, Arkansas
Back:	Mike Phipps, Purdue
	Steve Owens, Oklahoma
	Bob Anderson, Colorado
	Jim Otis, Ohio State

Defense:

End:	Jim Gunn, Southern California
	Phil Olsen, Utah State
Tackle:	Mike Reid, Penn State
	Mike McCoy, Notre Dame
Guard:	Jim Stillwagon, Ohio State
Linebacker:	Mike Ballou, UCLA
	Steve Kiner, Tennessee
	Dennis Onkontz, Penn State
Back:	Jack Tatum, Ohio State
	Buddy McClinton, Auburn
	Tom Curtis, Michigan
Kicker:	Bob Jacobs, Wyoming

1969 Heisman Trophy Vote

Steve Owens, senior tailback, Oklahoma	1488
Mike Phipps, senior quarterback, Purdue	1334
Rex Kern, junior quarterback, Ohio State	856
Archie Manning, junior quarterback, Mississippi	582
Mike Reid, senior defensive tackle, Penn State	297

Other Major Awards

Maxwell (Player)	Mike Reid, senior defensive tackle, Penn State
Walter Camp (Player)	Archie Manning, junior quarterback, Mississippi
Outland (Lineman)	Mike Reid, senior defensive tackle, Penn State
AFCA Coach of the Year	Bo Schembechler, Michigan

1970

The Year of The Year of the Quarterback, Bowl Upsets after Eleven Games, and Aeronautic Tragedy

The 1970s opened much the way the rollicking 1960s closed. Familiar names Texas (10-1), winners of 20 straight games, Ohio State (9-1), winners of 18 of 19 over two years, Southern California (6-4-1) and Arkansas (9-2) were considered the preseason cream of the crop. Penn State (7-3), with 22 straight wins and 30 games without a loss, was considered barely behind the top dogs.

With passing taking greater prominence in offensive game plans, 1970 became known as the "Year of the Quarterback." Among the strong-armed throwers were Lynn Dickey of Kansas State (6-5), Rex Kern of Ohio State, Archie Manning of Mississippi (7-4), Bill Montgomery of Arkansas, Jim Plunkett of Stanford (9-3), John Reaves of Florida (7-4), Pat Sullivan of Auburn (9-2) and Joe Theismann of Notre Dame (10-1).

The Year of the Quarterback contributed to a blizzard of Heisman preview attention, jump-starting a trend that made the Heisman the most prominent sports award in which advance media speculation grew to play an enormous role. Sports information directors of major football schools learned that successful candidates required campaigns be launched well in advance, almost like those of candidates for the U.S. Presidency. Heisman candidates had to stand on a strong record (Translation: The candidate must have flashy statistics from his sophomore and junior years.), have solid party backing (He must play on a team with a good record.), be able to carry their region (He must move ahead of other players as the top candidate from a given sector of the country.), look good in the primaries (He absolutely must play well in televised games.) and, lastly, have a good ad campaign. The latter often translated into the candidate becoming the subject of an appealing poster, an informative postcard, or three-dimensional graphic mailing to the voting media.

Plunkett had a superb year leading Stanford to the Rose Bowl and won the Heisman Trophy, partly because other candidates failed at critical moments of the election. Manning was assassinated—figuratively, of course—when he broke his arm in midseason. Kern peaked too soon because he had played his best ball in his sophomore year of 1968. Theismann peaked too late, playing his best ball in 1970.

Where did all this politicking begin? In a 1997 story in *The New York Times* that carped about how through "polls and beauty pageants…the news media assumes (sic) control of college football" near the end of every season, columnist William C. Rhoden revealed that Heisman hype had started at the U.S. Naval Academy, of all places. Budd Thalman, one-time sports information director for the Navy Midshipmen, admitted to Rhoden that, "In 1963, I did a mailing. It was four pages, the size of index cards. It said, 'Meet Roger Staubach.'" Each week Thalman would visit New York's football writers meeting and bring along a stack of Staubach stories and stats to sell his quarterback. Rhoden seemed affronted at hearing of the success of Thalman's campaign management, but no football observer could rightfully argue against the merits of Roger Staubach, who claimed the Heisman and a place in college football's pantheon in 1963.

By the end of the 1970 season, the highest individual honors may have gone to Plunkett, but championship team honors were captured by Nebraska (11-0-1), which, as the third-ranked team entering the bowl games, emerged as a surprise national champion in coach Bob Devaney's ninth year in Lincoln. Making Nebraska's title possible were two enormous bowl upsets.

The Cotton Bowl presented a rematch from the year before between No. 1 Texas and no. 6 Notre Dame. The Longhorns arrived at their quasi-home game in Dallas with 30 straight wins, the ninth longest streak in history at that time. Unlike the previous January when Texas prevailed, the Fighting Irish managed to knock the Horns from the top poll spot with a convincing 24-11 win.

No. 2 Ohio State, an undefeated, senior-dominated team that had won 31 of its last 32 games going back to the middle of the 1967 season, also was surprised, 27-17, in the Rose Bowl by Stanford. It was the Big Ten's third straight Rose Bowl loss, the onset of a painful 2-18 trend.

The upsets opened the throne room to the AP Poll. Could Notre Dame possibly leapfrog all the way from no. 6 to no. 1? After his team's 17-12 Orange Bowl win over no. 5 Louisiana State (9-3), Nebraska's Devaney quipped, "Even the Pope wouldn't vote Notre Dame no. 1." The Associated Press writers agreed, handing the Cornhuskers their first-ever, season-ending top vote.

A new issue developed that would continue to dominate the thinking of college athletic directors to the present day. The cost of athletics came under constant examination, and the NCAA convention voted in a referendum that passed with amazing ease. Starting in 1970, schools were allowed to schedule an eleventh game as a method of rescuing overtaxed athletic budgets. Ohio State, for one, still played an antiquated nine game slate in 1970. But most schools that added an extra game looked on them as an opportunity to daringly match themselves with powerhouses from other regions. This was a pleasant 1970s trend made evident in the season's first week as Southern California put a 42-21 whipping on Alabama (6-5) and Stanford beat Arkansas, 34-28.

The Trojans' convincing win over the Crimson Tide became a landmark contest in that USC's sophomore fullback Sam Cunningham, an African-American, played brilliantly, and his performance in the Deep South along with those of other black USC stars helped Alabama coach Bear Bryant convince his hierarchy that he needed to integrate his Crimson Tide with black players. Less than 10 years earlier, Alabama Gov. George Wallace had defiantly stated the Tuscaloosa campus would "never" be integrated, but within the next four years after 1970, the Crimson Tide squad boasted several stars of African heritage, including All-Americas in defensive end John Mitchell, linebacker Woodrow Lowe, and center Sylvester Croom, future head coach at Mississippi State. They were followed by greats Ozzie Newsome, Dwight Stevenson, E.J. Junior, Cornelius Bennett, and Derrick Thomas. It was said that Bryant cracked ironically, "Cunningham did more for integration in Alabama in 60 minutes than Martin Luther King did in 20 years."

Black players walked out because no black assistant coach had been hired at Syracuse (6-4). This action was surely a paradox since the school had been perhaps the nation's greatest champion of African-American athletes during the 1950s and 1960s. Animosity reigned and two former stars, militant Jim Brown and moderate Floyd Little, were pitted against each other during the conflict that boiled into a 0-3 start for the Orangemen. Still, Syracuse rallied for a big upset of Penn State to pave the way for a winning year.

Iowa (3-6-1) endured a nasty power struggle, ending in the firing of coach Ray Nagel and resignation of athletic director Forest Evashevski, once the highly popular coach who had taken the Hawkeyes to two Rose Bowls. When Bump Elliott was hired as new AD, he surprisingly rehired Nagel as coach.

It was a truly tragic year. Without discrimination, death claimed footballers young and old, famous and barely-known. By far, the most disquieting events came when separate airplane crashes wiped out significant numbers of the football squads of both Wichita State (0-9) and Marshall (3-6).

On Friday, October 2, one of two badly-overloaded propeller-driven planes chartered by Wichita State crashed into a mountainside near Silver Plume, Colo., on its way to Logan, Utah, for a game the next day against Utah State. The crash killed 30 people, including 13 Wichita football players as well as head coach Ben Wilson, assistant coaches, athletic staff, and boosters. The Federal Aviation Administration determined later that the Martin 404 aircraft, flying at 11,000 feet, was incapable of climbing quickly enough to clear the 11,990-ft. Continental Divide and that it was virtually impossible to turn around in narrow Loveland Pass. Nine players survived the crash, and 33 players, coaches, and fans were aboard the companion plane that landed safely. The Wheatshockers cancelled their Utah State date but voted to play out the string with a depleted and demoralized squad.

The Marshall Thundering Herd lost 17-14 to East Carolina in Greenville, N.C., on November 14, and a planeload of 70 players, coaches and boosters crashed in a ball of fire while on approach to landing at Tri-State Airport near the campus city of Huntington, W. Va. All aboard the chartered D-9 jet aircraft perished. Rescue efforts were hampered because the only access road had been turned to mud by a steady rain, although witnesses living nearby suggested no one could have survived the explosion.

Although neither school touched by aeronautic tragedy had ever challenged football's elite on the field, Wichita State had enjoyed a stronger football history than had Marshall. Wichita had won or shared five Missouri Valley Conference championships over a 10-year span starting in 1954, but the destruction of an already slipping team would bring on a 76-loss slump in the 1970s despite one remarkable year's winning record at 6-5 in 1972. The Shockers finally quit fielding football teams after 1986. Wichita State's

89 years of football—it played a major schedule starting in 1946—produced more wins (375) than any other discontinued program in NCAA history.

Marshall, known more for its basketball prowess in 1970, picked up the pieces in 1971 under Jack Lengyal, an unknown coach who was the only one willing to take on the challenge. In 2006, a major motion picture, "We are Marshall," starring Matthew McConaughey in the role of Lengyl told the story of a remarkable resurrection that the new Thundering Herd team created. Marshall softened its football schedule and eventually embraced 1-AA status when the lower division became available in the early 1980s. After building up to five trips to the 1-AA title game and becoming champions in 1992 and '96, Marshall reentered major status in Div. 1-A football in 1997, turning out such stars as wide receiver Randy Moss and quarterback Chad Pennington.

More than 30 years later, the plane crash memorial continues to emotionally galvanize Marshall's relatively-small Huntington community. On the other hand, the larger city of Wichita, ironically one of America's early aviation capitals, has moved on, hardly ever looking back, perhaps because the dead lost their lives not near home but far away in the Rocky Mountains.

Milestones

■ Athletic directors of major schools were allowed to add 11th game to schedules.

■ Two schools left small conferences to go independent: Cincinnati and Central Michigan.

■ Brian Piccolo, nation's leading rusher and scorer at Wake Forest in 1964, died on June 16 of cancer at 26. Piccolo was memorialized by ABC's made-for-TV movie "Brian's Song." On July 21, former Oklahoma tackle Bob Kalsu died in Vietnam military action at age 25. Severe headaches kept LSU quarterback recruit Herman Duhe Jr. on sidelines during preseason practice and youngster soon died of brain hemorrhage. On September 3, cancer claimed Vince Lombardi, 57, guard on famous mid-1930s "Seven Blocks of Granite" teams at Fordham. Lombardi gained everlasting fame as coach of five-time NFL champion Green Bay Packers, his image made stronger with his many quotes about desire and integrity. Lombardi made lesser known quote on value of college football: "A school without football is in danger of deteriorating into a medieval study hall." Rotary Club of Houston created Lombardi Award, which it presented for 1st time in 1970 to nation's top lineman. Also dying were highly-regarded coach Clark Shaughnessy, 78, reviver of T-formation during Stanford's undefeated season of 1940, Roger Hagberg, 31, fullback on Minnesota's 1960 national champion team who became victim of hit-and-run driver after being thrown from his car in auto accident, and Brooks Dawson, 23, Texas-El Paso quarterback in 1968, who died of heart attack. Airplane crashes in October and November tragically took considerable number of lives of Wichita State and Marshall players, coaches, and boosters.

■ Longest winning streaks entering season:

Penn State 22	Texas 20	San Diego State 12

■ Coaching Changes

	Incoming	Outgoing
Clemson	Hootie Ingram	Frank Howard
Colorado State	Jerry Wampfler	Mike Lude
Florida	Doug Dickey	Ray Graves
Miami (a)	Walt Kichefski	Charlie Tate
Purdue	Bob DeMoss	Jack Mollenkopf
Temple	Wayne Hardin	George Makris
Tennessee	Bill Battle	Doug Dickey
Texas Tech	Jim Carlen	J. T. King
West Virginia	Bobby Bowden	Jim Carlen
Wisconsin	John Jardine	John Coatta

(a) Kichefski (2-7) replaced Tate (1-1) after two games in 1970.

Preseason AP Poll

1 Ohio State (19)	646	11 Missouri	157
2 Texas (7)	599	12 Louisiana State (1)	131
3 Southern California (6)	551	13 Houston	123
4 Arkansas (1)	378	14 Kansas State	107
5 Mississippi (1)	361	15 Florida	84
6 Notre Dame	341	16 Alabama	49
7 Penn State (1)	308	17 South Carolina	40
8 Michigan	237	18 UCLA	38
9 Nebraska	216	19 Arizona State	35
10 Stanford	201	20t Auburn	28
		20t Oklahoma	28
		20t West Virginia	28

September 12, 1970

(Fri) MISSOURI 38 Baylor 0 (St. Louis): College football invaded St. Louis Cardinals' Busch Stadium as Missouri (1-0) HB Joe Moore (36/171y, TD) had big night. But, Baylor (0-1), trying to avoid SWC-record 11th straight defeat, held Tigers to 10-0 lead at H and dominated 3rd Q until 4:37 was left. At that point, Mizzou took over at its 28YL. Moore swept right and threw surprise pass to WR Mel Gray, who wiggled out of grasp of DB Ed Marsh and sprinted parallel to 50YL to pick up WB John Henley's block to break away for 72y TD. Bears sub QB Si Southall (2-7/25y, 2 INTs) was quickly picked off by Tigers DB Pete Buha, whose RET went to Baylor 18YL. Missouri backup QB Mike Farmer scored on sneak and rout was on.

NORTH CAROLINA 20 Kentucky 10: Charging to 48y TD, TB Don McCauley (27/157y) iced game for North Carolina (1-0) on 1st play of 4th Q. McCauley threw key block to enable Tar Heels WB Lewis Jolley to sprint 41y with QB Paul Miller's pass for 7-7 tie in 1st Q. Earlier, Kentucky (0-1) earned 7-0 1st Q lead and 10-10 H tie thanks to running of TB Cecil Bowens (5y TD run), passing of QB Stan Forston (12-22/108y), and punting of P Dave Hardt, who boomed 65y boot in 3rd Q.

Southern California 42 ALABAMA 21: Adding top-shelf foe as his 11th game, Alabama (0-1) coach Bear Bryant may have questioned his decision. Extending its unbeaten string to 22 games, no. 3 Southern California (1-0) used its big O line to roll back Crimson Tide for 485y rushing. FB Sam Cunningham's varsity debut was outstanding: His 1st carry went for 16y, and later on 4th-and-1, Cunningham (12/135y) tore through LT Marv Montgomery's block for 22y TD. Cunningham's 2nd TD came after DB Tyrone Hudson's 32y punt RET and provided 12-0 lead in 1st Q. Troy led 22-7 at H, and 89y TD trip after 2nd H KO wrapped it up. Trailing 32-7 in 3rd Q, Crimson Tide went to aerial attack (232y total) for TD catch by E David Bailey (7/101y). Bama TB Johnny Musso was held to 15/41y rushing, but scored twice.

FLORIDA 21 Duke 19: Gators (1-0) held on for win despite 2 late Duke (0-1) TDs in 4th Q. After having received doctor's approval to test his gout-plagued knees, superb Florida WR Carlos Alvarez returned 1st punt of his career and zigzagged 67y to TD which provided 21-6 lead late in 3rd Q. Earlier, Alvarez (4/70y) caught 46y toss by QB John Reaves (14-27/230y, 2 INTs) to set up 1st of 2 TD runs by TB Tommy Durrance. Blue Devils lost chance to add 10 pts in 1st H, but FB Steve Jones lost FUM at Gators 3YL and K David Wright missed 25y FG, although he made 2 on either side of H. Duke QB Leo Hart (21-36/228y, TD) broke Norm Snead's ACC career passing y record of 4,040y.

GEORGIA TECH 23 South Carolina 20: Soph Eddie McAshan ignored pressure of being 1st black football player at Georgia Tech (1-0) and 1st black QB in major southern program. He passed 20-38/202y, TD to beat Gamecocks (0-1). FB Steve Harkey was favorite target, catching Georgia Tech record to-date 14 passes. South Carolina earned 14-10 H and 20-17 3rd Q leads as RB Billy Ray Rice ran for 2 TDs after INTs, and QB Tommy Suggs flipped TD pass.

NEBRASKA 36 Wake Forest 12: Demon Deacons (0-1) scored 1st after S Frank Fussell recovered FUM by Nebraska (1-0) TB Jeff Kinney. Cornhuskers held, however, and Wake Forest K Tracy Lounsbury booted 35y FG. Nebraska's lightning O struck for 2 quick TDs: It went 63y as QB Jerry Tagge (9-12/168y, TD) passed 45y to WR Guy Engles to set up HB Joe Orduna's 5y TD. When Wake fumbled after next KO, Kinney made up for his bobble with TD plunge after 26y trip. Deacons authored 72y QK on next possession, and Nebraska's answering punt from EZ was blocked for safety by Wake CB Pat McHenry. Leading 14-5, Nebraska went 81y to Tagge's 13y TD run, followed by Tagge's 61y TD pass to WB Johnny Rodgers. Wake Forest gained 62y of its 222y total O in late going as soph QB Jim McMahen pitched 12y TD pass with 53 secs left.

Oklahoma 28 SOUTHERN METHODIST 11: It was bittersweet day for SMU (0-1) QB Chuck Hixson, who broke NCAA record for career completions to date with 506, previously held at 491 by Steve Ramsey of North Texas State. Despite 24 completions, Hixson suffered 4 damaging INTs in 1st H and was trumped by Oklahoma (1-0) QB Jack Mildren. Mildren sneaked 1y and passed 39y to WR Jon Harrison for TDs within 61-sec span. Each TD came after INTs by Sooners LB Jerry Backus and CB Geoffrey Nordgren. By season's end, Hixson would up his final record total to 642 completions.

Stanford 34 ARKANSAS 28: Indians (1-0) QB Jim Plunkett wowed Arkansas (0-1) with his short passes, mostly to RB Jackie Brown (11/130y receiving). And, it was Stanford LBs Jeff Siemon and Mike Simone who made game's key D plays. After Siemon roadblocked 3rd down play near his GL, Simone, playing on sprained ankle, stopped Porkers QB Bill Montgomery 4y shy of EZ on a 4th down keeper with time elapsing. Crafting nearly flawless 1st Q at 21-0, Plunkett (22-39/262y, 2 TDs, 3 INTs) had set up 2 TD runs by FB Hillary Shockley (23/117y, 3 TDs) and sandwiched 17y TD bullet to WR Jack Lasater in between. WR Eric Cross made brilliant 61y punt TD RET as Stanford built 27-0 lead in 2nd Q, but edge turned out less than safe. Ineffective until deep into 2nd Q, Montgomery passed for pair of TDs, each on 4th down that allowed Razorbacks to get back in game at 27-14 just before H. Stifling heat (more than 100 degrees), wore down O units in 2nd H, but decisive Tribe TD came early in 3rd Q as Shockley completed 86y drive with his 3rd TD run for 34-14 lead. Arkansas got back in game at 34-28 by going 83 and 84y for TDs by WR Chuck Dicus, on 8y pass from Montgomery, and TB Bill Burnett's 2y run.

Ucla 14 OREGON STATE 9: In 15 rapid-fire secs in 2nd Q, Beavers (0-1) grabbed 9-0 lead with safety on EZ sack by DT Mike Shannon and NG Bob Jossis, followed by QB Steve Endicott's 52y play-action TD bomb to E Jeff Kolberg, instantly after receiving free-kick. Power runs up middle set up pair of 3rd Q TD passes from UCLA (1-0) QB Dennis Dummit to TE Bob Christiansen. Bruins gained 269y rushing and got key break in 3rd Q when Beavers FUM was heading OB, but hit official which slowed it for REC by UCLA LB Tom Daniels. OSU DB Jack Faulkender had INT deep in own territory in 1st H.

AP Poll September 14

1 Ohio State (24)	728	11 Arkansas	148
2 Texas (6)	657	12 Louisiana State	139
3 Southern California (7)	644	13 Kansas State	134
4 Stanford	481	14 Florida	94
5 Mississippi (1)	432	15 Houston	91
6 Notre Dame	364	16 UCLA	70
7 Penn State (1)	316	17 West Virginia	44
8 Michigan (1)	307	18 Oklahoma	40
9 Nebraska	299	19 Georgia	21
10 Missouri	260	20 Arizona State	16

September 19, 1970

NORTH CAROLINA 19 North Carolina State 0: In blazing September heat, deep North Carolina (2-0) squad threw fresh reserves at tiring NC State (0-2) and extended 6-0 lead with 2 TDs in 4th Q. Tar Heels TB Don McCauley (22/171y) missed most of 2nd

H with heat exhaustion, but still spearheaded 411y ground attack. McCauley made brief bows in 4th Q: McCauley's ball-carrying fake into EZ allowed sub QB Johnny Swofford to prance around LE untouched for TD that built 12-0 edge and his 2y slam provided TD with 3:34 left. Wolfpack gained only 11y rushing, thanks to work of DEs Bill Brafford and Judge Mattocks and LBs John Bunting (future UNC coach) and Ricky Packard. NC State's only O came from QB Pat Korsnick, who passed 14-26/123y.

CLEMSON 27 Virginia 17: Ground O of Virginia (1-1) gave Cavaliers 17-10 H lead and was keyed by HB Jimmy Lacey's 9y TD run around LE and his sprints of 19 and 15y to set up 20y TD pass by QB Larry Albert (13-26/136y, TD, INT). Feeding off DT B.B. Elvington's 8y sack of Albert early in 3rd Q, Clemson (2-0) D pushed Cav runners back for –9y in 2nd H. Virginia failed to make 1st down on its 1st 5 possessions as Lacey was stopped twice on 3rd-and-1 runs. Tigers QB Tommy Kendrick (13-21/156y) passed 17y TD to TE John McMakin in last min of 3rd Q and wrapped it up when sub WR Pete Galuska went high among Cavs defenders for Kendrick's TD lob with 6:46 on clock.

SOUTH CAROLINA 43 Wake Forest 7: South Carolina (1-1) QB Tommy Suggs (12-27/185y, 2 TDs, INT) rifled 31y scoring strike to WR Mike Haggard 1st time Gamecocks saw ball. FB Larry Hopkins (9/79y) soon scored on powerful 61y run to tie it 7-7 for Wake Forest (0-2), but that was Deacs' last peep. K Billy DuPre's 23y FG gave Carolina 10-7 H lead, and DuPre added another FG after early 3rd Q punt FUM by Wake Forest DB Terry Kuharchek. Suggs pitched 7y TD pass to WR Jackie Brown for 23-7 advantage.

FLORIDA 34 Mississippi State 13: Hometown coach Doug Dickey made his Florida Field debut successful as Gators (2-0) QB John Reaves (14-25/272y, 2 TDs) initiated WR Carlos Alvarez' acrobatic 35y TD catch and FB Mike Rich's more-pedestrian 27y TD grab. Florida K Richard Franco contributed 2 FGs in 1st H, and TB Tommy Durrance powered for 2 TDs in 3rd Q. Mississippi State (1-1) made 2 big plays that led to scores: HB Lew Grubbs broke away on 66y punt RET in 1st Q, and DB Emile Petro returned INT 25y to Gators 31YL in 4th Q. Bulldogs TB Jim Patridge dived over for 1st TD, and QB Joe Reed (17-32/163y) passed 11y to sub TB Ronnie Jones for TD with 3:42 left.

KENTUCKY 16 Kansas State 3: No. 13 Kansas State (1-1) saw high hopes for 1970 season upset by upstart Kentucky (1-1) D. K-State QB Lynn Dickey was sacked 4 times and pressured into 4 INTs by Kentucky front-4 DL, led by T Dave Roller and E Dave Hardt. Due primarily to sacks of Dickey, Wildcats ended with -91y rushing stats. Kentucky converted 2nd H INTs by LBs Arvel Carroll and Wilbur Hackett into TD runs by TB Cecil Bowens and QB Stan Forston.

GEORGIA TECH 23 Florida State 13: With Florida State (1-1) coach Bill Peterson bemoaning lack of dynamic player who "can break a game open," Georgia Tech (2-0) offered its own answer: QB Eddie McAshan (13-25/159y, TD, 2 INTs) was very sharp in decisive drive. He accounted for 68y of 81y drive and his 22y TD pass to WR Larry Studdard in 3rd Q upped tally to insurmountable 21-7. When game stood tied at 7-7 in 3rd Q, Seminoles QB Frank Whigham, who had come off bench to whip 5y TD pass to TE Jim Tyson late in 2nd Q, rushed handoff to FB Tom Bailey on broken play and lost big FUM at own 29YL. Yellow Jackets soph TB Bruce Southall scored his 2nd 1y TD on 6th play after McAshan hit 11y pass to FB Steve Harkey and TB Brent Cunningham dashed 10y on option pitchout. Whigham hit 38 and 32y passes to ignite 80y 4th Q TD drive to Bailey's 9y TD run.

ALABAMA 51 Virginia Tech 18: Crimson Tide (1-1) ended their 3-game losing streak, which would equal longest under coach Bear Bryant with its match coming in last year of his 1958-82 tenure. Using surprise-starter Neb Hayden at QB, Alabama scored 3 of 4 times it had ball in 1st Q as TDs came on FB Dave Brungard's 21y run and QB Scott Hunter's 14y pass to WR Jerry Cash. In 3rd Q, HB Johnny Musso (10/92y) pitched lefty HB pass to WR David Bailey for 14y TD, and DB Tommy Wade dashed 71y on punt TD RET. Virginia Tech (0-2) QB Gil Schwabe trimmed H deficit to 30-6 on 8y TD pass to TB Perry Tiberio. Gobblers bolted to 3rd Q TDs by FB John Dobbins and TB Rich Matijevich on pass from Schwabe, but Brungard put end to comeback with 59y KO RET followed by his 20y TD scamper for 38-18 lead.

Texas A&M 20 LOUISIANA STATE 18: By 3rd Q, LSU (0-1) built 12-0 lead on WR Andy Hamilton's 73y TD reception, bad snap safety, and 1st of K Mark Lumpkin's 3 FGs. Trailing 12-3 after 3 Qs, Texas A&M (2-0) made inspired comeback in 4th Q. K Pat McDermott knocked through his 2nd FG, and TE Homer May caught 11y TD pass, but K Lumpkin restored LSU's lead at 18-13 with 2 FGs. On 3rd down from his 21YL, Aggies QB Lex James threw last-min desperation pass to WR Hugh McElroy as Tigers DB Paul Lyons jumped up for INT that would clinch win. Lyons amazingly missed ball, and McElroy raced into EZ with shocking 79y TD with 13 secs remaining. It sent Bayou Bengals to 1st home-opener loss since 1957.

TULANE 17 Georgia 14: Soph K Lee Gipson's 1st collegiate FG try pushed Tulane (1-1) past favored Georgia (0-1). Scrappy veteran Green Wave D, led by LB Rick Kingrea, kept young Bulldogs O away from their EZ. Only Bulldogs TD came from soph UGa DB Buz Rosenberg's 62y punt RET in 2nd Q for 14-7 lead at H. Rosenberg came up with next threat as well, charging to Greenies 31YL in 3rd Q only to see his punt RET be pushed back to Bulldogs 37YL by clipping PEN. Tulane QB Greg Gleason tied it 14-14 with 3rd Q TD sneak after LB Glenn Harder's INT at UGa 27YL. Georgia advanced across midfield only once in 2nd H, but was turned back from 23YL by QB James Ray's bounding pitchout which cost Bulldogs 10y.

MICHIGAN 20 Arizona 9: *Chicago Tribune* called Michigan (1-0) win "rather laborious" as it took 10 late Wolverines pts that developed off INTs by DB Bo Rather and LB Mike Huff to pad 10-9 4th Q lead. FB Billy Taylor's 29y TD catch from QB Don Moorhead (11-24/168y, TD) provided 10-0 edge in 1st Q. Arizona (0-1) QB Brian Linstrom (15-32/143y, 4 INTs) overcame some bobbled passes to position accurate K Steve Hurley for FGs of 29, 44, and 33y that kept Wildcats in contention. Actually, Arizona had to be disappointed by Hurley's 3rd FG. After Wildcats blocked short UM FG try early in 4th Q, Linstrom hit WR Barry Dean long down sideline for 46y gain to 21YL. Wolverines held at 16YL, and Hurley kicked Wildcats within 10-9. It was Hurley's accuracy that influenced Michigan coach Bo Schembechler into going for 4-pt lead at 13-9 in 4th Q. Fans booed choice of K Dana Coin's FG on 4th-and-goal at 3YL with 3:49 to go, but Schembechler rationalized, "That kid Hurley could have won the game for them."

Notre Dame 35 NORTHWESTERN 14: Powerful blocking by Notre Dame (1-0) line, led by LG Larry DiNardo, translated into 330y rushing. ND went 75y after opening KO to 1st of HB Denny Allan's 3 TDs, then took trips of 75, 71, and 70y, which included both TD run and pass by QB Joe Theismann (8-19/128y, TD). Trailing 14-0 late in 1st Q, Northwestern (0-1) LB John Voorhees recovered FUM at Irish 23YL, and TB Mike Adamle scooted for 13y TD at start of 2nd Q. NW QB Maurie Daigneau (10-32/120y, INT) faked to Adamle on 4th-and-1 and circled E for TD. Wildcats thrilled home crowd by tying it 14-14 moments later when WR Barry Pearson found picket fence of blockers and roared 71y on punt TD RET. Blown coverage on FB Bill Barz late in 2nd Q allowed him loose for Theismann's go-ahead 17y TD pass. WR Tom Gatewood, sick with flu, still caught 7/111y for ND.

TEXAS 56 California 15: Any doubts about new-look Longhorns' capability to defend national title were dispelled as squadron of young Texans reloaded to trounce Golden Bears (0-2). Longhorns (1-0) QB Eddie Phillips replaced the departed James Street with aplomb, rushing 9/129y, 2 TDs, and igniting scores on 4 of 1st 5 Steer possessions. In early going, Phillips cut 10y upfield on option run to California 5YL and surprised everyone with late pitchout to FB Steve Worster (7/43y), who trotted into EZ to score 1 of his 3 1st Q TDs that provided 21-0 lead. "I tried that once in practice, but fumbled it," admitted Phillips. "I guess I just had more confidence today." Trailing 49-0, Bears finally scored in 4th Q on 33y pass by QB Steve Curtis (11-14/174y, TD) to WR Isaac Curtis.

ARKANSAS 23 Oklahoma State 7: SMU's Doak Walker's 21-year-old Southwest Conf rushing TD mark fell to Arkansas (1-1) TB Bill Burnett, who scored his record 39th and 40th to break open game in 2nd H. But, it wasn't easy for no. 11 Razorbacks. Oklahoma State (0-2) went 80y after 2nd H KO to gain 7-7 tie on HB Bobby Cole's 6y scoring run. Cowboys offered balanced attack with QB Tony Pounds (15-21/183y) enhancing Oklahoma State's 190y rushing game, led by FB Jesse Williams, but Oklahoma State killed 1 of their threats with PENs and were stopped twice deep in Hogs' end. Porkers went ahead 9-7 in 3rd Q when Cowboys C Tommy Noles snapped ball over P Jim Benien's head for safety, and Burnett later added his 1 and 11y TD runs.

SOUTHERN CALIFORNIA 21 Nebraska 21: Cornhuskers (1-0-1) kept scoring TDs, but USC (1-0-1) answered right back each time. Nebraska QB Jerry Tagge (11-17/140y, TD, 2 INTs) deftly led O despite spending most of week hospitalized with broken vein in leg. Soph WB Johnny Rodgers launched 1st Huskers scoring foray with 30y punt RET, scored in 2nd Q on 15y pass from Tagge. Nebraska TB Joe Orduna cut left, zoomed 67y for 21-14 lead in 3rd Q. K Paul Rogers could have put game away midway in 4th Q with 22y FG, but snap was bobbled, and Rogers' try was wide. Trojans followed with 80y drive which included sub WR Paul Morgan's 14y diving catch at Huskers 16YL among 3 defenders. Coach John McKay took post-game heat after opting for tie with conv kick after TB Clarence Davis' 9y TD run with 6:44 remaining, saying, "We would have gone for two (points) if there were five minutes or less."

OREGON STATE 21 Iowa 14 (Portland): Umbrellas were open, it was dandy weather for Great Northwest. Oregon State (1-1) scored 2 TDs in 1st Q and fended off Iowa (0-1) in rain-drenched night game at Portland. Beavers gained 319y rushing as big FB Dave Schilling pounded for 36/174y and clinching 1y TD blast in 4th Q. Oregon State QB Steve Endicott (7-11/69y, 2 TDs) twice found WB Bill Carlquist for scores in 1st Q. Hawkeyes depended on sleek TB Levi Mitchell (21/103y) for nearly all of its 128y rushing, although their 2nd H TDs came from FB Tim Sullivan on 2y run in 3rd Q and 48y TD pass in 4th Q.

WASHINGTON 42 Michigan State 16: Soph QB Sonny Sixkiller (15-35/276y, 3 TDs, INT), grandson of chief of Native American Cherokee tribe, made his debut by beating 20-year-old Washington (1-0) total O record with 313y. Sixkiller hit soph WR Ira Hammon with 59y TD pass on game's 4th play, indicating that Huskies had whole new O approach, wide-open passing attack, as coach Jim Owens changed his ways. Washington FB Bo Cornell caught 2nd Q TD pass from Sixkiller, and Hammon gave Huskies 21-7 in 3rd Q with 37y TD reception. Michigan State (0-1) managed only 1 O TD against undersized but quick Huskies, and it didn't come until Spartans trailed 35-9 in 4th Q: TB Henry Matthews ran 8y to score. Michigan State tied game in 1st Q when Sixkiller suffered soph mistake, and Spartans S Brad McLee returned INT 80y for TD and 7-7 deadlock.

AP Poll September 21

1 Ohio State (14)	728	11 Houston	168
2 Texas (16)	632	12 Arkansas	113
3 Stanford (1)	472	13 Florida	79
4 Penn State (2)	453	14 Oklahoma	56
5 Mississippi (1)	420	15 UCLA	54
6 Notre Dame	369	16 West Virginia	50
7 Southern California (2)	368	17 Tennessee	33
8 Nebraska	304	18 Colorado	27
9 Missouri	274	19 Georgia Tech	23
10 Michigan (1)	256	20 Air Force	21

September 26, 1970

Boston College 28 NAVY 14: Boston College (2-0) used runs of HB Fred Willis for 131y and 3 TDs to take advantage of each of 3 trips into Navy (1-2) territory in opening 3 Qs. Meanwhile, Midshipmen had ball inside BC 31YL 5 times in 1st H and only 3y TD plunge by FB Andy Pease (108y rushing) to show for it. Even that brief highlight was brought about by DE Tom O'Brien's FUM REC at Eagle 22YL. Navy O failed to

capitalize on INTs by LB Chuck Voith and DB Brad Stephan, each of whom returned into BC end. Middies WRs Tom Moore and Karl Schwelm dropped long, open passes in 2nd H, but it was soon 28-7 as Willis scored on 7y TD pass from QB Frank Harris, and Harris added TD run.

Kansas 31 SYRACUSE 14: Mayor of Syracuse considered cancelling game as ancient Archbold Stadium was heavily guarded because of black player protest and rumored, massive on-field sit-in by students. Mostly because jumpy Kansas (2-1) flubbed early plays, dispirited Syracuse (0-2) was able to score game's 1st TD on TB Roger Praetorius' 13y screen pass from QB Randy Zur. Typically unfazed, Kansas FB John Riggins (26/162y, 3 TDs) crashed for 3 short TDs to supply 8-7 H edge and ignite 20-pt outburst in 3rd Q. Riggins cantered 57y down sideline to 17YL to set up his 3rd TD. Jayhawks QB Dan Heck ran for 2 pts after Riggins' 1st TD and capped 3rd Q with 43y TD pass to WR Marvin Foster, who took pass in stride and ignored own bobble for TD and insurmountable 28-7 edge.

ALABAMA 46 Florida 15: In just 15th meeting between SEC schools, Crimson Tide (2-1) buried Gators (2-1) with 22-pt barrage in 4th Q. Alabama D allowed solo 9y TD pass by highly-pressured Florida QB John Reaves (24-44/238y, TD, 2 INTs) to FB Mike Rich in 2nd Q that kept Gators competitive for awhile at 10-7. Gators earned only 41y rushing. QBs Scott Hunter and Neb Hayden each threw TD pass in Alabama's balanced attack of 286y rushing and 200y passing. TB Johnny Musso (21/139y) was 1 of 7 different Tide players to score TD. Before getting nicked up, Bama QB Hunter hit 12, 11, and 33y passes on opening drive, which sub QB Hayden finished with TD sneak. Hunter hit his TD pass to FB Dave Brungard in 2nd Q that took Tide to 17-7 H edge. "We stunk," blurted irritated Florida coach Doug Dickey afterward. "He means 'stank,'" corrected sports writer, while another posed rhetorical question: "What do you want? Good grammar or good football?" "...We'll be back," added Dickey.

AUBURN 36 Tennessee 23 (Birmingham): QB Pat Sullivan threw 17-31/268y, TD and ran for 70y as Auburn (2-0) beat Volunteers (1-1) in sloppy, 14-TO match-up. Tigers used 2 INTs within min by DB Larry Willingham; 1st went for 52y TD RET and 2nd was 3rd straight INT thrown by Tennessee QB Bobby Scott. Scott's 1y TD run had built early 10-0 lead for Tennessee. After blowing that lead, Tennessee pulled within 29-23 in 4th Q on TD run by TB Don McLeary and TD pass by Scott.

Mississippi State 20 Vanderbilt 6 (Memphis): Undefeated Vanderbilt (2-1) had roared past 2 patsies and looked to launch good season, while Mississippi State (2-1) searched for its 1st SEC win since beating Florida in 1965. As evidence of how early season results can be so deceiving, Vandy came in with nation's no. 7 D, having allowed no TDs against Chattanooga and The Citadel, while State had managed only 163y rushing in 2 games. Bulldogs barreled for 272y on ground, led by QB Joe Reed, who raced for 54y TD in 1st Q and finished with 18/131y, 2 TDs. Reed also threw 5y TD pass to WR David Smith that provided 14-0 lead in 2nd Q. Later, Smith caught 25 and 20y passes to fuel clinching 4th Q march for Maroons. Commodores pulled within 14-6 as their only O threat, soph TB Steve Burger, romped for 13y TD late in 2nd Q, part of Burger's 14/61y on ground. But, Vandy QB Watson Brown (11-20/93y, INT), normally option running threat, could generate only –3y rushing, thanks to lame shoulder, and team totaled 88y running.

LOUISIANA STATE 24 Rice 0: K Mark Lumpkin surpassed Doug Moreau's LSU (1-1) career score-by-kicking record with FG and 3 conv kicks. Bengals' rushing total was fairly meager at 114y as Rice (1-1) D limited TBs Art Cantrelle and Tommy Casanova to 20/63y and 11/30y respectively, but each scored TD for Tigers. Owls got decent production from QB Phil Wood (7-17/90y, INT), but Wood spent considerable time on bench after being shaken up in 1st Q. Tigers D made INTs by CB Jim Earley, LB Mike Anderson, and S Craig Burns, while also recovering 2 FUMs to help frustrate Rice O. LSU sub QB Bert Jones fired 33y pass to WR Andy Hamilton to set up Casanova's 1st Q TD wedge. Tigers went 53y behind QB Buddy Lee to Cantrelle's score in 2nd Q before Lumpkin made 44y FG. In late going, Wood completed 15, 9, and 11y passes and added 12y keeper to move Owls to 1st-and-goal at 9YL but lost ball on downs at 16YL when Tigers reserves rose up to snarl.

NOTRE DAME 48 Purdue 0: Ending 3-year Purdue hex, Irish (2-0) hurled balanced 633y O at Boilermakers (1-1). Improving ND QB Joe Theismann (16-24/279y, 3 TDs, INT) pitched TD passes of 17, 7, 20y to E Tom Gatewood (12/192y), who was maneuvered among 4 receiver spots to confuse double-team D. Inexperienced Boilers were held to 144y, but sub soph QB Gary Danielson led 3rd Q drive to ND 15YL. On 4th down, HB Stan Brown's run was stacked up.

Air Force 37 MISSOURI 14 (St. Louis): Explosive Falcons (3-0) blitzed no. 9 Missouri (2-1) to earn 1st top 10 AP poll spot since 1958. Air Force QB Bob Parker threw for 295y, TDs of 44 and 67y to WR Ernie Jennings, while RB Brian Bream rushed for 3 TDs. Reeling from 30-0 1st H, Tigers managed to send QB Mike Farmer into EZ twice in 2nd H.

Oregon State 23 OKLAHOMA 14: Surprising Oregon State (2-1) overcame 14-13 H disadvantage with concerted 2nd H effort. Oklahoma (2-1) got TDs from TB Joe Wylie (32y run) and FB Roy Bell (10y pass from QB Jack Mildren) in 2nd Q, only portion of game Sooners were able to control. Beavers QB Steve Endicott (17-34/197y) threw 3 TD passes to lead O that outgained Sooners 450y to 190y, while D chipped in with 2nd H shutout. K Lynn Boston kicked go-ahead 21y FG in 3rd Q.

OKLAHOMA STATE 26 Houston 17: Cowboys (1-2) snapped 10-game winning streak of Houston (1-1) as special teams KR Dick Graham starred. Graham scored on 85y KO RET and set up clinching TD with 35y punt RET. Houston's last defeat also had been to Oklahoma State in 1969. Cougars had opened scoring on K Carlos Lopez's 43y FG and got 6y TD run from HB Tommy Mozisek.

COLORADO 41 Penn State 13: Scoring their 1st TD only 1:25 into game, stampeding Buffaloes (2-0) used FB John Tarver's 1y TD run after DB Pat Murphy's INT to start to unravel 23-game winning streak of Penn State (1-1). K Dave Haney kicked 2 FGs and Colorado went 71y to TD to more than compensate for Lions FB Franco Harris' 6y TD run in 2nd Q. Any 2nd H comeback hope harbored by Penn State was stomped by flying feet of Buffs WR Cliff Branch, who sped 97y to TD with 2nd H KO TD. That gave Colorado 22-7 lead. D punishment was delivered by Colorado DE Herb Orvis, LB Rick Ogle, and DB John Stearns as Bison forced 5 damaging TOs by Lions.

Texas 35 TEXAS TECH 13: In 1st Q, all seemed right with mighty Texas' world as FUM REC by LB Scott Henderson and short punt by Red Raiders (2-1) led to running TDs by QB Eddie Phillips (18/127y rushing) and FB Steve Worster (18/93y). But, Texas Tech took next KO and went 72y, including HB Larry Hargrave's 31y dash, to QB Charley Napper's 1y TD sneak. Napper ran 43y later in 2nd Q to set up 10y burst up middle for TD by FB Doug McCuthen (15/63y) that sent teams to H with Longhorns (2-0) leading only 14-13. Any anxiety Texas held in remembering its last loss had come on same field early in 1968 was wiped out as Horns went 72y after 2nd H KO to HB Jim Bertelsen's 4y TD run. Trailing only 21-13 early in 4th Q, Raiders QB Napper (4-14/51y, INT) arched long pass down left side to TE David May, who appeared open for TD. But, Texas S Rick Nabors made leaping INT at 10YL as pass hung up just long enough. Texas added TDs by HBs Billy Dale (22/114y) and Bertelsen, and Steers owned their 22nd straight victory, now nation's longest winning string.

Michigan 17 WASHINGTON 3: Stellar soph QB Sonny Sixkiller (19-33/181y, 3 INTs) passed 13-21/117y in 1st H, but all Washington (1-1) had to show for it was K Steve Wiezbowski's 35y FG midway through 1st Q. In 2nd H, Michigan (2-0) pressured Sixkiller relentlessly, throwing him for sizable losses. After Wolverines K Dana Coin tied it in middle of 3rd Q with 39y FG, Michigan D halted Sixkiller on consecutive sneaks at midfield. Michigan took over at Huskies 49YL after big 4th down stop, and HB Preston Henry sped 8y TD run on pitchout. Huskies' 4th Q PEN, that returned custody to Wolverines after punt, paved way for Henry (105y rushing) to blast off RT and cut back for 30y TD.

AP Poll September 28

1 Ohio State (25)	782	11 Arkansas	172
2 Texas (14)	758	12 Auburn	141
3 Stanford (1)	568	13 UCLA	99
4 Notre Dame	528	14 West Virginia	98
5 Southern California (1)	422	15 Georgia Tech	94
6 Nebraska	392	16 Penn State	60
7 Mississippi	368	17 Alabama	41
8 Colorado	346	18 Arizona State	37
9 Michigan (1)	260	19 North Carolina	36
10 Air Force	209	20 Missouri	32

October 3, 1970

MISSISSIPPI 48 Alabama 23: Throwing 3 TDs and running for 2 more, astounding QB Archie Manning led no. 7 Rebels (3-0) to only their 2nd victory over Alabama (2-2) in 60 years. Ole Miss WR Vernon Studdard also starred, scoring on 100y KO RET and 8y reception. Crimson Tide QB Neb Hayden, in for injured Scott Hunter, flipped TD pass in each of 2nd, 3rd, and 4th Qs, but could pull Bama no closer than 26-17.

North Carolina 10 VANDERBILT 7: Uncharacteristic 4th down gambles by North Carolina (4-0) coach Bill Dooley paid off in 4th Q. Dooley's Tar Heels trailed 7-0 with 11 mins remaining and hungered to complete 95y march for score. Dooley bypassed FG opportunity on 4th-and-5 at Vanderbilt (2-2) 16YL. Instead, WB Lewis Jolley got open at 8YL, took QB Johnny Swofford's short rollout pass, and shook off tackler for TD. Swofford completed 7-8/89y on UNC's long TD drive. Heels K Ken Craven's 18y FG won it with 5:36 to play after Jolley caught another 4th down pass for 14y to 8YL. In 2nd Q, Commodores QB John Miller, in for injured Watson Brown, had found FB Bill Young for 25 and 15y catches and completed 83y sortie with 23y TD pass to TE Karl Weiss, who benefitted from crisp block by WR Curt Chesley. Vandy's quick defenders thrice gained FUMs inside own 10YL

MICHIGAN 14 Texas A&M 10: After stopping early Michigan thrust, Texas A&M (2-2) converted strong run game, led by FB Doug Neill (17/99y), into 10y TD run by HB Steve Burks (15/70y, TD) for stunning 10-0 lead in 2nd Q. Trailing for virtually entire game, Wolverines (3-0) needed 63y drive for winning score with 3:00 left. Michigan coach Bo Schembechler turned to sub FB Fritz Seyferth (12/64y), who hammered 7/45y on march. QB Don Moorhead's 7y TD rollout to left side capped 62y drive and spoiled Aggies' determined upset bid. It had taken Aggies DB Dave Elmendorf's punt FUM at his 8YL well into 2nd Q for UM to get back in game. TB Billy Taylor scored on 4th down plunge.

West Virginia 16 INDIANA 10: Winless Hoosiers (0-3) limited nation's leading O to less than half (298y) its 602y early-season avg and held Mountaineers FB Pete Wood, country's leading rusher, to 21/44y. But, West Virginia (4-0) inherited 6 TOs, most notably Indiana sub QB Ted McNulty's FUM at his own 13YL late in 3rd Q. WB Jim Braxton soon accepted 1st of his 2 TD passes from QB Mike Sherwood to break 3-3 tie. Indiana managed to tie it at 10-10 on HB John Motil's 25y dash. Mountaineers HB Bob Gresham pounded for 27y of 62y drive to set up Braxton's 35y clinching TD catch.

OHIO STATE 34 Duke 10: For nearly entire 1st H, Duke Blue Devils (2-2) connived to spring upset of no. 1 Ohio State (2-0). Duke led 3-0 on K Dave Pugh's 38y FG in 1st Q and was intent on adding TD when on 2nd-and-goal at 1YL Buckeyes DT Mark Debevc snatched loose ball out of air as TB Bob Zwirko tried to power over GL. Blues still clung to 3-pt lead as FB-P Steve Jones tried to punt Buckeyes deep in their end of field in last half-min of 2nd Q. Ohio DT Ralph Holloway blocked Jones' punt, and DE Ken Luttner corralled high-hopping ball for 55y TD RET. Buckeyes came to their senses in 3rd Q as HB Larry Zelina caught 10y TD pass from QB Rex Kern (2-9/22y, TD), and

Kern (13/113y rushing) and FB John Brockington (28/117y) scored short TDs for 27-3 lead. Duke coach Tom Hart mused afterward on what might have been: "Our people gave maximum effort on all except 4 plays: the fumble, the blocked kick, and two plays where their Rex Kern got away for long gains when we had him trapped."

Southern Methodist 21 NORTHWESTERN 20: SMU (2-2) star QB Chuck Hixson suffered worst aerial game of his career on 6-20/54y, TD, INT. So, Hixson did what was needed: he ran for decisive TD and 2-pt conv in 3rd Q. Early on, Hixson completed 8y toss to Mustangs WR Ray Mapps, who went high in EZ traffic to haul in 1st Q TD for 6-0 lead. Northwestern (0-3) QB Maurie Daigneau (5-12/64y, TD) pitched 20y TD pass to FB Mike Adamle to trim deficit to 13-7 in 2nd Q, but Daigneau was knocked out of next drive with bad shoulder. Soph QB Todd Somers (3-9/96y, 2 INTs) finished TD drive as Adamle scored for 14-13 Wildcats H edge. Next came Hixson's 8-pt runs, and when NU scored late in 3rd Q after Somers' 49y connection with E Jim Lash, K Bill Planisek muffed tying x-pt.

WISCONSIN 29 Penn State 16: So unaccustomed to losing was Penn State (1-2) that suddenly it couldn't stop downward trend. Nittany Lions were plagued by 6 TOs, but their D trapped Badgers (1-1-1) QB Neil Graaf 14 times for -99y. Graff (8-14/220y, 3 TDs) fired 68y TD to TE Larry Mialik (3/142y) in 2nd Q. Penn State QBs Bob Parsons and Chuck Cooper each found E Greg Edmonds with TD pass, and teams found themselves in 16-16 tie entering 4th Q. After Badgers DB Danny Crooks' INT, Graff whipped 26y TD over middle to WR Terry Whittaker and followed later with another TD bomb to Mialik.

Nebraska 35 MINNESOTA 10: Big 10, once unparalleled in outside conf play, lost its 14th straight game to Big 8 opponent as Nebraska (3-0-1) bucked 23-mph wind in 1st Q, still slammed over 3 TDs on way to 28-10 H lead. WB Johnny Rodgers capped 77y move after opening KO with 6y TD run. Minnesota (1-2) FB Ernie Cook provided brief tie with 45y TD run, but Cornhuskers countered with TB Jeff Kinney's TD run. Next Nebraska KO hung high in wind and on-rushing Gophers T Bart Buetow on receiving squad couldn't hold it; DB Joe Blaha recovered for Huskers at Minnesota 34YL. HB Joe Orduna took pitchout 3 plays later and flipped 14y TD pass to WR Guy Ingles for 21-7 Nebraska edge. Huskers QB Jerry Tagge (12-21/148y, TD) scored on 1y sneak in 2nd Q and threw TD pass to Ingles in 4th Q.

TEXAS 20 Ucla 17: Having taken possession with 46 secs remaining, Texas was behind by by 4 pts when it reached Bruins 45 YL with 20 secs to play. Longhorns (3-0) QB Eddie Phillips lofted blind pass to WR Cotton Speyrer, who jumped, split 2 defenders, and scored brilliant TD that somehow preserved Texas' 23-game win streak. Only :12 showed on clock, and DB Allen Lowry made quick INT to end it. UCLA (3-1) used 3-4 D, led by NG Tim Oesterling and LBs Phil Hendricks and Rob Scribner to hold Longhorns' dynamic triple-option ground attack reasonably in check. Bruins QB Dennis Dummit threw for 340y, including terrific 2nd H of 15-17 with TD passes of 11y each to WB Terry Vernoy and TE Bob Christiansen in 3rd Q that gave UCLA 17-13 edge. Texas had overcome early 3-0 deficit on HB Jim Bertelsen's 2y TD run early in 2nd Q. K Happy Feller kicked important 55 and 48y FGs in 2nd Q to extend Steers' lead to 13-3 at H.

KANSAS STATE 21 Colorado 20: WB Henry Hawthorne amassed 225y in total O, including 75y TD reception late in 3rd Q, and QB Lynn Dickey tossed 2 TDs and 2-pt conv to spark Wildcats (2-2). FB John Tarver scored 3 TDs for Colorado (2-1), but late decision to kick for 21-21 tie backfired as K Dave Haney missed his 1st kick in 33 tries.

Arkansas 49 TEXAS CHRISTIAN 14: Traditional SWC opener for both teams turned into something else that was becoming traditional: Arkansas (3-1) won going away for its 12th straight victory over Horned Frogs (1-2-1). Hogs rolled on long drives of 74, 80, 84, and 80y. Although, Razorbacks' TD machine, known as TB Bill Burnett (22/93y), scored on runs of 13, 4, 2, and 3y, it was QB Bill Montgomery (13-20/265y, TD, INT) who made 2 of TD trips easy with 62 and 60y bombs to WRs Chuck Dicus (6/150y) and John Rees. Pair of INTs off hard-working Texas Christian QB Steve Judy (21-44/260y, 2 TDs and 3 INTs) also made short order of 2 TD drives by Arkansas. Judy threw his TD passes in 2nd H to WR Lane Bowen (5/74y, TD) and HB Lee Harris, while TE Frankie Grimmett snared 8/82y.

Purdue 26 STANFORD 14: Apparently, no. 3 Indians (3-1) paid too much attention to upcoming USC contest and film of Purdue's dreadful loss to Notre Dame. Boilermakers (2-1) QB Chuck Piebes outshone Jim Plunkett, completing 15-20/112y. Stanford's Plunkett threw 5 INTs, 3 by to alert DB Randy Cooper. Boilermakers cruised to 16-0 H lead as WB Stan Brown scored 1st of his 2 TDs. Plunkett finally scored from 1YL midway in 3rd Q and added late 44y TD pass to HB Jackie Brown.

October 10, 1970

Duke 21 WEST VIRGINIA 13: Coach Bobby Bowden's 1st Mountaineers (4-1) team had rolled to 4 easy wins and no. 11 ranking before stumbling to Blue Devils (3-2) on Homecoming in Morgantown. Normally pass-happy Duke used ball control runs to surprise their hosts. Blue Devils soph RB Steve Jones scored twice, and soph TB Bill Thompson added key runs. WVU QB Mike Sherwood's 1st of 2 TD keepers had provided short-lived 7-0 lead in 1st Q.

Tennessee 17 GEORGIA TECH 6: Yellow Jackets (4-1) stumbled after loss of leading rusher, RB Brent Cunningham, who displaced shoulder on opening KO. Georgia Tech managed only 54y on the ground, so it had to wait for late 4th Q TD pass by QB Eddie McAshan. Tennessee (3-1) turned to its air attack as QB Bobby Scott threw TD passes to WR Joe Thompson and WB Stan Trott.

Mississippi 31 GEORGIA 21: QB Archie Manning (16-30/244y, 3 TDs, 3 INTs) rallied Ole Miss Rebels (4-0) to 17 pts in 4th Q to win going away over stubborn Bulldogs (2-2). Afterward, Manning was shielded from media by his coach Johnny Vaught who claimed visitors' dressing room was too cramped. "This'll cost Archie 18 points on his Heisman Trophy vote!" bellowed unknown sportswriter. Georgia nearly cost Mississippi even more. UGa played its best game of season in eyes of coach Vince Dooley, even though QB James Ray was knocked out early. Sr QB Mike Cavan (9-17/160y, TD, 3 INTs), long forgotten since stellar soph season, was back in form as Bulldogs fought to 14-14 deadlock at H. Ole Miss made only single 1st down in 3rd Q as Cavan flipped swing pass to FB Julian Smiley for 6y TD and 21-14 lead. Early in 4th Q, Rebels WR Floyd Franks flew by Bulldogs DB Bill Darby (INT) for perfect 52y TD bomb from Manning, QB's 2nd long scoring toss. Key play came next: Georgia snoozed while KO bounced free at its 7YL, and Ole Miss came up with REC. UGa held, but K Cloyce Hinton put Rebs ahead at 24-21, and Manning soon found his big TE, Jim Poole, for 9y TD pass.

Houston 31 MISSISSIPPI STATE 14: Blistering from previous year's 74-0 pasting, Bulldogs (3-2) scored 1st and gave Houston (2-1) tough time until Cougars rode passes of QB Gary Mullins (11-16/173y, TD) to victory. LB Joel Holliman made FUM REC to spark Mississippi State in 1st Q, and QB Joe Reed hit 4 passes before TB Lewis Grubbs powered over from 3YL for 1st of his 2 TDs. Bad x-pt snap kept score at 6-0 entering 2nd Q. Bullish Houston FB Ted Heiskell closed 63y march with 1st of his 3 TD runs on initial play of 2nd Q, but kick was missed to start series of failed 2-pt tries by Cougars. After Houston HB Tommy Mozisek raced 39y to score for 18-6 H edge, Heiskell added his 3rd TD in 3rd Q for 24-6 edge. Mullins, who was tapped late for starting assignment after missing most of 2 games with injury, matched with WR Elmo Wright to bedevil Maroons secondary. Mullins threw 4th Q TD pass to TE Riley Odoms.

Ohio State 29 MICHIGAN STATE 0: Robust Ohio State (3-0) FB John Brockington (30/126y, 2 TDs) scored after LB Stan White fell on FUM at Michigan State (1-3) 20YL in 1st Q, carried 9 plays in row on 80y TD drive in 4th Q, and also burst 25y for game's final TD. Spartans soph QB George Mikaiu (5-14/48y) lost FUM that ignited Bucks' short opening drive to Brockington's 2y blast. With Buckeyes QB Rex Kern (0-5/0y, and 11/54y rushing) bothered by recurring shoulder injury, sub QB Ron Maciejowski (5-13/51y, INT) came in to score 2 running TDs in 2nd H. Michigan State coach Duffy Daugherty said, "We don't play well, but we sure play hard." Spartans' effort held down 9-0 H score, including Ohio K Fred Schram's 33y FG, but Spartans were ineffectual on O.

IOWA 24 Wisconsin 14: Buoyed by its upset over Penn State on previous Saturday, Wisconsin (1-2-1) was stunned by winless Hawkeyes (1-3). Badgers D, so effective week earlier, "had too many people standing around and watching," according to Wisconsin coach John Jardine. Iowa TB Levi Mitchell dashed through holes for 27/146y rushing, including 4y TD burst that built 14-0 H edge. Badgers had some good moments, namely 2-TD rally—QB Neil Graff (15-20/153y, TD) ran 16y and passed 28y to TE Larry Mialik—in 3rd Q to tie it 14-14. But, Wisconsin defenders left momentum built by Graff on table. Hawks came right back on FB Tim Sullivan's 2nd TD blast as new starting QB Kyle Skogman (5-12/66y) made key toss to WR Kerry Reardon. Mitchell turned E for 56y gain that set up K Marcos Melendez's 31y FG in 4th Q.

NEBRASKA 21 Missouri 7: Tigers (3-2) were hampered by loss of star back as TB Joe Moore separated shoulder in 1st Q. Teams were tied 7-7 at H as Cornhuskers (4-0-1) QB Jerry Tagge hit workhorse TB Jeff Kinney with TD pass, and Missouri matched it with scoring plunge by QB Mike Farmer. Nebraska unleashed its big-play arsenal as HB Joe Orduna's 41y run was key play in winning 56y 4th Q drive, and WB Johnny Rodgers added clinching 48y punt TD RET.

Texas 41 Oklahoma 9 (Dallas): Sooners (2-2) surprised crowd with debut of its Wishbone attack. Sooners took 3-0 2nd Q lead on K Bruce Derr's 51y FG, but still dropped their 12th in last 13 in Red River series. Mighty Texas (4-0) sent 6 different players into EZ as 3 FUM RECs and DT Ray Dowdy's INT created easy scores. Longhorns were dealt tough loss of previous week's hero: sr WR Cotton Speyrer went out with season-ending broken arm.

AIR FORCE 24 Tulane 3: Tulane (3-2), accustomed to muggy New Orleans weather, must have been meteorologically-distracted as it bobbled away 3 FUMs that led to Airmen scores. KO temperature was pleasant 54 degrees, but wind-whipped rain turned to snow as mercury plummeted to 21 by 4th Q when Air Force (5-0) put verdict away at 24-3 on TB Brian Bream's 2nd TD run. Green Wave fell behind 14-0 at H as Air Force QB Bob Parker sneaked in 23y TD pass with 37 secs remaining in 2nd Q. Tulane stayed within 14-3 thanks to K Randy Muse's 29y FG in 3rd Q, but lost 3 key FUMs and was stopped at Falcons 6YL on downs as QB Mike Walker's EZ pass barely slipped past its mark.

Oregon 41 UCLA 40: UCLA (3-2) got 3 2nd H TD passes from star QB Dennis Dummitt and seemed comfortably in front at 40-28 in 4th Q. With time elapsing, Bruins coach Tommy Protho rested Dummitt, and Prothro's decision unleashed stunning series of events that doomed UCLA. After Oregon (3-2) QB Tom Blanchard threw 29y TD pass to HB Bobby Moore, Bruins backup QB Ron Nader lost FUM to Ducks LB Delton Lewis at Uclan 40YL. It was followed immediately by Blanchard's TD pass to Moore with 2:24 to go. Ducks gained on-side KO, and QB Dan Fouts came off bench to fire 15y TD pass on 3rd-and-14 to TE Greg Specht to propel Ducks to wild victory and 3-0 conf record. It was 2nd straight last-sec defeat for UCLA.

STANFORD 24 Southern California 14: There was bomb threat at Stanford Stadium, but only detonations came on RB Jackie Brown's pair of 4th down TDs from USC (3-1-1) 1YL. Brown's scores provided Stanford (4-1) with leads of 14-7 at H and 21-7 in 3rd Q. QB Jim Plunkett (19-31/276y) had pitched 50y TD to TE Bob Moore on Indians' 3rd possession. Stanford D line, nicknamed "Thundering Chickens" by DG Pete Lazetich, spilled Trojans' Jimmy Jones (20-37/250y, TD) 6 times. Jones managed to complete TD pass to WR Bob Chandler, despite heavy pressure. Defeat ended Trojans' 12-game win streak in series and was their 1st defeat in their last 25 regular season outings.

California 31 WASHINGTON 28: Heralded Huskies (2-2) soph QB Sonny Sixkiller (20-43/257y, 3 TDs, 4 INTs) was outshone by Golden Bears (2-3) QB Dave Penhall, who played what his coach Ray Willsey thought was "Dave's best game at Cal." Penhall isolated RB Tim Todd (3/106y, TD) on LB and found Todd wide open for 68y TD pass in 1st Q. Penhall followed with his own TD run later in 1st Q. Washington enjoyed spectacular, if fortunate, play for its 1st TD in 2nd Q: Sixkiller threw deep for WR Jim Kreig, but California S Joe Acker dove to tip pass beyond Kreig. Ball landed in hands of FB Bo Cornell, who pranced for 48y TD, 1st of Cornell's 2 scoring catches that pulled Huskies within 21-7. Kreig added 97y KO TD RET in last 36 secs of 1st H, after Cal K Randy Wersching's 44y FG and Wersching's KO that went OB. TB Stan Murphy's 2nd TD run of 2y in 3rd Q put game out of reach for Cal at 31-14.

ARIZONA STATE 37 Washington State 30: Visit to desert by Cougars (1-3) brought surprising pressure on undefeated Sun Devils (4-0). Thanks to Arizona State's 4 FUMs, 3 INTs, and muffed punt snap, Washington State was able to stand tall in O shootout with 220y passing in its 322y O arsenal. Arizona State HB Davey Buchanan (22/161y, TD) scored on 20y run early in 1st Q, but had difficulty hanging onto ball. Sub FB Brent McClanahan scored twice in 2nd Q to overcome Cougars HB Bernard Jackson's 3y TD run, so that Devils led 21-17 at H. K Don Sweet's 2nd and 3rd FGs in 3rd Q pulled Cougars within 24-23 at end of 3rd Q. Early in 4th Q, Washington State QB Ty Paine (13-24/209y, TD, 4 INTs) clicked on 58y TD pass to WR Brock Aynsley. ASU went 95y in 8 plays to 31-30 lead as Buchanan's 48y run augmented WB J.D. Hill's 3 catches from QB Joe Spaganola (14-29/233y, 2 TDs, 3 INTs). Hill caught 7y TD in heavy EZ traffic with 2:36 to play. Paine made 2 attempts to lift Wazzu back to lead, but each was met with INT, including Devils DB Windlan Hall's 65y TD RET.

AP Poll October 12

1 Ohio State (20)	731	11 Southern California	194
2 Texas (13)	712	12 Arizona State	122
3 Notre Dame (4)	666	13 Colorado	112
4 Mississippi (1)	492	14 Tennessee	90
5 Nebraska (1)	473	15 Louisiana State	53
6 Michigan (1)	383	16 Georgia Tech	19
7 Air Force	334	17 Texas Tech	17
8 Auburn	329	18 Missouri	15
9 Stanford	328	19t Houston	14
10 Arkansas	218	19t UCLA	14

October 17, 1970

PITTSBURGH 36 West Virginia 35: Annual "Backyard Brawl" was all West Virginia (4-2) in 1st H as drives of 66, 67, 69, 59, 85y, and FB Eddie Williams' 3 TD runs materialized as 35-8 lead. Panthers never quit their power run strategy, rallied for quartet of 2nd H TD drives behind running of RBs Dennis Ferris, Dave Garrett, and Tony Esposito, each of whom scored. Key to Pitt comeback was QB Dave Halvern's pair of 2-pt passes to TE Joel Klimek and tenacious D, led by DL Lloyd Weston and LB Ralph Cindrich. Mountaineers earned only 3 1st downs in 2nd H.

WAKE FOREST 36 Clemson 20: FB Larry Hopkins set new ACC rushing mark on 20/230y as revived Wake Forest (3-3) won 3rd straight game. Demon Deacons rushed for school record 441y as Hopkins credited OL, led by G Bill Bobbora, T Vince Nedimyer, and C Nick Vrhovac. Wake jumped to 19-0 lead in building 232y to 26y rushing advantage. QB Larry Russell (18/94y running) scored twice in 1st H, including 2nd Q TD set up by his brilliant 62y weaving sprint on 3rd-and-20 from own 10YL. Clemson (2-4) had nothing to cheer about until DB Don Kelley cut back from his right and motored 67y to score on 4th Q punt RET. Hopkins quickly replied with 50y dash and took pitchout 10y to score. Hopkins later raced for 44y TD. Tigers now had allowed 146 pts in 4 losses in row.

TENNESSEE 24 Alabama 0: For 1st time in 115 games, Alabama (3-3) was shut out. Ruination for Crimson Tide came by way of 8 INTs, 1 of which was returned 22y for TD by Volunteers LB Jackie Walker. Vols DB Tim Priest also picked off 3 passes. Tennessee (4-1) TD scorers who helped young coach Bill Battle beat mentor Bear Bryant were QB Bobby Scott and TB Don McLeary. Tide E David Bailey maneuvered himself loose to catch 12/150y, but injured QB Scott Hunter threw 5 INTs.

AUBURN 31 Georgia Tech 7: Tigers (5-0) remained unbeaten behind emerging star QB Pat Sullivan. Sullivan was brilliant against solid Georgia Tech (4-2) D, completing 16-19/312y, 2 TDs. He added 7/42y, TD rushing. Engineers hung close at 14-7 at H on QB Jack Williams' TD pass to TE Steve Norris after he kept drive alive with 4th down throw.

Southern Mississippi 30 MISSISSIPPI 14: Facing opponent beaten by 62 pts in 1969, no. 4 Rebels (4-1) had reason for confidence. But, game played out as shocker. Southern Miss (4-2) outrushed Rebels 205y to 85y and neutralized Ole Miss QB Archie Manning with booming punts of P Ray Guy (49y avg). Manning whipped 2 TD passes for 14-7 1st Q lead, but Eagles caught fire in middle Qs. HB Willie Heidelburg scored twice from 11YL, and HB Gerry Saggus ambled 60y for punt TD RET. Disaster hit both schools following week: Rebel coach Johnny Vaught was hospitalized with circulatory problems, Eagles were walloped 51-15 by Mississippi State.

MICHIGAN 34 Michigan State 20: In 13-13 1st H deadlock, Spartans (1-4) line, led by G Joe DeLamieleure, sprung TB Eric Allen (23/156y) for 42y TD run and 38y sprint to set up 1st of 2 FGs by K Borys Shiapak. Michigan (5-0) O, outshining its vaunted D, employed former FB Billy Taylor (29/149y, 3 TDs) at TB and former TB Glenn Doughty (8/85y, TD rushing, 5/68y receiving) at WB in new, but spectacular spots. After 2nd H KO, QB Don Moorhead (12-19/156y, TD, INT) pitched 20y pass to Doughty to State 31YL and handed ball to Taylor 7 straight plays until TB had his 3rd score for 20-13 edge. QB George Miahiu suffered Spartans' only TO right after ensuing KO when Michigan DB Tom Darden ran back INT 18y to 31YL. FB Fritz Seyforth stumbled over GL with 8y TD pass on 4th down to build 27-13 edge for ravenous Wolverines, who gained 460y.

Notre Dame 24 MISSOURI 7: Who made Missouri (3-3) schedule Fighting Irish (5-0) just week after Nebraska? ND pounded out 280y rushing, but QB Joe Theismann (15-24/209y, 2TDs) put his stamp on Heisman race by leading 3 consecutive 2nd H TD drives to ice Tigers. Irish E Tom Gatewood (8/123y, TD) set up each of ND's 3 TDs, including his own. Missouri coach Dan Devine marveled at his banged troops, who were shorthanded 7 starters, including all 3 1st-team LBs: "I had no idea we could play this well." Mizzou earned 7-3 H lead after Irish P Jim Yoder sliced 19y punt. Tigers FB James Harrison's 41y charge to Irish 11YL was soon followed by QB Mike Farmer's 6y TD pass to WR Mel Gray, who squirted out of DB Clarence Ellis' tackle. Mizzou DB Henry Stuckey tipped pass for INT and wrapped his arms around FUM and INT in 1st H.

Arizona State 27 BRIGHAM YOUNG 3: Explosive Sun Devils (5-0) proved ability to score from anywhere on field at anytime. WR Steve Holden turned in 94y punt TD RET, DB Windlan Hall scored on 29y INT RET, and WR J.D. Hill added 69y TD on reverse run. Until 2nd Q, BYU (1-5) had stayed close at 7-3 on K Joe Liljenquist's FG.

Ucla 24 CALIFORNIA 21: Golden Bears (2-4) picked off 2 passes by UCLA (4-2) QB Dennis Dummit (25-51/316y, TD, 3 INTs) in 4th Q after Cal QB Dave Penhall completed 58y TD pass to WR Geoff DeLapp on last play of 3rd Q for 21-18 lead. But, Dummit had 1 more chance made possible by 85y drive on 4th down pass interference PEN. It was called on Bears DB Dave Lawson, in for injured DB Ray Youngblood, when he tangled with Bruins WB Brad Lyman at 9YL with 23 secs left. Dummit dashed 3y for right corner of EZ and game-winning TD with :04 on clock. Earlier, Cal led most of way as Penhall opened with TD pass to FB Tim Todd in 1st Q, and when UCLA's D had 5y offside PEN on 3rd-and-6 at their 10YL, it magically turned into 1st down, waiting for Todd's TD plunge.

AP Poll October 19

1 Ohio State (19)	668	11 Tennessee	153
2 Texas (9)	630	12 Arizona State	147
3 Notre Dame (4)	585	13 Mississippi	140
4 Nebraska (1)	477	14 Louisiana State	73
5 Michigan (1)	387	15 Houston	48
6 Auburn (1)	355	16 UCLA	26
7 Air Force (1)	354	17 San Diego State	16
8 Stanford	316	18 Pittsburgh	10
9 Arkansas	224	19t Colorado	8
10 Southern California	184	19t Toledo	8

October 24, 1970

North Carolina State 6 Maryland 0 (Norfolk): Oyster Bowl's 24th match-up found hard-luck Maryland (1-6) knocking at victory's door, trailing 6-0, with less than 3 mins to play. Terps soph HB Art Seymore (36/156y) charged at LG from 3YL, but officials ruled that he lost controversial FUM at North Carolina State (2-4-1) 1-ft line. REC was credited to Wolfpack NG George Smith, but officials scurried from stadium without stopping at their dressing room where media could query them. Maryland DT Pete Mattia ended Wolfpack's only TD threat by swiping ball from HB Butch Altman at 1YL in 2nd Q. K Mike Charron made 35y FG late in 2nd Q and bombed through 40y FG on last play of 3rd Q for all of NC State's pts.

WAKE FOREST 14 North Carolina 13: FB Larry Hopkins burst for 39y run, then scored 3y TD with 3:01 left to boost Deacons (4-3) past ACC favorite North Carolina (4-3). K Tracy Lounsberry's conv kick that followed was difference in game. Wake Forest rushing D concentrated on and fairly well contained star Tar Heels TB Don McCauley (31/125y), but he managed 2nd Q TD on 4y run. After E Tony Blanchard's 27y TD catch in 3rd Q, Tar Heels botched conv kick. Upset victory played huge role in propelling Deacons to their 1st and only ACC championship.

Louisiana State 17 AUBURN 9: Bayou Bengals (5-1) snatched SEC lead with bruising upset of high-flying Auburn (5-1). LSU scored for 15-6 H lead on QB Buddy Lee's 11y TD pass to WR Andy Hamilton and TB Art Cantrell's short TD plunge. Plainsmen entered game with 35 pt scoring avg, but could manage only 3 FGs by K Gardner Jett. LSU LB Mike Anderson preserved victory in 4th Q with 4th down stop of Auburn RB Wallace Clark at 1YL.

Ohio State 48 ILLINOIS 29: On Friday, Illinois (2-4) coach Jim Valek was fired but allowed to administer this game. Inspired Illini led no. 1 Ohio State 20-14 at H and 23-21 in 3rd Q. Illini HB Darrell Robinson rushed 43/187y, TD, and TE Doug Dieken caught 2 TD passes from QB Mike Wells (11-19/123y, 2 TDs, INT). Buckeye QB Rex Kern passed 11-15/123y, 2 TDs, INT and rushed 8/92y, including 76y TD dash in 2nd Q. Ohio FB John Brockington (21/76y) scored 3 times including 2nd H TDs that provided 27-23 and 34-23 leads. Post-game player revolt postponed Valek's firing until his contract was fulfilled at season's end. Buckeyes' win over fired-up foe failed to impress voters, and Ohio State tumbled from no. 1 as Texas boiled Rice 45-21.

MICHIGAN 39 Minnesota 13: In decade of 1970s, only 4 teams would finish ahead of either Michigan or Ohio State in any season's Big 10 standings. Coach Murray Warmath of Minnesota's overmatched Golden Gophers (2-4) spoke for conf's fast-submerging "Little Eight" when he said after game that "when they had the ball, they

237

could move. When we had it, we couldn't." Michigan (6-0) outgained Minnesota 518y to 283y and sent walk-on FB Fritz Seyferth (18/76y) powering for 4 short TDs. Wolverines TB Billy Taylor (26/151y) followed sharp blocks of Seyferth, G Reggie McKenzie, Ts Jack Harpring and Dan Dierdorf, and TE Paul Seymour to his rushing leadership. Michigan QB Don Moorhead (7-18/104y) made 39y sprint to poise Seyferth for his 4y TD late in 2nd Q for 18-7 lead. On previous series in 2nd Q, Minnesota TE Doug Kingsriter made pair of spectacular catches of 45 and 16y from QB Craig Curry (16-37/214y, TD, 3 INTs), latter for 1-handed TD grab.

NORTHWESTERN 38 Purdue 14: Surprising Northwestern (3-3) found itself tied atop Big 10 at 3-0 after thumping Purdue (3-3). Wildcats O enjoyed 464y to 206y advantage as it rode back of pint-sized FB Mike Adamle (39/154y, TD). Adamle also flipped 2 pass completions, including 26y TD to TE Jerry Brown to open 21-pt 2nd Q. Wildcats secondary stole 6 passes, 3 by DB Jack Dustin, who ran for 35y INT TD RET. Purdue led briefly at 7-6 on WB Stan Brown's 1y run in 2nd Q, but didn't score again until sub QB Gary Danielson (4-13/73y, TD, 4 INTs) pitched 23y TD to TE Ashley Bell to vainly trim margin to 35-14.

KANSAS STATE 19 OKLAHOMA 14: Kansas State (4-3) QB Lynn Dickey (27-46/384y, 2 TDs, 3 INTs) sparked 2-TD rally in last 4 mins for win over Oklahoma (3-3). It was Wildcats' 2nd in row and 11th victory over Sooners in 56 tries since 1908. Dickey completed 38y TD pass to WB Henry Hawthorne for 7-0 1st Q lead. Then, Oklahoma roared back on strength of running by Joe Wylie (23/133y, 2 TDs), who made 2 and 60y TD runs in 2nd Q for 14-7 lead at H. Wylie's 1st TD came on 12y sail after K-State returner Ron Coppenberger lost ball in sun and allowed it to bounce into him for REC by OU WR Everett Marshall. P Wylie boomed his 2nd very long punt, this of 67y, to Wildcats 17YL with 6:44 showing on 4th Q clock. After facemask PEN against Oklahoma on 3rd down from K-State 10YL gave drive its life, Dickey hit passes of 12, 18, 5, and 26y before HB Bill Butler dribbled ball into EZ where Cats WR Rick Fergerson recovered for TD. But, Sooners blocked x-pt and still led 14-13. State CB Clarence Scott, covering OU's fine WR Jon Harrison, soon tipped pass by Sooners QB Jack Mildren into arms of Wildcats LB Oscar Gibson at 30YL. With 3:03 to play, Hawthorne (6/138y, 2 TDs) won it, grabbing 28y TD pass from Dickey, his Big 8 career-record, to-date 26th TD throw.

AIR FORCE 35 Boston College 10: Air Force (7-0) came from behind to post best start in its history. Passing combination of QB Bob Parker (16-34/186y, 3 TDs, INT) and WR Ernie Jennings (8/80y) struck for 3 TDs. HB Fred Willis (18/86y, TD) zipped up middle on trap block and sped 55y for TD that gave Eagles (3-2) 10-7 lead in 1st Q. With 5:59 before H, Falcons regained lead at 14-10 as TB Brian Bream (32/150y, TD), injured on previous series, returned to crash over RT for 3y TD. From that point, Boston College D shut down Air Force and its O threatened often, only to be frustrated when Flyboy's maligned secondary came up with INTs of BC QB Frank "Red" Harris (21-37/195y, 4 INTs). Air Force's 3rd INT of 3rd Q, by DB Jimmy Smith, was returned 28y to Eagles 30YL, and Jennings' 2nd TD catch in last min of 3rd Q built 21-10 lead. BC wasn't broken until Smith's 90y INT TD RET in 4th Q, but Eagles were left fuming when Falcons tried to impress 4 bowl scouts with Jennings' 3rd TD catch (his 14th of season), which came on game's last play from 1YL.

OREGON 10 Southern California 7: Heavy rain and wind greeted USC (4-2-1) in Eugene, but weather couldn't stop Oregon (5-2) TB Bobby Moore (later known as Ahmad Rashad), who rushed school record 38 times/168y and TD in 4th Q. Trojans took 7-0 lead in 1st Q on 1y dive by FB Sam "Bam" Cunningham. Ducks LB Tom Graham made amazing 30 tackles as Oregon swept L.A. schools for 1st time since 1957, just 2nd time to date.

Stanford 9 UCLA 7: Prevented from throwing TD pass for 1st time in his Stanford (6-1) career, QB Jim Plunkett still managed key play in 4th Q: 42y 3rd down strike to WR Randy "The Rabbit" Vataha that allowed K Steve Horowitz's winning 30y FG. UCLA (4-3) got its TD in 3rd Q from TB Marv Kendricks after DL Craig Campbell fell on pitchout FUM by Indians FB Hillary Shockley at Tribe 15YL. Stanford D surrendered only 25y rushing and posted 5 sacks in completing its 1st sweep of USC and UCLA since 1957. L.A. Coliseum crowd at 83,518 was UCLA's largest to see any foe other than USC since 1947.

October 31, 1970

DARTMOUTH 10 YALE 0: Coach Bob Blackman's final Dartmouth squad was perhaps his finest as it breezed to Ivy title, Blackman's 7th in 16 years. Indians (6-0) finished 1970 season 9-0, including 6 shutouts, to become final Ivy team to win Lambert Trophy, symbolic of Eastern supremacy and last Ivy squad to finish in AP Top 20 (14th at season's end). Dartmouth rolled up 480y O, held star Bulldogs (5-1) RB Dick Jauron, nation's no. 5 rusher, to 17/50y. Big Green spent all afternoon marching up and down hallowed turf of Yale Bowl, but 5 times they failed to score from inside Yale 18YL. Dartmouth overcame 3 INTs and FUM from close range before HB Brendan O'Neill (77y rushing) made 3y TD run before H. Eli pick-off artists of Indians QB Jim Chasey (18-29/237y, 4 INTs) included DB Dave Holahan's 2 INTs in EZ. Big Green K Wayne Pirman, rushed by air in time for 2nd H from Saturday morning soccer game in Hanover, N.H., kicked 30y FG in 3rd Q.

BOSTON COLLEGE 21 Army 13: To this point in 10-game series between Eastern rivals, Boston College (4-2) had never defeated Army Cadets (1-7), and 1st H looked like more of same. K Arden Jensen sandwiched FGs of 27 and 36y around 11y TD burst up middle by Army RB Bill Roden, so Black Knights ran off at H with 13-0 lead. Eagles QB Frank Harris, who had miserable 1-6 passing stats in 1st H, was whole new man after H intermission with 12-13 accuracy. Harris led 78y march right after 2nd H KO, but BC had to relinquish ball at Army 2YL. But, next time BC took over, it went 58y to 1y TD push by Harris (13-19/145y, TD, 2 INTs). Early in 4th Q, Boston College got break on 4y punt by Cadets P Ron Danhof (6/35y avg) and took its 1st lead at 14-13 on WR John Bonistalli's 21y TD grab. Eagles wrapped it up with 60y drive to Harris' 10y bootleg TD.

SYRACUSE 43 Pittsburgh 13: After weathering turbulent, racially-torn September, Orangemen (4-3) gained 4th straight win in October's month of orange. Former starting QB Randy Zur, broken ribs now healed, came off Syracuse bench to lead 5 scoring drives during 2nd and 3rd Qs to damage bowl hopes of no. 15 Pittsburgh (5-2). Zur pitched 2 TD passes, with TB Roger Praetorius and sub E Dave Boyer on receiving end, and ran 7 and 10y for scores. Panthers holder Tom Hasbach missed snap on 41y FG try in 2nd Q, which cost Pitt 27y and opened Orange floodgates. Pitt RB Dennis Ferris caught TD pass from QB John Hogan to keep Panthers within 19-7 at H.

OHIO STATE 24 Northwestern 10: Hopeful Wildcats (3-4) got 1st Q TD from FB Mike Adamle (32/122y) as he piled up 102y in 1st H. Northwestern led 10-3 at H. Coach Woody Hayes scrapped balanced Buckeyes O, permitting only 2 passes in 2nd H and directing 30 rushes by FB John Brockington (42/161y, TD). Key was DL Jim Stillwagon's 3rd Q REC of Wildcats QB Maurie Daigneau's FUM of C snap at NW 18YL. Daigneau accepted blame and Northwestern coach Alex Agase shook his head over the fumble afterward: "It was a crucial part of the game." Ohio State QB Rex Kern (15/74y rushing) overcame 3 INTs—2 by Wildcats DB Rick Telander, future Sports Illustrated writer—in 2nd Q to score 2 TDs on ground in 2nd H.

TOLEDO 14 Miami (Ohio) 13: Toledo (8-0) won its 19th consecutive game, clinching 2nd straight MAC title, but not before hard-working Miami (5-2) allowed just 50/98y rushing, cashed 3rd Q break for 10-7 lead. On punt from midfield, Redskins DL Fred Brisker fell on loose ball in EZ after mixup at 5YL allowed punt to carom off back of Rockets returner Jim Banks. Toledo QB Chuck Ealey (17-25/167y, TD) hit passes of 11, 8, 12, and 5y, then skirted E for winning 3y TD with 2:44 left.

Oklahoma 29 IOWA STATE 28: QB Dean Carlson (11-25/227y, 2 TDs, 4 INTs) picked apart Oklahoma (4-3) secondary as Iowa State (3-4) jumped to 21-0 lead in 1st Q. Carlson threw 38y TD pass to WR Mike Palmer and ran across for 2 scores. HB Joe Wylie punched across TD for Sooners in 2nd Q to add to safety that pulled them within 21-9 at H. OU gained only 133y rushing in 1st H, but it got back in game on QB Jack Mildren's 75y TD bomb to WR Willie Franklin in 3rd Q. Wylie scored again early in 4th Q, but Oklahoma missed x-pt kicks on each of its 2nd H TDs and were in 21-21 deadlock. Cyclones came back on Carlson's 70y TD pass and 28-21 lead with 4:29 left. Sooners answered with 37y pass, caught by TE Al Chandler to Iowa State 15YL. Wylie scored his 3rd TD 3 plays later, and TB Greg Pruitt ran for winning 2-pt conv with 2 mins left.

KANSAS STATE 17 Missouri 13: Winning its 3rd game in row, Kansas State (5-3) beat Tigers (4-4) at home for 1st time since 1938. Dominating much of last 3 Qs, Missouri came from behind after Wildcats jumped to 10-0 lead on TE-K John Goerger's 23y FG and QB Lynn Dickey's 33y TD arrow to WR Mike Creed. K-State appeared ready to take 17-0 lead early in 2nd Q, but Tigers DB Henry Stuckey made INT at his 4YL and returned to 30YL. Another INT of Dickey, authored by Mizzou DB Pete Buha, went 38y down sideline to Wildcats 2YL and set up QB Chuck Roper for 6-inch TD sneak. Missouri K Jack Bastable tied it in 3rd Q on 25y FG and put Tigers ahead 13-10 on masterful 38y FG against wind past midway in 4th Q. With 4:07 left, Dickey (13-33/234y, 2 TDs, 4 INTs) rallied his Purple Cats for 70y in 10 plays, his decisive TD pass coming on 20y pitch over middle to Creed.

Nebraska 29 COLORADO 13: Giddy crowd, largest sports gathering to date in Rocky Mountain region, got slapped into 1st Q reality by 2 TD passes from Nebraska (7-0-1) QB Van Brownson to WB Guy Ingles. Rebounding, Colorado (3-4) pulled to within 15-13 on QB Jimmy Bratton's 5y TD run in 4th Q, but missed 2-pt run. Nebraska IB Jeff Kinney then stepped forward. Kinney roared 76y on KO RET to position Cornhuskers' 21y TD drive for 22-13 lead. FUM REC at Buff 40YL by Huskers DL Larry Jacobsen promptly set stage for Kinney's clinching TD run.

SAN DIEGO STATE 56 Fresno State 14: Aztecs (7-0) crushed Fresno State (6-2) as QB Brian Sipe tossed 3 TD passes. Coach Don Coryell's team would run unbeaten streak to 21 games before losing year's final 2 games, to Long Beach and Iowa State.

November 7, 1970

Louisiana State 14 ALABAMA 9: National top-ranked run D of LSU (6-1) shut down Alabama (5-4) star RB Johnny Musso, holding Crimson Tide's "Italian Stallion" to 44y rushing. Tigers D had to make up for sloppy O that wasted numerous opportunities. TB Art Cantrelle's 2y TD run provided LSU with 6-3 H lead, and Bengals' clinching pts came on QB Buddy Lee's 2y TD pass to WR Jimmy Ledoux.

Florida 24 Georgia 17 (Jacksonville): Georgia (4-4) sub QB Paul Gilbert started his 1st game in relief of injured Mike Cavan. Gilbert spiced opening ground-oriented TD drive, capped by TB Ricky Lake's TD leap, when QB tossed 15y pass to WR Rex Putnal. Bulldogs D held surprising run strategy of Florida (6-3) in check in 7-3 1st H. After Georgia went up 10-3 early in 3rd Q, Gators finally took shackles off QB John Reaves (9-14/156y, 2 TDs), who completed passes of 20, 22, and 8y to gimpy WR Carlos "The Cuban Comet" Alvarez, and soon it was deadlocked at 10-10. Trailing 17-10 early in 4th Q, Florida found itself defending at own 2YL. Bulldogs FB Robert Honeycutt bobbled pitchout, and Gators DE Jack Youngblood went for ball and blasted it free to end threat and turn affair in Florida's favor. Reaves found Alvarez (5/135y, 2 TDs) splitting 2-man coverage for tying 32y TD pass, and after Florida held at own 38YL, Reaves won it on 48y TD arrow to Alvarez, who got clearing block from WR Willie Jackson.

MISSISSIPPI 24 Houston 13: QB Archie Manning (14-25 passing) clicked on 2 TD passes in 1st Q, and all seemed right in Rebels (6-1) camp, even though FB Robert Newhouse blasted for 12y TD to keep Houston (3-3) within 14-7 at H. Cougars LB Charlie Hall made pass rush hit in 3rd Q and fractured Manning's left (non-throwing) forearm. With Manning sidelined apparently for season, Ole Miss future grew cloudy. Rebs O stalled with sub QB Shug Chumbler, but he managed TD pass to brighten 4th Q.

LOUISVILLE 40 Memphis State 27: Picked for last in preseason Mo Valley Conf coaches poll, upstart Louisville (5-3) won conf title with upset of Memphis State (4-3), team that had beaten it by 50 pts in 1969. Trailing 7-0, coach Lee Corso's Cards got flying on DB Greg Campbell's 96y punt TD RET in 1st Q. Louisville soph QB John Madeya ran for 2 TDs and his 25y TD pass gave Cards first lead at 13-7. LB Tom Jackson soon created FUM that led to FB Tom Jesukaitis and 20-7 H lead. Tigers edged within 27-20 and 34-27 in 2nd H on short TD runs by HB Jay McCoy and QB Rick Strawbridge. Jesukaitis clinched it with 3y TD run with 1:30 left after DB Paul Mattingly's INT.

NORTHWESTERN 28 Minnesota 14: Wildcat FB Mike Adamle set Big 10 record with 48 rushes in gaining 192y. Adamle scored all 4 TDs for Northwestern (4-4), but not before tough Golden Gophers (2-5-1) popped out for early 14-0 lead. Only 3:10 into 1st Q, Minnesota DB Jeff Wright carried blocked punt 35y to TD. QB Craig Curry closed 1st Q with 4y TD run at end of 77y Gopher TD drive. Adamle scored on 1y blast in 2nd Q, so NW trailed 14-7 at H. Wildcats opened 2nd H wirh good drive, but Minny DB Walt Bowser spoiled it with EZ INT. On its next series, Northwestern went 80y and really cranked up Adamle, who carried on 11 of 14 plays. Wildcats QB Maury Daigneau (7-19/129y, 3 INTs) opened go-ahead drive from own 23YL with 19y pass to TE Tom McCreight, but Adamle toted on 8 of next 10 plays for 1y TD and 21-14 lead. Adamle finished his day with 5y TD with 1:05 remaining.

Michigan 29 WISCONSIN 15: Record crowd packed camp Randall Stadium on Homecoming Saturday as Wisconsin (2-4-1) sought big upset and shot at winning season after 3 years with 3 wins. Hitting 9 of his 1st 12 passes and tossing in effective scrambling runs, QB Neil Graff (11-23/168y, TD, INT) kept Badgers from falling out of it with 77y TD trip that just barely beat H clock. FB Alan Thompson caught Graff's 17y TD pass to pull Badgers to within 21-6. Michigan (7-0), forced to throw ball by Wisconsin's 9-man front, did just that. After Michigan S Jim Betts recovered FUM at Badgers 32YL in 1st Q, QB Don Moorhead (11-22/223y, 2 TDs) hit WR Paul Staroba (6/178y, TD) for 19y and soon followed with 8y TD pass to FB Fritz Seyferth. Moorhead's 70y bomb to Staroba carried to 3YL in 2nd Q for Seyferth to slam it across. Wisconsin DB Danny Crooks broke Jug Girard's 12-year-old long-distance punt RET record by racing 87y up sideline followed later in 3rd Q by K Roger Jaeger's 32y FG to nip deficit to 21-15. Poor field position and Graff's passing hand turning cold (0-9) ruined 4th QW chances for Badgers, and Moorhead capped 54y drive with perfect 31y TD toss to Staroba.

Texas 21 BAYLOR 14: Winning their 27th game in row, Longhorns (7-0) remained perfect, but not without struggle. FB Steve Worster (25/97y) scored twice as Texas built 21-7 H lead. Then Baylor (2-6) D took command, completely shutting down Steers' Wishbone attack, and scoring sole TD of 2nd H on DL Ray Penn's blocked punt RET. Earlier, Bears QB Si Southall (5-15/111y, TD, INT) pitched 73y TD pass to WR Derek Davis (4/197y, TD) and had 76y TD throw nullified.

TEXAS TECH 22 Texas Christian 14: Red Raiders (7-2) stayed alive in SWC race with clutch 2nd H play to overcome stubborn TCU (3-4-1). Texas Tech TE Robbie Best, alone in Frogs secondary on Raiders' 1st scrimmage play, dropped pass, but he scored later on 35y TD pass from QB Charles Napper (9-18/145y, 2 TDs) in 1st Q. Texas Tech led 10-0 in 2nd Q when TCU QB Steve Judy, who had erratic day after sustaining ankle injury in 1st Q, threw 35y TD pass to sideline-slanting WR Lane Bowen. Slender, but quick HB Raymond Rhodes (22/155y, TD) gave Horned Frogs 14-10 H lead with breathtaking 22y TD dash through bewildered Tech secondary. Napper put Raiders ahead 16-14 with 3rd Q TD pass, but Judy cranked up TCU attack to try to overcome 19-14 deficit with less than 6 mins to play. On 3rd-and-1 at Tech 6YL, Judy ran keeper, but fumbled away to LB Larry Molinare at 4YL. Raiders used rugged RB Doug McCutchen, who rushed to within 2y of school mark with 32/204y, to bludgeon to K Dickie Ingram's clinching 3rd FG with 1:16 left.

OREGON 46 Air Force 35: Oregon soph QB Dan Fouts gave glimpse of future glory, completing 28-43/396y, 4 TDs as improving Ducks (6-3) knocked Air Force (8-1) from unbeaten ranks. Falcons TB Brian Bream maintained his national scoring lead with 3 TDs, while prolific passing combo of QB Bob Parker and WR Ernie Jennings clicked for 2 more scores.

STANFORD 29 Washington 22: Joyous Indians (8-1) clinched their 1st Rose Bowl berth in 19 years as QB Jim Plunkett overcame up-and-down day to fire 22-36/268y, 4 TDs, to break Steve Ramsey's NCAA career y record. Washington (4-4) WR Jim Krieg had charged 95y with opening KO for shocking 7-0 lead. Huskies QB Sonny Sixkiller (18-41/158y) threw TD pass in 2nd Q and scored on 9y run late in 3rd Q. After his TD run, Sixkiller hit TE Ace Bulger with 2-pt pass for 22-21 lead. Plunkett hit 3 passes on winning 78y drive midway in 4th Q, including 15y curl-in TD to WR Randy Vataha.

November 14, 1970

Georgia 31 AUBURN 17: Erratic Bulldogs (5-4) combined spirited D with strong rushing—longtime staples of coach Vince Dooley—to upset Auburn (7-2). Georgia TB Ricky Lake used fine blocking for 96y, 2 TDs, rushing, while DLs Royce Smith and Tom Nash excelled to shut out Auburn in 2nd H. Tigers QB Pat Sullivan had accounted for 205y O in 1st H for 17-14 lead. But Sullivan was contained in 2nd H as K Jim Braswell's 13th FG of year tied it at 17-17 for Bulldogs until Lake put Georgia ahead for good.

Ohio State 10 PURDUE 7: Stressed Buckeyes (8-0) survived another close call and tumbled to no. 5 in AP poll. Game's 2 teams were within 12 secs of each other. Ohio FB John Brockington (24/136y) accounted for entire 62y drive in 3 runs in 1st Q, his 26y TD run turned trick. Purdue (3-6) WB Stan Brown followed with a 96y KO TD RET, 4th TD runback of his career. Buckeyes' star-studded D, led by DL Jim Stillwagon, DBs Jack Tatum and Mike Sensibaugh, held Boilers to 3 1st downs, even though Purdue D, led by DLs Rick Tekavec and Steve Nurrenbern and DB Randy Cooper, gave it possession across midfield 7 times. Boilermakers blocked 2 punts and recovered 2 FUMs, but could make no headway against Buckeye D. When Ohio took over at own 23YL with 4 mins left, it took scrambling run of 23y and option run of 7y by sub QB Ron Maciejowski to set up K Fred Schram's winning 30y FG with 2:04 to go.

NOTRE DAME 10 Georgia Tech 7: Fighting Irish (8-0) gained 448y but repeatedly were denied EZ by Yellow Jackets (7-3). After scoreless 1st H, Georgia Tech QB Eddie McAshan overcame 3-0 3rd Q deficit with 66y TD bomb to WR Larry Studdard. Winning Fighting Irish TD finally came on 2y run by RB Denny Allen with 6:28 to go. It capped 7-play, 80y drive that was launched by HB Ed Gulyas' 46y pass reception, thrown against stiff wind by QB Joe Theismann (15-30/272y, 2 INTs).

Iowa State 31 MISSOURI 19: Struggling Missouri (4-6) was assured of coach Dan Devine's 1st losing season in 13 years at Columbia. Big soph QB George Amundson (14/135y, 3 TDs rushing) came off bench in 2nd H as Iowa State (4-5) coach Johnny Majors smartly switched away from erratic passer, QB Dean Carlson (8-21/100y, INT, and TD rushing), to start 2nd H's O against stiff wind. Amundson raced 77y to score on 4th play of 3rd Q to propel Cyclones past H deficit of 12-10. Amundson sneaked over for 24-12 edge after E Tom Lorenz made diving grab at Mizzou 1YL. Tigers, who had scored with ease in 1st Q on 24 and 23y TD runs by HB Bill Mauser (23/106y), had another effortless TD trip late in 3rd Q. Missouri's 72y march was aided by WR Mel Gray's only catch, worth 22y. But, Amundson answered with 33y, late-game TD sprint. Tigers rushed for 328y, including 123y by FB James Harrison, but lost partly because they went too often to inconsistent air attack of QB Chuck Roper (12-26/133y, 2 INTs).

NEBRASKA 51 Kansas State 13: With 3 major bowl reps watching, Nebraska's awesome weaponry was unleashed, although Kansas State (6-4) trailed in O only 361y to 325y. Difference was 7 INTs stolen from K-State QB Lynn Dickey (22-39/255y, TD) by Cornhuskers (9-0-1) D. DB Joe Blahak grabbed 3 INTs, and DB Dave Morock took another 43y for TD. Elusive Huskers HB Joe Orduna (27/105y) topped scoring with 4 TDs. TOs set up WB Johnny Rodgers' 30y TD run and half of Orduna's TDs. QB Jerry Tagge (13-19/162y, TD, INT) threw screen pass that brilliant Rodgers took 60y to place K Paul Rogers in position for 23y FG. Wildcats RB Mike Montgomery scored on 9y pass from Dickey in 2nd Q, and, when K-State trailed only 21-7, Montgomery went for pass at 2YL, but back judge Wayne Cooley failed to call what might have been pass interference. Frustrated Montgomery was banished for shoving Cooley.

ARKANSAS 36 Southern Methodist 3: Steady Arkansas (8-1) remained tied atop SWC with rout of TO-plagued Mustangs (4-5). SMU QB Gary Carter was highly taxed by Porker D in throwing SWC-record 8 INTs in relief of injured Chuck Hixson. Arkansas QB Bill Montgomery excelled (21-35/327y, 2 TDs). Arkansas K Bill McClard booted 29 and 37y FGs and, in 2nd Q, nailed 60y FG, new NCAA record for distance that broke year-old 59y FG of Mississippi K Cloyce Hinton.

AIR FORCE 31 Stanford 14: Frigid mountain air seemed to affect Stanford (8-2), accustomed to mild weather, more than acclimatized Falcons. Undaunted in facing 4th down situations, cool Air Force (9-1) QB Bob Parker (229y passing) pitched 3 TD passes to WR Ernie Jennings. Passes of Stanford QB Jim Plunkett (17-35/182y) positioned FB Hillary Shockley for 2 TD runs, but Parker found Jennings on 1y TD pass

239

on 4th down for 17-14 lead late in 3rd Q. Indian K Steve Horowitz missed tying 37y FG after 15y holding PEN pushed him back. Parker followed with another 4th down pitch (19y) and then another to Jennings to set up TB Brian Bream's cinching TD from 1YL.

ARIZONA STATE 37 Utah 14: Avenging 1969 upset loss to Utah, Sun Devils (8-0) piled up 526y for their 14th straight win. Arizona State WB J.D. Hill switched to WR and snared 7/110y, 34y TD from QB Joe Spagnola (17-28/242y, 2 TDs, INT), and HB Bobby Thomas rushed 15/110y, TD as Utah (5-4) was routed. Utes enjoyed brief 7-0 lead when HB Gene Belczyk bolted 59y to score in 1st Q. But that was shortlived as Devils quickly solved Redskins D, that hadn't allowed TD in their last 3 games, for 17 pts in 2nd Q. Soph WB Steve Holden was in Arizona State lineup only because Hill vacated spot to fill in for injured WR Ed Beverly, and Holden raced 73y on punt TD RET in 2nd Q while adding 4/42y receiving.

AP Poll November 16

1 Texas (26)	816	11 Stanford	206
2 Notre Dame (7)	705	12 Mississippi	126
3 Nebraska (5)	694	13 Auburn	119
4 Michigan (6)	682	14 San Diego State	73
5 Ohio State (1)	643	15 Toledo	71
6 Arkansas	413	16 Dartmouth	68
7 Louisiana State	399	17 Georgia Tech	39
8 Tennessee	324	18 Northwestern	20
9 Arizona State (1)	231	19 Texas Tech	19
10 Air Force	209	20 Penn State	16

November 21, 1970

Penn State 35 PITTSBURGH 15: Scoring all its 35 pts in 1st H, Penn State (7-3) cruised over rival Panthers (5-5). Nittany Lions led after 23 secs as Pitt RB Dennis Ferris lost ball on game's 1st snap. Penn State DB George Landis recovered at Panther 23YL, and HB Joel Ramich scored on 1st down run. Lion FB Franco Harris scored 3 TDs, including 39y dash to propel lead to 14-0 in 1st Q. Pitt's Ferris provided only score of 2nd H, going over from 6YL in 4th Q. Afterward, Nittany Lion coach Joe Paterno issued enthusiastic, but unrealistic Eastern playoff challenge to undefeated Lambert Trophy winner Dartmouth, 28-0 victor over Penn, which couldn't accept, even if it wanted to, because of Ivy League rules. In other locker room, Pitt coach Carl dePasqua was so distraught that he refused questions. "Call back in January," barked unnamed asst coach.

NORTH CAROLINA 59 Duke 34: TB Don McCauley closed his North Carolina (8-3) career with 47/279y and scored 5 TDs. McCauley's single season rushing total of 1,720y set new national record, besting Southern Cal's O.J. Simpson's 1968 mark by 11y. Duke (6-5) led 10-7 early in 2nd Q on FB Steve Jones' 1y plunge, but Carolina ran off 38 straight pts in middle Qs. UNC lefty QB Paul Miller (9-13/133y) contributed 18y TD pass to E Tony Blanchard (5/95y) and mystified entire stadium as he faked 4th straight handoff to McCauley inside 5YL and tiptoed 1y to score bootleg TD that put Tar Heels ahead 21-10. DT Flip Ray and DE Bill Brafford hounded Duke (6-5) QB Leo Hart (13-38/260y, 2 TDs, 2 INTs) all day, sacking him 5 times. But, Hart threw 2 TDs and 2 twin-pt conversions in Duke's 24-pt rally in 4th Q. Devils at 5-2 in league play were deprived of ACC crown as UNC's victory promoted surprise champion Wake Forest at 5-1. Wake Forest, playing at night in Houston, was defeated 26-2 long after it realized it had captured ACC championship.

OHIO STATE 20 Michigan 9: Revenge was on mind of sr-dominated Ohio State (9-0), looking to turn tables on Michigan (9-1) which in 1969 inflicted most painful defeat in Buckeye history. After exchange of FGs, odd facemask PEN during line blocking ruined 71y Michigan punt by E-P Paul Staroba late in 2nd Q. Do-over resulted in good field position that allowed Buckeyes to grab 10-3 H edge as QB Rex Kern (8-12/87y, TD, INT) fired 26y TD pass to E Bruce Jankowski. But, Kern bungled scoring chance late in 2nd Q when he expelled K Fred Schram (2 FGs) from Bucks huddle, thus overriding coach Woody Hayes. Kern threw short pass to FB John Brockington, and he was tackled inbounds to end H. This unnoticed illegality made Michigan coach Bo Schembechler livid: "There is no way you can go into the huddle and come out without running a play!" UM E Staroba caught 3rd Q TD pass of 13y from QB Don Moorhead (12-26/118y, TD, INT) and Wolverines moved to within 10-9. But, Buckeyes DB Tim Anderson knifed through to block Michigan K Dana Coin's tying kick. Ohio State's run game, which enjoyed astounding 242y to 37y advantage, dominated 4th Q as HB Leo Hayden (28/117y, TD) topped Schram's 2nd FG with 4y TD run. Now holding impressive 27-1 record over last 3 years, Buckeyes looked to capture their 2nd national title in 3 years for remarkable recruiting class of 1966 when they were to meet Stanford in Rose Bowl.

Northwestern 23 MICHIGAN STATE 20: Northwestern (6-4) shrugged off upset attempt by Michigan State (4-6) and completed its best Big 10 record at 6-1 since it posted 6-0 mark in 1936. Wildcats K Bill Planisek opened scoring in 1st Q with school's 2nd longest FG to-date at 45y and was clutch booter in 4th Q with 37y FG that tied it at 20-20 and 27y 3-ptr that provided winning margin with 37 secs to go. In between, NW clicked for 2 TDs on pass play newly installed for this game, only to see determined Spartans claw from 17-0 hole to within 17-13 at H and 20-17 lead in 3rd Q. Northwestern HB Barry Pearson was sprung unattended up middle seam in MSU secondary on 2 occasions in 1st H, and each was turned into TD by QB Maurie Daigneau (8-17/185y, 2 TDs, 2 INTs): 31y and 64y. Pass interference PEN infuriated Wildcats in 2nd Q and notched 36y against them, and suddenly game turned toward Michigan State as TB Eric Allen (32/108y, 2 TDs) scored his 1st 3y TD. Spartans ate 9 mins of 3rd Q, going 19 plays to Allen's 2nd TD and 20-17 lead. Before Planisek enjoyed his kicking heroics, Northwestern FB Mike Adamle set new Big 10 rushing record on last play of 3rd Q. Adamle finished with 137y and 1,053y for season.

NOTRE DAME 3 Louisiana State 0: Ferocious classic D struggle finally was won by Notre Dame (9-0) on K Scott Hempel's 24y FG with 2:54 to play. Undersized LSU (7-2) D held ND's nation-leading O to 227y, which was 313y under its avg. Fighting Irish runners could claw for only 78y, 231y below their game avg. Tigers maintained season-long streak of allowing no rushing TDs, while sacking Irish QB Joe Theismann 6 times. Indicative of prowess of both Ds came early when Irish HB Denny Allen was belted and LSU DB Jim Early pounced on FUM at ND 31YL, but 3 plays later Tigers were 4y farther from GL and had to punt. LB Dick Picou soon stopped Irish surge to 3YL with FUM REC. Bayou Bengals' 2-way HB-DB Tommy Casanova received national acclaim by holding elusive Irish E Tom Gatewood to 4/21y receiving, none in the 2nd H. Outstanding K Mark Lumpkin missed 2 FGs for LSU, including block by Irish DE Bob Neidert, which, after ND DB Mike Crotty's RET and Gatewood's spectacular FUM REC from hands of 4 Tigers at ND 26YL, set stage for P Jim Yoder's punt that pinned LSU at its own 1YL. Resultant good field position after Tigers' punt from their EZ led to Hempel's winning FG in late going.

NEBRASKA 28 Oklahoma 21: Cornhuskers (10-0-1) stretched their unbeaten record to 18 in row, but had trouble with Oklahoma (6-4). QB Jack Mildren's 5y TD run and TB Joe Wylie's 37y TD sprint gave Sooners 2nd Q leads of 7-0 and 14-7 before Nebraska knotted it at H on HB Joe Orduna's 3y TD run. With 7:42 to go, Nebraska QB Jerry Tagge squirmed across for 1y to provide 28-21 lead, but it took DB Jimmy Anderson's EZ INT to preserve win and coach Bob Devaney's 6th Big 8 championship in 9 years.

Arkansas 24 TEXAS TECH 10: After steady diet of weak sisters, Texas Tech (8-3) needed upset of Razorbacks (9-1) to stay within reach of SWC leaders Arkansas and idle Texas. Hogs TB Jon Richardson, sub for injured Bill Burnett, scored 3 TDs, including 2nd Q plunge to break 3-3 tie. Red Raiders failed to find paydirt until they trailed 24-3 in 4th Q. TB Doug McCutcheon blasted 9y for Texas Tech score.

Colorado 49 AIR FORCE 19: Falcons (9-2) were caught peeking at bowl bids as unpredictable Colorado (6-4) rolled up 357y O in 1st H and 482y overall. Led by C Don Popplewell, Bison O-line dominated smaller front of Air Force as Buffs built 35-7 H edge and 62 to 24 advantage in O plays. Colorado romped to 42y TD pass by QB Jimmy Bratten (3-6/62y, TD), who added 7y TD run among his 11/81y rushing before being hurt. There was no drop-off with Colorado sub QB Paul Arndt (4-10/115y, TD, 2 INTs), who rifled 63y TD and contributed 15y TD run. TB Jon Keyworth (18/124y) also scored twice for Buffs. Colorado could have been demoralized early when it took 6 plays after opening KO to drive to AFA 18YL. Without assistance of possession, Air Force grabbed surprise 7-0 lead as CB Jimmy Smith hit Buffs TB John Tarver at 15YL and ball squirted forward to open arms of Falcons S Scott Hamm, who galloped 90y with midair FUM. But, Buffs launched ruinous option runs to build drives of 75, 69, 60, 35, and 83y.

CALIFORNIA 22 Stanford 14: Stanford (8-3) QB Jim Plunkett was days away from claiming Heisman Trophy, but Bay Area rival Bears could have cared less. Outplaying Plunkett was California (6-5) QB Dave Penhall, who threw mostly on run for 18-26/231y, TD, and ran for go-ahead, E-sweep TD run for 19-14 edge in 4th Q. Winning TD was set up by controversial pass interference in EZ against Indians: Cal receivers Jim Brady and Jim Fraser went high with 2 Cardinal defenders, and Stanford DB Mike Ewing knocked down pass. While 1st official on scene picked up ball, trailing official tossed down PEN marker. Plunkett (20-37/280y, 2 TDs, 2 INTs) was no slouch himself, hitting TD passes to WR Randy Vataha (6/52y, TD) and HB Jackie Brown to erase early 13-0 Bears lead for 14-13 advantage in 3rd Q. However, Plunkett's big mistake came when he threw pass behind Brown on 4th-and-3 from Cal 9YL midway in 4th Q with Bears ahead by 5 pts. K Ray Wersching had opened scoring with 25y FG, added another 3-ptr in 2nd Q after successful on-side KO, and made 26y FG in last 52 secs for California. His successes gave Wersching to-date conf career mark with 25 FGs.

AP Poll November 23

1 Texas (20)	812	11 Auburn	202
2 Ohio State (14)	760	12 Air Force	124
3 Nebraska (6)	718	13 Stanford	90
4 Notre Dame (3)	676	14 Dartmouth	86
5 Arkansas	482	15 Toledo	68
6 Louisiana State	414	16 Georgia Tech	49
7 Tennessee	413	17 Penn State	40
8 Michigan	385	18 Northwestern	33
9 Arizona State (2)	311	19 Colorado	24
10 Mississippi	246	20 Washington	19

November 26-28, 1970

(Th'g) Houston 53 FLORIDA STATE 21 (Tampa): Wild Thanksgiving night before disappointingly small crowd saw Houston (7-3) explode for 41 pts in 2nd H to erase 21-12 H lead of Florida State (7-4). Cougars scored 1st on WR Elmo Wright's 13y TD catch from QB Gary Mullins (9-22/238y, 3 TDs) for 6-0 lead. Seminoles QB Tommy Warren 17-34/249y, 2 TDs, 4 INTs) pitched 12y TD for 7-6 lead in 1st Q after catching surprise 16y pass from FB Tom Bailey. Warren's 65y TD pass to WR Barry Smith finished FSU's H jamboree. Key play came from Houston DB Charles Ford, who made 40y RET of INT, was hemmed in, and flipped lateral to beefy LB Frank Ditto, who rumbled another 30y to score. Cougars RB Tommy Mozisek scored twice, including 70y sprint, and when Wright added his 2nd TD catch, he became NCAA's record-holding career TD catcher to date.

(Th'g) Mississippi State 19 MISSISSIPPI 14: Bulldogs QB Joe Reed flipped desperation 3rd-and-21 pass resulting in interference PEN on Rebels DB Danny Hooker at 5YL, then capped 71y drive with winning 1y TD plunge with 8:16 to play. Acting Ole Miss (7-2) coach Billy Kinard griped: "Hooker intercepted the ball and the receiver (Maroons E David Smith) tripped over his foot, so they called pass interference." Still, Reed's TD clinched 1st winning season for Mississippi State (6-5) in 7 years and Maroons' 1st Egg Bowl win over Rebels since 1964. Sub QB Shug Chumbler scored

on 1y sneak with 6 secs left in H to give Ole Miss 14-10 advantage. Big play came late in contest with Rebels driving for potential winning TD: outstanding Mississippi TE Jim Poole slipped past State DB Frank Dowsing into EZ, but swift-closing Dowsing leaped high to make 1-handed spear for touchback INT.

Navy 11 Army 7 (Philadelphia): Navy (2-9) had its own way in 1st H, but bungled scoring chances by fumbling handoff at Army (1-9-1) 6YL, missing FG try from 33YL, and helplessly watching H clock expire just as it reached 1YL. Cadets had crossed midfield only once in 1st H, and that on offside PEN. But, Black Knights were afire when they received 3rd Q KO, roaring 85y to score in 8 plays. Payoff came on 42y bomb from soph QB Dick Atha (13-30/151y, TD, 4 INTs) to star WR Joe Albano (6/96y). Army came right back after forcing Middies to punt, but lost FUM at Tar 33YL after making 3 1st downs. Game wore on at 7-0 late into 3rd Q when Navy faced 3rd-and-2 at Cadets 49YL, and, out of Wishbone, Middies HB Bob Elflein followed FB Andy Pease's big block on Army LB Chuck Blakley, broke tackle, and raced 49y to score. Navy coach Rick Forzano boldly called for 2-pt conv and QB Mike McNallen (10-18/131y) found WR Karl Schwelm for 8-7 lead. Navy added K Roger Lanning's 33y FG in 4th Q, and finally, in last min, DB Mark Schickner made his game-record 4th INT of Atha at Navy 12YL.

Auburn 33 ALABAMA 28: Tigers (8-2) won wild tilt, rallying from 17-0 deficit to top Alabama (6-5). QB Pat Sullivan hit TE Robby Robinett with 4th Q TD pass to put Auburn ahead for 1st time at 27-20. Bama answered with QB Scott Hunter's 54y TD pass to WR George Ranager and Hunter's 2-pt pass for 28-27 lead. Tigers ended it with 4-play drive, capped by TB Wallace Clark's 3y TD run. RB Johnny Musso ran for school record 221y, becoming 1st Tide back to crack 1,000y barrier in season as he finished with 1,137y.

Georgia Tech 17 GEORGIA 7: Coach Bud Carson's Yellow Jackets (8-3) sparkled on D, holding Georgia (5-5) to 53y rushing and setting up all 3 of its scores with INTs. Sr QB Jack Williams (10-18/95y 2 TDs) sparked Georgia Tech O, which received clutch running from HB Rob Healy (26/85y). Standout DT Rock Perdoni was anchor in middle of Engineers' D. Tech DB Gary Carden picked off pass on Bulldogs' 3rd play of game to set up Williams' 36y TD pass to WB Mike Wysong. Georgia answered with its best drive, 62y to TD and 7-7 tie in 13 plays keyed by tough y from TB Ricky Lake (16/56y). Tech D came up big right after 2nd H KO: Georgia got RET to its 36YL from HB Jack Montgomery, and 2 PENs moved Bulldogs past midfield, only to have Tech stiffen. Clinching TD at 14-7 followed DL Smylie Gebhart's INT of flea-flicker pass intended for Bulldogs QB Paul Gilbert from Montgomery. Win sent Georgia Tech to Sun Bowl and knocked Georgia out of Peach Bowl.

Tennessee 24 VANDERBILT 6: Using TB Don McLeary's TD run and QB Bobby Scott's TD pass in 1st Q, Volunteers (9-1) won handily over undermanned Vanderbilt (4-7). Still, Vandy trimmed margin to 14-6 in 3rd Q when QB Steve Burger hit WR Jeff Peeples with TD pass. DB Bobby Majors, Johnny's kid brother, made his 9th and 10th INTs of season, and Tennessee quietly worked its way into the nation's top 5.

Louisiana State 26 TULANE 14: LSU (8-2) FB Chris Dantin scored on 3 short TD runs, all following TOs created by Bayou Bengals D deep in Green Wave territory. Tulane (7-4) outgained Tigers 319y to 269y, got 2nd H TDs from WR Steve Barrios on 23y catch and QB David Abercrombie on 1y dive. Latter TD represented only score on ground all year against LSU. Despite its loss, Tulane headed for Liberty Bowl, its 1st post-season action since 1940 Sugar Bowl.

SOUTHERN CALIFORNIA 38 Notre Dame 28: Once again, coach John McKay's Trojans (6-4-1) eliminated Fighting Irish (9-1) from national title race. This time, Notre Dame seemed likely to be headed for Orange Bowl showdown vs. Nebraska. USC amazingly recovered 2 EZ FUMs for TDs by OTs Pete Adams and John Vella within 42 secs of each other in 3rd Q to go up 38-14. ND rallied behind brilliant performance by QB Joe Theisman (33-56/526y, 2 TDs, 4 INTs), but ran out of time after HB Larry Parker's 46y TD sprint with short pass in 3rd Q and Theismann's short TD run at end of 70y drive early in 4th Q. Trojan LB Willie Hall recorded 5 sacks forced 3 FUMs.

December 5, 1970

TENNESSEE 28 Ucla 17: Tennessee (10-1) scored 2 TDs in final 2:20 to send frustrated Bruins (6-5) to yet another bitter defeat. After DB Ron Carver's 85y INT TD RET put UCLA ahead 17-14 in 4th Q, Volunteers stormed 67y downfield for quick 19y TD burst by FB Curt Watson, and turned TO into TB Don McLeary's 2nd TD plunge.

LOUISIANA STATE 61 Mississippi 17: QB Archie Manning's surprise return to Ole Miss (7-3) lineup was to no avail as Bayou Bengals (9-2) mauled Johnny Reb's D, piling up 506y and 27 1st downs. Amazingly, LSU's special teams fashioned 3 TDs on punt RETs: DB Tommy Casanova's 61 and 73y RETs and DB Craig Burns' 66y RET. Manning, with bulky hand cast, could muster no miracles on 12-26/82y, 2 INTs passing with encouraging early 9y TD to TE Jim Poole. Manning was dropped for safety on twisting, almost acrobatic tackle by LSU DT Ronnie Estay, and he sat once Tigers' tally mounted to 33-10 in 3rd Q. Bengals fans chanted "Archie Who?," when not pelting field with oranges in anticipation of Tigers' bowl bid to New Year's Day classic in Miami.

Houston 36 MIAMI 3: Easy Houston (8-3) win over Miami (3-8) was highlighted by WR Elmo Wright's record-setting performance. Wright's 2nd Q TD reception placed his career TD catches mark at NCAA record 34 and his 135y gave him career total of 3347y, good for 2nd to date behind Florida State's Ron Sellers on all-time y list. Hurricanes held brief 3-2 1st Q edge on 34y FG by little-used K Barry Borowicz, but Cougars FB Robert Newhouse followed with 2 scoring runs.

TEXAS 42 Arkansas 7: Anyone hoping "Shootout II" would duplicate classic of prior year was highly disappointed as Texas (10-0) sliced Porkers into bacon. Game turned midway in 2nd Q when Arkansas (9-2), trailing by TD, was stopped on 4 straight line bucks inside Steers 3YL, then surrendered 99y Longhorn TD drive for 21-7 deficit. Earlier, Razorbacks TB Jon Richardson had escaped for 12y TD run. HB Jim Bertelsen rushed 30/189y, 3 TDs, and FB Steve Worster added 21/126y, 2 TDs as Texas earned Cotton Bowl spot, SWC title, and 2nd consecutive national title from UPI coaches board.

Arizona State 10 ARIZONA 6: Season's low number of pts previously had been 27 for undefeated Sun Devils (10-0). ASU's scoring dropoff was due to 5 lost FUMs, but Devils still secured national O title by gaining 370y. Superb D effort, keyed by LB Mark Arneson (11 tackles and 21 assists), allowed Arizona (4-6) to finish 1st H in scoreless tie, thanks to 2 FUM RECs at its 1YL. ASU got on board in 3rd Q as QB Joe Spagnola (14-23/136y, TD, 2 INTs) hit WR J.D. Hill with 7y TD pass, 11th play of 61y trip. K Don Ekstrand booted FG in 4th Q for 10-0 ASU lead. Arizona came alive with about 5 min to play as DL Bill McKinley fell on FUM. Wildcats QB Bill Demery (13-23/203y, TD, 2 INTs) hit E Hal Arneson (6/98y) for 45y, then passed 20y to WR Charlie McKee for TD. K Al Mendoza, who missed earlier FG tries of 32 and 38y, missed x-pt kick. It took INT in last 2 mins to seal 16th straight win and trip to Peach Bowl for emerging ASU.

1970 Conference Standings

Ivy League

Dartmouth	7-0
Harvard	5-2
Yale	5-2
Cornell	4-3
Princeton	3-4
Pennsylvania	2-5
Columbia	1-6
Brown	1-6

Atlantic Coast

Wake Forest	5-1
North Carolina	5-2
Duke	5-2
South Carolina	3-2-1
North Carolina State	2-3-1
Clemson	2-4
Maryland	2-4
Virginia	0-6

Southern

William & Mary	3-1
Citadel	4-2
Furman	3-2
Richmond	3-3
East Carolina	2-2
Davidson	2-4
Virginia Military	1-4

Southeastern

Louisiana State	5-0
Tennessee	4-1
Auburn	5-2
Mississippi	4-2
Florida	3-3
Georgia	3-3
Alabama	3-4
Mississippi State	3-4
Vanderbilt	1-5
Kentucky	0-7

Big Ten

Ohio State	7-0
Michigan	6-1
Northwestern	6-1
Iowa	3-3-1
Michigan State	3-4
Wisconsin	3-4
Minnesota	2-4-1
Purdue	2-5
Illinois	1-6
Indiana	1-6

Mid-American

Toledo	5-0
Miami	3-2
Ohio	3-2
Western Michigan	2-3
Bowling Green	1-4
Kent State	1-4

Big Eight

Nebraska	7-0
Oklahoma	5-2
Kansas State	5-2
Colorado	3-4
Missouri	3-4
Oklahoma State	2-5
Kansas	2-5
Iowa State	1-6

Missouri Valley

Louisville	4-0
Tulsa	3-1
Memphis State	2-2
North Texas State	1-3
Wichita	0-4

Southwest		Western Athletic	
Texas	7-0	Arizona State	7-0
Arkansas	6-1	New Mexico	5-1
Texas Tech	5-2	Utah	4-2
Rice	3-4	Texas-El Paso	4-3
Southern Methodist	3-4	Arizona	2-4
Texas Christian	3-4	Colorado State	1-3
Baylor	1-6	Brigham Young	1-6
Texas A&M	0-7	Wyoming	1-6

Pacific Eight

Stanford	6-1
Washington	4-3
UCLA	4-3
Oregon	4-3
California	4-3
Southern California	3-4
Oregon State	3-4
Washington State	0-7

1970 Bowl Games

Liberty Bowl (Dec. 12): Tulane 17 Colorado 3

No active Green Wave player even was alive when Tulane (8-4) played in its last bowl game in 1940. Solid 213y rushing O, led by TB David Abercrombie (25/128y, 2 TDs), made surprising Tulane's return to post-season play memorable affair. Favored Colorado (6-5) suffered another downturn in its rollercoaster season. K Dave Haney's 33y FG in 2nd Q earned 3-3 H tie for Buffs, but Abercrombie returned 2nd H KO 66y to set up his 1st TD run. Greenies LB Rick Kingrea's INT set stage for Abercrombie's 4y TD run in 4th Q. Colorado's Big 8-best O (424y avg) gained 175y, and its failure ruined its hopes for win.

Sun Bowl (Dec. 19): Georgia Tech 17 Texas Tech 9

Georgia Tech (9-3) went to 10-0 H lead, later needed chipshot FG miss to hold off Texas Tech (8-4). Engineers HB Rob Healy blasted in from 1YL at end of early 62y drive. Dominating 1st H, Georgia Tech still was unable to build bigger margin brought by K Jack Moore's FG in last 42 secs of H. After TB Doug McCutcheon scored to bring Red Raiders to within 10-7, DL Don Rives blocked punt for safety to cut Yellow Jackets' margin to 10-9. After free kick, Raiders moved inside 10YL, but K Dickie Ingram missed easy 24y FG. Engineers' nicely balanced O (186y rushing and 138y passing) helped them throughout and provided confidence to clinch it with 1:44 to play. Georgia Tech FB Kevin McNamara's 2y plunge followed LB Bill Flowers' FUM REC at Raiders 25YL.

Peach Bowl (Dec. 30): Arizona State 48 North Carolina 26

Out of desert stormed undefeated, underappreciated Arizona State (11-0), only to meet unaccustomed misery of rain, sleet, and mud of Atlanta. Still, speedy Sun Devils cruised to 14-0 lead on 8y and 33y TD runs by FB Bob Thomas. North Carolina (8-4), hot team in November stretch run, rebounded beautifully in 2nd Q, scoring all its pts for 26-21 H lead. Tar Heels used sharp cuts, crunching power of TB Don McCauley, who blasted for 3 TDs. D adjustments by Sun Devils at H, along with loss to injury of QB Paul Miller, cramped North Carolina's 2nd H effort. Arizona State eased to 4 more TDs, 2 on runs by TB Monroe Eley. Sun Devils rushed for 306y and compiled 451y total O.

Astro-Bluebonnet Bowl (Dec. 31): Alabama 24 Oklahoma 24

Despite 9 defeats between them, ordinary Crimson Tide (6-5-1) and Oklahoma (7-4-1) teams put on thrilling O show. Each school reflected its 1970 season mode: weaker than normal on D with Oklahoma rushing for 349y out of Wishbone O, and Alabama passing for 199y with 3 TD tosses. Alabama QB Scott Hunter flipped 2 TD passes in 1st H, but Sooners enjoyed 21-14 H lead thanks to soph HB Greg Pruitt's blazing 58 and 25y TD dashes with option pitchouts. FUM of 2nd H KO led to Bama FG by K Richard Ciemny. Tide TB Johnny Musso's left-handed throwback pass to Hunter resulted in 25y TD at end of 85y 4th Q drive. Alabama now led 24-21. Oklahoma marched from own 20YL to K Bruce Derr's tying 42y FG with 59 secs left.

Sugar Bowl: Tennessee 34 Air Force 13

Football News writers were unanimous in wishing Sugar Bowl had tapped undefeated Arizona State to meet dynamic Tennessee (11-1). The writers turned out to be profits as maligned Air Force (9-3) laid early-game egg. Volunteers TB Don McLeary scored on team's 1st possession, then Falcons quickly lost FUMs at own 34, 42, and 26YLs. Each bobble cost Flyboys pts: Tennessee K George Hunt made 30y FG, McLeary raced 20y to TD, and QB Bobby Scott hit wide-open TE Gary Theiler for 10y TD. Tennessee owned lopsided 24-0 lead, and 1st Q was yet to be completed. Vols coach Bill Battle admitted, "We had a hot hand out there early." Falcons seemed to get righted on DL Darryl Haas' EZ FUM REC, but Tennessee DB Bobby Majors returned punt for 57y TD in 3rd Q. Air Force rushing game netted -12y; but its passes gained 239y, with 4 INTs serving as demerits. Vols air game clicked for 24-46/306y.

GAME OF THE YEAR

Cotton Bowl: Notre Dame 24 Texas 11

Only twice in bowl history had 2 teams been tapped for consecutive-year matchups. History was stacked against Notre Dame (10-1), loser to Texas (10-1) in prior year's Cotton Bowl, because Santa Clara beat LSU in neither 1937 nor 1938 Sugar Bowls, and Nebraska lost to Alabama in both 1966 Orange and 1967 Sugar Bowls. To measure magnitude of Fighting Irish's upset win that ended 30-game win streak of Texas, historians need only compare 1970 season-ending results. Much had gone

wrong for ND, including its run game, in loss to USC, while Longhorns easily thrashed no. 4 Arkansas. Fighting Irish stuffed 9 men at scrimmage line to stop Wishbone O. In his worst career game, Texas' magnificent FB Steve Worster was held to 16/42y and lost 3 FUMs. Notre Dame DBs Clarence Ellis and Ralph Stepaniak were brilliant when Steers felt compelled to go to their aerial game uncharacteristically often (10-27/210y, INT). With Texas up 3-0 in 1st Q, Irish QB Joe Theismann (9-16/176y, TD) passed 26y to E Tom Gatewood for game's 1st TD. Longhorns DB Danny Lester lost FUM on own 13YL on ensuing KO, and Theismann scored on 3y rollout to right. Game's signature play came at end of ND's 52y march in 2nd Q. Theismann pranced down sideline for 17y TD, and smallish QB powered over tacklers for last few y. Texas' sole bright moment came on 86y drive ending in HB Jim Bertelsen's 2y TD run and QB Eddie Phillips' 2-pt pass. Smelling upset, Notre Dame D grew stronger in scoreless 2nd H.

Rose Bowl: Stanford 27 Ohio State 17

Virtually every prognosticator favored Ohio State (9-1) over Stanford (9-3), which closed its regular season with 2 losses. But, rarely in Buckeyes' great 3-year run had they faced passing attack as effective as that led by Indians QB Jim Plunkett (20-30/265y, TD, INT). Plunkett later said he gained pre-game confidence knowing Ohio State hadn't faced a top passer since Purdue's Mike Phipps in late 1969. Little Stanford WR Eric Cross launched TD drive from Tribe 41YL with 42y dash on reverse. Plunkett then fooled Ohio D with 8y draw run, and RB Jackie Brown swept to 4y TD. Plunkett connected on 3 passes to set up K Steve Horowitz's 37y FG, and Stanford leapt to early 10-0 lead. Buckeyes charged back, using E Bruce Jankowski's 37y reverse and QB Rex Kern's 23y sprint to poise FB John Brockington's short TD blast. On Bucks' next possession, Kern rolled out for 32y, and Brockington scored again for 14-10 2nd Q edge. Before H, maligned Stanford D made stand at its own 3YL as DB Benny Barnes blocked FG try. Ohio led 17-13 as Ks Horowitz and Buckeyes' Ron Schram traded 3rd Q FGs. Early in 4th Q, Brockington was stopped on 4th-and-1 at Indians 19YL, and critical Stanford drive was launched. TE Bob Moore took Plunkett's pass between star DBs Mike Sensibaugh and Tim Anderson to 2YL. Brown scored 3 plays later, and after INT by Indians DB Jack Schultz, Plunkett threw clinching TD to WR Randy Vataha. Modern football made landmark impression: It seemed that run-oriented Big 10 powers could no longer cope with swift, aerial-minded champions of West Coast. It would play out that way in most 1970s and 1980s Rose Bowl encounters.

Orange Bowl: Nebraska 17 Louisiana State 12

When Cornhuskers (11-0-1) charged onto floor of Orange Bowl, they knew they had been blessed by big upsets of no. 1 Texas and no. 2 Ohio State. Nebraska headed right on its mission, hopping on FUM near midfield in 1st Q. QB Jerry Tagge hit TE Jerry List twice, added draw run to set up K Paul Rogers' 26y FG. On 1st snap after KO, LSU (9-3) QB Buddy Lee was hit by Huskers DT Larry Jacobson, so that DE Willie Harper, D ringleader all night, could reach FUM at Tigers 15YL. HB Joe Orduna scored in 2 runs, giving Nebraska 10-0 edge in 1st Q. Lee hit WR Andy Hamilton with 4 passes to spark LSU to 10YL in 2nd Q, but Harper's 10y sack forced LSU to settle for K Mark Lumpkin's FG. Lumpkin added another 3-pts in 3rd Q to trim Cornhusker lead to 10-6. Late in 3rd Q, LSU made its best move, going 75y with Lee's 31y arrow to little SB Al Coffee providing TD and 12-10 lead. As 4th Q opened, Nebraska made clutch 67y march as Tagge hit key throws to FB Dan Schneiss, WB Johnny Rodgers, and IB Jeff Kinney. Tagge stretched his big frame through RG and across GL for winning TD on 1y sneak. Huskers earned their 1st-ever AP national championship.

Gator Bowl (Jan. 2): Auburn 35 Mississippi 28

These SEC neighbors had last met in 1965 Liberty Bowl and not since 1953 in regular season. Game quickly turned into expected aerial battle between QB Pat Sullivan (27-42/351y, 2 TDs, INT in air and TD on ground) of Auburn (9-2) and QB Archie Manning (19-28/180y, TD, INT passing, 10/95y, TD rushing) of Ole Miss (7-4). Sullivan completed 2 TD passes, ran for 37y TD, and Tigers jumped to 21-0 lead in 2nd Q. In his collegiate farewell, Manning answered with TD run and TD pass to trim Mississippi's H deficit to 21-14. Auburn owned most of 3rd Q as HB Mickey Zofko barreled 6y to score. But it was matched by Ole Miss sub QB Shug Chumbler's 23y TD pass to TE Jim Poole. Critical 3rd Q play came from Auburn DB Larry Willingham, who sped 55y to INT TD and 35-21 lead. After Rebels stopped drive deep in own end on INT, Manning hit pass to Poole, then made marvelous 37y scramble to set up Chumbler's 4th Q TD sneak. It was not enough.

1970 Top Performance Formula

1	Arizona State	1.7411
2	Texas	1.7175
3	Nebraska	1.6889
4	Notre Dame	1.6812
5	Tennessee	1.6769
6	Ohio State	1.5989
7	Auburn	1.5917
8	Michigan	1.5480
9	Arkansas	1.5287
10	Louisiana State	1.4753
11	Stanford	1.4346
12	Air Force	1.4016
13	Georgia Tech	1.3865
14	Houston	1.3748
15	Southern California	1.2990
16	Penn State	1.2971
17	North Carolina	1.2585
18	Colorado	1.2550
19	Florida State	1.2491
20	Alabama	1.2352

1970 Top Opponent Records

1	UCLA	.6404
2	Alabama	.6352
3	Wake Forest	.6308
4	Navy	.6125
5	Southern California	.6081
6	Auburn	.6062
7	Mississippi State	.6027
8	Georgia Tech	.6025
9	Oklahoma State	.5938
10	Iowa State	.5909
11	Kentucky	.5901
12	Louisiana State	.5820
13	Vanderbilt	.5814
14	Texas A&M	.5802
15	Oklahoma	.5779
16t	Kansas State	.57658
16t	Texas	.57658
18	Stanford	.5763
19	Southern Methodist	.5727
20	Colorado	.5714

1970 Out-of-Conference Records

	W-L	Percentage	Bowl W-L
Southeastern	31-14-1	.6848	3-2
Big Eight	21-11-2	.6471	1-2
Pacific-8	17-13-2	.5625	1-0
Southwest	15-14-1	.5167	0-2
Western Athletic	16-16	.5000	1-0
Big Ten	12-17-1	.6471	0-1
Atlantic Coast	10-26	.2778	0-1

1970 Individual Statistical Leaders

RUSHING YARDS

	Attempts	Yards	Avg.
Don McCauley, North Carolina	324	1720	5.3
Ed Marinaro, Cornell	285	1425	5.0
Phil Mosser, William & Mary	212	1286	6.1
Brian Bream, Air Force	294	1276	4.3
Mike Adamle, Northwestern	304	1255	4.1
Roger Lawson, Western Michigan	168	1205	7.2
Steve Cowan, Cincinnati	239	1197	5.0
Johnny Musso, Alabama	226	1137	5.0
John Riggins, Kansas	209	1131	5.4
Dave Schilling, Oregon State	254	1084	4.3

PASSING YARDS

	Completions	Attempts	Yards	Pct.
Bob Parker, Air Force	199	402	2789	49.5
Jim Plunkett, Stanford	191	358	2715	53.4
Brian Sipe, San Diego State	195	337	2618	57.9
Pat Sullivan, Auburn	167	281	2586	59.4
John Reaves, Florida	188	376	2549	50.0
Joe Theismann, Notre Dame	155	268	2429	57.8
Dennis Dummit, UCLA	175	344	2393	50.9
Dan Fouts, Oregon	188	361	2390	52.1
Sonny Sixkiller, Washington	186	362	2303	51.4
Leo Hart, Duke	180	308	2236	58.4

RECEIVING YARDS

	Catches	Yards
Mike Siani, Villanova	74	1358
Ernie Jennings, Air Force	74	1289
Bob Newland, Oregon	67	1123
Tom Gatewood, Notre Dame	77	1123
Wes Chesson, Duke	74	1080
Ed Puishes, Texas-El Paso	57	1000
David Smith, Mississippi State	74	987
J.D. Hill, Arizona State	58	908
Don Fair, Toledo	76	893
Tim Delaney, San Diego State	62	794

1970 Concensus All-America Team
Offense

End:	Tom Gatewood, Notre Dame
	Ernie Jennings, Air Force
	Elmo Wright, Houston
Tackle:	Dan Dierdorf, Michigan
	Bobby Wuensch, Texas
	Bob Newton, Nebraska
Guard:	Chip Kell, Tennessee
	Larry DiNardo, Notre Dame
Center:	Don Popplewell, Colorado
Quarterback	Jim Plunkett, Stanford
Running Back:	Steve Worster, Texas
	Don McCauley, North Carolina

Defense

End:	Bill Atessis, Texas
	Charlie Weaver, Southern California
Tackle:	Rock Perdoni, Georgia Tech
	Dick Bumpas, Arkansas
Nose Guard:	Jim Stillwagon, Ohio State
Linebacker:	Jack Ham., Penn State
	Mike Anderson, Louisiana State
Backs:	Jack Tatum, Ohio State
	Larry Willingham, Auburn
	Dave Elmendorf, Texas A&M
	Tommy Casanova, Louisiana State

1970 Heisman Trophy Vote

Jim Plunkett, senior quarterback, Stanford	2229
Joe Theismann, senior quarterback, Notre Dame	1410
Archie Manning, senior quarterback, Mississippi	849
Steve Worster, senior fullback, Texas	398

Other Major Awards

Maxwell (Player)	Jim Plunkett, senior quarterback, Stanford
Walter Camp (Player)	Jim Plunkett, senior quarterback, Stanford
Outland (Lineman)	Jim Stillwagon, senior nose guard, Ohio State
Lombardi (Lineman)	Jim Stillwagon, senior nose guard, Ohio State
AFCA Coach of the Year	Charlie McClendon, Louisiana State
	and Darrell Royal, Texas

1971

The Year of Nebraska's Game of the Century, Bear Learning New Tricks, and the Thunder Chickens

Lincoln, Nebraska, remained the focal point of college football as the hometown Cornhuskers rolled to their second consecutive national championship. Coach Bob Devaney displayed an enormous wealth of talent on both sides of the ball in taking on and beating the best teams in the college game. Oklahoma (11-1), Colorado (10-2) and Alabama (11-1), amazingly were all victims of Nebraska (13-0), yet the same trio was good enough to wrap up the 1971 season in second, third, and fourth spots respectively in the Associated Press post-bowl poll, behind the all-conquering Cornhuskers.

The Big Eight Conference offered a spectacular entry into the Game-of-the-Century archives that more than 30 years later still is considered by many college fans to be the greatest game ever played. Rivals Nebraska and Oklahoma hooked up on Thanksgiving Day, dwarfing the NFL's holiday football in Detroit and Dallas. The nation's two top-ranked teams played an offense-oriented, knockdown-filled blockbuster. The game was won by visiting Nebraska 35-31 and it lived up to every bit of pre-game hype as the two red-hued teams traded leads and spectacular plays all afternoon. The Huskers followed their Thanksgiving glory with a decisive whipping of Alabama, then the new no. 2 team, in the Orange Bowl, which wrapped up the national title. As the Orange Bowl telecast drew near its conclusion and the Crimson Tide was being drubbed 38-6, veteran NBC play-by-play announcer Curt Gowdy suggested that Nebraska, after its two-year run of 24-0-1, possibly could be the greatest college team of all time. Gowdy got few arguments; the print media seemed universally to share his belief.

By averaging more than 44 points a game, Oklahoma displayed a spectacular Wishbone attack. Led by QB Jack Mildren, with 1,140 yards rushing (5.9 yards per run average), and HB Greg Pruitt, who gained 1,665 yards (9.4 average), the Sooners scored more than 30 points against every team on the schedule except for a 20-3 victory over Missouri (1-10). Oklahoma laid 75 points on unsuspecting Kansas State (5-6) and 58 on Oklahoma State (4-6-1).

While Nebraska and Oklahoma were anticipated to be very good, Colorado surprised with its first 10-win season in school history. Wins over Ohio State (6-4), Louisiana State (9-3), Houston (9-3) and every team in the Big Eight not named Oklahoma or Nebraska, provided the Buffaloes with a truly special season. The Big Eight, or more accurately a defacto Big Three, copped an unprecedented top-3 national poll finish after Colorado beat home-standing Houston (9-3) in the Bluebonnet Bowl.

The Big Eight may have dominated the spotlight, but it did not overshadow fine seasons from myriad clubs. The match-up of undefeated Alabama and undefeated Auburn (9-2) for state bragging rights, the SEC championship, and the chance to meet no. 1 Nebraska in Orange Bowl was not even considered the Game-of-the-Day because it too was played on Thanksgiving as part of a day-night national television doubleheader. Thanksgiving Thursday marked the first time since 1943 that two confrontations of top-5 teams occurred on the same day. October 9, 1943, featured top-ranked Notre Dame beating no. 2 Michigan 35-12 and no. 4 Navy topping no. 5 Duke 14-13. This unusual intermingling of top-5 teams would not happen again until November 30, 1996.

Alabama's successful season suggested that perhaps new tricks could be taught to an old dog. The Crimson Tide had slipped in recent years from their lofty position of the early and mid-1960s; their last SEC title was in 1966 and the won-loss record since then was an unBama-like 26-15-2. So, coach Bear Bryant went for two huge changes. On offense, Alabama switched to an option-run Wishbone attack, which was developed during the off-season after Bryant visited Darrell Royal and his Wishbone innovators, the Texas Longhorns. The Tide's new Wishbone simply proved to be too much for SEC defenses. Bryant's other change affected both his lineup and all of Southern society. Bryant, arguably the most revered and respected man in the state, suddenly started recruiting black high school players after the SEC schools had wrestled profoundly with U.S. government-dictated racial integration. Halfback Wilbur Jackson was the first African-American to accept an Alabama scholarship, while junior college transfer John Mitchell, a defensive tackle, became the Tide's first black starter in 1971.

Alabama went on to a streak of eight SEC championships over the next nine years with its new offense and integrated roster. In setting a new national record for victories in a decade, Alabama would win 103 games during the 1970s, including 1971's season opener on Friday night,

September 10. The 17-10 victory over Southern California (6-4-1) made Bryant the sixth coach ever to reach the 200-career win plateau.

Alabama's easy 31-7 win in the regular season finale over the Auburn Tigers dulled the Heisman Trophy accomplishment of Auburn quarterback Pat Sullivan. Auburn's losses to Bama and in the Sugar Bowl to Oklahoma fueled the notion that a jinx frequently hovered over the teams that sported a Heisman winner. Since 1953, these teams had suffered through a relatively awful 7-9-1 record in the games immediately following the announcement of a Heisman winner. In Sullivan's case, he was tapped only two days prior to the Alabama game, in which he slumped to 121 yards passing. Sullivan had edged Cornell (8-1) tailback Ed Marinaro by only 152 votes despite being been outvoted in three of five voting regions by the Big Red's record-setting rusher. Marinaro gained 1,881 yards on the ground for a new rushing mark and brought national attention back to the Ivy League.

Michigan (11-1) also ran the table during the regular season, gaining its second Rose Bowl bid in three seasons. Upstart Northwestern (7-4) finished second in the Big Ten for the second straight year, managing its first victory over Ohio State since 1963. Ohio State faced a rebuilding year because the brilliant class that turned varsity during the autumn of 1968 had moved on, but the Buckeyes had Michigan on the ropes in their annual clash. Michigan prevailed 10-7, only to drop the Rose Bowl by 13-12 to unheralded Stanford (9-3).

It was the second straight Rose Bowl upset for the Indians, who won the Pacific-8 with efficient quarterback Don Bunce, who had the unenviable task of replacing legendary Jim Plunkett, and a surprisingly tough "Thunder Chickens" defense. Stanford, a school that would soon begin winning a considerable number of Sears Cup awards for all-around athletic achievement, was known as "The Harvard of the West." That image was tarnished when former Thunder Chicken defensive lineman Tim McClure wrote in *Look Magazine* that Stanford's new pressure-to-win environment had led some players to pop amphetamines during halftime of the previous January's Rose Bowl upset win over Ohio State. Interestingly, the scandal had little life, and people went on recognizing Stanford as an over-achieving school that featured academics first. A visit to the beautiful Palo Alto campus would reveal that it looks suspiciously like acres of athletic fields surrounded by classrooms, but that's another story.

Once again, Notre Dame (8-2) and Penn State (11-1) were dominant independents. Notre Dame was tabbed as preseason no. 1 and went 5-0 before losing to a young, up-and-down Southern California team that arrived for the match-up with an uncharacteristic 2-4 mark. The Fighting Irish were unsettled at quarterback after enjoying six seasons of field generalship by Terry Hanratty and Joe Thiesmann. A December loss to Tennessee kept the Nittany Lions from their third undefeated season in four years. Their halfback Lydell Mitchell set an all-time touchdown record at that time of 29.

The Atlantic Coast Conference could boast that half its members were elite academic institutions and chose to raise league-wide standards for inbound players. High school grads were required to meet an SAT minimum of 800 and project to a 1.6 freshman GPA. Two Clemson recruits sued the school and the conference, and a federal judge wiped out the new standards. Clemson, Maryland, North Carolina, and North Carolina State begin to recruit borderline players; Duke, Wake Forest, and Virginia chose not to and suffered the pigskin consequences for years. South Carolina had already packed its bags for independence over similar complaints about what it considered over-regulation by academic administers.

For the first time in four years, the Southwest Conference, which had enjoyed three straight top-3 finishes, including the 1969 national title for Texas (8-3), was shut out of any spots in final Top 10. The SWC's highest ranking was a dismal 16th by a mediocre Arkansas (8-3-1) club that lost to Tulsa (4-7).

Toledo (12-0) ran its win streak to 35 games with its second undefeated, 12-win season in a row. Quarterback Chuck Ealey, the Rockets' starter for all those games, set a new NCAA record for most wins by a quarterback without losses, topping the 25-0 mark established by Oklahoma's Jimmy Harris from 1954-56.

According to an NCAA survey released in 1973, two-thirds of all university-level athletic departments operated at a financial loss during 1971.

Milestones

■ To limit injuries, NCAA banned crack-back blocking on offense and spearing by defenders.

- South Carolina began play as independent after leaving ACC over dispute with conference's high academic requirements.

- Southwest Conference accepted Houston as its ninth member. Cougars had long wait for conference title eligibility, which came in 1976.

- Big 10 rescinded its no-repeat rule, allowing teams to go to consecutive Rose Bowls.

- Fiesta Bowl, which would grow magnificently into original cornerstone of BCS championship in 1990s, debuted modestly at Sun Devil Stadium in Tempe, Arizona.

- Safety Freddie Steinmark, inspirational leader of 1969 Texas Longhorns national champions, lost his battle with cancer on June 6. George Trafton, center for undefeated Notre Dame in 1919 and member of pro football Hall of Fame, died on September 8. North Carolina sophomore guard Billy Arnold collapsed and died during practice on September 20. Coach Jim Pittman, of TCU, was stricken with heart attack during win over Baylor on October 30 and died later that day. "Pitt", former assistant at Texas, had returned to SWC after successful rebuilding effort at Tulane. Cal State-Fullerton assistant coaches William Hannah, Joseph O'Hara, and Dallas Moon, along with pilot Ernie Mariette, died in plane crash on November 13. Mercy Bowl between Fullerton and Fresno State netted more than $60,000 for families' trust fund. Legendary announcer Bill Stern, who covered college football among many sports for NBC and ABC in early days of radio, died of heart attack at age 64 on November 20. Joe Guyon, teammate of Jim Thorpe at Carlisle and star of Georgia Tech team that beat Cumberland 222-0 in 1917, died on November 27. Guyon is member of pro football Hall of Fame. Kenny "Kingfish" Washington, running back star for UCLA, died of polyarteritis, heart and lung condition. Washington played 580 of possible 600 minutes in 1939 and, in 1947, he re-integrated NFL by signing with Los Angeles Rams. Interestingly, it was same year his former Bruins football teammate, Jackie Robinson, gained world-wide fame for breaking baseball's color line.

- Longest winning streak entering season:

| Toledo 23 | Arizona State 17 | Nebraska, Tennessee 10 |

- Coaching Changes:

	Incoming	Outgoing
Dartmouth	Jake Crouthamel	Bob Blackman
Duke	Mike McGee	Tom Harp
Florida State	Larry Jones	Bill Peterson
Harvard	Joe Restic	John Yovicsin
Illinois	Bob Blackman	Jim Valek
Iowa	Frank Lauterbur	Ray Nagel
Kansas	Don Fambrough	Pepper Rodgers
Miami	Fran Curci	Walt Kichefski
Mississippi	Billy Kinard	Johnny Vaught
Missouri	Al Onofrio	Dan Devine
NC State	Al Michaels	Earle Edwards
Pennsylvania	Harry Gamble	Bob Odell
Rice	Bill Peterson	Bo Hagan
Texas Christian	Jim Pittman (a)	Fred Taylor
Texas Christian	Billy Tohill (a)	Jim Pittman
Tulane	Bennie Ellender	Jim Pittman
UCLA	Pepper Rodgers	Tommy Prothro
Virginia	Don Lawrence	George Blackburn
Virginia Tech	C.E. Coffey	Jerry Claiborne
Wyoming	Fritz Shurmur	Lloyd Eaton

(a) Tohill (3-1) was named interim coach after death of new coach Pittman (3-3-1).

AP Preseason Poll

1 Notre Dame (15)	885	11 Ohio State	237
2 Nebraska (26)	870	12 Penn State	190
3 Texas (5)	662	13 Syracuse	165
4 Michigan (1)	593	14 Arizona State	154
5 Southern California (1)	525	15 UCLA	122
6 Auburn	434	16 Alabama	88
7 Arkansas	332	17 Georgia Tech	76
8 Tennessee	323	18 Georgia	71
9 Louisiana State	302	19 Stanford	62
10 Oklahoma	242	20 Northwestern (1)	58

September 11, 1971

(Fri) Alabama 17 SOUTHERN CALIFORNIA 10: With unheralded QB Terry Davis at helm, newly installed triple option ran beautifully as Alabama (1-0) gained revenge for its 1970 loss to USC. Tide rushed for 302y, led by HB Johnny Musso's 85y and his 2 TDs in 1st H. Best chance for Trojans (0-1) to tie game came on special teams play in 3rd Q as WR Lynn Swann broke free with punt RET. Bama WR David Bailey turned in play of game with diving hand tackle of Swann at Tide 29YL after Swann maneuvered 57y. Trojans were unable to convert that opportunity thanks in large part to controversial 15y PEN on USC T John Vella, who was tossed out for throwing elbow. Southern California gained 287y—272y fewer than in its 1970 win—with TB Lou Harris rushing for 116y. Win was Crimson Tide coach Bear Bryant's 200th of storied career, coming on eve of his 58th birthday.

WEST VIRGINIA 45 Boston College 14: Mountaineers FB Pete Wood was too much for bumbling Boston College (0-1) team. Wood bulled through BC for school-record 214y, while Mountaineers (1-0) turned 5 FUM RECs into scores. After WVU sped to 17-0 2nd Q lead, Boston College pulled to within 17-7 on 1y keeper by QB Ray Rippman. Any chance to narrow gap ended quickly in 2nd H when West Virginia LB Wib Newton caught FUM and returned it 11y for TD. After BC was stopped again, Wood then burst away for 64y romp to set up 1y scoring pass from WVU QB Bernie Galiffa to WR Harry Blake.

SOUTH CAROLINA 24 Georgia Tech 7: Gamecocks (1-0) celebrated 1st game as independent with convincing victory over Georgia Tech (0-1), school that would take their ACC spot 8 years later. South Carolina could muster only single TD by its O, but excelled on special teams, led by DB Dickie Harris. Two punts were blocked through EZ for safeties, Harris returned punt 77y for TD, and blocked another punt that was returned 11y for TD by DB Jimmy Nash. Jackets scored courtesy of 32y INT TD RET by DB Rick Lewis to trail only 10-7 at H, but were unable to spark much O in 2nd H.

Colorado 31 LOUISIANA STATE 21: Colorado (1-0) surprised many with ease in which it handled host Bengal Tigers (0-1). Returning only 2 starters from unit that led nation in run D, LSU could not handle visitors' triple option attack that amassed 293y rushing. Leading Buffalo stampede were soph TB Charlie Davis, who tallied 174y rushing in his debut, and WR Cliff Branch, whose 75y punt TD RET in 3rd Q upped lead to 17-7. S John Stearns led Colorado D by picking off 2 passes as team forced 6 TOs. Play of Davis turned out to be crucial as Buff starting HB Jon Keyworth was knocked out for season with fractured leg in 1st H. Alternate QB Paul Lyons led LSU with TDs both rushing and passing.

Michigan 21 NORTHWESTERN 6: Bruising, hard-fought contest was sealed by odd play. Ahead 7-0 in 3rd Q, Michigan (1-0) attempted 51y FG by K Dana Coin. Northwestern DB Jack Dustin slapped down short kick in EZ, but as ball bounced around in EZ, Michigan WR Bo Rather pounced on it. Coach Bo Schembechler strenuously straightened out confused officials: TD for Wolverines and 14-0 lead. Physical Wildcats (0-1), who did not allow single 1st down during game's beginning 21 minutes, could not overcome this freakish 2-TD deficit. Wildcats blew 1st H chances, missing FG and ending 2 other drives on downs deep in Michigan territory.

OHIO STATE 52 Iowa 21: Rebuilding Ohio State opened with surprising style. Despite losing 5 players drafted in NFL's 1st round and with graduation and injuries limiting their O to single returning starter, Buckeyes (1-0) gained 402y on ground. QB Don Lamka, backup S in 1970, rushed for 100y and scored 4 TDs, while FB John Bledsoe, who played all of 3 mins in 1970, added 151y and 2 TDs. Hawkeyes (0-1) managed only 21y rushing, although establishment of run game was prevented when they trailed 17-0 in 1st Q. Iowa QB Frank Sunderman passed for 216y, including 10y TD to TE Tom Cabalka. New Hawks coach Frank Lauterbur's 23-game win streak evaporated, which he had compiled at MAC powerhouse Toledo. Welcome to Big 10's version of Big 2, Coach!

NEBRASKA 34 Oregon 7: Defending champion Cornhuskers (1-0) showed no signs of letdown in pasting solid Oregon squad that returned 17 starters. Nebraska IB Jeff Kinney rushed for 124y, while backup IB Gary Dixon scored 3 times. QB Jerry Tagge became Huskers career passing leader with 34y completion to TE Jerry List on opening drive. DE Willie Harper and DT Larry Jacobsen led swarming Nebraska D that had Ducks (0-1) shut out until 4th Q when blocked punt led to 7y TD run by TB Bobby Moore. INTs of Oregon QB Dan Fouts set up 2 of Huskers' 1st 3 scores. Capable Oregon faced killer opening schedule with Stanford, Texas, USC, and Washington up next.

Stanford 19 MISSOURI 0: Stanford (1-0) QB Don Bunce eased concern over loss of Heisman star QB Jim Plunkett. Bunce displayed option ability with nifty pitch to FB Hillary Shockley, who bowled over Missouri (0-1) DB Lorenzo Brinkley at 30YL en route to 52y TD run. Bunce also threw 26y TD pass to WR John Winesberry for 16-0 H lead. Being shutout for 1st time since 1967, Tigers struggled against veteran D, not gaining 1st downs until their 8th possession. Mizzou made only 7 1st downs; 3 QBs totaled 65y passing. Stanford's win was only Pac 8 bright spot, which had 6 teams lose opener.

HOUSTON 23 Rice 21: Exciting 1st-ever meeting between schools had fans wondering what took so long. Actually, it was well-established Rice not seeing anything to gain by playing new in-city rival that was certain to be fired up. FB Mike Phillips gave Rice (0-1) 7-0 H lead on 1y run. Dependable Houston (1-0) QB Gary Mullins ran for TD and threw for 2 other scores, including 73y scoring strike to WR Del Stanley on 2nd play of 3rd Q. On drive that turned out to spark winning pts in 4th Q, Mullins was flushed left and threw INT to Owls S Bruce Henley. After 30y RET, Henley frustratingly lost FUM at Houston 15YL. Cougars regrouped and went 85y to Mullins' 2y keeper for 23-14 lead; it proved sufficient to overcome Owls' 2 TDs in 4th Q. Victory margin came on safety secured by Houston DE Butch Brezina, who forced FUM by FB Ray Phillips that Rice scrambled to recover in its own EZ during 16-pt surge by Houston in 3rd Q.

Pittsburgh 29 UCLA 25: Panthers (1-0) ruined debut of loquacious UCLA (0-1) coach Pepper Rodgers as critical Bruins FUM set up Pitt's 4th Q 40y drive for winning TD. After starting QB Mike Flores (15-22/164y) led UCLA to go-ahead TD at 25-23, and Bruins D forced Pitt to punt, Rodgers surprisingly turned to back-up QB Clay Gallagher on practice evidence that he had surer hands than Flores. However, Panthers DE Andy Mollura nailed Gallagher to force FUM, recovered by roaming Pitt LB Ralph Cindrich. Panthers reserve QB Dave Havern then led 6-play drive, capped by his 10y TD pass to fellow back-up, TE Leslie Block. Bruins then moved into Panther territory before fizzling out at Pitt 28YL, thanks in large part to sack by NG Jack Dykes for 19y loss.

AP Poll September 13

1 Nebraska (31)	931	11 Georgia	229
2 Notre Dame (10)	829	12 Colorado	194
3 Texas (5)	672	13 Stanford	167
4 Michigan (2)	630	14 Penn State	123
5 Ohio State	546	15 Syracuse	99
6 Arkansas	541	16 Arizona State	95
7 Auburn (2)	437	17 Southern California	70
8 Tennessee	364	18 Michigan State	60
9 Alabama	314	19 South Carolina	58
10 Oklahoma	265	20 Houston	46

September 18, 1971

SYRACUSE 20 Wisconsin 20: Trailing 20-14 with 2:18 remaining, Syracuse (0-0-1) took over on its own 13YL. Orangemen QB Bob Woodruff (16-28/217y, TD, 2 INTs) hit 8-11 passes including 12y TD to WB Brian Hambleton. Badgers (1-0-1) seemed doomed to defeat but salvaged tie as LB Ed Albright blocked Syracuse K Earle Baugher's x-pt attempt. Wisconsin had taken 20-14 lead as TE Larry Mialik scored on 21y reception, lugging defender over final 5y to EZ. QB Neil Graff (14-24/229y,

INT) and TB Rufus "Roadrunner" Ferguson, who rushed for 149y and 2 TDs, paced Wisconsin. Syracuse lost star DT Joe Erhmann, who led GLS in 2nd Q, to season-ending knee injury.

Wake Forest 20 VIRGINIA TECH 9: Battle of contrasting styles was won by Wake's ground-oriented Veer attack. QB Larry Russell rushed for 149y, and Deacons D picked off star Virginia Tech QB Don Strock 3 times. After Gobblers (0-1) struck 1st with 2y TD run by TB Rich Matijevich, HB Junior Moore returned ensuing KO 89y for Wake Forest's 1st KO TD RET since 1952. After scoring again to build 14-6 lead, Deacons (2-0) were able to keep ball on ground, rushing for 354y to offset Strock's 258-38y passing advantage. Wake CB Steve Bowden contributed key play of 2nd H with EZ INT to preserve 14-9 lead. Russell commenced to lead 80y Deacs drive to 3y TD run by rugged FB Larry Hopkins (26/109y).

Florida State 20 MIAMI 17: Fran Curci's coaching debut at Miami (0-1) got initial shock as Seminoles DB Eddie McMillan raced opening KO back 90y for TD. But, Canes RB Chuck Foreman scored twice in 2nd Q for 17-7 lead at H break. Deeper Florida State (2-0) squad overcame its 78y O in 1st H to dominate in 2nd H heat. K Frank Fontes pulled FSU within 17-10 late in 3rd Q, and WR Rhett Dawson's 5y TD grab of toss by QB Gary Huff (15-24/183y, TD, 2 INTs) tied it early in 4th Q. Fontes' 25y FG won it with 4:38 left.

GEORGIA 17 Tulane 7: Green Wave (1-1) was guilty of only 1 PEN all day, but their single foul came at wrong time. Late in 3rd Q, Tulane tied game 7-7 on 9y TD run by soph TB Rickey Hebert (30/88y) and then forced Georgia (2-0) to punt. But, Wave was called for personal foul. Bulldogs retained possession on their 40YL, and Georgia rambled on to winning TD by TB Ricky Lake (24/82y) with 8:54 to play in 4th Q. Bulldogs soon added insurance on K Kim Braswell's 31y FG after DT Milton Brice recovered Hebert's FUM at 14YL. UGa QB Andy Johnson rushed for 127y, TD, which resulted from FUM inducing tackle by DE Phil Sullivan at Tulane 31YL in 1st Q.

MISSISSIPPI STATE 13 Florida 10: Bulldogs (1-1) K Glen Ellis booted winning 29y FG with 5 mins left, just moments after PEN against Florida nullified his missed FG. Gators (0-2) grabbed 10-3 H lead as QB John Reaves, who broke former Mississippi QB Archie Manning's SEC career total O mark (5,576y), threw 5y TD pass to TE Jim Yancey. As Mississippi State D—which intercepted Reaves 4 times—posted 2nd H shutout, Maroon FB Wayne Jones tied game at 10-10 with 21y scoring run to set up Ellis' 3-pt heroics.

NEBRASKA 35 Minnesota 7: Pick your poison; Huskers (2-0) proved they could pounce on any weakness, in this case, stepping out of mode to throw for 226y. Doing most damage was WB Johnny Rodgers, who caught 6/126y, TDs of 28, 20, and 37y. QB Jerry Tagge kept pace, going 15-21/ 218y in air. Gophers (1-1) dug themselves early hole, allowing 2 TDs in 1st Q when managing no 1st downs. Minnesota bounced back with 79y drive ended by TB Jim Henry's 6y TD run. Tagge then fumbled, and Gophers LB Bill Light recovered at Huskers 39YL. Driving to 10YL, Gophers sniffed tie, but after 3 plays produced –3y, they missed FG. Nebraska responded with 80y voyage to 2nd 1y TD run by IB Jeff Kinney (16/79y), pretty well ending matters at 21-7.

ARIZONA STATE 18 Houston 17: High scoring clubs hooked up in surprising D struggle, which was decided by last-sec FG. Houston (1-1) started slowly with 14y in 3 1st Q possessions, but built 17-7 lead in 4th Q on TDs by RB Robert Newhouse and TE Riley Odoms. Arizona State (1-0) converted FUM REC into FB Brent McClanahan's 7y TD run and 2-pt conv pass by QB Danny White to cut deficit to 17-15 midway through 4th Q. Sun Devils mustered last drive to produce winning 46y FG by 27-year-old K Don Ekstrand. Exhausting victory stretched Sun Devils' win streak to 18 games.

Texas 28 UCLA 10: Shaking off injuries, Texas QB Eddie Phillips led devastating attack that amassed 443y in swamping Bruins (0-2). Phillips ran for 142y, TD and threw surprise 36y TD pass to WR Jimmy Moore. HB Jim Bertelson added 124y rushing as Texas (1-0) did not seem to miss 17 graduated starters from 1970. S Ron Carver's 3 INTs kept Bruins in game. Trailing 14-10 early in 4th Q, Bruins moved to Texas 42YL before missing 60y FG attempt by K Efren Herrera. Longhorns soon marched 87y to seal deal at 21-10 with 2y TD keeper by Phillips on 4th down. Sole Bruins TD had come in 1st Q for 7-0 lead: QB Mike Flores' 42y TD to WR Reggie Echols.

WASHINGTON 38 Purdue 35: Fans of big plays should rent this film. Boilermakers (0-1) scored on 39y run by HB Otis Armstrong, 80y catch by WR Darryl Stingley, and 43y scramble by QB Gary Danielson. Huskies (2-0) featured 60y TD run by WR Tom Scott (3 TDs) on reverse and winning 33y TD strike to Scott by QB Sonny Sixkiller, who threw for to-date school record of 387y. Danielson's pass to Stingley had given Purdue short-lived 35-31 lead moments earlier.

September 25, 1971

NORTH CAROLINA 35 Maryland 14: Dedicating their effort to G Billy Arnold, who died during practice on Monday, Tar Heels (3-0) looked in control until FUMs on 3 straight carries by TB Ike Oglesby (24/110y) set up 2 Maryland TDs for 14-14 tie. Oglesby's 3rd bobble returned possession to Terps early in 3rd Q, but star Carolina LB John Bunting's INT reversed momentum and set up 55y drive for go-ahead 7y TD run by QB Paul

Miller. Neither Tar Heel was done: Miller completed 62y scoring strike to WB Lewis Jolley, and Bunting returned INT 35y for another TD. QB Al Neville threw for 172y and 24y TD to WR Dan Bungori to lead Terps (1-2).

Army 16 GEORGIA TECH 13: Army Cadets (1-1) won their 1st game in last 12 outings as K Jim Barclay nailed 40y FG in last 4:14 at Atlanta. "He just wanted to come out and kick, so we let him," said coach Tom Cahill. Army QB Dick Atha hit 6-13 passes in 1st H as his throws, including 44y gain to WR Ed Francis, set up 2 FGs in 1st Q. Soon, Black Knights DB Matt Wotell blocked punt to allow Army RB Ray Ritacco to blast 4y off LT for TD. Georgia Tech (1-2) got off mat to tally on QB Eddie McAshan's 8y TD throw that was lobbed over defenders to TE Mike Oven in EZ in 2nd Q. Jackets tied it 13-13 on pair of FGs by K Cam Bonifay before 2 ill-advised PENs by Tech D helped position Army's Barclay for his late 3-pt heroics

FLORIDA STATE 30 Kansas 7: Throwing for 300y and 3 TDs, Florida State QB Gary Huff proved to be too much for Kansas D that majestically had posted shutouts in 2 previous games. Huff's 3rd TD arrow, 88y to WR Barry Smith, can play that Smith and O coordinator Steve Sloan had drawn up on sideline. It turned out to be game-clincher and was school record at that time for pass play distance. Also, it was longest play surrendered to date by any Jayhawks (2-1) team. Smith also caught 19y TD, while K Frank Fontes kicked 3 FGs. Kansas was hampered by 5 INTs thrown by QBs Dan Heck and David Jaynes, while Heck threw solo 7y TD pass to TE John Schroll.

Auburn 10 TENNESSEE 9: Watching 1st home loss since 1966, Tennessee (1-1) fans had to be happy that Auburn QB Pat Sullivan was playing his last collegiate season. Trailing 9-3 late in 4th Q, Tigers began moving from their own 14YL following crucial FUM by Vols. Alternating between WR Terry Beasley, who returned from being knocked out on hit by DB Bobby Majors in 1st H, and WB Dick Schmalz, Sullivan completed 5 straight passes to lead Auburn (2-0) to winning 5y TD run by TB Harry Unger with 2:24 left. Vols had time for K George Hunt's attempt at his 4th FG, but Tennessee was stopped instead as Auburn LB Mike Neel made 4th down ankle tackle of Vols TB Bill Rudder for 8y loss. Vols LB Jackie Walker excelled in defeat, making 16 stops, blocking 2 FGs, and forcing FUM.

Colorado 20 OHIO STATE 14: Buffs (3-0) laid claim to Top 10 spot with big road win. WR Cliff Branch's 6th career KO TD RET put Colorado up 13-0. Bison QB Ken Johnson added 39y TD scamper in 4th Q, TB Charlie Davis rushed for 135y, and stiff Buffs D, led by G Bud Magrum's 20 tackles, twice stopped Ohio State (1-1) threats inside 5YL. QB Don Lamka (20-33/255y, TD), despite shoulder separation in his non-throwing arm, rallied Buckeyes to 2 late TDs. Win marked 18th straight Big 8 win over Big 10.

MICHIGAN STATE 31 Oregon State 14: Coach Duffy Daugherty turned to 3rd string QB Frank Kolch to deliver his 100th coaching win, and break hold from S Brad Van Pelt. Kolch (10-17/144y, 2 TDs, INT) led O, while Van Pelt had 2 masterful INT TD RETs for Spartans (2-1). Beavers (1-2) had more 1st downs and 357 to 323y O advantage, but burned themselves with 3 INTs. FB Dave Schilling led Oregon State with 133y rushing, while HB Eric Allen paced Spartans with 119y rushing and 5/78y receiving.

MICHIGAN 38 Ucla 0: Wolverines (3-0) jumped to 17-0 lead with assists by Bruins, who coughed up 2 early TOs. TB Billy Taylor rushed for 91y to join Ron Johnson and Tom Harmon as 3rd Michigan back to top 2,000y in career rushing. Wolverines D was led by DT Dave Gallagher, whose 1st Q INT led to team's 2nd TD, LB Mike Taylor, who forced FUM that led to FG, and S Thom Darden, who returned INT 92y for 4th Q TD. Shutout was Wolverines' 2nd of 3 in row. UCLA (0-3), off to its worst start since 1943 war-time squad dropped its 1st 7 games, featured 177y passing and QB Mike Flores' 59y rushing.

Notre Dame 8 PURDUE 7: Notre Dame (2-0) slipped out of Ross-Ade Stadium with fortunate win in final mins. Ahead 7-0 with less than 3 mins left, Purdue (0-2) was forced to punt from deep in its own end. Trying to field wet ball, P Scott Lougheed fumbled bad snap into EZ after he was hit by Irish CB Clarence Ellis. Loose ball was recovered by DE Fred Swenson for TD. QB Pat Steenberge (7-25/105y, INT) salvaged Irish's long day—he had lost FUM on Purdue 8YL moments earlier—with successful 2-pt conv pass to TE Mike Creaney. Purdue's lone TD was earned on 25y pass from QB Gary Danielson (12-24/138y, TD, INT) to HB Otis Armstrong.

NORTHWESTERN 12 Syracuse 6: Purple run game raged in 1st H as long as FB Randy Anderson was on stage. Anderson ran for 43y until injured, banging away on 1st series by Northwestern (1-2) that led to FG. After Syracuse (0-1-1) bobbled ensuing KO, Wildcats K Bill Planisek kicked his 2nd FG. Anderson ran out of full-house on 2nd Q drive of 80y he climaxed with 1y plunge for 12-0 lead. Orangemen's pair of big backs, TBs Roger Praetorius (23/82y, TD) and Marty Januszkiewicz, powered to 3rd Q TD. NW's opportunistic 2nd H D came up with big play on 4th down in 4th Q when LB Jack Derning and DT George Keporos made stop of Praetorius.

Tulsa 21 ARKANSAS 20: Hogs (2-1) were shocked by Tulsa's late rally. Down 20-0, QB Todd Starkes fired 3 4th Q TD passes to lead Golden Hurricane (1-1) comeback against rather green Arkansas D. Winning drive lasted 87y, with final 21y coming on screen pass to FB Larry Frey. Tulsa faced 3rd-and-24 to keep things alive, and Starkes threw 22y pass to TE Jim Butler before Frey ran for 3y for 1st down. Porkers QB Joe Ferguson, doing his best without 3 injured backfield mates, had rough time in 2nd H against strong wind and Tulsa's preventive 3-8 D alignment. Arkansas FB Skipper DeBorde rushed for 2 TDs, and Ferguson threw 9y TD to WR Mark Hollingsworth for what looked like safe margin.

AP Poll September 27

1 Nebraska (32)	1064	11 Georgia	249
2 Michigan (3)	840	12 Tennessee	193
3 Texas (3)	835	13 Arizona State	155
4 Notre Dame (1)	710	14 Ohio State	120
5 Auburn (2)	649	15 Washington	98
6 Colorado (2)	638	16 Louisiana State	70
7 Alabama	542	17 Southern California	62
8 Oklahoma	411	18 Arkansas	52
9 Penn State	316	19 Duke	31
10 Stanford	303	20 North Carolina	22

October 2, 1971

PENN STATE 16 Air Force 14: In need of last-sec 22y FG, Penn State (3-0) coach Joe Paterno could not have been too confident when he sent in K Alberto Vitello, good on only 1-5 FGs on season and 1-2 x-pts in this game. Neapolitan soccer's contribution to college football came through and Nittany Lions (3-0) averted upset. Air Force (2-1) had taken 14-13 lead in 3rd Q on 19y TD pass lobbed from QB Rich Haynie to 6'5" TE Paul Bassa, who out-jumped shorter defenders. Haynie threw for 194y and 2 TDs, but was picked off 6 times with 2 INTs coming in closing moments. HB Lydell Mitchell gained 91y rushing and TD for Nittany Lions, 1 week after he torched Iowa for 211y.

ARMY 22 Missouri 6: Break up Cadets! Hero in upset win was soph QB J. Kingsley "King" Fink, who came off bench to throw 3 2nd H TD passes to spark Army (2-1). Cadets also rushed for 212y. After taking 6-3 lead on 56y TD run by QB Chuck Roper, Missouri (1-3) made things easy for Army with 7 TOs as sloppy play negated productive output of 380y on O. Black Knights LB Gary Topping had 12 tackles and 2 FUM RECs for home team, with 2nd REC setting up Fink's winning pass to TE Dave Sanders.

Wake Forest 18 MARYLAND 14: Surprising Demon Deacons (3-1) erased 14-0 downside with 11 pts in 4th Q. Wake Forest employed run attack for 222y (of 283y total) in 2nd H and made 4 INTs of Terrapins (1-3) QB Al Neville, including pair by DBs Frank Fussell and Steve Bowden at 7 and 15YLs in 4th Q. Neville had run 20y for TD and thrown 12y to WR Dan Bungori for TD for 14-0 lead in 1st H. Wake centered its 2nd H O on RBs Gary Johnson (130y rushing) and Larry Hopkins (125y).

North Carolina 27 NORTH CAROLINA STATE 7: Tar Heels (4-0) jumped to 20-0 H edge as TB Ike Oglesby (21/83y) scored twice, but he spent whole 2nd H on sideline with leg cramps. So, it was left to North Carolina S Richard Stilley to take on yeoman duty in snuffing rally by North Carolina State (0-4). First, Stilley made saving tackle on Wolfpack WB Mike Stulz after 50y RET of 2nd H KO. After NC State soph FB Charley Young racked up 36y TD run to narrow margin to 20-7, Stilley made 4th down stop inches from his GL as Wolfpack WR Steve Lester caught pass that every NC State fan thought was TD at end of 79y drive. Heels kept ball for 32 plays of 4th Q and added TE Johnny Cowell's diving 11y TD catch, 2nd scoring toss of game for QB Paul Miller.

ALABAMA 40 Mississippi 6: (Birmingham): Undefeated but untested Mississippi (3-1) failed miserably against Bama, allowing 531y rushing—504y more than in last year's tilt. Crimson Tide (4-0) HB Johnny Musso (22/193, TD) was beneficiary of blocks laid out by likes of G John Hannah. Ole Miss was close early, tying game 6-6 late in 2nd Q as QB Kenny Lyons connected with FB Gene Allen on 48y TD pass. Trailing 13-6 entering 3rd Q, Rebels marched to Bama 18YL, only to miss FG. From then on it was all Tide.

TOLEDO 31 Ohio University 28: Safeguarding the nation's longest winning streak at 27 games, Toledo (4-0) killed last 4 mins of clock to hold off late charge by Ohio (1-2). Bobcats scored 1st on 5y run by HB Chuck Gary, who would duplicate effort at end of 2-TD comeback in 4th Q. When Rockets QB Chuck Ealey threw his 2nd TD pass to WR John Fair in 3rd Q, Toledo lifted its lead to 24-14. Clinching score came as TB Joe Schwartz banged up middle and raced 80y to TD in 4th Q.

OKLAHOMA 33 Southern California 20: HB Greg Pruitt (16/206y, 3 TDs) fit prototype of great Southern California TBs, but sadly for USC coach John McKay, Pruitt gained his ground for Oklahoma (3-0). QB Jack Mildren rushed for 102y and TD at helm of O that toted up 516y on ground. Trojans (2-2) made 402y in their own right as FB Sam Cunningham's 123y rushing sparked attack. USC converted 2 FUMs by Sooners FB Leon Crosswhite into 1st H TDs but still trailed 19-14 at H as Pruitt scored twice. Pruitt then went 75y to paydirt midway through 3rd Q before INT deep in Sooner territory was turned into additional score on 72y TD drive capped by Mildren's 11y keeper.

Texas Tech 13 ARIZONA 10: Mistakes cost Wildcats, who lost ball 8 times on TOs to kill their own drives and set up every pt for Texas Tech (1-3). Opening Red Raiders TD was 69y INT TD RET by DB Marc Dove that tied game at 7-7 after Arizona (2-1) had scored on 73y punt RET by CB Jackie Wallace. After teams traded FGs for 10-10 H score, FUM by TB Bobby McCall set up 3rd Q drive to winning 28y FG by Raiders K Don Grimes. Cats answered with drive to Tech 1YL, before holding PEN forced QB Bill Demory's pass that was promptly intercepted by Raiders DB Don Rebold. Arizona outgained Red Raiders 302y to 222y, but lost 4 FUMs within Red Raiders 25YL.

Duke 9 STANFORD 3: Duke (4-0) coach Mike McGee used prevent-D to limit damage inflicted by Stanford (3-1) QB Don Bunce (16-34/229y). Bunce, who rashly predicted unbeaten Tribe would score 6 TDs to none for Duke, sparked 362y O and even threw pass for TD. Unfortunately that TD went to Duke CB Ernie Jackson, who scored on 54y INT RET early in 1st Q to launch upset. Indians cause also was damaged by 3 lost FUMs and 3 missed FGs. Without FB Steve Jones, nation's 2nd leading rusher who was injured in car crash 5 days before game, Blue Devils managed only 139y O but led 6-0 at H despite attaining only single 1st down in game's opening 30 mins.

AP Poll October 4

1 Nebraska (43)	1058	11 Washington	241
2 Michigan (5)	886	12 Arizona State	148
3 Texas (3)	818	13 Tennessee	140
4 Auburn (2)	654	14 Duke	139
5 Colorado (2)	616	15 Ohio State	125
6 Alabama	607	16 Louisiana State	92
7 Notre Dame	606	17 Arkansas	53
8 Oklahoma	592	18 North Carolina	38
9 Penn State	289	19 Stanford	30
10 Georgia	280	20 Toledo	25

October 9, 1971

Clemson 3 Duke 0 (Norfolk, Va): No. 14 Duke (4-1) seemed to have easy target for its 5th win of season in winless Clemson in Oyster Bowl. Blue Devils were so injury-riddled, however, that 3 players had to play both ways. Clemson (1-3) won game on K Eddie Seigler's 39y FG in 3rd Q. Tigers, rushing for 204y, were successful keeping ball out of hands of TB-DB Ernie Jackson, who had been scoring threat every time he touched ball so far in 1971. Closest Blue Devils got to Clemson EZ was 4th Q trip to 27YL, spot from which QB Dennis Satyshur—who was picked off 3 times—missed 4th down pass.

SOUTH CAROLINA 34 Virginia 14: Even stadium power outage could not prevent blowout by Gamecocks (4-1). Cavs turned ball over 7 times, setting up 2 of 1st 3 TDs as South Carolina DB Tyler Hellams recovered FUM and picked off pass, both in Virginia territory. DB Dickie Harris added 43y punt TD RET, and Gamecocks enjoyed 20-0 H lead. Any hopes for UVa comeback ended early in 3rd Q after blocked punt by Carolina MG Pat Kohout was recovered in EZ by teammate DT John Lehoup. Virginia (1-4) was shut out until scoring 2 TDs in 4th Q, including 41y run by TB Kent Merritt.

Tulane 37 NORTH CAROLINA 29: Another undefeated ACC team bit dust as Tulane (2-3) QB Mike Walker fired 4 TDs in 1st H and WR Coleman Dupre added 100y KO TD RET. Walker completed 9-15/267y in game's opening 30 mins, getting Wave on board early with 65y scoring strike to FB Bob Marshall. Marshall's TD marked 1st time North Carolina (3-1) had trailed all season. Green Wave increased lead to 28-11 with Walker throwing scoring passes of 26y to WR Maxie LeBlanc and 56y and 38y to WR Steve Barrios. Tar Heels rallied behind 2 4th Q TD runs by TB Geof Hamlin. Just when UNC seemed reinvigorated, Dupre took his KO RET to house to keep upset alive.

Georgia 38 MISSISSIPPI 7 (Jackson): It was time for Bulldogs (5-0) to gain revenge on QB Archie Manning-less Rebels. Behind TB Jimmy Poulos (15/116y), Georgia rushed for 355y and scored on 4 of its 1st 6 possessions. First TD scored by G John Jennings, who caught FUM on odd play and rumbled 39y. QBs Andy Johnson and James Ray played well for Bulldogs with Johnson rushing for 102y and Ray passing 5-5/48y. Ole Miss (2-3) QB Kenny Lyons hit only 3 passes in 1st H for –1y before being benched. Rebels scored late on backup QB Norris Weese's 1y scoring pass to TE Burney Veasey to avert shutout. Georgia's 5-0 start was its 1st since 1946 club went 11-0.

Michigan 24 MICHIGAN STATE 13: Down 10-7 early in 4th Q and having marched to Michigan 14YL, spunky Spartans (2-3) seemed poised for upset. Wolverines DEs Mike Keller and Butch Carpenter then sacked QB Frank Kolch on consecutive plays, 2nd of which by Carpenter produced FUM recovered by Keller. Run attack of Michigan (5-0), which totaled 322y, then went 53y to TD on 2y run by TB Billy Taylor (15/117y, 2 TDs). Shaking off effects of shoulder injury, Taylor rushed for 29y on clinching drive to 17-7 margin. Kolch's 3y TD run with time elapsing in 2nd Q kept Michigan State in contest. MSU's 13 pts nearly doubled total against Wolverines D: 29 pts allowed in 5 games.

Ohio State 24 ILLINOIS 10: Winless Illinois (0-5) outdistanced crippled—3 starters were lost for season—Ohio State (3-1) 414y to 292y, and perhaps it helped to turn year around for 1st-year coach Bob Blackman. Illinois would lose once more and beat last 5 foes. Big play came in 1st Q: Ohio MG Kevin Fletcher, who soon joined wounded Bucks on bench, blocked punt of Illini P Terry Masar to turn it over at 2YL, and Buckeyes FB Randy Keith scored his 2nd TD for 14-0 lead only 4:51 into game. Illinois botched 1st down opportunities at 4 and 6YLs, but escaped 1st H with FG after LB Chuck Kogat recovered FUM. Ohio State QB Greg Hare (2-7/8y), in for injured QB Don Lamka, raced 31y after 2nd H KO and scored on 3y option run for 21-3 lead. Illini QB-K Mike Wells (15-29/198y, 2 INTs and FG) hit 15 and 17y passes on 85y TD march in 4th Q.

Oklahoma 48 Texas 27 (Dallas): Sooners (4-0) tore page out of UT playbook as QB Jack Mildren and HB Greg Pruitt, both Texas natives, led Wishbone attack that had been introduced to college ball by Texas (3-1). Mildren's and Pruitt's heroics gave OU its 1st series win since 1966 and snapped Horns' impressive 33-game regular season win streak. Oklahoma rushed for 435y—344 in 1st H—as Pruitt sped to 214y himself. Pts were most scored on Longhorns since 1952, as Sooners avenged 41-9 beating of 1970. Texas was crippled at QB, with starter Eddie Phillips slowed by hamstring injury and backup Donnie Wigginton knocked out with separated ribs in 3rd Q; by game's end more opening day starters were sidelined than were playing against Sooners. Wigginton managed 2 TDs for Steers before departing, as did HB Jim Bertelson.

Colorado 24 IOWA STATE 14: DE-K J.B. Dean was hero for Buffs, who needed full effort to defeat pesky Iowa State (3-1). Dean's 37y FG put Colorado (5-0) up 17-14. Dean then picked off QB Dean Carlson to set up 8y TD run on reverse by WR Cliff Branch. Game-sealing TD by Branch came 2 plays after his 56y reception. ISU LB Matt Blair appeared to have put Cyclones in good shape by recovering FUM 2 plays before Dean's INT. Game had been tied at 14-14 entering 4th Q as Colorado had scored TDs on 7y run by TB Charlie Davis and 11y pass from QB Ken Johnson to WR Willie Nicholes. Iowa State earlier had cracked EZ on 28y pass from TB George Amundsen to WR Willie Jones and 9y keeper by Carlson. Buffs rushed for 314y in building 26 to 7 differential in 1st downs.

KANSAS 39 Kansas State 13: QB David Jaynes came off bench in 2nd Q to throw 3 TDs as Jayhawks (3-2) broke open 0-0 game. Jaynes hooked up on 9y TD pass with TB Delvin Williams, who added 46y 4th Q TD run. After Kansas State TD, Jaynes pitched 2 TDs within 3-min span of 3rd Q. Wildcats (2-3) never got closer than 10-7 deficit after 7y TD run by HB Isaac Jackson on 4-play, 57y drive after 2nd H KO.

Stanford 17 WASHINGTON 6: Stanford D shut down Huskies QB Sonny Sixkiller, and, therefore, shut down undefeated Huskies (4-1). Washington entered at 49.8 pts per game, but aggressive, blitzing D kept them blanked until 4th Q. When DB Benny Barnes wasn't blitzing—he had 2 sacks—he made 3 of Indians' 4 INTs. Meanwhile, Stanford DG Kevin Lazetich was in on 4 sacks. All of Stanford's pts came in 1st H on 20y catch by WR John Winesberry, 20y run by FB Reggie Sanderson, and 47y FG by K Rod Garcia. Both TD drives were short (32y and 34y) and were set up by Tribe's D forcing Huskies to punt from their EZ and making INT. Sixkiller completed only 12-46 attempts.

Oregon 28 SOUTHERN CALIFORNIA 23: At game's end, Trojans (2-3) QB Jimmy Jones threw perfect long ball to WR Edesel Garrison for apparent winning 77y TD, but play was called back because of ineligible-receiver PEN. So, Ducks (2-3) hung on for stunning upset. Oregon QB Harvey Winn (17-25/253y, INT), starting for injured QB Dan Fouts, threw 3 TDs and led 2 4th Q TD drives to erase 23-14 deficit. TB Bobby Moore proved to be Ducks' most effective weapon as he rushed for 145y, including game-winning 2y TD, and caught 6 passes, including 11y TD that pulled Oregon to within 23-21 early in 4th Q. USC was sparked by FB Sam Cunningham's 187y rushing, although he lost crucial FUM late in 3rd Q.

AP Poll October 11
1 Nebraska (40)	1056	11 Arizona State	208
2 Oklahoma (8)	888	12 Louisiana State	163
3 Michigan (4)	880	13 Ohio State	159
4 Alabama	668	14 Tennessee	151
5 Auburn (2)	620	15 Stanford	141
6 Colorado (1)	619	16 Arkansas	86
7 Notre Dame	575	17 Toledo	29
8 Georgia	404	18 Washington	28
9 Penn State	387	19 Florida State	26
10 Texas	314	20 Purdue	17

October 16, 1971

Penn State 31 SYRACUSE 0: Penn State's domination of East continued as QB John Hufnagel ran unbeaten streak to 10 games. Scoring twice, Hufnagel rushed for 71y before departing in 3rd Q, while HB Lydell Mitchell added 94y to Nittany Lions' ground total of 245y. Penn State (5-0) D allowed only 204y and posted consecutive shutouts for 1st time since its D of 1948 turned trick. Lions D also got into scoring fun on Orangemen punt play as DE Bruce Bannon blocked ball and quickly led interference for LB Gary Gray's 21y TD RET. Syracuse (2-2-1) QB Bob Woodruff completed 14-27/102y for much of its O.

Clemson 32 VIRGINIA 15 (Richmond): Tigers (2-3) continued their hex over Virginia (1-5) by breaking game open in 3rd Q. Clemson scored 3 TDs on drives totaling 234y to wipe away 7-3 H deficit. QB Tommy Kendrick set up 1st score with 53y connection with WR Don Kelley, found Kelley for 75y scoring pass for next score, and completed 40y pass to TE John McMakin to set up 3rd TD of 3rd Q. TB Kent Merritt scored both Cavaliers TDs, racing 71y for 7-3 lead in 2nd Q and catching 15y pass in 4th Q.

Auburn 31 GEORGIA TECH 14: Trailing 7-6 entering 4th Q, Tigers (5-0) finally took lead on 9y scoring run by TB Tommy Lowry (12/103y). Lowry added 2-pt conv run for 14-7 edge to jumpstart 25-pt 4th Q deluge. Auburn QB Pat Sullivan did his usual yeoman's work, throwing for 281y and 3 TDs, including 12y scoring pass to WB Dick Schmalz (7/101y) for 21-7 4th Q lead. Sullivan set new SEC standard with 13 straight completions. Yellow Jackets (2-4) had hung tough thanks to Auburn TOs: Tigers snuffed their 1st 4 possessions with frustrating TOs. Converting FUM REC on Auburn 6YL, Georgia Tech QB Tommy Turrentine threw 5y TD pass to FB Greg Horne for 7-0 lead.

ALABAMA 32 Tennessee 15: Combination of Alabama (6-0) Wishbone and Tennessee's 8 TOs were too much for Vols. Crimson Tide QB Terry Davis completed only 3-5 passes, but 2 completions went to WR David Bailey for TDs. Davis also ran for 6y TD, while HB Johnny Musso (22/115y) led rushing attack that totaled 283y. FB Curt Watson, who 1 week earlier had broken Beattie Feathers' school career rushing mark, scored both Tennessee (3-2) TDs. Win was 1st for Tide over Vols since 1966.

Louisiana State 17 KENTUCKY 13: Tigers (5-1) looked like they had rout going early, holding 10-0 lead after 2 possessions on 26y FG by K Jay Michaelson and 1y TD run by TB Chris Datin. Wildcats (1-5) then began to fortify their D, while cracking scoreboard late in 1st H on FB Arvel Carroll's 1y TD run. Score remained 10-7 for LSU until 4th Q when INT by Bengals S Joe Winkler was converted into 3y scoring run by QB Bert Jones for 17-7 lead. Kentucky CB Heff Woodcock returned favor with INT that set up 36y TD run by WB Doug Kotar. Tigers D made big play by stopping Wildcats' 2-pt attempt and kept them in check rest of game.

FLORIDA 17 Florida State 15: Florida (1-5) gained measure of pride amid dreadful season with its upset win over in-state rivals. Fans expected shootout between Gators QB John Reaves and FSU QB Gary Huff, but Florida Coach Doug Dickey opted for ball control with 54 rushing plays and 11 passes out of playbook. Dickey's strategy worked well as Gators built 17-7 lead. But big play came on KO that followed TB Mike Rich's opening TD run. Gators S Jimmy Barr nabbed mid-air FUM on KO and returned it 26y for 14-0 lead. Huff (22-40/184y, TD, INT) led late Florida State (5-1) rally with 6y TD pass to WR Rhett Dawson, but ensuing Seminoles drive stalled short of FG range.

NOTRE DAME 16 North Carolina 0: Chicago Tribune's subhead said it all: "Toe Not Heels." Soph K Bob Thomas tied 58-year-old Notre Dame (5-0) FG record with 3, all in 1st H for daunting 9-0 lead. Tar Heels (4-2), on their way to ACC title, arrived in South Bend with 400y avg on O, but were held to measly 149y and only 4 1st downs after 1st Q, and Irish D raised its TD-free skein to 14 Qs in row. North Carolina threatened only once: E Earle Bethea made 20y catch to give UNC 1st down at ND 4YL, but 3 runs went nowhere, and Irish DL Mike Kadish tipped away FG try. E Tom Gatewood (3/62y) became ND receiving king with 139 career catches and added 4th Q TD on 4y grab.

OKLAHOMA 45 Colorado 17: Sooners (5-0) swept through nightmarish 3-game stretch against Southern California, Texas, and Colorado in impressive fashion. Oklahoma's school-record-to-date 670y O, including 172 through air, overwhelmed D of no. 6 Buffaloes (5-1). HB Greg Pruitt (14/193y, 2 TDs) proved to be tough to stop, while QB Jack Mildren fired TD passes of 54y to WR Jon Harrison and 68y to WB Joe Wylie. Displaying feast-or-famine approach to things, Sooners scored 3 TDs and kicked FG on 7 1st H possessions, but also lost 3 FUMs. QB Ken Johnson threw for 241y, but could not pull Colorado within rally range of no. 2 Oklahoma's dynamic scoring machine.

ARKANSAS 31 Texas 7: One week after Oklahoma ran over Texas D, Arkansas (5-1) went to air with surprisingly similar results. Razorbacks QB Joe Ferguson (14-24/249y, 3 TDs) and WR Mike Reppond (8/171y, TD) starred as Hogs snapped Texas' 21-game conf win streak. Ferguson ran in score from 10y out, while TE Bobby Nichols caught 2 of his TD passes. Arkansas' 451y was 30-year high for any UT opponent. Texas (3-2) managed early 7-0 lead on HB Jim Bertelson's 1y TD run, which was set up by 56y punt RET by WR Dean Campbell. Hogs cut off up-middle and pitchout options, so Texas' banged-up QBs were forced in vain to try to beat Porkers' quick D.

OREGON STATE 24 Arizona State 18 (Portland): Although Arizona State was fast becoming breeding ground for NFL-caliber skill position athletes, Devils' lack of wide bodies cost them their 21-game winning streak. Oregon State (3-3) FB Dave Schilling hammered 47 times at middle of ASU D and gained 157y and all 3 Beavers' TDs. Schilling became school's all-time leading rusher in process with total of 2,352y in his career. Win was 5th straight for Beavers over Sun Devils (4-1), whose highlight was 73y scoring bomb from QB Grady Hurst to WR Steve Holden that gained 10-10 tie in 3rd Q.

AP Poll October 18
1 Nebraska (35)	1046	11 Colorado	267
2 Oklahoma (18)	1008	12 Ohio State	230
3 Michigan (1)	837	13 Louisiana State	209
4 Alabama	765	14t Arizona State	62
5 Auburn (1)	585	14t Toledo	62
6 Notre Dame	578	16 Texas	60
7 Penn State	479	17 Purdue	40
8 Georgia	460	18 Tennessee	37
9 Arkansas	331	19 Duke	34
10 Stanford	280	20 Air Force	23

October 23, 1971

FLORIDA STATE 49 South Carolina 18: South Carolina got rude welcome to its new status as independent. Florida State (6-1), which never in its history had conf status, whacked Gamecocks. QB Gary Huff threw 5 TDs and ran for 6th score with his best moments coming in 28-pt 2nd Q: 227y in air and 3 scoring passes. WR Rhett Dawson (9/140y) and WR Kent Gaydos each caught 2 TDs for Seminoles. Carolina (5-2), playing with sad knowledge that JV G Bill Sedivy had died in car accident that morning, converted 2 early FSU FUMs into 10-0 lead. Florida State answered with 98y drive, capped with Dawson's 32y TD catch. Huff actually threw for 104y on march because PENs extended distance FSU had to cover. If that wasn't enough to swing momentum in Noles' direction, South Carolina DB Dickie Harris fumbled next 2 KOs to set up TDs and fire up Florida State's big 2nd Q.

ALABAMA 34 Houston 20: Bama (7-0) held Houston's potent attack in check while unleashing blistering O. Once again, HB Johnny "The Italian Stallion" Musso (22/122y) led way; his 2 TDs lifted his career SEC pt total to 212, 8 more than Georgia Tech's QB Billy Lothridge made in 1961-63. Alabama QB Terry Davis connected with WR David Bailey on pair of scoring passes for 2nd straight week. Houston (4-2) FB Robert Newhouse rushed for 182y, while QB Gary Mullins connected twice with TE Riley Odoms for TDs.

ILLINOIS 21 Purdue 7: Fightin' Illini (1-6) earned 1st win for coach Bob Blackman as ground game (57/263y) established 24-9 1st down differential. After marching 80y with opening possession for 7-0 lead on 1st of 2 TD runs by HB John Wilson, Illinois could not crack scoreboard for rest of 1st H. Boilermakers (3-3) tied game in 2nd Q on 2y run by HB Otis Armstrong to cap 35y drive begun with Illinois FUM. That was it for Purdue team that struggled against Illinois D, led by DT Tab Bennett. Purdue QB Gary Danielson (8-18/104y, INT) played with separated shoulder, which contributed to his ineffectiveness.

Southern California 28 NOTRE DAME 14: Southern California did it again to Irish (5-1). Trojans (3-4), 21-pt underdogs, grabbed early lead, forcing ND into passing game. USC WR Edesel Garrison (5/127y) used his sprinter's speed to catch 2 TDs in 1st H: 31y from QB Jimmy Jones and 24y from QB Mike Rae against Notre Dame D that came in with streak of 14 shutout Qs. ND QB Cliff Brown (12-35/160y, 3 INTs) suffered long day, topped by USC DB Bruce Dyer's 53y INT TD RET in 2nd Q. Notre Dame's highlight was 66y KO RET by HB Gary Diminick's that set up 1y TD run by FB Andy Huff.

Nebraska 41 OKLAHOMA STATE 13: Cornhuskers (7-0) extended 17-game win streak as WB Johnny Rodgers busted loose for 232y all-purpose. Rodgers scored twice, including 92y punt RET, while Huskers enjoyed other big TDs as IB Jeff Kinney

scored on 25y gallop, DB Dave Mason on 27y INT RET, and TE Jerry List on 42y pass reception. Oklahoma State (3-2-1) waited until 4th Q to score on 1y run by RB Bill Heilman and 21y effort by RB Steve Elliott.

TEXAS A&M 10 Baylor 9: K Pat McDermott bombed to-date school record 53y FG midway in 4th Q to spark Texas A&M (2-5) to 1st conf win in 12 games and prompt 4-game win streak. McDermott's boot was helped by 20 mph wind and was made with 1 blocker short. Bears (1-4) K Mike Conradt missed 1st x-pt of his career in 1st Q after QB Randy Cavender slipped 27y to score after HB Tommy Stewart raced 60y on punt RET. Wind-shortened punt set up A&M for its TD in 1st Q: TB Mark Green pounded left side for 3y TD and 7-6 lead. Conradt added wind-aided FG in 3rd Q for 9-7 Baylor lead.

Washington State 24 STANFORD 23: Stanford's Pac 8 title aspirations took jolt on WSU (3-4) K Don Sweet's 27y FG on game's final play. Indians (5-2) had taken 23-21 lead on 36y FG by K Rod Garcia, his 3rd FG of day. Stanford then seemed safe when LB Jim Merlo recovered FUM by Washington State QB Ty Paine on Stanford 11YL with 5 mins left. Paine, who earlier had thrown 71y TD pass to WR Ike Nelson, got 1 more chance and drove Cougars 75y to set up Sweet's heroics. TB Bernard Jackson (24/141y) had 2 TDs for Washington State, which had been outscored by Indians 112-16 over 2 previous seasons and had not won in rivalry since 1964 or in Pac 8 since 1968. Stanford highlight was 97y KO TD RET off reverse by WR John Winesberry.

AP Poll October 25

1 Nebraska (31)	1044	11 Louisiana State	273
2 Oklahoma (21)	1020	12 Notre Dame	235
3 Michigan (1)	833	13 Arizona State	110
4 Alabama (1)	788	14 Texas	94
5 Auburn (1)	637	15 Toledo	80
6 Penn State	557	16 Tennessee	67
7 Georgia	503	17 Stanford	57
8 Arkansas	403	18 Air Force	44
9 Colorado	331	19 Florida State	16
10 Ohio State	305	20 Southern California	13

October 30, 1971

(Fri) MIAMI 24 Army 13: Alert Army (3-4) turned Hurricanes (4-2) DB Burgess Owens' punt FUM at Miami 29YL and 46y INT RET by Cadets LB Peter Bucha into pair of 2nd Q TDs. But, Miami HB Tom Sullivan roared scott-free down sideline for 99y KO TD RET right after TD run by Cadets FB Bob Hines. QB John Hornibrook (10-21/174y, INT) scored on 16y run for 1st of his 2 TDs for 16-13 lead for Canes before H. Miami suffered 4 lost FUMs, Bucha's INT, and blocked punt by Army LB Scott Beaty, but ran for 217y, including TB Chuck Foreman's 22/119y.

Penn State 35 WEST VIRGINIA 7: Nittany Lions (7-0) broke open 7-7 3rd Q slugfest with 4 TDs after fumbled punt by West Virginia DB John Billetz opened floodgates. From West Virginia 45YL, Penn State rode HB Lydell Mitchell (24/128y) and FB Franco Harris, who caught 7y TD pass from QB John Hufnagel (11-14/132y, 2 TDs). Mitchell added 2 TD runs for his 15th and 16th scores of season, new school record. Mountaineers (6-2) struggled to score without their version of Mitchell-Harris combo, injured backfield mates TB Kerry Marbury and FB Pete Wood. TB Mike Nelson scored sole TD for home team, tying score in 3rd Q on 8y TD run.

CORNELL 24 Columbia 21: TB Ed Marinaro rushed for 272y and scored 2 TDs to continue rewriting record books while leading Cornell (6-0) to victory. Marinaro broke national career rushing mark (3,867y) of Oklahoma's Steve Owens on his 2nd carry of game and later cracked elusive 4,000y barrier. Despite Marinaro's performance, Cornell could not subdue Columbia Lions (3-3) until K John Killian's 4th Q 37y FG. QB Don Jackson (14-28/235y, TD) kept Lions close with TD pass and completions that set up other 2 scores, but was picked off 4 times, 2 by standout Big Red LB Bob Lally.

MISSISSIPPI 24 Louisiana State 22: Ole Miss Rebels (6-2) gained revenge for 61-17 whipping in 1970 as QB Norris Weese led 3 scoring drives in 1st H to stake team to 21-0 lead. LSU (5-2) finished with wild rally, scoring 2 TDs before running out of time on 3rd drive to Rebels 36YL, all in last 3 mins. Mississippi scored quickly in 1st H as TB Greg Ainsworth and FB Rickey Havard each ran in 1y TDs and Weese completed 3 passes on 60y drive to 14y keeper for 21-0 bulge. Bengals rode twin QBs Bert Jones and Paul Lyons, who combined for 255y passing.

Michigan State 43 PURDUE 10: While other backs grabbed national spotlight, HB Eric "The Flea" Allen performed brilliantly, but somewhat quietly, for Spartans (4-4). Allen was fantastic against Purdue (3-4) with single-game record 350y rushing, 3 more than Michigan HB Ron Johnson had gained in 1968 game. He also caught 2 passes/47y for single-game, all-purpose record of 397y. Allen's main interference was All-Big 10 G Joe DeLamielleure, who helped spring Allen on 4 TD runs that averaged 34.5y. Purdue's 5 TOs were costly as Michigan State converted them into 31 pts.

NEBRASKA 31 Colorado 7: If only Buffaloes (6-2) could play in another conf, anywhere but Big 8 owned by mighty Nebraska and Oklahoma. Huskers' star-laden D sparkled, holding Colorado's O studs, QB Ken Johnson, TB Charlie Davis, and WR Cliff Branch, to 83y rushing and 52y passing. Nebraska (8-0) LB Bob Terrio (13 tackles) and NG Rich Glover (12 tackles) were leading punishers of Colorado. IB Jeff Kinney scored twice to set Huskers record for career TDs with 29.

Texas A&M 17 ARKANSAS 9: Arkansas (6-2) expected to walk away with SWC crown after beating Texas, but was stunned by Aggies. Abysmal rushing effort (32/50y) pressured Hogs' pass game that went nowhere. TB Mark Green (27/102, 2 TDs) led opportunistic Texas A&M (3-5) that scored off 3 TOs, without committing any errors. Green's 1st TD came after muffed punt by Porkers DB Jack Morris, which was recovered by A&M TB Steve Burks. Next Aggies scoring drive began on Hogs 47YL

after big hit by LB Grady Hoermann caused FUM by Hogs TE Bobby Nichols to set up 37y FG by K Pat McDermott. INT by S David Hoot 3 plays later was converted into 20y TD run by Green. QB Joe Ferguson threw for 345y to pace Razorbacks.

Texas Christian 34 BAYLOR 27: TCU coach Jim Pittman's death from heart attack overshadowed game. QB Steve Judy, who raced off field when Pittman collapsed less than 5 minutes into game, ran and passed for 4 TDs. HB Larry Harris rushed for 113y and TD for Horned Frogs (3-3-1). Baylor (1-5) led 27-20 early in 3rd Q on 34y TD run by HB Matthew Williams following INT by S Phil Beall. Judy then led 75y drive to tying 5y keeper before tossing winning 10y TD pass in 4th Q to TE Ronnie Peoples. Final Baylor drive ended with INT by CB Lyle Blackwood on TCU 19YL.

ARIZONA STATE 44 Air Force 28: High-powered Arizona State (6-1) exploded in 3rd Q for 4 TDs to break open tight game. Sun Devils HB Benny Malone (22/192y, 2TDs) and QB Danny White (17-37/334y, 3 TDs, INT) sparkled in 3rd Q with Malone scoring his 2nd TD and White throwing 2 scoring passes and running in another. White completed 10-16/243y in 3rd Q alone, with 76y coming in one chunk on screen pass that HB Woody Green took to EZ. Air Force (5-2) had jumped to 15-10 H lead behind QB Rich Haynie (13-30/215y, 2 INTs), who kept Flyboys alive with 2 TD passes.

AP Poll November 1

1 Nebraska (34)	1050	11 Tennessee	164
2 Oklahoma (17)	1010	12 Stanford	158
3 Michigan (2)	840	13 Colorado	130
4 Alabama	782	14 Toledo	129
5 Auburn (1)	617	15 Texas	126
6 Penn State (1)	595	16 Arkansas	115
7 Georgia	517	17 Southern California	54
8 Notre Dame	374	18 Louisiana State	49
9 Ohio State	354	19 Houston	36
10 Arizona State	251	20 Washington	17

November 6, 1971

NORTH CAROLINA 26 Clemson 13: Battle for 1st place in ACC went to Tar Heels (7-2) as K Ken Craven kicked school-record 4 FGs and team posted 472y to 255y O differential. Aggressiveness sparked 2 UNC TDs: DE Bill Brafford blocked punt and fell on it in EZ, while another followed INT by LB Terry Taylor. Taylor's picked pass set up 8y TD keeper by QB Paul Miller (12-19/175y) as Tar Heels grabbed 10-0 lead during 1st H that was more 1-sided than score indicated. Clemson (3-5) could manage only 2 1st downs to Carolina's 20. Down 20-0 in 3rd Q, Tigers scored 2 TDs, both on receptions by TE John McMakin. North Carolina TB Louis Jolley rushed for 105y.

Virginia Tech 6 VIRGINIA 0: K Dave Strock booted 31 and 30y FGs in 1st and 3rd Qs respectively to launch Virginia Tech (3-5). Scoring-challenged Virginia (2-7) bogged down 5 times in Gobblers territory but frustrated Virginia Tech QB Don Strock (18-28/175y), nation's pass leader who doubled as holder for his older brother, by intercepting him twice. Cavaliers DBs Bob McGrail and Steve Sroba made INTs, and McGrail's sent UVa to last chance, which failed in last 2 mins when QB Larry Albert sailed 4th down pass from Hokies 24YL over head of wide-open WR Bill Davis. Tech held at its 8, 13, 5, 13, and 24YLs. Cavs TB Kent Merritt rushed 26/121y.

DUKE 31 West Virginia 15: Thanks to injuries, DBs Rich Searl and Ernie Jackson lent helping hand to Blue Devils (6-3) O with Searl playing QB for 1st time in 3 years and Jackson rushing out of TB spot for 76y, 2 TDs. Fellow DB Mike Davies chipped in with 3 of his team's 5 INTs, while FB Steve Jones added 2 running TDs himself as Duke built commanding 24-7 H lead. Mountaineers (6-3) were knocked out early, but their 1st H was highlighted by 89y TD pass from QB Bernie Galiffa to WR Chris Potts.

Alabama 14 LOUISIANA STATE 7: Alabama's potent O was held to 214y, but managed 3 scoring drives, culminating in K Bill Davis' 2 FGs in 1st H and QB Terry Davis' decisive 16y scamper in 3rd Q. QB Paul Lyons led LSU (5-3) on TD march moments later, completing 6 passes for 44y and adding 11y run in 61y drive that ended with 7y TD pass to WR Andy Hamilton. Final Tigers threat died on FUM by backup QB Bert Jones on Bama 43YL. Victory gave Alabama (9-0) coach Bear Bryant his 208th career win, moving him past Jess Neely into 4th place to-date on all-time list.

Georgia 49 Florida 7 (Jacksonville): Gators (2-7) had hoped to salvage their miserable season with upset win, but Georgia simply was too good. Bulldogs (9-0) hammered Florida's D for 380y, 228 on ground, even without injured QB Andy Johnson. Georgia QB James Ray completed 7-12/127y, TD, while rushing for 43y and another score. Defensively Georgia was even more dominant in holding QB John Reaves (9-21/87y, TD, INT) to lowest output of his season and shutting out WR Carlos Alvarez, hero from last season's upset. Georgia DE Mixon Robinson matched Florida O with TD, returning INT 38y for Bulldogs' 3rd score.

Michigan State 17 OHIO STATE 10: Surging Spartans (5-4) opportunistically pulled upset. Ohio State suffered 2 damaging TOs deep in its own territory set up short Michigan State TD drives of 7y and 11y. Spartans HB Eric Allen was held to 79y, 271y fewer than week before, finishing off mini drives that were set up by S Brad Van Pelt's INT and FUM REC, as Michigan State melted 7-3 lead by Buckeyes (6-2). TB Morris Bradshaw scored Ohio TD on 11y run, while FB Rick Galbos led Bucks in rushing with 91y. Allen topped MSU records with 13 TDs and 80 pts for season.

Illinois 22 INDIANA 21: Suddenly-hot Illini (3-6) scored 15 pts in 4th Q to capture their 3rd straight Big 10 win. After QB Mike Wells threw 6y pass to WR Garvin Roberson to pull Illinois to within 21-14, HB Eddie Jenkins scored on 1y run with 4:08 left to cut deficit to 21-20. Jenkins then took pitchout and waltzed for game-winning 2-pt conv. Hoosiers (1-8) quickly answered with 37y pass from QB Ted McNulty to WR Charley Byrnes to masterfully convert 4th down, but that dandy effort was wiped out by Indiana PEN. Thanks to running of TB Ken Starling (15/146y, TD) and 2 INTs that set up short TD drives, Hoosiers (1-8) gained early lead that came close to providing upset.

Oklahoma 20 MISSOURI 3: Sooners (8-0) needed big plays to subdue lowly Missouri Tigers (1-8). Oklahoma LB Mark Driscoll made 70y runback of blocked FG, WB Roy Bell dashed 78y, and QB Jack Mildren hit 44y pass to TE Al Chandler, all reaching paydirt. Sooners CB Ken Pope blocked FG attempt by Mizzou K Greg Hill early in 1st Q that was scooped up by Driscoll. Hill put Tigers on scoreboard with 34y FG in 2nd Q, before Sooners answered 2 plays later with Bell's run. Mildren's TD pass came later in 2nd Q as both Ds dominated 2nd H.

Arkansas 24 RICE 24: Upset-minded Owls (2-5-1) sported 24-13 lead late in 4th Q in quest for their 1st series win since 1963. Hogs (6-2-1) drove to TD, cutting deficit to 24-21 after 2-pt conv. Arkansas subsequently marched to Rice 9YL before losing FUM. Rice punted with 9 seconds left, but Owls DB Carl Swierc rushed in to accidentally hit DB Jack Morris after fair catch. Crippling PEN moved ball to Owls 28YL, from which spot K Bill McClard drilled game-tying 45y FG, his 3rd 3-ptr of day. Rice had grabbed 10-0 lead in 1st Q by converting 2 FUMs by Hogs TB Dickey Morton. Arkansas scored 3 times to grab 13-10 lead before QB Bruce Gadd (12-15/178y) came off Owls bench to throw 53y TD to WR Bubba Berg and 34y TD to WR Bob Brown (6/99y, 2 TDs). Hogs TB Mike Saint scored 2 TDs, while WR Mike Reppond caught 12/204y.

November 13, 1971

DARTMOUTH 24 Cornell 14: Dartmouth (7-1) grabbed share of Ivy League crown by "holding" Cornell (7-1) star HB Ed Marinaro to 177y and 2 TDs on 44 tough carries. Home crowd ended up serenading Marinaro with "Good-bye Heisman" diddies. Big Green QB Steve Stetson became surprise starter when he was informed of nod only 90 mins before KO and provided Indians in air and on ground. Key Dartmouth drive occurred in 3rd Q after Cornell (7-1) had scored twice to cut deficit to 3 pts. Stetson then put Indians up 24-14, forcing Big Red running machine into vain catch-up mode.

Auburn 35 GEORGIA 20: Auburn QB Pat Sullivan (14-24/248y, 4 TDs) picked apart Georgia in performance that probably clinched Heisman Trophy. Sullivan overcame fearsome pass rush to lead Auburn (9-0) to 2 quick 1st Q TD drives. Bulldogs (9-1) answered with 2 TDs on short runs by TBs Jimmy Poulos and Donnie Allen. Sullivan tossed his 2nd TD pass in 2nd Q, 15y to WB Dick Schmalz, to go up 21-14 at H. After Georgia pulled to within 21-20, Sullivan connected with his favorite target, fleet WR Terry Beasley (4/130y), at UGa 44YL. Beasley collided with 2 defenders after his reception, but broke free for his 2nd TD, most decisive of contest.

Michigan 20 PURDUE 17: Boilermakers (3-6) battled to end, scoring more pts than any other team had accomplished all season against nation's top-ranked scoring D. Michigan (10-0) did not secure its win until K Dana Coin's 25y FG flew through uprights with 43 secs left. Purdue QB Gary Danielson had opened scoring in 1st Q with 9y screen pass TD to HB Otis Armstrong. After Wolverines took 10-7 lead at H, Danielson hooked up with WR Darryl Stingley (5/140y, TD) on 66y TD pass on 1st possession of 3rd Q. With help from PEN and runs of 23y and 13y by Billy Taylor (17/98y), Michigan drove to go-ahead TD at 17-14: 2y run by HB Glenn Doughty (16/93y). Purdue then shrugged off injury to Danielson as back-up QB Steve Burke (5-9/110y, 2 TDs) excelled in moving home team to tying 34y FG by K Mike Renie. "Hail to the Victors:" Wolverines wrapped up Big 10 title by rallying to Coin's winning 3-ptr.

TEXAS 31 Texas Christian 0: In game they emotionally dedicated to late coach Jim Pittman, Horned Frogs were booted from SWC race. TCU (4-4-1) looked to score 1st but missed 2nd Q FG attempt. QB Eddie Phillips (14/83y rushing) then marched Horns (7-2) 80y to 1st of 2 TDs by FB Dennis Ladd (15/89y). Phillips went down with injured shoulder, but replacement QB Donnie Wigginton rushed for 2 TDs in 2nd H. Thanks to Texas' fine D and long boots of P Alan Lowry, Frogs were pinned in own end for most of afternoon, crossing midfield only 3 times. HB Larris Harris led TCU ground game with meager 58y. Texas' win insured unprecedented 4th straight conf title.

Southern California 13 WASHINGTON 12: After USC (6-4) WR Lynn Swann lost midfield FUM, Huskies (7-3) FB Pete Taggares (12/39y) scored 2y TD with 4:42 left in 4th Q for 12-10 lead. Washington coach Jim Owens then gambled for 2 pts to avoid possibility of late FG by Trojans. Twin-conv backfired when Huskies QB Sonny Sixkiller (12-37/201y, TD, INT) was stopped on run-pass option, and, with 2:08 left, Southern California K Mike Rae banged through his 2nd FG (28y) after CB Skip Thomas swiped INT out of hands of Washington WR Jim Krieg at UW 40YL. Huskies had owned 6-3 lead in 1st Q on Sixkiller's 21y TD pass after DB Calvin Jones authored 66y INT RET to USC 31YL. But, K Steve Wiezbowski shanked kick, which turned out all-important.

ARIZONA STATE 52 Wyoming 19: ASU (8-1) exploded in 2nd H for 49 pts as Sun Devils secured their 3rd straight WAC title with 18th straight conf win. Trailing 6-3 in 3rd Q, Devils unleashed their stable of weapons. Arizona State scored on 2 punt RETs—90y by WB Steve Holden and 71y by HB Woody Green—as well as 41y INT TD RET by S Prentice McCray. Sun Devils topped 200y in each of passing, rushing, and on RETs. QB Danny White (13-17/260y, 2 INTs), WR Cal Demery (6/121y), and Holden (4/117y) led ASU passing game, while Green rushed for 88y. Wyoming (5-5) scored twice in 3rd

Q briefly to cut deficit to 24-19 on 14y TD pass from QB Gary Fox to WR Jerry Gadlin and 12y INT RET by S Mel Meadows of pass by Green. Green answered unfortunate INT with 2 TDs of own as Sun Devils romped to 28 unanswered pts in 4th Q.

Arizona 27 BRIGHAM YOUNG 14: Overcoming sloppy play, Cougars (5-4) drove deep into Arizona territory late in 4th Q with game tied 14-14, but QB Bill Gunderson lost FUM, 1 of 10 crippling TOs for BYU. After 2 downs netted –3y, Arizona (5-4) QB Bill Demory (12-24/217y, 2 TDs, INT) uncorked bomb to WR Charlie McKee who outfought 2 Cougars for ball. McKee raced to EZ for 92y scoring play and winning TD. Play's distance erased school and conf records. Wildcats added another wild score before it was over: S Greg Boyd's 48y RET of FUM by teammate CB Jackie Wallace after Wallace's 2nd of 3 INTs. Gunderson had come off bench to lead 2 scoring drives as Brigham Young grabbed 14-7 advantage on his 59y TD pass to WR Golden Richards and 31y TD run by FB Dave Coon (18/100y).

November 20, 1971

North Carolina 38 DUKE 0: Tar Heels (9-2) crushed in-state rivals to capture their 1st ACC title since 1963 and their 2nd since conf was created in 1953. TB Lewis Jolley ran 24/159y, 3 TDs behind O-line featuring all-ACC selections, C Bob Thornton, G Ron Rusnak, and T Jerry Sain. With stars like T Ed Newman and DB/WR Ernie Jackson playing 2-way most of season, Blue Devils (6-5) did not have sufficient energy to stay with deeper Tar Heels. UNC's perfect ACC record (6-0) was 1st in school history.

North Carolina State 31 CLEMSON 23: Tigers (4-6) could not keep WB Mike Stultz out of their EZ, and, with each of Stultz's 3 TDs, Clemson fell further and further out of race for ACC crown. After catching 2 TD passes from QB Bruce Shaw in 1st H, Stultz ran for 9y score for what proved to be game winner and 24-10 3rd Q lead. Stultz rushed 100y, while teammate HB Willie Burden led Wolfpack (3-8) with 145y. Clemson QB Ken Pengitore kept Tigers close, throwing 8-11/120y, TD, but Clemson lost lead in 2nd Q and never regained it.

Tennessee 21 KENTUCKY 7: With time elapsing, Wildcats (4-7) drove to Tennessee 9YL trailing by 7 before QB Bernie Scruggs made pitchout he'd soon regret. Vols DE Carl Johnson corralled ball and raced to distant EZ to wrap up game at 21-7. Volunteers (8-2) took 14-0 H lead on TD runs of 26y by FB Curt Watson (152y rushing) and 4y by QB Jim Maxwell. But, Kentucky, which outrushed Vols 179y to 167y, moved ball in 3rd Q before paring lead on 4th-and-goal 1y TD plunge by FB Arvel Carroll.

LOUISIANA STATE 28 Notre Dame 8: As soon as LSU (7-3) WR Andy Hamilton caught his 3rd TD pass with 20 secs left, Bayou celebration began. Tigers routed Irish (8-2) behind QB Bert Jones and D that bent but did not break. Jones, starting for 1st time since opener, connected with his cousin Hamilton for 1st H TD passes of 36y and 32y. Jones ran for score in 3rd Q that put away Notre Dame, while QB Paul Lyons threw final TD pass. LSU's 2nd H TDs were 1st allowed by Irish in any 2nd H all year. Notre Dame scored in 4th Q on LSU D that had stopped them 3 times on 4th down within LSU 10YL on WR Tom Gatewood's 7y TD catch. LSU LB Warren Capone set up 2 TDs with INTs.

MICHIGAN 10 Ohio State 7: Buckeyes (6-4) attempt to salvage disappointing season was thwarted by S Thom Darden's INT, his 2nd of game, that ended Ohio State's last drive. It came on play vehemently protested by Ohio State coach Woody Hayes to referee Jerry Markbreight. Michigan (11-0) remained perfect, while Ohio State suffered its 3rd straight loss for 1st time since 1966. Michigan had scored on previous possession as TB Billy Taylor ran in 21y TD, 1 play after FB Fritz Seyferth converted 4th-and-1 with dive over right side. Buckeyes had made it 7-3 in 3rd Q on TD scored on 85y punt RET by HB Tom Campana, whose 166y on punt RETs outgained Bucks' entire O output.

NORTHWESTERN 28 Michigan State 7: Wildcats (7-4) repeated their 2nd place Big 10 finish of 1970 with easy win over Michigan State. Northwestern dominated Spartans (6-5) at line of scrimmage as Cats TB Al Robinson outrushed MSU star HB Eric Allen, 131y to 112y, and NW FB Randy Anderson scored 3 short TDs. Big 10's rule preventing members outside 1st place from accepting bowl bids, kept Wildcats out of their 2nd bowl ever. They would have to wait until 1994.

COLORADO 53 Air Force 17: Buffaloes (9-2) stampeded Air Force (6-4) to close out notable season. WR Cliff Branch scored twice—on beautiful 34y E-around and on 65y punt RET—while TB Charlie Davis rushed for 196y and 2 TDs. Colorado built 27-10 H lead. Falcons pulled to within 10 on QB Rich Haynie's 1y QB keeper early in 3rd Q. Colorado answered that with 26-pt explosion to blow open game.

SOUTHERN CALIFORNIA 7 Ucla 7: Bruins (2-7-1) finished their worst season since 1963 by capitalizing on short USC (6-4-1) punt in 3rd Q to spring upset tie. UCLA took over at Trojans 30YL after standout DE Fred McNeill (12y sack) pressured Southern California P Dave Boulware into 17y punt. It took UCLA only 4 plays for HB Marv Kendricks to crash over from 7YL to tie it. Trojans TB Lou Harris (29/118y) had scored from 2YL in 2nd Q to provide 7-0 lead at end of 85y drive that was started by INT by DB Eddie Johnson and featured TB Manfred Moore's 57y gallop. Bruins went 0-8, 4 INTs in air.

STANFORD 14 California 0: Sporting 1-3 home record, Indians (8-3) surprisingly donned road uniforms for game that clinched Pac-8 title. Overpowering performance by Stanford's Thunder Chickens D-line made everyone forget about previous home losses as Cal Bears (6-5) were held to measly 123y total O. QB Don Bunce (18-24/211y, TD) was equally overpowering in leading Stanford to easy victory and its 2nd straight Rose Bowl berth. HB Jackie Brown rushed for 56y and caught 7/119y, with 58y TD coming on swing pass he took to paydirt for Stanford's opening score.

Oregon State 30 OREGON 29: Beavers (5-6) won their 8th straight over in-state rival Ducks (5-6), riding broad back of FB Dave Schilling who plowed for 3 TDs. Oregon enjoyed 14-3 lead as DB Bill Drake raced 43y for punt TD RET in 2nd Q. Schilling scored 2 TDs for 17-14 lead and made it 24-21 after Ducks QB Dan Fouts hit short TD pass. Winning TD for Oregon State came at end of 61y trip with 1:40 to play as HB Billy Carlquist ran 6y after fake up middle to Schilling.

AP Poll November 22

1 Nebraska (40)	1024	11 Tennessee	236	
2 Oklahoma (8)	976	12 Texas	229	
3 Alabama (1)	740	13 Notre Dame	116	
4 Michigan (3)	695	14 Toledo	106	
5 Auburn (1)	653	15 Houston	82	
6 Penn State (2)	625	16 Stanford	73	
7 Georgia	445	17 Arkansas	71	
8 Colorado	356	18 Mississippi	56	
9 Arizona State	338	19 North Carolina	53	
10 Louisiana State	273	20 Washington	50	

November 25-27, 1971

(Th'g) Georgia 28 GEORGIA TECH 24: Trailing 24-21 with 1:29 remaining, Georgia (10-1) was led to Georgia Tech 1YL by QB Andy Johnson. TB Jimmy Poulos (19/152y) dove in from there as Bulldogs snapped 2-game series losing streak. Yellow Jackets DB Dave Beavens had stopped Johnson (107y passing and 99y rushing) on 4th-and-1 keeper on Tech 9YL only 2 mins earlier. Georgia Tech (6-5) opened with 2 long TD drives to grab 14-0 lead on 31y pass from QB Eddie McAshan to WR Jim Owings and 11y scoring run by TB Rob Healy. Johnson then flanked Yellow Jackets FG with 1y TD run and 23y TD pass for H deficit of 17-14. After scoreless 3rd Q, Johnson and Healy (24/130y) traded scores to keep Jackets ahead by 3 pts, with each scoring his 2nd TD.

(Th'g) Alabama 31 Auburn 7 (Birmingham): Game featured brilliant performance from star superstar, but star shining brightly was Alabama HB Johnny Musso, not Auburn's Heisman Trophy winning QB Pat Sullivan. Despite sprained toe, Musso rushed 33/167y and scored twice in 4th Q on 1-play drives set up by INTs. LBs Chuck Strickland and Jeff Rouzie authored INTs that each returned to within 10y of Tigers GL to help Tide (11-0) turn 17-7 struggle into rout. Musso's running and Bama D helped limit Auburn (9-1) to 18:11 time of possession, 7 1st downs, 27y rushing and 27 fewer pts than its avg. Alabama pushed in QB Terry Davis' 2 TD runs on its opening 2 possessions for 14-0 lead that was halved by Tigers' trick play. In 2nd Q, Auburn FB Harry Unger took pitchout from Sullivan and threw 31y scoring pass over 2 defenders to WR Terry Beasley. It was only catch of Beasley's 143 career grabs that came from someone other than Sullivan. Sullivan threw for 121y and gained 40y on single throw but only 81y on his 13 other completions.

GAME OF THE YEAR
(Th'g) Nebraska 35 OKLAHOMA 31:

Longtime rivals hooked up in contest that was worthy of pre-game accolades. To stop Sooners (9-1), who averaged NCAA-record 566y per game, Nebraska DEs Willie Harper and John Adkins were deployed wide in attempt to keep ball away from HB Greg Pruitt and WB Joe Wylie. Pruitt and Wylie significantly were negated (only 70 total y combined), but QB Jack Mildren produced 267y in total O and 4 TDs, 2 passing. With so much action in middle of line, Cornhuskers NG Rich Glover responded with 22 tackles. Nebraska (11-0) enjoyed 174y rushing and 4 TDs from IB Jeff Kinney, who ended game with Huskers career rushing record. Despite number of stars, 1 player shone most of all. Nebraska WB Johnny Rodgers opened scoring with amazing punt RET: With 6 Sooners surrounding him on Huskers 28YL, Rodgers took high boot by P Wylie, taking chance that lesser men would have fair-caught. Pruitt hit Rodgers with hard shot that spun him away from precarious situation—G Ken Jones was about to nail him. Several nifty moves later, Rodgers was off to 72y TD, with Wylie being bumped aside by Nebraska DB Joe Blahak. There was plenty of time left and OU wiped out 14-3 deficit as Mildren ran for TD and teamed up with WR Jon Harrison for TD. It was Huskers' turn and QB Jerry Tagge led them on 2 drives to Kinney TDs for 28-17 lead. Sooners mustered magnificent rally to regain lead at 31-28 as Mildren ran for score and threw his 2nd TD to Harrison. Nebraska's winning march featured more Kinney and Rodgers. Kinney bulldozed into OU territory, where drive reached crucial 3rd-and-8. Tagge was forced out of pocket before throwing to Rodgers, who made incredible catch between 2 defenders while sliding to knee. Kinney crashed off tackle for winning score 6 plays later. It truly was memorable "Game of the Century."

(Th'g) Texas 34 TEXAS A&M 14: Host of mistakes did in fired-up Aggies (5-6) as fumbled punt, short punt, and INT off deflection were all converted into Texas TDs. Closest Texas A&M came to scoring in 28-0 1st H was missed 52y FG. HB Jim Bertelsen and QB Donnie Wigginton each scored twice, and FB Dennis Ladd added another, all on 1y TD runs to launch Longhorns (8-2) to 34-0 lead. When Texas A&M finally scored, on 12y TD pass from QB Joe Mac King to WR Billy Joe Polasek, it was 1st TD surrendered by Texas D in previous 13 Qs. Aggies TB Mark Green rushed 104y and 2y TD. Longhorns were headed back to Cotton Bowl for conf-record 4th time in row.

Army 24 Navy 23 (Philadelphia): Navy (3-8) scored what appeared to be winning TD on HB George Berry's run in closing moments, but QB Fred Stuvek's knee was ruled down before he pitched ball to Berry. Alert Army D held after Navy refused tying FG try. Army (6-4) took safety on final play as game ended with 1-pt margin for 1st time in 72-game history of rivalry. Winning TD was 3y completion from QB Kingsley Fink to WR Ed Francis in back of EZ, followed by Fink 2-pt conv pass to WR John Simar. Cadets had taken 16-0 1st Q lead—with help from 3 Navy FUMs—as HB Bob Hines scored 2 TDs and K Jim Barclay booted 42y FG. Midshipmen rallied in 2nd Q on 2 Stuvek TD runs, and in 3rd Q, Navy took 21-16 lead on Stuvek's 12y TD pass to TE Steve Ogden.

Florida 45 MIAMI 16: This game left bad taste for long time. Gators (4-7) were so caught up in having QB John Reaves (33-50/348y, 4 TDs, 3 INTs) break Stanford QB Jim Plunkett's year-old record for career pass y, that their D chose to fall on turf near game's end to allow Miami cheap, but quick, 8y TD run to get ball back in Reaves' hands. This charade was perpetrated amid chants of "Let them score!" by Gator fans. After nearly throwing INT, Reaves would gain 18y to set new mark of 7,549y. With only 1 healthy starting DB and hastily employed Wishbone O, Miami (4-6) never had much chance. In his memorable finale, Reaves made 17y TD catch of pass from HB Tommy Durrance and set SEC record of 54 TD passes, topping Auburn QB Pat Sullivan's 53.

Texas Christian 18 SOUTHERN METHODIST 16: K Berl Simmons did it again, booting 29y FG with 13 secs left for Horned Frogs (6-4-1) same week after doing same versus Rice. Mustangs (4-7) had just driven 70y to take lead on 2y TD run by QB Gary Hammond, but missed 2-pt conv with incomplete pass after PEN wiped out successful 2-pt run. Visitors then moved ball 49y, with 40y on 3 passes by QB Steve Judy, to set up Simmons' winning boot. TCU, which came away empty on 3 drives that reached at least SMU's 10YL, gained 234y on ground while Mustangs were led by soph TB Alvin Maxson, whose 96y rushing gave him 1,012y for season.

AP Poll November 29

1 Nebraska (48)	1086	11 Texas	245	
2 Alabama (4)	938	12 Tennessee	220	
3 Oklahoma	851	13 Toledo	128	
4 Michigan (2)	764	14 Notre Dame	122	
5 Penn State (1)	740	15 Houston	104	
6 Auburn	478	16t Arkansas	46	
7 Georgia	458	16t Stanford	46	
8 Colorado	397	18t Mississippi	24	
9 Arizona State	380	18t North Carolina	24	
10 Louisiana State	319	20 Washington	19	

December 4, 1971

Syracuse 14 MIAMI 0: Orangemen (5-5-1) gift-wrapped 50y pass interference PEN and 2 lost FUMs in last 3 mins, but injury-ravaged Miami (4-7) couldn't avoid its 5th loss in row. Hurricanes penetrated to Syracuse 17, 20, 32, 30, 21, and 39YLs without managing single pt. Syracuse smashed 58y to 2nd Q TD on 10y TD run by TB Roger Praetorius (24/104y). Sub TB Ron Page added 7y TD sweep at end of 84y trip in 3rd Q. Miami QB Kelly Cochrane came off bench to pass 9-22/111y, 3 INTs in vain.

TENNESSEE 31 Penn State 11: After being honored with brother Johnny and late brother Billy for familial contributions to Tennessee (9-2) football, sr S Bobby Majors celebrated his final home game with 44y punt TD RET. Majors added another 38y punt RET, 2 KO RETs/113y, and contributed stellar DB play. Oddly, mighty Penn State (10-1) totaled 0y on all its RETs, and that became symbolic of surprisingly feeble effort. Vols sr LB Jackie Walker also scored in his final home game, capping outstanding game with 43y INT TD RET in 4th Q, while CB Conrad Graham began string of TDs by Tennessee D players with 76y RET of FUM for 7-0 lead in 1st Q. Loss completely snuffed Penn State's national title hopes and ended Lions' 15-game win streak. Lions HB Lydell Mitchell upped his record TD total to 29 with 4th Q 14y scoring catch.

AP Poll December 6

1 Nebraska (48)	1086	11 Louisiana State	307	
2 Alabama (4)	954	12 Texas	262	
3 Oklahoma	880	13 Notre Dame	142	
4 Michigan (3)	797	14 Toledo	129	
5 Auburn	581	15 Houston	81	
6 Georgia	480	16 Stanford	40	
7 Colorado	432	17 Mississippi	34	
8 Arizona State	394	18 Arkansas	28	
9 Tennessee	385	19 Northwestern	16	
10 Penn State	334	20 Washington	15	

1971 Conference Standings

Ivy League			Atlantic Coast	
Dartmouth	6-1		North Carolina	6-0
Cornell	6-1		Clemson	4-2
Columbia	5-2		Duke	2-3
Harvard	4-3		Virginia	2-3
Princeton	3-4		Wake Forest	2-3
Yale	3-4		North Carolina State	2-4
Pennsylvania	1-6		Maryland	1-4
Brown	0-7			

Southern

Richmond	5-1
William & Mary	4-1
Citadel	4-2
East Carolina	3-2
Furman	2-3
VMI	1-4
Davidson	0-6

Southeastern

Alabama	7-0
Georgia	5-1
Auburn	5-1
Mississippi	4-2
Tennessee	4-2
LSU	3-2
Vanderbilt	1-5
Florida	1-6
Kentucky	1-6
Mississippi State	1-7

Big Ten

Michigan	8-0
Northwestern	6-3
Illinois	5-3
Michigan State	5-3
Ohio State	5-3
Minnesota	3-5
Purdue	3-5
Wisconsin	3-5
Indiana	2-6
Iowa	1-8

Mid-American

Toledo	5-0
Bowling Green	4-1
Ohio U	2-3
Western Michigan	2-3
Miami (O)	2-3
Kent State	0-5

Big Eight

Nebraska	7-0
Oklahoma	6-1
Colorado	5-2
Iowa State	4-3
Oklahoma State	2-5
Kansas State	2-5
Kansas	2-5
Missouri	0-7

Missouri Valley

Memphis State	4-1
Louisville	3-2
Tulsa	3-2
North Texas State	3-2
Drake	2-3
West Texas State	1-4
Wichita State	0-5

Southwest

Texas	6-1
Arkansas	5-1-1
TCU	5-2
Texas A&M	4-3
SMU	3-4
Rice	2-4-1
Texas Tech	2-5
Baylor	0-7

Western Athletic

Arizona State	7-0
New Mexico	5-1
Arizona	3-3
Utah	3-4
BYU	3-4
Wyoming	3-4
Colorado State	1-4
Texas El Paso	1-6

Pacific Eight

Stanford	5-1
Oregon State	3-2
Washington	3-3
Southern Cal	2-2-1
Oregon	2-3
Washington State	2-4
UCLA	1-3-1
California	ineligible

Pacific Coast Athletic

Long Beach State	5-1
San Jose State	4-1
Fresno State	3-2
San Diego State	2-3
UC Santa Barbara	2-3
Pacific	1-4
L.A. State	0-3

1971 Major Bowl Games

Sun Bowl (Dec. 18): Louisiana State 33 Iowa State 15

After teams combined for 3 1st H FGs, Louisiana State and Iowa State entertained El Paso crowd with 2nd H explosion—6 TDs with 5 coming through air. LSU (9-3) stretched its 6-3 H lead to 19-3 as QB Bert Jones (12-18/227y, 2 TDs, INT) threw 2 3rd Q TDs, including 37y pass to WR Andy Hamilton. Iowa State QB Dean Carlson (18-32/230y, 2 TDs, INT) countered with 30y scoring pass to FB Larry Marquardt and 1y TD pass to TE Keith Krepfle—1 play after Krepfle broke numerous tackles for big play—to cut deficit to 19-15. Jones, game's MVP, passed and ran for 4th Q insurance TDs. Monster-man LB Matt Blair made tackles all over field for ISU (8-4), which was playing its 1st-ever bowl game. Winning coach Charlie McClendon had turned down $1 million dollar offer to try to right floundering ship as coach of Texas A&M.

Liberty Bowl (Dec. 20): Tennessee 14 Arkansas 13

To say game ended in controversy would understate how officials were chased off field in post-game fury by Razorbacks. Ahead 13-7 late in 4th Q, Hogs (8-3-1) had 48y FG by K Bill McClard—set up by DB Louis Campbell's 3rd INT—nullified by holding PEN called against Arkansas TE Bobby Nichols. On Arkansas' next drive, RB Jon Richardson lost ball, and possession was given to Tennessee on Razorbacks' 37YL by same official (Preston Watts) who had called earlier holding PEN. Arkansas was livid. Vols (10-2) needed only 3 plays to score TD as FB Curt Watson, playing with cracked ribs, scored on 17y scamper. K George Hunt made his 62nd straight x-pt for Tennessee's margin of victory. Arkansas had taken lead at 7-0 and extended it on FGs by McClard of 20y and 30y earlier in 4th Q, scores that had each followed INTs by alert Campbell. Razorbacks QB Joe Ferguson threw for 200y, including 36y TD pass to WR Jim Hodge in 2nd Q, but also threw 3 INTs as both teams were plagued by sloppy play, committing 9 TOs in all.

Fiesta Bowl (Dec. 27): Arizona State 45 Florida State 38

Game helped establish Fiesta Bowl's reputation as wide-open and unpredictable. Team that had ball at end of game came out winner, as HB Woody Green scored from 2YL with 34 secs remaining to win game for hometown Sun Devils (11-1). Finish was wild as Arizona State WB Steve Holden broke 31-31 tie with 69y punt TD RET with 6 mins left. Florida State (8-4) quickly answered with 24y scoring pass from QB Gary Huff, nation's leader in total O, to WR Rhett Dawson for Dawson's 3rd scoring reception. QB Danny White then led winning 58y drive for Sun Devils. Green scored 3 TDs and rushed for 101y to lead ASU's ground attack, while White threw for 250y and 2 TDs. Huff finished with 347y in air, but was picked off 3 times.

Peach Bowl (Dec. 30): Mississippi 41 Georgia Tech 18

Rebels (10-2) raced to 10-0 lead before Georgia Tech O even saw action, thanks to 2 scoring drives sandwiching fumbled KO by Jackets. Four TOs later, Ole Miss had rout going, despite finishing game with narrow 318y to 317y O advantage. Rebs alternated soph QBs Norris Weese (7-14/116y)—who opened scoring with 1y keeper—with fellow soph Kenny Lyons (2-4/23y, INT), and both led multiple scoring drives. Each QB threw TD as Rebels built mammoth 38-0 lead in 2nd Q. Georgia Tech TB Rob Healy managed rushing TDs in 2nd, 3rd and 4th Qs, but by then, Ole Miss' margin was too great for Yellow Jackets comeback. Invaders of Atlanta sent TB Greg Ainsworth rushing for 119y, while FB Jim Porter scored 2 TDs for Ole Miss. Final tally represented most pts ever scored in bowl game by Rebels, which evened it post-season record to 9-9.

Astro-Bluebonnet Bowl (Dec. 31): Colorado 29 Houston 17

Houston native TB Charlie Davis (37/202y, 2 TDs) scorched his home town Cougars (9-3) for Colorado (10-2) by breaking Astro-Bluebonnet game rushing mark. Game was pretty well wrapped up late in 4th Q when Colorado S John "Bad Dude" Stearns knocked down 4th down pass in EZ with Buffs ahead only 23-17. Buffaloes then took over on their own 10YL, wanting to run down clock. Houston D held and Buffs soon had to punt from deep in own territory. P Stearns received low snap and drastically eschewed punt plan to run 12y for 1st down. Bison continued on for 91y march to clinching TD, which became 1y keeper by QB Ken Johnson. Another Houston-born player, FB Robert Newhouse, rushed for 168y and 2 TDs, but for Cougars.

Gator Bowl (Dec. 31): Georgia 7 North Carolina 3

Attention was drawn to game's sideline tacticians as Gator Bowl featured conservative showdown of Dooley coaching brothers: Georgia's Vince and North Carolina's Bill. Vince of Bulldogs (11-1) won bragging rights in mighty D struggle. Teams ended up 1st H in 0-0 tie, before "opening things up" in 3rd Q with 10 combined pts on 35y FG by Tar Heels (9-3) K Ken Craven and 25y scoring run by Georgia TB Jimmy Poulos (161y rushing). Georgia marched 80y for winning TD after Craven missed 45y FG attempt that might have launched Carolina to strong 6-0 edge. North Carolina managed only 181y of total O with TB Lewis Jolley leading team with 77y rushing. Teams each matched prior Gator Bowl record of 10 punts.

Cotton Bowl (Jan. 1): Penn State 30 Texas 6

Texas O was mistreated in Cotton Bowl as Longhorns (8-3) were kept out of EZ for 1st time in any game since 1964. Good D play allowed Texas to enjoy 6-3 H lead, but that quickly became history as alert Nittany Lions (11-1) converted 3 Texas FUMs to pts. HB Lydell Mitchell, who rushed for 146y, scored from 1y out early in 3rd Q to cap short 41y drive that followed FUM by Texas QB Eddie Phillips. Penn State upped lead to 17-6 as QB John Hufnagel hit open WR Scott Skarzynski for 65y TD. Skarzynski beat injured DB Mike Bayer, who unknowingly for Texas was in game despite being, as coach Darrell Royal described it: "out of his head, out on his feet." DE Bruce Bannon led Lions D that held Longhorns to 159y rushing, significant 132y below its avg. Outgained 376y to 242y and scoring their only pts on 2 FGs by K Steve Valek, Longhorns apparently were affected by departure of coach and Wishbone guru Emory Bellard, who left in December to become head coach at rival Texas A&M.

Rose Bowl (Jan. 1): Stanford 13 Michigan 12

For 2nd straight Rose Bowl game, Stanford (9-3) upset undefeated Big 10 powerhouse. Heroics were spread among K Rod Garcia, QB Don Bunce, HB Jackie Brown and "Thunder Chickens" D. Trailing 10-3 in 4th Q and facing 4th-and-10 situation, Brown raced for 31y gain on trick play out of punt formation: Ball was snapped to FB Jim Kehl, who handed it forward through Brown's legs to speedy HB. Moments later, Brown tied game at 10-10 with 24y TD run. Michigan (11-1) quickly moved into position, hoping to at least make go-ahead FG. But odd play unfolded, and Wolverines came away with 12-10 lead not 13-10 lead. FG try came up short, and was brought out of EZ by Stanford HB Jim Ferguson. Michigan FB Ed Shuttlesworth met Ferguson at 6YL, chased him back to 3YL, and then flung him into EZ. Officials seemed to ignore forward-progress rule and, oddly, awarded safety to Wolverines for 2-pt lead with 3:18 left. Stanford's D then held after free-kick, and Indians—this was their last game with controversial nickname—entrusted ball and game to reliable Bunce (24-44/290y). Bunce was sharp on critical 64y drive, hitting 5-6, with 2 going to WR John Winesberry (8/112y) to move Stanford to Michigan 14YL. K Garcia nailed winning 31y FG with 12 seconds left. Big moment for Stanford D had come on opening drive of 2nd H after Michigan marched to 1st-and-goal at 8YL. Four downs later, Stanford regained ball as LB Jim Merlo and DB Bennie Barnes stopped TB Billy Taylor on 4th down run at 1YL. Wolverines later broke 3-3 tie early in 4th Q on 1y TD plunge by FB Fritz Seyferth that capped 71y drive. But, Michigan never made another 1st down.

Sugar Bowl (Jan. 1): Oklahoma 40 Auburn 22

Sooners routed Auburn (9-2), building somewhat shocking 31-0 H lead over SEC runners-up. Frustrated Tigers QB Pat Sullivan was outshone by Oklahoma (11-1) QB Jack Mildren, who led juggernaut O that amassed Sugar Bowl-record 439y rushing on whopping 87 carries. Mildren ran for 149y and 3 TDs, all in explosive 1st H when

OU converted 3 Auburn TOs in Tigers territory into big TDs. OU DE Ray Hamilton fell on FUM at Auburn 41YL to set up Mildren 5y TD run, S Geoff Nordgren picked off Sullivan's pass that led to Mildren's 2nd TD run, and LB Mark Driscoll added INT of trick pass attempt by Auburn A-A WR Terry Beasley that led to another Mildren score. Sullivan threw for 250y, much of it on 2 late window-dressing scoring drives, while Beasley caught 6/117y for Tigers. Sooners WB Joe Wylie contributed 71y punt TD RET, and K John Carroll added 53y FG to set record for longest FG in Sugar history.

Orange Bowl (Jan. 1): Nebraska 38 Alabama 6

Facing Wishbone O he felt was inferior to Oklahoma's bode well for no. 1 Huskers (13-0) coach Bob Devaney, who was looking to avenge blowout losses to Crimson Tide in 1966 Orange and 1967 Sugar Bowls. Most memorable play of this rout was WB Johnny Rodgers' 77y punt TD RET on final play of 1st Q that put Nebraska up 14-0 en route to 28-0 H lead. IB Jeff Kinney rushed for 99y and opened scoring with 2y TD run, while QB Jerry Tagge completed 11-19/159y and added 1y TD keeper for team's 3rd TD. Alabama (11-1) did not score until late in 3rd Q on QB Terry Davis' 3y TD run. Alabama toted up more rushing yards and led in 1st downs by 16 to 15, but surrendered 166y in RETs—to 36y for Tide—and handed over 2 more TOs. Huskers outgained Alabama 225y to 96y in 1st H when game was decided, with help from lost Bama FUMs on their own 27 and 2YLs to make Nebraska TDs easy. After his team stretched their unbeaten streak to 32 games, Nebraska's Rodgers gave game ball to Rex Lowe, who earlier had to leave team due to Hodgkin's Disease. Game marked 1st match-up of undefeated, untied teams in any bowl since January 1956 when Orange Bowl pitted Oklahoma and Maryland. It was only 3rd time teams ranked no. 1 and no. 2 had ever met in post-season (USC-Wisconsin occurred in 1963 Rose Bowl and Texas-Navy in 1964 Cotton). It was worst Alabama defeat to date for Bear Bryant, who agreed with media saying Nebraska "might be the best" he'd ever encountered.

Final AP Poll January 3

1 Nebraska (55)	1100	11 Louisiana State	324	
2 Oklahoma	990	12 Auburn	282	
3 Colorado	746	13 Notre Dame	164	
4 Alabama	674	14 Toledo	126	
5 Penn State	666	15 Mississippi	104	
6 Michigan	479	16 Arkansas	39	
7 Georgia	471	17 Houston	37	
8 Arizona State	414	18 Texas	31	
9 Tennessee	379	19 Washington	15	
10 Stanford	347	20 Southern California	9	

1971 Top Performance Formula

1 Nebraska	1.9154
2 Alabama	1.8025
3 Oklahoma	1.7667
4 Penn State	1.6875
5 Arizona State	1.6713
6 Georgia	1.6517
7 Colorado	1.5969
8 Michigan	1.5914
9 Auburn	1.5020
10 Tennessee	1.4773
11 Louisiana State	1.4768
12 Houston	1.4724
13 Notre Dame	1.4320
14 Stanford	1.3886
15 Texas	1.3616
16 Mississippi	1.3610
17 North Carolina	1.3550
18 Iowa State	1.3476
19 Arkansas	1.3309
20 Washington	1.3097

1971 Top Opponent Records

1 Alabama	.6825
2 Mississippi State	.6466
3 Colorado	.6411
4 Georgia Tech	.6260
5 Iowa State	.6200
6 Nebraska	.6185
7 Southern California	.6171
8 Missouri	.6150
9 Oregon	.6071
10 Houston	.6057
11tOklahoma	.60000
11tPittsburgh	.60000
13 Auburn	.5930
14 Florida	.5913
15 Kentucky	.5885
16 Kansas State	.5833
17 Navy	.5811
18 Oklahoma State	.5733
19 UCLA	.5686
20 California	.5636

1971 Out-of-Conference Records

	W-L	Percentage	Bowl W-L
Southeastern	32-9-1	.7738	4-2
Big Eight	28-8-1	.7703	3-1
Pacific-8	19-15	.5588	1-0
Western Athletic	13-18-2	.4242	1-0
Southwest	11-19-1	.3710	0-2
Atlantic Coast	14-25	.3590	0-1
Big Ten	8-17-1	.3269	0-1

1971 Individual Statistical Leaders

RUSHING YARDS	Attempts	Yards	Avg.
Ed Marinaro, Cornell	356	1881	5.3
Robert Newhouse, Houston	277	1757	6.3
Greg Pruitt, Oklahoma	178	1665	9.4
Lydell Mitchell, Penn State	254	1567	6.2
Eric Allen, Michigan State	259	1494	5.8
Howard Stevens, Louisville	250	1429	5.7
Charlie Davis, Colorado	219	1386	6.3
George Amundson, Iowa State	271	1260	4.6
Larry Hopkins, Wake Forest	249	1228	4.9
Rufus Ferguson, Wisconsin	249	1222	4.9

PASSING YARDS	Completions	Attempts	Yards	Pct.
Gary Huff, Florida State	184	327	2736	56.3
Don Strock, Virginia Tech	195	356	2577	54.8
Brian Sipe, San Diego State	196	369	2532	53.1
Gary Fox, Wyoming	171	328	2336	52.1
Don Bunce, Stanford	162	297	2265	54.5
Joe Ferguson, Arkansas	160	271	2203	59.0
John Reaves, Florida	193	356	2104	54.2
Sonny Sixkiller, Washington	126	297	2068	42.4
Jerry Tagge, Nebraska	143	239	2019	59.8
Pat Sullivan, Auburn	162	281	2012	57.7

RECEIVING YARDS	Catches	Yards
Tom Reynolds, San Diego State	67	1070
Mike Reppond, Arkansas	56	986
Mike Siani, Villanova	49	960
Johnny Rodgers, Nebraska	53	872
Bob Wicks, Utah State	58	862
Terry Beasley, Auburn	55	846
Rhett Dawson, Florida State	62	817
Don Fair, Toledo	49	673
Bill Davis, Virginia	49	617
Leland Glass, Oregon	46	584

1971 Consensus All-America Team

Offense

End:	Terry Beasley, Auburn
	Johnny Rodgers, Nebraska
Tackle:	Jerry Sisemore, Texas
	Dave Joyner, Penn State
Guard:	Royce Smith, Georgia
	Reggie McKenzie, Michigan
Center:	Tom Brahaney, Oklahoma
Quarterback:	Pat Sullivan, Auburn
Running Back:	Ed Marinaro, Cornell
	Greg Pruitt, Oklahoma
	Johnny Musso, Alabama

Defense

End:	Walt Patulski, Notre Dame
	Willie Harper, Nebraska
Tackle:	Larry Jacobson, Nebraska
	Mel Long, Toledo
	Sherman White, California
Linebacker:	Mike Taylor, Michigan
	Jeff Siemon, Stanford
Backs:	Bobby Majors, Tennessee
	Clarence Ellis, Notre Dame
	Ernie Jackson, Duke
	Tommy Casanova, Louisiana State

1971 Heisman Trophy Vote

Pat Sullivan, senior quarterback, Auburn	1597
Ed Marinaro, senior tailback, Cornell	1445
Greg Pruitt, junior halfback, Oklahoma	586
Johnny Musso, senior halfback, Alabama	385
Lydell Mitchell, senior tailback, Penn State	251

Other Major Award Winners

Maxwell (Player)	Ed Marinaro, senior tailback, Cornell
Walter Camp (Player)	Pat Sullivan, senior quarterback, Auburn
Outland (Lineman)	Larry Jacobson, senior defensive tackle, Nebraska
Lombardi (Lineman)	Walt Patulski, senior defensive end, Notre Dame
AFCA Coach of the Year	Paul "Bear" Bryant, Alabama

1972

The Year of Southern California Sunshine, Archie Leads Freshmen Back into Fray, and BYU's Rushing King

Sweeping every poll including unanimous acclaim from the AP voters, Southern California (12-0) offered perhaps its greatest team and clearly was the dominant outfit of 1972. After two sub-par seasons in which coach John McKay retooled his Trojans, his changes paid off handsomely. McKay installed a new conditioning program, worked on mental preparation, and packed his offense with experience and his defense with speed. A star-studded sophomore class checked in, and it included tailback Anthony Davis, who became the leading rusher, and All-America linebacker Richard Wood, who stepped right in to call the defensive signals.

After blitzing Arkansas (6-5) in the opener and having cross-town rival UCLA (8-3) defeat Nebraska (9-2-1) on one of the greatest regular season days in Los Angeles college football history, USC took over no. 1 in the AP Poll and liked the view from the mountaintop. The Men of Troy coasted from there, trailing in any game for the final time on October 7 when recent nemesis Stanford (6-5) went ahead 10-7 in a contest the Trojans went to win 30-21.

Freshman eligibility was returned nationally for first time since the Korean War days of the early 1950s. In January of 1972, the NCAA passed legislation to allow freshmen athletes to play varsity football and basketball, the only sports not covered by a 1968 rules change that first reopened athletics to the frosh. Ohio State (9-2) freshman tailback Archie Griffin made the biggest splash of all the 18-year-olds now on the varsity. Coach Woody Hayes recognized Griffin's talents and switched his attack to a Power-I after long embracing his Robust-T offense that featured fullback blasts by the likes of Jim Otis, Bob Ferguson, Matt Snell, Will Sander, and Bob White.

The mantle of nation's best team was passed from Nebraska early on during coach Bob Devaney's last year. Despite two losses and a tie, the Huskers proved their mettle with a 40-6 whipping of Notre Dame (8-3) in the Orange Bowl. Big Eight rival Oklahoma (11-1) was upset by Colorado (8-4), but parlayed wins over Nebraska, Texas (10-1), and its Sugar Bowl victory over Penn State (10-2) to land the poll's second place finish. The conference of the Great Plains may have surrendered defending national champion Nebraska's title, but the talent level remained extremely high. For example the top three in the Heisman Trophy balloting were all members of the Big Eight: trophy-winner, wingback Johnny Rodgers of Nebraska, halfback Greg Pruitt of Oklahoma, and Huskers' nose guard Rich Glover. More amazing was that all three were beaten out for the conference player of the year award by Iowa State (5-6-1) QB George Amundsen, who also went higher in the NFL draft than any of his more famous Big Eight brethren.

Although Tennessee (10-2) failed to win a national title during a wonderful span in the late 1960s and early '70s, this season marked the eighth straight in which the Volunteers won at least eight games. No other school, least of all one in the tough SEC, achieved so consistent a record during the same time period. The Vols sported a 73-15-3 mark since 1965.

Auburn (10-1) was expected to rebuild in 1972 without quarterback Pat Sullivan and wide receiver Terry Beasley, among others. Tigers surprised the experts to earn the nickname, "The Amazins."

Alabama (10-2) experienced an odd opening two weeks in beating both Duke (5-6) and Kentucky (3-8). In the first quarter versus both opponents, the Tide rolled for 14 points. In second quarter against both opponents, they failed to score. In the third period versus both Duke and Kentucky, Alabama tallied seven, and in the final quarter against both teams they made two touchdowns. Seeking more success, identical or not, the Crimson Tide won 10 straight but lost its final two games, including an incredible defeat to a punt-block by the rival Auburn Tigers.

Arizona State (10-2) had another excellent year under coach Frank Kush, setting a new school season points standard of 513. Led by quarterback Danny White and halfback Woody Green, the Sun Devils never scored less than 31 points in a game.

Miami (5-6), still several years from its future glory days, benefited from an official's blunder to gain an extra down during a winning drive versus Tulane (6-5) on October 14. Like Notre Dame in 1961 and Missouri in 1990—but unlike Cornell in 1940 which abdicated a 7-3 win over Dartmouth when films proved the decisive touchdown came on a fifth down—Miami kept its victory, much to the displeasure of the Green Wave.

Coach LaVell Edwards arrived for his first year at the coaching helm of Brigham Young (7-4). In the storied career that followed, Edwards would create an innovative aerial game at BYU and showcase a parade of brilliant quarterbacks, including Gifford Nielsen, Marc Wilson, Jim McMahon, Steve

Young, Robbie Bosco, and Ty Detmer. But, BYU's biggest claim to fame in Edwards' first season was tailback Pete Van Valkenburg, who would amaze current-day football historians because he led the nation in rushing, of all things. Van Valkenburg's BYU single season rushing record of 1,386 yards would stand for nearly 30 years.

Oddly enough, a passing record did fall in a game in Utah, but it was Utah State (8-3) quarterback Tony Adams setting a new single game standard with 561 yards that included five touchdowns in a 44-16 rout of Utah (3-8) on November 11.

Rushing for 204 yards against Tulsa (4-7) on November 4, Louisville (9-1) tailback Howard Stevens became the first player to break the 5,000-yard career rushing barrier with 5,058 yards, but was never recognized as the NCAA all-time rushing leader. Mighty-mite Stevens was a running force for the best team to date at Louisville in 1972, but he had gained a huge chunk of his yards while playing for Randolph-Macon against lesser competition in the College Division.

Oh, those campus hi-jinks! This was especially true in the Big Eight. During halftime of a 62-0 whipping of Missouri on October 14, the Nebraska card section was supposed to salute the United States Navy's 197th birthday. Instead, the messages came out as "Screw Missouri," "Johnny Rodgers is Shifty," and "Devaney for President." Meanwhile, ex-Oklahoma defensive back Steve O'Shaughnessy, who was a Colorado Law School grad student, was caught spying on the Buffs' practices. The ruse backfired as the Colorado team was motivated to a 20-14 triumph, the only loss of the season for the powerful Sooners.

Milestones

■ Stanford dropped politically-debated nickname of Indians in favor of Cardinals, later adjusted to Cardinal, its official school color.

■ By 94-67 vote, NCAA announced that freshmen would be eligible to play beginning with 1972 season. Ruling was proposed by ACC and WAC conferences but decried by many coaches.

■ Army won first Commander-in-Chief Trophy, emblematic of football supremacy among three major service academies. All three service academies played each other for first time in same season.

■ University of San Francisco dropped football.

■ Harry Kipke, head coach at Michigan from 1929-37, died after short illness on September 14. Jackie Robinson, who first earned athletic fame as fleet halfback for UCLA in 1939-40) before breaking baseball's color barrier, died of heart attack at age of 53 on October 24. Mississippi halfback (1952-54) and New York Giants safety (1955-66) Jimmy Patton died in car accident on December 22. Dayton defensive end Matt Dahlinghaus died on December 28 at age 20 from complications (massive pulmonary clot to lungs) from broken neck he suffered in November 11 game versus Bowling Green.

■ Longest winning streaks entering season:

Toledo 35	Nebraska 23	Arizona State, Mississippi, Tennessee 7

■ Coaching changes:

	Incoming	Outgoing
Baylor	Grant Teaff	Bill Beall
Brigham Young	LaVell Edwards	Tommy Hudspeth
California	Mike White	Ray Willsey
Georgia Tech	Bill Fulcher	Bud Carson
Maryland	Jerry Claiborne	Roy Lester
Minnesota	Cal Stoll	Murray Warmath
North Carolina State	Lou Holtz	Al Michaels
Oklahoma State	Dave Smith	Floyd Gass
Oregon	Dick Enright	Jerry Frei
Rice	Al Conover	Bill Peterson
Stanford	Jack Christiansen	John Ralston
Texas A&M	Emery Bellard	Gene Stallings
Texas El Paso	Tommy Hudspeth	Bobby Dobbs
Wake Forest	Tom Harper	Cal Stoll

AP Preseason Poll

1 Nebraska (28)	920	11 Louisiana State	257
2 Colorado (13)	746	12 Arizona State	221
3 Ohio State (4)	620	13 Notre Dame	205
4 Arkansas (2)	578	14 Texas	202
5 Penn State	550	15 Tennessee	163
6 Oklahoma (2)	538	16 Mississippi	88
7 Alabama	410	17 Georgia	79
8 Southern California	299	18 Purdue	67
9 Washington (1)	294	19 Florida State	40
10 Michigan	266	20 Stanford	27

September 9, 1972

Florida State 19 PITTSBURGH 7: At least briefly, it was whole new season for Seminoles (1-0) QB Gary Huff, last year's national total O leader. Pitt (0-1) LB George Feher intercepted season's 1st pass by Huff (11-24/242y, 2 TDs). But, Feher's early

TO did little to spark Panthers' new, but ineffective, Wishbone attack. QB John Hogan came off bench in 2nd Q to ignite Pitt with option runs totaling 28y on 67y trip he ended with 15y TD pass to WR Rod Huth for 7-3 lead. Huff quickly cranked it up to pitch 71y TD to WR Barry Smith and followed with 54y scoring arrow to WR Joe Goldsmith for 19-7 margin in 4th Q.

Tennessee 34 GEORGIA TECH 3: Tennessee Volunteers (1-0) turned 6-3 struggle into rout by converting 8 Georgia Tech TOs into 3 TDs. Reserve TB Bill Rudder scored 1st TD in 2nd H on 7y scoring run following INT. Now up 13-3, Tennessee forced FUM to set up another TD that came 71 secs later on 16y scoring pass from Rudder to WB Chip Howard, who leapt in back of EZ for catch. Game was 1st-ever to feature match-up of black starting QBs: Condredge Holloway of Tennessee and Eddie McAshan of Georgia Tech. McAshan threw for 124y to spark Yellow Jackets (0-1), but was picked off 3 times.

Auburn 14 MISSISSIPPI STATE 3: Coaches have to win with what they have and Tigers (1-0) quickly transformed themselves from 1971's passing game to power rushing attack. TB Terry Henley (32/136y) led charge that out-rushed Bulldogs 230y to 98y. Henley's 2y TD run in 2nd Q opened scoring as Auburn took 7-0 lead to H. K Glenn Ellis put Mississippi State (0-1) on board with 43y FG in 3rd Q. Tigers answer was 70y march to 15y TD run by FB James Owens that featured 2 broken tackles.

ALABAMA 35 Duke 12 (Birmingham): Crimson Tide (1-0) FB Paul Spivey rumbled up middle behind blocks of C Jim Krapf and Gs John Hannah and Buddy Brown, while QB Terry Davis passed with near perfection at 6-7/73y. Spivey made Bama's 1st TD on 8y run in 1st Q and contributed to subsequent TD drive. Duke (0-1) trimmed 2nd Q margin to 14-12 as poised, young QB Bob Albright nailed 2 TD passes after FUM REC by DL Ernie Clark and at end of 68y drive. Tide's Davis scored 3rd Q TD before HB Steve Bisceglia got loose for 39y TD romp that made it 28-12 in 4th Q.

Southern California 31 ARKANSAS 10: With 17 returning starters Razorbacks (0-1) were national contenders, until they played 2nd H of this opener. Trojans QB Mike Rae (18-24/269y) led rout, outshining Arkansas QB Joe Ferguson (19-36/223y, 2 INTs). After throwing 43y bomb to WR Edesel Garrison, Rae broke 3-3 tie with 5y keeper in 3rd Q. Southern California (1-0) soph LB Richard Wood debuted with 18 tackles, 2 sacks, and fortuitous INT that set up 3y TD run by TB Rod McNeil (28/117y, TD) for 17-3 lead that broke Hogs' hope. Arkansas TB Jon Richardson scored solo TD with 1y dive in 4th Q, while WR Jim Hodge contributed 7/127y in receptions.

RICE 14 Houston 13: Owls (1-0) won city championship as they stopped Houston twice on GL as time expired. FB Leonard Parker, who had scored on 2 short runs earlier, and QB D.C. Nobles were halted as Cougars (0-1) decided to skip FG attempt after having messed up snap on potential game-tying missed x-pt earlier in 4th Q. SS Preston Anderson made final game-saving tackle for Owls, nailing Nobles for 4y loss on 1st-and-goal play from 1YL. Rice had scored both its TDs on QB Bruce Gadd-to-WR Edwin Collins passing connections of 30y and 5y. Cougars vainly won O y battle with 354y to Owls' 230y.

COLORADO 20 California 10: Listless performance kept no. 2 Buffs (1-0) from pouncing on nation's top spot about to be vacated by Nebraska. It was not until Colorado LB Ed Schoen returned INT for TD late in game that unheralded Golden Bears (0-1) were put away. Schoen's 48y scoring RET gave Bison 17-3 lead in 3rd Q. Bears cut deficit in half on 9y TD pass from QB Steve Bartkowski (24-50/261y, TD, 2 INTs) to WR Steve Sweeney, but that was as close as they would come. Cal outgained Colorado 377y to 283y and picked up 9 more 1st downs (23 to 14), but failed twice on 4th-and-1 in 4th Q. Buffs K Fred Lima made 46y and 53y FGs.

UCLA 20 Nebraska 17: It might have been his bloodlines (son of former Heisman Trophy winner (Tommy) of Michigan), but UCLA (1-0) QB Mark Harmon made dandy debut throwing and running for TDs and hitting crucial pass for 1st down to set up Bruins' winning FG. Bruins had won only 2 games in 1971, but they were capable of ending Nebraska's 23-game win streak. Harmon, future actor, became star over-night. After K Efren Herrera opened with 27y FG, Harmon threw 46y TD pass to WR Brad Lyman to stretch lead to 10-0. Huskers (0-1) rallied to tie it 10-10 at H behind WB Johnny Rodgers, who returned punt 50y to set up FG and scored on 11y run. Uclans regained lead in 3rd Q following CB Jimmy Allen's 37y INT RET to Huskers 15YL, as Harmon scored on 2y keeper. After Nebraska TE Jerry List tied game on 44y scoring pass from QB David Humm, Harmon led 57y drive—during which he threw 13y bullet to TE Jack Lassner on 3rd-and-11—to Herrera's winning 30y FG with 22 secs left. Underestimated Bruins played heads-up, converting 5 TOs into 17 pts.

AP Poll September 11

1 Southern California (13)	779	11 Michigan	199
2 Colorado (12)	769	12 Washington (1)	186
3 Ohio State (5)	710	13 Arizona State	174
4 Oklahoma (12)	694	14 Notre Dame	162
5 Alabama	528	15 Texas	132
6 Penn State (1)	473	16 Georgia	81
7 Tennessee (1)	426	17 Arkansas	79
8 UCLA	415	18 Purdue	55
9 Louisiana State	375	19 Mississippi	43
10 Nebraska (1)	344	20 Florida State	40

September 16, 1972

North Carolina 31 MARYLAND 26: Ambitious Tar Heels (2-0) won their 10th straight ACC game against improved Maryland squad. UNC QB Nick Vidnovic (8-12/153y, TD, INT) passed for TD and ran for 2 others, while FB Dick Oliver capped 80y drive with 1y scoring plunge for eventual winning pts with 6 mins left to play. Terps mounted late drive, but FUM REC by Heels LB Jimmy DeRatt with 35 secs left on UNC 37YL killed

Turtles' hope. Slumbering Maryland (0-1-1) had awoken in time to rally from 17-3 deficit and tie game with 72y punt TD RET by DB Bob Smith and 10y TD run by RB Jamie Franklin that came moments later.

Florida State 37 MIAMI 14: Seminoles (2-0) won easily as QB Gary Huff (22-34/329y, 4 TDs, 2 INTs) made Hurricanes (0-1) pay for their sloppy play (7 TOs). Florida State WR Barry Smith (5/108y) caught 3 scoring passes, including 43y 2nd Q bomb for 10-7 lead that Noles would not relinquish. FSU LB John Murphy recovered 3 Miami FUMs. Canes had scored 1st on 3y TD run by HB Chuck Foreman and closed out scoring with 14y TD run by sub QB Ed Carney, who went in after QB Kary Baker broke ankle in 3rd Q.

TENNESSEE 28 Penn State 21: Between QB Condredge "Thisaway-Thataway" Holloway and HB Haskel "Snap Back" Stanback (3 TDs), Vols (2-0) had too many nicknames and too much speed for Penn State (0-1). At 1st night game ever played at Neyland Stadium, Stanback rushed twice for TDs as Tennessee built 21-0 H lead. QB John Hufnagel (12-29/192y, 2 TDs, 2 INTs), who was held to 3-10 passing in 1st H, rallied Nittany Lions with 2 TDs after H, including 69y scoring pass to WR Jim Scott. After Scott's TD, Vols led only 21-14 but then marched 80y to clinching 2y TD run by Stanback in 4th Q. Scoring drive not only doubled Tennessee's lead but ate 7 mins.

INDIANA 27 Minnesota 23: Relentless Golden Gophers (0-1) tallied 3 spectacular TDs in 1st H to come from behind for 20-13 H lead. Minnesota QB Bob Morgan breezed through enormous hole and dashed away for 46y TD that tied game 7-7 in 1st Q. Gophers FB John King took 2nd Q pitchout and raced 70y in 2nd Q, while LB Mike Steidl soon blocked punt which he chased to EZ where he fell on it for TD. Indiana (1-0) switched to effective stunting 6-man D line in 2nd H but allowed 3rd Q's only pts for 23-13 deficit. Final period then belonged to home team as Hoosiers QB Ted McNulty (17-29/198y, INT) led 2 scoring drives, both capped by TB Ken Starling (28/130y) TD runs.

Bowling Green 17 PURDUE 14: With last season's Big 10 leading passer, future pro Gary Danielson, returning, switch to Wishbone would seem odd choice for Boilermakers (0-1). Yet there was QB Bob Bobrowski (40y passing; 31y rushing) trying vainly to lead bumbling attack that lost 5 of 6 FUMs, while making Danielson (0-2/0y, INT) talented clipboard holder. Meanwhile Bowling Green enjoyed 1st-ever game versus Big 10 opponent and largest crowd to witness MAC conference team to date (51,859) by scoring 2 1st Q TDs and then winning game with only pts scored in 2nd H on 29y FG by frosh Don Taylor early In 4th Q. All 3 Bowling Green scores converted Purdue FUMs. Winning kick capped drive salvaged when P Ed McCoy picked up punt blocked deep in own territory and ran for 21y and 1st down. Falcons needed 7 more plays to drive to winning kick by Taylor, who joined team Wednesday and has yet to begin classes. Boilermakers HB Otis Armstrong rushed for 105y, with 16y on 2nd Q TD that tied game at 14.

Arizona State 33 HOUSTON 28: HB Woody Green (36/195, TD) made name for himself as Sun Devils (1-0) sent Houston to 2nd loss. QB Danny White threw 1st Q TD passes of 55y and 52y to WB Steve Holden as ASU built 20-0 lead. Cougars (0-2) answered with 2 TDs, including 20y INT TD RET by LB Harold Evans. It was now Arizona State's turn to score and they reeled off 10 pts for 30-14 H lead. Pace slowed down in scoreless 3rd Q before Cougars QB D.C. Nobles wrapped 2 TD passes around Devils' FG. Houston seemed to get go-ahead TD with 4 mins left, but it was erased by PEN.

CALIFORNIA 37 Washington State 23: After spotting Cougars (1-1) ample 17-0 lead by 2nd Q, Cal turned to its bench to jump-start rally. Back-ups, QB Jay Cruze (10-17/151y) and RB Fred Leathers, teamed up on 42y scoring pass play to put Golden Bears on board. Cruze then pulled Bears (1-1) to within 17-14 on 2y TD run. Then it was Leathers' turn, and he put home team in front for good at 21-17 with his 3rd Q 41y scoring jaunt. Now trailing, Washington State had to go to air with painful result: Cougars QB Ty Paine, who rushed for 68y and threw for 162y, tossed INT that California CB Bob Curry returned 60y to EZ.

AP Poll September 18

1 Southern California (28)	920	11 Penn State	180
2 Oklahoma (11)	840	12 Michigan	162
3 Colorado (7)	769	13 Notre Dame	156
4 Ohio State	622	14 Texas	109
5 Tennessee (2)	615	15 Washington	86
6 UCLA	490	16 Georgia	59
7 Alabama	463	17 Florida State	58
8 Louisiana Sate	392	18 Michigan State	54
9 Nebraska	377	19 Stanford	50
10 Arizona State	190	20 Mississippi	38

September 23, 1972

Nebraska 77 ARMY 7: Truly ugly result began shaping debate over whether Cadets should be asked to compete with larger programs. Huskers (2-1) broke record for most pts ever allowed by Army by whopping 26. WB Johnny Rodgers scored twice in 1st Q, on 3y run and 26y reception, but Nebraska led by only 14-0 until it staged 21-pt spurt late in 2nd Q that put nail in Black Knights' coffin. Huskers QB David Humm threw 14-18/169y with TDs both passing and running. Army (0-1) was able to avoid shutout on late 9y scoring pass from QB Dick Atha to WR Barry Armstrong. Week later, Cadets beat Texas A&M 24-14 on road to quiet some of their doubters.

PENN STATE 21 Navy 10: On day that rival Army lost by 70 pts, Midshipmen (1-1) acquitted themselves well against Penn State. Navy led 3-0 at H on 38y FG by K Roger Lanning and then 10-7 in 3rd Q after 1y TD run by FB Andy Pease that was set up by 56y KO RET by KR Ike Owens. Penn State (1-1) took control with long drive to its 2nd TD run from TB John Cappelletti. Down 14-10 throughout most of 4th Q, Navy

255

finally made fatal mistake that ended its upset chances as QB Fred Stuvek threw INT to brilliant LB John Skorupan (17 tackles and 3 sacks), who returned it 32y for clinching score. Nittany Lions lost 5 FUMs and had INT in sloppy 1st H.

NORTH CAROLINA 34 North Carolina State 33: Coach Lou Holtz faced late 2-pt decision in his young career at NC State (1-1-1), but he had no doubt: "We took the field to win, not to tie." So, after Wolfpack TE Pat Kenney made astounding TD catch with 10 secs to play, Holtz followed with 2-pt pass for HB Willie Burton, which was well-covered by North Carolina (3-0). There were 7 lead changes with biggest falling to Wolfpack when DB Mike Stultz found gap and charged 80y on punt RET for 19-10 H edge. Heels went ahead with 2 TDs in 3rd Q and took lead for good in 4th Q on TB Billy Hite's 2nd TD and K Ellis Alexander's 3rd x-pt.

LOUISIANA STATE 42 Texas A&M 17: Using 4-TD 2nd H burst, Bengal Tigers (2-0) blew away A&M as QB Bert Jones threw 3 TD passes and D contained Aggies' embryonic Wishbone. As Jones threw 2nd H TD passes of 13y and 26y to WR Gerald Keighley to help LSU pull away, Texas A&M (1-2) was stumbling to 7y net O in 2nd H. LSU D outscored Aggies over final 30 mins when CB Norm Hodgins returned INT—1 of 6 TOs for visitors—45y to score. Frosh WR Carl Roaches had 97y KO TD RET to highlight Texas A&M's effort.

FLORIDA STATE 27 Virginia Tech 15: Seminoles (3-0) QB Gary Huff (19-37/253y, TD, INT) got knocked silly late in 1st Q, so sub QB Mike Cadwell threw 40y TD pass, bobbled several times, to WR Joe Goldsmith for 14-0 lead. Gobblers (0-2) rallied to 14-9 on K Don Strock's 48y FG and TB James Barber's 3y TD run. Back came FSU to 20-9 H edge as resuscitated Huff fired 38y pass to WR Barry Smith to set up his TD sneak. When Huff followed with 3rd Q TD pass, it was all but over.

TULANE 24 Georgia 13: Big upset propelled Green Wave (2-0) into top 20 at no. 18 in Monday's vote for 1st time in regular season since 1956. Two 80y drives in 2nd Q put Tulane out in front 17-7 at H; they later added 57y punt TD RET by S George Ewing to ice contest. Georgia (1-1) running attack managed only 131y on 46 rushes, while opportunistic Tulane D came up with 3 INTs. Bulldogs opened scoring on 7y TD run by HB Jimmy Poulos, set up by controversial ruling. Tulane S David Lee appeared to not touch punt that bounded away from him, but refs ruled that he made contact and that Georgia had possession at Tulane 25YL.

WASHINGTON 22 PURDUE 21: K Steve Wiezbowski's 25y FG with 2:04 remaining enabled Huskies (3-0) to survive major road test. Purdue (0-2) earned 21-0 H lead before generously offering TO-sparked drives of 36, 48, and 34y to visitors in 2nd H. Boilermakers QB Gary Danielson rushed 16/213y, leading 3 drives of more than 80y in 1st H. Huskies were held to 88y in 1st H before exploding for 248y in 2nd H. QB Sonny Sixkiller (17-30/222y, TD, 4 INTs) led UW rally, running and pitching for TDs.

NOTRE DAME 37 NORTHWESTERN 0: Notre Dame (1-0) opened its season in fine fashion, scoring on 1st 5 possessions and allowing only 184y on D side. Score mounted to 30-0 by H, and Irish next marched 81y to 9y TD run by HB Eric Penick. Best opportunity for Northwestern (0-2) came in 1st Q, when QB Mitch Anderson connected with WR Jim Lash on passes of 22y and 20y to move into ND territory. Drive stalled and Fighting Irish LB Tim Rudnick blocked FG attempt. Irish HB Darryl Dewan rushed for team-high 105y.

Southern California 55 ILLINOIS 20: High-spirited Illinois (0-2) led 7-0 and 14-7 on HB Bob Hayes' 5y burst after E Joe Lewis' 21y E-around and HB George Uremovich's 5y sweep after WR Garvin Roberson's spectacular 41y catch he snatched off hands of USC defenders. No. 1 Trojans (3-0) quickly countered with tying TDs and went ahead just before H on 2nd of pair of TD passes by QB Mike Rae (9-13/178y, 2 TDs) which came after Illini howled over pass interference no-call at USC 5YL. Illinois was still in it, down 28-20, when roof fell in with 4th Q deluge of 20 pts that included Trojans' TD punt block and WR J.K. McKay's 2nd TD reception.

Michigan 26 UCLA 9: Wolverines (2-0) knocked out Bruins QB Mark Harmon in 1st Q and then knocked around his UCLA mates rest of way. FB Ed Shuttlesworth led Michigan rush attack, churning up 115y and 2 TDs as Michigan team won for 22nd time in last 23 regular season games. Bruins (2-1) clearly were pushed around, surrendering 389y rushing and 28 1st downs. Michigan QB Dennis Franklin enjoyed his 1st start and rushed for 75y and leading sharp O that committed no TOs. QB Rob Scribner came off UCLA bench to replace Harmon and vainly rushed for 90y.

AP Poll September 25

1 Southern California (28)	940	11 Arizona State	242
2 Oklahoma (14)	894	12 Texas	131
3 Colorado (5)	728	13 Penn State	130
4 Tennessee (1)	622	14 Washington	103
5 Ohio State (1)	544	15 UCLA	69
6 Alabama	468	16 Florida State	64
7 Nebraska	465	17 Mississippi	50
8 Michigan (1)	429	18 Tulane	34
9 Louisiana State	396	19 Stanford	29
10 Notre Dame	319	20 West Virginia	20

September 30, 1972

PRINCETON 7 Rutgers 6: Tigers (1-0) waited until last min to score, winning game on 2y TD run by FB Howard Baetjer and x-pt by K John Bartges. Baetjer (19/75y) was Princeton's leading rusher, subbing for starting FB Bob Harding who left game with leg injury. Rutgers (1-2) had better of play in 1st H, driving 66y with 3rd possession to score TD on 2y run by HB Ron Shycko. Tigers DE Barry Richardson then made crucial block of K John Pesce's x-pt ATT. Knights missed huge chance in 2nd Q to increase lead when they were unable to corral Princeton P Bruce Hennemuth after snap cleared

him and rolled to EZ. Hennemuth avoided 2 tackles before getting punt off to 30YL with PEN on Rutgers sending ball back to midfield. Drive failed and then best chances for both teams ended on missed FGs in rain. Shycko rushed for 111y on 20 carries.

Rice 36 GEORGIA TECH 36: Trailing by 8 with time elapsing, Georgia Tech (2-1-1) needed school-record 5th TD pass from QB Eddie McAshan, this from 2y to WR Jim Owings, and then successful 2-pt conv on another McAshan-to-Owings hook-up to pull out unlikely tie. Yellow Jackets had 21-9 2nd Q lead as McAshan, who also set school game yardage record with 371y on 23-38 passing and school career TD pass with 24, threw 1st 3 TDs, 2 to WR Jimmy Robinson (7/146y). Owls (2-0-1) QB Bruce Gadd then threw his 2nd TD pass, 28y to WR Carl Swierc, as Rice trailed 21-16 at H. Visitors then dominated 3rd Q, scoring twice for 10 pts and 26-21 lead with TD coming on S Bruce Henley's 52y punt RET. McAshan then led Tech deep into Rice territory before stunning 99y INT TD RET by SS Preston Anderson, 5th pick on day for Owls. With Rice K Mark Williams booting 47y FG and McAshan tossing 1 more TD, Rice was left with 36-28 lead. Final tying drive began for Georgia Tech on their own 39YL, facing stiff wind. CB Randy Rhino had 3 INTs for Yellow Jackets.

AUBURN 10 Tennessee 6 (Birmingham): New-look Auburn (3-0) snapped Vols' 10-game win streak as Tigers D surrendered only 80y rushing and 109y passing. TB Terry Henley (29-74y) was bullish on decisive 2nd Q TD drive, carrying ball final 10 plays for 52y and TD. K Gardner Jett added 30y FG for 10-0 lead. Auburn DE Danny Sanspree and CB Dave Beck led outstanding D performance, helping to force 4 TOs. Tigers finally allowed late TD on 30y pass from backup Vols QB Gary Valbuena to WB Chip Howard. Tennessee (3-1) coach Bill Battle stood at that moment with 24-4 career coaching record, but with 3 annoying losses to Auburn.

Indiana 35 KENTUCKY 34: Indiana passing duo of QB Ted McNulty and WR Glenn Scolnik burned Wildcats (1-2) for 3 TDs, including 43y TD effort to open scoring and 19y TD pass to win game in 4th Q. Hoosiers (2-1) rode wind in 1st Q to 20-0 lead, including school-record FGs of 51y and 52y by K Chris Gartner. When teams traded sides, Kentucky roared back with 19 pts. QB Dinky McKay (14-22/200y) had hand in 4 Wildcat TDs, rushing for 3 and throwing 10y scoring pass to TE Ray Barga. After being trapped in early deficit, Cats scored 34 pts until McNulty led winning 4th Q drive.

OHIO STATE 29 North Carolina 14: Ohio State (2-0) took advantage of new frosh eligibility rule by unveiling newcomer TB Archie Griffin and new Power-I attack. Tar Heels (3-1), having prepared for old Buckeye FB-focused Robust T, were ill prepared as Griffin rushed 27 times for 239y to break Ollie Cline's 27-year-old school record by 10y. Backup TB Elmer Lippert added 116y rushing against dazed visitors. North Carolina had opened scoring when LB Jimmy DeRatt blocked punt in 1st Q that was recovered in EZ by DE Gene Brown. Heels surrendered 29 straight pts before scoring on 37y pass from QB Nick Vidnovic to WR Earle Bethea.

OKLAHOMA STATE 31 Colorado 6: Only Wishbone Colorado (3-1) could snap was its own as Bison coughed up 10 FUMs, losing 3. Cowboys (2-1) held TB Charlie Davis, who entered contest with 6 straight 100y games, to 58y, while Oklahoma State HB Alton Gerald scored 3 TDs. Cowboys QB Brent Blackman rushed for 70y and threw 16y pass to WR Steve Pettes for opening score. Colorado sorely missed starting QB Ken Johnson, absent due to death of his father. Score signified significant reversal of 40-6 whipping administered by Colorado in 1971.

Texas 25 TEXAS TECH 20: Longhorns (2-1) reminded overflow crowd, including former Pres Lyndon B. Johnson, that TDs were better than FGs. Red Raiders (2-1) marched to Texas 4, 14, 17, and 15YL on drives that ended with quartet of FGs by K Don Grimes, which tied SWC record. So, Texas Tech led 12-7. CB Adrian Ford then launched Texas' 42y drive to go-ahead TD with INT of Raiders QB Joe Barnes. Texas converted on 8y run by QB Alan Lowry and his 2-pt conv pass to FB Roosevelt Leaks (23/107y). Lowry, who rushed for 103y, added insurance TD run of 7y.

WYOMING 45 Arizona State 43: Behind QB Steve Cockreham, who accounted for 4 TDs, Wyoming Cowboys (2-2) scored most pts ever against Frank Kush-coached squad. Cockreham rushed for 177y as Cowboys gained 472y on ground with FB Steve Brown (27/144y) and RB Charlie Shaw (10/117y) also topping century mark. Sun Devils (2-1) had their 19-game WAC win streak snapped even though HB Woody Green scored 4 TDs while rushing for 11/198y. Arizona State QB Danny White threw scoring passes of 23y to TE Joe Petty and 9y to WB Morris Owens to cut deficit to 45-43 with 51 secs left, but Sun Devils could not recover onside-KO.

OREGON STATE 29 Brigham Young 3: Beavers (1-3) opened with 22 straight pts as QB Scott Spiegelberg threw and ran for TDs. Cougars (1-2) found answers difficult because they fumbled 6 times, losing 2, and threw 6 INTs. Oregon State DB Bill Bartley (3 INTs) and LB Steve Brown (2 INTs) were leading thieves, and they set up 2 TDs with their pickoffs. BYU managed 23y FG by K John Monahan as 1st H ended 22-3, but were unable to mount attack in 2nd H. Beavers rushed for 241y.

SOUTHERN CALIFORNIA 51 Michigan State 6: Struggling Spartans (1-2) could not get its Wishbone attack in gear against 8-man and sometimes 9-man fronts that USC employed to force 7 FUMs. Trojans (4-0) recovered 5 FUMs and picked off 3 passes, converting 6 TOs into TDs including INT TD RET of 25y by LB Richard Wood. Despite final score, Spartan D played well in containing Southern California backs and forcing 6 TOs before being completely worn down: USC scored 27 pts in 4th Q. WR Lynn Swann opened scoring with 92y punt RET in 1st Q and closed it with 30y TD reception in 4th Q. Southern California QB Mike Rae threw 4 INTs, but completed 12-26 for 172y and was team's leading rusher with 53y. Loss was worst for Michigan State since 1947. Taking advantage of Trojans' D formations, MSU TE Billy Joe Dupree caught 8 passes for 134y.

October 7, 1972

Florida 42 FLORIDA STATE 13: TOs—10 in all—did in Seminoles (4-1) as in-state rival Gators converted 6 of them into TDs. FSU QB Gary Huff (26-59/325y) entered game as nation's leading passer but was left humbled by 33 incompletions and 4 INTs. Huff threw 2 TD passes, but gave score back on INT that Florida LB Ralph Ortega took 29y to EZ in 3rd Q. HB Nat Moore swept around E for 2 TDs to lead Gators (2-1), while QB David Bowden threw 2 TDs in 2nd Q as Florida took 14-0 lead. FSU had 423y O, 100y more than Florida, but Gators suffered only solo TO.

Alabama 25 GEORGIA 7: Not playing Georgia on annual basis, coach Bear Bryant had to bide time to gain revenge for Bulldogs' upset of his 1965 club. Alabama (4-0) would win, but not without struggle as O needed 2 long yd TD drives. QB Terry Davis took Tide on 78y march to open 2nd H, ending it with 39y TD pass to WR Wayne Wheeler (2/50y), and then moved Bama 80y to 1y scoring keeper. Davis audibled on scoring pass, taking advantage of S moving up to stop run which left Wheeler wide open. Bulldogs (2-2) did not give up, scoring on 17y run by HB Jimmy Poulos, but later lost 4th Q chances on downs and INT by Bama S David McMackin of Tucker, Ga. Georgia had 6 TOs, 4 lost FUMs.

Auburn 19 MISSISSIPPI 13: Tigers' 2nd straight upset was in doubt until game's end. On Auburn 15YL with time elapsing, Ole Miss (3-1) QB Norris Weese's last pass was deflected to end drive. TB Terry Henley led Auburn (4-0) with 139y rushing, while QB Randy Walls contributed 43y TD pass to WB Tommy Gossom and 5y TD run. Weese (21-38/249y, 2 INTs) threw TD passes of 38y and 10y to WR Burney Veazey. Last Rebs score was set up by blocked punt by LB Bob Bailess that gave Ole Miss ball on Auburn 5YL, but it was not enough to keep Rebels 10-game win streak alive.

Notre Dame 16 MICHIGAN STATE 0: Bare-knuckled D brawl went to Notre Dame's inexperienced defenders because they allowed only 6 1st downs and single penetration inside their territory to 44YL. That probe came midway through 4th Q and was terminated by Irish S Ken Schlezes when he stepped in front of Michigan State (1-3) TE Billy Joe DuPree to snatch INT thrown by new QB Mark Niesen (3-9/28y, 3 INTs, and 95y rushing), switched from DB as part of wholesale changes following 51-6 loss to USC week before. Irish led just 6-0 at time. ND K Bob Thomas booted FGs in 1st, 2nd, and 4th Qs before FB Andy Huff ran 8y for TD in game's last min.

KANSAS 34 Minnesota 28: With 38 total pts set up by FUMs, game was not pretty, but it was exciting presentation of 2 completely different styles of O. Pass-happy Jayhawks (2-2) rode QB David Jaynes (16-29/229y), who threw 3 TD passes, 2 to WR Bruce Adams (3/89y), as Kansas took leads of 24-7 and 34-21. Minnesota's Veer O is not designed for rallies, so QB Bob Morgan (9-18/173y, 2 INTs), 0-2 passing in 1st H, followed Jaynes' lead by throwing more often in ATT to comeback. Best he could do was throw 39y TD pass to WR George Honza (5/91y) with 3:30 left 1 play after Kansas FUM. Gophers (0-4) had 1 final possession, but pass interference PEN on Honza after Minnesota reached KU 20YL deflated matters. Gophers FB John King rushed for 93y and 3 TDs.

ARIZONA STATE 38 Oregon State 7: Arizona State (3-1) entered contest with 31 wins in past 32 games, and then they gained revenge for sole loss by beating Beavers. Oregon State won last year's game 24-18, but this year they never had chance against inspired Sun Devils. ASU D allowed only 135y, 1y on ground, and forced 3 TOs in throttling Pac 8 visitors. Sun Devils also struggled with TOs, 7 in all, but won game with rush attack that produced 324y and 4 TDs, including 181y and 2 TDs by HB Woody Green. Ahead 10-0 at H, Arizona State blew game wide open with 3 TDs within 5 min under part of 3rd Q, including LB Bob Breunig's recovery of Oregon State FUM in OSU EZ. Down 30-0 in 4th Q, Beavers (1-4) finally reached scoreboard on QB Scott Spiegelberg's 11y TD pass to WR Roger Hall. ASU QB Danny White struggled, throwing for only 19y with 2 INTs, but was not needed.

Southern California 30 STANFORD 21: Tired of watching Stanford (3-1) play in Rose Bowl, Troy asserted itself in hard-fought contest. Game turned on high snap that sailed over Stanford P Dave Ottmar's head 36y to own 5YL to set up 1y TD run by USC (5-0) TB Anthony Davis (20/60y, 2 TDs) that snapped 13-13 tie. Stanford had long completion to Southern California 7YL brought back due to PEN moments before ill-fated punt snap. Stanford C Bill Reid injured left hand play before punt, but had to remain in game to punt as Cardinals had already substituted then-maximum 2 players for punt including Ottmar. QB Pat Haden (8-14/97y, TD, INT) came off bench to lead 2 USC scoring drives as O gained 407y, which made up for 5 lost FUMs. Harassing Trojans D only allowed 1 TD as Stanford, who managed only 183y, gained score on FUM REC in EZ by DB James Ferguson. QB Mike Boryla (20-36/199y, TD, INT) was valiant in defeat. Proving that no love was lost between rivals, Trojans contemptuously threw into EZ without success with 10 secs left. Stanford's early 10-7 edge was last lead anyone would own against 1972 Trojans. "I'd like to have beaten them by 2,000 points," said Southern California coach John McKay. "They have no class. They're the worst winners we've ever gone up against." Stanford coach Jack Christiansen replied: "I have no comment on that. I don't want to get into a urinating contest with a skunk."

WASHINGTON 23 Oregon 17: Game ended in controversy as striving Ducks (1-4) reached Washington 10YL with time elapsing before QB Dan Fouts' pass to WR Greg Lindsey was ruled incomplete despite Lindsey being tackled well before ball arrived. Huskies (5-0) QB Sonny Sixkiller (11-27/148y) tossed 3 TD passes to counterbalance Fouts, who threw for 229y and 27y TD pass to WR Bob Palm late in 4th Q. Palm's TD, which was set up by Huskies FUM, was followed by successful onside-KO to launch final Ducks' drive. Sixkiller's last TD pass, 4y effort to TE John Brady, his 2nd scoring catch, came in 3rd Q and notched 23-10 lead.

October 14, 1972

VIRGINIA TECH 34 Oklahoma State 32: There were too many Strocks on field for Cowboys (3-2) to handle. While star QB Don Strock, nation's leading passer, threw for 355y and 2 TDs, K Dave Strock, his brother, booted winning FG for Virginia Tech (2-2-1) from 18y out and 12 secs remaining. Cowboys DB Darryll Stewart had blocked Strock's FG attempt 4 plays earlier, but OSU FB George Palmer lost FUM on own 3YL, recovered by LB Donny Sprouse. Teams did not disappoint on O as Cowboys rushed for 356y, 1y more than total reached through air by Don Strock.

MIAMI 24 Tulane 21: Winning 32y TD pass from QB Ed Carney, his 2nd of day, to WR Witt Beckman with time dying was thrown on mistaken 5th down. Refs literally called Miami (1-3) O back on field to give them 5th down, saying it was 4th-and-24 on call by head linesman John Duval, who started as clock operator before replacing injured D.L. Claborn. Play brought back memories of 1940 Cornell victory over Dartmouth that was aided by extra down. Unlike Cornell, Miami did not hand back victory. Game was virtual deadlock as teams each had 16 1st downs, identical 8-21 passing and 3 FUMs, while Tulane (3-2) had 239y to 234y rushing edge and Miami nipped Greenies with 99y to 98y RET advantage.

LOUISIANA STATE 35 Auburn 7: QB Bert Jones tossed 3 TDs and ran in another as Louisiana State easily won battle of unbeatens. LSU (5-0) gained 477y with Jones completing 10-14/179y and rushing for 61y more. Tigers WR Gerald Keigley caught all 3 TDs, 2 for 19y and another for 27y. Auburn (4-1) managed 211y total O. Tigers TB Terry Henley (20/57y) scored in 2nd Q, but Auburn failed at catch-up with little passing attack. Henley, SEC's leading rusher, carried only once in 2nd H. Coach Charlie McClendon became LSU leader in career coaching wins with 84.

MICHIGAN 10 Michigan State 0: Spartans (1-4) were again heroic in defeat on D, while O squandered at least 2 TDs with PENs and TOs and remains scoreless through 10 Qs. Only big play for either side was WB Gil Chapman's 58y scoring run on reverse for Wolverines (5-0) in 4th Q. Block by T Paul Seymour set Chapman free. With his Wishbone O sputtering, coach Duffy Daugherty turned once again to DB Mark Niesen—option QB in HS—to helm attack. Niesen, who had 23y scoring run wiped out by clipping PEN, led O to only 180y as Michigan posted its 1st series shutout since 1947. Game set passing back 20 years in Wolverine State as Niesen was 0-10 with 3 INTs and Michigan QB Dennis Franklin completed 3-8 for 37y. Runners fared better as Wolverines FB Ed Shuttlesworth bulled 28 times for 107y, while HB David Brown led Spartans with 77y on 17 carries. Brown lost FUM into Michigan EZ for touchback in 3rd Q after hit by CB Dave Brown.

OHIO STATE 26 Illinois 7: Pattern in Ohio's 346y rush attack was developing with TB Archie Griffin doing bulk of work between 20YLs and FB Champ Henson bulling his way into EZ. Griffin rushed for 192y to help set up 3 rushing TDs by Henson, who now owned 9 TDs in 4 games, as Buckeyes (4-0) led throughout. Illini (0-5) highlights came in 2nd Q when LB Tom Hicks made 4th-and-1 stop of Henson on Illinois 18YL, which was followed 5 plays later with 60y option pass from Illini HB Lonnie Perrin to WR Joe Lewis for team's sole TD. Unfazed, Buckeyes took ensuing drive 79y, keyed by 41y romp by Griffin, to Henson's 3rd TD and 19-7 lead.

COLORADO 34 Iowa State 22: Buffaloes (5-1) never looked back after early 78y punt TD RET by WR Steve Haggerty and 5y TD run by TB Charlie Davis, who rushed for 135y and 2 TDs. Haggerty also caught 41y TD pass from QB Ken Johnson (15-24/197y), while K Fred Lima kicked conf record 57y FG. Baffled Cyclones (3-1) rushed for 3 TDs, including 2 by TB Mike Strachan, but fell victim to their own 5 TOs, 121y in PENs, and season-ending injury to DB Matt Blair.

Oklahoma 27 Texas 0 (Dallas): Sooners (4-0) posted 1st shutout against Texas in 101 games (1963 Cotton Bowl against LSU), exploiting inexperience of Horns attack. Unable to run, Steers passed 32 times—completing 11 with 4 INTs—for most ever tries by any team coached by Darrell Royal. Sooners D posted their own TDs by DTs Lucious Selmon and Derland Moore. Texas (3-1) was effective on D, holding Sooners' powerful rushing attack to 245y, 253y below avg. Somewhat later, in 1976, Royal accused OU of spying on his practices for this game, his suspicions centering on 3rd down QK by Texas QB Alan Lowry that was blocked by Moore and recovered by Selmon in EZ for key 3rd Q TD. Oklahoma asst coach Larry Lacewell later confirmed truth of espionage charge.

ARKANSAS 31 Baylor 20: With help from Baylor sideline, Hogs (4-1) opened 21-0 3rd Q lead as Bears coach Grant Teaff was tipping plays he was signaling to QB. Once Bears (2-2) realized their problematic revelations, they scored 20 of next 27 pts,

boosted by DE Roger Goree's 2 blocked punts. Razorbacks D permitted 139y rushing and 124y passing, with most of Baylor's damage done in 4th Q. Arkansas O needed little help in gaining 400y as TB Dickey Morton rushed for 157y and 2 TDs.

STANFORD 24 Washington 0: Stanford QB Mike Boryla threw for 293y and 2 TDs to snap shaky unbeaten string of Huskies (5-1). Cardinals (4-1) grabbed 21-0 H lead as Boryla, who completed 14-26/191y in 1st H, threw TD passes of 23y to WR Eric Cross and 30y to WR Don Alvarado. Cards S Steve Murray tossed 13y scoring pass to WR Miles Moore off fake FG play. TE John Brady, who caught 7/96y, led Huskies O. Washington's chances fizzled with QB Sonny Sixkiller's 1st H knee injury. Afterward, Sixkiller claimed Stanford defender was "going for my knee."

October 21, 1972

DUKE 20 Maryland 14: Completely dominating opening 30 mins, Duke (3-4) sent QB Mark Johnson (5-8/54y, TD, INT) dashing for 100y of Devils' 178y rushing in 1st H they won 20-0. Johnson's big play came in 2nd Q on 68y option run on which he broke 4 tackles. Maryland (3-3-1) D, which hadn't allowed single pt in previous 10 Qs, awoke in 2nd H, while soph QB Bob Avellini (21-31/314y, 2 TDs, 2 INTs) set new school game pass y mark in his 1st starting assignment. E Frank Russell (4/113y) caught 76y bomb from Avellini, while TB Louis Carter carried home 28y TD in 4th Q. Avellini threw well but was dismayed to have tossed INTs to Duke DBs Ronnie Hoots at 3YL and Ben Fordham at GL. Duke TB Steve Jones gained 92y and scored on 6y run.

CLEMSON 37 Virginia 21: Tigers (2-4) ran lopsided series record to 14-0 as QB Ken Pengitore opened scoring with 5y keeper and hooked up with WR Dennis Goss on 60y scoring pass. After 15 mins, Clemson had already topped pt total of any of its previous 5 games. Lead was upped to 24-0 at H as Clemson K Eddie Seigler kicked 1st of 3 FGs and FB Heide Davis scored on 1y run. Cavaliers (3-4) closed deficit to 24-14 in 3rd Q as QB George Allen, Jr.—son of Redskins coach—threw 14y TD to WR Dave Sullivan and scored on 1y keeper. Self-destructive Virginia had 6 TOs.

Alabama 17 TENNESSEE 10: No. 3 Crimson Tide (6-0) thwarted brilliant Tennessee D by scoring 2 TDs within 36 secs in game's final 2 mins. After Alabama scored on HB Wilbur Jackson's 2y plunge, coach Bear Bryant went for tying x-pt kick. Whatever controversy might have been laid in Bryant's lap was erased when Vols (4-2) quickly lost FUM by QB Condredge Holloway to Tide DT John Mitchell at own 22YL. Tide QB Terry Davis then faked both handoff and pitchout before scampering 22y to lock it up. Volunteers D, led by DT Carl Johnson and LB Art Reynolds, held Tide's vaunted rushing attack to 135y and set up both their scores with FUM RECs.

Florida 16 MISSISSIPPI 0: Florida coach Doug Dickey knew shutout of Rebels (3-3) was possible; his 1968 Tennessee squad was last to blank Ole Miss. With aggressive D led by DE Preston Kendrick (12 tackles, 6 sacks), Gators (3-2) allowed only 50y rushing and 78y passing, while Florida O ate up clock with 252y rushing. HB Nat Moore had most spectacular play with nifty 46y scoring run for clinching 4th Q TD that closed scoring. Ole Miss' poor play began at get-go as 2 FUMs by FB Paul Hofer were turned into 10 early pts. Unable to move ball, Rebs could not rally.

MINNESOTA 43 Iowa 14: Minnesota FB John King crowned Hawkeyes, rushing 29 times for 173y and 4 TDs, which tied school record for 6-pters. Gophers (2-4) pounded to 402y rushing in making 21 1st downs without completing single pass in 4 tries. Iowa (2-4) hung tough early, matching King's 1st 2 scores with 15y TD run by TB David Harris (21/92y) and QB Bobby Ousley's 15y TD pass to WR Brian Rollins. Both teams were efficient early on O, as Minnesota scored on 3 of 1st 4 possessions and Hawkeyes reached EZ twice on 1st 3 drives. Then it was all Minnesota as D shut down Harris (3/-1y) in 2nd H, while visitors contributed 5 TOs, including 4 INTs thrown by Ousley. S Steve Politano came up with 2 picks for Gophers.

Missouri 30 NOTRE DAME 26: Just week after losing 62-0 to Nebraska, Mizzou Tigers (3-3) shocked Notre Dame, scoring all 3 of their TDs on 4th down plays. Irish (4-1) rallied with 2 4th Q TDs, but were stopped on final drive by INT. Game proved surprisingly wide open in 1st H as neither team dominated. Missouri took 21-14 lead at H as TB Leroy Moss rushed in 16y TD and FB Don Johnson (26/87y) cashed in twice from short range. Notre Dame drove 66y and 81y for 1st H TDs, but soon found rain-slicked ball hard to hold. Missouri converted 2 TOs into 2 FGs in 2nd H for 30-14 lead. Soph QB Tom Clements (7-17/108y, 2 INTs) led Fighting Irish to 2 late TDs, including his 13y TD run. He rushed for team-high 94y. Tigers had 0 TOs in slop, Notre Dame 5.

COLORADO 20 Oklahoma 14: Sooners (4-1) looked nothing like juggernaut on O, cracking Colorado 40YL just twice. Buffs (6-1) enjoyed brilliant 43y TD run down sideline by TB Gary Campbell—for 1st TD surrendered by Sooners to-date this season—and nifty 6y TD catch by WB Jon Keyworth in taking 14-7 3rd Q lead. After K Fred Lima added 2 4th Q FGs for Buffs, Sooners marched to their final score on 10y scoring pass from QB Dave Robertson to HB Greg Pruitt. Colorado held Sooners to 238y, while forcing 4 TOs. Colorado DB Cullen Bryant made INT at OU 18YL of odd pass forced by HB-P Joe Wylie, who was desperate after bad punt snap.

TEXAS 35 Arkansas 15: Texas (4-1) broke from its slump with 28-pt 2nd H. QB Alan Lowry (22/156y rushing) had 2 scoring keepers within 92 secs, turning 9-7 deficit into 21-9 lead early in 4th Q. After Lowry capped 51y drive with 6y scoring run, 2 Arkansas backs failed to cover ensuing KO. Texas HB Tommy Landry pounced on loose ball on Hogs 26YL to set up Lowry's 1y TD run for 12-pt lead. FB Roosevelt Leaks joined Lowry as Texas rushing star with 154y and 2 TDs as run attack totaled 394y. Razorbacks (4-2) inadvertently helped by playing only 10 men on 2 Longhorn TDs. After game got out of hand, Porkers QB Joe Ferguson (14-38/143y, 2 INTs) capped 80y drive with 5y scoring pass to WR Mike Reppond.

Navy 21 AIR FORCE 17: Sub QB Allen Glenny entered game with Midshipmen (3-3) trailing 10-0 and spearheaded upset. Winning 80y TD drive was capped by RB Dan Howard's 5y run with 31 secs left to play. Falcons (5-1) had grabbed 17-14 lead with 6:36 left on 60y scoring pass from QB Rich Haynie to WR Bob Farr. Haynie passed for 72y, but was picked off 3 times, while Navy did its damage with 271y rushing.

OREGON 15 Stanford 13: Upset-minded Ducks (2-5) built 15-0 H lead on 85y TD scamper by TB Don Reynolds and 3 FGs by sub K Hugh Woodward. QB Dan Fouts threw for 158y while steering Ducks attack. Cardinals (4-2) crammed their 3 scores into 3rd Q, but also were halted in 3rd Q by 2 INTs. Stanford K Rod Garcia missed 4 FGs, including potential game-winner in 4th Q, but he hit school-record 54y boot. Cards QB Mike Boryla (23-55/290y) suffered through 4 INTs. Oregon frosh S Mario Clark had 2 INTs, including nail-in-coffin INT at Oregon 26YL with 35 secs left, and classmate LB Bobby Green had 2 of Ducks' 6 sacks.

October 28, 1972

Penn State 28 WEST VIRGINIA 19: Penn State's balance was too much for Mountaineers (5-3), who hadn't beaten Lions since 1955. Although QB Bernie Galiffa threw for 341y to lead West Virginia, Nittany Lions (6-1) featured QB John Hufnagel's 2 TDs passing and TB John Cappelletti's 154y rushing. West Virginia's only lead of game came on 1st play: 100y KO TD RET by TB Kerry Marbury. Penn State quickly turned 2 INTs into 10-7 lead and built to 25-7 margin. Galiffa pulled West Virginia to within 25-19 on 18y TD pass to WR Danny Buggs before Lions went on clock-eating drive to clinching 25y FG by K Alberto Vitiello.

SYRACUSE 10 Pittsburgh 6: D struggle was built on D play that steady Orangemen (4-4) converted for 10-0 lead in 4th Q. After teams finished 1st H deadlocked at 0-0, K Bernie Ruoff nailed 34y 3rd Q FG for 3-0 Syracuse lead. Game's big play was turned in by LB Chuck Boniti, who returned 4th Q INT 8y to Pitt 2YL. Syracuse FB Roger Praetorius then bulled in for 2y TD run for squad that managed meager 132y rushing and 15y passing. Panthers (1-7), who themselves rushed for only 20y, were hard-pressed to rally with little O threat, but scored on blocked punt recovered in EZ by CB Ed Marstellar with 36 secs left.

Maryland 24 VIRGINIA 23: There is something about home teams blowing 20-pt leads that just wreck homecomings. Yet there was UVA, ahead 23-3 in 3rd Q before collapse as Maryland (4-3-1) converted 3 of 5 INTs into TDs, including 2 by TB Louis Carter. Cavaliers (3-5) built big lead with help of 1 of 4 INTs they managed as DE Billy Williams returned 1st Q pick 36y to Maryland EZ. Other TD came on 4y TD pass from QB George Allen to WR Dave Sullivan. With leading rusher TB Kent Merritt knocked out of game in 1st H, Cavs threw more in 2nd H than preferable. Terp DBs Ken Schroy and Bob Smith each had 2 INTs. "This was the greatest team win I have ever been associated with," said Terps coach Jerry Claiborne. "It was a tremendous comeback."

NORTH CAROLINA STATE 42 South Carolina 24: Wolfpack (6-2-1) ground up Gamecocks—rushing for 330y—and withstood rally that assured 1st winning season since 1968. Frosh FB Stan Fritts rushed for 130y to lead NC State O, while D unit overcame tougher-than-expected Gamecocks to blank South Carolina when it counted in 4th Q. South Carolina (2-5) wiped out 14-3 deficit when DB Tom Zipperly returned KO 98y for TD and S Alex Dobson's INT was converted into short scoring run. After Wolfpack answered with QB Bruce Shaw's 1y TD keeper, Gamecocks scored on 30y pass by QB Dobby Grossman (20-39/228y, 2 INTs) to take 24-21 lead. From there it was all Pack, with 3 straight TDs including 2nd by Fritts on 2y run for his 13th score of year.

Louisville 38 CINCINNATI 13: Angry at departure of assistant coach Joe Perella last spring to staff at Cincinnati (2-5) and subsequent transfer of QB Mike Campbell to Bearcats, Louisville head man Lee Corso poured it on in retribution. Corso called timeouts at game's end, winning 31-13, to get ball back 1 last time before scoring final TD on 27y pass off screen to WR Steve Jewell that beat expected blitz. U of L (6-0) RB Howard Stevens set up final score with 30y punt RET. Despite 4th Q commotion, Stevens was focus of game, shrugging off 3 FUMs to rush school-record 38 times for 258y with 3 TDs. He set all-college career rushing record with 4,854y, breaking mark set by Panhandle A&M's Jerry Linton (4,839y) and all-time TD record with 66, 2 more than Dale Mills of Northeast Missouri. Highlight for Bearcats came in opening Q when RB Reggie Harrison (22/165y) raced 79y for short-lived 6-0 lead.

Ohio State 28 WISCONSIN 20: Up 28-7 in 1st H, Buckeyes (6-0) cruised into neutral and almost blew game. Badgers (3-4) QB Rudy Steiner (16-27/252y, INT) led comeback with 2 TDs throwing and another rushing. Wisconsin earned last chance from Ohio 33YL with 6 secs left, but CB Neal Colzie batted down pass at GL. Ohio State FB Champ Henson rushed for 122y and scored his 12th and 13th TDs of season, while QB Greg Hare (9-12/120y, TD) threw 37y TD to FB Rick Galbos to open scoring and rushed for 8y of his 118y rushing for 4th TD. Wisconsin TE Jack Novak caught both TD passes from Steiner.

Texas Tech 17 SOUTHERN METHODIST 3: Red Raiders (6-1) displayed awesome D, holding SMU running mates, HB Alvin Maxson and FB Wayne Morris, to combined 83y rushing, forcing 4 TOs, and sacking Mustangs QB Keith Bobo 7 times. Southern Methodist (4-2) had averaged 34 pts per game, but in face of stern D pressure reached Texas Tech 10YL only once: K Clint Hackney made 38y FG but Ponies never came close again. Red Raiders did little on O themselves, earning only 11 1st downs, but QB Joe Barnes rushed for 129y and pitched 42y scoring toss to WR Calvin Jones. NG Donald Rives led Texas Tech D with 20 tackles and added important save: his REC of fumbled punt by Red Raiders on own 10YL.

MISSOURI 20 Colorado 17: Tigers (4-3) K Greg Hill did it again with last-sec FG, this time scoring upset on late 33y FG. Hill had beaten Oregon earlier in season on last-sec 3-ptr. Moments earlier, Colorado D had FUM REC taken away by controversial face mask PEN. Missouri TB Tommy Reamon, who rushed for 87y and TD, was key to winning drive as he gained 22y and earned 2 1st downs. Buffaloes (6-2) had rallied from 10-0 and 17-10 deficits, but never led despite gaining 319y. Injured Colorado TB Charlie Davis returned to lineup in 2nd H with his team trailing 10-0 and scored on 3y run, but was not enough of factor to prevent loss.

Air Force 39 ARIZONA STATE 31: QB Rich Haynie threw for 332y and 4 TDs and WR Frank Murphy (7/198y) caught 3 scores, as Falcons (6-1) handed Arizona State its 1st home loss in 3 years. Key Air Force play turned on 4th down by P Jerry Olin on fake that set up go-ahead TD: 26y catch by Murphy for 28-23 lead in 3rd Q. QB Danny White threw 3 TDs for Sun Devils (5-2), but was picked off 4 times. White averaged 55y on 5 punts. Arizona State WB Steve Holden (7/170y) went catch-for-catch with Murphy, grabbing all 3 of White's scoring passes. Air Force racked up 481y to 344y advantage, and key stats were dominant time of possession in 2nd H and overall TOs. Air Force had ball 22:22 to ASU's 7:38 in game's final 30 mins, and Falcons lost single TO to 6 handed away by Arizona State.

AP Poll October 30
1 Southern California (41)	980	11 Auburn	238
2 Alabama (3)	811	12 Notre Dame	196
3 Nebraska (4)	750	13 Tennessee	122
4 Michigan (1)	694	14 Iowa State	112
5 Ohio State (1)	629	15 Colorado	92
6 Louisiana State	558	16 Missouri	26
7 Oklahoma	471	17 Louisville	20
8 UCLA	379	18 Texas Tech	19
9 Texas	301	19 Air Force	17
10 Penn State	290	20 Arkansas	10

November 4, 1972

ARMY 17 Air Force 14: West Point heroes abounded as Cadets (4-3) picked off 6 Air Force aerials, and HB Bob Hines, who scored game-winner on 49y run in 4th Q, rushed for 202y. When not throwing INTs, QB Rich Haynie passed for 179y and pitched go-ahead 12y TD to WR Bob Farr as Falcons (6-2) took 14-10 lead in 3rd Q. His repeated ATTs on long patterns, however, were largely unsuccessful, while Falcons run game managed just 119y. WR Greg Smith was Haynie's favorite target, catching 6 passes for 109y with 42y TD grab in 2nd Q. Cadets QB Kingsley Fink played 2nd fiddle to Hines, but he did complete 15-28 for 164y and 0 INTs and scored opening TD on 1y keeper.

Houston 31 FLORIDA STATE 27: Houston (3-4-1) ground game outlasted Seminoles passing in hostile environment. Trailing 31-14 in 4th Q, Florida State (6-3) QB Gary Huff (17-51/409y) had crowd's hostility directed at him because he gave away 2 INTs and FUM. But, Huff shrugged off critics to lead rally that came up 6 pts short. QB D.C. Nobles paced Cougars' rushing attack that churned up 345y. Houston's big run went 80y on scoring romp by WR Marshall Johnson. Teams traded TDs most of 2nd H with Houston FB Puddin' Jones scoring game winner from 1y out.

Tennessee 14 GEORGIA 0: Redoubtable Volunteers (6-2) QB Condredge Holloway flipped pair of 2nd Q scoring passes to FB Bill Rudder and TE Sonny Leach for all pts team would need. Georgia (5-3) was held well in check by Tennessee's swift D and could mount only 2 threats: K Kim Braswell missed 44y FG on last play of 1st H, and Bulldogs ventured to 18YL early in 4th Q only to have Tennessee CB Conrad Graham make INT in EZ. Vols TB Haskel Stanback had pounded for 43y of 11-play, 74y TD drive in 2nd Q before Holloway hit Rudder from 7y out. TB Paul Careathers tight-roped sideline for 56y gain that led to Holloway's 13y TD pass to Leach.

LOUISIANA STATE 17 Mississippi 16: LSU QB Bert Jones led winning 80y TD drive that began with 3 mins remaining and ended as clock struck 0:00. Jones' winning throw—10y pass to TB Brad Davis in left corner just over GL—began at 0:01 as Bayou Bengals (7-0) needed entire clock and x-pt by K Rusty Jackson to stretch winning streak to 11 games. Rebels (4-4) used 3 FGs by K Steve Lavinghouze and 1y scoring keeper by QB Norris Weese to forge 16-10 lead, but later strong-legged Lavinghouze barely missed 27y FG that could have put Ole Miss out of reach.

Michigan 21 INDIANA 7: In game of red zone TO conversion—avg for all 4 scoring drives was only 20y—Michigan clicked more often. Wolverines (8-0) scored 1st after DT Fred Grambau recovered 2nd Q FUM on Indiana 13YL to set up 9y TD run by QB Dennis Franklin. Hoosiers (4-4), who committed 7 TOs, tied game 7-7 early in 4th Q as

FB Dennis Cremeens converted FUM by Franklin at his 14YL into 11y scoring romp. Michigan CB Dave Brown soon recovered FUM at Indiana 23YL to set up winning 12y TD run by Franklin (2-14/27y), who rushed for 92y, 2 TDs. Finally, Hoosiers botched punt that Michigan turned into 10y insurance TD run by TB Chuck Heater, who was part of phalanx of Wolverine backs rushing for 253y.

MICHIGAN STATE 22 Purdue 12: Even though Purdue (4-4) arrived in East Lansing with piece of Big 10 lead, coach Bob DeMoss had tough week. While battling pneumonia, DeMoss realized he'd face fired-up Spartans squad because longtime Michigan State coach Duffy Daugherty announced on Friday that 1972 would be his final year. Boilermakers simply could not check Michigan State (3-4-1) QB Mark Niesen as Daugherty's Wishbone operative burst loose for TD runs of 57y and 61y. MSU D was heroic too, sacking Purdue QB Gary Danielson 8 times, picking him off twice, and holding HB Otis Armstrong, Big 10's leading rusher, to 74y. Both Spartan INTs were manufactured by quick hands of CB Bill Simpson, who nabbed pass deflections. Purdue, who trailed entire game, managed TD runs of 4y by HB Darryl Stingley and 1y by FB Skip Peterson.

TEXAS 17 Southern Methodist 9: Mustangs (4-3) knew who they had to stop, but were unable to do so as big Texas FB Roosevelt Leaks banged out 175y to spur Longhorns. Leaks gained 115y in 1st H as Texas (6-1) grabbed 14-3 lead. Texas TDs were provided by HB Don Burrisk on 15y run and QB Alan Lowry on 1y effort. SMU went 51y early in 3rd Q to cut deficit to 14-9 on 3y TD run by FB Wayne Morris. After 33y FG by Steers K Billy Schott, SMU moved to UT 34YL before Longhorns LB Glen Gaspard pounced on FUM to end Ponies threat.

TEXAS A&M 10 Arkansas 7: Lowly Aggies (2-6) wrecked Arkansas' Cotton Bowl hopes for 2nd straight year, picking off 6 passes by QB Joe Ferguson. DT Boice Best and his Texas A&M linemates supplied pass-rush heat, while CB Ralph Murski and S Larry Ellis each had 2 INTs. Ellis set up lone Aggies TD, 2y run by FB Brad Dusek, with 26y INT RET to Arkansas 26YL. Hogs (5-3) answered with 11-play, 76y drive that ended on FB Marsh White's 2y TD run. Razorbacks would come no closer to scoring again as Texas A&M captured its 1st series win at home since Bear Bryant's 1956 SWC champions turned trick against Razorbacks.

Nebraska 33 COLORADO 10: Dazzling Nebraska (7-1) WB Johnny Rodgers darted and dodged his way to 266y all-purpose and tallied 2 TDs. Huskers notched TDs on their 1st 3 possessions for 19-0 1st Q lead and took crowd right out of game. After Buffs (6-3) scored 10 pts in 2nd Q to re-energize fans, Rodgers reached EZ with 1y run and 11y reception from QB David Humm (11-16/130y, INT). Colorado scored TD on drive prolonged by lucky break on Bison punt: ball was partially blocked by Huskers and recovered for handy 19y gain by Colorado G Chuck Mandril. Buffaloes FB Bo Mathews (16/67y) scored on 18y run 9 plays later. Facing intense pressure, Buffs QB Ken Johnson managed only 85y on 11-29 passing. "Their defense is far and away the best we have ever played against," said Johnson. "There's no comparison."

Oklahoma 20 IOWA STATE 6: Using power ground game, Oklahoma (6-1) pounded increasingly-impressive Cyclones (5-2), but had only 13-6 lead to show for its effort with 4 mins left. FB Leon Crosswhite gained 113y, while HB Greg Pruitt chipped in with 102y as Sooners rolled up 300y rushing. After Crosswhite put Oklahoma up 7-0 on 7y TD run, Ks Rick Fulcher of OU and Tom Goedjen of Iowa State each booted 2 FGs. Sooners then marched 87y—with QB Dave Robertson contributing brilliant 54y scramble—for clinching 2y TD run by Pruitt late in 4th Q. With Sooners D holding TB Mike Strachan, Big 8's leading rusher, to 50y, Cyclones capably went to air attack for 200y passing by QB George Amundson.

UTAH 28 Arizona 27: Ute fans could not be blamed for leaving early as Arizona (3-5) smartly built 27-10 lead through 3 Qs. Arizona built its edge on HB Bobby McCall's 183y rushing, big chunk of team's 357y, and FB Marty Shuford's 2 TD runs. Redskins (5-3) exploded in final Q, scoring 2 quick TDs on 52y and 36y passes to WR Steve Odom from QB Don Van Galder, who was able to shake off 4 INTs. Utah was spared when Cats K Charlie Gorham missed FG that could have put margin out of reach, then caught bigger break when Redskins DB Steve Marshall came up with INT he returned 68y for TD that pulled them to within 27-21. Utah marched 66y to game-winner as Van Galder completed 4 straight passes to set up 5y QB keeper with 10 secs left.

UCLA 28 Stanford 23: No. 8 Bruins (8-1) used QB Mark Harmon's late TD run to recapture lead and employed fierce pressure from front-7 to keep it. Stanford (5-3) had scored 2 TDs in 4th Q to take 23-21 lead, but allowed UCLA to drive 75y to Harmon's winning 11y TD run. Stanford K Mike Boryla (26-50/316y) then whipped his team to Bruins 29YL before sack by UCLA DT Tom Waddell brought FUM REC by LB Steve Hookano. Bruins rushed for 313y, while Harmon threw 2 TDs and ran for 2 others. Game's oddest play was 87y KO TD RET by Stanford HB Reggie Sanderson, during which last Bruin, K Efren Herrera, with chance to tackle Sanderson was busy arguing with Cardinals LB John Snider as Sanderson roared by. Stanford TE Bill Scott caught 7/143y.

AP Poll November 6
1 Southern California (40)	978	11 Auburn	225
2 Alabama (3)	821	12 Notre Dame	221
3 Nebraska (5)	797	13 Tennessee	165
4 Michigan (1)	708	14 Missouri	65
5 Ohio State (1)	600	15 Texas Tech	50
6 Louisiana State	524	16 Colorado	48
7 Oklahoma	485	17 Iowa State	45
8 UCLA	381	18 North Carolina	15
9 Texas	308	19 Arizona State	5
10 Penn State	304	20t Stanford	3
		20t Yale	3

November 11, 1972

PENN STATE 37 North Carolina State 22: Nittany Lions (8-1) roared out to 8th straight win, scoring 23 pts on 315y in 1st H while blanking North Carolina State on 53y. PSU QB John Hufnagel (10-19/210y) ran for 2 TDs and threw another, while TB John Cappelletti finished with 129y rushing. Hufnagel and Cappelletti hooked up on 33y TD pass for game's opening score. Wolfpack (6-3-1) rallied in 4th Q for 3 TDs as QB Bruce Shaw threw for 2 scores, including 98y pass to WR Pat Kenney.

ALABAMA 35 Louisiana State 21: Alabama QB Terry Davis, native of Louisiana, tossed 2 TDs and ran for another as Crimson Tide (9-0) won SEC showdown. After Tigers (7-1) scored 1st, on 21y QB Bert Jones (18-32/242y, 2 TDs, 2 INTs) to WR Jimmy LeDoux pass, Davis tied game with 25y scoring bullet to WR Wayne Wheeler after Tide CB Bobby McKinney took punt 57y into LSU end. Game remained tied until Bama's opening possession of 2nd H, which ended with another Davis-to-Wheeler TD pass, this time for 29y. Tide then rolled behind powerful rushing attack, gaining 335y with 52y coming on HB Joe LaBue's scoring run. Davis was leading rusher with 92y and threw for 10-18/157y.

Georgia 10 Florida 7 (Jacksonville): Bulldogs (6-3) needed 10 4th Q pts to pull out win, with winning 37y FG by K Kim Braswell with less than min remaining. Gators held 7-0 lead from early in 2nd Q when HB Nat Moore was on receiving end of 47y TD pass by QB David Bowden. Georgia used own big play to tie game as QB Andy Johnson threw 44y TD to WR Rex Putnal. Late TO opened door for Georgia as Florida (3-4) lost FUM—1 of 4 TOs for Gators—on handoff on own 31YL. UGa NG Joe McPipkin made REC. After 3 runs came up short, Braswell booted winning FG.

MICHIGAN STATE 19 Ohio State 12: Spartans (4-4-1) continued to draw inspiration from retiring coach Duffy Daugherty and shocked Ohio State (7-1) behind D that thoroughly blunted 2nd H efforts of Buckeyes' 31-pt-per-game scorers. MSU used old Ohio formula: rushing ball (74/334y), forcing TOs (5), and hitting timely FGs (4 by 6'4, 165-lb Dutch native K Dirk Krijt in debut). S Bill Simpson, who owned 1 of Spartans' 2 INTs, continued big-play season with FUM REC at Buckeyes 6YL that set up QB Mark Niesen's winning 6y TD run. Bucks' only TD came on 20y scoring pass from QB Greg Hare to TE Ted Powell. Spartans held frosh sensation TB Archie Griffin to 42y rushing, which was topped by 4 Michigan State players led by HB Mike Holt's 93y. After game, fed-up Ohio coach Woody Hayes shoved camera into face of Los Angeles Times photographer Art Rogers.

IOWA STATE 23 Nebraska 23: Expectant Iowa State lost chance to beat Huskers (7-1-1) for 1st time since 1960 when K Tom Goedjen painfully missed last-sec x-pt. QB George Amundson was star for Iowa State (5-2-1), throwing for 235y and 3 TDs. Amundson fashioned brilliant 70y drive in 35 secs to tie game on 24y TD pass to WR Willie Jones. Cyclones TE Keith Krepfle caught 2 TDs, while DE Merv Krakau was magnificent with 11 tackles, 3 pass knockdowns, 2 forced FUMs, 2 FUM RECs, and 3 sacks. Nebraska's performance was marred by 8 TOs and was far cry from normal championship caliber, although QB David Humm threw for 246y with TDs to WB Johnny Rodgers (9/113y) of 35y and 4y.

Texas 17 BAYLOR 3: With score tied at 3-3 entering 4th Q, Texas T Jerry Sisemore returned to lineup despite badly sprained ankle, and his presence lifted teammates. Behind Sisemore's blocking, Longhorns (7-1) drove 70y and 85y on ground to 2 TDs to put away pesky Baylor Bears. FB Roosevelt Leaks (35/162y), who gained 92y on decisive TD drives, capped each with short TD run. Baylor (4-4) D, under 1st year coach Grant Teaff, held Longhorns to only 4 1st downs through opening 3 Qs as DE Roger Goree sparkled, while TB Gary Lacy gained 60y rushing to lead O.

Texas Christian 31 TEXAS TECH 7: Horned Frogs (5-3) were on fire behind QB Terry Drennan, scoring on 1st 4 possessions and adding safety in forging 18-0 lead early in 2nd Q. After Drennan opened scoring with 6y pass to WR Steve Patterson, Purple D sacked Texas Tech (7-2) QB Joe Barnes in EZ for 2 pts. After free-kick, Horned Frogs sent FG unit onto field on 4th down at Tech 25YL, but QB Perry Senn, former starter and team's holder, sprinted right on fake before throwing screen to HB Mike Luttrell, who broke 2 tackles en route to TD. Luttrell (17/94y), who added 20y TD run in 4th Q, and HB Bill Sadler (19/100y) led TCU ground effort that gained 358y. Barnes threw for 144y for Red Raiders.

ARIZONA 21 Brigham Young 7: Win by Wildcats (4-5) boosted them closer to break-even mark and kept tied for WAC lead with 4-1 mark. All scoring occurred in 1st H, and Arizona grabbed 14-7 lead as QB Bill Demory's TD passes of 20y to WR Theopolis Bell and 41y to WR Barry Dean sandwiched 1y TD run by Cougars TB Pete Van Valkenburg (30/155y). Then it was BYU's turn and QB Bill August, who earlier had led 92y scoring drive, pushed Cougars (5-4) downfield until Arizona S Bob White picked off pass at own 22YL and set new school RET record with 78y TD sprint. Wildcats were then content handing off to TB Bobby McCall (34/151y).

WASHINGTON 30 Ucla 21: QB Sonny Sixkiller returned from 3-week absence to lead Huskies (8-2) with 212y passing, which set table for 4 TD runs by FB Pete Taggares (22/75y). Bruins (8-2) negated 348y in Wishbone rushing by turning ball over 5 times. Still, UCLA looked capable of maintaining its no. 8 ranking in early going when it forged 76y and 80y drives for 14-7 lead in 1st Q. Washington reeled off 17 straight pts for 24-14 H lead with both Huskies TDs following UCLA FUMs, Huskies D held off any 2nd H comeback by permitting Bruins only 118y rushing in final 30 mins. Washington also halted 2 4th Q drives with INTs by CB Roberto Jourdan. Leading UCLA rusher was FB Randy Tyler (13/108y) as Huskies' D alignment forced Bruins into frequent inside runs.

November 18, 1972

WEST VIRGINIA 43 Syracuse 12: Orangemen preferred low-scoring tilts during 1972, but West Virginia (8-3) subdued its Eastern rival by unleashing big plays for scores. Mountaineers QB Bernie Galiffa threw TD passes of 77y to WR Danny Buggs and 61y to TE Nate Stephens in 1st H. Buggs scored 2 TDs on reverses in 2nd H, including 80y gallop. Buggs' bursts helped West Virginia break open 14-12 game with 4 TDs in 2nd H. In losing, Syracuse (5-6), relegated to its 1st losing season in 23 years, scored on runs of 11y by QB Rob Sutton and 7y by FB Marty Januszkiewicz. West Virginia racked up 559y total O, including 292y rushing.

NORTH CAROLINA 14 Duke 0: North Carolina (8-1) finally broke up 0-0 wrestling match as QB Nick Vidnovic connected with TE Ken Taylor on 4th Q TD passes of 17y and 16y. Both TDs were set up by INTs—UNC had 6 in all—as Tar Heels won 15th straight in conf play. TB Steve Jones paced Blue Devils (4-6) attack with 102y of team's 146y total. LBs Mike Mansfield, Jimmy DeRatt and Mark DiCarlo led Tar Heels D, which enjoyed late-season brilliance with 1 TD allowed in past 4 games.

MICHIGAN 9 Purdue 6: Making amends for earlier missed x-pt, K Mike Lantry extended win streak of Michigan (10-0) with 30y FG with 1:04 on clock. Tie-breaking drive began after S Randy Logan picked off Purdue QB Gary Danielson (9-18/141y) near midfield. Purdue embraced 3-0 lead until opening drive of 2nd H when Michigan capped 80y voyage with QB Dennis Franklin's 11y scoring pass to TE Paul Seal. Lantry missed x-pt, which allowed Boilermakers (5-5) to knot things up at 6-6 on K Frank Conner's 2nd FG. Purdue, now eliminated from Rose Bowl contention, fought hard and held Michigan's running machine to only 100y.

NOTRE DAME 20 Miami 17: Poor 4th Q by Fighting Irish (8-1) almost allowed Miami to steal win. Notre Dame took 20-3 lead after TD runs by FB Andy Huff and QB Tom Clements (8-16/131y) and 10y scoring grab by WR Willie Townsend. Miami (4-5) QB Ed Carney (19-42/202y, 4 INTs) came alive in 4th Q, completing 6-8/76y on 78y drive for 1st TD—his 14y scoring pass to WR Walt Sweeting—before leading 68y drive to his TD keeper. Time dwindled, but Clements lost FUM to Miami DE Mike Barnes on ND 35YL. Irish D stiffened before trying 46y FG attempt by K Mike Burke flew wide to right. Teams combined for 9 TOs, including 3 lost FUMs and INT for Irish. Carney led all rushers with 50y on 15 carries.

Kent State 27 TOLEDO 9: Coach Don James led Kent State (6-4-1) to 1st-ever MAC title, in 22nd year of play, with complete reversal from last season's last place finish. Flashes did damage in 2nd H, expanding 6-3 lead to 20 -3 in 3rd Q on TDs of 95y on KO RET by WR Eddie Woodard and 1st of 2 scoring runs by RB Larry Poole. Rockets (6-5) marched 96y in final period for sole 6-pter, scored on 19y pass from QB Gene Swick to FB Bob Vickers. Poole rushed for 144y to lead Kent O, which gained 462y, while 5'7 K Herbie Page finished 2 1st H drives with FGs. With win, Flashes went to sole bowl game in school history, losing Tangerine Bowl 21-18 to Tampa.

MISSOURI 6 Iowa State 5: After teams exchanged FGs during 3-3 1st H, Iowa State (5-3-1) forged unusual 5-3 lead as LB Brad Storm blocked punt through EZ. Then, for 3rd time this season, K Greg Hill booted late FG for Missouri (6-4) victory, this from 22y out with 87 secs left to play. Slim win earned Fiesta Bowl berth for Tigers. Key play on winning drive, which began after DB Gary Anderson's clutch INT at his 23YL, was SB Chuck Link's diving 18y catch of pass from QB John Cherry that moved Tigers to ISU 27YL. FB Don Johnson then ran 4 times for 21y to set up Hill's FG.

Southern California 24 UCLA 7: Trojans (10-0) jumped to quick 10-0 lead and coasted home from there to clinch Pac 8 title and return to Rose Bowl after 2-year absence. Top-ranked Southern California sent TB Anthony Davis winging for 178y rushing and TD, while versatile QB-K Mike Rae (7-12/95y) ran for TD and kicked FG and 3 x-pts. Trojans D destroyed every dodge and dart executed by nimble Bruins QB Mark Harmon, who had miserable day rushing for only 3y and completing 3-9/38y passing. Young LB Richard Wood again led USC D with INT and 18 tackles, none more spectacular than his chase-down of speedy HB James McAlister from behind to spoil opportunity for UCLA (8-3). With outside lanes sealed, Bruins rushed more up middle than to their liking in finishing with 198y rushing, 170y less than 2nd-in-country average. FB Randy Tyler led way with 81y on 17 carries. "They were fantastic," said losing coach Pepper Rodgers. "I've never seen anyone better."

CALIFORNIA 24 Stanford 21: Despite sloppy field, 75th "Big Game" was classic, ending in riotous final-play 7y TD pass from Cal frosh QB Vince Ferragamo (8-23/98y) to WR Steve Sweeney on 4th down. Cal Bears (3-8) drove from own 38YL with 1:13 left as Ferragamo, who shrugged off 3 INTs swiped by Stanford S Steve Murray, hit key passes of 18y to WR Dave Bateman and 20y to Sweeney. Cardinals (5-5) had grabbed 18-14 lead on 3y scoring run by HB Reggie Sanderson in 4th Q, with key play on drive QB Mike Boryla's 25y completion to WR Eric Cross. California won yardage battle 213y to 169y, while teams combined for 7 TOs in swampy conditions. Stanford's 2nd TD came on miscue: 71y INT RET by LB Gordon Reigel. Winning TD was 13th 6-pter for Sweeney for season.

Oregon 30 OREGON STATE 3: Ducks (4-7) ended 8-game series losing streak with vengeance, crushing hometown Oregon State with explosive O and stingy D. Webfoots stormed out of gate, jumping out to 7-0 lead with 1st possession, 60y TD run by former Corvallis High School star TB Donnie Reynolds (9/79y). They then dropped 17 pts on Beavers (2-9) in 2nd Q, scoring TDs on 65y bomb from QB Dan Fouts (7-20/133, INT) to WR Greg Lindsey and DE Tim Guy's recovery of his blocked punt in OSU EZ. Ducks D held Oregon State to 179y in rain, allowing sole pts on 28y FG by K Ken McGrew. With Oregon K Hugh Woodward booting 3 FGs and Oregon State O losing 3 of 11 FUMS, rally was impossible. Losing Oregon State coach Dee Andros, who guaranteed win, is now 7-1 in "Civil War" series.

AP Poll November 20

1 Southern California (44)	988	11 Notre Dame	266
2 Alabama (5)	874	12 Tennessee	189
3 Michigan (1)	744	13 Colorado	128
4 Oklahoma	689	14 UCLA	73
5 Nebraska	608	15 North Carolina	72
6 Penn State	454	16 Missouri	62
7 Texas	414	17 Iowa State	36
8 Louisiana State	388	18 Arizona State	30
9 Ohio State	350	19 Washington State	16
10 Auburn	307	20 Texas Tech	15

November 23-25, 1972

(Th'g) Oklahoma 17 NEBRASKA 14: Sooners (9-1) roared back from 14-0 deficit by using passing attack, of all things. Game was supposed to feature duel between Heisman Trophy candidates Nebraska WB Johnny Rodgers, who was ineffective, and Sooners HB Greg Pruitt, who was hurt. So, Oklahoma QB Dave Robertson took center stage, throwing for 186y, mostly to frosh WR Tinker Owens (5/108y), as OU scored 17 straight pts. Pruitt's roommate, CB Ken Pope, placed Rodgers in his crosshairs, leading remarkable effort that held him to 53y total. In losing in Big 8 for 1st time in 36 contests, Nebraska (8-2-1) handed its lead away in storm of 6 TOs. Cornhuskers had built lead with Oklahoma miscues, converting 2 fumbled punts by OU into TDs, but then breaks went other way. Sooners fueled their anger over Huskers having received Orange Bowl bid before game into inspired play.

Dartmouth 31 PENNSYLVANIA 17: Big Green (7-1-1) won their 4th straight Ivy title (2 shared) on strength of 2 quick TDs in 4th Q. Go-ahead score at 24-17 came on 1y plunge by FB Steve Webster and was set up by QB Steve Stetson's clutch passing. HB Rick Klupchak, leading rusher with 143y, added 50y TD run after FUM to close scoring. Quakers (6-3) had grabbed 14-0 lead in game's initial 20 mins as QB Marc Mandel scored on 8y keeper and RB Johnny Sheffield added 2y TD run. Dartmouth rallied as Stetson ran and passed for TDs, and foes matched 2 H FGs for 17-17 deadlock midway through 4th Q. Stetson soon delivered clutch throw on 3rd-and-10 from his 30YL: 45y completion to WR Jack Thomas.

FLORIDA 3 Louisiana State 3: Very few games with 6 total pts—dictated in this instance by driving rainstorm—would produce wild finish, yet this supposed mismatch was exciting. Early on, Bengals DB Mike Williams somehow ran down speedy Florida (4-4-1) HB Nat Moore at 1YL and, when winded Moore was removed, sub Andy Summers lost FUM to Williams on next play. Gators (4-4-1) used field position advantage to soon tie game at 3-3 on 35y FG by K John Williams. Highly-favored LSU Tigers (8-1-1) marched to Florida 27YL in 4th Q and into position for potential winning FG by K Juan Roca, who already had missed 7 FG tries. Gators LB Fred Abbott blocked Roca's 44y effort, but ball bounced crazily downfield for 1st down REC by LSU at Florida 20YL. After short gain, LSU coach Charlie McClendon went to his kicking "bullpen" for K Rusty Jackson, who was summoned to try winning FG from 32y out. Jackson misfired, LSU's 9th missed 3-ptr of game.

GAME OF THE YEAR
OHIO STATE 14 Michigan 11:

Two mighty GLSs—featuring 6 unsuccessful Wolverines plays launched from Buckeyes 1YL—propelled Ohio State (9-1) past Michigan into Rose Bowl. Michigan (10-1), who reached Buckeye territory on 9 of its 10 drives, frustratingly won stat battle 344y to 192y, but could not seize necessary turf—in some cases necessary inches—to pull ahead. Michigan's final drive reached Ohio 41YL before stalling on downs, with DT George Hasenohrl authoring sack of QB Dennis Franklin (13-23/160y). TB Archie Griffin (17/75y) helped Buckeyes to 14-3 lead as he set up 1st score with 18y run and then scored himself from 30y out behind opening block by T John Hicks in 3rd Q. Those 2 TDs wrapped up Bucks' brilliant 4-down GLS from their 1YL at end of 1st H. Michigan then cut deficit to 14-11 on FB Ed Shuttlesworth's 1y run and subsequent 2-pt conv pass to WB Clint Haslerig. S Randy Logan soon picked off pass to give Wolverines ball on Ohio 29YL. Wolverines marched quickly to GL, but were thwarted on line cracks from 1YL with coach Bo Schembechler deciding to pass up tying FG attempt. Interestingly, had game ended in tie, it would have meant Pasadena roses for Michigan. Instead, 4 Buckeyes tacklers stood up Franklin for no gain on 4th down.

IOWA 15 Illinois 14: Hawkeyes (3-7-1) won evenly matched struggle by 3 conv pts to 2 as QB Butch Caldwell ran in 2-pt conv with 4:10 left for win. Iowa FB Frank Holmes had just scored 1y TD run to cap 67y drive. Iowa's 1st TD came on TB Royce Mix's 92y romp at end of 1st H. Illinois (3-8) pulled themselves to attention to gain 149y of their 296y total O on consecutive drives in 2nd H. Illini capped those trips with short rushing TDs by FB Steve Greene and HB Lonnie Perrin.

Arkansas 24 TEXAS TECH 14: It was last college game for NFL-bound Arkansas (6-5) QB Joe Ferguson, but back-up QB Scott Bull received starting nod. With game tied at 7-7 entering 4th Q, Bull moved Razorbacks 81y to go-ahead TD on 1y run by FB Marsh White. Red Raiders (8-3) soon lost FUM, and Bull capitalized with quick 26y drive to

his 1y scoring run for 21-7 lead. Texas Tech cut deficit on 2y keeper by backup QB Jimmy Carmichael, but came no closer. TB Dickey Morton rushed for 135y to lead Hogs, while TB George Smith led Red Raiders with 101y on ground.

Kansas 28 MISSOURI 17: Emergence of Kansas pass attack, coupled with 7 Jayhawks take-aways, ruined Tigers (6-5), who nonetheless edged ahead 17-16 early in 3rd Q. Kansas (4-7) QB David Jaynes (16-36/259y, 2 TDs, INT) was just warming up, leading 2 more scoring drives to pull off upset. Jaynes capped winning drive for Jayhawkers with 20y scoring pass to WR Bruce Adams before adding 1y TD run later in 3rd Q. Mizzou struggled with mud and Kansas D, except when throwing to WR Jack Bastable who caught 2 TD passes—67y bomb from QB John Cherry and 15y toss from HB Chuck Link. Kansas DE Pat Ryan (13 tackles) led Jayhawks D. Field at Memorial Stadium was renamed for former Missouri coach Don Faurot.

Arizona State 38 ARIZONA 21: Sun Devils (9-2) simply would not be denied unprecedented 4th straight conf title nor in-state series' 8th straight win. HB Woody Green rushed for 172y and FB Brent McClanahan gained 153y, 2 TDs as Arizona State totaled 555y. Wildcats (4-7) hung tough, trailing 31-21 after QB Bill Demory (17-31/238y, 3 TDs, INT) threw his last TD, 1y pass to WR Theopolis Bell (6/102y), that was set up by 38y punt RET by nimble CB Jackie Wallace. Sun Devils ended Arizona's upset bid with 82y drive that killed clock before reaching EZ on 8y pass by QB Danny White (8-12/192y, 2 TDs, INT) to WR Ed Beverly.

AP Poll November 27

1 Southern California (46)	990	11 Louisiana State	249
2 Alabama (4)	890	12 Tennessee	215
3 Oklahoma	790	13 Colorado	151
4 Ohio State	597	14 North Carolina	81
5 Penn State	563	15 UCLA	70
6 Texas	494	16 Arizona State	50
7 Michigan	487	17 Louisville	22
8 Nebraska	419	18 West Virginia	13
9 Auburn	323	19 Washington State	11
10 Notre Dame	306	20 Oklahoma State	10

December 2, 1972

Army 23 Navy 15 (Philadelphia): Army (6-4) swept its service academy rivals to win 1st-ever Commander-in-Chief Trophy as HB Bob Hines rushed for 172y, including 43y TD run for Army's opening pts. Play of day came on blocked FG by Army LB Tim Pfister that CB Scott Beaty returned 83y for TD that put Cadets up at 13-12. Navy (4-7) then marched deep into Army territory before failing on 4th down from Black Knights 5YL. In 4th Q, Army HB Bruce Simpson added 21y TD run that provided to be winning pts. TB Cleveland Cooper tallied 135y in becoming 1st running back to crack 1,000y season total (1,046y) for Navy.

Auburn 17 ALABAMA 16: Alabama (10-1) fell from unbeaten ranks in bizarre fashion as, amazingly, CB David Langner (2 INTs) scored both TDs for Tigers (9-1) on RECs of punts blocked by LB Bill Newton. Crimson Tide built 16-0 lead behind solid ground game that reached 235y total, but Auburn CB Roger Mitchell's block of K Bill Davis x-pt attempt in 2nd Q, proved to be difference by game's end. Auburn was inspired by Tide coach Bear Bryant's infamous reference to his rival as "cow college." K Gardner Jett began 4th Q comeback with 42y FG for cardiac Tigers, who went on to win 6th year as underdogs in 1972. Both punt blocks by Tigers occurred in 4th Q, inside game's last 5:30, and result was so shocking that 33rpm recording of game's play-by-play eventually sold more than 20,000 copies to rabid Auburn fans. Newton, dreamer who originally walked on at Auburn at 175 lbs, lived up to his fantasy by taking part in 22 tackles, while Langner's 45y on RETs practically amounted to Tigers' whole O. Auburn passed for only 30y and rushed for 50y against Alabama's mighty D.

Georgia 27 GEORGIA TECH 7: Bulldogs won battle of sub signal-callers as Georgia (7-4) QB James Ray led 17-pt surge at end of 1st H for commanding 20-0 lead. Ray connected with WR Rex Putnal on 37y TD pass that helped bury Yellow Jackets (6-4-1). With QB Eddie McAshan suspended, Georgia Tech sub QB Jim Stevens was thrust into starting role. Stevens threw for 202y, but 2 drives into Georgia territory ended on downs and another was halted by CB Buzy Rosenberg's INT.

OKLAHOMA 38 Oklahoma State 15: Sooners (10-1) buried in-state rivals to claim Big 8 title. QB Dave Robertson threw 2 1st Q TDs, including 68y bomb to TE Al Chandler, and frosh HB Joe Washington rushed for 1st of his 2 TDs as Oklahoma built commanding 24-0 H lead. OU notched 519y O, but upped its staggering season FUM total to 51, losing 2 on this day. Cowboys (6-5) had 206y rushing, with most damage inflicted after verdict was sealed. OSU QB Brent Blackman hustled for 3y and 24y TD runs.

SOUTHERN CALIFORNIA 45 Notre Dame 23: TB Anthony Davis built his reputation as Irish poison by playing 1-man wrecking crew for Trojans (11-0). Davis scored 6 TDs—twice on KO RETs exceeding 90y—to have game for ages. Davis' 2nd scoring RET, 96y effort, helped break open close 25-23 contest late in 3rd Q. What especially scarred Notre Dame was that Fighting Irish (8-2) had just rallied as QB Tom Clements (14-24/199y, 3 TDs, 2 INTs) followed CB Mike Townsend's 2 INTs with TD passes to bite into USC's once-prodigious lead. Less than 2 mins after Davis scored on his crucial TD RET, Clements threw INT to DB Artimus Parker on ND 26YL to set up 8y TD run by Davis for 39-23 lead. Davis finished game with all-purpose y total of 368y: 218y on RETs, 99y rushing, and 51y receiving. Davis, who was 3rd string at beginning of season, became USC's 1st soph in its storied history to rush for more than 1,000y (1,034y).

AP Poll December 4

1	Southern California (50)	1000	11	Tennessee	259
2	Oklahoma	878	12	Notre Dame	227
3	Ohio State	666	13	Colorado	174
4	Alabama	606	14	UCLA	79
5	Penn State	554	15	Arizona State	68
6	Auburn	536	16	North Carolina	60
7	Texas	484	17	Louisville	22
8	Michigan	467	18	West Virginia	18
9	Nebraska	385	19	Washington State	10
10	Louisiana State	273	20	Purdue	3

Conference Standings

Ivy League

Dartmouth	5-1-1
Yale	5-2
Pennsylvania	4-3
Cornell	4-3
Harvard	3-3-1
Princeton	2-4-1
Columbia	2-4-1
Brown	1-6

Atlantic Coast

North Carolina	6-0
North Carolina State	4-1-1
Maryland	3-2-1
Duke	3-3
Clemson	2-4
Virginia	1-5
Wake Forest	1-5

Southeastern

Alabama	7-1
Auburn	6-1
Louisiana State	4-1-1
Tennessee	4-2
Georgia	4-3
Florida	3-3-1
Mississippi	2-5
Kentucky	2-5
Mississippi State	1-6
Vanderbilt	0-6

Southern

East Carolina	6-0
Richmond	5-1
William and Mary	4-2
Citadel	4-3
Davidson	2-3-1
VMI	1-5
Furman	1-6
Appalachian State	0-3-1

Big Ten

Michigan	7-1
Ohio State	7-1
Purdue	6-2
Michigan State	5-2-1
Minnesota	4-4
Indiana	3-5
Illinois	3-5
Iowa	2-6-1
Wisconsin	2-6
Northwestern	1-8

Mid-American

Kent State	4-1
Bowling Green	3-1-1
Western Michigan	2-2-1
Miami (Ohio)	2-3
Toledo	2-3
Ohio	1-4

Big Eight

Oklahoma *	6-1
Nebraska	5-1-1
Colorado	4-3
Oklahoma State	4-3
Missouri	3-4
Iowa State	2-4-1
Kansas	2-5
Kansas State	1-6

* Oklahoma later forfeited three wins

Missouri Valley

Louisville	4-1
Drake	4-1
West Texas State	4-1
Memphis State	3-2
Tulsa	3-2
Wichita State	2-4
New Mexico State	1-4
North Texas State	0-7

Southwest

Texas	7-0
Texas Tech	4-3
SMU	4-3
Baylor	3-4
Rice	3-4
Arkansas	3-4
Texas A&M	2-5
TCU	2-5

Western Athletic

Arizona State	5-1
BYU	5-2
Utah	5-2
Arizona	4-3
Wyoming	3-4
New Mexico	2-4
Colorado State	1-4
Texas El Paso	1-6

Pacific Eight

Southern California	7-0
UCLA	5-2
Washington	4-3
Washington State	4-3
California	3-4
Stanford	2-5
Oregon	2-5
Oregon State	1-6

Pacific Coast Athletic

San Diego State	4-0
Pacific	3-1
Fresno State	1-3
Long Beach State	1-3
San Jose State	1-3
Los Angeles State *	0-2

* Ineligible

1972 Major Bowl Games

Liberty Bowl (Dec. 18): Georgia Tech 31 Iowa State 30

Exciting Liberty Bowl game came down to incomplete 2-pt conv pass by ISU QB George Amundson. Cyclones (5-6-1) enjoyed slim 21-17 lead at H after nifty 93y KO TD RET by WR Willie Jones. Yellow Jackets QB Jim Stevens (12-15/157y, INT), subbing for suspended QB Eddie McAshan, then threw his 2nd and 3rd TD passes to give Georgia Tech (7-4-1) late 31-24 lead. Stevens almost grew goat horns in late going as his lost FUM at Tech 33YL led to Amundson's quick 5y TD pass to WR Ike Harris, which proved to be Iowa State's final TD. Amundson, who received little national attention during season, threw for 153y and rushed for team-high 78y as Cyclones played without injured TB Mike Strachan. Area civil rights leaders organized

peaceful protest before game in honor of McAshan, who claimed that racism was at heart of his suspension. Some black players on both sides wore arm-bands in support of McAshan, who earlier had become 1st African-American to start at QB for any major college in South.

Fiesta Bowl (Dec. 23): Arizona State 49 Missouri 35

High-octane Sun Devils (10-2) dazzled in national showcase. Gaining school-record 718y, ASU had plenty of stars: QB Danny White threw for 266y, HB Woody Green rushed for 202y and FB Brent McClanahan chipped in with 171y rushing. Green scored 4 times, while White and WR Ed Beverly hooked up on 2 scoring passes. After 2 possessions, ASU had 156y and 14-0 lead on Green's opening 2 TD runs. Missouri DB John Moseley ended next possession with INT, which led to 8y TD run by FB Don Johnson to halve deficit. McClanahan then set up own 1y scoring run with 55y burst up middle. Sun Devils squeezed in another TD before H ended on 34y pass from White to Beverly, who out-fought Tigers DB Mike Fink in EZ, for solid 28-7 lead. Tigers (6-6) rallied behind HB Tommy Reamon (17/155y, TD) and scored twice on TD passes from QB John Cherry to WR Chuck Link to pull to 28-21. Teams traded TDs with Fink returning kickoff 100y to cut deficit again to 35-28. Devils roared as White threw 53y TD to Beverly, and D made 3 picks of Cherry.

Peach Bowl (Dec. 29): North Carolina State 49 West Virginia 13

Tight 14-13 game at H was blown open by Wolfpack's dominating 3rd Q performance. QB Dave Buckey led 3 TD drives—2nd only went 6y after blocked punt—as NC State (8-3-1) pulled away. Buckey (8-13/139y) ran for score and threw 2 others. His twin brother WR Dan Buckey (4/70y) caught 37y TD beauty. NC State's rushing attack gained 337y as TB Willie Burden for 116y and FB Stan Fritts cracked EZ on 3 occasions. Mountaineers (8-4) were frustrated for most of 2nd H, gaining only 86y as Wolfpack D posted shutout after opening period. In 1st Q, West Virginia grabbed 13-7 lead on 2 FGs by K Frank Nester and 37y pass from QB Bernie Galiffa (16-34/184y, TD) to slender WR Danny Buggs.

Astro-Bluebonnet Bowl (Dec. 30): Tennessee 24 Louisiana State 17

Volunteers (10-2) rode legs and right arm of masterful QB Condredge Holloway to 24-3 H lead before having to withstand LSU 2nd H rally. Holloway rushed for 96y and 2 scores—on runs of 15y and 10y—and threw 6y scoring pass to WR Jimmy Young. Tigers D found some energy to shut down Holloway and his mates in final 30 mins, which allowed LSU O to mount comeback. LSU (9-2-1) scored TDs on 2y run by QB Bert Jones and 1y run by TB Brad Davis to tighten game at 24-17 in 4th Q. Jones led late drive to Tennessee 22YL, where Bengals were halted on downs as Tennessee A-A DB Conrad Graham batted down final pass intended for LSU WR Gerald Keigley with less than 2 mins remaining. Tennessee gained 232y and 14 1st downs in 1st H, but only 41y and 3 1st downs in 2nd H. LSU was held to 0y net and 5 1st downs in 1st H, but improved its numbers to 197y total O and 13 1st downs.

Gator Bowl (Dec. 30): Auburn 24 Colorado 3

Auburn's hopes got emotional boost from oddsmakers, who pegged Colorado (8-4) as 11-pt favorites, despite success no. 6 Tigers enjoyed all season in their accustomed role as underdogs. Once again, Auburn D led way, limiting Buffs to 63y rushing, which included virtual whitewash of Bison TB Charlie Davis, who managed only 12y. Also, Auburn forced 4 TOs. Stumbling Colorado needed 20 mins to earn its initial 1st down. Auburn (10-1) scored 10 pts off miscues, while also stopping Colorado threat with EZ INT. After taking 3-0 lead on 27y FG by K Gardner Jett, Auburn recovered FUM on Buffs 16YL. Substituting for injured QB Randy Walls, QB Wade Whatley scored on 1y keeper for 10-0 lead, which SEC runners-up maintained to H. Tigers stretched their lead on 2 scoring passes from non-traditional, but adventurous sources: WB Mike Fuller threw 22y TD to TE Rob Spivey and, on fake FG, CB Dave Beck threw 16y TD to TE Dan Nugent. Colorado K Freddie Lima made 33y FG in 4th Q to avert shutout,

Sun Bowl (Dec. 30): North Carolina 32 Texas Tech 28

QB Nick Vidnovic (14-26/215y, INT) led Tar Heels (11-1), to late TD that finished off topsy-turvy contest. Vidnovic's 13y TD pass to WB Ted Leverenz, who earlier caught 62y TD strike, was game winner with min left. North Carolina opened with 9-0 lead on 32y FG by K Ellis Alexander and 22y TD run by FB Dick Oliver. Texas Tech (8-4) roared back with 21 pts, including scoring runs of 65y and 46y by TB George Smith, who rushed for game-record 172y. Tar Heels rebounded to 24-21 edge on Leverenz's long TD catch and 3y TD run by TB Billy Hite. It was Tech's turn to take lead and after WR Lawrence Williams returned punt 38y, Smith obliged with his 3rd TD on 5y run. Exchange of punts left Carolina fairly close in at Red Raiders 37YL, and Vidnovic went to work. Vidnovic converted 4th-and-1 with 4y keeper to set up his winning pass. Any chance for Texas Tech ended 2 plays later with sack of QB Joe Barnes in EZ for safety.

Sugar Bowl (Dec. 31): Oklahoma 14 Penn State 0

In bruising battle of unbending lines, it took 160-lb frosh WR Tinker Owens to turn game for Oklahoma (11-1). Owens had 27y TD catch in 2nd Q and added spectacular diving catch in 4th Q to set up another TD in earning game's outstanding player award. Penn State (10-2) was in trouble before opening KO as star TB John Cappelletti was knocked out with flu. QB John Hufnagel, forced to throw 31 passes, was sacked 3 times and harassed all day by Sooners DL featuring DE Ray Hamilton and DTs Lucious Selmon and Derland Moore. Oklahoma had to overcome 5 FUMs, but HB Greg Pruitt rushed for 86y to lead ground attack. Loss snapped Penn State's 10-game unbeaten streak, 4-game bowl win streak, and induced Sooner faithful to root for Ohio State to upset top-ranked Southern California in Rose Bowl.

Cotton Bowl: Texas 17 Alabama 13

Texas coach Darrell Royal remained undefeated (3 wins and tie) against Alabama (10-2) coach Bear Bryant as Horns survived matchup billed as "battle of the wishbones." Texas (10-1) won on strength of QB Alan Lowry's 2 TD runs in 2nd H. Questionable after bout of tonsillitis, Lowry (16/117y rushing) led attack that gained 317y rushing with nary FUM, nor PEN. Win wasn't finalized until Longhorns LB Randy Braband halted Alabama HB Wilbur Jackson (10/64y) on 4th-and-1 at Texas 43YL in closing moments. Jackson had put Tide in front 10-0 in 1st Q with 31y TD run, after K Greg Gantt kicked game-record 50y FG, his 1st FG of season. Alabama S Steve Wade set up both scores with INTs, 1 he returned 42y. Tide led until Lowry's 2nd TD on 34y bootleg run down left sideline with 4:22 left, which featured both brilliant running and controversial no-call as he appeared to have stepped out at 10YL trying to avoid tackle by Bama CB Mike Washington. DB Terry Melancon chipped in with 2 INTs for Steers, including 1 in EZ early in 4th Q to end threat. Texas FB Roosevelt Leak gained 120y rushing, his 7th 100y game of season. Alabama QB Terry Davis shook off 2 INTs to throw for 174y, but was less effective in 2nd H. Bryant, who selected game when Tide was ranked no. 2, was lambasted for bypassing higher ranked opponents that awaited him in Sugar and Orange Bowls.

Orange Bowl: Nebraska 40 Notre Dame 6

After failing to contain Southern California TB Anthony Davis in season finale, Fighting Irish (8-3) D now had to tangle with Heisman Trophy-winning Johnny Rodgers. WB Rodgers was placed in IB position in I formation for most of game and scored 4 TDs, while throwing for another: 52y pass to WR Frosty Anderson. Final TD—50th overall including bowls—of Rodgers' glorious career came on 50y dash after nabbing quick sideline pass from QB Dave Humm (13-19/185y). That score capped 20-pt burst in opening 9 mins of 3rd Q that cancelled Irish comeback plans. In addition to successful passing effort, Rodgers overcame flu bug, which had knocked 10 lbs off his 178-lb playing weight, to lead Huskers (9-2-1) in scoring (game-record 24 pts), rushing (15/84y), and receiving (3/71y) despite sitting out last 21 mins. Notre Dame QB Tom Clements suffered 3 INTs, while ND was held to 104y rushing. Early in 4th Q, Clements moved Irish 77y for their only score: 5y TD pass to WR Pete Demmerle. Rolling up 560y, Nebraska became 1st school to win 3 straight Orange Bowls while handing coach Ara Parseghian his worst loss in 9 years at Notre Dame.

Rose Bowl: Southern California 42 Ohio State 17

Once USC (12-0) FB Sam Cunningham went airborne, it was close to impossible for college players, even Ohio State's exemplary GL D members, to prevent him from his patented TD-landing in EZ. Cunningham dove 4 times and scored 4 times, and Trojans (12-0) blew open 7-7 H contest to win 3rd national championship in coach John McKay's 13 years. Southern California scored on its initial 5 2nd H possessions to eliminate any chance of upset. TB Anthony Davis rushed for 157y and explosive tandem of QB Mike Rae (18-25/229y, TD) and WR Lynn Swann (6/108y, TD) nearly were unstoppable as Trojans scored most pts ever allowed by any Ohio State team coached by Woody Hayes. Fear of Davis' KO RET abilities forced Buckeyes to kick short, which got Trojans rolling to TD scoring drives of 57y and 56y in 3rd Q. Rae completed 23y pass to Swann on 3rd-and-17 to keep go-ahead drive in gear, while big play on next possession—which ended on 20y TD pass to Swann—was 22y completion to Swann. Buckeyes were now beaten, but still fighting as they did in 1st H struggle when they had tied game at 7-7 on 1y run by FB Randy Keith. Bucks TB Archie Griffin rushed 20 times for team-high 95y.

Final AP Poll January 3

1	Southern California (50)	1000	11	Louisiana State	209
2	Oklahoma	872	12	North Carolina	179
3	Texas	667	13	Arizona State	158
4	Nebraska	665	14	Notre Dame	75
5	Auburn	631	15	UCLA	71
6	Michigan	502	16	Colorado	58
7	Alabama	453	17	North Carolina State	35
8	Tennessee	409	18	Louisville	19
9	Ohio State	372	19	Washington State	9
10	Penn State	340	20	Georgia Tech	5

1972 Top Performance Formula

1	Southern California	1.8483
2	Oklahoma	1.7577
3	Texas	1.6871
4	Alabama	1.6581
5	Nebraska	1.6280
6	Auburn	1.6244
7	Michigan	1.5955
8	North Carolina	1.5778
9	Tennessee	1.5763
10	Penn State	1.5269
11	Arizona State	1.4761
12	Ohio State	1.4618
13	UCLA	1.4361
14	North Carolina State	1.4265
15	Louisiana State	1.4120
16	Notre Dame	1.3423
17	Colorado	1.2908
18	Washington	1.2804
19	Georgia	1.2614
20	West Virginia	1.2467

1972 Top Opponent Records

1	Auburn	.6535
2	Florida	.6486
3	Texas	.6416
4	Kansas State	.6239
5	Alabama	.6148
6	Tennessee	.6121
7	Oklahoma	.6210
8t	Oregon State	.620536
8t	Texas A&M	.620536
10	Georgia	.6150
11	UCLA	.6116
12	Illinois	.5982
13t	California	.5840707
13t	Rice	.5840707
15	Miami	.5827
16	Southern California	.5792
17	North Carolina State	.5774
18	Nebraska	.5738
19	Oregon	.5714
20	Kentucky	.5702

1972 Out-of-Conference Records

	W-L	Percentage	Bowl W-L
Southeastern	29-10	.7436	1-2
Pacific-8	22-10	.6875	1-0
Big Eight	24-12	.6667	2-3
Southwest	20-11-1	.6406	1-1
Atlantic Coast	16-18	.4706	2-0
Western Athletic	13-18-2	.4242	1-0
Big Ten	8-17-1	.3269	0-1

1972 Individual Statistical Leaders

RUSHING YARDS	Attempts	Yards	Avg.
Pete Van Valkenburg, Brigham Young	232	1386	6.0
Bob Hitchens, Miami (Ohio)	326	1370	4.2
Woody Green, Arizona State	209	1363	6.5
Otis Armstrong, Purdue	243	1361	5.6
Mark Kellar, Northern Illinois	285	1314	4.6
Carlester Crumpler, East Carolina	340	1309	3.9
Howard Stevens, Louisville	259	1294	5.0
Jim Jennings, Rutgers	287	1262	4.4
Mike Strachan, Iowa State	267	1260	4.7
Steve Jones, Duke	287	1236	4.3

PASSING YARDS	Completions	Attempts	Yards	Pct.
Don Strock, Virginia Tech	228	427	3243	53.4
Gary Huff, Florida State	206	385	2893	53.5
Tony Adams, Utah State	204	351	2797	58.1
Bernie Galiffa, West Virginia	148	302	2312	49.0
Vince Boryla, Stanford	183	350	2284	52.3
David Jaynes, Kansas	153	287	2253	53.3
Joe Pisarcik, New Mexico State	182	382	2179	47.6
David Humm, Nebraska	140	266	2074	52.6
Bruce Gadd, Rice	170	322	2064	52.8
Dan Fouts, Oregon	171	348	2041	49.1

RECEIVING YARDS	Catches	Yards
Barry Smith, Florida State	69	1243
Tom Forzani, Utah State	85	1169
Johnny Rodgers, Nebraska	55	942
Jeff Calabrese, Toledo	62	886
Greg Taylor, Texas-El Paso	53	878
Rhett Dawson, Florida State	62	817
Clint Graves, Temple	63	707
Louis Regine, Brown	51	681
Gary Barnes. Louisville	52	655
Lee Calland, Navy	61	650

1972 Consensus All-America Team

Offense

Wide Receiver:	Johnny Rodgers, Nebraska
Tight End:	Charles Young, Southern California
Tackle:	Jerry Sisemore, Texas
	Paul Seymour, Michigan
Guard:	John Hannah, Alabama
	Ron Rusnak, North Carolina
Center:	Tom Brahaney, Oklahoma
Quarterback:	Bert Jones, LSU
Running Back:	Greg Pruitt, Oklahoma
	Otis Armstrong, Purdue
	Woody Green, Arizona State

Defense

End:	Willie Harper, Nebraska
	Bruce Bannon, Penn State
Tackle:	Greg Marx, Notre Dame
	Dave Butz, Purdue
Middle Guard:	Rich Glover, Nebraska
Linebacker:	Randy Gradishar, Ohio State
	John Skorupan, Penn State
Back:	Brad Van Pelt, Michigan State
	Cullen Bryant, Colorado
	Robert Popelka, SMU
	Randy Logan, Michigan

1972 Heisman Trophy Vote

Johnny Rodgers, senior wingback, Nebraska	1,310
Greg Pruitt, senior halfback, Oklahoma	966
Rich Glover, senior nose guard, Nebraska	652
Bert Jones, senior quarterback, Louisiana State	351
Terry Davis, senior quarterback, Alabama	338

Other Major Award Winners

Maxwell (Player)	Brad Van Pelt, senior safety, Michigan State
Outland (Lineman)	Rich Glover, senior nose guard, Nebraska
Lombardi (Lineman)	Rich Glover, senior nose guard, Nebraska
Walter Camp (Player)	Greg Pruitt, senior halfback, Oklahoma
AFCA Coach of the Year	John McKay, Southern California

1973

The Year of Ara's Era's Big Play, Big Ten's Vengeful Vote, and Something for Joey

The 1973 season may best be remembered for a game played on the last day of the calendar year. It was a classic New Year's Eve Sugar Bowl match-up, pitting undefeated Alabama (11-1) and undefeated Notre Dame (11-0) in the first meeting between the tradition-rich schools. The game featured coaching legends, Bear Bryant of Alabama and Ara Parseghian of Notre Dame, and two distinct styles of play. The Crimson Tide already had wrapped up the UPI national championship behind a Wishbone attack that had crushed opponent after opponent. Alabama's biggest rout was 77-6 over Virginia Tech (2-9) in a game in which the offense set modern NCAA records for total yards (828) and rushing yards (743). Continuing with their do-not-make-mistakes-but-let-defense-win-game offense, Notre Dame entered the game in the enviable position as a talent-laden underdog. With the help of an adventurous late-game play call, a pass from deep in Notre Dame territory to substitute tight end Robin Weber, the Fighting Irish kept possession to edge Alabama for the AP half of the national championship. It was the ninth-ever meeting of undefeated teams in a bowl game and Notre Dame's ninth national title.

Brilliant seasons by Ohio State (10-0-1) and Michigan (10-0-1) ended in controversy after a 10-10 tie could not separate the rivals. The Rose Bowl bid was determined by a vote of athletic directors, as dictated by Big Ten rules. The vote went to the Buckeyes 6-4, despite their presence in Pasadena the year before. Michigan cried foul, saying that the main reason Ohio State got the nod was the broken collarbone suffered by Wolverines quarterback Dennis Franklin, which made Michigan less likely to win in Pasadena. It certainly was a factor. Of course, Michigan ignored the fact that the Buckeyes were ranked higher all year, occupying the nation's top spot for eight weeks, and had tied their rivals in Ann Arbor. Michigan State's Buckeye vote exacted revenge for Michigan's having worked at keeping the Spartans out of the conference years earlier. Illinois, Northwestern, Purdue, and Wisconsin joined the Spartans and Buckeyes in voting for OSU. If the vote had been 5-5, Michigan would have been the Rose Bowl choice. In the end, the Buckeyes beat Southern California (9-2-1), 42-21, to snap the Big Ten's four-game Rose Bowl losing streak.

Oklahoma (10-0-1) was put on two-year probation (no bowls in 1973 or 1974, no television in 1974 or 1975, among other penalties) for altering quarterback Kerry Jackson's transcript. The Sooners, their fans, and state legislators fought the penalty to no avail. After routing Texas 52-13, Oklahoma gave the game ball to former assistant coach Bill Michaels, who resigned because of the recruiting scandal.

Tom Osborne debuted as head coach of Nebraska (9-2-1). Osborne and new Sooners coach Barry Switzer shaped the conference's identity for many years, with Switzer winning or sharing 12 titles in 16 years and Osborne 14 in 25. Osborne had bigger shoes to fill as new athletic director Bob Devaney had won 101 games in 11 years at Nebraska with two national titles amid a 33-2-2 mark over his final three seasons.

USC entered 1973 as defending champions and preseason no. 1. Troy fell from the top spot with a 7-7 tie against Oklahoma on September 29 and dropped further with a loss to Notre Dame. The Trojans managed their sixth Pac-8 title in eight years before losing to Ohio State.

While Penn State (12-0) was the East's top team yet again, the region's coaches made news: Penn State's Joe Paterno turned down a $1 million dollar offer to jump to the New England Patriots, while Johnny Majors debuted as head coach at moribund Pittsburgh (6-5-1). Majors already had beaten the Nittany Lions in recruiting tailback Tony Dorsett, who had a brilliant freshman year. Dorsett was the most dynamic player in the Northeast, and possibly the country, but he would not become a factor in the race for the Heisman Trophy until he aged a bit. Penn State tailback John Cappelletti won the honor—when early favorites fell to the curb—and became the first player from that school to do so. His emotional acceptance speech, which ended with the recognition that his young brother Joey's fight against leukemia had been a great inspiration to him, made the attendees shed a few tears. It was a landmark moment for a new, softer society's acceptance of grown men crying in public.

Oklahoma State (5-4-2) guard Deacon Stephens did his best imitation of the infamous 1954 Cotton Bowl gaffe by Alabama's Tommy Lewis when he jumping from the sidelines to tackle an Iowa State (4-7) runner on November 24. Cyclones QB Buddy Hardeman had broken free and was heading for a score until meeting up with Stephens. Hardeman was credited with a 74-yard touchdown, and Iowa State went on to win 28-12.

Rice (5-6) finished with a losing record, but it was not for lack of trying. Against Notre Dame, Owls coach Al Conover brought more than 100 local Roman Catholic priests to the game to root for his team. Owls held the Fighting Irish to 28 points, but the priests must have been on the concession line when Rice had ball; the sleepy Owls were shut out.

In a disturbing episode of disloyalty at Hawaii (9-2), quarterback Casey Ortez quit the team in late November due to pressure from defensive players who accused Ortez of poor play because they claimed he had bet against Hawaii. After the Rainbows lost to Pacific 28-3 on November 24 for their first loss of the season, defensive lineman Cliff Laboy struck Ortez.

In better news in the West, BYU (5-6) wide receiver Jay Miller became the second player to nab 100 receptions in a season and he set a new record for catches in a game with 22 against New Mexico (4-7).

Milestones

■ Rules Committee first allowed either team to use ball of their choice when in possession.

■ Legendary Tennessee G Bob Suffridge died on February 3. Suffridge was thrice All-America as part of all-time great defense that helped win 30 of 30 regular season games, three SEC crowns, and share of 1938 national title. Vols of 1939 were unbeaten, untied and unscored upon in regular season. Frank Leahy, coach with 2nd-best all-time winning percentage, died of congestive heart failure at 65 on June 21. Leahy (107-13-9) played for and coached under Knute Rockne at Notre Dame, was line coach of Fordham's Seven Blocks of Granite, and took Boston College to Cotton and Sugar Bowls before winning four national championships at Notre Dame. Elmer Layden, one of Four Horsemen of Notre Dame, died on June 30. Fast fullback arguably was best of backfield stars for Irish from 1922-24 before coaching career that took him back to South Bend (47-13-3). Layden was NFL commissioner during WW II. George P. "Icehouse" Wilson, star HB for St. Mary's in 1933-34, died on October 13. Greasy Neale, member of both NFL and college football halls of fame, died on November 2. Neale coached seven colleges, including Washington & Jefferson squad that shockingly tied California's "Wonder Team" in 1922 Rose Bowl. Emil "Six Yards" Sitko, twice All-America back for Notre Dame's title teams of 1946-49, died on December 15. Sitko, four-year starter for teams that went 36-0-2, won 1949 Walter Camp Trophy. Wally Butts, who won 140 games as coach of Georgia from 1939-60, died of heart attack at age 68 on December 17. Known for high-scoring passing attacks, Butts had best success in 1940s when 1942 team won share of national title and 1946 squad went 11-0.

■ Longest winning streaks entering season:

Southern California 13	North Carolina 8	Texas, Oklahoma, Tampa 7

■ Coaching Changes:

	Incoming	Outgoing
Arizona	Jim Young	Bob Weber
Brown	John Anderson	Len Jardine
Clemson	Red Parker	Hootie Ingram
Colorado State	Sarkis Arslanian	Jerry Wampfler
Indiana	Lee Corso	John Pont
Iowa State	Earle Bruce	Johnny Majors
Kentucky	Fran Curci	John Ray
Louisville	T.W. Alley	Lee Corso
Miami	Pete Elliott	Fran Curci
Michigan State	Dennis Stolz	Duffy Daugherty
Mississippi	Johnny Vaught (a)	Billy Kinard
Mississippi State	Bob Tyler	Charley Shira
Navy	George Welsh	Rick Forzano
Nebraska	Tom Osborne	Bob Devaney
Northwestern	John Pont	Alex Agase
Oklahoma	Barry Switzer	Chuck Fairbanks
Oklahoma State	Jim Stanley	Dave Smith
Pittsburgh	Johnny Majors	Carl de Pasqua
Princeton	Bob Casciola	Jake McCandless
Purdue	Alex Agase	Bob DeMoss
Rutgers	Frank Burns	John Bateman
San Diego State	Claude Gilbert	Don Coryell
Southern Methodist	Dave Smith	Hayden Fry
Vanderbilt	Steve Sloan	Bill Pace
Wake Forest	Chuck Mills	Tom Harper

(a) Kinard (1-2) was replaced by Vaught (5-3) after three games.

AP Poll Preseason

1 Southern California (55)	1238	11t Colorado	265
2 Ohio State (2)	896	11t Oklahoma	265
3 Texas	785	13 Auburn	224
4 Nebraska (2)	763	14 Arizona State	220
5 Michigan (2)	712	15 Florida	102
6 Alabama	673	16 Louisiana State	89
7 Penn State (1)	558	17 North Carolina State	62
8 Notre Dame	534	18 Houston	54
9 Tennessee	449	19 North Carolina	40
10 UCLA	427	20 Texas Tech	23

September 8, 1973

NEBRASKA 40 Ucla 13: Huskers (1-0) replaced coaching legend (Bob Devaney), Heisman Trophy winner (Johnny Rodgers), and Outland Trophy winner (Rich Glover) without missing beat. Coach Tom Osborne's era began with whipping of Bruins (0-1) that avenged opening loss of 1972. Nebraska IB Tony Davis rushed for 147y and 2

TDs, while QB Steve Runty, in relief of injured starter QB David Humm, completed 9-11/105y and was responsible for TDs rushing and throwing. Huskers CB Randy Borg added 77y scoring run with punt RET for 14-0 1st Q lead. Bruins hung tough early as HB Kermit Johnson scored TD on 8y run and set up another with 43y scamper, but being UCLA's inability to throw (2-9/20y) made comeback unlikely.

September 15, 1973

Bowling Green 41 SYRACUSE 14: Coach Ben Schwartzwalder's final season at helm of Orangemen (0-1) began on sour note as MAC power Falcons (1-0) soared. LB John Villapiano was D star for Bowling Green, piling up 19 tackles, INT and forced FUM, while TB Paul Miles appeared headed for 3rd straight 1,000y season with 113y rushing and 2 TDs. Syracuse was shut out until 4th Q, when WB Brian Hambleton caught 2 TD passes. Falcons had wide y discrepancy: 406y to 162y.

Pittsburgh 7 GEORGIA 7: Coach Johnny Majors was as close as 34y FG from stunningly successful debut at Pitt (0-0-1), yet he could not have been too upset. Tie in Athens was good building block for program that had registered 1-10 record in 1972. Dazzling frosh TB Tony Dorsett debuted too, rushing for 101y, and drawing D away from fake by QB Bill Daniels that allowed Daniels to romp 17y to open game's scoring. Georgia (0-0-1) QB Andy Johnson knotted matters in 2nd Q as he capped 53y drive with 4y keeper. Neither team came close to scoring in 2nd H until Panthers' final 64y drive ended on missed attempt by frosh K Carson Long.

South Carolina 41 GEORGIA TECH 28: QB Jeff Grantz shone in new Veer O as he threw 2 TD passes and rushed for 111y in leading Gamecocks (1-0). Grantz's 2 TD runs allowed South Carolina to build 21-0 2nd Q lead, while DB Mel Baxley's 100y INT RET bumped lead up to 34-7 in 3rd Q as they caught Yellow Jackets looking ahead to college football's other USC, no. 1 Trojans from Los Angeles. Georgia Tech (0-1) rushed for 218y and threw for 200y more, but did most of its damage during 21-pt 4th Q spree that only made score look more respectable.

LOUISIANA STATE 17 Colorado 6: LSU (1-0) QB Mike Miley looked every bit worthy successor to QB Bert Jones as he hit 7-10/140y and 30y TD to Jones' brother, WR Ben Jones. LSU D held Colorado to solo 1st down in opening H, which went scoreless as Tigers O fared little better. Jones' TD catch was opening score, followed by K Rusty Jackson's 25y FG. Buffaloes (0-1) scored later in 3rd Q on 37y reverse by WB Larry Ferguson, but were thwarted on 2-pt conv attempt. Unable to throw consistently, Colorado ended its own chances with 3rd INT—matched by only 3 completions—which was returned for 25y TD by Bengals LB Gary Champagne.

OHIO STATE 56 Minnesota 7: *Chicago Tribune* writer Bob Markus wrote that Buckeyes (1-0) "unleashed so many weapons they should be included in the next round of SALT (Strategic Arms Limitation Talks)." Ohio State FB Champ Henson bulled over for 1st of his 3 TDs at end of opening drive, and when touted Minnesota (0-1) HB Rick Upchurch fumbled ensuing KO, Bucks QB Cornelius Greene scored to put Gophers behind 14-0 before they even ran their 1st snap. Even when Ohio lined up for late 2nd Q FG, its snap was bad so WB-holder Brian Baschnagel picked it up and dashed for 5y TD as time expired on 35-7 H edge.

Michigan 31 IOWA 7: Butter-fingered Iowa (0-1) lost 4 FUMs in 1st H, and poor coach Frank Lauterbur had to be happy that his D held Michigan (1-0) to K Greg Lantry's 39y FG after bobbling opening KO. After all, Lauterbur had lost 63-7 and 31-0 in his 1st 2 cracks at Wolverines coach Bo Schembechler. Michigan rolled for 440y rushing, but their coach had promised to open up his attack. That plan didn't work as QB Dennis Franklin was intercepted in 2nd Q by Hawkeyes DB Earl Douthitt, who scrambled 47y for Iowa's only TD. So, Wolverines went back to grinding it, and by game's end could count TD drives of 80, 76, 75, and 66y. TB Chuck Heater gained 133y rushing and scored 1st Q TD for Michigan.

NORTHWESTERN 14 Michigan State 10: Northwestern (1-0) rolled dice and it came up 1st win in season opener in 6 years. Wildcats gambled successfully on 3 4th downs, including 1y run by HB Stan Key (31/107y, TD) to Michigan State 13YL, to continue their winning drive in 4th Q. March began when DB Pete Wessel stepped in front of pass by Spartans (0-1) QB Charley Baggett and raced 24y to Michigan State 40YL. Win was secured by 10y TD pass from NW QB Mitch Anderson to TE Steve Craig. Baggett had given Spartans 10-7 lead in 3rd Q with 8y keeper, capping 80y drive keyed by his 35y pass to WR Dane Fortney.

Oklahoma 42 BAYLOR 14: Tenure of Sooners coach Barry Switzer began appropriately with easy win as Oklahoma (1-0) rushed for 480y. Scoring 3 times in 1st Q and twice again in 2nd Q, Sooners clobbered Baylor early. OU QB Steve Davis rushed for 110y, HB Joe Washington motored to 113y, and FB Waymon Clark added 113y more, while Davis and Washington each scored 2 TDs. Turning ball over 5 times, Bears (0-1) had trouble moving their O but managed to get passing TDs from QBs Neal Jeffrey and Robert Armstrong in 2nd H.

KANSAS 29 Washington State 8: Kansas QB David Jaynes was held to 93y passing, but rushed for 2 TDs in leading win. Jaynes had Jayhawks (1-0) on board 1st with 28y scoring pass to WR Bruce Adams, which was countered by safety by Wazzu on

blocked punt. Up 7-2 at H, Kansas put game away with 3 straight TDs, including Jaynes' 2 QB runs and 23y INT RET by LB Steve Towle. Cougars (0-1) answered with their only TD on 1y run by TB Ken Grandberry. Neither team showed much O, as Cougars led by 215y to 205y, but crucial stat was Washington State's 5 TOs.

Colorado State 21 BRIGHAM YOUNG 13: While Rams (1-1) pulled off upset, outcome was not too shocking with BYU QB Gary Shiede out with injury. Game was scoreless at H and 7-7 after 3 Qs until K Dev Duke had 2 FGs for Cougars (0-1). Colorado State rallied with 14 pts, converting flea flicker (QB Jan Steubbe passed into flat to WR Willie Miller who lateralled to RB Tom Wallace for 45y gain) and INT by LB Greg Battle. Rams scored 4th Q TDs on short runs by RBs Kim Jones and Scott McLachlan, his 2nd on day. WR Jay Miller (6/63y) was leader of BYU O.

Arizona State 26 OREGON 20: Oregon (1-0) started and finished well, but had plenty of problems in between. Ducks shut out high-flying Arizona State in 1st Q and then grabbed 14-7 2nd Q lead on 13y TD run by TB Rick Kane and 8y scoring pass from QB Norval Turner to WR Bob Palm. Sun Devils (1-0) took control for balance of 1st H and most of 2nd H, scoring 3 straight TDs including scoring passes of 39y and 70y by QB Danny White (10-15/282y). Oregon had last gasp as Palm caught his 2nd TD pass with 44 secs remaining and then recovered onside-KO. Ducks reached ASU 28YL before time expired.

Penn State 20 STANFORD 6: That sound of bones crunching rung in ears of Stanford (0-1) QB Mike Boryla (17-29/188y), who was sacked 7 times by Nittany Lions D. Penn State forced Stanford to settle for -8y rushing. LB Doug Allen put Penn State on board 1st with blocked punt for safety. On next Stanford possession, DB Jim Bradley, who earlier had INT at Lions GL to stop Cardinals threat, scooped up FUM by TB Scott Laidlaw to set up 14y TD catch by Mount Nit WR Gary Hayman. Penn State QB Tom Shuman tossed 2 TDs, but TB John Cappelletti was held to 76y rushing, although he set up his own 2y TD run with 17y pass, his first-ever completion, to WR Chuck Herd. Battered Boryla climbed off canvas to throw late 8y scoring pass to TE Glen Stone.

SOUTHERN CALIFORNIA 17 Arkansas 0: Trojans (1-0) opened up defense of their national championship with 1st shutout of Arkansas in 73 games. Young Porkers (0-1) hung tough despite new USC QB Pat Haden sparking his troops to 452y O. Trojans led only 7-0 after 3rd Q because pair of long TDs by WR Lynn Swann had been wiped out by plethora of PENs. Arkansas D keyed on TB Anthony Davis, who struggled for his 96y with 1y TD run. Haden completed 12-20/143y and tallied clinching 4th Q TD run of 14y. Arkansas, led by TB Dickey Morton's 12/73y rushing, drove twice before missing 2 FGs in 1st H.

September 22, 1973

(Fri) MIAMI 20 Texas 15: Hurricanes (1-0) stunned no. 6 Texas in coach Pete Elliott's debut. QBs Coy Hall and Kary Baker combined 12-18/118y, INT passing, while TB Woody Thompson (25/80y) banged for 3 TDs. Also, Miami converted its share of 3rd-and-long situations while keeping ball for 37 mins. Longhorns (0-1) rushed for 287y, but contributed 5 lost FUMs to their downfall. Most harrowing was HB Joey Aboussie's baffling bobble without being touched on 24y run to Miami 30YL in 2nd Q. Longhorns QB Marty Akins lost pair of 4th Q FUMs at Hurricanes 29 and 34YLs. Big Texas FB Roosevelt Leaks rushed 30/153y and 2 TDs, but also bobbled away FUM at his 14YL that led to Thompson's 3rd TD early in 3rd Q that upped score to 20-6.

(Fri) HOUSTON 27 South Carolina 19: In battle of Veer Os, it took awhile before originator Houston (2-0) got going, but fakes by QB D.C. Nobles helped RBs Leonard Parker (24/135y) and Reggie Cherry (23/102y) to TD each. Gamecocks (1-1) led 6-3 early on couple of FGs by K Bobby Marino. Nobles and Parker soon scored for Cougars, but HB Jay Lynn Hodgin burst 93y up middle on KO TD RET to keep South Carolina within 17-13 at H. Cherry scored key TD 5 mins into 3rd Q that upped Houston's margin to 24-13 before Hodgin tacked on 4y TD for Carolina in 4th Q.

Maryland 23 NORTH CAROLINA 3: Terps (1-1) got leg up in ACC race by halting Tar Heels' 15-game conf win streak. QB Al Neville tossed 2 TD passes, but bruising D did most damage as Maryland looked for its 1st winning record since 1962. Tar Heels (1-1) led 3-0 in 1st Q on 32y FG by K Ellis Alexander, but Carolina gained only 210y and lost 5 TOs. Maryland took lead for good in 2nd Q as HB Louis Carter capped 89y drive with 3y TD run. Neville dominated 76y drive for next Terps score, rushing for 22y and hitting WR Frank Russell twice, including 23y TD pass.

Alabama 28 KENTUCKY 14: Coach Bear Bryant's 1st trip to school he coached from 1946-53 was triumphant visit, but tougher than expected. Crimson Tide (2-0) was slow out of gate, trailing 14-0 at H with 4 TOs spoiling their O. HB Willie Shelby returned 2nd H KO 100y for TD that sparked Bama's ensuing domination. Tide D allowed only 1 1st down rest of way. Wildcats (1-1) had scored 1st H TDs on 3y run by TB Sonny Collins and 14y pass from QB Ernie Lewis to WR Jack Alvarez.

Memphis State 17 MISSISSIPPI 13 (Jackson): Fortunes of Rebels (1-2) were sinking quickly, for only 2nd time in 28-game series they lost to Tigers (3-0). Winning TD drive was led by RB Dan Darby and capped by FB Clifton Taylor's 5y run. Tigers exploited

poor Mississippi passing attack (4-16/57y, 2 INTs) to score game's final 17 pts. Last Rebels threat reached Memphis 9YL, where it ended on incomplete pass in EZ. Ole Miss' slow start cost coach Billy Kinard his job on Monday along with that of AD brother Bruiser Kinard. Clean sweep meant legendary Rebs coach Johnny Vaught returned from retirement to take over both roles.

Miami (Ohio) 24 PURDUE 19: FB Chuck Varner rushed for 3 TDs as Miami (2-0) rallied, scoring 2 TDs late in 4th Q. Purdue (1-1) owned 19-10 lead after QB Bo Bobrowski threw 34y TD to TE Barry Santini early in 4th Q. Turning point took Miami to within 19-17 on 29y scoring pass from QB Steve Sanna to Varner moments after MG Brad Cousino's RET of blocked punt. Varner scored on 3y run for game-winner.

NOTRE DAME 44 Northwestern 0: On day 13-year-old sister, Alice, died of injuries sustained when struck week earlier by car, QB Tom Clements led Notre Dame (1-0) to easy victory. Clements (9-12/152y) threw 9y TD pass to WR Pete Demmerle to close 16-0 1st Q and then added 2 rushing TDs in 21-pt 2nd Q as Irish reached H with 37-0 lead. Frosh DE Ross Browner had started onslaught with blocked punt for 2 pts. ND HB Art Best then capped ensuing short 56y drive with 2y scoring run and rout was on. Wildcats (1-1) struggled to 9y O in 1st H, while snake-bit P Dave Skarin suffered Browner's punt block, had another deflected, and, after few near-misses, was hit on punt attempt and suffered compound fracture of left leg.

Oklahoma State 38 ARKANSAS 6: QB Brent Blackman was moving Cowboys (2-0) Wishbone attack well early on but had to settle for FGs. Ahead 8-0 in 2nd Q on 2 FGs by K Abby Daigle and 1st of 2 safeties on bad snaps to P Tommy Cheyne, Blackman (13/82y) took matters into his hands, or feet to be exact, in sprinting to 35y score. QB Mike Kirkland got TD back for Hogs (0-2) with 6y keeper, but Porkers were shut out 23-0 in 2nd H. Oklahoma State rushed for 213y, including FB George Palmer's 2 TDs, and held Arkansas to 17y on ground.

Michigan 47 STANFORD 10: Wolverines (2-0) steamrolled Stanford, scoring 3 TDs in 1st Q to pull away early. Michigan went 85y for opening score, 8y TD run by TB Chuck Heater, and then set up short TD drives by recovering FUM on Stanford 15YL and forcing botched punt snap at Stanford 6 YL. FB Ed Shuttlesworth and TB Gil Chapman scored 2 TDs apiece, while K Mike Lantry booted 50y and 51y FGs to establish school long-distance records. Stanford (0-2) got 222y passing from QB Mike Boryla, but managed only 95y rushing.

Illinois 27 CALIFORNIA 7: Golden Bears (0-2) were whipped at home, twice failing to score after TOs inside Illinois 25YL. Fighting Illini (2-0) jumped to 14-0 H lead on 1y TD runs by QB Jeff Hollenbach and TB George Uremovich (149y rushing). California halved deficit to 14-7 on 1y TD run by QB Vince Ferragamo before Uremovich blew open game on 35y TD run, and DB Mike Gow cantered 46y on INT TD RET in 4th Q.

Southern Methodist 35 OREGON STATE 16: Mustangs (2-0) took not 1 but 2 INTs for TDs in 2nd H to break open 14-10 game. S Andy Duvall roared 49y with INT for eventual winning TD in 3rd Q, while, early in 4th Q, DE Clarence Dennard grabbed pass for 11y insurance TD. Oregon State (0-2) QB Alvin White got up off mat to throw 29y TD pass to WR Grant Boustead, but 28-16 was as close as Beavers would get. QB Keith Bobo ran for 2 TDs and threw 3rd to pace SMU O, which overcame 6 FUMs with 370y rushing.

September 29, 1973

VIRGINIA 7 Duke 3: WR Kent Merritt used every bit of speed that had earned him ACC sprint crown in catching 65y TD pass from QB Scott Gardner. Virginia's big TD came on game's 3rd play. Merritt caught pass at midfield and raced away from 3 defenders to give Cavaliers (2-2) quick lead at 7-0. Gardner played artiste by building 259y total O, with 226y coming through air. Gardner led Virginia into Blue Devils territory 6 more times to no avail. Duke (1-2) could arrange no more than K David Malachek's FG in 1st Q and were otherwise blanked. Midway through 3rd Q, Blues drove to UVa 8YL, before stops by Cavs LBs Dick Ambrose and Jim Grobe produced –8y in 4 snaps. Final Duke drive reached Virginia 13YL before last-play incomplete pass fell harmlessly to ground.

TENNESSEE 21 Auburn 0: Tigers (2-1) were ambushed in Knoxville, managing only 110y total O. Up 13-0 at H in downpour, Vols (3-0) continually punted on 1st down with P Neil Clabo making 71y boot to Auburn 5YL. Tennessee LB Hank Walter contributed only pts of 2nd H when he added 38y INT TD RET to his 20 tackles and FUM REC. Tennessee HB Haskel Stanback rushed 22/96y despite taking tough hits. In handing Auburn its 1st shutout loss since 1967, Vols snapped 3-game series losing streak.

MISSISSIPPI STATE 33 Florida 12: Bulldogs (2-0-1) rolled up 403y and forced 7 TOs in handing Florida its 1st loss. Mississippi State FB Wayne Jones rushed 132y, and killing 29y TD in 21-6 4th Q lead. Miss State QB Rockey Felker added 153y passing—with 36y coming on 2nd Q TD pass—and 9y TD run. Bulldogs DB Larry Bouie added insult to injury by taking INT back for 96y TD on game's final play. Gators (2-1) lost HB Nat Moore to ankle injury in 1st Q after bruising tackle by DT Jimmy Webb. Sub HB Larry Brinson scored early 4th Q TD to cut deficit to 14-6.

Ucla 34 MICHIGAN STATE 21: Bruins (2-1) held give-away, losing 6 FUMs in alien wet conditions, but sent their backs scurrying for 286y to still come away from East Lansing as winners over Michigan State (1-2). Spartans coach Denny Stolz was impressed: "That's a 440-yard relay team they (Bruins) have in that backfield!" FB James McAlister rambled for 108y, but it was UCLA HB Kermit Johnson who scored 3 TDs on runs of 6, 18, and 9y that pretty well buried Spartans at 27-10. Michigan State had carved 10-6 lead early in 2nd Q on 44y FG by K Dirk Kryt and 1y TD plunge by TB Tyrone Wilson. QB John Sciarra (4-6/71y, TD) came off bench to spark Bruins, but starting QB Mark Harmon returned to score TD late in 4th Q before Spartans TB Mike Holt returned following KO 95y for TD in last 7 secs.

Notre Dame 20 PURDUE 7: HB Art Best, wackiest ball-carrier at Notre Dame (2-0) since George Gipp, smiled at TV camera during starter introduction and gave silly wave with his thumb in his mouth and pinky extended. "This ain't death row, you know," explained Irish's free-spirit, who proceeded to ramble 64y on his 1st play to set up K Bob Thomas' 22y FG. Purdue (1-2) went ahead 7-3 in 2nd Q on perfect 53y TD bomb from QB Bo Bobrowski (11-26/153y, 2 INTs) to WR Larry Burton. Back came Best (16/125y) for go-ahead 9y TD run behind great blocking in 3rd Q. ND D permitted only 33y rushing to Boilermaker runners and 4 1st downs in 2nd H.

Boston College 32 TEXAS A&M 24: Eagles (2-1) wiped out 7-pt deficit with 2 TD runs by HB Mike Esposito sandwiching INT within 2-min span in 4th Q. Texas A&M had led early as WR Carl Roaches took opening KO back for 100y. BC answered with 17 straight pts, before Aggies (1-2) did same, score 17 pts in row for 24-17 lead. Esposito's 1st TD run, from 3y out, pulled Boston College to within 24-13. QB Gary Marangi kept for 2-pt conv, and demoralized Aggies allowed 36y TD run by Esposito.

TEXAS 28 Texas Tech 12: Texas Longhorns (1-1) bounced back from opening week loss to hand Texas Tech what would be only blemish on 11-1 season. Texas DB Jay Arnold made 2 big plays: his INT set up early TD on 18y drive, but even bigger was Arnold's REC of KO FUM in EZ. Red Raiders (2-1) had trailed 14-0 at H before QB Joe Barnes led 2 TD drives, capping 1st with 12y TD pass to WR Lawrence Williams. Texas Tech FB James Moseley provided some hope with 21y TD scamper on opening play of 4th Q. But, Texas QB Marty Akins drove Longhorns downfield to clinching 3y TD run by HB Tommy Landry.

SOUTHERN CALIFORNIA 7 Oklahoma 7: Calling game their "Coliseum Bowl," Sooners, ineligible for post-season play, dominated stats but not scoreboard against top-ranked Trojans (2-0-1). Oklahoma (1-0-1) found itself in 7-0 hole as they blew opportunities and lost 3 early FUMs, 2 among team's 1st 4 plays. OU's 3rd FUM, on punt RET, set up 25y Trojans TD drive, capped by 15y pass from QB Pat Haden to WR J.K. McKay. QB Steve Davis (21/102y rushing) tied game at 7-7 on 2y TD run. Oklahoma enjoyed 339y to 161y advantage, with FB Wayman Clark rushing for 126y. OU D held TB Anthony Davis to 57y rushing and Haden to 59y passing. USC's 14-game win streak was snapped, but its unbeaten run was extended to 20.

October 6, 1973

NORTH CAROLINA STATE 28 North Carolina 26: QB Dave Buckey (7-10/130y, TD) tossed 36y TD to WR Paul Havance and ran in another score in leading Wolfpack (3-2). Game turned on FUM by North Carolina TB Billy Hite on NC State 1YL after he made 18y run. Riding strong backs of TB Willie Burden and FB Stan Fritts, NC State pounded 99y for TD and 14-3 lead it held at H. After Havance's TD upped Wolfpack advantage to 21-3, Tar Heels (1-3) rallied behind QB Bill Paschall (12-17/140y, 2 TDs, INT). UNC scored 2 TDs, each with 2-pt conv to pull within 21-19. State TB Roland Hooks then returned KO 39y that, with ensuing 15y PEN against UNC for piling on, set up clinching 1y TD run by Burden. Paschall closed scoring with 2nd TD pass to TE Charles Waddell.

ALABAMA 28 Georgia 14: Final result did not tell entire story as Crimson Tide (4-0) stunningly scored 15 pts in final 2:22. Alabama QB Gary Rutledge capped winning 3-play, 59y TD drive, that included 36y run by HB Willie Shelby, with his 7y TD run, and HB Randy Billingsly scored from 17y out with 34 secs remaining to provide final margin. Georgia (2-1-1) had scored go-ahead TD in 4th Q on 8y run by TB Jimmy Poulos to cap 33y drive set up by 35y punt RET by WB Glynn Harrison. K Allan Leavitt made 2 FGs for Bulldogs, including 54y effort that tied school record. Tide rushed for 345y with 8 players toting ball led by QB Gary Rutledge (12/74y).

AUBURN 14 Mississippi 7: Needing depth at RB, Tigers (3-1) switched DB Rick Neel prior to game. Not even getting in game until 2nd H, Neel (10/77y) still proved to be Auburn hero, racing for winning 33y TD with 90 secs left and becoming team's leading rusher. Persistent Rebels (2-3) countered with trip to Auburn 10YL with 11 secs remaining before Tigers DB Roger Mitchell picked off pass in EZ. Auburn had scored 1st H's only pts on 3y run by QB Wade Whatley. Mississippi had tied it 7-7 in 4th Q on 20y pass from QB Stan Bounds to WR Rick Kimbrough.

TENNESSEE 28 Kansas 27: It appeared that Kansas (3-1) QB David Jaynes (35-58/394y, 3 TDs, INT) would scoop up upset victory. But after throwing 17y TD to WR Bruce Adams to pare deficit to 1 pts with 3:15 remaining, Jaynes could not find open receiver on 2-pt conv and was forced to run. Tennessee (4-0) stopped Jaynes

on 1YL to remain undefeated. Leading stop on Jaynes was Vols S Eddie Brown, who had brilliant game. After blocking FG attempt with his face, effort that cost him 3 teeth, Brown added 74y INT RET, 48y KO RET that set up TD, and FUM REC that led to TD. TB Haskel Stanback rushed for 2 TDs for Volunteers.

OHIO STATE 27 Washington State 3: Woody Hayes' "I told you so" Ohio State (3-0) juggernaut stayed no. 1 in country even after slow, 1st down-free start by its O. FB Bruce Elia, filling in for FB Champ Henson who was out with torn knee that would prevent his playing again in 1973, rumbled 17y for TD in 2nd Q and 9y TD in 3rd Q. These bullish runs enhanced swift gait of TB Archie Griffin, who rushed for 128y, as he roared through Cougars (1-3) D for 16y TD run in 3rd Q after having fielded 6y TD pass in 2nd Q. Washington State gained reasonably effective 246y O but had only K Joe Danelo's 41y FG late in 2nd Q to show for it.

Missouri 17 SOUTHERN METHODIST 7: Ferocious Tigers D held nation's top-rated rushing attack in check as early-season surprise foes battled. Twice, Missouri (4-0) stopped SMU on 4th-and-2 deep in Tiger territory. TB Tommy Reamon rushed for 119y to lead Missouri, while DB Johnny Moseley took punt RET 74y for TD early in 4th Q. Moseley bounced off 6 would-be tacklers to ice game at 17-7. After averaging 438y of O in opening 3 wins, SMU (3-1) was held to 168y and lost 4 FUMs. TE Oscar Roan scored SMU's TD with 9y catch in 2nd Q.

Texas Tech 20 OKLAHOMA STATE 7: Cowboys (3-1) fumbled away their 11th ranking, dropping ball 8 times and losing 4 FUMs. Oklahoma State twice fumbled punts that led to Texas Tech (3-1) TDs, and 2 other FUMs led to FGs. Both Raiders TDs were scored by backup QB Jimmy Carmichael, who replaced injured starter QB Joe Barnes in 2nd Q. QB Brent Blackman (17/97y) scored sole OSU TD on 9y run that briefly tied game at 7-7 in 2nd Q. Blackman left with separated shoulder and Cowboy O left with him. Red Raiders rushed for 277y, with FB John Garner leading way with 16/119y.

Penn State 19 AIR FORCE 9: Penn State TB John Cappelletti piled up 184y rushing and 2 TDs in game decided within 31-sec span of 2nd Q. Moments after Nittany Lions (4-0) QB Tom Shuman hit WR Gary Hayman on 38y TD toss, Air Force QB Mike Worden lost FUM. Penn State recovered to poise Cappelletti for 4y TD run and 13-3 lead. Cappelletti's 2nd TD run, 8y effort in 3rd Q, bumped lead up to 19-3. Air Force (2-1) highlight was 45y TD pass from QB Rich Haynie to FB Bill Berry.

Arizona State 67 NEW MEXICO 24: Romp by Sun Devils (4-0) maintained their pace with nation's football elite. QB Danny White (18-28/344y, 4 TDs) led Arizona State O that racked up 709y. ASU HB Woody Green rushed for 119y and TD, while FB Ben Malone added 116y and TD. White hooked up with WB Morris Owens (7/168y) for 3 TDs, including 60y bomb, as Sun Devils built 28-3 3rd Q lead. QB Don Woods threw 2 TDs to WR Ken Lege as Lobos rallied to 35-17 before ASU left 32-pt avalanche in 4th Q. New Mexico (1-3) gained 405y in defeat. Sun Devils reached 67-pt total for 2nd straight week.

CALIFORNIA 54 Washington 49: Depth at QB was on display as teams poured it on. Cal starter QB Vince Ferragamo left due to injury in 2nd Q with Bears (2-2) up 21-7; replacement QB Steve Bartkowski quickly threw 75y bomb to WR Mike Shaughnessy. Bartkowski threw another TD pass of 52y to TB Howard Strickland on screen pass that bumped lead up to 37-7. By that point, desperate Washington (1-3) had turned to 3rd-string QB Chris Rowland. All Rowland did was set school record, while tying conf mark of Cal's Craig Morton in 1963, with 5 TD passes to rally Huskies. Cal TB Chuck Muncie rushed for 126y, 3 TDs as Bears gained 625y and scored just enough to win. Bears hurt their cause with 18 PENs/194y.

October 13, 1973

Pittsburgh 35 WEST VIRGINIA 7: Pitt TB Tony Dorsett marked his 1st game against bitter rival in "Backyard Brawl" by rushing for 150y and 3 TDs. Panthers (2-2-1) D also earned kudos with 2 INTs that led to Dorsett TDs and extra hard hitting, including blow that knocked Mountaineers QB Abe Dillon out of game with separated shoulder in 3rd Q. Pitt QB Bill Daniels scored 2 short TDs in 1st H as it built 14-7 H lead. Mountaineers (3-2) had scored TD on 8y pass from Dillon to WR Marshall Mills, but were hampered by QB injuries as they were shut out in 2nd H.

NORTH CAROLINA STATE 24 Maryland 22: Wolfpack (4-2) devoured 3 FUMs and INT by Maryland (3-2) sub QB Ben Kinard—in for injured QB Bob Avellini—to jump to 17-0 lead. QB Dave Buckey fired 39y TD to WR John Gargano and scored himself to put NC State ahead. "We couldn't keep going the way we were," said Terps coach Jerry Claiborne, so he reluctantly went with QB Al Neville, who had dislocated his non-throwing elbow 2 weeks earlier. Neville (19-32/212y, TD) sparked comeback with 10y TD pass to TE Walter White (8/112y) late in 2nd Q, but K Steve Mike-Mayer missed critical x-pt. Maryland TB Louis Carter wrapped pair of 2nd H TDs around TD by NC State RB Willie Burden, so Terps trailed 24-22 after Mike-Mayer made 32y FG, 18th of his career, with 4:20 left. In trying for new school FG record and win with 16 sec left, Mike-Mayer badly hooked 40y FG try, thanks to bad snap.

Louisiana State 20 AUBURN 6: Pts would be hard to come by as respective Ds had allowed combined 78 pts entering contest. With LSU (5-0) trailing 6-0, QB Mike Miley connected with WR Al Coffee for 51y pass to set up 5y TD run by TB Brad Davis. Davis' scoring run marked 1st time all season Auburn (3-2) had surrendered rushing TD. On next possession, Miley and Davis teamed up for 28y scoring pass. Auburn had taken early lead on 2y scoring run by TB Rick Neel, on drive set up by blocked punt by DE David Hughes at LSU 30YL. Bengals D was so dominate from that point, that Auburn managed only 90y for game, compared to LSU's 357y.

Michigan 31 MICHIGAN STATE 0: Wolverines (5-0) DB Dave Brown set game's tone with 53y punt TD RET for 7-0 lead in 1st Q. With Brown and his D mates blanking Spartans (1-4), Michigan slowly stretched its lead. K Mike Lantry booted 35y FG for 10-0 1st Q lead, and TB Gil Chapman busted loose for 53y scoring run and 17-0 H lead. At that point, Michigan State had been limited to 2 1st downs and was on way to losing 6 FUMs for game. Wolverines tacked on 2 insurance TDs in 4th Q, including 6y scoring pass from QB Dennis Franklin to TE Paul Seal.

Ohio State 24 WISCONSIN 0: Buckeyes (4-0) beat up Badgers behind their rushing attack and D, exploiting 423y to 104y run advantage. Ohio TB Archie Griffin rushed for 169y and FB Bruce Elia pounded for 2 short TDs, while D held nation's 8th-best run attack in check. Closest Wisconsin (1-4) got to Ohio State EZ was 34YL, midway through 4th Q. On next play, LB Rich Middleton picked off pass to end threat. Badgers TB Billy Marek rushed for meager 49y to lead O that mustered only 202y.

MISSOURI 13 Nebraska 12: Heroic Missouri (5-0) soph DE Bob McRoberts tipped vital 2-pt pass to teammate DB Tony Gillick in closing secs to seal win. Huskers (4-1) had pulled within 13-12 on 22y pass from QB David Humm to WB Rich Bahe that capped blistering 4-play, 72y drive. Game's turning point occurred moments earlier when Nebraska FB Randy Borg fumbled punt on his 4YL. Tigers C Scott Anderson recovered it with 2:10 left to set'up FB Tom Mulkey's 1y plunge to raise score to 13-6. Earlier in 2nd H, MG Harris Butler blocked 18y FG attempt by Nebraska K Rich Sanger to end big Huskers threat at Tigers 2YL. Mizzou earned only 7 1st downs and 170y to Nebraska's 21 and 444y, still avenged 62-0 defeat in 1972.

Oklahoma 52 Texas 13 (Dallas): Sooners (3-0-1) racked up most pts scored on Texas since 1908 by going to air game more than usual and completing 6-7/225y and 3 long TDs. OU HB Joe Washington opened scoring with option pass of 40y to WR Tinker Owens (4/163y). After 2 FGs for Texas (2-2) trimmed things to 7-6, Sooners QB Steve Davis (5-6/185y) hooked up with Owens on 63y scoring pass and threw 47y TD WR Billy Brooks. Davis added 2 rushing TDs in 3rd Q as Oklahoma stretched lead to 35-6. Texas FB Roosevelt Leaks bulled his way to 82y rushing, but became less threatening with each Sooner TD. Longhorns hurt their chances with 5 TOs in 2nd H. Frightening reality for Oklahoma opponents would be play of youngsters as soph Washington led OU with 117y rushing and every TD was scored by players with at least 2 years of eligibility left.

Arkansas 13 BAYLOR 7: Baylor (2-3) amazingly managed only single TD on 507y total O. Arkansas TB Dickey Morton was amazing as well with 271y rushing, highest single-game total in school history, with highlight-reel TD runs of 68y and 81y. QB Neal Jeffrey threw for 342y, completing 15-17 in 1st H when Bears reached scoreboard on 7y TD run by TB Gary Lacy. Razorbacks (3-2) held on when Jeffrey whipped late Baylor drive to Arkansas 8YL before CB Rollen Smith ended threat with GL INT he returned to 25YL.

Ucla 59 STANFORD 13: Bruins (4-1) O onslaught continued as they piled up school-record 621y rushing, scoring on 6 of 7 1st H possessions. HB Kermit Johnson rushed 11/168y, including 51y scoring jaunt 1st time he touched ball, and FB James McAlister rushed 14/117y, 3 TDs before he left game in 2nd Q with bruised knee. Johnson and McAlister had been dazzling tandem since days together at Blair High School in California. Cards were led by QB Mike Boryla, who threw for 18-29/151y. UCLA had historical shadow over Stanford (2-3): 59 were most pts permitted by Cardinals since 72-0 loss to Bruins in 1954.

October 20, 1973

(Fri) Houston 30 MIAMI 7: Cougars (6-0) scored twice within 20 secs in 3rd Q to turn fortunes their way. On go-ahead score, Houston QB D.C. Nobles (13-22/223y, TD) threw across middle into Miami (3-2) territory but ball was deflected—right to RB Reggie Cherry as he fell into EZ. On ensuing KO, Canes DB Greg Ingram lost FUM with Cougars special teamer Tommy Kaiser making REC, 1 of 5 Miami TOs. Nobles then tossed 20y pass to WR Bryan Willingham to set up insurance 1y TD dive by RB Leonard Parker. Houston's Cherry rushed for 104y with 66y coming on 4th Q TD run. Canes' big play was QB Ed Carney's 71y TD pass to TE Phil August in 3rd Q.

Pittsburgh 28 BOSTON COLLEGE 14: Eagles (3-2) made frosh TB Tony Dorsett earn every bit of his 109y, but O could not keep up with Pitt. Dorsett's 11y scoring run in 2nd Q bumped Panthers to 14-0. After BC TB Mike Esposito scored from 1y out to halve deficit, Pitt QB Bill Daniels scored 2nd TD on 1y keeper for 21-7 H lead. Dorsett scored again in 2nd H on 1y run to clinch matters. BC QB Gary Marangi finished scoring with 26y pass to WR Bob Watts in 4th Q.

RUTGERS 24 Delaware 7: Scarlet Knights ended Delaware's 20-game win streak as TB J.J. Jennings, nation's leader in rushing (738y) and scoring (86pts), gained 131y on ground with TD. Game was tied 7-7 late in 2nd Q when Blue Hens (6-1) marched downfield. S Tony Pawlik made crucial INT at GL for 1st of his 3 key INTs that also halted 2 3rd Q Delaware drives on Rutgers' 9YL and 20YL. QB Gary Smolyn had big game at helm of Scarlet Knights attack, hitting 7-10/105y, TD and rushing for 8y TD.

NAVY 42 Air Force 6: Game was expected to be close, but that changed with Middies' 21-pt burst in 2nd Q for 28-0 H lead. Navy (3-3) TB Cleveland Cooper rushed for 3 TDs and QB Al Glenny threw 41y scoring pass to WR Larry Van Loan. Glenny was not through, passing for 2 more TDs in 2nd H and leading O that gained 243y on ground and 230y in air. Air Force (2-3) TB Chris Milodragovich scored on 1y run in 4th Q to prevent shutout.

Clemson 24 DUKE 8: Blue Devils (1-5) built up y, but were scoreless in 1st H despite having 4 of 5 possessions reach at least Clemson 35YL. Tigers (3-3), on other hand, tallied 3 TDs and FG. Clemson opened with 78y scoring drive that featured QB Ken Pengitore passes of 40y to TE Bennie Cunningham and 28y to WR Gordy Bengel. HB Smiley Sanders finished that voyage with 1y TD run for 1st of his 2 scoring runs. Later in 1st Q, Sanders scored again, capping 36y drive set up by Duke's 2nd of 6 TOs. Devils finally scored in 4th Q when 3rd-string QB Roger Neighborhall connected with WR Troy Slade on 59y TD pass.

ALABAMA 42 Tennessee 21 (Birmingham): Battle of unbeatens was fittingly tied until 4th Q, when 3-TD blowout within 5-min span put Tennessee (5-1) away. S Robin Cary took punt 63y for TD and then HB Wilbur Jackson went 80y for TD that broke open game for Alabama (6-0). Cary added FUM REC of KO on Vols 3YL to set up Bama's final score. QB Condredge Holloway accounted for all Tennessee pts, throwing TD passes of 64y to TE Mitchell Gravitt and 20y to WR John Yarbrough and running 6y for another. Tide had scored on its opening 2 possessions, but became bogged down against Vols' excellent D. Loss snapped Vols' 11-game win streak.

VANDERBILT 18 Georgia 14: Commodores (4-2) snapped 12-game conf losing streak as K Hawkins Golden booted 4 FGs and QB Fred Fisher threw 15y TD to TE Barry Burton. Vandy TB Lonnie Sadler rushed for 109y. Bulldogs (3-2-1) had built 14-3 advantage at H behind QB Andy Johnson, who threw and ran for TDs. Vanderbilt D allowed only 2 1st downs after H and picking off 2 of Johnson's passes in game's final 5 mins. Special team play was crucial for more than FGs as P Burton nailed 79y punt to Bulldogs 1YL in 3rd Q, thus killing field position for Georgia for rest of 2nd H. For 1st time since 1963, Vanderbilt owned 3-game win streak, while Georgia coach Vince Dooley considered outcome "one of the most disappointing losses, if not the most disappointing loss, we have had."

OKLAHOMA 34 Colorado 7: Sooners (4-0-1) talent pool was quickly becoming too deep for their opponents. This game's hero was FB Waymon Clark, who rushed for 172y, TD. Oklahoma D excelled, turning game around on S Randy Hughes' 96y INT RET and finishing off Buffs (4-2) with GLS in 3rd Q. Most dazzling play from Sooners O was 37y scoring pass from QB Steve Davis to TE Wayne Hoffman for 1st TD, with Davis opening play by pitching to HB Joe Washington who then returned favor. Washington added 188y rushing and team's 3rd TD on 1y run in 3rd Q. Colorado had taken 7-0 lead on 3y run by FB Bo Matthews.

NEBRASKA 10 Kansas 9: Although Huskers shut down Kansas (4-2) QB David Jaynes (10-32/90y), they trailed until late FG. Key play was Nebraska LB Bob Nelson's 4th Q INT, which was converted into K Rich Sanger's winning 28y FG. Cornhuskers (5-1) had grabbed 7-0 lead on early 80y drive to IB Tony Davis' 2y TD. Mistakes then set up all pts for Jayhawks. Nebraska FB Maury Damkroger's FUM on own 36YL was converted into 26y FG by K Bob Swift, and in 3rd Q DB Randy Borg lost ball on punt that KU TE Ken Saathoff nabbed on Nebraska 18YL. TB Delvin Williams made 4y TD run, but Nebraska DB Ardell Johnson made crucial x-pt block.

KANSAS STATE 21 Iowa State 19: TB Isaac Jackson put on big show, rushing for 157y and scoring 3 TDs to lead Wildcats (4-2). Kansas State jumped to 14-6 lead in 2nd Q by trading Jackson's 2 TDs for FGs from ISU K Tom Goedjen. Cyclones (2-3) then marched 75y to 5y scoring pass from QB Wayne Stanley to TE Keith Krepfle that cut deficit to 14-12 after failed conv. After teams traded 3rd Q TOs, Jackson iced game with 28y romp to EZ with 3 mins left, which would serve to offset 3y scoring run by Iowa State TB Mike Strachan that came moments later.

Texas 34 ARKANSAS 6: Teams battled to 6-0 Texas (3-2) lead at H, but FB Roosevelt Leaks scored on TD runs of 43y and 59y as Longhorns broke open game with 21-pt 3rd Q burst. Leaks rushed 24/209y, 3 TDs of his team's 416y rushing. Longhorns also scored on other 2nd H big plays: WR Jimmy Moore took punt RET to 73y TD, and HB Raymond Clayborn raced 85y to tally. Arkansas (3-3) avoided shutout by blocking punt deep in Texas territory that CB Rollen Smith returned 1y for score. TB Dickey Morton rushed for 68y to lead Hog O that gained 304y, but failed to penetrate Texas GL. Arkansas' best opportunity died at Texas 5YL when LB Glen Gaspard halted Morton on 4th-and-1.

Texas Tech 31 ARIZONA 17: Ranks of unbeaten teams were thinned as Wildcats (5-1) stumbled against determined Texas Tech (5-1). Red Raiders DE Tommy Cones set up winning TD with blocked punt early in 4th Q, which was recovered on Arizona 21YL. HB Lawrence Williams (9/78y) scored his 2nd TD 4 plays later on 8y run. FB James Mosley added clinching 41y scoring run later in 4th Q. Raiders had opened 16-0 2nd Q lead, with Williams tallying on 18y run. Wildcats then ran off 17 straight pts to wrest lead away as HB Willie Hamilton (17/113y) scored Arizona's 1st TD on 4y run in 2nd Q. Cones' blocked punt and 5 TOs spelled difference for Cats.

Ucla 24 WASHINGTON STATE 13 (Spokane): Wishbone O of nation's top scoring team, UCLA (5-1), was nearly wrecked by hustling and gambling D of Cougars (1-5), led by LBs Gary Larsen, Clyde Warehime, and Tom Poe. FB Charlie "Choo Choo" Schuhmann (13/105y) filled in admirably for injured FB James McAlister and scored decisive 53y weaving TD in 3rd Q that provided 17-7 lead for Bruins. Washington State held UCLA to meager 3-0 lead in 1st H, and trimmed it to 10-7 in 3rd Q as Wazzu's 80y TD drive was spiced by 18 and 12y bursts by FB Andrew Jones (24/124y). HB Kermit Johnson mined his 92y rushing into 2 TDs while going past Kenny Washington (1937-39) as UCLA's all-time leading rusher to date.

ARIZONA STATE 52 Brigham Young 12: Arizona State (6-0) unleashed its potent O as QB Danny White threw for 17-25/303y, 3 TDs and rushed for 66y and another TD. Not to be outdone by his teammate, HB Woody Green rushed for 128y, while catching 2 scoring catches, and FB Ben Malone added 2 TD runs. After surrendering 36 straight pts, BYU (1-4) finally scored on 9y pass from QB Gary Shiede to redoubtable WR Jay Miller. Sun Devils played up to their nickname, gaining 652y despite 95-degree heat as afternoon game was played for TV.

AP Poll October 22

1 Ohio State (35)	1126	11 Arizona State	283
2 Alabama (12)	1042	12 Houston	280
3 Oklahoma (8)	953	13 UCLA	207
4 Michigan (1)	857	14 Tennessee	148
5 Penn State (4)	709	15 Tulane	88
6 Southern California	629	16 Miami (Ohio)	31
7 Missouri (1)	541	17 Kansas	21
8 Notre Dame	508	18 Texas Tech	20
9 Louisiana State	402	19 Texas	16
10 Nebraska	300	20 Richmond	13

October 27, 1973

Dartmouth 24 HARVARD 18: In storming to 24-3 H lead, aroused Big Green (2-3) took 2nd step in season-closing 6-game victory skein that reaped Ivy League crown. Unbeaten Harvard (4-1) was limited to 39y rushing in 1st H, but mustered its forces in 2nd H only to be discouraged thrice within Dartmouth's 10YL. After recovering early FUM at 11YL, Crimson settled for small lead on K Bruce Tetirick's 28y FG. QB Tom Snickenberger combined with HB John Souba on 74y run-and-lateral play to set up Snickenberger's TD sneak, soon followed by Snickenberger's 8y TD pass. Harvard finally got going behind FB Neal Miller (16/114y) who ran for 37, 31, and 21y gains. HB Alky Tsitsos ran for and caught TDs, but Crimson botched its chances later.

Louisiana State 33 SOUTH CAROLINA 29: LSU QB Mike Miley's 2y run with 1:03 remaining prevented upset in exciting game featuring 5 lead changes. Winning drive took Miley less than 2 mins to achieve, key play being his 48y completion to WR Ben Jones. Gamecocks (4-3) had snatched lead moments earlier on QB Jeff Grantz's 9y TD pass to WR Scott Thomas with 3:26 left. South Carolina had earned early 12-0 lead on 2 TD runs by RB Lynn Hodgin, before LSU (7-0) reeled off 16 straight pts. Teams then traded TDs, FGs, and then TDs again to wrap up thriller.

AUBURN 7 Houston 0: Cougars (6-1) O entered contest with 31-pt scoring avg, but were blanked by inspired effort by Auburn D. LB Ken Bernich led way with 22 tackles, as Auburn (5-2) became 1st team in 89 games to whitewash Houston. Thanks to 241y rushing, Houston had 3 opportunities when it cracked Auburn 20YL. Cougars failed to score in clutch and K Ricky Terrell missed 2 FGs. Final Cougars threat ended on Auburn 12YL when Tigers LB David Langner broke up 4th down pass. Auburn TB Mitzi Jackson rushed for 21/112y to lead O that scored on its 1st possession: 7y run by frosh QB Chris Vacarella.

TULANE 23 Georgia Tech 14: Quarter-century after his father starred for Tulane, backup TB Eddie Price, Jr., rushed for 2 TDs including 19y game-winner in 3rd Q. By game's end he was backup no more. Green Wave (6-0) rode their ground game for 260y. QB Jim Stevens sparked Georgia Tech (2-5), throwing for 211y and launching 69y scoring strike to WR Jimmy Robinson.

Michigan 34 MINNESOTA 7: Wolverines (7-0) needed only 5 possessions in 1st H to grab 24-0 H lead and end Little Brown Jug upset hopes of improved Minnesota. Golden Gophers (3-4) proved to be gracious hosts by losing FUMs on 2nd and 3rd plays from scrimmage to put themselves in 10-0 hole from outset. Michigan FB Ed Shuttlesworth and TB Gordon Bell each scored 2 TDs as Wolverines rushed for 275y. Minnesota used trick play to score its sole TD in 3rd Q as HB Rick Upchurch tossed 36y pass to WR Vince Fuller to cut deficit to 27-7 entering 4th Q.

NOTRE DAME 23 Southern California 14: Notre Dame (6-0) Gs Gerry DiNardo and Frank Pomarico, HS teammates from Brooklyn, pulled out of line and delivered punishing blocks all game. Duo sprung HB Eric Penick, who had been benched for fumbling in 1972 loss to USC, on game-breaking 85y TD run on opening play from scrimmage in 2nd H. Penick's score made it 20-7 for Fighting Irish, enough for their inspired D. Notre Dame defenders swarmed over Trojans (5-1-1) TB Anthony Davis, limiting him to 55y rushing and forcing crucial 4th Q FUM. Davis scored TD, but it was far cry from 1972's 6-TD scorching. USC's passing attack also was held in check as frosh CB Luther Bradley keyed aggressive Irish secondary with 2 INTs. Notre Dame churned up 316y rushing compared to 68y on ground for Trojans, and it showed in ND's 39:36 possession time total. Defeat snapped Trojans' impressive 23-game unbeaten streak.

COLORADO 17 Missouri 13: Missouri (6-1) scored 10 straight 4th Q pts on 22y run by QB John Cherry and 21y FG by K Greg Hill to take 13-10 lead. But, Tigers fumbled away chance to remain undefeated just when it seemed they were on verge of clinching victory. Colorado (5-2) D stiffened, forcing FUM at its 24YL; O then marched 76y to victory. Buffs FB Jim Kelleher delivered winning play on 4y run that capped 5-play drive. March was highlighted by 40y scramble by QB Clyde Crutchmer on play in which he was nearly sacked. Before being injured in 3rd Q, new Colorado career rushing leader TB Charlie Davis rushed for 76y and TD.

Nebraska 17 OKLAHOMA STATE 17: Shunning FG late in 4th Q, Nebraska (5-1-1) went on 4th-and-goal from 1YL only to be stopped. Huskers IB Tony Davis was nailed by Oklahoma State D, led by LB Cleveland Vann, who had scored 1st Q TD on 25y INT RET. Vann's TD gave Cowboys (3-2-1) 10-3 lead after teams had traded early FGs, including 51y effort by OSU K Abby Daigle. Foes alternated 1y TD runs, but try for 4th such score was no charm for Davis. Oklahoma State QB Brent Blackman rushed for 141y.

AP Poll October 29

1 Ohio State (36)	1148	11 Tennessee	287
2 Alabama (12)	1052	12 Missouri	243
3 Oklahoma (9)	961	13 Nebraska	196
4 Michigan (1)	876	14 Tulane	185
5 Notre Dame	754	15 Texas Tech	79
6 Penn State (4)	740	16 Miami (Ohio)	54
7 Louisiana State	518	17 Colorado	50
8 Arizona State	432	18 Houston	46
9 Southern California	331	19t Auburn	33
10 UCLA	307	19t Texas	33

November 3, 1973

Georgia 35 TENNESSEE 31: Embattled Vols coach Bill Battle took heat for his losing gamble. Ahead 31-28 late in 4th Q and with ball on its own 28YL, Tennessee (6-2) unaccountably tried fake punt. FB Steve Chancey, in at up-back blocking position, received direct snap, but was swarmed over for 2y loss. Georgia (4-3-1) scored winning TD 5 plays later on 8y scramble by QB Andy Johnson. Johnson improvised winning play when he was unable to get handoff to RB. Vols led 31-21 after 3 Qs as QB Condredge Holloway threw TD and ran for another before leaving with injury.

Florida 12 AUBURN 8: Win at Auburn was 1st-ever for Gators (3-4) and was sweet as soph QB Don Gaffney won his 1st start. Although Gaffney threw 22y TD pass to WR Joel Parker, his biggest contribution was handing off to FB Vince Kendrick. Kendrick bulled way to 119y and winning 5y TD in 3rd Q, while setting up Florida's 1st score with 40y run. Tigers (5-3) gained only 119y and were hampered by loss for season of leading rusher, TB Mitzi Jackson, to 2nd Q knee injury.

KENTUCKY 34 Tulane 7: Kentucky RB Sonny Collins surpassed 1,000y mark, racking up 176y rushing and 3 TDs. Kentucky (4-4) proudly reached 4-win mark for 1st time in 8 long years. Tulane (6-1) entered game with high hopes, but its O was prevented from entering Wildcats territory until late in 3rd Q. Green Wave was able to score their sole TD after recovering FUM on Kentucky 11YL. Even with that break, Green Wave need 6 plays to reach EZ.

Ohio State 30 ILLINOIS 0: Inspired Illini (5-3) put up strong 1st H fight against top-ranked Buckeyes on "Ray Eliot Day," but could muster little O. Ohio State (7-0) was held to only 3 pts at H and 10 after 3rd Q, but Bucks busted out for 20 pts in 4th Q against tiring Illinois D. Ohio QB Cornelius Greene made 2 TD runs in 4th Q. In no way did it help Illini that they lost TOs deep in their own territory on consecutive plays. Ohio State LB Randy Gradishar led D that held Illinois to 74y and 5 1st downs. TB Archie Griffin rushed for 108y and TD as Buckeyes gained 341y rushing.

NEBRASKA 28 Colorado 16: IB Tony Davis ran for 2 TDs and QB David Humm threw for 2 others as Nebraska (6-1-1) delighted Lincoln home crowd. Huskers marched 75y for opening TD, 10y pass to TE Brent Longwell, but most of all took advantage of 2 FUM RECs and blocked punt to break open game. Colorado (5-3) trailed 28-3 at H before rallying with 2 TDs, including 73y TD pass on flea-flicker from TB Billy Waddy to QB David Williams.

Texas 42 SOUTHERN METHODIST 14: Longhorns (5-2) all but locked up Cotton Bowl berth as FB Roosevelt Leaks bulled way to single-game conf rushing record 342y, breaking mark of Texas A&M's Bob Smith, who made 297y in 1950. Leaks had 206y rushing in 2nd H, 53y on final TD run busting up middle behind C Bill Wyman when he simply was trying to break Smith's mark; he finished 8y shy of NCAA record set by Michigan State's Eric Allen in 1971. Texas actually trailed 14-0 at H as SMU (4-3) scored on big plays by TE Oscar Roan on 74y reception and HB Alvin Maxson on 67y run. Ponies twice stopped Texas at their 1YL. Longhorns would not be denied in 2nd H, scoring 3 quick TDs including 94y punt RET by WR Jimmy Moore.

Texas Christian 34 BAYLOR 28: Bears (2-5) QB Neal Jeffrey threw for 339y in defeat, but Jeffrey's final incomplete would overshadow anything else he did. With 22 secs left, Jeffrey stopped clock with team on TCU 4YL by throwing ball away. Unfortunately it came on 4th down, and game was over. TB Mike Luttrell ignored his banged up leg to rush for 133y and 2 TDs to power Horned Frogs (3-4), who led 34-7 in 4th Q. Jeffrey then led 21-pt 4th Q surge, throwing 2 TDs before his final misstep.

HOUSTON 34 Florida State 3: Winless Seminoles (0-8) were ripped for 606y O by rampaging Houston (7-1). On Cougars' 1st series, QB D.C. Nobles (7-11/189y) scampered 56y to set up 1st of 2 TDs by RB Leonard Parker (24/151y). Florida State, which was to be limited to 188y O, countered with its only pts. FSU K Ahmet Ashin made 52y FG after frosh DL John Thomas recovered FUM at own 42YL. Parker scored at end of 60y trip midway in 2nd Q, and Nobles made it 20-3 at H with 83y bomb to WR Bryan Willingham.

UTAH 36 Arizona State 31: Utes (5-3) withstood near freezing conditions and 3 Arizona State TDs in 2nd H to snap 12-game win streak of Sun Devils. QB Don Van Galder ran for 2 TDs and passed for 2 others as Utah jumped out to comfy 30-10 H lead. ASU (7-1) made 10 ugly TOs. Especially painful was 3 lost FUMs turned into TDs during 2-min span of 2nd Q. Clinching score, Van Galder's 9y pass to WR Steve Odom, came on 95y drive after heroic GLS. Trailing by 5 pts, Sun Devils had 1st down on Utah 4YL, but lost 1y on next 4 plays. Arizona State closed scoring when QB Danny White hit WR Greg Hudson with 51y TD strike with 9 ticks left.

AP Poll November 5

1 Ohio State (35)	1146	11 Nebraska	310
2 Alabama (14)	1096	12 Texas Tech	133
3 Oklahoma (7)	910	13 Texas	129
4 Michigan (1)	888	14 Arizona State	126
5 Notre Dame (1)	746	15 Houston	112
6 Penn State (4)	714	16 Tennessee	80
7 Louisiana State	580	17 Miami (Ohio)	75
8 Southern California	450	18 Kansas	15
9 UCLA	431	19 Kent State	14
10 Missouri	352	20 Pittsburgh	13

November 10, 1973

PENN STATE 35 North Carolina State 29: Penn State (9-0) needed every single y of TB John Cappelletti's 220y rushing to overcome Wolfpack. Cappelletti's biggest play, worthy of Heisman he would soon earn, was 27y scoring burst for his 3rd TD to break 29-29 deadlock. Lions WR Gary Hayman (6/112y) contributed to win with 83y punt TD RET and clutch catches to set up other scores. NC State (6-3), which enjoyed 14-9 H lead, rushed for 245y and scored 4 running TDs.

Notre Dame 31 PITTSBURGH 10: TOs, 7 in all, did in Panthers (5-3-1), who outgained Irish with 383y as frosh TB Tony Dorsett tallied 209y rushing. FB Wayne Bullock answered call for Notre Dame (8-0) with 4 TDs among his 167y rushing. Dorsett's total was highest ever recorded against any Fighting Irish edition. ND O was hampered by QB Tom Clements' pulled stomach muscle, but DB Mike Townsend sparkled, catching Dorsett after 65y run to save TD, breaking up 2 passes in EZ, and picking off pass to stop another long Pitt drive.

Florida 11 Georgia 10 (Jacksonville): Soph QB Don Gaffney upped record to 2-0 as new Florida (4-4) starter, throwing 18y TD pass to WR Lee McGriff and then hitting TE Hank Foldberg for winning 2-pt conv with 3:48 left. Gaffney was 4-5/66y of clutch 80y drive. Bulldogs (4-4-1) had taken 7-3 H lead on 1 of QB Andy Johnson's 3 completions: 15y pass to TE Richard Appleby. Georgia pushed lead to 10-3 on 42y FG by K Alan Leavitt, who missed 60y effort at game's end.

OHIO STATE 35 Michigan State 0: There were 2 telling tales of Ohio State's massacre of Michigan State (3-6): Spartans were nearly error-free with no PENs, no INTs, and only 1 lost FUM. Still, they lost 35-0 because only 11 plays were run on Buckeyes (8-0) side of 50YL. Ohio CB Neal Colzie returned 8 punts/170y, including 43y TD in 2nd Q. Buckeyes T John Hicks hammered blocks so well that FB Bruce Elia had no resistance in scoring 3 short TDs. Spartans O, run by future coach, slender QB Tyrone Willingham (1-2/6y), could manage only 94y.

Michigan 21 ILLINOIS 6: Although Fighting Illini (5-4) put Wolverines behind for 1st time all season with 41y FG by K Dan Beaver in 2nd Q, home team simply could not compete at line of scrimmage. After allowing Beaver's 2nd FG, Wolverines soon grabbed 7-6 lead by converting FUM into 1y TD run by FB Ed Shuttlesworth. Michigan (9-0) pulled away, taking opening possession of 2nd H 67y to 33y TD run by WR Gil Chapman. Illinois had chances to stay in game thanks to 4 FUM RECs, but could manage no pts in 2nd H. Final TD smacked of pure luck as TE Paul Seal snared deflected pitchout on Wolverines running play and raced 20y to EZ.

RICE 17 Arkansas 7: Rice (2-6) continued recent mastery of series in stretching unbeaten string against Hogs to 4 games. Arkansas (5-4) lost despite outgaining Owls 404y to 138y as Rice took advantage of 5 to 1 TO differential. Owls started scoring after CB Cullie Culpepper returned INT 55y to set up QB Tommy Kramer's 15y scoring run. Arkansas QB Mike Kirkland then lost FUM on own 31YL, which led to 46y FG by K Alan Pringle. Down 10-0 at H, Hogs marched 92y in 3rd Q to score their sole TD on 18y run by TB Dickey Morton. Arkansas would not reach EZ again, while Rice D finished off game with 29y INT return for TD by LB Richard Hollas.

SOUTHERN CALIFORNIA 27 Stanford 26: Indonesian K Chris Limahelu nailed 34y FG with 3 secs remaining to lift Trojans (7-1-1) past Stanford in another hotly-contested chapter of rivalry. FG was set up by clutch passing of QB Pat Haden, who hit 3 passes, 2/49y to TE Jim Obradovich, to move Southern California from its 30YL to Stanford (5-4) 17YL in less than 30 secs left. Cardinals had built 26-17 lead late in 4th Q as K Rod Garcia booted 4 FGs, including school-record 59y effort. Trojans quickly responded to draw within 26-24, needed only min to position Haden's 10y keeper.

AP Poll November 12

1 Ohio State (35)	1130	11 Texas	188
2 Alabama (13)	1068	12 Texas Tech	176
3 Oklahoma (10)	966	13 Arizona State	167
4 Michigan (1)	834	14 Missouri	115
5 Notre Dame (1)	767	15 Houston	112
6 Penn State (1)	648	16 Tennessee	80
7 Louisiana State	572	17 Miami (Ohio)	71
8 UCLA	469	18 Kansas	44
9 Southern California	407	19 Arizona	16
10 Nebraska	358	20 North Carolina State	15

November 17, 1973

SYRACUSE 24 Boston College 13: Orangemen (2-8) surprisingly won for outgoing coach Ben Schwaltzwalder, rushing for 332y as QB Bob Mitch gained 98y on ground and scored 2 TDs. Syracuse held 10-0 H lead, which they expanded by 7 pts before TB Mike Esposito rushed in 2 TDs for Eagles (5-4) to make things interesting. Mitch answered with his 2nd TD run to finish off Boston College, which gained 353y but 5 TOs prevented any hopes of staging rally.

Maryland 28 CLEMSON 13: Maryland (7-3) grabbed its 1st bowl bid since 1956 Orange Bowl as TB Louis Carter rushed for 127y, 3 TDs, including 50y burst that opened scoring. Tigers (5-5) answered with QB Ken Pengitore's 19y pass to WR Gordy Bengel to tie game. Despite edging Terps in O by 336y to 331y, Clemson self-destructed on Pengitore's 3 INTs, even though he hadn't thrown INT in last 6 games. Maryland made INT deep in Clemson's end, and another set up Terps TD.

North Carolina State 21 DUKE 3: Liberty Bowl came knocking for North Carolina State (7-3), which was on verge of clinching undefeated ACC crown. Wolfpack rebounded from stinging loss to Penn State and led all game against Devils. DB Eddie Poole made key INT, and TB Willie Burden scored twice. Fading Duke (1-8-1) could count only tie against Wake Forest among its last 8 tilts and clearly had worst record in its history to that point. Devils managed only FG by K Dave Malechek.

ALABAMA 43 Miami 13: Bama (9-0) scored twice on punt RETs to stretch score against hard-nosed Hurricanes. DT Rubin Carter's 16 tackles led Miami (5-4) D that contained awesome Crimson Tide rushing attack, surrendering "only" 282y, which was 233y below Tide's avg. Alabama QB Gary Rutledge threw 2 TDs: 69y effort to WR Johnny Sharpless and 9y pass to HB Randy Billingsley. Tide built 22-0 H lead, but Miami scored twice in 2nd H, including 78y pass from QB Coy Hall to WR Steve Marcantonio, but was victimized by 4 INTs, 2 nabbed by Bama CB Mike Washington.

MISSISSIPPI 28 Tennessee 18 (Jackson): Using new week, Mississippi coach Johnny Vaught installed new O, an offshoot of Wishbone called "L," that Vols (6-3) could not contain. TB Jim Reed, who came off bench in 2nd Q to rush for 137y, led Ole Miss rush attack. Reed's 2nd TD run put Rebels (5-5) up 21-3 in 3rd Q. Vols reserve QB Gary Valbuena—in relief of injured QB Condredge Holloway—threw 2nd H TDs of 23y to TB Paul Careathers and 31y to WR Stanley Morgan.

MICHIGAN STATE 10 Indiana 9: East Lansing crowd transformed from comfortable to nervous in short order in 4th Q. Long before that TB Mike Holt (16/99y) delighted fans with 54y romp for 2nd TD as Spartans (4-6) grabbed 7-0 H lead. K Dirk Kryt booted 33y kick for 10-0 lead early in 4th Q. Rally by Hoosiers (2-8) was sparked by booming 52y FG by K Frank Stavroff, but with O that gained only 175y they would need break to fully close deficit. State FB Clarence Bullock (19/80y) gave it to them, losing FUM on 1st play of next series. Indiana frosh FB Courtney Snyder took it from there, rushing 4/22y on drive to score 1y TD run. Indiana WR Mike Flanagan caught 2-pt ATT pass but was tackled before reaching EZ.

Oklahoma 48 KANSAS 20: Big 8's other 7 teams were growing fast, but were still not up to level of Sooners (8-0-1). Oklahoma scored 27 1st Q pts and then added 2 TDs in 2nd Q. OU was up 7-0 before its O got on field: CB Clyde Powers took INT of Kansas (6-3-1) QB David Jaynes 45y to score. Jaynes answered with 57y scoring pass to WR Emmett Edwards, but then Sooners' rout heated up. OU K Tony DiRienzo hit 60y FG to set Big 8 distance record, HB Joe Washington scored 1st of his 2 rushing TDs and QB Steve Davis got into mix with 48y scoring strike to TE Steve Hoffman. Soon Oklahoma had 41-12 lead. Jayhawks (6-3-1) prevented further damage with 4th Q INT by CB James Bowman, returned 92y for closing TD.

IOWA STATE 17 Missouri 7: Cyclones (3-6) won D struggle in upset as they held Missouri (7-3) to 119y O. Iowa State led 3-0 at H before QB Buddy Hardeman found TE Keith Krepfle for 9y TD pass. Down 10-0, Tigers concocted trick TD play: TB Chris Hoskins threw 4y scoring pass to WR Jim Sharp. But, Iowa State DE Lon Coleman finished off Mizzou with FUM REC at Tigers 18YL late in game. FB Phil Danowsky scored on 3y run 4 plays later.

RICE 24 Texas A&M 20: With only 2:27 remaining, Texas A&M (5-5) sent much of big Rice Stadium crowd sadly to exits by punching across FB Bucky Sams' 2y TD run for its only lead of day. Not so fast, Owls friends. It took only 13 secs for former Texas HS hurdles champ, Rice (3-6) HB Carl Swierc, to corral ensuing KO, sneak out of pack of players and roar 95y for winning TD with 2:14 left. Aggies young QB sensation, David Walker, then came off bench and passed A&M to 10YL with help from interference PEN on Owls. But with less than 30 secs left, Aggies inexplicably went with 2 runs that made it only to 5YL where Rice DL Cornelius Walker put final clamps on Walker. Although Rice gained only 160y on 50 O plays, it led 17-0 at H thanks to QB Fred Geisler's 2 TD passes, including beautiful 38y hookup with WR Ed Lofton. Owls were inspired to win twice more to finish 1973 on 4-game victory streak.

Air Force 27 ARIZONA 26: Wildcats (8-2) drove 83y in final 90 secs to pull within 27-26 on 14y TD pass from QB Bruce Hill (17-29/262y, 2 TDs, INT) to TE Tom Campbell. Hill pitched to HB Willie Hamilton on 2-pt conv ATT, but Falcons S Steve Heil came up to make tackle to end game. Air Force (6-3) K Dave Lawson's 28y 4th Q FG provided winning pts, set up by INT by LB Dennis Collins. Falcons QB Rich Haynie completed 20-32/243y, 2 TDs, both caught by WR Frank Murphy.

November 22-24, 1973

(Th'g) Alabama 21 LOUISIANA STATE 7: Big plays were deciding factor in clash of Top 10 teams as Crimson Tide (10-0) parlayed QB Gary Rutledge's 19y TD sprint, 49y TD pass play to TE George Pugh and 77y TD pass to WR Wayne Wheeler into 21-0 lead. Alabama D bent but did not break in allowing 212y rushing and 21 1st downs, but only Bengals TB Brad Davis' 40y TD run. LSU (9-1) could not keep 15-game win streak alive as it turned ball over 5 times, but became only team to outrush Tide during regular season. Davis led way with 143y on ground. Win was 500th in Alabama history and wrapped up its 3rd straight SEC title.

(Th'g) Texas 42 TEXAS A&M 13: Longhorns (8-2) easily won their 6th straight SWC title, although star FB Roosevelt Leaks badly sprained his knee in 3rd Q. Game was no longer in doubt; big Texas lead had been built on 373y rushing without passing attack. Steers QB Marty Akins rushed for 3 TDs, and frosh HB Raymond Clayborn chipped in with 2 TDs. Texas A&M (5-6) QB David Walker threw for 164y in defeat.

(Fri) OKLAHOMA 27 Nebraska 0: Years later, Nebraska coach Tom Osborne might still have nightmares about Selmon family. Brothers formed 3-man interior line that harassed Cornhuskers (8-2-1) all day, helping prevent visitors from crossing 50YL but once (Nebraska lost FUM on that penetration.). Sooners forced 5 TOs and held Huskers to 10 1st downs and measly 74y rushing. QB Steve Davis rushed for 114y and 3 TDs to lead Sooners, racing 47y on game's most explosive score when he burst through short-yardage D to find no defender between him and Nebraska EZ. When prairie dust had settled, bowl-ineligible Oklahoma (9-0-1) had registered combined 82-13 score over projected New Year's Day Cotton Bowl participants: Nebraska and Texas.

PENN STATE 35 Pittsburgh 13: Nittany Lions (11-0) retained dominance of rivalry for another year as TB John Cappelletti won rushing duel with Pitt's TB Tony Dorsett. Cappelletti outrushed future fellow Heisman winner 161y to 77y as Nittany Lions recovered from 13-3 deficit by posting 32 unanswered pts in 2nd H. K Carson Long's 2 FGs and Dorsett's 14y TD run in 1st H had young Panthers (6-4-1) thinking upset. But, Penn State D shut down option attack, punishing Dorsett and sacking QB Billy Daniels 3 times in holding Panthers to 7y rushing and 41y passing after H. Penn State LB Tom Hull added 27y INT TD RET.

MICHIGAN 10 Ohio State 10: Ohio State (9-0-1) built 10-0 lead in titanic struggle as TB Archie Griffin ran for 99 of his 163y in 1st H, before leg injury hampered him, and frosh FB Pete Johnson bulled in from 5y out. K Blair Conway added 31y FG. Michigan tied up matters in 4th Q on K Mike Lantry's 30y FG and gutsy 4th down keeper from 10y out by QB Dennis Franklin (7-11/99y, INT), who set up his TD with 27y completion to TE Paul Seal. After rallying from 10-pt deficit, Wolverines were hit by disaster: Franklin broke collarbone of right (throwing) arm and Lantry missed 2 potential game-winning FGs. It got worse for Michigan as Big 10 ADs broke conference 1st-place tie and voted Rose Bowl nod to healthier Buckeyes, whom they felt would have better chance of snapping Big 10's 4-game losing streak. Michigan felt it deserved to go based on better performance in this deadlock, and that Ohio State had gone to Pasadena last year. Also, it was not as if Buckeyes much used their QBs: Ohio chose to run on 49 straight plays until backup QB Greg Hare threw potentially-disastrous INT that set up Lantry's last FG try, from 44y with 28 secs left.

MINNESOTA 19 Wisconsin 17: Surprising Gophers (7-4) wrapped up 3rd place in Big 10, using fleet TB Rick Upchurch to gain 167y and 2 TDs rushing. Upchurch opened scoring in 1st Q with 16y run, matched by 2y TD run by Badgers TB Billy Marek (31/131y). Wisconsin led 7-6 at H. Badgers (4-7) upped their lead to 10-6 on 23y FG by K Vince Lamia. Upchurch took another pitchout to paydirt with 14y scoring run, and Minnesota would not relinquish its hard-earned 13-10 lead. Upchurch, who set up each of his scores with long runs, then contributed 35y rushing on clinching 4th Q drive to set up 2y scoring run by TB Larry Powell. Marek set Wisconsin school to-date records for season TDs (14) and pts (84).

KANSAS 14 Missouri 13: Surprising Jayhawks (7-3-1) continued their winning ways as QB David Jaynes continued to plague Missouri by hitting WR Emmett Edwards for winning score. Confident Tigers (7-4) had built 13-0 3rd Q lead as QB Ray Smith ran for 45y TD and DB John Moseley returned punt 53y for TD. Jaynes then threw 2 TD passes in 4th Q to pull out victory. Kansas earned 2nd place tie with Nebraska in conf, while Missouri stumbled to its 3rd straight loss. Remarkable Jayhawks set new NCAA "cliffhanger" record by playing their 6th game of season decided by 2 pts or less. Kansas had defeated Iowa State, Colorado, and Missouri, while losing to Tennessee and Nebraska by single pt, and tying Oklahoma State.

ARIZONA STATE 55 Arizona 19: Highly anticipated desert match-up turned out to be disappointing. Arizona State (10-1) coach Frank Kush unleashed cadre of future NFL players on Wildcats: HB Woody Green (25/192y), FB Ben Malone (26/147y), QB Danny White (22-36/333y, 4 TDs), WB Morris Owens (7/128y, 3 TDs) and LB Bob Breunig (13 tackles, blocked punt and INT) all excelled. Arizona (8-3) remained in contention at H, trailing 28-19, thanks to FB Jim Upchurch's 2 TD runs. Sun Devils dominated 2nd H, with final TD scored by WR Greg Hudson when he recovered EZ FUM coughed up by Arizona WR Theo "T" Bell, bobbled when Bell tried to field 50y punt by White. Green finished his Devils career with school rushing record of 4,188y. That total broke mark set by Whizzer White (3,174), father of QB Danny.

SOUTHERN CALIFORNIA 23 UCLA 13: UCLA's vaunted rushing attack, which was leading nation with 415.4y avg, crashed into Trojans' new 3-4 D and was found lacking. Bruins (9-2) scratched to earn 249y with its option assault and committed 4 crucial FUMs and tossed up 2 INTs. TB Anthony Davis led Rose Bowl-bound Trojans (9-1-1) with 145y rushing and scored TD as USC copped its 6th trip to Pasadena in 8 years. Game's big play probably could be traced to Troy LB James Sims' hit on Bruins QB John Sciarra with Trojans up 20-13 in 3rd Q. It forced FUM that was recovered by USC LB Dale Mitchell.

STANFORD 26 California 17: Cardinals (7-4) took control of Big Game thanks to 6 California TOs and other mistakes that set up every score except final TD. With efficient QB Mike Boryla out by H with shoulder injury, Stanford needed all help they could muster. Winning TD, frosh RB Ron Inge's 3y run, began after 29y punt by Bears QB-P Steve Bartkoski, who was subbing for injured P Scott Overton. Stanford then went 81y with ball on next drive to clinch game on 10y scoring run by FB Scott Laidlaw. TB Chuck Muncie led Bears (4-7) with 129y, TD rushing.

December 1, 1973

Navy 51 Army 0 (Philadelphia): West Point was unpleasant place to be in 1973. With international military events overshadowing team's on-field performance, Cadets (0-10) posted its 1st-ever truly winless season (they went 0-1 in 1890 when Army lost only game on its schedule to Navy). This Navy (4-7) debacle was most 1-sided game in series history. Verdict was over by H as Midshipmen scored 31 pts in 2nd Q, all coming during 9:37 stretch. Navy coach George Welsh tried to limit damage by using all 59 of his players, but rout could not be prevented. TB Cleveland Cooper rushed for 3 TDs to pace Midshipmen. Previous widest margin of victory in series had come on Army's 38-0 win in 1949.

Notre Dame 44 MIAMI 0: Hurricanes' (5-6) brutal schedule finally concluded as Notre Dame clinched its 1st perfect regular season since 1949. Fighting Irish (10-0) racked up 448y rushing, led by FB Wayne Bullock's 117y, 2 TDs. Irish stayed on ground for all of its 1st drive of 82y that featured 40y run by HB Art Best. Ground game clicked again after Miami missed FG try; ND surprisingly built 13-0 lead without bothering to throw pass. Miami soon changed its D, and Irish QB Tom Clements went to air following Hurricane FUM, hitting WR Pete Demmerle for 21y TD, 1st of his 2 scoring catches. Notre Dame finished 1st H with 24-0 lead and 291y to 83y difference in O.

Georgia 10 GEORGIA TECH 3: Tied at 3-3 at H, Yellow Jackets (5-6) moved deep into Georgia territory in 3rd Q before TB Greg Horne lost FUM. Bulldogs (6-4-1) then marched 94y for winning TD on 12y pass to FB Bob Burns, gaining 28y on run by QB Andy Johnson. Georgia's attempts to score insurance pts failed with missed FG try and Georgia Tech S Randy Rhino's 14th career INT, which tied him for school record. Tech marched late in 4th Q to Georgia 9YL. Two rushes gained 6y, but, from 3YL, Jackets QB Jim Stevens was dropped for losses on 3rd down by DE Jim Baker and 4th down by DG Danny Jones and LB Sylvester Boler. Bulldogs TB Jimmy Poulos paced his team with 108y rushing.

ALABAMA 35 Auburn 0: Crimson Tide (11-0) celebrated its emergence to spot atop both polls with rout of in-state rivals that avenged 1972's unlikely loss. Alabama QB Gary Rutledge ran Wishbone to perfection as O gained 405y, while HB Wilbur Jackson added 89y rushing and 14y TD run. Tigers (6-5) rushed for 149y with frosh TB Secdrick McIntyre chipping in 59y. Far-ranging Bama LB Woodrow Lowe led fabulous D with 10 tackles and 10 assists.

TENNESSEE 20 Vanderbilt 17: After blowing 14-0 lead in big 4th Q lapse, Tennessee (8-3) had to rally behind K Ricky Townsend, who made 2 late FGs, including 36y game-winner. Vanderbilt (5-6) scored 17 pts in 4th Q to wrestle lead away from Tennessee as HB Martin Garcia scored twice on 1y runs to project Commodores to 17-14 advantage. Volunteers QB Condredge Holloway left game with injury and seemingly safe 14-0 lead, but had to re-enter to lead drive to tying FG. Next, Commodores P Barry Burton was unable to get punt away from deep in own territory, giving Vols ball on Vandy 24YL. Townsend's FG soon sealed win. Tennessee had scored 2 TDs in 1st Q, including S Eddie Brown's 78y punt RET.

TULANE 14 Louisiana State 0: Tulane (9-2) marched to its 1st win over LSU in 25 years in front of largest crowd (86,598) to date to watch game in South. Winning TD proved to be QB Terry Looney's 36y pass to TE Darwin Willie late in 1st H. Ahead 7-0 at H, Green Wave D had enough pts to win as they overall held Tigers to 12 1st downs and 220y, while picking off 3 passes. Tulane S David Greiner authored 2 INTs. FB Lyndon Lassiter added clinching 1y run on TD drive that featured 53y run by TB Doug Bynum. LSU (9-2) limped into Orange Bowl on 2-game losing streak.

Oklahoma 45 OKLAHOMA STATE 18: Oklahoma (10-0-1) completed undefeated season in convincing fashion, yet soon realized that national title would be long shot. With undefeated Alabama facing undefeated Notre Dame in Sugar Bowl, chances were slim for Sooners to win title without benefit of bowl win. Oklahoma QB Steve Davis concluded his soph season with 3 TD runs, while 1st-team D allowed just 2 FGs. Frosh QB Charlie Weatherbie added 2 late TD runs for Cowboys (5-4-2).

Conference Standings

Ivy League

Dartmouth	6-1
Harvard	5-2
Pennsylvania	5-2
Yale	5-2
Brown	4-3
Cornell	2-5
Columbia	1-6
Princeton	0-7

Atlantic Coast

North Carolina State	6-0
Maryland	5-1
Clemson	4-2
Virginia	3-3
Duke	1-4-1
North Carolina	1-5
Wake Forest	0-5-1

Southeastern

Alabama	8-0
LSU	5-1
Mississippi	4-3
Tennessee	3-3
Florida	3-4
Georgia	3-4
Kentucky	3-4
Auburn	2-5
Mississippi State	2-5
Vanderbilt	1-5

Southern

East Carolina	7-0
Richmond	5-1
William & Mary	3-2
Furman	3-3
Appalachian State	2-2
VMI	2-4
Citadel	1-6
Davidson	1-6

Big Ten

Michigan	7-0-1
Ohio State	7-0-1
Minnesota	6-2
Michigan State	4-4
Illinois	4-4
Northwestern	4-4
Purdue	4-4
Wisconsin	3-5
Indiana	0-8
Iowa	0-8

Mid-American

Miami (Ohio)	5-0
Kent State	4-1
Bowling Green	2-3
Ohio	2-3
Western Michigan	1-4
Toledo	1-4

Big Eight

Oklahoma	7-0
Nebraska	4-2-1
Kansas	4-2-1
Oklahoma State	2-3-2
Missouri	3-4
Kansas State	2-5
Colorado	2-5
Iowa State	2-5

Missouri Valley

Tulsa	5-1
North Texas State	5-1
Louisville	3-2
New Mexico State	3-2
Wichita State	2-4
West Texas State	1-5
Drake	1-5

Southwest

Texas	7-0
Texas Tech	6-1
Rice	4-3
SMU	3-3-1
Arkansas	3-3-1
Texas A&M	3-4
TCU	1-6
Baylor	0-7

Western Athletic

Arizona State	6-1
Arizona	6-1
Utah	4-2
New Mexico	3-4
Brigham Young	3-4
Wyoming	3-4
Colorado State	2-4
Texas El Paso	0-7

Pacific Eight

Southern California	7-0
UCLA	6-1
Stanford	5-2
Washington State	4-3
Oregon	2-5
Oregon State	2-5
California	2-5
Washington	0-7

Pacific Coast Athletic

San Diego State	3-0-1
San Jose State	3-0-2
Pacific	2-1-1
Fresno State	1-3
Long Beach State	0-4
Los Angeles State *	0-1

* Ineligible

1973 Major Bowl Games
Liberty Bowl (Dec. 17): North Carolina State 31 Kansas 18

Wolfpack (9-3) broke open 10-10 contest with 3 straight 2nd H TDs, with 31y RET of INT by DT Jim Henderson serving as final clincher. FB Stan Fritts led NC State with 83y rushing, 2 TDs, as he started 21-pt outburst with 8y run that capped short 19y drive after Kansas WR Bruce Adams fumbled punt. A-A QB David Jaynes threw for 218y and TD pass in his final game as Jayhawks leader, while FB Robert Miller rushed for 104y and scored both Kansas (7-4-1) TDs on 12y reception in 2nd Q and 12y run in 4th Q.

Fiesta Bowl (Dec. 21): Arizona State 28 Pittsburgh 7

Game was tight throughout with Arizona State leading 10-7 in 4th Q until 1 of game's many miscues allowed Sun Devils (11-1) to pull away. Fuse was lit when ASU QB Danny White connected with WR Greg Hudson (8/210y) on 62y scoring strike to pad lead to 16-7. Panthers (6-5-1), who suffered 8 TOs to 6 by ASU, failed to gain 1st down, and P Larry Swider muffed snap before getting off 5y punt. On next play—only 76 secs after Hudson's TD catch—HB Woody Green raced 23y to EZ and 22-7 lead. Green finished with another TD, his 3rd of game, as he won private duel with Panther TB Tony Dorsett 131y to 100y, 3 TDs to single TD. Sun Devils were angry week of game that Dorsett was named 1st-team AP over Green. CB Mike Haynes had 2 INTs and set up go-ahead 30y FG by K Frank Kush in 3rd Q.

Tangerine Bowl (Dec. 22): Miami of Ohio 16 Florida 7

Redoubtable Redskins (11-0) completed perfect season behind FB Chuck Varner's running and resourceful D that won TO battle by 7 to 1 to help contain Florida's potent attack. Varner gained 156y rushing with scoring TD, and Gators, playing in mid-20s temperature, were frozen with 90y rushing and 99y passing. K David Draudt kicked 3 FGs for Miami. HB Nat Moore rushed for 101y to pace Florida. Redskins led only 3-0 at H, but bumped their edge up to 13-0 after 3rd Q. Win was 1st for Miami of Ohio in bowl game since 1950.

Peach Bowl (Dec. 28): Georgia 17 Maryland 16

DB Dick Conn recovered 2 FUMs to help propel Bulldogs to victory. Conn scooped bad pitch by Terps QB Ben Kinard on Maryland 8YL in 3rd Q to set up winning 1y TD dive by QB Andy Johnson moments later. Bulldogs (6-4-1) were now ahead 17-10, lead that was whittled to 17-16 on 2 FGs by Maryland K Steve Mike-Mayer. Each team scored its 1st TD on long pass play: 62y from Johnson to TB Jimmy Poulos to open scoring for Bulldogs and TB Louis Carter's 68y scoring connection to TE Walter White to tie game at 7-7. Then game settled into expected struggle. Terrapins (8-4) threw for 242y but could not overcome 3 crucial FUMs.

Gator Bowl (Dec. 29): Texas Tech 28 Tennessee 19

Texas Tech sr QB Joe Barnes finished up heady season with 2 TD passes and scoring run to lead Red Raiders (10-1). Barnes hit on 8-11/154y as he led Texas Tech on TD-scoring drive in each Q. His most spectacular pass was 79y connection to WR Lawrence Williams in 2nd Q for 14-0 lead. QB Condredge Holloway of Tennessee (8-4) threw for 190y but was less able to reach EZ. Vols were able to pull within 14-10 in 3rd Q before Barnes threw his 2nd TD pass, 7y effort to TE Andre Tillman. Tennessee was not done yet, scoring 9 straight pts, including 2nd TD run by HB Haskell Stanback (19/95y) to jump within 21-19. Vols soon appeared on their way to go-ahead FG attempt, which would have provided their only lead. Instead, Tennessee K Ricky Townsend missed 32y FG with 3:36 remaining, and that was all she wrote. Dejected Tennessee D then allowed 70y romp by FB James Mosley to set up superfluous 3y TD run by Texas Tech TB Larry Isaac to wrap things up.

Sun Bowl (Dec. 29): Missouri 34 Auburn 17

Tigers A-A DB John Moseley's 84y KO TD RET came as 1st H ended and broke Auburn's back. Moseley's TD put Missouri (8-4) out front by 28-10. Auburn (6-5) had appeared to get back into it moments earlier at 21-10 on scoring pass by frosh QB Phil Gargis. Mizzou stayed on ground, gaining 295y to 113y rushing advantage, as FB Ray Bybee rushed for 127y and TB Tommy Reamon ran for 110y. Auburn contributed mightily to its downfall, losing 5 TOs and foolishly kicking to Moseley with only 8 secs remaining in 2nd Q. Earlier in 2nd Q, Missouri TB Chuck Link threw option pass to TE John Kelsey for 35y score.

Astro-Bluebonnet Bowl (Dec. 29): Houston 47 Tulane 7

Houston totaled 656y in routing Tulane (9-3), scoring on 5 drives, each measured more than 80y in length. Cougars RB Marshall Johnson (5/114y) opened with 75y scoring run on game's 3rd play. Houston QB D.C. Nobles, who threw for 201y, followed with 60y pass to TE Miller Bassler that set up FB Leonard Parker's 1y TD run for 14-0 lead in 2nd Q. Verdict soon was banked as Cougars (11-1) scored 5 more TDs, including 2nd from Parker and 2 from FB Donnie McGraw (13/108y). Cougars D held Tulane to fewer than 200y and had 4 INTs. Lone Green Wave TD was delivered by QB Buddy Gilbert on 32y pass to WR Tom Fortner in 2nd Q.

GAME OF THE YEAR
Sugar Bowl (Dec. 31): Notre Dame 24 Alabama 23

Needing 1st down to seal win and national title, Notre Dame (11-0) turned to unlikely hero: backup TE Robin Weber. On 3rd down-and-8, deep in his own territory, Irish QB Tom Clements found wide-open Weber for 35y completion, which matched TE's number of receptions in entire regular season. Primary target on play was other TE, star Dave Casper, but Weber, who needed cortisone shot prior to game for his ailing knee, was too free to ignore against Crimson Tide's D which totally expected Irish to call conservative running play. With Alabama (11-1) O nailed in place with no positive y in 1st Q, Irish sprung misdirection elements of Delaware's Wing-T formation and opened scoring with FB Wayne Bullock's 1y TD run on drive that featured 3 straight completions/59y to WR Pete Demmerle. After exchange of TOs, Alabama QB Gary Rutledge led 52y drive that netted 7-6 lead. It was short-lived as ND frosh HB Al Hunter raced 93y with ensuing KO, and 2-pt conv pass to Demmerle gave Notre Dame 14-7 edge. Tide added FG before H and then took their opening possession of 2nd H to 5y TD run by HB Wilbur Jackson that climaxed 93y drive in 11 plays. Trailing 17-14, ND regained lead after LB Drew Mahalic returned FUM 9y to Alabama 12YL.

Misdirection TD run by HB Eric Penick following huge block by Casper gave Irish 21-17 lead. Later, with Tide on ND 25YL, alternate QB Richard Todd handed off to HB Mike Stock, who threw back to Todd, all alone in left flat. Todd scored easily for 23-21 lead, but K Bill Davis missed crucial x-pt. Notre Dame next drove behind Clements—game's MVP with 74y rushing and 169y passing—who lugged it 3/25y and completed 30y pass to Casper (3/75y). K Bob Thomas then booted winning 19y FG, although Tide still had time to rally. Irish D held and forced punt, which was boomed 69y by P Greg Gantt to ND 1YL. At that juncture, Clements and Weber prepared to run out clock and enter ND lore. Alabama's mysterious bowl winless streak had reached 7 games.

Cotton Bowl: Nebraska 19 Texas 3

Nebraska (9-2-1) turned to backup QB Steve Runty in 2nd H to bail out sluggish O and, with help from D, he did just that. With game tied at 3-3 early in 3rd Q, Huskers 1st had to stop Texas that was marching with opening drive of 2nd H. DB Bob Thornton made EZ INT of Longhorns QB Marty Akins on play he was beaten by HB Lonnie Bennett, but was redeemed by Akins' under-thrown ball. Later in 3rd Q, Thornton returned short FG attempt to Nebraska 41YL. Runty needed 8 plays to move Huskers to winning TD: 12y run by WB Ritch Bahe. Longhorns then lost FUM on their 18YL, recovered by Nebraska NG John Bell. IB Tony Davis (28/106y) ran 3y score soon thereafter. Foes traded FGs in 1st H, both resulting from TOs. Texas (8-3) had opened with FG—marking 5th straight Cotton Bowl that losing team took 3-0 lead—on 22y boot by K Billy Schott 8 plays after LB Wade Johnston's FUM REC. Nebraska knotted things in 2nd Q after DE Steve Manstedt caught mid-air FUM by FB Roosevelt Leaks (48y rushing), which bounced off Leaks' foot, and returned it 65y to Texas 8YL. Longhorns surrendered only 1y in 3 downs and K Rich Sanger's 24y FG. At H's end, Nebraska was near Texas GL again, but was stuffed on 4 downs as time ran out. Texas LB Johnston, in on all 4 stops, led heroic GLS. Texas dropped 3rd of last 4 Cotton Bowls.

Rose Bowl: Ohio State 42 Southern California 21

Calling it "greatest victory I ever had, or we have ever had," coach Woody Hayes of Ohio State (10-0-1) was giddier than ever after big win. Hayes, with advice from Notre Dame coach Ara Parseghian, passed more than usual in subduing Trojans. QB Cornelius Greene threw 6-8/129y, and shrugged off INT by CB Danny Reece on his very 1st attempt. Interestingly, Hayes beat Trojans (9-2-1) having already adopted USC coach John McKay's modern I-formation attack, and, for this game, Troy's 3-8 D alignment. USC entered locker room at H tied 14-14 and moved 84y behind QB Pat Haden for 21-14 lead early in 3rd Q. After that flurry, Buckeyes completely dominated, pulling within 21-20 on 67y TD drive that featured Greene's 39y completion to TE Fred Pagac. Then DB Neal Colzie's 56y punt RET propelled them to 27-21 lead on Greene's 4th down keeper near end of 3rd Q. Ohio added 2 TDs in 4th Q, including TB Archie Griffin's scintillating 47y scoring run that closed scoring. Using variety of zones, Bucks D allowed Haden (21-39/229y) to throw short passes, but denied him long scoring connections. USC's sole scoring pass was thrown by TB Anthony Davis to WR J.K. McKay. Meanwhile, Griffin raced for 149y, more than doubling Davis' 74y, to set up 4 TDs by Ohio FBs, including 3 by FB Pete Johnson. Big 10's 4-game Rose Bowl losing streak ended.

Orange Bowl: Penn State 16 Louisiana State 9

Big, bruising Penn State (12-0) turned to 2 smaller, quicker players to pull out victory. WR Chuck Herd gave Nittany Lions lead they would never relinquish with 72y scoring reception in 2nd Q, and WR Gary Hayman set up other Lions TD with 36y punt RET later in 2nd Q. LSU (9-3) held Penn State to 9 1st downs, limiting Heisman Trophy winner, TB John Cappelletti to 50y, and TD. Cappelletti played on ankle that he sprained earlier in week. Tigers looked poised for upset following 46y RET of opening KO by frosh WR Robert Dow. With TB Brad Davis rushing 5/39y, Tigers quickly moved 51y to TD: TB Steve Rogers' 3y run. LSU O did not score again, but result might have been different had time not expired at end of 1st H with Tigers on Penn State 5YL. Only scoring of quiet 2nd H occurred when Penn State allowed safety on bad punt snap. Down by only 7 pts, LSU threatened once in 4th Q until Lions LB Doug Allen spilled Davis for 4y loss on 4th-and-3 at Penn State 27YL.

Final AP Poll January 3

1 Notre Dame (33)	1128	11 Texas Tech	336
2 Ohio State (11)	1002	12 UCLA	251
3 Oklahoma (16)	965	13 Louisiana State	179
4 Alabama	834	14 Texas	150
5 Penn State	709	15 Miami (Ohio)	125
6 Michigan	702	16 North Carolina State	94
7 Nebraska	430	17 Missouri	52
8 Southern California	386	18 Kansas	11
9t Arizona State	349	19 Tennessee	10
9t Houston	349	20t Maryland	3
		20t Tulane	3

1973 Top Performance Formula

1 Oklahoma	1.8007
2 Notre Dame	1.7913
3 Penn State	1.7632
4 Alabama	1.7572
5 Ohio State	1.6964
6 Michigan	1.6563
7 Houston	1.6378
8 Arizona State	1.6237
9 Texas Tech	1.6159
10 Nebraska	1.5646
11 UCLA	1.4913
12 Southern California	1.4834
13 Louisiana State	1.4717
14 North Carolina State	1.4593
15 Texas	1.4555
16 Maryland	1.3244
17 Missouri	1.2916
18 Georgia	1.2797
19 Arizona	1.2580
20 Kansas	1.2372

1973 Top Opponent Records

1 Nebraska	.6545
2 Louisiana State	.6400
3 Kansas State	.6167
4 Iowa	.6126
5 Rice	.6107
6 Iowa State	.6071
7 Georgia	.6063
8 Oklahoma	.6053
9 Miami	.6027
10 Auburn	.5976
11 North Carolina State	.5960
12 Southern California	.5917
13 Stanford	.5893
14 Alabama	.5880
15 Navy	.5856
16 Kansas	.5847
17 Mississippi	.5826
18 Oklahoma State	.5814
19 Florida	.5806
20 Colorado	.5796

1973 Out-of-Conference Records

	W-L	Percentage	Bowl W-L
Big Eight	24-7-1	.7656	2-1
Southeastern	31-11-2	.7273	1-5
Southwest	14-15	.4828	1-1
Western Athletic	16-20	.4444	1-0
Big Ten	12-17	.4138	1-0
Pacific-8	11-20-1	.3594	0-1
Atlantic Coast	11-20	.3548	1-1

1973 Individual Statistical Leaders

RUSHING YARDS	Attempts	Yards	Avg.
Mark Kellar, Northern Illinois	291	1719	5.9
Tony Dorsett, Pittsburgh	288	1586	5.5
John Cappelletti, Penn State	286	1522	5.3
Archie Griffin, Ohio State	225	1428	6.3
Roosevelt Leaks, Texas	229	1415	6.2
Jim Jennings, Rutgers	303	1353	4.5
Willard Harrell, Pacific	209	1319	6.3
Dickey Morton, Arkansas	226	1298	5.7
Mike Esposito, Boston College	254	1293	5.1
Walter Peacock, Louisville	290	1291	4.5

PASSING YARDS	Completions	Attempts	Yards	Pct.
Jesse Freitas, San Diego State	227	347	2993	65.4
Danny White, Arizona State	146	265	2609	55.1
Gary Sheide, Brigham Young	177	294	2350	60.2
Gene Swick, Toledo	165	301	2234	54.8
David Jaynes, Kansas	172	330	2131	52.1
Bill Hatty, Villanova	172	341	1947	50.4
Craig Kimball, San Jose State	165	305	1940	54.1
Jan Steubbe, Colorado State	146	310	1938	47.1
Marty Vaughn, Pennsylvania	114	206	1926	55.3
Neal Jeffrey, Baylor	132	251	1897	52.6

RECEIVING YARDS	Catches	Yards
Jay Miller, Brigham Young	100	1181
Hank Cook, New Mexico State	65	1111
Morris Owens, Arizona State	50	1076
Darold Nogle, San Diego State	59	945
Charles Dancer, Baylor	53	927
Don Cline, Pennsylvania	53	882
Emmett Edwards, Kansas	49	802
Willie Miller, Colorado State	53	793
Greg Hudson, Arizona State	54	788
Pat McInally, Harvard	56	752

1973 Consensus All-America Team
Offense

Wide Receiver:	Lynn Swann, Southern California
Tight End:	Dave Casper, Notre Dame
Tackle:	John Hicks, Ohio State
	Booker Brown, Southern California
Guard:	Buddy Brown, Alabama
	Bill Yoest, North Carolina State
Center:	Bill Wyman, Texas
Quarterback:	Dave Jaynes, Kansas
Running Back:	John Cappelletti, Penn State
	Roosevelt Leaks, Texas
	Woody Green, Arizona State
	Kermit Johnson, UCLA

Defense

Line:	John Dutton, Nebraska
	Dave Gallagher, Michigan
	Lucious Selmon, Oklahoma
	Tony Cristiani, Miami
Linebacker:	Randy Gradishar, Ohio State
	Rod Shoate, Oklahoma
	Richard Wood, Southern California
Back:	Mike Townsend, Notre Dame
	Artimus Parker, Southern California
	Dave Brown, Michigan
	Randy Rhino, Georgia Tech

1973 Heisman Trophy Vote

John Cappelletti, senior tailback Penn State	1057
John Hicks, senior tackle, Ohio State	524
Roosevelt Leaks, junior fullback, Texas	482
David Jaynes, senior quarterback, Kansas	394
Archie Griffin, sophomore tailback, Ohio State	362

Other Major Award Winners

Maxwell (Player)	John Cappelletti, senior tailback, Penn State
Walter Camp (Player)	John Cappelletti, senior tailback, Penn State
Outland (Lineman)	John Hicks, senior tackle, Ohio State
Lombardi (Lineman)	John Hicks, senior tackle, Ohio State
AFCA Coach of Year	Paul "Bear" Bryant, Alabama)

1974

The Year of Oklahoma's Half-Ignored Title, Rose Bowl Rubber Match, and Michigan's Bowl-Less Seniors

Oklahoma (11-0) went undefeated in becoming the first preseason no. 1 team in the AP poll to go on to win the title since 1956, the year when the Sooners last won a national championship. This edition of the Pride of Norman failed to go wire-to-wire however, dropping out of the top spot by September 16 due largely to the weakness of its early schedule.

In probationary jail levied after the faulty recruitment of quarterback Kerry Jackson, the Sooners were a troublesome choice for some voters, especially because they weren't able to risk their flawless record in a bowl game. In the end, Oklahoma was the last undefeated team standing. While the high-powered Oklahoma offense, led by quarterback Steve Davis and halfback Joe Washington, received the bulk of the publicity—averaging 508 yards per game and scoring 63 points against both Wake Forest (1-10) and Kansas State (4-7) and 72 against Utah State (8-3)—the Sooners defense was equally fantastic. With Dewey and Lee Roy Selmon leading the defensive line and Rod Shoate continuing as a dominant linebacker, Oklahoma posted three shutouts and held every opponent to 14 points or fewer.

Oklahoma was ineligible for the UPI title, which for the first time was awarded after the New Year's bowl games. It seemed awfully odd to have the Sooners heading the AP list when the coaches voting in the UPI half of the national polls were required to completely ignore Oklahoma.

Recovering well after an opening loss to Arkansas (6-4-1), Southern California (11-1) won the UPI championship as Alabama (11-1), which would have won a pre-bowl title, lost to Notre Dame (10-2) in the Orange Bowl. The Trojans coach, John McKay, joined Frank Leahy and Bear Bryant as the only coaches to win or share four titles since the AP and UPI began polling in 1936 and 1950 respectively. USC, featuring 14 players drafted by the NFL the following season, needed a late two-point conversion pass by Rhodes Scholar-earning signal-caller Pat Haden for a 18-17 win over Ohio State in the Rose Bowl. The play brought back memories of USC's failed attempt in the 1967 Rose Bowl loss to Purdue.

The Orange Bowl also was notable for being the final contest coached by Ara Parseghian, who resigned as an exhausted, if highly successful coach at Notre Dame in December. He finished his coaching career at 170-58-6 at Miami of Ohio, Northwestern, and Notre Dame after the Fighting Irish's emotional Orange Bowl victory over then top-ranked Alabama. The Irish had been expected to challenge for a second straight national title, but were limited before the season began by the loss of 10 players, including seven starters, to major injuries and suspensions.

Former Arizona State and Missouri coach Dan Devine was hired almost immediately to fill Parseghian's void in South Bend. Devine, who was rumored to be heading to the University of Washington after three years as coach of Green Bay in the NFL, never really escaped the shadow of Parseghian even though his 1977 team would win the national title. Meanwhile, Washington (5-6) made a great hire in Don James.

Ohio State (10-2) coach Woody Hayes suffered a heart attack on June 6, but he still led his Buckeyes to a season-end fourth place in AP balloting, although behind a Michigan (10-1) team he beat 12-10 in November. Hayes felt he had a squad that "could be the greatest college football team of all-time." Hayes faced Southern California in Rose Bowl for a third straight year, and this year's tense rubber match—after USC won easily in 1972 and Ohio State easily in 1973—went to the Trojans. The Rose Bowl also featured another Hayes anger-control adventure: he punched his own linebacker, Arnie Jones, during USC's late game-winning drive. Hayes, and for that matter Jones, downplayed the punch but it stuck as an example of Hayes becoming more out-of-touch with 1970s athletes. Before the decade was over, Hayes' use of physical force on players would cost him his job.

Michigan graduated a remarkable senior class that powered its way to a 30-2-1 record for three seasons without ever playing in a single bowl game. Although Big Ten reform came too late for the Wolverines, the conference agreed in December to a list of tiebreakers to determine its Rose Bowl representative in the future. Most notably, the conference eliminated the controversial decree that had athletic directors voting to break league title ties for selection of Rose Bowl participation. Such votes had cost Michigan when it tied Ohio State following the 1973 and 1974 seasons. In a significant change, permission was granted to worthy non-championship teams to go bowling, a decision that took root in 1975 and in time for Michigan to go to the Orange Bowl that year.

Texas (8-4) struggled but welcomed heralded freshman fullback Earl Campbell to its backfield. Surprising Baylor (8-4), under young head coach Grant Teaff, became the first Southwest Conference team to follow up a season in which they lost every conference game with the league title. The Bears won their first SWC crown since 1924 and made their first-ever Cotton Bowl appearance. Shut out of any other bowls bid, the Bears needed to beat Rice (2-8-1) in the finale to wrap up the conference crown and its automatic Cotton Bowl berth or be forced to stay home. They happily packed their bags for the short trip to Dallas.

Tailback Archie Griffin of Ohio State won the Heisman Trophy to become only the fifth junior to do so, and first since Roger Staubach in 1963. Griffin already owned the Big Ten career rushing record of 4,064 yards, breaking the mark of former Purdue running back Otis Armstrong on October 19 versus Indiana (1-10). Griffin, who owned a per-game rushing average of 147.3 yards, ended the regular season with his 22nd straight 100-yard rushing effort. USC Trojans tailback Anthony Davis finished a distant second, although the majority of Heisman ballots were sent in before an incredible four-touchdown game against Notre Dame on November 30. Davis finished as the Pac-8's all-time leading rusher with 3,657 yards and tops with 52 touchdowns. Davis, with 314 points scored, also held the career NCAA record of six kickoff return touchdowns.

Milestones

■ Blocking below waist was better defined by Rules Committee, and goalposts offset behind end-line were allowed.

■ UPI coaches board decreed that teams on probation were ineligible for consideration in weekly polls, thus eliminating Oklahoma as candidate for UPI national title.

■ TCU tailback Kent Waldrop broke his neck on October 26, suffering paralysis below neck.

■ Legendary Ohio State back Charles "Chic" Harley, died in Illinois VA hospital on April 21 of long-standing medical issues originating in World War I. Harley was thrice All-America who led Buckeyes to first Big 10 title (1916) and first Michigan win (1919), scoring 201 points in career. Dr. Eddie Anderson, All-America end for Notre Dame whose record as player was 28-1, and hall of fame head coach at 4 schools for 39 years died on April 26. Practicing physician Anderson was AFCA coach of year for 1939 Iowa team featuring Nile Kinnick. Johnny Mack Brown, All-America halfback at Alabama (1925) and hero of Rose Bowl upset over Washington with pair of touchdown catches before embarking on long Hollywood acting career, died from kidney ailment on November 15. After first working with stars like Mary Pickford, Brown became famed star of Westerns. November 15 heart attack took Jimmy Phelan, 1915-17 Notre Dame quarterback and coach at four schools including Washington (1930-41), where he led Huskies to 1937 Rose Bowl.

■ Longest winning streaks entering season:

| Penn State 12 | Miami (Ohio) 12 | Notre Dame 11 |

■ Coaching Changes:

	Incoming	Outgoing
Army	Homer Smith	Tom Cahill
Colorado	Bill Mallory	Eddie Crowder
Columbia	Bill Campbell	Frank Navarro
Florida State	Darrell Mudra	Larry Jones
Georgia Tech	Pepper Rodgers	Bill Fulcher
Hawaii	Larry Price	Dave Holmes
Iowa	Bob Commings	Frank Lauterbur
Mississippi	Ken Cooper	Johnny Vaught
New Mexico	Bill Mondt	Rudy Feldman
Oregon	Don Read	Dick Enright
Syracuse	Frank Maloney	Ben Schwaltzwalder
Texas Christian	Jim Shofner	Billy Tahill
Texas-El Paso	Gil Bartosh	Tommy Hudspeth
UCLA	Dick Vermeil	Pepper Rodgers
Utah	Tom Lovat	Bill Meek
Virginia	Sonny Randle	Don Lawrence
Virginia Tech	Jimmy Sharpe	C.E. Coffey

■ AP Preseason Poll

1 Oklahoma (23)	976	11 Houston	241
2 Ohio State (14)	907	12 UCLA	182
3 Notre Dame (13)	864	13 Pittsburgh	141
4 Alabama (6)	859	14 Maryland	137
5 Southern California (1)	752	15 Arizona State	88
6 Michigan (1)	586	16 Tennessee	79
7 Nebraska	472	17 Arizona	76
8 Penn State	451	18 North Carolina State	50
9 Louisiana State	360	19 Arkansas	45
10 Texas	328	20 Texas A&M	33

September 7, 1974

SYRACUSE 23 Oregon State 15: Syracuse (1-0) remained conservative under new coach Frank Maloney, passing only 3 times with 1 completion—5y TD toss from QB Jim Donoghue to TE Bob Petchel. Orange took lead with 16 4th Q pts, set up by 2 INTs of Beavers QB Alvin White, including 1 returned 17y for TD by S Tim Moresco. Oregon State (0-1) had opened scoring with 3y TD run by FB Dick Maurer before Syracuse scored 23 straight pts, due in part to Beavers handing out 5 TOs. Orangemen TB Ken Kinsey rushed for 169y.

North Carolina State 33 WAKE FOREST 15: QB Dave Buckey led explosive 2nd H performance for Wolfpack (1-0), who led only 3-0 at H. Buckey threw 2 TD passes, 10y to TE B.J. Lyttle and 31y to WR Mike Hardy, and ran for another. Wake Forest (0-1) tried mightily with 70y TD passing connection between frosh QB Mike McGlamry and TE Tom Fehring, but it could not maintain pace. State dominated stats, outgaining Deacons 429y to 196y, but also had 14 PENs/115y.

TENNESSEE 17 Ucla 17: Banged-up QB Condredge Holloway returned from emergency room late in 3rd Q to rally Volunteers (0-0-1) with tying 80y scoring drive, capped by his bad-shoulder-be-damned dive into EZ on 12y run. Holloway—who threw 74y TD pass to TB Stanley Morgan (4/139y) on game's 2nd play before suffering shoulder injury later in 1st H—also took hit that tore knee cartilage. Bruins (0-0-1) K Brett White had opportunity for hero's call, but shanked 40y FG attempt with 9 secs left. Bruins QB John Sciarra rushed for 178y and completed 15-21/212y, TD to set school's single-game total O record. On 1st play of 2nd H, Sciarra raced 71y to Vols 2YL, but UCLA was stopped on 4 plays on vital GLS. Injuries forced Tennessee frosh QB Pat Ryan into game and regrettably he flipped 10-0 Vols lead into 17-10 deficit with series of miscues, including FUM into his EZ recovered by Bruin DT Rick Kukulica for TD. Game marked something new in TV: debut of sideline reporter Jim Lampley, who provided ABC with 11 on-air segments.

ARIZONA STATE 30 Houston 9: Having lost explosive backfield to pro football, Sun Devils (1-0) were expected to have to rebuild their O. Tell that to Houston (0-1) after Arizona State soph FB Freddie Williams torched them for 178y rushing and TDs on 69y and 4y runs, latter set up by his 73y romp. ASU D helped in scoring as CB Bo Warren and LB Bob Breunig scored TDs only min apart in 3rd Q: Warren on 17y INT RET and Breunig on 25y FUM RET. Houston (0-1) won y battle 362y to 320y, but suffered 7 TOs to none for ASU. Cougars had pulled within 9 pts in 3rd Q as QB Chuck Fairbanks led 72y drive to 8y scoring run by FB Donnie "Quick Draw" McGraw.

(Mon) Notre Dame 31 GEORGIA TECH 7: Georgia Tech (0-1) had its fans smelling upset with TD on opening drive, but what they smelled after that was their team's poor performance. QB Tom Clements completed 10-14/170y, TD for Irish (1-0), who tied game at 7-7 on 1y run by FB Wayne Bullock following FUM by Yellow Jackets on their 14YL. With O gaining 441y, Notre Dame easily pulled away despite losing HB Art Best to injury, 3rd HB lost to Fighting Irish since April. Tech was held to 174y as coach Pepper Rodgers debuted at alma mater, with TB David Sims rushing for 77y.

September 14, 1974

PENN STATE 24 Stanford 20: Nittany Lions (1-0) withstood Stanford's big passing attack, winning game on 1y TD run by TB Woody Petchel with 2:19 remaining. Stanford (0-1) QB Mike Cordova, battling 2 others for starting job, threw for 301y and 2 TDs as Cardinals rallied from 14-0 deficit to go ahead 20-17. Cordova completed 6 passes on 80y drive to tying 10y reception by WR Eric Test and then 4 more on downfield trip that produced go-ahead 18y FG by K Mike Langford. To win its 13th straight, Penn State also were required to march 80y, which Lions accomplished as QB Tom Shuman threw for 49y to set up winning TD.

NAVY 35 Virginia 28: Midshipmen (1-0) built 35-7 lead early in 4th Q and then had to hold on. QB Phil Poirer led Navy team that managed only 10 1st downs but scored 5 TDs, getting help from LB Tom Gardner's TD REC of blocked punt in EZ, TB Gerry Godwin's 83y scoring run, and CB Len Moken's 66y INT TD RET. Cavaliers (0-1) rallied as combination of QB Scott Gardner and WR Ken Shelton exploded for 3 TDs in 4th Q until Navy S Gene Ford ended Virginia's final bid with EZ INT. Middies DT Dave Papack hit Virginia QB Gardner (25-43/264y, 4 TDs, 2 INTs) as final pass flew.

Alabama 21 MARYLAND 16: Alabama coach Bear Bryant returned to campus where he began his coaching career in 1945 and faced his former player and asst Jerry Claiborne, Game launched Claiborne's new Terps (0-1) coaching career. Crimson Tide (1-0) never trailed, but DT Randy White-led Maryland D let them know this was more than easy tune-up. Play of game was 4th-and-5 run by Bama QB Richard Todd for 1st down on fake punt from Tide 25YL, play he ran on his own. Costly 2nd H TOs prevented Maryland's upset chances: Terps QB Ken Kinard's FUM on his own 37YL led to Bama's 3rd TD, DB Bob Smith's punt FUM on his own 44YL and TE Walter White's bobble of pass that turned into Tide INT. HB Calvin Culliver compiled 169y rushing and 2 TDs for Bama, although he was held to 15y in 2nd H. Maryland K Steve Mike-Mayer booted 3 FGs.

FLORIDA 21 California 17: After talking about Veer attack all off-season, Florida (1-0) lined up in Wishbone, but trickery didn't help so much as having 6 possessions begin in California (0-1) territory. Bears led 9-7 at H on FG at end of 74y trip in 1st Q and 17y TD pass from QB Steve Bartkowski (12-28/162y, INT) to TB Chuck Muncie (14/71y), who scored twice. Gators young QB Jimmy Fisher tried only 5 passes, and 2 of them truly mattered. Fisher clicked with WR Lee McGriff (3/53y) for 19y TD in 3rd Q and same combo connected for 27y gain to set up winning 4th Q TD.

Ohio State 34 MINNESOTA 19: Ohio State QB Cornelius Greene totaled 213y, while TB Archie Griffin rushed for 134y to set new school career rushing record of 2,577y, 35y more than former FB Jim Otis. Greene and Griffin's play highlighted otherwise stale performance by Buckeyes (1-0), who opened on road for 1st time since 1894. Gophers (0-1) scored 16 straight pts in 4th Q behind 36y scoring run by TB Rick Upchurch, QB Tony Dungy's 6y TD run and pair of 2-pt conv passes to pull within 28-19. Greene ended Minnesota's comeback hopes with seal-up 57y TD burst.

Wisconsin 28 PURDUE 14: Badgers (1-0) opened conf play with 1st Big 10 road victory since 1970. Wisconsin TB Ron Pollard rushed for 2 TDs and team rushed for 252y despite injury to leading rusher, TB Billy Marek. Wisconsin D contributed with 3 INTs, with 2 setting up both Pollard TD runs. Boilermakers (0-1) scored twice in 4th Q including 64y TD catch by WR Larry Burton (8/180y).

ARKANSAS 22 Southern California 7: Home-standing Razorbacks (1-0) shocked Trojans, converting 6 TOs into 17 pts. Hogs D dominated, holding QB Pat Haden to only 6-18/59y, 4 INTs passing and not surrendering any pts. TB Anthony Davis delivered only Trojans (0-1) TD on 106y KO TD RET. Playing behind banged up O-line, Haden did not complete pass until 3rd Q. Best drive for USC was its 1st as Haden moved team to Arkansas 12YL before throwing INT to S Floyd Hogan. That was key play as Hogan returned INT 66y to set up 27y TD run by FB Ike Forte. Hogs rushed for 262y and became 1st Wishbone team to score more than 20 pts on Trojans in 7 previous opportunities: USC had allowed only 40 total pts in 6 previous games against Wishbone foes. Porkers LB Dennis Winston contributed 19 tackles.

OKLAHOMA 28 Baylor 11: Oklahoma's relative difficulties against Bears (0-1) cost them top spot in AP poll. Ahead only 7-5 entering 4th Q, Oklahoma (1-0) finally broke through with 3 quick TDs. Bears D forced 4 FUMs, including 1 on own 2YL, stopped Sooners on 4th-and-1 on their 7YL, and knocked OU QB Steve Davis out of game. Davis returned in 4th Q to jumpstart Sooners O, scoring game-winner on 1y keeper. Sooners rushed for 438y as HB Joe Washington gained 156y and FB Jim Littrell added 125y. HB Steve Beaird led Baylor with 54y rushing, 37y receiving with TD, and created safety with his FUM-inducing tackle of Sooners CB Tony Peters after latter had made INT deep in his own territory.

September 21, 1974

Navy 7 PENN STATE 6: Huge upset was orchestrated by Navy coach George Welsh, asst under Penn State coach Joe Paterno for 10 years. Navy (2-0) scored on game's only real drive: 80y effort in 2nd Q that was capped by FB Bob Jackson's surprise 4y TD pass to WR Robin Ameen. Victory by Midshipmen was due in part to Penn State (1-1) mistakes in heavy rain: 5 lost FUMs (1 at Navy 12YL and another at 9YL), 4 missed FGs by usually reliable K Chris Bahr (including 43y attempt at game's end), and late failed 2-pt conv. Nittany Lions, who lost 13-game unbeaten streak, had 20-8 advantage in 1st downs and 267y rushing but could not overcome errors.

WEST VIRGINIA 16 Kentucky 3: Wildcats (1-1) looked dandy when they buried West Virginia (2-0) at 1YL on opening KO. But, Mountaineers reversed field position on TB Artie Owens' 75y gallop to 10YL. WVU FB Heywood Smith scored on 4th down. Rainy slop contributed to pair of bad pitchouts by Kentucky QB Mike Fanuzzi (9-20/119y, 2 INTs) which helped Mountaineers to 16-0 lead by middle of 2nd Q. After that, Cats controlled action until they got close to WVU GL, where DT John "Tree" Adams and NG Jeff Morrow keyed pair of GLSs.

MISSISSIPPI STATE 38 Georgia 14: Sr QB Rocky Felker orchestrated upset as Bulldogs (2-0) scored 6 times and outgained Georgia 399y to 251y. Felker, who threw for 107y and TD and rushed for 59y and TD, opened scoring with 1y 1st Q TD pass to TE Bob Bozeman as MSU cruised to 24-0 H lead. RB Walter Packer rushed for 148y and TD, gaining 28 of 42y on opening scoring drive for Bulldogs (1-1) and added 25y burst for 24-0 lead in 2nd Q. Maroons enjoyed 283y to 96y advantage in dominant 1st H as they were on way to handing Georgia coach Vince Dooley his worst conf loss since his 1st year in 1964, 31-7 defeat to Alabama.

Texas A&M 21 LOUISIANA STATE 14: Punishing rush attack enabled Aggies (2-0) to top 7th-ranked LSU in game that was not as close as score might indicate. HB Skip Walker (16/130y), HB Bubba Bean (14/127y), and FB Bucky Sams (16/107y) all cracked century rushing mark—and all scored TDs—as Wishbone O was in full gear with 417y rushing. Bean personally outgained Tigers in 1st H, 113y to 89y, and made 50y TD run for 14-7 lead. Sams scored game-winner on 1y run in 4th Q to cap 37y drive after FUM REC by LB Garth Ten Napel. Tigers (1-1) had just single TO, but it was costly. LSU had opened scoring on 46y run by TB Brad Davis, but was forced to punt 7 times. Bengals' 2nd TD came on EZ FUM REC by WR Robert Dow.

MICHIGAN STATE 19 Syracuse 0: Spartans (2-0) racked up 391y (317y rushing) but it took QB Charley Baggett's 30y blitz-beating pass to WR Mike Jones inside last 1:30 of 2nd Q. Syracuse (1-2) D hung in well until TB Rich Baes (16/97y) scored 1st of his pair of 4th Q TDs at end of 70y drive early into Q. Orange coach Frank Maloney said, "Our defense played a tough, gritty game…Our offense gave us no help at all, our blocking was terrible." Syracuse made only 142y O, with 2.5 per run avg.

WISCONSIN 21 Nebraska 20: Highly memorable game played at Camp Randall Stadium was decided in 2-min span of 4th Q when Nebraska (1-1) had to settle for FG and 20-14 edge after having established 1st-and-goal at Wisconsin 2YL. Badgers (2-0) completely turned tables by scoring 2 plays later on 77y pass play from QB Gregg Bohlig to WR Jeff Mack with 3:29 left. Mack caught ball at own 35YL, racing 65y to winning score. Huskers were crippled by loss of QB David Humm, who left contest in 1st Q with hip injury, and loss of IB John O'Leary, who missed half of game after blow to head. O'Leary had given Nebraska 14-7 H lead on 6y scoring run, but with injuries mounting Nebraska managed only 2 FGs by K Mike Coyle in 2nd H while surrendering 2 TDs. Badgers had built confidence after 1973's 20-16 loss in Lincoln.

IOWA 21 Ucla 10: Hawkeyes (1-1) became perhaps day's most unlikely winner on Saturday rife with upsets: 4 top-10 and 8 top-20 teams went down to defeat. Iowa entered game with 12-game losing streak, but Hawks' "Bubble 50" D held QB John Sciarra and Bruins' Veer attack in check, limiting Sciarra to 113y total O. Iowa's wing-T O was led by unheralded 5th-year sr QB Rob Fick, who had been cut during previous year. Fick tossed 2 TDs within 52 secs of each other in 2nd Q for decisive pts. Iowa FB Mark Fetter, who broke 3 tackles on 30y scoring reception in 2nd Q, rushed for 4th Q TD to cap 91y drive and seal unlikely victory. Bruins (0-1-1) fumbled 6 times, losing 3, while being outrushed 241y to 194y.

Miami 20 HOUSTON 3: Hurricanes (1-0) were led by punishing DL featuring NG Rubin Carter, DT Bruce Ely and DT Eddie Edwards, and completely swamped Houston (1-2). Miami took lead for good with 35y scoring drive in 1st Q to 5y TD run by TB Don Martin, which came after Ely recovered FUM by Cougars RB Donnie McGraw. Miami TB Woody Thompson rushed for game-high 85y and clinching 4th Q 1y TD, while Canes D amassed 5 sacks. Houston D forced 4 FUMs, but its O could convert them only into 3 pts on 22y FG by K Lennard Coplin.

Oklahoma State 26 ARKANSAS 7: Coming off emotional win over Southern Cal, Arkansas was flat as prairie versus regional rival Oklahoma State (2-0). Special teams dominated for Cowboys as they got school-record 4 FGs from soph K Abby Daigle and 83y punt TD RET by frosh TB Wes Hankins. That helped build commanding 19-0 4th Q lead. Oke State O contributed 285y rushing as O-line dominated at scrimmage. Using 5-man front led by DTs James White and Phil Dokes, Cowpokes prevented Razorbacks (1-1) from crossing midfield until 4th Q while forcing 5 TOs and surrendering only 125y rushing. Hogs HB Barnabas White's 11y scoring run in 4th Q prevented shutout.

AP Poll September 23

1 Ohio State (23)	1110		11 Wisconsin	200
2 Notre Dame (26)	1104		12 Oklahoma State	192
3 Oklahoma (8)	913		13 North Carolina State	191
4 Alabama (4)	896		14 Tennessee	171
5 Michigan	756		15 Arizona	135
6 Texas	588		16 Illinois	115
7 Arizona State	477		17 Louisiana State	109
8 Pittsburgh	273		18 Southern California	103
9 Texas A&M	256		19 Penn State	97
10 Nebraska	237		20 Miami	95

September 28, 1974

TEMPLE 34 Boston College 7: Temple (2-0) QB Steve Joachim (21-33/205y, INT) ripped apart Eagles, tossing 3 TD passes, while Owls RB Walt Hynoski rushed for 138y. Owls D contributed 6 sacks in holding BC to 173y total O and 11 1st downs. Boston College (0-2) scored its sole TD on run by FB Keith Barnette (64y rushing). After 10th straight victory since last season's 45-0 loss to BC, Temple coach Wayne Hardin called win, "biggest I've ever been associated with."

Southern California 16 PITTSBURGH 7: Fast-rising Pitt (2-1) program had already climbed to top 10 ranking, but was no match for Trojan squad that torched them for 28 1st downs and 452y. USC (1-1) won battle of RBs as TB Anthony Davis rushed for 149y, 90y more than Panthers TB Tony Dorsett. Pitt's scrappy D hung tough, holding USC to 3 pts after 3 Qs and knocking out QB Pat Haden in 2nd Q. Despite gaining only 111y, Pitt actually took 7-3 lead in 2nd Q on 9y scoring pass from QB Bill Daniels to WR Karl Farmer. USC finally mounted 2 TD drives of 80y and 78y in 4th Q behind QB Vince Evans. In defeat, Dorsett set all-time rushing record at Pitt with 1,994y, eclipsing mark of 1,957y held by FB Marshall Goldberg since 1938.

AUBURN 21 Tennessee 0: Reborn Tigers (3-0) thrust themselves into SEC race behind D that remained unscored upon. With DEs Rusty Deen and Liston Eddins pinching Tennessee's Veer attack, Auburn surrendered only 153y of O and 8 1st downs, only 2 in 2nd H. Offensively Tigers racked up 319y, with 3rd-string FB Kenny Burks scoring all 3 TDs. Volunteers (1-1-1) trailed only 6-0 entering 4th Q, but being able to cross midfield once entire game—that drive ended at close of 1st H on missed FG—prevented rally. Vols QB Condredge Holloway managed 41y passing and −1y rushing as he was sacked 5 times.

KENTUCKY 28 Indiana 22: Wildcats (2-1) QB Mike Fanuzzi threw for 2 TDs and ran for 114y and 2 more scores as home team built 28-7 lead before Indiana rallied. Hoosiers (0-3) scored 15 4th Q pts to make game interesting with FB Reggie Holmes catching 2nd TD pass and QB Terry Jones throwing 3y TD pass to WR Mike Flanagan. HB Sonny Collins rushed for 160y for Kentucky team that gained 382y on ground. Collins

had been doubtful for game with knee injury until coach Fran Curci's wife located acupuncturist. Hoosiers Jones and QB Bob Kramer combined to pass for 286y, with school record 8/178y contributed by TE Trent Smock.

Purdue 31 NOTRE DAME 20: Huge underdog Purdue (1-1-1) rose up to smite mighty Notre Dame for 1st time since 1969. Boilermakers scored on 1st 3 possessions and returned INT by LB Bob Mannella for TD to build insurmountable 24-0 lead. ND (2-1) lost FUM on 2nd play and had 1st pass returned for TD. Closest Irish could get was 24-14 after FB Wayne Bullock scored twice on short runs. But having 4 drives halted on downs deep in Purdue territory prevented comeback. ND QB Tom Clements threw for 264y but also 3 INTs. Loss snapped Notre Dame's 13-game win streak and 14-game win streak over Big 10 opponents.

MISSOURI 9 Arizona State 0: Shutout of Arizona State (2-1) for 1st time since 1965, was surprise, although Missouri (2-1) had to share credit with muddy, swamp-like conditions in Columbia. Game's only TD unfolded on 18y pass from QB Ray Smith to WR Mark Miller at end of 1st H, while K Tim Gibbons added 21y FG in 4th Q. Unaccustomed Sun Devils could rush for only 117y in muck and had 4 of their passes picked off.

RICE 10 Louisiana State 10: Owls played like, well, Rice (0-2-1) in gaining 10 1st downs on 77y rushing. Thanks to 7 LSU TOs, however, Rice had 10-7 lead in game's final min. Tigers (1-1-1) prevented total shocker on 27y FG by K Rusty Jackson. Owls put up 10 pts in 1st H on 9y scoring pass from QB Claude Reed to TB Kenneth Roy and 35y FG by K Alan Pringle with both drives being converted from TOs. Tigers made 172y by H with 5 drives entering Rice end, but had no pts to show for effort. LSU, rushing for 260y, scored TD in 3rd Q on 1y run by TB Terry Robiskie.

TEXAS TECH 26 Texas 3: Red Raiders stunned Texas (2-1), sending Horns to 1st conf defeat since 1971 (20 games). Texas Tech (2-0-1) jumped out to 23-pt margin in 1st H and ate clock in 2nd H, defeating Texas for 1st time since 1968. Soph QB Tommy Duniven threw 3 TDs to WR Lawrence Williams, 1 for 77y, and completed 7-7/145y. Longhorns had 3 more 1st downs, 16-13, but could not punch ball in EZ behind QB Marty Akins, who rushed for team-high 71y. Texas fell behind 26-3 at H as they managed only 58y, all on ground.

AP Poll September 30

1 Ohio State (25.2)	1044		11 Auburn	224
2 Oklahoma (24.2)	1002		12 Arizona	210
3 Alabama (3.2)	898		13 Florida	191
4 Michigan (4.2)	878		14 Illinois	183
5 Texas A&M (1.2)	554		15 Penn State	168
6 Nebraska	452		16 Miami (Fla.)	144
7 Notre Dame	406		17 Pittsburgh	77
8 North Carolina State	344		18 Arizona State	74
9 Southern California	258		19 Texas	72
10 Texas Tech	257		20 Arkansas	44

October 5, 1974

Penn State 21 ARMY 14: Penn State coach Joe Paterno would rather not see another service academy anytime soon. Two weeks after losing to Navy, Nittany Lions (3-1) fell behind 14-0 to Cadets as RB Brad Dodrill and QB Scott Gillogly scored on short TD runs. Both Army (1-3) scores followed Penn State FUMs deep in own territory. Lions D never let Army cross midfield from that point on, while O scored 2 TDs in 2nd Q to slip ahead 15-14 by H. Frosh TE Randy Sidler caught 1st collegiate reception for go-ahead 18y TD late in 1st H on pass from QB Tom Shuman.

NORTH CAROLINA 45 Pittsburgh 29: Tar Heels (3-1) obliterated precarious 21-20 Pitt H lead with 22-pt 3rd Q outburst. TB Mike Voight scored 2 of 3 UNC TDs during decisive opening of 2nd H, while QB Chris Kupec led O that gained 550y. Panthers (2-2) had marched downfield with opening possession, which ended on TB Tony Dorsett's 3y scoring run. Kupec answered with 43y TD pass to WB Jimmy Jerome, 1st of 6 TDs for Tar Heels as TB James Betterson joined Voight with 2 rushing TDs. Dorsett finished with 57y rushing.

DUKE 16 Purdue 14: Coming off its big upset of Notre Dame, Boilermakers (1-2-1) killed themselves with 10 PENs/109y, including double foul at end when they could have had 1 more chance to pull out win. Duke (3-1) forged 10-0 lead but then gave away pts with special teams blunder. Purdue got break in 2nd Q on bad punt snap by Duke and went 29y to 1y TD by FB Pete Gross. TB Scott Dierking (19/122y) keyed 86y drive in 4th Q to Purdue's only lead at 14-10. Devils' winner was set up by WR Troy Slade's 16y punt RET for TB Tony Benjamin's 2nd TD run with less than 9 mins to play.

CLEMSON 28 Georgia 24: Behind rushing attack that gained 299y, Tigers (2-2) beat Georgia for 1st time in 19 years. Alternate QB Mike O'Cain rushed for 2 2nd H TDs as Clemson won topsy-turvy game that witnessed 5 lead changes. Bulldogs (2-2) took 10-0 lead, in part by containing Clemson O. QB Mark Fellers came off bench to run for Tigers TD and throw another—8y to TE Bennie Cunningham—as home team grabbed 14-10 H lead. Georgia HB Horace King and O'Cain then alternated 2nd H TDs as neither team could pull away.

FLORIDA 24 Louisiana State 14: Mighty Gators (4-0) D, led by roaming LBs Ralph Ortega and Glenn Cameron, bowed its back inside its 10YL thrice to never allow single pt while shielding 7-0 lead during 1st 3 Qs. "It looked like the ball was on our 20 yard-line for three hours,'" said Florida coach Doug Dickey. After frosh HB Tony Green (13/78y) dodged for 25y to set up his short TD run in 1st Q, Florida held on as LSU (1-2-1) dominated play until its fumbled punt late in 3rd Q resulted in Florida K David Posey's chipshot FG, to be followed by WR Lee McGriff's 16y TD grab that vaulted

Gators to 17-0 lead. McGriff would add 62y lightning bolt TD in 4th Q, but not before Tigers growled 83y on 10 plays, capped by QB Billy Broussard's 21y TD dash. But, LSU couldn't score again until TE Brad Boyd's 10y catch in last 2 secs.

Alabama 35 MISSISSIPPI 21: Overcoming 2 huge TOs that propelled Rebels (2-2) into 21-14 lead, Alabama rolled with 3 straight TDs. Down 14-7 entering 3rd Q, Mississippi quickly scored following recovered FUM on Tide 15YL as QB Kenny Lyons rushed in 2nd score of day. Moments later, Alabama (4-0) QB Richard Todd attempted pitchout that was grabbed by Rebs DE Gary Turner and returned 42y for go-ahead TD. HB Willie Shelby quickly knotted score with 58y scoring jaunt as Alabama scored TDs on consecutive drives to regain lead for good. Alabama S Ricky Davis finished things by returning INT 67y to set up Todd's clinching 1y TD run.

Notre Dame 19 MICHIGAN STATE 14: Home-standing Spartans (2-2) saddened their 77,431 crowd by giving away 2 FUMs in their territory and compounding these errors by adding pair of roughness PENs to assist Notre Dame (3-1) in putting FB Wayne Bullock (36/127y) in position to power for pair of short TDs in 1st H. Bullock was stopped inches short of TD with score at 16-0 in 3rd Q, and it inspired Michigan State to ramble 99y in 11 plays (extended by ND's roughing P foul) to QB Charley Baggett's 26y TD to WR Mike Jones. After 2nd FG by ND, Michigan State TB Richard Baes trotted 9y for TD with 3:49 to play, but DB Randy Payne's INT of Baggett (4-11/102y) wrapped it up for Irish few mins later.

California 31 ILLINOIS 14: Fightin' Illini (3-1) could not contain Cal's high-powered attack as QB Steve Bartkowski (14-19/244y) hooked up with WR Steve Rivera (8/158y) for 2 TDs. Cal (3-1) spotted Illini TD before reeling off 31 straight pts with TB Howard Strickland on 35y run and TB Chuck Muncie with 12y run joining Rivera in EZ, while K Ron Vander Meer tied school record with 54y FG. Illinois rushed for 255y and threw for 168y more but lost 3 FUMs and were burned by 8 PENs/85y. Bartkowski had been ready to give up football for baseball, but changed his mind when drafted in lowly 19th round of June's pro baseball draft.

KANSAS 28 Texas A&M 10: Kansas (3-1) ran Aggies from ranks of unbeaten as FB Robert Miller and HB Laverne Smith rushed for 142y and 135y respectively, while QB Scott McMichael completed 12-14/178y, 2 TDs in 2nd H. Texas A&M (3-1), held to just 173y rushing, took 10-7 lead at H with FB Bucky Sams scoring TD on 1y run following punt block by CB Tim Gray, that was returned 21y to Kansas 4YL by DT Edgar Fields. McMichael put Jayhawks in front for good early in 3rd Q on 61y bomb to WR Emmett Edwards, who then juked out DB James Daniels to cover final 30y untouched. Kansas gained 453y in its surprisingly convincing win.

Michigan 27 STANFORD 16: Cardinals (0-3-1) were down to their 3rd QB—Jerry Waldvogel—in last 4 games, but he turned out to put scare into Wolverines. By keeping Michigan (4-0) from making any 1st downs in 1st Q, Stanford used K Mike Langford's 3 FGs to build 9-6 H edge. Waldvogel (21-40/229y, TD, INT) threw for 114y in 1st H. Wolverines got down to business and went 94y to QB Dennis Franklin's 12y option keeper. Just secs after Stanford FB Scott Laidlaw (TD catch) laid ball on grass at 9YL, Franklin had another TD run for 20-9 lead. Action in 4th Q saw UM answer Waldvogel's TD toss to Laidlaw with 78y drive to FB Scott Corbin's 2y TD run. Michigan's only TD in 1st H had come on TB Gordon Bell's 1y sweep after Stanford's disastrously short punt in middle of 2nd Q.

COLORADO STATE 33 Brigham Young 33: For 15 mins, officials huddled before disappointing home crowd, ruling that Colorado State K Clark Kemble's last-sec x-pt try was no good following QB Mark Driscoll's 15y TD pass to WR Willie Miller that tied game. Driscoll threw 4 TD passes in match-up with Cougars (0-3-1) QB Gary Shiede, who tossed 3 scores of his own. Shiede had lost FUM on own 15YL while BYU was running out clock to set up Rams' wild finish. After Miller's TD, Colorado State (1-2-1) was hit with unsportsmanlike PEN to force Kemble, who kicked 2 FGs including school-record 59y effort, to try conv kick from farther out.

AP Poll October 7

1 Ohio State (33)	1144	11 North Carolina State	327
2 Oklahoma (24)	1124	12 Arizona	229
3 Alabama (1)	958	13 Wisconsin	174
4 Michigan (2)	893	14 Arkansas	133
5 Nebraska	664	15 Penn State	98
6 Notre Dame	485	16 Texas A&M	95
7 Southern California	431	17 Texas	71
8 Florida	418	18 Arizona State	51
9 Texas Tech	411	19 Kansas	34
10 Auburn (1)	395	20 Miami (Ohio)	20

October 12, 1974

MARYLAND 41 Clemson 0: Terps (3-2) brought Clemson down to earth as QB Bob Avellini completed 14-22/213y, while D forced 6 TOs in posting shutout. Maryland raced out to 20-0 H lead on 2 short TD runs by WB John Schulz and 2 FGs by K Steve Mike-Mayer. Terps used INT, FUM, and long punt RET to set up 17 of those 20 pts. Tigers (2-3) then managed to hold onto ball for long 3rd Q drive that ended on 1YL thanks to Terps' magnificent GLS. Game was over then, even without Maryland's 21-pt 4th Q. Tigers gained 240y, not enough to overcome mistakes.

Virginia Tech 31 SOUTH CAROLINA 17: QB Bruce Ariens kept ball on ground to mastermind pair of Gobblers (1-4) 2nd H drives that ate 78 and 84y respectively. Virginia Tech's 24-pt explosion in 2nd H created walk-away defeat of forlorn South Carolina (0-5) that had its Homecoming spoiled. Ariens wiffed on all his passes (0-6) but found strong running up middle in leading carrier, HB Phil Rogers (20/120y, 2 TDs), as well as HBs Roscoe Coles (111y) and George Heath (104y). Gamecocks had built 17-7 H lead on passing by QB Ron Bass (8-17/103y, INT), even though TDs were scored on runs by HBs Randy Chastain and Jay Lynn Hodgin.

ALABAMA 8 Florida State 7: Miserable Seminoles (0-5), losers of 17 straight games, came so close to copping huge upset. Ahead 7-3, FSU's 1st-year coach Darrell Mudra elected to take safety with Seminoles buried deep in own territory. Alabama (5-0) shook off doldrums after free-kick and marched 33y before K Bucky Berrey booted game-winning 36y FG. FG was set up by 32y completion by backup QB Jack O'Rear to WR Ozzie Newsome. Florida State, which outrushed (207y to 157y) and outpassed (138y to 72y) Crimson Tide, had K Ahmet Askin miss 2 FGs, and had another blocked. Noles TB Larry Key offered game's only TD on 6y run, which came at end of 9-play, 78y drive to give Florida State 7-0 lead in 1st Q. Tide was held without TD at Denny Stadium for 1st time in coach Bear Bryant's 17-year tenure.

VANDERBILT 24 Florida 10: Vandy grounded high-flying Gators (4-1) as backup QB David Lee sparked 18-pt 2nd H performance. After running in 7y TD in 3rd Q, Lee connected on 2-pt pass with TE Barry Burton, who ignited drive with 32y run on trick play, for 14-7 lead for Vanderbilt (3-1). After 32y FG by Florida K David Posey, Lee threw 5y scoring pass to Burton to put away Gators. Any chance to rally ended on INT by Vandy DB Scott Wingfield deep in own territory in 4th Q. Gators, outrushed 263y to 170y, scored their TD on 8y run by HB Tony Green in 2nd Q.

LOUISIANA STATE 20 Tennessee 10: QB Billy Broussard led Tigers (2-2-1) to must win with 3 TD drives, including 75y effort in 1st H and 80y march to clinch game in 4th Q. Vols (2-2-1) led 10-7 at H with QB Condredge Holloway throwing 33y scoring pass to WR Larry Sievers while LSU was losing 4 FUMs. Tigers started holding onto ball, taking lead for good in 3rd Q on 7y scoring run by TB Terry Robiskie. With D posting its 2nd H shutout, Tigers beat Tennessee for only 2nd time against 13 defeats.

OHIO STATE 52 Wisconsin 7: Wisconsin (3-2), victors over Missouri and Nebraska, marched 80y on opening drive to take 7-0 lead. Badgers were probably feeling pretty good about themselves. Buckeyes (5-0) then scored on their next 9 possessions to crush any good feeling on Wisconsin sideline. TB Archie Griffin rushed for 18/112y—16th straight 100y game—and QB Cornelius Greene rushed for 146y and 2 TDs to pace Buckeyes attack that gained 359y on ground. Greene also threw 6y TD to WB Brian Baschnagel, who also scored twice. Sole Badgers TD came on 38y reception by WR Ron Pollard of pass from QB Gregg Bohlig, who threw for 125y but was picked off 4 times—3 by Ohio S Bruce Ruhl.

MICHIGAN 21 Michigan State 7: Wolverines (5-0) won 5th straight in series as D forced 6 TOs in setting up 2 short scoring drives, while DE Dan Jilek scored 2nd TD on EZ REC of muffed punt snap he helped create with hard rush. Michigan built 21-0 H lead as TB Gordon Bell scored on 13y run and QB Dennis Franklin and WB Jim Smith hooked up on 44y TD pass with time elapsing in 1st H. Spartans (2-3), held to 45y during 1st H, did not score until 4th Q on 4th down 15y scoring pass by QB Charlie Baggett to TE Mike Cobb.

Baylor 21 ARKANSAS 17: Bears (3-2) shook up SWC with stunning result. Recovering FUM on Arkansas 36YL late in 4th Q, Baylor used methodical 7-play drive to score winning 1y TD run by HB Steve Beaird with 1:08 remaining. Hogs (3-2) had gone ahead 17-14 on 3y scoring run by WB Barnabas White with 7:42 left for last of their 17 consecutive pts. Baylor had enjoyed early 14-0 lead on TD run of 25y by WB Philip Kent and his reception of 16y scoring pass by QB Mark Jackson. QB Mark Miller led rally for Arkansas with 2nd Q 41y TD pass to WR Freddie Douglas, but Miller lost FUM of snap to set up Baylor's winning TD.

Oklahoma 16 Texas 13 (Dallas): Game's biggest play featured two eventual all-time greats as Sooners DT Lee Roy Selmon's bone-crushing, FUM-causing tackle on 4th-and-1 buck in 4th Q by Longhorn frosh FB Earl Campbell halted Texas (3-2) with score knotted at 13-13. Campbell, it appeared, had gained necessary y for 1st down. Oklahoma LB Rod Shoate, who was in on 25 tackles, broke up 2 passes and caused FUM recovered at midfield soon after K Tony DiRienzo kicked winning 37y FG. Sooners (4-0), who outrushed Texas 353y to 162y, took 7-0 lead on 22y scoring run by QB Steve Davis before Horns reeled off 13 straight pts. Steers K Billy Schott kicked 2 FGs and Campbell scored on 12y run to cap 33y drive set up by short OU punt. Oklahoma WR Billy Brooks scored on 40y run on E-around in 4th Q but missed x-pt kept game tied. HB Joe Washington rushed for 122y for Sooners.

Missouri 21 NEBRASKA 10: Tigers (3-2) D returned to form after debacle in Madison to stun Huskers, ranked 2nd in total O and scoring in NCAA. Nebraska (3-2) could manage only 54/101y rushing, but had 10-0 lead on QB Terry Luck's 10y scoring pass to WB Don Westbrook with 11:26 left in 4th Q. Tigers then exploded behind backup QB Steve Pisarkiewicz, who led 3 TD drives in 4th Q, Mizzou twice converting TOs. Pisarkiewicz rushed for 2y TD to cap 71y drive and put Tigers on board. Huskers FB Gary Higgs then lost FUM on own 25YL to set up 9y scoring pass to SB Mark Miller and 14-10 lead for aroused Missouri. Deep in his own territory, Luck then threw foolish INT, returned 6y by DB Steve Yount to Nebraska 5YL. FB Tony Galbreath scored on next play to stunningly end matters.

OREGON STATE 23 Washington 9: Game ended wildly as Beavers (1-4) scored 2 TDs in final 66 seconds. It was tied at 9-9 when Oregon State stopped Huskies on 4th down incompletion at Beavers 41YL. State marched 59y to winning 2y TD run by FB Dick Maurer on drive keyed by HB Ray Taroli's 22y sprint. Desperate Huskies (2-3) were then pinned in own territory, surrendering ball on downs on own 3YL to set up unneeded 1y TD run by Beavers HB Bill Cecil with 10 ticks of clock left. Washington had not trailed until game's end, scoring for 6-0 lead on 1y run by FB Robin Earl in 1st Q. Beavers' 1st TD came as result of trick play as QB Alvin White handed off to TB Elvin Momon, who handed to WR Chuck Gardner, who pitched back to White, who threw 47y TD pass to wide-open WR Grant Boustead.

Stanford 13 UCLA 13: Battle of contrasting styles ended in tie as Bruins K Brett White booted 37y FG as time expired. UCLA (2-1-2) rushed for 320y with HB Russel Charles (17/109y) and HB Wendell Tyler (16/106y) topping 100y barrier, while Cardinal QBs Mike Cordova and Guy Benjamin each led TD drives. Benjamin put Stanford (0-3-1) in

front 13-10 at H with 79y drive, completing 6 passes/58y including 11y TD pass to WR Bill Singler. To knot it up, Bruins drove 78y—including Tyler's 28y run—as 4th Q wound down.

AP Poll October 14

1 Ohio State (51)	1160	11 Penn State	244
2 Oklahoma (5)	1040	12 Nebraska	169
3 Michigan (1)	924	13 Kansas	141
4 Alabama (1)	814	14 Florida	107
5 Auburn (1)	636	15 Arizona State	73
6 Southern California	574	16 Texas	69
7 Notre Dame	506	17 Texas Tech	59
8 Texas A&M	425	18 Maryland	41
9 Arizona	394	19t Miami (Ohio)	39
10 North Carolina State	323	19t Tulane	39

October 19, 1974

NORTH CAROLINA 33 North Carolina State 14: Tar Heels (4-2) roared out of blocks, scoring 3 TDs within 6-min span of 1st Q in snapping State's 14-game ACC win streak. Still, Wolfpack (6-1) held brief 7-0 lead as TB Roland Hooks (14/75y) scored 1st of his 2 TDs to cap 40y drive set up by UNC FUM. Tar Heels then scored rapid-fire: 36y run by TB Mike Voight, 3y keeper by QB Chris Kupec after successful onside-KO, and 10y run by TB Jim Betterson after D recovered FUM on NC State 40YL. Kupec accounted for 3 TDs, while Voight rushed for 111y.

Michigan 24 WISCONSIN 20: Tied at 7-7 at H, Wolverines (6-0) took control at opening of 2nd H with 2 long TD drives while, in between, Badgers (3-3) were held to 3 plays and punt. Michigan QB Dennis Franklin led both drives, capping 1st with 8y pass to TE Greg DenBoer. Badgers managed 2 surplus TDs in 4th Q, including QB Gregg Bohlig's 26y pass to WR Jeff Mack. Wisconsin was hampered by 1st Q injury to its 1,000y rusher, TB Bill Marek, but walked away feeling respectable, having emerged from season's halfway mark against formidable slate that featured Michigan, Ohio State, Missouri, Colorado, and Nebraska.

ILLINOIS 21 Michigan State 21: Honoring 50th anniversary of Memorial Stadium and HB Red Grange's 5-TD performance against Michigan on October 18, 1924, Illinois (4-1-1) grabbed 7-0 lead after opening possession as TB Jim Phillips scored from 1y out. Spartans (2-3-1) ignored program, which included introduction of Grange at H, and reeled off 3 TDs in 2nd Q. Michigan State QB Charlie Baggett ran for 2 TDs and threw another of 16y to Dane Fortnoy. Illini scored 2 TDs in 2nd Q themselves, with 45y pass from QB QB Jeff Hollenbach to TE Joe Smalzer. Illini led 21-14 at H, foes were knotted 21-21 at H. Oddly, presence of Grange, great scorer of yore, seemed to inspire both Ds, which both posted 2nd H shutouts.

TEXAS 38 Arkansas 7: Texas FB Earl Campbell dominated 2nd Q with 68y run for eventual winning pts and then blocked punt that was returned for 1y TD by teammate DT Doug English and 17-0 lead. Rushing up middle, Campbell blocked P Tommy Cheyne deep in Arkansas (3-3) territory, with ball snared in mid-air by English. Longhorns (4-2) outrushed Arkansas 385y to 176y despite 50y scoring run by Razorbacks RB Rolland Fuchs that prevented shutout. Longhorns received 109y rushing from Campbell on only 8 rushes, while FB Roosevelt Leaks added 58y.

SOUTHERN METHODIST 19 Rice 14: With 35 secs left, Rice (0-4-1) K Alan Pringle booted FG that appeared to win game at 14-13, prompting team and coaches to pour onto field in celebration. Resultant 15y PEN helped Mustangs (5-1) SB Arthur Whittingham return KO 70y to set up 13y TD pass from QB Ricky Wesson to WR Freeman Johns for shocking win. SMU had built 13-3 lead on 4y and 50y TD runs by Wesson (22/149y). Owls then brought QB Tommy Kramer off bench, and he led early 4th Q scoring drive he capped with 8y pass to TE Kenneth Ray. Kramer then threw 2-pt conv pass to WR Ed Lofton to pull to within 13-11.

TEXAS TECH 17 Arizona 8: After starting QB Tommy Duniven was injured in 1st H, Coach Jim Carlen turned to inexperienced soph QB Don Roberts to lead Red Raiders (4-1-1). Roberts threw 6y TD for eventual winning pts in 2nd Q to WR Lawrence Williams that gave Texas Tech 10-0 lead at H. Hampered by 4 TOs, Wildcats (5-1) could not score until 4th Q on 5y pass from QB Bruce Hill to WR Theo Bell. Texas Tech D held Arizona to 273y, 162y less than its avg. Red Raiders K Brian Hall, who had artificial right leg, opened scoring with 1st Q FG.

Nebraska 56 KANSAS 0: Cornhuskers (4-2) took out frustrations over mediocre record with whipping of 13th-ranked Kansas. QB David Humm was healthy, completing 23-27/230y, 3 TDs, all to WB Don Westbrook, as Nebraska scored on 6 of its 7 2nd H possessions while Jayhawks could not muster even single 1st down. Humm saddened Lawrence crowd by breaking 2 conf records set in 1973 by former Kansas QB David Jaynes: Humm hit 15 straight completions and 36 career TD passes. IB John O'Leary and WB Jeff Moran each added 2 TD runs for Huskers. Jayhawks (4-2) hung within 7-0 until late in 2nd Q, but suffered 4 TOs and dented superior Nebraska D for only 71y rushing and 72y passing.

STANFORD 34 Washington 17: On hot seat all year, Stanford (1-3-2) QB Mike Cordova (23-37/284y, 3 TDs) carved apart Huskies (2-4) and silenced his critics. Washington turned ball over 6 times and was never in it. FB Scott Laidlaw scored early, and Cordova hit WR Billy Singler on 31y go-pattern for TD and 14-0 lead. Washington made some noise with 80y drive to QB Denny Fitzpatrick's 1y sneak, but Fitzpatrick (6-14/97y, 2 INTs) and his successors pitched INTs by Stanford CB Paul Skrabo, DL Drew Palin, and S Doc Blanchard that set up 13 pts.

AP Poll October 21

1 Ohio State (50)	1196	11 Texas Tech	188
2 Oklahoma (8)	1082	12 Florida	184
3 Michigan (1)	923	13 Texas	182
4 Alabama (1)	887	14 Arizona State	125
5 Auburn (1)	699	15 Maryland	94
6 Southern California	628	16 Arizona	88
7 Notre Dame	529	17 North Carolina State	55
8 Texas A&M	507	18 Tulane	46
9 Nebraska	355	19 Miami (Ohio)	35
10 Penn State	314	20 California	28

October 26, 1974

RUTGERS 20 Air Force 3: Taking advantage of 2 Air Force FUMs, Scarlet Knights (4-1-1) grabbed 10-3 lead and never looked back. FB Curt Edwards rushed for 147y and QB Bert Kosup scored 2 TDs to lead Rutgers. Falcons (2-5) had tied score at 3-3 on 24y FG by accurate K Dave Lawson, but could not overcome 4 INTs, 2 by Rutgers S Ed Jones. Starting Falcons QB Ken Vaughn had awful start, passing 1-7/0y, 2 INTs before finding bench. TB Ken Wood rushed for 87y to lead Air Force.

MARYLAND 20 North Carolina State 10: It took Wolfpack (6-2) almost 2 years to lose ACC game, and suddenly they could not stop. In becoming school's all-time rusher, Terps (5-2) TB Louis Carter rambled for 180y and 4th Q game-clinching 6y TD run. Maryland gained 441y, while its D held Wolfpack to 288y, far below 440y avg. Maryland QB Bob Avellini threw for 137y and scrambled for 30y scoring run that put Terps ahead 7-3 in 2nd Q. NC State QB Dave Buckey threw for 156y, but was picked off 3 times. Game film probably inspired Terps: camera caught NC State laughing at Maryland K Steve Mike-Mayer after his FG miss at end of last year's Wolfpack win.

GEORGIA TECH 26 Tulane 7: After racing out to 5-0 record and no. 18 ranking against so-so competition, Tulane (5-1) still had lots to prove. Even though they jumped to brief 7-3 lead on TD by RB Steve Trueting, Green Wave failed to swamp Atlanta, gaining only 88y rushing and 186y total O against Yellow Jackets (4-4), while losing QB Steve Foley to fractured right fibula. QB Rudy Allen was forced out of game with diabetes complications, but led Georgia Tech on 3 scoring drives with 1 ending with Allen's 2y keeper for 10-7 lead. Backup QB Danny Myers twice led 4th Q TD drives as Tech pulled away. Tulane had enjoyed brief 7-3 lead.

VANDERBILT 24 Mississippi 14: With S Jay Chesley opening scoring with 66y INT TD RET, Vanderbilt (4-2) was well on way to 1st win over Rebels since 1951. HB Jamie O'Rourke ran for 92y, 2 TDs to pace O; his 10y TD run in 2nd Q gave Dores 14-0 lead. Thanks to 2 Vanderbilt FUMs, Mississippi (2-5) tied game 14-14 as QB Kenny Lyons threw and ran for TDs. But, Vandy outclassed Rebs in 2nd H, getting key 38y FG from K Mark Adams and adding insurance on 2nd TD run by O'Rourke.

NOTRE DAME 38 Miami 7: Irish (6-1) rout was on early as WR Pete Demmerle caught 47y bomb from QB Tom Clements (13-19/154y) for TD less than 3 mins into 1st Q. Clements threw another scoring pass in 1st H and ran for score, while S Randy Harrison returned INT 44y for another TD. Notre Dame 1st-teamers scored 38 pts in 1st H before retiring to bench to spectate in 2nd H. Hurricanes (4-2) D allowed 423y and could force no TOs, while managing solo TD: 2y TD pass from QB Frank Glover to TE Phil August in 3rd Q.

IOWA 14 Illinois 12: Hawkeyes (3-4) HB Eddie Donovan's last-sec 8y scoring reception stunned over-achieving Illini (4-2-1). Iowa QB Rob Fick led his O deep into Illinois territory twice in 4th Q only to be denied, but he made last 49y trip work with screen pass to Donovan. Donovan skipped past tackler to joyfully reach EZ. Illini had scored 12 straight pts as K Dan Beaver kicked 2 FGs, including 50y effort in 2nd Q, and QB Jeff Hollenbach threw 19y TD to TE Joe Smalzer.

Miami (Ohio) 38 TOLEDO 22: Redskins (6-0-1) extended unbeaten streak to 19 games with win that cleared way for MAC title. FB Rob Carpenter pounded for 181y rushing, 3 TDs against D focused on QB Sherman Smith and TB Randy Walker. Still, Smith threw 2 TDs including 37y effort to Carpenter that tied game at 7-7 in 1st Q. Game was tied 14-14 at H before Miami blew it open with 21-pt barrage in 4th Q. Toledo (5-2) QB Gene Swick ran for 2 TDs and threw 12y TD to TE Don Seymour.

Texas A&M 20 BAYLOR 0: Key SWC match-up was won easily by Aggies as their D was awesome, preventing Baylor (3-3) ever from crossing Texas A&M's 40YL and adding INT TD on amazingly nimble play by DT Warren Tarahan. Texas A&M (6-1) rushed for 310y but needed odd play to score its only O TD as WR Carl Roaches scooped up FUM on 1 bounce and raced 56y with FUM dropped by Aggies HB Bubba Bean (15/77y). A&M K Randy Haddox added 2 FGs and leaping Tarahan fell into EZ with INT caught on 1YL for final TD. Bears managed just 4 1st downs on 149y with 4 TOs. HB Steve Beaird rushed for 71y to pace Baylor.

NEBRASKA 7 Oklahoma State 3: Trailing 7-3 in 4th Q, Cowboys (3-3) marched 70y to Nebraska 1YL, but QB Charlie Weatherbie lost FUM recovered by CB Ardell Johnson with 3:22 left. Huskers (5-2) were pinned deep and forced to punt, but Cowboys failed to move, and final try ended with Nebraska CB Jim Burrows' INT. All scoring occurred in 3rd Q as Nebraska went 79y to IB Tony Davis' 4y run. QB David Humm kept drive alive with 30y pass to WB Rich Bahe, while OSU K Abby Daigle booted 32y FG.

Brigham Young 37 ARIZONA 13: Magic number was 5 in aerial war that shook up WAC. BYU sr QB Gary Shiede (20-35/267y) tossed 5 TD passes, while D turned in 5 INTs for Cougars (3-3-1). Shiede turned to WR John Betham—only other sr in starting lineup—in absence of injured WR Jay Miller, and combination sparkled. Betham caught 10/144y, 3 TDs. After teams exchanged opening scoring drives for 7-7 tie, INTs on consecutive Arizona drives were converted into TB Jeff Blanc's TD catch for commanding 21-7 lead in 1st Q. While Arizona (5-2) QB Bruce Hill threw for 200y, he hit only 9-29 with 5 INTs. Wildcats FB Jim Upchurch rushed for 106y.

WASHINGTON 66 Oregon 0: In true reversal, Huskies (3-4) wiped out memory of 58-0 beating at hands of Oregon in 1973 to end patience-trying 10-game conf losing streak. Huskies QB Dennis Fitzpatrick rushed for 105y, TD, and alternate QB Chris Rowland added 2 running TDs and 12y scoring pass to WR Scott Phillips before he broke left ankle. Washington ground game churned up 338y as TB Mike Vicino and FB Robin Earl each scored 2 TDs. Huskies D also dominated, holding Ducks to 55y O and 2 1st downs and preventing them from crossing midfield until 4th Q.

AP Poll October 28			
1 Ohio State (45)	1222	11 Florida	236
2 Oklahoma (14)	1123	12 Texas	214
3 Michigan (2)	969	13 Texas Tech	198
4 Alabama (1)	887	14 Arizona State	175
5 Auburn (1)	765	15 Maryland	159
6 Southern California	584	16 Miami (Ohio)	59
7 Notre Dame	559	17 Mississippi State	28
8 Texas A&M	513	18 UCLA	24
9 Nebraska	353	19 Temple	16
10 Penn State	336	20t San Diego State	13
		20t Wisconsin	13

November 2, 1974

Pittsburgh 21 SYRACUSE 13: With TB Tony Dorsett (16/67y, TD) on shelf in 3rd Q with ankle injury, Panthers (6-2) turned to QB Bill Daniels and TB Elliott Walker to hold off Syracuse. Daniels threw TD of 11y to TE Jim Corbett to give Pittsburgh 14-13 lead in 3rd Q. Then, looking for 4th Q insurance, Daniels completed 19y pass on 3rd-and-12 to Corbett that set up Walker's 1y scoring plunge with 4:36 left. Orangemen (2-6) gained 207y on ground and FB Mark Bright had 2y TD run in 1st Q

BOSTON COLLEGE 35 West Virginia 3: FB Keith Barnette (20/91y, 4 TDs) ruined West Virginia for high-flying Eagles (4-3). Mountaineers (2-6) scored early on 36y FG by K Emil Ros that got them within 7-3 in 1st Q but could cross midfield only twice more. Boston College lost TB Mike Esposito with dislocated shoulder in 2nd Q, but BC had answer in sub TB Earl Strong, who carried 19/118y and scored 14y TD.

PENN STATE 24 Maryland 17: DB Jim Hite, starting due to injury to DB Jim Bradley, was surprise scoring leader for Nittany Lions (7-1) with 2 TDs. Hite's 1st score was traditional 79y INT RET, his 2nd was 21y special teams run with INT of lateral that came on Maryland's KO RET following Penn State's only O TD. Fans celebrating back-to-back TDs were shocked into reality as they witnessed Terps (5-3) score 18 secs later on 66y QB Bob Avellini to TE Walter White TD pass, duo's 2nd scoring hook-up of day. That was heart-racing 3 TDs hitting scoreboard in 25 secs.

FLORIDA 25 Auburn 14: Florida's O-line opened up holes against Tigers (7-1) that had not been seen all year. FB Jimmy DuBose was chief beneficiary, rushing for 143y to lead unit that churned up 324y. Florida QB Don Gaffney opened scoring with 7y pass to WR Lee McGriff as Auburn trailed for 1st time all season. Gators (7-1) finished 1st H in front 16-14 and then shut out Auburn in 2nd H, although Tigers once made it downfield but failed on dropped pass in EZ by WB Mike Gates. QB Phil Gargis (7-14/129y) had led Auburn to early 14-13 lead by throwing 6y TD pass to WR Ed Butler and setting up TB Mitzi Jackson's 1y TD run by completing 43y pass to WR Thomas Gossom.

Houston 31 GEORGIA 24: Texan invaders spoiled 3-game win streak of Georgia (5-3). Cougars (6-2) prowled early at Athens, riding RB Marshall Johnson's 76y gallop to 12YL with short pass from QB Bubba McGallion (4-5/96y, TD). McGallion soon scored on 5y slant through LT, and when Houston LB Bubba Broussard followed with INT, Johnson scored on 17y TD counter for 14-0 lead. Georgia fought back with 89 and 77y TD trips, highlight of which was TD pass to HB Glynn Harrison from QB Matt Robinson (16-30/281y, 2 TDs, 4 INTs). Odd sequence ended 1st H and benefited Cougars with RB Reggie Cherry's tie-breaking 7y TD run: Bulldogs DB Larry West intercepted Houston backup QB David Husmann but coughed up FUM at UGa 7YL before West was downed. Late in 3rd Q, Cougars tallied important TD at end of 2-play, 80y bolt: FB John Housman (17/92y) sliced over RT from 3YL.

OHIO STATE 49 Illinois 7: Ohio coach Woody Hayes earned his 200th win in easy fashion as Buckeyes (8-0) set school record with 644y. TB Archie Griffin rushed for 144y, for NCAA record 18th straight regular-season 100y rushing tally, and QB Cornelius Greene threw for 127y and rushed for 127y. Griffin opened scoring with 16y run in 1st Q. Illini (4-3-1) made brief surge and tied game at 7-7 on fancy 5y scoring pass from SB Tracy Campbell to WR Frank Johnson. It served only to anger Ohio State, which methodically scored 2 TDs in each of next 3 Qs. Greene rushed for TD and threw 2 others, Griffin added another TD in 3rd Q on 22y run, and his brother, TB Ray Griffin, scored in 4th Q on 39y run with pitchout.

Michigan State 28 WISCONSIN 21: Michigan State (4-3-1) won its 2nd straight in Big 10 to position itself for bigger things. Wisconsin (4-4) put itself behind conf 8-ball by losing at home. Confident QB Charley Baggett was all over field, scooting and throwing, blocking on broken play TB Richard Baes took for 22y TD in 3rd Q for 21-14 lead, even rejecting Spartans' coach Dennis Stolz's play call for his own that resulted in 3y TD pass to TE Larry Bethea. Baggett stated afterward he thought he was conf's best QB. Badgers tied it 14-14 in 3rd Q on HB Billy Marek's 4y run and lucky 2-pt conv FUM REC by G Rick Koeck. After Baes' TD, Badgers went 77y to tie it again at 21-21 on 77y drive. Baggett's 5y wide sprint for TD after fake into line to FB Levi Jackson proved to be winning pts with 9:12 to play.

Oklahoma 28 IOWA STATE 10: Sooners (7-0) led by only 7-0 as frosh HB Elvis Peacock opened scoring with 9y run in 2nd Q. Lead expanded in 25-sec span of 3rd Q when 2 Iowa State FUMs were converted into TDs for 21-0 lead. Cyclones (4-4) ended up with D effort that held powerful Oklahoma attack to 329y, considerably below 532y norm. Still, Cyclones couldn't prevent 4 TDs. On O side of things, Iowa State

twice drove into Sooners territory trying to tie game in 2nd Q, but was stymied by PENs. After Sooners scored their 3 straight TDs, 2 on passes by QB Steve Davis, Cyclones rebounded for game's final 10 pts with backup QB Tom Mason tallying TD.

SOUTHERN CALIFORNIA 15 California 15: As pro he would be known for his accuracy but against Trojans in last min of play, Cal (5-2-1) K Jim Breech was wide right on 34y attempt. Moments earlier, USC K Chris Limahelu missed from 39y out as neither team could score in 4th Q. Trojans (5-1-1) had tied game in 3rd Q on QB Pat Haden's 1y keeper and his 2-pt pass to TE Jim Obradovich. Bears had built 12-0 lead in 2nd Q behind QB Steve Bartkowski, who threw for 141y and 16y TD to WR Steve Rivera. Trojans S Marvin Cobb ended Bartkowski's string of 135 INT-free passes, returning his 2nd Q pick-off to Cal 14YL to set up USC's 1st score: 1y TD run by TB Anthony Davis. Both Davis and backup TB Allen Carter rushed for 119y.

WASHINGTON 31 Ucla 9: With injuries to top 2 QBs, Bruins (4-2-2) were forced to turn to 17-year-old frosh QB Steve Bukich to end 16-year losing streak in Husky Stadium. Thanks to harassing Washington (4-4) D, Bukich never had much chance, completing as many passes to his receivers (5) as to Huskies defenders, and being sacked 5 times as well. Huskies gained 428y, with 314y from ground attack keyed by 240-lb FB Robin Earl, who bulled his way to 152y. Sub QB Jeff Dankworth led Bruins to 2 scoring drives in 2nd H before re-injuring his ankle. UCLA, however, could mine only single TD on HB Carl Zaby's 1y run in 4th Q.

AP Poll November 4			
1 Ohio State (49)	1212	11 Southern California	344
2 Oklahoma (10)	1090	12 Texas	324
3 Alabama (2)	918	13 Miami (Ohio)	149
4 Michigan (1)	850	14 Maryland	54
5 Texas A&M	643	15 Houston	42
6 Florida	531	16 Arizona State	36
7 Penn State	522	17 Oklahoma State	33
8 Notre Dame	503	18 California	20
9 Nebraska	464	19t Pittsburgh	19
10 Auburn	381	19t Texas Tech	19

November 9, 1974

ARMY 17 Air Force 16: Cadets (3-6) looked to their bench for late win, needing backup QB and backup K for winning FG at end. Frosh QB Leamon Hall completed 3 passes/57y and induced pass interference PEN to take Army to Air Force 16YL. K Mike Marquez then kicked 33YL FG—1st ever in career for soph—with 17 secs remaining at Michie Stadium to end evenly-matched game. Falcons (2-7) rushed for 249y and scored on 3 FGs by K Dave Lawson and 5y run by TB Ken Wood. Army opened scoring with 1y scoring run by QB Scott Gillogly, but then surrendered 13 straight pts to trail entering 4th Q. HB Willie Thigpen's 4y rushing TD regained lead for Army at 14-13 early in 4th Q before teams traded FGs to end scoring.

NORTH CAROLINA STATE 12 Penn State 7: Nittany Lions (7-2) took 7 snaps from within NC State 8YL in 3rd period and 7 times were denied. QB Tom Shuman threw 13y TD pass to WR Jim Eaise in 4th Q to get Penn State on scoreboard but also threw costly INT earlier in Q to NC State S Bob Divens. Wolfpack (8-2) had success running against nation's stingiest rush D, gaining 215y on ground. FB Stan Fritts rammed for 112y and TD, then turned passer in flipping 22y TD to TE Pat Hovance. NC State scored TDs in 2nd and 3rd Qs to make Lions squirm under 12-0 shortfall.

CLEMSON 54 North Carolina 32: Scoring its most-ever pts in ACC game, Tigers (5-4) routed UNC as HB Ken Callicutt rushed for 3 TDs and threw another. Clemson QB Mark Fellers threw 2 TDs and ran for 2 others. Clemson rung up 38 pts and 322y by H, scoring game's opening 4 TDs. Tigers ended with 522y, with Callicut rushing for 170y and Fellers accounting for 171y in O. Bright spot for Tar Heels (5-4) was duo of QB Chris Kupec and TE Charles Waddell, who connected for 3 TD passes.

Florida State 21 MIAMI 14: Seminoles (1-8) snapped 20-game losing streak with newfound O power, gaining 404y over stunned Miami. FSU grabbed 14-0 lead at H with TDs on 14y run by TB Leon Bright and 48y catch by TE Joe Goldsmith from QB Steve Mathieson. Winning TD came on 1y run by Jeff Leggett in 4th Q that was sandwiched between 2 long-range TD missiles by Canes (5-3). TE Witt Beckman caught 77y scoring pass from QB Frank Glover for 1st Miami TD and TE Phil August caught razzle-dazzle 80y pass from WR Steve Marcantonio.

Georgia 17 Florida 16 (Jacksonville): Gators (7-2) happily accepted Sugar Bowl bid and promptly lost to Georgia (6-3), with difference being successful 2-pt conv by Bulldogs and similar failed try by Florida. Wining pts came on QB Matt Robinson conv pass to WR Richard Appleby following HB Horace King's 5y TD run in 4th Q. Gators then pulled to within 17-16 in game's waning moments on 4y run by resourceful QB Don Gaffney before missing 2-pt conv. Florida dazzled with footwork, outgaining Bulldogs 420y to 263y, but fell short on final incomplete pass, while Bulldogs' best play—87y romp by HB Glynn Harrison—came back because of PEN.

MICHIGAN STATE 16 Ohio State 13: Spartans' victory was as controversial as it was stunning. Game ended with Ohio State (8-1) WB Brian Baschnagel prone in EZ having scored apparent winning TD. Officials, however, ruled that time had elapsed just before snap, decision that had coach Woody Hayes screaming. Later referee Gene Calhoun not only confirmed call, but said that O had committed game-ending PEN too. Moments before final play, Michigan State was hopping mad over pass ruled incomplete that LB Terry McClowry appeared to have intercepted. Teams had played evenly in 3-3 1st H before Spartans (5-3), building confidence, hit 2 big home runs in 4th Q: 44y TD reception by WR Mike Jones and 88y TD burst by TB Levi Jackson to hammer home upset. Jackson's run, with Michigan State trailing 13-9 and game clock showing 3:30 to play, clearly was 1 of great moments in Spartans football history. Ohio

had forged ahead 13-3 on K Tom Klaban's 2 FGs and TD run by FB Champ Henson, but only had 3 pts to show for trio of 2nd H drives that probed MSU 10YL. Spartans' win was their 3rd in last 4 games of less-than-frequent series.

OKLAHOMA 37 Missouri 0: Sooners (8-0) steamrolled another Big 8 opponent as FB Jim Littrell bulled his way to 155y for buzz-saw O that made 571y. HB Joe Washington added 143y in becoming 2nd all-time rusher in OU history, while HB Grant Burget scored twice. Ahead 17-0 at H, Sooners limited Tigers (5-4) to –7y on 1st 3 drives of 3rd Q to guarantee their 17th straight win and propel team to nation's top-ranking with Ohio State's loss. Missouri gained 241y as QB Steve Pisarkiewicz threw for 145y.

COLORADO 17 Kansas 16: Buffs (4-5) bounced back from 13-0 H deficit by dominating 2nd H, even answering Jayhawks' only score—23y FG by K Mike Love for his 3rd of game—with 94y KO TD RET by TB Melvin Johnson. HB Laverne Smith had sparkled in 1st H for Kansas (4-5), rushing for 10/150y including 72y jaunt to open scoring in 1st Q. FB Terry Kunz (24/126y) was star of 2nd H for Colorado, rushing for 64y of 84y drive that he capped with 1y scoring run and then for 22y on short drive to K Tom MacKenzie's winning 24y FG. So different was 2nd H that Smith could add only 32y to his rushing total, and he lost key FUM on his own 40YL to set up Colorado's trip from midfield to winning FG.

SOUTHERN METHODIST 18 Texas A&M 14: Aggies (7-2) stumbled in Dallas because they could not block SMU's gigantic man in middle. NG Louie Kelcher, all 6'5, 275lbs of him, wreaked havoc for Mustangs (6-3) as he recorded 24 tackles. Mustangs held surprising 16-0 lead at H as TE Oscar Roan grabbed FUM by his teammate, FB David Bostick, and ran 14y to EZ for opening TD, K Ted Thompson added 21y FG, and QB Ricky Wesson raced 20y for TD. Aggies, who stubbornly outrushed SMU 230y to 225y, answered in 2nd H with 2 TDs by little-used FB Jerry Honore. Needing only FG to win because they trailed 16-14, Texas A&M took over on its 13YL late in game. Ponies DT Steve Morton then finished off visitors with safety by sacking A&M QB David Walker as Aggie desperately looked for receiver.

BAYLOR 34 Texas 24: Fast-starting Longhorns (6-3) wasted 24-7 H lead in losing to Baylor for 1st time since Bears were Sugar-Bowl-bound in 1956. HB Raymond Clayborn, FB Earl Campbell, and FB Roosevelt Leaks all scored 1st H TD runs, but Texas was outscored 27-0 in 2nd H. Baylor (5-3) QB Neal Jeffrey (20-31/ 351y, 2 TDs) had great day passing and ran for TD. Game actually turned on special teams play: Bears DB Johnny Greene blocked punt deep in UT territory, and Jeffrey's QB sneak cut deficit to 24-14 in 3rd Q. Jeffrey soon hit WR Ricky Thompson for 54y TD pass. Baylor D, which strategically sent its CBs charging at QB Marty Akins to stop Wishbone run, forced critical TO: Baylor's go-ahead TD was set up on big hit by frosh CB Ronald Burns on Akins to force FUM. WB Philip Kent's 6y TD run placed Bears ahead and in driver's seat for their 1st SWC crown since way back in 1924.

BRIGHAM YOUNG 21 Arizona State 18: Despite allowing 2 RETs of INTs for TDs, Cougars (5-3-1) hung on in sloppy WAC contest that all but ended ASU's hopes for 6th straight conf crown. BYU QB Gary Shiede threw 5 INTs, but also threw 2 TDs to FB Tim Mahoney, including 8y scoring pass for winning TD in 4th Q. Sun Devils (5-3) nearly matched Cougars' 8 TOs with 6 of their own, and only gained 186y to BYU's 363y. But, Arizona State rode star CB Mike Haynes for big play that allowed them to cling to 18-14 lead entering 4th Q. Haynes made 55y INT TD RET.

Southern California 34 STANFORD 10: Trojans (6-1-1) finally put aside recent so-so performances against Stanford to break 1st place tie in Pac-8. TB Anthony Davis—who passed former TB Mike Garrett (1963-65) for 2nd place on school career rushing list with 3,267y—rushed for 119y and 2 TDs as USC gained 295y on ground. Ahead by 17-3 at H, Trojans put game away with devastating 92y TD drive to open 3rd Q. It was capped by Davis' 21y scoring dash. Trip featured 15y run by Davis, 20y burst by FB Ricky Bell, and 26y romp by FB Dave Farmer. Cardinals (3-4-2) struggled as QB Mike Cordova (9-23/89y, 2 INTs) was harried all day by Troy DTs Art Riley and Gary Jeter.

AP Poll November 11

1 Oklahoma (48)	1198	11 Penn State	245
2 Alabama (10)	1102	12 Miami (Ohio)	160
3 Michigan (4)	1014	13 Maryland	139
4 Ohio State	877	14 Houston	117
5 Notre Dame	668	15 Michigan State	110
6 Nebraska	577	16 North Carolina State	103
7 Auburn	552	17 Pittsburgh	65
8 Southern California	487	18 Oklahoma State	63
9 Florida	318	19 California	55
10 Texas A&M	306	20 Texas Tech	48

November 16, 1974

KENTUCKY 41 Florida 24: Florida's Sugar Bowl bid did nothing to intimidate Wildcats (6-4), who scored game's final 20 pts to outlast Gators. After K John Pierce tied it at 24-24 with school-record 52y FG, Kentucky scored winning TD on 1y run by HB Steve Campassi early in 4th Q. Pierce then added insurance 37y FG, while HB Bill Bartos scored from 4y out to close scoring. Gators (7-3) did most damage during 5-min period in 2nd Q, scoring 17 pts with FB Jimmy DuBose reaching EZ on 18y run and WR Lee McGriff hauling in 42y TD pass from QB Don Gaffney.

AUBURN 17 Georgia 13: Tigers (9-1) posted 2nd H shutout that was tested to very end. Georgia marched to 10YL early in 4th Q before HB Horace King lost FUM, recovered by Auburn LB Johnny Sumner, and Bulldogs (6-4) soon moved within Auburn 5YL before being stopped on downs. QB Phil Gargis sparked Auburn O, rushing for 159y, as Tigers gained 343y on ground. Gargis scored 2nd TD on 2y run while TB Secdrick McIntyre added 112y and had tilt's 1st TD on 1y blast. Georgia scored only TD on 50y pass from QB Matt Robinson to WR Gene Washington.

MISSISSIPPI STATE 7 Louisiana State 6 (Jackson): Bulldogs (7-3) took advantage of disastrous punt miscue by LSU (3-5-1) in 2nd Q to score on QB Rocky Felker's short rollout and then turned 2nd H over to their solid D unit. Tigers P Rusty Jackson could not launch punt from his 11YL, and it all blew up when he threw panicked pass to ineligible receiver. LSU tallied mostly-fruitless 215y until WR Brad Boyd (5/85y) made terrific 25y catch at Mississippi State 18YL in 4th Q. Three plays went only 2y, but Boyd slanted between DBs to grab lob to EZ with 2:43 to play. LSU opted for potential win, but QB Billy Broussard (7-22/93y, TD, INT) tried to nail TB Brad Davis with GL pass but it was behind blanketed receiver.

NOTRE DAME 14 Pittsburgh 10: Fighting Irish (8-1) continued to struggle, blowing 7-0 lead thanks to 2 FUMs, INT, and blocked punt, but forging victory with 55y scoring drive late in 4th Q. FB Wayne Bullock (25/124y) barreled for 10y on 4th-and-4 play to Panthers 22YL that kept drive alive, before QB Tom Clements scored winning TD on 3y run. Panthers (7-3) converted Irish mistakes into only 10 pts—with 3 on go-ahead 52y FG by K Carson Long in 3rd Q—as TB Tony Dorsett was held to 61y, 148y less than he gained versus ND in 1973. Pittsburgh threatened at end, marching to Irish 22YL before 2 final passes were batted down in EZ.

Oklahoma 45 KANSAS 14: Difference between Sooners (9-0) and rest of Big 8 continued to exaggerate as Kansas allowed 444y at home. QB Scott McMichael gave Jayhawks (4-6) early 7-0 lead with 73y scoring run. Oklahoma QB Steve Davis shrugged his shoulders and tied game in 2nd Q with 72y pass to WR Billy Brooks. Davis then ran for go-ahead score before throwing his 2nd TD, 14y effort to WR Tinker Owens, as OU started to pull away for 18th straight win. McMichael was not through, completing 14y TD to WR Emmett Edwards for 21-14 H deficit. Kansas D was valiant in 0-0 3rd Q, but then Oklahoma beat it down with 24 pts in 4th Q. Davis rushed for 129y to lead O, while DT Lee Roy Selmon had 13 tackles and blocked FG.

Colorado 37 OKLAHOMA STATE 20: Buffs (5-5) ran over Oklahoma State, gaining 283y on ground with FB Terry Kunz (18/80y) leading way with 3 TD runs. Colorado built 20-0 H lead as D, ranked last in conf, held Cowboys to 5y rushing. Oklahoma State (5-4) was capable of 3 TDs in 2nd H, including 30y run by WB Skip Taylor (8/66y), but surrendered Buffs' 91y TD drive in 3rd Q that ate more than 9 mins.

BAYLOR 17 Texas Tech 10: Red Raiders (6-3-1) grabbed 7-0 H lead as TB Larry Isaac capped 61y drive with 1y scoring run, and D used 8-man front to limit Bears. Baylor CB Ronald Burns turned game around with hit that sent Raiders QB Dave Roberts to sideline and INT that was converted into TD, 1y run by HB Steve Beaird. Tech took 10-7 lead after blocked punt by DE Tommy Cones set up 26y FG by K Brian Hall. Bears (6-3) knotted game on 32y FG by K Bubba Hicks, and their D made stop to position 55y drive led by QB Mark Jackson. FB Pat McNeil's 20y romp was winning score as Bears kept SWC title hopes alive and moved into AP Poll.

CALIFORNIA 37 Washington State 33: Bears CB (and future NFL coach) Herm Edwards finally ended lead-change madness with his 4th INT of game as time expired. QB Chuck Peck (3-12/26y, 6 INTs) sparked Washington State's 442y run game with 27/135y, including 35y TD dash to open scoring. Cougars (2-8) HB Ron Cheatham (29/194y) scored twice, including 1y smash nearly midway in 4th Q that provided 31-29 lead. Meanwhile, California (7-2-1) TB Chuck Muncie scored twice, rushed for 70y and caught 7/90y, and QB Steve Bartkowski (21-30/304y, INT) placed himself at top of school's single season passing y list, his 2,262y surpassing Craig Morton's 2,121y in 1964. It was Bartkowski's 42y throw to WR Wesley Walker that set up TD run by FB Howard Strickland (19/112y) to make 7th lead change hold up for Cal at 37-31 with 7:17 to play. Still, Bears weren't out of woods just yet. Wazzu advanced to Cal 2YL with 1:39 showing on clock, but Cal LB Kim Staskus forced Peck to fumble, and Bears took intentional safety on C Jack Harrison's high punt snap through EZ with 7 secs left.

AP Poll November 18

1 Oklahoma (45)	1198	11 Maryland	227
2 Alabama (9)	1078	12 Miami (Ohio)	187
3 Michigan (8)	1040	13 North Carolina State	168
4 Ohio State	874	14 Michigan State	113
5 Notre Dame	639	15 Houston	105
6 Nebraska	630	16 Baylor	63
7 Auburn	560	17 Texas	50
8 Southern California	542	18 Pittsburgh	42
9 Texas A&M	375	19 California	41
10 Penn State	311	20 Florida	36

November 23, 1974

HARVARD 21 Yale 16: Once again "The Game" decided Ivy League championship as upset lifted Crimson (7-2) into tie with Yale for title. Harvard's final 95y drive ate up last 5 mins and produced QB Milt Holt's winning 1y TD run. Holt, nicknamed "The Pineapple" simply because he was from Honolulu, threw for 212y and 2 TDs in leading Crimson to sweet win in 100th anniversary of Harvard football. Yale (8-1) entered contest having surrendered only 46 pts during season. Crimson WR Pat McInally finished with 6 catches to up his career reception total to 108.

MARYLAND 10 Virginia 0: Cavaliers were closing 3rd straight 4-win season but had plenty of fuel left to frustrate Liberty Bowl-bound Maryland (8-3) for much of 1st H. In fact, Cavs (4-7) twice set up 1st down camp inside Terrapins 10YL but pts failed to materialize when Maryland DB Jim Brechbiel blocked FG try and DE Rod Sharpless ruined 2nd chance with 2 sacks and FUM REC. Meanwhile, Terps failed even to nose into Virginia territory until last 30 secs of 1st H. TB Louis Carter, who set Terps' single game record with 213y rushing, transformed simple dive play into cut-back 45y gain that somehow converted 3rd-and-41 from Maryland's 17YL. QB Bob Avellini (11-22/97y, 2 INTs) quickly hit pass to set up K Steve Mike-Mayer's 33y FG and 3-0 lead. Carter boomed 44y for TD in 3rd Q to lock it up and unleash Terps' D, led by DT Randy White, that visited 4 sacks on UVa QB Jim Pruner (11-30/171y) in 2nd H.

North Carolina 14 DUKE 13: Blue Devils (6-5) S Laniel Crawford blocked punt early in 61st meeting of ACC neighbors, and TB Art Gore soon skied over North Carolina (7-4) D-line for 1y TD. Tar Heels tied it early in 2nd Q as DB Bobby Trott started methodical 78y TD advance by snatching INT of Duke QB Hal Spears. Devils answered with 86y trip to game's 3rd 1y TD run, this by FB Mike Bomgardner. However, Carolina special teamer Kirt Wilson blocked K Rich McInturff's x-pt try to keep score at 13-7. Each team wrestled with scoring frustration, including McInturff's controversial, wide-by-whisker FG try, until Duke had possession and 6-pt edge at its 19YL with 5:57 to go. Gore (31/171y) caught swing pass but was clobbered into FUM, and Heels TB Mike Voight's 17y sweep set up QB Chris Kupec's TD pass for 14-13 lead. In 2 late tries, Duke made it to UNC 34 and 42YLs to no avail.

OHIO STATE 12 Michigan 10: Right foot of Czech walk-on K proved to be decisive for Rose Bowl-bound Buckeyes (10-1). K Tim Klaban's 4 FGs earned his team trip to Pasadena in yet another Big 10 tie decided by vote of ADs. Michigan K Mike Lantry lost chance for series immortality by missing 33y effort with 18 secs remaining. Wolverines (10-1) jumped to 10-0 lead, with WB Gil Chapman catching 42y TD throw on game's 1st series. Buckeyes methodically came back as D clamped down, posting shutout over final 3 Qs. Meanwhile Klaban booted 3 3-ptrs in 2nd Q and then winning 45y FG in 3rd Q. Both teams rushed for exactly 195y with top performances coming from TB Archie Griffin (111y) of Ohio and TB Gordon Bell (108y) of Michigan.

WISCONSIN 49 Minnesota 14: TB Billy Marek, 1 of Wisconsin's all-time best artists, put incredible cap on his November romp with 304y rushing and 5 TDs to win war for Paul Bunyan's Ax. Marek scored game's final 4 TDs and matched year-old record of Penn State's John Cappelletti for consecutive games with at least 200y rushing. They each had 3. Marek finished his season with 740y in final 3 games to boost year's total to 1,215y rushing. Game looked like shootout after Minnesota (4-7) TB Rick Upchurch took opening KO 100y for thrilling TD. Gophers went up 14-7 in 2nd Q, but Wisconsin (7-4) alertly recovered 3 Minnesota FUMs inside Badgers 15YL.

Oklahoma 28 NEBRASKA 14: Sooners unleashed awesome rushing attack in overcoming 14-7 3rd Q deficit to stretch unbeaten streak to 28 games. Oklahoma (10-0) tallied 482y on ground, led by FB Jim Littrell's 147y and HB Joe Washington's 142y. Nebraska (8-3) had taken 14-7 lead on trick play as IB John O'Leary took pitch from QB David Humm and then threw back to Humm for 11y score. OU HB Elvis Peacock then lost FUM on ensuing KO, but Huskers squandered chance to add to lead and following missed FG by Nebraska K Mike Coyle, Sooners marched 80y to tying 4y TD by Washington. Huskers especially suffered in 4th Q as they threw 3 INTs—2 picked off by S Randy Hughes—and surrendered 2 TDs: runs by Peacock and QB Steve Davis, which proved to be margin of victory.

KANSAS STATE 33 Colorado 19: Late-blooming Wildcats (4-7) ended 7-game losing streak as QB Steve Grogan completed 9-13/120y and 9y scoring pass to TE Dave Chambliss for 14-0 lead in 2nd Q. Kansas State upped lead to commanding 26-3 as TBs Kerwin Cox (14/76y) and Jim Couch rushed for TDs. Buffaloes (5-6) outgained Cats by 507y to 340y, but could not crack EZ until 4th Q on TD runs of 12y by TB Melvin Johnson and 1y by FB Terry Kunz (17/77y).

Baylor 31 SOUTHERN METHODIST 14: Surprising Baylor (7-3) caught Texas A&M for 1st place in SWC, casting O stars in little TB Steve Beaird (26/133y, 3 TDs) and QB Neal Jeffrey (11-17/166y), who slipped by Don Trull as Bears' leader in career pass y. Baylor overcame early FUM to cruise 80y as Beaird zipped away from SMU (6-4-1) star NG Louie Kelcher for 19y TD. Jeffrey hit 4 passes to lead Bears to 14-0 lead on another TD by Beaird in 2nd Q. Mustangs finally broke loose on next series, clicking along for 89y on QB Ricky Wesson's arm to 14y slant-in TD catch by WR Freeman Johns 16 secs before H. K Don Bockhorn drilled 59y FG to highlight Bears' 10-pt 3rd Q and just about lock up matters at 24-7.

Southern California 34 UCLA 9: Trojans (8-1-1) won 3rd straight trip to Pasadena with easy victory as TB Anthony Davis rushed for 195y to break former Trojan O.J. Simpson's team and conf rushing marks with 3,609y. Davis scored on 8y run to open 3rd Q, capping 81y drive that clinched win. K Chris Limahelu made Trojan-record 50y FG in 3rd Q. WR J.K. McKay added 17y scoring reception with brilliant behind-back grab, and DB Dennis Thurman closed scoring with 80y RET of FUM as USC enjoyed greatest series margin of victory since 40-13 win in 1944. Over-matched Bruins (6-3-2) trailed only 17-9 at H, behind QB Jeff Dankworth, who threw for 188y and rushed for 66y, as Bruins actually outgained rivals 370y to 349y.

Stanford 22 CALIFORNIA 20: As Cal QB Steve Bartkowski (20-41/318y, INT) threw go-ahead 13y pass to WR Steve Rivera (9/205y) with 26 secs left, Bears (7-3-1) had to like their chances. But, backup Cardinals QB Guy Benjamin (5-10/129y)—rumored to be transferring to San Diego State—went to work, throwing for 18y to TE Ted Pappas and 25y to TE Brad Williams, who fought through DB Herm Edwards to get to sideline with 2 secs left. K Mike Langford then booted winning 50y FG. Stanford (5-4-1) had built 19-10 lead late in 4th Q as Benjamin came off bench to lead visitors to 16 straight pts, including 61y scoring hookup with WR Tony Hill 1 play after LB Jeff Siemon's INT halted imposing Cal drive. Teams combined for 29 pts in 4th Q.

AP Poll November 25

1 Oklahoma (49)	1134	11 Maryland	222
2 Alabama (10)	1036	12 Miami (Ohio)	184
3 Ohio State	968	13 North Carolina State	172
4 Michigan	795	14 Michigan State	158
5 Notre Dame	641	15 Houston	96
6 Southern California	584	16 Baylor	95
7 Auburn	560	17 Texas	60
8 Texas A&M	384	18 Pittsburgh	35
9 Nebraska	371	19 Wisconsin	17
10 Penn State	362	20 Brigham Young	15

November 28-30, 1974

(Th'g) PENN STATE 31 Pittsburgh 10: Penn State was fired up for start of game: so much so that FB Tom Donchez accidentally knocked out LB Greg Buttle with his helmet while trying to exhort his mates in locker room. For 2nd straight season Nittany Lions (9-2) had to go back to locker room at H to find way to bounce back to blow out Pitt in 2nd H. For 2nd straight season, they did so by first stopping TB Tony Dorsett, who was limited to 65y rushing. Penn State QB Tom Shuman led 2nd H outburst by hooking up with WR Jim Eaise on 2 TD passes. Eaise's TDs made up for his twice fumbling on 1st H RETs, 1 of which set up Dorsett's 2y TD run as Pitt (7-4) ended H with 7-6 lead. Penn State G Tom Williams added TD on FUM REC in EZ, while K Chris Bahr kicked 4 FGs, including one from 50y. Win was 9th straight in series for Nittany Lions.

(Fri) Alabama 17 Auburn 13 (Birmingham): Despite squandering numerous opportunities, Crimson Tide (11-0) held on for 3rd perfect regular season in past 4 years. In control entire game, Alabama, nonetheless, was forced to punt from deep in own territory with time winding down. FUM at midfield—Tide DE Mike Dubose, future Bama coach, tipping away handoff from QB Phil Gargis to WR Dan Nugent on E- around—and it doomed Auburn (9-2). Controversy arose around potential Auburn TD in 3rd Q as 41y TD pass from Gargis to WR Tom Gossom was ruled incomplete because Gossum stepped OB at beginning of route. Tide had opened scoring with QB Richard Todd's 45y completion, 1 of only 2 successes on day for Todd, to HB Willie Shelby in closing moments of 1st Q. Tide then took advantage of muffed punt to stretch lead to 10-0 on K Bucky Berrey's 36y FG, before Auburn marched 71y to score on 1y TD run by Secdrick McIntyre (16/99y). Bama scored winning pts in 3rd Q on 13y run by FB Calvin Culliver.

(Fri) TEXAS 32 Texas A&M 3: Aggies (8-3) spit bit in losing 2 FUMs deep in own territory during game's 1st min to fall immediately behind by 14-0. Longhorns (8-3) scored on 18y run by HB Ray Clayborn and then 28y FUM RET by DE Lionell Johnson 12 secs later. Amazingly, Aggies lost FUM on 3rd possession, setting up 33y FG by K Billy Schott that created deficit too big for Texas A&M to overcome. A&M settled down to score on 25y FG by K Randy Haddox before Texas QB Marty Akins rushed for 2 TDs. Texas FB Earl Campbell rushed 28/127y. Aggies' previously great rush attack was held to 152y with HB Bucky Sams leading with 53y.

Navy 19 Army 0 (Philadelphia): For 2nd straight year, Navy (4-7) not only beat Army, but kept them off scoreboard. Navy rushers gained 290y with FB Bob Jackson scoring both TDs on runs of 3y and 6y, and TB Cleveland Cooper rushing for 105y. It was Cooer's 3rd straight 100y performance in series, and no back had ever done that before in history of Army-Navy. DE Tim Harden closed scoring with safety-producing sack of Army QB Scott Gillogly in 3rd Q. Cadets (3-8) managed only 145y rushing.

Georgia Tech 34 GEORGIA 14: Ignoring heavy rain, Yellow Jackets (6-5) upset Georgia as QB Danny Myers scored 2 TDs and led O that enjoyed 23 to 11 1st down advantage. Georgia Tech TB David Sims seemed best suited for weather, rushing for 110y and 2 TDs. Bulldogs (6-5), unable to get anything going to outside, were shut out at H 20-0 and did not reach paydirt until QB Matt Robinson's 1y keeper in 3rd Q following HB Glynn Harrison's 30y burst to 1YL. Tech coach Pepper Rodgers ran his record against Georgia as player and coach to 11-1.

Tennessee 21 VANDERBILT 21: HB Stanley Morgan's 3y run with 7 secs to play brought Vols (6-3-2) to 21-19 before QB Condredge Holloway hit WR Larry Sievers with tying 2-pt conv pass. TD was set up by FUM by Commodores P Barry Burton that put Tennessee on Vandy 11YL with 1:07 remaining. Tennessee had grabbed 13-0 lead in 1st Q on TD runs by Morgan and HB Mike Gayles, before momentum swung Vandy's way with TD in each of 1st 3 Qs. Vanderbilt (7-3-1) ground game was led by HB Jamie O'Rourke's 152y and HB Lonnie Sadler's 130y. Commodores won more than 5 games for 1st time since 1955. On other hand, Vols failed to win as many as 8 games for 1st time since 1965.

BAYLOR 24 Rice 3: On Golden Anniversary of their last SWC title, Bears (8-3) cruised to undisputed league championship. Workhorse TB Steve Beaird (28/134y) got Baylor off to good start with 6 carries that made up all of 58y TD drive in 1st Q. Beaird swerved to outside for 20y TD, small part of his new conf season record for rushing attempts (267). QB Neal Jeffrey keyed 80y TD drive in 2nd Q with 25y chuck to WR Ricky Thompson. Trailing 14-0, Rice (2-8-1) finally made some noise in 3rd Q. Owls K Alan Pringle, who missed 62y FG try in 2nd Q, made 29y chipshot after Rice squandered 1st-and-goal opportunity at 10YL. Bears backup QB Mark Jackson raced 14y for clinching score in 4th Q.

TULSA 30 Houston 14: Tulsa (8-3) surprised Cougars with stingy D that kept high-powered attack off board until well into 3rd Q. Meanwhile, opportunistic Golden Hurricane recovered FUM in EZ on 1st play of game for TD. RB Thomas Bailey added 2 TDs including 87y run. Houston (8-3), who last lost in September, trailed 13-0 at H and then 30-6 in 4th Q before scoring late TD on 31y pass from QB David Husmann to TE Don Bass. Cougars had 332y rushing, but could not overcome 4 lost FUMs. Despite 8 wins and MVC championship, Tulsa was shut out of bowls.

ARIZONA 10 Arizona State 0: Punting duel turned late in 4th Q when Sun Devils (6-5) threw costly INT, which LB Mark Jacobs returned 15y to ASU 19YL to set up winning 36y FG by K Lee Pistor. Wildcats (9-2) added late 4y TD run by HB Willie Hamilton on E-around to halt 9-year series losing streak. Arizona DE Willis Barrett led D, causing and recovering FUMs, deflecting 2 passes, and making 12 tackles. Arizona State matched Wildcats with 259y, with FB Mark Lovett gaining 81y rushing to pace Devils. Rivals combined for 21 punts with Arizona P Mitch Hoopes averaging 44.5y.

SOUTHERN CALIFORNIA 55 Notre Dame 24: USC TB Anthony Davis turned in 1 of football's greatest performances, and yet it may not have even been his best game against Notre Dame (9-2). Moments before H, Davis scored on 7y pass against nation's top rated D that cut into Irish's commanding 24-0 lead. With opening KO of 2nd

H, everything changed. Davis scampered 100y to Irish EZ. Moments later he scored his 3rd TD on 6y run. Next, he made 4y TD run which he followed up with 2-pt conv tally. Before incredible 3rd Q had ended, rest of Trojans (9-1-1) O, namely passing combo of QB Pat Haden and WR J.K. McKay (4/110y), managed 2 scores themselves as USC amazingly took 41-24 lead. Dazed Irish (9-2) surrendered 8 TDs over 17-min span from end of 2nd Q to beginning of 4th Q. Apparently beaten just before H, Trojans went on to outscore their rivals 49-0 in 2nd H. Notre Dame had given up only 8 TDs on season, but relinquished same number in short timeframe. Davis' performance came too late for many Heisman balloters, who had been rushed to vote by this weekend. Haden completed 11-17/225y, 4 TDs in becoming school's career leader with 31 TDs, while DB Charles Phillips contributed 3 INTs, including TD RET. Trojans, who had ball on ND 8YL as time expired, were 4 pts shy of most ever surrendered by Irish, which occurred in 59-0 loss to Army in 1944. In 3 career games against Irish, Davis scored 11 TDs, including 3 of his NCAA-record 6 KO TD RETs. Irish QB Tom Clements threw for 180y and 29y TD to WR Pete Demmerle, but was picked off 3 times. For 3rd straight year, winner of this game went on to win at least share of national title.

AP Poll December 2

1	Oklahoma (49)	1198	11	Texas	254
2	Alabama (12)	1112	12	Baylor	239
3	Ohio State	982	13	North Carolina State	228
4	Michigan	828	14	Michigan State	197
5	Southern California	616	15	Miami (Ohio)	154
6	Auburn	544	16	Texas A&M	79
7	Penn State	502	17	Brigham Young	31
8	Nebraska	500	18	Florida	28
9	Notre Dame	369	19	Arizona	20
10	Maryland	258	20t	Pittsburgh	18
			20t	Wisconsin	18

Conference Standings

Ivy League

Yale	6-1
Harvard	6-1
Penn	4-2-1
Brown	4-3
Princeton	3-4
Dartmouth	3-4
Cornell	1-5-1
Columbia	1-7

Atlantic Coast

Maryland	6-0
North Carolina State	4-2
Clemson	4-2
North Carolina	4-2
Duke	2-4
Virginia	1-5
Wake Forest	0-6

Southeastern

Alabama	6-0
Auburn	4-2
Georgia	4-2
Florida	3-3
Mississippi State	3-3
Kentucky	3-3
Vanderbilt	2-3-1
Tennessee	2-3-1
LSU	2-4
Mississippi	0-6

Southern

VMI	5-1
Appalachian State	4-1
East Carolina	3-3
Richmond	3-3
Citadel	3-4
William & Mary	3-3
Furman	2-4
Davidson	0-3

Big Ten

Ohio State	7-1
Michigan	7-1
Michigan State	6-1-1
Wisconsin	5-3
Illinois	4-3-1
Purdue	3-5
Minnesota	2-6
Iowa	2-6
Northwestern	2-6
Indiana	1-7

Mid-American

Miami (O)	5-0
Toledo	3-2
Ohio U	3-2
Kent State	2-3
Bowling Green	2-3
Western Michigan	0-5

Big Eight

Oklahoma	7-0
Nebraska	5-2
Missouri	5-2
Oklahoma State	4-3
Colorado	3-4
Iowa State	2-5
Kansas State	1-6
Kansas	1-6

Missouri Valley

Tulsa	6-0
Louisville	3-2
West Texas State	3-3
New Mexico State	2-3
Drake	2-3-1
North Texas State	1-3-2
Wichita State	1-4-1

Southwest

Baylor	6-1
Texas	5-2
Texas A&M	5-2
SMU	3-3-1
Arkansas	3-3-1
Texas Tech	3-4
Rice	2-5
TCU	0-7

Western Athletic

Brigham Young	6-0-1
Arizona	6-1
Arizona State	4-3
New Mexico	3-4
Texas El Paso	3-4
Colorado State	2-3-1
Utah	1-5
Wyoming	1-6

Pacific Eight

Southern California	6-0-1
Stanford	5-1-1
California	4-2-1
UCLA	4-2-1
Washington	3-4
Oregon State	3-4
Washington State	1-6
Oregon	0-7

Pacific Coast Athletic

San Diego State	4-0
San Jose State	2-2
Pacific	2-2
Long Beach State	1-3
Fresno State	1-3
Fullerton State *	0-3
* Ineligible	

1974 Major Bowl Games

Liberty Bowl (Dec. 16): Tennessee 7 Maryland 3

Struggle went way of Volunteers (8-3-1) on special teams play late in game. Ahead 3-0, Terps tried punt but C Marion Koprowski's snap went over head of P Phil Wagenheim, and ball went over to Tennessee at Maryland 7YL. With Terps DT Randy White causing havoc, Tennessee needed 3 downs to score winning TD, on 11y pass from backup QB Randy Wallace to WR Larry Sievers. Wallace, who shook off White's sack attempt on previous play, had replaced injured starting QB Condrede Holloway. Holloway was hurt on earlier 31y FG attempt, which was blocked by White. After Sievers' TD catch, Maryland (8-4) drove to Vols 20YL before Tennessee DB Ernie Ward picked off deflected pass by QB Bob Avellini. One play earlier, Maryland TB Louis Carter had thrown option pass to WR Frank Russell that was caught just out of EZ. Maryland's earlier FG, 28y effort by K Steve Mike-Mayer, was set up by 63y punt RET by DB Bob Smith.

Tangerine Bowl (Dec. 21): Miami of Ohio 21 Georgia 10

Redskins (10-0-1) dominated from outset as LB John Roudabush's FUM REC on Georgia's 1st play from scrimmage was converted quickly into 1y TD run by FB Rob Carpenter. Bulldogs (6-6) answered with scoring drive ended with 20y FG by K Allan Leavitt, but then Miami drove 78y for commanding 14-3 1st Q lead as QB Sherman Smith threw 7y TD pass to TE Ricky Taylor. Roudabush was up to old tricks in 2nd Q to further deflate Georgia's chances, recovering another FUM deep in Georgia territory. Smith scored on 8y keeper after Redskins took over on 22YL. Bulldogs managed 41y TD drive midway through 3rd Q, but damage was already done by underrated Miami. Carpenter rushed for 114y and Smith 90y, while QB Matt Robinson threw for 190y for Bulldogs. Victory over high-profile program earned eventual 10th place ranking in AP Poll for Miami.

Bluebonnet Bowl (Dec. 23): Houston 31 North Carolina State 31

Game would explode in 2nd H after North Carolina State held 10-3 lead after 1st 30 mins. Wolfpack's 17-10 advantage entering 4th Q was erased by 3-TD explosion by Houston (8-3-1), with go-ahead score coming on 73y pass from QB Bubba McGallion to WR Eddie Foster. Soon after Foster's TD, Houston S Joe Rust returned INT 43y to set up 5y TD run by FB John Housman (21/134y, 2 TDs). So, Cougars led by 14 pts. With less than 8 mins remaining, Wolfpack (9-2-1) begin 70y march to EZ. TB Tommy London's 9y scoring run pulled State to within 31-23 with incomplete pass on 2-pt conv spoiling victory ambitions. Wolfpack then recovered onside-KO with C Louis Alcamo pouncing on loose ball on Houston 47YL. QB Dave Buckey, who threw for 200y, led tying drive, capped by his 1y keeper. Clutch NC State FB Stan Fritts rushed for tying 2-pt conv.

Fiesta Bowl (Dec. 28): Oklahoma State 16 Brigham Young 6

Cougars (7-4-1) disliked result of their 1st-ever bowl trip, especially after crushing hit by Oklahoma State DT Phil Dokes dislocated QB Gary Shiede's shoulder late in 1st Q. BYU led 3-0 at that time and were driving to 2nd score behind Shiede (4-5/43y), nation's 2nd-ranked passer. Cowboys (7-5) rallied with help from 3 INTs thrown by BYU replacement QB Mark Giles. HB Kenny Walker's 12y TD run in 2nd Q proved to be game-winner, it coming after INT by Cowboys DE Tony Buck. Oke State piled on double indemnity insurance: 42y FG by K Abby Daigle and 40y scoring pass from WB Leonard Thompson to WR Gerald Bain in 2nd H. Interestingly, Cowboys had ball in Cougars territory only once in 1st Ho after Buck's INT RET to BYU 27YL. Brigham Young D continued strong play in 3rd Q by thwarting 2 Cowboy scoring chances with strong stops within their 10YL. Cowboys LB Larry Carr and DT Wayne Baker halted QB Charlie Weatherbie on 4th down at BYU 2YL to end 1st chance, CB Mike Russell stopped QB Jimmy Derrick on 4th down at 8YL to stop another. Cougars saw their 7-game win streak snapped despite having outgained Pokes 301y to 221y.

Sun Bowl (Dec. 28): Mississippi State 26 North Carolina 24

Bulldogs (9-3) edged North Carolina by unleashing awesome rush game, bulldozing way to 455y rushing and 25 1st downs. Mississippi State RB Walter Packer, who quietly led SEC in rushing with 994y, made noise in El Paso with game-record 183y rushing and 2 TDs. Tar Heels (7-5) hung tough with 402y of their own and took 24-20 lead in 4th Q on 26y FG by K Ellis Alexander. It was time for game's 4th and final lead change as QB Rockey Felker drove Bulldogs to winning 2y TD run by RB Terry Vitrano, who rushed for 164y and grabbed game MVP. Felker had biggest carry of night, converting 4th-and-2 on winning drive with 15y run, following block of FB James Smith to UNC 10YL. Tar Heels had final drive in motion, TB Mike Voight leading them to midfield before being halted on 4th-and-1 stand at own 48YL. Bulldogs ran out clock for 1st bowl victory in 11 years. UNC TB James Betterson (84y, 2 TDs rushing) returned 2nd H KO 45y to set up his own 6y scoring sweep for brief 14-10 lead.

Peach Bowl (Dec. 28): Vanderbilt 6 Texas Tech 6

Texas Tech (6-4-2) needed 35y FG by K Brian Hall with 2:21 left to tie game they should have won long before. Red Raiders rushed for 306y to control matters between 20YLs, but were unable to reach EZ. Best chance to score TD occurred late in 1st

H when Red Raiders marched to 1YL. Vandy's GL D twice stopped TB Larry Isaac (101y rushing), named game's outstanding O player, and then on 3rd down, QB Tommy Duniven was cut down on rollout as clock expired. Vanderbilt (7-3-2) led 3-0 at H on 31y FG by K Mark Adams. Red Raiders tied game 3-3 in 3rd Q on Hall's 26y FG, but had next scoring attempt die on blocked FG by burly Commodores frosh DT Dennis Harrison. Tie was soon broken as Red Raiders Duniven and Isaac fumbled away pitchout deep in own territory to set up 26y FG by Adams. Backs against wall, Texas Tech answered with WR Lawrence Williams' 54y KO RET to Vanderbilt 40YL, which led to Hall's tying FG. Tech FB Cliff Hoskins rushed for 116y, while Vandy was led by HB Jamie O'Rourke's 76y.

Gator Bowl (Dec. 30): Auburn 27 Texas 3

Once Longhorns (8-4) fell behind they were in trouble as playing catch-up was not their forte. Tigers (10-2) scored 2 quick TDs as QB Phil Gargis capped opening drive with 7y TD pass to WB Ed Butler and after REC of Texas FUM led to quick drive to 2y TD run by TB Mitzi Jackson. Gargis and Butler connected on another scoring pass (14y) in 2nd H. Best chance for Steers' comeback, when they trailed 16-3 late in 2nd Q, died on 4th-down keeper when QB Marty Akins slipped on Auburn 10YL for loss of 1y. Akins appeared to have had opening for TD. In sloppy game each team had 7 TOs, but unlike Longhorns, Auburn scored 20 pts off Texas largesse.

Sugar Bowl (Dec. 31): Nebraska 13 Florida 10

Trailing 10-0 entering 4th Q, partly because of 5 TOs, Cornhuskers (9-3) needed 3 scores to pull out their 6th straight bowl victory. FB Tony Davis contributed hard run after hard run, totaling 17/126y. IB Monte Anthony pulled Nebraska within 10-7 on 2y TD run early in 4th Q, capping 99y drive that began after tremendous GLS. Davis then set up K Mike Coyle's 2 FGs, 2nd coming from 30y out with 1:46 remaining. Davis broke free for 40y run on winning drive to set up FG. Gators (7-4) had taken 10-0 lead in 1st H on 21y run by frosh TB Tony Green and 40y FG by K David Posey, then looked to put game away late in 3rd Q after INT by DB Alvin Cowans set up 33y drive to Nebraska 1YL. Huskers D grimly held, with CB Jim Burrows stopping TB James Richards on 4th down sweep. Nebraska suddenly benched star QB David Humm—who had thrown 4 INTs—turning instead to QB Terry Luck who whipped his team 99y for momentum-swinging TD by Anthony. Huskers tied Georgia Tech (1951-56) for longest post-season win streak to date.

Cotton Bowl: Penn State 41 Baylor 20

Cinderella Baylor (8-4) squad in no way looked overmatched in 1st Q. It displayed spirited D play and had 84y march for opening score: 4y TD run by HB Steve Beaird (21/84y). Nittany Lions (10-2) dominated play for rest of 1st H, but could only manage 25y FG by K Chris Bahr. Penn State did better with opening drive of 2nd H, needing only 9 plays to travel 80y with FB Tom Donchez (26/116y) taking it 1y for 10-7 lead. Bears (8-4) took advantage of good field position later in 3rd Q to regain lead as QB Neal Jeffrey found WR Ricky Thompson for 35y scoring pass. It took State QB Tom Shuman (10-20/226y) less than min before striking back, connecting with frosh WB Jimmy Cefalo (3/102y) on 49y TD pass for 17-14 lead. Early in 4th Q, Cefalo scored on 3y run, and Penn State, which would set Cotton Bowl record for pts, started to pour it on. Bahr kicked another FG, and Shuman turned DB Mike Johnson's INT into 18y drive he capped with 2y TD run. Sub QB Mark Jackson led final 70y Baylor TD drive, but Penn State DB Joe Jackson returned onside-KO 50y to close scoring.

GAME OF THE YEAR
Rose Bowl: Southern California 18 Ohio State 17

QB Pat Haden had some terrific sr year. Fresh off being named Rhodes Scholar, Haden produced Rose Bowl's final 8 pts on TD pass and 2-pt conv pass as Trojans (10-1-1) claimed UPI national title. Trailing by 7 after brilliant Ohio State (10-2) drive for go-ahead TD and subsequent FG following Haden's FUM, Southern California flew up field behind their heady QB. Haden completed drive with 38y TD pass to longtime target WR J.K. McKay (5/104y). Then facing stiff Bucks pass rush, Haden rolled right and threw winning conv pass to WR Shelton Diggs, out of same formation that had produced Trojans' 1st TD. Game was supposed to be showcase for Ohio TB Archie Griffin (20/75y, 2 lost FUMs) and USC TB Anthony Davis, players chosen 1st and 2nd in Heisman balloting. But, neither TB dominated, thanks to punishing Ds and their own injuries. Trojans trailed 7-3 entering 4th Q, but went on march without Davis, out with bruised sternum and ribs after gaining 67y in 1st H. Big runs by sub TB Allen Carter and FB Dave Farmer brought USC to 9YL, where Haden hit TE Jim Obradovich for TD, beating A-A DB Neal Colzie, who had 2 INTs earlier. Buckeyes were not through, despite having been outgained by more than 200y at time of Obradovich's TD. QB Cornelius Greene's nifty 24y scramble and his 22y dump-off pass to Griffin propelled Buckeyes into Trojan country. Drive produced Greene's 3y TD run for 14-10 edge. Ohio K Tom Klaban stretched lead to 17-10 on 34y FG, but when it came time for even bigger boot at game's end, sack by Troy DT Gary Jeter forced Bucks to attempt 62y FG by P-K Tom Skladany, which was short. Ohio State coach Woody Hayes was criticized for striking LB Arnie Jones in chest during USC's winning drive.

Orange Bowl: Notre Dame 13 Alabama 11

Retiring Notre Dame coach Ara Parseghian went out winner in his last nail-biter. Crimson Tide (11-1) cracked 1st, losing FUM on punt RET by HB Willie Shelby deep in own territory, which Irish (10-2) converted into 4y TD run by FB Wayne Bullock (24/83y). That made it 7-0 in 1st Q. Traditional 77y drive in 2nd Q was capped by 9y TD run by HB Mark McLane, so ND was up 13-0 after missed conv kick. Tide closed 1st H by scoring on 21y FG by K Dan Ridgeway, but, because they trailed throughout, Tide was forced to attempt uncharacteristic 29 passes. ND kept Bama out of EZ until 4th Q when QB Richard Todd threw 48y scoring strike to WR Russ Schamun. After successful 2-pt conv pass to TE George Pugh trimmed margin to 13-11, Alabama forced punt and had ball for last drive from own 38YL. After 2 completions moved ball

into ND territory, Irish CB Reggie Barnett intercepted pass to end threat. Fighting Irish D had something to prove after 55 pts had been surrendered to USC. It forced 5 FUMs and grabbed 2 INTs, while holding Tide's Wishbone runs to 62y. Loss was 8th straight for Bama in bowl games, surprising flaw on coach Bear Bryant's ledger.

Final AP Poll January 2

(a) 1 Oklahoma (51)	1162	11 North Carolina State	223
(a) 2 Southern California (6)	1050	12 Michigan State	198
3 Michigan (2)	788	13 Maryland	105
4 Ohio State	778	14 Baylor	102
5 Alabama	761	15 Florida	91
6 Notre Dame	675	16 Texas A&M	58
7 Penn State	567	17t Mississippi State	57
8 Auburn (1)	555	17t Texas	57
9 Nebraska	440	19 Houston	51
10 Miami (Ohio)	231	20 Tennessee	46

(a) Oklahoma was ineligible for UPI Coaches Poll, which was won by Southern California.

1974 Top Performance Formula

1 Oklahoma	1.8484
2 Alabama	1.6889
3 Michigan	1.6244
4 Southern California	1.6067
5 Ohio State	1.5890
6 Auburn	1.5147
7 Notre Dame	1.4969
8 Penn State	1.4545
9 Miami (Ohio)	1.4313
10 Nebraska	1.4289
11 North Carolina State	1.4116
12 Maryland	1.4096
13 Tennessee	1.4015
14 Texas	1.3688
15 Mississippi State	1.3683
16 Florida	1.3390
17 Texas A&M	1.3233
18 Michigan State	1.2911
19 Houston	1.2874
20 Boston College	1.2832

1974 Top Opponent Records

1 Tennessee	.6492
2 Iowa	.6372
3 Florida	.6190
4 Georgia	.6160
5 Mississippi	.5957
6 Stanford	.5929
7 Florida State	.5913
8 Pittsburgh	.5885
9 Alabama	.5880
10 Auburn	.5872
11 Rice	.5870
12 Arkansas	.5833
13 Texas	.5813
14 Baylor	.5766
15 Colorado	.5759
16 Maryland	.5754
17 Syracuse	.5752
18 Mississippi State	.5750
19 Wake Forest	.5746
20 Kansas State	.5708

1974 Out-of-Conference Records

	W-L	Percentage	Bowl W-L
Southeastern	39-11-3	.7642	3-3-1
Big Eight	23-11	.6765	2-0
Atlantic Coast	18-15-1	.5441	0-3
Southwest	16-14-3	.5303	0-2-1
Big Ten	14-15-1	.4833	0-1
Pacific-8	14-17-2	.4545	1-0
Western Athletic	10-23-1	.3088	0-1

1974 Individual Statistical Leaders

RUSHING YARDS	Attempts	Yards	Avg.
Archie Griffin, Ohio State	236	1620	6.9
Louie Giammona, Utah State	329	1534	4.7
Dave Preston, Bowling Green	324	1414	4.4
Anthony Davis, Southern California	288	1354	4.7
Joe Washington, Oklahoma	194	1321	6.8
Willard Harrell, Pacific	224	1308	5.8
Freddie Solomon, Tampa	193	1300	6.7
Freddie Williams, Arizona State	249	1299	5.2
Billy Marek, Wisconsin	205	1215	5.9
Laverne Smith, Kansas	176	1181	6.7

PASSING YARDS	Completions	Attempts	Yards	Pct.
Steve Bartkowski, California	182	325	2580	56.0
Craig Kimball, San Jose State	175	356	2401	49.2
Gene Swick, Toledo	178	287	2235	62.0
Mark Driscoll, Colorado State	122	246	2016	49.6
Steve Joachim, Temple	128	221	1950	57.9
Bruce Hill, Arizona	132	249	1814	53.0
Craig Penrose, San Diego State	132	235	1683	56.2
Alvin White, Oregon State	120	256	1662	46.9
Kevin Sigler, Cornell	143	248	1648	57.7
Rick Costello, Wyoming	118	249	1639	47.4

RECEIVING YARDS	Catches	Yards
Willie Miller, Colorado State	53	1193
Dwight McDonald, San Diego State	86	1157
Steve Rivera, California	56	938
John Ross, Toledo	77	866
Steve Largent, Tulsa	52	844
Jimmy Jerome, North Carolina	47	837
Dave Quehl, Holy Cross	62	801
John Mastronardo, Villanova	46	739
Theo Bell, Arizona	53	700
Don Seymour, Toledo	43	673

1974 Consensus All-America Team
Offense

Wide Receiver:	Pete Demmerle, Notre Dame
Tight End:	Bennie Cunningham, Clemson
Tackle:	Kurt Schumacher, Ohio State
	Marvin Crenshaw, Nebraska
Guard:	Ken Huff, North Carolina
	John Roush, Oklahoma
	Gerry DiNardo, Notre Dame
Center:	Steve Myers, Ohio State
Quarterback:	Steve Bartkowski, California
Running Back:	Archie Griffin, Ohio State
	Joe Washington, Oklahoma
	Anthony Davis, Southern California

Defense

Line:	Randy White, Maryland
	Mike Hartenstine, Penn State
	Pat Donovan, Stanford
	Jimmy Webb, Mississippi State
	Leroy Cook, Alabama
Middle Guard:	Rubin Carter, Miami
	Louie Kelcher, Southern Methodist
Linebacker:	Rod Shoate, Oklahoma
	Richard Wood, Southern California
	Ken Bernich, Auburn
	Woodrow Lowe, Alabama
Back:	Dave Brown, Michigan
	Pat Thomas, Texas A&M
	John Provost, Holy Cross

1974 Heisman Trophy Vote

Archie Griffin, junior tailback, Ohio State		1920
Anthony Davis, senior tailback, Southern California		819
Joe Washington, junior halfback, Oklahoma		661
Tom Clements, senior quarterback, Notre Dame		244
David Humm, senior quarterback, Nebraska		210

Other Major Award Winners

Maxwell (Player)	Steve Joachim, senior quarterback, Temple
Walter Camp (Player)	Anthony Davis, senior tailback, Southern California
Outland (Lineman)	Randy White, senior defensive tackle, Maryland
Lombardi (Lineman)	Randy White, senior defensive tackle, Maryland
AFCA Coach of the Year	Grant Teaff, Baylor

1975

The Year of Passing Dodo-Birds, Archie's Heisman Double, and Arizona State's Broken Hearts

With Wishbone and Veer offenses en vogue, the run game regained its preeminence in offenses around the country. The proof was in the numbers as NCAA teams averaged 51.9 rushing plays per game to only 18.4 passes, statistics reminiscent of an earlier age. The top six finishers in the Heisman Trophy balloting all were running backs, and perhaps even more revealing was that the consensus All-America quarterback, John Sciarra of UCLA (9-2-1), was the mastermind of a Veer attack and threw only a handful of passes per game. Even in the 1950s heyday of the run-oriented Split-T offense, the All-America quarterbacks of that age were pass masters, such as Stanford's Bobby Garrett in 1953, Notre Dame's Ralph Guglielmi in 1954, Michigan State's Earl Morrall in 1955, and Stanford's John Brodie in 1956. But in option-conscious 1975, strong-armed passers were nearly as extinct as the Dodo-Bird.

At the forefront of the era's new breed of strong, fleet runners was Ohio State (11-1) tailback Archie Griffin, who led the Buckeyes to an 11-0 regular season. Ranked first entering the bowl season, Ohio State sported a magnificent backfield of Griffin, who became the first and history's only two-time Heisman Trophy winner, fullback Pete Johnson, who scored 25 touchdowns, and quarterback Cornelius Greene, who beat out Griffin for both the team and conference most valuable player awards. Of course, to win the national title, the Buckeyes had to win the Rose Bowl. Ohio State did not win the national title.

Griffin easily took the Heisman Trophy, but was he the nation's best back? Southern California (8-4) tailback Ricky Bell and California (8-3) tailback Chuck Muncie had better statistics, but had the misfortune of representing the same conference and voting area. West Coast votes cancelled out the pair. Oklahoma (11-1) halfback Joe Washington was both nicked up and considered a product of his system, while Pittsburgh (8-4) tailback Tony Dorsett needed his team to have won another game or two as the Panthers were not even ranked late in November.

Washington and his fellow Sooners won the biggest prize, Oklahoma's second straight national title as the Sooners celebrated the lifting of the previous year's probation to sweep both polls. Oklahoma was allowed to go to a bowl after a two-year absence and took advantage of Big Ten's poor bowl showing by beating Michigan (8-2-2) hours after top-ranked Ohio State lost the Rose Bowl. Baptist preacher and Wishbone quarterback Steve Davis, who ended his career with a 32-1-1 record as starter led the offense, and defensive tackle Lee Roy Selmon, winner of both Outland and Lombardi trophies, led the defense. The Sooners' sole loss was a 23-3 upset in Norman by Kansas on November 8 that snapped a 28-game win streak and, temporarily at least, knocked OU down to sixth in the rankings. Despite a loss that late in the season, the Sooners worked their way back to the top when it counted most: in January.

It appeared that Ohio State coach Woody Hayes would win his fourth national title—and possess at least one in each of the past three decades—as the undefeated Buckeyes faced a UCLA squad in the Rose Bowl that they had trounced 41-20 earlier in the season. But UCLA bounced the Buckeyes 23-10 as Sciarra proved his All-American mettle.

Ohio State's appearance in Pasadena was its fourth straight, all corresponding to Griffin's four years in the starting line-up. But in one of the most frustrating spells of Ohio State history, the Bucks won only one of those bowls and in the process lost out on two likely national titles.

With Ohio State's loss, only one team was left unscathed. Ambitious Arizona State (12-0) ended the season with a 17-14 win over Nebraska (10-2) in the Fiesta Bowl. The Sun Devils, winners of six of the last seven WAC titles, came from the still relatively-obscure Phoenix area and had been making noise under tough coach Frank Kush for years (86-15 since 1968). After its emotional Fiesta Bowl win over Nebraska, hearts were shattered in Tempe because Arizona State was so easily outdistanced in the season-end championship balloting by once-beaten Oklahoma. It remained a sore point in Tempe for years. Being a program that hungers for national recognition can have its frustrating moments: ask Michigan State in the late 1940s and early '50s and Penn State in the late 1960s and early '70s.

Texas A&M (10-2) rode its Wishbone attack, coached by the offense's founder Emory Bellard, to a 10-0 mark and second-place national ranking on December 1. Unfortunately, the Aggies had one more regular season game to play, and on December 6, they were routed by Arkansas 31-6, thus ending their national championship and Cotton Bowl dreams. Arkansas (10-2) won a three-way tiebreaker with Texas A&M and Texas (10-2) to go to

the Cotton Bowl as the Razorbacks were the least recent of the threesome to have won the Southwest Conference title. Arkansas routed Georgia 31-10 in Dallas in what would prove to be the final bowl game coached by Frank Broyles, who retired to become Arkansas athletic director a year later after the 1976 season.

Alabama (11-1) finally won a post-season game to end a stunningly inept 0-7-1 streak. The Crimson Tide topped Penn State (9-3) by 13-6 in the first Sugar Bowl to go indoors at the Louisiana Superdome. Alabama took its fifth straight SEC title, and it wouldn't have coach Shug Jordan of Auburn (3-6-2) to suit up against any longer. The legendary coach finished a fine 25-year run at the helm of the Tigers.

It was the end of an era in the Pac-8 as half of the coaches were gone after the season. The Los Angeles scene changed the most as UCLA coach Dick Vermeil took advantage of his team's stunning Rose Bowl win by accepting the invitation of the NFL's Philadelphia Eagles. Vermeil was greeted by his USC nemesis, John McKay, as rookie pro coaches. McKay could not keep quiet mid-season rumors of his departure to the expansion Tampa Bay Buccaneers, and his Trojans suffered for it. Southern California began November ranked fourth in country with a 7-0 record. But, November dragged to an end with the Trojans standing at 7-4 with no ranking and the Liberty Bowl, not the Rose Bowl, awaiting them. USC did manage to send off McKay with a victory, 20-0 over Texas A&M, but the NFL would be an awful dose of reality: McKay's Bucs went 0-14 in 1976. Longtime coach Dee Andros of Oregon State (1-10) retired, while Jim Sweeney was done with Washington State (3-8).

For the first time, the Pac-8 conference allowed teams other than their champion to go bowling, but this practice revealed a measure of reluctance in the rest of the nation to accept West Coast teams. No bowl committee was willing to hold a slot for co-champion California, which had a shot at Pasadena if USC had beaten UCLA on Thanksgiving weekend. The Golden Bears led the nation in total offense and featured a balanced attack with quarterback Joe Roth, big, bespectacled runner Chuck Muncie, and wide receivers Steve Rivera and Wesley Walker. Still, they received no bid.

Michigan coach Bo Schembechler won his 100th game, a 31-7 romp over Missouri (6-5) on October 5, which marked freshman quarterback Rick Leach's first start in his illustrious career. The Wolverines also increased the capacity of Michigan Stadium to a then-record 98,000, which they had no difficulty filling.

Milestones

■ UPI Coaches' Poll moved final vote from end of regular season to conclusion of bowl season.

■ College Football Association (CFA) was formed by many of nation's powers—Big 10 and Pac 10 schools notably absent—in fight over television money and in power struggle with NCAA.

■ NCAA set 60 (home) and 48 (away) squad sizes in effort to limit expenses. Alabama coach Bear Bryant, with Auburn and Missouri, sued to change to 60-60. On September 3, federal judge ruled against NCAA, but in appeal NCAA won in U.S. Circuit Court to revert to 60-48 for 1976.

■ Pac-8 and Big 10 agreed to accept bowls other than Rose for worthy non-champions.

■ After 41 years, Sugar Bowl moved from Tulane Stadium to new Louisiana Superdome.

■ Biggie Munn, player, coach and administrator, died on March 18 of effects of stroke. Munn was All-America guard and fullback at Minnesota before 22-year coaching career highlighted by his 54-9-2 record at Michigan State from 1947-53, with 1952 national title. Coaching great Carl Snavely, "The Grey Fox," who won 180 games at schools including Cornell and North Carolina, died on July 12. Innovator in studying game film, Snavely never gave up single wing offense he used at Cornell to upset Ohio State 23-16 in 1939. Elmer Oliphant, star halfback with both Purdue and Army, died on July 31. Two-time All-America, Oliphant set Army records for points in game (45) and season (125). Akron tight end Chris Engeloff, 20, collapsed on field and died from heart attack during game with Marshall on September 6. Joe Alexander, twice All-America guard at Syracuse (1918-19) and first-ever player signed by New York Giants, died on September 12 at age of 77. Alexander became specialist in treatment of lung diseases. Jack Mollenkopf, who coached Purdue to 84 wins from 1956-69, died of cancer on December 4 at age 70. Mollenkopf led 14-13 win over USC in 1967 Rose Bowl, went 10-4 vs Notre Dame, and coached trio of Heisman Trophy runners-up: Bob Griese (1966), Leroy Keyes (1967) and Mike Phipps (1969).

■ Longest winning streaks entering season:

Oklahoma 20	Tulsa 7	Boston College 6

	Incoming	Outgoing
Cornell	George Seifert	Jack Musick
Kansas	Bud Moore	Don Fambrough
Kansas State	Ellis Rainsberger	Vince Gibson
Louisville	Vince Gibson	T.W. Alley
Miami	Carl Selmer	Pete Elliott
Notre Dame	Dan Devine	Ara Parseghian
South Carolina	Jim Carlen	Paul Dietzel
Texas Tech	Steve Sloan	Jim Carlen
Vanderbilt	Fred Pancoast	Steve Sloan
Washington	Don James	Jim Owens
Wyoming	Fred Akers	Fritz Shurmur

AP Preseason Poll

1 Oklahoma (54)	1184		11 Texas	308	
2 Alabama (1)	914		12 Michigan State	304	
3 Michigan (1)	842		13 North Carolina State	135	
4 Ohio State (3)	814		14 UCLA	113	
5 Southern California	734		15 Florida	92	
6 Penn State (1)	469		16 Arizona	63	
7 Nebraska	457		17 Maryland	52	
8 Auburn	422		18 Tennessee	51	
9 Texas A&M	378		19 Arkansas	48	
10 Notre Dame	339		20 Stanford	42	

September 6, 1975

PENN STATE 26 Temple 25: Seeking return to major college football, Owls (0-1) refurbished their weight room, added artificial turf, hired coach Wayne Hardin from Navy, and scheduled Penn State. Temple desperately wanted upset of in-state monsters and nearly got it. RB Bob Harris put Temple on scoreboard with 76y TD run on game's 1st play from scrimmage. Owls led 13-12 at H and then 23-18 in 4th Q on K Don Bitterlich's 3rd FG and 6y scoring run by RB Anthony Anderson. Penn State (1-0) saved itself with 2 big RETs: TB Rich Mauti's 100y KO TD in 1st Q and TB Woody Petchel's 66y punt RET in 4th Q that set up FB Duane Taylor's winning 3y TD. Owls doubled Penn State's O 402y to 201y.

Pittsburgh 19 GEORGIA 9: TB Tony Dorsett's jr season started slowly as he gained only 17y in 1st H against Georgia's "Junkyard Dogs" D as Pitt (1-0) trailed 7-0. Georgia (0-1) scored on 2y run by HB Kevin McLee during 1st Q in which it moved deep into Panther territory on 3 occasions. Dorsett (15/104y) came back strong in 2nd H, setting up TDs with runs of 27y and 36y as Panthers scored all their pts. Score was 12-7 in 4th Q when snap to Pitt P Larry Swider sailed toward EZ. Swider prevented serious damage by fielding ball and accepting safety. Panthers D then stiffened, and Pitt drove to clinching 3y scoring run by Atlanta native QB Robert Haygood.

Grambling 27 Alcorn State 3 (New Orleans): Grambling QB Doug Williams (9-18/171y) sparkled in showcase game, tossing 4 TDs—2 to WR Sammie White—as Grambling (1-0) coasted in 1st-ever college football game played in Superdome. Braves (0-1) contributed to their own downfall with 6 TOs, while Grambling defenders caught twice as many Alcorn State passing attempts (4) as did Braves receivers (2). Tigers' victory avenged only loss of 1974 season.

(Mon) Missouri 20 ALABAMA 7 (Birmingham): That team scored on 4 of its 1st 5 possessions was not surprising, that upstart Missouri (1-0) did so, was stunning. Tigers 230-lb TB Tony Galbreath rushed for team-high 89y of 120y in 1st H as Tigers pawed 20-0 lead. Galbreath opened scoring with 3y TD run in 1st Q to cap 58y drive that featured his 48y rushing. FB John Blakeman scored on 9y run and K Tim Gibbons added FGs of 44y and 46y. DT Keith Morrissey keyed Mizzou D that held Alabama to 56y in 1st H, including miserly 3y total after Tide's opening 3 possessions. Alabama's TD came courtesy of 14y TD pass from QB Richard Todd to WR Ozzie Newsome. Surprising loss canned Bama's 22-game regular season win streak.

AP Poll September 8

1 Oklahoma (51)	1108		11 Michigan State	280	
2 Michigan (1)	918		12 Texas	257	
3 Ohio State (3)	787		13 Alabama	196	
4 Southern California	746		14 Maryland	125	
5 Missouri (1)	579		15 North Carolina State	124	
6 Nebraska	528		16 UCLA	85	
7 Auburn	397		17 Arizona	71	
8 Texas A&M	382		18 Pittsburgh	63	
9 Notre Dame	300		19 Florida	59	
10 Penn State	282		20 Tennessee	50	

September 13, 1975

PENN STATE 34 Stanford 14: After not playing in Penn State's opener and not appearing on pre-game depth chart, frosh WB Tom Donovan replaced injured WB Jimmy Cefalo to rush for 114y, scoring eventual winning TD with 61y 2nd Q burst. TB Rich Mauti added pair of 1y TD runs as Nittany Lions (2-0) rushed for 330y. Stanford (0-1) pulled no surprises on O, using passes by QB Mike Cordova for 2 TDs, both in 2nd Q, as Cardinals trailed 21-14 at H. Penn State scored 13 pts in 3rd Q to ice game.

Wake Forest 30 NORTH CAROLINA STATE 22: After averaging 7.6 pts per game during awful 1-10 record in 1974, Wake Forest (1-1) stunned North Carolina State (1-1) for its 1st ACC win since 1972. Deacs scored TDs in each Q as QB Jerry McManus (8-12/102y, 2 TDs) accounted for 3 TDs, and RB Clark Gaines rushed for 123y and 9y TD. Wolfpack (1-1) QB Dave Buckey (13-26/182, INT) also tossed 2 TD passes—including 43y effort to his brother, WR Don Buckey, at end of 1st H—and ran for another. NC State could not overcome its 3 TOs, all of which were converted into pts. Demon Deacons drearily reverted to form following week: 19-17 loss to Appalachian State.

TENNESSEE 26 Maryland 8: Maryland (1-1) must have had nightmares about Volunteers TB Stanley Morgan after this game. In addition to conventional 1y TD run, Morgan scored on 50y run and 70y punt RET as Tennessee (1-0) coasted. Terps earned only 2 1st downs in 1st H and then lost starting QB Mark Manges to separated shoulder. Sub QB Larry Dick (15-24/164y) threw Maryland's only TD, 3y to WR Kim Hoover in 4th Q, but Terps failed to overcome both 5 TOs and rash of injuries. Manges became 5th starter lost since August camp.

Ohio State 21 MICHIGAN STATE 0: Buckeyes (1-0) gained revenge for sole loss of 1974 while getting leg up in conf race. S Craig Cassady, son of Ohio State great "Hopalong" Cassady, picked off 3 passes to spark Ohio D that prevented Michigan State (0-1) from getting any closer than Ohio 32YL. FB Pete Johnson scored twice, sandwiching QB Cornelius Greene's 64y TD pass to WR Lenny Willis, and TB Archie Griffin went over 100y rushing mark for 23rd straight regular season game. Spartans were limited to 80y on ground and 93y through air, while surrendering 5 TOs, but kept down score, thanks to tough D.

NORTHWESTERN 31 Purdue 25: Being tied with Ohio State atop Big 10 standings must have seemed pretty good to Wildcats (1-0). TB Greg Boykin returned from year lost to injury to rush for 122y and 3 TDs to pace upset. With game knotted at 3-3 in 2nd Q, Boykin rambled into EZ on 21y jaunt. Purdue answered with QB Mark Vitali's 25y scoring pass to WR Paul Beery for 10-10 tie at H. After K Steve Schmidt gave Boilermakers (0-1) 3-pt lead in 3rd Q on 37y FG, Boykin scored 1 of 2 Wildcat TDs as NW took lead for good at 24-13. TB Scott Dierking pulled Purdue to within 24-19, but Boykin scored his 3rd TD in 4th Q to ice game.

Rice 24 HOUSTON 7: Rice (1-0) stunned cross-town rivals with series of big plays. Only 96 secs into game, Owls DB Gary Cox fielded punt and returned it 70y for opening score. Later in 1st Q, Houston (1-1) FB John Houseman lost 1st of 3 FUMs that was recovered on Cougars 20YL by Rice CB Ron Vaughan. Owls needed only 4 plays to double lead, scoring on 9y run by FB James Sykes. In 2nd Q, Houston's philanthropic spirit continued as pass by Cougars QB Bubba McGallion was tipped into hands of LB Larry Brune, who raced 86y for clinching TD. After trailing 24-0 at H, McGallion ended shutout in 3rd Q with 6y TD pass to WR Robert Lavergne.

(Mon) Notre Dame 17 BOSTON COLLEGE 3 (Foxboro): Billed as "Catholic Super Bowl" and "Frank Leahy Bowl," 1st-ever meeting of 2 of America's leading Catholic schools was won by Notre Dame (1-0) in coach Dan Devine's debut. Browner brothers led Irish to victory as DE Ross led aggressive D that shut down BC (0-1) QB Mike Kruczek (50y passing) and recovered FUM to set up winning 10y TD run by frosh FB Jim, who led team with 95y rushing. Later in 3rd Q, Notre Dame DB Randy Harrison's INT set up insurance 24y TD run by HB Al Hunter, who, like Ross Browner and 3 other key ND players, was returning from 1-year suspension. TB Glenn Capriola led Eagles with 107y rushing.

AP Poll September 15

1 Oklahoma (53)	1138		11 Texas A&M	272	
2 Michigan (2)	931		12 UCLA	217	
3 Ohio State (2)	922		13 Florida	205	
4 Southern California	685		14 Alabama	109	
5 Missouri	632		15 Pittsburgh	71	
6 Nebraska	478		16 Arkansas	64	
7 Penn State	433		17 Arizona	56	
8 Texas	427		18 Arizona State	51	
9 Notre Dame	392		19 Miami (Ohio)	42	
10 Tennessee	310		20 West Virginia	29	

September 20, 1975

West Virginia 28 CALIFORNIA 10: Cal Bears (0-2) must have felt embarrassed about their run D. After surrendering 467y rushing to Colorado prior week, Cal allowed Mountaineers (2-0) to gain 337y: WVU FB Heywood Smith went for 146y and 2 TDs, and TB Artie Owens added 118y. Owens finished off Bears with 52y run in 4th Q that set up his 4y TD run after West Virginia D stopped Cal on 25YL. TB Chuck Muncie led California with 107y rushing. With Cal trailing 14-10, Muncie surprised with 50y pass to WR Wesley Walker to WVU 16YL. Drive ended on DB Chuck Braswell's INT of Bears QB Joe Roth on fake FG. Mountaineers then marched 88y for TD.

NORTH CAROLINA STATE 8 Florida 7: Ahead 7-0 in 1st Q after 17y scoring run by HB Larry Brinson, Gators (1-1) were hoping to hang on. QB Dave Buckey, well contained all day, hit pass when it counted—38y strike to WR Elijah Marshall for TD—that pulled Wolfpack (2-1) to within 7-6 with 3:15 left. NC State went for 2 pts and RB Johnny Evans rushed in for game-winning pts on disputed play. Florida griped that Evans lost ball at GL, but officials ruled that he broke plane before losing possession. Florida reached Wolfpack 33YL on 36y pass from QB Don Gaffney to WR Wes Chandler, but next play was marred by lost FUM by A-A FB Jimmy Dubose on 21YL. Game over! Dubose's FUM was 3rd for Gators, negating 329y rushing.

OHIO STATE 17 Penn State 9: FB Pete Johnson's 11y TD blast late in 4th Q, his 2nd score of game, closed out Nittany Lions (2-1). Controversial play on final drive occurred when Ohio State (2-0) was pinned deep in its territory: Penn State CB John Bush was called for interference, saving Buckeyes with 1st down out at 33 YL. Moments later, Bucks star TB Archie Griffin made brilliant catch for 23y gain to move ball past midfield. Griffin added 128y and Johnson added 107y as Ohio snapped Penn State's undefeated series mark of 4-0. K Chris Bahr, fresh off being named Rookie of Year in North American Soccer League, kicked 3 FGs for Lions, including 55y effort that tied his own school mark and set Ohio Stadium record. FB Duane Taylor rushed for 113y to help set up Bahr.

Texas A&M 39 LOUISIANA STATE 8: Rout was established early as Tigers (0-2) could not stop Aggies' Wishbone O, allowing 390y rushing and giving up most pts since 1956. Texas A&M (2-0) QB David Shipman (17/99y rushing) led attack, while

FB George Woodard rushed 6/106y, and HB Bubba Bean added 79y on ground. All 3 reached EZ, with Bean bursting through LSU D for 46y run to open scoring in 1st Q, Shipman scoring on 42y romp in 3rd Q, and Woodard doing so twice in 4th Q on 66y burst and 20y run. Tigers meanwhile managed only 38y rushing and 114y total against LB Ed Simonini and rest of Aggie D. DE Butch Knight scored LSU's TD on REC of blocked punt in EZ.

MICHIGAN 19 Stanford 19: Bouncing back after opening loss, Stanford (0-1-1) shocked Wolverines on K Mike Langford's 33y FG with 9 secs left. QB Mike Cordova (24-44/285y, 2 TDs) sparkled. After teams matched 1st H aerial TDs—Cordova's 25y strike to WR Tony Hill and QB Rick Leach's 48y scoring toss to WB Jim Smith on final play of H—Michigan (1-0-1) was forced to finish up 4 scoring drives in 2nd H with K Bob Wood FGs. Cordova's 2nd TD pass ended up in arms of C Todd Anderson on deflection, for very odd way to tie game 13-13. After that, game came down to Langford's and Wood's kicking clinic.

OKLAHOMA 46 Pittsburgh 10: In tale of great RBs, Sooner HB Joe Washington was clear winner, with help from friends. "Little Joe" rushed for 166y and 3 TDs, and swarming Oklahoma D held Pitt TB Tony Dorsett to 17y rushing. Sooners (2-0) jumped to 23-0 H lead in preserving 23-game win streak. Panthers (1-1) managed TD on QB Robert Haygood's 53y scoring strike to WR Karl Farmer, but could not overcome 79y rushing, their 4 TOs and disastrous −2y on RETs. Oklahoma HB Elvis Peacock added 2 TD runs, while D was inspired by DE Jimbo Elrod's all-over-field performance: 17 tackles (5 for losses) and 2 FUM RECs.

OKLAHOMA STATE 20 Arkansas 13: Cowboys (2-0) celebrated having their 1st home game in series since 1951 with their 3rd straight win over Arkansas (1-1). With game knotted 13-13 in 4th Q, CB Clifton Sullivan picked off pass by QB Mike Kirkland to give Oke State ball at own 44YL. From there Oklahoma State marched to winning 1y TD run by FB Robert Turner (20/107y). Hogs skillfully advanced to OSU 32YL before Little Rock native DT Phil Dokes of Cowboys pounced on Razorbacks RB Jerry Eckwood to turn screen pass into 8y loss. Hogs chances ended with 4th down incompletion. OSU D earlier had turned in GLS with stop of FB Ike Forte on 4th-and-goal from 1YL. Arkansas' Eckwood (20/156y) had blistering 68y scoring run in 2nd Q, while HB Terry Miller led Cowboys with 130y rushing.

UCLA 34 Tennessee 28: Bruins (2-0) Veer attack proved to be difference in shootout, piling up 486y and several big plays. RB Wendell Tyler's 82y TD run put UCLA up for good at 14-7, and QB John Sciarra, who ran O to perfection, connected with WR James Sarpy on 47y pass to set up TD for 21-13 lead. WR Wally Henry scored on 45y run to up Bruins' lead to 27-13 in 3rd Q. Volunteers (1-1) trailed 34-20 after 3 Qs before getting QB Gary Roach's 2y TD to WR Larry Seivers (9/145y) on 4th down pass and adding 2-pt conv. Tennessee marched to Bruins 9YL before UCLA D stiffened. Vols totaled 459y, with 290y coming through air as QB Randy Wallace threw for 183y and Roach came off bench to throw for 107y more and 2 TDs.

September 27, 1975

(Fri) Oklahoma 20 MIAMI 17: Despite lackluster performance that cost them 26 1st place votes in AP poll, Sooners (3-0) stretched unbeaten streak to 32 games. Underdog Hurricanes (0-2) jumped to 7-0 1st Q lead with 74y drive capped by 19y scoring run by WB Larry Cain. OU exploded for 20 2nd Q pts—scoring on TDs set up by blocked punt and FUM by Miami TB Otis Anderson—as rout appeared to be on. Sooners snoozed in 2nd H as Miami made game interesting with 53y FG by K Chris Dennis and 72y scoring bomb by QB Kary Baker to WR Mike Adams in 4th Q. Sooners held on for win despite being outgained 289y to 176y. Interestingly, Miami's brilliant football future may have been have been saved by this night's performance because talk of dropping sport virtually ended after this game.

WEST VIRGINIA 35 Boston College 18: Mountaineers (3-0) sub FB Ron Lee may not have worked up sweat on his 3 TD runs: Lee's 3 TDs totaled only 4y. Lee's fellow backup TB Dwayne Woods rushed 7/102y. West Virginia built 21-0 lead on Lee's 2 TD runs and FUM REC in EZ by WR Steve Lewis. Eagles (1-2) scored next 10 pts on 2y TD run by QB Mike Kruczek and 27y FG by K Fred Steinfort, but they would get no closer.

Georgia 28 SOUTH CAROLINA 20: Bulldogs held on to win game they thought easily was salted away. Offsetting 2 FGs by South Carolina K Bobby Marino with TD runs by HB Kevin McLee, Georgia (2-1) built 14-6 H lead. QB Ray Goff added 3y scoring run in 3rd Q for eventual winning pts as Georgia built 28-6 lead before Gamecocks (2-1) rallied in 4th Q behind QB Jeff Grantz (14-24/180y). Grantz threw 44y TD pass to WR Phil Logan before running in last score from 3y out. But, Gamecocks comeback was too little, too late. Georgia rushed for 403y, with 160y being contributed by HB Glynn Harrison and 111y by McLee.

TENNESSEE 21 Auburn 17: Tennessee's balance withstood Auburn's bruising rushing attack. TB Kenny Burks rushed for 122y and 2 TDs for Tigers (0-2-1), with both his TDs coming in 14-14 1st H standoff. Vols (2-1) QB Randy Wallace (8-16/135y) hooked up with WR Larry Seivers (6/109y) twice for TDs, including winning 37y strike in 4th Q. On winning drive that brought Tennessee from 17-14 deficit, Wallace thrice completed 3rd down passes of at least 10y to Seivers. Seivers' best catch was on 1st

TD when he emerged from crowd to catch what Wallace described as "wounded duck coming down." TB Stanley Morgan rushed for 138y to lead Tennessee rush attack that amounted to 220y.

MICHIGAN 14 Baylor 14: Amazingly both squads played to tie for 2nd straight week as Baylor K Bubba Hicks missed 39y FG with 10 secs left. Bears (1-0-2) won statistical battle, outgaining Michigan 338y to 219y, but surrendered tying TD when they lost FUM in their own territory in 4th Q. Wolverines MG Rick Koschalk's REC was converted 11 plays later into 1y TD run by Michigan (1-0-2) TB Gordon Bell (26/89y, 2 TDs). Baylor TB Cleveland Franklin, game's leading rusher with 135y, had scored go-ahead 2y TD run at 14-7 in 3rd Q.

MISSOURI 27 Wisconsin 21: Tigers (3-0) were able to maintain no. 5 ranking with come-from-behind win. Missouri WR Henry Marshall got behind Badgers secondary for 66y scoring pass from QB Steve Pisarkiewicz late in 3rd Q to turn things for good at 24-21 in Tigers' direction. Wisconsin (1-2) had built 21-17 lead behind TB Bill Marek, who rushed for 117y and 2 TDs. Mizzou TB Tony Galbreath gained 104y rushing and threw 11y TD pass to Marshall in 2nd Q.

TEXAS 42 Texas Tech 18: Texas (3-0) unleashed inside-outside combination in gaining 411y rushing as FB Earl Campbell rushed for 150y and 2 TDs and QB Marty Akins ran for 114y and TD. Longhorns built 36-0 lead with help from Texas Tech (2-1) as TOs led to 3 Texas TDs and death of Red Raiders' drive at Texas 7YL. Horns also had scoring drives of 93y and 89y in dominating game from get-go. Raiders gained 397y, but more than half of total came on 3 window-dressing TD drives in 4th Q. Victory was 100th for Darrell Royal in SWC, although Texas' 16 PENs/169y may have dampened coach's celebration.

ARIZONA STATE 20 Brigham Young 0: Cougars (0-3) romped to 22 1st downs and gained 311y, but could not crack ASU's EZ in suffering 1st shutout in 40 games. Most of BYU's y came on 3 possessions: missed FG ended 1 threat, blocked FG try halted another, and still another drive died on INT by Sun Devils LB Larry Gordon late in game. Gordon's heroic effort had odd end: play was mistakenly whistled dead when unidentified Cougar player jumped off bench to confront Gordon as he raced toward BYU EZ. QB Dennis Sproul (9-20/190y) led Sun Devils (3-0), throwing 16y scoring pass to WB Larry Mucker (6/133y) and opening scoring with 1y TD run. Leading gainer for BYU was WR John Van Der Wouden with 5/60y receiving. Amazingly, shutout would be last visited upon BYU until 2003.

AIR FORCE 20 Ucla 20: Air Force (0-2-1) rallied with 17 pts in 3rd Q and scored tying TD when backup QB Rob Shaw hit TE Frank Cox from 6y out. UCLA O suffered through shoulder injury to QB John Sciarra, who nonetheless ran for TD. Sciarra also threw 3 INTs, including Falcons CB Ray Wild's 32y TD RET that tied game at 13-13 early in 3rd Q. Bruins (2-0-1) built 13-3 and 20-13 leads behind run game that sped to 322y: HB Wendell Tyler led way with 142y and opening 16y scoring jaunt. Falcons LB-K Dave Lawson had INT and 2 FGs, to tie Stanford K Rod Garcia for career 3-ptrs with 42. Lawson, whose 2nd FG was big 58y boot, finished his career at season's end with 51 FGs.

San Jose State 36 STANFORD 34: Spartans (3-0) had been winning behind D that posted shutouts in their 1st 2 games, but this win came from O which exploded for 30 pts in 2nd Q. San Jose QB Roger Profitt hooked up with WR Gary Maddocks (5/140y) on 52y pass to set up 1y QB sneak, and then threw TD passes of 12y to WR Maurice Hill and 39y to Maddocks as Spartans built 30-7 H lead. Cardinals set up 2 San Jose TDs with costly TOs: FUM on own 18YL by DB Ray Anderson on KO RET and INT thrown by QB Mike Cordova to SJS LB Rick Booth on own 36YL. Stanford (0-2-1) rallied late as backup QB Guy Benjamin connected with WR Tony Hill on 2 short TD passes.

October 4, 1975

NAVY 17 AIR FORCE 0 (Philadelphia): Midshipmen TB Gerry Goodwin ripped apart Falcons (0-3-1) for 132y and TD, while D posted shutout with spectacular effort. Navy (3-1) win was special for MG Jeff Sapp, who hailed from Colorado Springs, as he led effort that stymied Falcon rush attack and prevented Air Force from crossing midfield any time in 2nd H. Soph Goodwin did yeoman's work on opening 83y drive as his 34y romp and 20y catch set up his 10y scoring run. Air Force squandered 1st H scoring opportunities that ended with missed 49y and 55y FGs by K Dave Lawson.

MARYLAND 24 Syracuse 7: Previously unbeaten Orangemen (3-1) saw special teams wilt in 1st H as it permitted 42y punt RET by Maryland (3-1-1) DB Jim Brechbiel to set up 1st Q FG, had punt snap sail over Syracuse P Larry King's head that led to QB Larry Dick's 5y FG scramble for 17-0 deficit in 2nd Q and allowed Brechbiel to block Orange FG ATT. That turned fortuitous, at least, as Dick fumbled ball right back to Orangemen, which was converted into sole Syracuse TD. Maryland D took over in 2nd H, especially in 3rd Q when it permitted only 39y, and touted Terps frosh TB Steve Atkins lugged ball 5 times on 38y drive to his 1y TD after DG Paul DiVito's FUM REC.

ALABAMA 32 Mississippi 6: After scoreless 1st Q, Crimson Tide (3-1) forged lead thanks to 2 FUMs by Rebels deep in own territory. Bama moved 14y for opening 29y FG by K Bucky Berrey and moments later FUM REC on Rebels 5YL led to 4y TD run by HB Willie Shelby and 10-0 lead. Managing only 78y rushing while losing 4 TOs, Rebels (1-4) failed to rally and did not score until Alabama had erected 32-0 lead. Ole Miss got TD with 3 secs left on 1y pass from QB Tim Ellis to TB Michael Sweet. Alabama rushed for 274y and had 4 different scorers.

Florida 34 LOUISIANA STATE 6: Gators (3-1) kept pace with Alabama atop SEC standings with 2nd conf win in as many games. This was easy as Florida QB Don Gaffney threw 2 TDs in 1st Q and added 2nd Q rushing TD, helping to build 27-0 H lead. WR Wes Chandler caught 20y scoring pass in game's opening 2 mins to lead charge. Tigers (1-3) could not crack EZ until 4y TD pass from QB Pat Lyons to WR Carl Otis Trimble came with 36 secs left. That TD only matched LSU O with Gators D: Florida DE Jeff Kanter had caught Bengals FUM in mid-air and raced 9y to EZ for final score of 1st H.

Virginia Tech 23 AUBURN 16: Tigers (0-3-1) continued nightmarish start with loss to 21-pt underdog Virginia Tech. Hokies (2-2) QB Phil Rogers rushed for 128y and ran and threw for TDs. Tech trailed 10-9 at H, but grabbed control of game in 3rd Q with 2 TDs, including 89y scoring romp by HB Roscoe Coles (14/129y). Tigers drove to Gobblers 5YL at game's end, but gained only 1y in 4 plays to surrender ball with 28 secs left. Coached by former Alabama assistant Jimmy Sharpe, Hokies used Wishbone attack for 337y on ground. Auburn TB Mitzi Jackson rushed for 100y.

Michigan State 10 NOTRE DAME 3: With score knotted at 3-3 late in 4th Q and its O struggling, Spartans (3-1) received big play to gain road upset. TB Tyrone Wilson (12/117y) burst 76y to Irish (3-1) 4YL to set up FB Levi Jackson's TD rush on next play. Meanwhile, Fighting Irish moved ball all day—ending drives on downs, missed FG, EZ INT, and FUM deep in Spartan territory in 1st H—-but could not score TD for 1st time in 49 games. ND lost 2 more FUMs in 3rd Q, finishing game with 5 TOs. Without single pass completion, Michigan State rushed for 241y. Spartans won despite making only 11 1st downs.

MICHIGAN 31 Missouri 7: After two straight ties, Michigan coach Bo Schembechler turned to frosh QB Rick Leach to straighten out ship. Leach led rout of 5th-ranked Missouri (3-1) as O piled up 400y against D that had contained Alabama. Wolverines (2-0-2) set tone early with 77y drive with opening possession, but led only 10-0 at H. With Tigers stalled without injured TB Tony Galbreath, Michigan added 3 2nd H TDs to blow game open as FB Rob Lytle rushed for 19y TD, Leach raced 12y for team's 3rd TD, and frosh TB Harlan Huckleby added 11y scoring run for 31-0 4th Q lead. TB Gordon Bell (24/119y) led Michigan rushing attack that gained 372y. Mizzou averted shutout on 5y TD pass from backup QB Pete Woods to TE Charley Douglass.

OKLAHOMA 21 Colorado 20: Colorado coach Bill Mallory defended his decision to go for tying x-pt with 1:23 left. Unfortunately, Buffs K Tom MacKenzie, who earlier missed FG, shanked his tying try. Colorado QB David Williams had just thrown 8y TD pass to WB Billy Waddy to pull Buffs (3-1) to 21-20. HB Joe Washington (16/89y) was Oklahoma (4-0) star with TDs on 11y run and 74y punt RET for 14-0 2nd Q lead. Sooners blew lead with FUMs deep in own territory late in 1st H that were converted into 14-14 tie on 3y scoring run by Waddy and 2y TD run by Williams. Late in 3rd Q, Sooners marched 80y to regain lead on 2y scoring run by HB Elvis Peacock. Sooners DE Jimbo Elrod dominated D play again with 19 tackles.

Ohio State 41 UCLA 20: Bruins (2-1-1) could do nothing to stop backfield of QB Cornelius Greene, FB Pete Johnson, and TB Archie Griffin, which combined for 5 TDs. Johnson scored twice, Greene added 120y rushing, and Griffin led way with 160y for Buckeyes (4-0) who leapfrogged past Oklahoma into top spot in AP poll. UCLA opened well by stopping Buckeyes drive after NG Cliff Frazier forced Griffin into FUM. Bruins answered with 73y march for opening 7-0 lead on 13y QB John Sciarra to WR James Sarpy TD pass. Ohio then marched 92y to tie things up, recovered onside-KO to propel another TD, and was off and running. Buckeyes built 38-7 lead. During Ohio State scoring spree, Bruins could gain only single 1st down on 16 plays.

AP Poll October 6

1 Ohio State (47)	1178	11 Arizona State	179
2 Oklahoma (14)	1072	12 Missouri	175
3 Southern California (1)	975	13 Colorado	153
4 Nebraska	858	14 Oklahoma State	144
5 Texas	722	15t Michigan State	141
6 Texas A&M	657	15t Notre Dame	141
7 Alabama	451	17 Arizona	116
8 Michigan	444	18 Florida	98
9 Penn State	383	19 Tennessee	66
10 West Virginia	321	20 Miami (Ohio)	17

October 11, 1975

PENN STATE 39 West Virginia 0: Nittany Lions (5-1) generally did not take well to others occupying their accustomed spot atop weekly Lambert Trophy voting for Eastern supremacy. Rout of then Eastern no. 1 West Virginia (4-1) was devastating, even though Mountaineers entered game with 35-pt scoring avg. Penn State D forced 5 FUMs and held WVU to 200y, 241y below avg. Lions O racked up 372y rushing with TB Woody Petchel leading way with 120y. Petchel was 1 of 4 different players to rush for PSU TDs, while K Chris Bahr kicked 3 FGs. Bahr opened scoring with 52y effort early in 1st Q. Visitors meanwhile were dropping ball, losing 6 FUMs and throwing INT, to facilitate 5 Penn State scores. WVU's best scoring opportunity came in 2nd Q when 30y pass to WR Scott McDonald ended with FUM on Penn State 2YL.

MARYLAND 37 North Carolina State 22: Beating coach Jerry Claiborne's Terps (4-1-1) was tough anywhere, but playing on road and twice losing 2nd H FUMs deep in their own territory made it impossible for Wolfpack (3-3). Maryland led 17-14 entering 3rd Q when NC State unraveled. Pack D allowed Terps to march 68y to what proved to be winning TD, scored by WR Kim Hoover on 7y pass catch from WB John Schultz. NC State then lost FUMs on own 19 and 22YLs to set up Terrapin insurance TDs. Outlook had been brighter for visitors after QB Dave Buckey marched them 60y to frosh TB Scott Wade's 9y TD run and 7-3 lead in 1st H. Terps TB Ricky Jennings took ensuing KO 96y for go-ahead TD and permanent lead.

Notre Dame 21 NORTH CAROLINA 14: QB Joe Montana's legendary story added early chapter as soph QB replaced injured QB Rick Slager in 4th Q with Fighting Irish (4-1) trailing 14-7. Montana quickly led ND to 2 TDs. Key play on 1st drive was 38y pass to WR Don Kelleher that set up HB Al Hunter's 2y TD run, his 2nd of game. Montana (3-4/128y) hit TE Doug Buth with 2-pt conv pass to tie game. Winning TD was recorded as 80y pass, but WR Ted Burgmeier raced full distance after taking short sideline throw with min left. After scoreless 1st H, North Carolina (2-3) had grabbed 14-0 lead in 3rd Q behind TB Mike Voight, who rushed for 169y and game's opening score on 12y TD run.

Michigan 16 MICHIGAN STATE 6: With game knotted at 6-6 late in 3rd Q, Michigan QB Rick Leach put his stamp on in-state rivalry with huge 4th down run to Michigan State 28YL. Wolverines TB Gordon Bell followed Leach's 2y run for 1st down with 18y TD run 3 plays later. K Bob Wood did rest of scoring for Wolverines (3-0-2) with 3 FGs, while Spartans' pts came by way of K Hans Nielsen's 2 FGs. FB Rob Lytle rushed for 111y to pace Michigan O, while Michigan State (3-2) was led by QB Charley Baggett (10-16/162y). Wood took ownership of Michigan season FG mark with his 11th.

ILLINOIS 42 Minnesota 23: Fightin' Illini (3-2) ran all over Minnesota, compiling 417y and rushing for 6 TDs. TB Lonnie Perrin rushed for 90y and 3y TD that gave Illinois 7-3 lead in 1st Q, while TB Jim "Chubby" Phillips added 3 TDs in 2nd Q for 28-17 H lead. Golden Gophers (3-2) were led by future NFL coach, QB Tony Dungy, who threw for 216y and 3 TDs, including 4y effort to FB John Jones in 3rd Q that pulled Minnesota to within 28-23. Illinois kept ball on ground and added 2 TDs for safe margin that improved conf record to 2-0.

NEBRASKA 16 Kansas 0: It took 4th Q TD drive to finally put away Jayhawks (3-2) as Nebraska managed only 3 FGs by K Mike Coyle through 3 Qs. Cornhuskers backup QB Terry Lusk led 64y drive that took only 5 plays for game's sole TD, only 4th surrendered through 5 games by Kansas D. TE Brad Jenkins caught Lusk's 26y pass. Kansas was limited to only 7 1st downs, with QB Nolan Cromwell gaining 62y of team's 121y rushing. Best scoring threat for Jayhawks occurred at end of 1st H when Cromwell completed 50y pass to WR Waddell Smith to 3YL. After HB Bill Campfield's run lost 3y, Jayhawks attempted FG by K Dennis Kerbel that was blocked. Huskers romped for 258y rushing.

Oklahoma 24 Texas 17 (Dallas): Sooners HB Horace Ivory—1 of 19 Texas natives sprinkled throughout Oklahoma roster—raced through hole for 33y scoring run late in 4th Q for winning TD. OU (5-0) had 10-0 lead on K Tony DiRienzo's 45y FG and DE Mike Phillips' EZ REC of faulty pitch by Texas QB Marty Akins. Undaunted, Akins pulled Longhorns (4-1) to within 10-7 on 38y scoring pass to WR Alfred Jackson. Teams traded rushing TDs before Texas tied game at 17-17 on K Russell Erxleben's 43y FG. Sooners then marched 79y to winning score, aided by face mask PEN called on S Steve Collier. Later in 4th Q, HB Joe Washington helped seal Oklahoma's win with 76y QK that pinned Longhorns on 14YL with 2:30 left. Sooners' win was 25th straight and 5th in row in Red River Rivalry.

Texas A&M 38 TEXAS TECH 9: HB Bubba Bean stylishly gave Texas A&M (5-0) some 3rd Q breathing room, taking pitchout deep in own territory and racing to 94y TD run. With Bean's jaunt coming only 3 plays after Aggies DB Jackie Williams leapt for INT at his 1YL, A&M went from dodging bullet to firing fatal shot. Red Raiders (2-3) quickly stalled, and A&M was on move again, going 62y to insurance TD on 5y run by HB Skip Walker. Texas Tech gained 319y on nation's top D, with FB Rufus Myers scoring on 3y run. Raiders limited themselves with 5 TOs and bad snap that gave Aggies gift possession on Texas Tech 4YL. Bean's 180y rushing with 2 TDs paced Texas A&M attack that gained 343y on ground.

Arkansas 41 BAYLOR 3: Arkansas (4-1) vaulted into SWC lead with rout of FUM-prone Bears, who dropped ball 9 times with 8 being recovered by Hogs. QB Scott Bull rushed for TDs of 4y and 67y as Razorbacks gained 460y on ground against vaunted Baylor D. Bull (10/116y rushing), FB Ike Forte (22/106y, 2 TDs) and RB Jerry Eckwood (15/120y, TD) provided trio of century mark rushers. Baylor (1-2-2) had edge in 1st downs, 21-20, and gained 344y, all of which was done in by 10 TOs.

North Texas State 28 Houston 0 (Irving): North Texas reserve QB Ken Smith tore apart Cougars in 3rd Q, leading 3 TD drives. Starting QB Kenny Washington had marched Mean Green (3-3) to 1YL in 2nd Q before being knocked out of game on hit by Cougars S Gary Drake. North Texas scored winning pts on next play with 1y run by FB Brad Hammit. Houston O had trouble against coach Haden Fry's North Texas D, led by NG Walter Chapman (13 tackles), which forced 6 TOs. Youthful Cougars (1-3) gained 241y, but managed only 1 real drive that ended on downs at NTS 11YL. Mean Green proved win to be no fluke with 21-14 win over Tennessee later in year.

AP Poll October 13

1 Ohio State (42)	1066	11 Arizona State	226
2 Oklahoma (12)	982	12 Colorado	220
3 Southern California (1)	844	13 Arizona	134
4 Nebraska	762	14 Florida	130
5 Texas A&M	649	15 Notre Dame	117
6 Alabama	486	16 Tennessee	61
7 Michigan	449	17 Michigan State	33
8 Texas	445	18 UCLA	26
9 Penn State	434	19 Maryland	22
10 Missouri	241	20 Arkansas	15

October 18, 1975

DUKE 25 Clemson 21: Game came down to final drive that was set up by weak 18y Clemson punt. Blue Devils (3-3) took over on Tigers 33YL, trailing 21-19 with 2 mins left. Duke RB Chuck Williamson raced through middle for 14y, and FB Tony Benjamin then shot through similar hole for TD that ended streaky game. Blue Devils opened with 10-0 1st Q lead before Clemson (1-5) reeled off 3 TDs. Tigers QB Willie Jordan (11-14/202y) had led burst, throwing 67y scoring pass to WR Joey Walters for 14-10 lead. Duke then scored game's final 15 pts as O gained 456y, with TB Mike Barney making 103y..

ALABAMA 30 Tennessee 7: Crimson Tide (5-1) dominated in every way to topple Tennessee. Alabama QB Richard Todd ran for 3 TDs and passed for another—even though he had another scoring throw dropped—and totaled 90y rushing and 62y passing. FB Johnny Davis added 112y as Bama rushed for 318y. Tide D may have been even better, holding Vols to paltry 117y and sacking Vols QBs 10 times with DE LeRoy Cook bringing down QBs 4 times and DTs Bob Baumhower and Charley Hannah each recording 3 sacks. Volunteers (3-2) had trailed only 13-7 at H, scoring on 29y pass from QB Randy Wallace to WR Larry Seivers. Tennessee was hampered by ankle injury to TB Stanley Morgan.

South Carolina 35 MISSISSIPPI 29: After leading entire way, Gamecocks (5-1) suddenly were on short end of score after Mississippi rally. With 97 clock ticks left, South Carolina QB Jeff Grantz led 84y scoring drive that he topped off with 22y TD pass to WR Phillip Logan. Grantz had rushed for 1y TD in 1st Q before throwing 2 TDs as Carolina took 21-0 lead. Rebels (2-5) then scored 4 TDs on TB Michael Sweet's 2 runs and running and aerial TDs by QB Tim Ellis. Gamecocks' go-ahead score came on 10y TD reception by WR Rick Kimbrough, which was followed by 2-pt conv pass thrown by Grantz to FB James Storey.

Texas 24 ARKANSAS 18: Razorbacks (4-2) seemed to give it all away, losing 8 TOs in falling behind 24-3 before rallying for some late glory. With FB Earl Campbell (20/83y) leaving early with injured shoulder, QB Marty Akins had to lead Texas (5-1) with 135y rushing and 74y passing. Steers DT Brad Shearer contributed with INT and FUM REC, each of which led to Texas TD. Hogs fashioned rally, but it was too little, too late. Arkansas QB Scott Bull hit WR Teddy Barnes with 5y TD pass with only 19 secs remaining.

RICE 28 Southern Methodist 17: Owls (2-3) ground up SMU, rushing 72 times for 309y in earning school's 300th win. HB John Coleman rushed for 142y and HB James Sykes added 128y as Rice scored TDs in each Q. QB Tommy Kramer, who ran in 2 TDs, also threw 13y scoring pass—1 of only 2 completions on day—to TE Kenneth Roy for 7-3 lead in 1st Q. Mustangs (3-3) trailed by only 21-17 after 3 Qs, but special teams made costly clipping PEN that negated 63y punt RET by RB Arthur Whittingham in 4th Q. SMU QB Ricky Wesson (8-16/207y) threw TD passes of 52y to WR Kenny Harrison and 39y to HB Wayne Morris. Owls won their opening SWC game for 1st time since 1967.

Nebraska 28 OKLAHOMA STATE 20: QB Vince Ferragamo (10-16/140y) responded to his 1st start at helm of Huskers (6-0) with 4 TDs, 2 passing and 2 rushing. Nebraska held leads of 14-0, 21-7, and 28-14, but had to withstand rally by Oklahoma State (4-2) that was keyed by HB Terry Miller. Miller, who rushed for 90y, scored on TDs runs of 5y, 4y and 23y. But, Miller failed to get vital 2y late in game that could have tied it after Oke State recovered bad snap on Nebraska 23YL and marched to 2YL. Facing pressure, Nebraska CB Dave Butterfield made game-saving tackle of Miller for 3y loss with OSU sitting only 2YD and 2-pt conv away from tie game. QB Scott Burk rushed for 107y for Cowboys, while IB Monte Anthony led Huskers ground game with 117y.

COLORADO 31 Missouri 20: With QB Steve Pisarkiewicz tossing 2 TD passes, Tigers (4-2) jumped ahead 17-3 in 3rd Q. Lead was fleeting as stampeding Buffaloes (5-1) scored 4 TDs in 2nd H, 2 by TB Tony Reed. Reed's 2nd score, 42y scamper, sealed Missouri's fate. Colorado D had jump-started rally as DE Troy Archer forced Pisarkiewicz to lose FUM with jarring hit and recovering ball at midfield to set up 1st TD. Colorado LB Brian Cabral forced FUM on ensuing kickoff to set up tying TD, and later S Tom Tesone ended Mizzou's chances with clutch INT.

Arizona State 33 COLORADO STATE 3: QB Dennis Sproul may not have started for Sun Devils (6-0), but he played well enough off bench to earn player-of-game kudos. Sproul completed 8-12/140y, TD in leading Arizona State to 24-0 2nd H advantage. WR John Jefferson caught 6/107y, and HB "Fast" Freddie Williams rushed for 111y for ASU. Although Colorado State scored 1st on 21y FG by K Clark Kemble, Rams (4-2) shorted out on O, gaining 263y and punting 12 times. Colorado State LB Kevin McLain was all over field making 18 tackles.

AP Poll October 20

1 Ohio State (51)	1164	11 Arizona State		290
2 Oklahoma (8)	1053	12 Florida		221
3 Southern California	851	13 Arizona		178
4 Nebraska	828	14 Notre Dame		84
5 Texas A&M	616	15 Missouri		59
6 Alabama	572	16 Michigan State		50
7 Michigan	555	17 Pittsburgh		43
8 Texas	478	18 Maryland		42
9 Penn State	418	19 UCLA		39
10 Colorado	367	20 South Carolina		23

October 25, 1975

Navy 17 PITTSBURGH 0: Playing with broken thumb, S Chet Moeller (INT and FUM REC) inspired Midshipmen (5-2) D that handed Pitt its 1st shutout since 1968. Navy O was decidedly unexciting, but running of TB Gerry Goodwin (20/109y) and FB Bob Jackson (8/80y) got job done. Both scored as Navy held 2-TD lead in 3rd Q, which

was more than enough against Pitt (5-2) team that lost 3 FUMs deep in Navy territory. Panthers TB Tony Dorsett rushed for 122y, but lost 2 FUMs, and managed 36y through 3 Qs. Panthers' best chance to score occurred in 4th Q when they drove to 4th down at 1YL. Middies LB Andy Bushak and CB John Sturges nailed Pitt QB Robert Haygood to halt GL TD attempt.

FLORIDA 24 Duke 16: Gators (6-1) FB Jimmy DuBose rushed for 141y and 3 short TDs to celebrate his 21st birthday and title as UF's leading single season rusher. But overall, Florida was uninspired with 3 big SEC games coming up. Duke (3-4) had opened scoring on K Vince Fusco's 37y FG—after WR Troy Slade's 47y punt RET—gained 227y, and rallied for 13 pts in 4th Q, highlighted by QB Bob Corbett's 22y TD pass to WR Ed Hornberger. DuBose's 3rd TD that claimed 21-3 lead came courtesy of 56y 2nd H KO RET by HB Tony Green, Gators' previous seasonal rush king.

Southern California 24 NOTRE DAME 17: Trojans (7-0) did what they do best to pull out road win. Trailing 17-14 early in final period, USC displayed its rushing prowess on 71y drive as TB Ricky Bell carried ball 5/47y, and FB Mosi Tatupu rushed 3/22y to set up 2y TD keeper by QB Vince Evans. Notre Dame knew what was coming but could not stop it, although Trojans T Mervin Johnson came up with big FUM REC just before Evans' winning TD. Bell rushed 40/165y. Fighting Irish (5-2) had turned to big plays to take 14-7 H lead as HB Al Hunter raced 52y TD to paydirt, and DB Tom Lopienski returned blocked punt by CB Luther Bradley 13y to score. ND QB Joe Montana suffered poor introduction to national rivalry, hitting 3-11/25y, 2 INTs.

Miami (Ohio) 20 BOWLING GREEN 17: Miami Redskins (6-1) cleared biggest hurdle in their quest to win 3rd straight MAC crown, scoring 20 straight pts to erase 10-0 deficit. Miami tied game at 10-10 by H on 4y TD run by WB Mickey Green and 44y FG by K Fred Johnson. QB Sherman Smith then led Redskins to 1st 2 scores of 2nd H, including 14y TD pass to WR Steve Joecken. Suddenly trailing by 10, Falcons (6-1) pulled to within 20-17 on TB Dave Preston's 2nd TD of game on 5y pass from QB Mark Miller. But, Bowling Green could get no closer.

NEBRASKA 63 Colorado 21: Huskers (7-0) scored 3 TDs in each of opening 3 Qs to rout no. 10 Colorado (5-2). QB Vince Ferragamo completed 8-10/118y, 2 TDs as Nebraska capitalized on particularly sloppy performance by Bison. Buffaloes (5-2) turned ball over 8 times—6 TOs were converted into Husker scores—and committed 8 PENs. Fortunate Nebraska began drives at Buffs 31, 23, 1, 33, 10, 21, 14 and 27YLs. Colorado gained 454y with 74y coming on TD run by QB David Williams on game's 4th snap for 7-0 lead. Huskers then answered with 9 straight crushing TDs.

UCLA 28 California 14: Two high-powered Os moved ball—both topping 400y—but only UCLA succeeded at scoring. QB John Sciarra ran for 2 TDs and threw for another, while HB Wendell Tyler rushed for 143y to lead victorious Bruins (5-1-1). TB Chuck Muncie paced California (4-3) with 126y rushing, but his 4th down pass drop at Bruins 6YL late in game ended matters. Muncie did well enough to pass Johnny Olszewski (1950-52) by 8y for top spot on Bears' all-time rushing list with 2,512y. Golden Bears WR Steve Rivera caught 10/154y from QB Joe Roth (17-31/236y, INT), and his effort included 10y TD grab in 4th Q.

New Mexico 44 ARIZONA 34: For 3rd straight year, Arizona (5-1) marched into its 6th game of season with 5-0 record only to stumble. New Mexico surprised hosts as QB Steve Myer (26-38/351y) threw TDs to 4 different Lobos. His favorite target was WR Preston Dennard (8/141y), whose 15y TD reception put Lobos up 20-7 in 2nd Q. Wildcats QB Bruce Hill was excellent in defeat, completing 21-34/school-record 406y passing and 451y total O. Hill hooked up with WR Theo "T" Bell (7/217y) for scoring passes of 72y and 80y, while HB Dave Randolph rushed for 3 TDs. Loss snapped 9-game, school-record win streak for Wildcats, whose last loss was administered by BYU on October 26, 1974.

AP Poll October 27

1 Ohio State (50)	1190	11 Florida	293
2 Oklahoma (8)	1084	12 Missouri	183
3 Nebraska (2)	939	13 UCLA	151
4 Southern California (1)	890	14 Maryland	108
5 Texas A&M	632	15 Notre Dame	62
6 Alabama	609	16 Colorado	52
7 Michigan	584	17 Arizona	41
8 Texas	516	18 San Diego State	34
9 Penn State	459	19t Miami (Ohio)	33
10 Arizona State	342	19t Oklahoma State	33

November 1, 1975

GEORGIA TECH 21 Duke 6: Georgia Tech (6-2) used Wishbone attack to subdue Duke, churning up 376y on ground to control game throughout. Frosh HB Bucky Shamberger rushed for 124y to lead way, with HB Adrian Rucker adding 94y and TD. Also, Yellow Jackets overcame odd 15y PEN that was called when Homecoming festivities at H went over allotted time. Shamberger raced 68y soon after H, but Yellow Jackets were halted at 1YL by Duke GLS. Scoring for Blue Devils (3-5) was left to K Vinnie Fusco, who hammered home 2 FGs. Duke QB Bob Corbett completed 11-20/106y, but failed to complete anything long and threw 2 INTs.

VANDERBILT 17 Virginia 14: Cavaliers (1-7) had their chances, ending final opportunity on INT thrown to Vanderbilt DB Steve Curnutte after UVa had reached Vanderbilt 7YL in game's closing moments. QB Scott Gardner (19-23/105y) threw and ran for TDs and used short pass and run game to lift Virginia to 328y. HB Lonnie Sadler led Commodores (4-4) with 147y on ground and 2 TDs as Vandy used 10 pts in 4th Q pts to cinch win. Victory margin came on 44y FG by K Mark Adams.

Florida 31 AUBURN 14: Balanced attack behind backup QB Jimmy Fisher led Gators (7-1) to easy victory. Fisher (6-11/71y), replacing injured QB Don Gaffney, threw for 2 scores, while FB Jimmy DuBose ran for 149y and TD. Fisher's most impressive

play came on 34y scoring pass to WR Wes Chandler for 14-0 lead, which converted 1 of Tigers' 3 TOs. QB Clyde Baumgartner came off Tigers bench to hit 6-8/66y, TD, but was picked off once and could not sufficiently rally his charges. Auburn (3-4-1) D manfully made 2 GLS to keep score faintly respectable. Starting QB Phil Gargis led Tigers in rushing with 50y as Auburn was trampled in ground war by 341y to 180y.

Alabama 21 MISSISSIPPI STATE 10: Ferocious Bulldogs took it to Alabama (7-1) in upset attempt. MG Harvey Hull put Mississippi State (5-3) on scoreboard with 45y TD on play when ball was picked off, fumbled and then popped up to Hull, whose charge to GL tied game at 7-7. Another Tide TO, INT by Maroon CB Henry Davison, had Bulldogs driving again. QB Bruce Threadgill threw 2 passes for 51y to set up 22y go-ahead FG by K Kinney Jordan at end of 1st H. Turning point came in 3rd Q with Bulldogs ahead 10-7 when Alabama QB Richard Todd's 2nd FUM led to State's 57y drive to Bama 1YL. On 4th down, Bama DT Bob Baumhower and LB Woodrow Lowe nailed FB Clarence Harmon for 1y loss to halt hungry MSU. After exchange of punts, Alabama came up with vital play: CB Tyrone King returned INT for TD that pulled out Tide win.

Iowa 24 NORTHWESTERN 21: Hawkeyes (2-6) used only 2nd completion of day to subdue Northwestern as QB Butch Caldwell hit WR Bob Schultz with 22y TD pass with 40 secs left. Caldwell contributed masterful 20y run on broken play earlier in drive. Wildcats (3-5) had scored go-ahead TD with 2:26 left as TB Greg Boykin ran in from 1YL to cap 70y march featuring 13y pass from QB Randy Dean (13-24/164y, TD) to HB Mark Bailey that converted 4th-and-5 predicament. Game had started with bang as Iowa HB Dave Schick returned opening kickoff 97y for TD.

KANSAS 28 Kansas State 0: Jayhawks (5-3) tuned up for Oklahoma with laugher against in-state foes. KU QB Nolan Cromwell led 94y drive on opening possession that ended with 4y TD run by HB Laverne Smith. Cromwell and Smith hooked up for 11y TD pass in 2nd Q as Jayhawks began to pull away. Wildcats (3-5) managed only 102y against strong Kansas D, with deepest penetration reaching only Kansas 44YL. Score could have been lots worse as Kansas gained 516y, but allowed 2 drives within KSU 5YL to die with FUMs.

Arizona 36 BRIGHAM YOUNG 20: By controlling both lines, Wildcats (6-1) topped BYU. Cougars TB Jeff Blanc was held to 68y, barely half his 126y avg, while Arizona rushed for 235y. Cats, who held 19-0 H lead, rode strong leadership of QB Bruce Hill (10-15/168y), who added to his aerial exploits by rushing for 54y and another TD. Arizona led throughout, although BYU (3-4) rallied to 19-14 with 2 TDs in 3rd Q. Cougars QB Gifford Nielsen (27-44/387y, 2 TD, 2 INT) rushed for TD from 3y out and then threw 66y TD pass to WR John Van Der Wouden. K Lee Pistor's 3rd FG gave Arizona some breathing room, which was expanded when Hill threw his 2nd TD pass to WR Theo Bell (23y). Bell had KO RETs of 71y and 66y to launch scoring drives. Sure-handed BYU FB Todd Christensen caught 12/146y.

CALIFORNIA 28 Southern California 14: Cal TB Chuck Muncie, not Trojans TB Ricky Bell, was most explosive player on field as Golden Bears (5-3) snapped USC's 18-game win streak. Muncie ran for 143y, with key gains on Cal's 1st 3 scoring drives. QB Joe Roth (19-31/244y, INT) ended those opportunities with 2 TD tosses and TD run. Cal FB Tom Newton converted FUM by USC QB Vince Evans deep in own territory into clinching 11y TD run. Bears outgained USC by 477y to 296y, with Bell rushing for 121y. Trojans (7-1) had to weather volatile week as coach John McKay announced he would leave at season's end to become coach for NFL's expansion Tampa Bay Buccaneers.

Washington 17 UCLA 13: Bruins (5-2-1) blew chance for Pac-8 lead as Huskies FB Robin Earl bulldozed for 169y to set up 2 TDs by TB James Anderson. Earl went straight up gut for 56y run to set up team's 1st score: 3y pass by QB Chris Rowland to Anderson that tied game at 7-7 in 2nd Q. Washington (4-4) then marched 78y—shortest of 3 Huskies drives—to 4y scoring run by Anderson. Washington employed disguised 8-man front to neutralize UCLA's high-powered O. Bruins QB John Sciarra rushed for 70y and 2 TDs and passed for 117y, but was intercepted twice.

November 8, 1975

WEST VIRGINIA 17 Pittsburgh 14: He was walk-on K with 2 good FGs in 5 attempts when sent out to beat arch-rivals at game's end. Enter K Bill McKenzie's name in annals of Mountaineer (7-2) heroes with successful 38y FG, straight through uprights. "I was shaking," McKenzie admitted after game. "I couldn't feel a thing on that last play." On prior snap, QB Dan Kendra hit TE Randy Swinson with clutch 26y pass with Swinson just managing to get OB to stop clock. West Virginia had built 14-7 lead on 23y TD run by TB Artie Owens (102y), who led rush attack that topped Panthers 385y to 281y. Pitt (6-3) TB Tony Dorsett (22/107y) caught 9y TD pass to knot things up at 14-14 and make amends for FUM that led to 1y TD run by West Virginia FB Ron Lee.

North Carolina State 15 PENN STATE 14: Penn State was expected to exact revenge after Wolfpack (7-3) had sprung upset in 1974. All proceeded to form as Nittany Lions (8-2) cruised to 14-0 edge in 2nd Q. FB Larry Suhey scored on 14y run, and QB John Andress on 1y keeper for Penn State TDs. NC State fashioned rally to within 14-12 on 2 TD runs by TB Ted Brown, driving 65y at end of 1st H and 76y on its opening

possession of 2nd H. After missing 1st conv kick and 2-pt try, Wolfpack still trailed until 24y FG by K Jay Sherrill split uprights early in 4th Q. Penn State's best chance to score in 4th Q came on last-sec FG attempt by K Chris Bahr that was missed from 46y.

Georgia 10 Florida 7 (Jacksonville): Although it turned out to be D slugfest, Southern border war was memorable for winning TD: Bulldogs' flea flicker pass with less than 4 mins to play that left Gators stunned. From own 20YL, Georgia (7-2) TE Richard Appleby curled back into backfield to throw long, wounded-duck pass to wide-open WR Gene Washington at Florida 35YL. Washington waltzed into EZ and Florida's hopes for its 1st-ever SEC crown went with him. Gators (7-2) had 2 chances to reverse outcome, but QB Don Gaffney (8-16/150y, INT) was stripped at midfield by DE Dicky Clark to end 1st drive and Florida missed FG at game's end. Florida moved to UGa 21YL, but after 3 incompletions coach Doug Dickey surprisingly opted for long FG try. Snap was bad and 3-ptr missed, but 2nd-guessing had just begun. Gators FB Jimmy DuBose rushed for 96y, while HB Kevin McLee paced Bulldogs with 71y.

Ohio State 40 ILLINOIS 3: Illini D was valiant in defeat, holding Ohio State (9-0) to 10 1st H pts before finally wearing down. Illinois (4-5) took early lead on 36y FG by K Dan Beaver, but when its O was held to 9 1st downs and 156y O for game, it was clear only way to win was to post shutout. Buckeyes TB Archie Griffin (23/127y), who became 1st player ever to top 5,000y career rushing, burst free for 30y TD run. K Tom Skladany then added 2 FGs, including conf-record 59y boot that broke 57y mark set by Beaver earlier in season. Ohio DB Tim Fox got in on scoring with 20y INT TD RET before FB Pete Johnson rushed for 2 TDs to break former teammate Champ Henson's Big 10 record of 21 TDs in season. Illini TB Lonnie Perrin rushed for 60y.

Kansas 23 OKLAHOMA 3: Visiting Norman and facing Sooners (8-1), winners of 28 straight games, made it unnecessary to say that Kansas (6-3) was huge underdog. Special players play launched upset: blocked punt by Jayhawks CB Eddie Lewis in 1st Q set up QB Nolan Cromwell's 6y run that put Kansas up for good at 7-3. That score held up until 3rd Q, when Sooners lost FUMs on all 3 drives to set up 9 Kansas pts as nary single drive was longer than 40y. Jayhawks' insurance TD in 4th Q came on HB Laverne Smith's scoring run, from 18y out, and upset was secured. Oklahoma's 328y were negated by 8 TOs: all 7 2nd H possessions ended in either INT or FUM. This sloppiness led to Sooners' lowest scoring output since being shutout on road by Notre Dame's great D in 1966. "This isn't just the greatest victory of my career or of our players' career," said thrilled Kansas coach Bud Moore after game. "It's got to be the greatest victory in football."

TEXAS 37 Baylor 21: Longhorns (8-1) bulled over Bears in taking 37-7 lead by 4th Q, rushing 68/311y. Texas FB Earl Campbell (31/133y) topped 1,000y for season while scoring game's 1st 2 TDs. Baylor (2-4-2) put up little challenge, losing 4 of 8 FUMs and throwing 2 INTs, including important EZ INT by Steers LB Bill Hamilton when Texas led only 10-0. Bears' comeback hopes ended early in 3rd Q as FUM by Baylor QB Mark Jackson on his own 23YL was converted into Campbell's 21y scoring run. Texas reserve QB Charlie Parker then came off bench to lead 3 TD drives, including march punctuated by his 30y scoring pass to WR Alcy Jackson.

CALIFORNIA 27 Washington 24: Leading Golden Bears' O to 522y, QB Joe Roth (24-36/385y, INT) fired 4 TD passes as California (6-2) maintained Pac-8 lead. Despite gaining little more than half as many y (266y), Huskies (4-5) had shot to win with ball on Bears 24YL late in 4th Q. Cal D held on downs as Huskies scrapped tying FG try and missed 4th down pass. WR Steve Rivera had another huge game for Cal, catching 10/183y, 2 TDs and lifting his recent 3-game receiving totals to 29/468y. FB Robin Earl rushed for 130y for Washington, while Cal TB Chuck Muncie rushed for 87y and caught 5/48y with 3y TD reception.

OREGON STATE 7 Washington State 0: Beavers (1-8) won game for retiring coach Dee Andros in his final game at Parker Stadium. Oregon State DE Ernie Richardson had INT and 2 FUM RECs to lead D; his 28y RET of INT set up game's lone TD on 7y run by FB Ron Cuie. Cougars (2-7) moved ball much better than Beavers, but lost FUMs on OSU 5 and 27YLs and threw INTs at GL and 5YL, while also missing FG. QB John Hopkins threw for 121y for Washington State, but also 3 INTs. TB Rich Dodge paced Beavers with 96y rushing.

Stanford 13 SOUTHERN CALIFORNIA 10: Stanford (5-3-1) bounced free-falling Trojans from Rose Bowl race on 37y FG by K Mike Langford with :05 left on 4th Q clock. USC (7-2) was hoping last-sec FG could have been theirs, but INT by frosh CB Savann Thompson gave Cardinals ball at USC 38YL with 59 secs left. Cards QB Guy Benjamin (15-29/161y) immediately hit TE Ted Pappas for 14y gain and then ran for 9y himself to set up winning FG, Langford's 2nd FG in 5 tries. USC TB Ricky Bell was magnificent in defeat, rushing for 195y, while QB Vince Evans threw 68y TD pass to WR Junior Lee in 2nd Q. Interestingly, defender burned on Lee's TD catch was Stanford's Thompson, who more than made up for it in late going.

November 15, 1975

PITTSBURGH 34 Notre Dame 20: It was TB Tony Dorsett's fabulous show in Pittsburgh as speedy and shifty ace raced for 303y, 2 TDs rushing and caught TD pass. After only 4 carries, Dorsett had amazing 151y and TD, and Pitt (7-3) owned

14-10 lead for good. Notre Dame (7-3) dropped its 1st game in series in 12 years despite having nearly 16-min time advantage. On other hand, speedy Dorsett needed very little time to break off his big plays. Irish had led 10-7 early as QB Rick Slager converted KO FUM by Pitt WR Gordon Jones into 1y TD dive. Dorsett, who cracked career 4,000y barrier, busted away for 71y scoring romp moments later.

Miami 24 FLORIDA STATE 22: Canes (2-7) answered late Florida State rally with 29y FG by K Chris Dennis that came with 13 secs left. Having scored TDs in each of game's 1st 3 Qs, Miami entered final Q with 21-6 lead. Seminoles (2-8) then scored TD on 1y run by TB Rudy Thomas before QB Clyde Walker threw 2-pt conv pass to TE Ed Beckman to pull within 21-14. FSU DT Billy McPhillips then recovered FUM by Miami QB Kary Baker to set up blistering 31y TD romp by FB Larry Key to pull home team to within single pt. Going for 22-21 lead, Florida State's Walker completed go-ahead conv pass to WB Mike Shumann. Hurricanes soon took advantage of miserable 17y punt by P Bill Duley to go 29y to winning FG.

FLORIDA 48 Kentucky 7: Gators (8-2) were never challenged, grabbing 27-0 H lead behind 2 TD passes by QB Don Gaffney (4-8/123y). Florida totaled 487y, with 309y on ground behind host of fleet backs. Gators sub HB Willie Wilder romped with 7/78y, while HB Tony Green caught 19y TD pass and ran for 10y TD. Wildcats (2-7-1) gained 320y, with 75y coming on 4th Q drive capped by FB Rod Stewart's 3y run.

Mississippi State 16 LOUISIANA STATE 6: Tone of game was set early when Mississippi State (6-3-1) TB Walter Packer, who became 1st Bulldogs player to top 2,000y career rushing, raced 85y for opening score. Suffering from 5 TOs, Tigers fell behind 13-0 at H and could not answer until 3rd Q. QB Pat Lyons then put LSU (3-7) on board with 2y TD run, but K Mike Conway missed x-pt. He also missed 2 FGs. Conversely Mississippi State K Kinney Jordan booted 3 FGs to tie SEC record with 13 on season. HB Terry Robiskie rushed for 90y to lead Tigers.

Oklahoma 28 MISSOURI 27: Sooners (9-1) prevented 2nd straight upset as HB Joe Washington scampered 71y to score on 4th-and-short and followed it up with winning 2-pt conv run. Tigers (6-4), who had scored 27 straight pts to wipe out early 20-0 OU lead, had chance for late victory but K Tim Gibbons missed 40y FG with 1:02 remaining. Gibbons had missed his 1st x-pt in 31 attempts after final Tigers score, 2y FUM run by SB Randy Grossart with 5:35 left. Sooners had built 20-pt 1st H lead behind unbalanced O-line that had Tigers scrambling to adjust for 2nd H.

San Jose State 31 SAN DIEGO STATE 7: San Diego State enjoyed headlines for PCAA in 1975, but it was Spartans (9-1) earning conf crown with upset. San Jose won with D that allowed no pts, but scored on 2 INT TD RETs and safety, all in 22-pt 4th Q. Trailing 9-7, Aztecs (8-2) QB Craig Penrose, 2nd in NCAA passing, had thrown INT returned 53y by DB Gerald Small for TD. Penrose moved team again, only to throw EZ pick to Small, which eventually was converted into 28y TD run by TB Rick Kane (144y rushing). Near game's end, San Jose LB Vance Topps scored on 22y INT RET and special teams added safety on following KO RET. San Diego State's TD came on 1st Q blocked punt REC in EZ by CB Ken Hinton.

November 22, 1975

Harvard 10 YALE 7: Crimson captured 1st outright Ivy League title in league's 20 official years as K Mike Lynch booted winning FG with 33 secs left. QB Jim Kubacki (11-27/118y, 3 INTs) could manage only 2 long drives all day, but Harvard (7-2) capitalized on both. On winning 72y effort, Kubacki set up FG with 21y pass on 4th-and-12 to TE Bob McDermott that moved ball to Yale 13YL. D shut down Yale (7-2) O led by QB, and future TV news talent, Stone Phillips (2-13/20y, INT). Phillips scored TD on 5y run in 2nd Q, matched in 3rd Q by 2y run by Harvard WB Tommy Winn. HB Don Gesicki rushed for 80y to lead Bulldogs. Lynch snapped string of 4 missed FGs with his game winner. Lusty crowd of 66,846 converged on Yale Bowl.

Penn State 7 PITTSBURGH 6: It was day of mixed blessings for Pitt (7-4) K Carson Long, who missed 2 last-min FGs on day his wife gave birth to baby girl. Long missed chip-shot from 23y with 1:31 left, and, redeemed, he missed 45y kick with :09 on clock. It was not to be for Long on field: earlier he had missed 51y FG attempt and had x-pt blocked. Frosh QB Chuck Fusina was at helm for winning Penn State (9-2) drive, culminated by frosh TB Steve Geise's 29y run. Long's long night began after 37y TD run by TB Elliott Walker had given Panthers 6-0 lead. Penn State DB Tom Odell, long jumper in HS, leaped over middle of line to block x-pt try with his chest. Odell also got piece of Long's 23y attempt.

Ohio State 21 MICHIGAN 14: With Michigan (8-1-2) stopping brother Archie's 31-game 100y rushing streak, Ohio State (11-0) S Ray Griffin simply had to come up as hero. In addition to making 14 tackles, Griffin picked off critical 4th Q pass by QB Rick Leach that Buckeyes converted into FB Pete Johnson's winning 3y TD run. Johnson had scored only min earlier to tie game at 14-14. Johnson's tying TD capped 80y drive led by QB Cornelius Greene. Michigan, needing win for Rose Bowl bid, suddenly had to pass, with poor results. Wolverines D delivered masterful job in holding Ohio TB Archie Griffin to 46y rushing. Michigan TB Gordon Bell rushed for 124y and also threw

surprise 11y TD pass—on his 1st attempt as collegian—to WB Jim Smith that had tied game at 7-7 in 2nd Q. Michigan suffered 3 TOs in OSU end and missed 1st H FG, so it could not prevent end of 41-game home unbeaten streak.

Purdue 9 INDIANA 7: Hoosiers (2-8-1) wasted 2 late opportunities to regain Old Oaken Bucket after 3 straight series losses, losing FUM on Purdue 19YL with less than 2 mins remaining and again at Purdue 7YL with 9 ticks left. IU finished with 5 TOs, including 4 FUMs. Boilermakers (4-7) drove 82y midway through 4th Q to take 9-7 lead on 3y run by WR Paul Beery. For 2nd straight week, TB Courtney Snyder (34/211y) broke Indiana's single-game rushing record. FB Mike Pruitt proved to be rushing bulwark for Boilermakers with 121y.

OKLAHOMA 35 Nebraska 10: Unleashing awesome depth, Sooners (10-1) captured share of Big 8 title with 28 unanswered pts in 2nd H. Oklahoma backup HBs Horace Ivory, Billy Sims and Elvis Peacock all scored TDs. Oklahoma happily converted TOs as all 5 of its TDs followed Nebraska miscues. No. 2 Huskers (10-1) were held to 70y rushing and had something brewing. After being stopped at GL at end of 1st H on hit on IB Monte Anthony by Sooners MG Dewey Selmon, Nebraska took 10-7 lead in 3rd Q on Anthony's 1y TD run. Nebraska QB Vince Ferragamo (13-25/146y, 2 INTs) was separated from ball on next possession by Sooners DT Lee Roy Selmon to set up Ivory's 5y go-ahead TD run. QB Steve Davis led Oklahoma attack with 130y rushing. OU coach Barry Switzer labeled outcome "greatest win I've ever been associated with."

ARKANSAS 31 Texas Tech 14: With starting RBs Ike Forte and Jerry Eckwood out injured, QB Scott Bull took it upon himself to lead Arkansas O. Bull ran for 3 TDs and threw another to lead Razorbacks (8-2) to easy win. Score was 24-0 at H as Bull threw 44y scoring pass to TE Marvin Daily and rushed twice for 1y TD keepers. Red Raiders (6-5) made constant mistakes, setting up all 4 of Hogs' 1st H scores. Tech errors included 2 FUMs, 11y punt, and poor decision by S Curtis Jordan to go for INT and miss, which left Daily all alone for his TD dash. Texas Tech QBs Tommy Duniven and Rodney Allison combined for 173y passing as Allison scored running TD and Duniven passed for score.

TEXAS CHRISTIAN 28 Rice 21: Snapping 20-game losing streak, Horned Frogs (1-10) surprised Rice and home crowd with 28-7 3rd Q lead. QB Lee Cook (15-24/239y, INT) threw for 2 scores and ran for 3rd tally. But, perhaps Cook's biggest play was his launching of 68y punt from his GL with 2 mins to go. That boot quelled rally of Owls (2-8). Rice QB Tommy Kramer had led late surge, throwing 2 4th Q TDs, but he also made 5 INTs. CB Allen Hooker had 3 picks for Horned Frogs, who played prevent D in 4th Q, strategy they have had little use for over past 2 seasons.

California 48 STANFORD 15: TB Chuck Muncie had Big Game to remember for California (8-3), rushing for 166y and 3 TDs, catching TD and throwing 46y scoring pass to WR Wesley Walker (5/125y). For its part, Stanford scored on 38y QB Guy Benjamin (17-30/236y, 2 TDs, 3 INTs) pass to WR Tony Hill (7/138y) to briefly trim deficit to 14-6. Cal added 13 pts to its lead in 2nd Q and pulled away as Muncie scored 3rd TD and K Jim Breech kicked 2 FGs. Early in 4th Q Cardinals (6-4-1) rallied with safety and TD to get within 27-15 before surrendering 3 TDs. Mercury-swift Walker caught 2 scoring passes in 4th Q. Cal's Big Game win brought with it new series pts record. Still, Bears had to await result of following week's UCLA-Southern California clash to see if they had secured Rose Bowl spot.

November 29, 1975

(Th'g) Georgia 42 GEORGIA TECH 26: Bulldogs (9-2) completely routed Georgia Tech, building 42-0 lead against team that had topped 30 pts 4 times in 1975. Game started ominously for Yellow Jackets (7-4) as QB Danny Myers threw INT on 1st play, and it was returned to Tech 12YL by Georgia DB Bobby Thompson to set up QB Ray Goff's 2y scoring run. After Georgia Tech blocked FG to remain down only 7-0, HB Bucky Shamburger appeared gone on 68y dash toward tying TD before Thompson reeled him in to prevent score. Jackets HB Adrian Rucker lost FUM at 3YL on next play, and Georgia HB Glynn Harrison, who rushed for 139y of team's 431y, followed 2 plays later with crushing 78y TD run. Later in 1st H, DE Lawrence Craft added another TD to Georgia's total, catching FUM by TB David Sims and returning it 20y for 21-0 lead. Georgia Tech made things look better with 26-pt burst in 4th Q as reserve QB Rudy Allen rushed for 3 TDs.

(Fri) TEXAS A&M 20 Texas 10: Aggies (10-0) beat Texas for 1st time since 1967 as their D was brilliant, allowing only 6 1st downs and 179y. Twice they stopped Longhorns on 4th-and-short attempts in 3rd Q. It took reserve QB Mike Jay to get A&M rolling as he upped early lead to 10-0 with 4y TD pass to WR Richard Osborne. Texas (9-2) FB Earl Campbell was held to 40y rushing, while A&M knocked out QB Marty Akins on hit by CB Pat Thomas on opening play of 2nd Q. DB Raymond Clayborn scored sole TD for Texas on 64y punt TD RET. Aggies racked up 316y rushing, 203y more than Texas, as HB Bubba Bean excelled with 17/126y.

(Fri) Ucla 25 SOUTHERN CALIFORNIA 22: Bruins (8-2-1) headed to Rose Bowl, despite losing 8 of 11 FUMs. When not dropping ball, UCLA rushed for 328y, while QB John Sciarra threw 2 TDs to TE Don Pederson—2nd for eventual winning pts as UCLA

went up 25-14 in 3rd Q. Trojans finished game's scoring on 3y TD run by TB Ricky Bell (36/136y), but could not cash in 3 late FUM RECs against heroic Bruins D. UCLA HB Wendell Tyler rushed 130y and 57y 2nd Q TD, while Sciarra threw for 86y and ran for 85y. Seemingly out of nowhere, once high-ranked Trojans had lost 4 straight conf games for 1st time in their long history. Bell (36/136y) finished year with 1,875y, agonizing 6y short of former Cornell HB Ed Marinaro's single season record.

RUTGERS 21 Syracuse 10: Red-hot Scarlet Knights (9-2) won 7th straight game in convincing fashion. FB Curt Edwards bulled his way to 149y of team's 273y rushing, QB Jeff Rebholz connected with WR Mark Twitty on 41y TD pass to pace Rutgers O. Syracuse (6-5) scored TD when DB Tim Moresco recovered blocked punt by NG Bernie Winters in EZ. Rutgers D, ranked 6th in nation, held Orangemen to 117y and scored TD by CB Hank Jenkins on 59y INT RET. Jenkins' pick was 1 of team's 3 that came in 4th Q to preserve win. Knights celebrated 1st ever win over Orangemen in 10-game series after suffering 8 losses and tie.

Navy 30 Army 6 (Philadelphia): Army (2-9) could manage only single TD, but that was enough to prevent its 3rd straight shutout in what suddenly had become lopsided series. Midshipmen (7-4) completed their best record since 1963 as FB Bob Jackson rushed for 133y and 2 TDs and TB Gerry Goodwin gained 117y on ground. Jackson finished career as Navy's 2nd best ground gainer with 1,667y, while scoring 5 TDs in 3 wins over Cadets. Any chance of competitive game ended in 2nd Q when MG Jeff Hoobler blocked Cadet punt, which was returned 42y for TD and 17-0 lead by Navy DE Bob DeStafney. Navy finished with 302y rushing, while soph QB Leamon Hall (7-25/83y, 2 INTs) provided Army's only bright spot by scoring on 1y run.

Alabama 28 Auburn 0 (Birmingham): Ralph "Shug" Jordan's final game as college coach went pretty much way his final season had gone: miserable. Alabama QB Richard Todd had hand, and two legs, in on every Bama (10-1) score as he threw 2 TD passes and ran for 2 others. Todd finished with 90y rushing, scoring on runs of 33y and 14y, while FB Johnny Davis added 98y on ground as Tide gained 430y. Auburn (3-6-2) could manage only 144y, with 45/94y rushing. Tigers' best scoring chance ended with missed 44y FG by K Neil O'Donoghue early in 4th Q. Alabama recorded its 5th straight SEC title, mark later equaled by Florida Gators in 1996. Also, it was 20th straight conf win, matching record set by Tennessee 35 years earlier.

Vanderbilt 17 TENNESSEE 14: Having last won rivalry game in 1964 when their current players were in grade school, Commodores (7-4) took strong resolve to Knoxville. Vanderbilt D made difference, allowing only 89y rushing and 202y overall. Each squad made drive past midfield and each made them count for 7-7 H tie. Vanderbilt HB Lonnie Sadler scored on 1y run, and Tennessee QB Randy Wallace threw 3y scoring pass to TE Tommy West. Vols (6-5) took 14-7 lead on HB Stanley Morgan's 4y TD run in 3rd Q before surrendering 10 pts in 4th Q. TB Adolph Groves tied game at 14-14 for Commodores with 9y TD run. S Ed Oaks then made game-changing INT midway through 4th Q to give Vandy ball on Tennessee 6YL. K Mark Adams kicked winning 18y FG soon after, and Vandy D made played well to have 3-pt lead stand up for upset.

ARIZONA STATE 24 Arizona 21: With WAC title and Fiesta Bowl berth on line, Sun Devils (11-0) pulled out victory. Arizona State QB Dennis Sproul (13-24/139y, 2 TDs) led 80y winning drive early in 4th Q, capped by his 1y TD run. ASU's "Crunch Bunch" D made Sproul TD stand up and was especially effective against passing of Arizona (9-2) QB Bruce Hill (8-23/130y). Hill, who led Wildcats on the ground with 74y, was forced into 4 straight incompletions on final possession from Arizona 44YL. Sun Devils TB Freddie Williams rushed for 153y. Game's most spectacular play was ASU WR John Jefferson's diving 8y scoring catch late in 1st H that pared it to 14-10.

AP Poll December 1

1 Ohio State (50)	1144	11 UCLA	240
2 Texas A&M (7)	1038	12 Georgia	202
3 Oklahoma (1)	890	13 Florida	179
4 Alabama	761	14 California	174
5 Michigan	619	15 Arizona	66
6 Nebraska	612	16 Miami (Ohio)	64
7 Arizona State	553	17 Maryland	57
8 Penn State	382	18 Arkansas	53
9 Texas	353	19 Kansas	43
10 Colorado	340	20 Pittsburgh	16

December 6, 1975

ARKANSAS 31 Texas A&M 6: No. 2 Texas A&M (10-1) saw national title and Cotton Bowl dreams go up in smoke. Hogs (9-2), returning to Cotton Bowl for 1st time since January 1966, scored 17 more pts on Aggies than had any other team this season. Arkansas QB Scott Bull threw for TD and ran for another, although his most important duty was his successful limitation of mistakes. Razorbacks built 24-0 3rd Q lead as D held Aggies to 149y and forced 6 TOs. A&M scored its only pts on 24y TD run by back-up QB Keith Baker.

Conference Standings

Ivy League

Harvard	6-1
Brown	5-1-1
Yale	5-2
Dartmouth	4-2-1
Princeton	3-4
Penn	2-5
Columbia	2-5
Cornell	0-7

Atlantic Coast

Maryland	5-0
Duke	3-0-2
North Carolina State	2-2-1
Wake Forest	3-3
Clemson	2-3
North Carolina	1-4-1
Virginia	0-5

Southeastern

Alabama	6-0
Georgia	5-1
Florida	5-1
Mississippi	5-1
Tennessee	3-3
Vanderbilt	2-4
Mississippi State	1-4-1
Auburn	1-4-1
LSU	1-5
Kentucky	0-6

Southern

Richmond	5-1
East Carolina	4-2
Appalachian State	3-2
Citadel	4-3
William & Mary	2-3
Furman	2-4
VMI	2-4
Davidson	0-3

Big Ten

Ohio State	8-0
Michigan	7-1
Michigan State	4-4
Illinois	4-4
Purdue	4-4
Wisconsin	3-4-1
Minnesota	3-5
Iowa	3-5
Northwestern	2-6
Indiana	1-6-1

Mid-American

Miami (Ohio)	6-0
Central Michigan	4-1-1
Ball State	4-2
Bowling Green	4-2
Toledo	4-4
Ohio	3-3-1
Northern Illinois	2-3
Kent State	1-6
Western Michigan	0-7

Big Eight

Nebraska	6-1
Oklahoma	6-1
Colorado	5-2
Kansas	4-3
Oklahoma State	3-4
Missouri	3-4
Iowa State	1-6
Kansas State	0-7

Missouri Valley

Tulsa	4-0
West Texas State	2-2
New Mexico State	2-2
Drake	1-3
Wichita State	1-3

Southwest Athletic

Texas A&M	6-1
Arkansas	6-1
Texas	6-1
Texas Tech	4-3
SMU	2-5
Baylor	2-5
Rice	1-6
TCU	1-6

Western Athletic

Arizona State	7-0
Arizona	5-2
Colorado State	4-2
Brigham Young	4-3
New Mexico	4-3
Utah	1-4
Wyoming	1-6
Texas El Paso	0-6

Pacific-Eight

UCLA	6-1
California	6-1
Stanford	5-2
Washington	5-2
Southern California	3-4
Oregon	2-5
Oregon State	1-6
Washington State	1-7

Pacific Coast Athletic

San Jose State	5-0
Long Beach State	4-1
San Diego State	3-2
Pacific	2-3
Fresno State	1-4
Fullerton State	0-5

1975 Major Bowl Games

Liberty Bowl (Dec. 22): Southern California 20 Texas A&M 0

Coach John McKay went out as winner in final game at helm of Trojans (8-4) as team used big plays to overcome Aggies (10-2). QB Vince Evans (6-13/174y) hit WR Randy Simmrin with 65y pass that set up 1y scoring plunge by FB Mosi Tatupu, and TB Ricky Bell (28/82y) displayed his finest moves on 76y TD run with screen pass. Both plays occurred in 17-pt 2nd Q as Trojans padded K Glen Walker's 2 FGs to take 20-0 H lead. In 1st H, Texas A&M (10-2) twice drove into Southern California territory, but shot itself in foot with crucial TOs as FUM was lost at 3YL and trip to Trojans 26YL ended with INT. Aggies D, which led nation in total D and rushing D, played well save for 2 long scoring pass plays in 2nd Q, while it limited Troy rush attack to 80y. A&M HB Bubba Bean rushed 16/80y. Match-up took on "Disappointment Bowl" complexion as both teams had been in nation's top 5 as late as November 1. McKay finished run at Southern California with 127-40-8 record, while USC became 1st school ever to win 15 bowl games even though this was USC's 1st win at any bowl other than Rose Bowl.

Sun Bowl (Dec. 26): Pittsburgh 33 Kansas 19:

Post-season win was long time coming for Panthers (8-4) since their last victory had come in 1937 Rose Bowl. Pitt D perfectly neutralized Kansas Wishbone in building 19-0 H lead. Pitt O rushed very well with 3 Panthers topping 100y mark, so Pitt won clock battle and forced KU (7-5) to play catch up. That was tough task considering Jayhawks were virtually without passing attack: QB Nolan Cromwell threw 6 times without making single completion. Game's crucial play came early in 1st Q as MG Al Romano stopped Cromwell (24/99y rushing) on 4th-and-1 at Pitt 16YL. Four plays later, Pitt went up 7-0 on back-up TB Elliott Walker's 60y burst with option pitchout. Starting TB Tony Dorsett added 2 2nd Q TD runs to give Pitt commanding 19-0 lead. Dorsett rushed 17/142y, while Walker (11/123y, 2 TD) and QB Robert Haygood (14/104y) also topped 100y rushing. HB Laverne Smith rushed for 113y to pace Jayhawks, including 55y scoring jaunt in 3rd Q for Kansas' 1st pts.

GAME OF THE YEAR
Fiesta Bowl (Dec. 26): Arizona State 17 Nebraska 14

Trailing 14-6 early in 4th Q, Arizona State (12-0) faced 4th-and-1 at Huskers 13YL. QB Dennis Sproul kept for 2y for 1st down but temporarily injured his wrist. Sub QB Fred Mortenson entered game and promptly hit WR John Jefferson for 10y TD and WB Larry Mucker for tying 2-pt conv. After 2 Huskers (10-2) punts wrapped around INT by ASU, Sun Devils began winning drive at midfield with starter Sproul back in action. They marched to 12YL—with Sproul and Jefferson connecting on 16y pass—where K Danny Kush, coach Frank's son, booted game-winning 29y FG with 4:50 left. Cornhuskers then drove deep into Devils territory until FUM by FB Tony Davis at ASU 21YL after 10y completion ended any chance of Nebraska continuing its consecutive bowl win streak of NCAA record-tying 6. As clock ticked down, grateful Devils were near tears. Huskers rushed for 198y, led by Davis who finished with 60y, while IB Monte Anthony scored both TDs with short runs.

Astro-Bluebonnet Bowl (Dec. 27): Texas 38 Colorado 21

Griffins of Ohio State were rivaled by another dynamic brother combination: FB Earl Campbell rushed for 95y against Buffs (9-3) to earn game's best back honors, while brother Tim earned best lineman honors for play as DE and scored TD. Colorado had 21-7 H lead on 225y to 89y advantage as QB David Williams (17-25/177y, 2 INTs) tossed 2 TDs. Longhorns (10-2) answered with 31-0 2nd H effort, scoring 24 in 3rd Q alone. Early in 3rd Q Colorado, FB Terry Kunz lost FUM on own 34YL, which was recovered by Texas LB Bill Hamilton to set up 3y TD run by HB Jimmy Walker. Buffs then went 3-and-out, which led to blocked punt TD by DE Tim Campbell. Brother Earl then caught 2-pt conv pass to tie game 21-21 early in 3rd Q, deflating Colorado. Winning pts came later in 3rd Q on 55y FG by Horns K Russell Erxleben, while HBs Ivey Suber and Johnny Jones added TDs to stretch lead.

Gator Bowl (Dec. 29): Maryland 13 Florida 0

Terps (9-2-1) felt as though they officially were back from 20-year exile from power. Maryland forced 4 TOs in handing Gators their 1st shutout in 55 games. Frosh TB Steve Atkins sparked O with 127y, including 118y in 2nd H when Maryland played keep away. By that point, Terps had 10-0 lead on 19y TD pass from QB Larry Dick to WR Kim Hoover and 1st of 2 FGs by K Mike Sochko, of 20y. That was more than enough for D that allowed 210y and had as many catches of 19 Florida passes (3) as Gators (9-3). Both of Maryland's 1st H scores were set up by INTs. P Sochko, who had great duel with Florida P Tom Dolfi added insurance 24y FG for only pts of 2nd H, as Gators had only 2 drives across midfield. Maryland DG Paul Divito, who recovered FUM in 1st H, was particularly devastating on Florida's last threat with 3 sacks. FB Jimmy DuBose fought his way to 95y rushing for Gators.

Peach Bowl (Dec. 31): West Virginia 13 North Carolina State 10

Mountaineers (8-3) turned to passing duo of QB Dan Kendra (12-28/202y) and WR Scott MacDonald to pull out win. MacDonald (5/110y), who spent 4 years with hoop team before turning to football, caught 50y TD pass as WVU rallied from 10-0 deficit. Wolfpack (7-3-1) looked good early as QB Dave Buckey (11-24/103y) hit brother, WR Don Buckey, 2/29y total on 73y drive to 1st score: 1y TD run by TB Ricky Adams. Pack upped lead to 10 pts on 21y FG by K Jay Sherrill with under min to go in 1st H, but then allowed 75y West Virginia drive in 41 secs to Kendra's 39y scoring pass to TB Artie Owens that changed momentum. Each team had 3rd Q threats end on TOs, which allowed Kendra and MacDonald to pull off their magic. NC State had difficult time with inspired Mountaineer D until final drive moved from own 6YL to West Virginia 33YL before 2 sacks by LB Ray Marshall forced 4th down desperation pass that S Tom Pridemore picked off. TB Ted Brown rushed for 159y for Wolfpack. Win avenged 49-13 loss to North Carolina State in 1972 Peach Bowl.

Sugar Bowl: Alabama 13 Penn State 6

In 1st Sugar Bowl played in Louisiana Superdome, Alabama (11-1) used passing to snap 8-game bowl winless streak. QB Richard Todd threw for 10-12/210y—more than 100y better than his season average of 83.7y—against Penn State D that focused on running game. Nittany Lions (9-3) held Tide to 106y rushing, but Todd burned them with superb passing accuracy. Bama led 3-0 at H on K Danny Ridgeway's 25y FG that capped drive featuring 54y connection between Todd and WR Joe Dale Harris. Nittany Lions tied score on K Chris Bahr's 42y effort early in 3rd Q before Todd beat them with 55y pass to WR Ozzie Newsome (4/97y) that led to 14y scoring run by HB Mike Stock. Teams traded FGs after that. With O generating only 214y, Penn State was unable to rally. Last Alabama win in post-season had been 34-7 rout of Nebraska in 1967 Sugar Bowl. Bryant was conspicuous without his houndstooth hat, but as he said, "Momma taught me never to wear a hat inside a building."

Cotton Bowl: Arkansas 31 Georgia 10

Looking to run out clock late in 1st H, Georgia (9-3) looked comfortable with 10-0 lead, but disaster struck. QB Matt Robinson lost ball deep in his territory, and Arkansas had FUM REC by LB Hal McAfee to set up 39y FG by K Steve Little with 36 secs left. Moments later Bulldogs went for flea flicker: QB Ray Goff tried to surprise Hogs (10-2) by nonchalantly snapping ball to WR Gene Washington, but Washington lost ball when he ran into teammate Al Pollard. McAfee scooped up loose ball again. Razorbacks FB Ike Forte (24-119y) gained 12y with catch and plunged 1y for TD to quickly tie score at 10-10. Shocking turn-around crushed Georgia, which mustered marginal O in 2nd H. With 3 missed FGs in 3rd Q, Hogs had to wait until 4th Q to finish off Georgia. Finish them they did as QB Scott Bull completed 35y pass to WR Freddie Douglas to set up RB Rolland Fuchs' 5y TD run for 17-10 lead. DB Howard Sampson ended next Bulldogs drive with INT, and Arkansas scored 6 plays later on 1y run by FB Micheal Forrest. Forte added his 2nd TD to close scoring. Early Georgia pts had come on K Allan Leavitt's 35y FG and 21y pass from Robinson pass to Washington. Bulldogs O

made do with single 1st down from 2nd Q until late in 4th Q. Hogs" 1st 4 scoring drives averaged 22y in length.

Rose Bowl: UCLA 23 Ohio State 10

It was not supposed to end this way for coach Woody Hayes and Buckeyes (11-1). Fielding what he felt may have been his best squad, Hayes was optimistic after perfect regular season in which team led nation in scoring with 34 pts per game. Helping them reach that lofty average was UCLA (9-2-1) squad that was beaten 41-20 earlier in season. Bruins reversed that outcome with 23-pt 2nd H, keyed by newfound passing attack. Ohio had 174y to 48y O advantage in 1st H but suffered because star TB Archie Griffin broke hand on game's 3rd play. In final appearance for Ohio State, Griffin remained in game and rushed for 93y but was unable to bust long runs. Bucks led 3-0 at H on 42y FG by K Tim Klaban. UCLA made 2 adjustments at H, opting to have QB John Sciarra (13-19/212y, 2 INTs) pass more, and disguising its D to confuse Buckeyes QB Cornelius Greene. Bruins opened 3rd Q with drive to K Brett White's tying 33y FG. With D switching coverages to match Greene's audibles, Bruins began to take over. Sciarra and WR Wally Henry hooked up on 2 TD passes, including 67y effort, as UCLA forged ahead 16-3. With national title hopes fading, Buckeyes pounded ball downfield to pull within 16-10 as FB Pete Johnson bulled way into EZ from 3y out—26th time he crossed GL during season. That was as close as nation's no. 1 team could get as UCLA CB Barney Person and S Pat Schmidt picked off Greene passes, and HB Wendell Tyler (21/172y) raced 54y for clinching score. Bruins had big O differential (366y to 124y) in 2nd H. Game was reminiscent of Bruins' last bowl appearance, when UCLA upset undefeated and top-ranked Michigan State in 1965 Rose Bowl after Spartans had beaten them in regular season.

Orange Bowl: Oklahoma 14 Michigan 6

Following Ohio State's Rose Bowl loss, Sooners (11-1) knew national championship could be theirs with win in 1st bowl after 3 years of probation. OU needed only 2 plays to move 79y for 7-0 2nd Q lead as QB Steve Davis completed 40y pass on 2nd-and-22 to WR Tinker Owens, who quickly replaced Owens—went 39y to EZ on reverse. K Tony DiRienzo's x-pt provided eventual winning margin. Michigan (8-2-2) O had some opportunities, even though it gained only 202y, but could not score as frosh QB Rick Leach was 0-7 passing in 1st H, before being knocked out momentarily after hit by CB Jerry Anderson. Sooners started moving ball on ground in 3rd Q, losing FUM by HB Elvis Peacock at Michigan 34YL before going 67y for their 2nd TD on 10y run by Davis. Walk-on FB Jim Culbreath, who lost 2 FUMs as replacement for suspended FB Horace Ivory, redeemed himself with 33y rushing on clinching drive. Wolverines answered with 2y TD run by TB Gordon Bell (18/53y), who with fellow 1,000y back FB Rob Lytle was held well in check by Oklahoma. HB Joe Washington rushed for 73y in his final game as Sooners star.

Final AP Poll January 2			
1 Oklahoma (54.5)	1257	11 Texas A&M	260
2 Arizona State (5)	1038	12 Miami (Ohio)	194
3 Alabama (3.5)	964	13 Maryland	192
4 Ohio State	957	14 California	175
5 UCLA	658	15 Pittsburgh	144
6 Texas	542	16 Colorado	90
7 Arkansas	534	17 Southern California	64
8 Michigan	528	18 Arizona	58
9 Nebraska	456	19 Georgia	57
10 Penn State	319	20 West Virginia	32

1975 Top Performance Formula

1 Ohio State	1.7158
2 Oklahoma	1.6786
3 Alabama	1.6696
4 Arizona State	1.6620
5 Texas	1.5887
6 Arkansas	1.5515
7 Nebraska	1.5481
8 Penn State	1.4745
9 Arizona	1.4512
10 Texas A&M	1.4467
11 Michigan	1.4342
12 UCLA	1.4324
13 West Virginia	1.4234
14 Georgia	1.4042
15 Pittsburgh	1.4035
16 Florida	1.4033
17 Maryland	1.3936
18 Colorado	1.3774
19 California	1.3725
20 Oklahoma State	1.3352

1975 Top Opponent Records

1	Missouri	.6509
2	Washington	.6435
3	Miami	.6311
4	Penn State	.6270
5	Oklahoma State	.6261
6	Mississippi	.6217
7t	Oklahoma	.61600
7t	Pittsburgh	.61600
9	Texas Christian	.6155
10	Kansas State	.6000
11	West Virginia	.5976
12	Kentucky	.5983
13	Texas	.5887
14	Auburn	.5877
15	Louisiana State	.5862
16	Michigan State	.5789
17	Ohio State	.5766
18	Syracuse	.5746
19	Georgia	.5726
20	Purdue	.5702

1975 Out-of-Conference Records

	W-L	Percentage	Bowl W-L
Big Eight	29-7	.8056	1-2
Southeastern	31-18-2	.6275	1-2
Southwest	17-19-2	.4737	2-1
Pacific-8	14-16-2	.4688	2-0
Big Ten	13-16	.4483	0-2
Western Athletic	15-20	.4286	1-0
Atlantic Coast	13-27-1	.3293	1-1

1975 Individual Statistical Leaders

RUSHING YARDS

	Attempts	Yards	Avg.
Ricky Bell, Southern California	357	1875	5.3
Herb Lusk, Long Beach State	310	1596	5.1
Tony Dorsett, Pittsburgh	228	1544	6.8
Chuck Muncie, California	228	1460	6.4
Louie Giammona, Utah State	303	1454	4.8
Archie Griffin, Ohio State	245	1357	5.5
Gordon Bell, Michigan	255	1335	5.2
Freddie Williams, Arizona State	248	1316	5.3
Jimmy DuBose, Florida	191	1307	6.8
Billy Marek, Wisconsin	272	1281	4.7

PASSING YARDS

	Completions	Attempts	Yards	Pct.
Craig Penrose, San Diego State	198	349	2660	56.7
Gene Swick, Toledo	190	308	2487	61.7
Steve Myer, New Mexico	190	353	2501	53.8
Joe Roth, California	126	226	1880	55.8
Steve Pisarkiewicz, Missouri	113	232	1792	48.7
Pat Degnan, Utah	140	289	1621	48.4
Clyde Walker, Florida State	117	203	1619	57.6
Scott Gardner, Virginia	133	272	1547	48.9
Tony Dungy, Minnesota	123	225	1515	54.7
Don Buckey, North Carolina State	113	201	1511	56.2

RECEIVING YARDS

	Catches	Yards
Preston Dennard, New Mexico	59	962
Dave Quehl, Holy Cross	63	959
Pat Tilley, Louisiana Tech	53	926
Tony Hill, Stanford	55	916
Duke Fergerson, San Diego State	57	886
Larry Seivers, Tennessee	41	840
Mike Renfro, Texas Christian	49	810
John Jefferson, Arizona State	44	808
Steve Rivera, California	57	790
Philip Logan, South Carolina	39	716

1975 Consensus All-America Team

Offense

End:	Steve Riviera, California
	Larry Seivers, Tennessee
Tackle:	Bob Simmons, Texas
	Dennis Lick, Wisconsin
Guard:	Randy Johnson, Georgia
	Ted Smith, Ohio State
Center:	Rik Bonness, Nebraska
Quarterback:	John Sciarra, UCLA
Running Back:	Archie Griffin, Ohio State
	Ricky Bell, Southern California
	Chuck Muncie, California

Defense

End:	LeRoy Cook, Alabama
	Jimbo Elrod, Oklahoma
Tackle:	Lee Roy Selmon, Oklahoma
	Steve Niehaus, Notre Dame
Middle Guard:	Dewey Selmon, Oklahoma
Linebacker:	Ed Simonini, Texas A&M
	Greg Buttle, Penn State
	Sammy Green, Florida
Back:	Chet Moeller, Navy
	Tim Fox, Ohio State
	Pat Thomas, Texas A&M

1975 Heisman Trophy Vote

Archie Griffin, senior tailback, Ohio State	1800
Chuck Muncie, senior tailback, California	730
Ricky Bell, junior tailback, Southern California	708
Tony Dorsett, junior tailback, Pittsburgh	616
Joe Washington, senior halfback, Oklahoma	250

Other Major Award Winners

Maxwell (Player)	Archie Griffin, senior tailback, Ohio State
Walter Camp (Player)	Chuck Muncie, senior tailback, California
Outland (Lineman)	Lee Roy Selmon, senior defensive tackle, Oklahoma
Lombardi (Lineman)	Lee Roy Selmon, senior defensive tackle, Oklahoma
AFCA Coach of the Year	Frank Kush, Arizona State

1976

The Year of the Panthers' American Success Story, Coaching Greats into the Sunset, and Cougar SWC Debut

As America celebrated its bicentennial year, the University of Pittsburgh celebrated an American success story. How far had the Pittsburgh (12-0) football program fallen before the arrival of coach Johnny Majors and tailback Tony Dorsett for the 1973 season? From 1964 through 1972, the Panthers compiled a 22-68-2 record, had as many winning seasons as they had All Americans (none), labored through four one-win seasons, and beaten rival Penn State only once—and that was back in 1965. Hiring Majors, who had rebuilt Iowa State, was coup number one. Recruitment of Dorsett—and a raft of stars including Randy Holloway, Matt Cavanaugh, Gordon Jones, Tom Brzoza, and Bob Jury—was coup number two. In 1973, the Panthers won six games and qualified for their first bowl game since 1956. In 1974, Pitt won seven, which was improved to eight the following year including a Sun Bowl victory. With Majors' four full recruiting classes on board, Pitt was primed for 1976. The championship year began ominously as Notre Dame (9-3) drove to a touchdown on its opening series of the first game, but Dorsett soon raced 61 yards to jumpstart a 31-10 road romp. Eleven more teams fell—all but rival West Virginia (5-6) by double figures—with SEC champion Georgia (10-2) becoming the victim in the Sugar Bowl for the national title.

The national title going to Pittsburgh was a thorn in the sides of the major conferences that had become accustomed to championships being their birthright. Since 1950, Syracuse in 1959 and Notre Dame in 1966 were the only independents to snatch a national title before Pitt's triumph. As proof that 1976 would be a different year was made clear by the results of the opening week when no. 6 Alabama (9-3), no. 7 Texas (5-5), no. 8 Southern California (11-1) and no. 11 Notre Dame (9-3) all lost, while no. 1 Nebraska (9-3-1) suffered a tie. Those schools had won 12 of the previous 15 Associated Press national championships.

Pitt spent most of the season ranked behind Michigan (10-2), but Purdue (5-6) sprung an upset in early November. Still, a lot of people felt the Panthers were paper tigers with a weak Eastern schedule. Despite an opening loss to Missouri (7-4), third-ranked Southern California felt as Rose Bowl winner over second-ranked Michigan it was more deserving of the title than Pittsburgh. Not many people bought that argument, however.

Coaching changes were brewing in some large programs. The Southwest Conference was stunned by announcements from Arkansas coach Frank Broyles and Texas coach Darrell Royal that they each would retire after Texas' 29-12 win in the rivals' annual clash on December 4. Royal, who won 14 of 19 battles with Broyles, left with 167 wins and 11 conference championships, while Broyles won 144 games with seven SWC crowns. The loss of these two legends added to a growing trend as within five years Duffy Daugherty of Michigan State, Bob Devaney of Nebraska, Ben Schwartzwalder of Syracuse, Ara Parseghian of Notre Dame, Shug Jordan of Auburn, John McKay of Southern California, Broyles and Royal, all of whom coached teams to national titles, moved on.

Plenty of good coaches remained, including Vince Dooley of Georgia who won the SEC title behind a tremendous defense known as the "Junkyard Dawgs" and the heady play of quarterback Ray Goff, the SEC Player of the Year. Inspired by the death of lineman Hugh Hendrix in the off-season, the Bulldogs motivated themselves by shaving their heads. With one member of his coaching staff shaving after each win, Dooley promised to do the same if his team won the SEC. He whipped off a wig at the celebration dinner in December to show off his clean dome.

Other big winners in 1976 were Maryland (11-1), undefeated in the regular season en route to a third straight ACC title, and Houston (10-2), which debuted in the SWC by sharing the conference title with Texas Tech (10-2). Leading the charge for coach Bill Yeoman's Cougars was a defense led by Lombardi winner Wilson Whitley at tackle and the nation's top interceptor in Anthony Francis in the secondary and an electric offense built around quarterback Danny Davis, runner Alois Blackwell, and receivers Don Bass and Eddie Foster. The Cougars' 10 wins was a stark improvement over the 2-8 mark of 1975. At that time in football history, a mere two teams had shown better turnarounds: Stanford in 1940 and Purdue in 1943. The Cougars' 7-1 conference record was the best to that date in history for any new member entering an established league. Maryland and Houston met in the Cotton Bowl with the Cougars prevailing 30-21 after jumping to a 21-0 lead in the first quarter.

Another on the verge of a brilliant future was Florida State (5-6), which welcomed Bobby Bowden, who was beginning a remarkable record.

There was change afoot with another pride of Cougars as Brigham Young (9-3) coach LaVell Edwards hired former San Francisco 49er coach Doug Scovil, the quarterback coach at Navy when quarterback Roger Staubach won the Heisman Trophy, as offensive coordinator. Scovil pumped up BYU's pass-happy attack that made the university the breeding ground of record-breaking quarterbacks and pushed the Cougars into the nation's rankings by 1977. In each of his four seasons at the helm of the offense, Scovil's Cougars lead the NCAA in passing.

Woody Hayes of Ohio State (9-2-1) had an up-and-down year, worst of all, losing to Michigan for the Rose Bowl bid. Woody was all smiles, however, on January 1 after his Buckeyes visited a 27-10 Orange Bowl defeat upon Colorado (8-4), one of three teams to tie for the Big Eight title.

Missouri (7-4) had an odd season, beating USC, Ohio State, and Nebraska on the road but losing to Illinois (5-6) and Kansas (6-5) at home.

In September, a federal district court judge in Washington D.C., William Bryant, declared the pro football player draft illegal for violating antitrust laws and restricting the ability of players to bargain. Bryant was hearing the case of former Oregon defensive back Jim "Yazoo" Smith, who won his suit against the Washington Redskins and the NFL. The league eventually won a higher court battle, and the draft stayed in place.

Ticket scalping became the infraction of the year when the *Oklahoma Journal* printed a story about the selling or trading of complimentary football tickets that players received for each game. Former college greats like Michigan State's George Webster and Oklahoma's Joe Washington detailed the scalping practices. Eventually the NCAA changed the rule regarding complimentary tickets so that players no longer received paper tickets, but had to submit a list of family and friends to the stadium will-call window for each game.

Milestones

■ New rule aimed at favoring passing game allowed blockers to extend their arms in pass protection.

■ Independence Bowl in Shreveport, La., debuted with McNeese State defeating Tulsa.

■ Michigan Stadium (103,159 capacity) became first on-campus facility to top 100,000 seats.

■ Paul Robeson, All-America Rutgers halfback before embarking on controversial career as actor, singer and activist, died at age 77 on January 23 after suffering stroke. Famous his for portrayal of Othello, Robeson's acting career was overshadowed by his support of Soviet Union. Ernie Nevers, 73, legendary Stanford fullback died of kidney disease on May 3. Two-time All-America in 1924-25, Nevers led Stanford to 1925 Rose Bowl versus Notre Dame and then became pro star with barnstorming teams and NFL. He set NFL record for points in single game with 40 with 1929 Cardinals. Bill Swiacki, All-America end at Columbia, best known for his miraculous receptions in 1947, died at home aged 53 on July 7. Swiacki's diving end zone catch helped spark 21-20 upset of Army that stopped 32-game win streak. Georgia junior guard Hugh Hendrix died of rare blood infection during summer.

■ Longest winning streaks entering season:

Arizona State 13	Alabama 11	Miami (Ohio) 10

■ Coaching Changes:

	Incoming	Outgoing
Auburn	Doug Barfield	Ralph Jordan
Florida State	Bobby Bowden	Darrell Mudra
Michigan State	Darryl Rogers	Dennis Stolz
North Carolina State	Bo Rein	Lou Holtz
Oregon State	Craig Fertig	Dee Andros
Rice	Homer Rice	Al Conover
Southern California	John Robinson	John McKay
Southern Methodist	Ron Meyer	Dave Smith
Tulane	Larry Smith	Bennie Ellender
UCLA	Terry Donahue	Dick Vermeil
Virginia	Dick Bestwick	Sonny Randle
Washington State	Jackie Sherrill	Jim Sweeney
West Virginia	Frank Cignetti	Bobby Bowden

AP Preseason Poll

1 Nebraska (25)	961	11 Notre Dame	319
2 Michigan (10)	918	12 Maryland	211
3 Arizona State (7)	780	13 Arkansas	193
4 Ohio State (3)	749	14 Texas A&M	136
5 Oklahoma (6)	683	15 California	121
6 Alabama (3)	624	16 Georgia	108
7 Texas (3)	610	17 UCLA	102
8 Southern California (2)	517	18 Florida	101
9 Pittsburgh (1)	416	19 Kansas	37
10 Penn State	348	20 Miami (Ohio)	32

September 4, 1976

Furman 17 NORTH CAROLINA STATE 12: Wolfpack (0-1) rallied from early 10-0 deficit, but then could not stop Furman TB Harry King when it counted. After K Jay Sherrill kicked 2nd FG, from 26y out, to give NC State 12-10 lead, Paladins (1-0) marched 80y to King's winning 6y TD run. King rushed 4/36y on winning drive. Furman enjoyed 387y to 305y advantage, but almost lost its chance for upset by committing 5 TOs. Paladins QB David Whitehurst opened scoring with 25y TD pass to WR Angus Poole, while Wolfpack TD came on 1y run by TB Ted Brown.

Kansas 28 OREGON STATE 16: Coach Craig Fertig's debut at helm of Oregon State (0-1) started well. Thanks to 2 Kansas FUMs, Beavers grabbed 10-0 lead on 2y TD run by TB James Fields and 22y FG by K Kieron Walford. Jayhawks (1-0) then reeled off 28 pts as ground game exploded for 321y rushing. Kansas did not take lead for good until HB Laverne Smith's 1y scoring run in 3rd Q for 14-10 advantage. Kansas DT Franklin King set up winning TD—22y run by HB Billy Campfield—with 38y INT RET in 4th Q. Sub QB Kyle Grossart then pulled OSU to 21-16 with 9y TD pass to WR Lee Overton, before Kansas QB Nolan Cromwell added clinching TD.

September 11, 1976

(Th) Ucla 28 ARIZONA STATE 10: Returning 15 starters from 12-0 club, no. 3 Sun Devils (0-1) looked to compete for national crown. Opening with UCLA (1-0) on national TV proved disastrous, however, as Bruins, insulted as 1-TD underdogs, ran up 509y total O in coach Terry Donahue's debut. FB Theotis Brown (22/127y) and QB Jeff Dankworth (19/155y rushing) looked sharp behind sr-laden O-line, while speedy UCLA D dominated after Arizona State opened with 3-0 lead. Devils were held to 45y rushing in 1st H and did not cross GL until 4th Q on 15y catch by WR John Jefferson. Bright spot for ASU was emergence of HB Arthur Lane (11/74y).

BOSTON COLLEGE 14 Texas 13: Longhorns (0-1) had two late scoring chances to avert upset, but BC LB Gene Brown tackled HB Johnny Jones on 2-pt conv run short of EZ after final TD, and Texas K Russell Erxleben narrowly missed 53y FG attempt as game ended. Eagles (1-0) came out flying as TB Neil Green ran for 74y TD on game's 2nd play. In 2nd Q, BC D forced FUM on its 4YL which O converted into 96y TD drive. Texas QB Mike Cordaro threw 35y TD pass to WR Alfred Jackson to halve lead before H and then Jones, fresh off gold medal in 400-meter relay at Montreal Olympics, pulled Texas to within 14-13 on 18y TD run in 4th Q. Boston College's win was trumpeted as program's greatest since 1941 Sugar Bowl victory over Tennessee.

PENN STATE 15 Stanford 12: Capitalizing on 3 Stanford TOs, Nittany Lions (1-0) opened up with 15 pts before hanging on for win. Cardinals (0-1) fumbled 2 KO RETs, 1st recovered by Lions LB Joe Lally on 34YL and other by LB Joe Diange on Stanford 19YL. Penn State converted those FUMs into 10 pts on 1y scoring run by TB Steve Geise and 33y FG by K Matt Bahr. FUM by QB Mike Cordova then set up 1st career TD run, from 6y out, for frosh FB Matt Suhey (23/119y), subbing for injured brother Larry. Cordova rallied Cards to 3 scores, trimming H mark to 15-12 on 2 FGs by K Mike Michel, and tossing 48y TD pass to WR Tony Hill. Closest Stanford got was Penn State 14YL before PEN and sack finished off drive.

North Carolina 24 FLORIDA 21 (Tampa): Relying on mistaken scoreboard posting, Florida (0-1) QB Jimmy Fisher (13-21/247y) lost track of downs in throwing ball away to stop clock on 4th down with Gators on UNC 3YL. Tar Heels (2-0) had just converted their own 4th down as frosh QB Bernie Menapace—playing because 5 other QBs were hurt—completed 10y pass to diving frosh FB Billy Johnson on 4th-and-6 from Florida 16YL. Two plays later TB Mike Voight (35/142y) scored on 3y run. Gators paid for sluggish start, as North Carolina built 10-0 2nd Q lead behind Voight, who reached rushing century mark by H, while Florida failed to earn 1st down until midway through 2nd Q. Superb Gators WR Wes Chandler caught 8/187y including 42y TD in 2nd Q.

MISSISSIPPI 10 Alabama 7 (Jackson): Although graduation had taken its toll on no. 6 Crimson Tide, loss to Rebels (1-1) still was shock. Frosh K Hoppy Langley booted 34y game-winning FG as Ole Miss handed Alabama (0-1) its 1st conf loss since 1972 after 20 straight wins. Alabama threw 3 INTs, 1 returned 24y for 7-0 Ole Miss lead by DE Gary Turner after deflection by LB George Stuart in 1st Q. Score remained 7-0 until 3rd Q, when Tide HB Calvin Culliver (16/55y) capped 55y drive with 3y TD run. That was it for Bama O that never got untracked, rushing only 49/145y with 2 FUMs marring its efforts. TB Michael Sweet (13/65y) led ground game for Ole Miss that struggled as well (46/110y), but was able to move into position for Langley's heroics.

LOUISIANA STATE 6 Nebraska 6: Botched x-pt following TD on no. 1 Nebraska's opening drive was not considered too serious, at least until LSU DT A.J. Duhe and D mates shut out explosive Huskers (0-0-1) rest of way. Nebraska TD came on 3y pass from QB Vince Ferragamo (13-25/125y, INT) to TE Ken Spaeth that capped 65y drive, aided by 39y interference PEN. Huskers finished with 265y total for game, with mere 80y in final 2 Qs. Tigers (0-0-1) moved ball throughout 2nd H but were held to 2 FGs by K Mike Conway; his near miss from 44y out with 34 seconds left was LSU's final stab at victory. TB Terry Robiskie rushed for 75y to lead Tigers.

GEORGIA 36 California 24: Bulldogs (1-0) limited explosive Cal passing attack in 2nd H, to allow their O to rally from 21-12 H deficit. It helped that Georgia passed better than Bears (0-1) were capable of running ball, while Bulldogs D picked off 3 passes by QB Joe Roth (21-36/379y, 2 TDs) to turn tide. Roth was unstoppable in 1st H, especially when connecting with WR Wesley Walker on TD passes of 69y and 88y. Georgia then used better balance to score 2 TDs in 3rd Q for 27-24 lead as HB Kevin McLee capped 1st drive with 1y scoring run before QB Matt Robinson tossed 33y TD to WR Gene Washington to end 2nd, set up by INT.

Pittsburgh 31 NOTRE DAME 10: Opening-game win in South Bend by 3-TD margin gave Pitt's national title hopes boost, while 181y rushing by TB Tony Dorsett kept Heisman in focus. Dorsett upped 4-year rushing total against Notre Dame (0-1) to incredible 754y as Panthers handed Irish 1st loss of opener since 1963. He answered Notre Dame's opening drive for TD with 61y romp with 1st carry that propelled O to tie game. Pitt D set up go-ahead TD as pressure by DT Don Parrish forced Irish QB Rick Slager into INT that CB LeRoy Felder took 28y to ND 2YL. Pitt (1-0) scored TD soon after to take lead for good. Slager was 3-3/52y on opening drive, 3-19 afterwards for 33y. Irish did gain 290y, with FB Jerome Heavens rushing for 93y.

Houston 23 BAYLOR 5: After spotting Baylor Bears (0-1) 5 pts in 1st Q, Houston celebrated its SWC debut with 23 2nd H pts. Cougars (1-0) FB Dyral Thomas tallied on 2 TD runs, QB Danny Davis kept for 7y scoring run, and K Lennard Coplin booted 22y FG. Bears had 4 TOs and each was costly: FUM by QB Mark Jackson ended 2nd Q drive at Houston 14YL, FUM on bad pitchout was converted into 55y Houston TD, INT by CB Anthony Francis stopped Baylor drive on Houston 13YL and jumpstarted 87y march to TD, and finally INT by LB David Hodge set up Cougars FG. Bad punt snap had led to Baylor safety, and Bears went 45y with ensuing possession to 36y FG by K Lester Belrose. FB John Housman rushed for 85y to pace Cougars, while HB Gary Blair ran for 68y to top Bears.

Missouri 46 SOUTHERN CALIFORNIA 25: Blaming team's lack of desire on stellar previews, Trojans (0-1) looked pathetic in coach John Robinson's debut. Tigers QB Steve Pisarkiewicz (9-16/171y) read no clippings, tossing 3 TDs against D crammed with NFL prospects. Missouri (1-0) also featured TB Curtis Brown, who rushed for 101y and 5y TD, caught 49y TD reception, and scored on 95y KO RET that gave Tigers lead for good at 13-7 in 1st Q. All 3 of Brown's TDs were in 1st H as Mizzou scored stunning 30 pts in opening 30 mins. Southern California TB Ricky Bell rushed 29/172y, while his backup, frosh TB Charles White, closed scoring with 79y TD run in 4th Q.

AP Poll September 13

1 Michigan (28)	1077	11 Texas A&M	281
2 Ohio State (18)	1076	12 Arkansas	268
3 Pittsburgh (9)	892	13 Kansas	153
4 Oklahoma (4)	865	14 Alabama	108
5 UCLA (2)	731	15 Boston College	101
6 Missouri	480	16 Louisiana State	84
7 Penn State	464	17 North Carolina	72
8 Nebraska	446.5	18 Arizona State	66
9 Georgia	376	19 Texas	57
10 Maryland	370	20 Mississippi	54

September 18, 1976

BROWN 14 Yale 6: Bruins (1-0) held on for victory behind bend-but-don't-break D. Yale (0-1) made no 2nd H scoring despite marching into Brown territory 5 times, past Brown 30YL 4 times. Bruins converted 1 of 4 Eli FUMs into 15y drive to 11y TD pass by QB Paul Machalko to HB Bill Hill and then marched 74y to 33y scoring run by WR Charlie Watkins in 3rd Q. Sole Yale TD, 3y keeper by QB Stone Phillips, was set up by blown Bruin punt as snap was sent wrongly to TE Fred Polacek, who fell on it on own 15YL. Yale TB John Pagliaro rushed for 114y as O gained 320y.

Maryland 24 WEST VIRGINIA 3: QB Mark Manges led Maryland (2-0) to easy win, throwing 31y scoring pass to WB Chuck White and rushing for 2y TD. Terps totaled 422y, with 133y rushing by TB Steve Atkins who scored team's 2nd TD on 15y run. Mountaineers (1-1) were stumped by Maryland D, rushing for 25y and scoring only on 29y FG by K Bill McKenzie. QB Dan Kendra completed 12-19/132y, but was picked off twice and lost FUM on Terps 27YL when hammered by Maryland DE Chip Garber.

SOUTH CAROLINA 24 Duke 6: Frosh QB Steve Swinehart came off Gamecocks (3-0) bench to spur victory, throwing 36y scoring pass to WR Phil Logan and racing 57y to set up own 1y TD keeper. South Carolina QB Ron Bass had led team to 10 1st Q pts before succumbing to knee injury. Blue Devils (1-1) TB Art Gore scored 10y TD run to pull within 10-6 before Swinehart took over. Gore rushed for 105y for Duke O that finished with 182y total. USC TB Clarence Williams added 91y rushing.

Ohio State 12 PENN STATE 7: Ohio State (2-0) made smooth transition from 4 years of Archie Griffin to new TB Jeff Logan, who rushed for 160y behind big boys up front. Logan logged 48y run to set up 1st Buckeyes TD, 8y run by QB Rod Gerald. Ohio State had only 35y to travel for its winning score after Penn State DB Neil Hutton foolishly returned short FG try from his EZ to 3YL, spot from which Lions punted 4 downs later. Bucks sub WB Bob Hyatt scored on 8y run with pitchout for 12-0 lead in 4th Q. Nittany Lions (1-1) marched 87y to FB Matt Suhey's 1y dive, but could not overcome vital blown chances: lost FUM and EZ pick by S Ray Griffin to kill 2 drives that reached Ohio 5YL. Penn State offset 280y rushing by Buckeyes by having QB John Andress (16-29/178y) pass more than normal.

MICHIGAN 51 Stanford 0: Can Wolverines (2-0) play any better? They had 2 TOs, but considering how often they pitched ball, that was to be expected. HB Harlan Huckleby (16/157y, TD) led rushing attack that gained 531y with 5 different players topping 70y. FB Russell Davis (7/116y, 2 TDs) and HB Rob Lytle (19/101y, 2 TDs) also topped 100y mark. Michigan D posted shutout, although it allowed 314y with Stanford (0-2) QB Guy Benjamin returning from injury to throw for 236y. Michigan S Dwight Hicks was Benjamin's chief nemesis, with INT, deflection that prompted another INT, 3 pass break-ups, forced FUM, and 5 tackles. Although Benjamin drove Cardinals into Michigan red zone 3 times, he could not prevent school's 1st shutout since 1967.

NOTRE DAME 23 Purdue 0: Fighting Irish (1-1) bounced back from opening loss with rout of in-state rivals. Notre Dame HB Al Hunter rushed for 96y and threw 33y TD pass to HB Mark McLane. TD followed failed fake punt by Boilermakers (1-1) that ended on tackle by CB Luther Bradley of P Dave Eagin for 12y loss at Purdue 38YL. Purdue's best chance to score came at end of 1st H when time expired with WR Reggie Arnold falling after 30y catch. ND pulled away with 2 TDs in 2nd H, including 2y scoring run by Hunter. Boilermakers TB Scott Dierking rushed for 93y.

Illinois 31 MISSOURI 6: Missouri Tigers (1-1) unaccountably followed up their upset of USC with flat performance at home. Illini (2-0) TB James Coleman rushed for 152y, 2 TDs, and QB Kurt Steger (10-18/160y) twice threw scoring passes to WR Eric Rouse. Rouse supplied exclamation point when he caught ball at Illinois 45y and raced to EZ for 74y scoring play that gave Illinois 24-6 lead in 3rd Q. Missouri was outgained 418y to 257y as QB Steve Pisarkiewicz (7-18/64y) was hampered by injured shoulder. FB Packy Watson led Tigers with 10/67y.

ARKANSAS 16 Oklahoma State 10: It's not often kickers dominate games, but Arkansas P-K Steve Little was no run-of-mill kicker. Little beat Cowboys (1-1) with FGs of 57y, 53y, and 20y. He punted for 46y avg and hit 5 unreturnable KOs. Little sandwiched his 2 longest-to-date FGs around 16y TD run by RB Jerry Eckwood for 13-3 3rd Q lead. RB Ben Cowins led Razorbacks (2-0) ground game with 17/163y. Hogs D, led by 17 tackles from LB Curtis Townsend, held OSU HB Terry Miller to 47y rushing and allowed its only TD with only secs left in game on 7y run by FB Skip Taylor. Cowboys' 5 TOs contributed to failure to extend 3-game series win streak.

Colorado 21 WASHINGTON 7: It was downhill from opening KO for Huskies (1-1), which, as it turned out, they fumbled. Colorado S Chuck McCarter recovered FUM by Washington TB Stan Wilson on 17YL to set up opening 1y TD run by FB Jim Kelleher. Buffs (1-1) doubled their scoring total on QB Jeff Austin's 1y run and behind rush attack that churned up 256y. Huskies made short trip (34y) to FB Robin Earl's 1y TD dive in 2nd Q. Huskies needed possession to rally, but Colorado held it for most of 2nd H as Buffs had no TOs. Colorado WB Emery Moorehead scored clinching TD on pitchout he took to EZ from 12YL.

AP Poll September 20

1 Michigan (47)	1156	11 Penn State	285
2 Ohio State (3)	998	12 Arkansas	262
3 Pittsburgh (7)	947	13 Alabama	186
4 Oklahoma (3)	820	14 Illinois	122
5 UCLA	761	15 Louisiana State	94
6 Nebraska	511	16 North Carolina	85
7 Georgia	510	17 Mississippi	61
8 Maryland	412	18 Boston College	60
9 Texas A&M	373	19 Southern California	49
10 Kansas	288	20 Texas Tech	32

September 25, 1976

Iowa 7 PENN STATE 6: Home-standing Nittany Lions (1-2) could not muster sufficient pts against Big 10 opponent for 2nd straight week as Iowa frosh TB Tom Renn's 2y TD run in 1st Q stood up. Penn State pulled within 7-6 in 4th Q on 1y TD dive by FB Matt Suhey (19/74y), but could not complete 2-pt conv pass to WR Jimmy Cefalo. Lions had final chance with FUM REC with 2:09 remaining and ensuing march to Iowa 8YL before frosh K Herb Menhardt—with K Matt Bahr on bench—missed 25y FG. QB Butch Caldwell led meager Hawkeyes (2-1) O, rushing for 57y and passing for another 52y. Said losing coach Joe Paterno after game, "We were not ready mentally or tactically. Iowa outplayed us and outcoached us."

Clemson 24 GEORGIA TECH 24: Clemson (1-1-1) grabbed 24-13 lead as QB Steve Fuller, who threw for 164y and rushed for 111y more, looked like South's next great QB. Georgia Tech (0-2-1) made small progress toward righting its ship by rallying behind new starting QB Mike Jolly (11-18/177y). It looked as if Fuller would have last laugh in battle, marching Tigers to Tech 6YL once game was tied. LB Lucious Sanford made game-saving play for Yellow Jackets, nailing Fuller on 1st down to force FUM recovered by LB Mackel Harris. Both QBs passed and ran in TDs, with Fuller supplying game's most spectacular play: 59y scoring bomb to WR Jerry Butler.

AUBURN 38 Tennessee 28 (Birmingham): Tigers (1-2) QB Phil Gargis was on fire, completing 10-13/224y. Go-ahead TD came on Gargis' 33y pass to WR Chris Vacarella (4/141y), who had competed as Gargis for QB job but now made circus catches. Auburn rush game added 250y as Gargis ran for team-high 73y and FB Williams Andrews opened scoring with 7y run. Vols (1-2) had taken 21-17 lead at H, with dazzler coming on 73y scoring pass play from QB Randy Wallace to WR Stanley Morgan. RB Kelsey Finch rushed for 124y to lead Tennessee rush attack.

Missouri 22 OHIO STATE 21: Unpredictable Tigers (2-1) did it again, snapping Ohio's 25-game home win steak. QB Pete Woods led rally, culminating in 2y TD pass to WR Leo Lewis with 12 secs left to pull Tigers to 21-20. Going for 2 pts, Missouri failed on 1st conv attempt on overthrow, but Buckeyes (2-1) were called for holding. With reprieve, Woods fought his way into EZ for winning 2-pt run. In 1st H, FB Pete Johnson (23/119y) rushed for 103y, thrice scoring on 2y runs as Ohio State built 21-7 H lead.

HOUSTON 21 Texas A&M 10: Cougars (2-1) turned to air to top big Aggies D, as QB Donnie Davis (11-19/173y, INT) tossed 1st H TD passes: 2 to TE Eddie Foster and 50y effort to WR Robert Lavergne. Houston D, that had been sliced up by Florida's Wishbone attack in prior week, swarmed Texas A&M (2-1), allowing 115y rushing and forcing 4 TOs. Cougars DT Wilson Whitley was magnificent in stopping FB George Woodard (9/15y, TD), Aggies leading rusher, on big FB's runs up middle. HB Curtis Dickey managed 54y rushing to lead A&M. Cougars, 2-8 in 1975, surprisingly jumped to 2-0 in conf play in their 1st stab at SWC.

Tulsa 9 ARKANSAS 3: Tough scheduling made Razorbacks (2-1) suffer: Tulsa (3-1) arrived as fired-up rival on heels of Hogs' emotional game with Oklahoma State. K Steve Cox booted 3 FGs (39y, 28y, 40y) to account for all scoring by Golden Hurricane. Porkers' highlight came on 61y FG by K Steve Little for SWC record, although Little wouldn't keep record for long. Hogs made 306y on O, but QB Ron Calcagni, who rushed for team-high 81y, hit only 4-23/98y, INT passing. Although poor punt and INT set up 2 of Cox's FGs, game-winner followed impressive 91y drive with opening possession of 2nd H.

Brigham Young 23 ARIZONA 16: Wildcats played good, tough football until game's final 23 secs when 2 crucial mistakes allowed Cougars (2-1) chance to steal late victory. Unable to get 1st down late in game, deep in its territory, Arizona sent in P Wid Knight, who shanked 18y punt only to Arizona 43YL. Then Wildcats (1-2) dropped 8 men into coverage and put pressure on BYU QB Gifford Nielsen, who was able to scramble to find WR George Harris open behind CB Van Cooper. Nielsen (18-28/200y, 2 TDs, INT) hit Harris with 43y TD pass. Arizona had battled back on strength of 2 FGs by K Lee Pistor to tie it from 16-10 H deficit.

California 31 ARIZONA STATE 22: Sun Devils (0-2) dropped 2nd game to Pac-8 foe, despite handling Golden Bears QB Joe Roth (10-27/104y, 2 INTs). While ASU was focused on Roth, California (1-2) turned to its run game to produce 276y, led by TB Markey Crane's 102y. Sun Devils grabbed 6-0 lead on 47y INT RET by S Johnnie Harris, his 1st of 2 pick-offs. Cal dominated rest of 1st H with 3 TDs, including score set up by LB James Reed INT. Arizona State rallied to pull within 24-22, scoring its final TD on 93y pass from QB Dennis Sproul (12-23/232y, 2 TDs, 2 INTs) to WB Larry Mucker (6/178y). Sproul then overthrew 2-pt conv pass, and Bears moved to clinching 11y TD run by FB Tom Newton (15/97y) late in 4th Q. Arizona State TB Freddie Williams rushed for 123y.

AP Poll September 27

1 Michigan (56)	1208	11 Louisiana State	264
2 Pittsburgh (2)	972	12 Missouri	222
3 Oklahoma (2)	912	13 Southern California	156
4 UCLA	888	14 North Carolina	133
5 Nebraska	690	15 Boston College	114
6 Georgia	597	16 Mississippi	84
7 Maryland	491	17 Texas Tech	59
8 Ohio State	426	18 Notre Dame	32
9 Kansas	385	19 Florida	29
10 Alabama	325	20 Penn State	28

October 2, 1976

ARMY 21 Stanford 20: Rallying from 20-pt deficit, Cadets (3-1) stunned visiting Stanford with 3 2nd H TD drives of 80y or longer. Army QB Leamon Hall (14-36/214y) threw and ran for TDs, and then whipped winning 2-pt conv pass to TE Clennie Brundidge with 1:18 remaining. Army had given itself some anxious moments after missing x-pt after its 2nd TD, Hall's 11y scoring pass to HB Tom Kuchar. Hall started poorly, missing 15 straight attempts and throwing 3 INTs as Cardinals (1-3) built their big lead on strength of Cards QB Mike Cordova (15-33/212y, 2 TDs). Suddenly, Hall became as hot as he had been cold, hitting 11 of his final 17 passes with 52y bomb to WR George Dunaway to set up Army's 2nd TD. Stanford K Mike Michel (52y FG in 3rd Q) missed 4-6 FG attempts, including 42y try into wind at game's end.

GEORGIA 21 Alabama 0: Dedicating its effort to G Hugh Hendrix, who had died from rare blood infection in summer, Georgia (4-0) beat Alabama in front of raucous "Hedges" crowd. Current edition of Junkyard Dogs D was nicknamed "The Runts" for their slight builds—only 1 player topped 210lbs—and their hard-nosed style of play. Ask Tide (2-2) QB Jeff Rutledge, who was sacked 6 times in 4th Q as he attempted to prevent his team's 1st shutout loss since 1970. Slow-footed QB Matt Robinson led Bulldogs O, scoring on 3y keeper—to surprise of Crimson Tide and Georgia coaching staff—right before H and throwing 6y TD pass to TE Ulysses Norris in 4th Q to seal matters. Rutledge threw for 141y in defeat. Crimson Tide's record string of 5 straight SEC championships appeared to be all but over.

FLORIDA 28 Louisiana State 23: Last chance for LSU (2-1-1) ended on Gators 5YL, as Tigers were victimized by saving GLS by Florida D. Bengals had driven to Florida 9YL, where they had 1st-and-goal with time elapsing. Three rushes netted 4y and then QB Pat Lyons (9-20/125y) missed WR Bruce Hemphill in EZ. Reserve QB Bill Kynes (5-6/50y) had led Gators (3-1) on 2 scoring drives in relief of injured QB Jimmy Fisher, who earlier tossed 16y TD pass to WR Wes Chandler. Florida enjoyed 28-14 lead in 3rd Q on 2y TD run by HB Willie Wilder. LSU answered with 40y FG by K Mike Conway and 5y TD run by TB Terry Robiskie (22/64y), his 3rd of game.

OHIO STATE 10 Ucla 10: Conservative play was theme as these foes battled for 3rd time in 365 days. Buckeyes (2-1-1) managed 0y in 1st Q, but Bruins could not take advantage. OSU scored 1st on 4y run by FB Pete Johnson for 2nd Q lead that held up until 2nd H. Bruins (3-0-1) drove twice for 10-7 lead, 65y to 47y FG by K Frank Corral and 83y to 1y keeper by QB Jeff Dankworth. Highlight of UCLA's TD drive was fake punt on 4th-and-1—game's only bit of imagination—in which ball was snapped to FB Theotis Brown (20/102y), who rambled 25y. K Tom Skladany booted 25y FG to tie game in 4th Q before each team played not to lose. When faced with 4th-and-inches at Buckeye 43YL with less than 4 mins left, UCLA coach Terry Donahue punted. Ohio then marched to Bruins 47YL, where coach Woody Hayes also opted for punt on 4th-and-4, much to displeasure of home crowd. LB Jerry Robinson had 21 tackles for UCLA, but he could not get another against much bigger Johnson on 2nd Q TD run.

KANSAS 34 Wisconsin 24: Numbers 1-2-3 were lucky for Kansas (4-0) QB Nolan Cromwell, who rushed for 123y and threw for 123y in subduing Badgers. Cromwell completed only 3-15, but each success was big gainer to WR Waddell Smith, while fleet Cromwell also ran for 3 TDs including 64y dash in 2nd Q for 21-7 Kansas lead. Jayhawks HB Laverne Smith added 115y rushing, with 79y coming on nifty 3rd Q scoring run. QB Mike Carroll led balanced Wisconsin (2-2) attack that rushed for 246y and passed for 231y, but his 2 TD tosses couldn't overcome his 4 INTs.

NEBRASKA 17 Miami 9: Huskers (3-0-1) crushed Miami statistically, but needed late 10-pt surge to defeat Hurricanes. Roughing P PEN against Miami allowed Nebraska to keep ball on winning FG drive in 4th Q that ended on 32y boot by K Al Eveland for 10-9 lead with 6:30 left. QB Vince Ferragamo (17-22/264y, 2 TDs, INT) added 23y TD pass

to WB Dave Shamblin to seal it. Nebraska finished with 471y to 168y for Miami as IB Monte Anthony rushed for 109y and caught 5/60y. FB O.J. Anderson rushed for 58y for Hurricanes (1-2), with 5y on TD run for 6-0 1st Q lead.

Oklahoma 24 IOWA STATE 10: Sooners (4-0) broke open 10-10 game with 62y TD run to daylight by HB Horace Ivory on draw play with 4:08 left. CB Jerry Anderson then iced win with 58y INT TD RET. TB Dexter Green led Cyclones (3-1) with 101y rushing and short TD run in 3rd Q that ended 80y drive for 10-10 tie. ISU had 1st crack at breaking tie, but short drive set up by FUM REC by LB Tom Boskey near midfield ended with missed 34y FG. Iowa State outgained Sooners 315y to 215y and held vaunted OU rushing attack to 194y, well below its 321y avg for season.

SOUTHERN CALIFORNIA 55 Iowa 0: Hawkeyes (2-2) entered game with D ranked 1st in Big 10, but left with tails between their legs. With Iowa keying on TB Ricky Bell (28/119y), Trojans (3-1) took to air for 5 TDs, 4 by backup QB Rob Hertel (10-13/167y, INT). WRs Shelton Diggs (6/106y) and Randy Simmrin (4/71y) each caught 2 TD passes. Win was so complete that final y differential was astounding 512y to 77y. Leading gainer for Hawkeyes was TB Ernie Sheeler with 41y rushing. Trojans backup TB Charles White (15/120y) topped that on his 60y scoring romp. Southern California spotted Iowa 169y in PENs, but still enjoyed largest margin of victory since 1931.

AP Poll October 4

1 Michigan (52)	1182	11 Southern California	314	
2 Pittsburgh (3)	992	12 Florida	207	
3 Oklahoma (3)	914	13 Boston College	165	
4 Georgia (2)	870	14 Notre Dame	142	
5 UCLA	658	15 Texas Tech	106	
6 Nebraska	648	16 Texas	43	
7 Maryland	515	17 Texas A&M	27	
8 Kansas	500	18 Arkansas	22	
9 Missouri	389	19 North Carolina	20	
10 Ohio State	324	20 Louisiana State	17	

October 9, 1976

Florida State 28 BOSTON COLLEGE 9: Bobby Bowden's 1st upset as Florida State (2-3) coach occurred at expense of Eagles, team he was familiar with from his days at West Virginia. QB Jimmy Black took advantage of 2 BC PENs and his scrambling ability to move FSU to 1st TD on 12y run by TB Rudy Allen. Lead was expanded thanks to Boston College FUMs: REC at BC 15YL set up Black's 10y scoring run, another on 13YL was converted into 1y TD run by FB Mark Lyles. Seminoles DE Rudy Maloy contributed finishing touch by returning bobble by Eagles QB Ken Smith 65y for final TD. BC (3-1) had taken 6-0 lead on 1st pair of 3 FGs by K Tim Moorman.

MISSISSIPPI 21 Georgia 17: QB Tim Ellis rallied Rebels (4-2), running and passing for TDs within 6-min span of 2nd Q. Earlier, Georgia (4-1) had grabbed 14-3 lead on strength of 2 huge plays by QB Ray Goff, who broke free for 70y scoring run and tossed 75y bomb to WR Gene Washington. DT James Pittman turned game in Rebels favor with FUM-producing hit on HB Rayfield Williams that gave Ole Miss ball on Bulldogs 25YL. Soon after, Ellis (6-10/114y) kept for 5y TD and threw 2-pt conv pass to TB Michael Sweet (24/117y) to cut deficit to 14-11. Georgia then botched punt just before Ellis' 36y TD strike to TB Reg Woullard for 18-14 lead. Teams traded FGs in D-dominated 2nd H as Rebs earned 2nd straight series upset.

MISSISSIPPI STATE 14 Kentucky 7: Fresh off upset of Penn State, Wildcats (3-2) wanted to make waves in SEC. Bulldogs (4-1) burst their bubble as D surrendered paltry 222y, while State O scored 2 1st H TDs and committed no TOs. Nonetheless, game was not secured until late when LB Jim Kovach blocked punt to give Kentucky ball on MSU 27YL with time expiring. Bulldogs PEN then moved ball to 13YL with 41 secs left. Loss of 5y on scramble, PEN, incomplete pass, and sack ended threat as Maroons D preserved win. Mississippi State had scored on 3y keeper by QB Bruce Threadgill (24/105y rushing) and 29y run by FB Dennis Johnson.

MICHIGAN 42 Michigan State 10: Wolverines (5-0) easily maintained top ranking with abuse of in-state rivals. FB Rob Lytle rushed for 180y, TB Harlan Huckleby added 126y, 3 TDs, and TB Russell Davis chipped in with 91y as Michigan outrushed Spartans (1-3-1) 442y to 98y. Lytle gave Wolverines lead for good with 75y scoring romp in 1st Q that answered 24y FG by State K Hans Nielsen. Thanks to 2 Michigan FUMs, which set up both scores, Spartans trailed only 14-10 after 1st Q. Even with 2 GLS by Michigan State, Wolverines added 4 more TDs for school's highest series pt-total in 29 years. Michigan DB Jerry Zuver closed scoring with 60y INT TD RET. Michigan State QB Ed Smith passed for 198y.

MINNESOTA 29 Illinois 14: Golden Gophers (4-1) dominated from opening KO, building 29-0 lead behind rush attack that gained 251y rushing. Minnesota FB Jim Perkins rushed for game's 1st 3 TDs, while QB Tony Dungy passed for 76y and rushed for 89y with 7y TD scamper. Fighting Illini (2-3) RB James Coleman rushed for 77y and 2 TDs and caught 2/61y.

Nebraska 24 COLORADO 12: Injuries gave backup IB Rick Berns opportunity to shine and he took over in leading Cornhuskers (4-0-1). Berns rushed for 127y and clinching 1y TD, set up by his own 48y run, as Nebraska overcame 4 FGs by Buffs K Mark Zetterberg. QB Vince Ferragamo threw 9y TD pass to WB Curtis Craig as Nebraska regained lead at 14-12 in 3rd Q, lead which held up as D posted 2nd H shutout. TB Tony Reed led Colorado (3-2) rushers with 79y and receivers with 3/25y.

Texas 6 Oklahoma 6 (Dallas): Bad snap at game's end prevented winning x-pt for Sooners (4-0-1) in nasty edition of rivalry. Oklahoma had just traveled 37y in 11 plays to tie score on HB Horace Ivory's 1y TD run. Drive began after FUM by Longhorns (2-1-1) HB Ivey Suber, who was stripped by OU DL Dave Hudgens, with REC by CB Zac Henderson. With 5:23 left in game, Sooners had managed only 2 1st downs and 97y against inspired Texas D, led by LB Lionell Johnson's 23 tackles. Texas had built

6-0 lead on strength of 2 FGs by K Russell Erxleben—who also punted for 48.5y avg—riding FB Earl Campbell's 91y on 27 tough carries. Controversial week of practice featured accusation by Longhorns coach Darrell Royal that Sooners spied on his preparations. Royal offered $10,000 to OU coach Barry Switzer, assistant coach Larry Lacewell, and OU's "spy" if any of them could pass lie detector tests. Spying later was confirmed, although at much later date. Royal, who sported 12-6-1 record against Sooners, was feeling tension and vomited on way to locker room. Royal's decision to retire was taking root.

Texas Tech 27 TEXAS A&M 16: Raiders (3-0) pulled upset behind backup QB Rodney Allison, who relieved injured QB Tommy Duniven in 1st Q. Allison threw 2 TD passes to WR Sammy Williams and plowed into EZ from 1YL within 8-min span of 1st Q as Texas Tech grabbed 21-0 lead. Aggies (3-2) rallied with 52y FG by K Tony Franklin and 2 3rd Q TDs, but deficit was too great. With sub QB David Walker at helm of attack, A&M drove 3 times into Tech red zone before finally scoring TD on 2y run by HB Curtis Dickey (18/127y). Walker also hit WR Randall Teate for 76y TD. Williams' TD receptions were of 22y and 56y and came 3 mins apart.

Rice 26 TEXAS CHRISTIAN 23: With popularity of Wishbone and Veer, Owls (2-2) passing game was becoming more difficult to defend out of sheer novelty. Rice QB Tommy Kramer, who set 3 school records previous week vs. Texas, completed 27-46/342y, 2 TDs. Teams combined for 29 pts in 1st H pts as Kramer and TCU QB Jimmy Dan Elzner (13-27/256y) exchanged TD passes, and Rice DE Brian Seely speared FUM in midair and raced 19y to EZ. While HB Tony Accomando scored on 2 short 2nd H runs for Horned Frogs (0-5), Kramer's 6y TD pass to TE Kenneth Roy was game-winner. Rice WR Doug Cunningham had 10/175y receiving.

Southern California 23 WASHINGTON STATE 14 (Seattle): Bell rung loud and clear in new Kingdome, but it was not for Cougars (1-4) victory. Trojans TB Ricky Bell rushed 51/346y, both school and Pac-8 records. Game was tied at 14-14 in 4th Q until Southern California (4-1) converted FUM to 26y FG by K Glen Walker for 17-14 edge. Under 1st-year coach Jackie Sherrill, Washington State hung tough as QB Jack Thompson (26-50/341y) nearly matched Bell's run y with his passes. It was believed Bell had set new single-game NCAA record, but adding error prevented USC from giving him sufficient carries needed to eclipse 350y mark set by Michigan State's Eric Allen in 1971.

CALIFORNIA 27 Oregon 10: Despite being legally blind in 1 eye, WR Wesley Walker set California record with his 22nd career scoring reception: 33y catch of QB Joe Roth pass that gave Bears (3-2) commanding 20-3 lead in 4th Q. Roth threw for 208y, with 12y on TD pass to WR Leon Washington, and ran in 1y TD as Bears led throughout. Ducks (3-2) were disadvantaged in every stat, but K Roy Geiger nailed 51y FG.

AP Poll October 11

1 Michigan (57)	1194	11 Georgia	302	
2 Pittsburgh (3)	1057	12 Florida	230	
3 Nebraska	848	13 Texas	174	
4 UCLA	834	14 Notre Dame	158	
5 Maryland	660	15 Kansas	130	
6 Oklahoma	611	16t Louisiana State	42	
7 Missouri	485	16t Mississippi	42	
8 Southern California	418	18 Arkansas	37	
9 Ohio State	406	19 Houston	28	
10 Texas Tech	309	20 Alabama	18	

October 16, 1976

PENN STATE 27 Syracuse 3: Orangemen (2-4) had more 1st downs (19-17), more rushing yards (257-250), more passing yards (68-53), better punting average (36-26) and less penalty yards (48-61), but no TDs to Penn State's 4. Nittany Lions (3-3) did what it took to score as TB Steve Geise rushed for 98y and 27y TD and frosh TB Mike Guman gained 89y on ground with 2 TDs. Converting 2 FUMs, Penn State opened with 10-0 lead—enough pts against TD-challenged Orange. K Dave Jacobs kicked 24y FG for Syracuse pts.

PITTSBURGH 36 Miami 19: Panthers (6-0) may have been running out of healthy QBs, but as long as jersey no. 33 ran out to TB position they were okay. TB Tony Dorsett rushed 35/227y, 2 TDs, plus he caught scoring pass to lead undefeated Pitt. With QBs Robert Haygood and Matt Cavanaugh injured, sr QB Tom Yewcic orchestrated Panthers O that grabbed 22-0 H lead. Final 1st H was Yewcic's screen pass to Dorsett taken 40y to EZ. Dorsett, who breezed past 5,000y career rushing barrier, added 53y TD run in 4th Q. Panthers D forced 9 TOs and scored safety on tackle by DB LeRoy Felder of Miami QB George Mason. Hurricanes (1-4) rallied to make result appear more presentable with 3 late TDs, including 75y TD from QB Frank Glover to WB Larry Cain.

Virginia Tech 14 VIRGINIA 10: Cavaliers (0-6) were 7 mins away from ending nation's longest losing streak at 14 games after taking 10-7 lead on 1y TD run by TB Raymond Keys. Hokies (4-2) wouldn't stand for that, marching 70y in 16 plays to winning TD on 1y run by HB Roscoe Coles (18/86y) with just over min remaining. FB Paul Adams (26/86y), who scored Virginia Tech's 1st TD on 7y run in 1st Q, provided Tech with tough 1-2 tandem on winning drive. UVa P Russ Henderson had brilliant day, averaging 48.7y on 6 punts and pinning Gobblers 4 times within their own 4YL.

North Carolina State 21 NORTH CAROLINA 13: Led by QB Johnny Evans, Wolfpack (2-4-1) roared to 21-0 2nd Q lead with 98y and 97y TD drives. After TB Ted Brown (21/125y) scored on 1y run to cap 30y drive set up by S Richard Wheeler's INT, NC State was pinned twice in own territory. From own 2YL, Evans (8-14/129y) passed from EZ for 38y gain to WR Dave Moody to begin drive he ended with 1y sneak. Next long march featured runs of 27y by Brown and 31y by FB Billy Ray Vickers before

Brown's 8y TD run. Tar Heels (4-2) stopped bleeding with QB Matt Kupec's 32y TD pass to WB Wayne Tucker, but could get no closer than 8 pts. TB Mike Voight, who became all-time ACC rusher with 3,173y, was held to 84y and TD.

MARYLAND 17 Wake Forest 15: No. 5 Terps (6-0) had little relief until their REC of late 4th Q onside-KO by Deacons. Following 27y FG by Maryland K Mike Sochko that lifted margin to 17-7, Wake Forest (3-4) flew up field before QB Mike McGlamry (11-24/183y, INT) hit WR Bill Millner on 29y TD pass and added 2-pt pass to WR Solomon Everett. Terps had scored 1st on 47y screen pass to FB Tim Wilson. After Deacs tied game at 7-7 on 2nd Q 1y run by TB James McDougald, Maryland waited until 4th Q to take lead. TB George Scott (17/83y), elevated from 3rd string due to injuries, became 4th different back in 4 weeks to lead Maryland rushers, ran for 1y TD 5 plays after Terps G Ed Fulton recovered 3rd down FUM by QB Mark Manges for 8y gain and 1st down at Wake 32YL.

KENTUCKY 21 Louisiana State 7: Wildcats (4-2) rode 2 TD runs by FB Rod Stewart and 56y INT TD RET by S Dallas Owens for upset. Tigers (3-2-1) dominated O stats, 355y to 210y, but couldn't reap its rewards. At H, LSU trailed 14-0 despite having run 45 plays to 19 for Cats. Rally chances died when Kentucky TB Chris Hill raced 51y to set up clinching 10y scoring run by Stewart. TB Terry Robiskie, future frequent interim NFL coach, rushed for 126y for LSU.

Alabama 20 TENNESSEE 13: Volunteers (3-3) coach Bill Battle was victimized by his alma mater, Alabama (4-2), for 6th time in row. As he put it later, there was long shadow cast from Tennessee grad working in Pennsylvania: "the local press was writing more about what Johnny Majors and (eventual national champion) Pittsburgh were doing than what we were doing at Tennessee." Tide DB Mike Kramer, who had removed cast from his wrist just before KO, made big play by blocking Vols P Craig Colquitt's punt early in 3rd Q. That led to 15y TD run by Bama QB Jack O'Rear (119y rushing), which broke 6-6 deadlock. Tennessee managed to tie it on FB Bobby Emmons' 2y TD run before end of 3rd Q. UT LB Greg Jones participated in 25 tackles, but was hard pressed to halt Tide's winning 79y ride in 4th Q.

GAME OF THE YEAR
Florida 33 FLORIDA STATE 26:

As much as any game, this heart-breaking defeat proved that Florida State (2-4) was on its way. Afterward, coach Bobby Bowden told his players, "I think you're awfully close to being a good football team." No. 12 Gators (4-1) jumped to 10-0 lead in 1st Q, but FSU QB Jimmy Black (14-17/211y, INT) was sharp with his opening 12 passes to launch Seminoles to 17-13 lead in 2nd Q. FSU's 2nd TD came on terrific high grab by WR Kurt Unglaub. Just as quickly, QB Jimmy Fisher (139y passing) fired Florida's air game and whipped Gators 82y with go-ahead TD at 20-17 coming in last 10 secs of 1st H as WR Wes Chandler caught 23y pass and faked his way into EZ. After trade of 3rd Q TDs, Gators sprung HB Tony Green for 58y dash to set up TD run for 33-23 lead in middle of 4th Q. Even with Black out injured, Seminoles had plenty left: frosh QB Jimmy Jordan (6-13/109y) sparked FSU 73y to K Dave Cappelen's 27y FG and, with last-min connections to Unglaub and TE Ed Beckman, to Gators 9YL. Jordan barely overshot Unglaub, and, with 7 secs left, rolled out only to be dumped by hard-charging Florida DE Mike Dupree as clock ran out.

Oklahoma 28 KANSAS 10: Coach Barry Switzer avenged his only loss in 3 years as Sooners (5-0-1) converted 4 TOs into 2nd H scores. While QB Thomas Lott (19/104y rushing) may have completed none of his 5 pass attempts, he ran for 2 TDs. Jayhawks (4-2) QB Nolan Cromwell (12/83y), whom coach Bud Moore described as greatest Wishbone QB he had ever seen, was knocked out for season with knee injury after leading Kansas to 10-3 H lead on 24y TD run by HB Bill Campfield and 37y FG by K Mike Hubach. Lott quickly tied game in 3rd Q after Kansas FUM on 1st play of 2nd H, racing for 13y TD. Lott then put Sooners in front for good with 33y burst following INT by S Scott Hill of 1st pass thrown by Kansas sub QB Scott McMichael.

Iowa State 21 MISSOURI 17: Wins over USC and Ohio State had shot Missouri (4-2) into AP top 10 entering Cyclones (5-1) hit Columbia. TB Dexter Green (37/214y) scored twice, once on 65y jaunt, as Iowa State built 14-0 lead. Tigers managed FG before Iowa State scored again, on nifty pass from RB Buddy Hardeman back to QB Wayne Stanley for 36y TD. QB Steve Pisarkiewicz threw TD as Mizzou ended 1st H trailing 21-10. Cyclones D blanked Tigers in 2nd H until FB Rich Dansdill gave Missouri 56y scoring jaunt. Later in 4th Q, speedy Missouri WR Leo Lewis had 77y punt TD RET wiped out by clipping PEN. Cyclones CB Mike Clemons soon sealed it with INT.

TEXAS A&M 24 Baylor 0: As Texas A&M (4-2) defenders earned high marks by allowing only 48/93y rushing, K Tony Franklin earned national publicity by twice breaking NCAA record for long-range FGs of 64 and 65y. On same day elsewhere in Texas, K Ove Johannson of Abilene Christian, cousin of former heavyweight champion Ingemar, booted NAIA-record 69y FG. Meanwhile, Baylor (4-2) suffered 5 TOs, although it managed to lead Aggies in 1st downs by 16 to 12. Texas A&M scored 2 TDs, with QB David Walker throwing 15y scoring pass to TE Gary Haack, and HB Curtis Dickey (17/85y) racing 35y.

OREGON STATE 10 California 9: Inept game featured 9 TOs and 24 PENs as foes struggled to reach EZ. Bears (3-3) won FG battle by 3 to 1, taking 9-3 lead in 4th Q after K Jim "Into The" Breech's trio of 3-ptrs gave him school career FG mark (28). Oregon State (1-5) TB James Fields finally scored TD with less than 4 mins left on 1y run to cap 65y drive. Beavers D shackled Bears QB Joe Roth (13-28/119y), sacking him 3 times and picking off 3 passes. On final sack of game, Roth was carried off field with injured knee. Bumbling California suffered 16 PENs/172y.

STANFORD 34 Washington 28: Stanford (2-4) QB Guy Benjamin put on passing clinic to outduel Huskies QB Warren Moon. Benjamin completed 14-22/270y with 35y TD pass to WR James Lofton and scored on 2 short rushes. Washington (3-3) held brief

7-3 lead on 1y TD run by TB Joe Steele, but faced deficit rest of way after Cardinals reeled off next 24 pts. HB Gary Lynn scored TD on 2y run that gave Stanford lead for good at 10-7, capping 31y drive begun with REC of Moon's FUM. Moon (15-28/209y, INT) led 4th Q rally, throwing TD passes of 38y to WR Spider Gaines and 4y to WR Scott Phillips until Cards recovered late onside-KO.

October 23, 1976

Pittsburgh 45 NAVY 0: Game's sole excitement concerned moment when Pitt (7-0) TB Tony Dorsett would break Ohio State's Archie Griffin's year-old NCAA career rushing mark. Record-setting run was fittingly spectacular, as Dorsett raced 32y for his 3rd scoring jaunt of day and 11th of season. Gaining 180y, Dorsett put career mark at 5,206y and became 1st player to rush for more than 1,000y in each of 4 seasons. QB Tom Yewcic (8-10/97y), 2nd generation signal-caller, had opened Pitt's scoring with 30y TD pass to TE Jim Corbett. While Navy (1-6) D fought hard, its O had trouble penetrating Panthers' front-7 and finished with only 106y total O.

NORTH CAROLINA 12 East Carolina 10: Pirates (6-1) lost for 1st time despite not surrendering TD as Tar Heels used 2 kickers to boot 4 FGs. K Tom Biddle made FGs from 31y and 24y to give North Carolina (5-2) 6-0 H lead. In 3rd Q QB Matt Kupec led UNC into FG range again, but distance was 49y, so in came long-range K Jeff Arnold, who kicked it true. East Carolina Wishbone then got into gear, scoring on 15y run by QB Mike Weaver and, after 75y run by HB Eddie Hicks (17/129y), on 19y FG by K Pat Conaty for 10-9 lead in 4th Q. Tar Heels then marched 70y to winning FG, with Kupec's 24y pass to WR Walker Lee serving as drive's big blow. TB Mike Voight rushed for 112y for UNC.

Florida 20 TENNESSEE 18: Gators (5-1) held off Volunteers as QB Jimmy Fisher ran in 2y TD to tie score at 10-10 and hit WR Wes Chandler on 41y pass play that set up HB Willie Wilder's 7y scoring run for solid 20-10 lead. Vols (3-4) had come out flying, holding 10-0 lead after 2 possessions on 32y FG by K Jim Gaylor and 11y TD run by HB Stanley Morgan. Gators then moved LB Steve Hutchinson over C, and Vols O slowed under increased pressure. Florida attack began moving, tying game 10-10 at H on 42y FG by K David Posey after having scored TD on Fisher's 2y keeper. Gators HB Tony Green rushed for 124y, while Vols WR Larry Seivers caught 8/128y.

Notre Dame 13 SOUTH CAROLINA 6: Irish (5-1) won old-fashioned way, with stifling D and power run game. Notre Dame D made 10-pt 1st Q lead hold up by stretching string of Qs without allowing TD to school-record 20. In its 5 wins, Notre Dame D had allowed only 4 FGs. Irish O featured HB Al Hunter again and again for 32/181y rushing. Gamecocks (5-3) managed just 2 FGs by K Britt Parrish, with WR Philip Logan leading y-maker with 78y on 6 catches. Another ND record bit dust as K Dave Reeve booted FGs number 22 and 23 for new Notre Dame career mark.

Missouri 34 NEBRASKA 24: Play of game occurred in 4th Q, when, on 3rd-and-14 from his own 2YL, Missouri (5-2) QB Pete Woods (6-15/191y) connected with WR Joe Stewart on incredible 98y TD pass play. Big-8 distance record for pass, Stewart's TD gave Tigers 31-24 lead in front of shocked Lincoln crowd. Huskers (5-1-1) had last 2 drives end on FUM and INT, while K Tim Gibbons clinched 34y FG. Woods accounted for 4 TDs, while QB Vince Ferragamo (13-22/191y, 2 INTs) of Nebraska was unable to throw TD but ran for score. Tigers' giant-killer season continued as they had now conquered USC, Ohio State, and Nebraska.

Oklahoma State 31 OKLAHOMA 24: Cowboys (4-2) pulled stunner behind unlikely hero, QB Charlie Weatherbie, who bounced back from 1st H benching. Weatherbie sparked Oklahoma State to 18 2nd H pts to send Sooners (5-1-1) to only 2nd loss in past 41 games. Oklahoma had scored 1st H TDs on 37y run by FB Jim Culbreath, 21y run with FUM REC by T Richard Murray, and HB Elvis Peacock's blistering 84y scamper. Cowboys D held Sooners to 3 pts in 2nd H, while O scored TDs on 6y run by FB Skip Taylor and 5y TD catch by WR Ricky Taylor. OSU HB Terry Miller rushed for 159y, with 72y on spectacular run in 1st Q to open scoring. Win was 3rd in series for Cowboys in past 30 years. Last time Oklahoma and Nebraska both lost Big 8 games on same day was October 28, 1961.

Arkansas 14 HOUSTON 7: Hogs (4-1) got on board 1st with 8y keeper by QB Ron Calcagni to cap 59y drive that converted Cougars TO. Later, Arkansas got big play needed to pull out win as RB Ben Cowins (21/186y) raced 89y off guard for stunning 2nd Q TD. Forcing 5 TOs, including 3 FUMs by Houston QB Danny Davis (13-21/171y, INT), Razorbacks D kept Houston (4-2) off scoreboard until FB Dyral Thomas' 6y TD run in 4th Q.

AP Poll October 25

1 Michigan (53)	1184	11 Notre Dame	292
2 Pittsburgh (6)	1068	12 Florida	287
3 UCLA	944	13 Oklahoma	268
4 Southern California	707	14 Arkansas	159
5 Maryland	705	15 Texas	81
6 Texas Tech (1)	618	16 Oklahoma State	33
7 Georgia	483	17 Alabama	29
8 Ohio State	475	18 Mississippi State	25
9 Nebraska	368	19 Colorado	12
10 Missouri	293	20 Cincinnati	10

AP Poll November 1

1 Michigan (57)	1228	11 Notre Dame	290
2 Pittsburgh (5)	1076	12 Arkansas	267
3 UCLA	976	13 Oklahoma State	180
4 Southern California	758	14 Colorado	146
5 Texas Tech	703	15 Alabama	83
6 Maryland	668	16 Missouri	31
7 Georgia	547	17 Oklahoma	26
8 Ohio State	497	18 Texas A&M	19
9 Nebraska	451	19 Houston	18
10 Florida	342	20 Texas	10

October 30, 1976

PITTSBURGH 23 Syracuse 13: Orangemen (3-5) had fallen on hard times, but upset of no. 2 Pitt (8-0) would have sparked turn-around hope. Syracuse QB Bill Hurley, who threw for 203y and ran for 112y, led Orange to 13-10 lead, with last pts coming on booming 55y FG by K Dave Jacobs. Syracuse had no answer for great Panthers TB Tony Dorsett, who rushed for 242y and 2 TDs, scoring on 33y run to give Pitt lead for good at 17-13. Panthers K Carson Long added his 2nd and 3rd FGs for insurance. Syracuse drove twice into Panthers territory in 4th Q without scoring.

MARYLAND 24 Kentucky 14: Unbeaten Terps (8-0) were floundering in late stages of 1st H, down 7-6, when WB Dean Richards exploded for 49y punt RET, and when personal foul PEN was tacked on, Maryland found itself at Kentucky (4-4) 11YL. FB Tim Wilson (81y) scored 3 plays later, and QB Mark Manges ran for 2 pts, so Terps were on their way at 14-7. When Maryland converted quartet of 3rd downs on 77y drive to open 3rd Q, Wilson scored again for 21-7 lead. Wildcats QB Derrick Ramsey pitched his 2nd TD pass in 4th Q, 52y connection to RB Randy Brooks.

ALABAMA 34 Mississippi State 17: Bulldogs (6-2) started beautifully as QB Bruce Threadgill passed 16y and ran 12y for TDs. Trickery led to Alabama's 1st score as HB Tony Nathan pitched ball back to QB Jeff Rutledge (6-9/120y), who threw 62y scoring bomb to WR Ozzie Newsome. Mississippi State added on 22y FG by K Kinney Jordan to extend lead of 17-12 at H. Alabama (6-2) decided it was time to impress bevy of bowl scouts: HB Johnny Davis scored on 27y dash at end of 82y march after 2nd H KO, and QB Jack O'Rear scrambled for 2 pts. Bama's rout of Bulldogs was on. Bama D allowed only 54y in 2nd H and held MSU TB Walter Packer to 27y rushing for game.

TEXAS TECH 31 Texas 28: As soaring FB Billy Taylor finally landed in Texas EZ for 1y TD, Red Raiders (6-0) continued winning ways. Texas Tech QB Rodney Allison rushed for 106y and hit 10-11/87y, while contributing key 22y run on 3rd-and-long to keep winning drive alive. With FB Earl Campbell (7/65y) knocked out mid-game with hamstring injury and WR Alfred Jackson curbed with broken ribs, Texas O was out of sorts. Backup QB Ted Constanzo came forward, rallying Longhorns (3-2-1) to 4th Q lead with help from FB Jimmy Johnson (11/101y) who scored 3 TDs.

OKLAHOMA STATE 20 Missouri 19: Cowboys (5-2) stormed back from 16-0 deficit to chase Mizzou from nation's top 10. WR Joe Stewart, hero of Nebraska win, put Tigers (5-3) up by 16-0 with 100y KO TD RET to open 2nd H. Oklahoma State HB Terry Miller, who rushed for 228y, then took game over, exploding for 3 2nd H TDs. Miller scored twice in 3rd Q and then tallied game-winning 10y scoring effort in 4th Q. Game was 3rd straight that witnessed Miller set personal best for rushing, while FB Skip Taylor contributed 106y. Tigers rushed for 197y, led by TB Dean Leibson's 97y.

COLORADO 42 Oklahoma 31: Buffaloes (6-2) sent suddenly reeling Oklahoma to 2nd straight defeat, scoring game's final 22 pts. Colorado FB Jim Kelleher rushed for 3 short TDs, while QB Jeff Knapple (11-23/191y, 2 INTs) hooked up with WB Billy Waddy on 70y TD pass that pulled Buffs within 31-26. Less than min later, Colorado MG Charlie Johnson stripped OU HB Elvis Peacock late in 3rd Q to set up 27y drive to winning 1y TD run by Kelleher. Buffs followed by sucking life out of Sooners with 85y drive to 2y TD by Kelleher. With 2 TOs in final 10 mins, Sooners found rallying impossible. FB Kenny King rushed for 119y to lead Oklahoma and had raced 71y for 7-3 lead in 1st Q. Buffs TB Tony Reed logged game-high 136y rushing.

BRIGHAM YOUNG 43 Arizona State 21: BYU's dismantling of Sun Devils (2-5) made changing-of-guard in WAC complete. QB Gifford Nielsen threw for 339y and 2 TDs as Cougars (6-2) overcame Arizona State's 21-pt 1st Q. Sun Devils came out firing behind QB Dennis Sproul, who hooked up with WB Larry Mucker (6/ASU-record 206y) for TD passes of 80y and 43y and rushed for 3rd score from 1y out. Cougars stayed close, scoring on 3y run by WR John Van Der Wouden on fake FG, followed by 21y FG by K Dave Taylor and 35y TD pass to WR George Harris. BYU continued to score, including 2y 2nd Q TD run by FB Dave Lowry and 81y bomb to WR Mike Chronister in 3rd Q. At this point, ASU became plagued by 3 INTs.

UCLA 30 WASHINGTON 21: UCLA Bruins (7-0-1) dominated Washington but had difficult time putting away Huskies. FB Theotis Brown busted loose for school-record 220y, including TD runs of 29y, 15y, and 51y. Roommate and world-class hurdler HB James Owens chipped in with 123y rushing as Bruins won 1st game in Seattle since 1958. Huskies (4-4) trailed throughout, but close thanks to 89y KO TD RET by TB Joe Steele and 80y scoring drive in 4th Q. Drive ended on 28y TD pass from QB Warren Moon (11-27/132y) to TE Scott Greenwood that cut Bruins lead to 24-21. UCLA answered with 85y drive featuring Brown's blistering 51y TD run.

November 6, 1976

RUTGERS 34 Louisville 0: Louisville (3-5) represented step up in class for Scarlet Knights, who handled visitors with ease. Rutgers (9-0) pulled out all stops, scoring 1st on reverse by WR Mark Twitty and, before 1st H ended, on 35y pass to DB-turned-WR Henry Jenkins, used on no huddle play with 27 secs left in 2nd Q. Spirited Rutgers D never gave Cardinals chance to organize, even when Louisville recovered 3 Rutgers FUMs in 1st Q. RBs Mark Lassiter and Glen Kohler rushed for 94y each for Knights, while Louisville TB Calvin Prince struggled to gain 48y.

Georgia 41 Florida 27 (Jacksonville): "Cocktail Party" fans had fascinating game to watch as both teams entered with Top 10 rankings. QB Ray Goff was difference as he led Bulldogs (8-1) to 28 pts in 2nd H, rushing for 124y, 3 TDs. Florida (6-2) built 27-13 H lead before collapsing during game's final 30 mins. After Bulldogs scored TD on 1st possession of 3rd Q, Florida faced 4th-and-1 from own 29YL. To surprise of all, Gators went for 1st down. Bulldogs S Johnny Henderson made tackle on HB Earl Carr that set up tying 2y TD run by FB Al Pollard. "When I was running the play I was asking myself why in the world we were running this play," said Carr after game. HB Kevin McLee rushed for 198y to lead Bulldogs run game that totaled 432y, while QB Jimmy Fisher and WR Wes Chandler hooked up on 2 TD passes for Florida.

GEORGIA TECH 23 Notre Dame 14: Week after 31-7 loss to Duke, Yellow Jackets returned to Wishbone O and made wreck of vaunted Irish (6-2) D with 368y rushing. Georgia Tech (4-4-1) D got into act too, holding Notre Dame to 34y total O and 4 1st downs in 2nd H as Tech scored last 20 pts of game. Key drive occurred with less than 2 mins left in 1st H when Tech marched 84y to 8y TD run by frosh QB Gary Lanier. That cut deficit to 14-10. Turning point on drive was 46y E-around run by WR Drew Hill. TB David Sims tallied 122y rushing and scored twice in 2nd H in becoming Georgia Tech's career rushing leader. Jackets coach Pepper Rodgers received 3-year extension from his alma mater after thrilling upset.

PURDUE 16 Michigan 14: Roadblock for no. 1 Michigan's title aspirations was supposed to be Ohio State as Wolverines (8-1) had not lost to any other member of Big 10 since 1969. But as K Bob Wood's 37y FG attempt at game's end sailed wide, so too did Michigan's championship hopes. Purdue (4-5) TB Scott Dierking rushed for 162y and 2 TDs, while K Rock Supan booted winning 23y FG with 4 mins left. Michigan had scored 1st on 8y TD run by QB Rick Leach before Boilermakers answered with scoring runs of 4y and 25y by Dierking. Purdue now led 13-7 and used GLS early in 3rd Q to preserve lead. Wolverines broke through on next series as Leach tossed 64y scoring pass to WB Jim Smith. After gaining possession on TO, Michigan marched again until TB Rob Lytle (21/153y) lost FUM on Boilermakers 29YL, which launched long drive to Supan's winning FG.

Houston 30 TEXAS 0: Cougars (6-2) put stamp on debut SWC season with lopsided win over traditional conf juggernaut. After facing Florida's and Texas A&M's Wishbone attacks, Houston was more than ready for struggling Longhorn O, minus injured FB Earl Campbell. Texas (3-3-1) finished with 24y rushing, Horns' lowest total ever, while suffering worst conf loss in tenure of coach Darrell Royal. Cougars racked up 370y, with 267y on ground. RB Alois Blackwell made 7y TD run to cap 79y drive that began after DB Elvis Bradley's EZ INT had snuffed out Texas' early and only scoring opportunity. WR Alfred Jackson was Steers' O star with 6/93y in receptions, but he couldn't salve pain of end of Texas' 42-game home winning streak.

NEBRASKA 14 Oklahoma State 10: QB Vince Ferragamo (17-25/235y) twice tossed 2nd H TDs to lead Nebraska (7-1-1) past upstart Cowboys (5-3). HB Terry Miller (30/149y) played well in defeat, but Oklahoma State hardly could finish its drives. Cowboys opened 3-0 lead at H on 37y FG by K Abby Daigle, and later went up 10-7 in 3rd Q on Miller's 15y TD run. Ferragamo overcame 2 INTs to throw 34y TD to WR Chuck Malito and 6y score to TE Ken Spaeth. OSU rushed for 291y, number that would have been higher if not for Nebraska LB Clete Pillen's 30 tackles.

Wyoming 26 ARIZONA 24: Cowboys (7-2) moved step closer to Fiesta Bowl with win. Wyoming HB Latrail Jones took opening KO 81y to set up his 1y TD dive. Wildcats (4-4) answered as QB Marc Lunsford (15-29/358y, 3 TDs, INT) found WR Keith Hartwig (8/203y) for 44y TD pass. Cowboys regained lead on 56y romp by FB Robbie Wright (22/144y), before Lunsford threw 2 more TD passes. Wright scored again, on 6y run to cap 82y drive that nibbled at Arizona's 21-19 H margin. Wyoming converted FUM by Wildcats TB Derriak Anderson on 1st play of 3rd Q, moving 23y to Jones' 2y TD run. Except for successful FG, Cats spent drive after drive in Cowboys territory only to fail on downs or missed FG until reaching Wyoming 5YL when time expired.

Southern California 48 STANFORD 24: With Troy TB Ricky Bell out with ankle injury, Southern California (7-1) showed another side of its O with 5 TD passes, 4 by QB Vince Evans (7-15/131y). From game's 3rd play, 59y bomb to WR Shelton Diggs (3/100y, 3 TDs), rout was on, and tally reached 34-3 by H. Although Stanford D keyed on Trojans TB Charles White early, youngster still rushed 136y, 2 TDs. Cardinals (4-5) were not able to score TD until trailing 41-3 as USC D excelled with CB Ricky Odom leading way with 3 INTs. Cardinals QB Guy Benjamin threw for 144y, while QB Mike Cordova came off bench to hit 6-6/74y.

301

November 13, 1976

PITTSBURGH 24 West Virginia 16: Grateful Pittsburgh retired TB Tony Dorsett's no. 33 jersey at H, and Dorsett celebrated by rushing for 199y, 3 TDs in his final appearance in front of home fans. QB Matt Cavanaugh added 127y rushing as Panthers (10-0) gained 350y on ground. Although West Virginia (4-6) managed only 169y, they stayed close largely on strength of 2 TD passes from QB Dan Kendra to WR Steve Lewis. Marking 32nd time Dorsett topped 100y barrier, game ended with fight started by Dorsett after what he felt was latest in series of cheap shots by Mountaineer defenders.

Georgia 28 AUBURN 0: Bulldogs (9-1) grandly grabbed share of 1st SEC title since 1968 as O ran wild and D posted 4th shutout in 10 games. Georgia HB Kevin McLee increased his school single-game rushing record to 203y, and FB Al Pollard added 158y, 2 TDs as Bulldogs gained 470y on ground. Tigers (3-7) crossed midfield just 4 times and lost their best threat on 3rd Q FUM by QB Phil Gargis, recovered by Bulldogs DT Jeff Sanders at Georgia 12YL. Bulldogs experienced early FUM problem as their 1st 2 possessions ended on TOs in Auburn territory, but soon ball carriers held on and Tigers were caged. Frosh TB Joe Cribbs led Auburn rushing with 64y.

NOTRE DAME 21 Alabama 18: Coach Dan Devine's patience with QB Rick Slager paid off as besieged QB completed 15-23/235y and 56y TD pass to WR Dan Kelleher to lead Notre Dame (7-2). Twice Alabama (7-3) threw EZ INTs, including QB Jeff Rutledge's forced pass to double-covered WR Ozzie Newsome while wide-open HB Pete Cavan occupied other side of EZ. S Jim Browner picked off that pass with 4:17 left in game to end last good threat. HB Vagas Ferguson rushed for 107y in 1st start in his Irish career as Notre Dame gained 484y with 365y in decisive 1st H. Crimson Tide had 401y, 231y through air. Coach Bear Bryant's inability to beat Irish continued; he had suffered through 3 losses to ND by total of 6 pts.

Ohio State 9 MINNESOTA 3: With neither team scoring in 2nd H, Ohio State (8-1-1) was able to remain Big 10 frontrunners. Buckeyes QB Jim Pacenta's 4y TD run in 2nd Q proved to be winning score, after teams traded FGs earlier in 1st H. Gophers (6-4) drove deep into Ohio State territory on 2 occasions in 2nd H before INT by DT Nick Buonamici ended threat, and 4th down incompletion killed another. TB Jeff Logan (30/116y) converted critical 3rd-and-13 late in game with 14y run that helped Buckeyes run out clock. QB Tony Dungy threw for 201y for Minnesota.

NORTHWESTERN 42 Michigan State 21: Wildcats (1-9) joyfully snapped 15-game losing streak with 3 4th Q TDs, 2 on passes from QB Randy Dean (12-23/272, INT) to WR Mark Bailey. Northwestern S Malcolm Thomas set up 2 TDs with FUM RECs and recorded INT as MSU had 5 TOs. Spartans (4-5-1) TB Rich Baes rushed for 134y and QB Ed Smith threw for 188y. TB Pat Geegan rushed for 107y for Wildcats, and Bailey caught 6/108y, both contributing to 512y total O.

Iowa State 37 NEBRASKA 28: Upstart Cyclones (8-2) upended Nebraska behind stunning rushing differential of 321y to 77y. Teams combined for 24 1st Q pts, none more dramatic than TD put on board by WR Luther Blue on 95y KO RET for 17-7 Cyclones lead. Huskers eventually tied contest at 20-20, on QB Vince Ferragamo's 2nd TD pass to WR Bobby Thomas, early in 4th Q. ISU then reeled off 17 straight pts to secure upset, 10 pts of which came on short drives following Nebraska TOs. Losing 6 FUMs, Cornhuskers (7-2-1) lost to Iowa State for 1st time since 1960. TB Dexter Green led Cyclone rushing with 109y. Ferragamo passed for 199y.

TEXAS TECH 34 Southern Methodist 7: Not even snow could halt Texas Tech's best start since 1938, year school last appeared in Cotton Bowl. Despite November snowstorm, Red Raiders (8-0) rushed for 401y in crushing SMU from get-go. Winning pts came quickly on 20y FG by K Brian Hall. QB Rodney Allison scored 2 TDs, and TB Larry Isaac crossed GL to increase lead to 24-0 at H. Mustangs (2-8) made game interesting for about 2 mins of 2nd H as QB Tony Black threw short pass to WR Emanuel Tolbert, who raced 76y past fallen CB Craig Harris to EZ. SMU LB Putt Choate then picked off Allison's pass, but Ponies O lost ground and never threatened again. Forced to start 8 1st-year players, Mustangs had no chance to keep up.

Texas A&M 31 ARKANSAS 10: Arkansas found 2nd Q costly, allowing 24 pts and losing QB Ron Calcagni to injury. Within 59-sec span, Texas A&M HB Curtis Dickey (20/92y) scored on 3y TD run on 4th down and threw 41y TD pass to WR Randall Teate following INT by CB Lester Hayes for 14-3 Aggies (7-2) lead. Texas A&M then marched to 32y FG by K Tony Franklin and converted subsequent FUM into 1y scoring run by FB George Woodard, his 1st of 2. Arkansas (5-2-1) used HB option pass, scoring TD on 29y pass from RB Jerry Eckwood (20/74y) to WR Donny Bobo.

November 20, 1976

CLEMSON 28 South Carolina 9: Disappointing season ended well for Tigers (3-6-2) as soph QB Steve Fuller led O that started quickly for change, scoring 2 1st Q TDs for 14-0 lead. South Carolina (6-5) could have matched that score as 2 1st H drives cracked Clemson 10YL and Gamecocks made FUM REC at Tigers 6YL. But, thanks to EZ INT by DB Brian Kier and 2 GLSs by Clemson, Gamecocks could manage only 3 pts during those 3 threatening possessions. Tigers upped lead to 21-3 in 3rd Q after bad snap on Carolina punt set them up for 16y drive to Fuller's TD run. Fuller added 27y scoring run later. Fuller sparked young Tigers backfield, featuring soph RB Warren Ratchford (10/127y) and frosh RB Tracy Perry (16/98y). QB Ron Bass (16-39/261y, 3 INTs) provided Cocks' sole TD on 17y pass to WR Phil Logan.

NORTH CAROLINA 39 Duke 38: Tar Heels (9-2) edged rivals in wild game, riding TB Mike Voight to victory. Voight rushed 47/261y, raising career total to 5th-most ever at 3,971y, and running in winning 2-pt conv to cap his illustrious tenure at UNC. He added 4 TDs to break Choo Choo Justice's school career TD mark with 42. Matching Voight TD for TD was Duke (5-5-1) QB Mike Dunn, who rushed for 130y and passed for 109y. Dunn's 4 TD runs all were 9y or longer. Duke TB Art Gore rushed for 109y and twice made 50y KO RETs to set up scores. Neither team ever took more than 7-pt lead, while UNC had 450y to 434y edge in O. Heels QB Matt Kupec threw TD that set up winning 2-pt conv, 7y to FB Billy Johnson with :37 left.

Kentucky 7 TENNESSEE 0: Despite low score, Kentucky dominated Vols (5-5) for 1st series win in 12 years, share of SEC title, and 1st bowl bid since 1952. Wildcats (7-4) D held Tennessee to 166y, forced 14 punts, and shut down scoring chances. Cats O spent most of game ramming ball down Vols' throats, rushing 72/279y, but used rare pass play to score TD. QB Derrick Ramsey, who rushed for 77y, burned Tennessee blitz by hitting RB Greg Woods with pass down right sidelines that went for 68y TD. Vols D made 2 GLSs in 2nd Q, but there was little to cheer about in Knoxville as Big Orange suffered through worst W-L mark since 1964.

Michigan 22 OHIO STATE 0: Wolverines (10-1) left nothing to chance—even remote possibility of last-sec FG—as they whipped Ohio State (8-2-1) for 1st victory in series since 1971. Buckeyes (8-2-1) endured 1st shutout since 1964, streak of 122 games that came within 1 game of present-day record set by Oklahoma from 1946-57. TB Rob Lytle led Michigan O with 164y rushing and TD. Score was 0-0 at H until Wolverines option attack produced 257y and 3 TDs in final 30 mins. FB Russell Davis chipped in with 2 TDs, while QB Rick Leach orchestrated O and had 20y scamper to help set up 1st TD. Bucks wasted best opportunity as QB Jim Pacenta, harried all day, threw EZ INT to DB Jim Pickens in 2nd Q. Ohio State rushed for only 104y, so it created few chances. Michigan DT Greg Morton led way with 14 tackles. Ohio's finest performance may have come from P Tom Skladany, who averaged 52.2y on 8 punts. Loss snapped Buckeyes' streak of 4 straight Rose Bowl appearances.

Houston 27 TEXAS TECH 19: Cougars (7-2) dispatched Texas Tech (8-1) from ranks of unbeaten while vaulting themselves into 1st place in SWC. Houston enjoyed 24-5 lead, but had to pick off pass by Raiders QB Rodney Allison on own 2YL to halt nerve-wracking final drive. Houston QB Danny Davis (9-13/159y, INT) led way, throwing TD passes of 39y to WR Ricky Maddox and 7y to TE Eddie Foster. With run game struggling, Allison rallied Tech with 284y of his aerial 327y coming in catch-up 2nd H. Allison pulled Raiders within 27-19 with 16y TD pass to FB Billy Taylor, but his last assault died short. RB Alois Blackwell rushed for 103y for Houston squad that would capture conf lead with 42-20 win over Rice following week.

OKLAHOMA STATE 42 Iowa State 21: Oklahoma State (7-3) earned share of its 1st Big 8 title by halting Cyclones (8-3). Once again, Cowboys HB Terry Miller dominated stats, rushing for 199y and 2 long TDs, while QB Charlie Weatherbie ran for 2 TDs and threw for another to account for all of OSU's 21 pts in 1st H. Cowboys lead was 21-14 at H intermission, but soon Oke State dropped heavy hammer: LB John Weimer gobbled up FUM REC at Iowa State 1YL to set up FB Skip Taylor's TD blast, and Miller broke loose for 33y scoring jaunt, which also converted 1 of Cyclones' 5 TOs. TB Dexter Green rushed for 154y as Iowa State vainly outgained Oklahoma State 433y to 368y.

Colorado 35 KANSAS STATE 28: Buffaloes (8-3) picked up 1st piece of Big 8 title since 1961 and avoided 3rd straight upset loss to Kansas State (1-10). S Mike Davis' late INT on own 16YL sealed Colorado's victory. Buffs stayed in hunt for Orange Bowl as FB Jim Kelleher rushed for TDs in each of 1st 3 Qs, while Buffs D set up 2 scores in 2nd H with FUM RECs. TB Tony Reed paced Colorado O with 36/140y. HB Tony Brown carried Wildcats O, rushing for 84y and 3 TDs and adding team-high 6 catches/47y.

AIR FORCE 42 Wyoming 21: Falcons (4-7) eagerly earned 100th coaching win for Ben Martin with upset of Fiesta Bowl-bound Wyoming (8-3). Air Force flew to 27-0 lead behind frosh QB Dave Ziebart (19-26/339y), who tossed 89y TD to WR Paul Williams (5/148y, 2 TDs), and 3 TD runs by frosh FB David Thomas. Once Cowboys (8-3) began scoring, Ziebart threw 2 insurance scores to keep Wyoming at bay. FB Robbie Wright produced all 3 Wyoming TDs, while rushing for 84y.

SOUTHERN CALIFORNIA 24 Ucla 14: With Rose Bowl berth on line, Trojans (9-1) D reigned supreme with shutout of UCLA deep into 4th Q. USC D even scored momentum-swinging TD as DB Dennis Thurman caught FUM by FB Theotis Brown—ball was knocked loose by Brown's own Bruin teammate—and returned it 47y for game's opening score. Southern California strongly stretched lead to 24-0 as TB Ricky Bell totaled 167y rushing, and QB Vince Evans added nifty 36y TD run. Bruins (9-1-1), who came in averaging 37 pts per game, closed things up with 2 late window-dressing scores on 9y TD run by Brown and QB Jeff Dankworth's 1y keeper.

Stanford 27 CALIFORNIA 24: Cardinals (6-5) won Big Game for outgoing coach Jack Christiansen, who was fired on Friday. Stanford used late FUM REC to pull out win. Ahead 24-19 with less than 3 mins remaining, Golden Bears (5-6) were trying to run out clock from deep in own territory when TB Markey Crane fumbled pitchout. As was his custom, DE Duncan McColl was man-on-spot for Stanford D, recovering big-break FUM on 2YL. Bears D manfully stopped 2 runs before Stanford TB Ron Inge scored winning TD on 1y run. Cal's Crane had scored earlier in 4th Q on 13y run only single play after 24y INT RET by S Mike O'Brien. Both teams alternated QBs with Cal QB Joe Roth throwing for 100y and TD in his final appearance, while Cards QBs Guy Benjamin and Mike Cordova combined for 297y with each throwing TD pass.

November 27, 1976

(Th'g) Texas A&M 27 TEXAS 3: Texas (4-5-1) lost 2nd straight to rivals in painful fashion, losing 7 TOs, committing 11 PENs, rushing for 73y, and completing only 4-17 passes. Texas A&M (9-2), led by 109y rushing and 2 TDs by FB George Woodard, scored TDs on drives of 20y and 6y following Texas TOs. HB Johnny "Lam" Jones was leading gainer for Longhorns with 20/54y. Texas had not lost 2 straight to Aggies since 1909-10.

(Fri) Pittsburgh 24 PENN STATE 7: TB Tony Dorsett added 224y to all-time total (6,082y) as Pitt (11-0) topped in-state rivals for 1st time since 1965. Penn State (7-4) drew 1st blood as it scored on QB Chuck Fusina's 21y TD pass to FB Bob Torrey. Lions were done scoring, but Dorsett was just getting warmed up. In 2nd Q Dorsett tied game with 6y run. Panther coach Johnny Majors next surprised Nittany Lions by switching Dorsett to FB, from where he exploded in 2nd H with 173y behind unbalanced line. Majors then stunned everyone by taking Tennessee job after game.

(Fri) Oklahoma 20 NEBRASKA 17: Nebraska (7-3-1) faithful were grumbling after preseason no. 1 Huskers lost 5th straight to Oklahoma (8-2-1) and dropped 3rd home game of season. With time elapsing Sooners turned to trickery to pull out late win. Two huge plays set up winning score: 47y pass from HB Woody Shepard to WR Steve Rhodes and 32y pass play featuring lateral from Rhodes to HB Elvis Peacock. Peacock then scored on 2y run. Trick plays were only passes attempted by OU all day. Peacock rushed for 88y and all 3 OU scores, including 50y jaunt early in 4th Q, while HB Horace Ivory had game-high 101y rushing. Nebraska had taken 17-7 lead entering 4th Q on TD runs of 7y by WB Curtis Craig and 4y by IB Rick Berns.

Navy 38 Army 10: TB Joe Gattuso, Jr. scored 3 TDs and rushed for 128y in helping his father's old teammate, coach George Welsh, go 4-0 vs. Army (5-6). Gattuso became 5th Navy (4-7) back to score 3 TDs versus Army, while Midshipmen totaled 428y with no TOs. Army QB Leamon Hall was harassed into 13-31 passing with 3 INTs. Telling drive for Cadets was opener they took from own 4YL to Navy 9YL before losing FUM. It was that kind of day. Gattuso scored later in period from 2YL before Army tied game at 7-7 on 11y run by HB Greg King. Navy took lead for good in 2nd Q on 11y TD pass from QB Bob Leszczynski to WR Phil McConkey before breaking it open with 17 pts in 3rd Q.

GEORGIA 13 Georgia Tech 10: Bulldogs (10-1) needed K Allan Leavitt's last-sec 23y FG to pull out win. Game was scoreless until QB Ray Goff capped 80y drive with 3y TD run late in 2nd Q. After 2nd H KO, Bulldogs went to Georgia Tech 5YL before settling for FG and 10-0 edge. Yellow Jackets (4-6-1) answered with FG set up by INT and fashioned 79y drive that featured QB Gary Lanier's 14y run on which his lateral to TB David Sims tacked on 14y more. TB Eddie Lee Ivery's 26y TD run came on next play. Tie was broken after exchange of FUMs in Tech territory with Georgia gaining ball with less than 3 mins remaining. Goff's sneak on 4th down kept drive going and after 3 more rushes, Leavitt booted game-winner. Both FB Al Pollard (24/112y) and HB Kevin McLee (30/103y) topped century mark rushing for Georgia.

SOUTHERN CALIFORNIA 17 Notre Dame 13: Trojans (10-1) used pass game to win 50th anniversary of rivalry. Backup QB Rob Hertel's timely tossing broke 0-0 tie on 6y TD pass to WR Shelton Diggs late in 1st H. It capped 67y drive featuring Hertel's 6 completions. Starting USC QB Vince Evans followed with 63y TD strike to WR Randy Simmrin (6/121y) early in 3rd Q that drowned Irish (8-3). Notre Dame blew 6 chances in Trojans territory that came up empty, but scored 2 4th Q TDs to rally. Southern California TB Ricky Bell, still gimpy with ankle injury, rushed for 75y in final regular season game. He gamely played some FB and made key block on DE Ross Browner that allowed Hertel to get off 27y pass to TE William Gay on 1st TD drive. Browner was smidgeon late reaching Evans on 63y TD pass. Irish HB Al Hunter rushed for 115y. USC was now 7-2-1 in last 10 games of famed intersectional series.

December 4, 1976

TEXAS 29 Arkansas 12: Final game of legendary careers of Arkansas coach Frank Broyles and Texas coach Darrell Royal was anti-climatic as Longhorns (5-5-1) led throughout in what proved to be humble battle for 5th place in SWC. Texas FB Earl Campbell rushed for 131y and 2 TDs and K Russell Erxleben chipped in 3 FGs. Hogs (5-5-1) trailed 13-6 entering 4th Q before allowing 3 scores. Razorbacks RB Ben Cowins gained 87y to win SWC rushing title. Meeting at midfield post-game, coaches simply said "I love you" to each other before final exiting of field.

TEXAS TECH 24 Baylor 21: Red Raiders (10-1) gained tie for 1st place in SWC. After breaking free for 77y TD run in game's 1st min, Texas Tech QB Rodney Allison scored again and directed late winning drive. In opening Q, Red Raiders marched 90y to QB sneak and 14-0 lead. Bears (7-3-1) refused to fold, tying game at 14-14, including 50y pass from QB Sammy Bickham to WR Tommy Davidson. Baylor took 21-17 lead on 1y TD run by TB Gary Blair, who set school record with 199y rushing. Tech regained lead with 89y drive early in 4th Q that TB Larry Isaac ended on 5y TD run. Bears' final drive ended on short 48y FG try by K Lester Belrose.

Conference Standings

Ivy League
Brown	6-1
Yale	6-1
Harvard	4-3
Dartmouth	4-3
Columbia	2-5
Penn	2-5
Cornell	2-5
Princeton	2-5

Atlantic Coast
Maryland	5-0
North Carolina	4-1
Wake Forest	3-3
Duke	2-3-1
North Carolina State	2-3
Virginia (a)	1-4
Clemson	0-4-1

(a) Loss to Virginia Tech counted in ACC standing

Southeastern
Georgia	5-1
Alabama	5-2
Mississippi State	4-2
Florida	4-2
Kentucky	4-2
Mississippi	3-4
LSU	2-4
Tennessee	2-4
Auburn	2-4
Vanderbilt	0-6

Southern
East Carolina	4-1
William & Mary	3-2
Appalachian State	2-2-1
Furman	2-2-1
VMI	2-3
Citadel	1-4

Big Ten
Michigan	7-1
Ohio State	7-1
Minnesota	4-4
Illinois	4-4
Indiana	4-4
Purdue	4-4
Iowa	3-5
Michigan State	3-5
Wisconsin	3-5
Northwestern	1-7

Mid-American
Ball State	4-1
Kent State	6-2
Ohio U	6-2
Western Michigan	6-3
Central Michigan	4-3
Bowling Green	4-3
Miami (O)	2-4
Toledo	2-6
Eastern Michigan	1-5
Northern Illinois	0-6

Big Eight
Oklahoma	5-2
Oklahoma State	5-2
Colorado	5-2
Iowa State	4-3
Nebraska	4-3
Missouri	3-4
Kansas	2-5
Kansas	0-7

Valley
Tulsa	2-1-1
New Mexico State	2-1-1
Wichita State	2-2
West Texas State	1-1-2
Drake	1-3

Southwest
Texas Tech	7-1
Houston	7-1
Texas A&M	6-2
Baylor	4-3-1
Texas	4-4
Arkansas	3-4-1
Rice	2-6
SMU	2-6
TCU	0-8

Western Athletic
Brigham Young	6-1
Wyoming	6-1
Arizona State	4-3
Utah	3-3
Arizona	3-4
New Mexico	3-4
Colorado State	2-4
Texas El Paso	0-7

Pacific Eight			Pacific Coast Athletic	
Southern California	7-0		San Jose State	4-0
UCLA	6-1		Fresno State	3-1
Stanford	5-2		Long Beach State	2-2
California	3-4		Fullerton State	1-3
Washington	3-4		Pacific	0-4
Washington State	2-5			
Oregon	1-6			
Oregon State	1-6			

1976 Major Bowl Games

Tangerine Bowl (Dec. 18): Oklahoma State 49 Brigham Young 21

Rematch of 1974 Fiesta Bowl won by Cowboys (9-3) as TB Terry Miller rushed for 173y and 4 TDs and Oklahoma State D forced 5 TOs. Miller led ground game that churned up 375y to BYU's 46y. Cougars, behind QB Gifford Nielsen, won aerial game 209y to 27y, but lost war. Nielsen's 4 INTs did not help, especially 1 returned 36y by Oke State DT Chris Dawson that opened scoring. Brigham Young (9-3) answered Dawson's TD with 1y TD run by FB Todd Christensen. Oklahoma State took lead for good on scoring runs of 1y by QB Charlie Weatherbie and 3y by Miller. Nielsen then threw his only TD of game, 27y pass to TE Tod Thompson, as Cougars stayed within striking distance at 21-14. It was Miller time, and Miller raced 78y for TD to close 1st H. Although Brigham Young FB Dave Lowry took 2nd H KO 102y to pull Cougars within 7 pts again, Cowboys ran off 3 TDs in 3rd Q, 2 coming from fabulous Miller.

Liberty Bowl (Dec. 20): Alabama 36 UCLA 6

Crimson Tide won 2nd straight bowl game with ease, posting largest margin to date in 18-year Liberty Bowl history. Alabama (9-3) blew game open early with 17-pt 1st Q, including 44y INT TD RET by LB Barry Krauss (10 solo tackles, 8 assists). In 2nd Q, HB Tony Nathan (67y rushing) faked run, then downfield pass before throwing to wide-open QB Jack O'Rear for back-breaking 20y TD. Bruins (9-2-1) topped Alabama in O, 380y to 372y, but were awful once they smelled Tide EZ, despite entering game with 35-pts per game avg. Krauss had something to do with that as he keyed 2 GLS, including GLS he finished with 4th down tackle. Bruins also had 4 TOs to none by Alabama. Bruins FB Theotis Brown was game-high rusher with 102y including 61y on powerful 4th Q TD run.

Fiesta Bowl (Dec. 25): Oklahoma 41 Wyoming 7

Wyoming (8-4) had absolutely no answer for Oklahoma team desirous of returning to playing on New Year's Day in 1977. Sooners (9-2-1) could have left their punt unit back home in Norman as they were not needed at all. Oklahoma rushed for 415y with 16 backs getting piece of action, under guiding hand of QB Thomas Lott (13/79y). Backup HB Woody Shepard (7/85y) topped y chart and scored team's final TD on 8y run. That gave Oklahoma 41-0 lead, but shutout was denied when Cowboys FB Robbie Wright scored with 22 secs remaining. Starting OU HB Elvis Peacock rushed for 77y and 2 TDs. Sooners D made 5 INTs and forced FUM.

Gator Bowl (Dec. 27): Notre Dame 20 Penn State 9

Match-up of nation's power independents went way of Irish (9-3), who scored 20 1st H pts and held Penn State off from there. Notre Dame HB Al Hunter (102y rushing), who became 1st Irish back to top 1,000y (1,058) in season, stamped his name on 1st H: he gained 76y and scored 2 TDs. Nittany Lions (7-5) had gotten off to good start with 55y drive to K Tony Capozzoli's 26y FG. HB Terry Eurick quickly got Notre Dame going with 65y RET of ensuing KO. QB Rick Slager (10-19/141y) then moved O to 1st of 2 short TD runs by Hunter for 7-3 lead. Irish scored 3 more times in 2nd Q, twice on 23y FGs by K Dave Reeve. Penn State improved its play in 2nd H, but Lions rally was snuffed by Notre Dame D that picked off QB Chuck Fusina (14-33/118y) twice in 4th Q. Fusina reached EZ on 8y pass to FB Matt Suhey. As usual, TE Ken MacAfee (5/78y) was Slager's favorite target, while Penn State WR Jimmy Cefalo caught 5/60y.

Peach Bowl (Dec. 31): Kentucky 21 North Carolina 0

With huge support of Wildcat fans that flocked to Atlanta after 25-year bowl absence, Kentucky (8-4) routed Tar Heels (9-3) in 2nd H as FB Rod Stewart rushed for 104y, 3 TDs. Wildcats D surrendered only 108y and 5 1st downs. Teams combined for scoreless 1st H before Cats converted FUM by Carolina QB Matt Kupec on his 21YL into Stewart's 1y TD run early in 3rd Q. Kentucky added TD drives of 57y and 47y in 4th Q to finish off fading Tar Heels. North Carolina O was highly limited by loss of TB Mike Voight, 5th all-time rusher in NCAA history, who was felled by ankle injury in practice. Without him, Tar Heels O was swamped by Kentucky D, led by outstanding DE Art Still. Wildcats used ball control throughout game, rushing 70/318y.

Bluebonnet Bowl (Dec. 31): Nebraska 27 Texas Tech 24

Game turned in 3rd Q when Huskers (9-3-1) wiped out 24-14 deficit on strength of 2 quick TDs. Nebraska pulled within 24-20 on IB Rick Berns' 18y scoring jaunt, which followed 49y pass from WB Curtis Craig to WR Chuck Malito (3/107y). After Huskers D held, Nebraska DBs Ted Harvey and Kent Smith partially blocked punt to provide possession at Texas Tech 23YL. QB Vince Ferragamo (13-23/183y) quickly took reigns, tossing 23y scoring pass to Malito for what proved to be game-winning pts. Nebraska D dominated 4th Q, with big play turned in by DE Reg Gast with FUM REC that ended final Red Raiders (10-2) threat with 1:34 left. QB Rodney Allison (15-23/193y) was brilliant in defeat, rushing for 89y to enhance pair of TD passes. Texas Tech TB Billy Taylor caught both of Allison's TD passes and rushed for another score. Berns finished with 118y rushing to lead Cornhuskers.

Sugar Bowl: Pittsburgh 27 Georgia 3

Sure TB Tony Dorsett rushed for 202y, but Panthers (12-0) proved they were more than 1-man team with decisive championship-producing victory. QB Matt Cavanaugh (10-18/192y) displayed aerial skills in leading Panthers to 2 early TDs, firing 36y pass to TB Elliott Walker to set up 6y TD keeper and hitting WR Gordon Jones with 59y TD pass for 14-0 lead. Bulldogs (10-2) had to fight to gain 1st downs against Pitt D and did not come close to scoring any 1st H pts. Panthers LB Jim Cramer set up 3rd TD with INT that started 67y drive. Dorsett, who broke free for 22y run, scored from 11y out for 21-0 lead. Georgia was just about done at that point, scoring its only pts on 25y FG by K Allan Leavitt after taking advantage of Pitt FUM. QB Ray Goff led Georgia with 76y rushing, but he passed meager 1-4. Throwing specialist, QB Matt Robinson, couldn't rally Bulldogs as team's passing stats were awful 3-22/46y, 4 INTs. As Georgia coach Vince Dooley confirmed after game, "My hat's off to them (Pitt). They proved today they are the best team in the country."

Cotton Bowl: Houston 30 Maryland 21

Cougars (10-2) came out flying against Maryland, jumping to 21-0 lead in 1st Q despite losing FUM on 1st possession. After missed FG by Terps (11-1), QB Danny Davis marshaled Houston's Veer attack 80y to FB Dyral Thomas' 11y TD run. Cougars CB Mark Mohr set up next 2 TDs with blocked punt and FUM REC, both occurring in Maryland territory. Houston RB Alois Blackwell scored twice for 21-0 edge, his 2nd score coming from 33y out. QB Mark Manges (17-32/179y) finally put Maryland on board with 6y TD run. Houston matched that with 33y scoring pass to WR Don Bass to cap 97y drive. Although trailing 27-7 at H, Terps had 1 thing in their favor: Houston's propensity to drop ball. Houston lost pair of FUMs that were translated into Maryland TDs to trim margin to only 21-15. With time elapsing, Davis (5-8/108y) marched Cougars 81y—with Thomas converting 4th-and-1 with 32y run—to set up clinching 28y FG by K Lennard Coplin. Early in vital drive, Davis shook off 5 defenders to complete key 3rd down pass. Blackwell rushed for 149y and Thomas for 104y as Cougars surprisingly shredded nation's 2nd best rush D for 428y.

Rose Bowl: Southern California 14 Michigan 6

Teams were evenly matched except for Trojans' solid passing game. Southern California QB Vince Evans (14-20/181y, INT) was difference-maker in leading 2 TD drives. Wolverines (10-2) drew 1st blood on 1y TD run by TB Rob Lytle (18/67y) in 2nd Q, but could not muster power thereafter against USC's stingy D. Troy DT Walt Underwood's block of x-pt after Lytle's TD allowed Trojans (11-1) to take 7-6 edge later in 2nd Q on 1y run by Evans on 4th down rollout. With TB Ricky Bell out of game in 1st Q with concussion, super-sub TB Charles White rushed 32y/114y. Wolverines, nation's O leader with 448y avg, were hard-pressed to move. Michigan QB Rick Leach completed only 4-12/76y and was harassed all day by LB Rod Martin, who forced 2 FUMs and added 4th quarter sack. Leach hit 32y pass to WB Jim Smith early in 4th Q as Michigan moved to Trojans 33YL, but lost ball on downs as Trojans LB Eric Williams and DT Gary Jeter made tackles for losses. Wolverines, who finished with 231y, had final drive end on downs at USC 17YL. Southern California added insurance TD on 7y run by White late in 4th Q to cap 58y drive that featured Evans' 27y pass to WR Randy Simmrin. USC coach John Robinson won 1st Rose Bowl as head coach and USC propelled its impressive all-time Rose Bowl record to 15-6.

Orange Bowl: Ohio State 27 Colorado 10

Buffaloes returned to Orange Bowl for 1st time since 1961, but found little joy in visit. Colorado (8-4) started fast with 10-0 lead, but Ohio State (9-2-1) turned to its bench for game-changing sub. QB Rod Gerald, former starter who missed 4 games with back injury, came in to ignite Buckeyes attack with 81y rushing as Ohio ground out 271y, twice as many as Colorado's 134y. On his 1st play, Gerald dashed 17y, and Buckeyes took off from there. Ohio State took lead at end of 1st H as FB Pete Johnson capped 99y drive with 3y TD run, his 58th career TD. By then Buckeyes D was controlling field position, with help from booming KOs and punts by K-P Tom Skladany (2 FGs). After throwing 1st Q TD pass of 11y to WB Emery Moorehead, QB Jeff Knapple (8-22/137, 2 INTs) could not rally Buffs. Game marked return of hosting agreement with Big 8 Conf after 11-year absence.

Sun Bowl (Jan. 2): Texas A&M 37 Florida 14

While Aggies O gained 365y behind 124y by FB George Woodard, more impressive unit for Texas A&M (10-2) was D that shutout prolific Gators in 1st H. By game's end, A&M had held Florida (8-4) to 172y rushing and 53y passing. Florida trailed 24-0 by time WR Wes Chandler scored on 29y run in 3rd Q. Texas A&M answered with 4y TD run by Woodard, his 2nd score. Later, Woodard added TD on 15y pass from QB David Walker (11-18/122y, INT). Just as impressive was Aggies' kicking game as, in 2nd Q, K Tony Franklin booted all-bowl record 62y FG, with plenty of distance to spare. HB Larry Brinson was useful to Florida with 10/64y rushing.

Final AP Poll January 4

1 Pittsburgh (59)	1234		11 Alabama	331
2 Southern California (3)	1118		12 Notre Dame	321
3 Michigan	847		13 Texas Tech	276
4 Houston	804		14 Oklahoma State	190
5 Oklahoma	638		15 UCLA	172
6 Ohio State	510		16 Colorado	52
7 Texas A&M	487		17 Rutgers	50
8 Maryland	445		18 Kentucky	30
9 Nebraska	422		19 Iowa State	14
10 Georgia	388		20 Mississippi State	13

1976 Top Performance Formula

1 Pittsburgh	1.7271
2 Southern California	1.6425
3 Michigan	1.6286
4 Maryland	1.5946
5 Georgia	1.5647
6 Texas A&M	1.5205
7 Ohio State	1.5144
8 Texas Tech	1.4936
9 UCLA	1.4767
10 Houston	1.4742
11 Rutgers	1.4729
12 Oklahoma	1.4674
13 Alabama	1.4316
14 Oklahoma State	1.4288
15 Nebraska	1.4067
16 Notre Dame	1.4042
17 Iowa State	1.3972
18 Mississippi State	1.3895
19 Kentucky	1.3302
20 Florida	1.3247

1976 Top Opponent Records

1 Missouri	.6822
2 Kansas State	.6410
3 Florida	.6280
4 Miami	.6271
5 Kentucky	.6151
6 Auburn	.6018
7 Navy	.5991
8 Ohio State	.5927
9 West Virginia	.5885
10 Texas	.5877
11 Georgia	.5847
12 Colorado	.5833
13 Oklahoma State	.5827
14 Southern Methodist	.5746
15 California	.5652
16 Oklahoma	.5640
17 Illinois	.5619
18 Vanderbilt	.5614
19 North Carolina State	.5540
20 Southern California	.5524

1976 Out-of-Conference Records

	W-L	Percentage	Bowl W-L
Big Eight	28-7-2	.7838	3-1
Southeastern	34-16-1	.6765	2-2
Southwest	17-11-1	.6034	2-1
Atlantic Coast	19-19-1	.5000	0-2
Pacific-8	16-17-1	.4853	1-1
Big Ten	14-15-2	.4839	1-1
Western Athletic	12-24	.3333	0-2

1976 Individual Statistical Leaders

RUSHING YARDS	Attempts	Yards	Avg.
Tony Dorsett, Pittsburgh	338	1948	5.8
Terry Miller, Oklahoma State	268	1541	5.8
Jerome Persell, Western Michigan	269	1505	5.6
Rob Lytle, Michigan	221	1469	6.6
Mike Voight, North Carolina	315	1407	4.5
Mike Williams, New Mexico	258	1240	4.8
Ben Garry, Southern Mississippi	236	1236	5.2
Tony Reed, Colorado	264	1210	4.6
Jeff Logan, Ohio State	204	1169	5.7
Ben Cowins, Arkansas	183	1162	6.3

PASSING YARDS	Completions	Attempts	Yards	Pct.
Tommy Kramer, Rice	269	501	3317	53.7
Gifford Nielsen, Brigham Young	207	372	3192	55.6
Jack Thompson, Washington State	208	355	2762	58.6
Leamon Hall, Army	162	344	2174	47.1
Vince Ferragamo, Nebraska	145	254	2071	57.1
Guy Benjamin, Stanford	170	295	1982	57.6
Steve Haynes, Louisiana Tech	120	216	1981	55.6
Mark Miller, Bowling Green	126	245	1839	51.4
Joe Roth, California	154	295	1789	52.2
Dennis Sproul, Arizona State	111	243	1751	45.7

RECEIVING YARDS	Catches	Yards
Billy Ryckman, Louisiana Tech	77	1382
Keith Hartwig, Arizona	54	1134
Mike Levenseller, Washington State	67	1124
Wes Chandler, Florida	44	967
David Houser, Rice	52	931
Joe Stewart, Missouri	45	834
Preston Dennard, New Mexico	42	783
Mike Renfro, Texas Christian	42	773
Doug Cunningham, Rice	57	770
Kirk Gibson, Michigan State	39	748

1976 Consensus All-America Team
Offense

Tight End:	Ken MacAfee, Notre Dame
Split End:	Larry Seivers, Tennessee
Tackle:	Mike Vaughan, Oklahoma
	Chris Ward, Ohio State
Guard:	Joel Parrish, Georgia
	Mark Donahue, Michigan
Center:	Derrel Gofourth, Oklahoma State
Quarterback:	Tommy Kramer, Rice
Running Back:	Tony Dorsett, Pittsburgh
	Ricky Bell, Southern California
	Rob Lytle, Michigan
Placekicker:	Tony Franklin, Texas A&M

Defense

End:	Ross Browner, Notre Dame
	Bob Brudzinski, Ohio State
Tackle:	Wilson Whitley, Houston
	Gary Jeter, Southern California
	Joe Campbell, Maryland
Middle Guard:	Al Romano, Pittsburgh
Linebacker:	Robert Jackson, Texas A&M
	Jerry Robinson, UCLA
Back:	Bill Armstrong, Wake Forest
	Gary Green, Baylor
	Dennis Thurman, Southern California
	Dave Butterfield, Nebraska

1976 Heisman Trophy Vote

Tony Dorsett, senior tailback, Pittsburgh	2357
Ricky Bell, senior tailback, Southern California	1346
Rob Lytle, senior halfback, Michigan	413
Terry Miller, junior halfback, Oklahoma State	197
Tommy Kramer, senior quarterback, Rice	63

Other Major Award Winners

Maxwell (Player)	Tony Dorsett, senior tailback, Pittsburgh
Walter Camp (Player)	Tony Dorsett, senior tailback, Pittsburgh
Outland (Lineman)	Ross Browner, junior defensive end, Notre Dame
Lombardi (Lineman)	Wilson Whitley, senior, defensive tackle, Houston
AFCA Coach of the Year	Johnny Majors, Pittsburgh

1977

The Year of the Underdogs, the Tyler Rose Blooms at Tailback, and Wearing of the Green

In many ways 1977 was an odd year for college football. The head coach of the eventual national champions was underappreciated and seemingly in an underdog fight for his job at mid-season. The Heisman Trophy winner, who soon was considered to be an all-time great player, started the season as a Heisman underdog and did not even win his region in balloting for the award. The biggest favorites in the major bowls not only lost, they were manhandled by underdogs. When all was said and done, Notre Dame (11-1) and its embattled head coach Dan Devine were champions, edging Alabama (11-1), and Texas (11-1) back Earl Campbell was the Heisman Trophy winner.

Prior to his senior season of 1977, Campbell, the highly-recruited big back from Tyler, Texas, was considered something of an underachiever out of the fullback slot in the Longhorns' Wishbone. He was then moved to I-formation tailback by new Texas coach Fred Akers. Suddenly, Campbell and the Longhorns became dominant, especially after beating Oklahoma (10-2) for the first time since 1970. Akers seemed ready to become one of only three rookie coaches at that point in history to go undefeated, and he was in an excellent position to win a national championship during the first year on the job after taking over for Darrell Royal. Akers had served nine years as an assistant under Royal and two years as head coach at Wyoming. But in the Cotton Bowl, Notre Dame easily ended the dream, routing Texas 38-10 by forcing six turnovers.

The bowl loss by favored Texas opened the door for the second-ranked Oklahoma Sooners, who were facing Arkansas (11-1) on New Year's night in the Orange Bowl. The game was wrapped in controversy from the beginning as the Orange Bowl selection committee chose Arkansas over Penn State (11-1) out of fear that a Penn State loss in the last game regular season game against Pittsburgh (9-2-1) would ruin the match-up in Miami. The Nittany Lions nipped the Panthers in snowy Pittsburgh, but it was too late for them to renegotiate the Orange Bowl bid. The Arkansas Razorbacks, not the big, bad Sooners, were soon embroiled in a scandalous week prior to the game. Coach Lou Holtz, in his first year at Arkansas, suspended three players, including his leading rusher Ben Cowins, his back-up, Michael Forrest, and standout wide receiver Danny Bobo. The players, who had been caught in a room with a partially unclad female student, first sued the university for re-instatement, then dropped the suit. All three players were African-American and the remaining black players talked of a strike in solidarity for their teammates. The preparation for the Orange Bowl continued, and Oklahoma became more and more confident. Whether the Sooners were overconfident or overrated remains to be debated as the Razorbacks administered a completely unexpected 31-6 whipping.

The other underdog to pull a January upset was Washington (8-4), which stunned a Michigan (10-2) team that had been ranked no. 1 until late October when rival Minnesota (7-5) sprung an upset shutout. Huskies quarterback Warren Moon orchestrated an unpredictable offense that built a 24-0 lead in the Rose Bowl before holding on for 27-20 victory. His team's rally helped Michigan coach Bo Schembechler deal with yet another final-game disappointment.

The only favorite to win a major bowl was Alabama, which beat Ohio State (9-3) with surprisingly ease by a 35-6 margin. Bear Bryant's charges were passed in the final vote by a Notre Dame squad that was able to rout the undefeated no. 1 team. Crimson Tide fans were frustrated by the final vote, but myriad talent returned to launch successive national titles in the next two years.

Notre Dame pulled a little mysticism out of its leprechaun's bag as Devine decided to surprise his players by clothing them in old-school Kelly green jerseys for what turned out to be a momentous win at mid-season over Southern California (8-4). Newspapers reported with some dismay that the Fighting Irish, as Cotton Bowl visitors, couldn't wear green jerseys on New Year's Day, but Notre Dame did the next best thing. The Irish's white jerseys sported green numerals, and that Luck o' the Irish seemed to carry them over Texas for the national title.

A blue-clad school made waves in 1977. With only two winning seasons since 1965, Kentucky (10-1) knocked off ACC champion North Carolina (8-3-1) and dropped the season's only defeat on Penn State. The Wildcats were undefeated in SEC play, but Alabama had one more win to take the conference title. Unfortunately, Kentucky was on probation and ineligible to attend a bowl game, and a dark shadow soon engulfed the program and helped usher out coach Fran Curci, who had rebuilt the Wildcats.

While favorites won most of the big conference races, the Pacific-8 proved to be the wildest race, going down to the final play of the final game. A last-second field goal by Southern California knocked UCLA (7-4) out of the Rose Bowl and sent Washington to Pasadena for the first time in 14 seasons.

The Pac-8 also featured the debut of dynamic Stanford back Darrin Nelson, who became the first offensive player ever to rush for 1,000 yards and catch 50 passes in one year. The best back not named Campbell was Terry Miller of Oklahoma State (4-7), who actually beat Campbell in the southwest region voting and finished as runner-up in the Heisman balloting despite the Cowboys' disappointing season. Miller rushed for 4,581 yards in his career, fourth all-time at that point, and was twice named Big Eight player of the year. Finishing fourth in Heisman voting was Grambling quarterback Doug Williams, who became the first player from a predominantly black school to be named first-team Associated Press All-America.

Milestones

■ Rules Committee made major change to passing game, allowing offensive linemen downfield to block when receiver caught ball behind neutral zone.

■ Hall of Fame Bowl debuted in Birmingham, Ala., as Maryland defeated Minnesota. Name was changed to All-American Bowl in 1985.

■ Notre Dame became first school ever to collect $ 1 million payday for bowl game (Cotton Bowl).

■ Davey O'Brien, winner of 1938 Heisman Trophy in leading TCU to national championship, died at age 60 after long illness on November 18. Despite his 5'7", 155-lb frame, O'Brien was fearsome quarterback as runner, passer, kicker, and team leader. He set NFL record with 33 completions in 60 attempts as his Philadelphia Eagles beat Washington Redskins in 1940. Davey O'Brien Memorial Trophy was unveiled in 1977 to acknowledge best player in Southwest Conference. In 1981, format was changed to recognize best quarterback in nation.

■ Joe Roth, 21, who quarterbacked California to share of 1975 Pac-8 crown, died of melanoma on February 19. Dying at age 88 was Earle Edwards, coach with longest tenure (17 years) at North Carolina State. Edwards, who died on February 25, won 77 games from 1954-70 and beat Georgia in 1967 Liberty Bowl. Bernie Bierman, who coached Minnesota to national titles in 1936, 1940 and 1941, died at 82 on March 7. Bierman was back at Minnesota (1915) before embarking on coaching career, going 163-57-11 at four schools in 26 years. After leading Tulane to three straight SEC titles (1929-31), Bierman moved to his alma mater where he had five undefeated seasons. Long-time coach Buck Shaw died at age 77 on March 19. Although best known for his final game when his Philadelphia Eagles beat Green Bay Packers 17-13 for 1960 NFL championship, Shaw played for Knute Rockne at Notre Dame, coached Santa Clara to upset wins over LSU in 1936 and 1937 Sugar Bowls and, after stints at California and N.C. State, established new program at Air Force. West Virginia's Joe Stydahar, star tackle on college and pro levels (Chicago Bears), died at age 65 on March 24. Frosh FB Bob Vorhies, 18, of Virginia Tech died November 21 of heart failure in his sleep, after disciplinary drill for off-field issue.

■ Longest winning streaks entering season:

Rutgers 18	Pittsburgh 13	Southern California 11

■ Coaching Changes:

	Incoming	Outgoing
Arizona	Tony Mason	Jim Young
Arkansas	Lou Holtz	Frank Broyles
Clemson	Charley Pell	Red Parker
Cornell	Bob Blackman	George Seifert
Hawaii	Dick Tomey	Larry Price
Illinois	Gary Moeller	Bob Blackman
Miami	Lou Saban	Carl Selmer
Oregon	Rich Brooks	Don Read
Pittsburgh	Jackie Sherrill	Johnny Majors
Purdue	Jim Young	Alex Agase
Stanford	Bill Walsh	Jack Christiansen
Tennessee	Johnny Majors	Bill Battle
Texas	Fred Akers	Darrell Royal
Texas Christian	F.A. Dry	Jim Shofner
Texas-El Paso	Bill Michael	Gil Bartosh
Utah	Wayne Howard	Tom Lovat
Washington State	Warren Powers	Jackie Sherrill
Wyoming	Bill Lewis	Fred Akers

Preseason AP Poll

1 Oklahoma (23)	1068	11 UCLA	324
2 Michigan (19)	1020	12 Colorado	313
3 Notre Dame (10)	948	13 Penn State	238
4 Southern California (3)	766	14 Houston	219
5 Ohio State (2)	673	15 Nebraska	190
6 Alabama (1)	541	16 Mississippi State	124
7 Pittsburgh (2)	408	17t Arizona State	69
8 Texas Tech (1)	388	17t Florida	69
9 Texas A&M (1)	376	19 Georgia	40
10 Maryland	361	20 Oklahoma State	37

September 10, 1977

Notre Dame 19 PITTSBURGH 9: In defense of national title, Pittsburgh (0-1) scored early on 12y TD pass from QB Matt Cavanaugh to WR Gordon Jones, play that highly affected season. Notre Dame DE Willie Fry knocked down Cavanaugh as Pitt QB was throwing. Cavanaugh landed on his non-throwing hand, breaking his forearm. Panthers O unraveled without him, losing 4 FUMs deep in their own territory and managing only 6y O, 4 1st downs, and 7 TOs over final 3 Qs. Spirited effort by Pitt D held off Irish (1-0) until K Dave Reeve's 2 FGs in 4th Q gave ND lead of 12-9. Notre Dame had scored earlier on 5y TD pass from QB Rusty Lisch to TE Ken MacAfee. DE Hugh Green debuted for Panthers with 11 tackles, 2 sacks, and blocked punt.

Maryland 21 CLEMSON 14: Tigers (0-1) D was on prowl until Terps QB Larry Dick (5-7/118y) came off bench to throw 2 TD passes to pull out win. In relief of injured QB Mark Manges, Dick tied game on 25y pass to WB Chuck White on 3rd-and-19. Tying drive started with DB Lloyd Burruss' blocked FG. Maryland (1-0) D checked Tigers, and Dick delivered 3-play, 62y drive needed for 21st straight ACC victory. WR Jim Hagan, making 1st road trip in his 5th year, gobbled most of y when he caught short pass and raced 43y to EZ. Big play for Clemson had been 2nd Q 93y INT TD RET by CB Rex Varn to tie game at 7-7. Terps TB Steve Atkins rushed for 88y, TD.

California 27 TENNESSEE 17: Triumphant return of new Vols coach Johnny Majors to Knoxville took rude derailment as Cal (1-0) WR Charlie Young (11-25/154y, INT) broke 10-10 3rd Q tie with 58y scoring strike to frosh WR Floyd Eddings. Juco transfer Young also scored twice on runs, while Tennessee (0-1) QB Jimmy Streater (15/150y rushing) raced 80y to EZ to tie school record set by Majors in 1954. FB Paul Jones rushed for 128y for opportunistic Bears, who converted 4 Tennessee (0-1) FUMs into 17 pts en route to 1st win of season opener since 1968.

Michigan 37 ILLINOIS 9: Former Michigan asst coach Gary Moeller was brought to Champaign to build Illini (0-1) into something resembling program he left behind. His old team, however, spoiled debut of what would turn out to be Moeller's 3-year nightmare. Wolverines (1-0) TB Harlan Huckleby's FUM, after hit by LB John Sullivan, led to Illinois' early 3-0 lead, but he atoned for mistake with 128y rushing and 2 TDs, while QB Rick Leach threw 2 TDs. RB Clarence Baker scored Illinois' sole TD on 1y run late in 4th Q.

Washington State 19 NEBRASKA 10: After years of serving as Nebraska asst, new Cougars (1-0) coach Warren Powers knew how to win at Lincoln. Washington State QB Jack Thompson (18-30/174y) earned attention with 2 TD passes of 19y to WR Brian Kelly (8/102y). NG George Yarno finished off Nebraska with safety-producing sack of QB Randy Garcia in 4th Q. Cornhuskers (0-1) gained 470y, but self destructed with 3 lost FUMs inside Wazzu 10YL. They lost another FUM at own 25YL that set up Kelly's 1st TD grab. Huskers IB Rick Berns ran for 153y, 20y TD.

Texas Tech 17 BAYLOR 7: Teams traded spectacular scoring runs as QB Rodney Allison (14/85y) put Red Raiders (1-0) up with 54y run after faked pitchout before Baylor FB George Hawthorne tied things up with 80y jaunt. Allison then led backup unit on 75y drive that he capped with winning 4y TD throw to FB Jimmy Williams. Earlier in drive, Williams took pitch from Allison and raced 38y down sideline for 1st down at Bears (0-1) 12YL. Tech K Don Adams' 24y FG provided 2nd H insurance.

Mississippi State 27 WASHINGTON 18: Mississippi State (2-0) dominated Huskies, gaining 485y total O with 340y on ground. State FB Dennis Johnson rushed for 113y and caught 1 of 2 TDs thrown by QB Bruce Threadgill. After Bulldogs HB Len Copeland caught 44y scoring pass for 17-6 lead, Threadgill reached EZ again, tossing short pass to Johnson that went 81y for TD pass play. Washington (0-1) K Steve Robbins tied school mark with 4 FGs, while TB Joe Steele had 73y and 58y KO RETs and 1y TD run.

(Mon) HOUSTON 17 Ucla 13: "Veer" vs. "Son of Veer" meeting was won by undervalued Houston, originators of Veer O. Game turned on injuries to Bruins RB Theotis Brown and K Frank Corral 4 plays apart in 2nd Q with UCLA (0-1) comfortably ahead 13-3. Bruins backup K Michael Coulter missed FGs of 23 and 27y, while S Ken Easley had to replace Corral as P to poor reviews. Houston QB Danny Davis (11-18/147y) led 2 long TD drives in 2nd H to pull out victory. Davis nearly was game's goat with lost FUM, Cougars' 6th, on his own 38YL with 4:49 left. Bruins QB Rick Bashore (16-27/245y), who had thrown 19y TD pass to WR Homer Butler in 1st H, came up 1y short on 4th-and-10 pass to HB James Owens.

AP Poll September 12

1 Michigan (42)	1162	11 Maryland	298
2 Southern California (4)	980	12 Colorado	261
3 Notre Dame (9)	894	13 Mississippi State	150
4 Alabama (1)	771	14 UCLA	111
5 Oklahoma (2)	701	15 Oklahoma State	86
6 Ohio State (1)	647	16 Pittsburgh	78
7 Texas A&M	502	17 Georgia	73
8 Texas Tech (1)	498	18 Texas (1)	72
9 Houston (1)	422	19 Florida	42
10 Penn State	375	20 Brigham Young	34

September 17, 1977

West Virginia 24 MARYLAND 16: Upset victim Terps (1-1) dug hole with 4 1st H TOs that contributed to 24-0 West Virginia lead. Mountaineers (2-0) scored on 2 TD runs by TB Dave Riley (15/108y) and 54y TD bomb from QB Dan Kendra (11-18/160y, INT) to WR Cedric Thomas. After scoring twice in 3rd Q to pull within 24-14, Terps scored 2 pts after WVU botched punt snap. WR Vince Kinney (7/121y) then took free-kick to 5YL to leave 4 cracks for TD. But, Maryland gained only 3y to end threat and wasted another chance inside West Virginia 20YL in 4th Q. Final desperation pass by Terps QB Larry Dick (18-24/234y, INT) fell incomplete in EZ.

PENN STATE 31 Houston 14: Nittany Lions (2-0) unleashed balanced attack on weary Houston squad playing its 2nd game in 6 days. Penn State rushed for 276y, and QB Chuck Fusina completed 15-23/245y. Cougars (1-1) had game tied 7-7 on RB Alois Blackwell's 1st of 2 TDs, but Lions reeled off 13 straight pts to take control. Houston lost Veer magician, QB Donnie Davis, with shoulder separation, and was blanked in 2nd H. Afterward, coach Bill Yeoman answered question about injuries beyond that of Davis: "That's like asking Mrs. Lincoln if anyone else was hurt."

Grambling 35 Morgan State 19 (New York): Big Apple spotlight was on Grambling (2-0) QB Doug Williams, and he excelled in it. Williams (21-36/370y, 4 TDs, INT) lifted his TD pass total to 9 in 2 games and established credentials as Heisman candidate. Most of Williams' passes found either TE Mike Moore (7/142y, TD) or WR Robert Woods (6/106y), who opened scoring with catch of 51y bomb. Morgan State (1-1) QB Allen Rose threw for 201y, but had his 2 TD tosses overshadowed by 3 INTs.

Clemson 7 GEORGIA 6: Tigers (1-1) won for 1st time in Athens since 1914 behind brilliant D effort. Both Ds excelled in 1st H that ended 0-0. Bulldogs (1-1) forced punt from deep in Clemson's territory on Tigers' 1st series of 2nd H. But, Georgia CB Billy Woods fumbled punt right back to Tigers at his 48YL. Clemson QB Steve Fuller used his NFL-bound receiving corps to move into scoring position, hitting WR Jerry Butler with 15y pass and WR Dwight Clark with 17y effort. Clemson scored on 2y run by TB Lester "Rubber Duck" Brown. Georgia was kept off scoreboard until very late: QB Jeff Pyburn flipped 8y TD to TE Ulysses Norris with 6 secs left, only 2 plays after Norris threw 50y pass to WR Jesse Murray (6/112y). Bulldogs went for win, but game ended on overthrown 2-pt pass. TB Warren Ratchford rushed for 77y for Clemson.

MISSISSIPPI 20 Notre Dame 13: For all its bumbling—5 TOs, blocked punt, and myriad PENs—Notre Dame (1-1) took 13-10 lead with 4:53 left on K Dave Reeve's 28y FG. With Ole Miss (2-1) Bobby Garner wilting in high humidity, coach Ken Cooper turned to former starter, QB Tim Ellis, hero of Alabama upset in 1976. Ellis hit for 68y on winning 80y TD drive and delivered 10y TD to FB Jim Storey, who had caught 10y scoring pass from Garner earlier. Notre Dame's final 2 hollow drives ended on FUM by FB Jerome Heavens (70y, TD rushing), which set up Ole Miss K Hoppy Langley's 27y insurance FG, and on INT by QB Rusty Lisch.

INDIANA 24 Louisiana State 21: Traveling 88y and 70y to pull out upset win, Hoosiers (1-1) rallied in 4th Q. Indiana scored on 19y TD pass from QB Scott Arnett to TE Dave Harangody and 11y run by TB Ric Enis. Confident LSU (0-1) had built 21-10 lead behind TB Charles Alexander, who rushed for 122y and 2 TDs. With Indiana rushing for 282y to 280y for Tigers, difference was Arnett's 148y passing.

IOWA 12 Iowa State 10: Bitterness had ended in-state rivalry, but calmness and Ds reigned in series revival after 43 years. Hawkeyes upset Iowa State (1-1) behind quick D that held Cyclones to 96y total O. Iowa (2-0) was not much better, gaining 192y, but managed to score 2 early TDs. Bucking for spot in starting line-up, Iowa TB Dennis Mosley raced 77y for his team's 1st TD, while steady FB Jon Lazar added eventual winning TD later in 1st Q on 10y run. Lazar's TD was set up by FUM by Iowa State QB Terry Rubley after being hit by Hawks DE Jim Molini. Cyclones DB Tom Buck scored on 63y punt RET.

NEBRASKA 31 Alabama 24: Nebraska (1-1) righted its season, using 5 INTs to upend Crimson Tide. Despite TOs, Alabama (1-1) tied it at 24-24 early in 4th Q on 1y TD run by HB Tony Nathan (16/90y). Huskers responded with 80y drive, keyed by QB Tom Sorley's 33y pitch to WR Tim Smith, that ended on winning 1y scoring dive by IB Rick Berns (23/128y). Nebraska DB Jim Pillen was hero with 2 late INTs of Bama QB Jeff Rutledge, who would not throw another pick until 2nd week of 1978, school-record 100 straight passes. Berns scored 3 TDs, 2 on short runs and 7y reception, while Alabama WR Ozzie Newsome caught 8/132y.

ARKANSAS 28 Oklahoma State 6: Although Cowboys (1-1) TB Terry Miller gained 24/132y, Razorback (2-0) RB Ben Cowins was dominant player, scoring twice among his 21/203y rushing. Cowins opened scoring with 1y TD run in 1st Q that was matched by teammate QB Houston Nutt for 14-0 lead. Hogs went 80y on 2nd Q drive, capped by WR Danny Bobo's 22y run on reverse for commanding 3-TD lead. Cowins added 72y scoring burst in 3rd Q, while Cowboys finally mustered 4th Q drive to 1y TD keeper by QB Jimmy Derrick. LB Larry Jackson sparked Arkansas D with 20 tackles.

Oregon 29 TEXAS CHRISTIAN 24: Ducks (1-1) won for 1st time under coach Rich Brooks despite blowing 3-TD lead. Oregon S Kenny Bryant returned INT 97y early in 4th Q for 24-3 lead. Actually Bryant never reached EZ, but was credited with TD as TCU LB Steve Barker came off bench to tackle him midway downfield. Horned Frogs (0-2) rallied behind backup QB Don Harris, who threw TDs of 17y to WR Tony Accomando and 23y to WR Mike Renfro. With lead cut to 24-17, Ducks went to air with disastrous results as QB Jack Henderson (12-22/115y) threw INT returned 39y for TD by DB Barry Crayton. With game tied, Oregon DT Neil Elshire made clutch sack of Harris for safety, but in doing so was lost for season with knee injury. Ducks K Roy Geiger added 39y insurance FG.

AP Poll September 19

1 Michigan (42)	1094	11 Notre Dame	206
2 Southern California (5)	1032	12 Mississippi State	204
3 Oklahoma (7)	955	13 Florida	190
4 Ohio State (2)	877	14 Nebraska	161
5 Penn State (5)	717	15 Washington State	129
6 Texas A&M	708	16 Arkansas	108
7 Texas Tech	631	17 West Virginia	83
8 Colorado	435	18 UCLA	80
9 Texas (1)	287	19 Houston	73
10 Alabama	219	20 Brigham Young	64

September 24, 1977

SYRACUSE 22 Washington 20: Orangemen (1-2) shook off 6-game losing streak on K David Jacobs' 31y FG with 23 secs left. Syracuse QB Bill Hurley (20/118y rushing) led winning 57y drive, busting runs for 3/42y. Washington had taken late 20-19 lead on QB Warren Moon's 4y run, but his subsequent 2-pt pass conv sailed incomplete. Moon was Huskies' dominant force, completing 16-25/257y with TDs of 25y and 51y to WR Spider Gaines (7/169y) that built 14-10 H lead.

Florida 24 MISSISSIPPI STATE 22 (Jackson): Bulldogs (2-1) overcame 17-0 deficit with 22 straight pts and were poised to deliver deathblow on 4th-and-1 at Gator 33YL. But, Florida MG Scott Hutchinson (18 tackles) stacked up run to end threat. Gators (2-0) answered with 67y march to QB Terry LeCount's winning 16y TD run with 57 secs left. Gators had used 2nd Q burst to build early lead, scoring 1st on 80y run by HB Tony Green and doubling lead on 13y scoring lob pass from sub QB John Brantley to WR Wes Chandler. Bulldogs responded to 3 FUM RECs deep in Florida end, setting up 2 TD runs by HB James Jones and another by FB Dennis Johnson.

Auburn 14 TENNESSEE 12: While hiring of Tennessee (1-2) coach Johnny Majors was major news in off-season, it was an Auburn newcomer, frosh TB James Brooks, who dominated this match-up. Brooks dashed Vols' hopes with 112y as Auburn (2-1) rallied for game's final 14 pts. Tigers scored late in 2nd Q on 78y drive to QB John Crane's 25y TD pass to WR Byron Franklin. Auburn then took lead in 3rd Q after Brooks raced 40y to Vols 4YL, to set up 5y TD run by FB William Andrews. Tennessee had entire 4th Q to answer, but lost FUM on Tiger 1YL and missed late 36y FG by K Jim Gaylor. Two botched punts contributed to Auburn's early deficit.

Miami 23 FLORIDA STATE 17: Canes (1-2) surged early and late to win in-state rivalry. Miami took 10-0 1st Q lead on 24y TD pass from QB E.J. Baker to RB Ken Johnson and 17y FG by K Chris Dennis. Seminoles (2-1) reeled off next 17 pts as QB Jimmy Jordan (13-38/131y) found his moment of success against Hurricanes D with 27y pass to TB Larry Key to set up FG and 19y TD pass to WR Kurt Unglaub. With Baker and FB Ottis Anderson knocked out with injuries, Miami found answers in backups and alert D that picked off Jordan 4 times. Miami frosh QB Kenny McMillian (8-10/80y) threw 3y TD to TE Karl Monroe to tie game early in 4th Q and led drives to 2 more FGs by Dennis, both from 47y away.

MINNESOTA 27 Ucla 13: In shutting down Bruins high-powered O, Minnesota (2-1) pulled off stunning upset. Gophers' 1st-team D posted shutout as UCLA (1-2) scored TDs on 95y INT RET by LB Jerry Robinson and 1y TD run by HB Freeman McNeil against Minnesota reserves. By time McNeil scored late in 4th Q, Gophers had all its 27 pts. Minny FB Jeff Thompson (18/68y) scored 2 TDs; his 2nd score following poor Bruins punt snap deep in their territory. Later in H, Bruins QB Rick Bashore made bad pitchout to McNeil that was recovered in UCLA EZ by Gophers DT Steve Midboe.

Notre Dame 31 PURDUE 24: Legend of QB Joe Montana began to bloom. Montana, who missed 1976 season with injury, entered game in relief of ineffectual QB Rusty Lisch and soon-to-be-injured replacement QB Gary Forystek—yes Montana was 3rd string—with ND trailing 24-14 in 3rd Q. Montana (9-14/154y) rallied Irish (2-1) to 17 pts and victory, tossing game-winning 13y TD pass to TE Ken MacAfee (9/114y) with 1:39 left. Purdue (1-2) had built lead behind spectacular frosh QB Mark Herrmann, who threw school record 51 passes, of which he completed 24/351y, 3 TDs. He was picked off 4 times. Herrmann, native of Carmel, Indiana, had topped 300y passing in all 3 of his games to date.

GAME OF THE YEAR
Oklahoma 29 OHIO STATE 28:

Yes, that was Oklahoma K Uwe Von Schamann egging on all 88,119 Buckeye fans before making his last-min winning FG. While crowd was making usual big noise to bother kicker and Ohio State coach Woody Hayes was calling timeout to add pressure, West German-born, Texas-raised Sooners K was on his hands and knees doing deep breathing exercises. Von Schamann got up, briskly lifted both arms up-and-down to rile up Buckeye fans, even feigning concert conductor motions, and then drilled 41y FG. First-ever match-up of 2 winningest programs of past 25 years, was exciting, if sloppy. Oklahoma (3-0) opened with 20-0 lead early in 2nd Q lead on 33y TD run by HB Elvis Peacock, 14y TD run by HB Billy Sims (11/60y) and 2 FGs by Von Schamann. But 6 TOs over an 8-possession stretch put OU on its heels, prompting D coordinator Larry Lacewell to call for new stat: "pitchouts attempted and pitchouts completed." Buckeyes (2-1) then rode 80 in 7 plays to TB Ron Springs' 30y TD run. Then after recovering 1 of those missed pitchouts on Sooners 19YL, Ohio State quickly scored on QB Rod Gerald's 19y run. Ohio, however, squandered 3 other chances following OU FUMs deep in Oklahoma territory. With both starting QBs (Gerald and OU's Thomas Lott) knocked out of bruising game, Ohio State sub QB Greg Castignola fired 16y TD to TE Jimmy Moore for 28-20 lead in 3rd Q. Castignola lost 4th Q FUM when NG Reggie Kinlaw stripped him. Sooners backup QB Dean Blevins converted TO into 43y drive that ended with Peacock's 2nd TD, tackle-induced flip into EZ on 4th down from 1YL. Peacock's tying 2-pt conv run was halted, but Ohio State was not yet off hook. Oklahoma DB Mike Babb grabbed onside-KO for last chance: Blevins hit WR Steve Rhodes for 18y gain that set up Von Schamann's dramatic FG.

Texas A&M 33 TEXAS TECH 17: After getting excited early by TB Mark Julian's nifty 51y TD run with screen pass, Red Raiders (2-1) faithful fell silent when star QB Rodney Allison was carted off in 1st Q with broken leg, courtesy of hard hit by blitzing Aggies S Carl Grulich. Texas Tech stayed in contention through 3 Qs, helped by GLS against 280-lb Aggies FB George Woodard (nicknamed "Winnebago" by Tech coach Steve Sloan). Texas A&M (3-0) prevailed, thanks to 4 FGs by K Tony Franklin in 4th Q. A&M HB Curtis Dickey was held to 48y rushing, but caught 6/117y, including 68y TD catch in 3rd Q. Red Raiders FB Billy Taylor rushed for 65y.

October 1, 1977

(Fri) SOUTHERN CALIFORNIA 41 Washington State 7: As Trojans D handled Washington State (2-2) QB Jack Thompson (10-21/136y, 2 INTs), Southern California O took control with 494y. USC (4-0) mounted 24-0 H lead, which was stretched to 41-0 by early 4th Q, as alternating TBs Charles White (27/128y) and Dwight Ford (13/118y) each scored 2 TDs, and QB Rob Hertel completed 11-18/182y. Cougars, losers of 5 TOs, finally scored in 4th Q on Thompson's 6y TD pass to WR Brian Kelly.

Kentucky 24 PENN STATE 20: QB Derrick Ramsey and DE Art Still were HS teammates from Camden, N.J., normally Penn State's recruiting territory, but they turned tables to spark upset by Wildcats (3-1). Ramsey surprised Nittany Lions (3-1) by passing on 1st down, doing so 5 times during 3rd Q when Kentucky ate up 10 mins to score 10 pts including Ramsey's winning 1y TD run. Ferocious Still led Kentucky D that limited Lions to only 41y O in decisive 2nd H. Penn State had enjoyed 10-0 lead after WR Jimmy Cefalo's 75y punt TD RET, but Kentucky got 7 pts back when DB Dallas Owens took INT 23y for TD and took 14-10 lead on FB Chuck Servino's 1y TD run after Lions FUM. Penn State QB Chuck Fusina completed 17-32/230y.

DUKE 28 Navy 16: Blue Devils (2-2) eschewed long drives for big-play TDs from each of their units. Duke led 14-3 at H on special teams TDs scored on S George Gawdun's 47y punt RET and blocked punt returned 35y by CB Earl Cook. FB Steve Broadie (11/106y) then iced game for Duke with 63y scoring romp in 3rd Q. With Navy (2-2) now forced to throw more, Duke's D got into scoring act with 44y INT TD RET by LB Bill King. Midshipmen scored twice in 4th Q, including 19y TD reception by WR Phil McConkey (6/125y).

NORTH CAROLINA STATE 24 Maryland 20: As QB Johnny Evans ran in winning 2y TD run with 11 secs left, Wolfpack (3-1) ended Maryland's 21-game ACC win streak. Winning drive was aided by 2 Maryland (1-3) PENs and saving FUM REC by ace NC State C Jim Ritcher. Wolfpack TB Ted Brown (110y, 2 TDs rushing) threw key block on Evans' TD run. Terps TB Preacher Maddox came off bench to rush for 113y and 2 TDs. NC State won despite being outgained 377y to 328y. Maryland had not lost in ACC action since being defeated by Wolfpack 24-22 in 1973.

ALABAMA 18 Georgia 10: SEC slugfest was for fans of D as both teams found moving football difficult at best. Thanks to 56y punt by P Buddy Holt that pinned Bulldogs (2-2) on own 1YL, Alabama scored 1st when fumbled snap by Georgia P Mike Garrett produced safety. Crimson Tide (3-1) then took over at own 41YL before marching to 2y TD run by FB Johnny Davis for 9-0 lead. Georgia's only answer in rest of 1st H came on K Rex Robinson's 53y FG, which he booted against wind. Tide controlled 3rd Q, with help from Georgia TOs, 5 in all, to increase their lead to 15-3 on 2 FGs by K Roger Chapman. Led by LB Ben Zambiasi, who was in on 15 tackles, Bulldogs D played heroically in defeat.

LOUISIANA STATE 36 Florida 14: Ferocious Louisiana State (2-1) ground game and 4 Gator TOs were ingredients for surprisingly easy 29-0 lead in 2nd Q. Florida (2-1) woke up to score 2 TDs, including 85y scoring pass from QB Terry LeCount to WR Wes Chandler, before LSU slammed shut comeback door with TD drive to close scoring. Tigers TB Charles Alexander enhanced his fame, scoring twice and rushing 31/170 of Tigers' 385y, while having no run longer than 34y.

MICHIGAN 41 Texas A&M 3: Texas A&M (3-1) got its only pts early on as K Tony Franklin followed FUM REC with 24y FG. Wind-swept 1st H ended in favor of Michigan (4-0) at 7-3, but much-anticipated match-up had turned quiet with Wolverines QB Rick Leach (6-18/106y) misfiring on his passes, and A&M game plan being stuck in 1st gear. Aggies seemed content with plenty of handoffs to FB George Woodard (39/153y), but gained little. Flood gates opened for Michigan in 2nd H when FUM REC by LB Dom Tedesco set up 1y TD run by FB Russell Davis (19/110y). Rout was on when DB Jim Pickens took blocked punt into EZ for score and DB Mike Jolly scored on 50y INT RET.

NOTRE DAME 16 Michigan State 6: Finally, heeds of many Notre Dame fans were heard: jr QB Joe Montana was given 1st starting nod. Although Montana completed only 9-24 and was intercepted 3 times, he threw for effective 233y in game dominated by Fighting Irish (3-1) D. ND defenders, with 18 tackles, sack, and INT being contributed by LB Bob Golic, held Spartans (2-2) to 92y rushing, sacked QB Ed Smith and his replacements 8 times, and picked off 4 passes. Michigan State S Mark Anderson did his part to limit ND's attack, picking off 3 passes by Montana. FB Jerome Heavens rushed for 136y and K Dave Reeve booted 3 FGs to pace Irish. Notre Dame DT Ken Dike had 4 sacks.

TEXAS 72 Rice 15: When team scores 9 TDs it is difficult to get excited over single FG, but when Texas (3-0) K Russell Erxleben booted 67y FG he set new NCAA distance record. His 3-ptr had no meaning whatsoever for game's outcome; it boosted Steers' lead to 57-7. Dynamic Horns TB Earl Campbell rushed 13/131y, 4 TDs for O that gained 617y. Under pressure all day, new starting QB Randy Hertel finally put Owls (1-3) on scoreboard in 3rd Q with 16y TD pass to WR Joey Diquinzio.

Missouri 15 ARIZONA STATE 0: Stumbling, bumbling Sun Devils (2-1) were blanked at home due to host of TOs and other mistakes. Missouri frosh QB Phil Bradley, future Seattle Mariners baseball starter, led 2 80y scoring drives. Bradley capped marches with 33y TD pass to WR Joe Stewart and 1y TD run. Arizona State continually marched into Tigers territory only to lose 2 FUMs and throw 5 INTs, 4 by starting QB Dennis Sproul, who had 1st Q 1y TD run eliminated by PEN. TB Earl Gant led Tigers with 110y rushing, while Sun Devil WR John Jefferson caught 6/66y.

October 8, 1977

FLORIDA 17 Pittsburgh 17: QB Matt Cavanaugh returned to Pitt (3-1-1) lineup, but soft cast on left arm led to his 8 FUMs, 3 of which were lost. Gators (2-1-1) D carried team's effort, scoring on DE Richard Ruth's REC of Cavanaugh FUM in EZ, after ball was slapped away by DE Michael Dupree. Florida led 7-0, but Cavanaugh (8-19/160y, INT) led Panthers to tying TD, which he scored from 3y out. Pitt took lead in 3rd Q on pass from HB Jo Jo Heath to WR Willie Taylor for 34y TD. Dominating Pitt D looked to make 14-7 lead hold up, but Gators DB Tim Aydt blocked punt near midfield that rolled and rolled into Pitt EZ for DB Chuck Hatch to snatch for 4th Q TD. Teams traded FGs, with Florida K Berj Yepremian kicking tying 28y FG with 1:26 left.

WISCONSIN 26 Illinois 0: For low-down Badgers (5-0), undefeated record felt great even without big-name win. Wisconsin D posted its 1st shutout since 1966, while sub QB Charles Green (11-16/148y, TD, 2 INTs) sparkled in 1st start with 9 completions in 1st 10 tries and scored running TD. Illini (1-4) trailed 26-0 by time they managed initial 1st down, and game-end O was pathetic 78y total.

Michigan 24 MICHIGAN STATE 14: Wolverines (5-0) may not have earned style pts, but they were facing better-than-advertised and fired up Spartans. Michigan State (2-3) grabbed 7-0 lead on 19y TD pass from QB Ed Smith to WR Kirk Gibson in 2nd Q. Michigan responded to 10-7 lead, using 40y and 41y passes from QB Rick Leach to WB Ralph Clayton to set up 50y FG by K Gregg Willner and 12y TD pass to WR Rick White. Wolverines increased lead to 17pts, converting 2 Spartan TOs into TDs. TB Harlan Huckleby rushed for 146y to pace Wolverine attack, while Smith, who became Michigan State career passing leader, threw for 147y.

OHIO STATE 46 Purdue 0: Buckeyes crushed visitors with 29 pts in 1st Q. From very 1st play—45y completion from QB Rod Gerald to WR Herman Johns—rout was on. Ohio reserve FB Joel Payton scored 4 TDs. Payton's 1st score gave Buckeyes 2-TD lead as CB Mike Guess had already scored on 65y INT RET. Ohio State D held Purdue (2-3) QB Mark Hermann to 117y passing. Buckeyes TB Ron Springs rushed for 151y, including 66y TD run in 2nd Q. Boilermakers coach Jim Young had rough return to Columbus; he played for coach Woody Hayes on 1954 national championship club before transferring.

Texas 13 Oklahoma 6 (Dallas): Texas (4-0) overcame early misfortune to beat Red River rivals for 1st time since 1970. On game's opening play, TB Earl Campbell's ill-fated pass was picked off by Oklahoma DT David Hudgens, giving Sooners (4-1) ball at Texas 14YL only 6 secs into game. Oklahoma managed only FG, but Texas had not seen end to bad luck yet as its 2 top QBs, Mark McBath and Jon Aune, were knocked out for season. Sub QB Randy McEachern played well as Texas built 10-3 lead by H on 64y FG by K Russell Erxleben and brilliant 24y TD run by Campbell (23/124y). Campbell reversed field and hurdled defender before racing to EZ. Horns D, subbing only single defender in entire game, limited OU to 2 FGs by K Uwe Von Schamann and halted Sooners on 4YL with 4 mins left. Steers S Johnnie Johnson made 4th down tackle on QB Thomas Lott. Erxleben then sealed win with soaring 69y punt.

OREGON STATE 24 Brigham Young 19: Beavers (2-3) eliminated 19-pt 2nd H deficit as its LB unit became TD-crazy. After Oregon State broke through with 40y TD pass from QB John Norman to WR Dwayne Hall, LBs Kent Howe (32y) and Gene Dales (79y) returned INTs for TDs. By time Cougars (3-1) QB Gifford Nielsen threw decisive INT to Dales, he was playing on partial tear of knee ligament that would end his season. Nielsen still threw 3 TD passes, including 2 to WR Mike Chronister.

Alabama 21 SOUTHERN CALIFORNIA 20: Game pitted 2 storied programs and came down to Trojans' 2-pt pass attempt with 35 secs left. Alabama (4-1) DE Wayne Hamilton made disruptive pass rush, promoting INT by LB Barry Krauss. Hamilton had huge game; his earlier pass tip was picked off by linemate, DT Curtis McGriff, on Trojans' 8YL. McGriff's INT set up 13y TD run by HB Tony Nathan (12/76y, 2 TDs) for 21-6 Tide lead. QB Rob Hertel rallied Trojans (4-1) for TD drives of 91 and 79y, capping 1st with 10y pass to WR Calvin Sweeney and 2-pt conv pass to FB Mosi Tatupu. FB Lynn Cain scored USC's final TD on 1y sweep to set up Hertel's ill-fated conv pass. Trojans' TB combination of Charles White (15/63y) and Dwight Ford (13/22y) were held well in check, forcing Hertel (18-30/239y, 2 INTs) to rally his troops. Hertel united with WR Randy Simmrin (6/120y) to create most of damage.

STANFORD 32 Ucla 28: Cardinals (4-1) hopes seemed dim with QB Guy Benjamin on sideline. But, Stanford backup QB Steve Dils (24-37/287y) threw winning 27y TD to WR James Lofton (5/126y), who, as he neared GL, pulled away from UCLA DBs Kenny Easley and Levi Armstrong to score with 37 secs left. Bruins (2-3) flew up field to Stanford 15YL before time expired. Cards used sparkling performance by frosh HB

Darrin Nelson (23/189y) for early 16-0 lead, but UCLA HB Theotis "Big Foot" Brown returned from injury to spark 2 TD drives. Brown's thunderous 75y TD run cut deficit to 16-14 before FG by K Ken Naber sent Stanford to locker room with 5-pt lead. UCLA scored in 3rd Q on another long run, 78y by frosh HB Freeman McNeil, as Bruins took 21-19 lead that would not last.

October 15, 1977

Penn State 31 SYRACUSE 24: With coach Joe Paterno in hospital with son David, who injured himself in trampoline accident, Nittany Lions (5-1) won emotional road battle. They did so despite heroics by Syracuse QB Bill Hurley, who threw for school-record 329y and ran for 55y despite 7 sacks. Hurley could not overcome 31-10 deficit, created when Lions scored on 4 of 1st 5 possessions and again in 3rd Q. QB Chuck Fusina (14-25/160y) led O that enjoyed easier time in 1st H. Orangemen (2-4) rallied with 14 4th Q pts, including 11y TD pass from Hurley to WR Mike Jones.

Boston College 28 WEST VIRGINIA 24: Boston College (3-3) D decided game was theirs to win. After allowing 10 pts in 1st H—game was tied 17-17 at H as BC allowed INT TD RET—Eagles D got even tougher in 2nd H in allowing only 6y. Even so, West Virginia (4-2) took 24-17 lead on blistering 88y punt RET by TB Fulton Walker. Eagles D needed to produce, so DTs Fred Smerlas and Chuck Morris forced TB James Tackett to FUM, REC being made by LB Rich Scudellari on WVU 20YL. Four plays later, Boston College FB John Cassidy scored on 2y run, which was followed up by 2-pt conv pass from QB Ken Smith (17-25/183y, TD, INT) to WR Mike Godbolt.

North Carolina 27 NORTH CAROLINA STATE 14: Tar Heels (4-2) grabbed 1st place in ACC as TB "Famous" Amos Lawrence celebrated 1st start with 216y rushing. North Carolina built 27-0 lead before Wolfpack (5-2) could answer with 2 TD passes by QB Johnny Evans (17-35/196y, 2 INTs) in 4th Q. NC State fell behind early, not getting 1st down in 1st Q, and trailing for good on 38y FG by UNC K Tom Biddle. Tar Heels bumped lead to 10-0 with 6y TD pass from QB Matt Kupec to TE Brooks Williams, on drive featuring 19y pass from holder Jimmy Rouse to Williams on fake FG. Lead soon was increased as Heels LB Buddy Curry returned INT 31y for TD. Wolfpack meanwhile found denting UNC territory difficult, not crossing 50YL until late in 3rd Q.

GEORGIA TECH 38 Auburn 21: Yellow Jackets (4-2) didn't wear 28-0 lead well. Georgia Tech became TO-prone in its 4-TD glory, allowing Auburn to cut it to 28-14. Tigers (3-3) then recovered FUM by HB Bucky Shamburger at Tech 33YL, moving to 5YL before Jackets CB Donnie Patterson made GL INT off QB John Crane to stop rally. Sloppy Tigers cost themselves early TD as mishandled punt coughed up ball at 3YL, where Tech TB Gary Lanier scored. Later in 1st H, INT by Patterson set up 5y HB pass from Eddie Lee Ivery to WR Drew Hill. Tech FB Rodney Lee rushed for 112y, while TB Joe Cribbs got 89y of Auburn's 259y rushing.

Kentucky 33 LOUISIANA STATE 13: No. 12 Wildcats (5-1) were running on all cylinders and SEC was taking notice. Tigers (3-2) trailed 13-7 in 3rd Q before Kentucky exploded for TD variety, posted by its O, special teams, and D. Cats TB Randy Brooks (17/121y) took advantage of dominant O-line, rambling 53y to set up 4y TD run by QB Derrick Ramsey. LSU tried FG, blocked by Cats NG Richard Jaffe with DE Art Still scooping up ball and returning it 52y for TD. Stunned Tigers gave up 81y INT TD RET by Kentucky DB Dallas Owens. LSU QB David Woodley accounted for throwing and running TDs.

MICHIGAN 56 Wisconsin 0: Last thing a Big 10 team needed to do was to make Wolverines (6-0) take notice. By opening at 5-0, Badgers (5-1) were making noise in Big 10, but this thrashing quickly quieted Wisconsin. Michigan TB Roosevelt Smith rushed for 157y and 2 TDs in place of injured TB Harlan Huckleby, while QB Rick Leach (10-16/127, 2 TDs, INT) was sharp. Wolverines gained 546y and allowed only 126y. HB Ira Matthews was mildest of Wisconsin's weapons with 5/27y rushing.

Iowa State 24 NEBRASKA 21: Nebraska IB with peculiar and wonderful name, I.M. Hipp (25/165y), raced 59y to EZ on 2nd play from scrimmage, so it looked like Huskers (4-2) would avenge rare series loss lingering from 1976. Iowa State (5-1) QB Terry Rubley answered with 3y TD run to cap 76y drive to prove Cyclones came to win. Hipp tallied again at end of 1st Q, which at 14-7 was last time Nebraska led. ISU wiped away deficit with 2 TDs in 2nd Q. After 32y FG by K Scott Kollman extended Cyclone lead to 24-14 early in 2nd H, Hipp scored his 3rd TD. That proved to be Nebraska's last surge as Cyclones D posted 4th Q shutout. Iowa State TB Dexter Green (33/139y) and FB Cal Cummins (20/115y) each riddled Huskers D and scored TD.

Colorado 17 KANSAS 17: Rallying from 14-pt deficit in 4th Q, Jayhawks (1-4-1) almost pulled off miracle with final drive into Colorado (5-0-1) territory. After Kansas DB LeRoy Irvin's late INT, O marched to Colorado 22YL until FUM ruined everything with 14 secs left. TB Howard Ballage (19/91y) rushed for 2 TDs to build Colorado's lead to 17-3 in 4th Q, despite fact that Buffs registered only 259y O. Backup QB Brian Bethke, with help from Jayhawks' 344y rush attack, moved Kansas on short 29y and 21y drives, 1st capped by FB Norris Banks' 1y dive following FUM REC.

Texas 13 ARKANSAS 9: What ultimately proved to be battle for SWC crown went down to wire, with Longhorns (5-0) driving 80y in 4th Q for game's sole TD. With less than 7 mins left, QB Randy McEachern hit 3 passes for 72y—he completed only 4-10 for game—to set up HB Johnny "Ham" Jones' winning 1y TD. Prior to Jones' score, K Russell Erxleben of Texas and K Steve Little of Arkansas (4-1) waged magnificent kicking duel. Erxleben put Texas ahead 6-0 on 58y and 52y FGs, while Little nailed 33y, 67y and 25y FGs, his 67y boot tying Erxleben's 3-week-old NCAA distance mark. Texas HB Earl Campbell rushed for 188y and added 31y screen pass to set up winning score. Arkansas could not convert late 3rd-and-3 play and paid for it.

Southern Methodist 37 HOUSTON 23: Astrodome fans never witnessed ending like this. Up 23-17, Cougars (3-2) attempted FG with 4 mins left. SMU (3-3) CB David Hill blocked kick to spark rally. Pass-happy Mustangs surprisingly ground out 80y drive, scoring on 14y TD run by TB Art Whittingham (26/136y). Whittingham's TD was scored with 39 secs remaining. Amazingly, Mustangs scored 2 more TDs as Houston QB Delrick Brown lost FUM on own 2YL to set up TB Tennell Atkins' 2y TD run and CB D.K. Perry returned INT 37y for closing score. Brown threw for 145y and 2 TDs, while SMU QB Mike Ford gained 259y in air.

Brigham Young 63 COLORADO STATE 17: Brigham Young (4-1) QB Marc Wilson shed his backup role with big performance. With QB Gifford Nielsen out with long-term injury, Wilson (15-25/332y, INT) enjoyed new status by setting WAC record with 7 TDs. Cougars opened scoring with 37y TD pass to TE Tod Thompson to cap 92y drive. Rams (5-1) RB Ron Harris answered with 100y KO TD RET. BYU then marched 82y to 25y TD pass to WR George Harris to take lead for good. Thompson caught 2 more TD passes to help build 42-10 H edge for BYU. CSU K Erling Holly booted 47y FG.

WASHINGTON 45 Stanford 21: Long play TDs ruined Cardinals (4-2), who wasted big effort by QB Guy Benjamin (28-47/376y) in return from injury. Washington (3-3) scored 6 TDs, including 83y run on sweep by TB Joe Steele (29/177y, 2 TDs), 59y burst up middle by FB Ron Gipson, 73y punt RET by DB Nesby Glasgow, 26y TD pass by QB Warren Moon (10-14/147y) to WR Spider Gaines, and 29y INT RET by DB Greg Grimes. WR James Lofton scored Stanford's TDs on catches of 10y, 42y, and 19y. Teams combined for 916y, with Huskies gaining 507y, 360y rushing.

AP Poll October 17

1 Michigan (47)	1100		11 Notre Dame	296
2 Texas (8)	1014		12 Texas A&M	220
3 Alabama	811		13 Texas Tech	151
4 Ohio State	700		14 Pittsburgh	143
5 Southern California	689		15 California	111
6 Oklahoma	638		16 Iowa State	44
7 Colorado	431		17 Brigham Young	40
8 Kentucky (1)	369		18 Nebraska	38
9 Arkansas	340		19 Florida	33
10 Penn State	328		20 Clemson	31

October 22, 1977

PITTSBURGH 28 Syracuse 21: Orangemen (2-6) nearly dealt upset card to Panthers (5-1-1), who trailed at home for most of game. Syracuse led 3-0, 10-3, and 18-14 at H until adding K Dave Jacobs' 2nd FG over 40y for 21-14 edge at end of 3rd Q. In 2nd Q, Syracuse QB Bob Avery had scored on 3 and 1y runs, and QB Bill Hurley (13-26/203y, 2 INTs) pitched 2-pt pass. Pitt FB Freddy Jacobs took short pass from QB Matt Cavanaugh (332y passing) and turned it into tying 58y TD with 9:52 left. There was slightly more than 2 mins to go when Cavanaugh arched 45y pass to WR Gordon "Too Much" Jones that carried to 1YL, from where Cavanaugh wedged behind RG Walter Link on 3rd down for winning pts.

Kentucky 33 GEORGIA 0: Kentucky (6-1) upped ante for special season with convincing road win. Wildcats D held Georgia (4-3) runners to 38/47y (1.2y avg). Kentucky dominated normally tough Georgia D, rolling up 392y with 3 TD passes being tossed by QB Derrick Ramsey (11-17/107y). Kentucky K Joe Bryant opened scoring with 51y FG, and Cats' lead would reach 10-0 by H. Georgia DB Scott Woerner, 1 of nation's top returners, provided 209y on 9 punt and KO RETs.

MINNESOTA 16 Michigan 0: Michigan natives K Paul Rogind (3 FGs) and TB Marion Barber (3y TD run) did all scoring as Minnesota stunned no. 1 Wolverines (6-1). Gophers (5-2) D excelled, limiting usually strong Wolverine rushing attack to 33/80y and posting 1st shutout of Michigan since Michigan State turned trick in 1967. Wolverines suffered 3 FUMs and 2 INTs, while Gophers were TO-free in reversal of form. Key play came in 3rd Q when score was 13-0: pass interference PEN was called on Michigan S Dwight Hicks that eliminated his INT that he had returned to Minnesota 5YL. Michigan FB Russell Davis rushed for 55y and caught 3/30y. Game may have been decided in spring, when Minnesota returned to natural grass at "Brickhouse" after 7-year-old artificial turf wore out. Since beginning of last season, Michigan was 16-0 on artificial turf, now 0-3 on grass. In addition to this defeat, Wolverines lost on grass at Purdue and in Rose Bowl during 1976 season.

NOTRE DAME 49 Southern California 19: Sporting Kelly green jerseys for 1st time since 1963, Irish (5-1) energized Notre Dame Stadium fans with blowout win. Game was close early as Trojans NG Ty Sperling forced FUM by HB Terry Eurick, with ball caught mid-air by LB Mario Celotto for 5y TD and 7-7 tie. Irish DB Ted Burgmeier then sprung 2 special team surprises late in 2nd Q: shotputting 2-pt conv pass to diving WB Tom Domin for 15-7 lead and racing 19y on fake FG that was followed by 13y TD pass from QB Joe Montana (13-24/167y, 2 TDs, INT) to TE Ken MacAfee (8/97y). ND then poured it on, even adding 30y TD RET of blocked punt by DE Jay Case. Punt was blocked by LB Bob Golic, who also forced 2 FUMs. Trojans (5-2) scored 2 meaningless TDs in 4th Q, including 4y run by FB Lynn Cain for 1st rushing TD allowed by Irish D so far this season.

TEXAS CHRISTIAN 21 Miami 17: Break up those red-hot Horned Frogs (2-4), winners of 2 straight after 15-game losing streak. DB Steve Barnes was hero with blocked punt that gave TCU ball on Miami 36YL late in 4th Q, trailing by 17-14. With 1:08 left, QB Steve Bayuk scored winner from 1YL, for his 2nd 1y TD keeper. It came right after pass interference PEN against Canes (3-3). Miami had scored 11 straight pts to take lead on 74y tackle-breaking run with screen pass by FB Ottis Anderson (20/86y rushing). Earlier, Frogs had grabbed 14-6 H lead with both TDs following FUM RECs by DE Daron Mosley. TCU WR Mike Renfro caught 28y scoring pass, while Hurricanes K Chris Dennis kicked 3 FGs. Teams combined for 9 TOs.

ARKANSAS 34 Houston 0: Razorbacks (5-1) routed stumbling Cougars as Arkansas QB Ron Calcagni produced 232y total O. Calcagni rushed for career-high 127y, while accurately pitching 10-15/105y. Houston (3-3) lost 5 FUMs and INT to make any comeback impossible. Arkansas gained 442y, while allowing Cougars mere 144y. Razorbacks TE Charles Clay caught 2 TD passes and RB Ben Cowins rushed for 2 TDs. With leading rusher RB Alois Blackwell held to 24y, Houston had to count on alternating QB Darrell Shepard's 46y for rushing leadership.

NEBRASKA 33 Colorado 15: Nebraska (5-2) IB I.M. Hipp was all legs in leading win over undefeated no. 7 Buffs (5-1-1), rushing for 172y with TDs of 28y and 4y. Hipp's 28y scoring run in 2nd Q pulled Nebraska to 15-10. QB Tom Sorley threw 22y TD pass for winning pts to WB Kenny Brown later in 2nd Q. Huskers outgained Buffaloes 480y to 266y, while D allowed single TD. Colorado got its pts early as FB James Mayberry rushed for 113y and TD and TB Howard Ballage made 98y KO TD RET.

OKLAHOMA 35 Iowa State 16: Sooners (6-1) jumped into 1st place in Big Eight as QB Thomas Lott ran in 2 TDs and threw 23 scoring pass to HB Elvis Peacock. Oklahoma scored 3 straight TDs, including 85y punt RET by HB Freddie Nixon, to counteract Cyclones QB Terry Rubley's 12y TD pass to TE Guy Preston in 3rd Q for 16-14 lead. Recovered from myriad injuries, FB Kenny King led Oklahoma with 146y rushing, and TB Dexter Green paced Iowa State (5-2) with 177y and 44y TD.

UCLA 21 California 19: Bruins (4-3) woke up in 4th Q, scoring 2 TDs to wipe out 16-7 deficit. UCLA QB Rick Bashore, who rushed for team-high 90y, ended 80y drive with 5y TD pass to wide-open WR Homer Butler, to pull within 16-14. Bruins took lead when reserve NG Marvin Morris blocked Cal punt and returned it 26y for inspiring game-winning TD. QB Charlie Young (25-44/299y) led Bears (5-2) to 387y, to 262y for UCLA, while K Jim Breech booted 4 FGs. Young moved Bears to UCLA 42YL before throwing his 2nd INT of game, caught by LB Jeff Muro, to kill late chance.

AP Poll October 24

1 Texas (65)	1336		11 Texas A&M	285
2 Alabama	1077		12 Nebraska	260
3 Ohio State (1)	963		13 Pittsburgh	194
4 Oklahoma	952		14 Texas Tech	177
5 Notre Dame	740		15 Colorado	132
6 Michigan	719		16 Clemson	94
7 Kentucky (1)	610		17 Brigham Young	60
8 Arkansas	505		18 Florida	24
9 Penn State	484		19 Minnesota	22
10 Southern California	315		20 Florida State	14

October 29, 1977

Louisiana State 28 MISSISSIPPI 21: After spotting Rebels (4-5) 21 pts, Louisiana State roared back behind QB Steve Ensminger (14-27/181y). Tigers (5-2) drove 84y for TD, TB Charles Alexander's 1y run, to trail 21-7 at H. Ensminger truly sparkled in 2nd H, leading 3 TD drives that he capped with 2 scoring runs and 8y TD pass to SB Mike Quintela. LSU's winning pts came on 3y QB keeper with 1:25 left, and were set up by clutch INT that DB Willie Teal returned from midfield to Mississippi 10YL. Ole Miss had used 2 long runs to forge early lead as HB Freddie Williams opened scoring with 42y run, and HB Leon Perry gave team 21-0 lead with 69y run. Rebels rushed for 321y.

Nebraska 31 OKLAHOMA STATE 14: Although OSU (4-4) star HB Terry Miller won his rushing battle against Nebraska IB I.M. Hipp by 116y to 71y, it was Huskers O that moved ball with ease. QB Tom Sorley converted 1 3rd down after another for Nebraska (6-2). Huskers rushed 318y, with WB Curtis Craig leading way with 82y and 16y TD, while Hipp also scored twice. Cowboys had taken early 7-0 lead as Miller sped 7y for TD after INT by CB Gregg Johnson. Oke State closed scoring with 55y TD pass from QB Harold Bailey to WR Gerald Bain.

MISSOURI 24 Colorado 14: Tigers (3-5) came close to fumbling away game early before rallying behind QB Pete Woods and hard-hitting D. Mizzou self-destructed with 3 FUMs, 2 on opening 2 plays, so Colorado (5-2-1) took 14-0 1st Q lead as QB Jeff Knapple threw and ran for TDs. Tigers D then blanked Buffs, allowing only 13 game-end 1st downs. Woods led TD drives in each of final 3 Qs, scoring on 1y run and throwing TD passes of 33y to WR Joe Stewart and 8y to TE Kellen Winslow. Buffs FB James Mayberry rushed 136y, while Tigers TB Earl Gant led with 112y.

TEXAS 26 Texas Tech 0: With focus on TB Earl Campbell (27/116y), other Longhorns (7-0) took spotlight. QB Randy McEachern (4-8/137y) opened scoring with 57y TD pass to WR Johnny "Lam" Jones, while HB Johnny "Ham" Jones added 2 rushing TDs in 2nd H. K Russell Erxleben was not to be outdone, booting 2 FGs, including 60y effort that gave Horns 10-0 H lead. Texas Tech (5-2) had best drive fizzle when Earl's brother, LB Tim, recovered FUM by QB Rodney Allison on sack by DT Steve McMichael. Allison led 2 drives that crossed Texas 15YL in 1st H before fizzling, but Raiders managed only 60y in 2nd H as Texas posted 3rd shutout of season.

BRIGHAM YOUNG 34 Arizona 14: Taking advantage of wind was at their backs in 1st Q and magically changed direction as they did for 2nd Q, Cougars (6-1) romped behind dominant passing attack. BYU QB Marc Wilson (23-43/334y, 2 TDs, 2 INTs) built

17-0 lead in 1st Q, which improved to 27- 0 by H. Arizona (2-5) suffered worst loss of season, committing 6 TOs but managing 2 scoring runs in 2nd H to make score more respectable. Cougars finished with 554y of O, but suffered 4 TOs.

CALIFORNIA 17 Southern California 14: With game dedicated to late QB Joe Roth, Golden Bears handed Southern California (5-3) 1st conf loss. Cal S Anthony Green set up 1st score by returning INT 43y to USC 3YL, from where FB Paul Jones scored, and made clinching INT of QB Rob Hertel late in 4th Q. Bears (6-2) increased lead to 17-7 on K Jim Breech's 18y FG and QB Charlie Young's 1y keeper as 4th Q opened. Trojans, who outgained Cal 433y to 282y but repeatedly misfired in scoring position, closed scoring on 31y TD pass to WR Calvin Sweeney. USC TB Charles White rushed for 154y.

UCLA 20 Washington 12: Bruins (5-3) season recovery continued as each team scored 4 times, but UCLA reached EZ twice while holding Huskies to 4 FGs by K Steve Robbins. Washington (4-4) crossed UCLA 25YL 5 times, and 5 times it finished short of EZ. Bruins drove 74y after 2nd H KO for what proved to be winning score, taking 13-6 lead on 3y TD run by QB Rick Bashore. Although Washington cut deficit to 13-12 late in 3rd Q, UCLA D prevented more damage, and HB Theotis Brown added insurance 13y TD run. With half of Pac-8 in running for Rose Bowl, UCLA made its own statement with win. Huskies QB Warren Moon threw for 146y.

AP Poll October 31
1 Texas (57)	1176	11 Nebraska	255
2 Alabama (1)	953	12 Pittsburgh	253
3 Oklahoma	882	13 Clemson	160
4 Ohio State	868	14 Brigham Young	127
5 Notre Dame	652	15 Florida State	76
6 Michigan	592	16 Southern California	36
7 Kentucky (1)	569	17 California	32
8 Arkansas	465	18 Louisiana State	24
9 Penn State	448	19t Iowa State	18
10 Texas A&M	309	19t Arizona State	18

November 5, 1977

Penn State 21 NORTH CAROLINA STATE 17: Penn State (8-1) had to work hard for this win. QB Chuck Fusina (22-37/315y, 2 TDs) closed 83y winning drive with 11y TD strike to WR Scott Fitzkee with 58 secs left to prevent 3rd Wolfpack series upset in 4 years. Fusina set up winner with 3 passes/43y to WR Jimmy Cefalo. TB Ted Brown had put Wolfpack (6-4) in lead with highlight producing efforts as he rushed for 251y, to reach school-record 1,110y for season. His 3rd Q 7y TD run put Wolfpack up 10-7. Fusina, who hit his 1st 9 passes, set Penn State single-game marks for attempts, completions and y. Brown's rushing total was most-ever to-date by Lions opponent.

NORTH CAROLINA 13 Clemson 13: Tar Heels (6-2-1) gladly accepted tie to remain ACC front-runners on K Tom Biddle's 30y FG with 58 secs left. With starting QB Matt Kupec knocked out in 3rd Q with broken collarbone, 3rd-string QB Clyde Christensen drove North Carolina to FG. Thanks to 11y gain on 4th-and-1 by TB Amos Lawrence and 24y burst up middle by FB Bob Loomis, Heels did just that. Lawrence rushed for 17/150y and scored 59y TD in 2nd Q. Tigers (7-1-1) scored TDs on 12y run by TB Tracy Perry and 2y run by TB Lester Brown for 13-10 lead with K Obed Ariri missing crucial x-pt after Brown's TD.

Florida State 23 VIRGINIA TECH 21: Seminoles (7-1) almost threw away successful season, needing late 30y FG by Dave Cappelen to avoid upset. Flea-flicker set up winning FG as WR Mike Shumann threw shaky 40y pass to WR Roger Overby. Hokies (1-6-1) scored TDs early on runs of 19y by TE-turned-FB Mickey Fitzgerald and 5y by HB Roscoe Coles for 14-3 lead. QB Wally Woodham then marched FSU 80y to pull within 14-10 at H on 10y TD pass to Shumann, before taking 3rd Q lead on 1y sneak to cap 87y drive. Gobblers regained lead on 4y TD run by QB Dave Lamie.

ALABAMA 24 Louisiana State 3: Tide (8-1) captured 6th SEC title in 7 years as HB Tony Nathan displayed myriad skills, running in 2 TDs and throwing for another. Nathan broke 3-3 tie with 1y run to cap 94y drive. Alabama D held SEC's top rated O to 183y as LSU (5-3) managed only 47y rushing in 1st H and made no completions until midway through 4th Q. LSU, playing 1st home day game in 8 years, tied game at 3-3 in 2nd Q on 31y FG by K Mike Conway, Tigers' 1st successful FG of season. They moved deep into Tide territory twice in 3rd Q with score 10-3, but came up short both times. Bengals TB Charles Alexander rushed for 110y, while FB Johnny Davis gained 126y on ground for Bama. Coach Bear Bryant won his 21st straight over 1 of his "pupils"; LSU coach Charlie McClendon was last "student" to beat master in 1970.

Florida 22 Georgia 17 (Jacksonville): It was tale of 2 Hs for Bulldogs (5-4) O, rushing for 225y in taking 17-10 H lead as HB Willie McClendon gained 153y with TDs of 2y and 75y. Without QB Jeff Pyburn, who reinjured his knee in 2nd Q on 11y scramble, Georgia O disappeared in 2nd H in rushing for 33y and going 0-8 passing. With Bulldogs O basically done for afternoon, Gators (4-2-1) O reasserted itself as WR-HB Wes Chandler scored 2nd and 3rd TDs in 2nd H. Chandler even ran on 4 straight downs from within Georgia 8YL for final score, while QB Terry LeCount raced 49y to set up 3rd Q TD by Chandler.

Texas 35 HOUSTON 21: Wanting revenge for 30-0 Houston whipping in 1976, Longhorns (8-0) exploded in 2nd H. TB Earl Campbell rushed for 173y and 3 TDs, including 39y burst for 21-13 lead in 3rd Q. Texas QB Randy McEeachern (11-25/161y) followed up with 1y scoring run and 16y TD pass to WR Ronnie Miksch. Cougars (4-4) had been within 14-13 at H after 44y scoring sprint by RB Alois Blackwell (21/100y) became 1st rushing TD allowed by Texas D all year. Campbell, Texas' "Tyler Rose," blasted for 1 of his TDs and ran smack into mascot Bevo, knocking huge steer mascot to ground.

BRIGHAM YOUNG 38 Utah 8: Brigham Young (7-1) QB Marc Wilson continued to rewrite record books, throwing for single-game national record 571y to top Tony Adams' old mark by 10y. Adams, of Utah State, also had achieved record against Utes. Wilson offset 3 INTs with 5 TDs on 26-41 passing. Cougars enjoyed 17-0 lead after 1st Q, with most spectacular score coming on 72y catch by WR Mike Chronister. Utah (2-6) rallied with 8 pts to enter 4th Q down 17-8 before Wilson threw 3 TDs, 2 to WR John Van Der Wouden. FB Rocky Liapis scored Utes TD on 12y run in 3rd Q.

AP Poll November 7
1 Texas (61)	1307	11 Texas A&M	331
2 Alabama (2)	1072	12 Nebraska	324
3 Oklahoma	1020	13 Brigham Young	163
4 Ohio State	908	14 Southern California	94
5 Notre Dame (2)	798	15 Clemson	87
6 Michigan	688	16 Florida State	80
7 Kentucky (1)	568	17 Arizona State	54
8 Arkansas	536	18 Texas Tech	24
9 Penn State	464	19 North Carolina	16
10 Pittsburgh	339	20 Colgate	8

November 12, 1977

SYRACUSE 20 Boston College 3: Awful weather in Syracuse's northern climes was motivation for building dome someday, although Orangemen (5-5) won easily in horrible conditions. Syracuse QB Bill Hurley threw for 104y and rushed for 85y. Eagles (5-4), forced to play without nation's 2nd-ranked passer, QB Ken Smith, and D leader, LB Rich Scudellari, managed 179y while allowing 412y. BC backup QB Jay Palazola threw INT to Orange LB Chris Shaffer, and TO was converted 5 plays later on diving 28y TD catch by TB Art Monk. Syracuse FB Bob Avery rushed for 144y, while FB Dan Conway paced BC rushing with 54y.

Pittsburgh 52 Army 26 (East Rutherford, NJ): Panthers' (8-1-1) strength was evident from start as QB Matt Cavanaugh marched Pitt 98y for 1st TD: 38y TD pass to WR Willie Taylor. Pitt then blew game open in 2nd Q with 31 pts as Cavanaugh (11-17/197y) threw 2nd and 3rd TD passes, FB Elliott Walker scored on 14y run, and TB Larry Sims added 7y TD run. Army (6-4) rallied with 3 of game's final 4 TDs, with sole Pitt TD during streak coming on WR Gordon Jones' blistering 93y KO RET. Army QB Leamon Hall threw for 226y with TE Clennie Brundidge nabbing 9/167y.

NAVY 20 Georgia Tech 16: With President Jimmy Carter—who matriculated at both Georgia Tech and Naval Academy—in attendance, Midshipmen (5-5) dominated time of possession (more than 41 mins), but could not seal win until last-sec INT at GL by DB Glenn Flanagan. Navy TB Joe Gattuso paced O with 147y rushing and 3/36y receiving. Yellow Jackets (5-5) rushed for 238y behind QB Gary Hardie, who also threw 51y TD pass to TB Eddie Lee Ivery, high man with 91y rushing.

South Carolina 24 WAKE FOREST 14: Gamecocks (5-5) ground out win, rushing 75/343y in windy conditions. FB George Rogers led way with 97y, TB Spencer Clark rushed for 87y, and TB Johnnie Wright added 82y. Despite conditions, Wake Forest (1-9) QB Mike McGlamry went to frequent short passes, completing 22-38/154y and 13y TD to WR John Zeglinski. Wake's chances to rally were dimmed by Zeglinski when he fumbled twisting, wind-blown punt on own 12YL to set up Wright's clinching 2y TD run.

North Carolina 35 VIRGINIA 14: That's why he's called "Famous Amos." Carolina (7-2-1) TB Amos Lawrence of Virginia Beach rushed for conf-record 286y and scored on runs of 6 and 21y. Virginia (1-8-1) allowed 588y, but recovered 5 UNC FUMs—3 bobbled by Lawrence—to keep score down. Tar Heels in fact led only 7-0 at H, scoring with 44 secs left in 2nd Q on Lawrence's 1st TD. "Famous Amos" busted 46y run to set up Carolina's 2nd TD, 2y run by FB Doug Paschal, for 14-0 lead early in 3rd Q. Cavs QB Chip Mark threw TDs of 12y to WR Tom Champlin and 41y to TE Mark Newhall. Tar Heels QB Matt Kupec completed 12-16/155y and 28y TD to WR Walker Lee.

Notre Dame 21 CLEMSON 17: QB Steve Fuller (13-20/185y, INT) led Clemson (7-2-1), scoring on 10y TD run for 10-7 H lead, and then marching 48y early in 3rd Q for 17-7 lead. QB Joe Montana led 2 late drives, both capped by 1y QB runs, to rally Irish (8-1). Montana's 2nd TD, 2y run by FB Vegas Ferguson, came as Irish overcame 15y PEN, incurred by coach Dan Devine. Montana (9-21/172y) completed passes of 27y and 16y to TE Ken MacAfee. Following 2nd FUM REC by Irish DT Mike Calhoun, ND drove to Montana's winning 1y TD plunge; drive's big play was 36y pass to HB Vegas Ferguson.

Auburn 33 GEORGIA 14: Auburn (5-5) FB William Andrews, native of Georgia, rushed for 142y and 2 TDs as Tigers took advantage of Georgia's 6 lost FUMs. TBs Joe Cribbs and James Brooks added 83y and 75y rushing respectively as Tigers gained 357y. Andrews acknowledged brilliance of Auburn O-line with game ball he presented to them. Debuting no-huddle O, Auburn took 16-0 lead early in 2nd Q, which was enough against bumbling Bulldogs (5-5). Georgia was in trouble all day at QB position as starter Jeff Pyburn was already lost for year and backups QB Steve Rogers and Randy Cook (16/86y rushing) were knocked out of game. Frosh QB Chris Welton, who had to wear Pyburn's tear-away jersey, was unable to rally troops.

Kentucky 14 FLORIDA 7: Trailing 7-6, Wildcats (9-1) big QB Derrick Ramsey ran in 1y TD and ensuing 2-pt conv to keep probation-levied Kentucky undefeated at 5-0 in SEC. Ramsey had completed only 2-12 prior to winning 76y drive, during which he hit 3 passes/44y to set up his 4th down TD sneak. Gators (4-3-1) were led by QB Terry LeCount, who threw for 99y and rushed for 52y, including 1y TD run for 7-6 lead late in 2nd Q.

OHIO STATE 35 Indiana 7: Game was tight at 7-7 in 1st H, but Ohio State (9-1) coach Woody Hayes was not in business of providing tight, exciting contests against Big 10 foes. Buckeyes WR Jim Harrell jump-started 28-0 2nd H by returning KO 46y and then catching 29y TD pass with EZ leap. Ohio chose to do what it did best: it kept ball on

ground as TB Jeff Logan rushed for 113y of his 148y in 2nd H. Hoosiers (4-5-1) had to be content with early 7-0 lead, with TD scored on short 4th down pass from QB Scott Arnett to WR Keith Calvin to cap 80y drive.

OKLAHOMA 52 Colorado 14: Sooners (9-1) gained 478y O and grabbed at least share of Big 8 title in convincing fashion as HB Billy Sims scored TDs on 3 of his 1st 6 carries, and FB Kenny King rushed for 121y. QB Thomas Lott tossed in 6y TD run and 28y scoring pass to WR Steve Rhodes only 1 play after OU D had recovered FUM. Buffaloes (6-3-1) FB James Mayberry rushed for 108y and scored on 3y run that halted 35-pt beginning for Oklahoma.

Arkansas 26 TEXAS A&M 20: With game tied at 20-20 late, Hogs (8-1) QB Ron Calcagni hooked up with WR Robert Farrell on 58y scoring pass play to stun Aggies (6-2). Texas A&M used remaining time to race to Arkansas 14YL before Razorbacks DB Patrick Martin came up with game-ending EZ INT. A&M FB George Woodard (28/116y) and HB Curtis Dickey (20/101y) topped 100y rushing barrier, so too did RB Ben Cowins (30/111y) of Hogs. Cowins scored 2 TDs in 1st H, and K Steve Little nailed 2 FGs as Arkansas grabbed 20-10 H lead. Texas A&M came back with 10 straight pts to tie it as Woodard scored from 1y out and K Tony Franklin hit 2nd FG.

AIR FORCE 34 Vanderbilt 28: With Air Force (2-7-1) looking to snap 6-game losing steak and win for retiring coach Ben Martin, TB Mark Bushell got team off on right foot with 98y TD RET of opening KO. Falcons went to air for 249y by QB Dave Ziebart, and winning TD was his 4th to WR Steve Hoog, duo's 3rd scoring hookup. Despite being outgained 430y to 356y, Commodores (1-8) forced 6 TOs and were able to cut into 21-0 deficit as QB Mike Wright (19-37/204y, TD) rushed for 2 TDs. Vandy reeled off 21 pts to catch up and later tied it again at 28-28 on Wright's 33y TD pass to WR Martin Cox.

ARIZONA STATE 24 Brigham Young 13: Battle for WAC crown was taken by Sun Devils (8-1) as handsome parting gift. QB Dennis Sproul (14-25/142y) threw and ran for 1st H TDs as Arizona State built 17-0 H lead. Amazingly, Arizona State D held vaunted BYU passing attack to 14y in 1st H. QB Marc Wilson (21-38/283y) hit 20y TD pass to WR Chris DeFrance to get Cougars (7-2) on scoreboard in 3rd Q, but it was not enough to overcome his 3 INTs and team's 5 lost FUMs. HB Arthur Lane also scored in 3rd Q, and it maintained ASU's 17-pt edge.

WASHINGTON 28 Southern California 10: Washington (6-4) QB Warren Moon used his swift feet and right arm to subdue Trojans, throwing 19y TD to WR Spider Gaines and running in 2 TDs. Southern California (6-4) was bounced from Rose Bowl contention, and in no way did it help to have 6 TOs, contrasted with Huskies' none. Washington converted 4 errors into its 4 TDs: FUM by USC TB Charles White (101y rushing), roughing PEN whistled against USC S Dennis Smith, blocked punt by Huskies LB Mike Rohrbach, and FUM by Trojans QB Rob Hertel (14-28/144y, 3 INTs). Hertel INT ended 1 Trojans threat, and soon was followed by Moon's brilliant 71y TD run. Huskies TB Joe Steele contributed 106y and TD rushing.

AP Poll November 14			
1 Texas (58)	1214	11 Nebraska	306
2 Alabama (1)	983	12 Arizona State	165
3 Oklahoma (1)	962	13 Florida State	162
4 Ohio State	819	14 Texas A&M	111
5 Michigan	655	15 Clemson	86
6 Notre Dame	639	16 Texas Tech	59
7 Kentucky (1)	548	17 Brigham Young	31
8 Arkansas	529	18 North Carolina	28
9 Penn State	458	19 Washington	24
10 Pittsburgh	377	20 UCLA	21

November 19, 1977

Clemson 31 SOUTH CAROLINA 27: With cozy 24-0 3rd Q lead, Tigers (8-2-1) began bowl planning. Out of nowhere, South Carolina (5-6) RB Spencer Clark (18/157y) started rally with 77y scoring romp in 3rd Q, and Gamecocks exploded for 27 straight pts in 16-min span for 3-pt lead and kicked off with less than 2 mins left. With 49 secs left, Clemson players earned place in Tiger-Gamecock lore: QB Steve Fuller (14-20/178y) threw for WR Jerry Butler's lunging 20y TD catch. Gamecocks QB Ron Bass had been hero for 40y TD pass to pass to WR Phillip Logan that provided 1st lead at 27-24.

KENTUCKY 21 Tennessee 17: Ineligible for bowl game, Wildcats (10-1) had final chance for both 10th win and perfect SEC run, while motivation for 3-win Tennessee was simple—something to build on for 1978. Volunteers (3-7) TB Kelsey Finch scored 2 TDs in 1st H as visitors proved no easy target. Injured Kentucky QB Derrick Ramsey went beyond call of duty to prevent upset. Despite injured shoulder that made passing impossible, sr signal-caller scored 2 TDs including game-winner from 1YL with 5:29 left in his final game. Vols twice had ball in Cats territory after Ramsey's heroics, ending 1 drive on downs and other on QB Jimmy Streater's FUM after being walloped by ace DE Art Still.

MICHIGAN 14 Ohio State 6: With game once again deciding Rose Bowl, Ohio State (9-2) went out and earned 23 1st downs to only 10 for Michigan, while out-rushing Wolverines 208y to 141y and out-throwing them by 144y to 55y. Bucks failed to click when it mattered: last and most crucial drive ended when Ohio QB Rod Gerald (13-16/144y) fumbled when hit by LB John Anderson, with REC by Michigan (10-1) S Derek Howard. Telling stat: Buckeyes' net for 19 plays within Michigan 20YL was −14y. Game began with mini altercation between some of largest regular season crowd to date and Buckeyes team after coach Woody Hayes had squad touch "Go Blue" banner upon taking field. Buckeyes churned up big y on opening drive employing nation's leading ground attack to grab 3-0 lead on K Vlade Janakievski's 29y FG. Wolverines were frustrated on O until swing in field position. Michigan TB Roosevelt Smith capped 46y drive with 1y TD drive that put it ahead 7-3, before 3rd Q FUM by Ohio TB Ron

Springs (14/89y) at his 20YL allowed Michigan to go up 14-3 on QB Rick Leach's 2y keeper. Ohio State could only manage FG after that. Near end of game, frustrated Hayes did it again: he punched ABC sideline cameraman Mike Freedman.

Michigan State 22 IOWA 16: Spartans (7-3-1) continued winning ways in D game, featuring wind-affected stats and near-darkness at end. Michigan State QB Ed Smith was held to 9-22 passing, but threw 2y TD pass to FB Jim Early. Spartans leading rusher was FB Lonnie Middleton with only 71y, which was 23y better than Iowa (5-5) leader TB Dennis Mosley. Hawkeyes managed only single QB—25y pass from QB Tom McLaughlin to TE Jim Swift—but K Dave Holsclaw made 3 FGs of 47y or longer. MSU K Hans Nielsen kicked 2 FGs to increase Big 10 career record to 44.

INDIANA 21 Purdue 10: Dedicating game to DB Scott Etherton, walk-on who lost life in car accident week earlier, Indiana (5-5-1) rode TB Darrick Burnett to emotional win. Burnett rushed IU-record 43 times/196y, as Hoosiers played keep-away from Purdue (5-6) QB Mark Herrmann (10-22/164y). Indiana DBs picked him off 3 times, twice by S Dale Keneipp and twice in 4th Q. Indiana QB Scott Arnett sneaked for pair of TDs, 1st for winning pts in 3rd Q, other to cap 84y drive that clinched verdict in 4th Q. Boilermakers had opened scoring on 4y run by FB John Skibinski to cap 80y drive after Purdue CB Jerome King halted early Hoosiers march with EZ INT.

HOUSTON 45 Texas Tech 7: Much to chagrin of Tangerine Bowl committee, invitee Red Raiders were waxed by Houston (5-4) on same day that their Orlando foe, Florida State, got blitzed by San Diego State, 41-16. Rout was so profound that Cougars rushed for 345y to −7y by Texas Tech (7-3). Ten sacks recorded by Houston clearly affected that stat. Cougars RB Alois Blackwell rushed for 136y—71y on opening scoring run—and QB Delrick Brown (6-10/124y) tossed 2 TDs at helm of attack that gained 485y and mowed Raiders D down to tune of 26 1st downs. Red Raiders tied game 7-7 on 15y keeper by QB Mark Johnson after Houston CB Anthony Francis briefly knocked out starting QB Rodney Allison with hard hit. Texas Tech fell behind by 14-7 at H, then 35-7 after 3 Qs.

COLORADO STATE 25 Arizona State 14: Snow was not going to dampen spirits of unsung Rams, who rallied from 14-3 2nd Q deficit for 1 of biggest wins in program history. Colorado State (8-2-1) won game behind D that held O nation's 4th ranked O (457.9y avg) to 146y, rung up 8 sacks, scored TD on 15y INT RET by LB Dana Isoline, and added 2 pts on safety by DT Mike Bell. Bell (17 tackles, 6 for losses) had great game despite suffering from pinched nerve. Rams K Tom Drake kicked 3 FGs as they won for 1st time in 16-game series. When Arizona State (8-2) QB Dennis Sproul was able to get pass launched, he found WR John Jefferson, bright spot for Sun Devils with 6 catches/102y.

WASHINGTON 35 Washington State 15: Huskies (7-4) completed turnaround from 1-3 start as QB Warren Moon (12-18/159y, INT) threw 3 TDs, 2 to TB Joe Steele. Moon led sky-high O that scored TDs on 1st Q drives of 79, 50, and 80y, with Steele scoring on 33y catch and 3y run. Washington State (6-5) could not prevent blitzing Huskies D (14 times) from dominating QB Jack Thompson (17-38/178y, TD, 2 INTs) in decisive 1st H. Thompson, nation's 3rd-ranked passer, was limited to 4-13/9y passing in 1st H. FB Dan Doornink (26/104y) finally put Cougars on scoreboard in 4th Q with 4y TD run.

STANFORD 21 California 3: Cardinals (8-3) won with D for 1st time in recent memory as California (7-4) was frustrated in Stanford red zone in 2nd H. Cards opened up 14-0 1st H lead as FB Phil Francis capped drives of 78 and 80y with short TD runs. Bears moved ball, gaining 317y, until sniffing Cards EZ. Stanford QB Guy Benjamin (16-27/211y) was brilliant throughout, closing scoring with 12y TD pass to WR James Lofton (5/92y). All-around star HB Darrin Nelson was prime Stanford contributor: 23/116y rushing and 4/50y receiving. Nelson became 1st rusher in school history to reach 1,000y (1,069y) in single season. Cal QB Gary Graumann threw for 147y.

AP November 21			
1 Texas (60)	1272	11 Nebraska	324
2 Alabama	1044	12 Texas A&M	238
3 Oklahoma (1)	998	13 Clemson	164
4 Michigan	912	14 Washington	80
5 Notre Dame (1)	732	15 North Carolina	76
6 Arkansas	606	16 San Diego State	49
7 Kentucky (1)	600	17 UCLA	45
8 Ohio State	486	18 Brigham Young	29
9 Penn State	483	19 Arizona State	19
10 Pittsburgh	398	20 Florida State	18

November 24-26, 1977

(Th'g) Arkansas 17 TEXAS TECH 14: Clutch QB Ron Calcagni did it again, throwing 4th Q TD pass, his 2nd of 2nd H, to pull out victory for Razorbacks (10-1). Red Raiders (7-4) had roared to 14-3 H lead as FB Billy Taylor (34/104y) scored twice on 1y runs. Calcagni, who rushed for 85y and threw for 97y, pulled Hogs to within 14-9 on 11y TD pass to WR Danny Bobo and hooked up with WR Bobby Duckworth on 59y scoring blitz with 6:18 left. K Steve Little's 50y FG in 1st H had put Arkansas on scoreboard.

(Fri) OKLAHOMA 38 Nebraska 7: Oklahoma (10-1) opened gates with 1 of fastest backfields in history, running at, around, and past Huskers for 417y rushing. QB Thomas Lott (22/143y rushing) made it look easy, rushing for 119y in 1st H in leading Sooners to easy win. Lott's heroics set up pair of short TD runs by HB Elvis Peacock (20/123y) and his own 11y scoring dash 29 secs before H. Oklahoma D forced 5 TOs and held Nebraska (8-3) IB I.M. Hipp to 33y rushing, 94y below his avg. Huskers managed only IB Rick Berns' 2y run that had cut margin to 14-7 in 2nd Q. Lott then led Sooners on 80y drive to his TD keeper that dimmed Huskers' hopes. "The offensive team is the best I've ever coached," said OU coach Barry Switzer.

(Fri) ARIZONA STATE 23 Arizona 7: In final WAC game for each rival, Arizona State (9-2) unleashed "Tri-Harris team" to earn Fiesta Bowl berth. Sun Devils DE Al Harris, with 6 tackles, FUM REC, pass deflection, and loads of pressure, dominated line of scrimmage. DB John Harris dazzled with 55y punt TD RET, FUM REC, and 3 INTs. FB Mike Harris (16/109y) was leading rusher and chipped in 31y TD run in 2nd Q. Sun Devils built commanding 21-0 lead in 2nd Q before Wildcats broke onto board with 1y run by WR Harry Holt, set up by 57y pass from QB Marc Lunsford (14-31/222y, 2 INTs) to WR Reed May. Arizona (4-7) was hard pressed to rally, as Arizona State "Crunch Bunch" D only allowed trio of FG attempts that K Lee Pistor failed to make.

(Fri) SOUTHERN CALIFORNIA 29 Ucla 27: K Frank Jordan's 36y FG with 2 ticks remaining booted Bruins (7-4) out of Rose Bowl and made Washington fans happy with their team's improbable comeback. UCLA had rallied from 26-10 deficit and took 27-26 lead with 80y drive behind QB Rick Bashore (11-18/136y, 2 TDs, INT), who heroically returned from broken ribs and collapsed lung suffered 3 weeks earlier. Trojans (7-4) gained possession with less than 3 mins left, worked sidelines and profited from controversial interference PEN on Bruins S Johnny Lynn to move past midfield. Southern California QB Rob Hertel (15-24/254y, 3 TDs, 2 INTs), whose trio of TDs for season school-record 15, quickly hit WR Randy Simmrin (6/108y) with 18y pass that set up Jordan's winning boot.

Army 17 Navy 14 (Philadelphia): Before season began, Cadets sr players met in secret and vowed to beat Navy at year's end. Their vow was realized as Army (7-4) snapped 4-game losing streak to George Welsh-coached Midshipmen (5-6) as Cadets D held near GL at game's end. On option pass play, TB Joe Gattuso, Jr., (23/123y, TD) ended his fine career with incomplete pass to WR Phil McConkey on 4th-and-2 from Army 9YL. QB Leamon Hall, never much of runner, had scored on QB keeper for Army TD and directed 80y drive for other. MG George Mayes sparked Black Knights D with 3 sacks and constant pressure, while LB John Hilliard had 2 INTs to set up his team's opening 10 pts. Gattuso made 2y TD run in 3rd Q.

Penn State 15 PITTSBURGH 13: DT Matt Millen stood up Pitt TB Elliott Walker inches from GL to prevent tying 2-pt conv as game ended. Snow forced Pitt (8-2-1) to keep 2-pt try between hashmarks. Moments before, QB Matt Cavanaugh (14-29/204y, 3 INTs) had hit WR Gordon Jones with 17y TD pass capping 53y drive in 22 secs that featured 3 straight completions. Twice, Cavanaugh suffered EZ INTs by LB Ron Hostetler, brother of Cavanaugh's future pro teammate Jeff. Hostetler's 2nd came with just over 2 mins left. Nittany Lions (10-1) scored sole TD on reverse punt RET as TB Mike Guman took handoff from WR Jimmy Cefalo and scored from 52y. Home team Pitt chose to move game later for TV; choice earned Penn State $250,000 but cost it Orange Bowl bid as committee did not wait to see if Lions would win.

GEORGIA TECH 16 Georgia 7: Yellow Jackets (6-5) were ready from opening KO, grabbing 16-0 H lead with 201y to 73y O edge. Georgia Tech TB Eddie Lee Ivery, who rushed for 112y, and QB Gary Hardie each ran for TD. Georgia used blocked punts in Tech territory by S Bill Krug and CB Bobby Thompson to help its banged-up O; 2nd block set up FB James Womack's 1y TD with 6:02 left. Bulldogs (5-6), who suffered 1st losing year under coach Vince Dooley, continued to lose QBs, with 2 more knocked out and preseason 6th string QB Davey Sawyer, who played in frosh game 2 days earlier, calling signals by game's end. Win marked 1st time in 23 years that Jackets had swept traditional rivals Tennessee, Auburn, and Georgia.

Alabama 48 Auburn 21 (Birmingham): Crimson Tide (10-1) used 3-TD explosion to rack up most pts against arch rivals in Bear Bryant's gloried tenure. Alabama QB Jeff Rutledge (9-13/193y) threw TDs of 42y to WR Bruce Bolton and 30y to WR Ozzie Newsome, FB Johnny Davis added 104y rushing and 12y TD run, while HB Tony Nathan chipped in 2 short TDs to give him 92 pts for season. Most spectacular TDs were turned in by Auburn (5-6) TB Joe Cribbs, who went 85y for 7-0 lead, and WR Byron Franklin, who later hauled in 72y scoring pass from QB Charlie Trotman.

Texas 57 TEXAS A&M 28: Aggies (7-3) grabbed 7-0 lead but could not match pts with Texas O that scored 1st 4 times it had ball. Longhorns (11-0) built 33-14 H lead, but had to withstand rally that brought Aggies to within 40-28. Texas HB Earl Campbell opened 4th Q with 23y TD run on counter-option pitchout. He scored 4 TDs, including 60y reception, while rushing for 222y to finish as nation's leader in rushing (1,744y) and scoring (114 pts). Longhorns QB Randy McEachern returned from injury to complete only 6 passes, but 4 went for TDs to tie Clyde Littlefield's 62-year-old school record. Texas A&M FB George Woodard rushed for 81y and 2 TDs.

AP Poll November 28

1	Texas (49)	1124	11	Clemson	198
2	Oklahoma (5)	940	12	Nebraska	128
3	Alabama (1)	895	13	Washington	124
4	Michigan	771	14	North Carolina	118
5	Notre Dame (1)	666	15	Arizona State	109
6	Arkansas	568	16	San Diego State	78
7	Kentucky (1)	527	17t	Brigham Young	48
8	Penn State	467	17t	Texas A&M	48
9	Ohio State	437	19	Florida State	35
10	Pittsburgh	299	20	Southern California	31

Conference Standings

Ivy League

Yale	6-1
Brown	5-2
Dartmouth	4-3
Pennsylvania	4-3
Harvard	4-3
Princeton	3-4
Columbia	1-6
Cornell	1-6

Atlantic Coast

North Carolina	5-0-1
Clemson	4-1-1
Maryland	4-2
North Carolina State	4-2
Duke	2-4
Virginia	1-5
Wake Forest	0-6

Southeastern

Alabama	7-0
Kentucky	6-0
Auburn	4-2
Louisiana State	4-2
Florida	3-3
Georgia	2-4
Mississippi State	2-4
Mississippi	2-5
Tennessee	1-5
Vanderbilt	0-6

Mid-American

Miami (Ohio)	5-0
Central Michigan	7-1
Ball State	5-1
Eastern Michigan	4-3
Bowling Green	4-3
Kent State	5-4
Western Michigan	3-5
Northern Illinois	2-5
Toledo	2-7
Ohio	0-8

Southwest

Texas	8-0
Arkansas	7-1
Texas A&M	6-2
Texas Tech	4-4
Houston	4-4
Baylor	3-5
Southern Methodist	3-5
Texas Christian	1-7
Rice	0-8

Pacific-8

Washington	6-1
Stanford	5-2
Southern California	5-2
UCLA	5-2
California	3-4
Washington State	3-4
Oregon	1-6
Oregon State	0-7

Big Ten

Michigan	7-1
Ohio State	7-1
Michigan State	6-1-1
Indiana	4-3-1
Minnesota	4-4
Purdue	3-5
Iowa	3-5
Wisconsin	3-6
Illinois	2-6
Northwestern	1-8

Big Eight

Oklahoma	7-0
Iowa State	5-2
Nebraska	5-2
Colorado	3-3-1
Missouri	3-4
Kansas	2-4-1
Oklahoma State	2-5
Kansas State	0-7

Western Athletic

Arizona State	6-1
Brigham Young	6-1
Colorado State	5-2
Wyoming	4-3
Arizona	3-4
New Mexico	2-5
Utah	2-5
Texas-El Paso	0-7

Pacific Coast Athletic

Fresno State	4-0
Pacific	3-1
San Jose State	2-2
Long Beach State	1-3
Fullerton State	0-4

1977 Major Bowl Games

Liberty Bowl (Dec. 19): Nebraska 21 North Carolina 17

Back-up QB Randy Garcia became latest Nebraska bowl hero by throwing pair of 4th Q TD passes in relief of starting QB Tom Sorley (11-14/105y). Huskers (9-3) pulled within 17-14 on WB Curtis Craig's diving catch of 10y throw to cap 74y drive. Later in 4th Q, Garcia (3-3/56y) narrowly avoided blitz to hit WR Tim Smith for winning 34y TD pass. It came 6 plays after Huskers gained FUM REC by DT Dan Pensick on own 43YL. Tar Heels (8-3-1) led most of way as QB Matt Kupec finished opening drive with 12y TD pass to TE Brooks Williams. Later, Kupec followed tying 15y TD run by Nebraska FB Dodie Donnell (9/59y) with his 2nd TD pass in 1st Q: 10y to FB Bob Loomis. UNC K Tom Biddle increased lead to 17-7 on Liberty-record 47y FG in 3rd Q, but its limited O (262y) failed to compete with Nebraska's 367y. Tar Heels missed TB Amos Lawrence (8/35y), who injured his ankle in 2nd Q.

Hall of Fame Bowl (Dec. 23): Maryland 17 Minnesota 7

Returning to post-season action after 16-year absence, Minnesota (7-5) arrived smartly by driving 66y on 1st possession to TB Marion Barber's 1y TD run. Terps (8-4) sent Golden Gophers back to hibernation from that point forward, building 17-7 H lead as TB George Scott rushed for 2 TDs. Maryland D posted 2nd H shutout as DT Charlie Johnson had brilliant game with 17 tackles and 4 sacks. Scott rushed for 75y, QB Larry Dick threw for 211y, and WB Chuck White caught 8/126y. Gophers FB Kent Kitzmann, who earlier in season lugged ball 58 times in 1 game, gained 76y.

Tangerine Bowl (Dec. 23): Florida State 40 Texas Tech 17

Florida State (10-2) QB Jimmy Jordan in no way looked like alternating starter as he ripped Red Raiders (7-5) for 18-25/311y passing without INT. But big play for Seminoles came on TB Larry Key's 93y KO TD RET, and Jordan followed quickly with 2 TD throws during 24-pt scoring spree that broke open 3-3 game. Jordan's 37y scoring strike to WR Roger Overby made it 16-3 at H. Stunned Texas Tech allowed another 11 pts to open 3rd Q, including 40y TD pass from Jordan to WR Mike Schumann, before finally breaking streak with 44y TD pass from QB Rodney Allison (17-27/243y, 2 INTs) to WB Brian Nelson (4/99y). FSU QB Wally Woodham (7-10/144y) mopped up, throwing 2 4th Q TDs. Key added 83y rushing and 6/100y receiving, while Red Raiders FB Billy Taylor rushed for 63y, 21y on 4th Q TD romp.

Fiesta Bowl (Dec. 25): Penn State 42 Arizona State 30

Special teams of Penn State (11-1) made Sun Devils pay as they scored TD on blocked punt and set up FG with long punt RET. DE Joe Lally opened scoring with 21y RET of blocked punt in 1st Q. Nittany Lions D recovered FUM to set up 3y scoring pass from QB Chuck Fusina to FB Bob Torrey for 14-0 lead. Sun Devils (9-3) jumped back into fray behind QB Dennis Sproul (23-47/336y, 3 TDs, 2 INTs), who threw 2 TDs in 2nd Q: 11y to HB Arthur Lane and 13y to WB Ron Washington, which sandwiched

Penn State's 23y FG set up by 67y punt RET by WR Jimmy Cefalo. Lions run attack controlled 2nd H as TB Steve Geise (26/111y, TD) and Torrey (9/107y) topped 100y barrier, and FB Matt Suhey (13/76y) added 2 TDs. Loss was 1st for ASU coach Frank Kush after 5 bowl wins, while Penn State coach Joe Paterno upped his post-season record to 6-3-1.

Gator Bowl (Dec. 30): Pittsburgh 34 Clemson 3

Pittsburgh (9-2-1) showcased talent on both sides of ball in handing Tigers their worst bowl defeat. Pitt TB Elliott Walker (4/83y receiving, 3 TDs) displayed his receiving skills, caught 39y pass for opening score and 34y pass to set up 24y FG by K Mark Schubert for 10-0 lead. Clemson (8-3-1) had its hopes to stay in game dashed when Pitt DE Dave DiCiccio picked off QB Steve Fuller with Tigers threatening on Panthers 18YL. Pitt QB Matt Cavanaugh (23-36/387y, 4 TDs) immediately launched 82y scoring drive for commanding 17-0 lead on Walker's 10y TD grab. Clemson K Obed Ariri needed game-record 49y FG to prevent shutout, and another INT, this time in EZ, finally killed Tigers' chances. WR Gordon Jones caught 10/163y and TD. Panthers' snarling D authored 4 INTs, 2 by ace S Bob Jury.

Sun Bowl (Dec. 31): Stanford 24 Louisiana State 14

In match-up of high-powered rushing and high-powered passing, Stanford's air attack won out as QB Guy Benjamin (23-36/269y) threw TD passes in final 3 Qs to prompt Cardinals (9-3) to overcome 14-10 H deficit. His play topped brilliant performance by Tigers (8-4) TB Charles Alexander, who rushed for 196y and 7y TD. WR James Lofton caught pair of Benjamin's TD throws, 49y strike on fly pattern to tie game 7-7 and 2y effort for go-ahead pts in 3rd Q. LSU QB Steve Ensminger (7-21/55y, 3 INTs) opened scoring with 3y scoring pass to SB Mike Quintela, but was shut down rest of way by Stanford's suddenly-rigid pass D.

Peach Bowl (Dec. 31): North Carolina State 24 Iowa State 14

N.C. State (8-4) emerged from wild 1st Q with lead, at 7-0, it would maintain throughout. Iowa State (8-4) D enjoyed 1st highlight with GLS at its own 1YL that jump-started O to 76y drive. Wolfpack halted that with forced FUM, recovered on NC State 25YL, which in turn was converted into 77y TD pass from QB Johnny Evans to WR Randy Hall. Evans added 5y scoring pass and 32y TD run in 2nd Q for 21-0 H lead. Iowa State was kept off scoreboard until 4th Q when backup QB John Quinn ran in from 1y out and then closed scoring with 10y pass to TE Greg Meckstroth. Wolfpack TB Ted Brown was all-around threat, rushing for 114y, throwing 2 passes/47y and catching 7/47y. Cyclones so Evans focused on Brown, so Evans burned them with 202y, 2 TDs passing and 62y rushing. Evans punted 6/44.6y avg. TB Dexter Green rushed for 172y to lead Iowa State, while QB Terry Rubley was sharp in air with 10-12/133y before being pulled for inability to get Cyclones into EZ.

Bluebonnet Bowl (Dec. 31): Southern California 47 Texas A&M 28

Southern California (8-4) TB Charles White continued to step out of shadow of his illustrious predecessors, rushing 21/186y and making 25y TD catch for 14-14 2nd Q tie. Aggies (8-4) had opened up 2-TD lead as biggest weapons, FB George Woodard (27/185y) and frosh QB Mike Mosley (20/180y), both scored on TD runs en route to big rushing totals. Stat that mattered was FUMs as TO-free Trojans began to pull away thanks to 5 lost FUMs by Texas A&M. Southern California converted those FUMs, most on faulty pitchouts, into 28 pts. Balance also paid off for Trojans, who rushed for 246y and passed for same number. QB Rob Hertel (11-15/246y) threw 4 TDs, 2 to WR Calvin Sweeney, against secondary unaccustomed to bevy of swift receivers. Nail in Aggies' coffin was driven by USC TB Dwight Ford (14/157y) raced 94y to EZ with 4th Q carry that was school's longest run from scrimmage ever.

Cotton Bowl (Jan. 2): Notre Dame 38 Texas 10

With no. 2 Oklahoma, no. 3 Alabama, and no. 4 Michigan contracted to play in other bowl games, no. 1 Texas (11-1) was pitted against 5th-ranked Notre Dame (11-1) in Dallas, which gave talented Fighting Irish outside shot at national title. Longhorns wilted under pressure and hard hits from likes of DE Ross Browner, DE Willie Fry, and LB Bob Golic (18 tackles) and coughed up ball 6 times. While longest of Notre Dame's 6 scoring drives was 50y—and that came in 4th Q with 3-TD lead in place—Irish still dominated Longhorns. Texas managed its TD, with no time left on 1st H clock, after PEN on Irish D allowed QB Randy McEachern to throw 13y scoring pass to WR Mike Lockett. McEachern still gave away 3 TOs in 1st H. Texas' Heisman-winning TB Earl Campbell rushed for 116y, but he was kept out of EZ and was no factor once it got out of hand. Irish G Ernie Hughes dominated DT Brad Shearer, winner of Outland Trophy, who had ridiculed Hughes in press prior to game. ND's O-Line paved way for pair of useful rushers: FB Jerome Heavens (101y) and HB Vagas Ferguson (100y). Ferguson ran for 3 TDs, HB Terry Eurick added 2, and heroics from QB Joe Montana (10-25/111y) were unneeded. With its significant victory margin, Irish vaulted past Alabama, only team from top 4 to win, to claim national title. Texas swapped positions with 5th-ranked Irish, losing as no. 1 team for 2nd time to Notre Dame in 3 Cotton Bowls over 9 years.

Sugar Bowl (Jan. 2): Alabama 35 Ohio State 6

Contest pitting legendary coaches turned into rout as Alabama (11-1) placed its claim on national championship. Tide QB Jeff Rutledge won MVP honors, completing 8-11/109y and 2 TDs, against Buckeyes D that had 22 INTs during regular season. He led 2 76y drives to TDs for 13-0 H lead, throwing 27y pass to WR Bruce Bolton for 2nd score. Bama drove 67y in 3rd Q to 3y TD catch by TE Rick Neal to seal win against Buckeye team that struggled when Ohio State (9-3) QB Rod Gerald was sacked 9 times. Gerald (7-17/103y) finally put Ohio State on scoreboard in 4th Q on 38y pass to WB Jim Harrell, which was too little, too late against Tide O that gained 25 1st downs and punted only once. Alabama coach Bear Bryant won 1st match-up with Ohio coach Woody Hayes, who stood 2nd to Bryant in active wins.

Rose Bowl (Jan. 2): Washington 27 Michigan 20

Facing unheralded Husky team, Michigan (10-2) must have felt that long-awaited Rose Bowl victory would be theirs—feat school has not accomplished since 1965. Instead, Washington (8-4) threatened to blow Wolverines back to Midwest with wild O, grabbing 17-0 H lead and 24-0 3rd Q advantage before Michigan woke up. What happened to favored Michigan was Husky QB Warren Moon (12-23/188y, 2 INTs), who scooted for both TDs as underdogs threw reverses, rollout draw plays, and 4th down passes at Wolverines. Game was seemingly over when Moon followed his D's GLS with 97y drive, hitting WR Spider Gaines (4/122y) for 28y TD and 24-pt 3rd Q lead. Michigan QB Rick Leach (14-27/239y) showed his mettle by completing 10-16/195y, 2 TDs passing in 2nd H. He connected with WR Curt Stephenson on 76y scoring pass, longest to date in Rose Bowl history. Down 27-20 with time elapsing, Leach led Wolverine O to Washington 8YL with 88 secs left. Leach hit frosh TB Stanley Edwards in hands at 2YL, with Huskies LB Mike Jackson trailing. Edwards bobbled ball, however, and Jackson swiped it off TB's shoulder for game-saving INT. After time-killing runs, UW P Aaron Wilson got ball away to midfield, and Leach threw desperate pass picked off by CB Nesby Glasgow. With loss, Wolverines slumped to confounding 0-8-1 mark in season-ending games under coach Bo Schembechler.

Orange Bowl (Jan. 2): Arkansas 31 Oklahoma 6

Perhaps Oklahoma coach Barry Switzer should have been careful about what he wished for. He had pushed for alma mater Arkansas (11-1) to replace Penn State in at-large berth in Orange Bowl. Over-confident Switzer reportedly did not even look at Arkansas game film until 2 days before game, and highly-favored Sooners (10-2) seemed to get extra advantage from Arkansas coach Lou Holtz. Although confident because Orange Bowl Stadium had grass surface to slow down Sooners' flyers, Holtz was forced to suspend his leading rusher, TB Ben Cowins, back-up RB Michael Forrest, and leading WR Danny Bobo for "dormitory incident involving coed." Led by FB Roland Sales, black players threatened boycott and suspended players (all black) threatened suit, neither of which materialized. With its big A-A G Leotis Harris also out of Arkansas line-up with injury, pointspread zoomed upward. Holtz kept team in locker room for extra 15 minutes before game, during which Holtz and DT Dan Hampton told jokes to break ice. Game began, and Sooners HB Billy Sims lost FUM on own 9YL, recovered by Hogs DT Jimmy Walker, which led to Sales' 1y TD run. Sooners lost another FUM later in 1st Q, when FB Kenny King lost it to Hampton. Sales burst through huge hole for 38y ramble to set up 3y QB keeper. Key for Razorbacks' O was ability for QB Ron Calcagni to get outside, which opened middle that its line could seal with influence blocking. On 22 occasions, Calcagni feigned sprintout or pass before quickly handing off to his FBs. Sales benefited by rushing for 205y, new Orange Bowl record. His 3rd Q TD run from 4YL finished off Sooners at 24-0 and capped 82y drive, during which he burst for 38y. OU's only—and long overdue—TD came on 6y pass from QB Dean Blevins to TE Victor Hicks at end of 95y trip in 4th Q. Oklahoma HB Elvis Peacock rushed 15/117y.

Final AP Poll January 3

Rank	Team	Pts	Rank	Team	Pts
1	Notre Dame (37.33)	1180	11	Ohio State	242
2	Alabama (19.33)	1132	12	Nebraska	240
3	Arkansas (5.33)	1011	13	Southern California	140
4	Texas (2)	797	14	Florida State	138
5	Penn State	768	15	Stanford	68
6	Kentucky	605	16	San Diego State	62
7	Oklahoma	592	17	North Carolina	53
8	Pittsburgh	508	18	Arizona State	39
9	Michigan	443	19	Clemson	37
10	Washington	437	20	Brigham Young	23

1977 Top Performance Formula

Rank	Team	Score
1	Notre Dame	1.7519
2	Penn State	1.7375
3	Texas	1.6887
4	Arkansas	1.6703
5	Alabama	1.6517
6	Pittsburgh	1.6333
7	Kentucky	1.5904
8	Oklahoma	1.5462
9	Michigan	1.5446
10	Florida State	1.5107
11	Ohio State	1.4574
12	Brigham Young	1.4468
13	Washington	1.4278
14	Nebraska	1.4222
15	North Carolina	1.3748
16	Southern California	1.3628
17	Arizona State	1.3354
18	Colorado	1.3201
19	North Carolina State	1.3071
20	Clemson	1.3062

1977 Top Opponent Records

1	Penn State	.6533
2	Mississippi State	.6447
3	Pittsburgh	.6341
4	Notre Dame	.6210
5	Miami	.6147
6	Southern California	.5920
7	Oregon State	.5877
8	Nebraska	.5806
9	Kansas State	.5789
10	Auburn	.5783
11	Oklahoma	.5760
12	North Carolina State	.5754
13	Southern Methodist	.5739
14	Texas	.5720
15	Baylor	.5696
16	Houston	.5652
17	Washington	.5645
18	Texas Tech	.5630
19	Florida State	.5574
20	Missouri	.5565

1977 Out-of-Conference Records

	W-L	Percentage	Bowl W-L
Southwest	19-12	.6129	1-3
Pacific-8	20-13	.6061	3-0
Southeastern	29-19-1	.6020	1-1
Big Eight	18-16	.5294	1-2
Big Ten	16-15	.5161	0-3
Atlantic Coast	17-18-1	.4861	1-1
Western Athletic	16-17-1	.4853	0-1

1977 Individual Statistical Leaders

RUSHING YARDS	Attempts	Yards	Avg.
Earl Campbell, Texas	267	1744	6.5
Charles Alexander, Louisiana State	311	1686	5.4
Terry Miller, Oklahoma State	314	1680	5.4
Jerome Persell, Western Michigan	264	1339	5.1
Bobby Windom, Eastern Michigan	246	1322	5.4
I.M. Hipp, Nebraska	197	1301	6.6
James Mayberry, Colorado	246	1299	5.3
Joe Gattuso, Jr., Navy	266	1292	4.9
Charles White, Southern California	264	1291	4.9
Ted Brown North Carolina State	218	1251	5.7

PASSING YARDS	Completions	Attempts	Yards	Pct.
Guy Benjamin, Stanford	208	330	2521	63.0
Mark Herrmann, Purdue	175	319	2453	54.9
Marc Wilson, Brigham Young	164	277	2418	59.2
Keith Thibodeaux, Louisiana Tech	137	260	2384	52.7
Jack Thompson, Washington State	192	329	2372	58.4
Joe Davis, San Diego State	174	290	2360	60.0
Chuck Fusina, Penn State	142	246	2221	57.7
Randy Gomez, Utah	155	315	2126	49.2
Ken Smith, Boston College	149	257	2073	58.0
Mike Ford, Southern Methodist	153	301	2064	50.8

RECEIVING YARDS	Catches	Yards
Rod Foppe, Louisiana Tech	59	1274
Emanuel Tolbert, Southern Methodist	64	996
John Jefferson, Arizona State	58	968
Rick Morrison, Ball State	59	908
James Lofton, Stanford	53	931
Clennie Brundidge, Army	51	842
Randy Simmrin, Southern California	41	840
Reggie Arnold, Purdue	44	840
Ernest Gray, Memphis State	28	826
Jerry Butler, Clemson	47	824

1977 Consensus All-America Team
Offense

Wide Receiver:	John Jefferson, Arizona State
	Ozzie Newsome, Alabama
Tight End:	Ken MacAfee, Notre Dame
Tackle:	Chris Ward, Ohio State
	Dan Irons, Texas Tech
Guard:	Mark Donahue, Michigan
	Leotis Harris, Arkansas
Center:	Tom Brzoza, Pittsburgh
Quarterback:	Guy Benjamin, Stanford
Running Back:	Earl Campbell, Texas
	Terry Miller, Oklahoma State
	Charles Alexander, Louisiana State
Placekicker:	Steve Little, Arkansas

Defense

Line:	Ross Browner, Notre Dame
	Art Still, Kentucky
	Brad Shearer, Texas
	Randy Holloway, Pittsburgh
	Dee Hardison, North Carolina
Linebacker:	Jerry Robinson, UCLA
	Tom Cousineau, Ohio State
	Gary Spani, Kansas State
Back:	Dennis Thurman, Southern California
	Zac Henderson, Oklahoma
	Luther Bradley, Notre Dame
	Bob Jury, Pittsburgh

1977 Heisman Trophy Vote

Earl Campbell, senior tailback, Texas	1,547
Terry Miller, senior halfback, Oklahoma State	812
Ken MacAfee, senior tight end, Notre Dame	343
Doug Williams, senior quarterback, Grambling	266
Ross Browner, senior defensive end, Notre Dame	213

Other Major Award Winners

Maxwell (Player)	Ross Browner, senior defensive end, Notre Dame
Walter Camp (Player)	Ken MacAfee, senior tight end, Notre Dame
Outland (Lineman)	Brad Shearer, senior defensive tackle, Texas
Lombardi (Lineman)	Ross Browner, senior defensive end, Notre Dame
Davey O'Brien (SWC Player)	Earl Campbell, senior tailback, Texas
AFCA Coach of the Year	Don James, Washington

1978

The Year of the Goal-Line Admonition, Chicken Soup Comeback, and Woody's Punch Bowl

It was the goal-line stand of all goal-line stands, memorable because of the game's importance, the sharp quality of play, and the distinguished men running the sidelines. The match-up was top-ranked Penn State (11-1) and second-ranked Alabama (11-1) in the Sugar Bowl: coach Joe Paterno versus coach Bear Bryant. The teams knocked heads all night in a terrific defensive confrontation, with the biggest moment coming in the fourth quarter when Alabama stopped not one, but two dives from the one yard-line by Penn State backs. As Penn State came to the line of scrimmage for its fourth down play, Alabama linebacker Barry Krauss shouted to Nittany Lions quarterback Chuck Fusina: "You'd better pass!" When tailback Mike Guman leapt for the end zone, Krauss was the first to slam him back. Penn State had other fourth quarter chances, but Krauss' stop became the signature play of a famous game. The Crimson Tide held on to win 14-7 to take the AP national title, the fifth national crown won outright or shared during the Bryant era.

Southern California (12-1), victor over Alabama in September and five other ranked opponents, won the UPI final poll by five votes. The choice was the closest since 1966 when Notre Dame edged Michigan State by the same margin. USC's 17-10 Rose Bowl win over Michigan (10-2) was dominated by one play, a diving touchdown scored by Trojans tailback Charles White that was proven via multiple television replays to have properly been a fumble recovered by Michigan short of the end zone.

Notre Dame (9-3) found defending its national title difficult, but ended the season on a remarkable high note. The setting was a frigid New Year's Day at the Cotton Bowl. Despite icy conditions and a small turnout that created almost a surreal atmosphere, Houston (9-3) dominated early in building a 34-12 lead. Notre Dame quarterback Joe Montana had already established a reputation for comebacks, and with some hot chicken soup forced down at halftime to warm up his chilled body, Montana led his greatest collegiate comeback. The Irish won 35-34 and the Montana legend grew to proportions only a magnificent NFL career could expand upon.

Bowl season had another incident that went down in history, but for all the wrong reasons. Even though the 1978 Ohio State (7-4-1) season began with the exciting arrival of freshman passing star Art Schlichter, it totally was overshadowed by a punch thrown by coach Woody Hayes at the end of a heart-breaking loss in the Gator Bowl. Hayes' uppercut punch was there for all America to see on ABC television, and not only did he land a hard shot on Clemson (11-1) defender Charlie Bauman, but the blow was the last straw for a university embarrassed by it all. Ohio State's pink slip ended Hayes' brilliant, but often stormy, coaching career. At that point in history, Hayes was fourth all-time in wins with 238, but was known as much for cantankerous behavior as for his teaching ability.

Hayes' demise was sad. He was a tremendous coach who commanded incredible loyalty from his players. He was a gifted teacher who clearly cared about the young men who played at Ohio State. No matter the extent of negativity expressed about Hayes, the fan or writer making the accusation never could claim that Hayes was anything less than a great football coach.

"The Ten-Year War" between Hayes and Michigan (10-2) coach Bo Schembechler came to an abrupt end with Schembechler clinching the upper hand at 5-4-1 when he beat Hayes in Columbus 14-3 to cap the regular season. The win over Ohio State gave the Wolverines a tie with Michigan State (8-3) for first place in the Big Ten, and they got the Rose Bowl nod over the ineligible Spartans, a team that beat Michigan 24-15 in October to launch a seven-game win skein. With another controversial loss in Pasadena, the Wolverines unaccountably ended their season without a win in all of Schembechler's first 10 years as coach.

Penn State was led by quarterback Chuck Fusina, who finished second in Heisman balloting to Oklahoma (11-1) running back Billy Sims by the second-closest margin to-date despite receiving 12 more first place votes. Penn State seemed headed to the Orange Bowl to face once-beaten Nebraska (9-3) until Missouri (8-4) dispatched the Huskers on November 18. Alabama was next in line, but they faced being closed out of the Sugar Bowl if an unheralded Georgia (9-2-1) squad remained perfect in SEC play. If Georgia had won its final game against Auburn (6-4-1), Alabama, the eventual national titlist, would have been stuck in the Bluebonnet Bowl with no chance of winning the crown, while the Nittany Lions would have headed to the Cotton Bowl to face Houston (9-3). The Bulldogs tied Auburn, passing up a late two-point conversion attempt, so Alabama ended up

packing for the title game in New Orleans. Georgia's "Wonderdogs" finished a half-game out of first place in the SEC with young players picked to finish eighth in preseason prognostication.

The Pacific-10 debuted with the addition of Arizona (5-6) and Arizona State (9-3). Even with added competition--and ASU beat the Trojans--Southern California won its fifth crown in seven years. Jack "The Throwin' Samoan" Thompson of Washington State (3-7-1) became the NCAA career passing leader with 7,571 yards, while UCLA (8-3-1) linebacker Jerry Robinson became the first three-time consensus All-America since SMU's Doak Walker in the 1940s. One player who nearly got undeserved credit was UCLA center Brent Boyd, who was to be named All-Pac-10 at year's end until it was pointed out that he missed the season with injuries.

Nebraska finally beat Oklahoma, after six straight losses, and it was the first win by Tom Osborne over Barry Switzer. What reward did Nebraska get as it was basking in the delight over its big win? The Huskers got a rematch with Oklahoma, which went on to victory in an Orange Bowl that smacked of redundancy and lacked zing.

Colorado's successful pursuit of former Oklahoma and then-curent New England Patriots coach Chuck Fairbanks earned a great deal of attention. The AFC East champion Patriots were miffed and first suspended Fairbanks for the playoffs, but reinstated him in time for an opening round loss to the Houston Oilers. Oklahoma State's hiring of Jimmy Johnson was much quieter. Fairbanks was a bust at Colorado, while Johnson later became a coach who defined a generation.

Another former Oklahoma coach returned to the sidelines with disappointing results. Out of football for 15 years, Bud Wilkinson was named head coach of one of the NFL's most-frequent losers, the St. Louis Cardinals. Wilkinson's comeback failed as the Cards begin 0-8 before beating Philadelphia on October 29. He was fired toward the end of the 1979 season with a 9-20 record.

Southern football featured two record-breaking rushing performances, as North Carolina State (9-3) tailback Ted Brown became the all-time ACC rusher and finished fifth on the all-time list, passing Texas' Earl Campbell. Eddie Lee Ivery of Georgia Tech (7-5) set a new single-game rushing mark of 356 yards against Air Force (3-8) in November.

A record total of 34,251,606 spectators attended college football games for all 643 four-year colleges.

Milestones

■ New rule was established that had missed field goals from outside 20 yard-line placed at kicking team scrimmage line, with possession going to defending team. Other rule changes redefined roughing-the-passer and intentional grounding, allowance of free time-out to replace injured player, consideration of players being blocked into kick returner, and regaining of eligibility of offensive players pushed out of bounds.

■ Arizona and Arizona State joined Pac-8 to form new Pac-10. Georgia Tech, after 14 years of independent status, became member of ACC. Hawaii joined WAC.

■ Garden State Bowl, which would last four years, and Holiday Bowl were sanctioned.

■ In March, 139 schools applied for membership in NCAA's newly-designated Division 1-A.

■ National Football Foundation's College Football Hall of Fame opened in Kings Mills, Ohio.

■ Paul Governali, All-America passer-runner at Columbia died at 57 on February 14. Governali, also all-time Lions baseball player, won Maxwell Award and was Heisman runner-up in 1942. Heartley "Hunk" Anderson, four-year starting G and head coach at Notre Dame, died on April 29 at age of 80. Anderson led Knute Rockne-coached teams that won 20 straight games from 1919-21, and replaced his mentor as Irish coach (16-9-1 in three years) after Rockne's death in 1931. Earl "Dutch" Clark, All-America quarterback at Colorado College before heralded NFL career, died on August 5 of cancer at age 71. Clark rushed for 1,349 yards in 1928, including 381 yards in game versus Wyoming in which he also threw for 200 yards and scored 36 points in 48-25 win. He led Detroit Lions to 1935 NFL title. Ernest "Pug" Rentner, All-America Northwestern halfback in 1931, died at 67 on August 24. Arnie Galiffa, All-America quarterback for Army's 1949 undefeated squad, died of cancer at age 51 on September 5. Chris Golub, former Kansas safety (1976), was killed in car accident outside Olathe, Kansas, on November 11. Texas Tech receiver Michael Morris suffered heart attack during thyroid operation on December 11, went into coma before dying December 27.

■ Former Purdue halfback and active New England Patriots receiver Darryl Stingley was paralyzed on August 12 after hit by Raiders safety and former Ohio State star Jack Tatum.

■ Longest winning streaks entering season:
Alabama, Notre Dame 10   Kentucky, Miami (Ohio) 9

	Incoming	Outgoing
Air Force	Bill Parcells	Ben Martin
Boston College	Ed Chlebek	Joe Yukica
California	Roger Theder	Mike White
Clemson	Danny Ford (a)	Charley Pell
Dartmouth	Joe Yukica	Jake Crouthamel
Kansas State	Jim Dickey	Ellis Rainsberger
Mississippi	Steve Sloan	Ken Cooper
Missouri	Warren Powers	Al Onofrio
North Carolina	Dick Crum	Bill Dooley
Northwestern	Rick Venturi	John Pont
Princeton	Frank Navarro	Bob Casciola
Rice	Ray Alborn	Homer Rice
Texas Tech	Rex Dockery	Steve Sloan
Virginia Tech	Bill Dooley	Jimmy Sharpe
Wake Forest	John Mackovic	Chuck Mills
Washington State	Jim Walden	Warren Powers
Wisconsin	Dave McClain	John Jardine

(a) Ford (1-0) replaced Pell (10-1) prior to Gator Bowl game.

Preseason AP Poll

1 Alabama (31)	1215	11 Washington	546
2 Arkansas (13)	1111	12 UCLA	494
3 Penn State (5)	1013	13 Louisiana State	486
4 Oklahoma (1)	997	14 Pittsburgh	434
5 Notre Dame (9)	987	15 Kentucky	419
6 Michigan	908	16 Texas A&M (1)	410
7 Ohio State	884	17 Florida State	192
8 Texas (1)	759	18 Clemson	152
9 Southern California (2)	747	19 North Carolina	150
10 Nebraska	563	20 Iowa State	148

September 2, 1978

Penn State 10 TEMPLE 7: Give underdog Owls (0-1) credit for working mightily for upset, maintaining 7-7 deadlock until its only TO of night at Veterans Stadium gave Nittany Lions (1-0) chance to kill last 5 mins until K Matt Bahr nailed 23y FG to win it with 10 secs to play. Penn State TB Booker Moore scooted 26y for TD, and Temple QB Brian Broomell hit WR Zachary Dixon for tying 21y TD with 10:49 to go. Owls repeated their TD pass call from Lions 30YL, but Penn State DE Larry Kubin pounced on Broomell with big 23y sack, and TB Anthony Anderson fumbled at his 42YL on next play. From there, Lions moved in for Bahr's kill. Temple P Casey Murphy punted brilliantly for field position, including bombs of 64, 55, and 51y.

ALABAMA 20 Nebraska 3: After taking early 3-0 lead on K Billy Todd's 48y FG, Nebraska (0-1) surrendered 99y drive that showcased Bama's backfield depth. FB Billy Jackson ran for 29y and HB Tony Nathan rushed for 36y on drive that ended with 4y TD pass to another RB: HB Major Ogilvie. Cornhuskers' TOs aided Crimson Tide (1-0) cause as INT by CB Don McNeal led to Nathan's 2y TD run, and FU Ricky Gilliland recovered FUM at Nebraska 3YL that prompted QB Jeff Rutledge's 3y scoring keeper. Alabama's swift D held Huskers to only 110y rushing, with no ground y gained at all in 3rd Q, while allowing only 4 Nebraska 1st downs in 1st H.

September 9, 1978

PENN STATE 26 Rutgers 10: Philadelphia Inquirer called them "Listless Lions" as no. 3 Penn State (2-0) stumbled through its 2nd dull win. Even coach Joe Paterno saw handwriting on wall: "We have to get good or we have to stop talking." Lions K Matt Bahr punched through 4 medium-range FGs. QB Chuck Fusina (12-20/173y, 2 INTs) fired sideline pass to WR Scott Fitzkee, who spun away for 53y TD in 1st Q for 10-0 lead. Rutgers (0-1) gained only 189y and didn't cross GL until QB Ed McMichael's TD pass in 4th Q. Lions mustered long drive of 82y to TB Matt Suhey's 1y blast in 4th Q.

DUKE 28 Georgia Tech 10: Blue Devils (1-0) lost starting QB Mike Dunn to jammed thumb during practice, but it allowed backup QB Stanley Driskill to throw 65y TD pass to WR Derrick Lewis in 1st Q. Driskill set up another TD with 37y pass to Lewis in 3rd Q and added 46y TD run in 4th Q. Duke displayed balance as TB Greg Rhett rushed for 154y. Georgia Tech (0-1) got rough introduction as new member of ACC, but got 111y rushing from star TB Eddie Lee Ivery. Sole Georgia Tech TD was thrilling 90y pass play from QB Ted Peeples to WR Drew Hill in 4th Q.

Northwestern 0 ILLINOIS 0: There was little to savor in this battle of Big 10 bottom dwellers, which was played in intense heat. Illini (0-0-1) took 5 trips across Wildcats 20YL but lost 2 FUMs, missed 2 FGs, and failed on downs. Illinois TB Vince Carter managed 107y rushing, while QB Rich Weiss completed 8-13/109y. Northwestern (0-0-1) had its best scoring bid end with missed FG, and was led by QB Kevin Strasser's 137y passing. Illinois LB John Sullivan roamed for game-high 15 tackles.

Missouri 3 NOTRE DAME 0: Tigers (1-0) stunned defending champs with 1st shutout of Notre Dame since 1965. Irish (0-1) passed up FGs thrice in 4th-and-1 spots in Mizzou territory, none they converted. Notre Dame QB Joe Montana (13-28/151y, 2 INTs) completed only 4-17 in 1st H, losing FUM and throwing 2 INTs. In 2nd H, Notre Dame was stopped twice on downs in red zone and lost FUM on Tigers 25YL. Mizzou HB Earl Gant rushed for 102y, and led drive to K Jeff Brockhaus' 33y FG.

COLORADO 24 Oregon 7: Buffs (1-0) dominated with D that set up 2 2nd H TDs with INTs and posted shutout until final 2 mins. In 3rd Q, Buffs LB Bill Roe returned INT 48y to Oregon 9YL, and DT George Visger returned another INT 6y to Ducks 14YL as Colorado bumped 10-pt lead to 24-0. Colorado also rushed for 256y, with 3 backs scoring TDs. Oregon (0-1) marched 74y late in game to 11y TD pass from QB Mike Kennedy to WR Ken Page. Ducks FB Vince Williams rushed for game-high 105y.

SOUTHERN METHODIST 45 Texas Christian 14: In front of largest home crowd (41,112) since 1950s, Mustangs (1-0) dominated from start. DB D.K. Perry took opening KO 94y to give SMU lead it would never relinquish. Despite sore arm from dove hunting, SMU QB Mike Ford completed 17-26/280y, 2 TDs. Opportunistic Ponies got TDs from TE Elton Garrett, who made FUM REC in EZ, and DE Jerry Kovar, who dashed 70y with INT for score. Horned Frogs (0-1) QB Steve Bayuk threw 2 TD passes in 2nd Q, but was picked off 3 times.

Iowa State 23 RICE 19: Cyclones (1-0) TB Dexter Green (28/165y) tip-toed through raindrops for 3 TDs, but lowly Rice gave Iowa State fits. Owls (0-1) led 7-0 in 1st Q on 1st of 2 TD passes by accomplished QB Randy Hertel (15-27/149y, 2 INTs). Owls still led 7-3 at H until Green marked off his 1st spot in EZ. Rice FB Earl Cooper made like jack-knife for 3rd Q TD and 13-10 edge. WR David Houser nabbed Hertel's 2nd scoring throw in 4th Q for 19-10 until Green did his thing twice again.

Ucla 10 WASHINGTON 7: New-look Pac-10 debuted with rainy, low-scoring match-up in Northwest. Bruins (1-0) scored TD on blocked punt by S Kenny Easley (2 INTs), recovered in EZ by CB Brian Baggott. Washington (0-1) scored on QB Tom Porras' 6y pass to TE Scott Greenwood, after Huskies LB Bruce Harrell snatched FUM by HB James Owens. UCLA K Peter Boermeester made winning 37y FG, also set up by TO as Bruins DB Johnny Lynn had FUM REC on UCLA 41YL. UCLA maintained 10-7 H lead as D allowed no penetration past its 44YL in 2nd H.

AP Poll September 11

1 Alabama (51)	1247	11 Missouri	516
2 Arkansas (11)	1128	12 Nebraska	469
3 Oklahoma	1044	13 Louisiana State	460
4 Michigan	933	14 Pittsburgh	394
5 Penn State (1)	922	15 Notre Dame	379
6 Ohio State	891	16 Florida State	353
7 Texas	833	17 Kentucky	299
8 Southern California	780	18 Washington	235
9 UCLA	777	19 Iowa State	142
10 Texas A&M	544	20 Maryland	132

September 16, 1978

Navy 32 VIRGINIA 0: Balanced Naval attack swamped Cavaliers (0-2) as Midshipmen rushed for 229y and threw for 218y. QB Bob Leszczynski (9-13/210y, INT) led rout, running for TD and connecting with WR Phil McConkey (5/149y) on 3 long passes to set up 17 pts. TB Steve Callahan (21/100y) powered Navy (1-0) rush game with 2 TDs. On bright side for Virginia was play of 3rd-string QB Joe Mark (8-12/62y), albeit against Navy scrubs. "I apologize to you for having to watch that," Cavs coach Dick Bestwick proclaimed. "I hated to watch it myself."

Ucla 13 TENNESSEE 0: UCLA (2-0) FB Theotis Brown (15/105y) broke 0-0 tie in 3rd Q with 54y scoring run. UCLA threatened late in 2nd Q by running ball deep into Tennessee territory, but officials did not grant noise timeout and then, after Bruins ran play, strangely disallowed standard timeout. Brown's TD run, which padded his team's 303y on ground, and was followed by 4th Q plunge by QB Rick Bashore, was all scoring needed against young Vols (0-1) squad. S Kenny Easley had 2 INTs to lead UCLA D, while Tennessee QB Jimmy Streater had 58y sprint in 2nd Q among his 95y rushing.

LOUISIANA STATE 24 Indiana 17: Record Tiger Stadium crowd marveled at late D heroics of LSU (1-0), even though Hoosier invaders made things sticky. Thanks to pass interference, Indiana (0-1) was set up at Tigers 12YL in last 2 mins of 4th Q. But, Hoosiers QB Scott Arnett (3 INTs) had his pitchout swatted back to 34YL where he recovered, and Bayou Bengals LB Tommy Frizzell picked him off on next play. Indiana had owned early action, going into Tigers territory without results but responding with 83y TD drive to HB Darrick Burnett's 6y TD leap. But, FUM REC by LSU S Marcus Quinn signaled Tigers were ready for revival and it prompted tying TD run by TB Charles Alexander (32/144y, 2 TDs). After Alexander made it 14-7 in 2nd Q, LSU DE John "Thunderfoot" Adams stepped in front of TE Dan Powers, who later would score 4th Q TD for Indiana on EZ FUM REC, and rambled 73y for INT TD RET that vaulted Tigers to 21-7 lead in 2nd Q.

Penn State 19 OHIO STATE 0: Ballyhooed frosh QB Art Schlichter joined Buckeyes squad already led on O by sharp sr QB Rod Gerald. Who would start for Ohio State? Little did fans know, but coach Woody Hayes had switched to more open passing attack during closed practices and moved speedy Gerald to WR. Element of surprise did not help: Schlichter had rough intro as Ohio State (0-1) suffered 9 TOs at hands of hungry and already battle-hardened Nittany Lions (3-0) D. Penn State picked off 5 passes by Schlichter and forced 5 FUMs, 4 of which it recovered. K Matt Bahr booted 4 FGs, all following INTs, while FB Matt Suhey scored TD on 3y run in 3rd Q to boost Penn State lead at that time to 10-0.

PURDUE 21 Michigan State 14: Fast-starting Spartans (0-1) scored twice in 1st Q on 4y TD pass from QB Ed Smith to WR Kirk Gibson and on Smith's keeper, but were blanked rest of way. Boilermakers (1-0) rallied behind their rushing game as TB John Macon (19/120y) scored winning TD on 33y run in 4th Q after TB Russell Pope (7/102y) had scored on dazzling 62y run in 3rd Q. Spartans handled QB Mark Herrmann, who completed 7-23/85y, 2 INTs, with 1y TD pass to TE Dave Young. Michigan State struggled once Smith was lost in 1st H with hairline fracture of throwing hand. Spartans also committed 13 PENs/107y, while conversely, Purdue was not flagged for single PEN for 1st time in 30 years.

Alabama 38 MISSOURI 20: Scoring 20 straight pts, tiger-striped upset specialists from Columbia grabbed 20-17 H lead. Missouri (1-1) emphatically marked scoreboard in 2nd Q via HB Earl Gant's 4y run, QB Phil Bradley's dazzling 69y scamper, and DB Russ Calabrese's 20y INT RET to erase 17-pt deficit. Momentum abruptly shifted early in 3rd Q when Crimson Tide (2-0) DE E.J. Junior blocked punt that was returned 35y for TD

by LB Ricky Gilliland. Tigers fell apart, losing 2 TOs in own territory to set up 14 more pts for Tide. Alabama QB Jeff Rutledge threw 2 TDs, but saw end of his school-record streak of 100 straight throws without INT.

ARIZONA STATE 24 Brigham Young 17: Sun Devils (2-0) may have moved to Pac-10, but they proved they still could beat old WAC foes. Frosh QB Mike Pagel rallied Arizona State from 17-6 shortfall. Replacing QB Mark Malone in 3rd Q, Pagel threw 63y TD bomb to WR Melvin Hoover and immediately ran in 2-pt conv to pull ASU to within 17-14. Pagel led 2 scoring drives in 4th Q, with help from Malone, for clinching margin. Sun Devils set up for tying FG attempt early in 4th Q when holder Malone sprinted to his right and lofted 27y TD pass to TE Henry Pollard. ASU LB Bob Carl soon picked off BYU QB Marc Wilson for team's 4th INT, 3 by S Kim Anderson. Cougars (1-1) QB Wilson had something of off-game, throwing for 261y in vain.

September 23, 1978

PENN STATE 26 Southern Methodist 21: Nittany Lions (4-0) scored game's final 14 pts to outlast SMU. QB Mike Ford (18-36/289y, 2 INTs) had staked Mustangs (2-1) to 21-12 lead, with CB David Hill spicing up matters with 40y INT TD RET for final SMU TD. Shaking off INT, Penn State QB Chuck Fusina led 2 late TD drives, 69y to 16y TD pass to WR Scott Fitzkee and 73y to FB Matt Suhey's 3y TD run. K Matt Bahr supplied all of Penn State's 1st H scoring with 4 FGs. Ford was most impressive on Ponies' 2nd TD drive of 69y, going 3-3/52y, including 12y TD to WR Emanuel Tolbert.

Maryland 21 NORTH CAROLINA 20: QB Tim O'Hare marched Terps 68y, with 5 completions along way including miraculous 28y connection to FB Gary Ellis on 2nd-and-28, to winning 6y TD run by TB Steve Atkins. Powerful Atkins rushed for 162y and 2 earlier scores to spark Maryland. Terps D held Tar Heels TB Amos Lawrence to meager 38y on ground. North Carolina's on-going experiment with Veer attack continued to show cracks, although backup QB Clyde Christensen was able to put Heels (1-1) ahead 20-15 with 5y deflected TD pass to WR Wayne Tucker.

Florida State 31 MIAMI 21: Forcing 6 TOs, Seminoles (3-0) held off rivals with gutsy play. Thanks to TDs by DT Mark Macek on blocked punt, WR Jackie Flowers on 3y pass, and QB Wally Woodham on 1y sneak, Florida State held 24-21 lead in 4th Q. Save of game then belonged to CB Bobby Butler, who picked off Miami QB Mark Richt in FSU territory and returned ball 40y. That allowed Noles to add insurance TD as FB Mark Lyles took 4th down screen pass 22y to EZ. Hurricanes (0-2) were led by FB Ottis Anderson, who rushed for 137y, 80y of which were contributed to opening TD voyage. FSU NG Ron Simmons blocked punt, returned 48y by Macek to tie game at 7-7. Miami used big play to regain lead as WR James Joiner raced 48y on reverse. Win was 1st in series for Florida State coach Bobby Bowden after 2 losses.

GEORGIA 12 Clemson 0: Bulldogs (2-0) won hard-hitting affair as HB Willie McClendon rushed for 122y, K Rex Robinson hit 2 FGs, and QB Jeff Pyburn led 80y drive with opening possession of 3rd Q to finish off Clemson Tigers (1-1). Pyburn shook off pressure to fire 11y TD pass to WR Carmon Prince to cap victory drive. Georgia D limited Tigers QB Steve Fuller's passing to 10-22/137y, 2 INTs. Outstanding UGa CB Scott Woerner had INT on own 14YL in 4th Q, recovered FUM, and broke up crucial pass to Clemson RB Warren Ratchford. DB Ben Kelly, who had INT in EZ, wrapped up Bulldogs win on game's final play by recovering FUM on own 19YL.

KENTUCKY 25 Baylor 21: Hard-fought Kentucky (1-0-1) win was secured with 10y TD pass from QB Mike Deaton to TE Greg Nord late in 4th Q. Best chance for Bears (0-2) to answer came after deflected punt gave them ball at Wildcats 39YL. Cats LB Lester Boyd deflected final passing attempt at GL. Baylor had scored 1st on 33y pass from QB Steve Smith to TE Ronnie Lee. FB Randy Brooks then scored 2 TDs for Kentucky on short runs, 2nd being set up by LB Jim Kovach's INT. Baylor used INT to tie game, converting short-range pick-off by glue-pawed DT Joe Campbell into 1y TD run by HB Greg Hawthorne.

Southern California 24 ALABAMA 14: Trojans (3-0) made unthinkable advances right on Bama's back porch, gaining 417y against nation's no. 1 team. USC TB Charles White was main culprit, rushing for 199y. USC D chipped in with 2nd H GLS and 6 forced TOs including 4 INTs. Following huge blocks by G Brad Budde and WR Calvin Sweeney, White opened scoring with 40y TD run midway through 1st Q. But, Trojans led only by 10-7 in 3rd Q after 42y TD jaunt by Alabama (2-1) HB Major Ogilvie. Troy's left-handed wizard QB Paul McDonald (9-16/113y, INT) and WR Kevin Williams then burned Tide for 2 TD passes, 2nd for 40y after Bama CB Don McNeal accidentally tipped ball into WR's hands.

Michigan 28 NOTRE DAME 14: Wolverines (2-0) were determined to throw, and it paid off with 3 TD passes in 2nd H, all following TOs, to win 1st match-up of powerful Midwestern neighbors in 35 years. Inconsistent QB Rick Leach shook off 3-14 passing performance in 1st H to complete 5-6 after half. Notre Dame (0-2) QB Vagas Ferguson lost FUM at Michigan 26YL in 3rd Q with Irish up 14-7, and his bobble right away changed complexion of game. Leach threw 5y TD pass to TE Doug Marsh to tie game, 1st of his 2 TD connections with Marsh. INTs of QB Joe Montana set up Michigan's

next 2 scores, including Leach's 40y TD pass to WB Ralph Clayton. Notre Dame had 6 disastrous possessions in 2nd H, 5 ending in TOs and another going haywire when UM DL Curtis Greer earned safety with sack.

KANSAS 28 Ucla 24: Special teams carried day for Jayhawks (1-2) as LB Buford Johnson forced 2 FUMs on KOs, and WR Jimmy Little returned punt 66y, all of which set up 3 TDs. Bruins (2-1) were buried in stunning 3-min span of 2nd Q when KU QB Jeff Hines completed 51y pass to WR Kevin Murphy to set up TD, Johnson's 2nd forced FUM was converted into TD, and Little's RET led to TD for 28-7 lead. UCLA rallied behind D that allowed only 32y in 2nd H, and powerful runs of FB Theotis "Big Foot" Brown (23/148y, 2 TDs). Down 28-21 with ball on Kansas 8YL and 4:49 remaining, Bruins opted for FG on 4th-and-6. As coach Terry Donahue had hoped, his D quickly held, but Jayhawks P Mike Dumbach boomed punt for 58y to put UCLA at its own 17YL. Kansas then sacked QB Rick Bashore twice to finish off Bruins.

September 30, 1978

ARMY 21 Washington State 21: On Earl Blaik Day at West Point, visiting Cougars (3-0-1) exploded for 21 pts in 2nd Q and easy win seemed in offing. Blaik, in his H speech to capacity crowd at beautiful Michie Stadium, suggested that Washington State be chased "back to the Pacific Northwest." Indeed, Wazzu O seemed to leave early as it was outgained 377y to 297y by game's end. Army (1-1-1) stormed back to tie it on 2nd and 3rd Q TD runs by HB Jimmy Hill (23/88y). Washington State star QB Jack Thompson had thrown 2 short TD passes during 2nd Q uprising. His 1st TD followed KO to Army that was left uncovered, and WSU LB Scott Pelluer recovered ball to set up 6y TD catch by WR Jim Whatley. Cadets picked off Thompson 3 times, including 1 by DB Phil Macklin in 3rd Q that set up Hill's 2nd TD. Cadets QB Earle Mulrane looked for several receivers before hitting star TE Clennie Brundidge for slow-developing 2-pt pass that knotted score.

PITTSBURGH 20 North Carolina 16: QB Rick Trocano (16-27/220y) drove Panthers (3-0) 80y for winning TD in 4th Q, gaining last 13y on his 3rd scoring pass to TB Fred Jacobs. TB Doug Paschal scored both TDs for Tar Heels (1-2), catching 11y pass from QB Clyde Christensen for 9-7 3rd Q lead and then running in 2y score for 16-13 4th Q advantage. Trocano, who might have been game's goat with 3 FUMs, including 1 at UNC 1YL to halt Pitt drive and 2 others that set up Tar Heel scores, made up for his errors with final drive.

SOUTH CAROLINA 27 Georgia 10: Gamecocks (2-1-1) topped Georgia for 1st time since 1959 behind unstoppable run game. TB Johnnie Wright burst on scene with 156y rushing while fellow soph TB George Rogers added 128y. Bulldogs (2-1) had gone up 10-7 in 2nd Q on 81y scoring jaunt by HB Willie McClendon (20/150y). USC took lead on 8y TD pass from QB Garry Harper (9-12/103y) to TE Willie Scott, and dominated 3rd Q with 2 more TDs and rationing Georgia just 7 plays including 2 FUMs and INT. South Carolina ended game with telling stat edge: 40:15 to 19:45 time-of-possession advantage.

AUBURN 29 Tennessee 10: Rout came down to Auburn's ability to run and Vols' inability to do same. Gaining 372y on ground, Tigers (3-0) displayed depth as TB James Brooks rushed for 156y and alternating TB Joe Cribbs added 2 TD runs. Tennessee (0-2-1) was held to 69y on ground, with 24y gained on single TD run by HB Frank Foxx in 3rd Q. In helping to build 16-0 H lead, Auburn K Jorge Portela kicked 3 FGs in 2nd Q, 1 set up by blistering 70y run by Brooks. Vols scored 10 straight pts in 2nd H, with QB Jimmy Streater throwing for 63y of 85y TD drive before Tigers pulled game away on Cribbs' TDs.

OKLAHOMA 45 Missouri 23: Tigers D must have had nightmares about vainly chasing Sooners HB Billy Sims after this game was over. There went Sims (14/166y, 4 TDs) for 42y on 1st Q TD run. Then he dashed for 50y score moments later. In 3rd Q, he broke free for 78y romp, but wait, that was nullified by PEN. Sims scored 2 more TDs, mere 1y efforts, to lift Sooners (4-0). HB David Overstreet added 153y as team rushed for 484y, while OU K Uwe von Schamann hit record 93rd straight x-pt as well as 54y FG. Missouri (2-2) too was potent on O, gaining 463y, with HB Earl Gant rushing for 149y and QB Phil Bradley passing for 200y. So far in 1978, Tigers had lost to no. 1 Alabama and subsequent no. 1 Oklahoma, while beating defending champion Notre Dame.

Texas 24 TEXAS TECH 7: Powerful Longhorns ground game ate up Texas Tech (1-2) with 312y rushing, led by HB Johnny "Ham" Jones' 128y and TDs of 14y and 16y. Nation's top-ranked D held Texas Tech QB Ron Reeves (9-24/151y, 2 INTs) in check until meaningless 47y TD pass to WR Godfrey Turner in 4th Q. Texas (3-0) converted 1st INT of Reeves, by LB Bruce Scholtz on Red Raiders 39YL, into opening score on 19y run by HB LeRoy King. Texas took lead for good in 2nd Q following another TO, FUM by Tech FB James Hadnot on own 21YL. Ham Jones scored his 1st TD 2 plays later.

KANSAS STATE 34 Air Force 21: QB Dan Manucci went beyond call of duty in delivering coach Jim Dickey his 1st win at helm of Wildcats (1-3). Kansas State's Manucci completed 10-12/221y and 2 TD passes in 1st H, while going land-bound in

2nd H for 3 TDs. HB Mack Green chipped in with 123y rushing as Wildcats snapped 11-game losing streak. Falcons (2-2), who gained 401y O, trailed only 14-9 at H after QB Dave Ziebart's 6y scoring pass to WR Cormac Carney.

October 7, 1978

MARYLAND 31 North Carolina State 7: Winning 9th straight, Terrapins (5-0) used special-teams flurry for pair of TDs in 9-sec duration of 3rd Q. No. 19 North Carolina State (4-1), tried to go it without brilliant HB Ted Brown, whose cantaloupe-sized knee kept him on sideline in 1st Q. Brown (19/78y) gamely returned to spark short TD drive in 3rd Q that pulled Wolfpack within 10-7 on FB Scott Smith's 2y run, but Byrd Stadium immediately and figuratively collapsed on NC State. Maryland TB Steve Atkins (26/132y) roared through big hole near left sideline for 98y KO TD RET, and when LB Todd Benson forced FUM on ensuing KO, DB Steve Trimble fell on rolling ball in EZ for another quicksilver TD and 24-7 lead.

Miami 17 AUBURN 15: Miami FB Ottis Anderson (18/104y) burst through Auburn (3-1) line for 42y run on 4th-and-5 with less than min to go to set up frosh K Dan Miller's winning 24y FG. Auburn had just taken lead at 15-14 on 1y TD run by TB Joe Cribbs and 2-pt conv pass from QB Charlie Troutman to WR Mark Robbins. Anderson's run allowed Miami (2-2) to overtake Tigers in rushing 243y to 204y, partly because Auburn lost TB James Brooks (16/50y) to 3rd Q injury. Hurricanes enjoyed 7-0 and then 14-7 leads, with their 2nd TD coming on QB Ken McMillian's 70y pass to WR Jim Joiner.

PURDUE 14 Wake Forest 7: Former Purdue asst John Mackovic returned to West Lafayette at helm of Wake Forest (1-4) team in search of its 2nd win. Deamon Deacs struggled on O (42y rushing, 89y passing) but forced 4 Purdue TOs to help frustrate home team. Boilermakers (3-1) drove to Wake Forest 10YL 3 times, but were held to 2 FGs and TO in falling behind 7-6 in 3rd Q. Wake Forest had taken lead on TB James McDougald's 9y TD run. Purdue QB Mark Herrmann (16-21/188y, INT) led 63y drive late in 4th Q that cracked EZ on TB Russell Pope's 2y scoring run.

WISCONSIN 34 Indiana 7: TB Ira Matthews, nation's best RET-artist, opened scoring with 71y punt RET and kept on scoring with TD runs of 6y and 26y as Wisconsin (4-0) built 21-0 lead at H. Matthews rushed for 87y to lead Badger attack that gained 238y on ground. Hoosiers (1-3) got scant 37y rushing, while QB Tim Clifford passed for 108y with 2 INTs. Game ended amid charges of score run-up as backup Wisconsin QB Charles Green threw 16y TD pass with 13 secs left.

OHIO STATE 35 Southern Methodist 35: Buckeyes (2-1-1) squandered 2-TD lead in 4th Q as SMU QB Mike Ford (36-57/341y, TD) scored twice. Bucks D failed to account for Ford, despite his 3 TD runs, and he zipped into EZ for game-tying 2-pt conv. SMU's final drive ended with missed 47y FG try by K Eddie Garcia. Ohio's 21-0 3rd Q built bulge with started with TD by LB Alvin Washington, who made EZ REC of blocked punt. Mustangs (2-1-1) gained 31 1st downs on whopping 501y.

MICHIGAN 21 Arizona 17: With EZ INT by LB Corky Ingraham to open 4th Q, Arizona (3-2), leading 17-14, began believing in upset. Next time Michigan (4-0) was in red zone, it needed 4 downs before finally regaining lead on FB Russell Davis' 4th-and-inches carry for TD. Wildcats' 17-pt barrage in 1st H had afforded 17-7 edge on TD runs by TB Larry Heater and FB Hubert Oliver (25/99y), and adding K Bill Zivic's 21y FG. Michigan pulled within 17-14 at H on 30y TD pass from QB Rick Leach to TE Doug Marsh. Wolverines TB Harlan Huckleby rushed 104y and 2y TD.

Nebraska 23 IOWA STATE 0: With surprising 2-game series win streak, Cyclones (4-1) were confident in front of largest home crowd to-date (56,450). But, Huskers D held them to 82y total O. ISU TB Dexter Green, Big 8's leading rusher, was blanketed at 46y rushing, while QB Terry Rubley faced unrelenting pass-rush pressure. Nebraska (4-1) was more workmanlike with ball, led by sharp passing of QB Tom Sorley (11-22/112y, TD).

Oklahoma 31 Texas 10 (Dallas): Sooners (5-0) had Heisman winner in waiting (HB Billy Sims), while Longhorns were missing their Heisman winner (Houston Oilers rookie TB Earl Campbell), so Oklahoma was able to dominate Texas (3-1), which had held it to 6 pts in each of last 2 games. Sims ran for 135y to lead attack that outgained Texas 410y to 191y. Once Sims scored 2 1st H TDs, Longhorns were in trouble against Sooners D that forced 5 TOs. OU eventually pushed its lead to 24-3 before Texas WR Johnny "Lam" Jones raced for 25y score.

TEXAS A&M 38 Texas Tech 9: QB Mike Mosley and HB Curtis Dickey took turns running by Red Raiders defenders as formidable Aggies (4-0) easily erased 6-0 1st Q deficit. Mosley rushed for 99y of his 115y total in 1st H, including 64y scoring romp that gave A&M 14-6 lead in 2nd Q. Dickey had only 18y rushing at H, but he finished with 161y. Dickey dominating opening series of 3rd Q, pounding and dashing for 65y of 67y needed to give Aggies TD for 24-6 lead. Texas Tech (1-3) never crossed GL, and could only score on K Bill Adams' 3 FGs.

Navy 37 AIR FORCE 8: Midshipmen (4-0) K Bob Tata kicked 3 FGs and felt Navy got little respect: "If our name was Notre Dame or Pittsburgh, with what we're doing, we'd be no. 1 or no. 2. As it is, we're no. 50." Navy WR Phil McConkey made his future pro coach with New York Giants, Air Force's Bill Parcells, feel "embarrassed" with 19y

E-around and 36y catch for TDs that helped build 23-0 H edge. Great blocking by Gs Frank McCallister and Tom Feldman allowed Navy to spring TB Steve Callahan for 39y TD bolt in 2nd H. Overwhelmed Falcons (2-3) may have blushed when 2 returners collided under punt in 4th Q, but they recovered to move 60y to TB Mike Fortson's 11y draw run for TD. QB Dave Ziebart followed with 2-pt pass.

UCLA 27 Stanford 26: K Peter Boermeester provided late heroics with 37y FG to end game that featured style of whomever-has-ball-last-wins. Miscues had led to 3 1st H TDs as UCLA (4-1) converted FUM and shanked punt into 14 pts on 2 TD runs by HB James Owens (23/102y). Cardinals scored 7 pts after they blocked FG. In 3rd Q, QB Steve Dils tied game with 55y TD pass to WR Andre Tyler, and Stanford (3-2) next took lead on K Ken Naber's 21y FG. Naber then kicked off to UCLA FB Theotis Brown, who raced 93y for TD. Stanford had time for 12y TD pass to RB Gordon Banks to regain lead, but missed x-pt. Ks took over 4th Q, and UCLA had 1 more FG than rivals.

Alabama 20 WASHINGTON 17: Rare trip west found Crimson Tide (4-1) having to play unaccustomed deep pass D against Washington (2-3) QB Tom Porras (7-15/204y, 2 TDs). Porras hit WR Spider Gaines with 74y TD bomb in 1st Q on way to 10-7 H edge. After Alabama DE E.J. Junior swarmed Huskies P Aaron Wilson at UW 16YL, HB Tony Nathan banged across for go-ahead TD halfway through 3rd Q. Tide QB Jeff Rutledge (3-9/35y, TD) upped margin to 20-10 in 4th Q on his only effective pass of afternoon: 36y score to wide-open TE Rick Neal. Porras and Gaines struck again for 58y TD with 5:54 to play, and Washington got it last chance with 3:37 remaining. Aided by pass interference PEN, Huskies went to Bama 36YL, but TB Joe Steele (30/82y) lost FUM to Alabama S Murray Legg at 32YL to end it.

October 14, 1978

VIRGINIA TECH 16 West Virginia 3: Frosh QB Steve Casey sparked Hokies (3-3) in his 1st start, leading O to 493y. Virginia Tech cooked after H, scoring TD in 3rd Q on 2y run by TB Scott Dovel and in 4th Q on 2y run by TB Mike Romagnoli. K Steve Sinclair kicked 29y FG for Mountaineers (1-5), who rushed for 202y but had 5 TOs.

MISSISSIPPI STATE 55 Florida State 27: Bulldogs (4-2) routed Florida State with 41 2nd H pts to obliterate 7-pt deficit. TB James Jones rushed for 2 TDs, caught 2 TDs and threw another, while QB Dave Marler (17-31/307y, INT) threw 3 TDs at helm of O that gained school-record 596y. QB Jimmy Jordan threw 3 TDs in defeat, 2 in 2nd Q as Seminoles (4-2) converted 14-0 deficit into 21-14 lead. Bulldogs scored 3rd Q TDs of 12y by Jones and 29y by FB James Otis Doss to take lead for good. Jones added option pass for 34y TD to WR Mardye McDole (9/175y, 2 TDs) that ended 3rd Q.

Georgia 24 LOUISIANA STATE 17: WR Lindsay Scott jump-started Georgia's 2nd H comeback by taking KO 99y to EZ to cut LSU (4-1) lead to 17-14. After 29y FG by Bulldogs K Rex Robinson tied game at 17-17, HB Willie McClendon (27/144y) scored TD, his 2nd, from 6y out, to vault Georgia (4-1) into lead. Tigers had final chance to score on pass from QB David Woodley that was dropped by wide-open WR Carlos Carson in Georgia territory with min left. Earlier, Woodley and Carson collaborated on 82y scoring pass. LSU TB Charles Alexander rushed for 81y and TD before leaving game in 3rd Q with injury.

ALABAMA 23 Florida 12: Gators (1-3) O stumbled from start, but was able to take 3-0 1st Q lead without 1st down. Despite playing down to level of competition, Tide (5-1) started to pull away in 2nd Q on 13y TD run by QB Jeff Rutledge and 87y burst by FB Billy Jackson (13/147y). Upset-minded Florida did not give in, trading FGs with Bama and then pulling to within 17-12 on 19y scoring pass from QB John Brantley to WR Tony Stephens. Alabama HB Tony Nathan added 9y insurance TD, so Florida would get no closer against D that allowed 8 1st downs and 194y.

NOTRE DAME 26 Pittsburgh 17: As Notre Dame (3-2) maintained its season-long funk for 3 Qs, Panthers QB Rick Trocano opened 4th Q with 4y TD run for seemingly sturdy 17-7 lead. QB Joe Montana (15-25/218y, 2 TDs) and FB Jerome Heavens (30/120y) answered with 86y drive that invigorated Irish. After D held, Montana needed only 4 plays to travel 59y for 19-17 lead. Pitt fell apart, surrendering ball on own 29YL on FUM by TB Rooster Jones, team's 5th TO. Montana, who completed 7 straight passes/110y in 4th Q, sealed matters with 3y TD pass to HB Vagas Ferguson. Heavens became Fighting Irish's career rushing leader, surpassing George Gipp, who had held mark since way back in 1920.

Michigan State 24 MICHIGAN 15: Spartans (2-3) used balanced attack, 248y passing and 248y rushing, to spring upset. Michigan State built 17-0 H lead behind QB Ed Smith (20-36/248y, 2 TDs) and opportunistic D that bent to tune of 331y O for Michigan, but did not break. Three INTs, 2 by CB Mike Marshall, spoiled Wolverines QB Rick Leach's day as he completed only 5-15/98y. With Leach ineffective, Michigan (4-1) rallied around its ground game, led by TB Harlan Huckleby's 98y, for 15 pts in 2nd H. FB Lonnie Middleton scored both 1st H TDs for Spartans on 10y catch and 1y run. Michigan State's total O, 496y, represented most to-date permitted by Michigan team coach by Bo Schembechler.

PURDUE 27 Ohio State 16: Calling outcome "biggest win in my coaching career," coach Jim Young steered Boilermakers (4-1) to 1st win over Ohio State since 1967 and into 1st place in Big 10. QB Mark Herrmann threw for 210y and clinching 19y TD pass to WR Mike Harris late in 4th Q. Buckeyes outgained Purdue, 507y to 328y, but could not overcome 5 TOs or 116y in PENs. Ohio FUMs set up all 10 insurance pts scored by Purdue in 4th Q. Ohio State QB Art Schlichter (20-34/289y, INT) threw well in defeat, connecting with WR Rod Gerald on 60y TD pass.

Oklahoma 17 KANSAS 16: Jayhawks (1-5) went down to wire, scoring with 15 secs left and then failing twice while trying to win game with 2-pt conv. After Kansas QB Harry Sydney hit WR Kevin Murphy with 5y TD pass, confusion over going for kicked pt or for 2 pts cost Kansas delay of game PEN. Sydney threw incomplete pass, but Oklahoma was flagged for offside. Finally, Sydney misfired again, and Sooners dodged upset bullet. Playing without injured QB Thomas Lott and FB Kenny King, OU relied more than usual on HB Billy Sims (30/192y), and his 9y TD run gave Oklahoma 17-7 lead in 4th Q.

HOUSTON 33 Texas A&M 0: Houston O got rave reviews, but D was devastating against Aggies (4-1), holding HB Curtis Dickey to 25y rushing while forcing 5 TOs. Texas A&M QB Mike Mosley coughed up ball 4 times himself in 1st H with Cougars (4-1) converting each miscue into TD. All 33 pts of Houston's pts were scored in 1st H with QB Danny Davis tossing 2 scoring passes and FB Randy Love rushing for 2 more. Texas A&M's proud D had surrendered only 7 pts in team's 1st 4 games.

ARIZONA STATE 20 Southern California 7: Sun Devils (5-1) manhandled Southern Cal, forcing 6 TOs and pitching shutout until 4th Q. Arizona State QB Mark Malone took full advantage of TOs, marching O 28y after FUM for FG, 34y after FUM for TD, 46y after INT for TD, and 19y after FUM for FG. Malone rushed for 139y and TD and passed for 167y with 16y TD to WR John Mistler. Trojans (4-1) were hampered by injuries at C position, but inability to block Devils DE Al Harris hurt as well. USC TB Charles White was held to only 59y rushing, and QB Paul McDonald's 180y passing was offset by his 2 INTs and 4 FUMs.

AP Poll October 16

1 Oklahoma (40)	1137	11 Houston	593
2 Penn State (11)	1085	12 Texas A&M	352
3 Arkansas (7)	1072	13 Missouri	343
4 Alabama	947	14 Arizona State	327
5 Nebraska	875	15 Pittsburgh	316
6 Maryland	815	16 Louisiana State	239
7 Southern California	792	17 Navy	216
8 Texas	661	18 Georgia	198
9 Michigan	644	19 Purdue	189
10 UCLA	610	20 Notre Dame	181

October 21, 1978

North Carolina State 34 NORTH CAROLINA 7: Rushing 36/189y for 3 TDs, North Carolina State HB Ted Brown not only led rout but also became 6th player ever to rush for 4,000y. Brown also set new ACC rushing record with 4,135y. Brown capped team's 3rd and 4th possessions with TDs and after K Nathan Ritter kicked FG after 5th possession, he went 10y to score to end 6th as Wolfpack (4-1) took 24-0 H lead. After not reaching NC State territory in 1st H, North Carolina (2-4) received punt midway through 3rd Q at midfield and scored only TD on 34y pass from QB Matt Kupec to TE Bob Loomis. Banged-up Tar Heels HB Amos Lawrence rushed 5/12y.

Georgia Tech 24 AUBURN 10: Reeling Tigers fell victim to WR Drew Hill, who scored twice as Yellow Jackets (5-2) flipped 7-0 deficit into 21-7 3rd Q lead. Hill caught 32y TD pass from QB Mike Kelley to tie game in 1st Q, then took 2nd H KO 97y for 21-7 lead. TB Eddie Lee Ivery rushed for 127y and threw 17y TD pass to WB Bucky Shamburger for Tech's 2nd score. TB Joe Cribbs led Tigers (5-2) with 144y rushing, while QB Charlie Troutman capped opening 80y drive with 5y TD run. With 3rd straight over Auburn, Georgia Tech had won 5 in row for 1st time since 1966.

SOUTH CAROLINA 18 Mississippi 17: Gamecocks (4-2-1) pulled stunner as QB Garry Harper threw 80y TD pass to WR Horace Smith with 9 secs left and then threw 2-pt conv pass to WR Zion McKinney. Harper was flushed out of pocket on his TD toss, scrambling to find Smith down left sideline behind S Jerry Spore. Rebels (2-4) rushed 275y and had 10 more 1st downs, 21-11, with QB Roy Coleman running for 73y and both TDs. With leading rusher, TB George Rogers, injured, TB Johnnie Wright led limited Gamecock rush attack with 63y and TD. Game featured punting duel between Carolina P Max Runager (10/47y avg) and P Jim Miller (10/45.5y avg).

Michigan 42 WISCONSIN 0: Badgers (4-1-1) picked bad time to play Michigan, after rare Big 10 loss. Wolverines (5-1) scored TDs on 3 of their 1st 4 possessions to quickly disappoint record crowd of 80,024 at Camp Randall Stadium. QB Rick Leach threw for 101y, including 65y TD strike to WB Ralph Clayton, and rushed for pair of scores to lead Michigan O. TB Harlan Huckleby added 98y rushing. TB Ira Matthews rushed for 61y to lead Badgers, who were hampered by punting that averaged mere 21y for each of 10 punts.

Nebraska 52 COLORADO 14: Up 14-3 early, Buffs fans were optimistic. But, Colorado (5-2) scored its TDs with little participation by its O: 100y KO RET by WR Howard Ballage and 1y run by TB James Mayberry after 45y RET of Huskers FUM by S Tim Roberts. Huskers (6-1) crushed crowd mood quickly, running off 49 straight pts to dominate Big 8's top-ranked O. After scoring 11 pts in 2nd Q to tie game at 14-14, Huskers took lead on 10y TD run early in 3rd Q by IB Rick Berns (17/132y, 2 TDs). Huskers QB Tom Sorley (11-17/178y, TD, INT) sparked O that tied mark for most y allowed by Colorado with 641y.

Houston 42 SOUTHERN METHODIST 28: Teams matched TD for TD until 21-pt stretch in 2nd H allowed Houston (5-1) to pull away. Cougars corralled Mustangs behind D that enjoyed 5 INTs and O that featured 2 100y backs as RB Emmett King rushed for 161y and FB Randy Love rushed for 121y. Houston QB Danny Davis threw 2 TD passes and ran for another, all in 1st H as Cougars built 21-14 lead. Backup QB Delrick Brown orchestrated winning drive for Cougars that he capped with 12y run and later threw 5y TD pass. QB Mike Ford threw for 357y for SMU (3-2-1), including TDs of 77y and 26y to WR Emanuel Tolbert, but was picked off 5 times.

TEXAS 28 Arkansas 21: Coach Lou Holtz's record stood at 15-2 at helm of Hogs, but both losses had come against Texas. Proliferation of Longhorns' Joneses made it sound like grocery store: HB Jam Jones led team in rushing with 69y, FB Ham Jones scored TD and vital 2-pt conv in 4th Q, and WR Lam Jones scored 2 TDs. Lam's last TD proved to be winning margin and was executed on 4y catch of pass from QB Randy McEachern. Arkansas had taken 21-20 lead after it scored 2 TDs in 3rd Q: QB Ron Calcagni capped 69y drive with 1y run and pitched 27y pass to WR Bobby Duckworth. Texas S Johnnie Johnson authored 2 INTs.

Stanford 43 WASHINGTON STATE 27: QB Steve Dils ended up on winning end of confrontation with QB Jack Thompson (24-35/275y, 2 TDs, INT), throwing Pac 10 record 430y and 5 TDs. After throwing 13 INTs on season, Dils went without miscue as Cardinal built 27-7 and 40-14 leads. In scoring on its 1st 4 possessions, Stanford efficiently converted 12 consecutive 3rd downs. Teams combined for 1133y, with 95y rushing coming from HB Darrin Nelson to become all-time Stanford rusher, surpassing Ray Handley (1,768y in 1963-65). Nelson scored 3 times, twice on receptions. Dils broke old conf record of 401y in air, mark set by Stanford QB Dick Norman against Cal in 1959.

Ucla 45 CALIFORNIA 0: Golden Bears (5-2) receivers may have finished with more pass catches than did Bruin defenders, but it surely did not seem that way. UCLA (6-1) picked off 10 California passes, returning 3 for TDs, to turn battle of early-season Pac 10 unbeatens into rout. CB Brian Baggott returned 2 INTs for TDs to tie NCAA record. Cal QB Rich Campbell entered game as Pac 10's leading passer, but was pulled after throwing 5 INTs; backup QB Eric Anderson threw 4 more. Bruins FB Theotis Brown rushed for 113y and HB James Owens added 2 TDs.

AP Poll October 23

1 Oklahoma (54)	1270	11 Houston	617
2 Penn State (10)	1203	12 Arizona State	460
3 Alabama	1073	13 Missouri	456
4 Nebraska	1065	14 Louisiana State	405
5 Maryland	938	15 Pittsburgh	372
6 Southern California	926	16 Georgia	334
7 Texas	893	17 Purdue	266
8 Michigan	767	18 Navy	237
9 Arkansas	760	19 Notre Dame	204
10 UCLA	757	20 Clemson	77

October 28, 1978

NAVY 21 Pittsburgh 11: Midshipmen (7-0) entered with perfect record but without any billboard wins. Forcing Pittsburgh (5-2) into 34/-28y rushing disaster gained attention for coach George Welsh's outstanding D, already topping nation statistically. Navy vaulted to no. 11 ranking with this impressive win. Navy QB Bob Lesczynski threw TD pass of 4y to TE Curt Gainer, WR Phil McConkey made alert TD FUM REC in EZ after 1st Q run by TB Steve Callahan (20/71y), and FB Larry Klawinski ran for 3y TD. With Panthers' running game clogged, QB Rick Trocano was forced to throw uncharacteristic 25-51/275y, and Pitt didn't cross GL until HB Freddie Jacobs wedged over late. Trocano was sacked 7 times and picked off once. Led by LB Al Chesley's 15 tackles, Pitt D deserved better, allowing 179y and 9 1st downs while forcing 4 TOs.

Clemson 33 NORTH CAROLINA STATE 10: Featured school color for Clemson was orange, but brown dominated day as TB Lester Brown rushed for 117y and 2 TDs and LB Bubba Brown took part in 17 tackles. NC State's own Brown, outstanding HB Ted Brown, was held to 70y as Tigers (6-1) kept pace in ACC race. Wolfpack (5-2) gambled late in 1st H when, down 10-3, they attempted fake punt on pass from P John Isley that was incomplete. Clemson quickly moved 58y for clinching score on 2y pass from QB Steve Fuller to WR Jerry Butler. Highlight of 2nd H was 94y INT TD RET by Tigers DB Rex Varn.

ALABAMA 35 Virginia Tech 0: Alabama (7-1) uncharacteristically went to air to wallop Virginia Tech (3-5). QBs Jeff Rutledge (7-9/160y, INT) and Steadman Shealy (4-5/73y) lit up Gobblers' pass D, Rutledge hitting WRs Keith Pugh (5/148y) and Brice Bolton for 45 and 27y TDs respectively. Crimson Tide gained 444y, but its alert D squashed 3 Hokie threats to maintain shutout. Virginia Tech K Paul Engle missed 1st Q FG, and QB David Lamie threw 42y pass and scrambled 26y to 4YL only to see series die in PENs and losses at 13YL. Tide DB Allen Crumbley's INT quickly ended another threat after Va Tech DL Chris Albrittain fell on FUM right after Alabama took over.

MICHIGAN 42 Minnesota 10: QB Rick Leach (9-13/143y and 14/62y rushing) rifled trio of left-handed TD passes and ran for 2 scores to spark Michigan (6-1) to Little Brown Jug win in which it savaged Minnesota (3-4) for previous year's shutout upset. Frosh TB Butch Woolfolk sliced through Gophers for 131y rushing, including 49y sprint late in 4th Q. Woolfolk, just weeks from having left his New Jersey home, was forced into his 1st start when raft of injuries knocked starter Harlan Huckleby and 2 others from Wolverines lineup. Leach led 21-pt explosion in 3rd Q with pair of TD throws and runs of 13 and 17y that extended lead to 35-3. Minnesota scored on FB Kent Kitzmann's 2y blast at end of 58y trip that was extended by Michigan's roughing PEN against Gophers P.

Colorado 28 MISSOURI 27: Things looked bleak for Buffs (6-2) in 3rd Q, trailing 27-7 with TB James Mayberry injured and QB Bill Solomon struggling (3-8/24y in 1st H). Solomon woke up, hitting 9-14/157y in 2nd H to lead largest comeback in school history. Solomon rushed in his 2nd TD of day in 4th Q, while sub FB Eddie Ford scored twice in relief of Mayberry at TB. QB Phil Bradley (15-22/241y) led Tigers (5-3), hitting TDs of 14y to TE Kellen Winslow and 60y to FB James Wilder.

HOUSTON 20 Arkansas 9: Houston (6-1) coach Bill Yeoman's Veer O was wildly copied in 1978, but no team did it better than originators. FB Randy Love rushed for 120y and RB Emmitt King added 123y as Cougars, playing error-free ball, sent Razorbacks (4-2) to 2nd consecutive loss. Hogs opened game with 3 straight FGs by K Ish Ordonez as they dominated 1st Q. Houston D adjusted, surrendering only 6 1st downs rest of way. Love scored twice on TD runs in 2nd and 3rd Qs, and QB Danny Davis threw 4y scoring pass to WR Willis Adams as Cougars pulled away.

WASHINGTON 41 Arizona State 7: Huskies (5-3) devastated Devils with quick D and pounding rush attack. Washington grabbed 20-0 H lead on 21y scoring pass from QB Tom Porras to WR Spider Gaines, 4y by FB Toussaint Tyler, and 2 FGs by K Mike Lansford. Forcing 7 TOs for game, Huskies D never let ASU back in game. Subbing for injured TB Joe Steele, TB Kyle Stevens rushed for 101y and TD to pace Washington O, while Tyler added 53y and 2 TDs. Sun Devils (5-2) had only single highlight: QB Mark Malone's 80y TD connection to WR Chris DeFrance.

AP Poll October 30

1 Oklahoma (52)	1228	11 Navy	549
2 Penn State (10)	1168	12 Louisiana State	477
3 Alabama	1074	13 Georgia	475
4 Nebraska	995	14 Purdue	452
5 Maryland	966	15 Notre Dame	339
6 Southern California	948	16 Clemson	311
7 Texas	835	17 Arkansas	298
8 Michigan	783	18 Michigan State	101
9 UCLA	761	19 Pittsburgh	80
10 Houston	759	20 Washington	75

November 4, 1978

PENN STATE 27 Maryland 3: Battle of hottest teams in country—Maryland entered with win streak of 12 while Penn State (9-0) sported nation's longest streak at 16—went to Nittany Lions with ease. Penn State QB Chuck Fusina continued his fine year with 234y passing, including 63y TD strike to WR Tom Donovan (4/113y). Fusina read Maryland (8-1) D on each play and called audibles to take advantage of mismatches. For example, standup DE Jimmy Shaffer had to make difficult coverage on Donovan when WR scored his long TD. Lions' D roared as usual, contributing 10 sacks and 5 INTs, while allowing 32y rushing. S Pete Harris had pair of 2nd H INTs.

FLORIDA 31 Auburn 7: With heat on coach Doug Dickey, Gators (3-4) rolled behind QB John Brantley. Brantley opened scoring with 11y run and threw 33y TD pass to WR Cris Collingsworth to close 1st H scoring with Florida in lead at 24-7. Gators FB David Johnson rushed for 2 short TDs, and CB Bill Fiorillo keyed D effort with 2 INTs. TB Joe Cribbs was just about only able hand on Auburn (5-3) O (195y), running 30/111y, catching 2 passes/16y, and even throwing pass for 13y.

MINNESOTA 32 Indiana 31: This result must have been what drove Indiana coach Lee Corso to ESPN. Hoosiers used big plays to build 24-0 lead in 2nd Q, only to allow Gophers (4-4) to gain 577y and rack up game's final 18 pts. Minnesota K Paul Rogind nailed 31y FG to win it with 2 secs left. Sub QB Wendell Avery (8-14/85y) led Minny's 4th Q rally with 2 TD passes, while Gophers TB Marion Barber was steady throughout with 177y and 2 TDs rushing and TD pass reception. Indiana (3-5) scored TDs on 62y pass from QB Tim Clifford to WR Mike Friede, 92y FUM RET by S Dale Keneipp, and 2 runs by quick little TB Mike Harkrader (32/113y).

Notre Dame 27 Navy 7 (Cleveland): Interestingly, undefeated Navy (7-1) was ranked higher entering game, which clearly registered attention of Fighting Irish. Notre Dame (6-2) gained 530y and scored 27 pts against Middie D that had allowed only 35 pts all season. HB Vagas Ferguson shredded Midshipmen for Irish single-game mark of 219y. Navy lost FUMs on its 1st 2 possessions, leading to 10 Notre Dame pts. Irish added 2 more TDs before H, including Ferguson's 80y scoring scamper. Middies backup QB Bob Powers found WR Phil McConkey for 13y TD pass with time elapsing to prevent shutout. McConkey's score beat Irish starters who had been rushed back in to preserve shutout. Coach Dan Devine also raised eyebrows by having his charges throw some late-game passes.

IOWA STATE 24 Kansas State 0: Cyclones (6-3) took control in 1st H, during which they built 17-0 lead. TB Dexter Green (29/105y), who topped 100y for 17th time in his career, opened scoring with 1y run. After Iowa State K Brian Johnson's 30y FG, backup QB Vinny Cerrato scored on 36y run to lock it up. TE Guy Preston (7/103y) closed scoring with 15y scoring catch. Woeful Wildcats (2-7) were held to 162y, compared to 439y by Cyclones, as QB Dan Manucci passed for skimpy 23y before leaving game.

Texas A&M 20 SOUTHERN METHODIST 17: Aggies K Tony Franklin chose excellent time for his record-breaking 54th career FG to best Arkansas' Steve Little. Franklin booted 29y game-winning 3-ptr with 55 secs left. Texas A&M (6-2) never trailed, opening scoring on 5y pass from QB Mike Mosley to reserve TE Phillip Simpson and then taking 14-7 lead on 15y run by HB Curtis Dickey (33/143y). QB Mike Ford threw for 290y, including 25y TD pass to TE Elton Garrett in 2nd Q, to keep Mustangs (3-4-1) competitive.

BRIGHAM YOUNG 48 Wyoming 14: Not many teams could bench future NFL QB (Marc Wilson) for another (Jim McMahon), but BYU (6-2) had such luxury. McMahon (24-36/317, TD) ripped apart WAC's top-ranked D through air and ground as he also

rushed for 49y and 2 TDs. Cowboys (4-4), who took 14-10 2nd Q lead, sorely missed top gainer, RB Myron Hardeman, out with knee injury. Cougars would stay hot, grabbing 3rd conf title in row with 21-3 win over San Diego State following week.

Oregon State 32 WASHINGTON STATE 31: Beavers (2-5-1) stunned Pullman crowd with 10-pt 4th Q rally, ended on last-sec 27y FG by K Kieron Walford. Oregon State QB Steve Smith (11-17/177y) led 87y drive to FG, converting 4th down with 8y run. Smith earlier threw 2 TD passes and ran in another score. Cougars QB Jack Thompson threw for 223y and TD. Wazzu RB Mike Washington scored on 72y run, but team paid for 3 blown x-pts, 2 on missed kicks and another on fumbled snap.

AP Poll November 6

1 Oklahoma (50)	1247	11 Georgia	584
2 Penn State (13)	1193	12 Purdue	538
3 Alabama	1110	13 Maryland	512
4 Nebraska	1072	14 Notre Dame	484
5 Southern California	993	15 Clemson	391
6 Texas	889	16 Arkansas	319
7 Michigan	855	17 Michigan State	186
8 Houston	840	18 Navy	183
9 UCLA	745	19 Washington	123
10 Louisiana State	618	20 Pittsburgh	96

November 11, 1978

Dartmouth 31 BROWN 21: Big Green (5-3) raised their Ivy League mark to 5-1 and broke 1st place tie with Bruins (5-3) by breaking open 21-21 deadlock in 4th Q. Brown QB Mark Whipple (11-28/158y, TD, 2 INTs) broke into scoring column with 4y TD run in 1st Q, but Dartmouth FB Jeff Dufresne (31/127y) tied it on 1st of his 3 TD runs. Dartmouth WR Dave Shula, son of Miami Dolphins coach Don, made several fingertip catches over middle from QB Buddy Teevens (16-22/169y, TD), future coach of Tulane and Stanford.

RUTGERS 13 Temple 10: Owls (5-3-1) lost bid for Garden State Bowl with mistake-filled play. Temple outgained Scarlet Knights (8-1) 425y to 219y, but 3 TOs deep in Rutgers territory clipped wings. They reached Rutgers 18YL before suffering EZ INT, 30YL before another pass went awry for INT, and to GL where RB Anthony Anderson bobbled away FUM. Still down late at 10-10, Temple QB Brian Broomell lost FUM on own 29YL, recovered by Knights LB Jim Hughes. Rutgers quickly converted TO into victory on 31y FG by K Ken Startzell with 38 secs left. Owls RB Anthony Dixon rushed for 135y, while Rutgers HB Ted Blackwell ran for 83y.

PITTSBURGH 52 West Virginia 7: Long year for West Virginia (2-9) got longer as Pitt took them to woodshed. TB Rooster Jones rushed for 169y and 2 TDs as Panthers (7-2) built 21-0 H lead and then answered 1 West Virginia TD with 3 of own in 3rd Q. WR Steve Lewis caught 5y TD pass for Mountaineers on pass that gave him 104 career receptions, tied for school lead. Pitt FB Larry Sims added 2 TDs.

PENN STATE 19 North Carolina State 10: Penn State (10-0) was unable to get into EZ until FB Matt Suhey (24/97y) provided clinching TD with 43y punt RET. K Matt Bahr supplied all of Lions' 12 pts prior to Suhey's dash with 4 FGs. Always troublesome in series of 10 games with Penn State since 1967, Wolfpack (6-3) held Lions QB Chuck Fusina to 85y passing with 2 INTs. Penn State D limited NC State's star TB Ted Brown to 71y rushing, year after he ripped Lions for 251y. Brown scored on 2y run at end of 1st H for short-lived NC State lead at 7-3. Penn State controlled 3rd Q, driving to 3 FGs by maneuvering 168y. When Oklahoma lost later in day, Penn State took over top spot in Monday's AP Poll.

ALABAMA 31 Louisiana State 10: With team trailing 7-0 and in need of spark, Tide coach Bear Bryant turned to bench. Backup QB Steadman Shealy quickly led 2 scoring drives that gave Alabama (9-1) lead for good. Shealy tied game at 7-7 with 29y keeper down left sideline. He then marched Bama to 1y TD run by HB Major Ogilvie. In winning 16th straight SEC game, Alabama held TB Charles Alexander to 46y. Sole LSU (6-2) TD came on 25y pass from QB David Woodley to WR Carlos Carson.

Georgia 24 Florida 22 (Jacksonville): Rallying with 9 pts in 4th Q, Gators (3-5) pulled within 2 pts on 36y pass from former QB, WR Cris Collingsworth, to TE Ron Enclade. Bulldogs (8-1) halted 2-pt conv when LB Steve Dennis tipped pass to S Chris Welton. Georgia, needing to eat clock, marched into Florida territory on memorable non-scoring drive. QB Jeff Pyburn led march that wiped out remaining 6:56, with FB James Womack gaining 22y and HB Willie McClendon rushing for 20y on 76y trip. Georgia had scored winning pts on 2nd Q trick play: WR Anthony Arnold's 44y pass to WR Lindsay Scott. Collingsworth caught 4/97y including 33y TD in 2nd Q.

Purdue 24 WISCONSIN 24: Badgers (4-3-2) rallied for 2nd tie of their season. QB Mike Kalasmiki threw 3y TD pass to WR David Charles with 25 secs left before hitting lunging WR Wayne Souza for 2-pt conv. Boilermakers (7-0-1) had time to try 50y FG, which fell short. Purdue had 24-6 lead early in 4th Q pegged on QB Mark Herrmann (18-29/262y, 2 TDs) and FB John Macon (117y and 4y TDs rushing). Kalasmiki (9-20/166y) threw 3 TD passes, with his tying TD coming after blocked punt by DT Kasey Cabral. Bounding ball was recovered by Badgers LB Dennis Christenson at Purdue 12YL with 1:33 left.

MICHIGAN STATE 33 Minnesota 9: Spartans (6-3) routed Gophers behind passing attack, featuring QB Ed Smith (26-42/296y), WR Kirk Gibson (8/122y), and WR Eugene Byrd (6/81y). Smith and Byrd hooked up on 2 scoring passes as State led 17-3 at H and 24-3 after 3 Qs. Minnesota (4-5) finally penetrated EZ when QB Wendell Avery, harassed all afternoon, threw 15y TD pass to WR Elmer Bailey. Gibson, future baseball star, became school's all-time leading receiver with 107 catches.

Houston 10 TEXAS 7: Largest crowd (83,053) to date for athletic event in Texas was treated to impressive D display. Teams were scoreless until Houston (8-1) drove 57y in 3rd Q behind QB Danny Davis, who ran for 29y gain and completed 25y pass to TE

Garrett Jurgajtis to position RB Emmett King for 2y TD. Cougars K Kenny Hatfield hit 33y FG as 3rd Q ended to bump lead to 10-0. Texas (6-2) mounted 11-play, 72y drive, highlighted by passes of 27y and 29y from frosh QB Donnie Little to fellow frosh TE Lawrence Sampleton. Trip ended on HB Jam Jones' 1y TD run. Longhorns later misfired at midfield in 4th Q, and Houston embarked on time-killing 6 min drive.

Arkansas 27 BAYLOR 14: Warning to coaches everywhere: watching this game could be hazardous to one's health. Hogs (6-2) won contest featuring 17 FUMs, 11 becoming TOs, and 3 INTs as teams refused to hold on to ball. Arkansas gripped it more often, losing 4 of 6 FUMs. Razorbacks built 24-0 lead entering 4th Q. By then, Baylor (2-7) figured out how to hold ball long enough to score as QB Steve Smith tossed 2 TD passes. HB Ben Cowins rushed for 125y and QB Ron Calcagni completed 7-10/116y for Arkansas.

Nebraska 17 OKLAHOMA 14: HB Billy Sims had marvelous season, except for disastrous 4th Q against Nebraska (9-1). Sims (25/153y), who had TD runs of 44y and 30y, lost 2 FUMs deep in Huskers territory. Last FUM came at Nebraska 6YL with less than 4 mins left, to prevent Sooners (9-1) from authoring rally. Sims had burst free for 17y run to Huskers 6YL and was fighting for more y when hit by 2 defenders. Nebraska DB Jim Pillen made vital FUM REC. Usually it was Nebraska that pulled 4th Q fold-up in this series: in losing 6 straight to Oklahoma, Huskers had been outscored 79-0 in 4th Qs. They had been ahead or tied in 4 of those bitter games. This time, only 4th Q score came from Huskers K Billy Todd for winning 24y FG. IB Rick Berns rushed for 113y as Huskers won O y battle 361y to 319y. Sooners lost 6 of 9 FUMs, and their bobbles set up both Nebraska TDs.

Stanford 21 ARIZONA STATE 14: Cardinals (6-4) tempered pass-happy O in desert slop, rushing 59 times to control game. Stanford built 18-0 H lead by pounding Sun Devils (6-3) D, rushing 15 straight times on 76y drive for 2nd TD: 4y pass from QB Steve Dils (11-20/153y) to TE Marty Smith. HB Jim Brown rushed for 108y to lead effort, while HB Darrin Nelson gained 80y on ground before leaving in 3rd Q with knee sprain. Arizona State got TD passes from QBs Mark Malone and Mike Pagel. Devils WR John Mistler caught odd 23y TD pass from Pagel while lying in EZ and having deflection land in his lap. By throwing 2 scoring passes, Dils established Pac-10 single-season mark of 21 TDs.

OREGON STATE 15 Ucla 13: Oregon State K Kieron Walford did it again, winning game with 4th Q FG for 2nd straight week, this time from 36y out. Foes were tied 10-10 at H as Oregon State (3-5-1) scored on only 2 series in which they gained 1st downs, while UCLA drove into OSU territory 5 times but had 2 TOs and missed FG. INT by S Kenny Easley set up K Peter Boermeester's 2nd FG for 13-10 lead but only pts Bruins (8-2) would manage in 2nd H. Beavers held FB Theotis Brown to 6y rushing after H, after he gained 84y in 1st H. They also prevented QB Rick Bashore from completing any of his 10 pass attempts in 2nd H. Soon after Oregon State's 4th Q punt pinned Bruins at 1YL, UCLA P Matt McFarland stepped on end line for important safety that pulled Beavers within 13-12. Returning ensuing free-kick to UCLA 43YL, Beavers needed to move ball 24y for Walford's winning 3-ptr.

SOUTHERN CALIFORNIA 28 Washington 10: Huskies (6-4) keyed on USC TB Charles White (21/47y), who had problems in mud, but Washington could not stop FB Lynn Cain (25/128y) running up middle or QB Paul McDonald (12-16/192y) passing over top. Trojans (8-1) did their damage in 2nd Q, scoring 3 TDs with McDonald twice exploiting man-to-man D for TD passes. Washington QB Tom Porras, whose FUM and INT set up 2 Trojan scores, had highlight-reel play in him: 72y TD pass to WR Spider Gaines. White scored in 4th Q with 2nd TD, ending 64y drive with 8y run.

AP Poll November 13

1 Penn State (55)	1296	11 Maryland	640
2 Nebraska (6)	1209	12 Clemson	555
3 Alabama (4)	1203	13 Arkansas	461
4 Oklahoma	1092	14 UCLA	414
5 Southern California (1)	1071	15 Purdue	406
6 Houston	975	16 Michigan State	337
7 Michigan	965	17 Louisiana State	295
8 Georgia	803	18 Pittsburgh	251
9 Texas	733	19 Ohio State	142
10 Notre Dame	662	20 Georgia Tech	141

November 18, 1978

Syracuse 37 BOSTON COLLEGE 23: Future NFL stars TB Art Monk and FB Joe Morris dazzled, scoring Syracuse (3-7) TDs on spectacular plays. Monk knotted score at 7-7 with 65y punt TD RET, and Morris broke through Eagles D for 71y scoring romp in 4th Q. Orangemen did all their damage on ground, rushing for 364y while attempting only 1 pass, which fell uncaught. BC (0-8) managed 50y rushing, while throwing for 216y but was most damaged by 4 TOs, to none by visitors.

Clemson 28 MARYLAND 24: ACC showdown was big-play caravan. Teams were headed to 7-7 H until special teamer Mike Carney recovered blocked Clemson punt for Terps TD. Tigers (9-1) tied game in 3rd Q on 87y TD pass from QB Steve Fuller (8-17/216y) to WR Jerry Butler to cap 98y drive. Maryland (9-2) answered quickly when TB Steve Atkins raced 98y, shaking off 2 tackles, for longest TD run in ACC history. It was Fuller's turn and he hit WR Dwight Clark over middle for 62y TD to tie game again at 21-21. Clemson forced punt and took over on own 30YL. Tigers took 10 plays to go distance, scoring game-winner on TD run by TB Lester Brown.

AUBURN 22 Georgia 22: Tigers matched Georgia pt for pt, although their 502y to 268y O advantage left them wanting more. Auburn (6-3-1) TB Joe Cribbs was big gainer; he was close to matching Georgia with 34/school-record 250y. Bulldogs (8-1-1) pulled within 22-21 on 1y scoring run by HB Willie McClendon with 5:18 left, but coach Vince Dooley, thinking his charges would get another chance, opted for x-pt kick by K Rex Robinson. Win would have given Bulldogs Sugar Bowl berth. McClendon, SEC's

leading rusher, gained only 28/48y. Cribbs had scored on 60y run in 2nd Q and 2y run in 3rd Q, while catching 2-pt conv pass from QB Charlie Troutman after Troutman's 60y scoring run in 3rd Q.

MISSISSIPPI STATE 16 Louisiana State 14: Bulldogs (6-4) knocked off Bengals (6-3) as QB Dave Marler threw 2 TDs and D held LSU TB Charles Alexander to 57y rushing. Mississippi State took 13-0 H lead on Marler's scoring passes of 20y to WR Mardye McDole and 18y to TB James Jones (30/162y). Alexander answered in 3rd Q on 1st of his 2 short TD blasts, but Bulldogs K Rusty Martin's 21y FG bumped lead back to 16-6 in 4th Q. QB David Woodley ran in 2-pt conv after Alexander's 2nd TD as Tigers still had chance at 16-14 with 3:40 left. MSU simply ran out clock.

MICHIGAN 24 Purdue 6: Purdue's Rose Bowl hopes died quickly as QB Mark Herrmann left game early with concussion while Michigan (9-1) jumped to 10-0 lead in 1st Q. Wolverines scored 24 pts before having to punt, their running game totaled 343y with FB Russell Davis gaining 134y. QB Rick Leach sparked Michigan, rushing for 90y and throwing 2 TDs. With frosh QB Chuck Oliver (6-16/54y) forced into relief of Herrmann before 105,410 screaming Michigan fans, Purdue (7-2-1) never had much chance. Boilermakers crossed midfield only once in each H and didn't score until special teams blocked punt in 4th Q for DB Mark Adamle's TD.

Missouri 35 NEBRASKA 31: Alumni should support good ol' alma mater, but 1st-year Missouri (7-4) coach Warren Powers completely turned tables for his 2nd straight win in Lincoln. Powers, former Huskers HB (1960-62), masterminded Tigers to knockout of Nebraska (9-2) from potential national title bowl clash with Penn State. FB James Wilder led way with 188y rushing and 4 TDs, scoring Mizzou's final, winning TD to cap 74y drive. QB Phil Bradley (10-21/187y) set up Wilder's TD with 33y completion to TE Kellen Winslow (6/138y). IB Rick Berns had great game in losing effort, rushing for 255y to break by 1y Huskers' single-game mark held by his teammate, IB I.M. Hipp, who accomplished his big numbers against Indiana in 1977. Berns also set Nebraska career rushing mark of 2,605y. Powers had coached Washington State to victory over Huskers in 1977 season opener in Lincoln.

Iowa State 20 COLORADO 16: Cyclones (7-4) blew past Colorado as QB Walter Grant tossed 27 scoring pass to WR Ray Hardee and ran for another score from 5YL. Grant enjoyed total O of 237y (159y passing), while TB Dexter Green ran for 85y. Green, however, fell 11y short in his quest for 3rd straight 1000y season. Buffs (6-5), who never led, rushed for 181y with TB James Mayberry gaining 26/103y and both Colorado TDs. ISU D featured 4 different players with 15 or more tackles, led by LB John Less' 16.

OKLAHOMA 62 Oklahoma State 7: Oklahoma (10-1) rushed for whopping 629y as HB Billy Sims led way with 209y and 4 TDs, all in 1st H. Making matters worse for Oklahoma State, Sims broke Big 8 record for season rushing with 1,762y, 82y better than conf mark set by Cowboys HB Terry Miller in 1977. Oklahoma State (3-8) game tied early at 7-7 after 1y run by FB Worley Taylor capped 74y drive. Sooners QB Thomas Lott contributed to 2nd H onslaught with 49y TD pass to TE Victor Hicks and 50y scoring scamper.

ARKANSAS 26 Texas A&M 7: With QB Ron Calcagni scoring 3 TDs, FB Ben Cowins (17/74y) becoming school's all-time rusher (3,361y), and Arkansas (7-2) earned Fiesta Bowl berth. Hogs (7-1-2) outrushed Texas A&M 202y to 80y and won TO battle 3-0 as their active D truly sparkled. HB Curtis Dickey led Aggies (6-3) with 104y rushing, but he needed 28 tough carries.

UTAH 23 Brigham Young 22: Utes QB Randy Gomez threw for 265y and 3 TDs in 2nd H as Utah (6-3) rallied with 16 late pts for upset. Cougars (7-3) opened with 10-0 lead as QB Jim McMahon raced 56y on draw to set up 20y FG by K Brent Johnson and threw 37y TD pass to WR Lloyd Jones. Johnson booted 2 more FGs for 16-0 H lead, and Cougars seemed to be sitting pretty. Gomez got rolling in 3rd Q on 25y TD pass to WR Jim Teahan, before throwing ball deflected to BYU CB Dave Francis and returned 20y for TD. Gomez shook that off to toss 2 TDs, including 42y scoring pass to RB Tony Lindsay. McMahon threw for relatively low 249y.

SOUTHERN CALIFORNIA 17 Ucla 10: Trojans (9-1) had to love 2nd Q every week, this time outscoring UCLA 14-0 for 17-0 H edge and lifting their season-long 2nd Q total to 117 pts for and 6 pts against. USC TB Charles White rushed for 145y, while QB Paul McDonald threw 36y TD pass to WR Calvin Sweeney and 10y TD to WR Kevin Williams. Decisive score was set up by Bruins FB Theotis Brown's FUM, recovered by LB Gary Cobb on UCLA 17YL. Bruins (8-3), held to only 62y rushing, finally reached EZ on 81y TD pass from QB Rick Bashore to WR Severn Reece. White (3,739y) passed former Trojans Ricky Bell and Anthony Davis (3,724y) to become Pac 10's all-time rusher. UCLA LB Jerry Robinson had 21 tackles, but lost to USC in all 3 of his seasons as consensus A-A.

Stanford 30 CALIFORNIA 10: Stanford O piled up 538y against worn-out D of rival Bears (6-5). Cardinals (7-4) WR Ken Margerum (7/141y) served as prime target for QB Steve Dils (19-33/297y), nation's top-rated passer, while both HB Darrin Nelson (17/177y) and FB Jim Brown (22/101y) topped 100y rushing barrier. Cal's only TD, on 9y pass from QB Rich Campbell to FB Paul Jones, came in 4th Q after Stanford (7-4) already owned 30 pts.

AP November 20

1 Penn State (59)	1306	11 Arkansas	619
2 Alabama (3)	1213	12 Georgia	609
3 Southern California (2)	1152	13 Maryland	411
4 Oklahoma (2)	1150	14 Michigan State	403
5 Houston	1025	15 Pittsburgh	377
6 Michigan	1015	16 Ohio State	344
7 Nebraska	880	17 UCLA	309
8 Notre Dame	797	18 Purdue	179
9 Texas	794	19 Missouri	140
10 Clemson	749	20 Iowa State	82

November 23-25, 1978

(Fri) PENN STATE 17 Pittsburgh 10: Facing 4th-and-2 on Pitt 4YL in 4th Q, Nittany Lions (11-0) went for 1st down and got winning TD to boot. HB Mike Guman cut outside to score for 14-10 lead. QB Chuck Fusina (12-20/107y, INT) pushed for decision against FG try by fibbing to coaches by indicating that Lions needed only ft to gain 1st down. Later, K Matt Bahr added 38y FG, boosting season total to 22 to break NCAA record at that point of 21 set by Temple's Don Bitterlich in 1975. Penn State managed only 230y, but its D kept Pitt (8-3) in check by forcing 6 TOs, including 4th Q INTs by LBs Rich Milot and Lance Mehl. Panthers' sole TD was delivered on 16y pass from QB Rick Trocano to TE Steve Gaustad.

CLEMSON 41 South Carolina 23: Tigers (10-1) unleashed power running game to wear down in-state rivals, rushing 70/397y. Clemson needed 8 plays to score TD on opening possession, when QB Steve Fuller kept from 1y out. After FUM on ensuing KO, Clemson scored again on TB Lester Brown's 1y TD for 14-0 lead before Carolina O even saw action. Gamecocks (5-5-1) rushed for 310y themselves, but suffered 3 TOs to none by Tigers, keeping Carolina behind all game. For 1st time in school history, Tigers had 3 players top 100y rushing as Fuller went for 108y, Brown for 121y and 3 TDs, and FB Marvin Sims added 104y. Gamecocks TB George Rogers rushed for 123y.

FLORIDA STATE 38 Florida 21: After each team delivered knockdown, Seminoles (8-3) delivered final knockout punch. Florida State jumped out to 21-0 lead with help from 3 TOs as FB Mark Lyles (13/100y) ran in 2 TDs and QB Wally Woodham (16-24/179y) hooked up with WR Sam Platt on 40y scoring pass. QB John Brantley (18-33/242y, 3 INTs) rallied Florida to 3 TDs in 2nd Q, including 2 short runs by HB David Johnson. Woodham was not done, leading 3 scoring drives after H, while Noles D posted shutout over final 2 Qs. FSU DE Scott Warren grabbed 2 INTs in 4th Q.

MIAMI 21 Syracuse 9: Hurricanes (5-5), while still deciding about their QB, positioned themselves for victory following week over Florida for Miami's 1st winning season since 1974. Syracuse (3-8) never crossed GL and settled for 46, 50, and 36y FGs in middle Qs by K Dave Jacobs, who closed his 4th straight year as Orange's leading scorer. Orangemen rushed 52/196y, led by TB Joe Morris (25/110y), but QB Tim Wilson connected on only 3-10/60y, INT. Miami FB Ottis Anderson rushed 22/150y and scored go-ahead TD at 14-9 in 4th Q. Pair of Canes QBs, Kenny McMillian (5-12/70y, TD, 2 INTs) and Mike Rodrique (5-6/68y), split duties.

Michigan 14 OHIO STATE 3: Michigan (10-1) QB Rick Leach took Ohio State frosh QB Art Schlichter to Big 10 how-to school, completing 11-21/166y and 2 TDs despite having pulled his hamstring. Schlichter led Buckeyes (7-3-1) into Michigan territory 3 times during 1st H, but Ohio State managed only 3 pts. Schlichter struggled rest of way against mighty Michigan D that allowed only single 1st down in 2nd H. Leach had quickly moved his charges 70y on 3 passes to open scoring on 30y TD pass to WR Rodney Feaster. Leach added 11y TD pass to TB Roosevelt Smith in 3rd Q to finish off Buckeyes. Leach's 81 total TDs, throwing and rushing, became new NCAA record, while wins as starting QB reached then-record 38. Ohio, led on O by TB Ron Springs' 63y rushing, had to live with knowledge of having scored no TDs in last 3 games in bitter series.

MICHIGAN STATE 42 Iowa 7: Strong-closing Spartans (8-3) clinched share of Big 10 title with romp. Scoring TDs on its opening 2 possessions in rolling to 35-0 H lead, Michigan State never was challenged. QB Ed Smith (12-30/144y, 3 TDs) set new school and Big 10 single-season records with 16 TDs and finished his career with 5,606y and 43 TDs. TB Steve Smith rushed for 131y, 2 TDs to pace Spartans run attack. Ineligible for Rose Bowl due to 3-year probation, Spartans were sky high for final game. Iowa (2-9) forced 3 TOs, but O was blanketed for entire game.

TEXAS TECH 22 Houston 21: Clad in black jerseys for 1st time since early 1940s, Red Raiders (7-3) stunned Houston (8-2) as QB Ron Reeves scored late 1y keeper and threw winning 2-pt conv to FB James Hadnot. Cougars had opened scoring with 72y punt TD RET by WR Eric Herring and tied game at 14-14 on 4y pass from QB Danny Davis to TE Garrett Jurgajtis in 2nd Q. Earlier, Hadnot (111y rushing) had provided Tech with 1y TD run in 2nd Q for 14-7 lead. FB Randy Love regained lead for Cougars with 1y scoring run in 3rd Q, but Houston could not overcome 7 TOs.

BAYLOR 38 Texas 15: It was different way to fire up his team, but as worm dropped into coach Grant Teaff's mouth, Bears (3-8) had all inspiration they needed to vanquish Texas (7-3). Scoring 4 TDs in 1st H in taking 28-0 lead, Baylor was led by reserve QB Mickey Elam who entered game in 1st Q. Elam promptly scored on 2y run and threw 3y TD to WR Mike Fisher and Bears were off to 14-0 lead. Most spectacular TD came on HB Walter Abercrombie's 36y run in 2nd Q. Horns struggled on O, rushing for only 95y and lost 7 TOs, 6 of which were INTs. Highlight for Texas D was CB Ricky Churchman's 52y INT TD RET.

Arizona State 18 ARIZONA 17: Arizona State (8-3) dominated O stats (440y to 162y), but needed rally to win. Despite driving deep into Arizona territory numerous times, Sun Devils trailed 14-3 at H as Wildcats scored on QB Jim Krohn's 2 TD passes. Devils took 1st possession of 3rd Q and went 57y to paydirt, scoring on QB Mark Malone's 4y TD pass to WB Chris DeFrance. ASU finally took lead on next drive, using trick play to do it: 54y TD pass from frosh HB Alvin Moore to WR Bernard Henry. Devils D held, and K Bill Hicks added insurance in form of 42y FG. Meanwhile, Arizona missed 2 FGs. LB Sam Giangardella roamed all over field for Wildcats D, notching 14 tackles, INT, 2 pass deflections, and FUM REC.

SOUTHERN CALIFORNIA 27 Notre Dame 25: One of finest finishes in storied rivalry followed 3 Qs of domination by Trojans (10-1). Entering 4th Q with 24-6 lead, USC was on 96y march to finish FG attempt that K Frank Jordan missed. QB Joe Montana (20-41/358y, INT), "Comeback Kid" for Notre Dame (8-3), sparked 19 straight pts, hitting WR Kris Haines (9/179y) for 57y TD, completing 4 to Haines to set up 1y TD run by FB Pete Buchanan, and throwing go-ahead 2y TD to WR Pete Holohan with 46 secs left. Irish led 25-24 and nearly ended it on USC's 2nd play after KO as DT Jeff Weston recovered what appeared to be FUM by QB Paul McDonald (17-29/281y, 2 TDs). Controversial play was ruled incomplete pass. WR Calvin Sweeney (5/105y) then caught 35y pass, and TB Charles White (37/205y) gained 5y before Jordan booted winning 37y FG. USC gained 538y, most ever allowed to date by Notre Dame.

AP Poll November 27

1 Penn State (52)	1256	11 Georgia	658
2 Alabama (2)	1173	12 Michigan State	548
3 Southern California (7)	1145	13 Maryland	519
4 Oklahoma (3)	1133	14 Texas	396
5 Michigan	1028	15 UCLA	367
6 Nebraska	940	16 Pittsburgh	310
7 Clemson	864	17 Purdue	297
8 Arkansas	722	18 Missouri	200
9 Houston	698	19 Iowa State	98
10 Notre Dame	689	20 Ohio State	96

December 2, 1978

(Fri) TEXAS 22 Texas A&M 7: Texas (8-3) K Russell Erxleben put on amazing show, kicking 2 FGs, including 59y effort, and averaging 48y on 8 punts with 74y punt to his credit. Texas D was equally amazing in holding Aggies to 42y rushing. Texas QB Mark McBath threw for 88y and rushed for 3y TD while keeping mistakes to minimum. Texas Aggies (7-4) pulled within 10-7 on 9y TD scramble by QB Mike Mosley (14-26/154y) in 3rd Q. Key play of 2nd H helped seal deal for Texas as LB Bruce Scholtz caught HB Curtis Dickey (15/11y) in EZ for safety. After free-kick, Longhorns took possession, and McBath tossed 47y pass to WR "Lam" Jones to set up clinching 5y TD run by HB "Ham" Jones.

Navy 28 Army 0 (Philadelphia): Navy (8-3) broke out of its late-season 3-game slump in fine fashion, blanking Cadets for its 4th shutout of season. Middies QB Bob Leszczynski led attack, rushing for 2 TDs while tossing another score. Midshipmen scored TDs on 3 of their 1st 5 possessions for 21-0 H lead. Navy TB Steve Callahan caught 18y TD pass for sole 2nd H score, and it came on botched FG when holder Leszczynski picked up low snap and ended up improvising his 26th career TD pass for new Navy career record. Army (4-6-1) QB Earl Mulrane threw for 190y, but was picked off 3 times. TE Clennie Brundidge, Army's career leader in receptions, receiving y, and TD receptions, did his part with 6/92y catches.

GEORGIA 29 Georgia Tech 28: QB Buck Belue came off bench to lead greatest comeback in Georgia (9-1-1) history. Yellow Jackets (7-4) exploded for 20-0 lead, converting LB Al Richardson's FUM REC into 4y TD run by TB Eddie Lee Ivery (25/160y). Tech recovered onside-KO, which led to 1y TD run by FB Rodney Lee for 14-0 lead. WR Lindsay Scott promptly fumbled KO—Georgia O could not get on field—recovered by Tech special teamer Shelton Fox on UGa 16YL. K Johnny Smith booted FG, as he did after another FUM halted Bulldogs deep in Tech territory. Late in 1st H, Belue was summoned for QB Jeff Pyburn and moved Bulldogs 55y to TB Willie McClendon's 1y TD run to cut deficit to 20-7. In 3rd Q, Georgia converted DB Scott Woerner's INT into another McClendon TD, and Woerner took punt 72y for TD for sudden 21-20 lead for Georgia. Georgia Tech regained lead as quickly as it took WR Drew Hill to explode 100y with KO. At end of 3rd Q, Ivery, who became 1st to score TD in 4 series games, injured ankle to end his glorious career. Bulldogs twice converted 4th downs late in 4th Q, including memorable play as Belue scrambled and got hit as he threw pass to open WR Amp Arnold for 42y TD. Arnold scored winning 2-pt conv as D engulfed Belue after his toss-off, and Arnold waltzed into EZ.

Alabama 34 Auburn 16 (Birmingham): With Bama's Sugar Bowl bid on line, QB Jeff Rutledge (13-21/174y, 3 TDs, INT) sparkled, his 3 TD passes tied school game mark. Rutledge's 30 TD passes were 2 more than former career leader Joe Namath (1962-64). Rutledge's first 2 TD passes were of 33y and 17y to WR Bruce Bolton and gave Crimson Tide (10-1) 17-13 H lead. Auburn (6-4-1) hung tough early, converting fake punt and Rutledge FUM into TDs. Rutledge added 11y TD pass to TE Rick Neal early in 3rd Q to stretch Alabama's lead as Tide won their 7th SEC title in 8 years. TB Joe Cribbs rushed for 118y to lead Tigers.

Tennessee 41 VANDERBILT 14: With QB Jimmy Streater's O matching all Vandy could muster, Volunteers (5-5-1) ripped rivals. Commodores (2-9) had no such go-to man, gaining only 235y and 10 1st downs. Streater meanwhile threw for 163y and rushed for 72y and 2 TDs. Vandy did, however, score twice in spectacular fashion as QB Scott Madison threw 47y TD pass to WR Martin Cox, and LB Lyle Kilpatrick added TD on blocked punt.

HOUSTON 49 Rice 25: Cougars (9-2) shook off error-plagued start to score 5 TDs in 2nd H and clinch SWC title. After 5 FUMs and QB Delrick Brown off Cougars bench to lead onslaught, scoring on 5y run 1st time he touched ball for 21-13 3rd Q lead and throwing 19y TD pass to TE Hubert Miller. Difference was run game, which rung up 493y and had 2 players, RB Emmett King (11/147y) and FB Randy Love (17/90y), pass season's 1,000y barrier for 1st time in school and SWC history. QB Rob Hertel (27-51/368y, 3 TDs, 2 INTs) provided much of punch for Owls (2-9).

1 Penn State (48)	1159		11 Georgia	615
2 Alabama (5)	1091		12 Michigan State	516
3 Southern California (3)	1058		13 Maryland	442
4 Oklahoma (3)	1027		14 Texas	401
5 Michigan	950		15 UCLA	355
6 Nebraska	856		16 Pittsburgh	271
7 Clemson	775		17 Purdue	256
8 Arkansas	733		18 Missouri	173
9 Houston	682		19 Iowa State	86
10 Notre Dame	630		20 Ohio State	60

Conference Standings

Ivy League
Dartmouth	6-1
Brown	5-2
Yale	4-1-2
Cornell	3-3-1
Harvard	2-4-1
Columbia	2-4-1
Princeton	1-4-2
Pennsylvania	1-5-1

Atlantic Coast
Clemson	6-0
Maryland	5-1
North Carolina State	4-2
North Carolina	3-3
Duke	2-4
Wake Forest	1-5
Virginia	0-6
Georgia Tech *	0-1
* ineligible	

Southeastern
Alabama	6-0
Georgia	5-0-1
Auburn	3-2-1
Louisiana State	3-3
Tennessee	3-3
Florida	3-3
Mississippi State	2-4
Mississippi	2-4
Kentucky	2-4
Vanderbilt	0-6

Big Ten
Michigan	7-1
Michigan State	7-1
Purdue	6-1-1
Ohio State	6-2
Minnesota	4-4
Wisconsin	3-4-2
Indiana	3-5
Iowa	2-6
Illinois	0-6-2
Northwestern	0-8-1

Mid-American
Ball State	8-0
Central Michigan	8-1
Miami	5-2
Western Michigan	5-4
Bowling Green	3-5
Ohio University	3-5
Northern Illinois	2-4
Kent State	2-6
Toledo	2-7
Eastern Michigan	1-5

Big Eight
Oklahoma	6-1
Nebraska	6-1
Iowa State	4-3
Missouri	4-3
Kansas State	3-4
Oklahoma State	3-4
Colorado	2-5
Kansas	0-7

Southwest
Houston	7-1
Arkansas	6-2
Texas	6-2
Texas Tech	5-3
Texas A&M	4-4
Southern Methodist	3-5
Baylor	3-5
Rice	2-6
Texas Christian	0-8

Western Athletic
Brigham Young	5-1
Utah	4-2
Wyoming	4-2
New Mexico	3-3
San Diego State	2-4
Colorado State	2-4
Texas-El Paso	1-5
Hawaii *	2-1
* Ineligible	

Pacific-10
Southern California	6-1
UCLA	6-2
Washington	6-2
Arizona State	4-3
Stanford	4-3
California	3-4
Arizona	3-4
Oregon	2-5
Oregon State	2-6
Washington State	1-7

Pacific Coast Athletic
Utah State	4-1
San Jose State	4-1
Pacific	3-2
Fullerton State	2-3
Long Beach State	1-4
Fresno State	1-4

1978 Major Bowl Games

Hall of Fame Bowl (Dec. 20): Texas A&M 28 Iowa State 12

Texas A&M (8-4) TB Curtis Dickey could not be stopped, rushing for 276y against depleted Iowa State (8-4). Cyclones, with 10 players absent due to academic ineligibility including 2 starters, were hard-pressed to stop fleet Dickey, who scored TD on 19y run and set up 3 others. Cyclones managed 6-0 2nd Q lead on 5y pass from QB Walter Grant to TB Dexter Green (148y rushing) and pulled within 2 pts in 3rd Q after Green's 28y TD run. That was as close as ISU could get.

Holiday Bowl (Dec. 22): Navy 23 Brigham Young 16

Holiday Bowl debuted to unsuspecting world and delivered on what would become annual promise of hard-fought, exciting matchup. San Diego wanted wholesome atmosphere, but surprisingly Donny and Marie Osmond were booed during national anthem. Navy (9-3), playing in its 1st bowl since 1964, scored 13 4th Q points to upset Cougars with WR Phil McConkey's winning TD coming on 65y reception. After teams traded FGs, QB Jim McMahon threw 10y TD to WR Mike Chronister as BYU (9-4) grabbed 9-3 H lead. McMahon added 2y TD run for 16-3 lead that was short-lived. Midshipmen answered with TD and 2 FGs to tie game at 16-16 midway through 4th

Q. McConkey caught 4/88y and rushed twice for 42y in final game, while QB Bob Leszczynski completed 7-13/123y. Navy D only allowed 181y passing.

Sun Bowl (Dec. 23): Texas 42 Maryland 0

Too much Ham, Lam and Jam overwhelmed Maryland (9-3) in biggest-ever Sun Bowl rout. HB Ham Jones rushed 14/104y, WR Lam Jones scored 2 TDs, and FB Jam Jones gained 19/100y as Texas (9-3) jumped on Terps early and never let them up. Lam scored 1st on 7y run with reverse. After Jam doubled lead with 1y TD run, Lam caught 29y TD pass from QB Mark McBath. McBath ran in 2y scoring run in 2nd Q as Horns upped lead to 28-0 at H. Jam and Ham each added insurance TDs in 2nd H, with Ham's coming on 32y run. Wind played factor as Maryland had to travel into gusts sometimes reaching 45 mph in 1st Q, during which Texas built 21-0 lead. Texas D held TB Steve Atkins to 15y rushing, while forcing 5 TOs. Terps QB Tim O'Hare threw for 146y, but also tossed 3 of team's 4 INTs.

Liberty Bowl (Dec. 23): Missouri 20 Louisiana State 15

Battle of Tigers was won by Missouri (8-4) on strength of 20-pt 1st H as its D held off LSU's late rally, thanks in part to 5 TOs. FB James Wilder rushed for 115y and TD and QB Phil Bradley threw for 117y and 16y TD pass to TE Kellen Winslow as Missouri used all its weapons in scoring 3 TDs. Louisiana State (8-4) rallied behind TB Charles Alexander, who rushed for 133y and team's 1st TD. Alexander's score capped 80y drive that featured A-A TB's7/52y rushing. LSU, who outgained Missouri 364y to 317y, came no closer, with key hit coming from NG Norman Goodman on LSU QB David Woodley after Bengals reached Missouri 26YL. It forced FUM recovered by Mizzou LB Eric Berg. Missouri DE Kurt Pederson added INT later in 4th Q to help Big 8 Tigers hold their lead.

Tangerine Bowl (Dec. 23): North Carolina State 30 Pittsburgh 17

Right after game, NC State's magnificent TB Ted Brown had his jersey number retired. Brown finished Wolfpack career as 4th leading rusher in NCAA history, gaining 126y against good D that was stacked against him. Brown opened scoring with 1y run in 1st Q for 7-0 lead NC State (9-3) would not relinquish. After K Nathan Ritter hit 51y FG, QB John Isley threw 55y TD pass to WR Lee Jukes as Wolfpack led 17-0 at H break. Panthers (8-4) finally got on board in 3rd Q with 37y FG by K Mark Schubert, but Ritter topped that effort with 2 more FGs. After 1y TD run by TB Fred Jacobs pulled Pitt to within 23-10 early in 4th Q, Pack S Mike Nall ended comeback hopes with 66y scoring RET of INT. It was 1 of 3 picks by NC State in 4th Q. Pitt QB Rick Trocano finished with 182y passing and 3 INTs.

Peach Bowl (Dec. 25): Purdue 42 Georgia Tech 21

Boilermakers (8-2-1) went into Georgia Tech's Atlanta backyard and administered whipping. Purdue went to H, dominant at 34-7, thanks to QB Mark Herrmann (12-24/166y, 2 TDs, 2 INTs) throwing for 117y and TD, while TB Wally Jones enjoyed his 1st H with 2 TDs. It had taken little more than 5 mins for Boilers to score as Yellow Jackets (7-5) lost FUM on own 5 YL to set up Jones' 1st TD. Then, less than min later, Purdue LB Mike Marks set up another Jones scoring run with INT. Herrmann then led quick 80y march that he capped less than 4 mins later with 10y TD pass to WR Raymond Smith. With Tech hampered by absence of its all-time leading rusher, TB Eddie Lee Ivery—out with severe ankle injury—team managed just 12y on ground. Facing D backups, Georgia Tech scored twice at end of 4th Q on 2 TD passes from QB Mike Kelley.

Fiesta Bowl (Dec. 25): UCLA 10 Arkansas 10

Hard-knuckle battle produced no winner, as evenly matched teams labored to score pts. After Arkansas (9-2-1) downed punt on Bruin 1YL, UCLA marched 92y on its 1st possession, using its rush game featuring HB James Owens (17/121y) and FB Theotis Brown (11/84y). Bruins (8-3-1) missed FG, however, and game remained scoreless. Razorbacks jumped on board 1st as FUM REC led to hard-won 11-play, 37y drive, culminating in 4y TD run by FB Roland Sales. Hogs DE Jim Howard forced FUM with brutal hit on surprise starter, Bruins QB Steve Bukich, with ball pounced on by NG Dale White. Enjoying great field position entire 1st H, Arkansas pushed lead to 10-0 by H on 37y FG by K Ish Ordonez. UCLA drove after 2nd H KO to K Peter Boermeester's 41y FG. Owens rushed for 3/46y during drive that featured 4th-and-7 conv with fake punt 14y run by FB Toa Saipale. In 4th Q, punt and PEN gave Bruins ball at midfield, where Bukich set up own 14y scoring run with 36y pass to WR Severne Reece. Despite impressive TD throw, Bukich struggled against Hogs D, completing 4-11/61y. He was sacked 8 times, threw 2 INTs, and lost FUM. Arkansas DT Jimmy Walker had 13 tackles, 5 for losses, and 1 sack. LB Ben Cowins led Razorbacks with 89y rushing. LB Jerry Robinson had 15 tackles in final game of his brilliant Bruins career, while teammate S Kenny Easley had 11 tackles, FUM REC, and INT.

Gator Bowl (Dec. 29): Clemson 17 Ohio State 15

Clemson MG Charlie Bauman was solid contributor for Tigers (11-1), but his place in college football history will forever be immortalized by aftermath of his INT late in 33rd Gator Bowl. Bauman's unusual INT clinched Tigers' win, but, when he was knocked OB at Ohio State sideline, he was punched by Bucks coach Woody Hayes. Volcanic Hayes had violent legacy that he never apologized for. He also punched 1 of his own players, G Ken Fritz, when Fritz tried to restrain him. Game ended 2 mins later and so too Hayes' career. Buckeyes frustratingly lost 2 early drives to 4th down failures before K Bob Atha hit 27y FG for 3-0 lead. Tigers bounced back with 80y drive to take 7-3 lead on QB Steve Fuller's 4y keeper. Ohio (7-4-1) answered with 78y drive to 4y QB keeper by QB Art Schlichter (16-19/205y, INT). X-pt was blocked, however, and it would haunt Buckeyes. Eventual 47y FG by K Obed Ariri gave Clemson 10-9 H lead. Tigers moved out ahead 17-9 in 3rd Q on 1y run by frosh TB Cliff Austin that capped 19-play, 84y drive. Schlichter showcased his skills on 12-play, 87y drive that featured his 2nd rushing TD of game. Ohio felt compelled to try 2-pt conv, and Clemson DE Jim

Stuckey made biggest play of game, halting Schlichter short on 2-pt run. With game winding down, Fuller fumbled pitchout on Buckeyes 36YL, recovered by Bucks with 4:23 left. Ohio State moved to Clemson 24YL, but then Hayes drew 2 unsportsmanlike PENs, and Schlichter threw ill-fated INT that ended matters on Bauman's play at Buckeyes sideline. Few would remember, but when Charlie Pell skipped for Florida job on December 4, Clemson introduced 30-year-old former asst, Danny Ford, who became youngest coach in Div. 1. Ford could always say he opened his career with win over coaching legend.

Bluebonnet Bowl (Dec. 31): Stanford 25 Georgia 22

Final 2 games of 1978 season for Georgia (9-2-1) had sharply contrasting results. After biggest comeback in school history versus Georgia Tech ended regular season, Bulldogs suffered biggest blown lead in its history against Stanford (8-4). QB Steve Dils threw 3 TDs in less than 5 mins of 3rd Q to wipe out 22-pt deficit and then led short drive to 24y FG by K Ken Naber for winning pts early in 4th Q. Georgia's best chance to score in 4th Q ended on downs at Stanford 10YL. Bulldogs used blitzing D and efficient O to forge 15-0 H lead on 2 TD catches by WR Carmon Prince and 31y FG by K Rex Robinson. QB Jeff Pyburn then scored 1y TD in 3rd Q for 22-0 lead, but thanks to 2 missed x-pts by Robinson, Cardinal could tie score with 3 TDs and 2-pt conv. That they did as 2 FUMs by Bulldogs and short punt set up TD passes of 32y to WR Ken Margerum, 19y to HB Darrin Nelson, 14y to Margerum, and, lastly, tying 2-pt pass to Nelson. Another FUM—Georgia lost 5—set up Naber's game-winner as Georgia could not overcomes TOs despite 525y in O to only 311y for Stanford. TB Willie McClendon rushed for 115y for Bulldogs, but lost 3 FUMs.

Cotton Bowl: Notre Dame 35 Houston 34

QB Joe Montana's legend grew, although 23-pt 4th Q comeback was truly team effort by Fighting Irish. Amidst absolutely frigid conditions, Houston ran up 34-12 lead, scoring 34 straight pts thanks to host of Notre Dame (9-3) miscues. With shivering Montana out of action due to low body temperature, Notre Dame seemed unlikely to thwart Cougars (9-3). But, Montana gulped down hot chicken soup and summoned comeback effort once he returned from H. Irish special teams struck 1st as frosh LB Tony Belden blocked P Jay Wyatt's punt and S Steve Cichy caught ball in mid-air and raced 33y for TD. With 2-pt conv, Notre Dame trailed by 34-20 with more than 7 mins left. Irish D then did it part, and Montana went to work, completing 2 passes for 47y to set up own 2y scoring run, bouncing off big hit at GL. Pass to WR Kris Haines scored another 2-pt play, so Irish trailed 34-28 with 4:15 left. After PEN wiped out key 1st down, Cougars were forced to punt again. Snap was rolled to Wyatt who got off 26y punt to own 49YL. Montana now went for kill, but lost FUM—team's 7th TO—on Houston 20YL with 1:50 left on hard hit by LB David Hodge. With less than 1 min left, Houston was forced to punt, but offside PEN on Notre Dame gave Cougars 4th-and-ft with 35 secs left on own 29YL. Convinced his punting game was big risk, coach Bill Yeoman decided to go for risky 1st down. DT Joe Gramke stood up RB Emmett King, and Notre Dame had ball with 28 ticks left. Montana scrambled to 18YL. Then with 15 secs to go, he hit Haines for 10y, with WR finishing play by lowering shoulder into defender. Irish now faced 1st-and-goal from 8YL with 6 secs left. After incompletion, Montana rolled right and threw low quick out-pattern to Haines at right pylon of EZ. Haines slid his knees to turf and made catch before toppling OB. K Joe Unis, from Dallas, booted winning x-pt twice, due to PEN, for largest bowl comeback to date. Cougars QB Danny Davis rushed for 76y with 2 TDs and threw for 60y and TD.

Rose Bowl: Southern California 17 Michigan 10

Did he fumble or didn't he? Head linesman (Gilbert Marchman) said no, umpire (Don Mason) said yes, and referee (Paul Kamanski) deferred to Marchman by allowing Southern California (11-1) TB Charles White's 2nd Q 3y dive to count as TD even though ball ended up in arms of Michigan LB Jerry Meter on 1YL. Although replays indicated that White indeed lost ball, on strip by LB Ron Simpkins, before breaking plane of GL, his TD stood up for what proved to be winning pts. Trojans grabbed share of 8th national title by sending Michigan to its 3rd straight Rose Bowl defeat and 5th of 1970s. Wolverines (10-2) had begun poorly as QB Rick Leach, starting his 3rd Rose Bowl in as many years, threw INT to S Ronnie Lott that set up USC's 1st score: 9y TD pass from QB Paul McDonald to TE Hoby Brenner. From then on, Trojans O was mostly White (32/99y) and FB Lynn Cain (14/90y). Wolverines O didn't get going until 2nd H, when Leach (10-21/137y, 2 INTs) completed 8-11/109y and 44y TD pass to TB Roosevelt Smith. Frosh LB Riki Gray had 15 tackles for Trojans, despite playing on bum knee that later required surgery. In November, referee Kamanski had been official who allowed Trojans to keep possession late in game in win over Notre Dame when it appeared McDonald fumbled. Earthquake that measured 4.6 struck during Rose Bowl, but barely was noticed.

GAME OF THE YEAR
Sugar Bowl: Alabama 14 Penn State 7

It would not completely shape Sugar Bowl battle, but series of plays, "The Stand," went down in football history. It was strength versus strength, with Alabama (11-1) prevailing. On 3rd down from 1YL, LB Rich Wingo stood up FB Matt Suhey. On 4th down LB Barry Krauss did same to HB Mike Guman to stop Nittany Lions' 4th Q scoring threat. Penn State (11-1) had entered game ranked no. 1, and Alabama stood at no. 2. While game was not pretty, it was tightly contested. Krauss earned MVP honors, although entire Alabama D (5 sacks, 4 INTs, 19y rushing allowed) deserved credit. Crimson Tide took 7-0 lead late in 2nd Q after 80y drive with H clock elapsing. Penn State called 2 timeouts in assumption of getting ball back but 30y run by HB Tony Nathan (21/127y) changed matters. QB Jeff Rutledge found diving WR Bruce Bolton in EZ for 30y TD pass. With its O struggling, Nittany Lions D gave them break needed to tie game midway through 3rd Q as S Pete Harris picked off Rutledge pass at Alabama 48YL. QB Chuck Fusina (15-30/163y) took 5 plays to move Penn State in for score on 17y pass to WR Scott Fitzkee. Tide later used special teams to break tie as HB Lou

Ikner raced 62y with punt RET to Penn State 11YL. HB Major Ogilivie took pitchout 4 plays later and rushed for TD. Tide P Woody Umphrey shanked 12y punt to Alabama 29YL, but Penn State had this great scoring threat annihilated by PEN for 12 men on field. Alabama retained possession and ate up clock before Umphrey punted again. This time ball went to Penn State on own 21YL, cost of 50y because of PEN. Contest was 5th bowl meeting of top 2 teams, 1st since January 1, 1972, when Nebraska beat Bama 38-6 in Orange Bowl.

Orange Bowl: Oklahoma 31 Nebraska 24

Sooners (11-1) wanted this rematch, as Nebraska (9-3) had eliminated them from national title race with November win. Huskers had short-lived 7-0 lead on 21y TD pass from QB Tom Sorley (18-31/220y, 2 TDs, 2 INTs) to WR Tim Smith. HB Billy Sims (25/134y) and QB Thomas Lott each rushed for 2 TDs as Oklahoma built 31-10 4th Q lead, scoring 24 straight pts between Nebraska's TD and FG. Huskers rallied in 4th Q, marching 78y for 1y TD run by IB Rick Berns and then recovering Lott's FUM at OU 42YL. But, Sooners D stopped IB Craig Johnson on 4th-and-1 from 7YL to snuff rally. Nebraska closed scoring with TD at game's end. Lott's FUM was sole TO for Sooners, who lost 6 FUMs versus Nebraska in earlier meeting. This 1st-ever match-up of Big 8 teams in bowl game featured pre-game controversy as diagrams of special plays put in for game by Nebraska were found at Oklahoma's hotel.

Final AP Poll January 2

1 Alabama (38)	1317		11 Arkansas	689
2 Southern California (19)	1285		12 Michigan State	525
3 Oklahoma (1)	1251		13 Purdue	493
4 Penn State	1168		14 UCLA	487
5 Michigan	989		15 Missouri	434
6 Clemson	950		16 Georgia	312
7 Notre Dame	914		17 Stanford	306
8 Nebraska	865		18 North Carolina State	214
9 Texas	708		19 Texas A&M	128
10 Houston	698		20 Maryland	112

1978 Top Performance Formula

1 Southern California	1.7412
2 Alabama	1.7150
3 Penn State	1.6816
4 Oklahoma	1.6731
5 Michigan	1.5916
6 Clemson	1.5762
7 Notre Dame	1.5432
8 Nebraska	1.5313
9 Texas	1.4766
10 Arkansas	1.4757
11 Michigan State	1.4523
12 Houston	1.4343
13 Georgia	1.3939
14 Stanford	1.3762
15 Maryland	1.3744
16 Purdue	1.3684
17 Florida State	1.3616
18 Arizona State	1.3520
19 North Carolina State	1.3457
20 Missouri	1.3303

1978 Top Opponent Records

1 Notre Dame	.7132
2 Southern California	.6912
3 Alabama	.6508
4 Stanford	.6220
5 Nebraska	.6080
6 Oklahoma State	.6043
7t Penn State	.603175
7t Texas	.603175
9 Florida	.5929
10t Kansas	.590517
10t Rice	.590517
12 Duke	.5776
13t Oregon State	.57265
13t Texas Tech	.57265
15 Houston	.5725
16 Missouri	.5720
17 Mississippi State	.5703
18 Southern Methodist	.5647
19 Syracuse	.5565
20 Baylor	.5560

1978 Out-of-Conference Records

	W-L	Percentage	Bowl W-L
Pacific-10	18-10-3	.6290	2-0-1
Big Eight	22-14	.6111	2-2
Southwest	17-12-2	.5806	2-1-1
Southeastern	28-20-2	.5800	1-2
Atlantic Coast	24-22	.5217	2-2
Western Athletic	17-22	.4359	0-1
Big Ten	13-17-1	.4355	1-2

1978 Individual Statistical Leaders

RUSHING YARDS	Attempts	Yards	Avg.
Billy Sims, Oklahoma	231	1762	7.6
Charles White, Southern California	342	1760	5.1
Eddie Lee Ivery, Georgia Tech	267	1562	5.9
Bernard Jackson, North Texas State	269	1453	5.4
Joe Holland, Cornell	273	1396	5.1
Nathan Poole, Louisville	212	1394	6.6
James Hadnot, Texas Tech	251	1369	5.5
Ted Brown, North Carolina State	302	1350	4.5
Willie McClendon, Georgia	287	1312	4.6
Theotis Brown, UCLA	211	1283	6.1
Allen Harvin, Cincinnati	233	1283	5.5

PASSING YARDS	Completions	Attempts	Yards	Pct.
Mike Ford, Southern Methodist	224	389	3007	57.6
Steve Dils, Stanford	247	391	2943	63.2
David Spriggs, New Mexico State	169	317	2558	53.3
Dave Marler, Mississippi State	163	287	2422	56.8
Jack Thompson, Washington State	175	348	2333	50.3
Rich Campbell, California	164	293	2287	56.0
Ed Smith, Michigan State	169	292	2226	57.9
Joe Montana, Notre Dame	141	260	2010	54.2
Brad Wright, New Mexico	126	251	1925	50.2
Mark Herrmann, Purdue	152	274	1904	55.5

RECEIVING YARDS	Catches	Yards
Dave Petzke, Northern Illinois	91	1217
Emanuel Tolbert, Southern Methodist	62	1040
Mardye McDole, Mississippi State	48	1035
Vernon Henry, Long Beach State	60	985
Ken Margerum, Stanford	53	942
Jeff Evans, New Mexico State	48	926
Jerry Butler, Clemson	58	908
Jeff Groth, Bowling Green	56	874
Cormac Carney, Air Force	57	870
Mike Chronister, Brigham Young	52	850

1978 Consensus All-America Team
Offense

Tight End:	Kellen Winslow, Missouri
Wide Receiver:	Emanuel Tolbert, SMU
Tackle:	Keith Dorney, Penn State
	Kelvin Clark, Nebraska
Guard:	Pat Howell, Southern California
	Greg Roberts, Oklahoma
Center:	Jim Ritcher, North Carolina State
Quarterback:	Chuck Fusina, Penn State
Backs:	Billy Sims, Oklahoma
	Charles White, Southern California
	Ted Brown, North Carolina State
	Charles Alexander, LSU

Defense

Line:	Hugh Green, Pittsburgh
	Al Harris, Arizona State
	Bruce Clark, Penn State
	Mike Bell, Colorado State
	Marty Lyons, Alabama
Linebacker:	Bob Golic, Notre Dame
	Jerry Robinson, UCLA
	Tom Cousineau, Ohio State
Backs:	Johnnie Johnson, Texas
	Kenny Easley, UCLA
	Jeff Nixon, Richmond

1978 Heisman Trophy Vote

Billy Sims, junior halfback, Oklahoma	827
Chuck Fusina, senior quarterback, Penn State	750
Rick Leach, senior quarterback, Michigan	435
Charles White, junior tailback, Southern California	354
Charles Alexander, senior tailback, LSU	282

Other Major Award Winners

Maxwell (Player)	Chuck Fusina, senior quarterback, Penn State
Outland (Lineman)	Greg Roberts, senior guard, Oklahoma
Lombardi (Lineman)	Bruce Clark, junior defensive tackle, Penn State
Walter Camp (Player)	Chuck Fusina, senior quarterback, Penn State
Davey O'Brien (Southwest)	Billy Sims, junior halfback, Oklahoma
AFCA Coach-of-the-Year	Joe Paterno, Penn State

1979

The Year of the Tide Topping the Big Three, Mount Kush Toppled, and the Greatest Offensive Line

Alabama (12-0), which won more games (103) during the 1970s than any other school, fittingly finished the decade as national champions by winning its second straight national title. There was very little comment about the back-to-back championships at the time, but no school would be able to turn a similar trick again until Nebraska achieved consecutive titles in 1994-95. With a 24-9 Sugar Bowl win over Arkansas (10-2), the Crimson Tide completed a fantastic three-year run that saw them win three Southeastern Conference titles, three Sugar Bowls, and have three straight legitimate claims to the national championship. Their won-loss record over this period was 34-2. Featuring a seemingly endless supply of talented players, Alabama had reached a pinnacle of success under legendary coach Bear Bryant that perhaps has been matched by a select few championship-caliber teams, but never surpassed. The 1979 championship, however, would prove to be Bryant's last in coaching.

Alabama, Southern California (11-0-1), and Oklahoma (11-1) finished one-two-three in the final Associated Press Poll for the second straight year, an unprecedented feat that demonstrated just how superior these wide-spread "Big Three" programs were in the late 1970s. In fact, the trio of teams was ranked in the top three of the preseason poll with USC receiving top billing at the time. Although each had talented quarterbacks, there was no mistaking what they had in common on offense. They planned to run the ball, and defenses knew the run was coming, even expected specific plays, but were powerless to stop them.

Alabama almost stumbled in sloppy conditions in the unfriendly atmosphere of Tiger Stadium, winning 3-0 on November 10. The near upset could not save the job of Louisiana State (7-5) head coach Charlie McClendon, let go after 18 years at the helm of the Tigers. Ever since then, McClendon has held the distinction of being the LSU coach with the most wins with his record of 137-59-7.

The departure of another long-time coach dominated headlines. Frank Kush, highly successful football chief at Arizona State (6-6, but Pac-10 wins were forfeited) since 1958, was ousted at mid-season. There were a host of charges against the school regarding the runaway power of its boosters and an almost equal number of allegations against Kush for his physical abuse of players. The university suspended him for punching punter Kevin Rutledge during the previous year's Washington game and then lying about the incident. Rutledge transferred to UNLV (9-1-2), but not before suing the coach and school. The youngster faced threats from angry fans, and his father's insurance company building was set on fire. Kush himself sued the school for $1.1 million after being dismissed October 13 by athletic director Dr. Fred Miller, and later settled for six figures. Scandalous details came out about "Mt. Kush," an 800-ft path with a fierce 50-degree angle that players were forced to run in desert heat to overcome poor on-field performances or off-field transgressions. Out of control boosters, meanwhile, threatened to pull the plug on donations for a new golf course and Sun Devil Stadium expansion unless Kush was reinstated. The situation worsened when the school had to forfeit its first five victories of the season due to academic discrepancies. It was revealed that eight players, including starters Ron Washington, Ben Apuna, and Kani Kauahi, were found not to have taken a make-up math course over the summer that they supposedly passed at Rocky Mountain College. It was a very long year in Tempe.

Life was much better in Columbus, Ohio, where new Ohio State (11-1) coach Earle Bruce led his charges to a perfect regular season. The Buckeyes enjoyed a two-point lead over Alabama in the final regular season AP poll before losing a Rose Bowl thriller to Southern Cal, 17-16. The loss was the ninth in the last 10 Rose Bowls for the so-called "Big Two" of the Big Ten: Ohio State and Michigan (8-4). Ohio State was one of eight major college teams to make it to November with an unblemished record, the most since 1915. Two of those teams, Florida State (11-1) and Brigham Young (11-1), likewise did not lose until the bowl season and gave a preview of things to come in the 1980s.

Rushing for 247 yards in the Rose Bowl, his final game, Southern California tailback Charles White had one of the best bowl performances ever by a Heisman winner, an award that seemed more often than not to jinx its winners. White handily out-polled reigning Heisman incumbent Billy Sims of Oklahoma, even though Sims rushed for 529 yards in his final two regular season games. Of course, many voters already had cast their ballots for White as the Heisman Trophy continued to honor, in effect, the best player for the opening three-quarters of a season. White was

a deserving candidate, however, and became the third Trojan to win the award following Mike Garrett in 1965 and O.J. Simpson in 1968.

The Big Eight welcomed the return of coach Chuck Fairbanks as one conference team after another whipped his Colorado (3-8) squad. Fairbanks' return to the college game was controversial as his most-recent employer, the New England Patriots, sued him for breach of contract, thus preventing the new coach from stepping on campus until April. Colorado forked over $200,000 to settle and went on to post its worst record since 1964. His team became part of television history as ESPN, the new all-sports cable network that was eager to provide morning-to-midnight football in the future, televised its first football game on September 8 with Oregon (6-5) beating the Buffaloes by 33-19.

Nebraska (10-2) coach Tom Osborne waited for the Oklahoma game to unleash a new play, the "Fumblerooskie," a trick he learned by watching a high school game. The Fumblerooskie, had the center fake a snap to the quarterback and, instead, place the ball on the ground. The line pulled from its positions as if to block a wide play, but a tricky guard would scoop up the unattended ball and ramble in the opposite direction of the offensive flow. The Fumlerooskie was used twice against the Sooners, including Randy Schleusener's 15-yard touchdown run.

Lowly Wake Forest (8-4) enjoyed a renaissance under second-year coach and former Demon Deacon quarterback John Mackovic. Wake Forest opened 7-1, and even their loss was only by three points. Passer Jay Venuto and runner James McDougald were leaders in taking the Deacs to the Tangerine Bowl but Wake's winning ways were short-lived.

Although Houston (11-1) represented the Southwest Conference in the Cotton Bowl for the third time in the school's five years as a conference member, it was SMU (5-6) that created the biggest stir with the successful recruiting of a pair of talented high school backs, Eric Dickerson and Craig James. The signing of Dickerson, the most sought-after high school player in the country, attracted doubters, a situation that worsened when he showed up at school driving a sports car. The Mustangs were headed up, but a devastating crash was in their future.

After the season, Southern California guard Brad Budde was selected in the first round of the NFL draft by the Kansas City Chiefs, which had drafted his father Ed in 1963. The younger Budde was a member of what might have been the greatest offensive line in college football history. It was made up of fellow guard Roy Foster, center Chris Foote and tackle Keith Van Horne, plus three future NFL stars sharing time in staffing the other tackle spot. Anthony Munoz began the year as the returning starter at tackle, but was lost for the season with a knee injury in the opener. Freshman Don Mosebar replaced him until he was hurt prior to the UCLA (5-6) game. The Trojans then turned to another freshman, Bruce Matthews, and it was no surprise with such talent up front that White became the school's and conference's all-time leading rusher, surpassing Anthony Davis, who had preceded him at both San Fernando High and at USC. Also of note was White's mostly-blocking fullback, Marcus Allen, who himself would go on to the Heisman Trophy and NFL fame. It was more proof that for the top teams of 1979, the rich were getting richer.

Milestones

■ Rules were considerably toughened against intentional rough play: striking of opponent's head, neck, or face, use of helmet in tackling, kicking opponent, chopping potential receivers below waist, roughing passers, and roughing kickers.

■ Longtime coach Andy Gustafson died on January 7 at age 76. After playing halfback at Pittsburgh for both Pop Warner and Jock Sutherland, Gustafson became head man at Virginia Tech for four years, assistant at three schools for 18 years, and finally head coach for 16 years at Miami. He brought Hurricanes to four bowls and won 115 games. Beattie "Big Chief" Feathers, 71, star halfback at Tennessee from 1931-33, died on March 11. Vols went 25-3-2 during All-America Feathers' stint, when he rushed for 1,888 yards and scored 32 TDs. Coaching great Lou Little died on May 28 at age 85. After playing at Penn and professionally for four years, Little coached at Georgetown for six years and Columbia for 27. Jerry Anderson, starting cornerback for 1975 Oklahoma national champions, drowned on Memorial Day saving two boys from river in native Mufreesboro, Tenn. John Wayne, whose 50-year acting career overshadowed his line play at Southern California, died of cancer at age 72 on June 11. Known as Duke Morrison while playing tackle at USC, Wayne remained football fan while becoming huge Hollywood star. Former Colorado tight end J.V. Cain, 28, died July 22 during St. Louis Cardinals training camp. Cause was myocardial fibrosis, form of heart disease. Don "Midnight" Miller, all-America halfback in Notre Dame's Four Horsemen backfield of 1922-24, died at age 77 on July 28. Walter Gilbert, All-America center for Auburn (1934-36) and Texaco executive, died at 64 on August 19. New York University fullback Ken Strong, All-America in 1929 before all-pro career with New York Giants died October 5 of heart attack at 73. Ed Garbisch, who played four years at Washington and Jefferson and four more at Army, died at 79 on December 13. All-America center and guard Garbisch drop-kicked 4 field goals in 12-0 win over Navy in 1924.

■ Coaching Changes:

	Incoming	Outgoing
Air Force	Ken Hatfield	Bill Parcells
Arizona State	Bob Owens (a)	Frank Kush
Army	Lou Saban	Homer Smith
Colorado	Chuck Fairbanks	Bill Mallory
Duke	Red Wilson	Mike McGee
Florida	Charley Pell	Doug Dickey
Iowa	Hayden Fry	Bob Commings
Iowa State	Donnie Duncan	Earle Bruce
Kansas	Don Fambrough	Bud Moore
Miami	Howard Schnellenberger	Lou Saban
Minnesota	Joe Salem	Cal Stoll
Mississippi State	Emory Bellard	Bob Tyler
Ohio State	Earle Bruce	Woody Hayes
Oklahoma State	Jimmy Johnson	Jim Stanley
Stanford	Rod Dowhower	Bill Walsh
Texas A&M	Tom Wilson	Emory Bellard
Vanderbilt	George MacIntyre	Fred Pancoast

(a) Owens (3-4) replaced Kush (3-2) in October.

Preseason AP Poll

1 Southern California (47)	1242		11 Georgia	471
2 Alabama (11)	1141		12 Missouri	426
3 Oklahoma (4)	1058		13 Stanford	331
4 Texas (1)	1008		14 Texas A&M	326
5 Penn State	858		15 Washington	299
6 Purdue	856		16 Houston	292
7 Michigan	749		17 Pittsburgh	283
8 Nebraska	701		18 Arizona State	266
9 Notre Dame	633		19 Florida State	250
10 Michigan State	496		20 Arkansas	231

September 8, 1979

NORTH CAROLINA 28 South Carolina 0: Tar Heels (1-0) unleashed talent on both sides of ball as HB Amos Lawrence rushed for 134y and 2 TDs and D held South Carolina (0-1) to 149y rushing while forcing 3 TOs. Units combined for opening score as North Carolina S Ricky Barden picked off his 4th career INT against Gamecocks, returning it 28y to Cocks 40YL to set up 29y TD run by Lawrence. "Famous Amos" added 5y scoring run before H to put away visitors. Best drive for Gamecocks reached UNC 28YL before INT spoiled it. South Carolina TB George Rogers powered for 97y on ground.

Alabama 30 GEORGIA TECH 6: After 15 years of series dormancy, Tide routed Georgia Tech (0-1) in renewal of once fierce rivalry. Alabama (1-0) DE E.J. Junior, who opened scoring with 1st Q 59y INT TD RET, led D that allowed only 41y and sole 1st down in 1st H. Bama was quiet, however, on O, finally scoring with only 11 secs left in H on HB Major Ogilvie's 1y run. Engineers D collapsed under weight of Tide Wishbone in 3rd Q as they allowed 54y and 91y TD drives and final-game 312y rushing total. Home team averted shutout on 36y TD pass from QB Mike Kelley (15-27/160y, 4 INTs) to WR Leon Chadwick. Tide QB Steadman Shealy (9-11/108y, TD) rushed for 79y TD.

OHIO STATE 31 Syracuse 6: Columbus had not witnessed debut of new coach since arrival of Woody Hayes in 1951, but Buckeyes (1-0) made it seem like old hat with easy victory. Coach Earle Bruce's team ground out 383y rushing and played superb D. QB Art Schlichter led way with 172y total O, marking new era in Buckeyes football by throwing on 1st play from scrimmage. Nimble-footed Schlichter led Ohio with 91y rushing, while TB Calvin Murray added 86y. QB Bill Hurley threw for 158y and rushed in 3y TD for Orangemen (0-1).

Indiana 30 IOWA 26: Hoosiers (1-0) spotted Iowa 23-6 H lead before erupting for 27 pts in 2nd H. QB Tim Clifford (19-28/316y, 3 INTs) completed comeback for 123y and TD pass to TB Lonnie Johnson with 58 secs left. In coach Hayden Fry's debut, Iowa (0-1) lead seemed safe at 26-23 when IU K Steve Straub missed 22y FG with 2:41 left. But Hoosiers forced punt, and Clifford threw winning pass on 1st play of drive. Johnson rushed for 74y and caught 5/123y, scoring 3 TDs. TB Dennis Mosley rushed for 142y and tied school record with 4 TDs for Hawkeyes.

SOUTHERN METHODIST 35 Rice 17: Debuts of TB Eric Dickerson and FB Craig James for Mustangs (1-0) went well as expected. Dickerson rushed for 123y and 3 TDs, while James scored winning TD on 10y run in 3rd Q. SMU LB Byron Hunt then grounded Owls with 23y INT TD RET. Owls (0-1), who led 17-7, won rushing battle 224y to 208y, but had 6 TOs. Mustangs D kept Rice in check while O rallied for game's last 28 pts. Rice QB Randy Hertel (16-35/152y) threw and ran for 1st H TDs.

Brigham Young 18 TEXAS A&M 17 (Houston): BYU (1-0) CB Tim Halverson and QB Marc Wilson provided needed late heroics. Down 17-10, Halverson blocked punt by P David Appleby to give Brigham Young ball on Aggies 19YL. Wilson (17-35/165y, 3 INTs) threw 9y pass to TE Mike Lacey, induced 7y interference PEN and hit TE Clay Brown with 3y TD pass. He then threw winning 2-pt conv pass to Lacey. Texas A&M raced into FG range, but K David Hardy narrowly missed 3-ptr from 51y out. Aggies QB Mike Mosley earlier ran in 7y TD for 14-7 lead in 3rd Q. TB Curtis Dickey rushed for 143y to become Texas A&M's career rushing leader with 2,998y.

Southern California 21 TEXAS TECH 7: Could Trojans subs finish in top 20? USC (1-0) did not miss beat despite injuries to T Anthony Munoz (knee) and TB Charles White (shoulder). As featured runner, FB Marcus Allen rushed for 105y and 1y TD, and TB Michael Hayes added 84y behind O-line that now included T Don Mosebar. Southern California QB Paul McDonald threw for 133y and 2 TDs. Texas Tech (0-1) QB Ron Reeves capped 80y trip with 1y keeper, while FB James Hadnot rushed for 94y.

Houston 24 UCLA 16: Cougars (1-0) overcame slow start with 17 points in 4th Q to upend UCLA. Bruins (0-1) grabbed 9-0 H lead on K Peter Boermeester's 3 FGs, but they were frustrated by 2 stalled drives that crossed Cougars 10YL. Houston could not be contained for long, exploding for 4 scores as QB Delrick Brown threw and ran for 2nd H TDs. Brown set up by FB John Newhouse's winning 16y run with 67y scamper. Bruins' only TD came on QB Rick Bashore's 22y pass to TE Tim Wrightman. TB Freeman McNeil rushed for 119y; Bruin totaled 410y with 3 TOs.

California 17 ARIZONA STATE 9: Amid lawsuits and criminal charges, Sun Devils (0-1) had to focus on football. Cal (1-0) QB Rich Campbell (23-30/271y, INT) threw and ran for TDs as Bears wiped out 9-7 H deficit. Campbell, who threw 32y TD pass to WR Michael Buggs to open scoring in 2nd Q, hit 4-5/57y on 3rd Q drive to set up go-ahead 24y FG by K Mick Luckhurst. Later, Bears LB Greg Bracelin had 1st of 2 INTs of ASU QB Mark Malone to set up 29y drive to Campbell's 5y insurance TD run. Malone threw for 146y and ran for 45y more including 1y TD run in 2nd Q.

AP Poll September 10

1 Southern California (45)	1222		11 Missouri	575
2 Alabama (14)	1172		12 Georgia	521
3 Oklahoma (2)	1068		13 Houston	477
4 Texas (1)	962		14 Washington	444
5 Purdue	931		15 Ohio State	342
6 Michigan	898		16 Pittsburgh	278
7 Penn State	823		17 Arkansas	241
8 Nebraska	742		18 Florida State	170
9 Notre Dame	644		19 North Carolina State	163
10 Michigan State	594		20 Southern Methodist	118

September 15, 1979

Maryland 19 CLEMSON 0: Rugged Terps (2-0) D threw shutout to halt Clemson's 11-game win streak as TB Charlie Wysocki ran wild for 178y. TB Tim Wingfield scored game's sole TD on 31y run late in contest, while K Dale Castro propped up Maryland with 4 FGs. Terps S Ralph Lary had 3 INTs against Tigers' weak passing game that sorely missing departed QB Steve Fuller. Maryland avoided any TOs despite 6 FUMs it claimed of its own, while Tigers lost 4 TOs. Clemson struggled all game to move ball as proven by QB Bill Lott's 87y total O leadership.

Wake Forest 22 GEORGIA 21: Demon Deacons, coming off dreadful 1-10 mark in 1978, shocked no. 12 Georgia (0-1). QB Jay Venuto (20-34/283y, 3 TDs) passed for all his team's scores, and squat TB James McDougald rushed for 189y as Wake Forest (2-0) romped for 570y. Wake scored final 9 pts of game, with Venuto's winning 9y TD pass to McDougald coming early in 4th Q. Deacs DB Larry Ingram then halted 2 Georgia (0-1) drives with INTs. Late in game, Bulldogs QB Buck Belue threw 41y pass to WR Lindsay Scott with 4 secs left to set up 58y FG ATT missed by K Rex Robinson. Wake coach John Mackovic expelled local media from post-game locker room for its disparaging pre-game remarks.

Notre Dame 12 MICHIGAN 10: Known for his tackling, Notre Dame LB Bob Crable used jumping ability, with help of "stair-climbing" up backs of teammates, to block K Bryan Virgil's last-sec 42y FG attempt. No Wolverines were in position to block any 3-ptrs when Fighting Irish (1-0) K Chuck Male booted school-record 4 FGs. Crable and his D mates posted 2nd H shutout and forced TOs to set up 3 of Male's kicks. HB Vagas Ferguson rushed for 118y to lead O. Michigan (1-1) had scored on its 1st 2 possessions, moving 84y to FG and 80y to TD on 1y run by TB Stan Edwards. Loss was 1st by Michigan in regular season against team from outside Big 10 since 1969 defeat at hands of Missouri, team then led by current ND coach Dan Devine.

Southern Methodist 27 TEXAS CHRISTIAN 7: During rout of Dallas Metroplex rival, SMU (2-0) was dealt blow to SWC hopes as QB Mike Ford was lost for season with knee injury. Sub QB Jim Bob Taylor threw 15y TD pass to TE Robert Fisher on 1st play for 7-0 lead. He gave that back in 3rd Q when INT to TCU (0-1) CB Ray Berry was returned 41y to EZ. K Eddie Garcia kicked 44y FG for winning pts later in 3rd Q before Mustangs pulled away with 17 pts including LB Byron Hunt's 2nd TD of season on EZ FUM REC. Mustangs TB Eric Dickerson managed only 15y on ground before leaving with minor injury.

OKLAHOMA 21 Iowa 6: Oklahoma HB Billy Sims' campaign to repeat as Heisman winner was off to sluggish start as he rushed for 106y and 2 TDs, but did not break any highlight-reel runs. Sooners (1-0) held meager 7-6 lead at H, it stayed same after 3 Qs against Hawkeyes' hard-hitting D, led by LB Todd Simonson. Oklahoma scored twice in 4th Q on Sims' 2nd TD and 1y keeper by QB J.C. Watts, who also threw for 157y. Hopeful Iowa (0-2) had scored 1st on 10y TD pass from QB Phil Suess to TB Dennis Mosley, who rushed for 79y and had 41y receiving.

UCLA 31 Purdue 21: Purdue (1-1) QB Mark Herrmann entered with glowing press clippings, but Bruins QB Rick Bashore left with win on his 2 TDs passing and 2 running. Hermann (14-24/191y, 3 INTs) eventually was knocked out of game. S Ken Easley's 1st H INT gave him UCLA career INT record of 13 and set up 2nd of 3 straight Bruin TDs that opened game. Herrmann got off mat to throw 2 TD passes as Purdue trailed 21-14 at H. Bruins (1-1) stretched lead to 24-14 before backup QB Larry Gates drove Boilermakers 73y to TD that again shaved deficit to 7 pts. Bashore crafted clinching 87y drive that he ended on 1y TD run. UCLA TB Freeman McNeil rushed for 176y.

1 Southern California (49)	1227	11 Michigan	527
2 Alabama (12)	1153	12 Washington	514
3 Oklahoma	1017	13 Pittsburgh	406
4 Texas (1)	976	14 Florida State	386
5 Notre Dame	953	15 Arkansas	384
6 Penn State	947	16 Ohio State	364
7 Nebraska	815	17 Purdue	293
8 Michigan State	781	18 Southern Methodist	204
9 Missouri	613	19 North Carolina State	198
10 Houston	578	20 UCLA	162

September 22, 1979

Texas A&M 27 PENN STATE 14: TB Curtis Dickey kept turning corner for Aggies (1-2), to tune of 184y rushing and 3 TDs. Nittany Lions (1-1) had no answer for Dickey, who scored on runs of 69, 11, and 21y. QB Mike Mosley, on bench with injuries, quickly replaced QB Gary Kubiak after sub QB went down with early elbow injury. Mosley sparked Texas A&M to 298y and 4 TDs. Penn State had taken 7-0 lead on 3y run by TB Booker Moore, converting FUM pounced on by DT Matt Millen at Aggies 24YL. Only 28 secs later, Dickey took off behind pulling G Ed Pustejovsky on 69y TD run as A&M started unanswered run of 27 pts. Penn State TB Curt Warner rushed for 65y, week after he had torched Rutgers for 281y in his debut. It was 1st-ever loss to SWC team for Penn State coach Joe Paterno after 6 wins.

NORTH CAROLINA 17 Pittsburgh 7: Tar Heels (2-0) won D duel, controlling Pitt O and fashioning opportunistic TOs. North Carolina QB Matt Kupec threw 43y TD pass to TB Phil Farris to open scoring and added 1y scoring keeper for 14-0 1st Q lead. UNC LB Buddy Curry had 2 INTs for Carolina D that forced 7 TOs and helped hold FB Randy McMillan to 34y rushing. QB Rick Trocano threw for 204y, 3 INTs and sole Panthers (1-1) TD on 13y pass to TE Ken Bowles.

FLORIDA STATE 40 Miami 23: After falling behind 7-3, Florida State (3-0) scored 30 straight pts to blow away rivals for 1st series win at home in 6 tries. FSU swamped Miami QB Mark Rodrigue (5-18/67y, 4 INTs), giving Tallahassee native rude welcome home. Seminoles rushed for 205y, with FB Mark Lyles (25/85y) and TB Greg Ramsey (18/76y) each scoring 2 TDs. QB Jim Kelly (6-14/66y) made his debut for Hurricanes (1-1), running in team's 2nd TD from 2y out.

CLEMSON 12 Georgia 7: Tigers (2-1) avenged only 1978 loss as FB Marvin Sims rushed for 146y in leading O that ground out 306y. Hard-fought game remained scoreless until TB Lester Brown's 1y TD run gave Clemson 7-0 lead in 3rd Q. Tigers D, which held Georgia (0-2) to 68y rushing and had 3 INTs, sacked QB Jeff Pyburn in EZ for 2 more pts. After Clemson K Obed Ariri added 24y insurance FG for 12-0 edge, Bulldogs finally scored on 21y run by QB Buck Belue.

ALABAMA 45 Baylor 0: Despite playing hard, Baylor (2-1) D could not make up for inept O and were finally worn down late as Alabama scored 28 pts in 4th Q. Bama (2-0) held 15-0 lead at H on 3 FGs by K Alan McElroy and 1y TD plunge by HB Major Ogilvie. With 3 Bears QBs combining for 6 INTs to go with 2 lost FUMs, Baylor managed just 90y rushing and 72y passing. Closest Baylor got to Tide EZ was Alabama 38YL, but that advance came only 1 play before another INT landed in Tide hands. Alabama typically rolled up 453y rushing, using 11 different ball carriers.

Missouri 33 MISSISSIPPI 7: Inspired Ole Miss D contained Missouri's high-powered attack through opening H in taking 7-3 lead. Tigers (3-0) quickly scored 3 times in 3rd Q to spark rout as bullish RB tandem of Gerry Ellis and James Wilder each scored. Mizzou QB Phil Bradley (8-21/170y) and WR Ken Blair hooked up on 69y TD. Bradley led O that gained 198y on ground and 170y through air. Rebels (1-1) QBs John Fourcade and Roy Coleman combined for 155y passing, but no pts as team was held to 68y rushing and lost 4 FUMs. Frosh WR Michael Harmon opened scoring for Ole Miss with 54y punt RET in 1st Q.

PURDUE 28 Notre Dame 22: Boilermakers (2-1) enjoyed leadership of QB Mark Herrmann, who threw 158y and TD passes of 15y to TE Dave Young and 6y to WR Bart Burrell. Meanwhile, Notre Dame (1-1) experimented with 4 different passers and lost 20-7 lead in 2nd H. Purdue erased deficit with 3 TDs within 9-min span. Rugged Purdue D held HB Vagas Ferguson to 79y rushing, with only 24y in decisive 2nd H. With running game in check, Notre Dame (1-1) had to pass more than usual and had success with QB-variety-pack hitting 11-24/199y, 2 TDs.

ARKANSAS 27 Oklahoma State 7: Hogs (2-0) put away Oklahoma State early, scoring on 4 straight 1st H possessions to build 24-0 lead. Arkansas gained 336y in earning 18 1st H 1st downs, while not surrendering 1 until ahead 14-0. QB Kevin Scanlon rushed for 2 TDs, while backup QB Tom Jones threw 1y scoring pass to TE Darryl Mason. Cowboys (2-1) were held scoreless until 4th Q when QB Harold Bailey threw 11y TD pass to TE Don Echols.

Army 17 STANFORD 13: TB Gerald Walker capped 17-pt surge for Cadets (2-0) with 71y scoring romp in 4th Q. QB Turk Schonert had another bullet in his gun's chamber, tossing 24y TD pass to WR Ken Margerum with 1:44 left to pull Cardinals to within 17-13. Onside-KO went OB, however, to end Card hopes. Stanford (1-2) had opened scoring after forcing FUM on opening KO that set up 1y TD run by HB Mike Dotterer. Army D tightened, sacking Schonert 7 times, picking off 3 of his throws, and stopping 3 drives that cracked Army 10YL. Cadets took 10-7 lead at H on 30y FG by K Dave Aucoin and 2y TD run by HB Jimmy Hill.

Washington 21 OREGON 17: Huskies (3-0) stunned 1st Eugene sellout in 8 years with game's final 21 pts, including 53y punt TD RET by CB Mark Lee with 1:59 left. Ducks (1-2) enjoyed 17-0 lead on 35y FG by K Doug Jollymour, 2y TD catch by TE Greg Hogensen and, after QB Reggie Ogburn's injury, 5y TD pass from sub QB Tim

Durando to TB Dwight Robertson. TB Joe Steele answered with short TD runs late in 2nd H to pull Washington within 17-14. Oregon P Mike Babb got off 34y punt to Lee, who was trapped at sideline before reversing field and racing untouched to EZ.

1 Southern California (51)	1286	11 Michigan	564
2 Alabama (13)	1235	12 Florida State	556
3 Oklahoma	1122	13 Arkansas	519
4 Texas (1)	1040	14 Ohio State	458
5 Missouri	898	15 Notre Dame	436
6 Nebraska	862	16 North Carolina State	293
7 Michigan State	816	17 UCLA	280
8 Houston	755	18 Penn State	261
9 Washington	635	19 Southern Methodist	246
10 Purdue	599	20 Louisiana State	184

September 29, 1979

NORTH CAROLINA STATE 17 Wake Forest 14: Wolfpack (4-0) remained unbeaten in rainy, muddy conditions as K Nathan Ritter broke 14-14 tie with 41y FG with 5:13 left. Kick was set up by FUM REC as final 3 Wake Forest (3-1) drives ended on TOs. QB Jay Venuto (21-35/203y, 2 TDs, INT) led Deamon Deacs, passing team into North Carolina State territory late before Wolfpack DT Bubba Green recovered bad snap. QB Scott Smith (7-11/112y) ran for 2 TDs for NC State, with his 2nd coming on 27y sprint to give NC State 14-7 lead. With rain halted, Deacs rallied through air with Venuto tying game on 27y scoring pass to TE Mike Mullen.

KENTUCKY 14 Maryland 7: Wildcats (1-2) knew target and in holding TB Charlie Wysocki to 60y rushing, they held Maryland to single TD. Kentucky allowed Terps (3-1) O to gain 174y, only 46y in 1st H when Wildcats took 14-0 lead. Kentucky QB Randy Jenkins led early drive, completing 23 pass to WR Felix Wilson on 3rd down, until suffering broken ankle. QB Mike Shutt came in to lead Cats to TD, scoring himself from 3y out. TB Chris Jones added 1y TD run in 2nd Q for winning pts. Maryland was not able to score until 4th Q. All-Tice-combo of QB Mike Tice and brother TE John Tice did honors with 5y TD pass. QB Tice stormed Terps downfield to Kentucky 44YL before throwing INT to S Larry Carter with 22 secs left.

Southern California 17 LOUISIANA STATE 12: Rabid crowd was quieted late as Trojans (4-0), trailing 12-10, marched to LSU 8YL with 33 secs left. QB Paul McDonald, who hit 4-5 on drive, found WR Kevin Williams for game-winner on play called "55 double rollout." USC TB Charles White gained 185y and scored on 4y TD run in 4th Q to put Troy up 12-10. TB LeRoid Jones propelled Tigers (2-1) with 67y rushing and caught 13y TD pass in 2nd Q. Southern California was ragged when it 1st got off bus: it opened with 6 PENs and 2 TOs to trail 9-3 at H despite White having gained 100y on ground. Odd missed PEN cropped up as LSU coaching staff watched post-game film: USC FB Ricky Johnson had come off bench, without his helmet, to help tackle QB David Woodley, but Trojans were not penalized.

Navy 13 ILLINOIS 12: Navy (3-0) stepped up in class against marginal Big 10 team and narrowly avoided loss. After Illinois QB Lawrence McCullough (18-30/184y) threw 10y TD pass to TE Lee Boeke to pull team within 13-12 with 3:51 left, Illini (1-3) went for 2 pts. McCullough pitched to RB Mike Holmes, whose attempt to throw back to QB was picked off. Holmes had thrown 3y TD pass to TE Mike Sherrod. Middies rushed for 222y with TB Steve Callahan leading way with 117y.

NOTRE DAME 27 Michigan State 3: Irish (2-1) completed Big 10 tour with display of their trusty staples: running of HB Vagas Ferguson (28/169y) and hard-hitting D. While being blocked on INT RET, Michigan State QB Bert Vaughn was knocked out in 1st Q, and whatever O vitality State had went with him. At that time, Notre Dame led 7-0 on 14y TD pass from QB Rusty Lisch to WR Tony Hunter. Irish then added 2 FGs by K Chuck Male and 2 TDs by Ferguson, who carried on 28 of his team's 1st 36 plays. Spartans TB Steve Smith rushed for 103y, but Michigan State saw end of its 10-game win streak.

NEBRASKA 42 Penn State 17: Nittany Lions (1-2) jumped out to quick 14-0 lead before surrendering 4 TDs in 2nd Q avalanche. Nebraska (3-0) mined 2 TDs on passes from QB Tim Hager (14-22/215y, INT) to swift TE Junior Miller. Things were brighter for Penn State in 1st Q when QB Dayle Tate threw 19y TD pass to TE Brad Scovill, and CB Tom Wise returned INT of Hager 30y to EZ. IB Jarvis Redwine gained 124y for Huskers, but that only scratched surface of stat nightmare for Penn State. Nebraska outgained Lions 530y to 183y, with surprising 232y gained through air. Equally surprising was Lions' inability to run, held to 60y on ground with TB Curt Warner leading team with only 19y. On Monday, Penn State dropped out of AP top 20 for 1st time since 1976.

Ohio State 17 UCLA 13: QB Art Schlichter (13-22/159y) sparkled late, hitting 6-6 in marching Buckeyes (4-0) 80y to winning, last-min 2y TD pass to wide-open TE Paul Campbell. Bruins (2-2) scored early when LB Billy Don Jackson blocked punt to set up QB Rick Bashore's 10y TD pass to leaping WR Willie Curran, and K Peter Boermeester hit 27y FG for 10-0 lead. Ohio was not able to crack EZ until late in 2nd Q when TB Calvin Murray (18/117y) raced 34y to cap 70y drive. Teams traded FGs in 2nd H before Bruins marched to Bucks 15YL, where they facing 4th-and-1. Left side of UCLA line jumped offside, and resultant missed FG launched Ohio on its winning drive.

1 Southern California (47)	1222	11 Michigan	654
2 Alabama (14)	1180	12 Purdue	648
3 Oklahoma	1080	13 Arkansas	619
4 Texas (1)	1053	14 North Carolina State	388
5 Nebraska	999	15 Missouri	342
6 Houston	838	16 Michigan State	290
7 Washington	777	17 Louisiana State	266
8 Ohio State	683	18 North Carolina	256
9 Florida State	662	19 Tennessee	174
10 Notre Dame	656	20 Brigham Young	122

October 6, 1979

Temple 41 RUTGERS 20: Temple (4-1) romped as QB Brian Broomell (14-20/246y, 2 TDs) added to his scoring output with 2 TD runs. Owls also had other weapons: FB Mark Bright rushed for career-high 159y, and WR Gerald "Sweetfeet" Lucear (7/142y) was recipient of both TD throws. Rutgers (3-2) pulled to within 21-14 midway through 3rd Q on 2y TD run by TB David Dorn (22/100y). Owls O could not been stopped, however, and soon capped 58y drive with Broomell's 1y TD keeper. Owls gained 243y rushing and earned 29 1st downs.

Penn State 27 MARYLAND 7: Penn State (2-2), continually fortunate against southern border rival, easily won 17th straight in series, but look at stat sheet would argue otherwise: Lions hit less than half their passes, made only 11 1st downs, and rushed for less than 4y per attempt. Penn State excelled on D with 6 sacks and 7 forced TOs, allowing only 153y O and late 24y TD pass by backup QB Bob Milkovich. TB Booker Moore rushed for 2 TDs of 3 scored after Maryland FUMs, which occurred at Terps 2, 14, and 39YLs. Penn State FB Matt Suhey rushed for 95y and TD, while S Giuseppe Harris had 2 INTs and blocked punt. Terps (3-2) TB Charlie Wysocki was held to 51y rushing.

AUBURN 44 North Carolina State 31: Auburn (3-1) pounded Wolfpack on ground for 407y in chasing NC State from ranks of unbeatens. Tigers had 2 backs top 100y: reserve QB Charles Thomas garnered 113y and 2 TDs, and TB Joe Cribbs added 104y and 3 TDs. Wolfpack (4-1) opened with 14-0 lead as QB Scott Smith (9-15/221y) threw 25y TD pass to WR Mike Quick (6/106y) and RB Billy Ray Vickers rushed for 1y TD. Auburn scored 44 of game's next 47 pts with virtually all damage done on ground; Tigers bothered to go airborne infrequently for 4-6/39y.

Mississippi State 28 Tennessee 9 (Memphis): Mississippi State (2-2) overwhelmed Vols, forcing 5 TOs and outgaining SEC rivals 428y to 330y. Bulldogs QB Tony Black was superb early, rushing for 72y and passing for 66y more before leaving with injury in 2nd Q. By then Mississippi State had 14-3 lead on 33y TD pass to WR Mardye McDole and 1y scoring plunge by FB Fred Collins. QB Jimmy Streater led Tennessee (3-1) with 150y passing but was picked off 3 times.

MINNESOTA 31 Purdue 14: Gophers (3-2) had QB Mark Herrmann's number, picking off 4 passes with TB Marion Barber's 3 short TD runs being set up by INTs. Purdue (3-2) held Barber to only 38y, but Minnesota managed 343y total as QB Mark Carlson threw for 152y, and FB Garry White rushed for 94y. Game's turning point arrived early in 3rd Q when Purdue DB David Hill fumbled punt into own EZ, where Gophers DE Tom Murphy covered it for TD and 17-7 lead. Herrmann was far from being embarrassed, throwing for 235y but no TDs. TB Wally Jones rushed for 81y and 2 TDs for Boilermakers.

Michigan 21 MICHIGAN STATE 7: Michigan (4-1) QB B.J. Dickey pulled off stunner, stopping on fake option rollout to hurtle ball downfield to WB Ralph Clayton. Play, used against Michigan week before by California, went 66y to break up 7-7 tie in 3rd Q. Dickey (8-13/147y, 2 TDs) added 7y TD pass to WR Anthony Carter. TB Stan Edwards rushed for 139y, including 25y run during Wolverines' 96y drive to their 1st TD. Michigan State (3-3) tied game at 7 at start of 3rd Q on 6y run by TB Derek Hughes. Win was 100th at Michigan for coach Bo Schembechler.

OHIO STATE 16 Northwestern 7: Wildcats (1-4) came to fight Ohio State to very end. Despite starting 5 frosh, Northwestern D held QB Art Schlichter to 5-16/77y passing. Wildcats managed only 194y themselves, yet were down only 13-7 late after FB Dave Mishler's 1y TD run. Ohio finally iced game on 50y FG by K Bob Atha. Buckeyes (5-0) rolled up 357y featuring FB Paul Campbell's 113y rushing.

HOUSTON 13 Baylor 10: Cougars (4-0) won D battle on K Kenny Hatfield's 2 FGs in 4th Q. Houston LB David Hodge, in on 19 tackles, 2 sacks, INT, and FUM creation, led D that held Baylor to 37y O in 2nd H. Sole mistake by Cougars was allowing 78y TD pass between QB Mickey Elam and TB Walter Abercrombie for Bears' 10-7 H lead. Win was propelled by Houston rush game that produced 2 100y backs: RB Terald Clark (28/135y) and FB John Newhouse (16/104y).

OKLAHOMA 49 Colorado 24: Former Oklahoma coach Chuck Fairbanks returned with Colorado (1-4) for rude Norman homecoming. Game was over by H as Sooners (4-0) scored 4 TDs in 2nd Q to take 28-7 lead. Oklahoma HB Billy Sims (18/118y, 4 TDs) earned his 13th straight 100y game and scored 3 of his 4 TDs in 1st H. Sims compiled 11 TDs in season's initial 4 games. Buffs managed 277y O, but were never in contest once 2nd Q began. DT Richard Turner had 3 of OU's 7 sacks.

STANFORD 27 Ucla 24: Wild finish featured blocked FG attempt and successful 56y kick, all in final 71 secs. K Peter Boermeester, who won 1978 match-up with late FG, attempted 40y kick for Bruins (2-3) with game tied as it approached last min. Stanford RB Gordon Banks got piece of ball to keep it at 24-24. Frosh QB John Elway then marched Cardinals (3-2) to long winning FG by K Ken Naber, which was good despite bouncing off left upright. TB Freeman McNeil did yeoman's work for Bruins, rushing for 197y and 16y TD run that had knotted game at 17-17 in 4th Q. Elway (16-23/178y),

who combined with QB Turk Schonert to throw for 330y, answered with 80y drive to 17y TD pass to TB Vincent White (7/113y). UCLA then deadlocked it at 24-24 on 34y run by nimble QB Rick Bashore.

OREGON 19 California 14: Ducks (2-3) used big plays to pull out 1st win against any Golden State school in last 6 years. Trailing 7-3 at H, Oregon took lead on 60y TD pass from QB Reggie Ogburn, who rushed and passed for 100y each, to WR Don Coleman. Ducks then forced California (3-2) punt, which was returned 62y by CB Rock Richmond for 16-7 lead. Bears QB Rich Campbell (20-28/187y, 2 INTs), who threw 16y TD pass to WR Michael Buggs in 1st Q, managed another scoring drive in 4th Q, but it was not enough.

1 Southern California (53)	1285	11 Michigan	648
2 Alabama (11)	1248	12 Arkansas	629
3 Oklahoma	1126	13 Louisiana State	504
4 Texas (1)	1101	14 North Carolina	455
5 Nebraska	1059	15 Missouri	414
6 Washington	889	16 Brigham Young	323
7 Houston	884	17 North Carolina State	100
8 Ohio State	781	18 Auburn	98
9 Florida State	756	19 Michigan State	77
10 Notre Dame	664	20 Purdue	62

October 13, 1979

West Virginia 20 BOSTON COLLEGE 18: Oppressed Eagles (1-4), losers of 16 of last 17 games, came close to victory before allowing late TD pass. Mountaineers (3-3) QB Oliver Luck, who threw for 97y and rushed for 94y, tossed winning 9y TD pass to WR Darrell Miller with 3:50 left. Boston College had final chance at end on K John Cooper's missed 38y FG attempt, even though he had hit 2 3-ptrs earlier. Cooper's FG attempt was set up by frustrating FUM at BC 1YL, just when it seemed West Virginia TB Robert Alexander (20/100y) would ice it with TD. QB Jay Palazola, who rushed for 134y, then quickly hit 2 passes/76y to bring Eagles into FG range.

Wake Forest 24 NORTH CAROLINA 19: Demon Deacons (5-1) were enjoying magical year with no win any sweeter than upset of undefeated North Carolina . Wake Forest D shone, forcing 5 TOs and holding HB Amos Lawrence to 24/34y on ground. After TB James McDougald (26/61y) scored twice for visitors, FB Albert Kirby scored winning TD with 60y catch of pass from QB Jay Venuto (15-27/236y) in 4th Q. Tar Heels (4-1) rallied with game's final 9 pts before being finished off by late FUM. North Carolina QB Matt Kupec (24-41/267y, INT) threw 2 TDs to TE Mike Chatham (10/144y). Wake would soon be ranked for 1st time since 1950.

FLORIDA STATE 17 Mississippi State 6: Seminoles (6-0) were outgained, but controlled scoreboard in defeating Bulldogs. QB Jimmy Jordan came off bench due to injuries to lead 2 TD drives in 1st H that took advantage of good field position. Pass interference PEN set up 1y run by Florida State TB Mike Whiting's TD run. Jordan's alley-oop pass to WR Jackie Flowers for 17y TD gave FSU 14-0 lead in 2nd Q. Mississippi State (2-3) O struggled, gaining only 50y in 1st H and suffering 5 TOs. Bulldogs scored TD in 4th Q on 2y run by HB Michael Haddix, but 2-pt try failed.

GEORGIA 21 Louisiana State 14: LSU (3-2) continually shot self in foot until its final drive ended with FUM to Bulldogs omnipresent DB Scott Woerner on 22YL. Georgia (2-3) had built 21-7 lead behind efficient O that converted opportunities, scoring twice within 4-min duration early in 3rd Q to break 7-7 tie. Tigers cut into 21-7 deficit on 24y scoring run around LE by QB David Woodley (7-11/101y), but were weighted down by 5 TOs. S Jeff Hipp had 2 big 2nd H plays for Bulldogs D, setting up go-ahead TD with INT and preserving lead by forcing FUM with huge hit on LSU TB LeRoid Jones. TB Matt Simon rushed for 128y and 11y TD for Georgia.

WISCONSIN 38 Michigan State 29: Revenge is sweet: after losing to Spartans 55-2 in 1978, returning Wisconsin (2-4) players had this date circled in advance. Heroes abounded for Badgers as DE Guy Boliaux recovered 2 FUMs to set up TDs, fellow DE Dave Ahrens returned INT 55y for TD, K Steve Veith kicked 3 FGs, and FB Dave Mohapp (12/65y, TD) led rush attack that gained 238y. Michigan State (3-3) trailed only 24-21 in 3rd Q with help of 2 strikes: 79y TD run by sub TB Bruce Reeves in 1st Q and 98y KO TD RET by TB Derek Hughes in 3rd Q. Badgers quickly answered Hughes with TB Troy King's 41y KO RET to set up 29y TD run by FB Gerald Green.

OHIO STATE 47 Indiana 6: Buckeyes (6-0) dominated O, rushing for 347y and 6 TDs. QB Art Schlichter continued to put his stamp on 1979 season, passing for 136y and TD and rushing for 68y and TD. Ohio State TB Ric Volley, moved from FB due to injuries, was leading rusher with 97y, while WR Doug Donley (5/103y, TD) was Schlichter's favorite target. Hoosiers (4-2) managed 269y, and their only TD was delivered by QB Tim Clifford on 2y keeper.

Oklahoma State 14 MISSOURI 13: Cowboys (3-2) wiped out 13-0 H deficit behind play of little-used reserve players, QB John Doerner and RB Terry Suellentrop. Doerner replaced injured QB Harold Bailey to throw 2 TD passes, capping drives of 80y and 84y that featured some of 146y rushing that Suellentrop (22/152y) gained in 2nd H. Tigers (3-2) had taken 13-0 H lead on 1y TD run by FB James Wilder and 2 FGs by K Jeff Brockhaus, but Brockhaus missed 3 FG tries to regain lead in 4th Q. Passing of Mizzou QB Phil Bradley (21-27/209y) did everything but deliver win.

Texas 16 Oklahoma 7 (Dallas): Bruising Horns D earned spurs by holding HB Billy Sims to 73y with no TDs, Oklahoma O to 158y and 6 1st downs, while forcing 3 TOs. Only score for Sooners (4-1), 11y TD pass from QB J.C. Watts to FB Stanley Wilson, came as result of lost FUM at Texas 16YL on punt RET by S Johnnie Johnson. Texas HB Jam Jones rushed for 127y, while K John Goodson kicked FGs of 37, 18, and 38y for margin of victory. Longhorns (4-0) TD came on 5y QB Donnie Little-to-WR Steve Hall pass, which followed DB Derrick Hatchett's 36y INT RET.

Stanford 21 SOUTHERN CALIFORNIA 21: Cardinals shockingly tied top-ranked USC (5-0-1) with 21 unanswered 2nd H pts. QB Turk Schonert (16-27/163y, 2 TDs) had hand in all 3 TDs with 2 passes and TD run. Stanford (3-2-1) had pair of 4th down convs during its 2nd drive and another on tying 86y march. Latter conversion was exciting: Cards HB Mike Dotterer took pitch on 4th-and-1 on USC 11YL, fumbled but picked up ball, reversed field, and raced for 1st down. Southern California TB Charles White rushed for 221y and 2 TDs, but it wasn't enough to pull it out because QB Paul McDonald threw INT late in 4th Q. Stanford moved to Trojans 29YL before Schonert's 7y loss forced K Ken Naber to try 53y FG, which he missed. Trojans raced into final FG attempt, but botched snap.

ARIZONA STATE 12 Washington 7: Emotions ran high in Tempe as dismissed Arizona State (3-2) coach Frank Kush was carried onto field *before* game. Charged-up Sun Devils scored 2 TDs in 1st Q, while D dominated Huskies (5-1). Devils QB Mark Malone capped 1st drive with 3y TD run. Later in 1st Q, ASU P Mike Black pinned Washington on own 2YL. Devils LB Gary Padjen nailed Washington TB Toussaint Tyler to force EZ FUM REC for TD by DE Bob Kohrs. ASU thwarted Washington drive that reached Sun Devils 1YL on EZ INT by S Kendall Williams. Washington scored on TB Joe Steele's 3y run late in 2nd Q but mustered little in 2nd H.

October 20, 1979

North Carolina 35 NORTH CAROLINA STATE 21: North Carolina (5-1) built 28-7 lead as FB-TB Doug Paschal, subbing for injured TB Amos Lawrence, rushed for 2 TDs, and QB Matt Kupec (7-11/144y) threw 2 others. Tar Heels then withstood 2-TD North Carolina State (3-3) rally, with key play early in 4th Q turned in by LB Lawrence Taylor. Taylor nailed Wolfpack QB Scott Smith, ball popped loose and was pounced upon by UNC DE Jeff Pierce on State 12YL. Pack claimed Smith was passing, but officials ruled FUM, and soon Paschal (32/117y) had scored clinching 1y TD run. Smith had sparked rally with 203y passing and 63y rushing, but finished with 3 TOs.

ALABAMA 27 Tennessee 17: Crimson Tide (6-0), winners of 15 straight, did not panic after falling behind 17-0 early. Instead, Bama methodically marched up and down field, showcasing rush attack that gained 313y. HB Major Ogilvie rushed for 109y and 2 TDs for Alabama team that overcame 5 TOs. Several of those TOs contributed to Vols (4-2) racing to big early lead, with versatile QB Jimmy Streater throwing and running for scores. Alabama now had won 20 straight SEC games, tying record held by Tennessee from 1937-40 and Alabama from 1973–75.

Minnesota 24 IOWA 7: Hawkeyes' active D had answer for run game of Minnesota (4-3), so Gophers QB Mark Carlson took to air, completing 14-17/230y and TDs of 50y and 57y to WR Elmer Bailey in 3rd Q. Gophers TB Marion Barber was held to 38y rushing, but scored 1y TD run in 1st Q when Minnesota took 10-0 lead. Iowa (3-4) answered with 19y scoring run by TB Dennis Mosley (19/74y, TD), but shot itself in foot by committing 4 TOs.

Southern California 42 NOTRE DAME 23: Teams erupted in 2nd H for 51 pts between them as each D took day off: foes combined for 1,126y total O. TB Charles White set double career-highs by rushing 44/261y, 4 TDs to lead Trojans (6-0-1). QB Paul McDonald also set personal mark of 311y on 21-32 passing with 2 TDs. Irish (4-2) had their own fast-charging backfield combo as TB Vagas Ferguson, who became all-time Irish rusher, gained 185y and 2 TDs, and QB Rusty Lisch threw for 286y. Notre Dame could not keep up with USC O that scored 5 TDs in 2nd H, including all 4 of White's scores on short runs. Southern California WR Dan Garcia (8/149y) caught 12y TD pass, while ND WR Tony Hunter nabbed 5/131y.

ARKANSAS 17 Texas 14: Hogs (6-0) earned win and measure of respect with 31y FG in 4th Q by K Ish Ordonez, his record 15th straight. Texas (4-1) had taken 7-0 lead on 37y TD run by HB Jam Jones in 1st Q. Hogs converted TOs into 2 TDs to take 14-7 lead in 3rd Q after QB Kevin Scanlon pitched to HB Gary Anderson for 28y TD and passed 7y to TE Darryl Mason for go-ahead score. Arkansas stepped it up again as it marched from its 20YL to winning FG, converting 3rd-and-16 along way on FB Roland Sales' catch. Horns gained proximity TD on from QB Donnie Little 35y pass to TE Lawrence Sampleton to close scoring.

Nebraska 36 OKLAHOMA STATE 0: Huskers D earned kudos as scoreless streak stretched majestically to 16 Qs. Nebraska (6-0) was just as dominating on O against coach Jimmy Johnson's first OSU squad, rushing for 433y as IB Jarvis Redwine gained 104y and WB Kenny Brown added 110y. Redwine scored twice, cracking EZ from 29y out for team's 1st TD, and QB Tim Hager (10-17/163y) got into act with 42y TD pass to WR Tim Smith. WR Ron Ingram led Cowboys (3-3) with 3/49y receiving. IB I.M. Hipp (12/54y) became all-time Huskers rushing leader with 2,719y.

Pittsburgh 26 WASHINGTON 14: Huskies (5-2) dropped ball over and over and, in doing so, dropped 2nd straight game. Robust Pitt (5-1) had something to do with that, forcing 6 TOs with 3 created by super DE Hugh Green. FB Randy McMillan (22/92y, 2 TDs) paced Panther O that only gained 249y but still scored 5 times thanks to TOs that set up 23 of team's 26 pts. Washington scored TDs on 1y run by TB Joe Steele (28/113y) and 99y KO RET by WR Anthony Allen.

October 27, 1979

PITTSBURGH 24 Navy 7: Frosh QB Dan Marino hit 22-30/227y and 2 TDs to send Midshipmen (6-1) reeling with 1st loss. Marino entered game in 1st Q when starting QB Rick Trocano pulled hamstring, and Trocano would never regain starting job from phenom Marino. Navy went 50y in 2nd Q to go-ahead TD at 7-0 on 27y pass from QB Bob Powers to TE Carl Hendershot. But, injury-depleted Middies could gain only 116y trying to penetrate Pitt's bruising D. Panthers (6-1) took 10-7 lead in 3rd Q on 3y scoring pass to TB Freddy Jacobs, 1st of Pitt's 3 TDs in 2nd H.

North Carolina State 16 CLEMSON 13: Wolfpack (6-2) D had 2 memorable stops at game's end to preserve key win. Tigers (5-2) drove to NC State 4YL after 39y run by QB Billy Lott, FB Tracy Perry's 4 smashes could not penetrate Pack GL. Clemson soon marched to NC State 18YL before INT by Wolfpack S Mike Nall sealed deal with 58 secs left. Winning pts had come on 25y FG by K Nathan Ritter, his 3rd of game, with 4:47 left. Tigers gained 356y—to 148y by winners—but lost thanks to performance of Wolfpack D, which was terrific under pressure.

WAKE FOREST 42 Auburn 38: Auburn (5-2) erupted for 38 1st H pts behind TBs Joe Cribbs (16/88y, TD) and James Brooks (17/117y, TD), but failed to find EZ in 2nd H. Deamon Deacons (7-1) erased 18-pt H deficit to take lead, but needed LB Carlos Bradley's FUM REC deep in Wake Forest territory and DB Larry Ingram's INT to close out Tigers. QB Jay Venuto (23-43/258y, INT) and TB James McDougald (30/147y), who rushed thrice for 2nd H TDs, sparked surprising Wake Forest.

Florida State 24 LOUISIANA STATE 19: Hard-fought game went way of Florida State on strength of aerial wizardry of QB Jimmy Jordan (14-31/312y, 3 TDs, 2 INTs), who enjoyed being able to play entire game for change. Seminoles (7-0) went deep on LSU with scoring passes of 53y to WR Hardis Johnson and 40y to WR Jackie Flowers in 2nd H. TB Hokie Gajan led Tigers (4-3) with 103y rushing, scoring on 1y run in 2nd Q to tie game 7-7. LSU presented balanced attack (177y rushing and 175y passing) to take 13-7 lead after QB David Woodley's 2y TD. FSU then jumped on Tigers by scoring 17 straight pts.

MICHIGAN 27 Indiana 21: Number of exceptional plays by WR Anthony Carter during his Hall of Fame career at Michigan (7-1) were too many to count, but none was better than this game's winning play versus Indiana. With 6 secs left and game tied at 21-21, Michigan had ball at Hoosier 45YL. Carter caught 20y pass from QB John Wangler at Hoosiers 15YL, evaded what seemed like entire D and scored winning TD. Play was possible due to FB Laurence Reid's throwing ball OB on previous play to stop clock: illegal, but not called. Hoosiers (5-3) had just tied game on 3y TD pass from QB Tim Clifford (12-26/232y) to TE Dave Harangody.

Houston 13 ARKANSAS 10: For 5th time in 1979 Cougars (7-0) came from behind in 4th Q in winning battle of unbeatens on K Kenny Hatfield's late 19y FG. Arkansas (6-1) then drove 55y to attempt tying 42y FG with 4 secs left. Porkers K Ish Ordonez—who had NCAA record 16 straight FGs—kicked low off head of Cougars DT Hosea Taylor. Blocked FG left Houston as frontrunner for SWC crown. Razorbacks were led by QB Kevin Scanlon's 120y passing and 66y rushing, but his INT jump-started Houston's winning drive and his 1st H FUM set up Houston TD. FB Terald Clark rushed for 135y for Houston, which now had opened with 7 wins for 1st time ever.

OREGON STATE 33 Stanford 31: Crazy finish chased Cardinals (4-3-1) out of 1st place tie in Pac-10. Beavers (1-6) scored on 1y run by TB Jeff Southern and 2-pt conv pass from QB Scott Richardson to FB Tony Robinson (25/89y, 2 TDs) to tie game 31-31 with 1:13 left. On ensuing KO, Stanford CB Steve Gervais fielded ball clearly in field of play, on his own 2YL, and stepped back into EZ to take knee for what he thought would be touchback. Officials correctly ruled it as safety that was margin of victory for Oregon State. Stanford QB Turk Schonert (17-20/238y, 2 TDs) was brilliant in defeat. Win was sweet for Beavers coach Craig Fertig, who had been fired Monday effective at season's end.

November 3, 1979

Yale 23 CORNELL 20: Unbeaten Yale (7-0) took lead in Ivy race with rally in Ithaca. With its win, Yale, in its 107th season, became 1st school ever to reach 700 victories. Bulldogs enjoyed 70-win lead over Princeton, which was 2nd on all-time list. Victory over Princeton 35-10 following week coupled with Brown's loss gave Ivy League title to Elis. Cornell (4-3) QB Mike Tanner twice connected with TE Brad Decker for TDs to

take 20-17 lead with more than 6 minutes left. Winning drive featured 4th down tipped pass play to TB Ken Hill that helped set up winning 12y TD pass from QB John Rogan to TE Bob Rostomily with 47 seconds left.

Miami 26 PENN STATE 10: This game became renowned for coming-out party of former East Brady, Pa., prep star, Miami QB Jim Kelly (17-30/280y), who famously had rejected Penn State because he did not wish to play LB. Penn State (5-3) had won 4 straight games before running into hot Kelly, who threw 3 TDs in his 1st start. Canes (4-4) scored 10 pts before Lions got ball. Kelly led drive for TD, and Canes recovered loose ensuing KO and scored FG. WR Jim Joiner (6/177y) caught 2 TD passes as Miami stretched its 13-10 H lead to 26-10. LB Scott Nicolas (26 tackles) and DT Tim Flanagan (25 tackles) led Hurricanes D that forced 4 TOs and posted 2nd H shutout. FB Matt Suhey was Nittany Lions' leading rusher with 110y.

PITTSBURGH 28 Syracuse 21: At end of game's 1st possession, Syracuse (5-4) P John White spun punt dead at Pitt 1YL, but PEN forced him to reboot. This time, Panthers (7-1) DB Terry White ran it back 85y for TD and 7-0 lead. Orange QB Bill Hurley (80y passing, and 72y, 3TDs rushing) scored 1st Q TD and later would surpass 2,000y rushing and 3,000y passing, only 3rd player in history to do so in career. Pitt frosh QB Dan Marino clicked on 2 short TD passes in 2nd Q for 21-6 H edge. Hurley got Syracuse back in game at 21-13 with his 2nd TD run in 3rd Q, but Marino connected on 36y screen pass and 33y rope to WR Ralph Still at sideline to set up TB Rooster Jones' 3y TD run for commanding 28-13 lead late in 3rd Q.

Clemson 31 WAKE FOREST 0: Cinderella's slipper, which had been clutched all season by Wake Forest (7-2), was smashed by Clemson (6-2). TO-happy Tigers D picked off 3 passes by Wake QB Jay Venuto (16-36/114y) that were converted into TDs, including 17y INT TD RET by LB Jeff Davis. Additionally, DB Terry Kinard's 31y INT RET set up QB Billy Lott's 10y TD pass to WR Perry Tuttle, and DB Eddie Geathers' nifty 43y INT RET led to 1y TD run by TB Chuck McSwain (11/60y, 2 TDs). With these gifts, Tigers enjoyed 24-0 H lead and coasted from there.

Virginia 31 GEORGIA 0: Cavs (5-3) stunned SEC frontrunner for most impressive win in more than decade. Early on, upset bid began rolling in UVa's direction as its much-improved D unit forced 3-and-out on 1st possession for Georgia (4-4). Virginia then needed only 2 plays to score TD as QB Todd Kirtley threw 12y completion to WR Teddy Marchibroda before hitting 53y scoring pass to RB Greg Taylor. Bulldogs dug in heels and trailed only 10-0 after 3 Qs. Virginia roared to 21 in 4th Q, and Cavaliers posted their 3rd blanking on season. Kirtley finished with 215y passing, while Georgia rushed for 172y as TB Matt Simon gained 93y on ground.

Rutgers 13 TENNESSEE 7: "What's a Rutgers?" That was headlined joke in Knoxville before State University of New Jersey's Scarlet Knights (6-2), AKA Rutgers, shocked 17th-ranked Vols (4-3) in front of 84,265 at Neyland Stadium. TB James Berry scored Tennessee's sole TD on 1y run in 1st Q, but thereafter Rutgers ruled. Knights LB Ed Steward's 2 INTs set up 10 pts, including 37y scoring pass from QB Ed McMichael (11-12/174y) to TB David Dorn. K Kennan Startzell's 2 FGs proved to be scoring difference, although Vols had last gasp when special teamer Johnny Watts returned blocked FG to midfield. Clock expired, however, after Vols' PEN, long incompletion, and short completion.

Louisiana State 28 MISSISSIPPI 24 (Jackson): Scoring 28 of game's final 35 pts, Tigers (5-3) stunned fast-starting Mississippi (2-6). Winning 4y TD run by WR Tracy Porter with 2:29 left—which also gave Bengals 1st lead—was set up by Porter's 52y punt RET. Rebels responded by marching 82y to LSU 3YL before INT by Bengals DB Willie Teal ended Reb hopes. Ole Miss opened with 17-0 advantage as QB John Fourcade started with 24y TD pass to TE Billy Wise for lead. LSU rallied with 4 TDs, 2 scored by TB Hokie Gajan on 1y run and 54y catch. Rebels P Jim Miller averaged 47.9y on 7 boots.

Nebraska 23 MISSOURI 20: Trailing 23-20 late, Tigers (4-4) passed up FG ATT from Nebraska 11YL to go for win. Huskers (8-0) DE Derrie Nelson ended Mizzou's hopes with sack of QB Phil Bradley as time expired. Nebraska had built 20-6 3rd Q lead behind rushing attack that gained 291y. Tigers rallied for 2 TDs within 8 secs of each other in 3rd Q: frosh TE Andy Gibler caught 4y pass on 4th down to cap 90y drive, and on ensuing KO, DB Orlando Pope galloped 17y on FUM RET. Pope's TD was realized when Missouri WR Ron Fellows made crushing hit on Nebraska WB Anthony Steels to send ball into air for Pope to catch. Teams remained tied until 4th Q when Huskers K Dean Sukup booted game-winning 19y FG.

KANSAS 36 Kansas State 28: Spirited Sunflower State match-up was won by Jayhawks (3-5) as TB Mike Higgins led way with 165y rushing and 3 TDs. When QB Brian Bethke threw 43y TD pass to WR David Verser to add to Higgins' scores, Kansas led 27-14. Wildcats (3-5) stormed back on 2 TD runs by HB L.J. Brown to take 28-27 lead early in 4th Q. Kansas K Mike Hubach, who earlier missed x-pt, booted vital 37y FG for 30-28 edge with 4:24 remaining. Before it was over, FB Harry Sydney added Jayhawks' clinching TD run from 35y.

SOUTHERN CALIFORNIA 34 Arizona 7: Displaying fabulous balance, Southern California (8-0-1) methodically won behind superior weaponry. USC QB Paul McDonald was brilliant, passing for school-record 380y on 25-35. TB Charles White fully contributed with 167y rushing and 4/44y receiving. White dominated on opening 75y drive, he capped with 1y TD run. McDonald took over for 80y drive to 2nd TD, completing 5-6 against man-to-man D for 71y to reach EZ on 18y pass to WR Kevin Williams (5/110y, 2 TDs). FB Hubert Oliver led Arizona (4-3-1) O, rushing for 68y and adding 5/28y in receptions.

November 10, 1979

Pittsburgh 24 WEST VIRGINIA 21: With QB Dan Marino throwing for 232y, Panthers (8-1) grabbed 10-0 H lead and never looked back. In sloppy affair with each team having 6 TOs, Mountaineers (5-5) hung tough, despite falling behind 17-3 in 4th Q. QB Oliver Luck pulled West Virginia to within 17-10 on 19y TD pass to WR Cedric Thomas and had his O moving for potential tie. But, S Jo Jo Heath saved Pitt with INT that he returned 46y to West Virginia 4YL. TB Fred Jacobs scored from there for needed insurance.

VIRGINIA 20 Virginia Tech 18: Hokies (4-6) rallied from 17-0 deficit with 18 pts in 2nd H, but could not complete 2-pt conv pass in game's final secs. Virginia Tech had marched 75y behind QB Steve Casey, converting 4th down plays 3 times, with WB Sidney Snell leaping to catch 2y TD. On 2-pt try, pass was behind FB Tony Blackmon as Virginia (6-3) embraced victory that guaranteed its 1st winning season in 11 years. Cavs' lead was set up by D: CB Bryan Shumock returned FUM 89y for TD and 14-0 lead. Shumock's RET set new school and ACC records for distance. UVa LB Bryan Holoman recovered FUM to set up FG, and CB Bobby Call picked off pass to set up final FG by K Wayne Morrison for winning pts.

FLORIDA STATE 27 South Carolina 7: Clever coach Bobby Bowden and Florida State's flashy O hogged attention, but it was superb D that retained Noles' perfect record. FSU (9-0) held Gamecocks (6-3) to paltry 9 1st downs and single big play: 80y scoring jaunt by TB George Rogers (21/186y). Florida State got 4 FGs from accurate K Dave Cappelen, who included 50y 3-ptr among his successes. Seminoles received TDs from FB Mark Lyles (135y rushing) on 1y run and TE Sam Childers on 7y pass from QB Jimmy Jordan.

Alabama 3 LOUISIANA STATE 0: While it never was easy playing in Tiger Stadium, Crimson Tide had to be worried with Tigers (5-4) gunning for nation's top-rated team and looking to win for embattled coach Charlie McClendon. Torrential downpour helped to lessen Alabama's O advantage. Bama (9-0) ran for 252y, but blew several scoring chances. Crimson Tide D was superb in holding LSU to 83y rushing and 81y passing and permitting no advances inside Tide 41YL. Bama K Alan McElroy's 27y FG in 3rd Q—he missed 2 earlier—proved to be enough scoring as coach Bear Bryant won his 100th game in last 10 years.

PURDUE 24 Michigan 21: By November, bench strength often shows itself for top teams. Reserve TB Ben McCall started for Purdue (8-2) due to injuries and came through with 98y and 2 TDs. Boilermakers D had to use some subs, but limited Michigan (8-2) to 99y on ground and 159y through air. Starting CB Bill Kay had 3 of Boilers' 4 INTs and made FUM REC to help thwart Wolverines time and again. Michigan was kept off scoreboard until 6y TD pass from QB John Wangler to TE Doug Marsh finally was created in 3rd Q. Purdue methodically put 10 pts on board for 24-7 lead in 4th Q. Michigan TB Butch Woolfolk rushed for 105y and made 2y TDs to help 4th Q rally to pull within 24-21, but could do nothing with its final drive.

Texas 21 HOUSTON 13: After being yanked from prior week's game for missed assignments, Longhorns QB Donnie Little gained redemption with win. Little scored 2 TDs, including 15y scamper with 1:25 left that iced game for Texas (7-1). Houston had clawed within 1 pt on K Kenny Hatfield's 36y FG, but was stopped on downs on own 45YL against Steers D that allowed only 84y in 2nd H. Cougars (8-1) could not overcome 3 INTs—2 swiped by Texas CB Derrick Hatchett—FUM, and 2 blocked punts. Late in 1st H, blocked punt by special teamer Conny Hatch was recovered on Houston 27YL to set up Longhorn score: 6y TD run by HB Jam Jones for eventual winning pts. Earlier in 2nd Q, Cougars' TD was delivered by FB Terald Clark on 46y run.

ARKANSAS 29 Baylor 20: Upset-minded Bears (6-3) built 17-0 lead as HB Walter Abercrombie had 2 rushing TDs. Hogs (8-1) then roared back with 20 straight pts, including 32y scoring pass from QB Kevin Scanlon to WR Bobby Duckworth and DT Danny Phillips' EZ FUM REC. Baylor did not quit, tying game on 35y FG by K Robert Bledsoe. Winning TD came through air as Razorback Scanlon hit WR Robert Farrell down right sideline for 60y TD pass with 3:22 left.

Southern California 24 WASHINGTON 17: In dealing Huskies (7-3) what was thought to be killing 2nd Pac 10 defeat, Trojans (9-0-1) presumably wrapped up 10th Rose Bowl berth in last 14 years. But when Arizona State was forced to forfeit several wins, Washington picked up extra victory that dealt it right back into title race, half-game back. USC TB Charles White was brilliant as he rushed 38/243y, including 58y on winning 80y drive capped by FB Marcus Allen's 10y TD run. On White's 4th carry of game he passed TB Archie Griffin of Ohio State (1972-75) as 2nd all-time leading rusher in NCAA history. There was plenty of time for rally by Huskies, who then marched to Troy 1YL behind QB Tom Flick (18-28/245y, TD, 2 INTs), before Trojan D stopped TB Vince Coby (18/103y) on 3 runs to snuff out comeback.

1 Alabama (34)	1262	11 Pittsburgh	661
2 Ohio State (14)	1218	12 Purdue	614
3 Nebraska (5)	1209	13 Michigan	464
4 Southern California (12)	1164	14 Clemson	359
5 Florida State	983	15 Auburn	338
6 Texas (.33)	981	16 Washington	295
7 Oklahoma	960	17 Wake Forest	214
8 Arkansas (.33)	859	18 Temple	162
9 Houston (.33)	788	19 Tennessee	123
10 Brigham Young	705	20t Baylor	99
		20t Tulane	99

November 17, 1979

Harvard 22 YALE 7: Largest crowd in 25 years (72,000) packed Yale Bowl to see mighty Elis cap perfect season with rout of lowly Crimson. Instead, Harvard turned tables on Yale coach Carm Cozza yet again. Yale (8-1) seemed to be resting on laurels of Ivy title as Harvard (3-6) marched 74y on opening drive and then recovered FUM to halt home team and start 70y drive for 13-0 lead in 2nd Q. Bulldogs trimmed it to 13-7 in 3rd Q, but found extension of rally difficult because they suffered 6 TOs and 5 sacks. Crimson QB Burke St. John tossed 39y TD pass to FB Jim Callinan and added clinching 2y TD run in 4th Q.

PENN STATE 22 Temple 7: Coach Wayne Hardin's best Temple (8-2) squad had 7-6 lead late in 2nd Q as TB Kevin Duckett scored on 64y run. Although it took Penn State (7-3) O until 2nd H to get rolling, its burly D was sharp from get-go. Owls QB Brian Broomell, nation's pass percentage leader, hit only 4-16/46y, while being picked off 3 times and sacked 4 times. Sack total equaled number of sacks previously permitted by Owls O-line all season. Led by FB Matt Suhey's 87y and 2 TDs, Nittany Lions outrushed Owls 270y to 88y in compiling 24 1st downs to 6 for Temple.

Clemson 16 NOTRE DAME 10: QB Billy Lott went around RE for 26y TD, and K Obed Ariri kicked 3 FGs as snarling Clemson Tigers (8-2) erased 10-0 H deficit. Notre Dame (6-4) HB Vagas Ferguson (22/110y) had scored TD on 2y run, but his 2nd H FUM in Irish territory set up Lott's TD. Another key ND miscue came in form of Irish WR Ty Dickerson's punt FUM that was recovered by Clemson LB Chuck Rose and converted into Ariri's 1st FG and 10-10 tie. Tigers S Terry Kinard silenced 2 late ND drives with INTs as Notre Dame finished with 5 TOs and fell out of bowl consideration.

Auburn 33 GEORGIA 13: To pleasure of Alabama and Sugar Bowl officials, Bulldogs (5-5) got spanked. Victory would have given Georgia 6-0 SEC record and spot in Sugar Bowl on tiebreaker. Auburn (8-2), who knocked Bulldogs out of Sugar Bowl in 1978 with tie, rushed for 392y as TB James Brooks gained 200y, including TDs of 67y and 44y, and TB Joe Cribbs totaled 166y and 2 TDs. Both backs topped 1,000y for season, to become 1st SEC tandem to do so. Georgia turned to QB Jeff Pyburn (17-26/179y, INT) after QB Buck Belue was knocked out in 1st Q with ankle injury. Bulldogs managed to snare 10-9 H lead as FB Jimmy Womack ran for 12y TD.

Ohio State 18 MICHIGAN 15: Michigan P Bryan Virgil never had any chance. With Wolverines (8-3) up 15-12 early in 4th Q, Virgil faced 10-man rush. Ohio State (11-0) LB Jim Laughlin swooped in from RE to block punt—he blocked Virgil as well—and ball was picked up by LB Todd Bell on Michigan 18YL. Bell ran in winning TD. Ohio State had enjoyed 12-7 3rd Q lead after 19y TD pass from QB Art Schlichter (12-22/196y, INT) to WR Chuck Hunter off deflection by CB Mike Jolly, which snapped streak of 15 Qs without Ohio TD against northern rivals. Michigan went up 15-12 on 3y TD run by FB Roosevelt Smith after 66y pass from QB John Wangler to WR Anthony Carter. Wangler and Carter had hooked up on 59y TD in 1st H, but Ohio maintained proximity by stopping Michigan on 4th-and-goal from within 1YL.

Purdue 37 INDIANA 21: Boilermakers (9-2) had much too much balance for Indiana (7-4)—rushing for 270y and passing for 269y—and never trailed in battle for Old Oaken Bucket. Purdue QB Mark Herrmann (26-40/269y, INT) out-dueled QB Tim Clifford (15-35/171y, 2 INTs), who received upset help from Hoosiers run game (27/49y). Purdue TB Ben McCall rushed for 148y and TD, while FB Mike Augustyniak (76y rushing) scored 3 times. Hoosiers trailed 27-21 after 3 Qs with help from 15 PENs/158y by Purdue, with 2 scores set up by pass interference calls.

Oklahoma 24 MISSOURI 22: Despite amazing performance by HB Billy Sims, who rushed for career high 282y, Sooners (9-1) needed missed 37y FG by Missouri K Ron Verrilli late in contest to keep lead. Sims gained 206y in 2nd H—154y in 3rd Q alone—in last-ditch effort to win 2nd straight Heisman Trophy. His 70y TD run on 3rd play of 2nd H gave OU 14-9 lead it would never relinquish. On his 70y canter, Sims was hit on 30YL by CB Johnnie Poe, spun, and remained on his feet. QB Phil Bradley kept Tigers (5-5) close, completing 16-23/222y, while rushing for 74y, including 68y on 4th Q TD run. Tigers then went for 2-pt conv that might have tied it at 24-24, but Oklahoma CB Jay Jimerson broke up Bradley's pass.

BRIGHAM YOUNG 27 Utah 0: Domination of WAC by BYU (10-0) continued as Cougars crushed in-state rival. QB Marc Wilson, nation's total O leader, threw for 23-37/374y, with 18y TD to WR Matt Braga. Braga added 14y TD run on reverse as BYU scored 17 pts in 1st Q. Cougars dominated on D, holding Utes (6-6) to 59/167y rushing and 4 -12/59y passing. Wilson became 1st WAC player to top 7,000y total O.

WASHINGTON 17 Washington State 7: Huskies (9-2) put themselves in position to go to Rose Bowl should Southern California lose to UCLA on following Saturday. Washington had narrow stat edge: 284y to 261y total O with 19-15 advantage in 1st downs. For all their marching up and down field, Cougars (4-7) were held out of EZ until 4th Q. By that time, Huskies led 17-0 with their TDs coming on 3y run by TB Vince Coby (26/112y) and 20y pass from QB Tom Flick to WR Paul Skansi. QB Steve Grant finally put Washington State on board in 4th Q with 19y TD keeper.

California 21 STANFORD 14: Aerial circus was ultimately frustrating for Cardinal (5-5-1), who fell 1 bomb short. Stanford QB Turk Schonert threw 2 TDs but his final 4th down pass into EZ was knocked away with 40 secs left. Schonert twice had converted 4th downs on last drive, but Cards drive died 2y short. California's winning TD was thrown by QB Rich Campbell (23-33/314y, 3 TDs) earlier in 4th Q on ball caught by TE Bob Rose (8/121y, 2 TDs) that 1st was ruled OB before officials reversed call. Bears (6-5) Campbell set Pac 10 record of 67.1% for single season, mere 1 percentage pt better than Schonert's mark.

1 Alabama (32)	1238	11 Pittsburgh	652
2 Ohio State (18)	1214	12 Purdue	598
3 Nebraska (4)	1157	13 Clemson	487
4 Southern California (10)	1151	14t Washington	376
5 Florida State	1019	14t Auburn	376
6 Texas (.33)	959	16 Michigan	357
7 Arkansas (.33)	865	17 Baylor	215
8 Oklahoma	848	18 Tulane	184
9 Houston (.33)	811	19 South Carolina	124
10 Brigham Young	705	20 Penn State	93

November 24, 1979

(Fri) Florida State 27 FLORIDA 16: Although Gators (0-9-1) were having dreadful season, Florida State (11-0) had to fight to remain undefeated. After blowing 10-pt lead, Seminoles marched 80y to go up 17-10 early in 4th Q on 20y run by FB Mark Lyles (27/151y). Gators then lost ball on controversial play as QB Larry Ochab (22-54/270y) threw pass that DT Walter Carter came up with on Florida 10YL. Play was ruled INT—1 of 5 Ochab threw—despite TV replays showing that ball clearly hit ground before Carter caught it. K Bill Capece soon hit 18y FG to bump FSU's lead back up to 20-10.

(Fri) HOUSTON 14 Texas Tech 10: As FB James Hadnot (21/199y) burst down right sideline on 3rd play of 2nd H for 61y TD run and 10-0 Texas Tech lead, Cougars (9-1) must have felt they were reliving last season's upset. Houston responded with 2 TDs: 14y run by FB Terald Clark and backup QB Terry Elston's breathtaking 72y romp for game winner with 11:21 left. Clark rushed career-high 171y, while Hadnot set Texas Tech single season and career rushing marks as Raiders ran for 349y.

SOUTH CAROLINA 13 Clemson 9: For 1st time, both major schools from Palmetto State were bowl-bound. Gamecocks (8-3) TB George Rogers (27/102y) topped 100y for 9th straight game, and TE Ben Cornett scored on 2y pass from QB Garry Harper (7-11/112y). Tigers (8-3) showcased 3 FGs by K Obed Ariri, although team marched to Carolina 5YL at game's end where QB Billy Lott (14-21/199y) frustratingly overthrew 4th down pass to WR Perry Tuttle.

TULANE 24 Louisiana State 13: That Tulane (9-2) had beaten LSU so infrequently—Tulane won for only 2nd time in 31 years—just made win so much sweeter. QB Roch Hontas threw for 248y and 3 TDs as Green Wave built 24-0 H lead. Tigers (6-5) rebounded in 2nd H with 2 late TDs on short runs by QBs David Woodley and Steve Ensminger. Game was won with field position as longest drive for Tulane's 4 scores was 67y in 2nd Q to 17y TD pass by Hontas to WR Alton Alexis (9/115y), while Tigers continually started drives deep in their own territory. LSU's passing game gained 354y, but suffered 4 INTs.

OKLAHOMA 17 Nebraska 14: Big 8's showdown of undefeated 1st place teams was hard-hitting affair, but Huskers had tricks, but no answers for Oklahoma HB Billy Sims. Sims rushed for 247y against nation's best statistical rush D (67.2 y avg), including 71y on brilliant run during decisive 94y march in 4th Q. Drive ended with 3y TD run by QB J.C. Watts on 4th down that gave Sooners (10-1) 17-7 lead with 8 mins left. Watts earlier hooked up with TE Forrest Valora on 58y TD pass. Huskers (10-1) closed scoring when G Randy Schleusener ran in "Fumblerooskie" from 15y out, trick play that coach Tom Osborne had debuted earlier in game. In 7 years at OU, coach Barry Switzer had notched 4 outright Big 8 titles and shared 3 others.

ARKANSAS 31 Southern Methodist 7: It was downhill for Mustangs (5-6) from very 1st play with FUM REC swallowed up by Razorbacks DE Jeff Goff on SMU 34YL. Arkansas QB Kevin Scanlon threw 8y scoring pass to TE Steve Clyde 3 plays later for 1st of 3 TD passes thrown by Scanlon. Later in 1st Q, another FUM by SMU led to FG as Hogs (10-1) scored on 3 straight possessions for 24-0 lead in 2nd Q. Highlight for Mustangs was SWC record of 2,777y career receiving Y posted by WR Emanuel Tolbert (5/74y). SMU FB Craig James rushed for 149y.

Brigham Young 63 SAN DIEGO STATE 14: BYU QB Marc Wilson continued to rewrite record books as 278y passing pushed his season total to NCAA-record 3720y and his total O number to 3,604y, another record. It took Cougars (11-0) exactly 6 plays and 8:12 to effectively end maters as they ran up 21-0 lead. Wilson (13-21/278y, 4 TDs, 3 INTs) threw TDs of 25y to WR Danny Plater, 42y to WR Bill Davis, and 57y to TB Eric Lane. BYU scored so quickly in what would turn out to be 35-7 H that Aztecs (8-3) actually had ball for 21 of 30 mins. That possession time produced only RB Steve Fogel's 1y TD run as San Diego State suffered its worst loss since 66-0 pasting by Fresno State in 1942. Rare switch in killing clock had Cougars O gaining more rushing (320y) than passing (293y).

SOUTHERN CALIFORNIA 49 Ucla 14: Trojans (10-0-1) coach John Robinson ran record to 4-0 against cross-town rivals with laugher that was over by H at 35-0. TB Charles White slipped and jabbed for 194y and 4 TDs despite bell-ringing 4th Q hit by host of Bruins. White staggered around woozy and did not remember his opening 2 TDs. Although Trojans QB Paul McDonald had Pac-10 record streak for consecutive ATTs without INT halted at 143, he was brilliant throughout, completing 17-23/199y. USC D was equally terrific, holding UCLA frosh QB Tom Ramsey to 3-13/34y and 2 INTs passing. Trojans CB Ronnie Lott (2 INTs) made 30y INT TD RET that provided

14-0 lead in 1st Q. White's TDs gave him 52 for his career. HB Freeman McNeil gained 120y rushing to reach UCLA (5-6) single season mark of 1,396y, 8y more than Wendell Tyler had in 1975. Coach Terry Donahue dropped to 0-4 against USC. He vowed to reverse that trend, and he would with 5 wins in next 7 cross-town bouts.

Arizona 27 ARIZONA STATE 24: Frosh K Brett Weber was not listed as top kicker for Wildcats (6-4-1)—he was not on scholarship, nor even on roster—but Weber became hero for Arizona after last-second 27y FG for 1st successful 3-ptr. Weber missed wide right with 5 secs to go but was roughed by ASU CB Ron Brown, allowing unknown Wildcat another chance to become known. LB Jack Housely set up FG with INT of Sun Devils (6-5) QB Mark Malone (189y passing) with 33 secs left. Two plays later, Arizona QB Jim Krohn completed 43y pass to WR Greg Jackson, who won fight for ball with CB Ralph Dixon. Sun Devils lost 3 FUMs that Cats converted into 17 pts. FB Hubert Oliver rushed for 95y and 2 TDs for Arizona.

AP Poll November 26

1 Alabama (34)	1193	11 Pittsburgh	611
2 Southern California (12)	1142	12 Purdue	544
3 Ohio State (13)	1141	13 Washington	454
4 Florida State	997	14 Auburn	392
5 Oklahoma (1)	963	15 Michigan	376
6 Texas (.33)	934	16 Tulane	354
7 Nebraska	850	17 South Carolina	266
8 Arkansas (.33)	848	18 Clemson	122
9 Brigham Young (1)	760	19 Penn State	114
10 Houston (.33)	751	20 Baylor	73

December 1, 1979

Pittsburgh 29 PENN STATE 14: Panthers (11-1) easily captured Lambert Trophy for Eastern supremacy as their D held Penn State (7-4) to 40y rushing and 237y overall O. QB Dan Marino (17-32/279y, TD, INT), FB Randy McMillan (26/114y, TDs rushing and receiving), and K Eric Shubert (3 FGs) led victors who racked up 464y. Pitt DE Hugh Green dominated with 3 sacks. Score would have been more lopsided if not for 2 big plays for Penn State: FB Matt Suhey's 65y rumble for short-lived 7-0 lead and 95y KO TD RET by TB Curt Warner.

Navy 31 Army 7 (Philadelphia): TB Eddie Meyers—son of retired *Army* chief warrant officer—set Navy (7-4) game rushing records for carries (43) and yards (279y), while scoring 3 TDs. Continuing meteoric rise from 4th team to stardom, Meyers would go on to rewrite Navy single season and career marks as well. Injuries forced Army (2-8-1) to turn to JV for starting QB T.D. Decker, who promptly threw INT on 1st pass. By H, Midshipmen had 248y and 17 1st downs in building 17-7 lead. Army got its TD on 8y run by HB Bobby Crompton, converting S Chris Zawic's FUM REC on Navy 16YL. With its 6th win in last 7 service tilts, Navy knotted series at 37-37-6.

Alabama 25 Auburn 18 (Birmingham): Trailing in 4th Q for 1st time all season, Alabama (11-0) drove 82y behind QB Steadman Shealy, who scored from 8y out for his 2nd TD. Shealy rushed 99y for game, while completing 5-6/64y. Tigers (8-3) took advantage of Bama's 4 FUMs in 2nd H to forge 18-17 lead on 2 TD passes by QB Charlie Trotman. After Tide regained lead, TB James Brooks returned KO 64y, but following drive died on dropped 4th down pass by TE Mike Locklear near Alabama GL. Tide D had allowed only 40 pts through its 1st 10 games. This time it couldn't completely stonewall its GL, but allowed Auburn to rush for 161y rushing, 154y below its avg. Rivalry had extra heat as Auburn, losers of 7 straight in in-state series, felt Tide had fingered it for recruiting violations that earned 2-year probation.

TENNESSEE 31 Vanderbilt 10: Shaking off knee injury, QB Jimmy Streater would not let Tennessee (7-4) lose. Commodores (1-10) grabbed 10-0 lead in 1st H against bumbling rivals, who lost 2 FUMs and rushed for only 100y. Streater (13-23/221y, INT) launched Vols' rally with 41y TD pass to WR Anthony Hancock (6/163y), shortest of Streater's trio of 3rd Q TD passes. Vols took lead when S Roland James went 89y with punt RET. Later in 3rd Q, Streater found Hancock all alone for longest pass (85y) in Tennessee history. RB Terry Potter rushed for 127y to lead Vanderbilt attack that gained 278y on ground.

TEXAS A&M 13 Texas 7: HB Curtis Dickey's 20y TD run and K David Hardy's 2 FGs produced all pts needed by upset-minded Aggies (6-5). Longhorns (9-2) were victimized by inequity between their struggling O and exemplary D. Texas TD was set up by DT Steve McMichael's jarring hit on Aggies RB Johnny Hector that produced FUM REC by DE Ron Bones on Texas A&M 15YL. Texas FB Carl Robinson ran in only score moments later from 1y out. Longhorns fumbled 2 KOs and 2 punts.

AP Poll December 3

1 Ohio State (16)	1267	11 Texas	677
2 Alabama (29)	1265	12 Purdue	606
3 Southern California (19)	1257	13 Washington	489
4 Florida State	1103	14 Michigan	452
5 Oklahoma (1)	1068	15 Tulane	376
6 Arkansas (.5)	951	16 South Carolina	287
7 Nebraska	908	17 Auburn	244
8 Houston (.5)	893	18 Clemson	222
9 Brigham Young (1)	848	19 Baylor	106
10 Pittsburgh	728	20 Temple	65

Conference Standings

Ivy League

Yale	6-1
Brown	5-2
Princeton	5-2
Cornell	4-3
Dartmouth	4-3
Harvard	3-4
Columbia	1-6
Pennsylvania	0-7

Southeastern

Alabama	6-0
Georgia	5-1
Auburn	4-2
Louisiana State	4-2
Tennessee	3-3
Kentucky	3-3
Mississippi	3-3
Mississippi State	2-4
Vanderbilt	0-6
Florida	0-6

Mid-American

Central Michigan	8-0-1
Toledo	7-1-1
Western Michigan	5-4
Ball State	4-4
Ohio	4-4
Northern Illinois	3-3-1
Miami	3-4
Bowling Green	3-5
Eastern Michigan	1-6-1
Kent State	1-8

Southwest

Arkansas	7-1
Houston	7-1
Texas	6-2
Baylor	5-3
Texas A&M	4-4
Southern Methodist	3-5
Texas Tech	2-5-1
Texas Christian	1-6-1
Rice	0-8

Pacific-10

Southern California	6-0-1
Washington	5-2
Arizona	4-3
Oregon	4-3
California	5-4
Stanford	3-3-1
Arizona State (a)	3-4
UCLA	3-4
Washington State	2-6
Oregon State	1-7
(a) forfeited all games	

Atlantic Coast

North Carolina State	5-1
Clemson	4-2
Wake Forest	4-2
Maryland	4-2
North Carolina	3-3
Virginia	2-4
Duke	0-6

Big Ten

Ohio State	8-0
Purdue	7-1
Michigan	6-2
Indiana	5-3
Iowa	4-4
Minnesota	3-5-1
Michigan State	3-5
Wisconsin	3-5
Illinois	1-6-1
Northwestern	0-9

Big Eight

Oklahoma	7-0
Nebraska	6-1
Oklahoma State	5-2
Missouri	3-4
Colorado	2-5
Iowa State	2-5
Kansas	2-5
Kansas State	1-6

Western Athletic

Brigham Young	7-0
San Diego State	5-2
Utah	5-2
Hawaii	3-4
New Mexico (a)	3-4
Colorado State	3-4
Wyoming	2-5
Texas-El Paso	0-7
(a) forfeited all games	

Pacific Coast Athletic

Utah State	4-0-1
San Jose State (a)	4-0-1
Long Beach State	3-2
Fresno State (b)	2-3
Fullerton State	1-4
Pacific	0-5
(a) forfeited 3 conference wins	
(b) forfeited 1 conference win	

1979 Major Bowl Games

Holiday Bowl (Dec. 21): Indiana 38 Brigham Young 37

Led by QB Marc Wilson's 380y passing, Cougars (11-1) came just short of undefeated season as K Brent Johnson missed 27y FG with 11 secs left to preserve Indiana's 1st-ever bowl victory. Game-winning pts for Hoosiers (8-4) came courtesy of CB Tim Wilbur, who returned punt 62y for TD midway through 4th Q. BYU's next possession ended on INT by Hoosiers LB Marlin Evans—1 of 3 pickoffs for Indiana—which sent it on FG drive that was muffed on fumbled snap. Cougars then drove 69y in game's final moments before missing FG. As befitting Holiday Bowl, teams exchanged lead 8 times. BYU TE-P Clay Brown caught 9/142y, but he also had misfortune of punting ball to Wilbur. Indiana QB Tim Clifford (11-29/171y, TD) wedged over for pair of 1y TDs.

Liberty Bowl (Dec. 22): Penn State 9 Tulane 6

With many of best Penn State players injured or suspended, final hero became unknown 4th-string TB Joel Coles. With game tied 6-6 with less than min remaining, Penn State (8-4) faced 3rd-and-2 at midfield. Coach Joe Paterno went for unusually wild call: Coles took pitch and appeared to be running for 1st down when he abruptly pulled up and threw 39y pass to wide-open WR Tom Donovan. Soon after, K Herb Menhardt, who earlier made FGs of 33y and 27y, booted winning 20y FG with 18 secs left. QB Roch Hontas (21-39/210y) had rallied Green Wave (9-3) to tie game on K Ed Murray's 2nd 26y FG. In 1st H, Tulane managed only 63y against Nittany Lions D and were unable to convert any of Penn State's 3 early TOs. FB Matt Suhey (19/112y) committed 2 FUMs in 1st Q, but led attack that gained 242y on ground.

Sun Bowl (Dec. 22): Washington 14 Texas 7

Converting 3 TOs into scores, teams combined for 21 2nd Q pts but then settled into D struggle. Washington (10-2) managed only 165y of O, but only needed drives of 42y and 23y to score its TDs following Texas FUMs. Longhorns (9-3), who saw long 1st Q drive end on GL tackle by Huskies S Greg Grimes, converted FUM REC into 44y

drive to halve deficit. Washington's 1st scoring drive began when NG Stafford Mays recovered FUM late in 1st Q before facing 3rd-and-11 at Texas 18YL. QB Tom Flick threw pass to WR Tom Skansi in EZ for TD on diving catch. Using back-ups due to injuries, Horns then fumbled away next possession when frosh FB Darryl Clark lost ball on own 23YL. Grimes recovered FUM and 4 plays later Huskies had 14-0 lead on 4y TD run by frosh TB Willis Mackey. Texas reversed trend after DE Tim Campbell nailed Flick, with ball bouncing to DT Kenneth Sims, to set up 11 play drive to 5y scoring pass from QB Donnie Little to HB Brad Beck (16/98y). Each team posted 2nd H shutout as every play was hotly contested.

Tangerine Bowl (Dec. 22): Louisiana State 34 Wake Forest 10

Tigers (7-5) made sure "Cholly Mac," lovable coach Charlie McClendon, went out as winner. McClendon ended his final game riding on shoulders of players. LSU QB David Woodley (11-19/199y, INT) rushed for 68y and 2 scores. He threw 19y TD pass to WR Jerry Murphree (5/60y). Tigers D sacked QB Jay Venuto (10-20/165y) 3 times, while picking him off thrice. Eventually, Venuto was knocked out of game by Bengals DE Lyman White, who authored 3rd Q sack. Defeat could not dampen amazing year turned in by annual doormat Wake Forest (8-4). Deacons won more games (8) in 1979, coach John Mackovic's 2nd season, than they had in previous 3 seasons combined (7).

Fiesta Bowl (Dec. 25): Pittsburgh 16 Arizona 10

Although pts came at premium, Panthers (10-1) scored just enough to win as QB Dan Marino threw TD pass and K Mark Schubert booted 3 FGs. Drive to Marino's 12y scoring pass to TE Benjie Pryor was bright spot for Pitt O as Marino (15-29/172y, 2 INTs) completed passes of 34y to TE Mike Dombrowski and 24y to WR Ralph Still to turn around difficult 2nd-and-36 situation. Drive also featured 4th down conversion of 1y run by TB Fred Jacobs. Wildcats (6-4-1) scored TD in 4th Q on 1y run by FB Hubert Oliver that he set up with surprise 46y pass to WR Greg Jackson (5/89y). QB Jim Krohn completed 17-34/180y, 3 INTs for Cats, who came up empty on 1st H drives that reached Pitt 37, 26, and 22YLs.

Gator Bowl (Dec. 28): North Carolina 17 Michigan 15

Last chance to win bowl game in 1970s ended for Michigan (8-4) coach Bo Schembechler with disastrous 4th Q that pivoted on 4 TOs and, after Wolverines TD, dropped 2-pt conv pass. Finest moment for Tar Heels (8-3-1) arrived earlier as QB Matt Kupec (19-28/161y) led 97y drive, completing 6-7/49y including 12y TD pass to TB Phil Farris, in 3rd Q for 14-9 lead. Michigan had been ahead 9-0 in 2nd Q when red-hot starting QB John Wangler (6-8/203y, TD) was injured on sack. Wangler was never same gifted QB after injury, but heroically led Wolverines to Rose Bowl win in January 1981. After K Jeff Hayes kicked 32y FG in 4th Q to up Carolina's lead to 17-9, Wolverines drove 74y to QB B.J. Dickey's 30y TD pass to WR Anthony Carter (4/141y, 2 TDs) with 1:28 left. Dickey and Carter were unable to connect for tying 2-pt conv pass, and then Michigan illegally touched onside-KO before it traveled 10y. UNC TB Amos Lawrence rushed for 118y.

Hall of Fame Bowl (Dec. 29): Missouri 24 South Carolina 14

After Gamecocks (8-4) went distance with 1st possession, scoring on 20y QB Garry Harper pass to WR Zion "Mr. Clutch" McKinney, Missouri took control of game with 17-pt 2nd Q surge. K Ron Verrilli 1st put Tigers (7-5) on board with 22y FG, which was followed moments later by lost FUM on Gamecocks KO RET. QB Phil Bradley (7-11/72y) gave Mizzou lead it would not relinquish on next play, throwing 28y TD pass to WR David Newman. Bradley scored next on 1y run later in 2nd Q for 17-6 lead. Harper (13-19/172y, INT) answered in 3rd Q with 11y TD run and 2-pt conv pass to McKinney to pull within 17-14. Led by LB Eric Berg, Mizzou D shut out Gamecocks from then on, while O added HB Gerry Ellis' s11y TD run. South Carolina TB George Rogers rushed for 25/133y.

Peach Bowl (Dec. 31): Baylor 24 Clemson 18

Dedicating game to DB Kyle Woods, who had broken his neck in preseason, Baylor (8-4) pulled glorious upset. After emotional pre-game speech by Woods, Bears forged 24-10 lead on 3 aerial TDs and 2 blocked punts. Clemson (8-4) had opened scoring with 1y TD run by TB Lester Brown, but Bears QB Mike Brannan threw 2 TD passes and back-up QB Mickey Elam added 3rd after Brannan left with injury. In 4th Q, revitalized Tigers twice marched to within Baylor 24YL but came up empty. Then, Clemson LB Andy Headen blocked punt that was recovered at Baylor 1YL with 22 secs left. TB Chuck McSwain scored, and QB Billy Lott (17-34/204y) threw 2-point conv pass to FB Jeff McCall. Alert Headen recovered onside-KO, and Lott tossed 30y pass to WR Perry Tuttle (8/108y) to Baylor 23YL. That was as close as Tigers could get as PEN and INT ended matters.

Bluebonnet Bowl (Dec. 31): Purdue 27 Tennessee 22

Purdue (10-2) jumped out to big early lead, but had to withstand Vols' rally. QB Mark Herrmann (21-39/303y) hit 3 TDs in sparking Boilermakers, including comeback strike of 17y to TE Dave Young for game winner with 90 secs left. Herrmann had thrown TDs of 12y to WR Bart Burrell (8/144y) and 12y to Young as Purdue built 21-0 lead in 3rd Q. Tennessee (7-5) came back as D bent but did not break, and O started hitting passes. QB Jimmy Streater (16-34/218y) put Vols on board with 8y TD pass to sub TB Glenn Ford. Tennessee used trickery for next score on 15y option TD pass from TB James Berry to WB Phil Ingram. Vols scored next when FB Hubert Simpson ran 1y for TD that cut deficit to 21-20. Vols coach Johnny Majors went for lead, and Streater threw 2-pt conv pass to Simpson in 2nd H, reacted to late turn in fortune with winning 80y drive.

Cotton Bowl: Houston 17 Nebraska 14

For 2nd straight year Cotton Bowl went down to wire, but this time Houston (11-1) came out on top as WR Eric Herring caught winning 6y TD pass from backup QB Terry Elston with 12 secs left. Elston (9-16/119y, TD), who added 87y rushing, entered game after woeful 1st Q by Cougars O, which totaled only 28y. Nebraska (10-2) had chewed up 85y on opening drive that ended with IB Jarvis Redwine's 9y TD run. Elston got his team moving, leading 71y drive with 27y completion to WR Lonell Phea and 24y rushing, including 12y scoring run. Both teams concentrated on punting until midway through 4th Q when Houston grabbed 10-7 lead on 41y FG by K Ken Hatfield. Houston's "Mad Dog" D, which surrendered only 227y to Nebraska O that averaged more than twice that amount, held again, but Houston O gave away ball. FB John Newhouse lost FUM to Nebraska DT Bill Barnett on Houston 31YL. It took 6 plays—including tricky 13y pass from Redwine to QB Jeff Quinn—for Huskers to regain lead at 14-10, on 6y pass from Quinn to TE Jeff Finn. Houston then began victory drive, needing 66y to score. Elston completed 5-7/45y and rushed 3/10y. On winning play, Elston threw bullet pass past 3 defenders to Herring. Herring bobbled tipped ball slightly, but made catch for Cougars win.

Orange Bowl: Oklahoma 24 Florida State 7

Speed kills: lesson Florida State coach Bobby Bowden learned all too well against Sooners (11-1). While HB Billy Sims (24/164y) and QB J.C. Watts (16/127y) ran with abandon, it was quick Sooners D that truly dazzled. LB George Cumby—as fast as Florida State's backs—helped stop Seminoles rush attack while S Bud Hebert helped limit FSU passing game with 3 INTs, including pickoff that set up Sooners' 2nd TD for 14-7 edge. FB Stanley Wilson scored that TD from 5YL for eventual winning pts. Noles (11-1) managed only 182y and couldn't expand early 7-0 lead. FSU TD had come on 1y run by FB Mike Whiting in 1st Q at end of 74y drive. CB Bobby Butler blocked punt by K-P Michael Keeling to give Seminoles ball on Oklahoma 17YL. Florida State drove to 2YL before stumbling on PENs and bobbled hold on FG try. Sooners made them pay, needing only 4 plays to travel 81y, with Sims launching drive with 25y run and Watts ending it with 16y sprint to EZ. Wilson's TD gave OU lead that Keeling stretched to 17-7 at H on 24y FG. Watts and Sims combined for 2nd H score when Watts went around RE for 12y before pitching to Sims for 22y more and TD. Sims' TD highlighted wild 4th Q that produced 3 TOs on consecutive plays. Sooners romped to 411y total O.

Sugar Bowl: Alabama 24 Arkansas 9

Alabama (12-0) had just too much for Razorbacks, too much for all of college football, in fact, in taking win that assured another perfect season and national title. As if Arkansas (10-2) did not have enough to handle, Crimson Tide even used some double-wing formations to confuse Hogs D. HB Major Ogilvie (14/69y) ran for 2 TDs, HB Billy Jackson rushed for 13/120y, and nation's top-rated D excelled in easy win. Tide actually allowed 4 pts more than their amazing season avg, while holding Hogs to 97y rushing. Shaking off effects of 5 sacks, Arkansas QB Kevin Scanlon threw for 245y and 3y TD to WR Robert Farrell that cut deficit to 17-9 in 3rd Q. Teams then traded punts, with P Steve Cox pinning Alabama on own 2YL early in 4th Q. With A-A C Dwight Stephenson anchoring line, Tide answered with 98y TD drive. Jackson keyed drive with opening runs of 14y and 35y that set up FB Steve Whitman's 12y TD run right up middle. With DEs Wayne Hamilton and E.J. Junior putting pressure on Scanlon and DBs like CB Don McNeal laying out Arkansas receivers as they caught passes, Hogs comeback was impossible.

GAME OF THE YEAR
Rose Bowl: Southern California 17 Ohio State 16

Although Ohio State (11-1) entered game as nation's top-rated team, it clearly was underdog against Trojans squad that resembled NFL team. Buckeyes had to prove themselves all season, so they were ready for worthy effort. Ohio State D earned honors early in 1st Q as it stopped high-powered Southern California O at Ohio 5YL. Trojans (11-0-1) got on board later in 1st Q on 41y FG by K Eric Hipp. Buckeyes moved ball behind QB Art Schlichter, who completed 53y strike to WR Gary Williams (3/131y) on 3rd down to advance to 2YL. Passing game may have brought them there, but Bucks reverted to old style. USC stopped 4 runs—3 from 1YL—as Trojans preserved season-long streak of not giving up any 1st Q TDs. LB Riki Gray made key plays on 2nd and 3rd downs, with S Dennis Smith standing up Schlichter on 4th down. Midway through 2nd Q, Trojans upped lead to 10-0 as QB Paul McDonald beat Buckeyes blitz by hitting WR Kevin Williams for 53y score. Bucks, or at least Schlichter, were not done just yet as they rallied for 10 pts before end of 1st H. Schlichter connected on 67y TD pass to Gary Williams with 40 secs remaining. Bucks trotted off with momentum. Both teams adjusted for 3rd Q play, and Ohio took 16-10 lead as K Vlade Janakievski booted his 2nd and 3rd FGs of game. Up until 5:21 mark of 4th Q, game had been classic struggle; it then came down to talent of Troy TB Charles White and ability of USC O-line to wear down their talented foes. Beginning at own 17YL, Trojans marched to winning score as White would not be denied. Despite battling flu, White—whose 39 carries and 247y rushing were both Rose Bowl records—gained 71y on winning drive on 6 attempts. Included among those carries were 32y run on 1st play, 28y run on "student body right", and winning 1y run following G Roy Foster and FB Marcus Allen. It was as if entire game had been prelude to White's moment of greatness. Ohio had time for last drive, which ended when Schlichter (11-21/297y, INT) missed 4 passes from his 20YL. Teams combined for 931y, with 519y for Trojans. USC coach John Robinson upped his Rose Bowl mark to 3-0.

1 Alabama (46)	1317	11 Washington		690
2 Southern California (21)	1289	12 Texas		484
3 Oklahoma	1163	13 Brigham Young		474
4 Ohio Sate	1160	14 Baylor		358
5 Houston	1084	15 North Carolina		311
6 Florida State	893	16 Auburn		263
7 Pittsburgh	872	17 Temple		213
8 Arkansas	857	18 Michigan		207
9 Nebraska	852	19 Indiana		206
10 Purdue	739	20 Penn State		168

1979 Top Performance Formula

1 Alabama	1.7239
2 Oklahoma	1.6762
3 Brigham Young	1.6666
4 Southern California	1.6568
5 Pittsburgh	1.6379
6 Ohio State	1.6305
7 Nebraska	1.5773
8 Houston	1.5591
9 Arkansas	1.5520
10 Florida State	1.5516
11 Texas	1.4388
12 Washington	1.4356
13 North Carolina	1.4028
14 Penn State	1.4014
15 Purdue	1.3801
16 South Carolina	1.3249
17 Michigan	1.3196
18 North Carolina State	1.3077
19 Auburn	1.3021
20 Notre Dame	1.2989

1979 Top Opponent Records

1 Penn State	.6680
2 UCLA	.6581
3 North Carolina State	.6304
4 South Carolina	.6240
5 Notre Dame	.6207
6 Rice	.6197
7 Florida	.6018
8 Texas A&M	.5991
9 Texas Tech	.5940
10tArkansas	.59200
11tNorth Carolina	.59200
12 Texas	.5913
13 Wake Forest	.5831
14 Clemson	.5806
15tKansas	.577586
15tWest Virginia	.577586
17 Pittsburgh	.5754
18 Texas Christian	.5730
19 California	.5714
20 Minnesota	.5696

1979 Out-of-Conference Records

	W-L	Percentage	Bowl W-L
Atlantic Coast	23-11-2	.6667	1-2
Southwest	19-10-1	.6500	2-2
Big Ten	18-14	.5625	2-2
Big Eight	19-16	.5429	2-1
Pacific-10	21-18-1	.5375	2-2
Western Athletic	16-18-1	.4714	0-1
Southeastern	22-29-1	.4327	2-1

1979 Individual Statistical Leaders

RUSHING YARDS	Attempts	Yards	Avg.
Charles White, Southern California	293	1803	6.2
George Rogers, South Carolina	286	1548	5.4
Billy Sims, Oklahoma	224	1506	6.7
Vagas Ferguson, Notre Dame	301	1437	4.8
Freeman McNeil, UCLA	271	1396	5.2
Joe Morris, Syracuse	238	1372	5.8
James Hadnot, Texas Tech	273	1371	5.0
Dennis Mosley, Iowa	270	1267	4.7
James McDougald, Wake Forest	275	1231	4.5
James Brooks, Auburn	163	1208	7.4

PASSING YARDS	Completions	Attempts	Yards	Pct.
Marc Wilson, Brigham Young	250	427	3720	58.6
Rich Campbell, California	216	322	2618	67.1
Jay Venuto, Wake Forest	198	367	2432	54.0
Mark Carlson, Minnesota	177	300	2188	59.0
Brian Broomell, Temple	120	214	2103	56.1
Mark Herrmann, Purdue	182	309	2074	58.9
Paul McDonald, Southern California	153	240	1989	63.8
Turk Schonert, Stanford	148	221	1927	67.0
Eric Hipple, Utah State	144	238	1924	60.5
Tim Clifford, Indiana	149	259	1907	57.5

RECEIVING YARDS	Catches	Yards
James Murphy, Utah State	63	1067
Wayne Baumgartner, Wake Forest	55	1000
Gerald Lucear, Temple	45	964
Ken Thompson, Utah State	48	918
Steve Coury, Oregon State	66	842
Preston Brown, Vanderbilt	52	786
Ken Margerum, Stanford	41	733
Matt Bouza, California	52	717
Art Monk, Syracuse	40	716
Sidney Snell, Virginia Tech	43	706

1979 Consensus All-America Team

Offense

Wide Receiver:	Ken Margerum, Stanford
Tight End:	Junior Miller, Nebraska
Tackle:	Greg Kolenda, Arkansas
	Jim Bunch, Alabama
Guard:	Brad Budde, Southern California
	Jim Fritz, Ohio State
Center:	Jim Richter, North Carolina State
Quarterback:	Marc Wilson, BYU
Running Back:	Charles White, Southern California
	Billy Sims, Oklahoma
	Vagas Ferguson, Notre Dame
Placekicker:	Dale Castro, Maryland

Defense

Line:	Hugh Green, Pittsburgh
	Steve McMichael, Texas
	Bruce Clark, Penn State
	Jim Stuckey, Clemson
Middle Guard	Ron Simmons, Florida State
Linebacker:	George Cumby, Oklahoma
	Ron Simpkins, Michigan
	Mike Singletary, Baylor
Back:	Kenny Easley, UCLA
	Johnnie Johnson, Texas
	Roland James, Tennessee
Punter:	Jim Miller, Mississippi

1979 Heisman Trophy Vote

Charles White, senior tailback, Southern California	1695
Billy Sims, senior halfback, Oklahoma	773
Marc Wilson, senior quarterback, Brigham Young	589
Art Schlichter, sophomore quarterback, Ohio State	251
Vagas Ferguson, senior halfback, Notre Dame	162

Other Major Award Winners

Maxwell (Player)	Charles White, senior tailback, Southern California
Outland (Lineman)	Jim Richter, senior center, North Carolina State
Lombardi (Lineman)	Brad Budde, senior guard, Southern California
Walter Camp (Player)	Charles White, senior tailback, Southern California
Davey O'Brien (Southwest)	Mike Singletary, junior linebacker, Baylor
AFCA Coach of Year	Earle Bruce, Ohio State

1980

The Year of "How 'Bout Dem Dawgs!?," Holiday Miracle Pass, and Controversy for the Big Ten and Pac-10

"How 'bout dem dawgs!?" How about Herschel's debut? Herschel Walker burst onto the scene between the hedges in Athens, Georgia, with possibly the greatest offensive season ever contributed by a freshman. All Walker did was lead Georgia (12-0) to an undefeated record, the school's first-ever national title, run for a class record 1,616 yards, and finish third in balloting for the Heisman Trophy. Walker topped the 200-yard rushing barrier four times with a high of 283 yards coming against Vanderbilt (2-9). In a year when George Rogers, Hugh Green, John Elway, Lawrence Taylor, Ken Easley, Jim McMahon, and other stars played very well, Walker was the season's dominant figure.

Georgia was no one-man band. The Bulldogs' fine season finally brought coach Vince Dooley out from under Bear Bryant's considerable shadow, giving him recognition as a premier coach. In December he turned down an offer from his alma mater, Auburn, where he had played quarterback in the mid-1950s. The spotlight also shined on Walker's talented teammates, and the nation's fans learned of quarterback Buck Belue's baseball prowess and defensive back Scott Woerner's kickoff and punt return skills. The defense, still known as the "Junkyard Dawgs" from the mid-1970s, was much bigger than those teams but still superb, and the familiar shout around Sanford Stadium was, "How 'bout dem Dawgs!?" And there was the most memorable single play in school history, a 93-yard connection between Belue and wide receiver Lindsay Scott that beat rival Florida (8-4) when Georgia's backs were to the wall. Without that pass, Bulldogs still may have pulled out a victory against the Gators, but Scott's sprint for paydirt remains very special in Bulldog lore.

The best previous national finishes for Georgia were second in 1942 and third in 1946. Those squads featured the Bulldogs' only two previous consensus All-America running backs before Walker: Frankie Sinkwich in 1942 and Charlie Trippi in 1946.

The Bulldogs had to beat Notre Dame (9-2-1) in the Sugar Bowl to lock up the national title, which they did 17-10, as Walker rushed for 150 yards. The Sugar Bowl was the end for Fighting Irish coach Dan Devine, who earlier had announced his retirement effective at season's end. He was second in wins among active coaches and won the 1977 national championship, but Devine never was embraced by the Irish faithful. The rumor mill speculated that Don Shula, George Welsh, Lou Holtz, Lee Corso, Joe Restic, or Terry Donahue might be headed to Notre Dame. The wealth of quality candidates made the final selection, Cincinnati-Moeller High School coach Gerry Faust, all the more puzzling. Faust was a wonderfully upbeat man, but Dan Devine would be missed.

Florida State (10-2) played a tough schedule that included dates at Miami (9-3) and Nebraska (10-2), and at home against Pittsburgh (11-1). The Seminoles inflicted the season's only defeat on eventual runner-up Pitt, and, as bowl season opened, both the Seminoles and Panthers were waiting in the wings for shots at the title. Pitt pummeled South Carolina (8-4) by 37-9 in a Gator Bowl rout and slipped past Florida State in the final AP Poll when Oklahoma (10-2) rallied with a last-minute two-point conversion pass to beat Florida State 18-17 in the Orange Bowl. Florida State fared poorly with conversions in Miami's "Little Havana" stadium; its two losses coming by one point each. The Seminoles lost 10-9 during the season to improved Miami (9-3) because FSU could not convert a two-pointer at game's end. The New Year's night loss would be the last in any bowl game for Florida State until January 1997, a span of 14 games in which it would go 13-0-1.

While the Orange Bowl certainly was exciting and the Sugar Bowl wrapped up a national championship, the most thrilling bowl game was played on December 19 between Brigham Young (12-1) and Southern Methodist (8-4) in San Diego's Holiday Bowl. The Cougars rallied from a 20-point deficit in final the 3:57 to win on a 41-yard miracle pass from quarterback Jim McMahon to tight end Clay Brown. It took several seconds for officials to confirm Brown's catch amid an end zone pile of players. The game was over, BYU winning by a staggering 46-45 score.

Bear Bryant's 23rd Alabama (10-2) squad, the two-time defending national champions, occupied the nation's top spot for most of the season until dropping two games by 10 total points in November to Mississippi State (9-3) and Notre Dame. Bryant got his 300th victory, by 45-0 over Kentucky (3-8), in October. He finished the year with 10 wins after a Cotton Bowl rout of Baylor (10-2), which was pretty good considering he suffered a stroke in August that was withheld from the public.

The Pacific-10 suffered with half its teams ineligible for the Rose Bowl, either because of improper or phony course credits for some players. The firestorm burned hot in Los Angeles when Southern California (8-2-1) admitted that athletes were given preferential treatment for admission and that some players received credit for classes they did not take. The question soon centered on whether black athletes really were being helped to become student-athletes or being exploited in the Pac-10. The situation at Oregon (6-3-2) escalated when fullback Dwight Robertson and three former members of the team were indicted on sodomy and sexual coercion charges and others were implicated on rape and burglary charges. The Pac-10, or perhaps the "Pac-5," fortunately found a champion in probation-free Washington (9-3).

Cheating was so widespread that even the United States Military Academy received a reprimand from the NCAA for recruiting violations. The questions raised at Army (3-7-1) were instigated after former coach Homer Smith blew whistles after his dismissal following the 1978 season.

The Big Ten had a tough year, going a combined 10-17-1 in non-conference games and having only one team in the Top 20 at midseason. September 20 was the nadir as Big Ten teams combined to go 1-7; the sole victory was Indiana's 36-30 win over Kentucky on a last-second touchdown. The Big Ten also battled Illinois QB Dave Wilson in court over his junior college transcript and the number of eligible years left to him. Wilson won the right to play for two seasons, but in the off-season that was overturned and he was done after one record-filled season. Meanwhile, Northwestern (0-11) fired coach Rick Venturi after the season because of his 1-31-1 mark over three years.

Not all news was bad for the Big Ten as Michigan (10-2) finally won a Rose Bowl, its first New Year's win in Pasadena since January 1965. Senior Purdue (9-3) quarterback Mark Herrmann became the NCAA career passing leader with 9,188 yards.

Other records fell, as Brigham Young quarterback Jim McMahon became the first to pass for more than 4,000 yards (4,571) in a season, and Neil Lomax put Portland State on the map when he became the all-division career passing leader with 13,220 yards. California (3-8) signal-caller Rich Campbell, whose season ended early with a knee injury, set accuracy records for career completion percentage (64.4%) and season (70.7%). Washington quarterback Tom Flick set the single game mark (94.1%) on 16 of 17 passing versus Arizona (5-6) on November 8.

Although for the eighth straight season a running back, South Carolina's George Rogers, won the Heisman Trophy, passing was definitely on the rise as other records fell. Wilson of Illinois (3-7-1) threw for 621 yards against Ohio State (9-3) on November 8 to break the single-game mark by 70 yards. On the same day, Duke (2-9) freshman Ben Bennett broke the ACC record with 469 yards. The passing boom of the early 1980s was in full swing.

Running the football was not dead, however. Proving that, Oklahoma beat Colorado 82-42 on October 4 to set records for combined points by two teams in a modern contest and for team rushing yards with 758.

In addition to another fine year by Pittsburgh, Eastern football made plenty of news in 1980. Penn State (10-2) coach Joe Paterno proposed a regional football conference that was shot down by Boston College and Syracuse, who were enjoying the new basketball-driven Big East. Penn State applied for Big East membership but missed acceptance by one vote. Eastern football would forever feel the effects of that vote.

Milestones

■ Rules Committee further defined "chop block" for safety purposes, and "retreat block" now allowed pass protection blockers to extend their arms fully.

■ Air Force Academy joined Western Athletic Conference.

■ Recently-hired LSU coach Robert "Bo" Rein died on January 11 when private plane taking him from Shreveport to Baton Rouge crashed in Atlantic Ocean. It was assumed that Rein and pilot of plane were unconscious from hypoxia (lack of oxygen) as plane drifted off course. Rein played at Ohio State and went 27-18-1 in four years as coach of North Carolina State. Coaching great Dana X (for Xenophon) Bible died on January 19 at age 88 from complications of stroke. Bible retired from coaching in 1947 with lifetime record of 205-73-20, winning 14 major conference titles during stops at Texas A&M, Nebraska, and Texas. Long-time Auburn coach (1951-75) Ralph "Shug" Jordan died on July 17 of leukemia at age 69. Jordan went 175-83-7 at Auburn with 10-0 record in 1957 when Tigers won national championship behind defense that surrendered only 28 points. Jim Tyrer, All-America tackle for Ohio State in 1960, who played 13 years with Kansas City Chiefs, shot his wife to death and then killed himself on September 15.

■ Former Arkansas All-America K Steve Little, age 24, was paralyzed in auto accident hours after being waived by St. Louis Cardinals. At that time, Little shared NCAA record for distance with 67-yard field goal set in 1977.

■ Longest winning streaks entering season:

Alabama 21	Pittsburgh 10	Oklahoma, Purdue 7

■ Coaching Changes:

	Incoming	Outgoing
Arizona	Larry Smith	Tony Mason
Arizona State	Darryl Rogers	Bob Owens
Boston College	Jack Bicknell	Ed Chlebek
Columbia	Bob Naso	Bill Campbell
Georgia Tech	Bill Curry	Pepper Rodgers
Illinois	Mike White	Gary Moeller
Louisiana State	Jerry Stovall	Charlie McClendon
Louisville	Bob Weber	Vince Gibson
Michigan State	Frank Waters	Darryl Rogers
New Mexico	Joe Morrison	Bill Mondt
North Carolina State	Monte Kiffin	Bo Rein
Oregon State	Joe Avezzano	Craig Fertig
Stanford	Paul Wiggin	Rod Dowhower
Tulane	Vince Gibson	Larry Smith
West Virginia	Don Nehlen	Frank Cignetti
Wyoming	Pat Dye	Bill Lewis

AP Preseason Poll

1 Ohio State (36)	1253		11 Notre Dame	556
2 Alabama (24)	1217		12 Michigan	441
3 Pittsburgh (3)	1102		13 Florida State	439
4 Southern California (1)	1030		14 North Carolina	393
5 Oklahoma (1)	1009		15 Stanford	337
6 Arkansas	850		16 Georgia	333
7 Nebraska	812		17 Missouri	308
8 Houston	774		18 Penn State	280
9 Purdue	654		19 Auburn	261
10 Texas	580		20 Washington	200

September 6, 1980

(Mon) TEXAS 23 Arkansas 17: Facing 4th down at 2YL with Arkansas (0-1) ahead 7-3, Texas (1-0) coach Fred Akers passed up FG attempt and gave ball to his best O player, TB A.J. "Jam" Jones. Jones (29/165y) ran in 1st of his 2 TDs in 2nd Q as Longhorns went up for good. Hogs had taken lead, in earliest scheduled SWC game ever, on 39y TD reverse run by ever-dangerous WB Gary Anderson (9/103y). Jones' 2nd score—1y run that put Texas up 17-7—was set up by 30y pass interference PEN and QB Donnie Little's 28y throw to TE Lawrence Sampleton.

Virginia Tech 16 WAKE FOREST 7: Virginia Tech (1-0) employed stifling D to hold Deacons QB Jay Venuto (12-30/125y) in check, flooding passing lanes with defenders to prevent completions and make 7 coverage-sacks. Virginia Tech surprised with its passing, too, as QBs Steve Casey (10-19/162, INT) and Jeff Bolton (3-5/43y, INT) each threw TD passes to WB Sidney Snell (8/138y). Hokies sent TB Cyrus Lawrence rushing for 182y. Venuto was able to throw 13y TD pass to leaping WR Kenny Duckett that briefly gave Wake Forest (0-1) 7-3 lead in 2nd Q.

Florida State 16 LOUISIANA STATE 0: Seminoles (1-0) D posted shutout and set up every pt by forcing TOs. LSU (0-1) lost ball on season's 1st play as star Florida State NG Ron Simmons nailed RB Hokie Gajan to cause FUM, recovered by Noles DB Bobby Butler. Florida State K Bill Capece kicked 34y FG, 4 plays later. On LSU's next possession, QB Alan Risher (9-14/129y) lost FUM, recovered by omnipresent Simmons. This time it took 6 plays before Capece booted another 34y FG. Down 6-0, Tigers went TO-free until 2nd H when FUM and INT were converted into 10 pts by FSU: another FG by Capece and 3y TD run by TB Sam Platt. Seminoles O was less than stellar: it gained 187y rushing and only 35y passing.

Georgia 16 TENNESSEE 15: Georgia's high-flying season was almost grounded at start as Vols (0-1) jumped out to 15-0 lead behind QB Jeff Olszewski (15-20/186y), who ran for TD and threw 36y scoring pass to WR Mike Miller. Bulldogs (1-0) rallied behind ballyhooed frosh TB Herschel Walker (24/84y, 2 TDs), who made his debut in 2nd Q. After Georgia scored safety, Walker made impact with game-turning play: he scored inspiring 16y TD run that would have ended on 10YL if not for Walker putting his head down and ramming future pro S Bill Bates to turf. After breaking 2 more tackles, Walker scored. Georgia's deficit was now 15-9. Olszewski made costly mistake with his 4th Q FUM, 4th FUM lost by Tennessee, recovered on Vols 36YL. It set up winning 9y TD run by Walker.

NOTRE DAME 31 Purdue 10: With QB Mark Herrmann and backup QB Larry Gates injured, frosh QB Scott Campbell was thrust into starting job for Purdue (0-1). Although Campbell (17-26/178y) acquitted himself well, Boilermakers never led as Fighting Irish (1-0) showed surprising firepower. Notre Dame TB Phil Carter emerged with 142y rushing, 3y shy of his entire 1979 total, while QB Mike Courey (10-13/151y, INT) threw 9y TD to TE Tony Hunter and rushed for 63y. Courey tallied Notre Dame's final 6-ptr from 14y out. Trailing 17-0 in 2nd Q, Campbell completed 10 straight throws to rally Boilermakers to 17-10 H deficit before ND D adjusted, pressuring teenager and sacking him 7 times.

Texas A&M 23 MISSISSIPPI 20 (Jackson): Jackson had been Ole Miss' season-opener home-away-from-home, but Aggies (1-0) handed Rebs 1st loss after 8 straight wins in Magnolia State Capital. Win came because Texas A&M QB Mike Mosley barely outbattled Rebels (0-1) QB John Fourcade. Mosley completed 11-19/128y and rushed for 116y, while opening scoring with 43y run and later boosting A&M's lead to 23-14 with 40y TD scamper in 3rd Q. Fourcade did his best to match Mosley, going to air for 219y with TD passes of 8y and 49y to WR Ken Toler. Fourcade also dashed for 25y TD, but threw 4 INTs including crippling one returned 11y for TD by Texas A&M CB Dan Davis.

NEW MEXICO 25 Brigham Young 21: Perhaps day's most stunning result was registered in low-profile Albuquerque. New Mexico (1-0) QB Brad Wright passed and ran for 2 TDs to trigger huge upset of 4-time defending WAC champions. Brigham Young (0-1) QB Jim McMahon threw TDs of 9y and 21y to TE Clay Brown, but Lobos team, that had whole summer to prepare, was able to build game plan that slowed high-powered Cougars O. Lobos K Pete Parks had ultimate up-and-down day, missing x-pt and shanking subsequent KO, but he nailed 4 critical FGs.

AP Poll September 8

1 Ohio State (33)	1140		11 Michigan	465
2 Alabama (22)	1121		12 Georgia	452
3 Pittsburgh (3)	1009		13 Stanford	428
4 Oklahoma (1)	928		14 Penn State	414
5 Southern California	920		15 North Carolina	395
6 Texas	864		16 Arkansas	356
7 Notre Dame	733		17 Missouri	238
8 Nebraska	726		18 Auburn	203
9 Houston	723		19 Washington	182
10 Florida State	577		20 Purdue	107

September 13, 1980

PITTSBURGH 14 Boston College 6: Still shedding early-season kinks, foes combined for 16 ugly TOs. Unevenness seemed to help Boston College (0-1), which pulled close in 3rd Q on QB John Loughery's 35y TD pass to WR Jon Schoen, 1 play after LB Jerry Stabile's FUM REC. Panthers then stopped 2-pt conv effort, and Pittsburgh (1-0) D blanked Eagles rest of way. Sandwiching Schoen's TD were 2 TD passes by QB Dan Marino (23-43/221y, 5 INTs) to TE Benjie Pryor (10/110y), that each went 8y. "It certainly wasn't a pretty win, but a win is a win is a win," said Pitt coach Jackie Sherrill of team's 11th straight.

OHIO STATE 31 Syracuse 21: Using array of formations and pre-snap motion, Syracuse (0-1) confused top-ranked Buckeyes enough to take 21-3 lead in 2nd Q. Ohio State's advantages in size, speed, and depth finally wore down New York upstarts: QB Art Schlichter (7-13/107y, 2 INTs) led comeback with 47y TD pass to WR Doug Donley and 10y TD run. Ohio TB Cal Murray rushed for 117y of team's 301y. QB Dave Warner, who threw 2 TD passes and ran in 3rd score, led Orangemen, who also reaped TB Joe Morris' 150y rushing.

Iowa 16 INDIANA 7: Iowa TB Jeff Brown ran for 31/176y, 55y on single burst in 4th Q that set up FB Dean McKillip's clinching 1y TD run. QB Phil Suess (13-19/138y, INT) also played well for Iowa (1-0), throwing TD pass of 24y to WB Doug Dunham off flea-flicker. Indiana (0-1) QB Tim Clifford, Big 10's O MVP in 1979, threw for 205y, but Hoosiers were held to lone TD: Clifford's 7y pass to WR Nate Lundy in 4th Q that pulled Hoosiers to within 9-7. Indiana blew early chances, not scoring even though it cracked Iowa 30YL on 3 early drives, including trip to 7YL.

North Carolina 9 TEXAS TECH 3: Winning play was highlight reel stuff: shifty North Carolina (2-0) TB Kelvin Bryant caught flat pass from QB Rod Elkins, after Elkins deftly dodged blitz, and avoided 3 defenders to race for 58y TD. Tar Heels kept Red Raiders out of EZ, despite 5 drives reaching Carolina 25YL. Late in 4th Q, UNC LB Lawrence Taylor preserved win by forcing and recovering FUM at Tar Heels GL doorstep. Red Raiders (1-1) had moved to 2YL after S Tate Randle returned INT to Tar Heel 18YL. Texas Tech QB Ron Reeves threw for 191y, but had 2 costly INTs.

ARIZONA STATE 29 Houston 13: Heroes abounded for new Arizona State (1-0) coach Darryl Rogers. Devils WR John Mistler made 2 brilliant, glue-fingered TD receptions of 12y and 18y, K Scott Lewis booted 3 FGs, LBs Vernon Maxwell and Mark Hicks each recovered 2 FUMs, and CB Ron Brown returned his 2nd INT for 40y TD. Houston's normally-explosive Veer attack was contained throughout game, except for HB Terald Clark's 43y TD run that briefly cut deficit to 10-7. Cougars (0-1) O struggled throughout and would get no closer than that 3-pt margin.

AP Poll September 15

1 Alabama (30)	1232		11 Stanford	464
2 Ohio State (30)	1216		12 Penn State	440
3 Oklahoma (2)	1077		13 North Carolina	427
4 Southern California (2)	1011		14 Michigan	397
5 Pittsburgh (1)	996		15 Missouri	338
6 Nebraska	957		16 Washington	334
7 Texas	949		17 Arkansas	306
8 Notre Dame	790		18 Houston	202
9 Florida State	740		19 Auburn	183
10 Georgia	717		20 South Carolina	117

September 20, 1980

BOSTON COLLEGE 30 Stanford 13: At H, 2 Boston College (1-1) students paraded with banner that read: "Stanford, the BC of the West." It was hard to tell whether it was intended as insult to Stanford (often called "The Harvard of the West") or Harvard, Boston-area neighbor of Eagles. No matter; BC got fired up in 2nd H. After no. 11 Cardinals (2-1) took 13-9 lead early in 3rd Q when QB John Elway (21-36/259y) hit HB Darrin Nelson for 19y TD pass, QB John Loughery (8-15/145y, 2 TDs, INT) suddenly made like Elway: he threw 25y TD pass to TE Tim Sherwin (5/95y), scored on 1y plunge on 4th down following DE Greg Storr's INT, and pitched to TB Shelby Gamble, who raced 25y to EZ. Gamble played workhorse, totaling 32/154y with 2 TDs as BC ground game churned out 260y. BC D also contributed with 4 important INTs of bewildered Elway.

GEORGIA 20 Clemson 16: It would be difficult to find better games than what Bulldogs CB Scott Woerner delivered in 1st Q. Woerner scored TD on 67y punt RET and then made INT in EZ that he returned 98y—caught by Tigers TB Chuck McSwain—to set up 1y TD buck by QB Buck Belue as Georgia (3-0) took unlikely 14-0 lead. Clemson (1-1) actually would dominate 1st H, outgaining Bulldogs 239y to 33y and not surrender 1st down, yet still trail 14-10 thanks to Woerner's heroics. Teams swapped 2nd H FGs before Tigers' final drive ended with Bulldogs S Jeff Hipp's INT of QB Mike Gasque pass at Georgia 1YL. TB Edgar Pickett led Tigers ground game with 75y, while Georgia TB Herschel Walker carried 23/121y.

NOTRE DAME 29 Michigan 27: It didn't seem possible: Notre Dame (2-0) K Harry Oliver lined up 51y FG against wind. But, breeze suddenly went still, and Oliver became last-sec hero because his long 3-ptr barely cleared crossbar with time expiring. It sent Wolverines (1-1) to heart-breaking loss for 2nd straight year in heated series. Michigan had retaken lead at 27-26 only 41 secs earlier: Wolverines QB John Wangler, who replaced QB Rich Hewlett with Irish up 14-0 and pitched 3 TDs, fired pass to TB Butch Woolfolk that was tipped in air and caught inches from ground for score by TE Craig Dunaway. Only 3 mins earlier, HB Phil Carter (103y rushing) scored his 2nd TD of game for 26-21 ND lead. Irish QB Blair Kiel led winning drive, hitting WR Tony Hunter with 5y pass on 4th-and-1 to set up Oliver's miraculous FG.

Ucla 23 PURDUE 14: Game of missed chances unraveled for Boilermakers (1-2) as they were stopped deep in UCLA territory 3 different times, twice on INTs by CB Jimmy Turner. Purdue scored TDs on passes by QB Mark Herrmann (25-42/282y) to WR Bart Burrell (6/69y), his former HS target. Bruins (2-0) built 16-7 H lead: TB Freeman McNeil (29/117y), who struggled on poor turf, ran 2y TD and K Norm Johnson kicked 3 FGs. S Kenny Easley set up Johnson's 2nd FG with 25y run on fake punt. Easley set up and prevented TDs by forced FUM in 1st Q and pouncing on FUM in his EZ in 4th Q. UCLA QB Tom Ramsey (8-16/170y) added late 9y TD pass to WR Cormac Carney. Loss snapped Boilers' 12-game home winning streak.

SOUTHERN CALIFORNIA 23 South Carolina 13: Strong D ruled 1st H as Trojans led 10-6, scoring season's 1st pts against spirited Gamecocks' D in Its 3rd game. Battle of USCs was broken open in 3rd Q as no. 4 Trojans (2-0) scored 2 TDs within 3 mins to go up 23-6. Southern California QB Gordon Adams hit WR Kevin Williams for 9y TD pass moments before INT by S Dennis Smith at Gamecocks 17YL set up 7y scoring run by TB Marcus Allen (11/107y, 2 TDs). South Carolina (2-1) also enjoyed good moment in 3rd Q as LBs Walt Kater and Ed Baxley (14 tackles each) led GLS. Carolina TE Willie Scott hauled in 6/88y and TB George Rogers rushed 26/141y, including 34y on nifty TD jaunt with 1:30 left to play.

AP Poll September 22

1 Alabama (34)	1215	11 Penn State	569
2 Ohio State (26)	1183	12 Missouri	535
3 Nebraska (2)	1053	13 Washington	462
4 Oklahoma	1018	14 North Carolina	434
5 Southern California	999	15 Arkansas	326
6 Pittsburgh (1)	913	16 UCLA	280
7 Texas	902	17 Michigan	259
8 Notre Dame	835	18 Auburn	216
9 Florida State	770	19 Maryland	83
10 Georgia	718	20 Arizona State	76

September 27, 1980

Nebraska 21 PENN STATE 7: Stat sheet was filled with negatives for Penn State: 7 TOs, 9 surrendered sacks, 189y rushing with 2 TDs for Husker IB Jarvis Redwine. Score could have been worse. Nebraska (3-0) QB Jeff Quinn completed 12-17/158y and tallied 1y TD keeper. Huskers DEs Jimmy Williams and Derrie Nelson each had 2 sacks, while Nelson also pounced on nervous QB Jeff Hostetler's 2nd FUM of snap to set up Quinn's TD that opened scoring. Nebraska D set up another score as DB Sammy Sims returned 1st of his 2 INTs to Penn State 20YL 3 plays before Redwine scored on 3y run for 14-0 lead. Penn State (2-1) soon marched 76y behind frosh QB Todd Blackledge to 3y TD run by Curt Warner (16/84y) that halved deficit at 14-7.

NORTH CAROLINA 17 Maryland 3: Impressive Tar Heels (3-0) D held Maryland star TB Charlie Wysocki to 17y rushing and forced him into 3 FUMs. Gun-shy Wysocki lost FUMs on team's 1st 2 plays and another late in 1st H by North Carolina LB Lee Shaffer, with REC being made by CB Greg Poole on Terrapins 35YL. This troublesome TO set in motion odd PEN against Maryland: It appeared UNC TB "Famous" Amos Lawrence fumbled possession right back, so Terps O raced on field. Maryland (3-1) was assessed 15y PEN on no-call, and 1st H TD pass from QB Rod Elkins to Lawrence quickly followed for 10-0 lead. Terps QB and future NFL coach Mike Tice (14-22/179y) moved O to 50y FG by K Dale Castro in 3rd Q, but then lost FUM in 4th Q that Tar Heels converted into clinching 6y TD run by TB Kelvin Bryant. On Monday, North Carolina entered AP's Top 10 for 1st time since its 1949 team, featuring HB Charlie "Choo Choo" Justice, was ranked no. 6 for 3 weeks.

MIAMI 10 Florida State 9: Miami's best start since 1954 was preserved by hard-working NG Jim Burt, who deflected pass by QB Rick Stockstill on 2-point conv attempt after late TD by Florida State (3-1). Stockstill had just thrown 11y TD pass to TE Sam Childers to trim deficit to 10-9. Burt (9 tackles) led nation's top-ranked rushing D (65y total in 4 games), that allowed only 25y rushing. His harassment of Florida State Cs led to 10 botched snaps, 5 lost as FUMs. Miami (4-0) QB Jim Kelly ran in 1y TD late in 2nd Q, and K Dan Miller kicked 26y FG late in 3rd Q to provide scoring. Kelly's TD was set up by controversial interference PEN on Seminoles S Gary Henry, while Miller's FG was partially blocked by CB Bobby Butler. For 1st time since 1969, Canes outdrew NFL Dolphins on mutual home weekend.

South Carolina 17 MICHIGAN 14: South Carolina (3-1) TB George Rogers earned national acclaim by rushing for 142y and TD against highly reputable D. Still, Michigan Wolverines (1-2) led 14-3 at H on pair of TD passes by QB John Wangler to WR Anthony Carter. Michigan took its opening drive of 3rd Q to Carolina 8YL, but, in critical reversal, FB Stan Edwards lost FUM that bounded into EZ for touchback. Gamecocks countered with 80y drive that featured pass interference PEN that negated INT by UM S Tony Jackson. Rogers capped this voyage with 2y TD run that brought Cocks to within 14-10. What happened next would have been surprising for most teams, stunning for conservative Michigan: coach Bo Schembechler, apparently fearing Rogers, called fake punt from his 29YL. But, South Carolina DB Chuck Finney stopped Edwards on 4th-and-1 run to take possession. It took 7 plays for Gamecocks TB Johnnie Wright to score winning 1y TD run. Wolverines drove to Carolina 3YL before throwing incomplete pass on game's final play.

Stanford 31 OKLAHOMA 14: QB John Elway (20-34/237y, 3 TDs) engineered 1 of his most memorable collegiate wins, leading rebounding Cardinals (3-1) to road upset that snapped Oklahoma's 20-game home win streak. Despite absence of HB Darrin Nelson, out with bruised hip, Stanford built 17-0 H lead that they stretched to 31-0 as Sooners (1-1) committed 7 TOs in rainy conditions. Elway threw for 187y in 1st H, scoring TDs running and passing. Cards WR Andre Tyler (6/78y) caught 2 TD passes. It took most of day, but QB J.C. Watts (6-12/153y, 2 INTs) finally cranked up O and ran for pair of 4th Q TDs to get Oklahoma on board.

Oregon 34 WASHINGTON 10: QB Reggie Ogburn ran for 2 TDs and passed for 3rd for Oregon (2-1) team that erupted for 21 pts in 4th Q. Game started well for Huskies as S Ken Gardner took punt 65y to EZ for opening score, and K Chuck Nelson provided 10-3 Washington lead by matching FGs with Oregon K Pat English. Held to 187y in total O, Huskies were hard-pressed to add to pt-total as Ducks completely eliminated big plays. Ogburn threw 6y TD pass to WR Curt Jackson and ran in TD keepers of 3y and 1y. CB Steve Brown added to Oregon's 4th Q scoring explosion with 36y INT TD RET.

AP Poll September 29

1 Alabama (36)	1254	11 UCLA	615
2 Ohio State (22)	1245	12 Oklahoma	489
3 Nebraska (7)	1181	13 Miami	399
4 Southern California	1061	14 Arkansas	360
5 Texas	1004	15 Stanford	342
6 Pittsburgh (1)	992	16 Florida State	308
7 Notre Dame	895	17 Penn State	294
8 Georgia	864	18 South Carolina	269
9 Missouri	755	19 Florida	151
10 North Carolina	649	20 Baylor	120

October 4, 1980

YALE 17 Air Force 16: Was it last hurrah for Ivy League, creators of grand game of football? "Ancient Eight" soon would sequester itself in Div 1-AA, but Yale (3-0), conf's defending champion, would strike blow for Old Blues. Air Force (0-4-1) failed primarily because it tried tricky 2-pt conv after WR Denny Moore caught 47y TD pass to pull within 17-16 in 3rd Q. Holder Bob Renaud took snap on quick signal but was buried by Bulldogs defenders. Yale WR Curt Grieve had snared 20y TD pass from QB John Rogan (9-18/130y, 2 TDs, INT) to tie it 10-10 only 1:02 before H. Eli TB Rich Diana (136y rushing) caught 25y pass in 3rd Q for deciding pts.

PITTSBURGH 38 Maryland 9: Shaking off knee sprain, Pittsburgh QB Dan Marino completed 16-34/282y, 3 TDs. Pitt (4-0) D sacked Maryland QBs 7 times in surrendering 22y rushing to Terps, who featured TB Charlie Wysocki (19/40y), nation's 13th leading rusher. Panthers DE Hugh Green contributed 10 tackles and 2 sacks. TD by Terrapins (3-2) represented only 2nd 6-ptr Pitt D had allowed all season, it coming on 12y pass from QB Mike Tice to WR Chris Havener to cap 21y drive following overanxious Panthers S Tom Flynn's FUM of punt.

LOUISIANA STATE 24 Florida 7: Despite ungodly 12 FUMs, 5 of which were lost, Tigers (3-2) won as RB Jesse Myles rushed for 148y and scored twice. Bengals' decisive TD came when QB Alan Risher hooked up with WR Tracy Porter for 31y TD pass. Risher had replaced starting QB Robbie Mahfouz after latter bobbled 2 FUMs on LSU's 1st series. Hampered by loss of QB Bob Hewko, who left with knee injury in 1st Q, Florida (3-1) managed only 10 1st downs, rushed for 23y, and trailed 17-0 before WR Cris Collinsworth caught 7y TD pass from QB Larry Ochab in 3rd Q.

Ucla 17 OHIO STATE 0: UCLA's nemesis from 1979 loss, Bucks QB Art Schlichter, was swamped by Bruins (4-0) D that engineered 5 sacks, 4 by DE Irv Eatman, in posting UCLA's 2nd straight shutout. Schlichter (5-12/59y) went to bench early in 4th Q with slight concussion, although his poor play called for change. Schlichter's crucial EZ INT came in 2nd Q when he tried to throw through Bruins S Tom Sullivan and no. 2 Ohio State (3-1) trailed only 3-0. Bruins efficient QB Tom Ramsey completed 8-11/92y and 14y TD pass to WR JoJo Townsell for 10-0 lead early in 3rd Q. UCLA TB Freeman McNeil (31/118) added 4y TD run on following series, and S Kenny Easley led brilliant D before being thumbed for striking sideline photographer.

Penn State 29 MISSOURI 21: Improving QB Todd Blackledge (9-19/92y) ran for 2 TDs, including clinching 43y scamper, and threw 24y to TE Brad Scovill for 3rd score as Penn State (3-1) edged Mizzou (3-1). Nittany Lions S Paul Lankford chipped in with 2 INTs in 3rd Q that set up K Herb Menhardt FGs for decisive 22-21 lead. Tigers QB Phil Bradley threw for 214y and 2 TDs, including 53y effort to WR Ron Fellows, while also dashing for TD.

Florida State 18 NEBRASKA 14: Florida State (4-1) LB Paul Piurowski (17 tackles) capped huge game by forcing FUM by Nebraska QB Jeff Quinn (15-30/167y, 2 INTs), recovered by DT Garry Futch on FSU 10YL with 12 secs left. Quinn had marched Huskers 77y to FSU 3YL before sack by Piurowski, who was supposed to drop into

coverage. Nebraska (3-1) led 14-3 at H behind Quinn's 2 TD passes to SE Todd Brown. Setting them up were runs of IB Jarvis Redwine (25/145y) and D that held FSU to -7y in opening 21 plays with 4 sacks. In decisive 3rd Q, Seminoles ripped 12 pts out of Nebraska TOs, including TB Sam Platt's 6y TD run. Florida State D tossed shutout over final 36 mins, while kicking game excelled: K Bill Capece booted 4 FGs, all 6 KOs produced touchbacks, and P Rohn Stark averaged 48.4 on 7 punts while Nebraska could gain only 2y in punt RETs.

BAYLOR 24 Houston 12: Tongue-in-cheek, "that's how we drew it up" play occurred with score 17-12 and Bears (4-0) trying to muster clinching drive. Baylor frosh HB Alfred Anderson picked up FUM and heaved pass downfield to WR Gerald McNeil, whose diving catch secured 1st down and continued drive that ended with Anderson's 10y TD run. Bears QB Jay Jeffrey led O with 146y passing and 85 rushing, while spectacular LB Doak Field contributed 17 tackles, FUM REC, INT, and blocked FG. Cougars (1-3) enjoyed early 6-0 lead on 2 FGs by K David Humphreys.

SOUTHERN CALIFORNIA 23 Arizona State 21: With both Os outfoxing D tendencies, game proved more competitive than advertised. Trojans (4-0) built 20-7 H lead as QB Gordon Adams (20-29/226y, TD) took advantage of Arizona State D overplaying run. Sun Devils (2-2), using draw plays to offset USC pass rush, rallied as TB Willie Gittens (15/98y) eluded USC LB Riki Gray and S Dennis Smith to race 59y to EZ, and QB Mike Pagel tossed his 2nd TD pass, 14y to TE Ron Wetzel. Southern California managed only single 2nd H score, K Eric Hipp's 3rd FG, which was enough to hold on to victory. USC TB Marcus Allen (36/132y) did most of his damage in 2nd H, but also lost 2 FUMs.

AP Poll October 6

1 Alabama (60)	1252	11 Florida State	609
2 Southern California (1)	1127	12 Oklahoma	563
3 Texas	1088	13 Miami	519
4 Pittsburgh (1)	1087	14 Penn State	424
5 UCLA (1)	991	15 Arkansas	353
6 Georgia	896	16 Stanford	351
7 Notre Dame	882	17 South Carolina	323
8 North Carolina	731	18 Baylor	252
9 Ohio State	705	19 Missouri	205
10 Nebraska	635	20 Southern Methodist	66

October 11, 1980

Alabama 17 RUTGERS 13 (East Rutherford, NJ): Unheralded Scarlet Knights (4-1) became 1st team this season to take lead on Crimson Tide (5-0) after 44y FG by K Alex Falcinelli in 1st Q. Alabama's 26-game win streak was saved as QB Don Jacobs hit WR James Mallard with 49y TD pass in 3rd Q for 17-6 lead. Rutgers pulled within 17-13 on 9y TD pass from QB Ed McMichael to TB Albert Ray and had ball in Bama territory once more before blitzing CB Mike Clements made Tide's 5th sack of game to snuff threat. In holding Crimson Tide 25 pts below season scoring avg, Rutgers D was led by LB Mike Knight, who was in on 13 tackles. Perhaps Rutgers was too high for this effort because it lost following week to William & Mary.

FLORIDA STATE 36 Pittsburgh 22: Not bad October fortnight for Seminoles (5-1), following up win over no. 3 Nebraska with victory over no. 4 Pittsburgh (4-1). Scoring 36 pts against fabled Panthers (4-1) D was surprising. FSU stars included QB Rick Stockstill (10-20/127y, 3 TDs), who was assigned to choose play's direction at line of scrimmage upon reading D, and TB Sam Platt (26/123y). Pitt suffered 7 TOs, including 3 INTs by QB Dan Marino (18-34/286y, 2 TDs), while Seminoles lost none. FSU took advantage of field position to fashion 23 straight pts in between Marino's 2 TD passes to WR Dwight Collins (6/183y). Lead was stretched to 29-15 on final pair of Florida State K Bill Capece's school-record 5 FGs.

NOTRE DAME 32 Miami 14: Facing Miami (4-1) D that had surrendered only 62y total rushing without country's 2nd leading ground gainer (HB Phil Carter) should have been cause for concern. No worry: Notre Dame (4-0) O-Line opened holes for backup HB Jim Stone to gain 224y, more than he notched in all of 1979. QB Blair Kiel became 1st frosh since QB Ralph Gugliemi in 1951 to start at QB for Irish, and K Harry Oliver kicked school-record-tying 4 FGs. Notre Dame D had Hurricanes blanked until 4th Q and did not allow single 1st downs in either 2nd or 3rd Qs. Miami QB Jim Kelly, who passed for 220y, threw 3 passes for TDs in 4th Q, 2 to teammates but another to Notre Dame DB Tom Gibbons on INT RET.

Texas 20 Oklahoma 13 (Dallas): For years Oklahoma had dipped into Texas for star players; this time Oklahoma native starred for Longhorns (5-0). HB Rodney Tate, jr from Beggs, scored 2 TDs, including 4th down, 1y game-winner with little more than 8 mins left. Oklahoma (2-2) was kept off scoreboard in 1st H, while FUMs by QB J.C. Watts deep in his own territory set up Tate's 3y TD run and K John Goodson's 18y FG for 10-0 lead for Texas. Sooners stormed back in 2nd H despite suffering raft of TOs and having to battle formidable Texas D, led by DL Kenneth Sims' 3 sacks and forced FUM. Oklahoma took 13-10 lead on 2 FGs by K Mike Keeling and 36y TD run by FB Stanley Wilson (18/172y). Texas QB Donnie Little, who rushed for 110y and threw for 99y, sparkled on game-winning 76y drive, hitting WRs Les Koenning and Maurice McCloney for 25y and 32y respectively.

BAYLOR 32 Southern Methodist 28: Featuring 2 undefeated teams for 1st time in 63-year rivalry, game was more significant than usual. Mustangs (4-1) built 21-0 lead as TB Eric Dickerson (22/112y) had TD run, QB Mike Ford threw TD pass, and CB John Simmons returned INT 32y for TD. Baylor (5-0) rallied with 2 TDs before H as HB Alfred Anderson raced 22y for TD and QB Jay Jeffrey rushed for 1st of his 3 TDs. CB Reg Phillips turned momentum back SMU's way in 3rd Q with blocked punt in Baylor territory that set up Ford's 14y TD pass to TE Clement Fox. So, SMU led 28-14. Jeffrey then sparked Bears to clutch revival: 3 straight scoring drives that counted 18 pts. SMU's final effort went 66y before Ford frustratingly lost snap on 4th down on Bears 8YL with 18 secs left. Baylor DT Joe Campbell recovered FUM.

Rice 28 TEXAS CHRISTIAN 24: Pair of depressed teams totaling 1 win still produced exciting conclusion. Scoring 21 straight pts, Owls (2-3) rallied from 24-7 H deficit with 9y TD pass from QB Randy Hertel (13-27/195y, 2 INTs) to WR Hosea Fortune with 43 secs left. Hertel hit 9-9/79y on last drive to cover its entirety. QB Steve Stamp (15-27/175y) then led Horned Frogs (0-5) 66y to Rice 3YL before throwing EZ INT to Rice LB Richard Gray. Earlier, Stamp had thrown 2 TDs to WR Phillip Epps and run for TD. Unfortunately, Stamp also threw 3 INTs, 1 of which was returned 56y by Owls DB Rickey Thomas to TCU 19YL to set up Rice's 3rd TD on 1y run by QB Doug Johnson. It narrowed Frogs' margin to 24-21.

UCLA 35 Stanford 21: It was good old days for 2 foes: UCLA QB Tom Ramsey and Stanford QB John Elway had been HS rivals in San Fernando Valley at Kennedy and Granada Hills respectively. Clearly, Ramsey was flourishing under new O-coordinator Homer Smith. After slow start (28y O in 1st H) during which Bruins (5-0) trailed 21-7, TB Freeman McNeil busted out for 220y and 4 TDs in 2nd H. In garnering his 7th straight 100y game (and school-record 13th overall), McNeil racked up 146y and 2 TDs all in 3rd Q, including 72y play that tied score at 21-21. Cardinals (4-2) HB Darrin Nelson (17/102y) rushed for TDs of 17 and 30y, while Elway (20-34/204y) shook off 5 sacks during 1st H to forge 21-7 lead. Even with Stanford's 3 TDs, Bruins' D had surrendered only 49 pts in 5 games.

AP Poll October 13

1 Alabama (52)	1327	11 Pittsburgh	615
2 Southern California (8)	1224	12 Penn State	549
3 Texas (4)	1201	13 Baylor	472
4 UCLA (4)	1186	14 Arkansas	463
5 Notre Dame	1052	15 South Carolina	461
6 Georgia	1028	16 Missouri	319
7 Florida State	921	17 Oklahoma	229
8 North Carolina	856	18 Miami	179
9 Ohio State	819	19 Iowa State	129
10 Nebraska	811	20 Stanford	84

October 18, 1980

PENN STATE 24 Syracuse 7: QB Todd Blackledge (8-13/108y) upped his record as Penn State (5-1) starter to 3-0, sparking O that gained 308y. Nittany Lions TB Curt Warner scored game's opening 2 TDs on runs of 3y and 6y, and Blackledge hit WR Kenny Jackson for 13y TD to close scoring. Syracuse (3-3) was hard-pressed to stay in game without injured TB Joe Morris. Leading rusher in his absence was FB Ken Mandeville, with 57y, while LB Mike Zunic scored team's TD on 11y INT RET. Penn State DE Gene Gladys led D with 5 tackles and 2 sacks.

PITTSBURGH 42 West Virginia 14: Former starting Pittsburgh (5-1) QB Rick Trocano moved from S in relief of injured QB Dan Marino (left knee) to lead 28 quick pts in 2nd Q. Trocano (11-18/150y, 2 TDs) tossed TD passes of 53y to WR Dwight Collins and 25y to WR Willie Collier, while FB Randy McMillan scored twice on 1y runs. It was 5th straight series win for Panthers (5-1), most since 1946. Pitt D forced 4 TOs, clamped down on West Virginia (4-3) TB Robert Alexander (14/37y), and put constant pressure on QB Oliver Luck, who still was able to pitch 2 TDs to WR Cedric Thomas.

Mississippi State 34 MIAMI 31: Hurricanes' improved D surprisingly was ripped asunder as Mississippi State (5-2) racked up 404y, 339y of which came on ground. Maroons frosh QB John Bond rushed for 92y and directed sharp O. Miami (4-2) mounted rally from 24-10 deficit to knot game up at 31-31 as HB Mark Rush took KO 92y for tying TD. K Dana Moore's 37y FG gave Bulldogs renewed lead at 34-31, but Miami raced down to Mississippi State 3YL. Trio of Canes plays produced -2y and K Jeff Davis missed 22y FG. "We gave it away early, we tried to recapture it, but then we were not men enough to take it," said Miami coach Howard Schnellenberger.

Alabama 27 TENNESSEE 0: Vols (3-3) were fired up to break 9-game series losing streak, and WR Anthony Hancock nearly hauled long pass to EZ by QB Steve Alatorre in early moments. It was all downhill from there as Alabama D added own thunder to driving rain, holding Tennessee to 5 1st downs and only 59y total O in posting 3rd shutout of season. Crimson Tide (6-0) surprised by showing jazzed-up O with Shotgun formation, HB pass, and flea-flicker pass. Bama K Peter Kim booted 4 FGs, and QB Ken Coley and TB Major Ogilvie added TD runs to lead Tide to 27th consecutive win. Volunteers finished 1st H with –2y, but had ball 3 times in Bama territory in 3rd Q. Alabama D turned back 2 of those drives with INTs by LB Mike Pitts and DB Ricky Tucker, while DB Jeremiah Castille ended 3rd with blocked FG.

OHIO STATE 27 Indiana 17: TB Calvin Murray was too much for Hoosiers (4-2), who dropped 17th straight in 1-sided series. Murray ran 35/224y and 2 TDs, with 149y coming in 1st H as Buckeyes (5-1) built 17-10 lead. Indiana found 2nd H penetration of Ohio State D difficult, gaining but 5y and making no 1st downs in 3rd Q. But, Hoosiers TB Mike Harkrader (18/117y) became school's all-time leading rusher and 7th player in conf history to crack 3,000y mark. Ohio State K Vlade Janakievski booted 2 FGs, but missed 39y attempt that snapped his consecutive streak at 12.

IOWA 25 Northwestern 3: Wildcats (0-7) dropped 16th straight despite hard-nosed D that did not allow any 2nd H pts, even though Iowa scored 2 on safety. Hawkeyes (2-5) coach Hayden Fry demoted starting TB Jeff Brown, conf leader in rushing, and opted for TB Phil Blatcher, who must have coveted job as he rushed for 148y and made 7y TD catch. Northwestern FB Dave Mishler rushed for team-high 54y.

KANSAS 28 Iowa State 17: Teenagers ruined unbeaten Cyclones (5-1) as Kansas frosh TB Kerwin Bell (35/156y) had TD each of rushing and receiving, and classmate QB Frank Seuer came off bench to throw important TD pass that cut Iowa State lead to 17-14 in 3rd Q. Jayhawks (2-3-1) went ahead after recovering FUM by ISU QB John Quinn and moving ball 37y for Bell's 1y TD run. Cyclones TB Dwayne Crutchfield rushed for 117y and 3y TD. Kansas later forfeited victory for using ineligible players.

OREGON 7 Southern California 7: Despite losing FUM on Southern California 14YL at end of 1st H, Ducks (2-2-2) did not become disheartened, tying Trojans on 3y TD run by FB Terrance Jones in 3rd Q. Backup QB Kevin Lusk's 68y completion to WR Greg Moser put Ducks in scoring position. Trojans (5-0-1) had scored TD on brilliant catch by WR Jeff Simmons of QB Gordon Adams' 38y pass. Simmons was parallel to ground as he caught ball before sliding out of corner of EZ. Following late INT by Trojans DB Ronnie Lott, who was burned on Moser's long reception, Southern California had final chance for win. After reaching Oregon's 30YL, personal foul PEN wiped out USC's advance. Southern California TB Marcus Allen rushed for 159y, but lost FUM on Oregon 24YL in 1st Q and was stopped on 4th-and-1 in 4th Q.

Washington 27 STANFORD 24: Game was won by 25y FG by Washington (5-1) K Chuck Nelson moments after Cardinals K Ken Naber's tying 26y FG. QB Tom Flick completed 6-7 passes to drive Huskies 72y for winning pts. Washington had built 13-0 lead as Flick hooked up with WR Aaron Williams (5/117y) for TD passes of 41y and 28y, then stretched its edge to 24-7 before Stanford (4-3) rallied. QB John Elway (18-37/275y, 2 INTs), who had run for Cards' opening TD, threw 42y TD pass to HB Darrin Nelson and 13y TD to HB Vincent White.

AP Poll October 20

1 Alabama (57)	1250	11 Baylor	595
2 Texas (2)	1147	12 Pittsburgh	571
3 UCLA (4)	1108	13 Penn State	508
4 Notre Dame	1042	14 South Carolina	447
5 Georgia	990	15 Arkansas	426
6 Florida State	901	16 Missouri	334
7 North Carolina	833	17 Oklahoma	238
8 Southern California	817	18 Washington	147
9 Nebraska	735	19 Brigham Young	106
10 Ohio State	728	20 Southern Mississippi	71

October 25, 1980

NORTH CAROLINA STATE 24 Clemson 20: Tigers (4-3) shot themselves in paw, surrendering TDs after INT and blocked punt. Opportune Wolfpack (4-3) trailed 14-7 before CB Perry Williams returned INT 19y to Clemson 17YL to set up 11y TD pass from QB Tol Avery to WR Mike Quick. NC State K Nathan Ritter missed x-pt—his 1st miss in 47 attempts—but Pack took 1-pt H lead at 15-14 after DE Darryl Harris earned safety with tackle of Clemson P David Hendley in EZ after bobbled snap. In 3rd Q, Hendley received high snap in same EZ and had punt blocked by Wolfpack LB Vaughn Johnson with ball caught by DE James Butler and returned 5y for TD. Ritter kicked 24y FG to increase lead to 24-14 before K Obed Ariri booted his 3rd and 4th FGs. Clemson QB Homer Jordan rushed for 65y and passed for 93y.

PURDUE 36 Michigan State 25: QB Mark Herrmann broke NCAA career passing record while directing late victory as Boilermakers (5-2) scored game's final 17 pts. Herrmann surpassed Washington State's Jack Thompson (1974-78) early in 2nd Q, finishing game with 8,087y to 7,818y for Thompson. Herrmann completed 24-46/340y, with favored receiver TE Dave Young nabbing 12/172y. Not all was rosy for Herrmann, who threw 3 INTs, including TD taken back 56y by CB Mike Marshall in 1st Q, but he was bailed out by D that picked off 5 of QB John Leister's 54 passes. Leister had given Spartans (1-6) 25-19 lead early in 4th Q with 31y TD pass to WR Jim Williams.

Southern Methodist 20 TEXAS 6: After 2 straight losses, Southern Methodist (5-2) coach Ron Meyer benched longtime starting QB Mike Ford and boldly scrapped multiple O for ball-control attack that showcased talents of TBs Craig James and Eric Dickerson. SMU frosh QB Lance McIlhenny completed only 1-8/3y but clicked as option ground magician: James led Ponies with 143y rushing, including 53y TD run for 10-6 lead in 3rd Q. Mustangs D finished off Longhorns (5-1) as S James Mobley returned INT of overthrown pass by Texas QB Donnie Little for 22y TD. Texas still had chances, but lost ball on downs on SMU 3YL and later on INT by CB John Simmons. Win was Mustangs' 1st in series in 14 years and vaulted them back into AP Top 20.

HOUSTON 24 Arkansas 17: Houston (4-3) QB Brent Chinn shook off thigh bruise to rush for 137y and go-ahead 11y TD. QB Audrey McMillian had replaced Chinn in starting lineup before injuring his collarbone at end of 30y run on 1st scrimmage play. He joined original starting QB Terry Elston as lost for season. Razorbacks (4-2) had jumped to 14-3 lead on 93y KO RET by WR Derek Holloway and 17y TD pass from QB Tom Jones to WR Bobby Duckworth. Chinn led 2 TD drives in 2nd Q, capping latter with keeper that gave Houston 17-14 lead. Cougars added another TD in 3rd Q as INT by S Calvin Eason set up 58y drive to clinching 4y TD run by RB Terald Clark.

Oklahoma 42 IOWA STATE 7: Cyclones (5-2) started strongly with 69y TD drive on 1st possession and employed strong D that surrendered only single 1st H TD to Oklahoma (4-2). But, Sooners could not be contained for long and soon were on way to registering 19th straight series win. Oklahoma QB J.C. Watts began 2nd H deluge when he faked handoff, keeping for 45y TD scamper. Later, Watts would add pair of 4th Q TD runs. OU FB Stanley Wilson (24/160y) added 53y TD scamper and suddenly rout was on. Sooners rushed for 269y in 2nd H, 388y overall as Wilson totaled his career-high running number as did Iowa State counterpart TB Dwayne Crutchfield with 179y rushing.

Navy 24 WASHINGTON 10: Navy (5-2) QB Fred Reitzel sparked big upset, scoring 3 TDs including EZ REC of TB Eddie Meyers' FUM. Reitzel, who shifted from S to QB before season, threw for 104y and rushed for 54y, while Meyers rushed for 114y. Navy D spectacularly contained no. 18 Huskies who came in with 37 pts per game scoring avg. Washington (5-2) scored its TD on 69y pass from QB Tom Flick (19-29/228y, INT) pass to WR Aaron Williams. "Like they (Huskies players) said in the paper, it was nice for them to have an easy game after they beat Stanford," said Reitzel. "I don't think they were ready for us."

AP Poll October 27

1 Alabama (57)	1289	11 Pittsburgh	644
2 UCLA (8)	1222	12 Texas	623
3 Notre Dame	1141	13 Penn State	539
4 Georgia	1105	14 South Carolina	493
5 Florida State	985	15 Missouri	387
6 North Carolina	940	16 Oklahoma	310
7 Southern California	859	17 Brigham Young	197
8 Nebraska	852	18 Michigan	135
9 Ohio State	771	19 Southern Methodist	131
10 Baylor	719	20 Purdue	90

November 1, 1980

VIRGINIA TECH 34 West Virginia 11: Hokies (7-2) started smelling bowl bid after sending West Virginia to its 4th straight loss and all but ruining its season. Virginia Tech TB Cyrus Lawrence rushed for 173y of team's 294y rushing, while QB Steve Casey tossed 3 TD passes. Mountaineers (4-5) QB Oliver Luck was held to 137y in air, with 2 crucial INTs including pick-off returned by S Mike Scharnus for 44y INT in 1st Q. Luck managed dandy 80y drive late in 3rd Q that wrapped up with 17y TD pass to WR Cedric Thomas. Virginia Tech topped 30 pts for 5th time at home this season.

MARYLAND 24 North Carolina State 0: Terps' rousing win was launched by Maryland (6-3) TB Charlie Wysocki, who rushed for 132y and opening 1y TD run. Its D forced 4 TOs and scored TD, while K-P Dale Castro booted 48y FG and punted well. Shut out for 1st time since 1970, Wolfpack (4-4) reached Maryland 9YL in 3rd Q before Terrapins S Lloyd Burress blocked 21y FG attempt by K Nathan Ritter. Later in 3rd Q, P Castro pinned NC State at 1YL, from where pressure on QB Tol Avery forced bad throw picked off for TD by DE Mark Wilson while latter pass-rushed into EZ. That gave Maryland 17-0 lead. NC State TB Wayne McLean rushed for team-high 43y, but overthrew TE Todd Baker in EZ on drive that ended with Burress' blocked FG.

Virginia 16 TENNESSEE 13: Somehow, things got worse for Vols (3-5), who lost 5th home game for 1st time in history as Virginia K Wayne Morrison booted game-winning FG early in 4th Q. Cavs (4-4) grabbed 7-3 H lead on great catch by TE Kevin Riccio for 6y TD. Although Virginia controlled game throughout, Tennessee was able to tie it at 13-13 on 44y reverse run by WR Anthony Hancock. QB Todd Kirtley (11-18/181y) answered with 64y drive to set up Morrison's heroics. UVa notched season-high 375y, with sub HB Quentin Walker pacing run game with 114y.

GEORGIA 13 South Carolina 10: Battle of TBs George Rogers and Herschel Walker was showcased, with Walker (43/219y) outshining Carolina's upperclassman, especially with 76y scoring burst in 3rd Q that put Georgia (8-0) out in front, 10-0. Rogers rushed 35/168y, but lost FUM on Georgia 16YL with 5:18 left that was recovered by Bulldogs S Chris Welton. South Carolina (6-2) appeared on national TV, and George Rogers, Sr., just released from prison after 8 years, got to watch his son play. Georgia K Rex Robinson took away some of attention with FGs of 57y and 51y. South Carolina scored on 39y run by FB Carl West.

MISSISSIPPI STATE 6 Alabama 3: Mississippi State (7-2) sprung upset as D—led by LB Johnnie Cooks (13.5 tackles)—excelled, holding Alabama's Wishbone O to 116y rushing, down from avg of 349y. Crimson Tide (7-1) had final chance to win snuffed out as QB Don Jacobs lost FUM, after ferocious hit by DE Tyrone Keys, on Maroons 3YL with 6 secs left. Bobble was recovered by frosh DE Billy Jackson (12 tackles, 3 sacks). Nervous but fortunate Mississippi State promptly fumbled next snap, but it was recovered by FB Donald Ray King inside his 1YL as game ended. Jackson's earlier FUM REC led to tying FG by K Dana Moore. QB John Bond, game's high rusher on 20/94y, led winning FG drive of 67y to give Bulldogs 1st win over Bama since 1957 and snap Alabama's 28-game win streak. Only 3 members of its team were alive when Mississippi State last won against neighboring Alabama.

Michigan 35 INDIANA 0: Hoosiers (5-3) were gracious hosts, losing 3 FUMs and throwing 4 INTs to aggressive Michigan (6-2) D. With aid of takeaways, Wolverines burst to 21-0 1st Q lead as TB Lawrence Ricks (23/123y) scored twice within 28 secs on 29y and 3y runs, and QB John Wangler connected with WR Anthony Carter on 34y TD pass, Carter's school-record 9th TD catch of season. Michigan's other TB, Butch Woolfolk, rushed for 152y, including 64y scoring burst in 4th Q, while FB Stan Edwards chipped in with 16y scoring run of his own. Indiana QB Tim Clifford completed 14-27/117y, 4 INTs. Interestingly, Hoosiers' 7 TOs were in marked contrast to 13 they had committed in previous 7 contests in 1980.

OKLAHOMA 41 North Carolina 7: Sooners (5-2) made mockery of Tar Heels D ranked 3rd in rushing (76.9y per game) by totaling 495y on ground. No. 6 North Carolina (7-1) had surrendered only 538y total rushing in previous 7 games. Oklahoma QB J.C. Watts paced way with 139y rushing and 3 TDs, including 42y run to retake lead for good at 14-7 in 1st Q. TB Amos Lawrence led Tar Heels, who had 10-game win streak snapped, with 109y rushing, but 62y came on single dash that set up his own 1st Q TD dive of 1y. HB David Overstreet added 2 rushing TDs for Sooners, while FB Weldon Ledbetter rushed for 19/122y.

NEBRASKA 38 Missouri 16: IB Jarvis Redwine (129y rushing) scored TDs on Nebraska's 1st 2 possessions to chase Tigers out of tie for 1st place in Big 8. Cornhuskers (7-1) added two more TDs in opening H, including LB Kim Baker's 77y INT TD RET. QB Phil Bradley, who became Big Eight's all-time career total O leader, rallied Tigers (6-2) to within 28-13 on 4y TD pass to WR Ron Fellows, but it was too little, too late. FB Andra Franklin chipped in with 122y as Nebraska rolled up 331y rushing, while QB Jeff Quinn hit 11-16/151y. TE Jeff Finn caught 17y TD pass from Quinn, to pleasure of rhyming poets everywhere.

TEXAS TECH 24 Texas 20: Red Raiders (4-3) built 24-0 lead early in 2nd Q, scoring 17 pts within 4:06 span that featured 2y keeper by QB Ron Reeves (10-17/102y), 34y INT TD RET by S Ted Watts, and 31y FG by K John Greve. Longhorns (5-2) roared

back with 20 pts before H, including 56y TD pass from QB Rick McIvor to TE Lawrence Sampleton. Each team's D took over, with game-saving play turned in by Tech S Tate Randle—who had been burned on Sampleton's TD catch—with INT of tipped ball at Red Raiders GL. McIvor passed for 189y before leaving game after being poked in eye in 4th Q.

San Jose State 30 BAYLOR 22: Undefeated teams should put away games they lead 15-0 against lesser competition, especially in front of home folks. Baylor (7-1) opened scoring with 12y TD run by FB Dennis Gentry (12/103y) and increased lead on 41y TD pass from QB Jay Jeffrey to WR Mike Fisher and 22y FG by K Tim Strong. But, underrated San Jose State (5-3) rallied as QB Steve Clarkson threw for 201y and nifty TB Gerald Willhite (20/83y) scored 3 times, including 52y TD catch off ricochet pass from shoulder pads of teammate WR Rick Parma.

Boston College 23 AIR FORCE 0: Eagles' return from depths of winless 1978 season continued with road win. Taking advantage of 6 TOs, Boston College (4-4) converted INT, fumbled punt, and roughing PEN on its missed FG into 17 pts. Falcons (1-6-1) were able to mount 10-play, 94y drive in 3rd Q, but it ended on EZ INT by Boston College S Rich Dyer, his 2nd of game. TB Shelby Gamble paced Eagles O with 107y rushing and 11y TD run that opened scoring. Air Force QB Scott Schafer rushed for 103y, but completed only 2-10/12y, 3 INTs.

ARIZONA 23 Ucla 17: Although he hailed from Burbank, Cal., Arizona (3-4) frosh QB Tom Tunnicliffe (12-18/217y, 2 TDs) never made UCLA's recruiting list. He made Bruins pay, passing Wildcats to 21-17 3rd Q lead with 39y TD to TE Bill Nettling, right after hooking up with TB Brian Holland on 41y screen pass. Walk-on P Sergio Vega was not recruited by anyone, and he also helped Arizona with school-record 54.9y avg, including crucial 80y bomb in 2nd H. UCLA's poor field position allowed Cats D to tee off on QB Tom Ramsey (12-22/197y, 2 TDs). Arizona had 7 sacks, 2 by LB Ricky Hunley, to frustrate 2nd H possessions for Bruins (6-1) and to limit Ramsey to only 58y passing in 2nd H. DT Mike Robinson added late safety and S Dave Liggins snuffed out Bruins' last chance with INT at GL. No. 2 UCLA had taken leads of 7-0 and 17-7 in 1st H, before self-destructing to blow chance to capture nation's top spot.

AP Poll November 3

1 Notre Dame (47)	1281	11 Oklahoma	612
2 Georgia (15)	1238	12 Michigan	420
3 Florida State (1)	1094	13 Brigham Young	395
4 Southern California (1)	1077	14 North Carolina	357
5 Nebraska	1025	15 South Carolina	354
6 Alabama	986	16 Baylor	335
7 Ohio State (1)	908	17 Purdue	260
8 UCLA	867	18 Southern Methodist	242
9 Pittsburgh	812	19 Mississippi State	209
10 Penn State	717	20 Florida	138

November 8, 1980

Wake Forest 27 DUKE 24: Despite record-setting performance by Duke QB Ben Bennett, Deacons (4-5) prevailed by scoring game's final 10 pts. Blue Devils (2-7), who had blown 2-TD leads to Maryland and Virginia, ran out of steam in 4th Q with missed FG and INT ending their final 2 drives. Duke put on O show as Bennett threw 38-62/469y, all ACC records. Bennett also suffered 4 INTs. Wake Forest QB Jay Venuto—who held ACC completion and attempts records for all of single week—was no slouch, hitting 23-50/291y, TD, INT. Winning TD was scored on 3y run by Wake Forest FB Henderson Threatt early in 4th Q.

GEORGIA TECH 3 Notre Dame 3: It apparently didn't pay to own AP top spot this November. With 4:44 left, no. 1 Fighting Irish (7-0-1) needed tying 47y FG by K Harry Oliver, who earlier hit crossbar from 27y out, to keep alive their quickly fading national title aspirations. Notre Dame O moved into Georgia Tech (1-7-1) territory on numerous occasions before stalling or turning ball over: Irish lost 3 FUMs in 4th Q alone and had 5 TOs overall. Yellow Jackets K Johnny Smith had given his upset-focused teammates 3-0 lead with FG. Alert Georgia Tech S Mark Sheffield authored INT and recovered Irish HB Jim Stone's FUM on Tech 39YL with 2:08 left. Stone was game-high rusher with 85y. Notre Dame finished 1-13 on 3rd down, with Yellow Jackets LBs Steve Mooney and Duane Wood each in on 13 tackles.

GAME OF THE YEAR
Georgia 26 Florida 21 (Jacksonville):

"World's largest outdoor cocktail party" sobered up as quickly as it took WR Lindsay Scott to score last-sec, winning TD for Georgia (9-0). With 95 secs left to play, Florida (6-2) safely punted OB at Bulldogs 8YL. After 2 plays Georgia was on its 7YL and in need of miracle, trailing 21-20. On 3rd down, QB Buck Belue called "Left 76" in hopes of getting 1st down. Gators rush chased Belue to right while Scott found seam. Thanks to block by T Nat Hudson, Belue had time to fire most memorable pass in Bulldogs history. Scott caught ball on UGa 26YL, stumbled but then spun to elude 4 Gators. Once S Tim Groves fell, Scott was gone for glory. That Scott had lost his scholarship due to shoving match with academic counselor and was benched for 2 recent games was now forgotten. Florida had made its own comeback—engineered by 17-year-old frosh QB Wayne Peace—to erase 10-pt margin. Peace (20-37/282y, TD) hit WR Tyrone Young with 54y pass to set up FB James Jones' 11y TD run, and subsequent Peace-to-Young 2-pt conv pulled Gators within 20-18. Young (10/183y), surprise starter with no catches coming into game, took advantage of double coverage that limited WR Cris Collingsworth (3/29y). K Brian Clark hit 40y FG with little over 6 mins left to give Florida 21-20 lead. Also eclipsed by Scott's catch was brilliant performance by Georgia TB Herschel Walker, who rushed 37/238y, including 72y TD run on 4th play of game. Bulldogs CB Mike Fisher contributed 2 INTs, with 2nd off tip to end game. Win and LSU's loss guaranteed Georgia share of SEC crown. Georgia Tech's tie with Notre Dame allowed Georgia to occupy no. 1 for 1st time since November 1942.

ALABAMA 28 Louisiana State 7: Sloppy game went way of Alabama (8-1) as it did better job converting mistakes than did LSU (6-3). Crimson Tide scored on their opening possession on 35y TD run by QB Ken Coley, who left game with wrist injury on next series. Converting INT, with help from 45y run by new QB Don Jacobs, Alabama increased lead to 14-0 on 2y TD run by HB Major Ogilvie. Game's 2nd H was particularly painful to Louisiana State as Tigers drive that reached Alabama 24YL died on downs and subsequent FUMs killed advances to Bama 40YL and 36YL. Meanwhile, Alabama took advantage of Tigers' 1y punt to push lead to 21-7 in 4th Q on Ogilvie's 2nd TD run of day. QB Alan Risher had scored sole TD for Tigers with 1y keeper in 2nd Q.

OHIO STATE 49 Illinois 42: Buckeyes survived record onslaught by Illinois (3-6-1) QB Dave Wilson, who simply kept pitching passes. Equaling NCAA records for attempts (69, by Chuck Hixson of SMU in 1968), completions (43, by Rich Campbell of Cal earlier in 1980) and total plays (76, by Mike Stritling of Tulsa in 1968), Wilson passed for 621y to break 1977 record of 571y by Marc Wilson of BYU. He pitched 6 TDs and received standing ovation from Columbus crowd. Ohio State (8-1) QB Art Schlichter played well too, throwing 4 TD passes and eclipsing Archie Griffin as Bucks' career total y leader. Schlichter completed 17-21/284y, including school-record 11 straight completions in 1st H. Big 10 and NCAA records fell, 10 in all.

BAYLOR 42 Arkansas 15: Bears (8-1) continued march to SWC crown as TB Walter Abercrombie rushed for 128y and 3 TDs and FB Dennis Gentry added 100y. QB Jay Jeffrey added passing and running TDs as Baylor jumped to 35-7 H lead. Hogs finally stopped string of Bears' 28 straight pts as S Keith Burns recovered blocked punt in EZ. Arkansas (4-4) managed only 116y rushing in losing its 3rd straight game and 1st in Waco since 1963. Win clinched share of conf crown for Baylor.

Oregon 20 UCLA 14: Bruins (6-2), sudden losers of 2 straight in Pac 10, were hampered by 1st Q injury to star TB Freeman McNeil. With UCLA's big gun out, Oregon (5-2-2) built 17-7 H lead as QB Reggie Ogburn (11-19/142y, TD) sparkled through air and ground (18/83y). Bruins pulled within 17-14 on QB Tom Ramsey's 4y TD run and then—after surrendering FG to Oregon—marched to Ducks' 6YL, where they faced 1st-and-goal. Ramsey swept right on 1st down, right into arms of Ducks DT Vince Goldsmith. Ramsey then missed 3 straight passes, and Bruins were losers.

WASHINGTON STATE 28 Oregon State 7: Cougars (3-6) took control of contest with 21-pt 2nd Q as QB Samoa Samoa (9-13/150, INT) ran for 7y TD and threw 25y TD pass to TE Pat Beach. Rushing for 263y, Washington State prevented rally by retaining ball. RBs Tim Harris (12/114y) and Mike Washington (16/102y) led ground Cougars onslaught. QB Ed Singler put Beavers (0-8) on board in 3rd Q with 5y TD pass to WR Victor Simmons.

AP Poll November 10

1 Georgia (54.5)	1299.5	11 Michigan	577
2 Southern California (6)	1180	12 Baylor	550
3 Florida State (3)	1172	13 Brigham Young	464.5
4 Nebraska (2)	1105	14 South Carolina	455
5 Alabama	1067	15 North Carolina	454
6 Notre Dame	1045	16 Purdue	339
7 Ohio State (.5)	924.5	17 UCLA	251
8 Pittsburgh	868	18 Southern Methodist	243
9 Penn State	765	19 Mississippi State	225
10 Oklahoma	618	20 Florida	90.5

November 15, 1980

Georgia 31 AUBURN 21: Facing Auburn team that had knocked them out of Sugar Bowl in 1977 and '78, Bulldogs (9-0) clearly were inspired. Auburn (5-5) refused to let TB Herschel Walker beat them, holding frosh sensation to 77y rushing and single spectacular moment: 18y TD run that began as sweep to left, but ended up with Walker in right side of EZ. Georgia QB Buck Belue carried day, completing 10-19/99y, TD and adding 77y on ground. Play that blew game open was blocked punt by Bulldogs LB Greg Bell that was returned 27y by DE Freddie Gilbert for 10-7 lead. Bulldogs later raced upfield, with aid of 2 interference PENs, at close of 1st H. With 9 secs, left Belue fumbled at 1YL, and while refs determined possession, lined up O, and Belue beat clock—1 sec remained—throwing TD pass to TE Norris Brown, who later admitted he had never practiced pattern he ran. Protesting, Auburn bench was assessed 15y PEN that encouraged Georgia to successfully try onside-KO to open 2nd H. Belue scored from 1y out, moments later, and Georgia went on to build 31-7 lead. Tigers QB Charles Thomas twice made TD passes to WR Byron Franklin to made score representative; after all, Georgia dominated only in big play category. Bulldogs K Rex Robinson became SEC's all-time leading scorer with 261 pts.

Notre Dame 7 ALABAMA 0: Neither O seemed to want to win game, with contest's only TD occurring after QBs lost FUMs on 3 straight possessions. Notre Dame (8-0-1) QB-P Blair Kiel punted Alabama deep, and QB Don Jacobs lost handoff FUM. Kiel then turned ball over on Bama 1YL with Irish knocking on door. Moments later, Jacobs lost 2nd FUM before ND finally scored, on 2y run by HB Phil Carter. Frosh QB Walter Lewis led Crimson Tide (8-2) downfield before LB Bob Crable made brilliant stop of HB Linnie Patrick for no gain on 4th-and-1 sweep. Crable, in on 20 tackles, led way for inspired Notre Dame D that posted 1st shutout of Tide in Alabama since 1958 (0-0 vs Vanderbilt) and stretched streak to 5 games in which it had not surrendered TD. Bama D shone as well, surrendering only gift TD and mere 192y as LB Thomas Boyd and S Tommy Wilcox each had 19 tackles. Irish moved to 4-0 all-time vs Alabama, with outcome becoming biggest margin of victory after 3 prior wins by total of 6 pts.

MICHIGAN 26 Purdue 0: Passing combination of QB John Wangler and WR Anthony Carter (8/133y) produced Michigan (8-2) TDs on passes of 22y and 20y, while Wolverines D coordinator Bill McCartney devised 4-1-6 formation that thwarted Purdue QB Mark Herrmann. Herrmann completed 21-34, but could amass only 129y, while

throwing 3 INTs—2 to S Tony Jackson—in being kept off scoreboard in Michigan's 3rd straight shutout. Boilermakers (7-3) failed to make 1st down in 2nd H as Herrmann threw for only 25y while being sacked 3 times. FB Stan Edwards paced Wolverines ground attack with career-high 164y with 3y TD.

TEXAS TECH 14 Southern Methodist 0: Odd season for Red Raiders (5-4) continued as they wrapped wins over bowl-bound Texas and SMU around loss to lowly TCU. Texas Tech D, led by DT Gabriel Rivera and S Tate Randle, dominated Mustangs (7-3) O that had 27+ pts-per-game avg. Balance—Red Raiders rushed for 140y and QB Ron Reeves passed for 143y—produced pair of 2nd Q TDs that stood up once 4th Q snowstorm blew in. Reeves opened scoring with 12y TD pass to WB Jamie Harris before setting up 2nd score with 38y completion to diving Harris off tip by Ponies CB John Simmons. FB Freddie Wells followed with 1y TD run. TB Eric Dickerson rushed for 91y to lead Mustangs, while D prevented further damage with 3rd Q GLS.

OKLAHOMA 17 Missouri 7: It was Oklahoma (8-2) frosh HB Buster Rhymes' turn to shine as he rushed for 132y and 2 TDs. Sooners grabbed 10-0 lead in 2nd Q as Rhymes scored from 5y out and K Michael Keeling connected on 35y FG. Score remained 10-0 until 4th Q when Rhymes burst for 55y scoring jaunt, and Missouri (7-3) scored late to avoid shutout on 12y QB Phil Bradley-to-HB Bob Meyer TD pass with just more than 1 min left. Bradley threw for 105y and rushed for 41y.

BRIGHAM YOUNG 45 Colorado State 14: QB Jim McMahon (23-33/441y, 5 TDs) set 4 NCAA records and tied 2 others as Cougars beat Colorado State (6-4-1) to wrap up WAC title. McMahon, who hit his 1st 7 ATTs including 71y TD pass to WR Lloyd Jones, set marks for passing y (3,834) and total O in season. He extended records of consecutive 300y games (9) and 400y games (5). BYU (10-1) TE Clay Brown caught 2 TDs and DE Brad Arnae added 45y INT TD RET.

Washington 20 SOUTHERN CALIFORNIA 10: CB Ray Horton's 3rd Q 73y punt TD RET snapped 3-3 tie and propelled Huskies (8-2) to Pac 10 title. Washington D allowed 216y rushing to TB Marcus Allen and 404y to USC O—to 212y totaled by Huskies—but countered with 8 forced TOs, including 2 INTs by LB Tony Caldwell. Allen had well-rounded day for Trojans (7-1-1) as he threw for team's sole TD, 36y scoring pass to WR Jeff Simmons, but he injured right arm with 8 mins left. Trojans reserve TB Anthony Gibson lost 4th Q FUM at Huskies 8YL. USC QB Gordon Adams had already been knocked out with knee injury and his replacement QB Scott Tinsley threw 3 INTs and lost FUM at Washington 29YL in 4th Q. Loss snapped Troy's 28-game unbeaten streak and marked Huskies' 1st win in L.A. Coliseum since 1964.

AP Poll November 17

1 Georgia (55)	1306	11 Baylor	682
2 Notre Dame (4)	1188	12 Southern California	650
3 Florida State (3)	1175	13 Brigham Young	469
4 Nebraska (4)	1173	14 South Carolina	452
5 Ohio State	1012	15 North Carolina	436
6 Pittsburgh	978	16 Washington	347
7 Penn State	896	17 Mississippi State	346
8 Alabama	735	18 UCLA	239
9 Oklahoma	719	19 Florida	141
10 Michigan	685	20 Texas	124

November 22, 1980

CLEMSON 27 South Carolina 6: Halloween came late for Gamecocks as Clemson (6-5), wearing all-orange uniforms for 1st time in school history, delivered plenty of tricks to in-state rivals. Tigers D matched South Carolina (8-3) O in pts as S Willie Underwood's 37y INT TD RET equaled 2 FGs by Carolina K Eddie Leopard. Underwood also returned INT 64y to set up TD that broke 6-6 tie. Despite being 4-year starter at strong safety, Underwood had no career INTs before this day, his final game. K Obed Ariri booted 2 FGs for Tigers to give him NCAA record 23 for season and added to career mark of 60. South Carolina TB George Rogers rushed for 168y.

Michigan 9 OHIO STATE 3: Michigan's power rushing game and stingy D dominated Buckeyes (9-2), but game remained knotted at 3-3 at H as Wolverines (9-2) QB John Wangler suffered 2 INTs. Wangler, who audibled more than half of plays, made up for INTs in 3rd Q with 56y drive he began and ended with 13y passes to WR Anthony Carter. In between, he handed off to TB Butch Woolfolk (31/141y). Michigan S Tony Jackson had set up drive with FUM REC. Conservative Buckeyes never threatened in 2nd H against Michigan D that hadn't surrendered TD in 18 Qs. Buckeyes QB Art Schlichter completed 8-26/130y, including 38y pass to TB Calvin Murray in 2nd Q that set up K Vic Janakievski's 33y FG.

WISCONSIN 25 Minnesota 7: Wisconsin frosh QB Jess Cole enjoyed his 2nd career start by running for 4 TDs. Cole (15/92y) gave Badgers (4-7) lead for good when he raced 52y for 12-7 lead late in 3rd Q. Minnesota (5-6) soon lost FUM, recovered by Badgers LB Dave Levenick on Gophers 33YL, and Cole converted TO into 1y TD plunge for 18-7 lead. Gophers scored their only TD on 1y run by QB Tim Salem, who completed 5-5/70y before having to leave game with injury.

Oklahoma 21 NEBRASKA 17: QB Julius Caesar Watts lived up to his heroic name as he led gritty 80y winning drive in final 3 mins for as big road victory as his namesake managed in Gaul. Big gainer in drive was Watts' nimble pitchout to HB Buster Rhymes that went for 43y. Rhymes later scored game-winner for Sooners (9-2) with 1y dive over top. Huskers (9-2) had led 10-0 as IB Jarvis Redwine (21/152y) enjoyed 89y TD run and K Kevin Seibel booted 47y FG. Watts next led 2 scoring drives, 1st which he capped with 3y TD run and other that featured him racing 14y before pitching to Rhymes for 17y more. Nebraska marched to 1YL in 4th Q before losing FUM that seemed to be game-ender, until bad OU punt gave Huskers possession at Sooners 17YL. Nebraska quickly moved in for QB Jeff Quinn's go-ahead 1y TD run. Cornhusker fans then prematurely threw oranges on field, but Watts still had something to say. Win was Sooners 9th in last 10 games in heavyweight series.

BAYLOR 16 Texas 0: Baylor (10-1) dream year continued as it compiled most single-season wins in school history and went undefeated in league at 8-0 for 1st time since 1922. Bears FB Dennis Gentry rushed for 130y—his 64y 2nd Q scoring run broke 0-0 tie—and RB Walter Abercrombie added 109y for his school-record season total of 1,187y. Baylor D added to its nation's leading total of 29 INTs by picking off 4 passes. Most important INT was CB Cedric Mack's pick of Longhorns QB Rick McIvor with Texas (7-3) on Bears' doorstep, down only 7-0 in 4th Q. Bears had wrapped up SWC title week before by beating Rice, 16-6.

SOUTHERN METHODIST 31 Arkansas 7: Mustangs (8-3) routed Arkansas as 3 Ponies runners topped 100y rushing. As Hogs tried to mount D-plan to thwart double-TB combo of Eric Dickerson (18/107y) and Craig James (23/102y), WR Mitchell Bennett burned them for 106y on 3 reverses, including early 55y TD run on his 1st try. Arkansas (5-5) trailed only 10-7 at H following Hogs QB Tom Jones' 10y TD pass to WR Gary Stiggers. Razorbacks failed to stop SMU's "Pony Express" backfield in 2nd H and surrendered 3 TD runs to James (2) and Dickerson (1).

UCLA 20 Southern California 17: Los Angeles schools were humbled into playing "Probation Bowl," which was won on huge, "hot potato" play by Bruins (8-2) TB Freeman McNeil. Southern California (7-2-1) CB and future NFL coach Jeff Fisher tipped pass by UCLA QB Jay Schroeder (9-11/165y), and McNeil also tipped ball himself before grabbing it and racing down sidelines for 58y winning TD. McNeil, who earlier scored on 6y run, out-gained TB Marcus Allen by 111y to 72y in part because UCLA was able to construct 8-man D front. Superb UCLA D had set up McNeil's heroics moments earlier by stopping USC deep in Bruins territory on DB Lupe Sanchez's INT. Sweet victory served as Bruins 1st in series since 1975 but was not wrapped up until Trojans ran out of time on UCLA 29YL.

CALIFORNIA 28 Stanford 23: With this odd rivalry, experts could toss out W-L records and point spreads, even QB pedigrees. California (3-8) QB J Torchio (11-22/186y, TD) scored winning 3y TD run with 4:41 left. Torchio faked handoff to TB John Tuggle (27/110y, 2 TDs) and ran around E untouched. It cost Stanford (6-5) possible bowl bid and sent star QB John Elway to his 2nd straight series loss. Elway completed 28-44/257y and scrambled for 74y rushing, but his final attempt was pass he wished he could have had back. In face of pressure by Cal S Kevin Moen, Elway misfired on 4th down pass from Bears 6YL in game's final moments. Elway and HB Vincent White, standard-bearers of Cards rally from 21-7 deficit to 23-21 lead, messed up handoff deep in their own end that DT Dupre Marshall recovered to set up Torchio's winning TD. White rushed for 83y and caught 9/109y, scoring 3 TDs.

AP Poll November 24

1 Georgia (59)	1311	11 Ohio State	582
2 Notre Dame (3)	1222	12 Brigham Young	534
3 Florida State (4)	1206	13 North Carolina	521
4 Pittsburgh	1079	14 UCLA	502
5 Penn State	990	15 Washington	460
6 Oklahoma	940	16 Mississippi State	378
7 Michigan	902	17 Southern California	282
8 Baylor	863	18 Florida	213
9 Alabama	784	19 South Carolina	85
10 Nebraska	728	20 Southern Methodist	75

November 29, 1980

(Fri) Pittsburgh 14 PENN STATE 9: Panthers (10-1) earned 2nd straight Lambert Trophy as QB-turned-S-turned-QB Rick Trocano threw and ran for TDs. TE Benjie Pryor's leaping 16y TD reception from Trocano, which was set up by 32y screen pass to FB Randy McMillian, put Pittsburgh ahead 7-3 in 1st H. Eventual winning pts followed Pitt DE Ricky Jackson's strip of Nittany Lions (9-2) TB Curt Warner after 16y gain on 1st play of 2nd H, with Panthers recovering on Penn State 36YL. Ensuing 35y FG by K Dave Trout was good but roughing K PEN allowed coach Jackie Sherrill to take pts off board, and 2 plays later Trocano scored on naked bootleg from 9y out. Penn State clicked on 13y TD pass to frosh WR Kenny Jackson, but missed 2-pt try. Pitt S Carlton Williamson made 2 big D plays: he stopped Warner on 4th down to end threat and picked off Lions QB Todd Blackledge's attempt to throw away pass on State's final scoring opportunity.

Navy 33 Army 6: Mastery of series by Navy (8-3) continued as QB Fred Reitzel (12-18/138y) had 2 short TD runs before tossing 9y TD pass to SE Dave Dent. Middies K Steve Fehr kicked series record-tying 4 FGs and TB Eddie Meyers rushed for 144y to give him career series record to-date of 428y. HB Gerald Walker was bright spot for Cadets (3-7-1), rushing for 77y, including 25y sweep for Army's only TD. Navy, winners of 7 of last 8 tilts against Army, took 38-37-6 series advantage, 1st rivalry lead Midshipmen had enjoyed in 59 years.

GEORGIA 38 Georgia Tech 20: TB Herschel Walker rushed for 205y to set frosh rushing record of 1,616y and eclipse Pittsburgh's Tony Dorsett's 1973 mark of 1,586y. Walker's record run was spectacular: 65y TD scamper in 4th Q for his 3rd TD of afternoon. QB Buck Belue threw TD pass and dove in for another score as Georgia (11-0) built 17-0 lead. After QB Mike Kelley (27-46/333y, 2 TDs, 2 INTs) threw 47y TD pass to WR Leon Chadwick to pull Georgia Tech (1-9-1) within 10pts, Jackets foolishly attempted to force UGa CB Scott Woerner, beaten on play, into celebration. Yellow Jackets were penalized for excessive fun, and Woerner made them pay for insult with 71y RET of ensuing KO. It set up 23y TD run by Walker to re-establish 17-pt lead at 24-7. Bulldogs K Rex Robinson booted 57y FG and pushed his successful x-pt streak to 101: he missed his 1st as frosh and hadn't missed since.

Miami 31 FLORIDA 7: Game ended on sweet note for Miami as Canes (8-3) scored 9 pts in game's final min in effort to punish Florida fans for throwing oranges at them. Gators (7-3) owned short-lived 7-0 lead after 1st possession went 80y to QB Wayne Peace's 15y TD pass to WR Tyrone Young. Miami answered on its opening series

as QB Jim Kelly (13-21/192y, INT) came out firing. Kelly threw for 61y on drive with final 15y coming on TD strike to WR Jim Joiner. It was Florida's turn and Peace (19-41/239y, 3 INTs) hit WR Cris Collingsworth (8/114y) with 42y pass, but then threw INT to LB Scott Nicholas to end threat. Hurricanes converted Nicholas' INT into FG and rout was on.

Texas A&M 24 TEXAS 14: After 1st H in which they trailed 7-0 and gained only 51y O with single 1st down, Aggies (4-7) transformed themselves. QB David Beal (7-13/153y) led new-look Texas A&M, which gained 256y in 2nd H, by completing 56y pass to WR Mike Whitwell to set up team's 1st TD, 5y run by RB Johnny Hector. Beal lofted 50y pass to HB Earnest Jackson to set up his 5y TD pass to TE Mark Lewis. Longhorns (7-4) knocked out Beal during A&M's final drive, but were thanked for bruising play when Aggies sub QB Gary Kubiak threw 28y TD pass to HB Thomas Sanders. Texas added 57y TD pass from QB Rick McIvor to WR Herkie Walls, but could not prevent only 4th loss to Aggies in Austin since 1915.

AP Poll December 1

1 Georgia (54)	1187	11 Ohio State	550
2 Notre Dame (4)	1116	12 North Carolina	498
3 Florida State (4)	1092	13 Brigham Young	491
4 Pittsburgh	1007	14 UCLA	459
5 Oklahoma	926	15 Washington	437
6 Michigan	865	16 Mississippi State	359
7 Baylor	843	17 Southern California	265
8 Alabama	728	18 South Carolina	135
9 Nebraska	682	19 Southern Methodist	124
10 Penn State	627	20 Miami	73.5

December 6, 1980

FLORIDA STATE 17 Florida 13: Brushing aside rust—team had not played since November 8—Seminoles (10-1) rallied from 13-3 H deficit as QB Rick Stockstill (11-18/137y, 2 INTs) and WR Hardis Johnson (7/107y) teamed up for TD passes of 19y and 20y. Gators (7-4) had taken H lead as QB Wayne Peace hit WR Tyrone Young (5/109) with 53y TD pass in middle of stretch in which Florida reeled off 13 straight pts. Gators were mangled in 2nd H and managed only 31y O as Florida State added to its yearlong domination of 2nd H play in which it outscored opponents 186 to 21, 96-0 in 4th Qs. This defeat marked 5th straight loss for Gators in series that was once dictated by state legislature.

SOUTHERN CALIFORNIA 20 Notre Dame 3: No. 2 Notre Dame's weak O was no match for revitalized Trojans, gaining only 95y rushing and paltry 25y passing as both Irish QBs, Blair Kiel (0-5) and QB Mike Courey (3-8, 2 INTs), struggled. Trojans (8-2-1) built 10-0 2nd Q lead before they even allowed single 1st down in handing Fighting Irish (9-1-1) 4th defeat in L.A. Coliseum when ND entered with unbeaten record. In 3rd Q, USC D had 2 GLSs to preserve lead: CB Ronnie Lott nailed Courey on 4th down to stop 1st threat. Trojans next lost FUM deep in their territory, but Irish were pushed back and had to settle for 30y FG by K Harry Oliver. Southern California TB Michael Harper (20/87y) subbed for injured TB Marcus Allen and delivered both of team's TDs. USC converted FUM by Notre Dame HB Phil Carter, 49y INT RET by LB Chip Banks, and roughing K PEN into 13 pts in handing departing ND coach Dan Devine his 5th defeat in 6 series tries.

AP Poll December 8

1 Georgia (60)	1274	11 Ohio State	578
2 Florida State (4)	1208	12 Southern California	563
3 Pittsburgh	1127	13 North Carolina	495
4 Oklahoma	1027	14 Brigham Young	470
5 Michigan	947	15 UCLA	464
6 Baylor	914	16 Washington	439
7 Notre Dame	860	17 Mississippi State	343
8 Nebraska	801	18 South Carolina	177
9 Alabama	800	19 Southern Methodist	123
10 Penn State	644	20 Miami	67

Conference Standings

Ivy League

Yale	6-1
Cornell	5-2
Harvard	4-3
Princeton	4-3
Brown	4-3
Dartmouth	4-3
Pennsylvania	1-6
Columbia	0-7

Atlantic Coast

North Carolina	6-0
Maryland	5-1
North Carolina State	3-3
Clemson	2-4
Wake Forest	2-4
Virginia	2-4
Duke	1-5
Georgia Tech	0-2

Southeastern

Georgia	6-0
Mississippi State	5-1
Alabama	5-1
Louisiana State	4-2
Florida	4-2
Tennessee	3-3
Mississippi	2-4
Kentucky	1-5
Auburn	0-6
Vanderbilt	0-6

Big Ten

Michigan	8-0
Ohio State	7-1
Purdue	7-1
Iowa	4-4
Minnesota	4-5
Indiana	3-5
Wisconsin	3-5
Illinois	3-5
Michigan State	2-6
Northwestern	0-9

Mid-American

Central Michigan	7-2
Western Michigan	6-3
Northern Illinois	4-3
Miami (Ohio)	4-3
Ball State	5-4
Ohio	5-4
Bowling Green	4-4
Toledo	3-6
Kent State	3-6
Eastern Michigan	1-7

Big Eight

Oklahoma	7-0
Nebraska	6-1
Missouri	5-2
Kansas	3-3-1
Oklahoma State	2-4-1
Iowa State	2-5
Kansas State	1-6
Colorado	1-6

Southwest

Baylor	8-0
Southern Methodist	5-3
Houston	5-3
Texas	4-4
Rice	4-4
Arkansas	3-5
Texas Tech	3-5
Texas A&M	3-5
Texas Christian	1-7

Western Athletic

Brigham Young	6-1
Colorado State	5-1-1
Hawaii	4-3
Utah	3-3-1
Wyoming	4-4
San Diego State	4-4
New Mexico	3-4
Air Force	1-6
Texas-El Paso	1-6

Pacific-10

Washington	6-1
UCLA	5-2
Southern California	4-2-1
Arizona State	5-3
Oregon	4-3-1
Stanford	3-4
Arizona	3-4
Washington State	3-4
California	3-5
Oregon State	0-8

Pacific Coast Athletic

Long Beach State	5-0
Utah State	4-1
San Jose State	3-2
Fresno State	1-4
Fullerton State	1-4
Pacific	1-4

1980 Major Bowl Games

Holiday Bowl (Dec. 19): Brigham Young 46 Southern Methodist 45

Time had already elapsed on Brigham Young (12-1) sr TE Clay Brown's fine collegiate career when he leapt in EZ amid 4 defenders to haul in winning 41y TD catch. Brown's brilliant TD grab allowed Cougars to complete unbelievable rally from 45-25 deficit in game's final 3:57 and win for 1st time in their post-season history. BYU QB Jim McMahon (32-49/446y, 4 TDs, INT) performed for ages at game's end as he completed 18-25/239y in 4th Q to lead rally. Score was 38-19 when mercurial McMahon mounted 90y drive, on which he completed 10 passes, to 1y TD run by TB Scott Phillips. After BYU missed 2-pt conv, SMU still led 38-25. Mustangs (8-4) recovered Cougars' onside-KO, and, on next play, SMU TB Craig James capped his outstanding game with 45y scoring romp for 45-25 lead. James rushed for 225y as SMU gained 393y on ground. Now facing 2nd-team D, McMahon led desperate 72y drive to WR Matt Braga's 15y, possibly-trapped, TD catch that cut lead to 45-31 with 2:33 left. Next, BYU LB Todd Shell recovered onside-KO, leading to another 1y TD run by Phillips, following McMahon's 49y bomb to WR Bill Davis. After Phillips caught 2-pt conv pass, SMU's lead was down to 45-39 with 1:58 remaining. Worried Mustangs seemed to eat enough clock before sending out punting unit. But, BYU DB Bill Schoepflin blocked punt at 41YL with 13 secs remaining. After 2 quick incompletions, McMahon threw last play "Hail Mary" pass that Brown (5/155y) ripped away from defender. K Kurt Gunther booted x-pt for unfathomable Cougars win. James' rushing total—including 45y run on fake punt for team's 2nd TD—set game record, while fellow SMU TB Eric Dickerson added 110y rushing. Cougars finished with −2y on ground as Ponies D sacked McMahon 7 times. Ponies A-A CB John Simmons had left game with 1st H injury, and his usual heady play was missed during Brigham Young's late comeback.

Fiesta Bowl (Dec. 26): Penn State 31 Ohio State 19

Trailing 19-10 at H, Penn State (10-2) unleashed its shown-up D, which promptly held Buckeyes to 0y in 3rd Q. Lions O, with TB Curt Warner rushing for 155y, did its part with 3 TD runs in 2nd H, including 4y effort by TB Jonathan Williams for eventual game-winner and 37y romp by FB Booker Moore to clinch matters. QB Art Schlichter led Ohio State (9-3) with career-high 302y passing on 20-35, but he completed only 5-13/58y against constant rush pressure in 2nd H. He was sacked 4 times in 2nd H after getting through 1st H unscathed. While trailing 24-19, Schlichter was thrown for 20y loss by DL Greg Jones on 4th-and-3 after Buckeyes reached Penn State 27YL. Scores in 1st H had come quickly as Warner tallied on 64y run on Penn State's 1st play from scrimmage, and Schlichter threw 3 TD passes to cap drives of at least 77y that each took no more than 3 mins each. Buckeyes WR Gary Williams (7/122y) caught 33y TD pass, and WR Doug Donley (5/122y) hauled in TDs of 23y and 19y.

Liberty Bowl (Dec. 27): Purdue 28 Missouri 25

Purdue (9-3) QB Mark Herrmann, college football's new leader in all-time passing y, fittingly ended his excellent career by completing 22-28/289y, 4 TDs. Herrmann, who started from his 1st game as frosh in 1977, won for 33rd time, most-ever wins for Purdue's pantheon of great QBs. Herrmann found fellow A-A, TE Dave Young, for 5y score to end 1st H, up by 21-12. WR Bart Burrell caught 8/113y and 2 TDs, including 27y scoring reception in 3rd Q that put Boilermakers ahead by 28-12. Missouri (8-4) WR Ron Fellows had scored Tigers' 1st TD on 92y KO RET in 2nd Q, but x-pt was messed up. FB James Wilder scored on 1y run moments later as Tigers pulled within 14-12, but they failed on 2-pt pass. Missouri QB Phil Bradley (16-29/210y, INT) led rally for game's final 13 pts, but it came up short.

Hall of Fame Bowl (Dec. 27): Arkansas 34 Tulane 15

RB Gary Anderson added to personal highlight reel by setting up Razorbacks' 1st TD with 44y run, taking punt 80y for TD, and racing for 46y TD for commanding 28-0 lead in 1st H. Anderson ended with 11/156y rushing—126y contributed in decisive 1st H—as Arkansas (7-5) dominated run game with 383y to157y advantage. Green Wave (7-5) could not penetrate Arkansas D until 4th Q, scoring 2 TDs including 62y scoring pass from QB Nickie Hall (16-37/241y, 2 INTs) to WR Marcus Anderson.

Sun Bowl (Dec. 27): Nebraska 31 Mississippi State 17

It appeared that Nebraska (10-2) used December to work on trick plays, uncapping full arsenal to beat Bulldogs (9-3). Cornhuskers WR Todd Brown opened scoring with 23y reverse run on team's 1st scrimmage play that converted Bulldogs FUM. Nebraska later used flea-flicker, laterals off pass receptions, and fake FG to move ball against tough D geared to stop Huskers' ample rushing attack. Mississippi State surrendered mild 56/161y rushing and allowed Nebraska's star IB Jarvis Redwine to gain only 42y. Still, Huskers earned 17-0 lead entering 2nd H and finished off State with 2y TD run by FB Andra Franklin in 3rd Q and 52y TD pass by QB Jeff Quinn (9-19/159y, 2 TDs, INT), to WB Tim McCrady in 4th Q. Nebraska D was stalwart, too, pressing QB John Bond into 7-19/102y, 2 INTs, while recovering 4 FUMs. Bond ran for 1y TD and threw 11y TD pass to FB Michael Haddix in 4th Q.

Gator Bowl (Dec. 29): Pittsburgh 37 South Carolina 9

No. 3 Pittsburgh (11-1) met its mission to encourage national championship voters—win and win big. QB Rick Trocano (10-21/155y, 2 INTs) ran for opening TD and later threw screen pass that FB Randy McMillan turned into 42y TD in leading easy victory. In match-up of Heisman winner, South Carolina (8-4) TB George Rogers (27/113y), and award's runner-up, DE Hugh Green, Rogers won battle by topping century rushing mark. But, Green won war by sparking D that kept Rogers out of EZ and forced 5 TOs, including 2 FUMs by Rogers. Green was double-teamed most of game, finishing with 5 tackles while bookend linemate, DE Ricky Jackson, was free to make 19 tackles. Pitt S Tom Flynn recovered Rogers' FUM on very 1st play of game—Talk about Heisman jinx!—which set up Trocano's 3y TD keeper moments later. Panthers never looked back, building 34-3 2nd H lead in dominating game. Recovering from knee injury, Pittsburgh QB Dan Marino led 2nd TD drive by throwing 3y TD to WR Willie Collier late in 2nd Q for 17-3 H lead. Gamecocks had opportunities to stay in game, but let time ran out in 1st H with ball on Pitt 2YL and lost FUM on Panther 8YL in 2nd H. South Carolina sub QB Gordon Beckham threw 14y TD pass to WR Tim Gillespie in 4th Q.

Bluebonnet Bowl (Dec. 31): North Carolina 16 Texas 7

Holes were there for North Carolina (11-1) TB Amos Lawrence (18/104y), who knew what to do with them, rambling for 59y TD in 1st Q. Tar Heels muffed x-pt and Texas (7-5) grabbed lead 7-6 as HB Mike Luck went over from 1y out. WR Herkie Walls raced 42y with E-around to set up Longhorns' TD. North Carolina got ball back, but was forced to punt, and S-P Steve Streater booted 63y beauty. Streater continued to single-handily swing momentum back to Tar Heels with INT of QB Rick McIvor (11-27/128y). Tar Heels scored on ensuing drive as TB Kelvin Bryant (15/82y) ran in 1y TD to regain lead at 13-7. It was enough as Heels D shut out Horns rest of way. QB Rod Elkins passed 11-18/121y as Carolina finished with 355y O.

Cotton Bowl: Alabama 30 Baylor 2

Behind dominating D and efficient O, Crimson Tide (10-2) handed coach Bear Bryant his 1st Cotton Bowl win since 1951, when his Kentucky team had beaten TCU by 20-7. Alabama grabbed 13-2 H lead as D held Baylor (10-2) to 36y O and stopped best Bears drive at Bama 9YL on LB Randy Scott's FUM REC resulting from hit by DB Jim Bob Harris on Bears FB Robert Gentry. Alabama forced 7 TOs during game, including 2 FUMs on punt RETs that were converted into FGs by K Peter Kim. Alabama HB Major Ogilvie, game's leading rusher with 74y, scored on 1y dive in 1st H to become 1st back in NCAA history to run for TDs in 4 straight bowl games. He led attack that totaled 241y on ground, 187y more than Bears could muster. Leading SWC rusher, HB Walter Abercrombie, was held to 9y rushing. Baylor's only pts came on DT Tommy Tabor's safety-producing tackle of QB Walter Lewis in 1st Q. In his final college game, LB Mike Singletary sparkled for Bears with 30 tackles.

Rose Bowl: Michigan 23 Washington 6

Finally: "Hail to the Victors!" After 7 bowl losses, 5 in Rose Bowl, Michigan (10-2) coach Bo Schembechler won his 1st post-season game and 1st for Michigan since January 1965 Rose Bowl triumph over Oregon State. After Wolverines D bent without breaking in 1st H, Michigan O marched for 3 scores in 2nd H to trump Huskies (9-3). Troika of QB John Wangler (12-20/120y), TB Butch Woolfolk (26/192y, TD), and WR Anthony Carter (5/68y) simply was too much for Washington D. Carter made key receptions on each 2nd H scoring drive, and his 7y TD catch in 3rd Q capped 84y drive and provided Michigan with 17-6 lead. Huskies O was kept off field for most of 2nd H, but had had numerous chances to score earlier in game: QB Tom Flick (23-39/282y, 2 INTs) threw for 189y in 1st H without getting his team into EZ. Washington had sniffed paydirt early on when on 4th down FB Toussaint Tyler dived from Michigan 1YL. Tyler fumbled ball, with refs ruling he had not broken plane before losing possession. Michigan D, which had not surrendered TD since October 25 game against Illinois, allowed no 2nd TD chances to Huskies. In 2nd H, Washington was held to 6 1st downs and 93y passing as Wolverine LBs dropped into coverage to clog opportunities. Rose win was only Big Ten's 2nd in past 12 years.

Sugar Bowl: Georgia 17 Notre Dame 10

With national title on line for Bulldogs, it was Notre Dame (9-2-1) that made crucial errors under pressure in 1st-ever meeting of storied programs. Georgia (12-0), which led country with +33 takeaway margin, converted 2 huge Irish TOs into short TD drives

of 2y and 22y. Although TB Herschel Walker rushed for 150y, Bulldogs in fact did little on O to earn their 1st national championship. Walker was named game MVP, but he was unable to break anything long and was reasonably contained by Irish D that ranked 4th nationally and had enjoyed string of 23 Qs without surrendering TD during regular season. QB Buck Belue provided leadership, but not by example, completing no passes in 11 attempts until his crucial 1st down-gaining 7y throw to WR Amp Arnold to help Georgia run out clock at game's end. Irish had come out throwing and moved to 3-0 lead on 50y FG by K Harry Oliver, who later missed 3 ATTs, including block by UGa DB Terry Hoage. After Hoage's FG block, Georgia moved downfield behind Walker for K Rex Robinson's tying 46y FG late in 1st Q. Game turned immediately thereafter as Robinson sent KO high and deep, and both ND returners shied away until it landed short of EZ. Bulldogs DB Bob Kelly beat ND HB Jim Stone to loose ball, recovering on Irish 2YL. Walker leapt over top for 1y TD 2 plays later. Notre Dame's next costly miscue occurred moments later as FB John Sweeney lost FUM to DB Chris Welton on own 22YL. Georgia needed 3 plays to score this time, with Walker running it in on sweep right for 3y TD. Bulldogs went conservative, and Notre Dame controlled most of last 3 Qs without much to show for it. Irish pulled within 17-10 late in 3rd Q on 1y TD run by HB Phil Carter (27/109y), but rest of their drives ended in missed FGs or TOs. Entering 4th Q, Irish had 199y advantage, 9 more 1st downs, and had held ball nearly 10 mins more than Georgia, but came no closer. Irish coach Dan Devine then let frustration get better of his play-calling late in his last game of Hall of Fame career: he desperately called 4th-and-1 pass that was picked off by CB Scott Woerner, his 2nd of game. Bulldogs ran out clock to seal victory.

Orange Bowl: Oklahoma 18 Florida State 17

There were QBs with bigger reputations tossing pigskins in college ranks in 1980, but Oklahoma (10-2) coach Barry Switzer would not have wished to replace his QB J.C. Watts with any of them before team's final Orange Bowl possession. Watts ended his collegiate career with heroics, needing only 46 secs to march OU 78y to TD on 11y pass to WR Steve Rhodes. Watts, who finished with 128y passing and 48y rushing, then threw winning 2-pt conv pass to TE Forrest Valora with 1:27 left. On final drive, Watts (7-12/128y, TD) completed 4 passes that gained 73y, including 42y strike to Rhodes that took Sooners to Florida State 35YL. Seminoles (10-2) had taken 17-10 lead with 3:53 left when CB Bobby Butler pounced on flub of snap by K-P Michael Keeling in Sooners EZ. Game had been scoreless until final min of 1st H when TB Ricky Williams (19/99y) gave Noles 7-0 lead with 10y TD run. Sooners had time for quick drive to 53y FG by K Keeling as time elapsed in 2nd Q. Oklahoma took its 1st lead at 10-7 by cashing in opening possession of 3rd Q with 78y march to 4y TD run by HB David Overstreet. Florida State K Bill Capece kicked tying 19y FG at end of 3rd Q. Florida State surprisingly won rushing battle 212y to 156y, which happened infrequently in victories by Oklahoma. Sooners had now notched 3 straight Orange Bowl wins, while Watts had pair of wins and 2 Orange Bowl MVPs.

Peach Bowl (Jan. 2): Miami 20 Virginia Tech 10

Miami's opening 68y scoring drive was good, capped by QB Jim Kelly's 15y TD pass to WR Larry Brodsky (4/80y), but its 99y drive that crossed into 2nd Q was magnificent. Kelly (11-22/179y, TD, INT) threw for 66y on drive to set up 12y TD draw run by FB Chris Hobbs as Hurricanes (9-3) led 14-0. It all began when Virginia Tech (8-4) TB Cyrus Lawrence threw surprise pass that was intercepted by Canes S Fred Marion at his 1YL. Hokies QB Steve Casey later ruined another chance when his pass was picked off by Hurricanes CB Ronnie Lippett at GL. Virginia Tech rallied with 10 straight pts, pulling to within 14-10 on 1y TD run by Lawrence (27/134y) early in 2nd H. Casey (9-23/119y) had set up Lawrence's TD with 42y pass to TE Rob Purdham. Miami soon stopped bleeding, and K Dan Miller added insurance FGs of 31y and 37y. Swift Tech LB Ashley Lee was in on 15 tackles.

Final AP Poll January 4

1 Georgia (58.5)	1251.5	11 Southern California	610
2 Pittsburgh (3.5)	1187.5	12 Brigham Young	584
3 Oklahoma	1100	13 UCLA	502
4 Michigan	1033	14 Baylor	494
5 Florida State (1)	970	15 Ohio State	389
6 Alabama	928	16 Washington	253
7 Nebraska	879	17 Purdue	198.3
8 Penn State	797	18 Miami	192
9 Notre Dame	699	19 Mississippi State	159
10 North Carolina	665	20 Southern Methodist	98.3

1980 Top Performance Formula

1 Pittsburgh	1.7291
2 Florida State	1.7205
3 Brigham Young	1.7159
4 Nebraska	1.6798
5 Georgia	1.6161
6 North Carolina	1.6006
7 Alabama	1.5966
8 Penn State	1.5768
9 Oklahoma	1.5548
10 Michigan	1.5298
11 Notre Dame	1.5177
12 Southern California	1.5083
13 UCLA	1.4853
14 Baylor	1.4581
15 Ohio State	1.4172
16 Miami	1.4165
17 Purdue	1.3453
18 Washington	1.3356
19 Southern Methodist	1.3184
20 Missouri	1.3134

1980 Top Opponent Records

1	Florida State	.6905
2	Penn State	.6468
3	Southern California	.6283
4	Notre Dame	.6260
5	Miami	.6181
6	Pittsburgh	.6040
7	Kentucky	.6000
8	Georgia Tech	.5983
9	Stanford	.5885
10	Texas Christian	.5862
11	West Virginia	.5847
12t	Maryland	.58400
12t	Nebraska	.58400
14	South Carolina	.5823
15	Texas A&M	.5812
16	Arizona State	.5783
17	Mississippi	.5776
18	Clemson	.5765
19	Syracuse	.5739
20	Oklahoma	.5732

1980 Out-of-Conference Records

	W-L	Percentage	Bowl W-L
Southeastern	31-18	.6327	3-1
Pacific-10	21-15-1	.5811	0-1
Southwest	15-15	.5000	2-3
Big Eight	15-17-1	.4697	2-1
Western Athletic	18-23-1	.4405	1-0
Big Ten	12-18-1	.4032	2-1
Atlantic Coast	15-23-1	.3974	1-1

1980 Individual Statistical Leaders

RUSHING YARDS	Attempts	Yards	Avg.
George Rogers, South Carolina	297	1781	6.0
Herschel Walker, Georgia	274	1616	5.9
Marcus Allen, Southern California	354	1563	4.4
Charlie Wysocki, Maryland	334	1359	4.1
James Brooks, Auburn	261	1314	5.0
Dwayne Crutchfield, Iowa State	284	1312	4.6
Cyrus Lawrence, Virginia Tech	271	1221	4.5
Gerald Willhite, San Jose State	245	1210	4.9
Calvin Murray, Ohio State	185	1192	6.4
Walter Abercrombie, Baylor	229	1187	5.2

PASSING YARDS	Completions	Attempts	Yards	Pct.
Jim McMahon, Brigham Young	284	445	4571	63.8
Mark Herrmann, Purdue	220	340	2923	64.7
John Elway, Stanford	248	379	2889	65.4
Ricky Hardin, Utah	179	290	2459	61.7
Bob Gagliano, Utah State	184	346	2361	53.2
Tom Flick, Washington	168	280	2178	60.0
Kevin Starkey, Long Beach State	138	248	1955	55.7
Mark O'Connell, Ball State	175	295	1921	59.3
Oliver Luck, West Virginia	135	254	1874	53.2
Ed McMichael, Rutgers	146	235	1761	62.1

RECEIVING YARDS	Catches	Yards
Rainey Meszaros, Pacific	68	1062
Keith Chappelle, Iowa	64	1037
Clay Brown, Brigham Young	48	1009
James Murphy, Utah State	66	966
Mike Fahnestock, Army	47	937
Dave Young, Purdue	67	917
Perry Tuttle, Clemson	53	915
Bart Burrell, Purdue	58	888
Sam Greene, UNLV	43	859
Ricky Martin, New Mexico	43	850

1980 Consensus All-America Team

Offense

Wide Receiver:	Ken Margerum, Stanford
Tight End:	Dave Young, Purdue
Line:	Mark May, Pittsburgh
	Keith Van Horne, Southern California
	Nick Eyre, Brigham Young
	Louis Oubre, Oklahoma
	Randy Schleusener, Nebraska
Center:	John Scully, Notre Dame
Quarterback:	Mark Herrmann, Purdue
Running Back:	George Rogers, South Carolina
	Herschel Walker, Georgia
	Jarvis Redwine, Nebraska

Defense

Line:	Hugh Green, Pittsburgh
	E.J. Junior, Alabama
	Kenneth Sims, Texas
	Leonard Mitchell, Houston
Middle Guard:	Ron Simmons, Florida State
Linebacker:	Mike Singletary, Baylor
	Lawrence Taylor, North Carolina
	David Little, Florida
	Bob Crable, Notre Dame
Back:	Kenny Easley, UCLA
	Ronnie Lott, Southern California
	John Simmons, SMU

1980 Heisman Trophy Vote

George Rogers, senior running back, South Carolina	1128
Hugh Green, senior defensive end, Pittsburgh	861
Herschel Walker, freshman tailback, Georgia	657
Mark Herrmann, senior quarterback, Purdue	405
Jim McMahon, junior quarterback, Brigham Young	189

Other Major Awards

Maxwell (Player)	Hugh Green, senior defensive end, Pittsburgh
Walter Camp (Player)	Herschel Walker, freshman tailback, Georgia
Outland (Lineman)	Mark May, senior tackle, Pittsburgh
Lombardi (Lineman)	Hugh Green, senior defensive end, Pittsburgh
Davey O'Brien (Southwest)	Mike Singletary, senior linebacker, Baylor
AFCA Coach of the Year	Vince Dooley, Georgia

1981

The Year of Bear's Stagg Party, Allen's Run to Daylight, and Tigers Prowl as Last Number One

One of the most memorable seasons in college football history, 1981, featured a fascinating prowl for no. 1 as a record seven teams occupied the top AP Poll spot during the course of the season, and yet, an unranked team at season's start captured the national title as the last unbeaten team in the land. On display were a multitude of stars such as Marcus Allen, Herschel Walker, Anthony Carter, and Dan Marino, although not one of them could upstage a 68-year-old man in a checkered fedora. Alabama (9-2-1) coach Paul "Bear" Bryant became the all-time leader in coaching wins with his 315th career victory, earned in a 28-17 triumph over archrival Auburn (5-6) on November 28. The Crimson Tide's quest for the nine victories necessary for Bryant to surpass first Pop Warner (313 wins) and then leader Amos Alonzo Stagg (314) became a national curiosity. Earlier in the year, the NCAA had rejected a request by Amos Alonzo Stagg, Jr. that his father receive credit for half of the 21 wins achieved as head coach at Susquehanna between 1947 and 1952. Stagg, Jr. claimed that his father shared head coaching duties, but he picked the wrong year to make his complaint known. This was the year of Bear's party.

Another head coach received an enormous amount of attention in 1981, albeit under far different circumstances. Likeable Gerry Faust, who had built a powerhouse program at Cincinnati's Moeller High School, was entrusted with perhaps the most difficult job in collegiate sports—running the Notre Dame (5-6) football team—without any college head coaching experience. An excellent recruiting class and an easy opening win against Louisiana State (3-7-1) seemed to bode well for Faust's future. The Fighting Irish took over the top ranking in the country on September 14, but lost three of their next four games, and a five-year free fall had begun for the Irish. They would complete the year with their first losing mark since 1963.

One of the teams that beat Notre Dame was Southern California (9-3), which became the third team to occupy no. 1 in consecutive September weeks following losses by pre-season no. 1 Michigan (9-3) and Notre Dame. Trojans tailback Marcus Allen led the way with a magnificent season, tying or setting 13 NCAA records as he became the first college back to break the 2,000-yard rushing barrier. Allen began the season in the shadow of the sensational sophomore running back of Georgia (10-2), Herschel Walker, but a record eight 200-yard games by Allen handed another Heisman Trophy to a Trojans tailback. Allen broke former Pittsburgh standout running back Tony Dorsett's single-season rushing record of 1,948 yards when he rushed for 243 yards against California (2-9) on November 7 to advance his yardage total to 1,968. He finished with 2,342 yards, which stood until Oklahoma State's Barry Sanders broke it seven years later.

Allen's heroics did not translate into an unbeaten season, however, and USC was upset by Arizona (6-5) on October 10. Three consecutive weeks with a different top-ranked team ensued as Texas (10-1-1) lasted one week before losing to Arkansas (8-4) and being replaced by Penn State (10-2). Virtually even with the Nittany Lions were their Eastern rivals, the Pitt Panthers, thus creating hope for a Keystone State battle of unbeaten teams at the end of the regular season. Upstart Miami (9-2) put a swift end to that idea with an upset of Penn State. Pittsburgh (11-1)—which had impressively replaced 15 graduated starters (12 of whom were drafted by the NFL)—was thrust into the nation's top spot. That would last until a stunning 48-14 loss to Penn State after the Panthers had jumped out to a 14-0 lead.

With all the national powers having beaten each other, one undefeated team was left hiding in the weeds. It was surprising Clemson (12-0), which occupied the top spot for the final regular season poll. Clemson was the seventh team to prowl as no. 1. The Tigers, for years a regional power with little pizzazz on the national scene, were so overlooked early on that they became the first team to go from unranked in preseason to the national title since the 1962 Southern California Trojans. Clemson coach Danny Ford's charges had to start the season with three wins and upset Georgia (10-2) 13-3 on September 19 even to squeeze into the poll at no. 19. They efficiently ran the table against their ACC foes, gaining attention by putting up some ridiculously high point totals. Clemson's 82-point total against Wake Forest (4-7) garnered much more attention to the private school from western South Carolina than their hard-fought 10-8 victory over a good North Carolina (10-2) team. Despite upholding their ranking with an Orange Bowl victory over a Nebraska (9-3) squad that was undefeated in Big Eight play, to win their first-ever title, Clemson was never accepted as a legitimate champ by national college fans grown accustomed to the same powers winning on an annual basis. The scandal that erupted soon thereafter

seemed to prove that point. A lot of people felt that an upstart like Clemson surely had to be cheating to beat the big boys of college football. At 33, Ford was youngest coach ever to win a national title; by 1989 he was gone from Clemson.

Dennis Green since has proven to have far more staying power in the coaching fraternity than Ford, and in 1981, he became the first African-American coach in the Big 10 by taking over hapless Northwestern (0-11). Green won no games his first year, but three wins in 1982 broke a 34-game losing streak. The Wildcats set the mark for futility with their 29th straight defeat, being trounced 62-14 by Michigan State (5-6) on November 7. One mark for failure the Wildcats were able to avoid was football's first-ever 12-loss season, turned in by Colorado State (0-12).

Known for its stellar academic standards, the Ivy League entered a new chapter of its remarkable football history. On the same day, December 5, that Allen won the Heisman Trophy, the Ivy League members were among 25 schools that lost Division 1 football status (not counting the MAC that lost such rank for only one season). NCAA schools voted to require members to fulfill one of two necessities: a minimum average home attendance or a home stadium capacity of 30,000. Four Ivy League schools failed to meet either requirement and the league decided to stay together. Ivy schools once defined the sport of college football; now they were assigned lesser status in Division 1-AA.

Cynics had long renamed the Big Ten as the "Big Two and Little Eight" in recognition of the stranglehold Michigan (8-3) and Ohio State (8-3) had held on the conference title. The two had enjoyed a 14-year run of trips to the Rose Bowl as Big Ten representative. From the depths of the Big Ten was where Iowa (8-4) returned, as coach Hayden Fry's Hawkeyes entered the season with the nation's longest string of losing seasons (19), and amazingly finished it in the Rose Bowl as Iowa bombed Michigan State (5-6) on the last Saturday and Ohio State helped out by nipping Michigan in the last three minutes. That the Hawkeyes lost to Washington (10-2), making its third appearance in five years in the Rose Bowl, removed little luster from Iowa's story. The match-up marked the first time the game did not feature at least one of the traditional powers—USC, UCLA, Michigan, or Ohio State—since January 1, 1964, when Illinois beat Washington 17-7. The Huskies' 28-0 win was the Pac-10's 11th in the last 13 Rose Bowls.

Florida State (6-5) sought to build its reputation in coach Bobby Bowden's sixth season in Tallahassee and embarked on what Bowden called a "Death March" schedule. FSU won its first two games, but starting with a September 19 loss at Nebraska, the Seminoles played five straight road games (with one Saturday off) against famous stalwarts that had compiled a combined 46-12-1 record in 1980. Surprisingly, Florida State beat Ohio State (9-3), Notre Dame, and LSU, while being trounced by Pittsburgh. The Seminoles emerged from the Death March with a 5-2 record, but seemed pretty well tuckered out for late season losses to Miami, Southern Miss (8-2-1), and Florida (7-5).

Southern Methodist (10-1) was another team that emerged from recent periods of mediocrity to excel in 1981. Although put on probation in the summer, the Mustangs regrouped to win the Southwest Conference crown as their "Pony Express" backfield of tailbacks Eric Dickerson and Craig James excelled. The SMU defense forced a national-best 49 turnovers. Dickerson rushed for 1,428 yards and 19 touchdowns, while James gained 1,147 yards with nine scoring runs. SWC runner-up Texas beat SMU, Oklahoma (7-4-1), and, in Cotton Bowl, Alabama, to finish as AP's no. 2 despite its Arkansas loss and a tie with Houston (7-4-1).

Another of a new breed of national powers, Brigham Young (11-2) won at least 11 games for the third straight year. Despite numerous injuries, quarterback Jim McMahon became the nation's all-time passing yardage leader with 9,536 yards.

The battle for control of television rights continued with the NCAA signing with ABC and CBS for $264 million over 4 years. The elite College Football Association (CFA) members agreed on a $180 million contract with NBC as follow-up to a suit against the NCAA by CFA members Georgia, Texas, and Oklahoma. The NBC deal fell through by the end of the year because the NCAA was able to win this round in the courts. But, legal action had just begun.

Finally, historians should note October 31 as (perhaps) a scary moment in sports history. University of Washington alumnus Robb Weller and the school's band director Bill Bissell debuted "The Wave" at the Huskies'

42-31 home victory over Stanford (4-7). Although others claim creation of the popular cheer, in which whole sections of fans would rise in unison and whole stadiums looked like rolling waves of people, this birthdate of the wave remains college football's entry.

Milestones

■ Rules now required one team to wear white uniform jerseys. In 1983, visiting team would be required to wear white, but by 1995, home teams regained the option of wearing white if both teams agreed. Rule governing attempts to block kicks was tightened to exclude stepping, jumping, or standing on teammate or being picked up by teammate.

■ Big Sky, Ohio Valley, and Yankee Conferences began to use overtime to break ties. Weber State edged Northern Arizona, 24-23, on October 31 to win first-ever regular season OT game.

■ Sugar Bowl moved to night of January 1, thus freeing Fiesta Bowl to move from late December. It marked 1st change to New Year's Day slate since Sun Bowl left January 1 in 1959.

■ California Bowl debuted on December 19, pitting Big West and Mid-American champions.

■ Retired Marine Brigadier General John W. Beckett, standout halfback and defensive tackle for Oregon and player of game in Ducks' only Rose Bowl victory in 1917, died at age 88 on July 26. Jack Green, All-America guard and captain of Army's 1945 national champions, died after long illness at 57 on August 4. Green was head coach at Vanderbilt from 1963-66. Coaching great Pappy Waldorf died at age 78 on August 15. Waldorf won 170 games during 30-year career as head coach at five schools. Waldorf led Oklahoma State to four Missouri Valley titles in five years before moving to Kansas State for its Big 6 title with in 1934. He earned first AFCA coach of the year award for rebuilding effort at Northwestern in 1935, and led California to three PCC crowns in 1948-50. Waldorf was personnel director for NFL's 49ers from 1957-72. Longtime University of Michigan announcer Bob Ufer died of cancer on October 26. Bobby Grayson, twice All-America back at Stanford and member of "Vow Boys" teams in 1933-35, died at 66 on November 21. Star of 1932 frosh team that vowed to never lose to Southern Cal, Grayson kept pledge with two-way play that triggered three straight wins over USC and Cal and 3 straight Rose Bowl appearances. Team went 25-4-2 during string, while Grayson set then Rose Bowl record with 152 yards rushing in 1934. Former Iowa QB Aubrey Devine died at age 84 on December 15. Devine led coach Howard Jones' Hawkeyes to 17 wins from 1919-21, including 7-0 mark in 1921 All-America season when Hawkeyes won Western Conference crown and snapped Notre Dame's 20-game win streak.

■ Longest winning streaks entering season:

Georgia 13	Brigham Young 12	Michigan 9

■ Coaching changes:

	Incoming	Outgoing
Army	Ed Cavanaugh	Lou Saban
Auburn	Pat Dye	Doug Barfield
Colorado State	Chester Caddas (a)	Sarkas Arslanian
Northwestern	Dennis Green	Rick Venturi
Notre Dame	Gerry Faust	Dan Devine
San Diego State	Doug Scovil	Claude Gilbert
Syracuse	Dick MacPherson	Frank Maloney
Texas-El Paso	Billy Alton (b)	Bill Michael
Texas Tech	Jerry Moore	Rex Dockery
Wake Forest	Al Groh	John Mackovic
Wyoming	Al Kincaid	Pat Dye

(a) Caddas (0-6) replaced Arslanian (0-6) after loss to Utah on October 17.
(b) Alton (1-8) replaced Michael (0-2) after loss to Texas A&I on September12.

Preseason AP Poll

1 Michigan (38)		1183	11 Ohio State (1)		594
2 Oklahoma (7)		1100	12 North Carolina		462
3 Notre Dame		1050	13 UCLA		454
4 Alabama (3)		1020	14 Mississippi		359
5 Southern California		1014	15 Washington		272
6 Nebraska		768	16 Brigham Young		269
7 Penn State (1)		716	17 Florida		268
8 Pittsburgh		686	18 Stanford		205
9 Texas		647	19 Florida State		198
10 Georgia		624	20 Arizona State		158

September 5, 1981

Rutgers 29 SYRACUSE 27: Overcoming its own special teams breakdowns, Rutgers (1-0) sealed win with 80y scoring drive in 4th Q capped by 1y TD keeper by QB Ralph Leek. Rutgers had taken 15-3 H lead as Leek threw 2 TD passes, including 56y scoring hookup with WR Andrew Baker. Behind 29-20 in 4th Q, Syracuse (0-1), debuting under coach Dick MacPherson, could manage only 7y TD run by TB Joe Morris (21/100y) that was set up by 56y punt RET by DB Ed Koban. Slippery Morris earlier had scored on 95y KO RET.

PITTSBURGH 26 Illinois 6: Although neither team was mid-season sharp, Pittsburgh (1-0) was at least opportunistic in converting its numerous chances. QB Dan Marino (14-33/204y, 2 TDs) shook off dismal 2-14 numbers in 1st H, but didn't need to be hot in building 14-6 H lead: Illinois TO and short punt led to Pitt scoring drives of 11y and 19y. Fighting Illini (0-1) were held to 48y rushing by Panthers' still-dominant D, led by DT Bill Maas, who outscored Illinois himself in 2nd H with 4th Q sack for safety of Illinois QB Tony Eason (23-37/204y). Unknown Eason, who eventually would grow into stardom, had been brought in from American River JC as coach Mike White continued to sort through California JCs for his team's QB talent.

MIAMI 21 Florida 20: Lucky number for Miami (1-0) was 55 as Canes rallied from 20-11 deficit. All of Hurricanes' 10 pts in 4th Q pts were scored on 55y TD pass from backup QB Mark Richt to WR Rocky Belk and K Danny Miller's game-winning 55y FG with 40 secs left. Miller's FG—8y longer than his previous best—careened off left upright, while Richt, future head coach at Georgia, was subbing for injured QB Jim Kelly (14-22/218y). Gators (0-1) had time to reach Miami territory at game's end thanks to 26y

pass from QB Wayne Peace (17-28/189y, 3 INTs) to WR Broughton Lang, but 59y FG attempt by K Brian Clark was short. Before leaving with calf injury, Kelly succumbed to 3 INTs in 1st H, but drove Miami 83y to his 1y QB keeper that cut deficit to 14-11. Clark answered with 2 FGs for Florida team that had converted INTs of Kelly into pair of 1st H TDs for early 14-3 lead.

Alabama 24 LOUISIANA STATE 7: Alabama coach Bear Bryant's ballyhooed 9-win quest for record 315 victories got off on impressive note as Crimson Tide (1-0) cruised to 11th straight series win. Speed advantage for Bama was in evidence early as FB Kenny Simon raced 51y in 1st Q to open scoring. QB Ken Coley (14/108y) had runs of 51y and 42y to aid scoring drives as Alabama racked up 333y in 1st H to take 17-0 lead. Tide rotated 3 QBs—Coley, Walter Lewis and Paul Fields—who combined for 4-4/102y passing that included Fields' 44y TD pass to HB Mark Nix. LSU (0-1) managed no pts until game's end when sub QB Tim Byrd threw 5y TD pass to TE Malcolm Scott.

GEORGIA 44 Tennessee 0: Only 1-TD favorite, Georgia (1-0) looked primed for defense of its national title as Bulldogs inflicted worst defeat on Volunteers in 58 years (Vanderbilt had swamped Tennessee 51-7 in 1923). Bulldogs TB Herschel Walker continued where he left off in 1980, gaining 161y and TD, while QB Buck Belue passed 10-15/140y, 2 TDs. WR Lindsay Scott (6/95y) snared both of Belue's TD passes. Frosh K Kevin Butler had record-breaking debut as his 3 FGs and 5 x-pts totaled school-record 14 pts. Tennessee (0-1) could only muster 152y—to 563y for Georgia—and make 11 1st downs—to 30 for Georgia—against D led by DE Freddie Gilbert. Vols QB Jeff Olzewski completed 12-20/109y.

Lamar 18 BAYLOR 17: Defending SWC champion Baylor (0-1) opened new season with perceived laugher against Southland Conference member Lamar (1-0), which posted 3-8 record in 1980. But it was Cardinals who had last laugh as K Mike Marlow drilled 42y FG with 3 secs remaining. Baylor, which had to convert Lamar miscues to score both its TDs, had gone ahead 17-15 on K Marty Jimmerson's 41y FG with 2:53 left. In critical mistake, Bears RB Walter Abercrombie bobbled away FUM on Lamar 1YL and was held to 16/50y on ground, while QB Jay Jeffrey managed only 16y passing. Lamar QB Fred Hessen hit 18-35/168y and 7y TD to WR Herbert Harris.

AP Poll September 7

1 Michigan (37)	1184	11 Ohio State	538
2 Alabama (11)	1110	12 UCLA	466
3 Oklahoma (3)	1049	13 North Carolina	440
4 Notre Dame (4)	1024	14 Mississippi State	438
5 Southern California (3)	1009	15 Brigham Young	373
6 Georgia (4)	929	16 Miami	356
7 Nebraska	779	17 Washington	222
8 Texas	747	18 Florida State	186
9 Penn State	742	19 Stanford	180
10 Pittsburgh	724	20 Arizona State	173

September 12, 1981

Georgia Tech 24 ALABAMA 21: Stunning! Georgia Tech (1-0), winners of only 1 game previous season and on its way to 1-10 campaign, shocked Crimson Tide as frosh TB Robert Lavette scored his 2nd TD, from 2y out, to cap 80y drive in 4th Q that sealed Yellow Jackets' 1st opening game win in 11 years. It also was Tech's 1st victory over Alabama (1-1) since 1962, when Yellow Jackets' coach Bill Curry played important role as C-LB. Georgia Tech QB Mike Kelley, who hit 2 clutch passes on winning drive, threw for 137y, including 22y TD pass to FB Ronny Cone. Alabama's last-ditch effort to tie game failed as K Peter Kim's 50y FG try fell short. Tide HB Linnie Patrick made 78y with 4y TD in 3rd Q for short-lived 21-14 lead.

VANDERBILT 23 Maryland 17: Debut of Vanderbilt Stadium inspired Commodores (1-0) to upset. QB Whit Taylor (26-41/259y, 2 TDs, INT) hit WR Phil Roach with 5y game-winning TD pass with 5:11 remaining to cap 86y drive. Taylor completed 6-7 on winning march. Maryland (0-1) QB Bob Milkovich threw 2 TDs, but lost FUM—1 of Terps' 3 lost FUMs—on own 26YL, recovered by Vandy CB Leonard Coleman to set up K Mike Woodard's clinching 3rd FG that closed scoring. TB Charlie Wysocki rushed for 104y for Terps, but only 23y in 2nd H.

WISCONSIN 21 Michigan 14: Badgers (1-0) stunned top-ranked Michigan behind big-play O and stingy D that looked nothing like recent Wisconsin units. QB Jess Cole led way with 182y passing and 41y rushing as Wisconsin posted 1st victory over Michigan (0-1) since 1962, while scoring its 1st pts in series since 1976. Cole threw 2 TDs, including 71y effort to TB John Williams for winning TD in 3rd Q. Badgers S Matt Vanden Boom picked off QB Steve Smith pass at Badgers 17YL with 2 secs left to seal game and cap weak performance by Smith, who completed as many passes to Wisconsin (3) as he did to own team. WR Anthony Carter was held to single reception, while TB Butch Woolfolk rushed for 119y for Michigan with 89y coming on TD romp in 3rd Q.

IOWA 10 Nebraska 7: Iowa City was ecstatic over upset, sparked by Hawkeyes (1-0) D that allowed only 150y rushing and 231y overall. Hawkeyes quickly erased memories of last year's 57-0 loss to Nebraska (0-1) by scoring on 1st possession on 2y run by TB Eddie Phillips (9/94y). Iowa then added K Lon Olejniczak's 35y FG later in H before turning game over to its D. Fingernails were nibbled as Nebraska's last 3 drives ended on FUM recovered by Iowa DT Mark Bortz, downs, and CB Lou King's diving INT that sealed win with 39 secs remaining. Huskers IB Roger Craig rushed for 74y to lead O.

PURDUE 27 Stanford 19: In another performance typical of his collegiate days, Cardinals QB John Elway (33-45/418y, TD, INT) truly was brilliant—in ignominious defeat. Stanford (0-1) scored on its opening possession on FB Mike Dotterer's 3y TD run. Purdue (1-0) TB Jimmy Smith matched that with 100y KO TD RET. Smith scored twice more on 1y rushes, while Boilermakers QB Scott Campbell completed lofty 14-18/177y, including 28y scoring pass to WR Steve Bryant to ice game. Hampered by

1st H loss of HB Darrin Nelson to hip pointer, Cardinals twice lost FUMs at Purdue 1YL in 2nd H and squandered 2 drives in 4th Q that cracked Purdue's 20YL. Cards K Mark Harmon booted school-record 59y FG.

NOTRE DAME 27 Louisiana State 9: Coach Gerry Faust's debut at Notre Dame (1-0) fared well and offered no clue to his unfortunate future in South Bend. Faust unleashed his former Moeller High School standouts, WB Tony Hunter, QB Tim Koegel, WR Dave Condeni, and LB Bob Crable, on reeling Bayou Bengals (0-2). Hunter scored on ground and on pass, rushing for 42y and catching 2/40y, while Crable made 13 tackles and was especially magnificent during 2nd GLS when he contributed 3 stops. Koegel came off bench to hit 6-7/101y and 7y TD pass to Condeni. Notre Dame D forced 4 TOs, had 5 sacks, and allowed only 61y passing. Tigers sub RB Eric Martin rushed for 50y, including 26y scoring jaunt in 4th Q.

KANSAS 19 Oregon 10: Ahead 7-0 on early 6y TD run by TB Kerwin Bell (21/91y), Jayhawks (2-0) D came through with 4th down stop of Oregon (0-2) FB Terrance Jones on Ducks 29YL. Oregon's decision to go for 1st down in its territory proved costly: Kansas QB Frank Seurer threw 22y TD pass to WR Bob Johnson for 2-TD lead. Oregon rallied to 31y FG by K Doug Jollymour and 1y TD run by TB Reggie Brown for 14-10 H deficit as sharp QB Kevin Lusk (17-29/133y) completed 12-15 in 1st H. Despite gaining only 102y O in 2nd H, Kansas added pts on 32y FG by K Bruce Kallmeyer, while Oregon was blanked and surrendered safety on sack of Lusk.

1 Notre Dame (24)	1233	11 Michigan	560
2 Southern California (12)	1181	12 Alabama	538
3 Oklahoma (12)	1153	13 Brigham Young	439
4 Georgia (12)	1113	14 Mississippi State	397
5 Penn State (1)	996	15 Washington	313
6 Texas (1)	963	16 Miami	311
7 Pittsburgh	763	17 Nebraska	276
8 Ohio State	710	18 Arizona State	275
9 UCLA	690	19 Florida State	232
10 North Carolina	661	20 Wisconsin	174

September 19, 1981

BOSTON COLLEGE 13 Texas A&M 12: Wild 4th Q ended with Boston College (1-0) in front by slimmest of margins. With 11:30 left and Texas A&M (1-1) leading 12-7, Aggies HB Johnny Hector lost FUM deep in own territory after strip by Eagles DT Joe Ferraro, recovered by LB Jim Budness. TB Leo Smith's 5y TD run 2 plays later put Eagles up by 13-12, but that hardly was end to excitement. Later in 4th Q, BC botched punt that Aggies recovered on 17YL. A&M gained 7y but blew winning 27y FG attempt with high snap that allowed Eagles DB Vic Crawford split-second he needed to block 3-ptr. Texas A&M had another stab at victory, but DB Tony Thurman picked off desperation pass to seal win in coach Jack Bicknell's 1st game. Aggies FB Earnest Jackson led runners with 98y, 1y more than total of BC's Smith.

CLEMSON 13 Georgia 3: For Bulldogs (2-1), disastrous 9 TOs meant end to their 15-game win streak. TB Herschel Walker gained 111y on 28 tough carries, but was kept out of EZ and lost 3 FUMs. Walker's 1st Q FUM at Clemson (3-0) 13YL was most crucial. Walker credited Death Valley faithful for disrupting his concentration. QB Buck Belue needed someone to blame after tossing 5 INTs, 2nd of which was returned by S Tim Childers to Georgia 18YL to set up game's only TD. Four plays later, Tigers QB Homer Jordan threw 8y TD pass to WR Perry Tuttle, who brilliantly kept his feet inbounds as rest of his body veered OB. Tigers K Donald Igwebuike added FGs of 30y and 39y, while K Kevin Butler's 40y FG provided all of Georgia's scoring. Tigers lifted their record to 2-0 when inspired by wearing of orange pants to match jerseys, including win over South Carolina at end of 1980 season.

OHIO STATE 27 Michigan State 13: Although there was confusion over who called play, Ohio State (2-0) clinched win when QB Bob Atha went 27y to EZ on sneak up middle to close scoring late in 4th Q. Buckeyes received big plays from QBs throughout game as QB Art Schlichter (12-22/155y, INT), who left game late in 3rd Q with ankle sprain, threw picture-perfect 46y TD pass to WR Gary Williams (5/104y) to open scoring in 1st Q. Ohio State soon converted pair of INTs into 10 pts and commanding 17-0 H lead. Spartans (0-2) looked sharp on 84y drive in 3rd Q that QB John Leister (15-37/213y, 3 INTs) capped with 4th down 38y TD pass to wide-open TE Terry Tanker. Other bright spot for Michigan State was K Morten Andersen's Big 10 record 63y FG, his 2nd of game, to erase 59y best of former Ohio State K Tom Skladany, which he set in 1975.

MICHIGAN 25 Notre Dame 7: Michigan (1-1) WR Anthony Carter (3/99y) was unstoppable, catching 2 TD passes and dominating on returns. Carter's 1st score was 71y catch of QB Steve Smith's throw on 3rd-and-20 early in 2nd Q for 7-0 lead. Carter doubled score to 14-0 in 3rd Q with 16y TD reception. Notre Dame found it difficult to rally thanks to poor field position: nearly dozen possessions for Fighting Irish (1-1) began, at best, from their 25YL. To blame were Carter's brilliant RETs, TB Butch Woolfolk's rushing (23/139y), and Michigan's stifling D. Wolverines easily won y battle by 407y to 213y. Notre Dame WB Tony Hunter caught 5/72y.

IOWA STATE 23 Iowa 12: Iowa State (2-0) TB Dwayne Crutchfield (36/147y) sparkled in front of largest home crowd to date in Ames. On 1st play of game, Crutchfield blasted for 40y, to jumpstart 71y drive to QB John Quinn's 7y scoring keeper. Cyclones built 17-0 lead in 2nd Q on 1 of 3 FGs by K Alex Giffords and Crutchfield's 3y TD run, which was set up by 44y completion to TE Dan Johnson from Quinn (6-8/106y). Iowa (1-1) managed 1y TD run by TB Eddie Phillips on final play of 1st H but Iowa State D permitted only 79y rushing which ended rally hopes.

NEBRASKA 34 Florida State 14: Nebraska (1-1) avenged 1980 upset as IB Roger Craig rushed 20/234y. Craig's biggest play closed scoring and put dagger in heart of hopeful Florida State (2-1). Craig's magic came on 94y TD scamper, only 1 play

after he mistakenly stepped OB on KO RET. Another key stretch occurred in 3rd Q as Nebraska special teams transformed 10-7 struggle into 17-pt lead at 24-7: Seminoles P Rohn Stark bombed 63y punt only to have Nebraska WB Irving Fryar return it 82y for TD, and on ensuing KO, Huskers DE Tony Felici made TD RET of TB Greg Allen's FUM, caused by jarring hit by LB Mike Knox. FSU QB Rick Stockstill threw for 173y in futile attempt to rally his team in opening chapter of Seminoles' "Death March" road schedule that would take them to 5 tough venues: Lincoln, Columbus, South Bend, Pittsburgh, and Baton Rouge.

SAN JOSE STATE 28 STANFORD 6: Superb Stanford (0-2) QB John Elway's jr season quickly turned into nightmare as his badly sprained right ankle prompted 6-24 /72y, 5 INTs passing performance. Without his usual mobility, Elway was sacked 7 times, 4 by San Jose State LB Bob Overly. Benefiting from injury, oddly, was Elway's father, Jack, who was victorious Spartans (2-1) coach. HB Gerald Willhite (28/116y) and QB Steve Clarkson (19-32/181y, 2 TDs, INT) led Spartans' winning O. Game marked 1st time in 37 games that Stanford failed to score on any pass play. Afterwards, Elway announced his signing with New York Yankees that allowed him to retain his football eligibility at Stanford while playing minor league baseball. Elway's baseball deal later allowed him room to negotiate when he balked at signing with NFL Colts, who tapped him in 1983 draft.

1 Southern California (46)	1258	11 Brigham Young	554
2 Oklahoma (15)	1203	12 Mississippi State	549
3 Penn State (1)	1092	13 Notre Dame	548
4 Texas (1)	1038	14 Miami	439
5 Pittsburgh	976	15 Nebraska	412
6 UCLA	912	16 Washington	378
7 Michigan (1)	903	17 Georgia	365
8 Ohio State	832	18 Arizona State	265
9 North Carolina	806	19 Clemson	227
10 Alabama	556	20 Southern Methodist	125

September 26, 1981

MISSISSIPPI STATE 28 Florida 7: Bulldogs (3-0) O and special teams each scored twice and blitzing D sparkled. HB Michael Haddix had 2 rushing TDs, WR Glen Young returned punt 49y to Gator (2-2) EZ and special teamer Bobby Jenkins added 3y TD RET of blocked punt. Gators were held to 146y passing, -10y rushing, and meager 9 1st downs under pressure from Mississippi State, which blitzed Florida's Run-and-Shoot O about half of time. D recorded 10 sacks and 5 INTs. Florida QB Wayne Peace (15-26/117y, TD, 2 INTs) slipped in TD pass to WR Spencer Jackson.

IOWA 20 Ucla 7: Aggressive Hawkeyes (2-1) D overwhelmed Bruins, who played without injured TB Kevin Nelson and WR Cormac Carney. UCLA (2-1) could manage paltry 121y O with 35y rushing, and 7 1st downs, while committing 5 TOs. Iowa sacked QB Tom Ramsey 6 times, but produced TD when LB Andre Tippett and DE Brad Webb converged to create EZ FUM that DT Mark Bortz pounced on for TD. Although producing only 16y TD run by QB Pete Gales, Iowa O ate lots of clock and dominated field position with help from long skyward parabolas of P Reggie Roby.

PENN STATE 30 NEBRASKA 24: Shorty Miller's 1912 Penn State record for single game rushing of 250y (against Carnegie Tech) remained intact. But not without threat by TB Curt Warner, who exploded for 238y in leading Nittany Lions (2-0) back thrice from deficits. K Brian Franco set Penn State school record with 5 FGs, while FB Joel Cole scored winning TD on 2y run in 4th Q. Teams combined for 811y—414y by Penn State—but each also lost 3 FUMs. Nebraska (1-2) IB Roger Craig rushed for 124y and QB Mark Mauer came off bench to throw 2 TDs, but neither could prevent loss that marked Cornhuskers' poorest start since 1960.

SOUTHERN CALIFORNIA 28 Oklahoma 24: Southern California (3-0) rallied with 2 4th Q TDs to beat Sooners in highly-anticipated but sloppy match-up of teams ranked nos. 1 and 2, 1st such meeting since 1979 Sugar Bowl. Also, coaches Barry Switzer (.894) of Oklahoma and John Robinson (.850) of USC entered game as top 2 active coaches in win-percentage. TE Fred Cornwall went from goat to hero as Trojans frantically marched toward Oklahoma GL at game's end. Moments after he inadvertently deflected pass that was headed for open TB Marcus Allen, Cornwall caught 7y TD pass from QB John Mazur (13-25/149y 2 TDs) with 2 secs left for win. It was Cornwall's 2nd career reception. Allen topped 200y-rushing (208y) for 3rd straight game and added 2 TDs. Sooners (1-1) were self-destructive in 4 FUMs—often with no Trojan anywhere nearby—losing 5, while focused USC went entire game without TO. Nonetheless powerful Oklahoma led 24-14 in 4th Q as its dynamic run game totaled 307y and WR Bobby Grayson had 4/118y.

WASHINGTON STATE 24 Arizona State 21: K Kevin Morris booted 29y FG with 5:18 left for winning pts as Cougars (3-0) continued outstanding start to season. Washington State raced to 21-6 lead before Arizona State (2-1) rallied with 2 TDs in 3rd Q to tie it 21-21. QB Clete Casper (8-14/110y) marched Cougars from own 31YL to Arizona State 13YL, from where Morris supplied his kicking heroics. Big plays set up Wazzu for 3 TDs in 1st H, 2 following pair of Sun Devils TOs and another after Cougars WR Paul Escalera threw surprise 45y pass. Devils, now 0-4 all-time when playing in state of Washington, gained 478y with majority coming in 14-pt 3rd Q: HB Willie Gittens scored on 21y run, and FB Gerald Riggs (13/136y) raced 59y to set up 9y TD pass from QB Mike Pagel (12-26/159y, INT) to WR Eric Redenius.

October 3, 1981

West Virginia 38 BOSTON COLLEGE 10: QB Oliver Luck threw and ran for TDs as Mountaineers (4-0) had their 1st 4-0 start since 1975. Luck's accuracy was off (10-25/161y, INT), but West Virginia rushers gained 243y. WVU D picked off 4 BC (1-2) passes, even though Eagles began by converting their own INT by S Vic Crawford into 48y FG by K John Cooper for 3-0 lead. Riding TB Shelby Gamble (21/97y), Boston College began moving smoothly until disaster struck: QB John Loughery tried to force screen pass that was picked off by LB Jeff Seals and returned 41y for 7-3 lead. Mountaineers then exploded for 31 straight pts to put away mistake-riddled BC.

Missouri 14 MISSISSIPPI STATE 3: Battle of early-season unbeatens went way of Tigers (4-0) as HB Bobby Meyer and QB Mike Hyde sparkled. Meyer (26/122y) scored both TDs, on 4y run in 1st Q and game-sealing 2y reception in 4th Q with only 1:31 left. Hyde (20-34/191y) threw TD in engineering upset of Bulldogs (3-1), completing 7y pass on 4th-and-2 to WR James Caver to keep clinching drive alive. No. 9 Mississippi State (3-1), which took short-lived 3-0 lead in 1st Q on 42y FG by K Dana Moore, struggled to gain 237y O with FB Al Rickey Edwards toting 99y rushing.

Florida State 36 OHIO STATE 27: Florida State (3-1) QB Rick Stockstill returned victoriously to his home state, exacting revenge against Ohio State (3-1) coaching staff that neglected to recruit him. Stockstill (25-41/299y, 2 TDs) led balanced attack in school's 1st match-up against Big 10 opponent. Buckeyes QB Art Schlichter's 453y passing set school mark for game y, eclipsing John Borton's 312y in 1952. That was all well and good but Ohio's ground game, its normal bread-and-butter, could only muster 38y—to 197y for FSU—and Buckeyes were sent packing. Ohio State WR Gary Williams caught 13/220y, including 52y TD catch in 2nd Q.

OKLAHOMA 7 Iowa State 7: TB Dwayne Crutchfield bulled his way in from 3YL in 4th Q to tie game and keep upstart Cyclones (3-0-1) undefeated. Crutchfield did yeoman's work, rumbling for 43/171y as Iowa State did its best to keep ball away from Sooners. Once again, TOs did in Sooners (1-1-1), who lost 5 FUMs and had 2 passes picked off by aggressive Cyclones D. Cyclones S John Arnaud's INT RET to OU 46YL set up tying TD. K Alex Giffords blew 23y FG attempt at 1:08 left, and last-sec 62y FG try went wide for ISU. FB Stanley Wilson led Oklahoma with 157y rushing, while HB Steve Sewell scored Sooners' sole TD on 16y run in 1st Q.

TEXAS CHRISTIAN 28 Arkansas 24: QB Steve Stamp hooked up with WR Stanley Washington on 2 TD passes within 80 secs in 4th Q to produce upset for Horned Frogs (2-2) that broke 22-game series losing streak. Trailing 24-13 with less than 5:20 remaining and ball on its own 1YL, TCU's prospects looked bleak. Stamp came out firing, hitting WR Phillip Epps twice to get past midfield, and Washington, who previously had been shut out, for 2 straight completions including 22y TD. Arkansas (3-1) quickly fumbled, and moments later Stamp found Washington in EZ for 15y TD. Hogs QB Tom Jones had tossed 2 TDs to build once-comfortable lead.

HOUSTON 24 Baylor 3: Defending against unknown players never was easy, and Baylor (4-2) was forced to adapt to Cougars (3-1) newcomers. Houston FB David Barrett, who had total of 8 carries in 1st 3 games of season due to foot injury, dusted himself off to rush 25/104y, while QB Lionel Wilson (12-17/142y), in only his 2nd start, threw 5y TD pass to FB Alan Polk and rushed for 79y. Cougars O played clutch ball, converting 8-9 3rd downs in 1st H and 14-20 overall. Houston D excelled against Bears (4-2) O, holding HB Walter Abercrombie to 34y and team that scored at least 4 TDs in its past 3 games to K Marty Jimmerson's 28y FG. "It doesn't take a genius to see that they physically whipped us," said losing coach Grant Teaff.

BRIGHAM YOUNG 32 Utah State 26: With QB Jim McMahon out with knee injury, Cougars' 16-game win streak appeared vulnerable. Upstart Aggies (2-3) drove 65y to take 7-0 lead on QB Chico Canales' 14y TD pass to WR Nate Jones. At this point, Brigham Young (5-0) was losing for 1st time in 1981 and had to rally behind untested, backup QB. Of course, sub QB in question was none other than QB Steve Young—yes, Cougars had 2 future Super Bowl-winning QBs on roster—and this great-great-great-great grandson of Brigham Young threw for 307y and ran for 63y. In 4th Q, Young audibled into play that sprung FB Waymon Hamilton on 42y run that tied game at 26-26. BYU D then turned in game-winning TD as LB Todd Shell picked off screen pass and ran 12y for TD with 3:30 left.

Arizona State 26 WASHINGTON 7: Frosh K Luis Zendejas nailed school-record 4 FGs to lead Arizona State (3-1) past defending Pac 10 champs. Zendejas, perfect on season on 8 FG and 11 x-pt tries, stole spotlight from Huskies (3-1) K Chuck Nelson, who missed only attempt and lost NCAA record-tying streak of 14 games in row with at least 1 FG. Sun Devils QB Mike Pagel was non-kicking star, completing 13-23/183y and 4y TD pass to WR Willie Gittens as Arizona State glided to 16-0 H lead. Washington cracked EZ in 3rd Q on 20y TD pass by QB Steve Pelluer to WR Aaron Williams.

October 10, 1981

NAVY 30 Air Force 13: TB Eddie Meyers was back from injury list to spark Navy (3-2) coach George Welsh's school-record 51st win. Workhorse Meyers rushed 38/179y as Welsh passed 50 wins of Eddie Erdelatz, his coach when he was Navy QB in mid-1950s. QB Marco Paganelli added 106y rushing and aerial TD as Middies built 17-0 lead and scored game's final 10 pts to quell brief Air Force (1-4) rally. Falcons HB George James rushed for team-high 75y and 1y TD run in 4th Q that pulled Air Force to within 20-13. Navy K Steve Fehr made 3 FGs and 3 x-pts.

Pittsburgh 17 WEST VIRGINIA 0: With QB Dan Marino, nation's leading passer, sidelined with bruised right arm, Panthers (4-0) were in bind going into annual "Backyard Brawl" to be played in front of largest-ever West Virginia sports crowd to date. Pitt O proved adaptable to any situation by staying on ground—rushing 59 times while completing no passes in 6 tries—while Panthers D excelled as usual. S Tom Flynn had 2 INTs and forced crucial FUM that helped Pitt defend its 3YL. Pitt FB Wayne DiBartola led way with 33/103y. Mountaineers (4-1) QB Oliver Luck's fortune was mostly bad as he completed 16-36/92y while on run from pursuers.

ALABAMA 13 Southern Mississippi 13: Odd late decision by legendary coach Bear Bryant cost Alabama (4-1-1) dearly. With time elapsing, QB Reggie Collier (14-25/202y) completed 4 passes to move Southern Miss (4-0-1) from own 20YL to Alabama's 24YL, whereby K Steve Clark booted tying 40y FG. Eagles may not have had time for Clark's kick had Bryant not taken timeout with 8 secs left. Crimson Tide rushed for 273y, with sole TD coming in 3rd Q on 32y run with pitchout by HB Joe Carter. Collier tied game in 4th Q with 5y scoring run before teams traded FGs.

WISCONSIN 24 Ohio State 21: Badgers (4-1) QB Jess Cole made infrequent passes, but he made them count. Wisconsin snapped 21-game losing streak to Ohio State as Cole's only two completions went for TDs. Buckeyes (3-2) blew 14-6 lead, surrendering 11 pts in 18-sec black hole at end of 1st H; as it happened all 4 Badgers scores followed Ohio State TOs. Go-ahead pts at 17-14 came on K Wendell Gladem's 50y FG. Badgers stretched lead to 24-14 in 4th Q on Cole's 10y TD pass to WR Thad McFadden. QB Art Schlichter threw for 151y but was held without TD and intercepted twice. Ohio State scored on pass play when backup QB Bob Atha, lining up at WR, threw 34y TD to WR Gary Williams. For 1st time ever, Wisconsin had beaten Ohio State, Michigan, and Purdue in same season.

Texas 34 Oklahoma 14 (Dallas): Was Wishbone dead? Longhorns (4-0) D stymied Oklahoma's attack by surrendering only 194y, 64y in 2nd H they dominated 31-0. Both Sooners (1-2-1) TDs came on short drives (16 and 34y) following Texas TOs, so Oklahoma's ball control O indeed was out of whack. Play of game was turned in by Texas DT Kenneth Sims and DE Eric Holle, who combined to stop Sooners QB Kelly Phelps on 4th-and-1 keeper from Texas 27YL with Oklahoma ahead 14-13 in 3rd Q. Longhorns then marched 69y to winning 36y TD pass from QB Rick McIvor to WR Maurice McCloney. Texas TB A.J. Jones was leading rusher with 134y, while FB Stanley Wilson led Sooners with 85y on ground. Oklahoma fell below break-even W-L record for 1st time under coach Barry Switzer.

Oklahoma State 20 KANSAS 7: With O-line held together by band-aids, Jayhawks (4-1) managed only 125y O in dropping from ranks of unbeatens. Cowboys took advantage of injuries to 2 starters along Kansas O-line by sacking QB Frank Seurer 7 times and holding him to only 93y passing. Oklahoma State (3-1) enjoyed short TD runs by TB Shawn Jones and QB John Doerner and 2 FGs by frosh K Larry Roach, including school-record 56y effort. "This was the worst we have ever been," said losing coach Don Fambrough. "This was embarrassing."

Nevada-Las Vegas 45 BRIGHAM YOUNG 41: Coming in, Cougars owned their highest ranking to date, 8th in AP Poll. Last-sec 20y TD pass by QB Sam King to TE Jim Sandusky vaulted UNLV (4-2) to upset over depleted Cougars (5-1), who missed 7 starters. Rebels rallied from 41-24 deficit behind King, who completed 31-54/473y and 2 TDs. BYU QB Steve Young threw for 269y and TD. Loss snapped Brigham Young's 17-game win streak, longest current streak in country. Each QB had 4 INTs, while BYU added 4 FUMs to losing mix. Both team also had 12 PENs.

Arizona 13 SOUTHERN CALIFORNIA 10: Wildcats, 3-TD underdog, stunned top-ranked USC (4-1) behind passing of Burbank native QB Tom Tunnicliffe (21-37/293y, TD, 2 INTs) and inspired Arizona D. Vaunted Trojans O could not score if it was not on field, and Arizona (3-2) did its best to keep them off by winning time of possession battle by 14 mins. Tunnicliffe hit WR Vance Johnson on 13y winning TD pass in 3rd Q in which Southern California could only manage 7 plays on O. TB Marcus Allen (26/211y) went past 200y rushing level for record-extending 5th straight game, but he was fairly well contained after 74y TD gallop in 1st Q.

AP Poll October 12

1 Texas (35)	1274	11 Florida State	591
2 Penn State (24)	1262	12 Iowa	558
3 Pittsburgh (3)	1192	13 Miami	481
4 North Carolina (4)	1126	14 Wisconsin	427
5 Michigan	898	15 Alabama	358
6 Clemson	889	16 Mississippi State	344
7 Southern California	874	17 Brigham Young	220
8 Missouri	824	18 Washington State	195
9 Georgia	765	19 Nebraska	161
10 Southern Methodist	629	20 Arizona State	125

October 17, 1981

PITTSBURGH 42 Florida State 14: QB Dan Marino threw for 251y and 3 TDs and TB Bryan Thomas rushed for 217y as Pittsburgh (5-0) erased memories of upset to Florida State in 1980, which was last time Panthers had lost. Panthers built 21-0 lead in 1st H with unconventional TDs: bruising FB Wayne DiBartola's 22y run after catching short pass, LB Sal Sunseri's 22y INT RET, and S Tom Flynn's 83y punt RET. DiBartola's TD was game's 1st, and it capped 99y drive that was launched after 4th-and-goal stop by Pitt D on Florida State (4-2) FB Mike Whiting. Ahead 21-7 at H, Marino jumped on Seminoles in 3rd Q with 2 TD passes to WR Julius Dawkins. Featuring near-perfect balance, Pitt gained 252y rushing and 251y passing. QBs Rick Stockstill and Blair Williams combined for 235y passing for Florida State, but were sacked 8 times by Panthers D that forced 5 TOs. Marino set Pitt career marks for completions (308) and passing y (4219y).

North Carolina 21 NORTH CAROLINA STATE 10: Trailing for 1st time all season, Tar Heels (6-0) rode HB Tyrone Anthony, subbing for injured HB Kelvin Bryant, to win. Anthony rushed for 133y and TD, while Wolfpack contributed to own demise with series of 2nd H boners. Failed onside-KO, lost FUM, and blocked punt all led to North Carolina TDs. By game's end, NC State (4-2) easily had outgained it rivals, 376y to 288y, and had enjoyed 10-0 lead at H after 46y TD pass from QB Tol Avery (20-34/204y, INT) to TE Rufus Friday and 19y FG by K Todd Auten. In its exuberance, Wolfpack opened 2nd H with ill-fated onside-KO that jumpstarted UNC, which immediately drove 51y in 10 plays to FB Alan Burrus' 1y TD run.

Iowa 9 MICHIGAN 7: Surprising Hawkeyes passed Michigan (4-2) in Rose Bowl race. QB Gordy Bohannon (10-19/127y) engineered Iowa's victory, driving his charges to 3 FGs by frosh K Tom Nichol. It was Iowa's 1st series win since 1962. Iowa (5-1) held ball for almost 37 mins, preventing Wolverines TB Butch Woolfolk and WR Anthony Carter from doing much damage. Woolfolk tallied only 56y rushing, and Carter broke no big plays, although he scored on 17y TD pass from QB Steve Smith. Coupled with Wisconsin's 33-14 loss to Michigan State, win put Hawkeyes atop Big 10 standings.

IOWA STATE 34 Missouri 13: Despite sprained ankle and twisted knee, TB Dwayne Crutchfield rushed for 3 TDs and 98y to lead Iowa State (4-1-1). QB John Quinn was brilliant (20-32/226y, INT) as Cyclones bounced back from 52-31 loss to San Diego State week before. Iowa State came out on fire, running up 180y in 1st Q, including 41y TD pass by Quinn to future NFL personnel guru WR Vinny Cerrato for 14-0 lead. Tigers (5-1) lost 5 TOs—4 leading to scores—with QB Mike Hyde tossing 3 INTs. Missouri was at its best on 98y drive in 2nd Q that was capped by Hyde's 2y TD run.

Southern Methodist 38 HOUSTON 22: Southern Methodist (6-0) used pair of 4th Q INT TD RETs to break open close game in grabbing SWC lead. S Wes Hopkins and S James Mobley each scored in 4th Q as SMU stretched 17-14 lead to 38-14. Houston (3-3) negated its 25 1st downs and 296y rushing and 159y passing—easily topping Ponies in each category—with whopping 9 TOs (4 FUMs, 5 INTs). Hopkins had year's worth of picks himself with 4. TB Eric Dickerson rushed for 109y and 2 TDs to lead Mustangs O that converted only once in 15 tries on 3rd down. Cougars QB Lionel Wilson rushed for 120y and passed for 159y.

ARKANSAS 42 Texas 11: Longhorns (4-1) enjoyed brief stay atop national rankings as they were ambushed by Arkansas (5-1), falling behind 15-0 before registering single 1st down. Hogs showcased opportunistic O and punishing D that kept Texas out of EZ until 4th Q. By that time, Razorbacks were romping with 39-3 advantage: QB Tom Jones ran for 2 TDs and threw for another, while RB Gary Anderson scored twice. Field position killed Texas, whose starting point on O averaged own 12YL. Falling behind forced Horns to throw 51 times, of which they completed only 21. Texas suffered 7 TOs, including 4 INTs of QB Rick McIvor. Loss was worst to Arkansas in 43 years, prior damage coming in 1938 by 42-6.

AP Poll October 19

1 Penn State (36.5)	1283.5	11 Alabama	559
2 Pittsburgh (26.5)	1277.5	12 Arkansas	479
3 North Carolina (3)	1155	13 Brigham Young	413
4 Clemson	1033	14 Iowa State	410
5 Southern California	994	15 Nebraska	346
6 Iowa	928	16 Washington State	335
7 Georgia	902	17 Arizona State	326
8 Southern Methodist	848	18 Michigan	298
9 Mississippi State	641	19 Missouri	267
10 Texas	618	20 Florida State	147

October 24, 1981

PENN STATE 30 West Virginia 7: Newly anointed no. 1 Penn State (6-0) looked part, especially in 2nd H when it outscored visitors 20-0. While O adjusted to absence of TB Curt Warner (pulled hamstring), Nittany Lions D sparkled in holding Mountaineers (5-2) rushers to 38y and containing damage done by QB Oliver Luck (24-39/226y, INT). Penn State O eventually came around as soph TB Jon Williams rushed for 140y, TD, in sub role. West Virginia tied game 7-7 in 2nd Q on 54y TD pass to WR Rich Hollins from Luck, who set school records for career pass completions (360) and TDs passes (47).

MARYLAND 24 Duke 21: Despite absence of 5 injured D starters, Duke (3-4) nearly overcame 21-7 deficit when K Scott McKinney missed tying 42y FG attempt with 2 secs left. Blue Devils grabbed 7-0 lead as QB Ben Bennett (31-46/397y) threw 28y TD pass to WR Cedric Jones (6/183y). Terps (3-3-1) answered as DB Tim Quander raced 92y with KO RET. Maryland took 2-TD lead before 1st Q ended as TB Charlie Wysocki, who ignored bruised shoulder to rush for 143y, burst for TD runs of 54 and 17y. Each team scored again before end of 1st H as Maryland took 24-14 lead. Bennett rallied Duke in 4th Q, throwing 23y TD pass to Jones and moving Devils to Terps 26YL at game's end. Wysocki became Maryland's all-time rusher with 3045y.

CLEMSON 17 North Carolina State 7: Wolfpack (4-3) converted early FUM into 7-0 lead against no. 4 Clemson (7-0). That score, RB Larmount Lawson's 13y run, represented 1st rushing TD to be allowed by Tigers D so far this season. As game wore on, Tigers D dominated to prompt their taking 10-7 H lead on 39y FG by K Donald Igwebuike and 1y TD run by TB Cliff Austin, that came with only 13 secs left in 2nd Q. NC State, sharp in 1st Q with 100y O and 7 1st downs, was held without another 1st down for 35-min stretch in middle of game. Clemson failed to pull away because of 5 TOs, which hindered attack that mounted 304y rushing. Clemson LB Jeff Davis paced D, participating in 19 tackles.

South Carolina 31 NORTH CAROLINA 13: North Carolina's numerous injuries finally took toll as Gamecocks (5-3) convincingly won battle of Carolinas. Starting without injured RBs Kelvin Bryant and Tyrone Anthony and D leader, LB Darrell Nicholson, was bad enough, but Tar Heels (6-1) lost QB Rod Elkins to ankle injury in 1st Q. New UNC faces translated to committing 5 TOs—to none for Gamecocks—by Heels team that made only 8 to date. South Carolina QB Gordon Beckham (16-17/195y) was perfect in 1st H, completing 11-11 passes with TD. TB Johnnie Wright added 115y rushing, while frosh LB James Seawright sparkled with 12 unassisted tackles and INT. Tar Heels had to get tricky to break 70y TD on run by P Jeff Hayes.

Minnesota 12 IOWA 10: Premature Rose Bowl talk for Iowa was put on hold as Minnesota (5-2) K Jim Gallery's 4 FGs, including 52y boot, proved to be difference. Gallery's final FG success, from 27y out with 2:22 remaining, won game for Gophers. Behind throwing of QB Mike Hohensee (16-28/171y, INT), Minnesota led 9-0 at H as its D held Iowa (5-2) to 45y total O and pair of 1st downs. Hawkeyes quickly scored 10 pts in 3rd Q, with TD from TB Paul Blatcher on 2y run, but could then only threaten to stretch slim lead until Gallery ended it. Iowa K Tom Nichol, who hit 34y effort earlier, missed 2 late attempts. Most predictable of all collegiate leagues recently, Big 10 could boast of 9 teams still in hunt for title. Fans clearly were enjoying newfound parity; all 5 conf games on this Saturday were sold-out.

ILLINOIS 23 Wisconsin 21: Illinois (4-3) QB Tony Eason (26-38/357y) dazzled with 3 TDs, including 86y scoring hook-up in 2nd Q with WR Oliver Williams (7/142y) that gave Illini lead for good at 10-7. On that big play, Badgers CB Von Mansfield and S Matt Vanden Boom collided going for ball, leaving Williams alone at Badgers 45YL. Eason was perhaps at best on 5y pass later in same Q, converting 4th down with TD toss to RB Darrell Smith (9/76y receiving) as Illini ignored chance for chip-shot FG. Smith later caught 16y TD pass in 3rd Q for eventual winning pts. Wisconsin QB Jess Cole threw for 169y and 2 TDs, but lost 2 crucial 2nd H TOs. Eason now had topped 300y for all 5 Big 10 games he has started, tying conf career record.

Southern California 14 NOTRE DAME 7: Fighting Irish (2-4) nearly pulled upset, but their relative containment of Trojans (6-1) TB Marcus Allen was used against them. Over-zealous Notre Dame D that held Allen to 147y, his lowest rushing output of year, was fooled on 4th Q counter play that FB Todd Spencer (7/74y) took to winning 26y TD run. Notre Dame had tied game at 7-7 in 3rd Q on 5y run by TB Phil Carter, game's leading rusher with 161y, but blew other opportunities as K Harry Oliver missed FG attempts of 20 and 24y. Also, each of ND's last 2 drives was stopped on 4th-and-1: Carter's run to USC 33YL and QB Blair Kiel's lost FUM at Trojans 25YL with 11 ticks left. Both TD drives for Southern California featured big plays: QB John Mazur's 24y dash was big part of 69y trip to Allen's 14y TD run, and Allen's 21y jaunt led to Spencer's game-winning gallop.

Nebraska 6 MISSOURI 0: Big 8 hadn't seen scoreless impasse since Oklahoma State tied Air Force in 1967. This 0-0 struggle was knotted until last series by Nebraska (5-2). Cornhuskers QB Turner Gill hit 3 passes in row that ended with FB Phil Bates scoring from 3YL with 23 secs left. Gill's throws included 24y strike to WR Todd Brown when Huskers faced 3rd-and-10 from midfield. Missouri (5-2) D did fairly well against prolific Nebraska run attack, holding it to 222y, that was led by IB Roger Craig's 94y. Tigers netted only 85y on ground, thanks in large part to 10 sacks by Nebraska D. Huskers K Kevin Seibel had rough day in stiff wind: he missed x-pt and 3 FGs, including 16y 3-pt try into strong zephyr. HB Bobby Meyer paced Tigers O with 87y rushing and 4/38y receiving.

Texas 9 SOUTHERN METHODIST 7: SMU (6-1) entered key SWC contest scoring 39 pts per game, but became all too familiar with DT Kenneth Sims (15 tackles, 4 sacks) and his friends on Longhorns D. Texas (5-1) dominated line of scrimmage to hold TB Eric Dickerson to 18/33y with 2 lost FUMs and QB Lance McIlhenny to 5-15 passing with 2 INTs. Texas O was not whole lot better, gaining only 177y, but managing 3 FGs by K Raul Allegre, including 52y effort. Pair of Allegre's FGs followed FUMs by Dickerson. Horns P John Goodson also excelled, booming 3 punts more than 50y to significantly influence field position. Texas became 7th school in college history to reach 600 victories.

Houston 20 ARKANSAS 17: Cougars (4-3) scrambled SWC race by scoring game's final 13 pts. Decision-maker came on K Mike Clendenen's 17y FG with 5:16 left to play. Arkansas (5-2) QB Bill Pierce entered game in 1st H after QB Tom Jones sprained

his knee, and Pierce suffered INT by Houston CB Butch LaCroix to poise McClenden for winning FG. When he was in there, Jones had led Arkansas on scoring drives capped with TD passes of 17y to RB Gary Anderson and 3y to WR John Mistler. Houston QB Lionel Wilson threw for 141y, TD, and rushed for 87y, TD. Arkansas continued to have never beaten both Texas and Houston in same season.

WYOMING 33 Brigham Young 20: Cowboys (5-2) ran roughshod over BYU in Rockies snowstorm, totaling 350y on ground—more than 3 times amount averaged against Cougars D. QB Phil Davis rushed for 140y, including TD runs of 28, 30, and 32y, and teamed with WR James Williams on 81y passing play that gave Wyoming its 1st lead at 21-14. BYU (6-2) had scored opening 2 TDs behind QB Jim McMahon (29-47/393y, INT), who set 3 more NCAA records to push count to 41 in his illustrious career. Taking to running ball, Cowboys next reeled off 5 straight TDs.

October 31, 1981

YALE 24 Dartmouth 3: Although these Ivy League rivals would end up sharing conf crown because Yale would later be upset by Princeton, Elis (7-0) easily defeated Dartmouth (3-4), which lost for 1st time in conf play. Bulldogs 6'4" WR Curt Grieve (6/72y) twice soared over Big Green 5'11" DB Charles Williams to snare short TD passes from QB John Rogan (12-21/115y, INT). Grieve's 2nd scoring reception came at end of 89y drive in 2nd Q and broke 3-3 deadlock. Dartmouth made it thrice inside Yale's 10YL in 2nd Q, only to make K Tim Geibel's FG, lose EZ INT, and cough up FUM by QB Frank Polsinello (9-20/95y, 3 INTs).

MIAMI 17 Penn State 14: There were no Halloween treats for coach Joe Paterno in Orange Bowl stadium as his Nittany Lions (6-1) became 5th team to lose this season while occupying top-ranked spot in AP poll. Miami (5-2) QB Jim Kelly (13-25/220y) posted his 2nd win against Penn State, hooking up with WR Larry Brodsky on 80y TD pass in 1st H that produced 17-0 lead when added to K Danny Miller's 3 FGs. Hurricanes D-line was impressive, holding banged-up TB Curt Warner to 21y on ground and entire Penn State team to uncharacteristic 69y rushing. Lions rallied behind QB Todd Blackledge (26-41/358y, 2 INTs), who threw 2 TD passes within 2 min span of 4th Q, but were hindered by K Brian Franco's missing 4 FGs. Penn State's final drive was ended by INT by ball-hawking Miami DB Fred Marion.

CLEMSON 82 Wake Forest 24: Coach P Rich Hendley could have stayed in bed. Scoring 11 TDs and 2 FGs on 13 of 15 possessions—failures ended in TOs—Tigers put up ACC pts record on 756y O against overmatched Wake Forest (3-6). TB Chuck McSwain led scoring barrage with 3 TDs, while TB Cliff Austin and WR Perry Tuttle added 2 apiece. So exhausted was Tiger mascot Ricky Capps after having to do more than 600 pushups—his total increased geometrically after each Clemson score—that Deacons cheerleaders comically took up his effort.

Virginia Tech 29 KENTUCKY 3: With help from Kentucky's 4 TOs, Hokies (6-2) ruined Homecoming in Lexington as K Don Wade connected on school-record 5 FGs and TB Cyrus Lawrence rushed for 160y. Lawrence had 100y by H as Tech built 13-0 lead. Virginia Tech's 1st score, 3y TD run by WB Billy Hite, was set up by Wildcats (1-7) QB Randy Jenkins' FUM. Kentucky was outrushed 339y to 109y, so pressure was put on Jenkins (11-21/129y, INT), who was unable to get Wildcats into EZ.

ALABAMA 13 Mississippi State 10: Frosh K Terry Sanders booted Crimson Tide (7-1-1) past Mississippi State (6-2), sending coach Bear Bryant into 2nd place tie on all-time victory list with Pop Warner at 313, just single win behind leader Amos Alonzo Stagg. Subbing for injured K Peter Kim, Sanders kicked winning 29y FG late in 4th Q, although game was far from over. QB John Bond completed 3 passes/69y to march Bulldogs downfield before INT by Alabama LB Tommy Wilcox at 1YL with 18 secs left halted rally. Sloppy, but hard-hitting, game featured 13 TOs: Tide lost 7 FUMs. Although Alabama rushed for 256y, game's leading ground gainer was Mississippi State HB Michael Haddix (9/71y).

ILLINOIS 24 Iowa 7: Illinois farmed 3 TDs from 6 Iowa TOs to bounce Hawks (5-3) out of Big 10 top spot. Illini (5-3) LB Pete Burgard recovered FUM—1 of 4 by blitzing D—in Iowa EZ for TD; ball coughed up by LB Ron Ferrari's hit on Hawkeyes QB Pete Gales (11-19/117y, INT). Illini QB Tony Eason (22-34/263y) followed INTs by his defenders with TD passes of 56y and 4y to WR Oliver Williams. Iowa D also was aggressive, sacking Eason 7 times but without TOs. QB Gordy Bohannon put Iowa on scoreboard by throwing 12y TD pass to WR Jeff Brown in 2nd Q.

KANSAS STATE 10 Iowa State 7: Kansas State (2-6) snapped 6-game losing streak as its swarming D forced 3 TOs and limited Iowa State's bulwark TB Dwayne Crutchfield to career-low 46y. Wildcats S Gary Morrill paced D with 12 tackles and FUM REC, while TB Mark Hundley rushed for 109y and 2y TD. Cyclones (5-2-1) had opened scoring on QB John Quinn's 6y run at end of 34y drive set up by FUM REC. K-State began scoring drive in same FUM REC fashion, getting 35y FG by K Steve Willis at end of 1st H. Wildcats opened 2nd H with winning 80y drive that featured 25y run by FB Masi Toluao and Hundley's 14y pass to WR Rick Manning.

Southern Methodist 27 TEXAS A&M 7: No one could fault Texas A&M (5-3) for not being prepared for SMU's passing attack. Mustangs (7-1) rarely threw, but resourceful QB Lance McIlhenny passed for 108y, all in 1st H Ponies led 12-0. With passes keeping D honest, rush attack chewed up 254y, 123y by TB Eric Dickerson, who ran for 3 TDs. Aggies were forced to air themselves, and while QB Gary Kubiak reached 257y passing, he was picked off 3 times without tossing any TDs. Game was marred by ugly incident in 2nd Q when Texas A&M's "Officer of the Day" pulled his sword while trying to kick SMU's cheerleaders off field following TD by Mustangs.

SOUTHERN CALIFORNIA 41 Washington State 17: Trojans (7-1) attack, aka TB Marcus Allen's Heisman Trophy tour, derailed upstart Washington State's Rose Bowl plans as Allen tallied 44/289y, both career highs, en route to 4 TDs, including 17y scoring reception. Washington State (6-1-1) trailed by only 17-10 at H in its biggest game in many years, but eventually was worn down by USC rush attack. Trojans marched 76y on their 1st possession of 2nd H to Allen's 1y TD run and then, after INT by LB Chip Banks, added clincher at 31-10 on Allen's TD catch. Cougars QB Clete Casper threw and rushed for TDs. Allen topped 200y rushing for 6th game of season, besting record set by Cornell RB Ed Marinaro.

CALIFORNIA 45 Oregon State 3: Bears (2-6) unleashed balanced attack on Oregon State, rushing for 275y and passing for 293y. RB Carl Montgomery rushed for 113y and 4 TDs to pace California attack, while QB J Torchio completed 17-25/234y. When FB John Tuggle opened scoring with 2y run, Cal had all pts it would need. Beavers (1-7) were balanced too, rushing for 146y and passing for 147y, but it was not enough to overcome 4 TOs. Bears nimble WR Mariet Ford caught 8/105y.

November 7, 1981

Clemson 10 NORTH CAROLINA 8: Tar Heels (7-2) entered game with 36 pt-per-game scoring avg. They left with respect for Clemson's D. Each team managed single FG in 2nd H, with Tigers (9-0) K Donald Igwebuike's 39y boot producing margin of victory. Late drives by North Carolina into Tigers territory ended on sack by MG William Perry (5 tackles, 2 sacks) and, on last possession, fumbled pitchout that was recovered by DT Jeff Bryant. Game's sole TD came on 7y run in 2nd Q by Clemson FB Jeff McCall, who was top rusher with 84y. HB Kelvin Bryant (13/31y) returned to UNC lineup after 4-game absence with knee injury, but was largely ineffective.

Miami 27 FLORIDA STATE 19: Miami (6-2) had excuses for any lack of focus, but pulled off road win despite euphoria over Penn State victory and mid-week decision by NCAA to put team on 2-year probation for recruiting violations. Hurricanes broke 13-13 4th Q tie with 6y TD run by HB Smokey Roan following passes by QB Jim Kelly (22-41/273y, INT) of 33y to FB Speedy Neal and 17y to WR Rocky Belk. Miami LB Greg Brown set up winning drive with blocked FG attempt, as Canes special teams sparkled with 3 kick blocks and 2 FGs by K Danny Miller including school-record 57y effort. Florida State (6-3) QB Rick Stockstill then threw pass tipped to Miami CB Ronnie Lippett that set up 23y TD pass by Kelly to Neal for 27-13 lead. On scoring play, 247-lb Neal caught short pass, hurdled CB Harvey Clayton at 10YL, and raced into EZ. Seminoles, who lost 19-game home winning streak, answered with 7y TD pass to TE Sam Childers on drive set up by 50y KO RET by TB Greg Allen (23/109y) after backward pass by TB Cedric Jones. FSU would get no closer as final drive reached Miami 29YL before time ran out. "In 23 years that I've been coaching, I've never been prouder of a team," said Miami coach Howard Schnellenberger.

Georgia 26 Florida 21 (Jacksonville): Perhaps not as great as 1980 edition of rivalry, contest nonetheless featured another terrific 4th Q drive for victory by Georgia (8-1) by same score as previous year. Trailing 21-20, Georgia embarked on 17-play, 95y drive to 1y TD run by TB Herschel Walker with 2:31 left. Walker lugged ball 11 times on drive. He rushed for 192y on SEC-record 47 carries and scored all 4 TDs for Georgia, 2 on pass receptions. Florida (5-4) had just taken 21-20 lead on 10y TD pass from QB Wayne Peace (21-37/272y, INT) to WR Spencer Jackson. Gators, with help by botched KO RET by Walker, owned 14-0 2nd Q lead with Peace opening scoring with 54y TD pass to TB Steve Miller. Walker tied game with 2 TD catches, on 24y pass from QB Buck Belue (13-22/187y) to close 1st H and 16y toss in 3rd Q. His 4y TD run capped 48y drive for 20-14 lead early in 4th Q.

SOUTHERN MISSISSIPPI 7 Mississippi State 6: Largest-to-date football crowd in Magnolia State history (64,112) witnessed battle of resurgent programs. Both teams gave little quarter, with Golden Eagles (7-0-1) making late clinching D stop. Bulldogs (6-3) trailed by 7-6 with 1:26 left and faced 4th-and-1 at Southern Miss 33YL. Eagles knocked Mississippi State back, nailing backup QB Tim Parenton short of 1st down to preserve victory. TB Sammy Winder had scored from 1y out in 2nd Q for 7-6 lead after 2 FGs by Bulldogs' K Dana Moore. Moore missed 30y FG try early in 4th Q.

MINNESOTA 35 Ohio State 31: Minnesota (6-3) QB Mike Hohensee ripped Ohio State D for 444y and 5 TDs, including winning 28y pass to TE Jay Carroll with 2:38 left. Hohensee broke Gophers records for single game attempts (67), completions (37) and y, while Carroll caught 3 TD passes. WR Chester Cooper caught 12/ school-record 182y. Buckeyes (6-3) QB Art Schlichter threw and ran for TDs but could not help

Ohio's leaky pass D. Ohio State FB Tim Spencer rushed for 135y and 2 TDs including 73y run in 1st Q for 14-0 lead. Loss ended 15-game series win streak for Buckeyes, who blew 21-7 and 31-21 leads.

Michigan State 61 NORTHWESTERN 14: Any chance of preventing NCAA record 29th straight loss died quickly for Northwestern (0-9), who trailed 21-0 after 1st Q and 41-0 at H. Michigan State (4-5) scored on its 1st 7 series, gaining 352y and 24 1st downs in 1st H. Spartans QB Bryan Clark led way, completing 11-15/118y, 3 TDs in 1st H, while K Morten Anderson kicked 2 PATs to set Big 10 career mark with 45. Wildcats finally scored cosmetic 2 TDs in 3rd Q on passes by QB Mike Kerrigan.

HOUSTON 14 Texas 14: Texas (6-1-1) rallied behind walk-on QB Robert Brewer to score game's last 14 pts, with K Raul Allegre's 47y FG tying it with 2:40 left. Converting twosome of 1st H INTs by starting Texas QB Rick McIvor, who was slowed by shoulder injury, Cougars (5-3-1) enjoyed 14-0 edge. Houston O faced short field for both TDs as CB Butch LaCroix returned his 7th INT of year 10y to Horns' 22YL and DE Kelly McDonald made 30y INT RET to Texas 16YL. McIvor's day ended at H, with Brewer coming in to throw for 93y and lead 3 scoring drives.

UCLA 31 Washington 0: QB Tom Ramsey hooked up with WR Cormac Carney on 2 TD passes in 2nd Q to lead Bruins (6-2-1) to rout of generous Huskies. All 5 UCLA scores followed TOs by Washington (7-2) as longest scoring drive for Bruins was only 51y and 3 trips were of 14y or less. DT Irv Eatman led ferocious Bruins D with 2 sacks, while NG Karl Morgan forced FUM and recovered FUM in 17-pt 1st H. Small highlights for Washington were 2 INTs in 1st Q by CB Bill Stapleton.

AP Poll November 9

1 Pittsburgh (53)	1343	11 Michigan	738
2 Clemson (7)	1272	12 Miami	670
3 Southern California (8)	1232	13 North Carolina	509
4 Georgia	1129	14 Southern Mississippi	465
5 Penn State	1043	15 Oklahoma	358
6 Alabama	935	16 Arkansas	355
7 Nebraska	793	17 Washington State	222
8 Southern Methodist	791	18 UCLA	180
9 Arizona State	783	19 Hawaii	127
10 Texas	754	20 Florida State	113

November 14, 1981

Alabama 31 PENN STATE 16: Emotionally charged Alabama (8-1-1) squad won another for coach Bear Bryant, no. 314 to tie Amos Alonzo Stagg's career win record. While Tide's Wishbone attack rushed for 279y, it was surprising aerial game that did in Nittany Lions (7-2). QB Walter Lewis (6-10/167y) stunned Penn State with 2 TD passes to WR Jesse Bendross and 57y completion to WR Joey Jones to set up another 3 pts as Bama built 24-3 H lead. Crimson Tide enjoyed 334y to 70y advantage by H. Nittany Lions gained 294y in 2nd H, with Warner leading way with 69y rushing. Alabama D sparkled, highlighted by GLS in 2nd H after Penn State moved to 1st down at Bama 1YL. DE Mike Pitts' ankle stop of TB Curt Warner on 4th down was final TD-saving play. Said Penn State coach Joe Paterno, who dropped to 0-3 vs Bryant, "It's a historic moment in football and I'm glad for him."

CLEMSON 21 Maryland 7: Clemson (10-0) captured its 8th ACC title with win over nemesis. QB Homer Jordan (20-29/270y, INT) had huge game in completing 15-18/214y with 3 TDs in 1st H. WR Perry Tuttle (10/151y) was on receiving end of 2 scores among his 8 receptions in 1st H against largely single coverage. Terps (3-6-1) finally scored in 4th Q by converting Tigers FUM into 7y TD run by TB Charlie Wysocki. Maryland QB Boomer Esiason threw for 167y in losing effort.

North Carolina 17 VIRGINIA 14: Lowly Cavaliers (1-8) came close to upset with air show rarely seen by its fans. With QB Gordie Whitehead (18-31/243y, INT) throwing 2 TD passes in 2nd Q, Virginia surprised Tar Heels (8-2) with 14-7 H lead. Whitehead was out of game by end of 3rd Q with shoulder injury and so too were Cavs as Carolina took lead with 10-pt 3rd Q. TB Tyrone Anthony scored on 2y run for tying TD and K Brooks Barwick booted 34y FG late in 3rd Q for win. Sub QBs Mike Eck and QB Todd Kirtley, in for Whitehead, combined for 4 INTs, while Tar Heels kept ball on ground behind HB Kelvin Bryant, who rushed for 171y and TD.

MIAMI 21 Virginia Tech 14: In rematch of 1980 Peach Bowl, Hurricanes (7-2) jumped to 2-TD lead in 1st Q but had to hold on against resurgent Virginia Tech. Hokies (6-3) RB Bob Thomas fumbled opening KO to set up 1st of 2 scoring passes by QB Jim Kelly (20-27/209y, 2 INTs). TB Cyrus Lawrence (17/84y) and QB Steve Casey (13-24/172y) led Hokies rally, each rushing for TD. Best chance for Virginia Tech to secure 4th Q table-turner ended on Casey's FUM after he moved his troops to Miami 17YL.

TENNESSEE 28 Mississippi 20: With momentum swinging from fast-starting Vols (6-3) to rallying Rebs, Tennessee WR Willie Gault returned punt 66y for big TD late in 2nd Q. Gault's heroics boosted Tennessee's lead to 28-7 at H. Thanks to 2 short TD runs by TB James Berry and 13y TD pass by QB Steve Alatorre to WR Anthony Hancock, Tennessee had held commanding 21-0 lead. Mississippi (3-6-1) QB John Fourcade (21-34/243y) kept his Rebs in game, passing and running for TDs. Vols LB Mark Burns helped keep Rebels at bay with 2 INTs off deflections, 1st INTs of Fourcade after he had thrown 104 straight passes without being picked off.

MISSOURI 19 Oklahoma 14: Tigers (7-3) bounced Oklahoma (5-3-1) from Big 8 title race as HB Bobby Meyer ran for 108y and 19y TD. Mizzou, winning for 1st time in series since 1969, took 13-7 lead at H on 2 FGs by K Bob Lucchesi and QB Brad Perry's 1y TD run. Meyer's TD run in 3rd Q, featuring several broken tackles, upping lead to 19-7. Oklahoma rallied as HB Steve Sewell's 46y TD catch off tip was followed by profitable onside-KO. But Tigers D stiffened to secure win. Oklahoma finished with 296y rushing, led by 127y by FB Stanley Wilson and 123y by QB Darrell Shepard. Tigers DT Jeff Gaylord authored 12 tackles and 3 FUM RECs.

Brigham Young 13 HAWAII 3: Have you heard joke about WAC teams playing D? There was nothing funny here for Hawaii (7-1), which lost its unbeaten slate, 11-game win streak, 1st-ever poll ranking, and conf title hopes. QB Jim McMahon paced Brigham Young (9-2) with 269y passing, but was held without TD pass as BYU WR Neil Balholm recovered FUM by FB Waymon Hamilton in EZ for only TD of game. Cougars K Kurt Gunther booted 2 FGs. Cougars D shackled top WAC rusher, Rainbows RB Gary Allen, to −1y. Game had morning start for mainland TV.

WASHINGTON 13 Southern California 3: Trojans (8-2) of sunny California had to be anxious arriving at windy, gloomy Husky Stadium. Facing wind gusts up to 60 mph, Southern California was blown away. Key play occurred after 46y FG by K Chuck Nelson put Washington (8-2) up 6-3 late in 4th Q, when ensuing KO bounced over USC TB Fred Crutcher's head. Ball was knocked crazily into EZ and recovered by Washington LB Fred Small for clinching TD. Facing wind and Huskies D that held TB Marcus Allen to 155y rushing—after 7 games in row over 200y—Trojans had no chance for comeback. But, Allen cracked 2000y season rushing mark early in game to become 1st collegian ever to do so. Winning Huskies managed only 120y of O.

UCLA 34 Arizona State 24: QB Mike Pagel was driving Arizona State (7-2) for tying TD late in game when his pass was tipped by UCLA NG Karl Morgan and picked off by DE Joe Gary. Bruins (7-2-1) converted TO—7th in 44y FG by K Norm Johnson to seal win. TB Kevin Nelson rushed for 111y and 28y TD run, while QB Tom Ramsey threw and ran for TDs to lead UCLA. Sun Devils (7-2) took 14-0 lead, thanks in part to Ramsey's FUM on own 1YL. Ramsey evened things up at 14-14, Bruins' 2nd TD following FUM by Pagel after brutal hit by LB Brad Plemmons. Teams swapped FGs, and Bruins scored 2 TDs in 2nd H to open 31-17 lead. ASU cut lead with 81y drive that ended with 1y TD run by FB Gerald Riggs.

AP Poll November 16

1 Pittsburgh (63)	1354	11 Miami	661
2 Clemson (5)	1290	12 North Carolina	521
3 Georgia	1169	13 Penn State	509
4 Alabama	1128	14 Washington State	461
5 Nebraska	972	15 UCLA	457
6 Southern Methodist	924	16 Arkansas	443
7 Michigan	875	17 Washington	320
8 Texas	873	18 Brigham Young	184
9 Southern Mississippi	810	19 Iowa	166
10 Southern California	678	20 Arizona State	165

November 21, 1981

North Carolina 31 DUKE 10: TB Kelvin Bryant slammed ahead for 36/247y and scored 2 TDs to spark North Carolina (9-2) to big win and Gator Bowl invitation. It was 3rd-best rushing performance in Tar Heels' history. After K Jeff Hayes' 1st Q FG, Bryant tallied his 1st TD early in 2nd Q on way to 10-3 H lead. Carolina dismissed Duke's trick pass at its 10YL in 3rd Q and went 90y to QB Rod Elkins' 15y TD pass to WR Jon Richardson. Blue Devils (6-5) gained late TD on sub QB Ron Sally's pass.

Ohio State 14 MICHIGAN 9: Sr Buckeyes (8-3) QB Art Schlichter finished his up and down Big 10 career by scoring amazing 6y run for winning TD. Michigan (8-3) led 9-7 on 3 chip shot FGs by K Ali Haji-Sheikh as clock wound down in 4th Q. Starting at own 20YL, Schlichter (12-24/132y, 2 INTs) connected on 2 key passes: 10y lob to TB Tim Spencer (25/110y) on 3rd-and-7 while backpedaling from pass rush and 17y to WR Gary Williams. On 3rd down at Michigan 6YL, Ohio State went for run-pass option. Wolverines had pass target, TE John Frank, covered in EZ and encircled Schlichter with 4 defenders. But, FB Vaughn Broadnax, all 252 lbs of him, cleaned out 2 with thunderous block, while shifty Schlichter "jigged" and "jitterbugged" his way to memorable TD, his 2nd of game. With loss, Michigan, who crossed Ohio 30YL on 6 drives, 3 which ended with INTs, was bounced from Rose Bowl. Amazingly, Iowa, with 19 straight losing seasons behind it, beat Michigan State 36-7 to earn Pasadena trip. Wolverines' triple-teamed WR Anthony Carter (4/52y) still gained 206y on receptions and RETs.

Wisconsin 26 MINNESOTA 21: Notre Dame transfer QB Randy Wright was thrust into Wisconsin (7-4) lineup with less than 2 mins remaining, ball on own 15YL and trailing 21-20. In snowy air, Wright coolly led Badgers 85y, completing 4-5/82y with winning 7y TD pass with 65 secs left to frosh WR Michael Jones. Gophers (6-5) did most damage with aerial attack as QB Mike Hohensee threw for 254y and TD passes of 41y and 4y to WR Chester Cooper. Win propelled Wisconsin to Garden State Bowl, its 1st postseason tilt since 1963 Rose Bowl.

Southern Methodist 32 ARKANSAS 18: lashing back at their probation, Mustangs (10-1) won 1st SWC title in 15 years. Pony Express backfield excelled as TBs Eric Dickerson (25/140y) and Craig James (18/118y) each topped 100y. SMU D scored on DE Russ Washington's 10y INT RET and set up TD as LB Eric Ferguson returned INT to Arkansas 14YL. James needed 2 runs from there for winning TD midway through 4th Q. Arkansas (8-3) became years' only team to score 1st Q TD on Ponies when RB Gary Anderson caught 7y pass by QB Tom Jones to cap 80y drive. Gaining 259y, Hogs had insufficient O to rally. SMU K Eddie Garcia booted 4 FGs in setting SWC mark for career 3-pters with 132, passing K Happy Feller of Texas (1970). Texas, 34-12 winners over Baylor, grabbed Cotton Bowl bid.

WASHINGTON 23 Washington State 10: Needing win and loss by UCLA to earn Pac-10 title and back-to-back trips to Pasadena, Washington (9-2) took care of their end. Huskies TB Cookie Jackson rushed for 103y with 23y on winning 3rd Q TD run. Run capped 80y drive that featured 74y on ground with Jackson's 5/50y. Huskies K Chuck Nelson also made 3 FGs, and scored on WR Paul Skansi's diving 15y TD catch with 8 secs left in 1st H. Dropping 8th straight Apple Cup game, Cougars (8-2-1) lost 6 TOs and QB Clete Casper and RB Tim Harris (16/64y) to injuries.

353

SOUTHERN CALIFORNIA 22 Ucla 21: USC (9-2) TB Marcus Allen would not be denied as his 5y TD run with 2:14 left iced UCLA (7-3-1) out of Rose Bowl. UCLA's last chance was ended by Troy NG George Achica's block of 46y FG try by K Norm Johnson. Allen gained 219y for his 8th 200y game of season. But, Bruins converted Allen's 2 FUMs into 10 pts in 1st H for 18-12 edge. UCLA upped its lead to 21-12 in 3rd Q, before Allen led Trojans comeback that produced 77y drive for FG and 39y drive to Allen's winning score, following DB Troy West's INT.

AP Poll November 23

1 Pittsburgh (60)	1294	11 Penn State	645
2 Clemson (5)	1234	12 Washington	604
3 Georgia	1157	13 Iowa	491
4 Alabama	1054	14 Brigham Young	377
5 Nebraska	1015	15 Ohio State	330
6 Southern Methodist	965	16 Michigan	292
7 Texas	907	17 Southern Mississippi	264
8 Southern California	797	18 Arizona State	253
9 Miami	708	19 UCLA	199
10 North Carolina	656	20 Washington State	139

November 26-28, 1981

(Th'g) Texas 21 TEXAS A&M 13: TB John Walker, subbing for injured TB A.J. Jones, rushed for 178y and clinching 60y TD run as Texas (9-1-1) subdued Aggies (6-5). Longhorns scored all 3 TDs in crucial 2nd Q, during which D knocked A&M QB Gary Kubiak out of game. Kubiak, who led home team to 2 FGs in 1st Q, entered game with bruised shoulder that became target of Texas defenders. Aggies managed only 7 pts with backup QB John Elkins. Texas QB Robert Brewer (8-10/134y) ran in score and hit WR Herkie Walls on post pattern for 38y TD.

GAME OF THE YEAR
Penn State 48 PITTSBURGH 14:

With both rivals ranked no. 1 at different times during season, battle for Pennsylvania had extra juice. No. 1 Panthers, sporting 17-game win streak, jumped to 14-0 lead as QB Dan Marino hooked up with WR Dwight Collins (6/110y) on TD passes of 28y and 9y in 1st Q. At end of 1st Q, Pitt (10-1) D had allowed −1y O, and Marino was throwing 9-10/121y. Did Pitt relax itself into complete reversal? Perhaps so; Panthers bobbled away 7 TOs, including EZ INT thrown early in 2nd Q to Lions DB Roger Jackson that prevented 3rd TD that might have launched Pitt to national title. Penn State (9-2) soon got its O in gear as combo of QB Todd Blackledge (12-23/262y, INT) and WR Kenny Jackson (5/158y) caught fire. Blackledge led couple of 80y drives to tie game at 14-14 by H and found Jackson for 42y and 45y TD receptions in 3rd Q. Meanwhile, Penn State D swarmed Marino (22-45/267y, 2 INTs), holding him to 80y passing in 2nd H. Lions rolled on as G Sean Farrell scored TD on FUM REC, and DB Mark Robinson returned INT 91y for another. TB Curt Warner gave Lions O some balance with 104y rushing. Pitt's loss left top ranking to Clemson as only remaining undefeated team.

FLORIDA 35 Florida State 3: To winner went Peach Bowl invitation, to loser nothing. Determined Florida (7-4) QB Wayne Peace completed 20-33/275y and 4 TDs as Gators snapped 4-game series losing streak. Florida led 13-3 at H, same margin as in 1980 when Seminoles rallied for win. This time, pass to TE Mike Mularkey's 27y TD catch on 4th down in 3rd Q broke game open. Florida State (6-5) gained only 210y to 437y for home team in dropping 3rd game in late season, with lone bright spot being P Rohn Stark, who punted 6/54.8y avg. "This has to be the greatest victory I've ever had in football," said winning coach Charley Pell.

Alabama 28 Auburn 17 (Birmingham): Crimson Tide's big day finally arrived as they gave Bear Bryant his record 315th win in sweet fashion by topping rival. Led by TB George Peoples' 155y rushing, Auburn (5-6) converted 2 FUMs on punt RETs by Alabama (9-1-1) WR Joey Jones into 10 pts for 17-14 lead early in 4th Q. Using play action to fake Tigers, Bama QB Walter Lewis hit WR Jessie Bendross for 38y TD pass to grab 4th Q lead. Tide HB Linnie Patrick added 15y insurance TD run. "This was one of the greatest games ever played," said contented Bryant afterward.

ARIZONA STATE 24 Arizona 13: QB Mike Pagel (9-28/193y) threw 3 TDs in decisive 2nd Q as Sun Devils (9-2) won 15th of last 17 in bitter series. Arizona (6-5) grabbed early 6-0 lead on QB Tom Tunnicliffe's 8y TD pass to TE Bill Cook following INT by NG Gary Shaw. In 2nd Q, Pagel went deep to TE Jerry Bell for 44y TD and hit WR Bernard Henry twice for TDs, 2nd following INT by CB Mike Richardson. Sun Devils intercepted 5 passes by Tunnicliffe, while Pagel was picked off 4 times.

AP Poll November 30

1 Clemson (63)	1351	11 North Carolina	653
2 Georgia (1)	1255	12 Washington	614
3 Alabama	1188	13 Iowa	537
4 Nebraska (1)	1104	14 Brigham Young	397
5 Southern Methodist (1)	1050	15 Ohio State	364
6 Texas	959	16 Michigan	284
7 Penn State (1)	918	17 Arizona State	280
8 Southern California	844	18 Southern Mississippi	278
9 Miami (1)	827	19 UCLA	190
10 Pittsburgh	796	20 Washington State	132

December 5, 1981

Army 3 Navy 3 (Philadelphia): Heavily-favored Navy (7-3-1) felt like it lost, managing only 3 FG tries by K Steve Fehr: Army blocked 1, Fehr hit from 35y out just before H, and missed from 49y late in 4th Q. Cadets (3-7-1), who scored on 27y FG by K Dave Aucoin early in 3rd Q, had time for final, missed 55y FG. Army missed golden, early

chance when TB Gerald Walker fumbled near Middies GL. Revved-up Black Knights benefited from P Joe Sartiano's 5/57.6y avg to set NCAA record. TB Eddie Meyers (119y) set Navy single-season records for attempts (277) and y (1318y).

Georgia 44 GEORGIA TECH 7: On day he finished 2nd in Heisman balloting, Georgia (10-1) TB Herschel Walker (225y, 4 TDs) finished regular season with SEC-record 1,891y, 3rd highest to date. Bulldogs WR Lindsay Scott (5/154y) corralled QB Buck Belue (11-17/220y, INT) pass for 80y TD on game's 1st snap as Jackets bit on fake to Walker. Bulldogs scored on 6 series in row for 34-0 H lead. Georgia Tech (1-10), losers of 10 straight since opening day shocker of Alabama, averted shutout with TB Robert Lavette's 3rd Q TD. Due to abuse from Tech crowd, Georgia coach Vince Dooley brought back regulars late to add final TD, Walker's 4th.

Conference Standings

Ivy League

Yale	6-1
Dartmouth	6-1
Princeton	5-1-1
Harvard	4-2-1
Brown	2-5
Cornell	2-5
Columbia	1-6
Pennsylvania	1-6

Atlantic Coast

Clemson	6-0
North Carolina	5-1
Maryland	4-2
Duke	3-3
N.C. State	2-4
Wake Forest	1-5
Virginia	0-6
Georgia Tech *	0-2
* Ineligible	

Southeastern

Georgia	6-0
Alabama	6-0
Mississippi State	4-2
Florida	3-3
Tennessee	3-3
Auburn	2-4
Kentucky	2-4
Mississippi	1-4-1
Louisiana State	1-4-1
Vanderbilt	1-5

Big Ten

Iowa	6-2
Ohio State	6-2
Michigan	6-3
Illinois	6-3
Wisconsin	6-3
Minnesota	4-5
Michigan State	4-5
Purdue	3-6
Indiana	3-6
Northwestern	0-9

Mid-American

Toledo	8-1
Miami (Ohio)	6-1-1
Central Michigan	7-2
Bowling Green	5-3-1
Western Michigan	5-4
Ohio	5-4
Kent State	3-6
Ball State	2-6
Northern Illinois	2-7
Eastern Michigan	0-9

Big Eight

Nebraska	7-0
Oklahoma	4-2-1
Oklahoma State	4-3
Kansas	4-3
Missouri	3-4
Iowa State	2-4-1
Colorado	2-5
Kansas State	1-6

Southwest

Southern Methodist	7-1
Texas	6-1-1
Houston	5-2-1
Arkansas	5-3
Texas A&M	4-4
Baylor	3-5
Rice	3-5
Texas Christian	1-6-1
Texas Tech	0-7-1

Western Athletic

Brigham Young	7-1
Hawaii	6-1
Utah	5-1-1
Wyoming	6-2
New Mexico	3-4-1
San Diego State	3-5
Air Force	2-5
Texas-El Paso	1-6
Colorado State	0-8

Pacific-Ten

Washington	6-2
Arizona State	5-2
Southern California	5-2
Washington State	5-2-1
UCLA	5-2-1
Arizona	4-4
Stanford	4-4
California	2-6
Oregon	1-6
Oregon State	0-7

Pacific Coast Athletic

San Jose State	5-0
Utah State	4-1
Fresno State	2-3
Pacific	2-3
Fullerton State	1-4
Long Beach State	1-4

1981 Major Bowl Games
Independence Bowl (Dec. 12): Texas A&M 33 Oklahoma State 16

Balance was theme for Aggies (7-5), who totaled 223y rushing and 225y passing in easily topping Oklahoma State. QB Gary Kubiak (15-20/225y) twice hit WR Jimmie Williams for TDs, while completing 7 straight at 1 point and 10-11 in decisive 1st H, led by Aggies 20-10. Cowboys (7-5) had taken early 7-0 lead, converting FUM by Texas A&M HB Johnny Hector on game's 1st play from scrimmage into 25y scoring drive that TB Ernest Anderson capped with 1y TD run. Teams traded 1st Q FGs before combo of Kubiak and Williams struck for TDs of 50y and 38y. With injury-plagued rush attack finishing with 70y, Cowboys were hard-pressed to stay in game.

Garden State Bowl (Dec. 13): Tennessee 28 Wisconsin 21

In last Garden State Bowl, clash of styles between speedy Volunteers (8-4) and brawny Badgers (7-5) went to sleek team. Swift Tennessee WRs Anthony Hancock caught 11/196y and 43y TD and Willie Gault gave team lead for good at 10-7 with explosive 87y KO TD RET. QB Steve Alatorre happily passed to these 2 future NFL 1st rounders,

ringing up 315y in air. Vols built 21-7 H lead, forcing Badgers to give up ground game. Playing in 1st bowl game in 19 years, Wisconsin O sputtered until sub QB Randy Wright (9-21/123y, INT) tossed 2 TDs in 4th Q comeback bid.

Holiday Bowl (Dec. 18): Brigham Young 38 Washington State 36

All-Cougar match-up looked like rout for BYU (11-2) until formula was renewed for always-entertaining Holiday Bowl, decided by 4 pts in last 3 years. Playing in 1st bowl since 1931, Washington State (8-3-1) scored trio of 3rd Q TDs to cut deficit to 31-28. Starting on own 18YL, BYU QB Jim McMahon (27-43/342y, 3 TDs) swung momentum on 3rd-and-12 pass to TE Gordon Hudson (7/126y, TD) for 45y en route to clinching TD: TB Scott Pettis' 11y catch early in 4th Q. Wazzu scored once more, on 1y run by FB Mike Martin, but went nowhere on final series. WSU QB Ricky Turner was game-high rusher with 92y and 2 TDs. "I guess we had to keep the tradition of the Holiday Bowl alive," said BYU coach LaVell Edwards on close finish.

Sun Bowl (Dec. 26): Oklahoma 40 Houston 14

Perhaps Houston coach Bill Yeoman didn't have to be so nice. After illegal recruitment loan to QB Darrell Shepard put Cougars on probation, Yeoman helped him transfer to Oklahoma (7-4-1). Rushing for 107y, Shepard earned MVP honors in scoring twice. Houston (7-4-1) trailed only 10-7 early in 4th Q when Cougars RB Robert Durham raced 60y towards Sooner EZ with swing pass from QB Lionel Wilson (17-21/216y, INT). Oklahoma DB Elbert Watts caught him at 3YL and stripped him of ball, which rolled through EZ for touchback. Sooners went 80y, 42y on Shepard's brilliant run, to his 1y keeper that started 30-pt deluge. Subbing for injured FB Stanley Wilson, Sooners FB Fred Sims rushed 15/181y, TD after only 179y in regular year. Houston made 385y, but still suffered its worst bowl loss ever.

Gator Bowl (Dec. 28): North Carolina 31 Arkansas 27

Emerging from heavy Jacksonville fog, North Carolina's 2-headed TB duo must have seemed unworldly to Arkansas (8-4): TB Kelvin Bryant rushed for 148y and TD, while TB Ethan Horton added 144y and 2 TDs as Tar Heels (10-2) built commanding 31-10 lead. Arkansas rallied behind QB Brad Taylor, scoring game's final 17 pts as he threw for 307 and 2 TDs. Fog affected UNC's 1st TD as Hogs RB Gary Anderson lost sight of punt that then hit up-man Mike Harris. DB Larry James recovered for Tar Heels at Arkansas 6YL to set up Bryant's 1y TD for 10-7 lead. After Razorbacks tied game 10-10, Horton scored twice as Heels opened up 3-TD lead. North Carolina finished with no. 9 ranking as ACC put 2 teams in final top 10 for 1st time ever.

Liberty Bowl (Dec. 30): Ohio State 31 Navy 28

George Welsh would have liked win in his last game as Navy coach, but he had to be proud of team's effort. Navy (7-4-1) tested favored Buckeyes, grabbing 20-17 3rd Q lead on LB Ken Olson's 20y TD RET of blocked punt. Ohio State (9-3) answered with 2 TDs. Miracle finish was not to be as Navy's final TD, 1y TD pass by QB Marco Pagnanelli (14-27/201y, 2 TDs, INT) to TE Greg Papajohn and 2-pt conv connection by same combination, could narrow deficit only to 31-28 with 8 secs left. Ohio recovered onside-KO. QB Art Schlichter had thrown 2 TDs and sub TB Jimmy Gayle (15/88y) ran for 2 TDs for Bucks, who converted TOs into 24 pts. Middies TB Eddie Meyers ran for 117y. "We played as well as we can," said Welsh.

Peach Bowl (Dec. 31): West Virginia 26 Florida 6

Underdog Mountaineers rode devastating D to rout, holding Gators (7-5) to 105y O, with mere 27y in 1st H. Led by FB Dane Conwell's 97y, West Virginia (9-3) surprised Florida by rushing for 194y. Mountaineers did not completely abandon pass, but QB Oliver Luck (14-23/107y, INT) took what D gave him and connected 8 times with TB Mickey Walczak, including 7y TD pass for 7-0 1st Q lead. Frosh walk-on K Paul Woodside also excelled, booting 4 FGs including game and school record 49y 3-ptr. Florida, suffering 6 TOs and allowing 6 sacks, may have lost game before opening KO. "We might have been overconfident," said Gators LB Wilber Marshall. "We didn't think they were as good as some of the teams we played."

Hall of Fame Bowl (Dec. 31): Mississippi State 10 Kansas 0

Fans had to be on time as winning pts were scored when Mississippi State (8-4) QB John Bond raced 17y to EZ on option keeper on 1st play from scrimmage. Play followed FUM by Kansas (8-4) KR Darren Greene on opening KO after being stripped of ball with REC by Bulldogs S Rob Fesmire. Game's only other score was 22y FG by K Dana Moore. Thanks to 7 sacks by D, 236y rushing by O and 49y punting avg by Moore, Bulldogs controlled field position. Jayhawks missed injured QB Frank Seuer as reserve QBs Steve Smith and Mick Frederick managed 171y passing, but were unable to move Kansas past Miss State 35YL until late in 4th Q.

Bluebonnet Bowl (Dec. 31): Michigan 33 UCLA 14

Like May Day in Moscow, Michigan's weaponry was on full display: at 1 point it enjoyed 212y to 0y edge in O. Wolverines (9-3) TB Butch Woolfolk ran for 186y, TD, WR Anthony Carter caught 6/127y, TD, and QB Steve Smith completed 9-15/152y, TD, with another TD running. In end, Michigan outgained UCLA 488y to 195y and nearly doubled UCLA's 1st downs. Bruins QB Tom Ramsey (12-25/162y, INT) fired 2 TD passes in 2nd H. Game had been delayed as coaches argued over use of visible 25-sec clock. Big 10 rules prevailed; clock went unused. Michigan won its 2nd bowl game in same calendar year, including past January's Rose Bowl, after dropping 1st 7 bowl games under coach Bo Schembechler.

Fiesta Bowl: Penn State 26 Southern California 10

Outstanding back was showcased in Fiesta Bowl, but not Heisman winner, TB Marcus Allen of USC (9-3). As Allen was held to 30/85y, new low for season, Penn State (10-2) TB Curt Warner raced to 145y and 2 TDs. Allen also coughed ball up twice, which

led to 10 pts for Lions. Without being hit, Allen lost FUM on game's opening play. Warner bolted 17y for TD 2 plays later for 7-0 lead. Warner's feat was no surprise—not after torching Nebraska for 238y—but he proved to be recovered from hamstring that hobbled him. Meanwhile, Penn State D was slowing Southern California with 5 sacks, 4 INTs, 2 FUM RECs, and 1 QB knocked out: LB Chet Parlavecchio (15 tackles) sent QB John Mazur (11-23/123y, 3 INTs) to sidelines with slight concussion. Lone USC TD came on LB Chip Banks' 20y INT RET. That TD tied score at 7-7. Lions took lead for good at 14-7 on QB Todd Blackledge's 52y TD pass to WR Gregg Garrity, who used all of his ability to reel in pass.

Cotton Bowl: Texas 14 Alabama 12

Alabama (9-2-1) could not hold off Longhorns, who scored twice in 4th Q. Texas (10-1-1) QB Robert Brewer took advantage of over-aggressive Bama D, which had 10 sacks, with 30y TD scamper on delayed draw for TD no. 1. On winning drive, Brewer (12-21/201y) hit TE Lawrence Sampleton twice for 37 and 19y and WR Donnie Little (7/92y) for 8y to set up FB Terry Orr's 8y TD run—his only score of year—for 14-10 lead with 2:05 left. WR Joey Jones put Tide back in business with 61y RET of ensuing KO. QB Walter Lewis, who rushed for 79y in 3 Qs, soon threw INT to S William Graham on 1YL. After playing man coverage all day, Longhorns secondary went to zone and Graham surprised WR Tim Clark by reaching out at last moment for INT with 1:48 to go. Texas then ran 3 QB sneaks, surrendered safety, and punted out of danger. Bama's sole TD had been Lewis' 6y pass to WR Jesse Bendross (5/78y) in 2nd Q. Both teams were at less than full strength due to injuries and suspensions, so when LB Robbie Jones left with hand injury, Tide was without its 3 leading tacklers. Bama DE Russ Wood made 4 sacks. Texas raised its record to 7-0-1 all-time against Alabama, while Brewer joined father Charlie as victors over coach Bear Bryant: elder Brewer led Horns over Bryant's Texas A&M squad in 1955.

Rose Bowl: Washington 28 Iowa 0

Frosh RB Jacque Robinson threw coming out party and 100,000 attended. Robinson had gained only 177y rushing during season, but came off bench to race through Iowa (8-4) for 142y and 2 TDs. Huskies (10-2) piled up 186y on ground against nation's 5th-ranked run D that had surrendered 87y avg. After 0-0 1st Q, Robinson, who had zoomed up depth chart during USC practice week with his impersonation of Marcus Allen, ran 7 times in 11-play, 65y TD drive. Huskies scored again later in 1st H after Hawkeyes failed to convert 4th-and-7 pass at Washington 40YL. QB Steve Pelluer (15-29/142y, INT) hit passes of 18y and 20y to favorite target WR Paul Skansi and drew pass interference PEN in EZ. FB Vince Cosby scored from 1y out. Despite every trick play coach Hayden Fry could muster, Iowa never threatened in 2nd H and had its best drive end on INT after reaching Huskies 29YL. Iowa QB Gordy Bohannon suffered terribly in return to native Pasadena, completing 6-14/33y with 2 INTs and 2 lost FUMs. FB Norm Granger was team's leading ground gainer with 13/80y. Fry called it an "old-fashioned rump-kicking."

Sugar Bowl: Pittsburgh 24 Georgia 20

Georgia coach Vince Dooley decided to blitz Pitt (11-1) QB Dan Marino (26-41/261y, 3 TDs, 2 INTs) on late 4th down play and paid same price NFL coaches would pay in future. As his O-line helped pick up blitzers, Marino found TE John Brown alone for perfect 33y TD pass with 35 secs left to cap winning drive. Bulldogs (10-2) were secs away from victory in game in which they were outgained 469y to 224y and had 16 fewer 1st downs. Although held to under 100y for only time this season, Georgia TB Herschel Walker (25/84y) scored 2 TDs for opportunistic O that converted FUM RECs deep into Panther territory into both Walker TDs. Bulldogs saved best drive for late in 4th Q, taking 20-17 lead on QB Buck Belue's 6y scoring pass to TE Clarence Kay. Panthers should have been well ahead but for 5 TOs and 14 PENs/96y. Marino's cool demeanor prevailed: he ran for 8y on 4th-and-4 during winning drive. TB Bryan Thomas led Panthers rush attack with 129y, making up for his lost FUM.

Orange Bowl: Clemson 22 Nebraska 15

Ready or not, out of ACC, considered to be "basketball conf," stormed no. 1 Clemson (12-0) going for national title. Clemson, unbeaten for 1st time in 33 years, had wins over Top 10 teams Georgia, North Carolina, and, now, Nebraska. Once again Tigers' punishing D set tone, while unheralded QB Homer Jordan (11-22/134y, TD, INT, and 46y rushing) played his typically solid game in winning MVP. Cornhuskers (9-3) QB Mark Mauer entered with banged up arm and threw for only 5-15/38y. That wasn't good enough against Clemson D that trumped running attacks (88.7y per game avg). Nebraska's frustrated O was able to produce score in 1st Q as IB Mike Rozier pulled up on sweep and threw 25y TD to WB Anthony Steels over surprised Tigers S Terry Kinard. Tigers took advantage of good field position to grab 12-7 H lead behind 2y TD run by TB Cliff Austin and pair of K Donald Igwebuike's 3 FGs. Winning pts came on 13y hookup in 3rd Q between Jordan and WR Perry Tuttle. Clemson stretched lead to 22-7 before Huskers woke up with their best drive: 69y that was capped by 26y TD sweep by IB Roger Craig. Then, Nebraska still earned 2-pt conv on Craig's run even though PEN pushed them back to 8YL. Clemson ate up 5:18 of last 5:24, with Jordan scrambling for 23y on 3rd-and-4 in own territory in final 2 mins. By game's end, Tigers D could count 8 of 12 Huskers' series ending in 3-and-outs. Clemson, season's 7th different top-ranked team, became only school from ACC to win national title since Maryland captured it in conf's inaugural 1953 season.

Final AP Poll January 3

1 Clemson (47)	977	11 Nebraska	535
2 Texas	862	12 Michigan	416
3 Penn State (1)	845	13 Brigham Young	388
4 Pittsburgh	834	14 Southern California	325
5 Southern Methodist (1)	774	15 Ohio State	310
6 Georgia	691	16 Arizona State	245
7 Alabama	638	17 West Virginia	111
8 Miami	594	18 Iowa	103
9 North Carolina	590	19 Missouri	85
10 Washington	587	20 Oklahoma	76

1981 Top Performance Formula

1 Clemson	1.7203
2 Pittsburgh	1.7121
3 Penn State	1.6749
4 Georgia	1.5696
5 Nebraska	1.5445
6 Texas	1.5416
7 Miami	1.5352
8 Southern Methodist	1.5206
9 North Carolina	1.5180
10 Arizona State	1.5162
11 Brigham Young	1.4974
12 Alabama	1.4686
13 Michigan	1.4393
14 Southern California	1.4049
15 Washington	1.3887
16 West Virginia	1.3566
17 Ohio State	1.3498
18 Oklahoma	1.3236
19 Missouri	1.2997
20 Iowa	1.2926

1981 Top Opponent Records

1 Penn State	.6774
2 Miami	.6261
3 Nebraska	.6220
4 Pittsburgh	.6179
5 California	.6154
6 Boston College	.6026
7 South Carolina	.5927
8 Kentucky	.5897
9 Oklahoma	.5827
10 Texas	.5800
11 UCLA	.5794
12 Syracuse	.5777
13 Florida State	.5774
14 Colorado	.5672
15 North Carolina State	.5658
16 Northwestern	.5609
17 Iowa	.5600
18 Alabama	.5560
19 Notre Dame	.5526
20 Illinois	.5522

1981 Out-of-Conference Records

	W-L	Percentage	Bowl W-L
Southwest	15-10-1	.5962	2-2
Southeastern	29-21-1	.5784	2-3
Big Ten	15-11	.5769	2-2
Big Eight	19-14	.5758	2-3
Pacific-10	20-17	.5405	1-3
Western Athletic	18-17	.5143	1-0
Atlantic Coast	17-24-1	.4167	2-0

1981 Individual Statistical Leaders

RUSHING YARDS	Attempts	Yards	Avg.
Marcus Allen, Southern California	403	2342	5.8
Herschel Walker, Georgia	385	1891	4.9
Barry Redden, Richmond	335	1629	4.9
Eric Dickerson, Southern Methodist	255	1428	5.6
Cyrus Lawrence, Virginia Tech	325	1403	4.3
Eddie Meyers, Navy	277	1318	4.8
Butch Woolfolk, Michigan	226	1273	5.6
James Bettis, Cincinnati	246	1226	5.0
Joe Morris, Syracuse	261	1194	4.6
Joe McIntosh, North Carolina State	222	1190	5.4

PASSING YARDS	Completions	Attempts	Yards	Pct.
Jim McMahon, Brigham Young	272	423	3555	64.3
Tony Eason, Illinois	248	406	3360	61.1
Matt Kofler, San Diego State	262	436	3337	60.1
Steve Clarkson, San Jose State	206	402	2906	51.2
Scott Campbell, Purdue	185	321	2686	57.6
John Elway, Stanford	214	366	2674	58.5
Dan Marino, Pittsburgh	200	339	2615	59.0
Jim Kelly, Miami	168	285	2403	59.0
Art Schlichter, Ohio State	172	324	2392	53.1
Sam Shon, Ohio University	175	320	2366	54.7

RECEIVING YARDS	Catches	Yards
Jim Sandusky, UNLV	68	1346
Chester Cooper, Minnesota	58	1012
Darius Durham, San Diego State	65	988
Steve Bryant, Purdue	60	971
Gordon Hudson, Brigham Young	67	960
Jeff Spek, UNLV	54	895
Dan Plater, Brigham Young	62	891
Jeff Champine, Colorado State	66	882
Gary Williams, Ohio State	48	880
Darrin Nelson, Stanford	67	846

1981 Consensus All-America Team
Offense

Wide Receiver:	Anthony Carter, Michigan
Tight End:	Tim Wrightman, UCLA
Line:	Sean Farrell, Penn State
	Roy Foster, Southern California
	Terry Crouch, Oklahoma
	Ed Muransky, Michigan
	Terry Tausch, Texas
	Kurt Becker, Michigan
Center:	Dave Rimington, Nebraska
Quarterback:	Jim McMahon, BYU
Running Back:	Marcus Allen, Southern California
	Herschel Walker, Georgia

Defense

Line:	Billy Ray Smith, Arkansas
	Kenneth Sims, Texas
	Andre Tippett, Iowa
	Tim Krumrie, Wisconsin
Linebacker:	Bob Crable, Notre Dame
	Jeff Davis, Clemson
	Sal Sunseri, Pittsburgh
Back:	Tommy Wilcox, Alabama
	Mike Richardson, Arizona State
	Terry Kinard, Clemson
	Fred Marion, Miami
Punter:	Reggie Roby, Iowa

1981 Heisman Trophy Vote

Marcus Allen, senior tailback, Southern California	1,797
Herschel Walker, sophomore tailback, Georgia	1,199
Jim McMahon, senior quarterback, Brigham Young	706
Dan Marino, junior quarterback, Pittsburgh	256
Art Schlichter, senior quarterback, Ohio State	149

Other Major Award Winners

Maxwell (Player)	Marcus Allen, senior tailback, Southern California
Walter Camp (Player)	Marcus Allen, senior tailback, Southern California
Outland (Lineman)	Dave Rimington, junior center, Nebraska
Lombardi (Lineman)	Kenneth Sims, senior defensive tackle, Texas
Davey O'Brien (QB)	Jim McMahon, senior quarterback, BYU
AFCA Coach of the Year	Danny Ford, Clemson

1982

The Year of the Ironic National Title, Herschel Leaves for "The Donald," and Elway's Strange Finale

For 57 days, college football was the greatest football available as the first-ever, in-season player strike plagued the National Football League. Players held out for a bigger piece of the pie, demanding both a percentage of gross income, and an improved wage scale. Near the end of the stalemate, former University of Pittsburgh player Paul Martha, who played in the NFL for seven years before becoming an attorney, served as intermediary to help negotiate a final agreement. Upon returning to the field, the pros played a truncated nine-game schedule and full playoffs. Before the strike was settled on November 16, attendance for college football increased across nation, and fans enjoyed an exciting season. Ted Turner, the maverick of broadcasting, even made a failed attempt to air college games on Sundays.

After many close calls and controversial final ballots, Penn State (11-1) and coach Joe Paterno finally won a national title, and they did it, ironically, by shaking off a single loss. After absorbing an early-season thrashing by Alabama (8-4), the Nittany Lions rode the offensive abilities of quarterback Todd Blackledge and tailback Curt Warner and their usual tough defense to a championship match-up with Herschel Walker and top-ranked Georgia (11-1) in the Sugar Bowl. Penn State won the game 27-23 to become national champions for the first time in school history.

Paterno had lobbied loudly in vain attempts to sway voters during three previous undefeated seasons. It was odd to see Penn State win it all, despite having one loss in a year that another major team went undefeated.

Featuring the tailback combination of Eric Dickerson, who rushed for 1,617 yards, and Craig James, Southern Methodist (11-0-1) finished as the only undefeated team after beating Pittsburgh (9-3) in the Cotton Bowl. The Mustangs did, however, suffer a 17-17 tie against a good Arkansas (9-2-1) team. "No one will ever be able to explain to me how a team (Penn State) that has lost a game to another team (Alabama) that in turn lost four times can be ranked ahead of one that has not lost at all," said SMU coach Bobby Collins. But accusations of recruiting violations centered on SMU's program, and it was impossible to measure the impact the investigation had on poll voters. It didn't help the Mustangs' case that Clemson (9-1-1) had been put on probation less than a year after winning the 1981 national title. The worse possible scenario for SMU was around the corner.

Although Georgia failed to win a second national title in three years, junior tailback Walker gained 1,752 yards and finally won the Heisman Trophy as the nation's premier player. He had been third in voting as a freshman and runner-up in 1981. Walker was the seventh junior to win the award and second Georgia player after the selection of Frankie Sinkwich in 1942. Although Walker needed only 823 yards in his senior year to pass both Charles White of Southern California (5,598 yards) and Tony Dorsett of Pittsburgh (6,082 yards) to become the career rushing leader in college football, he felt he had accomplished enough at Athens. Walker became the first superstar to test the legality of being forced to stay in school. He opted for the United States Football League's New Jersey Generals, owned by real estate tycoon and self-promoter Donald Trump, who was whimsically referred to as "The Donald." Running backs Kelvin Bryant of North Carolina, James of SMU, Tim Spencer of Ohio State, and Michigan wide receiver Anthony Carter were some of the members of a very talented senior class who opted for the new league.

Alabama was expected to be Georgia's chief rival for the Southeastern Conference crown. Indeed on October 11, the Crimson Tide sat at 5-0, with a 42-21 win over Penn State under their belt and a no. 2 national ranking. But, Alabama went on one of the greatest free falls in school history, dropping four of their next six games including their first loss in Tuscaloosa since 1963. The Tide lost their first game to Auburn (9-3) since 1972 to drop completely out of the rankings by November 15.

After deflecting rumors from mid-season on, Alabama coach Bear Bryant retired after the regular season. Bryant, who finished with 323-85-17 record, ended on a high note with a Liberty Bowl win over Illinois (7-5). One month later, on January 26, Bear passed away from a heart attack. It was revealed at time that he had been sick for some time. Ray Perkins, coach of the New York Giants and a former Alabama end, took over the unenviable position as successor to Bryant.

Coaches were in the news throughout the season as Jackie Sherrill made a splash by leaving Pittsburgh, after 50 wins in five years, for the head position at Texas A&M (5-6). Sherrill received an astounding 10-year, $1.6 million dollar package after Michigan (8-4) coach Bo Schembechler turned it down.

The U.S. economy was making baby steps toward boom years, and coaches seemed to be the only ones reaping the benefits. Academic budgets were in delicate balance in the early 1980s, so coaches' salaries became controversial. Academia was perturbed that coaches now earned more than department heads or even some school presidents. Despite the consternation, the pay gap widened as the years went by.

There was a big-time debut in 1982, but this was by one of the most heralded high school players ever. Famously recruited out of Philadelphia, Miss., after rushing for 5,283 yards with 87 touchdowns in high school, Marcus Dupree began a star-crossed career at Oklahoma (8-4), that coaches and fans there hoped would be as fruitful as the three years spent at Georgia by Walker. Dupree teased fans during the regular season with his 905 yards rushing and 13 touchdowns. What he did to the Arizona State (10-2) defense in a Fiesta Bowl loss was both a glimpse into his incredible potential and a warning sign of problems to come. Dupree carved up the Sun Devils to the tune of 239 yards rushing. Amazingly, he reached that total despite missing most of the fourth quarter with a hamstring pull, although the real culprit was his being overweight. That a teenaged Dupree was in questionable shape for his first bowl game was startling, but things would get worse. By mid-season of 1983, Dupree was gone, leaving Norman for a variety of reasons including homesickness. It was alarming that he could not cut it with coach Barry Switzer, whom it was thought could coach any personality. Dupree ended up in the USFL in 1985 with the New Orleans Breakers, but never fulfilled his immense promise. Instead of bringing back memories of great Oklahoma backs like Billy Vessels, Steve Owens, Greg Pruitt, and Billy Sims, Dupree's saga reminded some OU fans of Joe Don Looney, a promising but troubled back of the early 1960s. Oklahoma failed to win the Big Eight conference in either year that Dupree played.

Northwestern (3-8) certainly was no threat to eventual Big Ten winner Michigan, but the "Mildcats" beat Northern Illinois 31-6 on September 25 to snap an NCAA-record 34-game losing streak. Coach Dennis Green's purple charges won their first Big Ten game after 38 straight losses on October 9, beating Minnesota (3-8) and went on to defeat Michigan State (2-9) to earn a very surprising tie for eighth place in the conference.

In the West, Stanford (5-6) had a much better chance to earn a Rose Bowl berth, but ended up with unbelievable heartache that even Northwestern couldn't comprehend. The Cardinal was unable to convert an early upset over Ohio State (9-3) with a title run in an exciting Pacific Ten race eventually won by UCLA (10-1-1).

It was the final year for one of Stanford's finest players, quarterback John Elway, and a team goal had been to secure a bowl bid as a gift for Elway, who was still looking for his first post-season action in a four-year career. Despite his passing for 3,242 yards with 24 touchdowns and leading a late drive to apparent victory over California (7-4), Elway would end his collegiate football days on the sideline as the strangest finish to a game developed before his disbelieving eyes. The "Big Game," the California-Stanford rivalry, became national news when the Bears pulled out a win on a game-ending kickoff return that featured five desperate laterals and ended with Bears safety Kevin Moen scoring a touchdown by running through the Stanford band. Cal students woke up the following day to read in the school paper, *The Daily Californian,* that the NCAA had reversed the decision and awarded the game to Stanford. The newspaper was a hoax, perpetrated by the *Stanford Daily* and did much to highlight the uniqueness of the wacky rivalry between schools known for their academic values. Air Force (8-5) was tapped for the Hall of Fame Bowl bid that would have gone to Stanford had Elway's late-game heroics withstood the strange kickoff return by the Cal Bears.

Milestones

■ Whopping 32 rules changes were implemented, including face-mask penalties differentiated between incidental (5-yard) and deliberate (15-yard) fouls, allowance of intentional grounding to stop clock, and stipulation that pass interference could occur only on catchable throws.

■ September 25 game pitting Southern California and Oklahoma was scheduled as first to break from NCAA TV contract after court ruling declared individual schools were clear to set up their own contracts. Oklahoma City station KOCO-TV was selected to broadcast game. Stay to prevent telecast was granted to NCAA on September 23 by three-judge panel in Denver.

■ In January, NCAA voted in Proposition 48 to take effect in 1986. It required minimum scholastic requirements for incoming freshmen to receive financial aid and be eligible to play.

■ UNLV joined Pacific Coast Athletic Association.

■ Aloha Bowl debuted in Honolulu.

■ UCLA began playing regularly in Rose Bowl stadium, ending 52-year association with L.A. Coliseum.

■ Tailback Derek Singleton, Colorado's leading rusher when he was struck down with meningitis on October 24, 1981, died at age 19 on January 1. While being operated on for knee injury suffered in varsity-alumni football game, former Oklahoma defensive back Mike Babb died from cardiac arrest on May 3 at age 23. Two-time All-America quarterback Irvine "Cotton" Warburton, who later became Academy Award-winning film editor, died at age 70 on June 21. Warburton led 1932 Southern California Trojans to 10-0 record and national title, beating Pittsburgh 35-0 in Rose Bowl. Warburton won 1964 Oscar for Mary Poppins. Jackie Jensen, Cal's "Golden Boy," died of heart attack at age 55 on July 14. Jensen helped lead Golden Bears to 1949 Rose Bowl, memorably bursting for 67 yard run in loss to Northwestern. After pitching and hitting Bears to their first NCAA baseball title in 1947, Jensen prospered in 11-year major league baseball career with Yankees, Senators, and Red Sox, for whom he won 1958 American League MVP award. H.O. "Fritz" Crisler, who played for Amos Alonzo Stagg at Chicago and won 116 games as coach of Minnesota, Princeton, and Michigan, died on August 19 at 83. Crisler won 71 games at Michigan in 10 years, where he coached 1940 Heisman Trophy winner Tom Harmon. He was pioneer in developing two-platoon football in 1945 to make up for war-time player shortages, and was athletic director for 28 years. Crisler's separate offensive and defensive units went undefeated in 1947 and beat USC 49-0 in Rose Bowl. Referee Rich McVay, 55, collapsed and died of massive heart attack while working Illinois-Michigan State game on September 11. Bill George, eight-time All-Pro with Chicago Bears who was credited with creating MLB position after days as All-America tackle with Wake Forest, died at age 51 of injuries suffered in car accident on September 30. Coaching great Ray Morrison died at 97 on November 19. All-Southern Conference quarterback at Vanderbilt (1911), Morrison became head coach for 4 different schools from 1915-51, most notably at SMU where his 1923 squad went 9-0. Morrison was early innovator of wide-open passing game. Benny Friedman, All-America quarterback at Michigan and NFL star, died of self-inflicted gunshot on November 23 at age 76. Teaming with E Bennie Oosterbaan, Friedman led Wolverines to 1926 Big 10 title. Leo "Dutch" Meyer, who won 109 games in 19 years as TCU coach, beginning in 1934, died at 84 on December 3. Meyer coached Frogs team led by Heisman Trophy winner Davey O'Brien to national title in 1938. Under Meyer, TCU won SWC titles in 1938, 1944, and 1951. Pitt linebacker Todd Becker died at age 20 after falling from third story window on December 16.

■ Longest winning streaks entering season:

Clemson 13	Miami 6	BYU, Toledo 5

■ Coaching Changes:

	Incoming	Outgoing
California	Joe Kapp	Roger Theder
Colorado	Bill McCartney	Chuck Fairbanks
Colorado State	Leon Fuller	Chester Caddas
Kentucky	Jerry Claiborne	Fran Curci
Maryland	Bobby Ross	Jerry Claiborne
Navy	Gary Tranquill	George Welsh
Pittsburgh	Serafino "Foge" Fazio	Jackie Sherrill
Purdue	Leon Burnett	Jim Young
South Carolina	Richard Bell	Jim Carlin
Southern Methodist	Bobby Collins	Ron Meyer
Texas A&M	Jackie Sherrill	Tom Wilson
Texas-El Paso	Jim Yung	Billy Alton
Utah	Chuck Stobart	Wayne Howard
Virginia	George Welsh	Dick Bestwick

AP Preseason Poll

1 Pittsburgh (36)	1092	11 Clemson (1)	561
2 Washington (15)	1064	12 Michigan	552
3 Alabama (3)	966	13 Arkansas	471
4t Nebraska (2)	949	14 Ohio State	423
4t North Carolina (2)	949	15 Miami	396
6 Southern Methodist	743	16 Florida	357
7 Georgia	698	17 Texas	236
8 Penn State	682	18 Notre Dame	157
9 Oklahoma	638	19 Arizona State	155
10 Southern California	624	20 UCLA	150

September 4, 1982

(Fri) Syracuse 31 RUTGERS 8 (East Rutherford, NJ): Orange (1-0) flexed muscles in controlling Rutgers for 4 Qs. HB Jamie Covington rushed for 64y and TD runs of 1y and 18y, while QB Steve Peach (12-20/209y, INT) threw and ran for TDs at helm of Syracuse O. Peach's 34y scoring pass to WR Mike Morris late in 2nd Q gave visitors 17-3 lead at H. Rutgers (0-1) surrendered 380y, while managing 273y but losing 4 TOs. QB Jacque LaPrarie threw for 119y and rushed for 58y to pace Scarlet Knights.

FLORIDA 17 Miami 14: As temperatures cooled in 2nd H to 102 degrees, Gators (1-0) turned to O stars to snap 4-game series losing streak. Flushed right, QB Wayne Peace (18-24/220y, INT) threw 17y to FB James Jones, who had run wrong pattern but was open, for TD on 1-handed, tumbling catch. TD capped late 4th Q, 61y drive. QB Jim Kelly (18-30/170y, 2 INTs) had completed 9 straight passes to open 2nd H as Hurricanes (0-1) took 14-10 lead on 1y TD dive by HB Mark Rush to end 86y drive. Miami D then held off Gators until very end, stopping Florida on 4th down run midway through 4th Q. Florida D excelled, led by LB Wilber Marshall's 17 tackles.

GEORGIA 13 Clemson 7: Georgia TB Herschel Walker may have only gained 20y but because of playing with broken thumb, he inspired mates in match-up of past 2 national champs. Bulldogs (1-0) could muster only 2 FGs by K Kevin Butler and DE Stan Dooley's 2y RET of DE Dale Carver's blocked punt for 2nd Q TD, but that was enough. Athens native, Clemson QB Homer Jordan, was forced into 4 INTs by Georgia D, which allowed sole TD after Bulldogs O lost FUM on own 10YL. Jordan scored on 6y draw as Tigers (0-1) took 7-0 lead. Walker had 2nd H TD nullified by PEN, so UGa great would close his career scoreless in 3 tries against Clemson.

Duke 25 TENNESSEE 24: Blue Devils (1-0) pulled upset by rallying from 10-0 and 24-12 deficits behind QB Ben Bennett (18-29/288y, TD), who came off bench late in 1st Q. Volunteers (0-1) had 10-0 lead as QB Alan Cockrell (20-25/239y, INT) completed 1st 8 passes including 17y TD pass to WR Mike Miller. K Ken Harper kicked 2 FGs as Duke trailed 10-6 at H. Tennessee opened 2nd H with 65y drive to 1st down at Duke 7YL, but 4 plays ended inside 1y. Bennett soon threw 88y TD pass to WR Chris Castor that pulled Blue Devils to within 12-10 while setting Duke long-distance mark. Bennett stumbled, losing 2 FUMs in own end to set up Vols TDs for 12-pt Tennessee lead. Duke FB Greg Boone raced 100y with KO as Duke now trailed 24-18 entering 4th Q. Only 1 TD would be squeezed out, scored by Devils TB Joel Blunk (13/101y) on 13y run at end of 83y drive. Duke D then made stop before O marched 98y from own 1YL to Tennessee's 1YL to eliminate clock.

Boston College 38 TEXAS A&M 16: In moving to SWC, coach Jackie Sherrill probably welcomed chance to escape Northeast passing attacks. But 1st, he had to debut against familiar face, Boston College (1-0) QB Doug Flutie, who lit up Texas A&M for 18-26/346y, 3 TDs, with another on ground. Pair of Flutie's TDs found WR Jon Schoen for 45 and 16y, both during 24-pt 1st H when BC scored on 1st 4 possessions. Aggies (0-1) opened 2nd H with 10 pts, with TD scored on 4y pass from QB Gary Kubiak (23-43/260y, 2 INTs) to TE Mark Lewis to pull within 24-16. Flutie next led 80y drive, capped by his 32y TD pass to WR Brian Brennan (4/119y) to quiet Aggies. Sherrill had been 5-0 versus Eagles while coaching Pittsburgh.

Arizona State 34 OREGON 3: Sun Devils (1-0) broke open 3-3 game in convincing fashion, and, once dam broke, Ducks were drowned. LB Willie Green jump-started Arizona State romp with INT returned 43y to Oregon (0-1) 20YL that set up 1y TD run by FB Dwaine Wright (15/70y) for 10-3 2nd Q lead. Arizona State scored trio of 2nd H TDs as NG Mitch Callahan recovered FUM in EZ and sub QB Todd Hons (12-18/98y, TD) directed 2 scoring drives. Best chance for Ducks to stem tide came while trailing 13-3 early in 3rd Q on drive deep into ASU territory. HB Ladaria Johnson (8/53y) lost FUM on ASU 8YL, recovered by Devils LB Greg Battle to kill Oregon's chances.

AP Poll September 6

1 Pittsburgh (33)	1082	11 Florida	549
2 Washington (16)	1007	12 Michigan	538
3 Nebraska (2)	918	13 Arkansas	492
4 Alabama (2)	916	14 Ohio State	394
5 North Carolina (2)	825	15 Arizona State	306
6 Georgia (1)	811	16 Clemson	236
7 Penn State	731	17 Texas	181
8 Southern Methodist	722	18 UCLA	173
9 Oklahoma	593	19 Miami	162
10 Southern California	573	20 Notre Dame	112

September 11, 1982

(Th) PITTSBURGH 7 North Carolina 6: As North Carolina D manhandled O of no. 1 Pitt, pressure was on Panthers (1-0) D to keep team's high hopes alive. With D coordinator Foge Fazio elevated to head job, his inspired charges kept Tar Heels (0-1) out of EZ and held them to 132y in 2nd H, 247y overall. Panthers D had to play its best as Pitt QB Dan Marino threw for only 125y with 4 INTs, although he was 4-4/45y on winning 69y TD drive in 3rd Q. Marino finished drive with 4y scoring pass to TB Bryan Thomas. While Panthers gained only 197y, Thomas rushed for 58y and caught 7/42y. Committing 15 PENs/133y served as poison for Carolina.

PENN STATE 39 Maryland 31: Strike up band for QB Todd Blackledge (19-30/262y, 2 INTs), who threw 4 TDs for 2nd game in row as Nittany Lions (2-0) won 19th straight in series. Maryland led 24-23 after 3rd Q TD passes of 50y and 60y from QB Boomer Esiason (18-36/276y, 2 INTs) to WR Russell Davis (7/188y). Blackledge followed with 2 TDs passes—23y to WR Greg Garrity and 10y to WR Kenny Jackson—for 36-24 lead. Terps (0-1) pulled within 36-31 on 10y TD run by TB Willie Joyner, but after Penn State kicked FG, they were snuffed by late INT by DE Walker Lee Ashley.

NAVY 20 Virginia 16: Midshipmen (1-0) did not offer former coach George Welsh happy homecoming, and Cavs above all were unwelcome near Navy's GL. Virginia (0-1) cracked Navy 10YL on 6 occasions only to make 3 FGs with 2 TOs and missed FB. Cavs managed 54y TD bomb from backup QB Wayne Schuchts (6-11/168y) to WR Nick Merrick, but it could not overcome missed opportunities. Middies scored 2 TDs, both on passing plays from QB Marco Pagnanelli to TB Rich Clouse. Virginia won y battle handily but for naught, 430y to 226y.

FLORIDA 17 Southern California 9: Gators (2-0) D halted USC run attack, allowing only 84y on ground and recovering 2 of 4 FUMs. QB Wayne Peace led balanced attack that truly shone on 97y drive in 2nd Q that put Gators up 14-0 on 22y TD run on draw by FB James Jones (16/81y). Earlier, Peace threw 1y TD pass to WR Spencer Jackson, who made brilliant 4th-and-goal catch. Trojans (0-1) were led by 222y passing by QB Sean Salisbury, but he threw 3 INTs. Florida LB Wilber Marshall had 14 tackles and 4 sacks, earning post-game kudos by USC coach John Robinson.

GEORGIA 17 Brigham Young 14: Right after snapping Clemson's 13-game win streak, Bulldogs (2-0) extinguished 6-game run of Cougars. Georgia D handled BYU (1-1) aerial game, picking off 6 passes by QB Steve Young (22-46/285y, TD), final INT coming from by CB Ronnie Harris at UGa 25 YL with 43 secs left. Moments earlier, K Kevin Butler drilled winning 44y FG after 23y run by TB Herschel Walker (31/124y). Bulldogs G Mike Weaver turned in play of game when recovering 4th-and-1 FUM by QB John Lastinger for 1st down with BYU up 14-7. Walker crashed into EZ 4 plays later from 1YL to tie game. Cougars TE Gordon Hudson caught 10/127y, while CB Tom Holmoe scored 2nd TD on 63y INT RET.

MICHIGAN 20 Wisconsin 9: Wolverines (1-0) played off par, but were sharp enough to beat Wisconsin (0-1). TB Lawrence Ricks led Michigan attack that totaled 377y with 153y rushing and opening 4y TD run. Ricks did well in part because Badgers D keyed

on WR Anthony Carter, holding him to 1 catch/10y and 35y total on RETs and single rushing try. With coverage doubled on Carter, QB Steve Smith (12-29/207y) looked elsewhere but was picked off twice while Wolverines also lost 2 FUMs. Wisconsin QB Randy Wright threw for 198y but only 70y in 2nd H.

West Virginia 41 OKLAHOMA 27: West Virginia QB Jeff Hostetler (17-37/321y) burst on national scene with 4-TD performance against Sooners (0-1). Hostetler, transfer from Penn State, helped send OU to 1st opening loss in coach Barry Switzer's tenure by leading O that scored most pts against Oklahoma in Norman since Nebraska made 44 in 1928. Hostetler's last TD, 9y strike to WR Wayne Brown, snapped 27-27 tie midway through 4th Q. Mountaineers TB Curlin Beck scored 2 big TDs, catching 30y TD for 27-21 lead and rushing 43y for clincher with 3 mins left. Sooners had opened with 2 TDs for 14-0 lead. Mountaineers then reeled off 20 pts before H, including 10 in final min of H as K Paul Woodside followed 38y FG with squib KO, recovered by West Virginia LB Brad Minetree at OU 33YL. Soon after, WR Darrell Miller caught 27y TD pass.

NEBRASKA 42 Iowa 7: It was sweet revenge for Huskers (1-0) as they paid Iowa back for 1981's 10-7 upset and manner in which Hawkeyes handled it. Nebraska TE Jamie Williams said of 1981 game, "I hate to see any team get its head inflated when it more or less sneaks by an opponent." Iowa heads clearly were not inflated after this contest, won in 1st H when Nebraska scored 4 TDs while Hawks earned only single 1st down. QB Turner Gill (9-16/144y, 2 TDs) led rout by throwing TD passes of 41y to WB Irving Fryar (6/127y) and 9y to WR Todd Brown, while IB Mike Rozier rushed for 127y. Iowa scored in 4th Q on 4y run by sub QB Tom Grogan.

September 18, 1982

Boston College 17 CLEMSON 17: After blowing 14-0 H lead, Clemson (0-1-1) almost pulled out late win. Boston College scored 17 straight pts to go up by 17-14 late, before Tigers tied game on 43y FG by K Donald Igwebuike. Clemson squeezed out last-sec FG try that flew wide left. Eagles (1-0-1) QB Doug Flutie, who frustrated Tigers with scrambles, threw for 242y and 15y TD pass to TB Jon Schoen early in 4th Q that tied it 14-14. Tigers RB Steve Griffin fumbled KO, which set up go-ahead 37y FG by K Kevin Snow and forced Clemson to rally with tying 53y drive. Tigers did most of its damage on ground, rushing for 254y, topped by TB Cliff Austin's 20/94y.

Pittsburgh 37 FLORIDA STATE 17: Ignoring heavy tropical storm, QB Dan Marino (13-22/133y, INT) powered Panthers (2-0) by throwing 2 4th Q TDs. Winning TD came on special teams as DE Art Lowery caught punt that was blocked and ran it in 5y for 24-17 lead. FB Marlon McIntyre scored twice for Panthers in 1st H, as Pitt wiped out 10-0 Noles lead with 17 straight pts. Florida State (1-1) tied it on 1y scoring run by TB Ricky Williams (16/83y), but that would be final pts for Seminoles as 2nd H storms slowed their speedy attack. "There's no doubt the rain was the difference," said Pitt coach Foge Fazio. "If it hadn't rained, the score might have been 50-50."

Alabama 42 MISSISSIPPI 14: Crimson Tide (2-0) coach Bear Bryant won 30th straight game over former coach or player, in this case Mississippi (2-1) coach and former Alabama QB Steve Sloan. Bama QB Walter Lewis sparked O for 484y, threw for 2 TDs and rushed for another, while FB Craig Turner tallied on 3 runs. Tide gained 296y rushing. Lewis (6-10/178y) broke open 14-7 game in 2nd Q with 80y TD bomb to WR Jesse Bendross (3/125y), and his 16y TD dash in 3rd Q put dagger in Rebs' hearts. QB Kent Austin (15-28/153y, 2 TDs, 2 INTs) collaborated with WR Michael Harmon on both Ole Miss TDs, but could not overcome 5 TOs.

NOTRE DAME 23 Michigan 17: Irish (1-0) used 1st-ever night game at Notre Dame Stadium to show that 1981's losing record was aberration. Converting pair of FUMs into 10-0 lead, Irish never trailed. ND FB Larry Moriarty rushed for 116y, scoring on 24y burst and bulling his way for 37y on big play that helped field position after Wolverines (1-1) had pulled to within 23-17. Notre Dame D had 7 sacks of QB Steve Smith in holding Michigan to 41y rushing. When Michigan scored its TDs, it was in wild fashion as WR Anthony Carter returned punt for 72y TD in 3rd Q, and TB Rick Rogers scored on 29y pass play when Smith's throw was batted by Irish CB Dave Duerson onto back of S Stacey Toran. Rogers snatched it and took off.

Iowa State 19 IOWA 7: For 3rd straight year, Cyclones K Alex Giffords made Iowa (0-2) rue day they did not get him signed to letter of intent. Iowa State (1-1) now had won 3 straight in series: Giffords kicked winning FG in 10-7 win in 1980, 3 FGs and 2 x-pts in 23-12 win in 1981, and now 4 FGs in this game to tie school and Kinnick Stadium records. Iowa State QB David Archer contributed 46y TD pass to WR Frankie Leaks in 4th Q. Archer's TD overcame 1st Q mistake, INT nabbed by Hawkeyes DE Tony Wancket that was returned 26y for opening score. Cyclones dominated their rivals, holding Hawkeyes to 102y and 5 1st downs. Best stat for Iowa was 45y punting average on 6 kicks by P Reggie Roby.

Colorado 12 WASHINGTON STATE 0: Buffs K Tom Field had stranglehold on tilt's scoring, kicking 4 FGs to tie school record. Back-up QB Steve Vogel was thrust into starting role for Colorado (1-1) and led 4 scoring drives, while D handed Cougars 1st shutout in 7 years. Washington State (1-1) managed only 182y and 1 good drive. It

came on 1st possession of 2nd H, which ended with GLS by Buffaloes D as LB Dave Alderson stopped Wazzu FB James Matthews on 4th-and-goal from 1YL. Colorado's ground game earned 241y as HB Lee Rouson led way with 22/97y.

San Jose State 35 STANFORD 31: Coach Jack Elway's Spartans upset Stanford for 2nd straight year as San Jose QB Steve Clarkson (21-40/285y) threw 3 TDs and converted late Cardinal FUM into winning 3y keeper. Stanford QB John Elway fell to 1-2 as starter versus father's team despite passing 24-36/382y, 3 TDs. Final drive summed up frustration of Elway's time in Palo Alto as he drove O to SJSU 26YL before being sacked on last 4 plays. Spartans WR Tim Kearse was splendid, catching 6/163y, 2 TDs, and throwing surprise 84y TD pass to WR Tony Smith.

September 25, 1982

PENN STATE 28 Nebraska 24: Controversial finish kept Penn State's national title hopes alive while dimming those of Huskers (2-1). On 1y sneak late in 4th Q, Nebraska QB Turner Gill (16-34/239y, 2 TDs, INT) capped rally from 2-TD deficit to take 24-21 lead. QB Todd Blackledge (23-39/295y, INT) then hit 4 passes, including 11y strike to WR Kenny Jackson to convert 4th-and-11 and out-pattern to TE Mike McCloskey, who caught ball as he was going OB at Huskers 2YL. Line judge ruled that McCloskey got 1 foot in, which TV replays showed was questionable decision. With 9 secs left, Penn State coach Joe Paterno passed up tying FG attempt, calling for pass play. Blackledge tossed pass into back of EZ to sub TE Kirk "Stonehands" Bowman, who dove and came up with ball. Was it trapped or caught? Play ruled catch, and Penn State escaped with win. Bowman earlier caught 14y TD pass to give Penn State 14-0 lead and hopefully earned himself new nickname. Alas, Bowman did not catch another pass all season. WB Irving Fryar (7/112y) caught 30y scoring pass for Huskers. At Boys Town, Neb., athletic banquet in 1998, McCloskey admitted, for 1st time, that it was true: he was OB on his big catch. Ironically, McCloskey was on hand to introduce main banquet speaker, Nebraska's Gill.

AUBURN 24 Tennessee 14: Auburn (3-0) HB Bo Jackson gave evidence of his future glory, rushing for 129y with TD runs of 20y and 32y. Tigers held slim 17-14 lead in 4th Q when Jackson made twisting, diving catch of pass by fellow HB Lionel James for 43y gain to propel clinching TD drive. James capped 86y drive with 2y TD dive. Volunteers (1-2) drove into Auburn territory late in contest, but lost ball on FUM by QB Alan Cockrell. Cockrell (16-28/212y, 2 INTs) had hooked up with WR Willie Gault for both Tennessee TDs, on 38y and 78y passes. Tigers rushed for 357y.

Pittsburgh 20 ILLINOIS 3: Match-up of Heisman candidate QBs was dominated by D as Pitt (3-0) sacked QB Tony Eason (30-58/275y) 9 times/82y and intercepted 5 passes, while Illini D had 4 INTs of QB Dan Marino (18-35/215y, TD). Unsung DT Dave Puzzuoli had moment to remember with 95y scoring RET of INT to put Panthers up 7-3 when they easily could have trailed 10-0. "I caught it before I had a chance to think about it," said Puzzuoli of INT. "And then there was nothing ahead of me but green." K Eric Schubert booted 1st of his 2 FGs, from 37y out, as Panthers took 10-3 H lead, and Marino threw 15y TD pass to TE John Brown to clinch matters in 3rd Q. Illinois (3-1) O had rough game but D played well, with frosh S Craig Swoopes having 1 pick for 4th on season. Pitt WR Dwight Collins caught 6/117y.

Ucla 31 MICHIGAN 27: Bruins (3-0) rallied from 21-0 deficit to post thrilling win. QB Tom Ramsey (22-36/311y, INT) led 2 quick drives for TDs on 46y bomb to WR Dokie Williams and 1y QB plunge to cut into Michigan's edge. Wolverines (1-2) K Ali Haji-Sheikh then booted 47y FG for 10-pt H lead. Bruins regained momentum early in 3rd Q on INT by S Don Rogers that set up 6y TD pass to WR Jojo Townsell (7/108y). Michigan upped lead to 6 with another FG, but kicked off to Williams, whose 65y RET set up winning 2y TD run by TB Kevin Nelson. UCLA K John Lee added FG, while D ended next 2 Michigan drives with INTs. QB Steve Smith then marched Wolverines to Bruins 8YL with 11 secs to go before 3 straight incompletions ended game. WR Anthony Carter was brilliant in defeat, with 8 catches/123y, TD.

Stanford 23 OHIO STATE 20: With help from Ohio State tacticians, Stanford (2-1) QB John Elway secured 1 of his finest victories with late 80y TD drive. Elway hit 4-6 on winning drive, including 18y TD pass to WR Emile Harry with 34 secs left. Buckeyes (1-2) had ball on Stanford 27YL and were primed to run out clock. Instead Ohio State went to air and QB Mike Tomczak, who had woeful passing day with 6-19/71y, 4 INTs, threw EZ INT to S Charles Hutchings. Elway completed 35 of his school-record 63 attempts/407y, 2 TDs, 3 INTs.

Southern California 12 OKLAHOMA 0: There would be changes coming to Norman after hometown Sooners (1-2) suffered 1st shutout since 1966, span of 181 games. USC D held Oklahoma to paltry 43y rushing as Sooners were forced to air more than usual, passing 8-23/168y, 2 INTs. Trojans (2-1) passed for both of their TDs, including 67y completion on trick play when WR Timmy White took 2nd handoff from TB Fred Crutcher and hit WR Jeff Simmons with TD pass. Crutcher rushed for 92y to lead Trojans, but lost 2 FUMs deep in own territory that Southern California D prevented from being costly.

SOUTHERN METHODIST 16 Texas Christian 13: Number 10 was lucky for SMU (3-0), who rallied with 10 4th Q pts for 10th straight series win. Ponies tied score at 13-13 with 85y drive, capped by 5y scoring run by TB Eric Dickerson (27/160y, 2 TDs) who rushed for 58y on drive. Winning 19y FG by K Jeff Harrell came 5 plays after Mustangs D stripped Frogs (1-2) HB J.C. Morris, FUM REC going to LB Gary Moten. Frogs had taken 13-6 lead as RB Egypt Allen forced FUM with hard hit on SMU S Blane Smith as Smith fielded punt on own 20YL. TCU C Mike Flynn recovered loose ball on SMU 4YL. On next play QB Reuben Jones rushed for 4y TD.

Air Force 39 BRIGHAM YOUNG 38: Task facing Air Force (2-2) O was great: march 99y in final 90 secs or lose. Trailing 38-31, QB Marty Louthan led stunning drive to 22y TD pass to HB Mike Brown with 6 secs left. Having gone that far, team went for win and got it when Louthan and Brown hooked up again on 2-pt conv pass. Biggest play on winning drive went awry as roughing PEN negated Cougars' INT and gave Falcons ball at BYU 22YL. QB Steve Young (19-28/215y) led Cougars (1-2), throwing 15y TD to WR Kirk Pendleton and running for 3 others. Air Force's final trip allowed Air Force to win O battle by 489y to 460y.

Arizona State 15 CALIFORNIA 0: Sun Devils (4-0) swept aside California (2-1) behind D that put heat on QBs Gale Gilbert and J Torchio, who were sacked 12 times. Blitzing Arizona State LB Vernon Maxwell led way with 3.5 sacks. Bears gained only 130y and initiated only 5 plays in Sun Devils' territory, 2 nullified by PENs and 2 others knocked back into Cal territory by sacks. Arizona State D made more big plays as CB Mike Richardson upped his career INT record to 18 by nabbing pair of pickoffs. Sun Devils QB Todd Hons threw 43y TD to WR Doug Allen in 2nd Q, K Luis Zendejas added 2 FGs, and punt blocked through EZ by LB Jimmy Williams registered safety. Cal TE David Lewis caught 7/75y.

October 2, 1982

PITTSBURGH 16 West Virginia 13: With prospects high for both squads, rivalry had extra juice. Mountaineers (3-1) built 13-0 4th Q lead after LB Darryl Talley recovered own punt block in EZ. Pitt (4-0) QB Dan Marino (20-41/211y, 2 INTs), unproductive for 3 Qs, drove Pitt O to 2 late TDs, ending with 8y TD pass to WR Julius Dawkins for 14-13 lead. Panthers S Dan Short set up winning TD with his FUM REC by near midfield. Now trailing, West Virginia gave up 2 more pts when pass-rushing Pitt DT Bill Maas forced QB Jeff Hostetler (19-39/214y, INT) out of EZ. Last chance for WVU ended when K Paul Woodside barely missed 52y FG attempt at game's end: his 1st miss after 15 straight. Marino became Pitt's career total O leader.

Navy 27 DUKE 21: As QB Ben Bennett exploded in 4th Q, completing 20-25/259y, 3 TDs, Blue Devils (3-1) almost rallied from 27-pt deficit. Bennett (32-53/363y, 3 INTs) even drove Duke deep into Navy territory in search of winning TD until he was hit hard on keeper and lost FUM at 5YL, recovered by Navy DL Steve Peters. Midshipmen (2-2) used balanced attack to forge lead as TB Napoleon McCallum rushed for 211y and QB Marco Pagnanelli (15-17/171y) threw for 2 TDs.

Louisiana State 24 FLORIDA 13: Any questions about LSU's rebirth were answered as Tigers (3-0) came out roaring. QB Alan Risher (9-14/148y, 2 INTs) completed 1st 7 pass attempts in leading LSU to scores on opening 3 possessions. Risher, who passed Bert Jones (1970-72) as school's all-time y leader, completed 9-14/148y and TD passes of 41y and 3y to TB Dalton Hilliard (26/127y, TD). Hilliard's 41y scoring run with screen pass displayed array of broken tackles and nifty feints. Florida (3-1) rushed for only 106y, while its sole TD came late in 4th Q, when trailing 24-5, on 5y pass from QB Wayne Peace (18-29/149y, 2 INTs) to TE Mike Mularkey.

Georgia 29 MISSISSIPPI STATE 22: Ignoring broken right thumb, TB Herschel Walker rushed for 215y in leading Georgia (4-0). Walker gained 55y of 65y drive that ended on winning 1y TD run by QB John Lastinger early in 4th Q. Mississippi State (3-2) built 19-14 2nd Q lead on pair of TDs by HB Michael Haddix (13/89y), including 40y run after lateral from QB John Bond (60y, 3 INTs passing), who had gained 14y before pitching out, and another on 40y catch of pass by P-K Dana Moore on fake punt. Mississippi State FB Al Rickey Edwards rushed for 92y, with 65y coming on 1st Q TD, but Bond was held in check and lost late FUM in QB match-up versus former Valdosta High School teammate Lastinger. Key Georgia score came on 80y voyage to TB Barry Young's 10y TD run for 22-19 lead.

Florida State 34 OHIO STATE 17: With temperatures high, heat on beleaguered Ohio State (2-2) coach Earle Bruce intensified as D surrendered 476y to Seminoles. After TB Tim Spencer (16/99y) gave Bucks 7-0 lead on 8y run in 1st Q, Florida State (3-1) scored on trick play as QB Kelly Lowrey (14-23/130y) caught 11y TD pass from FB Cedric Jones. Buckeyes answered with 40y FG by K Rich Spangler, but Seminoles scored 2 TDs to grab lead for good. Game's leading rusher, TB Greg Allen (18/104y) scored TD on 7y run. With heat taking more out of OSU than FSU players, Noles posted 2nd H shutout and secured win with 2 4th Q TDs.

Wisconsin 35 PURDUE 31: In 1 of oddest finishes in Big 10 history, Badgers (2-2) shocked Purdue when LB Jim Melka scooped up miss-hit Purdue punt and raced 30y for winning score with 21 secs left. After catching high snap, Purdue P Matt Kinzer rushed his kick that went straight to surprised Melka, who raced untouched to EZ.

Boilermakers (0-4) led for most of contest as TB Mel Gray rushed for 3 TDs, including 80y romp for team's 1st TD. QB Randy Wright (20-30/303y) excelled for Badgers, throwing TD passes of 54y and 28y to WR Michael Jones. Purdue's balanced attack had it out front until very end, rushing for 232y and passing for 233y.

ARIZONA STATE 30 Kansas State 7: Sun Devils (5-0) D was dominant again, scoring TD and setting up 2 others with forced TOs, while holding Kansas State (3-1) to 152y. Arizona State DE Bryan Caldwell scored on 20y INT RET and fell on FUM that was converted into 15y TD run by TB Darryl Clack (11/78y). QB Todd Hons (14-32/153y, 2 INTs) added 34y TD pass to WR Ron Brown. Wildcats prevented shutout thanks to D unit as DE Vic Koenning returned INT 43y to TD with 68 secs left.

October 9, 1982

WEST VIRGINIA 20 Boston College 13: Knotted at 13-13, game turned on punt FUM by Boston College CB George Radachowsky, recovered by West Virginia (4-1) at BC 13YL with 1:26 left. Moments later, QB Jeff Hostetler (11-29/98y) ran in winning TD from 2y out with 28 secs remaining. LB Darryl Talley (15 tackles) harassed Eagles (3-1-1) QB Doug Flutie (9-33/98y, 4 INTs) all afternoon. BC scored sole TD on fake FG as holder-QB John Loughery threw 8y pass to TE Scott Nizolek.

Rutgers 24 Army 3 (East Rutherford, N.J.): Scarlet Knights (3-2) CB Carl Howard returned punt blocked by DB Joe Corbin 12y for opening TD and Rutgers never looked back. Rushing for 200y and taking 4 TOs, Rutgers controlled game from 1st Q. Knights increased lead to 14-0 by H when QB Jacque LaPrairie (9-15/129y) threw tipped TD pass to WR Eric Johnson. Army (2-3) wasted best chance to score TD late in 1st H when WR Billy Noble was nailed for 3y loss at Rutgers 6YL as time expired. Cadets, who ended with just 6y rushing, finally scored in 3rd Q on 35y FG by K Craig Stopa. Sub Rutgers K Peter Konczylo, 1-year removed from club football and not listed in media guide, kicked 22y FG and all 3 x-pt attempts.

North Carolina 24 WAKE FOREST 7: Tar Heels (4-1) QB Scott Stankavage (11-19/113y, INT) capitalized on rush game and tossed pair of 2nd H TDs to WR Mark Smith. North Carolina TBs Tyrone Anthony (179y) and TB Kelvin Bryant (151y) dominated, save for 2 FUMs. Carolina, which held 481y to 188y advantage and 18-min edge in time of possession, never trailed after Anthony burst 40y to opening TD in 1st Q. Wake Forest (3-3) QB Gary Schofield threw for 156y, but Deacs failed to take advantage of TOs, including FUM REC on Tar Heels 7YL that produced no pts during 7-7 1st H. Deacons were able to convert Bryant's lost FUM into 45y drive to 1y TD by TB Michael Ramseur. Carolina completely dominated 2nd H by 17-0.

ALABAMA 42 Penn State 21: Coach Bear Bryant's mastery over Penn State (4-1) reached 4-0 mark as Crimson Tide (5-0) picked off 5 passes, including LB Eddie Lowe's 31y TD that wrapped up rout. Alabama's 2nd-to-last score was Nittany Lions gift: up-back Mike Suter backed into P Ralph Giacomarro, blocking own team's punt. Bama recovered at Penn State 11YL for 40y reversal and scored 2 plays later. Tide earlier had blocked punt by Giacomarro, recovering at State 14YL to set up opening TD on 4y keeper by QB Walter Lewis (86y rushing, 96y passing). Lions surrendered most pts since 49 to UCLA in 1966, but scored twice on TD passes by QB Todd Blackledge (20-36/234y, 4 INTs), who had new school season TD pass mark with 17.

VANDERBILT 31 Florida 29: These were your grandfather's Commodores (3-2). QB Whit Taylor ripped through Florida D by completing 30-47/287y, 3 TDs. Led by QB Wayne Peace (28-36/285y, TD, INT), Gators (3-2) gained 540y and 30 1st downs. None of that made much difference when time elapsed as TE Mike Mularkey was unable to get OB on final play at Vanderbilt 38YL. Vanderbilt had taken 21-14 H lead after pair of 2nd Q TD passes by Taylor, who led O to 226y in opening H. Florida tied game on 4y TD run by FB James Jones (26/146y), but fell behind for good in allowing 10 straight pts with final TD coming on EZ FUM REC by Vandy T Rob Monaco.

Tennessee 24 LOUISIANA STATE 24: When final bell rang this fight produced draw: Volunteers (2-2-1) tied it when K Fuad Reveiz hit 52y FG with 2:07 left. Tennessee CB Carlton Peoples next came up with INT to set up Reveiz for another 52y attempt at game's end, which missed by foot. Tigers (3-0-1) QB Alan Risher threw for 192y, but also tossed 3 INTs and lost 4th Q FUM that led to tying FG. After Risher's 24y TD run gave LSU 7-6 lead, LSU D scored TD when CB James Britt took INT 44y. With game about to get away, Vols WR Willie Gault took ensuing KO 96y to tie game at 14-14. Tigers answered with 10 straight pts, including 3y run by TB Dalton Hilliard for his 9th TD of season. Tennessee pulled within 24-21 midway through 4th Q on 9y TD pass by QB Alan Cockrell (21-37/213y, 3 INTs) to WB Darryal Wilson. Special teams were special indeed for Vols in negating LSU's 434y to 268y O advantage as Gault scored TD, P Jimmy Colquitt averaged 5/53y, and Reveiz nailed 3 FGs.

Wisconsin 6 OHIO STATE 0: With QB Randy Wright completing his 1st 5 passes, Badgers (3-2) drove 80y with opening possession to score on 1y run by TB John Williams (17/70y). And then, Ds and rain took over. Wright completed only 3 of remaining 15 passes, yet led Wisconsin to its 1st win in Columbus since 1918. Badgers D dominated throughout as LB Jim Melka led way with 15 tackles, while LB Jody O'Donnell had 12 tackles and forced FUM to end 356 final threat by Buckeyes (2-3).

Ohio State had driven to Wisconsin 22YL on that last possession, while 3rd Q drive ended on 4th down stop by 4 Badgers defenders at own 19YL. Ohio State TB Jimmy Gayle rushed for 108y.

Oklahoma 28 Texas 22 (Dallas): Red River rivalry, meet Oklahoma TB Marcus Dupree. Dupree (9/96y) came to Norman with high expectations and he certainly sparkled on his 1st collegiate TD, 63y score on fake reverse. FB Weldon Ledbetter, Dupree's less-acclaimed running mate, added 2 TDs and 144y as Sooners (3-2) rushed for 384y to snap 3-game losing streak. Texas (3-1) did better in air as QB Robert Brewer threw for 235y and 2 TDs to WR Herkie Walls. After using I-formation in 1st H, Sooners surprisingly switched to Wishbone early in 3rd Q to score on 59y run by Ledbetter. Dupree accused Texas of providing him with $143 cowboy boots during recruiting process; Longhorns ended up with year's probation for that and selling of complimentary tickets.

Missouri 7 KANSAS STATE 7: Game may have been off national radar, but featured amazing TD. Facing 4th-and-32, Kansas State (3-1-1) QB Doug Bogue threw 33y pass to WR Mike Wallace in EZ to tie game early in 4th Q. S Chris Erickson, like Bogue in lineup due to injury, tipped ball to Wallace who juggled it before securing TD. Tigers (3-1-1) had last chance, moving to K-State 30YL in game's final secs. After procedure PEN cost 5y, K Brad Burditt—team's 4th K this season—was short by 5y on 52y try. Mizzou had scored 1st Q TD on 2y run by FB Tracey Mack (18/89y).

Southern Methodist 22 BAYLOR 19: With Baylor (2-2-1) D focusing on SMU run attack, Mustangs QB Lance McIlhenny (7-16/134y, INT) burned them with trio of 2nd H TD passes. SMU (5-0) TBs Eric Dickerson (22/73y) and Craig James (9/22y) may have been held to 180y less than combined avg, but presence opened up passing lanes due to 8-men fronts Bear D often employed. Baylor took 13-0 H lead on 2 FGs by K Ben Perry and 1y run by FB Allen Rice, set up by S Ron Francis' punt FUM REC of Ponies WR Keith Brooks' bobble at SMU 12YL. By H, Mustangs managed only 44y of O against Bears D led by DE Charles Benson (3 sacks). McIlhenny changed that with 2 3rd Q TD passes, including 78y bomb to WR Jackie Wilson. After Baylor regained lead on QB David Mangrum's 38y TD pass to TE Sam Houston, McIlhenny went to air again for winning 3y TD pass to TE Rickey Bolden, his 2nd TD catch followed by 2-pt conv, with 3 mins left. Winning 75y drive featured 45y rushing by Dickerson. P James averaged 8/47.7y, including 75y boot.

Brigham Young 40 NEW MEXICO 12: Off to their best start since 1945, Lobos (4-1) fumbled away WAC lead with quartet of 2nd H TOs, converted into 26 3rd Q pts by Brigham Young. FB Casey Tiumalu scored 2 TDs in 3rd Q as Cougars (3-2) obliterated 12-7 H deficit. BYU QB Steve Young (18-28/335y) threw 2 TDs and ran in another. New Mexico had scored in 1st H on 1y runs by QB David Osborn and RB Carl Raven as rush attack gained 266y.

ARIZONA STATE 21 Stanford 17: Sun Devils (6-0) escaped with victory as FB Dwaine Wright, whose FUM moments earlier had halted previous drive, scored from 1y out in closing 13 secs. Needing only 38 secs to move team 80y, QB Todd Hons (12-22/187y) completed 4-5 throws to set up Wright's TD. Stanford (3-2) QB John Elway (18-33/209y, INT) seemed to own hero's role after hitting WR Mike Tolliver on go-ahead 15y TD with 49 secs left to cap 9-play, 80y drive. Card drive began after S Vaughn Williams recovered Wright's FUM in EZ for touchback. TB Darryl Clack rushed for 112y as ASU gained 223y on ground. Elway passed Jack Thompson of Washington State (1975-78) as Pac-10 career pass y leader with 7837y.

UCLA 24 Arizona 24: Yet another Pac 10 game went down to wire as K Max Zendejas booted 43y FG with 36 secs left to give Wildcats (1-2-1) 24-21 lead. UCLA (4-0-1) QB Tom Ramsey (29-43/345y) then completed 3 quick passes to march Bruins 61y. Wildcats S Alfred Gross dropped Ramsey's next throw in EZ before frosh K John Lee kicked 36y FG with 2 secs left to tie it. Ramsey threw 2 TD passes but had 2 picked off with score tied 21-21, 1st in EZ to Cats CB Randy Robbins to kill scoring chance, 2nd to LB Cliff Thorpe that set up go-ahead FG. Ramsey rubbed Dennis Dummitt out of Bruins record book, breaking Dummitt's records for completions in game, y in game, and career y with 4,664y. QB Tom Tunnicliffe (13-20/187y) led Arizona on 3 TD drives of 80y or more, capping 2 with scoring passes including perfectly-thrown 28y pass to WR Jay Dobyns.

October 16, 1982

NORTH CAROLINA 41 North Carolina State 9: In 1 of most lopsided games in series history, Tar Heels (5-1) dominated as QB Scott Stankavage (11-18/203y)—now 3-0 as sub for injured QB Rod Elkins—tied school record with 4 TD tosses. TB Kelvin Bryant chipped in with 107y rushing and 56y TD catch as UNC compiled 438y to 103y for Wolfpack (4-2) and picked up 20 1st downs to 6 for State. Tar Heels D, led by 5-man front, allowed TB Joe McIntosh only 61y rushing and posted shutout as all of NC State's pts came on blocked punt and 44y INT RET by CB Dee Dee Hoggard.

AUBURN 24 Georgia Tech 0: South's 2nd-oldest rivalry proved uncompetitive as very good Auburn (5-1) D easily won match-up with Georgia Tech's mediocre O. Tigers used big plays to produce 1st H pts as QB Randy Campbell (7-13/132y) threw 60y TD pass to WR Clayton Beauford and HB Lionel James took punt 62y to set up 28y FG by

K Al Del Greco for 10-0 H lead. Beauford's TD came on 3rd play at WR after previous week's move from QB. With TB Robert Lavette (15/28y) shackled, Yellow Jackets (3-3) managed only 36y and measly pair of 1st downs in 1st H. Tigers took opening possession of 2nd H 80y to 10y TD run by James (15/75y). Only bright spot for Georgia Tech was P Ron Rice, who averaged 45.4y on 10 punts.

TENNESSEE 35 Alabama 28: Sporting orange pants, Vols (3-2-1) had to sweat out 1st series win since 1970 as game was not sealed until EZ INT by DE Mike Terry came with 17 secs left. Tennessee QB Alan Cockrell (18-29/192y) threw TD passes of 52y to WR Willie Gault and 39y to WR Mike Miller, while K Fuad Reveiz kicked 4 FGs. Tennessee scored 22 straight 2nd H pts for 35-21 lead. Alabama (5-1), which converted 2 of 3 INTs by CB Jeremiah Castille into 1st H TDs, marched to 14y TD run by HB Linnie Patrick, and when Tide got ball back, drove to Vols 17YL with 30 secs left. QB Walter Lewis (10-22/200y, 2 TDs, 2 INTs) fired pass to WR Jesse Bendross in EZ that was deflected away. On next play, he threw to WR Darryl White, who was hit by 2 defenders with ball bouncing to Terry for victory-saving result.

Ohio State 26 ILLINOIS 21: Buckeyes (3-3) had to go to wire to snap 3-game losing streak, scoring 5 pts in final 8 secs of game. After K Rich Spangler, who missed 3 earlier FG tries, booted go-ahead 27y FG, Ohio D sacked QB Tony Eason in EZ as time elapsed. QB Mike Tomczak threw for 247y and TB Tim Spencer rushed for 151y as Ohio used big plays to launch 21-7 lead: Its 1st score was Tomczak's 74y pass to WR Cedric Anderson. Bucks' 2nd TD was 44y E-run by Spencer. Buckeyes D turned in GLS in 3rd Q as CB Shaun Gayle and S Lamar Keuchler stopped Illini FB Mike Murphy 1y short of Ohio goal on 4th down. Eason (25-44/284y, 2 TDs) led Illinois (5-2) on 4th Q rally to tie it 21-21. Pass-happy Illini coach Mike White even fooled Bucks on tying drive by often running against 3-man line. Tying score came on FB Thomas Rooks' 21y TD burst. After Illinois K Mike Bass hit crossbar on 56y FG try late in 4th Q, Buckeyes went 69y to turn Spangler from goat into hero.

Michigan 29 IOWA 7: Wolverines (4-2) won 4th straight to grab lead in Big 10 race as TB Rick Rogers rushed for pair of 4th Q TDs. Michigan scored for 2-0 edge on safety when LB Carleton Rose blocked punt by Iowa P Reggie Roby through EZ in 2nd Q. Ensuing free-kick led to 44y FG by K Ali Haji Sheikh. Wolverines had time for 1 more 1st H score as QB Steve Smith (13-24/172y) threw 11y TD pass to WR Vince Bean for 12-0 H lead. QB Chuck Long (19-32/220y) finally put Hawkeyes (3-3) on scoreboard with 8y TD pass to TE Mike Hufford in 4th Q. Michigan TB Lawrence Ricks rushed for 120y.

Arizona 16 NOTRE DAME 13: Ignoring history of Notre Dame Stadium, frosh K Max Zendejas, 2nd in line of kicking brothers, booted winning 48y FG into wind as time ran out. "I was a little nervous, but I like it when I'm nervous because that's the only way I can concentrate," said Zendejas, who was knocked down and never saw FG fly through uprights. Wildcats (2-2-1) had tied game 13-13 on TB Phil Freeman's 1y run for 1st rushing TD allowed by Irish D in 1982. Arizona QB Tom Tunnicliffe (19-38/199y) threw for 78y on tying drive and hit 19y pass to WR Brad Anderson to set up winning FG. Notre Dame (4-1) owned 10-0 H lead, but its O could gain 52y in 2nd H and lost 4 TOs that killed 2 1st H drives and set up 6 of Arizona's 2nd H pts. TB Phil Carter led ND rush attack with 55y, while TB Allen Pinkett scored on 25y TD run.

SOUTHERN METHODIST 20 Houston 14: SMU (6-0) TB Eric Dickerson (27/241y) had incredible game, monster 2nd H (206y), and 62y scoring romp in 3rd Q for 17-7 lead that was 1 of greatest runs ever. Dickerson took off down sideline, ran over 1 defender at midfield, before leaping another 25y downfield, and avoided 3rd Cougar with move of his body—in mid-air no less—that was truly stunning. Dickerson's magnificent run turned out to be winning TD. SMU coach Bobby Collins said of his star TB's run, "I just wish everybody in the country could have seen it. I had a good look at it and I don't see how he stayed on his feet." Cougars (2-3-1) were held to 75y and 4 1st downs in 2nd H, but scored on 5y TD run by QB Lionel Wilson to cap 38y drive that was set up by Mustangs' FUM.

NEBRASKA 42 Kansas State 13: Unstoppable Nebraska (5-1) IB Mike Rozier was suffering from hip-pointer, so when he rushed for 204y and TDs of 27y and 46y, fans were left to wonder what he have done if healthy. Huskers gained 496y O with 384y coming from ground attack to rout Wildcats (3-2-1). Nebraska QB Turner Gill nearly was perfect in passing 11-12/101y, although 3 of host team's 4 lost FUMs came after receptions. Also, Gill audibled from pass play to pitchout run that produced Rozier's 46y dash that exploited Kansas State's blitz. Wildcats QB Darrell Ray Dickey completed 8-17/93y, leading 255y O that had some good moments in defeat.

Southern California 41 STANFORD 21: Once again Stanford QB John Elway (27-41/239y) starred in losing effort. Although Elway notched his NCAA record-best 26th 200y aerial game, he couldn't play both ways and stop Trojans O. USC (4-1) outlegged Stanford 227y to 43y on ground to enhance QB Sean Salisbury's 17-30/201y, INT passing. Trojans TB Anthony Gibson led way with 120y and 3 TDs in relief of TB Todd Spencer (14/99y), who left with sprained knee in 2nd Q. Southern California D chipped in with 6 sacks and 3 INTs in harassment of Elway.

October 23, 1982

Penn State 24 WEST VIRGINIA 0: Record crowd of 60,958 packed Mountaineer Field in hopes of watching WVU snap longest current losing streak between annual opponents. But Nittany Lions (6-1) convincingly ran streak to 24 wins as D outscored its former teammate, QB Jeff Hostetler (19-37/250y, 2 INTs), with LB Scott Radecic returning INT 85y for TD. West Virginia (5-2) coach Don Nehlen's decision to come out in nickel-D to stop QB Todd Blackledge (11-21/118y, INT) backfired as Penn State rushed for 225y. Lions D also twice stopped WVU deep in Penn State territory.

Clemson 38 NORTH CAROLINA STATE 29: With 259y rushing, Clemson (5-1-1) built 22-pt 3rd Q lead and then held off NC State's rally. Tigers TB Cliff Austin rushed for 109y and 2 TDs, TB Chuck McSwain gained 129y and TD, and FB Jeff McCall added 2 TDs. Wolfpack (4-3) scored tilt's final 13 pts as TB Joe McIntosh (20/113y) scored his 2nd 4y TD, and QB Tol Avery (22-33/246y, INT) threw his 2nd TD pass to WR Stanley Davis. Clemson K Donald Igwebuike had kicked 55y FG to close 1st H.

GEORGIA TECH 31 Tennessee 21: Just week after awful performance against Auburn, Yellow Jackets (4-3) pulled upset as TB Robert Lavette ran for 139y and 3 TDs and QB Jim Bob Taylor threw for 202y. Georgia Tech was frothing at mouth after rough week of practice and started hot with drives of 61y and 75y that Lavette capped with TDs. After Tennessee (3-3-1) scored on 10y TD run by TB Johnnie Jones (9/63y), Yellow Jackets regained 2-TD lead on CB Jack Westbrook's 72y punt RET. Tennessee owned next highlight as K Fuad Reveiz booted SEC-record 60y FG to close 1st H. Foes traded FGs and TDs in 2nd H as QB Alan Cockrell (20-33/220y, TD, INT) could only keep Vols close against Jackets D that sacked him 5 times.

LOUISIANA STATE 14 South Carolina 6: Sometimes top teams can't help but struggle against supposedly easy foes. Tigers (5-0-1) duet of QB Alan Risher (12-22/127y) and WR Eric Martin (8/81y) connected on dual 1st H TD passes. But LSU seemed to coast, relying on D to make 14-0 lead hold up. Tigers won despite gaining only 256y and having miserable 2-17 3rd down conversions. Gamecocks (3-4) RB Thomas Dendy scored Carolina's sole TD on 6y run, right after 40y pass from QB Gordon Beckham to WR Ira Hillary. LB Al Richardson (18 tackles) keyed Tigers D that allowed 263y and forced 4 TOs. Risher became school's all-time career total O leader with 4147y to vault past RB Charles Alexander (1975-78).

Illinois 29 WISCONSIN 28: Wild finish featured Badgers' TD on flea flicker with less than min remaining, followed by winning 46y FG by Illini (6-2) K Mike Bass as time expired. Wisconsin (4-3) QB Randy Wright (13-28/198y, 2 INTs) purposely bounced lateral to WR Al Toon, slowing down D that was then burned by Toon's 40y TD pass to TE Jeff Nault. Toon made play work with good acting job in receiving lateral, pretending to be disappointed that play did not work with bounced ball. QB Tony Eason led Illinois 51y to Bass' 5th FG, setting up 3-ptr with 23y pass to TE Tim Brewster (8/154y). Eason threw 37-51/479y, TD, 2 INTs. Wright and Toon (2/86y) hooked up on 46y TD pass in 3rd Q for 20-15 lead for Badgers.

Southern Methodist 30 TEXAS 17: SMU (7-0) extended nation's longest current win streak to 11 games as it continued its best start since halcyon days of Doak Walker in 1947. Mustangs surprised Texas (3-2) with formation that featured 3 TBs in backfield: Eric Dickerson, Craig James, and frosh Reggie Dupard. Dickerson rushed for 118y and 60y TD and James ran for 57y and caught 46y TD pass, while punting beautifully all game. Texas D adjusted to hold SMU to 12 1st downs and Texas tied game 10-10 in 4th Q when QB Robert Brewer (186y, 2 TDs, 3 INTs passing) hit TE Bobby Micho for 51y TD—1st scored by Longhorns in series since 1979—and K Raul Allegre hit 41y FG. Freak play soon turned tide as QB Lance McIlhenny's (4-9/188y, 3 TDs) pass bounced off Horns CB Jitter Fields' shoulder to Ponies WR Bobby Leach, who scored on 79y play. Instead of earning INT, Texas had fallen back 17-10. SMU CB Russell Carter made INT to set up 33y TD catch by WR Jackie Wilson for 2-TD lead.

Arkansas 38 HOUSTON 3: Coming into Houston on what coach Lou Holtz termed "crusade," Hogs (6-0) snapped 4-game series losing streak. Arkansas, ranked 1st in nation in scoring D, held Cougars (2-4-1) to 44y FG by K Mike Clendenen, picked off 4 passes, including CB Danny Walters' 93y TD RET for Razorbacks' 1st TD. Soon after, QB Brad Taylor (6-13/107y) threw 56y TD pass to WR Derek Holloway (4/99y) for 14-3 lead. By H, Arkansas had built 28-3 lead on strength of 2 TD runs by Taylor. Hogs rushed 62/299y, without losing FUM. Houston WR David Roberson caught 6/99y, with pair of 30y receptions on Cougars' lone scoring drive.

NEBRASKA 23 Missouri 19: Tigers (3-2-2) enjoyed slim 10-9 lead after 3 Qs with their sole TD courtesy of 1y catch by TE Andy Gibler. After Missouri K Brad Burditt booted 51y FG to increase lead to 13-9, things looked even brighter. But, Missouri D wilted under pressure from Huskers O-line and IB Mike Rozier (17/139y). Nebraska (6-1) marched 79y to take 16-13 lead on 1y TD run by FB Mark Schellen. Huskers converted 3rd INT by QB Brad Perry (18-34/150y) into clinching 16y TD run by QB Bruce Mathison. Gibler caught his 2nd TD pass, thrown by reserve QB Mike Hyde from 24y out, to close scoring. Mathison replaced star QB Turner Gill, who left with concussion in 2nd Q after being hit away from ball by DT Randy Jostes.

WASHINGTON 10 Texas Tech 3: Struggling Huskies (7-0) fell from nation's top spot due to lackluster win. With heavy winds limiting passing, Red Raiders (3-4) took 3-0 lead on 39y FG by K Ricky Gann, and their D, led by DT Gabe Rivera, carried O that made only 147y with 4 TOs. Meanwhile, TB Jacque Robinson was sole Husky to sparkle, gaining 35/203y and scoring Washington's TD on 19y run with 9:35 left. Huskies S Vince Newsome (11 tackles, INT, 2 sacks) set up TD with FUM REC at Texas Tech 32YL. With 7-3 lead in 4th Q, Huskies went for on-side KO, recovered by Washington S Vince Albritton even though it appeared Huskies illegally touched ball before it went 10y. Robinson, who gained 104y in 4th Q, then burst through line for 42y run to Tech 2YL to set up FG by K Chuck Nelson, his 25th straight.

Ucla 47 CALIFORNIA 31: Looking to snap 10-game series losing streak, Bears (4-3) entered 4th Q tied at 31-31 before running out of gas. QB Tom Ramsey led Bruins (6-0-1), completing 17-23/322y, 2 TDs, while sub QB Rick Neuheisel completed 75y scoring bomb to WR Dokie Williams on play he devised on sideline. UCLA eschewed long drives, scoring on big plays or when set up by Cal TOs. DB Lupe Sanchez had 2 INTs, 1 of which poised K John Lee for winning 20y FG, and 25y punt RET that was converted into final TD. Bears were forced to go with 2 QBs as QB Gale Gilbert (126y passing) left in 1st H after hit by NG Karl Morgan. Reserve QB J Torchio (197y passing) threw California to pair of TDs in 2nd H.

AP Poll October 25

1 Pittsburgh (21)	1109	11 UCLA	610
2 Washington (28)	1105	12 Southern California	542
3 Georgia (3)	1010	13 Louisiana State	401
4 Southern Methodist (2)	976	14 Florida State	314
5 Arkansas (4)	909	15 Clemson	307
6 Nebraska	824	16 Miami	286
7 Arizona State	784	17 Oklahoma	194
8 Penn State	763	18 West Virginia	135
9 Alabama	740	19 Auburn	124
10 North Carolina	642	20 Michigan	118

October 30, 1982

Penn State 52 BOSTON COLLEGE 17: Both teams showed ton of O with BC winning that battle by 656y to 618y, but only Penn State scored ton of pts. QB Doug Flutie passed for Boston College record 520y, but managed only 1 TD as 6 TOs hurt Eagles (5-2-1). Penn State (7-1) TB Curt Warner rushed for 183y and 3 TDs, and QB Todd Blackledge threw for 243y and 3 TDs. Flutie opened scoring with 18y TD pass to TE Scott Nizolek (11/229y). Lions then reeled off 38 of next 41 pts, by scoring on 5 of 6 possessions with Blackledge passing 59y for go-ahead TD to WR Kenny Jackson (4/104y, 2 TDs). Lions won with exceptional balance, rushing and passing for 309y each. Warner became school's all-time leading rusher with 3,031y.

Maryland 31 NORTH CAROLINA 24: Both teams came out passing and Tar Heels (5-2) built 14-10 H lead as QB Rod Elkins (10-21/163y, INT) threw TD passes of 9y to TB Kelvin Bryant (130y rushing) and 68y to WR Mark Smith. Terps (6-2) took hold of 2nd H as TB Willie Joyner dazzled with 240y rushing and TD runs of 49y and 84y against nation's top-rated rush D. Joyner's dashes eliminated Carolina's last lead, 24-17, built upon Bryant's 2nd receiving TD. Win was 6th straight for Maryland team that gained 486y, with QB Boomer Esiason throwing for 166y and TD.

VIRGINIA TECH 29 Kentucky 3: Leading O that gained 379y, Hokies (5-3) soph QB Mark Cox (12-17/181y) threw 3 TDs. Virginia Tech had 7-0 edge in 1st Q on Cox's 26y TD pass to WR Mike Giacolone, right after punt FUM by Kentucky S Andy Molls. Next mistake by Wildcats was QB Doug Martin's snap FUM from 2nd-string C Jerry Klein at own 9YL. This time it took 2 plays for Hokies to score, on 3y run by WB Billy Hite. Cox ended hope for Kentucky (0-7-1) with 2nd H TD throws of 14 and 52y. Wildcats had 17y rushing and 6 TOs, with pts coming on K Chris Caudell's 25y FG.

FLORIDA 19 Auburn 17: K Jim Gainey was Gators (5-2) hero as he kicked 4 FGs, including 2 3-ptrs in final 3 mins. Gainey kicked 31y FG with 2:51 left to pull Florida within 17-16. Florida LB Leon Pennington grabbed ensuing on-side KO, and QB Wayne Peace (23-30/250y, INT) led 7-play, 20y drive that wiped out clock before Gainey booted game-winner from 42y with 1 sec left. Gators had owned 10-0 2nd Q lead on 9y TD run by FB James Jones (16/107y) and Gainey's FG. Auburn (6-2) got TD help from 2 unsportsmanlike PENs on Florida D and scored TD on 13y pass from QB Randy Campbell to WR Mike Edwards late in 1st H. Tigers took their 1st lead in 3rd Q on 7y TD run by TB Bo Jackson to cap short drive set up by HB Lionel James' 63y punt RET. Gators won subsequent FG battle by 3 to 1, and therefore won game.

Florida State 24 MIAMI 7: With more national implications than usual, this match-up meant more than Sunshine State pride. Seminoles (6-1) looked to clinch matters with 24y TD pass from QB Kelly Lowrey (9-21/127y) to TE Orson Mobley that converted 4th-and-4. Mobley shook off 3 would-be tacklers to score. Florida State TB Greg Allen rushed for 72y and 2 TDs, including 2y run with 41 secs left to close scoring. After being halted on GLS late in 2nd Q to trail 10-0 at H, Miami (5-3) managed 3rd Q TD on 1y run by HB Keith Griffin to cap 80y drive. Canes QB Mark Richt offset his 273y passing with 4 INTs, but he spotted HB Mark Rush for 5/124y.

IOWA 14 Illinois 13: Chicago native TB Eddie Phillips rushed for 158y to lead Iowa (5-3) to hard-fought win. Phillips scored on 2y run in 1st H, but his biggest play was 30y scamper when Iowa faced 3rd-and-29 at own 32YL with less than 2 mins left in game. Illinois (6-3) O, in anticipation of getting ball back before Phillips' clutch run, already had scripted its plays. When Hawkeyes finally did punt, P Tom Nichol pinned Illini inside 1YL with 24 secs left. Illinois owned 10-7 lead in 3rd Q on 47y TD pass from QB Tony Eason (31-46/292y, INT) to diving WR Oliver Williams and 1st of 2 FGs by K Mike Bass, both in 1st Q. Eason hit 14 straight passes during 2nd H. QB Chuck Long put Iowa in front for good with 8y TD pass to WB Ronnie Harmon early in 4th Q. "I've got the most beautiful team in the world," said Iowa coach Hayden Fry. "They keep fightin' and scratchin' and that's what life's all about."

Michigan State 22 INDIANA 14: Taking advantage of numerous Indiana mistakes, Spartans (1-7) rallied with 13 straight 3rd Q pts to win 1st game of season. Hoosiers (3-5) took 7-6 H lead with 2y TD run by TB Orlando Brown offsetting 2 FGs by Michigan State K Ralf Mojsiejenko. Michigan State LB Jim Neely started rally with INT returned to Indiana 20YL to set up 11y TD run by HB Tony Ellis. Later in 3rd Q, frosh QB Dave Yarema (10-18/116y, 2 INTs), in his debut for Spartans, made Hoosiers pay for short punt with 35y TD pass to WR Otis Grant for 19-7 lead. Indiana was able to score TD on 26y pass from QB Babe Laufenberg (23-45/307y, 4 INTs) to Brown, but could get no closer than 19-14.

OKLAHOMA STATE 30 Missouri 20: Cowboys (2-3-2) had simple plan: run TB Ernest Anderson until he scored or set up FGs by K Larry Roach. Anderson rushed for 227y and winning 11y TD run in 3rd Q, and Roach kicked 5 FGs to set Oklahoma State game-record. Tigers (3-3-2) held 20-19 H lead, scoring TDs on 55y pass from QB Brad Perry to WR Wallace Snowden, special teamer Ricky Doby's 85y run with lateral to complete 99y KO TD RET, and Perry's 1y keeper. Unable to stop Cowboys' running game, which torched Mizzou D for 343y, Tigers failed to hold lead. In only 7 games, Anderson has topped 200y 4 times to tie Big 8 season record held by Billy Sims of Oklahoma (1978).

ARKANSAS 24 Rice 6: FB Jessie Clark scored twice within 51 secs of 3rd Q as Hogs (7-0) pulled away. Following 80y punt by Rice P Dale Walters, Arkansas marched 20y to 2y TD run by Clark. Then, Arkansas LB Milt Fields' INT and add-on facemask PEN set up Clark's 2nd TD, 6y run. Razorbacks clicked 5 mins later on 8y TD pass from QB Brad Taylor to TE Eddie White. Owls (0-8) had notched 6-0 H lead on dual FGs by K Joel Baxter, but went south in 2nd H, finishing with 6 1st downs, 32y rushing, and 54y passing against D that had allowed no TDs in 15 Qs. Arkansas gained 370y. "I bet that halftime score shocked a lot of people," said Rice coach Ray Alborn.

STANFORD 43 Washington 31: For something different, QB John Elway (20-30/265, 2 TDs, INT) received boost from typically quiet Stanford (5-3) run game. With HB Mike Dotterer rushing for 106y and 2 TDs, including 46y scamper that burned Huskies blitz in 2nd Q, Cardinal had pass-run combo that stunned Huskies (7-1). Washington held 17-7 2nd Q lead before Cardinal scored on 5 straight series over 13-min span—with Elway hitting 12 straight passes—to forge ahead 37-17 late in 3rd Q. Stanford HB Vince White added 76y scoring punt RET in final Q. Stanford LB Garin Veris (4 sacks) led D that forced 5 TOs. UW TB Jacque Robinson rushed for 132y, 2 TDs.

ARIZONA STATE 17 Southern California 10: Arizona State (8-0) D presented non-stop blitzing to sack Southern California (5-2) passers 6 times. Trojans QB Sean Salisbury left in 3rd Q with sprained knee, although his sub, QB Scott Tinsley, nearly rallied USC. Twice Tinsley passed USC into Arizona State territory, reaching 8YL on 1st drive before failing on downs. Second drive ended fittingly on sack as Sun Devils went to 2-0 all-time vs. Trojans in Tempe. USC WR Jeff Simmons caught 11/173y and 21y TD, but Troy managed only 20y rushing against aggressive Devils. ASU QB Todd Hons (14-22/165y, INT) threw 29y TD pass to TB Darryl Clack in 1st H and set up winning 6y TD run by TB Alvin Moore with 2 passes/48y to TE Ron Wetzel.

November 6, 1982

Air Force 27 ARMY 9: Rushing for 367y, Falcons (6-4) were able to pull away with 20 straight pts in capturing Commander-in-Chief trophy outright for 1st time in trophy's 11-year history. HB Jody Simmons, who rushed for 100y, opened scoring with 37y TD run. Army (4-5) then marched 80y on its best drive to deadlock game at 7-7 on 6y TD run by HB Gerald Walker. Air Force scored 10 pts in 2nd Q on 1y TD run by HB Mike Brown and 1st of 2 FGs by K Sean Pavlich. With Walker (12/64y) departing in 3rd Q to recurring shoulder injury, Cadets lost their O linchpin.

Notre Dame 31 PITTSBURGH 16: Earning coach Gerry Faust his finest victory, Irish (6-1-1) upset top-ranked Pitt with trick plays and funky alignments. After taking 10-6 H lead by traditional means—FG and short TD run—Notre Dame found itself trailing when Pitt TB Bryan Thomas (27/93y) scored on 1y run in 3rd Q. Notre Dame went for flea flicker as QB Blair Kiel (6-15/126y) handed off to TB Phil Carter, who pitched ball back to Kiel, who threw 54y TD pass to WR Joe Howard for 17-13 lead. TB Allen Pinkett (10/115y) did his best to keep Panthers down, answering 3rd FG by Pitt K Eric Schubert with 76y scoring romp for 1st of his pair of decisive 4th Q TD runs. Pitt QB Dan Marino threw for 314y, but was held without TD pass for 1st time in 19 games by stellar Irish D, led by DE Kevin Griffith's 14 tackles, that sacked him 3 times.

CLEMSON 16 North Carolina 13: What proved to be ACC semi-final went down to wire as Tigers (6-1-1) stopped North Carolina on downs in closing secs. After driving 65y to Clemson 15YL, Tar Heels (5-3) stopped themselves with pass drops on 1st down in EZ by WR Mark Smith and on 4th down by FB Tyrone Anthony 4y shy of 1st down. Anthony, moved from TB due to injuries, admitted to having eye off ball to check "surroundings." Carolina had 389y O as QBs Scott Stankavage and Rod Elkins combined for 280y passing, with Stankavage's 3y TD toss to TE Arnold Franklin that tied game 13-13 in 3rd Q. Clemson K Bob Paulling hit 43y FG for lead preserved with 4th Q shutout. Tigers rushed for 176y, led by TB Cliff Austin (24/82y).

Louisiana State 20 ALABAMA 10 (Birmingham): Tigers (7-0-1) had lot to prove after weak 1st H schedule, and prove it they did. LSU prevented Tide (7-2) from earning any 1st downs in 1st H, holding them to 45y rushing overall. QB Alan Risher led Tigers, completing 20-26/182y and taking advantage of strong D for 17-0 H lead. Tide rallied with 10 straight 3rd Q pts, scoring on 28y TD pass from QB Walter Lewis to WR Joey Jones. Tigers D halted rally, setting up clinching 20y FG by K Juan Betanzos. While LSU celebrated its 1st series win since 1970, Alabama coach Bear Bryant admitted, "I think that's the best beating we've had since the '60's."

Georgia 44 Florida 0 (Jacksonville): Georgia (9-0) TB Herschel Walker's final game against rivals was brilliant as he rushed for 219y and 3 TDs. Walker's 30y TD run up gut of Florida D in 1st Q produced enough pts for Bulldogs victory. Georgia won rushing battle 391y to 34y and enjoyed 38:28 to 21:32 advantage in possession time. Gators (5-3) QB Wayne Peace (10-19/102y) was pounded, losing 2 INTs, and getting sacked 4 times. Gaining 649y in 3 games versus Florida, Walker, with 4,920y, passed Cornell HB Ed Marinaro into 5th place on all-time rushing list, while passing QB Zeke Bratkowski for school's career total O lead. With 5th straight series win, Georgia coach Vince Dooley ran his Gators mark to 13-5-1.

Michigan 16 ILLINOIS 10: Stirring GLS in last secs preserved win for Michigan (7-2) as Illini HB Dwight Beverly was stonewalled at 2YL on 4th down. Illinois (5-3) attack gained 515y—most by any Michigan opponent—but came up 2y short at end of 90y drive in front of largest Champaign crowd to date (75,256). Wolverines countered with inspired games by WR Anthony Carter (5/125y), who caught 40y TD pass from QB Steve Smith, and TB Lawrence Ricks, who rushed for 177y. Michigan K Ali Haji-Sheikh added 3 FGs. Illinois QB Tony Eason (28-47/272y) threw 7y TD to WR Mike Martin (8/81y) to tie game at 10-10 by H, but was picked off twice. Illinois coach Mike White took criticism for his play call on Beverly's final run, but was more concerned about his team: "I'm just sick of it. The kids wanted this game so badly."

BAYLOR 24 Arkansas 17: Bears (3-5-1) earned measure of satisfaction for their miserable year by shocking undefeated Arkansas (7-1) with HB Alfred Anderson (24/84y) scoring winning 4y TD run with 2:38 left. Razorbacks opened scoring when TB Gary Anderson caught 24y TD pass from QB Brad Taylor. After increasing lead to 14-0 on TD blast by FB Jessie Clark, Arkansas seemed to be in good shape. Bears revved up and marched 80y to 1st TD allowed by Hogs D in 17 Qs: Anderson scored from 2y out to halve deficit before H. After scoreless 3rd Q, Baylor tied game on 12y TD pass from QB Mike Brannan (10-20/230y, INT) to FB Allen Rice to cap 77y drive. Teams exchanged FGs before flea flicker went wrong for Hogs as WR Mark Mistler threw INT corralled by Baylor CB Preston Davis at midfield, 10 plays before Bears made winning TD. "With all the problems we've had, this would have to rank up there with our win over Texas in 1974," said Baylor coach Grant Teaff.

WASHINGTON 10 Ucla 7: Bruins (7-1-1) literally bobbled away Pac 10 lead: TB Frank Cephous lost FUM at Washington 5YL after hard tackle by Huskies S Vince Newsome, WR Cormac Carney dropped ball without getting hit at Huskies 20YL when on his way unmolested to EZ after pass reception, and TB Danny Andrews lost FUM at Washington 30YL. UCLA QB Tom Ramsey (18-31/248y), who threw 39y TD pass to WR Jojo Townsell, also gave up 2 INTs, 1 to Newsome that set up 18y FG by K Chuck Nelson for winning pts. Huskies had managed good drive in 1st Q, marching 70y to 4y TD run by TB Jacque Robinson.

November 13, 1982

Clemson 24 MARYLAND 22: Maryland (7-3) was on roll in scoring 14 straight 4th Q pts and moving ball back deep in Clemson territory. Up 2, Tigers (7-1-1) needed big play to save 7th straight win and got it once S Terry Kinard forced FUM after catch by TE John Tice (11/113y). DB Reggie Pleasant recovered with 3:48 left. Terrapins had scored in 4th Q on 37y scoring pass from QB Boomer Esiason (24-39/279y, 2 INTs) to WR Greg Hill and 1y blast by FB Rick Badanjek. Maryland D forced punt that traveled 4y thanks to strong winds, giving it ball on Clemson 21YL. Kinard's FUM REC was 4th of 5 TOs, which offset Terps' 342y to 231y edge.

Georgia 19 AUBURN 14: Objective of TB Herschel Walker's career became perfect; he led Bulldogs (10-0) to 3rd SEC title and 3rd Sugar Bowl in as many years. Walker rushed for 177y and 2 TDs, passed 5,000y career barrier with 5,097y, and scored game-winning TD on 3y run midway through 4th Q. His TD capped 80y drive. Auburn (7-3) had taken 14-13 lead on 87y scoring burst by nifty HB Lionel "Little Train" James (8/111y). Late in game, Tigers reached Georgia 20 and 14YLs, but both drives failed on downs. Bulldogs K Kevin Butler booted FGs of 20y and 50y. Walker, who scored on 47y run in 2nd Q, passed former South Carolina star George Rogers (1977-80) into 4th place on all-time rush list.

Southern Mississippi 38 ALABAMA 29: QB Reggie Collier showcased SEC-worthy skills, rushing for 88y and 3 TDs, as Golden Eagles (7-3) surprisingly snapped Crimson Tide's 57-game win streak in Tuscaloosa. "He broke our defense," said Alabama (7-3) DE Mike Pitts. "He was catching us off guard in bad positions." Southern Miss TB Sam Dejarnette, Selma, Ala. native, rushed for 153y and 2 TDs to lead ground gainers. Tide FB Ricky Moore rushed for 109y, FB Craig Turner scored 2 TDs, and QB Walter Lewis threw for 197y with 33y TD to HB Joe Carter. Key stat, however, was football poison: 4 Tide TOs to none for Southerners. Loss, which cost Bama possible Fiesta Bowl bid, was 1st on campus since 10-6 Florida defeat in 1963.

MISSISSIPPI STATE 27 Louisiana State 24: Unable to catch Georgia for SEC title, demoralized LSU (7-1-1) was ripe for picking. Maroon Bulldogs (4-6) certainly had something to do with outcome as K Dana Moore booted winning 45y FG at game's end. Nimble Mississippi State QB John Bond gave team 24-17 lead on 64y TD pass to WR Danny Knight, before LSU tied game on 35y TD run by FB Mike Montz. Tigers

QB Alan Risher completed 25-34 for 308y in losing cause. He threw TDs of 69y to WR Eric Martin to open scoring and 11y to TB Garry James to tie score at 14 at H. Mississippi State HB Michael Haddix rushed 15 times for 112y and 6y TD.

Ohio State 40 NORTHWESTERN 28: Former Big 10 laughingstock Northwestern (3-8) put up struggle, forcing Buckeyes to fight. TB Tim Spencer rushed for 190y to lead Ohio State (7-3) O that gained 605y to overcome record-breaking performance by Wildcats QB Sandy Schwab (27-43/393y, 3 INTs). Schwab, who threw 3 TD passes, set NCAA frosh records for game total O and passing y. He connected with WR John Harvey 6/160y with 80y TD bomb. Ohio State had record-setter of own as WR Gary Wellman set mark of 43 consecutive games with at least 1 reception. Resourceful QB Mike Tomczak threw for 222y at helm of Buckeyes attack.

Penn State 24 NOTRE DAME 14: Trailing 14-13 in 4th Q, Penn State (9-1) QB Todd Blackledge (11-27/189y, INT) burned run-conscious Irish D by connecting on pass to TB Curt Warner that resulted in winning 48y TD. Even keying on run, Notre Dame (6-2-1) allowed Warner to ramble for 145y. Irish was struggling without QB Blair Kiel, injured in 1st Q, but had taken lead on electrifying 93y KO TD RET by TB Allen Pinkett (19/70y). Nittany Lions WR Kenny Jackson caught 6/114y.

Oklahoma State 24 KANSAS STATE 16: Oklahoma State (3-4-2) pulled off road upset as TB Ernest Anderson, nation's leading rusher, simply wore out Wildcats. Anderson rushed for 175y and 2 TDs, gaining 97y in 4th Q with 15y scoring run for cincher. Cowboys FB Kelly Cook lumbered 40y for 17-10 lead midway through 4th Q. Oklahoma State maintained lead at 17-16 despite K-State TE Eric Bailey's 2nd TD reception—his 1st career TDs—as QB Darrel Ray Dickey's 2-pt conv pass was tipped away. Dickey (17-35/200y, 2 TDs, 2 INTs) had driven Wildcats (5-4-1) 80y to before boldly going for win to enhance possibility of Cats' 1st-ever bowl bid. Cowboys had led 7-3 at H, but were thrown back at 1YL on Kansas State's plucky 1st Q GLS.

OKLAHOMA 41 Missouri 14: When things went well for Sooners (8-2) TB Marcus Dupree, they were very good. Shaking off flu bug, Dupree toyed with Tigers by rushing for 166y and 2 TDs, including 70y burst in 4th Q. On his long run, Dupree ran over Mizzou S Raymond Hairston and outran CB Terry Matichak. Game featured Oklahoma's 1st TD pass in 1982 as QB Kelly Phelps pitched 11y pass to TE Johnny Fontenette to cap 80y drive for 28-14 beginning of 3rd Q. Phelps also scored on 38y run as Oklahoma rushed for 483y. Tigers (4-4-2) passed for 149y, but rushed for only 86y, thanks to 7 sacks by Sooners D. Missouri enjoyed 2nd Q success, scoring their 2 TDs, including 42y TD pass from QB Marlon Adler to WR Craig White.

Southern Methodist 34 TEXAS TECH 27: Important win in Southern Methodist's quest for SWC title ended in bizarre fashion, but odd closing play soon would become forgotten when California and Stanford overshadowed it week later. Tilt was tied 27-27 with 17 secs left when SMU (10-0) S Blane Smith bobbled snap, but recovered in time rising up to throw 1-bounce cross-field lateral to WR Bobby Leach at Ponies 9YL. Leach was alone near left sideline and raced 91y for TD. "It was a miracle," said eager Leach, "It never worked in practice." Red Raiders (4-6) K Ricky Gann had just tied game with 28y FG. Texas Tech TB Anthony Hutchison rushed for 206y to top SMU's Pony Express backfield, which also ran well. Mustangs TB Eric Dickerson (21/115y) broke his own single-season school rushing mark with 1536y and scored 2 TDs, while TB Craig James (19/97y) added another TD. Hutchison raced for 71y TD to tie it 24-24 early in 4th Q but was halted on 3rd-and-1 run at SMU 10YL just before Gann made his tying FG. Victory was SMU's 1st in Lubbock since 1968.

Washington 17 ARIZONA STATE 13: Bouncing no. 3 Arizona State from top of tight Pac-10 race, Huskies (9-1) were in driver's seat for 3rd straight Rose Bowl. Washington won by playing TO-free ball against aggressive Arizona State (9-1) D, while forcing 4 TOs. Huskies converted pair of those TOs into 32y and 25y TD drives. Ahead 10-3 entering 3rd Q, Huskies recovered Sun Devils frosh TB Darryl Clack's FUM of 2nd H KO. TB Jacque Robinson, who rushed for 124y, scored on 4y run moments later for 17-3 lead. Clack later raced 50y for TD—longest run against Huskies all season—but Sun Devils could not rally and wasted 360y in O. ASU QB Todd Hons passed for 206y, but was sacked 3 times. "The loss is devastating in our minds," said Arizona State coach Darryl Rogers. "It may take awhile for us to recover."

November 20, 1982

LOUISIANA STATE 55 Florida State 21: Resurgent Tigers (8-1-1) secured Orange Bowl bid with impressive win. LSU gained 602y, with TB Dalton Hilliard bumping and twisting for 36/183y. Scoring 4 TDs—3 on runs and 46y reception—Hilliard broke Georgia TB Herschel Walker's 2-year-old frosh record for TDs with 16. Tigers QB Alan Risher (8-12/212y, 3 TDs) pitched scoring strikes of 34y and 70y to WR Eric Martin. Seminoles (8-2) QB Kelly Lowrey (13-24/172y) threw and ran for TDs and alternate QB Blair Williams (10-14/135y) threw 21y TD to WR Jesse Hester, but it was heady and insurmountable pace set by LSU's O.

OHIO STATE 24 Michigan 14: Ohio State (8-3) could do no better than come within half game, at 7-1 in conf play, of Wolverines. For 1st time since 1971, rivalry had no bearing on Rose Bowl berth because, at 8-0, Michigan (8-3) already was guaranteed Pasadena trip. Still, Bucks had plenty of incentive, and TB Tim Spencer rushed for 124y and 2

TDs as Ohio took advantage of 6 TOs to set up each Buckeye pt. Key TO was FUM by WR Anthony Carter (7/78y) with score tied 14-14 after he took option pitchout on own 14YL. Ohio S Doug Hill pounced on FUM after combining with LB Rowland Tatum on tackle. Spencer scored vital, short TD soon thereafter for 21-14 lead midway through 4th Q. Michigan QB Steve Smith struggled with 3 INTs and 2 FUMs, but TB Lawrence Ricks sparked Michigan O with 110y rushing.

Arkansas 17 SOUTHERN METHODIST 17: Needing tie to clinch 2nd straight SWC title and 1st Cotton Bowl appearance since 1966, Mustangs (10-0-1) drove 80y behind QB Lance McIlhenny (7-9/98y) to tie it on 2y QB option keeper. Controversial pass interference PEN contributed 40y to SMU's cause. Hogs CB Nathan Jones was flagged, but did he pull up when pass was overthrown only to have WR Jackie Wilson run into him, or did he shield Wilson away from pass? Ponies' Wilson admitted later that he was acting on play. Razorbacks (8-1-1) TB Gary Anderson scored 2 TDs on 3y runs and caught 5 passes/82y to lead O that gained 330y. Mustangs TB Eric Dickerson rushed for 81y in becoming all-time SWC rushing leader with 4,450y, passing Earl Campbell (1974-77) of Texas.

AIR FORCE 30 Notre Dame 17: Falcons (7-4) chased Notre Dame out of rankings as Wishbone fooled Irish's bigger defenders. QB Marty Louthan rushed for 115y and 2 TDs, and K Sean Pavlich added 3 FGs to pace Air Force's 1st series win in 12 tries. Air Force converted TOs into 2 TDs for 17-0 H lead. After 3rd-string QB Jim O'Hara (14-23/216y) led Irish to FG, Louthan finished them off with 80y drive to HB Jody Simmons' 3y TD run. Louthan paced drive with 55y burst up middle. O'Hara threw 2 TDs with 55y pitch to WR Joe Howard. "When we walked into the stadium, we all knew that we would win the game," said AFA coach Ken Hatfield. "We were ready."

Brigham Young 17 UTAH 12: Cougars (8-3) held on after QB Steve Young (24-34/254y) threw 2 TD passes for 7th WAC title in row. Young hit WR Mike Eddo on 6y scoring pass in 1st Q and FB Casey Tiumalu on 16y game-winner in 3rd Q. With QB Ken Vierra passing for 155y and TB Carl Monroe rushing for 147y and 2 TDs, Utah (5-6) outgained BYU 468y to 300y, but wasted its edge with 4 TOs.

UCLA 20 Southern California 19: With no time left, game and possible Rose Bowl berth came down to 2-pt conv try by Southern California (7-3). Trojans had just scored on 1y TD pass to TE Mark Boyer. QB Scott Tinsley (14-23/137y, INT) dropped back but was hammered by NG Karl Morgan, whose sack preserved Bruins (9-1-1) win. Pressure had been on UCLA D entire 2nd H as O, which had scored TDs on 1st 2 possessions of 1st H, managed only 1 1st down in 2nd H. Bruins managed winning 3 pts in 2nd H on K John Lee's 45y FG in 3rd Q, set up by Tinsley's FUM at USC 29YL, recovered by DT Mark Walen. Lee's 3-ptr bumped lead to 20-10, but Trojans dominated 4th Q, marching 55y to 22y FG by K Steve Jordan and 66y to Boyer's TD.

WASHINGTON STATE 24 Washington 20: Logjam atop Pac 10 standings was freed of 1 Rose Bowl aspirant as Washington (9-2) was chopped down in Apple Cup rivalry. Huskies, down 21-20, had late chance to take lead, but very reliable K Chuck Nelson—with NCAA record 30 straight FGs to his credit—missed 32y FG with 4:35 left. Washington State (3-7-1) preserved its win as S Rob Treece blindsided Washington QB Tim Cowan (19-29/241y) to force FUM REC by Cougars S Gerald Waters at Washington 28YL. K John Traut soon added insurance 38y FG in final min. Wazzu TB Tim Harris rushed for 124y, including 8y TD in 3rd Q for 21-17 lead, and FB James Matthews added 112y, TD, rushing. WR Anthony Allen caught 9/140y and TDs of 24y, to open scoring, and 16y to give Huskies 17-7 lead late in 1st H, while TB Jacque Robinson rushed for 137y. Ecstatic Washington State fans not only tore down goalposts but sent them floating down Palouse River.

GAME OF THE YEAR
CALIFORNIA 25 Stanford 20:

Game's final play has been seen over and over, and still it remains difficult to fathom: multiple laterals—some blind—all hitting their mark, Stanford's band assembling on field in apparent victory, and California (7-4) S Kevin Moen running over trombone player Gary Tyrell in EZ. Forgotten is that Golden Bears, behind QB Gale Gilbert (17-31/289y), led for most of game on way to capping stormy but successful 1st season for coach Joe Kapp. Stanford (5-6) rallied as QB John Elway (25-39/330y), who needed win in his final game to go to 1st bowl game, threw for 260y in 2nd H, clicking on TDs of 2y and 43y to HB Vincent White in 3rd Q. On late, go-ahead FG drive, Elway marched Cardinal 70y to Cal 17YL, hitting 4th-and-17 pass of 29y to WR Emile Harry early in last desperate series. Stanford K Mark Harmon's 35y FG with 4 secs left set off wild celebration that cost Stanford important 15y PEN. Walk-off forced Harmon to kick off from his 25YL and enabled Moen to begin final play with catch of squibbed KO at Cal 46YL. Moen quickly whipped overhand lateral to DB Richard Rodgers, who pitched to HB Dwight Garner. Controversy set in next as Garner was swarmed over by Cardinal and was nearly tackled: if his knee did not touch ground it came close. He flipped ball back to Rodgers, who lateralled it to WR Mariet Ford (7/132y). All of that mischief gained less than 10y, but Ford ran to Stanford 20YL and attracted 6 defenders before blindly flipping ball over his head to Moen as Ford was hit by 3 tacklers. Moen encountered sea of Stanford red between him and EZ, but mob was celebrating band members. After all, several Stanford players had left bench too, thinking Garner had been stopped. Moen sliced through students in front of him and scored winning TD, jubilantly lofting ball above his head before running over Tyrell, who became minor celebrity. Officials huddled for 5 mins before allowing Bears' TD. "This was an insult to college football. There's no way it should have happened. They (the officials) ruined my entire college career," griped Elway.

AP Poll November 22

1 Georgia (52)	1133	11 Oklahoma	551
2 Penn State (2)	1057	12 West Virginia	449
3 Nebraska (3)	1018	13 Washington	444
4 Southern Methodist	969	14 Texas	333
5 Pittsburgh	898	15 Florida State	323
6 Arizona State	817	16 Maryland	253
7 Louisiana State	749	17 Southern California	245
8 UCLA	706	18 Ohio State	143
9 Arkansas	676	19 Tulsa	129
10 Clemson	654	20 Michigan	125

November 25-27, 1982

(Th'g) VIRGINIA TECH 21 Virginia 14: To win 100th career victory at Virginia Tech (7-4), coach Bill Dooley turned to backup QB Mark Cox (14-24/121y) to rally troops. Cox cut team's deficit to 7-6 with 6y scoring pass to TE Mike Shaw. Hokies took lead in 3rd Q with 9 straight pts on 1y TD run by TB Otis Copeland and 44y FG by K Allen Talbott. Cavaliers (2-9) bounced back with TD on 39y pass from QB Wayne Schuchts to WR Henry Johnson, duo's 2nd scoring hookup of day before Cox ran in insurance TD run from 1y out. Schuchts had difficulty rallying his team, throwing 5 INTs including 4 in 4th Q. Va Tech's Copeland ran for 124y to lead ground gainers.

(Th'g) TEXAS 53 Texas A&M 16: Texas (8-2) evidently was in hurry to get to Thanksgiving table, routing rivals as TB Darryl Clark connected with WR Herkie Walls on 87y TD pass on team's 1st snap. Longhorns were not through, scoring thrice more in 1st Q—all on runs by FB Ervin Davis—to build 27-0 lead. In addition to his passing prowess, Clark rushed for 137y as Horns gained 501y total O. Trailing 34-10, Aggies (5-6) QB Gary Kubiak (10-34/128y, INT), who had to run for life most of game, led 70y drive to open 3rd Q that ended on missed FG. His sole TD pass went 3y to WR John Kellen early in 2nd Q. Walls caught 2nd TD pass, 32y from QB Robert Brewer, to set Texas single-season record of 9 TD catches, while Longhorns DE Kiki DeAyala had his 19th and 20th sacks of season.

(Fri) PENN STATE 19 Pittsburgh 10: Wind-affected win allowed Penn State (10-1) to set up national title showdown with top-ranked Georgia as Lions QB Todd Blackledge topped Panthers QB Dan Marino for 2nd straight year. Marino (18-32/193y, INT) was held without TD pass, Pitt TB Bryan Thomas (143y), game's leading rusher, scored only TD for Panthers (9-2) on 4y run in 2nd Q. With wind in 3rd Q, Blackledge (10-24/149y, INT) threw 31y TD to WR Kenny Jackson on crossing pattern to give Nittany Lions 10-7 lead. Penn State K Nick Gancitano, who ignored wind and rain all game, upped lead to 16-7 on 2 of his 4 FGs. Marino led Panthers downfield, but with 8:04 left and Pitt facing 4th-and-goal at 1YL, coach Foge Fazio opted for 17y FG by K Eric Schubert. Pitt was able to created scoring opportunity once more, which ended on missed FG. Penn State TB Curt Warner rushed for 118y.

(Fri) NEBRASKA 28 Oklahoma 24: Gaining 409y, Cornhuskers (10-1) proved to be Big 8 kingpin as nation's top-rated O delivered. QB Turner Gill led 3 TD drives in 1st H as Nebraska built 21-10 H lead. Huskers' 2nd TD, on 1st of 2 scores by FB Doug Wilkening, was set up by trick play as Gill threw lateral to WB Irving Fryar that bounced before Fryar caught it. Fryar pretended that play was dead, before throwing 37y pass to TE Mitch Krenk to Sooners' 14YL. Without IB Mike Rozier (15/96y), injured in 2nd Q, Huskers struggled in 2nd H and surrendered TD on 3rd play of 3rd Q when Oklahoma TB Marcus Dupree (25/149y) raced 86y to score. TDs were traded, and Oklahoma (8-3) was forced into unfamiliar airways in 4th Q. QB Kelly Phelps completed only 1 of 13 4th Q attempts as Sooners showcased worst-ranked passing O in college football. On last good drive, Sooners marched to Nebraska 39YL before 3 straight incompletions ended possession with less than 3 mins left. "The offense did what it usually does," said Nebraska coach Tom Osborne. "But it was the defense that saved our bacon."

GEORGIA 38 Georgia Tech 18: On day Tennessee lost to Vanderbilt and Louisiana State was upset by Tulane, top-ranked, nervous Georgia (11-0) led rival Georgia Tech by only 7-6 at H. TB Herschel Walker, who scored in 1st H on 59y canter, led Bulldogs to 31-pt 2nd H. Walker rushed for 162y and 2 TDs, becoming 3rd all-time rusher in NCAA history with 5,259y to pass Ohio State's Archie Griffin. Yellow Jackets (6-5) featured game's leading rusher, however, as TB Robert Lavette gained 203y and tallied 2 TDs to finish season with school-record 19 TDs.

Tulane 31 LOUISIANA STATE 28: For 2nd straight season, Tulane (4-7) turned tables on its rival as QB Mike McKay (23-31/233y) threw 3 TDs. McKay's winning TD, with 5 mins left, went 31y to FB Reggie Regginelli. TB Garry James (18/166y, 3 TDs) sparked Tigers (8-2-1) by galloping 68y early in 4th Q for 28-24 lead. LSU QB Alan Risher (13-22/122y) saw his SEC-best streak of 137 passing attempts without INT end with desperation throw with 23 secs remaining. Tulane, 4-TD underdog, last had 2-game win streak in series in 1939. "It was the greatest victory of my life, anywhere, anytime," said Tulane coach Vince Gibson, who soon quit before he could be fired.

VANDERBILT 28 Tennessee 21: Commodores (8-3), enjoying highest win total since 1955, won 1st series game in 7 years when QB Whit Taylor ran in winning 1y TD with 2:53 left. Taylor was singing in rain, throwing for 391y and 3 TDs and setting up his winning TD with 65y pass to WR Phil Roach. Tennessee (6-4-1) had taken 7-0 lead on 3y TD run by TB Chuck Coleman—lead they held for all of 1:33 as Taylor soon threw 42y TD to WR Arnaz Perry. Vols went up by 14-7 in 2nd Q on 1y TD run by TB Johnnie Jones, but, once again, Taylor ignored rain with 6y TD pass to WR Chuck Scott late in 2nd Q. When 2nd H began, Vandy took lead when Taylor and Scott hooked up on 42y TD pass. It soon was Vols' turn to score, and Jones raced 42y to paydirt. Tennessee was done then, but Taylor was nowhere near finished.

Auburn 23 Alabama 22 (Birmingham): After 9 straight series wins, Crimson Tide (7-4) lost hard-fought game in coach Bear Bryant's final regular season contest. Entering 4th Q, Alabama led 22-14 behind O that rolled up 445y and 23 1st downs to 132y and 6 1st downs for Tigers. HB Bo Jackson (17/114y) jumpstarted Tigers' rally by racing 53y to set up K Al Del Greco's 23y FG. Auburn (8-3) soon drove 66y, including QB Randy Campbell's 16y pass to WR Mike Edwards on 3rd-and-14, to Jackson's 1y TD dive. Bo went over top of stack with 2:26 left for his 2nd TD of day. Jackson almost went from hero to goat as he followed Auburn DB Bob Harris' 2nd INT with FUM that gave Bama its last chance with 1:09 left. Alabama marched 25y before sack and PEN pushed it well beyond striking distance. Auburn coach Pat Dye became 1st Bryant disciple to beat master in 30 opportunities since 1970

SOUTHERN CALIFORNIA 17 Notre Dame 13: It was fitting finale for outgoing USC (8-3) coach John Robinson as Trojans won 5th straight, controversially, over rivals. It was Robinson's 67th win in 7 years at Troy. Looking like TB Charles White in 1979 Rose Bowl, TB Michael Harper dove into EZ from 1YL with 48 secs left to cap 60y drive, but landed without ball. Replays were inconclusive, but officials allowed TD to stand. QB Scott Tinsley (24-37/243y, INT) had rallied Trojans, connecting time and again with WR Jeff Simmons (11/149y), who set school records for career receptions (106), catches in season (56), and receiving y in season (973y). Led by QB Blair Kiel and D that allowed 54y rushing, Irish (6-4-1) took 10-3 H lead and tacked on another FG for 13-3 edge in 3rd Q. Notre Dame outgained USC by 392y to 297y. After being carried off field by his players, Robinson said, "It was a magnificent win for USC—in the USC tradition. This exemplifies what USC football is more than anything else."

ARIZONA 28 Arizona State 18: Needing win for Rose Bowl trip proved to be too much pressure for no. 6 Sun Devils (9-2) as D allowed 92y TD on short pass to Wildcats (6-4-1) TB Brian Holland and 50y run-after-catch by WR Brad Anderson on 65y TD. Arizona State's special teams also collapsed: blocked punt set up Arizona K Max Zendejas' 37y FG and ill-advised KO RET resulted in safety for Wildcats. These blunders added up to 19-0 deficit, and ASU O got into ugly mix when TB Alvin Moore's FUM at own 29YL led to 1y TD run by Holland. TB Darryl Clark scored on 2 short TDs to rally Sun Devils, but they were in hole too deep. Arizona State QB Todd Hons threw for 296y, while QB Tom Tunnicliffe led Wildcats with 270y passing. Sun Devils' loss projected idle UCLA into Rose Bowl.

AP Poll November 29

1 Georgia (52)	1115	11 Arizona State	494
2 Penn State (2)	1047	12 Texas	481
3 Nebraska (2)	1004	13 Louisiana State	478
4 Southern Methodist	975	14 Oklahoma	409
5 UCLA	863	15 Florida State	348
6 Arkansas	831	16 Southern Cal	332
7 Pittsburgh	727	17 Maryland	240
8 Clemson	706	18 Ohio State	167
9 Washington	543	19 Auburn	124
10 West Virginia	509	20 Michigan	116

December 4, 1982

Navy 24 Army 7 (Philadelphia): Anyone hoping to see some solid football was disappointed by annual rivalry, at least by both Os. Teams combined for 17 1st Q pts, with all of them set up by TOs. DB Dee Bryant began Army (4-7) freefall with FUM of punt at own 24YL, recovered at 8YL by Middies DE Rick Pagel. Navy (6-5) TB Napoleon McCallum (25/88y) quickly converted it into 2y TD run. S Brian Cianella (10 tackles) picked off Army pass moments later to set up 24y FG by K Todd Solomon, and Midshipmen had all pts they would need 5 mins into game. Cadets stayed close thanks to FUM by Navy TB Rich Clouse, which led to 15y drive to Army QB Rich Laughlin's 3y scoring keeper. After that, Cadets only had 1 more scoring opportunity, which ended on missed 49y FG attempt by K Craig Stopa. Navy proceeded to finish off Black Knights with pair of 2nd H TDs including 17y TD pass by QB Ricky Williamson to WR Bill Cebak on Williamson's only pass try of 2nd H.

Florida 13 FLORIDA STATE 10: Even though he would end game riding bench, Florida (8-3) QB Wayne Peace hit 7-13/109y in becoming 2nd-most proficient y-maker in SEC history and setting NCAA record with 70.73 percentage to top California's Rich Campbell's mark (70.70) from 1980. Florida State (8-3) jumped to 10-0 lead by marching 44y on 1st series to K P.M. Hall's 37y FG and 75y in 2nd Q to 3y TD run by TB Greg Allen (13/81y). After 5 years of injuries, QB Bob Hewko (6-10/66y) entered in 2nd Q and led drive, with TB Lorenzo Hampton (23/138y) rushing for 57y, to Hewko's 10y TD keeper. Florida kept momentum after H, tying it early in 3rd Q on K Jim Gainey's 23y FG. Gainey capped 69y 4th Q drive with 22y FG. Seminoles had their last opportunity end on downs after QB Kelly Lowrey moved O to Florida 31YL.

TEXAS 33 Arkansas 7: Arkansas (8-2-1) season ended with thud as 6 TOs led to 21 pts by Longhorns. First mistake was INT thrown by Hogs QB Tom Jones, who later left game with broken arm, that Texas (9-2) converted into 1y TD run by FB Ervin Davis. Arkansas sub QB Brad Taylor soon lofted 46y TD pass to TB Gary Anderson for 7-7 tie, but fumbled to set up 37y go-ahead TD pass by Longhorns QB Robert Brewer (8-14/144y) to WR Herkie Walls. Hogs' 3rd miscue came late in 2nd Q when fumbled punt RET was recovered by Horns special teamer Ronnie Mullins, which led to TD for 21-7 lead. With Arkansas held to 68y rushing, pressure was on Taylor, who was unable to muster 2nd H scoring drive. Texas TB Darryl Clark rushed for 97y.

AP Poll December 6

1 Georgia (46)	995	11 Arizona Sate	474
2 Penn State (2)	952	12 Oklahoma	385
3 Nebraska (2)	894	13 Louisiana State	383
4 Southern Methodist	869	14 Arkansas	381
5 UCLA	792	15 Southern California	301
6 Pittsburgh	719	16 Maryland	238
7 Clemson	635	17 Ohio State	182
8 Texas	622	18 Auburn	162
9 Washington	564	19 Michigan	120
10 West Virginia	511	20 Tulsa	85

Conference Standings

Atlantic Coast

Clemson	6-0
Maryland	5-1
North Carolina	3-3
Duke	3-3
North Carolina State	3-3
Virginia	1-5
Wake Forest	0-6
Georgia Tech *	2-2
* Ineligible	

Southeastern

Georgia	6-0
Louisiana State	4-1-1
Auburn	4-2
Vanderbilt	4-2
Tennessee	3-2-1
Florida	3-3
Alabama	3-3
Mississippi State	2-4
Mississippi	0-6
Kentucky	0-6

Big Ten

Michigan	8-1
Ohio State	7-1
Iowa	6-2
Illinois	6-3
Wisconsin	5-4
Indiana	4-5
Purdue	3-6
Northwestern	2-7
Michigan State	2-7
Minnesota	1-8

Mid-American

Bowling Green	7-2
Western Michigan	5-2-2
Miami	5-3
Central Michigan	5-3-1
Ohio	5-4
Toledo	5-4
Northern Illinois	5-4
Ball State	4-4
Eastern Michigan	1-7-1
Kent State	0-9

Big Eight

Nebraska	7-0
Oklahoma	6-1
Oklahoma State	3-2-2
Kansas State	3-3-1
Missouri	2-3-2
Iowa State	1-5-1
Kansas	1-5-1
Colorado	1-5-1

Southwest

Southern Methodist	7-0-1
Texas	6-1
Arkansas	5-2-1
Houston	4-3-1
Baylor	3-4-1
Texas A&M	3-5
Texas Tech	3-5
Texas Christian	2-6
Rice	0-8

Western Athletic

Brigham Young	7-1
New Mexico	6-1
Air Force	4-3
San Diego State	4-3
Hawaii	4-4
Utah	3-4
Colorado State	3-5
Wyoming	2-6
Texas-El Paso	1-6

Pacific-10

UCLA	5-1-1
Washington	6-2
Arizona State	5-2
Southern California	5-2
Arizona	4-3-1
California	4-4
Stanford	3-5
Washington State	2-4-1
Oregon	2-6
Oregon State	0-7-1

Pacific Coast Athletic

Fresno State	6-0
Long Beach State	5-1
San Jose State	4-2
Utah State	2-4
Pacific	2-4
Nevada-Las Vegas	1-5
Cal State-Fullerton	0-6

1982 Major Bowl Games

Independence Bowl (Dec. 11): Wisconsin 14 Kansas State 3

After 4 post-season losses, Badgers (7-5) won 1st bowl game in school history against Kansas State squad making bowl debut. Wisconsin QB Randy Wright threw 2 TDs, and D held Kansas State (6-5-1) to lonely 29y FG by K Steve Willis, which was scored after Badgers lost FUM at own 18YL. Wright shook off 9-24 air stats to hook up with WR Tim Stracka for play of game: 87y TD strike, longest pass on school ledgers, to close scoring in 3rd Q. Earlier, Wright had thrown 16y 2nd Q TD to WR Michael Jones for game-winner. K-State managed only 192y against Badgers D led by NG Tim Krumrie (13 tackles), who successfully clogged middle of line. Wildcats QB Darrell Ray Dickey threw 13-35/127y with EZ INT in 2nd H. Frigid conditions contributed to teams combining for 5 TOs, 14 punts and 14 PENs.

Holiday Bowl (Dec. 17): Ohio State 47 Brigham Young 17

Playoff pundits must have loved Ohio State (9-3) which closed with its 7th win in row. Buckeyes (9-3) erupted for 30 pts in 2nd H as they spaded 66/345y along ground, and D forced rout-building TO deep in Cougars territory in 3rd Q. BYU (8-4) QB Steve Young (27-45/341y, 2 TDs, INT) pitched 7y TD pass in 2nd Q, and Cougars led 7-3. But, Buckeyes TB Tim Spencer (21/167y, 2 TDs) exploded on 61y TD run in 2nd Q for 10-7 lead. By time Spencer scored again, on 18y rush midway through 3rd Q, Ohio State had built 24-10 lead: Buckeyes marched with 2nd H KO to short TD blast by FB Vaughn Broadnax, and CB Garcia Lane picked off Young soon after to set up Spencer's 2nd TD. Next KO was fumbled to Ohio to poise it for K Rich Spangler's 2nd FG. LB Marcus Marek made 8 tackles to launch himself to top of Ohio's career list.

Tangerine Bowl (Dec. 18): Auburn 33 Boston College 26

With each team featuring high-powered Os that showcased future Heisman Trophy winners, game was thriller. Boston College (8-3-1) scored 1st on 79y drive that displayed QB Doug Flutie's scrambling ability; he capped drive with 5y TD run. Auburn (9-3) stormed back with its option attack showing surprisingly balance as game MVP,

QB Randy Campbell (10-16/177y, INT), completed 8-10/146y in 1st H to lead Tigers to 23-10 H lead. Auburn still ran, gaining 313y on ground and scoring TDs on 1y and 6y runs by HB Bo Jackson, 2y run by HB Willie Howell and 15y run by FB Greg Pratt. Top Tigers ground gainer was HB Lionel James with 17/101y. Tigers deployed 5 and at times 6-man D backfield to limit damage by Flutie's aerial antics. Flutie still completed 22-38/299y, 2 TDs, but threw 2 INTs and was sacked 4 times. After their opening possession, Eagles were unable to return to Auburn's EZ until late in 4th Q. By then, Flutie's TD passes of 2y to TE Scott Nizolek and 16y to WR Brian Brennan (7/149y) were too little, too late.

Sun Bowl (Dec. 25): North Carolina 26 Texas 10

With terrific wind at backs, Tar Heels (8-4) scorched Texas for 23 4th Q pts on 4 scoring drives and TD by D. Sticking with ground game—sparked by 119y from TB Ethan Horton—and D that changed momentum of game with GLS early in 3rd Q, North Carolina set up 47y FG by K Rob Rogers, who had hit 53y effort in 2nd Q, on 1st play with wind in 4th Q. Down 10-6, Rogers then recovered own onside-KO at Texas (9-3) 47YL to set up 23y FG by short-distance K Brooks Barwick. Ahead 10-9, Longhorns were unable to move ball. Texas was limited, even with wind, as QB Robert Brewer broke thumb 5 days earlier and was replaced by soph QB Todd Dodge, who managed only 6-22/50y. Carolina moved to winning 42y FG by Barwick, before adding 2 insurance TDs in final 2:17 as LB Chris Ward's INT set up Horton's TD run and LB Micah Moon sacked Dodge to force FUM REC in EZ by LB Thomas Wilcher. Held to 48y in 2nd H, Texas gained only 130y total, to 234y by North Carolina. Longhorns special teams ace Ronnie Mullins had scored TD on EZ REC of punt block in 1st Q. Key to game was Tar Heels' ability to handle snow and wind. "Believe it or not, we practiced in weather worse than this back home preparing for the game," said UNC coach Dick Crum, now 6-0 career in bowls.

Aloha Bowl (Dec. 25): Washington 21 Maryland 20

Maryland's possible victory in inaugural Aloha Bowl went south quickly in 4th Q. Ahead 20-14 with less than 5 mins left, Terrapins (8-4) K Jeff Atkinson missed what could have been clinching 32y FG. Huskies (10-2) took over and marched 80y to score on 11y pass from QB Tim Cowan to WR Anthony Allen with 6 secs left. Washington A-A K Chuck Nelson added winning x-pt. Cowan, who threw for 33-55/369y, hooked up with Allen on 8/152y and 3 TDs, including 27y pass to open scoring in 1st Q. Maryland scored next by converting FUM by Washington TB Sterling Hinds on Huskies 19YL into 6y TD pass from QB Boomer Esiason (19-32/251y, INT) to FB Dave D'Addio. Terps settled for 7-6 deficit as x-pt was missed. After teams traded TDs—with Allen catching 71y pass and Terps TE John Tice (6/85y) catching 36y TD—Esiason led 86y drive to go-ahead 2y TD run by RB John Nash (11/41y) early in 4th Q. Cowan owned possession last, running or passing on 15 of winning drive's 16 plays. Cowan thrice converted 4th downs, twice on runs, in leading winning rally.

Liberty Bowl (Dec. 29): Alabama 21 Illinois 15

Illinois (7-5) picked wrong bowl in which to return to post-season action after 19-year absence. Fired-up Alabama (8-4) looked to send coach Bear Bryant out as winner of his final game. Big hits by Crimson Tide D forced Illini QB Tony Eason from game on 3 different occasions, and backup QB Kris Jenner saw all 3 of his pass attempts intercepted. When Eason was in play, he set Liberty Bowl records for total O (413y), passing yards (423y), attempts (55) and completions (35). He also set INT mark with 4. Illinois trailed 7-6 at H as O blew numerous chances, with 4 drives ending on INTs deep in Alabama territory and another on missed FG. Tide star CB Jeremiah Castille had 3 INTs, 2 coming deep in his end: 13 and 22YLs. Bama upped lead to 14-6 in 3rd Q on 8y reverse run by WR Jesse Bendross. Illinois got act together and reeled off next 9 pts on Eason's 2y TD pass to WR Oliver Williams and K Mike Bass' 23y FG. Alabama simply was not going to accept defeat, and QB Walter Lewis led winning drive to 1y TD run by FB Craig Turner, scored with 7:34 left. Illinois had plenty of time left, but Tide D came up with 2 big INTs. Final drive began at Illini 18YL, and Eason completed 3-3/47y before exiting again with wooziness. Jenner came in, and LB Robbie Jones sealed verdict with INT with 16 secs left. Illinois WR Mike Martin tied Liberty Bowl records with 8 catches/127y. Bear Bryant was escorted reverently off field afterward as team messed up opportunity to carry him to retirement on its shoulders. Regrettably, Bryant would die within month.

Gator Bowl (Dec. 30): Florida State 31 West Virginia 12

Was it Florida State (9-3) D or was it driving rain that stopped Mountaineers QB Jeff Hostetler? Hostetler completed only 10-28/118y, 2 INTs as West Virginia (9-3) was swamped. Seminoles' surprise starter at QB, Blair Williams (16-30/204y, INT), ignored weather, to throw 27y TD to skying WR Dennis McKinnon and lead O to 461y. McKinnon ran 65y on E-around, while HB Greg Allen (15/138y), who led nation with 20 TDs, scored twice in 3rd Q. Special teams came up big for each as 27-year-old soph HB Billy Allen returned 2nd Q KO 95y to EZ to give Florida State 10-3 lead, and West Virginia WR Willie Drewrey returned punt 82y to FSU 7YL. Drewrey pulled muscle on play, however, which prevented him from scoring, and Mountaineers were unable to cash in because K Paul Woodside missed FG. Both RETs set Gator Bowl records. WR Darrell Miller (5/100y) scored sole TD for West Virginia on 26y pass from reserve QB Kevin White. FSU S Brian McCrary twice intercepted Hostetler.

Hall of Fame (Dec. 31): Air Force 36 Vanderbilt 28

Vandy was hoping to win 9 games for 1st time since 1915, and turned things over to their best shot. As any good gunslinger must, Vanderbilt (8-4) senior QB Whit Taylor went out with guns ablazing. Taylor threw 38-51/452y and 4 TDs, but when that many balls go airborne bad things also happen. Taylor threw 3 INTs, with none more damaging than pick-off by Air Force (8-5) DE Carl Dieudonne early in 4th Q at Vandy 40YL. Dieudonne returned ball 19y to set up FB John Kershner's 5y TD run 5 plays later for 29-28 lead. Score was 2nd of 3 TDs for Falcons, whose punishing run game

wore down Commodores D. Kershner led attack that made 315y by rushing up gut for nearly half of its total. AFA QB Marty Louthan (11-17/136y) added 74y and 2 TDs on ground, including 46y romp that clinched game later in 4th Q. Other key stat was Falcons' lack of TOs. Taylor's leading target was TB Norman Jordan, who caught 20/173y and 3 TDs. Jordan's impressive reception total tied bowl game record set by Richmond WR Walker Gillette in 1968 Tangerine Bowl

Peach Bowl (Dec. 31): Iowa 28 Tennessee 22

Using 3-TD 2nd Q to jump on Tennessee, Hawkeyes (8-4) built lead big enough to withstand Volunteers' rally. With near perfection from QB Chuck Long, Iowa took 21-7 H lead as Long (19-26/304y, INT) completed 1st 11 attempts and ended 1st H with 229y and 3 TD passes. Vols cut into deficit with opening series of 2nd H, which took 9 plays to move 80y to 10y TD run by TB Chuck Coleman (11/103y). Long answered with 75y drive to what proved to be winning TD on 2y run by TB Eddie Phillips. Vols QB Alan Cockrell (22-41/221y) later threw 19y TD pass to WR Willie Gault and led 4th Q drive to 27y FG by K Fuad Reveiz, but 2 other 4th Q trips were halted by Iowa D. On final march, Vols advanced to Hawkeyes 39YL, before sack and 2 incompletions forced 4th-and-25 play. DE Shaun Joseph squelched that with FUM-inducing hit on Cockrell. WR Dave Moritz was Long's favorite target with 8/168y with 57y TD. WB Ronnie Harmon caught Long's other 2 TD passes on plays of 18y and 8y.

Bluebonnet Bowl (Dec. 31): Arkansas 28 Florida 24

Arkansas (9-2-1) QB Tom Jones made sure his final game was successful as he sparked Hogs to his 4th Q passing and running TDs that pulled it out. In closing, Jones led 78y march that eliminated final 6:29 of clock. After dust had settled, Arkansas' 2nd H surge had been built on 302y O for 3 TDs. Gators (8-4) had built 10-pt lead as QB Bob Hewko (19-28/234y), given start in final game, and WR Dwayne Dixon (8/106y) combined on 3 TD passes, all capping drives of at least 74y. Hogs converted FUM by Gator FB James Jones (12/89y) at midfield into 1st scoring drive, capped by 17y run by TB Gary Anderson (161y, 2 TDs). Gators then scored 17 pts to close out 1st H scoring on 2 Hewko TD passes and 34y FG by K Bobby Raymond. After trade of 3rd Q TDs, Hogs stalked 85y to 5y scoring catch by FB Jessie Clark and on next series, held Florida on downs before ripping off 80y drive to winning TD on Jones' 1y keeper. Arkansas D, led by A-A DE Billy Ray Smith (2 sacks), held again to set long time-killing possession. Win was 100th in career for Arkansas coach Lou Holtz, and he could thank O for totaling 480y.

Cotton Bowl: Southern Methodist 7 Pittsburgh 3

Undefeated Mustangs (11-0-1) looked to claim share of title with impressive win in sleet and rain. Pitt (9-3) was too good for that, however, especially with talent-laden D that promised that Pony Express TB tandem of Eric Dickerson (27/124y) and Craig James (14/54y) would earn every y. It was same for dominating SMU D, which played in shadow of O. Panthers came out with redesigned O—offering QB Dan Marino (19-37/181y) 4 outside targets—that surprised SMU enough to allow opening drive to reach its 1YL. FB Joe McCall then lost FUM to ball-hawking Pony S Wes Hopkins. It was Mustangs' turn to display new O, albeit formation they used in big Texas win at midseason. Playing Dickerson and James together, with 1 as power back, SMU moved 92y against D intent on leveling punishment—Panthers committed 2 personal foul and face mask PENs. Finally on Pitt 7YL, QB Lance McIlhenny was stripped with FUM REC by Pitt NG J.C. Pelusi. Game continued as slugfest, with missed 26y FG by Pittsburgh K Eric Schubert maintaining 0-0 score for H. Schubert made amends with 43y FG that ended 3rd Q drive. McIlhenny then began to emulate Marino, his more-famous Pitt counterpart, completing 2/62y to WR Bobby Leach that moved ball to Pitt 20. From there, 2 runs by Dickerson and 1 by James put ball on 9YL. McIlhenny then ran option to right, saw D covering James, turned downfield and avoided S Tom Flynn for TD. Pitt's best chance to retake lead ended with Marino's EZ INT, as throwing on run, he was picked off by S Blane Smith off deflection by Hopkins. For 5th time on season, Mustangs had rallied to win surprising D battle.

Fiesta Bowl: Arizona State 32 Oklahoma 21

For Arizona State (10-2) to win, it seemed, its top-ranked D would have to carry low-scoring game. Oklahoma (8-4) was having none of it, gaining 457y. Surprisingly, Sun Devils outscored OU in shootout as QB Todd Hons threw for 329y in leading O to 21 2nd H pts, while ASU D recovered 4 FUMs. Riding heralded, but chubby TB Marcus Dupree—who finished with 239y rushing despite missing most of 4th Q with hamstring pull—Sooners raced out to 7-0, 13-11, and 21-18 leads, but could not hold off better-conditioned Arizona State in 4th Q. Sun Devils had kept pace in 1st H with 3 FGs by K Luis Zendejas and safety earned when DE Jim Jeffcoat trapped Oklahoma QB Kelly Phelps in EZ. Teams traded 3rd Q TDs before Sun Devils took control of 4th Q, scoring TDs on 1y run by TB Alvin Moore and 52y pass from Hons to WR Ron Brown. Arizona State D had allowed avg of 95.4y rushing and 228.9y total during regular season, marks Dupree and OU obliterated. Dupree simply was unstoppable, despite being overweight and banged up.

Rose Bowl: UCLA 24 Michigan 14

Rubber game of 3-game mini-series played out between teams after Michigan (8-4) had beaten Bruins 33-14 in 1981 Bluebonnet Bowl before losing at home to UCLA in September. Position of S rarely makes highlight reel, but UCLA (10-1-1) S Don Rogers clearly was Rose star. First, Rogers intercepted pass by QB Steve Smith—1 of 4 Michigan TOs to none for UCLA by game's end—at Bruins 12YL that knifed Wolverines' finest drive of 1st H. Midway through 2nd Q, Rogers unloaded on Smith after QB gained 8y on option run and sent Smith to sideline with separated shoulder. In came raw QB Dave Hall (13-24/155y, 2 TDs, 2 INTs) and out went option portion of Michigan's O. Also, Rogers was instrumental in blanketing WR Anthony Carter. Carter caught 5 passes/only 59y, his 3 E-around runs were well defended, and he was forced into punt FUM. Carter's FUM led to 39y FG by K John Lee, and UCLA was

up 10-0 at H. Michigan refused to fold, scoring on 1y reception by FB Eddie Garrett. Bruins QB Tom Ramsey (18-25/162y), who had scored team's 1st TD on 1y keeper, motivated his Bruins 80y downfield to regain 10-pt edge. Ramsey completed 4-5 on said TD drive TB Danny Andrews finished with 9y dash. Bruins D fittingly iced game as LB Blanchard Montgomery returned INT 10y for TD and commanding 24-7 lead, 2 plays after Michigan D had halted TB Kevin Nelson on 4th-and-goal from 1YL. Hall threw another TD pass, 4y to FB Dan Rice, but game was all over. Pair of MVPs was selected: Ramsey, who rewrote UCLA record book, and Rogers, 1st D player so honored since 1967. Bruins coach Terry Donahue won his 1st bowl after going 0-2-1.

Orange Bowl: Nebraska 21 Louisiana State 20

Game looked to be no contest early on as LSU went 3-and-out on opening drive only to allow Cornhuskers (12-1) to march 51y in 6 plays to FB Mark Schellen's 5y TD run. For sake of competition, Nebraska handed ball back to Tigers 6 times, 4 on FUMs. They also muffed FG attempt and failed to gain 1st down on fake punt. FUMs by IB Mike Rozier (26/118y) and WB Irving Fryar led to 2 1y TD runs by TB Dalton Hilliard and Tigers (8-3-1) had 14-7 lead at H. LSU added 3 more in 3rd Q, converting yet another FUM into 28y FG by K Juan Betanzos. QB Turner Gill (13-22/184y, 2 INTs) then rallied Tigers surge, marching Huskers to 11y TD run by Rozier. Ahead 17-14, LSU was soon forced to punt. On 4th-and-19 from own 36YL, P Clay Parker was spooked by Nebraska rush and took off. He gained 12y, which was 7y shy of 1st down. Sparked by 30y pass to Fryar (5/84y), Gill had Nebraska in EZ soon after on 1y keeper and game was 21-17. Later in 4th Q after Fryar returned punt 43y, Huskers went for kill and faked FG on LSU 17YL, but WR Tim Brungardt dropped Gill pass. Another Gill pass was picked off and QB Alan Risher (14-30/173y, 2 INTs) led Tigers downfield before Betanzos kicked 49y FG. Huskers then ran out final 5:05.

Sugar Bowl: Penn State 27 Georgia 23

After undefeated teams in 1968, 1969 and 1973 went title-less, Penn State (11-1) finally won national championship with victory over top-ranked Georgia (11-1). Bulldogs TB Herschel Walker was focus of match-up, and he faced determined Penn State D, featuring many players who had shut down Heisman winner USC TB Marcus Allen (85y rushing) in last season's Fiesta Bowl. They also had stopped future Heisman winner, Mike Rozier (86y rushing) earlier in 1982. Walker topped both those totals, but he had to earn every bit of his 28/103y. Penn State QB Todd Blackledge (13-23/228y, TD) came out firing, completing 4 straight/74y of 80y opening drive against UGa secondary that had led nation in INTs with 35. Drive ended on 2y TD run by TB Curt Warner (18/117y, 2 TDs) for 7-0 lead. With Blackledge continuing to fling passes and WR Kevin Baugh returning 3 punts/100y, Lions quickly added another TD by Warner, from 9y out, and 2 FGs by K Nick Gancitano for 20 pts. Georgia could muster only 3 pts on its 1 threat until just before H. Suddenly, as clock neared 0:00 in 2nd Q, Bulldogs QB John Lastinger (12-27/166) performed his best impersonation of San Diego Chargers' Dan Fouts. Lastinger hit passes of 17, 13y, and 16y to 3 different receivers. Just like that, Georgia was downfield and on scoreboard again as WR Herman Archie caught 10y lob in left corner of EZ with 5 secs left in H. Bulldogs were back in business. Lastinger, completing passes of 25y and 11y to WR Kevin Harris, took O 69y on opening drive of 3rd Q to Walker's 1y TD. Penn State led 20-17 but had stalled O because Warner was on sideline with leg cramps, and Bulldogs D rattled Blackledge with sacks that would total 5 by game's end. After punt, Penn State D came through again with INT by S Mark Robinson to begin game-clinching drive late in 3rd Q. Warner limped on and off field, running brilliantly when called on as he outrushed current Heisman Trophy winner in 2nd straight bowl game. Lions moved to Georgia 47YL as 3rd Q ended. Then Blackledge went deep on play that would make unheralded WR Gregg Garrity all-time Lion hero. Beating frosh S Tony Flack, Garrity dove to catch ball at GL and land in EZ for big TD for 27-17 lead. Baugh's punt RET FUM was collared at Penn State 43YL, and Lastinger soon completed 9y TD pass to TE Clarence Kay. Bulldogs opted for 2 pts with Walker being stuffed by Lions D, led by DE Walker Lee Ashley. There was 3:54 left, which Lions killed as Blackledge and Garrity teamed up for 5y pass for 1st down.

1982 Top Performance Formula

1	Penn State	1.7587
2	Nebraska	1.7474
3	Georgia	1.6457
4	UCLA	1.5997
5	Southern Methodist	1.5399
6	Pittsburgh	1.4987
7	Florida State	1.4858
8	Arizona State	1.4857
9	Arkansas	1.4812
10	Washington	1.4765
11	Clemson	1.4676
12	Southern California	1.4621
13	West Virginia	1.4390
14	Texas	1.4341
15	Auburn	1.4243
16	North Carolina	1.4080
17	Ohio State	1.3586
18	Alabama	1.3461
19	Maryland	1.3455
20	Brigham Young	1.3450

1982 Top Opponent Records

1	Penn State	.6875
2	Oregon	.6491
3	Florida State	.6408
4	Kentucky	.6314
5	Pittsburgh	.6270
6	Stanford	.6228
7	Florida	.6135
8	Alabama	.6111
9	Auburn	.6102
10	West Virginia	.6040
11	Southern California	.5921
12	Texas Tech	.5913
13	Nebraska	.5882
14	North Carolina	.5880
15t	Maryland	.584677
15t	UCLA	.584677
17	Georgia	.5840
18	Syracuse	.5838
19	Notre Dame	.5783
20	North Carolina State	.5781

1982 Out-of-Conference Records

	W-L	Percentage	Bowl W-L
Pacific-10	25-10-1	.7083	3-0
Southeastern	35-17-1	.6698	2-5
Western Athletic	19-17	.5278	1-1
Atlantic Coast	16-16-1	.5000	1-1
Big Eight	16-16-1	.5000	1-2
Southwest	11-14	.4400	1-1
Big Ten	11-16	.4074	3-1

1982 Individual Statistical Leaders

RUSHING YARDS	Attempts	Yards	Avg.
Ernest Anderson, Oklahoma State	353	1877	5.3
Herschel Walker, Georgia	335	1752	5.2
Mike Rozier, Nebraska	242	1689	7.0
Eric Dickerson, Southern Methodist	232	1617	7.0
Sam DeJarnette, Southern Mississippi	311	1545	5.0
Carl Monroe, Utah	309	1507	4.9
Michael Gunter, Tulsa	195	1464	7.5
Tim Spencer, Ohio State	252	1371	5.4
Lawrence Ricks, Michigan	243	1300	5.3
Robert Lavette, Georgia Tech	280	1208	4.3

PASSING YARDS	Completions	Attempts	Yards	Pct.
Todd Dillon, Long Beach State	289	504	3517	57.3
Tony Eason, Illinois	278	450	3248	61.8
John Elway, Stanford	262	405	3242	64.7
Steve Young, Brigham Young	230	367	3100	62.7
Ben Bennett, Duke	236	374	3033	63.1
Randall Cunningham, UNLV	200	381	2847	52.5
Tom Ramsey, UCLA	191	311	2824	61.4
Jeff Tedford, Fresno State	153	298	2620	51.3
Tom Tunnicliffe, Arizona	176	328	2520	53.7
Steve Clarkson, San Jose State	196	340	2485	57.7

RECEIVING YARDS	Catches	Yards
Henry Ellard, Fresno State	62	1510
Mark Clayton, Louisville	53	1112
Darral Hambrick, UNLV	60	1060
Jeff Simmons, Southern California	56	973
Mike Martin, Illinois	69	941
Gordon Hudson, Brigham Young	67	928
Jeff Campine, Colorado State	54	904
Gerald McNeil, Baylor	52	822
Waymon Aldridge, UNLV	49	810
Jon Harvey, Northwestern	52	807

1982 Consensus All-America Team
Offense

Wide Receiver:	Anthony Carter, Michigan
Tight End:	Gordon Hudson, BYU
Line:	Don Mosebar, Southern California
	Steve Korte, Arkansas
	Jimbo Covert, Pittsburgh
	Bruce Mathews, Southern California
Center:	Dave Rimington, Nebraska
Quarterback:	John Elway, Stanford
Running Back:	Herschel Walker, Georgia
	Eric Dickerson, SMU
	Mike Rozier, Nebraska
Placekicker:	Chuck Nelson, Washington

Defense

Line:	Billy Ray Smith, Arkansas
	Vernon Maxwell, Arizona State
	Mike Pitts, Alabama
	Wilber Marshall, Florida
	Gabriel Rivera, Texas Tech
	Rick Bryan, Oklahoma
Middle Guard:	George Achica, Southern California
Linebacker:	Darryl Talley, West Virginia
	Ricky Hunley, Arizona State
	Marcus Marek, Ohio State
Back:	Terry Kinard, Clemson
	Mike Richardson, Arizona State
	Terry Hoage, Georgia
Punter:	Jim Arnold, Vanderbilt

1982 Heisman Trophy Vote

Herschel Walker, junior tailback, Georgia	1926
John Elway, senior quarterback, Stanford	1231
Eric Dickerson, senior tailback, Southern Methodist	465
Anthony Carter, senior wide receiver, Michigan	142
Dave Rimington, senior center, Nebraska	137

Other Major Awards

Maxwell (Player)	Herschel Walker, junior tailback, Georgia
Walter Camp (Player)	Herschel Walker, junior tailback, Georgia
Outland (Lineman)	Dave Rimington, senior center, Nebraska
Lombardi (Lineman)	Dave Rimington, senior center, Nebraska
Davey O'Brien (QB)	Todd Blackledge, senior quarterback, Penn State
AFCA Coach of the Year	Joe Paterno, Penn State

1983

The Year of a Hurricane Hitting the Orange Bowl, Georgia's Senior Mission, and Auburn's Best-Ever Factor

When south Florida big shots donned their orange blazers to plan the golden anniversary of the Orange Bowl Classic, no one in their right mind would have expected the hometown Miami Hurricanes (11-1) to play in, let alone, win the 50th game to nab a surprise national championship in one of the greatest games ever played. Miami may have been in the final year of coach Howard Schnellenberger's trumpeted five-year plan, but summertime expectations were modest with the departure of quarterback Jim Kelly to the professional ranks and the overall youth of a team that featured 57 freshmen and sophomores. Miami was unranked in the preseason top 20, which seemed completely justified after Florida (9-2-1) administered a 28-3 opening-game loss. Miami then went under the radar with a winning streak that readjusted its evaluation.

Meanwhile, mighty Nebraska (12-1) occupied the nation's top spot from the preseason, and the Cornhuskers set free a powerful offense featuring a troika of star players: quarterback Turner Gill, I-back Mike Rozier, and wingback Irving Fryar. After crushing the defending national champion, Penn State (7-4-1), by 44-6 in the Kickoff Classic opener that was played within earshot of the New York City media hub, the Cornhuskers became separated, in the nation's mind, from every other top team. By the end of September, they had scored 56 points against Wyoming (7-5), dropped 84 points on shell-shocked Minnesota (1-10), and delivered 42 points on eventual Pac-10 champion UCLA (7-4-1). This barrage made the Huskers the first unanimous no. 1 in both polls since Southern California turned the trick in 1972. The Cornhuskers later poured 63 points on Syracuse (6-5), torched Colorado (4-7) for 69, blasted Iowa State (4-7) with a 72-point volley, and bled Kansas (4-6-1) for 67. A 14-10 hiccup against Oklahoma State (8-4) almost derailed Nebraska in midseason, but once Oklahoma (8-4) was stopped 28-21, the national title seemed all but assured for Tom Osborne's Cornhuskers.

One task remained for Nebraska: defeating Miami on the Hurricanes' home field in the Orange Bowl. The Hurricanes not only had to come back from their opening loss to Florida, but also had to pass any team that could be invited to play no. 1 Nebraska. October 29 had turned out to be the day when everything came together for Miami. It beat West Virginia (6-5) 20-3 to improve to 8-1, no. 3 North Carolina (8-4) lost to Maryland (8-4), and no. 5 Florida was defeated by Auburn (11-1). The Orange Bowl path had cleared for Miami, now no. 5, because every team ranked in front of it would be forced to play in a bowl other than the Orange due to pre-arranged conference tie-ins.

Miami ran the table to clinch the Orange Bowl invitation, but it had to outlast another upstart, East Carolina (8-3), by a narrow 12-7 score. So, very few outside the Hurricane football family fostered national title hopes. Even if they could beat Nebraska, the Canes needed Cotton Bowl help from Georgia (10-1-1), which faced an undefeated Texas (11-1) squad that boasted one of the great defenses in recent memory. The Longhorns were ranked second from September 19 on, and people who clamored for a playoff system surely wanted to see Nebraska's top-rated offense play Texas' top-rated defense (212 yards per game). Ironically, neither team won the bowl games they were contracted to play.

For its part, the talented Georgia Bulldogs were hankering for respect. Herschel Walker, Georgia's all-time great running back, had left school early after the 1982 season to sign with the United States Football League (USFL). The pundits virtually wrote off the Bulldogs for 1983. Forever after, coach Vince Dooley sang the praises of the pride and talent displayed by his 1983 senior class, led by quarterback John Lastinger, offensive linemen Jimmy Harper and Guy McIntyre, tight end Clarence Kay, defensive end Freddie Gilbert, and safety Terry Hoage.

If ever a season appeared perfect for a bracketed playoff, 1983 would have served as a template. Nebraska, Miami, Texas, and Georgia surely would have qualified. Illinois (10-2), Auburn, Brigham Young (11-1) and Southern Methodist (10-2) were four schools that deserved title shots off their regular season deeds.

SMU lost only once, by three points to Texas, in the regular season but was snubbed by the major bowls and had to play Alabama (8-4) in the Sun Bowl. The uninspired Mustangs lost 28-7 in El Paso.

Auburn also suffered only one defeat despite playing the fifth toughest schedule after 1953. No major team in all those years and beyond posted so good a record as 11-1 against opponents exceeding .7000 in collective winning percentage. The Tigers' foes were .7016 in all games other than the Auburn match-up.

By comparison, Miami's opponents had a somewhat typical winning percentage of .514. Auburn's claim to the title was based on wins over Tennessee (9-3), Florida State (7-5), Florida, Maryland, Georgia, Alabama, and Michigan (9-3), with its sole loss coming to Texas. But, Auburn was afforded no crack at Nebraska and became an afterthought on the heels of its 9-7 win over Michigan in the Sugar Bowl.

Illinois became the first Big Ten team to beat all nine conference opponents in the same year, but that did little good when UCLA routed the Illini in the Rose Bowl despite the Bruins having sneaked into Pasadena with the worst-ever record of any Rose contestant.

No bowl team would have been favored over Nebraska, but of all the contenders, Miami had unique advantages well suited for an upset. The Hurricanes were playing at home, where they had been 24-2 under Schnellenberger. Nebraska likely would be more overconfident against them than the others. Also, Miami had a quarterback—redshirt freshman Bernie Kosar, who threw for 300 yards and two touchdowns in the bowl—capable of exploiting Nebraska's weakest link, its relatively slow-footed secondary. Even so, Miami won by a single point, and that occurred only because Nebraska coach Tom Osborne opted for a win for his rallying team on a last-moment two-point conversion instead of going for the tie, which almost certainly would have guaranteed the national title. It took winning national titles near the end of Osborne's career to finally put to rest his two-point decision in the magnificent 1984 Orange Bowl.

Nebraska's post-season loss was not the only dark moment for the Big Eight. Sophomore tailback Marcus Dupree quit Oklahoma in mid-season due to unhappiness with coach Barry Switzer. He also was homesick and seemed to lack the desire to become as good a player as expected. By the time he quit he had already missed a great deal of schoolwork and likely was facing flunking grades. One class he skipped on a regular basis was a philosophy course taught partially by the school president. Dupree rushed for 905 yards as a freshman and 369 yards in 1983. He ended up at Southern Mississippi with the possibility of eligibility in October 1984, but the NCAA ruled he could not play until 1985. So, Dupree signed a contract with the USFL; within a year the upstart league inked Dupree, Rozier, and Georgia's Walker.

Football legend Bear Bryant had died in January, shortly after his retirement, and his passing stunned the Alabama faithful and the sports world. His successor, former Alabama wide receiver and coach of the New York Giants, Ray Perkins, faced intense pressure. In March, Perkins made the task of replacing Bryant more difficult by adding the athletic directorship. While the Crimson Tide notched a so-so 4-2 record in the SEC, it was hard to fault Perkins' performance given the checked history of coaches who followed true legends.

The Atlantic Coast area made news as Duke (3-8) quarterback Ben Bennett grabbed the career pass yardage record with 9,614, trumping Jim McMahon, formerly of Brigham Young. Also on Tobacco Road, East Carolina made a splash with wins over North Carolina State (3-8) and Missouri (7-5), and close losses to Florida State, Florida, and Miami. There would be no bowl, however, awaiting the Pirates.

Milestones

■ NCAA approved new requirements for incoming freshmen athletes. Standards, known as Proposition 48, demanded that athletes post minimum high school or prep school GPA and score on either SAT or ACT test. Standards were to go into effect in 1986 and by 1988 scale up to 2.0 for GPA and 700 SAT or 15 ACT.

■ Georgia Tech began its first year of ACC eligibility; New Mexico State joined PCAA.

■ Kickoff Classic, created to benefit National Football Foundation and Hall of Fame, debuted on August 29 with game pitting defending champ Penn State and preseason top-ranked Nebraska.

■ Legendary coach Paul "Bear" Bryant died of massive heart attack at age 69 on January 26, only 37 days after retiring as all-time leader in coaching wins. Coaching for 38 years with Maryland, Kentucky, Texas A&M, and Alabama, Bryant compiled 323-85-17 record. Bryant was best known for his tenure with Crimson Tide, for whom he was three-year starting end during 23-3 won-loss stretch with upset over Stanford in 1935 Rose Bowl. Bryant won or shared six national titles at Alabama. On March 7, Charles "Rip" Engle, who coached Penn State to 104 wins and trio of Lambert Trophies from 1950-65, died at 76. Engle was coach at Brown and took his former quarterback, Joe Paterno, with him to join Penn State's coaching staff. One of great two-way players in SWC history, Charles "Ki" Aldrich died at 66 on March 12. Aldrich was center-linebacker for TCU's undefeated national titlist in 1938, beating Carnegie Tech 15-7 in Sugar Bowl. Aldrich went on to seven-year NFL career. Coaching great Jess Neely, who won 207 games in 40-year career, died on April 9 at 85. After successful nine years as coach of Clemson, including 6-3 Cotton Bowl win over Boston College in 1939, Neely began 27-year reign as coach at Rice. Neely coached Owls to four SWC championships. Norm Van Brocklin, All-America quarterback at Oregon in 1948, who went on to lead both Los Angeles Rams and Philadelphia Eagles to NFL titles, died of heart attack at age 57 on May 2. "The Dutchman" was famous for his surliness, which eventually cost him both pro coaching jobs he held after retirement in 1960 following title win with Eagles. He later became pecan farmer and TV analyst. Arizona State All-America (1975) and Miami Dolphins linebacker Larry Gordon, died at 29 on June 25 while jogging in desert near Phoenix. He unknowingly suffered from idiopathic cardial myopathy, which limited heart development. Gordon hailed from Monroe, Louisiana, which was scene of more tragedy days later when Joe Delaney, Kansas City Chiefs pro bowl running back, drowned while trying to save three boys, two died, who had gone under water in a pond in Monroe. Delaney went into the water despite not knowing how to swim. Delaney had been All-America back for I-AA Northwestern State. Matty Bell, coaching legend who won 153 games for four schools, died on June 30 at 84. "Moanin Matty" was best known for his SMU career, winning share of 1935 national title and taking Mustangs to Rose Bowl. Although Mustangs lost to Stanford 7-0, they helped put SWC on football map. Auburn fullback Greg Pratt collapsed after running sprints for fall physical on August 20, dying at age 20. While returning from memorial service for Joe Delaney on September 4, Claude "Buddy" Young, former All-America halfback at Illinois, who rushed for 9,419 yards with three pro teams and was NFL director of player relations at that time, died at 57 after driving off road early in morning. Young was an instant star with Illini, rushing for 13 touchdowns to tie Red Grange's freshman school record. He led Illinois to Big 10 title in 1946.

■ Gabe Rivera, All-America defensive tackle at Texas Tech and 22-year-old rookie with Pittsburgh Steelers, was paralyzed in car crash on October 20.

■ All-time LSU great, halfback Billy Cannon, 1959 Heisman Trophy winner, was arrested on October 9 on counterfeiting charges. He was convicted, received five-year sentence, and had recent election to College Football Hall of Fame rescinded.

■ Longest winning streaks entering season:

Nebraska 10	Tulsa 9	Ohio State, Penn State 7

■ Coaching Changes:

	Incoming	Outgoing
Alabama	Ray Perkins	Paul "Bear" Bryant
Army	Jim Young	Ed Cavanaugh
Duke	Steve Sloan	Red Wilson
Indiana	Sam Wyche	Lee Corso
Iowa State	Jim Criner	Donnie Duncan
Kansas	Mike Gottfried	Don Fambrough
Michigan State	George Perles	Frank Waters
Mississippi	Billy Brewer	Steve Sloan
New Mexico	Joe Lee Dunn	Joe Morrison
North Carolina State	Tom Reed	Monte Kiffin
South Carolina	Joe Morrison	Richard Bell
Southern Cal	Ted Tollner	John Robinson
Temple	Bruce Arians	Wayne Hardin
Texas Christian	Jim Wacker	F.A. Dry
Tulane	Wally English	Vince Gibson

AP Preseason Poll

1 Nebraska (30)	976	11 North Carolina	497
2 Oklahoma (11)	860	12 Louisiana State	394
3 Texas (3)	857	13 Alabama	376
4 Penn State (2)	756	14 Arizona	279
5 Auburn (2)	749	15 Georgia	246
6 Notre Dame	617	16 Iowa	218
7 Florida State (1)	575	17 Maryland	210
8 Southern California	553	18 Washington	199
9 Ohio State	518	19 Southern Methodist	191
10 Michigan (1)	515	20 UCLA	189

September 3, 1983

(Mon) Nebraska 44 Penn State 6 (East Rutherford, NJ): While gaining revenge for controversial loss to Penn State in 1982, Nebraska (1-0) romped in 1st-ever Kickoff Classic and made case as nation's best team. Huskers unleashed wing-T and triple option O on young, outclassed foe to tune of 500y, 211y by QB Turner Gill (158y passing, 53y rushing) and 71y rushing by IB Mike Rozier. Huskers pinned worst defeat in 17 years on Penn State (0-1), equaling 49-11 loss margin versus UCLA in 1966, coach Joe Paterno's 1st year as head man in State College. Nittany Lions were able to prevent whitewash only in last 20 secs on QB Dan Lonergan's 35y TD pass. Neither Lonergan nor starting QB Doug Strang effectively replaced graduated Todd Blackledge as Lions O gained only 93y against rugged and fast D of Cornhuskers, led by LBs Mike Knox and Mark Daum.

(Th) Houston 45 RICE 14: TB Donald Jordan rushed for 138y—with 1st H TD runs of 47, 45, and 1y—as Cougars (1-0) handed Rice 13th straight loss, 3 having been delivered by Houston. Cougars scored on 4 straight possessions in 1st H to easily top cross-town Owls (0-1), who managed 221y O. Rice's only 1st H exploit came on 65y INT TD RET by DB Donahue Walker. Houston QB Lionel Wilson shook off INT to lead O that gained 464y, and S Albert Pope made 32y INT TD RET in 3rd Q.

FLORIDA STATE 47 East Carolina 46: Seminoles (1-0) won barnburner featuring 7 lead changes that proved both teams needed work on D. Florida State TB Greg Allen rushed for 154y, 3 TDs, and QB Kelly Lowrey (28-35/322y, 3 TDs) threw winning 5y TD to TE Tom Wheeler with 4:36 left. Nine different players scored, although none more spectacular than East Carolina (0-1) WR Henry Williams, who had 56y punt RET—on game's only punt—and 98y KO RET TDs. Pirates fell 3 shy of then pts record scored by losing team, set by Washington in 1973 vs. California.

Pittsburgh 13 TENNESSEE 3: QB John Cummings (9-13/110y, INT) had up-and-down debut at helm of Pittsburgh (1-0). Panthers struggled in 1st H, gaining only 27y, but broke through with trio of 2nd H scores, including Cummings' 56y TD pass to WR Dwight Collins. But with time running out, Cummings suffered broken collarbone on QB keeper tackle by LB Alvin Toles. Tennessee (0-1) lost 6th season opener in 7 tries under coach Johnny Majors, who fell to 0-2 vs. school he led to 1976 national title. Vols K Fuad Reveiz nailed 49y kick, but missed efforts from 51 and 57y—longer try hit crossbar—while Panthers K Eric Schubert hit FGs from 47 and 45y. P Tony Recchia (8/46.4y avg) saved Pitt in 1st H, while D unit came up with INTs of QB Alan Cockrell (18-34/169y) by CB Melvin Dean at Pitt 5YL and LB Troy Benson at own 10YL. Vols FB Sam Henderson rushed for 108y.

FLORIDA 28 Miami 3: Never again would loss by Miami (0-1) receive such little national attention. Proving to be fully recovered from July surgery for herniated disc, Florida (1-0) QB Wayne Peace (18-32/146y) completed 1st 8 passes, with 2 TDs to FB Joe Henderson, as Gators took 13-0 H lead. Florida TB Neal Anderson loped 8y for TD in 3rd Q in which Florida upped lead to 25-0 to end matters. Hurricanes could not overcome 7 TOs, 4 which set up 16 pts for Gators. Miami frosh QB Bernie Kosar (24-45/223y, 3 INTs) threw 2 INTs deep in Florida territory, but it would turn out that this would be only game without TD pass in his remarkable opening campaign. Only score for Miami was K Jeff Davis' 41y FG at end of 4th Q.

GEORGIA 19 Ucla 8: Defense was back at center stage in Athens as Bulldogs (1-0) moved on without incomparable runner Herschel Walker. Georgia D was nicked for y but not scores and even sealed it with 69y INT TD RET by S Charles Dean when Bruins threatened late. UCLA (0-1) QB Rick Neuheisel threw for 203y, but was intercepted 4 times. Georgia O was unexciting, managing 50/169y rushing and only 59y passing. Leading ground gainer for Bulldogs was FB Scott Williams, who made 46y. K Kevin Butler of Georgia and K John Lee of UCLA each hit pair of FGs.

California 19 TEXAS A&M 17: California (1-0) raced to 17-0 lead, helped by A&M coach Jackie Sherrill's decision to go for onside-KO to open game, which was recovered by Bears. Cal TB Dwight Garner soon scored on 43y run. QB John Mazur (20-33/243y) led Aggies (0-1) rally, throwing 2 TDs to TE Rich Siler. Cal coach Joe Kapp made his own odd move late in 4th Q, taking go-ahead pts off board after successful FG temporarily put Bears up 20-17. After accepting PEN for 1st down, Kapp had to grimace when Cal QB Gale Gilbert (22-40/256y, INT) fumbled on next play, recovered by Texas A&M LB Mike Ashley. Kapp was saved when LB Ron Rivera tackled RB Jimmie Hawkins in EZ for winning safety with 57 secs left.

Air Force 34 COLORADO STATE 13: Knowing Falcons (1-0) attack was quite different than stopping it. HB Mike Brown rushed for 131y and FB John Kershner added 130y—each scoring twice—as Air Force ground up Rams with 397y rushing. Both backs made early splashes with Kershner scoring on 70y burst on game's 2nd play and Brown racing 69y to EZ on team's next possession. Rams (0-1), outgained 502y to 427y, had success through air as QB Terry Nugent (27-43/312y, 2 INTs) threw 7y TD pass to WR Jeff Champine and became State's career pass leader with 4,096y. Falcons fumbled 4 times, but recovered them all, while Rams lost 3 TOs.

AP Poll September 4

1 Nebraska (44)	993	11 Arizona	459
2 Oklahoma (3)	868	12 Florida State	408
3 Texas (2)	865	13 Louisiana State	400
4 Auburn (1)	757	14 Alabama	340
5 Notre Dame	659	15 Southern Methodist	250
6 Michigan	593	16 Iowa	215
7 Ohio State	586	17 Maryland	193
8 North Carolina	568	18 Florida	179
9 Southern California	560	19 Washington	152
10 Georgia	528	20 Penn State	148

September 10, 1983

BOSTON COLLEGE 31 Clemson 16: QB Doug Flutie led Boston College (2-0) on 4 2nd H TD drives to shock Tigers, who sat on 16-3 3rd Q lead. Eagles gained 504y and 29 1st downs against vaunted Clemson (1-1) D, with TB Troy Stradford rushing for 179y. Flutie (20-36/223y, INT) capped 93y drive with 6y scoring pass to TE Scott Gieselman for 1st TD of 2nd H and led Eagles to FB Bob Biestek's 4y run for decisive TD in 4th Q. Now trailing 17-16, Clemson's inability to pass doomed them as QB Mike Eppley hit only 2-10/21y. Stradford added 9y TD run, while Flutie threw 40y TD to WR Gerard Phelan. Clemson, with only 9 1st downs and 180y—42y on TD run by FB Kevin Mack (11/92y)—lost for only 2nd time in 26 games.

Cincinnati 14 PENN STATE 3: What was thought to be bad spot for Bearcats (1-0)—facing Penn State club seething over loss to Nebraska—proved anything but. New coach Watson Brown's passing attack helped deal Penn State 1st 0-2 start for coach Joe Paterno. Cincy JC transfer QB Troy Bodine hit 25-36/261y and 11y TD to WR Bill Booze to easily outpace 3 State QBs, who combined for meager 7-25/112y with 3 INTs. Cincinnati scored twice in 1st H when they outgained Lions 207y to 57y, with both scores set up by FUMs on RETs by WR Kevin Baugh in his own end. Nittany Lions, who beat Cincinnati 52-0 in 1981, scored in 3rd Q on 39y FG by K Nick Gancitano. Team's dreadful start continued following week with 42-34 loss to Iowa.

Wake Forest 13 VIRGINIA TECH 6: After missing 1st H with bad back, QB Gary Schofield (9-15/181y) came to rescue of moribund Wake Forest (1-1). Schofield hit 3 passes on winning 61y drive, capped by 7y TD pass to WR Duane Owens early in 4th Q. Deamon Deacs' other score came on 1st Q blocked punt by special teamer

Ronnie Grinton, which was scooped up by LB Scott Roberts for 14y TD RET. With x-pt missed, Hokies (0-1) were able to knot it on K Don Wade's 2 FGs. Wade's 1st FG came on drive that stalled at Wake 2YL. Despite gaining 437y—with 132y rushing by TB Otis Copeland—Tech trailed in 4th Q when they took final drive to Wake Forest 5YL before coughing up FUM by backup QB Todd Greenwood.

East Carolina 22 NORTH CAROLINA STATE 16: There was reason ACC teams feared Pirates (1-1). In front of state-record 57,700, East Carolina scored pair of 4th Q TDs for upset. TB Tony Baker scored on 6y run to pull Pirates within 16-14, before TB Ernest Byner (17/97y) capped 83y drive with winning 5y run with 3 mins left. Pirates D had to withstand dual Wolfpack (0-1) scoring threats, stopping 1 with forced FUM at ECU 9YL and other at 17YL after Byner fumbled it back to NC State. Wolfpack TB Joe McIntosh rushed for 160y to contribute to NC State's 398y O and to help establish lead that carried most of way.

ALABAMA 20 Georgia Tech 7: Alabama (1-0) coach Ray Perkins enjoyed fine debut in place of Bear Bryant, who was honored with houndstooth hat decals on team helmets. Bama's new pro-style O sputtered at times, but was bailed out by D and special teams. Crimson Tide LB Emanuel King set up 1st score by forcing FUM by Georgia Tech (0-1) QB Stu Rogers, recovered by DT Randy Edwards. Moments later, QB Walter Lewis, who threw for 204y, found TB Joe Carter for 15y TD and 7-0 lead. K Van Tiffin upped lead to 10-0 after Georgia Tech CB Jake Westbrook fumbled INT back to Tide. Another Tiffin FG and CB Stan Gay's 32y RET of punt blocked by LB Todd Roper pushed lead to 20-0. TB Robert Lavette (23/84y) broke shutout spell with 1y 4th Q TD, his school-record 27th TD.

Florida State 40 LOUISIANA STATE 35: Gaining 536y, Seminoles (2-0) won 2nd consecutive shootout as QB Kelly Lowrey (19-31/233, 2 TDs, INT) accounted for 3 TDs. TB Dalton Hilliard ran wild in 1st Q, totaling 89y of his 128y and scoring twice to help LSU (0-1) grab 14-0 lead. Florida State TB Greg Allen then took over as premier back, rushing for 201y including 28y TD run as FSU scored 33 straight pts. LSU, which wasted 490y O effort, tightened score behind 2 late 4th Q TD runs by TB Garry James—both in game's final min—but ran out of time. Tigers QB Jeff Wickersham debuted with 274y with 3 INTs, while being sacked 4 times.

MISSOURI 28 Illinois 18: Tigers (1-0) set early tone, playing ball possession in building 21-0 lead midway through 2nd Q. Missouri QB Marlon Adler (10-14/163y) threw TDs of 13y to TE Joe Close and 45y to WR Andy Hill (4/94y), while Tigers pass D—ranked 1st in nation in 1982—frustrated Illinois (0-1) QB Jack Trudeau. Trudeau (26-38/293y) put Illini on board with 45y bomb to WR Mitch Brookins, but without balanced attack—Illinois rushed for only 64y—there would be no comeback.

Iowa 51 IOWA STATE 10: Scoring on 4 of 1st 5 possessions, Hawkeyes (1-0) put away Iowa State (0-1) in most lopsided win in series. At H, score was already 31-3 as Iowa easily snapped 3-game losing streak to Cyclones. Iowa QB Chuck Long (13-17/204y) threw 2 TDs, while TB Owen Gill added 136y rushing. Gill tied Iowa record with 4 TDs, including 31y jaunt in 1st Q for 17-0 lead. Iowa State did not reach EZ until back-up QB Alan Hood's 65y pass to WR Mike Posey in 4th Q.

Baylor 40 BRIGHAM YOUNG 36: Baylor (1-0) won wild game as TB Alfred Anderson (25/144y) leapt to his 2nd TD, from 2y out, for winning score with 49 secs left. That left QB Steve Young (23-38/351y) plenty of time to get Cougars (0-1) into scoring position. Young, who also rushed for 113y and 2 TDs, moved BYU to Baylor 30YL before 4th down incompletion ended game. Baylor's 2-pronged field generals, QBs Cody Carlson and Tom Muecke, combined for 187y passing as they selected WR Gerald McNeil (6/113y) as prime target. Teams combined for 27 PENs/262y.

SOUTHERN CALIFORNIA 19 Florida 19: Game's end was not for weak of heart. Trailing 19-13, thanks largely to 4 FGs by Gators K Bobby Raymond, USC (0-0-1) failed on 4th down incompletion by QB Sean Salisbury. Florida (1-0-1), however, was penalized for 12 players on field, giving Trojans 15y and last chance. Salisbury (15-26/229y, 2 TDs, INT) made Gators pay with 25y TD pass to WR Timmie Ware (4/117y) with no time left for 19-19 tie. Delirious fans, about to celebrate win, were shocked by ensuing bad snap, which forced holder QB Tim Green to throw desperate incompletion. Led by QB Wayne Peace (13-22/148y), Florida's ball-control O outrushed Trojans 233y to 92y, held ball for 10 extra mins and held 22 to16 advantage in 1st downs. Each team lost 3 of 6 FUMs.

AP Poll September 12

1 Nebraska (51)	1114	11 Georgia	568
2 Oklahoma (2)	1034	12 Alabama	452
3 Texas (2)	964	13 Iowa	427
4 Notre Dame	909	14 Southern California	353
5 Auburn (1)	903	15 Florida	319
6 Ohio State	756	16 Washington	236
7 Arizona	667	17 Maryland	211
8 Michigan	624	18 Southern Methodist	196
9 Florida State	623	19 Pittsburgh	193
10 North Carolina	622	20 West Virginia	180

September 17, 1983

CLEMSON 16 Georgia 16: Clemson blew another 2nd H lead as backup QB Todd Williams (11-18/169y) rallied Bulldogs (1-0-1) to dual 4th Q scoring drives. K Kevin Butler's 31y FG with 38 secs left capped final drive, while earlier in 4th Q, Williams hit TE Clarence Kay with 8y TD pass. Clemson (1-1-1) K Bob Paulling also clicked on 3 FGs, but had 2 tries blocked by DB Terry Hoage including 38y try late in 3rd Q with Tigers up 16-6. Georgia's largesse helped Tigers build early lead as FUM by Bulldogs TB David McCluskey at own 16YL in 2nd Q led to 16y TD run by TB Kenny Flowers, and KO FUM by TB Melvin Simmons at 7YL in 3rd Q led to Paulling's 3rd FG.

TULANE 34 Florida State 28: After 2 close victories and with games against Auburn and Pittsburgh upcoming, Florida State (2-1) was ripe for picking. Tulane (2-1) turned to QB Jon English (16-29/210y)—coach Wally English's son—after starting QB Bubby Brister quit team. Green Wave flamed upset with big plays: 99y INT TD RET by S Treg Songy and 77y punt TD RET by DB Curt Baham for 1st 2 scores. Seminoles managed 3 2nd Q TDs to take 21-14 lead as TB Greg Allen (26/115y) tallied twice and QB Kelly Lowrey (15-31/241y, 2 INTs) threw 55y TD pass to WR Jesse Hester (5/126y). English threw 15y TD pass to WR Wayne Smith and HB Elton Veals (15/112y) dashed for 39y TD as Tulane outpaced Florida State in 2nd H.

Texas 20 AUBURN 7: Longhorns D showed Auburn (1-1) reason their O abandoned Wishbone, holding Tigers' 1-2 running punch of HB Bo Jackson and HB Lionel James to 35y and 33y respectively. Texas (1-0) dominated from outset, leading 20-0 at H behind devastating D and O that scored 4 times with help from special teams that earned 132y in RETs. Highlight of 1st H was 80y scoring hook-up between QB Rick McIvor, 1 of 2 QBs replacing injured starter QB Todd Dodge, and WR Kelvin Epps. Longhorns' other QB, Rob Moerschell, led 84y drive in 1st Q, converting 4 1st downs en route to 1y QB TD keeper. Tigers were held to 130y rushing by Texas team that eliminated pitchouts from attack options and forced Auburn to run up middle and into arms of DT Tony Degrate and his mates. After gaining only 51y and 2 1st downs in 1st H and losing ball on downs in Texas territory early in 3rd Q, Tigers turned to sub QB Pat Washington. He did lead 95y drive to Jackson's 2y TD run late in 4th Q.

Michigan State 28 NOTRE DAME 23: Teams battled back and forth until Spartans (2-0) S Phil Parker's 42y INT RET set up QB Dave Yarema's 5y pass to TE Butch Rolle midway through 4th Q for winning TD. Yarema (15-23/165y) had thrown 2 other TDs, including 81y pitch to WR Darryl Turner. Key to win for Michigan State was P Ralf Mojsiejenko (9/48.8y avg), Notre Dame fan spurned as recruit, who offset ND's 446y to 225y O advantage with booming punts, including 71y boot. Irish (1-1) had pair of runners top 100y in TB Greg Bell (18/114y) and TB Allen Pinkett (25/104y).

Ohio State 24 OKLAHOMA 14: As temperature rose, Ohio State (2-0) QB Mike Tomczak (15-25/234y, INT) heated up with pair of TD passes to TE John Frank (7/108y) for 14-0 2nd Q lead. Frank's 1st TD grab, from 16y out, capped 80y opening drive, and his 2nd, of 15y, followed FUM REC by Ohio LB Rowland Tatum of bobble by Oklahoma (1-1) TB Marcus Dupree (6/30y) at Sooners 15YL. Dupree left in 2nd Q with bruised knee, but FB Spencer Tillman (13/83y) raced 37y for 2nd Q TD that halved Sooners' deficit to 14-7. Oklahoma would get no closer as Buckeyes took 2nd H KO 57y to key 2y TD run by TB Roman Bates. Ohio State even outrushed

Sooners 178y to 177y in winning 17th consecutive road opener, despite obvious upgrade in facing nation's 2nd-ranked team. Frank, of Jewish heritage, was in spotlight for choosing to play on solemn holiday of Yom Kippur.

COLORADO 31 Colorado State 3: Under pressure from state legislature, rivalry was renewed after 25 years, and it turned out positively for Colorado (1-1), school that felt it had nothing to gain in playing Colorado State. Buffs dominated with 384y O, including 233y rushing. Buffs QB Steve Vogel (11-19/137y, INT) opened 1st Q scoring with 7y TD pass to WR Loy Alexander (7/96y, 2 TDs). Colorado upped lead to 24-0 in 2nd Q before Rams (0-3) scored on 53y FG by K Jon Poole. Colorado State QB Terry Nugent—who became school's career total O leader with 4,062y—threw for 192y, but was picked off twice.

WASHINGTON 25 Michigan 24: Washington (2-0) QB Steve Pelleur (27-33/269y, 2 TDs, INT), benched in 1982, was perfect on 14 tosses in 4th Q as Huskies wiped out 24-10 deficit with 2 long drives. He completed all 9 of his attempts on winning 80y drive, including 7y TD to WR Mark Pattison with 34 secs left. Huskies went for 2pts, and Pelleur connected on conv pass to TE Larry Michael for dramatic win. Despite his brilliance, Pelleur opened 4th Q poorly, losing FUM in own territory that was recovered for TD by Wolverines LB Mike Mallory. QB Steve Smith (18-26/225y) later drove Michigan (1-1) 65y to 32y FG try that was missed by K Todd Schlopy.

UCLA 26 Arizona State 26: Taking full advantage of pair of TDs with 2-pt convs, Bruins (0-1-1) scored 16 pts in 4th Q to tie Arizona State (1-0-1). Sun Devils chose to run out clock, despite having 96 secs available to move into FG range for K Luis Zendejas, who had been 4-4 on 3-ptrs including 51y boot. QB Rick Neuheisel (20-30/335y, 3 TDs, INT) had driven Bruins 80y to pull team within 26-17 on 7y TD pass to WR Karl Dorrell. After Sun Devils PEN, TB Kevin Nelson ran for 2-pt conv. UCLA S Joe Gasser soon picked off QB Todd Hons (26-39/319y, TD, 3 INTs) to jumpstart 53y drive. Neuheisel hit WR Mike Young for 19y TD before Nelson ran in another 2-pt conv for tie. Hons opened scoring for Sun Devils team that never trailed, throwing 8y scoring pass to WR Doug Allen. UCLA WR Mike Sherrard caught 7/140y.

AP Poll September 19

1 Nebraska (57)	1178	11 Auburn	525
2 Texas (2)	1112	12 West Virginia	506
3 Ohio State	1038	13 Notre Dame	378
4 Arizona	933	14 Georgia	375
5 North Carolina	847	15 Florida	362
6 Alabama	790	16 Pittsburgh	347
7 Iowa	732	17 Michigan	319
8 Oklahoma	700	18 Southern Methodist	315
9 Washington	662	19 Boston College	165
10 Southern California	535	20 Florida State	157

September 24, 1983

West Virginia 27 BOSTON COLLEGE 17: One week after upsetting Maryland, West Virginia (4-0) posted 2nd key road win of young season. Opening KO put Eagles (3-1) behind 8-ball early as TB Troy Stradford sprained his knee in losing FUM at own 16YL. QB Jeff Hostetler soon converted TO into 10y TD pass to TB Tom Gray. WVU doubled lead on 67y run with short snap on fake punt by FB Ron Wolfley. After allowing FG,

West Virginia scored eventual winning TD on 15y run on reverse by WR Gary Mullen. In catch-up mode, BC QB Doug Flutie threw for 418y, no TDs while throwing 4 INTs. Eagles thrice reached West Virginia 5YL without scoring.

MARYLAND 13 Pittsburgh 7: Walk-on LB Doug Cox entered annals of Maryland (2-1) heroics with 49y RET of his blocked punt in 2nd Q for Terps' sole TD in upset of Panthers (2-1). "I was thinking 'Please, nobody catch me,'" said Cox. "I had both hands on the ball and didn't want to look behind me." Cox's TD was only 1 allowed by Pittsburgh in 3 games so far. Replacing injured QB Boomer Esiason, QB Frank Reich threw for 155y as Terps made Cox's score stand up. Pitt had final chance for TD end after reaching Terps 7YL when pitchout was deflected by Maryland DE Brian Baker to hungry hands of LB Chuck Faucette with 1:14 left. Pitt had driven 56y on 11 straight runs, riding blocks of T Bill Fralic.

MIAMI 20 Notre Dame 0: Despite outgaining foe that beat them for 2nd straight week (305y to 296y), Notre Dame (1-2) suffered 1st shutout loss since 1978. Miami (3-1) QB Bernie Kosar (22-33/215y, INT) threw 12y TD pass to WR Eddie Brown for 14-0 2nd Q lead, capping 1 of 3 Canes scoring drives of 30y or less thanks to ND TOs. In posting 2nd straight shutout, D held Irish TB tandem of Allen Pinkett and Greg Bell to 62y rushing, 4y by Bell who left with season-ending injury. Irish bright spot was frosh QB Steve Beuerlein, who came off bench to hit 13-23/145y. Canes entered AP poll for 1st time in 1983 as Nebraska became unanimous no. 1.

Alabama 44 VANDERBILT 24: Apparently happy not to see coach Bear Bryant on opposing sideline, Commodores (1-2) raced to 17-0 lead. Slapped to senses, Crimson Tide (3-0) rode 274y of O by QB Walter Lewis to victory. Lewis, who rushed for 90y and passed for 184y, scored 2 TDs as Bama tied game by H. Lewis' 2nd TD, from 11y out, was brilliant. There was 27-pt Crimson explosion in 2nd H, with rushing TDs by TB Linnie Patrick (24/118y) of 2y, TB Joe Carter of 6y, and FB Ricky Moore of 37y. Vandy QB Kurt Page completed 25-44/347y but was pressured by Alabama D, which was unfazed by Commodores' 56y run game. WR Chuck Scott caught 6/150y including 59y reception for Vanderbilt's opening TD.

Auburn 37 TENNESSEE 14: Auburn stormed to 2nd H fury of 27 pts in subduing Tennessee (1-2), which trailed only 10-7 at H. Tigers (2-1) QB Randy Campbell shook off poor performance in previous week's loss to Texas by completing 10-16/118y, while HB Bo Jackson (15/91y) led run game that earned 273y. Volunteers wasted early opportunities with missed 33y FG by K Fuad Reveiz and lost FUM by QB Alan Cockrell at Auburn 7YL. Cockrell (18-33/195y, INT) got Tennessee on board in 1st H with 30y TD pass to WR Tim McGee. After 2 FGs by K Al Del Greco, Tigers finished job with 2 TDs scored in 3:04 span as Campbell scored on 2y keeper, D held, and frosh WR Trey Gainous loped 81y on punt TD RET for 27-7 lead early in 4th Q.

LOUISIANA STATE 40 Washington 14: Tigers (2-1) appeared unimpressed by Washington's prior upset of Michigan. LSU QB Jeff Wickersham (16-27/259y) ran for 3 TDs and passed for another while getting help from rush attack featuring TB Dalton Hilliard, who ran for 122y, and TB Garry James, who added 87y. Huskies (2-1) QB Steve Pelluer threw for 312y, with WR Mark Pattison nabbing 7/114y. Without help from Huskies run game—limited to 28y—Pelleur was picked off twice and saw his NCAA record-tying streak of consecutive completions snapped at 16. LSU WR Eric Martin had 7 catches/134y with 18y TD in 4th Q that stoked 34-7 lead.

IOWA 20 Ohio State 14: Hawkeyes D rose to occasion, holding QB Mike Tomczak—nation's leader in passing efficiency—to 13-34/121y, TD. Iowa (3-0) picked off 3 of Tomczak's throws to beat Buckeyes for 1st time since 1962, span covering 16 games. Ohio State (2-1) was limited by strained left knee ligaments suffered by TB Keith Byars, who rushed 9/98y and TD before leaving in 1st H. Vital play came on 73y TD pass from QB Chuck Long (16-26/276y, 2 TDs, 2 INTs) to WR Dave Moritz, who with 4:25 left to play, weaved to frustrate pursuing defenders. Iowa LB Larry Station roamed field for 13 tackles.

NEBRASKA 42 Ucla 10: Bruins (0-2-1) were whistling in dark as D brought end to Nebraska's opening 3 drives by forcing FUMs in UCLA territory. Even on 1st successful drive by Nebraska (4-0), QB Turner Gill (8-10/123y) fumbled forward on play that gained 29y with REC made by IB Mike Rozier (159y rushing). Rozier soon scored on 2y TD in which he ran from sideline to sideline before cracking GL. Gill rushed for 79y and found WB Irving Fryar for 6 catches/100y as Huskers racked up 477y rushing, 600y in total O. Bruins QB Rick Neuheisel hit 9-14/144y as UCLA built temporary 10-0 lead.

Oklahoma State 34 TEXAS A&M 15: Cowboys (3-0) made statement, blowing game open in 2nd Q with 80y TD run by TB Shawn Jones and 2 TD passes by QB Rusty Hilger (9-16/137y) to WR Jamie Harris (6/107y). With TB Earnest Anderson out with injury, Jones rambled for 37/203y, while Oklahoma State D enjoyed 4 INTs including DE James Ham's 69y TD RET. Aggies (1-2) had owned 6-0 lead on 2 FGs by K Alan Smith, but momentum swung on EZ INT of QB John Mazur just as Texas A&M appeared to be on verge of padding its lead. Jones' explosive go-ahead TD run followed on next play. Both of Hilger's subsequent TD passes were set up by TOs by generous Aggies. Jones was far from perfect himself, losing 3 FUMs.

Texas Tech 26 BAYLOR 11: Taking advantage of Baylor's 6-fold generosity, Red Raiders (1-1) scored all 26 pts following TOs. Of 6 TOs, Bears lost 5 FUMs. Texas Tech QB Jim Hart (11-18/131y) rushed for 2 scores, while K Ricky Gann kicked 3 FGs including personal-best 52y bomb. Texas Tech DT Brad White's safety-producing sack in 2nd Q started 26-pt surge. Baylor passed 315y passing, including its only TD: QB Tom Muecke's 10y toss in 4th Q to TB Ralph Stockemer.

Brigham Young 46 AIR FORCE 28: Cougars (2-1) QB Steve Young put on some road show, completing 39-49/486y and 3 TDs, including NCAA record 18 straight connections. TE Gordon Hudson (12/172y) caught 2 of Young's TDs, including 63y connection in 2nd Q, which foreshadowed 34-pt BYU explosion in 2nd H. Falcons (2-2) gained 402y as QB Marty Louthan threw for 223y, but they could not match Young's heady pace. BYU FB Casey Tiumalu rushed for 119y.

Kansas 26 SOUTHERN CALIFORNIA 20: QB Frank Seurer, California native from Huntington Beach turned proud Jayhawk, engineered upset for Kansas (2-1-1) by throwing for career-best 385y and TD. Seurer enjoyed his return by hitting 26-38 with 7 of his passes finding WR Darren Green for school-record 197y. Jayhawkers K Bruce Kallmeyer also excelled, booting 4 FGs. His 2 FGs were only pts scored in 4th Q as Trojans' final drive reached Kansas 35YL before stalling on downs. USC (1-1-1) QB Sean Salisbury (19-35/233y) produced rare Troy highlight by pitching 54y TD pass to TE Joe Cormier in 2nd Q. Seurer, who wanted to play for Trojans, had more to play for than hometown pride, having dedicated 1983 season to memory of his father who had been murdered on August 2.

AP Poll September 26

1 Nebraska (60)	1200	11 Georgia	619
2 Texas	1138	12 Florida	586
3 Arizona	1001	13 Southern Methodist	385
4 Iowa	998	14 Michigan	384
5 North Carolina	917	15 Miami	310
6 Alabama	880	16 Louisiana State	284
7 West Virginia	750	17 Florida State	215
8 Ohio State	709	18 Washington	179
9 Oklahoma	695	19 Maryland	157
10 Auburn	693	20 Arizona State	114

October 1, 1983

WEST VIRGINIA 24 Pittsburgh 21: With nearly 14,000 more fans (64,076) than capacity, Mountaineer Field was jumping as West Virginia (5-0) rallied for 1st series win since 1975. QB Jeff Hostetler (15-32/164y) led 90y drive to winning TD, his 6y scoring keeper, with 6:27 left. WVU D set up Hostetler's heroics, holding Panthers to 61y in 2nd H to allow rally from 7-pt H deficit. Pittsburgh (2-2) had taken 21-14 lead on big play TDs: 75y FUM RET by DT Tim Quense, 21y run by TB Chuck Scales, and 35y pass from QB John Congemi (15-27/148y, TD, 3 INTs) to WR Bill Wallace. Mountaineers pulled to 21-17 on K Paul Woodside's 49y FG in 3rd Q.

MARYLAND 23 Virginia 3: Dominant Maryland (3-1) halted coach George Welsh's Cavaliers (4-1) rebuilding job, at least for this week. Maryland's underrated rushing attack earned plaudits as FB Rick Badanjek (23/89y) scored twice and TB Willie Joyner rushed for 116y of team's 272y total. Passing of QB Boomer Esiason (13-26/190y, 2 INTs) and Terps' kicking game also sparkled as K Jess Atkinson kicked 3 FGs and P Alan Sadler enjoyed 52.2y avg for 4 punts. Virginia racked up only 37y FG by K Kenny Stadlin, following Maryland TO, and wasted 91y KO RET by WR Malcolm Pittman that produced no pts. Although UVa struggled to gain 214y on O, Cavs displayed growing poise by committing only 1 PEN/5y, and lost single TO.

AUBURN 27 Florida State 24: Auburn (4-1) dramatically marched 74y to win game, converting pair of 4th down plays including QB Randy Campbell's 15y TD on 4th-and-8 swing pass to HB Lionel James with 1:59 to go. There was time enough for Florida State (2-2) to drive into Auburn territory, but DT Donnie Humphrey's pass rush prompted LB Gregg Carr to clutch clinching INT at his 22YL with 50 secs left. QB Kelly Lowery (21-38/243y, 2 INTs) had rallied Seminoles with dual 4th Q TD runs. Tigers built 20-10 H lead, scoring on final play of 2nd Q when never-say-die FB Tommy Agee took short pass 27y to TD as time expired—he broke multiple tackles and nearly was stopped at 1YL. Campbell (12-20/152y) threw 2 other TD passes for Auburn, while HB Bo Jackson led Tigers with 123y rushing. Florida State TB Roosevelt Snipes, starting for injured TB Greg Allen, rushed for 11/100y.

Florida 31 LOUISIANA STATE 17: Another All-SEC LB clinched key win with INT as Gators (4-0-1) LB Wilbur Marshall picked off QB Jeff Wickersham at Florida 2YL with 1:30 left and LSU (2-2) trailing 24-17. Gators TB Neal Anderson (15/149y) soon raced 76y for TD, his 2nd of game. Florida's other TB, Lorenzo Hampton, made 2 big plays, scoring TD on 58y blitz-burning pass from QB Wayne Peace (15-23/186y, 2 INTs) for 14-0 lead and rushing for 51y to set up another score on 1y run by FB John L. Williams. Williams' score gave Florida 24-10 lead, and matters were turned over to Gators D, which held Tigers' powerful run attack to 99y and made big plays in 4th Q: early GLS and Marshall's INT. Wickersham passed for 271y, with WR Eric Martin hauling in 5/106y including nifty 52y catch to set up his 17y 2nd Q TD grab.

ILLINOIS 33 Iowa 0: That must have been some pre-game pep talk. Sporting all blue uniforms, fired up Illini (3-1) jumped all over Iowa for 27-0 H lead as QB Jack Trudeau (23-32/286y, INT) tossed 3 TDs, 2 set up by Iowa FUMs, during game's 1st 13 mins. Illinois' stunting D shut out Hawkeyes (3-1) who entered game with 38-pt scoring avg, locking it up with late GLS. Iowa QB Chuck Long (12-27/224y, 2 INTs) was sacked 7 times—including once in threatening position from Illini 12YL on 4th-and-10—and held to less than 50% completion rate for 1st time as starter. Trudeau's most spectacular scoring pass was 54y strike to WR Mitch Brookins (4/131y) for 10-0 lead, while K Chris White booted 4 FGs. WR Dave Moritz was Long's favorite target, with 6 catches/92y.

PURDUE 29 Michigan State 29: It took Purdue (1-2-1) entire game to take its 1st lead and only 29 secs to lose it. Boilers QB Scott Campbell (30-50/300y) threw 15y TD pass to WR Rick Brunner with 30 secs left for 29-26 lead. QB Clark Brown in turn moved Spartans (2-1-1) 38y—with big play coming on Brown's 30y pass to TE Butch Rolle—to set up K Ralf Mojsiejenko's heroic 59y FG to tie it with 1 sec to play. Mojsiejenko redeemed himself for shanked 23y punt that set up Purdue's last score. Brown, in his 1st start, led Spartans to 26-16 lead through 3 Qs, throwing TD passes of 82y to FB Carl Butler and 44y to WR Daryl Turner. Boilermakers made pair of 81y 4th Q TD drives, ending in TB Lloyd Hawthorne's 10y catch and Brunner's TD.

East Carolina 13 MISSOURI 6: After years as fodder for bigger programs, East Carolina (3-1) suddenly became outfit nobody wanted to play: Pirates added Missouri pelt to that taken against North Carolina State. ECU QB Kevin Ingram broke 6-6 deadlock by throwing 27y winning TD pass to WR Ricky Nichols in 4th Q. Tigers (2-2) built 6-0 lead by scoring on 1st 2 possessions, but had to settle for FGs by K Brad Burditt. Mizzou's only other flurry ended on missed FG after officials ruled that TE Greg Krahl's 34y catch was nullified by QB Marlon Adler having crossed line of scrimmage before launching throw. Later in 1st H, Carolina tied game on pair of FGs by K Jeff Heath.

CALIFORNIA 33 Arizona 33: As Wildcats (4-0-1) LB Ricky Hunley raced 57y to EZ with INT to take commanding 26-3 lead, whiff of rose petals seemed to descend upon Arizona bench. Pasadena dream turned into 7-min nightmare: California (2-1-1) rallied, scoring 4 TDs, including 3 scores of at least 60y. When Golden Bears K Randy Pratt slipped through tying 22y FG with 48 secs left, game was tied. During quick turn-around in 3rd Q, Cal went on scoring spree, begun with 80y TD catch by TE David Lewis (10/158y). After Bear D held, TB Dwight Garner scored on 67y punt RET. Wildcats clawed with 60y bomb to WR Brad Anderson for 33-17 lead. In 4th Q, WR Andy Bark caught 61y TD, and FB Scott Smith scored 3y TD run to pull Cal to within 33-30. Bears LB Hardy Nickerson recovered FUM to set up Pratt's big FG. Teams did most damage through air as Arizona QB Tom Tunnicliffe threw for 317y and Cal QB Gale Gilbert passed for 344y. Wildcats K Max Zendejas nailed 4 FGs.

AP Poll October 3

1 Nebraska (60)	1200	11 Georgia	677
2 Texas	1138	12 Miami	506
3 Alabama	982	13 Southern Methodist	485
4 North Carolina	981	14 Michigan	457
5 West Virginia	943	15 Iowa	395
6 Ohio State	779	16t Maryland	243
7 Auburn	761	16t Washington	243
8 Oklahoma	754	18 Arizona State	231
9 Florida	687	19 Illinois	101
10 Arizona	680	20 Brigham Young	64

October 8, 1983

ARMY 20 Rutgers 12: Black Knights (2-3) stunned Rutgers, no more so than on 1st play of 2nd H when RB Elton Akins threw 78y TD pass to WR Jarvin Hollingsworth for 14-6 lead. Army QB Rich Laughlin (5-7/51y) led way with opening TD run, while Akins rushed for 128y. K Craig Stopa added 2 3-ptrs including 50y FG as Cadets took 20-6 lead in 4th Q. Scarlet Knights (1-4) rushed for 270y, led by HB Albert Smith's 94y, but were handcuffed by 6 TOs, including 4 FUMs, while Army never relinquished ball. Rutgers' sole TD came in 4th Q on 2y pass from QB Jacque LaPrarie to TE Alan Andrews.

Air Force 44 NAVY 17: Midshipmen (1-4) made game of it early—holding 10-7 lead after 1st play of 2nd Q—but were swamped by Air Force's flexbone attack that toted up 340y rushing, 510y overall. Falcons (3-2) regained lead at 14-10 on 1y TD run by QB Marty Louthan (8-15/130y, INT), who rushed for 91y and 5 TDs. HB Mike Brown (10/136y) set up Louthan's go-ahead pts with 74y jaunt to Navy 2YL. HB Napoleon McCallum rushed for 211y and had spectacular 60y scoring burst to open 2nd Q, but was sole threat for Navy. Military series win was 1st-ever on road for Air Force. "That's what you call an old-fashioned butt kicking," said losing coach Gary Tranquill. "I knew we were going to have trouble stopping them, but this was ridiculous."

PENN STATE 34 Alabama 28: Penn State (3-3) may have escaped with narrow win but restored some of its pride. Game went to wire as reserve CB Mark Fruehan and LB Greg Gattuso halted Alabama (4-1) TB Kerry Goode on short side sweep at 2YL as time elapsed. One play earlier, Bama TE Preston Gothard's apparent EZ catch was ruled incomplete. Frosh TB D.J. Dozier paced Nittany Lions with 163y rushing, his 4th straight 100y game, while underrated QB Doug Strang (13-21/241y, 3 TDs, INT) played with zest. After Alabama opened scoring with WR Joey Jones' 8y TD catch, Strang struck deep with 80y TD pass to TE Dean DiMidio and then threw 38y TD strike to WR Kevin Baugh for permanent lead. Crimson Tide, which suffered 1st loss to Penn State in 5 games, rallied from 34-7 4th Q deficit behind QB Walter Lewis (25-35/336y, 3 TDs, 3 INTs), who passed 15-18 in rally including 2 TDs to WR Jesse Bendross (8/145y). Tide could not overcome 6 TOs, with 4 paving way for 20 pts.

NORTH CAROLINA 30 Wake Forest 10: Game was tied at H until North Carolina (6-0) began dominating both sides of ball. Tar Heels reeled off 20 unanswered pts in 2nd H, while limiting Wake Forest (3-3) to single 1st down in 2nd H. Three UNC rushers topped 100y: TB Tyrone Anthony (19/157y), FB Eddie Colson (13/119y), and TB Ethan Horton (13/116y), with Colson and Horton each scoring twice. TB Topper Clemons led Deamon Deacons with 111y rushing, big chunk of Wake's 235y.

Michigan 42 MICHIGAN STATE 0: Michigan (4-1) enjoyed in-state laugher, scoring 1st 4 times it had ball for 25-0 lead. QB Steve Smith (11-16/149y) threw and ran for TDs while besting Rick Leach's school career completion record (150) by 9. Spartans (2-2-1), playing without injured QB Dave Yarema (shoulder separation), managed only 111y O. Michigan State TE Butch Rolle was lone bright spot with 5 catches/51y. Wolverines coach Bo Schembechler became 3rd Big 10 coach to reach 100 wins after Amos Alonzo Stagg (Chicago) and Woody Hayes (Ohio State).

Nebraska 14 OKLAHOMA STATE 10: Cornhuskers (6-0) knew they were in for battle on opening possession as Cowboys (4-1) stopped IB Mike Rozier (146y rushing) for loss on 1st down and then sacked QB Turner Gill twice. Oklahoma State's blitzing D forced 5 FUMs, recovered 4, and gave up no rushing TDs. Pokes DT Rodney Harding recovered 2 FUMs, including Rozier's bobble at OSU 1YL as Huskers lost 4 2nd H TOs in OSU territory. Gill (10-19/172y, INT) buckled down, throwing TDs of 62y to WB Irving Fryar and 32y to TE Todd Frain. Frain's winning catch capped 92y 3rd Q

drive. Huskers D had to hold on, not securing win until S Bret Clark's EZ INT of QB Ike Jackson in EZ on final play. Jackson had come off bench in 2nd Q to quickly lead drive capped with 15y TD pass to WR Jamie Harris for 10-7 lead. TB Shawn Jones stirred in 125y rushing to Oke State's O. Coach Tom Osborne passed Bob Devaney in Nebraska wins with his 120th.

Texas 28 Oklahoma 16 (Dallas): Billed as best in country, Longhorns D held TB Marcus Dupree to 50y rushing and Sooners (3-2) to 197y. Even so, Texas (4-0) trailed 10-7 at H before getting untracked in 3rd Q with 3 TDs. Longhorns FB Ronnie Robinson began surge with 2y TD run, set up by brilliant 32y catch by FB Mike Luck. Horns scored again 3 mins later—following INT by CB Mossy Cade—on 2y run by FB Ervin Davis. Min later, TB Edwin Simmons (14/100y) ended matters with 67y TD run, his 2nd TD of game. Scoring all its pts following TOs, Oklahoma enjoyed 7-0 lead on 8y TD pass from QB Danny Bradley to WB Steve Sewell. OU DT Rick Bryan had 19 tackles, forced 2 FUMs, and added 2 sacks. Dupree quit team soon after game, complaining that coach Barry Switzer was too hard on him.

SOUTHERN METHODIST 42 Baylor 26: SMU (5-0) ran unbeaten streak to 21 games as QB Lance McIlhenny (10-15/183y) overwhelmed Bears, throwing 4 TDs and running for another. Ponies WR Marquis Pleasant (6/152y) was on receiving end of 3 scoring passes. Not all damage came way of pass as both SMU TBs, soph Reggie Dupard (22/133y) and frosh Jeff Atkins (14/125y), each topped century mark in rushing y. Bright spot for Baylor (3-2) was 99y KO RET by WB Bruce Davis that tied game 7-7 in 1st Q. Bears QB Cody Carlson threw for 206y and 3 TDs—2 to WR Gerald McNeil (7/141y), but was picked off twice.

AP October 10

1 Nebraska (55)	1195	11 Alabama	588
2 Texas (5)	1144	12 Southern Methodist	583
3 North Carolina	1014	13 Michigan	515
4 West Virginia	983	14 Iowa	416
5 Auburn	866	15 Oklahoma	314
6 Ohio State	861	16 Maryland	277
7 Florida	836	17 Washington	246
8 Georgia	725	18 Arizona State	245
9 Arizona	702	19 Illinois	209
10 Miami	600	20 Brigham Young	96

October 15, 1983

WEST VIRGINIA 13 Virginia Tech 0: Hokies D, ranked 2nd nationally, did all it could to hold West Virginia (6-0) to its lowest output of season, forcing FUM at own 1YL and later picking off EZ pass. Unfortunately Virginia Tech (4-2) had to tangle with equally strong Mountaineers D, which turned in 9 sacks—6 by LB Steve Hathaway—and held Hokies to 0-13 on 3rd down tries. West Virginia QB Jeff Hostetler threw for 156y and posted 1y TD run, set up by FUM REC by NG Dave Oblak at Va Tech 23 YL. K Paul Woodside kicked 2 FGs for good measure. Hokies QB Mark Cox managed 11-18/97y passing.

North Carolina 42 NORTH CAROLINA STATE 14: In front of state-record football crowd (57,800), Tar Heels (7-0) and Wolfpack battled to 14-14 H tie that featured hard-hitting action. North Carolina blitzed NC State (2-4) 28-0 in 2nd H as QB Scott Stankavage (12-22/136y) threw for 2 TDs, including winning 19y scoring pass to WR Mark Smith early in 3rd Q. Tar Heels TB Ethan Horton rushed for 122y and 2 TDs and TB Tyrone Anthony added 130y. Playing from behind, Wolfpack QB Tim Esposito (31-48/294y, INT) set school records for completions and attempts.

Tennessee 41 ALABAMA 34: Fleet-footed Tennessee handed Crimson Tide (4-2) 2nd straight loss as TB Johnnie Jones (14/112y) raced 66y for winning score with 3 mins left. Volunteers (4-2) QB Alan Cockrell threw for 217y of his 292y on 3 long TDs, connecting with WR Lenny Taylor for 80y on Vols' 1st play of game and WR Clyde Duncan for pair of scores totaling 137y. Despite early setback, Alabama fought throughout to take 34-24 lead after bruising 6y TD run by FB Ricky Moore (17/85y, 2 TDs). Vols next rattled off 17 pts without blinking eye. Tennessee D ended matters with sack of QB Walter Lewis on Bama's last O play. Lewis (19-34/245y) became school's total y leader with 4,880y—95y more than Scott Hunter (1968-70). Total of 75 pts represented most pts scored in 66 years of series.

ILLINOIS 17 Ohio State 13: With game on line, Illinois (5-1) needed only 37 secs to score on 5-play, 83y TD drive that snapped its 15-game Illi-Buck series losing streak. QB Jack Trudeau (24-38/234y) completed passes of 24y and 22y to WR Scott Golden and ran for 16y himself before final-play pitchout to FB Thomas Rooks, who scampered in from 21y out. Drive began after Illini D halted Ohio State (4-2) 1st play of game as QB Jim Karsatos 2y shy of 1st down on 4th-and-4 bootleg at Illinois 17YL. Karsatos had replaced QB Mike Tomczak, who left game with concussion but not before throwing INT to Illini S David Edwards 2 plays after injury-causing hit by DE Terry Cole. Edwards returned that INT 47y for game's opening score, and he made cinching INT at game's end. Bucks TB Keith Byars rushed for 168y, including 35y TD that tied it.

Oklahoma 21 OKLAHOMA STATE 20: In trouble at 20-3 early in 4th Q, Sooners (4-2) simply exploded. Oklahoma WB Derrick Shepard turned short pass into 73y TD drive with 9:37 left. Later it pulled within 20-18: QB Danny Bradley drove OU 47y to 5y scoring run by FB Spencer Tillman and 2-pt conv pass to TB Earl Johnson. Sooners S Scott Case then recovered onside-KO that even surprised coaching staff. Oklahoma drove to K Tim Lasher's 46y winning FG with 1:14 left. OU had fallen thanks to 7 TOs and school-record 15 PENs, while botched punt led to Cowboys DB Ken Montgomery's 14y scoring RET. Oklahoma State's 2nd TD also resulted from Oklahoma boners as Case lost punt FUM at own 15YL and Sooners went offside on Pokes' missed 25y FG try. With new life, Cowboys (4-2) scored TD on TB Shawn Jones' 5y run for 14-3 lead. Cowboys stretched lead to 17 pts despite its dreadful game-end O totals of 5 1st downs and 120y.

Nebraska 34 MISSOURI 13: Recently, Tigers (3-3) had played Nebraska (7-0) tough but were no match this time for no. 1 team. Trailing 20-13, Mizzou lost upset bid when opening 2 possessions of 2nd H stalled deep in Huskers territory. On 1st drive, FB Eric Drain was halted on 4th-and-1 at Nebraska 10YL. Missouri soon marched to Huskers 1YL before QB Marlon Adler lost FUM, recovered by Nebraska DT Mike Keeler. QB Turner Gill (14-18/151y) marched Nebraska 97y to clinching TD, scored on 4y pass to WB Irving Fryar. Huskers IB Mike Rozier added to his nation's leading rushing total with 159y and 2 TDs, while D sacked Adler 5 times and twice picked him off.

Texas 31 ARKANSAS 3: Razorbacks (3-2) decided to force Texas to beat them with pass by playing 8-man D front, and beat them with pass Texas did. Longhorns (5-0) WR Brent Duhon caught scoring throws of 54y and 43y from QB Rob Moerschell (6-15/216y) to help Longhorns stretch 7-3 H lead to final blowout score. Horns even broke big run—TB Mike Luck's 54y scoring burst—against Arkansas' stacked D. With 17-0 advantage in 3rd Q, Texas had now outscored 5 opponents by 66-3 in 3rd Qs played to date in 1983. Texas TB Edwin Simmons sprained knee in 1st Q and missed rest of season, never to reach stardom expected of him.

BRIGHAM YOUNG 66 New Mexico 21: Game's excitement proved to be whether Cougars (5-1) could maintain national y lead over Nebraska, which they did with WAC-record 777y. QB Steve Young picked apart Lobos, completing 24-30/340y and 4 TDs. Young's favorite target was WR Kirk Pendleton (9/183y), who caught all 4 scoring passes. New Mexico (3-4) QB Buddy Funck (14-29/206y, 2 INTs) threw for and ran in TDs but could not compete with BYU O that ripped Lobos' 7th-ranked D. Backup QB Robbie Bosco joined BYU's fun, completing 6-6/128y and TD.

Arizona State 34 SOUTHERN CALIFORNIA 14: Rarely had Trojans (2-3-1) been outrun by another team's TB. Arizona State (4-0-1) TB Darryl Clack rushed for 116y and added 134y more on receptions, including 80y run with short pass that opened 2nd H and extended lead to 34-0. USC could not muster ground attack as TBs Fred Crutcher and Michael Harper managed only 36y apiece. QB Todd Hons threw for 346y as Sun Devils gained 571y. Amid boos by home crowd, Trojans scored pair of 2nd H TDs to make score more respectable.

Oregon 19 ARIZONA 10: Even though Wildcats entered with Pac 10's leading O, all 4 starting DBs for Ducks made INTs of Arizona (5-1-1) QB Tom Tunnicliffe (13-35/137y) to lead to 2nd straight series upset. Big moment came on Oregon (3-3) S Doug Judge's 91y KO RET that set up TB Kevin McCall's 1y TD plunge for 9-7 H lead. Arizona secondary was flagged for 2 PENs, and it set up 1y scoring run by FB Todd Bland as Ducks went ahead 16-7 in 3rd Q. Teams then traded FGs, 47y by Oregon K Paul Schwabe and 50y by Wildcats K Max Zendejas. Oregon DT Dan Ralph had 12 tackles, 2 sacks, and 3 pass deflections as Arizona was limited to 229y O. Wildcats LB Ricky Hunley countered with 19 tackles, forced FUM, and 5th INT of season.

AP Poll October 17

1 Nebraska (52)	1154	11 Illinois	555
2 Texas (6)	1107	12 Iowa	526
3 North Carolina	997	13 Arizona State	422
4 West Virginia	978	14 Washington	359
5 Auburn	888	15 Maryland	336
6 Florida	861	16 Oklahoma	253
7 Georgia	795	17 Ohio State	243
8 Miami	722	18 Brigham Young	237
9 Southern Methodist	657	19 Arizona	186
10 Michigan	625	20 Alabama	84

October 22, 1983

PENN STATE 41 West Virginia 23: Penn State (5-3) showed that it was in no way ready to hand over mantle as best team in East. QB Doug Strang (16-26/220y, 3 TDs, INT) was red hot out of gate, hitting 1st 11 passes including 2 TDs as Nittany Lions built 21-10 lead after 3 possessions. Sacked twice and harried all day, QB Jeff Hostetler (18-29/273y, INT) still brought Mountaineers (6-1) to within 21-17 on 2y scoring pass to TB Pat Randolph. Penn State distanced itself again with 57y punt TD RET by exciting WR Kevin Baugh.

GEORGIA 47 Kentucky 21: In winning its 22nd straight SEC contest, Georgia (6-0-1) exploded for 23 pts in 3rd Q and 37 pts over 15-min span of 2nd H to erase 14-10 H deficit. Most spectacular TD was 53y bomb from QB John Lastinger to WR Jimmy Hockaday. Kentucky (5-2) contributed to its own downfall with 3 FUMs and INT during disastrous 3rd Q. Bulldogs D held TB George Adams to 34y rushing, although Wildcats threw for 253y. Georgia rushed for 362y with TB Keith Montgomery leading with 98y, while TBs David McCluskey and Tron Jackson each scored twice.

MICHIGAN 16 Iowa 13: After years of back-up work, sr walk-on K Bob Bergeron earned Michigan (6-1) scholarship with 45y FG with 8 secs left. Iowa (5-2) had just rallied to 13-13 tie, turning 2 TOs into 10 pts, and were moving again until TB Owen Gill (20/120y) fumbled at Michigan 29YL with 1:30 left. Wolverines LB Rodney Lyles recovered to set up winning 43y drive. Michigan D sparkled, holding Hawkeyes star QB Chuck Long to 91y passing and no TDs. Iowa's TD came on fake FG as backup QB Tom Grogan threw 3y TD to TE Lon Olejniczak. Michigan TB Rick Rogers rushed for 129y and 4y TD in 3rd Q. Iowa K Tom Nichol booted 2 FGs, including school-record 56y 3-ptr.

WISCONSIN 45 Indiana 14: It was momentous day for Wisconsin (5-2) QB Randy Wright (12-19/199y, 4 TDs), who became school's all-time passing leader to date with 3,783y, topping Neil Graff, while tying Graf for most TDs in game. TB Gary Ellerson set no records but contributed 136y rushing and 2 TDs as Wisconsin gained 572y. Thorny Hoosiers (3-4) had tied game at 14-14 in 2nd Q as QB Steve Bradley (15-29/159y, 2 TDs) led 2 scoring drives, capping 1st with 4y TD pass to WR Stephan Benson. Wright connected with WR Al Toon for 37y scoring pass and 21-14 lead at H. Badgers owned 2nd H, outgaining Indiana 298y to 68y in last 2 Qs.

NOTRE DAME 27 Southern California 6: Despite Southern Cal's recent struggles, Fighting Irish (5-2) took no chances against school they had not beaten since 1977. They dusted off inspirational green jerseys that had worked so well 6 years earlier. By H, score was 17-0 and Trojans (2-4-1) were well on way to defeat. Notre Dame TB Allen Pinkett rushed for 122y and 3 TDs, while throwing 59y pass to TE Mark Bavaro that set up 1st TD, on Pinkett's 11y run. ND scouts had noticed HB-pass had burned Trojans D prior week in loss to Arizona State. LB Rick Naylor led Irish D with 2 INTs. Bright spot for USC was extension of NCAA-record streak of not being shutout to 184 games, this consolation having been earned on TB Michael Harper's 1y TD run. Harper was USC's leading rusher with 64y.

Texas 15 SOUTHERN METHODIST 12: With neither team able to hold onto ball—foes combined for 10 TOs with 7 arriving in 2nd Q alone—battle of SWC unbeaten teams was knotted 6-6 late in game. Longhorns (6-0) turned to backup QB Todd Dodge, whose 7y alley-oop TD pass to WR Bill Boy Bryant with 7 mins left put them ahead 13-6. SMU (5-1) then marched 80y with final 16y on run by TB Reggie Dupard, who gained 52y rushing on drive. Mustangs went for lead, but harried QB Lance McIlhenny was forced to throw pass in ground in front of Dupard on 2-pt try. SMU got ball back, but Texas DE Ed Williams sacked McIlhenny for safety. Mustangs, held to only 8 1st downs by mighty Horns D, lost 21-game unbeaten string.

Washington State 31 ARIZONA STATE 21: Down 21-17 at H, Cougars turned to FB Kerry Porter (19/132y) to deliver upset of unbeaten Sun Devils (4-1-1). Porter capped 69y drive with 2y TD run as Washington State (3-4) took lead for good. Cougars then needed only 1 play to score insurance TD: 68y romp by Porter. Arizona State tried to rally behind QB Todd Hons (29-42/321y), who threw 3 1st H TDs but was picked off 2nd and 3rd times. Devils, who managed only 52y rushing, were hampered by injury to TB Daryl Clack (9/23y), conf's leading rusher, who left in 2nd Q with bruised left hip. Washington State QB Ricky Turner completed 11-15/119y, 2 TDs.

STANFORD 31 Arizona 22: Heralded frosh QB John Paye arrived, rallying Cardinal (1-6) from 10-pt deficit to snap losing streak. Paye (22-28/280y) threw 3 TDs, with 2 to WR Emile Harry (10/179y) on passes of 35y and 27y—2nd proving to be game-winner. Arizona (5-2-1) managed only 82y rushing, which put pressure on QB Tom Tunnicliffe (18-30/201y, INT). Tunnicliffe led Wildcats to 17-7 2nd Q lead, but then bottom dropped out for visitors as Paye proved unstoppable.

AP Poll October 24

1 Nebraska (54)	1156	11 Washington	545
2 Texas (4)	1106	12 West Virginia	513
3 North Carolina	1010	13 Maryland	452
4 Auburn	944	14 Oklahoma	370
5 Florida	892	15 Brigham Young	350
6 Georgia	883	16 Ohio State	309
7 Miami	792	17 Iowa	283
8 Michigan	743	18 Alabama	92
9 Illinois	688	19t Boston College	79
10 Southern Methodist	602	19t Notre Dame	79

October 29, 1983

BOSTON COLLEGE 27 Penn State 17: Upgrade in Boston College (6-1) program now seemed legitimate with 1st-ever series win after 11 losses. BC QB Doug Flutie completed 25-43/380y, 2 TDs, with 1 score coming on deflected pass to TB Troy Stradford for 67y. Flutie's biggest sequence clearly came in 4th Q after Nittany Lions (5-4) cut 21-pt deficit to 24-17 with TDs from TB D.J. Dozier (16/113y) on 42y run and TE Brian Siverling on 20y catch of 4th down pass by QB Doug Strang (16-35/168y). Boston College FUMs had contributed to both Penn State TDs. Flutie then went to air and moved Eagles 59y to clinching 40y FG by K Kevin Snow. Eagles WR Brian Brennan had 12 catches/172y and 10y TD. With wins over Penn State and Clemson, BC had notched victories over most-recent 2 national champs.

MARYLAND 28 North Carolina 26: Breezy, seesaw game ended in Terps (7-1) favor as LB J.D. Gross broke up North Carolina QB Scott Stankavage's 2-pt conv pass attempt with 22 secs left. Stankavage (19-35/211y, 2 TDs, INT) had just marched Tar Heels (7-1) 90y to pull within 2 pts on 1y scoring run by TB Tyrone Anthony. Maryland had taken 10-0 lead with wind at backs in 1st Q, but saw Tar Heels reel off 17 straight pts with 2nd Q wind advantage. It was Terps' turn in 3rd Q and they answered with 18 straight pts—using successful onside-KO to score back-to-back TDs on passes from QB Boomer Esiason—before North Carolina scored last 9 in 4th Q.

MIAMI 20 West Virginia 3: After allowing 3 pts on West Virginia's opening drive to trail for 1st time since 9/10, Miami (8-1) D clamped down, allowing only 2y rushing in sacking QB Jeff Hostetler 5 times. QB Bernie Kosar (19-36/211y, INT) led Canes to 20 straight pts, connecting with TE Glenn Dennison (7/72y) on 19y TD for 7-3 lead in 1st Q and 5y to HB Keith Griffin that closed scoring in 4th Q. Hostetler threw for 166y for Mountaineers (6-2) before being pulled in 4th Q for his own protection.

AUBURN 28 Florida 21: Riding rush attack that scored 3 TDs, including 55y romp by HB Bo Jackson (16-196y), Tigers (7-1) held 21-7 lead at H. QB Wayne Peace then lead Gators on drive that reached 8YL before handoff to TB Neal Anderson, who was stripped before reaching EZ, with ball ruled touchback. On next play Jackson went 80y for clinching score for Tiger squad that churned up 316y on ground. Florida (6-1-1) rallied in 4th Q with 2 TDs before running out of time. Peace (29-41/336y) threw 2 TDs, including 41y hookup with WR Ricky Nattiel in 2nd Q, while WR Dwayne Dixon was favorite target with 9 catches for 123y and TD.

ILLINOIS 16 Michigan 6: Engineering 1st win over Michigan in Champaign since 1957, QB Jack Trudeau (21-31/271y, 2 TDs) put Illini (7-1) in driver's seat for 1st Rose Bowl appearance since 1963. After opening 38y FG by K Michigan Bob Bergeron, Illini took lead after tipped Michigan punt gave them ball at Wolverines 49YL. From there, Trudeau moved charges to lead they would not relinquish on 9y TD pass to FB

Thomas Rooks. After another Bergeron FG—which capped final Wolverines (6-2) thrust—teams fought for every yard until 1st play of 4th Q, when Trudeau threw 46y TD pass to WR David Williams (6/127y).

UCLA 27 Washington 24: UCLA (4-3-1) QB Rick Neuheisel (25-27/287y, TD) had to be nearly perfect to beat Huskies (6-2), and nearly perfect he was. Neuheisel, future head coach at Washington, completed last 17 attempts to lead pair of 4th Q drives that Bruins TB Frank Cephous capped with TD runs. S Don Rogers preserved win with 1st INT of Steve Pelleur (19-25/305y, 2 TDs) in Huskies QB's last 137 pass attempts. TB Kevin Nelson rushed for 146y and WR Mike Sherrard caught 8/136y as UCLA gained 531y. After teams combined for 3 FGs for UCLA's 6-3 H lead, Pelleur and Neuheisel volleyed 2nd H lead with each sparking 3 TD drives of 80y or longer. Most spectacular was Washington's swift 99y trip that ended with Pelleur's pass to WR Danny Greene near midfield that Greene took for 70y TD. Neuheisel set record for percentage (92.6), breaking mark set by Stanford's Dick Norman, who hit 34-39 (87.2) versus California in 1959. This day saw many coincidences: Homer Smith, Neuheisel's O coordinator at UCLA, had coached Norman, who was in attendance for this thriller at Rose Bowl stadium.

AP Poll October 31

1 Nebraska (57)	1178	11 Oklahoma	526
2 Texas (2)	1123	12 Brigham Young	446
3 Auburn	1048	13 Michigan	404
4 Georgia	954	14 Ohio State	398
5 Miami	952	15 Iowa	391
6 Illinois	895	16 Boston College	326
7 Maryland	754	17 West Virginia	213
8 Southern Methodist	750	18 Notre Dame	179
9 Florida	676	19 Alabama	171
10 North Carolina	620	20 Washington	128

November 5, 1983

Clemson 16 NORTH CAROLINA 3: Probation-shackled Clemson (7-1-1) effectively treated match-up as its bowl game, much to chagrin of Tar Heels. Led by DT William Perry, Tigers D stuffed nation's 3rd best ground attack, holding North Carolina (7-2) to 111y rushing. QB Mike Eppley threw 6y TD pass to TE K.D. Dunn and K Bob Paulling kicked 3 FGs as Tigers won 18th straight ACC contest, having not lost to Tar Heels in Chapel Hill since '71. TB Stacey Driver was leading rusher for Tigers with 98y, while UNC TB Ethan Horton gained just 47y. Tar Heels QB Scott Stankavage threw for 222y, with 108y on 7 catches by WR Mark Smith. Clemson had extra incentive after Carolina coach Dick Crum implied, earlier in week, that 1981 national title had been bought.

MIAMI 12 East Carolina 7: Hurricanes (9-1) retained their high bowl aspirations with come-from-behind victory. Miami QB Bernie Kosar (15-25/207y), 6 plays after hitting WR Eddie Brown with 52y strike, lunged in from 1y out with 1:04 left to cap 80y drive. Earlier, he threw 4y TD pass to FB Albert Bentley for Miami record 14th scoring throw of season. QB Kevin Ingram (12-22/151y) led Pirates (6-3) to 7-0 lead in 2nd Q, completing 18y TD pass to TE Norwood Vann. After 2 impressive wins, ECU narrowly lost to Florida, Florida State, and Miami by total of 13 pts.

AUBURN 35 Maryland 23: Auburn frosh FB Tommie Agee stole show from big-name players, rushing for 219y on 24 carries with TD runs of 61y and 44y. Tigers ran freely as HBs Bo Jackson (18/105y) and Lionel James (14/115y) joined Agee for run game that ground out 450y. Maryland (7-2) QB Boomer Esiason (23-37/355, 3 TDs), who set school game passing yardage record, led team to 17-14 lead entering 4th Q. Tigers then reeled off 2 straight TDs on 5y Jackson run and Agee's 44y burst for 28-17 4th Q lead. Esiason was not done, throwing 40y TD pass to WR Russell Davis (4/113y). Terps D then forced punt, but P Lewis Colbert (55.7y average on 3 punts) continued glorious day by pinning Maryland on its own 2YL with 38 secs left. DE Quency Williams then supplied coup de grace, sacking Esiason on 2nd down to force FUM on 2YL, recovered in EZ by DT Donnie Humphrey for final TD.

Georgia 10 Florida 9 (Jacksonville): Gators will have to wait another year for 1st SEC crown, as Georgia (8-0-1) won 6th straight in series and 23rd straight in SEC. Winning drive was brilliant 99y effort, led by QB John Lastinger and finalized by FB Barry Young's 1y TD run. K Kevin Butler's x-pt proved to be margin of victory; earlier he booted 51y FG. Drive's big play was 25y pass to TE Clarence Kay that, coupled with 15y PEN on LB Wilber Marshall, gave Dawgs 1st down on Florida (6-2-1) 30YL. Three plays later they faced 4th-and-2, which Lastinger converted with 4y run. K Bobby Raymond supplied team's pts with 3 1st H FGs as Gators took 9-3 H lead. He missed from 42y out midway in 4th Q, ending 1 of 3 drives to pass Georgia 25YL and not produce pts. Gators QB Wayne Peace's 186y passing put him at 6,923y for career, good for 2nd place in SEC and also in school history behind QB John Reaves (1969-71).

Iowa 34 WISCONSIN 14: Breaking 6 school records, Iowa (7-2) QB Chuck Long led road romp. Long (16-21/231y, INT) threw 4 TD passes, 3 in decisive 1st H won easily by Hawkeyes 27-0 as they scored TDs on 4 of 5 possessions in game's 1st 30 mins. TB Eddie Phillips, starting in place of injured TB Owen Gill, rushed for 162y. Badgers (5-4) had been averaging more than 35 pts per game, but were shutout until 4th Q. Wisconsin QB Randy Wright threw for 325y and 44y TD pass to WR Al Toon (6/136y), but was ineffective early when game was on line.

Pittsburgh 21 NOTRE DAME 16: Pitt TB Joe McCall stunned Irish (6-3) with 116y rushing and 2 TDs, setting up own game-winning 4th Q 1y TD run with 31y gain around end. Notre Dame put themselves in early 14-0 hole as Pitt (7-2) QB John Congemi hit WR Bill Wallace (5/90y) for 44y TD pass and soon after Notre Dame TB Allen Pinkett lost FUM on own 14YL. McCall made home team pay with 10y scoring run. FUM was

1 of 5 TOs for Irish, to 0 by Panthers. Pinkett (22/82y), whose streak of consecutive games with 100y rushing ended at 5, scored team's sole TD on 9y catch. Despite gaining 352 to 287y for Pitt, ND has begun another November swoon.

MISSOURI 10 Oklahoma 0: Defensive supremacy pushed upstart Tigers (6-3) into bowl picture. DT Bob Curry led D that sacked QB Danny Bradley (10-27/117y, INT) 5 times, forced 3 TOs, and shockingly held OU to 84y rushing in handing Sooners (6-3) 1st conf shutout since Mizzou turned trick in 1965. QB Marlon Adler capped 71y drive with 20y TD pass to FB Andy Hill for lone TD, while K Brad Burditt had booted 3-ptr from 37y on Tigers' 1st possession. Sooners had 2nd H TD reception by WR Buster Rhymes wiped out by PEN, while losing new starting TB Spencer Tillman (13/42y) to pinched nerve in 4th Q. Missouri's "Show Me" fans failed to sell out game despite Tigers having beaten Sooners last time they played in Columbia.

Kansas State 21 OKLAHOMA STATE 20: Wildcats (3-6) stunned home team with 77y drive to winning 3y TD run by TB Greg Dageforde with 11 secs left. On play before, passing combo of QB Stan Weber (12-27/172y, TD, 4 INTs) and WR Darrel Wild (6/102y) had just connected on 24y completion—5th time they connected for yardage on winning drive. Cowboys scrambled to 58y FG attempt by K Larry Roach at game's end, which came up straight but short. OSU QB Rusty Hilger (13-21/209y, INT) led Cowboys to 17-7 lead on TD runs of 20y by FB Arthur Price and 1y by Hilger along with 28y Roach FG. Unheralded KSU D held OSU to 75y rushing.

Baylor 24 ARKANSAS 21: Bears (6-2-1) sent home team to defeat with game-ending 24y FG by K Marty Jimmerson. QB Cody Carlson threw 33y pass to WB Bruce Davis (6/113y) to set up kick. Arkansas (5-3) missed 50y FG with 40 secs left and had 31y attempt by K Greg Horne blocked earlier in 4th Q. Carlson (14-21/217y, INT) threw 10y TD pass to WR Gerald McNeil (9/151y) to open scoring before TB Alfred Anderson (27/140y) rushed in 7y TD for 14-0 lead. Arkansas then FB Carl Miller changed momentum when he took ensuing KO 100y to cut team's deficit to 7. Hogs scored twice more for 21-14 lead, with TDs on 9y pass from QB Brad Taylor (15-26/195y) to WR Donnie Centers and 1y run by FB Derrick Thomas. FB Allen Rice then tied game with 1y TD run. Bears rung up 34 1st downs on 543y, but lost 4 FUMs.

Washington 23 ARIZONA 22: Husky CB Vestee Jackson had game DBs dream about. Jackson had 2 INTs, returning 1st 66y for TD, and then broke up late 2-pt conv pass to preserve victory. Jackson's picks—Arizona had 5 TOs including 4 in 1st H—and QB Steve Pelleur's (22-32/217y, TD, 2 INTs) passing helped Washington (7-2) build 23-3 lead late in 3rd Q. QB Tom Tunnicliffe led Wildcats (5-3-1) on 19-pt rally, throwing 34y TD to WR Vance Johnson with 2:53 left to pull team within 1. Tunnicliffe (21-43/296y) was injured on scoring toss so when Arizona went for 2 they did so with back-up QB Alfred Jenkins. Jackson then deflected Jenkins' pass. Tunnicliffe became career leader in Pac 10 for INTs.

AP Poll November 7

1 Nebraska (58)	1198	11 Maryland	530
2 Texas (2)	1140	12 Iowa	528
3 Auburn	1063	13 Boston College	508
4 Georgia	999	14 Florida	506
5 Illinois	975	15 West Virginia	298
6 Miami	951	16 Alabama	258
7 Southern Methodist	815	17 Clemson	257
8 Brigham Young	650	18 Washington	210
9 Michigan	642	19 North Carolina	207
10 Ohio State	557	20 Pittsburgh	199

November 12, 1983

SYRACUSE 21 Boston College 10: Blanketing Boston College QB Doug Flutie, Orange (5-5) pulled stunner. Flutie was sacked 3 times and picked off 3 times, while being held to 12-36 passing for 114y. Counterpart QB Todd Norley led Syracuse with 180y passing, throwing 26y TD to WR Mike Siano to open scoring and 28y TD toss to TE Marty Chalk to close scoring. TB Troy Stradford paced Boston College (7-2) with 147y rushing and tying 7y TD run in 2nd Q.

Miami 17 FLORIDA STATE 16: For 2nd straight week Hurricanes (10-1) needed late score to continue dream season. This time, K Jeff "Flea" Davis booted 19y FG—he earlier missed 2 FGs longer than 40y—as time expired to win in-state clash. Winning drive began at FSU 49YL after clutch 19y punt RET by WR Eddie Brown. Miami QB Bernie Kosar (21-35/243y, INT) connected with WR Stanley Shakespeare on 2 10y passes before HB Keith Griffin (13/74y) ran 20y to set up FG. Seminoles (6-4), who now had dropped 4 games by total of 11 pts, led for most of game behind solid ground game that totaled 202y with TB Roosevelt Snipes (17/94y) leading way. FSU D also sacked Kosar 4 times. Seminoles held 9-pt lead late in 3rd Q after reserve QB Bob Davis (14-24/146y) scored on 1y run to cap 76y drive. Canes scored contest's final 10 pts on 37y TD catch by Brown (8/150y) made up for earlier blunder. Florida State's 1st Q safety had resulted from Brown's fair catch of punt on own 2YL. "This was a fairybook story with a fairybook ending," said Miami coach Howard Schnellenberger of another chapter in Canes' magical season.

CLEMSON 52 Maryland 27: Despite being shellacked by ineligible Tigers (8-1-1), Maryland became ACC champs with North Carolina's 17-14 loss to Virginia. Clemson FB Kevin Mack rushed for 186y and 3 TDs as contributor to 350y ground game, while QB Mike Eppley (11-16/194y) threw 1st Q TDs of 64y to TB Kenny Flowers and 13y to TE K.D. Dunn to begin onslaught. Although QB Boomer Esiason (17-33/227y, TD) put up good aerial numbers, Maryland (7-3) never was competitive factor, trailing 42-7 in 3rd Q before Esiason ran for 2 TDs. "I think this does tarnish the title to some extent," admitted honest, losing coach Bobby Ross.

Auburn 13 GEORGIA 7: Georgia's knack for last-sec heroics ran dry, although not before giving Tigers (9-1) some worry wrinkles. Trailing 13-0, Bulldogs (8-1-) QB John Lastinger (12-23/110y) hit WR Herman Archie with 13y TD pass with 2:11 left to

cap 80y drive in which Lastinger connected on 7-8 aerial darts. Georgia recovered onside-KO before stalling on downs, with final pass broken up by Auburn CB Jimmie Warren. Auburn QB Randy Campbell (12-15/95y) led O that gained 356y, dealing option pitchouts brilliantly to HB Bo Jackson (18/115y), while D held Bulldogs to 168y, only 51y on ground. Taking advantage of field position, Tigers built 13-0 H lead on HB Lionel James' 4y run and 2 FGs by K Al Del Greco. Longest of Auburn's trio of 1st H scoring drives was 47y, while best starting point for Bulldogs in 1st H was own 34YL. Loss snapped 23-game SEC and 24-game home winning streaks for Bulldogs, while win clinched at least tie for SEC title for Auburn.

Mississippi 13 TENNESSEE 10: Maybe it was too easy for Tennessee, who took early lead and then went flat. In search of major bowl bid, Vols (6-3) went up 7-0 early in 1st Q as QB Alan Cockrell threw 20y TD pass to WR Lenny Taylor. That was it for Volunteers as Rebels D held them to 256y and 13 1st downs. Ole Miss (5-5) quickly reeled off 13 straight pts for 13-7 H lead. Rebs QB Kelly Powell threw 4y TD pass to WR Jamie Holder for TD, while K Neil Teevan added 2 FGs. Best Vols could do in 2nd H was 25y FG by K Fuad Reveiz, with near miss later in 3rd Q when Rebels DE Carl Lewis pounced on FUM by Tennessee FB Randall Morris after 25y sprint to Mississippi 5YL. "I've never been more proud of a bunch of kids," said tearful Ole Miss coach Billy Brewer after school's 1st win in Knoxville since 1969. "It is just unbelievable."

ILLINOIS 49 Indiana 21: Champaign was awash with roses as Illini (9-1) won 1st Rose Bowl bid since 1963. Strong air attack took backstage as Illinois ground game toted up 306y with FB Thomas Rooks (18/134, 2 TDs) and TB Dwight Beverly (17/79y, 3 TDs) showing way. Indiana (3-7) could muster meager running itself, gaining only 32/62y while losing 4 FUMs. Game was decided early as Illinois opened with 27-0 lead before Hoosiers scored on 28y 2nd Q pass from sub QB Cam Cameron (15-27/177y) to WR Duane Gunn. Any chance for Hoosiers' rally ended on Illini's 4-down GLS early in 3rd Q. Not since 1928 had Illinois won 9 in row.

TEXAS 20 Texas Christian 14: Despite gaining only 20y in 1st H, Horned Frogs (1-7-2) took 14-3 lead to locker room as LB Robert Lyles returned FUM 80y for TD and S Byron Linwood went 66y with INT to score. Inspired by FB Ronnie Robinson—who played in 2nd H with shoulder injury—Longhorns (9-0) rallied with FG and 2 TDs, including Robinson's 40y TD dash. Texas TB Michael Brown's winning TD came on 8y run by late in 3rd Q and followed punt FUM. Late in 4th Q, Horned Frogs, still struggling with less than 100y O, moved ball from own 45YL to Texas 11YL before stalling when CB Fred Acorn broke up 4th down pass aimed at TCU WR Dwayne May. Longhorns had now outscored opponents 90-6 in 3rd Qs during 1983.

TEXAS A&M 36 Arkansas 23: Razorbacks (5-4) had no answer for frosh QB Kevin Murray (21-29/194y, INT), who threw 4 TDs and ran in 5th score in leading Aggies (4-4-1) to 1st win over Arkansas since 1976. Hogs led 9-3 at H before Texas A&M exploded for 33 2nd H pts as 5 different players scored TDs, including Murray on 34y run that provided 30-17 lead in 4th Q. Aggies' wild 12th man KO unit quickly forced FUM by Arkansas WR James Shibest on hit by special teamers LeRoy Hallman and Tom Arthur, recovered by Arthur at Hogs' 30YL to set up Murray's final, clinching TD pass: 5y to TE Rod Bernstine. Arkansas QB Brad Taylor threw for 142y, but got little help from his team's 39y running game.

BRIGHAM YOUNG 24 Colorado State 6: Cougars (9-1) won 8th straight WAC crown despite sluggish effort. QB Steve Young completed 33-45/311y and 2 TDs, but he threw 2 INTs and BYU lost 3 FUMs, 2 near Colorado State's GL. Rams (5-6), who entered game with chance to wrest conf crown from BYU, could not capitalize on TOs, losing ball 4 times themselves. Colorado State QB Terry Nugent threw for 279y and FB Steve Bartalo rushed for 126y and TD. Young tied NCAA record set by former teammate, Jim McMahon, with 21st straight game of 200y or more passing.

ARIZONA 27 Ucla 24: Tie was all UCLA (5-4-1) needed to keep 1st place in Pac-10, but Wildcats (6-3-1) put dent in Bruins' Rose Bowl plans as game ended on missed 37y FG by near-perfect UCLA K John Lee. QB Rick Neuheisel (20-30/185y, TD, INT) had hit 2 passes to move Bruins 43y into FG range. Bruins' biggest failure came, however, when they had to settle for Lee's 22y FG even though they advanced to 1st-and-goal at 1YL. Arizona QB Tom Tunnicliffe (23-40/270y, INT) drove his charges 69y in 8 plays to winning 8y TD pass to WR Jay Dobyns with 1:01 left. Arizona K Max Zendejas kicked FGs of 53y and 51y. Wildcats WR Brad Anderson caught 9/140y, with his 32y effort setting up Tunnicliffe's winning TD toss.

AP Poll November 14

1 Nebraska (59)	1199	11 Iowa	590
2 Texas (1)	1137	12 Florida	508
3 Auburn	1072	13 Clemson	491
4 Illinois	990	14 West Virginia	425
5 Miami	985	15 Washington	388
6 Southern Methodist	882	16 Alabama	346
7 Georgia	754	17 Pittsburgh	304
8 Michigan	718	18 Boston College	107
9 Brigham Young	706	19 Missouri	84
10 Ohio State	657	20 Maryland	73

November 19, 1983

PITTSBURGH 24 Penn State 24: With clock showing 0:00 and Pittsburgh (8-2-1) sporting 24-21 lead, happy Pitt Stadium fans poured onto field to celebrate. But, as coaches were aware, 6 secs were left in official time—time used by Penn State (7-4-1) K Nick Gancitano, once fans were chased off, to kick tying 32y FG. Pittsburgh had taken lead 75 secs earlier on 3rd TD pass from QB John Congemi to WR Bill Wallace of 23y. Congemi had mixed performance, with 2 FUMs deep in his own territory that led to Penn State TDs. Lions were held to 78y rushing, none in 1st H, yet magically led 14-10 at H as QB Doug Strang (14-23/246y) threw TDs of 24y and 57y to WR Kenny Jackson (4/108y). TB Joe McCall rushed for 138y as Panthers outgained their rivals by 469y to 281y, but Pitt ruined its own day with 4 TOs.

SYRACUSE 27 West Virginia 16: Orangemen (6-5) secured 1st winning season in 4 years as FB Harold Gayden ran for 2 TDs, while notching 93y rushing and 55y receiving. Syracuse K Don MacAulay added pair of FGs. Syracuse grabbed 14-6 H lead by trading Gayden TDs for WVU K Paul Woodside's dual FGs. Winning margin was delivered in 3rd Q on 1y TD run by TB Jaime Covington. West Virginia (8-3) QB Jeff Hostetler led 2 drives in 4th Q to cut deficit to 21-16 including 42y TD pass to WR Gary Mullen. He then threw 3rd INT with less than 6 mins left to kill rally.

Harvard 16 YALE 7: Ancient rivals met for 100th time, with Crimson (6-2-2) prevailing to win share of Ivy title with Penn. Poorest season in Yale history ended valiantly as Eli (1-9) had game knotted at 7-7 entering 4th Q. Harvard won it on 2y TD run by WB Steve Ernst (16/113y) to cap 88y drive, followed by K Bob Steinberg's 35y FG. Harvard QB Greg Grizzi ran for 97y and passed for 94y, while its blitzing D earned 1st H shutout with 6 sacks of Yale QB Mike Curtin (11-21/117y, INT). Win was saved by 4th Q stop of 4th-and-1 run by Elis FB Jeff Bassette, who earlier scored on 1y run.

Virginia Tech 48 VIRGINIA 0: DT Bruce Smith-led D posted 4th shutout as Hokies (9-2) tied 1905 team for most wins in season. Virginia Tech O put 507y into record books with 372y on ground, unleashing stable of frosh TBs on unsuspecting Cavaliers (6-5) as Maurice Williams rushed for 97 and 2 TDs, Ricky Bailey added 2 TDs, and Eddie Hunter (7/83y) scored on 56y run. TB Howard Petty rushed for 66y to lead Virginia squad that gained only 189y—228y less than avg—and suffered 5 TOs, with QB Wayne Schuchts throwing 3 INTs. Despite its fine record, Virginia Tech was not invited to any bowl game.

NORTH CAROLINA 34 Duke 27: Duke QB Ben Bennett (27-35/323y, 2 TDs, INT) set NCAA record for career passing y (9,614y) and almost earned upset in process. Bennett threw pair of TDs to lead Blue Devils (3-8) to 27-20 edge in 4th Q before Carolina TB Tyrone Anthony (27/232y) scored on 54y run. Tar Heels (8-3) soon were back on O, with QB Scott Stankavage leading drive he capped with winning 3y TD run. Anthony's big game couldn't catch teammate TB Ethan Horton (20/107y), who finished with ACC rushing title of 1,107y, 3y more than Anthony. Bennett ended his career with NCAA records for attempts (1,375) and completions (820) while tying mark for consecutive completions in game with 15.

Clemson 22 SOUTH CAROLINA 13: Tigers (9-1-1) won Palmetto State crown as TB Stacey Driver rushed for 110y and K Bob Paulling booted 3 FGs. Clemson did its damage on ground with 222y rushing. DE Terrence Mack thwarted South Carolina rally with INT in EZ late in 4th Q. Sporting all black uniforms, Gamecocks (5-6) gained 317y and stayed close by offsetting speed of Tigers D with counters and reverses. Marred by PENs and sharp words, game ended with bench-clearing brawl.

MICHIGAN 24 Ohio State 21: Third time was charm for QB Steve Smith (11-20/207y) as he threw for 2 TDs and ran in 3rd to help Wolverines (9-2) win after 2 straight series losses. Four Ohio State TOs allowed Michigan to take 24-14 lead, including blown "fumblerooskie" recovered by Michigan DT Mike Hammerstein. Smith soon hit TE Eric Kattus from 8y out for eventual winning TD. Buckeyes (8-3) added 32y TD pass from QB Mike Tomczak (21-40/298y, 2 INTs) to WR Cedric Anderson with less than 2 mins to go but failed to recover onside-KO. Ohio TB Keith Byars (26/115y) set Big 10 season records with 19 TDs and 114 pts. His 2 TDs erased 10-0 Michigan lead, built on 26y FG by K Bob Bergeron and 67y TD catch by WR Triando Markray.

Air Force 23 NOTRE DAME 22: Another winless November for Notre Dame (6-5) was guaranteed by Falcons DT Chris Funk, who blocked last-second 31y FG try, his 2nd kick block of game. QB Blair Kiel (16-22/285y, INT), who earlier led 22-pt rally with 2 TD passes had led Irish to Air Force 14YL before Funk's heroics.. Falcons (8-2) finished with game's final 13 pts as HB Mike Brown rushed for 148y and QB Marty Louthan surprised with 118y passing, including 48y scoring pass to WR Mike Kirby (4/100y). TB Allen Pinkett rushed for 197y for Notre Dame. Despite 0-3 November, Notre Dame accepted Liberty Bowl bid in spite of protests of big bowl purists.

KANSAS 37 Missouri 27: Jayhawks (4-6-1) unleashed air attack on Missouri as QB Frank Seurer (20-35/354y, 2 TDs, 2 INTs) became to-date career Big 8 passer with 6,410y and single-season record holder with 2,789y. Kansas State's Lynn Dickey (1968-70) held both marks. Both TD passes were thrown to WR Bobby Johnson, who nabbed 8/175y. Tigers (7-4) tied game 27-27 early in 3rd Q on 39y FG by K Brad Burditt, but allowed 32y FG to Kansas K Bruce Kallmeyer, his 3rd, for winning pts. Later in 3rd Q, DE Elvis Patterson added insurance TD with EZ REC of blocked punt. Tigers QB Marlon Adler threw for 176y and rushed for 45y.

TEXAS 24 Baylor 21: Texas (10-0) clinched tie of SWC crown with win that was not locked up until CB Mossy Cade's INT, his 2nd of day, at Baylor (7-3-1) 43YL with 13 secs left. But, Longhorns' significant D reputation took some hits: Baylor QBs Cody Carlson and Tom Muecke combined for 320y passing when Texas averaged but 87y coming in. Bears' 29 1st downs turned out to be most ever recorded against Texas. Horns TB Ronnie Robinson, moved from FB due to injuries, rushed for 120y with 20y TD bolt. Texas QB Rob Moerschell earned running and passing TDs.

Ucla 27 SOUTHERN CALIFORNIA 17: Hearing that Washington State was leading Washington 14-6 in 3rd Q, Bruins (6-4-1) charged out for 2nd H to grab unlikely Rose Bowl berth. Opening 2nd H with 80y drive for 13-10 lead on 7y TD pass from QB Rick Neuheisel (13-19/154y, INT) to WR Karl Dorrell, UCLA began to put nail in coffin of Trojans (4-6-1). Bruins CB Lupe Sanchez soon returned punt 39y to set up 12y TD run by TB Kevin Nelson. Now down 20-10, USC lost FUM by TB Michael Harper (27/120y) at own 26YL. UCLA FB Bryan Wiley converted that TO with 17y run up middle for 27-10 lead. Having gained 262y in 1st H with just 10 pts to show for it, dispirited USC faced its demise despite QB Sean Salisbury's 218y in air.

OREGON 0 Oregon State 0: It took all day to unfold, but last play of scoreless battle was truly exciting as Oregon (4-6-1) QB Mike Owens (5-5/85y), from own 8YL, threw 25y pass to WR Kwante Hampton, who lateralled to FB Ladaria Johnson, who raced 43y down sideline before being tackled by Oregon State S Tony Fuller. Attempting to snap 8-game series losing streak, Beavers (2-8-1) had 4 drives deep into Ducks territory fail on 2 FUMs and 2 missed FGs. FB Bryce Oglesby rushed 31/96y to pace Oregon State, while Ducks TB Kevin McCall rushed for 100y. Teams combined for 11 TOs and 4 missed FGs in last 0-0 tie ever played in major college football. Interestingly, it was 6th such scoreless deadlock in series history.

Washington State 17 WASHINGTON 6: For Washington (8-3), it came down to win and start packing bags for Pasadena. Cougars (7-4) relished chance to dash plans of bitter rival, grabbing 14-3 lead at H and withstanding several good Huskies opportunities during 2nd H. Washington State P Glen Harper made good tackle on Washington WR Danny Greene who had broken free on RET. Harper admitted, "I just closed my eyes and went for him." Huskies K Jeff Jaeger kicked 2nd FG soon after, but that was all they would score. In 4th Q, Wazzu halted UW drive that reached Cougars 39YL. FB Kerry Porter rushed for 169y for his 6th straight 100y game and tallied 1,000y on season to lead Cougars, who also had 2-TD contribution from sub FB Richard Calvin. QB Steve Pelleur led Washington with 142y passing.

AP Poll November 21

1 Nebraska (58)	1179		11 Florida	572
2 Texas (1)	1118		12 Clemson	571
3 Auburn	1052		13 Alabama	440
4 Illinois	977		14 Ohio State	415
5 Miami	962		15 Boston College	318
6 Southern Methodist	878		16 Pittsburgh	235.5
7 Georgia	776		17 Maryland	209
8 Michigan	761		18 Air Force	105
9 Brigham Young	686		19 West Virginia	92
10 Iowa	647		20 East Carolina	58

November 24-26, 1983

(Fri) BOSTON COLLEGE 20 Alabama 13: Eagles (9-2) won by converting 2 FUMs by Alabama (7-3) deep in Tide territory into dual TDs within 83-sec span late in 4th Q. QB Doug Flutie threw tying 5y TD pass to FB Bob Beistek, and Biestek soon ran in other TD from 2y out. Crimson Tide had taken 13-6 lead with their only TD, LB Anthony Smiley's 58y RET of blocked punt. Rough conditions—harsh winds, driving rain, and raw temperatures—limited effectiveness of both Alabama QB Walter Lewis (4-12/81y, INT) and Flutie (14-29/198y, TD, INT). FB Ricky Moore (25/109y) led Bama run game that posted 246y, but lost 4 of 6 balls it bobbled.

(Fri) Navy 42 Army 13 (Pasadena): In service academy tilt's 1st visit to West Coast, Cadets (2-9) were sky high at opening KO—and paid for it. Navy (3-8) HB Napoleon McCallum caught KO and was soon swarmed over by Army tacklers. Between catch and tackle, however, McCallum had handed ball off to DB Eric Wallace, who raced 95y for TD. Things quickly got worse for Cadets, who fumbled twice on 1st 3 snaps. Navy LB Andy Ponseigo grabbed 2nd FUM to set up 14y TD run by McCallum (30/182y) and rout had begun. Soon after, Army QB Rob Healy threw INT to Middies S Steve Brady, who returned 65y for 21-0 lead. Army sub QB Bill Turner came off bench to throw for 171y and score on 1y run.

Georgia 27 GEORGIA TECH 24: Bulldogs (9-1-1) were huge favorites, but had to sweat out 6th straight series win. Georgia CB Tony Flack ended Georgia Tech (3-8) rally with INT deep in own territory late in 4th Q. QB John Lastinger, who scored earlier on 6y run, put Georgia ahead for good at 24-17 late in 3rd Q on 4y TD pass to WR Kevin Harris. K Kevin Butler kicked eventual winning FG from 36y out early in 4th Q. Georgia Tech QB John Newberry closed scoring with 30y scoring pass to TB Robert Lavette (26/158y), Georgia nemesis, who had earlier scored on 72y run.

Nebraska 28 OKLAHOMA 21: Even with star-filled roster, Nebraska (12-0) victory was not secured until little-known DB Neil Harris leapt high in EZ to deflect QB Danny Bradley's pass to WR Buster Rhymes with 32 ticks left. Rhymes (3/127y) earlier caught 73y TD pass. Oklahoma (7-4) had marched 72y to 2YL, before PEN and loss of 3y put ball at 10YL. Sooners had surrendered 14-7 and 21-14 leads to great plays by IB Mike Rozier (32/205y), who scored from 3y out to tie game at 14-14 and rambled 62y to set up QB Turner Gill's 1y keeper for 21-21 knot. Huskers' winner came on 17y run by FB Mark Schellen late in 3rd Q drive. Frosh TB Spencer Tillman (16/134y) scored on TD runs of 39y and 18y, latter ending with spectacular 6y leap over 2 defenders—as Sooners became 1st team to lead Huskers in any 2nd H this season. Victory marked 1st time coach any Tom Osborne-led Nebraska team had left Owen Field undefeated.

Texas 45 TEXAS A&M 13: Eruption heard in College Station did not come from Texas A&M's drill cannon, but from explosive O of long-quiet Longhorns (11-0). Texas obliterated 13-pt deficit and Texas A&M's upset hopes as QB Rick McIvor (8-12/170y) came off bench to ignite 45-pt outburst during 15-min span of middle Qs. McIvor threw for then school record-tying 4 TDs. Texas set record with 5 TD passes as WR Bill Boy Bryant launched 41y TD off reverse, while both WR Kelvin Epps (2/93y) and WR Brent Duhon (5/106y) caught 2 scoring strikes. In 3rd Q alone, Longhorns outscored Aggies by 31-0. After scoring 13 pts in 2nd Q on 2 FGs by K Alan Smith, who set single-season Texas A&M record with 18, and 24y TD run by RB Roger Vick (14/55y), Aggies (5-5-1) were finished touching scoreboard.

Southern Methodist 34 Houston 12 (Tokyo, Japan): In front of 80,000 polite Mirage Bowl fans, who had cued up early in morning to get tickets, SMU (10-1) completed another successful season. TB Reggie Dupard rushed for 70y in winning SWC rushing crown with 1,249y, while QB Lance McIlhenny threw 2 TD passes. Cougars (4-7) committed host of mistakes to set up 27 pts by Ponies. Houston QB Gerald Landry

threw 19-48/213y, INT. Win was 34th of McIlhenny's career, breaking SWC record he shared with Texas great Bobby Layne (1944-47), while CB Russell Carter's 18th career INT set Mustangs career mark.

Arizona 17 ARIZONA STATE 15: Battle of kicking Zendejas brothers came down to wire before K Max Zendejas drilled 45y game-winning FG for Arizona (7-3-1) as time expired. K Luis Zendejas hit 3 FGs himself to help Sun Devils (6-4-1) take 15-14 lead, their final score coming on TD pass from QB Todd Hons to TB Mike Crawford early in 4th Q. Hons (21-35/239y) then tried to run in 2-pt conv, but was stopped on 1YL to leave Arizona State with 15-14 edge. QB Tom Tunnicliffe (13-26/134y) had led Wildcats attack, throwing 4y TD pass to TB Vance Johnson for 14-13 lead in 2nd Q. Arizona State's Luis Zendejas set records for kicking pts in career with 295 and season with 112. In 1-AA playoffs on same day, cousin, Nevada-Reno K Tony Zendejas, kicked 4 FGs, including 56y and 53y boots, in 27-20 win.

AP Poll November 28

1 Nebraska (52)	1097		11 Clemson	548
2 Texas (3)	1048		12 Florida	521
3 Auburn	973		13 Boston College	425
4 Illinois	910		14 Ohio State	386
5 Miami	885		15 Pittsburgh	289
6 Southern Methodist	824		16 Maryland	223
7 Georgia	732		17 Air Force	149
8 Michigan	694		18 West Virginia	146
9 Brigham Young	649		19 Alabama	126
10 Iowa	586		20 East Carolina	93

December 3, 1983

FLORIDA 53 Florida State 14: Controlling ball for almost 38 mins, Gators (8-2-1) dominated every aspect of Sunshine State match-up. Scoring 10 pts in each of 1st 2 Qs and then busting game open with 20-pt 3rd Q, Florida kept pressure on Noles, who gave away 6 TOs. With QB Wayne Peace (14-20/190y) at helm, Gators O gained 509y, almost twice as much as Florida State (6-5), nation's 4th best O entering game, which managed (257y). K Bobby Raymond ended 6 of 11 Florida scoring drives with FGs to tie NCAA record, while TB Neal Anderson added 87y rushing, TD. TB Greg Allen rushed for 87y, including 32y scoring run in 4th Q, to lead Seminoles.

Auburn 23 ALABAMA 20 (Birmingham): There was too much HB Bo Jackson and too much 4th Q rain for Crimson Tide (7-4). Jackson ripped Alabama D for 256y, 71y on winning TD run in 3rd Q, as Auburn (10-1) won its 1st outright SEC title since 1957. Earlier, Jackson enjoyed 69y scoring jaunt for 7-0 lead in 2nd Q. Tigers S Vic Beasley had two INTs as D held QB Walter Lewis to 62y passing, none in 2nd H when he went 0-8. Lewis was victimized by torrential downpour that picked up soon after Jackson's 2nd TD. Suddenly, Alabama O that gained 333y through 3 Qs, managed only 18y in 4th Q. Lewis had thrown 2 TD passes as Tide grabbed 14-10 H lead. Tigers answered with 2 FGs by K Al Del Greco, before Bama retook lead on FB Ricky Moore's 57y scoring run late in 3rd Q. Jackson answered immediately with winning TD on 1st play following KO. Using draw effectively, TB Kerry Goode (17/142y) and Moore (12/109y) each topped century mark rushing for Crimson Tide.

AP Poll December 5

1 Nebraska (51)	1077		11 Florida	560
2 Texas (3)	1028		12 Clemson	536
3 Auburn	961		13 Boston College	385
4 Illinois	889		14 Ohio State	368
5 Miami	875		15 Pittsburgh	308
6 Southern Methodist	813		16t Air Force	217
7 Georgia	731		16t Maryland	217
8 Michigan	671		18 West Virginia	146
9 Brigham Young	619		19 East Carolina	89
10 Iowa	566		20t Oklahoma	41
			20t Baylor	41

Conference Standings

Atlantic Coast

Maryland	5-0
North Carolina	4-2
Georgia Tech	3-2
Virginia	3-3
Duke	3-3
Wake Forest	1-5
North Carolina State	1-5
Clemson *	7-0
* Ineligible	

Southeastern

Auburn	6-0
Georgia	5-1
Alabama	4-2
Florida	4-2
Tennessee	4-2
Mississippi	4-2
Kentucky	2-4
Mississippi State	1-5
Louisiana State	0-6
Vanderbilt	0-6

Big Ten

Illinois	9-0
Michigan	8-1
Iowa	7-2
Ohio State	6-3
Wisconsin	5-4
Purdue	3-5-1
Michigan State	2-6-1
Indiana	2-7
Northwestern	2-7
Minnesota	0-9

Mid-American

Northern Illinois	8-1
Toledo	7-2
Bowling Green	7-2
Central Michigan	7-2
Ball State	4-4
Western Michigan	4-5
Miami	3-5
Ohio	3-6
Kent State	1-8
Eastern Michigan	0-9

Big Eight

Nebraska	7-0
Oklahoma	5-2
Missouri	5-2
Oklahoma State	3-4
Iowa State	3-4
Kansas	2-5
Colorado	2-5
Kansas State	1-6

Southwest

Texas	8-0
Southern Methodist	7-1
Baylor	4-3-1
Texas A&M	4-3-1
Arkansas	4-4
Texas Tech	3-4-1
Houston	3-5
Texas Christian	1-6-1
Rice	0-8

Western Athletic

Brigham Young	7-0
Air Force	5-2
Wyoming	5-3
New Mexico	4-3
Hawaii	3-3-1
Utah	4-4
Colorado State	4-4
San Diego State	1-6-1
UTEP	0-8

Pacific-10

UCLA	6-1-1
Washington	5-2
Washington State	5-3
Southern California	4-3
Arizona	4-3-1
Arizona State	3-3-1
Oregon	3-3-1
California	3-4-1
Oregon State	1-6-1
Stanford	1-7

Pacific Coast Athletic

Cal State-Fullerton	5-1
Nevada-Las Vegas	4-2
Long Beach State	3-3
Utah State	3-3
San Jose State	3-3
Fresno State	2-4
Pacific	1-5
New Mexico State *	0-0

* Ineligible

1983 Major Bowl Games

Independence Bowl (Dec. 10): Air Force 9 Mississippi 3

With TDs absent, due in part to muddy field, Air Force (10-2) won FG war as K Sean Pavlich made trio of 3-ptrs to solo FG by Rebels K Neil Teevan. Paced by 91y by HB Mike Brown, Falcons rushed for 277y in outgaining Mississippi (6-6) 348y to 244y. QB Marty Louthan rushed for 67y and threw 6-7/71y passing, leading Falcons 64y on opening possession to Pavlich's 44y FG. Air Force doubled its lead on 39y FG, set up by 35y punt RET by WR Mike Kirby. Ole Miss scored on Teevan's 39y FG after recovering FUM on errant pitchout by Louthan. Using run on fake punt, Falcons followed 2nd H KO with Pavlich's 3rd FG. Excitement in 2nd H came on GLS stand by Mississippi D in 4th Q, with DT Andre Townsend making stop of Louthan on 1YL, to keep Rebs' chances alive, but their final 2 possessions ended on downs. Ole Miss TB Buford McGee rushed for 111y. Falcons enjoyed 1st-ever 10-win season.

Florida Citrus Bowl (Dec. 17): Tennessee 30 Maryland 23

Tennessee TB Johnnie Jones sparked upset with several clutch runs, gaining 154y and scoring on 2 runs in 4th Q. Vols (9-3) entered 4th Q trailing 20-16, but were on move to Jones' 1y TD run for 23-20 lead. Tennessee LB Alvin Toles soon picked off pass by Maryland (8-4) QB Frank Reich and returned it 26y to 14YL. Moments later, Jones, who rushed for 1,116y in 1983 in becoming 1st 1,000y back in school history, scored on 2y run to boost lead to 30-20. Reich (14-22/192y), who replaced injured QB Boomer Esiason (4-6/61y) in 2nd Q, led last scoring drive for Terps that reaped K Jess Atkinson's 5th FG. Atkinson's longest FG was of 48y, which set new game record as did his total 3-ptrs. Esiason left with separated shoulder after hit by DT Reggie White and LB Dale Jones on 2nd play of 2nd Q.

Hall of Fame Bowl (Dec. 22): West Virginia 20 Kentucky 16

Mountaineers (9-3) rallied with 17 2nd H pts after being sparked by successful onside-KO to open 3rd Q. QB Jeff Hostetler (10-23/88y), who started dreadfully, missing all his 10 passes with INT in 1st H, needed 8 plays of 3rd Q to tie score at 10-10 on 16y TD pass to WR Rich Hollins. West Virginia took 17-10 lead later in 3rd Q, marching 81y before Hostetler's 2nd TD pass, 2y to TE Rob Bennett. Mountaineers soon converted INT by S Tim Agee into 23y FG by K Paul Woodside and 10-pt lead. QB Bill Ransdell (9-15/117y) came off bench to lead Wildcats (6-5-1) on 92y drive, with last 13y coming on TD pass to WR Joe Phillips. Kentucky missed seemingly important x-pt, but would advance no farther than its own 37YL. Year removed from 0-10-1 record, Cats had scored 1st TD with trick play as TB Tony Mayes threw back to circling QB Randy Jenkins for 26y TD. WVU TB Tom Gray rushed for 149y.

Holiday Bowl (Dec. 23): Brigham Young 21 Missouri 17

Yet another wacky Holiday Bowl went down to wire, won when all-time great QB *caught* TD pass to cap brilliant drive with 23 secs left. With less than 4 mins left, BYU (11-1) halted Tigers at Cougars 6YL with dramatic stand. QB Steve Young (24-36/314y, 3 INTs) then marched his O 94y for win, scoring himself with surprise catch of 14y flea flicker pass by HB Eddie Stinnett. Pass, 2nd TD thrown on season by Stinnett in as many chances, barely cleared outstretched fingers of DE Bob Bell (4 sacks), terror all day for Missouri (7-5). Biggest gainer on winning drive was 53y catch by WR Mike Eddo, while Young also converted 4th-and-10 at Missouri 25YL with 11y completion to FB Waymon Hamilton. Overall, Young threw, ran, and caught TDs, but threw 3 INTs in 1st H. TB Eric Drain (27/115y) rushed for both Tigers TDs, but could not gain 1y for 1st down with 4 mins left after being hit by DT Shawn Knight.

Sun Bowl (Dec. 24): Alabama 28 Southern Methodist 7

In early 1980s, SMU (10-2) won often—it entered game sporting 32-2-1 record during recent times—and when Mustangs did lose, it was close. So, SMU was ill-equipped for answering early 2-TD deficit, especially since it was not playing on New Year's Day. Crimson Tide (8-4) FB Ricky Moore (28/113y), who topped 100y for 6th straight game, scored for 1y and 11y runs for 14-0 lead in 1st Q. QB Walter Lewis ruled 2nd Q scoring as he capped Alabama's 86y drive with 1y run and later threw 19y TD pass to WR Joey Jones with 43 secs left in 2nd Q for commanding 28-0 H lead. To recap stunning 1st H, Lewis had completed 9-12/148y against Mustangs D ranked 2nd in nation against pass. Alabama enjoyed 303y total O in 1st H, while SMU managed only 105y and 4 1st downs during 1st H. Mustangs scored in 3rd Q on 15y pass from QB Lance McIlhenny to WR Marquis Pleasant. TB Jeff Atkins chipped in 120y rushing for obviously flat SMU squad. With win, Alabama tied Southern California for most to-date bowl victories with 20.

Aloha Bowl (Dec. 26): Penn State 13 Washington 10

Although not much O was produced, suspense came in spades as Penn State (7-4-1) rallied with 10 pts in 4th Q to pull out victory. Nittany Lions opened 4th Q with career-long 49y FG by K Nick Gancitano. Winning drive began 8 mins later from midfield. On 51y drive, Lions QB Doug Strang (14-34/118y, INT) completed passes of 19y to FB Jon Williams (12/48y) and 16y to WR Kevin Baugh to set up TB D.J. Dozier's 2y TD run. Running was at premium: Dozier was held to 37y rushing, while TB Ron "Cookie" Johnson led Washington with just 34y. With QB Steve Pelleur completing 19-40/153y, Huskies (8-4) outgained Penn State 279y to 213y, but could only reach EZ on 57y punt RET by WR Danny Greene in 2nd Q. It was 1st TD RET allowed by Lions in 22 bowl games. That RET notwithstanding, Penn State P George Reynolds was named D player of game for averaging 8/46.8y punting and later nailing Greene on RET that knocked out Greene for 2nd H. Greene was named outstanding O player as special teams sparkled.

Liberty Bowl (Dec. 29): Notre Dame 19 Boston College 18

Sr QB Blair Kiel (11-19/151y, INT) was tapped to start final game and responded by leading Notre Dame (7-5) to trio of 1st H TD drives and 376y in O. Final score came on Kiel's 14y scoring pass to WR Alvin Miller for 19-6 2nd Q lead. Boston College QB Doug Flutie would not go down without fight, however, throwing his 2nd and 3rd TDs to pull Eagles (9-3) to within 19-18. After both TD throws, Flutie (16-37/287y, INT) misfired on 2-pt convs, with Irish LB Tony Furjanic tipping away pass from Eagles TE Scott Gieselman after final TD. BC staked 2 more drives, ending 1st on INT by ND CB Stacey Toran and later on downs at Irish 35YL. Irish TB Allen Pinkett rushed for 111y and 2 TDs, and FB Chris Smith rushed for 104y of ND's 225y. Eagles WR Brian Brennan caught 4/91y. Game was played in horribly frigid weather in Memphis, but it was little factor for 2 cold-weather teams.

Gator Bowl (Dec. 30): Florida 14 Iowa 6

Facing Iowa team averaging 490y—3rd best in country—Gators D surprisingly dominated in forcing 5 TOs, holding Hawkeyes (9-3) to 114y rushing, 281y overall, and keeping them out of EZ. Special teams chipped in TD as well as LB Doug Drew pounced on EZ FUM by Iowa P Tom Nichol for Florida's key 2nd TD late in 1st H. Gators (9-2-1) had taken 7-0 lead on 1y TD by TB Neal Anderson (17/84y), who rushed for 61y on 87y drive. Hawkeyes' mined 2 FGs by K Nichol partly because Gators pressed QB Chuck Long (13-29/167y, 4 INTs) into poor game. Iowa TB Owen Gill rushed for 83y, while WB Ronnie Harmon caught 6/90y. Hawkeyes D was exemplary too, holding QB Wayne Peace to 9-22/92y passing with 2 INTs. Wind chill factor stood -13 degrees at game time.

Peach Bowl (Dec. 30): Florida State 28 North Carolina 3

Having nearly month to stew over 39-pt loss to Florida, Seminoles (7-5) took out frustration on North Carolina (8-4). Florida State QB Eric Thomas enjoyed 1st start with pair of 1st Q TD passes to WR Weegie Thompson and late TD sneak. Thomas' 2 TD passes came within 4 mins of each other as Noles pulled away early, building 21-0 H lead. Tar Heels clicked only on K Brooks Barwick's 36y FG, capping 71y drive. Trailing early, Carolina was forced to pass more than usual, and QB Scott Stankavage hit 17-39/150y. TBs Ethan Horton and Tyrone Anthony rushed for only 30y and 27y respectively, but each carried only 9 times. Florida State rushed well as TB Greg Allen's 97y led attack that gained 265y on ground. Loss snapped Carolina's 4-game postseason win streak.

Bluebonnet Bowl (Dec. 31): Oklahoma State 24 Baylor 14

Although knocked out with concussion by H, QB Rusty Hilger (12-17/137y) already had accomplished enough for Cowboys (8-4) by throwing 2 passes on way to 24-7 lead. Hilger was perfect at 4-4 on 1st drive which ended on 12y TD on screen pass to WR Malcolm Lewis. Oklahoma State TB Earnest Anderson (27/143y), who began 2nd drive with 39y burst, ran for 1y TD. Cowboys went up 21-0 midway through 2nd Q as Hilger hit WR Jamie Harris for 26y TD pass to cap 57y drive, set up by DB Rod Brown's REC of FUM by Baylor (7-4-1) WR Bruce Davis. Bears QB Cody Carlson threw 12y TD pass to WR Gerald McNeil to put team on scoreboard by end of 1st H, but Cowboys twice halted 4th Q drives with INTs. Baylor was able to add 28y option pass TD by HB Alfred Anderson (103y rushing) to McNeil in 2nd H. Oklahoma State LB Matt Monger led all defenders with 14 tackles and pair of his team's 5 sacks.

Cotton Bowl (Jan. 2): Georgia 10 Texas 9

For Texas (11-1) faithful, this defeat hurt for long time as potential national title blew up on single fateful play. Due to late-game concern over possible fake punt—although Georgia (10-1-1) was 17y away from 1st down—S Craig Curry was inserted into Longhorns' RET unit as up-man in receiving formation. P Chip Andrews kicked ball

and it found Curry, who amidst wind and pressure from Georgia TB Melvin Simmons and CB Gary Moss lost FUM to Moss on Texas 23YL. Opportunistic all season, Georgia needed only 3 plays to score and eliminate Texas from national title hunt as QB John Lastinger kept on 3rd-and-4 option run to right for 17y TD—digging behind blocks by G Guy McIntyre and FB Barry Young—for Bulldogs' only lead of game with 3:22 left. Texas went 3-and-out on only its remaining possession, and Bulldogs extinguished clock with drive that featured gutsy 4th down conv: they had converted only 2 of 15 on 3rd downs. Needing Cotton Bowl win and Nebraska loss in Orange Bowl that night, Texas had opened by marching into Georgia territory as QB Rick McIvor (7-16/153y, 2 INTs) threw 37y pass to TE Bobby Micho with bootleg before drive stalled at Bulldogs 8YL. Horns K Jeff Ward hit 1st of 3 FGs. Not scoring TDs became frustrating theme for Horns, who had 7 drives go inside Georgia 33YL with only 9 pts to show for them. This upset boosted Miami, which inherited national title opportunity in Orange Bowl. "They'll (his team) find a way to win," said Georgia coach Vince Dooley of his team. "It was fortune, luck—whatever you want to call it. We just had to somehow find a way to hang in there and keep it close."

Fiesta Bowl (Jan. 2): Ohio State 28 Pittsburgh 23

Buckeyes (9-3) won wild game as QB Mike Tomczak tossed 39y TD pass to WR Thad Jemison (8/131y) with 39 secs left. Pittsburgh (8-3-1) QB John Congemi had just led Panthers to go-ahead 37y FG by K Snuffy Everett with 2:39 left. After Ohio State's late TD, Congemi marched Panthers to Bucks 24YL in final, frantic secs. Tackle by DT Darryl Lee knocked Congemi out of game with 7 secs left, and backup QB Chris Jelic came in cold to throw 2 incompletions to end matters. Congemi played well in defeat, completing 31-46/341y, 2 TDs. Tomczak (15-32/226y, 2 TDs, INT) countered with clutch play, highlighted by 13y completion to TE John Frank on 4th-and-10 3 plays before winning TD. Teams combined for 30 pts in 4th Q with most spectacular TD coming on 99y KO RET by Ohio TB Keith Byars (15/73y) for 21-14 lead. Congemi then pulled Panthers to within 1 pt on 11y scoring pass to WR Dwight Collins, but 2-pt conv attempt was batted down by S Doug Hill. Pitt TB Joe McCall rushed for 115y, while TE Clint Wilson scored twice including EZ REC of McCall's forward FUM for 14-14 tie in 4th Q.

Rose Bowl (Jan. 2): UCLA 45 Illinois 9

Rose Bowl rematch of 1947's 1st official pairing of Big 10 and Pacific confs was disastrous for favored Big 10, losers of 9 of last 10 Pasadena contests. Bruins (7-4-1), sporting worst record ever of any Rose Bowl team, opened scoring after odd play. Illini (10-2) S Craig Swoope, returning blocked FG attempt, lost FUM at own 14YL after being tackled by UCLA TE Harper Howell. Bruins scored 4 plays later on 3y pass from QB Rick Neuheisel to TE Paul Bergmann. Neuheisel (22-31/298y) had just warmed up, throwing 3 more TD passes as UCLA scored 31 straight pts after Illinois made FG. UCLA's longest scoring pass was 53y effort to WR Mike Young (5/129y) for 28-3 H lead. Bruins also rushed for 213y against Big 10's best D, with 28y coming on TD run by TB Kevin Nelson (18/69y) for 14-3 2nd Q lead. Bruins prevented Illini from gaining any rushing y, while forcing 6 TOs. QB Jack Trudeau threw for 178y and 5y TD to FB Thomas Rooks, but was picked off 3 times, twice by UCLA S Don Rogers. Neuheisel, who tied Rose Bowl record for TD passes, was 1 of many Bruins who was suffering from food poisoning; he threw up 4 times before game. "I'd like to thank the person who wrote this story," said Neuheisel, who went from walk-on to starter to being benched as UCLA began season 0-3-1 to Rose Bowl hero. His future coaching career would feature similar peaks and valleys.

GAME OF THE YEAR
Orange Bowl (Jan. 2): Miami 31 Nebraska 30

Nebraska (12-1) coach Tom Osborne's controversial decision to go for 2-pt conv at game's close ended up overshadowing great effort on part of both teams. Entering with 22-game win streak, Cornhuskers seemed to have unbeatable O because they featured Heisman winner in IB Mike Rozier, Outland and Lombardi winner G Dean Steinkuhler, NFL's top pick in WB Irving Fryar, and QB Turner Gill, who may have been best of lot, directing O that ran up 624 pts against 12 opponents (52 avg) including UCLA, Penn State, and Oklahoma. Unexpectedly, it was O clad in white, orange, and green that opened 50th Orange Bowl in score-at-will style. Hurricanes (11-1) ripped apart Huskers through air, scoring 17 unanswered pts in 1st Q as QB Bernie Kosar (19-35/300y, INT) tossed TD passes of 2y and 22y to TE Glenn Dennison, and K Jeff Davis kicked 45y FG despite having hit only 1-10 from more than 40y in regular year. Miami's speedy D confused Huskers by getting to holes before RBs and preventing "home run" plays. Nebraska needed favorite trick play, "Fumblerooskie," to score as G Steinkuhler carried it across GL from 19y out. Steinkuhler's TD and scoring keeper by QB Turner Gill (16-30/172y, INT) brought H score to 17-14, as Nebraska adapted its pass D. (Nebraska got heat after game for switching jerseys between DBs Mike McCashland and Dave Burke to try to confuse Kosar's reading of coverage by inexperienced McCashland.) Miami countered by using FB Alonzo Highsmith (7/50y), FB Albert Bentley (10/46y), and HB Keith Griffin (9/41y) more as runners, with Bentley and Highsmith scoring in 3rd Q to extend lead to 31-14. Huskers were forced to rally without IB Rozier (25/147y), out in 3rd Q with injured ankle. Nevertheless, Nebraska used its size advantage to march 76y for 1y TD run by backup IB Jeff Smith. Davis missed 43y FG attempt, and Huskers took over on their 26YL with 1:47 left. They raced downfield, slowing down only when facing 4th-and-8 on Miami 24YL, 2 plays after Fryar dropped certain TD pass on GL. Having faith in O-line, Osborne kept ball on ground with Gill pitching to Smith who went for much more than 1st down, diving successfully for TD at pylon with 48 secs left. Hurricanes immediately readied 2-pt conv D, fully expecting Osborne's choice. Play call was rollout pass, with Gill running right and throwing to Smith—behind Smith actually—and Miami DB Kenny Calhoun tipped ball away.

Sugar Bowl (Jan. 2): Auburn 9 Michigan 7

Perhaps Auburn (11-1) needed blowout to impress voters, but since it was highest ranked team to win bowl game with toughest schedule by far of any contender—Tigers hoped to snatch 2nd national title. Michigan (9-3) QB Steve Smith scored game's only TD in 1st Q on 6y run but jammed finger on throwing hand in 2nd Q. Auburn K Al Del Greco booted 3rd 3-ptr, perfect 19y FG with 23 secs to register win. Tigers HB Bo Jackson earned MVP Award with 22/130y rushing, but was kept from big gains by Michigan's rubber band D, as too were backfield mates HB Lionel James (18/83y) and FB Tommie Agee (16/93y). However, James chipped in important play: 4y run on 4th-and-2 on winning drive, and Agee made 3 runs for 1st downs on same critical possession. After being shutout in 1st H, Tigers had turned to clever Wishbone counter plays. Meanwhile, Auburn D allowed not single 1st down in 2nd H until game's final moments. Making late spurt, Wolverines, who did not trail until Del Greco's final FG, almost pulled off upset as Smith (9-25/125y, INT) hit passes of 22y to WR Vince Bean and 38y to WR Triando Markey. Catch by Markey went to Auburn 25YL, and he almost broke away for stunning score as time elapsed.

Final AP Poll January 3

1 Miami (47.5)	1168.5	11 Clemson	585
2 Nebraska (4.5)	1109.5	12 Southern Methodist	540
3 Auburn (7)	1079	13 Air Force	354
4 Georgia	977	14 Iowa	341
5 Texas	954	15 Alabama	281.5
6 Florida	823	16 West Virginia	273
7 Brigham Young	804	17 UCLA	272
8 Michigan	649	18 Pittsburgh	189.5
9 Ohio State	640	19 Boston College	153
10 Illinois	594	20 East Carolina	127

1983 Top Performance Formula

1 Nebraska	1.7712
2 Auburn	1.7225
3 Brigham Young	1.6752
4 Miami	1.6396
5 Texas	1.6069
6 Georgia	1.5787
7 Florida	1.5058
8 Clemson	1.5045
9 Michigan	1.4802
10 West Virginia	1.4588
11 Ohio State	1.4401
12 Illinois	1.4370
13 Iowa	1.4339
14 Air Force	1.4077
15 Alabama	1.3694
16 Pittsburgh	1.3691
17 Southern Methodist	1.3597
18 Tennessee	1.32440
19 UCLA	1.32439
20 Oklahoma	1.3211

1983 Top Opponent Records

1 Auburn	.7016
2 UCLA	.6627
3 Missouri	.6310
4 Penn State	.6261
5 Mississippi State	.6250
6 Florida	.6242
7 Florida State	.6240
8 Vanderbilt	.6154
9 Georgia	.6071
10 West Virginia	.6055
11 Georgia Tech	.6026
12 Maryland	.6000
13 Alabama	.5885
14t Kentucky	.57600
14t Michigan	.57600
16 Miami	.5754
17 Nebraska	.5688
18 Pittsburgh	.5625
19 Purdue	.5603
20 Oklahoma	.5794

1983 Out-of-Conference Records

	W-L	Percentage	Bowl W-L
Southeastern	36-16-3	.6818	5-2
Big Eight	20-14-1	.5857	1-2
Big Ten	13-11	.5417	1-3
Western Athletic	16-18	.4706	2-0
Pacific-10	14-19-1	.4265	1-1
Southwest	10-14-1	.4200	0-3
Atlantic Coast	8-18-1	.3148	0-2

1983 Individual Statistical Leaders

RUSHING YARDS	Attempts	Yards	Avg.
Mike Rozier, Nebraska	275	2148	7.8
Shawn Faulkner, Western Michigan	394	1668	4.2
Napoleon McCallum, Navy	331	1587	4.8
Curtis Adams, Central Michigan	267	1431	5.4
Kirby Warren, Pacific	304	1423	4.7
Allen Pinkett, Notre Dame	252	1394	5.5
Reggie Dupard, Southern Methodist	197	1249	6.3
Bo Jackson, Auburn	158	1213	7.7
Michael Gunter, Tulsa	226	1198	5.3
Greg Allen, Florida State	200	1134	5.7

PASSING YARDS	Completions	Attempts	Yards	Pct.
Steve Young, Brigham Young	306	429	3902	71.3
Terry Nugent, Colorado State	275	433	3319	63.5
Brian McClure, Bowling Green	298	466	3264	64.0
Ben Bennett, Duke	300	469	3086	64.0
Gale Gilbert, California	216	365	2769	59.2
Doug Flutie, Boston College	177	345	2724	51.3
Randall Cunningham, UNLV	189	316	2545	59.8
Raphel Cherry, Hawaii	170	299	2478	56.7
Jack Trudeau, Illinois	203	324	2446	62.7
Chuck Long, Iowa	144	236	2434	61.0

RECEIVING YARDS	Catches	Yards
Jim Sandusky, San Diego State	69	1171
Brian Brennan, Boston College	67	1168
Bob Johnson, Kansas	58	1154
Dave Naumcheff, Ball State	65	1065
Eric Martin, Louisiana State	52	1064
Tracy Henderson, Iowa State	81	1051
Gerald McNeil, Baylor	62	1034
Larry Willis, Fresno State	63	1009
Chuck Scott, Vanderbilt	70	971

1983 Consensus All-America Team
Offense

Wide Receiver:	Irving Fryar, Nebraska
Tight End:	Gordon Hudson, Brigham Young
Line:	Bill Fralic, Pittsburgh
	Terry Long, East Carolina
	Dean Steinkuhler, Nebraska
	Doug Dawson, Texas
Center:	Tony Slaton, Southern California
Quarterback:	Steve Young, Brigham Young
Running back:	Mike Rozier, Nebraska
	Bo Jackson, Auburn
	Greg Allen, Florida State
	Napoleon McCallum, Navy
Placekicker:	Luis Zendejas, Arizona State

Defense

Line:	Rick Bryan, Oklahoma
	Reggie White, Tennessee
	William Perry, Clemson
	William Fuller, North Carolina
Linebacker:	Ricky Hunley, Arizona
	Wilber Marshall, Florida
	Ron Rivera, California
	Jeff Leiding, Texas
Back:	Russell Carter, Southern Methodist
	Jerry Gray, Texas
	Terry Hoage, Georgia
	Don Rogers, UCLA
Punter:	Jack Weil, Wyoming

1983 Heisman Trophy Vote

Mike Rozier, senior I-Back, Nebraska	1801
Steve Young, senior quarterback, BYU	1172
Doug Flutie, junior quarterback, Boston College	253
Turner Gill, senior quarterback, Nebraska	190
Terry Hoage, senior safety, Georgia	112

Other Major Awards

Maxwell (Player)	Mike Rozier, senior I-Back, Nebraska
Walter Camp (Player)	Mike Rozier, senior I-Back, Nebraska
Outland (Lineman)	Dean Steinkuhler, senior guard, Nebraska
Lombardi (Lineman)	Dean Steinkuhler, senior guard, Nebraska
Davey O'Brien (QB)	Steve Young, senior quarteback, BYU
AFCA Coach of the Year	Ken Hatfield, Air Force

1984

The Year of Flutie's Heroic Hail Mary, Television Frenzy Fed, and a Suitcase Full of Money

It was a rough year for college football. Off-field bickering and lawsuits showed the damage that greed over television money could do to a supposedly amateur sport. Many major college programs seemed to be either on probation, getting off probation, or under investigation. The game needed star power after having lost a host of top players to the pro ranks and a number of marquee names and Heisman hopefuls being injured and lost for most or all of the season. Another upstart team won the national championship, which ordinarily would have been good news, except that even the most dedicated fan of football outside the state of Utah failed to get terribly excited about the championship earned by Brigham Young (13-0). This was due in part to the Cougars wrapping up the title on December 21, long before the normally-crucial New Year's Day bowl games could unfold. Probably, unspoken religious prejudice against the Morman Church didn't make BYU warm and fuzzy either.

What the season needed was a hero like the old cartoon musical refrain, "…Mighty Mouse to save the day!" Fortunately, there was a thrilling quarterback at Boston College (10-2), Doug Flutie, who stepped into the role of pint-size hero, a real Mighty Mouse, if you will. Flutie became both the first quarterback to pass for more than 10,000 yards in a career and an inspiration to vertically-challenged sports fans everywhere. With the size of players getting larger all the time, the nation was enamored with Flutie for not only his lack of height, but his ability to dominate bigger players with talent, intelligence, and guts.

But not even Flutie could help a sport that seemed intent on shooting itself in the foot at every opportunity. The off-season started oddly when head coach Howard Schnellenberger of the defending national champion Miami Hurricanes found coaching in the United States Football League—for five years and $3 million—preferable to returning to Coral Gables. The situation became absurd as the Washington Federals, his new team, dissolved a few weeks after he signed. He resurfaced as an ESPN commentator, seemed in the running for the head job at Florida (9-1-1) that never came open, applied for a Notre Dame (7-5) job that was not yet available, and settled for trying to rebuild the Louisville (2-9) program.

Miami (8-5) turned to Oklahoma State (10-2) coach Jimmy Johnson for 1984 and painfully lost five games against a much more difficult schedule than the one faced by Schnellenberger's title team of 1983. Most incredible were two straight losses suffered by the Hurricanes at the end of the regular season. Miami followed up an amazing loss to Maryland (9-3), in which they squandered a record 31-point lead, with a 47-45 loss to Boston College that featured Flutie's storybook last-second, game-winning "Hail Mary" pass to wide receiver Gerard Phelan. Those back-to-back performances lived on in a 39-37 Fiesta Bowl loss to UCLA (9-3) that stamped Johnson's first team with question marks and cost the job of defensive coordinator Bill Trout. Johnson crafted a quick recovery from Miami's poor conclusion to 1984 by launching the foremost program of the next 10 years when it racked up a very impressive 107-13 record.

Not so easily repaired was the damage done to NCAA football by the legal squabbles over television rights. The NCAA had regulated a TV package with networks for 33 years, both in negotiating fees and presenting a schedule to the viewing public. After the NCAA was declared in violation of antitrust laws in 1982, Georgia and Oklahoma led a group of colleges that sued to allow individual schools more power in determining televised football. The U.S. Supreme Court ruled on June 27 that the NCAA could no longer control TV rights. With existing contracts with ABC and CBS now cancelled, each home-standing team had the right to negotiate its own deal as long as the visiting team approved. Without the power of the NCAA monopoly, the schools circled into two syndicates, but found the network money tight. The Big Ten-Pacific Ten syndicate signed on with CBS, while the 63-member College Football Association worked out a deal with ABC and ESPN. These deals were for rigidly-defined three-and-a-half hour periods each Saturday with the remaining time open for the individual 83 schools to sell their own rights. The result was that schools received less than half ($300,000 compared to $700,000) of per-team money for each televised game than they would have earned under the voided $263-million dollar agreement between the NCAA and the networks.

The immediate result was college football on TV roughly from noon to midnight on a host of networks, both national and local. What began as a blessing for the fanatic, turned a bit sour as only the most rabid fan could brave what turned out to be a glut of games with even Public Broadcasting airing a weekly Ivy League contest. Wall-to-wall football on TV would take some getting used to. The result was a cheapened product, with slumping ratings, that was a detriment to all. The biggest lunacy in the TV frenzy was that some attractive contests that pitted a CFA schools against a team from the Big 10-Pac 10 axis, like the attractive Miami-Michigan match-up, were not aired anywhere. UCLA and USC (9-3) had to sue to overturn a provision in the ABC contract with the CFA so that their big games against CFA members Nebraska (10-2) and Notre Dame, respectively, could be shown on CBS. Schools lost money, and some TV syndicators went bankrupt.

Ordinarily a new national champion for a fifth straight year would have been exciting. But, a lot of fans moaned about Brigham Young playing a weak schedule and clinching its national title in the Holiday Bowl by a mere touchdown margin over the Michigan (6-6) team with easily the worst record Bo Schembechler would have in 21 seasons. The Cougars' margin of victory in the closing AP Poll was a miniscule 20 points in the closest final AP poll ever. It surpassed the 28-point difference in 1978 between no. 1 Alabama and Southern California. It was the third time in four years that an unranked team in the preseason poll won the championship, but this time the Cougars sported the 96th most-difficult schedule of 98 Division 1-A schools. Detractors pointed out that although BYU beat everyone on their schedule, they did not beat any team that ended up in the Top 20. The lack of conviction in BYU as true champion might have served as the long-awaited spark to ignite interest in a playoff system. Despite support from coaches like Joe Paterno and Barry Switzer, the playoff idea remained doomed. A straw vote of Division 1 schools in June had gone overwhelmingly against any change to the existing bowl format.

Oklahoma (9-2-1) coach Barry Switzer was especially derogatory about BYU's worthiness, despite the Sooners facing a weak slate themselves. Oklahoma lost the Orange Bowl game to Washington (11-1), partly because Sooner cheerleaders drew a poorly-timed penalty by bringing the "Sooner Schooner" wagon onto the field when they thought the clock was stopped after a successful field goal. The Huskies had failed to win the Pac-10, and their New Year's win was somewhat irrelevant in terms of determining a champion. Washington finished second, even though it beat no Top 20 finalists either. Huskies coach Don James put an angry twist on the voting by ripping the six writers who voted bowl-ineligible Florida (9-1-1) as their no. 1 choice since the Gators had been charged with 107 NCAA infractions in September. "I don't think it's fair to vote for teams that have gotten to where they are in absolute violation of the structure of rules we're supposed to live with," said James at a press conference in Miami after the vote was tallied. "You give me a suitcase full of money," he continued, "and I can go out and develop a pretty good football team." Florida actually won *The New York Times* computer poll and an unofficial post-season poll by *The Sporting News*.

Of the charges against Florida, 59 of them stuck, and the NCAA gave the Gators probation for three years for abuses such as illegal recruiting, cash payments, phony jobs for players, even spying on opponents' practices. Former graduate assistant Mike Brown confessed to the last charge which prompted school president Marshall M. Criser to offer to forfeit five 1980 victories as well as a 1981 win over Florida State. He was ignored. As coach Charley Pell's empire crumbled—he announced he would leave at year's end but was forced out on September 16—the infractions brought into light the role of irresponsible school boosters.

The situation in Gainesville might have fizzled quietly but for the incredible job turned in by interim coach Galen Hall and his inspired team. The Gators reeled off eight straight wins to take their first league crown in 52 seasons in the SEC. Of course, the title was stripped in late season, and, after appeals, officially taken away in May 1985. Hall, an 18-year assistant at Oklahoma, was given the Florida head coaching job for the presumed long-term on November 17.

With Florida out of consideration for the Sugar Bowl, Louisiana State (8-3-1), in the first year under coach Bill Arnsparger, took the New Orleans stage instead of front-running Auburn (9-4), which fell all the way to the Liberty Bowl after losing its final game to Alabama (5-6) by two points.

Injuries also dampened spirits of the football faithful as Heisman candidates Bo Jackson of Auburn and Napoleon McCallum of Navy—the two leading returning rushers from 1983—missed most of the year with injuries. On the heels of the departure to the professional ranks of a host

of talented players over the first four years of the decade, the sport was lacking stars—at least west of Chestnut Hill, Massachusetts.

Milestones

■ Freedom Bowl in Anaheim, Calif., and Cherry Bowl in Pontiac, Mich., debuted.

■ NCAA rules changes included moving kickoffs that traveled beyond end zone to 30 yardline rather than standard touchback spot of 20 yardline.

■ Former Oklahoma standout and current Miami Dolphins back David Overstreet died at 26 when his car crashed into gas pump on June 24. He rushed for 1,806 yards with Sooners in 1977-80. Zygmont "Ziggy" Czarobski, starting T for three Notre Dame national championship teams, died at 61 on July 1. Czarobski anchored right side of line for coach Frank Leahy's Irish in 1943, 1946-47. Ricky Bell, one of great Southern California tailbacks and runner-up for 1976 Heisman Trophy, died at 29 from cardiac arrest on November 28. Bell suffered from cardiomyopathy, muscular disease of heart, and dermatomyositis, an inflammation of skin and muscles. Bell rushed for 3,689 yards at USC, including nation's best 1,875 yards in 1975, before five year career with Tampa Bay Buccaneers.

■ Colorado tight end Ed Reinhardt was knocked unconscious versus Oregon on September 15 and lapsed into coma after blow to head caused blood clot in brain. Reinhardt came out of coma in November.

■ Longest winning streaks entering season:
Brigham Young 11   Miami 11   Auburn 10

■ Coaching Changes:

	Incoming	Outgoing
Air Force	Fisher DeBerry	Ken Hatfield
Arkansas	Ken Hatfield	Lou Holtz
Florida	Galen Hall (a)	Charley Pell
Indiana	Bill Mallory	Sam Wyche
LSU	Bill Arnsparger	Jerry Stovall
Memphis State	Rey Dempsey	Rex Dockery
Miami	Jimmy Johnson	Howard Schnellenberger
Minnesota	Lou Holtz	Joe Salem
Northern Illinois	Lee Corso	Bill Mallory
Oklahoma State	Pat Jones	Jimmy Johnson
Rice	Watson Brown	Ray Alborn
Rutgers	Dick Anderson	Frank Burns
Stanford	Jack Elway	Paul Wiggin

(a) Hall (8-0) replaced Pell (1-1-1) after Pell's ouster due to NCAA violations.

Preseason AP Poll

1 Auburn (30)	1057	11 Penn State	589
2 Nebraska (5)	922	12 Iowa (1)	581
3 Pittsburgh (2)	890	13 Arizona State (2)	578
4 Clemson (11)	817	14 Michigan (1)	453
5 UCLA (5)	816	15 Southern Methodist	419
6 Texas	734	16 Oklahoma	374
7 Ohio State	661	17 Florida	295
8 Notre Dame (1)	639	18 Washington	285
9 Alabama (1)	632	19 Boston College	184
10 Miami (1)	602	20 Florida State	119

September 1, 1984

(Mon) Miami 20 Auburn 18 (East Rutherford, N.J.): At 2nd Kickoff Classic, Hurricanes (1-0) beat nation's top-ranked team for 2nd straight game (8 months apart) in extending win streak to 12 and ending Auburn's string at 10. Fourth Q turned into FG contest, won by Miami frosh K Greg Cox 2-1, with his 2nd from 25y counting as game-winner with 6:08 left. Canes QB Bernie Kosar (21-38/329y, 2 INTs) threw 2 TDs to WR Stanley Shakespeare, WR Eddie Brown made 8 receptions/157y, and FB Alonzo Highsmith rushed for 146y to outdistance Auburn star HB Bo Jackson (20/96y). Jackson's 4th Q FUM, after hit by Miami LB Bruce Fleming (15 tackles), led to Cox's 1st FG of 4th Q, from 45y. Tigers (0-1) had last chance end on poor pitchout by QB Pat Washington that was bobbled by HB Brent Fullwood (11/54y) and recovered by DE Julio Cortes. Miami squandered fast opening act—they outgained Tigers 190y to 38y in 1st Q—with INT and failed 4th down try, both within Auburn 15YL, and found themselves down 15-14 early in 3rd Q. Auburn frosh K Robert McGinty kicked 3 FGs, but never got last chance for win.

Brigham Young 20 PITTSBURGH 14: Cougars, long considered too weak to tangle with big boys, shocked no. 3 Pittsburgh (0-1), which would turn out to be pivotal road victory in Brigham Young's search for 1st national title. BYU (1-0) QB Robbie Bosco completed 25-43/325y and winning 50y TD pass to WR Adam Haysbert (9/141y) with 1:37 left. Bosco had suffered shaky start—he made only 1 of his 1st 8 passes—and threw twin 3rd Q INTs that led to both Panthers TDs, 1 coming on 78y INT RET by S Bill Callahan. Pitt's final drive, led by backup QB John Cummings after QB John Congemi (17-32/171, 2 INTs) left game with bruised thigh, ended on downs at Cougars 29YL.

Miami 32 Florida 20 (Tampa): Scoring 2 TDs in final 7 secs, Miami (2-0) escaped 2nd scrape with ranked team within week. Avenging sole loss of 1983, Hurricanes scored winning TD on 12y pass by QB Bernie Kosar (25-33/300y) to double-covered WR Eddie Brown that capped brilliant drive. Kosar took O 72y in 29 secs, with 36y coming on pass to TE Willie Smith (11/152y). With score 26-20, Gators (0-1) had remote chance die on INT by Miami frosh CB Tolbert Bain, returned 59y for final TD. Moments earlier, QB Kerwin Bell (15-30/159y, INT) hit WR Frankie Neal with 5y TD—1 play after converting 4th-and-5 with 7y run—that put Gators up 20-19 with 41 secs left. Florida had big play TD earlier in game when TB Lorenzo Hampton, following big block by G Jeff Zimmerman, raced 64y. Hurricanes K Greg Cox booted 4 FGs to tie school

record. Kosar also tied Miami record with 25 completions, while Smith set mark with 11 catches. While Miami played 2nd tough game in 6 days, Florida had to overcome frenzy regarding coach Charley Pell's possible resignation.

TENNESSEE 34 Washington State 27: TB Johnnie Jones would not be denied as his 203y rushing and 3 TDs led Volunteers (1-0) to 1st opening win since 1979. Cougars (0-1) built 16-14 H lead behind 3 FGs by K John Traut and 12y TD pass by QB Mark Rypien (17-32/220y, 2 TDs, INT) to WR Michael James. Tennessee took lead for good 5:15 into 3rd Q on 1y run by QB Tony Robinson (13-16/125y, TD) to cap 80y drive, before whipping up 10 more pts in 3rd Q. Vols eventually build lead to 34-16 before Washington State rallied for game's final 11 pts. Wazzu's Traut booted 4 FGs, with 3 as chip shots after O bogged down in Tennessee red zone.

Fresno State 27 ARIZONA 22: Upset featured amazing finish as Fresno State (1-0) QB Kevin Sweeney, after being flushed out of pocket, hit WR Vince Wesson for 80y scoring pass play with 35 secs left. Sweeney (13-28/204y) had scored on 9y run at 4:50 mark to put Fresno up 21-16. QB Alfred Jenkins (13-15/152y) soon threw 28y TD to WR Jon Horton on 4th down to give Wildcats (0-1) lead with 51 secs left. Bulldogs gained only 211y—to Arizona's 338y—but converted 2 FUMs inside 20YL to score TDs and tallied another on 52y INT RET by DB Roark Kelly.

AIR FORCE 34 San Diego State 16: Coach Fisher DeBerry's Air Force (1-0) debut was successful as QB Brian Knorr (8-10/110y) tossed 2 TD passes and FB Pat Evans rushed for 121y. Falcons clinched 9th straight WAC game early, converting 2 fumbled KOs by San Diego State (0-1) returners into TDs within 51 secs of 1st Q for 17-0 lead. Now able to tee off on frosh QB Todd Santos, Falcons built lead to 31-3 before H as D forced 5 TOs. Air Force won y battle 485y to 216y. Santos threw for 154y and 47y scoring pass to WR Vince Warren in his debut.

AP Poll September 3

1 Miami (36)	1040	11 Penn State	570
2 Nebraska (7)	949	12 Arizona State	541
3 Clemson (2)	900	13 Brigham Young	438
4 UCLA (6)	866	14 Michigan (1)	400
5 Texas	783	15 Southern Methodist	309
6 Ohio State	696	16 Oklahoma	302
7 Notre Dame (1)	619	17 Pittsburgh	273
8 Auburn	602	18 Boston College	257
9 Alabama (1)	595	19 Washington	213
10 Iowa (1)	581	20 Florida State	202

September 8, 1984

Syracuse 23 MARYLAND 7: Playing disastrous 2nd H, Maryland (0-1) lost 5 of its 6 total TOs in 3rd and 4th Qs and gained only 61y as 7-7 H tie became painful memory. Syracuse (1-0) converted 4 TOs into 16 pts, with 9 coming on FGs by K Don McAulay, while HB Jamie Covington rushed for 97y and scored final TD on 1y run. Orange D sparkled, recovering 3 FUMs—with another on special teams—picking off 2 passes, sacking QB Frank Reich 4 times and permitting -1y rushing in decisive 2nd H. Maryland's only score came on 14y TD pass from Reich to WR Greg Hill, although team had 67y TD catch by WR Azizuddin Abdur-Ra'oof wiped out by PEN.

Boston College 38 ALABAMA 31: Road to Heisman began in Birmingham as QB Doug Flutie (19-34/254y, 2 TDs, 3 INTs) accounted for 3 TDs, and heroically led Boston College (2-0) back from 31-14 deficit despite playing final 20 mins with injured left shoulder. BC D set up 1st score in comeback as S Tony Thurman's INT was converted into Flutie's 5y TD run. After 28y FG by K Kevin Snow, game was tied 31-31 when Flutie faked handoff and threw to open FB Jim Browne on 4th-and-1 from Alabama 12YL. TB Troy Stradford (24/106y) supplied winning pts with 42y romp for his 2nd TD. Thurman wrapped up game with diving INT—his 3rd—In EZ of pass by Tide HB Paul Carruth. Alabama (0-1) not only blew game but lost TB Kerry Goode for season. Goode scored 3 TDs including 99y KO RET to open of 2nd H.

FLORIDA 21 Louisiana State 21: With 4:55 left and Gators (0-1-1) riding high after 75y drive that ended with TB Lorenzo Hampton's 15y TD run, coach Charley Pell opted for tying x-pt. LSU (0-0-1) then lost chance for win in coach Bill Arnsparger's debut as K Juan Betanzo missed 46y FG into wind with 41 secs left. Tigers had rallied from 2-TD deficit, taking 21-14 lead early in 4th Q on 24y TD pass from QB Jeff Wickersham (29-42/271y, 2 TDs, 2 INTs) to TB Garry James and 2-pt conv pass to WR Rogie Magee, who leapt over Florida CB Ricky Easmon to reach EZ. Florida had taken early 14-0 lead by driving 83y to 9y TD run by frosh QB Kerwin Bell (14-24/194y, 2 INTs) and, after Wickersham's FUM, scoring on Bell's TD pass to WR Ray McDonald. WR Eric Martin nabbed 9/111y to become LSU's career leader in receiving y.

MICHIGAN 22 Miami 14: It was not surprising that Miami (2-1) could not go 3-0 against Auburn, Florida, and Michigan in 12-day span, but what was shocking was ease with which Wolverines D swamped QB Bernie Kosar (16-38/228, 2 TDs, 6 INTs), who lost FUM, and was sacked 3 times. Michigan (1-0) LB Rodney Lyles, Miami native who once committed to Canes, had 3 INTs, 2 on consecutive 4th Q passes that crushed Miami, while his 1st Q stripping of HB Darryl Oliver led to Michigan's 1st TD: 6y run by FB Bob Perryman. Kosar managed 4th down, 4y TD pass to WR Stanley Shakespeare that cut it to 19-14 with 6:25 remaining. Perryman scored 3 TDs for O led by QB Jim Harbaugh (11-21/163y) in 1st career start.

Purdue 23 Notre Dame 21 (Indianapolis): Coach Gerry Faust's 4th season in South Bend opened feebly as 3-TD underdog Purdue (1-0) smote Irish in dedication game of Hoosier Dome. With 17 returning starters, Notre Dame (0-1) had high hopes for season, which soured thanks to costly TOs, 5 in all, and play of Boilermakers QB Jim Everett (20-28/255y, INT). Everett threw 2 TD passes to WR Jeff Price, including 14y score to cap 88y drive early in 4th Q. Final Fighting Irish's play was controversial as QB Steve Beuerlein (13-20/233y, 3 INTs) threw INT to Purdue DE Don Baldwin, with Notre Dame arguing that 12 D players were on field.

Oklahoma State 45 ARIZONA STATE 3: Coach Pat Jones' era at Oklahoma State (1-0) began in fine fashion as Cowboys handed Arizona State 1 of worst beatings ever suffered in Tempe. Sun Devils (0-1)—who finished with 212y—had high expectations for season, but would have to rebound without QB Jeff Van Raaphorst, who strained knee and would miss next 4 games. Cowboys finished with 475y behind QB Rusty Hilger, who threw and ran for TDs. Oklahoma State DE Leslie O'Neal caused 1st TD with blistering hit on Van Raaphorst to force FUM, with ball popping into hands of DT Rodney Harding, who ran 36y for score.

WASHINGTON 26 Northwestern 0: Huskies (1-0) posted 3rd straight shutout in opener as LB Tim Meamber picked off 3 passes and recovered blocked FG. Northwestern (0-2) had 7 TOs, which led to 23 pts, as Wildcats O struggled to gain 226y. Considering that 6 series started in Wildcats' territory, Washington should have scored more pts for its 347y O. Huskies settled for 5 FG attempts by K Jeff Jaeger, 4 of which were good to tie school record. Huskies QB Hugh Millen threw for only 103y, while TB Ron Jackson was leading rusher with 68y. Cats QB Sandy Schwab threw for 132y, but was picked off 4 times.

AP Poll September 10

1 Nebraska (35)	1150	11 Auburn	664
2 Clemson (15)	1100	12 Penn State	489
3 Michigan (3)	948	13 Oklahoma State	456
4 Texas (1)	922	14 Southern Methodist	443
5t Iowa (2)	824	15 Oklahoma	409
5t Miami (1)	824	16 Washington	352
7 UCLA (2)	800	17 Pittsburgh	219
8 Brigham Young (1)	749	18 Florida State	196
9 Ohio State	693	19 Alabama	192
10 Boston College	668	20 Southern California	97

September 15, 1984

Oklahoma 42 PITTSBURGH 10: Oklahoma (2-0) QB Danny Bradley sparkled at helm of new Wishbone variation, running in 2 TDs and passing for 2 others. Bradley surprisingly threw 12-18/145y, in attack that showcased his many skills. By converting pair of Pitt (0-2) special teams blunders, FUM on punt RET and failed fake punt, into early TDs, Sooners were able to force bigger Panthers to throw more than desired. Pitt QB John Congemi (11-27/149y) had to leave his 2nd straight contest with injured groin. Oklahoma FB Lydell Carr rushed for 137y. On other side, WR Bill Wallace excelled for Panthers with 9 catches/135y.

West Virginia 14 VIRGINIA TECH 7: Mountaineers scored on consecutive 1st Q possessions and held off Virginia Tech (1-1) for win that propelled them into AP rankings. West Virginia (3-0) QB Kevin White (9-16/111y) led scoring drives of 39y and 45y, but White didn't throw WVU's sole TD pass. It came on trick play as TB Tom Gray opened scoring by pulling up after handoff and throwing 13y TD to TE Rob Bennett (5/90y). Once again D set up good field position, and Mountaineers soon scored on 1y TD run by FB Ron Wolfley. QB Mark Cox put Hokies on scoreboard with 5y TD run in 3rd Q, before Mountaineers D picked off pass by QB Todd Greenwood in EZ. Virginia Tech TB Maurice Williams rushed for 109y.

Navy 33 NORTH CAROLINA 30: Up by 30-25 late, North Carolina D front had ears pinned back, targeting Navy (1-0) QB Bill Byrne (13-28/171y, 3 TDs, 2 INTs). Midshipmen went to air anyway to move 80y for upset. Byrne completed 19y pass to WR Chris Weiler and, under intense pressure, lofted "fluttering duck" to TB Rich Clouse for 60y TD pass. TB Napoleon McCallum, who rushed for 117y, ended scoring with 2-pt conv run as Midshipmen handed Tar Heels (0-1) 1st opening loss since 1968. After Navy had rallied from 15-pt deficit for 25-24 lead, Tar Heels marched 83y to 2y TD run by TB Ethan Horton (26/96y) with 4 mins left. UNC finished with 456y O, but Navy darkened its Carolina blue sky with 4 TD passes.

GEORGIA TECH 16 Alabama 6: Georgia Tech (1-0) dominated throughout as TB Robert Lavette rushed for 128y and 1y TD, while K David Bell kicked 3 FGs. Yellow Jackets D was especially sharp in decisive 1st H, controlled 13-0 by Georgia Tech, by allowing Alabama (0-2) only 65y in 1st H, 213y overall. Crimson Tide, who lost opening pair of games for 1st time since 1956, marched 85y with 1st possession of 2nd H to score on 3y TD toss by QB Mike Shula (8-13/80y) to FB Ricky Moore. On next possession they reached Tech 43YL before P Terry Sanders shanked punt for momentum-killing 2y. Omnipresent LB Cornelius Bennett led Tide with 13 tackles.

ARKANSAS 14 Mississippi 14: Old rivals battled to 14-14 H tie, then settled down to lesson on how to blow clutch FGs. Foes combined to miss 5 2nd H FG attempts, 3 by Mississippi (1-0-1) K Bill Smith, including desperate 54y effort in final secs, and 2 by Hogs K Ernie Villarreal. Rebels jumped to 14-0 lead as QB Kent Austin (20-34/233y, INT) completed 11-16/129y in 1st H setting up FB Arthur Humphrey for 2 1y scoring blasts. Arkansas (0-0-1) debuted new flexbone O that featured more passing than expected as QB Brad Taylor (10-21/204y) tied game with 8y TD pass to WR Donnie Centers to cap 80y drive that featured 35y completion to Centers.

Penn State 20 IOWA 17: Game came down to 4th-and-1 for Iowa (1-1) at Penn State 29YL with less than 2 mins left. Sure-tackling Nittany Lions (2-0) S Mike Zordich made win-preserving play as he brought down TB Ronnie Harmon for no gain to finish off Hawkeyes. Iowa had advantage in experience, but its butter-fingered O lost 3 FUMs and threw INT. Penn State built 13-3 H lead, with 1st H's big play coming on 24y TD pass by QB Doug Strang (11-27/157) to WR Herb Bellamy. Harmon reignited Iowa's hopes by taking 2nd H KO back 50y and scoring moments later on 15y run. Teams then swapped short QB sneaks to close out scoring.

Washington 20 MICHIGAN 11: Wolverines (1-1) were doomed from beginning by inability to contain Huskies' puzzling but speedy 2-5-4 D. Backbreaker whisked through quickly: 73y TD pass from Washington QB Hugh Millen (13-16/165y) to WR Mark Pattison that lifted 3rd Q lead to 17-3. Huskies (2-0) forced 5 TOs in beating

Michigan for 2nd straight year and allowed only 52y FG by K Bob Bergeron until Wolverines' last-sec TD. Millen, who grew up as Michigan fan, was highly efficient in early going, completing 8-8 on 73y drive to K Jeff Jaeger opening 25y FG. Huskies D prompted 1st TD when LB Joe Kelly picked off QB Jim Harbaugh (17-37/183y, TD, 3 INTs) to set up 25y drive to 2y TD run by FB Rick Fenney. "I've seen us play worse, but I can't remember when," said Michigan coach Bo Schembechler. "We didn't do anything right. It was one mistake after another."

TEXAS 35 Auburn 27: Nightmare start for preseason no. 1 Auburn (0-2) worsened at game's end when it was learned shoulder injury suffered by HB Bo Jackson (14/103y, TD) in 3rd Q turned out to be separation, thus sidelining him for much of remaining schedule. Jackson had cantered 53y when knocked down on shoulder by Texas (1-0) S Jerry Gray. Longhorns enjoyed Tigers by gaining more yards through air (215y) than ground (126y) as QB Todd Dodge (15-24) thrived on good field position. Dodge, who passed for more y than he managed in part-time work in all of 1983, opened scoring with 10y TD run and threw 32y TD pass to WR Brent Duhon for 21-13 lead in 3rd Q. After Texas D recovered FUMs deep in Auburn territory, Horns scored last 2 TDs on runs by FB Jerome Johnson of 10y and 14y. Tigers gained 436y, but were short-circuited at end by Gray's INT.

AP Poll September 17

1 Nebraska (37)	1151	11 Oklahoma	663
2 Clemson (15)	1083	12 Oklahoma State	585
3 Texas (4)	1046	13 Southern Methodist	522
4 Miami (1)	897	14 Iowa	398
5 Ohio State	860	15 Florida State	360
6 Brigham Young	817	16 Michigan	352
7 Penn State	745	17 Southern California	173
8 UCLA (2)	726	18 West Virginia	100
9 Washington	718	19 Auburn	94
10 Boston College	698	20 Georgia	57

September 22, 1984

Florida State 38 MIAMI 3: After winning 1983 national title, Miami (3-2) was in center of target. Seminoles (3-0) handed Hurricanes worst beating since 1977, scoring 29 pts in 2nd H against exhausted rivals. Florida State enjoyed 9-0 H lead, earned on K Derek Schmidt's 3 FGs, including 54y effort in 1st Q. FSU WR Jesse Hester ran 77y on reverse early in 3rd Q to break open game. Seminoles D then focused on Miami's pass game, putting heat on QBs Bernie Kosar (11-19/154y) and Vinny Testaverde (7-15/83y), who were sacked 8 times with each throwing INT. Versatile Hester rushed for 102y and had 5 catches/116y.

GEORGIA 26 Clemson 23: All K Kevin Butler had to do to beat Clemson (2-1) in last 11 secs was kick school-record 60y FG. Butler, 4-5 on 3-ptrs, did just that to tie SEC record, set week before by Florida's Chris Perkins, and propel Bulldogs (2-0) to 26th win in past 27 home games. Clemson had grasped 20-6 H lead, thanks to 2 TD passes by QB Mike Eppley (11-28/161y), but gave it away, thanks to 2 FUMs by Eppley. Tigers K Donald Igwebuike knotted it at 23-23 with 2:10 left on his 3rd FG of game (48y). Bulldogs had rallied to 20-20 on 1y TD run by TB Cleveland Gary (17/61y) before FG kicking took over. Both QBs had it rough as Georgia QB Todd Williams threw 5 INTs, and embattled Eppley threw 3 INTs and lost 4 FUMs.

Army 24 TENNESSEE 24: It was new ballgame with new faces for Black Knights (1-0-1) under coach Jim Young, who implemented Wishbone O. Two O backfield starters had played D in 1983 (QB Nate Sassaman and HB Dee Bryant), and another intramurals (FB Doug Black). Sassaman, 1 of group of srs whom had lost 24 of 33 in 3 years, scored on 1y keeper with 1:17 left to tie it, capping 80y drive. Black charged up middle for 120y to lead all rushers. Vols (2-0-1), who were paced by TB James Jones' 118y rushing, took 24-17 lead early in 4th Q on FB William Howard's 1y TD.

OHIO STATE 45 Iowa 26: Hawkeyes (1-2) had no answer for TB Keith Byars' running, Keith Byars' receiving, or even Keith Byars' passing. Byars led Buckeyes (3-0) with TDs of 50y and 7y among his 120y rushing and 5 catches/55y, including 14y TD. He even launched left-handed 35y TD pass to WR Mike Lanese. After Ohio scored 3 TDs in 86-sec span of 1st H to forge 31-10 lead, Iowa rallied with 16 straight pts, including 2y TD run by QB Chuck Long (22-35/275y, 2 TDs, 2 INTs) and his 30y TD pass to TE Mike Flagg. Buckeyes squelched reversal with game's final 14 pts. Thanks, in part, to 4 TOs, Hawkeyes lost 2nd straight game in which they outgained opposition. Iowa TB Ronnie Harmon rushed for 132y.

Nebraska 42 UCLA 3: UCLA had to feel shell-shocked. Rushing for 364y, Nebraska (3-0) kept on sending fleet back after another to slice through Bruins' buttery D. IB Jeff Smith was main man in 1st H, rumbling for 123y and 8y TD before leaving with ankle injury. No worry, Nebraska had 5 other players to run for TDs, including IB Doug Dubose (8/104y), who dashed 64y to EZ in 4th Q. Huskers D front also dominated, sacking 2 UCLA QBs 8 times. Bruins (2-1) were hampered by absence of starting QB Steve Bono, out with sprained ankle, but he couldn't have helped. Thanks to pounding, UCLA lost 9 more players to injury. Bruins QB Matt Stevens survived to pass for 119y, but lost FUM at Nebraska 6YL on sack by DT Jim Skow that ended UCLA's best chance to score TD. More TV issues: CBS coverage hinged on Nebraska's permission, which, at 1st, was withheld because of AD Bob Devaney's desire not to share national audience with Ohio State-Iowa game.

Southern California 6 ARIZONA STATE 3: Southern California (2-0) won kicking battle as K Steve Jordan booted 2 50y FGs, while Arizona State K Luis Zendejas hit 20y boot but missed 47y kick in 2nd Q and chip-shot 28y try with 58 secs left. Zendejas would finish his career with more kicking pts in history to date, but might have traded some pts for 3 here. Sun Devils (1-2) coach Darryl Rogers went for FG facing 4th-and-5 at

USC 10YL because O was 1-14 converting 3rd downs. Jordan's winner was kicked early in 4th Q, set up by 33y run by TB Zeph Lee. ASU LBs Brian Noble and Jimmy Williams each had 13 tackles, with Noble adding 3 sacks and FUM REC.

AP Poll September 24

1 Nebraska (52)	1116	11 Southern Methodist	560
2 Texas (2)	1027	12 Georgia	557
3 Ohio State (2)	995	13 Clemson	473
4 Penn State	834	14 Michigan	366
5 Boston College	831	15 Southern California	341
6 Washington	830	16 Miami	200
7 Oklahoma	797	17 UCLA	153
8 Brigham Young	781	18 Georgia Tech	100
9 Florida State	665	19 Notre Dame	96
10 Oklahoma State	597	20 Auburn	94

September 29, 1984

SYRACUSE 17 Nebraska 9: Orangemen, week removed from 19-0 loss to Rutgers, shocked college football with yeoman D effort. With 30 members of 1959 national champion squad in attendance, Syracuse (3-1) wiped out 7-3 H deficit with 2 TDs, including WR Mike Siano's nifty, leaping 40y catch between Huskers DBs Bret Clark and Dennis Watkins from QB Todd Norley. FB Harold Gayden's clinching 1y TD sweep in 4th Q put wraps on game won by D: DT Tim Green (2 sacks, 2 caused FUMs), LB Rudy King (14 tackles), LB Bernard King (13 tackles), and mates held Cornhuskers O, averaging 40.7 pts and over 500y, to 214y. Orange O contributed by holding ball for 37 mins. Nebraska (3-1) received 107y rushing from IB Doug Dubose, who had been heavily recruited by Syracuse out of Connecticut.

Texas 28 Penn State 3 (E. Rutherford, NJ): In Penn State's unofficial backyard, Texas' wide-open O got better of Nittany Lions (3-1). QB Todd Dodge (7-11/167y), made half his y on 84y TD pass to TE William Harris that put Longhorns up 14-3. Texas (2-0) did not forsake run, gaining 263y on ground with FB Terry Orr (15/108y) racing 51y to TD in 1st Q. Texas used effective "Mash" O: 3 Ts in unbalanced line. Lions QB Doug Strang (9-26/113y) was pounded all day by quick Horns D, while TB D.J. Dozier rushed for 43y before being sent to sidelines after hard hit.

Virginia 26 VIRGINIA TECH 23: Trailing by 23-13 in 4th Q in stadium they had not won in since 1970 and facing 4th-and-1 at Virginia Tech 34YL, Cavaliers (3-1) ignored conservative play calling. QB Don Majkowski (10-17/154y) went to air and connected with diving frosh WR John Ford for 33y gain. TB Howard Petty soon scored on 1y run, and Virginia trailed by 4 after failed 2-pt conv. Cavs went to same combination for winning TD as Majkowski hit Ford with 14y TD pass for winner with 5:07 left. Duo had hooked up on 1st H TD pass, but Majkowski gave that back with INT returned 17y for TD by Va Tech S Bob Thomas. Hokies (2-2) took 23-13 lead early in 4th Q after 78y drive—with 43y on run by QB Mark Cox (20-34/219y, INT)—capped by TB Eddie Hunter's 17y scoring bolt. Hokies K Don Wade had 11 pts to become school's career pts leader with 182, while UVa K Kenny Stadlin hit school-record 56y FG.

SOUTH CAROLINA 17 Georgia 10: Reserve QB Mike Hold hooked up in 4th Q with WR Ira Hillary on 62y pass to set up Hold's 1y sneak 2 plays later that propelled Gamecocks (3-0). Despite leading South Carolina to 10-3 edge, banged-up QB Allen Mitchell (8-14/107y, INT) was pulled after dishing 2 errant pitchouts. Together, Mitchell and Hold sparked O that gained 360y. Carolina D featured 2 GLSs as Bulldogs (2-1) had 2 drives reached South Carolina 5YL without cracking EZ, reaping only 3 pts. Georgia converted only 4-16 3rd downs, but tied it 10-10 in 3rd Q when QB Todd Williams (10-20/125y, TD, INT) threw 17y scoring pass to WR Jimmy Hockaday.

GEORGIA TECH 28 Clemson 21: It must have been "reserve day" in South as Georgia Tech (3-0) turned to bench player for winning pts. Backup FB Chuck Easley scored on 1y plunge with 33 secs left as Georgia Tech was off to best start in 14 seasons. Led by TB Stacey Driver (26/131y), Tigers (2-2) rallied from 21-0 deficit, with tying TD coming early in 4th Q on 13y pass from QB Mike Eppley (14-22/160y, 2 TDs, 2 INTs) to WR Terrance Roulhac. Yellow Jackets nervously went 3-and-out, but P Mike Snow's 46y punt pinned Tigers at their 3YL. Clemson was forced to punt 6 plays later, and QB John Dewberry (10-20/188y, TD) led Tech's winning 54y drive that snapped Clemson's 20-game ACC win streak, 1 shy of record.

IOWA 21 Illinois 16: Iowa's New York City combination was too much to handle for Illini (3-2) as TB Ronnie Harmon of Queens ran for 191y and 3 TDs, and Brooklyn native FB Owen Gill chipped in 16/115y. Rushing for 313y, Hawkeyes (2-2) need no heroics from QB Chuck Long (7-14/73y, 2 INTs). With glue-fingered assistance from WR David Williams (11/131y), QB Jack Trudeau (26-33/230y, 2 TDs) was brilliant in defeat, completing 10 straight 4th Q passes in an attempt to rally Illinois to 13th straight Big 10 win. Illinois fell in early hole when its onside-KO backfired at game's opening. Iowa recovered it to launch 52y trip to 2y TD run by Harmon. Hawkeyes scored 2nd TD, on Harmon's 8y run, after Illini failed on 4th-and-2 on Iowa 42YL. Illinois also ran out of time in 1st H after reaching Hawks 8YL.

SOUTHERN METHODIST 26 Texas Christian 17: Largest crowd (58,206) to watch rivals since 1948 saw Mustangs (3-0) score 10 4th Q pts to win 13th straight in series. SMU TB Reggie Dupard rushed for 153y and clinching 25y TD run, while WR Ron Morris had 5 receptions/120y and rushed for 53y. Morris scored twice, and came up with clutch catch: 38y grab on 3rd-and-33 in 3rd Q. SMU, which also counted key 4th Q FG of 24y by K Tomas Esteve, outflanked TCU's "Purple Reign" O by 501y to 347y. Horned Frogs (2-1) rushed for only 151y, but were able to tie score 10-10 in 3rd Q on TB Tony Jeffrey's 2y run and trailed only 19-17 late after QB Anthony Gulley (14-28/196y, INT) threw 22y TD to TE Dan Sharp.

Louisiana State 23 SOUTHERN CALIFORNIA 3: Inability to score TDs doomed Trojans (2-1) in intersectional clash. LSU (3-0-1) had no such problem as TB Dalton Hilliard (28/81y) hurried for 2 1st H TDs, while QB Jeff Wickersham (14-27/171y) hit WR Glenn Holt with 34y TD pass late in 3rd Q. Tigers scored 1st TD on Hilliard's 2y run after Trojans FUM, 1 of 5 TOs by USC. Their 79y drive to another 2y score by Hilliard was kept alive when P Clay Parker—who wore only 1 shoe—ran 16y for 1st down after high snap. Tally had reached 14-3, and Trojans were in trouble and on way to 8 Qs without TD. Troy O struggled without QB Sean Salisbury, who was injured in 1st H of prior week. TB Fred Crutcher led USC with 97y rushing.

AP Poll October 1

1 Texas (51)	1183	11 Penn State	502
2 Ohio State (5)	1113	12 Georgia Tech	474
3 Washington (1)	1008	13 Michigan	462
4 Boston College (2)	1005	14 Miami	382
5 Oklahoma (1)	959	15 Louisiana State	319
6 Florida State	846	16 Notre Dame	206
7 Brigham Young	836	17 UCLA	198
8 Nebraska	794	18 Auburn	179
9 Oklahoma State	751	19 Vanderbilt	134
10 Southern Methodist	691	20 Georgia	97

October 6, 1984

North Carolina State 27 GEORGIA TECH 22: Recovered from hamstring pull, TB Joe McIntosh rushed for 138y and TD to lead N.C. State (3-2) to upset. QB Tim Esposito completed 15-19/143y, TB Vince Evans ran for 2 TDs, and K Mike Cofer added FGs of 35y and 22y for Wolfpack who gained 333y. Georgia Tech (3-1) struggled with 4 TOs, including 3 INTs thrown by QB John Dewberry (15-24/225y, TD), while TB Robert Lavette could penetrate Wolfpack Flex-D for only 76y rushing. Yellow Jackets did tighten it up late with 2 TDs in game's final mins. NC State CB Nelson Jones had 2 INTs. "They took us kind of lightly," said Esposito. "In fact, they took us as kind of a joke. I think the joke's on them."

KENTUCKY 27 Rutgers 14: Kentucky (4-0) TB Mark Higgs, at 5'7" and 187 lbs, may not fill uniforms like Bo Jackson and Herschel Walker, but he knew how to hit open hole. Higgs scored winning TD in 3rd Q on 29y run, breaking 3 tackles en route. He later added incredible 76y TD run in 4th Q to clinch game and give heralded frosh 29y avg on 4/116y. Starting Wildcats TB George Adams rushed for 116y and scored on short run and pass. Rutgers (3-2) took 14-13 H lead, scoring late in 1st H on 66y drive capped by 20y TD pass from QB Rusty Hochberg (25-45/241y, INT) to WR Andrew Baker. Scarlet Knights TE Alan Andrews caught 9 passes/127y.

Georgia 24 ALABAMA 14: That Bear Bryant had been unable to bring in level of talent once enjoyed in Tuscaloosa in final years was all too evident as Crimson Tide (1-4) was unable to continue school's streak of 26 straight winning seasons and 25 bowl games. Georgia FB Andre Smith (12/117y) raced 44y and 34y for early 1st Q TDs as Bulldogs went for kill before 1st Q ended. With lead, Georgia D blitzed frosh QB Vince Sutton (14-30/120y) often, forcing 4 INTs and sacking him 3 times. Alabama was able to pull within 17-14 on Sutton's TD runs of 32y on 4th down in 2nd Q and 3y following TB Paul Ott Carruth's 59y run in 3rd Q. Georgia QB Todd Williams clinched game with 31y TD pass with 4:45 left.

Tulane 27 VANDERBILT 23: Tulane (1-4) ended 7-game losing streak in sending high-flying Vandy team back to earth. Notre Dame transfer QB Ken Karchner (24-39/316y) threw 39y TD pass to TE Larry Route (8/97y) as Green Wave grabbed 24-13 3rd Q lead. After 32y FG by K Tony Woods wrapped up Tulane's scoring, Commodores (4-1), rallied for 10 straight pts. Using 5 and at times 6 DBs, but Tulane D targeted QB Kurt Page (20-47/247y), who entered as SEC's leading passer but left with 4 INTs, 2 each by DB Benny Burst and S Kevin Tate. Page had streak of 117 consecutive passes without INT broken. Tulane RB Mike Jones rushed for 93y and 2 TDs, while Vanderbilt's main weapon was WR Chuck Scott (8/147y).

PURDUE 28 Ohio State 23: Purdue (4-1) S Rod Woodson, future 3-time All Big 10 player and NFL star, made 1st national splash with 55y INT RET for clinching TD. QB Jim Everett completed 17-23/257y and 3 TDs as Boilermakers grabbed sole possession of 1st place in Big 10. Go-ahead drive began on Purdue 21YL following INT, this time by Boilers CB Don Anderson, and featured Everett's 46y completion to WR Rick Brunner that led to his 4y TD pass that made score 21-17. Loss wasted incredible effort by TB Keith Byars, who gained 191y rushing, with 2 TDs, and 102y receiving. He even took 2nd H KO 61y, running over Woodson in process.

Michigan State 19 MICHIGAN 7: Michigan's hopes for season were dashed significantly in 3rd Q when, in scramble to recover FUM by TB Jamie Morris, QB Jim Harbaugh broke left (non-throwing) arm. Backup Wolverines (3-2) QBs Russ Rein and Chris Zurbrugg combined for 3 INTs and only single 1st down. Michigan State (2-3) QB Dave Yarema completed 18-27/180y, with 5-5/63y during 85y TD drive with opening possession that dictated tone of game. Spartans upped lead to 13-0 when WR Bobby Morse returned punt 87y for TD, 1st punt RET scored against Wolverines since 1971. Michigan cut lead to 13-7 at H on FB Eddie Garrett's 1y run to cap 75y drive.

NEBRASKA 17 Oklahoma State 3: Teams combined for 18 punts throughout D struggle. Nebraska (4-1) WB Shane Swanson restored normalcy by racing 49y on punt TD RET in 4th Q that snapped 3-3 tie. Huskers added insurance TD when QB Travis Turner (5-10/100y), who replaced QB Craig Sundberg after starter's 3rd INT, hooked up with WR Jason Gamble on 64y pass. Nebraska CB Dave Burke gave superb effort with 7 tackles, blocked FG, FUM REC, INT, and block that helped spring Swanson. Cowboys (4-1) had taken 3-0 lead on 40y FG by K Larry Roach, 62nd of his career, that was set up by CB Mark Moore's INT. OSU QB Rusty Hilger threw for 242y, while Nebraska IB Doug DuBose came off bench to rush for 157y.

Texas Tech 30 TEXAS A&M 12: Frosh QB Aaron Keesee (6-8/78y) had efficient game, throwing 3 TDs and running in 4th, to lead Texas Tech (2-2) to surprisingly easy win. With help from IB Timmy Smith (19/139y), Keesee led Red Raiders to 20 4th Q pts, jump-started by 23y QB draw run for winning pts. Smith set up TD with 43y scamper.

Aggies (3-1) lost stat battle by only 286y to 266y, but struggled to reach EZ in settling for 4 FGs by K Alan Smith. Texas A&M QB Craig Stump threw for 137y, but Red Raiders D consistently pressured him. Victory was sweet for teary-eyed Tech assistant Tom Wilson, who was fired by Texas A&M after 1981 season.

Texas Christian 32 ARKANSAS 31: Horned Frogs (4-0) pulled stunner with 15 pts in final 10 mins, including winning 2-pt conv with 15 secs left. Twice TCU drove 80y to score, with WR James Maness providing heroics with catch worth 2 pts. Frog QBs Anthony Gulley and Anthony Sciaraffa each had hand in win as Sciaraffa scored final TD on 1y run—2 plays after EZ PEN on Arkansas CB Greg Gatson—before Gulley threw winning pass to Maness in back of EZ. Hogs (2-1-1) took 17-10 2nd Q lead with 2 late TDs, including controversial 27y scoring catch by WR James Shibest, who tipped ball before rolling on ground to catch it—replays showed that ball hit ground. TCU tied game when CB Garland Littles returned INT 67y. Arkansas run game, which gained 361y, was sparked by RB Bobby Joe Edmonds (13/124y) who scored on 37y run to open 4th Q, and FB Marshall Foreman (21/150y), who went 59y for 2-TD lead. With 4 wins, TCU already had topped win total for every season since 1972.

Stanford 23 UCLA 21: Without injured QB John Paye, Cardinal (3-2) turned to D to lead way, and it responded, holding Bruins to 66y rushing and forcing 4 TOs. Frosh FB Brad Muster rushed for 82y and sub QB Fred Buckley hit only 9-21/83y, INT, he provided leadership during 20-0 onslaught in game's initial 20 mins. Bruins (3-2) scored TD right before H on 4y pass from QB Matt Stevens (17-32/271y, 3 INTs) to WR Mike Young. After Stanford K Mark Harmon hit 3rd FG, UCLA rallied in 4th Q as INT by CB Ronnie Pitts was converted into 6y TD run by FB Bryan Wiley followed by 2-pt conv run by TB James Primus. Cardinal, now up 23-15, answered with RB Kevin Scott's 89y KO RET, but S James Washington picked off Buckley in EZ, returning INT 4y. With 2nd life, Bruins marched 96y—with 60y TD pass to WR Mike Sherrard—but then failed on 2-pt try as Primus was halted on sweep right. Stanford ate up 4 mins, before PEN and sack halted UCLA's final attempt.

ARIZONA 28 Oregon 14: Wildcats (4-2) snapped Oregon's 4-game win streak as QB Alfred Jenkins (14-25/230y) rushed for TD, and K Max Zendejas tied NCAA record with FG in 18th straight game. Oregon (4-1) had come out firing, scoring 1st TD on 80y bomb from QB Chris Miller (11-32/205y, 3 INTs) to WR Lew Barnes. Arizona scored next 21 pts including 6y run by Jenkins, while Arizona D was holding Ducks to pair of 3-and-out series in 3rd Q. Ducks came alive in 4th Q when Miller capped 72y drive with 11y scoring pass to TB Kevin McCall, and soon moved Oregon to Arizona 17YL with less than 5 mins left. LB Byron Evans came through with INT to halt rally and propel Wildcats to TB David Adams' clinching 11y TD run.

October 13, 1984

SOUTH CAROLINA 45 Pittsburgh 21: Gamecocks (5-0) added to Pitt's woes as "Fire Ants" D, led by LB James Seawright (14 tackles), held Panthers (1-5) to 108y rushing. South Carolina's Veer O made 443y by out-running bigger Panthers. QB Mike Hold (8-12/124y) played well off bench, tossing 2 TD passes, as Carolina opened with 5 wins for 1st time since 1928. Hold's scoring strikes found WR Chris Wade (3/88y) for 31 and 33y connections, as Cocks built 28-14 lead in 3rd Q. Panthers cut deficit in half on 5y TD run by TB Craig Heyward, before Carolina turned back to starting QB Allen Mitchell, who sparked 17 straight pts to end it. WR Chuck Scales was bright spot for Pitt, catching 4/125y including 60y TD.

ALABAMA 6 Penn State 0: Despite starting 13 frosh and sophs, young Crimson Tide (2-4) posted 1st shutout over Penn State (4-1) since 1966. QB Vince Sutton, recently removed from 18th birthday, directed O that gained 218y rushing and, most importantly, committed no TOs. Alabama K Van Tiffin won kicking contest with 2 FGs, including school-record 53y effort, while Penn State K Nick Gancitano missed 1st H attempts, from 51 and 42y. Thereafter, Nittany Lions (4-2) penetrated no farther than Bama 45YL. Game's leading rusher was Alabama HB Don Horstead, who edged Penn State TB D.J. Dozier by 59y to 58y.

Auburn 42 FLORIDA STATE 41: Barnburner went down to wire, with Auburn (4-2) scoring winning TD with 48 secs remaining on HB Brent Fullwood's 3rd TD, 4y run that capped 76y drive. Big play was QB Pat Washington's 35y completion to WR Freddie Weygand (4/147y), who in 1st Q had caught 51y pass from Fullwood to set up TD. Florida State (4-1-1) gained 591y as QB Eric Thomas threw for 357y and 4 TDs, with 52y on final pass to WR Herb Gainer, who went OB as time expired but before FSU could attempt FG. Thomas launched 73y bomb to WR Jesse Hester (4/143y) in 2nd Q and spun 14y TD pass to WR Hassan Jones (7/101y, 2 TDs) with 7:44 left that gave Seminoles 41-36 lead. Tigers also scored on big-play TDs as HB Collis Campbell raced 69y in 2nd Q, and when Fullwood fumbled 2nd H KO, ball popped to Auburn special teamer Ed Graham, who streamed remaining 60y to EZ. "This was probably the greatest game I've ever been associated with," said winning coach Pat Dye. "An all-timer. Lord have mercy."

Iowa 40 PURDUE 3: Hawkeyes (4-2) easily grabbed share of Big 10 lead as QB Chuck Long (17-21/369y) threw 4 TDs of 30y or longer. WR Robert Smith nabbed 3 TDs/120y. Long's 4th TD went 56y to WR Scott Helverson. Trailing 19-3 at H, Purdue

---

(4-2) blew chance to rally after it made 2 FUM RECs off hands of Iowa TB Ronnie Harmon deep in Hawks territory, opportunities ended on missed FG and lost EZ FUM by TE Marty Scott. Boilermakers QB Jim Everett threw for 228y, but was picked off 3 times. Said Long, "(Purdue) didn't adjust, and we just picked them apart in every way."

OHIO STATE 45 Illinois 38: Unable to stop Ohio State TB Keith Byars, Illini (4-3) blew early 24-pt lead. Despite big deficit, Ohio State (5-1) kept delivering ball to its meal ticket, and Byars rushed for school-record 274y—breaking TB Archie Griffin's mark of 246y set in 1973—and scored 5 TDs as Buckeyes posted 28 straight pts. After Illinois tied game 38-38 late in 4th Q on 16y FG following failed 4th down try from 1YL—Ohio State began final drive at own 20YL. Bucks marched 80y on 7 carries by Byars among 11 plays to win game on 3y run with 36 secs left. Byars' most impressive TD was 67y effort during which he lost his left shoe 27y into run. His performance gave him 1,076y for season and extended scoring streak to 12 games. Scoring 1st 4 times it had ball, Illinois was led by QB Jack Trudeau, who air it out for 313y and 4 TDs, and FB Thomas Rooks (28/168y). Ohio QB Mike Tomczak threw for 236y, with WR Cris Carter catching 7/134y.

Oklahoma 15 Texas 15 (Dallas): Ranked 1st and 2nd by UPI, rivals battled to controversial finale. With Sooners leading 15-12, Texas (3-0-1) QB Todd Dodge, who played despite hyperextended knee, threw to WR Bill Boy Bryant in EZ. Oklahoma (4-0-1) CB Andre Johnson tipped ball into hands of S Keith Stanberry, who appeared to catch it before toppling over sideline. Official Ed Clark ruled that pass was incomplete as Stanberry was OB. Longhorns K Jeff Ward then booted tying 32y FG as time expired. Replays clearly showed that Stanberry had possession of ball in bounds—league later admitted call was blown. Also blown was Texas' 10-0 H lead—built on 25y TD pass to Bryant and 40y Ward kick—as OU LB Brian Bosworth made early splash, forcing FUM by FB Terry Orr at Horns 6YL that led to 5y TD run by HB Steve Sewell. Ninety secs later, Texas botched punt snap deep in own territory for 2 more pts for Sooners, who then scored on ensuing drive with Sewell catching 24y TD pass from QB Danny Bradley. Sooners D, which allowed only 96y rushing on wet turf, surrendered 58y on 1 play by backup TB Kevin Nelson to put ball, 1st-and-goal, on 2 YL. Four plays later ball was on 3YL and going over to Sooners on downs. Oklahoma coach Barry Switzer soon opted for conceded safety and booted ball away, giving Texas ball on own 44YL with 2:04 to go for final drive.

Southern Methodist 24 BAYLOR 20: Bears (1-4) blew 20-10 lead in 4th Q by allowing 80y and 85y drives within game's final mins. Mustangs (4-0) QB Don King led rally, completing 3 passes/57y on drive to set up his 3y TD run and finishing 2nd drive with 27y scoring pass to WR Ron Morris (8/100y) with 49 secs left. King (19-31/285y, 2 TDs, INT) was 3-3/all 85y on winning trip. Baylor D had played well up until end, limiting potent Mustangs to 180y rushing. Baylor TB Ron Francis ran for 112y and snared 3y scoring reception.

BRIGHAM YOUNG 41 Wyoming 38: Brigham Young (6-0) QB Robbie Bosco's 14y TD pass to TE David Mills (7/136y) with 4:16 left secured come-from-behind victory. Bosco (29-44/384) threw 5 TD passes, 3 to Mills as Cougars continued win streak to nation's best 17 games. Cowboys (3-4) had scored 19 straight pts to take 26-21 lead in 3rd Q. Scoring string included TD on 77y punt RET by PR Oliver Davis late in 1st H. Teams then traded scores until HB Kevin Lowe scored on 61y run late in 3rd Q to give Cowboys last lead at 38-33. WR Allyn Griffin (5/148y) caught 64 and 37y TDs for Wyoming.

October 20, 1984

WEST VIRGINIA 21 Boston College 20: West Virginia (6-1) coach Don Nehlen continued mastery over Eagles, winning 5th straight on 2nd H rally. Boston College (4-1) grabbed 20-6 H lead as QB Doug Flutie (21-42/299y)—0-4 career record against West Virginia—threw 42y TD pass to WR Kelvin Martin, and FB Steve Strachan ran for 24y TD, while Mountaineers could manage only 2 FGs. Mountaineers woke up with 52y pass from QB Kevin White (17-30/227y, INT) to WR Willie Drewrey that set up FB Ron Wolfley's 1y plunge. As West Virginia D proved impenetrable in 2nd H, TB John Gay (17/71y) ran for winning 5y TD early in 4th Q.

Louisiana State 36 KENTUCKY 10: TB Dalton Hilliard continued his excellent season with 164y rushing and school record-tying 4 TDs as Tigers (5-0-1) overcame 5 1st H TOs to rout previously undefeated Kentucky. Cats (5-1) more than made up for LSU's mistakes with 4 lost FUMs and 5 INTs of own, while D allowed visitors to gain 506y. Tigers led by only 9-3 at H despite 301y in O, but exploded in 2nd H as Hilliard scored his TDs including 2 runs of 14y apiece. Wildcats had own 1st H chances, twice losing ball within LSU 10YL, but had only FG to show for these opportunities as CB James Pierson picked off trick pass on 1YL to kill chance. By time Wildcats cracked LSU GL, on 1y run by TB George Adams (23/76y), score was 29-10 against them in 3rd Q. Tigers QB Jeff Wickersham threw for 221y.

South Carolina 36 NOTRE DAME 32: No one expected coach Joe Morrison to turn things around at South Carolina (6-0) so quickly. Great start in 2nd year included wins over Georgia, Pittsburgh, and Notre Dame. Fighting Irish (3-4) held 26-14 lead entering 4th Q as TB Allen Pinkett (25/100y) ran in 2 TDs and passed 6y for TD to QB

Steve Beuerlein on flea-flicker. Gamecocks raced for 22 pts during 6-min span of 4th Q as relief QB Mike Hold scored twice, including 33y run that put Carolina up 29-26. Final Gamecocks' TD, on 4y run by backup HB Quinton Lewis, was set up by FUM REC by DB Rick Rabune on Notre Dame 17YL.

IOWA 26 Michigan 0: Coach Bo Schembechler suffered worst loss at Michigan as Iowa (5-2) D stretched TD-free streak to 3 straight Big 10 games. Critical stop occurred with score at 12-0 in 4th Q—Wolverines (4-3) driving—as Iowa S Devon Mitchell picked off his 2nd pass at 1YL and returned it 75y to set up FB Owen Gill's backbreaking 10y TD run. Wolverines D did good job of holding TB Ronnie Harmon (27/63y, TD) and QB Chuck Long (14-20/146y) in check, but could not prevent Hawkeyes' 1st win over Michigan at home since 1962. Also, it was 1st shutout in series since 1929. Michigan O had something to do with that, gaining only 187y with TB Rick Rogers' 55y leading run game, and special teams lost 3 FUMs.

Nebraska 24 COLORADO 7: Yeoman D effort gave Buffs (1-6) slim 7-3 lead entering 4th Q, but 15 mins was all Huskers needed to win. Nebraska (6-1) QB Travis Turner, native of Colorado, ran for 2 TDs and threw 11y scoring pass to TE Brian Heimer to lead Huskers' 4th Q blowout. Prior to 4th Q, Buffs gamely employed "tilt" D with 2 NGs to frustrate Nebraska and set up sole TD. QB Steve Vogel's 16y TD pass to WR Loy Alexander followed FUM REC by Colorado LB Danny McMillen (2 sacks). Huskers IB Jeff Smith rushed for 165y, 28y more than registered by all Buff runners.

Houston 29 SOUTHERN METHODIST 20: Never trailing, Cougars (4-2) scored on 6 of 1st 7 possessions in snapping 11-game losing streak to Top 20 teams. Houston K Mike Clendenen booted school-record 5 FGs, and QB Gerald Landry (12-17/193y, INT) threw 68y TD pass to TE Carl Hilton for 26-7 lead in 3rd Q. Mustangs (4-1) scored 2 TDs to pull within 26-20 late in 4th Q before forcing punt. SMU PR Franky Thomas fumbled punt, recovered by Houston DE Gary McManus at 16YL to set up clinching FG. SMU TB Reggie Dupard rushed for 114y, with 71y TD jaunt, and caught 5/90y. Defeat was Mustangs' 1st in SWC to any team other than Texas since 1980. Ponies permitted 430y despite tower of strength in middle, NG Jerry Ball, who participated in 19 tackles. Houston D held Mustangs to 325y, with 4 sacks of QB Don King and 2 INTs, both by CB DeWayne Bowden.

TEXAS 24 Arkansas 18: PEN by Texas (4-0-1) as time elapsed allowed Razorbacks to launch 1 more attempt at victory from Steers 20YL. With extra chance, Arkansas QB Brad Taylor threw slant pass to WR Jamie Lueders, who spooked Memorial Stadium crowd by darting to 4YL before being halted by Longhorn CB Tony Tillmon. Razorbacks (3-2-1) had rallied from 24-3 deficit as Taylor (201y passing) shook off awful start. Taylor went 0-10, 4 INTs from opening whistle but eventually launched 54y TD to WR James Shibest (7/128y) in 4th Q. Steady Texas QB Todd Dodge threw 2 TD passes, tossing 22y to WR Brent Duhon to open scoring in 1st Q and 5y to TE William Harris in 3rd Q. Rain contributed to both teams coughing up 6 TOs.

Brigham Young 30 AIR FORCE 25: Cougars (7-0) won contrast of O styles as QB Robbie Bosco (28-41/484y), nation's total O leader, threw 4 TD passes. While Cougars' top-rated passing attack clicked beautifully, Falcons, with country's top ground attack, were held to 219y rushing, more than 100y less than avg. Winning pts at 27-19 were delivered in 3rd Q by Bosco's 54y pass to TE David Mills (10/225y), which dug BYU out of 3rd-and-21 hole. In 4th Q, QB Bart Weiss led 76y drive to 2y TD keeper to pull Air Force (5-3) to within 27-25, but he misfired on 2-pt conv pass. BYU D had made 2 big plays in 2nd Q by stopping Air Force's 4th down rushes, including tackle of FB Pat Evans (20/105y) at Cougar 1YL by DE Larry Hamilton.

WASHINGTON 17 Oregon 10: Washington (7-0) maintained top spot in AP ranking despite abysmal O performance. Incredibly, Huskies earned 3 1st downs—total—on 109y and still won. Huskies counted TDs on 42y punt TD RET by CB Ron Milius and WR Mike Gaffney's EZ REC of punt blocked by S Tim Peoples. Ducks (4-3) endured other special team struggles with bad punt snap and 2 missed FGs. Oregon created 17 1st downs and 268y, but found penetrating Washington GL difficult. Huskies O found everything difficult as QB Hugh Millen passed for microscopic 36y, and TB Jacque Robinson (12/36y) found holes hard to maneuver. Oregon made its TD in 2nd Q on 1y run by FB Alex Mack, and it capped 35y excursion set up by S Dan Wilkin's INT. Washington LB Reggie Rogers knocked Ducks QB Chris Miller out of action with concussion on late hit, and Miller would be troubled by head injuries rest of his college and pro careers.

AP Poll October 22

1 Washington (30)	1161	11 Boston College	512
2 Oklahoma (7.5)	1121.5	12 Auburn	500
3 Texas (3.5)	1096.5	13 Georgia	486
4 Nebraska	980	14 Southern Methodist	370
5 Brigham Young	926	15t Florida State	328
6 Ohio State	842	15t Florida	328
7 Louisiana State	829	17 Iowa	319
8 Miami	752	18 West Virginia	308
9 South Carolina	719	19 Penn State	122
10 Oklahoma State	613	20 Southern California	60

October 27, 1984

WEST VIRGINIA 17 Penn State 14: Having not witnessed win over Penn State (5-3) since 1955, Mountaineer fans were justifiably excited as DB Larry Holley picked off Nittany Lions QB John Shaffer (12-22/167y, 2 INTs) on West Virginia 18YL with 35 secs left. Although time remained, fans poured onto field and tore down goal posts—coach Joe Paterno pulled Lions off field, conceding defeat—and congratulated opposing players in their locker room after game. West Virginia (7-1) K Paul Woodside's 49y FG early in 4th Q had broken 7-7 tie. WVU sub TB Pat Randolph's 22y TD run was added needed insurance as Penn State TB D.J. Dozier (20/108y) later raced 51y to close out scoring.

Georgia 37 KENTUCKY 7: Bulldogs (6-1) won game in trenches, dominating Kentucky with blocks that sprung runners for 307y to 10y ground advantage. Even when rush game made mistake, team profited as TE Scottie Williams scored team's and his career's 1st TD with 16y advance of FUM by TB Tron Jackson. By themselves, Georgia special teams outscored Kentucky: RB Jimmy Harrell added 76y punt TD RET for 1st-ever score, while tough K Kevin Butler, who was expected to miss game with stained knee ligament, booted 3 FGs with his bad leg. Wildcats (5-2) needed 59:50 to score as backup QB Kevin Dooley threw 16y TD pass to WR Cisco Bryant at game's end to wipe out shutout.

Notre Dame 30 LOUISIANA STATE 22: It was probably best for Notre Dame (4-4) to get out of South Bend, where rumors of possible coaching change swirled amid 3-game home losing streak. Even Death Valley looked good to Irish, who rode TB Allen Pinkett to upset. Pinkett (40/162y) set school record for carries on his way to 2 TDs. Other Irish stars were K John Carney, who kicked 3 FGs, and QB Steve Beuerlein, who hit 16-23/168y. Tigers (5-1-1) were held to 9y rushing in 1st H but wiped clean that slate with 66y TD explosion in 3rd Q by TB Dalton Hilliard (13/118y) that cut deficit to 20-14. QB Jeff Wickersham (19-27/213y, 2 TDs, INT) could not get Tigers to score again until closing moments on hopeful 50y EZ toss-up to WR Rogie Magee.

WISCONSIN 16 Ohio State 14: There was 200y rusher in game, but it wasn't star Ohio State (6-2) TB Keith Byars (142y, TD). Bench-warming Wisconsin TB Marck Harrison, sr ironically from Columbus who started in place of injured TB Larry Emery, rushed 31/203y, 143y more than his previous best game. Badgers (5-3) also got 3 FGs from K Todd Gregoire, and QB Mike Howard threw 34y TD pass to WR Thad McFadden. Another unheralded Wisconsin player, LB Craig Raddatz, made 2 INTs and 11 tackles in his 2nd start.

KANSAS 28 Oklahoma 11: Kansas (3-5) scored as many pts as pundits predicted Jayhawks to lose by. In shocking Oklahoma for 1st series win in Lawrence since 1964, Jayhawks took 7-3 lead on TB Lynn Williams' 1y run in 2nd Q and never trailed again. They added 4 FGs by K Dodge Schwartzburg and 63y INT TD RET by S Wayne Ziegler. Sooners (5-1-1), who were limited to pair of 1st downs in 2nd H, did not score TD until 3 secs remained on RB Kyle Irvan's 1y plunge. Of frosh and future star QB Troy Aikman, who was forced to enter game when QB Danny Bradley was injured, Sooners coach Barry Switzer said, "The boy was scared to death. It's not all his fault, not at all". Weekend worsened for OU when starting DBs Keith Stanberry and Andre Johnson were seriously injured in horrific car accident that night.

Iowa State 14 MISSOURI 14: Tigers (3-4-1) blew chance to stay in Big 8 race as sloppy conditions played into hands of underdog Iowa State. Cyclones (2-5-1) backup QB Alan Hood, who entered game in 2nd H when QB Alex Espinoza was knocked out with broken leg, led dual 4th Q scoring drives. Hood, Missouri native not recruited by Tigers, ignored 6 sacks to lead Iowa State to 27y FG by K Marc Bachrodt and 7y TD pass to TE Dave Smoldt. On his 2 series, Hood completed 7-9/66y and succeeded on all-important 2-pt conv pass to TE Jeff Wodka to tie game. Mizzou had ball twice more, but both possessions ended in INTs by QB Marlon Adler as Tigers finished with 6 TOs, 3 on KO RET FUMs. Cyclones played TO-free ball. Adler threw 31y TD pass to WR George Shorthouse and scored Missouri's other TD on 16y run.

TEXAS 13 Southern Methodist 7: Mustangs (4-2) twice drove deep into Texas (5-0-1) territory in game's closing moments, losing possession after 1st drive on controversial no-call against CB James Lott's tight 4th down coverage against WR Marquis Pleasant and later on Lott's INT of QB Don King's pass into EZ with 1 min to go. Longhorns D allowed only 221y and no pts as SMU's sole TD was delivered by 42y INT RET by S Keith Brooks. Texas K Jeff Ward kicked FGs of 41 and 35y for 1st H scoring, and QB Todd Dodge led 10-play, 71y drive in 3rd Q that ended with FB Jerome Johnson's 7y TD run.

WASHINGTON 28 Arizona 12: Top-ranked Huskies (8-0) won sloppy game—teams combined for 19 TOs and 13 PENs—in muddy conditions behind D, special teams play, and 3 2nd H runs by TB Jacque Robinson (25/119y). Huskies QB Hugh Millen was benched at H for 3 INTs and 2 lost FUMs as Arizona (4-4) took 6-0 lead on 89y INT RET by S Lynnden Brown. Led by QB Paul Sicuro, Washington scored next 28 pts before Arizona LB Byron Evans recovered FUM in EZ for final TD. Cats TB David Adams rushed for 52y, while QB Alfred Jenkins hit 9-25/92y passing.

AP Poll October 29

1 Washington (50)	1184	11 Auburn	558
2 Texas (3)	1121	12 West Virginia	540
3 Nebraska (3)	1076	13 Florida	425
4 Brigham Young (4)	970	14 Florida State	406
5 South Carolina	919	15 Louisiana State	357
6 Miami	872	16 Ohio State	341
7 Oklahoma State	741	17 Iowa	272
8 Georgia	714	18 Southern California	233
9 Boston College	703	19 Southern Methodist	166
10 Oklahoma	586	20 Texas Christian	113

November 3, 1984

ARMY 24 Air Force 12: In 1st night game at Michie Stadium and under ESPN's cameras, Cadets (5-2-1) closed out 1st perfect home mark since 1966 with 19-0 2nd H performance. Game got off to unusual, big-play beginning when Army DE Kurt Gutierrez sped through blockers to nail Air Force HB Jody Simmons for safety on wide backwards pass. Black Knights sub QB Rob Healy sparked win with 73y of team's 261y rushing, while D held Air Force rushers to 177y, 34y in 2nd H. K Craig Stopa booted 4 of his 5 FGs in 2nd H, including 50y effort, while WR Scott Spellman scored Army's sole TD on 41y run. Falcons (5-4) QB Bart Weiss (10-14/173y, 2 INTs), threw

more than usual, but team's 408y were limited by 5 TOs. After Stopa had provided 5-0 lead with his 1st FG (48y), Air Force scored final 12 pts of 1st H on 2 FGs by K Carlos Mateos and Weiss' 39y pass to WR Eric Pharris.

PENN STATE 37 Boston College 30: Although Eagles (5-2) QB Doug Flutie became 1st player ever to crack 10,000y in career total O, he was in no mood to celebrate as he lost 2 FUMs, threw 2 INTs, and was sacked 4 times. Nittany Lions (6-3) ran well as TB D.J. Dozier rushed for 143y, including 39y late TD dash that upped lead to 37-23, and FB Steve Smith added 126y and 2 TDs. Play of game was turned in by QB Doug Strang, who set up Dozier's TD with Flutie-like 28y run on 3rd down. He also ran for 6y to gain clinching 1st down as Penn State ran out clock after BC had scored TDs on its last 2 opportunities. Flutie (29-53/447y, TD) went past BYU's Jim McMahon (9,723y) in total O with 20y pass to roommate WR Gerard Phelan (8/110y). He also set mark for career y against 1 team: 1,445y versus Penn State. Flutie gained 203y of his total in 4th Q despite slightly separating left shoulder in 3rd Q.

Virginia 27 WEST VIRGINIA 7: Cavs (6-1-1) dominated both lines of scrimmage in amassing 351y to 51y rushing advantage. Virginia took 10-0 H lead as QB Don Majkowski threw 17y TD pass to TE Geno Zimmerlink, and K Kenny Stadlin kicked 40y FG. FB Steve Morse (18/141y) then raced 51y to EZ in 3rd Q to wrap things up for Virginia, whose relentless D was led by LB Charles McDaniel's 11 tackles. Mountaineers (7-2) prevented shutout with 44y TD pass from reserve QB Tony Reda to WR Gary Mullen. UVa remained undefeated since opening 55-0 loss to Clemson.

Maryland 34 NORTH CAROLINA 23: FB Rick Badanjek (16/68y) powered for 4 TDs as Terps (5-3) shook off slow start to continue ACC domination. North Carolina (3-5) controlled ball for 18 of 1st 20 mins, taking 10-0 lead when TB Ethan Horton (35/126y) scored on 5y run early in 2nd Q. Maryland reeled off 34 of game's next 40 pts. Terps QB Stan Gelbaugh passed for 269y, including 10y TD to Badanjek that tied it 10-10. Terps S Keeta Covington kept UNC in game with 2 consecutive FUMs of KOs deep in own zone, and each set up FGs by K Kenny Miller. It was all Maryland from then on as its O, that gained 395y, cashed in 4 straight drives.

FLORIDA 24 Auburn 3: HB Bo Jackson's surprise return from shoulder injury could not lift Tigers, as Florida (6-1-1) continued its march to SEC glory. TB Neal Anderson (15/108y) ran 36y for TD that put Florida up 10-3 in 3rd Q and added 15y TD in 4th Q, both on same misdirection play. Gators used that play, "36 Tack," to also score 3rd TD on 43y run by TB Lorenzo Hampton. Anderson gained redemption for 2 costly FUMs in last season's 28-21 loss to Auburn. Gators P Ray Criswell contributed big play early in 2nd Q when he retrieved high snap in own EZ and punted ball to 43YL. Jackson was able only to rush 5/16y as Auburn (6-3), strangely 6-0 in games without Bo, lost 10-game SEC win streak. Auburn rushed for 117y—to Florida's 264y—with QB Pat Washington (10-22/111y, 2 INTs) leading with 34y. "Other teams have scored points against us," said Auburn LB Ben McCurdy. "But nobody's taken the ball and driven it the way Florida did. Basically, they whipped us."

IOWA 10 Wisconsin 10: Hard-hitting game was not for meek as rugged D dominated, Iowa (6-2-1) stars TB Ronnie Harmon (broken fibula) and QB Chuck Long (bruised knee) were being knocked out with injuries. Before departing, Long tied game with 11:54 left on 1y TD run, but he was held to 111y passing with 4 INTs. Wisconsin (5-3-1) took 10-0 1st Q lead on 25y FG by K Todd Gregoire and 1y TD run by TB Marck Harrison (23/76y) before finding y tough to come by. Hawkeye D allowed only slim pair of 1st downs in 2nd H. Harmon, nation's 2nd-leading all-purpose runner was finished for season.

Texas Christian 21 HOUSTON 14: CB Sean Thomas bailed out high-scoring Horned Frogs (7-1) by ending not 1, but 2 Cougar drives in final 3 mins with INTs at TCU 37YL and 13YL. His INTs gave Thomas personal best 3 INTs for year. Horned Frogs RB Kenneth Davis (22/131y) scored winning TD, breaking 14-14 tie with 2y TD run in 3rd Q to cap 70y drive. With its Veer attack held to 52/179y on ground, Houston (4-4) tried to retaliate through air, but QB Gerald Landry (10-21/115y) had no answer for Thomas' interventions.

Oregon 20 UCLA 18: Ducks (5-4), who followed opening 4-game win streak with 4 straight losses, reverted to winning ways as spoiler that eliminated any chance of UCLA (6-3) going to 3 straight Rose Bowls. Oregon QB Chris Miller (20-30/200y, INT) threw pair of 3rd Q TD passes to break 3-3 tie, putting Ducks up for good with 35y scoring pass to WR Scott Holman. QB Steve Bono (26-44/282, 3 INTs), who had been 6-0 as starter, answered with 2 TD passes of his own to rally Bruins (6-3), but they bracketed Oregon's 75y drive to winning 26y FG by K Matt MacLeod. TB Kevin McCall (17/71y) led Oregon attack that outran Bruins 251y to 106y.

WASHINGTON STATE 20 Oregon State 3: Facing struggling Oregon State (2-7), Cougars did not have to be perfect to win. So while they fumbled 8 times, losing 3, they still won by 17 pts. TB Rueben Mayes rushed 31 times for 141y as Washington State (5-4) gained 341y in miserable conditions that prevented them from reaching 49.5-pt average from past 2 games. QB Mark Rypien threw for only 82y but opened scoring with 1y TD run to cap 15y drive begun after WSU S Jeff Dullum recovered FUM by Beavers QB Steve Steenwyk. Rypien also booted 76y quick kick with score 13-3 in 2nd H. TB Donald Beavers rushed for 53y to lead OSU, with 47y run in 2nd Q.

AP Poll November 5

1 Washington (50)	1147	11 Florida State	509
2 Nebraska (4)	1062	12 Louisiana State	481
3 Texas (1)	1032	13 Ohio State	467
4 Brigham Young (3)	1008	14 Southern California	403
5 South Carolina	921	15 Texas Christian	310
6 Miami	832	16 Boston College	258
7 Oklahoma State	781	17 Southern Methodist	164
8 Georgia	719	18 Iowa	159
9 Oklahoma	686	19 West Virginia	102
10 Florida	665	20 Auburn	92

November 10, 1984

RUTGERS 23 West Virginia 19: Mountaineers (7-3) had beaten best of East in Pittsburgh, Syracuse, Boston College, and Penn State in successive weeks before stumbling against Rutgers (6-3). TB Albert Smith (23/120y) ran for 2 TDs and QB Eric Hochberg (9-13/163y) hit WR Andrew Baker with 36y TD pass to trigger upset. TB Tom Gray's 1y TD run brought West Virginia (7-3) within 23-19 with 1 min left but Scarlet Knights thwarted 2-pt conv try and recovered onside-KO. Mountaineers QB Kevin White (18-28/247y) connected with WR Gary Mullen 7/152y.

Wake Forest 20 DUKE 16: Deacons (6-4) assured themselves of 1st winning season in 5 years as QB Foy White led 93y drive to winning 7y TD pass to frosh WR Greg Scales with 16 secs left. White, who threw for 288y, completed 8 passes on drive, 4 to WR Duane Owens (8/134y), who had caught 42y TD pass to open scoring in 1st Q. Duke (1-8), playing better than record would indicate, ran for 214y as TB Julius Grantham gained 117y on ground. Grantham scored on catch of 7y pass from QB Steve Slayden (14-24/142y, 2 INTs) for brief 16-13 lead.

Maryland 42 MIAMI 40: Terrapins QB Frank Reich, foreshadowing similar playoff performance for Buffalo Bills in 1992, engineered greatest comeback in NCAA history. Maryland (6-3) was transformed into whole new team under Reich's leadership and erased 31-0 H deficit with 6 consecutive scoring drives in 2nd H. Replacing QB Stan Gelbaugh, Reich (12-15/260y, 3 TDs) threw 2 TDs and ran in 3rd in 3rd Q as Terps cut deficit to 34-21. TB Tommy Neal ran for 14y TD, and WR Greg Hill (8/182y) caught 68y TD off tipped pass for 35-34 lead. Terps added yet another score on 4y run by FB Rick Badanjek, but Hurricanes (8-3) crawled off mat as QB Bernie Kosar (30-53/363y, 2 INTs) threw his 4th TD, 5y pass to WR Eddie Brown. Miami's tying 2-pt conv failed when Maryland S Keeta Covington smothered HB Melvin Bratton after he caught pass short of GL. Biggest comebacks in college ball had been 28 pts, achieved by Oregon State against Fresno State in 1981 and equaled by Washington State against Stanford earlier this season. "I can see them scoring a few points in the second half," said losing coach Jimmy Johnson. "But so many, so quick? And shutting us down like that? Unbelievable!"

CLEMSON 17 Virginia Tech 10: Winning TD, scored by Clemson (7-2) WR Ray Williams on 17y reverse in 3rd Q, was set up by roughing-K PEN against Virginia Tech (7-3) on what simply would have been tying 49y FG by Tigers K Donald Igwebuike. Clemson coach Danny Ford gambled by taking 3 pts off board, which paid off for Tigers' 5th win in row. Hokies, who entered with 5-game win streak themselves, allowed 66y TD pass from QB Mike Eppley to WR Terrance Roulhac early in game, but settled down to allow only 165y apart from Roulhac's TD. Virginia Tech marched 96y to tie game in 2nd Q on TB Maurice Williams' 1y run and took 10-7 lead on 26y FG by K Don Wade after S Ashley Lee returned INT 26y to Clemson 9YL. Hokies QB Mark Cox threw for 233y but was unable to produce 2nd H pts.

SOUTH CAROLINA 38 Florida State 26: Bidding for Orange Bowl berth, Gamecocks (9-0) exploded out of gates for 38-7 lead as HB Thomas Dendy (14/113y) scored on TD runs of 57y and 2y, and HB Raynard Brown returned 2nd H KO 99y for another TD. Seminoles O, hampered by season-ending knee injury to TB Greg Allen and revolving door at QB, committed 9 TOs, including 7 INTs. Trailing 24-7 after Brown's TD, FSU proceeded to lose possession on 1st 4 series of 2nd H. Gamecocks S Bryant Gilliard led D with 4 INTs. Seminoles (6-2-1) made some noise behind TB Roosevelt Snipes (19/151y) and WR Jesse Hester (10/170y), but did most damage after game was long decided, scoring final 19 pts. For 1st time ever, South Carolina had won 9 games in 1 season.

Florida 27 Georgia 0 (Jacksonville): Amazing Gators (7-1-1) grabbed 7th victory in row and snapped 6-game series losing streak. QB Kerwin Bell (8-17/178y) teamed with WR Ricky Nattiel on 96y TD pass for 24-0 lead moments after Florida D, led by LB Alonzo Johnson, stopped 4 thrusts by Bulldogs (7-2) at 1YL. Gators D impressed throughout as it allowed only 59y passing, 186y overall in handing Georgia 1st shutout since 1979 and 1st loss in SEC to any team other than Auburn since 1978. Bell was walk-on frosh who would go on to win SEC Player of Year over more illustrious names. Georgia had only 46y O in 1st H, which was led 14-0 by Gators on 25y catch by TB Lorenzo Hampton and 2y vault by TB Neal Anderson. FB Andre Smith was Georgia's most effective runner with 74y rushing. Florida had not achieved 7 straight wins since 1966. It also was only 5th time in 33 tries that Florida had beaten Auburn and Georgia back-to-back.

Houston 29 TEXAS 15: Where was Texas legend Bobby Layne when you need him? QB Todd Dodge (2-16/23y) missed his 1st 13 pass attempts, 4 of which were indeed caught but by Cougars (5-4) defenders. Dodge's performance brought down boo birds, and he eventually was benched after 5th INT, which tied school record. Longhorns replacement QB Bret Stafford fumbled 1st snap, which led to Houston FG. Nine TOs in all did in unbeaten Longhorns (6-1-1), squelching national title aspirations and 18-game conf win streak. Houston QB Gerald Landry (4-17/123y, INT) did not throw much better but tossed 2 TDs, including 79y pass to WR Anthony Ketchem during 17-pt 2nd Q. Cougars CB DeWayne Bowden had excellent day, intercepting pass in his EZ and taking another INT all way to 62y TD to end scoring.

SOUTHERN CALIFORNIA 16 Washington 7: Trojans (8-1) knocked off top-ranked Huskies and grabbed Rose Bowl berth for 1st time since 1979. First H ended with Washington (9-1) scoring late in 2nd Q on 4y run by TB Jacque Robinson (15/57y) for 7-6 lead. QB Tim Green (13-28/161y)—now 6-0 as Trojan starter—led winning 68y drive that ended with TB Fred Crutcher's 2y scoring run. USC scorers were Crutcher (35/116y) and K Steve Jordan, who booted 3 FGs of 46, 47, and 51y. Huskies D entered game averaging 5 forced TOs per game, but could not jar loose FUM and picked off only 1 of Green's pass attempts. Nebraska, 41-7 conquerors of Kansas, became AP's new no. 1 team come Monday.

AP Poll November 12

1 Nebraska (37)	1148		11 Ohio State	636
2 South Carolina (11)	1104		12 Texas Christian	567
3 Brigham Young (11)	1096		13 Boston College	412
4 Oklahoma State	949		14 Miami	347
5 Florida	892		15 Georgia	321
6 Oklahoma	870		16 Southern Methodist	311
7 Southern California	805		17 Florida State	219
8 Washington	754		18 Auburn	203
9 Louisiana State	693		19 Virginia	167
10 Texas	643		20 Clemson	102

November 17, 1984

BOSTON COLLEGE 24 Syracuse 16 (Foxboro, Mass.): Memorable season for Boston College (7-2) continued as S Tony Thurman came up with his 10th INT of season with less than 2 mins left to both clinch win and deliver Cotton Bowl bid. BC last played on New Year's Day in 1943 Orange Bowl. With help from fierce wind, Syracuse (6-5) held QB Doug Flutie to season-low passing marks of 136y and no TDs. Trying vainly to force passes in 1st H, which they trailed 10-7, Eagles went to run game in 2nd H, rushing 28/178y—74y by fleet Flutie. TB Troy Stradford (21/102y) made go-ahead 5y TD late in 3rd Q. Flutie led drive to 25y FG by K Kevin Snow before Eagles D forced punt that WR Kelvin Martin took for 78y TD for 24-10 lead. Final TD came on 49y pass by Syracuse QB Mike Kmetz (10-17/200y, 2 INTs) to WR Scott Schwedes.

NAVY 38 South Carolina 21: Navy (4-5-1) sunk no. 2 Gamecocks' magical season behind D that shut down run and forced 6 TOs. Middies' banged up O played inspired ball to score on 3 straight 2nd H possessions—2 following INTs—to expand 14-7 H lead. QB Bob Misch (10-21/114y, 2 INTs), in for injured Bill Bryne, hit Middies WR Chris Weiler (6/108y) with pair of 2nd H TD strikes, while FB Mike Smith (18/96y) twice ran for TDs. Injured Navy TB Napoleon McCallum's replacement, TB Rich Clouse (12/97y), added 53y TD run. Gamecocks (9-1) had tied game 7-7 in 2nd Q on QB Allen Mitchell's 2y keeper, but were unable to score again until 4th Q after Navy had built 31-pt lead. Carolina D sorely missed injured LB James Seawright.

MISSISSIPPI STATE 16 Louisiana State 14: Upset loss and Florida's 25-17 win over Kentucky temporarily cost LSU (7-2-1) SEC crown until Tuesday's vote booted Gators from throne room. Still, Tigers had to be disappointed with loss as they surrendered 24y FG by K Artie Cosby, his 3rd of game, with 1:15 remaining. Mississippi State (4-6) backup QB Orlando Lundie threw for 157y and rushed for 115y, including wild 8y TD as Bulldogs snapped 4-game losing streak. QB Jeff Wickersham (12-27/195y, 3 INTs) threw 41y TD to WR Eric Martin (6/123y) to give Tigers, aiming for 1st SEC title since 1970, thin 14-7 lead in 2nd Q. LSU gained only 95y during decisive 2nd H in losing 5th straight to State, which had bounced Bayou Bengals from Sugar Bowl 2 years earlier on another late FG.

OHIO STATE 21 Michigan 6: Despite 2 conf losses, Buckeyes (9-2) were Rose Bowl-bound, thanks to 3 more TDs scored by TB Keith Byars on rushes totaling 5y. Michigan D held Byars (28/93y) to rare day with less than 100y rushing, but let QB Mike Tomczak (11-15/139y) find key completions. Ahead 7-6 after failed Michigan FG attempt, Buckeyes drove to TD as Tomczak hit WR Mike Lanese for 17y on 3rd-and-12 and WR Cris Carter for 15y moments later. Wolverines (6-5), who completed their worst regular season under coach Bo Schembechler, soon lost FUM by TE Sim Nelson (7/77y), recovered by Ohio CB William White at Michigan 37YL. Four plays later Byars scored his 22nd TD of season, and Buckeyes were Pasadena-bound. K Bob Bergeron did scoring for Michigan with FGs of 37 and 45y. In 6 seasons, Ohio State coach Earle Bruce led 3 Rose Bowl teams and compiled higher winning percentage than Woody Hayes, yet still lacked respect in Columbus.

NOTRE DAME 44 Penn State 7: TB Allen Pinkett (34/189y) and QB Steve Beuerlein (20-28/267y, INT) led Notre Dame (6-4) rout that easily snapped 3-game losing streak to Nittany Lions. Irish scored on their 1st 5 possessions to grab 31-7 H lead, with most impressive TD coming on 66y burst by Pinkett. With TB D.J. Dozier (10/44y) well-contained, rally chances were limited for Penn State (6-4) as its 3-headed pass game managed only 58y. Lions did, however, march 90y in 1st Q for TB Tony Mumford's 2y TD. Leading O that won y battle 543y to 169y, elusive and determined Pinkett scored 4 TDs to earn school's career mark of 40, 4 more than scored by "Red" Salmon (1901-03).

Oklahoma 17 NEBRASKA 7: Little-known Oklahoma (8-1-1) CB Brian Hall turned in play of game by stopping IB Jeff Smith head-on inches from GL on 4th down in 4th Q to preserve Sooners' 10-7 lead. Trying to extend 27-game Big 8 win streak and keep its national title hopes alive, no. 1 Nebraska (9-2) had marched from own 11YL to OU 1-foot-line, where it passed on game-tying FG after having missed 3 earlier tries. Smith, who scored Huskers TD, started up middle before running toward left sideline and unwelcome arms of Hall. GLS and 29y insurance TD run by QB Danny Bradley—set up later by Smith's punt FUM—propelled Oklahoma to 1st series win since 1980 and Huskers to "as disappointing a loss as we've had," as coach Tom Osborne observed. Considering past Orange Bowl, that was big. Huskers lost despite 19-9 1st down advantage and making whopping—for them—236y passing. Brigham Young, 24-14 winners over Utah, stepped up as new no. 1 in AP Poll.

Texas 44 TEXAS CHRISTIAN 23: Horned Frogs (8-2) had chance for 1st SWC crown in 25 years, and nervousness showed for TCU squad that had secured its 1st winning campaign in 13 years. Playing in front of largest crowd (47,280) in school history, TCU coughed up ball 6 times, losing 4, with 3 lost by RB Tony Jeffrey. Meanwhile, Longhorns (7-1-1) were paced by FB Terry Orr, who ran for 18/195y and scored 4 TDs, including 82y run and 63y pass-run with QB Todd Dodge (6-9/173y, 2 TDs). Dodge ran for 2 scores, while not throwing INT after pitching disastrous 5 against Houston week earlier. TCU RB Kenneth Davis ran for 16/102y, while WR James Maness caught 9/131y and 2 TDs.

UCLA 29 Southern California 10: Ask South Carolina; it was bad day for those with initials U-S-C. USC Trojans (8-2), who clinched Rose Bowl berth in previous week's win, fell to their cross-town rivals for 3rd straight year due to 5 TOs and UCLA K John Lee's 5 FGs. Bruins (8-3) scored 16 pts following TOs, including 63y INT TD RET by CB Dennis Price, and 10 more pts after short punts. Lee set single-season record for 3-ptrs with 29. USC QB Tim Green (18-39/226y), who gabbed about whipping UCLA in days prior, was sacked twice, pressured into 3 INTs, and involved in shouting matches. Injuries to TBs Danny Andrews of UCLA and Fred Crutcher of USC gave frosh, Gaston Green (18/134y) and Ryan Knight (25/100y), chances with Green becoming 1st back to crack 100y barrier against Trojans during 1984 season.

AP Poll November 19

1 Brigham Young (40)	1124		11 Southern Methodist	470
2 Oklahoma (7)	1053		12 Miami	466
3 Oklahoma State (3)	1042		13 Auburn	430
4 Florida (7)	1015		14 Southern California	381
5 Washington (1)	874		15 Florida State	350
6 Texas	830		16 Louisiana State	309
7 Nebraska	826		17 Texas Christian	277
8 Ohio State	768		18 Maryland	176
9 South Carolina	706		19 UCLA	97
10 Boston College	611		20 Georgia	76

November 22-24, 1984

GAME OF THE YEAR
(Fri) Boston College 47 MIAMI 45:

Behold "Hail Mary." Facts of Boston College (8-2) QB Doug Flutie's miracle pass have remained as follows: 6 secs were left; play call was "Flood Tip 55" as 3 WRs flooded GL and tipped ball to 4th receiver in EZ; line of scrimmage was Miami 48YL but Flutie dropped back to own 37YL to evade rush; pass was thrown into wind (although Miami faithful swear wind died down just as he threw); Miami defenders blanketed area between GL and 5YL (not believing that Flutie could throw pass as far as he did); WR Gerald Phelan was Flutie's roommate and best friend; Phelan was there to tip ball (until, of course, it hit him in hands in EZ); Flutie and Phelan had hooked up on successful "Flood Tip" 67y TD pass at end of 1st H of 24-10 win over Temple earlier in season; closest Miami player, DB Reggie Sutton, was hit as he attempted to bat down ball; Phelan was *falling backwards* as he reeled in biggest catch of his life, biggest catch in school history, and probably most replayed catch ever. Eagles usually practiced their special play on Thursdays, but did not on day before game as it rained. Flutie (34-46/472y, 3 TDs) was amazing, completing his 1st 11 attempts en route to his creating 4 TDs. Redoubtable Miami (8-4) QB Bernie Kosar (25-38/447y, 2 TDs) passed right with him, as teams combined for 1,282y in total O with 919y coming through air lanes. Each QB had favorite target in BC's Phelan (11/226y) and Miami WR Eddie Brown (10/220y). HB Melvin Bratton (16/134y) scored 4 times, including 52y run early in 4th Q and 1y scoring dive with 28 secs left to cap 79y drive that seemingly won game for Canes at 45-40. After game, Bicknell admitted that after Bratton scored he was thinking of how he would console team.

Maryland 45 VIRGINIA 34: FB Rick Badanjek stamped his name on 1984 by banging for 217y to lead Terps (8-3) to ACC sweep. Badanjek led powerful O that torched Virginia (7-2-2) D for 575y in topping 40-pt barrier for 5th time in 6 games. Maryland did its most damage with home run bursts: Badanjak had 65y TD run and another 72y run to set up score, while TB Alvin Blount (9/104y) added 72y TD run. Cavaliers' 9-game unbeaten streak went by boards even though they gained 527y in scoring 5 TDs. Virginia QB Don Majkowski threw for 219y and ran for early 3y TD. UVa led 7-3 when its D was stymied by loss of all-ACC DT Ron Mattes, who left at end of 1st Q with broken arm. Badanjek made his 65y TD on very next play.

Kentucky 17 TENNESSEE 12: Battle of bowl teams went way of Kentucky (8-3), which converted 1st of 4 TOs to take lead it would never relinquish. Tennessee (6-3-1) TB Charles Wilson lost FUM on 1st play from scrimmage that Wildcats turned into TD on 2y run by TB George Adams (30/110y), who topped 1,000y rushing for 3rd straight season. Vols managed rest of 1st H scoring with 2 FGs by K Fuad Reveiz, his 17th and 18th consecutive 3-ptrs, before Adams cashed in 1y scoring run in 3rd Q for 14-6 lead. Tennessee QB Tony Robinson (17-28/204y, 2 INTs) answered with 11y TD pass to WR Eric Swanson, but tying 2-pt conv run was stuffed. On Vols' last series, they marched to Kentucky 13YL before time expired.

OKLAHOMA 24 Oklahoma State 14: Cowboys (9-2) tied game 7-7 when QB Rusty Hilger (14-26/202y, 2 TDs, INT) hit diving WR Jamie Harris for 1y TD pass as 1st H ended. Oklahoma State doubled lead on 3rd play of 2nd H as Hilger clicked with WR Malcolm Lewis for 77y TD pass. Sooners (9-1-1) needed to rally to keep Orange Bowl and national title hopes alive. Soon after, HB Spencer Tillman (30/102y) ran in option pitchouts for 3 and 20y TDs in 2nd H, while OU D posted shutout over last 25 mins. Oklahoma State TOs led to Oklahoma's final 10 pts including game-winning 27y FG by K Tim Lashar late in 3rd Q. Sooners D shut down TB Thurman Thomas (11/29y), surrendering –4y net rushing while sacking Hilger 5 times.

BAYLOR 24 Texas 10: Baylor coach Grant Teaff did it again, beating Longhorns (7-2-1) for 5th time in past 6 games played in Waco to severely damage Texas' Cotton Bowl hopes. Texas QB Todd Dodge had mixed day, setting and tying school records for season passing yardage (1,441y) and completions (91), but throwing 3 INTs to break school season record with 17. Bears (5-6) scored 3 TDs, driving 18y and 24y after TOs, and later reaching EZ on 46y INT RET by S Thomas Everett. Game's leading rusher was Baylor FB Broderick Sargent with only 50y.

SOUTHERN METHODIST 31 Arkansas 28: Battle for share of SWC title went down to wire as Hogs (7-3-1) scored 3 4th Q TDs to nearly pull off miracle. SMU (8-2) had built 24-7 lead after 3 Qs as K Brandy Brownlee kicked 3 FGs and TB Reggie Dupard

rushed for 2 TDs. In explosive 4th Q, Arkansas QB Brad Taylor (20-28/261y, 2 INTs) threw his 2nd and 3rd TD passes of game and hustled for TD from 3YL. After Hogs pulled to within 24-20, Mustangs QB Don King (6-11/146y) answered with 79y pass to WR Ron Morris to set up winning 1y TD run by Dupard. Arkansas WR James Shibest caught 13/199y. SMU NG Jerry Ball had 13 tackles.

Notre Dame 19 SOUTHERN CALIFORNIA 7: Prepping for wet-ball snaps might have earned Fighting Irish 1st win in L.A. in 18 years. ND (7-4) had no snapping mishaps, while Trojans—who did not practice wet snaps—fumbled snap between C Tom Cox and QB Tim Green 5 times, 4 of which were recovered by Notre Dame. All 12 pts scored by ND after game was tied 7-7 in 2nd Q came after FUM RECs. ND TB Allen Pinkett made 98y on field that was in horrible condition, while Irish D, contained USC sweeps. Green threw for 179y to lead Trojans. Notre Dame K John Carney ignored pouring rain to boot pair of 45y FGs to produce only 2nd H pts.

AP Poll November 26

1 Brigham Young (34.5)	1148.5	11 Auburn	539
2 Oklahoma (18.5)	1128.5	12t Florida State	430
3 Florida (5)	1048	12t Texas	430
4 Washington (1)	991	14 Louisiana State	427
5 Nebraska	939	15 Maryland	391
6 Ohio State	837	16 Miami	325
7 South Carolina	830	17 UCLA	222
8 Boston College	764	18 Georgia	163
9 Oklahoma State	762	19 Notre Dame	116
10 Southern Methodist	612	20 Southern California	83

December 1, 1984

Army 28 Navy 11 (Philadelphia): Resurgent Cadets (7-3-1) won in series for 1st time since 1977 by unleashing potent Wishbone. Army marched 80y with 1st possession, which ended on 6y TD run by HB Clarence Jones, to take lead for good. Black Knights went 71y to 1y TD run by FB Doug Black for 14-0 lead. After Navy got on scoreboard with 40y FG by K Todd Solomon, Army CB Kermit McKelvy made huge play to help prevent rally. With QB Bob Misch (22-39/280y) driving Navy to possible TD, McKelvy separated WR Mark Stevens from ball with CB Eric Griffin recovering FUM in EZ. QB Nate Sassaman tallied 2 TDs in 2nd H as Army pulled away. Black rushed for 155y to set new Army single-season record of 1,148y, while Sassaman added 154y to finish with 1,002y rushing.

Georgia Tech 35 GEORGIA 18: Yellow Jackets (6-4-1) easily snapped 6-game series losing streak, blowing game open with 21-pt 2nd Q. TB Robert Lavette keyed rout with 109y rushing as he became 20th rusher in NCAA history to reach 4,000y. He finished with 4,066y, 17th best. Georgia Tech QB John Dewberry—who had turned down Georgia recruiters when told he might be moved from QB—burned blitzing Bulldogs with 2 TD passes to WR Gary Lee and 30y scoring draw in. Georgia (7-4) had early 3-0 lead on 57y FG by K Kevin Butler, his 1st of 3 as he finished with SEC record 353 pts. With 3 QBs combining for 4 INTs, while being sacked 4 times, Georgia would not score TD until 4th Q on WR Fred Lane's 72y punt RET. Georgia LB Knox Culpepper had 14 tackles, while Georgia Tech LBs Ted Roof and Jim Anderson each made 10 tackles.

Florida 27 FLORIDA STATE 17: Florida (9-1-1) completed its most successful season ever in grand, albeit wet, style, winning 4th straight against Seminoles (7-3-1). Heavy rain dictated better running team would win, and Gators clicked with 273y as TBs Neal Anderson and Lorenzo Hampton each rushed for 94y. Although Florida QB Kerwin Bell threw for only 71y, he produced team's 1st 2 TDs with scoring passes of 33y to WR Frankie Neal and 5y to FB John L. Williams. Trailing 17-3 at H, Florida State tapped 23y FG by K Derek Schmidt after Florida S Roger Sibbald lost FUM of punt on own 9YL. Hampton scored on 8y run in 3rd Q for commanding 24-7 lead. Seminoles TB Roosevelt Snipes rushed for 108y. Having been forced out of bowl system due to NCAA PENs, Gators wished to make statement for AP Poll with as impressive win as possible.

Alabama 17 Auburn 15 (Birmingham): Auburn, pack your bags for Memphis and Liberty Bowl. Needing win to secure Sugar Bowl berth, Tigers (8-4) passed on short FG try with 3:27 left—they had blown 3-pt try earlier on bad snap—to go for TD on 4th-and-goal from 1YL. Coach Pat Dye decided to use HB Bo Jackson (22/118y) as blocker, calling for pitchout to HB Brent Fullwood. Play blew up when Jackson went wrong way—depending on read play call could go either way—and bumped Fullwood, who was soon corralled at 4YL by trio of Alabama defenders: LB Randy Rockwell, CB Vernon Wilkerson and wrap-up tackler, frosh S Rory Turner. Auburn was able to get ball back for late missed 42y FG attempt by K Robert McGinty. After Jackson had opened scoring with 2y TD run, Crimson Tide (5-6) scored 17 straight pts, with HB Paul Ott Carruth (23/97y) sweeping for 2 TDs. Tigers made it 17-15 on Fullwood's 60y TD run with 9:11 left.

Tennessee 29 VANDERBILT 13: Emergence of Tennessee (7-3-1) QB Tony Robinson (20-31/273y, 2TDs) continued. Both of Robinson's scoring passes were to WR Tim McGee of 19y and 55y, and they came within 3 mins in 3rd Q for 26-0 lead. McGee collared 10/190y. When Vanderbilt (5-6) finally dusted off QB Kurt Page (11-22/111y), who was on sideline with bruised shoulder, he connected on 2 4th Q TDs, including 6y effort to WR Chuck Scott (10/121y). Vols TB Johnnie Jones rushed for 119y, including 57y TD run in 2nd Q, to claim SEC rushing crown for 2nd straight year at 1,290y. Robinson broke his coach Johnny Majors' Vols season completion percentage record with 61.7% to Majors' 61% toted up in 1956.

Texas A&M 37 TEXAS 12: Texas A&M (6-5) eliminated any suspense with dominating 1st H in which it invaded Austin for quick 20-0 tally en route to scoring most its most pts to date versus Texas. Aggies QB Craig Stump (11-22/168y, INT) led 4 scoring drives in opening 1st H, including 1st of 2 TD passes, 7y to WR Jeff Nelson. Led by FB Thomas

Sanders (15/83y), run game chugged for 287y to keep Longhorns at bay. Texas (7-3-1) used 2 QBs to throw for 248y and pair of 2nd H TDs, highlighted by QB Bret Stafford's coming off bench to throw 14y TD pass to TE William Harris (5/93y) in 3rd Q. Texas A&M K Eric Franklin kicked 3 FGs.

HOUSTON 38 Rice 26: With most of regular suspects back in mid-pack, Cougars (7-4) sewed up Cotton Bowl berth by tying SMU for SWC title and winning tiebreaker with victory over Mustangs on October 20. Houston became 1st SWC champion ever to have 2 losses. Cougars almost blew chance by allowing Rice (1-10) frosh QB Mark Comalander to throw for 357y off bench. Houston owned 13-0 lead on TD runs by HB Raymond Tate, who rushed for 205y, and HB Mat Pierson before Comalander entered in 2nd Q. He threw for 108y in 2nd Q to lead Owls to 1y TD run by TB Marc Scott. CB Dwayne Holmes then gave Rice lead with 43y INT TD RET, but Houston QB Gerald Landry made up for that mistake with 14y 3rd Q TD run, before Comalander threw 76y TD pass to WR Tony Burnett (6/139y). Rice now led 20-19, but Tate took over, rushing for TDs of 27y and 72y.

AP Poll December 3

1 Brigham Young (33.5)	1091.5	11 Louisiana State	525
2 Oklahoma (16.5)	1083.5	12 Maryland	484
3 Florida (6)	1033	13 Miami	416
4 Washington (1)	963	14 UCLA	342
5 Nebraska	888	15 Florida State	271
6 Ohio State	811	16 Auburn	213
7 South Carolina	808	17 Notre Dame	210
8 Boston College	767	18 Southern California	191
9 Oklahoma State	725	19 Texas	136
10 Southern Methodist	608	20 Wisconsin	74

Conference Standings

Atlantic Coast

Maryland	5-0
Virginia	3-1-2
North Carolina	3-2-1
Wake Forest	3-3
Georgia Tech	2-2-1
N.C. State	1-5
Duke	1-5
Clemson	5-2

Note: No games against ineligible Clemson were counted in ACC standings

Southeastern

Florida*	5-0-1
Louisiana State	4-1-1
Auburn	4-2
Georgia	4-2
Kentucky	3-3
Tennessee	3-3
Vanderbilt	2-4
Alabama	2-4
Mississippi	1-5
Mississippi State	1-5

* Florida's SEC championship was vacated

Big Ten

Ohio State	7-2
Illinois	6-3
Purdue	6-3
Iowa	5-3-1
Wisconsin	5-3-1
Michigan	5-4
Michigan State	5-4
Minnesota	3-6
Northwestern	2-7
Indiana	0-9

Mid-American

Toledo	7-1-1
Bowling Green	7-2
Central Michigan	6-2-1
Ohio	4-4-1
Northern Illinois	3-5-1
Miami	3-5
Ball State	3-5
Western Michigan	3-6
Kent State	3-6
Eastern Michigan	2-5-2

Big Eight

Oklahoma	6-1
Nebraska	6-1
Oklahoma State	5-2
Kansas	4-3
Kansas State	2-4-1
Missouri	2-4-1
Colorado	1-6
Iowa State	0-5-2

Southwest

Houston	6-2
Southern Methodist	6-2
Texas Christian	5-3
Arkansas	5-3
Texas	5-3
Baylor	4-4
Texas A&M	3-5
Texas Tech	2-6
Rice	0-8

Western Athletic

Brigham Young	8-0
Hawaii	5-2
Air Force	4-3
Utah	4-3-1
San Diego State	4-3-1
Wyoming	4-4
Colorado State	3-5
New Mexico	1-7
Texas-El Paso	1-7

Pacific-10

Southern California	7-1
Washington	6-1
UCLA	5-2
Arizona	5-2
Washington State	4-3
Arizona State	3-4
Oregon	3-5
Stanford	3-5
Oregon State	1-7
California	1-8

Pacific Coast Athletic

Nevada-Las Vegas*	7-0
Cal St.-Fullerton	6-1
San Jose State	5-2
Fresno State	3-4
Long Beach State	3-4
Pacific	2-5
New Mexico State	1-6
Utah State	1-6

* Championship vacated, all of UNLV's games forfeited

1984 Major Bowl Games

Independence Bowl (Dec. 15): Air Force 23 Virginia Tech 7

While pre-game attention centered on whether Virginia Tech DT Bruce Smith would play—he did, thanks to restraining order after NCAA had made him ineligible and had 8 tackles and sack—presence of Air Force (8-4) QB Bart Weiss was true key to game. Weiss rushed for 93y against nation's 2nd-ranked rush D, scoring on 13y run in 4th Q while hitting 6-7/49y. Hokies (8-4) enjoyed early 7-3 lead after 3y TD run by TB Maurice Williams (12/60y). In 2nd Q, Virginia Tech squandered lead after FUM by FB Nigel Bowe deep in its territory, which led to 3y TD run by Air Force HB Jody Simmons 1 play later. Sloppy Virginia Tech had 4 TOs, to none for disciplined Falcons. Hokies also committed 11 PENs/112y, to 4/30y by Air Force. In addition to Smith, who was ticketed for top spot in NFL draft, bright spot for Hokies D was LB Vince Daniels, who totaled 15 tackles.

Holiday Bowl (Dec. 21): Brigham Young 24 Michigan 17

National championships were meant to be secured on New Year's Day, but undefeated BYU (13-0) took command of top honors with win over so-so Michigan (6-6) Wolverines, who had finished tied for 6th in Big 10. Win was never sure thing, especially in 1st Q when QB Robbie Bosco left game with severely sprained ankle, sprained ligaments in left knee, and bruised ribs, all result of late hit by Wolverines DT Mike Hammerstein. Bosco soon returned and finished with 30-42/343y, 2 TDs passing despite being unable to plant left (front) foot firmly. With Cougars' O switched to Shotgun to save him stressful movement, Bosco led 80y drive, hitting 5-7/43y, to 5y TD run by HB Kelly Smith (10/88y) that started scoring. Wolverines knotted game 7-7 with their own 5y TD run, by TB Rick Rogers, before Cougars took 10-7 lead into H break on 31y FG by K Lee Johnson. Despite being outgained 483y to 202y for game, Michigan began to take over, thanks in part to 6 BYU TOs including 3 INTs by Bosco and his FUM into EZ that killed 1 BYU drive. Wolverines took 14-10 lead early in 4th Q on 10y TD pass from QB Chris Zurbrugg to FB Bob Perryman (13/110y) that capped 46y drive began after blocked FG by Michigan LB Tim Anderson that S Erik Campbell returned 25y. Only 65 secs later, Wolverines scored again as quick BYU FUM set up 32y FG by UM K Bob Bergeron. Gimpy Bosco had more left, completing 6 straight passes for last 59y of 80y drive to his tying 7y scoring pass to WR Glen Kozlowski. With game now knotted 17-17, teams suddenly found it difficult to score. Down to 1 last chance, BYU couldn't afford deadlock and sent Bosco out to be hero with his 13y TD pass to Smith with 83 secs to play. His TD throw became most important pass in history of Cougars, who since 1970s had given college football glimpse of its O future: QBs winging passes over every part of field. When it mattered, Cougars gained 184y to Michigan's –5y in 4th Q. Maligned BYU D came up with 2 big sacks on 3rd down in late-game series. "If you're number one going in, you're number one coming out," said Brigham Young coach LaVell Edwards. "Anybody that saw us win tonight, the way we won with such adversity, knows we earned it."

Cherry Bowl (Dec. 22): Army 10 Michigan State 6

In Army's heyday, it always snubbed bowl invitations. So, Cadets (8-3-1) of 1984 made 1st bowl appearance enjoyable with impressive win in Michigan State's backyard of Pontiac, Mich. Taking advantage of 2 Spartans FUMs, Army grabbed 10-0 lead on 4y run by HB Clarence Jones and 38y FG by K Craig Stopa. QB Dave Yarema (11-25/155y, 3 INTs) pulled Michigan State (6-6) to within 10-6 on 36y TD pass to WR Bob Wasczenski on 4th Q drive begun by FUM REC. With Cadets O playing ball control—dominating possession time by 34:05 to 25:55—and D containing TB Lorenzo White (23/103y) and forcing 5 TOs, Spartans were going nowhere. Army D also sacked Yarema 4 times. Black Knights QB Nate Sassaman, playing with flak jacket protecting cracked ribs, endured hamstring pull in 3rd Q, but his 136y still led running attack that gained 256y. "I was really sucking it down for a while, but I have the rest of my life to heal," said happy Sassaman. Bowl invitation was 1st for Michigan State since 1965 season.

Citrus Bowl (Dec. 22): Georgia 17 Florida State 17

Shaking off effects of both 3-game losing streak that ended season and NCAA investigation, Georgia (7-4-1) gave performance that worked everywhere but on scoreboard. It looked bad early for Bulldogs when QB Todd Williams left team's 2nd possession with toe injury, but frosh QB James Jackson—who was playing CB earlier in season—came off bench to earn MVP honors at head of O that gained 367y to 246y for Florida State. Jackson passed for 159y and added 36y rushing in leading Bulldogs to 17-9 lead in 4th Q, which was not quite enough to cement matters. Earlier, Seminoles (7-3-2) had rallied from 14-0 H deficit on 32y FG by K Derek Schmidt and 1y TD run by TB Tony Smith (10/65y), before Georgia K Kevin Butler nailed 36y FG. Trailing 17-9, Florida State forced punt near midfield and its punt-block specialist, NG Lenny Chavers, succeeded for 5th time this season. Ball bounced toward Bulldogs GL, and S Joe Wessel scooped it up for 13y TD RET. FSU used trick play for tying 2-pt conv, with WR Darrin Holloman scoring on reverse as he nabbed misdirected pitchout toward Smith. Georgia had time for just 70y FG attempt by Butler, which was short. Georgia TB Lars Tate (11/75y) scored TDs on runs of 4 and 2y, and CB Kevin Harris had 2 INTs to pace D.

Sun Bowl (Dec. 22): Maryland 28 Tennessee 27

Tennessee (7-4-1) knew that 21-0 H lead was not safe against comeback-confident Terps, who month earlier staged greatest comeback in college history. Sure enough, 3rd Q began, and Maryland (9-3) ran up 22 straight pts to take lead. With Vols O struggling—it gained only 82y in 2nd H—Tennessee needed big play to regain lead, getting it from TB Pete Panuska on 100y KO TD RET. Reversal proved no problem for Maryland O, which had entire 4th Q to score TD, doing so on 1y run by FB Rick Badanjek (21/90y, 2 TDs) that capped 12-play, 57y drive. Tennessee authored 1 more drive, marching into FG range before CB Keeta Covington ended matters with brutal hit on QB Tony Robinson (15-24/132y), forcing FUM to Keeta's brother, S Al Covington, on Maryland 30YL. Robinson's 6y TD pass to WR Tim McGee late in 2nd Q had capped Vols' great 1st H, in which they outgained Terps 195y to 55y. Maryland TB Tommy Neal (12/107y) began rally with 57y scoring run to end 1st possession of 2nd H. FUM by Robinson at Vols 23YL set up 1y TD run by Badajek as Terps trailed 21-15 after 2 straight failed 2-pt conv tries. On next series, Maryland earned brief go-ahead pts at 22-21 as QB Frank Reich (17-28/201y, INT) burned blitz with 40y TD pass to TE Ferrell Edmunds. "I had some real doubts that we could come back this time," said Terps coach Bobby Ross. "But somehow we keep doing it and doing it against some pretty good football teams."

Freedom Bowl (Dec. 26): Iowa 55 Texas 17

It was hard to imagine that Texas (7-4-1) was ranked 3rd as late as November 5, before its stunning freefall that ended with embarrassing Freedom Bowl rout. Despite rain in Anaheim, Hawkeyes (8-4-1) QB Chuck Long ripped apart Longhorns D, completing 29-39/461y and all-bowl record 6 TDs. Remarkably, Long missed his 1st 4 attempts and amazingly hit nearly 83 percent rest of way. Thanks to encouraging 17-pt flurry in 2nd Q, Texas trotted to locker room at H trailing only 24-17. Adjustments made by Hawkeyes worked to charm in 3rd Q, won by Black-and-Gold with 31 pts that got no answer from Texas. Long completed 12-14/241y, 4 TDs—excellent work for whole game—but achieved in 3rd Q alone. Five different targets caught scoring passes from Long, with TE Jonathan Hayes snaring pair, while both WR Bill Happel (8/104y) and WB Robert Smith (4/115y) exceeded 100y receiving. Texas QB Todd Dodge (16-32/180y, 2 INTs) threw for both Texas TDs, 11y to WR Bill Boy Bryant and 1y to TE William Harris. Iowa pt total represented 2nd most surrendered by Longhorns and most since 68-0 loss to University of Chicago way back in dusty days of 1904.

Liberty Bowl (Dec. 27): Auburn 21 Arkansas 15

Arkansas (7-4-1) D may have held Auburn (9-4) HB Bo Jackson (18/88y, 2 TDs) in check but couldn't keep good man down for long. Jackson burst through line for 40y TD run that clinched game in 4th Q. Razorbacks had pulled to within 14-9 earlier in 4th Q on 2y TD run by FB Marshall Foreman (15/62y), 3 plays after brutal hit by Hogs S Nathan Jones forced Tigers HB Brent Fullwood to fumble away to Jones at Auburn 6YL. Razorbacks soon forced punt and faced 4th-and-2 at Auburn 46YL. Surprise pass call was perfect as HB Bobby Joe Edmonds was wide open down right sideline, perfect except Edmonds dropped ball with no one near him. Instead of go-ahead TD, Arkansas was back on D and Jackson smartly burned Hogs after taking pitchout. After Jackson's TD, Arkansas scored again as QB Brad Taylor (17-34/201y, 2 INTs) threw 25y TD pass to WR James Shibest on 4th-and-18 with 3:10 left. Even though Auburn struggled on O (242y) throughout game, it was able to eliminate most of remaining time. Tigers CB Kevin Porter chipped in with key TD on 35y INT RET.

Gator Bowl (Dec. 28): Oklahoma State 21 South Carolina 14

Beginning last drive at own 12YL and trailing 14-13, Cowboys (10-2) moved to late victory behind QB Rusty Hilger (24-41/205y, INT). Although needing only FG, Hilger took Oklahoma State entire length of field, throwing 13y pass to TE Barry Hanna (8/92y) on 4th-and-6 at USC 49YL. TB Thurman Thomas (32/155y) then ran for 11y to set up Hilger's 25y TD pass to Hanna with 64 secs remaining. Hanna ran through tacklers to score 1st TD on season. Hilger threw for 2 more pts, hitting WR Jamie Harris on 2-pt conv. Gamecocks (10-2) rallied in 3rd Q to take lead after trailing 13-0 at H. Team then scored twice in 3rd Q despite holding ball for only 1:42 in period as HB Quinton Lewis threw 24y TD pass and then QB Mike Hold (7-20/170y, INT) tossed 57y scoring pass to WR Ira Hillary. That was it for struggling USC O that fumbled 6 times, losing 3, and finished with only 103y rushing. OSU scored twice in 1st H as Thomas ran in 1y TD and threw 6y scoring pass to Hilger.

Hall of Fame Bowl (Dec. 29): Kentucky 20 Wisconsin 19

Game came down to 4th Q FG contest as Kentucky (9-3) K Joe Worley booted 52y effort for 1-pt lead midway through final period that held up when Badgers holder Bob Kobza threw desperate EZ INT after bobbling snap on 26y attempt by K Todd Gregoire with 1:58 remaining. Winning FG was longest Worley would ever kick. Badgers' Gregoire kicked 4 FGs, with Wisconsin (7-4-1) building 13-0 lead on his initial 2 FGs and 3y TD pass from QB Mike Howard (19-29/203y) to WR Thad McFadden, who later set up FG with 67y punt RET. Wildcats rallied as TB Marc Logan scored 2 TDs and Worley kicked 2 FGs. Logan's 1st TD, on 9y run, had followed Kentucky S Paul Calhoun's INT late in 2nd Q. Badgers then raced downfield, scoring on Gregoire's 3rd FG for 16-7 H lead. Opponents traded 3rd Q FGs before Logan took screen pass from QB Bill Ransdell (18-34/188y) 27y for TD and 2-pt deficit. On Kentucky's next possession, TBs Mark Higgs and George Adams combined for 44y rushing to set up Worley's game-winner. Badgers next went to Kentucky 8YL in late going until botched FG try. "I wasn't really nervous," said Worley. "I wasn't thinking about it being the game-winner or anything like that. It was just another kick."

Aloha Bowl (Dec. 29): Southern Methodist 27 Notre Dame 20

Mustangs (10-2) jumped to 14-0 lead behind TBs Reggie Dupard (23/103y) and Jeff Atkins (17/112y, TD), who energized drives of 78y and 80y. Irish (7-5) answered with star TB of own, Allen Pinkett (24/136y), who scored on 17y TD reception. After teams traded long FGs—51y by ND K John Carney and 47y by SMU K Brandy Brownlee—Mustangs took 17-10 lead into H break. Notre Dame pulled even in 3rd Q as FB Mark Brooks plowed into EZ on 11y run. Ponies trotted to next 10 pts, but not without controversy. Brownlee kicked 30y FG following Dupard's FUM that was given back to SMU despite EZ REC by ND DB Pat Ballage. Dupard held onto ball on next possession, with his 2y scoring run that proved to be winning pts. After 31y FG by K John Carney, Irish's last chance began on own 23YL with 2:42 left, but after 14-play possession went over on downs at SMU 16YL as QB Steve Beuerlein's 3rd straight incompletion overshot WR Milt Jackson in EZ on 4th down. SMU won 10 games for 4th year in row.

Bluebonnet Bowl (Dec. 31): West Virginia 31 Texas Christian 14

Mountaineers (8-4) applied knockout punch early, scoring 31 1st H pts to end suspense. West Virginia gained 355y in opening H in scoring on 5 of 7 possessions. QB Kevin White (16-30/280y, INT) threw 3 TD passes, including 62y beauty to WR Gary Mullen that gave Mountaineers lead for good at 14-7 in 1st Q. TCU (8-4) could not maintain pace, especially when A-A RB Kenneth Davis (6/19y) went down with bruised calf early in contest. With deficit, Davis injury, and speedy Mountaineer D limiting their Veer O, Horned Frogs chose aerial route behind QB Anthony Gulley (9-14/150y). Both TCU scores came on passes by Gulley, but 2 of his late drives past West Virginia 25YL were halted: RB Barry Riddick fumbled, and other ended on downs. Elusive West Virginia WR Willie Drewery ran free in Frogs secondary all game to catch 6/152y.

Peach Bowl (Dec. 31): Virginia 27 Purdue 24

Cavaliers (8-2-2) celebrated 1st-ever bowl appearance with exciting victory, rallying to score game's final 13 pts. Purdue (7-5) scored 2 TDs in final 6 mins of 2nd Q to earn 24-14 edge at H break. Keyed by D that posted 2nd H shutout, Virginia scored on 2 early possessions of 2nd H to tie game on 1y TD run by QB Don Majkowski (8-17/118y, TD, 2 INTs) and 19y FG by K Kenny Stadlin. Purdue TB Ray Wallace soon lost FUM on own 42YL, recovered by UVa DT Scott Matheson with 9:50 left to play. On move, Cavs faced 4th-and-goal from 1YL and opted for go-ahead 22y FG by Stadlin. QB Jim Everett (2-42/253y, 3 INTs), who threw 3 1st H TDs, rekindled Boilermakers for 42y advance to Virginia 25YL until Cavs CB Ray Daly picked off pass intended for WR Steve Griffin. Daly (2 INTs), who had surrendered TD to Griffin on same pattern in 1st H, adjusted beautifully to make game's big D play. Riding O-Line and TB Howard Petty (21/114y), Virginia happily churned out 4 1st downs to wipe out remaining 5 mins of contest.

Fiesta Bowl: UCLA 39 Miami 37

Wild offensive show ended on, of all things, big hit by D player as Bruins (9-3) NG Terry Tumey forced FUM by Hurricanes QB Bernie Kosar (31-44/294y, INT), recovered by LB Eric Smith near midfield to end Miami's final series. Moments earlier, K John Lee kicked game-winning 22y FG with 51 secs left to boost UCLA to 3rd straight bowl win. Canes (8-5) opened with 21-7 lead with long TDs by: 34y run by HB Darryl Oliver, 68y punt RET by WR Eddie Brown, and 48y pass from Kosar to WR Brian Blades. With 10 mins left in H, it was UCLA's turn to score in highlight reel manner, as TB Gaston Green (144y, 2 TDs) raced 72y for score. Bruins D came up with safety and Lee booted 2 FGs for 22-21 lead. After K Greg Cox put Miami out front with 31y FG in 3rd Q, Bruins leapt ahead 36-24 early in 4th Q as QB Steve Bono (18-27/243y) threw 2 TD passes. Hurricanes answered with 2 TDs themselves when HB Melvin Bratton capped 60 and 79y drives with 19y run and 3y catch for 37-36 lead with just less than 4 mins left, which was sufficient time enough for Bono and Lee.

Cotton Bowl: Boston College 45 Houston 28

On Eagles' 2nd possession, Boston College (10-2) QB Doug Flutie (13-37/180y) hooked up with WR Kelvin Martin for 63y scoring bomb, and Eagles never looked back. Boston College NG Mike Ruth soon pounced on FUM, and BC had another TD on 8y catch by TB Troy Stradford, who rushed for 198y. CB Earl Allen quickly cut Houston's deficit in half with 98y KO RET, but 1st Q scoring reached 24 combined pts when INT by BC S Tony Thurman set up 31y FG by K Kevin Snow. Eagles upped lead to 31-7 on Flutie's 13y pass to WR Gerard Phelan (7/94y) and 2y TD run by FB Steve Strachan. Houston (7-5) was too explosive to keep down for long, and QB Gerald Landry, who rushed for 100y and threw for 154y, tossed 15y TD to WR Larry Shepherd late in 1st H. In 3rd Q, he then led 65y drive that ended with RB Raymond Tate's 2y TD run. Flutie had poor 2nd H as attested by 2-13 with 2 INTs, and his INT on next series by S Audrey McMillian was returned 25y for Houston's 2nd TD within min. Suddenly, BC led only 31-28. Boston College O-Line proved itself by dominating 4th Q with rushing TDs by Strachan (23/91y) and Stradford to set Cotton Bowl records for pts and total yards (537y) and secure 1st bowl win since 1941. "BC is just a real good football team," said Houston coach Bill Yeoman. "It was evident today that there is a lot more to BC than just Doug Flutie."

Rose Bowl: Southern California 20 Ohio State 17

Champion of Pac-10 won another Rose Bowl as underdog Trojans (9-3) built 17-6 H lead and held on down stretch. Ohio State (9-3) QB Mike Tomczak (24-37/290y) threw 18y TD pass to WR Cris Carter midway through 4th Q and ran for 2 pts as Buckeyes pulled to within 20-17. Ohio State had final chance as Tomczak drove into USC territory until 3 straight incompletions ended drive on downs. USC D had set game's tone by holding Ohio to 113y rushing—including 4 sacks of Tomczak—and picking him off thrice. Troy CB Tommy Haynes made 2 INTs. Trojans also forced FG when Buckeyes had 1st-and-goal at 5YL. On O, Southern California enjoyed 2 TD passes from QB Tim Green (13-24/128y) in 1st H: 3y to TE Joe Cormier and 19y to WR Timmie Ware. Trojans K Steve Jordan proved to be difference with pair of 51y FGs, 1st of which set Rose Bowl record for distance until Ohio State K Rich Spangler kicked 52y FG for new mark. Carter, who caught 9/172y, and TB Keith Byars, who rushed for 109y, were top performers for Buckeyes. Byars, however, was held in check after 50y run in 1st Q.

Orange Bowl: Washington 28 Oklahoma 17

Which team was no. 2 Oklahoma (9-2-1) more worried about, Washington or no. 1 Brigham Young? Huskies (11-1) took advantage of what might have been loss of focus by Sooners by using 2 TDs scored within min of 4th Q to earn upset. They got some unusual help from OU cheerleaders as well. Teams were tied 14-14 at H, and score remained same entering 4th Q. Sooners advanced into Washington territory and opted for go-ahead 22y FG attempt by K Tim Lashar. FG flew through uprights, but OU was penalized 5y for illegal procedure. Onto turf came Oklahoma cheerleaders driving "Sooner Schooner" wagon, which officials flagged for being on field illegally in prematurely celebrating ill-fated FG. This flag cost additional and embarrassing 15y. Lashar now faced 42y attempt, which was blocked by Washington S Tim Peoples. Sooners D forced punt, and Lashar got his FG, from 35y, for 3-pt lead. Somehow, air was escaping from Sooners' balloon. It was Washington's turn, and Huskies reached EZ on 12y pass from QB Hugh Millen to WR Mark Pattison. Only 54 secs later, UW LB Joe Kelly sealed deal with INT that set up 6y TD run by FB Rick Fenney. Millen had come off bench to replace QB Paul Sicuro, who had started scoring with 29y pass to WR Danny Greene, but endured 3 INTs. TB Jacque Robinson led Washington O with 135y, TD, rushing. QB Danny Bradley had role in both TDs by Oklahoma, rushing 1y and throwing 61y pass to WR Derrick Shepard to end 1st H. "We're number one," said Huskies coach Don James. "When you beat a team like Oklahoma, your kids deserve to be number one." Poll voters felt otherwise.

Sugar Bowl: Nebraska 28 Louisiana State 10

In home state, LSU Tigers really came to play in opening H, scoring on 2 of 1st 3 possessions for 10-0 lead. Bayou Bengals did most damage through air as QB Jeff Wickersham threw for 17-25/212y in 1st H, but largely was frustrated near Nebraska's GL. Most painful was LSU drive that reached 1-inch-line before PEN forced missed FG. Cornhuskers O showed no panic, getting on scoreboard before H on IB Doug DuBose's 31y TD reception. Nebraska QB Craig Sundberg (10-15/143y, 2 INTs), returning to lineup after midseason injury, added 9y scoring run in 3rd Q for permanent lead and threw 2 more TD passes in 4th Q. Facing D that began to drop extra defender into coverage, Wickersham was picked off 4 times in completing only 3-12/9y in 2nd H against Huskers D that forced 6 TOs overall. DuBose (20/102y) and IB Jeff Smith (17/84y) led rushing attack that boasted 280y, while Tigers TB Dalton Hilliard gained 86y and 2y TD.

Final AP Poll January 2

1 Brigham Young (38)	1160	11 South Carolina	557
2 Washington (16)	1140	12 Maryland	552
3 Florida (6)	1092	13 Ohio State	497
4 Nebraska	1017	14 Auburn	432
5 Boston College	932	15 Louisiana State	314
6 Oklahoma	883	16 Iowa	228
7 Oklahoma State	864	17 Florida State	207
8 Southern Methodist	761	18 Miami	166
9 UCLA	613	19 Kentucky	152
10 Southern California	596	20 Virginia	119

1984 Top Performance Formula

1 Brigham Young	1.6611
2 Florida	1.6139
3 Washington	1.6044
4 Nebraska	1.5860
5 Oklahoma State	1.5086
6 Boston College	1.4958
7 Oklahoma	1.4365
8 Southern Methodist	1.4217
9 Maryland	1.3934
10 Ohio State	1.3840
11 South Carolina	1.3797
12 Southern California	1.3771
13 Louisiana State	1.3591
14 West Virginia	1.3456
15 Auburn	1.3241
16 Virginia	1.3228
17 Florida State	1.3162
18 Arkansas	1.3123
19 Kentucky	1.3010
20 Tennessee	1.2985

1984 Top Opponent Records

1 Syracuse	.6404
2 Tennessee	.6310
3 Georgia	.6280
4 West Virginia	.6048
5 Penn State	.6043
6 Boston College	.6016
7 Texas	.5969
8 Florida	.5966
9 Baylor	.5958
10 Notre Dame	.5930
11 Stanford	.5921
12 Southern California	.5880
13 Michigan	.5878
14 Pittsburgh	.5855
15 Louisiana State	.5766
16 Alabama	.5690
17 Auburn	.5657
18 Clemson	.5643
19 Houston	.5635
20 Miami	.5612

1984 Out-of-Conference Records

	W-L	Percentage	Bowl W-L
Southeastern	36-15-2	.6981	2-2-1
Pacific-10	24-12	.6667	3-0
Southwest	14-11-2	.5556	1-4
Atlantic Coast	15-14	.5172	2-0
Big Eight	14-17-1	.4531	2-1
Big Ten	12-15	.4444	1-5
Western Athletic	13-17	.4333	2-0

1984 Individual Statistical Leaders

RUSHING YARDS	Attempts	Yards	Avg.
Keith Byars, Ohio State	313	1655	5.3
Rueben Mayes, Washington State	258	1637	6.3
Kenneth Davis, Texas Christian	211	1611	7.6
Johnnie Jones, Tennessee	229	1290	5.6
George Swarn, Miami (Ohio)	269	1282	4.8
Dalton Hilliard, Louisiana State	254	1268	5.0
Ethan Horton, North Carolina	238	1247	5.2
Curtis Adams, central Michigan	222	1204	5.4
Robert Lavette, Georgia Tech	260	1189	4.6
Reggie Dupard, Southern Methodist	196	1157	5.9

PASSING YARDS	Completions	Attempts	Yards	Pct.
Robbie Bosco, Brigham Young	283	458	3875	61.8
Bernie Kosar, Miami	262	416	3642	63.0
Doug Flutie, Boston College	233	386	3454	60.4
Kevin Sweeney, Fresno State	227	421	3259	53.9
Doug Gaynor, Long Beach State	248	385	3230	64.4
Jim Everett, Purdue	227	389	3003	58.4
Brian McClure, Bowling Green	263	414	2951	63.5
Jack Trudeau, Illinois	247	378	2724	65.3
Bob Frasco, San Jose State	221	387	2688	57.1
Randall Cunningham, UNLV	208	332	2628	62.7

RECEIVING YARDS	Catches	Yards
David Williams, Illinois	101	1278
Larry Willis, Fresno State	79	1251
Eddie Brown, Miami	59	1114
Charles Lockett, Long Beach State	75	1112
Steve Griffin, Purdue	60	991
Gerard Phelan, Boston College	64	971
Tracy Henderson, Iowa State	64	941
James Shibert, Arkansas	51	907
Glen Kozlowski, Brigham Young	55	879
Willie Smith, Miami	66	852

1984 Consensus All-America Team
Offense

Wide Receiver:	David Williams, Illinois
	Eddie Brown, Miami
Tight End:	Jay Novacek, Wyoming
Tackle:	Bill Fralic, Pittsburgh
	Lomas Brown, Florida
Guard:	Del Wilkes, South Carolina
	Jim Lachey, Ohio State
	Bill Mayo, Tennessee
Center:	Mark Traynowicz, Nebraska
Quarterback:	Doug Flutie, Boston College
Running Back:	Keith Byars, Ohio State
	Kenneth Davis, Texas Christian
	Reuben Mayes, Washington
Placekicker:	Kevin Butler, Georgia

Defense

Line:	Bruce Smith, Virginia Tech
	Tony Degrate, Texas
	Ron Holmes, Washington
	Tony Casillas, Oklahoma
Linebacker:	Gregg Carr, Auburn
	Jack Del Rio, Southern California
	Larry Station, Iowa
Back:	Jerry Gray, Texas
	Tony Thurman, Boston College
	Jeff Sanchez, Georgia
	David Fulcher, Arizona State
	Rod Brown, Oklahoma State
Punter:	Ricky Anderson, Vanderbilt

1984 Heisman Trophy Vote

Doug Flutie, senior quarterback, Boston College	2240
Keith Byars, junior tailback, Ohio State	1251
Robbie Bosco, junior quarterback, BYU	443
Bernie Kosar, sophomore quarterback, Miami	320
Kenneth Davis, senior running back, TCU	86

Other Major Awards

Maxwell (Player)	Doug Flutie, senior quarterback, Boston College
Walter Camp (Player)	Doug Flutie, senior quarterback, Boston College
Outland (Lineman)	Bruce Smith, senior defensive end, Virginia Tech
Lombardi (Lineman)	Tony Degrate, senior defensive tackle, Texas
Davey O'Brien (QB)	Doug Flutie, senior quarterback, Boston College
AFCA Coach of the Year	LaVell Edwards, Brigham Young

The Year of Back to Basics after Aikman's Knockout, Close Heisman Shave, and Eddie Winning his 324th

Back in 1982, Oklahoma's big-shot running back recruit Marcus Dupree sufficiently turned coach Barry Switzer's head to prompt experimentation with Dupree as featured back in a power-I attack. Dupree had a remarkably short career, but the Sooners soon adapted their offensive scheme to the skills of another touted newcomer, quarterback Troy Aikman, who was possibly the best passer ever recruited to Norman.

There was every reason to believe Oklahoma (11-1) was entering a new era as Aikman was named starter for 1985. But, Aikman was knocked out for the season in the fourth game, and Switzer had little choice but to return full-time to the basic Wishbone offense with which the Sooners had become the scourge of college football in the 1970s. With gifted 5'9" QB Jamelle Holieway at the helm, the Sooners took off on the 500-yard offensive clip of old, and, thanks also to their explosive defense led by All-America linemen Tony Casillas and Kevin Murphy and linebacker Brian Bosworth, opponents began to fall. A surprisingly easy win over Nebraska (9-3) thrust them into an Orange Bowl showdown with undefeated Penn State (11-1). The Nittany Lions' rugged defense gave Oklahoma a tough time for awhile in the bowl game before succumbing by 25-10. Thanks to Tennessee (9-1-2) routing second-ranked Miami (10-2) in the Sugar Bowl, Oklahoma's sixth national title became the first championship claimed by an Associated Press pre-season number one team since Alabama turned the trick in 1978.

Meanwhile, Aikman was on the mend but had become all but forgotten. He transferred to UCLA after the season, and when he became an instant passing star for the Bruins in 1987, he qualified as perhaps the greatest college player ever to transfer from one major school to another.

Miami was the Sooners' only master as it inflicted the only regular season defeat on Oklahoma for each of the next three years. The Hurricanes' use of a high-octane passing attack featuring quarterback Vinny Testaverde to compliment a speedy defense seemed like kryptonite to Oklahoma's Superman. It was all the more intriguing that Miami was coached by brash Jimmy Johnson, a friend of Switzer's from their days together at Arkansas.

Standing in contrast to the perceived win-at-all-costs philosophy of Switzer and Johnson was Penn State coach Joe Paterno, who celebrated his 20th season as head man in State College with his fifth perfect regular season. His Nittany Lions were not flashy, attracted low-level attention, and seemed to like it that way.

As the race for the national title went down to the wire, so too did the battle for the Heisman Trophy. Magnificent Auburn (8-4) tailback Bo Jackson edged the sharp-passing Iowa (10-2) quarterback Chuck Long by 45 points (1,509 to 1,464) to win the closest vote ever staged by New York's Downtown Athletic Club. Jackson won his own South region, while also grabbing the Mid-Atlantic and Southwest. Long was first in the Midwest, Northeast, and West regions. Each had flashy numbers, but Jackson shaved Long despite his missing time with injuries in losses to Tennessee and Florida (9-1-1). He also lost the national rushing crown to Lorenzo White of Michigan State (7-5) by 1,908 yards to 1,786. The Heisman's previous tightest race had come in 1961, when Syracuse's halfback Ernie Davis edged Ohio State fullback Bob Ferguson by 53 points.

Long's heady career signaled a new era of Big Ten play. Long, Jack Trudeau of Illinois (6-5-1), Jim Everett of Purdue (5-6), Jim Harbaugh of Michigan (10-1-1), and Jim Karsatos of Ohio State (9-3) all had big years throwing the ball in a conference made famous by its power football of olden days. That Illinois and Purdue would have good passers was to be expected, but it was surprising to see the Wolverines' Harbaugh lead the nation in passing efficiency with Long third and Karsatos fourth. The injured foot that ruined most of running back Keith Byars' season allowed the Buckeyes passing game to edge the rushers in yardage, something that would have been unthinkable in the Ohio State program of the past. As for Long, he led Iowa to the Hawkeyes' first no. 1 ranking since 1961—they held the top spot for five weeks beginning on September 30—and into the Rose Bowl, where their hopes for national title consideration were dashed by UCLA (9-2-1).

The Southeastern Conference may not have turned pass-crazy, but it featured a wild race that ended with Tennessee and Florida tied for first place with 5-1 records. Although Tennessee lost to the Gators, it was awarded the conference crown due to probation that shackled Florida. The Sugar Bowl appearance was the first for the Volunteers since 1970. Euphoria over the SEC title and subsequent 35-10 pasting of Miami was lost in January of 1986 when talented quarterback Tony Robinson was busted on drug charges. Steroids continued to dominate headlines, with Southern schools like Tennessee, Vanderbilt (3-7-1), and Clemson (6-6) among many dealing with the problem. The investigation at Clemson began after the drug-related death of Augustinius Jaspers of the Tigers' track team.

On a more positive note in the South, Eddie Robinson, who began coaching at Grambling (9-3) in 1941, entered the season with a 320-106-15 mark—three wins short of Bear Bryant's record total. Robinson, the son of a sharecropper, tied Bryant's career mark with a 23-6 win over Oregon State (3-8) on September 28. One week later, he passed Bryant with his team's 27-7 win over Prairie View A&M (2-9). With a legacy that included a 95 percent graduation rate and former players dotting both the rosters of the NFL and the National Honor Roll, Robinson, who finished the season with 329 wins, was showered with well-deserved national attention. Of course, a scant number of his victories were recorded over Division 1-A competition, so Bryant remained in the coaching pantheon for subsequent assaults by Paterno and Bobby Bowden.

One coach was on the other end of the victory spectrum. Gerry Faust, Mr. Nice Guy of Notre Dame (5-6), ended his short run with a crushing 58-7 rout administered by Miami. Faust finished with a 30-26-1 record with the Fighting Irish, losing more games in five seasons than had been visited upon legends Knute Rockne and Frank Leahy in a combined 24 years. George Welsh, Jack Bicknell, Don Shula, Dick Vermeil, Jim Young, Howard Schnellenberger, and Terry Donahue all were mentioned as candidates to replace Faust before Lou Holtz got the job one day after Faust resigned on November 26.

Schnellenberger was busy trying to rebuild at Louisville (2-9). The Cardinals dropped their opener 52-13 to West Virginia (7-3-1) and things got no better. The pipe-smoking coach of Miami's 1983 national champions would never approach the same success at Louisville or at any of his future stops, which briefly would include Oklahoma.

The Southwest Conference continued on a path to self-destruction as the NCAA capped a 29-month investigation of pre-season no. 3 Southern Methodist (6-5) by levying severe reductions in scholarships, denial of television money, and limitation of eligibility for both conference titles and bowl games. The Mustangs' juiciest rule violation was cash payoffs to players of up to $11,000. The severity of the punishment was due to a repeated pattern of wrongdoing: SMU had been penalized four times in 11 years and been found guilty of infractions during 11 of 14 years. During the season, word broke of "sugar daddies" taking care of Texas A&M (10-2) players. TCU (3-8) coach Jim Wacker suspended seven players, including star running back Kenneth Davis, for accepting cash payments while being recruited during the days of past coach F.A. Dry. Davis lost a lawsuit to try to immediately turn professional.

The service academies had up and down seasons as Air Force (12-1) finished eighth in the final poll, while Army (9-3) won nine games for the first time since 1949. Navy (4-7) was held back by injuries that slowed star back Napoleon McCallum. Navy beat Army, however, and McCallum finished his illustrious career with 7,172 all-purpose yards and finished seventh in Heisman balloting.

A horrible accident at The Citadel (5-5-1) occurred when linebacker Marc Buoniconti, son of former NFL star Nick, was paralyzed while making a tackle. Marc and Nick soon launched The Miami Project to Cure Paralysis, and since then have raised millions of dollars to help fund medical research for paralyzed people of all sorts.

Milestones

■ Orlando's Downtown Athletic Club created annual Butkus Award to nation's best linebacker.

■ For first time, NCAA allowed players to insure themselves from injury. In rules committee changes, pass blocking was liberalized to allow better protection of passers.

■ Denver judge invoked separation of church and state law to restrict Colorado coach Bill McCartney's ability to lead pre-game prayers as he was considered to be state employee.

■ Former Notre Dame star Paul Hornung won $1.16 million lawsuit against NCAA for refusal to allow him to work as broadcaster for WTBS in 1982-83 due to his promotional ties to gambling services and beer companies.

■ Jerome "Brud" Holland, two-time All-America end at Cornell in 1938-39 and president of both Delaware State College and Hampton Institute, died of cancer at age 69 on January 13. Holland served on numerous boards, including American Red Cross, and was ambassador to Sweden in 1970-'72. Notre Dame all-time great center Adam Walsh, captain of 1924 national champions, died at 83 on January 31. Leader of "The Seven Mules" line, Walsh helped pave way for "Four Horsemen" backfield before becoming coach at Bowdoin College (34-15-6) and then NFL Rams, where he won title in 1945. Francis "Whitey" Wistert, first of 3 brothers to have hall of fame careers at Michigan, died on April 23 at age 75. Wistert was dominant tackle for 1937 Wolverines that went 7-0-1. Gene "Wild Bull" McEver, 1st All-America for Tennessee as halfback in 1929, died on July 12 at age 76. Leading Vols to 27-0-3 record in his 3 seasons (1928-29, '31), McEver led nation with 130 pts in his sophomore season. Apparently due to financial plight of his family's farm, Nebraska tight end Brian Heimer, former 10th-string, walk-on player who worked himself up to co-starter status, died on August 14 from self-inflicted gunshot to head. Heimer had 12 catches for 174 yards in 1984. Nebraska halfback Bobby Reynolds, who set NCAA record for points per game in season with 17.4 in 1950, died of cerebral hemorrhage on August 19 at age 54. Rushing for 1,342y in 1950, Reynolds was named All-America in leading Cornhuskers to first winning season at 6-2-1 since 1940. He scored 211 points and rushed for 2,196 yards in his career. Frank "Bruiser" Kinard, legendary tackle who was Mississippi's 1st All-America in 1936, and 5-time All-Pro in NFL, died September 8 at age 70. Iron man Kinard averaged 55 mins per game for Rebels. Two-time All-America Don Stephenson, part of Georgia Tech's heritage of great centers under Bobby Dodd, died in car accident at age 50 on November 25.

■ Longest winning streaks entering the season:
Brigham Young 24　　Florida 9　　Maryland 7

■ Coaching Changes:

	Incoming	Outgoing
Arizona State	John Cooper	Darryl Rogers
Ball State	Paul Schudel	Dwight Wallace
East Carolina	Art Baker	Ed Emory
Louisville	Howard Schnellenberger	Bob Weber
Missouri	Woody Widenhofer	Warren Powers
Northern Illinois	Jerry Pettibone	Lee Corso
Oregon State	Dave Kragthorpe	Joe Avezzaro
Tulane	Mack Brown	Wally English
Utah	Jim Fassel	Chuck Stobart

AP Preseason Poll
1 Oklahoma (23)	1090	11 Illinois (2)	599
2 Auburn (13)	1027	12 Washington (2)	578
3 Southern Methodist (13)	924	13 Louisiana State	447
4 Iowa (7)	837	14 Notre Dame	426
5 Florida (4)	788	15 Arkansas	378
6 Southern California	754	16 Oklahoma State	319
7 Maryland (3)	738	17 South Carolina	309
8 Ohio State	609	18 Penn State	218
9 Nebraska	676	19 Florida State	195
10 Brigham Young (1)	608	20 UCLA	175

August 31, 1985

(Th) Brigham Young 28 Boston College 14 (East Rutherford, NJ): Cougars (1-0) won 25th straight game in Kickoff Classic as QB Robbie Bosco completed 35-53/508y, 3 TDs. BYU WR Glen Kozlowski (10/241y, TD) made play of game with backward-falling 40y catch that set up 2nd TD. Boston College (0-1) drove 80y to tie score 14-14 in 3rd Q on 5y TD run by TB Troy Stradford (21/104y). After trade of TOs, Bosco fired 51y pass to Kozlowski on 12y toss to WR Mark Bellini (9/111y) for winning TD. Eagles D had 4 INTs and NG Mike Ruth ignored double teams to make 4 sacks, 8 tackles, and INT. BC QB Shawn Halloran threw for 165y with 3 INTs in starting debut. Game marked 4th straight year Eagles had met defending national championship team: they tied Clemson in 1982 and knocked off Penn State in 1983 and Miami in 1984.

PITTSBURGH 31 Purdue 30: Purdue (0-1) came, oh, so close with 49 secs left: QB Jim Everett completed desperation pass to FB Ray Wallace for 31y TD to pull Boilermakers to within 31-30. Purdue opted to try for win, running play that left TE Jack Beery open in EZ. Everett (34-53/398y, 2 INTs) threw low pass into turf, ending any chance at victory. QB John Congemi (10-19/110y) threw 2 TD passes in helping Pitt (1-0) build 21-10 H lead that was erased when Everett threw 2 TD passes in 3rd Q. Panthers regained lead as TB Charles Gladman (24/163y, 2 TDs) ran for 10y TD, and K Mark Brasco booted 43y FG that proved to be game-winner.

Oregon 42 WASHINGTON STATE 39: Ducks (1-0) unleashed "Quack Attack" as QB Chris Miller threw for 259y, 3 TDs, TB Tony Cherry rushed for 143y, TD, and WR Lew Barnes caught 8/120y, 2 TDs. Oregon D held TB Rueben Mayes—who had tattooed it for NCAA-record 357y rushing in 1984—to comparably paltry 84y. With Ducks focused on ground D, Cougars (0-1) went to air as QB Mark Rypien threw 21-38/403y, 4 TDs. But Rypien also lost 3 FUMs, including pair that set up Oregon TDs, including winning 5y pass to TE Bobby DeBisschop with 6:46 left.

(Mon) Alabama 20 GEORGIA 16: It looked like Georgia (0-1) had stolen late win as LB Terrie Webster blocked punt of Alabama P Chris Mohr, which was recovered by DE Cal Ruff in EZ for go-ahead TD with 50 secs left. Suddenly, Crimson Tide (1-0) QB Mike Shula—who had thrown for only 65y to that moment—directed 71y drive without timeouts to stun Stanford Stadium faithful. After missing his 1st pass, Shula hit WRs Greg Richardson and Albert Bell with 3 passes/54y. That took Bama to Georgia 29YL with 20 secs left. Shula soon avoided blitz to hit Bell over middle for winning 17y TD. With top 3 QBs hobbled with injuries, frosh QB Wayne Johnson had directed Bulldogs' sole TD drive, throwing 11y TD pass to WR Jimmy Hockaday to pull Georgia to within 13-9 with 4:21 left.

AP Poll September 3
1 Oklahoma (27)	1149	11 Illinois (1)	559
2 Auburn (10)	948	12 Washington (1)	521
3 Southern Methodist (2)	834	13 Louisiana State	383
4 Iowa (5)	810	14 Notre Dame	367
5 Florida (2)	735	15 Arkansas	307
6 Southern California (1)	715	16 Oklahoma State	301
7 Maryland (3)	701	17 Florida State	291
8 Brigham Young (3)	691	18 South Carolina	286
9 Ohio State	645	19 Penn State	145
10 Nebraska	640	20 UCLA	142

September 7, 1985

Penn State 20 MARYLAND 18: Even though Maryland (0-1) was Sport Magazine's choice for no. 1 in nation, Penn State (1-0) still had Terps' number. For 21st straight time, Nittany Lions beat Maryland, but needed K Massimo Manca's 30y 3rd Q FG after blowing 17-0 lead. On blazing hot day, Nittany Lions D launched 7-0 lead on S Mike Zordich's 32y INT TD RET on game's 2nd play and put wraps on Terps QB Stan Gelbaugh. Penn State marched 80y to QB John Shaffer's 2y TD pass to TE Bob Williams. Terps rallied as rugged FB Rick Badanjek slammed in 2 TDs. After Badanjek's 8y scoring effort in 3rd Q, backup QB Dan Henning then hit TE Chris Knight with 2-pt conv pass for 18-17 lead. After Lions took 20-18 lead, Maryland K Ramon Paredes missed 2 FGs and TB Alvin Blount lost FUM at Penn State 22YL.

Florida 35 MIAMI 23: No. 5 Gators (1-0) quickly lived up to billing by winning 11th straight behind 4 TD passes by QB Kerwin Bell (20-28/248y). Florida WR Ricky Nattiel (4/79y) corralled pair of scores in front of record Orange Bowl stadium crowd of 80,227. Game 1st turned in Florida's favor on 10 pts scored late in 1st H for 20-7 lead: Gators converted Miami's FUM and followed with on-side KO REC in closing 31 secs of 1st H. Hurricanes (0-1) answered for 21-20 lead on strength of 2nd H TD drives led by QB Vinny Testaverde (24-40/278y, 2 INTs) in starting debut. With 7:50 left, Florida went ahead for good at 28-21 on Bell's 16y TD pass to Nattiel as Bell pitched 5-6/74y on winning 79y drive. Displaying naiveté earlier in week, Testaverde predicted Hurricanes to win by 24-0.

Florida State 17 NEBRASKA 13: It was hot in America's Heartland, which bothered both teams. QB Danny McManus completed 15-27/172y, TD, as Seminoles (2-0) built 17-13 H lead that stood up in heat of Lincoln. While more than 100 fans were treated for heat-related problems, each team's attack wilted in scoreless 2nd H. Cornhuskers ground out 372y rushing, including 60y on FB Tom Rathman's TD run on 4th play of game, but could not overcome miscues. None was more damaging than bad punt snap that gave possession to Florida State at Nebraska 6YL to set up winning 2y TD run by FB Cletus Jones. IB Doug DuBose led Huskers with 129y rushing and 1y TD run in 2nd Q.

Oklahoma State 31 WASHINGTON 17: Oklahoma State (1-0) TB Thurman Thomas put on show, rushing for 237y and TD, while even throwing 3rd career TD pass—in 3 attempts—for winning score early in 4th Q. Pulling up after rolling right on apparent sweep, Thomas hit SE Bobby Riley for 6y TD. Washington (0-1) attempted to rally before OSU S Mark Moore turned in his 2nd INT of QB Hugh Millen (21-38/232y, 2 TDs). Earlier, Moore returned INT for 49y TD, 1st of 2 scores by Cowboys D. Win was costly for Cowpokes as QB Ronnie Williams was knocked out until midseason with broken jaw.

Ucla 27 BRIGHAM YOUNG 24: Bruins (1-0) continued great weekend for visiting teams in snapping BYU's 25-game win streak. UCLA's sole O TD, TB Gaston Green's 2y TD run, proved to be game-winner and capped drive that featured 62y pass by backup QB Matt Stevens to WR Mike Sherrard (6/102y). QB Robbie Bosco had just put Cougars (1-1) up 24-19 with 1y keeper—which may or may not have broken plane of GL. Although Bosco (29-41/340y) threw 2 TD passes, his 2 INTs included Bruins S Craig Rutledge's 65y TD RET and frosh CB Marcus Turner's pickoff that ended BYU's final drive. Bruins K John Lee booted 4 FGs in game for 7th time in his illustrious career, while Terry Donahue tied Bill Spaulding for most all-time coaching wins at Westwood with 72.

AP Poll September 10
1 Auburn (16)	1118	11 Penn State	516
2 Oklahoma (28)	1116	12 Louisiana State	476
3 Florida (3)	974	13 Notre Dame	456
4 Southern California (6)	970	14 Arkansas	439
5 Iowa (5)	911	15 South Carolina	329
6 Southern Methodist (2)	908	16 Brigham Young	294
7 Florida State	755	17 Maryland	251
8 Oklahoma State	741	18 Nebraska	240
9 Ohio State	686	19 Illinois	198
10 UCLA	612	20 Alabama	175

September 14, 1985

Georgia Tech 28 NORTH CAROLINA STATE 18: Yellow Jackets (1-0) earned 500th all-time win as QB John Dewberry (10-20/197y, INT) threw 3 TDs for O that gained 411y. Georgia Tech DE Pat Swilling made 6 of team's 7 sacks. NC State (0-2) opened scoring with 52y TD strike from QB Erik Kramer (15-35/181y, INT) to WR Haywood Jeffires. Dewberry answered with his trio of TDs, with pair of scoring passes being caught by WR Gary Lee. Tech built 21-7 H lead. Georgia Tech added insurance TD on CB Reggie Rutland's block and REC in EZ of punt early in 3rd Q, which was 1st such TD for Ga Tech in 19 years. Wolfpack rallied with 11 pts in 4th Q, with TD coming on Kramer's 28y pass to WR Phil Brothers.

Bowling Green 30 KENTUCKY 26: Falcons (2-0) earned respect with road win over Kentucky, 1984 bowl winner, as sr QB Brian McClure (30-48/309y) played brilliantly. He threw 3 TDs and directed 76y drive to win game on 11y TD pass to WR Greg Meehan with 23 secs to go. McClure would finish his career 2nd all-time to date in passing y behind former Boston College great Doug Flutie. Wildcats (0-1) QB Bill Ransdell threw for 313y, but Kentucky had to settle for K Joe Worley's 4 FGs.

Louisiana State 23 NORTH CAROLINA 13: Unleashing balanced O, Louisiana State (1-0) looked to build on coach Bill Arnsparger's 1st-year success in 1984. Teams were knotted at 13-13 until Bengals K Ron Lewis nailed school-record 54y FG. LSU QB Jeff Wickersham (23-34/206y, INT) led air attack, while TB Dalton Hilliard rushed for 142y and clinching 3y TD. Tigers TB Garry James added 97y rushing and 8/72y receiving. Tar Heels (1-1) relied on QB Kevin Anthony (31-53/302y), who broke raft of school aerial records, with WR Earl Winfield on receiving end for 11/133y. FB Brad Lopp scored both of North Carolina's TDs on 2y run and 5y catch, both set up by Heels D that forced TOs by LSU's Wickersham deep in Tigers' territory.

Rutgers 28 FLORIDA 28: Tale of 2 back-up QBs was dominated by underdog Scarlet Knights (0-0-1), who rallied from 21 pts behind to shock Florida. After Gators (1-0-1) QB Kerwin Bell threw for 256y and 3 TDs to build 28-7 lead, coach Galen Hall, Penn State teammate of his Rutgers counterpart Dick Anderson 24 years earlier, turned to QB Rodney Brewer. Brewer promptly threw INT to Knights DT Todd McIver, who rumbled 48y for score to pull Rutgers within 28-14. Brewer later lost FUM and threw 2nd INT. Anderson went with reserve QB Joe Gagliardi (10-18/120y, INT), who led TD drives of 65y and 86y to tie game. Even after Gagliardi hit TE Bruce Campbell for 16y TD and FB Curtis Stephens scored 2-pt conv, Rutgers had chance to win after recovering its short KO at Florida 31YL. But, TB Albert Smith, who scored 2 TDs and made 53y KO RET, soon lost FUM. Tie snapped Florida's 10-game win streak.

TENNESSEE 26 Ucla 26: Sub QB rallied Bruins (1-0-1) for 2nd week in row, but this time it was former starting QB David Norrie (10-15/138y, INT). Trailing 26-10 in 4th Q, Norrie led 97y drive capped with 8y TD pass to WR Al Wilson and 2-pt conv pass to TE Jeff Nowinski. Norrie sparked UCLA with 25y TD pass to WR Willie Anderson with 37 secs left before TB Gaston Green—who rushed for 194y including 72y scoring romp on game's 3rd play—ran in tying 2-pt conv. Bruins WR Mike Sherrard (7/120y) got loose for key receptions in both 4th Q TD drives. Vols (0-0-1) QB Tony Robinson (25-35/387y) set school records for passing y and total y (417y) and threw 2 TDs, including 68y pass to WB Joey Clinkscales. Vols WR Tony McGee received 5/142y. Tennessee D had 4 INTs with 3 by S Chris White.

MISSISSIPPI STATE 30 Syracuse 3: Maroon Bulldogs (2-0) were off to 2-0 start for 6th straight year, and it would show mixed results once again in 1985. Balanced Mississippi State attack ground out 439y, while D frustrated Syracuse (0-1) to tune of 200y. RB Rodney Peters scored on short run in 1st Q for Bulldogs, but when K Artie Cosby hit pair of FGs, they led only 13-3 by end of 3rd Q. Syracuse K Don McAulay had made 22y FG in 1st Q, but it would be Orange's last score. Peters added another TD run in 4th Q, and QB Don Smith (17-24/226y) pitched 21y TD.

MICHIGAN 20 Notre Dame 12: Conservative described Notre Dame (0-1); Irish seemed to think handoffs to TB Allen Pinkett (22/94y) were only sensible plays near Michigan EZ. On 1st 10 plays snapped within Michigan 15YL, Pinkett ran ball on each of them for total of 12y, converting 4 drives that reached red zone into K John Carney's FGs. Trailing 9-3 at H, Michigan (1-0) scored 1st of 2 TDs—QB Jim Harbaugh's 10y run—3 plays after ND TB Alonzo Jefferson lost FUM of 2nd H KO. After Carney booted Irish back into lead, Wolverines answered with 3y TD run by FB Carl White for 17-12 edge. When on final drive, Notre Dame QB Steve Beuerlein (11-23/160y) finally dropped back to throw when deep in Michigan territory, Wolverines D was ready and struck with its 6th sack—3rd by DT Mike Hammerstein—before grabbing INT. Wolverines TB Jaime Morris rushed for 121y.

MICHIGAN STATE 12 Arizona State 3: Mid-September game looked more like mid-August scrimmage as teams combined for 208y in PENs. Spartans (1-0) TB Lorenzo White rushed for 174y, with 127y in 1st H including 42y for game's sole TD and 6-0 lead for Michigan State. K Chris Caudell added 2 FGs for Spartans. Sun Devils (0-1) QB Jeff Van Raaphorst threw for 228y, but could not get team in EZ and threw 2 INTs during Arizona State's woeful 1st H. Devils were still in game until late in 4th Q and had 60y punt RET by CB Anthony Parker wiped out by PEN, that would have given them 1st down at Spartans 19YL trailing 9-3 with 5 mins left.

BRIGHAM YOUNG 31 Washington 3: Washington (0-2) coach Don James couldn't be blamed for canceling subscription to *Sports Illustrated* after magazine tapped Huskies as its preseason choice for no. 1. James' Huskies dropped their 2nd straight. Cougars (2-1) proved not only that they could play with big boys, they could beat them with balanced O that included 168y and 4 TDs rushing. BYU QB Robbie Bosco (23-37/279y, 2 INTs) played well but failed to click on single TD pass—to snap Cougars' remarkable streak of 38 games with aerial TD. FB Lakei Heimuli rushed for 112y and 2 TDs to pace Cougars' ground game, doing most of his damage on draws that were barely contested by Washington's D. Huskies O gained 382y, with QB Hugh Millen throwing for 202y, but squandered chances with 5 TOs, trio of 4th down failures in BYU territory, and 9 PENs/88y, 2 of which wiped out TDs.

September 21, 1985

ARMY 20 Rutgers 16: Although game was played in 1985, not 1385, Black Knights (2-0) topped Scarlet Knights behind rush game that churned up 230y. Army's winning TD was scored late in 3rd Q on 10y sweep by HB William Lampley to cap 71y drive. Cadets used sweep to tack on 2 more pts as HB Clarence Jones ran for twin conv. Army QB Bob Healy rushed for team-high 81y, TD, and passed for 85y. Rutgers (0-1-1) built 13-12 H lead as starting QB Rusty Hochberg drove team to his 2y TD pass to TE Scott Drake on opening possession, and QB Joe Gagliardi (15-23/178y) came off bench to throw 36y TD to WR Greg Raffaelli.

Boston College 29 PITTSBURGH 22: After blowing 21-3 lead to trail by 22-21, Eagles (2-2) pulled out win behind QB Shawn Halloran. Faking handoff to FB Ken Bell on 4th-and-1, Halloran (25-33/400y) threw 51y TD pass to WR Kelvin Martin (7/172y, 2 TDs) with 1:21 left. TB Jim Bell (14/94y) rushed for 2 TDs as BC built its 18-pt lead by 3rd Q. Panthers (1-2) rallied behind highly recruited frosh TB Brian Davis (15/100y), who replaced injured TB Charles Gladman (14/121y). After Davis scored on 26y run late in 3rd Q, QB John Congemi ran and threw for 4th Q TDs to construct 22-21 lead for Pitt.

MARYLAND 28 West Virginia 0: Earning their 1st home win, after 5 losses against West Virginia (2-1) since 1966 was easy for Terps (2-1), who outgained Mountaineers by 518y to 271y and scored TDs on 3 of 1st 4 possessions. QB Stan Gelbaugh (15-23/263y, INT) threw 2 TDs and TB Tommy Neal added 90y, 2 TDs rushing to lead O, while Maryland D posted its 1st shutout since 1982. Maryland WR Azizuddin Abdur-Ra'oof (5/90y) had key catches on opening pair of scoring drives. Bright spot for Mountaineers was play of reserve QB Tony Reda, who completed 8-10/127y.

Virginia 24 GEORGIA TECH 13: Beating Georgia Tech for 1st time in 8 attempts, Cavaliers (2-0) rode back of TB Barry Word (17/188y) to take lead and rugged D to preserve it. Word scored on 79y burst 5 mins into game and later raced 52y to set up Cavs' 2nd TD, 3y run by QB Don Majkowski (10-16/150y) near end of 1st Q. Yellow Jackets (1-1) had opened scoring with 47y FG by frosh K Thomas Palmer and led 10-7 on 5y TD pass by QB John Dewberry to TE Tim Manion. Virginia took control by tallying next 17 pts, including 15y TD reception by TE Geno Zimmerlink. Teams did all scoring in 1st H. Dewberry threw for 190y, but suffered 3 INTs.

Georgia 20 CLEMSON 13: Georgia (2-1) wiped out 7-pt deficit with dominating 4th Q to win in Clemson (1-1) for 1st time since 1976. Bulldogs held ball for more than 11 mins of 4th Q in outscoring Tigers in 4th Q by 17-3. Georgia option attack piled up 360y to tire out Tigers, and S John Little (9 tackles) swooped in to steal 2 passes in 4th Q. After his 11y TD run tied game 10-10, Bulldogs QB James Jackson led 80y drive to winning TD, oddly scored by C Peter Anderson on REC of FB Keith Henderson's FUM into EZ. Clemson QB Randy Anderson threw for 183y, including 43y TD to TE Jim Riggs for 7-3 lead in 1st Q.

Michigan 34 SOUTH CAROLINA 3: Big 10 fans might have been saying ominous, "They're baaaack!" Memories of 1984's 6-6 record were snuffed as Michigan (2-0) routed no. 15 Gamecocks. South Carolina (2-1) entered game with O avg of 557y and 38 pts. Employing its great size edge, Michigan D held Carolina to 202y O and limited scoring to K Scott Hagler's FG. Wolverines rushed for 324y, led by TB Thomas Wilcher's 106y, while QB Jim Harbaugh threw for 183y. Forced to hang onto ball more than usual, Cocks option QB Mike Hold ran for team-high 78y.

Texas Christian 24 KANSAS STATE 22: Texas Christian (2-0) S Garland Littles came up big at game's end, breaking up Kansas State QB John Welch's 2-pt conv pass to preserve win. Wildcats (0-3) had converted FUM at Cats 15YL by TCU QB Scott Ankrom into 6 pts on 1y TD run by HB Tony Jordan. TB Tony Jeffrey rushed for and received TDs for Horned Frogs, who overcame 16-7 H deficit. Game was 1st since Horned Frogs coach Jim Wacker suspended 6 players, including star TB Kenneth Davis, for illegally accepting money from boosters.

Baylor 20 SOUTHERN CALIFORNIA 13: No. 3 Trojans' season soured as Baylor (2-1) used late GLS to preserve win. With 3:16 left, USC (1-1) had 1st down at Bears 6YL. Four straight running plays later, Baylor took over on its 4YL. Southern California wasted fine game by QB Sean Salisbury (20-29/235y, 2 TDs), which was marred only by EZ INT early in game. USC WR Hank Norman caught 10/132y, including 9y TD in 2nd Q. Bears sprung rush attack that used 7 runners to gain 203y.

September 28, 1985

Navy 17 VIRGINIA 13: It was bad news for Virginia when, for 1st time ever, Naval Academy (1-3) granted 5th year to midshipman. Man in question, TB Napoleon McCallum, was no ordinary Middie, something he proved with 139y rushing and 2 TDs. TB Barry Word rushed for 110y for Virginia (2-1), but Navy D held QB Don Majkowski to 108y passing and intercepted him twice. He scored team's sole TD on 5y run in 2nd Q. McCallum had suffered season-ending injury year ago versus Cavs.

Georgia Tech 14 CLEMSON 3: Yellow Jackets (2-1) QB John Dewberry shook off shoulder injury to lead clinching drive that opened 3rd Q. After being knocked out in 2nd Q, Dewberry returned, setting up TD with 32y completion of wobbly pass to TE Tim Manion. He also was able to catch as demonstrated on TD play: Georgia Tech TB

Jerry Mays took pitchout, ran right before pulling up to throw wounded duck back to Dewberry for score. That finished scoring as Clemson (1-2) was held without TD for 1st time since 1979. Not only did gimmicks victimize Tigers, but also so did TOs. They gave away 4 in all. QB Randy Anderson threw for 125y at helm of Clemson O.

FLORIDA STATE 24 Kansas 20: Frosh QB Chip Ferguson salvaged day for Florida State (4-0), coming off bench to rally Noles with pair of 4th Q TD drives. Resurgent Jayhawks (3-1) had entered 4th Q with 20-10 lead as QB Mike Norseth (28-44/308y) threw 2 TDs. On his 4th play, Ferguson got 1 TD back, hooking up with WR Phillip Bryant (4/113y, 2 TDs) on 68y pass. Florida State CB Martin Mayhew picked off Norseth 4 plays later to set up winning 6y TD run by FB Victor Floyd. Seminoles needed only 8 plays to gain 130y on its 2 TD drives in 4th Q. Norseth had set Big 8 record with 175 straight passes without INT before throwing quartet in 2nd H. Seminoles TB Tony Smith rushed for 132y, while WR Hassan Jones caught 7/107y.

TENNESSEE 38 Auburn 20: Inspired Tennessee (1-0-1) outclassed nation's top team, Auburn (2-1), by jumping to 24-0 lead. Vols QB Tony Robinson (17-30/259y) threw 4 TDs, WR Tim McGee nabbed 6/163y, and frosh TB Keith Davis rushed for 102y. Vols D contained Auburn TB Bo Jackson (17/80y) before he left in 3rd Q with strained knee ligament. Tigers (2-1) trailed by 24 pts before scoring 3 TDs in 4th Q, with 7y scoring run by backup TB Brent Fullwood (15/96y). Robinson, who, as usual, called 70 percent audibles, was still slinging it in 4th Q, throwing 2 TDs. Auburn S Tom Powell made 3 INTs, his 3rd was returned 50y to set up TD.

Oklahoma 13 MINNESOTA 7: With 5 mins left, Oklahoma (1-0) had as dominating 13-0 lead as imaginable, with Gophers held to 3 1st downs deep into 4th Q. But, Sooners S Sonny Brown lost punt FUM at 19YL, which Minnesota (2-1) turned into QB Ricky Foggie's 12y TD pass to TE Kevin Starks. Gophers got ball back on own 30YL with 65 secs left. Two passes later, ball was on Oklahoma 32YL. Sooners D forced incompletion, sacked Foggie, knocked ball away in EZ, and picked off pass—Brown losing his goat horns with INT. OU had built 10-0 H lead on 1st of 2 FGs by K Tim Lashar and HB Earl Johnson's 1y TD run, while D allowed only 30y.

ARIZONA STATE 24 Southern California 0: Prospects for Trojans' glory may have gone up in smoke during crucial few moments of 2nd Q. Trailing 7-0 and having marched to Arizona State 2YL, USC (1-2) TB Fred Crutcher lost FUM to Sun Devils S David Fulcher. After 2 running plays netted 3y, Devils (2-1) went to air for QB Jeff Van Raaphorst's pitch to WR Aaron Cox at 30YL. Cox beat CB Matt Johnson and eluded S Tim McDonald to race to crushing score. Making matters worse, ASU NG Dan Saleaumua stripped Trojans QB Sean Salisbury—Troy lost 7 TOs—on next possession, which was converted into FG at end of 1st H for commanding 17-0 lead. Southern California rushed for 197y, led by TB Aaron Emanuel (14/76y).

WASHINGTON 21 Ucla 14: Trailing 14-3 near end of 1st H, Huskies (2-2) grabbed momentum for good as QB Hugh Millen (19-27/185y) arched 31y TD to WR Lonzell Hill. Ensuing 2-pt pass to WR David Trimble cut deficit to 14-11, which vanished on K Jeff Jaeger's 37y FG early in 3rd Q. Bruins (2-1-1) followed with lost FUM by TB James Primus. It led to 46y drive late in 3rd Q to winning 1y TD run by Huskies TB David Toy, on his only play. Washington LB Joe Kelly recovered Primus' FUM and later added key INT. Bruins turned to backup QB, which worked twice this early season, but failed as NG Jim Mathews injured QB Matt Stevens on pass attempt. UCLA outgained Huskies 303y to 263y, scoring pair of 26y TDs on 1st H passes from QB David Norrie (13-20/152y, INT) to WRs Mike Sherrard and Karl Dorrell.

AP Poll September 30

1 Iowa (35)	1111	11 Florida	561
2 Oklahoma (13)	1046	12 Alabama	532
3 Southern Methodist (6)	1001	13 Nebraska	526
4 Florida State	928	14 Auburn	482
5 Ohio State	921	15 Brigham Young	463
6 Oklahoma State (1)	850	16 Tennessee	393
7 Michigan (3)	842	17 Air Force	282
8 Louisiana State	670	18 Georgia	116
9 Penn State	640	19 Baylor	94
10 Arkansas	616	20 Texas	84

October 5, 1985

Florida 20 LOUISIANA STATE 0: Although QB Kerwin Bell and TB Neal Anderson get lion's share of press, Gators (3-0-1) D was very good, proving it with decisive road performance. LSU (2-1) picked off 3 of Bell's passes, but its O could do nothing with them, being blanked at home for 1st time since 1980. Florida sacked QB Jeff Wickersham 7 times, held TB Dalton Hilliard to 35y rushing, and allowed Tigers past midfield twice. Gators' 1st Q TD came on 51y pass by Anderson to WR Ray McDonald. Anderson rushed for 123y to become school's career leader with 2,670y.

ILLINOIS 31 Ohio State 28: Fighting Illini (2-2) K Chris White made his dad, coach Mike White, happy with last-sec 38y FG for victory. Illinois took early 14-0 lead on short TD runs by HB Keith Jones and FB Ray Wilson. Buckeyes (3-1) tied game on 2 long TD drives, 2nd following EZ INT by S Terry White on ball thrown by Illinois' Jones on trick sprung at Ohio 5YL. Buckeyes pushed to 28-14 edge with pair of 3rd Q TD passes from QB Jim Karsatos to WR Cris Carter (7/147y), who caught all 7 of Karsatos' completions of game. Illinois woke up with 2 TDs to knot it at 28-28 as QB Jack Trudeau (28-40/294y) scored on 1y wedge with 6 mins left. Illinois WR Stephen Pierce had 7 catches/131y. "I don't remember a sweeter victory in my coaching career, and you know why," said White.

IOWA 35 Michigan State 31: QB Chuck Long threw 4 TDs and ran in 2y winner for Hawkeyes (4-0) with 27 secs left. Long slickly faked hand-off to TB Ronnie Harmon (20/84y) and waltzed into EZ. WR Robert Smith and TE Mike Flagg each caught pair of TD passes from Long (30-39/380y, 2 INTs). Loss was tough for Spartans (2-2), who gained 580y and scored 24 pts in row in taking 24-13 lead in 3rd Q. Michigan State TB Lorenzo White rushed for 226y and 2 TDs, QB Bobby McAllister (18-27/275y) threw TD in his 2nd start, and WR Mark Ingram caught 7/148y.

INDIANA 26 Northwestern 7: Recalling memories of glorious 1967 season, Hoosiers (4-0) romped as QB Steve Bradley, school's all-time O leader, threw for 257y and TDs of 37y to WR Ernie Jones and 57y to WR Kenny Allen (6/115y). Allen's score gave Hoosiers 14-0 lead, which ballooned to 26-0 within 3 min-span of 2nd Q on safety, TB Bobby Howard's 59y scamper for TD, and K Pete Stoyanovich's 28y FG after TO. Wildcats (2-2) prevented shutout with 11y TD catch by HB Brian Nuffer. Northwestern QBs Mike Greenfield and Sandy Schwab threw for 237y, but also 3 INTs. Indiana D broke up 7 passes, had 9 tackles for loss, and authored 2 GLSs.

Texas A&M 28 TEXAS TECH 27: On his only carry of game, Red Raiders (3-2) TB Bouvier Dale scored on 9y run to pull within 28-27 with 42 secs left. There was no shortage of courage as Raiders went for winning 2-pt conv, and Texas A&M (3-1) called for blitz on play. Texas Tech QB Aaron Keesee dropped back, but was nailed by CB Terrance Brooks to end game. Conv was made more difficult by delay-of-game PEN as Tech 1st decided on tying x-pt and sent out K Marc Mallery. Game was knotted 21-21 entering 4th Q after Texas Tech S King Simmons' 42y INT TD RET. That INT was 1 of few mistakes by Texas A&M QB Kevin Murray (14-20/181y). Aggies regained lead for good at 28-21 on 8y run by TB Roger Vick (37/135y, 2 TDs).

ARIZONA 28 Southern Methodist 6: After scoring 13 TDs in opening 2 games, SMU (2-1) looked for more with 99y TD drive to open scoring at 6-0. After Wildcats (4-1) blocked x-pt, it was all Arizona as QB Alfred Jenkins (13-26/177y) threw 3 TD passes, 2 to WR Jon Horton (7/119y). Wildcats D forced 4 TOs in handing Mustangs worst loss since 1979. TB David Adams rushed for 136y to overshadow SMU TBs Reggie Dupard (17/82y, TD) and Jeff Atkins (14/56y), while LBs Danny Lockett (10 tackles, 3 sacks) and Byron Evans (15 tackles and INT) paced Cats D. With QB Don King throwing for 247y, Mustangs actually won y battle, 388y to 345y.

UCLA 40 Arizona State 17: Bruins (3-1-1) gained 460y and whipped Arizona State (2-2) team that had surrendered only 12 pts in 3 games. UCLA K John Lee enhanced aerial performance of QB David Norrie (14-24/215y, 2 TDs) by booting 4 FGs in stretching consecutive FG streak to 15, while his x-pt streak went to 81. Sun Devils (2-2) QB Jeff Van Raaphorst threw for 230y, but O gained only 248y. UCLA WR Mike Sherrard (6/89y) caught 36y TD pass before exiting with broken collarbone after 19y catch that briefly earned him school career receiving y. "They had a great game plan," said losing coach John Cooper. "They picked us like a chicken."

AP Poll October 8

1 Iowa (34)	1137	11 Brigham Young	529
2 Oklahoma (14)	1106	12 Auburn	514
3 Michigan (7)	1037	13 Air Force	452
4 Florida State (3)	993	14 Tennessee	442
5 Oklahoma State (1)	986	15 Ohio State	430
6 Arkansas	806	16 Southern Methodist	300
7 Florida	779	17 Texas	170
8 Penn State	745	18 Georgia	161
9 Nebraska	656	19 Baylor	159
10 Alabama	650	20 Louisiana State	115

October 12, 1985

PENN STATE 19 Alabama 17: Penn State (5-0) remained unbeaten as coach Joe Paterno pulled out all stops in nail-biter: Nittany Lions WR Michael Timpson raced 29y on reverse, and, on same drive, sub QB Matt Knizner bootlegged before pulling up to hit TE Brian Siverling for 11y TD pass. Siverling's TD followed 4 FGs by K Massimo Manca as Penn State built 19-10 lead. Crimson Tide (4-1) QB Mike Shula (16-27/211y) led late TD drive, throwing 14y TD pass to TE Thornton Chandler to pull to 19-17 with 14 secs left. Alabama's REC of onside-KO was wiped out by PEN. Tide WR Al Bell caught 6/112y with 19y on opening TD. "It was," said Paterno, "the kind of game you go somewhere like Penn State or Alabama to play."

Air Force 24 NAVY 7: Air Force (6-0) had bumpy takeoff before straightening things out for smooth flight. After sluggish start, in which Air Force had no 1st downs after 1st Q—QB Bart Weiss jumpstarted O with 60y pass to WR Ken Carpenter to set up 3y TD run by FB Johnny Smith. Weiss went on to rush for 102y and complete another pass to set up TD: Later in 2nd Q Weiss hooked up with TE Hugh Brennan for 53y gain to set stage for 14-0 lead. Navy (1-4) went to bread-and-butter TB Napoleon McCallum for 67y rushing to cut deficit in half on QB Bill Byrne's 15y pass to TE John Sniffen, but could not continue rally as Flyboys ran off 10 4th Q pts.

AUBURN 59 Florida State 27: Separation between Auburn (4-1) TB Bo Jackson and mortal players was wide in this game as he scored on 53y run in 1st Q and 35y romp in 3rd Q for eventual winning pts. Jackson rushed for 176y, inspiring Auburn to blow open 31-27 game with 4 TDs scored within 4:08 of 4th Q, including INT TD RETs by CB Kevin Porter of 33y and DT Ron Stallworth of 22y. Close entering 4th Q, game went Tigers' way as WR Freddie Weygand began scoring burst with 13y TD reverse, 2 plays after FB Tommie Agee burst through line for 68y. Seminoles (4-1) lost 5 TOs, including 3 INTs thrown by QB Eric Thomas (6-16/165y). Thomas had replaced QB Danny McManus, who left with dizzy spells in 2nd Q with Florida State ahead 14-7. FSU had to turn to 3rd-string QB Chip Ferguson, who, on his 1st play, was nailed by DT Tracy Rocker to force Stallworth's INT. On Ferguson's 2nd play, he lost FUM that led to final TD on 8y run by FB Demetrius Threatt.

FLORIDA 17 Tennessee 10: Gators (4-0-1) stretched their unbeaten streak to 15 games with 2 nearly identical 3rd Q drives. After 3-3 draw in 1st H, Florida twice stopped Volunteers (2-1-1) deep in Tennessee's end to force short punts by P Bob Garmon. Each punt allowed Gators to profit by great field position at Florida 49 and 38YLs. Florida TB Neal Anderson (26/160y) capped short drives with TD runs of 9y

and 1y for 17-3 lead late in 3rd Q. Vols QB Tony Robinson was able to throw for 300y, including 20y TD pass to WR Tim McGee (6/91y), but was intercepted twice. McGee's 4th Q TD was 1st allowed by Gators D in most-recent 9 Qs, while Vols DT Mark Hovanic achieved 3 sacks of Gators QB Kerwin Bell (12-17/143y, INT).

Michigan 31 MICHIGAN STATE 0: Giving away 2 quick TDs within game's 1st 4 mins was no way to upset in-state rival. Michigan State (2-3) QB Bobby McAllister's FUM on game's 2nd play was converted into 9y TD pass from Wolverines QB Jim Harbaugh to TE Eric Kattus. Michigan (5-0) D held, and LB Dieter Heren blocked punt, which he returned to 1YL before fumbling into EZ, where special teamer Ed Hood pounced on it for TD and 14-0 advantage for Michigan. Spartans staunched their bleeding until 4th Q, when Michigan turned 2 INTs into TDs. Harbaugh threw for 149y and 2 TDs, but 3 INTs. Michigan State TB Lorenzo White was held to 47y rushing as Spartans O went flat with only 139y total O and 6 1st downs.

Nebraska 34 OKLAHOMA STATE 24: Cowboys (4-1) had improved to level that annual loss to Nebraska was now disappointing instead of inevitable. With IB Doug DuBose rushing for 139y and QB McCathorn Clayton passing for 161y, Huskers (4-1) used more O balance than usual to win their 24th straight of series. Clayton ran for 2 TDs and threw for another as Nebraska built 20-3 lead in 3rd Q. With TB Thurman Thomas held to 71y rushing, Cowboys rallied for 2 TDs behind QB Ronnie Williams, who was forced to aerials and surprised by throwing for school-record 363y. Pokes outgained Huskers 420y to 417y, but lost 4 TOs including Huskers LB Marc Munford's INT at Oke State 7YL. FB Tom Rathman soon scored on 4y run for 27-17 lead in 4th Q. Cowboys WR Bobby Riley caught 5/131y.

IOWA STATE 22 Kansas 21: Efficient Cyclones (3-2) TB Don Poprilo rushed only twice, both for 3y TDs, including game-winner with 2:45 left. Poprilo's key TD was set up when Kansas (4-2) was trying to clinch game: FB Mark Henderson lost FUM to Iowa State DT Bill Berthusen at Cyclones 26YL. Iowa State QB Alex Espinoza (21-35/262y, 2 INTs) then led 10-play drive, completing 3 passes/53y. QB Mike Norseth threw for 182y at controls of Jayhawks' attack.

Oklahoma 14 Texas 7 (Dallas): Longhorns (3-1) probably caught break when knee sprain sent Sooners star NG Tony Casillas to bench in 1st Q. After all, if Casillas had stayed on field, Texas may not have earned even 1 of 4 1st downs with which it finished. Sooners (3-0) sacked Horns QB Todd Dodge 6 times and picked him off twice, while Texas could manage only 17y rushing and 70y total O. Texas actually led 7-0 on 7y FUM TD RET by DE Kip Cooper in 1st Q after DE Thomas Aldridge stripped Oklahoma FB Lydell Carr. Oklahoma tied game with 80y drive in 2nd Q that ended on 1y TD run by Carr (23/80y). With Longhorns limited to -24y in 2nd H, Oklahoma needed to score only once to win, which it did when HB Patrick Collins broke majestically down left sideline for 45y TD run on triple-option sleight of hand.

Baylor 21 SOUTHERN METHODIST 14: Bears (5-1) came out slugging for 14-0 lead as K Terry Syler booted 2 FGs and QB Tom Muecke (8-13/135y, 2 INTs) hit HB Ralph Stockemer with 26y TD pass. SMU (2-2) answered with pair of 80y drives, capped by TD runs of 16y by TB Reggie Dupard (14/98y) and 1y by TB Jeff Atkins for 14-14 H tie. Mustangs marched again late in 3rd Q, only to have Dupard lose controversial FUM at Bears 2YL after hit by Baylor S Thomas Everett that popped ball into EZ for REC by DE Eugene Hall. Having gained 2nd life, Bears themselves marched 80y, scoring winning pts on Muecke's 2y keeper with 9:18 left. Muecke completed 3 passes/70y on drive, including 34y hook-up with TE Jay Kelly. Ponies were unable to earn single 1st down on any of their final 3 possessions. Ranked 3rd in preseason, SMU now was off to its worst start since 1977.

AP Poll October 14

1 Iowa (27)	1146	11 Ohio State	522
2 Michigan (20)	1126	12 Oklahoma State	493
3 Oklahoma (12)	1124	13 Florida State	459
4 Arkansas	936	14 Baylor	375
5 Florida	905	15 Alabama	364
6 Penn State (1)	902	16 Georgia	336
7 Nebraska	868	17 Louisiana State	212
8 Auburn	777	18 UCLA	182
9 Brigham Young	685	19 Army	146
10 Air Force	624	20 Tennessee	141

October 19, 1985

Penn State 24 SYRACUSE 20: After being temporarily sidelined with injury, Penn State (6-0) QB John Shaffer (10-20/115y) returned in 2nd H to throw winning 8y TD pass to FB David Clark with 1:53 left. Trying to snap 14-game series losing streak, Syracuse (2-3) had late lead, but FB Roland Grimes lost FUM, recovered by Lions DE Don Graham (forced FUM, 2 sacks) to launch winning TD. Syracuse won y battle by 304y to 231y, but lost 4 TOs. All of Penn State's 3 TD drives were short: 43y following Grimes' FUM, 19y set up by 78y KO RET by WR Jim Coates, and 26y after 48y punt RET by WR Michael Timpson. Orange QB Don McPherson, who passed for 173y, ran for 26y TD in 3rd Q and hit WR Mike Siano on 44y TD pass for 20-17 lead with 10:19 left. D-minded Nittany Lions now owned 6 wins by total of 24 pts.

Virginia Tech 28 VIRGINIA 10: It wasn't flashy, but Hokies (3-4) jammed ball down throats of Virginia (3-3), rushing 55/236y in reversing 10-0 deficit with quartet of 2nd H TD drives. Virginia Tech TBs Eddie Hunter (21/107y) and Maurice Williams (17/93y, 2 TDs) and big O-line wore down Cavaliers as Va Tech held ball for nearly 21 mins of 2nd H. After gaining only 49y in opening H, Hokies reset tone in 3rd Q with 18-play, 80y drive—converting 4 times on 3rd down—to Hunter's 1y TD dive. With next possession, Tech needed to travel only 59y to score decisive TD on 1y run by Williams. He added 25y TD run on next series. TB Barry Word finished with 104y rushing, but after gaining 241y in 1st H, Cavaliers could assemble only 57y thereafter.

VANDERBILT 13 Georgia 13: As Vanderbilt K Alan Herline missed 44y FG attempt at game's end, highly-favored Bulldogs (4-1-1) escaped with tie. Near upset by Commodores (2-4-1) was orchestrated by dynamic duo of frosh QBs. Vandy starting QB John Gromos (8-11/84y, INT) left with bruised sternum in 2nd Q, and QB Tim Richardson (17-24/181y, INT) took O reins. Bulldogs did most damage on ground with 215y, but Dores D shut them out in 2nd H. Each team found EZ once: Vandy FB Carl Woods scored on 12y run, and Bulldogs QB James Jackson tallied on 7y keeper. Also, each K, Herline and Georgia K Steve Crumley, booted dual FGs. "Vanderbilt battled us down to the wire," said Georgia coach Vince Dooley. "They should have had a better fate. They should have won."

Tennessee 16 ALABAMA 14 (Birmingham): Tennessee (3-1-1) won game, but Crimson Tide (4-2) LBs Cornelius Bennett and Wayne Davis tackled QB Tony Robinson (10-19/130y, INT)—heart of Vols' O—on 1st play of 4th Q, sending him to sideline with knee injury. Vols were leading 16-7 at time, but soon surrendered 61y drive that ended with QB Mike Shula's 19y TD pass to TB Bobby Humphrey. Shula, who threw for 216y, had Tide on move again until clutch INT by Vols LB Dale Jones. Final Alabama drive ended with short kick by K Van Tiffin on 61y FG attempt. Frosh TB Keith Davis rushed for 141y for Vols. "When Tony went out, we knew every play might make the difference," said Jones, who gave game ball he was awarded to D coordinator Ken Donahue, who had coached for 21 years at Alabama.

GAME OF THE YEAR
IOWA 12 Michigan 10:

Battle of nos. 1 and 2—19th such match-up since AP started polling in 1936 and 1st since Sugar Bowl following 1982 season pitted Penn State and Georgia—featured Iowa's top rated O and Michigan's top rated D. Hawkeyes (6-0) were kept out of EZ, but moved ball as QB Chuck Long threw for 297y and HB Ronnie Harmon rushed for 134y. Harmon became 1st back to top 100y rushing against Michigan in 6 games. Iowa appeared to score TD in 1st H as Long found WR Scott Helverson deep in EZ with 18y pass, but officials ruled Helverson failed to get foot down. Iowa settled for 35y FG by K Rob Houghtlin. Michigan (5-1) answered quickly as TB Jamie Morris took KO 60y to poise QB Jim Harbaugh's 6y TD pass to FB Gerald White. Harbaugh was flushed out of pocket by DE Jeff Cross and shoveled ball to White, who knifed in from 2YL. Later in 1st H, Long's 25y pass to Harmon led to another FG by Houghtlin to cut margin to 7-6. Early in 3rd Q, Long drove Hawkeyes to Michigan 22YL before INT by LB Dieter Heren. In 4th Q, Harbaugh lost FUM in Michigan territory, which set up 36y FG by Houghtlin for 9-7 Iowa lead. Hawks had 12-min time advantage but only 2-pt lead, which Wolverines wiped out with 40y FG by K Mike Gillette. Iowa forced punt and took over at own 21YL with less than 6 mins left. Drive began poorly as Harmon dropped pass, but Long completed 11y pass to TE Mike Flagg, who alternated with Harmon on 4 1st down-gaining plays as Iowa went to Michigan 26YL. Teams exchanged PENs, and Iowa reduced clock with short runs before Houghtlin took another FG try. His 29y effort was true.

Miami 27 OKLAHOMA 14: Although Miami QB Vinny Testaverde and Oklahoma QB Troy Aikman both would become top overall NFL picks, their highly-anticipated battle of young gunslingers fizzled due to injury that had surprising national championship consequences. Nation's top D was no match for passing of Miami (5-1) as Testaverde threw for 270y and 2 TDs, while scoring team's other TD on bootleg run. Score was 14-7 at H as Testaverde hit WR Michael Irvin with 56y TD pass and ran in score from 4y out, while Oklahoma (3-1) countered with 14y TD pass from Aikman to WR Derrick Shepard. Sooners, however, lost Aikman (6-7/131y) with broken ankle in 2nd Q and found catching up tough without him. Hurricanes scored 13 pts in 3rd Q on 2 FGs by K Greg Cox and WR Brian Blades' 35y scoring reception. With Aikman out for year, Sooners turned to frosh QB Jamelle Holieway, whose speed would energize Oklahoma's march back to top of rankings.

Nebraska 28 MISSOURI 20: Benched earlier in season after missing 5 straight FG attempts, Nebraska (5-1) jr K Dale Klein proved to be over his slump with NCAA record-tying 7 made FGs as Huskers did just enough to win. Amazingly, Klein entered game with only 6 career FGs. With IB Doug Dubose rushing for career-high 199y, Huskers O took advantage of opportunities presented by Tigers to score 8 times. Missouri (0-6) D played inspired football behind DE Dick Chapura (21 tackles) and S Erik McMillan (10 tackles, 2 INTs). But Mizzou O self-destructed, losing 4 TOs to negate its 401y. Loss was 9th straight for Tigers for new school record.

Texas 15 ARKANSAS 13: Longhorns K Jeff Ward put on clinic, but Arkansas (5-1) K Greg Horne missed his lesson. Ward booted 5 FGs, including career-best 55y 3-ptr, to score all pts for Texas (4-1), while Horne missed all 3 attempts for Hogs, from 48y, 40y, and 33y. Texas QB Bret Stafford scrambled to throw for 137y and TB Edwin Simmons rushed for 86y. Razorbacks received TDs from WR James Shibest on 30y catch and TB James Rouse on 20y run. After Rouse's TD, Hogs went for 2 pts but QB Mark Calcagni's pass was incomplete. Arkansas' final drive ended with INT by S John Hagy on own 22YL with clock expiring. "I hurt more at this moment than I ever have in my life," declared defeated Arkansas coach Ken Hatfield.

BAYLOR 20 Texas A&M 15: Second time was charm for Baylor (6-1) HB Ralph Stockemer, who scored on 4th-and-goal from 1YL after being halted on 4th-and-1 in 3rd Q. TD capped 75y drive after Aggies (4-2) had taken 15-14 lead. Bears' key play was 25y pass from QB Tom Muecke (7-14/110y, INT) to WB Glenn Pruitt on 3rd-and-25, to Texas A&M 21YL. In front of 1st home sellout in 11 years, Bears took 14-6 H lead on TD runs by QBs Cody Carlson (11y) and Muecke (6y). Aggies pulled within 14-12 on S Kip Corrington's 40y INT TD RET in 3rd Q, before taking lead on K Eric Franklin's 3rd FG. Texas A&M FB Anthony Toney rushed 10/74y.

Oregon State 21 WASHINGTON 20: Having lost last 2 games by combined 97-0, Beavers—37-pt underdogs—pulled off 1 of great upsets in Pac-10 history. DE Andre Todd blocked Washington punt with 1:46 to go that was recovered in EZ for winning TD by CB Lavance Northington. Oregon State (3-4) owned 14-10 H lead behind frosh QB Rich Gonzales (26-42/298y, INT), who threw and ran for 1st H TDs. Huskies (4-3) bounced back with 14y TD run by TB Tony Covington and 43y FG by K Jeff Jaeger for 20-14 lead. Beavers then marched 70y before turning ball over on downs to Washington, who was soon forced to punt late in 4th Q.

STANFORD 28 Arizona 17: Recovering from partially separated shoulder, Stanford (2-5) QB John Paye (12-14/116y, TD) came off bench in 2nd H to lead upset. Trailing 17-7 at H, Cardinal erupted for 3 TDs, including Paye's 14y pass to TB Thomas Henley and 1y keeper. In between, Card TB Brian Morris scored key TD on 5y run to cap 74y drive. Wildcats (5-2) contributed 2 huge mistakes to Stanford's cause: QB Alfred Jenkins' INT by Stanford CB Toi Cook at Wildcats 25YL set up Paye's scoring pass and KO FUM by TB David Eldridge in 4th Q, gave ball at Arizona 19YL. Five plays later, Paye scored Cardinal's final TD. Cats Jenkins threw for 177y.

October 26, 1985

PENN STATE 27 West Virginia 0: QB John Shaffer did not rack up huge passing stats each week for Penn State (7-0)—he just won. Shaffer, now 50-0 since 7th grade, completed only 4 passes, but 2 went for TDs to WR Ray Roundtree. Healthy after hamstring injury, Lions TB D.J. Dozier rushed for 125y and 14y TD. West Virginia (4-2-1) QB John Talley ran for 85y and threw for 106y but was picked off 3 times. Win was 600th in Penn State history, 5th Div. 1-A school to top mark.

MIAMI 45 Louisville 7: Excitement generated by return of Louisville coach Howard Schellenberger to Orange Bowl dissipated under weight of rout by Hurricanes (6-1). While there was some booing, Schnellenberger's former players kept their mouths shut (for once). Miami QB Vinny Testaverde completed 13-21/295y with TD passes of 48y to TE Willie Smith, 5y to WR Brian Blades, and 78y to WR Michael Irvin (5/145y). Irvin's TD marked 6th straight game in which he scored, tying Eddie Dunn's school record set in 1938. Canes D chipped in with 6 sacks and S Bennie Blades' 33y INT TD RET. Cardinals (1-7) managed only 158y, scoring TD on 39y reverse run by WR Ernest Givens.

Ohio State 23 MINNESOTA 19: With Gophers (5-2) facing 4th-and-1 on Ohio State 12YL with 52 secs left, reserve QB Alan Holt was forced into game as ref sent off banged-up QB Ricky Foggie (2 TD runs) despite Minnesota calling timeout. Buckeyes (6-1) halted play to seal win. Ohio State had erased 19-10 4th Q deficit as QB Jim Karsatos converted 4th-and-goal from 1YL with pass to TE Ed Taggart, while TB Vince Workman scored winning TD moments later on 16y run. Workman's TD was set up by CB William White's INT, 1st by Foggie all season. TB Keith Byars started 1st game for Buckeyes in returning from broken foot, rushing for 67y and team's 1st TD before leaving game when his 7th ranked foot stepped on.

NOTRE DAME 37 Southern California 3: Even with 27-0 H lead, Notre Dame (3-3) came out for 2nd H dressed in inspirational green jerseys. WR Randy Tanner put Trojans (3-3) in hole by losing FUM on opening KO after punishing hit by S George Streeter; in Tanner's defense he tore tendon in left knee on hit. Moments later, TB Allen Pinkett scored from 2y out for decisive TD. Pinkett rushed for 110y against nation's 7th ranked rush D. Although Southern California QB Sean Salisbury threw for 191y, Trojans never got much O stoked.

NEBRASKA 17 Colorado 7: Buffaloes (5-2) coach Bill McCartney ran out of QBs at worst time. Backup QB Rick Wheeler's torn knee ligament in 1st Q put him on sideline with injured starting QB Mark Hatcher already there. Third-string QB Craig Keenan was able quickly to lead TD drive for 7-0 lead, even though he had missed time during week with appendix attack. But, Colorado was shut down rest of way. Outgaining Buffs 445y to 218y, Huskers (6-1) pushed series win streak to 18 games. Nebraska IB Doug DuBose (26/125y) tied game in 2nd Q with 1y scoring run, and FB Tom Rathman scored winning TD with 84y run late in 3rd Q. One week after setting record by hitting 7-7 FGs, Nebraska K Dale Klein missed 2 of 3 FG attempts.

SOUTHERN METHODIST 44 Texas 14: Trailing 13-6, Longhorns (4-2) marched 75y with 2nd H KO to SMU 3YL, where they faced 4th-and-1. HB Eric Metcalf took pitchout but was stopped by Ponies LB Kit Case (2 INTs) and S Darrell Reese, who each would tally 11 tackles. GLS and lost FUM on punt RET by Metcalf moments later completely deflated Texas, which then was scorched for 31 pts. After Metcalf's FUM—1 of 6 Texas TOs—SMU (4-2) QB Don King hit WR Jeffrey Jacobs with 45y pass to set up 3y TD run by TB Reggie Dupard (25/117y, 3 TDs, TD receiving). Mustangs next scored on odd play as FB Cobby Morrison ran 65y before being

stripped by Longhorns CB Tony Tillmon, with ball caught by trailing WR Jacobs, who went 30y to EZ. Horns scored on 15y 4th Q TD pass from QB Bret Stafford to WR Russell Hays, but could not prevent worst loss in series history.

TEXAS-EL PASO 23 Brigham Young 16: In 1 of biggest stunners in WAC history, lowly Miners (1-6) shocked BYU (6-2). Coach Bill Yung went with unusual 2-9 D alignment against O averaging 507y and 32 pts. Texas-El Paso's odd D held QB Robbie Bosco to 151y passing with 4 INTs. DB Danny Taylor took decisive INT back for 100y TD that put Miners up 17-10. Heroes abounded for UTEP team winning for only 14th time in 11-year span. Frosh TB John Harvey rushed for 102y, QB Sammy Garza threw for 146y, including 52y TD strike to WR Clarence Seay, and K Hugo Castellano kicked 50y FG. Forced into run strategy, BYU completed only 4-13 passes in 2nd H, while FB Lakei Heimuli rushed for 154y. Clearly caught napping, Cougars had to accept end to 25-game conf winning streak.

November 2, 1985

PENN STATE 16 Boston College 12: Penn State (8-0) continued to sputter, needing 262-lb DT Mike Russo's winning TD on 21y INT RET. Russo caught ball off deflection by DT Tim Johnson. Lions D also had GLS in 2nd Q as LB Shane Conlan's hit forced FUM on 1YL by FB Ken Bell (13/76y), 1 of 4 TOs for Boston College (3-7). Eagles had 12-3 lead late in 3rd Q when Bell scored on 54y run, but this thunderbolt seemed to wake up Lions. Facing 4th-and-1 on own 46YL, Penn State went for it: TB D.J. Dozier (21/91y) slipped wide against stacked D and rambled around LE for 42y to set up 1y TD keeper by QB John Shaffer. Russo scored moments later as Lions pulled out another squeaker. BC QB Shawn Halloran (24-48/245y) led O that gained 359y, but was sacked 3 times and threw 2 INTs. "When was the last time I scored a touchdown?" asked Russo after game. "Never. That's it right there."

MARYLAND 28 North Carolina 10: In winning 15th straight ACC game Terps (6-2) overwhelmed North Carolina with 2y TDs, scoring 4 of them on 3 runs by FB Rick Badanjek (24/88y) and pass from QB Stan Gelbaugh (16-25/197y, 3 INTs) to TE Chris Knight. Maryland D sparkled with 2 stops on 4th down, 4 forced TOs, and made 6 sacks. Tar Heels (4-4) trailed 14-0 at H, but pulled to 14-10 as INTs set up 43y FG by K Kenny Miller and 15y TD pass from sub QB Jonathan Hall to WR Eric Streater (6/73y). Terps settled down with 87y drive to Badanjek's 2nd TD run. After UNC failed to gain 1st down, Gelbaugh led 4th TD drive, hitting 31y pass to WR Eric Holder on 4th down to set up yet another TD by Badanjek, his 46th career TD.

Miami 35 FLORIDA STATE 27: Daring in face of pressure, Miami (7-1) QB Vinny Testaverde stood tall to deliver team's 9th straight road win. Seminoles (6-2) threw everything at Testaverde (23-41/339y), sacking him 7 times, but were unable to prevent his 4 TD passes. Go-ahead TD came with 9:55 to go on 30y pass to Canes WR Michael Irvin, who burned CB Martin Mayhew, for 28-27 lead. Irvin had set it up with 22y reception. Testaverde added 1y TD pass to WR Brett Perriman. Florida State had opened scoring on 8y TD pass from QB Chip Ferguson (14-28/158y, 2 TDs, 2 INTs) to WR Hassan Jones. Miami countered with pair of 1st Q TD catches by WR Brian Blades (5/129y), but Seminoles tied it on blocked punt REC in EZ and built 27-21 lead on Ferguson's 2nd TD pass and 2 FGs by K Derek Schmidt.

Florida 14 AUBURN 10: Coach Galen Hall was cruising at helm of Gators (7-0-1), advancing to 15-0-1mark. It helped that thigh bruise suffered by Auburn (6-2) TB Bo Jackson (16/48y) limited him to only 3 plays in 2nd H. Florida's main weapons, TB Neal Anderson (23/84y) and QB Kerwin Bell (9-20/121y), were banged up but playing, and they sparked Gators to winning 69y TD trip realized, with 7:18 left, on 8y fingertip reception by WR Ray McDonald off fade pattern for his 2nd scoring catch. Big play of drive was 36y draw run by FB John L. Williams (9/82y). After scoring their sole TD on 2y run by QB Pat Washington early in 4th Q, Tigers managed only single 1st down on final 2 possessions. Led by frosh DT Tracy Rocker, Auburn D had 4 sacks/−53y. Gators improved their gruesome record at Auburn to 3-21.

Louisiana State 14 MISSISSIPPI 0: For 2nd straight game Bengals (5-1) D posted shutout, with help from rainstorm that turned SEC battle into punting contest. Despite needing 13 punts from P Matt DeFrank (37.6y average) and gaining only 245y, LSU won by reaching EZ twice in 5-min span of 1st H. TB Dalton Hilliard (30/91y) was big scorer with 1y and 4y TD runs to end consecutive possessions. Mississippi (3-4-1), restricted by knee injury suffered by QB Kent Austin in 2nd Q, gained 149y and suffered 4 TOs. Hopeful Rebels switched from Navy blue jerseys to cardinal for 2nd H without success. Ole Miss improved in 2nd H, but saw 2 drives end on INTs inside LSU 10YL and were stacked up by Tigers GLS at 2YL.

OHIO STATE 22 Iowa 13: Thanks to yeoman effort by Ohio State D, Hawkeyes (7-1) left rainy Columbus without its no. 1 ranking. With LBs Chris Spielman and Pepper Johnson spilling ball carriers all over gridiron, Iowa was in trouble. Each LB registered 19 tackles, while Spielman also contributed 2 INTs. They stopped Hawkeyes' tying attempt in 3rd Q when, with Buckeyes (7-1) up 15-7, Iowa called for TB Ronnie Harmon (26/127y, TD) to run 4 straight times inside Ohio 10YL. Johnson nailed him on 3rd-and-2 after 1y gain, and Spielman crushed him on 4th down for no gain. Ohio State shut down Iowa aerial ace QB Chuck Long, forcing 4 INTs and limiting him to 169y, no TDs. Crowd noise eliminated audibles, key to Long's attack management. Meanwhile, Buckeyes featured balanced attack behind QB Jim Karsatos (10-17/151y, 2 INTs) that converted 3 TOs into 17 pts, including 57y TD run by TB John Wooldridge in 2nd Q.

ILLINOIS 3 Michigan 3: Coaches' sons played key roles as LB Andy Moeller, son of Michigan D coordinator Gary, made 19 tackles, and K Chris White, son of Illini (4-3-1) coach Mike White, hit crossbar on possible winning 37y FG try at game's end because Michigan LB Dieter Heren got finger on it. Both teams scored in 3rd Q as White booted 36y FG and Wolverines K Mike Gillette matched it from 49y. In 4th Q, Michigan drove to Illinois 12YL when FB Gerald White lost FUM, recovered by Illini LB Bob Sebring. Illinois QB Jack Trudeau (27-36/238y), although kept out of EZ by Michigan D that also frustrated Iowa's Chuck Long and Purdue's Jim Everett, surpassed Tulsa's Jerry Rhome (1964) for NCAA mark for consecutive passes without INT, eventually stretched to 215. Michigan WR Paul Jokisch caught 6/130y of his team's 142y passing. White would end season as Illinois' all-time top scorer.

TEXAS A&M 19 Southern Methodist 17: SWC foes combined for 16 pts in final 6:38 with winning 3-ptr coming on 48y FG by Texas A&M (6-2) K Eric Franklin with 1:46 left. Earlier, Franklin missed x-pt and FG. SMU (4-3) had scored 1st on 4y run by TB Reggie Dupard (19/69y) to cap 47y drive kept alive with Dupard's 3y run on 4th-and-1. Franklin then kicked 38y FG in 2nd Q after O PEN wiped out TD pass. After WR Rod Harris galloped 71y on RET of 2nd H KO, Aggies took 3rd Q lead on 2y TD run by FB Anthony Toney (21/117y), who cracked 100y rushing barrier with teammate TB Keith Woodside (12/104y). After Mustangs tied game with FG, Texas A&M regained lead on WR Shea Walker's 5y TD catch from QB Kevin Murray (12-23/107y). Missed x-pt allowed SMU to take lead at 17-16 as it marched 91y—29y on pass from QB Don King (12-27/172y, INT) to WR Jeffrey Jacobs—to score on 4y run by TB Jeff Atkins with 4:46 left. Aggies then went 50y to Franklin's winning FG.

AP Poll November 5

1 Florida (42)	1159	11 Baylor	597
2 Penn State (15)	1113	12 Arkansas	556
3 Nebraska	1027	13 Auburn	462
4 Ohio State (1)	958	14 UCLA	452
5 Air Force	882	15 Louisiana State	359
6 Iowa	834	16 Florida State	243.5
7 Oklahoma (1)	821	17 Georgia	228
8 Miami	815	18 Brigham Young	193
9 Michigan	685	19 Tennessee	158
10 Oklahoma State	600	20 Alabama	94

November 9, 1985

WAKE FOREST 27 Duke 7: Frosh QB Mike Elkins (13-21/119y, INT) emerged as leader of Wake Forest (4-6) by throwing 3 TDs, 2 in 17-pt 2nd Q. Elkins was aided by rushing attack that gained 272y, led by RB Michael Ramseur's 149y. After scoreless 1st Q, during which Duke (2-7) reached Wake 4YL before losing FUM by TB Stanley Monk, Elkins opened scoring with 12y TD pass to WR James Brim. On Duke's next play, QB Steve Slayden (16-26/166y) threw INT to S Dexter Victor to set up 32y FG by Wake Forest K Doug Illing. Wake D forced punt, and Elkins provided imposing 17-0 lead on 5y TD pass to WR Greg Scales. Blue Devils marched 79y on next series to 22y TD pass to WR Doug Green, but were blanked beyond that point.

Miami 29 MARYLAND 22 (Baltimore): Oddly, jittery Miami (8-1) had to endure frustrating TOs that ended its opening 4 possessions. Ultimately, Terrapins (6-3) were ready to crawl back into shells after blowing 13-0 and 22-13 leads. With game knotted at 13-13 at H, Maryland scored 9 straight pts on 2y TD run by FB Rick Badanjek (16/79y) and safety after punt blunder by Miami (8-1) P Jeff Feagles. WR Brett Perriman brought Canes to within 22-20 on 74y punt TD RET, and then K Greg Cox kicked winning 20y FG with 8:13 left, after having had his 19y 3-pt try blocked earlier in 4th Q. HB Melvin Bratton added his 2nd soaring TD for final score. Miami TE Willie Smith caught 8/140y as QB Vinny Testaverde threw for 298y, including 35y on 2nd Q TD pass to WR Michael Irvin (5/82y).

Georgia 24 Florida 3 (Jacksonville): Bulldogs (7-1-1) put end to Florida's unbeaten ride, knocking off rival for 11th time in last 14 contests. Gators (7-1-1) QB Kerwin Bell surprisingly was unable to penetrate Georgia EZ despite throwing for school-record 408y. One reason was Florida's meager 28y net rushing because of 5 sacks of Bell. Bulldogs, meanwhile, rushed for 344y. Leading way for Georgia was frosh FB Keith Henderson, who dashed 9/145y, with 2 TDs, including 76y burst up middle in 1st H. Fellow frosh TB Tim Worley (7/104y) raced 89y in 4th Q to close scoring. Georgia DE Greg Waters contributed 13 tackles and sack, while breaking up 2 passes. FB John L. Williams led Gators with 42y rushing and 12 catches/103y, but lost 4th Q FUM at Georgia 8YL. Florida was able to keep 1st-ever no. 1 ranking for only 1 week. "We were a total team today," said winning coach Vince Dooley. "I don't know how you play any better. Everybody was superb."

LOUISIANA STATE 14 Alabama 14: With 1:24 left, Alabama (6-2-1) coach Ray Perkins settled for tying x-pt by K Van Tiffin. Tigers (5-1-1) then raced downfield, with QB Jeff Wickersham (12-23/214y) hitting 4 passes/55y, to set up 24y FG attempt by K Ron Lewis, who promptly missed for 3rd time. Deadlocked outcome overshadowed fine 1st start by Alabama frosh RB Gene Jelks (14/95y), who ran for 33y TD for 7-0 H lead and displayed passing prowess in 4th Q with 2y TD toss to QB Mike Shula (13-24/153y). One play earlier, Shula converted 4th-and-19 with 29y pass to WR Albert Bell. In between Jelks' scoring efforts, LSU scored dual 3rd Q TDs on 49y run by TB Garry James and 67y catch by WR Wendell Davis (3/119y).

IOWA 59 Illinois 0: Hawkeyes (8-1) easily bounced back from 1st loss, blowing open game with 5 TDs in 1st Q. QB Chuck Long passed 10-12/188y in 1st Q alone, connecting with WB Robert Smith on TDs of 49y and 43y. Illinois native Long—passed over by Illini despite hailing from Wheaton, Red Grange's hometown—soon toned down aerial efforts and finished with 289y passing and 4 TDs. Iowa FB David Hudson plowed for 2 TDs and TB Ronnie Harmon added 46y scoring run. Illini (4-4-1) turned ball over 9 times and rushed for 5y. Illinois QB Jack Trudeau threw for 208y, but had NCAA record string of passes without INT end at 215 on INT by Iowa S Jay Norvell off deflection in 1st Q.

ARKANSAS 20 Baylor 14: Arkansas (8-1) TE Luther Franklin, with 1 career catch, surprised Bears with winning 50y TD grab with 6:09 left. It was only completion in 4 tries by QB Greg Thomas, coming on "117-pass," put into playbook for game. Baylor (7-2) led entire way behind QBs Tom Muecke and Cody Carlson, who combined for 311y passing and accounted for TD each for 14-0 lead. Muecke's TD was dramatic, as he connected with WR Matt Clark (6/153y) for 88y pass—longest ever to date against Arkansas. Hogs admirably clamped down Baylor's Veer, allowing 118y on ground and forcing 5 TOs, including 4 INTs—2 off each QB. Razorbacks converted pair of INTs into TDs, on trips of 29y and 25y, to tighten game at 14-12 in 4th Q.

AIR FORCE 45 Army 7: Both teams were prospering with Wishbone O, but Falcons (10-0) had better talent including WR Ken Carpenter, son of former Army hero Bill. Carpenter caught 64y TD pass from QB Bart Weiss in 2nd Q to begin rout. Weiss (4-9/105y) ran for 114y, with 56y TD romp in 3rd Q, to lead 396y ground game. Air Force reclaimed Commander-in-Chief trophy by rolling up 501y and 24 1st downs to 186y for Army (7-2). Cadets had entered game tops in nation in scoring avg, but had to settle for late 7y TD run by HB Clarence Jones, Army's leading rusher with 39y.

Ucla 24 ARIZONA 19: Wild contest went to UCLA (7-1-1). Big special team plays set up opening scores as bad punt snap by Arizona led to 27y drive for Bruins' 1st TD, 7y run by TB Gaston Green (29/78y), and S Chuck Cecil's punt block did same for Wildcats (6-3), who tied game on 2y run by TB James DeBow. Back from injury, Green rushed for 3 TDs, including score that followed, by 2 plays, his amazing REC of downfield FUM by WR Karl Dorrell. Ball was loose near 4 Arizona defenders, yet trailing Green came up with it on Arizona 4YL. Ensuing TD put Bruins up 24-7, but they almost blew it. CB Dennis Price lost FUM after his INT in 4th Q, and it gave Wildcats new life on Bruins 24YL. DeBow, who recovered Price's FUM, ran for his 2nd TD to pull Cats within 24-13. QB David Norrie committed next Bruins' boner. While extinguishing clock, he threw ball to avoid sack and was picked off by DT Dana Wells, who rumbled 61y for TD. UCLA D finally calmed down Cats' rally.

CALIFORNIA 14 Southern California 6: Unable to score TD for 3rd time in 1985, Southern California (4-4) reached new low in falling to California, Pac-10 cellar-dweller. Golden Bears (4-6) frosh TB Marc Hicks (22/113y) scored twice, on 26y pass play that featured nifty running, and 16y run with botched handoff. QB Kevin Brown (9-16/156y) lost ball on play on hit by LB Marcus Cotton, with FUM being picked up by Hicks who raced to EZ. Triple-threat Hicks also punted for Bears and ran 26y for 1st down after low punt snap in 1st Q. USC managed 2 FGs by K Don Shafer, while rushing for 130y and passing for 166y against D that allowed 20 or more pts in 9 previous games. TB Ryan Knight led Trojans with 62y rushing.

AP Poll November 11

1 Penn State (44)	1143	11 Florida	577
2 Nebraska (9)	1083	12 Georgia	548
3 Ohio State (2)	1021	13 UCLA	494
4 Air Force (2)	941	14 Auburn	436
5t Iowa	891	15 Florida State	323
5t Miami	891	16 Brigham Young	238
7 Oklahoma (2)	883	17 Baylor	225
8 Michigan	744	18 Tennessee	204
9 Arkansas	662	19 Louisiana State	172
10 Oklahoma State	646	20 Alabama	82

November 16, 1985

PENN STATE 36 Notre Dame 6: Avenging 44-7 loss in 1984, Penn State (10-0) finally looked like 1984's no. 1 team with easy win. Building 23-0 H lead that grew to 36-0 after 3 Qs, Nittany Lions were led by QB John Shaffer, who was at Cincinnati's Moeller High when coach Gerry Faust left for Notre Dame. Shaffer and backup QB Matt Kinzner led scoring drives on 8 of Lions' 1st 9 possessions, with 5 ending on FGs by K Massimo Manca. TB Hiawatha Francisco's 2y TD in 4th Q run broke shutout for Irish squad that bumbled away 5 TOs. Penn State D held TB Allen Pinkett to 61y rushing, 127y less than he racked up in 1984 tilt. With ND's worst defeat since 1974, Faust now had suffered more defeats (24) than any Irish coach.

Maryland 34 CLEMSON 31: Maryland (7-3) won 3rd straight ACC title as walk-on frosh K Dan Plocki booted 20y FG with 3 secs left. For his effort, Plocki was awarded scholarship. Clemson (5-5) had built 24-14 H lead, converting 2 blocked punts into TDs including CB Perry Williams' 30y TD RET. Terps QB Stan Gelbaugh (23-35/361y, INT) led rally to tie game 24-24 on his 2nd TD pass, 20y to TE Ferrell Edmunds (6/101y). Teams then traded TDs, but not without controversy. Trailing by 7, Maryland faced 3rd-and-goal at Clemson 2YL. With 1:18 left, Gelbaugh threw into EZ for Edmunds, who dropped ball. Refs ruled TE had possession for TD, while Clemson argued against both ruling and that 25-sec clock expired before snap. Terps then forced punt before Gelbaugh's 3 pass connections set up Plocki's winning 3-ptr. Game ended unfortunately as Clemson players angrily jumped CB Lewis Askew after his tackle on final KO.

Auburn 24 GEORGIA 10: Auburn (8-2) TB Bo Jackson (19/121y) added to highlight reel with 67y scoring burst, breaking 2 tackles en route, in 2nd Q, and 6y insurance TD run in 4th Q on play in which he ran over Bulldogs S Miles Smith. Jackson unleashed his speed and power on Georgia's SEC-best rush D (85.5y avg). Bulldogs (7-2-1) had 7-3 lead on 4y run by QB James Jackson (11-22/162y, INT), but could not contain Bo Jackson and fell behind in time it took him to race 67y. Tigers went up 17-7 at H as WR Freddy Weygand went 8y on reverse, leaping into EZ for score. Tigers QB Pat Washington threw for 122y in support of O that gained 336y with no TOs, while DT Tracy Rocker led spirited D with 15 tackles and 2 sacks.

Iowa 27 PURDUE 24: Hawkeyes (9-1) moved into 1st place in Big 10, needing 64y drive late in 4th Q for winning 25y FG by K Rob Houghtlin. Boilermakers (4-6) then drove to Iowa 20YL before time expired; on final play TB Rodney Carter (8/77y) was unable to get OB to stop clock. Time ran out before QB Jim Everett threw pass away, which drew ire of coach Leon Burnett for lack of home-field clock advantage. Iowa TB Ronnie Harmon excelled both rushing (25/122y) and receiving (9/118y), while FB David Hudson ran for 118y and 2 TDs. Passing duel between Everett (23-32/325y, TD, INT) and Iowa QB Chuck Long (20-33/268y, INT) was virtual standoff.

Wisconsin 12 OHIO STATE 7: Wisconsin (5-5) won in Columbus, once Badger graveyard, and it was Buckeyes' 4th loss in last 5 games to Wisconsin. Badgers LB Mike Reid had big hand in upset, recovering trio of Ohio State (8-2) FUMs after Bucks had lost only 2 in 9 prior games. Biggest FUM REC came in 3rd Q with Badgers trailing 7-6, when Buckeyes QB Jim Karsatos (20-31/263y) lost ball on own 22YL. FB Marvin Artley's 1y TD run was scored 4 plays later. Ohio State's next drive ended with 4th-and-2 stop by LBs Russ Fields and Craig Raddatz of TB Vince Workman on Badgers 11YL, and next Ohio possession was halted when Reid recovered FUM by TB Roman Bates on Wisconsin 3YL. Visitors had 6-0 lead on 2 FGs by K Todd Gregoire before Ohio WR Cris Carter (7/131y) caught 37y TD pass.

OKLAHOMA 31 Colorado 0: Injured Oklahoma QB Troy Aikman and replacement QB Jamelle Holieway do not seem to have much in common, except for 1 thing—both know how to beat you. Holieway rushed for 79y and TD runs of 2y and 20y to lead rout as Sooners (7-1) gained 360y on ground. Sooners D held Buffs (6-4) to measly 109y total, dominating Wishbone O inferior to 1 faced in practice. Colorado could not crack midfield until midway through 4th Q, when they reached OU 46YL. S Rodney Rogers made 14 tackles for over-worked Colorado D.

TEXAS A&M 10 Arkansas 6: With SWC lead in balance, teams slugged it out in fog-shrouded Kyle Field. After 32y FG in 1st Q by K Eric Franklin, Aggies (7-2) went up 3-0, which went to 10-0 on 18y 3rd Q TD pass from QB Kevin Murray to FB Roger Vick. Arkansas (8-2) O found responding arduous, rushing for 141y, which was barely more than half its 278y avg. Miscues cost Razorbacks as QB Greg Thomas threw EZ INT to A&M S Kip Corrington at end of 1st H and HB Bobby Joe Edmonds lost FUM to set up Aggies' TD. Hogs scored late in 4th Q on CB Kevin Anderson's EZ REC of punt blocked by DE Rickey Williams, but they failed on 2-pt attempt.

BRIGHAM YOUNG 28 Air Force 21: Match-up of 4th-ranked Air Force (10-1) and BYU, WAC's glamour team, brought large attention to conf. BYU (9-2) QB Robbie Bosco (29-49/343y) came out rusty, completing 2-9 to start before straightening himself out; he was 12-15/198y in 2nd H. Bosco finished by allowing 4 INTs, 2 returned for TDs as Falcons grabbed 21-7 lead without much help from O, which was held significantly below, at 136y, its accustomed high rushing level. Bosco overcame 7 sacks to throw 3 TDs, with pair going to WR Mark Bellini (9/143y) and another of 69y to TB Vai Sikahema for game-winner with 5:41 left. Sikahema earlier made 72y punt TD RET to cut it to 21-14. Trailing late, Air Force drove to BYU 7YL before Cougars S Rob Ledenko picked off QB Bart Weiss (9-18/101y) in EZ to preserve win.

AP Poll November 19

1 Penn State (46)	1180	11 Brigham Young	518
2 Nebraska (12)	1122	12 Ohio State	509
3 Iowa	1020	13 Air Force	492
4 Miami	1011	14 Florida State	436
5 Oklahoma (2)	992	15 Baylor	316
6 Michigan	923	16 Tennessee	310
7 Oklahoma State	769	17 Louisiana State	217
8 UCLA	720	18 Arkansas	186
9 Florida	700	19 Texas A&M	183
10 Auburn	646	20 Georgia	135

November 23, 1985

Penn State 31 PITTSBURGH 0: Penn State (11-0) was on mission to both prove doubters wrong and avenge 1984 loss. Any chance Panthers (5-5-1), had to stay competitive, in coach Foge Fazio's final game, ended in 2nd Q when Lions FB Tim Manoa (7/91y, 2 TDs) burst through 3 defenders on right side of line for 60y TD run and, 19 secs later, LB Pete Giftopoulos fell on EZ FUM by Pitt QB John Congemi. Penetrating DE Don Graham forced Congemi's FUM. Congemi threw for only 75y, while TB Charles Gladman rushed for 81y. Rout was costly as Lions TB D.J. Dozier (57y, TD) dislocated elbow in 3rd Q, but win wrapped up 5th perfect regular season for coach Joe Paterno in 20 years as Penn State head coach.

MICHIGAN 27 Ohio State 17: Wolverines (9-1-1) QB Jim Harbaugh put stamp on rivalry with near-perfect performance, completing 16-19/230y, 3 TDs. Harbaugh finished off Ohio State (8-3) in 4th Q with his most memorable throw: 77y strike to Ohio native, frosh WR John Kolesar. Beating blitz, Harbaugh's pass was perfect, and it had to be as Kolesar lost contact lens in looking up for ball. Moments earlier, Buckeyes pulled within 20-17 on 36y TD pass on 4th-and-15 from QB Jim Karsatos (17-31/179y, INT) to WR Cris Carter (5/90y). Michigan FB Gerald White added 110y rushing and caught 4y TD pass. Harbaugh set season school records for pass y (1,913y) and TDs (18). Point total was most in series for Michigan since 1946.

IOWA 31 Minnesota 9: After passing up NFL last winter to have another shot at trip to Rose Bowl, Iowa (10-1) QB Chuck Long (21-31/268y, INT) wrapped up school's 4th-ever Pasadena berth with record-setting performance. Long became 1st Big 10 QB to surpass 10,000y (10,052y) passing, while throwing 26th TD pass of season for another conf mark. Long's scoring pass, 4y to TE Mike Flagg, gave Hawkeyes commanding 17-3 lead they took to H. Gophers (6-5) were not able to crack Iowa EZ until late in game on QB Alan Holt's 16y TD pass to WR Eugene Gailord. Hawkeyes won 1st outright Big 10 title since 1958—they shared crown in 1981—and Iowa won 10 games for 1st time ever.

OKLAHOMA 27 Nebraska 7: Great rivalry fizzled as Oklahoma (8-1) dominated on both sides of ball. QB Jamelle Holieway rushed for 110y and 2 TDs, including 43y TD run in 1st Q, while TE Keith Jackson, little used as receiver since injury to QB Troy Aikman, carried ball 3/136y on E-arounds to surprisingly lead Sooners in rushing. Jackson raced 88y on TE reverse for 1st Q TD as OU logged 246y rushing in 1st Q of its 423y game-end total. WB Von Sheppard ran 52y on reverse to Sooners 6YL in 2nd Q to breathe some life into Nebraska (9-2). But after 3 plays, Huskers were still on 6YL, and K Dale Klein then missed chip-shot FG. DT Chris Spachman scored Nebraska's sole TD on 76y FUM RET with 26 secs left, much to chagrin of shutout-hungry Sooners D which permitted 161y rushing and 224y total.

IOWA STATE 15 Oklahoma State 10: Snow, frigid wind, and occasional 11-man D front stopped TB Thurman Thomas (21/54y), and so Oklahoma State (8-2) was stopped. Iowa State (5-6) TB Andrew Jackson rushed for 93y, while WR Hughes Suffern scored Cyclones' TD on 13y pass from QB Alex Espinoza for 9-0 1st Q lead. K Rick Frank supplied ultimate margin with 3 FGs. Cyclones dared Oklahoma State QB Ronnie Williams to pass, and he threw badly: 14-44/206y, 3 INTs. "Basically they just lined up against us and whipped us," said Cowboys coach Pat Jones.

TEXAS 17 Baylor 10: Must-win game for both went to Longhorns (8-2) as blitzing D neutralized Baylor. Texas owned 2-TD lead in 4th Q, but Bears (8-3) halved deficit on 14y TD run by RB Randy Rutledge and took over late in 4th Q on Texas 10YL after stellar DB Ron Francis' INT. Longhorns stuck with blitz, holding Bears to 5y on 3 downs before coming up with 4th down sack: DE James McKinney finishing what heavy pressure by DT Rocky Reid and LB Ty Allert had started. Texas TB Edwin Simmons bulled his way to 90y rushing and 8y TD, while Baylor TB Derrick McAdoo reached same total with 59y having come on run that set up TD.

ARKANSAS 15 Southern Methodist 9: With time running out, Arkansas (9-2) needed big play, and HB Bobby Joe Edmonds delivered. Down 9-7 and facing 3rd-and-23 from their own 27YL, Hogs got speedy Edmonds isolated on Mustangs LB Kit Case (13 tackles), who soon slipped on fake, to burn SMU (6-4) for 48y pass play. Razorbacks needed 4 plays to travel remaining 25y to 4y TD keeper by QB Mark Calcagni, with 3:47 left. FB Derrick Thomas scored 2 on conv run, and Arkansas' lead grew to 15-9. Mustangs soon stalled on downs, but would have been hard-pressed to score against D that did not allow rushing TD to any SWC opponent all year. All 3 of Ponies' scoring drives ended on FGs by K Brandy Brownlee. Hogs' winning 77y drive was achieved despite Mustangs LB Ben Hummel's 2 sacks.

SOUTHERN CALIFORNIA 17 Ucla 13: Bruins (8-2-1) did everything they could to blow Rose Bowl bid, turning ball over 5 times and allowing USC to travel 56y in final 2 mins for winning TD. Trojans (5-5) frosh QB Rodney Peete scored that TD on 1y run after gaining 1st down 4 plays earlier on 3y run on 4th-and-2 from 6YL. UCLA lost 3 FUMs within Trojans 20YL, including TB Eric Ball's bobble on 1YL. Peete completed 8-15/101y, with all 8 caught by TE Joe Cormier, including 34y TD in 1st Q. TB Ryan Knight rushed for 147y against UCLA's top-notch rushing D to offset 145y gained by Bruins TB Gaston Green. UCLA K John Lee set NCAA record with his 79 career FGs, converting both attempts. Bruins could still capture Rose Bowl berth, but needed Arizona State to lose in Tempe.

Arizona 16 ARIZONA STATE 13: Wildcats (8-3) happily bounced bitter rivals from Rose Bowl as K Max Zendejas booted 32y FG with 1:43 left to supply winning pts over Arizona State (8-3) for 3rd straight year. Game turned on hit by Arizona LB Byron Evans that forced punt FUM by Sun Devils CB Anthony Parker, recovered in EZ for TD by Arizona CB Don Be'Ans. Arizona had been outplayed to that moment, yet now trailed only 13-10. Sun Devils QB Jeff Van Raaphorst (19-41/209y, 2 INTs), who threw for team's only TD on 7y pass to FB Vince Amoia, lost FUM to Cats DT Stan Mataele to set up winning FG on sack by DT Dana Wells. Tie would have sent ASU to Rose Bowl, but Sun Devils decided to keep passing to try to win. Van Raaphorst later threw INT to S Chuck Cecil to end final threat. Zendejas also booted 42y and 57y FGs for 77 3-ptrs in his career, 1 short of brother Luis' former NCAA record. Max could not match UCLA's John Lee, who set career FG mark and, thanks to Max's last FG, was Pasadena-bound with Bruins.

AP Poll November 25

1 Penn State (49)	1186	11 Air Force	583
2 Iowa (3)	1082	12 Florida State	581
3 Oklahoma (6)	1074	13 Louisiana State	425
4 Miami (1)	1058	14 Arkansas	370
5 Michigan (1)	971	15 Texas A&M	367
6 Florida	848	16 UCLA	286
7 Auburn	761	17 Oklahoma State	269
8 Nebraska	722	18 Texas	238
9 Brigham Young	631	19 Ohio State	196
10 Tennessee	590	20 Georgia	168

November 28-30, 1985

(Th'g) TEXAS A&M 42 Texas 10: Thanks to 3 TD passes by slick QB Kevin Murray (10-17/146y), Aggies (9-2) no longer had to wait for next year. They were packing bags for 1st trip to Cotton Bowl since 1967. Up 7-0 at H, Texas A&M exploded for 21-pts in 4-min span of 3rd Q as Murray threw pair of TDs to WR Rod Harris (3/61y), and FB Roger Vick (19/87y) scored on 11y run with Longhorns presenting TO gifts to set up 2nd and 3rd scores. Texas (8-3), which gave away 6 TOs total and allowed 6 sacks, finally scored in 4th Q on K Jeff Ward's titanic 57y FG. Following successful onside-KO, Texas scored again on 10y pass by QB Todd Dodge to WR Russell Hays. Texas A&M answered with 2 more TDs, still throwing passes with big lead. Aggies WR Jeff Nelson caught 7/107y and opening 10y TD.

West Virginia 13 SYRACUSE 10: It was not Syracuse's fault that Mountaineers (7-3-1) were denied bowl bid, but they sure did pay for it. Inspired by snub, West Virginia pulled out win with last min TD drive. QB Mike Timko, who threw for 198y, drove WVU 75y to score on 5y pass to WR Grantis Bell with 36 secs left. On drive, Timko hit WR Harvey Smith with passes of 44, 30, and 14y. Orangemen (7-4) QB Don McPherson (14-21/186y) led O with help from WR Scott Schwedes (6/79y), who contributed 38y punt RET to set up FG and 20y TD reception in 3rd Q. Syracuse suffered 9 FUMs in 1st H, losing 3, before tightening its grip to go FUM-free in 2nd H.

MIAMI 58 Notre Dame 7: Notre Dame (5-6) coach Gerry Faust's 5-year run at school ended with horrid 4th Q that included TD passes by back-up QB, last-sec reverse runs, and blocked punt by merciless Canes. With QB Vinny Testaverde (22-32/356y) throwing 2 TDs, Miami (10-1) built 30-0 3rd Q lead en route to scoring on 8 of 10 possessions and handing Notre Dame its worst defeat since Army won 59-0 in 1944. Canes had showboating skills on display, with S Bennie Blades slowing down near GL to high-five teammate near end of 61y INT TD RET in 2nd Q. Irish TB Allen Pinkett rushed for 77y and scored TD on 3y run. Rout was impressive: Miami jumped from no. 4 in country to no. 2, thus proving that some voters clearly rewarded teams for running up score. As it happened, Notre Dame's men's basketball team surrendered fewer pts in same day's 87-56 win over Butler.

GEORGIA TECH 20 Georgia 16: Georgia Tech (8-2-1) WR Gary Lee raced 95y with winning KO RET late in 3rd Q, adding another chapter to great rivalry. Facing possibility of 2-game series losing streak, Bulldogs (7-3-1) thought they had momentum with 39y FG by K Davis Jacobs for 16-10 lead. After Lee's heroics, Yellow Jackets blanked Georgia in 4th Q while adding 46y insurance FG by K David Bell. Lee's TD helped neutralize 371y to 188y advantage for Bulldogs, who were led by fierce ground game featuring TB Lars Tate (18/120y) and FB Keith Henderson (17/111y). Georgia Tech had not won back-to-back games in 15 years against Georgia, which swept 6 straight victories through 1983.

FLORIDA 38 Florida State 14: Treating game like bowl invite, Florida (9-1-1) won unofficial championship of Sunshine State with surprisingly easy win. Gators QB Kerwin Bell (14-22/343y) was unstoppable in leading school to 5th straight series win. In building 28-0 lead, Gators piled up more yards in 1st H (328y) than Florida State (8-3) earned in whole game (292y). TB Neal Anderson chipped in with 95y rushing and 2 1st Q TDs for Florida, while Bell and WR Ricky Nattiel collaborated for 2nd Q TD passes of 75y and 14y, with 2nd being set up by Nattiel's 48y catch. Florida State rallied with 2 TDs in 3rd Q, with CB Deion Sanders taking punt 58y to EZ, but Florida answered with 10 more pts, including 82y TD pass to WR Frankie Neal, to quell momentum switch.

ALABAMA 25 Auburn 23 (Birmingham): Alabama (8-2-1) walk-on K Van Tiffin won classic Iron Bowl with 52y FG at game's end, capping wild 4th Q that witnessed 4 lead changes in final 7:03. Crimson Tide jumped to 13-0 and 16-7 leads before Tigers (8-3) rallied, thanks in part to Alabama's 4 lost FUMs in 3rd Q. Early in 4th Q, Tide suffered EZ INT by Tigers CB Kevin Porter, and Auburn marched 80y, with TB Bo Jackson (142y, 2 TDs) running for 41y and catching pass for 21y, to take 17-16 lead on Jackson's 1y vault with 7:03 left. Alabama needed only 66 secs to regain lead as 74y of 82y drive were gained on TD run by HB Gene Jelks (18/192y), who hit huge hole and was sprung by WR Greg Richardson's downfield block. Bama's 2-pt try failed, and they led 22-17 with shade less than 6 mins left. Tigers went 70y, capped by FB Reggie Ware's 1y TD run for 23-22 lead with 57 secs left. Key plays on drive were WR Freddy Weygand's 21y catch and 15y late-hit PEN incurred by Alabama S Kermit Kendrick. Tide LB Cornelius Bennett batted down 2-pt conv pass. Game's final min belonged to Alabama QB, and future coach, Mike Shula (14-28/195y, INT), who led memorable march. It looked grim early when Auburn NG Harold Hallman sacked Shula, forcing Tide to use final timeout on own 12YL with 47 secs left. Shula threw both 14y pass to Jelks and key block on 20y reverse run by WR Al Bell. With 15 secs left, he threw 19y pass to Richardson, his 3rd choice of receivers on play, and Richardson wriggled OB at Auburn 35YL with 6 secs to play. It set up Tiffin's 4th FG and marked 1st last-sec, game-deciding FG in series history. Alabama LB Thomas Boyd had 12 unassisted tackles as Tigers were held to 161y, less than half their 315y O avg. Jackson played well on his 23rd birthday despite 2 broken ribs suffered in Georgia game. Tigers had extra incentive in 50th annual match, feeling that Alabama blew whistle for recruiting violations that led to 2-year probation.

Oklahoma 13 OKLAHOMA STATE 0: Icy conditions and Sooners (9-1) D conspired to make Oklahoma State (8-3) Oklahoma's 2nd shutout victim of 1985. TB Thurman Thomas fought his way to 100y—only player to achieve century mark versus Sooners all season—but Cowboys finished with 99y on ground and QB Ronnie Williams' 5-25/32y in air. Oklahoma won game on 27y FG by K Tim Lashar in 1st H, pushing lead to 10-0 on 3y scoring run by HB Spencer Tillman. Sooners finished 2nd in country in run D, 1st in pass D, and 1st in fewest avg y allowed.

Houston 24 RICE 20: Houston (4-7) QB Gerald Landry ended season on high note, rushing for 104y and passing for 144y. He rushed for all 3 Cougars TDs, including 1y effort that capped 55y drive early in 4th Q for 24-14 lead. But, Cougars barely held on against Rice (3-8) team that outgained Houston 336y to 323y. Rice QB Quentis Roper ran and passed for TDs before being pulled in 2nd H in favor of backup QB Kerry Overton, who flipped 2y TD pass to WR Eddie Burgoyne, late in 4th Q. Owls quickly recovered onside-KO, but ball was 1y short of necessary 10y, and Houston ran out clock.

December 7, 1985

Navy 17 Army 7 (Philadelphia): On day he finished 7th in Heisman vote, Navy (4-7) TB Napoleon McCallum completed illustrious career with award-worthy show. McCallum rushed for 217y as Midshipmen outgained Army (8-3) on ground by 313y to 192y. Middies' finest moment was 58y drive on last possession that ate more than 5 mins of clock and ended with clinching 26y FG by K Todd Solomon. Navy D's highlight came late in 1st H with GLS that cost Army services of QB Rob Healy, who suffered separated shoulder on 4th-and-1 rush for no gain from Navy 2YL. GLS kept score tied at 7-7, where it stayed until 4th Q when Navy FB Chuck Smith scored winning 5y TD run with 8:26 left. Cadets FB Doug Black was held to 64y rushing to fall 50y short of consecutive 1,000y seasons. McCallum set NCAA records with 7,172y all-purpose and 1,137 all-purpose plays.

Conference Standings

Atlantic Coast

Maryland	6-0
Georgia Tech	5-1
Clemson	4-3
Virginia	4-3
North Carolina	3-4
Duke	2-5
North Carolina State	2-5
Wake Forest	1-6

Southeastern

Tennessee	5-1
Louisiana State	4-1-1
Alabama	4-1-1
Georgia	3-2-1
Auburn	3-3
Mississippi	2-4
Vanderbilt	1-4-1
Kentucky	1-5
Mississippi State	0-6
Florida*	5-1

*Not eligible for championship

Big Ten

Iowa	7-1
Michigan	6-1-1
Illinois	5-2-1
Ohio State	5-3
Michigan State	5-3
Minnesota	4-4
Purdue	3-5
Wisconsin	2-6
Indiana	1-7
Northwestern	1-7

Mid-American

Bowling Green	9-0
Miami	7-1-1
Central Michigan	6-3
Western Michigan	4-4-1
Northern Illinois	4-4
Eastern Michigan	3-6
Ball State	3-6
Toledo	3-6
Kent State	2-6
Ohio	2-7

Big Eight

Oklahoma	7-0
Nebraska	6-1
Oklahoma State	4-3
Colorado	4-3
Iowa State	3-4
Kansas	2-5
Kansas State	1-6
Missouri	1-6

Southwest

Texas A&M	7-1
Arkansas	6-2
Baylor	6-2
Texas	6-2
Houston	3-5
Rice	2-6
Texas Tech	1-7
Texas Christian	0-8
Southern Methodist*	5-3

*Not eligible for conference championship

Western Athletic

Air Force	7-1
Brigham Young	7-1
Utah	5-3
Hawaii	4-3-1
Colorado State	4-4
San Diego State	3-4-1
New Mexico	2-6
Wyoming	2-6
Texas-El Paso	1-7

Pacific-10

UCLA	6-2
Arizona	5-2
Arizona State	5-2
Washington	5-3
Southern California	5-3
Oregon	3-4
Washington State	3-5
Stanford	3-5
Oregon State	2-6
California	2-7

Pacific Coast Athletic

Fresno State	7-0
Cal State-Fullerton	5-2
Nevada-Las Vegas	4-2-1
Long Beach State	4-3
Utah State	3-4
San Jose State	2-4-1
Pacific	2-5
New Mexico State	0-7

1985 Major Bowl Games

Cherry Bowl (Dec. 21): Maryland 35 Syracuse 18

Floundering Cherry Bowl staged its final game before less than half-house, and it turned sour for Syracuse (7-5) as Terps scored 29 straight pts during middle of game to build commanding 35-10 lead. QB Stan Gelbaugh (14-20/223y, INT) threw 2 TDs and ran for 3rd as Maryland (9-3) took advantage of 5 TOs. Winning pts came courtesy of Maryland DT Scott Tye, who grabbed midair punt FUM by Syracuse WR Scott Schwedes and ran 8y for TD to provide 21-10 lead in 2nd Q. Throwing for 204y and rushing for 111y, Syracuse's star QB Don McPherson couldn't single-handedly overcome Terps' 467y to 445y O advantage. However, McPherson threw 3 INTs and lost FUM on Terps 35YL on vital drive that might have reversed fortunes after Tye's TD. Maryland TB Alvin Blount rushed for 132y and 20y TD.

Independence Bowl (Dec. 21): Minnesota 20 Clemson 13

Despite having lost coach Lou Holtz to Notre Dame, Minnesota (7-5) rallied for 1st bowl win since 1962 Rose Bowl and victory in new coach John Gutekunst's debut. Gophers started well: 9y TD pass from QB Ricky Foggie (9-21/123y) to WR Mel Anderson capped 91y drive for 10-0 lead in 2nd Q. Powered by TB Kenny Flowers (27/148y), Tigers (6-6) scored next 13 pts on 2 FGs by K David Treadwell and 3y TD pass from HB Stacey Driver to WR Keith Jennings. Driver later misfired on 4th down pass to QB Rodney Williams from Gophers 12YL, as Clemson tried to stretch lead in 2nd H. Minnesota scored next as K Chip Lohmiller tied game at 13-13 with his 2nd FG early in 4th Q. After Minny D held, TB Valdez Baylor (13/98y) scored winning TD with 4:56 left. Clemson had 4 TOs, including ends to each of its 1st 3 possessions.

Holiday Bowl (Dec. 22): Arkansas 18 Arizona State 17

Frosh K Kendall Trainor was summoned to boot 37y FG with 21 secs left to lift Razorbacks (10-2) to stunning victory. Thanks to 37y RET of ensuing KO by TB Darryl Clack and 21y pass from QB Jeff Van Raaphorst (14-27/167y, INT) to WR Aaron Cox, Arizona State (8-4) dealt itself into FG range in final secs, but 59y effort by K Kent Bostrom, who earlier kicked 3 FGs, was short. Arkansas had taken 15-14 lead earlier in 4th Q on QB Mark Calcagni (10-17/117y) 2-pt conv keeper following 17y TD run by HB Bobby Joe Edmonds. Sun Devils marched 68y to regain 17-15 lead on 28y FG by Bostrom. Edmonds then supplied more heroics on winning drive, converting 4th-and-1 with dive and catching 21y pass.

Liberty Bowl (Dec. 27) Baylor 21 Louisiana State 7

Liberty Bowl was not as close as score would indicate. Underdog Bears (9-3) dominated, outgaining LSU 489y to 192y and earning 26 1st downs to 9 for Tigers. They also trailed 7-0 after Louisiana State (9-2-1) CB Norman Jefferson scored TD on 79y punt RET down left sideline; team's sole highlight, coming midway through 1st Q. Baylor answered with 80y drive—fueled by 59y pass to WR John Simpson (3/117y, TD)—to 5y TD pass from QB Cody Carlson (9-12/167y, 2 TDs) to diving WR Matt Clark. K Terry Syler's 29y FG in 2nd Q proved to be winning pts as Bears D allowed only 72y in 2nd H, 11y in 3rd Q. Syler added 2nd FG, and Carlson hit his 2nd TD. Bears star CB Ron Francis was outstanding with recovered FUM, INT, and 6 tackles. RB Dalton Hilliard led LSU in rushing with 66y.

Florida Citrus Bowl (Dec. 28): Ohio State 10 Brigham Young 7

After holding powerful Brigham Young O in check, it was fitting that Buckeyes (9-3) D would score winning TD. LB Larry Kolic, positioned all about to confuse Cougars (11-3), returned INT of BYU QB Robbie Bosco (26-50/261y, TD, 4 INTs) 14y for 10-7 lead in 3rd Q. Ohio D posted 2nd H shutout to secure win. Cougars committed 6 TOs, with Kolic and S Terry White each coming up with 2 INTs. Bucks K Rich Spangler provided victory margin with 47y FG in 2nd Q that was only score allowed by Cougars D. BYU answered with long drive that ended on lost FUM by TB Vai Sikahema at GL. Later in 2nd Q, BYU was able to crack scoreboard on Bosco's 38y strike to WR David Miles. That would be it for Cougars, held to lowest pt total since 1978. QB Jim Karsatos led Ohio State O with 196y passing.

Sun Bowl (Dec. 28): Georgia 13 Arizona 13

If there was OT in 1985, they might still be playing this tight Sun Bowl. Arizona (8-3-1) grabbed 13-3 lead after 3 Qs on 2nd FG by K Max Zendejas and 35y INT TD RET by CB Martin Rudolph. INT was 1 of only 8 passes attempted by Georgia. Bulldogs (7-3-2) answered with 52y drive to 2nd FG by K Dave Jacobs, subbing for injured K Steve Crumley. Georgia forced FUM by Wildcats TB James DeBow 2 plays later, recovered by S Tony Flack to set up tying 2y dive by TB Lars Tate (22/71y). Each team had chance to win late in 4th Q, but Jacobs missed 44y 3-pt try with 69 secs left and Zendejas missed 39y FG try with 4 ticks left. Zendejas' try was set up by blistering 25y run on 4th down by shifty Arizona TB David Adams (13/51y). Ironically Zendejas was named player of game as balloting took place before late miss. Even though he was 3rd on all-time career FGs list with 79, Zendejas was in no mood for acceptance speeches. LB Byron Evans' 23 tackles sparked Wildcats D.

Aloha Bowl (Dec. 28): Alabama 24 Southern California 3

By whipping them on field, Alabama (9-2-1) tied Trojans, with 21 overall bowl wins. Crimson Tide succeeded with what worked in many past bowl games: powerful rushing attack and unrelenting D. This was especially true in 2nd H that was controlled 21-0 by Tide, during which Alabama rushed for 141y and Trojans (6-6) ended up with −10y on ground. Helped by USC's ineptitude, Alabama began 1st TD drive at Trojans 42YL after 14y punt RET by WR Greg Richardson, 2nd TD drive at Trojans 44YL after INT by S Kermit Kendricks, and 3rd TD drive at Trojans 44YL after short punt. QB Mike Shula led Bama with 112y passing, including 24y TD toss to WR Clay Whitehurst, while HB Gene Jelks paced rushing attack with 79y.

Freedom Bowl (Dec. 30) Washington 20 Colorado 17

Nip-and-tuck game went down to wire, with Washington (7-5) holding off Buffs in showdown at its GL at game's end. After pulling within 20-17 on P Barry Helton's 31y TD pass to TE Jon Embree on fake punt early in 4th Q, Colorado marched toward Huskies GL late in game. Rally ended when HB Mike Marquez (10/80y) lost FUM on 2YL, although Colorado felt ground had caused FUM. LB David Rill, who led Washington with 17 tackles, pounced on FUM. Huskies had taken lead for good at 17-10 on 1y TD dive by frosh TB Tony Covington late in 3rd Q. On 1st play of 4th Q, K Jeff Jaeger made his 2nd FG, from 18y out, to supply Huskies with winning pts.

Gator Bowl (Dec. 30): Florida State 34 Oklahoma State 23

Seminoles (9-3) returned to pass-happy O, flinging ball all over field against D built to play run game. Florida State QB Chip Ferguson completed 20-43/338y—with 12 throws coming on game's 1st 13 snaps to quickly test soon-to-be shell-shocked secondary of Cowboys (8-4). Once Oklahoma State adjusted, TB Tony Smith ran wild for Florida State, to tune of 201y. What was surprising about number of FSU passes was the absence of starting WRs Hassan Jones, to suspension, and Phillip Bryant, to injury. Seminoles reserve WR Herb Gainer stepped up with 7/148y and TDs of 39y in 2nd Q and 19y in 3rd Q. He caught 1st TD on bounce off shoulder of Pokes CB Demise Williams. With Noles focusing on TB Thurman Thomas (26/97y), Cowboys were forced to pass more than usual. QB Ronnie Williams also threw 43 times, with 21 completions/251y and 29y TD pass on screen pass to Thomas. Williams and Thomas reversed roles as Thomas tossed 12y TD pass in 3rd Q to QB.

Peach Bowl (Dec. 31): Army 31 Illinois 29

Army (9-3) needed full game of big plays to win, with S Peel Chronister (2 INTs), in lineup due to injury to S Darold Londo, capping great game by breaking up late conv pass to seal win. Illinois (6-5-1) had pulled within 31-29 on 54y TD pass by QB Jack Trudeau to WR David Williams (7/109y, 2 TDs) with 34 secs left. Cadets had built lead on pair of HB-option passes: TDs on 33y pass from HB William Lampley to WR Benny White in 2nd Q and 26y pass from HB Clarence Jones to WR Scott Spellmon in 3rd Q. Spellmon's great catch of wobbling throw gave Army lead for good at 28-23. K Craig Stopa added 39y FG in 4th Q for what proved to be winning pts. Army QB Rob Healy rushed for 107y, with 22y on 1st Q TD, despite lingering effects of dislocated left shoulder suffered in Navy game. Illinois lost 4 TOs that led to 24 pts by Army. Trudeau set 3 game records with 38-55/401y passing.

Bluebonnet Bowl (Dec. 31): Air Force 24 Texas 16

Longhorns were expected to exploit size advantage, but Air Force (12-1) proved stalwart indeed. Texas (8-4) D focused on Falcons QB Bart Weiss, who had become 3rd QB ever to exceed 1,000y both rushing and passing in season, and he was held to 41y rushing and 5y passing. Weiss took what D presented and inside handoffs to FB Pat Evans (18/129y) proved to be Falcons' best strategy. Evans scored on 19y run in 3rd Q for 21-10 lead that proved sufficient. TD capped 23y drive that began after INT by CB Tom Rotello—ever efficient, Air Force converted 2 INTs and KO FUM REC into 17 pts. Texas had 2nd H chances, but could only manage 3 FGs by K Jeff Ward. Longhorns won rushing battle, 214y to 189y, as QB Bret Stafford gained 63y on ground. Outcome was consistent with both teams' recent bowl performances as Air Force won its 4th straight in postseason, while Texas lost its 4th in row.

All American Bowl (Dec. 31): Georgia Tech 17 Michigan State 14

With suspensions to 4 players, including QB John Dewberry, Georgia Tech (9-2-1) was expected to struggle. Instead, Yellow Jackets edged Spartans (7-5) 281y to 233y in total O, with 115y coming on pair of 4th Q scoring drives for comeback victory. Jackets QB Todd Rampley led O in his 1st-ever start, modestly completing 12-23/99y. He led 57y drive to 40y FG by K David Bell early in 4th Q. Ahead 14-10, Michigan State looked to eat clock behind TB Lorenzo White (158y rushing), but he lost FUM with 5:32 to go after hit by S Riccardo Ingram. Tech DE Pat Swilling recovered FUM at own 42YL. Ensuing drive began poorly as Rampley soon threw INT, but was reprieved by roughing PEN. Seven plays later, FB Malcolm King followed block by T John Ivemeyer to score on 5y TD run for game-winner with 1:50 left to play. MSU WR Mark Ingram (3/70y) caught TD passes of 6y and 27y from QB Dave Yarema (6-15/85y, 2 TDs, INT). Ingram was left uncovered by confused D on 6y TD catch.

Cotton Bowl: Texas A&M 36 Auburn 16

With help from D, Texas A&M (10-2) QB Kevin Murray upstaged Heisman Trophy winner, Auburn TB Bo Jackson. Murray threw for Cotton Bowl record 292y on 16-26 as A&M finished off Tigers with 15 unanswered pts in 4th Q. Aggies TE Rod Bernstine (6/108y) was Murray's favorite target. Auburn (8-4) had drawn 1st blood, converting LB Neal Vinson's FUM REC into 5y TD run by Jackson (31/129y). A&M answered with 11y TD run by FB Harry Johnson to cap short drive that began with FUM REC by DB Monty Jay. Aggies added TB Keith Woodside's 22y TD run—that featured 3 broken tackles—before end of 1st Q, but had only 12-7 lead after missing x-pt and 2-pt pass.

Early in 2nd Q, Jackson took screen pass and turned upfield for 73y TD to give Tigers 1-pt lead as they too missed 2-pt conv attempt. K Scott Slater's 26y FG right before H gave Texas A&M lead for good at 15-13. By end of 3rd Q lead was 21-16, but Tigers had driven from their 6YL to 4th-and-goal at 2YL. Auburn handed ball to Jackson for 4th straight play, but, instead of cracking GL, he was dropped for 1y loss by Aggies frosh LB Basil Jackson. Teams traded possessions and Auburn faced 4th-and-2 on Aggies 27YL, from where Jackson again was stopped short. Texas A&M directly put game away with 72y drive that ended with 9y TD pass to Woodside.

Fiesta Bowl: Michigan 27 Nebraska 23

Michigan (10-1-1) erased 14-3 H deficit with 24 pts in 3rd Q, thanks in large part to Huskers' miscues. IB Doug DuBose (17/99y), who scored 2 TDs in 1st H, lost ball on opening Nebraska (9-3) possession of 2nd H, recovered by Wolverines LB Jeff Akers at Huskers 21YL. Michigan scored moments later on FB Gerald White's 1y TD run. On next series, Nebraska QB McCathorn Clayton fumbled on own 38YL, with REC by DT Mark Messner. Runs of 18y by TB Jamie Morris—who led with 156y rushing—and 19y by White set up 1y sneak by QB Jim Harbaugh (6-15/63y) for 17-14 lead. Nebraska next had P Dan Wingard's punt blocked by Michigan CB David Arnold, which led to 19y FG by K Pat Moons. Wolverines were not done: D stiffened, and Harbaugh led drive to his 2nd TD run. Backup Huskers QB Steve Taylor scored on 1y keeper late in 4th Q to tighten it to 27-21, and Michigan conceded safety rather than punt from deep in own territory. Wolverines CB Garland Rivers' EZ INT ended it. "Obviously we had a letdown in intensity," said Nebraska coach Tom Osborne. "The first eight or nine minutes of the third quarter killed us."

Rose Bowl: UCLA 45 Iowa 28

UCLA (9-2-1) TB Eric Ball was introduced to America in big way. With TB Gaston Green knocked out late in 1st Q with hamstring pull, Ball came in to rush for 227y, 2nd most in Rose Bowl history. He ran for game record-tying 4 TDs in becoming 2nd frosh to win MVP. Hawkeyes (10-2) scored 1st, converting INT into 29y TD drive capped by FB David Hudson's 1y TD run. Bruins knotted score on 30y run by Ball. Focus of game then became slippery hands of Iowa star TB Ronnie Harmon (14/55y), who lost 4 FUMs in 1st H alone and dropped what appeared to be TD pass as UCLA pulled away to open 24-10 H lead. Harmon, who fumbled once during regular season, was 1 of few Hawkeyes who could stay with swift Bruins, who sacrificed size for speed. Iowa QB Chuck Long (29-37/319y, TD, INT) played well, but could not overcome his team's 5 TOs. Long's 4y scoring keeper to cap 1st possession of 2nd H cut Hawkeyes deficit to 24-17. Bruins answered with 73y drive that QB Matt Stevens (16-26/189y, INT) ended with 9y TD pass to WR Mike Sherrard. Later in 2nd H Iowa K Rob Houghtlin had 1 of team's few highlights with 52y FG that tied Rose Bowl record. UCLA became 3rd school ever to win 4 straight January 1 bowl games.

Sugar Bowl: Tennessee 35 Miami 7

Miami's national title hopes were chased away in time it took Tennessee blitzers to run down Hurricanes (10-2) QB Vinny Testaverde. Miami scored 7 pts on opening possession, traveling 48y to 18y TD catch WR Michael Irvin (5/91y) that followed 25y run by HB Melvin Bratton on fake punt. Vols (9-1-2) D keyed upset by completely thwarting Testaverde (20-36/216y, TD) by sacking him 7 times, intercepting 3 of his passes, and forcing him to fumble twice. Canes had 6 TOs in all, with FUM REC by Vols LB Darrin Miller setting up 1y TD run early in 3rd Q for 21-7 lead. On Tennessee's next possession, TB Jeff Powell (11/102y) raced 60y for clinching TD. Powell led rush attack that gained 211y against stout Miami D. Sixth-year sr QB Daryl Dickey (15-25/131y, INT) was not threat Testaverde was, but he ran his record to 6-0-2 as team's starter and earned MVP honors with steady performance. Teams combined for 245y in PENs, with Tennessee setting Sugar Bowl record with 125y.

Orange Bowl: Oklahoma 25 Penn State 10

No. 1 Penn State (11-1) headed into bowl season knowing Orange Bowl victory guaranteed them national title, but for Oklahoma (11-1) all incentive it needed came with Tennessee's humbling of 2nd–ranked Miami earlier in evening. It ensured title would go to Orange Bowl winner. Sooners D forced 5 TOs in shutting down unbeaten Nittany Lions even though Penn State had committed only 20 TOs during perfect regular season. Oklahoma LB Brian Bosworth made 13 unassisted tackles, while S Sonny Brown had 2 INTs and broke up 2 passes. Meanwhile, Penn State D took away option runs of QB Jamelle Holieway (17y rushing), but he hooked up with A-A TE Keith Jackson on 71y TD pass on 3rd-and-24, with OU trailing 7-3 in 2nd Q. Sooners K Tim Lasher bumped lead to 19-10 by adding 3 of his game-record 4 FGs. His 4th 3-ptr came on 3rd drive that continued after controversial no FUM call on play in which WR Derrick Shephard caught pass and lost ball, recovered by Penn State S Ray Isom. In 4th Q, FB Lydell Carr (19/148y) ended it with 61y scoring run. Nittany Lions had opened scoring with 1y TD run by FB Tim Manoa and trailed only 16-10 in 3rd Q when they drove to OU 21YL. Brown then picked off QB John Shaffer (10-22/74y, 3 INTs) at 1YL to kill rally. Later in 4th Q, trailing 19-10, Lions drove 50y to OU 10YL before stalling and missing FG. National title was 6th ever for Oklahoma and 3rd under coach Barry Switzer.

Final AP Poll January 2

1 Oklahoma (55)	1138	11 Nebraska	500
2 Michigan (1)	1032	12 Arkansas	495
3 Penn State	980	13 Alabama	484
4 Tennessee (1)	957	14 Ohio State	409
5 Florida	929	15 Florida State	359
6 Texas A&M	792	16 Brigham Young	288
7 UCLA	767	17 Baylor	184
8 Air Force	755	18 Maryland	158
9 Miami	699	19 Georgia Tech	128
10 Iowa	621	20 Louisiana State	126

1985 Top Performance Formula

1 Oklahoma	1.7395
2 Michigan	1.7015
3 Air Force	1.6423
4 Florida	1.6270
5 Tennessee	1.5978
6 Penn State	1.5864
7 Miami	1.5754
8 Alabama	1.5673
9 Iowa	1.5390
10 Texas A&M	1.5202
11 UCLA	1.5151
12 Arkansas	1.5001
13 Nebraska	1.4812
14 Brigham Young	1.4588
15 Auburn	1.4569
16 Auburn	1.4490
17 Baylor	1.4347
18 Ohio State	1.4331
19 Georgia	1.3960
20 Florida State	1.3799

1985 Top Opponent Records

1 Notre Dame	.6933
2 Auburn	.6706
3 Alabama	.6614
4 Florida	.6552
5 Michigan	.6299
6 Tennessee	.6120
7 Oklahoma	.6094
8 UCLA	.6000
9 Boston College	.5969
10 Rice	.5966
11 Rutgers	.5957
12t Georgia	.595238
12t Maryland	.595238
14 Ohio State	.5898
15 Illinois	.5858
16t Michigan State	.579365
16t Texas	.579365
18 Penn State	.5680
19 Texas A&M	.5768
20 Miami	.5754

1985 Out-of-Conference Records

	W-L	Percentage	Bowl W-L
Southeastern	35-10-5	.7500	2-2-1
Big Ten	24-9	.7273	3-3
Southwest	17-10	.6296	3-1
Big Eight	17-14	.5484	1-3
Pacific-10	17-16-2	.5143	2-2-1
Western Athletic	16-18	.4706	1-1
Atlantic Coast	11-14-1	.4423	2-1

1985 Individual Statistical Leaders

RUSHING YARDS	Attempts	Yards	Avg.
Lorenzo White, Michigan State	386	1908	4.9
Bo Jackson, Auburn	278	1786	6.4
Thurman Thomas, Oklahoma State	302	1553	5.1
Paul Palmer, Temple	279	1516	5.4
George Swarm, Miami (Ohio)	309	1511	4.9
Steve Bartalo, Colorado State	338	1368	4.0
Napoleon McCallum, Navy	287	1327	4.6
Reggie Dupard, Southern Methodist	235	1278	5.4
Rueben Mayes, Washington State	228	1236	5.4
Barry Word, Virginia	207	1224	5.9

PASSING YARDS	Completions	Attempts	Yards	Pct.
Robbie Bosco, Brigham Young	338	511	4273	66.1
Jim Everett, Purdue	285	450	3651	63.3
Doug Gaynor, Long Beach State	321	452	3563	71.0
Vinny Testaverde, Miami	216	352	3238	61.4
Chuck Long, Iowa	231	351	2978	65.8
Todd Santos, San Diego State	226	357	2877	6.31
Kerwin Bell, Florida	180	288	2687	62.5
Brian McClure, Bowling Green	226	371	2674	60.9
Kevin Sweeney, Fresno State	177	295	2604	60.0
Erik Kramer, North Carolina State	189	339	2510	55.8

RECEIVING YARDS	Catches	Yards
Marc Zeno, Tulane	73	1137
Richard Estell, Kansas	70	1109
Rodney Carter, Purdue	98	1099
Webster Slaughter, San Diego State	82	1071
David Williams, Illinois	85	1047
Mark Bellini, Brigham Young	63	1008
Walter Murray, Hawaii	66	973
Loren Richey, Utah	73	971
Charles Lockett, Long Beach State	69	949
Ken Allen, Indiana	55	929

1985 Consensus All-America Team
Offense

Wide Receiver:	David Williams, Illinois
	Tim McGee, Tennessee
Tight End:	Willie Smith, Miami
Line:	Jim Dombrowski, Virginia
	Jeff Bregel, Southern Cal
	Brian Jozwiak, West Virginia
	John Rienstra, Temple
	J.D. Maarleveld, Maryland
	Jamie Dukes, Florida State
Center:	Pete Anderson, Georgia
Quarterback:	Chuck Long, Iowa
Running Back:	Bo Jackson, Auburn
	Lorenzo White, Michigan State
	Thurman Thomas, Oklahoma State
	Reggie Dupard, SMU
	Napoleon McCallum, Navy
Placekicker:	John Lee, UCLA

Defense

Line:	Tim Green, Syracuse
	Leslie O'Neal, Oklahoma State
	Tony Casillas, Oklahoma
	Mike Ruth, Boston College
	Mike Hammerstein, Michigan
Linebacker:	Brian Bosworth, Oklahoma
	Larry Station, Iowa
	Johnny Holland, Texas A&M
Backs:	David Fulcher, Arizona State
	Brad Cochran, Michigan
	Scott Thomas, Air Force
Punter:	Barry Helton, Colorado

1985 Heisman Trophy Vote

Bo Jackson, senior tailback, Auburn	1509
Chuck Long, senior quarterback, Iowa	1464
Robbie Bosco, senior quarterback, BYU	459
Lorenzo White, sophomore tailback, Michigan State	391
Vinny Testaverde, junior quarterback, Miami	249

Other Major Awards

Maxwell (Player)	Chuck Long, senior quarterback, Iowa
Walter Camp (Player)	Bo Jackson, senior tailback, Auburn
Outland (Lineman)	Mike Ruth, senior nose guard, Boston College
Lombardi (Lineman)	Tony Casillas, senior nose guard, Oklahoma
Davey O'Brien (QB)	Chuck Long, senior quarterback, Iowa
Dick Butkus (Linebacker)	Brian Bosworth, sophomore linebacker, Oklahoma
AFCA Coach of the Year	Fisher DeBerry, Air Force

1986

The Year of the Prime-Time Showdown in the Valley of the Sun, Steroids for Sale, and Lockbaum for Heisman

The Fiesta Bowl in Tempe, Arizona, had been created 15 years earlier as way to keep local favorite Arizona State active in the post-season. The upstart Fiesta Bowl stunned the college football world in 1986 by securing the top two teams, Miami (11-1) and Penn State (12-0), for a defacto national championship game. The contest was moved for prime-time television as a stand-alone game on January 2. In many ways, the concept for the Bowl Championship Series (more than 10 years in the future) was born with the Fiesta Bowl coup, made possible by two circumstances. Neither team was in a conference tied to a traditional New Year's Day bowl, so their independence allowed each to shop around. Secondly, the Fiesta, located in Arizona's fast-growing Valley of the Sun, was able to provide a record $2.4 million purse to each school. The match-up would be the first in a post-season bowl of unbeaten no. 1 and 2 teams since Oklahoma and Maryland met in the 1956 Orange Bowl and the first that left New Year's Day traditional powers—Cotton, Sugar, Orange and Rose Bowls—out of the title picture.

The Hurricanes were big favorites in the Fiesta, after knocking off then no. 1 and defending champion Oklahoma (11-1) on September 27. Also, Miami's outlaw reputation was firmly secured during the season as four star players were caught driving expensive cars leased by a pro agent, 34 players were caught using an illegal telephone access card for more than $5,000 worth of calls, running back Melvin Bratton was arrested for shoplifting, and leading tackler, linebacker George Mira, Jr., was arrested for battery against his girlfriend and unlawful possession of steriods. Although a university committee found that the number of such incidents were no higher than the general student body, the impression was of a program out of control. Arriving in Phoenix in battle fatigues and storming out of a dinner with Penn State players a few days before the game did nothing to endear the Hurricanes to average sports fans.

The game was terrific, however, going down to the wire as a goal-line interception by little-known Nittany Lions linebacker Pete Giftopoulos, his third of the game, sealed a 14-10 triumph for Penn State. The national title was the second in five years for a Penn State program at the pinnacle of success under head coach Joe Paterno. His counterpart, Miami coach Jimmy Johnson, saw his bowl record fall to 1-4, while the upset prevented quarterback Vinny Testaverde from becoming the first Heisman-winning signal-caller from a national champion team since 1947, when Notre Dame's Johnny Lujack pulled off the double delight.

Bowl news was dominated by drug testing as at least 21 of 720 tested players received a 90-day ban, thereby missing bowl games. Most players were caught using steroids. Earlier in the year, the NCAA began testing of any team entered in its championships, including bowl games. Oklahoma linebacker Brian Bosworth was the biggest fish caught, although fellow All-Americas, Southern California (7-5) offensive tackle Jeff Bregel and LSU (9-3) defensive lineman Roland Barbay, also were nailed. Barbay took the NCAA to court, saying that his steroid use occurred in the spring before the NCAA banned steroids in August. He lost his appeal. Bellicose Bosworth further disgraced himself with a pathetic defense of his drug use at a press conference. He then turned pro with a season of eligibility remaining. Former Cornhuskers guard Dean Steinkuhler, 1983 winner of the Outland Trophy, confessed to his steriod use while in college. Nebraska (10-2) coach Tom Osborne then admitted that he knew some players had used drugs.

Adding to Osborne's woes was the suspension of 60 of his Cornhuskers for misuse of their complimentary game tickets. All of this came down the week of a big match-up with Florida State (7-4-1); a stay of suspension allowed everyone to play in that game but there was talk of the Seminoles being handed a forfeit victory. The investigation included players at other schools, but the NCAA restored eligibility to all players, while taking heat for potentially meting out such excessive penalties.

The other drug plaguing college sports was cocaine, brought to light in the summer with the sad cocaine-related deaths of basketball star Len Bias of Maryland and Don Rogers, safety for the Cleveland Browns who once starred for UCLA. Tennessee quarterback Tony Robinson, who had led the Vols to a 9-1-2 record and final no. 4 ranking in 1985, was arrested and charged with selling cocaine early in 1986. He served jail time with roommate, fullback Kenneth Cooper. Vols coach Johnny Majors once called Robinson "the best talent I've seen since I've been around college football." Majors had coached Tony Dorsett in 1973-76.

Controversial Proposition 48 set minimum requirements for incoming freshman that, if not met, would mean loss of athletic scholarships. Its biggest controversy centered on inclusion of standardized tests, which advocates for African-American players felt were racist in nature. The goal was noble: to force high school athletes to focus more on grades at a younger age in anticipation of college work. Student-athletes who did not reach standards, which at first were a 1.8 grade-point average with minimum test requirements, were forced to pay tuition at the colleges that recruited them. They had to hope to become academically eligible to play athletics. The oft-used alternative was to attend junior college.

With too much discussion centered on drugs, ticket misuse, and suspended players, Gordie Lockbaum of Division 1-AA Holy Cross (10-1) became a breath of fresh air and famous as a true throwback player. Lockbaum was profiled in *Sports Illustrated* as a superb player at a school where academics came first. Playing both on offense and defense, Lockbaum caught 57 passes for 827 yards, scored 22 touchdowns, and made 46 tackles to spark the Crusaders to their best mark since 1938. There was another all-around talent playing spectacularly in 1986: Purdue (3-8) defensive back Rod Woodson. In his final collegiate game, a 17-15 win over rival Indiana (6-6), Woodson excelled as usual on returns and defense—his seven tackles lifted his school career record to 320—and chipped in on offense with three catches for 67 yards and 97 yards rushing, a season high for Purdue, on 15 carries. He was on the field for 137 plays, more than 90 percent of the game's total. On the Boilermakers track team, Woodson also was three-time conference champion at the high hurdles.

The biggest individual NCAA record to fall was Doug Flutie's two-year-old career passing yardage mark of 10,579, broken by Fresno State (9-2) quarterback Kevin Sweeney with 10,623 yards.

The coaching Dooley brothers were in the news for more than on-field work. Virginia Tech (10-1-1) head Bill Dooley led the Hokies to the Peach Bowl despite having been fired in February. Dooley was allowed to coach one more season and no one other than the principals was made aware of the firing until after the season's third game when Dooley began a lawsuit for wrongful termination. Hokies players rallied around the coach, who was knocked for his boring offense and weak schedule. During the season, Dooley became Tech's all-time leader in wins with a 62-38-1 record, but was gone by year's end with an out-of-court settlement. Brother Vince's Georgia Bulldogs (8-4) were rocked by a lawsuit and subsequent trial brought by former professor Jan Kemp, who eventually won a $2 million lawsuit after being fired in 1982 for speaking out against preferential treatment given athletes.

Of course, no program had it tougher than Southern Methodist. Linebacker David Stanley, who dropped out in December of 1985, admitted he received $750 a month in payments that continued after NCAA sanctions had been applied to SMU for improper recruiting. He stated that he was paid $25,000 dollars to sign with the Mustangs. Paying players was a second offense and it resulted in the famous "Death Penalty." By year's end, coach Bobby Collins, athletic director Bob Hitch, and school president L. Donald Shields all resigned.

Major conference members that had not been penalized by the NCAA since 1952 made up a rather short list: Stanford in the Pac-10, Rice in the Southwest, Tennessee and Vanderbilt in the SEC, Michigan and Northwestern in the Big 10, Air Force, Brigham Young, and Colorado State in the WAC, and Georgia Tech, Virginia, and Wake Forest in the ACC. Members of the entire Big 8 Conference had been penalized at one point or another.

Milestones

■ Kickoff position was moved from kicking team's 40 yard-line to its 35 yard-line.

■ On September 23, NCAA announced drug testing for collegiate sports, limited to playoffs in NCAA's wide range of sports and Division 1 football bowl games.

■ Last surviving member of Notre Dame's Four Horsemen backfield, Jim Crowley, died at age 83 on January 15. Crowley was fleet halfback for national champion Notre Dame team that went 10-0 in 1924, including Rose Bowl win over Stanford. In October of that year, *New York Herald Tribune* writer Grantland Rice famously compared Irish backs to "Four Horsemen of the Apocalypse." Crowley was noted as quick-witted coach, achieving great success with Fordham in 1930s as his 1937 team, led by "Seven Blocks of Granite" line, ranked 3rd in final AP poll. Holy Cross coach Rick Carter committed suicide by hanging on February 2 at age 42. Carter had 137 career wins, going 9-1-1 in 1983 and 14-0 in winning Division III title at Dayton in 1980. Frederick Douglass "Fritz" Pollard, All America back for Brown in 1916, died at 92 on May 11. Pollard was 1st African-American to play in Rose Bowl, following 1915 season, before breaking color barriers in NFL as player and later coach of Hammond Pros. Following football career, he owned coal companies, movie studio, newspaper, and an investment company. Bill Murray, star Duke halfback and winner of 93 games in 15-year coaching tenure at alma mater died March 29 at age 77. Murray won 49 games at Delaware before leading Duke to 7 conference titles and wins in Orange and Cotton Bowls as successor to Wallace Wade, who himself died on October 7 at 94 of complications from pneumonia. Teammate of Fritz Pollard at Brown, Wade became 1st to play in Rose Bowl and later coach team in Pasadena when his 1925 Alabama squad became 1st southern team invited to Rose Bowl. Wade won 61 games at Alabama with pair of national titles before moving to Duke, where he won 110 games and had trio of Top 10 teams. Kent State coach Dick Scesniak died of heart attack on April 1 at age 45. Wisconsin coach Dave McClain, who won 46 games in 8 years at Madison, died April 28 of heart attack at age 48. Jack Christiansen, six-time All Pro S for Detroit Lions and later head coach of San Francisco 49ers and Stanford Cardinal, died at age 57 on June 29. Christiansen went 30-22-3 in five years at Stanford. Former UCLA S and current Cleveland Brown Don Rogers died June 30th of cocaine poisoning at age 23. Coming 11 days after death of basketball star Len Bias, Rogers' death helps push NCAA to begin tests for cocaine at bowl games. Alabama DL Willie Ryles died at 19 of blood clot to brain on August 23 after taking blow to head in practice 5 days prior, while Crimson Tide back George Scruggs died in auto accident on April 26. Former Arizona State and Washington Redskins tight end Jerry Smith, 43, died on October 15 of complications from HIV/AIDS. On September 13 Florida State tackle Pablo Lopez, 21, was shot dead during on-campus argument. Bobby Layne, known for his intensity on field and carousing off it, died of cardiac arrest at age 59 on December 1. Layne starred for Texas, leading Longhorns to SWC title and Cotton Bowl win as soph tailback in 1945 and 10-win season as All-America quarterback in 1947. Layne set 11 Texas records before having top-notch 15-year pro career primarily with Detroit Lions and Pittsburgh Steelers.

■ Hall of Fame Bowl was resumed, while Cherry Bowl was cancelled.

■ Season marked debut of Jim Thorpe Award, given annually to nation's best defensive back.

■ Longest winning streaks entering season:
Fresno State, Oklahoma 8 Tennessee, Texas A&M 6

■ Coaching Changes:

	Incoming	Outgoing
Akron	Gerry Faust	Jim Dennison
Bowling Green	Moe Ankey	Denny Stolz
Kansas	Bob Valesente	Mike Gottfried
Kansas State	Stan Parrish	Jim Dickey
Kent State	Glen Mason	Dick Scesniak
Memphis State	Charlie Bailey	Rey Dempsey
Minnesota	John Gutekunst	Lou Holtz
Mississippi State	Rockey Felker	Emory Bellard
North Carolina State	Dick Sheridan	Tom Reed
Northwestern	Francis Peay	Dennis Green
Notre Dame	Lou Holtz	Gerry Faust
Pittsburgh	Mike Gottfried	Foge Fazio
Rice	Jerry Berndt	Watson Brown
San Diego State	Denny Stolz	Doug Scovil
Vanderbilt	Watson Brown	George MacIntyre
Wisconsin	Jim Hilles	Dave McClain

Preseason AP Poll

1 Oklahoma (44)	1171	11 Florida State	422
2 Michigan (6)	1016	12 Baylor	404
3 Miami (1)	976	13 Florida	396
4 UCLA (3)	972	14 Auburn	269
5 Alabama	911	15 Louisiana State	229
6 Penn State (3)	892	16t Georgia	220
7 Texas A&M (1)	871	16t Washington	220
8 Nebraska (1)	826	18 Brigham Young	210
9 Ohio State	673	19 Arkansas	188
10 Tennessee	578	20 Michigan State	182

August 27, 1986

Alabama 16 Ohio State 10 (East Rutherford, NJ): Ohio State had late rally fail in losing Kickoff Classic that was anything but classic with neither team looking sharp. On strength of 3 completions and 2 pass interference calls on Alabama LB Derrick Thomas, QB Jim Karsatos (20-31/191y, 2 INTs) marched Buckeyes (0-1) to Bama 18YL. He then threw high into EZ on final pass to WR Cris Carter, who was unable to come down with it. After TOs on 3 straight 3rd Q possessions, Crimson Tide (1-0) scored 10 straight 4th Q pts to grab lead, with winning TD coming on 3y pass from QB Mike Shula to WR Albert Bell. Alabama later added 28y K Van Tiffin FG, 3rd of game. Game's key play was Buckeyes FB George Cooper's FUM at Alabama 9YL with Ohio ahead 10-6 in 3rd Q. Ohio LB Chris Spielman had 16 tackles in losing effort.

September 6, 1986

Rutgers 11 BOSTON COLLEGE 9: It was looking bad early for Rutgers (1-0) as QB Joe Gagliardi was sacked 3 times in 1st Q and D was forced to stop numerous BC scoring chances. But Boston College (0-1) missed 2 FGs and was held on downs at 11YL. Rutgers O made sufficient adjustments to march 80y in 2nd Q to 4y TD pass to HB Henry Henderson. Knights then went for 2 pts, surprising Eagles with snap to FB Curt Stephens, who waltzed into EZ. K Doug Giesler added 23y FG in 3rd Q to push lead to 11-0. Eagles scored on odd play as Rutgers LB Tyronne Stowe nailed BC QB Shawn Halloran at Rutgers 17YL, ball popping into arms of TB Troy Stradford, who waltzed 20y into EZ. Eagles missed 2-pt conv to trail by 11-6 and could only add 29y FG by K Brian Lowe midway through 4th Q.

Miami 23 FLORIDA 15: In snapping Florida's 21-game home win streak, Miami (2-0) D held QB Kerwin Bell to 137y passing and sacked him 6 times. Miami's O was contained most of night, losing 7 TOs, while QB Vinny Testaverde (12-25/163y, TD) threw 3 INTs. WR Michael Irvin caught his only pass, TD for Canes, while flat on his back in EZ. LB Winston Moss (11 tackles) and DE Daniel Stubbs (2.5 sacks) shone for Miami, while Gators (1-1) DB Jarvis Williams sparkled with 2 INTs, sack, FUM REC, and hit on HB Melvin Bratton that broke up pass. Bratton did fine himself with TD runs of 20y and 24y. Gators had 3 scoring drives in 1st H, but all ended with FGs by K Jeff Dawson for 9-7 lead. Florida lost quartet of 2nd H FUMs to blow 15-9 lead.

OKLAHOMA 38 Ucla 3: Sooners were in midseason form in administering Bruins' worst opening game loss in 56 years. UCLA (0-1) D had surrendered 855y rushing in all of 1985, but Oklahoma (1-0) ran roughshod for 470y. Sooners D contributed 5 INTs and allowed only 34y rushing. QB Jamielle Holieway led way with 83y rushing, while backup QB Eric Mitchel ran in 2 TDs. Bruins CB Darryl Henley prevented shutout by returning INT 72y to set up 28y FG by K David Franey. Even on that play, Oklahoma looked good as Sooners FB Lydell Carr caught fleet Henley from behind. TB Gaston Green led Bruins rushing with only 40y.

NEBRASKA 34 Florida State 17: Lights needed for 1st night game in Lincoln shone brightly on hometown QB Steve Taylor (10-16/130y), who rushed for 139y and 2 TDs and added 2 more TDs passing in his 1st start. Taylor threw 12y TD pass to TE Todd Millikan and 46y TD pass to WB Von Sheppard to cap consecutive 3rd Q possessions that reversed momentum after Seminoles (0-1) grabbed 14-10 lead at H. Huskers (1-0) D then held FSU to –2y throughout 2nd H, finishing with 24-8 advantage in 1st downs. Florida State scored both its TDs on big plays in 1st H as frosh TB Sammie Smith ran 57y for TD and QB Chip Ferguson threw 30y scoring strike to WR Victor Floyd.

AP Poll September 8

1 Oklahoma (55)	1175	11 Brigham Young	425
2 Miami (1)	1050	12 Baylor	422
3 Michigan (1)	1026	13 Florida	366
4 Alabama	986	14 Louisiana State	362
5 Penn State (1)	952	15 Florida State	300
6 Nebraska (1)	896	16 UCLA	298
7 Texas A&M	868	17 Washington	253
8 Tennessee	713	18 Arkansas	250
9 Auburn	509	19 Georgia	235
10 Ohio State	502	20 Michigan State	196

September 13, 1986

Virginia Tech 20 CLEMSON 14: It took 32 years for Hokies (1-1) finally to leave Clemson as winner and reaching 20 pts vs. occasional rival for 1st time in 22-game series. Tigers (0-1) had entered season with punting worries as coach Danny Ford had to advertise before finding former high school P in Tigers' baseball player, Bill Spiers. Spiers' debut blew up in his face in 1st Q: Virginia Tech got on scoreboard as S Mitch Dove recovered blocked punt in EZ for 7-0 lead. Hokies QB Erik Chapman (13-23/242y) quickly became game's dominant player, increasing team's lead to 17-7 in 3rd Q on 5y TD pass to TE Steve Johnson. Clemson rushed for 215y, scoring both TDs on ground as TB Terrence Flagler scored from 13y out in 2nd Q and TB Kenny Flowers (22/87y) capped 80y trip in 3rd Q to cut deficit to 17-14.

Mississippi State 27 TENNESSEE 23: Brilliant performance by Mississippi State (2-0) QB Don Smith (15-30/231y, 3 TDs) was crowned by winning 62y TD run with 4:40 left. Taking option to left, Smith—who rushed for 102y—kept ball and broke into clear when Volunteers LB opted to cover RB. Tennessee (1-1) QB Randy Sanders (10-14/146y), who replaced injured QB Jeff Francis in 2nd Q, had chance to be late hero, but overthrew WR Terence Cleveland in EZ before suffering INT. Vols wasted effort by TB William Howard, who moved from FB to replace injured TB Keith Davis and bulled his way to 195y and 3 TDs.

LOUISIANA STATE 35 Texas A&M 17: LSU (1-0) QB Tommy Hodson electrified home crowd by completing 15-22/193y, 2 TDs. Texas A&M (0-1) had controlled ball in building 14-7 lead on 2 TD passes by QB Kevin Murray (24-35/209y): 5y to WR Shea Walker and 13y to TE Rod Bernstine. Tigers D then stiffened, surrendering only 143y rushing for game and picking off 5 passes. LB Michael Brooks returned final INT 36y to EZ. WR Wendell Davis (10/132y) formed nice tandem with Hodson.

Michigan 24 NOTRE DAME 23: Notre Dame (0-1) outgained Wolverines (1-0) 455y to 393y and never had to punt. Still, Lou Holtz became 1st ND coach to lose debut since Elmer Layden in 1934. QB Steve Beuerlein (21-33/263y), who broke Fighting Irish career passing y mark of QB Joe Theismann (1968-70), neatly operated different formations, including Wishbone. However, Irish lost 2 FUMs within Michigan 20YL, had INT in EZ, and missed FG and x-pt kick. ND had marched 75y on opening drive to WR Tim Brown's 3y TD run and then took ball to Michigan 7YL on 2nd drive before losing TO. Michigan took 24-14 lead by scoring 2 TDs in 6-sec span of 3rd Q, 2nd following REC of KO that blew away from Irish returners. Beuerlein answered with drives to 9 pts: Irish had to settle for K John Carney's 23y FG on 2nd trip to cut deficit to 24-23. Michigan QB Jim Harbaugh completed 15-23/239y and 27y TD pass to TB Jamie Morris, while throwing no INTs for 8th straight game. For 1st time in 22 years Notre Dame was unranked in preseason, but actually became ranked after losing, which had never happened under present polling system.

IOWA 43 Iowa State 7: Hayden Fry became tops among Iowa coaches. Fry won his 53rd game with Hawkeyes (1-0), passing Forest Evashevski for most wins in school history. QB Mark Vlasic helped him achieve that honor, passing for 286y with 5/149y going to WR Jim Mauro. Mauro set Iowa record with 3 TD receptions, while FB

David Hudson rushed for 120 and 1y TD run as Hawks O gained 580y. Iowa State (0-1) gained but 125y, finishing with –11y net rushing, thanks in large part to 7 sacks. Dropping 4th straight in series, Cyclones scored sole TD on 21y pass from backup QB Brett Sadek to WR Eddie Brown in 4th Q.

Stanford 31 TEXAS 20: Longhorns (0-1) could not cover WR Jeff James (9/162y) and paid for it with 1st loss in home opener since 1966. QB John Paye, who threw for 241y, hooked up with James for 3 TDs, including passes of 56y and 45y as Stanford (1-0) took 14-0 lead. By 3rd Q, Cardinal led 31-9. Texas QB Bret Stafford set school records for completions (20) and attempts (41) and threw 3 INTs. Teams combined for 229y in PENs. Fred Akers had won his 1st 21 September games as Texas coach.

WASHINGTON 40 Ohio State 7: For 1st time since way back in 1894, Ohio State (0-2) opened with 2 losses as they allowed 24-pt bonanza in 2nd Q, with 21 pts coming in 3-min span that blew game open. QB Chris Chandler (14-21/204y) led Huskies (1-0) O that compiled 408y to 186y advantage. Chandler threw 2 TDs to WR Lonzell Hill, son of former NFL receiver J.D. Hill. QB Jim Karsatos threw for only 85y, 9y of which came on Buckeyes' only TD: pass to WR Cris Carter. K Jeff Jaeger's 2 FGs and 4 x-pts enabled him to set Washington's all-time scoring mark of 275 pts.

OREGON 32 Colorado 30: Ducks (2-0) won wild finish as teams combined for 16 pts in last 4 mins, with Oregon tallying TD and FG in final min. After QB Mark Hatcher (15/176y, 2 TDs rushing) gave Buffs (0-2) 30-23 lead with 55y scoring run, QB Chris Miller (28-42/262y) drove Ducks to TD on 1y run by TB Derek Loville (17/88y, 3 TDs). When Ducks' 2-pt failed, Oregon S Tim Cooper pounced on onside-KO. Miller quickly threw into FG range, and K Matt MacLeod delivered winning 35y 3-ptr. MacLeod tied Oregon school record with his 4 FGs as did Miller for completions.

AP Poll September 15

1 Oklahoma (55)	1175	11 Brigham Young	441
2 Miami (1)	1099	12 Arkansas	402
3 Michigan	1000	13 Florida	396
4 Alabama	992	14 Georgia	383
5 Penn State (1)	938	15 Florida State	298
6 Nebraska (1)	924	16 Texas A&M	218
7 Washington (1)	751	17 Arizona	199
8 Louisiana State	747	18 Arizona State	187
9 Baylor	629	19 UCLA	169
10 Auburn	615	20 Notre Dame	143

September 20, 1986

Penn State 26 BOSTON COLLEGE 14: Nittany Lions (2-0) ran series mark to 14-1 by forcing 7 TOs, each more crippling than next. Eagles (1-2) were hampered by 1st H thumb injury to QB Mark Kamphaus. Sub QB Shawn Halloran came off bench to complete 18-25/260y, 2 TDs, but his 3 INTs did not help. Halloran's 1st TD pass, 44y to WR Darren Flutie, cut deficit to 12-7. Penn State answered with 2 TDs by TB D.J. Dozier, on 17y reception from QB John Shaffer and 7y run, while D snuffed out big Boston College opportunity with LB Shane Conlan's EZ INT of pass by TB Troy Stradford. Dozier rushed for 78y and caught 3/50y.

FLORIDA STATE 10 North Carolina 10: Emotionally drained in wake of T Pablo Lopez's death, Seminoles (1-1-1) could not pull out victory. Florida State K Derek Schmidt missed 36y FG attempt—his 3rd miss of day—at game's end. Tar Heels (2-0-1) took 7-0 lead on QB Jon Hall's 1st Q 14y TD pass to WR Eric Streater. Florida State finally got on scoreboard in 3rd Q when DE Felton Hayes blocked UNC punt through EZ to cut deficit to 7-2. Noles then took lead on 28y scoring pass from backup QB Peter Tom Willis to WR Ronald Lewis. Subsequent 2-pt conv gave Florida State 3-pt lead until Tar Heels K Lee Gliarmis' 24y FG in 4th Q. Carolina coach Dick Crum had mixed day, remaining undefeated but suffering strained ligaments in right knee after sideline collision.

Clemson 31 GEORGIA 28: Tigers (1-1) enjoyed rare victory over bitter non-conf rival—2nd in 18 games—as K David Treadwell nailed 46y FG as time expired. Clemson drove 34y in 1:11 as TB Terrence Flagler had 16y run and QB Rodney Williams broke loose for 15y more. Bulldogs (1-1) had tied game 28-28 on QB James Jackson's 78y hookup with WR Fred Lane at end of 3rd Q. Later in 4th Q Georgia was back on O, moving into Clemson territory before Jackson (12-22/211y, 2 TDs, INT) lost FUM at 15YL. Tigers displayed RB depth as TB Kenny Flowers rushed for 72y in 1st H before departing with ankle sprain, and Flagler added 90y rushing and TD catch.

Alabama 21 FLORIDA 7: Crimson Tide (4-0) won early SEC showdown as TB Bobby Humphrey came off bench to rush for 114y, and QB Mike Shula (11-16/118y, 2 INTs) led 2 long scoring drives in 3rd Q to eliminate 7-0 H deficit. Humphrey tied game with 10y scoring reception and then added 1y TD run later in game. Alabama outgained Florida by 162y to 20y during decisive 3rd Q, with winning 91y drive being capped by FB David Casteal's 4y TD run. Despite strong pressure that resulted in 3 sacks by Bama, Gators (1-2) QB Kerwin Bell threw for 22-36/235y.

Miami (of Ohio) 21 LOUISIANA STATE 12: Tigers (1-1) failed to return to level shown previous week against Texas A&M as they lost 7 TOs, had punt blocked, and blew myriad chances in Redskins end. Miami (2-1) WB Andy Schillinger made his pair of catches count for 121y, 2 TDs. LSU D held Ohioans to 20y rushing and 9 1st downs, while QB Tommy Hodson threw for 183y. Miami raised its remarkable all-time mark against SEC, considered America's toughest conf, to 8-0-1.

Wyoming 23 AIR FORCE 17: Wyoming (2-1) LB Mike Schenbeck did his best to kill Air Force (2-1) hopes, returning 1st Q INT 17y for TD and picking off another QB Troy Calhoun pass deep in own territory with 34 secs left. QB Scott Runyan led Cowboys, throwing for 145y and 24y TD pass to WR Eric Loftus to open scoring before departing in 3rd Q with bruised shoulder. Wyoming held on with 2nd H shutout after Falcons rallied

to tie game 17-17 at H on 41y FG by K Mike Johnson. Falcons were held without 1st down and 24y in 2nd H won by Wyoming on 2 FGs by K Greg Worker. LB Terry Maki dominated for AFA, contributing 21 tackles, 3 sacks, and FUM REC.

WASHINGTON 52 Brigham Young 21: Brigham Young (2-1) scored on 94y RET of opening KO by HB Robert Parker, but Huskies (2-0) handed BYU its worst defeat since 1973 as QB Chris Chandler (13-22/202y) threw 4 TD passes and ran in another. LB Steve Roberts had 4 of Huskies' 10 sacks, leading D that held Cougars to only 225y, including -45y rushing. Gaining revenge for 31-3 blowout in 1985, Huskies effectively cast outcome by H as they led 42-7; 2nd Q alone featured all 4 of Chandler's TDs. WR Lonzell Hill (4/65y) caught 2 TDs for 2nd straight game. After Parker's long KO RET, BYU had to wait until 4th Q to score again as backup QBs Mike Young and Bob Jensen each threw TD pass.

AP Poll September 22

1 Oklahoma (55)	1175	11 Arizona State	544
2 Miami (1)	1104	12 Southern California	356
3 Alabama	1020	13 Maryland	321
4 Nebraska (1)	954	14 Texas A&M	312
5 Michigan	946	15 Iowa	307
6 Washington (1)	903	16 UCLA	304
7 Penn State (1)	878	17 Baylor	297
8 Auburn	722	18 Louisiana State	186
9 Arkansas	639	19 Michigan State	148
10 Arizona	583	20 Florida State	108

September 27, 1986

MIAMI 28 Oklahoma 16: "I don't want to play them again," admitted Oklahoma (2-1) coach Barry Switzer after Orange Bowl meeting of top 2 teams. Miami (4-0) showed nation who was best, locking up win in 3rd Q, as QB Vinny Testaverde (21-28/261y, 4 TDs) completed all 9 of his attempts with 3 TDs. Hurricanes D held no. 1 Sooners to 186y rushing by eliminating middle of field with stalwart line, while speedy DBs and LBs chased down outside runs. Sooners played inspired D in 1st H—LB Brian Bosworth finished with 14 tackles—and trailed 7-3. Miami marched to TD on opening possession of 2nd H and quickly set up another score by recovering HB Anthony Stafford's FUM of KO. Testaverde hit WR Michael Irvin with 5y TD pass for 21-3 lead, and outcome essentially was complete. QB Jamelle Holieway threw abnormal 13 times to spark short-lived rally by Sooners, including 54y TD pass to TE Keith Jackson. Brawl between hard-hitting teams erupted in 4th Q.

North Carolina State 28 MARYLAND 16: Cardiac Wolfpack (3-0-1) rallied from 16-7 deficit in 4th Q to snap Maryland's 17-game ACC win streak. QB Erik Kramer (18-30/297y, 3 INTs) led surge, throwing TD passes of 18y to FB Mal Crite and 25y to WR Haywood Jeffires, while running in another from 1y out. Terrapins (3-1) assisted with 5 TOs, 2 leading to decisive NC State TDs in 4th Q. School records dropped: WR Naz Worthen set NC State record with 187y receiving on 9 catches, while QB Dan Henning (27-54/300y) eclipsed Maryland marks for attempts and completions.

AUBURN 34 Tennessee 8: Reversing result from 1985, Auburn (3-0) routed Vols as TB Brent Fullwood (18/207y) ran all over Tennessee D, setting up TD with 85y run and scoring his own from 19y out. Fullwood's TD run, which gave Tigers 17-0 lead in 3rd Q, came right after ace DT Tracy Rocker stripped TB William Howard (25/86y) for Howard's 2nd lost FUM. Fullwood rushed for 131y in decisive 3rd Q. Tennessee's bright spot came on 60y TD pass from sub QB, and future O coordinator, Randy Sanders to WR Anthony Miller to mar shutout by Auburn D still steaming from 38 pts Vols scored on them in prior season. "Today we showed people we're ready to win the SEC," stated Fullwood.

Baylor 45 TEXAS TECH 14: Baylor D forced 6 TOs in routing Red Raiders (2-2), setting early tone as QB Cody Carlson converted 1st TO into 22y TD pass for 6-0 lead. Bears (3-1) needed only 13 secs to double lead as LB Aaron Grant took INT of QB Billy Joe Tolliver (12-34/143y, 3 INTs) 21y to EZ. Bears racked up 10 more pts in 1st Q to bury Texas Tech. Carlson finished with 309y passing, with 69y coming on 3rd Q TD pass to WR David Davis for 32-0 lead. Texas Tech FB Cliff Winston's 5y scoring run in 3rd Q ended notions of shutout.

ARIZONA STATE 21 Washington State 21: After being benched for throwing 4 INTs, Sun Devils (2-0-1) QB Jeff Van Raaphorst returned to throw 52y pass to WR Aaron Cox that set up FB Channing Williams' tying 1y TD run. Washington State scored go-ahead 1y TD pass from QB Ed Blount to TE Doug Wellsandt following INT by S Ron Collins, returned 25y to ASU 40YL. Cougars (1-2-1) RB Kerry Porter rushed for 131y and TD, while Sun Devils TB Darryl Harris gained 145y on ground with 2 TDs.

SOUTHERN CALIFORNIA 20 Washington 10: After impressive wins over BYU and Ohio State, Huskies (2-1) were primed for conf play. Trojans D, led by LB Marcus Cotton's 9 tackles, sack, and 4 deflected passes, had other plans, targeting UW QB Chris Chandler (12-25/120y, 2 INTs). Washington FB Rick Fenney rushed for 89y, with 25y coming on opening 80y drive for 7-0 lead on 1y TD dive by FB Aaron Jenkins. USC (3-0) O began slowly and needed trick play for spark: Catching lateral from QB Rodney Peete, WR Randy Tanner launched pass to WR Ken Henry that resulted in 67y TD that knotted score at 10-10 in 3rd Q. Peete (15-24/181y, INT) later added 13y TD pass to Henry (3/88y) as Trojans romped to 10 pts in 4th Q.

1	Miami (56)	1156	11	Iowa	510
2	Alabama (1)	1058	12	Washington	455
3	Nebraska	1020	13	Baylor	420
4	Michigan	953	14	Texas A&M	381
5	Penn State (1)	908	15	UCLA	290
6	Oklahoma	891	16	Arizona State	278
7	Auburn	819	17	Michigan State	259
8	Arkansas	716	18	Louisiana State	166
9	Southern California	707	19	Fresno State	85
10	Arizona	639	20	North Carolina State	62

October 4, 1986

(Fri) Colorado State 24 BRIGHAM YOUNG 20: Colorado State TB Steve Bartalo's 1-man highlight show continued as he rushed for 131y and 3 TDs, setting career conf rushing mark of 3,863y (topping mark set by New Mexico RB Mike Williams, 1976-78). Bartalo's 3rd score on 1y run won it with 46 secs left. QB Kelly Stouffer threw well for Rams (3-2), completing 26-37/262y. Cougars (3-2) QB Steve Lindsay (25-39/265y, 3 INTs) ran in 1 TD, but was unable to outlast Rams.

VIRGINIA TECH 13 West Virginia 7: Opponents of Virginia Tech (4-1) came to realize they shouldn't allow Hokies K Chris Kinzer to decide game. Kinzer kicked his 12th and 13th consecutive FGs—these from 50y out into wind—to break school record and hearts of West Virginia (2-3). TB Eddie Hunter led Tech with 102y and 1y TD run midway through 2nd Q, while D preserved win with pair of 4th down stops and 4th GLS. TB John Holifield led Mountaineers with 161y rushing. Committing no TOs to WVU's 4, Virginia Tech was now plus-10 in takeaways on season.

Nebraska 27 SOUTH CAROLINA 24: After surrendering 24 pts to pesky Gamecocks (1-4), Nebraska D came up with 2 late TOs to set up TD and preserve win. After TB Harold Green's 3rd TD gave South Carolina 24-20 lead with 5 mins left, Gamecocks O looked to run out clock. Cornhuskers (4-0) DE Broderick Thomas forced FUM, recovered by DB Brian Davis at Carolina 26YL. Nebraska QB Steve Taylor, who threw for 196y, hit TE Todd Millikan with winning 11y TD pass. Gamecocks QB Todd Ellis (26-38/286y), who performed brilliantly, then moved O downfield until Nebraska DB Bryan Siebler picked off Ellis' hurried throw at Huskers 10YL with 38 secs left.

Iowa 24 MICHIGAN STATE 21: "Greatest team victory I have ever been associated with," said Iowa (4-0) coach Hayden Fry, but win was not secured until DB Ken Sims' EZ INT of Spartans (2-2) QB Dave Yarema's last-ditch pass with 1:35 left. Yarema (23-36/271y, 3 INTs) had hooked up with WR Mark Ingram on all 3 Michigan State TDs. Iowa QB Tom Poholsky threw 2 long TDs, including 50y to WR Jim Mauro at beginning of 3rd Q, and K Rob Houghtlin followed with eventual winning FG from 42y out. Spartans lost TB Lorenzo White for season with sprained left knee.

ARKANSAS 34 Texas Christian 17: Horned Frogs (2-2) grabbed 17-14 H lead, then moved to Arkansas 8YL early in 3rd Q after TB Tony Darthard raced 54y. Hogs S Odis Lloyd quickly ended threat by stripping ball from TB Tony Jeffrey, and Arkansas D allowed no 76y rest of way. Arkansas (4-0) reeled off 20 pts with QB Greg Thomas (198y passing, 88y rushing) scoring on runs of 42 and 25y. Razorbacks WR James Shibest caught 5/121y, while FB Marshall Foreman rushed for 106y, TD.

Arizona State 16 UCLA 9: Sporting 0-6-1 mark against UCLA, Arizona State (3-0-1) was confident nonetheless. Sun Devils D was big reason, which held Bruins (2-2) to 167y. Early in 4th Q, QB Jeff Van Raaphorst (16-19/187y, INT) threw 11y TD pass to WR Bruce Hill to cap 73y drive that featured Hill's 48y catch. Luckless Bruins, now 0-3-2 in last 5 Pac 10 openers, were frustrated by dropped INT by LB Ken Norton, Jr. on 1st play of decisive drive. UCLA QB Matt Stevens was held to miserable 2-12/12y passing in 2nd H, so it was up to K David Franey to score 3 FGs. Sun Devils K Kent Bostrom also had booted trio of FGs.

SAN JOSE STATE 45 Fresno State 41: Wild West, indeed. Bulldogs (3-1) lost 15-game win streak on stunning pair of San Jose TDs in final 42 secs. QB Mike Perez's 5th TD pass, 22y to WR Lafo Malauulu, was game-winning bolt coming 2 plays after successful onside-KO that followed Perez's 4th TD pass. With help from WR Guy Liggins (15/203y), Perez (33-53/433y, 2 INTs) led Spartans (3-2) to 24-0 lead in 2nd Q. Fresno State, behind QB Kevin Sweeney (13-23/337y) and TB James Williams (28/141y), scored 31 straight pts to take lead as Sweeney threw 2 TD passes to WR Stephen Baker (4/170y) and Williams ran for 2 TDs. Spartans answered with 6y TD run by TB Kenny Jackson before Sweeney and Baker hooked up for 84y TD pass and K Barry Belli hit 49y FG for 10-pt lead.

1	Miami (55)	1155	11	Arizona	605
2	Alabama (2)	1084	12	Washington	504
3	Nebraska	988	13	Baylor	438
4	Michigan	959	14	Texas A&M	393
5	Penn State (1)	937	15	Arizona State	392
6	Oklahoma	867	16	Louisiana State	268
7	Auburn	828	17	North Carolina State	133
8	Arkansas	726	18	Stanford	111
9	Southern California	709	19	Mississippi State	86
10	Iowa	614	20	Clemson	77

October 11, 1986

Army 25 TENNESSEE 21: Cadets (3-2) pulled stunner in Knoxville with 18-pt 4th Q, capped by DB Reggie Fullwood's 2y RET of blocked punt by CB Charles Williams with 35 secs left. Tennessee (2-3) entered 4th Q with 21-7 lead as TB William Howard ran in 3 short TDs, and QB Jeff Francis helped with 24-33/334y in air. After Fullwood's TD,

Francis raced Vols to Army 15YL before his final pass was broken up in EZ by S Peel Chronister. QB Tory Crawford rushed for 112y as Black Knights beat Div 1-A program on road for 1st time since 17-13 win at Stanford in 1979.

GEORGIA TECH 59 North Carolina State 21: Georgia Tech (2-2-1) TB Jerry Mays—all 171 lbs of him—led surprisingly easy win with 188y rushing and 3 TDs, including 79y scamper on 3rd play of game. He even threw 30y TD pass to WR Toby Pearson for 35-7 lead in 2nd Q, which held to H. Jackets quickly answered Wolfpack (3-1-1) score with WR Gary Lee's 99y KO TD RET. QB Erik Kramer (13-28/207y, 2 INTs) led NC State to 2 TDs, once near end of 2nd Q and at opening of 2nd H, to pull to within 35-21. Yellow Jackets reeled off 24 pts to ice it. Gaining 565y, Georgia Tech scored on 9 of its initial 11 possessions and did not punt until 4th Q. Tech QB Darrell Gast (9-17/111y) threw 2 TDs as replacement for QB Rick Strom, who turned ankle.

LOUISIANA STATE 23 Georgia 14: Struggling Louisiana State (3-1) K Ron Lewis, who grew up as Georgia fan, nailed 3 FGs to supply victory margin. Tigers D posted 2nd H shutout—they had allowed no 4th Q pts all season—to boost O that took lead for good on 9y TD pass from QB Tommy Hodson (16-30/172y, INT) to WR Wendell Davis (8/108y) in 3rd Q. Georgia (3-2) QB James Jackson (15-23/235y) threw 31y scoring pass for 1st TD and ran in other from 10y out, both scored in 7-min span of 2nd Q. LSU TBs Harvey Williams (24/133y) and Sammy Martin (11/106y) shared rushing honors, while LB Toby Caston made 20 tackles and corralled late INT.

MISSISSIPPI 33 Kentucky 13: Rebels (3-2-1) crushed Cats behind O that gained 418y and D that allowed 203y. After Mississippi K Bryan Owen kicked 1st of his 4 FGs for 3-0 1st Q lead, Kentucky special teams scored 7-3 edge when S Tony Mayes pounced on fumbled punt in Ole Miss EZ. Lead was short-lived as Mississippi poured on 20 unanswered 2nd Q pts, with TD runs of 3y and 60y by TB Willie Goodloe and 2 more FGs. Wildcats (3-1-1) had no answer until 4th Q when QB Bill Ransdell (15-31/131y, 2 INTs) threw 18y TD pass to FB Marc Logan.

Ohio State 24 INDIANA 22: With K Pete Stoyanovich attending mother's funeral, Hoosiers (4-1) were hurt when frosh K Jay Tuttle missed 2 FGs. QB Brian Dewitz was knocked out in 1st H, so depleted, but game Hoosiers came up short trying for 1st series win since 1951. Converting Indiana FUM, Buckeyes (4-2) scored winning pts when QB Jim Karsatos tossed 21y TD pass to WR Cris Carter in 3rd Q. Sub IU QB Dave Kramme (10-16/118y, 2 INTs) led 95y drive that ended scoring with frosh TB Anthony Thompson's 1y TD run. Bucks TB Jim Bryant ran for 131y.

MICHIGAN 27 Michigan State 6: Wolverines (5-0) needed only 2 series to score 10 pts, enough to win. QB Jim Harbaugh orchestrated victory with 219y, 2 TDs passing—most ever in series for any Michigan QB—and scored on run. DT Mark Messner (2 sacks) led rush on Michigan State (2-3) QB Dave Yarema, who was sacked 6 times, while Wolverines secondary permitted future pro WRs Andre Rison and Mark Ingram only 1 catch between them. Spartans, who missed injured TB Lorenzo White, managed only K Chris Caudell's 2 FGs.

Oklahoma 47 Texas 12 (Dallas): Loss may have been final nail in coffin of Texas (2-2) coach Fred Akers, whose fast start in 1977 helped bring about avg of 9 wins per year and 9 bowl trips in row. Sooners (4-1) ended matters quickly by scoring on 5 of 6 possessions in building 31-0 H lead. QB Jamelle Holieway led attack that totaled 396y on ground by rushing for 95y before departing early. TB Patrick Collins ignited rout with pair of 1st Q TDs and finished with 3 TDs. Longhorns, meanwhile, managed but 29y rushing. Texas QB Bret Stafford threw for 199y.

NEBRASKA 30 Oklahoma State 10: Cornhuskers (5-0) won 13th straight in series as they rushed for 287y, and Huskers' D kept Oklahoma State out of its EZ. Nebraska jumped to 14-0 lead as leading rusher IB Keith Jones (14/85y) scored from 1y out and WR Rod Smith returned punt 63y for TD. Cowboys (2-3) answered with DE Jerry Deckard's 45y INT TD RET and K Joe O'Donnell's 27y FG. Huskers held on as Jones, who became starter in August when IB Doug DuBose went down with injury, added his 2nd rushing TD (5y) and D shut down TB Thurman Thomas (22/38y).

Southern Methodist 27 BAYLOR 21: Mustangs (4-1) hit 2 home runs early and held on for win. Ponies S Mitchell Price took handoff from WR Jimmy Young on opening KO and scored on 100y RET. After Bears tallied on 13y TD pass to FB Randy Rutledge, SMU FB Jed Martin scampered 74y to EZ for 14-7 lead. Bears (3-2) rallied as QB Cody Carlson (18-33/245y, 2 INTs), who became school's leader in career passing y and total O, led attackers to 31 1st downs. SMU D forced pair of 2nd H TOs and stopped drive on downs with 8 mins left, while O controlled final 4 mins.

Texas Tech 17 ARKANSAS 7: Red Raiders surprised 3-TD favorite Arkansas (4-1) as D held Hogs to 231y, 179y less than O avg. Texas Tech (3-3) DT Desmond Royal (11 tackles, 2 sacks) keyed unit that never let Razorbacks get comfortable. Tiny WR Tyrone Thurman's 27y punt RET set up 1y TD sneak by QB Billy Joe Tolliver for 17-7 lead that forced run-oriented Hogs to take to air. Comeback chances for Arkansas ended with 2nd H FUMs at Red Raiders 23 and 41YLs.

WASHINGTON STATE 34 Southern California 14: Cougars ripped Trojans (4-1) as TB Kerry Porter rushed for 164y of Wazzu's 309y to deliver 1st win over USC in 29 years. Ahead 17-0 at H, Washington State (3-2-1) drove 75y, final 42y on pass to WR Kitrick Taylor for TD, to go up 24-0 at open of 3rd Q. QB Ed Blount (13-20/201y) ran option perfectly in committing no TOs, rushing for 2 scores, and using play action to throw 2 TDs. Meanwhile, O-line, led by G Mike Utley, dominated USC as Cougars held 40:30 to 19:30 advantage in possession time. Trojans QB Rodney Peete threw for 253y, but also lost 2 FUMs and threw 2 INTs.

UCLA 32 Arizona 25: Bruins (3-2) exploded in 4th Q, scoring 25 pts to crush early 18-0 deficit. Wildcats (4-1) had profited by big plays: 2 blocked punts, safety, and 28y INT RET by LB Byron Evans. Bruins did not answer until 3rd Q when S James Washington picked off pass before being stripped by Cats TB David Adams, with ball caught by

CB Darryl Henley and advanced 54y for TD. Bruins completed rally when TB Gaston Green ran for 2 TDs in 4th Q, including winning 32y rumble in final min. Arizona scored its sole O TD with trick play as Adams surprised Bruins with 15y TD pass to WR Derek Hill (6/114y) midway through 4th Q.

Washington 24 STANFORD 14: After Stanford (4-1) QB John Paye (28-47/364y) tore apart Huskies in 1st H with 213y, 2 TDs passing, adjustments were made by UW. Pressure D blanked Cards in 2nd H, sacking Paye twice and gaining EZ INT by CB Tony Zachery on 4th-and-goal from 5YL. Washington (4-1) QB Chris Chandler (19-31/224y, INT) threw winning 42y TD in 3rd Q to WR Lonzell Hill (9/137y), and FB Rick Fenney added 9y insurance TD run. Fenney rushed for 79y and scored earlier TD on 6y reception. TB Vince Weathersby led Huskies rushers with 122y.

AP Poll October 13

1 Miami (56)	1175		11 Texas A&M	559
2 Alabama (2)	1099		12 Louisiana State	524
3 Nebraska	1018		13 Mississippi State	345
4 Michigan	986		14 Arkansas	338
5 Oklahoma	946		15 Southern California	325
6 Penn State (1)	892		16 Arizona	296
7 Auburn	861		17 Clemson	293
8 Iowa	753		18 North Carolina	147
9t Washington	676		19 UCLA	116
9t Arizona State	676		20t Baylor	94
			20t Southern Methodist	94

October 18, 1986

North Carolina State 35 NORTH CAROLINA 34: Hard-fought game went down to wire as Tar Heels (4-1-1) drove 68y to pull within 35-34, with QB Mark Maye (25-33/311y, 3 TDs) completing 5 passes in row. Eschewing tie, UNC lost 7-game series win streak when TE Dave Truitt was ruled down before catch in EZ on 2-pt conv try. Heels had ball deep in NC State (4-1-1) territory moments earlier before Wolfpack DT Ray Agnew recovered RB Eric Starr's FUM at 2YL. QB Erik Kramer (17-27/279y) then led 98y drive to winning 37y TD pass to WR Naz Worthen (8/160y). North Carolina WR Quinton Smith caught 9/126y, while Starr rushed for 102y, TD.

MICHIGAN 20 Iowa 17: In reversal of 1985 nail-biting outcome, Michigan K Mike Gillette booted last-sec 34y FG for win. Iowa (5-1) had 10-3 H lead, but failed to capitalize on 3 Michigan TOs in 2nd Q. Wolverines FB Gerald White scored twice in 3rd Q, on 25y TD catch and 10y run, for 17-10 lead. Iowa QB Mark Vlasic, who did not start due to separated shoulder, entered game to hit 4 passes including tying 15y TD pass to WR Robert Smith. Michigan QB Jim Harbaugh (17-28/225y, 2 INTs) authored 78y march to missed FG. But when Hawkeyes drove to Michigan 43YL with 2 mins left, Vlasic and FB Richard Bass messed up pitchout on 3rd-and-1, only to see Wolverines LB Andy Moeller pounce on it. Gillette followed with victorious FG.

MINNESOTA 19 Indiana 17: Despite outgaining Hoosiers 421y to 185y, Minnesota (4-2) needed late 21y FG by K Chip Lohmiller to pull out victory. Managing single TD, on 2y pass from QB Rickey Foggie (12-22/145y) to WR Mel Anderson, Gophers allowed Hoosiers (4-2) to take 17-10 lead in 2nd Q on TB Damon Sweazy's 2 TD runs and K Pete Stoyanovich's 52y FG. Along with Lohmiller, whose 4 FGs included 52y 3-ptr in 1st Q, TB Darrell Thompson was Minnesota's O dominator with 191y rushing.

TEXAS A&M 31 Baylor 30: Aggies (5-1) QB Kevin Murray was brilliant, completing 25-40/308y, 3 TDs, while running in another. Murray threw winning 4y TD pass to WR Tony Thompson with 3:48 left. On TD play, Bears LB Robert Watters, who had 2 sacks, was eyelash late, nailing QB just after throw. Baylor (4-3) had 2 final tries at end doomed by 4th down sack and INT. Bears jumped to 17-0 lead in 1st Q as QB Cody Carlson (15-28/273y, 3 INTs) threw 52y TD pass to FB Randy Rutledge and ran 58y to set up 2y scoring run by WR Matt Clark. K Terry Syler also hit 20y FG after FUM by Aggies. A&M D settled down, while Murray led 2nd biggest comeback in school history. "You can spell this win, M-U-R-R-A-Y," said losing coach Grant Teaff.

Arizona State 29 SOUTHERN CALIFORNIA 20: Sun Devils (5-0-1) took advantage of Trojan miscues to become 1st conf team ever to sweep UCLA and USC in Los Angeles in same season. Arizona State's final TD, on 9y pass from QB Jeff Van Raaphorst (13-22/184y, 2 TDs) to WR Jeff Gallimore, was set up by REC of FUM by Southern California TB Aaron Emanuel at his own 26YL. Trojans (4-2) failed to cover short KO to set up another TD drive, and roughing K PEN by S Tim McDonald on missed FG allowed another Devils drive to EZ. Trojans QB Rodney Peete passed for 226y, although his INT set up FG by Arizona State, team that was beginning to smell roses.

AP Poll October 20

1 Miami (55)	1174		11 Iowa	601
2 Alabama (3)	1111		12 Louisiana State	561
3 Nebraska	1024		13 Mississippi State	411
4 Michigan	997		14 Arkansas	388
5 Oklahoma	937		15 Arizona	348
6 Penn State (1)	902		16 Clemson	335
7 Auburn	861		17 UCLA	192
8 Washington	704		18 Southern Methodist	175
9 Arizona State	695		19 Stanford	93
10 Texas A&M	606		20 North Carolina State	71

October 25, 1986

Boston College 19 WEST VIRGINIA 10: Rivalry between schools had been heated but 1-sided of late as Mountaineers (2-5) sported 9-game series win streak. About to embark on year-closing winning streak, Eagles (4-3) had better material this year, but West Virginia QB Ben Reed put fear into Boston College by passing for 201y. Trailing 12-3 after Eagles K Brian Lowe booted school record 4 FGs, Reed led Mountaineers to BC 12YL before DB Ed Duran picked off tipped pass. After punt, Reed drove WVU

80y to 26y TD pass to WR Harvey Smith. In 4th Q, Eagles built on their 12-10 edge with 66y scoring drive, featuring 47y rushing and short TD dive by FB Jon Bronner. Reed was off again, hitting 3 passes to move Mountaineers to BC 12YL before DE Eric Lindstrom came up with important INT. TB Troy Stradford's 96y rushing allowed him to become Boston College's all-time rusher with 2,812y, 53y more than TB Mike Esposito (1972-74).

NORTH CAROLINA STATE 27 Clemson 3: Wolfpack (5-1-1) reversed Clemson's blueprint for success by rushing for 253y against nation's 4th-best run D and halting Clemson's string of 14 consecutive 200y rushing games. QB Erik Kramer threw 2 TDs and K Mike Cofer added 2 FGs to finish off what NC State rushers started. Tigers, who briefly enjoyed 3-0 lead, rushed for 141y, while passing for only 72y. NC State WR Haywood Jeffires scored TD on 2y reception and another on 62y run.

Penn State 23 ALABAMA 3: Nittany Lions (7-0) won with traditionally tough D, holding Tide to 44y rushing, 222y below avg. LB Shane Conlan and company stuffed Bama sweeps and pressed QB Mike Shula (14-30/172y), sacking him 5 times. Lions also had 2 INTs and 3 FUM RECs. Penn State gained 378y as steady QB John Shaffer (13-17/168y) ran his regular season mark to 18-0. Suffering worst loss since Georgia's 21-0 win in 1976, Alabama (7-1) still led 3-0 early on 40y FG by K Van Tiffin. Victory over marquee foe propelled Lions up to no. 2 spot in AP Poll.

Auburn 35 MISSISSIPPI STATE 6: Undefeated in conf, Bulldogs (6-2) looked to this game as statement to nation. It was unintentional negative as Tigers (8-0) rode 21-pt 2nd Q to blow-out win. Game was as good as over early in 2nd Q when Auburn TB Brent Fullwood (16/179y) took pitchout and rambled 88y for TD, 1st of his trio. Fullwood was battling flu but instead sickened Bulldogs. Auburn D held Mississippi State to 47y rushing and twice picked off QB Don Smith (19-31/153y). Bulldogs finally scored in 4th Q on 16y TD pass from QB Mike Davis to WR Jerry Myers.

COLORADO 20 Nebraska 10: Colorado fans could celebrate: 18-game losing streak to Huskers finally was over. Holding Nebraska to lowest rushing total in 8 years (123y), Buffs D earned kudos. Colorado O contributed 2 trick-play TDs as WR Jeff Campbell scored on 39y reverse in 1st Q and HB O.C. Oliver threw 52y to WR Lance Carl for clinching TD in 4th Q. QB Steve Taylor scored Husker TD, running in from 2y out to offset frustrating day in which he was held to 27y rushing and 7-21, 2 INTs passing. Buffs K Dave DeLine added 2 FGs, including 57y boot for 10-0 H lead.

TEXAS 27 Southern Methodist 24: K Jeff Ward's 40y FG with 40 secs remaining won game Texas (3-3) thought it had bagged while sporting early 21-0 lead. Ward's 3-ptr was set up by CB Eric Jeffries' INT at SMU 47YL and came after TB Edwin Simmons, starting his 1st game in 3 years, nearly earned goat horns in losing FUM at Ponies 15YL with 2:10 left. Simmons recovered for 85y, scored twice in 14-0 1st Q, and led Horns to 255y to 48y running edge. QB Bobby Watters shook off 3 INTs to rally Mustangs (5-2) by throwing for 285y and TDs of 66y and 19y to WR Ron Morris (16/162y) and 14y to WR Jeff Jacobs.

Air Force 22 SAN DIEGO STATE 10: Falcons (6-2) moved into 1st place in WAC as FB Pat Evans rushed for 116y of team's 314y. Ahead, Air Force was ahead 17-10 in 3rd Q when LB Trent Pickering was inserted. Only 2 plays after entering game, Pickering contributed crucial INT at own 21YL that he returned 41y to set up insurance TD. San Diego State (4-3) was held to 107y in 2nd H despite passing of QB Todd Santos (28-44/272y, TD). Santos was sacked 7 times by Flyboys' aggressive rush, with Air Force NG John Steed gaining 2 pts on safety in 4th Q.

Southern California 10 STANFORD 0: High-flying Cardinal was grounded as Trojans (5-2) D allowed 172y, with only 64y being earned in 2nd H. Stanford (5-2) FB Brad Muster led with 35y rushing, while QB John Paye, who opened game by completing 10-11, ended up with 23-37/172y, 3 INTs passing. USC used 5, sometimes 6, DBs in coverage, and Trojans DB Louis Brock, son of baseball Hall of Famer Lou Brock, returned INT 41y to set up game's only TD. It developed as 18y pass from Troy QB Rodney Peete to WR Erik Affholter. Stanford's best penetration was to 38YL, but that came on drive when USC chipped in with pair of 15y PENs. Stanford D had bright moment, posting GLS in 2nd Q as Trojans wasted 1st-and-goal from 1YL. Busy Stanford LB Dave Wyman logged 22 tackles and INT.

AP Poll October 27

1 Miami (55)	1174		11 Iowa	602
2 Penn State (4)	1107		12 Louisiana State	597
3 Michigan (1)	1081		13t Arkansas	467
4 Oklahoma	1017		13t Arizona	467
5 Auburn	986		15 UCLA	343
6 Washington	818		16 North Carolina State	262
7 Arizona State	798		17 Ohio State	188
8 Alabama	792		18 Southern California	173
9 Nebraska	684		19 Mississippi State	93
10 Texas A&M	679		20 Florida State	65

November 1, 1986

SYRACUSE 24 Pittsburgh 20: Syracuse (3-5) rallied behind QB Don McPherson, who threw 3 TD passes including 2y game-winner to leaping WR Scott Schwedes in back of EZ. McPherson was flushed out of pocket on play but scrambled until Schwedes, who earlier caught 11y TD in 2nd Q, came open. Panthers (4-3-1) built 10-0 lead in odd manner: 2 FGs and 2 safeties, both off Syracuse punts. Pitt's sole TD came on 75y scoring pass from QB John Congemi to FB Craig Heyward. Orange D posted 5 sacks, 3 INTs and FUM REC to fuel turnaround.

MIAMI 41 Florida State 23: Saving his best for last, Miami (8-0) QB Vinny Testaverde (21-35/315y, 3 TDs, 2 INTs) hit 10-11/185y, 2 TDs in 4th Q and scored his 2nd rushing TD. Florida State (4-3-1) had grabbed 20-14 H lead, scoring on wild 100y KO RET as RB Keith Ross ran to 10y then bounced lateral to CB Dexter Carter who raced final

90y. Hampered by 1st H injuries to QB Danny McManus and TB Sammie Smith, Boles stalled in 2nd H as Hurricanes pulled away with 20-pt 4th Q. "Wasn't he the stinking, cold-flat difference?" asked Bobby Bowden with admiration. "We played about as well as we can play, but Testaverde was just great."

Mississippi 21 LOUISIANA STATE 19: Ole Miss converted 2 GLSs and balanced attack to inflict upset and only SEC loss of year for LSU (5-2). QB Mark Young (18-31/171y, INT) led Rebels (6-2-1) to trio of 1st H TDs, running for 6 pts himself. Tigers (5-2) were able to move ball, but 6 drives were held to FG tries; K David Browndyke hit 4 FGs, including from 52y. Browndyke's misses came late in 4th Q, including 30y attempt that went wide left with 9 secs left. Loss wasted great effort by LSU WR Wendell Davis, who caught 14/208y, including 28y TD from QB Tom Hodson (21-39/251y) and 4/53y on final, futile drive.

FLORIDA 18 Auburn 17: Florida shocked Tigers (7-1) by overcoming 17-pt deficit for greatest comeback in school history to date. After Gators (4-4) helped Auburn race to 17-0 lead by turning ball over 6 times, QB Kerwin Bell (17-31/182, TD, 2 INTs) led 3 scoring drives to pull out win. Bell, wearing brace after missing 2 games with strained ligament, came in to start 79y drive in 3rd Q to his 1y TD run early in 4th Q. On next series, Bell drove Gators to 51y FG by K Robert McGinty, who had left starting job at Auburn after not receiving scholarship. Finally, Bell converted FUM by Tigers FB Reggie Ware into TD as WR Ricky Nattiel—playing with separated shoulder—caught 5y over-*shoulder* pass with :36 left. Bell made winning 2-pt conv by niftily avoiding DT Tracy Rocker. Tigers had time for 52y FG attempt by K Chris Knapp that was missed. Auburn TB Brent Fullwood rushed for 166y.

Ohio State 31 IOWA 10: By game's end it was difficult to remember that Hawkeyes (6-2) grabbed early 7-0 lead as S Kerry Burt returned tipped pass 17y for TD. Ohio State (7-2) scored 21 straight pts in 2nd Q, beginning with spectacular 72y hook-up between QB Jim Karsatos and WR Cris Carter (6/121y) that featured nifty spin at midfield by Carter to shake LB Ken Sims. Short Iowa punt set up short drive for 14-7 edge, and Bucks CB Greg Rogan nabbed FB Richard Bass' FUM, returning it 31y for TD. Buckeyes D chased QB Mark Vlasic all day, holding him to 46y passing.

Purdue 17 NORTHWESTERN 16: Losing streak of Wildcats (2-6) stretched to 5 games as Purdue (2-6) used 2 blocked punts to pull out win. Boilermakers K Jonathan Briggs kicked 25y FG with time elapsing to cap 37y drive after CB Brad Davis deflected Northwestern P Shawn Carpenter's punt. Purdue's 1st block, by LB Jerrol Williams in 1st Q, had set up 15y drive to RB Lorenzo McCline's 2y TD run for 7-3 lead. Wildcats scored 10 straight pts in 2nd Q for 13-7 H lead, which was given back in 3rd Q when Purdue uncovered WR Calvin Williams ran under 69y TD pass from sub QB Doug Downing. Northwestern QB Mike Greenfield passed for 195y.

Texas A&M 39 SOUTHERN METHODIST 35: Texas A&M (7-1) won shootout on QB Kevin Murray's 3rd TD pass, 34y to RB Keith Woodside (5/134y receiving) with 1:48 left. Lead changed 7 times, thrice in 4th Q as 23y TD run by SMU WR Ron Morris was sandwiched by Woodside's earlier 50y TD catch and his winning score. A&M FB Roger Vick rushed for 118y, 2 TDs, while Murray threw for 278y. Morris led SMU (5-3) with 140y all-purpose, and QB Bobby Watters passed for 173y.

TEXAS TECH 23 Texas 21: Game had future impact for coaches Fred Akers of Texas (3-4) and counterpart David McWilliams of Texas Tech (5-3). Red Raiders had control until Horns' 2-TD rally in 4th Q made it 2-pt nail-biter. WR Tyrone Thurman had taken punt 96y in 1st Q for Tech's 7-0 lead. IB James Gray bumped lead to 14-0 with 20y TD run later in 1st Q. After Texas QB Bret Stafford halved deficit with 20y scoring run, Tech K Scott Segrist booted 3 FGs for 23-7 lead in 4th Q. Stafford launched 2 TD passes in 2-min span, then had Longhorns driving to midfield. Facing 4th-and-3, Stafford was nailed for no gain by LB Brad Hastings and DT Desmond Royal. After season, Akers lost his job, replaced by McWilliams.

Southern California 20 ARIZONA 13: Trojans (6-2) QB Rodney Peete (14-23/179y, INT) returned to Tucson, where he played HS ball, to throw 2 TDs, while USC D held Pac 10's top O to 253y, 160y and 28 pts less than avg. Cashing in on 3 Arizona FUMs in 3rd Q, USC entered 4th Q with 20-6 lead. Wildcats (6-2) pulled within 20-13 on TB David Adams' 5y TD run, but had last drive halted when Trojans CB Greg Coauette's hit on FB Charles Webb forced FUM, recovered by S Cleveland Colter.

ARIZONA STATE 34 Washington 21: Attention centered on scrimmage line battle between Arizona State's massive O-line and Huskies' D that was surrendering 61.6y rushing per game. Sun Devils (7-0-1) won face-off with early knockout, rushing for 77y on way to demoralizing 1st Q TD. TB Darryl Harris (108y rushing) ended drive with 24y TD romp. ASU FB Channing Williams tallied 154y on ground against nation's 2nd rated D. Arizona State built 17-0 lead before end of 1st Q ended as D permitted single 1st down. Washington (6-2) rallied before H as REC of punt FUM set up TD, and QB Chris Chandler (20-41/231y) threw 38y scoring pass to WR Darryl Franklin to pull Huskies within 24-14. Devils LB Stacy Harvey ended rally with 2nd Q EZ INT, while his other INT in 3rd Q set up Arizona State's final score.

AP Poll November 3

1 Miami (53)	1153	11 Ohio State	535
2 Penn State (4)	1076	12 UCLA	500
3 Michigan (1)	1053	13 Washington	477
4 Oklahoma	953	14 Southern California	434
5 Arizona State	921	15 North Carolina State	343
6 Alabama	861	16 Iowa	260
7 Nebraska	793	17 Arizona	178
8 Texas A&M	740	18 Louisiana State	154
9 Auburn	660	19 Georgia	103
10 Arkansas	639	20 Clemson	56

November 8, 1986

ARMY 21 Air Force 11: With Hudson River tailgaters just settling into seats, Army (4-5) QB Tory Crawford burst through Falcons D on 65y opening-play run, and HB Benny Wright quickly ran for 1y TD as Cadets secured lead for good at 7-0. Soon thereafter, Crawford (26/165y) drove 72y driving with 1st of his 2 TDs on 4th down run for 14-0 lead. Air Force (6-3) reeled off 11 straight pts, capping 97y drive with HB Marc Munafro's 11y TD run. Falcons came no closer, gambling on 4th down at own 33YL, which set up Army's final TD. Falcons QB Jim Tomallo rushed for 92y.

VIRGINIA 20 North Carolina State 16: Some defenders could be happy to make 3 INTs in single season, Virginia (3-6) S Mike Pettine amazingly made 3 INTs in final 6 mins. They each halted drive by Wolfpack (6-2-1), and pair of Pettine's INTs came in Cavaliers EZ in final 1:11. Cavs FB Durwin Greggs rushed for 177y, while QB Don Majkowski threw and ran for scores. Hampered by leg injury to standout QB Erik Kramer, North Carolina State settled for 3 FGs off foot of K Mike Cofer and TD on CB Derrick Taylor's 88y INT RET. UVa coach George Welsh was in wheelchair after breaking leg at practice.

CLEMSON 38 North Carolina 10: Wearing orange pants for 12th time in history for 11-1 record, fired-up Tigers (7-2) grabbed ACC lead. Clemson TB Terrence Flagler rushed for 114y and 2 TDs, and QB Rodney Williams passed for 108y and rushed for 76y and 7y TD. TB Derrick Fenner rushed for 89y, but Tar Heels (5-3-1) failed to score TD until 4th Q on QB Mark Maye's 43y pass to WR Eric Streater. By then, Carolina down by 28 pts, having allowed 30 or more pts for 5th straight outing.

Louisiana State 14 ALABAMA 10: Alabama (8-2) was frustrated throughout, crossing LSU 30YL 6 times and going for score on 10 pts. TB Bobby Humphrey's 2 FUMs ended 4th Q drives ended deep into Tigers (6-2) territory: LSU CB Kevin Guidry made 1 REC in EZ. That FUM came on hit by S Greg Jackson, who also had an EZ INT and recovered FUM on his 18YL. Humphrey rushed for 134y and QB Mike Shula threw for 190y. LSU's passing attack was held in check, but QB Tommy Hodson managed 6y TD toss to WR Wendell Davis. Road team now had won every game in series since 1980.

Florida 31 Georgia 19 (Jacksonville): Scoring last 21 pts, Gators (5-4) engineered 2nd straight comeback over their heated rival. Florida QB Kerwin Bell (20-31/272y, INT) connected with WR Ricky Nattiel (7/97y), who had been questionable with bad shoulder, on 3 TD passes, 2 coming in 2nd H after Georgia (6-3) grabbed 19-10 lead. Winning score turned out to be 3y run by TB James Massey on 1st play of 4th Q. Drive of 41y was launched by FUM REC by Florida DE Steve Stipe. Gators D made rally possible with big 2nd H: it held Bulldogs to 58y O and 4 1st downs after H. Georgia TB Lars Tate rushed for 86y and TD, and K Steve Crumley added 4 FGs.

ILLINOIS 20 Iowa 16: With its run game vanishing (29/34y), Iowa (6-3) faded from Big 10 race. Before they swooned, Hawkeyes took 10-0 lead, as special teams blocked 3 placekicks and made punt FUM REC. QB Brian Menkhausen (10-19/134y) next ignited Illini by hitting WR Stephen Pierce on 54y TD pass, with Pierce dragging Hawks DB Ken Sims into EZ. Illinois (3-6) went up 14-10 in 4th Q on short TD run, and scored 20th pt in row on K Chris Siambekos' 2nd FG, both set up by Iowa TOs. Iowa scored again at game's end on 3y run by TB Kevin Harmon. Illini were edgy over 59-0 shellacking suffered in 1985. "This was a payback win," said LB Steve Glasson.

OKLAHOMA 77 Missouri 0: Destruction of Missouri (2-7) meant Sooners (8-1) had outscored opponents 301-25 during their 6-game win streak since September loss to Miami. Oklahoma QB Jamelle Holieway's 117y rushing led ground game that ground out incredible 681y and 10 TDs; backup QB Eric Mitchel added 122y and 2 TDs. Oklahoma scored TDs on its 1st 7 possessions, while K Tim Lashar's 11 x-pts set Big 8 record. Also, Lashar's 129 straight conv kicks set new school record. Tigers HB Vernon Boyd rushed for 72y for modest Mizzou O. Win was largest for Sooners since 157-0 pasting of little Kingfisher College in 1919.

BAYLOR 29 Arkansas 14: Despite knee injury, QB Cody Carlson (21-35/258y, 2 INTs) lifted Bears (6-3) past Arkansas. Baylor D also shone, holding Hogs to 112y rushing and 60y passing. Arkansas (7-2) had taken 14-12 H lead, with QB Greg Thomas hitting HB Joe Johnson for 38y go-ahead TD. Baylor had to wait until 4th Q to take lead for good on 36y FG by K Terry Syler. With Hogs held to 24y and 2 1st downs in 2nd H, 15-14 lead was enough although Bears tacked on 2 insurance TDs.

Stanford 28 UCLA 23: Stanford (7-2) eliminated UCLA from Rose Bowl race as FB Brad Muster rushed for 183y, 2 TDs. Muster gained 159y in 1st H as Cardinal took 21-16 lead. After Stanford CB Toi Cook's INT, Muster scored again on 4y run. TB Gaston Green's (26/142y) tallied his 3rd TD run to pull Bruins (6-3) to within 28-23 and later led final drive into Stanford territory that ended on downs. With banged up right shoulder, QB John Paye (17-22/147y) kept his passes short and effective.

AP Poll November 10

1 Miami (57)	1195	11 Alabama	560
2 Michigan (1)	1102	12 Louisiana State	529
3 Penn State (1)	1075	13 Southern California	506
4 Oklahoma	1041	14 Arizona	415
5 Arizona State (1)	973	15 Clemson	310
6 Nebraska	878	16 Stanford	249
7 Texas A&M	830	17 Arkansas	242
8 Auburn	782	18 Baylor	195
9 Ohio State	711	19 UCLA	95
10 Washington	606	20 Mississippi	68

November 15, 1986

MARYLAND 17 Clemson 17: Tie enabled Tigers (7-2-1) to wrap up ACC title in odd match-up of teams whose coaches were both banished from sidelines for arguing: Clemson's Danny Ford was out for actions in last season's match-up against Terps and Maryland's Bobby Ross for grabbing ref against North Carolina 2 weeks prior. Tigers,

who rushed for 254y, marched to Maryland 2YL in closing secs before sending in K David Treadwell for tying 21y FG that guaranteed conf title. Loss would have meant 3-way tie. FB Tommy Neal scored both of Maryland's TDs on short runs, 2nd following FUM by Clemson FB Tracy Johnson at own 6YL. But, Tigers won ground battle with 254y to Terps' 114y. Maryland QB Dan Henning threw for 195y.

Georgia 20 AUBURN 16: With QB James Jackson at his grandmother's funeral, QB Wayne Johnson led Bulldogs (7-3) to upset. Tigers (8-2) marched 84y to 4y TD run by FB Reggie Ware for 7-0 lead. Georgia answered as Johnson went on 3-3 on 75y drive he capped with 8y TD pass to TE Troy Sadowski. Auburn O was halted rest of 1st H, while Georgia added dual FGs by K Steve Crumley and added Johnson's 6y keeper for 20-10 lead in 3rd Q. Game seemed over when Bulldogs P Cris Carpenter pinned Tigers on own 1YL with 5:37 left, but Auburn QB Jeff Burger (19-36/233y, 3 INTs) threw for 99y on drive, including 13y TD pass to WR Lawyer Tillman (9/150y). Tigers had late chance but Burger, after passing for 56y, threw INT to LB Steve Boswell (19 tackles). Water cannons chased UGa celebrants off field after game.

Tennessee 22 MISSISSIPPI 10: Playing spoiler, Tennessee (4-5) displayed talent that made them SEC's preseason favorite. Down 10-9 entering 4th Q, Vols scored 2 TDs as QB Jeff Francis (16-27/183y) fired 38y scoring pass to WR Joey Clinkscales (6/92y) for game-winner and TB William Howard (17/74y) carried on 8 straight plays to ice game with 2y TD run. Rebels (6-3-1) scored 1st on FB Tony Dentley's 2y run, capping 44y drive set up by INT by CB Don Price. Held to 199y total O and dozen 1st downs, Ole Miss could add only 26y FG by K Bryan Owen.

Penn State 24 NOTRE DAME 19: Gaining 27 1st downs and 418y, Fighting Irish (4-5) seemed poised for upset, but Nittany Lions (10-0) made it well into 4th Q with 24-13 lead. Notre Dame began final drive at own 20YL with 2:29 left, and QB Steve Beuerlein (24-39/311y) hit 5 straight passes to Irish 6YL. Penn State CB Ray Isom dropped WR Tim Brown for 3y loss, LB Dan Graham and DE Bob White sacked Beuerlein, and CB Gary Wilkerson broke up pass to TE Joel Williams with well-timed hit. On 4th down, with receivers covered, Beuerlein threw to TB Mark Green, who fell well short of EZ for end rally. PSU was wise to pass near GL as Penn State has not allowed rushing TD for 21 Qs. Mt Nits QB John Shaffer (9-13/162y) threw TD and ran for another. He connected with WR Ray Roundtree 3 times: 34y key pass on 1st TD drive, 37y TD completion that put Penn State in front 17-13 in 3rd Q, and 24y hook-up that opened final TD drive.

Minnesota 20 MICHIGAN 17: On final play, Minnesota (6-4) K Chip Lohmiller booted 30y FG and booted no. 2 Wolverines from national title hunt. Michigan (9-1) had tied game moments earlier on FB Gerald White's 1y TD run, and coach Bo Schembechler opted to kick tying x-pt. Gophers' winning FG was set up by 31y run by QB Rickey Foggie, who earlier threw and ran for scores. Gophers' 1st win in Ann Arbor since 1962 was inspired by film of last Little Brown Jug win in 1977, and was assisted by Michigan's 5 TOs that led to 17 pts. Wolverines QB Jim Harbaugh (14-22/207y, INT) became school's all-time passing leader with 4,891y, while breaking own single-season mark with 2,171y. "They deserved the game," said Schembechler. "It just seemed like everything we did backfired."

Ohio State 30 WISCONSIN 17: Buckeyes (9-2) dashed upset bid early, scoring TD on 32y run by TB Vince Workman (29/172y) 19 secs into game. TD converted Wisconsin (3-7) CB Nate Odomes' FUM of opening KO. Ohio State finished with 10 more pts in 1st Q, including 2nd TD run by Workman. Badgers, who lately had owned rivalry with 4 wins in 5 games, got off mat to score 10 2nd Q pts, but rally soon died. Ohio WR Cris Carter (7/112y) finished off Badgers with 28y TD grab. Wisconsin TB Larry Emery rushed for 120y and 2y TD.

ARKANSAS 14 Texas A&M 10: Razorbacks (8-2) opted for ball-control, rushing 49/186y, to stay in SWC race. Arkansas grabbed 14-7 lead late in 3rd Q on 10y run by QB Greg Thomas (11-14/112y) and stopped Aggies (8-2) twice after long 4th Q drives. Texas A&M QB Kevin Murray threw for 180y, but Hogs S Nate White's 3rd Q INT—his 1st after 160 pass attempts— provided winning TD set-up. Murray drove Aggies to Hogs 12YL late in 4th Q before S Odis Lloyd deflected final pass in EZ.

Oklahoma 28 COLORADO 0: Completely ignoring its passing game, Sooners (9-1) ran roughshod over Colorado (5-5) with 344y. QB Jamelle Holieway led way with 126y rushing, taking Sooners 77y in 1st Q for 17y scoring run by HB Patrick Collins. Buffs then lost FUM on own 2YL when QB Marc Walters muffed handoff to FB Anthony Weatherspoon to set up 2y TD run by FB Lydell Carr. Colorado managed only 135y total O while losing 4 TOs to Oklahoma's none.

AP Poll November 17

1 Miami (56)	1196	11 Arkansas	546
2 Penn State (3)	1119	12 Washington	472
3 Oklahoma	1083	13 Texas A&M	455
4 Arizona State (1)	1025	14 Arizona	432
5 Nebraska	964	15 Auburn	405
6 Michigan	856	16 Stanford	321
7 Ohio State	842	17 Baylor	232
8 Louisiana State	730	18 UCLA	160
9 Alabama	707	19 Clemson	156
10 Southern California	641	20 Georgia	78

November 22, 1986

PENN STATE 34 Pittsburgh 14: Nittany Lions (11-0) easily finished undefeated regular season, 6th in coach Joe Paterno's 21 years. Panthers (5-5-1) had 7-3 lead wiped out on 91y KO TD RET by swift TB Blair Thomas. Starting Penn State TB D.J. Dozier ran 26y for TD, while back-up QB Matt Knizer hit WR Eric Hamilton with 82y TD pass. Knizer had another pass converted into 82y scoring play, but this came as reversal:

INT TD RET by Pitt S Troy Washington. FB Craig Heyward had bulled for 2y TD for Pitt's 1st score; it was 1st rushing TD surrendered by Lions D in 22 Qs. Win was coach Joe Paterno's 198th, tying him with Dana X. Bible for 9th all time.

Michigan 26 OHIO STATE 24: Michigan (10-1) effortlessly transformed 14-6 H deficit into 26-17 lead, scoring TDs on its 1st 3 series of 2nd H. Ohio State (9-3) struck back for TD on QB Jim Karsatos' 17y pass to WR Cris Carter. FUM REC allowed Bucks to attempt late 46y FG, but K Matt Frantz hooked it to seal Rose Bowl berth for Michigan. Perhaps inspired by Michigan QB Jim Harbaugh's guarantee of victory, Buckeyes looked like they were Pasadena-bound early on. Ohio scored on TDs by Carter and TB Vince Workman in 1st Q. Harbaugh (19-29/ 261y, 2 INTs) and TB Jamie Morris (29/210y) gradually sparked Wolverines' 529y O. They went ahead at 19-17 when Ohio LB Chris Spielman bit on fake to allow Morris to race 52y to set up own 8y TD run. Morris' runs quickly set up Wolverines' 3rd straight TD, scored by backup TB Thomas Wilcher on 7y run.

Oklahoma 20 NEBRASKA 17: Oklahoma (10-1) could pass after all. Completing Sooners' largest comeback during Wishbone era, QB Jamelle Holieway hit TE Keith Jackson from 17y out to tie game 17-17 with 1:22 left. Huskers (9-2), who had squandered 10-pt lead, soon punted. Jackson again got free, hauling in 1-handed 41y catch with 9 secs left to set up K Tim Lashar's winning 31y FG. Nebraska, who scored 1st rushing TD against Sooners D all season, had taken 17-7 lead when QB Steve Taylor threw 25y TD pass to WR Rod Smith.

Arkansas 41 SOUTHERN METHODIST 0: QB Greg Thomas rushed for 113y, 3 TDs to help Arkansas (9-2) keep its Cotton Bowl hopes alive. Thomas' 3 scores and 47y FG by K Kendall Trainor provided Hogs with 24-0 H lead. Arkansas rushed for 422y in earning its 1st victory at Texas Stadium. Mustangs (6-5) QB Bobby Watters threw for 191y in final game before NCAA lowered "Death Penalty" on SMU.

ARIZONA 34 Arizona State 17: Wildcats (8-2) won 5th straight in series, beating Pac 10's 1st place team in 50th edition of rivalry. Arizona's 1st score came after DT George Hinkle's FUM REC led to 97y trip to 18y TD pass from QB Alfred Jenkins (11-17/165y) to TB David Adams. Wildcats converted INT by CB James DeBow on own 27YL into TB Art Greathouse's 5y TD run. QB Jeff Van Raaphorst (38-55/437y) led 2 scoring drives to rally Sun Devils (9-1-1) to 14-10 H deficit, but his 3 INTs helped doom comeback bid. S Chuck Cecil's 100y INT TD RET in 4th Q highlighted Arizona's 20 2nd H pts. Cats logged 413y rushing, to 65y for ASU, and made no TOs to 4 for Sun Devils. ASU WR Aaron Cox caught 10/191y, including 20y TD.

UCLA 45 Southern California 25: Hot Bruins routed rivals, building 31-0 lead behind TB Gaston Green, who rushed for 224y, 4 TDs. Up by 24 pts as 1st H neared its end, UCLA (7-3-1) QB Matt Stevens (14-19/190y) lofted ball in EZ in hopes of lucky bounce. Southern California DBs Tim McDonald and Junior Thurman collided, inadvertently tipping ball to WR Karl Dorrell for eventual winning TD. Bruins had 308y to 52y advantage in 1st H. After 29y passing in 1st H, USC (7-3) QB Rodney Peete finished with 199y, but most padded 18 cosmetic pts into 4th Q.

CALIFORNIA 17 Stanford 11: Golden Bears (2-9) gave Joe Kapp fine send-off in fired coach's final game. California pulled game out on strength of 2 huge plays by frosh WR Mike Ford—only 2 times he touched ball during contest: Ford made lunging catch of 61y 2nd Q pass to set up team's opening TD and scored eventual game-winner on 47y run with 4th Q reverse. WR Wendell Peoples scored Bears' 1st TD with 5y catch from QB Kevin Brown (15-23/221y, 2 INTs). QB John Paye (23-35/224y) kept Stanford (7-3) close with late 69y TD bomb to WR Jeff James (7/138y). Cardinal D forced punt, and Paye moved Stanford into Cal territory before 2 sacks stalled drive on downs in last 2 mins.

AP Poll November 24

1 Miami (54)	1156	11 Ohio State	606
2 Penn State (4)	1090	12 Arizona	589
3 Oklahoma	1056	13 Washington	568
4 Michigan	878	14 Auburn	416
5 Louisiana State	862	15 UCLA	346
6 Nebraska	834	16 Baylor	315
7 Alabama	763	17 Southern California	168
8 Arizona State	723	18 Georgia	153
9 Arkansas	670	19 North Carolina State	66
10 Texas A&M	625	20 Iowa	63

November 27-29, 1986

(Th'g) Texas A&M 16 TEXAS 3: Aggies (9-2) grabbed Cotton Bowl bid and put Texas coach Fred Akers out of his misery as he was fired soon afterward. Texas A&M WR Rod Harris' diving catch of 6y TD pass from QB Kevin Murray (25-36/277y) broke 3-3 tie, capping drive that advanced after roughing-P PEN. FB Roger Vick (41/167y), 1st Aggie to lead SWC in rushing in 35 years, led ball control O for winners, who also received 3 FGs from K Scott Slater. Longhorns (5-6) QB Bret Stafford threw for 201y. Loss was 3rd straight to A&M, another reason Akers was handed pink slip.

GEORGIA 31 Georgia Tech 24: With Georgia (8-3) TB Tim Worley injured, 1-time heralded recruit TB Lars Tate rushed for 154y and 3 TDs, including game-winning 5y effort in 4th Q. FB Keith Henderson added 116y to Bulldogs rush attack that totaled 332y. Yellow Jackets (5-5-1) entered 4th Q with 24-21 lead as QB Rick Strom threw for 223y and 14y TD to WR Gary Lee (4/122y). Georgia Tech's last drive ended with :90 left when TB Jerry Mays was stopped for no gain on 4th-and-1 at Georgia 46YL.

Auburn 21 Alabama 17 (Birmingham): Auburn (9-2) won game on mistake: WR Lawyer Tillman scored on reverse meant for backup WR Scott Bolton, who was on bench. With coach Pat Dye and Tillman trying to call timeout, QB Jeff Burger (19-30/153, 3 INTs) was oblivious amidst raucous crowd. Once ball was snapped Tillman knew what he had to do, racing left to take handoff from TB Tim Jessie and head to EZ.

Play capped 67y drive that featured Burger's 9y completion to WR Trey Gainous on 4th-and-3. TB Bobby Humphrey rushed for 204y to lead Crimson Tide (9-3) to late 17-7 lead. Auburn TB Brent Fullwood, who rushed for 145y, went 26y for his 2nd TD to pull within 17-14. LB Kurt Crain led Tigers D with 22 tackles.

Rice 14 HOUSTON 13: Coach Bill Yeoman lost final game after 25 years at helm of Cougars (1-10). Houston led 13-0 well into 4th Q before Rice (4-7) QB Quentis Roper threw and ran for TDs in final 5:36. After scoring on 7y TD run, Roper led Owls back into Houston territory, throwing 11y TD pass to WR Darrell Goolsby with 18 secs left. K Glenn Ray Hines added winning x-pt. Rice managed just 225y, less than Houston gained on ground (252y). Cougars scored TD on 9y run by RB Mat Pierson, while K Chip Browndyke added 2 FGs. Houston RB Vernell Ramsey rushed for 149y.

Notre Dame 38 SOUTHERN CALIFORNIA 37: Crazy season for Notre Dame (5-6) ended on positive note as K John Carney's game-ending 19y FG—shown on videotape by CBS after game officials declined request for extra delay to finish airing commercials—capped 18-pt 4th Q comeback. USC (7-4) had built 37-20 lead behind QB Rodney Peete's 171y passing, K Don Shafer's 60y FG, and CB Louis Brock's 58y INT TD RET. Irish then scored 3 times in final 13 mins as QB Steve Beuerlein (18-27/285y, 4 TDs, INT) threw TD passes of 42y to WR Milt Jackson and 5y to FB Braxston Banks, while WR Tim Brown (252 all-purpose y) set up final 10 pts with 49y catch and 56y punt RET. Notre Dame's 2nd TD drive began after controversial spot on 4th-and-1 keeper by QB Rodney Peete on Irish 5YL: Trojans came up short. USC coach Ted Tollner's record against UCLA and Notre Dame dropped to 1-7.

SAN DIEGO STATE 10 Brigham Young 3: King is dead: all hail new king. After BYU (7-4) dominated WAC for 10 straight years, Cougars were dethroned by Aztecs (8-3). Each team had 8 sacks as Ds set game's tempo. Cougars were held to 73y passing because QB Steve Lindsley was knocked out in 2nd Q. With D playing so well, San Diego State O needed to contribute little, and QB Todd Santos delivered 43y completion to WR Alfred Jackson to set up 7y TD run by RB Chris Hardy. DT Jason Buck, who won Outland Trophy earlier in day, led Cougars D with 3 sacks. Win was San Diego State's 1st over BYU since 1970.

AP Poll December 1

1	Miami (53)	1155	11	Ohio State	578
2	Penn State (5)	1092	12	Washington	561
3	Oklahoma	1053	13	Alabama	452
4	Michigan	984	14	Baylor	337
5	Louisiana State	877	15	UCLA	316
6	Nebraska	861	16	Arizona	307
7	Arizona State (1)	777	17	Georgia	234
8	Texas A&M	710	18	North Carolina State	135.5
9	Arkansas	692	19	Iowa	127
10	Auburn	631	20	Stanford	125

December 6, 1986

Army 27 Navy 7 (Philadelphia): QB Tory Crawford rushed for 94y and brilliantly led Wishbone attack as Army (6-5) won Commander in Chief trophy for 4th time in trophy's 14-year history. After Navy pulled to within 13-7 with 3rd Q TD, Crawford led consecutive TD drives of 79y and 48y to finish off their rivals. Midshipmen (3-8), who dropped 7th straight game of season, had single good drive of 71y, featuring 10 straight rushes by sub TB Don Holl that included TD bolt of 3y.

Conference Standings

Atlantic Coast

Clemson	5-1-1
North Carolina State	5-2
North Carolina	5-2
Georgia Tech	3-3
Maryland	2-3-1
Wake Forest	2-5
Duke	2-5
Virginia	2-5

Southeastern

Louisiana State	5-1
Auburn	4-2
Alabama	4-2
Georgia	4-2
Mississippi	4-2
Tennessee	3-3
Florida	2-4
Mississippi State	2-4
Kentucky	2-4
Vanderbilt	0-6

Big Ten

Michigan	7-1
Ohio State	7-1
Iowa	5-3
Minnesota	5-3
Michigan State	4-4
Indiana	3-5
Illinois	3-5
Northwestern	2-6
Purdue	2-6
Wisconsin	2-6

Mid-American

Miami (Ohio)	6-2
Toledo	5-3
Kent State	5-3
Bowling Green	5-3
Eastern Michigan	4-4
Ball State	4-4
Central Michigan	4-4
Western Michigan	3-5
Ohio	0-8

Big Eight

Oklahoma	7-0
Colorado	6-1
Nebraska	5-2
Oklahoma State	4-3
Iowa State	3-4
Missouri	2-5
Kansas State	1-6
Kansas	0-7

Southwest Athletic

Texas A&M	7-1
Arkansas	6-2
Baylor	6-2
Texas Tech	5-3
Texas	4-4
Rice	2-6
Houston	0-8
Southern Methodist *	5-3
Texas Christian *	1-7
* Ineligible	

Western Athletic

San Diego State	7-1
Brigham Young	6-2
Air Force	5-2
Hawaii	4-4
Colorado State	4-4
Wyoming	4-4
New Mexico	2-5
Texas-El Paso	2-6
Utah	1-7

Pacific Ten

Arizona State	5-1-1
Washington	5-2-1
UCLA	5-2-1
Arizona	5-3
Stanford	5-3
Southern California	5-3
Oregon	3-5
Washington State	2-6-1
California	2-7
Oregon State	1-6

Pacific Coast Athletic

San Jose State	7-0
Fresno State	6-1
Long Beach State	4-3
Nevada-Las Vegas	3-4
Utah State	3-4
Pacific	2-5
Cal State-Fullerton	2-5
New Mexico State	1-6

1986 Major Bowl Games
Independence Bowl (Dec. 20): Mississippi 20 Texas Tech 17

Nip-and-tuck affair went to Rebels (8-3-1) as winning 48y FG by K Bryan Owen bounced off crossbar before flying true early in 4th Q. Ole Miss had squandered 14-0 and 17-7 leads, with biggest play by Red Raiders (7-5) coming on 33y scoring RET of INT by S Merv Scurlark in 3rd Q. Mississippi QB Mark Young shook off INT to finish with 31-50/343y passing, setting up winning FG with 13y completion to TE Mario Perry. Texas Tech DE James Mosley, despite not starting, did his best to disrupt Young by sacking him 3 times. Young's favorite target was WR J.R. Ambrose, who caught 8/102y—all in 1st H—and jump-started winning drive with 29y KO RET. Red Raiders rode balanced O, rushing for 175y, including 99y by IB Ervin Fariss, and 181y passing by QB Billy Joe Tolliver.

Hall of Fame Bowl (Dec. 23): Boston College 27 Georgia 24

It took Hall of Fame Bowl rally by Boston College (9-3) QB Shawn Halloran (31-52/316y, 2 INTs) to finally get out from under considerable shadow of former Eagles QB Doug Flutie. Halloran did so with winning 76y drive, hitting 5y TD pass to WR Kelvin Martin with 32 secs left. Martin (9/98y) was involved in controversial play moments before as 4th down pass to him sailed overhead, but LB John Brantley was flagged for D holding. Boston College had 20-7 H lead, scoring 14 pts within 2 mins of 2nd Q as 4y TD pass to TE Pete Casparriello (7/75y) and 1y TD run by TB Troy Stradford were sandwiched around KO TD FUM RET by Georgia FB Hiawatha Berry. Bulldogs (8-4) rallied with 17 straight 2nd H pts, keyed by D that sacked Halloran 4 times in 2nd H and picked him off twice including 81y TD RET by CB Gary Moss. Perhaps Halloran was groggy on Moss' pick-off, having just returned to game after brutal hit by DE Calvin Ruff. Georgia QB James Jackson (13-21/178y) scored go-ahead 4y TD run at 24-20 early in 4th Q. Boston College NG Dave Nugent had 12 tackles and 2.5 sacks and LB Bill Romanowski had 19 tackles to pace D, while Stradford contributed 122y rushing. Eagles' 8th straight win was most since 1940.

Sun Bowl (Dec. 25): Alabama 28 Washington 6

With surprising ease Alabama (10-3) crushed Huskies, unleashing speed advantage on bigger Pac 10 foes. Bama LB Cornelius Bennett ruled in his final game with 11 tackles, while TB Bobby Humphrey rushed for 158y and opened scoring in 2nd Q with 64y jaunt. Washington (8-3-1) answered with 2 FGs by K Jeff Jaeger to trail 7-6 at H. Alabama QB Mike Shula (15-26/188y) took over, connecting on TDs of 32y to WR Greg Richardson and 17y to Humphrey. Scoring pass to Humphrey capped 83y drive that included Shula passes of 27y to TE Angelo Stafford, 25y to Richardson, and TD. Shula led 92y drive—team's longest of year—to Humphrey's 3y TD run and 28-6 margin. Huskies QB Chris Chandler threw for 199y, but was intercepted twice, while rush attack was held to 68y. Alabama K Van Tiffin completed his career, making every x-pt try, 146 successful kicks. Rumors about Alabama coach Ray Perkins' departure to NFL, which dominated pre-game hype, were proven true when he took head coaching job with Tampa Bay Buccaneers soon after Sun Bowl date.

Gator Bowl (Dec. 27): Clemson 27 Stanford 21

Tigers (8-2-2) dominated 1st H as QB Rodney Williams (12-19/135y, INT) led option attack that scored 27 pts, while D posted shutout. Clemson gained 291y and scored on opening 5 possessions in dizzying display in game's 1st 30 mins, while Stanford struggled to gain 57y. Special teams contributed as well as LB Reggie Harris stripped ball away on KO RET to set up WR Ray Williams' 14y run on reverse for 24-pt lead. Cardinal (8-4) rallied in 2nd H behind FB Brad Muster, who rushed for 1 score and caught 2 TD passes from backup QB Greg Ennis (20-40/168y, INT), in for QB John

Paye who did not make trip due to injured right shoulder. Muster finished with 70y rushing and 53y on 4 receptions.

Aloha Bowl (Dec. 27): Arizona 30 North Carolina 21

Arizona (9-3) used complete team effort to build 30-0 lead and then held on for 1st post-season win in school's history after 4 losses and tie. Wildcats TB David Adams rushed for 81y and TD and caught 3/77y, while QB Alfred Jenkins passed for 187y and 13y TD to WR Jon Horton. Blocked punt by LB Boomer Gibson set up Adams' TD, while Wildcats D forced 5 FUMs including Heels QB Jonathan Hall's bobble that set up Jenkins' TD pass after huge hit by S Chuck Cecil. Finally, another FUM led to 5y TD run by TB Art Greathouse for 30-0 lead. North Carolina (7-4-1) scored 3 straight TDs, with TB Torin Dorn (7/101y) scampering to EZ from 58y out and QB Mark Maye (17-34/171y) throwing and rushing for scores. Tar Heels ran out of time and missed TB Derrick Fenner, academic casualty who led ACC in rushing with 1250y. Said winning coach Larry Smith, "At the half, we had controlled the game. Then the guys must have started thinking about (girls in) bikinis."

Liberty Bowl (Dec. 29): Tennessee 21 Minnesota 14

Minnesota (6-6) had no answer for Volunteers QB Jeff Francis, who completed 22-31/243y, 3 TDs. Tennessee (7-5) vaulted to 14-0 lead in 2nd Q as Francis hooked up with WR Joey Clinkscales (7/72y) and TB William Howard on TD passes of 18y and 23y. Behind TB Darrell Thompson (25/136y), Gophers bounced back to tie game at 14-14 in 4th Q as K Chip Lohmiller bracketed 11y scoring run by QB Rickey Foggie with FGs of 27y and 25y. Francis answered Minnesota's surge with his 2nd TD pass to Clinkscales, 15y effort early in 4th Q for winning score. On 66y drive, Francis hit TE Nate Middlebrooks with 20y pass and WR Anthony Miller on 24y completion before throwing over Minnesota CB Matt Martinez for TD.

Freedom Bowl (Dec. 30): UCLA 31 Brigham Young 10

Rushing for 266y, most ever in any bowl game, TB Gaston Green led Bruins (8-3-1) to theirs and coach Terry Donohue's 5th bowl win in row. UCLA finished with 423y on ground, including 49y run by WR Karl Dorrell to set up 1st TD and 70y romp by FB Marcus Greenwood that led to 2nd TD. UCLA had 9 sacks, while LB Ken Norton was leading tackler with 17. Cougars (8-5) took short-lived 3-0 lead on 32y FG by K Leonard Chitty, set up by FUM REC. BYU failed to score again until FB Bruce Hansen's 3y TD run in 4th Q. Despite 150y rushing by Green in 1st H, UCLA led only 7-3, but rolled up 17 pts in 3rd Q to break game open. Green was part of all 4 TDs, running for scores of 3, 1, and 79y and passing 13y to Dorrell in EZ. Green broke mark set by Rice's Dickie Moegle (265y rushing against Alabama) in infamous 1954 Cotton Bowl game: Moegle was awarded TD when Crimson Tide capt Tommy Lewis came off sideline to make tackle.

Holiday Bowl (Dec. 30): Iowa 39 San Diego State 38

Iowa (9-3) won thriller on last-sec 41y FG by K Rob Houghtlin, set up by TB Kevin Harmon's 48y KO RET. Aztecs (8-4) had just taken 2-pt lead on K Kevin Rahill's 21y FG. Hawkeyes rallied from 28-13 3rd Q deficit as QB Mark Vlasic (15-28/222y, INT) threw TD passes of 29y to backup TE Marv Cook and 4y to starting TE Mike Flagg in taking 36-35 lead. San Diego State was back on O with 4:20 left, moving into FG range as WR Alfred Jackson (44y TD catch) fought through double coverage to haul in 45y pass from QB Todd Santos (21-33/298y, 2 INTs). Iowa had little time left, but Harmon only needed 8 secs to reach San Diego State 37YL. Hawkeye gained 13y on 2 runs to 24YL with 4 secs left, close enough for Houghtlin's winning 3-ptr. Iowa TB Rick Bayless was leading ground gainer with 110y.

Peach Bowl (Dec. 31): Virginia Tech 25 North Carolina State 24

Teams scratched and clawed for 60 mins, with game decided by Hokies K Chris Kinzer's 40y FG as time expired, 6th time this season Kinzer provided late tying or winning pts. Virginia Tech (9-2-1) began final drive on own 20YL with 1:53 remaining. With 38 secs left, Tech was on NC State 36YL, facing 3rd-and-1 with no timeouts remaining. Pitch to TB Maurice Williams lost 1y, with Williams injured. Or was he? Refs stopped clock with 27 secs left. On 4th down, QB Erik Chapman (20-30/200y, TD, 2 INTs) hit 9y pass to TE Steve Johnson. Tech holding PEN pushed it out of FG range, but Chapman's pass drew interference PEN on Wolfpack S Brian Gay to set up Kinzer's heroics. NC State (8-3-1) QB Erik Kramer (12-19/155y) threw TD passes of 25y to WR Naz Worthen and 5y to TE Ralph Britt, while FB Mel Crite rushed for 101y. Hokies had 2 RBs top 100y in Williams (16/129y) and TB Eddie Hunter (22/113y). Win served as redemption for coach Bill Dooley, ending his 9th and final season with school's 1st-ever bowl victory after 5 losses.

Bluebonnet Bowl (Dec. 31): Baylor 21 Colorado 9

With both Ds begrudgingly surrendering y, Baylor (9-3) stretched its lead from 7-3 to 21-3 by converting 2 Colorado FUMs deep in Buffs territory into TDs. It became too much to overcome as Colorado (6-6) was stopped twice on 4th down deep in Baylor territory in 4th Q drawing to 21-9 on QB Mark Hatcher's 31y TD run. LB Ray Berry (12 tackles) led Bears D that was so dominant that at midway through 3rd Q Colorado had gained only 77y total O. Baylor's O went 64y for its 1st score—drive was aided by Buffs' PEN with Baylor set to punt—but then needed only 8y and 21y for decisive TDs. Bears TB Derrick McAdoo tallied 2 TDs, while QB Cody Carlson (11-22/136y, INT) threw 2y TD pass to WR Darnell Chase for other score.

All-American Bowl (Dec. 31): Florida State 27 Indiana 13

Playing what they hoped would not be final game for coach Bobby Bowden—he was rumored front-runner for Alabama's open job—Florida State (7-4-1) rode 205y rushing from frosh TB Sammie Smith to victory. Smith scored FSU's 1st pair of TDs as Seminoles led 13-3 at H. Florida State upped its lead to 20-3 in 3rd Q before Hoosiers (6-6) began clicking on O. Indiana bogged down in Noles territory, however, and K Pete Stoyanovich made matters worse by missing 3 FGs. IU finally pulled within 20-13 on 2y TD run by FB Andre Powell and Stoyanovich's 30y FG, but could get no closer before Holloman iced game with another TD run from 10y out. It was day for 1st-year backs as frosh TB Anthony Thompson rushed for 127y to lead Hoosiers. Birmingham native Bowden coached his 1st game at Legion Field, but stayed in Tallahassee as Alabama's head job went to Georgia Tech's Bill Curry.

Florida Citrus Bowl: Auburn 16 Southern California 7

Coach Ted Tollner's era at Southern California (7-5) ended fittingly with frustrating loss as Trojans managed 44y rushing and no pts on O. LB Marcus Cotton returned INT 24y for USC's only score. Tigers TB Brent Fullwood rushed 28/152y and 4y TD run, while LB Aundray Bruce menaced Trojans with 4 sacks and 2 forced FUMs. Thanks in large part to Bruce's unbridled pressure, Troy QB Rodney Peete hit only 12-31 passes and threw 4 INTs, 2 by Auburn S Chip Powell. Bruce rested once, but he returned when Trojans reached Auburn 29YL to immediately produce tackle, sack, and pressure on Peete that forced INT. Auburn DT Tracy Rocker also produced EZ sack for safety. Tigers D even kept USC off scoreboard following blocked punt by CB Louis Brock that gave Trojans ball at Auburn 7YL. USC gained 7y in 3 plays before FB LeRoy Holt was halted on 4th-and-goal.

Cotton Bowl: Ohio State 28 Texas A&M 12

After leading only 7-6 at H, Ohio State (10-3) began to flex muscles in 3rd Q behind its punishing D. Leader of that unit, LB Chris Spielman (11 tackles) started things off on 2nd H's 3rd play from scrimmage by picking off pass by Texas A&M (9-3) QB Kevin Murray and rambling 24y for TD. Buckeyes would pick off 4 more passes by Murray, who threw only 8 INTs during regular season, including S Sonny Gordon's pick on A&M's next series. That INT set up Ohio's 8-play, 59y drive capped by 8y TD run by TB Vince Workman for 21-6 lead. Aggies FB Roger Vick (24/113y) cut deficit to 21-12 with his 2y TD. Ohio State D put exclamation point on win with LB Mike Kee's late 49y INT TD RET. QB Jim Karsatos threw for 195y—including 6/105y to WR Nate Harris—and scored team's 1st TD on 3y run. In daring fashion statement, Ohio State switched to red shoes for Big 10's 1st-ever appearance in Cotton Bowl. Normally-sedate Bucks coach Earle Bruce was fashionably daring too; opting for unusual undertaker's black suit and fedora.

Rose Bowl: Arizona State 22 Michigan 15

Sun Devils (10-1-1) sparkled in their 1st Rose Bowl appearance in front of partisan crowd, scoring TDs on consecutive drives, 1st to close 1st H and other to begin 2nd H. Both TDs came on passes from QB Jeff Van Raaphorst (16-36/193y) to WR Bruce Hill, who snatched ball away from Wolverines S Doug Mallory in EZ for 1st score. Arizona State K Ken Bostrom added 3 FGs, TB Darryl Harris rushed for 112y, and WR Aaron Cox caught 6/104y. Devils committed 0 TOs, continuing season-long focus on error-free play. Michigan (11-2) had enjoyed 15-3 lead by traveling 66y with 1st possession to 18y TD run by TB Jaimie Morris (16/47y), followed by 2-pt conv pass from K Mike Gillette to FB Gerald White. Michigan QB Jim Harbaugh added 2y TD keeper in 2nd Q. From then on, quick ASU D dominated, holding UM to less than 10 mins possession in 2nd H, during which they held Morris to 4y rushing and team to –4y on ground. Harbaugh threw for 172y, but was picked off 3 times. Pac 10 won 6th straight Rose Bowl, leaving Wolverines coach Bo Schembechler at 3-11 in bowls.

Sugar Bowl: Nebraska 30 Louisiana State 15

Meeting Nebraska in bowl game for 3rd time in 5 years, LSU (9-3) needed only 54 secs to score on TB Harvey Williams' 1y TD run. Cornhuskers (10-2) answered with 30 straight pts, churning out 352y and allowing only 191y total. Nebraska QB Steve Taylor threw for 110y and rushed for 63y more, while IB Tyreese Knox chipped in with 84y and 2 TDs. Taylor's 2y run, capping 72y drive, put Huskers up for good at 10-7 in 2nd Q. Nebraska took 2nd H KO 78y in 9 plays to Knox's 1y TD run and commanding 17-7 lead. Huskers D had 3 sacks of QB Tommy Hodson and 6 other tackles for losses in winning scrimmage line battle. Williams was held to 48y rushing as team finished with 32y net on ground. In dirty game, teams combined for 17 PENs/208y with 3 personal fouls called against each team. Huskers were happy to leave New Orleans, feeling LSU fans and police had harassed them all week.

Orange Bowl: Oklahoma 42 Arkansas 8

Revenge for 1978 Orange Bowl was sweet as 2 explosive 2nd Q TD runs by Oklahoma (11-1) HB Spencer Tillman provided enough pts in rout of Razorbacks. Held without 1st down in 1st Q, Sooners needed none on 1st scoring drive as Tillman (7/109y) took pitchout and went 77y for score. Razorbacks (9-3) then marched to OU 25YL before INT ended matters. Another INT set up Tillman's 21y TD run for 14-0 H lead before Oklahoma QB Jamelle Holieway scored twice in 3rd Q. Sooners D contributed its part by holding Razorbacks to 48y rushing and 4 times picking off QB Greg Thomas (13-26/129y), who only once threw regular-season INT. Arkansas FB Derrick Thomas' 2y scoring run in 4th Q prevented shutout. Oklahoma LB Dante Jones played brilliantly in place of suspended A-A LB Brian Bosworth.

GAME OF THE YEAR
Fiesta Bowl (Jan. 2): Penn State 14 Miami 10

Fiesta Bowl boldly pitted undefeated teams in 1st bowl match-up of kind since Sugar Bowl arranged Notre Dame and Alabama in 1973. Prior to this game, there was some fan indifference to Penn State (12-0), but with Miami's boorish behavior, suddenly everyone was in Lions' corner, and hatred was building for Hurricanes (11-1). Mouthy Canes stormed out of promotional dinner wearing army fatigues. Miami DT Jerome Brown was quoted, "Did the Japanese sit down and eat with (the U.S. at) Pearl Harbor before they bombed them? No. We're out of here!" Once game was on, Miami gained 445y, but Penn State D coordinator Jerry Sandusky's schemes confused QB Vinny Testaverde (26-50/285y) with mixed zone coverages that featured LBs

dropping off and DBs walloping Canes' NFL-caliber WRs at every opportunity. Feeling heat, Testaverde threw 5 INTs—3 to unheralded LB Pete Giftopoulos—and his WRs dropped 7 passes. Game was tied at 7-7 at H after FUM led to Miami's 23y drive to HB Melvin Bratton's 1y TD run. Penn State answered with 74y drive to QB John Shaffer's 4y keeper. Hurricanes took 10-7 lead on 38y FG by K Mark Seelig in 4th Q. Game then turned in big way with key play supplied by leader of Penn State D, A-A LB Shane Conlan, who picked off his 2nd pass early in 4th Q, returning it 38y to Miami's 5YL. Penn State O, which had been slowed all night, punched ball into EZ as TB D.J. Dozier (20/99y) scored on 6y run. Miami and Testaverde were not through, however, keeping nail-biting final drive alive with 4th down completion of 31y to WR Brian Blades that catapulted it downfield. Quintet of completions, 3 to WR Michael Irvin, put Miami at Penn State 5YL. Decision time came for Miami O: Ride big FB Alonzo Highsmith (18/119y) or throw? Testaverde convinced coach Jimmy Johnson to keep ball in air, which led to huge sack by Lions DT Tim Johnson for 12y loss on 2nd down just as Irvin broke open in EZ. Canes faced 3rd down at 13YL, and incompletion later left national title on line with 4th down play with 18 secs left. Testaverde attempted to drill pass to WR Brett Perriman, but Giftopoulos cemented upset with 3rd INT, this time at 1YL. "This is a very big disappointment," said Testaverde. "I'm not very happy with the way I played."

Final AP Poll January 3

1 Penn State (54)	1137	11 Arizona	494
2 Miami	1064	12 Baylor	491
3 Oklahoma (3)	1045	13 Texas A&M	458
4 Arizona State	938	14 UCLA	439
5 Nebraska	937	15 Arkansas	342
6 Auburn	791	16 Iowa	247
7 Ohio State	762	17 Clemson	209
8 Michigan	758	18 Washington	206.5
9 Alabama	680	19 Boston College	140
10 Louisiana State	526	20 Virginia Tech	107.5

1986 Top Performance Formula

1 Oklahoma	1.7913
2 Penn State	1.7652
3 Miami	1.7190
4 Arizona State	1.5985
5 Nebraska	1.5585
6 Alabama	1.5306
7 Michigan	1.5304
8 Louisiana State	1.5052
9 Auburn	1.4703
10 UCLA	1.4635
11 Washington	1.4447
12 Ohio State	1.4413
13 Arkansas	1.4043
14 Arizona	1.3892
15 Texas A&M	1.3843
16 Iowa	1.3675
17 Clemson	1.3460
18 Boston College	1.3452
19 Florida State	1.3448
20 Stanford	1.3266

1986 Top Opponent Records

1 Florida	.6636
2 Louisiana State	.6602
3 UCLA	.6269
4 Notre Dame	.6197
5 California	.6186
6 Alabama	.6168
7 Oregon	.6059
8 Washington State	.5983
9 Penn State	.5927
10 Washington	.5923
11 Oklahoma	.5913
12 Oregon State	.5890
13t Colorado	.587302
13t Florida State	.587302
15 Stanford	.5866
16 South Carolina	.5863
17 Miami	.5806
18 Southern California	.5794
19 Mississippi State	.5792
20 West Virginia	.5789

1986 Out-of-Conference Records

	W-L	Percentage	Bowl W-L
Southeastern	35-15-2	.6923	4-2
Pacific-10	24-11	.6857	3-3
Big Ten	21-16	.5676	2-3
Atlantic Coast	14-14-4	.5000	1-2
Big Eight	15-16	.4839	2-1
Southwest	12-14	.4615	1-3
Western Athletic	15-20	.4286	0-2

1986 Individual Statistical Leaders

RUSHING YARDS	Attempts	Yards	Avg.
Paul Palmer, Temple	346	1866	5.4
Kelvin Farmer, Toledo	299	1532	5.1
Bobby Humphrey, Alabama	236	1471	6.2
Steve Bartalo, Colorado State	366	1419	3.9
Rick Calhoun, Cal. State-Fullerton	259	1398	5.4
Brent Fullwood, Auburn	167	1391	8.3
Reggie Taylor, Cincinnati	256	1325	5.2
Derrick Fenner, North Carolina	200	1250	6.3
Darrell Thompson, Minnesota	217	1240	5.7
Troy Stradford, Boson College	218	1188	5.4

PASSING YARDS	Completions	Attempts	Yards	Pct.
Sammy Garza, Texas-El Paso	258	410	3140	62.9
Todd Ellis, South Carolina	205	340	3020	60.3
Danny McCoin, Cincinnati	237	369	2831	64.2
Larry Egger, Utah	233	382	2761	61.0
Dave Yarema, Michigan State	200	297	2581	67.3
Jim Harbaugh, Michigan	167	254	2557	65.8
Vinny Testaverde, Miami	175	276	2557	63.4
Todd Santos, San Diego State	218	350	2553	62.3
Kevin Murray, Texas A&M	212	349	2463	60.7
Terry Morris, Miami (Ohio)	193	308	2365	62.7

RECEIVING YARDS	Catches	Yards
Wendell Davis, Louisiana State	80	1244
Sterling Sharpe, South Carolina	74	1106
Cris Carter, Ohio State	65	1066
Marc Zeno, Tulane	68	1033
Guy Liggins, San Jose State	72	983
Andre Rison, Michigan State	54	966
Terance Mathis, New Mexico	53	955
James Brim, Wake Forest	66	930
Michael Irvin, Miami	53	868
Dave Montagne, Oregon State	78	862

1986 Consensus All-America Team
Offense

Wide Receiver:	Cris Carter, Ohio State
Tight End:	Keith Jackson, Oklahoma
Line:	Jeff Bregel, Southern California
	Randy Dixon, Pittsburgh
	Danny Villa, Arizona State
	John Clay, Missouri
Center:	Ben Tamburello, Auburn
Quarterback:	Vinny Testaverde, Miami
Running Back:	Brent Fullwood, Auburn
	Paul Palmer, Temple
	Terrence Flagler, Clemson
	Brad Muster, Stanford
	D.J. Dozier, Penn State
Placekicker:	Jeff Jaeger, Washington

Defense

Line:	Jerome Brown, Miami
	Danny Noonan, Nebraska
	Tony Woods, Pittsburgh
	Jason Buck, Brigham Young
	Reggie Rogers, Washington
Linebacker:	Cornelius Bennett, Alabama
	Shane Conlan, Penn State
	Brian Bosworth, Oklahoma
	Chris Spielman, Ohio State
Back:	Thomas Everett, Baylor
	Tim McDonald, Southern California
	Bennie Blades, Miami
	Rod Woodson, Purdue
	Garland Rivers, Michigan
Punter:	Barry Helton, Colorado

1986 Heisman Trophy Vote

Vinny Testaverde, senior quarterback, Miami	2213
Paul Palmer, senior running back, Temple	672
Jim Harbaugh, senior quarterback, Michigan	458
Brian Bosworth, junior linebacker, Oklahoma	395
Gordie Lockbaum, junior RB-WR-DB, Holy Cross	242

Other Major Awards

Maxwell (Player)	Vinny Testaverde, senior quarterback, Miami
Walter Camp (Player)	Vinny Testaverde, senior quarterback, Miami
Outland (Lineman)	Jason Buck, senior defensive tackle, Brigham Young
Lombardi (Lineman)	Cornelius Bennett, senior linebacker, Alabama
Davey O'Brien (QB)	Vinny Testaverde, senior quarterback, Miami
Jim Thorpe (DB)	Thomas Everett, senior safety, Baylor
Dick Butkus (Linebacker)	Brian Bosworth, junior linebacker, Oklahoma
AFCA Coach of the Year	Joe Paterno, Penn State

1987

The Year of Raising Canes, "Tie Dye," and SMU Doomed to Death

Having lost three straight bowl games, including the Fiesta Bowl that followed the 1986 season and cost it the national championship, Miami (12-0) took no prisoners in winning its second title in five years in 1987. Coach Jimmy Johnson put his stamp on a team whose players had toughness, speed, and a strong measure of cockiness. He got the match-up he wanted in the bowl season when he greeted his friend from his playing days at Arkansas, coach Barry Switzer of Oklahoma (11-1). Johnson got the right setting, too, on his team's home field in the Orange Bowl. For a second straight year, the nation's top two teams were pitted in a bowl game, with Oklahoma the higher seed after being ranked no. 1 for most of the year. The Sooners pulled a rare feat by leading the nation in both scoring average (43.5) and scoring defense (7.5), all ingredients that copped a fourth straight Big Eight title. But, for the third straight year, the Sooners could not beat Miami's mighty Canes, losing 20-14. So, despite being ranked at the top of the polls for virtually the entire season, Oklahoma's season was doomed to end in Orange Bowl frustration.

The Hurricanes may have finished undefeated, but did nothing to improve their image. Not that they cared. Maryland (4-7) and South Carolina (8-4) vowed never again to schedule the Canes due to Miami's raising cane in most unsportsmanlike fashion. Miami's biggest victory came when it outlasted Florida State (11-1) 26-25, with safety Bubba McDowell eerily foreshadowing the biggest outcome of 1988 by breaking up a two-point pass at game's end. Miami had rallied from a 19-3 deficit behind gutsy quarterback Steve Walsh. The loss was the sixth in eight series games so far in the 1980s for the hard-luck Seminoles, who finished second in the state of Florida and second in the nation. The final poll positions of Miami and Florida State marked the first time that the top pair in the poll was filled by teams from the same state.

Florida State almost suffered a bigger loss in the off-season prior to the 1987 season: coach Bobby Bowden considered returning to his home state to take the Alabama (7-5) job. With unfinished business remaining in Tallahassee, namely a national title, Bowden stayed put, and the Crimson Tide job went to Bill Curry, who was treated as a second choice for all three years he held the position in Tuscaloosa.

Besides Curry, the newcomers attracting attention in the Southeastern Conference were a group of freshman backs who sparkled: Emmitt Smith of Florida (6-6), Rodney Hampton of Georgia (9-3), and Reggie Cobb of Tennessee (10-2-1). The SEC winner proved to be Auburn (9-1-2), behind a dominating defense and a "Comeback Kid," quarterback Jeff Burger, who shook off accusations of classroom plagiarism, an arrest for drunkenness, and eligibility issues that cropped up after a hosted hunting trip. Still, Burger led Auburn to the Southeastern Conference crown.

The Tigers, however, ended their season on a discouraging note for both themselves and their Sugar Bowl opponent, undefeated Syracuse (11-0-1). The Superdome match-up ended in a controversial 16-16 deadlock. Auburn coach Pat Dye's decision to kick a tying field goal at game's end not only earned him the nickname "Tie Dye", but prevented a perfect season for the surprising Orangemen, a team without so much as an eight-win season since 1967. Dye defended himself vigorously, but it seemed like the no. 6 Tigers had little to lose by going for a win. Dye never was able to shake the public's distaste for his tying decision.

Led by quarterback Don McPherson, Syracuse rode roughshod over the East, including a memorable 48-21 rout of a young Penn State (8-3) squad. Although coach Joe Paterno earned his 200th win, 45-19 over Bowling Green (5-6), the Nittany Lions had to defend their 1986 national title without 17 starters from the previous Fiesta Bowl.

One Eastern team inadvertently made it a specialty to get beaten. Columbia (0-10) saw its losing streak grow to 42 games, breaking Northwestern's mark of 34 by losing 38-8 to a Princeton (6-4) team featuring the three Garrett brothers, quarterback Jason, running back Judd, and wide receiver John. The vengeful trio had transferred from Columbia when their father Jim was forced to resign as coach in 1985. Princeton also featured a defensive back and future *Superman* actor, Dean Cain, who dated glamorous Princeton grad Brooke Shields. Columbia's Lions had last won on October 15, 1983, beating Yale 21-18.

But, no team ever had it worse than SMU, whose program was shut down in February for repeated violations of NCAA rules. The Mustangs became the first and only school ever to receive the NCAA's relatively new weapon known as "The Death Penalty." SMU was prevented from playing football in 1987 and voluntarily shut itself down for the 1988 season as well. Some alumni and students probably had their tongues in cheeks when they said they rather enjoyed Homecoming festivities that centered on a soccer game.

Those who hoped the Mustangs would rebound from two years of football abstinence were dead wrong. SMU never recovered from its "death penalty," and the shadow of guilt considerably affected the eventual break-up of the storied Southwest Conference. In fact, SMU's hopeless attempts at winning football since returning in 1989 probably have spared other schools from being sentenced to death by the NCAA. The governing body never realized the penalty really meant as close to death as a football program could get. Angry critics could say whatever they wished about SMU's transgressions—Mustang administrators and boosters were guilty as charged—but it was a sad two years for the private Dallas-based school that had given football the greatness of Doak Walker, Kyle Rote, Raymond Berry, Forrest Gregg, Don Meredith, Jerry LeVias, Louie Kelcher, Eric Dickerson, Craig James, and Russell Carter.

Ohio State (6-4-1) had a rough year as well. Former coach Woody Hayes died in March, which seemed to darken the entire season in Columbus. Wide receiver Cris Carter was ruled ineligible for his senior season for accepting money from an agent. The Buckeyes struggled on the field, losing conference games to Indiana (8-4), eventual champion Michigan State (9-2-1), Wisconsin (3-8), and Iowa (10-3). Coach Earle Bruce, who replaced Hayes after the 1978 season, lost his job during the week leading up to the Michigan rivalry game. The firing of the coach with the best winning percentage in the Big 10 during his nine-year tenure was handled so poorly that athletic director Rick Bay resigned in protest. Bruce's final game was an emotional win over Michigan (8-4), after which his players carried him off the field. Bruce brought suit against the school, which was settled before year's end. Bruce left Columbus with a record of 81-26-1 at Ohio State with five wins over Michigan.

Milestones

■ Citing repeated rule violations, NCAA shut down Southern Methodist football for 1987 season. Due to "death penalty" sanctions levied against program, SMU administrators decided 2 years were needed to comply and canceled 1988 season as well.

■ Johnny Unitas Golden Arm Award was first presented by Kentucky Chapter of National Football Foundation and College Football Hall of Fame.

■ Matt Hazeltine, All-America center-linebacker at California (1954) before embarking on 15-year NFL career, died at age 53 on January 13 from complications stemming from ALS, or Lou Gehrig's Disease. Legendary coach Woody Hayes died on March 12 of heart attack. Of his 238 lifetime coaching victories, Hayes won 205 games during his 28-season tenure at Ohio State (1951-78), where his Buckeyes shared national titles in 1954 and 1957 and won outright in 1968. Although best known for fiery temper that brought abrupt end to his career, Hayes was exceptional teacher, recruiter, tactician, and leader. Two-time consensus All-America middle guard Wayne Meylan died at age 41 on June 26. Meylan, who set records for single-season and career tackles at Nebraska (1967), died in crash of WW II plane at air show at Ludington, Michigan. Duffy Daugherty, who went 109-69-5 as head coach at Michigan State (1954-72), died of kidney failure September 25 after long bout with heart disease. Daugherty, skilled raconteur as well as coach, built Spartans into mid-1960s power, going 19-1-1 in 1965-66 with UPI national title in 1965. Peter "The Great" Pund, all-time great Georgia Tech center, died on October 17 at age 80. He led Georgia Tech to 9-0 record in 1928 and berth in Rose Bowl, where they beat California 8-7 in his final game. Virginia defensive end Craig Fielder died of cancer at 21 on October 16.

■ After 28 years, final Bluebonnet Bowl was played on December 21.

■ Longest winning streaks entering season:
Penn State 12   Oklahoma, San Jose State 9

	Incoming	Outgoing
Alabama	Bill Curry	Ray Perkins
Arizona	Dick Tomey	Larry Smith
California	Bruce Snyder	Joe Kapp
Duke	Steve Spurrier	Steve Sloan
Georgia Tech	Bobby Ross	Bill Curry
Hawaii	Bob Wagner	Dick Tomey
Houston	Jack Pardee	Bill Yeoman
Iowa State	Jim Walden	Jim Criner
Louisiana State	Mike Archer	Bill Arnsparger
Maryland	Joe Krivak	Bobby Ross
Navy	Elliot Uzelac	Gary Tranquill
New Mexico	Mike Sheppard	Joe Lee Dunn
Purdue	Fred Akers	Leon Burtnett
Southern Cal	Larry Smith	Ted Tollner
Texas	David McWilliams	Fred Akers
Texas Tech	Spike Dykes	David McWilliams
Tulsa	George Henshaw	Don Morton
Virginia Tech	Frank Beamer	Bill Dooley
Wake Forest	Bill Dooley	Al Groh
Washington State	Dennis Erickson	Jim Walden
Western Michigan	Al Molde	Jack Harbaugh
Wisconsin	Don Morton	Jim Hilles
Wyoming	Paul Roach	Dennis Erickson

Preseason AP Poll

1 Oklahoma (55)	1193	11 Penn State (1)	603
2 Nebraska (3)	1005	12 Arkansas	598
3 UCLA (1)	935	13 Washington	521
4 Ohio State	906	14 Arizona State	440
5 Auburn	835	15 Texas A&M	424
6 Louisiana State	789	16 Iowa	318
7 Michigan	754	17 Tennessee	231
8 Florida State	723	18 Notre Dame	207
9 Clemson	682	19 Southern California	141
10 Miami	676	20t Florida	127
		20t Georgia	127

August 30, 1987

Tennessee 23 Iowa 22 (East Rutherford, NJ): Volunteers (1-0) K Phil Reich booted 20y FG at game's end as 5th Kickoff Classic was 1st to end on game-winning kick. FG was former walk-on Reich's 3rd of game. Tennessee moved ball on ground for winning FG behind frosh TB Reggie Cobb, who debuted with 142y rushing, 123y coming in 2nd H. Vols took 14-10 lead at H as LB Darrin Miller raced 96y with FUM RET. Iowa (0-1) rallied with 9 pts in 3rd Q, although failure to convert 2-pt try following HB Kevin Harmon's 23y TD run proved costly. Despite using 3 different QBs, Iowa passed for 280y and outscored Tennessee O with WR Quinn Early serving as Hawks' leading target with 9/131y.

September 5, 1987

SYRACUSE 25 Maryland 11: Season began auspiciously for Orangemen (1-0) as HB Robert Drummond completed 55y option pass to WR Tommy Kane (4/125y) to set up 1st of 4 FGs for K Tim Vesling. Scoring on its 1st 4 possessions, including 1y TD runs by Drummond and QB Don McPherson, Syracuse held 22-0 H lead. Unable to run (48y) against Orange NG Ted Gregory (10 tackles, 1.5 sacks) and his mates, Maryland (0-1) finally penetrated EZ with 28 secs left on 42y pass from QB Dan Henning (19-36/241y, TD) to WR Vernon Joines.

MIAMI 31 Florida 4: Inspired by no. 10 pre-season ranking they felt disrespected them, Hurricanes (1-0) won big. In its 1st TV appearance in 3 years due to NCAA sanctions, Florida (0-1) could not protect QB Kerwin Bell, who had to duck often. Bell was sacked 5 times, pressured into 3 INTs and bobbled 3 snaps in face of Miami's quick D. Canes DE Daniel Stubbs stormed to 3 sacks. QB Steve Walsh was plugged right into Miami's aerial system and enjoyed his 1st start with 234y passing. Walsh pitched go-ahead 23y TD to WR Brian Blades in 1st Q. Oddly, Gators were spared shutout by 2 safeties on bad punt snaps by Miami DE-C Willis Peguese.

FLORIDA STATE 40 Texas Tech 16: Seminoles (1-0) looked like they were in for barn-burner as Texas Tech (0-1) matched them with 13 pts in 1st Q. After that, it was all FSU as QB Danny McManus (19-34/275y, 2 TDs) led 3 drives in 2nd Q. McManus scored on 6y run and pitched 37y TD to WR Herb Gainer (6/128y) for 30-16 H lead. Red Raiders IB James Gray rushed for 90y and 2 TDs to pace Tech O.

Louisiana State 17 TEXAS A&M 3: Youth was served in College Station as LSU coach Mike Archer, youngest in nation at 34, won debut behind swarming D that held Aggies to 3 1st downs and 67y in entire 1st H. Score favored Tigers (1-0) by 17-0 when Texas A&M (0-1) finally crossed midfield initially, on its 2nd possession of 3rd Q. FB Victor Jones rushed in both LSU TDs, while QB Tommy Hodson threw for 149y. Aggies scored on K Scott Slater's 41y FG, but even that tally was difficult: Texas A&M reached LSU 8YL before backpedaling to 24YL.

WASHINGTON 31 Stanford 21: QB Chris Chandler threw for career-high 314y as Huskies (1-0) won conf opener at newly expanded Husky Stadium. Stanford (0-1) was hindered by sprained ankle suffered by TB Brad Muster, 1986's Pac-10 Player of Year, who was finished after rushing stats of 3/-2y. Cardinal trailed only by single TD after CB Alan Grant's 69y punt TD RET in 3rd Q but came no closer as Washington FB Tony Covington added insurance TD on 1y run in 4th Q, and K Brandy Brownlee, transfer from SMU, booted his 3rd FG. Dependable Stanford WR Ed McCaffrey caught 4/108y.

(Mon) MICHIGAN STATE 27 Southern California 13: Just like his 4 predecessors, Larry Smith lost coaching debut at Southern California (0-1) as Spartans took advantage of Trojan miscues to stretch 10-6 H lead into 27-6 advantage. Michigan State (1-0) QB Bobby McAllister rushed for 63y, scored TD, and threw for 103y. Spartans TB Lorenzo White rushed for 111y and 2 TDs. USC QB Rodney Peete threw for 229y, but was intercepted twice, fumbled 3 times, and failed to get Troy into EZ. USC backup QB Kevin McLean threw for his team's only score: 26y pass to WR Randy Tanner (8/107y, TD). Trojans had owned impressive 17-game win streak against Big 10 foes, but suffered 1st such loss since January 1974 Rose Bowl, when they were beaten 42-21 by Ohio State.

AP Poll September 8

1 Oklahoma (54)	1154	11 Penn State	572
2 Nebraska (3)	1054	12 Washington	524
3 UCLA (1)	947	13 Arkansas	475
4 Auburn	937	14 Tennessee	417
5 Ohio State	857	15 Arizona State	391
6 Louisiana State	821	16 Notre Dame	198
7 Miami	793	17 Michigan State	161
8 Florida State	744	18 Pittsburgh	159
9 Michigan	723	19 Alabama	155
10 Clemson	674	20 Georgia	112

September 12, 1987

Alabama 24 PENN STATE 13: Hiring of coach Bill Curry may have been unpopular with Alabama (2-0) fans, but suddenly he stood undefeated with big road win over defending national champs. Workhorse Tide TB Bobby Humphrey busted out for 36/220y on ground and scored early on beautiful 73y cutback run. Half-dozen different Nittany Lions (1-1) defenders got hand on Humphrey during his long scamper. Humphrey also threw his 1st-ever pass, which gained 57y to set up Bama's 2nd TD for 17-0 lead. Alabama LB Derrick Thomas was outstanding, sacking QB Matt Knizer 3 times which skunked Penn State's run total at 88y. Lions WR Ray Roundtree (4/114y) had good game in scoring both his team's TDs.

Tennessee 38 MISSISSIPPI STATE 10: Avenging 1986 upset defeat, Tennessee (3-0) coach Johnny Majors gained his 1st win in 4 tries versus Mississippi State (1-1) in his 11th season since his return to Knoxville. Vols' big attack was sparked by QB Jeff Francis, who threw for 227y. Frosh TB Reggie Cobb added 3 TDs for Tennessee, rushing for 81y and catching 3/87y. Vols did not blow open game, however, until they mounted 3-TD surge in 4th Q. Bulldogs TB David Fair (12/133y) provided his team's highlight by breaking away for 80y TD run in 4th Q.

Notre Dame 26 MICHIGAN 7: Fighting Irish (1-0) celebrated opening of their 100th season with surprisingly lopsided margin, handing Bo Schembechler only his 2nd opening-game loss in 19 years at Michigan, and 1st-ever at home. Wolverines (0-1) committed 7 TOs, most in 27 years, in suffering their worst home licking since 1969. Notre Dame converted gifts into 23 pts, including WR Tim Brown's brilliant catch over double coverage of 11y pass by QB Terry Andrysiak (11-15/137y, TD). However innovative Michigan felt about its 2-headed QB strategy, it simply struggled: QBs Demetrius Brown (4-15/54y, 3 INTs) and Michael Taylor (4-8/72y, INT) hardly made Irish D sweat. TB Jamie Morris helped Michigan with 128y, but also had 2 FUMs.

OKLAHOMA 28 North Carolina 0: Top-ranked Sooners (2-0) dominated Tar Heels as QB Jamelle Holieway rushed for 170y and scored all 4 of Oklahoma's TDs. OU put game away with 21-pt 2nd Q explosion, as rushing advantage—Oklahoma outrushed North Carolina 405y to 29y—took toll on Blue D. Carolina (1-1) had 2 great opportunities, but misfired on fake FG in 1st Q and bungled 4th down play after having reached Sooners 4YL. On latter miscue, Tar Heels allowed Sooners DE Darrell Reed to roar in on UNC QB Mark Maye (16-35/168y, INT) for important sack. OU failed in 1 aspect of game; it had sloppy 19 PENs/125y.

NEBRASKA 42 Ucla 33: Lesser light of QB match-up won out as Huskers quick QB Steve Taylor surprised everyone with school-record 5 TD passes. UCLA QB Troy Aikman threw for 211y but could not find EZ, while being sacked 5 times. Bruins (1-1), led by LBs Ken Norton, Jr., and Carnell Lake, keyed on option run in holding Nebraska (2-0) to 117y rushing, but UCLA's strategy eventually opened airways for Taylor. Huskers only gained 30y rushing in 1st Q and dropped 3 FUMs, so at that stage, UCLA led 7-0 on TB Gaston Green's 1st of 3 TD runs. Taylor was taking his licks from Bruins D and injured his left shoulder. Only alternative was to have right-handed Taylor go to unexpected aerial attack, and Bruins could not adjust. Nebraska built 42-17 4th Q lead with Taylor (10-15/217y, 5 TDs) throwing his longest TD (48y) to WR Rod Smith in 3rd Q. Huskers D held UCLA to 94y rushing.

AP Poll September 15

1 Oklahoma (54)	1193	11 Alabama	563
2 Nebraska (6)	1127	12 Arkansas	556
3 Auburn	1027	13 UCLA	550
4 Louisiana State	926	14 Tennessee	525
5 Ohio State	908	15 Arizona State	434
6 Miami	873	16 Pittsburgh	286
7 Florida State	830	17 Michigan State	251
8 Clemson	689	18 Georgia	187
9 Notre Dame	619	19 Michigan	183
10 Washington	608	20 Penn State	140

September 19, 1987

WAKE FOREST 21 North Carolina State 3: Wake Forest coach Bill Dooley enjoyed his return to ACC after 10-year absence, and his Deacons manhandled NC State (0-3). After Wake (2-0) TB Darryl McGill (18/81y, TD) injured his ankle in 3rd Q, sub TB Mark Young took over. Young rushed for 144y and tallied 2nd H TDs of 1y and 28y. Margin

was more than enough for Deacons D, which held stumbling Wolfpack to 92y rushing, 130y passing, and 11 1st downs. NC State coughed up 5 TOs, which hurt performance of young QB Shane Montgomery (10-21/130y, INT).

Clemson 21 GEORGIA 20: Although 90-year-old Georgia-Clemson rivalry pitted opponents from different confs and different states, it was as intense as any competitive series. Bulldogs (2-1) took 20-16 lead with 8:59 left on 8y TD run by frosh TB Rodney Hampton and soon forced Clemson to punt. Tigers P Rusty Seyle hit biggest punt of his life, pinning Georgia on own 1YL. Bulldogs coach Vince Dooley admitted after game that he should have punted out of trouble on 1st down. On 2nd down, CB James Lott nailed QB James Jackson in EZ before being joined by what seemed like 10 Tiger teammates. Score was now 20-18. After free-kick, Tigers (3-0) stayed on ground for 9/53y; last carry of 16y by TB Terry Allen positioned K David Treadwell's winning 21y FG with 2 secs to play. Not since 1905-06 had Clemson won 2 straight in Georgia series.

Florida 23 ALABAMA 14: Florida TB Emmitt Smith made 1st start and rushed for 224y and 2 TDs in announcing to SEC that he would be fearsome player. Tide K Philip Doyle's 2 FGs had tied it 6-6 in 3rd Q when Smith burst up middle for 30y score. He added 1y TD midway through 4th Q. K Robert McGinty booted 3 FGs for Gators (2-1), whose last win over Bama had come in 1963, span of 8 games in infrequent series. Florida D pitched in with 5 sacks of Alabama (2-1) QB David Smith, while holding TB Bobby Humphrey to 73y rushing.

TEXAS A&M 29 Washington 12: Texas A&M (1-1) D was magnificent, holding Huskies (2-1) to 42y in 2nd H and forcing 4 FUMs that led to 22 pts. Huskies QB Chris Chandler (11-31/120y) was sacked 4 times and coughed ball up twice. Aggies managed only 3 1st downs in 1st H, but still led 14-9 thanks to long run and FUM REC. A&M TB Keith Woodside raced 77y to set up FB Matt Gurley's 2y TD run, and LB Tito Landrum recovered FUM on Washington 7YL 2 plays before QB Lance Pavlas threw 7y TD pass to WR Percy Waddle. K Brandy Brownlee booted 4 FGs to account for all of scoring for Huskies.

AIR FORCE 49 San Diego State 7: Passing heroics of San Diego State (1-2) QB Todd Santos dominated WAC headlines, but it did him no good against active Air Force (2-1) D, led by DT Chad Hennings. Santos was held to 258y in air, while QB counterpart, Falcons' elusive Dee Dowis, earned some press clippings himself with 188y rushing. HB Alfred Booker added 3 TD runs for Falcons, scoring twice in decisive 1st Q led 21-0 by home team.

AP Poll September 21

1 Oklahoma (53)	1193	11 Tennessee	587
2 Nebraska (7)	1129	12 Arizona State	547
3 Auburn	1028	13 UCLA	507
4 Louisiana State	995	14 Michigan	307
5 Miami	888	15 Penn State	231
6 Florida State	869	16 Texas A&M	223
7 Ohio State	867	17 Alabama	214
8 Notre Dame	788	18 Washington	176
9 Clemson	777	19 Iowa	164
10 Arkansas	643	20 Georgia	145

September 26, 1987

Penn State 27 BOSTON COLLEGE 17 (Foxboro, Mass.): After blowing 17-0 lead, Nittany Lions (3-1) regrouped to control decisive 4th Q. Penn State O was stopped early in 4th Q, but running-into-P PEN called against Boston College (2-2) NG Dave Nugent allowed Lions K Eric Etze to break 17-17 tie by hitting 46y FG. Penn State added insurance 4y TD run by FB John Greene. TB Blair Thomas led Lions with career-high 164y rushing, while Lions D sacked Eagles QB Mike Power 10 times. When Powers was able to stay upright, his passes connected with WR Darren Flutie for 7/103y and 2 TDs.

TENNESSEE 20 Auburn 20: Volunteers (3-0-1) coach Johnny Majors was happy to accept late-game tie that kept Tennessee in SEC race. But, he took some heat for sending in K Phil Reich to make tying x-pt after TB Reggie Cobb swept 7y on 4th-and-1 with 1:20 left. Having rallied from 20-10 down in 4th Q, Majors was happy to get deadlock. Neither team accomplished much in 1st H as Auburn (2-0-1) used FGs of 52y and 55y by K Win Lyle to take 6-0 lead. Reich opened 3rd Q with his own long-range FG of 51y, Vols their only lead to 10-6 as Cobb scored on 8y run moments after CB Victor Peppers' INT. Auburn answered with 80y drive, capped by QB Jeff Burger's 4y TD pass to RB James Joseph, and DT Nate Hill soon recovered Tennessee FUM at Vols 40YL to set up FB Reggie Ware's 2y TD run for 20-10 lead.

LOUISIANA STATE 13 Ohio State 13: Playing to win, Tigers (3-0-1) kept on throwing at game's end which led to INTs that ended their final 2 drives, 1 in Ohio State EZ and other in own territory that allowed late, desperate Buckeyes FG attempt. LSU DE Karl Dunbar got piece of that 3-pt try, which fell short as time elapsed. Bengals QB Tommy Hodson (15-45/267y) misfired often, including 2 late INTs. Hodson looked sharp early, throwing 24y TD to WR Rogie Magee on opening possession. Ohio (2-0-1) D then settled down, and teams traded FGs for 10-3 H score. QB Tom Tupa threw TD pass to TE Jay Koch for tying Buckeyes TD, which came after QB-holder Scott Powell's 11y pass to FB George Cooper on fake FG.

Florida State 31 MICHIGAN STATE 3: After observing moment of silence for late Spartans coach Duffy Daugherty, Michigan State (1-2) was battered by D and special teams of Florida State (4-0). LB Paul McGowan (9 tackles) and NG Odell Haggins (11 tackles) clogged middle, while CB Deion Sanders (1 INT) made 53y punt RET to set up FSU's 1st TD in 2nd Q. Spartans responded with 11-play drive to K John Langeloh's 35y FG. Ahead only 7-3 in 3rd Q, Seminoles sprung WR Ronnie Lewis (8y TD catch in 4th Q) for 56y TD reverse, and DB Eric Williams blocked punt to set up FG. MSU TB Lorenzo White was held to 88y rushing after starting 6/11y in 1st H.

Miami 51 ARKANSAS 7: In dealing Hogs their worst defeat since WW II, Miami (2-0) scored 5 TDs over 10-min span in 1st H that ended 38-0. Canes D held Arkansas (2-1) to 38y O in 1st H. Miami QB Steve Walsh threw for 215y as WR Michael Irvin caught 6/104y, including 21y TD. Miami HB Warren Williams contributed 108y rushing and 2 TDs. Razorbacks finally scored late in 4th Q on HB James Rouse's 7y run, gaining 80y of 188y total. Miami coach Jimmy Johnson showed no mercy towards alma mater, nor former teammate and Hogs coach Ken Hatfield.

Nebraska 35 ARIZONA STATE 28: Huskers (3-0) failed to secure win until IB Keith Jones burst 62y to set up QB Steve Taylor's winning 3y TD run with 3:37 left. QB Danny Ford, who led balanced attack that totaled 200y passing and 177y rushing, then moved Arizona State (2-1) to midfield before throwing his 3rd INT of game, to LB Steve Forch. Nebraska relentlessly plowed ahead as Jones (17/145y) and Taylor (19/122y) led option attack to 364y rushing. Trading TDs for FGs, Nebraska built 14-6 H lead that evaporated early in 3rd Q on Ford's 2y TD pass to WR Chris Garrett. Teams then traded rushing TDs by big guns, Jones and ASU's TB Darryl Harris (26/110y). Taylor added 12y TD pass to WR Rod Smith for 7-pt lead before losing FUM later in 4th Q on own 13YL to set up Harris's tying TD run. Taylor's 3 TOs—2 FUMs and INT—set up 17 pts for ASU.

AP Poll September 29

1 Oklahoma (44)	1181	11 UCLA	564
2 Nebraska (12)	1136	12 Michigan	452
3 Miami (4)	1088	13 Arizona State	445
4 Florida State	965	14 Penn State	372
5 Notre Dame	890	15 Texas A&M	320
6 Auburn	859.5	16 Washington	225
7 Louisiana State	821.5	17 Alabama	221
8 Clemson	810	17t Iowa	221
9 Ohio State	775.5	19 Florida	218
10 Tennessee	636.5	20 Georgia	179

October 3, 1987

GAME OF THE YEAR
Miami 26 FLORIDA STATE 25:

Wild affair ended on Florida State's failed 2-pt conv as Miami S Bubba McDowell broke up pass. Seminoles (4-1), who blew 19-3 lead, had marched downfield behind QB Danny McManus (16-24/201y, INT) who threw 18y TD to WR Ronald Lewis. With K Derek Schmidt having poor game—2 missed FGs and x-pt—coach Bobby Bowden called 2-pt pass for TE Pat Carter. Miami (3-0) rallied to TD on 49y QB Steve Walsh to FB Melvin Bratton pass. DE Daniel Stubbs' INT readied another TD pass: 26y to WR Michael Irvin (4/132y). Canes were successful on 2-pters after both TDs for 19-19 tie. Later in 4th Q, Miami S Bennie Blades made game's clutch play, with Noles threatening at Miami 16YL, by recovering FUM on C-QB exchange. Irvin quickly made great catch of Walsh's pass and waltzed for 73y scoring play. TB Sammie Smith led Florida State O that gained 426y—including huge loss of 51y on botched FG attempt—with 189y rushing, while Walsh threw for 254y to pace Hurricanes O that gained 306y. Although Miami did not commit TO, they had permitted Seminoles to score early on blocked punt as S Alphonso Williams picked up ball blocked by CB Martin Mayhew and raced 17y to EZ.

LOUISIANA STATE 13 Florida 10: As Florida (3-2) K Robert McGinty's tying 37y FG attempt sailed right at game's end, LSU won in series for 1st time since 1979. Tigers (4-0-1) scored all of game's 2nd H pts, 10 in all, in 4th Q on 2y run by TB Harvey Williams to tie game at 10-10 and then win it on 24y FG by K David Browndyke. LSU QB Tommy Hodson threw for 223y, while Gators were led by TB Emmitt Smith's 184y rushing. Smith's 7y TD run had given Florida 10-3 lead in 2nd Q; Smith outrushed Williams, touted as SEC's best back, 184y to 69y.

Georgia 31 MISSISSIPPI 14: TB Rodney Hampton stole spotlight for Bulldogs (4-1), rushing for 227y in his 1st start in place of injured TB Lars Tate. Hampton scored on 7y pass from QB James Jackson, who threw for 2 TDs and ran for another for 17-0 lead in 3rd Q. Staying ahead, Georgia was able to match 2 belated Rebel TDs that came in 2nd H: Ole Miss (4-1) QB Mark Young threw for 207y and 2 TDs to TE Shawn Sowder, but could not overcome 3 INTs.

Michigan State 19 IOWA 14: Brilliant 2nd H performance—following tongue lashing by coach George Perles at H—sparked upset as Spartans (2-2) blanked Iowa 12-0 over final 2 Qs. Hawkeyes (3-2), who led 14-7 at H on 2 TD passes by QB Dan McGwire (16-26/159y), could manage only 68y in 2nd H. Meanwhile, Michigan State QB Bobby McAlister threw game-winning TD pass of 8y to TE Mike Sargent in 4th Q. Spartans TB Lorenzo White was brilliant, rushing for 166y and 2y TD in 1st H.

NEBRASKA 30 South Carolina 21: Feeling effects of 6 sacks and relentless pressure, Gamecocks QB Todd Ellis threw 2 INTs late in game as Nebraska (4-0) held on. Ellis had thrown TDs of 35y to WR Ryan Bethea and 80y to WR Sterling Sharpe as South Carolina (2-2) built 21-13 lead in 3rd Q. Huskers drove 96y to pull within 21-19 on 3y TD run by IB Keith Jones (25/129y), who rushed for 51y on drive. Nebraska LB Steve Forch then forced FUM that set up Jones' 4y TD run and ensuing 2-point conv for sudden 27-21 lead. Ellis tried to rally his troops, but S Mark Blazek's 46y INT RET led to 43y FG by K Chris Drennan. Huskers S Bryan Siebler's INT with 38 secs left clinched it. Ellis finished with 256y passing with 2 TDs and 3 INTs.

TEXAS TECH 27 Texas A&M 21: He didn't like being called "Mighty Mite," but WR Tyrone Thurman, all 5'3 and 135 lbs of him, jump-started Red Raiders (3-2) with 74y punt TD RET. Texas Tech QB Billy Joe Tolliver threw for 272y and 76y TD to WR Wayne Walker that pushed Raiders to 14-0 lead. Aggies (2-2) converted 2 Tolliver INTs into TDs, including 66y dash by TB Keith Woodside. Red Raiders then took 27-14 lead as sub QB Scott Tolman threw 7y TD pass, and K Scott Segrist hit 2 FGs.

OREGON 29 Washington 22: Game ended nervously for Oregon crowd as bitter rival Huskies (3-2) cut into late 29-14 deficit: WR Brian Slater (8/165y) caught 7y TD pass with 1:43 left to get to 29-20. Washington could not convert 2-pt play, but scrambled to recover onside-KO. Washington QB Chris Chandler soon threw INT to Ducks DB Brett Young on 1YL, but Huskies DE Bob Willig tackled Oregon TB Russell Lawson for safety. Huskies took free-kick and drove to Ducks 32YL before Oregon (3-1) finally sealed victory with EZ INT by CB Ron Gould with 4 secs left. Ducks QB Bill Musgrave completed 17-23/282y and 2 TDs, with 83y effort to WR Terry Obee (4/133y). Chandler threw for 317y and 2 TDs.

October 10, 1987

PITTSBURGH 30 Notre Dame 22: Scoring on 4 straight 1st H drives for 27-0 lead, Panthers (4-2) had to sweat out Notre Dame's valiant rally that died when time expired with Irish on Pitt 42YL. Fighting Irish WR Tim Brown caught 6/156y, but his FUM led to Pitt's 3rd TD. Pitt RB Craig Heyward rushed for 42/132y, 2 TDs. Notre Dame (3-1) managed only 3 1st downs during 1st H with 2 TOs that Panthers converted into TDs. After QB Terry Andrysiak broke his collarbone on last play of 1st H, Irish rallied behind QB Tony Rice, who threw for 125y and ran for 16y TD.

CLEMSON 38 Virginia 21: Remarkable mastery of Tigers (5-0) over Virginia (3-3) continued as they ran series win string to 27 in row, longest active streak in Div 1-A. Clemson gained 403y rushing behind dominating line play. Tigers TB Terry Allen rushed for 183y, and TB Wesley McFadden added 119y. Cavaliers QB Scott Secules threw for 202y, with WR John Ford (5/109y) serving as his favorite target, in leading 3 long scoring drives against malleable Clemson D.

Louisiana State 26 GEORGIA 23: Someone had to lose. Bayou Bengals (4-0-1) built early lead on QB Tommy Hodson's 36y TD pass to WR Tony Moss and 3 of K David Browndyke's 4 FGs. Georgia (4-2) rallied from 16-3 H deficit to take 23-19 lead on 2 TD passes by QB James Jackson and 14y TD run by TB Rodney Hampton. Hodson answered with 5y TD pass to TE Brian Kinchen, capping drive that featured 2 diving receptions by WR Wendell Davis (11/128y). Georgia had more than 3 mins to retaliate but pass to Hampton glanced off TB's hands, only to be turned into game-sealing INT by LSU DB Kevin Guidry. Bulldogs' earlier rally had been helped by 2 TDs converted TOs. Georgia's most spectacular scoring play came from WR Cassius Osborn, who caught short pass and broke tackle to race 74y down sideline.

MEMPHIS STATE 13 Alabama 10: More stunning than Memphis State (2-3) K John Butler's winning 47y FG was that 8:28 remained, yet Crimson Tide could not score against inspired Tigers D. Alabama (4-2) scored 1st on 8y reception by TB Bobby Humphrey, who also gained 84y rushing. Tide fans felt Bama was killed by tough decisions: holding call wiped out Alabama's TD run early in 4th Q, and 2 interference PENs led to Memphis' only TD: 3y run by RB Gerald White. Teams traded FGs before Tigers scored game's final 10 pts to pull upset. Memphis D had fashioned GLS in 1st H and limited Tide to so-so 274y by game's end. Tigers FB Wayne Pryor rushed for 112y to help earn team's 3rd win in last 21 games.

Indiana 31 OHIO STATE 10: Hoosiers coach Bill Mallory, former Woody Hayes assistant, beat Ohio State (3-1-1) at own game. Indiana (4-1) QB Dave Schnell (15-23/200y) led O that did not turn ball over, while D copped 3 miscues by home team. TB Anthony Thompson bulled for 126y behind big Indiana O-line. Buckeyes were limited to 10y rushing in 2nd H while they made no 1st downs during 3rd Q. It was Buckeye football at its best, but played by IU. Ohio FB James Bryant had team-high 56y with 8y TD in 2nd Q to assist getting score to 10-10 at H. Hoosiers' victory was 1st over conf nemesis Ohio State since 1951, span of 31 games in which Indiana lost 30 times and tied once.

MICHIGAN STATE 17 Michigan 11: Wolverines (3-2) O stunk up East Lansing, where Michigan had not lost to in-state rival since 1969. While Michigan TB Jamie Morris was able to gain 31/108y on ground, QB Demetrius Brown threw 7 INTs, 4 pilfered by Spartans S John Miller. Spartans (3-2) TB Lorenzo White (185y rushing) passed Wolverines' Butch Woolfolk to become Big 10's 2nd all-time leading rusher and scored both green-clad TDs. White's 1st score deserved high praise as he broke 2 tackles and carried tough Michigan S Doug Mallory last 4y into EZ.

PURDUE 9 Illinois 3: New Purdue (1-3-1) coach Fred Akers finally posted win. While game may not have been pretty—it was far from that—but it counted in Big 10 standings. Boilermakers scored its pts in 5-min span of 2nd Q when K Jonathan Briggs booted 3 FGs. Purdue FB James Medlock rushed for career-high 131y. Fightin' Illini (1-4) were too inept to match that Boilers' humble pt total, losing 8 FUMs in rain, including frustrating bobble on Purdue 1YL in 3rd Q. Although he lost 4 FUMs, Illinois QB Scott Mohr threw for 206y with WR Darryl Usher grabbing 8/115y.

Oklahoma 44 Texas 9 (Dallas): Experts foresaw mismatch as Sooners had to cover 31-pt spread, highest ever in series. Longhorns (2-3) grabbed 3-0 lead on 52y FG by K Wayne Clements, but started misguiding passes throughout Cotton Bowl air. Oklahoma (5-0) took advantage of 7 INTs, and, in so doing, got chance to display depth. Sooners QB Jamelle Holieway rushed for 70y and passed for 76y, including 32y scoring throw to TE Keith Jackson. Holieway's backup QB Charles Thompson,

rushed for 114y, big chunk of which came on 55y TD run. Still, Texas trailed only 13-6 in 3rd Q before INTs led to 3 straight OU TDs: 44y catch by WR Carl Cabbiness, 32y romp by FB Lydell Carr, and 4y run by HB Patrick Collins.

OKLAHOMA STATE 42 Colorado 17: Newly-ranked Cowboys (5-0) opened season with 5 straight wins for 1st time since 1945 as TBs Thurman Thomas and Barry Sanders rushed for TDs, QB Mike Gundy threw 2 TD passes, and Sanders closed scoring on 73y punt TD RET. Gundy completed 21-28/257y, Thomas led rushers with 110y, and WR Hart Lee Dykes caught 8/114y. Buffaloes (3-2) were barely outgained, 394y to 341y, but lost 6 TOs which led to 21 pts for OSU. Colorado's chances were pronounced dead when Buffs FB Michael Simms dribbled away 2 FUMs that were turned into Cowboy TDs early in 3rd Q.

Wyoming 29 BRIGHAM YOUNG 27: Cowboys (4-2) stormed back from 14-0 H deficit as QB Craig Burnett finished game with 308y passing and 3 TDs. Wyoming blitzed Cougars (3-3) for 29 straight pts to wrest control of game. BYU rallied with 13 pts before game ended. QB Bob Jensen threw for 291y and 3 TDs to pace BYU attack.

OREGON 34 Southern California 27: QB Bill Musgrave led resurgent Ducks to 1st win over USC (3-2) since 1971, completing 22-33/287y, 3 TDs. Oregon (4-1) piled up 448y, 305y in 1st H in building 21-0 lead on 2 TD passes to TE Tim Parker and 1y TD run by TB Derek Loville. Two Trojans TDs in 3rd Q sandwiched 2 FGs by Ducks K Kirk Dennis as Southern California pulled to within 27-14. Musgrave then led 70y drive early in 4th Q to 18y TD pass to WR Terry Obee that closed out Southern Cal. QB Rodney Peete rebounded from awful 1st H in which he threw for only 70y and INT, to finish with 279y and 3 TDs. WR Erik Affholter (8/147y) caught 2 scores.

October 17, 1987

(Fri) Indiana 18 MINNESOTA 17: Indiana's giddy ride atop Big 10 standings continued as Hoosiers handed Minnesota (5-1) 1st loss. Golden Gophers K Chip Lohmiller had opportunity to beat Hoosiers (5-1) with late FG for 2nd straight year, but he missed left on 44y effort with 1:32 left. Gophers TB Darrell Thompson lost battle of Thompsons, rushing for 103y, although he broke loose for 42y for game's 1st score. TB Anthony Thompson continued his fine season for IU with 160y rushing. Indiana QB Dave Schnell threw for 250y and rushed for 2 TDs. Game was moved to Friday night to accommodate Twins' World Series game on Saturday.

SYRACUSE 48 Penn State 21: For Orangemen, 5-0 start felt meaningless without beating school that had replaced them as Eastern kingpins 2 decades earlier. Syracuse (6-0) snapped 16-game series losing streak by striking quickly, scoring on 1st play from scrimmage as QB Don McPherson completed 80y pass to WR Rob Moore. K Tim Vesling added 2 FGs for 13-0 1st Q lead for Syracuse squad that was just warming up. WR Tommy Kane caught 6/163y, 2 TDs, while McPherson (15-20/336y, 3 TDs) was brilliant, totaling 375y in total O and adding 2 rushing TDs to those he threw. Penn State (5-2) scored on big 2nd H plays—80y run by TB Gary Brown, blocked punt REC by DT Rich Shonewolf, and 59y pass to WR Ray Roundtree. But, Lions were never in contest in which they surrendered most pts since 1966 loss to UCLA. It was Orange's 1st 6-0 start since glorious 1959 national championship season.

RUTGERS 38 Boston College 24: Scarlet Knights (4-2) may not have won East's big game of week, but win was important nonetheless. Rutgers QB Scott Erney and WR Eric Young (9/136y) hooked up on TDs of 10y and 63y during 21-pt burst late in 1st H. Erney completed 18-26/234y, while TB Harry Henderson ran for 100y. Eagles (4-3) moved ball well but fell short on scoreboard: QB Mike Power threw for 262y, TB Mike Sanders rushed for 112y, and WR Tom Waddle caught 8/174y.

ALABAMA 41 Tennessee 22 (Birmingham): Kicking game always had been significant in this rivalry, and Alabama (5-2) DB Gene Jelks, converted this season from TB, got offensive again with 63y punt TD RET for vital score in 1st Q. With injuries to QBs David Smith and Vince Sutton, Bama had to turn to frosh QB Jeff Dunn. Cool-headed Dunn was magnificent, throwing for 10-17/229y in 1st-ever night game in series. Crimson Tide D also rose to occasion in holding Tennessee (4-1-1) to 51y rushing and intercepting 4 passes by QB Jeff Francis (26-44/358y). TB Bobby Humphrey made 23/127y rushing with TDs of 4 and 17y for victors.

MICHIGAN 37 Iowa 10: Wolverines (4-2) got back to winning as QB situation stabilized. QB Demetrius Brown ran for TD and threw for 3 scores, without throwing INT. Hawkeyes unsuccessfully tried onside-KO with 2 secs left in 1st H, and Brown launched 50y TD pass to WR Greg McMurtry, his 2nd scoring catch of day. That TD revved up Michigan, its lead reaching 30-10 at H intermission. Wolverines D contributed its part by teeing off on Iowa (4-3) QB Chuck Hartlieb (362y passing), sacking him 5 times. Hawkeyes' rushing game was hampered by injuries to top TBs Kevin Harmon and Rick Bayless.

Texas 16 ARKANSAS 14: With Arkansas (4-2) keying on HB Eric Metcalf, QB Bret Stafford (21-34/182y) found WR Tony Jones for 18y winning TD pass on game's final play. It was 1st-ever game in Texas (3-3) history decided on final play, and Jones hung on to ball despite taking hard hits. Longhorns' winning drive began with 1:48 left and was dominated by Stafford, who completed 6 straight, biggest for 19y to Metcalf on 4th-

and-10 from Arkansas 32YL. Metcalf rushed for 76y and caught 10/86y. His 1st Q 8y TD run was set up by S John Hagy's 50y INT RET, 1 of 4 Arkansas INTs. Hogs were effective on ground, with HB James Rouse rushing for 92y of team's 288y.

Texas A&M 34 BAYLOR 10: Winning in Waco for 1st time in 10 years, Aggies (4-2) went to ball control in rushing for 310y. Bears (5-2) managed only 38y on ground in earning only 8 1st downs to 27 for Texas A&M. HB Darren Lewis rushed for 103y and 2 8y TD runs, while frosh QB Bucky Richardson capped 1st career start with 71y scoring pass to WR Rod Harris that closed scoring. Baylor trailed only 12-10 at H as QB Brad Goebel hit WR Ben Baker on 28y TD pass, but came no closer.

Nebraska 35 OKLAHOMA STATE 0: Versatile Cowboys (5-1) O had been averaging 37.4 pts per game, but Nebraska D woke them up to reality. And reality reminded Cowboys they were 0-25-1 in series since 1961. Oklahoma State crossed midfield once in 1st H in falling behind 21-0. Nebraska (6-0) never let up, gaining 617y as QB Steve Taylor threw for 140y, and IB Keith Jones rushed for 115y and 2 TDs. Oke State QB Mike Gundy put up 20-43/221y passing, but his unit's best drive went to 2YL before ending on EZ INT by Huskers DB Charles Fryar. Huskers DE Broderick Thomas (9 tackles, 2 sacks, and 2 FUM creations) helped thwart his namesake, OSU TB Thurman Thomas, NCAA rushing leader, who gained meager 9/7y on foot.

Southern California 37 WASHINGTON 23: Featuring more option runs than ever for 319y on ground, Trojans' new O excelled as TB Steven Webster rushed for 182y and 2 TDs. Washington QB Chris Chandler threw for 181y but also suffered 2 INTs, including late pick-off by USC (4-2) CB Greg Coauette. Coauette returned it to Huskies 9 YL to set up clinching 1y TD run by Webster. Chandler was involved in odd play earlier that helped Washington (4-3) tie game at 7-7. Trojans S Mark Carrier nailed FB Aaron Jenkins on 1st Q carry, and ball crazily popped into hands of Chandler, who got over his shock in time to sprint 54y to set up his 2y TD run. Southern California quickly answered with 82y drive, aided by 46y Webster run, for go-ahead TD on his 1y run. Teams swapped lead until QB Rodney Peete took Trojans on 80y drive, capped by winning 9y TD pass to TE Paul Green.

UCLA 41 Oregon 10: Bruins (5-1) may have gained only 280y but thanks to fake punt and Oregon gifts—7 TOs in all—Bruins had all they needed. Scoring on drives of 47y, 23y and 19y, UCLA built 17-7 H lead thanks to 2 Oregon FUMs and 12y punt. Special teams finished off Ducks (4-2) in 3rd Q as special teamer Will Austin scurried down left sideline on fake punt. Bruins TB Gaston Green then took over with 1y TD run as he rushed for 83 of his 122y in 2nd H. Ducks QB Bill Musgrave threw for 195y, with 68y on quick pass to WR J.J. Birden to set up 1y TD run by TB Derek Loville. Bruins set NCAA record for scoring in 187 consecutive games, snapping streak set by rival Southern California from 1967 to 1983. UCLA had last been blanked in 1971, 38-0 to Michigan.

AP Poll October 19

1 Oklahoma (42)	1179	11 Florida	579
2 Nebraska (12)	1134	12 Georgia	436
3 Miami (6)	1106	13 Tennessee	370
4 Florida State	977	14 Michigan State	362
5 Louisiana State	923	15 Indiana	333
6 Auburn	893	16 Ohio State	294
7 Clemson	846	17 Alabama	171
8 UCLA	802	18 Penn State	170
9 Syracuse	722	19 Oklahoma State	154
10 Notre Dame	676	20 Michigan	142

October 24, 1987

North Carolina State 30 CLEMSON 28: Wolfpack (3-4) eliminated no. 7 Clemson from national title chase with convincing 1st H performance. NC State racked up 252y and took shocking 30-0 H lead. Wolfpack QB Preston Poag (11-17/118y) led attack, throwing and running for scores. Clemson (6-1) rallied behind QB Rodney Williams (21-53/271y, TD, 2 INTs), who threw NCAA record 46 passes in 2nd H, hardly typical for school with run-oriented history. Williams completed 21-46 to lead 4 TD drives in 2nd H, 3 in 4th Q. Last Tigers drive died on downs on NC State 44YL.

VIRGINIA 35 Wake Forest 21: Cavaliers QB Scott Secules was not going to be denied, completing 20-25/220y against Wake Forest (5-2) D that was ranked 6th in country in pass D. Virginia (4-4) was in control at H enjoying 25-7 lead built on 319y O. Deacons WR Ricky Proehl (7/129y) scored all 3 TDs, 2 on passes from QB Mike Elkins, including 60y catch for Wake's 1st score. Cavs finished with 438y total O.

GEORGIA 17 Kentucky 14: To snap 9-game series losing streak, Wildcats (4-3) simply had to hold on. Kentucky had built 14-0 1st Q lead, then blew opportunity to enhance lead with numerous PENs and costly INT deep in Georgia territory. With TB Rodney Hampton rushing for 123y, Bulldogs (6-2) scored TDs in 3rd and 4th Qs with winning tally coming on 5y run by TB Lars Tate with 1:08 left. Earlier in 4th Q, Cats GLS had stopped Hampton on 4th down at Kentucky 7YL. Georgia D held Wildcats' fading O to 33y in 2nd H, only 7y in 4th Q. Georgia coach Vince Dooley had angioplasty surgery 4 days earlier, but returned to sidelines for happy escape win.

INDIANA 14 Michigan 10: Hoosiers (6-1) fans were getting excited. They grabbed 1st place in Big 10 with 1st win over stumbling Michigan (4-3) since 1967 Rose Bowl team turned same tricks. Indiana QB Dave Schnell threw and ran for TDs to lead attack that could muster only 190y. With 152y rushing by TB Jamie Morris, Wolverines gained 300y, lost because blocked punt and batch of PENs set up 2 Hoosier TDs. IU S Bill Reisert made punt-block, recovered on Michigan 11YL to set up WR Ernie Jones' TD catch. Wolverines rallied for 10-7 H lead. Schnell scored winning 3y TD run in 3rd Q, capping 65y drive propelled by pair of 15y interference PENs. Indiana still needed 15 plays to scratch remaining 35y for TD. Rain in 2nd H helped prevent Michigan comeback; goal posts came tumbling down at Memorial Stadium.

NOTRE DAME 26 Southern California 15: Irish option attack was in full gear as they gained 351y rushing and churned out 90y and 88y drives for 2nd Q TDs. QB Rodney Peete (23-45/275y, INT) had taken Trojans (4-3) on opening 70y drive to grab 7-0 lead on 9y pass to WR John Jackson. Then it was all Notre Dame (5-1), as sr-laden O-line dominated on run of 26 straight pts. With Troy D front-7 manhandled, USC S Mark Carrier was forced to make 20 tackles. Trojans blew chances to rally in 2nd H as K Quin Rodriguez missed FG, and RB Steve Webster lost FUM at ND 5YL.

OKLAHOMA 24 Colorado 6: Despite treating ball as if it was on fire, Sooners remained unbeaten as D smothered Colorado (4-3) and allowed 213y. Oklahoma (7-0) fumbled 9 times, but alertly recovered ball all but 3 times. Frequent diving for loose balls somewhat limited O production, but it still reached 358y. Thanks to K Eric Hannah's 2 FGs, Buffs trailed only 10-6 at H but committed 2 PENs on opening KO of 2nd H to set up easy Sooners drive from midfield that turned game into waltz at 17-6. FB Lydell Carr scored TD that opened 3rd Q on 21y run. Carr (16/100y) and QB Jamelle Holieway (27/146y) were Sooners' top rushers.

Texas Christian 24 BAYLOR 0: Baylor Homecoming was ruined as Horned Frogs (4-3) stomped Bears on stat page: 485y to 106y. TCU TB Tony Jeffrey rushed for 174y and TDs on 80y jaunt and 2y run. Purple Frogs TB Tony Darthard added 101y rushing. TCU QB David Rascoe opened scoring with 14y TD run to cap drive he started with 27y scamper. Horned Frog D handed Baylor (5-3) its 1st shutout in 89 games, sacking QB Brad Goebel 10 times. Bears best penetration was to TCU 23YL, where they lost FUM by HB Jackie Ball, leading rusher with pale 29y. TCU DE David Spradlin spent game in Bears' backfield: 3 sacks and 10 tackles, 4 for loss.

WASHINGTON STATE 45 Arizona 28: Wildcats (3-3-1) tied game at 14-14 in 1st H on pair of TD throws from QB Ronald Veal to WR Derek "Thrill" Hill, but passing of Cougars (3-4) QB Timm Rosenbach (25-31/324y) proved to be difference. Wazzu win, however, was not guaranteed until late INT TD RETs by DL Dan Webber and CB Shawn Landrum. Washington State never trailed, and augmented Rosenbach's passing with strong run game. Cougars sub TB Richard Calvin rushed for 117y and top TB Steve Broussard scored 3 TDs. Broussard tallied on 42y pass play and 2y run in 1st Q, before he suffered shoulder separation. Sideline docs popped Broussard's shoulder back in, and he manfully returned in 2nd H to score on 1y run.

AP Poll October 27

1 Oklahoma (40)	1176	11 Indiana	546
2 Nebraska (13)	1134	12 Georgia	491
3 Miami (7)	1108	13 Tennessee	466
4 Florida State	986	14 Clemson	459
5 Louisiana State	952	15 Ohio State	327
6 Auburn	900	16 Alabama	279
7 UCLA	842	17 Oklahoma State	187
8 Syracuse	774	18 Penn State	184
9 Notre Dame	732	19 South Carolina	112
10 Florida	612	20 Michigan State	110

October 31, 1987

Syracuse 24 PITTSBURGH 10: QB Don McPherson threw 2 1st H TD passes and added another by land as Syracuse (8-0) built 24-3 H lead, gaining 301y with 3 masterful scoring drives that exceeded 80y. Orangemen D dominated despite loss of ace DT Ted Gregory with knee injury on game's 1st play. Syracuse DT Rob Burnett had 4 of team's 7 sacks, while DB David Holmes added 15 tackles and clinching 4th Q INT. TB Craig Heyward was top gainer for Panthers (5-3) with 141y and TD rushing. WR Tommy Kane (5/100y) and TE Pat Kelly (3/105y), who each caught TD pass, became 1st duo to reach 100y receiving in game for Syracuse.

PENN STATE 25 West Virginia 21: Penn State's ducking and diving TB Blair Thomas put on dazzling show, rushing for 36/181y to spark comeback from 21-10 deficit. Nittany Lions (6-2) needed 2 TDs in game's final 8 mins to pull out win that guaranteed school's remarkable 49th straight break-even or better season. Mountaineers (4-4) QB Major Harris did his best to dart all over Beaver Stadium, ending with 128y and 2 TDs passing while adding 40y and TD rushing. WVU led 21-10 before Thomas weaved his magic. He scored 1st TD on 1y run to cap 58y drive. He added 2-pt conv catch to pull Penn State to within 21-18. After forcing punt, Penn State launched 7-play, 62y drive that ended with frosh TB Gary Brown's 19y scoring run for game-winner.

DUKE 48 Georgia Tech 14: Yellow Jackets (2-6) knew Duke QB Steve Slayden would throw and throw, yet there was nothing they could do about it. Slayden completed 31-50/396y and produced ACC-record 6 TDs. Blue Devils (4-4) won rare "laugher" as their last win by more than 30 pts had been 51-17 victory over Virginia in 1982. Slayden passed for 396y with FB Roger Boone lugging pigskin for 169y on passes out of backfield. Magical WR Clarkston Hines caught 3 Duke scores. Georgia Tech QB Darrell Gast completed 24-49/416y, but with 3 costly INTs. Gast's big play was 87y TD hookup with WR Greg Lester in 3rd Q.

Michigan State 13 OHIO STATE 7: Spartans (5-2-1) got past early D letdown to slap Ohio State and grab 1st place in Big 10 race. After scoring long, early TD on 79y pass from QB Tom Tupa to WR Everett Ross, Buckeyes were shut out for game's final 59:45. Tupa's TD toss was more than half of team's yardage, as Ohio State (5-2-1) gained 147y total with only 2y rushing. Michigan State rushed for 247y as QB Bobby McAllister led way with 83y, including 15y TD run in 1st Q, and TB Lorenzo White added 80y. K John Langeloh's 2 FGs, which proved to be difference, were both set up by INTs. Michigan State DT Travis Davis had 5 sacks.

IOWA 29 Indiana 21: Hawkeyes (6-3) bounced Indiana from top of Big 10, but not before blowing cozy 20-7 H lead. Most of Iowa's damage came courtesy of QB Chuck Hartlieb (19-27/271y, TD), who threw 35y TD pass to open scoring and completed 5-6 passes on winning 86y drive in 4th Q. Iowa FB David Hudson capped that drive with 1y TD run for 26-21 lead. K Rob Houghtlin added insurance 28y FG, his 3rd of game, to

close scoring. Hoosiers (6-2) had rallied behind reserve QB Dave Kramme, who threw for 157y in relief of QB Dave Schnell, but also relinquished 2 critical INTs in decisive 4th Q. Indiana's normally consistent TB Anthony Thompson was held to 35y, but WR Ernie Jones caught 6/116y, 2 TDs.

TEXAS 41 Texas Tech 27: Late-arriving fans missed lots of action as SWC foes combined for 27 pts on series of big plays in 1st Q. Red Raiders (5-4) quickly blocked punt for DB Lemuel Stinson's EZ REC for TD. Texas answered with QB Bret Stafford's 33y TD pass to WR Gabriel Johnson, and took lead for good on 19y INT TD RET by S John Hagy. Texas Tech QB Billy Joe Tolliver bounced back to throw 10y TD pass to WB Eddy Anderson, but x-pt was missed. So, Texas held on to 14-13 lead after 1st Q. Longhorns (4-3) kept up onslaught with 27 straight pts including Hagy's 39y punt TD RET, TB Eric Metcalf's 27y run, and Metcalf's 19y TD pass to WR Tony Jones. Texas Tech added 2 window-dressing TDs for 4th Q respectability. Texas coach David McWilliams could brag about 2-0 mark in combative series, since he had coached Red Raiders to 23-21 win over Texas in previous season.

BRIGHAM YOUNG 24 Air Force 13: Sean Covey enjoyed debut as starting QB, throwing for 294y to lead slow-starting Cougars (5-3). Air Force (6-3) jumped out to 10-0 lead on 3y TD run by HB Anthony Roberson and 32y FG by K Steve Yarbrough. Just as quickly, Air Force had BYU pinned deep in own territory. Cougars TB Mike O'Brien burst free for 20y run to wake up home team, which then outscored Falcons 24-3. O'Brien rushed for 2 TDs, and Covey threw 5y scoring pass to FB Fred Whittingham.

AP Poll November 2
1 Oklahoma (38)	1173	10t Georgia	599
2 Nebraska (15)	1137	12 Oklahoma State	437
3 Miami (7)	1108	13t Alabama	393
4 Florida State	987	13t South Carolina	393
5 Louisiana State	943	15 Michigan State	386
6 Auburn	906	16 Penn State	309
7 UCLA	835	17 Florida	229
8 Syracuse	798	18 Indiana	224
9 Notre Dame	751	19 Tennessee	90
10t Clemson	599	20 Texas A&M	84

November 7, 1987

Clemson 13 NORTH CAROLINA 10: Showcasing dependability that kept him in NFL for more than decade, K David Treadwell booted Clemson (8-1) into no worse than share of ACC title with 30y FG with 32 secs left. Tigers ran 18 straight times on winning drive, which began on own 20YL and featured 6y run by TB Terry Allen on 4th-and-2 from UNC 38YL. Tigers QB Rodney Williams had hit WR Gary Cooper with 29y TD pass to open scoring in 2nd Q. TB Torin Dorn, who led Tar Heels (5-4) with 92y rushing, tied game at 7-7 with 20y run in 3rd Q. Teams then exchanged FGs. FB Tracy Johnson rushed for 124y to pace Clemson.

Florida State 34 AUBURN 6: After blowing big lead to Miami, Florida State (8-1) was not about to let 27-3 H margin slip away. Seminoles D continued to batter Auburn, holding Tigers (7-1-1) to less than 100y in 2nd H. Thanks to their balanced attack and Tigers' ill-timed TOs, FSU took 17-0 lead early in 2nd Q. Auburn's 1st play from scrimmage was pass by QB Jeff Burger (19-34/187y, 3 INTs) that was bobbled by WR Duke Donaldson into hands of Florida State LB Terry Warren. Soon after, Noles took lead for good at 7-0 on 2y run by FB Dayne Williams. Warren later recovered FUM by Auburn FB Reggie Ware that led to FG by K Derek Schmidt, who became all-time NCAA scoring leader. Schmidt's 370 pts topped Arizona State's Luis Zendejas (1981-84) by 2 pts. FSU WR Herb Gainer only caught 2 passes from QB Danny McManus, but both went for TDs, 5y in 1st Q and 19y in 2nd Q. Auburn's pts came on FGs by K Win Lyle.

Alabama 22 LOUISIANA STATE 10: With Alabama TB Bobby Humphrey rushing for 177y and D forcing 5 TOs, Crimson Tide (7-2) shook up SEC race. Tigers (7-1-1) entered game as tops in conf, but had to play without QB Tommy Hodson. Backup QB Mickey Guidry threw for 115y, which was deemed dissatisfactory. So, Hodson was summoned in 4th Q and immediately was intercepted by Bama CB Gene Jelks, who returned INT to LSU 30YL. Humphrey soon took 10y run to TD-house. WR Wendell Davis wriggled his way open in Bama secondary, regardless of who played QB for Bengals, and caught 9/101y. K Philip Doyle's 3 FGs were of considerable help to Tide, which remarkably ran record to 8-0-1 in most recent visits to Tiger Stadium. Tigers had been darlings of ESPN, and loss was 1st after 8 wins.

Georgia 23 Florida 10 (Jacksonville): Bulldogs (7-2) turned to basic football, controlling both lines of scrimmage in defeating border rivals. Georgia TB Rodney Hampton rushed for 103y to lead O that held ball for more than 37 mins, in gaining 306y rushing. Angry Bulldogs D ruled: it held TB Emmitt Smith to 46y, sacked QB Kerwin Bell (15-22/162y, TD) 5 times--3 by DE Richard Tardits--and garnered 2 INTs, both by CB Ben Smith. "Dawgs" were steaming over Jacksonville news suggestion their DBs were so bad they "couldn't cover their mouths when they coughed." Gators (5-4) had opened with 3-0 lead as wind aided 52y FG by K Robert McGinty, series-record and his personal-best. From then on, Florida spent frustrating game struggling just to get 1st downs. Georgia TB Lars Tate rushed for 86y and 2 TDs as attack kept ball away from Gators' O.

WISCONSIN 26 Ohio State 24: Sloppy Buckeyes (5-3-1) blew what might have been easy win as their 7 TOs negated 484y to 233y O advantage. Wisconsin K Todd Gregoire kicked 4th FG, all from 41y or farther out, to clinch game early in 4th Q. Ohio State QBs Tom Tupa (187y passing) and Greg Frey each threw 2 INTs as Badgers (3-6) D posted shutout in rainy 2nd H. Back-breaker was INT of Tupa midway through 3rd Q by S Greg Thomas, who returned it 37y to EZ to pull Wisconsin to 24-20. Next,

Badgers converted INT and FUM into Gregoire's 2 FGs for win. "It's a momentous day," said winning coach Don Morton. "We needed something good to happen to this football team."

COLORADO 27 Missouri 10: WB J.J. Flanigan only carried ball once for Buffs (6-3), but he made it count by racing 53y to kick-start victory in 1st Q. Colorado added 17 pts in 2nd Q to grab commanding 24-3 H lead, closing 1st H scoring on deceptive play. WR Lance Carl pulled up on what seemed to be reverse run, only to throw 34y TD pass to HB Eric Bieniemy over puzzled Missouri secondary. Tigers (4-5) were outgained 392y to 235y, but pulled within 24-10 on 5y TD pass from QB John Stollenwerck to TE Tim Bruton. Both Ks took advantage of light mountain air: Buffs K Ken Culbertson (52y) and Missouri K Tom Whelihan (54y) each made long FGs. FB Erich Kissick rushed for 129y for Colorado.

OKLAHOMA 29 Oklahoma State 10: Trailing 16-10 late in 4th Q, Cowboys (7-2) went to air with disastrous results. Oklahoma DE Troy Johnson and S Ricky Dixon each romped to INT TD RETs in last 4 mins of contest. Backup FB Rotnei Anderson rushed for 191y as Sooners (9-0) gained 413y on ground. Oklahoma State TB Thurman Thomas rushed for 25/173y, but QB Mike Gundy negated that effort by being picked off 4 times. It was costly win as QB Jamelle Holieway (123y rushing) and FB Lydell Carr, each were lost for season with knee injuries. Coach Barry Switzer supplanted Bud Wilkinson as winningest coach in Sooners history with 146.

ARKANSAS 10 Baylor 7: Riding punishing D, Razorbacks (7-2) pulled out late win on 1y TD run by HB James Rouse with 47 secs left. Arkansas D held Bears (5-4) to 27y rushing and picked off 3 passes by QB Brad Goebel. Arkansas S Odis Lloyd forced Baylor HB Jackie Ball's FUM that Hogs recovered on Baylor 39YL to set up winning score. Razorbacks rushed for 198y with Rouse leading with 91y. Highlight for Baylor was 80y drive to its TD on 1y run by HB Charles Perry.

AP Poll November 9
1 Oklahoma (36)	1164	11 Alabama	617
2 Nebraska (15)	1137	12 Auburn	567
3 Miami (9)	1111	13 Michigan State	460
4 Florida State	1021	14 South Carolina	450
5 UCLA	943	15 Penn State	328
6 Syracuse	902	16 Indiana	301
7 Notre Dame	856	17 Oklahoma State	258
8 Georgia	694	18 Tennessee	166
9 Clemson	646	19 Texas A&M	114
10 Louisiana State	632	20 Arkansas	58

November 14, 1987

SYRACUSE 45 Boston College 17: Eagles (5-6) soared to 17-0 lead early in 2nd Q on TD runs by TB Jim Bell (26/115y) and FB Bill Hislop, latter scoring on his only carry of game. Suddenly, Syracuse (10-0) seemed to reacquire sweet taste of Sugar Bowl prospects and exploded for 6 TDs and K Tim Vesling's 31y FG in its next 7 possessions. QB Don McPherson (10-19/211y) got Orangemen going in 2nd Q with 1st of 2 TD passes to his favorite target, WR Tommy Kane. HB Robert Drummond scored twice, including go-ahead TD before H for 21-17 edge.

PITTSBURGH 10 Penn State 0: Hungry Panthers (7-3) moved into Penn State territory on opening series before settling for 44y FG by K Jeff Van Horne. Fans of D should have been licking their lips, while fans of pts might have thought about going home. Score stayed 3-0 nearly all game as Pitt came up big, blocking 2 FG tries by K Ray Tarasi. Late in 4th Q, Penn State (7-3) moved into Pitt territory before QB Matt Knizner threw INT with 37 secs left, returned 69y for TD by Pitt S Billy Owens. Panthers TB Craig Heyward went past 100y rushing for 10th straight game as he totaled 160y. TB Blair Thomas led Penn State with hard-fought, but mild 87y rushing. Pitt beat Nittany Lions for 1st time in Pitt Stadium since 1965, shutting them out for 1st time since 1955.

Auburn 27 GEORGIA 11: Georgia was eliminated from SEC race by Tigers (8-1-1) strategy that dinked Bulldogs to death with short passes. QB Jeff Burger completed 22-32/217y and 2 TDs to lead Auburn that remained in driver's seat for title. Ahead 10-3 at H, Tigers converted 2 TOs forced by hard-hitting D, to score 17 pts in 3rd Q. Tigers' surge wrapped it up, but Bulldogs (7-3) closed scoring on 2y TD run by TB Lars Tate, followed by 2-pt conv. Rivalry, South's oldest, was now tied at 42-42-7.

NOTRE DAME 37 Alabama 6: By all accounts, Fighting Irish (8-1) had re-emerged among nation's elite in coach Lou Holtz's 2nd year. Notre Dame outgained Alabama (7-3) 465y to 185y, building 20-6 H lead as QB Tony Rice threw 2nd Q TD pass and ran for another. Irish employed dangerous WR Tim Brown in various manners: he caught 4/114y, while also gaining 111y on RETs and occasional scrimmage run. ND eliminated chance of rally when it prevented Bama for making any 1st downs in 3rd Q. Tide shuttled in 3 different QBs but could pass for only 50y. Worn-down Alabama D surrendered 4th Q TD runs of 74y by TB Mark Green (18/149y) and 81y by TB Ricky Watters. Tide TB Bobby Humphrey rushed for 94y.

MICHIGAN STATE 27 Indiana 3: Spartans (7-2-1) jumped on back of their star TB Lorenzo White to secure Rose Bowl berth. White carried near-record 56 times to gain 292y rushing and score 2 TDs. Hoosiers (7-3) grabbed 3-0 lead on 49y FG by K Pete Stoyanovich, but were stymied by nation's top rated rush D and gained only 33y on ground. Michigan State DB Todd Krumm had 2 of team's 3 INTs of QB Dave Kramme, who seemed to constantly face 3rd-and-long, deep in Indiana territory.

OKLAHOMA 17 Missouri 13: Averaging 49 pts per game, no. 1 Oklahoma (10-0) played without injured starters, QB Jamelle Holieway and FB Lydell Carr, and struggled on O with no TDs until last min of 2nd Q. It didn't help that sideline tackle injured knee of Sooners coach Barry Switzer, who missed some time being fitted for brace. HB Anthony Stafford scored for Sooners with 45 secs to go in 2nd Q to break 3-3 tie, and QB Charles Thompson scampered 14y for 3rd Q TD and 17-3 advantage. Key

contributor to both drives was FB Rotnei Anderson (17/118y), who ably replaced Carr. HB Michael Jones (5/32y, 20y TD run in 3rd Q) and FB Tommie Stowers (15/56y) led Missouri (4-6) O that eked out 13 pts against nation's top scoring D.

TEXAS A&M 14 Arkansas 0: With precarious 7-0 lead in balance, it took TD pass from 3rd-string Aggies QB to walk-on WR to finish off Arkansas (7-3). QB Craig Stump, who lost his starting job earlier in season, came off bench in 3rd Q and immediately led Texas A&M (7-2) 78y to clinching TD, his 3y pass going to WR Gary Oliver. Hogs coach Ken Hatfield changed his QBs often, but never found anyone who could move ball against Aggies D that had 10 sacks, and surrendered just 125y. A&M posted its 1st shutout of Arkansas since 1956. Aggies swift WR Rod Harris had opened scoring in 1st Q on 66y punt RET.

UCLA 47 Washington 14: Red-hot no. 5 Bruins (9-1) coasted to 8th straight win as QB Troy Aikman threw for 247y. Aikman registered TDs passing and rushing as UCLA topped 40 pts for 5th time in 6 games. Hip pointer suffered by QB Chris Chandler, who left in 2nd Q after completing 10-12/93y, hampered Huskies (5-4-1). Sub QB Cary Conklin drove Washington to 14-13 lead, but team's O stalled thereafter. Bruins took 16-14 lead at H and then blew Huskies out in 2nd H on Aikman's 2 TDs and 4y TD runs by TB Gaston Green and FB Brian Estwick. UCLA TB Eric Ball rushed for 99y and scored 2 TDs.

AP Poll November 16			
1 Nebraska (32)	1164	11 Michigan State	611
2 Oklahoma (20)	1128	12 South Carolina	530
3 Miami (8)	1101	13 Oklahoma State	405
4 Florida State	1025	14 Georgia	371
5 UCLA	958	15 Tennessee	332
6 Syracuse	894	16 Texas A&M	319
7 Notre Dame	834	17 Alabama	220
8 Clemson	714	18 Iowa	130
9 Louisiana State	697	19 Pittsburgh	103
10 Auburn	689	20 Indiana	81

November 21, 1987

SYRACUSE 32 West Virginia 31: Teams erupted for 36 pts in 4th Q as Syracuse (11-0) scored decisive 8 pts with secs to spare. Orangemen TE Pat Kelly brought in 17y TD pass, and TB Michael Owens made ensuing 2-pt conv run on wide pitchout race to left portion of EZ. Owens, who had 207y all-purpose, had tied score at 17-17 early in 4th Q on 65y TD reception. West Virginia (6-5) QB Major Harris answered with 3y TD run, before Syracuse FB Daryl Johnston broke tackles on 19y scoring run for 24-24 tie. Mountaineers then scored on 10y run by TB Undra Johnson, game's leading rusher with 119y. QB Don McPherson threw for 246y for Syracuse, although he was picked off 4 times.

PENN STATE 21 Notre Dame 20: Irish (8-2) failed on critical play because Lions DT Pete Curkendall halted QB Tony Rice on 2-pt conv attempt at game's end. Rice had moved Irish 62y to pull team within 21-20 on 1y TD run by FB Anthony Johnson. Penn State (8-3) DB Brian Chizmar made 2 clutch plays in 1st H, recovering fumbled QK by DB Brandy Wells at ND 19YL to set up opening score and preventing Irish from tying score with EZ INT of QB Kent Graham. Notre Dame tied it 14-14 in 3rd Q on Rice's 2nd rushing TD, before trading 4th Q TDs the ended in crucial 2-pt miss. Each team totaled 312y in O, with Penn State TB Blair Thomas rushing for 214y and scoring on 1y TD dive.

SOUTH CAROLINA 20 Clemson 7: Gamecocks (8-2) took in-state battle as their no.2-ranked D came through: S Brad Edwards picked off 2 passes late in 4th Q to end Tigers drives, and made TD RET to end Clemson's chances. Tigers' no. 4 D played well, but Clemson (9-2) O managed only 166y, lowest total so far under coach Danny Ford—as South Carolina held 9th opponent to 7pts or less. Carolina TB Harold Green rushed for 107y, scored winning 6y TD run late in 3rd Q.

Virginia 34 NORTH CAROLINA STATE 31: Cavs (7-4) won battle for 2nd place in ACC as QB Scott Secules threw for 269y and 2 TDs. QB Shane Montgomery threw for 402y as Wolfpack (4-7) tried to match pt for pt, but among NC State's 6 TOs, he was picked off 4 times including 3 by frosh CB Keith McMeans. Virginia jumped out to 24-0 2nd Q lead as WR John Ford scored twice—catching 10y TD pass and racing 44y to EZ on reverse. Montgomery then dominated rest of 1st H, rallying Wolfpack to 17 straight pts with 2 TD passes. Secules then led 2 scoring drives in 3rd Q to bump Virginia lead back to 34-17 edge, and its D had to struggle to hold on.

Ohio State 23 MICHIGAN 20: Wanting to win last game for fired coach Earle Bruce, Buckeyes received even more inspiration from coach himself. Pulled into traditional tackling drill for outgoing sr players, Bruce hammered dummy to pleasure of his team. Buckeyes (6-4-1) may have been too high early, trailing 13-0 in 2nd Q as Wolverines scored on 1y TD run by TB Jamie Morris (23/130y) and 2 FGs by K Mike Gillette. Ohio rallied to lead behind hot QB Tom Tupa (18-26/219y), who threw 2 TD passes, including 70y score to TB Carlos Snow, and ran for another. Michigan (7-4) stopped bleeding with 10y TD run by FB Leroy Hoard that knotted game at 20-20 late in 3rd Q. Go-ahead 26y FG with 5:18 left in 4th Q proved to be redemption for K Matt Frantz, who missed late 48y effort in 2-pt loss in 1986 to UM. In final game, Buckeyes legendary LB Chris Spielman contributed 29 tackles.

Oklahoma 17 NEBRASKA 7: With teams ranked no. 1 and no. 2, this game was trumpeted as "Game of Century II." Match-up did not reach level of 1971 classic, but top ranking was on line nonetheless. Sooners (11-0), who rushed for 419y, dominated more than close score might indicate. With game tied 7-7 late in 3rd Q, Oklahoma HB Patrick Collins (13/131y) took off down left sideline for 65y TD gallop. QB Charles Thompson (21/126y) and FB Rotnei Anderson (24/119y) were not outdone, helping to lug pigskin. Huskers (9-1) entered game with 525y O avg, but after IB Keith Jones'

early 25y TD run, they were held to 151y and did not gain another 1st down on their next 7 possessions. Sooners conspired to low victory margin with 6 TOs and 2 missed FGs.

OKLAHOMA STATE 48 Iowa State 27: Running at will, TB Thurman Thomas set new Oklahoma State (9-2) standards for game rushing with 293y and career rushing with 5,047y in final regular season tilt. Thomas added 4 TDs for good measure, including dazzlers of 58y and 66y. His sub, TB Barry Sanders, gave brief glimpse of his unbelievable future with 12/122y. Cyclones (3-8) trailed by only 27-24 in 3rd Q after QB Brett Sadek (19-36/265y, 2 TDs) hit WR Dennis Ross for his 2nd TD, from 34y out, but Cowboys sealed win with Thomas' final 2 TD runs. FB Joe Henderson rushed for 137y as Iowa State gained 477y, but its D permitted 540y.

SOUTHERN CALIFORNIA 17 Ucla 13: With teams battling for Rose Bowl, Southern California (8-3) surprised UCLA with 2nd H rally. Opening H came up anything but roses for Trojans who lost 3 potential TDs: scoring pass was brought back for PEN, FUM was lost on Bruins (9-2) 1YL, and INT was tossed from UCLA 5YL. That INT, by Bruins S Eric Turner, was nearly returned length of field for TD, but hustling Troy QB Rodney Peete overhauled Turner at USC 11YL as H clock expired. Ahead 13-0 in 3rd Q despite being outplayed, UCLA had ridden TB Gaston Green's 138y rushing and 6y TD run, but had to be smiling nervously. Smiles were turned to frowns by Trojans' 17-pt surge, which was led by Peete (23-35/304y, 2 TDs). Peete became school season record holder for completions (175) and y gained (2460y), and tied mark for TDs (19). USC WR Erik Affholter (9/151y, TD) caught winning 33y TD pass from Peete to end drive that began with 1st of 2 INTs by S Mark Carrier. USC upped its series record to 13-5-1 when Rose Bowl was on line for both teams.

AP Poll November 24			
1 Oklahoma (54)	1173	11 UCLA	620
2 Miami (4)	1108	12 Oklahoma State	478
3 Florida State (8)	1056	13 Clemson	347
4 Syracuse (1)	983	14 Georgia	344
5 Nebraska	979	15 Texas A&M	336
6 Louisiana State	830	16 Tennessee	320
7 Auburn	809	17 Southern California	213
8 South Carolina	711	18 Alabama	175
9 Michigan State	680	19 Iowa	156
10 Notre Dame	654	20 Pittsburgh	119

November 26-28, 1987

(Fri) Auburn 10 Alabama 0 (Birmingham): Giving true meaning to Iron Bowl, Auburn (9-1-1) and Alabama battled through hard-fought contest. Game turned on big plays midway through 2nd Q after LB Derrick Thomas' blocked punt gave Alabama (7-4) ball on Auburn 9YL. Three plays netted 8 tough y before 4th down incomplete pass turned over possession. With help from Tide PENs, Auburn then marched 99y, with 44y coming on pass from QB Jeff Burger to WR Lawyer Tillman, for 7-0 lead on 5y TD run by TB Harry Mose. Tigers rushed for 165y in 2nd H, controlling ball for over 23 mins. TB Stacy Danley was Tigers' leading rusher with 129y.

MIAMI 24 Notre Dame 0: Hurricanes (10-0) proved that Notre Dame still has talent gap, easily winning yardage battle (417y to 169y). After FB Melvin Bratton lost 1st Q FUM on ND 24YL, Miami forced ND punt and converted good field position into 35y drive that ended with 1st of Bratton's 2 redeeming TD runs. Fighting Irish (8-3) answered with their best drive—seemingly their only drive—that went to Miami 26YL before QB Tony Rice was picked off by Miami CB Bennie Blades. Canes marched to 30y FG by K Greg Cox, and ND was done at 10-0. Miami QB Steve Walsh (13-22/196y) paced O, while LB George Mira, Jr. and Blades sparkled on D that sacked Rice 5 times and controlled WR Tim Brown (3/37y) through intimidating hits. After 1st couple of hits, including shot by LB Rod Carter in 1st Q, Brown started dropping passes, 3 in all, or falling to ground after catch.

Florida State 28 FLORIDA 14: Doubts about FSU coach Bobby Bowden's ability to win big games was eased with 1st series victory since 1980. On strength of 2 TD runs by FB Dayne Williams and 4 FGs by K Derek Schmidt, Seminoles (10-1) overcame early 14-3 deficit to win Bowden's 100th as head coach of FSU. Gators (6-5) grabbed their 14-3 lead on 2 TD runs by TB Emmitt Smith, who rushed for 100y. Florida was outscored 19-0 in 2nd H. Florida State had 2 100y rushers leading ground attack for 279y as TB Sammie Smith rushed for 116y and TB Dexter Carter gained 111y. UF QB Kerwin Bell was held to 114y, but he went past former Gator John Reaves by 35y atop school and conf career passing y list with 7585y.

HOUSTON 45 Rice 21: Cougars (4-6-1) and high-powered O were getting in gear for future headlines. Houston QB David Dacus threw 34-58 passes for SWC-record 450y. WB Jason Phillips caught 12 passes to finish his season with conference record 99 catches. Cougars SB Kimble Anders contributed 13/147y and rushed for 88y and 2 TDs, while WB James Dixon joined fun with 8/203y and 2 TDs. Rice (2-9) provided its own air show as QB Mark Comalander threw 25-50/316y. TB Todd Jones caught 9/124y and rushed for 76y more to pace Owls. Rice fought hard from behind and nipped away to trail by only 28-21 early in 4th Q. Owls were on march, but threat died as Houston CB Johnny Jackson returned blocked FG 75y for TD.

AP Poll November 30			
1 Oklahoma (48)	1090	11 Oklahoma State	473
2 Miami (6)	1049	12 Notre Dame	417
3 Florida State (8)	985	13 Clemson	405
4 Syracuse (1)	914	14 Georgia	374
5 Nebraska	904	15 Texas A&M	371
6 Auburn	803	16 Tennessee	271
7 LSU	765	17 Southern California	267
8 South Carolina	708	18 Iowa	146
9 Michigan State	635	19 Pittsburgh	125
10 UCLA	573	20 Penn State	82

December 5, 1987

Army 17 Navy 3 (Philadelphia): Cadets (5-6) played near-perfect game in capturing 88th edition of rivalry. Army wore down Midshipmen (2-9) with flawless execution (no TOs and being penalized once for 5y) and powerful running: 72/315y. Rugged Cadets D permitted only 132y rushing. HB Mike Mayweather rushed for 119y to lead Army O that could not crack EZ until 4th Q, but still dominated. Navy managed only 30y FG by K Ted Fundoukas for school-record 11th straight 3-ptr. Middies were in no way helped by suspensions to C Matt Felt and G Joe Brennan.

MIAMI 20 South Carolina 16: Hurricanes (11-0) finished with perfect regular season for 2nd straight year, although expected blowout never materialized. Big play for no. 8 Gamecocks (8-3) was short pass WR Sterling Sharpe converted to 47y TD, and it provided 13-7 lead in 2nd Q. Miami QB Steve Walsh—who threw for career-high 310y—clicked on TDs of 46y to WR Michael Irvin (7/121y) and 56y to WR Brian Blades, while P Jeff Feagles set up other TD with 24y run on fake FG. That TD, 4y run by FB Melvin Bratton, gave Miami lead for good at 14-13 in 2nd Q. Canes D adjusted at H and held South Carolina's Run-and-Shoot O to single FG in 2nd H. It was 3rd of game for Carolina K Collin Mackie. Fight began in 4th Q after Miami DE Daniel Stubbs raced in after whistle and flung QB Todd Ellis to ground. South Carolina players immediately pounced on Stubbs, and proverbial "hockey game" broke out. Miami LB George Mira, Jr. picked off Ellis on next play, as if to rub salt in wound. Gamecocks TB Harold Green rushed for 108y.

AP Poll December 8

1 Oklahoma (47)	1129	11 Oklahoma State	509
2 Miami (9)	1088	12 Notre Dame	467
3 Florida State	1018	13 Texas A&M	400
4 Syracuse (1)	955	14 Clemson	392
5 Nebraska	926	15 Georgia	370
6 Auburn	847	16 Southern California	296
7 Louisiana State	794	17 Tennessee	274
8 Michigan State	687	18 Iowa	165
9 South Carolina	653	19 Pittsburgh	131
10 UCLA	642	20 Penn State	96

Conference Standings

Atlantic Coast

Clemson	6-1
Virginia	5-2
North Carolina State	4-3
Wake Forest	4-3
Maryland	3-3
North Carolina	3-4
Duke	2-5
Georgia Tech	0-6

Southeastern

Auburn	5-0-1
Louisiana State	5-1
Tennessee	4-1-1
Georgia	4-2
Alabama	4-2
Florida	3-3
Kentucky	1-5
Vanderbilt	1-5
Mississippi State	1-5
Mississippi	1-5

Big Ten

Michigan State	7-0-1
Iowa	6-2
Indiana	6-2
Michigan	5-3
Ohio State	4-4
Minnesota	3-5
Purdue	3-5
Illinois	2-5-1
Northwestern	2-6
Wisconsin	1-7

Mid-American

Eastern Michigan	7-1
Kent State	5-3
Miami	5-3
Bowling Green	5-3
Western Michigan	4-4
Central Michigan	3-4-1
Toledo	3-4-1
Ball State	3-5
Ohio	0-8

Big Eight

Oklahoma	7-0
Nebraska	6-1
Oklahoma State	5-2
Colorado	4-3
Missouri	3-4
Iowa State	2-5
Kansas	0-6-1
Kansas State	0-6-1

Southwest

Texas A&M	6-1
Arkansas	5-2
Texas	5-2
Texas Tech	3-3-1
Baylor	3-4
Texas Christian	3-4
Houston	2-4-1
Rice	0-7

Western Athletic

Wyoming	8-0
Brigham Young	7-1
Air Force	6-2
Texas-El Paso	5-3
San Diego State	4-4
Hawaii	3-5
Utah	2-6
Colorado State	1-7
New Mexico	0-8

Pacific-10

UCLA	7-1
Southern California	7-1
Washington	4-3-1
Arizona State	3-3-1
Oregon	4-4
Stanford	4-4
Arizona	2-3-3
California	2-3-2
Washington State	1-5-1
Oregon State	0-7

Pacific Coast Athletic

San Jose State	7-0
Fresno State	4-3
Cal St. Fullerton	4-3
Nevada-Las Vegas	4-3
Utah State	4-3
Pacific	3-4
Long Beach State	2-5
New Mexico State	0-7

1987 Major Bowl Games

Independence Bowl (Dec. 19): Washington 24 Tulane 12

Playing their best D, Huskies (7-4-1) held Tulane O to single FG, even though Green Wave had averaged 417y and 32 pts per game in regular season. Tulane's TD came on 44y punt RET by PR Mitchell Price, which tied game 7-7 in 1st Q. Washington flexed its muscles in 2nd Q as QB Chris Chandler sandwiched 2 drives around K Todd Wiggins' chip shot FG for Tulane (6-6), capping them with pair of 5y TD passes: caught by TE Bill Ames and WR Darryl Franklin. Both Ds dominated 2nd H as only pts scored came on 4th Q FG by Huskies K Channing Wyles and intentional safety taken by Washington with 7 secs left. Chandler threw 15-30/234y, 2 TDs, 3 INTs, and TB Vince Weathersby rushed for 84y and TD, while catching 5/64y. Green Wave WR Marc Zeno continued his brilliant year with 7/116y receiving.

All-American Bowl (Dec. 22): Virginia 22 Brigham Young 16

Cavaliers (8-4) may have had little postseason experience, but when on rare instance that they got to bowl game, they tended to win. QB Scott Secules led 3 TD drives as Virginia upped its bowl record to 2-0. Secules ran in 2y TD in 1st Q for 7-3 lead and threw 22y TD pass to WR John Ford for 22-9 lead in 4th Q. BYU QB Sean Covey threw whopping 61 passes in gaining 394y, but not enough of them found EZ. In team's 10th straight bowl appearance, Cougars (9-4) pulled to within 22-16 on Covey's 1y TD pass to TE Fred Whittingham. Later in 4th Q, Cavs D rose to occasion with 4th-and-1 stop of Covey at Virginia 46YL to halt last scoring chance. UVa used balance to offset Covey's big day, gaining 187y on ground and 162y in air. Cavs TB Kevin Morgan (82y rushing) went 25y for TD that gave Virginia 14-3 2nd Q lead. WR David Miles was leading target for Covey, catching 10/188y, while Whittingham scored both TDs for Cougars including 8y TD run in 3rd Q.

Sun Bowl (Dec. 25): Oklahoma State 35 West Virginia 33

Known for O firepower, Cowboys (10-2) needed D stop at game's end to win exciting Sun Bowl—that in reality was more like "Sleet and Snow Bowl." After Mountaineers (6-6) marched 58y late in 4th Q to pull within 35-33 on 6y TD run by FB Craig Taylor, Oklahoma State DT Shawn Mackey made tackle of TE Keith Winn on GL to stop 2-pt conv. Winn caught pass at 3YL, but could only lunge inside 1YL. West Virginia had enjoyed 24-14 H lead as TB Anthony Brown rushed for 2 TDs and 107y of his total of 167y. Cowboys rallied in 3rd Q as TB Thurman Thomas, who rushed for 157y and 4 TDs, scored from 4y out to cap 6-play, 56y drive that featured solely his rushing. Cowboys QB Mike Gundy hit TE J.R. Dillard on 6y TD pass for 28-27 lead.

Aloha Bowl (Dec. 25): UCLA 20 Florida 16

Bruins (10-2) won 6th straight bowl despite gaining only 221y—to 373y for Florida—and needing lucky bounce to score winning TD. UCLA TB Danny Thompson caught 5y TD pass from QB Troy Aikman on play in which he fell down in EZ but still caught ball after tip by Gators (6-6) DB Kerry Watkins. Watkins' deflection sent ball downward where Thompson waited, flat on his back. Bruins' decisive TD, which was set up by blocked punt by special teamer David Keating and returned 17y to Florida 17YL by DB Randy Beverly. It gave Bruins 17-10 lead. FUM REC set up next UCLA score, K Alfredo Velasco's 2nd FG, so Bruins were scoring without gaining much y. Florida QB Kerwin Bell (19-38/188y, 2 TDs) tossed 14y TD pass to FB Anthony Williams to close scoring. Final Florida threat expired at UCLA 20YL. Gators' front-4 sacked Aikman (19-30/173y, 2 INTs) 5 times and allowed Bruins—albeit without starting TB Gaston Green and FB Mel Farr—only 48y rushing. Florida O was led by TB Emmitt Smith, who rushed for 128y.

Liberty Bowl (Dec. 29): Georgia 20 Arkansas 17

For 3 Qs, Arkansas (9-4) QB Greg Thomas (13/79y rushing) played hero, with 2 rushing TDs that capped drives of 68y and 76y, before he threw 2 late killing INTs. Georgia (9-3) coach Vince Dooley had to know it would come down to last-sec FG attempt by unproven K John Kasay after K Steve Crumley had been suspended. Kasay, who hit 1 of 3 3-ptrs earlier, made 39y boot to ease Dooley's mind. It capped 13-pt Bulldogs rally in 4th Q. Georgia D contributed its late INTs that led to short drives for game's final 10 pts. After Georgia tied game 17-17 on 5y run by QB James Jackson to close 39y post-INT scoring drive, Arkansas marched 70y, but K Kendall Trainor missed 35y FG attempt with 1:42 left. There was plenty of action remaining. Hogs D forced punt and still had chance to pull out victory. Hero soon emerged, but he played for Bulldogs: CB Carver Russaw picked off pass in Razorbacks territory that Georgia converted into 3-play, 20y drive to Kasay's winning FG.

Freedom Bowl (Dec. 30): Arizona State 33 Air Force 28

Sun Devils coach John Cooper passed audition for Ohio State job, leaving Arizona State (7-4-1) after beating Air Force. Cooper had to sweat out final victory as his team almost blew 33-14 lead. Devils QB Daniel Ford threw for 272y to lead attack, with 61y coming on scoring pass to WR Aaron Cox at end of 1st H. Air Force (9-4) had just scored TD on HB Albert Booker's 3y run with 30 secs left in 2nd Q to cut deficit to 17-14. Air Force coach Fisher DeBerry elected to go for onside-KO, but it backfired on Ford's TD heave after CB Eric Allen recovered KO for Sun Devils. ASU opened 2nd H with 9

straight pts before Air Force rallied behind 3rd-string QB Lance McDowell, who threw 2 TDs to WR Steve Senn. Each team's star sr DT went out fighting: Falcons DT Chad Hennings made 12 tackles and 2 sacks, while Arizona State DT Shawn Patterson had 13 tackles and sack.

Holiday Bowl (Dec. 30): Iowa 20 Wyoming 19

Tough-luck Cowboys (10-3) shut down Iowa attack for 3 Qs, but allowed TDs on blocked punt and INT RET that keep Iowa in contention. Hawkeyes (10-3) trailed by only 19-14 early in 4th Q when they marched 86y to win game on 1y TD run by FB David Hudson. Winning drive featured 48y connection from QB Chuck Hartlieb to WR Travis Watkins. Wyoming then moved into Hawks territory before Iowa CB Merton Hanks blocked 52y FG attempt by K Greg Worker with 46 secs left. Hanks had made punt block earlier, stuffing P Tom Kilpatrick's boot that was pounced on by S Jay Hess for TD in 2nd Q. Still, Wyoming led 19-7 at H as Worker kicked 2 FGs, QB Craig Burnett (28-51/332y) threw 15y TD to WR James Loving and TB Gerald Abraham rushed for 3y score. Burnett set Holiday Bowl record for attempts, but had 1 regret: his overthrown pass on 2nd play of 4th Q that was intercepted by CB Anthony Wright and returned 33y for TD. Iowa secondary, playing without suspended starters CB Joe Mott and S Dwight Sistrunk, earned measure of redemption. Holiday Bowl was decided by 1 pt for 5th time in its 10-year history, 2nd straight such win by Iowa.

Gator Bowl (Dec. 31): Louisiana State 30 South Carolina 13

Gamecocks "Black Death D" surrendered only 10 pts per game in regular season, but allowed 2 TDs in game's opening 5 mins to Louisiana State (10-1-1). Both scores came on passes from QB Tommy Hodson (20-33/224y) to WR Wendell Davis (9/132y, 3 TDs) against blitzing D that assigned single DB—unlucky CB Robert Robinson—to speedy Davis. Davis caught TD passes of 39y and 12y in 1st Q and added 25y TD in 3rd Q. Tigers never looked back, in part because of beating they gave QB Todd Ellis (28-47/304y), who was sacked 7 times and hurried into 4 INTs. It didn't help that Ellis broke middle finger on non-throwing hand in 2nd Q. TB Harold Green (15/72y) scored sole TD for Gamecocks (8-4) on 10y run in 4th Q, not nearly enough to keep Carolina from falling to all-time 0-7 in bowl games.

Bluebonnet Bowl (Dec. 31): Texas 32 Pittsburgh 27

Texas (7-5) QB Bret Stafford (20-34/368y, 3 TDs, INT) and WR Tony Jones may not have been many people's prototypical unstoppable passing combination, yet they dominated Panthers (8-4) in last-ever Bluebonnet Bowl. By end of 1st Q, Longhorns had lead they would never relinquish at 14-7 as Jones scored on receptions of 77y and 60y against man-to-man D. After catching 36y pass with more than 8 mins left in 1st Q, Jones (8/242y) had already set game y record with 173y—10y more than previous mark—while Stafford finished with new pass y mark. Texas eventually built 32-14 lead in 4th Q as Stafford threw his 3rd TD pass and HB Eric Metcalf (18/95y) scored on 24y run. Frosh QB Larry Wanke threw 3 TD passes for Panthers—although he was also picked off 3 times—and TB Craig Heyward rushed for 136y.

Florida Citrus Bowl: Clemson 35 Penn State 10

Clemson surprised Nittany Lions (8-4) by going to air successfully behind MVP QB Rodney Williams, who completed 15-24/214y. Williams threw for 169y in 1st H to set up 2 TD runs by Tigers (10-2) FB Tracy Johnson (18/88y) for 14-7 H lead. On 1st scoring drive, Williams found WR Keith Jennings (7/110y) for 24y connection, and on 2nd he and Jennings hooked up on 35y pass. In between Johnson's TD runs, Penn State QB Matt Knizer (13-22/148y, 2 INTs) threw 39y TD pass to WR Michael Alexander. Early in 3rd Q, Penn State drove 50y to Clemson 10YL before settling on 27y FG by K Eric Etze. From that point on it was all Tigers, who reached EZ 3 more times on runs by Johnson, for his 3rd score of game, 25y for leading rusher TB Terry Allen (11/105y), and 4y by TB Joe Henderson. Penn State, hampered by absence of injured TB Blair Thomas, managed only 12 1st downs with 111y rushing.

Fiesta Bowl: Florida State 31 Nebraska 28

Florida State (11-1) QB Danny McManus turned in finest performance of his career, throwing for game-record 375y passing and heroically hitting WR Ronald Lewis with winning 15y TD pass on 4th down late in 4th Q. Last TD pass represented tremendous reversal: it capped 97y drive that began with DT Eric Hayes' REC of Nebraska (10-2) IB Tyreese Knox's FUM, just when Huskers were looking to finish off FSU. McManus went 5-7/95y on 97y winning drive, with big 43y pass to TB Dexter Carter to 2YL. Nebraska had 3 mins left after Lewis' TD, but drive stalled as QB Steve Taylor's 58y completion to WR Morgan Gregory was wiped out by PEN. Earlier, Nebraska had used great special teams play to grab 14-0 1st Q lead. WB Richard Bell's 27y punt RET set up 2y TD run by IB Keith Jones to open scoring, and WB Dana Brinson took another punt 52y all way for 2nd TD. Seminoles answered as QB Danny McManus hit WR Herb Gainer twice for TDs that sandwiched FB Dayne Williams' 4y TD run to grab 21-14 H lead. Taylor, who rushed for 75y and passed for 142y more, tied game with 2y scoring run early in 3rd Q. After Noles K Derek Schmidt hit 32y FG, Nebraska converted 5y punt by FSU P Rick Tuten into 52y drive for 4y scoring run by Knox. With 28-24 lead, Nebraska then moved downfield to FSU 2YL, before Knox's FUM set up winning drive by Seminoles.

Cotton Bowl: Texas A&M 35 Notre Dame 10

Making 3rd straight Cotton Bowl appearance, Aggies (10-2) showed young Notre Dame squad thing or 2 about postseason play. Dallas native and Heisman winner WR Tim Brown (6/105y) put Fighting Irish (8-4) up 7-0 with 17y scoring reception from QB Terry Andrysiak (15-25/203y). After spotting Irish 7-0 lead, Aggies began to take advantage of ND miscues to score 29 pts after TOs. Teams traded FGs before Irish moved again into Texas A&M territory on drive that ended when Aggies CB Alex Morris made momentum-swinging INT in EZ. At time, ND had gained 208y to 73y by A&M. Aggies roared 80y for score on 24y pass from HB Darren Lewis to WR Tony Thompson late in 2nd Q. Moments later CB Tony Jones recovered FUM by FB Braxston Banks, which led to 2y HB Larry Horton run with 26 secs left in 1st H that broke ND's back at 17-10. Texas A&M's "Wrecking Crew" D dominated 2nd H, shutting down ND rushers who made only 74y for game, 176y less than its avg. A&M also switched out of zone coverage to double cover Brown, while putting more pressure on Andrysiak. Notre Dame managed only 76y O in 2nd H, while frosh QB Bucky Richardson (13/96y rushing), who alternated with QB Lance Pavlas, ran for 2 TDs, capping short drives of 23y and 30y to stretch Aggies lead.

Rose Bowl: Michigan State 20 Southern California 17

Trojans (8-4) QB Rodney Peete (22-41/249y) led comeback from 14-3 H deficit with 2 TD passes to TB Ken Henry (3/66y), who capped frustrating, injury-plagued year with performance. In end, however, it was Spartans (9-2-1) who snapped Big 10's 6-game losing streak in Pasadena with bullpen TB strategy that featured TB Lorenzo White (35/113y) for 3 Qs and fresh back-up TB Blake Ezor for 4th Q. USC had gotten accustomed to White when Ezor pounded 6 straight times to set up winning 36y FG by K John Langeloh. Earlier on winning 54y drive, Spartans QB Bobby McAllister was chased to right sideline where he made miraculous leaping throw as he was heading OB: WR Andre Rison grabbed McAllister's 36y pass. McAllister and Rison had hooked up on 55y pass earlier in game to set up Michigan State's 2nd TD. Trojans traipsed to Michigan State 30YL trying for late-game reversal, but C John Katnik's Shotgun snap bounded off Peete's shin, rolling until recovered by Spartans S Todd Krumm. Southern California got ball back, but had only 31 secs from own 25YL. Peete threw his 3rd INT, nabbed by S John Miller to end game. Critical bad snap was 1 of many miscues for Trojans, who had 5 TOs that negated their 410y to 276y advantage. Michigan State's 2nd win over USC this season was team effort as White, McAllister (4-7/128y) and Rison (2/91y) made big plays. Spartans LB Percy Snow also excelled with 17 tackles.

Orange Bowl: Miami 20 Oklahoma 14

Beating Sooners for 3rd straight year, Miami (12-0) won rare bowl match-up of teams with perfect records. Hurricanes grabbed 2nd national title in 1980s and 1st under coach Jimmy Johnson after having suffered 3 straight bowl losses. Much is made of how Sooners (11-1) could not handle Miami passing, but speed on Canes D and coach Johnson's knowledge of OU Wishbone O had as much to do with win as anything. Miami held explosive Sooners Wishbone to 179y rushing, which in many ways marked philosophical end to Wishbone strategy in college ball. QB Steve Walsh (18-30/209y, INT) led Miami O with 2 TD passes, putting it in lead with 30y TD pass to FB Melvin Bratton to cap opening series. Bratton ran to open space to finish game with almost half of team's receiving y total with 9/102y. Opening drive was remarkable given that Miami had to shuffle O-line due to absence of 2 starters. Walsh's only INT, by S Rickey Dixon, sent Sooners on 49y drive to HB Anthony Stafford's tying 1y TD run late in 2nd Q. Walsh made amends in 3rd Q with clutch plays on 2 scoring drives. Walsh converted twice on 3rd-and-8 situations on 27y drive to booming 56y FG by K Greg Cox that put Canes ahead 10-7. Walsh soon took Miami 64y in 12 plays to his 23y TD pass in corner of EZ to WR Michael Irvin. Walsh threw 6y pass to Bratton on 4th-and-4 at OU 29YL, earlier in drive. Cox bumped lead to 20-7 with 48y FG before Oklahoma closed scoring with play borrowed from Nebraska: G Tom Hutson rumbling on 29y TD "Fumblerooskie" late in 4th Q. Hurricanes were only team to score 20 pts against Sooners in 1987 season. Drug testing had taken center stage prior to game as Miami LB George Mira Jr. and OT John O'Neil were ruled ineligible and fought in court all week. Mira's replacement LB Bernard Clark was named co-MVP, marking 2nd straight year sub LB won such award following Oklahoma's Dante Jones, who replaced ineligible LB Brian Bosworth year earlier. Meeting of top-rated 2 teams was 23rd such game, 8th in bowl game.

Sugar Bowl: Auburn 16 Syracuse 16

Only tie result in 54-year history of Sugar Bowl left bitter taste, especially for Syracuse (11-0-1) squad aiming for perfect season. With ball on Syracuse 13YL as clock wound down, Auburn (9-2-1) coach Pat Dye opted for tying FG, decision he would have to defend during entire off-season. Dye leapt in excitement when 30y kick by K Win Lyle cleared crossbar, while players—except for happy Lyle—on both sides looked disappointed. Many fans booed. Teams had matched each other TD for TD and FG for FG throughout game, with Syracuse taking its 1st lead at 16-13 on K Tim Vesling's 3rd FG with 2:04 left. Auburn QB Jeff Burger (24-33/171y, TD, INT) then led final drive, completing 10-11/62y before Lyle's final 3-ptr. Orangemen QB Don McPherson was named MVP, but Auburn D sacked him 5 times and held him to 140y passing. WR Lawyer Tillman caught 6/125y and Tigers' only TD, 17y effort after he nabbed 55y pass. Burger's TD pass gave Auburn 7-0 lead, but his INT to DB David Holmes set up 58y drive for Orange that tied game on 12y TD pass from McPherson to WR Deval Glover. Tigers took 10-7 lead at H on 40y FG by Lyle. Syracuse then marched to Auburn 1YL with opening possession of 3rd Q before stalling and settling on 1st of 3 FGs by Vesling. Interestingly, Syracuse left with Sugar championship trophy, while Auburn was sent replica hardware.

Peach Bowl (Jan. 2): Tennessee 27 Indiana 22

Tennessee (10-2-1) came out guns blazing behind O aces TB Reggie Cobb and QB Jeff Francis. Cobb scored from 6y out for early lead, and then after Indiana (8-4) K Pete Stoyanovich hit 52y FG, Francis (20-26/225y) threw 2 TD passes. Ahead 21-3 in 2nd Q, Vols looked to end matters after blocked punt by CB Preston Warren gave them ball on Indiana 9YL. Cobb fumbled, however, and S Brian Dewitz recovered to give Hoosiers new life. Indiana stormed 91y to tally 1st of 3 straight TDs on QB Dave Schnell's 43y pass to WR Ernie Jones (7/150y). Scoring spurt gave Hoosiers 22-21 lead, with go-ahead TD scored on well-designed 12y run by TE Tim Jorden on fake FG. Vols D later forced punt from EZ that turned out to be turning point: Tennessee was set up at IU 40YL, from where Francis led winning drive that Cobb capped with 9y TD run, his 2nd. Cobb galloped for 146y, while Indiana's Jones made 244y all-purpose.

Hall of Fame Bowl (Jan. 2): Michigan 28 Alabama 24

What was shaping up to be miserable game for Michigan QB Demetrius Brown (4-13/72y) ended beautifully as Brown threw winning 20y TD pass on 4th down to WR John Kolesar with 50 secs left. Earlier on winning 62y drive, Brown hit WR Greg McMurtry with 31y pass. Wolverines (8-4) had built 21-3 lead on superb running of TB Jamie Morris, who finished with career best 234y rushing and TD runs of 14y, 25y, and 77y. Crimson Tide (7-5) had great back of their own in TB Bobby Humphrey (27/149y) who—with help from QB Jeff Dunn (23-40/269y, INT)—led comeback from 18-pt deficit. Dunn threw 16y scoring pass to TE Howard Cross before Humphrey twice reached EZ on runs. Alabama finished with 28-12 advantage in 1st downs as they outgained Wolverines 460y to 346y. Michigan coach Bo Schembechler had to miss this 1st-ever match-up of traditional powers after undergoing his 2nd quadruple heart bypass surgery in mid-December.

Final AP Poll January 3

1 Miami (57)	1140	11 Oklahoma State	542
2 Florida State	1071	12 Clemson	537
3 Oklahoma	1008	13 Georgia	423
4 Syracuse	966	14 Tennessee	379
5 Louisiana State	864	15 South Carolina	306
6 Nebraska	825	16 Iowa	296
7 Auburn	795	17 Notre Dame	219
8 Michigan State	768	18 Southern California	158
9 UCLA	641	19 Michigan	137
10 Texas A&M	629	20 Arizona State	48

1987 Top Performance Formula

1 Miami	1.8290
2 Florida State	1.7828
3 Oklahoma	1.6776
4 Nebraska	1.6634
5 Louisiana State	1.5816
6 UCLA	1.5778
7 Auburn	1.5752
8 Texas A&M	1.4906
9 Michigan State	1.4855
10 Clemson	1.4315
11 Oklahoma State	1.4306
12 Notre Dame	1.4265
13 Georgia	1.4212
14 Tennessee	1.4076
15 Iowa	1.4068
16 South Carolina	1.3928
17 Michigan	1.3199
18 Syracuse	1.3168
19 Pittsburgh	1.3076
20 Southern California	1.2980

1987 Top Opponent Records

1 Notre Dame	.6615
2 Florida State	.6603
3 Florida	.6602
4 North Carolina State	.6395
5 Alabama	.6367
6 Maryland	.6336
7 Boston College	.6186
8 Nebraska	.6151
9 Texas	.6094
10 Michigan State	.6055
11 Oregon State	.6026
12 Miami	.6024
13 Auburn	.5977
14t California	.594828
14t Ohio State	.594828
16 Virginia Tech	.5855
17 Penn State	.5833
18 Georgia	.5820
19 Iowa State	.5785
20 Washington State	.5776

1987 Out-of-Conference Records

	W-L	Percentage	Bowl W-L
Southeastern	37-17-2	.6786	2-2-1
Big Ten	18-13-3	.5735	3-1
Pacific-10	21-17	.5526	3-1
Big Eight	17-15	.5313	1-2
Southwest	15-14	.5172	2-1
Western Athletic	12-22	.3529	0-3
Atlantic Coast	11-17	.3929	2-0

1987 Individual Statistical Leaders

RUSHING YARDS	Attempts	Yards	Avg.
Elbert Woods, UNLV	259	1658	6.4
Craig Heyward, Pittsburgh	357	1655	4.6
Thurman Thomas, Oklahoma State	250	1613	6.5
Jamie Morris, Michigan	259	1469	5.7
Lorenzo White, Michigan State	322	1459	4.5
Blair Thomas, Penn State	268	1414	5.3
Tony Jeffery, Texas Christian	202	1353	6.7
Emmitt Smith, Florida	229	1341	5.9
Dee Dowis, Air Force	194	1315	6.8
Mark Higgs, Kentucky	193	1278	6.6

PASSING YARDS	Completions	Attempts	Yards	Pct.
Todd Santos, San Diego State	306	492	3932	62.2
Mike Perez, San Jose State	243	408	3260	59.6
Scooter Molander, Colorado State	237	407	3168	58.2
Steve Slayden, Duke	230	395	2924	58.2
Chuck Hartlieb, Iowa	196	299	2855	65.6
Terrence Jones, Tulane	192	319	2551	60.2
Rodney Peete, Southern California	175	291	2460	60.1
Troy Aikman, UCLA	159	243	2354	65.4
Don McPherson, Syracuse	129	229	2341	56.3
Scott Secules, Virginia	174	296	2311	58.8

RECEIVING YARDS	Catches	Yards
Guy Liggins, San Jose State	77	1208
Marc Zeno, Tulane	77	1206
Terance Mathis, New Mexico	73	1132
Ernie Jones, Indiana	59	1115
Clarkston Hines, Duke	57	1093
Kendal Smith, Utah State	67	1048
Ron Jenkins, Fresno State	76	985
Hart Lee Dykes, Oklahoma State	61	978
Robb Thomas, Oregon State	58	891

1987 Consensus All-America
Offense

Wide Receiver:	Tim Brown, Notre Dame
	Wendell Davis, Louisiana State
Tight End:	Keith Jackson, Oklahoma
Line:	Mark Hutson, Oklahoma
	Dave Cadigan, Southern California
	John Elliott, Michigan
	Randall McDaniel, Arizona State
Center:	Nacho Albergamo, Louisiana State
Quarterback:	Don McPherson, Syracuse
Running Back:	Lorenzo White, Michigan State
	Craig Heyward, Pittsburgh
Placekicker	David Treadwell, Clemson

Defense

Line	Daniel Stubbs, Miami
	Chad Hennings, Air Force
	Tracy Rocker, Auburn
	Ted Gregory, Syracuse
	John Roper, Texas A&M
Linebacker:	Chris Speilman, Ohio State
	Aundray Bruce, Auburn
	Dante Jones, Oklahoma
Back:	Bennie Blades, Miami
	Deion Sanders, Florida State
	Rickey Dixon, Oklahoma
	Chuck Cecil, Arizona
Punter	Tom Tupa, Ohio State

1987 Heisman Trophy Vote

Tim Brown, senior wide receiver, Notre Dame	1442
Don McPherson, senior quarterback, Syracuse	831
Gordie Lockbaum, senior tailback-DB, Holy Cross	657
Lorenzo White, senior tailback, Michigan State	632
Craig Heyward, junior tailback, Pittsburgh	170

Other Major Awards

Maxwell (Player)	Don McPherson, senior quarterback, Syracuse
Walter Camp (Player)	Tim Brown, senior wide receiver, Notre Dame
Outland (Lineman)	Chad Hennings, senior defensive tackle, Air Force
Lombardi (Lineman)	Chris Spielman, senior linebacker, Ohio State
Davey O'Brien (QB)	Don McPherson, senior quarterback, Syracuse
Jim Thorpe (DB)	Bennie Blades, senior defensive back, Miami and Rickey Dixon, senior def. back, Oklahoma
Dick Butkus (Linebacker)	Paul McGowan, senior linebacker, Florida State
John Unitas (Quarterback)	Don McPherson, senior quarterback, Syracuse
AFCA Coach-of-the-Year	Dick MacPherson, Syracuse

1988

The Year of Third-Year Magic, Mainstream Negative Stories, and Records for Nebraska, Oklahoma, and Houston

Notre Dame Football was the story of the year, and no matter whether fans loved or hated the Irish—there hardly ever has been any neutrality—it was good for the college game. Like the excitement the New York Yankees can bring to baseball, Notre Dame has always been able to generate attention for college football like no other football program.

One piece of little-known Notre Dame (12-0) lore played out again in 1988: coaches in their third year on the job have had an uncanny ability to bring the national title to South Bend. Frank Leahy coached Notre Dame to the 1943 national title, three years after his arrival from Boston College. Ara Parseghian won in 1966, and so did Dan Devine in 1977. Even Knute Rockne, who led Notre Dame in the days prior to polls, saw his 1920 squad, his third at the helm, be selected as titlists years after the fact by Parke H. Davis, a former Princeton player who back-dated his champion selections in 1933. So an undefeated 1988 Notre Dame team, led by wisecracking, third-year coach Lou Holtz, was a good story, filling the coffers of the television networks and appeasing traditionalists.

Notre Dame played a challenging schedule with a host of memorable games, even got into some skirmishes that put the "fighting" back in the Irish nickname. They opened with a win against Michigan (9-2-1) on a last-second field goal. They knocked off defending champion Miami (11-1) in October in the famous "Catholics versus Convicts" game, and beat Southern California (10-2) in November in the first game of the storied rivalry ever to pit the nation's two top-ranked teams.

Only one other unscathed team remained as the bowls opened, unbeaten West Virginia (11-1), but Notre Dame whipped the Mountaineers in the Fiesta Bowl to claim the school's record eighth AP national title. As All-America tackle Andy Heck said after the bowl: "This is what is good and right in America: Notre Dame being number one."

Notre Dame's season helped overshadow a host of negative stories as the mainstream media expanded coverage of the unseemly aspects of football. College sports was rocked by scandal that put unsavory characters named Norby Walters and Lloyd Bloom into headlines for signing dozens of athletes to professional management contracts before completion of their NCAA eligibility. A host of former college stars, including Iowa's Ronnie Harmon, Purdue's Rod Woodson, and Ohio State's Cris Carter, were indicted to pressure them into testifying against their agents. Drug problems at South Carolina (8-4) and probation woes across the Southwest Conference received more attention than the exploits of star players like Alabama (9-3) linebacker Derrick Thomas, UCLA (10-2) quarterback Troy Aikman, or Auburn (10-2) defensive tackle Tracy Rocker.

No team epitomized the confluence of brilliant play and cynicism swirling around the sport in 1988 than Oklahoma State (10-2), champions of the Holiday Bowl. Cowboys tailback Barry Sanders rushed for an unworldly 2,628 yards and 39 touchdowns, each achievement obliterating standing NCAA records. While Sanders was easily winning the Heisman Trophy, All-America wide receiver Hart Lee Dykes was detailing to the NCAA the seedy bidding war over his recruitment four years earlier.

Because Oklahoma State lost twice it was no threat for the national title, a race which was dominated by two pairs of sun-baked rivals—Miami and Florida State (11-1), and UCLA and Southern California—plus that Irish team from South Bend. Preseason no. 1 Florida State fell quickly in September to Miami by a shocking 31-0 score. The Hurricanes held the top spot until they lost at Notre Dame. The Irish had to wait to become the nation's top team as UCLA, which had handed Nebraska (11-2) its only regular season loss early in the year, became no. 1 for the first time since 1967. With the USC Trojans also undefeated, the battle for Los Angeles bragging rights was shaping up as a national title tilt until Washington State (9-3) stunned the Bruins, 34-30, on October 29.

Suddenly, the Notre Dame-Southern California rivalry would help decide it all. On four occasions an unbeaten Notre Dame team had traveled to the L.A. Coliseum only to return with a loss and elimination from national title honors. Independent schools ruled the late 1980s and this year was no different, as the Fighting Irish won 27-10. The Fiesta Bowl against West Virginia was somewhat anti-climatic after the wars against Miami and USC, but Notre Dame prevailed 34-21. Notre Dame, Miami, and Florida State, independents all, finished 1-2-3 in the final AP Poll.

Finishing fourth was Michigan (9-2-1), which easily could have gone 12-0. The Wolverines lost 19-17 to Notre Dame as kicker Mike Gillette missed a long field goal on the last play. Michigan lost 31-30 to Miami in a game it led

by 16 points with seven minutes left. A likely win became a tie with Iowa (6-3-3) on a fumble at the Hawkeyes one yard-line with 1:21 remaining.

Winning the Big Eight with a 7-0 mark, Nebraska set a record of 27 straight winning seasons, breaking the mark the Cornhuskers shared with Penn State (from 1939-64) and Alabama (1958-83). But, the Huskers lost the Orange Bowl as they continued to earn trips to Miami only to be faced by a home-state juggernaut, in this year's case, Miami. Like old times, Oklahoma (9-3) rushed for a record 768 yards in a 70-24 romp over woeful Kansas State (0-11). But, the Sooners lost to ACC champion Clemson (10-2) in the Citrus Bowl.

The Southeastern Conference's two Tiger teams, Auburn and Louisiana State (8-4), tied for the conference title with 6-1 records, with Auburn getting the Sugar Bowl bid due to a better overall record. LSU was justifiably disturbed over being left out of New Orleans because it had won the regular season tilt against Auburn. The year was the final one for the dean of SEC coaches, Vince Dooley, who resigned at Georgia but stayed on as athletic director. After 25 years, Dooley sat 10th on the all-time victory list with 201.

The Southwest Conference had another rough season as it spun toward eventual deconstruction. Three-time defending champion Texas A&M (7-5) lost its first two games and was put on two-year probation, all by September 9. Houston (9-3) later would join the Aggies on probation, but its fabulous Run-and-Shoot attack blazed a new record: receivers Jason Phillips (108 catches) and James Dixon (102) became the first teammates to finish in the top two spots on the national receiving list.

After a record-setting 44 losses in a row, Division 1-AA Columbia (2-8) stunned Ivy rival Princeton (6-4) with a 16-13 win on October 8 in front of a Homecoming crowd that had gathered to honor the distant 1940s glory days of Columbia football. On the subject of losing, Penn State (5-6) suffered its first losing season in 50 years (the Nittany Lions were 5-5 in both 1965-66), a record run without a losing year, and Ohio State (4-6-1) had its first negative ledger since 1966.

Milestones

■ Pacific Coast Athletic Association changed its name to Big West Conference.

■ Coaching great Bobby Dodd, who won 165 games at Georgia Tech, died on June 21 of lung cancer at age 79. Dodd was quarterback leader for Tennessee (27-1-2) from 1928-30 before building Yellow Jackets program into early 1950s power, winning 31 straight from 1951-53 and six straight bowls. Dodd beat rival Georgia eight straight from 1949-56. After stepping down in 1967, he remained as athletic director until 1976. Wisconsin great Alan Ameche, 1954 Heisman Trophy winner, died of heart attack after bypass surgery at age 55 on August 8. Ameche rushed for 3,212 yards for Badgers before embarking on All-Pro career with Baltimore Colts for whom he scored famous overtime TD in 1958 NFL championship against New York Giants. Clark Hinkle, "The Lackawanna Express" and star halfback for Bucknell and member of both college football and pro football halls of fame, died November 9 at age 79. Hinkle scored 128 points in 1929 and led Bucknell to undefeated mark in 1931 before all-star career with NFL Green Bay Packers.

■ Boston College beat Army 38-24 in Emerald Isle Classic in Dublin on November 19. Contest was first major college game played in Europe.

■ Longest Winning Streaks Entering Season:

Miami 12	Texas A&M 8	Florida State 7

■ Coaching Changes:

	Incoming	Outgoing
Arizona State	Larry Marmie	John Cooper
Illinois	John Mackovic	Mike White
Kansas	Glen Mason	Bob Valesente
Kent State	Dick Crum	Glen Mason
Louisiana Tech	Joe Raymond Peace	Carl Torbush
North Carolina	Mack Brown	Dick Crum
Ohio State	John Cooper	Earle Bruce
Southern Mississippi	Curley Hallman	Jim Carmody
Tulane	Greg Davis	Mack Brown
Tulsa	Dave Rader	George Henshaw

Preseason AP Poll

1 Florida State (44)	1161	11 Michigan (1)	608
2 Nebraska (2)	952	12 Georgia	449
3 Oklahoma (2)	946	13 Notre Dame (1)	359
4 Clemson (3)	929	14 Alabama	342
5 UCLA (2)	818	15 Michigan State	307
6 Southern California (3)	775	16 West Virginia	285
7 Auburn	769	17 Tennessee	250
8 Miami (1)	747	18 Louisiana State	249
9 Iowa (1)	736	19 South Carolina	216
10 Texas A&M	659	20 Penn State	211

August 27, 1988

Nebraska 23 Texas A&M 14 (East Rutherford, NJ): Although Nebraska QB Steve Taylor (11-22/125y) threw well, he earned Kickoff Classic MVP honors by scrambling brilliantly in face of blitzing Aggies (0-1) D. After Taylor threw 20y TD pass to TE Todd Millikan for 20-14 lead, he saved game with nifty 18y run on 3rd-and-10 from Husker 35YL to continue drive that culminated with K Gregg Barrios' game-record 48y FG. That boot, 1 of 3 FGs for Barrios, subbing for injured K Chris Drennan, served as difference for Huskers (1-0). Texas A&M QB Bucky Richardson managed only 5-17/42y, while tossing 2 INTs. TB Larry Horton rushed for 81y to lead Aggies, while Husker IB Ken Clark rushed 20/87y, TD.

September 3, 1988

(Th) WYOMING 24 Brigham Young 14: Cowboys (1-0) D pounded BYU into submission, recording 9 sacks and 7 forced TOs. Wyoming QB Randy Weiniak threw 2 TDs and ran in 3rd score, while DE Dave Edeen had 5 sacks and INT. Cowboys D knocked out Cougars (0-1) QB Sean Covey with 2nd Q concussion-producing sack that caused FUM that they converted into 3rd TD. Redshirt frosh QB Ty Detmer threw 4 INTs in relief of Covey, arching 1st career TD in humble debut. BYU K Jason Chaffetz missed 2 FGs and temporarily lost his job.

MIAMI 31 Florida State 0: Some members of preseason no. 1 Florida State (0-1) celebrated with recording of self-glorifying rap song. Between song ringing in their ears and snub with no. 1 preseason rankings, defending champion Hurricanes had plenty to fire them up. Seminoles time atop polls was short-lived as Canes proved they simply had reloaded. Only 4 starters returned on Miami O, led by QB Steve Walsh, who passed for 228 and 2 TDs. LB Maurice Crum had 11 tackles and sack to lead Miami D that forced bitter rivals to swallow 1st shutout since 1976. TD that put Miami (1-0) up 10-0—capping 20y drive following S Bobby Harden INT—featured FB Cleveland Gary running over CB Deion Sanders for 2y TD. With 239y to 91y O differential in 1st H, Hurricanes took 17-0 lead with 11 secs left in H on 19y TD pass caught by TE Rob Chudzinski. With FSU QBs throwing 5 INTs and RB Sammie Smith being held to 6y rushing, 183y fewer than in 1987 match, Noles rally was impossible. Win was 13th straight for Miami, 33rd in row in regular season, and 6th straight vs. no. 1 ranked teams.

GEORGIA 28 Tennessee 17: Bulldogs had bundle of great backs to combat Vols (0-1) as TB Rodney Hampton rushed for 196y and 2 TDs and TB Tim Worley added 144y and 2 TDs. Georgia (1-0) ran ball 63/414y on ground and twice converted 4th downs on 87y drive to clinching 2y scoring dive by Hampton. On 19-play march, Bulldogs ran 18 times. Drive began after GLS by Georgia D, when DG Paul Giles stripping Vols QB Jeff Francis on 3rd-and-goal play. In addition to 6y TD run, Francis hit 25-39/354y and moved past Alan Cockrell (3989y) as Tennessee's career leader.

Western Michigan 24 WISCONSIN 14: Broncos (1-0) won 1st-ever game against Big 10 foe as they outscored Badgers 24-3 over final 3 Qs. RB Rob Davis ran for 136y, 2 TDs, and QB Dave Kruse threw for 247y and go-ahead 22y TD. Wisconsin (0-1) had opened with 11-0 edge on 52y FG by K Rich Thompson and 60y run by RB Steve Vinci, but let Broncos score 3 straight TDs. Season worsened as Badgers lost next game to Northern Illinois, who also beat Big 10 team for 1st time. "Being in the Big Ten, I thought they should be a little more tough," said Davis of Badgers.

Washington State 44 ILLINOIS 7: Illini had hired new coach John Mackovic for his O genius, but it was Washington State (1-0) that put on O clinic. WSU QB Timm Rosenbach (21-29/228y, INT) threw TD and ran in 3 others at helm of O that gained 601y and scored on 6 straight possessions. TB Steve Broussard rushed for 173y as Cougars piled up 382y on ground in winning 1st road game since 1985. Bright spots for Illinois were 53y TD run by FB Howard Griffith and highly-touted QB Jeff George, who debuted with 143y passing, after sitting out his transfer from Purdue.

September 10, 1988

(Th) BRIGHAM YOUNG 47 Texas 6: While missing suspended star TB Eric Metcalf (improper class credit), Longhorns (0-1) clearly revealed bigger problems. Brigham Young (1-1) QB Sean Covey threw for 323y and 2 TDs. On game's 1st play, Covey connected with WR Bryce Doman on 80y TD pass. Cougars WR Chuck Cutler (5/116y) caught 2 TDs, while CB Rodney Rice returned INT 70y for another score. Small spot for Texas was big boot: 55y FG by K Wayne Clements.

Duke 31 TENNESSEE 26: Week after Georgia wore down Tennessee D with run attack, Duke (2-0) QB Anthony Dilweg (19-30/278y, INT), who completed his 1st 10 attempts, blitzed reeling Volunteers (0-2) through air. With WR Clarkston Hines grabbing 8/112y, 3 TDs, Blue Devils built stunning 31-7 lead. Vols rallied as QB Jeff Francis (16-26/257y, INT) threw 2 TDs to WR Thomas Woods (7/128y), and TB Reggie Cobb (28/182y) scored another. Duke recovered Tennessee's late onside-KO to end comeback.

Oklahoma 28 NORTH CAROLINA 0: Coach Mack Brown's tenure in Chapel Hill began, ironically, with blowout by future Big 12 nemesis. Oklahoma (1-0) rushed for 391y, 216y in opening H when it took 21-0 lead. Sooners QB Jamelle Holieway led Wishbone attack that scored on drives ranging from 71y to 88y. Holieway closed scoring with 4y run in 3rd Q. Sooners LB Kert Kaspar paced D that held "Mack Attack" to 116y rushing and 139y passing. Tar Heels (0-1) QB Jonathan Hall had to run for his life and thus was turned into North Carolina's best rusher with 10/44y.

OHIO STATE 26 Syracuse 9: Coach John Cooper opened his stint in Columbus by snapping Syracuse's 14-game unbeaten streak. Buckeyes (1-0) QB Greg Frey handled liberalized playbook and beat blitzing of Orangemen (1-1) by hitting 12-17/141y, TD. Syracuse settled for 3 FGs by K Kevin Greene and committed 2 costly physical errors that Ohio State converted into 17-3 lead. First mistake was dreadful 8y QK by FB Daryl Johnston from his 22YL that set up 14y TD run by Bucks TB Carlos Snow. Later in 2nd Q, QB Todd Philcox threw INT in his territory that led to Frey's 3y TD pass to TE Jeff Ellis.

Rutgers 17 MICHIGAN STATE 13: QB Scott Erney threw for 239y and 2 TDs as Scarlet Knights (1-0) pulled stunner over no. 15 Spartans (0-1). Despite rushing for 33/196y, Michigan State TB Blake Ezor earned goat horns with FUM at Rutgers 11YL with 5:23 left, and Spartans never got ball back. Rutgers, playing 2nd Big 10 foe in history—previously it beat Northwestern 28-0 way back in 1919—were 18-pt underdogs, but built 17-0 lead as Erney hit WR Eric Young (9/124y) for 61y TD and WR Brett Mersola for 18y TD. Michigan State rallied as K John Langeloh booted 2 FGs, and QB Bobby McAllister (8-18/80y), tallied on 1y TD run.

NOTRE DAME 19 Michigan 17: Walk-on K Reggie Ho, all 5'5" of him, entered pantheon of Irish (1-0) heroes with school-record 4 FGs, including game-winner from 26y out with 1:13 left. Moments earlier, Wolverines had.gone ahead on K Mike Gillette's 49y boot, only to surrender ND's 10-play, 71y winning drive. Gillette had chance to be Michigan hero but missed 48y kick with time expiring. Special teams governed early part of game as ND WR Ricky Watters opened scoring with 81y punt TD RET. Ho made it 13-0 by kicking 2 FGs, his 2nd following FUM on KO RET by Michigan FB Leroy Hoard. Wolverines TB Tony Boles then flew 59y on KO RET to set up Hoard's 1y TD. Michigan took 14-13 lead in 3rd Q on 2y keeper by QB Michael Taylor, but Irish soon began to dominate line of scrimmage. Notre Dame rushed for 226y, averaging 5.3y, behind young O-Line.

UCLA 41 Nebraska 28: Coach Terry Donahue earned 100th win in surprisingly easy fashion over no. 2 Nebraska (2-1) as Bruins erupted for 28-0 lead in 1st Q. QB Troy Aikman (13-22/205y) went 5-5/101y, including 2 TDs, during UCLA's outburst. Big plays were norm as UCLA (2-0) scored on 57y catch-and-run by TE Charles Arbuckle (5/110y), 50y run by backup TB Shawn Wills, and 75y punt RET by DB Darryl Henley. Nebraska finally, and with good luck, broke negative stretch when S Mark Blazek, unbeknownst to refs, went to 1 knee to pick off pass, then, after loud encouragement from bench, ran 75y for TD. Bruins pushed lead to 38-14 as they scored on 6-8 possessions in 1st H. Huskers rallied behind QB Steve Taylor's 95y rushing and 125y passing and 2 TD passes. Pt total became most allowed by Tom Osborne-coached team, although Oklahoma State broke it later in season.

September 17, 1988

PENN STATE 23 Boston College 20: With game tied at 20-20 and less than 2 mins left, Nittany Lions (2-0) went for blocked punt. CB Eddie Johnson came in clean to smother punt, giving Penn State ball at BC 27YL. After Lions gained 6y, K Ray Tarasi delivered winning 27y FG. Eagles (1-2) had tied game on 19y pass from QB Mark Kamphous (20-29/257y, 2 TDs) to WR Tom Waddle (9/105y). Lions TB Gary Brown (12/83y) had game's big play, scoring on 43y run. "I came free, and my eyes lit up," said Brown of blocking ahead of him. "Nobody touched me."

PITTSBURGH 42 Ohio State 10: Panthers (2-0) beat Ohio State for 1st time since 1952 as TB Adam Walker rushed for 179y, 3 TDs, and QB Darnell Dickerson added 11/88y, 2 TDs. Pittsburgh totaled 363y rushing and 29 1st downs; Buckeyes (1-1) managed 91y running and only 10 1st downs. Pitt's aerial D was effective, permitting Ohio QB Greg Frey to complete only 9-29/142y. Buckeyes (1-1) had single great moment: 100y KO TD RET by TB Carlos Snow, who totaled 213y on RETs.

Florida State 24 CLEMSON 21: Only adventurous Florida State (2-1) coach Bobby Bowden would go for fake punt on 4th-and-4 on own 21YL, with score knotted at 21-21, 1:31 left. CB LeRoy Butler ran 76y with ball to set up 19y FG for K Richie Andrews with 32 secs left. On play, ball was snapped to FB Dayne Williams, while P Tim Corlew pretended it went to his right and over his head. Williams placed ball between Butler's

feet and then joined O-line in blocking formation to right to "protect" Corlew. Tigers fell for fake and went for Corlew, leaving entire left side open for Butler. Clemson returner-CB Donnell Woolford knocked down Butler at 1YL. Bowden later said he remembered play from Jerry Claiborne, and opted for unusual gamble because tie result would have eliminated FSU from national title picture. Tigers (2-1) had knotted game only 1 min earlier on FB Tracy Johnson's 19y run. Special teams were fruitful for Seminoles as CB Deion Sanders returned 3rd Q punt 76y for team's 2nd TD. Clemson's opening score also had been trick play: WR Chip Davis pulled up on apparent E-around run and threw 61y TD to WR Gary Cooper.

Miami 31 MICHIGAN 30: "It was an ungodly set of circumstances," coach Bo Schembechler said after Wolverines (0-2) blew 30-14 lead in game's final 5 mins and 30 secs. Miami (2-0) QB Steve Walsh hit 7-11 passes on drive that ended with 7y TD toss to TE Rob Chudzinski. After 2-pt conv pass to WR Dale Dawkins, Miami trailed 30-22 with 5:23 left. Miami scored soon after forcing punt as FB Cleveland Gary (9/162y, 2 TDs receiving) took pass on Michigan 35YL and rambled to EZ. CB David Arnold, who was annihilated on TD by Dawkins, then picked off 2-pt conv pass as Michigan held 30-28 lead. Hurricanes S Bobby Harden next recovered onside-KO at Michigan 47YL. Walsh (24-45/355y) then fired passes of 14y to WR Andre Brown and 18y to Gary to set up winning 29y FG by K Carlos Huerta with 43 secs left. Wolverines, opening with 2 losses for 1st time since 1959, had built lead behind QB Michael Taylor's 214y passing and 3 TDs and TB Tony Boles' 129y rushing.

Colorado 24 IOWA 21: QB Sal Aunese (5-8/116y) led Buffaloes (2-0) on 11-play, 85y drive to 1y game-winner keeper with less than 2 mins left. On drive, Aunese threw 23y pass to WR Jeff Campbell and TB Eric Bieniemy (25/153y) added 22y run. Hawkeyes (1-2) were threatening for clincher when Colorado LB Alfred Williams sacked Iowa QB Chuck Hartlieb (21-38/269, TD, INT) to force FUM. Iowa had taken 21-17 lead in 3rd Q on Hartlieb's 12y TD pass to WR Tom Ward (6/94y). Iowa's 1st TD had come courtesy of DB Merton Hanks, who fell on punt blocked by DE Tyran Beerie after Buffs had leapt to 14-0 lead on TD runs by Aunese and Bieniemy.

Oregon 43 WASHINGTON STATE 28: Pac 10 shootout, featuring combined 903y combined O, was won by Ducks (2-0) as QB Bill Musgrave (17-29/206y, INT) threw 3 TDs. Displaying notable balance, Oregon also had 2 rushers top 100y in TB Derek Loville (30/131y) and FB Latin Berry (16/115y), while K Kirk Dennis added school-record 5 FGs. QB Timm Rosenbach (21-30/261y) paced Washington State (2-1) with 2 TDs passing and another running, but Ducks converted his 3 INTs into 3 scores. Wazzu TB Steve Broussard rushed for 125y, TD. Cougars crept to within 30-28 at beginning of 4th Q, but allowed Ducks to hold ball for 11 mins in 4th Q. Turning point for this time-of-possession advantage was Oregon S Derek Horton's well-timed INT.

AP Poll September 19

1 Miami (52)	1171	11 West Virginia	609
2 UCLA (3)	1104	12 Clemson	577
3 Oklahoma (2)	1016	13 Alabama	455
4 Auburn	900	14 South Carolina	417
5 Southern California (2)	859	15 Penn State	354
6 Georgia	802	16 Pittsburgh	230
7 Louisiana State	794	17 Washington	229
8 Notre Dame	753	18 Oklahoma State	175
9 Florida State	739	19 Michigan	169
10 Nebraska	639	20 Florida	89

September 24, 1988

West Virginia 31 PITTSBURGH 10: Panthers (2-1) were haunted by 2 Mountaineers who got away. West Virginia (4-0) QB Major Harris, who grew up 5 mins from Pitt Stadium but turned down offer to be Panthers DB, ran for 55y and threw for 61y more. TB Anthony Brown, transfer from Pitt, added 17/110y rushing. Brown, who ran for 105y for Panthers against Mountaineers in 1985, easily outpaced Panthers TB Adam Walker, who was held to 17/39y, 126y below his early-season avg. Harris hit WR Reggie Rembert for 33y TD pass that opened scoring, while Brown added 64y romp in decisive 3rd Q when Mountaineers registered 17 pts.

Rutgers 21 PENN STATE 16: Facing QB, Scott Erney, who had completed 67% of his passes for 675y, Nittany Lions decided to force Rutgers to move ball on ground. So Rutgers (2-1) ran enough, 36/143y, to surprise Penn State (2-1) for its 2nd win in 17-game series, and 1st since days of A-A Paul Robeson in 1917. Scarlet Knights TB Mike Botti rushed 12/112y, 2 TDs, while Erney threw 38y TD to WR Eric Young. Penn State had more than twice as many 1st downs at 28 to 13, but was susceptible to big plays in Young's TD and Botti's 57y scoring romp in 3rd Q. Nittany Lions QB Tom Bill (11-24/127y) threw 38y TD pass to WR Dave Daniels.

SOUTH CAROLINA 23 Georgia 10: After 2 straight 300y passing games in losses to Georgia (3-1), 3rd time was charm for South Carolina QB Todd Ellis. Ellis hit 28-43/321y, TD to lead undefeated Gamecocks (4-0). Ellis' most accurate passing came on 2nd Q drive in which he hit 8 straight, last of which was 36y TD to frosh WR Robert Brooks that pushed lead to 17-3. Georgia's ground attack was hampered without injured TB Rodney Hampton, totaling 41/102y rushing, well below 355y avg for its opening 3 games. Carolina K Collin Mackie added 3 well-placed FGs.

OHIO STATE 36 Louisiana State 33: Buckeyes (2-1) fantastically wiped out 33-20 deficit in game's final 2 mins. Louisiana State (2-1) WR Alvin Lee caught tipped pass from QB Tommy Hodson (20-39/299y, 2 TDs) for 55y score to provide seemingly safe 13-pt lead. Then, Ohio State QB Greg Frey (24-37/281y, TD) led drive that ended with 5y TD run by TB Carlos Snow (21/90, 2 TDs). LSU, making its 1st visit to Columbus since 1935, was next held on downs deep in its end as clock ticked down. Bengals elected to take safety to maintain 33-29 lead. Bucks WR Bobby Olive returned ensuing free-kick 32y to LSU 38YL. Frey completed 3 straight passes, his 20y TD to Olive ending Tigers' 14-game road win streak.

SOUTHERN CALIFORNIA 23 Oklahoma 7: Oklahoma coach Barry Switzer fell to 0-3-1 lifetime against Trojans (3-0), as USC D allowed 89y rushing, 222y overall, and forced 6 TOs. Clash of powers ended early as Trojans built 20-0 lead in 1st H in which Sooners' avg starting point was own 14YL. Oklahoma (2-1) QB Jamelle Holieway lost 2 FUMs, 1 after nasty hit by LB Junior Seau, within own 20YL led to 10 pts, while his INT was converted into FG for USC. Trojans QB Rodney Peete (16-34/198y, INT) had brilliant 22y run on 3rd-and-20 in 1st Q to keep scoring sortie alive. Holieway's best moment occurred in 3rd Q, when brilliant fake allowed WR Eric Bross to get open for 48y pass that set up 2y TD run by FB Leon Perry. That was it for Oklahoma as Troy CB Chris Hale, beaten on Bross' catch, picked off 2 passes by QB Charles Thompson, 2nd of which led to another Trojans FG. Peete moved past Charles White (6,462y to 6,240y) to become USC's all-time total O leader to date.

Wyoming 48 AIR FORCE 45: Frosh K Sean Fleming hit 27y FG at clock's last tick to keep Cowboys (4-0) perfect 90 secs after coach Paul Roach conservatively opted for tying x-pt after FB Steve Bena's 9y TD run. Fortunately for Wyoming, Air Force QB Dee Dowis (27/208y, 2 TDs rushing) lost FUM on own 42YL with 45 secs left. Cowboys QB Randy Weiniak (28-43/359y, 3 TDs, and 108y, TD rushing), who set school-record with 467y total O, led winning drive that included 14y pass to WR Freddy Dussett. Dowis, who sparked suddenly-resilient Falcons (2-2) to 4 TDs in 3rd Q for 38-17 lead, had raced 69y for go-ahead TD with 2:42 left.

AP Poll September 26

1 Miami (55)	1193	11 Clemson	609
2 UCLA (3)	1130	12 Alabama	568
3 Southern California (2)	1050	13 Oklahoma State	407
4 Auburn	1001	14 Louisiana State	403
5 Notre Dame	902	15 Georgia	388
6 Florida State	815	16 Washington	286
7 West Virginia	791	17 Florida	240
8 South Carolina	742	18 Wyoming	160
9 Nebraska	727	19 Michigan	155
10 Oklahoma (2)	620	20 Oregon	82

October 1, 1988

FLORIDA 19 Louisiana State 6: Gators D, near perfect against weak competition, quieted its critics against LSU (2-2) team with 31-pt scoring avg. Florida held Tigers QB Tommy Hodson to 72y passing with 3 INTs, 2 contributed by CB Richard Fain, including 32y TD RET and other for 36y to set up FG. RB Emmitt Smith (27/132y) topped century mark for 8th straight game and became 2nd fastest to reach 2,000y in career rushing (16 games) behind Herschel Walker. K John David Francis kicked 4 FGs for Florida, while K David Browndyke accounted for 2 Tigers FGs. Gators enjoyed their 1st 5-0 start since 1969.

Illinois 31 OHIO STATE 12: Illini (2-2) gave coach John Mackovic great 45th birthday present with team's 1st win in Columbus since 1967. Illinois QB Jeff George threw for 224y, with 24y TD to WR Steven Williams. Buckeyes (2-2) QB Greg Frey threw 13y TD to WR Jeff Graham, but Illinois D held Ohio to 38y rushing. Illini S Mark Kelly blocked punt and made 2 sacks and FUM REC that set up 53y TD drive late in 3rd Q, capped by 5y run by FB Howard Griffith for 17-6 lead. Ohio was forced to punt on next series, but snap eluded P Jeff Bohlman deep in own end. Bohlman tried to kick ball through EZ for safety but Illini S Pat Donnelly fell on it for TD.

NOTRE DAME 42 Stanford 14: Rushing for 341y, Notre Dame (4-0) crushed Stanford as QB Tony Rice led Irish with 107y rushing with 2 TDs. Rice also surprised Cardinal (1-3) with his passing prowess, completing 11-14/129y, TD. Rice tossed 3y TD pass to TE Derek Brown for 35-7 lead early in 2nd H. Stanford QB Jason Palumbis threw for 158y and 27y TD pass to WR Henry Green.

Houston 27 BAYLOR 24: Wild game ended on Houston (3-0) CB Johnny Jackson's INT with 4 secs left to end late Baylor rally. Bears (3-2) had taken 14-10 H lead on 2 TD passes from QB Brad Goebel to WR John Simpson. After Baylor added 2 pts, Cougars (3-0) struck back for 17 pts in row: RB Chuck Weatherspoon scored on 13y run and QB David Dacus threw TD pass, 22y winner to WR Jason Phillips. Goebel's 3rd TD pass and Baylor's REC of onside-KO set up Jackson's late deeds.

Ucla 24 WASHINGTON 17: Favored Bruins (4-0) needed 2 TDs in 4th Q TDs, last on 48y QB Troy Aikman-to-WR Reggie Moore pass with 88 secs left. It was UCLA's 1st time in Seattle since 1978. On play before his late TD, Aikman scrambled for 9y on 3rd-and-8. He then avoided blitz to hit Moore on 32YL, with WR outracing CB Art Malone to EZ. Huskies (3-1) blew chance to take lead after reaching Bruins 19YL, where poor snap on 3rd down led to loss and then fake FG play produced disastrous -4y on pass from QB Cary Conklin (19-37/163y) to FB Tony Covington. UCLA TB Eric Ball ground out 107y rushing and scored TD.

AP Poll October 3

1 Miami (53)	1153	11 Clemson	574
2 UCLA (3)	1088	12 Alabama	501
3 Southern California (2)	1037	13 Oklahoma State	485
4 Auburn	959	14 Florida	424
5 Notre Dame	910	15 Georgia	395
6 Florida State	778	16 Wyoming	237
7 West Virginia	758	17 Michigan	196
8 South Carolina	732	18 Oregon	132
9 Nebraska	692	19 Washington	128
10 Oklahoma (2)	606	20 Arkansas	82

October 8, 1988

SYRACUSE 34 Rutgers 20: Big O show saw Syracuse (4-1) rack up 515y, and Rutgers (3-2) advance for 348y. All this was accomplished by leadership of team's QBs: Scarlet Knights QB Scott Erney pitched 204y, while his Orangemen opposite, QB Todd

Philcox, tied school record with 4 TD passes among his 268y in air. Neither team could get it into EZ in early going as Rutgers settled for K Carmen Sciafani's 24y FG for 9-6 lead late in 2nd Q. Then, Syracuse set sail as WR Rob Moore caught passes of 17 and 28y to boost 73y trip to TE Pat Davis' 4y catch of misdirection pass. INT by Orange DB Jeff Buskirk set up Moore's TD pass, Syracuse's 2nd TD in last 93 secs. Moore caught pair of scoring passes in 2nd H.

LOUISIANA STATE 7 Auburn 6: Auburn K Win Lyle kicked FGs of 41y and 33y, so "Blue Tigers" led 6-0 as time wound down. LSU (3-2) QB Tommy Hodson (17-38/167y, TD) had work cut out for him late in 4th Q. After moving ball 55y, Bengals faced 4th-and-9 at Auburn (4-1) 20YL on only their 2nd trip across midfield. Hodson hit clutch 10y pass to TE Willie Williams, before finding TB Eddie Fuller in back of EZ, but play was ruled OB. After 2 more incompletions, Hodson went back to Fuller for winning TD pass.

Mississippi 22 ALABAMA 12: Mississippi (2-3) pulled stunner, roaring back from 12-0 deficit with 3 TDs in 2nd H, 2 scores coming in game's final min. Rebels TB Shawn Sykes scored on 53y run in 3rd Q and added 12y TD run with 50 secs left for Ole Miss' 1st lead at 15-12. Alabama (3-1) QB Jeff Dunn then lost FUM, which led to 18y TD run by Rebs FB Joe Mickles. Ole Miss D kept its EZ clean: Bama's sole 6-pter came on 100y KO RET by WR Pierre Goode that opened 3rd Q after scoreless 1st H. Tide managed only 8 1st downs and did not complete pass as Dunn went 0-7 and backup QB Vince Sutton threw 0-4.

Memphis State 17 FLORIDA 11: Huge road upset was helped by decimation suffered by Florida backfield. Memphis D was aggressive against run, task made easier by left knee sprain suffered by Gators (5-1) RB Emmitt Smith (25/89y) in 3rd Q. Add QB Kyle Morris' broken finger, and Gators' O was hurting. Morris (10-24/125y, 3 INTs) injured himself knocking CB Glenn Rogers OB after Tigers DB returned clinching INT 49y. Gators trailed by 3 at that time, were within FG range, and gunning for TD. Memphis State (3-3) RB Xavier Crawford (13/76y) scored winning TD in 3rd on 11y run that capped 77y drive. Tigers head coach Charlie Bailey had been former D coordinator for Gators, and his knowledge fueled surprisingly result.

INDIANA 41 Ohio State 7: TB Anthony Thompson put on record-breaking show for Indiana (4-0-1), rushing for 190y and scoring 4 TDs in 1st H to set school game (24), season (86), and career (186) pt totals. QB Dave Schnell and WR Rob Turner added TD hook-ups of 31y and 38y, while Hoosiers D contributed 4 INTs. FB James Bryant led Buckeyes with 98y rushing and team's sole TD, but he could not prevent team's worst series loss ever. It was Ohio's 1st loss to Indiana in Bloomington since 1904, span of 14 visits. Indiana now had won consecutive series games for 1st time since 1913, while team enjoyed biggest margin of victory in conf game since 1945.

MICHIGAN 17 Michigan State 3: Spartans (0-4-1) continued their horrific start as team gained 151y and failed to add to its 3-TD total scored all year. Wolverines (3-2) rushed for 249y, while K Mike Gillette scored 11 pts—including TD on 40y run with fake punt—to overtake Tom Harmon and Anthony Carter as school's career pts leader with 247. Down 10-0 in 3rd Q, S John Miller gave Spartans hope with 48y RET of INT to Michigan 5YL. After 2 runs failed, QB Bobby McAllister scrambled to 1YL from where coach George Perles opted for FG. Michigan State got no closer than midfield rest of way.

Oklahoma 28 Texas 13 (Dallas): After Texas (3-2) cut Sooners (4-1) lead to 14-7, Oklahoma LB Kert Kaspar seemed to put Longhorns away with 26y INT TD RET. But, Horns concocted drives ending with 48y and 44y FGs by K Wayne Clements, to stay in game at 21-13. Oklahoma QB Charles Thompson, who entered game when QB Jamelle Holieway sprained his ankle in 1st Q, scored from 8y out with 6:53 left to cap 81y drive. FB Leon Perry rumbled for 118y for Sooners, while HB Anthony Stafford ran for 4/97y, mostly on 86y TD run in 1st Q.

Oklahoma State 41 COLORADO 21: Cowboys (4-0) reeled off 24 straight pts in 1st H, converting 7 consecutive 3rd downs en route to 3 TD runs by TB Barry Sanders. Buffaloes sandwiched that streak with pair of TDs of their own, both on runs by QB Sal Aunese, to trail by 24-14 at H. Sanders (24/174y, 4 TDs) was far from finished, however, racing 65y for score on early carry in 3rd Q. Colorado was victim of its own sloppy play, losing 6 TOs that led to 5 Oklahoma State scores.

SOUTHERN CALIFORNIA 42 Oregon 14: Trojans (5-0) avenged 1987 upset loss with wipeout of Oregon that played without injured QB Bill Musgrave. Southern California grabbed 21-0 H lead with each of its TDs following TO by Ducks (4-1). USC earned wide margin on O: 564y to 112y total O and 27 to 8 in 1st downs despite absence of top rushers, TBs Ricky Ervins and Aaron Emanuel. Trojans QB Rodney Peete (17-33/270y, INT) connected with WR John Jackson (7/155y) on 2 TDs. Oregon, who alternated QBs Pete Nelson (10-18/70y, INT) and Bob Brothers (3-11/19y, 2 INTs) with poor results, might have been shut out without its special teams. Ducks CB Chris Oldham had 99y KO TD RET, and WR Terry Obee set up TB Derek Loville's 1y TD run with 36y punt RET.

October 15, 1988

Syracuse 24 PENN STATE 10: After snapping 16-game losing streak to Penn State in 1987, Syracuse (4-1) claimed Beast of East status. Orange QB Todd Philcox threw for 286y and 2 2nd H TDs, while K Kevin Greene kicked 3 FGs. Philcox's 1st TD, 6y pass to WR Deval Glover, came moments after LB Roger Carges stripped ball away from Penn State (4-2) TB Gary Brown: Syracuse S Jeff Mangram recovered at Penn State 12YL. Nittany Lions had 7-6 H lead, but mustered little O all day. QB Tony Sacca was 15-27/209y, but suffered 5 sacks. Syracuse improved its regular season slate to 17 wins in last of 18 games.

CLEMSON 49 Duke 17: Tigers (5-1) jumped on upstart Duke and continued to build rout. Clemson D kept Duke (5-1) QB Anthony Dilweg (18-41/209y, TD, 2 INTs) well in check, holding him to under 300y for 1st time all season. Clemson FB Tracy Johnson scored twice, and TB Terry Allen rushed for 134y. WR Gary Cooper caught only 2 passes, but they both went for scores including 79y TD on trick-play throw from backup QB DeChance Cameron, who snuck into game at TB. CB Quinton McCracken returned kickoff 96y to put Blue Devils on scoreboard in 2nd Q.

Wake Forest 27 MARYLAND 24: Wake Forest (4-2) rallied with 2 TDs in 4th Q, including game-winning 1y plunge by TB Tony Rogers. On his way airborne to EZ, Rogers lost ball, recovered by T Rod Ferguson to set up presumed 4th down try, until officials surprised even Wake O with decision that Rogers had broken plane of EZ for TD. Deacons QB Mike Elkins (31-43/345y) followed with 2-pt conv pass to TB Mark Young for 27-24 lead with 86 secs left. Terps (3-3) had time to march upfield behind QB Neil O'Donnell (19-31/199y, INT), reaching Demon Deacons 7YL until time ran out. Maryland had built 17-6 H lead, with big strike TB Mike Beasley's 37y TD run. Wake D posted 2nd H shutout, as Terps scored on 86y INT RET by DB Irvin Smith.

GEORGIA TECH 34 South Carolina 0: Although it sported 15-game winless streak vs Div. 1-A opponents, Georgia Tech (2-4) owned nation's top-rated pass D. Yellow Jackets' aerial net sparkled, picking off 4 passes by South Carolina (6-1) QB Todd Ellis (151y passing), including 51y TD RET by S Andre Thomas (2 INTs, 9 tackles). QB Todd Rampley (14-22/170y) led scoring drives of 79y and 88y—with help from TB Jerry Mays (30/125y)—as Georgia Tech grabbed 31-0 H lead.

IOWA 17 Michigan 17: Tie could not be avoided as each team suffered huge 2nd H FUM near opponent's GL. Wolverines (3-2-1) were especially heartbroken as TB Tracy Williams lost ball on 1YL with 1:21 left. QB Chuck Hartlieb (26-33/263y, TD) then drove Iowa (3-2-2) downfield before final play, desperation pass to TE Marv Cook (9/111y), was batted down. Earlier, coach Haden Fry, with 17-10 lead, went for TD on 4th-and-goal from 1YL but RB Tony Stewart lost FUM in mid-dive, QB Michael Taylor (13-22/172y) led Michigan on tying, 13-play drive that culminated with Taylor's 24y pass to WR John Kolesar. Michigan TB Tony Boles rushed for 148y.

GAME OF THE YEAR
NOTRE DAME 31 Miami 30:

Game was billed as "Catholics vs. Convicts"—at least on Notre Dame's campus where many T-shirts carried slogan—although they all looked like convicts during pre-game shoving match. It prompted ND coach Lou Holtz to publicly question continuation of volatile series. Fighting Irish (6-0) victory was not secured until DB Pat Terrell knocked down 2-pt conv pass from Miami QB Steve Walsh (31-50/424y, 4TDs, 3 INTs) to FB Shannon Crowell with 45 secs left. Terrell had memorable day as he scored on INT RET for 21-7 lead in 2nd Q, INT coming on deflection by LB Frank Stams (2 forced FUMs, 8 tackles) that was 1 of 7 TOs on day for Hurricanes (4-1). Walsh quickly threw 2 TDs in final 2:30 of 1st H to tie score at 21-21. After Notre Dame increased lead to 31-24 late in 4th Q, converting INT by DT Jeff Alm into 27y FG by K Reggie Ho, Canes committed most controversial TO. Miami drove downfield until RB Cleveland Gary (11/130y receiving) caught ball near GL and was hit by DB George Streeter. Ball popped loose, was recovered as FUM by ND LB Michael Stonebreaker. Hurricanes felt it should have been ruled incomplete. Teams exchanged FUMs before Walsh, who set personal mark and record for Irish opponent for passing y, hit WR Andre Brown on 4th-and-6 for 7y TD to set up final 2-pt pass try that decided outcome. Notre Dame QB Tony Rice (8-16/195y, INT) had TDs passing and running. Miami's 36-game regular season win streak ended and it also was disappointed to allow Rice to score 1st running TD of season against D.

Texas Tech 38 RICE 36: Teams combined for SWC record 1,109y, although Rice needed few more to keep its late rally alive. Red Raiders (2-4) led 31-14 entering 4th Q, before Owls scored TDs on final 3 possessions. Texas Tech IB James Gray, who rushed for 181y, scored on 46y run midway through 4th Q for winning TD that lifted team's pt total to 38. Texas Tech QB Billy Joe Tolliver threw 3 TD passes, 2 to WR Tyrone Thurman, who also scored on 75y punt RET. QB Quentis Roper paced Owls (0-5) with 277y passing and 105y rushing.

NEBRASKA 63 Oklahoma State 42: Ds got workout as teams, 1-2 in pts per game, played to capabilities. Huskers (6-1) IB Ken Clark rushed 27/256y, 3 TDs, and QB Steve Taylor (11/140y rushing) accounted for 5 TDs. Cowboys (4-1) brilliant TB Barry Sanders rushed 35/189y and scored 4 TDs. But Sanders' scores came too late: Nebraska threw early KO punch to lead 42-0 early in 2nd Q. In 1st Q, both Taylor and Clark ran in 2 scores apiece, 3 of which were on runs of 43y and longer. Nebraska DB Charles Fryar took INT RET 86y for TD. Final score looked respectable, thanks to efforts of illustrious Cowboys trio of Sanders, QB Mike Gundy (17-30/247y, 2 TDs), and WR Hart Lee Dykes (7/125, TD).

SOUTHERN CALIFORNIA 28 Washington 27: Failed 2-pt conv was difference as Trojans (6-0) survived near-perfect 2nd H by Washington (4-2) QB Cary Conklin. Despite dislocated thumb, Conklin hit 15-19/239y, 3 TDs in 2nd H, but had pass he would take back. Conklin underthrew TB Vince Weathersby on 2-pt conv attempt after

late TD. USC led entire way as TB Scott Lockwood, subbing for 3 injured teammates, rushed for 133y with 4y TD run serving as ignition. QB Rodney Peete (16-22/186y, TD) excelled, although FUM on sack at own 2YL led to Huskies' 1st score: Conklin's 1y keeper cut lead to 14-7. Peete bounced back with TD pitch to TE Scott Galbraith, while Conklin hit WR Brian Slater (6/155y) with all 3 TD passes.

October 22, 1988

ARMY 34 RUTGERS 24: Riding wind to 3 straight TDs in 2nd Q, resurgent Cadets (6-1) knocked off favored Rutgers (4-3). HB Mike Mayweather rushed for 115y, 3 TDs as Army gained 378y on ground. Scarlet Knights (4-3) rallied with 24 pts in 2nd H, but had dug too big hole in 1st H. Said Rutgers coach Dick Anderson, "Army outplayed us in every phase. They played aggressive, physical, hustling, disciplined football."

WEST VIRGINIA 59 Boston College 19: That West Virginia (7-0) trailed 9-7 after 1st Q was easily forgotten after QB Major Harris (18-21/297y, INT) led easy romp. Boston College (2-5) had no answer for Harris, who led Mountaineers to 8 TDs including 3 he threw and 2 he ran in. Harris rushed for 75y and set school record total O mark with 372y. Eagles had taken early lead on 36y FG by K Brian Lowe and 63y TD run by FB Ed Toner. BC TB Mike Sanders rushed for 142y and 14y TD, while West Virginia TB Undra Johnson rushed for 111y, TD and had TD receiving.

NORTH CAROLINA STATE 10 Clemson 3: Wolfpack (6-1) had Clemson's number for 3rd straight season as TB Chris Williams ran in winning 5y TD early in 4th Q. Bad snap on Tigers P attempt set up Williams' TD as 35y loss on play gave Pack 1st down on Clemson 21YL. NC State needed that break as O gained only 185y. Tigers also struggled moving ball against nation's top-ranked D. Clemson QB Rodney Williams passed 4-23 with 3 INTs by NC State defenders. While Clemson K-P Chris Gardocki was blameless on punt snap snafu, he missed 2 40y FGs after kicking 35y effort in 1st Q. Tigers TB Terry Allen led ground attack with so-so 67y.

Virginia 34 WAKE FOREST 14: Virginia (3-4) QB Shawn Moore put on show, breaking Cavs' game total O record by 20y with 396y. Moore completed 14-22/315y and TDs of 28y to WR Herman Moore and 19y to WR Tim Finkleston, while rushing for 81y and 1y TD. Converting 3 of Wake Forest's 5 TOs into 17 pts in 1st H, Virginia pulled away. Deacons (4-3) had trailed only 10-7 after QB Mike Elkins (17-39/242y, 2 TDs, 4 INTs) hit WR Ricky Proehl for 36y TD in 2nd Q. Moore then ran for and threw TDs to grab 24-7 H lead.

ALABAMA 8 Penn State 3: It was day of frustration for Penn State (4-3), when even sole penetration of Tide EZ, 1st Q QB Tony Sacca pass to WR Michael Timpson, was nullified by PEN. Crimson Tide (5-1) O was not much better, managing 2 FGs by K Phillip Doyle, including 35y boot to snap 3-3 tie in 3rd Q. Bama D was brilliant, even scoring 2 on safety on sack by LB Derrick Thomas (8 tackles, 3 sacks) early in 4th Q. After losing 3-3 tie, Penn State managed pathetic -9y rest of game, only 169y on day. Alabama TB Murry Hill rushed for 137y, and QB David Smith threw for 186y.

KENTUCKY 16 Georgia 10: Georgia native TB Alfred Rawls (15/128y) rambled 48y for winning TD in 3rd Q as Wildcats (3-4) pulled stunner. Bulldogs (5-2) had 3 more series after Rawls' TD run, but managed only solo 1st down before Rawls rushed 5 straight times to eat clock at game's end. TB Tim Worley led way for Georgia with 99y rushing, but Kentucky won O battle, 368y to 224y. Rawls originally signed with Georgia, but was rejected due to HS grades and after 2 years at JC, spurned Bulldogs for matriculation in Lexington. Georgia LB Richard Tardits had 4 sacks.

Michigan State 28 ILLINOIS 21: Spartans (2-4-1) scored 28 straight pts to wrest control. QB Bobby McAllister threw 2 TD passes, including 63y bomb to WR Andre Rison (4/107y) that hit paydirt despite floating in breeze. TB Blake Ezor (30/113y) rushed for 2 scores as Michigan State majestically transformed 14-0 deficit into 28-14 lead. With meager running attack, Illinois (4-3) QB Jeff George had to throw 34-55/316y, including opening 4y TD pass to WR Shawn Wax. Michigan State P John Butland excelled with 7/47y avg.

MICHIGAN 31 Indiana 6: Wolverines (4-2-1) used trick play of all things to break open 10-6 ballgame. WR Greg McMurtry, who received ball from TB Tony Boles on what appeared to be reverse, threw 46y TD pass to WR Chris Calloway. Hoosiers (5-1-1) tried to rally behind QB Dave Schnell, who suffered bruised tailbone in 1st H; they could not add to 53y and 45y FGs kicked by K Pete Stoyanovich. While Wolverines were scoring 17 pts in decisive 3rd Q, Indiana was managing 4 punts, INT, and only single 1st down. Hoosiers TB Anthony Thompson, nation's 2nd leading rusher, was held to 20/68y by Michigan D. FB Leroy Hoard led Michigan with 128y rushing and 3 TDs, with all but 20y coming on two 54y scoring bursts in 2nd H.

Arkansas 26 HOUSTON 21: Arkansas (7-0) continued to slice through SWC, holding off Cougars thanks to brilliant 95y drive in 4th Q for clinching 9y TD run by RB Joe Johnson. Hogs QB Quinn Grovey, in relief of QB John Bland, led 16-play drive that took wind out of sails of Houston (4-2). Cougars scored once more on 1y TD pass from QB Andre Ware (20-32/245y, 2 INT) to WR Jason Phillips, before coming up with loose ball on onside-KO that frustratingly was ruled dead before FUM by Arkansas S

Steve Atwater. Although Cougars decried call and other PENs, Hogs won by controlled ball for more than 42 mins, keeping it away from potent Houston O. Razorbacks K Kendall Trainor booted 4 FGs for 15 straight.

Oklahoma 17 COLORADO 14: First night game in Folsom Field history ended with missed 62y FG attempt by Buffs (5-2) K Ken Culbertson. Winning FG, much more realistic 22y effort by Oklahoma (6-1) K R.D. Lashar with 8:15 left, was set up by crucial 3rd down runs of 21y by HB Eric Mitchel and 17y by QB Charles Thompson. Sooners (6-1) lost late FUM at midfield while trying to run out clock, recovered by Colorado S Bruce Young. Buffs PEN wiped out big gain, then sack pushed back Culbertson's 3-pt attempt. QB Sal Aunese threw for 184y, and TB Eric Bieniemy rushed for 114y to lead Colorado O, while 6 different players rushed for at least 40y to pace Sooners attack that gained 360y on ground.

IOWA STATE 42 Kansas 14: Appropriately, Cyclones (4-3) took advantage of severe windy conditions. Key may have been 3rd score for Iowa State, which, after scoring 2 TDs with wind, was able to reach EZ against it—only 1 of 8 TDs going into gales—for 21-0 lead. Kansas (0-7) scored twice with wind in 2nd Q but then allowed 21 pts in 3rd Q, with Cyclones TDs following punts of 9y and 13y. ISU FB Joe Henderson rushed for 141y and 4 TDs and added 3/52y in receptions including 19y TD. Kansas QB Kelly Donohue threw for 218y and rushed for both Jayhawks TDs.

Brigham Young 24 HAWAII 23: Hawaii (5-2) scored 2 TDs in final 4 mins, converting fumbled punt and onside-KO REC. Going for 2 after 38y TD pass from QB Warren Jones to WR Chris Roscoe, Rainbows handed off to TB Heikoti Fakava (126y rushing), who was halted by BYU DBs Troy Long and Scott Peterson. Cougars (6-1) had built lead as QB Sean Covey (10-16/130y) threw 2 TD arrows in 1st H before leaving with injury. BYU replacement QB Ty Detmer added 71y TD pass to WR Chuck Cutler (5/133y).

Ucla 24 ARIZONA 3: Bruins (7-0) celebrated no. 1 AP ranking, 1st since 1967, as QB Troy Aikman (20-29/283y, 3 TDs, INT) threw for at least 3 TDs for 5th time in 1988. By end of 1st Q, with UCLA driving to 2nd TD, Aikman had already thrown for 115y. Lead of 14-0 was plenty for Uclan D that allowed only 219y and last-min 35y FG by K Doug Pfaff. Arizona extended its scoring streak to 187 games on Pfaff's boot, 2nd active in country to UCLA's 200. Cats FB Art Greathouse rushed for 56y.

October 29, 1988

WEST VIRGINIA 51 Penn State 30: West Virginia (8-0) delighted record 66,811 crowd with 41-8 1st H lead, scoring on 7 of 8 drives, before settling for most pts scored against Penn State since 1944. WVU QB Major Harris (12-20/230y) set tone by scoring from 26y out on broken play during 1st possession. Harris hit on 2 long TD passes, 40y to WR Reggie Rembert and 49y to WR Calvin Phillips. With 49 secs left, joyous Mountaineers fans poured on field after CB Tim Newsom's 4th down sack of Penn State (4-4) QB Lance Lonergan, who ran and threw for TDs in valiant, but futile 22-pt spree in 2nd H. Mountaineers' win ended longest yearly, non-winning series streak in country: Penn State had defeated border rival WVU every year since 1956 with tie in 1958 as only bump in country roads.

South Carolina 23 NORTH CAROLINA STATE 7: With steroid scandal swirling, South Carolina (7-1) took its frustrations out on Wolfpack with 356y against nation's top-rated D. South Carolina LB Patrick Hinton (3 INTs, FUM REC) broke up 1st H punting show—teams combined for 11 punts in 30 mins—with INT he returned 83y for game's opening score. With robust Gamecocks D continuing to control game, they pulled away on strength of 3 FGs in 2nd H by K Collin Mackie and 20y TD pass by QB Todd Ellis to WR Eddie Miller. North Carolina State (6-2) WR Naz Worthen was brilliant in defeat, catching 10/141y before leaving with 3rd Q injury.

Auburn 16 FLORIDA 0: Auburn (7-1) TB Stacy Danley (29/131y) outgained and outscored depleted Gators O (116y) all by himself, scoring clincher from 10y out in 4th Q. Danley stumbled on TD run, which froze D waiting for him to fall. K Win Lyle had 3 FGs as Tigers won for 1st time in Gainesville since 1972. Auburn D, ranked 2nd in nation, surrendered only 13y rushing and had 3 INTs in tossing 3rd straight shutout. Florida (5-3) lost game of field position as Auburn P Brian Shulman pinned them within own 12YL on 5 occasions. Gators D pressured Tigers passing attack, sacking QB Reggie Slack 3 times and holding him to 35y passing.

INDIANA 45 Iowa 34: Red-hot Hoosiers (6-1-1) rode strong back of TB Anthony Thompson, who rushed for 168y and 3 TDs, to help build huge 35-3 lead in 1st H. Indiana QB Dave Schnell pitched in too, throwing for 185y and 2 TDs, while rushing for another score. Indiana needed all of those pts as Iowa (4-3-2) QB Chuck Hartlieb shook off 5 sacks to rally troops. Hartlieb set 3 school records by passing 44-60/558y and clicking on 3 TD throws. TB Nick Bell added 13 catches for Hawkeyes in setting another school record.

NEBRASKA 26 Missouri 18: Huskers (8-1) needed big blocks from mammoth O-line to pull out win in game's late going. Before that, Mizzou D, led by S Otis Smith, made Nebraska QB Steve Taylor miserable. Missouri (2-5-1) led 6-0 at H with Nebraska O amazingly held to 15y. After Taylor suffered his 2nd FUM on opening drive of 2nd H,

Tigers upped lead to 9-0 on K Jeff Jacke's 3rd FG. Broken play then got Big Red going as Taylor found TE Todd Millikan for 82y TD pass. Later in 3rd Q, Nebraska converted FUM into 1y TD run by IB Tyreese Knox for 14-9 lead. Mizzou answered with HB Michael Jones' 3y TD run on 4th down. Teams traded FGs, and Huskers burned blitz with 49y TD trap run by FB Bryan Carpenter.

Washington State 34 UCLA 30: Cougars (5-3) scored 28 pts in 2nd H to shock top-ranked UCLA. Bruins (7-1) drove to Washington State 6YL with 35 secs left, but could not score as QB Troy Aikman (27-44/325y, TD, INT) misfired on 4 straight passes after having been intercepted on previous drive. UCLA's most painful TO, however, probably was TB Eric Ball's FUM on own 37YL, with Bruins up 27-13, which led to 2nd of 4 straight Cougars TDs. Wazzu QB Timm Rosenbach threw for 272y, including 81y TD bomb to WR Tim Stallworth that later tied game at 27-27. Cougars TB Rick Swinton (117y rushing) scored winning 1y TD with 6:21 left.

Arizona State 21 OREGON 20: Arizona State (5-3) won nail-biter as TB Bruce Perkins rushed for 134y, including winning 39y TD burst in 3rd Q. Ducks (6-2) had been ahead 14-7 after 1st Q as QB Bill Musgrave (6-10/97y) threw 27y TD pass to WR Terry Obee (5/81y). But, reliable Musgrave left in 2nd Q with broken collarbone. Sun Devils tied game at 14-14 in 2nd Q on 2nd TD pass by QB Paul Justin (10-18/146y, INT) to TE Ryan McReynolds and then took 21-14 lead on Perkins' score. Oregon tallied on 27y TD pass from sub QB Pete Nelson to FB Latin Berry, but Nelson misfired on 2-pt try. Sloppy Ducks lost 7 TOs to only 1 for ASU.

AP Poll October 31

1 Notre Dame (44)	1144		11 Arkansas	564	
2 Southern California (11)	1097		12 Oklahoma State	490	
3 Miami (1)	1041		13 Louisiana State	379	
4 West Virginia (2)	950		14 Michigan	352	
5 Florida State	886		15 South Carolina	301	
6 UCLA	847		16 Syracuse	281	
7 Nebraska	835		17 Clemson	266	
8 Oklahoma	739		18 Alabama	216	
9 Auburn	715		19 Georgia	162	
10 Wyoming	658		20t Brigham Young	81	
			20t Indiana	81	

November 5, 1988

ARMY 28 Air Force 15: Neither wind nor rain could stop Black Knights (7-1) from bowl-clinching win. In battle of wishbones, Army dominated as HB Mike Mayweather rushed for 192y with 52y on run in 2nd Q that set up 1y scoring run by FB Ben Barnett. That TD gave Cadets lead for good at 14-7, with QB Bryan McWilliams making it 21-7 with 4y keeper. Mayweather added 1y insurance TD run before Air Force (5-4) QB Dee Dowis threw his 2nd TD pass—21y toss to WR Greg Cochrun—to close scoring.

Florida State 59 SOUTH CAROLINA 0: Florida State (8-1) QB Peter Tom Willis had enjoyable 1st start of season, throwing for 4 TDs as Noles handed Carolina its worst home loss ever. After 2 plays, Willis already had hit WR Terry Anthony with 44y bomb. Rolling out to avoid blitzing South Carolina D, Willis picked apart harried DBs to tune of 17-20/271y, 4 TDs passing. Florida State gained 638y and never had to punt. Gamecocks (6-2) QB Todd Ellis (9-22/79y) threw 2 picks in miserable afternoon, while TB Harold Green rushed for 77y and caught 3/39y.

Georgia 26 Florida 3 (Jacksonville): For stumbling Gators (5-4), this game was better left forgotten. Georgia (7-2) TB Tim Worley rushed for 135y and 2 TDs to break 1000y mark for season. Bulldogs D was keyed by LB Demetrius Douglas, in lineup due to injuries, and Douglas came up big with 2 INTs and forced FUM. Douglas' 1st INT set up winning pts: 22y TD pass from QB Wayne Johnson to WR John Thomas in 2nd Q. Florida TB Emmitt Smith returned from sprained knee to rush 19/68y.

Louisiana State 19 ALABAMA 18: It took entire game but Tigers (7-2) came back from 15-0 deficit to win on K David Browndyke's 34y FG with 28 secs on clock. Taking 7-0 lead, Tigers scored TD on 3y TD run by FB Jay Egloff, capping 69y drive led by hot backup QB Mickey Guidry (4-4/44y). Score favored Alabama (6-2) by 15-7 at H. Starting LSU QB Tommy Hodson (12-23/222, 3 INTs) returned to lead 3 scoring drives in 2nd H, including his 48y scoring toss to WR Tony Moss (6/133y). Hodson and Moss combined on 2/41y on winning drive. For 1st time since dreadful days of 1955, Crimson Tide had lost 2 games in Bryant-Denny Stadium in same season. Bama QB David Smith threw for 241y.

ILLINOIS 21 Indiana 20: It was amazing how quickly Rose Bowl hopes slipped away from Hoosiers (6-2-1). Ahead 20-9 with 3:33 to play after CB Erick Coleman returned FUM 47y for TD, Indiana was helpless to stop Illini (5-3-1) QB Jeff George from pulling it out with 2 TD passes. George led 80y drive in only 1:27 that he capped with 4th down, 21y TD to WR Shawn Wax. After missing 2-pt conv try that left it 21-15, Illinois turned to CB Chris Green, who separated Hoosiers QB Dave Schnell from ball at Indiana 30YL with 2 mins to play. With 26 secs left, George hit WR Mike Bellamy in EZ from 5y out for win. Illinois TB Keith Jones rushed for 149y, while Indiana TB Anthony Thompson gained 145y on ground.

Houston 66 TEXAS 15: Worst Texas loss in 85 years was decided early as QB Andre Ware threw 4 TDs as Cougars (6-2) built 35-3 H lead. RB Chuck Weatherspoon rushed 11/218y, including 60y TD run.. Weatherspoon also came up with TD on EZ REC of muffled punt. That play, controversially called in Houston's favor, pushed lead to 21-3 and essentially finished off reeling Longhorns (3-5), losers of 4 straight. Texas TB Eric Metcalf rushed for 104y.

Arkansas 33 BAYLOR 3: Undefeated Razorbacks (9-0) ruined Baylor's Homecoming and stadium renaming festivities—for philanthropist Floyd Casey—as Arkansas O scored on 4 of its 1st 5 possessions. Meanwhile, Razorbacks D kept Bears (4-5) bottled up in their own territory entire game. Arkansas rushing attack churned out 286y

in outgaining Bears 462y to 196y, while all 10 Baylor drives began at or inside own 36YL. Hogs FB Barry Foster scored 2 TDs, while, across way, LB Gary Joe Kinne was bright spot for Baylor D with 17 tackles.

Oklahoma 31 OKLAHOMA STATE 28: Oklahoma (8-1) QB Charles Thompson's excellent relief work continued as he capped winning 13-play, 80y drive with 18y TD run at 2:33 mark in 4th Q. Cowboys (6-2) then raced downfield behind, not TB Barry Sanders who rushed for 215y and 2 TDs, but passing combination of QB Mike Gundy and WR Hart Lee Dykes, who led Oklahoma State from own 9YL to Sooners' 20YL. After foolish 15y personal foul PEN set up 4th-and-16 from 34YL, Gundy threw howitzer to frosh WR Brent Parker that was dropped in EZ. HB Mike Gaddis led Sooners with 213y rushing to almost double his season output (234y). At 4:39 of 1st Q, fast-starting Gaddis already had gained 110y rushing and scored 2 TDs.

AP Poll November 7

1 Notre Dame (42)	1160		11 Arkansas	593
2 Southern California (15)	1122		12 Louisiana State	469
3 Miami (1)	1065		13 Michigan	425
4 West Virginia (1)	979		14 Oklahoma State	386
5 Florida State	933		15 Syracuse	384
6 UCLA	864		16 Clemson	321
7 Nebraska	840		17 Georgia	298
8 Oklahoma	752		18 Alabama	95
9 Auburn	719		19 Colorado	66
10 Wyoming	665		20 Washington State	61

November 12, 1988

West Virginia 35 RUTGERS 25 (East Rutherford, NJ): Despite QB Scott Erney's poor passing performance of 6-19/66y, 3 INTs, Rutgers (4-6) surprisingly led no. 4 Mountaineers by 10-7 midway in 2nd Q, thanks to DB Ron Allen's 92y KO TD RET and K Carmen Sciafani's 35y FG. West Virginia (10-0) QB Major Harris put on his usual spectacular show, rushing 11/71y and passing 7-14/130y, TD. FB Craig Taylor scored pair of key 2nd H TDs to extend WVU's lead to 35-13. Reserve QB Tom Tarver led Rutgers to 2 cosmetic TDs in 4th Q.

Pittsburgh 14 PENN STATE 7: It had been 50 years since Penn State (5-5) suffered losing season, but old rival Pittsburgh (6-3) forced Nittany Lions to brink. Early on, Lions inexperienced sr QB Lance Lonergan (8-19/114y, 3 INTs) was spilled for safety on LB Curtis Bray's blitz. Pitt TB Curvin Richards became 24th frosh to surpass 1,000y in season as he rambled for 31/159y and 6y TD in 2nd Q that provided 8-7 lead. Panthers K Scott Kaplan's 2nd FG wrapped up scoring in 3rd Q. It was Penn State's popgun O, totaling 220y, that left home fans snoozing.

Clemson 49 MARYLAND 25: Tigers (8-2) clinched 3rd straight ACC title in close game broken open by 3-TD spurt over 2:40 span of 4th Q. TB Terry Allen (19/110y) scored 2 of those as Clemson, which gained 373y on ground, took advantage of 2 TOs and blocked punt to put away Terps (5-5). WR Gary Cooper was highly efficient with 2 carries/72y rushing and 2 scores. Maryland QB Neil O'Donnell threw for 175y and TD. Clemson LB Levon Kirkland registered 13 tackles, sack, and INT.

Duke 43 NORTH CAROLINA STATE 43: Duke (6-3-1) scored what it thought was game-winner at 43-40 on 8y TD pass from QB Anthony Dilweg (33-56/357y, 2 INTs) to WR Clarkston Hines with 57 secs left. QB Shane Montgomery then took NC State (6-3-1) from its 11YL to Devils territory, where K Damon Hartman booted tying 37y FG. Montgomery threw for 205y and 3 TDs to WR Naz Worthen (6/140y) while alternating with QB Charles Davenport, who rushed for 66y. Blue Devils TB Roger Boone rushed for 131y and 2 TDs and caught 20y TD pass in 1st Q.

AUBURN 20 Georgia 10: Biggest crowd (85,214) ever in state of Alabama witnessed fine efforts by Auburn (9-1) TB Stacy Danley (172y rushing) and QB Reggie Slack (20-34/263, 2 TDs). Primed for upset, Bulldogs (7-3) marched 85y on 1st possession for 7-0 lead as QB Wayne Johnson's 27y TD strike to WR John Thomas became 1st TD allowed by Auburn D in 1st H all season. Slack tied game with 7y TD pass to WR Lawyer Tillman. Teams exchanged FGs before Tiger D, tops in nation in total y and rushing y, tightened up to punch Bulldogs. Slack threw decisive 6y TD pass to TE Walter Reeves that kept Tigers tied with LSU atop SEC. Georgia TB Tim Worley, SEC's leading rusher, was limited to 63y rushing.

MICHIGAN 38 Illinois 9: Wolverines (7-2-1) clinched conference title as FB Leroy Hoard ran for 137y and 2 TDs and QB Demetrius Brown, starting with QB Michael Taylor injured, completed 8-14 for 101y and TD. Using injuries as inspiration, Michigan marched to 6y TD pass to WR Chris Calloway. Drive included 22y run on faked punt by LB Erick Anderson. K Doug Higgins did scoring for Illini (5-4-1) with 3 FGs, as O moved ball but could not crack EZ. Illini TB Keith Jones rushed for 105y.

ARKANSAS 25 Texas A&M 20: With Texas A&M (5-4) ineligible for conference crown, game had no bearing on SWC race—just don't tell players that. Aggies gained 414y and 22 1st downs but could not pull upset as Arkansas (10-0) scored 25 pts without O TD. K Kendall Trainor led way with 5 FGs to tie SWC record and stretch consecutive mark to league-best 22 straight. A&M contributed to Hogs win by setting up 14 Arkansas pts with TOs, including INT returned 47y to EZ by DB Patrick Williams. Aggie TB Darren Lewis rushed for 192y for 7th straight 100y game.

HOUSTON 34 Wyoming 10: Houston (7-2) DT Glen Montgomery had 6 sacks and 14 tackles to lead D that had 16 sacks in pounding Cowboys out of ranks of unbeaten. QB Randy Welniak (14-31/163y, 2 INTs) went down 9 times in 1st H alone as Wyoming (10-1), leading nation in total O, finished with -37y rushing. Cougar CB Reggie Burnette turned in 3 sacks, INT and FUM recovery. Cougars grabbed 28-3 lead as QB Andre Ware (23-40/295y) threw TD passes of 15y to WR Patrick Cooper and 22y to WR Brian Williams, while K Roman Anderson added career-high 4 FGs.

NEBRASKA 7 Colorado 0: After gaining only 90y in smothering 0-0 1st H, Huskers (10-1) rolled up 101y-25y advantage in 3rd Q including 2y on IB Ken Clark (28/165y) TD. Buffs squandered best scoring opportunity in 1st H as HB J.J. Flanigan (27/133y) broke through Nebraska line seemingly en route to EZ 43y away. Inexplicably, he dropped ball on 19YL. Colorado (7-3) recovered, but lost 19y on reverse 3 plays later that moved them out of FG range, with LB Broderick Thomas snuffing out play.

Southern California 50 ARIZONA STATE 0: USC (9-0) QB Rodney Peete, Arizona native, threw for 23-33/361y, 3 TDs, to set school mark for single-game total O with 377y. Troy D also excelled, preventing Sun Devils (6-4), who had won last 5 of 7 in series, from crossing midfield until 4th Q. Peete continuously rolled out and used play action to free WRs John Jackson (8/86y, TD) and Erik Affholter (8/135y, TD). TB Aaron Emanuel rushed for 88y and TD as Trojans piled up 294y on ground. USC was successful on 15-19 3rd down conversions in handing ASU worst-ever home defeat and worst-ever Pac 10 loss. ASU QB Paul Justin tossed 11-22/104y.

AP Poll November 14

1 Notre Dame (42)	1156	11 Louisiana State	524
2 Southern California (18)	1131	12 Michigan	508
3 Miami (1)	1080	13 Oklahoma State	464
4 West Virginia (1)	977	14 Syracuse	476
5 Florida State	937	15 Clemson	377
6 UCLA	866	16 Wyoming	223
7 Nebraska	805	17 Houston	207
8 Auburn	769	18 Alabama	192
9 Oklahoma	750	19 Washington State	122
10 Arkansas	657	20 Georgia	57

November 19, 1988

WEST VIRGINIA 31 Syracuse 9: Mountaineers (11-0) wrapped up 1st perfect regular season since 1922 in style. QB Major Harris sparkled as usual, leading O that cracked 30-pt total for 10th time in 1988 and set new school record with 472 pts. Harris ran for 96y and picked up 9 of his team's 14 3rd down conversions on ground. Syracuse (8-2) misfired on numerous occasions, turning ball over 6 times including QB Todd Philcox's morale-killing FUM at WVU 1YL when Orangemen trailed only 7-0. Philcox, who later threw INT returned 49y by Mountaineers CB Willie Edwards for TD, found WR Rob Moore for 16y TD in 4th Q.

Miami 44 LOUISIANA STATE 3: Miami (8-1) handed 11th-ranked Tigers worst home loss since 1948, scoring on 11 of 2 possessions made for 10-0 lead. Hurricanes made Orange Bowl selection committee look good as QB Steve Walsh threw for 220y and 2 TDs, giving him school record with 28 on season. Miami RB Cleveland Gary officially scored twice, on 31y run and 8y reception, but earlier he also took 18y pass to GL before fumbling. WR Randal Hill made REC for Canes' opening TD. LSU (7-3) had 4 drives reach red zone, but produced only K David Browndyke's 27y FG. Bengals QB Tom Hodson threw for 238y.

NOTRE DAME 21 Penn State 3: Irish (10-0) put away game in 3rd Q as QB Tony Rice, who threw for 191y and rushed for 84y, hooked up with WR Raghib Ismail on 67y TD pass play. With young, struggling O, Nittany Lions (5-6) could not play catch-up football. Winners outgained Penn State 502y to 179y, gaining 84y on 1st possession capped by Rice's 2y keeper. Lions QB Lance Lonergan hit on only 3-16/39y. Penn State K Eric Etze's 52y FG prevented shutout, but couldn't avert Penn State's 1st losing season in 50 years.

Michigan 34 OHIO STATE 31: Wild game ended with Michigan LB Marc Spencer's saving INT in final min. It was all Wolverines (8-2-1) in 1st H as they took 20-0 lead. Buckeyes (4-6-1) roared back in 2nd H with 24 straight pts to take lead. Teams traded TDs before WR John Kolesar returned KO 59y and caught game-winning TD pass of 41y from QB Demetrius Brown (11-17/223y). Michigan FB Leroy Hoard rushed for 158y, 2 TDs, while TB Tony Boles added 103y. Ohio State TB Carlos Snow rushed for 170y, TD, but Bucks had to accept 1st losing season since 1966.

Nebraska 7 OKLAHOMA 3: Huskers (11-1) marched 80y with opening possession to go up 7-0 on QB Steve Taylor's 1y QB keeper. Like giving great starting pitcher early lead, Nebraska O deferred to its D, which held Sooners (9-2) to 137y, 98y of which came on ground. Oklahoma, which had owned 368y per game rush avg, managed only 8 1st downs against D that registered 10 sacks, 3 by Huskers LB LeRoy Etienne. K R.D. Lashar booted 29y FG, but OU was kept out of EZ for 1st time in 62 games. In critical 4th Q, Sooners failed to make even single 1st down and lost 11y in 4 possessions. IB Ken Clark pitched in with 167y rushing as Nebraska O gained 313y. Sooners' 31-game conf win streak, 2nd longest in Big 8 history was snapped as well as OU's 4-game series victory string.

Houston 30 TEXAS TECH 29: Driving snowstorm had greatest effect on game's end as short Texas Tech (5-5) punt led to 22y drive for winning 3y TD pass from QB Andre Ware (35-61/348y, 2 TDs, INT) to WR Jason Phillips (11/157y). Red Raiders outgained potent Houston (8-2) O by 49y and owned comfy 23-14 lead entering 4th Q. Cougars opened 4th Q with 10 straight pts to regain lead on Ware's 3y TD pass. QB Billy Joe Tolliver, who threw for 363y, needed less than 2 mins to lead Red Raiders to FB Ervin Fariss' 6y TD run. Versatile Fariss also caught 4/132y, TD.

WASHINGTON STATE 32 Washington 31: Snowy Apple Cup came down to 2 huge 4th Q plays by Cougars (8-3) as QB Timm Rosenbach scored on 5y run for late win. Facing 4th-and-2, Wazzu call was for bootleg by Rosenbach, who had thrown for 148y and rushed for 57y. He rolled left, then cut up middle. Play was set up by CB Shawn Landrum's punt block, recovered by S Jay Languien on Washington 13YL. Huskies (6-5) FB Aaron Jenkins rushed for 93y and 2 TDs, but missed final Q with injury. With Washington State TB Steve Broussard also leaving game with injury, TB Rich Swinton, who rushed for 155y and 2 TDs, led Cougars run game.

SOUTHERN CALIFORNIA 31 Ucla 22: Neither measles nor Bruins D could stop QB Rodney Peete, who threw for 2 TDs and had TDs running and passing to put Trojans (10-0) in Rose Bowl. QB Troy Aikman put up big numbers in defeat, passing 32-48/317y, but did not visit EZ often enough. Peete, who spent 2 nights in hospital under assumed name prior to game, threw 58y TD pass to WR Erik Affholter for 14-3 lead and added 1y TD keeper for 21-9 advantage. Bruins (9-2) cut into deficit before H as Aikman threw 10y TD pass to WR Reggie Moore. Trojans scored 10 straight pts in 3rd Q, which sealed Bruins' fate of 9th straight loss in series when Rose Bowl was on line. USC TB Aaron Emanuel chipped in with 113y and 2 TDs.

Oregon State 21 OREGON 10: Oregon (6-5) coach Rich Brooks' amazing Civil War game string ended. As player and asst coach for Oregon State he never lost to Ducks; as head coach with Oregon beginning in 1977 he raised his series unbeaten record to 19-0-1. That is, until this bit of revenge. With Ducks holding Oregon State (4-6-1) QB Erik Wilhelm (6-15/57y, INT) in check, Beavers turned to run game. Beavers FB Pat Chaffey rushed for 109y and 2 TDs in 4th Q, while TB Brian Taylor (9/61y) opened scoring with 27y TD run in 1st Q. Oregon took 10-7 H lead on 12y run by TB Derek Loville, who rushed for 117y. Despite poor results, Wilhelm upped his career passing to 9,393y and broke John Elway's Pac-10 mark by 44y.

AP Poll November 21

1 Notre Dame (35)	1167	11 Michigan	590
2 Southern California (22)	1158	12 Oklahoma State	558
3 Miami (1)	1081	13 Clemson	498
4 West Virginia (2)	1016	14 Houston	338
5 Florida State	954	15 Wyoming	291
6 Nebraska	883	16 Louisiana State	235
7 Auburn	846	17 Alabama	234
8 Arkansas	755	18 Washington State	207
9 UCLA	720	19 Syracuse	165
10 Oklahoma	637	20 Georgia	106

November 26, 1988

(Th'g) Texas A&M 28 TEXAS 24: Aggies (7-4) burst to 28-0 2nd Q lead behind 3 rushing TDs and LB John Roper's 48y scoring RET of blocked FG. Texas A&M TB Darren Lewis scored game's 1st TD from 15y out and his 36y sprint set up 2nd score. Texas DE Oscar Giles' FUM REC at A&M 14YL was converted into QB Mark Murdock's 8y TD pass to WR Kerry Cash to get Longhorns (4-7) on board late in 1st H. Murdock had 2 more TD passes in him, including short pass to WR Tony Jones that Jones took to house for 76y TD. After pulling to within 28-24 on 39y FG by K Wayne Clements, Texas (4-7) moved ball to Aggies 34YL before Texas A&M LB Dana Batiste ended rally by recovering fumbled pitchout.

(Fri) Auburn 15 ALABAMA 10 (Birmingham): Auburn (10-1) DT Ron Stallworth led ferocious D with 4 sacks, including safety, as Tigers squelched Crimson Tide and allowed only 12y rushing. Win gave Tigers share of SEC with LSU, which had beaten them by single pt. Auburn also was tapped for Sugar Bowl as Auburn's higher ranking swayed selection committee. Play of day was Tigers WR Lawyer Tillman's leaping 53y catch on 3rd-and-18 that set up game's sole TD: FB Vincent Harris' 1y TD run. Drive was helped by 12y pass by QB Reggie Slack (13-26/220y) to WR Freddy Weygand that replays indicated was caught OB. Harris' TD put Auburn up 15-3, nearly insurmountable edge against D that had allowed mere 79 pts all season. Alabama (7-3) made things interesting with 12y TD pass from QB David Smith (20-35/255y) to WR Greg Payne with 3:23 left. Tigers LB Quentin Riggins made EZ INT that wasted Tide's 74y drive. For 1st time in series tickets were not split evenly as Alabama received all but 10,000 tickets. Next season, series would move to Auburn's Jordan-Hare Stadium for 1st time.

FLORIDA STATE 52 Florida 17: With largest margin of victory in series, Florida State (10-1) was looking to take over in-state skirmish once dominated by rivals. QB Chip Ferguson (10-16/131y, INT) threw 3 1st Q TDs to light Seminoles' fire. After tying game at 7-7 in 1st Q on 1y TD run by RB Emmitt Smith, Gators (6-5) allowed FSU to score 45 of next 48 pts. Florida's feeble passing attack could not produce comeback: it was incapable of even single completion during 25-min stretch. Gators surrendered TD on 11y INT RET by, of all people, Seminoles NG Odell Haggins. FSU D keyed so effectively on Smith that he managed only 15/56y rushing. FSU TB Sammie Smith gained 20/109y rushing. Ferguson exploited absence of Florida A-A S Louis Oliver, out with injured elbow.

MIAMI 18 Arkansas 16: Hogs (10-1) came within whisker of avenging 1987's 44-pt loss to Miami (9-1). Had star Arkansas S Steve Atwater not dropped EZ INT of QB Steve Walsh (33-50/361y) with less than 6 mins it likely would have preserved 16-15 upset. But, Hurricanes K Carlos Huerta booted winning 20y FG with 5:38 left. Canes outgained Razorbacks 438y to 186y and made 26 lethal 1st downs to only 6, but failed to score TDs. Miami managed 1y TD run by RB Cleveland Gary for 10-3 lead. It capped drive kept alive by fake-punt run by LB Maurice Crum and 44y reception by WR Dale Dawkins. Moments later, Arkansas FB Barry Foster (8/103y) rumbled 80y to tie game at 10-10: 1st TD surrendered by Miami at home all season. Foster later scored another, catching QB Quinn Grovey's 2nd completion of day for 16y TD and 16-15 lead. Arkansas' other pts came on 58y FG by K Kendall Trainor. Huerta's 3 FGs gave him Miami school-record 19 for season.

Tennessee 14 VANDERBILT 7: Closing out lost season with 5 straight wins, Volunteers (5-6) salvaged bit of pride. TB Keith Davis led way with 162y rushing and 5y TD for winning score in 3rd Q. Davis, Nashville native, had 59y rushing on drive. WR Boo Mitchell led Vanderbilt (3-8) with 9/142y in setting new single-season school record for receiving yards with 1,312y. Commodores led 7-6 at H as QB Eric Jones (23-39/272y, INT) threw 5y TD pass to WR Tony Pearcey. Tennessee QB Jeff Francis completed 17-25/169y, but had 3 passes pilfered by Vandy. Vols P Kent Elmore kicked school-record 81y punt, along with 55y effort to keep Dores in check.

431

Notre Dame 27 SOUTHERN CALIFORNIA 10: Never in long history of "Rivalry that Rock Built" had teams occupied no.1 and no. 2 poll spots, and never had both been undefeated when they met. Game turned on huge play midway through 1st Q when Notre Dame (11-0) QB Tony Rice attacked nation's best rush D (68y per) with option run wide to left. Rice turned corner with trailing TB Mark Green to face Trojans (10-1) S Mark Carrier, sole D player on hand to take on Rice *and* Green. Carrier stopped Green, but Rice kept ball and went 65y for TD. Later in 1st H, Fighting Irish DE Frank Stams (9 tackles, 2.5 sacks) recovered FUM by TB Aaron Emanuel (18/95y) deep in USC territory to set up Green's 2y TD run. Trojans cut deficit to 14-7 on 1y run by TB Scott Lockwood, but lost momentum with QB Rodney Peete's 2nd INT, returned 64y for game-breaking TD by CB Stan Smagala. Stams threw crushing block on Peete (23-44/225y, 2 INTs) on INT RET, which was set up by Southern California WR John Jackson's slip on pass route. USC went on to gain 356y and 21 1st downs, easily outdistancing ND's 253y and 8 1st downs, but never could close gap in losing 6th straight in series. Irish played without leading rusher TB Tony Brooks and leading receiver Ricky Watters, who were suspended for excessive lateness.

AP Poll November 28

1 Notre Dame (57)	1197	11 Michigan	591
2 Miami (1)	1124	12 Oklahoma State	548
3 West Virginia	1069	13 Clemson	488
4 Florida State	1013	14 Houston	402
5 Southern California	946	15 Wyoming	306
6 Nebraska	891	16 Louisiana State	259
7 Auburn	865	17 Washington State	222
8 UCLA	733	18 Syracuse	170
9 Arkansas	731	19 Georgia	149
10 Oklahoma	649	20 Alabama	90

December 3, 1988

Army 20 Navy 15 (Philadelphia): Midshipmen (3-8) opened scoring with 44y FG late in 1st Q: K Ted Fundoukas' 1st of 3 FGs. Army (9-2) trailed only as long as it took to march 63y to go-ahead 1y TD run by FB Ben Barnett. Cadets never trailed again as K Keith Walker chipped in with 2 FGs and clincher was scored by QB Bryan McWilliams on 8y run. FB James Bradley scored on 2y run with 1:35 left to bring Navy within 20-15, but Middies were unable to recover onside-KO. Series was brought even at 41-41-7 as Cadets committed no TOs 4th straight time vs. Navy.

Oklahoma State 45 Texas Tech 42 (Tokyo): In contest marked by O firepower, no one stood out like Oklahoma State (9-2) TB Barry Sanders. Rushing for 44/332y to reach 2,628y for season, Sanders stormed past old single-season record set by Southern California's Marcus Allen (2,342) in 1981. Sanders scored 4 times to finish with 39 TDs, an amazing 10 more scores than anyone else in history. Texas Tech (5-6) IB James Gray matched Sanders with 4 TDs, 3 rushing, but he was held to minimal 23y on ground as Red Raiders did better through air. Teams combined for 1163y with Texas Tech QB Billy Joe Tolliver throwing for school-record 446y.

AP Poll December 5

1 Notre Dame (49)	1055	11 Michigan	534
2 Miami (1)	994	12 Oklahoma State	476
3 West Virginia (3)	950	13 Clemson	426
4 Florida State	900	14 Houston	340
5 Southern California	839	15 Wyoming	245
6 Nebraska	775	16 Louisiana State	225
7 Auburn	767	17 Syracuse	195
8 Arkansas	647	18 Washington State	174
9 UCLA	643	19 Georgia	122
10 Oklahoma	567	20 Alabama	118

Conference Standings
Atlantic Coast

Clemson	6-1
Virginia	5-2
North Carolina State	4-4-1
Wake Forest	4-3
Maryland	4-3
Duke	3-3-1
North Carolina	1-6
Georgia Tech	0-7

Southeastern

Auburn	6-1
Louisiana State	6-1
Georgia	5-2
Alabama	4-3
Florida	4-3
Mississippi	3-4
Tennessee	3-4
Kentucky	2-5
Vanderbilt	2-5
Mississippi State	0-7

Big Ten

Michigan	7-0-1
Michigan State	6-1-1
Illinois	5-2-1
Iowa	4-1-3
Indiana	5-3
Purdue	3-5
Ohio State	2-5-1
Northwestern	2-5-1
Wisconsin	1-7
Minnesota	0-6-2

Mid-American

Western Michigan	7-1
Eastern Michigan	5-2-1
Ball State	5-3
Central Michigan	5-3
Ohio	4-3-1
Toledo	4-4
Kent State	3-5
Bowling Green	1-6-1
Miami	0-7-1

Big Eight

Nebraska	7-0
Oklahoma	6-1
Oklahoma State	5-2
Colorado	4-3
Iowa State	3-4
Missouri	2-5
Kansas	1-6
Kansas State	0-7

Western Athletic

Wyoming	8-0
UTEP	6-2
Brigham Young	5-3
Hawaii	5-3
Utah	4-4
Air Force	3-5
San Diego State	3-5
Colorado State	1-7
New Mexico	1-7

Big West Conference

Fresno State	7-0
Cal State-Fullerton	5-2
Utah State	4-3
San Jose State	4-3
Nevada-Las Vegas	3-4
Long Beach State	3-4
Pacific	2-5
New Mexico State	0-7

Southwest

Arkansas	7-0
Texas A&M	6-1
Houston	5-2
Texas Tech	4-3
Baylor	2-5
Texas	2-5
Texas Christian	2-5
Rice	0-7

Pacific 10

Southern California	8-0
UCLA	6-2
Arizona	5-3
Washington State	5-3
Arizona State	3-4
Oregon	3-5
Washington	3-5
Oregon State	2-5-1
Stanford	1-5-2
California	1-5-1

1988 Major Bowl Games
Sun Bowl (Dec. 24): Alabama 29 Army 28

El Paso's Sun Bowl game featured contrast: QB David Smith's 412y passing for Crimson Tide (9-3) and Army's 350y rushing. FB Ben Barnett led Army (9-3) with 177y rushing, including 51y jaunt up middle on 1st drive that signaled 2-TD underdog Cadets came to play. Although Bama had nation's 5th best rushing D at 96y per, it was unfamiliar with Army's Wishbone tactics. Cadets gained 233y rushing in 1st H behind QB Bryan McWilliams, taking 14-13 H lead. Tide deficit would have greater had LB Derrick Thomas not blocked 2 FGs. With Smith and his favorite targets, WRs Greg Payne (9/107y) and Marco Battle (9/99y), heating up, teams matched score for score until late in 3rd Q, when Army S O'Neal Miller returned INT 58y for TD and 28-20 lead. Crimson Tide drove to 2 4th Q scores: K Phillip Doyle's 32y FG and FB David Casteal's 2y TD run. Bama S Charles Gardner made INT to seal win.

Aloha Bowl (Dec. 25): Washington State 24 Houston 22

Match-up of nation's 3rd and 4th-ranked Os (Washington State was averaging 494y per game, Houston 484y) provided close game if not expected O fireworks. Washington State (9-3) LB Tuineau Alipate turned in game-saving play as he knocked ball loose from Houston WR James Dixon at Wazzu 15YL with ball recovered by S Artie Holmes as clock was winding down. QB David Dacus (8-11/153y) had come off bench to rally Houston (9-3) to 2 TDs and put it into position for another when Dixon lost ball fighting for more y. Dacus, who threw TD passes of 53y to WR Kevin Mason and 2y to RB Chuck Weatherspoon, completed his throw to Dixon despite broken jaw suffered earlier in final drive on hit by WSU DT Mark Ledbetter. State scored all of its pts in 2nd Q as WR Victor Wood carried FUM 5y to EZ and caught 15y TD pass from QB Timm Rosenbach (19-36/306y, INT). After WSU K Jason Hanson increased lead to 17-3 with 33y FG, Houston scored its 1st TD on 1y Weatherspoon TD run moments after WR Jason Phillips threw 44y pass to WR Paul Smith. Rosenbach increased team's lead to 24-9 at H with 1y keeper that capped drive featuring TB Steve Broussard (33/139y).

Liberty Bowl (Dec. 28): Indiana 34 South Carolina 10

Playing great game from start to finish, Hoosiers (8-3-1) gained game-record 575y while D held South Carolina to 153y total O. Indiana QB Dave Schnell stepped out of TB Anthony Thompson's shadow to earn MVP honors as he threw for 378y and 2 TDs, including game-breaking 88y effort to WR Rob Turner. That TD, which opened 4th Q, bumped lead to 27-10 and squelched any comeback notions Gamecocks (8-3) may have entertained. Turner caught 5/182y, WR Tony Buford added 3/100y, and Thompson rushed for 140y and 2 TDs that opened and closed Indiana's scoring. Hoosiers D sacked QB Todd Ellis 6 times and intercepted 3 of his passes. Indiana LB Joe Huff earned D MVP honors with 10 tackles, 2 sacks. Play of game for Carolina was special teamer Mike Tolbert's 34y TD dash with blocked punt in 3rd Q that put team on board, trailing 17-7. Cocks would get no closer.

All American Bowl (Dec. 29): Florida 14 Illinois 10

Looking every bit like future NFL star, Florida (7-5) TB Emmitt Smith (28/159y) took off on 1st scrimmage for 55y TD. Illini (6-5-1) tightened up after that and tied it 7-7 in 2nd Q on TB Keith Jones' nifty 30y TD run. That was it until midway through 4th Q when Illinois K Doug Higgins knocked through 44y FG. Illini D held; O looked to run out clock before huge INT by Gators LB Owen Bartruff was returned to Illinois 26YL. Facing 3rd-and-2, Smith appeared to be held up for no gain before he bounced off tackle, reversed field, and took off until caught at 2YL. Smith quickly scored his 2nd TD for winning pts. QB Jeff George (20-37/194y, 2 INTs) drove Illini into Florida territory before holding PEN wiped out completion to Gators 17YL. Florida LB Huey Richardson then sealed win with 4th-and-1 stop of TB Lynn McClellan. Richardson led D that sacked George 4 times and picked him off twice.

Freedom Bowl (Dec. 29): Brigham Young 20 Colorado 17

Brigham Young (9-4) QB Ty Detmer made 1st national splash with off-bench heroics. After BYU O struggled to gain 127y in 1st H that ended with team trailing 14-7, coach LaVell Edwards turned to 21-year-old redshirt frosh Detmer to jumpstart high-powered attack. Detmer (11-17/129y) led 3 scoring drives in 2nd H to tie game at 14-14 on 14y pass to WR Chuck Cutler, then win game on 2 FGs by K Jason Chaffetz. After Cutler's TD, Buffaloes (8-4) had answered with 19y FG by K Paul Blottiaux to regain lead at 17-14. Detmer drove charges 78y to 31y FG that tied game at 17-17. BYU had shorter trip to win game as S Scott Peterson came up with INT near midfield to set up Chaffetz's game-winning 35y FG. Colorado TB Eric Bieniemy led Buffs with 144y and 2 TDs. Despite his kicking heroics, Chaffetz had experienced topsy-turvy year after serving as Utah co-chairman of Democrat Michael Dukakis' failed presidential bid.

Holiday Bowl (Dec. 30): Oklahoma State 62 Wyoming 14

However strong bowl game jinx that had haunted Heisman winners, it simply did not apply this time to Oklahoma State TB Barry Sanders. Sanders burned Wyoming (11-2) for 222y rushing and scored 5 TDs. He even completed 1st pass of college career with 17y sleight-of-hand to QB Mike Gundy. Sanders capped 1 of greatest single seasons in college football history with spectacular performance. Among his TDs was 33y run at end of opening possession and 67y romp in 3rd Q after Wyoming had cut into Cowboys (10-2) lead by 24-14. Gundy enjoyed supporting role with near-perfect pitching of 20-24/315y, 2 TDs. Oklahoma State WR Hart Lee Dykes was on receiving end of half of Gundy's completions, catching 10/163y, TD. Wyoming QB Randy Welniak threw for 164y and ran for 2 TDs at helm of O that managed only 204y, while D could not prevent OSU from topping 40 pts for 11th time this season.

Peach Bowl (Dec. 31): North Carolina State 28 Iowa 23

With sloppy conditions producing even sloppier game, North Carolina State (8-3-1) held on to win game for coach Dick Sheridan, who had turned down Georgia coaching offer. Wolfpack won despite 7 TOs, largely because Iowa (6-4-3) committed same number. Slow-developing Hawkeyes scored final 20 pts as QB Chuck Hartleib completed 30-51/428y, 4 INTs. NC State's key stop of charging Iowans came on group tackle of Iowa FB Richard Bass on 4th-and-2 at NC State 41YL midway through 4th Q. Wolfpack built big lead with help from special teams as 2 FUMs on KOs by Hawkeye returners led to TDs, while NC State QB Shane Montgomery (7-10/152y) additionally threw 75y TD bomb to WR Danny Peebles. Wolfpack TB Tyrone Jackson (17/86y) added 2 TD runs in 1ST H, and S Michael Brooks had 3 INTs. Iowa star TE Marv Cook caught 8/122y.

Gator Bowl (Jan. 1): Georgia 34 Michigan State 27

Georgia coach Vince Dooley's final game ended in victory but it was manner in which Bulldogs (9-3) won that was surprising. Georgia went to air behind QB Wayne Johnson, who threw career-high 227y, 3 TDs. Johnson's TD passes, 2 to TB Rodney Hampton and 1 to TE Kirk Warner, gave Bulldogs 24-7 advantage in 3rd Q. After Michigan State (6-5-1) rallied behind QB Bobby McAllister, who connected with WR Andre Rison on TD passes of 4, 55, and 50y, Georgia scored vital TD on Hampton's 32y run early in 4th Q. Hampton rushed for 109y and caught 4/71y, while Rison set Michigan State and Gator Bowl-record for receiving y with 9/252y, 3 TDs. Rison had hand in every Spartan TD, setting up 4th TD, 3y run by TB Blake Ezor (146y), with 51y reception. Dooley was rumored to be eyeing Georgia gubernatorial race, but run for office never materialized.

Hall of Fame Bowl (Jan. 2): Syracuse 23 Louisiana State 10

Holding up honor of Eastern football, Syracuse (10-2) D held Tigers to 76y rushing and picked off 3 passes of LSU QB Tommy Hodson. Syracuse QB Todd Philcox (16-23/130y) led efficient O that scored in each Q as HB Robert Drummond rushed for 122y of team's 208y with 2 TDs. Drummond opened scoring with 2y scoring run in 1st Q and then, after LSU (8-4) tied game 10-10 in 3rd Q, he scored on 1y run for winning pts. Drummond's 2nd TD capped 67y drive featuring WR Rob Moore, who made 2 catches/26y and ran for 8y on E-around. Philcox closed scoring with 4y pass to WR Deval Glover in 4th Q. Hodson threw for 192y, but could not overcome 3 picks, 2 by Orangemen DB David Holmes. Orangemen wore special "103" armbands to honor passengers who perished in December 20 crash of Pan Am Flight 103 over Lockerbie, Scotland. Crash, later proven to have been bombing by Middle East terrorists, ended lives of 38 Syracuse University students.

Citrus Bowl (Jan. 2): Clemson 13 Oklahoma 6

Bitter struggle ended with Oklahoma (9-3) running out of downs and time deep in Tigers territory. Sooners QB Jamelle Holieway (10-24/138y, INT) completed 7 passes in 40 secs and converted 4th-and-10 with 11y scramble to Clemson 14YL, but he misfired on final 3 attempts with Clemson (10-2) CB Dexter Davis tipping away last pass in EZ. Spending 1st 3 Qs pounding each other, teams combined for 6-6 deadlock on 4 combined FGs, 2 by Clemson K Chris Gardocki and 2 by Oklahoma K R.D. Lashar. Tigers O finally grouped behind QB Rodney Williams to march 80y to game-winning TD. Williams ran twice for 1st downs and completed 3-3/27y as Clemson marched to 4y TD run by TB Terry Allen (17/53y). Sooners, who only rushed for 116y, had 10 mins left to score, but managed only its final threat. Oklahoma dropped its 1st-ever game to ACC opponent after 16 straight wins.

Cotton Bowl (Jan. 2): UCLA 17 Arkansas 3

Winning bowl in record 7th straight season, UCLA Bruins (10-2) dominated like their mid-season top ranking. Matching up favorably to Arkansas' flexbone attack, Bruins D put on spectacular show and held Arkansas to all-time low 42y—21y passing and rushing each—in dominating time of possession by 42:43 to 17:17. After sluggish 1st Q, UCLA scored 2 TDs in 2nd Q on 93y and 74y drives, 2nd ending with QB Troy Aikman's 1y TD toss to TE Corwin Anthony with 21 secs left in H. Recovering midfield FUM midway through 3rd Q, Arkansas finally gave its 60,000 fans something to cheer about when it took 6 plays to move 14y to 49y FG by K Kendall Trainor. That was it for Hogs (10-2). Playing in his future pro city, Aikman completed 19-27/172y with passes to 13 different receivers. TB Shawn Wills rushed for 120y as bulwark of Bruins TD drives. Cotton Bowl appearance for Razorbacks was 1st in 13 years, but matters darkened because coach Ken Hatfield suspended his best linemen, G Freddie Childress and DT Wayne Martin, for rules violations.

Fiesta Bowl (Jan. 2): Notre Dame 34 West Virginia 21

Behind huge O-line, made up of 5th-year seniors, Mountaineers (11-1) and QB Major Harris accumulated impressive y and pt totals during undefeated regular season. But by H of Fiesta Bowl match-up with top-ranked Notre Dame (12-0), WVU trailed 23-6 and Harris was being chased all over gridiron by Irish DE Frank Stams (2 sacks) and cohorts. Harris suffered injured shoulder on game's 3rd play; he continued on but with limited pitching capability. Irish gained 455y total O as QB Tony Rice threw for 7-11/213y, 2 TDs. He ran for game-high 75y as well. Rice's sole mistake almost allowed West Virginia back into game in 3rd Q, throwing INT to DB Willie Edwards that gave Mountaineers ball on ND 26YL, while trailing 26-13. Irish blitz on 3rd down produced 12y sack by Stams and DE Arnold Ale and forced West Virginia to punt. Rice then marched Notre Dame 80y to clinching TD, running for 15y on 3rd-and-7 draw play, hitting WR Ricky Watters on 57y strike, and finding reserve TE Frank Jacobs for 3y TD pass to seal win and national title.

Rose Bowl (Jan. 2): Michigan 22 Southern California 14

What in name of Pasadena was going on? Suddenly, Big 10, now much deeper collection of bowl teams, had won consecutive Rose Bowls for 1st time since Illinois and Michigan turned trick in 1964 and 1965 to complete 9 of 12 run of Rose wins. Wolverines (9-2-1) needed 19 pts in 2nd H to win 75th Rose Bowl, while also posting 2nd H shutout. FB Leroy Hoard (19/142y) was virtually unstoppable in game's 2nd H, rushing for 113y and 2 TDs, both of which he set up with long runs. Michigan's 1st TD came in 3rd Q on 6y pass from QB Demetrius Brown to WR Chris Calloway that cut USC's lead to 14-9. With Trojans (10-2) prevented from gaining even single 1st down in 3rd Q, Michigan drove 92y to go up 15-14 on Hoard's 1st TD. Southern California then managed its best drive of 2nd H, moving to Michigan 30YL before stalling with 5:38 left in 4th Q. K Quin Rodriguez missed 47y FG attempt that would have regained lead for Trojans. Michigan made them pay soon enough as Brown handed off to Hoard who was immediately grabbed at ankles by LB Junior Seau. Hoard broke free and rambled 61y to set up his own 1y TD run on 4th down. This score wrapped up scoring. Both of Trojans TDs had come on QB Rodney Peete's runs, each culminating long drive. Peete was held in check thereafter, throwing for 158y with 2 INTs as Troy suffered 5 TOs.

Orange Bowl (Jan. 2): Miami 23 Nebraska 3

After playing for championships in past 2 seasons, Miami (11-1) wanted to prove to nation that they still consider themselves best in all land. Hurricanes looked as good as ever in routing Huskers (11-2) and holding Big 8 champs to 80y rushing and 55y passing, while gaining 354y on O. Canes D used speed to consistently thwart Nebraska, which came in averaging nation's best 382y rushing. Miami sacked QB Steve Taylor 6 times and picked off 2 of his passes, while making 3 INTs overall. Miami QB Steve Walsh led workmanlike O, completing to date Orange Bowl-record 21-44/285y with 2 TD passes to FB Leonard Conley. Despite his passing record, Walsh never truly reached his rhythm, as blitzing Huskers D picked him off 3 times, 2 by DB Charles Fryar. Miami received 3 FGs from K Carlos Huerta which was more than enough scoring. K Gregg Barrios' 50y FG in 3rd Q prevented shutout, but Nebraska still scored its fewest pts in 27-game bowl history. Said coach Jimmy Johnson after what would prove to be his final game at Miami: "That's what we wanted to prove tonight and to the country, that we were the very best." Still, Hurricanes finished 2nd in final AP Poll.

Sugar Bowl (Jan. 2): Florida State 13 Auburn 7

Teams grappled in D struggle which was ended appropriately by star defender: Florida State (11-1) A-A CB Deion Sanders, who had been twice burned on Auburn's ill-fated final drive for victory. Sanders came back to life by picking off pass in EZ with 5 secs left. Tigers (10-2) QB Reggie Slack (19-33/162y, 3 INTs) threw to WR Lawyer Tillman, Sanders stepped in front of taller target for decisive INT. Slack dramatically had marched Tigers from own 4YL to Florida State 22YL, completing 7 passes, including 3 that converted 4th downs along way. Seminoles had done their best O work in 1st Q in driving 84y to 2y TD run by FB Dayne Williams. TB Sammie Smith (24/115y) keyed drive with 3 runs of 9y or more. Noles S Stan Shiver made INT to set up 35y FG by K Bill Mason for 10-0 lead. Twice in 2nd H, FSU drove to Auburn 2YL without scoring, ending 1 drive with incomplete pass by QB Chip Ferguson (14-26/157y, INT) on fake FG and 2nd on bad 3rd down pitchout that was recovered by Tigers. Auburn had scored its TD in 2nd Q when Slack faked pitchout to pull Sanders away from TE Walter Reeves, who caught 20y TD pass.

Final AP Poll January 3

1 Notre Dame (58.5)	1198	11 Oklahoma State	671
2 Miami (1.5)	1141	12 Arkansas	489
3 Florida State	1073	13 Syracuse	469
4 Michigan	926	14 Oklahoma	438
5 West Virginia	917	15 Georgia	333
6 UCLA	864	16 Washington State	330
7 Southern California	803	17 Alabama	213
8 Auburn	801	18 Houston	147
9 Clemson	708	19 Louisiana State	92
10 Nebraska	704	20 Indiana	75

1988 Top Performance Formula

1 Miami	1.8395
2 Notre Dame	1.7860
3 Florida State	1.6776
4 West Virginia	1.6517
5 Southern California	1.6240
6 Nebraska	1.5948
7 UCLA	1.5863
8 Auburn	1.5811
9 Michigan	1.5441
10 Clemson	1.5425
11 Oklahoma State	1.5252
12 Arkansas	1.4956
13 Syracuse	1.4395
14 Oklahoma	1.4166
15 Washington State	1.4038
16 Houston	1.3949
17 Alabama	1.3817
18 Arizona	1.3229
19 Brigham Young	1.3123
20 Georgia	1.3109

1988 Top Opponent Records

1 Virginia Tech	.6667
2 Miami	.6512
3 Arizona	.6447
4 Southern California	.6440
5 North Carolina	.6304
6 Maryland	.6272
7 Florida State	.6267
8 Oregon State	.6140
9 UCLA	.6063
10 Penn State	.6053
11 Michigan	.6016
12 Louisiana State	.5992
13 Washington	.5991
14 Tennessee	.5957
15 Notre Dame	.5952
16 Stanford	.5948
17 Michigan State	.5898
18 Clemson	.5883
19 Kentucky	.5853
20 Missouri	.5847

1988 Out-of-Conference Records

	W-L	Percentage	Bowl W-L
Pacific-10	27-7	.7941	2-1
Southeastern	20-18	.5263	3-2
Western Athletic	17-16	.5152	1-2
Big Eight	16-17-1	.4853	1-3
Atlantic Coast	11-12-1	.4792	2-0
Southwest	12-17	.4138	0-2
Big Ten	13-22-1	.3750	2-3

1988 Individual Statistical Leaders

RUSHING YARDS

	Attempts	Yards	Avg.
Barry Sanders, Oklahoma State	344	2628	7.6
Darren Lewis, Texas A&M	306	1692	5.5
Anthony Thompson, Indiana	329	1546	4.7
Ken Clark, Nebraska	232	1497	6.5
Tony Boles, Michigan	248	1359	5.5
Blake Ezor, Michigan State	290	1358	4.7
Eric Wilkerson, Kent	247	1325	5.4
Eric Bieniemy, Colorado	219	1243	5.7
Don Riley, Central Michigan	215	1238	5.8
Curvin Richards, Pittsburgh	207	1228	5.9

PASSING YARDS

	Completions	Attempts	Yards	Pct.
Scott Mitchell, Utah	323	533	4322	60.6
Anthony Dilweg, Duke	287	484	3824	59.3
Chuck Hartlieb, Iowa	258	409	3310	63.1
Steve Walsh, Miami	233	390	3115	59.7
Billy Joe Tolliver, Texas Tech	190	354	2869	53.7
Timm Rosenbach, Washington State	199	302	2791	65.9
Rodney Peete, Southern California	208	338	2654	61.5
Randy Welniak, Wyoming	184	324	2627	56.8
Sean Covey, Brigham Young	174	319	2607	54.6
Troy Aikman, UCLA	209	327	2599	63.9

RECEIVING YARDS

	Catches	Yards
Jason Phillips, Houston	108	1444
Hart Lee Dykes, Oklahoma State	74	1278
Boo Mitchell, Vanderbilt	78	1213
Kendal Smith, Utah State	65	1196
Carl Harry, Utah	65	1145
James Dixon, Houston	102	1103
Clarkston Hines, Duke	68	1067
Chuck Cutler, Brigham Young	64	1039
Tim Stallworth, Washington State	55	1031
Tony Moss, Louisiana State	55	957

1988 Consensus All-America Team

Offense

Wide Receiver:	Jason Phillips, Houston
	Hart Lee Dykes, Oklahoma State
Tight End:	Marv Cook, Iowa
Line:	Tony Mandarich, Michigan State
	Anthony Phillips, Oklahoma
	Mike Utley, Washington
	Mark Stepnoski, Pittsburgh
Center:	Jake Young, Nebraska
	John Vitale, Michigan
Quarterback:	Troy Aikman, UCLA
Running Back:	Barry Sanders, Oklahoma State
	Anthony Thompson, Indiana
	Tim Worley, Georgia
Placekicker:	Kendall Trainor, Arkansas

Defense

Line:	Mark Messner, Michigan
	Tracy Rocker, Auburn
	Wayne Martin, Arkansas
	Frank Stams, Notre Dame
	Bill Hawkins, Miami
Linebacker:	Derrick Thomas, Alabama
	Broderick Thomas, Nebraska
	Michael Stonebreaker, Notre Dame
Back:	Deion Sanders, Florida State
	Donnell Woolford, Clemson
	Louis Oliver, Florida
	Darryl Henley, UCLA
Punter:	Keith English, Colorado

1988 Heisman Trophy Vote

Barry Sanders, junior tailback, Oklahoma State	1878
Rodney Peete, senior quarterback, Southern Cal	912
Troy Aikman, senior quarterback, UCLA	582
Steve Walsh, junior quarterback, Miami	341
Major Harris, junior quarterback, West Virginia	280

Other Major Award Winners

Maxwell (Player)	Barry Sanders, junior tailback, Oklahoma State
Walter Camp (Player)	Barry Sanders, junior tailback, Oklahoma State
Outland (Lineman)	Tracy Rocker, senior defensive tackle, Auburn
Lombardi (Lineman)	Tracy Rocker, senior defensive tackle, Auburn
Dick Butkus (Linebacker)	Derrick Thomas, senior linebacker, Alabama
Jim Thorpe (Defensive Back)	Deion Sanders, senior corner back, Florida State
Davey O'Brien (Quarterback)	Troy Aikman, senior quarterback, UCLA
Johnny Unitas (Quarterback)	Rodney Peete, senior quarterback, Southern Cal
AFCA Coach of the Year	Don Nehlen, West Virginia

1989

The Year of Sal's Memorial, Double Ericksons, and Run-and-Shoot's Heisman with No Prisoners

National newcomer Colorado (11-1) became the team of the year through inspiration from their cancer-stricken quarterback Sal Aunese. The Buffs posted a surprising undefeated regular season, outright Big Eight crown, no. 1 ranking at the close of the regular season, and Orange Bowl bid. Despite a bowl loss to Notre Dame (12-1) in Miami, which postponed the school's first-ever national title until 1990, Colorado enjoyed a great season played in teary-eyed honor of Aunese, who died in September.

What might have been a positive story about how sports could galvanize a community, how players could love a courageous teammate, and simply the greatness of college football, instead became a base tale the national media devoured. The story spoke of exploitation of minority players, an unwed mother who happened to be the coach's daughter, crimes of various sorts, and the infiltration of college football by gang members. Amidst as complicated and troublesome a situation as had occurred in recent times, the exciting football played by Colorado became practically a secondary story. In place of Aunese, quarterback Darian Hagan, for one, had a brilliant year in becoming the sixth player in history to rush (1,004) and pass (1,002) for more than 1,000 yards each. Tailback Eric Bieniemy added 1,628 yards rushing as the Colorado offense finished second nationally in rushing and third in scoring. The Buffaloes' defense featured a hard-hitting linebacking corps and dominated most of its foes.

For better or worse, Colorado's twisted tale was the story of the year, but the Buffs were unable to hold the top ranking in the final poll. With a third national title in seven years, Miami (11-1) became the fourth straight independent to win the title, following Penn State in 1986, Miami itself in 1987, and Notre Dame in 1988. Since 1982, only one conference team had won a national crown: Oklahoma in 1985. The 1989 edition of the big, bad Canes won with defense, going a stretch of 10 quarters without surrendering a single point and holding six teams without a touchdown. Miami's decisive 27-10 win over Notre Dame on Thanksgiving weekend opened the door for its third title once the Irish did their part by deflating Colorado in the Orange Bowl. That win also allowed Miami to continue its remarkable streak of beating top-ranked teams in each of seven straight seasons. That the Hurricanes achieved all of this with a new coach, Dennis Erickson, and won three titles with three different coaches, proved the system and talent base to be unparalleled. Miami closed the 1980s as the clear-cut team of the decade. It is likely no school ever dominated an entire decade as did Miami in the 1980s. It is even more remarkable that the program was in such poor shape in competition with the NFL Dolphins in the early 1970s that school administrators considered dropping football.

As well as things went for Miami, Florida State (10-2) rocked the Hurricanes in a late October game and completed 1989 with a 10-game winning streak. Still, the Seminoles had no shot at the title thanks to two upset losses to Southern Mississippi (5-6) and Clemson (10-2) to open the season. FSU's late charge netted the no. 3 spot in the final AP Poll.

Defending champion Notre Dame had an August to forget, losing four starters to injury, disciplinary decisions, or academic suspension. Nonetheless, the Irish increased their consecutive win streak to 23 before the Miami loss, whipping eight eventual bowls teams including the champions of the Big Eight (Colorado), Big Ten (Michigan), ACC (Virginia), and Pac-10 (Southern California). Having beaten top-ranked Colorado in the Orange Bowl—scene of the only loss in a two-year period—coach Lou Holtz wondered why his Irish were not champions. With the defeat to Miami so fresh in voters' minds a no. 1 finish was impossible, but the university succeeded in feeding the bottom line when it signed an exclusive $30 million television deal with NBC to broadcast every home game for six years (1990-95).

One coach who was denied the opportunity to stop Colorado's steam-roller was Barry Switzer, forced out at Oklahoma (7-4) in June after a rash of Sooner-involved incidents and accusations against the coach himself. Although the personal allegations went unsubstantiated, Switzer saw players jailed for attempted murder, gang rape, drug trafficking, and theft. The team also went on probation, as too did in-state rival Oklahoma State (4-7), which was nailed for 63 violations in narrowly avoiding the dreaded "Death Penalty." The NCAA used former Cowboy Hart Lee Dykes to bring down the program. Dykes set a record of sorts by getting four different schools in trouble with sordid tales of his recruitment.

Florida (7-5), meanwhile, saw coach Galen Hall resign on October 8 under pressure for financially helping a player who faced a court order for non-payment of child support and for supplementing assistant coaches' salaries. Both Ara Parseghian and Barry Switzer admitted on television that they had supplemented assistants' pay, while Bobby Bowden estimated that 90 percent of coaches did not realize there was a rule against it. The Gators suspended four players for the season for rule violations, including quarterback Kyle Morris, who bet on games.

On the subject of the "Death Penalty," Southern Methodist (2-9) returned to the playing field from the NCAA's only application of the sentence. On September 16, the Mustangs beat Div. 1-AA Connecticut (8-4) 31-30 for their first win since 1986. It was an exciting triumph as wide receiver Mike Bowen tallied on a five-yard scoring reception on the game's final play. With only seven Mustangs having previous college football experience, including senior wide receiver Mitchell Glieber, the only returnee from 1986, the 1989 season was a long one for alumni coach Forrest Gregg. On October 21, the Mustangs started 17 freshmen against the wicked Run-and-Shoot offense of Houston (9-2), which under coach Jack Pardee took no prisoners. SMU lost 95-21. The Cougars, the eventual national total offense (642.9 yards per game) champion, set or tied records for single-game passing (771 yards), total offense (1,021 yards) and touchdown passes (10). Quarterback Andre Ware established marks for passing yards in one quarter (340) and in one half (517) and for scoring passes in a quarter (5). Gregg was angry with his former NFL rival, Pardee, for piling it on. The Cougars would end up piling on 50 points or more in five games.

Houston quarterback Andre Ware won the Heisman Trophy, despite being an African-American quarterback whose team was on probation, and therefore not on television. No African-American quarterback had ever won the top prize in college football, and no player from a school on probation had ever won it. Of interest was that it universally was considered impossible to win the award without television exposure. Ware was helped by the sheer weight of his record-setting passing (4,699 yards and 46 touchdowns). The reality was that black signal-callers were here to stay. African-American quarterbacks Major Harris, Tony Rice, and Darian Hagan finished third, fourth, and fifth respectively in Heisman voting. Ware may not have won the award—246 of 743 ballots did not mention him at all—as much as everyone else lost it.

Proposition 42, surprisingly sponsored by the SEC, was passed at the NCAA convention to go into effect in 1990. It denied scholarships to students who could not meet standards (minimum score of 700 on SAT or 15 on ACT plus 2.0 GPA on core curriculum of 11 academic courses) set by Prop 48, which had allowed those students to be red-shirted. The only option for non-qualifying players now would be junior college. The NCAA Rules Committee had written 283 rules changes in the 1980s, most of any decade. In comparison, there were only 74 changes in the 1960s.

Tailback Anthony Thompson of Indiana (5-6) set records of 68 career touchdowns and 377 yards for single-game rushing against Wisconsin (2-9), but finished second in Heisman balloting due largely to the Hoosiers' inability to get to a bowl game.

The biggest week for the Big Ten came in mid-December, after the regular season. Bo Schembechler retired as Michigan (10-2) coach, effective after the Rose Bowl. He finished with a 234-65-8 overall record with Miami (Ohio) and Michigan, good enough for fifth all-time in wins at the time. Fittingly, Schembechler won the Big Ten with an 8-0 conference record and just as fittingly he lost the Rose Bowl to Southern California (9-2-1) 17-10 to run his record in Pasadena to a surprisingly dismal 2-8. Schembechler stayed on as Michigan athletic director. The next day, the conference invited Penn State (8-3-1) to join, which it did for football only at first. The Big Ten athletic directors, led by Schembechler, complained that conference presidents made the decision without their input. Ironically, the new active leader in coaching wins with Bo's retirement became Penn State coach Joe Paterno with 220 victories.

Milestones

■ With large-scale exodus of stars to NFL due to threatened wage scale for rookies, NFL changed draft eligibility policy to allow any player draft entry who had been on campus for three years.

■ Kicking tees were prohibited for field goal and PAT attempts. Also, rule was changed on offensive fumbles that go out of the opponent's end zone, which were now to be awarded to defensive team at spot of fumble. Fumbles that go out of bounds were now to be returned to spot of fumble.

■ College Football Association floated 16-team playoff plan to member schools, which voted it down by 3-1 margin.

- Associated Press expanded weekly poll to 25 teams.

- Copper Bowl debuted in Tucson with local Arizona as host team.

- Morley Drury, All-America halfback for Southern California in 1927, died at 85 years old on January 22. Drury rushed for 1,163 yards to become USC's first 1,000-yard back, and last until Mike Garrett in 1965. South Carolina head coach Joe Morrison, former star player at Cincinnati, died of heart attack on February 5 after racquetball game. His record at Tennessee-Chattanooga, New Mexico and South Carolina was 101-37-7. Col. Earl "Red" Blaik, who won 166 games as head coach of Dartmouth and Army with national championships at West Point in 1944 and '45, died in Colorado Springs nursing home at age 92 on May 5. Blaik was selected All-America end at Miami (Ohio) in 1919 and was assistant coach at Army from 1927-34 before taking Dartmouth head job where he won two Ivy League titles. He coached three Heisman Trophy winners at Army. All-time great Ohio State end Wes Fesler died on July 30 at age 81. Fesler was three-time All-America, who was Big 10 MVP in 1930. He was Phi Beta Kappa, basketball All-America, and baseball star. Fesler coached four schools, including Ohio State, whose 1949 team won Rose Bowl over California. Dan "Tiger" Hill, All-America center-linebacker for famous 1938 Duke team, died at age 72 on August 24. Iron Dukes were "undefeated, untied and unscored upon" before losing in Rose Bowl on Southern Cal's late TD. Georgetown great G Augie Lio, whose blocking, tackling and kicking led Hoyas on 23-game win streak, died on September 3 at age 71. Lio's most memorable game as defensive wrecking crew ironically occurred in 1940 19-18 loss to undefeated Boston College to snap Hoyas' streak. Colorado quarterback Sal Aunese died of cancer in September (see above).

- Longest winning streaks entering the season:

Notre Dame 12	Florida State 11	Fresno State, Miami 7

- Coaching Changes:

	Incoming	Outgoing
Colorado State	Earle Bruce	Leon Fuller
Cincinnati	Tim Murphy	Dave Currey
East Carolina	Bill Lewis	Art Baker
Georgia	Ray Goff	Vince Dooley
Kansas State	Bill Snyder	Stan Parrish
Miami	Dennis Erickson	Jimmy Johnson
Memphis State	Chuck Stobart	Charlie Bailey
Missouri	Bob Stull	Woody Widenhofer
Oklahoma	Gary Gibbs	Barry Switzer
Pacific	Walt Harris	Bob Cope
Rice	Fred Goldsmith	Jerry Berndt
San Diego State	Al Luginbill	Denny Stolz
South Carolina	Sparky Woods	Joe Morrison
Southern Methodist	Forrest Gregg	Bobby Collins (a)
Stanford	Dennis Green	Jack Elway
Temple	Jerry Berndt	Bruce Arians
Texas A&M	R.C. Slocum	Jackie Sherrill
Texas-El Paso	David Lee	Bob Stull
Washington State	Mike Price	Dennis Erickson

(a) Collins coached SMU during its most-recent season, 1986.

- Preseason AP Poll

1 Michigan (23)	1439	14 Colorado	630
2 Notre Dame (20)	1378	15 Oklahoma	620
3 Nebraska (10)	1333	16 Alabama	479
4 Miami (4)	1322	17 West Virginia	457
5 Southern California (1)	1288	18 Arizona	319
6 Florida State (2)	1202	19 Brigham Young	306
7 Louisiana State	1059	20 Pittsburgh	282
8 Auburn	1007	21 Houston	281
9 UCLA	996	22 Illinois	277
10 Arkansas	884	23 Iowa	250
11 Penn State	746	24 North Carolina State	238
12 Clemson	695	25 Ohio State	200.5
13 Syracuse	644		

September 2, 1989

(Th) Notre Dame 36 Virginia 13 (East Rutherford, N.J.): Kickoff Classic's 1st sellout in 7-year history watched impressive show by defending champions. Notre Dame (1-0) QB Tony Rice, who passed for 147y and rushed for 70y, engineered O that totaled 477y and enjoyed 33-0 H lead. Irish WR Rocket Ismail caught 5/121y, while TB Ricky Watters rushed for team-high 80y and opening 2y TD run. Cavaliers (0-1) were never in game, trailing 19-0 after 1st Q and not scoring until 4th Q on 2y TD pass from QB Shawn Moore (10-22/85y, 2 INTs) to TE Bruce McGonnigal that cut deficit to 33-7. "It could have been worse," said losing coach George Welsh. "We were dominated."

NORTH CAROLINA STATE 10 Maryland 6: Maryland (0-1) drove to NC State 17YL at game's end but could not reach EZ as final pass by QB Neil O'Donnell (22-34/211y, INT), who completed 5-6 on drive, was tipped away by CB Barry Anderson. Wolfpack TB Anthony Barbour's 7y TD run in 3rd Q proved to be game winner, capping 80y drive led by QB Shane Montgomery (13-23/161y) who completed 5 passes/54y. North Carolina State (1-0) did not commit single TO or PEN in winning key ACC battle.

SOUTH CAROLINA 27 Duke 21: TB Harold Green rushed for 160y and 2 TDs as Gamecocks (1-0) won in coach Sparky Woods' debut. Green set tone with 42y TD run on opening possession. Duke (0-1) WR Clarkston Hines caught 22nd and 23rd career TD passes. South Carolina K Collin Mackie became school's all-time leading scorer, surpassing George Rogers' 202 pts.

Southern Mississippi 30 FLORIDA STATE 26 (Jacksonville): Golden Eagles QB Brett Favre (21-39/282y, 2 TDs, 2 INTs) proved heroic, winning game with 2y TD pass to WR Anthony Harris with 23 secs left. Florida State (0-1) had taken controversial lead as Eagles LB Bryant Medders was flagged for illegally batting down ball on blocked FG. Seminoles K Bill Mason was true with 2nd chance for 26-24 lead. Southern Miss (1-0) turned ball over 3 times within FSU 15YL, which offset great deal of its impressive 427y O against touted D of no. 6 Florida State. QB Peter Tom Willis (25-40/269, TD) led Seminoles' attack.

TEXAS A&M 28 Louisiana State 16: Aggies' 1st game under R.C. Slocum—also 1st on probation—went well as Texas A&M (1-0) scored two TDs in 15-sec span late in 4th Q. After 20y run by FB Robert Wilson (15/121y) put A&M up 21-10 with 2:58 left, CB Kevin Smith returned INT 40y for 28-10 cushion. Tigers (0-1) mounted late drive to QB Tommy Hodson's 2nd TD pass. Aggies S Larry Horton had zipped 92y with opening KO. A&M TB Darren Lewis was held to 17/55y, and TB Harvey Williams of LSU was completely blanketed with 13/32y rushing. Win was 1st for Aggies since highly-competitive series resumed in 1986.

Rice 35 SMU 6: Mustangs (0-1) returned to playing football after 2-year absence, and new program opened with miserable results. On-campus Ownby Stadium hosted its 1st game since 1948. Lowly Rice (1-0), losers of 18 straight games, routed Ponies after slow start. QB Donald Hollas' 222y, 2 TDs passing and 82y, 2 TDs rushing led Owls, who had not beaten SMU since 1976. Mustangs managed short-lived 3-0 lead after REC of fumbled opening KO led to K Matt Lomenick's FG. With only 41 scholarship players and 18 frosh starters, Mustangs were in for long year. "I want to give SMU credit for fighting their guts out," said Rice coach Fred Goldsmith.

(Mon) Illinois 14 SOUTHERN CALIFORNIA 13: This inter-sectional tilt was originally scheduled for Moscow as "The Glasnost Bowl," but idea was nixed. Once Illini (1-0) switched to Shotgun O, QB Jeff George (27-43/248y, INT) heated up, throwing pair of 4th Q TD passes. Illinois WR Shawn Wax scored off tipped pass for 53y TD, and George capped 80y drive, in which he hit 6-8 throws, with 20y TD pass to WR Steven Williams. USC (0-1), whose only TD came on DB Marcus Hopkins' RET of blocked punt, featured debut of heralded frosh QB Todd Marinovich (14-27/120y, INT). After Illinois' go-ahead TD, Marinovich threw sole INT to Illini S Henry Jones in considerable reversal, Southern California now had been tagged with 4-game losing streak to Big 10 teams after having served up 17 straight wins.

(Mon) COLORADO 27 Texas 6: QB Darian Hagan was impressive in 1st Colorado (1-0) start, rushing for 116y and TD, while passing for 95y and another TD. Hagan raced 75y on game's 2nd play to set up opening score: TB Eric Bieniemy's 1y run. Moments later, Hagan found HB George Hemingway for 5y TD pass that gave Colorado 14-0 lead. Buffs D tallied 5 sacks in holding Longhorns (0-1) to 69y rushing. QB Mark Murdock threw for 148y, but Texas had 0y or less on 32 of its 68 snaps.

AP Poll September 6

1 Notre Dame (31)	1430	14 Syracuse	606
2 Michigan (18)	1419	15 Texas A&M	569
3 Miami (4)	1342	16 Florida State	548
4 Nebraska (6)	1335	17 West Virginia	515
5 Auburn	1149	18 Southern Mississippi	486
6 UCLA	1110	19 Alabama	434
7 Arkansas	968	20 Arizona	396
8 Oklahoma	886	21 Louisiana State	369
9 Colorado	860	22 Houston	326
10 Clemson	812	23 Pittsburgh	319
11 Illinois	811	24 Brigham Young	272
12 Penn State	774	25 North Carolina State	157
13 Southern California	650		

September 9, 1989

(Th) Washington State 46 BRIGHAM YOUNG 41: It was Western football at its finest. Washington State (2-0) QB Brad Gossen threw for 317y and 2 TDs. WSU TB Steve Broussard caught 66y TD pass and ran in 3 others, WR Tim Stallworth caught 6 passes for 121y, and K Jason Hanson kicked school-record 58y FG among 4 3-ptrs to tie mark. For BYU (1-1), QB Ty Detmer completed 34-53/537y, 4 TDs, with WR Mark Bellini (10/140y, 3 TDs) sparkling. Detmer also threw 3 INTs, 1 of which Wazzu S Jay Languein returned 78y to set up score.

PITTSBURGH 29 Boston College 10: Pittsburgh (1-0) dominated on both sides of ball as QB Alex Van Pelt was nearly perfect (15-18/216, 2 TDs) and Panthers D contributed 4 INTs, 3 sacks, and 57y FUM TD RET by DE Carnel Smith. Smith's TD, set up on hit by DT Marc Spindler on Boston College QB Mark Kamphaus (16-32/158y), gave Pitt 20-0 H lead. Eagles (0-1) made game of it with 10 pts in 3rd Q, including 1y TD run by FB Ed Toner, until Smith came through again with sack for safety that finished off BC.

CLEMSON 34 Florida State 23: Clemson inflicted on Seminoles (0-2) what FSU coach Bobby Bowden call "good whipping." Tigers (2-0) jumped out to 21-0 lead as TB Terry Allen (20/130y) scored 2 of his 3 TDs, and frosh LB Wayne Simmons raced 73y with INT for score. Clemson gained 148y before FSU could muster its opening 1st down. FSU hoped to turn momentum with 2y TD run by TB Dexter Carter near end of 1st H. Tigers, however, quickly answered when Allen raced 73y for TD and 28-10 H lead.

Mississippi 24 FLORIDA 19: Rebels (2-0) stole game in which they garnered 9 1st downs and were outgained 379y to 128y. Mississippi won by converting 4 TOs into scores. Former Mississippi HS star QB Kyle Morris had tough game for Gators, throwing 2 INTs and losing FUM. Both picks were by CB Chauncey Goodwin—HS all-star game roommate of Morris—who made 58y INT TD RET and went 19y with another to set up additional TD. Florida (0-1) TB Emmitt Smith rushed for 117y, 2 TDs.

Miami 51 WISCONSIN 3: New-look Hurricanes (1-0) debuted with double dose of Ericksons: new coach Dennis had QB Craig Erickson (17-37/281y, 4 TDs) running new single-back O. QB Erickson started slowly, but turned to another new face, WR Wesley Carroll, fresh out of JC, who caught 7/113y and pair of TDs in 2nd Q while totaling 235y topped by 122y in punt RETS. Still, Badgers (0-1) used 2 personal foul PENs by rambunctious Miami to move 37y to K Rich Thompson's 38y FG on opening possession. Carroll made punt RETs of 36 and 20y to set up 1st H TDs that extended Miami's 6-3 lead to 20-3 early in 2nd Q. Smallest crowd since 1943 turned out at Camp Randall Stadium and enjoyed itself with mocking chant: "We scored first!"

Tennessee 24 UCLA 6: Redshirt frosh TB Chuck Webb had 22/134y on ground to lead Tennessee (1-0) to surprisingly easy victory. QB Bret Johnson debuted at helm of Bruins (0-1) O and received mixed reviews. UCLA moved ball but could not muster any pts until 4th Q TD pass. Volunteers, whose 3 TD drives averaged 86y, rushed for 247y and pounded away on 20 straight runs at 1 point to wear down Bruins.

WASHINGTON 19 Texas A&M 6: QB Cary Conklin's arm, TB Greg Lewis' legs, and K John McCallum's foot were too much for Aggies (1-1). In new single-back O set, Conklin tossed for 224y, including 22y TD pass to WR Mario Bailey, Lewis rushed for 133y, and McCallum booted 4 FGs, shortest from 35y, to lead Huskies (1-0). Improved Washington D thwarted the strong Texas A&M rushing game, limiting Aggies to 2 FGs by K Layne Talbot. QB Lance Pavlas threw for 189y to lead A&M.

September 16, 1989

SYRACUSE 10 Army 7: Syracuse (2-0) tried best to blow game, but Cadets could not pull out win. Orangemen drove downfield with 1st possession until FB Duane Kinnon lost FUM in Army EZ. Syracuse O soon turned ball over on 2 INTs and had punt blocked. Army (0-1) converted punt block into 1y TD run by TB Mike Mayweather (17/102y), who led attack that outrushed 11th-ranked Orange by 212y to 118y. Syracuse righted itself, emerging with 10 pts in 3rd Q, including 23y TD run by TB Michael Owens.

WEST VIRGINIA 45 South Carolina 21: QB Major Harris led Mountaineers (3-0) to 14th straight win, completing 17-20/239y, 3 TDs, and rushing for 58y, 2 TDs. West Virginia outgained Gamecocks (1-1-1) by 589y to 338y margin, despite Carolina QB Todd Ellis' contribution of 256y passing. But, Ellis also was sacked 3 times and threw 2 INTs. West Virginia built 31-7 lead before Ellis threw his 2nd and 3rd TD passes.

Florida State 31 LOUISIANA STATE 21: Pressure was on Florida State after 2 straight defeats. QB Peter Tom Willis completed 25-35/301y, TD as Seminoles (1-2) scored 21 pts in 2nd H to win battle of early-season disappointments. Willis threw 32y TD pass to WR Terry Anthony in 3rd Q and added 7y scoring keeper for winning pts in 4th Q. Florida State outgained LSU (0-2) 522y to 362y, compiled 31 1st downs and spread O wealth. FSU TB Dexter Carter rushed for 95y, and 3 other backs scored TD. QB Tommy Hodson threw for 222y in Tigers' losing effort.

AUBURN 24 Southern Mississippi 3: FB James Joseph, rushed 23/career-high 149y, and devastating D led way for Tigers (2-0). D, which was led by extra-quick DE Lamar Rogers, continuously pressured Eagles QB Brett Favre (14-29/143y) and allowed measly 39y rushing. Southern Miss (1-2) could muster only 10 1st downs, having now followed big win over Florida State with consecutive losses. Mighty Auburn D had now played 11 Qs in row, including last season's Sugar Bowl, without surrendering TD.

Notre Dame 24 MICHIGAN 19: Last KO TD RET surrendered by Michigan (0-1) had occurred 32 years earlier. In wild affair, lightning struck twice. Notre Dame launched WR Raghib "Rocket" Ismail, who scored on dazzling KO RETs of 88y and 92y to lead Fighting Irish (2-0) to 14th straight win and 3rd in row in border rivalry. Both of Ismail's KO TDs featured crushing blocks by ND RB Rodney Culver. Overshadowed in loss was play of Michigan (0-1) soph QB Elvis Grbac (17-21/134y, 2 TDs), who relieved injured QB Michael Taylor. Grbac's TD pass to WR Greg McMurtry closed game's scoring as ND ran out clock thereafter by converting 4th-and-1 on FB Anthony Johnson run with 1:58 remaining. Game served up 25th matchup of AP's no.1 and 2 teams. It was earliest date in any season that such meeting had occurred.

Oregon 44 IOWA 6: Ducks chased Iowa (0-1) from AP rankings as QB Bill Musgrave (20-27/263y) threw 3 TDs, 2 to TE Kolya Tefft. Oregon (2-0) used speed advantage to hold Hawkeyes to 28/26y rushing with 7 hurtful TOs. Score reached 24-0 at H, 38-0 after 3rd Q—Iowa had only 74y when 3rd Q ended. QB Tom Poholsky completed 8-19/70y amid chorus of boos as Hawkeyes absorbed worst opening loss since 1970. Iowa sub QB Matt Rodgers scored TD on 4th down bootleg in 1YL. Ducks WR Terry Obee caught 5/126y, and S Derek Horton contributed 2 INTs and FUM REC.

COLORADO 38 Illinois 7: TB Eric Bieniemy (17/100y) rushed for 2 TDs and threw 48y TD pass to WR M.J. Nelson, as Buffaloes (3-0) roamed. Illinois (1-1) QB Jeff George was held to 99y passing, was sacked 4 times, and threw 2 INTs that were converted into TDs. Colorado QB Darian Hagan's 74y pass to WR Jeff Campbell on game's 3rd play set early tone and led to TD. Buffs gained 475y total O with whopping 223y coming on only 7 pass completions. Meanwhile, Fighting Illini were shut down after 80y voyage had tied matters at 7-7 in 1st Q on 2y run by FB Howard Griffith (16/87y).

ARIZONA 6 Oklahoma 3: Arizona (2-1) won war of attrition on K Doug Pfaff's 40y FG with 2 secs left, capping drive that featured FB Mario Hampton's 1y run that transformed 4th-and-1 challenge. Wildcats recovered 3 Oklahoma (2-1) FUMs and held Sooners to 0y passing and 222y rushing. Punt FUM by OU WR Otis Taylor led to Pfaff's 1st FG. Oklahoma FB Kenyon Rasheed and QB Chris Melson each lost FUM deep in Arizona territory in 2nd H to ruin strong Sooners threats. HB Mike Gaddis rushed for 88y to lead no. 6 Oklahoma's hindered rush attack.

September 23, 1989

PITTSBURGH 30 Syracuse 23: QB Alex Van Pelt (25-32/306y) was on fire, completing 13 straight passes at 1 point, to lead Panthers (3-0) to 1st series win since 1983. Pittsburgh TB Curvin Richards rushed for 100y, and TB Derrick Lewis added 3 TDs. Swarming Pitt D sacked Syracuse (2-1) QB Bill Schaar 8 times and picked him off twice. Each team had scored quickly as Orange WR Rob Carpenter threw 69y scoring pass to WR Rob Moore (6/170y), and Van Pelt hit WR Henry Tuten with 61y TD pass on Pitt's 1st play. That score represented 1st TD pass allowed by Orange secondary since 2nd game of 1988. It paved way for 24 more pts by Panthers, and gave inspiration to Pitt D to hold off late Syracuse rally.

ALABAMA 15 Kentucky 3: Crimson Tide D dominated, holding Kentucky (2-1) to 9 1st downs and 125y total O. Alabama sacked Kentucky QB Freddie Maggard 7 times. Wildcats did its best to keep team in game, holding Alabama (2-0) to 3 K Philip Doyle FGs. Tide had led 6-3 at H, until 1y TD run by Bama RB Martin Houston in 4th Q. Alabama QB Jeff Dunn (14-19/136y) played well until being knocked out with knee injury in 2nd H. When Maggard was able to avoid rush, he threw for 89y.

Arkansas 24 MISSISSIPPI 17: Arkansas (2-0) outlasted Ole Miss as HB E.D. Jackson (22/83y) rushed for 2 TDs and QB Quinn Grovey threw 7y game-winning TD pass to WR Derek Russell. Winning pass was thrown in 3rd Q only to see neither team able to score in 4th Q. Rebels (3-1) led 7-0 early on 21y INT RET by S Chris Mitchell, but surrendered Jackson's 2 TDs before tying game at 14-14 on 43y scoring pass from QB John Darnell to WR Pat Coleman (6/85y). Ole Miss had final march halted on EZ INT by Hogs CB Anthony Cooney with 13 secs left. Although throwing 2 INTs, Darnell passed for 149y and rushed for team-high 54y. Seesaw game was tied 3 occasions.

Rutgers 38 NORTHWESTERN 27: Rutgers QB Scott Erney and WR Randy Jackson (2/173y) teamed up on 2 bombs that served as centerpiece to Wildcats' submission. Trailing 10-6 in 2nd Q, Erney threw 90y TD pass to Jackson. Northwestern (0-3) regained lead on 10y run by HB Bob Christian, who rushed for career-high 162y. Teams slugged it out, trading TDs and FGs until 4th Q. Scarlet Knights (2-0-2) were up 32-27, but were pinned deep in own territory. Then, Erney (13-28/306y, 2 INTs) and Jackson struck again, with 83y TD connection. Wildcats QB Tim O'Brien, who threw for 222y and TD, could not rally his troops. Game was 1,000th played by Rutgers.

Nebraska 48 MINNESOTA 0: At least embarrassed Golden Gophers (1-1) still led all-time series record at 29-19-2. Huskers (3-0) had numerous stars with IB Ken Clark rushing for 100y and 2 TDs, QB Gerry Gdowski completing 10-15/180y, and WB Richard Bell catching 5/121y with 26y TD reception. Minnesota TB Darrell Thompson managed only 45y, and once Gophers fell behind 24-0 at H he became less of factor.

Michigan 24 UCLA 23: Michigan (1-1) overcame 8-pt deficit in final 95 secs to stun Bruins (1-2) as TD pass and 25y FG by K J.D. Carlson were sandwiched around successful onside-KO. Wolverines CB David Key forced FUM by Bruins TB Shawn Wills at 43YL, and it was converted into short TD pass by QB Elvis Grbac to TE Derrick Walker that pulled Michigan within 23-21. UCLA broke up ensuing 2-pt conv pass attempt. S Vada Murray, who blocked x-pt following last Bruins TD, recovered onside-KO to set up 7-play, 39y drive to winning FG. Murray then picked off Hail Mary pass by backup QB Jim Bonds at game's end. UCLA QB Bret Johnson had thrown 2 TD passes, and LB Marvcus Patton forced 2 FUMs with tough hits. Contest was 1st regular season game in Rose Bowl stadium for Michigan coach Bo Schembechler, who was 2-7 in same facility on New Year's Days.

SOUTHERN CALIFORNIA 42 Ohio State 3: Trojans (2-1) started slowly, but then exploded to hand Buckeyes worst defeat in 43 years. USC backup QB Shane Foley jump-started O in 2nd Q with 3y TD pass to TE Scott Galbraith. Starting QB Todd Marinovich (14-22/246y, INT) returned from injury to throw 87y scoring bomb to WR John Jackson, 1st of 4 TDs for young QB. TB Ricky Ervins added 117y on ground as Southern California featured balanced attack. Things had gone well in early going for Ohio State (1-1) because TB Carlos Snow rushed for 70y in 1st Q to prompt 3-0 lead on 45y FG by K Pat O'Morrow. Snow, however, soon was shut down, finishing with only 83y rushing as USC D helped Trojans to total O edge of 491y to 223y.

ARIZONA 20 Washington 17: Arizona (3-1) K Doug Pfaff did it again, booting 35y FG with 61 secs left to knock off Huskies (2-1). QB Ronald Veal (8-12/153y and 53y rushing) slowly moved Wildcats 38y, needing 18 plays including 1y keeper on 4th down at Washington 33YL. Arizona had taken 14-10 H lead on Veal's 43y TD pass to WR Melvin Smith, who was arrested later that day for firing gun into crowd. Huskies QB Cary Conklin led TD drive on 1st possession of 2nd H, completing 6-7/81y of his 354y total to set up 7y TD run by FB James Compton. Pfaff tied up game early in 4th Q with 19y FG after Arizona stalled on Husky 2YL. Washington WR Orlando McKay caught 6 passes for 110y and 38y TD.

STANFORD 18 Oregon 17: Trailing 17-0 in 4th Q, Stanford (1-2) needed 2 QBs to spark winning rally. Starting QB Brian Johnson (24-39/270y, 2 INTs) threw 21y TD pass to RB Gary Taylor to get Cardinal on scoreboard before injuring shoulder on next drive at Oregon 24YL. Stanford QB Steve Smith stepped in to run 1y TD keeper 5 plays later and pass for vital 2-pt conv. After onside-KO was recovered by Stanford TE Cory Booker, Smith (6-6/42y) needed 2 passes to set up winning 37y FG by K John Hopkins. QB Bill Musgrave (16-30/213y) had thrown 2 TDs to lead Ducks (2-1), whose D used 6 sacks, 3 by DE Andre Williams, and 3 TOs to forge shutout for 3 Qs. Even so, Stanford outgained Ducks 414y to 272y by day's end.

AP Poll September 25

1 Notre Dame (57)	1497	14 Houston	659
2 Miami (3)	1432	15 North Carolina State	565
3 Nebraska	1315	16 Oklahoma	544
4 Auburn	1284	17 Arizona	495
5 Colorado	1236	18 Syracuse	462
6 Michigan	1193	19 Washington State	422
7 Clemson	1186	20 Illinois	366
8 Arkansas	1030	21 Washington	320
9 West Virginia	955	22 Texas A&M	233
10 Pittsburgh	943	23 Georgia	213
11 Southern California	852	24 Air Force	163
12 Tennessee	803	25 Florida State	145
13 Alabama	725		

September 30, 1989

Pittsburgh 31 WEST VIRGINIA 31: Sloppy Pittsburgh spotted Mountaineers (4-0-1) 22-pt lead, but rallied for tie in 4th Q as K Ed Frazier booted 42y FG at game's end. Pitt (3-0-1) QB Adam Walker's 2y TD run capped 80y march that cut deficit to 31-15. TB Eugene Napoleon's lost FUM on West Virginia's next possession was converted into 9y TD pass from QB Alex Van Pelt to WR Henry Tuten (7/142y). Onside-KO led to FG attempt, but roughing K PEN allowed drive to continue to 5y TD run by TB Curvin Richards (20/128y) that made it 31-28. Fired-up Panthers soon forced punt, and Van Pelt, with 49 secs left, connected on 2 passes to set up Frazier's 3-ptr. West Virginia QB Major Harris had thrown 4 TDs, 2 to WR Reggie Rembert (5/145y), as Mountaineers converted 6 Panther TOs, including Van Pelt's 4 INTs, into 31-9 lead.

DUKE 21 Clemson 17: Coach Steve Spurrier enjoyed biggest win in Durham as Blue Devils (2-3) notched 1st win over Clemson since 1980 and 1st over Top 10 team since beating Stanford in 1971. Tigers (4-1) played favorite's role in 1st H, grabbing 14-0 lead on 2 TD runs by TB Terry Allen (32/143y). Duke QB Billy Ray (24-43/262y, 2 TDs), transfer from Alabama, overcame 5 INTs to throw 2 TDs in 2nd H including game-winning 7y TD pass to wide-open FB Chris Brown with 3:18 left. Stellar Duke WR Clarkston Hines caught 18y TD pass, while breaking conf record for career receiving yards (2,453y). "This is one all of us will remember the rest of our lives," said soon-to-be-ex-Duke coach Spurrier.

South Carolina 24 GEORGIA 20: Gamecocks (3-1-1) converted 2 TOs into 10 pts in 3rd Q in upsetting Georgia (2-1), which lost possession 3 straight times during crucial 3rd Q. South Carolina QB Todd Ellis (11-16/126y, 2 TDs) threw decisive 22y TD to WR Carl Platt late in 3rd Q to break 17-17 tie. TB Rodney Hampton paced Bulldogs with 104y rushing and 10y TD run, but Gamecocks D held Bulldogs to –21y during last 2 series. Carolina sacked QB Greg Talley on final 3 plays, 2 by NG Tim High.

TENNESSEE 21 Auburn 14: TB Reggie Cobb exploded for 225y, with 79y TD jaunt in 2nd Q, as Volunteers (4-0) dominated run game by 350y to 29y. Tennessee sandwiched pair of safeties around Cobb's run for 11-0 lead, as 2 different long snappers overshot frustrated Tigers P Chris Dickinson. Teams traded FGs before QB Reggie Slack, who threw for 285y, hit WR Alexander Wright (4/129y) with 83y TD pass. It pulled Auburn (2-1) to within 14-11 after profitable 2-pt conv. Vols LB Shazzon Bradley sealed matters with INT at Auburn 22YL to set up TB Chuck Webb's 8y TD run. "That's the worst we've been whipped in a long time," said Auburn coach Pat Dye.

OHIO STATE 34 Boston College 29: Scarlet and Gray rode TB Scottie Graham's 151y rushing and his 70y TD burst that gave Ohio State (2-1) commanding 31-7 lead at H. Three different Eagles (0-4) scored in 2nd H as Boston College rallied to claw within 31-23 and 34-29. Ohio D rose up to stonewall BC on 4th-and-1 at its 4YL in last min.

Miami 26 MICHIGAN STATE 20: With QB Craig Erickson leaving with hand injury, backup QB Gino Torretta led Hurricanes (4-0) to victory. Throwing for 134y, Torretta overcame INT returned 35y by Michigan State S Harlon Barnett for TD that tied game at 20-20 by leading drives for K Carlos Huerta's pair of FGs in 4th Q. Hopeful Spartans (1-2) were dismayed to lose FUM on last drive to end game. Michigan State QB Dan Enos completed 14-20/141y and ran for 19y TD. Huerta kicked 4 FGs, including 52y effort that ended day's scoring.

Penn State 16 TEXAS 12: With thanks to LB Andre Collins, Nittany Lions (3-1) escaped with road victory. CB Leonard Humphries returned Collins' 4th career blocked punt for winning TD, game's only 2nd H TD. Penn State TB Blair Thomas rushed for 90y to pace O that managed only 264y and 9 pts, with TD coming on 33y pass from QB Tony Sacca (9-20/129y) to WR David Daniels. Longhorns (1-2) switched QBs Peter Gardere (12-23/170y, INT) and Mark Murdock (7-13/74y) with moderate success. Texas took 7-6 lead in 1st Q on 30y TD pass from Gardere to WR Johnny Walker (8/120y) and led 10-9 at H and 12-9 after 3rd Q, but failed to penetrate inside Penn State 36YL in 2nd H.

Colorado 45 WASHINGTON 28: Inspired by memory of QB Sal Aunese, who died 8 days earlier, every Buffaloes player knelt in moment of silence for their fallen leader, lifted their helmets skyward in salute, and turned to business at hand: crushing Washington (2-2). Building 38-6 lead entering 4th Q, Colorado (4-0) ran roughshod in racking up 485y total O and frustrating Huskies passing with 3 INTs. Buffs QB

Darian Hagan led balanced rushing attack that gained 420y on ground, while TB Eric Bieniemy rushed for 2 TDs, including 35y romp for 1st of team's 6 rushing TDs. Huskies scored 3 TDs in 4th Q to make score appear more respectable.

AP Poll October 2

1 Notre Dame (57)	1497	14 North Carolina State	669
2 Miami (3)	1426	15 Clemson	665
3 Colorado	1344	16 Oklahoma	637
4 Nebraska	1324	17 Syracuse	496
5 Michigan	1234	18 Illinois	419
6 Tennessee	1193	19 Texas A&M	375
7 Arkansas	1118	20 Air Force	371
8 Pittsburgh	1061	21 Washington State	334
9t Southern California	939	22 Florida State	171
9t West Virginia	939	23 Oregon	162
11 Auburn	892	24 Michigan State	128
12 Houston	879	25 UCLA	103
13 Alabama	807		

October 7, 1989

Virginia Tech 12 WEST VIRGINIA 10: Relying on D and kicking game, Hokies (3-1-1) made news with upset of no. 9 West Virginia. In 1st start, Virginia Tech QB Cam Young (15-22/167y) directed O to trio of 1st H FGs for 9-0 lead. Mountaineers (4-1-1) stormed back in 3rd Q behind QB Major Harris, who overcame 3 sacks and 2 INTs to throw TD pass for 10-9 lead. Virginia Tech D stiffened, and frosh K Mickey Thomas, 1 of 2 straight-on kickers in NCAA, nailed his 4th FG, 24y effort to win game.

CLEMSON 34 Virginia 20: Tigers (5-1) ran all-time record vs Virginia to 29-0 as QB Chris Morocco (14-21/210y) threw 2 TDs and ran for another. Replacing injured QB Shawn Moore, QB Matt Blundin led Cavs (4-2) to 17-17 tie in 3rd Q with trick play: he faked reverse before hitting wide-open WR Herman Moore with 75y TD pass. Tigers answered with 80y scoring drive for Morocco's winning TD run. Clemson TB Joe Henderson (105y rushing) contributed 45y scoring burst in 1st Q for 10-7 lead.

TENNESSEE 17 Georgia 14: Vols (5-0) had only 1 scoring opportunity in 2nd H, but made it count with 26y TD run by TB Reggie Cobb (20/106y) for 17-6 lead in 4th Q. Georgia (2-2) sub QB Preston Jones followed with 39y TD to WR Arthur Marshall to close scoring. Tennessee had 10-0 1st Q edge on TB Chuck Webb's 8y TD burst and K Greg Burke's 37y FG. Bulldogs K John Kasay put his team on scoreboard to trim it to 10-3. Talented Cobb had been suspended in mid-week for failing drug test.

Michigan State 17 IOWA 14: With 29 secs on clock, Iowa coach Hayden Fry went for win, down 3 and facing 4th-and-goal at Michigan State 10YL. Under pressure from DT Travis Davis, Iowa (2-2) QB Matt Rodgers (21-35/214y) threw incomplete pass to end matters. Spartans (2-2) earned 17-7 lead behind 35y TD run by frosh RB Tico Duckett (175y rushing) and sharp passing of QB Dan Enos (20-25/217y, INT). Despite those sharp Spartan performances, Hawkeyes hung around within 17-14 after Rodgers hit WB Mike Saunders with 12y TD pass.

ILLINOIS 34 Ohio State 14: Illinois created 17-pt spurt keyed by surprise 34y TD pass from WR Steven Williams to WR Mike Bellamy (10/152y). FB Howard Griffith contributed 2 TDs from his 117y rushing as Illini (3-1) scored 24 pts in 2nd H. Illinois QB Jeff George (12-20/130y, 2 INT) returned from 1st H injury to help spark rally. Sub QB Jason Verduzco played well in George's absence, throwing for 126y in 1st H. WR Jeff Graham's 66y punt TD RET was highlight for Ohio State (2-2), whose O was limited to 10 1st downs.

TEXAS TECH 27 Texas A&M 24: QB Jamie Gill and WR Travis Price hooked up twice in 4th Q for TD passes to rally Red Raiders (4-1) from 10-pt deficit. Their 2nd connection covered 35y with 50 secs left to play. TB Darren Lewis rushed for 3 TDs for Aggies (3-2), who never trailed until final min. Game had to be halted in 3rd Q after brawl was triggered by Texas A&M LB Anthony Williams' hard hit on Red Raiders RB James Gray.

Washington State 51 OREGON 38: TB Steve Broussard rushed for 205y and 3 TDs as Cougars (5-1) amassed 503y. Washington State jumped to 20-6 H lead with key score coming from special teamer Paul Carr, who scored TD with blocked punt. Ducks (3-2) rallied behind QB Bill Musgrave, who threw for career-high 347y, to pull within 27-24. Broussard was not done, however, rushing for 2 TDs in 4th Q, while Cougars CB Ron Ricard made 2 INTs, including 74y TD RET that created potential 2-TD swing. Washington State QB Aaron Garcia (18-25/276y, INT) threw 36y TD to WR Calvin Griggs and K Jason Hanson added 3 FGs.

SOUTHERN CALIFORNIA 24 Washington 16: Trojans QB Todd Marinovich's coming of age continued, while frustration for Washington (2-3) saw no end. Down 10-0, Southern California (4-1) scored 17 straight pts behind Marinovich (23-35/284y), who started rally with 15y TD pass to WR John Jackson at close of 1st H. Huskies answered with 54y drive to pull within 17-16 on 31y TD catch by WR Andre Riley (8/143y). With ample time left (8:44), Washington coach Don James decided on try for 2 pts. It became déjà vu as Washington QB Cary Conklin threw incomplete 2-pt pass while trying for lead against USC in same northwest EZ corner of L.A. Coliseum. And to rub salt in Huskies' wounds, Troy immediately marched to clinching TD for 2nd straight season: 1y TD run by TB Ricky Ervins. WR Jackson's 7 catches/95y made him Trojans' leading career receiver with 124 receptions.

AP Poll October 9

1 Notre Dame (53)	1494	14 Clemson	684
2 Miami (4)	1428	15 Oklahoma	679
3 Colorado (2)	1371	16 Illinois	593
4 Nebraska	1298	17t Washington State	498
5 Michigan	1232	17t Air Force	498
6 Tennessee	1205	19 Florida State	470
7 Arkansas	1108	20 West Virginia	394
8 Houston	1002	21 Michigan State	273
9 Pittsburgh	994	22 UCLA	226
10 Southern California	951	23 Penn State	82
11 Alabama	888	24 South Carolina	77
12 Auburn	869	25t Florida	66
13 North Carolina State	727	25t Brigham Young	66

AP Poll October 16

1 Notre Dame (52)	1443	14 Florida State	644
2 Miami (3)	1374	15 Washington State	627
3 Colorado (3)	1352	16 Houston	611
4 Nebraska	1243	17 Penn State	434
5 Michigan	1187	18 West Virginia	419
6 Tennessee	1162	19 Air Force	317
7 Arkansas	1118	20 Florida	272
8 Pittsburgh	1011	21 Brigham Young	260
9 Southern California	983	22 Arizona	245
10 Alabama	900	23 Texas A&M	203
11 Auburn	873	24 South Carolina	173
12 North Carolina State	779	25 Oklahoma	151
13 Illinois	680		

October 14, 1989

Penn State 34 SYRACUSE 12: Ahead 7-6 in 2nd Q, Penn State blew open hard-fought game with 27 straight pts to halt 2-game series losing streak. Lions (5-1) did so with punishing ground attack that churned out 356y to 63y advantage. TB Blair Thomas rushed for 115y and 38y TD run, while WR O.J. McDuffie raced 84y with punt TD RET, using nifty spin to break free, to close 17-pt 3rd Q with 27-6 lead. Sole TD for Orangemen (2-3) came in 4th Q on QB Mark McDonald's 13y pass to WR Rob Moore.

Georgia Tech 30 CLEMSON 14: Improving Yellow Jackets (2-3) achieved breakthrough win, scoring on 5 1st H possessions to win 2nd straight ACC game after 16 straight losses. K Scott Sisson kicked 3 FGs and RB Jerry Mays scored TDs running and receiving as 20-pt underdog Georgia Tech grabbed 23-6 H lead. QB Shawn Jones (15-23/223y, TD) engineered victory, capping team's performance with 81y TD pass to WR Bobby Rodriguez for 30-6 3rd Q lead. Tigers (5-2) turned to reserve QB DeChane Cameron to lead rally and he moved them 69y, completing 5-5 passes, to 11y QB keeper. But, Tech D rose up to force 2 TOs and ended 2 drives on downs.

Michigan 10 MICHIGAN STATE 7: Spartans (2-3) probably wanted replay after series of mistakes: allowing FG to be blocked, going off-side to allow Michigan to have 2 tries for winning FG, failing to get TD from Wolverines 1YL in 4th Q, and missing 2 FG tries. Wolverines (4-1) scored TD on 1y run by FB Leroy Hoard on 4th down and took 10-0 lead on FG by K.J.D. Carlson. UM TB Tony Boles rushed for 100y. Michigan State drove to within few feet of Wolverines GL before DB Tripp Welborne stopped 188-lb TB Blake Ezor on 4th-and-goal on 1st play of 4th Q. On next possession, Spartans K Jon Langeloh missed 34y 3-pt try. Michigan State QB Dan Enos threw 4y TD pass to WR Courtney Hawkins on 4th down with slightly more than 5 mins left.

Texas 28 Oklahoma 24 (Dallas): Texas (3-2) redshirt frosh QB Peter Gardere earned state-wide adulation, completing 5 straight passes on final drive to pull out Texas win. Last 25y of 66y drive came on Gardere's pass to WR Johnny Walker, who had separated himself from OU secondary. Sooners (4-2) had rallied from 21-7 H deficit as QB Steve Collins threw 41y TD to WR Artie Guess and led marches that ended with 30y FG by K R.D. Lasher and 1y TD run by HB Ike Lewis. Lewis replaced HB Mike Gaddis (14/130y, 66y TD), who left in 3rd Q with knee injury. OU had trailed 15-7 on 2 odd plays as Sooners punt returner Otis Taylor lost FUM when he bumped into blocker, with ball popping up to hands of Texas LB Mical Padgett who returned it 44y for TD. Ensuing x-pt was blocked, but Longhorns K Wayne Clements alertly scooped up ball and threw adlibbed 2-pt conv pass to TE Curtis Thrift.

TEXAS A&M 17 Houston 13: Aggies (4-2) went to unusual 1-5-5 D alignment to check Houston's high-flying Run-and-Shoot O that already had topped 60 pts thrice in 1989. A&M sacked QB Andre Ware 6 times and picked him off 3 times, while allowing him only 247y, TD in air. Texas A&M O contributed attack that featured 2 backs topping 100y: FB Robert Wilson (22/115y, TD) and TB Darren Lewis (12/120y). Cougars (4-1) scored game's final TD on 1y run by RB Chuck Weatherspoon (17/147y), but were unable to spark late score as rally ended on sack by Aggie LB Aaron Wallace.

Notre Dame 41 AIR FORCE 27: Battle of unbeatens quickly proved no contest as Fighting Irish (6-0) vaulted to commanding 35-14 lead at H, scoring TDs on 4 of their 1st 5 possessions. Notre Dame WR Raghib Ismail scored on 24y reverse run and finished off Falcons (6-1) with 56y punt TD RET. ND's rampaging D held AFA's Wishbone attack to 168y rushing, nearly 300y less than avg, so Falcons QB Dee Dowis was forced to throw. Dowis uncharacteristically passed for 306y and 2 TDs, but Air Force's most exciting moment came on run in 4th Q: G Steve Wilson scored TD on "Fumblerooskie" play made popular by Nebraska's O-line earlier in 1980s.

ARIZONA 42 Ucla 7: With week off following frustrating loss to Oregon, Arizona (4-2) coach Dick Tomey switched his O to Colorado's I attack. Proving to be quick learners, Wildcats rushed for 480y to easily handle unprepared Bruins (3-3). Arizona authored 2 early marches of 80y and 82y, scoring on 19y and 54y runs by TB David Eldredge (20/205y). When Wildcats QB Ron Veal, who added 81y rushing and 2 TDs, scored for 21-0 lead in 2nd Q, Arizona had compiled 246y total O to only 21y for shell-shocked Bruins. Arizona led 28-0 by H. Sole consolation for UCLA was late 69y TD drive that continued nation-best 211-game streak of not being shut out.

October 21, 1989

CLEMSON 30 North Carolina State 10: Tigers remained big factor in ACC race by crushing undefeated North Carolina State (6-1) as D allowed paltry 99y in 1st H they led by 17-0. Clemson (6-2) FB Wesley McFadden's 9y TD run in 1st H turned out to be winning score. Wolfpack never got any closer than 17-7, which was achieved on 5y TD run by FB Todd Varn late in 3rd Q. Clemson ended NC State's next drive with frosh S Robert O'Neal's 5th INT of season, 1 of 5 TOs coughed up by visiting leaders of ACC.

FLORIDA STATE 22 Auburn 14: Rallying from 19-pt deficit in 4th Q, Auburn (4-2) scored 11 pts to get within 22-14 and then drove 72y in game's final moments before running out of time at FSU 11YL. Seminoles (5-2) had scored 22 straight pts to take commanding 22-3 lead as FB Edgar Bennett scored twice, from 1y and 7y out, and reserve K Bill Mason booted 3 FGs. Florida State's swift D, which sacked QB Reggie Slack (15-26/173y) 6 times, appeared to have clinched game in 4th Q in forcing incomplete pass on 4th down. However, roughing passer PEN kept Tigers drive alive, and FB James Joseph scored on 4y run. Noles TB Amp Lee (25/110y) lost FUM on Auburn 17YL to set up Tigers' final and vain threat.

ALABAMA 47 Tennessee 30: Both 3rd-Saturday-in-October foes arrived unbeaten for 1st time since 1973. Alabama (6-0) QB Gary Hollingsworth, in only his 4th start, brought back fond memories of Joe Namath and Scott Hunter, throwing for 379y and 3 TDs on school-record 32 completions in 46 tries. Tide TB Siran Stacy added his best impersonation of Bobby Humphrey or Johnny Musso in scoring 4 TDs, while rushing for 33/125y and catching 9/158y. Alabama opened game with TD on 1st possession, 4y catch by FB Kevin Turner, to take lead it would never relinquish. In 2nd Q, Hollingsworth dumped shovel pass to Stacy, who raced to 75y score to extend lead to 17-7 after Vols FB Greg Amsler powered over from 1YL. TB Chuck Webb led Tennessee (5-1) with 110y rushing, while QB Andy Kelly threw for 226y, 2 TDs, 3 INTs, including 33y pitch to WR Anthony Morgan that got it within 16-14 in 2nd Q.

INDIANA 28 Minnesota 18: Unfortunately for Indiana TB Anthony Thompson, few Heisman voters witnessed his 216y, 3-TD rushing act. Golden Gophers (4-2) were dominated throughout, gaining but 12 1st downs to 27 for Hoosiers (4-2). But, Minnesota trailed by slim 21-18 in 4th Q, thanks to spectacular 98y scoring RET of blocked FG by DB Fred Foggie, longest play in Memorial Stadium history. Indiana finally put win in vault on steady Thompson's 16y TD run in game's last secs. "Other" Thompson, Minnesota's TB Darrell Thompson, led Gophers with 117y rushing.

NOTRE DAME 28 Southern California 24: Pre-game fight could not overshadow thrill of nail-biting outcome. Trojans (5-2) marched to Notre Dame 12YL late behind QB Todd Marinovich (33-55/333y, 3 TDs, 3 INTs), but FG wouldn't do, Troy needed TD. After 5y run and 2 incompletions, Marinovich threw 4th down ball to WR Joel Scott broken up in EZ by ND DB D'Juan Francisco. Irish (7-0) QB Tony Rice had scored winning TD with 9:42 left on 15y run right after his 40y pass to WR Raghib Ismail. Trojans had owned 17-7 H lead on TD passes that converted FUMs by Ismail. USC WR John Jackson caught 15y TD on his way to 3 school records: 14 catches/200y and most career y with 2029y. Fighting Irish rallied, rushing for 266y against Southern California D that arrived with nation's best avg of 36.7y per game. TB Ricky Watters and FB Anthony Johnson each ran for 2nd H TDs as ND grabbed 21-17 lead. Johnson later lost FUM—5th TO for Irish—to set up USC's 40y drive for go-ahead TD at 24-21. All 3 TD drives for USC, none longer than 40y, followed FUMs by Notre Dame.

Missouri 21 KANSAS STATE 9: Tigers (2-5) grabbed hard-fought win, while leading from beginning: Missouri scored 1st H's sole TD on 64y INT RET by S Ted LePage. Late in 3rd Q, facing 3rd-and-1, Tigers QB Kent Kiefer lifted team's lead to 14-0 with 41y TD pass to WR Byron Chamberlin. Wildcats (1-6) rallied as QB Carl Straw (26-46/302y, 2 INTs), threw 25y TD to WR Frank Hernandez and converted TO into 32y FG by K David Kruger. HB Michael Jones (15/133y) broke backs of K-State with 67y romp on sweep down left sideline for 21-9 edge. WR Michael Smith was brilliant for Kansas State, catching school-record 13 passes/166y, despite dogged coverage by Mizzou CB Adrian Jones (1 INT).

Texas 24 ARKANSAS 20: Texas (4-2) QB Peter Gardere added another pelt with 3rd win in 3 games as starter. Gardere (16-20/247y), who threw 61y TD to WR Tony Jones (4/114y) in 1st H, sparkled in 3rd Q, completing all 7 of his passes in leading 2 scoring drives to turn 14-13 H deficit into 24-13 lead. Despite heading into wind, Texas outgained Razorbacks 130y to 26y in crucial 3rd Q. Arkansas (5-1) had taken 1st H lead on 9y TD pass from QB Quinn Grovey to TE Billy Winston.

TEXAS CHRISTIAN 27 Air Force 9: Backup QB Leon Clay and frosh WR Stephen Shipley (3/117y) connected on 2 TDs to lead Horned Frogs (4-3), while TCU D shut down QB Dee Dowis and Air Force's explosive attack. Replacing injured QB Ron Jiles in 2nd Q, Clay completed 10-11/165y including 86y on 3rd Q scoring pass to Shipley. RB Tommy Palmer rushed for 177y as Frogs controlled play. Dowis was limited to 28y rushing, while hitting 5-19/69y, INT. Falcons (6-2) were unable to penetrate EZ until 2y scoring run by HB Bill Wosilius with less than 2 mins left.

Nebraska 48 OKLAHOMA STATE 23: Oklahoma State won 70 games in 1980s but could never beat Nebraska (7-0), something it had not done since 1961. Huskers QB Gerry Gdowski rushed for career-high 125y and threw for 170y. Cowboys (2-5) had pulled within 20-16, in 3rd Q on K Cary Blanchard's 3rd FG, but got no closer. Nebraska S Reggie Cooper ended Oklahoma State drive with EZ INT, and Cowboys QB Mike Gundy, who eclipsed Missouri QB Phil Bradley to become Big 8's career total O leader with 6559y, was nailed by blitzing CB Bruce Pickens to force FUM recovered by Pickens at OSU 27YL. Gdowski ran twice, for 26y and 1y, to earn winning TD. Pokes WR Curtis Mayfield (6/208y) set school record for single-game receiving y.

Oklahoma 43 IOWA STATE 40: Cyclones (3-4) set free O that compiled 609y, most ever allowed in Oklahoma (5-2) history, but came up 2y short of 2-pt conv for tie with 1:57 left. Iowa State QB Bret Oberg, who threw for school record 411y, had just tossed 5y TD pass to WR John Glotfelty to pull within 36-34. Ensuing Cyclones onside-KO took unfortunate hop and was returned 42y for TD by Oklahoma WR Eric Bross. Oberg quickly led 76y scoring drive that ended with his 46y TD pass to Glotfelty as teams combined for 3 TDs in final 2 mins. FB Leon Perry led Sooners with 99y rushing.

Arizona 23 WASHINGTON STATE 21: Resurgent Wildcats (5-2) held off Washington State behind D that sacked QB Aaron Garcia (19-35/231y, TD) 6 times, nabbed 4 INTs, and limited Cougars to 67y rushing. Even when Washington State TB Steve Broussard broke through for 53y of his 96y, DB Richard Holt caught him from behind at 10YL to prevent TD. Cougars settled for FG, when more was needed at game's end. Settling for FGs were theme of game as K Jason Hanson kicked 4 FGs for Cougars (6-2) and Arizona K Doug Pfaff hit 3 FGs, including game-winner from 28y out with 5:03 left. Cats standout CB Darryl Lewis ended matters with his 2nd INT, coming with less than 2 mins remaining and Wazzu perched on Arizona 27YL.

October 28, 1989

Alabama 17 PENN STATE 16: Joe Paterno of Penn State (5-2) needed last-sec, chip-shot FG by K Ray Tarasi to prevent coach's 1st-ever 3-game losing streak to opponent. He did not get it. High C snap delayed Tarasi long enough for 6'7" Alabama DE Thomas Rayam to block 17y FG effort and preserve unbeaten season so far for no. 6 Crimson Tide (7-0). Alabama's winning TD came earlier in 4th Q on 12y run by TB Siran Stacy (19/106y). Overcoming 4 INTs, Bama QB Gary Hollingsworth completed 4 passes/55y on go-ahead trip. TB Blair Thomas kept Penn State's O humming with 160y rushing.

FLORIDA STATE 24 Miami 10: Red-hot Seminoles (6-2) put damper on awaited rematch between Miami and Notre Dame by forcing 6 TOs and converting GLS into magnificent clinching 99y TD drive in 3rd Q. Trailing 14-10, Hurricanes (6-1) drove to Florida State 2YL, from where HB Shannon Crowell lost FUM on 3rd down, recovered by LB Kirk Carruthers (16 tackles, 2 INTs). Noles then marched length of field to TB Amp Lee's 1y TD run. Any Miami rally would prove difficult without injured QB Craig Erickson. Sub QB Gino Torretta threw 4 INTs, and Miami frustratingly was shut out on 3 drives that reached FSU 1YL (by FUM, INT, loss of downs). TB Dexter Carter sealed Florida State's 1st series win in 5 years with 142y rushing—1y less than sloppy Noles were penalized—as FSU rushed for 220y against nation's top-ranked rush D (45.5y per game). Carter had opened scoring with 37y run on team's 2nd play after CB Terrell Buckley picked off Torretta's pass on game's 1st scrimmage. Miami WR Wesley Carroll fielded 10/119y.

NOTRE DAME 45 Pittsburgh 7: Playing like defending national champs, Notre Dame (8-0) posted easy win over recent nemesis Pitt, winners of 3 of 4 latest match-ups. Panthers (5-1-1) scored on 1st series on QB Alex Van Pelt's 8y pass to FB Ronald Redmon, but gained only 1y next 5 times with ball. Irish powered for 310y rushing against D that was surrendering only 92y rushing per game. WR-TB Raghib Ismail led ND rushers with 74y, including 50y on blistering TD run. Notre Dame D picked off 3 of Van Pelt's passes, with DB Pat Terrell roaring 54y with 1 INT for 1st H TD.

MICHIGAN 38 Indiana 10: Player named Anthony scored multiple TDs in Ann Arbor, but it wasn't Indiana (4-3) TB Anthony Thompson (30/90y), who managed to tie NCAA record with his 59th career TD. It was Michigan TB Tony Boles, who scored 3 times in 2nd Q despite hurting nerve in pinched nerve. Boles' 91y TD burst gave 24-3 H edge to Wolverines (6-1). Michigan gained 550y total O, including 347y on ground, as Boles rushed for 156y, and QB Michael Taylor threw for 165y and 2 TDs. Wolverines D crafted 6 sacks and 2 INTs while stretching streak of rushing TD prevention to 23 Qs, before allowing Thompson's late score. Hoosiers K Scott Bonnell kicked longest FG (55y) in school history in 2nd Q.

OHIO STATE 41 MINNESOTA 37: Talk about H adjustments. Spotting Gophers 31 pts, Ohio State (5-2) roared back with 41 pts in 2nd H to pull out amazing win on 15y TD reception by WR Jeff Graham with 41 secs left. Buckeyes' rally after H represented tie for biggest pt-margin comeback in NCAA history (Maryland's 42-40 win over Miami in 1984). Bucks QB Greg Frey shook off disastrous 1st H, in which he went 2-8/35y in air

with 3 TOs that Minnesota converted into 17 pts. In 2nd H, Frey authored 18-23/327y, 3 TDs passing, scored TD, and succeeded on trio of 2-pt conv passes. Golden Gophers (4-3) built early lead as TB Darrell Thompson (29/133y) scored on 12y TD run, K Brent Berglund kicked 1st of 3 FGs, and S Sean Lumpkin speared Frey's FUM pop-up and ran 85y for Minny's 2nd TD. Minnesota added 2 more TDs before Ohio finally scored on TB Carlos Snow's 1y run with 10 secs left in 1st H.

Colorado 20 OKLAHOMA 3: Changing of guard in Big 8 continued as Buffs (8-0) won opening 8 games for 1st time since 1937. Colorado D proved mettle by allowing only 169y rushing and 79y passing on combined 3-21 misfortunes of Oklahoma (5-3) QBs Steve and Tink Collins. Buffaloes rushed for 284y, with QB Darian Hagan gaining 107y and TB J.J. Flannigan adding 103y. Flannigan scored winning pts on 1y run late in 1st H at end of 53y drive that was jumpstarted by Hagan's 40y run. Sooners HB Ted Long caught 2/64y to become team's leading y-maker. Buffs' triumph was 1st over Sooners since 1976, 1st in Norman since 1965.

ARKANSAS 45 Houston 39: Matching career-high single-game passing y in 1st H, Arkansas (6-1) QB Quinn Grovey (11-14/256y, 2 TDs) led efficient O that stunned Cougars (5-2). Razorbacks racked up 647y total O and scored on 6 of last 7 possessions; RB James Rouse (19/114y) and FB Barry Foster (20/125y) were useful weapons. Erasing 28-24 deficit, Arkansas took lead on 1st play of 4th Q as Grovey hit WR Derek Russell for 51y TD pass. Strong-armed Houston QB Andre Ware rifled 34-46/352y, 3 TDs, and RB Benny Anders also threw TD pass, tricky 60y throw to WR Patrick Cooper that opened scoring for Cougars. It matched Grovey's 65y strike to Russell that had given Hogs early 7-0 edge.

ARIZONA STATE 44 Washington State 39: Despite school-record passing 534y passing by QB Paul Justin (33-47/534y, 4 TDs), assurance of Sun Devils (4-3-1) victory required 2y TD run by FB Kelvin Fisher with 1:02 left and INT by S Nathan LaDuke with 33 secs left. Arizona State WR Ron Fair set Pac-10 record with 19 catches/277y and registered 3 TDs. Washington State (6-3) owned leads of 17-13 at H and 24-23 after 3 Qs before teams combined for 36-pt explosion in 4th Q. Nifty Cougars TB Steve Broussard rushed for 97y and 2 TDs and added Wazzu's 3rd TD in 3rd Q on 98y KO RET. Cougars co-QBs Aaron Garcia and Brad Gossen combined for 24-31/419y and INT, with Gossen notching 334y in air. Game provided big O pyrotechnics as ASU racked up 651y total O, and Cougars romped for 566y.

November 4, 1989

PENN STATE 19 West Virginia 9: Mountaineers (6-2-1) should have used stick-um on their hands. Nittany Lions (6-2) scored all 19 pts after West Virginia suffered TOs. Penn State D recovered 5 WVU FUMs, intercepted pass, and sacked QB Major Harris 4 times. Lions D fairly well destroyed Mountaineers O that had averaged 35 pts per game. Penn State LB Andre Collins had 15 tackles, forced 2 FUMs, blocked x-pt kick, and raced 28y with fake punt to set up FG. Lions LB Mark D'Onofrio burst in for 2 sacks and forced pair of FUMs. Penn State TB Blair Thomas rushed for 150y and lifted his career rushing mark to 4,072y. K Ray Tarasi scored 13 pts for State as he kicked 4 FGs, including personal-best 49y effort. Harris threw for 166y and rushed for 135y.

Virginia 20 NORTH CAROLINA STATE 9: Cavaliers (8-2) won key ACC game despite being doubled in 1st downs and suffering through miserable passing game (3-10) by QB Shawn Moore. UVa CB Jason Wallace scored on 40y INT RET, while Moore overcame his inaccuracy to launch 32y TD to star WR Herman Moore. Virginia K Jake McInerney stretched his streak to 14 successful FGs when he nailed pair of 3-pters. Wolfpack (7-2) were limited by injury to QB Shane Montgomery (3-3/42y), who nonetheless quickly became school's all-time passing leader on opening possession that reached Cavs 3YL. NC State had to settle for 3 pts on that drive and dittoed that procedure on subsequent trip to Virginia's red zone, making FG for 6-0 lead.

AUBURN 10 Florida 7: In closing moments, all QB Reggie Slack faced was prospect of driving his Tigers (6-2) through Gators defenders, nation's top-rated D, that had been dominant for most of game. Slack (12-19/143y), booed throughout, remarkably threw 25y TD pass on 4th down to uncovered WR Shayne Wasden with 26 secs left to pull out victory. Florida (6-2) had grabbed 7-0 H lead as TB Emmitt Smith—held to 86y rushing, shadow of 161y per-game run avg—scored on 5y run. Tigers, unable to cross midfield for more than half of game, finally put vital pts on scoreboard in 3rd Q on K Win Lyle's 47y FG.

Illinois 31 IOWA 7: Illini (7-1) took no prisoners in racking up 507y Total O. Illinois QB Jeff George (28-44/302y) threw TD and RB Wagner Lester rushed in 2 scores. WR Mike Bellamy was George's favorite target, catching 8/108y and 25y TD. Iowa QB Matt Rodgers threw for 291y, but was picked off 4 times as Hawkeyes (4-4) committed 6 ugly TOs. Illinois LB Steve Glasson ranged all over field, making 11 tackles and 2 INTs.

GAME OF THE YEAR
COLORADO 27 Nebraska 21:

Focused mission of Colorado (9-0) continued as they won battle of conf unbeatens with determined performance. QB Darian Hagan led Buffs charge, rushing for 86y and TD, while WR Jeff Campbell made 3/108y on punt RETs to set up pair of TDs. Huskers (8-1) opened scoring with 51y TD on screen pass to FB Bryan Carpenter. Colorado HB J.J. Flannigan soon knotted game at 7-7 with 70y scoring dash. Teams then traded TDs again as Campbell's 47y punt RET set up Hagan's 1y TD run, matched by 2nd TD pass by Nebraska QB Gerry Gdowski (11-27/211y, 3 TDs): 12y to WR Morgan Gregory. K Ken Culbertson's 49y FG near end of 2nd Q gave Buffs lead for good at 17-14. Flannigan added another TD in 3rd Q, following pass interference PEN that was 1st ruled as INT by Nebraska. Huskers scored again, but then Buffs D blanked them in 4th Q with Colorado CB Dave McCloughan making EZ break-up of pass to WR Jon Bostick. "It's for Sal," Flannigan said afterwards. "We're doing this for Sal."

Texas Tech 24 TEXAS 17: Underrated Red Raiders (6-2) stunned Texas (4-3) as QB Jamie Gill (15-22/224y) connected with 5'9" walk-on WR Anthony Manyweather for 65y TD pass with 4:26 left. K Lin Elliott added 51y FG insurance as Texas Tech won in Austin for 1st time since 1967. TB James Gray paced Red Raiders rushers with 117y and 14y TD that gave 7-3 lead. Texas (4-3) profited from fine effort by WR Johnny Walker, who caught 8/142y. Longhorns suffered 5 TOs, including 4 INTs.

AIR FORCE 29 Army 3: Army (5-3) rushed for 195y, led by HB Mike Mayweather's 16/62y, but it wasn't enough to keep Falcons from easily snatching Commander-in-Chief Trophy. Air Force (7-2) QB Dee Dowis (5-9/107y, 2 TDs) accounted for 3 TDs and ran for 141y to set career QB rushing y mark of 3336y, 37y more than Tampa's Freddie Solomon (1971-74).

BRIGHAM YOUNG 45 Oregon 41: QB Ty Detmer rallied Cougars (7-2) from 33-19 deficit, throwing his 3rd TD pass, 15y effort, to WR Jeff Frandsen (10/188y) with 1:01 left. BYU's winning drive went 90y drive to pull out win. Ducks (5-4) permitted 19 straight pts and trailed 38-33 until they answered with QB Bill Musgrave's 15y TD and 2-pt conv passes to WR Terry Obee. TB Derek Loville rushed for 3 TDs for Oregon, while Musgrave (26-44/489y, TD, INT) and Detmer (29-47/470y, 3 TDs, 2 INTs) combined for 2-team passing record of 959y. North Carolina State's Shane Montgomery and Duke's Steve Slayden had shared old mark of 926y since 1987.

CALIFORNIA 29 Arizona 28: Having 3-TD lead apparently wasn't enough in high-scoring Pac-10. Wildcats (6-3) jumped out to 21-0 lead behind QB George Malauulu, who finished game with 112y rushing and 147y passing. Arizona smoothly drove 81y, 98y, and 63y to forge its lead. But, California (3-6) QB Troy Taylor had no intention of wasting game in which he supplanted Rich Campbell as Bears all-time passing leader. Taylor completed 28-44/372y and pair of TDs to WR Michael Smith (8/177y). Taylor drove team 83y for winning 6y TD run by TB Greg Zomalt as Cal scored game's final 19 pts. TB Anthony Wallace led Cal's rushing attack with 96y and 1y TD.

FRESNO STATE 31 San Jose State 30: Spartans (4-4) paid for late-game conservative call and blew upset chance. Backup QB Ralph Martini led 2 late TD drives as San Jose rallied from 31-17 deficit. Down by 31-30, Spartans went for tying kick only to bungle snap with 2:33 left. Fresno State (9-0) ran out clock to preserve its perfect record. Down 17-10 at H, Bulldogs scored 3 TDs in 3rd Q to wrest control of game including WR Dwight Pickens' 10y run on reverse for ultimately decisive pts. Each team enjoyed big RETs in 1st H as Fresno KR Kelvin Means took kick 90y to set up Bulldogs' 1st TD, and Spartans TB Sheldon Canley, nation's leader in all-purpose y, tied game moments later with thrilling 97y KO RET.

November 11, 1989

Miami 24 PITTSBURGH 3: With season-long injury bug limiting usually potent O, Hurricanes (8-1) counted on D to dominate. Panthers (5-2-1) were held to −10y rushing in 1st H and 28y for game, while QB Alex Van Pelt threw 2 INTs under intense pressure. Miami QB Craig Erickson returned from injury list to throw for 199y, TD, and FB Steve McGuire rushed for 114y, TD, in relief of injured leading rusher FB Leonard Conley. Canes converted 2 TOs into K Carlos Huerta FGs. K Ed Frazier scored Pittsburgh pts with 29y FG in 4th Q.

MARYLAND 13 Penn State 13 (Baltimore): After 24 straight series losses, tying Penn State seemed awfully attractive to Terrapins (3-6-1). Maryland knotted game with just under min remaining on K Dan DeArmas' 26y FG, even though it passed up last shot at winning TD in 4th-and-5 situation at Penn State 9YL. TB Blair Thomas rushed for 125y for Nittany Lions (6-2-1), while Terps QB Neil O'Donnell completed 14 straight passes to finish with 18-24/219y.

DUKE 35 North Carolina State 26: Arm-weary NC State (7-3) QB Shane Montgomery attempted NCAA-record 73 passes, but could not rally his charges. Duke (7-3) was led by record-setter of its own in WR Clarkston Hines (6/131y), who caught 2 TD passes from QB Dave Brown to set mark for career TD catches at 35, although his record was

tied later in same day by WR Terance Mathis of New Mexico. Brown threw for 374y and 4 TDs, while TB Randy Cuthbert added 158y rushing as Blue Devils O outlasted Montgomery's constant aerial barrage. WRs Reggie Lawrence (5/129y) and Al Byrd (5/126y) were NC State's leading targets as Montgomery ended his game with 37-73/535y.

VIRGINIA 32 Virginia Tech 25: Melee-filled battle, in which Hokies (5-4) coach Frank Beamer lost front tooth to inadvertent elbow, went to Virginia on strength of 24-0 lead built by H on 1st of 2 TD runs by FB Durwin Greggs and 11y TD draw run by QB Shawn Moore (12-21/188y). Cavaliers (9-2) WR Herman Moore spun away for 56y pass-run that positioned frosh TB Terry Kirby for TD leap before H. Virginia Tech QB Cam Young (7-15/54y) rallied his team to UVa 21YL after 2nd H KO but went down with broken arm at end of scramble. QB Rodd Wooten (9-16/102y, INT) flipped 4th down TD pass and followed with 2-pt pass to pull Hokies within 24-8. Greggs scored again on 22y run for 32-8 lead, but WR Marcus Mikel ran 14y reverse for TD and FB Rich Fox made 1y TD dive to rally Va Tech to within 32-22. When Kirby fumbled ensuing KO with more than 5 mins left, Hokies appeared to have chance. But they were held to FG, and Cavs DB Jason Wallace ended it with INT with 1:13 to go.

Georgia 17 Florida 10 (Jacksonville): Georgia TB Rodney Hampton scored 2 TDs during 3-min span of 3rd Q to turn 7-3 deficit into 17-7 lead. As Bulldogs (6-3) were scoring twice in 3rd Q, Florida was stopped on downs twice during 3rd Q. Georgia DB Ben Smith had 2 of his team's 3 INTs as Bulldogs won 14th series contest in last 18 games. Hampton outgained his Florida counterpart, TB Emmitt Smith, nation's rushing leader, by 121y to 106y. Sole Florida (6-3) TD provided 7-3 H edge. It came in 2nd Q courtesy of WR Ernie Mills' 19y catch—after 37y grab—from QB Donald Douglas (12-20/181y, TD, 3 INTs), making his 2nd collegiate start after regular QBs Kyle Morris and Shane Matthews were suspended. Big 3rd Q play came on 4th-and-1 at UGa 22YL as Bulldogs NG Robert Bell led stonewall that greeted Gators' Smith when he needed 1y. Although Florida quickly got LB Ephesians Bartley's INT, Gators handed ball right back on LB Matt McCormick's FUM REC that set Georgia sailing 76y to Hampton's 1st TD after his 29y gain with QB Greg Talley's "ugly" half-bobbled, half-thrown short pass.

MICHIGAN STATE 21 Minnesota 7: WR Courtney Hawkins had career day for Michigan State (5-4), catching 9/197y, including 3 and 47y TDs from QB Dan Enos (13-26/240y, 2 INTs). Still, Golden Gophers (5-4) led 7-6 at H, thanks to blown x-pt after Hawkins' short scoring catch. Minnesota scored its TD in 2nd Q on QB Scott Schaffner's 36y TD romp and K Brent Berglund's kick. Hawkins' long scoring grab broke open game in 4th Q at 12-7, and Spartans made up for missed convs by tacking on safety: DT Bobby Wilson nailed Gophers TB Darrell Thompson (23/73y) in EZ before big State TB Tico Duckett slammed 34y for late, clinching TD run.

Michigan 24 ILLINOIS 10: In battle for Big 10 supremacy, Illini (8-2) made crucial mistake: they failed to cash in all opportunities against Michigan's strong D. QB Jeff George (22-38/253y, INT) moved Illinois well in 1st H but trailed 17-10 at H after several blown chances, including odd jump-ball 4th down toss for FG would have brought score to 17-13. Wolverines (8-1) made D adjustments and shut down Illinois O in 2nd H, including stop on 4th-and-1 after George drove his charges to Michigan 5YL. Michigan, meanwhile, pounded ball as TB Tony Boles rushed for 115y—including 73y run in 1st Q to set up Wolverines' 1st score—and team compiled 266y on ground.

ARKANSAS 19 Baylor 10: Using script that had worked for years, Arkansas (8-1) deployed tough D, sound running game, and steady kicking to remain tied with Texas A&M for 1st place in SWC. Razorbacks TB James Rouse rushed for 133y and TD, while frosh K Todd Wright booted 4 FGs. Baylor (4-5), was held to 9 1st downs and 28y rushing and was finished as soon as QB Brad Goebel went down with injury in 3rd Q: Bears kept ball for only 7 mins in 2nd H and gained paltry 53y.

HOUSTON 47 Texas 9: Cougars (7-2) added to its treasure trove of records in easy win over once-formidable Longhorns (4-4). QB Andre Ware (27-49/411y, 4 TDs) set SWC records for completions in season with 292, breaking Tommy Kramer of Rice's mark of 269 from 1976, and career y of 7327y, surpassing SMU's Chuck Hixson 7179y accumulated from 1968-70. Houston WR Manny Hazard (19/226y) caught 2 TD passes to set NCAA record for TD receptions with 19, breaking record (18) set by Tom Reynolds of San Diego State in 1969. Texas trailed 27-9 at H, managing only K Wayne Clements' 3 FGs.

BRIGHAM YOUNG 44 Air Force 35: HB Stacey Corley kept Cougars in game early; QB Ty Detmer won game for Cougars late. Corley ran back opening KO 99y for 7-0 lead before Falcons (8-3) scored 17 straight pts. Corley then went 85y for 2nd KO TD RET to jump-start BYU (8-2). With Detmer (16-27/334y, INT, 4 TDs) getting hot hand, BYU stormed out to 38-20 lead. QB Dee Dowis answered with 2 TD drives, capping 2nd with 3y scoring run to pull Air Force to within 38-35. Cougars recovered onside-KO, leading to Detmer's 45y TD pass to TE Chris Smith (4/110y) to wrap up scoring. Corley became 7th player to return 2 KOs for TDs in single game, while Detmer's 25 TD passes established record for soph passers. Also, Air Force's clever Dowis became 5th player to rush and pass for 1000y in same season.

Southern California 24 ARIZONA 3: For coach Larry Smith, it was 3 Rose Bowls in as many years as his Trojans (8-2) dominated Arizona (6-4). Smith joined Stanford's Tiny Thornhill (1933-35) as only coach ever to open career with trio of Pasadena trips. QB Todd Marinovich (11-19/168y, TD, INT) and TB Ricky Ervins (21/151y, TD) paced Southern California's O, while D, led by rampaging LB Junior Seau and DT Tim Ryan (17 tackles, 2 sacks), bit into Arizona's I-Bone O to tune of 158y rushing and 16y passing. Arizona FB Mario Hampton was heroic in defeat, rushing for 9/team-high 62y despite broken hand. Trojans won for 19th straight time in Pac-10 play.

1 Notre Dame (57)	1497	14 Texas A&M	680
2 Colorado (3)	1439	15 Clemson	632
3 Michigan	1360	16 Virginia	564
4 Alabama	1312	17 Penn State	425
5 Florida State	1240	18 West Virginia	393
6 Nebraska	1197	19 Pittsburgh	379
7 Miami	1163	20 Texas Tech	334
8 Southern California	1076	21 Brigham Young	310
9 Tennessee	991	22 Ohio State	262
10 Arkansas	979	23 Fresno State	233
11 Auburn	866	24 Hawaii	131
12 Illinois	855	25 Duke	114
13 Houston	690		

1 Notre Dame (57)	1497	14 Texas A&M	716
2 Colorado (3)	1439	15 Clemson	670
3 Michigan	1359	16 Virginia	603
4 Alabama	1319	17 West Virginia	413
5 Florida State	1244	18 Texas Tech	390
6 Nebraska	1200	19 Pittsburgh	384
7 Miami	1169	20 Ohio State	375
8 Tennessee	1065	21 Brigham Young	330
9 Arkansas	988	22 Penn State	314
10 Auburn	925	23 Duke	231
11 Illinois	907	24 Hawaii	182
12 Southern California	815	25 Michigan State	131
13 Houston	730		

November 18, 1989

Notre Dame 34 PENN STATE 23: Fighting Irish (11-0) rolled on as its run game gained 425y to win for 1st time in State College in 76 years. QB Tony Rice reached career-high 141y on ground, while TB Ricky Watters went for 128y, and all-purpose WR Raghib Ismail added 84y on 9 carries. No. 17 Penn State (6-3-1) took early 7-0 lead on 2y run by TB Blair Thomas, who did best to keep pace with Notre Dame, finishing day with 133y and 2 TDs rushing. Rice tied game at 7-7 later in 1st Q on 5y run, and Irish gained control by H with 21-10 lead. Win was 23rd in row for Notre Dame and 11th straight vs opponents in Top 25.

Virginia 48 MARYLAND 21: Virginia (10-2) QB Shawn Moore was developing own highlight reel, throwing 3 TD passes and rushing for 2 TDs. Cavaliers earned 1st-ever 10 win season and copped share of 1st ACC title in 36 years of conf play. Game was tied 14-14 in 2nd Q when Moore cracked GL with 1y keeper. Later, he hooked up with WR Herman Moore on 36y TD pass for 28-14 H lead. Moore threw for 161y and rushed for 121y of his team's total O of 361y, while TB Marcus Wilson (23/95y) scored twice. QB Neil O'Donnell threw for 231y and TD for Terrapins (3-7-1).

TENNESSEE 33 Mississippi 21: Volunteers (8-1) spun Webb in erasing 21-17 deficit as TB Chuck Webb finished with 294y and 2 TDs rushing. Tennessee rode Webb on 80y and 82y TD drives in 4th Q. Rebels (6-4) O failed to score in 2nd H, although WR Tyrone Ashley took 2nd H KO back 90y for Ole Miss' 3rd TD. Mississippi QB John Darnell threw for 168y to become school's single-season passing leader with 2,128y.

Auburn 20 GEORGIA 3: Bulldogs (6-4) runners got bushwhacked as Auburn (8-2) D allowed only 48y rushing, while Tigers O held larger than 2-1 time of possession and 1st down advantages. QB Reggie Slack threw for 230y, while frosh TB Darrell Williams rushed for 128y, TD, as Tigers won 4th straight in series. K John Kasay's 23y FG in 3rd Q prevented shutout for Georgia.

NEBRASKA 42 Oklahoma 25: Even without Big 8 title in balance, which was secure already in Colorado, Nebraska (10-1) had to enjoy beating Sooners (7-4). QB Gerry Gdowski performed surgery on OU secondary with 12-15/225y, 4 TDs passing, while adding running TD. Huskers scored on 1st 4 possessions to tally 25 pts in 1st H. But, Sooners had 1st H answer: 82y TD catch by WR Arthur Guess, 1y TD run by FB Leon Perry—set up by G Mike Sawatzky's run with "Fumblerooskie"—and 26y FG by K R.D. Lashar. Oklahoma trailed only 25-18 at H. Gdowski quickly squashed any OU comeback ideas with 2 TD passes in 3rd Q. Sawatzky again rambled on Fumblerooskie to set up another Perry TD in 4th Q, but it came too late. Oklahoma HB Dewell Brewer rushed for 137y.

SOUTHERN CALIFORNIA 10 Ucla 10: Looking to end poor season on high note, Bruins (3-7-1) were unable to set up winning FG at game's end. K Alfredo Velasco had tied game at 10-10 earlier in 4th Q with 49y effort that converted Bruins DT Meech Shaw's REC of errant pitchout. Trojans (8-2-1) D held UCLA to 10 1st downs and 51y rushing—thanks in part to 5 sacks—but O committed uncharacteristic 6 TOs, including 3 INTs by QB Todd Marinovich. Marinovich started well with 78y passing on Troy's opening TD drive, which ended on 13y TD pass to WR Gary Wellman, who was controversially ruled as making catch in-bounds. TV replays showed officials' call was close, but nobody thought Trojans would fail to penetrate Bruins GL for rest of game. TB Kevin Williams (16/70y) scored 2nd Q TD for UCLA after it made INT, but Trojans K Quin Rodriguez glanced FG off and through uprights for 10-7 H edge. Pac-10 rushing champ, Southern California TB Ricky Ervins, chipped in with 28/173y on ground.

STANFORD 24 California 14: Where else could pair of teams with combined 6 wins battle for last place in conf standings and still draw 86,019 people? Cardinal (3-8) entertained its faithful as O stormed for 229y rushing, including FB Tommy Vardell's 22y romp for winning TD. Stanford TB J.J. Lasley rushed for 101y and opened scoring with 3y TD run. Sr QB Troy Taylor did great work for Bears (4-7) in his final game, throwing for career-best 377y and finding WR Brian Treggs open for 10/160y.

WASHINGTON 20 Washington State 9: Apple Cup tilt featured D struggle as O units could combine for only single TD: Washington (7-4) TB Greg Lewis' 21y run. Huskies D sacked QB Brad Gossen 8 times and picked off 2 passes, including S Eric Briscoe's 35y TD RET on game's 1st scrimmage play. Washington State (6-5) D picked off QB Cary Conklin 3 times. Lewis rushed for 115y for Huskies, while Wazzu TB Steve Broussard reached 29/153y on ground. Police sprayed tear gas at celebrating students, who nevertheless threw goal posts into Lake Washington. One would think Northwest environmentalists would reject such littering.

November 23-25, 1989

(Th'g) West Virginia 24 SYRACUSE 17: Mountaineers QB Major Harris received kudos for orchestrating road win with 95y rushing and 182y passing. West Virginia (8-2-1) posted 2nd H shutout while scoring 10 pts in 3rd Q to pull ahead. FB Rico Tyler scored winning 1y TD to cap 46y drive after DB Lawrence Drumgoole recovered FUM by Syracuse HB Michael Owens. WR Rob Moore starred for Orangemen (6-4) with 6/123y receiving, including 31y TD reception. Harris became 1st player ever to pass for 5,000y and rush for 2,000y in career.

(Fri) Arkansas 23 TEXAS A&M 22: Task was tough—Texas A&M had not lost conf home game since 1984—but Razorbacks (9-1) pulled out win as FB Barry Foster scored on 2y run with just less than 3 mins to play. Arkansas jumped to rapid-fire TDs, spaced apart by 52 secs, on QB Quinn Grovey's 25y TD romp and LB Mick Thomas' 23y INT TD RET. Aggies (7-3) scored 20 of tilt's next 23 pts behind QB Lance Pavlas, who threw 27y TD pass, and RB Darren Lewis, who finished game with 91y rushing. K Layne Talbot's 2nd FG gave A&M 20-17 lead with 8:14 left. Hogs then marched 70y for win, with FB E.D. Jackson rushing for 49y of his game-high 93y. Interference PEN on Texas A&M S Larry Horton kept drive alive on critical 4th-and-3 play from A&M 13YL.

Penn State 16 PITTSBURGH 13: With thoughts of last-sec blocked FG against Alabama in everyone's thoughts, Penn State (7-3-1) K Ray Tarasi booted winning 20y 3-ptr with 13 secs left. Moments earlier, Pitt (6-3-1) had played for tie with 3 straight short running gains up middle before K Ed Frazier booted 40y FG. TB Curvin Richards led Panthers with 152y on ground. QB Tom Bill, building reputation as inspirational Nittany Lions relief pitcher, sparked late 58y drive, completing 3rd down passes of 19y to WR Dave Daniels and 29y to FB Leroy Thompson. Lions TB Blair Thomas contributed with 131y rushing.

MIAMI 27 Notre Dame 10: Game's turning point came deep in Miami territory in 3rd Q: Ball popped up into air, and Notre Dame (11-1) DE Devon McDonald nearly caught it for what could have been short TD RET to tie it 17-17. Instead, Miami C Bobby Garcia fell on it at own 3YL to keep Hurricanes (10-1) up by 17-10. Play lost 23y and with earlier 15y PEN, Canes faced 2nd-and-48. After 4y run, Miami still faced 3rd-and-44 and somehow pulled 44y pass for 1st down to WR Randall Hill out of hat of QB Craig Erickson (16-26/210y, 2 TDs, INT). Hill admitted after game that he had no idea where 1st down marker was, but that he "had to go long". Miami continued downfield on runs of FBs Leonard Conley and Stephen McGuire until Erickson's clinching 5y TD pass to WR Dale Dawkins (7/123y, 2 TDs) capped 22-play drive that devoured nearly 11 mins of clock. Dawkins had worn Notre Dame baseball cap all summer to remember close loss to ND in 1988 and commitment needed to regain no. 1 spot. Miami LB Bernard Clark had 13 tackles and INT. Irish TD came on LB Ned Bolcar's 49y INT RET. ND WR Raghib Ismail separated shoulder and was no factor, and QB Tony Rice was all-but-eliminated from Heisman race with no TDs. Irish ended 1980s with disappointing 0-5 mark in Orange Bowl stadium.

Tennessee 31 KENTUCKY 10: It all headed downhill for Wildcats (6-5) once TB Alfred Rawls was halted on 4th-and-1 attempt at Tennessee 33YL in 3rd Q. Kentucky owned 10-9 lead at that time and nervously hoped for upset. Tennessee (9-1) took over and marched 61y for go-ahead on 1y run by TB Tony Thompson. Volunteers D allowed only 19y in 2nd H, so game was pretty well over before WR Alvin Harper and LB Shon Walker tacked on 22y TD catch and 18y INT TD RET respectively. Rawls had scored Kentucky's sole TD on 8y run in 1st H. TB Chuck Webb rushed for 145y to pace Vols. Tennessee's amazing November record jumped to 20 wins in row.

Mississippi 21 Mississippi State 11 (Jackson): Trailing 7-3 in 3rd Q, Bulldogs (5-6) went for it on 4th-and-1 at Rebels 7YL. Mississippi (7-4) held as pitchout from QB Todd Jordan misfired. Ole Miss snatched momentum to push for 2 TDs in 4th Q as RB Randy Baldwin (11/80y) capped 93y drive with 1y TD run and backup QB Russ Shows added 3y keeper. Rebels D also contributed 3 TOs, including FUM REC in 2nd Q to set up TD.

MICHIGAN 28 Ohio State 18: Michigan (10-1) reserves carried day. After Buckeyes (8-3) scored 12 straight pts to cut Wolverines' lead to 14-12, backup CB Todd Plate picked off Ohio State (8-3) QB Greg Frey on 1st play of 4th Q to give Michigan ball on Ohio 47YL. UM TB Leroy Hoard, starting in place of injured TB Tony Boles, rushed for 40y of his game-high 152y to set up QB Mike Taylor's 5y scoring pass to FB Jarrod Bunch. Frey then led 80y drive to cut deficit to 21-18, and, with Hoard on bench with injured ankle, Buckeyes (8-3) got ball back quickly. Plate came up big again, picking off another pass to set up clinching score, Bunch's 2nd TD on 23y run. In his final season, coach Bo Schembechler earned unshared back-to-back Big 10 championships for 1st time in his career, and it was 1st such occurrence in conf since Michigan State turned trick in 1965-66. TB Scottie Graham led Ohio State with 133y rushing.

Purdue 15 INDIANA 14: TB Anthony Thompson's inability to deliver bowl bid for Hoosiers (5-6) effectively doomed his Heisman Trophy candidacy. Boilermakers (3-8) knocked Indiana out of Freedom Bowl with upset win, scoring winning pts on K Larry

Sullivan's 3rd FG, from 32y away, with 2:51 left to go. Thompson was held to 97y rushing, but enjoyed final heroics with 64y RET of short ensuing KO to Purdue 15YL. Indiana K Scott Bonnell missed winning opportunity 4 plays later by missing 26y FG try. Indiana entered 4th Q with 14-3 lead, but Purdue frosh QB Eric Hunter (15-24/184y) hit WR Calvin Williams with 20y TD pass and Sullivan booted 2 FGs. In addition to late missed FG, Hoosiers exaggerated their doom by muffing punt that set up 1 of Sullivan's FGs and affecting facemask PEN on Purdue's go-ahead drive.

Minnesota 43 IOWA 7: Scoring midway through 3rd Q to pull within 13-7, Hawkeyes (5-6) hoped for momentum swing entering 4th Q. Instead Golden Gophers (6-5) exploded for 30 pts to blast Iowa and regain Floyd of Rosedale Trophy for 1st time since 1984. Minnesota picked off 5 Iowa passes, 2 by CB Fred Foggie, and another returned 35y for TD by DE Eddie Miles. Gophers TB Darrell Thompson rushed for 122y in his final game, while also providing game's 1st scoring with surprise 14y pass to WR Chris Gaiters. Iowa TB Nick Bell rushed for 133y.

HAWAII 23 Oregon State 21: Hawaii (9-2) K Jason Elam booted 3 FGs, stretching his consecutive 3-pt string to 20. His 3rd FG, early in 4th Q, gave Rainbows seemingly comfortable 23-7 lead. But Oregon State (4-7-1) rallied behind QB Nick Schichtle, who threw 2 TDs including 24y scoring pass to WR Reggie Hubbard (7/144y). Controversial call ended game as Beavers FB Pat Chaffey fumbled into EZ. Loose ball was recovered by Hawaii S Walter Briggs and was ruled touchback REC despite Beavers' claim that Chaffey's knee was down before ball came out. RB Jamal Farmer rushed for 101y for Rainbows, while QB Garrett Gabriel threw for 200y.

Brigham Young 48 SAN DIEGO STATE 27: Cougars clinched WAC title for 1st time since 1984 national title team earned conf crown. BYU QB Ty Detmer threw for 327y and 3 TDs, while running for 2 others, and just missed Jim McMahon's season's pass y record by narrow 11y. BYU jumped to 35-14 H lead as Aztecs QB Dan McGwire nursed bruised back that he suffered on 1st possession. McGwire (14-21/215y) returned to rally San Diego State to 10 straight pts before FUM on punt RET by WR Monty Gilbreath set up Cougars' 19y drive for clinching TD. It was scored on 1y keeper by Detmer. BYU FB Stacey Corley rushed for 121y.

Arizona 28 ARIZONA STATE 10: Sun Devils (6-4-1) trotted out in gold jerseys at start and grabbed 10-7 H lead behind QB Paul Justin, who threw for 307y. But, record crowd (74,926) witnessed Wildcats (7-4) continue their recent series domination—7-0-1 in past 8 years—by outscoring Arizona State by 21-0 in 2nd H. TB David Eldridge rushed for 104y and 2 TDs within 1:18 stretch of 3rd Q. Eldridge's scores sandwiched Justin's FUM at own 9YL when sacked by Wildcats DT Reggie Johnson. Arizona's run attack gained 285y and wore down Sun Devils D by controlling ball for 41 mins.

AP Poll November 27

1	Colorado (53)	1468	14	Clemson	684
2	Alabama (2)	1351	15	Virginia	640
3	Michigan (1)	1332	16	Texas A&M	534
4	Miami (3)	1319	17	West Virginia	499
5	Notre Dame	1231	18	Penn State	450
6	Florida State	1200	19	Brigham Young	401
7	Nebraska	1154	20	Duke	301
8	Tennessee	1045	21	Ohio State	264
9	Arkansas	1000	22	Michigan State	247
10	Illinois	913	23	Hawaii	197
11	Auburn	893	24	Pittsburgh	180
12	Southern California	802	25	Texas Tech	177
13	Houston	750			

December 2, 1989

GEORGIA TECH 33 Georgia 22: Georgia Tech TB Jerry Mays performed under national media radar, but he knew what to do when carrying pigskin. Mays rushed 39/207y, scoring on 7y run in 3rd Q for 20-14 Yellow Jackets lead and adding insurance TD on 22y TD pass from QB Shawn Jones. Bulldogs (6-5) had scored 2 TDs in 2nd Q—both by TB Rodney Hampton (16/96y)—to grab 14-10 lead. Georgia's chances suffered blow when Hampton left game with ankle injury late in 1st H. Yellow Jackets dominated game with Hampton on sideline, scoring 3 TDs, including pair by Mays who finished season with 1,349y rushing.

Florida State 24 FLORIDA 17: QB Peter Tom Willis led Seminoles (9-2) to 9th straight win by throwing for 319y and 3 TDs. Willis dynamically hit WR Terry Anthony (4/126y) for 62y score and 7-0 lead. After teams trotted off 10-10 at H, Willis hit 2 more TD passes to hand 24-10 advantage to Florida State. Gators (7-4) struck back behind TB Emmitt Smith, who rushed for 153y, scoring from 2y out with just over 4 mins remaining. But, Florida State hung on for 3rd straight series victory.

TENNESSEE 17 Vanderbilt 10: For 2nd straight week Volunteers (10-1) were required to rally in 2nd H, this time behind reserve TB Tony Thompson. Thompson rushed for 128y and capped 70y drive with winning 1y TD run with 7:11 left. Tennessee's march had begun with INT by S Carl Pickens. Versatile WR Pickens had scored tying TD at 10-10 on 4y pass from QB Andy Kelly in 3rd Q. After Thompson's TD, Vols CB J.J. McCleskey ended 2 straight Vandy series with INTs. Vanderbilt (1-10) had taken 10-3 H lead as RB Brad Gaines scored on 1y TD run and K Johnny Clark booted 35y FG. With win, Vols remained tied for 1st in SEC with Auburn and Alabama at 6-1, marking only 2nd time that SEC race had ended in 3-way tie. Since Pickens had started playing both ways, Vols won 4 straight games with his having plucked INT in each.

AUBURN 30 Alabama 20: Finally, after 45 series games in 2nd home, Birmingham, Crimson Tide had agreed to play at Auburn's Jordan-Hare Stadium, and they paid for it. Undefeated no. 2 Alabama (10-1) blew early chances, twice driving to within Auburn 10YL but coming away with only 3 pts. Auburn's O-line dominated, allowing little pass-rush pressure and paving way for TB Stacy Danley's 130y rushing. WR Alexander Wright contributed 7/141y to Tigers. Trailing 10-7 at H, Auburn (9-2) reeled off 20

straight pts in 2nd H to delight its home crowd. Alabama QB Gary Hollingsworth, who grew up Auburn fan, threw his 2nd TD pass to WR Marco Battle before Tigers nabbed onside-KO to nip rally. K Win Lyle booted clinching 34y FG. Auburn coach Pat Dye, who joined Gen. Bob Neyland, Bear Bryant, and Vince Dooley as coaches who shared or won 3 straight SEC titles, ran lifetime record against opposing coach Bill Curry to 10-0, spread across all of Curry's coaching stops.

AP Poll December 4

1	Colorado (55)	1492	14	Clemson	681
2	Miami (4)	1407	15	Virginia	657
3	Michigan (1)	1374	16	Texas A&M	570
4	Notre Dame	1323	17	West Virginia	490
5	Florida State	1265	18	Penn State	466
6	Nebraska	1198	19	Brigham Young	378
7	Alabama	1090	20	Duke	330
8	Tennessee	1069	21	Ohio State	298
9	Auburn	1024	22	Michigan State	271
10	Arkansas	983	23	Hawaii	207
11	Illinois	931	24	Pittsburgh	190
12	Southern California	831	25	Texas Tech	139
13	Houston	748			

December 9, 1989

Navy 19 Army 17 (E. Rutherford, NJ): Midshipmen (3-8) stunned Army (6-5) on 32y FG by K Frank Schenk with 11 secs left. Navy QB Alton Grizzard's run converted 4th-and-2 on winning drive, his notable 3rd conv of 4th down in game. HB Mike Mayweather added his name to West Point pantheon, rushing for 84y to become Army's all-time leader in career rushing with 2,960y. Mayweather's total broke by 3y Glenn Davis' 43-year-old mark, by far oldest such school record among major colleges. Mayweather also broke Doug Black's much more recent Cadets single-season mark with 1,176y. Navy's victory failed to save job of coach Elliot Uzelac.

HAWAII 35 Air Force 35: Air Force Falcons (8-3-1) converted 3 of 4 Hawaii TOs into TDs to forge high-scoring tie. Rainbows K Jason Elam missed 47y FG as time expired, breaking his string of 20 straight successful FGs. FB Rodney Lewis scored 4 TDs for Air Force, his final TD tying it with 3 mins left. Hawaii (9-2-1) had taken 35-28 lead 4 mins earlier on RB Jamal Farmer's 2nd TD run, 36y effort that helped vault Farmer to 242y rushing for game. Farmer finished season with frosh-record 18 TDs.

Conference Standings

Atlantic Coast

Virginia	6-1
Duke	6-1
Clemson	5-2
Georgia Tech	4-3
North Carolina State	4-3
Maryland	2-5
Wake Forest	1-6
North Carolina	0-7

Southeastern

Alabama	6-1
Tennessee	6-1
Auburn	6-1
Florida	4-3
Mississippi	4-3
Georgia	4-3
Kentucky	2-5
Louisiana State	2-5
Mississippi State	1-6
Vanderbilt	0-7

Big Ten

Michigan	8-0
Illinois	7-1
Ohio State	6-2
Michigan State	6-2
Minnesota	4-4
Indiana	3-5
Iowa	3-5
Purdue	2-6
Wisconsin	1-7
Northwestern	0-8

Mid-American

Ball State	6-1-1
Eastern Michigan	6-2
Toledo	6-2
Central Michigan	5-2-1
Bowling Green	5-3
Western Michigan	3-5
Miami	2-5-1
Ohio	1-6-1
Kent	0-8

Big Eight

Colorado	7-0
Nebraska	6-1
Oklahoma	5-2
Iowa State	4-3
Oklahoma State	3-4
Kansas	2-5
Missouri	1-6
Kansas State	0-6

Southwest

Arkansas	7-1
Houston	6-2
Texas A&M	6-2
Texas Tech	5-3
Baylor	4-4
Texas	4-4
Texas Christian	2-6
Rice	2-6
Southern Methodist	0-8

Western Athletic

Brigham Young	7-1
Air Force	5-1-1
Hawaii	5-2-1
Wyoming	5-3
San Diego State	4-3
Colorado State	4-3
Utah	2-6
Texas-El Paso	1-7
New Mexico	0-7

Pacific-10

Southern California	6-0-1
Arizona	5-3
Oregon	5-3
Washington	5-3
Arizona State	3-3-1
Oregon State	3-4-1
Washington State	3-5
Stanford	3-5
UCLA	2-5-1
California	2-6

Big West

Fresno State	7-0
Cal State-Fullerton	5-2
San Jose State	5-2
Utah State	4-3
Nevada-Las Vegas	3-4
Long Beach State	2-5
Pacific	2-5
New Mexico State	0-7

1989 Major College Bowls

Independence Bowl (Dec. 16): Oregon 27 Tulsa 24

Tulsa (6-6) authored inspired effort, playing without star WR Dan Bitson (broken legs) and leading tackler LB Matt Luke (suspension). But, Hurricane came up short on 2 4th Q plays: Tulsa FB Brett Adams' inability to secure 1st down on 4th-and-1 from Oregon 48YL and officials' no-call when Oregon QB Bill Musgrave appeared to have lost handle on ball deep in Golden Hurricane territory. Refs ruled that QB was down and K Gregg McCallum booted winning 20y FG on next play. Musgrave threw for 320y and 2 TDs for Ducks (8-4), while Tulsa QB T.J. Rubley threw for 184y. Golden Hurricane built 17-10 lead at H, scoring TDs on Adams' 1y run and LB Derrick Williams' 21y RET of blocked punt. Adams scored again in 3rd Q for 24-10 lead. It was wiped out by 9y TD pass from Musgrave to WR Joe Reitzug (6/121y) and Musgrave's 1st-ever rushing TD. Strong Ducks O topped 400y (460y) for 8th time this season.

Aloha Bowl (Dec. 25): Michigan State 33 Hawaii 13

Having lost to Miami, Notre Dame, Michigan, and Illinois by total of 21 pts, Spartans (8-4) were in different class than host Hawaii. Rainbows (9-3-1) proved gracious in losing 8 TOs, ending 1st 6 possessions with either lost FUM or INT. They had 4 of each by game's end. Michigan State TB Blake Ezor rushed for 179y and 3 TDs, leaving him with 19 for season. Hawaii's spread O thrice topped 60 pts during regular season but was manhandled by nation's 6th-ranked D. Michigan State LB Percy Snow led stunting 4-3 alignment with 9 tackles and INT, while DE Mark Vanderbeek recovered 3 FUMs and LB Carlos Jenkins had INT, FUM REC, and blocked x-pt. Rainbows QB Garrett Gabriel threw for 197y and 2 TDs, but also allowed 3 INTs while bungling 2 pitchouts on option plays in 1st Q.

Liberty Bowl (Dec. 28): Mississippi 42 Air Force 29

Team speed was key for easy victory as Rebels (8-4) built 42-15 lead in 2nd H behind QB John Darnell's 261y passing. Ole Miss RB Randy Baldwin rushed for 177y, 2 TDs, while WR Pat Coleman added scores on 58y punt RET and 11y reverse. Mississippi held dandy Falcons (8-4-1) QB Dee Dowis in check, allowing him to rush for 92y and 2 TDs but twice picking off his passes as he threw for only 184y. Trailing 14-9 after Dowis' 1st TD, Air Force went for 2 pts, but Rebs DB Jeff Carter made INT. Carter halted next Air Force series with another INT, which was altered to Baldwin's 21y TD run for 21-9 lead. Later in 2nd Q, Coleman took punt 58y for crushing TD and 28-9 lead. Air Force closed game with 14 pts in row as sub QB Lance McDowell (7-8/147y) hit WR Steve Senn (7/150y) for TD passes of 35y and 21y.

All American Bowl (Dec. 28): Texas Tech 49 Duke 21

With coach Steve Spurrier on way out, Duke was no match for TB James Gray and Red Raiders (9-3). Gray rushed for 280y and 4 TDs in setting personal and game bests. Blue Devils (8-4) fell behind by 28-0 in 1st H before QB Dave Brown threw 2 TD passes to halve deficit by H. Texas Tech had converted 2 TOs into TDs to take big lead, scoring on Gray's 3 runs, including 54y run right after S Brian Dubiski, who made earlier FUM REC to set up Raiders' opening TD.

Holiday Bowl (Dec. 29): Penn State 50 Brigham Young 39

Despite 576y passing by QB Ty Detmer—most ever in any bowl game until tied by Marshall's Byron Leftwich in 2001—BYU (10-3) fell to Nittany Lions, although Cougars seemed poised to tie it with 2-pt conv with 2:30 left. Active Penn State (8-3-1) LB Andre Collins picked off Detmer's EZ pass intended for WR Andy Boyce (8/127y) and returned it 102y for 43-39 lead. Brigham Young D held and Detmer had 2 mins to pull out win. Completions to 4 different receivers brought ball to Penn State 38 YL. On 3rd-and-3, Lions S Gary Brown blitzed, stripping Detmer, scooping ball, and looking every bit like RB he used to be in returning ball 53y for clinching TD with 45 secs left. Play of day for Nittany Lions was great juggling TD catch by WR Dave Daniels that put State up 41-26. Ball bounced twice off of DB Tony Crutchfield before being corralled by Daniels as he was on his back in EZ. Penn State TB Blair Thomas rushed for 186y to share MVP honors with Detmer, while Lions QB Tony Sacca added 206y passing and 2 TDs. Penn State FB Leroy Thompson rushed for TDs of 16y and 14y in 3rd Q, 2nd of which was set up by fake punt. Cougars had pair of receivers joined Boyce atop 100y peak: HB Matt Bellini (10/124y) and WR Brent Nyberg (8/117y). Pair of O-minded foes combined for 1115y, with BYU earning 651y total O. Teams also combined for 20 PENs/181y, 5 unsportsmanlike or personal fouls.

Freedom Bowl (Dec. 30): Washington 34 Florida 7

Scoring on 1st 3 possessions, Huskies (8-4) routed Florida from opening KO behind balanced attack that produced 217y rushing and 242y passing. Gators (7-5) were able to tie game at 7-7 in 1st Q on 67y TD run by QB Donald Douglas, but netting only 16y rest of way as star TB Emmitt Smith was held to 17y rushing. Once Florida fell behind by double digits, Smith, who averaged 126y per game this season, became nearly useless. Up 17-7 in 2nd Q, Washington went for kill with LB Chico Fraley blocking punt that was recovered in EZ by LB Jaime Fields for TD. Huskies QB Cary Conklin (21-39/217y, 2 TDs) engineered O that finished with nearly 42 mins of possession time.

UW TB Greg Lewis chipped in with 97y against nation's 5th-ranked rush D, while sub QB Mark Brunell scorched it for 20y TD sprint to end matters.

Peach Bowl (Dec. 30): Syracuse 19 Georgia 18

Trailing 18-7 in 2nd H, Syracuse (8-4) turned to backup QB Mark McDonald (10-13/135y) who rallied Orangemen with 3 scores, including his 19y TD pass to WR Rob Moore. Syracuse's rally became complete when K John Biskup ended 64y drive with 26y FG with 25 secs remaining. Big play of drive was McDonald's 29y connection with HB Michael Owens on 4th down from own 43YL. Owens rushed for 116y—and added 5/62y receiving—as Orange totaled 243y on ground. Syracuse D held Bulldogs (6-6) to 202y and limited TB Rodney Hampton to 32y on ground, although Hampton slipped out of backfield to catch 7/62y. Orange totaled 478y O, but was able to overcome 4 TOs as Georgia scored only 3 pts following takeaways. Bulldogs built 18-7 lead on QB Greg Talley's 2 TD passes.

John Hancock (Sun) Bowl (Dec. 30): Pittsburgh 31 Texas A&M 28

On day that Pittsburgh (8-3-1) dropped coach Paul Hackett's interim status, Panthers won hard-fought debut for mentor. Pitt QB Alex Van Pelt (20-40/354y, 2 TDs, INT) took advantage of Aggies blitz to hit WR Henry Tuten on 44y game-winning TD with 2:19 left. Van Pelt's pass went through hands of Texas A&M (8-4) CB Kevin Smith. Van Pelt's 1y TD run in 3rd Q had put Panthers up 24-10, but with QB Lance Pavlas returning from rib injury that knocked him out for 2nd Q, A&M rallied with 3 straight TDs. TB Keith McAfee ran for pair of those TDs to grab 28-24 lead as team failed on 2-pt conv following all 3 TDs. Van Pelt next led winning 84y drive. Pitt TB Curvin Richards rushed for 156y and opening 12y TD run, while FB Robert Wilson paced Aggies run attack with 145y on ground. WR Olanda Truitt led all receivers with 4/124y for Panthers.

Gator Bowl (Dec. 30): Clemson 27 West Virginia 7

QB Major Harris' great career at helm of Mountaineers attack ended poorly as Clemson D overwhelmed 3rd place finisher in Heisman Trophy balloting. West Virginia (8-3-1) scored TD on 1st drive, but crossed midfield on only twice thereafter with each drive being curtailed by TO by Harris on 1st play after crossing midfield. Tigers (10-2) held Harris to 119y passing and 17y rushing and recovered 3 of his FUMs, made INT, and sacked him 3 times. Clemson DT Chester McGlockton sealed deal midway through 4th Q by pouncing on last of Harris' FUMs in EZ for 24-7 lead. Tigers TB Joe Henderson and FB Wesley McFadden each rushed for TDs to help boost Clemson to its 4th straight bowl win.

Copper Bowl (Dec. 31): Arizona 17 North Carolina State 10

Quick glance at stats would have given evidence of romp by Wolfpack (7-5), but it never materialized. NC State gained 310y to Wildcats' 130y, but NC State lost by falling into early and insurmountable hole. Big play invisible on stat sheet was Arizona (8-4) S Scott Geyer's 85y INT TD RET in 2nd Q that followed WR Olatide Ogunfiditimi's beating double coverage to snare 37y scoring catch from QB Ronald Veal. QB Shane Montgomery (21-46/222y, INT) bounced back to throw 4y TD pass to FB Todd Varn. Teams traded FGs thereafter, but Montgomery led 1 last drive into Arizona territory before misconnecting with TB Chris Williams in EZ.

Florida Citrus Bowl: Illinois 31 Virginia 21

With QB Jeff George throwing for 26-38/321y, Illinois (10-2) finally won bowl game after 4 postseason losses in 1980s, and it was Illini's 1st since 1964 Rose Bowl. In what would prove to be final game of tumultuous college career on path to NFL's top draft pick, George threw 3 TD passes, 1st of which, 15y effort to WR Steven Williams, put Illinois up 7-0. Only 36y trip was required after Virginia (10-3) TB Marcus Wilson lost opening KO FUM, fallen on by Illinois LB Bill Henkel. Cavaliers tied it on 30y scoring pass from QB Shawn Moore (17-27/191y, 2 TDs, 2 INTs) to WR Tim Finkelston, but George quickly moved his O back to lead as he connected with WR Mike Bellamy (8/166y) on 68y completion to set up 1y, 4th down TD pass to TE Dan Donovan. Illini pushed lead to 17-7 by H on K Doug Higgins' 34y FG. Result was then put out of reach when Illini followed 2nd H KO with 84y drive to TD: 3y run by FB Howard Griffith. Bellamy made great grab of 24y scoring pass to wrap up Illinois' scoring in beautiful downtown Orlando.

Cotton Bowl: Tennessee 31 Arkansas 27

TB Chuck Webb blew through Arkansas D for 205y and 2 TDs, including 78y romp in 3rd Q that vaulted Vols (11-1) to 31-13 advantage. Hogs (10-2) came back behind O that earned Cotton Bowl-record 568y to make it interesting with less than 2 mins left: FB Barry Foster (103y, 2 TDs rushing) plunged for 1y TD run and TE Billy Winston fell on his own FUM in EZ after 67y catch and run. But, Tennessee recovered Hogs' onside-KO to end it. TB James Rouse was Arkansas' leading rusher with 134y and TD, and QB Quinn Grovey threw for 207y, but Razorbacks was forced to overcome 4 TOs. Biggest TO was TD-preventing EZ INT by brilliant Vols WR-CB Carl Pickens, that was followed 2 plays later by 84y TD pass from QB Andy Kelly to WR Anthony Morgan for 10-6 lead. Win was 150th for coach Johnny Majors and 600th all-time for Tennessee.

Fiesta Bowl: Florida State 41 Nebraska 17

Once again, Nebraska (10-2) was done in by superior speed of bowl opponent. Florida State's fleet receiving corps ran under passes of QB Peter Tom Willis for whopping 422y and 5 TDs. Aerial numbers by Seminoles (10-2) represented best passing stats racked up against Huskers to date. Willis led TD drives on 5 out of 7 possessions in middle of game by tossing all his scoring passes in 2nd and 3rd Qs. Nebraska had led 7-0 on QB Gerry Gdowski's 9y TD pass to WR Morgan Gregory to cap 69y trip on 1st possession that featured P Mike Stigge's 41y fake-punt pass to WB Mark Dowse. After Florida State (10-2) converted FUM REC into Willis' 14y TD toss to WR Terry Anthony, Huskers rode WB Tyrone Hughes' 68y KO RET to regain lead on 39y FG by K Chris

Drennan. Noles, who finished season on 10-game winning streak, proceeded to reel off 34 straight pts, taking advantage of 5 TOs by Huskers and blocked punt. Win was Florida State's 2nd in bowl game over Nebraska, which dropped to 0-4 in Fiesta Bowl.

Rose Bowl: Southern California 17 Michigan 10

Bo Schembechler's final game was hard-fought yet disappointing as Trojans coach Larry Smith finally won Rose Bowl battle in his 3rd straight appearance. After squandering early opportunities, Southern California (9-2-1) took 7-0 lead on keeper by QB Todd Marinovich (22-31/178y, INT) to cap 11y drive set up by DT Dan Owen's blocked punt. TD came on busted play where Marinovich made up for his inexperience by scoring when he was supposed to hand off. Wolverines (10-2) answered with 19y FG by K J.D. Carlson after FB Leroy Hoard (17/108y) made nifty 46y run to pick up where last season's Rose MVP performance left off. USC extended its lead to 10-3 at H on K Quin Rodriguez 34y FG moments after intentional grounding PEN against Marinovich moved ball from 1st-and-goal at 2YL to 2nd-and-goal at 19YL. Michigan dominated 3rd Q, tying game at 10-10 on TB Allen Jefferson's 2y run. Early in 4th Q, Wolverines faced 4th-and-2 at own 46YL and surprisingly went for fake punt. Call looked great as P Chris Stapleton rambled for 24y. Holding PEN, however, wiped out play, and forced Michigan to punt. Schembechler nearly fell down he was so mad. Southern California then marched from own 27YL behind short passes from Marinovich, who scrambled for drive's initial 1st down, to winning 14y run by TB Ricky Ervins (30/126y). In losing to his former assistant Smith, Schembechler finished career with 2-8 record at Rose Bowl.

Sugar Bowl: Miami 33 Alabama 25

Miami laid claim to 3rd national title in 7 years with convincing, yet hard-fought victory over Crimson Tide (10-2). Although Hurricanes (11-1) never trailed in front of decidedly pro-Alabama crowd, it took well into 2nd H to stab Bama's inspired underdogs. Teams traded early TDs on 3y run by Miami FB Stephen McGuire and 4y TD pass from Tide QB Gary Hollingsworth to WR Marco Battle. Miami went to air to take lead for good as QB Craig Erickson connected with WR Wesley Carroll on 3/50y, last on 18y TD pass. After Crimson Tide cut deficit with 45y FG by K Philip Doyle, Canes reserve TB Alex Johnson scored on 3y run for 20-10 lead late in 2nd Q. Alabama reacted with 11-play, 80y march that Hollingsworth capped with 7y scoring pass to TE Lamonde Russell. Bama TD that pared it to 20-17 with 40 secs left in 1st H, whipped crowd into frenzy. Thus challenged, Miami tried to pass on final drive on H, but INT by S Lee Ozmint set up Doyle for tying FG attempt which sailed wide. D dominated 3rd Q as neither team scored. With title in balance in 4th Q, Miami pulled away by air as Erickson threw TD passes of 11y to TE Rob Chudzinski and 12y to backup TE Randy Bethel. Hollingsworth threw late TD pass and 2-pt conv pass but Bama failed to cover onside-KO. Dennis Erickson became 2nd-ever coach to win national championship in 1st year with school; previous occurrence being Michigan's Bennie Oosterbaan in 1948.

Orange Bowl: Notre Dame 21 Colorado 6

Colorado (11-1) had brilliant, emotionally charged regular season, but it proved to be too much to play for national championship against Notre Dame (12-1), team that had occupied top ranking for most of season. After squads exchanged angry words at center of field before opening KO, they played to scoreless 1st H. It was 1st 0-0 H deadlock in Orange Bowl since Classic's 4th outing between Auburn and Michigan State way back in 1938. Buffs moved ball better during game's opening H, but were stopped on 3 drives deep into Notre Dame territory: FUM by TB Eric Bieniemy, missed 23y FG attempt by K Ken Culbertson, and GLS by Irish D. On last threat, QB Darian Hagan (19/106y rushing) marched Colorado to ND 1YL, but mid-air tackle by S D'Juan Francisco halted Bieniemy on 1st down. Hagan was then stopped by NT Chris Zorich, and, on 3rd down, Hagan was pushed OB on option run. Instead of taking game's 1st pts with bad-angle chipshot, Buffs went for fake FG, with holder WR Jeff Campbell being swallowed by CB Stan Smagala at 1YL after Colorado LB-WB Chad Brown failed to release to EZ as planned pass target. Irish then flew downfield behind own multi-dimensional QB, Tony Rice (99y passing and 50y rushing), before Buffs NT Garry Howe blocked K Billy Hackett's FG attempt. Colorado would rue missed 1st H opportunities as Irish took command in 3rd Q once Rice completed 27y pass to WR Tony Smith and FB Anthony Johnson raced 27y to set up his own 1y TD run. LB Ned Bolcar next picked off Hagan's tipped pass near midfield, and Notre Dame was on move again. Overcoming 1st-and-31 after PEN, ND scored on quick handoff to WR-TB Rocket Ismail (16/108y)—playing TB after 1st Q injury to TB Ricky Watters—who took advantage of blitz to race 34y down sideline for commanding 14-0 lead. On final play of 3rd Q, Hagan galloped 39y for Colorado's only score, but Culbertson, holder of school record 66 straight x-pts, missed kick. That miss was inconsequential once Irish embarked on 82y drive featuring 17 straight rushes that ate nearly 9 mins. One of most devastating drives in bowl history was culminated by Johnson's 7y TD.

Final AP Poll January 2

1 Miami (39)	1474	14 Houston	748
2 Notre Dame (19)	1452	15 Penn State	633
3 Florida State (2)	1384	16 Michigan State	507
4 Colorado	1320	17 Pittsburgh	478
5 Tennessee	1228	18 Virginia	455
6 Auburn	1161	19 Texas Tech	451
7 Michigan	1091	20 Texas A&M	330
8 Southern California	1067	21 West Virginia	260
9 Alabama	1029	22 Brigham Young	231
10 Illinois	1019	23 Washington	200
11 Nebraska	860	24 Ohio State	154
12 Clemson	820	25 Arizona	77
13 Arkansas	807		

1989 Top Performance Formula

1	Notre Dame	1.7466
2	Miami	1.7365
3	Colorado	1.7289
4	Florida State	1.6582
5	Tennessee	1.6368
6	Nebraska	1.6029
7	Houston	1.5894
8	Clemson	1.5743
9	Auburn	1.5634
10	Alabama	1.5628
11	Southern California	1.5530
12	Michigan	1.5350
13	Illinois	1.5295
14	Arkansas	1.5140
15	Penn State	1.3833
16	Michigan State	1.3686
17	Virginia	1.3546
18	Washington	1.3386
19	West Virginia	1.3337
20	Texas A&M	1.3334

1989 Top Opponent Records

1	Notre Dame	.6512
2	Florida State	.6457
3	Louisiana State	.6261
4	Virginia	.6153
5t	Auburn	.615079
5t	Tennessee	.615079
7	Alabama	.6120
8	Texas	.6087
9	Southern California	.6063
10	UCLA	.6059
11	Penn State	.6000
12	Maryland	.5932
13	Oregon State	.5913
14	Miami	.5906
15	Clemson	.5868
16	Colorado	.5847
17	Michigan	.5833
18	Washington	.5827
19	South Carolina	.5802
20	Illinois	.5787

1989 Out-of-Conference Records

	W-L	Percentage	Bowl W-L
Southeastern	31-13	.7045	3-3
Southwest	16-11-1	.5893	1-3
Pacific-10	20-15	.5714	4-0
Atlantic Coast	14-14-2	.5000	1-3
Big Eight	15-16	.4839	0-2
Big Ten	15-17	.4688	2-2
Western Athletic	17-21	.4474	0-3

1989 Individual Statistical Leaders

RUSHING YARDS	Attempts	Yards	Avg.
Anthony Thompson, Indiana	358	1793	5.0
Mike Pringle, Cal State-Fullerton	296	1727	5.8
Emmitt Smith, Florida	284	1599	5.6
Blaise Bryant, Iowa State	299	1516	5.1
James Gray, Texas Tech	263	1509	5.7
Stacey Robinson, Northern Illinois	223	1443	6.5
Jerry Mays, Georgia Tech	249	1349	5.4
Blair Thomas, Penn State	264	1341	5.1
Brian Mitchell, Southwest Louisiana	237	1311	5.5
Bob Christian, Northwestern	277	1291	4.7

PASSING YARDS	Completions	Attempts	Yards	Pct.
Andre Ware, Houston	365	578	4699	63.1
Ty Detmer, Brigham Young	265	412	4560	64.3
Peter Tom Willis, Florida State	211	346	3124	61.0
Dan Speltz, Cal State-Fullerton	214	309	2671	69.3
Tommy Hodson, Louisiana State	183	317	2655	57.7
Paul Justin, Arizona State	183	314	2591	58.3
Alex Van Pelt, Pittsburgh	172	307	2527	56.0
Jeff George, Illinois	216	348	2417	62.1
Todd Marinovich, Southern California	197	321	2400	61.4
T.J. Robley, Tulsa	155	308	2292	50.3

RECEIVING YARDS	Catches	Yards
Manny Hazard, Houston	142	1689
Dan Bitson, Tulsa	73	1425
Terance Mathis, New Mexico	88	1315
Clarkston Hines, Duke	61	1149
Richard Buchanan, Northwestern	94	1115
Dennis Smith, Utah	73	1089
Ron Fair, Arizona State	64	1082
Courtney Hawkins, Michigan State	60	1080
Ricky Proehl, Wake Forest	65	1053
Reggie Barrett, Texas-El Paso	58	1042

1989 Consensus All-America Team
Offense

Wide Receiver:	Clarkston Hines, Duke
	Terance Mathis, New Mexico
Tight End:	Mike Busch, Iowa State
Line:	Jim Mabry, Arkansas
	Bob Kula, Michigan State
	Mohammed Elewonibi, Brigham Young
	Joe Garten, Colorado
	Eric Still, Tennessee
Center:	Jake Young, Nebraska
Quarterback:	Andre Ware, Houston
Running Back:	Anthony Thompson, Indiana
	Emmitt Smith, Florida
Placekicker:	Jason Hanson, Washington State

Defense

Line:	Chris Zorich, Notre Dame
	Greg Mark, Miami
	Tim Ryan, Southern California
	Moe Gardner, Illinois
Linebacker:	Percy Snow, Michigan State
	Keith McCants, Alabama
	Alfred Williams, Colorado
Back:	Todd Lyght, Notre Dame
	Mark Carrier, Southern California
	Tripp Welborne, Michigan
	LeRoy Butler, Florida State
Punter:	Tom Rouen, Colorado

1989 Heisman Trophy Vote

Andre Ware, senior quarterback, Houston	1073
Anthony Thompson, senior tailback, Indiana	1003
Major Harris, junior quarterback, West Virginia	709
Tony Rice, senior quarterback, Notre Dame	523
Darian Hagan, sophomore quarterback, Colorado	292

Other Major Award Winners

Maxwell (Player)	Anthony Thompson, senior tailback, Indiana
Walter Camp (Player)	Andre Ware, senior quarterback, Houston
Outland (Lineman)	Mohammed Elewonibi, senior guard, BYU
Lombardi (Lineman)	Percy Snow, senior linebacker, Michigan State
Dick Butkus (Linebacker)	Percy Snow, senior linebacker, Michigan State
Jim Thorpe (Defensive back)	Mark Carrier, junior safety, Southern Cal
Davey O'Brien (Quarterback)	Andre Ware, senior quarterback, Houston
AFCA Coach of the Year	Bill McCartney, Colorado

1990

The Year of Helter Skelter Fifth Down and Cinderella in Atlanta, Dancing the Hokey Pokey, and Rocket's Near Glare

Eager bowl officials created unbelievable disruption of the 1990 post-season because more than ever they simply couldn't resist making early obligations to a number of teams that stumbled the moment they received an invitation from a major bowl. On the other hand, the Fiesta Bowl had trouble finding a match due to the political perception of the state of Arizona. Colorado (11-1-1) and Georgia Tech (11-0-1) shared the national title, a fitting finish to a helter skelter year in which hardly any team seemed capable of holding on to or eager to stake a claim to the no. 1 ranking.

Colorado handled several powerhouse teams, but a tremendous blunder by officials in a game against an ordinary, but fired-up Missouri (4-7) team, truly shaped the kind of season it would be. The late 33-31 win positioned Colorado for a title shot some felt was monumentally undeserved.

On October 6, confused officials allowed Colorado a fifth down late in a frenzied finish at Missouri's Faurot Field, and the Buffaloes scored the winning touchdown with two seconds left. Fifty years earlier, undefeated and second-ranked Cornell beat Dartmouth on a fifth down play, and the Big Red graciously conceded defeat the following day after reviewing film of the game. But 1990 was nothing like 1940, and with national honors and millions of bowl dollars at stake, Colorado was in no mood to hand back anything. Coach Bill McCartney tried to change the subject to bad artificial turf: "We slipped and slid all day, or we would have put more points on the board, I'll tell you that." Later, McCartney correctly pointed out that Cornell's 1940 situation was different in that the Big Red used all five plays to try to score, while Colorado spiked the ball twice to stop the clock. The Buffs wouldn't have run on third down nor spiked the ball on fourth down had they known it was something other than second or third down as the down markers showed. Regardless, the tainted win amazingly kept the Buffs alive in the national championship race at 4-1-1 which they would extend with six straight wins to finish the regular season. In fact, many Buffalo players credited their improved play to the furor over the fifth down that forced them to regroup in a mindset of us-against-the-world.

Meanwhile, Georgia Tech authored a genuine Cinderella story. Coach Bobby Ross had arrived in Atlanta in 1987 and weathered 13 straight ACC losses at one stretch. The Yellow Jackets had opened 1989 with three straight defeats, but won seven of their last eight. Still, they were unranked in the opening 1990 poll. They suffered an annoying tie against improved North Carolina (6-4-1) on October 20, a blemish AP media voters seemed never to forgive. In a November 3 showdown, Georgia Tech defeated no. 1 Virginia (8-4) in a memorable 41-38 game. Georgia Tech finished the regular season as the nation's only unbeaten—but once tied—team.

Virginia's top-ranking was its first in school history, but the Cavaliers crashed with three late losses, rendering their early Sugar Bowl selection highly dubious. At least Virginia made a competitive, if losing, 23-22 game of it against Tennessee (9-2-2) in New Orleans.

The weekly top-ranked team lost an amazing five times during the season. Only two other years in history—1981 and 1984—saw more (six) no. 1 teams knocked off. Preseason no. 1 Miami (10-2) was spilled by Brigham Young (10-3) and its Heisman-winner-in-waiting Ty Detmer on September 8. On October 6, Notre Dame (9-3) self-destructed in a raft of turnovers against Stanford (5-6). Michigan (9-3) held on to the top spot for one week, losing controversially to Michigan State (8-3-1) by a single point on October 13. Virginia enjoyed its top-ranking for three weeks until being beaten in the Georgia Tech thriller. And finally, Notre Dame, which had lost at home in Notre Dame Stadium only twice in its *entire history* while holding the no. 1 mantle, lost at home as no. 1 for the second time in the *same season* as Penn State (9-3) authored the upset on November 17.

Iowa (8-4) coach Hayden Fry welcomed back most of the same players who had delivered a weak 5-6 record in 1989, the Hawkeyes' worst ledger since 1980, the second season of Fry's Iowa City resurrection. Iowa received more intense play from their defensive unit, and quarterback Matt Rodgers, son of Boston Celtics basketball coach Jimmy Rodgers, and 255-lb. tailback Nick Bell considerably improved their play. Iowa won on the road at both Michigan State and Michigan and enjoyed its post-game celebrations with a favorite dance of Fry's, the always-silly, but always-fun Hokey Pokey. Iowa had the Big Ten championship all to itself after its 54-28 annihilation of the conference's best defense in Illinois (8-4) on November 4. The following week the Hawkeyes lost a heartbreaker to Ohio State (7-4-1) and, after losing to up-and-down Minnesota (6-5), they backed into the Rose Bowl as conference quad-champs because they had beaten the other title sharers.

Washington (10-2), beginning to gear up for a 1991 national title run, ran away by 33-7 in the first half of the Rose Bowl game, but some of Fry's trickery helped the Hawks make the score look respectable at the end. After all the cheering had stopped, Iowa could revel in having danced away an enjoyable year with lots of Hokey Pokey laughs, just the way coach Fry always wanted football to be.

For better or worse, the rest of the bowl games were far more serious.

Due to the failure of the Arizona electorate to vote a paid holiday for state workers on Martin Luther King Day, the Fiesta Bowl became a "politically-incorrect" hot potato. Several schools snubbed invitations to Tempe out of avowed respect for their black players. Fiesta Bowl participants by default were under-valued Louisville (10-1-1) and Alabama (7-5); a team simply grateful to have any New Year's Day invitation. The Cardinals proved their worth with a solid 34-7 win over the Crimson Tide.

Colorado met sometimes-disappointing Notre Dame in the Orange Bowl. The Fighting Irish were one of the early bowl invitees that tumbled from the title picture with a late loss, in their case, the 24-21 home defeat by Penn State.

Nursing a delicate 10-9 Orange Bowl lead, Colorado faced fourth down with 65 seconds left. A punt, which could have been aimed safely out of bounds, instead, was kicked directly to one of the all-time most dangerous returners, Raghib "Rocket" Ismail, undoubtedly the year's fastest player and the Heisman Trophy runner-up to BYU's Detmer. "The Rocket" raced 91 yards for an apparent winning touchdown and destruction of Colorado's championship dreams. But, officials caught Notre Dame's Greg Davis blocking the back of Buff tackler Tim James at the Irish 37 yard-line. Although TV replays indicated a genuine if marginal foul, James admitted afterward that even without hinderance of the illegal block he might have had difficulty halting Ismail's ruinous run.

Georgia Tech headed to the Florida Citrus Bowl. Despite little respect from oddsmakers, who favored Nebraska (9-3) by a narrow margin, the Yellow Jackets dismantled the Cornhuskers 45-21 to win the coaches' half of the national championship. Had Ismail managed to score in the Orange Bowl's dying moments, Georgia Tech, in 1990s vernacular, likely would have "had it all."

Massive aerial battles broke out all over in 1990. Not only did BYU's Detmer throw for 5,188 yards, but four of the 10 most prolific individual passing yardage efforts to date were proffered during the season. Leading the way was David Klingler, spotlighter of Houston's dynamic Run-n-Shoot offense, which gained few fans because of coach John Jenkins' perceived proclivity for running up scores on behalf of his NCAA-sanctioned school. Mean-spirited or not, the Cougars won games by 51-35, 44-17, 62-28, 56-35, and 62-35. Klingler set a record for completing 11 touchdowns against Div. 1-AA Eastern Washington as Houston (10-1) prevailed 84-21 on November 17, part of Klingler's record 54 passing touchdowns for the year. Klingler's 572 yards in the air in the Eastern Washington contest became the seventh-best in history by season's end. Just two weeks earlier, TCU succumbed 56-35, but in defeat Horned Frogs quarterback Matt Vogler set a new NCAA mark with 690 yards passing. In Tokyo on December 2 in a 62-45 win over Arizona State (4-7), Klingler pitched 70 passes, completing 41 for 716 yards and the all-time single-game yardage mark. Pacific's Troy Kopp threw for 564 yards against New Mexico State, the 10th-best game total to that point in collegiate history.

Milestones

● In February, Notre Dame announced its defection from College Football Association, group of major schools (excluding Big Ten and Pac-10) that had banded together primarily to formulate television policy. Notre Dame signed lucrative contract with NBC to telecast all its home games.

● Penn State jolted status quo and accelerated demise of most independent football programs when it accepted 11th membership in Big Ten with conference games starting in 1993. "Super Conferences" began to formulate. Arkansas bolted flagging Southwest Conference for Southeastern Conference, and South Carolina dropped independence to become 12th member of SEC. Each would begin play in 1992. Independent Florida State joined Atlantic Coast Conference and would compete for its first league title in 1992.

● Successful Big East basketball concept was extended to gridiron as football-playing members Boston College, Pittsburgh and Syracuse were joined by Miami of Florida (which in turn found high-profile setting for its fledgling basketball program), Rutgers, Temple, Virginia Tech and West Virginia. Full league play was slated to begin in 1992.

● Controversial Proposition 48 was modified, permitting athletes, who were partial academic qualifiers, to get financial aid previously unavailable to them.

● Testing for anabolic steroids and related masking agents became mandatory. Penalty for positive results would cost a player one year of eligibility.

● Famed for 222-0 loss to Georgia Tech in 1922, Cumberland University returned to competition for first time since 1949, losing its opener 34-0 to Campbellsville on September 15.

● Illinois senior fullback Howard Griffith set two scoring records on September 22 in a 56-21 win over Southern Illinois. Griffith's eight touchdowns bested Ole Miss' Arnold "Showboat" Boykin's seven in 1951, and his 48 points bettered the record of 43 set by Syracuse's Jimmy Brown in 1956.

● Michigan lost two greats in 1940 Heisman Trophy winner and scorer of 33 touchdowns and thrower of 16 more, Tommy Harmon, who died in Los Angeles on March 17, and Bennie Oosterbaan, who died at 84 on October 25. Oosterbaan was coach for 11 years (1948-58) at Michigan and one of its greatest athletes: Hall of Fame football end, basketball All-America (Big Ten scoring leader in 1928), and Big Ten batting leader in baseball. Former Texas Christian defensive lineman and Chicago Bears rookie, Fred Washington, died in car accident on December 21. Long-time pro coach George Allen returned to college ranks at Long Beach State. The 49ers closed with three wins for 6-5 record, but Allen died on New Year's Eve at age 72 before he could coach another season (55-36-7 collegiate mark). Long Beach dropped its financially-strapped program prior to 1992 season.

● Longest winning streaks entering season:
Florida State 10   Auburn, Michigan State, Northern Illinois, Tennessee 6

● Coaching Changes:

	Incoming	Outgoing
Alabama	Gene Stallings	Bill Curry
Arkansas	Jack Crowe	Ken Hatfield
Clemson	Ken Hatfield	Danny Ford
Duke	Barry Wilson	Steve Spurrier
Florida	Steve Spurrier	Gary Darnell
Houston	John Jenkins	Jack Pardee
Kentucky	Bill Curry	Jerry Claiborne
Miami (Ohio)	Randy Walker	Tim Rose
Michigan	Gary Moeller	Bo Schembechler
Navy	George Chaump	Elliot Uzelac
Ohio University	Tom Lichtenberg	Cleve Bryant
Pittsburgh	Paul Hackett	Mike Gottfried
Rutgers	Doug Graber	Dick Anderson
Toledo	Nick Saban	Dan Simrell
Utah	Ron McBride	Jim Fassel
Wisconsin	Barry Alvarez	Don Morton

Preseason AP Poll

1 Miami (24)	1431	13 Texas A&M	719
2 Notre Dame (22)	1406	14 Arkansas	629
3 Auburn (3)	1311	15 Virginia	575
4 Florida State (6)	1268	16 Brigham Young	557
5 Colorado (4)	1258	17 Ohio State	502
6 Michigan	1116	18 Pittsburgh	459
7 Nebraska	1019	19 UCLA	404
8 Tennessee	982	20 Washington	394
9 Southern California	977	21 Penn State	362
10 Clemson	919	22 Oklahoma	311
11 Illinois	900	23 Michigan State (1)	288
12 Alabama	728	24 Houston	195
		25 West Virginia	119

August 25, 1990

(Sun) Colorado 31 Tennessee 31 (Anaheim): After error-plagued opening to 1st-ever Disneyland Pigskin Classic, teams erupted for 35 pts in 4th Q. Tennessee (0-0-1) used QB Andy Kelly's passing (33-55/368y, 2 TDs) to overcome 24-10 Colorado (0-0-1) lead. Volunteers scored with 2:25 left, but chose to kick tying x-pt, thus passing up 2 pt conv that could have won it. Tennessee got ball back in late going and finished game at Buffs 16YL. In strategy switch, TB Chuck Webb advanced Tennessee to 16YL by running ball 3 straight times/46y in last 30 secs. Colorado TB Mike Pritchard, in place of suspended Buffs TB Eric Bieniemy, ran 20/217y, including 2nd H TD runs of 55 and 78y. Colorado DB Dave McCloughan had 55y punt TD RET in 3rd Q.

September 1, 1990

(Fri) Southern California 34 Syracuse 16 (E. Rutherford, N.J.): Blocked punt by Trojans DB Calvin Holmes and 12-men-on-field PEN against Syracuse (0-1) allowed Southern California (1-0) to wrestle away 2nd H control at 24-13 and 27-16. USC QB Todd Marinovich threw for 25-35/career-high 337y, 3 TDs, while his counterpart, Orangemen frosh QB Marvin Graves, in his 1st game, passed 15-30/191y and rushed 17/59y.

MARYLAND 20 Virginia Tech 13: Teams traded lead 5 times with Virginia Tech (0-1) going up by 3-0 in 1st Q and 10-7 in 2nd Q on 5y TD pass by QB Will Furrer (13-20/147y, TD). After Terrapins K Dan DeArmas made his 2nd and 3rd Q FGs, Hokies K Mickey Thomas tied it at 13-13 with 19y FG in 3rd Q. Maryland (1-0) turned it over 4 times, but Virginia Tech couldn't muster sufficient O (251y) to take advantage. With 1:01 to go, WR Gene Thomas took medium-length pass in stride at Tech 35YL, sprinted 51y to winning score for Maryland. Hokies countered with drive to Terps 33YL that died with Furrer's 4th down EZ incompletion. Terps QB Scott Zolak passed 28-46/303y, 2 TDs, INT, his completions setting new school single-game mark. Also setting Maryland game record was frosh H-back Frank Wycheck, who patrolled flanks to catch record 14 passes/106y.

CLEMSON 59 Long Beach State 0: Double coaching debut—Ken Hatfield at Clemson and Long Beach's George Allen, in 1st job since 1984 USFL—turned into early rout. Moving smartly in 1st Q, Long Beach (0-1) reached Tigers 48YL. But, swing pass by QB Todd Struder (8-19/70y, INT) was picked off by Clemson (1-0) DB Arlington Nunn, who raced 55y to score. TB Rodney Blunt soon scored at end of 68y drive as Tigers cruised to 28-0 H lead. Allen admitted long trip to soldout "Death Valley" stadium served as payday "to keep the program going." In its worst defeat in history, 49ers were held to –16y rushing and allowed Clemson WR Doug Thomas to return 2nd H KO for 98y TD.

Virginia 59 KANSAS 10: Sr QB Shawn Moore (16-27/254y) passed for 3 TDs, ran for 4th as Virginia (1-0) trounced Kansas (0-1) on artificial turf that reached 130 degrees in summer sun. Cavaliers piled up 564y O with no TOs and only single PEN. Still, coach George Welsh was dissatisfied, saying, "They (Kansas) did not execute that well, otherwise it would have been a lot closer game in the first half." Virginia led 31-0 at H, thanks in part to Moore's 2 tallies 16 secs apart in 2nd Q. Swift QB scored on 2y run and, when UVa DL David Ware forced FUM by Kansas QB Chip Hilleary (13-24/134y, INT), Moore hit WR Brian Satola on next play for 13y TD. Jayhawks were held to 235y, failed to score until nearly midway in 3rd Q when K Dan Eichloff made 46y FG. Cavs WR Herman Moore (4/97y) then answered with 59y TD reception for 38-3 lead.

NEBRASKA 13 Baylor 0: Top 10 Ds of 1989 squred off with no TDs scored until last 22 secs when Nebraska (1-0) IB Scott Baldwin (14/92y, TD) celebrated his 21st birthday with scoring run. Baylor (0-1) was limited to 164y O, including QB Steve Needham's dismal 2-8/28y in air. Huskers K Gregg Barrios had kicked 2 FGs in 2nd Q for 6-0 H margin.

AP Poll September 3

1 Miami (27)	1444	13 Alabama	704
2 Notre Dame (20)	1421	14 Virginia	668
3t Florida State (7)	1304	15 Arkansas	612
3t Auburn (4)	1304	16 Brigham Young	536
5 Michigan	1176	17 Pittsburgh	505
6 Colorado	1100	18 Ohio State	489
7 Southern California	1091	19 UCLA	420
8 Tennessee (1)	1073	20 Washington	358
9 Clemson	998	21 Penn State	309
10 Nebraska (1)	992	22 Michigan State	291
11 Illinois	896	23 Oklahoma	266
12 Texas A&M	806	24 Houston	184
		25 West Virginia	146

September 8, 1990

(Th) COLORADO 21 Stanford 17: Stanford (0-1) jumped to early TDs by QB Jason Palumbus and FB Tommy Vardell, but was held to 230y overall. Suspended by Colorado (1-0-1) coach Bill McCartney for opener, RB Eric Bieniemy returned to rush 32/149y, 3 TDs. Bieniemy made 18 and 36y TD runs in 3rd Q to overcome 14-0 deficit, and it was his diving TD from 1YL that won game with 12 secs left. But, Cardinal felt they received bad call on TD and successful GLS could have made winner out of K John Hopkins' FG earlier in 4th Q. "His (Bieniemy's) head came down first (in the end zone)," complained Stanford NG Frank Busalacchi, "Hell, it's not where his head is, it's where the ball is."

RUTGERS 24 Kentucky 8 (E. Rutherford, NJ): New coaches squared off, with Doug Graber watching his Scarlet Knights (1-0) dominate Wildcats (1-1) of Bill Curry. Rutgers alertly made 6 INTs and 2 FUM RECs. Tone was set on game's 1st snap as Knights RB Tekay Dorsey squirted off RT for 56y. In 2nd Q, DB Willie Wilkes returned INT of Wildcats QB Freddie Maggard 19y for Rutgers TD, sandwiched between 2 TD passes by QB Tom Tarver (9-15/172y, 2 TDs). Knights held Kentucky to 7y rushing, only losing its 1st shutout since 1987 in last min when Maggard hit WR Phil Logan with 36y TD.

Texas 17 PENN STATE 13: Nittany Lions (0-1) built perilous 7-6 H edge on TB Leroy Thompson's 2y TD run after TB Gary Brown (205y KO RETs) raced 95y with opening KO. Texas (1-0) soph RB Adrian Walker turned momentum by similarly taking 2nd H KO 88y to Penn State 6YL. RB Chris Samuels quickly scored, and QB Peter Gardere added 2-pt pass for permanent Longhorns lead at 14-7. In end, it was raft of blunders by Penn State that turned Joe Paterno into loser of 2 straight openers for 1st time in his career as coach. On game's last play, Lions QB Tony Sacca (13-32/243y, INT) lofted pass toward EZ for TE Al Golden, but DB Stanley Richard swatted it away. What sunk Sacca, however, was 0-8 passing ledger in 3rd Q when poised Texas added K Michael Pollak's 3rd FG to Samuels' TD for 17-7 lead.

Maryland 14 WEST VIRGINIA 10: Almost identical to previous week's late post-pattern, long TD that beat Virginia Tech, Maryland (2-0) again popped WR Gene Thomas for winning TD, this time on 3rd-and-10 for 59y with 2:22 left to play. Moving up and down field for 381y and 5 fruitless trips into WVU territory in 1st H, Terrapins made enough mistakes to squander victory. West Virginia (1-1), rallying behind back-up QB Darren Studstill (8-16/91y, TD), scored 10 pts in 4th Q. It was Studstill's 2y TD pass to RB Jon Jones with 4:21 remaining that gave Mountaineers their only lead at 10-7. After ensuing KO, Maryland QB Scott Zolak (23-42/313y, 2 TDS, INT) was sacked, for 6th time, on 3rd down but WVU pumped life into Terps by perpetrating holding PEN. That set stage for Zolak's winning toss.

VIRGINIA 20 Clemson 7: Since 1955, it had been Clemson 29 wins, Virginia none, but longest losing streak to single foe in college football history to date came to crashing end. Virginia (2-0) QB Shawn Moore passed 13-28/145y, TD. Cavaliers D, which allowed 304y, bent but broke only on early 80y Clemson (1-1) TD march that was capped by QB DeChance Cameron's 25y rollout TD run. Cavs DE Chris Slade (10 tackles, 2 sacks) forced Cameron's FUM late in 2nd Q that led to Virginia's 2nd FG and 7-6 H score. Vital play came in 3rd Q with Virginia ahead 13-7: DB Jason Wallace made 79y punt RET to Tigers 8YL to set up Moore's clinching 12y high TD toss to 6'5" WR Herman Moore.

GEORGIA TECH 21 North Carolina State 13: Typical opener was marked by TOs and PENs in 1st Q as new Georgia Tech (1-0) TB William Bell (18/68y) lost FUM on opening snap. That led to 24y FG by NC State (1-1) K Damon Hartman, and when Yellow Jackets FB Stefen Scotton lost handle in 2nd Q, Wolfpack DB Fernandus "Snake" Vinson provided 10-0 lead with uncontested 11y FUM TD RET. Georgia Tech was deeper team in broiling heat and tallied 2 TDs in 4th Q to lock it up after trailing 13-7 through 3 Qs. QB Shawn Jones (9-19/123y, 2 TDs, INT) passed 12y to TE Tom Covington and ran option for 21y before hitting Bell for 8y TD for 1-pt lead. Jackets went 54y for clinching score as frosh TB Jeff Wright came off bench to run 5/44y, including 9y sweep for TD.

LOUISIANA STATE 18 Georgia 13: Bulldogs (0-1) D was short-staffed as 3 veteran linemen were academically ineligible. So, LSU (1-0), trying to get coach Mike Archer off hot seat after disappointing 4-7 mark in 1989, opened holes for TB Harvey Williams, who rushed 24/132y, and protected for alternating QBs, Sol Graves and Chad Loup, who passed 11-17/155y, 2 TDs. Georgia was beneficiary of punt snap that sailed over P Brian Griffith's head that put the ball on LSU's 18YL. WR Sean Hummings soon scored for 10-6 Bulldogs lead, but Tigers WR Todd Kinchen beat Georgia DB Al Jackson for 15y TD pass from Graves to take lead for good at 12-10 in 2nd Q. LSU DB Ray Adams made INT 2 plays later, and K Pedro Suarez made 39y FG.

Southern Mississippi 27 ALABAMA 24: Gene Stallings, owner of just 1 winning record (1967 when his Texas A&M team beat Alabama in Cotton Bowl) in 11 years of college coaching, suffered embarrassing upset while opening his Alabama career. Southern Miss (2-0) got 75y INT TD RET from DB Kerrie Valrie and K Jim Taylor's winning 52y FG with 3:35 to play. Crimson Tide (0-1) squandered 2 late chances: QB David Hollingsworth's 3rd INT, by Southerner DB Simmie Carter, at Eagles 40 YL and long 4th down pass, which sailed harmlessly through EZ.

Texas Christian 20 MISSOURI 19: Tigers QB Kent Kiefer hit WR Linzy Collins for 2 long TD passes in 2nd Q, but Missouri (0-1) botched both conv attempts. TCU (1-1) QB Leon Clay came off bench to throw 3 TD passes, 2 to RB Cedric Jackson, in 4th Q. Horned Frogs' winning 52y drive was positioned by DB Tony Rand's INT.

SOUTHERN METHODIST 44 Vanderbilt 7: At least briefly climbing Dracula-like from its "Death Penalty" coffin, SMU (1-0) served opening rout, but it was brief glory. SMU was swept to defeat in 1990's last 10 games. Mustangs QB Mike Romo hit 31-41/342y, 6 TDs and moved past Don Meredith on school's career pass y list. For Vanderbilt (0-1), it was worst opening-game loss to-date in its 101-year football history.

Oklahoma 34 UCLA 14: Santa Ana winds, dreaded easterlies off California's desert, brought 120 degrees to floor of Rose Bowl stadium. UCLA (0-1) K Brad Daluiso provided 6-0 lead with early FGs of 30 and 39y, but Oklahoma (1-0) went ahead 14-6 when FB Kenyon Rasheed blasted over from 1YL after special teams ace Tony Levy fell on punt FUM by Bruins WR Sean LaChapelle at 6YL. UCLA TB Shawn Wills ran for 2nd Q TD, and TE Randy Austin caught 2-pt pass to earn 14-14 tie in 2nd Q. Then, Levy recovered his 2nd punt FUM in Bruins territory, and FB Mike McKinley ran 10y to 21-14 Sooners lead. Oklahoma (1-0) never trailed after H as QB Steve Collins (2-10/23y, INT) scored his 2nd TD on ground.

BRIGHAM YOUNG 28 Miami 21: Cougars (2-0) surprisingly dominated 1st H, but their ill-timed TOs kept edge over no. 1 Miami (0-1) merely at 17-14. BYU QB Ty Detmer (38-54/406y, 3 TDs, INT) hit RB Mike Salido for 7y TD and WR Andy Boyce for 2-pt conv to create 28-21 lead late in 3rd Q. This came after Cougars D stopped Canes FB Stephen McGuire (18/63y, 2 TDs) on 4th down at BYU 43YL. Hurricanes drove into BYU territory twice in 4th Q only to see QB Craig Erickson (28-52/299y) thwarted by DB Ervin Lee, who made EZ INT and broke up last gasp pass at GL with 1:49 to play. Bright performance came from BYU P Earl Kauffman, who enjoyed 53.8y avg on 4 punts deep into Miami territory. "If anyone had told me before the game that we would turn the ball over five times and win, I would have asked for a saliva test," gasped winning coach LaVell Edwards.

September 15, 1990

Clemson 18 MARYLAND 17 (Baltimore): Despite Tigers WR Doug Thomas' 98y KO TD RET, Maryland (0-1) led 14-10 at H, thanks in part to QB Scott Zolak's 43y scoring pass to WR Gene Thomas. But, Zolak completed only 18-43 and suffered 3 INTs. Key decision: With Terps up 17-12, coach Joe Krivak accepted 5y PEN instead of forcing Clemson (2-1) to deal with 4th down decision near midfield. Reprieved, QB DeChane Cameron (14-25/164y) led 68y TD drive, hitting Clemson's Thomas for 37y and FB Rudy Harris for 11y winner.

Florida 17 ALABAMA 13: Crimson Tide (0-2) built 10-0 3rd Q lead on QB Gary Hollingsworth's 15y TD pass to WR Craig Sanderson and K Philip Doyle's 41y FG. But, after QB Shane Matthews (21-37/267y, TD, INT) led Florida (2-0) to 3rd Q tie, DB

Jimmy Spencer blocked early 4th Q punt. DB Richard Fain recovered it in EZ for decisive Gators TD. Dating back to 1989, it was Bama's 4th loss in row, longest such streak since 1956.

Washington 20 PURDUE 14: Despite 2 early TD passes by Boilermakers (0-1) QB Eric Hunter (16-35/237y, 2 TDs), big and mobile D of Washington (2-0) nearly ran Purdue's Run-n-Shoot O out of Ross-Ade Stadium. Boilers finished with 0y rushing on 25 carries that included 6 sacks. Purdue scored on its 1st possession and led 14-7 after 1st Q as FB Tony Vinson (11y) and WR Rod Dennis (54y) caught scoring passes. Huskies QB Mark Brunell (11-24/150y, TD, INT) broke away for 47y of his 76y rushing to score in 1st Q. Brunell finally put Washington ahead with 35y TD pass to WR Orlando McKay at end of 66y trip with 10:02 to play. UW TB Greg Lewis rushed 26/101y.

Duke 27 NORTHWESTERN 24: WR Richard Buchanan (9/108y, TD) of loss-numbed Northwestern (0-1) said, "...this was like someone stealing your sucker when you were a little kid. The game was ours." Wildcats soph QB Len Williams (23-31/231y, TD) made outstanding debut and positioned NW for 24-20 lead in 4th Q that came on RB Eric Dixon's 24y TD run. Duke (1-1) QB Dave Brown (23-33/278y, 2 TDs) completed 7 passes on game-winning, 80y drive that ended with his 9y TD pass to WR Marc Mays (8/101y) with :38 left. Earlier, Mays dropped 4th down pass, which seemed to end Blue Devils' hope. But they forced punt with 3:04 to go, and, although Wildcats P Ed Sutter's 75y punt was nearly downed at 1YL, it went into EZ to set up Duke's late drive.

ILLINOIS 23 Colorado 22: Colorado (1-1-1), in on-going highwire act, built 17-10 H lead with QB Darian Hagan hitting WB Michael Simmons with 32y TD pass. Illini (1-1) QB Jason Verduzco (23-29/222y, 2 TDs) threw his 2nd scoring pass to tie it at 17-17 in 3rd Q. After Illinois RB Howard Griffith, just week away from his scoring of record 8 TDs against Southern Illinois, was trapped for safety and Buffalo K Jim Harper kicked FG, Colorado led 22-17 early in 4th Q. Verduzco's accurate passes drove Illini to Griffith's winning TD plunge with 1:18 to go.

NOTRE DAME 28 Michigan 24: Notre Dame (1-0) gained 4th victory in row over Michigan (0-1) as soph QB Rick Mirer made his 1st start, throwing winning 18y TD pass to WR Adrian Jarrell with 1:40 remaining. It overcame Wolverines' 24-14 edge, gained on WR Desmond Howard's 2nd TD catch from QB Elvis Grbac (17-30/190y, 2 TDs) with 7:33 left in 3rd Q. Soph TB Jon Vaughn rushed 22/201y, most y accumulated in last 3 years against Fighting Irish.

BRIGHAM YOUNG 50 Washington State 36: Could BYU let down after its big upset of Miami? That seemed likely thanks to QB Brad Gossen's 25-42/323y, 2 TDs passing that helped launch Washington State (1-2) to 29-14 lead at end of 3rd Q. But, Brigham Young (3-0) QB Ty Detmer (32-50/448y, 2 INTs) threw 3 of his 5 scoring passes in amazing 36-pt 4th Q. With score at 36-36, BYU went 68y in 3 plays, capped by 30 and 23y runs by RB Peter Tuipulotu (6/81y, TD). RB Shaumbe Wright-Fair had rushed 21/125y for Wazzu, including 42y TD run that provided 1st lead at 10-7 in 1st Q.

UCLA 32 Stanford 31: Frosh QB Tommy Maddox (13-20/244y, 2 TDs) passed 5-5/71y in barely more than min in closing drive that set up last-sec winning FG by UCLA (1-1). Bruins WR Reggie Moore caught all 5 of Maddox's throws on drive. Meanwhile, Stanford (0-2) WR Ed McCaffrey scored twice while catching 9/123y.

SOUTHERN CALIFORNIA 19 Penn State 14: For only 2nd time in coach Joe Paterno's 25 years at Penn State (0-2), Nittany Lions dropped their opening 2 games. Soph "Robo-QB" Todd Marinovich, so named because his father Marv virtually built him into passer from cradle to college, passed 22-34/240y, TD. He went toe-to-toe with slight advantage over Lions QB Tony Sacca (16-34/243y, TD, 2 INTs). Lions were held to 28/70y on ground with TB Gary Brown as shining star who gained 6/51y. Each QB hit TD pass on consecutive possessions in 1st and 2nd Qs, so tilt was tied 7-7 until Troy K Quin Rodriguez hit 26 and 46y FGs for 13-7 H bulge. Marinovich was superb on 3rd Q drive, hitting 5-5/55y until TB Ricky Ervins pushed across from 1YL. Paterno called that 15-play drive "very draining," and heat seemed to affect State on threat in 4th Q. Brown raced 32 and 8y to Trojans 1YL, but was pulled to keep him fresh. Runs went nowhere, and 4th down pass was blocked when prime receiver, TE Al Golden, was knocked down at line, and Sacca had to retreat. Lions scored 5 mins later, but by then were about out of gas.

September 22, 1990

SYRACUSE 20 Pittsburgh 20: For 2nd straight week, Syracuse (1-1-2) was tied late in game. Pittsburgh (2-1-1) QB Alex Van Pelt nailed WR Olanda Truitt with 25y 4th down TD pass with 1:30 left, then found FB Ron Redmon for 2-pt pass. Orangemen had built 14-3 and 20-10 leads as frosh QB Marvin Graves scored twice and threw TD pass. Panthers' surge was created by turnaround authored by DB Doug Hetzler. Syracuse K John Biskup tried to add x-pt to WR Shelby Hill's 4y TD grab for 21-10 lead 3 mins into 4th Q. Pitt DB Vernon Lewis blocked Biskup's kick, and Hetzler alertly

scrambled 90y for 2 ptsto pull outplayed Pitt to within 20-12. Orangemen fumbled for 3rd time, and Panthers flew downfield for tying 69y drive as Van Pelt connected with Truitt on 19, 20, and 25y passes.

Louisville 9 WEST VIRGINIA 7: Cardinals (3-0-1) K Klaus Wilmsmeyer booted 3 medium-to-long-range FGs, including 42y 3-pointer with 3:47 to go in 4th Q to win remarkably even contest against stubborn West Virginia (1-2). Squat Mountaineer FB Rico Tyler (7/24y) scored on 1y TD run in 2nd Q to provide 7-0 lead. Wilmsmeyer connected on 41y kick before H and 37y in 3rd Q to trim it to 7-6. Louisville outgained WVU by whisker: 289y to 286y. Each team tried 26 passes, and each was penalized 4 times. Biggest y maker was WVU QB Greg Jones, who passed 10-21/123y.

GEORGIA 17 Alabama 16: Behind K Philip Doyle's 3 FGs, Alabama (0-3) built 16-6 4th Q lead. Thwarted all day, Georgia (2-1) O came alive, going 71y on TB Larry Ware's 3y TD run and 2-pt pass catch by TE Chris Broom. Bulldogs now trailed 16-14 and started their winning drive at Bama 45YL with 4:10 to go. Georgia frosh TB Garrison Hearst contributed 17y run, and K John Kasay kicked 40y FG with :31 to play.

Mississippi 21 ARKANSAS 17: In 2nd Q, WR Vincent Brownlee caught TD pass and went 89y with punt RET to give Ole Miss (2-1) 14-6 lead. K Todd Wright's 3rd FG and QB Quinn Grovey's 11y TD gave Arkansas (1-1) 17-14 lead. But, Rebels RB Jim Earl Thomas scored in 4th Q, and DBs Chauncey Godwin and Chris Mitchell combined on game-saving tackle as clock expired.

MICHIGAN 38 Ucla 15: Nation's rushing leader, Wolverines (1-1) soph TB Jon Vaughn, ran 32/288y, 3 TDs, but losing UCLA (1-2) coach Terry Donahue chose to acknowledge Michigan's "very unusual" O line, led by G Dean Dingman, T Tom Dohring, G Matt Elliott, C Steve Everitt, and T Greg Skrepenak. Donahue: "...we got overwhelmed" to tune of 456y rushing. Bruins got within 21-12 in 2nd Q on TD pass by QB Tommy Maddox (26-47/353y, TD, 2 INTs) and 47y TD run by giant FB Kevin Smith. But then, Vaughn scored his 2nd TD on 23y run to pull Michigan away. Gary Moeller's 1st home game as UM coach was spiced by Vaughn's 63y TD run in 4th Q after he bounced along scrimmage line to find opening.

NOTRE DAME 20 Michigan State 19: *Chicago Tribune* writer Joseph Tybor suggested that Notre Dame (2-0) pulled win out of hat, "or wherever it gets these storybook endings." Before that ending, Spartans (0-1-1) stunned Irish with 12 pts in 5:20 span of 2nd Q, cashed in K John Langeloh's 43y FG, DB Todd Murray's blocked punt for safety, and TB Hyland Hickson's 1y TD run. Notre Dame trailed 19-7 early in 4th Q, but got 2y TD run from TB Ricky Watters thanks to FB Rodney Culver twisting for 1st down at Michigan State 18YL when his catch on 4th-and-8 appeared to come up short. Irish then went 81y in last 5 mins: poised QB Rick Mirer (14-21/155y) completed 5-6 until Culver's 1y game-winner. Big play started on State 36YL: Mirer fired bullet toward GL pylon, and ball hit CB Murray on shoulder pad so that ND WR Adrian Jarrell could grab it. MSU held thin stat edge 313y to 311y, thanks greatly to QB Dan Enos' 196y in air.

Colorado 29 TEXAS 22: Despite its opening win against Penn State, Texas (1-1) was unknown quantity. Still, Longhorns got 10 pts in 1st H thanks to 2 FUMs by Colorado (2-1-1) QB Darian Hagan (7-11/160y, TD) and dominated 3rd Q play to score on short TD run by TB Phil Brown (17/92y, TD). Texas took 19-14 lead to 4th Q and quickly padded it to 22-14 on K Michael Pollak's 22y FG, his 3rd 3-ptr. Buffaloes' O rallied immediately, going 60y in 9 plays to 1st of 2 short TD runs by TB Eric Bienemy (26/99y, 3 TDs) in 4th Q. Colorado trailed 22-20 when it missed 2-pt pass. After stopping surprise appearance of Texas' 2nd O unit, Buffs had their winning TD set up by DB Dave McCloughan's 31y punt RET to Longhorns 35YL. Bienemy and FB George Hemingway (130y of O, including 1st Q TD catch) powered to Bienemy's game-winning 2y score with 5:47 left. Gaining only 36y on last 3 series, Steers lost ball on downs and took over again at own 3YL, where Buff LB Alfred Williams tackled QB Peter Gardere (15-28/153y, TD, INT) for safety.

BRIGHAM YOUNG 62 San Diego State 34: Skies over Provo were obscured by airborne pigskins. Aztecs (1-2) QB Dan McGwire, brother of Oakland A's slugger Mark McGwire, attempted stadium-record 59 passes. McGwire completed 32 for 361y, 3 TDs. But, QB Ty Detmer of BYU (4-0) outdid McGwire with 26-38/514y, including 3 TDs to WR Andy Boyce. Cougars pounced to 21-0 lead early in 2nd Q as HB Stacey Corley tallied 1st of his 2 TD runs with 17y sprint. But, SDSU kept ball for all of 2nd Q except 1:13, and used K Andy Trakas' popup on-side KO to fuel 2nd of 3 TDs that pulled Aztecs within 28-24 at H. Still, Detmer outpassed McGwire 276y to 194y in 1st H. Through 3rd Q and into 4th Q, Cougars scored 3 TDs and held Aztecs only to Trakas' 2nd FG. Key score came with BYU ahead 35-24: S Derwin Gray blocked SDSU punt, and Cougars HB Matt Belini scored on next play from 1YL for 41-24 edge.

WASHINGTON 31 Southern California 0: Huskies (3-0) made 2 quick scores late in 2nd Q to embolden their 10-0 lead. They went 80y to FB Darius Turner's 1st of pair of 1y TDs, and S Tommie Smith picked off pass with 2:40 remaining in 1st H. QB Mark Brunell hit WR Mario Bailey with 12y TD pass for 24-0 lead. Trojans (2-1) QB Todd Marinovich felt disgusted after thrashing by Washington. "I've never been shutout in my life," said Marinovich (7-16/80y, 2 INTs), "It's pathetic. I'm embarrassed." Marinovich was pulled early in 4th Q, and USC had crossed midfield only once while he was in game, having probed to Huskies 45YL early in 2nd Q. On play that followed that advance, however, Washington D sacked Marinovich for 9y loss.

ARIZONA 22 Oregon 17: Wildcats (3-0) CB Darryl Lewis gave rise to several magnificent plays to build and preserve Arizona's victory over formidable Ducks (2-1). Oregon QB Bill Musgrave (22-41/258y, 2 TDs, 4 INTs), who had trouble delivering some throws because of sprained ankle, came back from 3-14 start to hit 2 TD passes in 2nd Q to TE Jeff Thomason. That gave Ducks 14-10 H edge after Arizona had dominated 1st Q with K Gary Coston's 23y FG, after bad Oregon punt snap and Cats QB Ronald Veal's 11y TD pass. Lewis (2 INTs) gave Musgrave rugged 3rd Q working-over: He sprinted 40y to 8YL with 1st INT thrown by Musgrave so far in 1990. That led to Coston's 2nd FG, and Lewis stole deflected pass and went untouched for INT TD RET 3 mins later. When UA DB Bobby Roland made another INT late in 3rd Q, Coston kicked another 3-ptr for Wildcats' 22-14 lead. K Gregg McCallum bounced successful 51y FG off crossbar in middle of 4th Q, so Ducks trailed by 5 pts. Musgrave launched last drive from his 29YL and it included 37y strike to WR Michael McClellan to Cats 3YL. Arizona stopped 3 runs, and on 4th down, Musgrave rolled out looking for receiver in EZ, but had to make dash for corner where Lewis made crushing stop short of GL with 13 secs left.

AP Poll September 24

1 Notre Dame (43)	1478	13 Houston	696
2 Florida State (11)	1397	14 Illinois	621
3 Auburn (3)	1384	15 Ohio State	595
4 Brigham Young (3)	1261	16 Arizona	582
5 Tennessee	1168	17 Florida	525
6 Michigan	1156	18 Southern California	518
7 Virginia	1106	19 Clemson	510
8 Nebraska	1082	20 Colorado	493
9 Oklahoma	1042	21 Arizona State	281
10 Miami	1034	22 Michigan State	212
11 Texas A&M	916	23 Arkansas	155
12 Washington	787	24 Fresno State	106
		25 South Carolina	64

September 29, 1990

West Virginia 38 PITTSBURGH 24: Panthers (2-2-1) D allowed 547y, most in rivalry game since 1971, as West Virginia (2-2) RB Michael Bentley (22/197y) led O that scored 1st 4 times it had ball. Mountaineers led 28-10 at H as Pitt "...looked like we set the NCAA record for missed tackles in the first half," according to D coordinator Fred VonAppen. RB Ricky Turner briefly thrilled Panther partisans with 100y KO TD RET in 2nd Q. With 16 secs left in 3rd Q, RB Jon Jones ran 29y to score for West Virginia's 35-16 lead. Pitt QB Alex Van Pelt pitched 9y TD to TE Dave Moore and 2-pt pass to FB Ronald Redmon to pull within 35-24 with 13:49 to go, but Van Pelt suffered EZ INT with 3:25 left.

MIAMI 48 Iowa 21: Miami (2-1) coach Dennis Erickson threatened to bench any player who celebrated excessively, and Hurricanes almost didn't get to celebrate at all. Miami lost 4 TOs and got jumpy when Iowa (2-1) crept to 24-21 in mid-3rd Q, but its O cruised magnificently to 542y. Canes FB Stephen McGuire (20/128y, 2 TDs) opened scoring in 1st Q, and QB Craig Erickson (17-33/360y, 3 TDs, 2 INTs) soon launched 73y TD pass to WR Wesley Carroll. Hawkeyes TB Nick Bell scored on 3y run at end of short drive that started on DB Gary Clark's INT of Erickson. Bell caught 53y TD from QB Matt Rodgers (21-36/275y, 2 TDs, INT), so Iowa trailed 24-14 at H. Rodgers struck again on 35y TD pass after McGuire fumbled in 3rd Q. But, McGuire redeemed himself on Miami's next scoring trip. McGuire touched it 6 straight times: runs totaling 33y and 10y catch to his 6y TD run. Icing was DB Ryan McNeil's 75y FUM TD RET with 1:34 to go.

North Carolina State 12 NORTH CAROLINA 9: Trailing 9-6 in tight D-dominated battle, Tar Heels (3-2) finally got their O to catch fire in 4th Q. QB Todd Burnett (6-19/71y, INT) hit 3 passes of 23, 8 and 20y for 1st-and-goal at NC State (3-2) 5YL with less than 2 mins to go. But, UNC coach Mack Brown took out Burnett for GL QB Steve Jerry and had to settle for K Clint Gwaltney's tying 21y FG with 1:06 to play. Wolfpack, which outgained North Carolina 244y to 169y, got to FG position on 15y pass interference PEN and 4 short completions by QB Charles Davenport (16-37/161y, 2 INTs). K Damon Hartman set NC State school distance record with 56y FG on game's last play, his 4th FG of day.

FLORIDA STATE 39 Virginia Tech 28: Gallant Hokies (2-3) pushed Seminoles (4-0) to ropes, leading 7-3 after 1st Q and 21-3 before receding to 21-18 advantage at H. Virginia Tech QB Will Furrer (21-37/194y, 3 TDs, INT) hit WR John Rivers with 2 TDs, and TB Tony Kennedy (13/60y) ran 26y for score in 1st H. Florida State took lead for good at 32-28 when DB Terrell Buckley scored on 53y INT RET in last min of 3rd Q. DB Errol McCorvey scooped up 4th Q FUM and went 77y for FSU's last score.

LOUISIANA STATE 17 Texas A&M 8: During 4th Q, LSU (3-1) WR Todd Kinchen took short pass from QB Chad Loup (10-13/152y, TD) and broke away for 79y TD, then set up RB Harvey Williams' clinching score with 60y punt RET. Aggies (3-1) were done in by 4 INTs, but got late TD pass and 2-pt play from QB Lance Pavlas.

AUBURN 26 Tennessee 26: FB Greg Amsler rushed for 2 TDs and WR Alvin Harper weaved 82y with pass as Tennessee (3-0-2) built 26-9 edge early in 4th Q. With QB Stan White (30-58/338y, 3 TDs) tying school completion record, Auburn (2-0-1) got within 26-19 on K Jim Von Wyl's FG and White's TD pass with 8:26 left. White hit WR Greg Taylor with TD with 1:56 to go, and coach Pat Dye opted for tying kick. Sack by Vols DL Darryl Hardy stopped Tigers late in game, but Tennessee K Greg Burke missed 34y FG with :15 to go.

Southern California 35 OHIO STATE 26: TB Ricky Ervins keyed overwhelming 331y Southern California (3-1) ground game with career-high 199y with 2 TDs on 28 tries. Trojans opened scoring with blocked punt for TD. Ohio State (2-1) got within 14-10 on 1st of 2 TD passes by QB Greg Frey, but Ervins provided 21-10 H lead on his 2nd TD. Frey (19-36/262y, 2 TDs, INT) pulled Buckeyes within 28-18 on 3rd Q TD pass to WR Jeff Graham and 2-pt pass to TE Bernard Edwards. Still struggling to catch up, Ohio made it 35-26 with 2:38 left. Heavy rain, near-striking lightning influenced game officials to suggest suspension of play until weather cleared. But, Buckeyes coach John Cooper informed officials his team intended to try on-side KO. Cooper was realistic with officials: "If we get it (on-side-KO), go ahead and suspend it. If not, you might as well call it off because they are going to win." USC covered KO, and play ended.

COLORADO 20 Washington 14: Before leaving with sprained shoulder, Colorado (3-1-1) QB Darian Hagan scored on 15 and 3y runs in 3rd Q for 17-14 lead. Huskies (3-1) counterpart, QB Mark Brunell (16-34/190y, TD, 3 INTs), scored only TD of 1st Q and tossed 3y TD to TE Aaron Pierce in 3rd Q. Washington D had arrived with minuscule 23.3y game rush avg, but Bison runners, led by TB Eric Bieniemy's 29/143y, totaled 183y. When Brunell drove Washington to 20YL early in 4th Q and to 7YL in closing mins, Buffs DBs Tim James and Deon Figures made INTs. Figures' pass snatch came in EZ on 4th down, when throw was aimed at UW WR Mario Bailey, who appeared woozy after earlier hit by James. "Everybody's been beating us in the fourth quarter," said Colorado LB Kanavis McGhee, "and we said, 'we've just got to stop it.'"

OKLAHOMA 31 Kansas 17: Jayhawks (1-3) dominated everywhere but scoreboard. "They were thinking: what's going on?," Kansas OT Chris Perez said of Oklahoma (4-0), which experienced reversal of series history's pattern for awhile. Sooners were outgained 396y to 261y despite enjoying solid early leads of 14-0 and 31-7. Edgy Jayhawks lost 4 TOs, which Sooners turned into 24 pts as Oklahoma FB Kenyon Rasheed scored thrice. Kansas QB Chip Hilleary (15-23/153y) rushed 11/76y.

HOUSTON 24 Rice 22: Cross-city rivals went after midnight before K Roman Anderson split uprights with 32y FG to win it for Houston (3-0) at Astrodome. Contest started late due to field conversion after Astros baseball in afternoon, and Owls (2-2) enjoyed early nighttime. Rice flew to leads of 3-0, 10-7, 13-7, and 22-7 before Cougars began to prowl late in 3rd Q. Owls QB Donald Hollas (21-33/269y, TD, 3 INTs) fired 2y slant-in TD pass to WB Eric Henley to wrap up 80y drive midway in 2nd Q, and then after wild exchange of INTs, FUM, and punt, Rice went from Houston 45YL to K Clint Parsons' 29y FG, 2nd of his 3, for 13-7 H edge. TB Trevor Cobb (28/136y), who left early in 4th Q with hip-pointer, carried load to Hollas' 3y TD run after 2nd H KO. Trailing 22-7, Houston woke up on QB David Klingler's 78y TD to WR Patrick Cooper when Owls DB Everett Coleman fell down. Klingler (34-56/454y, 2 TDs, 2 INTs) flipped 2-pt pass to WR Manny Hazard (8/82y). With 2:31 to play, Klingler and Cooper reconnected for 56y TD, but all seemed lost for Cougars when ILB O.J. Brigance batted down 2-pt throw to keep Owls up 22-21 until last-gasp 42y drive into FG position with 12 secs left.

California 30 ARIZONA 25: California (2-2) QB Mike Pawlawski accounted for 3 TDs, and TB Russell White broke 2 tackles in racing for his 2nd TD that created 28-13 lead in 3rd Q. Arizona (3-1) rallied with 11y TD run by TB Art Greathouse, but lost 2 pts when QB George Malauulu was trapped for safety that made score 30-19 for California. Wildcats failed on late drive that reached deep into Golden Bears territory.

OREGON 32 Brigham Young 16: Glance at BYU (4-1) schedule led some speculators to believe Oregon (3-1) was last possible obstacle between Cougars and undefeated season. Energetic Ducks built 12-0 early lead on TD pass by QB Bill Musgrave (23-37/286y, 3 TDs, INT) and DL Marcus Woods' EZ sack. Oregon led 12-10 in 3rd Q, but Musgrave hit 2 TDs to overcome heartbreak of previous week's 22-17 loss at Arizona when Musgrave was tackled inside Wildcats 1YL in final secs. BYU QB Ty Detmer (33-57/442y, 2 TDs) suffered 5 INTs, 3 by DB Daryle Smith for Ducks' record. Detmer was sacked 5 times as Cougars finished -47y rushing; 12 runs went for minus y.

AP Poll October 1

1 Notre Dame (49)	1489	13t Houston	748
2 Florida State (10)	1420	13t Illinois	748
3 Michigan	1296	15 Southern California	713
4 Virginia (1)	1244	16 Clemson	636
5 Auburn	1227	17 Washington	580
6 Tennessee	1217	18 Michigan State	342
7 Oklahoma	1129	19 Texas A&M	333
8 Nebraska	1106	20 Ohio State	280
9 Miami	1096	21 Arkansas	273
10 Florida	816	22 Oregon	257
11 Brigham Young	779	23 Georgia Tech	197.5
12 Colorado	777	24 Fresno State	193
		25 Arizona	191

October 6, 1990

MIAMI 31 Florida State 22: Emotionally-charged Miami (3-1) crushed Florida State (4-1) with surprisingly murderous 334y ground game and ended nation's longest win streak at 14 games. RBs Stephen McGuire (31/176y, TD) and Leonard Conley (16/144y, 2 TDs) posted their best career rushing days. Hurricanes scored 4 of 1st 5 times they had possession and cruised to 24-0 2nd Q lead. Seminoles rallied in 2nd H behind QBs Brad Johnson (26-37/251y, TD) and Casey Weldon (6-11/67y, TD). When TB Amp Lee scored on 2y run with 11:30 remaining, FSU had clawed back to within 24-16. Hurricanes answered with 13-play, 80y drive on which McGuire lugged ball 9/45y and clinching TD. Jumping back into title race, Miami rushed for more than 300y for 1st time since 1987. Its nation's leading run D held Seminoles to 57y on ground.

Georgia Tech 31 MARYLAND 3: Coach Bobby Ross returned to old College Park stomping grounds to administer lesson in what things used to be like there. Georgia Tech (4-0) D was led by 5 sacks by rampaging LB Marco Coleman and rattled Maryland (3-3) with 11 sacks. Terps' rushing total was -20y, while Atlantans' D continued its streak of 4 games without allowing single TD. Battered Terrapins QB Scott Zolak hit 16-33/192y, INT passing and was dumped 10 times before being relieved by QB Jim Sandwisch (4-9/63y, INT). Georgia Tech D set up 1st Q TD as it pushed back Maryland to its 7YL, and ensuing punt was returned to 39YL to launch short drive. Early in 3rd Q, it looked like Maryland might rally from 17-3 H score when DT Lubo Zizakovic made FUM REC at Tech 34YL. Instead, Coleman sacked Zolak, and 2 passes flew off mark. Soon thereafter, Yellow Jackets QB Shawn Jones (15-25/271y, TD) hit WR Greg Lester with 40y TD at end of blistering-quick 94y trip in 3rd Q.

FLORIDA 34 Louisiana State 8: Handed ball thrice inside LSU (3-2) 20YL on 2 FUMs and blocked punt in 1st H, Florida (5-0) had easy time of it. Gators QB Shane Matthews (12-22/157y, 3 TDs, INT) hit twice on TDs to WR Ernie Mills, and TB Errict

Rhett rushed 15/105y. Tigers trimmed margin to 20-8 in 3rd Q when they went 90y but had to settle for K Pedro Suarez's 23y FG. Florida came right back as TE Kirk Kirkpatrick shed 2 tacklers and rambled 42y with pass to LSU 6YL to poise Matthews for TD to Mills and 27-8 edge.

Illinois 31 OHIO STATE 20: For 1st time since 1927-29, Illinois (3-1) beat Ohio State (2-2) for 3rd time in row. Illini didn't take lead until late in 3rd Q when they forced 2 TOs. With Buckeyes up 20-17, Illini scored on short TD catch by TE David Olson. Then, Illini blocked FG, which was scooped by LB Romero Brice. Brice stumbled, but lobbed lateral to DB Quintin Parker who went 45y to TD and 31-20 lead. TV replays appeared to show Brice's pitch to be 3y ahead to Parker, but of course replay reversals were more than 10 years in future.

Iowa 12 MICHIGAN STATE 7: Hawkeyes (3-1) LB Melvin Foster made 2 big plays: his 14y INT RET to 44YL of no. 18 Michigan State (1-2-1) led to Iowa's 2nd Q TD, and he penetrated Spartans line on 4th-and-1 at Iowa 20YL early in 4th Q to spill TB Tico Duckett (23/121y) for loss and keep Michigan State off scoreboard at 9-0. Hawks QB Matt Rodgers (20-38/236y, TD) had found TB Nick Bell, who beat Michigan State DB Alan Haller in back of EZ, for 5y TD pass after Foster's INT, and K Jeff Skillett made FGs of 31y and 34y. After Foster stopped Duckett early in 4th Q, Michigan State got ball back on next series and converted 69y drive to TB Hyland Hickson's TD run with 4:06 to play. Win kept coach Hayden Fry remarkably undefeated (5-0-1) at Spartan Stadium in his 12-year career at Iowa, and he was so thrilled that he revived past tradition of having his players dance hokey pokey in winning locker room.

Stanford 36 NOTRE DAME 31: FB "Touchdown" Tommy Vardell's 4th TD run, each coming from 1YL, was accomplished with :36 left as Stanford (2-3) upset no. 1 Notre Dame (3-1). Looking for Irish's 3rd miracle finish so far, QB Rick Mirer (15-26/235y, 2 TDs) threw EZ pass that eluded TE Derek Brown's fingertips as time expired. Mirer hit WR Tony Smith with 2 TD passes within 3 mins and ND led 24-7 with 6:30 to go in 1st H. Stanford began throwing to 6'5" WR Ed McCaffrey (6/111y) who towered over his coverman, 5'10" DB Reggie Brooks. McCaffrey caught 2-pt pass after Vardell's 1st TD as Cardinal pulled within 24-15 at H. After Vardell and Irish FB Rodney Culver (104y rushing) traded 3rd Q TDs, McCaffrey caught 43y pass from QB Jason Palumbis to set up Vardell's score that pulled Stanford within range at 31-29 late in 3rd Q.

Colorado 33 MISSOURI 31: With 1st-and-goal at Tigers' 3YL with 31 secs to play, Buffaloes (4-1) backup QB Charles Johnson, in for injured QB Darian Hagan, spiked ball twice (on 1st and 4th downs) to stop clock in frantic 26-sec span after TB Eric Bieniemy (29/217y, TD) was stopped twice just short of GL. Johnson ran off T for winning TD on game's last play—erroneously-permitted 5th down play—so his TD should not have counted. Even then, Mizzou D coordinator Michael Church contended, "When we see the film, we'll see that he did not cross the goal line." Lost in game's confusion and controversy was QB Kent Kiefer's 19-34/326y, 3 TDs, INT passing for Missouri (2-3). Kiefer hit WR Victor Bailey for diving 18y TD in 1st Q and WR Damon Mays (5/153y) for 49 and 38y TDs. After 14-14 H tie, Mizzou trumped 35y FG by Buffs K Jim Harper with FB Michael Jones' 13y TD run for 21-17 lead in 3rd Q. Johnson threw 70y TD pass to WR Mike Pritchard early in 4th Q, but after exchange of FGs, Tigers took 31-27 lead on Kiefer's 3rd TD pass and 2nd scoring catch by Mays with 2:32 to play. Amazingly, it was 6th straight game in which Colorado had played with verdict hanging on last possession.

Houston 31 BAYLOR 15: Houston (4-0) QB David Klingler threw 68 passes, prompting local media to wonder if his arm would fall off. Klingler laughed it off, saying he threw 600 times every day. Writer might have wondered, then, if Klingler ever went to class. Klingler, nation's O leader, completed 35-68/405y, including decisive 2 TDs to WR Patrick Cooper in 3rd Q. FB Robert Strait scored on 3y run early in 3rd Q to bring Baylor (2-3) within 13-7, but Bears D couldn't hold off aerial assault. Baylor was outgained 467y to 289y.

WYOMING 52 San Diego State 51: Quesy winning coach Paul Roach of Wyoming (6-0) said, "There's not enough Maalox in Laramie to take care of my gut." QBs racked up big y: Cowboys QB Tom Corontzos threw 20-32/421y, 3 TDs, while Aztecs (2-3) QB Dan McGwire hit 27-42/415y, 5 TDs. Amazingly, there were no INTs despite 74 pass tries. SDSU WR Dennis Arey (8/171y) caught 3 of McGwire's TD throws. Arey's 2nd TD gave Aztecs 1st lead at 17-14, which carried into H. Break came after Wyoming tied 38-38 midway in 4th Q and its KO bounced off group of Aztecs to be recovered at 18YL. Wyoming FB Mark Timmer scored in 2 plays for 45-38 lead. Final lead change went to Pokes as WR Ryan Yarborough (2/88y) streaked to 80y TD. Verdict came down to failed 2-pt conv try: After 13y TD, McGwire was pressed by Cowboys DE Mitch Donahue into EZ overthrow.

AP Poll October 8

1 Michigan (34)	1453	13 Brigham Young	751
2 Virginia (14)	1384	14 Colorado	705
3 Miami (6)	1324	15 Clemson	690
4 Oklahoma (1)	1244	16 Southern California	667
5 Tennessee (1)	1235	17 Washington	648
6 Auburn	1176	18 Georgia Tech	451
7 Nebraska (2)	1145	19 Oregon	424
8 Notre Dame	1122	20 Texas A&M	395
9 Florida (1)	1017	21 Arizona	319
10 Florida State	993	22 Indiana	212
11 Illinois	796	23 Wyoming	132
12 Houston (1)	763	24 Mississippi	93
		25 Iowa	86

October 13, 1990

PENN STATE 27 Syracuse 21: In 68th and final (for time being) meeting against its old foe Syracuse (2-2-2), Penn State (3-2) rode QB Tony Sacca's 16y TD run and 36y TD pass to 40-23-5 edge in occasionally bitter Eastern rivalry. Series ended over home dates squabble in new contract. Trailing whole way, Orange got 36y TD run by frosh QB Marvin Graves and QB Mark McDonald's 23y TD pass in 4th Q to make it close.

GEORGIA TECH 21 Clemson 19: Yellow Jackets (5-0) won 9th straight over 2 years, jumping to 14-0 1st Q lead on 2 TD passes by QB Shawn Jones. Clemson (5-2) fought back on 4 FGs by K Chris Gardocki, his 44y boot narrowing gap to 14-12 in 4th Q. On following KO, Georgia Tech soph RET artist Kevin Tisdale went 87y to Tigers 13 YL to set up TD run by RB T.J. Edwards. Tech staged GLS when LB Calvin Tiggle (19 tackles) made 4th down stop, but later allowed their 1st TD all year when Clemson QB DeChance Cameron scored with 3:27 left. Gardocki missed 60y FG try with 1:00 to play.

TENNESSEE 45 Florida 3: Intense D battle unraveled when Tennessee (4-0-2) DB Dale Carter dashed 91y with 2nd H KO to provide 14-3 lead. Vols' 28-pt 3rd Q explosion was highlighted by rare TE pass: QB Andy Kelly handed to TE Von Reeves who threw 47y TD bomb to WR Carl Pickens for 28-3 Volunteers' margin. Florida (5-1) passers were picked off 4 times and Gators lost 2 FUMS as they lost for 1st time under new coach Steve Spurrier.

Michigan State 28 MICHIGAN 27: Another top-ranked team bit the dust, but not without considerable controversy over officials' no-call. Michigan (3-2) capped seesaw game with 70y drive ended by QB Elvis Grbac's 7y TD pass to WR Derrick Alexander to draw within 28-27 with :06 to go. Gambling for 2 pts, Grbac lofted pass to WR Desmond Howard, who was hit by DB Eddie Brown. Howard couldn't hold throw, and no flag was thrown. "...I couldn't believe it," said Howard, who earlier in 4th Q returned Spartans (2-2-1) KO 95y for 21-21 tie. TB Hyland Hickson (20/90y) scored twice for Michigan State.

INDIANA 27 Ohio State 27: Critics who would take Indiana (4-0-1) coach Bill Mallory to task for settling for FG tie in last 1:39 didn't see him gamble twice on 4th down in last 5 mins because "we played to win." Hoosiers led 17-14 at H with their big TD play coming on 64y pass from QB Trent Green (8-19/175y, TD, 2 INTs) to WR Rob Turner (4/134y, TD) in 2nd Q. Ohio State (4-0-1) dominated 3rd Q with 13-pt flurry and O fireworks that included 71y gain by TB Robert Smith (16/127y), 65y TD pass from QB Greg Frey (8-18/153y, 2 TDs) to WR Jeff Graham, and K Tim Williams' 2 FGs. Down 27-17 with 10 mins to play, Indiana looked to ace TB Vaughn Dunbar (30/188y, 2 TDs) to slam for 6y TD on 4th-and-2 with 9:21 on clock. Dunbar led 62y drive to Buckeyes 3YL in last 2 mins and scored on 2nd down. But, ref called holding PEN behind point of attack, of which Mallory said, "I hope he saw what he called." After incompletion, Dunbar gained 3y to 10YL, and, on 4th down, Mallory waved in K Scott Bunnell for tying 27y FG.

KANSAS STATE 23 Oklahoma State 17: Don't look now Big 8, but coach Bill Snyder's magic was beginning to brew for Kansas State (4-2). Wildcats rallied for their 1st conf win in 4 years (28 games) in defeating Oklahoma State (2-4), which had not been beaten on its visits to Manhattan since 1978. K-State frosh RB Kit Rawlings scored on short burst for 7-0 lead in 1st Q, teams traded FGs, and Cowboys QB Kenny Ford (5-13/13y, TD, 2 INTs) created 10-10 H deadlock with 3y TD pass in 2nd Q. Go-ahead TD from 17-17 tie came on 1y run from Wildcats QB Carl Straw (14-21/182y), who pushed into Cowboys EZ. Straw's 2-pt pass went astray. Cowboys threw late scare into K-State: They drove to 1st-and-goal at Wildcats 10YL late in 4th Q. Oklahoma State QB Kenny Ford appeared to cross GL on 3rd down run, but Wildcats DB Chris Patterson made dive for and strip of ball, and Ford's FUM was ruled in play for Kansas State S Danny Needham to scramble for REC at his 14YL.

TEXAS CHRISTIAN 38 Rice 28: Off to its best start since 1984, TCU (5-1) won 5th straight as soph QB Leon Clay (21-38/288y, INT) threw for 3 TDs and ran for another. But before their heroics, Horned Frogs were guilty of 6 PENs/45y in 1st Q they trailed 7-0, thanks to 2y TD run by Rice (2-4) QB Donald Hollas (23-39/250y, TD, INT). Owls RB Trevor Cobb rushed 26/90y and scored twice, including 3y run to create 14-14 H deadlock. DT Kenneth Walton got TCU rolling in 3rd Q with FUM REC at Owls 35YL, and 7 plays later, FB Cedric Jackson scored out of Wishbone formation. Clay threw 2 scores to complete 21-pt 3rd Q uprising in which Frogs broke open game at 35-14. Trailing 38-14, Rice made late TDs by Cobb and Hollas. Owls LB O.J. Brigance had 12 tackles.

Texas Tech 49 ARKANSAS 44: Texas Tech (2-4) got back starting QB Jamie Gill (15-18/337y, 3 TDs) and he sparked Raiders to 28-6 H lead with 2 TD runs and 69y TD pass to WR Anthony Stinnett. Arkansas QB Quinn Grovey (14-35/191y, 3 TDs, INT) passed for 2 TDs in 3rd Q, but Gill chimed in with 85y TD bomb to WR Rodney Blackshear (6/161y, 2 TDs). Teams had 14-14 standoff in 3rd Q, and when Gill threw another TD arrow to open 4th Q, Red Raiders led 49-20. Then out of nowhere came amazing comeback as Hogs ran off 25 plays and 24 pts before Tech saw ball again. In 4th Q alone, Grovey passed 9-21/110y, TD and rushed for 58y. Grovey's 1y TD run started avalanche, and it was fueled on next play as LB Darwin Ireland recovered on-side KO for Arkansas. Porkers TB Ron Dickerson scored on 5y reception and ran for 2 pts to cut ledger to 49-35 with 10 mins left. Raiders CB Ron Ferguson took KO at 2YL and mistakenly stepped back in EZ for touchback, which was scored as Porkers' safety. After free kick, Grovey registered 11y TD run to pull Razorbacks within 49-44. Tech had to punt, and Arkansas drove 73y to 4th-and-5 at Raiders 15YL. LB Charles Rowe got hand on Grovey's pass to end it.

HOUSTON 36 Texas A&M 31: RB Chuck Weatherspoon (27/131y), key runner in Run-and-Shoot O, vaulted Houston (5-0) past Texas A&M (4-2) with his 2nd short TD dive with 20 secs remaining. It was 9th straight win for Cougars, who were outgained 555y to 452y. TB Darren Lewis (21/124y, 4 TDs) helped Aggies to 17-0 and 24-7 leads in 1st H with TD dashes of 47, 9, and 4y. FB Robert Wilson rushed 15/111y to add to A&M's 314y ground total. Happiest Aggie had to be QB Bucky Richardson, who made his 1st start since being injured in November 1988. Although Richardson (15-30/241y) passed for to-date career-high y, he suffered 4 INTs, and it was 8 TOs by A&M that handed Houston frequent opportunities. Cougars QB David Klingler (24-51/352y, TD, 2 INTs) scored on 1y sneak with 10:37 left in 3rd Q to deadlock it at 24-24, and K Roman Anderson's 2nd of 3 FGs provided 27-24 lead late in 3rd Q. Lewis broke 3 tackles on 12y TD run as Texas A&M regained lead at 31-27 on 2nd play of 4th Q. But, after Anderson's FG pulled Cougars to within 1 pt, DB Kenny Perry made INT at his 5YL to launch winning drive.

Texas 14 Oklahoma 13 (Dallas): Sooners (5-1) rushed for effective 72/292y and carried fragile 13-7 lead into 4th Q. Determined Texas (3-1) took over on its 9YL and fabricated 12-play drive that included frosh RB Butch Hadnot's 21 and 16y runs. Faced with 4th-and-7 at Oklahoma 16YL, QB Peter Gardere hit WR Keith Cash with winning TD pass with 2 mins left. Game's drama closed with Oklahoma K R.D. Lashar dropping to knees in anguish as his 47y FG swerved left at 0:00.

WASHINGTON 38 Oregon 17: Enhancing their Rose Bowl chances, Huskies (5-1) became only Pac-10 team without league defeat and virtually eliminated up-and-down Oregon (4-2). Rival QBs Mark Brunell of Huskies and Bill Musgrave of Ducks traded 2nd Q rushing TDs in 14-10 1st H led by Washington. Brunell sealed Ducks' fate at 31-10 with 3rd Q 12y TD run and 4th Q 45y TD pass to WR Orlando McKay. Musgrave was thrown for 46y in losses as Washington D held Ducks to 7y on ground.

AP Poll October 15

1 Virginia (38)	1454	13 Washington	786
2 Miami (15)	1414	14 Colorado	762
3 Tennessee (2)	1354	15 Southern California	761
4 Nebraska (3)	1258	16 Oklahoma	724
5 Auburn	1238	17 Florida	485
6 Notre Dame (1)	1208	18 Mississippi	374
7 Florida State	1046	19 Texas	354
8 Illinois	971	20 Indiana	312
9 Houston (1)	963	21 Wyoming	291
10 Michigan	939	22tClemson	278
11 Georgia Tech	835	22tIowa	278
12 Brigham Young	830	24 Michigan State	193
		25 Texas A&M	116

October 20, 1990

TEMPLE 31 Virginia Tech 28: Temple (3-3) was inspired by WR Carlos Diaz, who after cancer diagnosis in previous spring, participated in every football practice until he was hospitalized earlier in week. Owls withstood 4 TOs and came from behind in 4th Q. Virginia Tech (3-4) played without injured TB Vaughn Hebron, team's leading rusher and receiver, but took 21-17 H lead because QB Will Furrer (12-21/135y, 2 TDs) ran 22y to score and threw 2 TD passes. After Hokies TB Tony Kennedy scored on 24y run in 3rd Q, Temple fought back to within 28-24 on TD run by TB Scott McNair (12/77y). Then, D-line coach Earle Mosley collapsed on Owls sideline, and, despite free-flowing tears, players sucked it up, especially WR Kevin McCoy (6/82y), whose supple 15y catch won game.

Louisville 27 PITTSBURGH 20: Bowl-hungry Louisville (6-1-1) coach Howard Schnellenberger suggested that "we didn't chase too many of those guys (bowl scouts) away." Pitt (3-3-1) fans booed coach Paul Hackett's play-calling and just about everything else, with many walking out on 24-6 deficit late in 3rd Q. Cardinals led 1st H 10-3, but Panthers spent much of 3rd Q on Louisville's doorstep, thanks to DB Doug Hetzler's 40y punt RET to 26YL and DB Derrick Hicks' FUM REC. All Pitt had to show for it was K Scott Kaplan's 32y FG. Panthers stopped next Cards possession, but Louisville DB John Gainey angled in front of out-pattern pass thrown by Pitt QB Alex Van Pelt (21-35/209y, 2 TDs, INT) and returned INT to Pitt 3YL. TB Curtis Lipsey then vaulted over from 2YL for Louisville's 16-6 lead. Trailing 27-6 early in 4th Q, Van Pelt rallied for 2 TD passes to FB Ron Redmon, but Cardinals maintained lead by running out clock with 3 1st downs when they needed them.

NORTH CAROLINA 13 Georgia Tech 13: Yellow Jackets (5-0-1) outgained Tar Heels (4-2-1) 435y to 151y, but suffered 4 damaging TOs. Looming largest was punt FUM by Georgia Tech DB Willie Clay at own 7YL early in 4th Q. Play was described as "best hit of my career" by sr North Carolina LB Reggie Clark, who forced Clay's 2nd FUM of game. TB Natrone Means (20/79y) quickly gave UNC its only TD for 13-10 lead. North Carolina LB Eric Gash led GLS that ended at Tar Heels 1YL before Georgia Tech settled for K Scott Sisson's tying FG on last possession.

Alabama 9 TENNESSEE 6: Bruising D battle turned into FG joust as Alabama (3-3) ground game was held to 2.4y avg, and Tennessee (4-1-2) air game totaled only 51y on 25 attempts. With score at 6-6, Volunteers K Greg Burke lined up his 3rd FG try, potential 50y winner with 1:35 to play. DB Stacy Harrison blocked it with his chest, and Crimson Tide recovered to set up K Philip Doyle's 3rd FG from 48y away as time expired.

AUBURN 20 Florida State 17: Auburn (5-0-1) dealt itself into national title picture and delivered blow to Florida State (4-2), which led 17-7 at H after scoring quick 17 pts in 2nd Q on relief pitching of QB Casey Weldon (20-30/244y, TD). Tigers TB Stacy Danley tied it 17-17 with TD run with 3:47 to play. Seminoles faced 4th-and-5 at Auburn 37YL with 1:10 on 4th Q clock, and gambling coach Bobby Bowden decided to go for it. But, Weldon stumbled as he backpedalled to pass and was in trouble before being sacked for 22y loss at his own 41YL by Tigers LB Ricky Sutton. "When we gave up field position, it was all they needed," said Bowden, castigating his decision not to punt. "That was just bad coaching, like playing with matches." Auburn K Jim Von Wyl soon kicked his 2nd game-winning FG of season: 38y boot with :02 to play was made

possible by frosh QB Stan White's 4th down 21y pass to WR Herbert Casey. Auburn's tying TD in 3rd Q by Danley also had been set up by FSU risk: Tigers DT Walter Tate noticed Weldon placing ball on ground for G Hayward Haynes' "Fumblerooski" run and gobbled up FUM at FSU 43YL. Seminoles gained 358y in pursuit of Bowden's 200th coaching victory, but 13 PENs/134y proved to be heavy burden.

Iowa 24 MICHIGAN 23: Precise Iowa (5-1) D made FUM REC and INT to lead Big 10 with 20 TOs, and defenders held Michigan (3-3) to only 3 1st downs in 2nd H. Wolverines TB Jon Vaughn was held down well as he gained 18/86y but scored game's opening TD in 1st Q. On O, Hawkeyes "scratched where it itches," coach Hayden Fry's term for taking what D gives you. In this case in Ann Arbor, it was short passes and dump-offs, which QB Matt Rodgers (27-37/276y, TD) executed to perfection. Iowa was behind 14-10 in 3rd Q when Michigan blocked punt and Wolverines DB Dwayne Ware took it 7y to score. Coach Gary Moeller had advised his x-pt team to look for 2-pt run if available, but Iowa was ready this time and stuffed it. Trailing 23-17 with 4:22 to play, Hawkeyes launched 85y drive on which Rodgers hit 5-6/67y in clutch. FB Paul Kujawa scored clincher from 1YL. It was 2nd Wolverines home loss in row, 1st such occurrence since 1967.

MINNESOTA 12 Indiana 0: Golden Gophers (4-2) coach John Gutekunst threw up his hands month earlier after Minnesota D was humiliated by Nebraska 56-0. Taking greater control of Gopher D strategy, Gutekunst honed his defenders into playing 3 solid weeks and capping it with their 1st whitewash victory since 1977. Indiana (4-1-1) entered game with 41.8 pts-per-game scoring avg and Big 10's leading run attack (280.4y). Stunningly, Hoosiers gained only 27/63y rushing, and star TB Vaughn Dunbar (7/11y) was smothered completely. Minnesota K Brent Berglund nailed FGs of 26 and 27y, while QB Marquel Fleetwood scored on sneak. Gophers suddenly found themselves tied for Big 10 lead with Illinois and Iowa at 3-0.

NOTRE DAME 29 Miami 20: Although Miami had taken 5 of last 7 meetings, finale in bitter series went to Notre Dame (5-1) when K Craig Hentrich kicked school-record 5 FGs and QB Rick Mirer kept his poise under fierce 4th Q pass rush. Fighting Irish WR Rocket Ismail took 1st Q KO 94y to create 10-10 tie, while enjoying career-high-to-date 268 all-purpose y, including 13/100y rushing. Dashed were Hurricanes (4-2) hopes for 3rd national title in 4 years. Miami led 7-0 in initial 3 mins on FB Stephen McGuire's 1st Q plunge and 17-13 in 2nd Q when QB Craig Erickson (20-36/355y, 2 INTs) hit 4 straight passes and finished 80y drive with 1y TD push. Hurricanes got within 22-20 early in 4th Q on K Carlos Huerta's 2nd FG, but were ruined by RB Leonard Conley's FUM at Irish 2YL when he was hammered by DB Greg Davis, and LB Steve Stonebreaker recovered FUM. Decisive Irish TD, which lifted them to 29-20, came on simple dump-off pass to FB Rodney Culver for 21y as Mirer (8-16/153y, TD, INT) was heavily blitzed and had DE Rusty Medearis in his face.

Iowa State 33 OKLAHOMA 31: Iowa State (3-3-1) beat Oklahoma (5-2) for 1st time since 1961. Cyclones QB Chris Pederson (TD pass) scrambled and ran draw plays magnificently all day (29/148y, 2 TDs rushing) and scored decisive TD with 35 secs left. Packing most of its scoring in 1st H, Oklahoma built 14-0 and 28-17 leads as TB Dewell Brewer (25/140y, TD) and FB Kenyon Rasheed (16/97y, TD) each scored on short TD run. Sooners DB Jason Belser made 2nd Q INT and raced to 42y TD. Trailing 31-20 entering 4th Q, Iowa State used QB Bob Seiler's 23y pass out of punt formation to spark 80y drive that made it 31-26 when sub TB Sherman Williams, in for injured regular Blaise Bryant, scored on 7y run. Oklahoma drove to Cyclones 6YL, but K J.D. Lasher missed chip-shot FG with 2:50 left, and set up Iowa State at its 20YL. Pederson daringly raced for 20y gain on 4th-and-8 from Cyclones 22YL and made 20y pass and 15y run to position himself for game-winning TD sneak.

RICE 42 Texas Tech 21: Ready-to-play Rice (3-4) scored its highest conf pt total since 1961, and nothing went right for Texas Tech (2-5), including loss of QB Jamie Gill to early injury. On Red Raiders' 1st scrimmage play, Gill suffered INT by Owls DB Antonio Wilson, and Rice went immediately to work: RB Trevor Cobb, who finished with 203y rushing, ran 5/43y, and QB Donald Hollas (4 TDs rushing) sped 8y to option run TD. Texas Tech's only long drive of game came next: RB Anthony Lynn scored on 2y run to tie it 7-7 after 81y drive. On 1st play of 2nd Q, Hollas hit TE Tim Winn at 3YL on post-pattern as Winn was belted by 2 Raiders defenders. Cobb skirted LE on next play for TD. Trailing 21-7 after another Hollas TD, Red Raiders WR Rodney Blackshear fumbled KO at his 22YL, and Rice WR Courtney Cravin soon made leaping EZ TD catch. Texas Tech got no closer than 28-14, margin it earned in 3rd Q when S Tracy Saul returned INT to Owls 3YL. Back-up QB Robert Hall, who replaced Gill after latter took hit in throat, scored 2 plays later.

Arizona 35 SOUTHERN CALIFORNIA 26: Wildcats QB Ronald Veal relieved faltering QB George Malauulu (4-15/69y, INT) in 2nd H and nearly disdained pass attack (2-4/31y). Instead, Veal scored 4 running TDs as Arizona (5-2) beat USC (5-2) for 1st time in 7 tries. Trojans had led 17-7 at H, highlighted by DB Calvin Holmes' 25y INT TD RET of Malauulu's pass. Veal scored on 19y run in 3rd Q to put Wildcats on top for good at 21-17. Southern California TB Scott Lockwood rushed 16/124y, including 30y TD run.

October 27, 1990

NORTH CAROLINA STATE 38 South Carolina 29: With nation's 7th- and 10th-best Ds pitted against each other, conservative D battle was expected. But when South Carolina (4-3) coach Sparky Woods uncharacteristically called fake punt from his 27YL on game's 1st series, every preconceived notion went out window. Gamecocks RB Bralyn Bennett soon scooped up blocked punt for 20y RET and 6-0 lead. Back came NC State (5-4) on TD pass by QB Terry Jordan (13-23/188y, TD) and TB Greg Manior's 1y TD run. When Wolfpack WR, and former QB, Charles Davenport launched reverse TD pass to WR Al Byrd and frosh TB Gary Downs (23/113y, 2 TDs) scored 1st of his 2 1y smashes, NC State led 28-15 at H. South Carolina QB Bobby Fuller, who threw for 356y, connected with RB Mike Dingle and WR Robert Brooks for TDs, so Cocks trailed 38-29 early in 4th Q. South Carolina drove to Wolfpack 20YL, but when Fuller threw for EZ, NC State DB Sebastian Savage made INT.

KENTUCKY 26 Georgia 24: After 10-10 H tie, Kentucky (3-5) jumped to 16-10 lead on 12y TD run by FB Al Baker (24/133y, 2 TDs) in 3rd Q. Wildcat K Doug Pelfrey's kick was deflected away. Just moments later, slender Georgia (4-4) WR Andre Hastings turned into Bulldog by breaking 5 tackles on way to 89y KO TD RET for 17-16 lead. Baker's 2nd TD that came with 4:31 left in 3rd Q regained 23-17 edge. Game marched past midway of 4th Q when Georgia CB Chuck Carswell took P Bill Hawk's boot at his 31YL and raced unheaded to 69y TD RET. With injured QB Brad Smith out, Wildcats rode with QB Freddie Maggard, and Maggard hit passes of 17 and 10y to Bulldogs 23YL. Cats went to 14YL, and K Pelfrey overcame icing timeout to make winning 32y FG with 7 secs left.

Auburn 17 MISSISSIPPI STATE 16: Auburn (6-0-1) got TD pass from QB Stan White (16-27/224y, TD) and TD run from frosh FB Tony Richardson to take 14-10 H edge. Ultimate winning margin came early in 4th Q when march stalled at Bulldogs 3YL, and K Jim Von Wyl made FG. Mississippi State (3-4) struck back with RB David Fair's 2y TD run with 2:33 left, but Tigers LB Darrel Crawford blocked K Joel Logan's conv attempt.

Illinois 21 WISCONSIN 3: Sputtering Illini (6-1) O turned ball over 5 times, but their rampaging D compensated with 18 tackles for 82y in losses and recovered 4 FUMs. DL Mel Agee returned to his natural position from LB and fell on FUMs after 2 of Illinois' 7 sacks. Short span of 2nd Q doomed Wisconsin (1-6) as Illinois scored 2 quick TDs for 14-0 lead. Illini QB Jason Verduzco (13-24/121y, 2 TDs, 2 INTs) hit WR Shawn Wax with 6y TD on 1st play of 2nd Q after Badgers P-K Rich Thompson (43y FG in 2nd Q) was spilled short of 1st down at his 18YL following bad punt snap to EZ. Wisconsin QB Tony Lowery lost snap FUM on his own 23YL just 3 plays later, and DL Erik Foggey recovered for Illinois. Illini RB Wagner Lester soon ran 6y for TD. Illini permitted only 43/15y rushing.

Nebraska 45 IOWA STATE 13: Fresh from upset of Oklahoma, Cyclones (3-4-1) made big mistake: they scored 1st: Cyclones QB Chris Pederson threw 64y TD pass to WR Brandon Hughes. Iowa State, playing before largest crowd in Cyclone Stadium to date, maintained 10-10 tie until final min of 2nd Q and laid on 3 TDs in 10-min span of 3rd Q. Big play for no. 4 Nebraska (8-0), which rushed for 70/557y, came on 70y TD run by IB Leodis Flowers (208y, 3 TDs) early in 3-TD explosion in 3rd Q. Flowers exceeded 100y barrier for 6th straight game, longest streak since Mike Rozier's 1983 Heisman Trophy year in 1983. Huskers frosh TE Johnny Mitchell caught TDs of 22 and 33y from QB Mickey Joseph (8/123y rushing). Pederson, effective with runs in previous week's win over Oklahoma, was forced wide into clutches of speedy Nebraska CBs. Without injured TB Blaise Bryant, Iowa State's run O fizzled.

KANSAS 27 Kansas State 24: In 1st Homecoming win since 1984, Kansas (2-5-1) K Dan Eichloff booted wind-aided, school-record 58y FG early in 4th Q to give Jayhawks 27-10 lead. Wildcats (4-4) rallied behind passing of QB Carl Straw (24-44/325y) for 2 4th Q TDs, and Eichloff's long FG, his 2nd of game, proved to be game-winner. TB Tony Sands (11/48y) got Kansas winging with 2 early TD runs in 17-7 1st H. Jayhawk QB Chip Hilleary passed 13-20/221y, INT and rushed 12/102y.

COLORADO 32 Oklahoma 23: Oklahoma (5-3) led 14-12 at H on TD run and pass by QB Cale Gundy. Tense game was broken open when Buffs TB Eric Bieniemy (28/188y) raced 69y for 3rd Q TD. In 4th Q, Colorado (7-1-1) clinched 6th win in row as QB Darian Hagan hit WR Rico Smith for 85y TD and added 3y run for 32-17 edge. For Sooners, it was 1st time in 25 years they had lost 3 in row.

WASHINGTON 46 California 7: Washington (7-1), on Pasadena cruise-control, built 24-0 H lead. Huskies piled up 597y with TB Greg Lewis rushing 29/205y, TD. QB Mark Brunell passed 10-21/181y, including 56y TD to Lewis, and caught 11y TD pass. Cal (5-3) gained 306y with TB Russell White (19/121y) and QB Mike Pawlawski (10-24/166y) leading way.

November 3, 1990

GAME OF THE YEAR
Georgia Tech 41 VIRGINIA 38:

Virginia (7-1) QB Shawn Moore set school record with 344y passing on 18-28, WR Herman Moore caught 9/234y, including fake-reverse 63y TD bomb in 3rd Q. All seemed in order for no. 1 Virginia in taking 10-0 lead in 1st Q, 28-14 lead by H. But, resourceful Georgia Tech (7-0-1) took advantage of 2 3rd Q errors to tie it at 28-28. Tech scored 4 plays after recovering FUM on opening possession of 3rd Q. LB Calvin Tuggle's INT at Jackets 10YL stopped ensuing Cavs drive; and Georgia Tech gained field position for QB Shawn Jones' (17-29/257y, 2 TDs) 26y scoring pass to WR Emmett Merchant. Virgina's Moores then countered with their long TD bomb, but RB William Bell tied it 35-35 with 8y run late in 3rd Q. Tech took its 1st lead on K Scott Sisson's 35y FG with 7:17 left. Back came Virginia, gaining 1st-and-goal 6 inches from GL, a move sparked by 48y Moore-to-Moore pass. But, Cavs were penalized twice in next 5 plays, once nullifying TE Aaron Mundy's TD catch. Virginia had to settle for K Jake McInerney's tying FG with 2:30 to go. Jackets went 56y in 5 plays to position Sisson for game-winning FG with 7 secs left, keys being Jones-to-Bell 23y pass, Bell's 13y run on which he fell on own FUM, and Jones-to-WR Greg Lester 15y pass.

FLORIDA 48 Auburn 7: Higher-ranked at no. 4, but underdog Auburn (6-1-1) held early 7-7 tie on WR Herbert Casey's 55y TD catch. But, no. 15 Florida (7-1) took advantage of 2 INTs of Tigers QB Stan White (10-27/135y, 2 INTs and 4 sacks) and Gators WR Terence Barber's 73y punt RET to compile 27 pts in 2nd Q. Thrown for -14y rushing, Auburn suffered its worst defeat in 40 years. Gators stayed tied with Ole Miss atop SEC, but their probation would prevent any official title claim.

Mississippi 19 LOUISIANA STATE 10: No. 17 Ole Miss (8-1) raised its conf mark to 4-1 and positioned itself for run at its 1st SEC title since 1963 as RB Randy Baldwin rushed 24/89y, 3 TDs. LSU (4-4) was stunned by Baldwin TDs on Rebels' opening 2 drives in 1st Q. Baldwin finished 84 and 45y trips with 1y smashes and tallied from 5YL midway in 2nd Q. Tigers trailed 19-7 at H, using trickery for its only TD in 1st Q: HB Harvey Williams (20/69y) pitched HB pass to WR Marcus Carter, who rambled 43y to score. LSU K Pedro Suarez's 51y FG represented only pts of 2nd H. Mississippi K Brian Lee hit upright with his 1st x-pt try and also validated his harmless bad day with 25y FG miss in 3rd Q.

Iowa 54 ILLINOIS 28: RB Wagner Lester's FUM on Illinois' (6-2) 1st possession allowed giant Hawkeyes TB Nick Bell (22/168y) to run 43y to set up 1st of 2 TD passes by QB Matt Rodgers (11-16/188y, 2 TDs). By time Illini got their 2nd 1st down of game, Iowa (7-1) led 28-0 early in 2nd Q. Illini turned to air game, and QB Jason Verduzco (32-51/358y, 4 TDs) threw 4 scoring passes, including WR Shawn Wax's 3 TD receptions of 20, 9, and 5y. Hawkeyes riddled Illini's top-ranked Big 10 D for 540y as they scored on their 1st 5 possessions. Iowa back-up TB Tony Stewart rushed 22/101y. However, Iowa decided to scrub their corny dance routine this time, according to CB Merton Hanks, who said, "This wasn't big enough; we're going to save the hokey pokey."

Colorado 27 NEBRASKA 12: Big 8 title fracas opened with Colorado (8-1-1) driving to Cornhuskers 2YL. But, Buffs RB Eric Bieniemy (38/137y, 4 TDs), nation's leading rusher, lost 1st of his 3 FUMs on hit by Nebraska LB Travis Hill. Impetus leaned to Nebraska (8-1) when it used gusty trailing wind in 2nd Q for K Gregg Barrios' 2 FGs for 6-0 lead. TE Johnny Mitchell's 46y TD reception from QB Mickey Joseph (2-9/69y, TD, INT) gave Nebraska 12-0 edge near close of 3rd Q. Early in 4th Q, Colorado came alive and marched 71y to 1st of Bieniemy's 4 TDs. After Bieniemy's 2nd short TD provided 13-12 Buffs lead, Huskers coach Tom Osborne turned to deperate fake punt that blew up at their 31YL. "I began to see that we weren't stopping them very well," Osborne explained. "We came up about a yard short (on 4th down run by FB Tim Johnk), and that was the game." Led by blocking of C Jay Leeuwenburg, Bieniemy split middle from 3YL for his 3rd TD. Another Nebraska TO at own 10YL led to Bieniemy's 4th and clinching TD.

HOUSTON 56 Texas Christian 35: Season's surprise individual performance came from TCU (5-3) sub QB Matt Vogler who threw for NCAA record 690y on 44-79, that included 5 TDs. Offsetting Vogler's fireworks was Houston (8-0) QB David Klingler, who pitched 7 TDs of his own. Frogs trailed 28-14 at H, but used INTs by DBs Tony Rand and Larry Brown to poise Vogler for 2 TD passes and 28-28 tie. But Klingler put Cougars ahead for good with TD pass to RB Chuck Weatherspoon. Teams combined for 1,563y, breaking 1981 record of Arizona State and Stanford.

COLORADO STATE 17 Wyoming 8: Rambunctious Rams (6-3) dealt 1st loss to soon-to-fade no. 19 Wyoming (9-1) as their stout D proved to be difference. Colorado State DT Robert Chirico notched safety in 1st Q on Cowboys QB Tom Corontzos and went on to author 3 sacks. Cowboys scored in 3rd Q to draw within 3 pts when Corontzos (22-37/299y, TD, 3 INTs) whipped 18y score to WR Shawn Wiggins and added 2-pt pass to WR Robert Rivers (6/91y). With score at 11-8 in Colorado State's favor with 6 mins left, Rams DB Harlan Carroll stopped Wyoming threat with EZ FUM REC after DB Adolf Reneaud (4th Q INT) made big hit on Cowboys RB Jay Daffer at 3YL. CSU RB Eric Tippeconnic weaved 33y for clinching TD with 1:29 left to play. Wyoming outgained Rams, but 3 FG tries went awry on wide try, bobbled snap, and blocked 3-ptr.

OREGON 28 Ucla 24 Beating UCLA (4-5) for 1st time at home since Autzen Stadium was constructed in 1967, Oregon (7-2) had to rally for 2 TDs in last half of 4th Q. Bruins dominated most of 1st H as its strategy of 1st down passes worked to perfection: QB Tommy Maddox (21-34/332y, 3 TDs, 2 INTs) hit 7-7/70y on 1st H 1st downs. UCLA led 17-7 at H break on TD catches by WR Scott Miller for 37y and WR Reggie Moore for 9y. K Brad Daluiso hit short FG, but another 3-pt chance, after dropped TD pass by Moore, blew up when ball stuck to artificial turf on FG snap. UCLA took 24-13 lead in 4th Q when Maddox and Miller united on 62y TD fling. With 6:25 to play, Bruins CB Dion Lambert was called for debatable pass interference on 4th down throw that landed near EZ, several y short of Ducks WR Anthony Jones. Reprieved, Oregon scored on FB Juan Shedrick's 2y run and added FB Ngalu Kelemeni's 2-pt bull-over to pull within 24-21. UCLA had to punt, and Ducks QB Bill Musgrave (14-23/224y, TD, INT) hit 28y screen pass to TB Sean Burwell and, from 16YL, he faked screen pass and hit TE Vince Ferry with winning TD with 2:01 left.

AP Poll November 5

1 Notre Dame (37)	1456	13 Nebraska	818
2 Washington (13)	1403	14 Texas	782
3 Houston (5)	1337	15 Auburn	650
4 Colorado (5)	1310	16 Mississippi	600
5 Miami	1228	17 Illinois	568
6 Iowa	1129	18 Clemson	509
7 Georgia Tech	1074	19 Michigan	438
8 Brigham Young	1039	20 Oregon	362
9 Tennessee	980	21 Penn State	279
10 Florida	949	22 Louisville	224
11 Virginia	924	23 Southern California	148
12 Florida State	845	24 Michigan State	106
		25 Wyoming	84

November 10, 1990

Air Force 15 ARMY 3: In driving rainstorm, Army (4-5) HB Arlen Smith gained only 1y on 4th-and-3 at Air Force (5-5) 47YL in 1st H, and Falcons took advantage with resultant TD trip to sub FB Jason Jones' 2y TD run. Trailing 9-0 at H, Cadets took 2nd H KO and drove to Air Force 17YL, where K Patmon Malcolm kicked 34y FG. Army HB Mike Mayweather rushed for 129y while making his farewell appearance at Michie Stadium as school's all-time leading career rusher (4122y to date). But, Army gambled and Mayweather was halted for no gain by Air Force LB Vergel Simpson and DB Shanon Yates on 4th-and-1 at own 20YL with 6:41 remaining in 4th Q. "I felt we had to go in that situation," said Cadets coach Jim Young.

Temple 28 PITTSBURGH 18: Panthers (3-6-1) cruised along at 6-0 after RB Larry Markel's opening series TD run when 10-min brawl broke out near end of 1st Q. Temple (5-4) DB Tony Schmitz had just made EZ INT and runback to own 26YL when fisticuffs erupted, and Owls suddenly were whole new team. Owls FB Conrad Swanson (15/56y, 3 TDs) scored his 1st TD with 3:36 left in 1st H. Temple took 2nd H KO and marched 80y to 14-6 edge. QB Anthony Richardson (15-20/241y, TD, INT) sparked that drive with 62y bomb to WR Rich Drayton. Pitt QB Alex Van Pelt (12-25/193y, TD, 3 INTs) bootlegged 11y to score with 5:36 left in 3rd Q, but missed 2-pt pass. Schmitz's 2nd INT and DB Mark Ellis' 1st paved way for pair of Owls TDs in 4th Q.

Penn State 24 MARYLAND 10: Penn State (7-2) QB Tony Sacca (8-16/162y, TD), who had been relieved by QB Tom Bill in previous pair of Lions wins, shrugged off 1-5 passing performance in 1st H to ignite 3rd Q charge with 7-9/151y and beautiful 30y TD pass to WR David Daniels on 4th down play that broke 10-10 tie. After suffering early 74y INT TD RET by Penn State DB Leonard Humphries, Maryland (5-5) QB Scott Zolak (14-37/137y, TD, INT) was harassed into terrible passing day despite setting school single season completion mark with 205. TB Leroy Thompson (26/132y) scored 3rd Q TD on 10y run that put Lions ahead 24-10.

Florida 38 Georgia 7 (Jacksonville): Winners of 10 of last 12 against Florida (8-1), Georgia (4-5) faced daunting task this time because of its considerable youth and injury decimation. Early on, Bulldogs FB Alphonso Ellis lost FUM at own 15YL, and Gators qucky scored on 2y blast by TB Willie McClendon. Deflected pass landed in hands of Florida LB Tim Paulk, who used wall of blockers to charge down sideline for TD and 14-0 lead. Georgia QB Greg Talley hit frosh WR Andre Hastings over middle late in 1st Q for 23y score that pulled Dogs within 14-7. DB Richard Fain's INT deep in UGa end set up TD pass by QB Shane Matthews (26-39/344y, 3 TDs) to WR Ernie Mills, and Florida led 24-7 at H, despite 5 pointless trips inside Georgia 20YL. Dogs failed to make single 1st down in 3rd Q against mighty Gators D, led by Es Huey Richardson and Mark Murray, and lost by most decisive score in "World's Biggest Outdoor Cocktail Party" series to date.

Notre Dame 34 TENNESSEE 29: Unhappy with Notre Dame (8-1) DB play, coach Lou Holtz held mid-week auditions among his TBs. In end, early-season DB Rod Smith, back in secondary, saved Fighting Irish with GL INT with 46 secs left. "I wasn't even supposed to be in that position," said Smith, "but I knew (WR Alvin Harper) would try to go deep and for the corner of the end zone." Lead changed hands 5 times with several heros: Notre Dame WR Raghib Ismail set up FG with outstanding punt RET and scored ND's TD on 44y run. Irish TB Ricky Watters (17/174y) scored twice: 66y run in 3rd Q that provided 17-13 lead and 10y run in 4th Q that gave ND lead for good at 27-23. For Volunteers (5-2-2), QB Andy Kelly hit Harper (7/110y) twice for TDs and passed 35-60/school record 399y despite 2 INTs in 2nd H. Notre Dame locked up Orange Bowl rematch with Colorado, 41-22 winners over Oklahoma State.

Southern Mississippi 13 AUBURN 12: It was time to send out bloodhounds to sniff out absent Auburn (6-2-1) O. In losing its 1st home game since 1987, Tigers scored FGs by K Jim Von Wyl on each of their 1st 4 possessions, but couldn't cash TD all game. Most painful failure came on opening snap of 2nd Q when Auburn FB Tony Richardson churned his way 63y to Southern Mississippi (8-3) 11YL, but Tigers had to settle for Von Wyl's shortest FG: 21y. With scouts from 6 bowls watching, Southern Miss enhanced its image with 4th Q rally, while crushing Tigers' hopes for 5th straight New Year's Day date. Eagles QB Brett Favre (24-40/207y, 2 TDs, INT) led 69y march midway in 4th Q to his 12y TD pass. With 5:53 left, Southern DB Pat Wynn blocked punt, but Auburn CB Eric Ramsey broke up 4th down pass in EZ. Eagles regained possession at its 42YL, and Favre hit TE Anthony Harris with winning 10y TD pass 6 plays later, but not before making miraculous scramble and successful heave.

LOUISVILLE 17 Boston College 10: DB John Gainey's leaping EZ INT of Boston College's "Hail Mary" as time expired preserved Louisville's best record (9-1-1) since 1972. In building 10-0 lead by 2nd Q, Cardinals benefitted from odd 48y "on-side" KO that landed short and bounced high so that Cards S Ricky McFadden could recover at Eagles (4-5) 18YL. Louisville QB Browning Nagle (6-11/101y, TD) connected on 5y TD pass, but was knocked from game by 1 of BC's 7 sacks soon thereafter. Eagle QB Glenn Foley (24-55/345y, TD, 5 INTs) completed 27y TD pass to RB Ed Toner (11/98y) in 2nd Q and broke Doug Flutie's frosh pass y record. But, Foley suffered LB Mark Sander's 29y INT TD RET, which gave Cards 17-7 lead with 8:30 left in 3rd Q. Additionally, Foley couldn't do much with crippled receiver corps that was down by game's end to 3 able bodies, including frosh and converted DB.

Michigan State 28 MINNESOTA 16: Powerful O line, staffed by Ts Roosevelt Wagner and Jim Johnson, Gs Eric Moten and Matt Keller and C Jeff Pearson, kept alive flickering Rose Bowl hopes of Michigan State (5-3-1) by paving road for TBs Tico Duckett (16/76y) and Hyland Hickson (16/97y). Duckett scored through huge hole from Gophers 14YL in 1st Q, and Hickson put Spartans ahead for good on untouched, 7y TD gallop in 2nd Q. Minnesota (5-4) was all but eliminated from bowl consideration, but managed to tie it 7-7 on 11y TD romp by QB Marquel Fleetwood early in 2nd Q. Fleetwood was Golden Gophers' brightest performer as he returned from injury list to pass 16-28/164y. MSU WR Courtney Hawkins sprinted 28y on reverse for 21-7 lead in 2nd Q, and QB Dan Enos (11-12/121y, INT) scored on sneak in 3rd Q to extend Spartans' lead to 28-10.

Ohio State 27 IOWA 26: Attempting to close in on Big 10 crown, Hawkeyes (7-2) seemed in full command at 26-14 with 11 mins to play after RB Lew Montgomery scored his 2nd TD. Instead, Ohio State (6-2-1) moved within half game of conf lead with fortuitous late rally. Buckeyes DB Foster Paulk blocked punt, and QB Greg Frey quickly nailed WR Bobby Olive with 21y TD with 6:34 to go. Ohio State got its last chance with min left when it took over at Hawkeyes 48 YL, and cool-headed Frey connected on 3 passes before finding Olive in EZ with :01 showing on 4th clock.

TEXAS 45 Houston 24: Texas (7-1) took command of SWC race by shutting down high-powered O of Houston (8-1) until late in game. Cougars' 12-game-win streak evaporated as Longhorns scored all 6 TDs on ground, 3 tallied by frosh RB Butch Hadnot (23/134y). Celebrated Houston QB David Klingler (22-52/299y, 2 TDs, 4 INTs) completed only 10 of his 1st 34 pass attempts (164y) in opening 3 Qs. Although Klingler managed 2 TD passes to WR Manny Hazard, he was kept under 400y for only 2nd time in 9 games in 1990. Cougars became last major team to fall from unbeaten ranks and their defeat meant that for 1st time since 1936 not single major school would go undefeated through regular season.

Brigham Young 45 WYOMING 14: QB Ty Detmer (35-50/484y, 2 TDs) moved past Jim McMahon as career BYU (8-1) pass y leader and he marked his 21st game in row with 300y passing. RB Peter Tuipulotu scored 3 Cougars TDs on ground. Fading Cowboys (9-2) fell out of WAC contention while being limited to 189y O.

Ucla 25 WASHINGTON 22: Hungry Bruins (5-5), in danger of suffering 2 straight losing years, made fewer mistakes than no. 2 Washington (8-2), which lost FUM and 2 INTs. Huskies, Pac-10 leaders in rushing (254.7y avg), could gain only 38/146y partly on account of TB Greg Lewis (12/50y) coming up lame in 1st H. UCLA TB Brian Brown (12/113y, TD) beat blitz in 1st Q to dash 88y for TD and 7-0 lead. UW QB Mark Brunell (10-34/137y, TD, 2 INTs) ignored his off-day long enough to run for TD and pass 47y to WR Orlando McKay to set up 14-13 lead after 3 Qs. In 4th Q, Bruins frosh QB Tommy Maddox (23-41/239y, 2 TDs, INT) completed 4 passes on 80y drive, and Bruins added FG after Brunell's FUM for 22-14 edge. UCLA WR Scott Miller, who had made brilliant catch for 4th Q go-ahead TD, muffed punt in last 4 mins. Brunell pitched 32y TD pass to WR Mario Bailey and tied it 22-22 on 2-pt run as Bruins were called for PEN. UCLA DB Eric Turner made INT at midfield on Washington's next series to set up K Brad Daluiso's winning 43y FG that bucked swirling wind with 10 secs to play.

November 17, 1990

Maryland 35 VIRGINIA 30: Cavaliers (8-2) blew 14-pt H lead and lost QB Shawn Moore (12-22/109y) with late-game dislocated throwing thumb. TB Nikki Fisher's 2 TDs keyed 21-7 Virginia lead. Little-used Terrapins (6-5) frosh TB Mark Mason (18/116y, 2 TDs) tied it at 21-21 with 59y TD run midway in 3rd Q, but Cav DB Jason Wallace quickly countered with 60y punt TD RET. Maryland knotted it 28-28 thanks to P Dan DeArmas' 13y surprise run on 4th down from own 41YL. When Virginia threatened, Maryland DB Scott Rosen made INT at his 13YL. Terrapins QB Scott Zolak (20-36/257y, 2 TDs) set up Mason's 8y 4th Q clinching TD run on 71y pass against wind to WR Marcus Badgett on 3rd-and-14. DeArmas ran into EZ to concede safety with 40 secs left, and Maryland DL Derek Steele made sack to end game after UVa sub QB Matt Blundin was able to hit 2 passes.

North Carolina 24 DUKE 22: In 77th series renewal, frosh North Carolina (6-4-1) TB Natrone Means pierced Duke (4-7) for 37/256y rushing, 7th-best in ACC history. On Carolina's 1st snap after early punt, Means swept left for 76y score. Duke came back to tie it 7-7 in only 5 plays: QB Dave Brown hitting WR Walter Jones for 42y TD, but Tar Heels retaliated on Means' 9y TD run. FG by K Clint Gwaltney provided UNC with 17-7 H lead. Means had 50y TD run called back by PEN in 3rd Q, and Duke DB Quinton McCracken quickly made INT to set up FB Randy Cuthbert's 21y TD run. In lightning flash, it was 17-14 instead of 24-7. Tar Heels P Scott McAlister pinned Devils deep in their territory early in 4th Q, creating field position for Means to sprint 28 and 9y, last run going for score. Another McAlister punt placed Duke at its 1YL, but Brown riddled UNC prevent D for 6 completions, including TD and 2-pt conv to WR Marc Mays.

Tennessee 22 Mississippi 13 (Memphis): Seeking its 1st SEC title since 1970, Ole Miss (8-2) bungled 3 chances inside Tennessee (6-2-2) 20YL in 1st H. Rebels made it to Volunteers 23, 20, and 16YLs and failed to get any pts because of 2 FUMs and INT. All TOs were committed by QB Tom Luke (5-10/67y, TD, 2 INTs), who still managed to provide 7-3 lead in 1st Q with 7y TD pass as counterpoint. Ole Miss WR Darrick Owens caught Luke's early TD throw and added late-game TD catch. Mississippi gained 451y to UT's 353y, but Volunteers QB Andy Kelly hit Rebels air D with 19-23/174y, TD passing. Tennessee took command by scoring 17 pts in row on TD pass to WR Alvin Harper by Kelly and short plunge by TB Tony Thompson (23/106y, TD). Still, Rebels had chance when QB Russ Shows (9-13/125y, TD) came off bench to throw Owens' 2nd scoring catch. Preparing to close within 20-14 with 2:02 to play, Mississippi had its x-pt blocked, and UT DB Floyd Miley raced 97y for 2 pts.

Florida 47 KENTUCKY 15: While it couldn't go to bowl game and couldn't officially embrace SEC title, Florida (9-1) finished with conf's best mark of 6-1. So, that seemed good enough for ecstatic Gators. Afterward Florida players brandished fan's sign that read: "Too Bad, Sugar Bowl, UF No. 1." Kentucky (4-6) led 9-7 at end of 1st Q. Gators rolled to 31-9 H margin with 24-pt burst in 2nd Q, led by WR Ernie Mills, who exploded against man-to-man coverage for 8/136y and 2 TDs from QB Shane Matthews (20-37/303y, 4 TDs). Wildcats had employed reliable run game to win 3 of last 4, but were shut down at 27/19y on ground. Early on, Kentucky LB Jeff Brady had trapped Matthews for safety and QB Freddie Maggard (19-31/192y, TD, 3 INTs) tossed screen pass to TB Al Baker who had clear path for 73y TD. But in between was symptom of more to come: Maggard overshot TE Rodney Jackson, and Gators DB Godfrey Myles picked it off and went 52y untouched for 1st Q TD.

Michigan State 29 NORTHWESTERN 22: Angling for possible Big 10 title tie, Michigan State (6-3-1) opened big holes for its TB-tandem of Tico Duckett (20/137y, TD) and Hyland Hickson (27/184y, 2 TDs) to rally in 4th Q. Northwestern (2-8) K Ira Adler trumped 2nd Q TD pass by Spartans QB Dan Enos (9-14/117y, TD, INT) with his 3rd FG (40y) as time expired in 1st H. So, Wildcats led 9-7. NW seemed on verge of monumental upset when FB Bob Christian's 5y TD run, after WR Richard Buchanan's exciting 48y punt RET, gave it 15-14 lead with 13 mins to play. State spoiled things with 2 drives that nearly made earth shake to Hickson's 1y TD blast, plus Enos' 2-pt run, and Duckett's 29y TD smash. Northwestern, 4-TD underdog, didn't quit, converting twice on 4th down to Buchanan's 15y TD catch from QB Len Williams (18-26/170y, TD). Over 4 years, Spartans remained undefeated in month of November.

Penn State 24 NOTRE DAME 21: Surreal season grew stranger as Notre Dame (8-2), undefeated at home while ranked no. 1 since 1954, lost in that role for 2nd time in 1990. ND WR Rocket Ismail compiled 109 total y in 1st H, but left with thigh bruise. Fighting Irish led 21-7 at H as fans tossed oranges on field in recognition of booked showdown in Miami with no. 2 Colorado. Notre Dame shredded Nittany Lions D as slippery TB Ricky Watters (19/114y, TD) raced 22y to score in 1st Q, and QB Rick Mirer (8-21/161y, 2 INTs) capped 92y march with 1y TD plunge in 2nd Q. Penn State (8-2) won its 8th tilt in row since September, coming alive after LB Mark D'Onofrio returned INT 38y to Irish 11YL in last min of 3rd Q. QB Tony Sacca (20-34/277y, 3 TDs) tied it 21-21 midway in 4th Q with his 3rd TD pass, 14y rollout to TE Al Golden. Later, Lions coach Joe Paterno, making nothing but right moves, decided to punt on 4th-and-2 at Irish 37YL, and P Doug Helkowski pinned ND at its 7YL. On 3rd-and-8 with just over 1:00 left, Mirer passed and was picked off by Penn State DB Darren Perry, who returned INT 20y to ND 19YL. Nittany K Craig Fayak followed with winning 34y FG with 4 secs to go.

Texas 38 TEXAS CHRISTIAN 10: Eyes of Texas (8-1) were on SWC crown and Steers moved to within 1 more win of Cotton Bowl berth as Cash brothers—WR Keith and TE Kerry—combined for 9 catches and 3 TDs. Injured TCU (5-5) QB Matt Vogler (20-51/208y, 2 INTs) made surprise start, but his hurried throws under pressure only hurt his stats. Longhorns broke up 17-10 game with 3 quick 4th Q scores, including frosh DB Van Malone's 21y scoring RET of DB Bubba Jacques' punt block.

Southern California 45 UCLA 42: Knock-down-drag-out battle of L.A. was so fiercely emotional that USC (8-2-1) coach Larry Smith said, "I felt like I was in the middle of a Rocky movie." Troy's plan was to control possession, and TB Mazio Royster's 31/157y, TD helped keep ball nearly 15 mins longer than Bruins (5-6). When frosh QB Tommy Maddox got his chances he passed 26-40/to-date UCLA game-record 409y and 3 TDs. Unfortunately, 2 of Maddox's 3 INTs were returned for scores by Trojan DBs Stephon Pace and Jason Oliver. Pace's 27y TD RET came in game's opening min for 6-0 lead, and Oliver's 34y RET gave USC 31-21 lead early in raucous 4th Q that would see 6 TDs, 3 apiece. Maddox rebounded from Oliver's score by hitting WR Scott Miller (8/175y that beat Kurt Altenberg's school record 166y) for TDs of 29 and 38y for 35-31 edge. FB Kevin Smith battered over at 75y drive from 1YL to give what seemed like game-winning TD to UCLA with 1:19 to play. Trailing 42-38, QB Todd Marinovich passed Troy 75y downfield in 5 plays with his winning peg going 23y to WR Johnnie Morton (4/70y, 2 TDs) with 16 secs left. Winning pass came on check-off at line to post-corner route that Morton acknowledged to Marinovich with wink from his flanked WR spot.

Stanford 27 CALIFORNIA 25: Like 1982, exhilarated fans impacted last-sec outcome, this time in Cardinal favor. Incident was far less famous this time. Stanford (5-6) cut deficit to 25-24 as QB Jason Palumbis threw 19y TD to WR Ed McCaffrey with 12 secs left. When Palumbis' desperate 2-pt pass attempt was picked off by DB John Hardy of California (6-4-1), thousands of Bear fans ran on field to rejoice. Officials threw flags. Delay PEN gave Cardinal midfield opportunity for on-side KO which LB Dan Byers successfully recovered. California then roughed Palumbis, and 15y PEN moved ball to 22YL. Stanford K John Hopkins booted winning FG with no time left.

Oregon 6 OREGON STATE 3: K Gregg McCallum made 43 and 28y FGs in 1st and 3rd Qs, respectively, and Oregon (8-3) D came up with big plays in 4th Q to nail down win over rival Beavers (1-10). Oregon State tied it at 3-3 in 1st Q on K Jamie Burke's 34y FG and threatened in 2nd H to no avail. With regular QB Bill Musgrave on shelf, Ducks used sub QB Bob Brothers (8-22/76y, 2 INTs) with few results. On other hand, Oregon State enjoyed most of its success in air as QB Matt Booher completed 14-22/171y, INT. Oregon's 8 wins were its most in regular season since 1959.

Washington 55 WASHINGTON STATE 10: Always rowdy Martin Stadium in Pullman, every visiting school's least favorite tourist trap in Pac-10, was site of half-hour KO delay because of bomb scare. Don James, coach of no. 10 Washington (9-2), was less concerned with fairly harmless, radio-controlled "flash powder" bomb found in grandstand than with his gladiators losing their edge. "We tried not to let them burn off nervous energy," said James, who had no reason to fuss after 24-pt Huskies explosion in 2nd Q. After Washington K Travis Hanson traded long 1st Q FGs with his brother, Washington State (3-8) K Jason Hanson, QB Mark Brunell (8-15/138y, 3 TDs) got Huskies started with 1st of his 2 TD throws to ace TE Aaron Pierce. Sub TB Beno Bryant, in for injured regular TB Greg Lewis, carried 23/112y for Washington, while his replacement, TB Jay Barry, plunged for 3 short TDs.

AP Poll November 19

1	Colorado (45)	1476	13	Iowa	810
2	Miami (3)	1344	14	Tennessee	791
3	Georgia Tech (8)	1333	15	Michigan	634
4	Brigham Young (2)	1263	16	Clemson	595
5	Florida (1)	1229	17	Virginia	533
6	Texas (1)	1228	18	Southern California	432
7	Notre Dame	1113	19	Ohio State	364
8	Florida State	1060	20	Louisville	330
9	Washington	1043	21	Mississippi	301
10	Nebraska	926	22	Illinois	290
11	Penn State	923	23	Auburn	205
12	Houston	839	24	Michigan State	168
			25	Southern Mississippi	124

November 22-24, 1990

(Fri) OKLAHOMA 45 Nebraska 10: Gary Gibbs of unranked Oklahoma (8-3) called this win his "biggest" in his 2 years as Sooners coach. OU held no. 10 Cornhuskers (9-2) to season-lows of 118y rushing and 229y total O, while scoring most pts allowed by Nebraska since Sooners beat Huskers 47-0 in 1968. Oklahoma turned 7 TOs into 4 TDs and FG as FB Mike McKinley (8/87y) scored 3 TDs, including 48y dash in 3rd Q on which he knocked down DB Tyrone Byrd with devastating stiff-arm along his sideline trip. OU QB Cale Gundy passed 5-8/119y, TD, while Nebraska, 1st Q leader at 3-0, lost QB Mickey Joseph early in game with deep cut in leg. Nebraska got within 21-10 with IB Leotis Flowers' 3rd Q TD, but McKinley quickly put game away with his 2nd and 3rd TD runs. In 4th Q, Sooners LB Greg DeQuasie returned Huskers' 4th INT of game for add-insult-to-injury 43y TD.

Temple 29 BOSTON COLLEGE 10: Even though they were passed over by Independence Bowl in mid-week, Owls (7-4) ripped Boston College (4-7) to complete their best season since 1979. On other hand, BC coach Jack Bicknell, on hot seat after 4 straight losing sesons, turned out to have coached his last game. Instrumental were 3 Temple sr players: QB Matt Baker passed 13-23/194y, TD, while WR Rich Drayton got loose for 6/133y receiving, including spectacular 72y play that set up FB Conrad Swanson's TD run for 23-3 lead early in 3rd Q, and K Bob Wright hit 5 FGs to finish his career with 12 straight FG successes. Eagles K Sean Wright briefly tied it at 3-3 with 25y FG in 2nd Q, and DB Jay Clark provided vain thrill with 80y KO TD RET in 3rd Q.

PENN STATE 22 Pittsburgh 17: Penn State (9-2) won its 9th straight game, but not before suffering some nervous moments after jumping out by 10-0 in 2nd Q. Lions FB Sam Gash added to K Craig Fayak's 26y FG with 1y TD bash in 2nd Q. Fired-up Panthers (3-7-1) took 17-16 lead with 8:48 to go when QB-turned-WR Darnell Dickerson took lateral and pitched his 1st pass in 2 years: 63y TD to wide open WR Olanda Truitt. At this moment, Pitt players "thought the game was over," said their fuming coach Paul Hackett. But, Penn State's little WR Tison Thomas took following KO 59y to Pitt 35YL. After Nittany Lions TB Gary Brown gained 19y on 3 tries, QB Tony Sacca (16-32/187y) hit WR David Daniels (9/119y) for winning 16y score. Sacca (6/113y rushing) scrambled for 50 and 55y gains, while Pitt QB Alex Van Pelt hit 22-44/264y, TD to Dickerson, but threw 4 INTs, including late picks by Nittany Lions DBs Leonard Humphries at own 10YL and Derek Bochna with 1:41 left.

MIAMI 33 Syracuse 7: After 1st play FUM by Syracuse (6-4-2) QB Marvin Graves (11-17/157y, 13/-10y rushing), Miami (8-2) turned TO gift into 3-0 edge. Hurricanes QB Craig Erickson (23-41/259y, TD) hit 5 passes in row/68y on 2nd possession and capped it with 15y TD run. Miami K Carlos Huerta upped it to 10-0 with kick, his NCAA-record 136th straight x-pt. Huerta added FGs of 52, 33, and 26y. Orangemen got their only tally on Graves' late 4y run after WR Qadry Ismail returned KO 37y to midfield.

Michigan 16 OHIO STATE 13: Tie would do no good for Buckeyes (7-3-1); they needed win and Iowa loss to gain berth in Rose Bowl. They got reprieve in 13-13 deadlock when Wolverines K J.D. Carlson missed 38y FG try with 4:16 to go. Ohio State had to gamble on 4th-and-1 at own 30YL with 1:38 left. Michigan (8-3) D halted Buckeyes QB

Greg Frey's option run to set up Carlson's winning 37y FG as time ran out. Ohio State had led much of way due in part to Frey (13-26/157y, TD), who threw TD pass in 2nd Q. Frosh TB Ricky Powers rushed 27/128y for Wolverines, who tied it at 13-13 when WR Desmond Howard caught 3rd Q TD fling. "I think this was a Woody Hayes-type game and the way it should be played," said Michigan's 1st-year coach Gary Moeller, who played under Hayes, Ohio's late coach.

Indiana 28 PURDUE 14: Purdue (2-9), suffering through its final season of ill-chosen coach Fred Akers, lost 7 TOs to Peach Bowl-bound Indiana (6-4-1). Boilermakers drubbed Hoosiers on stat sheet, outgaining in-state rival 393y to 187y, but RETs of 4 Purdue INTs proved fatal. Indiana DB Mike Dumas set school record with 99y TD RET of INT and added another that set up 3rd TD run of TB Vaughn Dunbar (105y rushing). All-Big 10 LB Mark Hagen scored on 21y INT RET and DB Damon Watts made 25y INT RET to set up Dunbar's 1st TD. Purdue WR Ernest Calloway let 3 FUMs get away. It was Hoosiers' 3rd win over Boilermakers in last 4 meetings and brought series mark to 57-30-6 for Purdue.

MINNESOTA 31 Iowa 24: Iowa (8-3) backed into Rose Bowl as Ohio State lost, and Hawkeyes had already defeated others that tied for Big 10 title. Sizable group of Hawkeye fans among 64,694 at Minneapolis' Metrodome gave mighty roar when news of Buckeyes' defeat came with 10:52 to go in 2nd Q. Spoil-sport Minnesota (6-5), perhaps irritated by Iowa fans celebrating share of their team's 5th Big 10 title, got lift from WR Keswic Joiner, who ran in TD of punt blocked by frosh WR Omar Douglas. Joiner snatched loose ball away from Hawkeyes DB Jason Olejniczak to give Gophers 21-10 H lead. Earlier, RB Mark Smith (25/80y, 2 TDs) had plowed over for 3 and 1y TD runs for Minnesota. Joiner added 28y TD catch from QB Marquel Fleetwood for 31-17 edge early in 4th Q. Iowa RB Nick Bell narrowed it to 31-24 when he ran 39y to score. Afterward, subdued Iowa was self-consciously proud of Rose Bowl achievement. "We defeated all those other teams head up," said coach Hayden Fry. "If those other teams would have been good enough to go to the Rose Bowl, they would have whipped us." Still, Hawkeyes DB Merton Hanks observed, "It probably was the quietest Rose Bowl presentation ever."

Texas 23 BAYLOR 13: Bears (6-4-1) scored 1st 2 times they had ball for 10-0 lead as FB Robert Strait (16/78y, TD) blasted for 15y TD. Texas (9-1) rallied from behind for 6th time this year to clinch its 1st outright SWC title in 7 years, its 22nd overall. In 17-pt 3rd Q, Longhorns WR Keith Cash took 31y TD pass, and RB Butch Hadnot followed with 19y TD run for decisive 17-10 advantage. Longhorns K Michael Pollak booted FGs of 57, 43, and 38y to pad winning margin. Before this defeat, Baylor had dismissed Independence Bowl because it still harbored hopes of winning conf title and going to Cotton Bowl. Instead, Bears were left out of post-season play. It was host Bears' 1st loss to Texas in Waco since 1982.

ARIZONA 21 Arizona State 17: Cats' 9 lives seemed to spell difference as Arizona Wildcats (7-4) stayed unbeaten against rival Arizona State (4-6) for 9th straight season (8 wins and tie). K Mike Richey's 43y FG gave Sun Devils 17-14 lead late in 3rd Q, and Arizona State sought to add to its margin. But, Wildcats frosh LB Jimmie Hopkins yanked ball away as Sun Devils TB Leonard Russell (1st Q TD run) neared midfield. Gimpy UA TB Art Greathouse (17/69y, TD) sucked it up and carried load, rushing 6/24y on Cats' 47y trip, including 1y TD plunge for 21-17 lead. With clock winding down, ASU QB Paul Justin (16-33/234y, TD, 2 INTs) hit 4 straight throws, but with 30 secs left, Arizona DB Bobby Roland stepped in front of Devils WR Eric Guliford (6/147y, TD) for INT at 4YL. Cats had opened scoring late in 1st Q with TD when LB Jey Phillips hustled to baseline of EZ to recover punt snap that sailed over head of ASU P Brad Williams. Devils had tied it at 7-7 in less than 4 mins on Russell's short TD run after Justin's 57y aerial to Guliford.

Notre Dame 10 SOUTHERN CALIFORNIA 6: Notre Dame (9-2) won its unprecedented 8th game in row of hard-fought series with no. 18 Southern California (8-3-1). Troy QB Todd Marinovich (26-39/273y) completed his 1st 4 passes/52y (3/44y to WR Gary Wellman) in opening drive to K Quin Rodriguez's 22y FG. But, before night was over Marinovich was sacked 6 times/-35y by ND's terrific D. Rodriguez broke 3-3 H tie with 30y FG at end of 57y drive that launched 3rd Q. TB Ricky Watters (16/61y) gained 41y on winning march, but Fighting Irish decoyed with Watters to convert 4 3rd downs, including TB Tony Brooks' 1y TD run for 10-6 lead with 3:14 to go in 3rd Q. After WR Rocket Ismail (2/70y and 6/39y rushing) took ND to 2YL early in 4th Q on 39y reverse run and 41y gain with short pass, USC held on downs, but couldn't cash its momentum.

AP Poll November 26

1	Colorado (41)	1468	13	Michigan	793
2	Georgia Tech (10)	1338	14	Clemson	707
3	Miami (2)	1332	15	Mississippi	487
4	Brigham Young (3)	1275	16	Illinois	449
5	Texas (3)	1260	17	Louisville	444
6	Florida (1)	1218	18t	Iowa	397
7	Notre Dame	1170	18t	Nebraska	397
8	Florida State	1060	20	Auburn	339
9	Washington	1051	21	Southern California	292
10	Penn State	1026	22	Oklahoma	259
11	Houston	862	23	Michigan State	230.5
12	Tennessee	856	24	Southern Mississippi	216
			25	Ohio State	194

December 1, 1990

ALABAMA 16 Auburn 7: Crimson Tide (7-4) ended string of 4 losses to chief rival Auburn (7-3-1). Alabama accepted Fiesta Bowl bid despite faculty senate's rejection due to Arizona voters' defeat of Martin Luther King Day paid holiday. Tigers edged within 10-7 at H on QB Stan White's TD pass to TE Fred Baxter. In 2nd H, K Philip Doyle added his 2nd and 3rd FGs of 40y to pad Crimson Tide pt total.

Georgia Tech 40 GEORGIA 23: Bulldogs (4-7) jumped to 9-0 1st Q lead, primarily on TD run by TB Garrison Hearst (13/53y) after early 49y drive. But Georgia lost its 4th game in row for 1st time since 1963. Georgia Tech (10-0-1) QB Shawn Jones (15-20/225y, 4 TDs) hit 12 passes in row to spark 23-pt 2nd Q outburst for 23-12 H lead. Catching Jones TD passes were WRs Bobby Rodriguez (49 and 25y), Emmett Merchant (21y), and TE James MacKendree (7y). WR Andre Hastings tallied Georgia's only 2nd H TD on 31y pass from QB Greg Talley.

FLORIDA STATE 45 Florida 30: Seminoles (9-2) easily beat Florida (9-2) for 4th time in row as Gators failed in bid to become 1st 10-win squad since 1906. Seminoles stars were TB Amp Lee, who rushed for career-high 147y, scored 3 TDs for season total of 18, QB Casey Weldon, who passed for 13-23/325y, 2 TDs, and WR Lawrence Dawsey, who tied Ron Sellers' school record with catch in 30th straight game while grabbing 76 and 71y throws. FSU DB Bill Ragans made early hit to cause FUM, later blocked conv kick. Florida QB Shane Matthews (29-48/351y, 2 TDs, 2 INTs) scored twice on runs that pulled Gators within 17-10 in 2nd Q and 38-24 in 4th Q. It was 1st of 14 coaching matchups between FSU's Bobby Bowden and Florida's Steve Spurrier. Bowden's record in matchups would become 8-5-1, but Spurrier would beat Bowden for 1996 national title.

TEXAS 28 Texas A&M 27: QB Peter Gardere ran for TDs of 50 and 11y and threw for another as Texas (10-1) set itself for possible national title consideration vs. no. 3 Miami in Cotton Bowl. With Longhorns up 28-21 with 8:30 to go, Aggies (8-3-1) went 80y, scoring on QB Bucky Richardson's 32y run. Texas DB Mark Berry dumped TB Darren Lewis on 2-pt run. Aggies coach R.C. Slocum was angered to learn CBS sideline mic had picked up 2-pt play call prior to attempt, but Texas coach David McWilliams claimed no knowledge of play call.

HAWAII 59 Brigham Young 28: Surrounded by teammates and wearing Hawaiian lei around his neck, grinning BYU (10-2) QB Ty Detmer accepted Heisman Trophy via satellite TV hook-up with New York's Downtown Athletic Club, prior to late game against Rainbows. True to mysterious Heisman jinx affecting award recipients' next games, Detmer threw 4 INTs. But, his passing stats (22-45/319y, 3 TDs) meant he had thrown for at least 300y in 23 games in row. Hawaii (7-5) sprung upset for 2nd straight year against Cougars by using almost constant blitzing and reliable passing of QB Garrett Gabriel (21-39/359y, 3 TDs, INT), who also scored TD. Hawaii jumped to 35-14 H edge as DB Kenny Harper made 3 INTs among BYU's 5 TOs. Detmer earned sufficient passing y to build season's total to 5187y and edge Houston's David Klingler by 47y, but he was disappointed: "It (losing) takes a lot away. You can't enjoy it (Heisman Trophy) like you should be able to because we're riding home on a long flight."

(Sun) Houston 62 Arizona State 45 (Tokyo): Unusual Heisman weekend ended as Houston (10-1), ineligible for bowl game, wrapped up its season on far side of world several hours after announcement that Cougars QB David Klingler finished 5th in voting. Klingler broke month-old NCAA record of TCU's Matt Vogler (690y passing vs. Houston) with 716y on all-out air effort of 41-70, INT. Klingler's 7 TD passes gave him 54, which broke mark of 47 set by BYU's Jim McMahon in 1980. Arizona State (4-7) went toe-to-toe with Cougars to gain 666y with its balanced attack. Sun Devils TB Leonard Russell (16/129y, 3 TDs) scored on runs of 42, 13, and 16y and caught 16y pass from QB Paul Justin (33-63/474y, 2 TDs, INT). Justin's 2nd TD pass of 4th Q, 19y to FB Kelvin Fisher (2 TDs), pulled Arizona State to within 55-45 with ample time left. Next, Sun Devils DB Phillippi Sparks picked off Klingler. But, ASU's Justin suffered INT at Cougars 5YL by S Jerry Parks with 2:27 to go, and Klingler rung curtain down on his record-setting season with electrifying 95y TD pass to WR Manny Hazzard (8/201y, TD) on 3rd down.

AP Poll December 3			
1 Colorado (42)	1476	13 Brigham Young	786
2 Georgia Tech (16)	1397	14 Clemson	737
3 Texas (2)	1338	15 Mississippi	535
4 Miami	1303	16 Illinois	500
5 Notre Dame	1252	17 Iowa	461
6 Florida State	1196	18 Louisville	450
7 Penn State	1125	19 Nebraska	406
8 Washington	1117	20 Oklahoma	360
9 Houston	945	21 Southern California	352
10 Tennessee	944	22 Michigan State	260
11 Florida	905	23 Southern Mississippi	226
12 Michigan	833	24 Ohio State	197
		25 Alabama	115

December 8, 1990

Army 30 Navy 20 (Philadelphia): Retiring coach Jim Young completed outstanding 51-39-1 record in 8 years at West Point. Army (6-5) used HB Mike Mayweather as decoy, springing QB Willie McMillian for career-high 195y rushing. McMillian hit his only pass attempt for 35y TD to WR Myreon Williams; interestingly it was Army's 1st TD pass vs. Navy since 1971. After trailing 17-0, Navy (5-6) rallied to within 17-14 as frosh FB Brad Stramanak charged 45y to score. U.S. military in Saudi Arabian "Desert Shield" operation paused to enjoy hard-fought tilt between traditional rivals.

1990 Conference Standings

Atlantic Coast

Georgia Tech	6-0-1
Virginia	5-2
Clemson	5-2
Maryland	4-3
North Carolina	3-3-1
North Carolina State	3-4
Duke	1-6
Wake Forest	0-7

Southeastern

Tennessee	5-1-1
Mississippi	5-2
Alabama	5-2
Auburn	4-2-1
Kentucky	3-4
Louisiana State	2-5
Georgia	2-5
Mississippi State	1-6
Vanderbilt	1-6
Florida *	6-1
*ineligible	

Big Ten

Iowa	6-2
Michigan	6-2
Illinois	6-2
Michigan State	6-2
Ohio State	5-2-1
Minnesota	5-3
Indiana	3-4-1
Purdue	1-7
Northwestern	1-7
Wisconsin	0-8

Mid-American

Central Michigan	7-1
Toledo	7-1
Western Michigan	5-3
Ball State	5-3
Miami (Ohio)	4-3-1
Bowling Green	2-4-2
Eastern Michigan	2-6
Kent	2-6
Ohio University	0-7-1

Big Eight

Colorado	7-0
Nebraska	5-2
Oklahoma	5-2
Iowa State	2-4-1
Kansas	2-4-1
Kansas State	2-5
Missouri	2-5
Oklahoma State	2-5

Southwest

Texas	8-0
Texas A&M	5-2-1
Baylor	5-2-1
Texas Christian	3-5
Rice	3-5
Texas Tech	3-5
Arkansas	1-7
Southern Methodist	0-8
Houston *	7-1
* Ineligible	

Western Athletic

Brigham Young	7-1
Colorado State	6-1
San Diego State	5-2
Wyoming	5-3
Hawaii	4-4
Air Force	3-4
Utah	2-6
New Mexico	1-6
Texas-El Paso	1-7

Pacific-10

Washington	7-1
Southern California	5-2-1
Oregon	4-3
California	4-3-1
Arizona	5-4
Stanford	4-4
UCLA	4-4
Arizona State	2-5
Washington State	2-6
Oregon State	1-6

1990 Major Bowl Games

Independence Bowl (Dec. 15): Maryland 34 Louisiana Tech 34

After trailing 31-20 early in 4th Q, Maryland (6-5-1) took 34-31 lead with 52 secs left on 4th down 15y TD pass by QB Scott Zolak (18-28/214y). Low-profile Louisiana Tech (8-3-1) happily settled for tie as frosh K Chris Boniol kicked 29y FG as time expired. Tying FG was set up by Techster LB Lorenzo Baker, D player of game with 9 tackles, when he rambled 41y with KO to Terps 40YL. Terrapins RB Mark Mason rushed 15/93y, and RB Troy Jackson scored 3 TDs.

Aloha Bowl (Dec. 25): Syracuse 28 Arizona 0

When Santa Claus arrived, Syracuse (7-4-2) frosh QB Marvin Graves opened all the gifts: 2 TDs by air and 2 TDs by ground, while he accounted for 190y total O. MVP Graves passed 10-19/145y, including 47y TD to wide-open TB Terry Richardson in 2nd Q and 6y TD to TE Chris Gedney in 4th Q. Under stress from Orangemen D, Wildcats (7-5) managed only 226y total O, 77y in air. Shut out for 1st time in 19 years, Arizona was provided its brightest moments by DB Todd Burden, who made 2 INTs.

Liberty Bowl (Dec. 27): Air Force 23 Ohio State 11

Buckeyes QB Greg Frey and his mates got slightly riled up over TV commercial that promoted ticket sales by suggesting Falcons had good chance to bump off Ohio State (7-4-1), which felt it was only 1y away from converted 4th down against Michigan that would have sent them to Rose Bowl. Locals didn't take well to Ohio players voicing their displeasure with trip to Memphis, so frayed rose petals greeted Buckeyes at luncheon table during pre-game festivities. Air Force (7-5), 17-pt underdog, fell behind 5-0 on bad punt snap that forced P Jason Curtis into EZ where he was felled by Ohio LB Craig Criffey. Bucks K Tim Williams made 28y FG. Ahead 6-5 at H, Falcons used Wishbone mastery of MVP QB Rob Perez for team rushing total of 61/254y. Perez scored twice, and DB Carlton McDonald twice picked off Frey (10-27/110y, 3 INTs), returning late 4th Q INT for 40y TD that iced victory cake. Ohio TB Robert Smith was held to 62y on 13 tries.

All-American (Dec. 28): No. Carolina State 31 Southern Mississippi 27

Last-ever All-American Bowl, which was soon discontinued, turned on late D stand at its 20YL by North Carolina State (7-5). Southern Mississippi (8-4) QB Brett Favre riddled Wolfpack's outstanding secondary for 28-39/341y, 2 TDs, INT in air, but could do no better than 6-0 lead in 1st Q and 14-14 tie in 2nd Q. Wolfpack QB Terry Jordan (15-25/166y, TD, INT) accounted for 2 TDs, and RB Greg Manior scored late, clinching

41y TD run. Manior's TD gallop for 31-21 lead happened in last 6 mins and came only single snap after NC State LB David Merritt made midfield INT of Favre. Dynamic Favre then drove his Eagles 86y in final mins to get within 4 pts. Problematic for Eagles, who were debuting under new head coach and former asst Jeff Bower, was that twice they failed on 2-pt tries. With time elapsing and needing TD, Southern Miss made it to NC State 20YL but Wolfpack OLB Mark Thomas sacked Favre as it ended.

Blockbuster Bowl (Dec. 28): Florida State 24 Penn State 17

Amid slow and bumbling early pace, nation's longest win streak owned by Penn State (9-3) ended at 9 games as Florida State (10-2) TB Amp Lee (21/86y, 2 TDs) scored twice. Nittany Lions WR David Daniels smoked away from FSU defenders late in 1st Q for 56y TD catch from QB Tony Sacca (12-25/194y, TD, 2 INTs). Seminoles QB Casey Weldon (22-36/248y, 2 INTs) was masterful with precise passes and added his team's 3rd TD on ground in 3rd Q to make score 24-10. QB Tom Bill, ace Lions relief pitcher, tried to spark 4th Q rally by leading off with 37y TD pass to WR Terry Smith, but strong FSU D rejected comeback story that had 2 chapters left that might have made dramatic headlines. Bill, former Penn State starting QB, was playing his last collegiate game and earlier in his career had lost his job because of bouts with alcoholism. Seminoles stopped next drive after Bill opened it with 25y completion to Smith, and later DB John Davis picked off Bill at FSU 1YL with 2:54 to play. Coach Bobby Bowden (0-6 vs. Penn State at West Virginia in 1970-75) enjoyed his 1st personal win over coach Joe Paterno, whose bowl record slipped to 13-7-1. "…Florida State is the best team I've seen," said Paterno afterward. Oddly enough, each team amassed exactly 400y total O.

Peach Bowl (Dec. 29): Auburn 27 Indiana 23

QB Trent Green (10-19/99y), who had regained his Indiana (6-5-1) starting job, scored his 3rd rushing TD from 11YL with 2:26 to play for 23-20 Hoosier lead, Indiana's 1st advantage of Peach Bowl game. "...We thought we had it sealed up," said Green, after directing 29y scoring drive that capitalized on punt snap FUM by Auburn (8-3-1) P Richie Nell. But, frosh QB Stan White (31-48/351y, TD), who set Tigers bowl passing y record, guided 72y trip to game-winning TD. Hoosiers rose up at end of march, and after Auburn FB James Joseph was stonewalled on 3rd-and-goal at 1YL, O coordinator Pat Sullivan called naked bootleg run to left. With Indy fooled, White easily scored 4th down game-winner with 39 secs on clock. "A guard would never have called that play," grinned Tigers head coach Pat Dye, who was topnotch G in his playing days at Georgia.

Freedom Bowl (Dec. 29): Colorado State 32 Oregon 31

Things started to go badly for Ducks (8-4) in middle of 3rd Q as mistaken check-off call resulted in EZ FUM by FB Ngalu Kelemeni that cost safety and narrowed Oregon's lead to 17-16. Then two truly clumsy moments on D by Oregon, that surrounded TB Sean Burwell's FUM at Colorado State (9-4) 26YL, added up to 4th Q nightmare for Ducks. Trailing 25-19 early in last Q, Rams QB Mike Gimenez completed 49y TD to WR Greg Primus when Ducks DB Eric Castle fell down. Colorado State FB Todd Yert (12/94y, TD) scored winning 52y TD when 2 Ducks defenders collided. QB Bill Musgrave (29-47/392y, 3 TDs) brought Oregon back to within 32-31 on Burwell's 1y TD run with 1:01 remaining, but his unsuccessful conv pass to WR Michael McClellan was halted at GL. Rams, improving from 1-10 record only 2 years ago under veteran coach Earle Bruce, made their 1st bowl appearance since 1949 Raisin Bowl.

Holiday Bowl (Dec. 29): Texas A&M 65 Brigham Young 14

Heisman Trophy bowl jinx remained painfully in force as BYU (10-3) QB Ty Detmer was battered by fierce Aggies (9-3-1) D. Detmer (11-23/120y, TD, INT) suffered his 2nd shoulder separation of game—this time on his right, throwing arm—early in 3rd Q when hit by A&M LB Anthony Williams just after releasing pass. Detmer's 1st Q TD throw to A-A TE Chris Smith (5/96y, TD) had earned brief 7-7 tie. Texas A&M scored 20 pts in 2nd Q and led 27-7 at H. A&M pounded beleaguered Cougars D, accumulating 680y to 185y O advantage as QB Bucky Richardson (9-11/203y, TD, and 12/119y, 2 TDs rushing) accounted for 4 TDs. Richardson was everywhere: he ran for TD from TB slot, even caught 22y option pass TD from TB Darren Lewis (25/104y, 2 TDs).

Copper Bowl (Dec. 31): California 17 Wyoming 15

California (7-4-1) won its 1st post-season game in 53 years by building 17-3 lead. Bears QB Mike Pawlawski (15-26/172y, TD) threw 2nd Q TD pass to WR Brian Treggs. When FB Greg Zomalt ran 4y at end of 11-play TD drive it gave Cal 17-3 lead with 3:38 remaining. But, Wyoming (9-4) fought back with 83y TD drive and WR Robert Rivers' 70y TD punt RET with 49 secs left. Cowboys QB Tom Corontzos (20-39/226y) failed to convert 2-pt passes after each late score. Sack by Golden Bears DL Joel Dickson snuffed Corontzos' 2nd try for twin conv. California's dual 1,000y TBs, Anthony Wallace and Russell White, managed only combined 31/94y.

Gator Bowl: Michigan 35 Mississippi 3

"We practiced so hard we were getting on each other's nerves," admitted Michigan (9-3) FB Jerrod Bunch. "We just exploded," he explained, once game started. Wolverines QB Elvis Grbac led pyrotechnics with career-high 4 TDs, including 63 and 50y scores to outstanding WR Desmond Howard. Wolverines amassed Gator Bowl-record 715y, but Ole Miss (9-3) coach Billy Brewer was philosophical: "We can't let one bad day spoil the entire year." Rebels finally scored midway in 4th Q on to-date Gator Bowl-record 51y FG by K Brian Lee, his 1st FG success since September.

Hall of Fame Bowl: Clemson 30 Illinois 0

Nation's top-ranked D and effective run-pass ball control delivered 4th straight 10-2 record to Clemson as Tigers blanked Illinois (8-4), Big 10 co-champs. First blow to Illini came on early FUM at own 14 YL by FB Howard Griffith (15/59y rushing), who earlier greeted legendary Red Grange, HB whose 66-year-old Illini TD records Griffith broke during regular season. Clemson quickly converted TD on pass by QB DeChance Cameron (14-20/141y, 2 TDs) to WR Doug Thomas. Tigers D added other score before H when DB Arlington Nunn returned INT of QB Jason Verduzco (13-25/121, 2 INTs) for 34y TD. Highly-efficient Nunn's INT was his 3rd of career and each had ended in TD RET.

Florida Citrus Bowl: Georgia Tech 45 Nebraska 21

Georgia Tech (11-0-1) staked its claim to national title by completing season's only undefeated run through major schedule. It was 1st such unblemished record for Tech since 1952. Playing early on New Year's Day, Yellow Jackets had to wait for late-night Orange Bowl result. When Colorado won in Miami, it meant shared national titles in 2 major polls, writers picking Colorado and coaches going with Georgia Tech by single pt over Colorado. Yellow Jackets went 70y on opening drive to FB Stefen Scotton's 2y TD run and eventually rolled to 21-0 lead in 2nd Q. QB Shawn Jones passed 16-23/277y, 2 TDs, and RB William Bell rushed 16/127y, 3 TDs, including 4th Q 57y charge after bouncing off scrimmage stack. Nebraska (9-3) played without injured QB Mickey Joseph and soon benched sub QB Mike Grant, who was hitless in 5 early passing attempts, in favor of little-used QB Tom Haase. Hasse's 1st handoff resulted in FUM recovered by DE Coleman Rudolph and it led to Georgia Tech's 2nd TD. Until Hasse's insertion, Huskers had gained only 34y in 1st 22 mins. Hasse threw 14-21/209y, including TDs of 30 and 21y that briefly encouraged Huskers and moved them to within 24-14 by H and 31-21 in 3rd Q. IB Derek Brown (11/99y, TD) had crammed 50y TD canter between Hasse's TD passes to TE Johnny Mitchell and WR William Washington respectively. Georgia Tech iced it with Bell's 2 TDs in 4th Q.

Cotton Bowl: Miami 46 Texas 3

In ferocious, PEN-filled attempt to sway pollsters in its favor, brash no. 4 Miami (10-2) ended national title dream of no. 3 Texas (10-2) with biggest rout in Cotton Bowl history. Miami spent most of day dancing and jiving to accentuate its superiority. Most observers could have lived without it. Hurricanes DT Russell Maryland's 3 sacks led 8 maulings of Longhorns QB Peter Gardere (7-16/40y, 3 INTs). Meanwhile, Miami QB Craig Erickson passed 17-26/272y, 4 TDs. Maryland summed up mood of game, which started when both teams taunted each other in tunnel: "Everybody hates the 'Canes. We're the team you love to hate." Miami overcame staggering 16 PENs/202y by forcing 5 TOs. Canes got 8/135y receiving from WR Wesley Carroll. Texas' only score came in 2nd Q when K Michael Pollak toed 29y FG at end of PEN-aided 46y drive.

Fiesta Bowl: Louisville 34 Alabama 7

Each team wore commemoration of Dr. Martin Luther King on their uniforms while NAACP waged small protest outside stadium over Arizona voters' rejection of paid state King holiday. Lost in furor was fact that city of Tempe and Fiesta Bowl already gave its employees paid King holiday and that Fiesta was 1st bowl to appoint African-American to its board and to have black president: Dr. Morrison Warren in 1982. Roaring out of locker room, underappreciated Louisville (10-1-1) scored 25 pts in 1st Q to complete its best record in school history. QB Browning Nagle (20-33, 3 TDs) threw for to-date Fiesta Bowl-record 451y. Alabama (7-5), which had allowed only 38 pts in previous 7 games, was burned for 2 Nagle TD throws of 70 and 37y, RB Ralph Dawkins' 5y TD run, and DB Ray Buchanan's blocked punt TD REC in 1st Q. DB Charles Gardner had 2nd Q 49y INT TD RET bringing Crimson Tide back to within 25-7. Held to 189y, bumbling Alabama O suffered 3 TOs and late-game safety.

Rose Bowl: Washington 46 Iowa 34

Highest scoring Rose Bowl match played to date saw Washington (10-2) shoot to 33-7 H lead. Huskies used 67y drive to K Travis Hanson's 27y opening FG. Then, disastrous Iowa (8-4) fake punt had to be aborted, and, in confusion, was blocked by Washington frosh LB Andy Mason: DB Dana Hall carried it 27y to TD. Alert Huskies DB Charles Mincy detected Iowa O audible, and, being certain that Hawks WR Dana Hughes had missed call, Mincy charged to reception spot and began 37y INT TD RET. Soph QB Mark Brunell (14-22/163y, 2 TDs) scored twice and hit WR Mario Bailey with TD for 39-14 lead going into 4th Q. Then, Hawkeyes coach Hayden Fry opened his marvelous bag of tricks with 2 on-side KO RECs to help tally 3 TDs against Washington's D subs, and make final score more respectible. Another on-side KO was collared by Huskies' fair catch, and it led to clinching TD that iced game amid Iowa comeback. Interestingly, Hawkeyes outgained Huskies 454y to 385y overall, but didn't make enough y when game was decided in 1st H.

Sugar Bowl: Tennessee 23 Virginia 22

Virginia (8-4) QB Shawn Moore returned from dislocated thumb but was ineffective in air (9-22/62y, 2 INTs, including 0-9 in 2nd H). Cavs still used 287y run attack to build 16-0 H lead and 16-3 edge at end of 3rd Q. When redemption for Virginia's poor late season seemed at hand, Tennessee (9-2-2) "...made a terrific comeback," according to coach Johnny Majors. QB Andy Kelly (24-35/273y, TD) created 3 TD drives in 4th Q, throwing 15y score to WR Carl Pickens between 2 TD runs by TB Tony Thompson. Thompson's last score came with 31 ticks of clock left and it come at end of 79y drive which consumed 1:53, on which Vols converted 4th down and 2 3rd downs. Still with 1:24 to go, Cavs DB Keith McMeans, early-game star, agonizingly allowed INT to slip through his hands which likely would have salvaged victory for Virginia.

Orange Bowl: Colorado 10 Notre Dame 9

Every top-ranked, bowl-winning team since AP began its procedure of post-bowl balloting in 1969 had been able to retain its no. 1 ranking. So, when Colorado (11-1-1) won its 1st bowl game in last 8 tries, it wrapped up school's 1st-ever national title. But, victory almost escaped its grasp in dying moments. Notre Dame (9-3) sputtered on O, suffering 5 TOs, but got 2nd Q 2y TD run from TB Ricky Watters and short 3rd Q FG from K Craig Hentrich. Buffs superb QB Darian Hagan ruptured his knee tendon just before H, and sub QB Charles "Fifth Down" Johnson took over to throw 5-6/80y,

including 3 completions on 80y TD drive in 3rd Q that overcame Irish's 9-3 lead. Johnson earned MVP accolades. Critical to outcome was blocked conv by Buffs DB Ronnie Bradford, but big play, or non-play, came in game's last min. Midfield punt by Colorado P Tom Rouen, which could have been angled safely OB, instead was booted directly at WR Raghib Ismail. "The Rocket" burst through several tacklers, and Colorado DB Tim James loomed from the right, but was cut down by block of Irish DB Greg Davis. Illegal blocking-from-behind was called against Davis, nullifying Ismail's stunning 91y TD RET. Davis was left to sadly ponder what James and others already wondered: "Would I have tackled him? That's a tough call. This *is* The Rocket we're talking about."

Final AP Poll January 2

1a	Colorado (39)	1475	13 Florida	863
2a	Georgia Tech (20)	1441	14 Louisville	775
3	Miami (1)	1388	15 Texas A&M	627
4	Florida State	1303	16 Michigan State	610
5	Washington	1246	17 Oklahoma	452
6	Notre Dame	1179	18 Iowa	370.5
7	Michigan	1025	19 Auburn	288
8	Tennessee	993	20 Southern California	266
9	Clemson	950	21 Mississippi	253
10	Houston	940	22 Brigham Young	246
11	Penn State	907	23 Virginia	188
12	Texas	887	24 Nebraska	185
			25 Illinois	146.5

a Coaches voted Georgia Tech no. 1 and Colorado no. 2 in UPI Poll.

1990 Top Performance Formula

1	Miami	1.6801
2	Georgia Tech	1.6706
3	Colorado	1.6452
4	Washington	1.6369
5	Florida State	1.5780
6	Texas	1.5763
7	Tennessee	1.5435
8	Clemson	1.5410
9	Florida	1.5213
10	Houston	1.5187
11	Notre Dame	1.4899
12	Michigan	1.4873
13	Nebraska	1.4836
14	Brigham Young	1.4712
15	Oklahoma	1.4518
16	Penn State	1.4491
17	Texas A&M	1.3935
18	Virginia	1.3917
19	Auburn	1.3419
20	Oregon	1.3082

1990 Top Opponent Records

1	Notre Dame	.6565
2	Colorado	.6460
3	Texas	.6389
4	Maryland	.6378
5	Miami	.6318
6	Virginia Tech	.6261
7	Kansas	.6207
8	Stanford	.6167
9	Georgia	.6121
10	Tennessee	.6058
11	Penn State	.6008
12	Washington	.5977
13	Virginia	.5859
14t	Auburn	.5852713
14t	California	.5852713
16	Georgia Tech	.5848
17	Michigan	.5781
18	Clemson	.5764
19	Florida State	.5764
20	Southern California	.5755

1990 Out-of-Conference Records

	W-L	Percentage	Bowl W-L
Atlantic Coast	18-7-1	.7115	3-1-1
Southeastern	25-17-1	.5930	2-2
Big Eight	18-13-1	.5781	1-1
Southwest	15-12	.5556	1-1
Pacific-10	19-18	.5135	2-3
Western Athletic	17-17	.5000	2-2
Big Ten	16-18	.4706	2-4

1990 Individual Statistical Leaders

RUSHING YARDS

	Attempts	Yards	Avg.
Darren Lewis, Texas A&M	291	1691	5.8
Gerald Hudson, Oklahoma State	279	1642	5.9
Eric Bienemy, Colorado	288	1628	5.7
Tico Duckett, Michigan State	249	1376	5.5
Roger Grant, Utah State	266	1370	5.2
Mike Mayweather, Army	274	1338	4.9
Trevor Cobb, Rice	283	1325	4.7
Greg Lewis, Washington	229	1279	5.6
Jon Vaughn, Michigan	201	1236	6.1
Vaughn Dunbar, Indiana	229	1143	5.0

PASSING YARDS

	Completions	Attempts	Yards	Pct.
Ty Detmer, Brigham Young	361	562	5188	64.2
David Klingler, Houston	374	643	5140	58.2
Dan McGwire, San Diego State	270	449	3833	60.1
Craig Erickson, Miami	225	393	3363	57.3
Troy Kopp, Pacific	243	428	3311	56.8
Shane Matthews, Florida	229	378	2952	60.6
Ralph Martini, San Jose State	204	362	2928	56.4
Garrett Gabriel, Hawaii	165	320	2752	51.6
Tommy Maddox, UCLA	182	327	2682	55.7
Jason Palumbis, Stanford	234	341	2579	68.6

RECEIVING YARDS

	Catches	Yards
Patrick Rowe, San Diego State	71	1392
Aaron Turner, Pacific	66	1264
Andy Boyce, Brigham Young	79	1241
Herman Moore, Virginia	54	1190
Chris Smith, Brigham Young	68	1156
Dennis Arey, San Diego State	68	1118
Keenan McCardell, UNLV	68	1046
Eric Morgan, New Mexico	80	1043
Lawrence Dorsey, Florida State	65	999
Gary Wellman, Southern California	63	996.

1990 Consensus All-America Team
Offense

Wide Receiver:	Raghib Ismail, Notre Dame
	Herman Moore, Virginia
Tight End:	Chris Smith, Brigham Young
Tackle:	Antone Davis, Tennessee
	Stacy Long, Clemson
Guard:	Joe Garten, Colorado
	Ed King, Auburn
Center:	John Flannery, Syracuse
Quarterback:	Ty Detmer, Brigham Young
Running Back:	Eric Bieniemy, Colorado
	Darren Lewis, Texas A&M
Placekicker:	Philip Doyle, Alabama

Defense

Linemen:	Russell Maryland, Miami
	Chris Zorich, Notre Dame
	Moe Gardner, Illinois
	David Rocker, Auburn
Linebacker:	Alfred Williams, Colorado
	Michael Stonebreaker, Notre Dame
	Maurice Crum, Miami
Backs:	Tripp Welborne, Michigan
	Darryl Lewis, Arizona
	Ken Swilling, Georgia Tech
	Todd Lyght, Notre Dame
Punter:	Brian Greenfield, Pittsburgh

1990 Heisman Trophy Vote

Ty Detmer, junior quarterback, Brigham Young	1,482
Raghib Ismail, junior wide receiver, Notre Dame	1,177
Eric Bieniemy, senior tailback, Colorado	798
Shawn Moore, senior quarterback, Virginia	465
David Klingler, junior quarterback, Houston	125

Other Major Awards

Maxwell (Player)	Ty Detmer, junior quarterback, Brigham Young
Walter Camp (Player)	Raghib Ismail, junior wide receiver, Notre Dame
Outland (Lineman)	Russell Maryland, senior defensive tackle, Miami
Lombardi (Lineman)	Chris Zorich, senior nose guard, Notre Dame
Doak Walker (Running Back)	Greg Lewis, senior tailback, Washington
Davey O'Brien (Quarterback)	Ty Detmer, junior quarterback, Brigham Young
Jim Thorpe (Defensive Back)	Darryl Lewis, senior cornerback, Arizona
Dick Butkus (Linebacker)	Alfred Williams, senior linebacker, Colorado
Johnny Unitas (Quarterback)	Craig Erickson, senior quarterback, Miami
AFCA Coach of the Year	Bobby Ross, Georgia Tech

1991

The Year of Wide Right Again, Shared Title in Distant Corners, and the Struck Pose

Short field goals had become "about as exciting as watching a man ice fishing," said Dave Nelson of the University of Delaware, longtime rules committee secretary, so the committee chose to narrow the goalpost gap from 23'4" to 18'6", the width of the posts prior to 1959. The wide position of the inbounds hashmarks (53'4" from each sideline) remained the same, however, and that circumstance created some uncomfortably narrow angles, especially on short kicks.

Regrettably, Nelson would die before the season was completed, and with his passing football lost a great supporter whose influence on the formation of rules was dramatic. One of the great features of college football has been its willingness to consider improvement and change every year. Not every new rule had been a good one, but, generally, the rules committee under Nelson's guidance maintained a highly open-minded approach to modifying existing statutes and implementing new ideas.

In mid-November, Florida State (11-2) coach Bobby Bowden might have preferred ice fishing with Dave Nelson to coaching football. The Seminoles had entered the 1991 season as a solid no.1 pick and spent 12 undefeated weeks atop the polls. The Seminoles found themselves trailing unbeaten Miami 17-16 with 25 seconds remaining. FSU's Gerry Thomas barely missed a 34-yard field goal, which flew wide to the right. The kick would have been successful with the previous year's wider posts. After Bowden watched yet another potential Florida State national championship evaporate, he lamented, "They're going to chisel on my tombstone: '...and he had to play Miami.' "

Two distant campuses on the football map, 3,303 miles apart, shared the national championship. Miami (12-0) took the AP writers poll while the coaches poll, under the new sponsorship banner of CNN/*USA Today*, went to the only other undefeated team, Washington (12-0), from the faraway corner of the nation.

As far apart as the two champions were located, they were oddly linked. Miami coach Dennis Erickson had grown up in Everett, Wash., had been head coach at Washington State during 1987-88, and would later coach the NFL's Seattle Seahawks. Husky coach Don James had played quarterback at Miami in the early 1950s. When the votes rolled in, each school was satisfied. The mutual sentiment was expressed by Erickson: "It would have been an injustice if one team was shut out."

The Cinderella story of the season belonged to East Carolina (11-1). Without a winning record since 1983, the Pirates lost their opener to Illinois by a touchdown, then surprised South Carolina (3-6-2), Syracuse (10-2) and Pittsburgh (6-5) on the way to 10 wins in a row, followed by a heart-stopping Peach Bowl win over North Carolina State (9-3).

Another surprise was California (10-2), which won the Citrus Bowl in its first post-season appearance since the 1951 Rose Bowl. Unfortunately for Golden Bears fans, coach Bruce Snyder, architect of the gradual rebirth, bolted Berkeley after the season for a lucrative offer at Arizona State (6-5).

Alabama (11-1), left for dead when it was shellacked 35-0 by Florida (10-2) early in the year, ran the table, 10 in a row, including a Blockbuster Bowl triumph over Colorado (8-3-1). Another rally came from BYU (8-3-2), which matured around All-America quarterback Ty Detmer (35 touchdown passes) after losing its first three games by a combined 104 to 58 score.

Wide receiver Desmond Howard of Michigan (10-2) all but clinched his Heisman Trophy on national TV on September 14. He thrilled the viewing audience and more than 100,000 at Michigan Stadium with a miraculous diving end zone catch on fourth down to seal a 24-14 victory over Notre Dame (10-3). After the last of Howard's 23 touchdowns of the year, which came against rival Ohio State (8-4), he fit right into 1990s lifestyle for young "Generation Xers." He "struck a pose" to promote his candidacy, that of the straight-arm runner of the Heisman Trophy.

Freshman back Marshall Faulk burst onto the scene for San Diego State (8-4-1). He set a single game rushing mark of 386 yards against Pacific on September 14 and finished the year as the nation's leading rusher (158.8 yards per game) and scorer (140 points), the first frosh to accomplish either feat. Faulk's game record lasted only two months. Tailback Tony Sands of Kansas made 396 yards against Missouri in his career finale. Called "Tuxedo Tony" because he wore formal wear to the locker room on game days, Sands had gotten few recruiting nibbles from big-time programs because of his 5'6" height. That small stature helped him on his big day. Missouri defensive tackle Mario Johnson said, "He's so small you don't see him. He's running by you before you even see him."

Star sophomore running back Robert Smith quit the Ohio State team in August, accusing assistant coach Elliot Uzelac of hindering his academic pursuits by demanding that Smith skip pre-med classes to attend football practice. Much publicity ensued, and Smith stood his ground. He was hardly missed by the Buckeye offense, however, as Butler "Mr. Apostrophe" By'not'e, Carlos Snow, and Raymont Harris sparkled in the tailback spot. In fact, in Ohio State's opener against Arizona (4-7), it rushed for a total of 325 yards, more than any game during 1990 when Smith broke Archie Griffin's Buckeye freshman rushing mark. After Uzelac was forced out in the following off-season, Smith returned to play his junior year in 1992. But, he opted to enter the NFL draft in the spring of 1993 rather than play or attend undergraduate pre-med classes during his senior year.

EDITOR'S NOTE: From this point forward in history this book will use the *USA Today* Coaches Poll as its featured method in college football polling.

Milestones

● NCAA Rules Committee voted to shrink width of goalposts from 23'4" to 18'6", same width as in National Football League.

● CNN/*USA Today* took over coaches poll, formerly administered by UPI.

● For first time since NCAA took control of college football telecasts from individual schools in 1950s, one school signed its own arrangement with individual network. NBC contracted to telecast all Notre Dame home games.

● Texas A&M kicker James Glenn collapsed and died before practice session in September. Sonny Werblin, 81, who signed Alabama quarterback Joe Namath to rich New York Jets contract after 1964 season and was instrumental in moving his alma mater Rutgers to higher level of football, died of heart attack on September 21. Mississippi State defensive lineman Rodney Stowers broke his leg in September 28 game against Florida and died five days later of complications from lung hemorrhaging. Secretary editor of NCAA Rules Committee, Dave Nelson, 71, died at home after watching Delaware, school he coached from 1951-65, lose double overtime 1-AA playoff game on TV.

● Awaited major Eastern conference took shape as Big East launched its first year with Pittsburgh opening at West Virginia and Boston College at Rutgers on August 31. Scheduling disparities in 1991 (West Virginia played seven Big East opponents, Miami only two) prompted league to settle its first title via *USA Today* coaches poll.

● Coaching Changes:

	Incoming	Outgoing
Army	Bob Sutton	Jim Young
Boston College	Tom Coughlin	Jack Bicknell
Bowling Green	Gary Blackney	Moe Ankney
Illinois	Lou Tepper (a)	John Mackovic
Kent	Pete Cordelli	Dick Crum
Louisiana State	Curley Hallman	Mike Archer
Mississippi State	Jackie Sherrill	Rockey Felker
Oregon State	Jerry Pettibone	Dave Kragthorpe
Purdue	Jim Colletto	Fred Akers
Southern Methodist	Tom Rossley	Forrest Gregg
Southern Mississippi	Jeff Bower	Curley Hallman
Syracuse	Paul Pasqualoni	Dick MacPherson
Toledo	Gary Pinkel	Nick Saban
Vanderbilt	Gerry DiNardo	Watson Brown
Wyoming	Joe Tiller	Paul Roach

(a) Tepper (0-1) replaced Mackovic prior to John Hancock Bowl.

● Longest winning streaks entering season:

Colorado 10	Louisville 7	six with 6

Preseason *USA Today* Coaches Poll

1	Florida State (42)	1428	14	Houston	693
2	Miami (Fla.) (3)	1298	15	Nebraska	646
3	Michigan (6)	1282	16	Auburn	572
4	Washington (3)	1235	17	Southern California	561
5	Notre Dame (1)	1085	18	Iowa	486
6	Georgia Tech (1)	1047	19	Brigham Young	383
7	Florida	1016	20	Texas A&M	380
8	Penn State	995	21	Ohio State	305
9	Clemson	934	22	Michigan State	297
10	Colorado (1)	855	23	Alabama	236
11	Oklahoma (2)	845	24	UCLA	169
12	Texas	758	25	Baylor	141
13	Tennessee	725			

August 31, 1991

(Wed) Penn State 34 Georgia Tech 22 (E. Rutherford, N.J.): Nation's longest unbeaten streak ended at 16 as Penn State (1-0) built 34-3 4th Q lead. QB Tony Sacca (13-24/206y) set school and Kickoff Classic records with 5 TD passes, 2 each to WRs Terry Smith and O.J. McDuffie. McDuffie's 2nd scoring catch, spectacular 39y juggling job, provided 31-pt lead. Yellow Jackets (0-1) got 3 TDs (2 from their back-up O squad) in last 4:40 of game, but earlier, behind young O-line, QB Shawn Jones suffered 4 FUMs and INT while running for his life from Nittany Lions defenders.

(Th) Florida State 44 Brigham Young 28 (Anaheim): Useful Seminoles (1-0) FB Edgar Bennett scored 3 short TDs: 3 and 2y runs and 4y pass from QB Casey Weldon. Bennett's 3rd tally iced it at 35-14 in 3rd Q. Weldon passed 21-28/268y, 2 TDs to outshine Heisman defender, QB Ty Detmer of Brigham Young (0-1), who managed ho-hum 229y, after passing for 300y in 24 straight games.

RUTGERS 20 BOSTON COLLEGE 13: Inaugural Big East game went to Rutgers (1-0) near spot where Scarlet Knights won 6-4 over Princeton in 1st American "football" game 122 years earlier. Rutgers, winners of only 3 games in 1990, played well on D behind S Malik Jackson and LB Shawn Williams. Opening under intense new coach coach Tom Coughlin, Boston College (0-1) lost ace KR-DB Jay Clark's FUM on opening KO, and quickly fell behind 7-0 as Knights TB Bill Bailey (74y rushing) scored from 1YL. BC tied it late in 1st Q as TE Mark Chmura worked his way open in Scarlet EZ for 15y TD reception from QB Glenn Foley. After all but squandering its domination of 2nd Q on way to 14-7 H edge, Rutgers gained 20-10 lead late in 3rd Q as QB Tom Tarver (21-30/275y, TD) earned game's only long score with 42y pitch to WR Chris Brantley.

Pittsburgh 34 WEST VIRGINIA 3: After 2 years of all-out aerial bombardment, Pitt (1-0) O settled into running game in its opener. Panthers D was again sharp after awful 1990 (397.6y avg), holding West Virginia (0-1) to 267y and allowing only K Mark Johnson's 21y FG. Behind 3-0, Panthers DB Steve Israel (INT) dashed 73y with ensuing KO to set up FB Glenn Deveaux's 1y TD. Mountaineers soph QB Darren Studstill left early in 2nd H with banged up shoulder and took WVU's O with him. Pitt QB Alex Van Pelt (12-20/152y, 3 TDs) pitched TDs to TE Eric Seaman and WR Chad Askew to elevate lead to 24-3 with 2:24 left in 3rd Q.

ILLINOIS 38 East Carolina 31: Leading 38-10 in 3rd Q on QB Jason Verduzco's 3 TD passes and FB Kameno Bell's 2 TD runs, Illinois (1-0) hung on in disputed finish. East Carolina (0-1) QB Jeff Blake (21-42/353y) fired up Pirates with 3 TD passes, last of which went 80y to WR Dion Johnson. Pirate WR Clayton Driver immediately fell on successful on-side KO, but was flagged for (debatably) excessive celebration. ECU never recovered from having to face 1st-and-25 at own 25YL with 1:46 to play.

Miami 31 ARKANSAS 3: Gino Torretta won Hurricanes (1-0) QB job from Bryan Fortay in spring, prompting Fortay to transfer to Rutgers and later sue Miami. Torretta opened season by arching 99y TD pass to WR Horace Copeland. Hanging tough at 14-3 at H, overmatched Arkansas (0-1) saw Torretta break it open with 3rd Q TD pass to RB Martin Patton. Hogs passed only 8-31/102y, suffering 3 INTs.

(Mon) Memphis State 24 SOUTHERN CALIFORNIA 10: USC (0-1) TB Mazio Royster rushed for 97y in 1st H and led 10-3 by Troy. But, Royster was shelved by sprained knee. Ultimately, Memphis State (1-0) coach Chuck Stobart thought "they might overlook us." Trojans did just that in 2nd H as Tigers QB Keith Benton threw 2 TD passes for 17-10 4th Q lead. Ensuing KO blooped in front of USC returners, and Memphis LB Rod Brown fell on it. RB Xavier Crawford scored clinching TD 3 plays later, and Trojan horse was left to head back to barn with its tail between its legs.

September 7, 1991

Michigan 35 BOSTON COLLEGE 13: Boston College (0-2) jumped to 10-0 1st Q lead on 24y TD pass by QB Glenn Foley (22-47/280y, TD, 3 INTs) and K Sean Wright's 34y FG. WR Desmond Howard caught 19y TD pass only 5 secs into 2nd Q to pull Wolverines (1-0) within 10-7. Howard's 93y TD RET of 2nd H KO finally ignited no. 2 Michigan (1-0). Howard caught his 2nd and 3rd TD passes from QB Elvis Grbac (14-25/178y, 3 TDs, INT) in last 8 mins to break open 14-13 game. Wolverines DB Lance Dottin polished things off with 50y INT TD RET with 55 secs left. BC showed some different D wrinkles and were evaluated by coach Tom Coughlin afterward: "We were about three quarters of the way there. We've still got another quarter to go."

MARYLAND 17 Virginia 6: FUMs, 4 of them, ruined Cavaliers (0-1) and Virginia FB Dave Sweeney dropped 1st FUM when he was hit by Terrapins DB Bill Inge at Maryland (1-0) 30YL in 1st Q. Terps then cranked up their run game, driving 70y to 4y TD run by TB Troy Jackson (22/96y). Although QB Matt Blundin (17-36/226y) whipped 40y pass to WR Terrence Tomlin after LB Curtis Hicks' INT, Virginia had to settle for K Michael Husted's 20y FG just before H. Virginia had ignored their outstanding TB Terry Kirby (13/73y) in 1st H as he touched ball only 3 times, but Cavs drove 55y to 1st-and-goal at Terps 8YL in 3rd Q. Kirby's 2 runs gained only 3y and group of defenders broke up 3rd down slant pass meant for Kirby. K Husted added another FG, this of 22y, in 4th Q to trim deficit to 10-6. Maryland locked verdict in last 1:50 as TB Mark Mason (21/96y) scored on 5y run.

NORTH CAROLINA STATE 7 Virginia Tech 0: NC State (1-0) secondary picked off 5 Virginia Tech (1-1) passes, and QB Terry Jordan (9-23/113y, 2 INTs) flipped scrambling 10y TD pass to WR Shad Santee just before H. It finished 80y drive on which Jordan completed 3-4 passes and was imperiled by loss of 8y from 2YL on rollout by Jordan. Hokies threw double scare into Wolfpack in late going. Tech QB Will Furrer (20-

37/198y, 5 INTs) threw INT to Wolfpack S Mike Reid in red zone that was returned 31y with 2:04 left. NC State fumbled ball right back, but, after Furrer made 2 completions to 25YL, Wolfpack LB Billy Ray Haynes made his team's 5th INT with 1:10 to go.

GEORGIA 31 Louisiana State 10: Alternating 5th-year sr Greg Talley and frosh Eric Zeier at QB, Georgia (1-0) broke Zeke Bratkowski's 40-year school pass attempt record with 42. Talley passed 10-22/137y and created 14 pts, while Zeier passed 11-20/168y to lead Bulldogs to 17 pts. Georgia TB Garrison Hearst rushed 12/56y in relief of TB Larry Ware (19/113y) and tallied TD runs in 1st and 4th Qs. LSU (0-1) went 20 mins without making 1st down and didn't cross GL until trailing 31-3 in 4th Q when QB Chad Loup (8-16/84y, TD, INT) found WR Todd Kinchen (5/83y) with 10y TD pass. Discouraged new Bengals coach Curley Hallman lamented, "We could've been beat by 60 or 70 to nothing."

MISSISSIPPI STATE 13 Texas 6: Bulldogs (2-0) D, which had allowed only 9 pts in 2 wins, forged upset of Texas (0-1) by holding Longhorns RB Butch Hadnot to 14/67y and QB Peter Gardere to 13-26/87y, 2 INTs. Mississippi State DL Rodney Stowers, who would sadly die before season end, highlighted 4th Q D stand with sack of Gardere. Trailing 3-0 on Texas K Jason Ziegler's 44y 1st Q FG, Maroons struck for 35y TD pass by QB Sleepy Robinson (8-19/119y, TD, INT) to TE Treddis Anderson.

NOTRE DAME 49 Indiana 27: Notre Dame (1-0) notched its 14th straight win over Big 10 foes. QB Rick Mirer (11-17/209y, TD, INT) ran for 3 TDs and connected with TE Irv Smith for notable TD: Smith carried Hoosiers DB Harry Winslow for 25y and dragged 3 tacklers into EZ for score that lifted ND's margin to 42-20 lead with 3 mins left in 3rd Q. Indiana (0-1) led 3 times in 1st H and got 2 TD runs from QB Trent Green, who passed 18-31/221y, but suffered 4 INTs. Behind 17-14 with 5 mins left in 1st H, Mirer went 46y for TD on option run, and when Irish quickly recovered on-side KO, Mirer hit 28y pass to set up TB Tony Brooks for 13y outside run for TD and 28-17 edge. Hoosiers TB Vaughn Dunbar rushed 33/161y and TE Rod Coleman caught 7/75y.

IOWA 53 Hawaii 10: Hawaii (1-1) had amassed 523y in opening win over Wyoming and managed 192y passing in this trip to Iowa City. But, Hawkeyes burst to 27-0 lead in 1st Q and finished off Rainbows with 277y to 150y rushing advantage, using only their most basic plays. In front of record opening game crowd, Iowa aggressively blocked punts for TD in 1st Q and safety on LB Matt Hilliard's block in 3rd Q. Hawkeyes QB Matt Rodgers (12-18/168y, 2 TDs) threw 1st Q TDs to WRs Danan Hughes and Jon Filloon. RB Lew Montgomery plunged for 3 TDs, all from Hawaii's 1YL, and his scores added up to 41-3 H edge. Hawaii K Jason Elam broke up Iowa's scoring party with 35y FG in 2nd Q, and SB Ivin Jasper flung surprise 35y TD pass in late going.

COLORADO 30 Wyoming 13: Cowboys (0-2) briefly stunned Buffs as WR Ryan Yarborough caught TD pass for 3rd Q 10-10 tie. Entering 4th Q, defending national champion Colorado (1-0) clung to mere 16-13 lead. QB Darian Hagan, fielding punts for 1st time in his career, ignited flagging Buffaloes O with 37 and 30y RETs that led to scores. Hagan passed 12-23/151y, TD.

Washington 42 STANFORD 7: Star Cardinal T Bob Whitfield had made stunning and wacky pre-game prediction of "biggest upset in history when we beat 'em by 60 points." Stanford (0-1) coach Dennis Green was more realistic as he told Cards they couldn't play like it was season's 1st game. Mighty Washington (1-0) was forced to punt after Stanford FB Tommy Vardell smashed for 1y TD with 2:02 left in 1st H. Trailing 14-7 at that key moment, Cardinal QB Jason Palumbis (14-33/141y, 2 INTs) suffered INT by Huskies DB Walter Bailey at midfield. Trying to throw away pass with only 9 secs left in 1st H, Washington QB Billy Joe Hobert (21-31/244y, 2 TDs, INT) was surprised to see his wind-blown rainbow be whiffed by well-positioned DB Vaughn Bryant in back of EZ and fall into hands of stunned Huskies WR Mario Bailey for TD that made it 21-7. Stanford D gained 2 TOs in 3rd Q to give opportunity to its bumbling O, which immediately suffered INT and 2 lost FUMs. Washington TB Jay Barry (8/81y, 2 TDs) enhanced Hobert's early 4th Q TD pass with 23y TD run barely 2 mins later to build 35-7 lead. TB Glyn Milburn (11/16y) was held in check by Washington D.

OREGON 40 Washington State 14: Touted soph QB Drew Bledsoe (13-35/213y, TD, 3 INTs) made mistake of leading Washington State (0-1) to 7-0 lead in 1st Q, registering 22y pass to WR C.J. Davis (8/118y). Bledsoe paid dearly rest of game against experienced Ducks (1-0) D as he was sacked 6 times and suffered 3 INTs. Oregon S Eric Castle turned in 2 INTs in 3rd Q, during which Ducks extended their 12-7 lead to 33-7 edge. Castle scored on 39y INT RET and set up another score with 30y RET to Cougars 3YL. Ducks frosh QB Danny O'Neil (10-23/129y, 2 TDs, INT) was excellent in his collegiate debut, and TB Sean Burwell rushed for career-best 30/189y, TD.

September 14, 1991

(Th) MIAMI 40 Houston 10: Space-age passing attack of no. 10 Houston (1-1), which had developed national curiosity with terrifyingly great stats, was crushed by superior Miami (2-0) D. Although he threw late-game TD pass, Cougars QB David Klingler (32-59/216y) was sacked 5 times by lightning-quick Hurricanes D-front. Coming off 9-TD

outing against Louisiana Tech, Klingler was upstaged by new Miami QB Gino Torretta, who passed 16-35/365y, 4 TDs. Miami built 30-3 H bonanza as it held Houston to 3 1st downs and 76y total O. Hurricanes sewed up 39th home win in row, to tie Notre Dame for 2nd longest such streak in NCAA history.

FLORIDA 35 Alabama 0: Florida (2-0) won 1st-ever home game against Alabama (1-1) after 6 losses. QB Shane Matthews passed 15-27/251y, 3 TDs, 2 INTs, including 3rd Q TD tosses to WRs Tre Everett (5/97y, TD) and Willie Jackson (2/25y, 2 TDs) that broke open tight 6-0 H struggle. Columnist Larry Guest in *Orlando Sentinel* called 1st H "a flashback …reminiscent of leather helmets and third-down punts." "The defense kept us alive until we could get some offense going," said Gators coach Steve Spurrier. Florida DB Will White picked off pass by frosh QB Jay Barker (4-11/62y, 2 INTs) on Alabama's 1st series of 3rd Q, and Florida scoring spree began on next 4 possessions. Gators TB Errict Rhett rushed 23/170y and scored 3y TD at end of 90y drive in 4th Q that iced it with 5:36 left. It would turn out to be Alabama's last defeat until late 1993.

TENNESSEE 30 Ucla 16: In oppressive heat and humidity, Tennessee (2-0) QB Andy Kelly (25-35/275y, TD, 3 INTs) pitched 34y TD pass to WR Carl Pickens (6/104y) in 1st Q, and DL Darryl Hardy blocked punt in 2nd Q to 3YL to set up another TD for 14-3 H advantage. "Still getting used to" his switch from TB to DB, Volunteers Tracy Smith stepped in front of Bruin WR Sean LaChapelle on 1st play of 4th Q and returned INT 38y for TD and 23-9 lead. UCLA (1-1) responded with QB Tommy Maddox's screen pass to TB Kevin Williams that went 74y to TD that got Bruins back in game at 23-16. What followed was 75y Tennessee (2-0) drive ended with WR J.J. McCleskey's 3y TD reverse run. This decisive Volunteers march was boosted by UCLA coach Terry Donohue's uncharacteristic 15y unsportsmanlike PEN for arguing call by officials.

MICHIGAN 24 Notre Dame 14: Playing without TOs and only 21y in PENs, flawless Michigan (2-0) built 17-0 lead, which included WR Desmond Howard's 29y E-around TD run. Notre Dame (1-1) closed to within 17-14 on QB Rick Mirer's 2 TD passes. In 4th Q, Wolverines faced 4th-and-1 at Irish 25 YL. QB Elvis Grbac (20-22/195y) executed coach Gary Moeller's gamble, perfectly arching clinching TD pass to EZ corner that Howard took in with majestic dive.

Central Michigan 20 MICHIGAN STATE 3: Labeling it "a lousy game for us," understating Michigan State (0-1) coach George Perles endured Chippewas TB Billy Smith's 40/162y rushing, with 15y TD for 7-0 lead 52 secs before H. Central Michigan (2-0-1) lost what would have been stunning shutout to K Jim Del Verne's 3rd Q FG, but coach Herb Deromedi called it his school's "greatest victory." Central QB Jeff Bender (10-22/144y, TD, 2 INTs) connected with WR Ken Ealy on 57y TD pass in 3rd Q.

Baylor 16 COLORADO 14: Leading 14-13 late in 4th Q, Colorado (1-1) recovered FUM at Bears 30YL and was ready for kill. But, Baylor (2-0) DT Santana Dotson blocked Buffaloes K Jim Harper's chip-shot FG, and ball bounced to midfield where LB Brian Hand advanced loose ball to Colorado 30YL. Bears TB David Mims (23/104y) gained 13y to prepare K Jeff Ireland's winning 35y FG with :51 left. Loss ended nation's longest win streak at 11 and Buffs' 15-game home winning string. Culprits were callow Colorado running game (168y) and young D that permitted 428y to Baylor. Bison QB Darian Hagan (11-19/154y, TD, INT) hit TE Sean Brown for 26y TD in 2nd Q and it held up until well into 3rd Q when Bears WR Melvin Bonner beat Buffs frosh CB Chris Hudson for 74y TD. Baylor QB J.J. Joe was sharp in passed 12-19/233y, TD, INT.

Air Force 24 UTAH 21: Kick-blocking ace, Air Force (3-0) CB Carlton McDonald, raced in to block Utah (2-1) K Chris Yergensen's chip-shot, tying FG try in last secs of game. Trying to reverse 6 straight losses to Air Academy, Utes drove to 5YL and called timeout for FG tie because deadlock in their 1st conf game of season wouldn't have harmed their record. But, bad snap and McDonald's speed ruined attempt. Air Force jumped to 14-0 lead in 1st Q, driving 81y on 1st possession to TD blast by FB Jason Jones (22/138y, TD) and blocking punt to set up QB Rob Perez's 38y pass to WR Scott Hufford and Perez's 2y TD keeper. Passing of Utah QB Frank Dolce (22-33/265y, INT) rallied home team to Yergensen's 27y FG and Dolce's TD sneak, followed by Dolce's 2-pt pass. Utah's 8-pt surge came with 7 secs before H and capped 95y drive. Utes dominated 1st 9 mins of 3rd Q to take 21-14 lead: RB Keith Williams reversed field, avoided McDonald's tackle for loss, and scored on 4y run. Air Force managed 78y drive to tying TD and K Joe Wood's winning 37y FG midway in 4th Q.

SOUTHERN CALIFORNIA 21 Penn State 10: Southern California presented quick, blitzing D which bothered Nittany Lions (2-1) throughout. USC (1-1) QB Reggie Perry was steady after previous week's Memphis State disaster and rushed 14/52y, including clinching 2y TD dash around E with 6:36 to play. Without injured top runner, TB Mazio Royster, Perry passed 10-20/123y, TD, 2 INTs. Trojans TE Yonnie Johnson caught 7y TD from Perry to open scoring in 1st Q. Lifeless Penn State allowed 5 sacks of QB Tony Sacca (18-40/236y, TD, 2 INTs), but Lions briefly tied game at 7-7 on Sacca's TD pass to WR Terry Smith in 2nd Q. Penn State WR O.J. McDuffie lost FUM, and personal foul PEN gave Trojans ball at 20YL in 2nd Q. In for Royster, TB Deon Strother (20/67y) plunged 1y for TD and permanent lead for USC at 14-7.

CALIFORNIA 42 Purdue 18: California (2-0) was off to its best start since 1982 as it forced 6 TOs in bedeviling Purdue (1-1). Cal scored 26 pts off 4 TOs that were gathered inside Boilermakers 30YL. Purdue scored 1st on 5y pass from QB Eric Hunter (10-27/165y, 2 TDs, 3 INTs) to WR Ernest Calloway for TD that closed 1st Q. Bears QB Mike Pawlawski (22-33/275y, 3 TDs, 2 INTs) threw TD passes to 3 different receivers, including 30y pitch to WR Sean Dawkins that provided Cal's 1st lead at 9-7 in 2nd Q. Bears TB Russell White (21/65y) scored on run and pass in 3rd Q, but Boilers got back within 28-18 near end of 3rd Q as Hunter and Calloway collaborated on another TD.

USA Today Coaches Poll September 16

1	Florida State (47)	1451	14	Penn State	699
2	Miami (Fla.) (6)	1401	15	Baylor	646
3	Michigan (4)	1353	16	Ohio State	569
4	Washington (1)	1270	17	Syracuse	449
5	Florida (1)	1239	18	Pittsburgh	412
6	Tennessee	1078	19	Georgia Tech	370
7	Clemson	1051	20	Houston	323
8	Oklahoma	1041	21	Colorado	316
9	Nebraska	934	22	Georgia	243
10	Iowa	915	23	Southern California	235
11	Notre Dame	774	24	Mississippi State	216
12	Texas A&M	738	25	California	118
13	Auburn	731			

September 21, 1991

(Th) GEORGIA TECH 24 Virginia 21: WR Greg Lester got loose for 76y TD bomb on game's 1st play for Georgia Tech (2-1). Sub Virginia (1-2) QB Bobby Goodman returned from 3rd Q shoulder sprain to throw 72y TD to frosh WR Tyrone Davis. Extra-man PEN sustained Yellow Jackets' tying 80y drive early in 4th Q, and TB Jimy Lincoln (31/229y) went 23y behind FB Michael Smith's block for 21-14 Georgia Tech lead. Gutty Goodman rallied Cavs to 21-21 tie on TD pass to TE Aaron Mundy with 1:56 to go, but QB Shawn Jones (14-29/214y) maneuvered Yellow Jackets for clutch K Scott Sisson's 33y FG, his 4th last-min career game-winner.

SYRACUSE 38 Florida 21: Launching upset was Orangemen RB Kirby Dar Dar's 95y opening KO TD RET off reverse. Syracuse (3-0) added TD within 5 mins for 14-0 lead. Florida (2-1) crawled as close as 28-21 with 4:56 to go in 3rd Q after Syracuse's only TO of game led to 4y TD pass from QB Shane Matthews (27-43/347y, 3 TDs, 2 INTs) to TE Terrell Jackson. Orange alternated QBs Marvin Graves and Doug Womack every few snaps on 11-play march to ice it at 35-21, Womack scoring on 2nd play of 4th Q. Syracuse rushed 250y, and its fired-up D threw Gators for 17y in losses.

TENNESSEE 26 Mississippi State 24: Tennessee (3-0) pillaged SEC's leading D for 516y, but had to drive 88y to QB Andy Kelly's 10y blitz-beating, winning TD pass to TE Mark Adams with 1:50 to go. Earlier, Volunteers had made highly profitable mistake: Thinking it was 3rd down instead of 4th, Tennessee called pass and WR Cory Fleming caught 3y TD to elevate score to 10-3 with only 2 secs left before H. "We were going to throw it in the end zone on third down and try for a field goal on fourth down," admitted sheepish coach Johnny Majors. WR Willie Harris' 63y TD run on reverse started Mississippi State (3-1) on rally from 17-3 2nd H deficit to 24-17 lead. Bulldogs QB Sleepy Robinson (7-14/102y, TD) hit 42y pass against blitz and put tying 4y TD pass in hands of WR Tony James. LB Keo Coleman helped Miss State to its 7-pt lead with 43y INT RET to Vols 3YL. But, QB Kelly (27-41/330y, 2 TDs, 3 INTs) came through to create 2 Volunteers scoring drives in last 12 mins.

ALABAMA 10 Georgia 0: Dealing 1st shutout suffered by Georgia (2-1) since 1984, Alabama (2-1) bumbled along, riding its D might until RB Siran Stacy scored game's only TD with 1:01 to go in 3rd Q. Myriad of Crimson Tide PENs, FUMs, and missed FGs precluded their successful 80y TD drive. Georgia K Todd Peterson missed chip-shot FG that launched winning march for Alabama.

OHIO STATE 33 Washington State 19: Unsinkable jr QB Kirk Herbstreit (8-13/158y, TD, INT), son of former Buckeyes player and asst coach Jim, finally got his chance to guide his beloved Buckeyes (3-0) in Ohio Stadium after 3 years of riding bench and contributing KO wedge-busting. Herbstreit, only few years away from stardom as Lee Corso's TV sidekick on ESPN's College Gameday, made most of QB Kent Graham being out with injury. On 1st series, Herbstreit faked handoff and whipped 20y completion, then faked option run and fired 39y TD to WR Bernard Edwards. Washington State (0-3) QB Drew Bledsoe (26-43/287y, TD, INT) suffered 1st Q INT that Ohio DB Roger Harper chugged back 42y for TD. TB Carlos Snow (18/97y, TD) scored for 21-0 Buckeyes lead in 3rd Q before Cougars K Jason Hanson belted 52 and 44y FGs. Not discouraged by being sacked 9 times, Bledsoe hit TE Calvin Schexnayder for 4th Q TD, but his 2-pt pass was picked off and returned 96y for 2 pts by Ohio LB Steve Tovar.

INDIANA 13 Kentucky 10: Fighting mightily but scorelessly over Beer Barrel trophy in 1st H, Kentucky (1-1) kicked off to start 2nd H. Hoosiers (1-1) consumed 7:55 in advancing to 1st-and-goal at 6YL, but Wildcats stacked up IU TB Vaughn Dunbar (39/147y, TD) inches short of GL on 4th down. Now inspired, Kentucky converted 3rd down 4 times in going 99y to score on frosh TB Donnie Redd's 13y sweep. Drive took nearly 9 mins, so 7-0 lead came early in 4th Q. Staying poised, Hoosiers rallied on 42y TD pass from accurate QB Tim Green (17-20/232y, TD) to WR Eddie Thomas. K Doug Pelfrey bombed Wildcat-record 53y FG for 10-7 advantage, but Dunbar lugged pigskin 4 straight plays, including 28y dash to set up his winning 1y TD with 1:52 to go. Hoosiers S Damon Watts picked off pass at his 13YL as time expired.

Washington 36 NEBRASKA 21: No. 9 Cornhuskers (2-1) led 21-9 with 5:32 left in 3rd Q, but lost their 6th in row to ranked opponent when Washington (2-0) TB Beno Bryant scored late in 3rd Q, and QB Billy Joe Hobert passed and ran for 4th Q scores. Nebraska had gained its lead on IB Derek Brown's short TD run after LB Mike Anderson's FUM REC at Huskies 2YL. Hobert passed 23-40/283y, including go-ahead 8y TD to WR Orlando McKay. TB Jay Barry burst 81y for Huskies clincher with 5:38 to go.

TULSA 35 Texas A&M 34: QB Jeff Granger threw 2 TD passes in 1st Q as Aggies (1-1) built 21-3 lead. But, Tulsa (3-1) refused to surrender, rushing for 240y, including 231y by TB Chris Hughley, to claw back with 19 pts in 3rd Q. Texas A&M briefly regained lead at 34-29 in 4th Q on Granger's 4th TD pass. But, strong-armed Tulsa QB T.J.

Rubley threw 63y bomb to WR Chris Penn to regain lead at 35-34. When Hurricane LB Billy Cole recovered Aggies FUM on ensuing KO, Hughley was able to run out clock.

Arizona State 32 SOUTHERN CALIFORNIA 25: Post-game concert by Beach Boys included their classic "Don't Worry Baby," but *Los Angeles Times* suggested that would be tough concept for Southern California (1-2) fans to swallow. , Arizona State (2-0) scored on 5 of its 1st 7 series to build 32-10 lead by end of 3rd Q. Trojan gift had come in last 4 mins of 1st Q as Sun Devils scored to go ahead 6-3: USC was offside on x-pt, so ASU sent FB Parnell Charles blasting for 2 pts and 8-3 edge. Devils rushed for 307y as TB George Montgomery (22/136y, 2 TDs) scored twice in 2nd Q on 43 and 2y trap runs. Trojans slipped back within 18-10 when versatile WR Curtis Conway switched to QB and gained 4/43y running on 73y drive late in 2nd Q, including 12y TD run. Troy QB Reggie Perry (13-28/136y, 2 INTs) got hot in 4th Q to lead 82 and 80y TD drives while USC D allowed no 1st downs to Sun Devils. Trojans TB Mazio Royster (16/78y) scored twice, but it was not enough.

September 28, 1991

PENN STATE 28 Boston College 21: Nittany Lions (4-1) trailed 7-6 at H to Eagles (0-4) who at that point "wanted it more than we did," or so said Penn State coach Joe Paterno. Penn State got big plays from 3rd-string TB Shelly Hammonds (56y TD run) and DB Darren Perry (45y INT TD RET). Still, Boston College rallied to within 28-21 on pair of 4th Q TD passes to dandy TEs Mark Chmura (7/118y) and Pete Mitchell by QB Glenn Foley (17-34/277y, 2 TDs, 5 INTs). Eagles mustered late drive from their own 33YL to Lions 17YL before Foley misfired on 2 EZ passes. Uncharacteristic 10 PENs, including 4 foolish personal fouls, bogged down Penn State, which meant referee would step off more y against Lions than they gained on ground: 95y to 78y, despite Hammonds' long TD run.

CLEMSON 9 Georgia Tech 7: Yellow Jackets (2-2) scored on 84y 1st Q sortie with TB Jimy Lincoln's 59y run serving as chief gain. After that, Clemson (3-0) D hunkered down; it held Georgia Tech to single 1st down on 5 possessions of 1st H. With 4th Q score at 7-3, Tigers DB Robert O'Neal's 23y punt RET to Georgia Tech 46YL set up TB Ronald Williams, who turned workhorse to carry 5/44y and scored on 2y TD run. Conv was blocked by Georgia Tech LB Tom Johnson, giving Yellow Jackets K Scott Sisson desperate chance for winning FG. But, Sisson missed from 44y with 3 secs left.

TENNESSEE 30 Auburn 21: No. 13 Auburn (3-1) played under cloud of accusations made by former players Eric Ramsey and Alex Strong, who contended in Friday story in *Montgomery (Ala.) Advertiser* that coaches had made payoffs on their behalf. Volunteers (4-0) were only too happy to fuel Tigers' misery: Tennessee bombardier WR Carl Pickens caught 87 and 67y TD missiles that QB Andy Kelly (23-35/355y, 3 TDs, INT) sent. Pickens' 1st TD was longest to date in Vols history and came early in 3rd Q for 17-7 lead. Pickens' 2nd TD grab required him to make excellent adjustment on short throw that got him free of Auburn S Mike Pina. Tennessee K John Becksvoort's 34y FG made it 20-7, but Auburn DB Fred Smith—who had been beaten by Pickens' 1st TD bomb—grabbed INT for 21y TD in 1st min of 4th Q. Tigers QB Stan White passed 11-26/222y, 2 INTs, and 78y TD to RB Joe Frazier that had opened scoring in 2nd Q. White also kept Vols fans gnawing their fingernails with 5y TD run midway in 4th Q that kept Auburn within 27-21 striking distance.

MISSISSIPPI 24 Arkansas 17: For 1st time in 30 years, Ole Miss (4-1) earned consecutive victories over Razorbacks (2-2). Aerial works of Rebels QB Russ Shows (11-16/193y, INT) made difference in outcome as his throws positioned FB Marvin Courtney (13/67y, 2 TDs) for critical TD runs of 1 and 9y in 1st and 4th Qs. Arkansas QB Jason Allen (8-14/123y, 2 TDs, INT) passed sparingly, but kept his Hogs within hailing distance by pitching 46y score to WR Tracy Caldwell in 1st Q to pull within 10-7 and 14y to WR Ron Dickerson Jr. (4/60y, TD) in 4th Q that capped contest's scoring.

Florida State 51 MICHIGAN 31: No. 1 Seminoles (4-0) enjoyed DB Terrell Buckley stealing INT from Michigan WR Desmond Howard and dashing 40y to early TD. After Howard responded with TD for 7-7 1st Q tie, FSU coach Bobby Bowden dusted off 2 trick plays: "Crocodile" play, in which sub QB Charlie Ward flanked left, then took long lateral from QB Casey Weldon and threw back to Weldon for 29y gain. That oddity set up fake FG TD by FB William Floyd. Outclassed, Michigan (2-1) still gained 357y and crawled to within 25-23 in 2nd Q as QB Elvis Grbac tossed 2 of his 4 TD passes.

Rutgers 14 MICHIGAN STATE 7: Sad Michigan State (0-3) dropped another surprising tilt to smaller program. Rutgers (3-1) used identical fake-dive, passes to flat to TB Antoine Moore (22/83y) for TDs in 1st and 4th Qs. QB Tom Tarver (19-33/182y, 2 TDs) pitched his 2nd scoring pass to Moore with only 46 secs to play. Spartans had tied game at 7-7 in 3rd Q as sub QB Jim Miller (8-16/165y, TD, INT) whipped medium pass to WR Courtney Hawkins (8/143y, TD), who broke tackle of Rutgers DB Ron Allen at 20YL and cantered in to score on 38y TD. Game-winning drive was launched by 20y

punt RET by Scarlet Knights CB Marshall Roberts that nearly went to midfield. Tarver hit passes of 15 and 6y to WR Jim Guarantano and pitched 26y to WR Chris Brantley, who beat MSU S Myron Bell's tight sideline coverage at Michigan State 7YL.

Pittsburgh 14 MINNESOTA 13: Golden Gophers (1-2) built 10-7 H lead on QB Marquel Fleetwood's short TD run and K Aaron Piepkorn's 52y FG. Meanwhile, Panthers (4-0) managed blocked point for TD. Held to 12y rushing in 1st H, Pitt RB Curtis Martin, went for 158y in 2nd H, with 36y TD. Martin added 5/42y receiving. Winning squeaker meant Pittsburgh (4-0) had opened with 4 wins for 1st time since 1982 Dan Marino era.

Texas Christian 30 TEXAS TECH 16: Unbeaten TCU (4-0) was off to its best start since its 1955 conf title, but it took 3-TD outburst in 4th Q to win in Lubbock for 1st time since 1972. Texas Tech (1-3) led 13-9 at H as QB Jamie Gill (26-50/293y, TD, 2 INTs) hit 2-3/37y on 80y trip to TD power off left side and hit 7-10/48y late in 2nd Q to lead to his 8y TD throw to Lynn. Frogs mounted 72y and 80y TD drives in 4th Q, but big play came in between: DE Roosevelt Collins dropped into zone pass coverage, picked off Gill's pass, and rambled 25y to TD that built 23-13 lead.

BRIGHAM YOUNG 21 Air Force 7: Unbeaten Air Force (4-1) managed 209y rushing, but it was not enough to overcome passing of Cougars fine QB Ty Detmer (20-30, 2 TDs, INT). BYU (1-3) got going in 2nd Q as QB Detmer found sub WR Otis Sterling for 2 TD passes. Falcons HB Antoine Banks (60y rushing), scored His team's only TD on 16y TD in 4th Q.

WASHINGTON 56 Kansas State 3: Of unbeaten Kansas State (3-1), Washington (3-0) QB Billy Joe Hobert said, "They're a pretty competitive team, but they picked a bad day to play us." Hobert passed 13-18/234y, 3 TDs, including 71 and 32y TDs to WR Mario Bailey. TB Jay Barry (9/62y, 2 TDs) got Huskies flying to 20-0 lead in 1st Q with game's 1st TD. By time Hobert threw his 2nd TD pass, to WR Orlando McKay for 28y in 2nd Q, Washington led 35-0. K Tate Wright salvaged some K-State respect by making 42y FG late in 2nd Q. Wildcat rushing total was -17y as its 2 QBs lost 43y, but starting QB Paul Watson was able to pass 17-23/232y, INT, 1 of 4 pick-offs by hungry Huskies D. Sub Washington TB Beno Bryant (14/85y, TD) scored on 4th Q punt TD RET of 53y to tie UCLA's Sam Brown (1954-55) for tops to date in conf history with 4 in career.

STANFORD 28 Colorado 21: FB Tommy Vardell (29/114y, 3 TDs) took sugared water at H to rehydrate himself and scored 2 of his 3 TDs in 4th Q to launch Stanford (1-2) back into winning side of ledger. Vardell broke 14-14 deadlock 2 mins into 4th Q and started upset downfall of no. 17 Colorado (2-2). Score had been tied at 7-7 by Buffs CB Chris Hudson, who steamed 40y with INT TD RET 1:01 into 2nd Q. On next drive, fired-up Cardinal coach Dennis Green called timeout after CU TB Lamont Warren (15/95y, TD) slipped tackle and raced 23y to Stanford 20YL. Green implored his D to step it up, and although defenders soon allowed Buffalo QB Darian Hagan (6-12/87y, TD) to slip 20y TD pass to WR Michael Westbrook, they closed scoring door except Warren's 10y TD run in last 4 mins of 4th Q. On 3rd-and-short early in 4th Q, Vardell broke outside T Bob Whitfield's block for 20y TD to close 83y trip on which RB Glyn Milburn (9/106y) added 55y sprint. Warren lost FUM at his 15YL, and Vardell scored from 7YL for 28-14 edge.

Nebraska 18 ARIZONA STATE 9: No. 16 Nebraska (3-1) survived its trek across desert, and K Byron Bennett had every reason to whimsically say, "I can't kick," or at least his blockers weren't helping. Bennett had arrived with 12 of 14 on x-pts and perfect 3 of 3 on FGs so far in 1991, but Sun Devils blocked 2 FGs and x-pt. Additionally, after making go-ahead FG in 3rd Q, Bennett plunked right and left uprights respectively on missed 31 and 23y FGs in 4th Q. After Nebraska QB Keithen McCant barely had edged into EZ on game's opening drive that followed WR Nate Turner's 42y KO RET, TE William Washington scored 2-pt conv with which he blasted across GL after scooping up Bennett's blocked conv kick. Arizona State (2-1) shaved it to 8-3 on K Mike Richey's 42y FG in 2nd Q and went up 9-8 early in 3rd Q after NG Arthur Paul blocked FG: QB Bret Powers (14-20/174y, INT) threw 39y pass to FB Kelvin Fisher, and TB George Montgomery (16/71y, TD) wedged over. IB Derek Brown (25/134y) and DB Steve Carmer (2 FUM RECs, INT) helped nurse Huskers through 11-9 advantage until McCant's 4th Q TD pass to WB Jon Bostick.

October 5, 1991

NORTH CAROLINA STATE 28 Georgia Tech 21: Opportunistic North Carolina State (5-0) D cashed in 2 vital TDs: LB Tyler Lawrence's 32y INT TD RET in 1st Q for 13-0 lead and DB Ricky Turner's 26y FUM TD RET in 3rd Q for 20-7 lead. Georgia Tech (2-3) had its own glorious D moments in 3rd Q that earned 21-20 advantage: DB Willie Clay pilfered pass by Wolfpack frosh QB Geoff Bender (17-32/138y, TD, 3 INTs) for 40y TD. NC State fashioned 12-play, 74y 4th Q drive for winning TD by Bender. Key play was 3rd down pass interference PEN called against Tech LB Marco Coleman.

Mississippi 35 KENTUCKY 14: Sr sub RB Darren Billings had never scored in his Ole Miss (5-1) career, but he burst off block by LT Wesley Melton in 1st Q for 10y TD. After Wildcats (2-2) S Brad Armstrong picked off pass at his 1YL and returned it 55y, FB

Terry Samuels roared up middle for tying 45y TD run in opening min of 2nd Q. Billings scored again on 13y run, so Ole Miss led 14-7 at H. Teams traded 3rd Q TDs as Rebels QB Hank Shows (13-27/292y, 2 TDs, 2 INTs) pitched 1st of his 2 scores and Kentucky's little frosh QB Pookie Jones (11-21/152y) raced 51y to set up TD. Wildcats, winners of their last 10 night games at home until this evening, hung within 7 pts until Shows lifted Rebels to 28-14 as he rifled 60y TD to WR Tyrone Montgomery with 9:11 on 4th Q clock.

GEORGIA 27 Clemson 12: Frosh QB Eric Zeier (15-33/249y, 2 TDs) came off bench, went immediately to air with 50y connection to WR Arthur Marshall and 8y TD to WR Andre Hastings with 32 secs left before H to give Georgia (4-1) 10-3 lead. K Kenon Parkman's 2nd FG gave Bulldogs 13-3 edge in 3rd Q. Clemson (3-1) QB DeChane Cameron (19-38/246y, TD, 3 INTs) pitched 24y pass to WR Larry Ryans to set up K Nelson Welch's 29y FG with 49 secs left in 3rd Q. Georgia came right back on Zeier's TD pass on next possession for 20-6 lead to end Tigers' 8-game win streak.

FLORIDA STATE 46 Syracuse 14: For 1st time in its last 11 games, no. 1 Florida State (5-0) found itself trailing. Late in 1st Q, Syracuse (4-1) WR Qadry "Missile" Ismail eluded 3 tacklers and raced 95y on KO RET to score his 2nd TD for 14-7 lead. Seminoles scored game's next 39 pts as they harvested 642y O. QB Casey Weldon passed 22-35/347y, 3 TDs, including 50y TD strike to WR Shannon Baker for 30-14 lead in 3rd Q. After gaining 80y on opening 2 snaps of game, Orangemen gained 105y on next 48 plays. "They (Florida State) are in the left (fast) lane on every play," said Orange coach Paul Pasqualoni.

Southern Mississippi 10 AUBURN 9: Underrated Southern Miss (3-2) got fired up for yet another unsuspecting SEC foe. FB Roland Johnson scored 1st Q TD, and Eagles led rest of game. No. 16 Auburn (3-2) got TD pass from QB Stan White (23-43/258y, TD, 2 INTs) with 1:33 left. Auburn coach Pat "Tie" Dye, who built reputation for accepting ties, instead gambled with 2-pt pass which Eagles DB Brian Wood knocked down. When Tigers on-side KO failed, Southern ran out clock. Auburn had 397y to 204y O edge.

OHIO STATE 31 Wisconsin 16: Upstart Wisconsin (3-1) was completely corraled until last part of 4th Q as it was limited in opening 53 mins to 17/-1y rushing and 134y passing despite TB Terrell Fletcher (7/33y) making 29y gain on Badgers' 2nd scrimmage play. Ohio State (4-0) led 14-2 as QB Kent Graham (9-12/119y, TD, INT) returned from mild shoulder injury to pitch 22y TD to WR Bernard Edwards in 2nd Q. Ohio lead went to 24-2 in 4th Q on K Tim Williams' 41y FG and sub QB Kirk Herbstreit's 32y TD dash. Buckeyes TB Raymont Harris added his 2nd TD run to offset Badgers O, which suddenly came alive against Ohio 3rd-teamers. Wisconsin sub QB Jay Macias (6-11/126y) threw 2 late TDs.

INDIANA 31 Michigan State 0: As defending co-champion of Big 10, Michigan State (0-4) continued to fall completely on its face in 1991. Losers of previous 4 games to Spartans by combined 161-55 pts, Indiana (2-1-1) turned tables, which was described by Hoosiers sr G Jim Hannon: "This is the greatest feeling I've had since I've been here." IU gained 446y O, led by QB Trent Green (20-29/241y, TD passing, and 10/46y, TD rushing). After Green opened scoring with 15y TD sprint, WR Scott McGowan's thrilling 79y punt TD RET provided 14-0 H lead. Michigan State was held to 31/33y rushing by stubborn Hoosiers D.

Michigan 43 IOWA 24: Wolverines (3-1) snared 1st score on DB David Ritter's 21y blocked punt TD RET, then bounced back from 18-7 deficit to take 19-18 H lead on 1st of 3 TD passes by QB Elvis Grbac (14-22/196y). Go-ahead TD was set up by Iowa's ill-advised fake punt at its 47YL with 1:40 before H. Leading 18-13, mostly because of QB Matt Rodgers' brilliant 1st H of 15-20/181y, TD passing, Hawkeyes turned it over at own 46YL. Coach Hayden Fry apologized to his troops at H for his error. Michigan WR Desmond Howard (4/47y) nabbed 2 scoring throws to extend lead to 33-18. Rodgers, who passed 26-42/275y, TD, INT, was outstanding for Iowa (3-1), scoring twice. His 2nd 8y TD gallop cut lead to 36-24 at end of 80y drive in 4th Q. Michigan sub TB Jesse Johnson, who caught Grbec's 28y TD pass late in 1st H for 19-18 lead, rushed 22/168y and scored on 2 TD runs.

Baylor 38 HOUSTON 21: Houston (1-3), combined 124-49 winners over Baylor (5-0) in previous 3 years, felt another sting by vengeful foe in 1991. Bears QB J.J. Joe (16-23/262y) pitched 2 TD passes and ran for 9y TD in 2nd H to extend 17-14 H edge. Cougars QB David Klingler passed 35-57/470y, 2 TDs, but had 3 INTs and lost 2 FUMs.

Texas A&M 37 TEXAS TECH 14: In its 6 most recent trips to Lubbock, Texas A&M (3-1) had lost 4 times, each settled by less than 7 pts. This time, Aggies cruised to 24-0 H lead as QB Bucky Richardson (6-13/121y) ran for 3 scores. Red Raiders (1-4) scored in 3rd Q on FB Louis Sheffield's 2y run to slice deficit to 27-7, and immediately recovered surprise on-side KO. But, when K Lin Elliott missed 34y FG, "...you could kind of see the blood run out of the faces of some of the guys," said defeated coach Spike Dykes.

California 27 UCLA 24: Despite having suffered 18 consecutive losses to UCLA (2-2), California (4-0) rallied from 24-14 4th Q disadvantage. K Doug Brien booted 33y FG, and RB Russell White (25/121y) tallied on short TD run to knot it at 24-24. Golden Bears took punt at own 40YL in late going and advanced to UCLA 29YL. With 30 secs to play, Brien kicked winning 47y FG, longest of his career to date. UCLA QB Tommy Maddox (19-33/251y, INT) had pitched 2 TD passes to WR Sean LaChapelle (8/136y).

WASHINGTON 54 Arizona 0: Fast-charging Washington (4-0) dropped largest defeat on Arizona (2-3) since 1949. Lefty QB Mark Brunell (5-7/93y), coming back from injured knee in spring drills, hopped off bench in 2nd Q for injured QB Billy Joe Hobert (5-15/72y) to pitch 2 TD passes to WR Mario Bailey (5/89y). Wildcats managed only 39/30y rushing.

USA Today Coaches Poll October 7

1	Florida State (55)	1468	14	North Carolina State	627
2	Miami (Fla.) (3)	1405	15	Clemson	602
3	Washington (1)	1370	16	California	592
4	Tennessee	1276	17	Iowa	578
5	Oklahoma	1203	18	Syracuse	539
6	Michigan	1108	19	Alabama	485
7	Baylor	1036	20	Illinois	403
8	Notre Dame	1022	21	Texas A&M	323
9	Penn State	976	22	Georgia	191
10	Florida	877	23	Mississippi	120
11	Ohio State	821	24	Auburn	114
12	Pittsburgh	728	25	Colorado	109
13	Nebraska	679			

October 12, 1991

East Carolina 23 SYRACUSE 20: Surprising Pirates (5-1) won 5th straight game as they overcame 20-10 H deficit, scoring on 3 of their 1st 4 possessions of 2nd H. Magical QB Jeff Blake passed 23-43/324y, TD, but it was his broken pass attempt in 4th Q, turned into 43y TD dash, that provided winning margin. K John Biskup, most accurate K in Syracuse (4-2) history, made 2 FGs in 1st Q for 6-0 lead, but missed 4th Q FGs of 27 and 42y. East Carolina piled up 423y total O while stifling Orangemen's mighty rush game by permitting only 66y on ground. Syracuse QB Marvin Graves posted career-high 295y passing on 20-25, with TD and INT. Critical sequence came barely into 4th Q when Biskup missed his 27y attempt, and Carolina answered with 80y drive capped by Blake when he looked long to pass but instead sprinted through huge gap to his left for long TD gallop and 3-pt lead. Orange answered with Graves throwing for 63y to camp at Pirates' 6YL with 1st-and-goal. But, ECU DL Greg Gardill sacked Graves on 3rd down to force Biskup's 42y miss. Sr WR Dion Johnson caught 7/136y, his best game ever for East Carolina.

NORTH CAROLINA 24 Wake Forest 10: Annoying Wake Forest (1-4) failed to score in 3-0 1st H but clearly had North Carolina (4-1) out of rhythm. In opening H, Demon Deacons' D held Tar Heels to 28y rushing, made 3 sacks, and knocked QB Chuckie Burnette from game with sore ribs and banged-up pitching paw. Wake's O, "best we've looked all year," according to QB Keith West (24-37/231y, INT), put it ahead at 7-3 with 55y drive midway through 3rd Q with TB John Leach finishing things up with 27y TD pass to WR Todd Dixon. West contributed 15y run to scoring trip. Then, in 2 swift strikes, Carolina turned momentum: backup TB Randy Jordan took screen pass from effective replacement QB Todd Burnett (6-9/116y, TD) and stepped out of tackle for 44y TD. When UNC got ball back less than 4 mins later, it sent TB Natrone Means (29/167y, 2 TDs) left with pitchout, and Means rambled 63y to score for 17-10 lead.

CLEMSON 20 Virginia 20: Try as they might, Cavaliers (3-2-1) could not crack Clemson (3-1-1), which rallied from 10 pts down in 4th Q. Virginia had tough time swallowing tie, but it was school's best result ever at "Death Valley" and would turn out to be only blemish on Tigers' ACC record. Virginia started smartly on TE Aaron Mundy's 15y TD catch from QB Matt Blundin (15-34/241y, 2 TDs) and K Michael Husted's 32y FG. Cavs could have all but put game away in 2nd Q as DB Keith Lyle botched FUM RET in his haste to score, and Clemson scored 3 plays later on 56y run by TB Ronald Williams (20/185y, TD). Husted tacked on line-drive 47y FG in 4th Q for 20-10 edge before Tigers FB Rudy Harris (26/102y, TD) slashed over for 1y TD with 3:33 to play. With 46 secs on clock, Clemson K Nelson Welch, who had missed 3 short FG tries, tied it from 40y out. Welch's FG became possible when UVa TB Terry Kirby appeared to have made run for clinching 1st down but frustratingly lost FUM to Tigers LB Kenzil Jackson at Cavs 49YL.

FLORIDA 35 Tennessee 18: Gators frosh DB Larry Kennedy didn't exactly shut down ace Volunteers WR Carl Pickens (7/145y), but batted away 3 bombs for Pickens, allowed no TDs, and sealed win with 44y INT TD RET in last 4 mins. Florida (5-1) used QB Shane Matthews' 2 TD passes and RB Errict Rhett's 2 TD runs to build 28-12 lead in 3rd Q. Rhett's 2nd score was set up by LB Carlton Miles' punt block. QB Andy Kelly (33-56/392y, TD) twice drove Tennessee (4-1) inside Gators 10YL, but each time it had to settle for FGs.

MIAMI 26 Penn State 20: After 6-6 1st H deadlock in south Florida heat, Miami (5-0) appeared to put game away with 2 lightning TDs within duration of 2:19 late in 3rd Q: WR Horace Copeland streaked 80y with TD pass from QB Gino Toretta, and WR Kevin Williams squirmed away from 6 tacklers to dash to school-record to-date 91y punt TD RET. Penn State (5-2) came back, however, on 72y drive as WR O.J. McDuffie caught passes of 28 and 18y to set up QB Tony Sacca's 2y TD toss in back of EZ to WR Terry Smith with 24 secs left in 3rd Q. Hurricanes WR Lamar Thomas got behind DBs for 42y TD catch early in 4th Q for 26-14 margin. Nittany Lions went 78y on PEN-aided drive as Sacca (24-38/263y, 2 TDs, but 8 sacks) threw TD pass to draw within 26-20. Late Penn State drive expired on DB Darryl Williams' GL INT as fatigued Sacca made desperate long fling while failing to notice yawning opportunity to scramble for big gain.

ILLINOIS 10 Ohio State 7: Illini coach John Mackovic likened game to heavyweight fight: "Boom, boom, boom. Back and forth." RB Darren Boyer gave Illinois (4-1) early 7-0 lead with 7y TD run at end of 88y drive, and Illini D maintained shutout, battling against Ohio State (4-1) run attack that totaled 199y. Twice Buckeyes advanced inside Illini 5YL only to lose possession. With 3:47 to play, it appeared decided when midfield Ohio pass fell incomplete. Illini FB Kameno Bell (7/48y and 12/89y receiving) barreled for 17y run, only to be stripped from behind. Bell lamented his elusive effort, "...Keep two hands on the ball, as if you didn't understand the situation, but you can't really make cuts with two hands on the ball." In 2 plays, Buckeyes QB Kent Graham (7-11/130y, TD) hit speedy WR Joey Galloway with 44y TD to tie it at 7-7. QB Jason Verduzco (28-41/272y, 2 INTs) took it upon himself to rally Illinois 49y to Ohio 24YL

with key gain coming on his 12y pass to WR Elbert Turner on 3rd down. With 36 ticks to go on clock, frosh K Chris Richardson kicked winning 41y FG, atoning for earlier chip-shot miss.

NOTRE DAME 42 Pittsburgh 7: Previously-unbeaten Pitt (5-1) was hanging with Notre Dame (5-1) at 0-0, but muffed punt set up 2nd Q TD run by big Irish FB Jerome Bettis (17/125y). On next series, Panthers P Leon Theodorou's punt was blocked by ND TB Reggie Brooks for TD. So, ND (5-1) led 14-0 at H. Rout was on when Irish QB Rick Mirer passed and ran for 3rd Q TDs. Pitt QB Alex Van Pelt (22-37/207y) launched 51y TD pass in 4th Q, but otherwise Pitt could gain only so-so 221y O.

KANSAS STATE 16 Kansas 12: Before packed house in "Little Apple," Kansas State Wildcats (4-1) won by overcoming 6 daunting TOs and scoring 2 TDs in last 8 mins to overturn Kansas (3-2). Jayhawks had used K Dan Eichloff's 24 and 47y FGs and short TD pass in 3rd Q by QB Chip Hilleary (13-27/155y, TD) to WR Jim New to enjoy 12-3 lead in 4th Q. When CB Robert Vaughn's 2nd INT put Jayhawks at 15YL, they appeared poised for tie bow on victory. But K-State D held at 6YL as coach Glen Mason chose to skip short FG try and Hilleary's 4th down pass fell incomplete. K-State QB Paul Watson (18-36/209y, TD, INT) returned to action and drove his club 94y to TD by RB Eric Gallon and 12-10 deficit. Kansas has 3:53 to kill, but gave ball back with punt to Cats 34YL with 2:48 left on clock. Watson, who connected on 10 of his last 15/136y, was about to be sacked by his friend, KU DT Lance Flachsbarth, but his scrambling 34y pass to WR Andre Coleman was collared inside 10YL and carried for winning TD. Kansas made it to KSU 8YL, but clock expired as Jayhawks scrambled to reassemble after WR Matt Gay's catch.

Texas 10 Oklahoma 7 (Dallas): Big rivalry contest at Texas State Fairgrounds often had carried multiple-year tendencies and now it was Sooners' turn to suffer trendy downswing. Oklahoma (4-1) lost another 4th Q lead to Texas (2-2) for agonizing 3rd successive year. . Sooners had 4 trips inside Longhorns 25YL, but managed only QB Cale Gundy's 24y TD pass to WB Ted Long in 1st Q. K Jason Post's 30y FG drew Texas within 7-3 at H. Gundy would pass 0-6 in middle Qs, and Oklahoma gained only 20y on 21 4th Q plays. In 4th Q, Sooners FB Mike McKinley ploughed ahead but was plastered, and ball squirted from stack of players to Texas DB Bubba Jacques, who dashed 30y to winning TD.

Rice 20 BAYLOR 17: Volatile Rice (3-2) coach Fred Goldsmith called it "biggest win in our program since the early '60s." Unbeaten Baylor (5-1) rolled up 531y O, but lost scoring chances in 1st H with FUMs at Owls 26 and 23YLs. Bears K Jeff Ireland missed 2nd H FGs of 43, 45, and 27y which allowed Rice K Darrell Richardson to break 17-17 tie with 33y FG with 2:39 left. Highly-valued Owls TB Trevor Cobb ran 34/171y and scored 1st Q TD.

USA Today Coaches Poll October 17

1	Florida State (55)	1471	14	Alabama	703
2	Miami (Fla.) (3)	1405	15	Penn State	688
3	Washington (1)	1369	16	Baylor	599
4	Michigan	1260	17	Georgia	490
5	Notre Dame	1226	18	Ohio State	416
6	Florida	1138	19	Texas A&M	376
7	Nebraska	1019	20	Pittsburgh	306
8	California	1008	21	Clemson	261
9	North Carolina State	954	22	Colorado	213
10	Tennessee	885	23	Auburn	152
11	Iowa	797	24	Arizona State	146
12	Oklahoma	773	25	Fresno State	145
13	Illinois	715			

October 19, 1991

VIRGINIA 14 North Carolina 9: Cavaliers (4-2-1) QB Matt Blundin (17-28/206y, 2 TDs) set school mark with 148 consecutive throws without INT, outstanding mark he eventually would extend to NCAA single season record of 224. WR Brian Satola caught 6y crossing-pattern TD pass on Virginia's 1st series, and Cavaliers' 7-0 lead held up until North Carolina (4-2) K Clint Gwaltney made 23y FG late in 3rd Q. Blundin answered right away with 3-4/54y passing to 14y score to Satola. UVa had mounted solid run D, limiting UNC TB Natrone Means to 22/65y rushing, but finally allowed backup TB Randy Jordan's 4y TD run with 4:34 remaining. Cavs DB Keith Lyle made INT at his 2YL to save win in last min.

Maryland 23 WAKE FOREST 22: On verge of being yanked at H for 6-16 passing effort, Terrapins (2-4) QB Jim Sandwisch (18-41/318y, 2 TDs) rallied Maryland from 19-7 H deficit to win 500th game in school history. In 1st H, Wake Forest (1-5) QB Keith West (20-39/249y, TD) threw 66y TD pass to WR Todd Dixon, who slipped behind defenders, and K Mike Green kicked 4 of his 5 FGs. After Sandwisch threw his 1st TD pass in 3rd Q, Green popped 19y FG for 22-17 edge for Wake with 13 mins to go. Demon Deacons punt barely hopped into EZ with 3:09 to play, so Maryland took possession at 20YL. In middle of Terps drive, Wake Forest had chance to force Maryland into 3rd-and-25, but PEN was declined against wishes of coach Bill Dooley, who set ACC record with his 174th game. On 4th-and-8, Sandwisch hit WR Marcus Badgett with 20y pass underneath coverage. Terps H-Back Frank Wycheck then spun away from 2 tacklers to tally winning TD on 35y catch.

ALABAMA 24 Tennessee 19 (Birmingham): Going into 4th Q, No. 8 Tennessee (4-2) was nursing 6-3 lead—thanks to K John Becksvoort's 2nd FG (43y) that came in last 20 secs of 2nd Q—when scoreboard at Legion Field exploded. With do-all speedster WR-QB David Palmer and QB Danny Woodson knocked out of game, Alabama (6-1) turned to TB Siran Stacy (22/77y, 2 TDs) to capture its 6th straight win over Volunteers. Stacy scored twice in 4th Q to gain 10-6 and 24-6 leads. TB Chris Anderson contributed 56y punt RET in between to position sub TB Derrick Lassic for short TD run. Frosh QB Jay Barker (2-3/26y) threw sparingly but directed all 3 TD drives in 4th Q in his 1st opportunity under pressure. It seemed Bama had locked it up with 18-pt bulge with

6:21 left. Tennessee TB Aaron Hayden (22/85y, 2 TDs) scored twice in 4th Q TDs, his 2nd score coming after profitable on-side KO and bringing Vols to within 24-19 with 2:25 to play. Then sure-handed Stacy lost FUM, but Crimson Tide DE John Copeland hauled down scrambling Vols QB Andy Kelly (19-32/229y, INT) as clock ticked to end.

VANDERBILT 27 Georgia 25: With 4:34 left in 3rd Q, Commodores (2-5) RB Corey Harris scooped up FUM as QB Marcus Wilson was sacked by 3 Georgia (5-2) tacklers and sprinted 51y for Vanderbilt's 3rd straight score to overcome 17-13 deficit. Wilson padded Vandy's lead to 27-17 with 4th Q TD run, but QB Greg Talley came off Bulldogs bench to pass for TD and 2-pt conv. UGa frosh K Kenon Parkman twice missed FG tries in last 2 mins that could have won game.

IOWA 24 Illinois 21: Fighting Illini (4-2) tumbled from Big 10 lead as Iowa (5-1) QB Matt Rodgers powered across GL on sneak with 2:39 left. It came on heels of controversial call. On prior play, Rodgers had run QB-draw to within inches of GL, but lost handle trying to stretch to score. Illinois S Mike Hopkins recovered loose ball in EZ, but it was ruled that Rodgers' knee had been down. Illini QB Jason Verduzco (20-27/240y, TD) hit 12 passes in row to start, and his 2nd Q TD was arched to WR John Wright (4/48y, TD) in EZ just as little QB was chopped down. Rodgers (24-32/281y, 2 TDs) had taken Hawkeyes to within 21-17 at H with 5y TD pass to RB Mike Saunders. Iowa's ferocious D dealt Verduzco -33y in sacks, prompting 6 Illinois punts in 2nd H. Rodgers faced his own difficulty in 3rd Q as he was picked off twice by Illini DB Filmel Johnson, and he also coughed up FUM. Illinois' frustration could be noted on series just before Hawkeyes' winning surge: With less than 10 mins left and milking 21-17 lead, Verduzco hit TE Ken Dilger with 9y pass on 1st down, but 2 runs went nowhere, and Illinois was forced to punt.

NEBRASKA 38 Kansas State 31: Cornhuskers QB Keithen McCant both passed and ran for 100y, and IB Derek Brown rushed 28/145y, 3 TDs. But it took GLS in final min for Nebraska (5-1) to escape with its 23rd Homecoming win in row. Dangerous Kansas State (4-2)—last to spoil Lincoln Homecoming in 1968 but saddled with 0-22 against Nebraska ever since—gained most y (452) it ever had against Huskers. Cats relished passing of QB Paul Watson (26-46/340y, 2 TDs) and receiving of WR Michael Smith (10/172y, 2 TDs). Watson had to endure 8 sacks, but put Wildcats on board at 7-0 in 1st Q, threw 2nd Q TD pass, and ran 3y keeper for score late in 3rd Q that provided 31-24 lead. Brown scored twice at end of 80 and 60y drives in last 7 mins.

Colorado 34 OKLAHOMA 17: Option wizard QB Darian Hagan turned to air for 3 TD passes in 3-min span of 1st Q as Colorado (4-2) claimed its 17th straight Big 8 victim. Hagan (10-15/151y, 3 TDs) created 2 brilliant and dominant Bison TD drives of 99y each. Runs of TB Mike Gaddis (17/120y, TD) helped pull no. 12 Sooners (4-2) to within 20-17 in 2nd Q, but Buffaloes D blanked Oklahoma rest of way. Colorado players wore "I accept the torch" T-shirts all weekend after having been visited by members of 1990 national championship team on Thursday. "They came in," said coach Bill McCartney, "and challenged our kids to keep the torch (of championship desire) lit." Against nation's 2nd-best statistical D, Buffs rolled to 219y on ground, 371y total O.

Texas A&M 34 BAYLOR 12: Savage Aggies (4-1) D sacked Baylor (5-2) QB J.J. Joe 6 times and forced him into INT and FUM. Ever-resourceful Texas QB Bucky Richardson (9-15/182y) ran for 2 TDs and caught throw-back 38y pass from WR Brian Mitchell to set up another score as A&M rolled to 34-0 lead in 3rd Q. Bears got 2 consolation TD runs in 4th Q from its bench players.

Notre Dame 28 AIR FORCE 15: No. 5 Fighting Irish (6-1) showed their mettle by scoring TDs on 4 of their 1st 5 possessions, and although, they gave up 354y rushing to Air Force's Wishbone attack, Notre Dame's GL wasn't crossed until 4th Q when result was well cinched at 28-9. Falcons (6-2) couldn't solve Irish D in close and had to accept K Joe Wood's 2 FGs, so they trailed only 7-6 as 2nd Q entered last 3 mins. Notre Dame QB Rick Mirer (6-12/151y, 2 TDs) then sprung 83y TD surprise with connection to WR Tony Smith. After Falcons QB Rob Perez lost FUM, Notre Dame FB Jerome Bettis (10/52y, 2 TDs) scored 2nd of his 3 TDs. Irish led 21-6 until Wood bombed career-high 58y FG through on 1st H's last play. Trying to turn momentum, Air Force tried on-side KO to start 2nd H, but its lack of success allowed Notre Dame to negotiate only 55y to Bettis' next TD and 28-9 lead. Falcons FB Jason Jones rushed 37/171y, TD, and Perez gained 26/125y rushing.

Washington 24 CALIFORNIA 17: Surprising Bears (5-1) tied it 17-17 on TB Lindsey Chapman's 68y TD dash with 1 sec to go in 3rd Q. But on-rolling Huskies (6-0) charged back on TB Beno Bryant's 65y TD run just 1:05 later. This punch-counterpunch sequence mirrored 1st Q when Cal took its only lead at 7-0 on 59y pass connection from QB Mike Pawlawski (18-41/215y, TD, 2 INTs) to WR Sean Dawkins. Washington gained 441y O, even though QB Billy Joe Hobert (15-34/189y, INT) said, "Our offense stunk it up." Huskies sub TB Jay Barry (19/143y) scored 9y TD that broke 2nd Q 10-10 tie. Despite Chapman's long run, Washington D maintained rush D avg of less than 2y per play. Even as California's last-play pass by QB Mike Pawlawski fell harmlessly near Huskies EZ, full-house crowd stood and cheered their Golden Bears as they walked off. Realistic Bears coach Bruce Snyder said, "It's difficult to get anything positive out of a loss....(but) I think our fans recognize these guys play very, very hard."

1	Florida State (53)	1465	14	Ohio State	687
2	Miami (Fla.) (4)	1406	15	Colorado	587
3	Washington (2)	1370	16	Tennessee	554
4	Michigan	1289	17	Illinois	463
5	Notre Dame	1228	18	Clemson	425
6	Florida	1193	19	Syracuse	370
7	Nebraska	1027	20	Oklahoma	349
8	Iowa	964	21	Auburn	225
9	Alabama	944	22	Fresno State	212
10	North Carolina State	933	23	Baylor	188
11	Penn State	902	24	East Carolina	164
12	California	804	25	Pittsburgh	126
13	Texas A&M	709			

October 26, 1991

(Fri) Michigan 52 MINNESOTA 6: Little Brown Jug game was moved to Friday night to accommodate Braves-Twins World Series game at Humphrey Metrodome on Saturday. It was Michigan (6-1) WR Desmond Howard's night to shine. Clobbered by early tackle, Howard (6/154y) came back to beat double coverage for 65y TD catch and added 41y score to break Big 10 TD catch record of Michigan's Anthony Carter. Wolverines QB Elvis Grbac (15-21/242y) also had TD pass to WR Yale VanDyne to set school career TD passing mark with 49. After score reached 35-0 in 3rd Q, Minnesota (5-2) made 73y TD march to QB Marquel Fleetwood's 12y pass to WR Keswic Joiner.

CLEMSON 29 North Carolina State 19: Clemson Tigers (4-1-1) donned purple jerseys for 1st time since 1939, and their passion resulted in scores on 7 straight series to thwart hopeful Wolfpack (6-1). Clemson frosh K Nelson Welch kicked school-record 5 FGs, and QB DeChane Cameron ran 11/83y and passed 11-17/122y in creating 23-7 H lead. NC State QB Geoff Bender (18-43/281y, TD) passed and ran for TDs, but it was too-little-too-late. Tigers' stout D permitted only 10y rushing. NC State coach Dick Sheridan said, "For the first time this year we really got kicked around on defense."

EAST CAROLINA 24 Pittsburgh 23: Early in 4th Q, Pittsburgh (5-3) took its 1st lead over Pirates (6-1) at 20-16 on RB Jermaine Williams' 1y TD run. Behind passing of QB Alex Van Pelt (29-43/369y), Pitt next reached Carolina 13YL. But on 3rd-and-1, LB Robert Jones nailed Panthers RB Tim Colicchio for loss. Panthers' FG followed, but ECU had stayed within reach at 23-16 with 3:22 left. QB Jeff Blake (21-31/247y, TD, INT) stirringly rallied Pirates on 80y trip, hitting pair of 3rd down passes, scoring on 2y option run, and adding 2-pt rollout for win.

Mississippi State 24 AUBURN 17: Homecoming weekend at Auburn (4-3), already soured because of allegations of player payments from Pat Dye's staff, turned bitter when Mississippi State (5-3) RB Kenny Roberts made his only carry of day count in 4th Q. Bulldogs had led 10-0 at H, primarily on FB Michael Davis' 15y TD run after WR Tony James raced 22y on punt RET. Tigers rallied with 2 TDs in 4th Q to tie it 17-17. They went 54y to 5y bootleg TD run by QB Stan White (14-34/130y, 3 INTs) and pulled to within 17-11 on TB Joe Frazier's 2-pt run. Auburn CB Mike Pina made FUM REC at State 11YL and FB Reid McMilion scored from 1YL with 4:09 left, but K Jim Von Wyl missed x-pt that could have provided lead. Bulldogs LB Danny Boyd said, "…Auburn gave us a lift by missing the extra point." Roberts burst around Auburn line on option call, which had been tested earlier, for 61y TD with 1:49 left to play and finished Auburn's 9-game win streak over Maroons. Afterward, Auburn coach Dye denied he called for boycott of Montgomery Advertiser, paper that broke former player Eric Ramsey's pay allegations.

Florida State 27 LOUISIANA STATE 16: Hard-hitting Tigers (3-4) knocked 17 Seminoles from game, held 13-0 1st Q lead in heavy rain at raucous Tiger Stadium. FSU DB Terrell Buckley bit on run fake on game's 2nd play, and LSU QB Chad Loup hit WR Todd Kinchen in clear for 63y TD. Florida State (8-0) TB Amp Lee rushed 112y, including 2 TDs, and caught 22y TD from QB Casey Weldon, who later was turned into knee sprain casualty. It took FB William Floyd's short TD run for Seminoles to gain their 1st lead 45 secs into 4th Q at 21-16. Result flew out of reach of Bengals when Noles tallied once more.

NORTHWESTERN 17 Illinois 11: "Some of us seniors talked coach (Francis) Peay into wearing the purple pants," said LB Tom Homco. "He said we looked like grapes, but they fired us up." Northwestern, clad all in purple for 1st time in more than decade, surprised no. 17 Illinois (4-3) for what became 1st win by Wildcats (2-5) over ranked team since 1971. QB Len Williams (10-19/141y) passed through driving rain to set up 1st Q TD by frosh RB Rodney Ray, and emotional D, led by LBs Ed Sutter (20 tackles) and Jason Cunningham and CB Willie Lindsay, stuffed 4 Illini run attempts from inside its 4YL late in 2nd Q. Williams ran for 4y TD to up margin to 14-0 in 3rd Q. Illini QB Jason Verduzco was picked off twice while throwing 14-33/153y. Trailing by 2 TDs, Illinois finally got on scoreboard on 40y FG by K Chris Richardson in 3rd Q and RB Steve Feagin's 2y TD dive in 4th Q. Verduzco pitched 2-pt pass to WR Elbert Turner, but Illini never came close again.

NOTRE DAME 24 Southern California 20: Irish FB Jerome Bettis ran for 2 TDs, including 53y 1st Q sprint. After 2 brilliant, tackle-breaking runs by Bettis, Notre Dame (7-1) QB Rick Mirer (10-19/166yTD, INT) hit 15y TD pass to TB Tony Brooks in 2nd Q, so ND led 14-0 at H. Injury-beset Notre Dame D that started 3 frosh in front-7 allowed 320y in 2nd H, Irish D fought in 3rd Q to hold on 4th down at own 6YL, and later frosh LB Justin Goheen stripped Strother for FUM to end tying threat. Irish WR Lake Dawson made stretch-out catch of 49y throw to set up Bettis' early 4th Q TD. Now trailing 24-14, Trojans got TD run from FB Raoul Spears with 1:50 to play. Then, hotly-disputed onside-KO was recovered by ND TE Irv Smith. It was 9th straight Irish win over USC, prompting coach Lou Holtz to say, "We've been the luckiest team in America against Southern Cal."

1	Florida State (47)	1459	14	Colorado	661
2	Miami (Fla.) (4)	1398	15	Tennessee	603
3	Washington (8)	1383	16	Clemson	547
4	Michigan	1290	17	North Carolina State	463
5	Notre Dame	1222	18	Syracuse	454
6	Florida	1186	19	Oklahoma	416
7	Nebraska	1057	20	East Carolina	383
8	Iowa	983	21	Baylor	309
9	Alabama	962	22	Georgia	230
10	Penn State	931	23	Fresno State	227
11	California	869	24	UCLA	140
12	Texas A&M	814	25	Arkansas	82
13	Ohio State	749			

November 2, 1991

Florida 31 AUBURN 10: Fading Auburn (4-4) lost its 3rd in row at home for 1st time since 1977. Florida (7-1) QB Shane Matthews (20-36/264y, 2 TDs, 2 INTs) ran 10y and threw 11y for TDs in 1st H led by Gators by 17-3. Tigers took 2nd H KO and drove to QB Stan White's 30y TD arrow to WR Herbert Casey. Even with score sliced to 17-10, "we weren't concerned," said Matthews as he soon followed with 28y TD strike to WR Harrison Houston. Gators WR Willie Jackson caught 12/157y, TD.

ALABAMA 13 Mississippi State 7: Heroic DB Stacy Harrison rescued stumbling Alabama (7-1) with his 64y INT TD RET for 7-0 H lead and his late EZ INT. Mississippi State (5-4) QB Sleepy Robinson (11-20/205y, 2 INTs) hit WR Treddis Anderson with tying 4y TD in 3rd Q. After 2 FGs in 4th Q by K Matt Wethington gave Bama 13-7 lead, Bulldogs drove all way to Crimson Tide 1YL, and on 4th down, Robinson threw Harrison's 2nd INT.

Iowa 16 OHIO STATE 9: On Friday, University of Iowa grad student killed 3 professors and classmate before turning gun on himself. Iowa (7-1) wore trimless black helmets as memorial to those slain and used QB Matt Rodgers' scoring run and pass for 13-9 H lead. Ohio State (6-2) had gotten 2y TD run from TB Carlos Snow (14/73y) and 2 pts from LB Jason Simmons, who scored on 85y RET of blocked conv after Rodgers had hit TD pass to TE Alan Cross. Buckeyes failed to score after H and were doubled up at game's end by Iowa in O: 443y to 221y. "The tragedy back in Iowa City…had a big part in us winning," said saddened coach Hayden Fry, who raised his career record against Ohio State to 3-9-1.

COLORADO 19 Nebraska 19: Big 8 deadlock at top between no. 15 Colorado (5-2-1) and no. 9 Nebraska (6-1-1) stayed intact, but Buffs' 18-game conf win streak came to end. With conf title likely to be shared, higher-ranked Huskers took inside track to Orange Bowl. Buffaloes QB Darian Hagan suffered mild concussion in 3rd Q, but returned later in 3rd Q to score his 2nd TD from 4YL for 19-12 edge. Huskers IB Derek Brown 30/96y) tied it on 7y TD run with 6:41 to play. Nebraska K Byron Bennett lined up last-play 41y FG for win, but Colorado iced him with 3 timeouts in minus-8 wind chill factor. Buffs DB Greg Thomas blocked FG as time expired, his 3rd such block of year.

TULSA 13 Southern Mississippi 10: With score at 10-10 and blowing snow coming sideways, Southern Miss (4-5) K Lance Nations slipped with his plant-foot and missed potential winning 35y FG with 12 secs to play. Tulsa (6-2) QB T.J. Rubley then tossed long pass that was batted several times until hauled in by WR Chris Penn for 65y gain. Hurricane K Eric Lange then missed 29y FG into wind, but Eagles were flagged for 12 men on field. With 2nd life, Lange connected on game-winner from 24YL.

CALIFORNIA 52 Southern California 30: California (7-1) TB Russell White rushed for career-high 23/229y, 3 TDs. It surpassed highest-to-date run total against tradition-steeped USC, set by UCLA's Gaston Green (224y) in 1986. WR Sean Dawkins caught 3 TDs as Bears amassed staggering 601y. Sub QB Rob Johnson (6-9/80y, TD) led 2 late Trojans drives for measure of respect.

1	Florida State (47)	1457	14	Colorado	668
2	Miami (Fla.) (4)	1395	15	Clemson	648
3	Washington (8)	1386	16	North Carolina State	550
4	Michigan	1295	17	Syracuse	497
5	Notre Dame	1231	18	Oklahoma	452
6	Florida	1192	19	East Carolina	446
7	Alabama	1033	20	Ohio State	363
8	Iowa	1013	21	Baylor	339
9	California	962	22	UCLA	251
10	Penn State	952	23	Georgia	226
11	Nebraska	864	24	Indiana	109
12	Texas A&M	846	25	Brigham Young	54
13	Tennessee	677			

November 9, 1991

MIAMI 27 West Virginia 3: Clearly, Miami (8-0) and its fans were looking past West Virginia (6-4) to showdown with no. 1 Florida State, 38-10 winners over South Carolina. Hurricanes led 10-3 at H on QB Gino Torretta's TD pass to WR Lamar Thomas, but "felt threatened," according to DE Rusty Medearis. Mountaineers had gotten 35y FG from K Mark Johnson in last 4 secs of 2nd Q as QB Darren Studstill (7-17/82y, 2 INTs) hit passes of 12 and 29y on 50y drive. In 3rd Q, Torretta (23-35/277y, TD, INT) used his less-than-swift legs for 16y to set up K Carlos Huerta's 2nd FG for 13-3 lead, and Torretta sneaked for clinching TD at 27-3 in 4th Q. Canes DB Ryan McNeil made INT at WVU 32YL in 3rd Q to poise WR Kevin Williams' 16y catch and FB Stephen McGuire's 4y TD.

Florida 45 Georgia 13 (Jacksonville): After 59 years as charter member of SEC, Florida (8-1) finally clinched tie for its 1st-ever valid conf title, those of 1984, '85, and '90 having been disallowed by sanctions. Domination started as soon as Gators went 74y with

opening drive, capped by WR Willie Jackson's 1st of 3 TD grabs. QB Shane Matthews passed 22-32/303y, 4 TDs in little more than 3 Qs to help Gators to 512y to 220y O edge. Florida TB Erict Rhett (25/124y, TD) capped 71y drive early in 2nd Q with 13y TD run that provided 14-3 lead. Georgia (6-3), held to 25y rushing, got its only TD when Gators personal foul PEN provided life to 64y drive in 3rd Q. Late in 3rd Q, Bulldogs went 64y in 11 plays to score: QB Eric Zeier (18-35/195y, TD, INT) flipped 5y pass to WR Andre Hastings (5/64y, TD) after PEN on 3rd down incompletion gave Georgia 1st down at 6YL. Georgia lost back-to-back to Florida for 1st time since 1963.

VANDERBILT 17 Kentucky 7: Resurgent Commodores (5-5) won their 4th tilt in row for 1st time since 1984. But, Vandy's dominating assembly of 243y and 13 1st downs in 1st H could reap only 3-0 lead. "I was concerned at halftime," admitted coach Gerry DiNardo. No reason for worry: RB Corey Harris (29/157y) and QB Marcus Wilson (20/107y, 2 TDs rushing) mounted 2nd H charge resulting in Wilson's 5 and 2y TD runs for Vanderbilt. Vandy D sniffed its 1st shutout since 1985, but it was ruined in last min when Kentucky (3-6) sub QB Ryan Hockman (10-21/146y, TD, INT) hit WR Kurt Johnson with 29y TD. Wildcats were limited to 216y total O, and afterward Cats coach Bill Curry tipped his hat: "Vanderbilt's defense was outstanding: They were as good as we were poor."

IOWA 38 Indiana 21: RB Mike Saunders became 5th Hawkeye ever to score 4 TDs, 3 scores coming in 1st Q, to boost Iowa (8-1) to handsome 31-6 H lead. Hawks QB Jim Hartlieb, making his 1st start, passed 11-18/170y, 2 TDs. His Indiana (5-3-1) counterpart, Trent Green, threw for 210y and 2 TDs but was picked off 4 times. Green was sacked 6 times, 2 posted by DE Leroy Smith, which gave him Iowa career record with 19. Iowa closed 1st H with WR Danan Hughes' 26y TD catch and added Saunders' 4th score in 3rd Q. Indiana TB Vaughn Dunbar (25/137y, TD), nation's leading rusher, was well cuffed in early going (6/15y) but broke out in 2nd H and scored 4th Q TD of 11y.

Tennessee 35 NOTRE DAME 34: Capitalizing on 3 TOs by Volunteers, Notre Dame (8-2) built 31-7 lead in 2nd Q. Just as K Craig Hentrich prepared to put polishing touch on runaway Irish win, LB Darryl Hardy blocked his FG, and DB Floyd Miley sparked Tennessee (6-2) with 85y TD RET with 14 secs left in H. Trailing 31-14, Volunteers QB Andy Kelly (24-38/259y, 3 TDs, INT) engineered 3-TD 2nd H miracle as TB Aaron Hayden scored twice. Hayden's 2nd TD and K John Becksvoort's kick provided 35-34 lead with 4:03 to play. ND drove from own 25YL to Tennessee 9YL with :04 showing on clock in hallowed Notre Dame Stadium. Walk-on K Rob Leonard, subbing for injured Hentrich, had his 27y FG blocked by backside of Vols DB Jeremy Lincoln, whose "big butt paid off for us." Coach Lou Holtz called it his "most difficult loss."

Nebraska 59 KANSAS 23: Improved Kansas (5-4) blocked early punt that led to FG. Jayhawks got 50y TD pass to TE Dwayne Chandler and 34y TD scramble from clever QB Chip Hilleary (11-25/210y, TD, INT) to stunningly 17-0 lead in 1st Q and 20-17 at H. Frosh IB Calvin Jones provided Huskers spark, in less than 3 Qs of play, rushing for Nebraska (7-1-1) records of 294y and 6 TDs in relief of IB Derek Brown, who was poked in eye in 2nd Q. Jayhawks' bid for 1st win over Huskers in 23 years was dashed as Jones put it away with 4 TDs. "People will look at this game, see the final score, and think it was a ho-hummer," said coach Tom Osborne. "It wasn't…I was worried."

Kansas State 37 IOWA STATE 7: Ending 30-game road losing streak, Kansas State (5-4) D made big INT and 4th down stop to launch burial of Iowa State (3-5-1). After Cyclones QB Kevin Caldwell (6-9/134y, TD, INT) tied game in 1st Q at 7-7 by throwing 41y TD to WR Lamont Hill, K-State lost FUM on KO. Caldwell pitched sideline pass, but Cats CB Rogerick Green stepped in to INT and return to 41YL. WR Michael Smith (5/38y, 3 TDs) speared 2 TDs in 2nd Q to put Wildcats in front 21-7 at H. In 3rd Q, Iowa State's midfield, 4th down gamble was stuffed by Purple Cats NG Evan Simpson's stop of FB Sundiata Patterson. Smith caught his 3rd TD from QB Paul Watson (20-27/209y, 3 TDs) in 4th Q which gave him Kansas State's single-season record for TD receptions.

BRIGHAM YOUNG 56 Wyoming 31: QB Ty Detmer (20-30/306y, 2 TDs) broke his 54th and 55th NCAA O records: most plays in 3-year-career (1,516) and 1st QB to gain 3000y in each of 3 seasons. Detmer scored 1st 2 TDs for Brigham Young (7-3), providing lead for good at 14-7 in 2nd Q. Wyoming (4-6-1) soph WR Ryan Yarborough was superb, catching 11/205y and TDs of 16, 3, and 72y, on his way to 53 receptions and 13 TDs for season. Canadian-born, Cowboys sub QB Peter Rowe pitched 3 TDs in late-game mop-up duty.

STANFORD 27 Ucla 10: Stanford (6-3) QB Steve Stenstrom earned his 5th win in row as starter as he threw TD passes to WRs Chris Walsh and Jon Pinkney. In 1st Q, FB "Touchdown" Tommy Vardell (24/109y) opened scoring with 2y run for Cards. UCLA (6-3) drew within 14-10 on TB Kevin Williams' 9y run in 3rd Q, but saw 4-game win streak evaporate when Pinkney went 66y to his score. Cardinal D had taken over during its winning streak and continued its fine play against UCLA, holding 5 foes to 76y per-game rushing avg. Bruins QB Tommy Maddox threw 21-38/214y, 3 INTs, but coughed up FUM.

Washington 14 SOUTHERN CALIFORNIA 3: Powerful Huskies (9-0) took 14-0 H lead on TD runs of TB Beno Bryant (26/158y), who blazed to 55 and 7y scores. Washington's snarling D was led by DL Steve Emtman and LBs Dave Hoffmann and Chico Fraley, and it held struggling USC (3-6) to 36/78y rushing. But still, Troy put together some big plays on O against nation's no. 1 D. Trojans went to Huskies 14YL on their 1st series and later to 1YL. What went wrong for USC was K J.J. Dudum's missed 33y FG in 1st Q, which was soon followed by Bryant's 55y dodge of Troy tacklers, and all Southern California could manage was Dudum's 3rd Q FG of 22y. QB Reggie Perry passed 14-29/196y, INT, and completed 46y strike to WR Curtis Conway in 3rd Q. Later in 3rd Q, Trojans' best Q of day, TB Estrus Crayton made 40y mad dash, and WR Johnnie Morton caught 3rd down GL pass that was ruled down inside 1YL. Trailing 14-0 with 7 secs before H, USC went to UW 9YL, and under heavy rush, Perry lost EZ INT to Washington S Shane Pahukoa.

ARIZONA STATE 24 Oregon 21: Up-and-down Arizona State (5-4) went back to basics, and although TO-bug—3 INTs in 1st H by QB Bret Powers—still bit Sun Devils, they ended 3-game skid with 4th Q win. Oregon (3-6) started its 5th different QB in 1991 as Bob Brothers (12-32/93y, TD, 2 INTs) could ignite only his 29y TD pass to TE Jeff Thomason after sub FB Donovan Moore ran 31y. Ducks' other scores came on DB Eric Castle's 2nd INT, which became 30y INT TD RET in 2nd Q for 14-7 lead, and CB Muhammad Oliver's acrobatic 21y RET of blocked punt in 3rd Q which provided 21-21 tie. Oliver's big play came with 4 mins left in 3rd Q as he got hand on punt, somersaulted under ASU P Paul Slabinski, and picked up ball 1-handed. Sun Devils WR Eric Guiliford (9/136y) took pass from QB Powers (14-34/196y, 2 TDs, 3 INTs) and twisted and spun for 39y to set up K Mike Richey's winning 33y FG less than min into 4th Q.

November 16, 1991

SYRACUSE 38 Boston College 16: No. 17 Orangemen (8-2) won their 4th in row as WR Antonio Johnson caught 55y TD pass from QB Marvin Graves for 17-10 lead 25 secs before H and put it away at 31-16 late in 3rd Q with his 63y run with TB David Walker's FUM. Johnson's TD catch notably hurt BC (4-6) because Syracuse went up for good at 17-10, and irritated BC coach Tom Coughlin: "Everyone in the stadium knew what they were going to try to do, and we go ahead and let them do it." BC's 3-game win streak was snapped, but early 10-0 lead came when TB Chuckie Dukes (26/201y) caught 1st Q TD pass from QB Glenn Foley (10-20/122y, TD, 2 INTs). "I never anticipated that we could have a back go for 200 yards against us," said Syracuse coach Paul Pasqualoni, "and we could win by that kind of score." Orange was helped by Walker's career game of 148y rushing and vital 7y TD run at end of 79y drive that opened 2nd H.

PENN STATE 35 Notre Dame 13: Penn State (9-2) QB Tony Sacca (14-20/151y, 2 TDs) threw 7-9 on early TD drives of 73, 73, and 53y as Notre Dame (8-3) was outgained 199y to 3y in 1st Q. Key play came after FB Jerome Bettis brought Fighting Irish within 21-7 with 2nd Q score: QB Rick Mirer (16-37/198y, TD, INT) overthrew FB Rodney Culver on 4th down pass at Penn State 2YL. When Sacca wasn't breaking Chuck Fusina's school single-year pass y record, he was throwing thunderous block to spring WR O.J. McDuffie on 37y reverse run that gave Lions 28-7 lead in 3rd Q.

GAME OF THE YEAR
Miami 17 FLORIDA STATE 16:

Entering game, Miami (9-0) owned remarkable 7 wins in row over top-ranked teams and bagged another in no. 1 Florida State (10-1). "They got touchdowns; we kicked field goals," lamented Seminoles DB Terrell Buckley. Canes FB Stephen McGuire (22/142y) opened with 1st Q TD run, but FSU took 10-7 H edge on 24y TD trip prepared by DE Henry Ostaszewski's FUM REC. Seminoles led 16-7 early in 4th Q as K Gerry Thomas added his 2nd and 3rd FGs after Hurricanes D crafted emergency stops. Miami made several clutch plays in 4th Q: K Carlos Huerta nailed 45y FG after McGuire's 27y burst, and QB Gino Torretta (14-27/145y, 2 INTs) keyed winning 58y TD drive with 21y strike to TE Coleman Bell and 9y toss to WR Horace Copeland on 4th down. Miami frosh FB Larry Jones stormed for 1y TD, and Huerta toed winning pt. FSU QB Casey Weldon (17-26/209y, INT) then sparked 63y march, but Thomas missed 34y FG with 25 secs to go. It was wide right by inches. Afterward, Thomas gamely said new, narrower uprights had no impact: "I started practicing on it last summer." Later, he admitted: "I kept my head down. I followed through. I didn't do my job."

NORTH CAROLINA 21 South Carolina 17: Ferocious pass rush of North Carolina (6-4), fueled by extra LB in 2nd H, spilled Gamecocks (3-5-2) QB Bobby Fuller (24-40/243y, 2 TDs, INT) 7 times/-45y. In 1st H, however, South Carolina pieced together drives that led to Fuller's 2 TD passes. Gamecocks WR Robert Brooks caught 10/97y and both short TD throws that created 7-0 edge in 1st Q and 14-14 tie in 2nd Q. UNC made its H adjustments and limited South Carolina to 4th Q FG and single last moment threat at Tar Heels 41YL that was spoiled by DL Troy Barnett's sack, and failed Hail Mary pass for Brooks. Meanwhile, UNC frosh QB Jason Stanicek (14-24/119y, 2 TDs) threw winning 9y TD pass after TB Natrone Means (20/144y) rambled 44y to 1YL in 3rd Q.

TENNESSEE 36 Mississippi 25: "We live a dangerous life," sighed coach Johnny Majors of his Volunteers (7-2), who built 26-0 lead then let Ole Miss (5-5) back into game in 2nd H. Tennessee D sparked 1st Q advantage as DL Chuck Smith sacked Rebels QB Tommy Luke (7-17/228y, 2 TDs, INT) for safety, and DB Jeremy Lincoln blocked punt for TD. TB James Stewart (38/215y) carried for 2 TDs for 26-pt lead in 3rd Q. Mississippi trimmed it to 36-25 as Luke pitched 2 TDs, and TB Dameion Logan scored from 7YL with 6 mins left. Tennessee dynamically killed clock with 12-play drive.

Mississippi State 28 LOUISIANA STATE 19: Bengal Tigers (4-6) gained 507y but were stopped twice inside 3YL in 2nd H and failed to contain 407y running game of Mississippi State (6-4) that was led by HB Kenny Roberts (22/156y) and QB Sleepy

Robinson (22/78y, 2 TDs). LSU practiced on Bulldogs' 1-back formation, and O-coordinator Watson Brown, previous year's Vanderbilt mastermind of Wishbone attack that devastated Tigers, surprised them again with Wishbone power that ran ball 71 times while Maroons QB Robinson passed only 3-4/64y, TD. Tigers scored 1st on 75y catch in 1st Q by WR Todd Kinchen, who set SEC record with 248y on 9 grabs. Back stormed Bulldogs who scored game's next 4 TDs, 3 on 11 and 16y runs and 11y pass by Robinson. Miss State led 28-7 with little more than 5 mins to go when LSU QB Jesse Daigle (25-44/394y, 3 TDs), in for injured QB Chad Loup, pitched 2 late TDs.

OHIO STATE 20 Indiana 16: Fans bid adieu to sr Buckeyes (8-2): TB Carlos Snow (32/124y, 2 TDs), who had been plagued by major surgery and occasional FUMs in his career, got biggest cheers in pre-game introductions. "This is how I always wanted to go out…as a winner," said Snow, whom at that time had become school's 4th all-time rusher. Hoosiers (5-4-1) answered with TB Vaughn Dunbar (28/125y, and 5/83y receiving), but their workhorse failed to land in EZ as Ohio D bent (356y) but broke only in 1st H. Indiana QB Trent Green (21-37/256y, 2 TDs, INT) had pitched 1st Q TD to TE Rod Coleman for 6-0 lead and, after LB John Miller raced to 13YL in last min of 1st H, Green hit WR Thomas Lewis with 9y TD and 13-7 lead. Bucks scored on opening possession of 3rd Q as Snow slanted left and cut back to prance untouched for 13y TD. Trade of FGs left Indiana with hopeful EZ throw by Green that frosh Ohio State DB Walter Taylor slapped down on game's last play.

PURDUE 27 Michigan State 17: Snapping 6-game losing streak to Michigan State (2-8), Purdue (4-6) used frosh QB Matt Pike (11-22/157y, TD, 2 INTs) to build 24-0 lead in 3rd Q. Pike had fumbled his 1st 3 collegiate snaps in September, but relieved starting QB Eric Hunter after woeful opening series. Michigan State rode spurting runs of TB Tico Duckett (31/126y, TD) to 17 unanswered pts in 2nd H, but Boilermakers K Joe O'Leary salted it away with 27y FG in 4th Q.

Michigan 20 ILLINOIS 0: No. 4 Michigan (9-1) sewed up Rose Bowl spot by blanking erratic Illinois (6-4). Dynamic WR Desmond Howard (7/80y, TD) scored both Wolverine TDs: very short pass from QB Elvis Grbac (16-20/133y, INT) after Illini lost FUM at their 6YL in 2nd Q and on 15y run in 4th Q. Outrushed 332y to 49y, Illini rode QB Jason Verduzco's 22-37/202y passing, but his only INT, when he tried to force throw to WR Elbert Turner, halted team's best scoring chance. Michigan LB Marcus Walker picked it off in EZ early in 4th Q. Verduzco also had TD pass to WR John Wright called back in 3rd Q because of holding PEN. Michigan sported pair of 100y rushers: TBs Ricky Powers (26/152y) and Jesse Johnson (21/106y).

COLORADO 30 Kansas 24: Plucky Jayhawks (5-5) worked for 10-3 2nd Q lead on 39y FG by Dan Eichloff and 3y TD run by TB Tony Sands (25/104y, TD). But, Colorado (7-2-1) TB Lamont Warren (20/94y) fired surprise 48y TD to WR Charles Johnson to tie it at H. Kansas QB Chip Hilleary (13-23/199y, 2 INTs, INT) flipped 2 TD passes in 3rd Q for 24-10 lead. Hilleary's 2nd score, 22y throw to WR Kenny Drayton, came after Kansas KO team recovered FUM, and Drayton delivered sensational EZ catch. Jayhawks special teams recovered another FUM at Colorado 39YL after Drayton's TD, and, while TD at this moment might have served as 3rd Q knockout punch, Buffaloes D held. Sub QB Vance Joseph, in for starting sr QB Darian Hagan who left his last home game early with ankle injury, rallied Buffs with 3 late TDs, including 20y TD pass to WR Michael Westbrook. Trailing 24-23, CU went 80y through snowstorm to win.

TEXAS A&M 13 Arkansas 3: Writer David McNabb suggested in *Dallas Morning News* that these teams were so conservative that they could have played in "winged-tipped shoes, serge blue suits and white shirts." Aggies (8-1) clinched at least tie for SWC crown as QB Bucky Richardson (19/83y, TD rushing) scored game's only TD in 3rd Q by slamming through 3 Arkansas (5-5) defenders. For their part, Razorbacks ran out of Wishbone, gained only 121y, and passed only 3 times without success. Meanwhile, Richardson (6-13/128y, INT) failed on all his passes in 6-3 1st H in which A&M K Terry Venetoulias hit 41 and 22y FGs to Hogs K Todd Wright's 45y FG. Arkansas' option O came as little surprise to Aggies. Hogs coach Jack Crowe complained, "It's disappointing to close practice and by Tuesday they (Aggies coaches) knew what we were doing on Monday. I don't know how they found out." Texas A&M LB Quentin Coryatt made 20 tackles, many by chasing down option runs with backside pursuit.

SAN DIEGO STATE 52 Brigham Young 52: Teams combined for amazing 1167y passing in NCAA history's highest scoring tie ever played. San Diego State (8-2-1) enjoyed 45-17 lead in 3rd Q behind QB David Lowery (26-39/568y, 5 TDs, INT) who found WR Darnay Scott (8/243y) for 1st H TD passes of 75 and 79y. BYU (7-3-1) QB Ty Detmer (31-54/599y, 6 TDs, 3 INTs) pitched 4 TDs from middle of 3rd Q. Deadlock ended BYU's 7-game win streak, but projected it to within single win of WAC title.

USA Today Coaches Poll November 18

1	Miami (Fla.) (44)	1459	14	Colorado	656
2	Washington (15)	1426	15	East Carolina	593
3	Michigan	1317	16	Oklahoma	568
4	Florida State	1292	17	Syracuse	540
5	Florida	1254	18	Ohio State	504
6	California	1087	19	Notre Dame	435
7	Penn State	1071	20	Virginia	310
8	Iowa	1039	21	Stanford	223
9	Alabama	1030	22	North Carolina State	215
10	Texas A&M	930	23	Fresno State	129
11	Nebraska	887	24	Brigham Young	109
12	Tennessee	850	25	UCLA	102
13	Clemson	750			

November 23, 1991

Miami 19 BOSTON COLLEGE 14: On 7th anniversary of Doug Flutie's famous "Hail Mary" winning pass over Hurricanes, no. 1 Miami (10-0) this time survived late EZ bomb to beat Boston College (4-7). Clock ticked down and with Flutie shouting encouragement from sideline, QB Glenn Foley lofted desperate pass that fell harmlessly in EZ. Leading 16-7 on TE Coleman Bell's 2y TD catch and FB Martin Patton's 3y TD run, Canes turned to QB Gino Torretta's passing (23-42/251y, TD) after loss of their top runner, FB Stephen McGuire, to 1st Q knee injury. Clutch Miami D stopped BC on 4th down plays at its 37 and 46YLs in 2nd H. Eagles' Foley (21-36/241y, 2 TDs, INT) trimmed it to 16-14 in 3rd Q with 20y TD pass to WR Clarence Cannon, who made diving corner grab.

VIRGINIA 38 Virginia Tech 0: Impeccable passing record of Virginia (8-2-1) QB Matt Blundin was extended. By completing 13-23/222y, 3 TDs, Blundin reached 231 straight attempts without INT, breaking Illinois' Jack Trudeau's season and career marks. Blundin's TD passes in 1st H to WR Larry Holmes and TE Aaron Mundy set career and season TD records respectively. TB Jerrod Washington streaked 90y with 2nd H KO to advance score to 24-0. On way to 4th loss in last 5 match-ups with Cavaliers, Virginia Tech (5-6) resorted to several unsuccessful trick plays. Hokies' O registered 308y despite superb effort by Cavs DE Chris Slade, who made 5 sacks, 2 pass knockdowns, and FUM REC.

Clemson 41 SOUTH CAROLINA 24: With both its lines playing superbly, Clemson (8-1-1) powered for 299y rushing while permitting South Carolina (3-6-2) only 15y on 19 run attempts. Telling events of 1st Q rang true: Gamecocks drove to Tigers 15YL on opening series, but short pass by QB Bobby Fuller (21-39/254y, TD, 2 INTs) was picked off by DB Tyrone Mouzon. When Carolina roughed P on 4th down at Clemson 16YL, Tigers were on their way to 84y TD drive capped by mammoth FB Rudy Harris' 1st of 2 TDs. But, South Carolina hung tough, trailing only 17-10 at H as Fuller connected with WR Robert Brooks (7/97y, TD) for 16y TD. On 1st snap of 2nd H, Clemson WR Terry Smith spun away from tackle after short catch and rambled 63y to set up K Nelson Welch's 22y FG. Tigers then went 81y to TB Rodney Blunt's acrobatic 16y sprint-and-launch TD and followed with 69y trip to Harris' 2nd TD. Suddenly, it was 34-10 for Tigers at end of 3rd Q. Key to Clemson was QB DeChane Cameron, who rolled up 322y total O, including 12-14/206y, INT passing and 31y TD run.

MISSISSIPPI STATE 24 Mississippi 9: For 1st time in 10 years, Mississippi State (7-4), magically revived under coach Jackie Sherrill, was bound for bowl game. "I really didn't know what it meant to win this game until the way everyone reacted when it was over," gushed Sherrill afterward. Bulldogs QB Sleepy Robinson (6-8/137y, TD, INT) passed 24y to WR Willie Harris for 1st Q TD and ran 4y in 3rd Q to build 21-0 lead. Mississippi (5-6) lost QB Tommy Luke with concussion in opening series and lost its 5th game in row. Rebels run game was massacred by relentless State D: Ole Miss rushed 29/33y and totaled only 160y O.

MICHIGAN 31 Ohio State 3: With new, rumor-squelching contract extension in his pocket, Ohio State (8-3) coach John Cooper went out and did what he usually did. His Buckeyes lost for 4th straight time to bitter rival Michigan (10-1). It was Ohio State's worst spanking by Michigan since 58-6 defeat in 1946. Successful fake FG provided 1st down at Ohio 3YL and allowed Wolverines FB Burnie Leggette's 1y TD run for 7-0 1st Q edge. Buckeyes K Tim Williams countered on 50y FG early in 2nd Q. But UM scored 10 pts off TOs before H: DB Lance Dottin returned INT 18y to 12YL and LB Brian Townsend (10 tackles) forced FUM by Bucks TB Carlos Snow (24/54y). Soon, Michigan WR Desmond Howard took punt near his left sideline, split 2 tacklers at 10YL, and burst 93y for school record RET. Howard, who accounted for 223y, struck Heisman pose before his happy teammates engulfed him in EZ to celebrate his 23rd TD of year. Result was sealed by 24-3 H score, and Michigan's mammoth D completed more than 22 Qs without allowing rushing TD.

INDIANA 24 Purdue 22: Indiana (6-4-1) was headed to Copper Bowl and it rolled up 18-pt H edge. Hoosiers QB Trent Green (18-33/258y, 2 TDs, 3 INTs) followed 13y TD run by TB Vaughn Dunbar (29/153y, TD) with scoring passes of 34y to WR Thomas Lewis and 13y to WR Eddie Thomas. So, Indiana's 21-pt 2nd Q meant 24-6 H lead. Purdue (4-7) fashioned comeback on K Joe O'Leary's 22y FG and 2 TD throws by QB Eric Hunter (9-12/133y, 2 TDs). Victory slipped through hands of Boilermakers when O'Leary missed 35y FG attempt with 24 secs on 4th Q clock.

KANSAS 53 Missouri 29: In 100th meeting of old rivals, Kansas (6-5) completed its 1st winning season in 10 years as stubby sr TB Tony Sands (58/396y, 4 TDs) broke NCAA records for rush y and attempts in single game. Missouri (3-7-1) faced its season-long injury jinx—only 7 players started all 11 games—as soph QB Phil Johnson suffered separated shoulder 3 plays into 1st Q. But, Tigers showed some resilience and trailed only 25-22 at H, and 32-29 in 3rd Q as frosh QB Jeff Handy (17-28/245y) launched 22-pt 2nd Q with TD run and later fired 2 TD passes. Sands broke open game with 9y TD run in last min of 3rd Q and, after K Dan Eichloff's squib KO was mishandled, Sands rammed for 7y TD run 4 plays later. Afterward, tearful Sands thanked God, his family, his coaches, and his teammates, saying it was tough to accept that he "might not see some of these guys the rest of my life." Sands did his damage against nation's worst run D.

TEXAS CHRISTIAN 49 Houston 45: Houston (4-6), which lived extravagantly by passing, died by passing, and punting too. Horned Frogs (7-4) finished their 1st winning season since 1984 partly because Cougars failed to launch punts on 3 occasions—bobbled or high snap—that led to short TCU TD drives of 2, 31, and 16y. Frogs led 14-0 in 1st Q, but Houston tallied next 4 TDs, 3 on passes by QB David Klingler (30-62/429y, 4 TDs, INT), so Cougars led 35-21 at H. Purple Frogs TE Kelly Blackwell (11/124y, 2 TDs) surpassed BYU's Gordon Hudson for NCAA career receptions for TEs with 181. Blackwell, who scored game's opening TD, also took shovel pass for 8y TD from holder Mike Noack on fake FG that tied it 35-35 with min left in 3rd Q. QB Matt Vogler (20-39/238y, 3 TDs, 2 INTs) pitched 15y TD to WR Stephen Shipley, who battled Houston DBs John Brown and Lorenzo Dickson for winning pass with 66 secs left.

STANFORD 38 California 21: Stanford (8-3) FB Tommy Vardell pounded mostly behind T Bob Whitfield for 39/182y and scored 3 TDs to upset California (9-2). Bears trapped themselves with 11/140y in PENs, and oft-reliable K Doug Brien missed 3 mid-range FGs. Cal QB Mike Pawlawski (21-35/312y, 3 TDs, INT) threw 3 TD passes, and WR Sean Dawkins caught 2 TDs, his 1st going for 66y to tie it at 7-7 in 2nd Q. When Pawlawski connected on his 3rd TD it brought Bears to within 17-14 at end of 3rd Q. Cardinal scored thrice in 4th Q as Vardell smacked for 1 and 13y TDs and TE Ryan Wetnight caught 6y score from QB Steve Stenstrom (21-35/213y, 2 TDs, 2 INTs).

Oregon State 14 OREGON 3: Oregon State (1-10) joyously broke nation's longest losing streak at 15 as it won in Eugene for 1st time since 1973. Ducks (3-8) went up 3-0 as K Gregg McCallum punched 37y FG late in 1st Q. Beavers went ahead 7-3 when QB Ian Shields romped 6y for TD at end of 64y voyage near end of 2nd Q. Frosh RB Chad Paulson (21/149y) became Beavers' 1st back in 2 years to rush for more than 100y and he tossed surprise 20y TD pass to WR Maurice Wilson with 10:32 left.

WASHINGTON 56 Washington State 21: Apple Cup saw its highest pt total since rivalry began in 1900. Washington (11-0) QB Billy Joe Hobert (16-26/236y, INT) pitched 3 TDs, but big Huskies play came when DB Walter Bailey added to 12-7 2nd Q lead with 37y INT TD RET. Washington State (4-7) QB Drew Bledsoe (18-35/295y, 2 INTs) fired 3 TDs attempting to rally Cougars from 6-0, 35-7, and 42-14 holes.

USA Today Coaches Poll November 25

1	Miami (Fla.) (32)	1442	14	Colorado	640
2	Washington (27)	1439	15	East Carolina	622
3	Michigan	1323	16	Oklahoma	583
4	Florida State	1295	17	Syracuse	563
5	Florida	1234	18	Notre Dame	468
6	Penn State	1108	19	Virginia	400
7	Iowa	1101	20	Stanford	384
8	Alabama	1069	21	North Carolina State	262
9	Texas A&M	1004	22	UCLA	158
10	Nebraska	958	23	Ohio State	148
11	Tennessee	892	24	Brigham Young	137
12	Clemson	802	25	Fresno State	97
13	California	666			

November 28-30, 1991

(Th'g) Penn State 32 PITTSBURGH 20: Unbelievably long at nearly 4+ hours, in-state rivalry saw 53 passes fall incomplete or be picked off. Penn State (10-2) jumped to 14-0 lead in 1st Q on TD pass by QB Tony Sacca (11-27/162y) and 1st of 2 TD runs by TB Richie Anderson (27/162y). Trailing 23-7 at H, Pitt (6-5) narrowed it to 23-14 and 26-20 on 2nd H TD passes by QB Alex Van Pelt (27-64/324y, 2 TDs, 5 INTs). Nittany Lions LB Reggie Givens' big INT halted Panthers and sent coach Joe Paterno to 239th win, ahead of Woody Hayes into 4th place on all-time major school coaches' win list.

(Th'g) TEXAS A&M 31 Texas 14: Aggies (10-1) had outscored foes 262-37 in 1st H. This time it was only 10-7 H bulge for Texas A&M thanks to fury of LB Marcus Buckley, who made 19y INT TD RET, 2 sacks, and FUM REC. Still, Texas (5-6) held firm, stayed within 17-7 until last 6 mins of 3rd Q. A&M DB Kevin Smith took punt, faked right, and darted 73y to score. Longhorns DB Grady Cavness' INT led to RB Roderick Walker's 2nd TD run which vainly trimmed Aggies' lead to 24-14 with 8:44 to go.

(Fri) NEBRASKA 19 Oklahoma 14: When chips were down, Nebraska (9-1-1) earned Orange Bowl trip by pounding out 159y rushing in 2nd H against nation's 5th best D. Oklahoma (8-3) enjoyed 14-3 H lead on short TD runs by QB Cale Gundy (5-14/40y) and TB Mike Gaddis (22/63y). Huskers moved within 14-13 in 4th Q as TE Johnny Mitchell (7/137y) caught 28y pass in double coverage to set up K Byron Bennett's 33y FG. Nebraska pounded 80y to win on frosh IB Calvin Jones' 15y TD with 2:57 to go.

MIAMI 39 San Diego State 12: Miami (11-0) dropped its scoring slump with QB Gino Torretta's 66, 30, 42, and 69y TD passes. Also, Miami DB Darryl Williams leapt high to snare INT and sped 27y for TD that built 10-0 lead in 1st Q. San Diego State (8-3-1) hung in at 17-7 deficit near end of 1st H because they fashioned 2 conversions of 4th downs on 64y drive in 2nd Q. Climatic play came on 24y pass from struggling QB David Lowery (22-53/213y, TD, 4 INTs) to WR Merton Harris with 57 secs left in H. But, Miami came right back with 42y TD arrow from Torretta (23-44/485y, 4 TDs) to WR Kevin Williams. SDSU TB Marshall Faulk (27/154y) never came close to scoring but his late-game surge made him 1st frosh ever to win NCAA season rushing title.

ALABAMA 13 Auburn 6 (Birmingham): While Alabama (10-1) K Matt Wethington and Auburn (5-6) K Jim Von Wyl traded 2 FGs each, versatile Tide frosh WR-QB David Palmer lay in waiting. Palmer caught 2nd Q pass for 47y, rushed 4/39y, and his only play at QB resulted in 10y TD run as he dodged 3 tacklers. QB Jay Barker hit FB Kevin Turner with 68y table-setter for Palmer's TD. Fading Tigers lost 4th of last 5 games and were doomed to their 1st losing season since 1981.

FLORIDA 14 Florida State 9: In just 2 weeks, Florida State (10-2) went from no. 1 in nation to 3rd-best in Sunshine State as Gators (10-1) won their 8th game in row. After K Gerry Thomas' short 2nd Q FG gave FSU 3-0 lead, Florida TB Erict Rhett (24/109y) scored on 3y run for 7-3 H lead. Gators QB Shane Matthews (13-30/208y, TD, 3 INTs) beat heavy pressure to find WR Harrison Houston streaking deep past LB Reggie Freeman for vital 72y TD in 3rd Q. Gaining only 37y rushing and failing to score twice from inside Gators 5YL, FSU finally dented EZ with QB Casey Weldon's late TD pass.

Georgia 18 GEORGIA TECH 15: Allowing just 100y rushing per game, Georgia Tech (7-5) D was riddled for 242y. Georgia (8-3) TB Garrison Hearst ran 21/175y, rocketing for 7-5 lead in 1st Q and dashing 30y to set up FG. Yellow Jackets QB Shawn Jones (11-26/87y) skipped to 4y TD run to tie it for Georgia Tech at 15-15 in 3rd Q. When K Kenon Parkman booted 34y FG in 3rd Q, Bulldogs took their final lead at 18-15 on way to ending Georgia Tech's 17-game home win streak.

USA Today Coaches Poll December 2

1	Miami (Fla.) (31)	1443	14	East Carolina	648
1	Washington (28)	1443	15	California	624
3	Michigan	1335	16	Syracuse	600
4	Florida State	1315	17	Stanford	468
5	Iowa	1138	18	Notre Dame	453
6	Penn State	1128	19	Virginia	403
7	Florida State	1102	20	Oklahoma	339
8	Alabama	1063	21	North Carolina State	266
9	Texas A&M	1049	22	UCLA	201
10	Nebraska	984	23	Ohio State	175
11	Tennessee	915	24	Brigham Young	139
12	Clemson	803	25	Georgia	114
13	Colorado	664			

December 7, 1991

Navy 24 Army 3 (Philadelphia): On 50th anniversary of Japanese attack on Naval Air Station at Pearl Harbor in Hawaii, winless but inspired Navy (1-10) rolled over Army (4-7). Alternating between TB and QB, Jason Van Matre sparked 76y Middies TD drive in 2nd Q that trumped K Patman Malcom's early 39y FG for Black Knights. After Cadets had to punt from own GL, resultant field position allowed Navy sub TB Billy James to blast over from 5YL for 14-3 H lead. Van Matre put game away in 4th Q with his only pass attempt: 12y TD to TE Kevin Hickman. Army QB Myreon Williams rushed 22/106y, but passed only 4-13/57y, INT.

1991 Conference Standings

Big East (a)

Miami	Poll: 1
Syracuse	Poll:16
Pittsburgh	
Rutgers	
West Virginia	
Virginia Tech	
Boston College	
Temple	

Atlantic Coast

Clemson	6-0-1
North Carolina State	5-2
Georgia Tech	5-2
Virginia	4-2-1
North Carolina	3-4
Maryland	2-5
Duke	1-6
Wake Forest	1-6

(a) Big East champion was determined by highest Coaches Poll ranking because of limited number of games that could be scheduled in 1991.

Southeastern

Florida	7-0
Alabama	6-1
Tennessee	5-2
Georgia	4-3
Mississippi State	4-3
Louisiana State	3-4
Vanderbilt	3-4
Auburn	2-5
Mississippi	1-6
Kentucky	0-7

Big Ten

Michigan	8-0
Iowa	7-1
Ohio State	5-3
Indiana	5-3
Illinois	4-4
Purdue	3-5
Michigan State	3-5
Wisconsin	2-6
Northwestern	2-6
Minnesota	1-7

Mid-American

Bowling Green	8-0
Central Michigan	3-1-4
Miami (Ohio)	4-3-1
Toledo	4-3-1
Ball State	4-4
Western Michigan	4-4
Eastern Michigan	3-4-1
Ohio	1-6-1
Kent	1-7

Big Eight

Nebraska	6-0-1
Colorado	6-0-1
Oklahoma	5-2
Kansas State	4-3
Kansas	3-4
Iowa State	1-5-1
Missouri	1-6
Oklahoma State	0-6-1

Southwest

Texas A&M	8-0
Baylor	5-3
Arkansas	5-3
Texas Tech	5-3
Texas Christian	4-4
Texas	4-4
Houston	3-5
Rice	2-6
Southern Methodist	0-8

Western Athletic

Brigham Young	7-0-1
San Diego State	6-1-1
Air Force	6-2
Utah	4-4
Hawaii	5-3
Wyoming	2-5-1
Texas-El Paso	2-5-1
Colorado State	2-6
New Mexico	2-6

Pacific-10

Washington	8-0
California	6-2
Stanford	6-2
UCLA	6-2
Arizona State	4-4
Arizona	3-5
Washington State	3-5
Southern California	2-6
Oregon	1-7
Oregon State	1-7

1991 Bowl Games

Aloha Bowl (Dec. 25): Georgia Tech 18 Stanford 17

In odd sense, Aloha Bowl took on NFL flavor as it was last college game before each coach headed to pro football: Georgia Tech's Bobby Ross to San Diego Chargers and

Stanford's Dennis Green to Minnesota Vikings. Valuable Cardinal (8-4) FB Tommy Vardell rushed 3/20y and caught 12y pass on opening TD drive. At end of long drive, Georgia Tech (8-5) QB Shawn Jones (14-29/61y, INT) pitched short TD pass in 1st Q. When Vardell (21/104y) tallied his 2nd TD, Stanford enjoyed 17-10 H lead. It looked like it would end that way until Cardinal punted to Tech 8YL with 1:42 to play. DB Willie Clay, who earlier dropped possible TD INT, authored 63y punt RET to Stanford 31YL. Jones scored TD, and TB Jimy Lincoln overcame sore ankles to stumble for 2-pt run.

Blockbuster Bowl (Dec. 28): Alabama 30 Colorado 25

Crimson Tide (11-1) was sparked by frosh sensations QB Jay Barker (12-16/154y, 3 TDs, INT) and WR-QB David Palmer, who was being trumpeted for 1992 Heisman by teammates in post-game glow. MVP Palmer burst through group of tacklers in 1st Q, sprinting 52y on punt TD RET. In middle of 4th Q, Palmer made diving grab of 5y TD pass for 30-19 lead. Colorado (8-3-1) abandoned its usual run O to showcase sr QB Darian Hagan to NFL. Hagan pitched 11-30/210y, INT and pair of TDs: 62y TD to WR Michael Westbrook and 13y TD to WR Charles Johnson. Alabama threw Buffs runners for 30/-11y rushing including WR Rico Smith's 33y loss on disastrous reverse.

Independence Bowl (Dec. 29): Georgia 24 Arkansas 15

Arkansas (6-6) previewed its 1992 venture into SEC play. Georgia (9-3) frosh QB Eric Zeier (18-28/228y) sparked 17-0 jump in 1st H by hitting WRs Arthur Marshall and Andre Hastings with 1st Q TD passes. TB E.D. Jackson (28/112y) found EZ on 7y run with 35 secs left in H to draw Razorbacks to within 17-7, but any comeback hopes were dashed by Marshall's 51y RET of 2nd H KO. After INT of Hogs QB Wade Hill, Hastings ran 53y reverse TD. Although Arkansas made 1st down at Bulldogs 3YL late in 3rd Q, it failed to score until Jackson's TD run and 2-pt conv that capped 81y drive with 1:19 to go.

Liberty Bowl (Dec. 29): Air Force 38 Mississippi State 15

Mississippi State coach Jackie Sherrill admitted afterward that "they (Air Force) played their style of football, and we just did not play ours." Falcons (10-3) played ball control, enjoyed 15-min possession advantage. After TD runs by Falcons FB Jason Jones and QB Rob Perez (26/114y rushing), DB Shanon Yates picked off option pitchout, dashing to 35y TD and 21-0 lead in 2nd Q. Bulldogs (7-5) retaliated with QB Sleepy Robinson's 4y TD pass at end of 76y drive. Air Force held ball for 13 min of 3rd Q, got K Joe Wood's 20y FG and added 2 4th Q TDs on 31y reverse and EZ FUM REC.

Gator Bowl (Dec. 29): Oklahoma 48 Virginia 14

Sooners (9-3) QB Cale Gundy came out firing, earning MVP honors with 25-34/329y, 2 TDs, most bowl aerial y to date by any Big 8 passer. It broke his brother Mike's y record with Oklahoma State. Oklahoma TB Mike Gaddis rushed for 104y, scored 3 times as Sooners built 34-7 H margin. Virginia (8-3-1) QB Matt Blundin completed 12-26/142y, 2 TDs, but absorbed his 1st INT of year after setting NCAA-record 224 attempts in season without being picked off. Sooners built 618y to 243y O edge.

Holiday Bowl (Dec. 30): Brigham Young 13 Iowa 13

Iowa (10-1-1) DB Carlos James picked off GL pass that deflected off hands of receiver to ruin collegiate farewell of BYU (8-3-2) QB Ty Detmer, all-time pass y leader to that point in history. Game was misadventure of failed placekicks: each team botched conv kick, and 3 FGs were missed in lowest scoring Holiday Bowl in history. Hawkeyes RB Mike Saunders (19/103y) scored 2 TDs for 13-0 edge in 2nd Q, but Detmer connected for TD passes in 2nd and 4th Qs, latter coming on 4th-and-4 from 29YL. BYU's last 7 possessions carried into Iowa territory, but Hawkeyes yielded only Detmer's 2 TD passes. Iowa closed door in last 16 secs with James' INT.

Freedom Bowl (Dec. 30): Tulsa 28 San Diego State 17

With starting TB Chris Hughley suspended for academic deficiency, Tulsa (10-2) reached to bench for sub TB Ron Jackson, who outshined San Diego State (8-4-1) frosh TB Marshall Faulk (30/157y, TD). Jackson rushed 46/211y and scored Freedom Bowl record 4 TDs. After Faulk opened scoring with 2y TD at end of 86y drive on 1st possession, Aztecs' on-side KO backfired. Jackson soon tallied twice to create 14-14 1st H tie. Hurricane D stiffened in 3rd Q, and Jackson put them ahead 21-14 late in Q. Faulk rushed for 61y of Aztecs' 65y 4th Q drive leading to K Andy Trakas' FG. Trailing 21-17, SDSU lost FUM at own 4YL with 4 mins to go. Hurricane LB Billy Cole recovered to set up clinching TD to pave way to Tulsa's 1st bowl win since 1964.

John Hancock (Sun) Bowl (Dec. 31): UCLA 6 Illinois 3

It took fine D to keep alive 8-game bowl winning streak of UCLA (9-3). Illinois (6-6) D made new coach and D coordinator Lou Tepper proud, allowing only 268y. Bruins (9-3) K Louis Perez opened scoring with 32y FG in 1st Q. Illini DB Mike Hopkins' 3rd Q INT of UCLA QB Tommy Maddox (17-28/176y, INT) set up K Chris Richardson's tying 27y FG. In end, it was UCLA's 3 INTs, blocked punt, and FUM REC that helped deliver field position that finally was converted on Perez's winning 4th Q FG.

Copper Bowl (Dec. 31): Indiana 24 Baylor 0

Choosing to run right at Baylor (8-4) A-A DT Santana Dotson, Indiana (7-4-1) mounted TD drives of 70y in 1st Q, 80y in 2nd Q, 60y in 4th Q. Hoosiers O stars were TB Vaughn Dunbar (28/106y, TD) and QB Trent Green (11-21/165y), who faked well while running for 2 TDs. Hoosiers LB Mark Hagen made 3 tackles for 17y in losses, and counted additional 8 stops near line of scrimmage to help hold Bear runners to 138y, 3.3y avg. Usually discreet coach Grant Teaff blurted, "They kicked our rear ends."

Peach Bowl: East Carolina 37 North Carolina State 34

Cinderella season of East Carolina (11-1) took another unbelievable twist. Pirates rallied in 4th Q for 5th time during season, this time coming back from early 4th Q deficit of 34-17. North Carolina State (9-3), like its ACC brethren, had been reluctant to schedule Pirates, finally accepted that it had to play hard and got hot hand after trailing 17-14 at H. Wolfpack notched 20 straight pts. QB Terry Jordan (15-23/145y, 2 TDs, INT) pitched his 2nd TD pass, RB Greg Manior plunged to TD at end of 71y march, and FB Ledel George threw 52y TD option pass to WR Charles Davenport (6/118y). Wolfpack cozily led 34-17 with 10 mins left. QB Jeff Blake (31-51/378y, 4 TDs, 3 INTs) rallied ECU, scoring from 2YL after hitting 3-6/30y on march and making TD throw after connecting on 8-10/70y on next series. Winning TD drive began with 2:37 to go, and Blake passed 4-5/29y, including winner to TE Luke Fisher (12/144y) with 1:32 on clock.

Hall of Fame Bowl: Syracuse 24 Ohio State 17

Just when 4th Q disaster struck, Syracuse (10-2) chose not to fold its tent, instead scoring game-winning 60y TD. Orange QB Marvin Graves (18-31/309y, 2 TDs, INT) tossed middle screen pass for 50y TD and ran for 3y TD for 14-0 lead in 1st Q. Behind 17-3 late in 3rd Q, Ohio State (8-4) came to life as TB Carlos Snow plunged 2y for TD to pare disadvantage to 17-10. Buckeyes LB Steve Tovar burst through to block P Pat O'Neill's punt, and DB Tito Paul fell on it in EZ to tie it at 17-17. But, just 2 plays later, Graves lofted 60y TD pass to WR Antonio Johnson to clinch victory for Syracuse.

Citrus Bowl: California 37 Clemson 17

Rough game had 3 ejections, including Clemson (9-2-1) DL Brentson Buckner, who helped stop 3rd-and-1 QB sneak at own 27YL in 1st Q. But, Buckner's roughing PEN on play gave new life to California (10-2) drive which led to K Doug Brien's 31y FG and 10-0 lead. Tigers had allowed only 86y on punt RETs all year, but Cal WR Brian Treggs had 108y by end of 1st Q, including 72y TD to extend lead to 17-0. Clemson managed to score on K Nelson Welch's 32y FG and QB DeChane Cameron's 62y TD sprint. But, Tigers trailed 27-10 at H. QB Mike Pawlawski (21-32/230y), whose passes softened up early-game Tigers D, capped scoring with 23y toss to WR Sean Dawkins. Bears TB Russell White (22/103y, TD) became 1st rusher to exceed 100y against vaunted Clemson run D since 1988.

Cotton Bowl: Florida State 10 Texas A&M 2

Florida State (11-2) QB Casey Weldon (14-32/92y, 4 INTs) called it "great win" vs. rampaging Aggies (10-2) D, but "it won't make up for (not) having that (national) championship ring." Texas A&M made costly errors. On their 1st possession, Aggies squeezed TB Greg Hill through line for 39y run, but he lost FUM at FSU 1YL that bounded into EZ for touchback. On next play, LB Quentin Coryatt sacked Weldon for safety and 2-0 A&M lead. Aggies WR Tony Harrison dropped EZ pass to spoil another threat, and PEN took K Terry Venetoulias' 47y FG off board. Weldon scored game's only TD in 1st Q after faking draw, rolling right for 4y after his 20y screen pass to TB Sean Jackson had converted 3rd-and-10. A&M lost 6 FUMs, and QB Bucky Richardson could complete only 6-24/57y, 2 INTs.

Fiesta Bowl: Penn State 42 Tennessee 17

Tennessee (9-3) controlled much of 1st H, coming back from 7-0 shortfall on TB James Stewart's 1st Q TD plunge and WR Cory Fleming's 44y TD reception from QB Andy Kelly (20-40/273y, TD, INT). Volunteers enjoyed final O advantage of 441y to 226y and also doubled Penn State's 1st downs with 25 to 12. Stats were all so misleading. Trailing 17-7 late in 3rd Q, Nittany Lions (11-2) exploded for 4 TDs within span of 3:59. WR O.J. McDuffie's 39y punt RET poised QB Tony Sacca (11-28/150y, 4 TDs) for short TD pass. DL Tyoka Jackson quickly made sack and FUM REC at Vols 13YL to set up TE Kyle Brady's TD grab on next play that earned Penn State lead of 21-17. Lions LB Reggie Givens made INT to set up TB Richie Anderson's 2y TD run and scored himself on 23y FUM RET. Out of nowhere, Nittany Lions suddenly led 35-17 on way to coach Joe Paterno's 14th bowl win.

Rose Bowl: Washington 34 Michigan 14

Mighty D of Washington (12-0) held Michigan (10-2) to practically microscopic 72y rushing, which included TB Tyrone Wheatley's late-game 53y TD spurt, stopped 13 of 15 3rd down plays by Wolverines, and put blanket over Heisman-winning WR Desmond Howard (1/35y receiving, 1/15y rushing, and 60y in RETs). In fact, Howard never touched ball after overthrow eluded him early in 3rd Q. Huskies CBs Walter Bailey and Dana Hall clamped down well on Howard and got help in double- and triple-coverage. Wolverines QB Elvis Grbac (13-26/130y, INT) flipped 9y TD pass to WR Walter Smith for brief 7-7 2nd Q tie, but K Travis Hanson's 2 FGs gave Huskies 13-7 H lead as QB Mark Brunell (7-8/89y, TD) came off bench, as planned, and completed his 1st 6 passes. Starting QB Billy Joe Hobert (18-34/192y, 2 TDs, 2 INTs) was back in 2nd H to hit frosh TE Mark Bruener for 3y TD at end of 80y drive and followed with 2-pt pass for 21-7 lead in 3rd Q. Washington locked it up with 2 TD passes in 1:09 duration of early 4th Q. WR Mario Bailey (6/126y) made diving TD catch from Brunell and mocked Howard by striking Heisman pose. Afterward Howard countered with: "He's invited over to my house to look at the real thing." Washington completed its 1st unblemished season in 76 years and awaited next day's poll results, where it came in as 2nd in AP media poll by mere 4 points and overtook Miami for 1st in coaches' tally.

Orange Bowl: Miami 22 Nebraska 0

When Washington's big margin in Rose Bowl was announced, "it was a footrace for points. We knew we had to get the points," said Canes DL Eric Miller. Miami (12-0) accomplished that, scoring on its 3 opening possessions to begin 1st Q in 13-0 fashion. Rain would cancel elaborate H show for 1st time in Orange Bowl history, and slippery footing stung Cornhuskers (9-2-1) right from start. On Miami's 2nd snap, Nebraska DB Curtis Cotton slipped, and WR Kevin Williams took 36y pass from QB Gino Torretta (19-41/257y, TD, 2 INTs) to set up his own 8y TD reception from Torretta for 7-0 lead. Hurricanes K Carlos Huerta quickly kicked pair of 24y FGs after Torretta's 38y connection with WR Lamar Thomas and after DB Ryan McNeil recovered FUM at Huskers 14YL. Miami D, led by LB trio of Jessie Armstead, Michael Barrow, and

Darrin Smith, held Nebraska to 82y rushing even though Huskers came in as leaders in national rushing (353y/game) and scoring (41 pts/game). IB Calvin Jones gained 15/69y, but QB Keithan McCants was swallowed by Miami's quick front-4, losing 32y. Top rusher for Hurricanes was FB Larry Jones with 30/144y, TD. It was Nebraska's 5th bowl loss in row and its 1st whitewash in any game since way back in 1973, 220 games ago. Huerta's 3rd FG came from 54y out in 3rd Q and helped Miami to its 45th win in row on its home turf.

Sugar Bowl: Notre Dame 39 Florida 28

Wearing green trim (numerals and socks) for 1st time in Lou Holtz's coaching regime, Notre Dame (10-3) got 3 TDs from FB Jerome Bettis in span of 2:44 late in Sugar Bowl to wrap up win. Florida (10-2) cruised to early 13-0 edge as QB Shane Matthews (28-58/370y, TD, 2 INTs) pitched 15y TD pass to WR Willie Jackson on game's 1st series. Ultimately, explosive Gators had to accept FGs after gaining 1st downs at Fighting Irish 9, 13, 15, and 12YLs. Irish's power running spiced 2 long drives to open 2nd H for 10 pts and 17-16 lead. K Arden Czyzewski's 5th FG, from 24YL, gave Gators 22-17 lead with 11:21 to play, but that series had started promisingly with 12YL sack of and lost FUM by Notre Dame QB Rick Mirer (14-19/154y, 2 TDs, INT). ND went up 25-22 on 14-play, 64y drive to Bettis' 3y TD run that ate more than 6 mins to dwindle clock to 4:48 to go. When Florida failed on midfield 4th down gamble, Bettis charged to 49y TD. Matthews countered with 36y TD to WR Harrison Houston, so Florida trailed 32-28, even though Gators failed on 2-pt pass try. Irish TB Rodney Culver fell on Florida's on-side KO attempt, and Bettis rambled 39y for TD to wrap up 16/150y rushing day.

Final AP Poll January 2

1	Miami (32)	1472	13	Notre Dame	848
2	Washington (28)	1468	14	Tennessee	716
3	Penn State	1342	15	Nebraska	666
4	Florida State	1310	16	Oklahoma	629
5	Alabama	1216	17	Georgia	428
6	Michigan	1151	18	Clemson	410
7	Florida	1119	19	UCLA	406
8	California	1039	20	Colorado	383
9	East Carolina	1024	21	Tulsa	348
10	Iowa	883	22	Stanford	262
11	Syracuse	876	23	Brigham Young	182
12	Texas A&M	870	24	North Carolina St.	109
			25	Air Force	87

Final USA Today Coaches Poll January 3

1	Washington (33.5)	1450	14	Oklahoma	694
2	Miami (Fla.) (25.5)	1441	15	Tennessee	617
3	Penn State	1321	16	Nebraska	608
4	Florida State	1292	17	Clemson	450
5	Alabama	1191	18	UCLA	443
6	Michigan	1071	19	Georgia	407
7	California	1027	20	Colorado	366
8	Florida	1020	21	Tulsa	233
9	East Carolina	1003	22	Stanford	216
10	Iowa	944	23	Brigham Young	149
11	Syracuse	891	24	Air Force	165
12	Notre Dame	815	25	North Carolina State	142
13	Texas A&M	799			

1991 Top Performance Formula

1	Washington	1.8618
2	Miami	1.8189
3	Florida	1.6688
4	Florida State	1.6311
5	Michigan	1.6157
6	Penn State	1.6022
7	Alabama	1.6018
8	Texas A&M	1.5658
9	Nebraska	1.5427
10	California	1.5369
11	Notre Dame	1.5046
12	Iowa	1.4961
13	East Carolina	1.494146
14	Syracuse	1.494133
15	Clemson	1.4140
16	Oklahoma	1.4035
17	UCLA	1.3952
18	Brigham Young	1.3861
19	Colorado	1.3628
20	Georgia	1.3448

1991 Top Opponent Records

1	Florida	.6705
2	Florida State	.6288
3	Southern California	.6271
4	South Carolina	.6237
5	Tennessee	.6250
6	Maryland	.6229
7	Oklahoma State	.6217
8	Michigan	.6124
9	Brigham Young	.6076
10	Notre Dame	.6000
11	Boston College	.5983
12	Miami	.5930
13	Nebraska	.5927
14	West Virginia	.5913
15	Arizona	.5862
16	Virginia Tech	.5839
17	Houston	.5826
18	Oregon State	.5776
19	Georgia Tech	.5745
20	Washington	.5726

1991 Out-of-Conference Records

	W-L	Percentage	Bowl W-L
Southeastern	30-11	.7317	2-3
Big East	29-17	.6304	2-0
Pacific-10	19-14	.5758	3-1
Atlantic Coast	16-12-1	.5690	1-3
Big Ten	17-14-2	.5455	1-3-1
Big Eight	15-14-1	.5167	1-2
Southwest	15-15	.5000	0-3
Western Athletic	14-18-2	.4412	1-1-1

1991 Individual Statistical Leaders

RUSHING YARDS	Attempts	Yards	Avg.
Vaughn Dunbar, Indiana	336	1699	5.1
Trevor Cobb, Rice	360	1692	4.7
Ryan Benjamin, Pacific	226	1581	7.0
Tony Sands, Kansas	273	1442	5.3
Billy Smith, Central Michigan	374	1440	3.9
Marshall Faulk, San Diego State	201	1429	7.1
Jason Davis, Louisiana Tech	244	1351	5.5
Chris Hughley, Tulsa	267	1326	5.0
Derek Brown, Nebraska	230	1313	5.7
Mike Gaddis, Oklahoma	221	1240	5.6

PASSING YARDS	Completions	Attempts	Yards	Pct.
Ty Detmer, Brigham Young	249	403	4031	61.8
Troy Kopp, Pacific	275	449	3767	61.3
Shane Matthews, Florida	218	361	3130	60.4
Gino Toretta, Miami	205	371	3095	55.3
Jeff Blake, East Carolina	203	368	3073	55.2
Tom Corontzos, Wyoming	203	363	2868	55.9
Andy Kelly, Tennessee	228	361	2759	63.2
David Lowery, San Diego State	176	311	2575	56.6
Casey Weldon, Florida State	189	313	2527	60.4
Bobby Fuller, South Carolina	202	340	2524	59.4

RECEIVING YARDS	Catches	Yards
Aaron Turner, Pacific	92	1604
Marcus Grant, Houston	78	1262
Carl Winston, New Mexico	76	1177
Ryan Yarborough, Wyoming	53	1081
Greg Primus, Colorado State	67	1081
Mario Bailey, Washington	62	1037
Eric Drage, Brigham Young	46	1018
Bryan Rowley, Utah	60	1011
Sean LaChapelle, UCLA	68	987
Wilbert Ursin, Tulane	70	969

1991 Consensus All-America Team
Offense

Wide Receiver:	Desmond Howard, Michigan
	Mario Bailey, Washington
Tight End:	Kelly Blackwell, Texas Christian
Tackle:	Greg Strepenak, Michigan
	Bob Whitfield, Stanford
Guard:	Jeb Flesch, Clemson
	Jerry Ostroski, Tulsa
	Mirko Jurkovic, Notre Dame
Center:	Jay Leeuwenburg, Colorado
Quarterback:	Ty Detmer, Brigham Young
Running Backs:	Vaughn Dunbar, Indiana
	Trevor Cobb, Rice
	Russell White, California
Kicker:	Carlos Huerta, Miami

Defense

Line:	Steve Emtman, Washington
	Santana Dotson, Baylor
	Brad Culpepper, Florida
	Leroy Smith, Iowa
Linebacker:	Robert Jones, East Carolina
	Marvin Jones, Florida State
	Levon Kirkland, Clemson
Backs:	Terrell Buckley, Florida State
	Dale Carter, Tennessee
	Kevin Smith, Texas A&M
	Darryl Williams, Miami
Punter:	Mark Bounds, Texas Tech

1991 Heisman Trophy Vote

Desmond Howard, junior wide receiver, Michigan	2,077
Casey Weldon, senior quarterback, Florida State	503
Ty Detmer, senior quarterback, Brigham Young	445
Steve Emtman, junior defensive tackle, Washington	357

Other Major Awards

Maxwell (Player)	Desmond Howard, junior wide receiver, Michigan
Walter Camp (Player)	Desmond Howard, junior wide receiver, Michigan
Outland (Lineman)	Steve Emtman, junior defensive tackle, Washington
Lombardi (Lineman)	Steve Emtman, junior defensive tackle, Washington
Doak Walker (Running Back)	Trevor Cobb, junior tailback, Rice
Davey O'Brien (Quarterback)	Ty Detmer, senior quarterback, Brigham Young
Jim Thorpe (Defensive Back)	Terrell Buckley, senior cornerback, Florida State
Dick Butkus (Linebacker)	Erick Anderson, senior linebacker, Michigan
Johnny Unitas (Quarterback)	Casey Weldon, senior quarterback, Florida State
AFCA Coach of the Year	Don James, Washington

1992

The Year of the First Conference Championship Game, Hurricane Andrew, and Alabama's Sugar Surprise

After two straight years of split decisions in the writers and coaches poll, the clamor for a post-season playoff was louder than ever in 1992. The bowl committees, fearing a loss of power, scurried to create a potential no. 1 vs. no. 2 matchup for the national title to be played in one of their bowls. Seven bowls (not including the Rose, which remained tethered to the Big Ten and Pac-10 champions) signed with the ACC, Big East, Big Eight, SEC, SWC and Notre Dame to arrange a system to encourage a matchup of first- and second-ranked teams in one of the bowls.

The masterplan succeeded in matching top-ranked Miami (11-1) with no. 2, SEC champion Alabama (13-0), which clinched its conference title with a win over SEC East champ Florida in college football's first-ever conference playoff game.

When the SEC commissioner Roy Kramer induced Arkansas and South Carolina to join the elite conference, it created the opportunity to split the league into two divisions and to play a championship game between the two titleists. It was instantly popular for the most rabid fans in any region, and served up plenty of cash for one of college football's most successful conferences. The SEC title game would serve, for better or worse, as the blueprint for other conferences.

The Miami Hurricanes survived an 8-7 home scare at the hands of Arizona's "Desert Swarm" defense as Steve McLaughlin's long, last-play field goal sailed wide. On consecutive weeks in October, Miami brushed aside Florida State (11-1), as the Seminoles again missed a vital late field goal against the Hurricanes, and Penn State (7-5) on the road. Those two wins were sufficiently impressive to place Miami no. 1 until its Alabama showdown.

The Hurricanes faced no easy task, especially in the early season when the irony of their nickname struck too close to home. Hurricane Andrew, the third most intense storm (22 millibars pressure) and the most costly ($26.5 billion of damage) to make landfall to date in the United States, wiped out the family homes of many players and that of head coach Dennis Erickson. It was clearly difficult for Miami players to bench their sorrow and play, but the shared devastation helped bond them in their quest for an unprecedented fourth national championship in six years during the school's remarkable recent run. Because of frequent on-field acts of arrogance, Miami was nearly every fan's favorite to hate, but the humbling experience of Hurricane Andrew did much to tone down that behavior in 1992.

In the Sugar Bowl, underdog Alabama combined a brilliant defensive scheme and rugged ground attack to utterly surprise the seemingly untouchable Hurricanes. Miami entered the game with a 29-game win streak and a record of 66-4 since its jolting loss in the 1987 Fiesta Bowl to Penn State. The Canes also had Heisman Trophy-winning quarterback Gino Torretta and three defenders, linebackers Michael Barrow and Darrin Smith and cornerback Ryan McNeil, who had earned All-America mention. Instead, coach Gene Stallings' blue-collar Crimson Tide prevailed in a fascinating game that ABC gladly broadcast in prime time on its own night.

The Rose Bowl exhausted some of its appeal when Big Ten champion Michigan (8-0-3) was tied by Illinois (6-5-1) and Ohio State (8-3-1) in its last two regular season games, and Pac-10 co-winner Washington (9-3) was beaten by Arizona (6-5-1) and Washington State (9-3) after entering November with an 8-0 slate. Washington's fall from the no. 2 spot made possible the coalition's 1 vs. 2 matchup in New Orleans. Otherwise, Washington would have ruined the plan since the Rose Bowl played no part in the major bowl agreement. The collapse came amid turmoil over a booster's loan to quarterback Billy Joe Hobert, and the issue seemed to tear down the Huskies.

Penn State, locked out of the bowl coalition and a year away from any Rose Bowl opportunity with the Big Ten, was left in bowl no-man's land. As a result, it cut an extraordinarily early deal in May with the Blockbuster Bowl. The scheme lost some fiz when the Nittany Lions lost four of their last six games. Stanford (10-3), celebrating the return of "genius" coach Bill Walsh, dominated the Blockbuster Bowl 24-3, using its notable defense, not always a highlight of Walsh-coached teams. The result enhanced a fine season for the Cardinal as they tied Washington as Pac-10 co-champions. It would turn out, however, to be Walsh's last fine season as a coach.

Out in the cold was no. 4 Texas A&M (12-1), which hoped for a longshot national title opportunity if it could win the Cotton Bowl over no. 3 Florida State and somehow the Sugar Bowl ended in an unsatisfying standoff. But, Cotton Bowl organizers ruffled coalition feathers by bypassing the

Seminoles and opting for Notre Dame's better TV appeal. Any hopes the Aggies harbored for a backdoor national championship crumbled when four players were suspended prior to the bowl for summer job irregularities, and the Fighting Irish taught them a stern 28-3 lesson in Dallas.

Two SEC coaches saw their stellar careers crumble with unbelieveable speed. A contract extension was drafted for Johnny Majors of Tennessee (9-3) the same summer day he underwent heart bypass surgery. After interim coach Phillip Fulmer opened 3-0, Majors returned to lose games to Arkansas (3-7-1) and Alabama. Suddenly, the new contract was withdrawn, and Majors was out of Tennessee's coaching picture, replaced by Fulmer in time for bowl season. Pat Dye of Auburn (5-5-1) faced player payment charges from former defensive back Eric Ramsey, and a second straight five-win season hastened Dye's departure from "The Loveliest Village on the Plain."

On the other hand, admired longtime coaching stalwarts, Bill Dooley of Wake Forest (8-4) and Grant Teaff of Baylor (7-5), guided their over-achieving teams to bowl wins over Oregon (6-6) and Arizona (6-5-1) respectively before they enjoyed their new-found retirement.

Milestones

● New rule allowed defenses to advance fumbles from any spot on field.

● Southeastern Conference added South Carolina and Arkansas as new members and split into six-team East and West divisions. Thus, college football's first-ever intra-conference championship game was contested between Florida and Alabama on December 5 in Birmingham.

● Western Athletic Conference added Fresno State, expanding its ranks to 10.

● No school entered season on probation—all 107 Division I-A schools were eligible for bowl games.

● Lou Groza Award was introduced by Palm Beach (Fla.) Co. Sports Commission to honor former Ohio State and Cleveland Browns kicker.

● Mel Hein, 82, star Washington State center who went on to become all-time NFL great with New York Giants, died on January 31. On June 25, former Miami All-America defensive tackle Jerome Brown, 27, was killed in auto accident in Brooksville, Fla. Alex Wojciechowicz, 76, center and most prominent player of Fordham's famed "Seven Blocks of Granite" line in 1930s, died on July 13. Skin cancer claimed John Bruno, punter for Penn State's 1986 national champions. Florida State freshman tight end Michael Hendricks was home in September after suffering knee sprain in practice and was fatally electrocuted while climbing a 100-ft power tower in Baytown, Texas.

● Auburn retired Heisman Trophy winner Bo Jackson's jersey no. 34 on October 31.

● Longest winning streaks entering season:

Miami (Florida) 18	Washington 14	East Carolina 11

● Coaching Changes:

	Incoming	Outgoing
Arizona State	Bruce Snyder	Larry Marmie
California	Keith Gilbertson	Bruce Snyder
Georgia Tech	Bill Lewis	Bobby Ross
Maryland	Mark Duffner	Joe Krivak
Minnesota	Jim Wacker	John Gutekunst
New Mexico	Dennis Franchione	Mike Sheppard
Northwestern	Gary Barnett	Francis Peay
Stanford	Bill Walsh	Dennis Green
Tennessee	Phillip Fulmer (a)	Johnny Majors
Texas	John Mackovic	David McWilliams
Texas Christian	Pat Sullivan	Jim Wacker

(a) Fulmer stepped in for ailing Majors for first three games of 1992, then formally replaced him on November 29 in time for Hall of Fame Bowl. Fulmer was credited with 4-0 record for 1992.

Preseason *USA Today* Coaches Poll

1	Miami (Fla.) (40)	1475	14	Colorado	695
2	Washington (14)	1365	15	Iowa	643
3	Notre Dame (3)	1267	16	Georgia	569
4	Florida State	1219	17	UCLA	482
5	Michigan	1184	18	Ohio State	400
6	Florida (1)	1156	19	Tennessee	351
7	Texas A&M	1151	20	Stanford	340
8	Penn State (2)	1104	21	Brigham Young	220
9	Alabama	981	22	California	205
10	Syracuse	829	23t	Georgia Tech	191
11	Nebraska	826	23t	Texas	191
12	Oklahoma	741	25	Southern California	170
13	Clemson	708			

August 29, 1992

(Wed) Texas A&M 10 Stanford 7 (Anaheim): Bill Walsh, highly successful Super Bowl coach for San Francisco 49ers, was back at Stanford (0-1) where he had led Cardinal to 17-7 record, including 2 bowl wins in 1977-78. Each D (which would finish season 9th and 18th in scoring prevention respectively) sparkled in Disneyland Pigskin Classic. Even though QB Steve Stenstrom had to run for his life from swift Texas A&M (1-0) D, Cardinal scored on FB J.J. Lasley's 5y run on 1st play of 2nd Q after RB Glyn Milburn's

27y punt RET. Aggies QB Jeff Granger, yanked for weak passing performance (6-20/66y) in 1st H, returned to heave tying 4th Q TD pass to TE Greg Schorp. A&M K Terry Venetoulias' 39y FG won it with 4:27 left after Stenstrom was picked off, and Granger contributed 33y scramble to Stanford 29YL.

North Carolina State 24 Iowa 14 (East Rutherford, N.J.): After Kickoff Classic officials attempted to match 1991 co-champs Miami and Washington, they had to settle for smallest attraction to Giants Stadium, 46,251, in preseason bowl's 10-year history. Iowa (0-1) QB Jim Hartlieb threw 23y and 9y TD passes to WR Danan Hughes in 2nd Q, tying it 14-14 just before H. It would stay that way until Wolfpack (1-0) soph K Steve Videtich's 46y FG broke it with 6:50 left. Happiest combatant had to be NC State QB Terry Jordan (15-24/160y, TD), who missed 7 games in 1991 with broken non-throwing arm. Jordan rushed 13/91y, including 33y option run that boosted game-opening 81y TD march to TB Gary Downs' 2y scoring run. Jordan's TD pass came after Videtich's 4th Q FG and clinched verdict for coach Dick Sheridan's Wolfpack.

USA Today Coaches Poll August 31

1	Miami (Fla.) (43)	1473	14	Clemson	711
2	Washington (12)	1386	15	Georgia	588
3	Notre Dame (3)	1297	16	UCLA	490
4	Florida State	1238	17	North Carolina State	460
5	Florida	1192	18	Ohio State	437
6	Michigan	1187	19	Tennessee	393
7	Penn State (2)	1143	20	Iowa	240
8	Texas A&M	1098	21	Brigham Young	233
9	Alabama	1012	22	Stanford	226
10	Syracuse	863	23	Texas	193
11	Nebraska	856	24	Georgia Tech	181
12	Oklahoma	774	25	California	175
13	Colorado	740			

September 5, 1992

(Th) Oklahoma 34 TEXAS TECH 9: Pre-game campaign stop in Lubbock by Pres. George Walker Bush failed to inspire Texas Tech (0-1). In 1st Q, Oklahoma (1-0) QB Cale Gundy hit FB Kenyon Rasheed with TD for 13-7 lead, but Red Raiders LB Ben Kirkpatrick took blocked kick for 2-pt conv to make it 13-9. That's as close as Tech would get as Gundy threw 13y 2nd Q TD pass to TB Earnest Williams. Gundy, with 1y TD keeper, and LB Aubrey Beavers, on 5y INT TD RET, iced game with 4th Q scores. Gundy broke his own Sooner passing y record with 341y.

BOSTON COLLEGE 37 Rutgers 20: Big East pair of teams, each hopeful, looked to improve on mediocrity under which each suffered in 1991. BC (1-0) used 3 TD passes from QB Glenn Foley (12-21/275y, INT) and 2 TD runs by TB Darnell Campbell (22/107y) to best Rutgers (0-1), which debuted Miami transfer QB Brian Fortay (19-40/175y, 3 TDs, 2 INTs). Eagles led only 10-7 late in 2nd Q when Foley hit diving WR Keith Miller for 45y TD. BC exploded with 20-7 margin in 3rd Q to lock up 1st season-opening win in 5 years. Fortay, who would later sue Miami for alleged broken promises and mishandling by coaching staff, passed for all of Scarlet Knights' TDs despite being under heavy pass-rush pressure. Fortay's career as Rutgers starter, however, would be short-lived.

Texas A&M 31 LOUISIANA STATE 22: TBs Greg Hill (21/98y) and Rodney Thomas combined for 194y rushing for Aggies (2-0) who padded 3-pt lead with 2-TD surge in 4th Q. Experimenting with 3 QBs, LSU (0-1) moved WR-turned-QB Jesse Daigle under center, and he rallied Tigers with 10-13/115y passing, including late-game 19y TD pass followed by 2-pt pass. In 2nd Q, Bayou Bengals starting QB Chad Loup (6-13/81y, 2 INTs) was pulled for QB Robert Huffman (2-4/19y), who immediately tossed pitchout to frosh TB Robert Davis (15/134y, TD) who hauled 76y before being brought down at Texas A&M 8YL by pursuing DB Aaron Glenn. Huffman scored on next play to tie it 7-7. With score in Aggies favor at 17-14 early in 4th Q, Loup was back in. Texas A&M blitzed Loup, who scrambled away from pressure, only to have Aggies DB Derrick Frazier make game-turning INT at LSU 22YL. Thomas scored on next play for 24-14 lead for A&M. Aggies went 80y to TD in 10 plays to 31-14 lead later in 4th Q.

The Citadel 10 ARKANSAS 3: DE Judson Boehmer of 1-AA Citadel (1-0) was alert to new collegiate rule allowing advancement of FUMs from any spot on field and picked up 4th Q bobble caused by teammate DE Garrett Sizer to go 34y to decisive TD. Game had rolled scoreless into 4th Q until Arkansas (0-1) K Todd Wright hit 25y FG at end of 68y march. Then, workhorse Razorbacks TB E.D. Jackson (29/167y) lost critical TD FUM when hit by Sizer. Later in 4th Q, Bulldogs DB Detric Cummings picked off deflected pass from Hogs QB Jason Allen (11-23/110y, INT) to set up clinching FG. It was Citadel's 5th win in last 6 games against Div-1A teams, but loss so distressed Arkansas AD Frank Broyles that he immediately dismissed coach Jack Crowe, despite Crowe's new contract.

Miami 24 IOWA 7: Highly-stressed Miami (1-0) left behind South Florida's heartbreak and devastation created by Hurricane Andrew, not to mention 2 months of player arrests, federal indictments, and injuries. Only few days earlier, Andrew's massive fury leveled home of coach Dennis Erickson and those of several players' families. Hurricanes dropped their own devastating landfall on Iowa (0-2) as Miami QB Gino Toretta passed 31-51/433y, 2 TDs, INT. WR Kevin Williams caught 11y TD and RB Darryl Spencer nabbed 35y TD pass, each from Toretta. Hurricanes D blanked Hawkeyes until 35y TD pass from QB Jim Hartlieb (26-38/266y, TD) to WR Harold Jasper in last 5:30. That score narrowed tally to 17-7, but Canes hurriedly went 46y in 5 plays to Toretta's TD throw to Spencer.

OHIO STATE 20 Louisville 19: Louisville coach Howard Schnellenberger eschewed tying kick in last 33 secs after RB Ralph Dawkins' 2nd TD run of game, saying his Cardinals (0-1) "came to win." Energetic DL Tim Wilkinson of Ohio State (1-0) made clutch play, pressuring QB Jeff Brohm on conv try, and Broehm's 2-pt pass for Dawkins drifted long. Buckeyes had burst to 10-0 lead in 2nd Q as WR Joey Galloway raced 50y on flanker-reverse. Broehm (20-32/230y, TD) found his brother, WR Greg Broehm, for 3y TD that pulled Cards to within 10-6 at H. Ohio, 88-11-4 all-time in season openers, lost its lead at 13-10 in 3rd Q but got back 10 pts on FB Jeff Cothran's 9y TD run and K Tim Williams' 26y FG.

SAN DIEGO STATE 31 Southern California 31: Super sophs RB Marshall Faulk (27/220y, 3 TDs) of Aztecs (0-0-1) and QB Rob Johnson (20-33/278y, 4 TDs) of Trojans (0-0-1) sparkled in 1st-ever meeting of California colleges. USC K Cole Ford booted tying FG with 5:36 left, and SDSU K Andy Trakas missed 2 FGs in game's last 54 secs. Trakas' 1st miss was from fairly short range (30y), and he hooked it left. Southern California had led 21-7 at H after Johnson connected on 3 scores. Trojans couldn't move at all on opening 3 possessions of 3rd Q, which allowed Aztecs nearly to catch up with Trakas' 37y FG and Faulk's 11y TD run. Johnson's FUM led to tall SDSU WR Darnay Scott's leaping TD catch over shorter USC CB Jason Oliver. Trojans WR Johnnie Morton made his 3rd scoring catch late in 3rd Q to regain lead at 28-24. Although deadlocked result may have been unfulfilling to Troy, it at least ended its school-record streak of 6 straight losses.

Hawaii 24 OREGON 21: Using its tricky spread option O, Hawaii (1-0) never trailed in its trip to mainland as QB Ivin Jasper (3-10/69y, TD, INT) rifled 49y TD pass to WR Darrick Branch in 1st Q, and ace K Jason Elam booted x-pt. WR Derrick Deadwiler scored on 1y wide run in 2nd Q to bring Ducks (0-1) to within 7-6, but conv kick was missed. Rainbow QB Mike Carter started at SB and scored on 3rd Q TD run that built 17-6 lead, but Carter went to QB when Jasper banged up leg in 3rd Q. Carter flipped 2y TD pass to WR Eddie Kealoha with 4:34 left in 3rd Q and it proved to be winning pts as Oregon rallied late. Ducks QB Danny O'Neil (26-40/312y, TD, INT) produced 15 pts in last 19 mins as he picked on Hawaii's pass D, nation's statistically-worst in 1991.

USA Today Coaches Poll September 8

1	Miami (Fla.) (45)	1482	14	Clemson	660
2	Washington (13)	1427	15	Georgia	627
3	Notre Dame (2)	1283	16	North Carolina State	497
4	Florida State	1281	17	Tennessee	479
5	Michigan	1180	18	UCLA	439
6	Florida	1172	19	Mississippi State	350
7	Texas A&M	1147	20	California	343
8	Alabama	1037	21	Ohio State	293
9	Syracuse	956	22	Brigham Young	235
10	Penn State	926	23	Virginia	178
11	Nebraska	913	24	Georgia Tech	167
12	Oklahoma	853	25	Stanford	159
13	Colorado	748			

September 12, 1992

(Th) San Diego State 45 BRIGHAM YOUNG 38: Superb Aztecs (1-0-1) RB Marshall Faulk rushed 35/299y and 3 TDs in ESPN TV bid for program acclaim. As usual Brigham Young (1-1) did its damage in airways: Cougars QB John Walsh threw 23-44/380y, 5 TDs, INT, and WR Eric Drage caught 9/198y, 3 TDs. But, Walsh's INT launched San Diego State as DB Darrell Lewis made 57y TD RET to open scoring at 7-0 in 1st Q. Aztecs led 24-17 at H, but pulled away in 21-pt 3rd Q when Faulk tallied on 10 and 65y runs. In most recent 4 games against each other since 1989, O-minded teams had totaled 358 points, or 44.75 avg for each side.

West Virginia 44 PITTSBURGH 6: Mountaineers (1-0-1) QB Jake Kelchner (9-12/168y, INT), transfer from Notre Dame, made his 1st start and came out as effective winner. West Virginia rolled up 21-0 lead with 3rd TD coming as fortuitous bounce: Kelchner threw 24y pass to TE John Cappa on 3rd down pass in 2nd Q. Cappa lost handle, and his FUM bounded into EZ where WVU WR Ed Hill fell on it just before it dribbled OB. Pittsburgh (1-1) QB Alex Van Pelt (16-31/193y, 2 INTs) was held in reasonable check, and Mountaineers DB Kwame Smith made 70y INT TD RET on 1 pick-off suffered by Van Pelt.

SYRACUSE 31 Texas 21: Texas (0-2) led 21-13 in 3rd Q on 2 TD passes by QB Peter Gardere (14-27/247y, 2 TDs, 2 INTs). Then, Orangemen (2-0) QB Marvin Graves (11-18/284y, TD) threw 10y score to WR Kerry Ferrell and caught 2-pt conv pass from TB David Walker for 21-21 tie late in 3rd Q. Graves' 51y toss to WR Shelby Hill was key to Syracuse's 13-play drive to set up go-ahead 20y FG by K John Biskup for 24-21 lead in 4th Q. WR Qadry Ismail caught 58y bomb from Graves to poise TB Al Wooten for clinching 1y TD run with 28 secs to play. Earlier, Longhorns appeared in great shape at midfield to overtake 3-pt deficit when LB Van Malone partially blocked punt with 2:57 left. But, Orange DB Bob Grosvernor quickly made his 2nd INT of Gardere.

Florida State 24 CLEMSON 20: New ACC member Seminoles (2-0) dethroned defending champion and chose to add Clemson (1-1) to their "Sod Cemetary," traditional uprooting of grass square from field of vanquished rival on road. Tigers took 13-10 lead 5 mins into 3rd Q as DB James Trapp authored 39y INT TD RET. FUM that FSU DB Clifton Abraham had carried 51y to Clemson 39YL set up QB Charlie Ward's 11y TD pass to WR Matt Frier for 17-13 edge late in 3rd Q. Tigers then answered to lead again at 20-17 on WR Terry Smith's 35y TD catch on underthrown pass. Despite 4 INTs during game, Ward (20-39/258y, 2 TDs, 4 INTs) staged winning, late-game 77y drive by passing 5-5/64y, including winning 9y TD to WR Kevin Knox (6/72y).

Tennessee 34 GEORGIA 31: Forced into annual battle by new SEC divisional setup, Volunteers (2-0) and Bulldogs (1-1) met for only 22nd time in 94 years. Georgia RB Garrison Hearst rushed 20/161y, including TDs of 4, 64, and 18y, his last provided 31-27 lead halfway into 4th Q. Tennessee QB Heath Shuler (12-22/152y, INT) hit WR Ronald Davis with 22y pass on 4th-and 13 and then dashed 3y to score game-winner at end of 80y drive with :50 left. Shuler rushed 19/81y, 2 TDs. Vols gained from 6 Georgia TOs, including clinching FUM at Vols 34YL after Bulldogs WR Andre Hastings (5/150y, TD) caught pass from QB Eric Zeier (18-26/354y, TD, 2 INTs) and dodged 2 tacklers to gain 38y with 14 secs left.

LOUISIANA STATE 24 Mississippi State 3: During week, coach Jackie Sherrill was highly criticized in media for his having castrated bull named "Willie," demonstration intended (successfully) to inspire Bulldogs (1-1) prior week against Texas Longhorns. Tigers (1-1) proved less passive, earning 3-3 tie in 4th Q. Mississippi State had taken 3-0 lead at H on K Chris Gardner's 47y FG. Then with its D yielding plenty of y but gaining 8 TOs, LSU QB Jesse Daigle fired 66y TD pass to WR Wesley Jacob in 4th Q, and TB Robert Davis and FB Germaine Williams added TD runs to complete runaway upset.

ALABAMA 17 Southern Mississippi 10 (Birmingham): Highly-favored Crimson Tide (2-0) made miscues that assisted Southern Miss (1-1) even though Bama's splendid D held Eagles to only 3 1st downs and 54y total O. Alabama pulled 1st Q surprise: P Bryne Diehl threw pass to wide open DB-special teamer Tommy Johnson, who raced to 73y TD on punt fake. SMU DE Bobby Hamilton accepted INT gift early in 3rd Q and ran 18y to tie it 7-7, and S Melvin Ratcliff recovered FUM at Tide 18YL, but they settled for FG. In 4th Q, Bama O managed 63y ground drive to TB Chris Anderson's TD that broke tie.

PURDUE 41 California 14: No. 17 California players got off their bus on Friday wearing straw hats and chewing on shoots of grass as method of delivering put-down to Boilermakers' rural Indiana homeland. Riled-up Purdue (1-0) scored 6 times in row to stun Golden Bears with 38-3 bludgeoning by H. While California (1-1) outgained Boilermakers 376y to 306y, it lost FUM and 3 INTs at wrong times. Young Purdue D, inspired by fierce sr NG Jeff Zgonina, held Bears' star TB Russell White to 18/79y, TD rushing. Purdue TB Jeff Hill (21/106y) scored on 8y run and 8y pass from QB Matt Pike (10-16/144y, TD) in 1st H. FB Arlee Connors tallied on 1 and 38y runs in 1st H.

Central Michigan 24 MICHIGAN STATE 20: It's not that Spartans (0-1) weren't warned: focused Chippewas (1-1) had upset Michigan State in 1991 opener, and this time Spartans vowed to block upset bid. Central Michigan scored 1st and never trailed as QB Joe Youngblood (17-22/163y, 2 TDs) twice connected with WR Bryan Tice (6/78y) for TDs in 14-7 1st H. Chippewa K Chuck Selinger booted 45y FG to lift lead to 17-7. Michigan State TB Tico Duckett (16/80y) scored twice and his understudy, TB Craig Thomas (16/87y) also blasted for TD. But, big break that went against Michigan State and prevented TD was Thomas' GL FUM that Central's D gobbled up in EZ.

ILLINOIS 24 Missouri 17: Illinois (2-0) QB Jason Verduzco (24-37/236y, TD, INT) had day's understatement: "We have to learn how to put people away." After building 24-0 lead by 2nd Q and 24-7 at H, Illini suffered through 2nd H of poor tackling and TOs when they drove into Missouri (0-1) territory. Todd Leach, part of Illinois' squadron of outstanding LBs, recovered bad pitchout at Tigers 16YL on game's 1st series, and RB Steve Feagin scored 4 plays later from 1YL. Illini FB Darren Boyer (24/92y) caught TD pass from Verduzco and plunged over for scores in 1st Q. After 2nd H KO, Illinois punted from Mizzou 28YL instead of trying 44y FG into stiff wind. Missouri went downfield for K Jeff Jacke's 51y FG with wind, and when Tigers smothered FG fake, momentum flipped to their side. But, Mizzou, which had no non-conf wins in 8 years, could get only 1 more score, TD pass by backup QB Jeff Handy (5-11/71y, TD, INT).

NOTRE DAME 17 Michigan 17: K Craig Hentrich's 32y FG gave Notre Dame (1-0-1) tie with 5:28 left. Michigan (0-0-1) had led 17-7 in 4th Q of sloppy game that offered shoddy tackling and several TOs on both sides. Fighting Irish lost 3 FUMs, and UM turned 2 of them into TD receptions by TB Tyrone Wheatley in 2nd Q for 27y and WR Derrick Alexander in 4th Q for 30y. Notre Dame drew within 17-14 on 2y TD run by FB Jerome Bettis (15/82y, TD). Wolverines appeared headed to late winning score, but ND DB Jeff Burris picked off pass by QB Elvis Grbac (17-28/242y, 2 TDs, 3 INTs) at Irish 12YL with 1:15 left. ND coach Lou Holtz was chided for killing clock with 2 runs, incompletion, and failed long bomb. Afterward, Holtz proposed little-accepted claim that Irish needed to read Michigan D before it could try passes.

Colorado 57 BAYLOR 38: New Colorado (2-0) air game sizzled, with QB Kordell Stewart passing 16-17/251y, 3 TDs, as big part of 33-10 H lead. Buffs' 57 pts were most allowed by Bears (0-2) at home in 21-year career of retiring coach Grant Teaff. Oddly enough, Baylor scored 1st on K Trey Weir's 28y FG in 1st Q it would exit trailing 7-3. Using 2 QBs in rout, Colorado achieved 26-32/405y passing, but had its only INT returned 48y for TD by Baylor DB Michael McFarland in 4th Q. Although Bears QB J.J. Joe (6-20/262y, 2 TDs) lost 2 pts in disastrous 2nd Q when he was called for intentional grounding in EZ, he threw 80y TD pass to TB David Mims and 30y TD pass to WR Reggie Miller.

Washington State 23 ARIZONA 20: Using DB Darryl Morrison's GL INT, P Josh Miller's 63 and 49y punts, and WR Troy Dickey's 29y TD catch, Wildcats (1-1) built handy 17-6 edge in 3rd Q, even though they would have only 24:37 in possession time by game's end. Reliable QB Drew Bledsoe (22-43/270y, 2 TDs, 2 INTs) rallied Cougars (2-0) with TD passes to WRs Deron Pointer and Phillip Bobo to pull them into 20-20 tie in 4th Q. Coach's son, K Aaron Price, nailed winning 47y FG for Washington State with :35 left, as drive was highlighted by Bledsoe's 14y pass to Bobo and 14y run by RB Shaumbe Wright-Fair (27/112y). Arizona TB Ontiwaun Carter was held to 22/40y on ground, but scored 7y TD in 2nd Q.

USA Today Coaches Poll September 14

1	Miami (Fla.) (47)	1486	14	Tennessee	696
2	Washington (13)	1437	15	North Carolina State	603
3	Florida State	1314	16	UCLA	513
4	Florida	1249	17	Clemson	449
5	Texas A&M	1166	18	Ohio State	406
6	Michigan	1083	19	Virginia	365
7	Notre Dame	1063	20	Georgia Tech	317
8	Penn State	1042	21	San Diego State	270
9	Alabama	1041	22	Stanford	258
10	Syracuse	1029	23	Georgia	253
11	Nebraska	935	24	Mississippi	137
12	Oklahoma	920	25	Illinois	80
13	Colorado	827			

September 19, 1992

Ohio State 35 SYRACUSE 12: Confident no. 8 Syracuse (2-1) harbored national title hopes as it hosted same team it had beaten in 1991's Hall of Fame Bowl. But, Orange dream was crumbled in strong hands of Buckeyes (3-0), who left boobirds of Ohio Stadium to ride QB Kirk Herbstreit's passing (10-19/154y, TD, INT) to TDs on 3 straight 1st H possessions. Well-covered WR Brian Stablein stretched out for 46y TD catch from Herbstreit, and it got Bucks rocking in 1st Q. FB Terry George (9/23y, 3 TDs) followed with 2 short TD runs. Ohio's D wrecked havoc on Syracuse's sharp QB Marvin Graves (12-25/158y), sacking him 6 times and forcing 4 INTs. Orange glimmered briefly in 3rd Q when Graves scored on 1y run to pull within 21-12. Speedy WR Qadry "Missile" Ismail (1/15y) was sent wide on 2-pt run try, but was walloped out of game with bad shoulder.

VIRGINIA 55 Georgia Tech 24: In 1st Q, Georgia Tech (1-1) scored on WR Bobby Rodriguez's 48y TD pitch to WR Jason McGill for 7-3 lead. Virginia (3-0) responded with 3 TD drives before 1st H was over. Cavaliers QB Bobby Goodman moved to top of national pass efficiency list with 11-15/177y, 3 TDs. Cavs TB Terry Kirby added 135y and 1 TD rushing, while also catching 7y TD pass. Virginia DE Chris Slade became all-time ACC sack leader with 29th of his career.

FLORIDA STATE 34 NORTH CAROLINA STATE 13: Floundering in its own mistakes, Florida State (3-0) had only 13y total O, and NC State (3-1) owned 3-0 lead with 6 mins remaining before H. Noles then woke up. After DB Corey Sawyer's acrobatic INT, Seminoles QB Charlie Ward (16-30/275y, 3 TDs, INT) found blazing-fast, frosh WR Tamarick Vanover for 60y TD pass and added 32y scoring pitch to WR Shannon Baker before H. Ward and Baker collaborated on 44y TD connection in 3rd Q, with all 3 of Ward's TD passes exploiting Wolfpack blitzes. NC State D couldn't stop inevitable, allowing scores on 6 of 7 Florida State possessions, and its O didn't score until it faced FSU's 3rd-string D: Wolfpack sub QB Geoff Bender hit his only pass try for 39y TD to WR Reggie Lawrence.

TENNESSEE 31 Florida 14: Gators RB Errict Rhett sprained ankle and left game with only 11/34y rushing, while Florida (1-1) bungled its way to 12 PENs and its high-tech O managed only 278y total O. Tennessee (3-0) used 56 running plays/250y to hand Florida coach Steve Spurrier only his 2nd SEC loss in 3 years. Volunteers QB Heath Shuler (3-9/94y, TD) passed sparingly and executed TD runs of 11 and 8y to enhance his short pass to FB Mose Phillips, which Phillips took 66y to TD for 24-7 lead in 3rd Q.

VANDERBILT 31 Mississippi 9: Teeming D of Vanderbilt (2-1) provided impetus for its O to overwhelm Mississippi (2-1). Ole Miss gained moderate 196y, but never saw EZ. Rebels K Brian Lee made 3 of 6 FGs, including 50y success that opened scoring in 1st Q. Commodores S Jeff Brothers led attacking D as he set up 3 TDs by netting 146y in RETs of his INT, blocked FG, and punt RET. Vandy led 7-6 with 3:07 left in 2nd Q as Lee lined up makeable FG for Ole Miss. CB Robbie Young blocked FG try, and Brothers scooped it up for 71y RET so that TB Tony Jackson could score on 11y run for Vandy's 14-6 H edge. In 3rd Q, Brothers' 29y INT RET and 15y PEN against Rebels set up QB Marcus Wilson's 39y TD pass to WR Clarence Sevillian. Ole Miss TB Cory Philpot rushed 20/112y.

Colorado 21 MINNESOTA 20: Although scoring took awhile to get going, geared-up Minnesota (0-2) was all over big favorite no. 11 Colorado (3-0). Gophers blocked 2nd Q punt, and CB Derek Fisher recovered it in EZ for TD. So, Minny trotted off with 7-0 H edge. Gophers QB Marquel Fleetwood (26-54/262y, TD, 4 INTs) executed 71 plays, including short TD pass to TE Steven Cambrice that built 17-0 3rd Q edge. Colorado QB Kordell Stewart was out injured and backup QB Duke Tobin was ineffective 2-10/21y throwing in 1st H. Buffaloes edged back on off-bench arrival of QB Koy Detmer (11-18/184y, 2 TDs), who linked with WR Michael Westbrook (8/135y) on 49y TD pass in 3rd Q. Coach Bill McCartney had planned to redshirt Detmer, but had little choice but to play younger brother of 1990 Heisman Trophy winner, Ty, as 2nd H wore on. Detmer hit 11-18/184y, 2 TDs, including game-winning 24y TD to WR Charles Johnson with 12:02 to play. Minnesota K Aaron Piepkorn had chance to win it, but his 55y attempt for his 3rd FG barely missed with 17 secs to go. "I'm not sad to lose his (Detmer's) redshirt year, not when we win a game like that," McCartney said afterward.

Southern California 20 OKLAHOMA 10: USC had not won since last October 12, beating Washington State 34-27 which meant its school winless record was nearly full year old. Even this wonderful road win required patience as Southern California (1-0-1) trailed 10-0 into 4th Q, but got big efforts on WR Curtis Conway's 51y TD catch from QB Rob Johnson (17-27/201y, TD, INT) and DB Stephon Pace's alert 19y FUM TD RET to quickly wipe out 10-pt deficit. Oklahoma (2-1) was held to 48y rushing, its lowest total since 12-0 loss to USC in 1982. Sooners QB Cale Gundy had thrown 25y TD pass to WR Corey Warren in 3rd Q, but his passing was less than great at 14-32/153y, TD, 2 INTs. Conway achieved career highs in catches and y with 9/115y receiving.

Ucla 17 BRIGHAM YOUNG 10: With top QB Wayne Cook out with season-ending knee injury, UCLA (2-0) tapped frosh QB Rob Walker (18-26/198y, INT) who had fine 1st H: 14-16/160y in air. Walker hit WR Sean LaChapelle with 30y pass on early FG drive and hit 5 straight, including 26 and 13y throws to WR J.J. Stokes, on 77y 2nd Q TD drive. TB Damon Washington (12/48y) scored again, 4 plays after UCLA DB Othello Henderson recovered Brigham Young (1-2) FUM of 2nd H KO. After K David Lauter's 42y FG put Cougars on scoreboard at 17-3, QB John Walsh (12-28/175y, TD, 2 INTs) drove BYU to Bruins 5YL. As UCLA S Tommy Bennett blitzed, Walsh suffered EZ INT by DB Michael Williams. But, when Cougars DB Derwin Gray turned INT tables on Walker, Walsh hit WR Eric Drage with 19y TD in last min of 3rd Q. Walsh was soon knocked out of game, and QB Steve Clements drove Cougars to 11YL but under pressure he suffered EZ INT by S Marvin Goodwin. DE Jamir Miller had 3 of UCLA's 5 sacks.

STANFORD 35 Northwestern 24: On their way to 513y total O, Cardinal (2-1) rode passing of QB Steve Stenstrom (21-29/297y, 2 TDs, 2 INTs) to 14-3 lead in 2nd Q. Then, Northwestern (0-3) special teams, that played well all day, broke shifty WR Lee Gissendaner for 53y punt RET that set up QB Len Williams (12/57y, TD rushing) for 22y TD run. Stanford boxed up win with TDs that ended 1st H and opened 2nd H: Stenstrom beat H clock on 80y trip capped by WR Justin Armour's 9y catch, and RB Ellery Roberts carried 7 plays in row for TD and 28-10 lead. When Card RB Glyn Milburn (19/111y, 2 TDs) scored his 2nd TD in 3rd Q, edge rose to 35-10. Cats rallied for "some self respect," according to coach Gary Barnett. Williams threw TD pass and Gissendaner raced 72y on punt TD RET. NW LB Steve Ostrowski made 14 stops.

WASHINGTON 29 Nebraska 14: Depth of Husky power was verified against no. 12 Nebraska (2-1), which sought revenge for 1991's blown 21-9 lead at home. Some had questioned Huskies D, but it registered safety on DB Tommie Smith's 1st Q sack and finished with 3 sacks, recovered 2 FUMs, and picked off INT. In 2nd Q, Cornhuskers closed to within 9-7 on IB Calvin Jones' 73y TD run with option pitchout. But, Washington (3-0) struck back with 2 TDs within 42 secs: TB Napoleon Kauffman's 1y run and QB Billy Joe Hobert's 29y pass to WR Joe Kralik right after CB Walter Bailey made INT of Nebraska QB Mike Grant. It was Cornhuskers' 10th loss in row when facing top-5 team, and that fact was beginning to get under their skin.

USA Today Coaches Poll September 21

1	Miami (Fla.) (45)	1485	14	Virginia	695
2	Washington	1447	15	Nebraska	599
3	Florida State	1353	16	Clemson	511
4	Texas A&M	1196	17	Syracuse	503
5	Michigan	1186	18	Georgia	470
6	Notre Dame	1156	19	Stanford	349
7	Penn State	1149	20	Oklahoma	343
8	Alabama	1103	21	San Diego State	326
9	Tennessee	1056	22	Southern California	278
10	Colorado	892	23	North Carolina State	273
11	Ohio State	810	24	Kansas	191
12	UCLA	779	25	North Carolina	144
13	Florida	715			

September 26, 1992

(Th) California 27 KANSAS 23: Jayhawks (3-1), proudly ranked in AP Poll for 1st time in 16 years, fell behind 10-0 as Golden Bears (2-1) WR Sean Dawkins caught 40 and 9y passes during 1st Q 78y TD drive. Kansas was slapped out of lethargy by QB Chip Hilleary's beautiful broken-field rollout TD run of 28y in 2nd Q. Golden Bears weathered fumbled punt near end of 2nd Q, costing them only FG, and TE Steve Stafford went 38y with dump-off pass in 3rd Q to set up QB Dave Barr's TD sneak. Trailing 20-17 late in 3rd Q, Kansas' outstanding K Dan Eichloff attempted to tie it up with his 2nd FG. Cal's 6'7 DE Brad Bowers blocked Eichloff's 47y FG try to set up Dawkins' clinching 11y TD catch from Barr (15-24/211y, 2 TDs, 3 INTs). Bears TB Russell White, still believing he had Heisman prospects, scored TD and rushed for 153y, often against 8-man D front.

BOSTON COLLEGE 14 Michigan State 0: In chilly rain, unbeaten Boston College (4-0) won its 4th at home. Eagles D, led by LB Tom McManus, DB Charlie Brennan, and DT Mike Marinaro, pitched its 3rd straight shutout. Big Michigan State (0-3) O-line ploughed 156y rushing, mostly by TB Tico Duckett (19/116y), but when QB Jim Miller (6-12/44y) suffered concussion, Spartans' weak air game went completely south. BC blockers also broke open big holes for their TB-duo of Chuckie Dukes (25/153y) and Dwight Shirley (24/159y, 2 TDs). Shirley raced 80y in 1st Q, and when K Jim Del Verne missed 39y FG on Michigan State's 1st series of 2nd H, BC responded with 16-play, 79y drive to Shirley's 2nd TD.

MIAMI 8 Arizona 7: Swarming D of Arizona (1-2-1) stuffed callow Miami line, and yielded amazing 22/2y rushing. But, Miami (3-0) took 2-0 lead on Arizona's 2nd series when star DE Rusty Medearis, whose career later was ended on 4th Q block to his knee, belted Wildcats RB Chuck Levy into EZ for safety. Arizona used power run attack to travel 80y in 10 plays in 2nd Q: FB Billy Johnson rammed for 9y score and 7-2 H edge. In 3rd Q, QB Gino Toretta's 2y TD pass to TE Dietrich Clausell (out of tight 3-TE formation) won it for Hurricanes, even though Wildcats K Steve McLaughlin barely missed 51y FG at gun. Style points do matter: Narrow escape cost Miami as it lost 31 1st place votes and dropped to no. 2 in AP poll. Idle Washington edged ahead, rare fall for no. 1 team that won its game, while no. 2 didn't play.

Virginia 55 DUKE 28: Recently-bitter rivalry bubbled more effusively as Virginia (4-0) piled it on in building 41-7 H lead on way to its 3rd straight 50-plus pt total of season. Virginia TB Terry Kirby rushed 28/207y and QB Bobby Goodman, nation's pass efficiency leader, threw for 15-26/226y, TD. When Duke saxophonist wandered inside 20YL during H show, disdainful home crowd at Wallace Wade Stadium howled at Blue Devils' deepest penetration into Cavalier territory. Devils' only score of 1st H had been DB Derrick Jackson's 38y RET of blocked punt. After tally mounted to 55-14, Duke (1-3) made mild 4th Q rally behind QB Spence Fischer (8-10/123y, TD, INT).

North Carolina State 27 NORTH CAROLINA 20: Winning its 5th in row in neighborhood rivalry, North Carolina State (4-1) left Chapel Hill in giddy mood. Brilliant QB Terry Jordan (23-25/361y) said, "It means a lot more than a win over Florida State (last week's conqueror)." Only TD scorers were FB Greg Manior for Wolfpack and QB Jason Stanicek for Tar Heels (3-1) as game turned into 4th Q, tied 13-13. Early in 4th Q, Jordan hit WR Eddie Goines for 46y gain to set up Jordan's short TD run. UNC came right back to knot it 20-20 on TB Natrone Means' 1y TD smash. NC State went 78y, using up 4 excruciating mins, as Jordan hit 23y pass on 3rd-and-10 to Heels 18YL and Manior (14/54y) carried on last 3 plays, flying over top of stack for winning 2y TD.

GEORGIA TECH 20 Clemson 16: Georgia Tech (2-1) upset Clemson (1-2) when QB Shawn Jones (21-34/260y, 2 TDs) opened game with 1y TD pass to WR Keenan Walker and closed 3rd Q with 36y toss to WR Bobby Rodriguez, who, after 10y curl pattern, squirmed away from several defenders. Tigers had gained only 72y O in 1st H against revitalized Yellow Jackets D, but made 69y on their opening possession of 3rd Q: Clemson burned 8:48 off clock on its march but had to settle for K Nelson Welch's 25y FG. That trimmed Tech's lead to 13-6. Jackets' O immediately went 3-and-out, and Tigers QB Richard Moncrief (6-22/82y) keyed tying TD drive with 2 effective QB-draw runs. Next came Rodriguez's TD after Jones' 18y scramble. When Tech stopped 3rd-and-10 run in 4th Q, Clemson had to settle for another FG by Welch, this from 32y.

MEMPHIS STATE 22 Arkansas 6: Frustrated by 3 tight losses to Southern Miss, Louisville, and Mississippi State, Memphis State (1-3) players boycotted coach Chuck Stobart's mid-week practices. Summit ended team discord, and emotions played out on field: Tigers DB Ken Ivan broke NCAA record with 4 blocked punts, and K Joe Allison, nephew of NASCAR legend Bobby Allison, booted 3 FGs, including 51y kick to open scoring. Arkansas (1-3) made only 157y O while alternating its QBs, Jason Allen (10-18/60y, INT) and Barry Lunney Jr (2-8/28y, INT). Hogs TD came in 4th Q on RB Oscar Malone's 99y KO TD RET after Memphis FB Marcus Holliday made his 2nd TD.

TEXAS TECH 36 Baylor 17: Undefeated at 8-0-1 in last 9 road games, Baylor (1-3) seemed unaffected by trip to Lubbock, but for change, Texas Tech (2-2) put solid performances together on both sides of ball. Bears opened game with 56y drive to FB Robert Strait's 13y TD run. Red Raiders turned on its balance attack (297y rushing and 231y passing) in 2nd Q as TB Byron "Bam" Morris (32/157y) slammed for 2 TDs. Tech completely flipped 14-10 H lead by scoring on its 1st 3 possessions of 3rd Q: K Jon Davis' 27 and 38y FGs and 7y TD pass by QB Robert Hall (17-27/213y, 2 TDs). QB J.J. Joe scored in 4th Q to get Baylor back to 27-17, but Raiders D slammed door.

HAWAII 36 Brigham Young 32: Picked near bottom of WAC, Hawaii (3-0) surprised Cougars as strong-legged K Jason Elam booted 3 FGs, including majestic 56y kick, to become all-time conf top scorer with 327 career pts. When BYU (1-3) lost QB Steve Clements to injury, they had to dig down to 3rd string QB Ryan Hancock.

USA Today Coaches Poll September 28

1	Washington (43)	1480	14	Nebraska	688
2	Miami (Fla.) (16)	1431	15	Florida	683
3	Florida State (1)	1338	16	Georgia	530
4	Michigan	1227	17	Syracuse	510
5	Texas A&M	1215	18	North Carolina State	444
6	Penn State	1183	19	Stanford	414
7	Notre Dame	1163	20	Oklahoma	356
8	Tennessee	1104	21	Southern California	340
9	Alabama	1064	22	Boston College	269
10	Colorado	922	23	Georgia Tech	138
11	UCLA	836	24	Clemson	104
12	Ohio State	821	25	West Virginia	93
13	Virginia	759			

October 3, 1992

(Th) MISSISSIPPI STATE 30 Florida 6: Bulldogs (3-1) slickered Gators (1-2) with opening 15-play, 86y drive in atypical no-back spread formation as Mississippi State QB Sleepy Robinson finished off TD drive by lobbing 10y TD to WR Olanda Truitt. Later, Robinson went down with bad knee. Florida (1-2) QB Shane Matthews (17-38/224y, 5 INTs) endured 5 pickoffs grabbed by aroused Maroon secondary. "It's a total embarrassment," said Matthews. Mississippi State entered 4th Q with 13-6 lead. DL Kevin Henry launched rout by rumbling 22y with INT to 1YL to set up sub QB Greg Plump's TD keeper. Bulldogs D completely hemmed in Gators RB Errict Rhett (20/38y) all game, and coach Steve Spurrier observed that "too many times we couldn't even get the ball back to the line of scrimmage."

MIAMI 19 Florida State 16: Frosh WR Tamarick Vanover sped 94y with opening KO as Florida State (4-1) built 13-10 margin entering 4th Q, and advanced lead to 16-10 with 9 mins left. Miami (4-0) QB Gino Toretta beat blitz on 33y streak pattern to WR Lamar Thomas for 17-16 lead. When FSU DB Corey Sawyer mistakenly drifted into own EZ on punt RET, he panicked and flipped illegal forward pass that gave safety to Miami and extended lead to 19-16. Seminoles answered with drive that ended when K Dan Mowery missed tying 39y FG on last play, which added to coach Bobby Bowden's bitter legacy of late, game-turning kicks that went "wide right."

GEORGIA TECH 16 North Carolina State 13: Sr K Scott Sisson, already owner of 6 last-min game-winning FGs in his Yellow Jackets (3-1) career, nailed 29y FG with no time on clock to nip North Carolina State (4-2). Wolfpack led 10-3 at H as QB Terry Jordan (18-24/164y, TD) hit WR Robert Hinton with 11y TD before spraining his ankle. Georgia Tech QB Shawn Jones (19-37/244y, TD, INT) threw TD pass to TE Jeff Papushak to tie it 10-10 late in 3rd Q, but NC State escaped 3rd Q with 13-10 lead as K Steve Videtich hit 31y FG. Sisson tied it 13-13 with 2:27 to play. Then, Videtich sailed

51y FG attempt just under crossbar with 11 secs left. Miraculously, Jones scrambled away from pass rush to fire 54y strike over middle to WR Keenan Walker with 0:01 on clock. Georgia Tech H Bill Weaver fielded low snap for Sisson's game-winning FG.

Northwestern 28 PURDUE 14: Coach Gary Barnett handed out black T-shirts emblazoned with "Expect Victory Purdue '92," and sure enough it worked as Northwestern (1-3) won its Big 10 opener for 1st time since 1983 and only 2nd time since 1975. Wildcats D, led by NG Nick Walker, DT Frank Boudreaux, and LBs Jason Cunningham and Steve Ostrowski, sacked Purdue (1-3) QB Matt Pike (7-20/95y, 2 INTs) in 1st min of game and forced each 3-and-out series each of Boilers' 1st 4 possessions. NW TB Dennis Lundy rushed 39/154y and scored game's opening TD in 2nd Q. Cats WR Lee Gissendaner dodged for 70y TD on pass reception for 14-0 lead, and, after Purdue FB Mike Alstott battered for 3y TD, Gissendaner found last 9 secs of H to pluck 21y TD pass from QB Len Williams (10-13/180y, 2 TDs) for 21-7 H edge. That TD was realized through big gamble with Williams as punt-formation up-back, throwing 29y pass to DB Willie Lindsey on 4th-and-1 from Northwestern 29YL. Gissendaner's 72y punt RET contributed to TD that made it 28-7 in 3rd Q. QB Scott Hoffman relieved Pike for Boilermakers in 2nd H, and thanks to superb D play by NG Jeff Zgonina (7 tackles for loss), Purdue crept back into game as Hoffman hit WR Jerome Ross with 43y TD pass. Boilermakers returned to Cats 10YL, but Hoffman was sacked on 3rd and 4th downs to keep Purdue down by 2 TDs.

WISCONSIN 20 Ohio State 16: Wisconsin (3-1) RB Brent Moss scored 2 TDs in 3rd Q to launch his upset-making team to 17-10 lead. QB Darrell Bevell, 22-year-old frosh, threw 12-16/140y in 2nd H to spark Badgers, team without winning season since 1984. When Ohio fell behind 20-10, QB Kirk Herbstreit (20-33/216y, TD) rallied no. 12 Buckeyes (3-1) on 76y drive to WR Brian Stablein's 3y TD catch with 4:29 to play. Ohio State kicked x-pt, but Wisconsin committed personal foul. Coach John Cooper took pt off board and ordered 2-pt play from 1YL. It became magic moment for Badgers: their D came up with 1st of 2 big plays: DB Korey Manley halted TB Raymont Harris's 2-pt conversion. Later Herbstreit was stopped by Badgers DB Reggie Holt on 4th-and-5 at Wisconsin 23YL with 2 mins left.

MINNESOTA 18 Illinois 17: Illinois (2-2) coach Lou Tepper was amazingly upbeat after his Tribe blew 17-3 4th Q lead to moribund Minnesota (1-3), saying, "I was awfully proud of the effort they (his players) gave us." Gophers led 3-0 when they lost 1st Q FUM to Illini DB Robert Crumpton, whose RET went to Minny 17YL. On 2nd down, Illinois QB Jason Verduzco was victimized by DB Sean McKinley's circus-catch 17YL INT. Verduzco immediately was benched in favor of sr QB Jeff Kinney (7-15/108y) by O coordinator Tom Beck. Kinney completed 6 passes in 3rd Q, leading Illinois to FB Darren Boyer's 2nd TD run for 14-13 lead. Down 17-3 in 4th Q, Minnesota caught fire as QB Marquel Fleetwood (20-49/245y, 2 TDs) led 81 and 54y drives that ended with Fleetwood clicking on TD passes each time. Gophers ended their 9-game losing streak as Fleetwood found WR Omar Douglas all alone in EZ for 2-pt pass with 3:54 remaining.

Stanford 33 NOTRE DAME 16: LB Demetrius DuBose's 1st play blitz gave Notre Dame (3-1-1) safety on way to 16-0 lead as TB Reggie Brooks (11/86y, TD) scored on 12y run after free kick and FB Jerome Bettis (17/54y, TD) added 2y TD run in 2nd Q. However, sloppy Irish lost 5 TOs and they led to 19 Cardinal pts. Stanford (4-1) went up 20-16 in 3rd Q on QB Steve Stenstrom's 20y pass to FB J.J. Lasley. Ballhawk DB John Lynch had vital GL INT early in 4th Q. Cardinal FG drive to 23-16 lead consumed 5:49 of early 4th Q. HB Glyn Milburn (20/119y, 2 TDs) added his 2nd TD on 14y run to put it out of reach. Teary-eyed Stanford coach Bill Walsh, who had served as NBC-TV analyst for Notre Dame games in 1991, called his team's effort as big as his 3 Super Bowl wins.

TEXAS A&M 19 Texas Tech 17: K Jon Davis' 30y FG at end of 67y march with 5:19 left gave Texas Tech (2-3) hard-fought 17-16 lead. QB Jeff Granger (8-18/86y) then methodically drove Texas Aggies (5-0) 76y to set up 21y FG, booted as time expired by K Terry Venetoulias, who made amends for his missed FG and conv kick earlier in 4th Q. On winning drive, Granger escaped seemingly certain sack by Red Raiders DE Dusty Beavers on 3rd-and-8 and fired 13y pass to TE Greg Shorp at Tech 29YL. A&M rode its twin TB terrors, Greg Hill (32/141y) and Rodney Thomas (24/179y), behind big blocks of C Chris Dausin and LG Tyler Harrison and each TB scored TD. Red Raiders had shown off their own O might: QB Robert Hall (17-30/228y, TD) hit nation's 2nd leading receiver, WR Lloyd Hill (6/117y), on 41y up-and-out TD pass on last play of 3rd Q for 14-10 lead.

OREGON 30 Arizona State 20: "We're a very aggressive team," said Arizona State (1-3) coach Bruce Snyder, "But we're not a very intelligent football team." Personal fouls, other PENs adding up to 122y, 3 TOs, and muffed punt killed Devils and aided Ducks (3-2), who won their 1st Pac-10 game since early 1991. Oregon QB Danny O'Neil (14-26/209y, TD) hit WR Ronnie Harris midway in 1st Q, and K Tommy Thompson kicked 1st of his 5 FGs, each aided by ASU PEN. TB George Montgomery set up Devils' 1st TD with 10y run and added 24y TD catch in 2nd Q. Trailing 16-14 at H, ASU LB Harlen Rashada muffed punt to set up Thompson's 4th FG, and TB Sean Burwell (25/115y, TD) raced 9y to score after ASU FUM in 3rd Q. So, Oregon had sizable 27-14 lead at end of 3rd Q.

WASHINGTON 17 Southern California 10: INT RET of 31y on game's 1st play to Trojans 1YL by S Shane Pakukoa set up 1st of 2 Billy Joe Hobert TD passes in 1st Q for top-ranked Washington (4-0). Huskies WR Joe Kralik also caught 18y TD after LB Dave Hoffman's FUM REC. USC (1-1-1) won game-end stat battle 332y to 271y despite having to use sub QBs when starter Rob Johnson suffered concussion and got back in contention, trailing 14-7, on deflected 53y TD catch by WR Curtis Conway from QB Reggie Perry in 2nd Q. Trojans staged late surge behind 3rd-team frosh QB Kyle Waccholtz, only to see it snuffed when frosh QB threw into double coverage and Washington DB Walter Bailey made EZ INT with 1:32 left.

October 10, 1992

Miami 17 PENN STATE 14: Rejuvenated Miami (5-0) run game (previously ranked 106th in nation) was led by TB Donnell Bennett (15/79y, TD) and FB Larry Jones (17/69y), who helped Canes past Penn State (5-1) despite being outgained in total O by 370y to 218y. Bennett scored on 10y run in 1st Q, and Miami led 10-0 at H. Key play came in 3rd Q: Hurricanes LB Jessie Armstead's pass rush prompted DE Darren Krein's 28y INT TD RET of QB John Sacca's screen pass. It put Miami ahead 17-7. Usually reliable Nittany Lions K Craig Fayak was suffering painful back injury and had miserable day: Miami DB Dexter Seigler blocked 49y FG try in 1st Q, Fayak shanked 20y FG try in 2nd Q, and he knuckled 36y miss in 4th Q. Behind by 10 pts, Penn State coach Joe Paterno had little option but to send TB Richie Anderson into line on 4th-and-2 from Hurricanes 5YL with 10 mins to play. Miami LB Michael Barrow stopped Anderson, who rushed 27/116y and earlier scored 3rd Q TD. Lions WR O.J. McDuffie ran away from Seigler to score on late 14y TD reception.

Clemson 29 VIRGINIA 28: QB Bobby Goodman's 4 TD passes gave Virginia (5-1) 28-0 lead by middle of 2nd Q. Then, Clemson (3-2) coach Ken Hatfield reached to bench for frosh QB Louis Solomon, who raced 64y to TD just before H. Solomon (16/116y rushing) ignited biggest comeback in school history as Tigers gained 375y (288y rushing) in 2nd H. Clemson TB Rodney Blunt (16/141y) scored on 53y dash and 245-lb FB Rudy Harris (12/96y) scored twice, including churning 27y charge off LT. That pulled Clemson within 28-26 with 5:31 to play, but sub FB Howard Hall failed on 2-pt run that started at 8YL due to PEN. Key to winning drive to K Nelson Welch's FG in last min was Solomon's 45y pass to WR Larry Ryans. Goodman's last moment, desperate 40y pass to try to pull off UVa win bounced off crowd of players in EZ. Cavs star TB Terry Kirby (26/132y) left game with injury, which turned out to be broken shoulder blade, with 10 mins to go.

Arkansas 25 TENNESSEE 24: Previously-floundering Porkers (2-4) took big Knoxville crowd out of game by scoring on 50y TD bomb from QB Barry Lunney (13-19/168y, TD) to WR Ron Dickerson in 2nd Q and gaining 13-7 edge. Relying on QB Heath Shuler's 2 TD runs, sluggish Vols (5-1) awoke to score on 3 straight possessions and led Arkansas by 24-16, with only 2:28 left. Shuler ran 14y on QB draw that seemed to put Vols in heart of Hogs, but PEN erased his gain, and Tennessee had to punt. Razorbacks DB Orlando Watters' 71y punt RET brought score to 24-22, even though Vols rose up to stop 2-pt run. Arkansas LB Darwin Ireland then alertly fell on Hogs' on-side KO, which led to K Todd Wright's 4th FG, game-winning 41y boot, which came with 2 secs left. Result was 1st chink in armor of coach Johnny Majors as Volunteer loyalists began to grumble.

Illinois 18 OHIO STATE 16: Illinois' season appeared doomed after previous week's 4th Q disaster, but its grand D came up with big plays to upset Ohio State (3-2). Birthday boy Jeff Arneson, Illini DB, had happy RET of early-game FUM for stunning 96y TD. Illinois (3-2) D forced 2 other TOs as Buckeyes neared its GL and also earned 2nd Q safety as Ohio TB Robert Smith (8/40y) tried to get out of his backfield and ran into brick wall posed by DT Ken Blackman. Illinois took 15-13 lead to H on QB Jeff Kinney's 3y run but might have second-guessed its 2-pt try (from short range after Ohio PEN) when Kinney's run failed. Ohio State made FG in 3rd Q for 16-15 lead. Huge tackle launched 15-play, 86y drive to Illini K Chris Richardson's 4th Q chip-shot FG that won it. It started when Buckeyes were driving for apparent winning TD: Ohio State TB Eddie George lost FUM at Illinois 10YL when hammered by LB Dana Howard. Buckeyes K Tim Williams, who made 3 FGs, was left pounding turf in frustration after he missed 44y FG in last min.

Indiana 28 NORTHWESTERN 3: Tough D of Indiana (3-2) sacked Wildcats (1-3) QB Len Williams (10-21/96y, INT) and his replacements 9 times in keeping Northwestern out of EZ. NW's D played well too, allowing only 278y and coming up with 3 INTs of Hoosiers QB Trent Green (9-22/104y, TD, 3 INTs), 2 by S Greg Gill. Wildcats had 2 potentially great gambles blow up because of poor execution: Trailing 7-3 in 2nd Q, P Matt Dzierwa passed on 4th-and-2 from Indiana 38YL, but wide open LB-E Steve Shine dropped pass inside 30YL. Green soon found WR Thomas Lewis (4/36y) for 16y TD for 14-3 IU H edge. Early in 4th Q, FG holder Dzierwa pitched out to Cats K Brian Leahy, who was halted 1y short of 1st down at Hoosiers 25YL by DB Chris Dyer.

IOWA 23 Wisconsin 22: At last, groggy Iowa (2-4) awoke from season-long slumber in 4th Q of contest it needed badly to win. Hawkeyes QB Jim Hartlieb passed 31-51/297y, 3 TDs, INT, including 2 clutch plays that won game in last 55 secs: 4y TD pass and 2-pt pass, each to WB Anthony Dean. TB Brent Moss rushed 25/158y and scored both TDs for Wisconsin (3-2), including 1y smash that provided 19-14 lead in 4th Q. Having not been defeated by Badgers since 1976, Iowa pulled out last-min victory for 2nd year in row over Wisconsin. But, it still took CB Carlos James taking advantage of bounced snap to swoop in to block 53y FG try by Badgers K Rich Thompson at end.

Texas 34 Oklahoma 24 (Dallas): Putting pressure on Sooners (3-2) QB Cale Gundy (17-41/276y, 3 INTs), Texas set throttle wide open for its pro-style O to build 34-10 lead in Cotton Bowl stadium. Before Texas' O explosion could occur, Gundy led Oklahoma 80y to 9y scoring pass to WR P.J. Mills (3/40y, TD) on opening series. Longhorns (3-2) QB Peter Gardere threw 20-32/271y, 2 TDs and became 1st QB to lead his team to 4 wins in storied 87-year history of hard-fought series. Gardere hit TE Jason Burleson with 31y TD pass to break 10-10 tie in 2nd Q after Oklahoma's roughing and unsportsmanlike PENs turned Texas' 4th-and-5 punt from its own 25YL into 1st down opportunity at Sooners 48YL. FB Phil Brown scored Longhorns' 1st rushing TD against Sooners since 1983 with 13y run that extended lead to 24-10 in 3rd Q. Longhorns LB Winfred Tubbs contributed 11 tackles and 2 INTs, both in Texas territory.

RICE 28 Southern Methodist 13: Playing without 5 starters and 5 reserves because of NCAA-mandated suspensions over abuse of book-card privileges, 15 available defenders of SMU (3-3) couldn't cope with 322y ground game of Rice (2-3). Shifty Rice TB Trevor Cobb rushed 33/210y and scored 2 TDs, and QB Bert Emanuel (5-12/123y) scored game's 1st 2 TDs on 10 and 7y runs on his way to 21/109y rushing. Mustangs were able to move ball for 472y, but lost FUMs at Owls 5 and 11YLs. SMU QB Dan Freiburger (36-55/393y, 2 TDs, 3 INTs) filled air with his passes, 2 of which were taken for TDs by WR Korey Beard.

AIR FORCE 18 Navy 16: Never before had Air Force (5-1) K Chris MacInnis attempted collegiate FG. He faced 38y try in last min with Falcons trailing 16-15, and made it. Navy (0-5) used 2 timeouts to ice MacInnis, but he claimed it had reverse effect: "…they helped me to get out on the field, get adjusted and have time to relax." Navy had led 10-9 at H, thanks primarily to QB Jason Van Matre's 63y TD pass to WR Michael Jefferson. Behind 15-13 in middle of 4th Q, Middies used personal foul PEN tacked on to Van Matre's 17y pass to WR Jimmy Screen to earn 1st down at Air Force 19YL. FB Cleavon Smith's 3 runs made 9y, and K Tim Rogers' FG gave Navy its 1st lead of season at 16-15. Held to single 1st down in 2nd H to this point, Falcons used 35y KO RET to launch 41y drive to MacInnis' winning FG, on which QB Jarvis Baker lost FUMs twice, but each was ruled after whistle.

October 17, 1992

Boston College 35 PENN STATE 32: Nittany Lions (5-2) led 10-7 late in 1st H when roughing punter PEN positioned Boston College (5-0-1) QB Glenn Foley (21-37/344y, 4 TDs) for comeback on 3 quick TD passes in 4-min span of 2nd Q. Eagles led 28-10 at H after WR Ivan Boyd caught 48y TD and TE Pete Mitchell grabbed 16 and 29y TDs. Trailing 35-16 in 4th Q, Lions rallied for 16 pts on 80 and 90y TD drives. Penn State WR O. J. McDuffie caught 11/212y, ran 43y with reverse, and scored on 7y TD pass and 2-pt pass from QB Tony Sacca (20-41/288y, TD, INT). TB Chuckie Dukes (29/149y) was relentless runner for BC, while backup TB Dwight Shirley added 19/56y.

Wake Forest 30 MARYLAND 23: Wake Forest (3-3) QB Keith West (17-30/331y, TD, INT) had his best passing game yet to help spoil Maryland (1-6) Homecoming. Among West's 7 best plays were completions ranging from 21y to 51y and they averaged 34.6y. Short TD runs by TB John Leach gave Wake 14-10 H lead, but Terps overhauled Deacons in 3rd Q as RB Doug Burnett scored on 15 and 6y runs. Then, with 35 secs left in 3rd Q, 2 Wake sub DEs, Glenn Hart and Willie Hall, injured their necks on Maryland running play. Medical service delayed game more than 20 mins, and Terrapins, facing 2nd-and-1, never warmed to task, had to punt, and didn't score again. Just 3 plays after gaining post-punt custody, West threw 49y TD to WR Todd Dixon for 27-23 lead. Maryland QB John Kaleo (30-48/405y, TD, 4 INTs), despite 9 sacks (3 by Wake DE Mike McCrary), nearly pulled out win at end as WR Marcus Badgett (11/187y, TD) just missed pulling in post-pattern pass inside Deacons 5YL in game's last min.

SOUTH CAROLINA 21 Mississippi State 6: Monday's player vote to oust Gamecocks (1-5) coach Sparky Woods eventually evolved into emotional win, its 1st-ever in SEC, over no. 15 Mississippi State (4-2) as tall, long-haired, fist-pumping frosh QB Steve Taneyhill (7-14/183y, 2 TDs, INT) sparked South Carolina to 2 early scores and 14-0 H advantage. Bulldogs opened 2nd H with signs they wanted back in contention, going 75y after KO to WR Orlanda Truitt's 15y TD reception from QB Greg Plumb (9-19/148y, TD, INT). Ahead 14-6, Taneyhill quickly reclaimed game's momentum with 43y TD bomb to leaping WR Don Chaney. Carolina frosh WR Asim Penny, who caught 1st Q TD pass, had punched another student during tumultuous days prior to game and he apologized after game, saying, "I guess we all learned something this week, didn't we?"

GEORGIA 30 Vanderbilt 20: Alerted by last year's upset loss to Vanderbilt (2-4), Georgia (6-1) jumped to 13-0 lead in 1st Q as TB Garrison Hearst (21/246y, 2 TDs) began day-long piercing of Commodore D. But, Vandy surged back in 2nd Q as FB Royce Love pushed over GL at end of 62y drive, K Robbie Chura chimed in with 22 and 19y FGs after Dores bungled GL opportunities, and QB Marcus Wilson scored from 4YL after LB Brad Brown's INT. Only interruption was Hearst's 71y TD

jaunt around LE. It was tied 20-20 at H. Meanwhile, according to *Atlanta Journal-Constitution,* "Vanderbilt grounded Air Georgia…only to get bombed by the ground game." Hearst's 55y bolt past C Jack Swan's block put Bulldogs in lead for good. After 1st Q, Vandy had crimped UGa QB Eric Zeier (9-20/107y, INT) to tune of 4-11/51y, INT, and had reason to gripe over illegal blocking call that nullified TB Tony Jackson's 99y KO TD RET, Chura's wide 29y FG that TV replays showed was good, and Wilson's 4th Q GL sneak that was ruled short.

Alabama 17 TENNESSEE 10: Alabama (7-0) used TB Derrick Lassic's pair of 1y TDs and 33/142y rushing to roll Tide to 7th straight win. Leading 17-3 and owning line of scrimmage well into 3rd Q, Alabama coach Gene Stallings kicked himself for not taking easy FG on 4th-and-2 at Vols 3YL. DB Steve Session firmly spilled Lassic for 1y loss, and Tennessee (5-2) suddenly was energized. "I made a silly mistake and they (Tide players) bailed me out," said Stallings afterward. Volunteers QB Heath Shuler's 3y TD flip to TE David Horn trimmed margin to 17-10 with 12:53 left in 4th Q. Even midfield FUM, lost by Bama FB Martin Houston to Tennessee DE Todd Kelly with 1:33 left, couldn't deter Crimson Tide D, top-ranked in nation. After Shuler (12-23/116y, TD, INT) was sacked for 5th time, DB Chris Donnelly's INT snuffed late hopes on next play.

Kansas 50 IOWA STATE 47: RB Sherman Williams (5/38y, 2 TDs) tallied on 18 and 12y TD runs and RB Jim McMillion rushed 10/119y, TD, including 62y sprint to set up Williams' 1st Q TD, to key 40 straight pt surge by Iowa State (2-4). Cyclones LG Jim Thompson scored on 25y "Fumblerookie" to tie it at 21-21 in 2nd Q on way to 47-21 edge in 3rd Q. Kansas (5-1) staged biggest comeback in school history as QB Chip Hilleary (16-27/239y, 4 TDs) ran for 17y TD and passed for 2 more scores to pull his team to within 47-42. Jayhawks D, shredded for 516y until it stiffened in 4th Q, chipped in with 2 FUM RECs, including LB Larry Thiel's winning 37y TD RET of bobble by ISU QB Bob Utter (11-16/212y). RB Maurice Douglas made 2-pt run to complete Kansas' comeback with 6:07 to play. It was enough for Jayhawks' 1st win in Ames since 1981.

COLORADO 24 Oklahoma 24: LB Aubrey Beavers' 58y FUM TD RET and RB Dewell Brewer's 72y TD run helped Oklahoma (3-2-1) to 17-7 lead in 3rd Q. Buffaloes (5-0-1) frosh QB Koy Detmer ignored unpleasantness of 5 INTs to toss 2 TDs and set up K Mitch Berger's final-play 53y FG. Berger replaced regular K Pat Blottiaux in 2nd H after Blottiaux was injured. Wrestling with yellow flags all night (more than 100y in PENs), Sooners seemed to have salted away game at 24-14 on DB Darrius Johnson's 17y INT TD RET. But, OU FB Kenyon Rasheed lost FUM at Sooners 38YL, and Detmer completed 17 and 18y passes to WR Charles Johnson to poise TB Lamont Warren's 3y TD run. With no timeouts left, Colorado clicked on Detmer's 23y pass and Berger blasted his long, line-drive FG to tie it.

Arizona 21 STANFORD 6: K Eric Abrams led off with 2 FGs for 6-0 lead in 2nd Q for no. 8 Stanford (5-2). Iron D of Arizona (3-2-1) limited Cardinal to 33y rushing, but most of all, it made 8 sacks, and knocked Cardinal QB Steve Strenstrom (13-26/133y) from game on 3 different occasions. Stanford backup QB Mark Butterfield was in action and cocking his arm in 2nd Q when swift Wildcats DE Tedy Bruschi forced FUM at Stanford 1YL, and Cards' only TO quickly paved way for QB George Malauulu's TD run for 7-6 lead. Arizona rushed 58/256y, adding middle-Q 45 and 33y TD runs by backup TB Chuck Levy (15/72y) and FB Billy Johnson (12/80y) respectively. TB Antiwaun Carter led with 20/97y.

WASHINGTON STATE 30 Ucla 17: Rose Bowl Fever suddenly ran rampant in The Paloose as Cougars ran record to 6 opening wins for 1st time since their last Pasadena visit in 1930. Keys to victory for surprising no. 22 Washington State (6-0) were LB Ron Childs' 17y INT TD RET and WR Deron Pointer's 98y TD RET of 2nd H KO. UCLA (3-3), winless in Pac-10, was forced to use 4th string, frosh QB Ryan Fien (5-20/55y, INT) because of earlier injuries to QBs Wayne Cook and Rob Walker and ineffectiveness of 1st-time starter John Barnes. Fien lost 2 FUMs deep in his end that set up Wazzoo TDs and was sacked 4 times for 35y. With its high-octane O somewhat struggling (QB Drew Bledsoe passed 9-25/108y, TD, 2 INTs), Cougars depended on their D, which, aside from Bruins TB Kevin Williams' 78y 1st Q TD run, completely stuffed UCLA. Childs made FUM REC at Bruins 5YL in 2nd Q that led to Bledsoe's 3y TD pass to TE Brett Carolan, and DE DeWayne Patterson's 3rd Q sack forced FUM at 2YL in 3rd Q.

October 24, 1992

NORTH CAROLINA 26 Georgia Tech 14: It had been 10 years since North Carolina (6-2) had beaten even 1 ranked foe. Tar Heels succeeded 2nd week in row, after having defeated no. 17 Virginia 27-7 previous Saturday. No. 19 Georgia Tech (4-3) was held to 175y O, including 5 of Shawn Jones's 11-27/106y, TD passing. Carolina QB Mike Thomas' 19y run keyed mid-4th Q FG drive that burned 7 mins and earned 20-14 lead.

WAKE FOREST 23 Army 7: Black Knights (2-4) arrived with nation's 2nd-best rushing O (292y per-game avg) in its Wishbone attack. Fast-improving Wake Forest (4-3) limited Army to 61/123y rushing as Demon Deacons DEs Mike McCrary and Maurice Miller combined for 17 tackles. High punt snap gave Army possession at Wake 19YL in 1st Q, and Cadets scored on QB Rick Roper's 3y run. Using balanced attack, Deacons built

10-7 H lead as WB Bobby Jones made 22y catch to set up TB John Leach's short TD run and terrific 35y grab in double coverage to poise K Mike Green's 34y FG. Wake DL Jay Williams made midfield FUM REC in 3rd Q, and backup TB Ned Moultrie, having career day with 20/149y rushing, scored from 1YL to up lead to 17-7.

ALABAMA 31 Mississippi 10: Holding Alabama (8-0) to only 83y rushing, Ole Miss (4-3) D blunted Bama's fine 241y per-game rushing avg. But, Crimson Tide QB Jay Barker had season highs in passing: 25-39/285y, TD, INT, with early 22y TD pass to WR David Palmer. Win all but clinched SEC West for Bama. Trailing 14-0 in 2nd Q, Rebels QB Russ Shows (7-19/93y, TD, INT) launched 53y TD pass to WR Eddie Small to stoke visitors' hopes, at 14-7, of springing upset. Alabama TB Derrick Lassic (8/18y, TD) sprained his ankle in 3rd Q and his replacement, Sherman Williams, made TD runs of 1 and 4y in 4th Q.

MICHIGAN 63 Minnesota 13: Michigan (6-0-1) celebrated its 1000th game with its 728th victory and retained Little Brown Jug trophy by walloping Minnesota (1-6). Wolverines QB Elvis Grbac (14-19/208y, 4 TDs) bested Jim Harbaugh's school career passing y record and WR Derrick Alexander (7/130y) became 1st UM player to score 4 receiving TDs in single game. Alexander tallied on plays of 52, 13, 3, and 32y. Michigan TB Tyrone Wheatley (24/148y) scored 2 TDs as Wolverines scored on 9 of 11 series through 3 Qs. Minnesota coach Jim Wacker was impressed: "There's nobody close to these guys; the NFL should give them a call." Gophers WR John Lewis dialed long distance for 2 TDs: He raced 92y on KO TD RET in 1st Q and turned short pass from QB Marquel Fleetwood (7-21/150y, TD, INT) into 94y TD in 3rd Q.

NOTRE DAME 42 Brigham Young 16: BYU (4-4) QB Ryan Hancock put up big pass numbers (28-56/339y, TD, 3 INTs), but Notre Dame (5-1-1) won this year's Holy War when QB Rick Mirer was equally effective in airways: 12-17/151y, 2 TDs. Fighting Irish earned TDs at beginning of each H: LB Demetrius DuBose recovered EZ FUM for 1st Q TD, and WR Ray Griggs took screen pass and raced 54y to advance lead to 21-9 in 3rd Q. After K David Lauder's trio of 1st H FGs, Hancock's TD pass pulled Cougars within 21-16. FB Jerome Bettis led ND with 21/113y rushing and scored twice as Irish pulled away with 21 pts in 4th Q. Virtually absent from 1st H Irish lineup, TB Reggie Brooks rushed 15/112y. Crowd chuckled in 4th Q as ND coach Lou Holtz drew PEN for demonstrating BYU technique with late game hammerlock on official's neck; victim had no post-game comment, but Holtz apologized. Coach Lavell Edwards downplayed Irish mystique after BYU's 1st visit to South Bend: "The biggest concern I had was Bettis, Brooks, Mirer, DuBose, and as it turned out, that was a lot more of a problem for us than ghosts."

KANSAS 27 Oklahoma 10: Goalposts were falling at Memorial Stadium and coach Glen Mason was riding shoulders of his players as clock ticked down on 1 of Kansas' greatest victories over longtime nemesis Oklahoma (3-3-1). Kansas (5-1) won for only 3rd time in 29 years over Sooners. Jayhawks TB Maurice Douglas and FB Monte Cozzens each went past 100y rushing barrier and each got TD: Douglas from 14YL for 17-7 lead in 2nd Q, and Cozzens broke through 4 tacklers running from 13YL to cap scoring in 4th Q. Kansas P-K Dan Eichloff had 48y avg on 5 punts and made FGs of 49 and 47y. QB Cale Gundy (18-30/233y, TD, INT) broke 3 Sooner career passing marks, but was knocked from game with separated shoulder in 3rd Q. Could it have been that riled-up Jayhawk D did not appreciated Gundy's "fat butts" comment during pre-game warmups? With Oklahoma gaining only 69y rushing and Gundy gone, it O was blanked in 2nd H.

COLORADO 54 Kansas State 7: It started as innocent compliment to Kansas 2 weeks earlier, which had thrashed K-State 31-7. At that time, Wildcats (3-3) coach Bill Snyder called Jayhawks D best he'd coached against since coming to Kansas State. Colorado (6-0-1) coach Bill McCartney tacked quote to wall of D meeting room, and Buffs D turned Cats into road kill. Kansas State made 3 1st downs, was stopped for no or negative y on 30 of 47 plays, and finished with 16y total O. Wildcats only TD came in 3rd Q on DB C.J. Masters's 52y INT TD RET. Colorado gained 514y O, but suffered some weak moments: In 5 trips to at least K-State's 11YL, it had to settle for 4 FGs by K Mitch Berger and suffered INT. Buffs QB Kordell Stewart (21-39/247y, TD, 2 INTs) opened scoring with 2y TD pass to TE Christian Fauria and built 27-0 lead in 2nd Q by scrambling from pass rush, breaking 3 tackles, and lunging into EZ. Colorado WR Charles Johnson caught 8/104y.

Texas A&M 19 BAYLOR 13: Aggies (7-0) TB tandem of Greg Hill (19/119y) and Rodney Thomas (9/116y) each topped 100y and scored TD as A&M propelled to its best start since 1975. Thomas opened scoring at 7-0 with 84y sprint in 1st Q. Baylor (4-4), relying on balanced 206y to 181y run-to-pass O, went ahead 10-7 by H on 26y TD arrow pitched by QB J.J. Joe (10-21/181y, TD, INT) to WR Melvin Bonner in 2nd Q. Bears K Trey Weir extended lead to 13-7 with his 2nd FG in 3rd Q, but Hill put lead back for Aggies at 14-13 with 40y TD dash before end of 3rd Q. FG and safety extended A&M's margin, but victory remained unsecured until CB Aaron Glenn picked off pass at his 25YL with 1:07 left.

Arizona State 20 UCLA 0: Another UCLA (3-4) QB went to injury list: frosh Ryan Fien (4-7/18y) banged up hip near end of 3rd Q as Bruins, with scant 48y O and only 2 trips past midfield, trailed 17-0 at that time. Sun Devils (4-3) had to dig deep down its depth chart and came up with TB Kevin Galbreath, who rushed 44/183y and scored 10y 2nd Q TD to end 66y drive for 14-0 H lead. Transfer QB John Barnes led UCLA on late-game drive from Bruins 20YL to Arizona State 1YL as he passed 6-7/79y, including 25y strike to WR J.J. Stokes. But, RB Daron Washington tried to leap for TD and lost FUM. With it went UCLA's NCAA-record 245 straight games, since early 1971, in which it had scored.

SOUTHERN CALIFORNIA 31 Washington State 21: Do-all WR Curtis Conway made 24y TD carry on wide reverse run in 1st Q to tie it 7-7, caught 27y TD pass in 2nd Q for 21-7 lead, and raced 58y to 12YL with pooched KO to set up victory-assuring 4th Q TD for Trojans (4-1-1). Washington State (6-1) QB Drew Bledsoe countered with

24-37/358y, 2 TDs, INT through air, while RB Shaumbe Wright-Fair added 15/103y rushing. Cougars valiantly rallied to within 24-21 as Bledsoe connected with TE Calvin Shexnayder on 9y TD pass at end of 58y drive in 3rd Q and WR Deron Pointer on 34y TD pass at end of 99y drive in 4th Q. TDs were set up respectively by CB Torey Hunter's 30y KO RET and Bledsoe's 4y midfield pass on 4th-and-2. No sooner had Wazzu taken 5 mins to finish its 99y trip, when on-side or squib KO was discussed with 3:19 to play. Instead, K Aaron Price, coach Mike's son, popped it up to left sideline. Conway raced upfield to make excellent catch and found hole for his 58y RET to set up FB Wes Bender's 8y TD run and bust comeback bid by Cougars.

October 31, 1992

RUTGERS 50 Virginia Tech 49: WR Chris Brantley's 8th catch, his 4th TD, at 0:00 of 4th Q squeaked Rutgers (5-3) past Hokies (2-5-1). QBs Brian Fortay (24-45/338y, 4 TDs, 5 INTs) of Rutgers and Maurice DeShazo (15-27/302y, 2 TDs, 4 INTs) of Virginia Tech staged air wars, while Scarlet Knights TB Chris Ritter ran 17/148y, 2 TDs. Tech led 28-13 at end of wild 1st Q, which included Hokies DE Cornell Brown's 18y INT TD RET. It was 35-23 at H, and after teams traded 3rd Q TD passes—1 for DeShazo and another for Rutgers backup QB Ray Lucas—Scarlet Knights erupted for 3 TDs in 4th Q.

North Carolina 31 MARYLAND 24: Massive Tar Heels TB Natrone Means (31/249y) wore down Maryland (2-7) with TD runs of 27 and 76y as Terps faded late. Still, with QB John Kaleo throwing school-record 58 times with 31 completions/255y, 3 INTs, Terrapins were able to lead twice at 14-7 and 21-14. WR-RB Frank Wycheck (19/102y rushing), who moved into lead RB spot to replace injured Doug Burnett in 2nd Q, made 20y TD run. North Carolina (7-2) used 46 secs that remained in 2nd Q after Wycheck's TD, and Heels scored in 4 plays to tie it 14-14 at H: Sub QB Jason Stanicek hit WR Steven Jerry with 28y TD pass. Terps went ahead 21-14 on Wycheck's 1y TD run that followed DB Bill Inge's REC of 2nd H on-side KO. Terps tied it at 24-24 on FG in 4th Q, but Carolina drove to 12YL with 4 mins left, and here came Means again, running to right. Maryland reacted that direction, only to have Means slip handoff to WR Randall Felton for 12y romp into EZ.

WAKE FOREST 18 Clemson 15: Wake Forest (5-3) won its 4th straight game when Deacons made most of only 21 2nd H plays. TB Rodney Blunt's 118y rushing powered Clemson (4-4), but he sat in favor of sub TB Greg Hood as Tigers regained 15-10 4th Q edge on Hood's 15y run. Key 4th Q moment for Wake: 42y pass from QB Keith West to TE John Henry Mills on 3rd-and-9. Winning tally soon came on WR Todd Dixon's diving TD catch, his 2nd of game, with 3:41 left.

SOUTH CAROLINA 24 Tennessee 23: Suddenly resurgent Gamecocks (3-5) beat 2nd top 20 team, win called by coach Sparky Woods "greatest I've ever been part of." No. 16 Tennessee (5-3) fell behind on early TD pass by South Carolina QB Steve Taneyhill, but surged back ahead 17-14 behind QB Heath Shuler's 20-28/296y passing. At 17-17 in 4th Q, each team scored: Gamecocks on 79y drive for 24-17 lead and Vols on FB Mose Phlips' 39y catch and magnificent run through 8 tacklers. Winning 2-pt try by Vols was thwarted by Carolina LB Hank Campbell.

Florida 26 Georgia 24 (Jacksonville): Gators (5-2) shut down Georgia (7-2) TB Garrison Hearst, nation's leading rusher, with 14/41y rushing, and UF defenders taunted Bulldog fans afterward by striking Heisman poses. Bulldogs 310-lb T Bernard Williams had cracked big block for sub FB Frank Harvey, who slipped 2 tackles near scrimmage and raced 80y to give Georgia short-lived 7-3 lead in 1st Q. Georgia could have clinched SEC East crown, but blocked punt by Florida CB Larry Kennedy and passing of QB Shane Matthews (28-45/301y, 2 TDs) helped build 23-7 Gatosr lead. But, Bulldogs QB Eric Zeier (15-28/238y, 2 TDs, 2 INTs) overcame 2 sacks by Gator DE Kevin Carter and INT by LB Ed Robinson late in 2nd Q to lead UGa to TD pass to WR Ha'son Graham and 49y FG by K Todd Peterson. Georgia was back in game at H, 23-17. K Bart Edmiston made 34y FG in 3rd Q to extend Florida's lead at 26-17. After Georgia recovered FUM at Gators 31YL, Zeier threw scrambling, tripped-up INT snatched by UF DB Ben Hanks to kill great chance before he narrowed gap to 26-24 with 4 mins left on TD pass to WR Brian Bohannon.

Michigan 24 PURDUE 17: Halloween brought out old "Spoilermakers" who nearly struck again as Purdue (3-5) QB Eric Hunter ran and passed for TDs to build 17-7 H lead, biggest margin faced by Michigan (7-0-1) since 1989 Rose Bowl. But, TB Jesse Johnson, part of stellar Wolverines TB trio, rushed for 111y in 2nd H in relief of injured TB Tyrone Wheatley, after spending 1st H in well-rested 2-carry role. Michigan stormed 92y on 10-play advance after 2nd H KO as TE Tony McGee caught 10y TD pass from QB Elvis Grbac (17-24/169y, 2 TDs). Purdue was halted on next series, and Wolverines went 76y, sparked by Johnson's runs, including his 3y TD dive. Wolverines copped Big 10 record with their 18th straight win, but to earn it, they had to come up with DB Pat Maloney's INT of Purdue QB Eric Hunter at 11YL with 2 secs left.

Michigan State 27 NORTHWESTERN 26: Northwestern (2-6) celebrated as K Brian Leahy's last moment FG try appeared to win Homecoming thriller, but it faded late against wind and officials called it wide. Wildcats QB Len Williams (28-35/465y,

TD, 2 INTs) passed brilliantly, while Michigan State (3-5) TB Tico Duckett rambled for 31/172y, TD in 267y ground game. Northwestern forged 17-10 H edge on 2 big plays: 56y TD run by TB Dennis Lundy (16/138y, TD) and 90y KO TD RET by WR Lee Gissendaner. Leahy's 28y FG with 10 mins left tied it at 20-20, but things turned bizarre after Spartans TB Craig Thomas scored on 7y run with 6:59 to play. Bad snap cost MSU x-pt, but K Bill Stoyanovich (2 FGs) got 2nd try when Cats needlessly committed facemask foul. Little Tar Pat Wright made 1-handed grab of Williams' lobbed TD pass, but NW failed on 2-pt pass try to stay down 27-26. Spartans couldn't move, so Williams had chance to complete 3 passes and scramble to 18YL before Leahy's miss, of which he said: "In my heart, I know it was good."

NEBRASKA 52 Colorado 7: Exorcizing its big game demons, Nebraska (6-1) ended Buffaloes' 25-game Big 8 unbeaten streak. Huskers frosh QB Tommie Frazier tossed 2 TD passes in 2nd H, and IB Calvin Jones (21/101y) ran for 3 TDs. Jones said it was "nice to win one of the so-called big ones." It was Huskers' 1st win after 7 losses dating back to 1988 against top 10 teams. Only time Colorado (6-1-1) O got cooking was in last 6 mins of 2nd Q when fierce pass rush pressure on QB Koy Detmer was relieved by strategy of no-huddle O. Reserve TB James Hill scored Buffalo TD on 3y run to slice Huskers lead to 17-7. On next Colorado series, however, Detmer was stripped of ball by Nebraska LB Travis Hill, who carried it to Buffs 27YL to set up TD for 24-7 H lead.

Utah 20 AIR FORCE 13: Soph DL Luther Elliss, playing his 2nd game in his home state of Colorado, made 4 tackles for losses as Utah (5-3) D bent, but failed to break against Air Force (6-3) Wishbone. Meanwhile, Falcons D, which had played so well against San Diego State's superb TB Marshall Faulk previous week, was trampled by 273y run game of Utes that featured nifty TBs Keith Williams (20/119y), Pierre Jones (17/84y, TD), and powerful TB Jamal Anderson (9/55y, TD). Falcons QB Jarvis Baker scored on 31y sprint in 1st Q, and HB Antoine Banks dashed 55y to set up K Chris MacInnis' 23y FG in 2nd Q. MacInnis had 27y FG try blocked with 44 secs to go in 2nd Q, so teams were knotted 10-10 at H. Vital TD came from Anderson from 1YL in 3rd Q as Utes went 68y for 17-13 lead.

WASHINGTON 41 Stanford 7: Huskies (8-0) raked ranked Stanford (6-3) D for 467y, prompting impressed Cardinal DB John Lynch to say: "I'd vote them no. 1." That is exactly what writers did in Sunday's AP poll. Huskies QB Mark Brunell, starting his 3rd game since replacing Billy Joe Hobert, threw for 161y, 2 TDs, and ran for another. Stanford owned stellar 120y rushing D avg, but relinquished 275y as T Lincoln Kennedy led Huskies O line, which felt it had "something to prove." Things had started well enough for Cardinal as they stopped opening 3 Huskies possessions and became 1st team this season to own lead over Washington at 7-0. Stanford's TD came when DB Darrien Gordon's INT set up Stenstrom's 31y scoring arrow to WR Justin Armour, only 3:04 into 1st Q. TB Napoleon Kaufman's 65y punt RET to 4YL soon turned momentum in UW's favor.

November 7, 1992

North Carolina State 31 VIRGINIA 7: With North Carolina's 40-7 loss to Clemson, Wolfpack moved into 2nd place in ACC. It was NC State's 1st win over Virginia (6-4) since 1985, season before coach Dick Sheridan came to Raleigh. Cavaliers benched QB Bobby Goodman after trailing 17-0 at H on 2 big plays by Wolfpack: DB Mike Reid blocked punt for DB Dewayne Washington's 6y TD RET in 1st Q, and TB Anthony Barbour (21/107y) raced 59y to score in 2nd Q. FB Charles Way battered to 1y TD in 3rd Q to pull UVa back into game, trailing 17-7 under direction of frosh QB Mike Groh. Wolfpack ran away in 4th Q on QB Terry Jordan's 65y TD pass and LB Tyler Lawrence's 8y INT TD RET.

Vanderbilt 20 KENTUCKY 7: Commodores (3-5) put end to 4-game losing streak as they banked on their aroused D. Wildcats (4-5) coach Bill Curry ended up frustrated by his O and angry at home crowd for catcalls aimed at up-and-down QB Pookie Jones (7-27/75y, 2 INTs): "…I don't see how you can boo the kid who last week just turned in the best game in school history." (Kentucky had gained 500y on October 31 in 37-36 loss to Mississippi State.) LB Shelton Quarles led Vandy D with 10 tackles as UK was held to 123y total O. Vanderbilt QB Marcus Wilson broke loose for 57y run to Kentucky 9YL in 1st Q to set up FB Royce Love's 1y TD smash. Cats tied it later in opening Q as S Brad Armstead scooped up FUM by Vandy WR Eric Lewis and charged 70y to score. Early in 4th Q, Dores LB Brad Brown evened up D TD count with his own: 13y INT TD RET to boost score to 17-7 in favor of happy Vandy, winners of 2nd SEC road game in its last 28.

FLORIDA 24 Southern Mississippi 20: It wasn't pretty for no. 14 Gators (6-2) as rain and chill mixed with rash of personal foul PENs to contribute to nasty day. To make matters worse, school song *We Are the Boys from Old Florida* was judged sexist by UF's Committee on Sexism and Homophobia. Still, Gators scored on game's 1st snap as TB handoff was returned to QB Shane Matthews (22-39/317y, TD, INT), who fired long to WR Willie Jackson for 70y TD. Big play for Southern Miss (6-4) came in 2nd Q as DB Perry Carter was only player in area as Matthews tried to unload pass, and

Carter returned his INT 52y for TD that pulled Eagles to within 17-10 with 11:26 left before H. Aided by personal foul PEN, Southern added FG by K Lance Nations to crawl within 17-13 at H. Eagles QB Tommy Waters (23-43/248y, TD, INT) capped 77y trip early in 4th Q with 17y TD pass that gained 20-17 lead, but Florida TB Errict Rhett (21/120y, TD) quickly took over with 5/22y and 8y reception culminating in his 3y TD run behind block of T Jason Odom.

NOTRE DAME 54 Boston College 7: No. 9 Eagles (7-1-1) had excellent statistical numbers—nation's 6th-ranked O and 7th-ranked D—as they arrived for matchup of Division I-A's only Catholic colleges. Boston College produced little of either on crisp autumn afternoon in Indiana. No. 8 Notre Dame (7-1-1) scored 5 straight times for 37-0 H lead, outgaining BC 347y to 11y. Scoring on 16y keeper for 21-0 lead in 1st Q, Fighting Irish QB Rick Mirer (13-18/180y, INT) also passed for 3 TDs. ND TB Reggie Brooks rushed 18/174y, 2 TDs, including 73y TD dash in 2nd Q. Boston College gained 165y in 2nd H and finally tallied in 4th Q, with score standing at 54-0, on TE Pete Mitchell's 4y catch from QB Glenn Foley (11-28/121y, INT).

NEBRASKA 49 Kansas 7: After its best start in 24 years, Kansas (7-2) got dose of reality on its prime-time TV visit to Lincoln. Frosh QB Tommie Frazier, new igniter of Nebraska O, passed for 3 TDs in 1st H, 2 to TE Gerald Armstrong as Huskers (7-1) brushed aside Kansas for inside track to Orange Bowl berth. Huskers Derek Brown (15/156y) and Calvin Jones (13/107y, 2 TDs) continued their 2-headed IB assault on twin 1,000y seasons. Nebraska's last 3 TDs of 1st H, which built 35-7 edge, came in sparkling stretch of 2:24. Folded into Husker spree was Jayhawks' only 1st H TD: 4y run by RB Maurice Douglas (17/63y, TD) that very briefly trimmed margin to 21-7.

TEXAS CHRISTIAN 23 Texas 14: Twenty-five years had passed since TCU (2-6-1) had last beaten Texas (5-3); not since 1958 had it occurred in Fort Worth. Tumbling from SWC lead, Longhorns were held to 52y rushing. Two keys: Texas DB Grady Cavness suffered safety by illegally batting his muffed catch of punt out of EZ, and TCU DB Tony Rand exploding 58y on INT RET for clinching TD.

WASHINGTON STATE 20 Arizona State 18: Rushing for only 29y, but utilizing QB Drew Bledsoe's 22-31/267y, 2 TDs, INT passing, Cougars (7-2) overcame early 10-0 Arizona State (4-5) lead. Bledsoe hit WRs Deron Pointer (25y) and C.J. Davis (31y) for long TDs. Washington State K Aaron Price made 2 FGs in 3rd Q to take lead at 13-10. Davis' 3rd Q TD catch put Wazzu up 20-10, and TD came after ASU players thought their K Mike Richey had tied it with 32y FG. Neither team had been able to score when it faced stiff wind, and Richey's FG would have bucked that trend. Sun Devils DE Shante Carver enjoyed magnificent game: Carver twice deflected Bledsoe's passes, once so that DT Greg Kordas could intercept to set up ASU's 1st Q TD, 9y run by TB Kevin Galbreath for 7-0 lead. Carver also blocked FG try, blocked punt through EZ for 4th Q safety, made FUM REC, made 2 tackles for -9y, and sacked Bledsoe once. With 2:29 to play in 4th Q, Arizona State scored on QB Grady Benton's 29y TD pass to WR Clyde McCoy, but TE Bob Brasher dropped tying 2-pt pass.

ARIZONA 16 Washington 3: "Who's no. 1?" debate between Washington and Miami that had raged for nearly 2 years was silenced as magnificent Arizona (6-2-1) D ended 22-game win streak of Washington (8-1). In 1st H led 3-0 by Wildcats, Huskies TE Mark Bruener dropped pass in EZ on botched FG try, and Arizona QB George Malauulu (5-12/54y) fumbled inside Washington 5YL. Huskies K Travis Hanson tied it 3-3 with 24y FG in 3rd Q. Using 17 plays, Wildcats went 74y in 4th Q to K Steve McLaughlin's 20y FG and 6-3 lead. QB Mark Brunell (25-41/243y, INT) lost FUM on next possession and McLaughlin's 3rd FG became prelude to Malauulu's clinching 1y TD run. P Josh Miller was crucial for Arizona as he booted 8/47.4 avg. Loss culminated bad week for Huskies as former starting QB Billy Joe Hobert was suspended for accepting booster's $50,000 loan, and Hobert was unavailable to replace ineffective Brunell as he had several times this year.

November 14, 1992

Syracuse 27 BOSTON COLLEGE 10: Stumbling Boston College (7-2-1) lost its 2nd straight big game when it couldn't mine several mid-game chances despite TB Chuckie Dukes' 19/108y rushing. Syracuse (9-1) effectively avoided any look-ahead to next week's Miami showdown and never trailed, although BC was able to create 1st H deadlocks at 7-7 on 10y TD pass by QB Glenn Foley (19-32/275y, TD, 3 INTs) and 10-10 on 22y FG by K Sean Wright. K John Biskup's 35y FG, his 2nd of 2nd Q gave Orangemen 13-10 H bulge. Nifty Syracuse QB Marvin Graves (13-19/138y, TD) threw for short TD pass in 3rd Q and salted away game at 27-10 with TD run in 4th Q.

RUTGERS 13 West Virginia 9: Surprising Rutgers (6-4) merged running of TB Bruce Presley (27/105y), QB Ray Lucas' 1st Q TD pass, and late-game D stand to keep its bowl hopes alive. Lucas (15-29/191y, TD) was surprise starter for QB Brian Fortay and his 33y scoring pass to WR James Guarantano in 1st Q helped to offset 3 FGs by West Virginia (4-4-2) K Mike Vanderjagt in 10-9 1st H. K John Benestad kicked his 2nd FG in 3rd Q from 26y out as Scarlet Knights moved to 13-9 edge. But, Mountaineers CB Harold Kidd blocked punt in final 3 mins to set up great opportunity at Rutgers 15YL.

Knights D allowed 1y in 2 plays, WVU QB Jake Kelchner missed on 3rd down pass in EZ, and FB Jim Freeman was dropped by Rutgers DB Marshall Roberts inside 10YL on 4th down.

Georgia 14 AUBURN 10: When Auburn (5-4-1) RB James Bostic lost 2nd down FUM at Georgia (8-2) GL in game's last 19 secs, both teams claimed possession amid chaos. Officials ruled Tigers made REC, but clock ticked to 0:00 during melee. Officials quickly exited as QB Stan White pleaded for ball to be marked and time reset on clock. Auburn FB Joe Frazier, who bumped White's arm to precipitate bobble, said afterward, "I do feel like we had this game taken from us; we were robbed." TB Garrison Hearst had scored twice for Bulldogs: on 1y run and 64y pass from QB Eric Zeier. Hearst's 2nd TD came in 3rd Q and provided 14-7 lead. Tigers, who scored on Bostic's 2nd Q smash and, amid several 4th Q chances, K Scott Etheridge's 25y FG. Subsequent opportunity for Tigers went wrong when, after Auburn drove from its 19YL, they had 3rd-and-goal at Georgia 8YL. But, Bulldogs DB Al Jackson outbid Tigers WR Orlando Parker for EZ pass with 3:52 to play. Wild finish was put in motion when Tigers regained possession at UGa 45YL with 2:36 remaining.

Alabama 30 MISSISSIPPI STATE 21: Early key was DB Antonio Langham's punt block and 24y TD RET to boost Alabama (10-0) to 14-0 1st Q lead. Bama led 20-3 at H. "We started out strong," said Crimson Tide QB Jay Barker (13-27/198y, TD, 2 INTs), "and then lost our poise a little bit in the third period." Bulldogs (7-3) DB Charlie Davidson made INT off Barker, returned to Bama 11YL, and Mississippi State frollicked for 18 3rd Q pts. Bulldogs QB Greg Plump (14-28/193y, TD, 2 INTs) threw 10y TD pass to WR Orlanda Truitt and 2-pt pass to TE Curt Clanton. Plump added 1y TD run, and State took 21-20 lead on K Chris Gardner's 27y FG. Odd double FUM punt RET allowed K Michael Proctor's FG to give lead at 23-21 back to Crimson Tide with 8:10 left.

MICHIGAN 22 Illinois 22: Clinching their 15th Rose Bowl berth, Wolverines (8-0-2) opened with 50y screen pass TD that TB Tyrone Wheatley carried away and closed with K Peter Elezovic's 39y FG with :16 left. In between, Michigan bobbled ball 10 times, losing 4. Illinois (5-4-1) came to Ann Arbor with fire in its eyes: coach Lou Tepper played tape of late coach Ray Eliot describing Illini's 1939 upset of 4-0 Michigan, led by future Heisman-winning Tom Harmon. Wolverines had slim 7-6 lead at H because of their dropped passes, INTs and FUMs and despite 309y to 106y O advantage. Illinois stayed in it with K Chris Richardson's 3 FGs, but Richardson missed x-pt after FB Darren Boyer's 3rd Q TD run. Still, Illinois earned 22-19 lead on QB Jason Verduzco's 2y run that split 2 defenders with 2-and-half mins left in 4th Q. Concerned about UM speed, Illini D conceded short passes on last drive, and QB Elvis Grbac (21-29/278y, TD) took 6 in row of them to place his team at 17YL. Illinois LB Dana Howard's tackle of Johnson spilled Wolverines back to 22YL, and Michigan coach Gary Moeller chose to tie it with Elezovic's FG on 4th-and-15, over protests of Grbac, saying, "I didn't want to risk (blowing) the Rose Bowl by throwing an interception."

NOTRE DAME 17 Penn State 16: After Nittany Lions TB Richie Anderson (26/73y, TD) dived for 1y TD in 1st Q to overtake Notre Dame (8-1-1) at 6-3, leaping Fighting Irish DB Bobby Taylor blocked K V.J. Muscillo's 1st Q conv kick. It proved vital. With 4:25 left to play, Penn State (6-4) took 16-9 lead on FB Brian O'Neal's weaving 13y TD run. Notre Dame responded with 60y drive to Lions 3YL, but faced 4th down with :25 left. QB Rick Mirer lobbed pass over middle to FB Jerome Bettis for TD, then scrambled to find stretching TB Reggie Brooks for 2-pt conv pass and win. With Nittany Lions headed to Big 10 Conf in 1993, series took hiatus with it knotted at 8-8-1. Truly spellbinding, uninterrupted 12-year run between 2 juggernauts ended with Penn State showing 8-4 edge in games that exactly spanned Presidencies of Ronald Reagan and George H. W. Bush. Even though it was beaten in wins-and-losses from 1981 to 1992 against Penn State, Notre Dame lost total pts battle during that time by only 271-260.

Colorado 25 KANSAS 18: Win would have kept hopeful Kansas (7-3) in midst of Big 8 title race with Nebraska, but Golden Buffaloes (8-1-1) came from behind in 4th Q for their 8th comeback win in last 3 years. DT Leonard Renfro chugged 18y with INT TD RET and FB James Hill (24/69y, 2 TDs) powered over for score in 1st Q, and Colorado led 17-7 at H. Jayhawks K Dan Eichloff booted 35y FG and QB Chip Hilleary (7-18/153y, TD, INT), who had run in TD in 2nd Q, pitched 66y TD pass to TE Dwayne Chandler. RB Maurice Douglas (23/102y) followed with 2-pt run, so Kansas suddenly held 18-17 edge in 3rd Q. Meanwhile, Jayhawker D-line had put tremendous pressure on Buffs QB Kordell Stewart (22-34/304y), sacking him 8/-74y. Still ahead by pt, Kansas P Eichloff got off poor 29y punt when trying to pin Colorado deep with 6 mins to play. Compounding matters was personal foul on Buffs' fair catch of Eichloff's pop-up punt. Colorado took over at its 42YL with 5:15 to play, and its O-line took charge. Key play in winning drive was Stewart's 24y pass to WR Charles Johnson (8/166y), which led to Hill's 8y TD run.

IOWA STATE 19 Nebraska 10: Amazing Iowa State (4-6) stunned no. 7 Nebraska (7-2) by limiting Cornhuskers to 192y rushing, 159y below their avg. Cyclones K Ty Stewart kicked 4 FGs, but big play came from 3rd string QB Marv Seiler, sr who received gratuitous start from coach Jim Walden because it was his last home game. Despite having only 31y career rushing, Seiler (24/144y rushing) dashed 78y on option keeper to set up FB Chris "The Groundhog" Ulrich for clinching 2y TD run. Huskers stayed in Orange Bowl picture, but their tumbling poll rank (12th after next day's AP vote) dictated no. 1 Miami would go elsewhere under bowl coalition rules. It was Iowa State's 1st series win after 14 losses in row and raised Cyclones to 15-70-2 all-time. Some astonishing facts about upset: Nebraska had outrushed ranked Colorado and Kansas in previous 2 wins by 724y to 136y, but was outrushed 373y to 192y; and ISU K Stewart, who hadn't made FG in nearly month's time, was unable to practice in Cyclone Stadium because of vandalized goalposts, but still made 4 of 5 tries.

RICE 34 Baylor 31: Rice (5-4) K Darrell Richardson, who had won this matchup last year with 3-ptr, ended wild, whoever-has-ball-last affair with triumphant 27y FG with :04 on clock. Owls' fabulous little TB Trevor Cobb (27/128y, TD) edged within range of SWC's all-time rushing leadership and added 21y TD catch from QB Bert Emanuel (15-24/223y, 2 TDs) in 2nd Q. Even though it trailed 28-24 at H, Baylor (5-5) racked up 24 pts in 2nd Q as FB Robert Strait (11/82y, 2 TDs) tallied twice and QB J.J. Joe (8-19/161y, TD, INT) hooked up with WR Melvin Bonner for 37y TD connection. Richardson's 33y FG was only score of 3rd Q and gave Owls 31-24 lead. Bears sub TB Kendrick Bell broke loose for 32y TD run in opening min of 4th Q to knot it at 31-31. Emanuel launched winning drive with 12y rollout run, Rice got 4th down break when Baylor DT Steve Strahan lined up offside, and Cobb's runs on 5 straight plays to 9YL set up Richardson's winner.

SOUTHERN CALIFORNIA 14 Arizona 7: Coupled with Washington's 45-16 win over Oregon State, loss eliminated up-and-down Wildcats (6-3-1) from Rose Bowl consideration. Southern California (6-2-1) D outshone that of highly-publicized Arizona defenders as USC S Jason Sehorn made 2 INTs and LB Mike Salmon recovered FUM. Stunningly, Wildcats gave up 3 big pass plays. Trojans QB Rob Johnson (12-24/213y) hit WRs Johnnie Morton for 19y and Curtis Conway for 29y to set up 2nd Q TD by TB Estrus Crayton. Conv snap was bobbled by holder Corby Smith, so USC led 6-0 at H. Arizona jumped to 7-6 lead early in 4th Q as QB George Malauulu hit WR Cary Taylor with 41y TD pass. Johnson and Morton connected on 65y play to UA 6YL 2 series later when Morton beat LB Jamal Lee. On 3rd down, Johnson, former 6'4" HS basketball forward, outjumped Arizona CB Jey Phillips to catch lofted 3y pass from TB Deon Strother for winning score in middle of 4th Q.

Ucla 9 OREGON 6: Oregon (5-5) K Tommy Thompson banged through FGs of 47 and 30y in 1st H for 6-0 lead, but when chips were down he missed shortest FG attempt (19y) of his career when he tried to break 6-6 tie with 3:17 to go in 4th Q. UCLA (5-5) had gone 80y earlier in 4th Q, mostly on 3 big plays: TB Kevin Williams (17/95y) raced 25 and 22y to position relief QB John Barnes (11-21/156y, TD) and WR J.J. Stokes (10/143y, TD) for improvised 28y TD pass. But, K Louis Perez, who has 38y FG attempt blocked in 1st H by Ducks DE Romeo Bandison, suffered same fate on x-pt kick. Stokes then caught 3 passes to allow Perez to make 40y game-winning 3-ptr on game's last play.

USA Today Coaches Poll November 16

1	Miami (Fla.) (59)	1499	14	Southern California	667
2	Alabama (1)	1431	15	Stanford	652
3	Texas A&M	1360	16	Ohio State	644
4	Florida State	1317	17	Arizona	542
5	Washington	1251	18	Mississippi State	370
6	Notre Dame	1146	19	Boston College	364
7	Syracuse	1125	20	Tennessee	363
8	Michigan	1124	21	Kansas	246
9	Colorado	926	22	North Carolina	222
10	Georgia	899	23	Penn State	165
11	Florida	881	24	Mississippi	132
12	Nebraska	843	25t	Washington State	89
13	North Carolina State	773	25t	Hawaii	89

November 21, 1992

Miami 16 SYRACUSE 10: While using superb D to hold Syracuse (9-2) to -1y O in 1st H, Miami (10-0) cruised to 16-0 lead on FB Larry Jones' TD run and 3 FGs by K Dane Prewitt. FGs came at times when Cane TDs could have put vice grip on outcome. In 2nd H, Orangemen changed key element of O to trap runs and mounted 92y drive to narrow score to 16-10 early in 4th Q. QB Marvin Graves (13-24/145y, 2 INTs) keyed drive with 21y pass to WR Qadry Ismail and scored from 1YL. Next Orangemen threat was halted at 19YL on INT by LB Rohan Marley, son of late Reggae music legend Bob. Last upset bid died at Miami 3YL where TE Chris Gedney was tackled by DB Casey Greer after taking 29y pass from Graves as clock struck 0:00. Graves was forced to take timeout on last drive because of his repeated vomiting. "We saw him throw up and we said, 'Yeah, we got him,'" said Hurricanes DT Warren Sapp (1.5 sacks). "Whenever the defense is on the field at the end of the game," Sapp continued, "we are going to come out with a 'W.'"

PENN STATE 57 Pittsburgh 13: FB Brian O'Neal gained 105y rushing, scored 4 TDs for Nittany Lions (7-4) as Pittsburgh (3-8) fell to its worst mark since 1972. Last meeting between long-time rivals—until renewal in 1997—turned in 2nd Q: QB Alex Van Pelt's short TD pass to TE Rob Coons brought Panthers to within 14-6, but Nittany Lions DL Tyoka Jackson blocked kick, and DB Lee Rubin took it coast-to-coast for 2 pts. WR O.J. McDuffie set 4 Penn State records, including most catches in season and career.

Southern Methodist 24 ARKANSAS 19 (Little Rock): Victory brought best W-L record to SMU (5-6) since its return to football in 1989. Thirty sr players had nearly upset Cotton Bowl-bound Arkansas as frosh in 1989, but absorbed 38-24 defeat. This time, Mustangs won when LB Drew Randall advanced fumbled punt to 20y TD to build 24-13 lead with 2:29 to play. SMU QB Dan Freiburger (31-45/275y, 2 TDs) overcame 5 sacks in 10-10 1st H to connect with WR Jason Wolf (14/144y, TD) on 19y TD pass. Wolf extended his SWC record to 235 career catches, while WR Korey Beard (8/76y, TD) advanced his games-with-reception to 23 in row and grabbed 6y TD pass in 4th Q that put Ponies ahead for good at 17-13. Trailing 24-13, Razorbacks (2-7-1) went 50y to WR Tracy Caldwell's 15y TD reception from QB Barry Lunney (20-36/177y, TD), but Caldwell spiked ball to draw 15y PEN that forced Hogs to try unsuccessful on-side KO from their 20YL.

OHIO STATE 13 Michigan 13: Ohio State pres Gordon Gee gleefully said, "This tie is one of our greatest wins ever." Gee's silly statement was prompted by his delight to be spared task of having to fire Buckeyes coach John Cooper, who never seemed able to beat Michigan. In fact, early-week media speculation had Cooper out if he failed to top Ohio State's biggest rival. Wolverines (8-0-3) QBs Elvis Grbac and Todd Collins each scored short running TD, but Michigan K Peter Elezovic missed conv in 2nd Q.

Buckeyes (8-2-1) seemed in deep trouble, trailing 13-3 in 4th Q. Ohio State K Tim Williams nailed his 2nd FG and QB Kirk Herbstreit, who attempted 2nd-most Buckeye passes ever (28-47/271y, TD), connected on game-tying 5y toss on 4th down to diving WR Greg Beatty with 4:24 left. While Buckeyes had upper hand in O stats at 362y to 271y, Wolverines TB Tyrone Wheatley (19/100y) outrushed Ohio TB Robert Smith (20/61y) on slick turf.

KANSAS STATE 10 Oklahoma State 0: Kansas State Wildcats (5-5) completed 1st undefeated home schedule at 5-0 since 1934 by playing tough D with 6 TOs and blocked punt and FG. K-State grabbed early 3-0 lead on K Tate Wright's 30y FG. At beginning of 2nd Q, Wildcats scored on 8y Fumblerooski TD run by 290-lb G Toby Lawrence. "My first…and my last," laughed Lawrence. Cowboys (4-6-1) opened their 1st 4 series of 2nd H In Cats territory. With 5 mins left in 3rd Q, K-State DB Thomas Randolph blocked 34y FG try by OSU K Lawson Vaughn. Oklahoma State challenged again early in 4th Q with 1st down at 12YL but, after sack and PEN, had to punt.

UCLA 38 Southern California 37: Crosstown rivals stayed tied 10-10 after 1st Q and 17-17 at H. USC (6-3-1) RB Estrus Crayton ran for 140y, including 32y TD run at 9-min mark of 3rd Q to put Trojans ahead 31-17. "Mystery Man" QB John Barnes, who at UCLA was enrolled at his 5th school, became instant Bruins (6-5) legend as former 4th-stringer passed 16-28/385y, 3 TDs. UCLA WR J.J. Stokes, who caught 6/263y with TD catches of 57, 29, and 90y, also owned place in spotlight by zipping between DBs for magnificent 90y TD on 3rd-and-4 pass from Barnes with 3:08 to play in 4th Q. K Louis Perez kicked pt that followed for 38-31 lead. USC QB Rob Johnson (16-32/166y) converted twice on 4th down passes on ensuing 69y drive before sneaking over. But, UCLA LB Nkosi Littleton knocked down pass in EZ corner for Troy TE Yonnie Jackson to bring failure to Trojans' 2-pt pass with 41 secs left. And so, thriller ended. City of Los Angeles sports fans had suffered in 1992, and *Los Angeles Times* columnist Mike Downey wrote: "After a year of misery, of injuries and illnesses and floods and riots and defeats, all we can say is thanks, guys."

Stanford 41 CALIFORNIA 21: Stanford (9-3) ace RB Glyn Milburn went 76y for his season's 3rd punt TD RET. Cardinal QB Steve Stenstrom threw 3 TDs to cap 34-pt flurry and provide 34-3 3rd Q lead. California (4-7) got 3 TD passes from QB Dave Barr in 4th Q. Fisticuffs erupted among fans over behavior of school bands, especially Cal band's reenactment of famous 5-lateral Kevin Moen KO TD RET of 10 years earlier.

WASHINGTON STATE 42 Washington 23: No. 5 Washington (9-2) saw its national title hopes freeze in miserable 3rd Q in The Palouse. In driving snowstorm, Cougars (8-3) fashioned upset with 4 TDs in 3rd Q. Trailing 7-6 at H, Washington State QB Drew Bledsoe (18-30/260y, 2 TDs, 2 INTs) enjoyed lack of pass rush and hit WR Phillip Bobo with 44y TD and TE Calvin Schexnayder with 15y TD. RB Shaume Wright-Fair (22/193y 3 TDs) slipped away for 51y score, and G Konrad Pimiskern recovered EZ FUM for sudden and overwhelming 35-7 lead. Too little too late, Huskies got TD run and 2 passes for 2 pts from QB Mark Brunell (11-25/122y). Afterward, happy Cougars coach Mike Price asked rhetorically: "Is there any bowl where there's snow?"

USA Today Coaches Poll November 23

1	Miami (Fla.) (60)	1500	14	Stanford	737
2	Alabama	1433	15	Ohio State	611
3	Texas A&M	1370	16	Boston College	499
4	Florida State	1327	17	Mississippi State	469
5	Notre Dame	1237	18	Tennessee	461
6	Colorado	1064	19	North Carolina	370
7	Georgia	1016	20	Washington State	364
8	Michigan	1013	21	Penn State	287
9	Syracuse	988	22	Arizona	257
10	Florida	980	23	Southern California	233
11	North Carolina State	895	24	Mississippi	202
12	Nebraska	882	25	Brigham Young	137
13	Washington	876			

November 26-28, 1992

(Th'g) ALABAMA 17 Auburn 0: Coach Pat Dye said goodbye to Auburn (5-5-1), and although Alabama (11-0) coach Gene Stallings was headed undefeated for 1st SEC championship game, he felt a twinge of sorrow for Dye. Tigers, 2-TD underdog, hung tough in scoreless 1st H, but early in 3rd Q, QB Stan White (14-23/119y, 2 INTs) aimed pass at WR Orlando Parker only to have Bama DB Antonio Langham tip it, catch it, and run with it for unmolested 61y TD. After K Michael Proctor nailed 47y FG in 3rd Q, Crimson Tide clinched it on 15y 4th Q TD scamper by TB Sherman Williams after Auburn managed weak 16y punt only to its 45YL. Bama's magnificent D sacked White 5 times and allowed only 139y to improve its national-best y-per-game avg.

(Th'g) Texas A&M 34 TEXAS 13: Texas Aggies (12-0), least respected unbeaten team in country at no. 4, brushed aside early 3-0 deficit and used 3rd Q surge for 17-13 lead in beating Texas (6-5). A&M TB Rodney Thomas scored 3 TDs, and DB Aaron Glenn punctuated victory with 95y INT TD RET. QB Peter Gardere caught 18y TD pass on lighthearted Longhorn flea-flicker.

(Fri) Nebraska 33 OKLAHOMA 9: Led by FB Kenyon Rasheed (15/60y), Sooners (5-4-2) opened with bruising run game and outgained Nebraska 142y to 6y in 1st Q. But, Huskers (8-2) came out of 1st Q with 7-3 lead as LB Ed Stewart made 50y INT RET for TD. Even though Oklahoma K Scott Blanton made 3 FGs, K Byron Bennett kicked 33y FG with :06 left in H for 10-9 lead for Nebraska. Exploding in 2nd H, Nebraska quickly started 2nd H with QB Tommie Frazier's 24y TD pass to TE Gerald Armstrong. Huskers LB Travis Hill sacked Oklahoma QB Cale Gundy (9-20/98y, 2 INTs) for 3rd Q safety, which prompted Owen Field boobirds. Nebraska IB Calvin Jones (22/137y, 2 TDs), added 2 scores in 4th Q. After their slow start, Huskers ended up with 400y O.

FLORIDA STATE 45 Florida 24: QB Charlie Ward passed for 331y, ran for 70y as Seminoles (10-1) drowned Gators (8-3) with 38 pts in 1st H. Saying he doubted anyone "is playing better than us right now," coach Bobby Bowden lobbied for rematch with Miami. Unfortunately, Bowden's hoped-for bowl date with no. 1 Miami would require Florida subsequently beating no. 2 Alabama in SEC title game. This game was never in doubt after Seminoles jumped to 24-7 lead early in 2nd Q as TB Sean Jackson ran in 10y, Ward hit WR Tamarick Vanover for 10y TD pass, and Ward scored on 3y run after Vanover returned KO 76y. With score at 38-17 at H, ABC commentator Dick Vermeil told partner Brent Musburger, "This is the best team in the country, Brent, it really is." Musburger questioned Vermeil about Miami's earlier win over Florida State and Alabama's unbeaten status, and still Vermeil insisted. It would not turn out that way as Seminoles were shut out of title match. Florida QB Shane Matthews (15-30/175y, 2 TDs, INT) was lifted for 2nd H because of beating he was taking, and QB Terry Dean (9-25/138y, TD, INT) connected on 4y TD pass to WR Willie Jackson in 4th Q.

GEORGIA 31 Georgia Tech 17: Making his late Heisman bid, TB Garrison Hearst rushed 31/169y, 3 TDs for Bulldogs (9-2). Hearst said, "…whatever happens, I know I gave the voters something to look at." He also struck Heisman pose in EZ after his late-game score. Bulldogs clinched it at 24-3 with Hearst's pair of TDs in 3rd Q. QB Shawn Jones gained some respectability for Georgia Tech (5-6) with 2 late TD passes to WR Bobby Rodriguez and RB Dorsey Levens to cut deficit to 24-17. But, Tech's on-side KO failed to travel 10y, and Georgia took over in Jackets end with 2:28 to go, and Hearst got his last TD with 29 secs to go. Hearst's 21 TDs broke SEC season mark, while Tech's K Scott Sisson tied ACC career FG record with his 60th 3-ptr which put Yellow Jackets within 10-3 at H.

MISSISSIPPI 17 Mississippi State 10: With both teams bowl-bound, LB Dwayne Dotson said Ole Miss (8-3) "saved best and most dramatic stand" for rival Bulldogs (7-4). Mississippi State led 10-0 in 2nd Q primarily on FB Michael Davis' 7y TD run in 2nd Q. Rebs steadily chipped away with 7y TD grab in 2nd Q by FB Marvin Courtney and 7y TD run in 3rd Q by TB Cory Philpot (19/107y, TD). Cliffhanging finish saw Miss State fail on 1st-and-goal tries at Rebels' 8, 8, and 2YLs near end of 4th Q. DL Chad Brown sparked Mississippi's late stand and finished with 13 tackles and 2 sacks.

HOUSTON 61 Rice 34: Owls (6-5) enjoyed their 1st winning season since 1963, but lost chance for bowl bid when high-scoring Cougars (4-7) lay in ambush. Rice pass D was totally incapable of dealing with Houston QB Jimmy Klingler, who passed 46-71/613y, 7 TDs. Rice TB Trevor Cobb gained 121y rushing, finishing season with 1386y and his marvelous career with 4948y.

Notre Dame 31 SOUTHERN CALIFORNIA 23: Fighting Irish (9-1-1) TB Tony Brooks (19/227y, 3 TDs) was sick to his stomach before game, but responded with 12y TD run with pitchout 1st time ND had ball and galloped 55 and 44y for scores that provided 17-13 and 24-16 leads. Southern California (6-4-1) opened game nicely on 4 completions by QB Rob Johnson (27-41/302y, TD, INT), but his only miss stalled drive, so K Cole Ford hit 1st of his 3 FGs. Trojans missed another chance when S Stephon Pace intercepted on Notre Dame 31YL, but FB Wes Bender was hammered on 3rd-and-1 by small Irish LB John Covington and Johnson overthrew open receiver on 4th down. USC edged to 24-23 late in 3rd Q on Johnson's TD pass, but ND sealed 10th straight win over Troy when Brooks' 44y sprint set up FB Jerome Bettis (18/89y, TD) for 8y TD run with 7 mins left.

Miami 63 SAN DIEGO STATE 17: Much anticipated Heisman showdown failed to materialize when Aztecs (5-5-1) RB Marshall Faulk, eventual Heisman runner-up, missed game with knee sprain. Still, he owned his 2nd straight national rushing title (1630y), becoming only 5th player to repeat. Meanwhile, Miami (11-0) QB Gino Toretta, eventual Heisman winner, passed 19-35/310y, TD in only 3 Qs of play. No. 1 Hurricanes extended nation's longest win streak to 29 games. Miami WR Lamar Thomas broke school career reception record of Michael Irvin with 144 and scored on TD passes of 68 and 24y. RBs Larry Jones and Stephen McGuire each scored twice as Miami gained 581y and built 28-3 H lead and 63-17 edge by end of 3rd Q. San Diego State QBs David Lowery and Tim Gutierrez each threw TD passes in 3rd Q when teams combined for 49 pts. Teams also combined for 2 bench-clearing brawls.

USA Today Coaches Poll November 30

1	Miami (Fla.) (59)	1499	14	Ohio State	651
2	Alabama	1429	15	Florida	639
3	Texas A&M (1)	1364	16	Boston College	541
4	Florida State	1323	17	Tennessee	499
5	Notre Dame	1247	18	North Carolina	434
6	Colorado	1097	19	Washington State	410
7	Michigan	1056	20	Mississippi	396
8	Georgia	1051	21	Penn State	302
9	Syracuse	1020	22	Arizona	240
10	Nebraska	976	23	Brigham Young	172
11	Washington	929	24	Southern California	144
12	North Carolina State	880	25	Hawaii	124
13	Stanford	760			

December 5, 1992

Army 25 Navy 24 (Philadelphia): With their win, Army Cadets (5-6) tied historic series at 43-43-7, rallying twice from 17-pt deficits. Navy (1-10), using RB Jason Van Matre at QB, enjoyed 17-7 edge in 1st H thanks to TB Duke Ingraham's TD runs of 24 and 7y. When Van Matre hit WR Tom Pritchard with TD pass to open 2nd H, Army's Wishbone O, bottled up so far by LBs Chris Beck and Javier Zuluaga, faced tough comeback task from 24-7 hole. After FUM RET by Black Knights DT Gary Graves to Navy 22 YL, Cadets QB John Roper pared score to 24-14 with naked sweep around RE for TD with 3:24 left in 3rd Q. Roper's 68y pass to WR Gaylord Greene and fake kick, 2-pt run by holder Chris Shaw moved Army within 24-22 with 7:23 left. P Patmon Malcom's punt to 1YL provided field position for his last-sec, 49y winning FG. Sr K Malcom's boot

showed notable concentration since he had to rekick it with swirling 35 mph wind after his 44y FG was ruined by delay PEN. "I was celebrating, and then my holder told me I had to do it again," said Malcom, whose career long had been 46y. "I turned around and saw the flags (blowing), and went back and kicked it again. I knew it was good, and it was the best feeling ever."

Alabama 28 Florida 21 (Birmingham): SEC championship playoff went to Crimson Tide (12-0) when DB Antonio Langham stepped in front of Gatosr QB Shane Matthews' pass in right flat, weaved 27y with INT RET for TD and 28-21 4th Q lead. Alabama LB Michael Rogers' INT iced it 22 secs later. Alabama appeared in charge at 21-7 when TB Derrick Lassic ran 15y for TD with 5:14 left in 3rd Q, but Florida (8-4) rallied to 21-21 deadlock on Matthews' 4y pass to WR Willie Jackson and RB Errict Rhett's 1y TD run with 8:09 to go.

HAWAII 36 Pittsburgh 23: Rainbows (10-2) achieved their 1st 10-win slate in school history by powering for 22 pts in 4th Q to break open relatively tight contest. Pitt (3-9) coach Paul Hackett resigned earlier in week, so asst Sal Sunseri took over Panthers' unsuccessful trip to Islands.

(Sun) Nebraska 38 Kansas State 24 (Tokyo): Traveling halfway around globe, Nebraska (9-2) cinched Big 8 title and 3rd trip to Orange Bowl in 5 years. QB Tommie Frazier ran for 3 TDs, passed for another in locking up Huskers' 24th straight 9 or more win season. Nebraska was stopped on its opening series, but got rolling on Frazier's perfect touch-pass for 18y TD to WR Corey Dixon. Frazier soon scored on 19 and 4y runs, before being positioned by IB Calvin Jones' 4th down dive for 1st down at Kansas State (5-6) 21YL. Wildcats had hoped for another winning season and felt letdown after its promising 7-4 ledger in 1991.

USA Today Coaches Poll December 7

1	Miami (Fla.) (59)	1499	14	Ohio State	690
2	Alabama	1431	15	Florida	595
3	Texas A&M (1)	1366	16	Boston College	540
4	Florida State	1343	17	Tennessee	515
5	Notre Dame	1250	18	Washington State	424
6	Colorado	1112	19	Mississippi	412
7	Michigan	1063	20	North Carolina	378
8	Georgia	1057	21	Penn State	324
9	Syracuse	1007	22	Arizona	231
10	Nebraska	977	23	Brigham Young	156
11	Washington	907	24	Hawaii	143
12	North Carolina State	877	25	Southern California	129
13	Stanford	764			

Conference Standings

Big East (a)

Miami (1st in Poll)	4-0
Syracuse (9th)	6-1
Boston Coll. (16th)	2-1-1
Rutgers	4-2
West Virginia	2-3-1
Pittsburgh	1-3
Virginia Tech	1-4
Temple	0-6

(a) Big East standings based on Coaches' Poll

Atlantic Coast

Florida State	8-0
North Carolina State	6-2
North Carolina	5-3
Virginia	4-4
Wake Forest	4-4
Georgia Tech	4-4
Clemson	3-5
Maryland	2-6
Duke	0-8

Southeastern

EAST
Florida	6-2
Georgia	6-2
Tennessee	5-3
South Carolina	3-5
Vanderbilt	2-6
Kentucky	2-6

WEST
Alabama	8-0
Mississippi	5-3
Mississippi State	4-4
Arkansas	3-4-1
Auburn	2-5-1
Louisiana State	1-7

Big Ten

Michigan	6-0-2
Ohio State	5-2-1
Michigan State	5-3
Illinois	4-3-1
Iowa	4-4
Indiana	3-5
Wisconsin	3-5
Purdue	3-5
Northwestern	3-5
Minnesota	2-6

Mid-American

Bowling Green	8-0
Western Michigan	6-3
Toledo	5-3
Akron	5-3
Miami (Ohio)	5-3
Ball State	5-4
Central Michigan	4-5
Kent	2-7
Eastern Michigan	1-7
Ohio	1-7

Big Eight

Nebraska	6-1
Colorado	5-1-1
Kansas	4-3
Oklahoma	3-2-2
Oklahoma State	2-4-1
Kansas State	2-5
Iowa State	2-5
Missouri	2-5

Western Athletic

Hawaii	6-2
Brigham Young	6-2
Fresno State	6-2
San Diego State	5-3
Air Force	4-4
Utah	4-4
Wyoming	3-5
Colorado State	3-5
New Mexico	2-6
Texas-El Paso	1-7

Southwest

Texas A&M	7-0
Baylor	4-3
Rice	4-3
Texas	4-3
Texas Tech	4-3
Southern Methodist	2-5
Houston	2-5
Texas Christian	1-6

Pacific-10

Washington	6-2
Stanford	6-2
Washington State	5-3
Southern California	5-3
Arizona	4-3-1
Oregon	4-4
Arizona State	4-4
UCLA	3-5
California	2-6
Oregon State	0-7-1

1992 Major Bowl Games

Aloha Bowl (Dec. 25): Kansas 23 Brigham Young 20

RB Hema Heimuli of BYU (8-5) went 94y with opening KO, only to be matched in 1st Q by Kansas (8-4) WR Rodney Harris' crude, but baffling 74y flanker TD reception from WR Matt Gay, who had accepted wide lateral. Brigham Young RB Jamal Willis was ambushed for safety by Jayhawks DT Chris Maumalanga in 2nd Q but gave Cougars 14-12 H lead with his 29y TD sweep. Despite that he "looked awful" to coach Glen Mason during pre-game warmups, Jayhawks K Dan Eichloff made 42y FG before H. Harris' 48y, jumpball catch at 8YL in 4th Q set stage for QB Chip Hilleary's gritty 1y TD run off RT and his play-action and rollout for 2 pts that earned 20-20 tie. Kansas got down to business with 7-min drive to set up Eichloff's 48y winning FG with less than 6 mins left. BYU QB Steve Young, brother of famed Cougars QB Steve, avoided game MVP, Jayhawks DT Dana Stubblefield (6 sacks), long enough to drive WAC tri-champs to 35YL. Kansas DB Charley Bowen's INT ended heroics by soph Young (15-31/262y, TD, INT), who made his only career start.

Copper Bowl (Dec. 29): Washington State 31 Utah 28

QB Drew Bledsoe, who threw for Pac-10 leadership in y with 2,770y, broke his own Washington State (9-3) school pass y record with 476y. But, it took Cougars DB Singor Mobley's 9y FUM RET to Utah 21YL to set stage for K Aaron Price's tie-breaking, winning FG with 5:08 left. Utah (6-6) then surged back behind pre-med student QB Frank Dolce (21-40/315y, 2 TDs) as he hit WR Sean Williams with 70y pass to Wazzu 5YL. Williams beat Mobley on his long catch–and-run, but was run down from behind by Cougars S John Rushing. After 3 Ute plays managed only 2y, K Chris Yergensen was called upon but yanked his tying FG try wide to left of posts.

Freedom Bowl (Dec. 29): Fresno State 24 Southern California 7

Thoroughly dominating legendary and proud down-state juggernaut Southern California (6-5-1), Fresno State (9-4) scored highest profile victory in its relatively short football history. Fresno gained 405y, with TB Ron Rivers rushing 19/104y, including TD. Bulldogs' D, ranked near bottom of 1-A stats, limited Trojans to 183y in total O. USC QB Rob Johnson offered pre-game insults in media such as wanting to put Fresno "in their place" and "beat them bad." Bulldogs subjected Johnson to 3 sacks and 3 INTs. Troy's loss, termed by some alumni as "greatest embarrassment in Trojan football history," sealed trembling fate of Southern California coach Larry Smith, who was soon fired.

Holiday Bowl (Dec. 30): Hawaii 27 Illinois 17

Hawaii (11-2) became 1st WAC champ to win as Holiday Bowl host team since BYU won 1984 national title in San Diego's bowl fest. Rainbow Warriors captured their 1st-ever bowl victory and finished with best record in school history. Hawaii Wishbone FB Travis Sims charged for 28/112y and 2 TDs, while MVP QB Michael Carter passed 6-16/115y and rushed 21/105y. Illinois (6-5-1) had 10-7 1st H edge as QB Jason Verduzco hit 16-21 passes, including TD to WR John Wright.

Independence Bowl (Dec. 31): Wake Forest 39 Oregon 35

Wake Forest's 1st bowl win in 46 years sent Bill Dooley into happy retirement as coach with most wins in ACC's 40-year history. Oregon (6-6) leaped to 29-10 lead as DB Herman O'Berry had 24y FUM RET for TD, recovered another FUM, and forced 2 others. DB Alex Moldren scored on 8y INT RET, and QB Danny O'Neil passed 227y, 2 TDs for Ducks. Deacons (8-4) tallied 29 straight points in 13:35 span of 2nd H. MVP WR Todd Dixon caught 5/166y, including 61y throw from WR Bobby Jones on razzle dazzle play that gave Wake Forest its 1st lead. Deacons RB John Leach rushed 21/116y, 2 TDs.

John Hancock (Sun) Bowl (Dec. 31): Baylor 20 Arizona 15

Baylor (7-5) turned robust D, Arizona's favorite weapon, back on Wildcats (6-5-1) as retiring coach Grant Teaff went out as winner. Teaff finished 21-year Bears career with 182-105-6 record. Arizona scored 10-0 2nd Q lead on K Steve McLaughlin's 22y FG and QB George Malauulu's 7y TD draw run. Wildcats D, which had 8.9 pts scoring avg, failed on 2 big plays by MVP Baylor WR Melvin Bonner, who took HB pass from Brandell Jackson for 61y TD in 2nd Q and 69y TD pass from QB J.J. Joe on 2nd play of 3rd Q. Bears gained only 119y on their other 65 plays. Turning point at 13-10 came early in 4th Q when 4th down sneak by Malauulu was stacked up at 1YL by Bears line

and polished off by LB Le'Shai Maston. Baylor K Trey Weir added 2 4th Q FGs after Cat FUMs. Bears conceded last min safety and allowed scary lob pass to GL which fell incomplete. Having lost 10-0 lead, Arizona still outgained Baylor 428y to 249y.

Gator Bowl (Dec. 31): Florida 27 North Carolina State 10

Dense fog rolled in from Atlantic Ocean, but couldn't shroud sparkle of Florida (9-4) RB Errict Rhett who rushed 39/182y (3rd-most running y in Gator Bowl history) and caught 7/60y. Florida QB Shane Matthews (19-38/247y) hit TDs to WRs Willie Jackson and Harrison Houston and scored on 1y run. Wolfpack (9-3-1) saw their 7-game win streak end and were forced into Gator Bowl-record 11 punts by P Tim Kilpatrick. NC State's sole TD came on QB Terry Jordan's 4th Q 11y pass, which briefly shaved it to 20-10.

Liberty Bowl (Dec. 31): Mississippi 13 Air Force 0

Mississippi (9-3) coaching staff allowed players to drive own cars on short trip to Memphis, but confiscated keys in final days of game prep. Air Force (7-5) drove its own ball control O car, holding pigskin for 4:08 longer than Ole Miss. But, Flyboys netted only 185y O, 26y passing and only 49y from leading rusher, FB Joe Pastorello. Rebels RB Dou Innocent scored on 1st Q 5y run, and K Brian Lee kicked FG for 10-0 lead at 3:49 mark of 2nd Q.

Blockbuster Bowl: Stanford 24 Penn State 3

"The Genius vs. The Legend:" marquee coaching matchup of Stanford's Bill Walsh against Penn State's Joe Paterno swung Walsh's way for surprising reason. Walsh, considered O genius, watched his superior D hold Nittany Lions (7-5) to 35/107y on ground and 13-40/156y in air. "I don't think this was one of Joe Paterno's best teams," said Walsh afterward. "He did well to win seven games." Leading receiver for Cardinal (10-3) was TE Ryan Wetnight (5/71y, TD), who caught 2y scoring pass from QB Steve Stenstrom, who completed 4 straight on impressive 71y drive to open game. Penn State got within 7-3 on K V.J. Muscillo's 33y FG in 1st Q, but QB Kerry Collins (12-30/145y, INT) suffered through tough game as Lions advanced inside Cardinal 30YL only once after Muscillo's FG. Even its own clumsy handoff went right for Stanford, as it enjoyed its 1st 10-win season since 1940. On that 2nd Q play, FB J.J. Lasley took awkward exchange and still scored 5y TD for 14-3 H edge. Stenstrom (17-28/210y, 2 TDs, INT) added 40y screen pass TD to speedy RB Glyn Milburn for clinching TD in 3rd Q.

Hall of Fame Bowl: Tennessee 38 Boston College 23

Poor punt snap on 1st possession grounded Eagles (8-3-1) at own 43 YL. Tennessee (9-3) QB Heath Shuler quickly threw 42y bomb to WR Ronald Davis and followed with 1y TD run. Shuler (18-23/245y) added TD throws of 27, 69y and 14y TD run in building 31-7 4th Q lead. Coach Phillip Fulmer, in his 1st game as official Vols coach, gushed about his QB's "tremendous character" as he handed Shuler MVP trophy. Perhaps distracted by rumors of coach Tom Coughlin's offer (ultimately rejected until many years later) from New York Giants, Boston College fell far behind before staging modest 16-pt late rally.

Florida Citrus Bowl: Georgia 21 Ohio State 14

Georgia (10-2) aces—TB Garrison Hearst, QB Eric Zeier, and WR Andre Hastings—sparkled for Bulldogs attack. Hearst rushed 28/163y and 2 TDs, while Zeier passed 21-31/242y. Hastings (8/113y) authored 49y KO RET to open 3rd Q to help break open 7-7 H knot. Hastings' clutch RET helped boost Bulldogs to 14-7 lead as Hearst burst for 5y TD. Battling poor field position most of day, Ohio State (8-3-1) used its star TB Robert Smith (25/112y, 2 TDs), for TD runs in 2nd and 3rd Qs to tie it 7-7 and 14-14. Smith produced 45y gain with screen pass to Georgia 15YL early in 4th Q, but, 3 plays later, Buckeyes QB Kirk Herbstreit and FB Jeff Cothran met in handoff collision that spoiled promising drive as UGa DT Travis Jones recovered. Last play of contest saw Herbstreit, who had so-so passing game with 8-24/110y, INT, suffer EZ pickoff by Bulldogs DB Mike Jones.

Cotton Bowl: Notre Dame 28 Texas A&M 3

Harboring outside hope that dud result in Sugar Bowl might give them argument for national title, Texas A&M (12-1) made it sadly moot by surrendering 290y rushing to well-prepared Notre Dame (10-1-1). Scoreless beginning was ended by ND QB Rick Mirer's 40y middle screen TD pass to WR Lake Dawson in final min of 1st H. After Mirer threw 26y TD to FB Jerome Bettis midway in 3rd Q, Irish turned to 28 running plays in row as O line smothered Aggies. Irish TB Reggie Brooks ran 11/115y, while powerful Bettis added 20/75y. Aggies gained only 165y, but K Terry Venetoulias made 41y FG in 4th Q.

Fiesta Bowl: Syracuse 26 Colorado 22

Desert warfare, waged on rutted, sand-covered playing surface, left Colorado (9-2-1) ahead 7-6 more than halfway into 3rd Q. Then scoreboard erupted with 29 pts in 7-min span. QB Marvin Graves scampered 28y to give Orangemen (10-2) 19-10 lead. Buffs countered with QB Kordell Stewart's 16y TD pass to WR Charles Johnson, but conv was missed. On last play of 3rd Q, Syracuse RB Kirby Dar Dar took KO handoff from WR Qadry Ismail and raced 99y for 26-16 lead. TB Lamont Warren pulled Colorado to within 26-22 with 4:28 left, but K Mitch Berger, filling in for suspended Pat Blottiaux, missed his 2nd kick. Afterward, coach Bill McCartney (1-6 in bowls at Colorado) angrily blamed his team's overall kicking game which cost 2 bad convs and missed chipshot FG by Berger, plus Dar Dar's crippling TD RET.

Rose Bowl: Michigan 38 Washington 31

Final episode of Washington's unraveling season was played out in Pasadena. After 2 late losses, Huskies (9-3) were forced to suspend players and withstand tough media scrutiny. Still, Washington contributed to exciting seesaw game that was decided in final moments. Michigan (9-0-3) led 10-7 in 1st Q as QB Elvis Grbac threw TD pass to TE Tony McGee into middle of secondary on 3rd-and-3 from Washington 49 YL. It was 17-7 when TB Tyrone Wheatley (15/235y, TD) raced 56y on trap behind G Doug Skene to score in 2nd Q. Back came Huskies as QB Mark Brunell (18-30/308y, 2 TDs) hit WR Jason Shelley for 64y and TE Mark Bruener for 18y scores. Wolverines seemed to gain control at 24-21 as Wheatley went up middle for Rose Bowl-record 88y TD on 1st scrimmage play of 2nd H. But, Huskies leapt ahead 31-24 in 3rd Q only to see Wheatley tie it at 31-31 with 24y run near end of 3rd Q. With Wheatley on sidelines with numb legs and back spasms, Michigan went 80y for winner in 4th Q. McGee beat LB Jaime Fields at flag to catch Grbac's 15y pass with 5:29 left. Washington threw 1 last scare at Michigan, blocking punt at 44YL with 1:03 left, but Brunell missed 4 straight passes.

Orange Bowl: Florida State 27 Nebraska 14

Seminoles (11-1) set NCAA record by winning 8th straight bowl game, eclipsing UCLA's mark of 7 set from 1983-89. Nebraska (9-3), fast becoming New Year's Day media punching bag, lost its 6th straight bowl and 3rd to Florida State. Seminoles built 20-0 1st H lead on QB Charlie Ward's 2 TD passes before Huskers QB Tommie Frazier found WR Corey Dixon for 41y TD pass late in 2nd Q. TB Sean Jackson's 11y 3rd Q TD was crippler. "We played well enough to win," sighed Nebraska coach Tom Osborne. "I imagine many people in the media won't see it that way." Meanwhile, Florida State's Bobby Bowden felt his team, winner of last 7 games, was as good as any in nation.

GAME OF THE YEAR
Sugar Bowl: Alabama 34 Miami 13

Heavy choice to take its 5th national title in 10 years, Miami (11-1) was thoroughly outplayed, even becoming rattled at times. Alabama (13-0) used tricky D alignments to thwart Hurricanes' prime weapon: short passes their speedy receivers could turn into long gainers. Tide D pressured and confused Heisman-winning QB Gino Torretta sufficiently to force 3 INTs, and each led to Bama score. FGs dominated 1st H with Alabama freshman Sherman Williams contributing 1st H to give Tide edge. In narrow span in 3rd Q, Bama put game away. After Tide punted, Torretta suffered INT by DB Tommy Johnson, returned 23y to Miami 20 YL. TB Derrick Lassic, who gained 28/143y rushing behind Bama's underrated line, leapt to TD 6 plays later. On next snap, confused Torretta tried to dump pass over middle, but it was picked off by DB George Teague, who raced 31y to TD. Suddenly, Alabama led 27-6. Teague authored game's signature play shortly thereafter, termed by Sports Illustrated as "one of the more spectacular comeuppances in the history of sport." Although it would be called back for Tide offside, play saw Miami WR Lamar Thomas, loudest pre-game trash-talker, take Torretta bomb and appear headed for 89y TD. But hustling Teague caught Thomas at Tide 15YL and stripped ball away from behind, a stunning theft at full speed. It considerably quieted Miami until WR Kevin Williams sped 78y with 4th Q punt for TD, but Lassic answered with 4y TD run to close scoring. "It was a blur," Torretta sadly said of game's tone afterward.

Peach Bowl (Jan 2): North Carolina 21 Mississippi State 17

Seemingly nervous Tar Heels (9-3) spotted Bulldogs (7-5) 14-0 H lead on QB Greg Plump's 2y pass to WR Olanda Truitt and RB Kenny Roberts' 22y run (set up by Roberts' catch of 21y shovel pass). North Carolina countered with 82y drive in 3rd Q, capped by short TD run by TB Natrone Means (21/128y). Game's big plays arrived next: 2 blocked punts by Heels DB Bracey Walker. Carolina failed to convert 1st blocked punt, but Walker made certain 2nd time, sprinting 24y for TD and 14-14 tie. Clinching TD came on DB Cliff Baskerville's 45y INT RET, play made possible by Walker's big hit on Mississippi State receiver.

1992 Top Performance Formula

1 Alabama	1.7679
2 Florida State	1.7130
3 Notre Dame	1.6548
4 Miami	1.6168
5 Michigan	1.5588
6 Texas A&M	1.5580
7 Syracuse	1.5138
8 Georgia	1.5019
9 Nebraska	1.4898
10 Stanford	1.4761
11 Washington	1.4539
12 Tennessee	1.4076
13 Ohio State	1.3857
14 Colorado	1.3779
15 Florida	1.3538
16 Mississippi	1.3278
17 North Carolina State	1.3151
18 Washington State	1.2904
19 Boston College	1.2856
20 Arizona	1.2537

1992 Top Opponent Records

1 Florida	.6377
2 Southern California	.6357
3 Arizona	.6220
4 Stanford	.6115
5 Florida State	.6055
6 Northwestern	.5975
7 Arkansas	.5983
8 Oregon	.5937
9 Nebraska	.5906
10 Georgia Tech	.5872
11 South Carolina	.5855
12t Louisiana State	.583333
12t Ohio State	.583333
14 Alabama	.5809
15 Vanderbilt	.5805
16 Notre Dame	.5789
17 Washington	.5781
18 Missouri	.5725
19 Miami	.5719
20 Syracuse	.5680

1992 Out-of-Conference Records

	W-L	Percentage	Bowl W-L
Southeastern	30-10	.7500	5-1
Atlantic Coast	18-8-1	.6852	3-1
Pacific-10	22-12-1	.6429	2-4
Big Eight	16-14	.5333	1-2
Big East	23-21-2	.5217	1-2
Southwest	16-15-1	.5156	1-1
Western Athletic	20-19-1	.5125	2-3
Big Ten	14-19-1	.4265	1-2

1992 Individual Statistical Leaders

RUSHING YARDS

	Attempts	Yards	Avg.
Marshall Faulk, San Diego State	265	1630	6.2
Garrison Hearst, Georgia	228	1547	6.8
Travis Sims, Hawaii	220	1498	6.8
Ryan Benjamin, Pacific	231	1441	6.2
Chuckie Dukes, Boston College	238	1387	5.8
Trevor Cobb, Rice	279	1386	5.0
Reggie Brooks, Notre Dame	167	1343	8.0
Greg Hill, Texas A&M	267	1339	5.0
LeShon Johnson, Northern Illinois	265	1338	5.0
Byron Morris, Texas Tech	242	1279	5.3

PASSING YARDS

	Completions	Attempts	Yards	Pct.
Jimmy Klingler, Houston	303	504	3818	60.1
John Kaleo, Maryland	286	482	3392	59.3
Shane Matthews, Florida	275	463	3205	59.4
Alex Van Pelt, Pittsburgh	245	407	3163	60.2
Gino Torretta, Miami	228	402	3060	56.7
Trent Dilfer, Fresno State	174	331	2828	52.6
Charles Puleri, New Mexico State	189	349	2788	54.2
Drew Bledsoe, Washington State	211	386	2770	54.7
Joe Hughes, Wyoming	216	373	2706	57.9
Charlie Ward, Florida State	204	365	2647	55.9

RECEIVING YARDS

	Catches	Yards
Ryan Yarborough, Wyoming	86	1351
Lloyd Hill, Texas Tech	76	1261
Marcus Badgett, Maryland	75	1240
Victor Bailey, Missouri	75	1210
Aaron Turner, Pacific	79	1171
Darnay Scott, San Diego State	68	1150
Charles Johnson, Colorado	57	1149
Bryan Reeves, Nevada	81	1114
Eric Drage, Brigham Young	56	1093
Dietrich Jells, Pittsburgh	55	1091

1992 Consensus All-America Team
Offense

Wide Receiver:	O.J. McDuffie, Penn State
	Sean Dawkins, California
Tight End:	Chris Gedney, Syracuse
Tackle/Guard:	Lincoln Kennedy, Washington
	Will Shields, Nebraska
	Aaron Taylor, Notre Dame
	Willie Roaf, Louisiana Tech
	Everett Lindsay, Mississippi
Center:	Mike Compton, West Virginia
Quarterback:	Gino Torretta, Miami
Running Backs:	Marshall Faulk, San Diego State
	Garrison Hearst, Georgia
Placekicker:	Joe Allison, Memphis State

Defense

Linemen:	Eric Curry, Alabama
	John Copeland, Alabama
	Rob Waldrop, Arizona
	Chris Slade, Virginia
Linebacker:	Marcus Buckley, Texas A&M
	Marvin Jones, Florida State
	Michael Barrow, Miami
Backs:	Carlton McDonald, Air Force
	Carlton Gray, UCLA
	Deon Figures, Colorado
	Ryan McNeil, Miami
Punter:	Sean Snyder, Kansas State

1992 Heisman Trophy Vote

Gino Torretta, senior quarterback, Miami	1400
Marshall Faulk, sophomore tailback, San Diego State	1080
Garrison Hearst, junior tailback, Georgia	982
Marvin Jones, junior linebacker, Florida State	392
Reggie Brooks, senior tailback, Notre Dame	294

Other Major Awards

Maxwell (Player)	Gino Torretta, senior quarterback, Miami
Walter Camp (Player)	Gino Torretta, senior quarterback, Miami
Outland (Lineman)	Will Shields, senior guard, Nebraska
Lombardi (Lineman)	Marvin Jones, junior linebacker, Florida State
Doak Walker (Running Back)	Garrison Hearst, junior running back, Georgia
Davey O'Brien (Quarterback)	Gino Torretta, senior quarterback, Miami
Jim Thorpe (Defensive Back)	Deon Figures, senior cornerback, Colorado
Dick Butkus (Linebacker)	Marvin Jones, junior linebacker, Florida State
Johnny Unitas (Quarterback)	Gino Torretta, senior quarterback, Miami
Lou Groza (Placekicker)	Joe Allison, junior kicker, Memphis State
AFCA Coach of the Year	Gene Stallings, Alabama

The Year of the Coalition Poll, the Team that Beat the Team, and Orange Bowl Thriller

The term Coalition Poll entered the college football lexicon in 1993, a year marked by ruthless criticism of the national championship process, which remained, well, mythical. After the AP writers poll had served to position Miami and Alabama in the bowl coalition Sugar Bowl matchup after the 1992 season, many journalists objected to their votes being used to determine bowl pairings. They argued their function was that of reporter, not that of newsmaker. So, a new poll, the Coalition Poll, was born, a ranking system that combined the vote totals for each school from both the AP writers and CNN/*USA Today* coaches polls, then used the results to seed the 1993 bowl coalition pairings.

The season started harmlessly enough, with Florida State (12-1) pegged as preseason no. 1. Many were pleased that popular coach Bobby Bowden might finally win a championship after several near misses. The undefeated Seminoles were a unanimous AP no. 1 as they entered a November 13 showdown with undefeated no. 2 Notre Dame (11-1) at South Bend, and the winner seemed set to take command of the race for no. 1. Unbeaten and lingering on the cusp were no. 4 Nebraska (11-1) and no. 9 West Virginia (11-1). The wildcard was unbeaten Auburn (11-0), omitted in the coaches poll and ineligible for a bowl, but inexplicably seeded nonetheless in the coalition poll by doubling its AP votes. An entertaining twist was that the first-year coach of the Tigers was Terry Bowden, son of Florida State's Bobby.

Notre Dame dominated Florida State, but a late Seminole rally brought the score to 31-24, prompting Bowden to say, "At least the score looked respectable." The rally was important; it simply saved Florida State's season. The writers dropped the Seminoles only to no. 2, and a week later, Boston College (9-3) came to Notre Dame and trumped the win by the Fighting Irish the week before. The Eagles won 41-39 on a last moment field goal.

BC's upset of Notre Dame put Florida State back in the picture and gave new life to Nebraska. Suddenly, the media began ripping the Cornhuskers, losers of six straight bowl games and whose coach Tom Osborne wore the never-won-a-title albatross that perfectly matched Bowden's. If he had an AP vote, brassy Michael Wilbon wrote in *The Washington Post*, he would place Nebraska so low it couldn't earn the coalition's top two. Because of bad recent bowl records, Nebraska was "the second biggest fraud (after Michigan) in college football," according to Wilbon.

Try as it might, the media couldn't ignore the Cornhuskers this time as they finished the regular season at 11-0, their 21st straight year of nine wins or more. The coaches voted the Huskers no. 1, while the writers kept Florida State on top. Coalition rules dictated the two meet in the Orange Bowl, while Notre Dame and West Virginia were left to lobby for votes. Each had a fair argument: the Irish had the same number of losses as the Seminoles and had beaten then-no. 1 Florida State head to head. West Virginia, victim of a very low preseason rating, argued that it deserved a shot at Nebraska because both were the last-standing unbeatens. After a closing win over Boston College, Mountaineer coach Don Neylan asserted that, "We beat the team (Boston College) that beat the team (Notre Dame) that beat the team (Florida State) that was number one." The debate raged over a backdrop of positive commentary about the college game's excitement, while the NFL was criticized for a multitude of dull, low-scoring games.

When the dust cleared on New Year's, Florida (10-2) silenced West Virginia with a Sugar Bowl thrashing, Notre Dame edged Texas A&M (10-2) in the Cotton Bowl, and Florida State claimed no. 1 in an 18-16 thriller that at least restored post-season pride at Nebraska. And, the image of Nebraska soon would turn in upcoming years to invincibility, mostly for the better but partly for the worse.

The Orange Bowl was a strange game that clearly could have left Nebraska highly frustrated. The Huskers could have and probably should have won. As it turned, Nebraska would win the next two national titles, so had "Can't-Win-the-Big-One" Osborne's Huskers gotten a few small breaks against Florida State, Osborne may well have earned a totally unprecedented three titles in a row. The Orange Bowl game was clearly one of the greatest games in a year packed with thrillers. It might be the best game ever played that no experts ever seem to cite as one of the greatest ever. It was full of tension and odd plays.

With passing offenses becoming a more mainstream mode in football there was a parallel consequences on defense. Maryland (2-9) used the Run-and-Shoot offense to fill the air with passes. Terps quarterback Scott Milanovich set a new Atlantic Coast Conference record with 26 touchdown passes, but, partly because the Terps' offense burned little time off the clock, Maryland became the first team in history to allow more than 6,000 yards on defense. Opponents gained 6,083 yards against the Terrapins.

Milestones

● Hashmarks (point from sideline at which wide-running or out-of-bounds plays were remarked) were moved closer to center of field to create more room for offenses on short side of field and for quarterbacks to make easier throw on out-patterns to wide side. "Fumblerooski, " trick play in which lineman ran with intentional fumble, was outlawed as too difficult to officiate.

● Penn State officially started play within Big Ten Conference as its 11th member.

● Just before openers, Pac-10 severely penalized Washington including two-year ban on bowls. Coach Don James (153-57-2) quit in anger, and was replaced by assistant coach Jim Lambright.

● TCU retired no. 49 jersey of 79-year-old quarterback great Sammy Baugh (1934-36).

● Roy Riegels, who pulled most famous "boner" in football history when he ran 69 yards in wrong direction on decisive play that lost 1929 Rose Bowl for California, died at age 84 on March 28. Riegels became well-known as frequent writer of uplifting letters to hundreds of athletes who blundered in game action. Ben Schwartzwalder, 83, coach of Syracuse's 1959 national champions, died on April 29. Dave Waymer, former Notre dame defensice back, died young at 34 on May 1. Bill Peterson, Florida State's most successful coach (62-42-11 in 11 years) before arrival of Bobby Bowden, died on August 6 at age 73. Jess Hill, 86, coach of Southern California (1951-56) and athletic director who hired coach John McKay in 1960, died on September 3. Jim Leonard, Notre Dame guard in 1931-33 and Pittsburgh Steelers coach in 1945, died at 83 on December 2. Jeff Alm, star defensive lineman on Notre Dame's 1988 champions and NFL's Houston Oilers, took his own life with firearm 25 minutes after death of friend in car driven by Alm that was involved in traffic accident in Houston.

● Longest winning streaks entering season:

Alabama 23	Bowling Green 9	Florida State, Notre Dame 7

● Coaching Changes:

	Incoming	Outgoing
Arkansas	Danny Ford	Joe Kines (interim)
Auburn	Terry Bowden	Pat Dye
Baylor	Chuck Reedy	Grant Teaff
Clemson	Tommy West (a)	Ken Hatfield
Colorado State	Sonny Lubick	Earle Bruce
Eastern Michigan	Ron Cooper	Jan Quarless (interim)
Houston	Kim Helton	John Jenkins
North Carolina State	Mike O'Cain	Dick Sheridan
Pittsburgh	Johnny Majors	Paul Hackett
San Jose State	John Ralston	Ron Turner
Southern California	John Robinsoh	Larry Smith
Temple	Ron Dickerson	Jerry Berndt
Wake Forest	Jim Caldwell	Bill Dooley
Washington	Jim Lambright	Don James

(a) Tommy West (1-0) replaced Hatfield (8-3) prior to Peach Bowl.

Preseason *USA Today* Coaches Poll

1	Florida State (47)	1523	14	Penn State	652
2	Alabama (8)	1423	15	Stanford	630
3	Michigan (5)	1414	16	Arizona	616
4	Miami (Fla.)	1259	17	Ohio State	497
5	Texas A&M (1)	1185	18	Southern California	436
6	Notre Dame (1)	1154	19	North Carolina	377
7	Syracuse	1137	20	Clemson	313
8	Nebraska	1054	21	Oklahoma	264
9	Tennessee	947	22	Brigham Young	246
10	Colorado	939	23	North Carolina State	230
11	Washington	900	24	Boston College	182
12	Florida	887	25	Mississippi State	150
13	Georgia	658			

August 28, 1993

Florida State 42 Kansas 0 (East Rutherford, N.J.): Hoping for early PEN-assisted TD, Jayhawks (0-1) took K Dan Eichoff's FG off board, never to score again. Wasn't Eichloff's day, for as Kansas P he saw Seminoles TE Lonnie Johnson block 1st Q punt for TD REC by DB Clifton Abraham. No. 1 Florida State (1-0) took control in 2nd Q, its D, inspired by LB Derrick Brooks, magnificently stonewalled 9 plays inside its own 3YL at end of 80y Kansas drive prolonged by PENs. Jayhawks' TD at that stage would have cut deficit to 14-7. Instead, FSU RB Sean Jackson, who scored twice on runs, threw 40y pass to WR Kevin Knox in middle of 99y TD drive that followed Seminoles'GL-protecting series, called by coach Bobby Bowden: "The best goal-line stand I've ever seen." Asst AD Gale Sayers had warned Kansas against accepting this momentous task, and he turned out to be correct. Although Kickoff Classic was big payday, Jayhawks, coming off 8-4 record in 1992, have never been same since.

(Sun) North Carolina 31 Southern California 9 (Anaheim): John Robinson, football's current winningest active coach, was back in Cardinal and Gold, but his Trojans (0-1) showed little of past prowess. Tar Heels (1-0) mounted fierce ground attack with new TB tandem of "Johnson & Johnson." TBs Curtis and Leon Johnson combined for 172y rushing, while each scored TD for 7-0 and 14-3 leads. USC, which nibbled to within 7-3 at H on K Cole Ford's 27y FG in middle of 2nd Q, was hurt when elusive soph TB

Dwight McFadden (7/44y) shattered his ankle in 1st Q and went down for season. It took until 3rd-string frosh TB David Dotson (9/48y) surfaced for Troy's run game to finally get moving on 71y drive to TD pass by QB Rob Johnson (21-28/167y, TD) in Disneyland Pigskin Classic's fading moments. North Carolina stepped to 21-3 in 3rd Q on WR Marcus Wall's 6y TD run after Tar Heels' recovered FUM at USC 20YL.

USA Today Coaches Poll August 30

1	Florida State (54)	1538	14	Stanford	683
2	Alabama (4)	1446	15	Arizona	636
3	Michigan (4)	1442	16	Ohio State	582
4	Miami (Fla.)	1242	17	Southern California	443
5	Texas A&M	1220	18	North Carolina	379
6	Notre Dame	1158	19	Oklahoma	329
7	Syracuse	1155	20	Brigham Young	296
8	Nebraska	1073	21	Clemson	292
9	Florida	1008	22	North Carolina State	263
10	Colorado	938	23	Boston College	250
11	Tennessee	939	24	Texas	178
12	Penn State	727	25	Mississippi State	163
13	Georgia	702			

September 4, 1993

(Th) Pittsburgh 14 SOUTHERN MISSISSIPPI 10: Coach Johnny Majors called his second debut at Pitt (1-0) "not a thing of beauty, but who cares." Afterall, his Panthers won as QB John Ryan (12-19/118y, TD) threw 4th Q TD pass to RB Curtis Martin, and LB Tom Tumulty (15 tackles) iced it with late INT of Southern Miss (0-1) QB Tommy Waters. DL Michael Tobias had 7 tackles, including 3 sacks for Eagles. Steady Martin (21/68y, TD) played big role in Pitt's TO-free O in Delta swelter and scored early on 2y run after Panthers DE Zatiti Moody stripped USM ball-carrier and recovered FUM at Eagles 40YL. Southern Miss tied it at 7-7 on TB Myreon McKinney's short TD run on ensuing series and went up 10-7 by H on K Johnny Lomoro's 42y FG.

Miami 23 BOSTON COLLEGE 7: Legacy of 1st-year Hurricanes (1-0) QBs hung heavy over newcomer Frank Costa because each of his 3 predecessors—Steve Walsh, Craig Erickson, and Gino Torretta—had guided Miami to national title in his maiden season. Canes built 23-0 lead and won their 28th regular season game in row as QB Costa threw 15-31/205, INT. Costa winged 63y pass that set up RB Donnell Bennett's 2nd Q TD run of 8y. Bennett (18/73y, 2 TDs) had scored in 1st Q on 12y dash. Boston College (0-1) kept stats close—trailing Miami 390y to 340y—but BC failed to score until Canes K Dane Prewitt's 3 long FGs gave them 23-0 lead. BC RB Darnell Campbell's 2y TD run came with 2:46 left in game. Miami halted Eagles runners to tune of 33/68y, so Boston College QB Glenn Foley (23-47/272y, 3 INTs) was forced to air with moderate success.

South Carolina 23 GEORGIA 21: Gamecocks RB Brandon Bennett rushed 24/108y and scored winning TD just as time expired. Unlike Georgia (0-1) win over Auburn in 1992 because Tigers couldn't get off last-sec play, South Carolina (1-0) succeeded. Wearing down Bulldogs D by controlling ball for 10:25 of 4th Q, Carolina went 55y on winning drive as QB Steve Taneyhill (12-26/190y, TD) hit passes twice on 3rd down to sustain march. WR Toby Cates had given Gamecocks 17-7 lead with heads-up play in 3rd Q: he fell on EZ FUM when teammate lost handle at GL. QB Eric Zeier (21-27/242y, TD) dashed 22y to TD and sparked tying 14-pt rally by Georgia in 4th Q. Taneyhill, Cocks' emotional leader, upped his record to 6-1 since taking over as QB.

PENN STATE 38 Minnesota 20: If Penn State (1-0) was nervous, as coach Joe Paterno claimed, about its 1st Big 10 game, jitters quickly were quieted with TD on 1st snap: WR Bobby Engram turned short catch into TD with blocking help from G Mike Malinoski after DB Derek Bochna's INT. QB John Sacca threw 4 TD passes to Engram, which set Nittany Lions game record. Sacca was perfect on his 1st 6 throws including 29, 31, and 20y TDs to Engram in 1st Q for 21-7 lead. QB Tim Schade, who played for coach Jim Wacker at TCU 2 years earlier and followed him to Minnesota (0-1), scored on 13y run in 1st Q, but his day reached other goals. Behind from start, Schade was forced to set Gophers school pass y record with 34-66/478y, 2 TDs. Score went to 31-13 at H as TB Ki-Jana Carter (15/120y, TD) made 2nd Q TD for Penn State. Engram (8/165y, 4 TDs) caught his last TD of 31y in 4th Q to cap scoring.

OHIO STATE 34 Rice 7: WR Joey Galloway (3/92y, TD), who missed most of 1992, returned with great flair, but it was dueling Ohio State (1-0) QBs that made news. QB Bobby Hoying (13-22/144y, TD), grandson of 1950s slugging Cincinnati Reds outfielder Wally Post, and QB Bret Powers (5-8/102y, TD, INT) performed in such harmonic manner that *Cincinnati Enquirer* columnist Tim Sullivan suggested that they were so frequently on same page "that they could share a bookmark." Buckeyes had modest rushing numbers (50/207y) as TB Raymont Harris led with 16/76y and TD that gave Ohio 10-0 lead in 2nd Q. Powers followed with 48y TD to Galloway on way to 20-0 H edge. Rice (0-1) QB Bert Emanuel (13-25/105y) gained 158y O, but his sub, QB Josh LaRocca (2-5/49y, TD, INT), supplied Owls' only score on 43y pass to WR Herschel Crowe in mop-up duty.

COLORADO 36 Texas 14: Colorado (1-0) QB Kordell Stewart passed 19-30/246y, 3 TDs, and TE Christian Fauria caught 9/97y, TD. RB Lamont Warren (23/110y, TD) also scored for Buffs to extend 4th Q lead to 34-14. Making 1st start for Texas (0-1) was frosh QB Shea Morenz, son of Brian Morenz, former penalty-killing hockey standout for New York Raiders of WHA and distant relative to Hockey Hall of Famer Howie Morenz. Younger Morenz lamented some bad throws but passed 23-42/347y, TD, 4 INTs and brought big play back to Longhorns O with 53y TD connection with WR Lovell Pinkney. Morenz suffered Colorado DB Chris Hudson's 2 INTs, 1 of which Hudson returned 21y for TD that, as only tally of 3rd Q, created insoluble 28-7 lead.

BAYLOR 42 Fresno State 39: Fresno (0-1) pass wizard QB Trent Dilfer completed 31-38/473y, 3 TDs in building 20-0 and 33-14 leads, but Baylor (1-0) counterpart J.J. Joe passed 12-16/283y, TD in stirring Bears comeback. Trio of players scored 2 TDs each: WR Charlie Jones and TB Ron Rivers for Bulldogs, and FB John Henry for Baylor. WR Marvin Callies caught 55y bomb form Joe for game winner in 4th Q.

WASHINGTON 31 Stanford 14: Infuriated by Stanford (0-1) coach Bill Walsh's off-season reference to Washington's "outlaw program," Huskies (1-0) debuted under new coach Jim Lambright. After pre-game helmet-raised salute to former coach Don James, Washington played clean D, but fell behind 7-3 in 2nd Q when Stanford (0-1) QB Steve Stenstrom hit FB Ellery Roberts with 7y pass at end of PEN-aided 86y drive. Huskies RB Napoleon Kaufman then unlimbered for 195y on ground, and soph QB Damon Huard threw 3 TD passes to TE Mark Bruener.

USA Today Coaches Poll September 7

1	Florida State (56)	1555	14	Ohio State	732
2	Michigan (2)	1441	15	North Carolina	699
3	Alabama (2)	1440	16	Oklahoma	562
4	Miami (Fla.) (2)	1297	17t	Clemson	417
5	Texas A&M	1233	17t	North Carolina State	417
6	Syracuse	1170	19	Brigham Young	402
7	Nebraska	1111	20	South Carolina	268
8	Florida	1042	21	Georgia	221
9	Colorado	1039	22	Stanford	202
10	Notre Dame	1038	23	Southern California	164
11	Tennessee	1009	24	Arizona State	133
12	Penn State	817	25	Baylor	129
13	Arizona	755			

September 11, 1993

NORTH CAROLINA 59 Maryland 42: Looking like scorers from D-free WAC, North Carolina (3-0) and Maryland (0-2) piled up pts like pinball wizards. Tar Heels took control by 38-21 in 1st H that featured TB Leon Johnson's 57y TD run that snapped 7-7 tie, QB Jason Stanicek's 56y TD pass to WR Bucky Brooks, and 90y TD dash by TB Curtis Johnson (168y rushing). Stanicek (14-17/288y, 2 TDs) completed his 1st 9 passes. For their contribution, Terrapins passed for 405y and QB Scott Milanovich completed 34 passes, new record allowed by UNC. Lightning-quick, little WR Jermaine Lewis (9/250y, 2 TDs) slipped out of Terps' Run-and-Shoot set to befuddle Carolina DBs Sean Crocker and Sean Boyd all afternoon. Tar Heels set school mark of 714y with avg of 9.3y per play.

FLORIDA STATE 57 Clemson 0: Florida State (3-0) administered worst defeat on Clemson (1-1) in 62 years. Tigers held ball for 20 min of 1st H, but failed to capitalize. Problematic for Tigers was inability to run ball; they rushed 38/73y. Seminoles QB Charlie Ward passed 25-33/318y, 4 TDs, then watched sub QB Danny Kanell (4-4/125y) toss 2 TDs. FSU LB Derrick Brooks blocked punt for TD and had 83y FUM TD RET.

Florida 24 KENTUCKY 20: Kentucky (1-1) D roamed for 7 INTs off Florida's famed Fun-n-Gun O, including 3 by DB Marcus Jenkins. Little QB Pookie Jones hit TD pass in 1st Q for Wildcats, but they trailed 9-7 at H. On 3rd play of 3rd Q, Cats frosh TB Moe Williams squirted up middle for 70y TD and 14-9 lead. K Juha Leonoff kicked short 4th Q FGs for 17-9 and 20-17 Kentucky leads, last, with 1:23 left, was set up by CB Willie Cannon's 5y INT RET to Florida 15YL. Gators WR Harrison Houston was unfazed in taking KO RET for 40y. In relief of QB Terry Dean, Gators (2-0) QB Danny Wuerffel suffered 3 of UK's INTs, but hit WR Chris Doering (6/95y, 2 TDs) with 28y post-pattern TD for winner with :03 left.

PENN STATE 21 Southern California 20: Superior O line play gave Penn State (2-0) 21-7 H lead, as its robust D, anchored by DL Lou Benfatti, held Trojans (1-2) to 34y on ground. But when Nittany Lions K Craig Fayak, trying to extend lead to 24-7, missed 18y FG late in 3rd Q, Southern California had new life. USC QB Rob Johnson threw TDs to WR Ken Grace for 30y and TE Johnny McWilliams for 2y, last score coming with 37 secs left. Identical play to McWilliams for 2 pts failed when pass bounced inches short.

Notre Dame 27 MICHIGAN 23: Few gave Notre Dame (2-0) much chance after humdrum opening win over Northwestern, but sr QB Kevin McDougal, default starter since frosh QB Ron Powlus was hurt, scored on 43 and 11y runs. In between, another Irish comeback, WR Mike Miller made 56y punt TD RET. Trailing 24-10 at H, Michigan (1-1) used TB Tyrone Wheatley's 146y rushing to build 2 late TDs.

OHIO STATE 21 Washington 12: Buckeyes (2-0) opened with 80y TD drive to TD run by TB Raymont Harris (23/102y, TD) on which WR Joey Galloway (4/104y, TD) caught 2 big passes. Ohio State led 14-3 in 2nd Q when QB Bobby Hoying (6-21/142y, TD, INT) hit Galloway with 4th down TD from 35YL. Huskies (1-1) had won 11 in row over Big 10 teams, but were swamped by Ohio State's big plays amid inconsistent O: 6 passes for 23y avg and runs of 10y or more. Washington QB Damon Huard (18-32/186y, TD, INT) battled his team back into game with 8y TD pass to WR Theron Hill before H. But 2-pt pass was missed. UW made it to Buckeyes 4YL in 3rd Q and had to settle for K Travis Hanson's 2nd short FG, so Huskies trailed 14-12. Breathing room for Ohio came in 4th Q lead on 49y TD sprint by sub TB Butler By'not'e (9/80y, TD).

MISSOURI 31 Illinois 3: Illinois (0-1) coach Lou Tepper, D-specialist, was highly disappointed in his touted D and suspected it threw in towel by H when it trailed 17-3. Missouri (1-0) piled up appalling 365y total O with Tigers QB Jeff Handy hitting 20-30/281y, 2 TDs. Illini frosh QB Scott Weaver (18-32/169y, 2 INTs) showed promise in his 1st collegiate start but squandered 2 TD opportunities: Weaver made 3y toss so soft to wide-open RB Rodney Byrd in EZ that Tigers DB Jerome Madison was able to break

it up, and, in 3rd Q, Weaver scrambled alone deep in Mizzou territory only to drop FUM which Tigers recovered. RB Michael Washington (15/56y, 2 TDs) scored from 2YL in 1st Q for 7-0 Missouri lead and capped scoring in 4th Q with 15y TD jaunt.

OKLAHOMA 44 Texas A&M 14: Just when *Dallas Morning News* suggested that Oklahoma coach Gary Gibbs had to get over his "blandness" in this important game, Sooners (2-0) beat top 5 team for 1st time since 1987. Veteran Oklahoma QB Cale Gundy (13-24/167y, 2 TDs) stood up to Texas A&M (1-1) blitz and guided option attack with short passing to 20-0 lead, achieved in 3rd Q when he hit frosh TB James Allen (21/98y) with 10y TD pass. A&M was feeble on O in 1st H with only 5 1st downs and when game ended it had suffered 6 TOs and blocked punt. It was hard-hitting game, and 3 Aggies defenders went out with concussions. Still, A&M clawed within 27-14 midway in 4th Q as TB Rodney Thomas (22/106y) scored in both 2nd H Qs.

Iowa 31 IOWA STATE 28: Hawkeyes (2-0) romped to scores on 5 of its 1st 6 possessions, but had to hold on at end to capture 11th victory in row against rival Iowa State (1-1). TB Ryan Terry (21/107y, TD) and his understudy, frosh TB Sedrick Shaw (17/82y, TD), keynoted Iowa's 287y running game, while QB Paul Burmeister (6-8/71y, TD) fit 6y TD pass into modest aerial attack. Iowa led 28-7 at H. Cyclones could offer only 35y passing, so it used short TD runs—making up game's last 3 scores—by QB Bob Utter and RBs Graston Norris and Calvin Branch.

BRIGHAM YOUNG 41 Hawaii 38: Rainbows (1-1), looking for 3rd win in 1990s over Brigham Young (2-0), ran for 472y out of coach Bob Wagner's unusual spread option O. Hawaii run leaders were RB Calvin Melvin (18/172y, TD), who got Warriors on scoreboard in 1st Q with TD that trimmed lead Cougars' lead to 14-7, and SB Brian Gordon (8/166y, 2 TDs), who tied it in 1st Q with 59y run and put Hawaii ahead 21-14 in 2nd Q with 30y TD sprint. Despite being booed by home crowd for several overthrows, BYU QB John Walsh (19-26/262y, 3 TDs) gave Cougars 31-21 H lead with 2 scoring tosses in 2nd Q, including 24y TD to WR Eric Drage (4/100y, TD). In 3rd Q, Hawaii blocked punt for TD and took 38-31 lead in 4th Q. Walsh tied it 38-38 with his 3rd TD pass, and, with 41 secs to play, Rainbows K Carlton Oswalt bounced chip-shot FG off left upright. Walsh found Drage for 58y aerial to poise K Joe Herrick for BYU's winning 40y FG with :19 on clock.

USA Today Coaches Poll September 13

1	Florida State (59)	1546	14	North Carolina	807
2	Alabama (1)	1451	15	Arizona	718
3	Miami (Fla.) (2)	1329	16	Texas A&M	614
4	Syracuse	1251	17	North Carolina State	562
5	Notre Dame	1229	18	Brigham Young	489
6	Nebraska	1208	19	Stanford	238
7	Tennessee	1174	20	Arizona State	217
8	Colorado	1146	21	California	212
9	Florida	999	22	Iowa	162
10	Michigan	924	23	Virginia	160
11	Ohio State	890	24	Boston College	122
12	Penn State	866	25	Wisconsin	81
13	Oklahoma	864			

September 18, 1993

(Th) Virginia 35 GEORGIA TECH 14: Hitting 10 of his 1st 12 passes, slick Virginia (3-0) QB Symmion Willis (16-21/185y, TD) returned to his hometown of Atlanta to win battle of young QBs as he outshone Yellow Jackets (1-1) QB Donnie Davis (17-33/177y, TD, 3 INTs). Leading 3-0 on 1st of 3 FGs by K Kyle Kirkeide, Cavaliers went 80y in 4 plays to Willis' 30y TD pass to WR Larry Holmes. After Davis' 20y TD pass pulled Georgia Tech within 9-7, Holmes sprinted 65y on KO RET to Tech 35YL, and UVa TB Kevin Brooks (17/74y, 2 TDs) quickly scored 1st of his 2 TDs. FB Charles Way (13/78y, TD) blasted 33y on 4th down to put game away at 28-7 for Wahoos 5 mins into 4th Q.

MIAMI 21 Virginia Tech 2: Miami (2-0) was stomping to opening TD drive of 85y on 20 plays when WR Chris Jones caught 21y pass and began prancing about in celebration. Unsportsmanlike excessive celebration PEN was called, Miami being prime target of new rule. Still, Hurricanes finished off their long march on FB Larry Jones' 1y dive into EZ on 4th down and 11 mins into game. At that point, Miami launched rock-hard D that threw Hokies (2-1) for losses on 14 plays. Virginia Tech, which itself held Miami runners to 34/54y while sacking QB Frank Costa (19-37/265y, TD) 3 times, rarely threated. Trailing 7-0 in 3rd Q, Hokies marched from own 20YL to UM 18YL. Frosh DE Kenny Holmes knocked Virginia Tech QB Maurice DeShazo out of game, and 2 plays later, QB Jim Druckenmiller was picked off in EZ by Canes CB Dexter Seigler. Miami WR A.C. Tellison suggested repeat of earlier play in 3rd Q and took Costa's pass for 45y TD. Hokies' only score came on safety when they pulled their typical blocked punt mischief.

Florida State 33 NORTH CAROLINA 7: Unbeaten in 10 ACC games so far, Florida State (4-0) fell behind for 1st time in 1993 when Tar Heels (3-1) WR Bucky Brooks made diving 28y TD catch. Seminoles turned to QB Charlie Ward (27-41/303y, 2 TDs) to break open 10-7 game with 17 pts in 3rd Q. LB Derrick Brooks scored on 49y INT RET, which amazingly upped Brooks' to-date TD margin over FSU foes to 3 to 1.

FLORIDA 41 Tennessee 34: Frosh QB Danny Wuerffel, who relieved QB Terry Dean week earlier as Gators (3-0) signal-caller, threw 19-38/213y, 3 TDs in his 1st start. Florida frosh LB James Bates created FUM when he walloped Volunteers WR Nilo Silvan on 2nd H KO RET that put halt to UT comeback. Bottom line: Florida's improving army of young stars was growing up. It wasn't all easy in "The Swamp," however. QB Heath Shuler (25-41/355y, 5 TDs) rallied Tennessee (2-1) from 21-0 deficit with 2 late 2nd Q bombs that brought much momentum and paring of 21-14 score by H. After Silvan's KO FUM at his own 30YL, Wuerffel audibled into arched sideline pass to WR Harrison Houston for vital TD. Tennessee WR Billy Williams (5/140y, 3 TDs) caught 3 of Shuler's TD passes as CB Anthone Lott was picked on for 3 scores. Another Williams TD pulled Vols to within 31-20, but they never got closer than 7 pts. Florida TB Errict Rhett added 30/147y, 2 TDs to move into 2nd on all-time school rushing list behind Emmitt Smith.

Auburn 34 LOUISIANA STATE 10: Night opener in Baton Rouge carried measure of optimism since Bayou Bengals (2-0) had scored upset over Mississippi State week earlier. But, coach Terry Bowden had his Auburn Tigers (3-0) snarling for 554y total O. Confident Auburn QB Stan White (20-28/282y, TD) mastered LSU's D as he vaulted past former Heisman winner, Pat Sullivan, for all-time school passing leader. Before that, LSU sent its faithful into 1st Q hysterics with frosh WR Eddie Kennison's 54y punt RET to Auburn 34YL, and QB Jamie Howard (9-36/103y, TD, INT), plagued all game with dropped passes, enjoyed his bright moment with 10y TD arrow to WR Scott Ray. Auburn answered with 21-pt 2nd Q as White capped 89y trip with TD sneak, TB James Bostic (13/110y, TD) ran 13y for score after Howard lost FUM at his 30YL, and White hit WR Thomas Bailey for 57y TD. Auburn added 87y TD drive in 3rd Q.

LOUISVILLE 35 Arizona State 17: Sun Devils (1-1), 19-0 winners over Cards in 1992, were dominated by vengeful Louisville (3-0) which was enjoying its best start since 1972. Operating out of Shotgun that afforded excellent protection, Cardinals QB Jeff Brohm passed career-high 26-38/331y and sparked drives of 66, 75, 92, and 80y. Louisville DE Joe Johnson delivered 4 sacks on Arizona State QB Grady Benton (17-34/273y, 2 TDs, 4 INTs), even though Benton put Devils on scoreboard with 51y TD bomb to WR Carlos Artis on opening drive. At end of 75y drive in 2nd Q, Cards WR Kevin Cook snared 28y TD from Brohm, who soon tallied himself on QB sneak for 21-10 lead at H. Louisville took 2nd H KO and went 80y, aided by ASU's roughing passer PEN, to HB Ralph Dawkins 25y TD catch. Louisville DB Anthony Bridges picked off pass in late moments and weaved through demoralized Sun Devils for 79y TD RET.

INDIANA 24 Kentucky 8: Superb D by Hoosiers (3-0) sent Kentucky (1-2) to sidelines after 3 plays on many occasions, while their O rushed for 224y—100y by reserve TB Michael Batts—among their 445y O. Conservative Indiana coach Bill Mallory threw caution to wind on 1st possession, calling doomed sneak on 4th-and-inches at IU 29YL. But, Hoosiers LB Charles Beauchamp sacked Wildcats QB Pookie Jones (12-21/125y, INT) on 3rd down and pretty well sent UK attack into slumber. Indiana led only 3-0 at H, but TB Jermaine Chaney (10/84y, 2 TDs) soon scored on 40 and 5y runs. Kentucky made only 65y until 4th Q. Down 24-0, Cats pieced together 80y TD drive on passing of QB Antonio O'Ferral, who hit 24y TD to FB Michael Woodfork.

NORTHWESTERN 22 Boston College 21: Eagles FB Darnell Campbell rushed 22/104y and scored 2 TDs in 1st H, only to see waterbug Wildcats (1-1) WR Lee Gissendaner (4/48y, 2 TDs) tie it in 3rd Q with 21y TD reception. When QB Glenn Foley (14-27/194y, TD, INT) rallied to throw 28y TD pass to TE Pete Mitchell in 4th Q, Boston College (0-2) felt its Chicagoland trip would end safely at 21-14. But, Northwestern (1-1) frosh WR Eric Scott authored 86y RET of ensuing KO to set up 9y TD pass by Wildcats QB Len Williams (17-21/125y, 2 TDs) to Gissendaner, which was followed by winning 2-pt conv run by RB Dennis Lundy (23/103y, TD). Eagles K David Gordon, who would enjoy November return to Midwest, shook his head this time, missing 40y FG with 1:07 left.

Arizona 16 ILLINOIS 14: Wildcats' O couldn't outscore its D, and Illini's O couldn't outscore its special teams. In end, Arizona (3-0) displayed such brilliant D that it hung on to remain undefeated. Desert Swarm D tossed Illinois (0-2) backs for 87y in losses (8 sacks) for net of -27y, and scored both Arizona TDs on FUM RETs in 1st H: On 1st Q sack of Illini frosh QB Scott Weaver (17-31/208y, TD) from UA 17YL, LB Sean Harris took FUM 74y to score, and midway in 2nd Q, DT Jim Hoffman was happy recipient of FUM for 46y TD after S Brandon Sanders blitzed Weaver. Wildcats almost did it again later in 2nd Q as Weaver was hit and lost ball in his EZ; Illinois T Mike Suarez recovered for safety. Arizona led 16-0 until Illini DB Rod Boykin recovered fumbled punt in EZ for TD that made it 16-7 late in 2nd Q. Early in 4th Q, Illinois eschewed FG—it suffered 2 earlier blocks and missed chip-shot—and RB Ty Douthard was stuffed for loss on 4th down from 1YL. Weaver later hit 25y pass to 4YL and 2y TD to TE David Olson.

TEXAS 21 Syracuse 21: Fortunate win seemed assured for highly-favored no. 6 Syracuse (2-0-1) as K Pat O'Neill lined up late 33y FG. But, O'Neill's boot sailed wide, his 2nd miss in last 3 mins of game. Texas (0-1-1) was outgained 429y to 201y, but profited from other Orange special teams failures: Texas WR Mike Adams' KO and punt RETs of 80 and 54y respectively built foundation for 15 pts. Late in 2nd Q, Adams authored his 80y KO RET to Syracuse 19YL, and it led to RB Phil Brown's 19y TD run up middle and 2-pt pass by QB Shea Morenz (14-24/80y, INT) that brought Longhorns to within 14-11 late in 2nd Q. Adams escaped 5 Orangemen, last tackler, TE Eric Chenoweth, was left diving at air, to churn 54y for punt TD RET and 18-14 lead early in 3rd Q. Orange QB Marvin Graves (15-26/181y, TD, 2 INTs) suffered his 2nd INT that led to Steers K Scott Szeredy's 27y FG, but Graves pitched tying 3y TD pass with 2:23 to play. Syracuse had late chance when LB Kevin Mitchell drilled Morenz as he threw and DB Tony Jones made INT RET to his 33YL. Ball was worked downfield, and, on 2nd down at Texas 19YL, Syracuse coach Paul Pasqualoni had FB Marcus Lee run right to 16YL but take spot away from middle of field to right hash mark. K Pat O'Neill pushed 33y FG to right with 8 secs to play.

San Diego State 38 AIR FORCE 31: QB Demond Cash made his 1st start for Air Force (1-2) and ran out of Wishbone for 18/172y and 18y TD that raised AFA's 4th Q lead to 31-14. Cash surprisingly outrushed SDSU RB Marshall Faulk, who finished with 24/106y, 3 TDs. Helping Falcons build 17-pt lead was DB Brian Watkins, who returned INT 30y for TD in 3rd Q. Aztecs (2-1) QB David Lowery (13-28/206y, INT) reinjured his calf with 12:40 left, so sub sr QB Tim Gutierrez (13-21/217y, 2 TDs) trotted off bench to inspire 4 scores: K Peter Holt booted 26y FG, and then, after Cash lost quick FUM on C-QB exchange, Gutierrez immediately pitched 19y TD to WR Darnay Scott (11/217y, 2 TDs). Faulk's 3rd TD run tied it 31-31 with 2:25 to play. Aztecs forced another Air

Force punt and advanced to 4th-and-5 at Falcons 36YL. Gutierrez skipped away from 2 D rushers and found Scott, who had dropped 2 EZ passes, streaking down sideline for winning TD pass.

Nebraska 14 UCLA 13: Frosh IB Lawrence Phillips from nearby West Covina, Calif., came off bench to spark fumbling Nebraska (3-0) as he rushed for 28/137y, TD. UCLA (0-2) had taken 10-0 lead on 39y FG by frosh K Bjorn Merten and TD run by TB Skip Hicks (19/148y, TD). Merten's FG was set up by 29y pass by QB Wayne Cook (11-22/134y), by Huskers NG Terry Connealy sacked Cook to force FG. Hicks' TD was poised by 18 and 12y runs by TB partner Sharmon Shah. Cornhuskers rolled 80y drive as Phillips replaced fumbling IB starter Damon Benning and scored his TD in 2nd Q. Nebraska QB Tommie Frazier (13-19/145y, TD, INT) hit 3 key throws including 11y TD to TE Gerald Armstrong to cap 14-play, 80y march that came midway in 3rd Q and provided 14-10 lead. Merten, who missed 53 and 44y FGs in 1st H, made 27y FG early in 4th Q.

STANFORD 41 Colorado 37: Stanford (2-1) leapt to 14-3 edge on WR Justin Armour's 48y catch from QB Steve Stenstrom, mantained 21-17 H lead. Colorado (2-1), playing its 3rd straight ranked opponent, clawed back to 24-21 and 37-27 leads as QB Kordell Stewart scored on 2 and 4y runs, 2nd TD coming on 4th-and-3 with 12:41 left in game. Amazingly, Cardinal struck for 2 late TDs, last on TE Tony Cline's catch with 13 secs left. Cline held ball only for instant, and officials ruled his reception legal after mutual discussion.

September 25, 1993

VIRGINIA 35 Duke 0: Virginia (4-0) QB Symmion Willis fired 2 TD passes late in 2nd Q for 28-0 H lead, while Blue Devil QBs Spence Fischer and Joe Pickens suffered 5 INTs. Bad blood between pillars of academia spilled into brawling 4th Q as 4 players were ejected. After rash of PENs, Duke (1-3) faced unusual 3rd-and-63 at own 8YL.

North Carolina 35 NORTH CAROLINA STATE 14: QB Mike Thomas started for injured North Carolina Tar Heels (4-1) QB Jason Stanicek. But, Thomas was knocked from game in 1st series, and Stanicek came in to hit 10-12 passing in 1st H. However, NC State (2-1) led 14-10 at H, which ended with helmet swinging fight. WR Marcus Wall had 41y KO RET to start 2nd H, and TB Curtis Johnson (18/153y) gave Heels lead for keeps with 50y TD run for 17-14 lead.

LOUISVILLE 41 Texas 10: Rout of Texas (0-2-1) was set in motion on game's 2nd play: Cardinals QB Jeff Brohm hit RB Ralph Dawkins with 80y TD. Louisville (4-0) showed variety pack to send Longhorns off to their worst start since 1938: Brohm passed 14-24/293y, Dawkins ran 13/117y and caught 3/95y, and RB Anthony Shelman ran for 2 TDs. Additionally, Cards K David Akers booted 43 and 25y FGs, and barrel-chested DT Jim Hanna rumbled 15y for 2nd Q TD when he scooped up Texas' only TO. Louisville took 24-0 at H, limiting Steers to 74y. Coach John Mackovic went to sub QB Chad Lucas in 2nd H, and although Lucas produced 25y TD pass to WR Lovell Pinkney, dropped passes and other miscues slammed door on Longhorns' hooves.

Wisconsin 27 INDIANA 15: Year 4 of Barry Alvarez coaching era had Wisconsin (4-0) off to its best start since 1978. Badgers burned Hoosiers (3-1) with big plays: TB Brent Moss (198y rushing) set up TD with 56y run, TB Terrell Fletcher scored on 57y dash, and, although QB Darrell Bevell hit only 5 passes, WR Lee DeRamus caught his big 39, 35, and 42y throws. Moss scored 1st TD, and Badgers shrugged off 2-pt kick-block RET by Indiana DB Lance Brown that made it 6-2.

Miami 35 COLORADO 29: Third "brawlgame" of day got most attention because it appeared on network TV. Miami's bad-boy image was magnified by 2nd Q donnybrook in which 12 players were ejected; which team started it was unknown. Brawl started after Hurricanes (3-0) scored for 21-6 lead with 20 sec left in H on WR Chris T. Jones' catch of QB Frank Costa's 25y toss. Colorado (2-2) tallied 2 TDs in 90-sec span of 4th Q, pulling within 35-29 on RB James Hill's 5y run with 5:04 left. But, QB Kordell Stewart's 4th down pass failed from Miami 17YL with :13 showing on 4th Q clock.

BAYLOR 28 Texas Tech 26: Bears (3-1) won their 7th in row in Waco by overcoming balanced 508y total O by Texas Tech (1-3) and rallying for 2 TDs in 4th Q. Forgotten Red Raiders TEs Jerod Fiebiger and Roger Corn caught their 1st passes of year, each for TD in 1st and 3rd Qs respectively. Meanwhile, Baylor WR Ben Bronson (3/104y) caught 36 and 44y TD passes from QB J.J. Joe (14-17/254y, 2 TDs). Tech TB Byron "Bam" Morris rushed for 174y, including 44y TD romp in 3rd Q for 23-14 lead. Raiders were on verge on controlling outcome late in 3rd Q when they reached 2YL, but Bears threw them back and forced K Jon Davis' 21y FG. That set stage for 74y march in 4th Q to Baylor FB John Henry's 3y TD run, and when Tech WR Lloyd Hill was stripped of ball after 35y catch by DB Phillip Kent, Bears went 45y to Henry's 2nd TD run.

Ucla 28 STANFORD 25: Erratic Cardinal (2-2) lost 3 FUMs, sustained mere 33y ground game, and allowed Bruins (1-2) to rack up 259y rushing, mostly from TB Sharmon Shah (40/187y) behind road-grader Ts Jonathan Ogden and Vaughn Parker. UCLA DB

Marvin Goodwin returned FUM 36y for TD, K Bjorn Merten kicked 3 FGs, but Stanford got late TD pass from QB Steve Stenstrom (22-24/313y) and made it close thanks to 2 blocked convs by NG Jason Fisk.

October 2, 1993

Boston College 33 SYRACUSE 29: Lead changed hands 4 times in 4th Q as Syracuse (3-1-1) QB Marvin Graves (17-24/200y, TD, INT) put Boston College down by 29-26 with 1y run with 8:56 left. QB Glenn Foley (22-29/423y, 3 TDs) moved Eagles (2-2) downfield in less than 4 mins to TB Darnell Campbell's winning 1y TD run. Boston College LB Brian Howlett sealed win with INT of deflected pass with 1:20 left. Foley had provided 10-7 and 19-14 leads with his 48 and 38y TD flings to WRs Clarence Cannon and Greg Grice, latter coming with 1:20 to go in 3rd Q.

WEST VIRGINIA 14 Virginia Tech 13: Surviving 5 TOs, West Virginia (4-0) held breath as breeze wafted Virginia Tech K Ryan Williams' 44y FG wide right with 1:10 left. Ahead 7-3 in 3rd Q, Virginia Tech (3-2) DB Tyrone Drakeford saved score by creating FUM at Hokies 1YL, but on next play Mountaineers DB Buddy Hager and LB Joe Pabian trapped Tech TB Brian Edmonds for safety. When Hokies went up 13-8 in 3rd Q, they tried but failed on 2-pt pass, and 5-pt edge was overcome by 15-play WVU drive capped by RB Rodney Woodard's TD run.

Alabama 17 SOUTH CAROLINA 6: Alabama (5-0) matched own school and SEC records for consecutive wins with 28, previously set by Bear Bryant's 1978-80 teams. RB Sherman Williams (106y rushing) scored twice in boosting Bama to 17-0 lead. South Carolina (2-3) QB Eric Brown's INT set up RB Brandon Bennett's 21y TD at opening of 4th Q, but Gamecocks blew chance to draw any closer than 17-6 when they couldn't convert FUM REC in Crimson Tide territory.

Auburn 14 VANDERBILT 10: Sneaking up on everyone was underrated Auburn (5-0), which got 1st Q 45y INT TD RET by DB Brian Robinson (10 tackles). K Steve Yenner followed FB Royce Love's short TD run at end of 72y drive by blasting 53y FG with 7 secs left to give Vanderbilt (2-3) 10-7 H edge. RB James Bostic (16/55y) scored winning TD in 3rd Q, but Tigers D had to make GLS early in 4th Q after Vandy set up shop with 1st-and-goal at Auburn 3YL. Tigers LBs Anthony Harris and Terry Solomon and DTs Damon Primus and Mike Pelton keyed GLS that included 3 tries from 1YL.

KENTUCKY 21 Mississippi 0: Posting 2nd shutout of year, Wildcats (3-2) held Ole Miss (3-2) to 201y O and held ball for 37:24. Kentucky's O kept ball for nearly 9 mins and going 77y to score on K Juha Leonoff's early 28y FG. Wildcats got 3y TD run by TB Moe Williams (18/73y, TD) and Leonoff's 2nd FG, thus tallying on each of its opening 3 possessions. Cats dominated in 1st H, running 43 snaps to 16 for Mississippi. Kentucky's D took over in 2nd H as futile Rebs employed 2 QBs, frosh Lawrence Adams (9-14/58y, INT) and soph Paul Head (8-13/65y, 2 INTs), throwing to overcome its inept 78y rushing output. Wildcats WR Mark Chatmon (6/79y, TD) caught 33y score from QB Pookie Jones (13-25/177y, TD) with 3:12 to play.

CALIFORNIA 42 Oregon 41: Oregon QB Danny O'Neil fired 3 1st Q TD passes as Ducks (3-1) built 30-0 lead in 2nd Q. Margin reached 38-14 in 3rd Q when suddenly QB Dave Barr (21-31/368y, 2 TDs) authored greatest comeback in California (5-0) history. Contributing to rally was DB Eric Zomalt's 15y punt block TD, and Bears' critical 85y drive ended with 1:17 left when Barr hit WR Iheanyi Uwaezuoke for 26y TD. Winning margin came on Barr's 2-pt pass to WR Mike Caldwell, gamble which asst coach Denny Schales had to coax coach Keith Gilbertson into trying.

OREGON STATE 30 Arizona State 14: Beavers' archaic Wishbone O rattled Arizona State (2-2) to tune of 419y rushing, and in so doing Oregon State (2-3) snapped 9-game conf losing streak. After losing FUM deep in Sun Devils territory on their opening series, Beavers scored 4 of next 5 times they had ball for 27-0 lead with 2:29 to go before H. Soph QB Donnie Shanklin (18/117y) ran perfect option O and scored on 1 and 31y runs to open 12-0 lead early in 2nd Q. HB J.J. Young (11/105y) raced 75y on option pitchout in 2nd Q. Devils rallied late in 2nd Q with 2 TDs. ASU FB Parnell Charles took 11y TD pass from QB Brady Benton (12-29/126y, TD, 2 INTs) and scored again quickly after fumbled KO. Benton was sacked from Oregon State 14YL on 2nd H's opening series and Sun Devils never threatened again.

ARIZONA 38 Southern California 7: QB Danny White (14-21/228y) energized Arizona (5-0) with 3 TD passes and 1y TD run. Wildcats TD drives were set in motion by 3 FUM RECs, as strong D held Trojans to 22/-3y rushing through 3 Qs. Southern California (2-3) failed to score until subs were playing deep in 4th Q: QB Kyle Wachholtz threw 11y scoring pass to FB Rory Brown. Trojans got 47y rushing, lifting Arizona's amazing total to mere 30y that it had relinquished for year to date.

USA Today Coaches Poll October 4

1	Florida State (57)	1544	14	California	639
2	Alabama	1477	15	North Carolina	593
3	Miami (Fla.) (2)	1398	16	Virginia	580
4	Notre Dame (1)	1319	17	Louisville	569
5	Nebraska	1229	18	Brigham Young	548
6	Florida	1208	19	Wisconsin	430
7	Ohio State	1177	20	West Virginia	380
8	Penn State	1135	21	Colorado	347
9	Oklahoma	1028	22	Syracuse	287
10	Michigan	1008	23	Fresno State	136
11	Arizona	952	24	Clemson	92
12	Tennessee	834	25	Indiana	58
13	Texas A&M	779			

October 9, 1993

WEST VIRGINIA 36 Louisville 34: Seesaw battle turned against Louisville (5-1) on special teams play and late TOs. Cardinals consistently lost field position with 29y punt avg vs WVU P Todd Sauerbrun's 49y avg, and by allowing 3 long KO RETs. West Virginia (5-0) RB Robert Walker rushed 25/161y, including 50y TD run in 3rd Q for 33-28 lead. Louisville rebuttal came early in 4th Q on QB Jeff Brohm's 32y TD pass to WR Kevin Cook (5/86y, 2 TDs), which was Brohm's 4th TD among his 22-39/270y, 2 INTs passing. Behind 34-33, Mountaineers sent WR Mike Bauer steaming 48y on subsequent KO RET, and on 9th play thereafter, K Sauerbrun won it with 36y FG with 10:49 remaining. Cards had chances thereafter but turned it over 4 times, including controversial play called against star DE Joe Johnson. Louisville blocked FG try, and Johnson foolishly tried to advance ball, but lost FUM for new set of WVU downs, even though he claimed he had knee down when hit.

FLORIDA STATE 28 Miami 10: After losing 7 of 8 to Miami with several late-game heartaches, Seminoles (6-0) finally beat Hurricanes (4-1) and took giant step toward national title. Florida State built 21-7 H lead on explosive TDs: TB Sean Jackson's 69y outside-breaking sprint and scramble by QB Charlie Ward (21-31/256y, TD and TD rushing) to find deep-dashing WR Matt Frier for 72y. Hurricanes had tied it 7-7 on 80y trip late in 1st Q as QB Frank Costa (21-43/193y, TD, INT) fired 40y pass to WR Chris T. Jones (7/86y) and found FB Donnell Bennett with 6y TD pass. With score at 21-10 and 5 mins left in 4th Q, Florida State DB Devin Bush darted in front of receiver and went 40y to TD with INT. Year earlier, Bowden wearily suggested his tombstone should read, "And he had to play Miami." This time he offered new saying for his headstone: "He finally beat 'em before he died!" Miami was hopeful while doubling Seminoles' possession time in 1st H, but FSU still led 21-7. Loss ended Hurricanes' 31-game regular season winning streak.

Tennessee 28 ARKANSAS 14: All-around O play of star Tennessee (5-1) QB Heath Shuler (19-26/307y, TD, INT) spelled difference with 3 TDs. Razorbacks (3-3) QB Barry Lunney (15-25/183y, TD, 2 INTs) matched Shuler's ice-breaking TD run with 6y scoring pass to FB Oscar Gray in 2nd Q. Shuler connected with WR Craig Faulkner to set up TB James Stewart's TD run for 14-7 H bulge, and Shuler and Faulkner teamed for 11y TD pass and 21-7 3rd Q edge. Arkansas went 74y to make it 21-14 and then held on 4th down at its 7YL in 3rd Q. Hogs CB Dean Peevy made INT at his 47YL early in 4th Q, but Arkansas went 3-and-out to set up Vols' 6:40 drive to Shuler's clinching TD.

MICHIGAN STATE 17 Michigan 7: Magnificent Spartans (3-1) D paved way for upset by sacking Michigan (3-2) QB Todd Collins 3 times, holding nation's highest all-purpose y-maker, TB Tyrone Wheatley, to 11/33y on ground, and blanking Wolverines at H for 1st time since 1987. FBs Brice Abrams and Scott Greene, normally called upon for fierce blocking, cashed Michigan State TDs: Abrams on 3y 1st Q run and Greene on 3y 2nd Q pass from QB Jim Miller.

Ohio State 20 ILLINOIS 12: Buckeyes (5-0) maintained their best start since 1979, beating Illinois (1-4) after 5 losses in row in Illi-Buck rivalry. Illini QB Johnny Johnson (15-32/126y, INT) lost early FUM at his own 14YL, and 3 plays later Ohio State QB Bobby Hoying (7-12/82y, TD) clicked with WR Joey Galloway on 11y TD pass. K Tim Williams made 52y FG in 1st Q, 1st of his pair of 3-ptrs, for 10-0 Buck edge. Illinois finally got going in 2nd Q, moving 68y in 11 plays but had to settle for K Chris Richardson's 29y FG. Late in 2nd Q, Ohio WR Terry Glenn recovered EZ FUM after DB Tito Paul so pressured Illini P Brett Larsen that he bobbled punt snap. Richardson kicked 3 FGs in 3rd Q as frustrated Illinois couldn't punch it in after 2 trips inside Buckeyes 10YL.

KANSAS STATE 10 Kansas 9: On its way to best to-date record, Kansas State (5-0) continued its fabulous turnaround and won 10th home game in row. Wildcats WR Andre Coleman caught 19y TD pass in 1st Q, and K Tate Wright followed with career-best 50y FG, enough to offset K Dan Eichloff's 3 FGs for Kansas (2-4).

RICE 34 Texas Christian 19: Horned Frogs (1-4) lost 9th straight road tilt as Rice (4-2) overcame early 6-0 deficit to mix runs (255y) with passes (229y) to swamp TCU in 2nd H. Although Owls led only 14-9 at H after Frogs QB Max Knake (15-30/147y, TD, INT) and Rice QB Bert Emanuel (13-18/221y, 2 TDs), Emanuel hit 9 passes in row in 3rd Q. Runs by TB Yoncy Edmonds (22/149y) helped Rice keep ball for 20:29 of 2nd H.

North Carolina State 36 TEXAS TECH 34: After busting 10-10 2nd Q tie, Red Raiders (1-5) led until last 2 secs. Texas Tech coach Spike Dykes painfully called game "toughest one I've ever been through." Tech players would unite to close 1993 with 5 straight wins, but had to endure this heartbreaker. RB Byron "Bam" Morris (27/141y) extended Tech's 4th Q lead to 34-24 with 5y TD run. As 4th Q clock rolled on, NC State (3-2) scored to make it 34-30 on 26y TD pass to TB Gary Downs (22/146y) from QB Terry Harvey (26-41/307y, 4 TDs, INT), who had left bench in 2nd Q to spark Wolfpack.

Morris' FUM with 1:23 left then gave NC State life at its own 34YL. Harvey ripped Raiders with 7-10 passing, including 11y winner to WR Eddie Goines (9/123y, 3 TDs) on game's last play.

Washington 24 CALIFORNIA 23: After huge comeback previous week vs. Oregon, California (5-1) saw fortunes reversed as Huskies (4-1) rallied from 23-3 deficit in 3rd Q. Golden Bears D forced 7 TOs as LB Jerrott Willard had INT and FUM REC for set up 10 pts. Washington QB Damon Huard (22-34/237y, 4 INTs) hit WR D.J. McCarthy with 29y TD pass to make it 23-17 with 2:06 to go, then, after on-side KO, Huard found TE Mark Bruener with 7y TD pass.

USA Today Coaches Poll October 11

1	Florida State (58)	1546	14	Virginia	703
2	Alabama (2)	1475	15	West Virginia	627
3	Notre Dame (2)	1399	16	Wisconsin	600
4	Florida	1289	17	Michigan	538
5	Nebraska	1261	18	Colorado	443
6	Ohio State	1228	19	Syracuse	369
7	Penn State	1184	20	California	352
8	Oklahoma	1113	21	Louisville	283
9	Miami (Fla.)	1070	22	Indiana	215
10	Arizona	1003	23	UCLA	199
11	Tennessee	934	24	Kansas State	147
12	Texas A&M	857	25	Michigan State	145
13	North Carolina	726			

October 16, 1993

Wake Forest 20 CLEMSON 16: It was thrilling moment for Wake Forest (2-4) as Jim Caldwell became 1st coach since Notre Dame's Dan Devine in 1977 to win in his initial visit to "Death Valley." Wake's 2nd win in row over Clemson (4-2) previously hadn't happened since 1946-47. Demon Deacons G Kevin Smith threw seal block for QB Jim Kemp's 2y TD keeper in 1st Q. Kemp provided 13-0 lead by hitting WR Todd Dixon with 2nd Q TD pass after bad snap trapped Tigers P Nelson Welch for 14y loss in his end. Clemson moved within 13-10 when K Welch hit 24y FG at end of 15-play drive in 3rd Q. Deacons reasserted themselves on FB Ned Moultrie's 48y burst that positioned 6y TD run for 20-10 lead by TB John Leach (18/82y, TD). Tigers coach Ken Hatfield was beginning to hear boo-birds at Clemson.

ALABAMA 17 Tennessee 17: Despite 11 running plays that lost y in opening 22 tries, Alabama (5-0-1) led 9-7 at H. After Tennessee (5-1-1) regained 17-9 advantage, RB Charlie Garner opened 4th Q with 73y TD run behind blocks of C Bubba Miller and G Kevin Mays. Now trailing 17-9, Crimson Tide started last drive at own 17YL with 1:44 to go. WR David Palmer made 3 straight catches and WR Kevin Lee grabbed 4th down pass to set up QB Jay Barker's TD sneak with :21 left. When Palmer lined up at QB post for tying 2-pt conv try, Vols called timeout. Coach Phillip Fulmer said, "I thought we were prepared for the perimeter play," but swift Palmer still knotted game with wide dash right.

AUBURN 38 Florida 35: Leading 10-0 in 1st Q, Florida (5-1) suffered 1st of 2 key INTs: Tigers DB Calvin Jackson made thrilling 96y TD RET. Midway in 4th Q, DB Chris Shelling dashed 65y with INT to set up WR Frank Sanders' 9y TD sweep and 35-27 Auburn (7-0) lead. Gators tied it 35-35 on QB Danny Wuerffel's TD throw and 2-pt pass, but K Scott Etheridge kicked winning 41y FG for ecstatic Tigers with 1:21 left.

Mississippi 19 Arkansas 0 (Jackson, Miss.): Mississippi (4-2) failed 3 times to earn TD from inside Arkansas (3-4) 15YL in 1st H. But, Rebels K Walter Grant came through with 3 FGs of 23, 31, and 30y for 9-0 H edge. Razorbacks were forced to use backup TBs Dexter Hebert and Carlton Calvin, and FB Oscar Gray, so their run attack (41/105y) was pretty well stonewalled by Rebs' pressure D, led by LB Abdul Jackson, DT Tim Bowens, and S Johnny Dixon. Hogs lost 4 TOs to further stymie their O. In 4th Q, Ole Miss scored on 23y run by FB Renard Brown, and Grant kicked his 4th FG, this time from longer range of 46y.

Michigan 21 PENN STATE 13: Miffed Michigan (4-2), somewhat resentful of attention paid Penn State's Big 10 entry, found itself floundering, down by 10-0 with 5:14 left before H. Then, WR Derrick Alexander's 48y punt TD RET righted ship of defending conf champs. Wolverines QB Todd Collins made 2 TD passes in 2nd H: 16y to WR Mercury Hayes and 5y swing toss to FB Che Foster for 21-13 clincher. Holding Nittany Lions (5-1) to 16y rushing in 2nd H, Wolverines D sustained its 14-10 lead and turned back Penn State momentum by stopping Lions inches from GL. After moving from its 20YL late in 3rd Q, Penn State made 3 thrusts: QB Kerry Collins (16-30/182y, TD, INT) ran 2 sneaks and TB Ki-Jana Carter (19/127y) took dive into line before 3rd Q ended. Lions had plenty of time to think about its 4th down call that opened 4th Q, but LB Jarrett Irons and SS Shonte Peoples put vice grip on Carter's TD run attempt.

OHIO STATE 28 Michigan State 21: WR Joey Galloway's 3 TD catches gave Ohio State (6-0) 21-10 H lead. Michigan State (3-2) drove all 12 of its possessions into Ohio territory, and finally cashed K Bill Stoyanovich's FG on 1st play of 4th Q. But, Stoyanovich missed 4 FGs, and WR Nigea Carter dropped certain TD pass. Spartans, however, came alive to tie it 21-21 when QB Jim Miller (31-42/360y) hit FB Scott Greene with 38y TD pass and WR Mill Coleman with 2-pt conv. Buckeyes TB Raymont Harris won it with 1:06 left on 7y run at end of 80y drive engineered by backup QB Bret Powers.

NEBRASKA 45 Kansas State 28: "There are no moral victories at Kansas State (5-1) any more," said LB Percell Gaskins. "We expected to win." Although Nebraska (6-0) rammed to 14-7 1st Q lead and 31-14 H lead on QB Tommie Frazier's TD pass and run and IB Calvin Jones' 2 TD runs, Wildcats clawed back to within 31-28 midway in 4th Q on 2nd long TD pass by QB Chad May (30-51/489y, 2 TDs, INT). Huskers responded with 76y trip to FB Cory Schlesinger's 13y TD sprint. Misbegotten trick play late in 2nd Q had helped seal K-State's case: Trailing 28-14 and having advanced to Nebraska

4YL, Cats TB J.J. Smith (23/102y, 2 TDs) tried sweep right with throw-back to QB May. Smith's poor lob was picked off by DB Tyrone Williams and it led to 48y FG by Huskers K Byron Bennett. So what might have been 7-pt deficit turned into 17-pt K-State shortfall.

UCLA 39 Washington 25: Trailing 15-0 in 1st Q, UCLA (4-2) turned to QB Wayne Cook-to-WR J.J. Stokes combo for 95y TD pass. Same TD battery connected thrice more: 18y in 2nd Q, 22y for 21-18 lead in 3rd Q, and 6y for 32-18 lead with 8:42 left. Sub QB Eric Bjornson got Huskies (4-2) back in game at 32-25 with TD pass with 4:38 left, but endured 2 INTs, 2nd of which went 36y by DB Teddy Lawrence to clinching Bruins TD.

USA Today Coaches Poll October 18

1	Florida State (59)	1547	14	Michigan	756
2	Notre Dame (3)	1472	15	West Virginia	718
3	Nebraska	1376	16	Colorado	665
4	Ohio State	1363	17	Oklahoma	617
5	Alabama	1297	18	UCLA	472
6	Miami (Fla.)	1186	19	Louisville	387
7	Arizona	1107	20	Virginia	376
8	Tennessee	1048	21	Syracuse	371
9	Texas A&M	1001	22	Indiana	306
10	Florida	949	23	Michigan State	100
11	North Carolina	870	24	Washington State	65
12	Wisconsin	798	25	Kansas State	64
13	Penn State	776			

October 23, 1993

VIRGINIA TECH 49 Rutgers 42: QB Maurice DeShazo (14-29/267y, 3 TDs) accounted for 4 TDs, including his 2y scoring run that gave Virginia Tech (5-2) 35-7 H bulge. Rutgers (4-3-1) TB Terrell Willis (21/155y, 3 TDs) had cut against grain for 35y run and game's 1st TD in 1st Q, but Hokies D held Knights to only 2 1st downs on next 7 possessions. Willis scored again to touch off 14-14 standoff in 3rd Q, but when DeShazo fumbled at midfield early in 4th Q, Rutgers rallied with 3 TDs capped by 8y TD throw by QB Brian Fortay (19-35/273y, 2 TDs) in contest's last min.

VIRGINIA 17 North Carolina 10: Virginia coach George Welsh thought his team played with more emotion than he had seen in years. Perhaps it was pre-game, on-field woofing by UNC that riled up UVa. As Cavaliers (6-1) LB Randy Neal put it: "They won the warm-up; they lost the game." Virginia fed run-oriented Tar Heels (7-2) their own ball control medicine, launching 3 drives that each burned in excess of 6 mins and resulted in 70y drive to FB Charles Way's go-ahead 4th down TD plunge late in 3rd Q. North Carolina had lost punt FUM at his own 20YL midway in 2nd Q, and Virginia quickly jumped to 10-0 lead on TB Kevin Brooks' 7y run. QB Jason Stanicek (14-27/172y, INT) had wedged over for short TD run just before H to climb his team back to 10-7. DL Mike Frederick and Ryan Kuehl helped hold UNC to season-low 101y on ground, while Virginia QB Symmion Willis hit 22-31/239y passing.

Illinois 24 MICHIGAN 21: Inconsistent Wolverines (4-3) lost at home to Illinois (3-4) for 1st time since 1966. With TB Tyrone Wheatley injured, Michigan tried to run out clock with 21-17 lead, but TB Ricky Powers had ball ripped away by Illini LB Simeon Rice. Illinois QB Johnny Johnson (22-38/265y, 2 TDs) scrambled away from 2 tacklers and hit WR Jim Klein with winning 15y TD with 34 secs left.

MINNESOTA 28 Wisconsin 21: When Ohio State defeated Purdue 45-28, Wisconsin lost Big 10 lead to Buckeyes. Minnesota (4-4) built 21-0 by H as outstanding RB Chris Darkins rushed 17/83y, 2 TDs, including 39y TD bolt that opened scoring at 7-0 in 1st Q. Falling so far behind forced Badgers (6-1) into uncharacteristic aerial game: QB Darrell Bevell was up to task, clicking on 31-48/school-record 423y and late 16y TD pass to WR J.C. Dawkins, who had career-best day with 9/131y, TD receiving. Unfortunately, Bevell suffered 5 INTs with Gophers DB Jeff Rosga returning INT 55y for 2nd Q TD to extend score to 21-0. TB Brent Moss (27/130y, 2 TDs) barreled over for 2 TDs in 3rd Q, but Wisconsin could never catch up.

NOTRE DAME 31 Southern California 13: Fighting Irish (8-0) leveled Trojans (4-4) for 11th straight time as RB Lee Becton burst away for 70y TD run on game's 2nd play and rushed for career-high 177y. Sub ND QB Paul Failla (6-9/78y, TD), in for ailing QB Kevin McDougall, threw modestly but effectively, while USC QB Rob Johnson (29-46/269y, 2 TDs, INT) threw TD passes to TB Deon Strother in 2nd Q and TE Johnny McWilliams in 4th Q, but suffered INT, and otherwise was controlled by Irish pass rush. Fighting Irish scored every time it had ball in 1st H for 28-7 lead at H break.

KANSAS STATE 16 Colorado 16: Wildcats (5-1-1) QB Chad May (17-31/273y, 2 TDs, 2 INTs) must have slipped into phone booth and donned Superman outfit: He went from dismal 35y passing in 1st H to 238y in air in 2nd H. Meanwhile Colorado (4-2-1) owned 1st H with 239y to 36y O advantage. But, when Buffs marched inside K-State 20YL on their 1st 3 series only to settle for K Mitch Berger's 3 FGs for H lead of 9-0. Fortune was on side of K-State QB May when he luckily guided 3rd Q pass through hands of Bison DB Chris Hudson and into arms of Wildcats WR Andre Coleman for 7y TD. But, Kansas State had vital x-pt blocked. Colorado, struggling with only 106y rushing against Big 8's 7th-worst run D, finally dented GL for 16-13 edge on TB James Hill's TD run with 3:57 left. When coach Bill Snyder chose to take K Tate Wright's tying 35y FG on 4th down with 21 secs left, he agonized over his decision: "I felt like the kids played hard, and I didn't want them to go to the locker room with a loss."

Texas A&M 38 RICE 10: TB Leeland McElroy electrified Texas A&M (6-1) by becoming 6th player in NCAA history to race back 2 KO RETs in single game for TDs. McElroy also was 2nd frosh to turn KO RET magic; Notre Dame's Rocket Ismail had other such lightning bolt, also, oddly, against Rice (4-4). Scrambling Owls QB Bert Emanuel (12-15/120y, TD) moved his team 72y to opening FG by K Johnny Bagwell, but McElroy answered with 93y KO RET. Rice went 80y to Emanuel's 14y TD pass to

RB Byron Coston, but again McElroy responded before 1st Q ended. Aggies QB Corey Pullig (12-19/145y, 2 TDs) threw his TD passes in middle Qs, and ace DE Sam Adams recovered last of Rice's 5 lost FUMs in EZ for 4th Q TD.

ARIZONA 9 Washington State 6: Marcia Hammond offered good lead paragraph in *Arizona Republic:* "There was little room to run against the two best defenses in the country, but there was plenty of room to kick." Arizona (7-0) became 1st team in school history to open with 7 wins, and it was accomplished on foot of K Steve McLaughlin, who powered 53y FG in 2nd Q that tied it 3-3, put Wildcats ahead 6-3 with 40y FG in 3rd Q, and nailed game-winner from 32y out with 1:33 remaining. Washington State (5-3) K Aaron Price had tied it at 6-6 in 3rd Q after Arizona WR Terry Vaughn (5/95y) fumbled reverse punt RET. Superb Cats DE Tedy Bruschi made 2 sacks near game's end of 3rd string Cougars QB Chad DeGrenier to force Price into tying 49y FG try, which he booted barely wide to left.

USA Today Coaches Poll October 25

1	Florida State (59)	1547	14	Virginia	696
2	Notre Dame (3)	1475	15	UCLA	658
3	Ohio State	1379	16	Louisville	555
4	Nebraska	1364	17	Indiana	515
5	Alabama	1259	18	Colorado	422
6	Miami (Fla.)	1226	19	North Carolina	415
7	Arizona	1179	20	Wisconsin	385
8	Texas A&M	1040	21	Michigan State	317
9	Tennessee	1028	22	Kansas State	210
10	Florida	1008	23	Michigan	208
11	West Virginia	882	24	Virginia Tech	134
12	Penn State	871	25	Wyoming	115
13	Oklahoma	819			

October 30, 1993

West Virginia 43 SYRACUSE 0: RB Robert Walker dashed for 198y, 2 scores, including 90y TD as undefeated West Virginia (7-0) finally grabbed nation's attention with its destruction of Syracuse (4-3-1). Mountaineers QB Jake Kelchner passed 12-18/191y, TD, and rushed for 51y to score TD. So badly crushed were Orangemen, with their 188y total O, that their only bright spots were QB Marvin Graves' 14-28/144y pasing and P Pat O'Neill's 51.7y avg. During 4 wins in month of October, WVU, which started season unranked, managed to jump from 25th to 11th in AP Poll.

Notre Dame 58 Navy 27 (Philadelphia): Middies (4-4) coach George Chaump called 1st H "as great a half as Navy has ever had." Score sent shock waves across America: Navy 24, Notre Dame 17. Midshipmen QB Jim Kubiak threw 12-19/193y, 2 TDs, including toss that nimble WR Jimmy Screen grabbed between 2 defenders and turned into 53y TD. Normalcy returned in 2nd H as Irish (9-0) scored 6 TDs, including WR Lake Dawson's 44y catch, TB Randy Kinder's 70y sprint, and CB Bobby Taylor's 31y INT RET.

Florida 33 Georgia 26 (Jacksonville): In Gator Bowl stadium quagmire, rivals traded scores all day. Winning edge was ability of Florida (6-1) to rush for 193y. Gators TB Errict Rhett ran 41/183y, 2 TDs. Georgia (4-5) QB Eric Zeier (36-65/384y, 2 TDs) was forced to fill air with passes. In final 6 secs, Zeier hit TD pass, but what went unnoticed was timeout called by panicky Bulldogs player just before snap. "Do-over" resulted in EZ interference against Florida, but Zeier followed by missing open receiver in EZ.

LOUISIANA STATE 19 Mississippi 17: LSU's K with hockey-sounding name, Andre Lafleur, couldn't "put the puck in the ocean" when he missed pair of x-pts in 2nd H. So, Lafleur was reduced to wishin'-and-hopin' in last 54 secs as Ole Miss (4-4) K Walter Grant missed 35y FG that could have won it for Rebels. Against nation's 3rd-leading D, LSU (3-5) scored when it needed to. Rebels QB Lawrence Adams (14-22/125y, TD, INT) opened with 18y TD arrow to WR Ta'boris Fisher at end of 69y advance in 1st Q. Tigers answered with 72y march to frosh WR Eddie Kennison's TD grab. LSU long-snap C Chris Watermeier fired punt snap all way to his 1YL in 2nd Q, and Mississippi QB Adams scored in 1 play for 14-7 H edge. Bengals TB Jay Johnson (15/104y, 2 TDs) scored on 36 and 4y runs in 2nd H, but Lafleur was wide with each conv kick. In between, Grant hit 34y FG for Ole Miss. So, LSU led 19-17 with nearly 12 mins to go, and it would end with fans finally happy in Bayou.

Auburn 31 ARKANSAS 21: Chilly conditions in Fayetteville greeted Auburn (8-0), and Hogs (3-5) scored 1st on 76y TD drive. Tigers WR Frankie Sanders (7/134y) nabbed 56y pass to help tie it at 7-7 before end of 1st Q. It stayed that way until early 3rd Q when Auburn DB Brian Robinson turned tide with 35y INT TD RET. Although Razorbacks QB Barry Lunney (17-41/286y, 2 TDs, INT) hit 1st of his 2 TD passes, 3rd Q closed with Tigers up 17-14. Auburn put it away with 4th Q TD runs for 12y by TB James Bostic and 16y clincher from FB Reid McMilion (12/91y, TD) that came with 4:30 to go.

OHIO STATE 24 Penn State 6: In Columbus' snow and rain, Ohio State (8-0) derailed any hope harbored by Penn State (5-2) that it might enjoy Rose Bowl trip in its 1 Big 10 season. For 8th straight time in 1993, Buckeyes tallied on their 1st possession: TB Raymont Harris (32/151y, TD) scored on 4y TD run after Nittany Lions K Craig Fayak had kicked 1st of his 2 FGs from 29y out. Fayak became his school's all-time leading scorer with 49y FG later in 1st Q, but that long 3-pt boot was matched by Ohio K Tim Williams from short range. Bucks QB Bret Powers (4-8/49y, TD, INT) left bench in relief of QB Bobby Hoying (4-11/107y) in 2nd Q and promptly gave great run fake on 3rd-and-2 at Penn State 25YL and lofted TD pass to WR Joey Galloway. TB Ki-Jana Carter rushed for 24/123y, but Lions' O derailed with dreadful aerial game: QB Kerry Collins (13-29/122y) was intercepted 4 times. Sub TB Butler By'not'e provided last TD in 3rd Q to extend Ohio State lead to 24-6.

WISCONSIN 13 Michigan 10: Badgers' 1st win over Wolverines in dozen years and its greatest victory in decades was marred by post-game celebration in which dozens of Wisconsin students were crushed against stadium fence in celebratory stampede to playing field from student section. There were more than 70 injured, some critically. As insignificant as game result would later seem, Badgers got started toward their upset as walk-on K Rick Schnetzky booted 25 and 26y FGs for 6-0 lead in 2nd Q. Wisconsin (7-1) jumped to 13-3 H edge as backup TB Terrell Fletcher (9/78y, TD), in for TB Brent Moss (26/128y), completed 80y drive by beating H clock with 12y TD run. Michigan (5-3) had gotten short FG from K Peter Elezovic, before Fletcher's TD, with 2:39 left in 1st H, but UM repeatedly squandered its 2nd H chances despite drawing to within 13-10 on QB Todd Collins' 7y TD pass to WR Derrick Alexander in 3rd Q.

Nebraska 21 COLORADO 17: Cornhuskers (8-0) were staked to 21-3 lead in 1st Q on IB Calvin Jones' 2 TDs and WR Corey Dixon's 60y catch from QB Tommie Frazier. Colorado (4-3-1) was held to 18y in 5 series in 2nd H, but finally propped itself up for 80y TD drive in 4th Q. It was on that trip that Buffaloes TB Rashaan Salaam (25/165y, 2 TDs) scored his 2nd TD to bring tally to 21-17. Late Colorado rally was snuffed by Nebraska DB John Reece's clutch INT.

KANSAS STATE 21 Oklahoma 7: QB Chad May threw 2 TDs and ran for another to lead Wildcats (6-1-1) past fumbling Oklahoma (6-2) for 1st time in 23 years. Kansas State completed 1-1-1 consecutive-week stretch vs. Big 8's "Big 3" and beat ranked team for 1st time since 1981. Down 14-0 in 3rd Q, Sooners had 3rd-and-1 at K-State 41YL, but lapsed into PEN and miserable 11y punt. May (13-31/203y, 2 TDs, 3 INTs) then capped 68y drive with his 2y TD run for formidable 21-0 lead. Oklahoma earned trifling 31y TD pass from QB Cale Gundy to WR P.J. Mills in last 5 mins.

UCLA 37 Arizona 17: Little went right for unbeaten Arizona (7-1) as UCLA (6-2) scored 27 pts off TOs. Wildcats QB Danny White had minor knee sprain; rusty QBs Brady Batten and Ryan Hesson—who was nicked for 64y INT TD RET by Bruins LB Nkosi Littleton in 4th Q—had rough time against inspired UCLA D. UCLA built 30-0 margin by middle of 3rd Q as QB Wayne Cook threw 14-29/166y and clicked on 2 TD throws at vital times, while WR J.J. Stokes caught 6/91y, including his 14th TD of season that provided 7-0 in 1st Q. Arizona TBs Chuck Levy and Gary Taylor scored ground TDs after it was too late.

USA Today Coaches Poll November 1

1	Florida State (59)	1547	14	Wisconsin	738
2	Notre Dame (2)	1456	15	Louisville	706
3	Ohio State (1)	1419	16	Penn State	534
4	Nebraska	1357	17	Kansas State	520
5	Alabama	1278	18	North Carolina	519
6	Miami (Fla.)	1244	19	Virginia	320
7	Tennessee	1108	20	Oklahoma	316
8	Texas A&M	1077	21	Wyoming	292
9	West Virginia	1041	22	North Carolina State	275
10	Florida	1032	23	Virginia Tech	266
11	UCLA	886	24	Colorado	156
12	Arizona	792	25	Boston College	130
13	Indiana	752			

November 6, 1993

DUKE 21 North Carolina State 20: "Gosh, it's been a long time since I've been carried off a field," said Barry Wilson, who revealed he would quit as Duke (3-7) coach at year's end. Blue Devils jumped to 21-0 H lead, outgaining Wolfpack 266y to 59y. Duke QB Spence Fischer, who passed for 229y and 2 TDs, said, "We felt pretty unstoppable in the first half." Rallying NC State (6-3) scored 3 TDs in 7:06 span of 4th Q, and, after their 3rd TD, Wolfpack went for 2 pts. Blitzing Duke LB Billy Granville and DB Tee Edwards swarmed to NC State QB Geoff Bender and forced incomplete conv pass.

NORTH CAROLINA 24 Clemson 0: Losers of 11 of past 12 tilts to Clemson (6-3), North Carolina (8-2) dominated game as it blanked Tigers for 1st time since 1964. Key to final result could be found in rushing totals: Tar Heels gained 53/194y, and Tigers managed but 32/3y out of its fairly new Flex-bone run-oriented O. It was Clemson's worst rushing total since 1947. UNC TB Leon Johnson (15/62y) scored 1st Q TD that tied Charlie "Choo Choo" Justice's school frosh record of 12 TDs. Score was produced when Heels D stopped Clemson cold and partially blocked punt at Tigers 43YL. QB Jason Stanicek (15-25/221y, TD) and TB Curtis Johnson (16/63y, TD) also produced scores for North Carolina before 1st H was over.

VANDERBILT 12 Kentucky 7: Dreaming about wrapping up bowl invitation before road game crowd that was dressed predominantly in Kentucky blue, Wildcats (5-4) got caught by 1st SEC win for Vanderbilt (3-5) this season. Commodores played brilliant pass D, limiting Cats QB Pookie Jones to 7-18/47y, INT in air and launching CB Robert Davis on 45y INT TD RET in 2nd Q for 7-0 lead. Vandy stopped 4th-and-1 sneak by Jones at its 21YL late in 2nd Q. Kentucky DB Adrian Sherwood put UK at Dores 30YL in 4th Q after his INT, and TB Moe Williams (21/91y, TD) scored 6 plays later to tie it 7-7. Vanderbilt TB Cliff Deese (8/62y) soon appeared to be stopped at his 41YL: shortly later, but broke 48y dash down right sideline to Wildcats 11YL. Kentucky held for 3 downs, but Vandy K Steve Yenner kicked winning 21y FG with 2:29 to play. Game ended with 3 straight sacks of Jones, last by DT Alan Young was chalked up as safety for Commodores.

Louisiana State 17 ALABAMA 13: Nation's longest unbeaten streak ended at 31 as LSU (4-5) forced 4 INTs by 3 different Alabama QBs who subbed for injured QB Jay Barker. WR David Palmer moved to QB for Crimson Tide (7-1-1) and threw 2 TD passes, but his mercury-footed efforts couldn't catch fired-up Tigers. LSU had gone up 14-0 on 3rd Q TD runs by RBs Jay Johnson (14/83y) and Robert Toomer (18/72y). Opening floodgates after scoreless 1st H was starting Tide QB Brian Burgdorf's INT by Bengals FS Anthony Marshall on opening series of 3rd Q, which led to Johnson's TD. Palmer (6-10/116y, 2 TDs, INT) finally put frustrated Bama on scoreboard in 4th Q as it trailed 14-7. But as LSU K Andre Lafleur succeeded on 36y FG game went out of reach at 17-7.

TENNESSEE 45 Louisville 10: Vols (7-1-1) scored on their opening 2 drives of 59 and 63y on way to posting remarkable 32-1 November record since 1985. QB Heath Shuler (21-30/215y) hit WR Cory Fleming with 3rd Q TD and 24-3 lead. Louisville (7-2) rallied on QB Jeff Brohm's hustling TD run to cut margin to 24-10 and then succeeded with on-side KO. At that point, Card wheels came off: Vols DB DeRon Jenkins snatched INT and scored on 22y FUM RET. Punt RET reverse from Fleming to WR Nilo Silvan covered 69y for Volunteers' 3rd TD within 3:30 time span.

WISCONSIN 14 Ohio State 14: Stunned Wisconsin crowd made no rush of field this week as it filed silently out of Camp Randall Stadium after sobering week. Increased security was in place, but event on field prevented repeat of student stampede that hurt 69 people after prior Saturday's win over Michigan. Ohio State (8-0-1) DB Marlon Kerner sobered crowd by blocking Badgers K Rick Schnetzky's potential winning 33y FG try with 7 secs left. Tie kept Buckeyes in Big 10 control, while Badgers (7-1-1) now needed help from Indiana or Michigan to qualify for Rose Bowl. Ohio QB Bret Powers left bench in 4th Q to spark 99y drive and throw tying 26y TD pass to WR Joey Galloway with 3:48 to play. Having not played since 1st H, Powers "went by the (bench-side) heater to loosen up" and then hit Galloway on 4 completions that comprised 88y of Bucks' length-of-field drive. Wisconsin TB Brent Moss (25/129y, TD) had broken 7-7 tie with 3y TD run in 3rd Q.

PENN STATE 38 Indiana 31: Hoosiers (7-2) entered game with worst passing stats in Big 10, but QB John Paci threw 20-37/379y and 3 TDs, while adding 4th Q TD on ground for 31-31 deadlock. Earlier in 4th Q, Indiana WR Thomas Lewis (12/285y, 2 TDs) raced 99y with pass from Paci that broke 38-year-old conf long-distance record held by Lenny Dawson and Erich Barnes of Purdue. Penn State (6-2) balanced its attack with 208y rushing and 215y passing. QB Kerry Collins (18-29/215y, 2 TDs) broke 31-31 tie with winning 45y TD pass to WR Bobby Engram (6/112y, 2 TDs) with 6:25 left. Indiana, which twice rallied from 14 pts down, appeared headed to tying score in last 2 mins, but Nittany Lions DB Tony Pittman took INT at his 7YL to break up rally.

Nebraska 21 KANSAS 20: Coach Glen Mason of Kansas (4-6) was asked when during this seesaw game that he decided to try for late winning 2-pt conv. His answer: "When I took the job and saw what a lopsided series it was!" With 52 secs to go, Huskers (9-0) forced Jayhawks QB Asheiki Preston into high and wide 2-pt pass after TB June Hensley's 3y TD run. So, Nebraska held its 1-pt edge. Kansas had scored 1st on TE Dwayne Chandler's 30y TD reception, but trailed 14-7 at H. Jayhawks tied it at 14-14 on Preston's 5y TD run in 3rd Q. Hard-fought win tarnished Nebraska's image as voters placed Miami, 35-7 winners over Pitt, no. 3 in poll, just ahead of Huskers. Nebraska IB Calvin Jones rushed for 195y and scored on 1st Q TD run that had tied it at 7-7.

ARIZONA STATE 41 California 0: Golden Bears (5-4) continued their steep slide to 4th straight loss, while Sun Devils (5-4) followed frosh QB Jake Plummer (16-27/265y, 2 TDs) to 574y total O. After scoreless 1st Q, K Jon Baker made long and short FGs for 6-0 Arizona State lead, and Plummer moved Devils 48y to slant-in TD pass to WR Johnny Thomas (6/123y, TD), who later scored on 68y reverse run early in 4th Q. ASU led 12-0 at H. In 1st H, California's banged up O was led by frosh QB Pat Barnes (10-33/125y, 3 INTs), who coach Keith Gilbertson had hoped to red-shirt. Barnes' ineffective play (7-21/64y, INT passing in 1st H) led to return in 2nd H of sore-shouldered regular QB Dave Barr. Barr faired little better with (7-12/46y), but drove Cal to 4th-and-3 at Devils 45YL in 3rd Q. Arizona State stopped 4th down run and marched to 4y TD catch to FB Parnell Charles, who slipped out of full-house jumbo backfield, enhanced by presence at HB of G Farrington "Taco" Togiai, to take Plummer's TD pass for 19-0 lead. It was 1st time Cal had been shut out since 1986.

ARIZONA 31 Oregon 10: Facing prospects of trying to run Pac-10's weakest O without his top 2 QBs, Wildcats (8-1) coach Dick Tomey reached into past for option attack that placed TB Chuck Levy (29/127y, 3 TDs rushing) at QB. Arizona rushed for 389y and bothered with only 1 pass, which fell incomplete. Levy's scoring runs of 1, 3, and 48y capped drives of 70, 79, and 65y for 21-0 H edge. Pass O of Oregon (5-4) was blasted by pressure (8 sacks), starting with S Brandon Sanders' blitz of Ducks QB Danny O'Neil (16-23/253y, TD, INT) on game's 1st snap. Outstanding K Tommy Thompson managed 54y FG against wind in 3rd Q for Oregon, and O'Neil and TB Ricky Whittle collaborated on 67y pass play to set up WR Cristin McLemore's 7y TD catch early in 4th Q.

USA Today Coaches Poll November 8

1	Florida State (60)	1548	14	Penn State	713
2	Notre Dame (2)	1471	15	North Carolina	692
3	Nebraska	1398	16	Virginia	553
4	Miami (Fla.)	1361	17	Oklahoma	489
5	Ohio State	1246	18	Indiana	464
6	Tennessee	1208	19	Wyoming	402
7	West Virginia	1129	20	Louisville	328
8	Texas A&M	1124	21	Boston College	324
9	Florida	1104	22	Colorado	303
10	UCLA	984	23	Kansas State	199
11	Alabama	925	24	Southern California	132
12	Arizona	840	25	Michigan State	99
13	Wisconsin	743			

November 13, 1993

CLEMSON 23 Virginia 14: Frosh Dexter McCleon became 5th Clemson (7-3) QB of season by taking field general reins after Patrick Sapp was benched after 2 series. On same play that launched previous year's 29-pt Tiger comeback, McCleon faked to his FB and darted outside for 29y TD and 7-0 lead in last 3 mins of 1st Q. Meanwhile,

young Virginia (7-3) QB Symmion Willis (13-26/157y, TD, 4 INTs) continued to slip badly after sharp early season play. Willis' INTs now reached 8 in last 2 contests, but he tied score at 7-7 in 2nd Q as WR Demetrius "Pete" Allen got loose for deep ball and 57y TD. McCleon (4-9/109y, TD, 3 INTs passing and 12/127y rushing) pitched short pass over middle to WR Terry Smith, who cut through Cav D for 73y TD and 17-7 lead early in 3rd Q. Virginia briefly got back in it at 17-14 on next series as TB Jarrod Washington (20/98y, TD) charged for 3y TD run up middle.

Auburn 42 GEORGIA 28: Season's most unlikely success story, Auburn (10-0), kept hopes alive of repeat of 1957, year in which Tigers went undefeated and won national title while probation kept them out of bowl play. RB James Bostic (19/183y) burst 41y in 2nd Q for 14-7 Auburn lead, then scored again after Bulldogs FUM. Georgia (4-6) QB Eric Zeier lit it up for 34-53/426y, 3 TDs, but allowed 2 costly INTs, including DB Chris Shelling's 73y TD RET.

OHIO STATE 23 Indiana 17: No. 5 Buckeyes (9-0-1) clinched at least share of their 1st Big 10 title since 1986 as TB Raymont Harris rushed for 162y on muddy gridiron of Ohio Stadium. Ohio State jumped to 10-0 lead after scoreless 1st Q, but was helpless to prevent Indiana (7-3) from tying it in 2nd Q on WR Thomas Lewis' 28y TD catch from QB Chris Dittoe (16-30/207y, TD). Bucks went to H ahead 17-10 when backup QB Bret Powers (9-15/124y, TD) rifled 5y score to WR Buster Tillman. K Tim Williams' 2 FGs made it 23-10 going to 4th Q, but Hoosiers misinterpreted coach Bill Mallory's plan and tried fake FG ("...a screwed-up mess," said Mallory) after Ohio DE Jayson Gwinn (5 tackles for loss) pushed them back from 9YL. Indiana still returned downfield for TB Jermaine Chaney's 21y TD romp, but Gwinn ruined IU's late possession with sack and forced incompletion. Surprisingly, it was Indiana's 12th loss in row on natural grass.

GAME OF THE YEAR
NOTRE DAME 31 Florida State 24:

Fighting Irish (10-0), 6-pt underdog, knocked off 1st top-ranked opponent ever at home. Seminoles (9-1) scored 1st on QB Charlie Ward's 12y pass to WR Kevin Knox. ND roared back for 21-7 H lead as holes were smashed by huge O line, led by T Aaron Taylor, C Tim Ruddy, and T Todd Norman. Irish WR Adrian Jarrell took misdirection pitch 32y to cap 80y drive. And there was more: HB Lee Becton (26/122y) scored at end of 60y drive, and DB-HB Jeff Burris powered for 6y TD run out of full-house backfield after S John Covington's INT. During fateful 2nd Q, Seminoles lost focus, tossing aimless passes, especially gimmick double cross-field lateral which lost 14y just prior to INT, 1st for Ward in 159 attempts. After being blanked for 32 mins, Florida State scored on RB Warrick Dunn's 6y catch to narrow score to 24-14. Irish stretched lead to 31-17 midway through 4th Q on Burris' 2nd score. That appeared to be it, but back roared Seminoles to 31-24, covering 45y in 1:39. TD came on 4th-and-goal from Irish 20YL with 2:26 left, as WR Kez McCorvey (11/138y) grabbed pass that slipped through grasp of ND DB Brian Magee. FSU got another chance after partially blocking punt, and Ward drove them deep into Irish end. His last play pass was knocked down at GL by DB Shawn Wooden. Comeback heartened Seminoles who spoke of bowl rematch with Irish. Had Magee held on to or knocked down McCorvey's 4th Q TD catch, Notre Dame would likely have won with 2-TD margin and pushed Florida State lower in polls than no. 2. Thus, during next 6 days, ND-FSU bowl rematch was highly anticipated by fans everywhere.

NEBRASKA 49 Iowa State 17: Clinching 3rd straight Orange Bowl berth, Nebraska (10-0) rolled for 438y rushing. Nebraska O stars were IB Calvin Jones, who rushed 26/208y, TD, and QB Tommie Frazier, who ran 13/125y, 3 TDs. Huskers DB Tyrone Williams grabbed 2 early FUMs to make 1y TD runs by Frazier and Jones very simple. Iowa State (3-7) fought back within 21-10 by H while forging 4.8y run avg. Cyclones RB Jim Knott scored 1y TD late in 1st Q, but Nebraska took over in 2nd H with only D blemish coming on TD pass from Iowa State QB Todd Doxson (4-6/60y, TD) to RB Calvin Branch.

NEW MEXICO 10 Wyoming 7: Coupled with BYU's annual pts war (45-44 win) with San Diego State, Wyoming (7-2) fell into 1st place WAC tie with BYU. New Mexico (5-5) WR Carl Winston lit up 5 passes for 69y and set NCAA record with receptions in 45 games in row. RB Ryan Christopherson rushed for 164y and lone Cowboys TD. Winning margin came on lucky bounce off goalpost of K Hugo Ojeda's 48y FG in 1st Q.

CALIFORNIA 24 Arizona 20: Wildcats (8-2) enjoyed good numbers with 434y total O, but saw their Rose Bowl hopes fizzle when they blew 20-0 H edge. RB Ontiwaun Carter rushed 21/122y, including 34y scoring romp that launched 3-TD 2nd Q for Arizona. Cats QB Dan White (12-25/175y, TD, 2 INTs) returned from knee injury to pitch 25y TD pass to WR Terry Vaughn. California (5-5) nipped away with TD pass by QB Dave Barr (20-33/263y, TD, 2 INTs) in 3rd Q, then narrowed it to 20-17 as TB Lindsey Chapman (20/80y, TD) scored in 4th Q. Nursing 3-pt lead, Arizona looked to make 1st down with less than 4 mins to play: White threw for Vaughn, but ball was deflected and grabbed in full flight by Bears DB Eric Zomalt. Zomalt raced 35y to winning TD, although 2 Arizona pass attempts died at Cal 14YL in closing moments.

Southern California 22 WASHINGTON 17: Trojans (7-4) rallied from 14-10 H deficit to keep Rose Bowl hopes alive as Cal upset Arizona and UCLA lost to Arizona State 9-3. Washington TB Napoleon Kaufman exploded in early going: he returned KO 45y, juked for 24y run, and scored on change-of-direction 12y masterpiece. Mysteriously thereafter, Kaufman shared lots of playing time with TB Beno Bryant, but finished with 18/119y, TD, for fading Huskies (6-4). All day long, however, Kaufman was within hare's breath of breaking long run. Trojans frosh TB Shawn Walters carried 25/116y, 2 TDs. It was 6th consecutive contest in which USC defenders had not permitted TD in 2nd H action, and much credit was handed to slumping P John Stonehouse, who pounded 4th Q punts of 44 and 50y and ended with 67y punt with 55 secs left to play.

USA Today Coaches Poll November 15

1	Notre Dame (60)	1548	14	Oklahoma	666
2	Nebraska (2)	1443	15	UCLA	653
3	Florida State	1433	16	Boston College	552
4	Miami (Fla.)	1343	17	Arizona	544
5	Ohio State	1301	18	Colorado	440
6	West Virginia	1194	19	Southern California	350
7	Tennessee	1175	20	Kansas State	338
8	Texas A&M	1120	21	Indiana	250
9	Florida	1097	22	Virginia	233
10	Alabama	977	23	Virginia Tech	210
11	Wisconsin	838	24	Michigan State	177
12	Penn State	827	25	Clemson	123
13	North Carolina	825			

November 20, 1993

WEST VIRGINIA 17 Miami 14: DB Mike Logan's opening 42y KO RET gave Mountaineers (10-0) field position which they clung to until K Tom Mazzone made 22y FG on 3rd trip inside Miami 30YL. That's how 1st H ended: 3-0. After gaining only 60y in opening 2 Qs, Hurricanes (8-2) went 80y to 7-3 lead after 2nd H KO on 1st of RB Donnell Bennett's 2 TDs. Miami pulled ahead 14-10 early in 4th Q as QB Ryan Collins' 42y pass off broken play fueled 80y scoring drive. WVU regained control on RB Robert Walker's 19y TD sprint off LT Rich Braham's block and later followed with QB Jake Kelchner's 42y pass to WR Jay Kearney to maintain possession.

Virginia Tech 20 VIRGINIA 17: Virginia Tech (8-3) enjoyed 1st winning trip to Charlottesville since 1985 as it earned 14-pt 2nd Q. After teams traded FGs, Hokies TB Dwayne Thomas (28/89y) scored TD early in 2nd Q. Then, on 3rd-and-10 at Virginia (7-4) 26YL, Tech DE Cornell Brown ploughed into Cavs QB Symmion Willis (11-28/189y, TD, INT) who lost FUM to Tech DT Jeff Holland. Holland rumbled 8y to score for 17-3 lead. Trailing 17-10 in 3rd Q, Cavaliers disdained FG and gambled on 4th-and-5 at Hokies 7YL. TB Jerrod Washington (21/129y, TD) was stuffed by Hokies LB George DelRicco, but when DeRicco screamed about lack of holding call, officials threw flag on him. From 3YL, Virginia ran Washington again, and again fired-up DelRicco slammed him back.

Tennessee 48 KENTUCKY 0: QB Heath Shuler (23-34/221y, INT) threw 3 TDs in launching no. 7 Tennessee (8-1-1) to 571y O and dominating win over Kentucky (7-4). Volunteers WR Cory Fleming caught 8 and 19y TD passes, and TB Charlie Garner (19/186y, TD) became 5th Vols back to gain more than 1000y rushing in season. Sub QB Jerry Colquitt threw only 1 pass, and it went for 70y TD to frosh WR Joey Kent that gave Tennessee 41-0 lead in 4th Q. Wildcats (6-5) tried 3 QBs to little avail as they passed only 9-20/54y to complement 190y rushing. Kentucky coach Bill Curry was convinced: "The Tennessee team that we saw is the best team that I've seen in a long time."

AUBURN 22 Alabama 14: Similar to its 1957 band of national champions, sanctioned Auburn (11-0) accomplished all it could by sweeping its schedule. Tigers had to wait and hope every unbeaten team would exit New Year's Day with loss. With QB Stan White out with bad knee, QB Patrick Nix sparked Auburn rally from 14-5 3rd Q deficit. On Nix's 1st play, he hit WR Frankie Sanders with 35y TD pass on 4th down. Tigers K Scott Etheridge booted FG for 15-14 lead, and RB James Bostic clinched it with 70y TD run. Alabama (8-2-1) got 2nd Q TD runs from WR Kevin Lee (63y) and RB Sherman Williams (19y).

MICHIGAN 28 Ohio State 0: With Rose Bowl fate in its own hands, no. 5 Ohio State (9-1-1) suffered INTs on 4 straight 1st H series. Michigan (7-4) WR Mercury Hayes twisted in EZ to make great catch of wind-swirled 25y pass late in 1st Q. Buckeyes soon switched QBs to late-year star relief pitcher Bret Powers, but he was picked off 3 times, 2 INTs leading to scores in Wolverines' 21-0 H lead. Ohio State lost any hope for reversal early in 2nd H when low punt snap forced TO at its own 32YL. Michigan soon scored on TB Ed Davis' 5y run and continued its 1990s trend of playing spoiler against its bitter rival.

Boston College 41 NOTRE DAME 39: Vengeful Boston College (8-2) retaliated for 1992 shellacking at hands of Fighting Irish, tossing giant wrench into national championship works. Eagles jumped to 24-14 H lead as QB Glenn Foley (30-48/315, 4 TDs) threw 3 TD passes. When RB Darnell Campbell scored from 21y (his 20th TD of season) midway through 3rd Q and TE Pete Mitchell (13/132y) caught Foley's 4th TD early in 4th Q, BC's lead seemed safe at 38-17. But, Notre Dame (10-1) scored just 1:01 later on RB Lee Becton's 29y run and his 2-pt pass to QB Kevin McDougal. When BC lost C-exchange FUM, Becton went behind T Aaron Taylor for 41y to set up FB Ray Zellars' 4y TD. Suddenly, it was 38-32 with 4:02 to go. With home fans waking up echoes, Fighting Irish WR Derrick Mays (7/147y) made brilliant, tumbling catch to set up McDougal's 4th down 4y TD pass to WR Lake Dawson, and ND had suddenly rallied to 39-38 lead with 1:09 left. Foley retaliated with 2 passes to Mitchell and inside screen to WR Ivan Boyd to reach Irish 24YL. Drive was aided by ND personal foul PEN on KO and LB Pete Bercich's dropped INT on 2nd play. Kick-holder Foley grabbed high snap as K David Gordon booted winning 41y FG. Upset loss cost Notre Dame top spot in AP Poll, and placed Florida State and Nebraska back in hunt for title.

Ucla 27 SOUTHERN CALIFORNIA 21: Little sr TB Ricky Davis, who seemed to be keeping UCLA TB seat warm for bigger, faster youngsters, rushed for 153y to guide Bruins (8-3) to their 1st Rose Bowl berth in 8 years. Mixing in Shotgun formations for effective runs and passes, UCLA burst to 17-0 H lead on TD runs by QB Wayne Cook (5y) and TB Skip Hicks (4y). But, QB Rob Johnson (23-36/307y, 2 TDs) brought back Trojans (7-5). With 2 quick TDs in 3rd Q, USC regained its composure in trying to keep alive 11th straight win over Bruins when Rose Bowl was on line for both teams. Bruins used another of their fake-runs out of Shotgun on 3rd-and-8 as quick-footed Cook faked handoff and rolled right to hit WR J.J. Stokes (6/53y), who caught his 17th TD

pass of season. Trailing 27-21, Trojans rallied again for 79y to 1st-and-goal at UCLA 3YL with 1:16 to go. Instead of it turning out as smashing TD for USC, long known as "Tailback U," Johnson had to pass on 3rd down after 2 runs by TB Shawn Walters made 1y. Johnson looked for TE Tyler Cashman, but Bruins DB Marvin Goodwin made game-saving INT in triple-coverage crowd in EZ. It was only 5th INT for Johnson during season in which he tried 405 passes. Superior line play meant UCLA outrushed Troy 230y to 7y.

November 25-27, 1993

(Th'g) Georgia 43 GEORGIA TECH 10: TB Terrell Davis gave Georgia (5-6) 10-3 2nd Q lead with wide TD sweep, but Georgia Tech (5-6) QB Donnie Davis retaliated with TD pass to TE Todd Vance with 20 secs left before H. But, Georgia was able to take 13-10 lead on K Kevin Parkman's 38y FG 2 secs before H because Tech's squibbed KO backfired. Bulldogs ran 7:02 off clock on 3rd Q FG drive. So, Yellow Jackets trailed only 16-10 as 4th Q opened, but in final 5:04, Georgia exploded for 3 TDs, including short drive after FUM REC and CB Greg Tremble's 20y INT TD RET. Throwing right to game's end, Georgia's QB Eric Zeier (28-41/328y, TD) broke SEC marks of Florida's Shane Matthews for season passing and total O and piled on his only TD pass in last 1:29. Zeier's late-game throwing when score was 36-10 angered Jackets, and tilt in Atlanta ended with several fights that prompted Tech coach Bill Lewis to say he was "embarrassed."

(Th'g) TEXAS A&M 18 Texas 9: For Texas (5-5-1), it was Cotton Bowl or no bowl, as Longhorns had chance to beat Aggies (10-1) for trip to Dallas. Instead, it was A&M that picked Cotton by winning 100th renewal of rivalry. Longhorns, 3-TD underdog, took 6-0 lead on 20 and 42y FGs by K Scott Szeredy. McElroy launched Aggies to decisive 2nd Q with 100y KO RET, his 3rd TD of season on KO RETs. Szeredy regained lead for Texas at 9-7 with 48y FG after QB Shea Morenz (10-30/124y, INT) connected with TE Jimmy Hakes in 2nd Q. Texas A&M took lead for good at 15-9 late in 2nd Q when QB Corey Pullig (9-21/154y, TD, INT) found WR Tony Harrison for 31 and 14y passes, latter for TD. Starting from its 34YL midway in 4th Q, Texas went to A&M 2YL where it faced 4th-and-1. Morenz rolled right and threw for EZ, but Aggies sub nickel-DB Dennis Allen stepped in to make crushing INT and launch 94y FG drive.

(Fri) West Virginia 17 BOSTON COLLEGE 14: Fresh from it major upset of unanimous no. 1 Notre Dame, Boston College Eagles (8-3) appeared to break open game with 2nd H TDs for 14-3 lead. West Virginia (11-0) drew to within 14-9 on 4th Q TD run by FB Rodney Woodard. Clutch DB Mike Logan grabbed BC RB David Green's late FUM at WVU 37YL. Super-sub QB Darren Studstill drove Mountaineers to game-winner, hitting WR Ed Hill for 24y TD as Hill outfought Eagles DB Eric Shorter in EZ. Studstill threw to WR Jay Kearney for 2-pt conv. Logan ended it with INT. Coach Don Nehlen made his "team that beat the team" post-game appeal on behalf of his Mountaineers: If West Virginia and Nebraska were prevented from playing for national title, it would be, as Nehlen said, "…the biggest crime ever perpetuated on a college football team. A team (Florida State) that loses doesn't do everything in its power to be no. 1." Nehlen's plea was to no avail; coalition poll tapped Nebraska and FSU for Orange Bowl showdown for national title.

(Fri) NEBRASKA 21 Oklahoma 7: Nervous Nebraska (11-0) started slowly as Oklahoma (8-3) marched 74y on its 1st possession, cashing FB Dwayne Chandler's 1y TD smash. Sooners corralled nation-leading run O, holding Nebraska runners to 72y through 3 Qs of 7-7 tie. Huskers D, playing without A-A LB Trev Alberts, still made enough big plays to maintain deadlock until QB Tommie Frazier passed 11y to WR Abdul Muhammad for go-ahead 4th Q score. When Sooners CB Darrius Johnson fumbled ensuing KO, Huskers recovered, and IB Calvin Jones dashed 20y for clinching score on next play. Nebraska polled 2nd with AP writers and topped coaches poll with 43 1st place votes.

(Fri) Arizona 34 ARIZONA STATE 20: D-dominant Arizona (9-2) and fast-closing Arizona State (6-5), winners of 4 straight coming in, slugged it out in 7-7 1st H stalemate. TBs Mario Bates of Arizona State and Chuck Levy of Arizona traded 1y TD runs in 2nd Q. Sun Devils led for only time at 10-7 in 3rd Q as K Jon Baker's 20y FG followed REC of Arizona WR Richard Dice's FUM at ASU 40YL. But, Dice soon made up for his gaffe by hauling in 13y TD pass from accurate QB Dan White (14-18/209y, 3 TDs) with 4:19 to go in 3rd Q. While Wildcats rushed for 237y, led by FB Billy Johnson (16/126y) and TB Ontiwaun carter (13/101y), game's biggest surprise became Wildcats' aerial game as White smoothly fired 31 and 51y TD passes to WR Troy Dickey (3/91y, 2 TDs) in 4th Q for 27-10 advantage.

TENNESSEE 62 Vanderbilt 14: No. 6 Tennessee (9-1-1) led 10-0 early in 2nd Q, thanks to DB Shawn Summers' 51y punt TD RET. Apparently edgy about his team's punt coverage, Vanderbilt (4-7) coach Gerry DiNardo called for fake on 4th-and-8 at own 35YL. Fake failed as Commodores P Bill Marinangel took handoff from BB Jeff Brothers, but was spilled short of 1st down. Floodgates opened: Volunteers scored on

3 straight plays from scrimmage in 2nd Q: TB James Stewart (11/91y, 3 TDs) on 7y run, WR Joey Kent on 47y pass from QB Heath Shuler (10-19/131y, TD, INT) after S Jason Parker's INT, and TB Charlie Garner (16/151y, TD) on 13y run after FUM REC. It was 48-0 by time Vandy scored on runs by QB Ronnie Gordon (11-24/120y, INT) and TB Cliff Deese early in 4th Q. With 471 pts (42.8 avg), Vols became highest scoring team in school history. Pt total broke Alabama's 20-year-old SEC scoring mark of 454.

MISSISSIPPI STATE 20 Mississippi 13: Both teams ended disappointing seasons, Mississippi State (3-6-2) was happy to regain Golden Egg Trophy it lost to Mississippi (5-6) in 1992. Bulldogs took 14-3 lead in 1st Q as workhorse RB Michael Davis (40/154y, TD) scored on 3y run, and, after Ole Miss FG, QB Todd Jordan (7-19/136y, TD, INT) lofted 49y TD pass to WR Eric Moulds. Mississippi (5-6) lost for 4th time in season's final 5 games, but closed to within 17-13 at H, primarily on 8y TD pass by QB Lawrence Adams (11-23/92y, TD, INT).

Florida State 33 FLORIDA 21: Coming in, Gators (9-2) had won 23 straight on their home field known thanks to coach Steve Spurier as "The Swamp." But, Seminoles (11-1) cruised behind QB Charlie Ward (38-53/446y, 2 INTs) with relative ease, building 13-0 2nd Q edge and 27-7 margin after 3 Qs. In fact, largest football crowd in state's history probably was eyeing exits when they heard stats after 3Qs: Seminoles had run 70 plays to 39 and outgained Florida 401y to 156y. Florida coach Steve Spurrier yanked starting QB Danny Wuerffel, and back-up QB Terry Dean rallied Gators, moving within 27-21 with 6 mins left. Dean (14-33/259y, 2 TDs, 2 INTs) hit TD throws to WRs Willie Jackson and Jack Jackson, on fabulous juggling catch. Then when needed most, Florida State frosh RB Warrick Dunn turned short Ward pass into 79y TD to provide late-game cushion. FSU pass rush forced Gators into -33y rushing total as Dean lost 19y and Wuerffel 24y.

Penn State 38 MICHIGAN STATE 37: Michigan State (6-4) scored TD on 28y catch by WR Mill Coleman (4/98y) for 6-0 lead, but its botched x-pt would haunt them. Foes traded 17 pts each in 2nd Q as Lions (9-2) left at H trailing 23-17 after TB Mike Archie's 24y TD run and QB Kerry Collins' 16y TD pass to WR Freddie Scott. Spartans went up 37-17 with 2:54 to go in 3rd Q as 320-lb T Bob Denton became eligible receiver at TE to catch 3y TD pass from QB Jim Miller (14-29/186y, 2 TDs, INT). Lions' comeback was triggered by DB Derek Bochna's INT late in 3rd Q, and Collins (23-42/352y, 3 TDs, INT) completed 18y pass to Scott and hit WR Bobby Engram with 40y TD to pull Penn State within 37-24 with 53 secs left in 3rd Q. Penn State LB Brian Gelzheiser's FUM REC prompted FB Brian O'Neal's 3y TD run. Finally, Collins hit Engram again for 52y TD, and K Craig Fayak nailed winning kick. "We used our two-minute drill a lot more than two minutes," said Collins. "It has never, ever gone as smooth as it did today, even as much as we practice it."

December 4, 1993

Army 16 Navy 14 (Meadowlands, N.J.): Army (6-5) used relentless option runs directed by QB Rick Roper to build comfortable 16-0 lead. Navy (4-7) QB Jim Kubiak rallied Middies with 4th Q TD run, 2-pt pass, and hit H-back Jimmy Mill with tricky 8y misdirection TD pass. Pushed to brink, Navy fell on FUM deep in its own end with 4:30 left. Midshipmen resolutely drove all way to Army 1YL, where FB Brad Stramanack was stopped tellingly on far right hashmark with 6 secs left. Navy called timeout and brought in frosh K Ryan Bucchaneri, who stunningly missed 18y FG from sharp angle. It only was Bucchaneri's 3rd career FG try and would painfully affect rest of his Naval Academy career.

Florida 28 Alabama 13 (Birmingham): SEC title game lacked some luster as argument could be made that best 2 teams were sitting at home. Undefeated Auburn of Western Divisions was ineligible, and AP Poll's no. 6 Tennessee finished half game behind no. 9 Florida in East. With QB Danny Wuerffel sidelined with knee injury, Gators (10-2) QB Terry Dean hit 20-37/256y, 2 TDs against Tide secondary playing without its A-A DB Antonio Langham, who was declared ineligible for signing with pro agent. Alabama (8-3-1) hung close at 14-13 late in 3rd Q when Gators P Shayne Edge took major gamble that paid off: With 4th-and-8 at his own 37YL, Edge ran 20y. Dean hit WR Jack Jackson with critical 43y TD on next play. With QB Jay Barker out, dangerous Crimson Tide WR David Palmer was at QB for most of 2nd H, but he was held to moderate 93y rushing and 90y passing.

(Sun) Wisconsin 41 Michigan State 20 (Tokyo): When game was scheduled 2 years earlier, little did Badgers AD Pat Richter know that it would decide Rose Bowl fate of Wisconsin (9-1-1). Thus, contest took on nickname of "Tokyo Rose Bowl." Trailing 7-3 to Spartans (6-5) QB Jim Miller hit WR Mill Coleman with 34y TD, but Badgers DB Scott Nelson stop another Michigan State threat with INT. TB Terrell Fletcher soon scored from 1YL, then quickly added 40y TD sprint for 17-7 H lead. Never headed, Badgers earned their 1st Pasadena trip in 31 years, where they had 0-3 record to date.

USA Today Coaches Poll December 6

1	Nebraska (41)	1519		14	Arizona	728
2	West Virginia (7)	1469		15	Boston College	654
3	Florida State (13)	1446		16	Oklahoma	501
4	Notre Dame (1)	1369		17	Colorado	490
5	Tennessee	1278		18	Alabama	481
6	Texas A&M	1238		19	Kansas State	443
7	Wisconsin	1089		20	Indiana	394
8	Florida	1075		21	Virginia Tech	394
9	Miami (Fla.)	1049		22	Michigan	306
10	Ohio State	951		23	Clemson	257
11	North Carolina	901		24	Fresno State	95
12	Penn State	884		25	Louisville	77
13	UCLA	808				

1993 Conference Standings

Big East

West Virginia	7-0
Miami	6-1
Boston College	5-2
Virginia Tech	4-3
Syracuse	3-4
Pittsburgh	2-5
Rutgers	1-6
Temple	0-7

Atlantic Coast

Florida State	8-0
North Carolina	6-2
Clemson	5-3
Virginia	5-3
North Carolina State	4-4
Georgia Tech	3-5
Duke	2-6
Maryland	2-6
Wake Forest	1-7

Southeastern

EAST	
Florida	7-1
Tennessee	6-1-1
Kentucky	4-4
Georgia	2-6
South Carolina	2-6
Vanderbilt	1-7
WEST	
Auburn (ineligible)	8-0
Alabama	5-2-1
Arkansas	3-4-1
Louisiana State	3-5
Mississippi	3-5
Mississippi State	2-5-1

Big Ten

Wisconsin	6-1-1
Ohio State	6-1-1
Penn State	6-2
Indiana	5-3
Michigan	5-3
Illinois	5-3
Michigan State	4-4
Iowa	3-5
Minnesota	3-5
Northwestern	0-8
Purdue	0-8

Mid-American

Ball State	7-0-1
Western Michigan	6-1-1
Bowling Green	5-1-2
Central Michigan	5-4
Akron	4-4
Ohio	4-5
Toledo	3-5
Eastern Michigan	3-5
Miami (Ohio)	3-6
Kent	0-9

Big Eight

Nebraska	7-0
Colorado	5-1-1
Kansas State	4-2-1
Oklahoma	4-3
Kansas	3-4
Missouri	2-5
Iowa State	2-5
Oklahoma State	0-7

Southwest

Texas A&M	7-0
Texas Tech	5-2
Texas	5-2
Rice	3-4
Baylor	3-4
Texas Christian	2-5
Southern Methodist	1-5-1
Houston	1-5-1

Western Athletic

Fresno State	6-2
Wyoming	6-2
Brigham Young	6-2
Utah	5-3
Colorado State	5-3
New Mexico	4-4
San Diego State	4-4
Hawaii	3-5
Air Force	1-7
Texas-El Paso	0-8

Pacific-10

Arizona	6-2
UCLA	6-2
Southern California	6-2
Washington	5-3
California	4-4
Arizona State	4-4
Washington State	3-5
Oregon	2-6
Oregon State	2-6
Stanford	2-6

1993 Major Bowl Games

John Hancock (Sun) Bowl (Dec. 24): Oklahoma 41 Texas Tech 10

Oklahoma (9-3) ended 5-game win streak of Texas Tech (6-6) and claimed Southwest Conf "championship" with its 4th convincing win over Texas-based team. Sooners TE Rickey Brady (4/35y) caught pair of QB Cale Gundy's 3 TD passes in 1st H charge to 28-3 lead. Red Raiders owned huge 3rd Q territorial edge, but TOs prevented all but HB Bam Morris' TD run. Sooners TB Jerald Moore ran for 6y TD at end.

Aloha Bowl (Dec. 25): Colorado 41 Fresno State 30

Colorado (8-3-1) mined 4 TOs into 24 pts, starting when DB Chris Hudson recovered FUM on own 47YL. MVP TB Rashaan Salaam (23/135y, 3 TDs) scored his 1st TD at 5-min mark of 1st Q and added 40 and 4y TD runs behind dominating Buffaloes O-line

in 3rd and 4th Qs respectively. Buffs created 20-3 lead in 2nd Q on K Mitch Berger's 2 FGs and 7y TD run by TB James Hill. Salaam's 2 TDs in 2nd H built 27-10 and 41-24 leads. Fresno State (8-4) QB Trent Dilfer passed 37-63/523y, 2 TDs, but when Colorado frosh DB Maurice Henriques made INT in 4th Q, it broke Dilfer's remarkable streak of 318 passing tries without INT. Buffs disguised their pass coverage well and frequently sent All-Conf CB Hudson on blitzes off corner, all to disrupt Fresno's aerial genius. Bulldogs had stayed competitive at 20-10 thanks to bizarre TD just before H. After Colorado's Berger made 49y FG in 2nd Q, he squibbed seemingly safe KO to Fresno 30YL with only single sec on 1st H clock. Bulldogs reserve FB Jamie Christian fielded slippery KO and was about to be snowed under when he threw desperate lateral pass to WR Malcolm Seabron, who bobbled ball but recovered en route to 68y TD.

Liberty Bowl (Dec. 28): Louisville 18 Michigan State 7

Michigan State (6-6) opened game with 79y TD drive and enjoyed tremendous field position advantage in 7-3 1st H. But, Spartans thwarted themselves with frequent O holding PENs. Louisville (9-3) entered game with 0-5-1 record vs. Big 10 teams, but won in 2nd H when QB Jeff Brohm overcame broken finger on passing hand to throw 19-29/197y. Brohm hit WR Reggie Ferguson with 25y TD with 12:05 left for 10-7 lead. Cardinals added late safety and TD to clinch win.

Copper Bowl (Dec. 29): Kansas State 52 Wyoming 17

Kansas State (9-2-1) revealed dazzling O in winning 1st-ever bowl game in 2 tries during its mostly-horrendous 97-year football history. Wyoming (8-4) opened game with FG drive, but lost TD when motion PEN nullified WR Ryan Yarborough's scoring catch. FB Ryan Christopherson's 2nd Q TD run got Cowboys within 16-10. Wildcats Gs Bryan Campbell and Eric Wolford and C Quentin Neujahr dominated scrimmage line for TB J.J. Smith to rush 20/133y, TD. K-State WR Andre Coleman broke 68y punt TD RET which padded lead to 24-10 just before H. Kansas State broke it open early in 3rd Q when Coleman took 61y TD pass from scrambling QB Chad May (19-28/275y, 2 TDs).

Holiday Bowl (Dec. 30): Ohio State 28 Brigham Young 21

Ohio State (10-1-1) DB Tim Patillo blocked early punt, returning it for TD and 7-0 Buckeyes lead. Ohio State O-line broke open big holes for TB Raymont Harris, who rushed for 2 Holiday Bowl records: 39 attempts and 235y. Harris scored 3 TDs, including game-winner with 4:11 left in 3rd Q that put Buckeyes up 28-21. Ohio coach John Cooper laughed with Harris afterward: "And don't say we didn't give you the ball." Brigham Young (6-6) had earned 21-21 H deadlock on 3 TD passes by QB John Walsh (25-44/389y, 3 TDs, INT). Cougars marched into Buckeye territory 3 times in 4th Q in search of tying TD, but failed each time on 4th down tries, including EZ overthrow by QB Walsh of WR Eric Drage in closing secs. Walsh hit Drage for 52y gain to Ohio 6YL with 32 secs to play, but Cougars bobbled 2 passes, and Buckeyes' pass rush forced last-play incompletion. With BYU finishing even in W-L record for season, it marked 1st time in 19 years without winning mark in Provo.

Freedom Bowl (Dec. 30): Southern California 28 Utah 21

Scoring 3 quick TDs enroute to 28-0 H lead, Southern California (8-5) held on as QB Mike McCoy rallied Utah (7-6) with 23-40/286y, TD passing. Trojans QB Rob Johnson threw 30-44/345y, 3 TDs, including 2 scores to A-A WR Johnnie Morton. Morton set Freedom Bowl catch with 10/147y, while Johnson tied Freedom record, hitting 9 passes in row. Troy DB Jason Sehorn made EZ INT with 35 secs to go in 2nd Q to preserve 1st H shutout. Utah scored twice in 3rd Q to peel deficit to 28-13 as WR Henry Lusk (6/140y, TD) caught 59y TD pass from McCoy, and TB Jamal Anderson charged 34y up middle to score. Ute D got into comeback act with 2 of its 5 sacks of Johnson in 3rd Q. TB Keith Williams scored with 3:56 left and McCoy hit 2-pt pass, but Utah got no closer.

Independence Bowl (Dec. 31): Virginia Tech 45 Indiana 20

Early fireworks from Indiana (8-4) came on 75y TD pass from banged-up QB John Paci to WR Thomas Lewis. Hokies TB Dwayne Thomas scored on screen pass behind block of A-A C Jim Pyne, and nearing end of H, Virginia Tech (9-3) enjoyed 14-13 lead. Then, 2 peculiar plays sealed Hoosiers' fate. With 35 sec left before H, Paci tried ill-advised pass and was sacked. Resultant FUM was returned for TD by DL Lawrence Lewis. Moments later, Hoosiers WR Eddie Baety caught pass, and officials ruled Indiana had called timeout with 1 sec to go, calling teams back to field as they headed to locker rooms. Indiana K Bill Manolopoulos tried 51y FG, which was partially blocked by Virginia Tech's special teamer Jeff Holland. Hokies DB Antonio Banks nabbed bounding ball on his 20YL, raced to TD, to effectively clinch it at 28-13.

Peach Bowl (Dec. 31): Clemson 14 Kentucky 13

Tommy West of Clemson (9-3), 1st-ever new coach tapped in time for bowl game who was not elevated from asst job. West made successful debut as replacement for Ken Hatfield, who was forced to resign in December after not receiving contract extension. Tigers were lucky to be trailing only 13-7 because officials made questionable no-TD call on Kentucky TE Alfonzo Browning's attempt at breaking GL plane at end of opening 79y drive in 1st Q. Browning's FUM set up 98y Clemson drive to FB Emory Smith's 2y TD blast. With 3:50 to play in 4th Q, Tigers took over on own 18YL and QB Patrick Sapp hit Smith with screen pass for 57y to Wildcat 25YL. With :42 left, Kentucky LB Marty Moore's INT seemed to save game, but he failed to protect ball as TB Rodney Blount hit him. Moore's excruciating FUM was fallen on by Clemson T Brent LeJuene at Wildcats 21YL. "I went from hero to chump; I made a great play and then I cost us the game," said Moore as on 4th down with 20 secs to go, Sapp hit WR Terry Smith with TD pass. K Nelson Welch followed with winning kick.

Gator Bowl (Dec. 31): Alabama 24 North Carolina 10

Teams were tied 10-10 at H with most exciting play having come on Alabama (9-3-1) QB Brian Burgdorf's 33y TD scramble. Powerful North Carolina (10-3) running game—it boasted twin 1000y TBs in Curtis and Leon Johnson—was shut down in 2nd H as Tar Heels were tossed for 19y in losses. Tide held ball for 11 mins of 3rd Q, and Burgdorf, making his 4th career start, drilled FB Tarrant Lynch with 8y TD pass. Roughing PEN on tackle of Alabama WR David Palmer moved ball into UNC territory in 4th Q, and Burgdorf took advantage by hitting WR Chad Key with TD to end 66y drive. Burgdorf passed 15-23/166y, 2 TDs as Bama, in defense of its national title, finally beat its 1st opponent that had posted winning record in 1993.

Alamo Bowl (Dec. 31): California 37 Iowa 3

In newly-built Alamodome, city of San Antonio hosted its 1st bowl game since 1947. Miscues cost early TDs for California (9-4), but K Doug Brien made 3 FGs for 9-0 lead in 2nd Q, at which point Bears had run 31 plays to only 6 by Iowa (6-6). With :35 to go before H, Bears QB Dave Barr (21-28/266y, 3 TDs) hit WR Mike Caldwell with 6y TD pass for 16-0 lead. Cal LB Jerrott Willard sacked Iowa QB Paul Burmeister (6-17/70y, INT) 3 times and went 61y with INT on last play of 1st H for 23-0 edge. Overmatched Hawkeyes were held to 90y total O, scoring only in 3rd Q on K Brion Hurley's 42y FG.

Hall of Fame Bowl: Michigan 42 North Carolina State 7

Warm Florida rain fell on KO as underachieving Michigan (8-4) had healthy squad for change and used it to dominate North Carolina State (7-5). Wolfpack stopped themselves with opening drive FUM for 5th time this season. Throwing ineffective passes early, Wolverines finally turned to TB Tyrone Wheatley (18/124y, 2 TDs) in 2nd Q as jr TB capped 80y drive with 26y TD run. WR Derrick Alexander took punt RET 79y to TD and 14-0 lead, and well-covered WR Amani Toomer added TD from QB Todd Collins (11-22/189y, TD) in EZ corner. Frosh DB Clarence Thompson dashed 43y with INT, helping Michigan to 35-0 lead in 3rd Q until QB Geoff Bender put Wolfpack on scoreboard with 12y TD pass to sub TB Brian Fitzgerald near end of 3rd Q.

Citrus Bowl: Penn State 31 Tennessee 13

Pre-game praise as "hottest team in country" positioned Tennessee (9-2-1) for big day. Meanwhile, Penn State (10-2) QB Kerry Collins was growing tired of hearing about greatness of Volunteers QB Heath Shuler. When QB Shuler (22-42/205y, TD, INT) engineered 10 quick pts including his 19y TD pass to WR Cory Fleming, Lions' worst fears seemed realized. But, Collins (15-24/162y, 2 TDs, INT) hit clutch inside screen to WR Bobby Engram for 36y to set up TB Ki-Jana Carter for 1st of 2 TDs in 1st H. Up 17-10, Penn State dominated 2nd H as DLs Tyoka Jackson, Eric Ravotti, and Lou Benfatti draping themselves all over Shuler. Vols had 6 pass drops, and TB Charlie Garner gained only 7y in 2nd H after he rushed for 82y in 1st H. Lions coach Joe Paterno tied Bear Bryant with 15 bowl wins, most by any coach in history.

Fiesta Bowl: Arizona 29 Miami 0

It had been 15 years since Miami (9-3) had been whitewashed, but Arizona (10-2) put net over every aspect of Hurricanes, limiting Miami's O to 182y. Wildcats QB Danny White hit WR Troy Dickey for opening 13y TD pass, and duo hooked up again for 14y TD in 4th Q. Coach Dennis Erickson yanked QB Ryan Collins after Miami gained only 20y in 1st Q as Collins passed 2-9, INT. Relief pitcher, QB Frank Costa, hit 3 of his 1st 4 passes, but suffered LB Brant Boyer's INT and was very nearly sacked for safety by Arizona A-A NG Rob Waldrop. Big Arizona score came with 3:39 left before H when RB Chuck Levy (17/142y, TD) raced 68y for TD and 16-0 lead. "Desert Swarm" D recovered FUM, forced 3 INTs, permitted only 20/35y rushing, and registered 4 sacks of Miami QBs, including 16y loss by kinetic DE Tedy Bruschi, who joined Levy as co-MVP.

Carquest Bowl: Boston College 31 Virginia 13

Runaway verdict in what was earlier known as Blockbuster Bowl swung on passes of Eagles MVP QB Glenn Foley (25-36/391y, 3 TDs, 2 INTs). Headed for its 4th straight bowl loss, Virginia (7-5) scored 1st on TB Jerrod Washington's up-middle 11y run after LB Randy Neal's 1st Q INT. Because of FB Charles Way's 7y TD run in 2nd Q, Cavs trailed only 17-13 at H despite Foley's 78y bomb to WR Clarence Cannon. Midway through 3rd Q, Boston College (9-3) went 70y in 5 plays, crowned by little WR Keith Miller blowing by former HS teammate, Cavs LB Tom Burns, for 46y TD catch. Boston College TB Darnell Campbell's 12y TD run early in 4th Q locked up verdict.

Cotton Bowl: Notre Dame 24 Texas A&M 21

Notre Dame (11-1) went 91y on opening march, turning it into QB Kevin McDougal's 19y option run for score. Underrated Texas A&M (10-2) responded with 1st TD in its last 3 Cotton Bowls: TB Greg Hill's 8y run. Aggies' successful gamble on 4th-and-1 at ND 15YL resulted in play-action pass from QB Cory Pullig (17-31/238y, TD) to FB Detron Smith for 14-7 H lead. Irish frosh FB Marc Edwards bulled over to tie it 21-21, and 3rd Q ended that way. Native Texan WR Mike Miller returned punt 45y to set up ND's winning FG from 31y out by K Kevin Pendergast. Coach Lou Holtz was left to argue that Notre Dame had beaten Florida State head-to-head, same logic that handed Miami its 1989 national title over Notre Dame. Because Irish failed to blow out Aggies, they were given little chance of taking national championship votes away from winner of Orange Bowl.

Rose Bowl: Wisconsin 21 UCLA 16

Playing in its home stadium, UCLA (8-4) must have felt strange to wear road white jerseys, dress in visitors' room, and look into sea of Wisconsin red in 80th Rose Bowl crowd. Atmosphere was so peculiar that Bruins, nation's leader in giveaway-takeaway ratio, embarrassingly lost ball 6 times to hungry Badgers (10-1-1). After K Bjorn Merten gave Bruins 3-0 lead, Wisconsin went 78y for 3y TD run by TB Brent Moss (36/158y).

It was Badgers' longest drive of day as UCLA's 95y in PENs aided other trips. Moss scored again for 14-3 edge after DL Lamark Shackerford recovered FUM by WR J.J. Stokes (14/176y) at UCLA 32YL midway in 2nd Q. Bruins opened 3rd Q with long drive from KO, but QB Wayne Cook (28-43/288y, TD, INT) lost FUM at Wisconsin 8YL when sacked by DT Carlos Fowler. Badgers answered in kind, going all way to UCLA 10YL where Bruins D held on 4th down. Fisticuffs ensued, and 2 players per side were shown way to showers. TB Ricky Davis (13/88y, TD) scored early in 4th Q to bring UCLA to within 14-10, but pattern of losing TOs continued: Bruins lost TOs on 4 of their 1st 5 possessions of 2nd H, including Davis' FUM on their next series. Snatched by Badgers DT Mike Thompson (2 FUM RECs), FUM REC poised QB Darrell Bevell (10-20/96y, INT) for his clinching 21y TD scramble. After trimming it to 21-16 on Cook's TD pass, Bruins moved to Wisconsin 15YL as time expired with Cook mistakenly trying to run instead of throwing it away to save 1 more try for winning TD.

Sugar Bowl: Florida 41 West Virginia 7

Associated Press revealed prior to game that former Florida coach Charley Pell had become so enraged over bombastic Gators' embarrassing loss to West Virginia in 1981 Peach Bowl that he burned and buried game film under small monument on UF practice field. AP reported that current coach Steve Spurrier had gotten rid of such things soon after his arrival in 1990. Spurrier said, "We removed that monument; West Virginia is not a part of our practice field anymore." Mountaineers (11-1) had more important things to worry about: win over Gators coupled with Nebraska loss in Orange Bowl could vault them into top spot in coaches' poll. Things started well with WVU scoring on its 1st possession as QB Jake Kelchner (13-27/123y, TD, INT) hit WR Jay Kearney with 32y TD pass to finish 80y drive. Key play came from TB Robert Walker (13/59y) who converted 4th-and-1 run of 3y to UF 35YL. From that point on, however, nothing went right for West Virginia. Florida (11-2) tied it on 1st of RB Errict Rhett's 3 short rushing TDs that were part of his 25/105y ground effort. Gators delivered 2 crushing scores in 2nd Q: DB Lawrence Wright made spectacular spinning 52y TD RET of INT, and QB Terry Dean (22-37/255y, TD) found WR Willie Jackson for 39y TD with 51 secs left in H. Coach Don Nehlen, forced for weeks to stump for West Virginia poll votes, fell silent as his 58th birthday was spoiled.

Orange Bowl: Florida State 18 Nebraska 16

Uproarious Orange Bowl matchup with odd twists determined national title for Florida State (12-1). Cornhuskers (11-1) WR Corey Dixon dashed 71y with 1st Q punt, but illegal block was called on Dixon's RET. Painstaking search of various angles of TV replays failed to locate any foul. After frosh K Scott Bentley put Seminoles ahead 3-0 with 34y FG in 2nd Q, QB Tommie Frazier had pass deflected into welcome arms of WR Reggie Baul, who sprinted 34y to TD and 7-3 lead. Heisman-winning Florida State QB Charlie Ward overcame inability to convert 3rd downs and drove team to Bentley's 2nd FG with :22 showing on H clock. Drive was aided by roughing passer call, 1 of several such fouls against Huskers. Seminoles abandoned use of I-formation for Shotgun and quickly scored to open 2nd H, but their TD was tainted. FB William Floyd smashed over from 1YL and lost ball. TV replays indicated Floyd may have dropped it before breaking plane of GL. When DB Toby Wright, night-long Huskers D star, knocked down 2-pt pass, Seminoles led 12-7. Nebraska lost top rusher Calvin Jones to 1st H injury and turned to IB Damon Benning. But Benning was ineffective, so coach Tom Osborne inserted 3rd string IB Lawrence Phillips, who ignited Nebraska after Bentley made it 15-7 for FSU with 39y FG late in 3rd Q. Phillips led 73y drive, scoring from 12YL on 1st play of 4th Q. Frazier's rollout run for 2 pts missed, so FSU still led 15-13. After Seminoles DB Richard Coes stopped Huskers drive with INT at own 8YL, Nebraska launched trip from own 20YL with 4:39 to go. Huskers went all the way to FSU 4YL as Frazier contributed 31y run, but DB Clifton Abraham and DL Jon Nance made big tackles to force FG try by Huskers K Byron Bennett, who hadn't made FG in 6 games. Bennett was true from 27y away, and Nebraska led 16-15 with 1:16 left. Cool Ward rallied Florida State with help of 2 big PENs: Bennett's KO went out of bounds, so FSU took over on own 35YL, and Huskers DB Barron Miles roughed RB Warrick Dunn after 20y catch. Frosh Bentley made 22y FG with 21 secs left, and FSU led again. Nebraska took over on own 46YL with 14 ticks left, and Frazier hit TE Trumane Bell with pass to Seminoles 28YL. Clock appeared to expire, and coach Bobby Bowden was doused with victory ice water as players dashed onto field. However, officials restored :01 to clock, and Bennett tried 45y kick toward same end of Orange Bowl where Osborne's 2-pt try had failed in 1984 and same goalposts where Bowden had suffered 1 of his miserable episodes of "wide right." This time, Nebraska's Bennett was wide left, and Florida State, less than 50 years removed from being all-female college, won its 1st-ever national championship.

Final AP Poll January 2

1 Florida State (46)	1532	13 Boston College	817
2 Notre Dame (12)	1478	14 Alabama	685
3 Nebraska	1418	15 Miami	611
4 Auburn (4)	1375	16 Colorado	574
5 Florida	1307	17 Oklahoma	521
6 Wisconsin	1228	18 UCLA	460
7 West Virginia	1090	19 North Carolina	447
8 Penn State	1074	20 Kansas State	444
9 Texas A&M	1043	21 Michigan	397
10 Arizona	992	22 Virginia Tech	321
11 Ohio State	971	23 Clemson	164
12 Tennessee	870	24 Louisville	159
		25 California	79

Final *USA Today* Coaches Poll January 3

1 Florida State (36)	1523	
2 Notre Dame (25)	1494	
3 Nebraska (1)	1441	
4 Florida	1313	
5 Wisconsin	1271	
6 West Virginia	1142	
7 Penn State	1132	
8 Texas A&M	1107	
9 Arizona	1094	
10 Ohio State	960	
11 Tennessee	891	
12 Boston College	828	
13 Alabama	742	
14 Oklahoma	636	
15 Miami (Fla.)	604	
16 Colorado	586	
17 UCLA	539	
18 Kansas State	523	
19 Michigan	496	
20 Virginia Tech	472	
21 North Carolina	452	
22 Clemson	240	
23 Louisville	214	
24 California	158	
25 Southern California	121	

1993 Top Performance Formula

1 Florida State	1.8831
2 Florida	1.6803
3 Auburn	1.6674
4 Notre Dame	1.6481
5 Nebraska	1.6431
6 West Virginia	1.6298
7 Tennessee	1.5806
8 Texas A&M	1.5637
9 Ohio State	1.5635
10 Miami	1.5202
11 Wisconsin	1.5195
12 Penn State	1.5130
13 Arizona	1.4559
14 Oklahoma	1.4528
15 Boston College	1.4316
16 Virginia Tech	1.4195
17 UCLA	1.4095
18 North Carolina	1.3983
19 Alabama	1.3899
20 Michigan	1.3879

1993 Top Opponent Records

1 Miami	.6744
2 Florida	.6533
3 Florida State	.6454
4 UCLA	.6395
5 Pittsburgh	.6368
6 Louisiana State	.6345
7 Maryland	.6333
8 Purdue	.6229
9 Michigan State	.6202
10 Northwestern	.6186
11 Southern California	.6179
12 Stanford	.6059
13 Missouri	.6026
14 Vanderbilt	.5862
15 Iowa State	.5812
16 Michigan	.5787
17 Nebraska	.5773
18 Kansas	.5744
19 Colorado	.5714
20 Syracuse	.5696

1993 Out-of-Conference Records

	W-L	Percentage	Bowl W-L
Southeastern	28-9-1	.7500	2-2
Pacific-10	24-10	.7059	3-1
Big Ten	26-13	.6667	4-3
Big East	22-11-1	.6618	2-2
Big Eight	20-12-1	.6212	3-1
Atlantic Coast	17-13	.5667	2-3
Southwest	11-20-2	.3636	0-2
Western Athletic	11-22	.3333	0-4

1993 Individual Statistical Leaders

RUSHING YARDS	Attempts	Yards	Avg.
LeShon Johnson, Northern Illinois	327	1976	6.0
Byron Morris, Texas Tech	298	1752	5.9
Marshall Faulk, San Diego State	300	1530	5.1
Brent Moss, Wisconsin	276	1479	5.4
Ron Rivers, Fresno State	216	1440	6.7
Junior Smith, East Carolina	278	1352	4.9
Napoleon Kaufman, Washington	226	1299	5.7
Errict Rhett, Florida	247	1289	5.2
Terrell Willis, Rutgers	195	1261	6.5
James Bostic, Auburn	199	1205	6.1

PASSING YARDS	Completions	Attempts	Yards	Pct.
Chris Vargas, Nevada	331	490	4265	67.6
Mike McCoy, Utah	276	430	3860	64.2
John Walsh, Brigham Young	244	397	3727	61.5
Eric Zeier, Georgia	269	425	3525	63.3
Glenn Foley, Boston College	222	363	3397	61.2
Rob Johnson, Southern California	278	405	3285	68.6
Trent Dilfer, Fresno State	217	333	3276	65.2
Danny O'Neil, Oregon	223	360	3224	61.9
Tim Gutierrez, San Diego State	208	341	3033	61.0
Charlie Ward, Florida State	264	380	3032	69.5

RECEIVING YARDS	Catches	Yards
Chris Penn, Tulsa	105	1578
Ryan Yarborough, Wyoming	67	1512
Johnnie Morton, Southern California	78	1373
Bryan Reeves, Nevada	91	1362
Darnay Scott, San Diego State	75	1262
Charles Johnson, Colorado	57	1082
Demond Thompkins, UNLV	62	1068
Michael Stephens, Nevada	80	1062
Isaac Bruce, Memphis	74	1054
J.J. Stokes, UCLA	68	1005.

1993 Consensus All-America Team
Offense

Wide Receiver:	J.J. Stokes, UCLA
	Johnnie Morton, Southern California
	David Palmer, Alabama
Tackle:	Aaron Taylor, Notre Dame
	Wayne Gandy, Auburn
Guard:	Mark Dixon, Virginia
	Stacy Steegers, Clemson
Center:	Jim Pyne, Virginia Tech
Quarterback:	Charlie Ward, Florida State
Running Back:	LeShon Johnson, Northern Illinois
	Marshall Faulk, San Diego State
Placekicker:	Bjorn Merten, UCLA
Kick Returner:	David Palmer, Alabama

Defense

Linemen:	Rob Waldrop, Arizona
	Dan Wilkinson, Ohio State
	Sam Adams, Texas A&M
	Kevin Patrick, Miami
Linebacker:	Trev Alberts, Nebraska
	Derrick Brooks, Florida State
	Jamir Miller, UCLA
Backs:	Antonio Langham, Alabama
	Aaron Glenn, Texas A&M
	Jeff Burris, Notre Dame
	Corey Sawyer, Florida State
Punter:	Terry Daniel, Auburn

1993 Heisman Trophy Vote

Charlie Ward, senior quarterback, Florida State	2310
Heath Shuler, junior quarterback Tennessee	688
David Palmer, junior WR-QB, Alabama	292
Marshall Faulk, junior running back, San Diego State	250
Glenn Foley senior quarterback, Boston College	180

Other Major Awards

Maxwell (Player)	Charlie Ward, senior quarterback, Florida State
Walter Camp (Player)	Charlie Ward, senior quarterback, Florida State
Outland (Lineman)	Rob Waldrop, senior nose guard, Arizona
Vince Lombardi (Lineman)	Aaron Taylor, senior tackle, Notre Dame
Dick Butkus (Linebacker)	Trev Alberts, senior LB-DE, Nebraska
Jim Thorpe (Defensive Back)	Antonio Langham, senior cornerback, Alabama
Davey O'Brien (Quarterback)	Charlie Ward, senior quarterback, Florida State
Doak Walker (Running Back)	Byron "Bam" Morris, junior RB, Texas Tech
Lou Groza (Placekicker)	Judd Davis, junior kicker, Florida
AFCA Coach of the Year	Barry Alvarez, Wisconsin

1994

The Year of the Only Game in Town, Slip in Bloomington Occasions the Doctor's Title, and the Five-Cornered Knot

College football celebrated its 125th season in 1994. Come September, both college and pro football completely took center stage in the American sports world because Major League Baseball ended its season in August over a salary cap squabble between players and owners. The World Series, which by some thinking could be portrayed as an annual autumn intrusion on 89 straight football seasons, was junked when baseball's acting-commissioner, Bud Selig, announced the death of the season on September 14. Hockey failed to open its season on time in October. Pro basketball had its share of labor rumblings; only an 11th hour accord saved the NBA season. For much of a wonderful autumn, football—college and pro—was the only game in town.

Florida (10-2-1) and Nebraska (13-0) were pre-season favorites and spearheaded a quickly-identified elite group, most of which piled up fabulous early-season point totals.

Colorado (11-1), one of the early elites, seemed touched by destiny. In consecutive games, the Buffaloes hammered Wisconsin (7-4-1) 55-17, beat Michigan (8-4) on an amazing, last-second Kordell Stewart "Hail Mary" pass caught by Michael Westbrook, and nipped Texas (8-4) on a last-play field goal by Neil Voskeritchian.

Meanwhile, Nebraska lost its spectacular option quarterback Tommie Frazier to a blood clot in his leg. When the no. 2 Huskers used backup quarterback Brook Berringer behind its great line to beat tough Kansas State (9-3) on October 15, and top-ranked Florida lost to Auburn (9-1-1), Penn State (12-0) stepped past Nebraska to no. 1.

But, the no. 3 Cornhuskers vaulted right back in the AP poll on October 29 when they dominated then-second-ranked Colorado by 24-7. On that same Saturday, Penn State walloped 21st-ranked Ohio State (9-4) by the overwhelming margin of 63-14 yet retained only its coaches' poll lead. A week later, the Nittany Lions also abdicated the coaches' admiration after an easy but deceptive win in Bloomington, Indiana. Hopelessly behind at 35-13, Indiana (6-5) snuck in two late touchdowns with two-point conversions against Penn State reserves for an artificially close 35-29 final score. Coach Joe Paterno justified his using substitutes to gain game-experience, but clearly Penn State made a costly slip in Bloomington.

The Nittany Lions went on to sweep the Big Ten in their second year in the league but wouldn't return to the conference throne room until 2005. Underrated Oregon (9-4) fell to Penn State in the Rose Bowl, and Paterno became the all-time bowl-winning coach with 16 victories. Oregon came into the Rose Bowl ranked only 12th in the AP Poll, so the victory did little to boost the national championship prestige of the Lions. Thus, Paterno had coached the third undefeated team of his career that failed to capture a writers or coaches national title. *The New York Times* Computer Poll, however, tapped Penn State as no. 1 after the bowl games had concluded.

Alabama (12-1) may have barely slipped by mediocre foes early in the year but grew into a late no. 1 candidate. The Crimson Tide finished the regular season with solid wins over Mississippi State (8-4) and Auburn to join Nebraska and Penn State as the only unbeaten teams heading into December. But, Florida ended the Crimson Tide's national title dream with a one-point win in the SEC title game.

No. 3 Miami (10-2) was poised as Nebraska's Orange Bowl foe, potentially a familiar mess for the visiting Huskers: drawing a top-flight Florida-based team playing in its own backyard. The game started like another rout in the Orange Bowl stadium, where the Hurricanes were 62-1 since the mid-1980s. This time, however, Nebraska wore down the Hurricanes and got two late scores from fullback Cory Schlesinger to win coach Dr. Tom Osborne's first national title. Conference bowl affiliations had prevented a Nebraska-Penn State match, so the Nittany Lions were left to finish second and ponder what might have been had they been able to keep the pressure on the Indiana Hoosiers nine weeks earlier.

The Southwest Conference staged a bizarre race for its championship. Texas A&M (10-0-1) enjoyed its first undefeated season in 38 years but was on probation for recruiting violations and forced to abdicate its conference crown. An unprecedented five teams ended up sharing first place in the SWC. The Aggies, led by members of its "Wrecking Crew" defense paced by end Brandon Mitchell, linebacker Reggie Brown, and cornerbacks Donovan Greer and Ray Mickens, ended up defeating each of the championship teams to no avail. It took some remarkable outcomes on Thanksgiving weekend to create the big knot at the top. Texas (8-4) trounced Baylor (7-5) on Thanksgiving Thursday to equal the Bears' 4-3

conference mark, and Texas Christian (7-5) upset Texas Tech (6-6) on Friday as each also finished 4-3 in the SWC. Finally, Rice (5-6) completed the five-cornered knot on Saturday by beating cross-city rival Houston (1-10). It was Rice's first whiff of the league title since its 1957 team, led by dual future NFL quarterbacks King Hill and Frank Ryan, built a 7-4 record and a Cotton Bowl appearance.

After his team's 24-17 loss to TCU, witty Texas Tech coach Spike Dykes observed, "It's like getting hit in the face with a dead fish. Once the smell's gone, you're okay." Dykes' Raiders were tapped for the Cotton Bowl this time around because they had played in Dallas' New Year's extravaganza only once in 1939 and never as a member of the frequently-unpredictable Southwest Conference.

The Heisman Trophy award took on unusual debate. Among many aspirants were running backs Rashaan Salaam of Colorado (the fourth-ever ballcarrier to gain 2,000 yards in a season) and Ki-Jana Carter of Penn State, and quarterbacks Kerry Collins of Penn State and Jay Barker of Alabama. High on many lists was quarterback Steve McNair of Division 1-AA, historically-black Alcorn State. McNair smashed the all-time NCAA career total offense record with 16,885 yards, but his credentials were debated on a daily basis. Some considered his opposition way too weak for him to be taken seriously, but other selectors were duly impressed by his magnificent stats. In the end, Heisman electors were taken off the hook by Salaam's magical 2,055 yards. He won the vote somewhat handily. McNair finished third behind Carter, but ahead of Collins, who was a surprise Maxwell Award winner, with Barker fifth.

Dark circumstances created world-wide publicity for one of football's all-time greatest stars. Movie and TV personality O.J. Simpson, the 1968 Heisman Trophy winner as tailback for Southern California and record-setting running back for the NFL's Buffalo Bills, went on trial for the knife-slashing murder of his estranged wife, Nicole, and Ron Goldman, a friend of hers. Simpson was named as a suspect shortly after the bodies were found at Nicole's house in upscale Bel Aire, Calif. Simpson responded with a bizarre low-speed "getaway" police-chase, which was broadcast by TV cameras capturing the drama from low-flying helicopters. A distraught Simpson supposedly held a gun to his head as friend and former teammate Al Cowlings was at the wheel of a Ford Bronco. Simpson turned himself in after hours on Los Angeles streets and freeways. Months of live TV coverage of the trial generated massive worldwide attention, and it ended with Simpson's stunning acquittal in the most famous celebrity murder case ever.

Milestones

⬤ Southwest Conference, in its 80th year, was dissolved effective after 1995 season. Baylor, Texas, Texas A&M and Texas Tech entered the Big Eight, expanded to Big 12. Rice, TCU and SMU linked with Tulsa to join expanded Western Athletic Conference. Houston joined Cincinnati, Louisville, Memphis, Southern Mississippi, and Tulane in new conference, later named Conference USA.

⬤ Florida State's 1993 Heisman winner Charlie Ward, snubbed in 1994 NFL draft when he tried to use basketball skills as bargaining wedge, was signed as guard by New York Knicks of NBA.

⬤ Cancer claimed former Texas A&M fullback-linebacker Lee Roy Caffey, 52, on January 18. Bob Bjorklund, co-captain of undefeated 1940 Minnesota Gophers died at 75 on January 28. On February 4, former UCLA Single Wing tailback Ronnie Knox died penniless at 57 in San Fransisco. Knox's wandering career, masterminded by stepfather Harvey, led him to three high schools, Cal-Berkeley, UCLA, and four pro teams, but his finest moment was 1956 Rose Bowl in Bruins' losing 17-14 effort. Oklahoma coaching legend Bud Wilkinson died of heart failure on February 9. Wilkinson, 77, earned spectacular 145-29-4 (.826) record during 1947-63 and won three national championships and 14 conference titles in 17 years. Francis "Pug" Lund, halfback on Minnesota's 1934 national champion, died at 81 on May 26. Pro stars of 1970s, tackle Jerry Mays of SMU and Kansas City Chiefs, and linebacker Bob Matheson of Duke and Cleveland Browns and Miami Dolphins, died at ages 54 and 49 respectively.

⬤ During September 3 season opener at Jones Stadium against New Mexico, Texas Tech's quarter horse mascot "Double T" threw its rider and died when its head hit a cement wall after slip off its hooves.

⬤ Longest winning streaks entering season:
Auburn 11   Cincinnati, Penn State 5

	Incoming	Outgoing
Boston College	Dan Henning	Tom Coughlin
Central Michigan	Dick Flynn	Herb Deromedi
Cincinnati	Rick Minter	Tim Murphy
Duke	Fred Goldsmith	Barry Wilson
Georgia Tech	George O'Leary (a)	Bill Lewis
Harvard	Tim Murphy	Joe Restic
Kent	Jim Corrigall	Pete Cordelli
Mississippi	Joe Lee Dunn (interim)	Billy Brewer
Missouri	Larry Smith	Bob Stull
Nevada	Chris Ault	Jeff Horton
Rice	Ken Hatfield	Fred Goldsmith
San Diego State	Ted Tollner	Al Luginbill
South Carolina	Brad Scott	Sparky Woods

(a) O'Leary (0-3) replaced Lewis (1-7) on November 12.

Preseason *USA Today* Coaches Poll

1	Florida (17)	1416	14	Southern California	692
2	Florida State (13)	1402	15	UCLA	677
3	Nebraska (12)	1375	16	Ohio State	644
4	Notre Dame (12)	1362	17	North Carolina	574
5	Michigan (3)	1302	18	Texas	466
6	Miami (Fla.) (2)	1148	19	Virginia Tech	301
7	Colorado	1097	20	Brigham Young	281
8	Arizona (2)	1037	21	Clemson	254
9	Penn State (1)	1022	22	Illinois	249
10	Alabama	964	23	West Virginia	209
11	Wisconsin	902	24	Georgia	161
12	Tennessee	878	25	Virginia	138
13	Oklahoma	746			

August 27, 1994

(Sun) Nebraska 31 West Virginia 0 (East Rutherford, N.J.): Contest that matched 1993 regular season unbeatens came 8 months too late for West Virginia (0-1) coach Don Nehlen: most of his team was gone. Splendid Cornhuskers (1-0) amassed 468y to 89y advantage as QB Tommie Frazier scored on runs of 25, 27, and 42y and passed for 4th TD. Weary WVU got 90y punt from P Todd Sauerbrun, who boasted 60.1y avg.

September 3, 1994

(Th) Arizona 19 GEORGIA TECH 14: Georgia Tech (0-1), hoping for turnaround season, got off on right foot: FUM REC and QB Tommy Luginbill's 14y TD pass to WR Derrick Steagall just 45 sec into game. No. 7 Arizona (1-0), named preseason no. 1 by *Sports Illustrated*, had to overcome 3 FUMs by rusty RB Ontiwaun Carter (30/151y), who had missed camp contact due to injury. Four min into 4th Q, Luginbill's 2nd TD pass put Georgia Tech ahead 14-13, and Wildcats seemed dumped when their short FG try was blocked by Jackets DL Elliott Fortune with 7:14 to play. But, frosh sub RB Kevin Schmidtke (17/92y) carried last 6/26y to complete 60y drive with 26 secs remaining.

Texas 30 PITTSBURGH 28: On Tony Dorsett Day, Panthers (0-1).RB Curtis Martin emulated the Hall of Fame runner by rushing 28/251y, most ever allowed in 101 years of Texas (1-0) football. But in dying moments, Pitt ignored Martin when it needed 2-pt conv to tie. Sub Longhorns DB Taje Allen knocked down Panthers QB Sean Fitzgerald's pass with :36 showing on 4th Q clock. Texas held ball for most of 4th Q after K Philip Dawson's 50y FG gave it 30-22 lead. Costly to Pitt were 2 botched conv kicks.

Oklahoma 30 SYRACUSE 29: Sooners (1-0) opened 24-0 H lead as QB Garrick McGee hit 2 TD passes. Midway in 3rd Q, WR P.J. Mills streaked for TD which probably would have created Sooners rout, but hustling lunge by Orange DB Bryce Bevill dislodged ball. It bounced through EZ; Syracuse (0-1) took over on own 1YL and turned game with 78y TD pass by QB Kevin Mason to WR Marvin Harrison. Orange followed with 2 more TDs. Leading by 6 pts with 2:01 to play, Sooners conceded safety for 27-23 lead. Oklahoma's strategy backfired min later when Mason hit Harrison for 48y TD and 29-27 Orange lead. But, SU was flagged for excessive celebration on TD play and woefully missed its conv kick. PEN was assessed on Syracuse's KO and gave OU ball at its 36YL. McGee's quick 2 completions to WR Albert Hall set up K Scott Blanton's winning 48y FG with 11 secs left.

DUKE 49 Maryland 16: Underdog Duke (1-0), playing 1st game under enthusiastic new coach Fred Goldsmith, surprised Maryland (0-1) with battering ram RB Robert Baldwin, who charged to 33/238y, 4 TDs on ground. Baldwin took charge on Duke's 2nd possession, powering up middle against Terrapins' depleted D-line that was missing regulars in Sharrod Mack and Johnnie Hicks, who were out for disciplinary and academic reasons respectively. Early on, Blue Devils TE John Farquhar caught 17y TD to open scoring when he barreled over Terps DB Wade Inge. Key play came soon thereafter when Duke QB Spence Fischer (15-24/197y, TD) converted 4th-and-3 at Terps 22YL with 19y pass to TE Bill Khayat. Maryland QB Scott Milanovich hit 20-31/230y, TD, but much of it came after feisty Devils built 28-3 H lead. Milanovich's TD pass went 43y to WR Geroy Simon in 3rd Q to briefly trim deficit to 28-10.

FLORIDA STATE 41 Virginia 17: Defending national champion Florida State (1-0) extended its ACC record to 17-0, but was most happy about chance to finally end its scandalous off-season. "The whole team was excited...to get on TV for something other than the (free shoes from sports agents) scandal," said QB Danny Kanell, who expertly racked up 32-48/330y, 4 TDs passing. Playing without 7 well-shod but suspended players, Seminoles fell behind 3-0 on Virginia (0-1) K Rafael Garcia's 40y FG in 1st Q and were behind for only 5th time in last 53. But, FSU exploded for 34 straight pts in middle Qs as Kanell hit 3 TD passes in 2nd Q, including 16y score to RB Warrick Dunn, who sat out last 41 mins due to sprained knee. WR Kez McCorvey (11/107y, 2 TDs) scored in 2nd Q to make it 20-3 at H and in 4th Q to raise count to

41-10. Virginia QB Symmion Willis had rough time, throwing for 9-24/66y, INT. Willis gave way to sub QB Mike Groh, who found WR Germane Crowell twice for scores in 4th Q.

MICHIGAN 34 Boston College 26: BC Eagles (0-1) exploded from gate under new coach Dan Henning, scoring on their 1st play: 74y pass from QB Mark Hartsell to WR Greg Grice. QB Todd Collins rescued Michigan (1-0) from 12-0 2nd Q deficit with 46 and 38y TD passes to WR Amani Toomer (7/179y, 2 TDs). TB Tshimanga "Tim" Biakabutuka, filling in for injured TB Tyrone Wheatley, rushed 12/128y in boosting Wolverines to 34-12 lead before Hartsell hit 2 late TD passes for Boston College.

SOUTHERN CALIFORNIA 24 Washington 17: Earthquake-ravaged L.A. Coliseum was refurbished at $60 million just in time for season opener. Southern California (1-0) trotted out old-fashioned array of TBs, including Shawn Walters, who ran for 2 TDs in 2nd H to tie it at 17-17 and put Trojans ahead by 7 pts with 7:14 left. USC frosh TB Delon Washington also rushed 10/109y. Washington (0-1) TB Napoleon Kaufman ran 26/152y and had 244 all-purpose y. Difference was 5 TOs suffered by Huskies.

UCLA 25 Tennessee 23: Sr Volunteers QB Jerry Colquitt, who waited 4 years for starting spot to open up, tragically tore up his knee on game's 7th play. Trio of young Tennessee (0-1) QBs followed Colquitt, including frosh Peyton Manning (who tried no passes), and were ineffective until 4th Q as UCLA (1-0) built 18-0 lead. QB Wayne Cook (25-38/295y, TD) had hit WR Kevin Jordan with 51y TD on Bruins' 1st possession, and K Bjorn Merten kicked 4 FGs. Bruins thought they were about to win their 1st opening game shutout in 25 years. Instead, Vols rallied to within 18-16 when QB Todd Helton (14-28/165y, TD, INT) returned in 4th Q to spark 76 and 57y TD drives that included his 10y TD pass to WR Courtney Epps and pair of throws for 2 pts. UCLA LB Donnie Edwards authored important INT just as Tennessee was brewing momentum. His pick-off of future baseball All-Star Helton set up Bruins TB Daron Washington's 30y clinching TD run that upped score to 25-16.

USA Today Coaches Poll September 6

1	Nebraska (20)	1463	14	Ohio State	755
2	Florida (23)	1449	15	Oklahoma	745
3	Florida State (6)	1385	16	North Carolina	634
4	Notre Dame (7)	1362	17	Texas	472
5	Michigan (3)	1242	18	Virginia Tech	457
6	Miami (Fla.) (2)	1209	19	Tennessee	413
7	Colorado	1138	20	Clemson	320
8	Penn State	1128	21	Brigham Young	283
9	Arizona (1)	1024	22	Georgia	274
10	Alabama	967	23	California	127
11	Wisconsin	894	24	Kansas State	121
12	UCLA	859	25	Stanford	98
13	Southern California	812			

September 10, 1994

RUTGERS 17 West Virginia 12: New Rutgers Stadium hosted its 1st Big East game, and Scarlet Knights (2-0) gleefully beat defending champion West Virginia (1-2). Rutgers staged 2nd H rebound after 1st H saw Mountaineers outgain it 193y to 61y and take 6-0 lead on FGs by K Bryan Baumann. WVU had reason to be frustrated by 1st H as it went inside Knights' 25YL 4 times. Rutgers copped control with 2 TDs in 6-sec span of 3rd Q. WVU RB Robert Walker lost FUM at own 35YL, and Knights QB Ray Lucas converted 4th down sneak before clicking on 4y TD pass to TE Jason Curry. On next series, Rutgers LB Alcides Catanho picked off pass by QB Eric Boykin for 24y sprint to paydirt. Sub West Virginia TB Jimmy Gary scored in last 2 mins, but LB Rusty Swartz batted down 2-pt pass and TE Marco Battaglia pounced on on-side KO.

Florida State 52 MARYLAND 20: Outmanned Maryland (0-2) stunningly led 13-3 early in 2nd Q and 20-17 at H, but heat and Florida State (2-0) depth steamrolled Terps in 2nd H. Seminoles took lead for good on their opening possession of 3rd Q, going 80y to TD run by TB Rock Preston (4/30y, 2 TDs). FSU settled in to score 35 straight pts in 2nd H as QB Danny Kanell passed 28-44/417y, TD, 2 INTs, part of FSU's total O of 731y. FB Zack Crockett rushed 19/123y, scoring in 2nd and 3rd Qs. QB Scott Milanovich went 17-34/188y, 2 TDs, INT in leading Terps to H margin, 1st time FSU had trailed at H during its 18 ACC wins in row.

North Carolina State 29 CLEMSON 12: So thorough was Clemson's worst home whipping in 14 years that it only gained 21y rushing. North Carolina State (2-0) coach Mike O'Cain, former Tigers QB in mid-1970s, became 1st ex-Tiger to beat his alma mater. In 2nd Q, Wolfpack QB Terry Harvey (12-17/167y, 2 TDs) faked Clemson (1-1) D into submission as WR Eddie Goines (3/108y, 2 TDs) went long for 76y TD pass. Tigers stayed within hailing distance at H by sacking Harvey in 2nd Q and having LB Chris Franklin, fomer FB who scored in 1992 vs. NC State, race 60y to score with scooped-up FUM. Leading 16-6 at H, Wolfpack added 2 FGs by K Steve Videtich and sub QB Geoff Bender's TD pass to Goines before Clemson tallied late on pass by QB Patrick Sapp (19-38/158y, TD, INT).

Tennessee 41 GEORGIA 23: No. 19 Tennessee (1-1) ignored its QB problems, passing only 9-13/110y by jr QB Todd Helton, future National League batting champion with Colorado Rockies. Helton fit 9y TD pass to WR Joey Kent into his infrequent array of tosses, but handed ball often to TBs James "Little Man" Stewart (24/211y, 4 TDs) and Aaron Hayden (25/113y) behind SEC's most powerful O-line. Volunteers enjoyed nearly 40 mins of possession time with 383y run attack. Meanwhile, Georgia (1-1) QB Eric Zeier fired 30-45/401y, and his 45y TD pass to WR Juan Daniels narrowed it to 24-15 by end of 3rd Q after DB Will Muschamp halted Vols with INT. Bulldogs could get no closer. Crushing blow came on Stewart's 71y TD run midway in 4th Q that made it 34-15 as he probed inside and bounced outside for TD trip down left sideline. Stewart scored again inside last 3 mins on 15y run.

SOUTH CAROLINA 14 Arkansas 0: Arkansas (1-1) coach Danny Ford, who led Clemson to 1981 national title, made his much-ballyhooed return to state of South Carolina, and it turned into nightmare of TOs: Razorbacks lost 3 FUMs and INT, missed 2 FGs, and suffered both blocked punt and FG. South Carolina (1-1) DE Stacy Evans made 8 tackles, including sack, and blocked punt. Gamecocks weren't too swift on O, being outgained 276y to 185y and making only 8 1st downs. However, Cocks' O managed 2 short drives: 32y to FB Stanley Pritchett's 1y TD and 51y midway in 4th Q as Pritchett took 7y shovel pass from QB Steve Taneyhill (15-28/165y, TD). Porkers threatened with last gasp: TB Marius Johnson rammed to GL, was hit hard by Carolina DB Reggie Richardson, and FUM was recovered by LB Hank Campbell.

ALABAMA 17 Vanderbilt 7: Symptomatic of its successful but unimpressive season in making, Alabama (2-0) was held to 151y O in opening 3 Qs as QB Jay Barker (9-15/88y, TD) was sacked 6 times but unfurled 8y TD pass in 1st Q to WR Curtis Brown. Fired-up Vanderbilt (1-1), 1-24 against Crimson Tide since 1960s, smelled blood and maintained 7-7 tie on TB Cliff Deese's 25y TD run in 2nd Q. Deadlock held up until last 7 mins of game when Bama K Michael Proctor kicked go-ahead 31y FG. TB Curtis Alexander added late TD run for Bama. Commodores outgained Tide 279y to 222y, but lost 4 critical TOs including 3 INTs by run-oriented QB Ronnie Gordon (9-17/131y).

PENN STATE 38 Southern California 14: Fast-starting Penn State (2-0) got explosive 32y TD run from TB Ki-Jana Carter (17/119y) and leaping and spin-away 44y TD catch from WR Freddie Scott to lead 14-0 just 2:05 into game. "Their execution was phenomenal," said Troy coach John Robinson of Nittany Lions' 35-0 H bulge. DB Quincy Harrison turned in best play for USC (1-1) when he raced 68y for TD with 3rd Q INT, but that accounted only for 35-7 improvement. Trojans QB Rob Johnson (18-30/221y) was sacked 6 times but managed 4th Q drive to TD.

Michigan 26 NOTRE DAME 24: Game was oddly like Notre Dame's last home game against Boston College in 1993 as last-moment loss spoiled earlier Fighting Irish rally. K Remy Hamilton's 42y FG, his 4th of game, completed miracle comeback for Michigan (2-0) with mere 2 secs left. Highly-touted Notre Dame (1-1) QB Ron Powlus (15-27/187y, 2 TDs) said, "I thought we had it won" after his 7y TD pass to WR Derrick Mayes with 52 secs left put Irish ahead 24-23. Wolverines QB Todd Collins (21-29/224y, TD) positioned Hamilton for his winning 3-ptr with 15y scramble and 3 completions, last of which came on desperate 9y toss to WR Seth Smith as Collins spun from grasp of pass-rushing Notre Dame DE Bert Berry. Irish TB Lee Becton's 2 FUMs and bobbled C-QB exchange set up trio of Hamilton's FGs: 32y in 2nd Q, 35y in 3rd Q, and 32y early in 4th Q for 23-7 Michigan lead. Wolverines TB Tim Biaukabutuka rushed 25/100y and scored 1st Q TD.

TEXAS A&M 36 Oklahoma 14: Revenge for 44-14 loss in 1993 was on Aggie minds as Texas A&M (2-2) blew open their 19-14 lead in 4th Q. Oklahoma (1-1) TB James Allen (15/66y) had caught short TD pass from QB Garrick McGee (11-34/118y, TD, 3 INTs) to trim margin to 19-14 but lost critical 4th Q FUM at own 8YL. Texas A&M QB Corey Pullig (17-30/191y, 2 TDs) quickly built score up to 26-14 with his 2nd TD pass with 5:13 to play. Another FUM led to FG by Aggies K Kyle Bryant, and DB Ray Mickens poured it on with 38y INT RET for TD.

UCLA 17 Southern Methodist 10: Still searching for post-Death Penalty glory (just 11 wins in 6 years), SMU (0-2) gained late 3rd Q 10-10 tie on TD pass from QB Ramon Flanigan (22-34/301y) to WR Mick Rossley. TB Sharmon Shah (24/158y) scored 4 mins later for 17-10 UCLA (2-0) lead. Bruins stopped 4 Mustang tries at UCLA 3YL with 1:47 left, including LB Donnie Edwards' 4th sack, 1 of 8 by fierce-rushing Bruins.

WASHINGTON 25 Ohio State 16: Huskies' quick, little TB, Napoleon Kaufman, rushed for career-high 211y and scored on 38y sprint. QB-turned-WR Eric Bjornson caught 25y TD pass as Washington (1-1) built 22-0 H lead. Huskies LB Richie Chambers had 3.5 sacks among 14 tackles. Buckeyes (1-1) rallied in 2nd H with 2 TDs, each followed by 2-pt sneak by QB Bobby Hoying (19-38/288y, TD). Ohio State got within 25-16 with 1:43 to play and recovered on-side KO. Hoying then hit TE D.J. Jones with 44y pass, but missed 3 passes and was sacked for 6th time on 4th down.

Miami 47 ARIZONA STATE 10: Early on, Miami's 3-loss Sun Devil Stadium curse looked like it might stay alive as exchange of INTs left Arizona State (1-1) at Hurricanes (2-0) 22YL after Devils CB Traivon Johnson's 16y RET. Miami held and forced Arizona State K Jon Baker's 1st of 2 FGs. Oddly, Sun Devils got 2 safeties near end of 1st Q as Canes QB Frank Costa (295y and 4 TDs passing) was called for intentional grounding in his EZ, and later punt snap was hiked through EZ. In between, Costa threw 2 TD passes, and RB James Stewart ran in from 9YL after DB Tremaine Mack made FUM REC at ASU 18YL. Costa threw his 3rd TD pass by beating Sun Devils blitz on dump over middle to WR Jonathan Harris. Stewart scored again after 74y drive was kept alive by roughing P PEN as Miami jumped to 33-10 H lead.

USA Today Coaches Poll September 12

1	Nebraska (34)	1501		14	Tennessee	693
2	Florida (18)	1483		15	Texas	687
3	Michigan (5)	1383		16	Virginia Tech	645
4	Florida State (1)	1366		17	Brigham Young	483
5	Penn State (2)	1260		18	Ohio State	355
6	Miami (Fla.) (2)	1259		19	Oklahoma	327
7	Colorado	1164		20	Southern California	273
8	Arizona	1060		21	Kansas State	248
9	Notre Dame	1015		22	Washington State	243
10	Wisconsin	1010		23	Kansas	195
11	Alabama	968		24	North Carolina State	152
12	UCLA	855		25	Indiana	97
13	North Carolina	763				

September 17, 1994

AUBURN 30 Louisiana State 26: Unbelievable finish allowed Auburn (3-0) to escape with its 14-game win streak intact. Long streak on The Plains seemed over as Bengals K Andre Lafleur made 39y FG early in 4th Q and LSU (1-2) led 23-9. Inexplicably, LSU passed when it needed to kill clock. QB Jamie Howard (18-41/280y, TD, 6 INTs) was picked off by Auburn DBs Ken Alvis and Fred Smith, each racing for TDs and 23-23 deadlock. Lafleur's 3rd FG put LSU back in front 26-23 with 5:26 left. With 2:06 to go on 3rd-and-4 at own 32YL, Howard suffered deflected INT, which Auburn DB Brian Robinson snared and returned 41y to winning TD.

Florida 31 TENNESSEE 0: Rampaging top-ranked Gators (3-0) inflicted worst home loss on Tennessee (1-2) in 70 years. Florida QB Terry Dean passed 18-26/303y, 2 TDs before stepping to sideline in 4th Q. Gators made 136y on ground, using 2 TEs at times, but also shifted into 5-WR set that seemed to puzzle Vols D. Gators DL Kevin Carter had 7 tackles and 2 of team's 5 sacks. Tennessee was held to 68y on ground, but threw for 235y.

Notre Dame 21 MICHIGAN STATE 20: Inspired Spartans (0-2) turned 3 TOs into pts on way to 20-7 H lead. WR Mill Coleman (30y) and QB Tony Banks (3y) had TD runs as 1st H stats read: MSU 270y, ND 114y. Irish QB Ron Powlus (10-30/161y, 2 TDs, 4 INTs) hit 4 key passes to keep alive 2 long TD dives in 2nd H. RB Lee Becton (12/90y) scored from 37y in 3rd Q as Irish (2-1) won school-record 16th road game in row.

NEBRASKA 49 Ucla 21: Nebraska (3-0) piled up 484y rushing, modern record allowed so far by out-classed UCLA (2-1). IB Lawrence Phillips (19/178y, TD) capped 89y 1st Q drive which gave Huskers 12-0 lead. Bruins came right back at 12-7, going 80y as QB Wayne Cook hit WR Kevin Jordan (7/129y) with 2/70y. QB Tommie Frazier, although held to only 88y total O, was master of option pitches, leading to 49-14 lead.

COLORADO 55 Wisconsin 17: Converting 4 1st H INTs, Colorado played its O aces: QB Kordell Stewart (301y total O and 2 TDs) and RB Rashaan Salaam (26/85y, 4 TDs). Wisconsin (1-1) QB Darrell Bevell was victim of all INTs of 1st H, and Buffs turned them into 17 pts. Bevell came back with 2 TD passes to TE Michael Roan, and Badgers TB Brett Moss rushed 21/118y, his 13th straight game with more than 100y.

Colorado State 28 BRIGHAM YOUNG 21: Furious Colorado State (3-0) D barred BYU (2-1) coach LaVell Edwards from his 200th career win. DB Greg Myers had 2 (including 30y TD RET) of Rams' 4 INTs, and they sacked Cougars QB John Walsh (27-57/358y, 2 TDs) 4 times. Rams QB Anthoney Hill hit 17-31/280y, and ran for TD as Colorado State opened 3-0 for 1st time since 1977.

Utah 34 OREGON 16: Crowd at disappointed Oregon (1-2) was smallest in 10 years as Ducks lost to 2nd WAC foe in 2 weeks (Hawaii won 36-16 on September 10). Utah (3-0) DB Kareem Leary had 2 INTs late in 2nd Q, returning 2nd 38y to TD for 21-10 H lead. Leary's 1st INT set up FG holder Jason Jones' race up middle on well-conceived fake for TD and 14-10 lead, Utes' 1st lead. Utah QB Mike McCoy (28-39/309y, 2 TDs) outdueled Oregon's QB Danny O'Neil (19-39/164y).

USA Today Coaches Poll September 19

1	Nebraska (33)	1501		14	Ohio State	617
2	Florida (20)	1495		15	Wisconsin	563
3	Florida State	1390		16	Oklahoma	551
4	Michigan (4)	1351		17	Kansas State	423
5	Penn State (3)	1327		18	Washington State	413
6	Miami (Fla.) (2)	1242		19	Southern California	361
7	Colorado	1201		20	UCLA	358
8	Arizona	1100		21	Indiana	331
9	Notre Dame	1028		22	North Carolina State	302
10	Alabama	1007		23	Tennessee	246
11	North Carolina	906		24	Baylor	218
12	Virginia Tech	806		25	Colorado State	125
13	Texas	768				

September 24, 1994

(Th) VIRGINIA TECH 34 West Virginia 6: High hopes of no. 14 Virginia Tech (4-0) were maintained by strong D, which permitted 91y rushing, had 8 sacks, and authored critical 2nd Q GLS. "I'm playing terrible," said Tech QB Maurice DeShazo, who had 3 INTs and 2 TDs among his 12-32/185y throwing. West Virginia (1-4), off to worst start in coach Don Neylen's 15 years, led 3-0 and got within 14-6 on K Bryan Baumann's 2nd FG.

Washington 38 MIAMI 20: Miami (2-1) had not lost in Orange Bowl since Florida won in September 1985, and history's longest consecutive home win streak ended at 58 as Hurricanes wilted under Washington's 2nd H heat. Huskies (2-1) went to H down 14-3, DB Russell Hairston having just been burned with 13 secs until H on 51y bomb by Miami QB Frank Costa (20-43/261y, TD, 2 INTs) to WR Yatil Green. But, after Washington FB Richard Thomas made 3 tacklers miss and churned 75y with screen pass TD early in 3rd Q, Hairston went 34y with INT RET that put Huskies ahead for good at 18-14 to stun Orange Bowl stadium crowd. Miami WR Jammi German fumbled away ensuing KO, and Washington T Bob Sapp recovered EZ FUM when QB Damon Huard (14-26/217y, TD, 2 INTs) lost handle near Canes GL. In less than 5 mins of 3rd Q, Huskies went from down 14-3 to up 25-14. They cruised from there on 2 FGs and Huard's 7y TD run.

FLORIDA STATE 31 North Carolina 18: Like clockwork, Florida State (4-0) hummed to 31-7 lead in 3rd Q as WR Kez McCorvey (5/83y) caught 31y TD at end of 79y drive. North Carolina (2-1) came back with 80y TD drive as QB Jason Stanicek hit 3 passes totaling 64y. After Tar Heels FG sliced margin to 31-18, DL Riddick Parker sacked FSU QB Danny Kanell, and DL Oscar Sturgis fell on FUM at Seminoles 6YL. On 2nd down, Carolina WR Octavus Barnes lost disputed catch-and-FUM, and FSU survived last 10 mins for its 20th ACC win in row.

MISSISSIPPI STATE 24 Tennessee 21: Volunteers (1-3) outgained Mississippi State (2-1) 464y to 294y behind relief pitching of frosh QB Peyton Manning, son of Archie, 1960s Ole Miss A-A QB. Replacing injured QB Todd Helton, Manning passed 14-23/256y, 2 TDs. But last 4 Vols possessions ended in TOs, allowing Bulldogs WR Eric Moulds to catch 3 clutch passes on 52y winning drive that was cashed with :36 to play.

Colorado 27 MICHIGAN 26: Buffaloes (3-0) led 14-9 at H on TD run by TB Rashaan Salaam (22/141y, 2 TDs) and TD pass by QB Kordell Stewart (21-32/294y, 2 TDs, INT). No. 4 Michigan (2-1) scored next 17 pts and seemed home free at 26-14 after shutting down Colorado's high-powered O in 2nd H. Wolverines TB Tyrone Wheatley (17/50y) returned from injury and scored on 5y run for 16-14 lead. After Michigan added 20y FG, Wolverines QB Todd Collins (17-24/258y) found WR Amani Toomer for 65y score. Stewart lost FUM at UM GL with 5:08 to play, but Buffs came back on 72y drive as Salaam scored his 2nd TD on 1y run with 2:16 left. Colorado trailed 26-21. After recovering Buffs' on-side KO try, Michigan was forced to punt thanks to procedure PEN. Only 6 secs remained when play unfolded that would be shown on TV many thousands of times: Buffaloes QB Kordell Stewart heaved 64y "Hail Mary" pass that was tipped before tumbling to WR Michael Westbrook, who miraculously grabbed it for winning TD in a crowd of players over shoulder of Michigan DB Ty Law.

Washington State 21 UCLA 0: Marvelous D of quiet Washington State (3-0), universally picked for Pac-10 cellar, finished September with no TDs allowed and 36y per game rushing D avg. Cougars RB Kevin Hicks scored at end of 85y drive in 1st Q, and made it 14-0 with TD that followed DB Terrell Henderson's block of punt late in 2nd Q. UCLA (2-2) QB Wayne Cook (11-25/90y) was tossed for 25y in losses and was exempted from wrath of Rose Bowl stadium boobirds in 2nd H by coach Terry Donahue's hook.

Arizona 34 STANFORD 10: Calling Arizona (3-0) D-front "best in country," Stanford (1-1-1) QB Steve Stenstrom said, "I got to know each of them pretty well," as he was sacked 7 times. Stenstrom passed 26-43/295y, 2 INTs but managed 2nd Q TD pass to TE Tony Cline. Before that, Wildcats used punt FUM REC and blocked FG to set up RB Ontiwaun Carter's 2 TDs, which served as lion's share of 24-0 lead.

CALIFORNIA 25 Arizona State 21: Still crabby 3 years later, Cal's alumni band formed "BS" at H for Bruce Snyder, Arizona State (1-3) coach and former Bears mentor, and transformed "S" into "$" to bitter cheers of Berkeley crowd of 37,000. California (1-2) rallied behind passes of QB Dave Barr (27-34/254y, TD, INT) and TB Tyrone Edwards (15/71y), who ran for 1 and 8y TDs at end of 63 and 60y drives in 4th Q. Sun Devils QB Jake Plummer (14-24/224y, 3TDs, INT) had thrown to WR Keith Poole for pair of TDs in middle Qs, including Poole's adjustment on slightly-underthrown ball for 66y TD in 2nd Q. When Plummer and Poole hooked up again in 3rd Q, ASU had 21-11 lead.

OREGON 40 Iowa 18: Hawkeyes (2-2), trying to rebound from previous Saturday's 61-21 pasting by Penn State, went to 12-7 lead in 1st Q as TB Sedrick Shaw (24/89y) pushed across TD and WR Harold Jasper eluded enough Oregon (2-2) tacklers to complete 68y punt TD RET. But, Iowa suffered blocked kick after each TD, symptomatic of rest of day: 4 TOs, 107y in PENs, and several dropped passes marked it for defeat. On its way to 34-12 lead in 3rd Q, Ducks tallied next 4 TDs, included 3 of 6, 2, and 9y by TB Ricky Whittle (14/66y). Oregon QB Danny O'Neill (7-17/74y) passed for 2 TDs despite Friday's treatment for infecting finger on throwing hand. Ducks backup TB Dino Philyaw (15/73y) scored twice.

October 1, 1994

SYRACUSE 28 Virginia Tech 20: RB Kirby Dar Dar's 34y run in 4th Q, his 3rd TD, gave Syracuse (4-1) lead for good at 21-20. Late Orange icing came on RB Malcolm Thomas' 42y TD run. Dar Dar and Thomas became 1st pair of Syracuse backs since 1980 to each exceed 100y rushing in same contest. Hokies (4-1) lost neat 7-game win streak, getting little besides K Ryan Williams' 4 FGs to support QB Maurice DeShazo's 20-37/290y passing. Va Tech frosh RB Ken Oxendine barreled 62y for 3rd Q TD for short-lived 20-14 lead.

ALABAMA 29 Georgia 28: Entering game, Alabama (5-0) had SEC's worst pass O, but always-resourceful QB Jay Barker threw for career-high 396y on 26-34. Clutch K Michael Proctor kicked winning 32y FG with 1:12 to play. Meanwhile, brilliant but frustrated QB Eric Zeier (25-33/263y, 4 TDs) passed Georgia (3-2) to leads of 7-0, 21-7, and 28-19 and said, "I do not know how we lost." Zeier set SEC career pass y record.

TENNESSEE 10 Washington State 9: Cougars (3-1) had allowed only 94/108y rushing all season, but were fooled on 3rd Q reverse by WR Nilo Sylvan, who ran untouched for 62y. "I must have asked him (coach Phillip Fulmer) to run that play 10 times," said Silvan. TD was 1st vs. Washington State in previous 16 Qs, but Cougars rallied and retook lead in 4th Q at 9-7 on K Tony Truant's 3rd FG. Frosh QB Peyton Manning, making his 1st start of career that would soon sparkle, hit WR Kendrick Jones with 41y pass to poise Volunteers (2-3) for K John Becksvoort's winning FG.

MICHIGAN STATE 29 Wisconsin 10: Michigan State's snarling D forced 4 TOs and held Badgers (2-2) to 297y, about half their O avg. Wisconsin QB Darrell Bevell had rare bad day: 4-7/3y and left with shoulder separation. Michigan State TB Duane Goolbourne (26/115y) scored 2 TDs, and frosh sub TB Marc Renaud wrapped it up with 41y TD burst on 4th-and-short

INDIANA 25 Minnesota 14: Minnesota (2-3) led 14-10 at H as valuable RB Chris Darkins (27/146y) scored on 20 and 2y runs in 2nd Q to overcome 10-0 Hoosiers (4-1) lead, which had carried over from 1st Q. Pulling away with 2 TDs, Indiana's alert D pounced on TOs on 4 of Gopher's 5 2nd H possessions. After Hoosiers K Bill Manolopoulos booted his 2nd FG, good for 33y, to draw within 14-13 in 3rd Q, DB Reggie Bryant (2 INTs) picked off pass and galloped 80y to score. Indiana QB John Paci (12-19/123y) scored clinching TD in 4th Q.

Purdue 22 ILLINOIS 16: Bidding for season's biggest turnaround from 1993's 1-10 mark was upset-minded Purdue (3-1). Boilermakers FB Mike Alstott opened scoring with 12y run in 1st Q and closed it with 2-pt run. TB Corey Rogers (28/103y) slammed for 2 Purdue TDs. Still, Illinois (2-2) had final chance: QB Johnny Johnson (19-25/244y, TD) found WR Jasper Strong at 10YL, then on game's last snap hit TE Ken Dilger who was stopped at 1YL by Purdue DB John Jackson's sure tackle.

NEBRASKA 42 Wyoming 32: With QB Tommie Frazier shelved at mid-week with blood clot in leg, Nebraska (5-0) turned controls to sub QB Brook Berringer, who scored 3 TDs before suffering collapsed lung. Huskers finally put it away in 4th Q with TD run by IB Lawrence Phillips (27/168y) as Wyoming (2-3) surprised with 21-7 H lead. Cowboys frosh QB Jeremy Dombeck threw 2 TDs in 1st Q, but standout FB Ryan Christopherson was held to 12/0y on ground.

Colorado 34 TEXAS 31: "Drama Buffs" were at it again, winning in last min. After Texas (3-1) tied game 31-31 on K Phil Dawson's 47y FG with 4:49 left, Buffaloes (4-0) went 73y in 13 plays for K Neil Voskeritchian's 24y FG with :01 to play. "I hope the guys don't think they need to make it exciting just for me," said coach Bill McCartney. "I've aged 10 years in 7 days (since Michigan win)." Colorado RB Rashaan Salaam (35/317y) rushed for most y ever vs. Texas, which lost at home for 1st time in 102 years when scoring more than 24 pts. Texas QB Shea Morenz hit 19-36/270y, 3 TDs, 2 INTs.

Baylor 42 TEXAS CHRISTIAN 18: Moving to plus-9 in season's TO ratio, Baylor (4-1) DB Tyrone Smith slammed ball loose from Texas Christian (2-3) TE Brian Collins (5/38y) on game's 1st snap, and Bears cashed over 28 pts on 3 TOs and blocked punt. Baylor leapt to 21-0 lead in 1st Q as QB Jeff Watson (5-8/46y, TD) threw 16y TD pass to WR John Stanley, and frosh DB Nikia Codie slipped up middle to block TCU punt that DB Smith took 2y to score. Horned Frogs trimmed deficit to 21-10 at H as TE Collins made amends for catching short TD pass from QB Max Knake (23-34/190y, 2 TDs, INT). Knake was involved in game's turning point in 3rd Q: After TCU went to Baylor 17YL on Knake's short passes, Bears secondary crept closer. Under pass-rush, Knake rolled out and threw for Collins, but Baylor SS Adrian Robinson broke into passing lane for INT that he returned 89y for TD and 28-10 lead. Bears scored 1st 2 TDs of 4th Q, including LB Glenn Coy's 15y FUM RET.

Oregon 22 SOUTHERN CALIFORNIA 7: QB Tony Graziani (16-31/287y, TD) filled in for Danny O'Neil and led Oregon (3-2) to 1st win in L.A. Coliseum since 1971. Ducks DB Ken Wheaton's 34y INT RET led to 1st Q FG and TB Dino Philyaw raced 49y through 3 tacklers for 10-0 edge. USC (2-2) QB Rob Johnson (20-30/237y) sliced 2nd Q score to 10-7 with TD pass, but left in 3rd Q with bad ankle after being victimized by 1 of Ducks' 9 sacks.

ARIZONA 30 Oregon State 10: Wishbone attack of Beavers (1-3) piled up 185y rushing, most against Wildcats (4-0) in 2 years, and managed 2 long drives in 2nd Q. Oregon State scored on FB J.D. Stewart's 3y TD run, which took bite out of Arizona's 13-0 lead. Beavers K Randy Lund's 26y FG cut H deficit to 20-10. After scoreless 3rd Q in which Arizona D clamped down on Beavers, Wildcats K Steve McLaughlin added his 3rd FG, and QB Dan White (14-21/194y) threw his 3rd TD pass, this of 34y to WR Richard Dice (7/136y, 2 TDs).

October 8, 1994

(Th) Kansas State 21 KANSAS 13: After early jousting that stayed between 20YLs, Wildcats (4-0) QB Chad May (33-44/379y) fired up air game for 21-0 3rd Q lead on way to K-State's 1st win in Lawrence in 25 years. Kansas (3-2) made things interesting in 4th Q with 2 scores, including 51y TD pass from QB Asheiki Preston to WR Ashaundi Smith. Kansas' home fans watched helplessly as Kansas State fans tore down goalposts of its in-state foes.

BOSTON COLLEGE 30 Notre Dame 11: After 16 road wins in row, it was harsh for Fighting Irish (4-2) to be dominated on both sides of ball by Eagles. "We got beat in every facet of the game," said coach Lou Holtz. Leading 7-3 at H, Boston College (2-2)

scored on its next 3 possessions: 2y run by RB Omari Walker after flea-flicker, 7y run by RB Justice Smith, and 37y FG by David Gordon, nemisis of ND in 1993's upset win for Eagles. BC harassed ND QB Ron Powlus (5-21/50y) into 4 sacks and loss of 39y.

MIAMI 34 Florida State 20: Apparently written off after last week's Washington loss, Miami (4-1) rebounded with superb D effort, led by T Warren Sapp. Hurricanes had 4 INTs, FUM REC, 5 sacks, and limited Florida State (4-1) to 47y on ground. Miami O line dominated, powering rejuvenated run game: FBs James Stewart and Danyell Ferguson combined for 176y rushing. Miami DB Carlos Jones ran back INT for 16y TD to knock favored Seminoles out of it at 31-17 in 3rd Q. Miami held FSU's vaunted O to 219y.

FLORIDA 42 Louisiana State 18: No. 1 Gators (5-0) rolled up 29-3 H lead, but coach Steve Spurrier was unimpressed: "We're not near as good as all you (media) guys think we are, so quit saying we are." Spurrier even suggested his O "may not have made a first down" without TB Fred Taylor. Frosh Taylor rushed 16/136y, and, with 2/48y receiving, he accounted for 45 percent of Florida's 408y O. Gators got 2 TDs in 1st H off special teams and D: DB Sam McCorkle's punt block and DB Anthony Lott's 88y INT TD RET. LSU (1-4), losers of 2 narrow results to Auburn and South Carolina, played virtually even by trailing 22-18 over last 3 Qs yet fell behind 20-0 in 1st Q, despite being outgained by only 91y to 88y. In end, LSU managed only 295y vs. Gators D, led by DE Kevin Carter, DT Ellis Johnson, and Lott.

Auburn 42 MISSISSIPPI STATE 18: Tigers (6-0) tied school record with 17th win in row as QB Patrick Nix threw 16-23/311y, 3 TDs, including 19 and 56y scores to superb WR Frankie Sanders (6/175y). Bulldogs (3-2) were outgained 554y to 338y, getting 107y in 4th Q as subs played for Auburn. DB Walt Harris contributed 46y TD run with FUM in 3rd Q, too little too late for Mississippi State as it trailed 35-12 by then.

LOUISVILLE 35 North Carolina State 14: TOs killed Wolfpack (4-1) as Louisville (3-2) LB Alan Campos (8 tackles) returned FUM 14y to set up Cards TB Anthony Shelman (27/139y, 2 TDs) for TD and 28-14 edge midway in 4th Q. Moments later, Campos picked up TB Brian Fitzgerald's 2nd FUM and dashed 20y to score. Game had been tied 14-14 at H largely on NC State LB Duan Everett's 66y INT TD RET.

Illinois 24 OHIO STATE 10: Illinois (3-2) won at Ohio Stadium for 4th time in row as far-roaming LB Dana Howard, who boldly guaranteed victory in Monday's media conference call, made 14 tackles and 2 sacks. Ohio State (4-2) broke on top 10-7 at H thanks to TB Eddie George's TD plunge. Illini broke 10-10 tie on 3rd Q's last play as WR Jasper Strong made 49y TD catch from QB Johnny Johnson (16-21/224y, 2 TDs).

CALIFORNIA 26 Ucla 7: Golden Bears (3-2) LB Jerrott Willard played spectacularly, rebounding from knee injury and flu bout to stir up O confusion of UCLA (2-4) with 14 tackles, including 2 sacks. Before he had his collarbone broken, California QB Dave Barr (7-12/116y, TD, INT) threw short 1st Q TD pass to wide-open TE Tony Gonzalez, after CB Artis Houston pranced 52y on INT RET to Bruins 11YL. Barr's replacement, much-maligned QB Kerry McGonigal (6-9/82y, TD), completed 2 passes on 60y drive to late 2nd Q score, his 20y pitch to WR Iheanyi Uwaezuoke providing 19-7 H lead. UCLA had tied it at 7-7 on TB Daron Washington's 26y TD run, capping 80y trip enhanced by WR Kevin Jordan's 3/56y catches from QB Wayne Cook (9-15/92y, INT). QB Ryan Fien went in to shake up Bruins' O late in 3rd Q. Instead, Fien's deflected pass was picked off by Bears LB Andre Rhodes, who took it 25y for TD in 4th Q.

USA Today Coaches Poll October 10

1	Florida (43)	1527	14	Virginia Tech	668
2	Nebraska (13)	1479	15	Syracuse	659
3	Penn State (5)	1417	16	Notre Dame	601
4	Colorado (1)	1387	17	Washington State	598
5	Michigan	1247	18	Utah	414
6	Alabama	1193	19	Baylor	361
7	Miami (Fla.)	1171	20	Wisconsin	328
8	Florida State	1050	21	Oklahoma	311
9	Texas	927	22	Ohio State	275
10	Arizona	903	23	Duke	259
11	Kansas State	894	24	North Carolina State	172
12	North Carolina	863	25	Brigham Young	154
13	Colorado State	775			

October 15, 1994

DUKE 19 Clemson 13: DB Ray Farmer blocked Clemson (2-4) P Nelson Welch's punt and recovered it for winning TD that broke 13-13 tie with 3:37 to play, and amazing Duke (6-0) stayed undefeated. On 2 plays prior to punt block, Blue Devils dusted off blitz it hadn't shown all day to twice sack Clemson QB Nealon Greene (16-30/172y). Earlier, Farmer blocked K Welch's FG try in 2nd Q to preserve 10-7 H advantage, but Welch hit 47 and 25y FGs in 3rd to give Tigers 13-10 lead. Devils QB Spence Fischer (25-39/240y, TD) had hit TE Bill Khayat (10/119y, TD) with 17y TD pass at end of 50y drive to open scoring in 1st Q.

Auburn 36 FLORIDA 33: Playing its "Super Bowl," bowl-banned Auburn (7-0) jumped to 1st H advantages of 10-0 and 22-14 primarily on discovery of TE Andy Fuller's catching skill. No. 1 Florida (5-1) changed signal-callers in 3rd Q as QB Danny Wuerffel relieved Terry Dean and hit his 1st 9 passes, giving Gators leads of 26-22 and 33-29 in 4th Q. Late in game, Florida needed to kill clock, but tried 3rd-and-15 pass that Tigers DB Brian Robinson (3 INTs) picked off and returned to his own 45YL with 1:20 to play. QB Patrick Nix converted 4th down pass to WR Thomas Bailey and found WR Frankie Sanders for winning TD with :30 to go. It was only 2nd loss at "The Swamp" for Florida coach Steve Spurrier, who took responsibility for ill-advised late throw. Auburn coach Terry Bowden said, "It ought to make us no. 1." It didn't; Tigers went to no. 4.

Alabama 17 TENNESSEE 13: In front of 96,856 at Neyland Stadium in Knoxville, Tennessee Volunteers (3-4) sought to stop 8-game winless streak against no. 11 Crimson Tide (7-0). "Third Saturday of October" rivals went off knotted 3-3 at H. With still teams tied 10-10 at end of 3 Qs, K John Beeksvoort gave Volunteers 13-10 lead with 22y FG early in 4th Q. Crimson Tide RB Sherman Williams (26/142y) took over next, scoring on 4y TD run to cap 80y drive that consumed 7:45 and ended with 3:04 left. Young QB Peyton Manning avoided Bama DT Dameian Jeffries, who had 3 sacks, long enough to look for his favorite target, WR Joey Kent, for connections of 17, 17, and 18y. After Tide LB Michael Rogers broke up pass, Tennessee faced 4th down at Bama 12YL. Manning's pass for WR Nilo Sylvan fell incomplete, and Alabama had its 8th win with tie in last 9 years against frustrated Tennessee. Vols TB Aaron Hayden rushed for 145y and caught 2/49y in losing effort.

ARKANSAS 31 Mississippi 7: Ole Miss Rebels (2-4) scored in 1st Q on 70y TD pass from QB Josh Nelson (12-27/143y, TD, INT) to WR Roell Preston (3/79y, TD). Shortly thereafter, Mississippi, which had won 4 straight from Razorbacks (3-4), lined up FG try for 10-pt lead. But holder Bubba Bonds couldn't haul down high snap and had to chase wrong-way dribble for 52y loss. "It was a backbreaker for them," said Arkansas LB Don Bray of FG miscue, because it opened floodgates for aerial game of Porkers QB Barry Lunney, Jr (7-13/92y, 3 TDs). Lunney soon hit TB Oscar Malone with 8y TD pass that tied it at 7-7. In 2nd Q, Arkansas went ahead 14-7 on Lunney's 34y TD pitch to WR J.J. Meadors (5/59y, TD). Arkansas added 10 quick pts in 3rd as DEs Marcus Adair and Steve Conley each created TO.

Penn State 31 MICHIGAN 24: Battle in "The Big House" drew 106,382, 3rd largest crowd to date in collegiate history. On the verge of putting verdict away, early-striking Penn State (6-0) collected mostly FGs and led 16-0 until K Remy Hamilton put Wolverines (4-2) on board at 16-3 before H. TB Tyrone Wheatley, who had only 9/11y rushing in 1st H, exploded for 67 and 21y TDs on consecutive series, and, in span of 4:19, Michigan suddenly jumped into 17-16 lead. Nittany Lions answered with QB Kerry Collins (20-32/231y, 3 TDs) passing for TD and 2-pt conv at end of 86y foray. After WR Amani Toomer (7/157y) set up 24-24 tie with 38y catch, Penn State forged ahead for good with 2:53 left: WR Bobby Engram made toe-in-bounds catch, TB Ki-Jana Carter ran 26y, and Engram caught 16y TD. Toomer maneuvered himself all alone at Lions 5YL, but lost his bearings and long pass drifted off his fingertips. Michigan soon evaporated possession on 4th down INT by Penn State CB Brian Miller.

Northwestern 37 MINNESOTA 31: With several Wildcats LBs on injury shelf, Northwestern (2-3-1) coach Gary Barnett, with new contract extension in his pocket, wanted to control ball against Minnesota (2-5). Wildcats failed somewhat, in as much as Golden Gophers ran 75 plays to Northwestern's 70. But, alternating Purple TBs, Dennis Lundy (34/213y) and Darnell Autry (15/100y), set personal-best rushing totals. Wildcats enjoyed 27-10 H lead as O-line, led by C Rob Johnson, G Matt O'Dwyer, and nicked-up T Todd Baczek, broke Lundy for 71y TD run and Autry for 47y TD dash. Staying just within striking distance, Minnesota QB Tim Schade (21-43/294y, 2 INTs) found WR Ryan Telwell (10/178y) for TDs of 80y in 2nd Q and 19y in 4th Q. WR Chris Gamble sped for 24y TD on reverse with 9:34 left, and NW seemed out of danger at 37-24. Gophers DB Rodney Heath's INT led to RB Chris Darkins' TD run, and Lundy's FUM forced Cats to have to halt Schade's 4th down run.

Brigham Young 21 NOTRE DAME 14: Injured Notre Dame (4-3) lost its 1st game ever to Brigham Young (6-1) and fell out of top 25 for 1st time since 1986. Keys to win: QB John Walsh passed 17-31/216y, TD, and BYU stopped ND twice inside its 10YL. Irish gained 436y as RB Randy Kinder opened scoring with 41y run and QB Ron Powlus passed 12-22/212y, TD. Cougars K David Lauder booted 1st H FGs of 49 and 48y.

Nebraska 17 KANSAS STATE 6: Going in, unbeaten Wildcats (4-1) were surprise no. 1 in *The New York Times* computer rankings. Meanwhile, Nebraska (7-0) was in dire QB straits: 3rd-string QB Matt Turman started, mostly handing off to IB Lawrence Phillips (31/126y, TD). Huskers D met daunting task of carrying their team, magnificently holding K-State to -7y rushing on 23 tries. Kansas State QB Chad May threw 22-48/249y and TD to WR Mitch Running that closed 2nd Q gap to 7-6. Even though its 1-pt lead would last precariously until 4th Q, Nebraska won its 26th in row over Wildcats going away. Despite its difficult win on road against opponent ranked 16th in AP Poll, Cornhuskers were leap-frogged by Penn State to no. 1 in AP Poll on Sunday.

Missouri 24 OKLAHOMA STATE 15: Victory represented 2nd straight conf road win for Mizzou (2-4), 1st such successes since 1983. Tigers coach Larry Smith jokingly griped about complexity of "Fight, Tigers," Missouri's fight song: "At Arizona, it was just, 'Bear Down.' That's all you'd have to say about 20 times. At Southern Cal, it was "Fight on," about 20 times. And this one, golly!" Missouri QB Jeff Handy (18-33/189y, 3 TDs, INT) pitched 2 TD passes in 1st Q for 14-0 lead, but Oklahoma State (3-3) came back with 15 unanswered pts in 2nd Q. Cowboys QB Tone Jones (15-34/132y, TD, INT) threw TD pass to WR Mark Cheatwood, and FB Geoff Grenier burst 50y to TD. When OSU went 66y in last 49 secs of 1st H to go-ahead 27y FG, it was fired up as clock struck 0:00. But, Tigers answered 2nd H bell with 5-min, 15-play drive to K Kyle Pooler's 30y FG and 17-15 edge. Handy's 3rd TD pass, coming in 4th Q to WR Frank Jones, gave sr signalcaller his school's career pass TD leadership with 34.

COLORADO 45 Oklahoma 7: Woody Paige in *Denver Post* opened his column with, "The last time I saw such an awful Oklahoma performance was at a dinner theater in Tulsa." Commanding Colorado (6-0) sent TB Rashaan Salaam behind vet line, led by C Bryan Stoltenberg, G Chris Naeole, and Ts Tony Berti and Derek West, to 25/161y rushing and he scored all 4 TDs Bison Herd got in 4 straight possessions in dominating 1st H at 28-0. S Donnell Leomiti made INT, WR Michael Westbrook lugged reverse run for 40y, and Salaam scored his 4th TD on 9y run. Colorado took advantage of over-reaction by Sooners LBs to succeed with cut-back runs that added up to 49/273y ground attack. Salaam's big night vaulted him ahead of Washington's Napoleon Kaufman for national rushing leadership at 175.7y per game. No. 4 Buffs maintained shutout until last 23 secs when no. 22 Sooners (3-3) QB Garrick McGee hit WR P.J. Mills with TD pass to avoid 1st shutout in 125 games. Oklahoma Wishbone run attack gained only 35/40y, while McGee (19-38/225y, TD, 4 INTs) suffered 3 INTs in 1st H.

OREGON 23 California 7: Ducks (4-3) came up with 304y rushing game to knock California (3-3) off its perch atop Pac-10 with Arizona. Oregon TBs Ricky Whittle (24/177y) and Dino Philyaw (21/130y) each scored TD, and Philyaw had 62y run. After Cal opened with TB Reynard Rutherford's 4y TD run for 7-0 lead, it was fully clamped down by Ducks' dominating D. Bears QB Kerry McGonigal (11-32/119y, 2 INTs), making his 1st start in 2 years, irritated Oregon by saying beforehand that he welcomed blitz because he expected to beat it with TD passes. "The guy hadn't played hardly any Pac-10 downs and he's coming in talking like that?" wondered Ducks DB Chad Cota.

Arizona 10 WASHINGTON STATE 7: Far West's best D teams butted heads, and Washington State (4-2) rushed only 37/5y. Still, Cougars took 7-0 1st Q lead as WR Albert Kennedy got deep for 85y bomb from QB Chad Davis. Arizona (5-1) tied in 2nd Q as QB Dan White executed perfect 3rd-and-short play-action fake and hit wide-open TE Tim Thomas. Wildcats K Steve McLaughlin kicked decisive 27y FG in 3rd Q after Nigerian Prince RB Frank Madu lost FUM. Cougars LB Mark Fields provided late chance with his FUM REC and would have scored on his RET but for hustling stop by Wildcats C Hicham El-Mashtoub. When Wazzu K Tim Turant lined up tying FG try, WSU was called for delay of game, and Turant missed left from 44y out.

(Sun) RICE 19 Texas 17: Not since Pres Lyndon Johnson was in White House in 1965 had Rice (3-2) defeated Texas (4-2). Starting on right foot, Owls opened with ball control drive for FG. Longhorns bobbled and lost ensuing KO when wind held it up, and Rice QB Josh LaRocca quickly hit HB Byron Coston with 33y misdirection TD pass. Owls out-gained Steers 122y to 8y in 1st Q on way to 12-10 lead. Texas QB Shea Morenz hit WR Matt Davis with 14y TD pass with 1:27 left, but on-side KO failed, and Owls killed clock.

USA Today Coaches Poll October 17

1	Penn State (22)	1504	14	Syracuse	729
2	Nebraska (31)	1498	15	Utah	623
3	Colorado (9)	1458	16	Kansas State	559
4	Miami (Fla.)	1283	17	Duke	543
5	Alabama	1271	18	Brigham Young	499
6	Florida	1254	19	Ohio State	424
7	Florida State	1188	20	Washington State	328
8	Arizona	997	21	North Carolina State	321
9	Texas	975	22	Virginia	223
10	North Carolina	935	23	Boston College	191
11	Colorado State	927	24	Indiana	124
12	Michigan	914	25	Illinois	123
13	Virginia Tech	745			

October 22, 1994

Miami 38 WEST VIRGINIA 6: Miami (5-1) had its team bus rocked and spit upon by fans in Morgantown after losing to WVU previous year. Hurricane players remembered, using their fabulous D to destroy West Virginia (2-5) on their revisit. Mountaineers gained only 23y rushing, 168y total, as Miami defenders, led by T Warren Sapp and CB Carlos Jones (INT), allowed no scoring. Canes scored on 3 of opening 5 possessions, including 2 long TD bombs by QB Frank Costa (14-29/266y, 2 TDs, INT) to WRs Chris T. Jones and Yatil Green. WVU TD came on odd punt play in 4th Q after trailing 32-0: Miami P Mike Crissy let snap get past him into EZ, where he tried to punt on run. Ball dribbled off his edge of his foot and was scooped up by Mountaineers DB Rodney Allen for 2y TD RET.

VIRGINIA 34 North Carolina 10: Cavaliers QB Mike Groh (15-21/256y) hit TD to WR Tyrone Davis while completing his 1st 9 passes and led Virginia (6-1) to 17-7 H lead. North Carolina (5-2) gained 169y on ground, 54y coming on single bruising play as FB William Henderson scored on seemingly-endless 2nd Q smash. It led to Henderson's 2y TD. Cavaliers LB James Farrier made INT RET to 13YL on 3rd play of 3rd Q, to set up FG for 20-7 edge. UVa WR Davis (5/124y, 2 TDs) caught 35y TD in 4th Q.

FLORIDA STATE 17 Clemson 0: Things were getting so bad for ACC teams other than all-triumphant Florida State, now 21-0 in conf games, that Tigers (2-5) fans cheered their favorites afterward because score was so close. Clemson coach Tommy West was having none of it: "I don't believe in moral victories. I believe you win or lose the ball game." Seminoles (5-1) lost 2 TOs, but more than doubled Tigers' O y, 393y to 149y, and FSU's D, led by DE Derrick Alexander and LBs Derrick Brooks and Daryl Bush, was brilliant. Slippery TB Warrick Dunn (17/133y, 2 TDs) scored on 5 and 4y runs as FSU went 70y early in 2nd Q and 66y on its next possession. Florida State QB Danny Kanell (17-32/181y, INT) made several mistakes near Clemson GL and was benched. Also, FSU missed 3 of 4 FG tries as rusty sr K Dan Mowrey missed from 29y, then made 22y FG in 3rd Q, in relief of soph K Scott Bentley, who missed from 32 and 28y.

ALABAMA 21 Mississippi 10: Lightning halted play for 25 mins during 1st H that was led by Mississippi (2-5) 10-0 on FB Dou Innocent's short TD run and K Tim Montz's 40y FG. Down 10-7 and facing 2nd-and-35 on its 36YL early in 4th Q, Alabama (8-0) reaped 1st down via interference PEN on Rebels DB Alundis Brice. When that drive stalled inside Ole Miss 1YL, Bama K Michael Proctor kicked FG to tie it 10-10, but overzealous Brice was called for roughing K Proctor. So, Alabama chose to take pts off board, and QB Jay Barker registered go-ahead TD instead. At 31-1-1, Barker became QB with best winning percentage ever at Bama.

OHIO STATE 48 Purdue 14: Ohio State (6-2) QB Bobby Hoying, grandson of former Cincinnati Reds slugger Wally Post, got considerable time to throw and sparkled with 20-24/304y passing, his 5 TD passes tying John Borton's 1952 school single-game record. WR Joey Galloway was Hoying's prime collaborator with 7/95y receiving that included TDs of 42, 2, and 11y. Hoying retired to bench in 3rd Q with tidy 48-0 lead.

Purdue (4-2-1) earned some measure of joy by setting school long distance pass mark with QB Rick Trefzger's 90y TD to WR Craig Allen. Allen added another TD catch later, but by then most of Columbus crowd was gone on mission of celebration.

Northwestern 20 INDIANA 7: TB Dennis Lundy became career rushing leader to date for Northwestern (3-3-1) with robust 174y performance. With Wildcats trailing 7-3 on 19y TD pass from Hoosiers (5-2) QB John Paci to WR Ajamu Stoner, Lundy, who earlier went 51y to set up K Sam Valenzisi's 1st Q FG, broke away on 35y TD gallop in 2nd Q for 10-7 lead. WR Brian Musso soon gave NW more breathing room with 56y punt TD RET. Indiana lost any comeback chance when it botched 1st-and-goal at 7YL Cats in 4th Q. Paci lost 3y, then holding PEN nullified his TD run, and Hoosiers' opportunity evaporated on his 2 incompletions.

COLORADO 35 Kansas State 21: Kansas State (4-2) opened with rapier-like TD drive from KO as RB J.J. Smith scored from 1y. Colorado (7-0) unleashed RB Rashaan Salaam for 28/202y, 3 TDs. But, K-State jumped on comeback wagon as Smith's 2nd and 3rd TD runs in 3rd Q tied it twice at 14-14 and 21-21. With 10 mins left, Buffs QB Kordell Stewart ran seemingly innocent keeper and broke away for 60y TD. Wildcats QB Chad May (23-40/356y, 2 INTs) missed 4 passes in row from own 15YL in last 2 mins, and Stewart tacked on insurance TD from short range.

TEXAS A&M 7 Rice 0: Texas Aggies (7-0), contemporary bullies of SWC's famous final scene, had to struggle to fend off Rice (3-3) and hand Owls their 1st conf loss of 1994. No. 6 A&M scored 1:59 into game as TB Rodney Thomas (21/136y) took off with screen pass from QB Corey Pullig, got clearing block from WR Chris Sanders, and dashed 60y to score. Rice threatened 4 times in 2nd H. Aggies DB Dennis Allen made INT and stepped in front of Owls WR Ed Howard to kill dangerous EZ play. Rice DE Andy Clifton returned FUM 23y to Texas A&M 43YL with 9:49 remaining, but A&M held. Rice made 1 more try in game's last min: QB Josh LaRocca (4-11/19y, INT) finally had to abandon Wishbone O on 4th down at Aggies 31YL. SS Michael Hendricks raced over to break up long pass, but LaRocca failed to see wide open RB Byron Coston on other side of field. Had Rice scored late TD, would it have tried for 2-pt conv? "Against these guys, a tie made the most sense," said Owls coach Ken Hatfield.

TEXAS TECH 38 Baylor 7: Texas Tech (3-4), which hadn't played in Cotton Bowl since 1939, reinvigorated its post-season chances for Dallas by using off-week to prepare for Baylor (5-3). Although Rice held best cards, 6 teams still retained hope of finishing 2nd behind ineligible Texas A&M with 60 mathematical title possibilities. Red Raiders scored 1st on 34y TD run by TB Byron Hanspard (11/83y). Bears couldn't get FB Bradford Lewis (11/13y) untracked, but soon sprung TB Brandell Jackson on 66y sprint to set up QB Jeff Watson's 2y TD run and 7-7 tie. Baylor D lapsed on 3rd-and-10 at its 44YL early in 2nd Q as Tech QB Zebbie Lethridge (14-34/194y, 2 TDs, INT) scrambled to 1YL, from where he scored to put Raiders ahead for good. Texas Tech kicked 3 FGs in middle Qs, and Lethridge pitched 2 TDs to complete rout.

Utah 45 COLORADO STATE 31: After Utah led 1st H 9-7, game evolved into old-style WAC shootout between surprising unbeatens. It turned on ability of Utah (7-0) to block 3 kicks, return 2 INTs for scores. Utes went up 16-7 on QB Mike McCoy's sneak, but Colorado State (6-1) rallied ahead at 17-16 on QB Anthoney Hill's TD pass and 28y FG by K David Napier. Utah surged back to 31-17, fooling Rams with overloaded formation for 2-pt pass. Rams FB Van Ward's 2 TDs tied it 31-31 early in 4th Q. Utah went ahead on McCoy's 8y pass to WR Curtis Marsh. Rams drove to Utes 10YL in final min, but DB Harold Lusk took INT 100y to clinch it for Utah.

OREGON 31 Washington 20: Wild finish saw Washington (5-2) rally to take 20-17 lead with 7:44 left on FB Richard Thomas' 10y TD run. But, unsinkable Ducks (5-3) created upset on 98y drive as FB Dwayne Jones burst up middle from 12YL with 2:40 to go. Huskies too seemed comeback-bound as QB Damon Huard directed sortie to Oregon 8YL in last min. But, Huard fired cross-field when Ducks frosh DB Kenny Wheaton stepped in front of WR Dave Janoski and went 97y to TD, longest RET to that point inDucks history. Outgained 386y to 202y, Ducks got 1st series win since 1988.

USA Today Coaches Poll October 24

1	Penn State (28)	1507	14	Ohio State	630
2	Nebraska (25)	1492	15	Texas	626
3	Colorado (9)	1459	16	Virginia	616
4	Miami (Fla.)	1318	17	Brigham Young	584
5	Alabama	1300	18	Colorado State	522
6	Florida	1245	19	Washington State	467
7	Florida State	1166	20	North Carolina	407
8	Arizona	1093	21	Kansas State	383
9	Michigan	979	22	North Carolina State	363
10	Virginia Tech	928	23	Southern California	159
11	Utah	879	24	Oregon	91
12	Syracuse	806	25	Oklahoma	77
13	Duke	717			

October 29, 1994

MIAMI 24 Virginia Tech 3: K Ryan Williams launched scoring for optimistic Virginia Tech (7-2) with 38y FG. But, Miami (6-1) D took over in 2nd Q, taking possession at Hokies 47YL after forcing punt and 13YL on FUM REC as Hurricanes got 17 quick pts before H. Miami forced 3 TOs, made 6 sacks, and held Hokies to -14y rushing. Intense LB Ray Lewis made 17 tackles, broke up 4 passes, and grabbed INT that led to 4th Q TD.

PENN STATE 63 Ohio State 14: Penn State (7-0) pasted Ohio State (6-3) with highest pt total Buckeyes had allowed since 1902. "I think we made a statement today," said QB Kerry Collins (19-23/265y, 2 TDs). "I'd be miffed if we weren't no. 1." Still, Lions slipped to no. 2 behind Nebraska. Penn State led 35-0 at H, and its 1st team O left at 49-7 in 3rd Q. By then, RB Ki-Jana Carter had rushed for 4 TDs on 19/137y. FUM REC at outset of 2nd H gave Ohio State its single bright spot: QB Bobby Hoying quickly threw TD pass.

Wisconsin 31 MICHIGAN 19: Sinking Badgers (4-3-1) dug deep for pride-filled effort that upset Michigan (5-3) and briefly ended Wisconsin's internal bickering. Return of TB Brett Moss (26/106y, TD) boosted Wisconsin, and Badgers D came up with 3 INTs and 3 sacks. WR Seth Smith had 100y KO RET that provided Wolverines with brief 7-3 lead. Afterward, euphoric Badgers made odd claim that win, which placed them 6th in Big 10, might have been more important than last January's Rose Bowl.

NEBRASKA 24 Colorado 7: So dominant was Nebraska (9-0) that its romp over Colorado (7-1) vaulted Cornhuskers past Penn State to no. 1 in AP poll. QB Brook Berringer, underestimated stand-in for injured QB Tommy Frazier, was efficient 12-17/142y, TD in air while running raft of new plays that puzzled Buffs. Berringer consistently found his TEs Eric Alford (30y TD catch) and Mark Gilman for combined 9/124y. Buffaloes' 1st 3 possessions were stuck in their own end of field and lasted total of 3:24. Colorado RB Rashaan Salaam was his team's only bright spot with 22/134y rushing and 3rd Q TD that came after it already stood 24-0 for Nebraska.

Texas A&M 21 Southern Methodist 21 (San Antonio): Season's only blemish cost on-probation Texas A&M (7-0-1) its only shot at top poll ranking. Dedicated SMU (1-7-1) jumped to 14-0 H lead. FUM REC at Texas A&M 29YL midway in 4th Q gave SMU QB Ramon Flanigan chance for his 2nd TD and 21-13 lead. Aggies TB Rodney Thomas (134y) scored 3 TDs in 2nd H, last of 3y came with 6:18 to play, and QB Corey Pullig added 2-pt pass to tie it. Ponies K Ben Crosland missed 43y FG in last 30 secs.

Arizona State 36 BRIGHAM YOUNG 15: Funny thing happened to Arizona State (3-5) on way to dreary 3-8 season in Pac-10 cellar. Coach Bruce Snyder identified BYU (7-2) secondary as its weak spot, and QB Jake Plummer threw for career-high to-date 327y and 3 TDs on 15-25. ASU surprisingly led 23-0 at H, but Cougars excited Homecoming crowd with 70y TD early in 3rd Q: QB John Walsh tossed 10y pass to TE Chad Lewis, who made impromptu pitch to streaking RB Jamal Willis. But, Plummer came right back with TD passes to TB Terry Battle for 44y and WR Keith Poole for 83y.

OREGON 10 Arizona 9: Surprising Ducks (6-3) matched their "Gang Green" D with Arizona's "Desert Swarm," emerging with Pac-10 1st place tie and inside track to their 1st Rose Bowl in 37 years. Wildcats (6-2) had led 9-0 on 3 FGs by K Steve McLaughlin, but earned only pair of 1st downs in 2nd H. Game's only TD came with 12:17 left, giving Oregon its eventual 10-9 margin. QB Danny O'Neil (15-28/161y, TD) twice hit 3rd down passes on 12-play, 53y drive, but big break came on 4th down pass interference call against Wildcats DB Mike Scurlock that moved Ducks to 16YL. O'Neil followed with winning TD pass to TE Josh Wilcox.

USA Today Coaches Poll October 31

1	Penn State (32)	1520	14	Washington State	745
2	Nebraska (30)	1518	15	Kansas State	693
3	Miami (Fla.)	1373	16	Virginia Tech	671
4	Alabama	1358	17	Oregon	520
5	Florida	1313	18	Michigan	492
6	Florida State	1251	19	Duke	388
7	Colorado	1189	20	Southern California	374
8	Utah	1074	21	Brigham Young	208
9	Syracuse	1014	22	Mississippi State	172
10	Virginia	896	23	Illinois	166
11	Colorado State	777	24	Ohio State	154
12	North Carolina	751	25	Notre Dame	147
13	Arizona	748			

November 5, 1994

Miami 27 SYRACUSE 6: Persistent LB Dan Conley, back from his 10th knee operation, made INT and deflected pass that created INT to spark Syracuse (6-2) in 1st H. Orange utilized option runs for pivotal 105y in 1st H, but their dominance realized measly 6-0 lead. Hurricanes (7-1) cranked up their ground game, scoring on 1st 3 series of 2nd H. RB James Stewart (20/100y) tallied on runs of 3 and 27y, while rugged Miami DL of Es Kenard Lang and Kenny Holmes and Ts Warren Sapp and Pat Riley never again allowed Orangemen to escape their own end.

DUKE 28 Virginia 25: Recent domination by Virginia (6-2) over Duke (232-59 scoring differential in last 5 games) seemed to bloom again as Cavs jumped to 17-7 2nd Q lead. UVa WR Tyrone Davis caught 65 and 6y TDs from QB Mike Groh. But, Blue Devils (8-1) got late 2nd Q TD from TB Robert Baldwin (28/67y) to narrow H score to 17-14. Duke ruled 3rd Q as QB Spence Fischer (18-35/234y, TD) threw and ran for TDs. Virginia failed to convert 1st-and-goal at 5YL after DL Mike Frederick's REC of batted Devils' lateral. But, Cavaliers were able to pull within 28-25 as QB Symmion Willis came off bench to pitch 69y TD bomb to WR Pete Allen.

Alabama 35 LOUISIANA STATE 17: Alabama (9-0) joined Michigan and Notre Dame as only schools in college history to date with 700 victories. Crimson Tide D provided lead that would never be relinquished when LSU (2-6) O-lineman accidently kneed ball from TB Robert Toomer on Tigers' 1st scrimmage play. Ball popped right to Bama DB Sam Shade who raced to 7-0 lead. Tide blocked 2 punts, DB Tommy Johnson's in 2nd Q allowed WR Roman Colburn to charge 33y to 14-3 lead. Last-min TD catch by LSU WR Brett Bech became 1st TD allowed in 4th Q by Alabama all season.

Penn State 35 INDIANA 29: Entering its trip to Bloomington as no. 1 in coaches' poll, Penn State (8-0) all but wrapped up game at 35-14 with 6 mins to play, but 2 closing TDs followed by 2-pt conv pass by Hoosiers (5-4) gave appearance of tight contest. Indeed, Hoosier fans hooted scornful "Over-rated!" at Nittany Lions near contest's end, and by Sunday, Penn State had fallen to no. 2 in both polls. Penn State had driven 96y to opening TD in 1st Q: 7y scoring catch by TE Kyle Brady. Lions closed their effort in 4th Q with 80y TD run by TB Ki-Jana Carter (20/192y). In between, Lions QB Kerry Collins (20-32/213y, 2 TDs, 2 INTs) hit his 2nd TD pass, but his 2 INTs made this his worst game of season. Coming off bench in 2nd Q, sub QB Chris Dittoe (21-35/279y, 4 TDs) had enlivened Indiana's attack and produced late-game 15 pts on his 2 TD

passes. Indiana's last TD came on 40y "Hail Mary" catch by WR Dorian Wilkerson with no time on clock. Interestingly, Hoosiers' late surge was intermingled with 90y punt RET and 89y FUM RET by Nittany Lions that would have launched rout, but both scores were nullified by PENs. Neutral observer Jason Whitlock of *Kansas City Star* wrote that he arrived "positive the high-scoring Lions were the best team in the country." In Sunday's column, Whitlock wrote, "Now I'm not so sure," but maintained he'd still vote Lions as no.1.

NEBRASKA 45 Kansas 17: No. 1 in AP Poll but no. 2 on *USA Today* coaches' ballot, Nebraska (10-0) opened game with sack and 3-and-out to set up scores on its next 6 possessions. Huskers QB Brook Berringer (13-18/267y, 2 TDs) threw for career-high y, including 51 and 64y scores. Jayhawks QB Asheiki Preston (7-18/107y, 2 INTs) missed wide open TE Brent Willeford and threw 1st of his 2 early INTs on Kansas' opening drive. Nebraska led 38-10 at H as IB Lawrence Phillips (21/153y, 2 TDs) scored his on 4y run and FB Cory Schlesinger burst 40y to score. TB June Henley (16/86y, TD) tallied on 6y run in 2nd Q that gave Kansas (5-4) some mild, but brief respectability.

Texas A&M 34 TEXAS 10: Coming off surprise tie with SMU, seemingly reluctant Aggies (7-0-1) broke out of their O slump by beating Texas (5-4) for 4th year in row. Longhorns' loss all but eliminated them from wide-open Cotton Bowl race. Texas A&M TBs Rodney Thomas and Leeland McElroy combined for 3 TDs, but crippling score against Texas came from 271-lb DL Brandon Mitchell, who rambled 48y with FUM REC for 2nd Q TD. Texas was limited to 51y rushing, but got 265y in air from QBs Shea Morenz and James Brown.

COLORADO STATE 35 Wyoming 24: Thanks to New Mexico's 23-21 upset of Utah, Colorado State (8-1) had chance to control own WAC destiny. Teams traded run-oriented 1st Q TD drives for 7-7 tie. Leading 10-7 at H, Cowboys (4-6) roared out of locker room with TDs on their 1st 2 series of 2nd Q as WR Marcus Harris' 13y flanker screen TD catch made it 24-7. Rams were halted on next possession, but turned their fortune in right direction on 35y fake-punt pass from soph P Matt McDougal to DB Andre Strode. Rams tallied 4 unanswered TDs, and fans happily cascaded onto field at end.

Southern California 23 WASHINGTON STATE 10: Always at his best against Cougars, USC QB Rob Johnson shook off ankle woes to throw 20-31/327y, 3 TDs. Aerial partner, WR Keyshawn Johnson (8/145y), caught 3 scores as Trojans (6-2) gained 395y on touted Cougars (6-3) D. Interestingly, it was Trojans D that matched Washington State's normal D numbers: 10 pts and 50y rushing. "Each snowball got us more fired up," said DL Matt Keneley of pre-game pelting by Martin Stadium fans.

USA Today Coaches Poll November 7

1	Nebraska (42)	1530	14	Utah	707
2	Penn State (20)	1503	15	Syracuse	685
3	Miami (Fla.)	1375	16	Southern California	661
4	Alabama	1365	17	Michigan	585
5	Florida	1322	18	Virginia	468
6	Florida State	1269	19	Brigham Young	439
7	Colorado	1183	20	Mississippi State	382
8	Arizona	982	21	Ohio State	322
9	Kansas State	897	22	Washington State	295
10	Colorado State	810	23	North Carolina	231
11	Oregon	801	24	Boston College	197
12	Virginia Tech	784	25	Illinois	188
13	Duke	753			

November 12, 1994

BOSTON COLLEGE 31 Syracuse 0: Fading Orangemen (6-3) went 2nd week in row without scoring TD. Boston College (6-2-1) got 3 TD passes in 2nd Q from QB Mark Hartsell and RB David Green's 70y TD run in 3rd Q. Ferocious Eagles D had 6 sacks and held Syracuse runners to 29y total gain. BC had set tone at game's very beginning by clawing 77y on 17 plays to K David Gordon's 20y FG.

VIRGINIA TECH 41 Rutgers 34: Virginia Tech (8-2) earned bowl spot by building big lead over Rutgers (5-4-1) as accurate QB Maurice DeShazo (12-15/186y, 2 TDs) set school mark with his 44th career TD pass in 1st Q: 44y to WR Bryan Still (3/89y, 2 TDs). DeShazo added another TD pass to Still and ran 4y to wrap up runoff of 20 straight pts, thus building 41-13 edge heading into 4th Q. Scarlet Knights QB Ray Lucas (26-44/374y, 4 TDs, INT) got hot early in 4th Q. Lucas hit frosh WR Chris Hutton with 15y TD pass with 13:41 left. Then, after FUM REC, Rutgers TB Terrell Willis scored with 9:11 to go, and Lucas found school career-leading TE y-maker, Marco Battaglia (6/110y), with 1y TD with 1:54 on clock. Hokies recovered Knights' on-side KO attempt and extinguished clock.

NORTH CAROLINA STATE 24 Duke 23: Devils' magical season lasted until H as Duke (8-2) led 20-7 thanks to 3 TOs suffered by Wolfpack QB Terry Harvey (16-30/262y, 2TD, INT). Devils LB John Zuanich recovered his 4th FUM of year, sprinting 21y to TD. After K Tom Cochran's 3rd FG gave Duke 23-7 lead in 3rd Q, NC State (7-2) roared back as Harvey redeemed himself by bombing to WR Adrian Hill for 82y gain late in 3rd Q. Harvey suddenly found consistency, flipping to Hill for TD, and after FG, to WR Mike Guffie for winning TD with 6 mins to go.

FLORIDA STATE 23 Notre Dame 16 (Orlando): Seeking revenge for physical beating it took in 1993, Florida State (8-1) powered Notre Dame (5-4) with 56/332y rushing. Oft-criticized Seminoles K Dan Mowrey made 3 FGs in 1st H, but fast-striking DB Bobby Taylor kept ND within 9-7 with 57y FUM RET for 2nd Q TD. When Irish QB Ron Powlus (9-22/83y, INT) passed to WR Derrick Mayes for 4th Q TD, game was tied at 16-16. ND K Scott Cengia missed go-ahead x-pt with 5:17 to go. Deflated ND allowed 49y catch by WR Kez McCorvey to poise RB Warrick Dunn for winning 5y TD run.

FLORIDA 48 South Carolina 17: Gators (8-1) launched their speed merchants in time to clinch SEC East title and overcome stubborn South Carolina (5-5), which enjoyed 10-7 lead as late as 5 mins into 2nd Q. Gamecocks slowed flashy Florida attack in early going with 7-DB setup and used pass interference PEN to keep alive opening TD drive to TB Stanley Pritchard's 12y scoring run. Gators QB Danny Wuerffel (20-32/357y, 4 TDs) quickly adjusted in 2nd Q, rifling his 2nd and 3rd TD passes, both to WR Jack Jackson (6/80y, 2 TDs) for 21-10 H edge. After Florida FG opened 3rd Q, Gators blocked Carolina punt, and special teamer Mike Harris trotted 40y to score for 31-10 lead. Gamecocks QB Steve Taneyhill hit 11-19, including 4th Q TD, but terrific Gators front-4 prevented him from going long and he managed only 87y passing.

AUBURN 23 Georgia 23: So stunning was effort by Georgia (5-4-1) that Sunday's *Atlanta Journal-Constitution* front page headline read: "Georgia 'Wins' 23-23." Stalemate halted nation's longest win streak at 20 as Tigers K Matt Hawkins' 44y FG try sailed wide right with 8 secs to go. Auburn (9-0-1) had built 23-9 lead on QB Patrick Nix's 1y TD run late in 2nd Q and TB Stephen Davis' 41y TD run early in 3rd Q. After INT by DB Robert Edwards saved UGa at its 10YL, WR Jeff Thomas made diving 3rd down catch. QB Eric Zeier (14-17/261y, 2 TDs, INT) quickly found WR Juan Daniels open for 79y TD and later followed with tying 4y TD pass to WR Brice Hunter early in 4th Q.

Alabama 29 MISSISSIPPI STATE 25: Ornery Bulldogs (7-3) used their huge O-line to batter Alabama (10-0) for 167y rushing in 1st H, and when dangerous WR Eric Moulds caught his 2nd TD pass in 3rd Q, Mississippi State enjoyed 25-15 lead that lasted as late as mid-4th Q. But, persistent Crimson Tide QB Jay Barker (26-35/325y, 3 TDs, INT) passed 7-11/120y on drives of 65 and 66y as Bama rallied to clinch SEC West title.

Penn State 35 ILLINOIS 31: In Pennsylvania, it will forever be known as "The Drive," indomitable 96y march by magnificent O of Nittany Lions (9-0) through nation's 4th-ranked D of Illinois (6-4). Late TD completed biggest comeback in any game of Joe Paterno's long coaching tenure in State College. *Chicago Tribune* had predicted this as tough spot for Penn State 3 weeks earlier. Right on cue, Illini LB Simeon Rice recovered FUM and DB Tyrone Washington made INT as home team jumped to 21-0 lead in 1st Q with QB Johnny Johnson (17-34/199y, 2 TDs, INT) throwing 2 scoring passes to exploit Lions' weak pass D. Lions QB Kerry Collins (24-38/300y, TD, INT) tossed 38y TD pass to WR Freddie Scott to pull within 21-14 in 2nd Q. Still trailing 31-21 midway in 4th Q, Penn State went 54y to FB Brian Milne's 2nd TD run. After Illinois P Brett Larsen's 75y punt, Lions took over on their own 4YL with 6:07 to go. Collins hit 7-7/59y on remarkable 14-play drive that clinched Big 10 title and trip to Rose Bowl. Milne capped it with 2y TD run behind blocks of G Jeff Hartings and FB Jason Sload with 57 secs left.

Kansas State 21 MISSOURI 18: When Mizzou Tigers (3-7) couldn't negotiate 3y for TD in final 46 secs, they knew they had failed for 11th straight year to post winning record. No. 11 Kansas State (7-2) frosh CB Chris Canty smacked Missouri QB Jeff Handy's 4th down pass away from WR Brian Sallee to preserve victory. Despite nearly equaling its 1st H O output (118y) with PEN y (115y), Missouri maintained 7-7 H deadlock, thanks to RB Brock Olivo (27/151y) squirting 21y to score after sub QB Brandon Corso briefly ignited Tigers with 39y completion to WR Lou Shepherd. TD pass by QB Chad May (8-20/163y, 2 TDs, INT) gave Wildcats 14-10 lead inside last 5 mins of 3rd Q. TB J.J. Smith (34/138y, TD) padded K-State lead with 5y TD on drive kept alive by personal foul PEN on Tigers. Handy, back in when Corso got hurt, soon hit 4-5 passes to K-State 18YL. Handy's flat pass and willed his way into EZ for TD, followed by Handy's 2-pt pass. K-State's lead now was down to 21-18. After Wildcats were stopped with 3:40 to play, Missouri took 7 plays to go inside Cats' 10YL, and team fully supported coach Larry Smith's disdain for tying FG. But Tigers failed from 3YL when Cats' ace Canty made his clutch EZ knockdown.

Baylor 19 RICE 14: Although 5 SWC teams remained in contention for Cotton Bowl, Baylor (7-3) and Texas Tech appeared to be sitting pretty. Bears held 13-0 lead when K Jarvis Van Dyke added his 2nd FG, from 35y, in 3rd Q. Rice (4-5) K Matt Huelsman hadn't fared so well: he missed 3 FG tries in swirling winds of 1st H. Owls struck back on unusually accurate arm of QB Josh LaRocca (11-12/127y, 2 TDs, INT). WR Ed Howard beat single coverage for 39y TD catch to pull Rice to within 13-7 in 3rd Q. In 4th Q, LaRocca hit Howard again for 23y TD and 14-13 edge, but when Rice regained possession, LaRocca was blind-sided by Bears LB Glenn Coy and FUM REC was made by Baylor DE Bryan Tanner at Owls 28YL. FB Bradford Lewis (13/56y, TD) burst up middle for Baylor's winning TD.

AIR FORCE 40 Utah 33: Soaring Air Force (7-3) won 7th straight in upset that seriously damaged WAC title hopes of no. 12 Utah (8-2). Utes led 17-0 in 2nd Q as QB Mike McCoy (25-45/238y, 3 TDs, 3 INTs) threw for 2 early TDs. Falcons soph QB Beau Morgan, making his 1st start, scored running TD and threw to HB Jake Campbell for 2 scores. Falcons took lead for good at 34-31 in 4th Q when K Randy Roberts hit 2 FGs into stiff wind.

SOUTHERN CALIFORNIA 45 Arizona 28: Dandy D reputation of Arizona (7-3) was built on low y per game avg. But, USC (7-2) ripped Arizona D for 550y and bruised Wildcats' self-esteem. Playing barely into 4th Q due to ankle sprain, Trojans QB Rob Johnson passed 25-35/390y, 3 TDs. His counterpart, Wildcats QB Danny White, threw for 370y, 3 TDs, and WR Richard Dice (9/171y) made sparkling TD catches that gave Arizona leads of 14-7 and 21-14. White's 3rd TD pass created 28-21 edge in 3rd Q, but Troy was able to tie it 28-28. Johnson scrambled to put USC ahead for good at 35-28, and Trojans made stirring GLS that prompted clinching 98y TD drive, finished by backup QB Brad Otton.

USA Today Coaches Poll November 14

1	Nebraska (41)	1525	14	Virginia	679
2	Penn State (21)	1504	15	Brigham Young	589
3	Alabama	1386	16	Ohio State	554
4	Miami (Fla.)	1339	17	Boston College	541
5	Florida	1309	18	Arizona	508
6	Florida State	1254	19	Duke	404
7	Colorado	1209	20	Utah	368
8	Kansas State	985	21	North Carolina	350
9	Oregon	983	22	North Carolina State	273
10	Colorado State	916	23	Mississippi State	250
11	Virginia Tech	896	24	Syracuse	200
12	Southern California	882	25	Baylor	125
13	Michigan	734			

November 19, 1994

Virginia 42 VIRGINIA TECH 23: Sloppy Virginia Tech (8-3) suffered 8 TOs, most lost in any game by Hokies since 1958, and Virginia (8-2) doused its reputation for major swoons in November. TB Kevin Brooks led Cavaliers' 249y ground assault with 23/108y, TD, and key score came in 2nd Q as FB Charles Way blasted over to give Cavs lead for good at 19-13. Virginia Tech QB Maurice DeShazo passed 22-34/235y, 2 TDs, 5 INTs.

North Carolina 41 DUKE 40: Blue Devils (8-3) survived 87y KO TD RET and 48y TD reception by Tar Heels WR Marcus Wall to maintain 24-17 H lead. Trailing 38-34 with 2:47 left, North Carolina (8-3) managed 71y miracle TD pass by sub QB Mike Thomas. Duke QB Spence Fischer (33-57/395y, 4 TDs, INT) hit favorite targets WR Jon Jensen (14/174y, TD) and TE Bill Khayat (8/104y, TD) all day, but suffered tipped pass picked off by DB Fuzzy Lee with 1:10 to play. It ended potential winning drive. North Carolina (8-3) still had to relinquish punt play safety and hold breath through wide 60y FG try by Devils K Tom Cochran on game's last play.

ALABAMA 21 Auburn 14: QB Jay Barker's pair of TD passes helped Alabama (11-0) to 21-0 H lead. When Tide reached 4th-and-1 at Tigers 16YL with 12:39 to play it led 21-7, but coach Gene Stallings turned down possible clinching FG. Bama made its 1st down, but Barker threw INT in EZ. Auburn (9-1-1) cut it to 21-14 on 1y run by QB Frank Nix (23-42/247y, INT). Faced with no timeouts, 1:57 left, and 99y for TD, Nix drove Tigers into Bama territory. On 4th-and-3, Nix found WR Frankie Sanders across middle, but Sanders was stopped inches from 1st down by DB Sam Shade's tackle, so Crimson Tide could breathe easier.

OHIO STATE 22 Michigan 6: Ohio State (9-3) finally beat Michigan (7-4) for coach John Cooper, who had been 0-5-1 since succeeding Earle Bruce in 1988. Michigan shot itself in foot twice in 2nd H when QB Todd Collins (13-22/160y, INT) overthrew open receivers in EZ. Trailing 12-6, Wolverines drove to 15YL at end of 3rd Q, but were forced into FG try when Collins had 1 of his misses. DB Marlon Kerner blocked that FG attempt, and Ohio soon banked K Josh Jackson's 36y FG for 15-6 lead. Just after Wolverines accepted KO, Ohio State DL Luke Fickell tipped Collins' pass and made lunging INT at Michigan 16YL. Buckeyes TB Eddie George (27/71y, TD) soon scored. Michigan failed to score TD for 1st time since 3-3 tie vs. Illinois in 1985.

Kansas 31 MISSOURI 14: Coach Larry Smith finished his 1st Missouri (3-8) season without home win: "We gave these people who showed up week-in and week-out... nothing!" he growled. He berated his team afterward. Kansas (6-5) romped for 365y rushing, including TB L.T. Levine's 25/221y, 2 TDs. Tigers, however, actually had led 14-7 for about 5 mins in middle of 1st Q as QB Jeff Handy (12-22/141y, TD) hit WR Brian Sallee (6/89y) with 28y TD on their 1st series. Tigers OLB Chris Singletary made INT on Jayhawks' next possession at KU 41YL, and Missouri RB Brock Olivo (20/78y) scored from 1y out 6 plays later. Levine tallied on 5y TD run, so Kansas knotted it 14-14 with 2:18 left in 1st Q. Jayhawks Gs Hessley Hempstead and John Jones led tremendous O-line push rest of game as Kansas wrapped it up with K Jeff McCord's 24y go-ahead FG late in 3rd Q, and went on to game's last 17 pts, including Levine's 26y TD run in 4th Q.

COLORADO 41 Iowa State 20: Iowa State (0-10-1) nearly had coach Jim Walden dreaming of wonderful going-away present as Cyclones drew within 20-13 in 3rd Q. Iowa State highlight came on frosh RB Troy Davis' 99y school-record longest KO RET. But, Buffaloes QB Kordell Stewart, who would set Big 8 career total O mark, soon raced 23y to TD. Trumping that was Buffs TB Rashaan Salaam, who ran wide for 67y TD, putting him over 2,000y rushing mark to become 4th such runner to that point in history. Salaam finished season with 2,055y rushing and soon won Heisman Trophy. Post-game shocker came from Colorado (10-1) coach Bill McCartney who announced his resignation: "I've been here 13 years; it's time."

TEXAS A&M 34 Texas Christian 17: If probation-scarred Aggies (10-0-1) couldn't go to Cotton Bowl, neither would TCU (6-4). Texas A&M QB Corey Pullig threw 25y TD pass to WR Chris Sanders for 24-10 lead, and Aggies D made 2 drive-stopping plays in 3rd Q. Frogs TB Andre Davis rushed 33/119y, TD. Aggies sr players finished careers with best-ever 4-year SWC record of 29-0-1. Texas Tech (6-4), never Cotton Bowl participant in its 35 years in SWC, became frontrunner for Dallas invitation with its 34-0 win over Houston.

Colorado State 44 FRESNO STATE 42: Questionable because of bad ankle, Colorado State (10-1) FB E.J. Watson ran for TDs of 2, 24, and 22y as Rams overcame 21-pt deficit to earn their 1st WAC crown since entering conf in 1968. Rams went ahead for 1st time late in 3rd Q at 31-27 as DB Ray Jackson blocked punt and ran 30y to score. Fresno State (4-7-1) suffered its 1st losing slate in 13 years, but twice cut margin to 2 pts in 4th Q on TDs by TB Reggie Brown and WR Michael Ross.

Oregon 17 OREGON STATE 13: USC needed upset by Beavers (4-7) for shot at Rose Bowl, and when Oregon (9-3) came from behind for its 8th win in last 9 trips to Corvallis, disappointed Trojans fell to UCLA 31-19. Oregon State WR Chris Cross recovered blocked punt for TD in 2nd Q, so Beavers trailed only 10-6 at H. Oregon State QB Don Shanklin sneaked over with 6:01 to go in 3rd Q to provide 13-10 lead. Ducks WR Cristin McLemore came back from X-ray infirmary to catch 31, 4, and 21y passes on winning 70y drive late in 4th Q as decisive score came on QB Danny O'Neil's 19y screen pass to TB Dino Philyaw who scored behind key blocks from TE Josh Wilcox, C Mark Gregg, and G Eric Reid. Happy Oregon, losers of 2 of opening 3 games of 1994, was off to its 1st Rose Bowl since January 1958.

USA Today Coaches Poll November 21

1	Nebraska (39)	1522	14	North Carolina	640
2	Penn State (22)	1504	15	Arizona	607
3	Alabama	1421	16	Virginia Tech	563
4	Florida	1334	17	Southern California	462
5	Miami (Fla.)	1330	18	Mississippi State	386
6	Florida State	1254	19	Brigham Young	376
7	Colorado	1206	20	Syracuse	364
8	Kansas State	1051	21	Michigan	362
9	Oregon	1032	22	Duke	286
10	Colorado State	916	23	Baylor	218
11	Virginia	924	24	Washington State	212
12	Ohio State	856	25	Boston College	185
13	Utah	710			

November 24-26, 1994

(Th'g) WEST VIRGINIA 13 Syracuse 0: Left for dead in September at 1-4, West Virginia (7-5) closed with 4 straight triumphs, including wins over ranked foes Boston College by 21-20 and this shutout of fading no. 22 Syracuse (7-4). Mountaineers gained 230y rushing led by TB Jimmy Gary (19/119y) and FB Kantroy Barber (17/70y, TD), who scored on 2nd Q TD run. Orange run attack was stopped at 32/51y as TB Kirby Dar Dar earned only 11/24y. Despite early 6-game win streak, Syracuse dropped its 3rd in last 4 games; scoring only 6 pts in those defeats.

(Fri) North Carolina State 30 VIRGINIA 27: Set to clinch 2nd place in ACC, Virginia (8-3) stumbled in 2nd H. North Carolina State (8-3) executed 3 long TDs: 62 and 69y catches by WR Adrian Hill and RB Tremayne Stephens' 84y blitz-burning draw run in 4th Q for 30-25 lead. On 2-pt try after Stephens' TD, Cavs DB Joe Crocker returned INT for 2 pts. Despite 4 TOs, Virginia was positioned for potential tying FG with 3:13 left. Coach George Welsh chose to run on 4th-and-1 at Wolfpack 19YL, and DB Duan Everett and DL Eric Counts stopped powerful Virginia FB Charles Way for no gain.

(Fri) Nebraska 13 OKLAHOMA 3: Less than overwhelming win still sent Nebraska (12-0) to Orange Bowl as no. 1 in both polls. Unemotional Huskers gained 136y on ground, far below their 358.5y avg. Clincher came when QB Brook Berringer finally scored game's only TD early in 4th Q. His 1y sneak expanded lead to 13-3. Time and again, Nebraska D came through: limiting Sooners (6-5) to 15y in 1st Q, stopping 64y 2nd Q drive on DB Barron Miles' FG block, and preventing any 1st downs in 4th Q.

(Fri) TEXAS CHRISTIAN 24 Texas Tech 17: With Baylor falling by Cotton Bowl wayside due to its 63-35 loss to Texas on Thursday, Texas Tech (6-5) inherited Dallas bid despite this upset loss to TCU (7-4). Red Raiders had built 14-10 and 17-16 leads in 2nd H, but TCU TB Andre Davis (23/107y), SWC rushing champion, ran for 63y of winning 69y drive that ended with 3:52 left. Davis sealed it with 9y TD dash and 2-pt blast. Frogs QB Max Knake threw 89 and 62y TD passes to WR Jimmy Oliver (7/school-mark 206y). Both schools were headed to unprecedented 5-way conf title tie behind undefeated but ineligible Texas A&M.

(Fri) ARIZONA 28 Arizona State 27: After TB Ontiwaun Carter, new Arizona (8-3) career rushing leader, was carted from field with neck sprain late in 3rd Q, Wildcats came alive for pair of 4th Q TDs to overturn 27-15 deficit. TE Lamar Harris grabbed 4 TD toss in back of EZ with 3:54 left to win it. Arizona State (3-8), QB Jake Plummer (12-25/180y, TD) scrambled for 2y TD and hit WR Keith Poole with 41y TD. Thanks to blocked punt TD, ASU led 20-9 late in 2nd Q, but at game's end, Devils K John Baker (2 FGs) was slightly wide right with 47y try.

MIAMI 23 Boston College 7: Eagles (6-4-1) opened game with impressive drive to QB Mark Hartsell's 6y pass to A-A TE Pete Mitchell. BC led 7-3 at H. Eagles D sacked Miami (10-1) QB Frank Costa (22-37/251y, 2 TDs) 6 times, but it was swirling Hurricanes D (nation's best in total and scoring D) that took command in 2nd H. TOs set up 2 TD passes by Costa: Miami A-A DT Warren Sapp deflected pass to DE Kenard Lang for INT at BC 47YL and LB Corwin Francis got FUM REC at own 33YL to stop BC threat.

FLORIDA STATE 31 Florida 31: Florida (9-1-1) cruised to 31-3 lead on 3 TD passes and TD run by QB Danny Wuerffel (21-36/304y, 2 INTs), but dramatic 4th Q completely turned around result. Clock read less than 13 min to play, but "we snatched a tie from the jaws of defeat," said Seminoles (9-1-1) coach Bobby Bowden. Gators dropped man-to-man pass D in favor of soft zone, and FSU QB Danny Kanell launched 4-WR O. Kanell (40-53/421y, TD, INT) had dazzling 4th Q: 18-22/232y, TD, amid scoring drives of 84, 60, 73, and 60y. After DB James Colzie made diving INT at own 40YL, Seminoles moved to within 31-30 on RB Rock Preston's 4y TD run with 1:45 to go. Bowden, oft-times great gambler, opted for K Dan Mowrey's tying kick. Bowden, still hoping for another possession, reasoned that his team had rallied from so far behind that he did not want to risk failed 2-pt play.

Rice 31 HOUSTON 13: Owls (5-6) may not have owned winning mark or be headed to bowl game, but Rice captured unprecedented 5-way share of Southwest Conf championship by virtue of their victory over Houston (1-10). With run-away 1st place Texas A&M ineligible, Baylor, Texas, TCU, and Texas Tech shared 4-3 league marks

with Rice, which had owned no conf titles since 1957. Texas Tech headed to Cotton Bowl, however, based on tie-breaker system. Rice frosh QB Chad Nelson (2-7/37y, TD, INT, and 14/109y rushing) barely lifted his arm all game but 1 of his completions went to WR Jeff Venghaus for 23y TD in 3rd Q that extended Owls' lead to 21-7 over their cross-city rivals. Nelson also had scored on 10y run that provided 14-7 H edge. Cougars QB Chuck Clements (20-34/188y, INT) made his 1st start since breaking his wrist in September and threw 4th Q TD pass. Houston WR Daniel Adams nabbed 5/87y and followed T Billy Milner's downfield blocking for 57y gain to set up Clements' TD pass.

SOUTHERN CALIFORNIA 17 Notre Dame 17: In biting night wind more typical of South Bend, 90,217 in L.A. Coliseum watched 11-game Irish (6-4-1) winning streak vs. USC (7-3-1) end on surprising 4th Q score by Troy. Tall LB Israel Ifeanyi blocked 37y FG try by ND K Stefan Schroffner with 6:43 left in game, and DB Sammy Knight raced 56y with loose ball to Notre Dame 16YL. In 4 runs, USC TB Shawn Walters crammed ball into EZ, and K Cole Ford's kick earned 17-17 deadlock with 4:53 to play. RB Lee Becton, 1 of Irish stars back off injury list, rushed 26/156y and made key gains to set up FG and 2 TDs authored by QB Ron Powlus.

USA Today Coaches Poll November 28

1	Nebraska (44)	1531	14	North Carolina	676
2	Penn State (18)	1502	15	Virginia Tech	630
3	Alabama	1424	16	Virginia	560
4	Miami (Fla.)	1351	17	Mississippi State	506
5	Colorado	1277	18	Brigham Young	460
6	Florida	1242	19	Michigan	433
7	Florida State	1211	20	Duke	388
8	Kansas State	1077	21	North Carolina State	364
9	Oregon	1028	22	Southern California	322
10	Colorado State	987	23	Washington State	287
11	Ohio State	910	24	Tennessee	103
12	Utah	780	25	Boston College	72
13	Arizona	715			

December 3, 1994

Army 22 Navy 20 (Philadelphia): For 3rd straight heart-breaking year, Navy (3-8) fell to Army (4-7) on late made-or-missed FG. Coming off 2 wins in row in November, Middies gained 20-19 lead as TE Kevin Hickman carried textbook 56y screen pass from QB Jim Kubiak (24-24/361y, 2 TDs). Kubiak set Army-Navy record with pass y, but threw 3 INTs, last on overthrow to Army DB Derek Klein at Middies' 1st down opportunity at Cadet 15YL late in 3rd Q. With 6:19 left, Army K Kurt Heiss set series record with 52y FG for 22-20 lead, and Cadets' Wishbone attack killed last 5 mins with ball control. Rushing heroes for West Point were QB Ronnie McAda (8/127y) and FB Joe Ross (22/120y).

Florida 24 Alabama 23 (Atlanta): In nerve-racking SEC title game, Florida (10-1-1) silenced lingering doubt about big game ability, and Alabama (11-1) saw national title shot evaporate. Crimson Tide opened scoring as QB Jay Barker (10-19/181y, TD, 2 INTs) passed 70y to WR Curtis Brown on perfectly-threaded arrow. But, Barker banged up his throwing shoulder as Gators took 17-10 H lead on 2 TDs by QB Danny Wuerffel. Bama K Michael Proctor made 47 and 48y FGs in 3rd Q, and when LB Dwayne Rudd ran in 23y INT in 4th Q, Tide led 22-17. Coach Gene Stallings was criticized for not trying 2-pt conv, but kicked instead for 23-17 edge. At this point, Gators dipped into coach Steve Spurrier's bag of tricks and came up with 20y lateral double-pass from Wuerffel to WR Chris Doering to WR Aubrey Hill, who carried to 2YL. Doering caught TD pass on next play, and K Judd Davis made winning kick with 5:29 to go.

USA Today Coaches Poll December 5

1	Nebraska (44)	1532	14	North Carolina	693
2	Penn State (18)	1505	15	Virginia Tech	641
3	Miami (Fla.)	1406	16	Virginia	572
4	Florida	1325	17	Mississippi State	523
5	Colorado	1317	18	Michigan	460
6	Alabama	1235	19	Brigham Young	454
7	Florida State	1218	20	North Carolina State	376
8	Kansas State	1076	21	Duke	352
9	Oregon	1051	22	Southern California	305
10	Colorado State	976	23	Washington State	261
11	Ohio State	915	24	Tennessee	137
12	Utah	792	25	Boston College	59
13	Arizona	766			

1994 Conference Standings

Big East

Miami	7-0
Virginia Tech	5-2
Syracuse	4-3
West Virginia	4-3
Boston College	3-3-1
Rutgers	2-4-1
Pittsburgh	2-5
Temple	0-7

Atlantic Coast

Florida State	8-0
North Carolina State	6-2
Duke	5-3
North Carolina	5-3
Virginia	5-3
Clemson	4-4
Maryland	2-6
Wake Forest	1-7
Georgia Tech	0-8

Southeastern

EAST

Florida	8-1
Tennessee	5-3
South Carolina	4-4
Georgia	3-4-1
Vanderbilt	2-6
Kentucky	0-8

WEST

Alabama	8-1
Auburn	6-1-1
Mississippi State	5-3
Louisiana State	3-5
Arkansas	2-6
Mississippi	2-6

Big Ten

Penn State	8-0
Ohio State	6-2
Michigan	5-3
Wisconsin	4-3-1
Illinois	4-4
Michigan State	4-4
Iowa	3-4-1
Indiana	3-5
Purdue	2-4-2
Northwestern	2-6
Minnesota	1-7

Mid-American

Central Michigan	8-1
Bowling Green	7-1
Western Michigan	5-3
Miami (Ohio)	5-3
Ball State	5-3-1
Toledo	4-3-1
Eastern Michigan	5-4
Kent	2-7
Akron	1-8
Ohio	0-9

Big Eight

Nebraska	7-0
Colorado	6-1
Kansas State	5-2
Oklahoma	4-3
Kansas	3-4
Missouri	2-5
Oklahoma State	0-6-1
Iowa State	0-6-1

Southwest

Texas A&M *	6-0-1
Baylor	4-3
Texas	4-3
Texas Christian	4-3
Texas Tech	4-3
Rice	4-3
Houston	1-6
Southern Methodist	0-6-1
*Ineligible	

Western Athletic

Colorado State	7-1
Utah	6-2
Brigham Young	6-2
Air Force	6-2
Wyoming	4-4
New Mexico	4-4
Fresno State	3-4-1
San Diego State	2-6
Texas-El Paso	1-6-1
Hawaii	0-8

Pacific-10

Oregon	7-1
Arizona	6-2
Southern California	6-2
Washington State	5-3
Washington	4-4
UCLA	3-5
California	3-5
Oregon State	2-6
Stanford	2-6
Arizona State	2-6

1994 Major Bowl Games

Aloha Bowl (Dec. 25): Boston College 12 Kansas State 7

RB David Green (28/121y) burst for 51y gain on Boston College's 1st scrimmage play, and Eagles (7-4-1) quickly scored on RB Justice Smith's short run. Kansas State (9-3) tied it when DB Chris Sublette recovered blocked punt in EZ. But, Wildcats QB Chad May (13-31/185y, 2 INTs) ran for his life all day as BC D ponied up its Big East pride, sacking May 8/-71y. Eagles LB Mike Mamula personally had 4 sacks, including key safety in 2nd Q for 9-7 lead. In 4th Q, Eagles QB Mark Hartsell threw 46y post pass to WR Kenyatta Watson that carried to 3YL. Watson's shimmy dance cost BC 15y PEN for excessive celebration, and Eagles had to settle for K David Gordon's 35y FG.

Freedom Bowl (Dec. 27): Utah 16 Arizona 13

Utah (10-2) won unusual D game in which it managed only 5 1st downs and gained 75y compared to its 448y avg. In 1st Q, Wildcats RB Ontiwaun Carter stole away 23y pass at GL from Utah DB Edwin Garette for TD and 7-0 lead. In 2nd Q, Utah DB Ernest Boyd made FUM REC at Arizona 4YL, and Utes quickly tied it at 7-7 on RB Chris Brown's 6y scamper. With Arizona (8-4) up 13-7 with 4:11 to play, it conceded safety rather than punt from EZ. But, maneuver backfired when Utah special teamer Cal Beck returned free-kick 72y to Cats 5YL. While being dragged down by DL Chuck Osborne (2 sacks) on 4th down, Utah QB Mike McCoy (11-25/69y, 2 INTs) flung winning TD pass to EZ corner to WR Kevin Dyson. It was McCoy's 19th straight game with scoring pass, even though he was sacked 6 times, 4 by Arizona DE Tedy Bruschi.

Independence Bowl (Dec. 28): Virginia 20 TCU 10

Thomas Jefferson, prime author of American Declaration of Independence, would have been proud of his other creation, University of Virginia (9-3), winning bowl named for his 1776 document. Cavaliers, prior losers of 4 straight bowls, got off to quick start with 2nd Q FG by K Rafael Garcia, and FB Charles Way scored from 6YL after TB Kevin Brooks (17/114y) raced 52y to start drive. Cavs DL Mike Frederick was selected D player of game thanks to his pressuring TCU (7-5) QB Max Knake into 8-24/65y passing performance. Sloppy conditions didn't prevent Knake from leading 48y drive to late TD. On 4th down at Cavs 1YL, Knake faked handoff to TB Andre Davis (24/97y) and flipped TD pass to wide-open TE Brian Collins.

Copper Bowl (Dec. 29): Brigham Young 31 Oklahoma 6

Try as they might to get up for coach Gary Gibbs' swansong, Sooners (6-6) turned flat as soon as BYU (10-3) QB John Walsh fired 43y pass to RB Jamal Willis on game's 1st play. Controlling clock with his air game, Walsh (31-45/454y) tossed 2 TDs each to WRs Bryce Doman and Mike Johnston and spread his throws among 8 receivers.

With future coach Howard Schnellenberger watching from private box, Oklahoma struggled behind sub QB-WR Terence Brown, who entered game with 8 catches as WR compared to 3 pass attempts as fill-in for ill QB Garrick McGee. TB Jerald Moore scored Sooners' only TD long after Cougars salted it away at 24-0.

Sun Bowl (Dec. 30): Texas 35 North Carolina 31

RB Priest Holmes (27/161y) wrapped up record-tying 4-TD performance with 5y somersault score with less than 2 mins left to bring Texas (8-4) its 1st bowl win for coach John Mackovic. Longhorns led 21-17 at H as Holmes scored twice, but its O sputtered for part of 2nd H. Meanwhile, North Carolina (8-4) jr WR Marcus Wall returned punt for 1st time in career and used DB Ronald Thomas' near-clip block to race 82y with line-drive punt to TD with 13:35 left. Tar Heels QB Mike Thomas (23-39/298y, 2 TDs, INT) then fired 50y TD to WR Octavus Barnes to build 31-21 lead. Next came 2 whirling TDs by Holmes, his game-winner described by Mackovic as "up there in the stratosphere."

Gator Bowl (Dec. 30): Tennessee 45 Virginia Tech 23

Golden Anniversary Gator Bowl was staged not in Gator Bowl stadium but in "The Swamp" as game moved to Florida Field in Gainesville. Normal Jacksonville site was being reconfigured for 1995 debut of NFL Jacksonville Jaguars. Tennessee (8-4), winners of its last 5 games, and Virginia Tech (8-4), losers of 3 of its last 4, combined for new Gator-Bowl-record pt total. RB James "Little Man" Stewart (22/87y), Vols' new career rushing leader, scored 3 TDs and tossed 19y TD pass to WR Kendrick Jones. Volunteers O stars were plentiful: QB Peyton Manning (12-19/189y, TD), SEC frosh of year, hit 6-7/123y in 14-pt 1st Q, Jones ran reverse 76y to TD behind devastating block by G Kevin Mays, and frosh QB Branndon Stewart led 2 scoring drives to build 35-7 lead in 2nd Q. Virginia Tech managed 426y and TDs by TB Dwayne Thomas, QB Maurice DeShazo, and WR Bryan Still, but much of Hokies' success came after result was settled.

Holiday Bowl (Dec. 30): Michigan 24 Colorado State 14

During season, Big 10 had best record in nation outside conf, and no. 20 Michigan (9-3) launched Big 10 to 4-1 bowl jam by besting solid WAC champ Colorado State (10-2). Forcing 4 TOs, Wolverines needed short trips on 2 TD drives wrapped around H to ice verdict. Leading 10-7 with 1:49 to go before H, Michigan RB Chris Howard blocked punt by P Matt McDougal, and QB Todd Collins (14-24/162y, 2 TDs, 3 INTs) hit WR Mercury Hayes in EZ corner for 17-7 lead. On 1st series of 2nd H, Michigan LB Woodrow Hankins stripped ball from Rams QB Anthony Hill with LB Jarrett Irons falling on it at 17YL. TB Tyrone Wheatley carried 4 straight plays to score. Shut off on ground with 51y, CSU relied on passing of Hill (22-40/289y, 2 TDs, 2 INTs), but Michigan's blitzes and fake blitzes caused considerable pressure and confusion.

Alamo Bowl (Dec. 31): Washington State 10 Baylor 3

Washington State (8-4) ate 7:32 to go up 7-0 on opening drive, aided by roughing punter PEN and questionable 3rd down catch. Key play was 33y pass from QB Chad Davis (27-35/286y) to WR Albert Kennedy. Young Bears (7-5) hit hard, but dissipated their chances, running slow-developing plays gobbled up by ace Cougars LBs Ron Childs and Ken Fields. WSU closed 1st H, in which it held Baylor to 41y O, with K Tony Truant's 37y FG. RB Clifton Rubin made 4th-and-1 at midfield in 3rd Q, poising Baylor K Jarvis Van Dyke for 36y FG. Frosh QB Jeff Watson (8-22/77y, 2 INTs) found RB Kalief Muhammad streaking up left sideline for 33y pass to take Bears to 10YL in last 3 mins, but Cougars DB Todd Jensen picked off Watson in EZ on 4th down.

Peach Bowl: North Carolina State 28 Mississippi State 24

Atlanta's Peach Bowl game suffered from low TV ratings, being up against Orange Bowl, but still served up its annual exciting Southern-fried matchup. Wolfpack (9-3) rallied behind QB Terry Harvey's passing to upset Mississippi State (8-4). Settling for 5 FGs by K Tim Rogers, Bulldogs never capitalized on numerous chances to wrestle away control of game. Mississippi State appeared to have made key play early in 3rd Q when DB Andre Bennett blocked NC State P Chad Robson's punt. Robson fought off several Bulldogs to make EZ REC. So, NC State suffered mere safety, instead of more damaging TD, that broke 13-13 tie at 15-13. Late in 3rd Q, Harvey passed for TD and ran for 2 pts for 21-21 tie. On Wolfpack's next series, Harvey took NC State 80y to TD on his 62y strike to WR Jimmy Grissett.

GAME OF THE YEAR
Orange Bowl: Nebraska 24 Miami 17

Much pregame analysis pointed to no. 1 Nebraska's recent Orange Bowl failures, 5 straight losses to Miami or Florida State. Also under microscope was coach Tom Osborne's interesting choice of Tommie Frazier as starting Cornhuskers (13-0) QB even though Frazier's last game appearance had been September 24. On its 1st series, Miami (10-2) went from own 42YL to K Dane Prewitt's 44y FG. Rusty or not, Frazier pegged ill-advised long pass into double coverage on 2nd possession, and DB Carlos Jones' INT put Hurricanes in position to launch quick 97y TD parade. Miami QB Frank Costa (18-35/248y, 2 TD, INT) fired to WRs Jammi German for 17y and A. C. Tellison for 44y, and frosh RB Trent Jones took swing pass for 35y TD as Huskies LBs were slow to react. Up 10-0, strutting Canes adopted their familiar, flamboyant posture of "nobody comes to our house and wins." Call it adjustment or panic, QB Brook Berringer replaced Frazier to open 2nd Q, although Osborne had announced beforehand that both would see action. Nebraska DB Kareem Moss made good punt RET, and Berringer rolled right, threw 19y TD pass to TE Mark Gilman. For remainder of H, O PENs hurt Miami, and DT Warren Sapp played havoc with Huskers O. Miami went 78y with 2nd H KO for 17-7 lead with RB Jonathan Harris taking short pass, cutting right for 44y TD. Another of Miami's 11 PENs soon set it back to own 4YL, and LB Dwayne Harris poured in on Costa to rack up safety. Slowly-turning momentum, superior Nebraska conditioning and Miami's energetic celebrations began

to wear down Hurricanes. Odd play came early in 4th Q. Hurricanes punt snap sailed over Prewitt's head, and with Huskers in hot pursuit, he soccer-kicked through own EZ. Nebraska took over on Miami 4YL, but in effort to throw away 1st down pass, Berringer permitted DB Earl Little's diving INT in EZ corner to kill golden chance. After Miami was forced to punt, Frazier was reinserted with 12:07 to go. Although Sapp sacked Frazier on 1st down, it was Canes' last hurrah. IB Lawrence Phillips (19/96y) dashed 25y on option pitchout by Frazier, and FB Cory Schlesinger blasted 15y for TD. Frazier tied it at 17-17 on misdirection 2-pt pass to TE Eric Alford. On Nebraska next possession, Frazier ran 21 and 6y before Schlesinger scored again for 24-17 lead with 2:46 left. On last series, battered Costa was sacked twice and threw INT as Nebraska D wrapped up 4th Q with -35y dominance and clinched national title for Osborne after 22 years of waiting.

Hall of Fame Bowl (Jan. 2): Wisconsin 34 Duke 20

On his team's opening 3 series, Duke (8-4) QB Spence Fischer lost INTs in disastrous beginning. Wisconsin (7-4-1) turned TOs into 13-0 lead as DB Jeff Messenger raced 19y with INT TD RET and K John Hall kicked 2 FGs. But, Messenger and others on Badgers D went down with injuries, and Fischer's passes (28-46/314y) began to take toll. Devils tied it at 13-13 early in 3rd Q. Badgers responded with 76y TD drive with TB Terrell Fletcher (39/241y) gaining 56y as workhorse runner. Former sub Fletcher had inherited role after TB Brent Moss was suspended during season for drug possession. Midway into 4th Q, Wisconsin made it 27-13 with 83y drive, crowned by 11y TD pass by QB Darrell Bevell (11-20/161y, TD, INT). Duke countered with RB Robert Baldwin's 2nd TD run, but Fletcher sealed it for Wisconsin with 49y TD burst on 4th down with 1:59 to play.

Carquest Bowl (Jan. 2): South Carolina 24 West Virginia 21

Trends were all against South Carolina (7-5), losers of all 8 previous bowl appearances, playing West Virginia (7-6), which came in winning 6 of last 7 games of 1994. Gamecocks QB Steve Taneyhill (26-36/227y) threw early TD to TE Boomer Foster, then made play of game just before H. Ducking between 2 defenders and faking pass at scrimmage line, Taneyhill leapt over group at GL for 4y TD that put Gamecocks ahead 17-7. WVU was own worst enemy with TOs and 4th down failures, but QB Chad Johnston hit WR Lovett Purnell with 2 TD passes. Down 17-14, Johnston maneuvered Mountaineers into Carolina territory, but frosh DB Ben Washington made INT and returned it 42y to make possible Gamecocks' last and clinching TD at 24-14.

Cotton Bowl (Jan. 2): Southern California 55 Texas Tech 14

SWC in 80th and next to last season had odd collection of teams. Probation-stained Texas A&M went 6-0-1 in conf, but was bowl ineligible. Texas Tech (6-6) was 1 of unprecedented 5 to tie for title despite last-game loss to TCU. Texas Tech was selected for Cotton Bowl by virtue of longest spell since its last appearance (1939). Showing no ill effects of landing in Dallas for 1st time ever instead of Pasadena, Southern California (8-3-1) ripped into Red Raiders for 48-0 lead as QB Rob Johnson (16-21/289y) threw 3 TD passes. WR Keyshawn Johnson (8/Cotton record 222y) had 3 TD catches, including 86y TD from sub QB Brad Otten as USC set Cotton Bowl records with 578y total O and 435y gained in air. Red Raiders didn't score until QB Zebbie Lethridge's 3rd Q run and found coach Spike Dykes grateful afterward: "A class man (John Robinson) is coaching that team; the score could have been a lot worse. It's not much fun to get your tail kicked like that." Southwest Conf went out with wimper, not bang: Result marked SWC's 7th consecutive and last Cotton Bowl.

Citrus Bowl (Jan. 2): Alabama 24 Ohio State 17

Usually reliable Alabama (12-1) fell into contagious 2-team comedy of errors as 2 punts were blocked, FG was blocked, 3 TOs occurred within 14 secs, and Bama's sure-footed K Michael Proctor missed chip shot 25y FG in 4th Q. For their part, Buckeyes handed Crimson Tide TD with 2 PENs including 12-men-on-field on 1 drive, and officials failed to see Ohio State WR Joey Galloway's foot OB on TD catch. Rising above mayhem was Tide RB Sherman Williams, who sparkled with 27/166y rushing, 8/155y receiving, and 2/38y on kick RETs. Williams caught short pass over middle from QB Jay Barker (18-37/317y) and raced away from out-of-position blitzing D for 50y winning TD with 42 secs left. Ohio State (9-4) slipped to 1-5 bowl record with coach John Cooper, but had grabbed 14-7 2nd Q lead as QB Bobby Hoying (11-27/180y, INT) hit Galloway (8/146y) twice for TDs. Buckeyes took 17-14 lead midway in 4th Q on K Josh Jackson's 34y FG. Eventually, Ohio was outgained 521y to 276y, and Hoying suffered 5 sacks.

Fiesta Bowl (Jan. 2): Colorado 41 Notre Dame 24

Notre Dame's good luck charm—green jerseys—failed to derail Colorado (11-1), which was intent on sending coach Bill McCartney out as winner. RB Rashaan Salaam was determined to break recent bowl jinx of Heisman winners and half succeeded. Salaam scored 3 TDs, but Irish (6-5-1) D held him to 27/83y rushing, considerably under his game avg. While ND concentrated on Colorado's left fist (Salaam), it was clobbered by right fist: QB Kordell Stewart, who set Buffs bowl record with 348y total. "As I said at the beginning of the year, they can't stop us all," explained Stewart, who accounted for 2 TDs as Buffs built 31-10 H lead. Irish QB Ron Powlus overcame 3 sacks by DE Shannon Clavelle to hit WR Derrick Mayes with TD pass 5 secs before H, then came back to slice deficit to 31-17 with 39y TD to Mayes in 3rd Q. Colorado answered with K Ted Voskeritchian's FG and LB Ted Johnson's INT to set up Salaam's last TD for 41-17 edge with 9:29 remaining.

Rose Bowl (Jan. 2): Penn State 38 Oregon 20

It was difficult to read mood of Penn State (12-0). On 1 hand, it's national championship dream seemed all but snuffed by Nebraska's Orange Bowl win on previous night. On other hand, Lions seemed focused on completing undefeated

season, 4th time (1968, '69, '73, and '94) coach Joe Paterno had accomplished feat without being selected as national champion. Oregon (9-4) clearly was better than its record and in perfect position to spring upset of year, but got quick slap in face. On Lions' 1st snap, RB Ki-Jana Carter rammed off T, caught several Ducks out of position, broke grasp of DB Herman O'Berry, and dashed 83y to TD. Oregon struck back quickly as QB Danny O'Neil (41-61/456y, 2 TDs, 2 INTs) completed all 4 of passes on drive that took 45 secs. TE Josh Wilcox (11/135y) caught 1y TD. Frosh WR Joe Jurevicius caught 44y pass in 2nd Q to set up FB Brian Milne's 1y TD behind G Jeff Hartings' block, Penn State led 14-7 late in 2nd Q. While Oregon was passing well in 1st H, it squandered chances to take command: 2 missed FGs by frosh K Matt Belden, and misadventure inside 10YL only to have clock expire. After LB Reggie Jordan had 48y INT RET, Oregon tied it 14-14 on O'Neil's TD pass to WR Cristin McLemore in 3rd Q. Soon came some key plays for Lions: Frosh RB Ambrose Fletcher's 72y KO RET and 3rd string DB Chuck Penzenik's pair of INTs to set up Carter (21/156y) for his 2nd and 3rd TDs as Lions took control at 28-14.

Sugar Bowl (Jan. 2): Florida State 23 Florida 17

Game became known as "Unfinished Business: The Fifth Quarter in the French Quarter," as Seminoles (10-1-1) and Gators (10-2-1) were rematched after epic 31-31 draw of November 26. For 9th time in bowl history, regular season opponents were matched up. Teams that had won regular season match-up only had 3-5 records vs. rematched foes. No tied opponents had ever been rematched before. Florida State picked up where it left off in November, jumping to 7-0 lead as RB Warrick Dunn fired 73y pass to WR 'OMar Ellison in 1st Q. K Dan Mowrey kicked 3 FGs, but missed when FSU could have put game out of reach. Seminoles D held Florida to its season-low in pts, stopping it twice on downs inside FSU 30YL and prompting some oddball sandlot plays. High on coach Steve Spurrier's play list were ill-advised flea-flicker out of Gators' own EZ and lateral-and-pass by WR Chris Doering from deep behind scrimmage line. Gators were able to score before H on K Judd Davis' FG and WR Ike Hilliard's Sugar Bowl-record to-date 82y TD catch. Florida QB Danny Wuerffel (28-39/394y, TD) threw INT with just over min left to kill any late hopes. Florida State QB Danny Kanell pitched 23-40/252y, TD.

Final USA Today Coaches Poll January 3

1	Nebraska (54)	1542	14	Colorado State	690
2	Penn State (8)	1496	15	Southern California	670
3	Colorado	1387	16	Kansas State	657
4	Alabama	1345	17	North Carolina State	627
5	Florida State	1325	18	Tennessee	517
6	Miami (Fla.)	1231	19	Washington State	453
7	Florida	1182	20	Arizona	402
8	Utah	1034	21	North Carolina	312
9	Ohio State	846	22	Boston College	301
10	Brigham Young	840	23	Texas	250
11	Oregon	834	24	Virginia Tech	188
12	Michigan	797	25	Mississippi State	149
13	Virginia	777			

Final AP Poll January 3

1	Nebraska (51)	1539	13	Southern California	691
2	Penn State (10)	1497	14	Ohio State	672
3	Colorado	1410	15	Virginia	648
4	Florida State	1320	16	Colorado State	630
5	Alabama	1312	17	North Carolina State	511
6	Miami	1249	18	Brigham Young	500
7	Florida	1153	19	Kansas State	496
8	Texas A&M	1117	20	Arizona	364
9	Auburn	1110	21	Washington State	344
10	Utah	955	22	Tennessee	303
11	Oregon	810	23	Boston College	236
12	Michigan	732	24	Mississippi State	160
			25	Texas	90

1994 Top Performance Formula

1	Penn State	1.8165
2	Nebraska	1.7935
3	Florida State	1.7018
4	Colorado	1.6642
5	Florida	1.6405
6	Texas A&M	1.6066
7	Miami	1.5629
8	Alabama	1.5506
9	Auburn	1.5081
10	Kansas State	1.4133
11	Virginia	1.4046
12	Southern California	1.3896
13	Michigan	1.3851
14	Ohio State	1.3694
15	Tennessee	1.3667
16	Wisconsin	1.3378
17	Oregon	1.3354
18	Brigham Young	1.3237
19	North Carolina State	1.3185
20	Duke	1.2889

1994 Top Opponent Records

1 Michigan	.6667
2 Florida State	.6385
3 Oklahoma	.6357
4 Florida	.6213
5 Notre Dame	.6094
6 Michigan State	.6078
7 Southern California	.6055
8 Tennessee	.6016
9 Oregon	.5993
10 Miami	.5913
11 Minnesota	.5870
12 Ohio State	.5833
13 Colorado	.5775
14 Northwestern	.5769
15 No. Carolina St.	.5768
16 Penn State	.5748
17 Louisiana State	.5733
18 Nebraska	.5719
19 Alabama	.5699
20 Arizona State	.5684

1994 Out-of-Conference Records

	W-L	Percentage	Bowl W-L
Southeastern	27-10-1	.7237	3-2
Big Ten	27-11-1	.7051	4-1
Big Eight	23-13-1	.6351	2-2
Atlantic Coast	16-10-1	.6111	3-2
Western Athletic	22-14-1	.6081	2-1
Big East	20-15	.5714	1-3
Pacific-10	18-14-2	.5588	2-2
Southwest	18-18	.5000	1-3

1994 Individual Statistical Leaders

RUSHING YARDS	Attempts	Yards	Avg.
Rashaan Salaam, Colorado	298	2055	6.9
Brian Pruitt, Central Michigan	292	1890	6.5
Lawrence Phillips, Nebraska	286	1722	6.0
Ki-Jana Carter, Penn State	198	1539	7.8
Andre Davis, Texas Christian	260	1494	5.7
Alex Smith, Indiana	265	1475	5.6
Ryan Christopherson, Wyoming	300	1455	4.8
Chris Darkins, Minnesota	277	1443	5.2
Napoleon Kaufman, Washington	255	1390	5.5
Billy West, Pittsburgh	252	1358	5.4

PASSING YARDS	Completions	Attempts	Yards	Pct.
John Walsh, Brigham Young	284	463	3712	61.3
Mike Maxwell, Nevada	271	447	3537	60.6
Eric Zeier, Georgia	259	433	3396	59.8
Stoney Case, New Mexico	233	409	3117	57.0
Mike McCoy, Utah	247	381	3035	64.8
Steve Stenstrom, Stanford	217	333	2822	65.2
John Gustin, Wyoming	181	306	2757	59.2
Kerry Collins, Penn State	176	264	2679	66.7
Max Knake, Texas Christian	184	316	2624	58.2
Chad May, Kansas State	200	337	2571	59.4

RECEIVING YARDS	Catches	Yards
Marcus Harris, Wyoming	71	1431
Alex Van Dyke, Nevada	98	1246
Kevin Jordan, UCLA	73	1228
Randy Gatewood, UNLV	88	1203
Keyshawn Johnson, So. California	58	1140
Justin Armour, Stanford	67	1092
Amani Toomer, Michigan	49	1033
Bobby Engram, Penn State	52	1029
Freddie Scott, Penn State	47	973
Richard Dice, Arizona	56	969

1994 Consensus All-America Team

Offense

Wide Receiver:	Jack Jackson, Florida
	Michael Westbrook, Colorado
Tight End:	Pete Mitchell, Boston College
Line:	Zach Wiegert, Nebraska
	Tony Boselli, Southern California
	Korey Stringer, Ohio State
	Brenden Stai, Nebraska
Center:	Cory Raymer, Wisconsin
Quarterback:	Kerry Collins, Penn State
Running Back:	Rashaan Salaam, Colorado
	Ki-Jana Carter, Penn State
Kick Returner:	Leeland McElroy, Texas A&M
Placekicker:	Steve McLaughlin, Arizona

Defense

Line:	Warren Sapp, Miami
	Tedy Bruschi, Arizona
	Luther Elliss, Utah
	Kevin Carter, Florida
Linebacker:	Dana Howard, Illinois
	Ed Stewart, Nebraska
	Derrick Brooks, Florida State
Back:	Clifton Abraham, Florida State
	Bobby Taylor, Notre Dame
	Chris Hudson, Colorado
	Brian Robinson, Auburn
	Tony Bouie, Arizona
Punter:	Todd Sauerbrun, West Virginia

1994 Heisman Trophy Vote

Rashaan Salaam, junior running back, Colorado	1743
Ki-Jana Carter, junior tailback, Penn State	901
Steve McNair, senior quarterback, Alcorn State	655
Kerry Collins, senior quarterback, Penn State	639

Other Major Award Winners

Maxwell (Player)	Kerry Collins, senior QB, Penn State
Walter Camp (Player)	Rashaan Salaam, junior RB, Colorado
Outland (Lineman)	Zach Wiegert, senior T, Nebraska
Vince Lombardi (Lineman)	Warren Sapp, junior DT, Miami
Doak Walker (Runner)	Rashaan Salaam, junior RB, Colorado
Davey O'Brien (Quarterback)	Kerry Collins, senior QB, Penn State
Fred Biletnikoff (Receiver)	Bobby Engram, junior WR, Penn State
Jim Thorpe (Defensive Back)	Chris Hudson, senior CB, Colorado
Dick Butkus (Linebacker)	Dana Howard, senior LB, Illinois
Lou Groza (Placekicker)	Steve McLaughlin, senior K, Arizona
AFCA Coach of the Year	Tom Osborne, Nebraska

1995

The Year of Northwestern's Purple Dream, Bowl Alliance, and Nebraska's Repeaters

The big story of 1995 came from long-deflated Northwestern (10-2), which owned a meager 46-203-4 record since its last winning season in 1971. The purple-hued Wildcats entered 1995 with the second-most losses (530) in NCAA history, but enjoyed a tremendous turnaround under fourth-year coach Gary Barnett. Northwestern began the year with a stunning 17-15 win at Notre Dame (9-3). After flopping against Miami of Ohio (8-2-1), the Wildcats snapped back to beat Michigan (9-4) and Penn State (9-3) while building an undefeated record in the Big Ten. However, the loss to Miami of Ohio hung like an albatross for a while on the Wildcats' overall record.

Ohio State (11-2) didn't meet Northwestern due to the Big Ten's rotating schedule so if it stayed undefeated was in position by winning out to block Northwestern from the Wildcats' first Rose Bowl since 1949. However, the Buckeyes saw their unbeaten season, share of the Big Ten title, and no. 2 national ranking ruined by Michigan 31-23 on November 25. The Buckeyes had been in line for their first Pasadena trip since 1985 because an overall record at 11-0, which was the conference's tie-breaking methodology, would have trumped Northwestern's 10-1. The Wildcats thoroughly enjoyed their trip to Pasadena, dominating pre-game media coverage, and turning New Year's purple, at least figuratively. But Northwestern's dream of Rose Bowl victory ended in an exciting 41-32 shootout with Southern California (9-2-1).

Ohio State charged through a very difficult schedule, counting six ranked foes among its first eight victims. Prime in those wins was a 46-28 verdict over Notre Dame, the first meeting between the titans since 1936.

Another happy recipient of the Michigan upset of Ohio State was the new Bowl Alliance. The Alliance's purpose was to build a championship game between the no. 1 and no. 2 teams in the AP Poll, drawn from the champions of the ACC, Big East, Big Eight, SEC, SWC, and Notre Dame. Notably absent were Rose Bowl affiliated Big Ten and Pacific-10 conferences. So, as long as Ohio State lingered in the top two, it had completely hindered the Bowl Alliance plan.

For most of the year, the Alliance appeared likely headed for a match between no. 2 Nebraska (12-0) and the winner of the late season game between no. 1 Florida State (10-2) and no. 3 Florida (12-1). Virginia (9-4) upset Florida State, and Florida finished off the Seminoles to earn the no. 2 spot behind Nebraska. By crushing the Gators 62-24 in the Fiesta Bowl, Nebraska became the first repeat champion since Alabama in 1978-79, and first undisputed back-to-back no. 1 team since Oklahoma in 1955-56.

For the first time, Kansas (10-2) and Kansas State (10-2) were in the top 10 for most of the year. The Jayhawks authored surprises over ranked teams Colorado (10-2) and Oklahoma (5-5-1), but received thrashings from Kansas State and Nebraska. Kansas State also lost handily to Nebraska. The Sunflower State teams ended up tied for second in the Big Eight's last season.

September proved to be a bit stormy. Rev. Jerry Falwell, chancellor of Baptist-oriented Liberty University, brought a short-lived suit against the NCAA for its enforcement of Rule 921, which included prayer among banned "prolonged" post-play demonstrations. ESPN anchor Chris Fowler called the rules enactment "typical NCAA overreaction." The issue quickly died except for previously-effusive Miami (8-3) players who blamed the rule for a loss to UCLA (7-5) at the outset of the Hurricanes' worst start of a season since 1976.

Top teams were chastised for trying to impress pollsters with huge point totals. On September 16, six teams in the top 10—Nebraska, Florida State, Penn State, Colorado, Florida, and Texas A&M (9-3)—rolled up winning point totals of 77, 77, 66, 66, 62, and 52 respectively, prompting many accusations of running up the score. While some coaches apologized, it was clear no team wanted any part of Penn State's 1994 pratfall, a drop from no. 1 when reserves allowed late-game scores to create the appearance of a tight game. Coaches tended to play starters the whole game, which sometimes fueled a big rout. Also, the over-matched teams frequently exacerbated their own plight by blindly launching all-out passing attacks. Poor passing by the defeated often built a wildfire of turnovers and even bigger margins of defeat.

The year's biggest negative news had nothing to do with blowouts. A firestorm of news centered on Nebraska star I-back Lawrence Phillips. The media also criticized Nebraska's Tom Osborne for his eventual reinstatement of Phillips after Phillips pleaded guilty to assault of his former girlfriend. Phillips played a diminished role in the Huskers championship run

until he starred as a starter in the Fiesta Bowl, but Osborne's program came under serious fire for the first time since he became head coach in 1973.

Eddie Robinson, 76-year-old who had coached at historically-black Division 1-AA Grambling State since 1941, beat Mississippi Valley State 42-6 on October 7 to win his 400th game, the most by any coach at any level in football history. A happy and teary Robinson said, "It could only happen in America."

Sharmon Shah, top running back for UCLA, reconfirmed his Muslim faith during the summer and returned to campus with an ironic new name—Karim Abdul-Jabbar—provided innocently by his religious mentor. It was amazingly similar to Kareem Abdul-Jabbar, who changed his name from Lew Alcindor after his spectacular basketball career at UCLA in the late 1960s. Adding to the coincidence was that both players wore no. 33.

The Southwest Conference, which gave the football world myriad great players and on-field thrills, played its 81st and last season. The modern fan who loves an all-out passing attack should thank the Southwest for having the gumption and foresight to have been the first region to truly air out the football in the early part of the 20th century. A few of the many great names the SWC contributed to football history were Sammy Baugh, Earl Campbell, Trevor Cobb, John David Crow, Eric Dickerson, Santana Dotson, Lawrence Elkins, Thomas Everett, Tony Franklin, E.J. Holub, Louie Kelcher, John Kimbrough, Bobby Layne, Bob Lilly, Steve Little, Don Meredith, Dicky Moegle, Tommy Nobis, Davey O'Brien, Loyd Phillips, Kenneth Sims, Mike Singletary, Jerry Sisemore, Billy Ray Smith, Jim Swink, Andre Ware, Doak Walker, Froggie Williams, Bobby Wilson, Steve Worster, and Elmo Wright.

At the outset of the 1995 season, there were high hopes for preseason no. 3 Texas A&M making a run at the league's ninth national title, but two early losses ended Aggie dreams for national honors. On December 2, Texas (10-2-1) beat Texas A&M 16-6 to clinch its 25th league crown, the most for any school in league history, as the curtain sadly fell on the Southwest Conference.

Milestones

⬤ NCAA rules committee voted to apply stronger enforcement of Rule 921 which prohibited on-field demonstrations by players such as removing helmets, non-spontaneous gestures, doing choreographed dances, or kneeling to pray. Enforcement was designed to penalize teams for "any prolonged act by which a player attempts to focus attention on himself."

⬤ Arizona tight end Damon Terrell died on September 7 of unknown causes after a practice field collapse in August. Head coach Dick Tomey missed his team's game on September 9 at Champaign, Ill., a 9-7 loss to Illinois, to attend Terrell's funeral in Los Angeles. Terrell's teammates called timeout on the opening kickoff to form the initials DT and hold their helmets to the sky. Don Faurot, coach at Missouri 1935-42, 46-56, died. Faurot built a 100-80-10 record and was considered the father of the Split-T which launched option offensive football in the 1940s. Also passing away was Les Horvath, Ohio State's 1944 winner of the Heisman Trophy.

⬤ Longest winning streak entering season:

Penn State 16	Nebraska 13	Tennessee 5

⬤ Coaching Changes:

	Incoming	Outgoing
Akron	Lee Owens	Gerry Faust
Ball State	Bill Lynch	Paul Schudel
Colorado	Rick Neuheisel	Bill McCartney
Eastern Michigan	Rick Rasnick	Ron Cooper
Iowa State	Dan McCarney	Jim Walden
Louisiana State	Gerry DiNardo	Curley Hallman
Louisville	Ron Cooper	Howard Schnellenberger
Memphis	William Scherer	Chuck Stobart
Miami	Butch Davis	Dennis Erickson
Michigan	Lloyd Carr	Gary Moeller
Michigan State	Nick Saban	George Perles
Mississippi	Tommy Tuberville	Joe Lee Dunn
Navy	Charlie Weatherbie	George Chaump
Ohio	Jim Grobe	Tom Lichtenberg
Oklahoma	Howard Schnellenberger	Gary Gibbs
Oklahoma State	Bob Simmons	Pat Jones
Oregon	Mike Bellotti	Rich Brooks
Stanford	Tyrone Willingham	Bill Walsh
Utah State	John Smith	Charlie Weatherbie
Vanderbilt	Rod Dowhower	Gerry DiNardo

Preseason *USA Today* Coaches Poll

1	Florida State (28)	1438	14	Alabama	572
2	Nebraska (17)	1437	15	UCLA	477
3	Texas A&M	1326	16	Virginia	470
4	Penn State	1298	17	Oklahoma	445
5	Florida	1293	18	Texas	427
6	Southern California	1240	19	Arizona	350
7	Auburn	1170	20	North Carolina	323
8	Notre Dame	941	21	Washington	307
9	Miami (Fla.)	906	22	Wisconsin	299
10	Ohio State	864	23	Boston College	291
11	Tennessee	852	24	Illinois	260
12	Michigan	788	25	North Carolina State	216
13	Colorado	771			

August 26, 1995

MICHIGAN 18 Virginia 17: In 1st on-campus Pigskin Classic, Lloyd Carr's Michigan coaching debut was awakened from 4th Q nightmare by arm of frosh QB Scott Dreisbach (27-52/372y, 2 TDs, 2 INTs). Confident Virginia (0-1) had bolted to 17-0 lead as DB Ronde Barber's INT RET to Michigan 29YL set up late 2nd Q TD by QB Mike Groh. TB Tiki Barber, Ronde's twin brother, raced 81y to 3rd Q TD, and K Rafeal Garcia added early 4th Q FG. Practically dead, Wolverines (1-0) made comeback from largest deficit in school history as Dreisbach pitched for 236y in 4th Q. WR Mercury Hayes caught 41 and 43y passes to set up TB Ed Davis' TD, then caught 31y TD to bring Michigan within 17-12 midway in 4th Q. Wolverines went 80y in last 2:35 as Cavs just missed downing punt inside 5YL. Dreisbach hit Hayes on corner route for winning TD as clock expired. Big Michigan break just before: It took WR Tyrone Butterfield's lucky and unintentional butter-fingered drop at 4YL to keep drive alive with 4 secs left. Butterfield almost certainly would have been tackled in field of play to end game.

(Sun) Ohio State 38 Boston College 6 (East Rutherford, N.J.): Ohio State (1-0) led 7-3 in 2nd Q after Buckeyes DB Shawn Springs answered 24y FG by Boston College (0-1) K Dan McGuire by going up sideline for 97y KO TD RET. Ohio State QB Bobby Hoying hit TB Eddie George (17/99y) with 14y pass and newly-found WR Terry Glenn for 46y on 99y TD march before H. McGuire made 50y FG in 3rd Q, but it was trumped by George's 2nd TD run for 31-6 Buckeyes lead. RB Justice Smith registered 24/119y on ground, but BC lost -6y rushing because of plethora of sacks. Eagles QB Mark Hartsell passed 17-31/187y, 2 INTs.

September 2, 1995

(Th) Nebraska 64 OKLAHOMA STATE 21: Defending national champion Nebraska (1-0) cooled Oklahoma State (0-1) with 30-pt 2nd Q in Stillwater's stifling heat. IB Lawrence Phillips (12/153y, 3 TDs) romped to his 13th 100y game of his career in only 26 mins. He and QB Tommie Frazier (6-10/120y, 2 TDs, and 10/64y, TD rushing) and rest of 1st team O packed up only 5 mins into 3rd Q after having built 50-7 lead. Phillips' TD runs came from 3, 80, and 27y out. Coach Bob Simmons made his debut with Cowboys and unveiled frosh-oriented lineup that allowed 671y on D. TB David Thompson rushed 16/128y and scored 3rd Q TD for Oklahoma State.

PITTSBURGH 17 Washington State 13: Neither team was capable of running ball very well: Washington State (0-1) picked up 47y in 4th Q, but made only 52y rushing in opening 3 Qs, and Pitt's run game vanished with TB Billy West's early 2nd Q shoulder separation. So, Panthers (1-0) QB John Ryan (27-47/266y, 2 TDs, 3 INTs) filled air with passes, many of them to WR Dietrich Jells (9/131y, 2 TDs). After 3-3 H deadlock, Pittsburgh came from behind twice in 4th Q to take 10-6 and 17-13 leads on scoring catches by slippery Jells. Now his school's all-time receiving y king, Jells' game-winning TD came on 8y slant-in pattern in front of Cougars DB Shad Hinchen with 1:41 to play, and after Pitt had converted miraculous twice-tipped 4th-and-7 pass to WR Curtis Anderson from its own 28YL. Wazzu had taken 13-10 lead on its only dent in Panthers D: Cougars went 80y in 7 plays to score on RB Frank Madu's 11y TD run.

Purdue 26 WEST VIRGINIA 24: Underdog Boilermakers (1-0) opened smartly with 19-0 H lead on TD run by TB Corey Rogers and TD pass by QB Rick Trefzger (15-22/187y, INT). Making good H adjustments, West Virginia (0-1) rallied with 17 straight pts in 2nd H, mostly on 2 TD runs by TB Robert Walker (28/137y), which were set up by catches by TE Lovett Purnell. In 4th Q, FB Mike Alstott (17/109y) dashed 39y to set up Rogers' 2nd TD, and Purdue enjoyed 26-17 advantage. Walker's 3rd TD drew Mountaineers within 26-24 with 5:39 left, but K Bryan Baumann missed short FG near end.

FLORIDA STATE 70 Duke 26 (Orlando): Bobby Bowden became only 5th Div. 1-A coach in history to win 250 games as Florida State (1-0) scored on 7 of its 1st 8 possessions. Seminoles led 27-10 in 1st Q and 54-12 at H. Scoring heroes included 280-lb FB "Pooh Bear" Williams with 3 scores, TB Rock Preston (6/126y) who had 85y in 1st Q TD, TB Warrick Dunn (9/124y) who had tackle-breaking 33y TD. Duke kick-blocking ace DB Ray Farmer succeeded twice, with DB Tawambi Settles taking blocked conv to 2-pt RET. Held to 167y in 1st H, Blue Devils (0-1) made 2 3rd Q TDs vs. Seminoles subs: 51y TD run by RB Charles London and 35y pass thrown by QB Spence Fischer.

Syracuse 20 NORTH CAROLINA 9: Teams of Tobacco Road were coughing and wheezing as North Carolina, Duke, and Wake Forest all lost their home openers. At end of 3 Qs, Tar Heels (0-1) led 9-3 on FGs by K Scott Capparelli of 21, 23, and 32y. Moreover, North Carolina had outdistanced Syracuse (1-0) by total O margin of 333y to 139y. Also, Heels had not as yet had to punt. Then, Orangemen S Darrell Parker made 30y INT RET of UNC QB Mike Thomas (25-42/284y, 2 INTs) that set up backup TB Tebucky Jones' go-ahead TD run at 10-9 in 1st min of 4th Q. Syracuse TB Malcolm Thomas, who rushed for 67y, wrapped it up at 17-9 with another 4th Q TD run.

GEORGIA 42 South Carolina 23: Gamecocks (0-1) appeared in command before and after H. Frosh WR Zola Davis caught 23 and 30y TDs from QB Steve Taneyhill (34-51/405y, 3 TDs, INT), his 2nd coming as time expired at H. When K Reed Morton kicked 27y FG 4:20 into 3rd Q, South Carolina led 17-7. Converted DB Robert Edwards (30/169y, 4 TDs) got Georgia (1-0) moving in 2nd H from TB position, scoring school-record 5 TDs. Edwards made 4 rapid-fire TDs, including 45y pass from scrambling QB Mike Bobo (13-28/250y, 2 TDs), then, after Carolina's Taneyhill slipped in 27y TD pass with 4:48 remaining, Edwards burst 58y with 3:01 to play in 4th Q.

AUBURN 46 Mississippi 13: Great expectations rode steadily on strong shoulders of no. 6 Auburn (1-0), for finally, Tigers were off probation and eligible for SEC championship, bowl games, and, dare loyal fans think it, national championship. Now 21-1-1 under coach Terry Bowden, Tigers fell behind early. Mississippi (0-1) mixed short passes with power runs of TB Dou Innocent (22/137y) to set up 33y FG by K Tom Montz. Auburn used similar O strategy to tie it on K Matt Hawkins' 44y FG. Innocent answered with 17y run and Ole Miss QB Josh Nelson (15-26/216y, INT) followed with 9y pass to WR Ta'Boris Fisher (7/101y) to Tigers' 32YL. On short y on 3rd and 4th downs, Auburn LB Jason Miska shot through to dump Ole Miss runners in their tracks. Only 9 plays later, Tigers TB Stephen Davis (14/70y, 2 TDs) cut through LT block for 4y TD and permanent lead at 9-3 midway in 2nd Q. QB Patrick Nix took it from there, breaking Pat Sullivan's 25-year-old school single-game passing y record with 28-39/382y, including 24y TD to FB Kevin McCleod.

Michigan 38 ILLINOIS 14: During off-season, Illini (0-1) coach Lou Tepper mentioned being disappointed to have Michigan (2-0) on schedule only once. Tepper claimed he meant no disrespect, but visiting Maize and Blue fans were chanting, "Let's play two!" as early as 3rd Q. Wolverines led 10-0 at H and struck quickly in 3rd Q: QB Scott Dreisbach (7-12/129y, TD) hit 46 and 39y passes to 5YL, and TB Tim Biakabutuka (10/97y, 3 TDs) scored. Illinois FB Robert Holcombe coughed up FUM right after subsequent KO, and Biakabutuka zipped 11y to score. It was 24-0 for Michigan, and Biakabutuka rambled 35y to score and Wolverines blocked punt for TD. Now down 38-0, Illinois salvaged pride with pair of 4th Q TDs and amazingly finished with more y than Wolverines: 352y to 330y. Illini LB Simeon Rice made 2 sacks.

Colorado 43 WISCONSIN 7: Rick Neuheisel debuted as Colorado (1-0) coach and welcomed back QB Koy Detmer (17-24/267y, 3 TDs), who had seen little action since 1992. Wisconsin (0-1) special teams fell apart early: K John Hall missed FG tries of 39 and 46y, and too-deliberate P Brian Alexander had punt blocked by Buffaloes DB Marcus Washington that led to K Neil Voskeritchian's 27y FG, all in 1st Q. WR Rae Carruth caught 17y TD pass from Detmer at end of 72y drive early in 2nd Q. Badgers responded with 82y trip as QB Darrell Bevell faked pass and dived across GL on 5y run. Wisconsin now trailed 10-7. Detmer and Carruth connected on 51y pass to set up TB Marlon Barnes' 6y TD run and they collaborated on 21y TD just 16 secs to H to bump lead to 26-7. In 2nd H, Detmer added his 3rd TD pass for 36-7 margin. Neuheisel's win made him 1st Buffaloes coach to win his opener since Jim Yeager, 8 coaches ago in 1946.

Northwestern 17 NOTRE DAME 15: Associated Press called it "one of the biggest upsets in college football history," but confident Northwestern (1-0) coach Gary Barnett said, "It's just got to send a message...that our kids can play with anybody." Midfield FUM REC gave Wildcats 1st Q chance for QB Steve Schnur's 7y TD pass to WR Dave Beazley, who spilled out of EZ into band's drum section. Notre Dame (0-1) moved within 10-9 in 2nd Q on TB Robert Farmer's 5y TD run, but try for tying kick was messed up. Northwestern went up 17-9 as TB Darnell Autry (33/160y) broke 2 tackles and charged 29y to position WR D'Wayne Bates for 26y TD catch. Irish finally seized momentum in 4th Q and got going on DL Paul Grasmanis' sack. TB Randy Kinder scored with 6:15 to go, but ND failed on tying 2-pt try as QB Ron Powlus tripped over teammate's foot. With classes not scheduled to begin in Evanston for 2 weeks, astounding victory was met with relative quiet in Chicagoland, yet to know extent of Northwestern's new profile.

SOUTHERN METHODIST 17 Arkansas 14: SMU (1-0) marked its return to Cotton Bowl stadium with encouraging crowd of 29,107 and used that spirit to surprise Razorbacks (0-1). Oddly enough, thin ranks of Ponies served to prod them to win. Fiery leader QB Ramon Flanigan dislocated his left hip on game's 1st play and was to miss most if not all of season. "Losing Ramon, that gave us more inspiration," said RB Donte Womack, who rushed 21/137y, including 37y romp off LT that served as winning TD in 4th Q. Arkansas fell behind 10-0 in 2nd Q, but TB Madre Hill (22/89y, TD) scored 3y TD. QB Barry Lunney (14-22/168y, TD) gave Hogs 14-10 lead with short TD pass to WR J.J. Meadors in 3rd Q. After Womack's go-ahead score, Arkansas roared back to 1st down inside Mustangs 1YL, but Lunney disastrously fumbled to SMU DE Wilbert Mitchell and upset was secured in last 56 secs. SMU coach Tom Rossley had told his troops at H that there "was no way we were leaving this stadium tonight without signing a winning game ball for No. 8 (Flanigan)."

TEXAS A&M 33 Louisiana State 17: TB Leeland McElroy, touted in preseason for Heisman consideration, started his 1st game for Texas A&M (1-0), scored 3 TDs and racked up 359y all-purpose y. McElroy rushed 35/229y and caught 5 passes/49y. Louisiana State (0-1) QB Jamie Howard overcame sack for safety by Aggies LB Keith Mitchell in 2nd Q to pass 21-38/131y, TD. Tigers frosh TB Kendall Cleveland scored twice in 3rd Q to lift LSU within 19-14, but McElroy scored 2 of his TDs in 4th Q as Aggies pulled away.

AIR FORCE 38 Brigham Young 12: Heat in 1st H caused rapid heartbeat for Air Force (1-0) QB Beau Morgan, but not before he led TD drive and positioned Falcons for another score. Sub QB Tom Brown completed 2nd TD march, and guided 3rd for Falcons' stunning 21-0 lead at H. Morgan (8-13/117y) opened 2nd H action, igniting Airmen's Wishbone O for 3 straight scoring possessions and 38-6 edge in 4th Q. BYU (0-1) QB Steve Sarkisian (25-42/346y, 2 TDs, 2 INTs) whipped 2 TD passes in 2nd H

in debut after Juco transfer. But, it couldn't keep emotional Falcons from their 1st-ever home win vs. Cougars and 1st anywhere in last 12 tries. "Any time anybody beats you 12 times in a row, it begins to eat at you," said proud Air Force coach Fisher DeBerry.

UCLA 31 Miami 8: Bruins (1-0) got great blocking from OT Jonathan Ogden and 2 TD runs in 2nd H from TB Karim Abdul-Jabbar (29/180y). Key UCLA score came early in 3rd Q when LB Abdul Jabbar McCullough fell on EZ FUM after Miami (0-1) DB Earl Little misplayed bounding punt near his GL. It gave UCLA 10-0 lead. Hurricanes miscued in many facets of play, managing their only TD drive of 84y midway in 4th Q as QB Ryan Collins (17-33/188y) threw 35y pass to RB Danyell Ferguson, then 10y TD to TE Syii Tucker. *Los Angeles Times* poked fun at Bruins coach Terry Donahue, who wore shorts for his 20th season opener: "(He) look(ed) more like a lifeguard on 'Baywatch' than like Bear Bryant."

September 9, 1995

(Th) Boston College 20 VIRGINIA TECH 14: Highly effective on 3rd down conversions, Boston College (1-1) QB Mark Hartsell (24-38/273y) threw 3 TD passes as Eagles topped jittery no. 20 Virginia Tech (0-1). Hartsell clicked on 5 straight passes, including 11y TD to TE Todd Pollack, to open game. Hokies appeared poised to tie it on 1st series of 2nd Q as they drove 70y to BC 24YL. Eagles D popped FUM from Tech FB Brian Edmonds (7/44y, TD), and S Terence Wiggins returned mid-air REC 53y. Just 6 plays later midway in 2nd Q, Hartsell hit frosh WR Dennis Harding with 4y TD pass for 14-0 lead. Right after KO, Hokies WR Bryan Still faked around DB at 30YL and sprinted distance to complete 80y TD pass-run from QB Jim Druckenmiller (21-42/296y, TD). Trailing 20-7 after Hartsell's TD pass in 3rd Q, Tech blocked x-pt, which loomed large when Edmonds scored early in 4th Q. On critical next-to-last possession, Va Tech suffered through myriad of problems: broken play, illegal procedure PEN, and Druckenmiller's bad lob of screen pass. Those miscues embellished 5 earlier pass-drops and missed 30y FG.

MARYLAND 32 North Carolina 18: Loser of 5 straight games to North Carolina (0-2), Maryland (2-0) collared biggest win so far at Mark Duffner's coaching regime. Terps D bagged 4 INTs of QB Mike Thomas as Heels now totaled 10 TOs in their 2 losses. Maryland QB Brian Cummings, who replaced Scott Milanovich while starter sat out 4-game gambling suspension, passed 10-18/180y, TD. Terps WR Mancel Johnson caught TD passes of 50 and 32y. TB Jonathan Linton went 22y for TD as Carolina tied it at 18-18 in 3rd Q, but Maryland answered with 79y drive on which WR Jermaine Lewis caught passes of 27 and 40y.

Virginia 29 NORTH CAROLINA STATE 24: In 2nd H, Virginia (2-1) blew leads of 20-7 and 23-21 built primarily on 52y TD pass, 1y TD run by QB Mike Groh (12-20/159y). NC State (1-1) had charged back on TD drives of 96 and 84y: TB Tremayne Stephens (27/103y) dove over from 1YL and QB Terry Harvey (18-27/195y, INT) fired 32y score to WR Jimmy Grissett. After trade of FGs, Wolfpack led 24-23 with 1:15 to go. Cavs pulled it out with 13 secs left as Groh completed 5 passes in row, 4 to WR Patrick Jeffers. TB Tiki Barber blasted over for winning TD.

Florida State 45 CLEMSON 26: Florida State (2-0) ran its ACC winning streak to 26 games but not without fight from slow-starting Clemson (1-1). Waterbug TB Warrick Dunn (12/180y, 2 TDs) was Florida State clutch player after FB Poo Bear Williams' 2 early TD runs. Dunn scored 3y TD to send FSU off at H with 21-7 lead and made key gains and long TD run in competitive 2nd H. Led by TB Raymond Priester's 22/111y and TD rushing, Tigers ground out 321y on ground. Clemson's rushing attack kept it within hailing distance at 28-17 and 31-20. After Clemson K Jeff Sauve's 31y FG in 3rd Q, Dunn spurted up middle for 41y to set up TD pass by QB Danny Kanell (13-27/170y, 2 TDs). Sauve kicked another FG to open 4th Q and pull Tigers within 31-20, but Noles responded with 80y trip to Kanell's 2nd TD pass. Dunn's 55y draw run clinched it at 45-20 in 4th Q.

TENNESSEE 30 Georgia 27: Bulldogs lost TB Robert Edwards (15/156y, 2 TDs) with broken foot, just beginning of long injury list for Georgia (1-1). But, Bulldogs put up fight, taking leads of 7-0 and 10-7 in 1st Q and 24-20 in 3rd Q. Tennessee (2-0) QB Peyton Manning (26-38/349y, INT) ran for 8y TD and passed for 2 scores. With score tied 27-27, Bulldogs K Dax Langley missed 53y FG try, and Vols took over on own 36YL with 1:29 to go. Manning hit TB Jay Graham (28/137y) with 29y pass and WR Joey Kent with 7y pass before Graham's 10y run set up frosh K Jeff Hall's winning 34y FG.

Florida 42 KENTUCKY 7: Coach Steve Spurrier had to look deep on Florida (2-0) depth chart to find TB in former-DB Terry Jackson (16/138y, 3 TDs) to fill in for injured TBs Fred Taylor and Elijah Williams. Gators QB Danny Wuerffel (21-28/253y, 2 TDs, INT) connected with WR Chris Doering for TD passes at end of 85 and 80y drives in 1st H. After WR Jacquez Green's punt block in 1st Q, Taylor made short TD run before his shoulder was separated. Another Gator who played well before being injured was

DT Keith Council who put considerable pressure on Kentucky (0-2) QB Jeff Speedy (6-21/40y, INT). Wildcats went 68y during "garbage time" in latter part of 4th Q as QB Billy Jack Haskins (5-5/82y, TD) hit 30y pass to WR Craig Yeast.

PENN STATE 24 Texas Tech 23: Beforehand, Penn State (1-0) coach Joe Paterno warned, "We're not very good," despite Lions owning nation's longest winning streak at 16 games prior to game. WR Bobby Engram, sr star usually to be counted upon, lost 2 FUMs that led to Texas Tech (0-1) TDs for stunning 20-7 H lead for Raiders: LB Shawn Banks had EZ FUM REC and QB Zebbie Lethridge threw 2 TDs. Engram made amends in 2nd H, catching 7/106y including 3 grabs on closing drive that led to K Brett Conway's winning 39y FG with 4 secs left.

OKLAHOMA 38 San Diego State 22: Despite 129y in PENs, Howard Schnellenberger won his coaching debut at Oklahoma (1-0), but he was unimpressed: "We have a long way to go..." Stout D keyed Sooners as it limited San Diego State (1-1) to 87y rushing and scored on 65y FUM RET in 4th Q by DB Maylon Wesley. FB Jerald Moore (14/159y) scored 3 TDs as Sooners built 31-0 lead in 3rd Q. SDSU DB Ricky Parker set up 2 TDs with long INT RETs in 4th Q. Aztecs' JC transfer sensation RB George Jones rushed only 21/89y, but tallied 2 TDs.

OREGON 34 Illinois 31: RB Ricky Whittle (24/108y, 3 TDs) scored 3 times for Oregon (2-0), but it was Ducks D that made biggest play in 4th Q. DB Jaiya Figueras blitzed Illinois (0-2) QB Johnny Johnson with 6:24 left, forced FUM, and recovered it in EZ to take 34-31 lead. Illini had constructed 19-7 H advantage on 41y TD pass by Johnson (14-30/129y, TD), 1st of 2 TD runs by RB Ty Douthard, and 2 FGs by K Bret Scheuplein. Whittle tallied his 2nd TD on 12y run early in 3rd Q, and it took his 3y run, followed by 2-pt pass by QB Ryan Perry-Smith (17-37/234y, 2 INTs), 2:46 into 4th Q to pull Ducks within 31-28 and give them shot at win in coach Mike Belotti's home debut.

September 16, 1995

(Th) KANSAS 38 Texas Christian 20: So confused were long-suffering Kansas (3-0) fans that they threw oranges on field during Jayhawks' 1st Q explosion, even though Big 8 champs were no longer contracted for Orange Bowl. Kansas RBs June Henley (13/160y, 2 TDs) and L.T. Levine (13/134y, 2 TDs) combined to romp over TCU (1-1) for 21-0 lead early in 2nd Q. Then, however, KU stumbled through 6 straight series without so much as single 1st down. Meanwhile, Horned Frogs QB Max Knake (32-57/391y, 2 TDs) was glad to shake sack-focused LB Keith Rodgers from nightmarish start in which TCU missed 7 3rd down tries in row. Just before H, Knake hit diving WR John Washington with TD, 40th TD of Knake's career that boosted him past legendary Sammy Baugh for school record. TCU nipped score to within 24-13 in 4th Q but soon was stopped on 4th down at Kansas 31YL. Henley took pitchout left and used TE Jim Moore's big block to canter 59y for important TD.

FLORIDA 62 Tennessee 37: Trailing 30-14 late in 1st H after Volunteers (2-1) DB Raymond Austin returned FUM 46y for TD, Florida (3-0) ran off 48 unanswered pts including 3 TDs from QB Danny Wuerffel (29-39/381y, 6 TDs, INT) to WR Ike Hilliard (9/112y, 4 TDs). Vols had silenced Florida Field crowd by building 23-7 lead in 2nd Q as QB Peyton Manning (23-36/326y) threw 2 TD passes to WR Marcus Nash. Gators O explosion registered 584y (7.8y per play), while Tennessee gained 460y.

Arkansas 20 ALABAMA 19: Winners of 7 games with 4th Q rallies in 2 years, Alabama (2-1) instead had tables turned by upset-hungry Arkansas (2-1), which won in closing moment. On 4th down at Bama 3YL, Razorbacks QB Barry Lunney (15-26/181y) rolled left, fired low pass to WR J.J. Meadors in EZ. Meadors made controversial, diving grasstop catch, and K Todd Latourette kicked winning pt with 6 secs left. Crimson Tide had come back from 10-3 deficit in 1st Q to lead 19-10 in 3rd Q as QB Brian Burgdorf threw 40y TD pass to WR Curtis Brown, but finished with only 6-17/90y, TD, INT in air.

LOUISIANA STATE 12 Auburn 6: Making good on his promise to return excitement to Saturday nights at Tiger Stadium, LSU (2-1) coach Gerry DiNardo used revenge for bizarre 1994 loss as inspiration for upset of Auburn (2-1). LSU got all pts in 1st Q on short TD pass by QB Jamie Howard (19-30/220y, TD, INT), K Andre Lafleur's 41y FG, and EZ sack of Auburn QB Patrick Nix (19-36/127y, INT). Auburn had late chance at LSU 11YL, but Bengals DB Troy Twillie made EZ INT of Nix.

OHIO STATE 30 Washington 20: Huskies (1-1) put 8 men up close and dared Ohio State (2-0) to run, and still Buckeyes TB Eddie George gained 36/212y, 2 TDs. QB Bobby Hoying threw early TD pass, but x-pt was blocked so that Ohio State led 6-0. Washington got its only lead at 7-6 when TB Rashaan Sheehee galloped 10y. George ran 12y to Huskies 12YL on fake FG run in 2nd Q to set up another TD pass by Hoying (18-25/192y, 2 TDs, INT), and George blasted 51y behind block of T Orlando Pace to set up his 7y TD run for 23-7 H edge. George scored on 16y run in 3rd Q, but as he put it later, "There was too much drama in the second half." In 4th Q, Buckeyes had bundle of miscues that allowed Washington to threaten with 2 TD passes, 1 each from QBs Shane Fortney and Damon Huard (19-26/192y, TD, INT).

Miami (Ohio) 30 NORTHWESTERN 28: When this score became final on crazy last-moment Miami (2-1) FG by K Chad Seitz, know-it-alls around nation began thinking win over Notre Dame had been total fluke for Northwestern (1-1). Wildcats had built comfortable 28-7 advantage at end of 3rd Q as QB Steve Schnur (13-26/187y, INT) threw 2 TD passes to WR D'Wayne Bates and TD pass to RB Darnell Autry (35/152y). Redskins rallied to wthin 28-27 as sub QB Sam Ricketts (13-26/190y, INT) threw 2 TD passes. In closing secs, NW's punting game went awry with sub snapper forced into action: his wild snap crushed Northwestern as it gave Miami possession at Wildcats 2YL. Seitz immediately kicked 20y, bad angle winner at final gun.

NEBRASKA 77 Arizona State 28: Matching no. 1 Florida State's pts from Seminoles' 77-17 win over NC State, no. 2 Nebraska (3-0) put aside distractions of IB Lawrence Phillips' suspension and national media spotlight. QB Tommie Frazier, who accounted for 4 TDs, curtly told media, "We made a statement today that even though we lost a great player, we're going to move on." Arizona State (1-2) coach Bruce Snyder called Huskers' school-record 63 pts in 1st H "an avalanche." It began on Nebraska's 1st snap as IB Clinton Childs (12/143y, 2 TDs) raced 65y for TD. Frosh IB Ahman Green added 13/111y, 2 TDs on ground. Sun Devils WR Keith Poole caught 6/200y, scored 3 TDs.

Iowa 27 IOWA STATE 10: TB Sedrick Shaw (32/178y, TD) and FB Rodney Filer (9/113y, TD) each had their best rushing totals to date for Iowa (2-0) as Hawkeyes rolled up 310y on ground. After Shaw's early TD, Iowa State (1-2) took 7-6 lead in 1st Q on TB Darren Davis' 63y sprint. When K Jamie Kohl made FG, Cyclones led 10-6 in 2nd Q, but they lost for 13th straight time to Iowa when they couldn't stop running game. Hawkeyes jumped to 18-10 edge in 3rd Q when backup TB Tavian Banks made 5y TD run.

Oregon 38 UCLA 31: Injury-riddled UCLA (2-1) compiled 460y O vs. Oregon (3-0), but TB Karim Abdul-Jabbar (32/127y), playing with sore back, couldn't make 1y for tying TD on game's last play. Ducks QB Tony Graziani riddled depleted Bruins D for 19-35/255y, 3 TDs passing and also ran 6y to give Oregon 31-24 lead early in 4th Q. Bruins knotted it at 31-31 on WR Derek Ayers' 29y reverse run. Oregon WR Cristin McLemore caught Graziani's game-winner with 1:02 to go, before UCLA went 92y to Ducks doorstep. Big play on UCLA's failed final drive was WR Kevin Jordan's 46y catch from frosh QB Cade McNown (12-24/183y, INT).

USA Today Coaches Poll September 18

1	Florida State (33)	1508	14	Virginia	752
2	Nebraska (24)	1493	15	UCLA	565
3	Texas A&M (4)	1400	16	Tennessee	550
4	Florida	1351	17	Miami (Fla.)	438
5	Southern California (1)	1227	18	Georgia	399
6	Penn State	1200	19	Kansas State	361
7	Ohio State	1186	20	LSU	330
8	Colorado	1143	21	Notre Dame	308
9	Michigan	1136	22	Washington	251
10	Texas	897	23	Alabama	225
11	Oklahoma	889	24	Arizona	197
12	Auburn	804	25	Maryland	127
13	Oregon	780			

September 23, 1995

VIRGINIA TECH 13 Miami 7: No. 17 Miami (1-2) hadn't lost to unranked foe since 1984, but Hurricanes were clearly slipping early in 1995. Score looked close, but Virginia Tech (1-2) gave thorough caning to Canes. "This game, to be honest with you, should have been over earlier," said Hokies coach Frank Beamer. Indeed, Virginia Tech K Atle Larson made FGs of 45 and 30y, but missed 4 others. And Virginia Tech dropped sure TD pass and failed to make TD when it had 1st-and-goal from Miami 9YL. Hokies QB Jim Druckenmiller (9-16/97y) pitched 47y pass to WR Bryan Still to set up short TD run by TB Dwayne Thomas (24/165y, TD) on their 2nd series. Greatest damage came from powerful 300y rushing, most Hurricanes had allowed since 1979 game against Syracuse.

SYRACUSE 27 Minnesota 17: WR Marvin Harrison scored vital TD on thrilling 94y punt TD RET and caught 8/184y passes to spark Syracuse (2-1) to 21 pts in row that sealed victory over frustrated Minnesota (1-1). After 3-3 tie in 1st Q, Gopher RB Chris Darkins (34/206y, TD) rammed across score for short-lived 10-3 lead. Despite his big run total, Darkins was angry: "This stinks. I'd rather have two yards rushing in a victory." Harrison authored his TD RET late in 2nd Q for 13-10 H edge, and Orangemen led 27-10 when he caught 30y TD pass from QB Donovan McNabb (11-16/216y, TD, INT). Syracuse's margin was sliced to 27-17 on 13y TD pass by Minnesota QB Cory Sauter (16-25/200y, TD, 2 INTs). Gophers threatened again, marching to Orange 7YL, but Sauter was intercepted in EZ by Syracuse CB Rod Gadson.

Penn State 59 RUTGERS 34 (E. Rutherford, N.J.): Penn State (3-0) and Rutgers (1-2) repeated O war of 1994 with 661y and 496y respectively. Prime weapons were Nittany Lions WR Bobby Engram, who caught 8/175y, 3 TDs, and Scarlet Knights TE Marco Battaglia, who grabbed 13/184y, 3 TDs. Engram also opened scoring with 58y run with 1-hop scoop of his open-field FUM, which launched Penn State to 17-0 edge in 1st Q. Story of game, however, became 42y TD pass by Lions sub QB Mike McQueary in game's last min. It prompted expletive-filled midfield exchange between coaches. Penn State's Joe Paterno conceded Doug Graber's right to be angry but later apologized only for his own words in response to Graber's confrontation.

MARYLAND 41 Duke 28: Maryland (4-0) knocked off Duke (2-2) to fashion its best start since 1978. Terps QB Brian Cummings (19-27/299y, 2 TDs), who could head to bench with starter Scott Milanovich's gambling suspension ended, hit WR Jermaine Lewis with 9/205y, TD. Maryland let 21-3 lead dwindle to 21-18 as Blue Devils TB Lamarr Marshall (30/115y, 2 TDs) scored twice in 2nd Q. But, Terps were alive in 3rd Q as they went 90y to score TD for 32-18 edge after K Joe O'Donnell had made 19y FG after 2nd H KO. Duke gained possession while trailing 35-28 with 4 mins to play, but failed to advance past Maryland 39YL where it lost ball on downs. TB Buddy Rodgers (13/103y, 2 TDs) scored Terps' clinching TD on 21y run.

Virginia 22 CLEMSON 3: After 19 tries, Virginia (4-1) finally ended "Curse of Death Valley," winning for 1st time ever on road at Clemson (2-2). Cavaliers jumped to 12-0 lead in 1st Q despite blocked and missed x-pt kicks: TB Tiki Barber (27/111y, TD) scored UVa's 2nd TD on 11y run. Tigers drove to Cavs 1YL late in 2nd Q, but TB Raymond Priester (27/111y) and gigantic FB Emory Smith each failed on GL smashes. Priester touched ball on 11 of 12 plays on 64y 3rd Q drive to 27y FG by Clemson K Jeff Sauve. Bust-out play came on Virginia WR Patrick Jeffers' slant-out long pattern to beat CB Dexter McCleon for 76y TD with 5 mins left in 3rd Q. It gave Wahoos insurmountable 19-3 edge that meant end of long defeat streak at Clemson.

Baylor 14 NORTH CAROLINA STATE 0: Never having been blanked at home since Carter-Finley Stadium opened 29 years earlier, North Carolina State (1-3) could fabricate only 138y in 51 O plays. Baylor (2-1) sent its trio of TBs pounding up middle for 224y in steady downpour of rain. On 4th-and-2 at NC State 34YL in 1st Q, Wolfpack DE Brad Collins jumped off-side to help advance Bears to their 1st TD on TB Anthony Hodge's 15y run. Baylor TB Shawn Washington added 1y TD run in 2nd Q. NC State had planned option attack, but bad footing and annoying groin injury to QB Terry Harvey (12-31/114y, 2 INTs) killed that idea, and Harvey could penetrate Bears territory only once with his so-so passing. That drive came in last 2 mins, but was crushed by Baylor LB Dean Jackson's sliding INT.

Kentucky 35 SOUTH CAROLINA 30: "We make an All-American out of every back in the SEC," moaned South Carolina (1-3) D coordinator Wally Burnham after witnessing Kentucky (2-2) TB Moe Williams rip for 40/299y and 4 TDs through Cocks' conf-worst (5.9y per carry) run D. Still, Gamecocks rallied from 14-0 deficit to trail 21-14 at H despite Williams' TD runs of 20, 43, and 2y. South Carolina FB Stanley Pritchett (9/131y, TD receiving) barreled 92y with pass from QB Steve Taneyhill (26-44/304y, 3 TDs, 2 INTs), but its O stopped itself with numerous dropped passes and 4 TOs. Behind 28-23 early in 4th Q, Taneyhill had to scramble on 1st down at UK 9YL and was picked off in EZ by DB George Harris. Wildcats scored on QB Billy Jack Haskins' TD run, and Harris fell on FUM to halt Cocks again.

MISSISSIPPI 18 Georgia 10: Ole Miss (2-1) D held injury-riddled Georgia (2-2) to 81y rushing, and K Tim Montz made FGs of 44, 42, 33, and 20y to secure upset. Bulldogs QB Brian Smith (18-32/219y, TD, INT) replaced QB Mike Bobo, who left with season-ending knee injury, and flipped 2nd Q TD pass to WR Brice Hunter for 7-6 H lead. TD pass was matched in 3rd Q by Rebels QB Josh Nelson (21-33/227y). Down 18-10 with 3:47 to go, Georgia moved 61y to 20YL, but Rebels LB Nate Wayne made INT. Georgia's last gasp try died at Ole Miss 7YL as Smith's 4th down pass failed to gain 1st down.

NOTRE DAME 55 Texas 27: Just 9 days after spinal surgery, Notre Dame (3-1) coach Lou Holtz returned to coach from press box and then made trip to bench in tilt's last min. Irish beat 1st ranked foe in 2 years though Texas (2-1) led 20-19 after QB James Brown (19-33/326y, 4 TDs, 2 INTs) pitched 1y TD to TE Steve Bradley on 1st series of 3rd Q. FB Marc Edwards then scored 3 of Notre Dame's 4 unanswered TDs. Irish DB Allen Rossum scored 2 pts on 80y run of blocked conv in 2nd Q and 29y INT TD RET in 4th Q.

COLORADO 29 Texas A&M 21: With 3 O stars and winningest coach in school history missing in 1995, Colorado (4-0) appeared to be headed for subpar season. But, backup QB John Hessler and suffocating Buffs D ruined no. 3 Texas A&M (2-1) in year's 1st big game. Buffs QB Koy Detmer injured knee late in 1st Q with A&M up 7-0 on EZ FUM REC by DL David Maxwell after sack by DL Brandon Mitchell, Aggies' bookend Ts in 3-4 D. Hessler (10-20/177y, TD) came off bench to run for 2 TDs to give Colorado 20-14 H lead. Aggies bounced back to lead 21-20 on QB Corey Pullig's 38y TD arrow to WR A.C. Connell. When Buffs went ahead 26-21 on Hessler's 4th Q TD pass, coach Rick Neuheisel cleverly forced Aggies to burn 2 timeouts as he used 2 odd formations for 2-pt play. A&M could have used those timeouts when its last drive failed on 4th down pass near midfield. Buffaloes' 5-man front frustrated A&M TB Leeland McElroy (23/52y).

Stanford 28 OREGON 21: Off to its best start since 1986, Stanford (3-0-1) used WR Marlon Evans' 96y KO TD RET to take lead for good just moments after Oregon (3-1) tied it at 14-14 in 3rd Q. Ducks QB Tony Graziani (26-50/292y, 2 TDs) was picked off 3 times in 1st H, 2 leading to Cardinal TDs by FB Greg Comella and RB Anthony Bookman. Oregon held total O edge 454y to 293y and got within 28-21 with 2:58 left. Ducks K Josh Smith then recovered his own onside KO, but last drive died at Stanford 39YL.

WASHINGTON 21 Army 13: "We took this game way too lightly," said Washington (2-1) QB Damon Huard, who lost 2 FUMs and threw INT in each of 1st 3 Qs during which huge underdog Army (1-2) built 10-7 lead. Huard rallied in 4th Q with 6-7/119y passing including early 49y TD to WR Andre deSaussure for 14-13 lead. Huard later added 2y TD run. Cadets, who by game's end would enjoy 13-min edge in possession time, next marched from own 27YL to Huskies 1YL, but time expired after 3 futile cracks at GL. Army FB John Conroy rushed 24/166y.

Southern California 31 ARIZONA 10: Revolving Trojan QB door allowed Kyle Wachholtz to enter with 8-9/138y, 3 TDs passing. On his receiving end in 2nd Q were WR Keyshawn Johnson (9/112y), who caught 28y TD, and TE Johnny McWilliams, who rambled 38y with TD pass. Southern California (3-0) D allowed only 1 penetration of its territory in 1st H. WR Richard Dice's 50y punt RET put Arizona (2-2) at USC 24YL in 3rd Q, but USC LB Izzy Ifeanyi sacked QB Dan White (22-40/176y) and DB Sammy Knight knocked down White's subsequent 4th down pass. Wildcats failed to score until after subs were protecting USC's 24-0 lead in 4th Q.

1	Florida State (35)	1514	14	Notre Dame	657
2	Nebraska (25)	1502	15	Kansas State	651
3	Florida	1397	16	LSU	618
4	Southern California (1)	1308	17	Maryland	491
5	Colorado	1275	18	Washington	353
6	Ohio State	1246	19	Texas	351
7	Penn State	1243	20	Oregon	327
8	Michigan	1139	21	Alabama	278
9	Oklahoma	998	22	Kansas	248
10	Texas A&M	971	23	Stanford	207
11	Virginia	897	24	Arkansas	172
12	Auburn	803	25	UCLA	129
13	Tennessee	720			

September 30, 1995

(Th) GEORGIA TECH 31 Maryland 3: Both schools looked at TV match to fuel their comeback seasons. Maryland (4-1) found itself in middle of inadvertent QB controversy and on doorstep of dreadful scoring slump. Soph QB Brian Cummings had played through injuries to guide Terps to undefeated record, and QB Scott Milanovich returned rusty from NCAA suspension, but still got start vs. Georgia Tech (2-2). Yellow Jackets took early command, their improving D sacked Milanovich 6/-51y, 3 times by LB Jimmy Clements. Georgia Tech TB C.J. Williams scored on runs of 37 and 14y.

SOUTH CAROLINA 20 Louisiana State 20: Maligned South Carolina (1-3-1) D held LSU (3-1-1) to 33y rushing in building 17-10 H lead. Embarking on fabulous 4-game passing surge (109-141/1333y, 13 TDs, 0 INTs), QB Steve Taneyhill (20-33/243y) hit WR Monty Means with 5y TD pass in 1st Q. Tigers WR Sheddrick Wilson (6/93y) had to be helped from field at H with severe knee sprain. But, Wilson returned limping in 2nd H and caught 19y TD pass from QB Jamie Howard (18-36/271y, TD) with 1:06 to play. Coach Gerry DiNardo chose to kick pt to keep Tigers within touch of SEC West leader Arkansas, 35-7 winner over Vanderbilt.

Wisconsin 17 PENN STATE 9: Lethargic Penn State (3-1) owned 20-game win streak, but fell behind 10-0 as efficient Wisconsin (2-1-1) crafted 2 faultless drives resulting in K John Hall's 26y FG and QB Darrell Bevell's 21y TD pass to TE Matt Nyquist. Lions edged within 10-3 as K Brett Conway atoned for early miss with 32y FG in 3rd Q. Master of 3rd down, Bevell (18-22/192y, 2 TDs) connected with leaping WR Tony Simmons for TD midway through 4th Q. Penn State QB Wally Richardson (33-48/259y) found WR Freddie Scott with 4th down TD pass, but Badgers thwarted FB Jon Wittman's 2-pt run off fake kick. Richardson missed 4th down pass in last min. "Even their band kicked our butts," muttered Penn State fan Fred Strouse.

NORTHWESTERN 31 Indiana 7: Surging Northwestern (3-1) broke into AP Poll after win over Indiana (2-2) and started season at 3-1 for 1st time since Ara Parseghian was coach in 1963. Interesting exchange occurred in 2nd Q as NW P Paul Burton bombed 90y punt to Hoosiers 3YL, and Indiana TB Alex Smith (23/136y) soon spurted 61y. Indiana didn't score on that series but took 7-3 lead in 2nd Q as QB Chris Dittoe (15-27/155y, INT) wedged in. Indiana held ball for 20:51 of 1st H, yet, thanks to 42y cutback TD run by TB Darnell Autry (28/162y, 2 TDs), Wildcats led 10-7. When WR Brian Musso broke through wide gaps in Hoosier punt coverage for 86y RET in 3rd Q, Autry scored on next play from 6YL. That TD and 2-pt pass by QB Steve Schnur (7-13/45y) provided 21-7 lead, and it was all she wrote even though Indiana finished with 401y to 258y total O advantage.

OHIO STATE 45 Notre Dame 26: Sixty years after its storied last visit (last-min, 18-13 victory once called greatest game ever by some observers); Notre Dame (3-2) returned to Columbus to take 10-0 and 17-7 2nd Q leads on 2 TDs by TB Randy Kinder (28/143y, 3 TDs). WR Dimitrious Stanley made magnificent EZ readjustment to QB Bobby Hoying's 17y pass with 44 secs before H to draw Ohio State (4-0) to within 17-14. Lou Holtz, coaching on ND sideline for 1st time since spinal surgery, was helpless to stop TOs on 3 straight series, and Buckeyes scored 3 TDs in less than 6 mins to erase 20-14 deficit. Killing error for ND came with it ahead 20-14 and 6:33 left in 3rd Q: KR Emmett Mosley, thinking punt would hit Irish teammate, tried to catch drifting ball. Ohio State's REC of muff quickly was turned into TE Rickey Dudley's 15y TD catch from Hoying (14-22/272y, 4 TDs). WR Terry Glenn soon took short pass from Hoying and streaked away from 2 Irish DBs for spectacular 82y TD. Ohio TB Eddie George rushed 32/207y, 2 TDs, but refused to campaign for Heisman: "All I know is I played a game against Notre Dame to the best of my ability…If I'm up for consideration, that's great."

MICHIGAN STATE 25 Boston College 21: Eagles (1-3) desperately wanted to win at least 1 of their 3-game sojourn into Big 10 opposition, and after losses to Ohio State and Michigan, this appeared to be it. But, sloppy tackling by Boston College and 2 INTs by alert Michigan State (2-1-1) defenders helped overturn BC's 15-9 H edge. Eagles had gone ahead late in 2nd Q on no-huddle drive that captured 64y and tallied on QB Mark Hartsell's 4y TD pass to WR Dennis Harding, followed by Hartsell's 2-pt pass. BC jumped to 21-9 lead when TE Michael Hemmert got all alone for 4y play-action TD catch. MSU QB Todd Schultz (20-28/210y, 2 TDs, 2 INTs) hit 2 big passes on 64y drive, including TD to TE Marcus Chapman. Spartans regained ball on S Rob Shurelds' INT for 46y march capped by FB Scott Greene's TD plunge to retake lead at 22-21. MSU K Chris Gardner hit 19y FG, his 2nd 3-ptr late in 4th Q.

Colorado 38 OKLAHOMA 17: Sooners (3-1) spoke confidently all week about upset of Colorado (5-0), which started sub QB John Hessler for 1st time in place of injured QB Koy Detmer. ESPN's Lee Corso got huge cheer from Sooner fans near on-campus TV stage after his prediction of 2-TD Oklahoma victory and Hessler's demise against rough D. But, after Oklahoma jumped to early 10-0 lead on K Jeremy Alexander's FG and QB Eric Moore's short TD run after LB Terrence Malone's blocked punt, Hessler went to work. He pitched 24-34/348y and school-record 5 TD. Bison WRs Phil Savoy

and Rae Carruth (5/112y, 2 TDs) each hauled in pair of scores: 19 and 42y and 11 and 71y respectively. After Sooners tapped 17-14 H edge on WR JaJuan Penny's TD grab from Moore (7-15/87y, TD), Colorado held Oklahoma to 28y O in 3rd Q and took command at 28-17, starting with Carruth's long TD.

SOUTHERN CALIFORNIA 31 Arizona State 0: Playing without 3 suspended starters—TB Shawn Walters, DL Israel Ifeanyi, and LB Errick Herron—Southern California (4-0) counted on stellar WR Keyshawn Johnson (13/171y, TD) to extend his streak of 100y receiving to 12 games, new NCAA record. Johnson was matched up against former JC teammate, Sun Devils (2-3) CB Traivon Johnson, and in days before game, he needled his pal, "I know what Traivon Johnson is doing at ASU this week, …telling people he can cover me when he knows he can't cover me." With USC up 16-0 in 3rd Q, Johnson took quick hitch pass, meant only to make 1st down, from QB Brad Otton (15-26/192y, 2 TDs) and streaked 60y to score. Arizona State QB Jake Plummer passed 17-35/148y, 2 INTs and Devils hung in at 10-0 H deficit even though they could total only 274y to USC's 517y at game's end. Walters' suspension allowed playing time for little, 3rd-team Trojans TB LaVale Woods (7/62y, 2 TDs).

1	Florida State (34)	1513	14	Oklahoma	625
2	Nebraska (24)	1500	15	Washington	555
3	Florida	1394	16	Texas	525
4	Southern California (2)	1323	17	Alabama	508
5	Ohio State (2)	1303	18	Oregon	423
6	Colorado	1291	19	Kansas	421
7	Michigan	1179	20	Stanford	352
8	Texas A&M	1054	21	Arkansas	335
9	Virginia	1014	22	LSU	328
10	Auburn	937	23	Notre Dame	160
11	Tennessee	909	24	Baylor	133
12	Penn State	830	25	UCLA	132
13	Kansas State	744			

October 7, 1995

Virginia Tech 14 NAVY 0: Midshipmen (2-3) played well on D, allowing 273y, but its woeful O could take no advantage of 4 TOs forced upon Virginia Tech (3-2). Navy made error in special team play to lead to Hokies' 2nd Q TD and 7-0 H score. Forced to punt from its 24YL, Virginia Tech P John Thomas was roughed, and Hokies kept possession at own 39YL. QB Jim Druckenmiller (10-19/88y, 2 INTs) then hit passes of 11, 31, and 7y to close 1st Q. On opening play of 2nd H, Druckenmiller lobbed 16y TD to WR Jermaine Holmes. On their last possession, Hokies went 85y to TB Dwayne Thomas' 28y tip-toe TD trip down left sideline with 1:55 on clock.

FLORIDA STATE 41 Miami 17: After many troublesome results vs. Miami, Florida State (5-0) kicked Hurricanes (1-3) when they were down. After slow start that resulted in 10-7 lead near H, Seminoles QB Danny Kanell (17-27/170y, 3 TDs, 3 INTs) clicked on scoring passes of 8 and 26y to WR Andre Cooper to boost edge to 24-7 at H. RB Warrick Dunn, submerged by Hurricanes D in 1994, resurfaced with career-high to-date 184y rushing to give him flashy 10.3y run avg for season. FSU D limited Miami to 223y O and put significant pressure on QB Ryan Clement (10-23/96y, 3 INT) in his 1st career start. Coach Bobby Bowden raised his career record against Hurricanes to 7-13.

Tennessee 49 ARKANSAS 31: Volunteers QB Peyton Manning (35-46/384y, 4 TDs, INT) was fooled on 1st series on which Tennessee (5-1) lost but, Volunteers scored on 6 of their next 8 possessions. Meanwhile, Arkansas (4-2) QB Barry Lunney also wielded hot hand, throwing TD passes that gave Hogs 1st H leads of 14-7 and 24-14. At game's end, Lunney had completed 22-27/276y, 3 TDs. Back ahead 28-24, Manning completed 3 passes on 3rd down on critical 77y TD drive that culminated in TB Jay Graham's 1y dive.

GEORGIA 19 Clemson 17: Slim, unknown frosh TB Torin Kirtsey slipped through gaping holes for 38/195y rushing as injury-riddled Bulldogs (3-3) came from behind to beat Tigers (3-3). Wearing replica jerseys from 1940 Cotton Bowl team, Clemson took 10-7 lead: FB Emory Smith (12/60y, 2 TDs) scored on 1y blast as Tigers burned half of 1st Q clock, and K Jeff Sauve belted 47y FG in 2nd Q. Georgia's outstanding O line, led by G Resty Beadles and T Adam Meadows, began carving big holes in 2nd Q. Bulldogs took 19-10 lead in 3rd Q, primarily on QB Brian Smith's 29y TD pass to WR Juan Daniels. Early in 4th Q, Clemson sparked briefly to life on 60y drive in 6 plays to Smith's 2nd TD, but UGa completely shut down Tigers' last 2 possessions. Clemson frosh LB Anthony Simmons had hand in 15 tackles.

Ohio State 28 PENN STATE 25: Inspired Penn State (3-2) rolled to 10-0 1st Q lead on sum of 3 TD plunges by FB Jon Witman and K Brett Conway's 40y FG. Then, Ohio State (5-0) WR Terry Glenn (9/175y, 2 TD) went to work, soaring for QB Bobby Hoying (24-35/354y, 3 TDs, INT) passes at each sideline and for 28y TD over middle. Buckeyes drilled 98y downfield to TE Rickey Dudley's 25y TD catch and 14-10 H lead. Featuring runs of TB Curtis Enis (25/146y) Lions went 85y in 3rd Q to Witman's TD, and when WR Joe Jurevicius caught QB Wally Richardson's 2-pt pass, Penn State was within 21-18. Lions went ahead 25-21 early in 4th Q, but their inability to move on last 2 possessions allowed Hoying to maneuver Buckeyes for TB Eddie George's winning 6y run behind T Orlando Pace's block with 1:42 left.

Northwestern 19 MICHIGAN 13: Pres Lyndon Johnson was in White House in 1965 last time Northwestern (4-1) beat Michigan (5-1). Wolverines had 4 TOs and 6 critical PENs to help Wildcats to K Sam Valenzisi's 4 FGs and FB Matt Hartl's short 4th Q TD pass from QB Steve Schnur (11-23/126y, TD). Northwestern LB Pat Fitzgerald, Wildcats' future coach, had 14 tackles and was instrumental in stopping late Michigan drive. Wolverines TB Tim Biakabutuka rushed 34/career high 205y.

Iowa 21 MICHIGAN STATE 7: Elusive TB Sedrick Shaw rushed for 250y and cinching 4th Q TD on 42 carries, and visiting Iowa (4-0) fans shouted "Heisman!" at him afterward. Modest Shaw waved off that talk: "I don't want any part of it. That's the offensive line, that's not me. It's a team thing." Hawkeyes thoroughly dominated both lines, holding Michigan State (2-2-1) to 42/31y rushing. Iowa took 14-7 lead in 3rd Q when QB Matt Sherman (13-26/213y, TD) hit WR Tim Dwight (6/115y, TD) with 11y score and followed with 2-pt pass to Shaw. Spartans had 2 fine opportunities in 4th Q to get back into contention: TB Marc Renaud (10/28y) lost FUM at Hawkeyes 9YL, and QB Todd Schultz (20-37/255y, 2 INTs) was picked off in EZ while throwing from 2YL. Rugged FB Scott Greene had given Michigan State 7-3 lead in 2nd Q on 2y TD run.

MINNESOTA 39 Purdue 38: RB Chris Darkins broke Clarence Schutte's 71-year-old Golden Gophers (3-1) school rushing record on 38/294y, of which 231y came in wild 2nd H. Darkins scored 3 TDs on runs of 7, 45, and 24y after H that had been led 17-7 by Boilermakers. It took QB Cory Sauter's 1y sneak and 2-pt pass to WR Ryan Thelwell for Minnesota to take long road to its 1st lead at 39-38 with 1:38 to play. It was 4th nail-biter of season for Purdue (2-2-1), which next got 45y KO RET from frosh TB Lee Johnson only to have K Brad Bobich miss 42y FG with 21 secs on clock. Boilers FB Mike Alstott (26/135y, 3 TDs) had scored on 11y run for 7-0 lead in 1st Q, 1y blast in 2nd Q for 17-7 edge in 2nd Q, and 3y run for 24-14 lead in 3rd Q. Purdue QB Rick Trefzger (13-24/264y, TD) pitched 78y score to speedy WR Brian Alford to close 3rd Q with 31-24 advantage.

KANSAS STATE 30 Missouri 0: Fleet, ferocious D of no. 13 Kansas State (5-0) posted its 3rd straight shutout of season in its Big 8 opener. TB Eric Hickson (17/86y) scored 2 TDs in 3rd Q to break open 7-0 game into 20-0 rout for Wildcats. Missouri (2-3) left Manhattan in considerable snit: It was angry over late TD pass by QB Matt Miller (12-21/185y, TD, 2 INTs, and 8y TD run), starter who was still in lineup in late going. Tigers' ineptitude on O eventually took its toll on D that had played well. Mizzou gained only 49y after 1st Q and went 32 snaps between 1st downs. It gained only 118y total as QB Brandon Corso (6-18/44y, INT) was sacked 5 times. K-State LB Travis Ochs stepped in front of Corso's forced pass on 2nd play of 3rd Q to put Cats at Tigers 23YL. Hickson quickly scored for 14-0 lead.

Kansas 40 COLORADO 24: With 2 weeks to prepare, confident Kansas (5-0) slipped into Boulder, piled up 495y, and stunned unbeaten Buffaloes (5-1). Inspired Jayhawks got winging early by scoring TD: special teamers Spencer Bonner and Manolito Jones combined to block punt by Colorado P Andy Mitchell, and Jones ran it in from 31y out. Jayhawks RB June Henley rushed 23/137y, 2 TDs, including 43y backbreaker after FUM REC for 33-24 lead in 4th Q. Colorado QB John Hessler threw 3 TD passes among his 15-32/253y, INT stats, and injured QB Koy Detmer courageously returned only to further damage his knee. Kansas QB Mark Williams pitched 25-35/299y and game-closing TD.

TEXAS TECH 14 Texas A&M 7: Aggies' streak of 29 SWC games without defeat came crashing down in 1 disastrous play. Tied at 7-7 in game's last min, Texas A&M (2-2) QB Corey Pullig (20-46/246y, 3 INT) threw pass over middle, only to have it picked off by Texas Tech (2-2) star LB Zach Thomas, who charged 23y for winning TD. Aggies TB Leeland McElroy (27/80y) had scored on 8y run in 1st Q, but was tackled for losses 7 times and hobbled off in 3rd Q with ankle sprain.

Notre Dame 29 WASHINGTON 21: Facing elimination from Bowl Alliance eligibility, Notre Dame (4-2) rallied in closing moments with 3 big plays. Trailing 21-14 thanks to 2 TD runs by Washington (3-2) TB Rashaan Shehee (32/191y), Irish WR Derrick Mayes lost FUM at Huskies 20YL with 3:43 left. But, ND held, and punt snap FUM by Washington P John Wales gave ND ball at Huskies 20YL. Irish TB Autry Denton quickly scored, and Mayes added 2-pt catch for 22-21 lead. After Huskies QB Damon Huard scrambled to ND 33YL with 44 secs left, Irish DB Allen Rossum made big INT and weaved to 76y TD RET.

USA Today Coaches Poll October 9

1	Florida State (33)	1513	14	Alabama	662
2	Nebraska (24)	1500	15	Oregon	629
3	Florida	1404	16	Virginia	536
4	Ohio State (3)	1372	17	Northwestern	530
5	Southern California (2)	1341	18	Texas A&M	453
6	Auburn	1160	19	Stanford	444
7	Tennessee	1136	20	Penn State	439
8	Kansas State	1015	21	Notre Dame	381
9	Kansas	976	22	Iowa	259
10	Colorado	930	23	Baylor	198
11	Michigan	852	24	Syracuse	153
12	Oklahoma	778	25	Wisconsin	140
13	Texas	670			

October 14, 1995

Notre Dame 28 ARMY 27 (East Rutherford, N.J.): Titans of 1940s played epic game just as they had contested in bygone days. Notre Dame (5-2) rolled to 28-7 lead in 3rd Q as FB Marc Edwards scored on both short run and 46y pass from QB Ron Powlus (8-19/189y, TD, INT). Army (3-1) FB John Conroy (31/104y, 2 TDs) scored 1st of his TDs to narrow it to 28-14 in 3rd Q. With 6:11 left, Cadets S Ray Tomasits made INT to poise Conroy's 2nd TD to draw within 28-21. ND gambled at own 40YL on 4th-and-1, but Powlus lost FUM on QB sneak. Coaching in press box because of his recent neck surgery, Notre Dame's Lou Holtz wanted his team to call timeout: "I was the most shocked person in the world when the ball was snapped." Army took over and dramatically drove to 7y TD pass from QB Ronnie McAda (5-9/42y, TD) to WR Leon Gantt with 39 secs left. *Newsday* writer John Jeansonne had glimpse of history: "Army had scored its second touchdown in less than four minutes and, with no timeouts remaining, was lining up for the two-point conversion that would blow Notre Dame clear back to the 1940s, when these two teams traded No. 1 rankings for five consecutive years." McAda called 2-pt pass, and 240-lb TE Ron Leshinski took pass at 1YL with his momentum slanting toward sideline. Fighting Irish DB Ivory Covington, only 161 lbs, tackled Leshinski just short of GL, bear-hugging him OB, to prevent upset loss.

Florida 49 AUBURN 38: Florida (6-0) moved into serious national title contention as coach Steve Spurrier ended his 7-game winless streak against Auburn (4-2) coach Terry Bowden and his father Bobby of Florida State. Gators QB Danny Wuerffel (20-34/380y, 4TDs, INT) got off to dreadful 1-9 aerial start with FUM that was returned 20y to TD by LB Anthony Harris and INT by DB Charles Rose that led to 10-0 Tiger lead in opening 3 mins. It didn't help that Gators WR Reidel Anthony dropped passes on game's 1st 2 plays, but he quickly made amends with 90y KO TD RET that pared Auburn's 1st Q lead to 10-7. Florida tallied 28 straight pts in 5:38 span of 2nd and 3rd Qs: TB Elijah Williams launched Gator spree with 1y TD for 21-10 lead with 3:32 to play before H. Wuerffel pitched 3 TDs, 2 to WR Chris Doering (5/76y, 3 TDs), during uprising that built 42-20 lead. Tigers TB Stephen Davis rushed 23/149y, including 46y TD that came with 2:01 left in 4th Q. Florida TB Fred Taylor (17/111y, TD) produced 155y O and had scored 10y TD for his team's 1st lead.

Tennessee 41 ALABAMA 14: Crimson Tide (4-2) went into rivalry contest with +22 TO ratio in 1st half of season, but lost 5 TOs as Tennessee (6-1) whipped Alabama for 1st time since 1985. Vols QB Peyton Manning (20-29/301y, 3 TDs) put game away early. On game's 1st play, Manning found WR Joey Kent streaking alone on slant pass for 80y TD. When Tide QB Brian Burgdorf lost FUM, Manning quickly scored for 21-0 lead in 1st Q. QB Freddie Kitchens (20-43/204y, TD, 3 INTs) relieved Burgdorf to muster 70 and 97y TD drives. TB Jay Graham (17/114y) raced to 75y TD getting Volunteers back on track to win 1st match since 1914 not to be played on traditional and famous "Third Saturday of October."

Ohio State 27 WISCONSIN 16: Twice in recent years (1985 and '93), Ohio State (6-0), ranked 4th this time around, came to Madison with top 5 ranking only to be sunk at Camp Randall Stadium's unfriendly confines. Badgers (2-2-1) almost carried off another upset, riding QB Darrell Bevell's TD pass and TB Carl McCullough's 14y TD dash to 16-13 lead at end of 3rd Q. Buckeyes TB Eddie George, held to 33y rushing in 1st H, took team on his back and rumbled 1y pitchout to score for 20-16 lead with 8:32 left. It was game's 5th lead change. Field position for this vital 46y drive had been gained when Badgers were pushed back on holding PEN called against OT Jerry Wunsch. Previously-bullish Wisconsin D-line made midfield miscommunication with 7 mins to go, and George (26/141y) burst through resultant big hole for clinching 49y TD run.

IOWA 22 Indiana 13: Quietly undefeated Iowa (5-0) managed meager 224y total O against aroused Indiana (2-4) D, but came up with clutch play when needed. Hoosiers sub TB Sean Glover (48/199y) plunged for 2nd Q TD to fuel 10-7 H lead. TD by Hawkeyes TB Sedrick Shaw (22/81y) provided 14-10 edge that lasted until little Hoosiers K Bill Manolopoulos made 23y FG in 4th Q. With 4:36 to go, Indiana drove to Hawkeyes 46YL, but Iowa DB Tom Knight picked off QB Adam Greenlee (12-29/111y, INT) and scurried 60y to clinching TD.

Oklahoma 24 Texas 24 (Dallas): Longhorns (3-1-1) stampeded to 21-0 1st Q margin on TE Pat Fitzgerald's short TD catch, LB Michael Boudoin's 1y TD RET of blocked punt, and RB Shon Mitchell's 69y TD sprint. Oklahoma (4-1-1) gradually sliced margin, moving to within 24-10 by H on TB Jerald Moore's 24y TD run. QB Eric Moore (7-15/48y) pitched 3rd Q TD pass to WR P.J. Mills to lift Sooners to within 24-17. OU TB Moore (21/174y, 2 TDs) tied it with his 2nd TD, right after DB Rod Henderson pounced on punt FUM by Texas WR Mike Adams at 22YL late in 3rd Q. Oklahoma DB Larry Bush halted Steers frosh FB Ricky Williams at OU 11YL when Texas decided to go for 1st down on 4th-and-1 with 9:17 to go. Steers coach John Mackovic later explained: "I thought we needed a touchdown (instead of FG)." Sooners then drove to 4th down at Longhorns 25YL with 26 secs to go, but K Jeremy Alexander, perfect 12-12 in FGs to date in 1995, hooked it in swirling wind after high snap from C.

Kansas State 23 OKLAHOMA STATE 17: Stubborn Oklahoma State Cowboys (1-5), who counted their season's only win over Div 1-AA SW Missouri State, still were able to press undefeated Kansas State (6-0) into 4th Q comeback. Showing scant regard for K-State's string of 3 straight shutouts, Oklahoma State rushed for 226y, including TB David Thompson's 17/181y, 2 TDs. Midway through 4th Q, Thompson slipped away for explosive 91y TD run and stunning 17-14 lead. Wildcats O, which had stumbled for much of day, responded with 80y drive: QB Matt Miller (17-21/261y, 2 TDs, INT) opened TD trip with 33y pitch to WR Mitch Running and finished with 18y scoring toss to TE Brian Lojka, who delayed underneath deep-running receivers. Lojka quipped: "I think I ran off 30 or 35 seconds from the time I caught it until I reached the end zone." Along way, Miller converted K-State's 5th of half-dozen 4th down tries. Miller squirted forward 3y on QB draw on 4th-and-3 at Oklahoma State's 21YL. Last-play EZ tackle of Cowboys QB Craig Strickland netted safety for Wildcats DE Nyle Wiren.

Texas Christian 33 RICE 28: TCU (4-1) hung on to hope for top spot in SWC thanks to season's best performance by QB Max Knake (18-25/167y, 2 TDs, INT). Horned Frogs hopped to 10-0 lead in 1st Q on Knake's TD pass to WR Chris Brasfield for 34y against soft coverage. Ace TCU K Michael Reeder's added 36y FG. Rice (1-4-1) rallied with its typical ground attack, scoring on HB Yoncy Edmonds' 8y run and, while ignoring tying FG opportunity, took 14-10 lead on last play of 1st H as HB Michael Perry plowed in from 1YL. Down 21-10 in 3rd Q, TCU used 3 TOs to regain momentum and score 10 pts. TB Andre Davis (34/144y, TD) piled over top from 1YL for 27-21 lead after Owls QB Josh LaRocca (14-23/208y, INT) lost FUM. Knake's TD pass to WR John Washington nailed it down.

SOUTHERN CALIFORNIA 26 Washington State 14: It started easily enough for no. 5 Southern California (6-0) as Trojans romped to 26-0 lead early in 3rd Q by scoring in myriad of manners: After alternate K Adam Rendon's 1st Q FG, Troy WR Larry Parker raced 63y on punt RET and soaring for EZ when he was met by tacklers. WR

Mike Bastianelli beat Cougars (3-3) to EZ TD REC. Double-barrel USC QBs Kyle Wachholtz (9-16/90y, TD) and Brad Otton (14-24/130y, TD, INT) hit 8 and 40y TD passes respectively. Otton's Pac-10-record string of 216 pass attempts without INT was ended when Cougars LB Johnny Nansen picked him off in 3rd Q. Despite facing robust Trojans D that was keyed by enormous soph DT Darrell Russell's 5 tackles for loss, Washington State QB Chad Davis (30-48/236y, TD, INT) masterminded 2 TDs in last 22 mins on drives of 43 and 66y. Lightweight RB Frank Madu scored on 12y run in 3rd Q after Davis hit 17 and 11y throws, and Davis pitched 4y TD in 4th Q to WR Chad Carpenter.

Washington 38 STANFORD 28: For 1st time in 1995, Stanford (4-1-1) scored game's 1st pts as K Eric Abrams booted 24y FG late in 1st Q. Newly-found Washington (4-2) TB Rashaan Shehee, making his 2nd start, scored on 7y run on 2nd play of 2nd Q. LB Ikaika Malloe's INT set up TD run by Huskies QB Damon Huard (20-30/295y, TD). Stanford tied it 14-14 in 3rd Q as QB Mark Butterfield (22-35/348y, 3 TDs, 2 INTs) tossed 16y TD to WR Andre Kirwan and 2-pt pass to WR Mark Harris. But Shehee (30/196y) leapt to 1y TD, later capped 24-pt spree with 80y TD dash.

October 21, 1995

SYRACUSE 22 West Virginia 0: Syracuse (6-1) had been blanked by Mountaineers in previous 2 meetings, but Orangemen returned favor to break 1st place tie in Big East. Frosh QB Donovan McNabb threw 16-23/308y, 2 TD, including school-record 96y bomb to WR Marvin Harrison (9/213y) in 4th Q. Orange D limited West Virginia (3-4) to 6 1st downs and 115y O through 3 Qs. WVU finished with 178y, but were denied late scoring bid by Syracuse's GLS.

Alabama 23 MISSISSIPPI 9: Rebels (3-4) did outstanding job on D, limiting Alabama (5-2) to 239y total O that included mere 34/82y rushing. TB Dennis Riddle (15/53y) was Crimson Tide's top ground gainer. But, Bama D scored 9 pts on way to 16-0 H edge: Rampaging Alabama LB Dwayne Rudd swooped in to sack Mississippi QB Josh Nelson (19-38/163y, INT) in EZ in 1st Q, and when Nelson lost FUM it trickled over backline for safety. Only 6:34 into game, Tide LB Ralph Staten picked off Ole Miss pass and rambled 61y to score for 9-0 lead. Ole Miss got on scoreboard in 3rd Q on K Tim Montz's 38y FG, but Bama QB Brian Burgdorf (13-24/157y, TD) put game out of reach with 20y scoring fling to WR Toderick Malone in 4th Q. TB Dou Innocent (20/52y, TD) was Rebs' best weapon; he caught 6/68y to contribute 120y in O and his 4th Q TD run.

NOTRE DAME 38 Southern California 10: Overconfident USC (6-1) fell flat at critical moments and failed to beat Notre Dame (6-2) for 13th straight year. Fighting Irish said they mustered inspiration from pre-game comments by Southern Cal's Keyshawn Johnson, which, it turned out, were complete fabrications. With Trojans ahead 7-6 in 2nd Q on 17y TD catch by WR Johnson (6/122y), Irish used 11 runs, mostly powerful traps, to go 60y to 2nd of FB Marc Edwards' 3 TDs. Playing perhaps his best game in his up-and-down 2-year ND career, QB Ron Powlus (18-29/189y, TD, INT) took control, and made 3 1st downs with passes to set up 7y TD delay run up middle by TB Autry Denson (27/95y). Irish led 21-7. K Adam Rendon's FG pulled Troy within 21-10, but its O finished with no pts in last 6 possessions. Johnson summed up USC's disappointment over its 4 TOs: "We were in the red zone five times and got three points. We played horrible."

NEBRASKA 49 Kansas State 25: Undefeated no. 8 Wildcats (6-1) turned out to be paper tigers after its series of wins against inferior foes: Kansas State's no. 1 scoring D (7.5-pt avg) allowed 24 of 49 pts and its no. 1 total D (199.8y avg) was shredded for 338y. DB Mike Fullman opened scoring for Nebraska (7-0) on 79y punt RET made possible by crushing block by LB Mike Rucker. PEN gave Kansas State good field position to get within 7-6 on QB Matt Miller's pass to WR Kevin Lockett. Huskers QB Tommie Frazier (10-16/148y, 4 TDs) pitched 3 scores to reach 42-6 advantage late in 3rd Q. That's when Husker starters exited to bench. K-State managed 19 pts in 7 mins sparked by DB Gordon Brown's punt block for TD. Nebraska's top O unit returned with narrowed 17-pt cushion and immediately scored. Imposing D held Wildcats to 128y O, including 7 sacks/-4y which prompted groggy Miller to be relieved by sub QB Brian Kavanaugh.

Kansas 38 OKLAHOMA 17: Underdog Kansas (7-0) squandered good field position early, made worse by allowing Sooners RB Jerald Moore (18/219y) to race for 60 and 72y TDs. Jayhawks, however, owned 2nd Q, going 80y in 12:22 to TE Hosea Friday's 4th down catch, Kansas' 4 conversion on 4th down. "We can't do that against air," joked coach Glen Mason. DB Dorian Brew's 41y INT RET and P Darrin Simmons' fake-punt run set up 10 pts for Kansas' 17-14 3rd Q lead. Oklahoma (4-2-1) opened 4th Q with K Jeremy Alexander's tying FG, but Kansas QB Mark Williams (18-26/163y, 3 TDs) hit TE Jim Moore for short TD and permanent 4th Q lead at 24-17.

TEXAS 17 Virginia 16: In last 25 years, only 3 other teams, Kentucky in 1980, Louisville in 1989, and Eastern Michigan in 1991, had lost 2 games in same season on last play. Virginia (6-3) became 4th such team, victimized by incredible 50y FG into stiff wind by Texas (5-1-1) K Phil Dawson. It was Longhorns' 700th win, but 1st-ever on last play FG. Texas QB James Brown (17-33/197y, TD, INT) hit 3 big strikes: 30y screen to RB Jeffrey Clayton for 1st Q TD and pair of 4th down connections of 12y each to WR Michael Adams. Brown's accuracy kept alive 10 pts worth of 2 marches for 10 pts. Strong leg of UVa K Rafael Garcia supplied FGs of 27, 45, and 56y, last of which gave Cavs 16-14 lead with 3:12 to go.

UTAH 22 Air Force 21: Seemingly assured of keeping top perch in WAC, Air Force Falcons (5-3) led 21-7 in last min of game. Air Force QB Beau Morgan had rushed 21/119y and thrown 2 TD passes. Suddenly, Utah (4-4) QB Mike Fouts, nephew of former Oregon and NFL great Dan Fouts, hit WR Rocky Henry with 17y TD pass with 41 secs left. After 2-pt run made it 21-15, K Dan Pulsipher's on-side KO was vacuumed up by Ute DB Artis Jackson. Fouts (20-38/355y, 3 TDs, INT) lofted 50y TD to WR Kevin Dyson, who stunningly ran alone down left sideline against snoozing Falcons' secondary. K Pulsipher's kick stole astonishing win.

Ucla 42 STANFORD 28: On UCLA's 1st series, frosh QB Cade McNown threw 3rd down pass from his 5YL, which was batted into jump ball. Stanford (4-2-1) DL Carl Hansen leaped higher than Bruins O-line behemoths for INT. Cardinal FB Greg Comella caught 1y TD pass 3 plays later. QB Mark Butterfield (17-39/221y, 4 TDs, 2 INTs) threw 2 more TD passes in 1st H, including WR Mark Harris' nifty EZ steal from DB Shaun Williams, so Stanford had 21-7 lead. In 2nd H, UCLA (5-2) RB Karim Abdul-Jabbar simply took over, rushing by game's end for 42/261y, 4 TDs, and was so ubiquitous that Stanford's witty PA announcer identified 1 of his runs with: "You know who!" McNown (15-27/150y, TD) opened 2nd H with 16y keeper run, plus personal foul PEN meted out to Cardinal moved ball to Stanford 11YL. McNown scored on option run on next play. After Abdul-Jabbar's 10y TD run provided 35-28 4th Q lead, Cardinal advanced to Bruins 4YL. But, Butterfield's pass was tipped high in air by Bruins CB Teddy Lawrence, and LB Abdul McCullough came down with it to launch UCLA's 15-play, 98y clinching drive fueled by Abdul-Jabbar's mighty runs.

October 28, 1995

Florida 52 GEORGIA 17: Moving game to Athens, while Jacksonville's Gator Bowl stadium was being refurbished, did nothing to help 6-year slide by Bulldogs (5-4) in rivalry. Florida (7-0) hadn't visited Georgia since 1932, had never won there, and, as Gator asst coaches had pointed out to head coach Steve Spurrier, no team had ever dropped 50 pts on Bulldogs at Sanford Stadium. "We wanted to do that," admitted Spurrier. "You always want to do something that hadn't been done before." Florida's 5 barely-answered TDs sent many home fans to exits with 3:31 to go in 3rd Q. Gators QB Danny Wuerffel (14-17/242y, 5 TDs, INT) clicked on his 5 TDs by late in 3rd Q with 3 being hauled in by WR Chris Doering. Former Georgia TB-WR, now at QB Hines Ward (20-33/226y, TD) rushed for 65y; his 291y total O outgained his team. Other backs lost 10y to account for UGa's 281y in final-game O tally.

ARKANSAS 30 Auburn 28 (Little Rock): Much like Ohio State's 56-35 win over Iowa, earlier in day, where Buckeyes took 56-0 lead in 2nd Q, Arkansas (6-2) dominated 1st H at 27-0, holding ball for 23:06. Hogs moved into SEC West driver's seat as QB Barry Lunney (17-24/199y) threw 2 TD passes, TB Madre Hill rushed 45/186y, TD, and K Todd Latourette booted 3 FGs. Auburn (5-3) suffered 3 TOs, never crossed Arkansas 25YL in 1st H, but QB Patrick Nix (34-52/387y, 2 TDs, 2 INTs) got hot in 2nd H. Nix completed 28-36 for 2 TDs, 2-pt play, and ran for 15y score. Tigers moved within 2 pts with 18 secs left, recovered on-side KO, completed pass to omni-present WR Willie Gosha (17/222y), but K Matt Hawkins' 52y FG was tipped by Razorbacks DL Junior Soli to preserve win.

Northwestern 17 ILLINOIS 14: No. 8 Wildcats (7-1) fell behind 14-0 as it appeared that their golden spell was to be broken by in-state rival Illinois (3-4). QB Scott Weaver and RB Robert Holcombe (27/100y) each scored 1st H TD for Illini, but Northwestern retaliated with 10 pts in 2nd Q and went ahead on 4th Q TD plunge by dependable RB Darnell Autry (41/151y), who contributed 37y on TD drive and exceeded 100y rushing for 9th straight game. suffered INT by Wildcats S Eric Collier. Illinois had late chance when Weaver rifled 37y pass to WR Jason Dulick to Northwestern 18YL on 4th down with 1:07 left. But Illini bungled it away when they suffered 13y loss on sack by NW DL Matt Rice, 10y PEN for holding, and Cats DB Eric Collier's leaping EZ INT.

KANSAS STATE 41 Kansas 7: Never had so much been at stake in 93rd battle of Sunflower State. Inspired no. 14 Kansas State (7-1) had lots to prove after its shellacking by Nebraska. QB Matt Miller (5-11/55y) threw 2 early TDs to WR Kevin Lockett, and K-State was off to its 1st win over Top 10 team since 1970. Rushing O told story: no. 6 Kansas (7-1) gained 76y after coming in with 232y run avg, while Wildcats rolled up 373y. K-State ground leaders were RBs Eric Hickson (15/121y, TD) and Mike Lawrence (20/118y, TD).

Nebraska 44 COLORADO 21: With no. 1 Florida State idle, Nebraska (8-0) staked its claim for no. 1 even though it had to overcome pounding Samoan war drums, unusual student-section greeting for entrance of their Colorado (6-2) team. Surprise was on

Buffs as Huskers QB Tommie Frazier used Shotgun formation to pass 14-23/241y, with TDs to each of his WBs Abdul Mohammad and Clester Johnson. Colorado QB John Hessler threw 2 TD passes among his 21-43/276y, but Buffs trailed 21-7 after 1st Q and 31-14 at H as Nebraska cruised to 467y O.

BAYLOR 27 Texas Christian 24: Bears (5-2) took 49-47-7 edge in apparently last game between long-time SWC foes. Taking spotlight were Baylor TB Jerod Douglas (21/149y, 2 TDs), WR Pearce Pegross (8/123y, TD), and S Adrian Robinson. Douglas scored on 28y run in 1st Q and built 14-3 lead in 2nd Q when he bolted 50y to 15YL before Pegross made his TD catch from QB Jeff Watson (13-22/167y, TD). Horned Frogs (5-2) went 93y to cut margin to 14-10 on 1st TD throw by QB Max Knake (27-46/265y, 2 TDs, 3 INTs). Douglas came back to make it 21-10 at H for Baylor as he slipped across for 7y TD run. Although Knake moved into 5th place all-time on Southwest completions list, TCU had to play without suspended TB Andre Davis, and Knake suffered 2 INTs by Robinson. Robinson's 2nd INT came in EZ when Knake tried to trim 27-17 deficit with 10 mins left.

UCLA 33 California 16: California (2-6), which was enjoying 5-game winning streak over its southern cousins, tied game at 7-7 in 1st H on WR Iheanyi Uwaezuoke's 17y TD reception from QB Pat Barnes. With 2nd Q clock ticking down, UCLA (6-2) coach Terry Donahue pulled regular K Bjorn Mertens, who had missed earlier from 49 and 40y out, and sent KO-specialist Greg Andrasick in for 34y FG and 10-7 H edge. "We looked as down as we ever have," said TB Karim Abdul-Jabbar, "and we were up by three." Opening snap of 2nd H rekindled Bruins as DL George Kase dislodged ball from Cal RB Reynard Rutherford, who later scored in 4th Q, and LB Tommy Bennett scooped up FUM for 22y TD RET. UCLA next turned O over to Abdul-Jabbar, who rushed for 217y, 122y of it in 4th Q.

WASHINGTON 21 Southern California 21: USC (6-1-1) regained some of its lost fire, rallying in 4th Q to frustrate Washington (5-2-1). Meanwhile, Oregon fell from Pac-10 race, beaten by Arizona State 35-24. Huskies built 21-0 lead through 3 Qs, chiefly on 3 and 46y TD runs by TB Leon Neal (31/152y and 5/65y receiving). With H tirade from coach John Robinson still ringing in their ears, Trojans got going on WR Larry Parker's 19y punt RET. Washington inadvertently helped by falling into soft zone on D. "Once we got them into a predictable passing situation, the game should have been ours," said Huskies S Lawyer Milloy. QB Brad Otton (21-36/251y, 2 TDs, INT), usually 4th Q spectator in USC QB rotation, led TD marches of 57, 73, and 79y, last ending in tying TD catch by TE Johnny McWilliams on 3rd down with 33 secs left. To kick tying pt was perfectly logical because deadlock helped USC in conf's hockey-like Rose Bowl pts formula.

November 4, 1995

GAME OF THE YEAR
(TH) VIRGINIA 33 Florida State 28

Starting fast, Florida State (7-1) QB Danny Kanell (32-67, 3 TDs, 3 INTs) threw for 454y, most ever vs. Virginia (7-3), but from late in 2nd Q when FSU trailed 24-21, it strangely failed to score for next 26 mins. Compiling 311y all-purpose, Cavs star TB Tiki Barber rushed 31/193y, including 64y TD sprint behind FB Darrell Medley's block in 1st Q. When K Rafael Garcia kicked his 4th FG 7 mins into 4th Q, Virginia seemed safely in upset territory, ahead at 33-21. Seminoles coach Bobby Bowden pulled Warrick Dunn's 33y HB pass out of his trick bag, and 3 plays later Dunn scored on 7y run to trim margin to 5 pts. With 1:44 left, desperate FSU surged back while Virginia held on. Seminoles reached Cavs 6YL with 9 secs left. After Kanell threw incomplete pass, FSU made interesting call. Dunn, aligned beside Kanell, took direct snap in Shotgun and shot through line and low toward EZ, but was halted inched from GL by frosh DB Adrian Burnim and LB Anthony Poindexter. Florida State's loss ended string of 29 ACC wins and ignited greatest festival in Virginia's previously sedate football history.

VIRGINIA TECH 31 Syracuse 7: Big East 1st place was annexed by Virginia Tech (7-2) as Hokies won their 7th game in row. Syracuse (6-2) opened scoring on FB Rob Konrad's 19y TD run, but Orangemen would gain only 167y all day. Virginia Tech's run D, nation's best statistically, held Syracuse to 54y rushing. Hokies QB Jim Druckenmiller pitched 16-27/224y, 3 TDs, including 25y TD to FB Brian Edmonds that gave them lead for good at 10-7 in 2nd Q. Syracuse lost FUM on 2nd H KO, and Druckenmiller quickly upped margin to 24-7 as TB Dwayne Thomas weaved 25y with scoring screen pass. Virginia Tech TB Ken Oxendine rushed 19/118y.

ALABAMA 10 Louisiana State 3: Rival Ks Andre Lafleur and Michael Proctor traded 20y FGs in 2nd Q of D battle spiced by frequent trips by both teams deep into opponent's end. Alabama (7-2) took possession on DB Deshea Townsend's INT at LSU (4-4-1) 22YL with 13:05 left, and TB Dennis Riddle (33/174y) followed with winning 2y TD on option run.

ARKANSAS 26 Mississippi State 21: Arkansas (7-2) grabbed SEC West title, but QB Barry Lunney had so-so game. Early on, Lunney's opening 3 completions were for TDs: His 1st was off-mark and returned 37y for Mississippi State (3-6) TD by DB Walt Harris. Lunney's other early tosses went 64y to WR Kotto Cotton and 29y to WR Anthony Eubanks, each for TD that granted Hogs 14-7 lead. Bulldogs tied it on RB Keffer McGee's short TD run, but gave away 3 1st downs by PEN on 3rd Q drive that ended with TD run by TB Madre Hill (30/80y) to extend Porkers lead to 24-14. After MSU blocked 4th Q FG to keep deficit at 24-21, QB Derrick Taite (18-35/133y, TD, 2 INTs) was sacked for safety by stork-like Razorbacks DE Steven Conley. Lunney said he had received odd looks before season when predicting crown for Hogs in their 4th year of SEC play.

MICHIGAN STATE 28 Michigan 25: Against stellar Michigan (7-2) D, QB Tony Banks (26-34/career-high 318y, TD) rallied Michigan State (5-3-1) from 4th Q deficits of 18-14 and 25-21. Spartans FB Scott Greene scored twice, while WR Derrick Mason (5/71y) went 70y on 2nd Q punt TD RET and, when it mattered, Mason made 2 critical catches on 4th Q drives. Winning TD came on Banks' 25y pass to WR Nigea Carter with 1:24 to play. Wolverines TB Tim Biakabutuka ran 37/191y, TD, while QB Brian Griese (16-26/140y, TD) threw 22y TD to WR Mercury Hayes for 25-21 lead with 3:38 left.

NORTHWESTERN 21 Penn State 10: "Purple Dream" continued on as Northwestern (8-1) won its biggest home game since whipping Notre Dame in 1962. TB Darnell Autry (36/147y, 3 TDs) set single-season school rushing record to put Wildcats ahead 14-0, but momentum changed when Penn State (6-3) scored in closing secs of 1st H on short TD pass from QB Wally Richardson (18-29/129y, TD, INT) to TE Keith Olsommer. Nittany Lions owned 3rd Q, limiting NW's O to mere 3 snaps. Strangely, though, Penn State could mine only K Brett Conway's 24y FG, which came after big break in kicking game. Lions P Darrell Kania's punt grazed Northwestern punt-receiving-teamer Matt Stewart, and Penn State recovered to set up Conway's FG that rimmed deficit to 14-10. Richardson's passing later took Lions to NW 7YL, but holding PEN and clutch sacks by Wildcats DE Casey Dailey and S Hudhaifa Ismaeli forced Conway into missed FG try. Now reprieved, Wildcats pounded 80y to Autry's clinching TD run, thanks mostly to WR Dave Beazley's 25y reverse run on 1st-and-19 and Autry's 23y dash.

SOUTHERN CALIFORNIA 31 Stanford 30: Relieved Trojans (7-1-1) moved within single victory of cinching their 20th Rose Bowl visit. Stanford (5-3-1) had jumped to 16-0 lead on K Eric Abrams' 3 FGs and 60y TD catch by WR Mark Harris (10/187y). Punt snap FUM led to Southern California TD, and 75y drive got Trojans within 24-17 at H. USC got its 1st lead at 25-24 when WR Chris Miller caught 2-pt pass with 7:42 remaining. Trailing 30-25 with 2:51 on clock after Cardinal traveled 80y to FB Greg Comella's 6y TD spurt up middle, USC went 80y mainly on WR Keyshawn Johnson's 32 and 8y catches and his winning reception with 39 secs to play. Switching to D as S, Johnson nearly caught INT, but knocked down Hail Mary pass by Cardinal QB Mark Butterfield (29-48/345y, TD) at Troy GL at 0:00.

Oregon 24 WASHINGTON 22: Tall and swift WR Pat Johnson strode 89y with opening KO for Ducks (7-2) TD. This score hatched 24-0 H lead for Oregon, which also enjoyed TB Ricky Whittle running for 4y TD and QB Tony Graziani (22-37/282y, 2 INTs) passing for vital 2-pt conv. Huskies (5-3-1) were booed in hapless 1st H by chilled crowd of 74,054, but no. 15 Washington rallied around QB Damon Huard (21-36/327y, TD, INT) and 2 TD runs by TB Rashaan Shehee (14/50y, 2 TDs). Huskies D permitted only 86y O in 2nd H in utter turnaround. However, Washington, with 4-1-1 Pac-10 slate, all but fell out of Rose Bowl consideration because of 2 late missed FGs. Oregon blocked K John Wales' 33y FG try with 3:02 to go, but Huskies regained possession on LB Ink Aleaga's FUM REC only to have Wales kick wide right on 36y try with strong breeze picking up at field level. "You can't say the wind or that kick cost us the game," said TE Ernie Conwell, who made long snap on last FG try. "We had plenty of other chances."

November 11, 1995

Miami 17 BOSTON COLLEGE 14: Miami (6-3) won its 5th in row, to get back into Big East race with 1st place Virginia Tech, 38-16 winner over Temple. RB Danyell Ferguson rushed 26/144y, including 85y TD romp in 3rd Q to provide 14-0 lead to Hurricanes. Boston College (3-7) clawed back to 14-14 tie on short TD pass to WR Steve Everson from QB Mark Hartsell (28-44/253y, INT) and RB Mike Cloud's 39y run to set up RB Omari Walker's tying score. Miami QB Ryan Clement hit 23y pass to position K Dana Prewitt's winning 24y FG. BC K Dan McGuire missed his 4th FG of day at final whistle.

Florida State 28 NORTH CAROLINA 12: Rebounding Florida State (8-1) stopped North Carolina (4-5) on 1st possession, and DB Mario Edwards blocked punt for 24y TD RET. RB Warrick Dunn (27/143y) followed quickly with 43y TD run for 14-0 lead. From that moment on, Seminoles' national-leading O somewhat slumbered vs. nation's no. 2 D, compiling 377y, far below their 594y avg. Tar Heels gained only 170y, had 2nd punt blocked, but UNC QB Mike Thomas' 63y pass to WR Octavus Barnes led to 4th Q TD pass by Thomas (10-24/146y, TD, INT). Failed 2-pt play left it at 28-12.

GEORGIA TECH 27 North Carolina State 19: Running for 111y and 3 TDs in 4th Q, soph Georgia Tech (6-4) TB C.J. Williams (23/143y, 3 TDs) became 4th Yellow Jacket back to top 1,000y mark in single season. Disappointing North Carolina State (2-7) had balanced 318y attack and found itself in Tech territory throughout 1st H. However, Wolfpack was "not taking care of the little things that you've got to do to win," according to coach Mike O'Cain, and had to settle for 4 FGs by superb K Mark Primanti. QB Terry Harvey (13-24/154y) became NC State's career passing and total O king, but his poor pitchout with 10 mins left allowed 19-13 lead get away. Yellow Jacket S Ryan Stewart (11 tackles) recovered pitch at Wolfpack 28YL, and Williams scored on 8y run in arms of DB Kenny Harris for 20-19 lead. Difference in 4th Q rally came from Tech O line that blew big holes in NC State D behind leadership of C Michael Cheever.

Auburn 37 GEORGIA 31: Auburn (7-3) led 20-7 in 2nd Q when plucky Georgia QB Hines Ward, playing with broken passing hand, scored on 11y demolition run to get Bulldogs (5-5) back in game. In 2nd H, Georgia fought back to within 27-24 and 34-31 as TB Torin Kirtsey scored on 18 and 36y runs. Seesaw affair pivoted on 4th Q decisions: Hines' failed 4th down pass at Auburn 10YL with 6:17 left and Tigers QB Dameyune Craig's 4th down sneak at own 42YL kept clock-killing drive alive. On next play after Craig's sneak, Auburn TB Stephen Davis (28/152y, 2 TDs) charged 42y to 16YL. It was Sanford Stadium's last game before famous hedges temporarily were removed for 1996 Olympic soccer.

OHIO STATE 41 Illinois 3: Illinois (4-5) had won 6 of last 7 against Ohio State (10-0) and arrived hoping to trump Buckeyes in Illi-Buck rivalry with its tough D. Instead, magnificent TB Eddie George put his name in Ohio State record book with 36/314y rushing, on his way to Heisman Trophy. After his runs of 39, 24, and 12y keyed 99y march in 1st H, George scored on 64 and 13y runs in 3rd Q to ice outcome at 38-3. George topped his performance with his 3rd TD of 3rd Q: toe-tapping reception in corner of EZ of lofted 13y TD pass by QB Bobby Hoying (8-13/109y, 2 TDs, INT). Illini converted only 1 of 11 3rd downs as they were held to 59y rushing and QB Johnny Johnson's 11-18/101y in air. Illinois scored only on K Bret Scheuplein's 42y FG early in 3rd Q.

NORTHWESTERN 31 Iowa 20: Hawkeyes (5-4) swooped in from west seeking its 22nd straight win over Wildcats (9-1). Iowa made it exceedingly difficult with 20-pt 2nd Q, but was blanked in 2nd H. Throughout bitterly cold afternoon, Hawkeyes enjoyed nearly 10 mins of extra possession time and outgained Wildcats 303y to 188y. Iowa built 14-3 lead in 2nd Q on 1y run by TB Sedrick Shaw (38/135y, TD) and DB Tom Knight's 28y INT RET. Northwestern regained 17-14 edge as QB Steve Schnur (6-12/82y, TD, INT) threw 21y TD pass to TE Darren Drexler, who dragged tacklers into EZ. "They kept hitting me toward the end zone," Drexler observed of defenders piling on. Then, Wildcats WR Brian Musso broke away for 60y punt TD RET before QB Matt Sherman's 39y TD pass put Iowa in lead at 20-17 at H. Northwestern's secondary played brilliantly in 2nd H, including S Hudfaifa Ismaeli's 4th Q 31y FUM TD RET. Wildcats TB Darnell Autry (32/110y, TD) scored winning TD in 3rd Q and wondered afterward about fuss over his having appeared on Sports Illustrated cover: "What jinx?"

Nebraska 41 KANSAS 3: Hopeful Jayhawks (8-2) eyed 1st Big 8 title since 1968, but sloppy Nebraska (10-0) was simply too tough. Nebraska lost 3 TOs, but Kansas had 5 TOs, including its bungled punt RET that turned into Nebraska special teamer Jon Vedral's early FUM REC in EZ. Huskers QB Tommie Frazier ran for 2 TDs and passed to TE Vershan Jackson for 3rd Q TD that pushed Kansas down by 21-3. DB Mike Fullman raced 86y for TD with 4th Q INT. Jayhawks were limited to 72y rushing, 271y in air.

Oklahoma State 12 OKLAHOMA 0: Sooners (5-4-1) were blanked for 1st time since Missouri turned trick in 1983 as their poor cousins, Oklahoma State (3-7), beat Oklahoma for 1st time in 19 years. Cowboys K Lawson Vaughn made 2 FGs, including 47y boot, that came in 2nd Q for 6-0 lead. After its O lost FUM at own 20YL, maligned Oklahoma State D made GLS with 7 mins left in 3rd Q, bending to its 2YL before forcing 2 losses and 4th down incompletion by OU QB Eric Moore (16-35/210y, 2 INTs). Game's only TD came on 2-play 48y charge with 6:24 to play: After Cowboys CB R.W. McQuarters made INT, QB Tone Jones (8-17/97y) scored from 1YL after hitting WR Terance Richardson for 47y on previous snap. Cowboys made another stand in last 2 mins: Sooners WR P.J. Mills took 34y completion to 3YL, but Moore (9/-16y rushing) threw wildly on 3 tries for EZ and was run OB for loss on 4th down.

Washington 38 UCLA 14: Bruins (6-4) TB Karim Abdul-Jabbar sought his 4th straight 200y rushing game, but when he was smacked on game's opening play he limped to sideline with sprained ankle. Since he was UCLA's O centerpiece, Bruins finished with only 68y rushing and suffered 4 INTs and FUM. Meanwhile, Washington (6-3-1) received good performances from QB Damon Huard (22-30/259y, TD) and TB Rashaan Shehee (20/72y, 3 TDs). Huard hit WR Fred Coleman for 6y TD 4:32 into 1st Q. Shehee added another 1st Q TD, but Bruins managed 55y trip to TB James Milliner's 3y score, and were hanging in at 14-7 in middle of 2nd Q. From his 2YL, WR Eric Scott was forced into trying 1-handed catch of quick slant pass from frosh QB Cade McNown (7-19/61y, 3 INTs). Instead Huskies LB Ikaika Malloe dropped into coverage and speared pass away from Scott for INT. FB Richard Thomas quickly scored for 21-7 UW lead.

Oregon 17 ARIZONA 13: Oregon's fine O-line, on its way to conf-low 17 sacks for season, kept Arizona (5-5) D out of sack column for 1st time in 1995. Motor-driven Wildcats DE Tedy Bruschi remained 3 sacks short of NCAA career record. Even though USC clinched Rose Bowl with 28-10 win over Oregon State, no. 17 Ducks (8-2) kept alive their hopes for major bowl bid when they marched 83y on drive with 6:06 left in 3rd Q to FB Aaron Jelks' 5y TD catch from QB Tony Graziano (10-26/147y, TD, INT). Game had been tied 10-10 at H, thanks to Arizona leaping to 10-0 lead on TB Gary Taylor's short TD run midway in 1st Q and K Jon Prashun's 50y FG 4 mins later. TB Ricky Whittle, who rushed 28/107y of Oregon's 195y on ground, scored Ducks' 1st TD in 2nd Q.

November 18, 1995

Virginia Tech 36 VIRGINIA 29: Bitter in-state battle went to fast-closing Virginia Tech (9-2) in last min. Virginia (8-4) sub QB Tim Sherman (8-10/129y) flipped 2 TD passes in 2nd Q in relief of injured Mike Groh. When TB Tiki Barber (18/58y) scored on 9y run in 3rd Q, Cavs enjoyed 29-14 lead heading into 4th Q. Hokies QB Jim Druckenmiller (17-36/230y, 3 INTs) threw TD pass to WR Jermaine Holmes, and K Atle Larsen kicked 35y FG to draw within 29-23. Virginia Tech took over on own 29YL with 2:12 to go and went ahead 30-29 on Druckenmeiller's pass to Holmes with 47 secs left. DB Antonio Banks added insult with 65y INT TD RET of Groh on game's last play.

Clemson 38 SOUTH CAROLINA 17: Tigers (8-3) broke open seesaw affair with vigorous 3 TDs in 4th Q. Although Clemson rolled to 60/323y rushing, it was 56y TD pass from efficient QB Nealon Greene (9-13/171y, TD) to WR Antwuan Wyatt that created 17-17 tie in 3rd Q. Then, Tigers were inspired by TB Raymond Priester coming off bench, after having pulled hamstring in 1st H, to rush for 80y in 4th Q and score go-ahead 6y TD early in that period. South Carolina (4-6-1), whose run game was limited to 90y, stayed competitive as QB Steve Taneyhill passed 28-43/307y, 2 TDs, INT. Taneyhill's scoring throws gave Gamecocks early 7-0 lead and 17-10 edge in 3rd Q.

AUBURN 31 Alabama 27: In 60th meeting of rivalry that split Heart of Dixie State, 1st H turned into surprising scoring festival. Auburn (8-3) QB Patrick Nix threw 2 TD passes for 21-14 lead as Alabama (8-3) WR Toderick Malone also was explosive with 52y TD bomb reception and 59y TD run around LE after taking pitch as motion man. Bama took charge in 3rd Q, holding Tigers to 22y. K Michael Proctor made 2 FGs, after 6 straight misses, sandwiched around Crimson Tide's 64y TD march. Frosh WR Robert Baker's good KO RET and 34y reception set up FB Fred Beasley's 22y TD run for 31-27 Auburn lead early in 4th Q. Tide got last chance on move to Tigers 22YL in last min. EZ pass found WR Curtis Brown just past EZ line.

LOUISIANA STATE 28 Arkansas 0: Having already cinched spot in SEC title game, Arkansas (8-3) started so flat that coach Danny Ford said, "I wish I would have called a timeout before we ever got off the bus." Underdog LSU (6-4-1) opened with 19-play TD drive that lasted 10 mins as frosh QB Herbert Tyler (9-13/131y) rifled pass-pattern to WR Sheddrick Wilson for 7-0 lead. In 2nd Q, Tigers romped to 3 TDs by RB Kendall Cleveland (24/102y). LB Pat Rogers made 37y INT RET to set up Cleveland for last TD, 28-0 H lead. Hogs were held to 21y O on 20 plays in 1st H.

PENN STATE 27 Michigan 17: With mountains of early-season snow on sidelines and in Beaver Stadium seating area, Penn State (7-3) led Michigan (8-3) 13-7 in 1st H featured by K Brett Conway's career-best 49 and 51y FGs for Lions and WR Amani Toomer's 18y TD catch for Wolverines. Ahead by 3 pts, Penn State was primed to take 20-10 lead, but fumbled handoff on 1st play of 4th Q was recovered in Michigan EZ by LB Clint Copenhauer. Lions came back on WR Bobby Engram's 11y fade-pattern TD catch. Midway in 4th Q, Michigan QB Brian Griese (24-46/323y, TD, 2 INT) hit 3 straight passes, and TB Tim Biakabutuka slipping 18y up middle for TD behind block of C Rod Payne. Up 20-17, Penn State sprung little-used sr TB Stephen Pitts (17/164y) for 54y run, leading to fake FG TD run by WR-holder Joe Nastasi. Needless to say, Wolverines were pelted with snowballs before afternoon was over.

Colorado 27 KANSAS STATE 17: Colorado (9-2) used late thunder to gain 3-way tie for 2nd in Big 8 with Kansas State (9-2) and Kansas. After tricky double pass-run between QB Matt Miller (15-29/206y, INT) and WR Mitch Running (3/74y) set up Wildcats for 17-13 lead with 2:24 left, Buffs went 80y as QB John Hessler (24-42/314y, 2 TD, 2 INT) hit WR James Kidd with 20y TD pass. Bad Shotgun snap 45 secs later resulted in TD for Colorado's D.

MISSOURI 45 Iowa State 31: In lower-tier Big 8 game, Iowa State (3-8) RB Troy Davis, little-known but prodigious runner who led nation in rushing in 1995, gained 181y to become only 5th collegiate player to rush for more than 2000y in single season, but Davis was outrushed this day by RB Brock Olivo (28/201y) as Missouri (3-8) beat Cyclones 45-31. Tigers snapped 6-game losing streak to climb out of Big 8 cellar and tie Iowa State for 7th in conf finale for both.

Notre Dame 44 AIR FORCE 14: Careful QB Thomas Krug (8-13/96y, INT) spelled injured Notre Dame (9-2) starter Ron Powlus in highly-publicized "$8 Million Game," meaning that if Irish won, they were guaranteed spot in Bowl Alliance. Air Force (7-4) QB Beau Morgan's 1st completion made him only 8th player all-time to compile more than 1000y in both rushing and passing in single season, but otherwise Falcons were shut down with 69y in 20-0 1st H runaway. When RBs Autry Denson and Randy Kinder added their 2nd TDs in 3rd Q, ND iced it at 37-7. Air Force TDs came on Morgan's pair of misdirection passes in 2nd H.

Ucla 24 SOUTHERN CALIFORNIA 20: Looking for 5th straight win over USC (8-2-1), UCLA (7-4) jumped to 21-0 lead on its 1st 3 possessions. Bruins' 3rd TD was pure razzle-dazzle: WR Jim McElroy took reverse, pitched 35y TD pass to wide-open WR Kevin Jordan. Earlier, McElroy had caught 59y pass, important cog in UCLA's 2nd TD

drive. Having locked up Rose Bowl trip week before, Trojans gradually clawed back to within 24-20 as QB Brad Otton (17-23/151y, 2 TDs) threw for 2 TDs, 2nd of which was fine-tuned lob to TE Tyler Cashman with 3:30 to go. Otton kept 82y drive alive by finding WR Keyshawn Johnson with 5y pass on 4th-and-3 from UCLA 29YL. Bruins coach Terry Donahue's Pac-10 career-record 151st win was secured when QB Cade McNown rambled 21y on 3rd down keeper to help kill clock. Trojans fell into conf championship tie with Washington, each with 6-1-1 records.

STANFORD 29 California 24: Seeking to regain The Ax after it had been displayed in Cal's trophy case for 2 years, Cardinal (7-3-1) took leads of 3-0 and 10-3 in 2nd Q and 17-10 in 3rd Q on K Eric Abrams' 41y FG and TD runs by FB Greg Comella and TB Mike Mitchell (26/138y, 2 TDs). Golden Bears (3-8) played their part in heated rivalry by rallying to ties at 3-3 and 10-10 by H, and 17-17 in 3rd Q. California scorers were K Ryan Longwell, TE Tony Gonzalez on 23y pass from QB Pat Barnes, and TB Reynard Rutherford (28/114y, TD). Mitchell started 4th Q with another TD run, but sr K Abrams left door open by chili-dipping x-pt try. On Bears' next possession, glue-fingered hoop star Gonzalez, caught 14y pass, but lost FUM at his 29YL. Card WR Mark Harris caught clinching 7y TD.

OREGON 12 Oregon State 10: Frosh K Joshua Smith, not even on Oregon (9-2) roster at season's beginning, booted 4 FGs, including game-winner of 35y with 9:21 left in 4th Q. Improving Beavers (1-10) D, defiantly labeled "best defense in Pac-10" by head coach Jerry Pettibone, allowed no TDs in staunchly holding whenever Ducks drove deep into Oregon State territory. Beavers had earned game's only TD for 7-0 lead in 1st Q when HB Cam Reynolds scored on 7y run out of Wishbone. Oregon State had to stick to modest 160y ground attack because its passing by 2 QBs reaped miserable 3-10/38y, INT. Still, Beavers were able to hold 10-6 lead after 3rd Q.

WASHINGTON 33 Washington State 30: It was rollercoaster ride in Apple Cup rivalry as Washington State (3-8) QB Ryan Leaf (22-33/291y, TD) ran for 2 scores for 14-6 H edge. In 3rd Q, Washington (7-3-1) TB Rashaan Shehee (26/212y, 2 TDs) rambled 85y to score, but 2-pt pass misfired. Also, maligned K John Wales kicked 38y FG in 3rd Q for 15-14 advantage for Huskies. Leaf threw 30y TD pass and 2-pt pass to provide Wazzu with 22-15 lead entering 4th Q. Huskies QB Damon Huard (20-34/276y, TD, 2 INTs) threw 42y TD pass to WR Dave Janoski (6/162y, TD), and UW led 30-22 after Shehee's 2nd TD. Cougars tied it as Leaf flipped 2-pt pass to WR Chad Carpenter after TD run by RB Miguel Meriweather (9/79y, TD). K Wales, Huskies' goat 2 weeks earlier in loss to Oregon, came through with 21y FG to win it with 1:02 to play.

USA Today Coaches Poll November 20

1	Nebraska (44)	1528	14	Kansas	764
2	Ohio State (16)	1482	15	Auburn	595
3	Florida (2)	1454	16	Penn State	580
4	Northwestern	1321	17	Southern California	545
5	Tennessee	1306	18	Syracuse	486
6	Florida State	1260	19	Virginia	404
7	Texas	1117	20	Michigan	370
8	Colorado	1092	21	Washington	319
9	Notre Dame	1022	22	Clemson	273
10	Kansas State	894	23	Alabama	237
11	Virginia Tech	848	24	Arkansas	235
12	Oregon	779	25	Miami (Fla.)	119
13	Texas A&M	769			

November 23-25, 1995

(Th'g) Georgia 18 GEORGIA TECH 17: Deposed Georgia (6-5) coach Ray Goff bid regular season farewell on shoulders of his players, saying afterward, "If you're going to leave, it's really hard to leave if you lose your last game to your biggest rival." Seeking bowl-clinching win, Georgia Tech (6-5) had cruised to 14-0 H lead. Key to Yellow Jackets' edge was precise 47y TD bomb to WR Harvey Middleton from QB Donald Davis (10-19/153y, 2 TDs). Georgia TB Torin Kirtsey, benched at outset for missed practices, scored both 2nd H TDs, and surprise 2-pt pass from QB Hines Ward (23-33/242y, INT) to WR Brice Hunter (7/93y) gave Bulldogs their 1st lead at 15-14. Down by 2 pts after Jackets' FG, K Kanon Parkman booted knuckleball 34y FG with :47 showing on clock to win it for Goff and Bulldogs.

(Th'g) Texas 21 BAYLOR 13: Longhorns (9-1-1) won smashmouth contest over Baylor (7-4) and clinched at least tie for conf title. Meanwhile, Bears lost their chance at SWC crown as they fell to 5-2 in league and were coincidentally bopped out of bowl picture. Texas played without QB James Brown, who stood around on crutches thanks to twisted ankle. With frosh QB Richard Walton (5-12/121y, TD) at helm, Longhorns O was pared down to extent that it had gained only 1y well into 2nd Q, but finished with 47/187y on ground. Key TD came on pass in 2nd Q as Walton flipped to TE Pat Fitzgerald over middle for short 2nd down pass. Fitzgerald broke tackle and charged 70y to score, his 8th TD of season. Texas run attack added 2 TDs, including 27y dash outside right by RB Shon Mitchell (20/106y, TD) for 21-0 lead with 9:21 left. Baylor TB Jerod Douglas was held to 14/72y rushing, and Bears couldn't earn their 2nd TD, 13y toss by QB Jeff Watson (16-27/228y, TD) to WR Dustin Dennard, until time expired.

(Fri) NEBRASKA 37 Oklahoma 0: Fading Sooners (5-5-1) suffered worst defeat in 30 years and was blanked by Cornhuskers (11-0) for 1st time since 1942. Nebraska QB Tommie Frazier's stats were so-so at 12-25/128y, TD, INT passing and 10/35y rushing, but Huskers D stepped up. It built 20-0 3rd Q lead on 2 TDs: DB Tyrone Williams stepped in front of pass by Sooners QB Eric Moore and returned it 36y, and DB Tony Veland scooped up FUM for 57y score. These scores augmented 3 FGs by K Kris Brown before Frazier came through by whipping 38y TD to WB Jon Vedral early in 4th Q. Oklahoma rushed for meager 30/51y.

MIAMI 35 Syracuse 24: Efficient Syracuse (8-3) tallied on 4 methodical drives for 24-14 lead at H. Key Orange gains were WR Jim Turner's 45y KO RET which led to QB Donovan McNabb's nifty 17y TD draw and FB Rob Konrad's 23y run which led to TB Malcolm Thomas' 2nd TD. Meanwhile, Miami (8-3) saw TB Danyell Ferguson become school's only rusher beside Ottis Anderson, in 1978, to gain more than 1000y in single season. Ferguson (29/163y) spurted up middle for consistent gains and 2 TDs in 1st H. Hurricanes broke on top 28-24 as they held ball most of 3rd Q. DB Tremain Mack made blocked Miami's 12th kick-block (FG) of year in 4th Q, and Canes sub frosh TB Dyral McMillan and WR Omar Rolle collaborated on 25y pass for TD. Mack's 2 INTs clinched Miami's 7th straight win and share of Big East title.

FLORIDA 35 Florida State 24: QB Danny Wuerffel passed 25-40/443y, 4 TDs to keep alive national title aspirations of no. 3 Florida (11-0). Florida State (9-2) stayed within 7-3 and 14-6 but trailed 28-6 at H. Seminoles TB Warrick Dunn set up his own TD with 30y run, trimming margin to 28-14 in 3rd Q. Gators answered with immediate 74y TD bomb from Wuerffel to WR Ike Hilliard (6/192y, 2 TDs) to restore 3-TD edge, but FSU inched back on TD pass by QB Danny Kanell (17-44/184y, TD, 3 INT) after bad punt snap. Big play came from Gators DB Anthone Lott who stripped away INT from receiver at GL, 1 of 3 Gators INTs in last 6 mins of contest.

Mississippi 13 MISSISSIPPI STATE 10: Resourceful Rebels (6-5) scratched out winning season on overland spark provided by TB Dou Innocent (39/251y, TD). Innocent's rushing y set new single-game school record. Home-standing Mississippi State (3-8) seemed on its way to win over its rival when it scored on both of its opening possessions: frosh TE John Jennings' 17y TD grab from QB Derrick Taite (13-29/179y, TD, INT) and K Brian Hazelwood's 49y FG. Ole Miss was 3 pts down and content to run out 1st H clock until personal foul PEN sparked drive to K Tim Montz's 46y FG on last play of 1st H. Montz booted winning pts from 29y out in 4th Q. On 4th down in waning secs, Bulldogs TB Keffer McGee caught 4th down pass in waning secs but was halted just short of 1st down to kill Miss State's last chance.

MICHIGAN 31 Ohio State 23: For 33rd time since 1935, rivalry game impacted Big 10 title. Dominating both scrimmage lines, spirited no. 18 Michigan (9-3) upset undefeated no. 2 Ohio State (11-1), sending idle Northwestern to Rose Bowl. Wolverines couldn't hear supportive roars of Wildcats players all way from Evanston, but TV viewers were hooked up by ABC for rich dose of yelling from Northwestern's team meeting room. Michigan's O-line blocked so well that TB Tim Biakabutuka rushed 37/313y, including nearly 200y in 1st H led by Wolverines 10-9. Michigan soph CB Charles Woodson, picked on by Ohio State passes somewhat in 1st H, made INT to open 2nd H, and QB Brian Griese soon sneaked over for 17-9 edge. Ohio DE Mike Vrabel dropped into flat for 3rd Q INT which he ran back to Michigan 27YL. TB Eddie George (21/104y) vaulted for Ohio TD, but was stopped trying for 2-pt run. Biakabutuka's 38y run keyed next Wolverines drive, ended by frosh TB Clarence Williams' early 4th Q TD run behind T Jon Runyan. Teams then traded TDs with George's 2-pt catch bringing Buckeyes to within 31-23, but Woodson's 2nd INT in late stages depressed any comeback plans of Ohio State QB Bobby Hoying (22-45/286y, TD, 2 INT).

Colorado State 24 SAN DIEGO STATE 13: Rams (8-3) slipped into 4-way cluster atop WAC, but grabbed Holiday Bowl honors by virtue of earlier wins over others sharing crown, including Brigham Young, 45-28 winner this day over Fresno State, and Air Force, 45-28 winner over Hawaii. Colorado State did most of its damage in 21-3 1st H as QB Moses Moreno (16-25/247y) threw dual TD passes. Also, S Greg Myers, soon to be named Thorpe Award winner, raced 84y on punt TD RET. San Diego State (8-4) lost its chance for conf title tie even though its O outgained Colorado State 425y to 401y. TB George Jones, who week earlier broke Marshall Faulk's single-season Aztec rushing record, was held well in check and gained 26/87y to finish with year's total of 1842y. Aztecs scored 1st on K Peter Holt's 1st of 2 FGs, but Rams led 21-3 at H as turning-point play for Colorado State was DB Greg Myers' 84y punt TD RET that upped lead to 14-3. SDSU QB Billy Blanton threw 55y TD pass in 4th Q to enhance his fine passing numbers to 33-48/311y, TD, 2 INTs.

USA Today Coaches Poll November 27

1	Nebraska (55)	1543	14	Kansas	749
2	Florida (7)	1494	15	Michigan	650
3	Northwestern	1410	16	Auburn	635
4	Tennessee	1316	17	Penn State	618
5	Ohio State	1295	18	Southern California	537
6	Texas	1175	19	Virginia	339
7	Colorado	1135	20	Washington	304
8	Florida State	1087	21	Miami (Fla.)	297
9	Notre Dame	1066	22	Clemson	284
10	Kansas State	911	23	Alabama	222
11	Virginia Tech	883	24	Arkansas	207
12	Oregon	788	25	Syracuse	157
13	Texas A&M	761			

December 2, 1995

Army 14 Navy 13 (Philadelphia): Early FUM REC gave Navy (5-6) chance for QB Ben Fay's TD pass to WR LeBron Butts. Army (5-5-1) tied it in 1st Q on TD burst by FB John Conroy (22/74y, 2 TDs). Although Middies had only 53y rushing through 3 Qs, sub QB Chris McCoy provided spark with 42y dash to Cadets 10YL early in 4th Q. Army held, and K Scott Vanderhorst booted his 2nd FG for Middies' 13-7 lead. Navy had chance to go up by more than TD later on but disdained short FG. On 4th down, McCoy missed quick EZ pass. Taking over just inches from own GL, Army went more than 99y as QB Ronnie McAda (5-9/74y, INT) overcame sack with desperate but dandy 28y connection on 4th-and-24 to WR John Graves which carried all way to Middies 1YL. Conroy blasted for TD, and K J Parker made winning pt. Navy coach Charlie Weatherbie later lamented his FG decision, calling it "very poor tactical error on my part."

Florida 34 Arkansas 3 (Atlanta): Oddsmakers pegged SEC Championship game as lost cause unless Arkansas (8-4) could manage ball control. With Florida (12-0) O serving as ticking timebomb on sideline, well-prepared Razorbacks read script and used up half of 1st Q to march downfield. But, Hogs were doomed by knee injury to TB Madre Hill and failed to convert TD. K Todd Latourette booted 36y FG instead. Coach Steve Spurrier's Gators O-machine scored on its 1st 2 tries: QB Danny Wuerffel's 22y pass to WR Chris Doering for his 17th TD catch of year and on Wuerffel's 1y sneak. Gators' 2nd TD came after midfield INT overthrow by harried Hogs QB Barry Lunney (17-27/170y, 2 INT), 1st of 4 disastrous TOs that led Hogs to slaughterhouse. Game's signature play came in 3rd Q when Hogs threatened GL with 4th down run. Lunney went left on option and pitched out as he was tackled. Florida LB Ben Hanks stepped in to pick off pitchout and charged 95y to TD that gave Gators safe lead at 31-3. Wuerffel (20-28/276y, 2 TDs) finished game with bandaged chin courtesy of 1st H hit, but he owned SEC career record for TD passes (75) and his year's pass efficiency rating (178.4) came out as highest since NCAA created system in 1979.

Texas 16 TEXAS A&M 6: Last-ever SWC title went to D-stout no. 9 Texas (10-1-1) as it ended 31-game home winning streak of Texas A&M (8-3). Both D squads dominated 1st H as Aggies lost 3 TOs. Longhorns led 6-0 at H when WR Michael Adams drew EZ interference PEN on Aggies DB Ray Mickens, and RB Ricky Williams followed with 21y draw for TD. A&M penetrated Steers territory several times in 2nd H, but 3 more TOs prevented all but K Kyle Bryant's 2 FGs. Williams (24/163y) scored another TD after 44y run in 3rd Q. A&M TB Leeland McElroy rushed 29/145y in losing cause.

USA Today Coaches Poll December 4

1	Nebraska (55)	1543	14	Michigan	676
2	Florida (7)	1494	15	Auburn	662
3	Northwestern	1412	16	Penn State	651
4	Tennessee	1315	17	Southern California	557
5	Ohio State	1305	18	Texas A&M	508
6	Texas	1213	19	Virginia	427
7	Colorado	1140	20	Washington	360
8	Florida State	1087	21	Clemson	344
9	Notre Dame	1068	22	Syracuse	223
10	Kansas State	963	23	Arkansas	143
11	Virginia Tech	888	24	UCLA	125
12	Oregon	847	25	Texas Tech	106
13	Kansas	805			

1995 Conference Standings

Big East

Virginia Tech	6-1
Miami	6-1
Syracuse	5-2
West Virginia	4-3
Boston College	4-3
Rutgers	2-5
Temple	1-6
Pittsburgh	0-7

Atlantic Coast

Florida State	7-1
Virginia	7-1
Clemson	6-2
Georgia Tech	5-3
Maryland	4-4
North Carolina	4-4
North Carolina State	2-6
Duke	1-7
Wake Forest	0-8

Southeastern

EAST	
Florida	8-0
Tennessee	7-1
Georgia	3-5
South Carolina	2-5-1
Kentucky	2-6
Vanderbilt	1-7
WEST	
Arkansas	6-2
Alabama	5-3
Auburn	5-3
Louisiana State	4-3-1
Mississippi	3-5
Mississippi State	1-7

Big Ten

Northwestern	8-0
Ohio State	7-1
Michigan	5-3
Penn State	5-3
Michigan State	4-3-1
Iowa	4-4
Illinois	3-4-1
Wisconsin	3-4-1
Purdue	2-5-1
Minnesota	1-7
Indiana	0-8

Mid-American

Toledo	7-0-1
Miami (Ohio)	6-1-1
Ball State	6-2
Western Michigan	6-2
Eastern Michigan	5-3
Bowling Green	3-5
Central Michigan	2-6
Akron	2-6
Ohio	1-6-1
Kent	0-7-1

Big Eight

Nebraska	7-0
Colorado	5-2
Kansas State	5-2
Kansas	5-2
Oklahoma	2-5
Oklahoma State	2-5
Missouri	1-6
Iowa State	1-6

Southwest

Texas	7-0
Texas A&M	5-2
Texas Tech	5-2
Baylor	5-2
Texas Christian	3-4
Houston	2-5
Rice	1-6
Southern Methodist	0-7

Western Athletic

Colorado State	6-2
Air Force	6-2
Brigham Young	6-2
Utah	6-2
San Diego State	5-3
Wyoming	4-4
Hawaii	2-6
New Mexico	2-6
Fresno State	2-6
Texas-El Paso	1-7

Pacific-10

Southern California	6-1-1
Washington	6-1-1
Oregon	6-2
Stanford	5-3
UCLA	4-4
Arizona	4-4
Arizona State	4-4
California	2-6
Washington State	2-6
Oregon State	0-8

1995 Major Bowl Games

Aloha Bowl (Dec. 25): Kansas 51 UCLA 30

Aloha Bowl was billed as Lame Duck Coaches Bowl as UCLA's Terry Donahue was leaving for CBS broadcast booth and Kansas' Glen Mason had accepted head job at Georgia. On morning of game, however, Mason announced he would stay at Kansas because of family matters. Uplifted Jayhawks (10-2) soared to 17-0 lead in 1st H on QB Mark Williams' 9y pass to TE Jim Moore, 49y sideline sprint by RB June Henley (13/107y), and Jeff McCord's 27y FG. Kansas scored on its 1st 3 possessions of 3rd Q as Henley registered his 2nd TD and Williams (18-27/288y, 3 TD) nailed TD passes to WRs Isaac Byrd, Andre Carter. Trailing 37-7, Bruins scored 3 TDs in 4th Q, including 5y run by TB Karim Abdul-Jabbar (26/152y).

Copper Bowl (Dec. 27): Texas Tech 55 Air Force 41

Texas Tech (9-3) became 1st team ever to relinquish 50 pts in bowl game (55 to Southern California in 1995 Cotton Bowl) and answer with 50 pts in its next bowl. Red Raiders surged to 28-7 lead in 2nd Q. Flash points of Tech O were RB Byron Hanspard (24/260y, 4 TDs) and QB Zebbie Lethridge (22-41/245y, TD, INT, and 10/85y, 2 TDs rushing). No. 3 in national rushing, Air Force (8-5) piled up 67/431y out of Wishbone ground attack. Falcons fought to within 31-28 in opening 7 mins of 3rd Q as Raiders fell victim to series of blunders. But, Hanspard scored his 3rd TD with 5:06 left in 3rd Q and dashed 63y to set up Lethridge's 3y TD run for formidable 45-28 edge.

Alamo Bowl (Dec. 28): Texas A&M 22 Michigan 20

Soon to announce his early NFL draft entry, Texas A&M (9-3) TB Leeland McElroy was out with bad ankle. In his stead, Aggies threw mixture of 3 frosh TBs—Sirr Parker (21/56y), Eric Bernard (15/40y, TD), and D'Andre Hardeman (6/41y)—who combined for 137y. QB Corey Pullig (12-22/136y) played virtually mistake-free, and "Wrecking Crew" D wrecked Michigan (9-4) when it had to. Early TO led to 9y TD run by Bernard for 7-0 A&M lead. Wolverines QB Brian Griese (9-23/182y, 2 TDs, INT) matched it with 41y connection with WR Amani Toomer. Then, A&M K Kyle Bryant, inconsistent all season, booted 1st of his FGs of 27, 49, 47, 31, and 37y. Griese opened 2nd H 1-10 in air as he had to dodge blitzers, but Michigan trailed only 19-13 in 4th Q when Aggies DB Andre Williams stepped in front of slipping WR Mercury Hayes to pick off Griese's pass. Williams' INT positioned Bryant for his last FG with 23 secs left. Toomer caught window-dressing TD from Griese with 5 secs left.

Sun Bowl (Dec. 29): Iowa 38 Washington 18

Grumpy Washington (7-4-1) coach Jim Lambright complained that his Pac-10 co-champs should have received Cotton Bowl bid but would have to "settle" for Sun Bowl. Upbeat Iowa (8-4) socked it right to Huskies. After early FUM REC, Hawkeyes sent RB Sedrick Shaw (21/135y) bursting through right side for 58y TD run. TO-plagued Washington lost ball twice more and suffered bad snap safety in 1st H dominated 21-0 by Iowa. TE-turned-FB Michael Burger smashed for 2 TDs out of Power-I setup, and Hawks kicked Sun Bowl record 5 FGs. Long specialist K Brion Hurley connected from 49, 47, and 50y, and K Zach Bromert made his from 33 and 34y. Huskies got brief spark in 3rd Q, going to sub QB Shane Fortney as relief for sr Damon Huard (14-26/194y, 2 TD). Fortney threw 30y TD to WR Jerome Pathon at end of 80y drive.

Independence Bowl (Dec. 29): Louisiana State 45 Michigan State 26

With LSU (7-4-1) playing near home in Shreveport, Tigers were given unwelcome welcome on game's 2nd snap. Michigan State (6-5-1) QB Tony Banks launched 78y TD pass to WR Muhsin Muhammad. After Tigers tied it 7-7, 2nd Q turned into shootout with 3 TDs traded in less than 2 mins. After FB Scott Greene had given Michigan State 13-7 lead with TD run on 1st play of Q, LSU WR Eddie Kennison took KO 92y to set new Independence Bowl RET record. Spartans WR Derrick Mason ignored extra ball tossed from grandstand and went 100y with ensuing KO to trump Kennison's record. LSU RB Kevin Faulk (25/234y, 2 TDs) soon raced 51y to TD, but K Chris Gardner's FG gave Spartans 24-21 H lead. LSU's speedy D collapsed on Spartans in 3rd Q as 3 big TDs decided contest at 42-24. Killing score came midway in 3rd Q as CB Greg Hill, on surprise blitz from edge, and DE Gabe Northern converged on Banks. Northern stripped ball, went 37y to TD which built 35-24 LSU advantage. Michigan State's 6 TOs proved deadly.

Holiday Bowl (Dec. 29): Kansas State 54 Colorado State 21

Kansas State (10-2) and Colorado State (8-4) traded opening drive TDs for 7-7 tie. Running aggressively, Wildcats QB Matt Miller struggled for extra y on 2nd Q scramble and had neck injured in helmet-to-helmet collision. Relief QB Brian Kavanaugh converted TDs in 12 and 32 secs for 19-7 lead when he inherited great field position on his 1st 2 series: DB Mario Smith's INT put K-State at Rams 24YL, and blocked punt turned ball over to Wildcats at 18YL. Kavanaugh (18-24/242y, 4 TDs, INT) had career game thereafter, building 33-7 3rd Q lead on 12y TD to TE Brian Lojka and TD to WR Tyson Schwieger on deflection by Rams A-A S Greg Myers. Bright spot for Colorado State came in 3rd Q as DB Ray Jackson corralled blocked punt at 3YL to lead to TD.

Liberty Bowl (Dec. 30): East Carolina 19 Stanford 13

Undervalued East Carolina (9-3) won without TD from its O, using 3 Stanford TOs and gadget plays to earn leads of 10-0 and 16-7 at H. Key TO came on INT TD RET by Pirates DB Daren Hart. Also, Pirates LB Morris Foreman set up FG with 22y run on punt fake in 2nd Q. Cardinal LB Nick Watts busted up middle to block punt early in 3rd Q, and DB Kwame Ellis ran it in for TD. Stanford (7-4-1) trailed 16-13 after missed conv. Cardinal made good D stand midway in 4th Q, but O failed to move from midfield. ECU QB Marcus Crandell (19-46/218y, INT) hit 3 late passes for 1st downs to set up K Chad Holcomb's 4th FG with 1:15 to go. WR Damon Dunn's 40y KO RET and 3 completions by QB Mark Butterfield (15-27/139y, 2 INTs) moved ball to Pirates 20YL, but possession was lost on downs after 2 incomplete passes.

Carquest Bowl (Dec. 30): North Carolina 20 Arkansas 10

Arkansas (8-5) WR Anthony Lucas took QB Barry Lunney's high, 25y pass off back of helmet of defender to score opening TD after 5:07 drive. North Carolina (7-5) used occasional Shotgun formation in drive that answered with WR Darrin Ashford's 18y TD catch midway in 1st Q. H score stayed knotted at 7-7 after DL Greg Ellis Conley made UNC's 2nd FG block with min to go. D-oriented game saw Heels DT Marcus Jones overcome double-team blocks to star. With Razorbacks up 10-7 late in 3rd Q, UNC QB Mike Thomas ran perfect blitz-beating option, pitching out to TB Leon Johnson (29/195y) for 28y TD. WR L.C. Stevens, who rode bench for much of game, hauled in 87y heave by harassed Thomas (10-23/177y, 2TDs) for clincher. So, Arkansas closed its season with 3 losses and still was looking for 1st bowl win since 1985.

Peach Bowl (Dec. 30): Virginia 34 Georgia 27

Peach Bowl was coaching swansong for Georgia's excitable, likable Ray Goff, who comically stuffed his head deep into his cap after being outraged by official's call. Virginia (9-4) got early boost from P Will Brice (8/42y avg), who made spectacular 41y punt with 3 on-rushing Bulldogs draped over him. Cavs soon turned INT and their own full-fledged punt block into TDs by TBs Tiki Barber (20/103y) and Kevin Brooks (7/23y). Bulldogs (6-6) K Kanon Parkman's 2 FGs shortened deficit to 14-6 in 2nd Q, but QB Mike Groh (10-20/156y, INT) pitched 83y bomb to WR Pete Allen for 24-6 Virginia lead late in 2nd Q. Suddenly, Georgia's harried QB Hines Ward (31-59/413y, 2 INTs) turned hot on way to career-best game. Ward's 1y TD run and 2-pt pass shaved deficit to 24-14 at H. Late in 3rd Q, Barber made 18 and 26y runs to set up K Rafael Garcia's 36y FG, and Cavs led 27-17. Trailing 27-20, Georgia launched 17-play drive on which Ward hit 5 passes, but missed on 3rd and 4th down throws from Cavs 13YL. Virginia surprisingly chose to pass on 2nd down even though it needed only to kill slightly more than min. Bulldogs DB Armin Love made huge hit, and after his reception TE Walt Derey coughed up FUM that Georgia DL Jason Ferguson ran to tying 10y TD with 1:09 left. Amazingly, Virginia, year-long masters of last-min decisions, broke Allen free for thrilling 83y KO TD RET on which he barely tight-rope-walked left sideline to win it.

Sugar Bowl (Dec. 31): Virginia Tech 28 Texas 10

Prior to Sugar Bowl, Texas (10-2-1) was stunned to learn it had imposter within its ranks. Reserve DB Joel Ron McKelvey was thrown off team (and later sued) for fraudulently playing under assumed name. Ron Weaver, 30-year-old who had previously exhausted his eligibility at small colleges, had borrowed social security number of California man. Longhorns found no imposters on Virginia Tech (10-2) D, which allowed only 78y rushing, 129y below Texas' avg. After Longhorns earned 10-0 lead on short TD pass by QB James Brown (14-36/148y, INT) and 52y FG by K Phil Dawson, Hokies inserted WR Bryan Still on punt RET. Still raced 60y to TD to provide spark Tech was missing. In 3rd Q, Still (6/119y) made twisting catch at Texas 2YL to set up FB Marcus Parker's go-ahead TD, and he caught 54y TD from QB Jim Druckenmiller in 4th Q. Next, Hokies D took over, scoring its 7th TD in last 6 games—while allowing just 9 TDs during same span—when DL Jim Baron took Brown's FUM 20y to score late in 4th Q.

Outback Bowl: Penn State 43 Auburn 14

Penn State (9-3) used half of 1st Q for 13-play FG drive, but back came Auburn (8-4). Pouring rain forced Tigers out of planned air game, but TB Stephen Davis ran 7/92y in 1st Q. But, on next-to-last play of 1st Q, Davis sustained head injury, missed most of 2nd Q, and gained only 22y rest of way. Auburn QB Patrick Nix (5-25/48y, 2 INTs) threaded 25y TD pass to WR Robert Baker for 7-3 lead in 2nd Q. Lions led only 9-7 on K Brett Conway's 3 FGs, but DB Kim Herring made INT of Nix in last 19 secs of 1st H. QB Wally Richardson (13-24/217y, 4 TDs, INT) launched 43y bomb to WR Joe Jurevicius to 8YL and found TB Mike Archie for TD with 5 secs left. Penn State WR Bobby Engram (4/113y) and FB Brian Milne (12/82y) sparked 27-pt surge in 3rd Q as Engram caught 2 TDs and Milne made key gains and threw hefty blocks. Lions outgained Tigers 375y to 79y in middle Qs.

Florida Citrus Bowl: Tennessee 20 Ohio State 14

Golden anniversary of Citrus Bowl turned into central Florida quagmire. Blocked punt by Ohio State (11-2) DB Central McClellion set up Heisman Trophy winner, TB Eddie George, for 2y TD run in 1st Q. Tennessee (11-1) made brilliant 4th down stop of George at 4YL in 2nd Q as DL Bill Duff made penetration. Vols appeared to be running out clock before H, but, with 23 secs left, TB Jay Graham broke 2 tackles to dash 69y to tying TD at 7-7. Roughing-punter PEN on Buckeyes gave Volunteers QB Peyton Manning (20-35/182y) chance to launch 47y TD pass to WR Joey Kent. Early in 4th Q, Ohio QB Bobby Hoying successfully sneaked on 4th-and-inches at own 41YL to keep alive 68y drive culminated in TE Rickey Dudley's 32y TD catch. Midway in 4th Q, K Jeff Hall's 29y FG gave Tennessee 17-14 lead. Buckeyes failed twice on 4th down: when Hoying's pitchout hit blocker's helmet on option and pass at own 25YL when hurried Hoying flipped ball to G Juan Daniels. Hall added FG with 27 secs on clock. Extending Heisman bowl jinx, George finished with solid 25/101y rushing, but it was his 2nd lowest total of season.

Gator Bowl: Syracuse 41 Clemson 0

Looking for 6-0-1 record in its most recent bowls, Syracuse (9-3) jumped to 20-0 lead in 1st Q as QB Donovan McNabb went for TD on option run and threw 38y TD pass to WR Marvin Harrison (7/173y, 2 TDs). Clemson (8-4) never was able to gear up its 4th-best-in-nation rushing O. On top of that, it was pass failure near Orangemen GL in 2nd Q that sealed Tigers fate: QB Nealon Greene (9-19/63y, 2 INTs) threw errant pass for TE Lamont Hall on 4th-and-2 from Orange 6YL. Intended as big surprise, it was only pass directed at any Tigers TE all season. McNabb (13-23/309y, 3 TDs, INT) set up 2nd H TD with his 39y pass and followed with TD aerials of 56 and 15y.

Cotton Bowl: Colorado 38 Oregon 6

Miserable cold, wet weather and lack of Texas-based host team kept Cotton Bowl turnout to its lowest since 38,000 sat in snow and ice for scoreless tie in 1947. Oregon (9-3) failed to cash numerous early chances, harvesting only 2 FGs by K Joshua Smith from 4 drives starting at midfield or inside Colorado (10-2) territory. QB John Hessler's 62y pass to WR James Kidd led to Hessler's 1y TD run for 7-6 edge for Buffaloes early in 2nd Q. Game's biggest play soon came when Ducks reached Colorado 9YL. Under duress, Oregon QB Tony Graziani threw into coverage, and extra DB Marcus Washington stuffed Ducks with 95y INT TD RET. Colorado TB Herchell Troutman raced 55y to set up another TD in 2nd H. Buffs missed 4 conv kicks, and their fake-punt pass angered Oregon because it set up game's last TD.

Rose Bowl: Southern California 41 Northwestern 32

Rarely has 1 team received so much pre-game attention—Cinderella Northwestern (10-2)—while its opponent stewed and plotted off-stage. Southern California (9-2-1) coach John Robinson said, "Most of our players have bruises from the media stepping on their toes to get to Northwestern." Overcoming bruised toes were O stars QB Brad Otton (29-44/391y, 2 TDs) and WR Keyshawn Johnson (12/Rose Bowl record 216y, TD). Opponents traded opening-drive TDs as Otton's throws led to TB LaVale Woods' 1y TD plunge at end of 83y march, and Wildcats answered with TB Darnell Autry's 3y TD run at end of 68y advance. Trailing 17-7 late in 2nd Q, Wildcats WR Brian Musso took pass over middle for good gain, but coughed up ball. Trojans DB Daylon McCutheon scooped it up and ran 53y to TD. Down 24-7, NW opened 2nd H with K Brian Gowins' FG, followed by Gowins' perfectly-bunted on-side KO. Autry (32/123y) soon scored to pull Wildcats within 24-19. Johnson broke away up middle with 56y scoring pass, but NW came back with QB Steve Schnur's TD sneak and Autry's 3rd TD gave Cats 32-31 lead early in 4th Q. After K Adam Abrams' career-best 46y FG regained lead for USC, Schnur (22-39/336y) overthrew wide-open FB Matt Hartl, and DB Jesse Davis' 39y INT RET set up clinching TD for Trojans. PEN Later nullified Schnur's TD pass, and when Gowins' 48y FG try hit upright, Northwestern coach Gary Barnett's wry smile indicated he had accepted his sad fate.

Orange Bowl: Florida State 31 Notre Dame 26

Momentum came in waves in last Orange Bowl game played in stadium of same name. Notre Dame (9-3) held ball for 11:03 of possession during 1st Q on way to 10-7 lead. Irish gained 178y on 1st 3 series, only 48y on next 3, but recaptured their edge during 3rd Q and early 4th Q. Florida State (10-2) relied on WR Andre Cooper (4/38y, 3 TDs) to catch 15 and 10y TD passes for 14-10 H lead. Cooper's 2nd grab was lovely leaping takeaway from Irish DB Allen Rossum. ND WR Derrick Mayes put his own stamp on highlight tape. Leaping high at GL with FSU DB Samari Rolle, Mayes tipped 33y throw to himself for TD that provided 17-14 3rd Q lead. ND's ground game took control, and when safety and TE Pete Chrylewicz's 5y catch from QB Thomas Krug (14-24/140y, 3 TDs, INT) were added, Irish led 26-14. QB Danny Kanell (20-32/290y, 4 TDs, 2 INTs) fired Seminole guns for 73y TD drive in 1:56, and after TB Dee Feaster's 48y punt RET, Kanell hit Cooper for his 3rd TD and duo added 2-pt conv. Florida State led 29-26 and added safety with 2:02 left when it pressured Krug into intentional grounding from own EZ.

Fiesta Bowl: Nebraska 62 Florida 24

Early going of Bowl Alliance's championship matchup in Tostitos Fiesta Bowl looked like it would be classic to remember. Each team roared from locker room to score on its opening series. Florida (12-1) QB Danny Wuerffel (17-31/255y, 2 TDs, 3 INTs) drilled WR Chris Doering with 4 passes, but missed twice in EZ. Gators settled for K Bart Edmiston's 23y FG. Nebraska (12-0) responded with QB Tommie Frazier's rollout right and throw-back left pass to IB Lawrence Phillips for 16y TD. Late in 1st Q, Gators regained lead at 10-6 when Wuerffel sneaked over at end of 54y advance started by DB Teako Brown's INT. But then onslaught began. Early in 2nd Q, Phillips broke 3 tackles to charge 42y on cutback TD run for permanent Huskers lead at 13-10. PENs and sack pushed Gators to within inches of own GL. With Florida aligned with no backs behind QB, Nebraska blitzed LB Jamel Williams, who smashed Wuerffel for safety. Frazier contributed 31y dash, leading to frosh IB Ahman Green's TD run for 22-10 edge. DB Michael Booker cut in to make 43y INT TD RET. When K Kris Brown kicked his 2nd FG just before H, Nebraska had created 29-pt 2nd Q storm and enjoyed 35-10 H lead. Precise cross block by Huskers C Aaron Graham and G Steve Ott allowed Frazier to zoom 35y to TD on QB draw late in 3rd Q. In dying moments of 3rd Q, Frazier created game's most memorable play: he broke 7 arm tackles by exhausted Gators to canter 75y down right sideline. It now stood 49-10 Nebraska, and victory was secure. Gators were so dominated that they ended with -28y rushing. Nebraska's 38-pt margin was 2nd largest in no. 1 vs. no. 2 matchups to Army's 48-0 win over Notre Dame in 1948. Nebraska became 1st repeat AP national champion since Alabama in 1978-79.

1 Nebraska (62)	1550	13 Penn State	867	
2 Florida	1474	14 Texas	724	
3 Tennessee	1428	15 Texas A&M	661	
4 Florida State	1311	16 Virginia	603	
5 Colorado	1309	17 Michigan	474	
6 Ohio State	1161	18 Oregon	416	
7 Kansas State	1147	19 Syracuse	382	
8 Northwestern	1124	20 Miami	352	
9 Kansas	1029	21 Alabama	313	
10 Virginia Tech	1015	22 Auburn	276	
11 Notre Dame	931	23 Texas Tech	197	
12 Southern California	886	24 Toledo	170	
		25 Iowa	133	

Final *USA Today* Coaches Poll January 4

1 Nebraska (62)	1550	14 Texas	768	
2 Tennessee	1438	15 Texas A&M	703	
3 Florida	1434	16 Syracuse	593	
4 Colorado	1308	17 Virginia	585	
5 Florida State	1280	18 Oregon	441	
6 Kansas State	1129	19 Michigan	426	
7 Northwestern	1121	20 Texas Tech	329	
8 Ohio State	1105	21 Auburn	292	
9 Virginia Tech	1101	22 Iowa	205	
10 Kansas	994	23 East Carolina	163	
11 Southern California	898	24 Toledo	150	
12 Penn State	857	25 LSU	110	
13 Notre Dame	813			

1995 Top Performance Formula

1 Nebraska	1.9434
2 Florida	1.7391
3 Tennessee	1.6789
4 Colorado	1.6163
5 Florida State	1.6062
6 Ohio State	1.6044
7 Kansas State	1.5715
8 Northwestern	1.5607
9 Notre Dame	1.5162
10 Virginia Tech	1.4823
11 Kansas	1.4513
12 Texas	1.4472
13 Penn State	1.4381
14 Southern California	1.4108
15 Texas A&M	1.3963
16 Syracuse	1.3962
17 Texas Tech	1.3817
18 Michigan	1.3635
19 Virginia	1.3180
20 Oregon	1.3071

1995 Top Opponent Records

1 Notre Dame	.6462
2 Colorado	.6230
3 Michigan State	.6229
4 Northwestern	.6190
5 Houston	.6144
6 Illinois	.6134
7 UCLA	.6071
8 Indiana	.6059
9 Vanderbilt	.6026
10 Georgia	.6024
11 Florida	.6014
12 Nebraska	.5984
13tWisconsin	.593220
13tPurdue	.593220
15Tennessee	.5930
16 Washington	.5893
17 Michigan	.5827
18 Penn State	.5814
19 Florida State	.5795
20 Oklahoma State	.5786

1995 Out-of-Conference Records

	W-L	Percentage	Bowl W-L
Big Eight	28-7-1	.7917	4-0
Southeastern	30-12	.7143	2-4
Big Ten	27-11-1	.7051	2-4
Pacific-10	17-15-1	.5303	1-4
Southwest	17-16-2	.5143	2-1
Western Athletic	17-18	.4857	0-2
Atlantic Coast	13-15	.4643	3-1
Big East	14-20	.4118	2-0

1995 Individual Statistical Leaders

RUSHING YARDS	Attempts	Yards	Avg.
Troy Davis, Iowa State	345	2010	5.8
Wasean Tait, Toledo	357	1905	5.3
George Jones, San Diego State	305	1842	6.0
Eddie George, Ohio State	303	1826	6.0
Tim Biakabutuka, Michigan	279	1724	6.2
Darnell Autrey, Northwestern	355	1675	4.7
Deland McCullough, Miami (Ohio)	321	1627	5.1
Moe Williams, Kentucky	294	1600	5.4
Charles Talley, Northern Illinois	285	1540	5.4
David Thompson, Oklahoma State	256	1509	5.9

PASSING YARDS	Completions	Attempts	Yards	Pct.
Mike Maxwell, Nevada	277	409	3611	67.7
Cody Ledbetter, New Mexico State	259	453	3501	57.2
Steve Sarkisian, Brigham Young	250	385	3437	64.9
Billy Blanton, San Diego State	243	389	3300	62.5
Danny Wuerffel, Florida	210	325	3266	64.6
Steve Taneyhill, South Carolina	261	389	3094	67.1
Bobby Hoying, Ohio State	192	303	3023	63.4
Danny Kanell, Florida State	257	402	2957	63.9
Peyton Manning, Tennessee	244	380	2954	64.2
Jake Delhomme, Southwest'n Louisiana	190	351	2761	54.1

RECEIVING YARDS	Catches	Yards
Alex Van Dyke, Nevada	129	1854
Marcus Harris, Wyoming	78	1423
Terry Glenn, Ohio State	57	1316
Chad Mackey, Louisiana Tech	90	1255
Keyshawn Johnson, Southern California	90	1218
Will Blackwell, San Diego State	86	1207
Charlie Jones, Fresno State	71	1171
Marvin Harrison, Syracuse	56	1131
Bobby Engram, Penn State	63	1084
Joey Kent, Tennessee	69	1055

1995 Consensus All-America Team
Offense

Wide Receiver:	Keyshawn Johnson, Southern California
	Terry Glenn, Ohio State
Tight End:	Marco Battaglia, Rutgers
Line:	Jonathan Ogden, UCLA
	Jason Odom, Florida
	Orlando Pace, Ohio State
	Jeff Hartings, Penn State
Center:	Clay Shiver, Florida State
	Bryan Stoltenberg, Colorado
Quarterback:	Tommie Frazier, Nebraska
Running Back:	Eddie George, Ohio State
	Troy Davis, Iowa State
Placekicker:	Michael Reeder, Texas Christian

Defense

Line:	Tedy Bruschi, Arizona
	Cornell Brown, Virginia Tech
	Marcus Jones, North Carolina
	Tony Brackens, Texas
Linebacker:	Zach Thomas, Texas Tech
	Kevin Hardy, Illinois
	Pat Fitzgerald, Northwestern
Back:	Chris Canty, Kansas State
	Lawyer Milloy, Washington
	Aaron Beasley, West Virginia
	Greg Myers, Colorado State
Punter:	Brad Maynard, Ball State

1995 Heisman Trophy Vote

Eddie George, senior tailback, Ohio State	1,460
Tommie Frazier, senior quarterback, Nebraska	1,196
Danny Wuerffel, junior quarterback, Florida	987
Darnell Autry, sophomore tailback, Northwestern	535

Other Major Award Winners

Maxwell (Player)	Eddie George, senior tailback, Ohio State
Walter Camp (Player)	Eddie George, senior tailback, Ohio State
Outland (Lineman)	Jonathan Ogden, senior tackle, UCLA
Vince Lombardi (Lineman)	Orlando Pace, sophomore tackle, Ohio State
Doak Walker (Runner)	Eddie George, senior tailback, Ohio State
Davey O'Brien (Quarterback)	Danny Wuerffel, junior quarterback, Florida
Fred Biletnikoff (Receiver)	Terry Glenn, junior wide receiver, Ohio State
Jim Thorpe (Defensive Back)	Greg Myers, senior safety, Colorado State
Dick Butkus (Linebacker)	Kevin Hardy, senior linebacker, Illinois
Lou Groza (Placekicker)	Michael Reeder, soph. kicker, Texas Christian
Johnny Unitas (Quarterback)	Tommie Frazier, senior quarterback, Nebraska
Chuck Bednarik (Defender)	Pat Fitzgerald, junior linebacker, Northwestern
Bronko Nagurski (Defender)	Pat Fitzgerald, junior linebacker, Northwestern
AFCA Coach of the Year	Gary Barnett, Northwestern

1996

The Year of Changing Landscape, Overtime Thrillers and Marathons, and Gators Aided by Gamesmanship

The landscape of college football changed considerably in 1996 with the actualization of the Big 12 and Conference USA and the expansion of the Western Athletic Conference from 10 to 16 teams in two divisions. Tie games, those long-time "kissing your sister" bugaboos, were eradicated by utilizing an overtime format much like baseball extra innings. After a coin toss determined one team's choice of first playing offense or defense (i.e., determining the top half of the "inning"), a four-downs-for-a-first-down offensive series was started at the 25 yard-line and the other team followed with a similar possession until one team outscored the other. In practice, the untimed overtime periods often ended in on-going outlandish scores.

Several wild overtime games occurred in 1996, none nuttier than California's 56-55 decision over Arizona (5-6) made possible when the Golden Bears (6-6) stopped the Wildcats' courageous two-point conversion run off a fake tying conversion kick. There would be far more of these overtime marathons over the coming years. Kansas (4-7), with 58 ties during its 106 years playing the sport, was locked in as the all-time leader of deadlocked games.

Was the occasional tie game all that awful? Some of the greatest games in football history earned their legendary status simply because they ended in deadlocks that could be debated into history. History points to the 33-33 tie between Yale and Dartmouth in 1931—which stood for 17 years as the highest scoring tie of all time—when a scoreboard error encouraged Dartmouth to adopt a fourth quarter kicking strategy it thought would end a long winless drought against the Bulldogs, when instead its field goal only created a tie. The greatest defensive teams of the 1930s, Pittsburgh and Fordham, tied each other in 0-0 knots for three straight years. There is the famous 1947 scoreless deadlock between Army and Notre Dame at Yankee Stadium which was loaded with "might-have-beens" that would have swung the national title to the winner. Every coach was impacted by Notre Dame coach Ara Parseghian's ridiculed, but right choice to accept a 10-10 tie with Michigan State in 1966. In 1968, Harvard tied Yale 29-29 by scoring 16 points in a matter of seconds to close the game. Would it have been the same if Harvard and Yale had battled on into the cold New England night through endless successions of overtime periods?

The advent of the two-point conversion in 1958 went a long way in curing the number of tie results. Occasionally, the opportunity to overtake an opponent with a two-point conversion set up spine-tingling, all-or-nothing play-calls at the end of games. These were far more fascinating than drawn-out overtime marathons that would produce basketball scores because defenses became so exhausted that they couldn't function properly. Especially ridiculous was the idea of counting overtime offensive statistics toward game stats, so that a quarterback might throw for two touchdowns in regulation only to end up with a new conference record of eight TDs because the opposing defense hadn't the strength to cover receivers or rush the passer. So, what exactly has overtime proved?

The 1996 early season was spiced by unusual happenstances. Struggling Pittsburgh (4-7) allowed a 66-yard punt return by freshman David Boston, the last score in a 72-0 thrashing by Ohio State (11-1), even though the Buckeyes had only eight men on the field at the time. Pitt turned around two weeks later to score 20 fourth-quarter points to nip Temple (1-10) 53-52. The winning touchdown in that one was set up by the Panthers stopping a foolish fourth down gamble by the Owls deep in their own territory. Taking the blame, Temple coach Ron Dickerson resigned only to change his mind on Monday. Navy (9-3), playing its part in a single-year renaissance of the military academies, scored its most points since 1953 in a 64-27 romp over Duke (0-11). The biggest shock was the upset on which votes at the top of the polls pivoted: Arizona State (11-1) used the popular "Press Defense" to stun two-time national champion and top-ranked Nebraska (11-2) 19-0 on September 21. Florida (12-1) defeated no. 2 Tennessee (10-2) earlier in the day, making it the first time nos. 1 and 2 were beaten on the same regular-season date since 1984.

Coach Steve Spurrier's Florida team showcased an explosive offense with quarterback Danny Wuerffel, tailback Fred Taylor, and wide receivers Reidel Anthony, Ike Hilliard, and Jacquez Green. The Gators piled up stunning scores in the normally-competitive SEC. Florida walloped Kentucky 65-0, LSU 56-13, Auburn 51-10, and Georgia 47-7.

Circled on calendars all year was November 30, a date for Florida and Florida State (11-1) which became no. 1 vs. 2 when yet another undefeated Ohio State team under coach John Cooper couldn't beat Michigan (8-4).

Underdog Florida State used a huge pass rush to craft a 24-21 upset and launch itself to no. 1. On-charging Nebraska was in position to slide into a national championship Sugar Bowl showdown against the Seminoles until a sensational December 7.

Pearl Harbor Day felt like an old-fashioned New Year's Day with four thrilling games. Army (10-2) rallied to beat Navy as both locked up bowl bids. Texas (8-5) coach John Mackovic used a stunning fourth down gamble to clinch a great upset over Nebraska in the Big 12 title game. That result put Florida, winner over Alabama (10-2) in the SEC title game, in the Bowl Alliance championship, and into a rematch in the Sugar Bowl that Florida State, recent victor over the Gators, understandably wanted no part of. BYU (14-1) won an overtime thriller from Wyoming (10-2) in the WAC title game, but was unfairly left out of an Alliance at-large spot.

Steve Spurrier, Florida's gifted coach, took up an intriguing bit of gamesmanship prior to the Sugar Bowl. In the late November loss to Florida State, Gators quarterback Wuerffel had spent a lot plays under a pile of hard-charging Seminole pass rushers. Seeking to gain even a split-second more passing time for Wuerffel, the recent Heisman Trophy winner, Spurrier launched a consistent barrage of complaints against FSU for late hits and dirty tactics. Whether Spurrier believed the "Dirty Football" image or not, he was hoping to get the Sugar Bowl referee to pay more attention to possible roughing-the-passer fouls and, even better, to force the Seminole defense into easing up slightly for fear of getting flagged. Spurrier's media strategy worked. Florida made significant strategic changes on both sides of the ball since its November defeat and won the Sugar Bowl rematch with surprising ease, 52-20 to claim its first-ever national title.

Squat Iowa State (2-9) tailback Troy Davis led the nation in rushing with 2,185 yards and, in so doing broke the consecutive-season rushing record of USC's Marcus Allen of 3,905, set in 1980-81. Davis earned a two-season total of 4,195 yards on the ground.

In the midst of a miserable season, Boston College (5-7) wrestled with an ugly situation. Rumors circulated about Eagle players wagering on college sports after a 45-17 thrashing by Syracuse (9-3) and a 20-13 upset at the hands of Pittsburgh. Thirteen players were suspended, two permanently for betting against the Eagles. Coach Dan Henning resigned at season's end.

Henning's departure was part of a huge late season change in the coaching ranks. High-profile coaches Lou Holtz of Notre Dame (8-3) and Gene Stallings of Alabama resigned, although neither convinced the media that he had a clear reason. Holtz, it turned out, had worn out his welcome at Notre Dame only to resurface at South Carolina in 1999 after a two-season stint as an in-studio analyst for CBS. Stallings, always straightforward, simply was interested in retirement, which is what he had stated.

Dozens of other coaches fell victim to win-or-else pressure. Even the legendary Eddie Robinson, in his 55th season at Grambling, fell under alumni scorn for recruiting violations, but survived for one last year in 1997. It was a cruel end for one of America's most gifted and admired molders of young men. Before the Southeastern Conference schools integrated their teams in the 1970s, Robinson all but cornered the recruiting market on black players from the Deep South. Robinson finished his career with 408 wins and sent stars to the NFL such as Willie Davis, Buck Buchanan, Gene Upshaw, and Doug Williams. Robinson, who coached the Tigers from 1941, except two years of World War II service, held the all-level coaching wins record until 2003. He enjoyed a .707 winning percentage and during his 1980-83 matchups with coach John Merritt of Tennessee State they set the mark for most confrontations between coaches with 200 wins each.

Milestones

● Rules committee created overtime format to eliminate tie games.

● Beloved Clemson coach Frank Howard (1940-69) died at age 90. Charlie Conerly, star Mississippi tailback (1942, 1946-47) and twice All-Pro quarterback with New York Giants, died on February 13 after long illness. Ernest "Pokey" Allen, 53, MVP in the 1964 Liberty Bowl for Utah, had been diagnosed with cancer two days after coaching Boise State in 1-AA title game in 1994. He coached in 1995, but had to step aside until final two games of 1996. Allen relapsed and died on December 30. Harry Babcock, All-America end at Georgia in 1952 and first overall selection by San Francisco 49ers in 1953 NFL draft, died at age 66. Crash of airliner in Florida Everglades took lives of former Notre Dame tailback and captain of 1991 squad, Rodney Culver, and former Miami (Florida) guard Robert Woodus (1992-94). Miami also mourned loss of linebacker Marlin Barnes, squad-member who was found murdered in his apartment.

● Miami of Ohio, one of last holdouts in politically-correct age, voted to drop its nickname of Redskins. Leaders of Miami native American tribe contributed input for new name: RedHawks.

● Coaching Changes:

	Incoming	Outgoing
California	Steve Mariucci	Keith Gilbertson
Georgia	Jim Donnan	Ray Goff
Hawaii	Fred vonAppen	Bob Wagner
Oklahoma	John Blake	Howard Schnellenberger
Rutgers	Terry Shea	Doug Graber
UCLA	Bob Toledo	Terry Donahue

● Longest winning streaks entering season:

Nebraska 25	Virginia Tech 10	Miami 7

Preseason *USA Today* Coaches Poll August 9

1	Nebraska (47)	1524	14	Alabama	603
2	Tennessee (6)	1398	15	Virginia Tech	562
3	Florida State (6)	1376	16	Miami (Fla.)	527
4	Florida (3)	1364	17	Auburn	432
5	Colorado	1231	18	Kansas State	407
6	Southern California	1121	19	Northwestern	363
7	Notre Dame	1094	20	LSU	359
8	Penn State	983	21	Virginia	347
9	Texas	968	22	Washington	346
10	Ohio State	958	23	Clemson	282
11	Michigan	866	24	Kansas	256
12	Texas A&M	774	25	Iowa	190
13	Syracuse	743			

August 24, 1996

BRIGHAM YOUNG 41 Texas A&M 37: In earliest opener in college history, BYU (1-0) QB Steve Sarkisian (33-44/536y, INT) tossed 6 TD passes in Pigskin Classic upset of Texas A&M (0-1). Aggies enjoyed 20-6 lead in 2nd Q as Tennessee transfer, QB Branndon Stewart (20-28/232y, 2 TDs), pitched 57y TD to WR Aaron Oliver, but Sarkisian hit 2 TDs in last 5:20 of 2nd Q to tie it. With score at 34-34 with less than 3 mins to play, Stewart connected with WR Albert Connell for explosive slant-in TD. But Texas A&M was penalized and had to settle for K Kyle Bryant's 3rd FG. Cougars WR K.O. Kealaluhi beat young Aggies DBs for deep game-winning TD with 1:03 to go.

(Sun) Penn State 24 Southern California 7 (East Rutherford, N.J.): Nittany Lions soph TB Curtis Enis blasted for 27/241y and 3 TDs rushing, highest ground total to date against Southern California (0-1). FUM at own 11YL midway in 2nd Q put Trojans in hole that K Brett Conway's 28y FG filled for 3-0 lead for Penn State. Next, USC was held at Penn State 3YL, and Trojans K Adam Abrams missed FG. Enis bounced 24y for TD at end of 80y drive for 10-0 H edge. Enis added 2 TDs in 4th Q, and it looked like 24-0 blanking until Lions' GL FUM was recovered for TD in last min by active USC LB Chris Claiborne.

August 31, 1996

WEST VIRGINIA 34 Pittsburgh 0: Coach Johnny Majors, in what would turn out to be his last year in coaching, promised vastly improved Panthers (0-1) team, but he was far from being correct in season opener. West Virginia (1-0) opened "Backyard Brawl," only 7th time rivalry had started season, by springing frosh TB Amos Zereoue for 69y TD romp on his 1st collegiate carrry. Zereoue (12/135y) broke 3 tackles on his initial scoring run that came on game's 4th snap, on his way to school rushing y record for frosh. WVU QB Chad Johnston (15-22/184y, 3 TDs) hit WR Rahsaan Vanterpool with 33y TD pass at outset of 2nd Q for 14-0 lead. Pitt QB Matt Lytle had miserable 5-16/68y, INT aerial game as Panthers were outgained 461y to 101y. It was West Virginia's 5th win in row over Pittsburgh, which now had 8-26 record since Majors' return as head coach.

NORTH CAROLINA 45 Clemson 0: Bested on both lines, Clemson (0-1) allowed most pts to date to North Carolina (1-0), only its 3rd loss in last 16 series games. After TB Leon Johnson (19/109y, 2 TDs) set up own short TD with 67y run in 1st Q, LB Brian Simmons created 10 pts for Tar Heels with FUM REC at Clemson 20YL and 13y INT RET to 21YL. New UNC QB Chris Keldorf (15-22/182y, 2 TDs, INT) pitched 45y score to WR L.C. Stevens in 21-pt 3rd Q, and game's body left for dead had Tiger stripes.

Southern Mississippi 11 GEORGIA 7: Bulldogs (0-1) debuted under coach Jim Donnan, who arrived with great success at Marshall. With only 227y O, Southern Miss (1-0) managed K Johnny Lomoro's 3 FGs and added 4th Q safety when Bulldogs QB Mike Bobo and TB Robert Edwards (34y TD catch) collided on GL handoff and were swarmed over by Eagles DL Jeffrey Posey. Georgia moved to 13YL in last min, but Bobo missed 4th down pass.

MICHIGAN 20 Illinois 8: Michigan (1-0) QB Scott Dreisbach (11-23/117y, TD) returned having missed last 9 games of 1995 with thumb injury. Dreisbach found himself alone on broken pass play early in 2nd Q and sprinted for 72y TD. Illinois (0-1) DL Paul Marshall called it "pathetic defense." Illini gained safety as Dreisbach fell on EZ FUM in 2nd Q. Key moment came late in 2nd Q as Illinois, trailing 10-5, was stopped by GLS and settled for K Bret Scheuplein's 2nd FG. Michigan WR Russell Shaw's 10y TD catch in 4th Q iced verdict. Wolverines LB David Bowens totaled 3 sacks.

MICHIGAN STATE 52 Purdue 14: Spartans (1-0) unveiled frosh TB Sedrick Irvin, cousin of former Miami WR Michael Irvin, who sprinted to TDs of 17, 5, and 5y and caught 12y TD pass from QB Todd Schultz. Irvin rushed for 13/73y and caught 7/59y. Despite gaining 397y on O things went terribly wrong for Purdue (0-1): even when Boilers blocked 1st Q x-pt kick it was mishandled by LB Noble Jones and turned into EZ REC by Spartans FB Travis Reece for 2-pt conv and 15-0 lead. Boilermakers trailed 35-0 before TB Edwin Watson (22/83y, TD) scored at end of 80y drive in 3rd Q.

KANSAS STATE 21 Texas Tech 14: Inaugural Big 12 game saw Kansas State (1-0) DB Mario Smith contribute 2 big plays. Smith made TD REC for 21-3 lead early in 4th Q when Red Raiders C Brad Spinks made bad punt snap, and later Smith broke up 4th down pass with thunderous hit with :44 to go. Earlier, K-State QB Brian Kavanaugh pushed over for

1y TD and flipped 17y score to WR Jimmy Dean. Texas Tech (0-1) came alive in last 6:39 as QB Zebbie Lethridge found wide-open FB Sammy Morris for 14y TD and added 2-pt pass. With 2:27 left, K Jaret Greaser nailed 53y FG to pull Raiders within 7 pts. Texas Tech TB Byron Hanspard (21/115y) chalked up his 7th 100y rushing game in row.

TEXAS 40 Missouri 10: At newly-named Darrell Royal-Texas Memorial Stadium, thunderstorm delayed 3rd Q action for 45 mins, but Longhorns (1-0) got electrified: "All week we practiced in storms," said Texas DB Bryant Westbrook, "The lightning fired us up. It felt great!" Longhorns led 27-10 at moment of game's delay, but Missouri (0-1) was looking good with 2 long drives to K Mark Norris' 30y FG and FB Ernest Blackwell barged ahead for 21y TD as he racked up 45y of 80y drive behind blocking of T Craig Heimburger, G Mike Morris, and C Russ Appel. But, Tigers were declawed by 3 FUMs that led to 13 pts by Texas. Steers QB James Brown (11-20/104y, 2 TDs, INT) threw 2 scoring passes in 1st H. Mizzou faced blinding rain on 1st series of 3rd Q, and muffed punt snap set up Texas TD before lightning halted things. After delay, Westbrook blocked punt for 35y TD RET. TB Ricky Williams (14/112y) scored his 2nd TD in 4th Q on 21y dash.

COLORADO 37 Washington State 19: Returning from injured list, Colorado (1-0) QB Koy Detmer pitched 20-33/254y, 3 TDs and rushed for another score against Washington State (0-1). Midway through 1st Q, punt FUM REC gave Buffs control at Cougars 27YL, and K Jason Leslie booted 31y FG. Colorado quickly made it 24-0 with 3 Detmer tallies. Down 37-6 midway in 4th Q, Washington State D again was stout but this time on 4th down 280-lb DE Dorian Boose scooped up FUM and rumbled 94y to score. On-side-KO led to Cougars TD pass by QB Ryan Leaf (13-33/163y, TD, INT).

USA Today Coaches Poll September 3

1	Nebraska (51)	1536	14	Virginia Tech	613
2	Tennessee (4)	1423	15	Kansas State	542
3	Florida State (3)	1399	16	Brigham Young	541
4	Florida (3)	1387	17	Auburn	439
5	Colorado	1303	18	Northwestern	421
6	Penn State (1)	1178	19	LSU	386
7	Notre Dame	1121	20	Virginia	345
8	Texas	1050	21	Southern California	340
9	Ohio State	1035	22	North Carolina	321
10	Michigan	951	23	Washington	286
11	Syracuse	851	24	Kansas	258
12	Miami (Fla.)	701	25	Texas A&M	247
13	Alabama	643			

September 7, 1996

North Carolina 27 SYRACUSE 10: Assertive D of aspiring North Carolina (2-0) gained 2nd straight win over tough foe. Thwarted by tight coverage by UNC DBs Robert Williams and Dre Bly, touted Syracuse (0-1) QB Donovan McNabb (11-32/125y, TD) failed to complete pass until just before H. Tar Heels QB Chris Keldorf (22-32/218y, 2 TDs) topped 17-0 H runaway with 3y TD pass to WR Na Brown. After Orangemen rallied to score 10 pts in 3rd Q, mainly on McNabb's TD pass, Keldorf sealed it with 18y TD pitch to TE Freddie Jones.

Georgia Tech 28 NORTH CAROLINA STATE 16: Wolfpack (0-1) scored early as QB Jose Laureano (16-23/242y) fired 29y pass to WR Torry Holt, and TB Tremaine Stephens (14/82y, TD) charged 40y to TD. Moments later, INT set up NC State K Marc Primanti for 1st of 3 FGs, career-long-to-date of 47y. Trailing 10-0, Georgia Tech (1-0) wasted little time in 2nd Q as TB C.J. Williams (28/148y, 2 TDs) caught 20y TD pass from QB Joey Hamilton (8-9/74y, TD, INT) and tallied from 1YL for 14-13 H margin. Game's big play came early in 3rd Q. As NC State QB Jimmy Grissett broke open, Laureano cocked arm to throw. Jackets DE Jermaine Miles knocked ball from Laureano and 290-lb DT Derrick Shepard took FUM on fancy cutback for 27y TD and decisive 21-13 edge.

WAKE FOREST 28 Northwestern 27: Last year's glass slipper was shattered by 1 of history's most downtrodden teams. Lowly Wake Forest (2-0) blew leads of 10-0 and 13-3, but upset no. 13 Northwestern (0-1), Cinderella team of 1995. Workhorse Wildcats TB Darnell Autry (32/173y) scored in each middle Q, and QB Steve Schnur (21-32/218y, TD, 3 INTs) tossed 33y TD for 24-13 edge in 4th Q. But, Deacons QB Brian Kuklick (12-25/172y, 2 TDs, INT) hit WR Desmond Clark with 7 and 30y TDs, last coming with 51 secs left. Winning 78y drive featured trio of 3rd-and-1 conversions. Last Wake Forest win over ranked team had come in October 1979, 30 losing games ago.

TENNESSEE 35 Ucla 20: Intersectional "pastels and punts" rivalry swung on late big gainers. After pale blue UCLA (0-1) got 3-0 jump on K Bjorn Merten's 50y FG and added 51y INT TD RET by DB Abdul McCullough, pale orange Tennessee (2-0) bounced to 14-10 lead with RB Mark Levine's 48y KO RET to launch QB Peyton Manning's 2nd TD run. In 4th Q, Vols added 86y punt TD RET and 53y TD strike from Manning (16-28/288y, 2 TDs, INT) to WR Joey Kent (7/114y) who set Vols career reception record. Bruins fitted in 88y TD bomb by QB Cade McNown (16-24/230y) to WR Danny Farmer to trim it to 28-20.

LOUISIANA STATE 35 Houston 34: Coach Gerry DiNardo reinstated LSU (1-0) TB Kevin Faulk when police dropped battery charges. Faulk responded by rushing 21/246y, 2 TDs and igniting 4th Q explosion with 78y rout TD RET. Hopeful Houston (1-1) had rare O mix: more rushing (162y) than passing (115y). Cougars built 20-7 H lead accented by TB Antowain Smith's 25y TD run, QB Chuck Clements' 24y TD pass. After Faulk ran 80y for TD in 1st min of 3rd Q, Cougars DB Stedmon Forman created 34-14 edge with 30y FUM TD RET. TB Rondell Mealey (14/161y), slated to start for Faulk, finished LSU's rally with winning 36y TD run with 3:22 to play.

IOWA 21 Arizona 20: Opportunistic Hawkeyes (1-0) took advantage of 4 FUM RECs, INT to nip Arizona (1-1). Iowa TB Sedrick Shaw rushed 23/115y, scored TD early in 3rd Q for 21-7 lead. Wildcats sub QB Keith Smith (former Detroit Tiger outfielder) accounted for his 2nd TD with 20y run, K Matt Peyton booted FGs of 50 and 39y to pull Wildcats within 21-20. Iowa weathered hard-hitting affair by killing last 6 mins with 15-play drive.

NEBRASKA 55 Michigan State 14: Cornhuskers (1-0) launched pursuit of national title "three-peat" with overwhelming D play. DB Mike Minter blistered 84y INT TD RET, and DL Grant Wistrom charged to 9y INT TD RET. DB Mike Fullman added 62y punt TD RET to enhance Nebraska's somewhat tentative 298y O behind new QB Scott Frost (5-12/74y, TD, and 10/58y rushing), who pitched 35y TD pass to WR Brendan Holbein. Michigan State Spartans (1-1) suffered injuries, but sub QB Gus Ornstein (11-18/133y, 2 INTs) flipped 3rd Q TD. This was Ornstein's biggest public moment since appearing on TV's "Regis and Kathy Lee" couple of years earlier when he was Notre Dame recruit tossing pass to Regis Philbin on New York City streets.

ARIZONA STATE 45 Washington 42: In early season Pac-10 showdown, Arizona State (1-0) exploded for 2 TDs in 2-min span of 3rd Q for 28-21 lead as WR Isaiah Mustafa fell on EZ FUM at end of RB J.R. Redmond's 61y punt RET. Sun Devils boosted edge to 42-21 with 12 mins left behind TB Terry Battle, who scored from 7YL and QB Jake Plummer (16-30/186y, 3 TDs). Washington (0-1) rode frosh sub QB Brock Huard's TD run and TD pass, and frosh RB Corey Dillon's TD run to tie it 42-42. Poor punt provided Sun Devils with late opportunity, and K Robert Nycz salvaged win with 38y FG with 2 secs to go.

USA Today Coaches Poll September 9

1	Nebraska (57)	1544	14	Kansas State	664
2	Tennessee (1)	1415	15	Brigham Young	649
3	Florida State (1)	1412	16	Auburn	614
4	Florida (3)	1391	17	Virginia	533
5	Colorado	1289	18	Southern California	491
6	Penn State	1206	19	Virginia Tech	457
7	Ohio State	1154	20	LSU	323
8	Texas	1119	21	Iowa	319
9	Michigan	960	22	Kansas	309
10	Notre Dame	856	23	Arizona State	227
11	Miami (Fla.)	847	24	Syracuse	214
12	Alabama	743	25	Texas A&M	189
13	North Carolina	672			

September 14, 1996

Virginia Tech 45 BOSTON COLLEGE 7: Using no-huddle attack in 1st Q, Virginia Tech (2-0) cruised to TDs on its 1st 3 possessions. Boston College (1-1) TE Todd Pollack caught 9y TD from QB Matt Hasselbeck (25-42/221y, INT), then Eagles had 1st-and-goal at 7YL after blocked punt. But Virginia Tech's superior D prevented any more pts. In winning school record 12th in row, Hokies offered balanced attack (215y rushing and 226y passing), got 2 TDs each from TE Brian Jennings and FB Brian Edmunds (5/45y).

WEST VIRGINIA 10 East Carolina 9: During spring, East Carolina (1-1) coach Steve Logan decided to play for late-game wins, not ties. "Overtime is an option, not a mandate," he said, reasoning that QB Marcus Crandall was potent weapon for 2-pt tries. When Crandall's 20y TD throw to WR Lamont Chappell drew Pirates within 10-9 with :22 to play, Logan ordered 2-pt pass for win. Crandall found WR Mitchell Galloway, but throw went OB. West Virginia (3-0) clung to win built on 3 INTs of Crandall (22-48/222y, TD) and TB Amos Zereoue's 3rd Q TD catch.

SOUTH CAROLINA 23 Georgia 14: Hardluck Bulldogs (0-2) continued to be barely bad enough to lose. In 1st Q, Georgia lost snap FUM after sub TB Torin Kirtsey's 20y run, WR Hines Ward's 45y TD catch was nullified, and TB Robert Edwards made 3 good runs only leading to lost FUM and missed FG. All along, South Carolina (2-0) built 16-0 lead on QB Anthony Wright's TD pass and TB Duce Staley's brilliant 51y TD run. Edwards' diving TD run before H ended 11-play UGa drive to narrow it to 16-7. Bulldogs cut it to 16-14 in 3rd Q as QB Mike Bobo (15-34/180y, TD, 2 INTs) found WR Juan Daniels for score. Staley's runs and catches led Gamecocks to hurry-up O set at GL that sent FB Steve Mixon crashing for clinching TD midway in 4th Q.

ALABAMA 36 Vanderbilt 26: Alabama (3-0) coach Gene Stallings mostly was happy with "big league plays" of his team, but it had some pratfalls, too. Behind 9-7, Vanderbilt (0-2) P Bill Marinangel faked punt and sprinted 81y, longest run to date in Commodores history. Vanderbilt RB Alvin Duke also raced 88y on punt TD RET in 2nd H. Vandy K Brett Speakman's 38y FG 4:22 into 3rd Q broke 15-15 H deadlock, but Crimson Tide QB Freddie Kitchens dashed 15y to put Alabama ahead for good at 22-18 in 3rd Q. Still, Kitchens suffered 2 INTs in 4th Q, 2nd of which by S Eric Vance brought Dores to Crimson Tide 42YL with 7:29 on clock. Vandy QB Damian Allen hit WR Billy Miller with 38y pass, but 2 plays later LB Ralph Staten rushed Allen into INT by Bama LB Dwayne Rudd. In Sunday's AP Poll, this result interestingly dropped Alabama to share of 13th place with its bitter rival Auburn.

NOTRE DAME 35 Purdue 0: Fighting Irish (2-0) QB Ron Powlus (19-32/238y, TD) had 1 of his best days in moderately disappointing career, but was already looking ahead to Texas and Ohio State games: "We must win the next two weeks," and then, in realization of Notre Dame's heady expectations, added, "But we need to win the next 10 as well." Irish's ferocious front-7 kept Purdue (0-2) from any effective running (26/44y), while DB Allen Rossum roared 99y with opening KO to put ND ahead 7-0. Interestingly, Lou Holtz, who would break Knute Rockne's ND record of coaching in 122 games this day, had predicted Rossum's KO TD RET during Friday's pep rally. With score at 7-0 late in 1st Q, Boilermakers enjoyed threat for instant: Powlus looked over middle for FB Marc Edwards (9/37y, TD), and Purdue LB Joe Hagins had INT in his hands until ball bounced away. ND TB Autry Denson rushed 15/66y, 2 TDs, and caught 10y TD from Powlus. Boilers QB Billy Dicken passed 14-31/150y, but lost 25y in sacks.

Michigan 20 COLORADO 13: Bitter memory of "Hail Mary" loss of 1994 was exorcised by Michigan (2-0), especially when last-play throw by Buffaloes to EZ was batted away harmlessly by UM DBs Chuck Winters and Charles Woodson. Roughing passer PEN had given Wolverines chance for K Remy Hamilton's 1st Q FG, but Colorado (2-1) came back for 13-10 H lead on TB Lendon Henry's 8y TD run and WR Phil Savoy's 5y TD catch from QB Koy Detmer (23-39/287y, TD, INT). Michigan tied it 13-13 midway in 3rd Q on Hamilton's 2nd FG after 3 straight completions by maturing QB Scott Dreisbach (13-23/108y, TD). Late in 3rd Q, Dreisbach pitched 3y TD after short Buffs punt, and Michigan D allowed only 11y on next 10 plays. Hampered by 14/99y in PENs, Buffs also failed twice on 4th down in 4th Q, once after 6-min drive achieved 1st-and-goal at Michigan 8YL.

SOUTHWESTERN LOUISIANA 29 Texas A&M 22: Since playing its 1st major foe in 1961, SW Louisiana (1-1) had never beaten ranked team. Ragin' Cajuns DB Damon Mason starred in upset of no. 25 Texas Aggies (0-2), making 2 INTs and creating 2 FUMs. Mason put SW Louisiana ahead early by authoring 42y INT TD RET, and his hit allowed 17y FUM TD RET by DB Charles Johnson for 14-7 lead in 1st Q. Aggies seemed out of woods with 3 straight scores starting late in 2nd Q: TB D'Andre Hardeman's 2nd TD on 39y run, QB Branndon Stewart's 46y TD run, and K Kyle Bryant's 48y FG. Texas A&M led 22-21 until Cajuns DB Britt Jackson's 30y INT TD RET ruined Aggies' Saturday.

WASHINGTON 29 Brigham Young 17: Huskies D made fine reversal from disappointing opener, sacking BYU (2-1) QB Steve Sarkisian (23-35/279y, 2 TDs) 8 times, including late-game safety by LB Jason Chorak (3 sacks). Washington (1-1) stuffed no. 14 Cougars' run O attack to tune of 27/14y. Washington rolled up 445y total O, relying on TB Rashaan Shehee (21/131y), who ran for 2 TDs in 14-0 1st Q, and QB Shane Fortney (16-24/172y, TD), who passed and ran for scores. BYU WR Kaipo McGuire caught 32y TD arrow from Sarkisian in 2nd Q, but Cougars trailed 21-7 at H and 27-10 at end of 3rd Q.

USA Today Coaches Poll September 16

1	Nebraska (58)	1546	14	Kansas State	728
2	Tennessee (2)	1437	15	Auburn	722
3	Florida State (1)	1421	16	Virginia Tech	599
4	Florida (1)	1395	17	Virginia	589
5	Penn State	1247	18	Southern California	557
6	Ohio State	1177	19	Iowa	410
7	Michigan	1150	20	Kansas	360
8	Texas	1135	21	LSU	324
9	Notre Dame	943	22	Arizona State	304
10	Miami (Fla.)	868	23	Washington	185
11	Alabama	786	24	Syracuse	177
12	Colorado	785	25	Brigham Young	142
13	North Carolina	776			

September 21, 1996

ARMY 35 Duke 17: Army (2-0) hadn't beaten ACC team since 1989 and was especially frustrated by Duke (0-3), frequent foe it hadn't beaten since 1984. Sr QB Ronnie McAda enjoyed big day, rushing 20/88y, 2 TDs, while passing 7-8/225y, including 82y TD bomb to WR Ron Thomas. McAda's 313y was 4th-best single game O total in West Point history. Blue Devils drew within 14-10 in 2nd Q on TD run by QB David Green (11-20/102y) and K Sims Lenhardt's 27y FG. Army HB Bobby Williams tallied twice in 2nd H.

NAVY 19 Southern Methodist 17: QB Chris McCoy (27/140y, TD rushing) sparked Navy (2-0) to 16-0 H lead. SMU (2-2) finally got on scoreboard on K Daniel Hernandez's 26y FG in 3rd Q. Mustangs suddenly took lead on 2 TD passes from QB Ramon Flanigan (13-23/232y, 2 TDs, 2 INTs) to WR Kevin Thornal. Flanigan's 2nd TD pass came from 35YL with 2:46 to play. Backup QB Ben Fay, better passer than McCoy, went in to lead Middies to sub K Tom Vanderhorst's winning 38y FG as clock expired.

Florida 35 TENNESSEE 29: Highly anticipated SEC showdown swung steeply and early toward no. 4 Florida (3-0) in thunderous 1st H. On-campus record crowd of 107,608 was barely in seats to see Gators go 80y to 35y TD pass on 4th down by QB Danny Wuerffel (11-22/155y, 4 TDs). Florida DB Teako Brown soon made INT RET to Volunteers 10YL and soon made hard hit to foil Vols 4th down pass. Florida DB Jacquez Green added INT, and each of 3 TOs guided Wuerffel to another TD pass. Gators led 35-6 at H and had career-high 4 INTs of Tennessee (2-1) QB Peyton Manning. Thanks to Manning's school record 492y passing on 37-65, 3 TDs, no. 2 Vols battled back with 23 unanswered pts in 2nd H. But result was never in doubt.

Louisiana State 19 AUBURN 15: With nearby arena fire lighting night sky, fierce D battle ended in scoring pyrotechnics. LSU (2-0) held 10-9 lead 6:41 into 4th Q thanks to block of Auburn (3-1) K Jaret Holmes' conv kick. Moments later, LSU DB Raion Hill picked off pass by Auburn sub QB Jon Cooley (14-21/145y, TD, 2 INTs) and dashed 39y to TD. Back came Auburn with TB Rusty Williams crashing over from 7YL to pull within 17-15 with :38 to go. Then, suddenly, Hill stepped in front of Cooley's try for tying 2-pt pass and went coast-to-coast for 2-pt reversal for LSU.

TULSA 27 Iowa 20: In season's 1st 2 games, Tulsa (1-2) QB John Fitzgerald couldn't nail down starting job, but against no. 19 Iowa (2-1) he completed 22-37/361y, TD, INT. Hawkeyes TB Sedrick Shaw helped build 17-10 2nd Q lead with his 19/123y, TD, rushing. Huge upset swung on 17 straight pts by Hurricane that built 27-17 edge at end of 3rd Q. Tulsa TBs Reggie Williams (24/106y) and Solomon White each scored 3rd Q TD.

Notre Dame 27 TEXAS 24: Notre Dame (3-0) overcame tough field position in 1st H for 17-14 lead, its running game taking over in 2nd Q. Irish QB Ron Powlus (13-24/127y) hit FB Marc Edwards with TD pass, and TB Robert Farmer slipped through for 18y TD run. Texas (2-1) scored on 2 long drives in 1st H, and K Phil Dawson tied it in middle of 3rd Q with 47y FG. Early in 4th Q, Steers RB Shon Mitchell burst for long run to set up TD by RB Ricky "Little Earl" Williams (17/107y) for 24-17 edge. Irish LB Lyron Cobbins caught ricochet INT to provide opportunity at Texas 34YL. On 4th-and-goal, TB Autry Denson (24/158y) tied it with 5y TD run with 2:54 to play. Texas P Mark Schultis' 21y punt put ND at own 44YL with :59 to go. Denson dashed 21y to 35YL, and Powlus hit WR Malcolm Johnson to 22YL. Frosh K Jim "Foul Ball" Sanson hit 39y FG at final gun for Irish win.

WASHINGTON STATE 55 Oregon 44: Washington State (2-1) presented balanced O with 234y on ground, 225y in air. Leaders were TB Michael Black (28/161y, TD) and QB Ryan Leaf (16-25/225y, 4 TDs, INT) who piled up 6 TDs for 52-14 lead in 3rd Q. Oregon (3-1) waged vain but impressive comeback: Ducks took advantage of 3 FUM RECs, got late 3rd Q FG from K Joshua Smith and TD pass in 27-pt 4th Q outburst from QB Ryan Perry-Smith (21-46/291y, 3 TDs, INT) and 2 TD runs from frosh TB Derien Latimer (9/64y).

ARIZONA STATE 19 Nebraska 0: It was "Frank Kush Day" in Tempe as new Hall of Famer--once disgraced but later exonerated--was welcomed back. Playing field at Sun Devil Stadium was named in honor. Mighty Cornhuskers (1-1) had won 26 games in row. With bevy of fans returning to Valley of Sun, site of previous year's national title Fiesta Bowl victory, no. 1 Nebraska looked invincible. But, improving Sun Devils (3-0) stunned Huskers early with QB Jake Plummer's scramble left for 25y TD pass to wide-open WR Keith Poole. Arizona State D rattled rookie QB Scott Frost (6-20/66y) into bad EZ pitchout that dribbled OB, inattention on Shotgun snap, and sack by DL Derrick Rodgers, all 3 of which resulted in safeties. Nebraska O endured night of frustration and was held to 226y O. Plummer threw 20-26/292y, TD, INT, and K Robert Nycz nailed FGs of 27 and 44y in 2nd Q.

USA Today Coaches Poll September 23

1	Florida (38)	1524	14	Texas	744
2	Florida State (22)	1494	15	Colorado	724
3	Penn State	1380	16	Virginia Tech	675
4	Ohio State (2)	1359	17	Virginia	614
5	Notre Dame	1197	18	Southern California	573
6	Michigan	1181	19	LSU	551
7	Nebraska	1166	20	Kansas	402
8	Tennessee	990	21	Washington	305
9	Miami (Fla.)	945	22	Auburn	245
10	Alabama	913	23	West Virginia	174
11	North Carolina	896	24	Brigham Young	172
12	Arizona State	821	25	Iowa	57
13	Kansas State	771			

September 28, 1996

SYRACUSE 52 Virginia Tech 21: Nation's longest winning streak of 13 came to end as ailing Syracuse (1-2) recovered from TO fever and won its 600th all-time game by shredding vaunted Virginia Tech (3-1) D for 338y rushing and converting 13-18 3rd down plays. QB Donovan McNabb returned to his 1995 brilliance, leading Orangemen to 461y O and game's final 28 pts. Each team scored on blocked punt in 1st H: Virginia Tech WR Cornelius White went 60y, and Syracuse DB Phil Nash had easier 4y RET for TD which provided 17-14 lead. TB Ken Oxendine scored his 2nd TD as Hokies closed to 24-21 early in 3rd Q, but then came key play. McNabb hit WR Jim Turner with 48y deep slant pass on 3rd-and-17 to set up score that launched late avalanche.

FLORIDA STATE 13 North Carolina 0: Coming into game, resurgent North Carolina (3-1) knew it had to pass-protect QB Chris Keldorf (16-35/147y, INT), but never did it expect 8 sacks/-42y. Florida State (3-0) counted on DLs Reinhard Wilson and Peter Boulware for their 11 combined sacks of year. K Scott Bentley made 2 FGs after FSU DB Dexter Jackson blocked punts in 1st and 4th Qs. Seminoles' only TD by TB Warrick Dunn came after excitable Heels DB Dre Bly lost FUM at own 11YL after his 5th INT of season.

VIRGINIA 37 Texas 13: Before game, Texas (2-2) RB Ricky Williams (19/44y) said he never heard of Virginia's "Barbers of C'ville." Dominating on sloppy field from opening KO, TB Tiki Barber rushed 25/121y, gained 311y all-purpose y, and scored on 1st Q runs of 16, 26, and 12y for 21-0 Cavaliers (4-0) lead. His twin, DB Ronde Barber, made INT to set up Tiki's 2nd TD and collaborated with LB James Farrier (11 tackles, INT, forced FUM) to lead D. Steers RB Priest Holmes scored early in 3rd Q, but Cavs put it away at 34-13 with QB Tim Sherman's 24y TD run at end of 72y drive early in 4th Q.

FLORIDA 65 Kentucky 0: Wildcats' eventual game-end O total of 67y turned out to have been trumped on Florida's 1st 3 plays. Gators (4-0) WR Jacquez Green (4/46y) may have exhausted himself with explosive 66 and 79y punt TD RETs within 3-min span of 3rd Q, but by then hapless Kentucky (1-3) had already imploded in 41-0 1st H in which it was outgained 392y to 23y. Making his 1st start, heralded Cats frosh QB Tim Couch (6-18/13y, INT) was not yet Blue Grass answer. Rushed unmercifully, Couch threw INT to Gators DB Fred Weary on his initial collegiate pass attempt. Florida QB Danny Wuerffel (21-31/279y, 3 TDs, INT) played barely more than H, and TB Fred Taylor returned from 3-game suspension for 21y TD run among his 6/45y rushing.

Ohio State 29 NOTRE DAME 16: Ohio State (3-0) became only 4th school to defeat Notre Dame (3-1) in consecutive years to date. Tone was set with 85y RET of opening KO by Buckeyes WR Dimitrious Stanley. TB Pepe Pearson (29/173y) soon scored 1st of 2 TDs. In 2nd Q, ND led 7-6 on short TD pass from QB Ron Powlus (13-30/154y, TD, 2 INTs) to FB Marc Edwards (2 TDs), but Ohio led 22-7 at H as its D began to dominate. Ohio TE D.J. Jones caught TD pass from QB Stanley Jackson (9-15/154y, 2 TDs, INT) late in 3rd Q for 29-10 edge. Any Irish comeback hope was dashed when holding PEN (brief grab of jersey) erased TB Autry Denson's 90y punt TD RET with 3:35 left.

Penn State 23 WISCONSIN 20: Fired-up Badgers (3-1) had never lost to Penn State (5-0), and Lions coach Joe Paterno felt "the kids won (school's 700th victory) in spite of me." Paterno's failed calls (fake FG and late EZ pass) kept Wisconsin close enough for K John Hall's game-ending 58y FG try to be agonizingly close. Frosh 260-lb TB Ron Dayne (24/129y) scored on 12y run in 4th Q rallying Badgers from 20-10 deficit to 20-20. K Brett Conway's 3rd FG from 25y turned out to be winning margin with 1:23 to go.

IOWA STATE 45 Missouri 31: Fresh from previous week's upset of Clemson, Missouri (1-3) looked for its 1st Big 12 win. Instead, Iowa State (2-2) sent star TB Troy Davis (41/378y, 4 TDs) to 3rd-best single game rush total in NCAA history. In 1991, Kansas' Tony Sands had gained 396y, and San Diego State's Marshall Faulk had made 386y. Davis tallied go-ahead TD on 40y run in 4th Q. Tigers had led 31-24 entering 4th Q thanks to 2 TD passes and TD run from QB Corby Jones (6-12/81y, INT).

UTAH 45 Kansas 42: Utah (4-1) QB Mike Fouts (21-35/476y, 4 TDs) weathered pair of 4th Q INTs to throw winning 5y TD pass to WR Rocky Henry at end of 82y drive with 1:39 to play. Kansas (2-1) used its most potent weapon, RB June Hensley (41/216y) for creative go-ahead TD at 42-38 with 4:09 to play. Jayhawks pretended they had 12 men on field for FG try, and Hensley ran toward sideline, acting as if he was extra player. Holder Matt Johner took snap, fired pass to Hensley, who was wide of D, alone to scamper for 20y TD. Utes FB Chris Fuamatu-Ma'afala rushed 17/103y.

USA Today Coaches Poll September 30

1	Florida (48)	1533	14	Notre Dame	784
2	Florida State (9)	1453	15	LSU	702
3	Ohio State (5)	1429	16	Southern California	660
4	Penn State	1361	17	North Carolina	585
5	Michigan	1281	18	Washington	387
6	Nebraska	1145	19	West Virginia	383
7	Arizona State	1101	20	Auburn	348
8	Miami (Fla.)	1086	21	Brigham Young	299
9	Tennessee	1001	22	Virginia Tech	223
10	Alabama	940	23	Texas	157
11	Virginia	863	24	Utah	124
12	Kansas State	841	25	Wyoming	106
13	Colorado	840			

October 5, 1996

GEORGIA TECH 13 Virginia 7: Resurgent Georgia Tech (4-1) projected itself back into top 25 with opportunistic D against frustrated Cavaliers (4-1). Yellow Jackets TB C.J. Williams (28/79y) tallied on 3y run in 1st Q and set up FG for 13-0 lead early in 2nd Q with 50y dash. Virginia TB Tiki Barber (24/123y) capped 65y drive in 2nd Q with 1y TD run, but possible winning drive was snuffed by Jackets DB Nathan Perryman's 4th Q INT.

FLORIDA STATE 34 Clemson 3: Florida State (4-0) got off to slow start, leading 6-3, but QB Thad Busby (16-29/304y, 4 TDs) overcame questions about his ability (5 INTs in 3 games up to this game) to fling TD passes of 37, 60, and 23y in 1st H. Busby also kept Seminoles drives alive by clicking on 50 and 42y connections. His favorite target was WR Ernie Green (5/156y) who caught TD passes in each Q in 1st H. Clemson (2-3) had moved well in 1st Q behind QB Nealon Greene (15-29/132y, INT), who shrugged off week-old knee injury. But, Tigers with little running threat (36/54y) had to settle for K Matt Padgett's 29y FG 10 secs into 2nd Q. Clemson TB Raymond Priester's runs were held to 18/27y by nation's top statistical D.

OHIO STATE 38 Penn State 7: For 1st time since 1980, single school beat top-5 foes in 2 consecutive weeks. So dominating was no. 3 Ohio State (4-0) D that 32-pt per game O of no. 4 Penn State (5-1) failed to cross midfield until 2nd H. In all, white-clad Lions gaining only 211y as QB Wally Richardson (14-30/105y) was blitzed unmercifully and completed no passes longer than 15y. Buckeyes racked up 565y as alternating QBs Stanley Jackson (11-22/169y, 2 TDs) and Joe Germaine (3-8/46y, 2 TDs) each tossed 2 scores. Score was 24-0 at H as Ohio WR Dimitrious Stanley (5/105y, 2 TDs) caught 42 and 34y scoring throws. TB Pepe Pearson (28/141y, TD) scored late in 3rd Q for 31-0 lead. Nittany Lions tallied in last 6 mins on FB Anthony Cleary's plunge.

NORTHWESTERN 17 Michigan 16: Michigan (4-1) moved to 16-0 lead at end of 3rd Q as K Remy Hamilton booted 3 FGs and TB Chris Howard (17/47y) scored on 3rd Q run. Determined Northwestern (4-1) outgained Wolverines 172y to 28y in 4th Q, got 3y TD run from FB Levelle Brown and 2-pt pass from QB Steve Schnur (20-35/246y) to halve margin to 16-8. K Brian Gowens' 2 FGs brought Wildcats within 16-14. Schnur's 12y pass on 4th down to WR Brian Musso sparked 80y drive to Gowens' winning 39y FG, which he had to make twice because it was ruled 1st try came before play was whistled ready.

Nebraska 39 KANSAS STATE 3: Fierce Huskers D completely left Kansas State (4-1) for dead in 1st H: Wildcats ran 27 plays, gained 0y, and had 2 punts blocked. Still, Nebraska (3-1) had fairly placid 18-3 lead at H as K-State D forced Husker K Kris Brown in making 4 FGs. Huskers frosh IB DeAngelo Evans (21/168y, 2 TDs) replaced injured IB Ahman Green (14/66y, TD) and dashed to 69y TD early in 3rd Q to get Big Red's runaway ignited.

TEXAS 71 Oklahoma State 14: Texas Longhorns (3-2), leaders of Big 12 South, broke 2-game non-conf losing streak by launching FB Ricky Williams to 13/156y rushing and 3 TDs. Oklahoma State (3-2) had its answer in under-valued TB David Thompson, who countered with 20/153y rushing, but that's all Cowboys had. Texas gained 624y, 2nd-highest O total in school history to date. It was Steers' highest pt total since they dropped 72 pts on Rice in 1977. Oklahoma State coach Bob Simmons found answer afterward: "Burn the film. We're not going to watch it." Texas coach John Mackovic lauded his line.

TEXAS TECH 45 Baylor 24: Texas Tech (3-2) rushing attack rolled up 482y, and TB Byron Hanspard (35/287y, 2 TDs) had his 5th straight 200y+ game. Trailing 17-0 in 2nd Q, Baylor (3-1) narrowed it to 17-10 on K Michael Benjamin's 45y FG and TD pass by QB Jermaine Alfred (14-27/249y, INT). In last min of 1st H, Red Raiders put it away at 31-10 with QB Zebbie Lethridge's TD pass and abrupt 21y FUM TD RET by DL Montae Reagor.

California 22 SOUTHERN CALIFORNIA 15: For 1st time since 1970, Golden Bears (5-0) visited L.A. Coliseum for winning result. California controlled clock for 17 mins more than USC (3-2) and jumped to 19-0 lead by end of 3rd Q. Bears QB Pat Barnes (19-31/229y, 2 TDs) threw scoring passes to WR Dameane Douglas and top-notch TE and basketball star Tony Gonzalez (5/74y). Playing without 4 suspended starters, Trojans got all their pts in 4th Q on passes by heavily-pressured QB Brad Otton (19-34/234y, 2 TDs, INT).

Washington 27 STANFORD 6: Stanford (1-3) had to settle for K Kevin Miller's chip-shot FGs at end of each of opening 2 Qs. But, frustrated no. 18 Huskies (3-1) could do no better than pair of longer FGs by K John Wales through 3 Qs. Then, Washington used spark provided by 2 O subs for 2 quick scores as part of 3-TD outburst in 4th Q: WR Jerome Pathon (6/128y, TD) worked himself completely free in Cardinal EZ to haul in QB Brock Huard's 45y TD 2 mins into 4th Q. Wales' ensuing KO soared high and slightly short and was recovered by Washington after ball bounced off Stanford FB Adam Salina. UW TB Corey Dillon (36/173y, TD), another backup, powered over GL on his 4th straight run to lift Huskies to 20-6 lead. Card rushing O was curbed as young QBs Chad Hutchinson (12-21/148y, INT) and Todd Husak were sacked 6 times.

October 12, 1996

Army 42 RUTGERS 21 (East Rutherford, NJ): Even with their top QB and leading rusher, Ronnie McAda, shelved with injury, Black Knights (5-0) rushed 78/546y to overwhelm Rutgers (1-5) for its 5th straight loss. Scarlet Knights started reasonably well, marching 48y before having FB Gary Fauntleroy stopped on 4th down at Cadet 24YL. On its next series, Rutgers converted 4th down twice and RB Chad Bosch took pitchout 9y to score for 7-0 lead at end of 1st Q. Army came back with 3 TDs in 2nd Q: Backup QB Adam Thompson (17/126y), 1 of 3 Cadets who rushed for 100y, chose to pass only 3 times, but completed 2, including tying 23y TD to TE Ron Leshinski. FB Joe Hewitt (14/117y) followed barely 4 mins later with 59y TD sprint, and HB Bobby Williams scored 1st of his pair of 3y TDs for 21-7 H lead for Cadets. Army HB Demetrius Perry (15/127y) raced 61y to score in 3rd Q before Rutgers QB Mike Stephans (16-34/246y) was able to throw 2 TDs.

Florida State 34 MIAMI 16: Hurricanes' 11-game win streak, built mostly vs. patsies, was crushed by no. 3 Florida State (5-0). Seminoles burst to 17-0 1st Q lead, highlighted by 54y FUM TD RET by DB Shevin Smith and 80y TD sprint by TB Warrick Dunn (22/163y, TD). Miami (4-1) rebounded in 2nd Q and trailed 20-16 at H after QB Ryan Clement (20-31/267y, 2 TDs, INT) hit WR Yatil Green for 31 and 5y TD passes. Florida State crafted 75 and 72y TD drives in 2nd H, and its marvelous D allowed 42y rushing and had 6 sacks.

FLORIDA 56 Louisiana State 13: Predatory Gators D snapped clamps on normal LSU (4-1) 280y-per-game rushing attack, holding it to 33/28y, especially throttling TB Kevin Faulk (13/26y). Florida (6-0) scotched any upset threat with 42-6 lead by H. Gators outgained Tigers 635y to 303y. Moving to 4th all-time on SEC TD catch list, Florida WR Ike Hilliard (8/145y, 2 TDs) grabbed 25 and 8y scores from QB Danny Wuerffel (17-27/277y, 3 TDs, INT). LSU's only bright spots came at end of 80y drive in 2nd Q and 70y drive in 4th Q: WR Larry Foster's TD catch and sub TB Rondell Mealey's TD run.

OHIO STATE 17 Wisconsin 14: In perfect spot for letdown, no. 2 Ohio State (5-0) was beaten at scrimmage line in 1st H. Wisconsin (3-2) moved 378-lb T Aaron Gibson in at TE, and despite being halted on 4th-and-1 from Ohio 1YL Badgers came back to slam to 7-3 H lead on FB Cecil Martin's 1y blast. Stymied all day, Buckeyes TB Pepe Pearson (24/56y) used WR Dimitrious Stanley's 21y catch to position 3rd Q TD run which regained 10-7 lead. Badgers DB Kevin Huntley scooped up FUM, raced 36y to TD for 14-10 lead early in 4th Q. Stanley (10/199y) took sub QB Joe Germaine's pass for decisive 48y TD with 9 mins left to play.

NORTHWESTERN 26 Minnesota 24: "It was kind of scary," said Northwestern (5-1) DT Matt Rice of comebacks from 23-0 and 26-11 engineered by Golden Gophers (3-2) in 2nd H. Previous week's hero in comeback win against Michigan, Wildcats K Brian Gowins nearly was goat with 3 missed FGs and x-pt. TB Darnell Autry (41/189y, TD) became Wildcat's all-time rushing leader, and his 11/57y helped consume 7 mins of 4th Q after Minnesota had nearly caught up. NW QB Steve Schnur (17-25/278y, TD) outpassed Gophers QB Cory Sauter, who slumped from his 265y passing avg to 17-31/154y.

NOTRE DAME 54 Washington 20: From outset, Fighting Irish (4-1) rolled over stunned Huskies (3-2). On 1st series, ND DB Deke Cooper picked off pass by Washington QB Brock Huard (8-26/99y, INT), and TB Autry Denson (14/137y) dashed 33y to score. Irish built 26-0 lead in 2nd Q, and QB Ron Powlus (8-14/194y, 3 TDs) extended advantage to 47-14 with 3 TD passes in 3rd Q. Huskies sub TB Corey Dillon (18/87y, 2 TDs) ran for 2 window-dressing scores. ND's back-to-basics O rushed for 397y and totaled 650y.

Oklahoma 30 Texas 27 (OT) (Dallas): Oklahoma (1-4), losers of school record 7 in row, responded against old rival Texas (3-3) in 1st mutual conf meeting since both were in SWC in 1919. Longhorns frosh WR Dustin Armstrong blocked and recovered punt for TD in 1st Q. When RB Ricky Williams (21/99y) scored from 7YL midway in 4th Q, Texas led 24-13. Sooners were ignited by 51y punt TD RET by frosh WR Jarrail Jackson, followed by 2-pt pass by QB Justin Fuente (15-34/165y, TD), and tied it on 44y FG by K Jeremy Alexander with 2:26 left. Down 27-24 in OT, Sooners QB James Allen (23/158y) twisted to critical 1st down on pass and scored winning TD from 2YL.

Kansas State 35 MISSOURI 10: Coming off its exciting 27-26 win over SMU previous week, Missouri (2-4) had high hopes but ended up with handful of miscues. Tigers soph QB Kent Skornia (12-29/142y, TD, 3 INTs) made his 1st start of season and drove his unit 80y on its opening possession to WR Jay Murchison's 3y TD catch. Meanwhile, Mizzou TB Brad Olivo (21/100y) piled up 65y in 1st Q, but 3 big plays by Kansas State (5-1) in same Q turned it into 14-7 advantage for Wildcats: K-State DB Chris Canty roared 44y on KO RET to launch 47y march to tying TD, K-State CB Lamar Chapman made brilliant INT at his 5YL to blunt Missouri's answering drive, and Canty soon raced 58y on punt TD RET to put Wildcats ahead for good at 14-7. Cats TB Mike Lawrence (25/168y, 2 TDs) scored his 2nd TD in 3rd Q for 28-7 edge, and DB Mario Smith raced 100y on INT TD RET in middle of 4th Q.

Arizona State 42 UCLA 34: Enjoying heady heights of top-5, Arizona State (6-0) went on road for 1st time this season. UCLA (2-3) QB Cade McNown (22-41/395y, INT) lofted 3 TD passes, but ASU QB Jake Plummer (19-36/275y, 3 TDs, INT) got his 1st TD pass to WR Keith Poole to trim it to 28-14 at H. Still, Sun Devils appeared in huge 34-21

jam when Bruins DB Javelin Guidry made INT with 10:38 left in game. But UCLA was forced to punt, and Plummer threw another TD pass to pull within 34-28. Bruins TB Skip Hicks (22/114y, 2 TDs) soon lost FUM deep in his own territory. Frosh Sun Devils RB J.R. Redmond took pitchout and swept right, stopping and throwing downfield to impulsive Plummer, who twisted through tacklers for 16y go-ahead TD for 35-34 lead.

STANFORD 27 Oregon 24 (OT): Pre-game dope indicated previously feeble O of Stanford (2-3) might be helped by Oregon's 38.2 pts-per-game D. Ducks' D inadequacies may have helped, but it took clutch D play by Cardinal to rally for OT win. After Stanford RB Mike Mitchell (10/121y, 2 TDs) had scored his 2nd TD on 42y run, Oregon (3-4) WR Pat Johnson provided immediate 24-14 lead with 95y KO RET with 9:21 to play in regulation. Stanford QB Chad Hutchinson (27-41/365y, TD) rifled 27y TD pass to WR Damon Dunn, and K Kevin Miller forced OT with 25y FG with 50 secs to go after well-covered WR Andre Kirwan made brilliant 49y catch on 4th-and-12. Cardinal DL Carl Hansen recovered Ducks QB Tony Graziani's FUM on 1st OT possession, and Miller soon won it with 27y FG.

October 19, 1996

East Carolina 31 MIAMI 6: Pirates DB Daren Hart was brilliant in surprisingly easy road win over dispirited Miami (4-2). Hart led East Carolina (4-2) with 8 tackles, including 2 for losses, positioned 2 TDs with INTs, and forced 2 FUMs. Pirates QB Marcus Crandell passed 17-27/230y, 3 TDs. QB Ryan Clement (9-13/120y, TD, INT) went out with non-throwing shoulder separation as Hurricanes lost their 2nd straight at home for 1st time in 12 years.

CLEMSON 28 Georgia Tech 25: TB Raymond Priester (25/175y) scored 5y TD and QB Nealon Greene (11-20/156y) tossed short TD pass to help Clemson (4-3) roll to 21-10 H benefit. Resourceful Georgia Tech (4-2) QB Joey Hamilton (13-19/180y) had great 3rd Q. Hamilton pitched 39y TD pass to WR Mike Sheridan, added 2-pt pass to TE Grant Baynham, and scored on 2y run to lift no. 22 Yellow Jackets to 25-21 lead that lasted into 4th Q. Greene nurtured 15-play winning drive old-fashioned Clemson way: by running. Greene chipped in with 25y run on 3rd down and converted 4th-and-1 run to Tech 41YL. Greene ended march with 1y run that had him ducking under Jackets' D line to score with 4:06 remaining. K David Frakas missed 51y FG for Jackets with 1:43 to play.

SOUTH CAROLINA 23 Arkansas 17: TB Duce Staley (105y rushing) of South Carolina (4-3) shrugged off bruised thigh after being held to 17y in 1st H by Arkansas (2-4) D, 1 of nation's best at stopping run, to accumulate 86y on ground in 4th Q to ice game. TB Chrys Chukwuma had scored on 4y run to give Razorbacks 17-10 lead in 3rd Q, but Hogs lost FUM on own 43YL next time they had ball. Gamecocks WR Zola Davis raced down sideline with 29y pass to 1YL, and TB Troy Hambrick pounded over. K Courtney Leavitt missed x-pt, so Carolina led 20-17. In clinching drive, Staley made runs of 20, 17, and 10y and caught 2y pass to position K Reed Morton for put-away 46y FG in waning mins.

ALABAMA 37 Mississippi 0: Flu-ridden Mississippi (3-3) QB Paul Head started in effort to pass Crimson Tide (7-0) D silly, but Head missed all his passes on 3 straight snaps after KO and headed for bench. More conservative O (that gained only 158y) under QB Stewart Partridge (10-22/132y) in no way helped Rebels, who became Alabama's 1st shutout victim since September 1995. Bama QB Freddie Kitchens (13-33/216y, 2 TDs, 2 INTs) flipped 10y TD pass to WR Michael Vaughn in 2nd Q, and Tide led 10-0 at H. Ole Miss FS Timothy Strickland picked off Kitchens on Alabama's 1st series in 3rd Q and returned 17y to Tide 41YL. But Rebs gained only 1y, and K Tim Montz was considerably short on 57y FG try. On next play, Kitchens tossed short pass to Vaughn over middle, who outlegged 2 defenders for 60y TD. Alabama TB Dennis Riddle (31/140y) scored 2y TD, and soph TB Montoya Madden added 2 TDs from 5YL in 4th Q.

Iowa 21 PENN STATE 20: Calling his Hawkeyes "happy group of young men," Iowa (5-1) coach Hayden Fry enjoyed locker room hokey pokey dance to celebrate 1st win in "Happy Valley" since 1983. Penn State (6-2) led 20-14 at H largely on efforts of FB Aaron Harris (11/152y, TD) who set up TD with 48y dash, scored his own 49y TD despite mid-run FUM. Hawkeye heroes included LB Matt Hughes and DB Damien Robinson, each with 14 tackles, WR Tim Dwight with 83y punt TD RET and 65y catch, and TB Tavian Banks, who rushed 26/116y, 2 TDs, including game-winner from 8YL early in 4th Q. FUM by Penn State QB Wally Richardson (10-30/106y, TD) recovered by Iowa DL Jared DeVries set stage for Banks' winning TD. Lions had late chance that went nowhere after they stopped Iowa's pass off fake 50y FG.

Ohio State 42 PURDUE 14: No. 2 Ohio State (6-0) had to climb out of 14-0 hole before trouncing Purdue (2-5) on 3 big gainers in 2nd H. Buckeyes FB Matt Keller snared screen pass and broke through tacklers for 63y TD, TB Pepe Pearson (26/152y, 2 TDs) made 64y TD run, and DB Rob Kelly scooped up FUM for 79y TD RET. Earlier, Boilermakers QB John Reeves (20-40/342y, 2 TDs, 3 INTs) shockingly had fired 2 TD passes: 86y to WR Isaac Jones and 55y to WR Brian Alford (8/129y). Ohio transferred 2nd H KO FUM by Purdue LB Joe Hagins into 21-14 lead on 9y TD scramble run by QB Stanley Jackson (9-22/162y, TD, INT), who was later ejected.

Northwestern 34 WISCONSIN 30: Wildcats (6-1) TB Darnell Autry (10/58y, TD) scored on 20y TD run in 1st Q, but went out with bad shoulder to end streak of 19 games of 100y rushing. NW QB Steve Schnur (25-41/310y, 2 TDs, INT) tossed TD pass to WR D'Wayne Bates (10/131y) for 14-13 H edge. Badgers (3-3) scored 2 straight TDs to open 30-20 lead in opening min-and-half of 4th Q and took over with 30-27 edge at own 38YL after Wildcats K Brian Gowins missed 55y FG in last min. It was debatable whether Wisconsin could have killed clock with 3 knee-to-ground plays, but its attempt to advance ball blew up on 2nd down as bobbled handoff to TB Ron Dayne (28/139y, TD) was caused by Northwestern DL Joe Reiff. Cats DB Eric Collier fell on FUM, and Schnur hit Bates for winning 20y TD 2 plays later.

Air Force 20 NOTRE DAME 17 (OT): Strong service academy revival (combined 14-3 to date in 1996 for Army, Navy, and Air Force) was hung on dominant run D of Air Force (4-2). Notre Dame (4-2) gained 67y, lowest rush total since 1985, and was forced to air as QB Ron Powlus pitched 16-24/268y. Falcons QB Beau Morgan (5-11/51y), who keyed 304y ground attack with 23/183y, scored TD in 10-10 1st H tie. Early in 4th Q, Irish FB Marc Edwards (7/29y) provided 17-10 lead with 1y blast, but Falcons HB Tobin Ruff tied it with 19y TD run. In OT, Powlus was sacked and lost his 4th FUM to LB Alex Pupich. Air Force K Dallas Thompson soon nailed winning 27y FG and was left to worry about stomped bare kicking foot amid celebrating Flyboys, who enjoyed showcase win.

Nebraska 24 TEXAS TECH 10: Red Raiders (4-3) capitalized on FUM REC and DB Robert Johnson's 9y INT TD RET to frighten Nebraska (5-1) with 10-10 H knot. Cornhuskers QB Scott Frost scored go-ahead TD in 3rd Q, and sub IB Damon Benning (4/32y) positioned his own short TD run with 51y punt RET. Nebraska D held Texas Tech's national rushing leader, TB Byron Hanspard, to relatively tame 31/107y.

UTAH 21 Texas Christian 7: In 1st-ever meeting between new WAC rivals, QB Mike Fouts (10-19/146y, TD, INT) produced less than normal air power, so Utah (6-1) turned to giant FB Chris Fuamata-Ma'Afala (20/182y) for spectacular 70 and 52y TD runs in 2nd H. Utes earned 6th straight win after 7-7 H tie. TCU (2-4) stayed close thanks to QB Fred Taylor's tying 13y TD pass to TE Mike Brown in 1st Q.

ARIZONA STATE 48 Southern California 35 (OT): Winning Arizona State (7-0) coach Bruce Snyder said, "...it would probably take two hours to analyze everything." Southern California (4-3) led 4 times: 14-0 after 2 INTs provided early edge, 21-14 early in 4th Q when Trojans WR Chris Miller made disputed catch, 28-21 when frosh WR R. Jay Roward motored 98y with KO TD RET with 6:56 left and 35-28 when QB Brad Otton (16-39/205y, 3 TDs, INT) put USC ahead in OT. Sun Devils QB Jake Plummer (26-44/277y, 2 TDs, 3 INTs) tied it in OT with 6y toss to WR Keith Poole (7/103y). ASU TB Terry Battle (30/192y) scored his 4th TD on 25y run over RT in 2nd OT, and DB Courtney Jackson iced it by dashing 85y with FUM which Otton argued was his incomplete pass.

WASHINGTON STATE 21 California 18: Rose-scented dream of California (5-1) expired in harsh cold of Palouse of Washington State (5-2). Loss sent Golden Bears on 2-game downward spiral. Cougars were ignited by early punt block by DB Ray Jackson, which was recovered for TD by DB Dee Moronkola. Wazzu QB Ryan Leaf threw and ran for TDs to jump to 21-3 H lead. Bears clicked in 2nd H, however, with QB Pat Barnes passing Cal to within 21-16 on his TD pass to TE Tony Gonzalez, but Barnes lost FUM at WSU GL in closing moments. Cougars RB Michael Black rushed 25/214y, but lost 3 FUMs that kick-started Bears in 2nd H. Still, difference was 3 critical FUMs by California, 2 leading to 1st H TDs by Cougars, and Barnes' late bobble.

USA Today Coaches Poll October 21

1	Florida (56)	1544	14	Kansas State	697
2	Florida State (5)	1466	15	LSU	690
3	Ohio State (1)	1440	16	Brigham Young	551
4	Arizona State	1326	17	Penn State	497
5	Nebraska	1286	18	Wyoming	461
6	Alabama	1200	19	Iowa	361
7	Tennessee	1187	20	Notre Dame	359
8	Colorado	1089	21	Virginia Tech	342
9	North Carolina	947	22	Utah	265
10	Michigan	915	23	Miami (Fla.)	178
11	West Virginia	902	24	Washington	173
12	Northwestern	806	25	California	160
13	Virginia	731			

October 26, 1996

Miami 10 WEST VIRGINIA 7: After rainy 0-0 1st H, Miami K Andy Crosland booted 31y FG with 10:35 left in 3rd Q. No. 12 West Virginia (7-1) held Hurricanes (5-2) to 58y rushing and 104y passing, but it took WVU DB Mike Logan's 32y INT RET to 3YL to set stage for TB Alvin Swoope's 2y TD run and 7-3 lead. Unruly Mountaineer fans were silenced with 29 secs left in game when Miami came up with its play-of-year: DB Tremaine Mack blocked P Brian West's punt, and DB Jack Hallmon avoided West's attempt at saving tackle with handoff to DB Nathaniel Brooks, who dashed 20y to stunning TD. WVU's Don Neylan, in football coaching since 1965, called it his toughest loss ever.

FLORIDA STATE 31 Virginia 24: Vengeful Florida State (6-0) provided payback to Virginia (5-2) for only ACC loss (1995), piling up 533y. FSU D put heavy pressure on twice-battered Cavs QB Tim Sherman (9-28/159y, TD, 2 INTs), but Virginia used 48y TD run by TB Tiki Barber (21/150y) to spark 10 pts in 2nd Q into 17-14 H lead. QB Thad Busby's 2nd TD pass early in 3rd Q gave Seminoles lead for good, and TB Rock Preston's brilliant 24y TD run put it away at 31-17 in 4th Q.

TENNESSEE 20 Alabama 13: Rugged Alabama (7-1) D had Tennessee (5-1) on ropes at 10-0 as Bama QB Freddie Kitchens (8-21/137y, 3 INTs) threw 40y TD pass to WR Marcell West on opening possession of 3rd Q. INT soon put Tide at Vols 13YL, but Tennessee D forced FG. WR Joey Kent's 54y TD catch against run-stacked D got Vols back into contention at 13-6 late in 3rd Q. Having suffered through heretofore sub-par season, Tennessee TB Jay Graham (14/128y, 2 TDs) scored twice in 4th Q. With 2:17 left, Graham's winning 79y TD run came behind blocks of FB Eric Lane and G Spencer Riley.

LOUISIANA STATE 28 Mississippi State 20: Drenching rain for 3 days and poor field position mired LSU (6-1) deep in its end in 2nd H in which it was blanked, but explosive 1st H had provided Bayou Bengals with 2-TD lead. Mississippi State (2-4) tricked Tigers' 5-DB set-up on opening possession as it used 7 runs in 8 plays to FB Nakia Greer's 3y TD run. After LSU TB Kevin Faulk (32/170y, 2 TDs) passed 7y to WR Larry Foster for tying TD, Bulldogs TB Robert Isaac set up 14-7 led by visitors with 60y KO RET. Faulk's 18 and 2y TD runs at end of 73 and 77y marches in 2nd Q gave 28-14 H edge to Tigers. Faulk bobbled away FUMs at his 36 and 21YLs in 3rd Q, but Mississippi State could gain only 3 pts on K Brian Hazelwood's 22y FG early in 4th Q. Tigers DB Greg Hill broke up 3rd down pass to force Hazelwood's FG, and then when LSU QB Herb Tyler (6-13/89y) lost FUM to Maroons SS Eric Brown at his 7YL, Tigers made their best stand. It was keyed by CB Denard Walker's pass breakup to force another Hazelwood FG with 6:59 to play.

Ohio State 38 IOWA 26: Resourceful Iowa (5-2) entered showdown game tied with mighty Ohio State (7-0) in TO margin. But, bumbling Hawks lost 4 INTs, suffered blocked punt for TD by Buckeyes DB Kevin Griffin, and butchered KO RET, all in disastrous 5-min span of 1st H that Ohio State owned by 31-6 tally. QB Stanley Jackson (8-18/91y) tossed 2 TD passes during Ohio's uprising. After TB Pepe Pearson's 4y TD run provided 38-6 lead early in 3rd Q, Buckeyes relaxed during 20-pt Iowa retaliation that included spunky WR Tim Dwight's 19y TD run on reverse and his 86y punt TD RET.

NORTHWESTERN 27 Illinois 24: "Cardiac Cats" won their 4th straight late-game decision. Inspired Illinois (2-5) led 17-7 in 2nd Q as RB Robert Holcombe (31/166y) scored on 3 and 45y runs. Northwestern (7-1) clawed its way to 20-17 edge, but allowed Illini to reclaim 24-20 advantage on Holcombe's 3rd TD midway in 4th Q. Wildcats traversed 48y, winning with 1:02 left as plunge by sub TB Adrian Autry (30/128y, 2 TDs) ended TD drive that was kept alive by 4th down pass by QB Steve Schnur (18-29/258y, 2 TDs, INT).

COLORADO 28 Texas 24: Faced with unraveling of its season, fading Texas (3-4) came up with striking effort. Longhorns led 10-0 and 17-7 on QB James Brown's 2 1st H TD passes and knocked Buffaloes (6-1) QB Koy Detmer (7-15/137y, 54y TD, 2 INTs) from game with 2nd Q sack. Colorado supersub QB John Hessler (11-19/158y) directed 66y 3rd Q TD drive capped by TB Herchell Troutman's 13y run and victorious 90y TD march ended by his 1y sneak with 3:10 left. In between, Steers had regained lead at 24-21 on 3rd TD pass by Brown (16-35/224y, 2 INTs).

Arizona State 41 STANFORD 9: Sun Devils (8-0) cruised to 21-0 lead at end of 1st Q as QB Jake Plummer (21-34/316y, 2 TDs, INT) fired 2 scoring passes. Stanford (2-5) bounced back on TE Greg Clark's 45y scoring reception from QB Todd Husak (17-34/173y, TD, 2 INTs) and 27y FG by K Kevin Miller after Arizona State CB Courtney Jackson committed pass interference near GL only 2 secs before H. "We went up 21-0, and we threw out an anchor. I was not happy at all at halftime," said ASU coach Bruce Snyder of Cardinal comeback to within 21-9. Devils D put up roadblock in 2nd H, allowing only 93y after Stanford had gained 206y in 1st H. Arizona State went 75y on its opening series of 3rd Q to FB Jeff "Jurassic" Paulk's 1y TD blast. CB Jackson made amends for his earlier gaffe with INT at Card 40YL, and Plummer hit WR Keith Poole for 29y before skipping 4y to score himself.

Washington 33 OREGON 14: For player who had labored on 2nd O unit until season's 4th game, Huskies (5-2) TB Corey Dillon (32/259y, 3 TDs) continued his assault on Pac-10 rushing leadership. Dillon scored on 1st H runs of 1, 7, and 2y for 21-0 lead, while, in 3rd Q, he broke loose for 75y run that set up K John Wales' 19y FG. Later in 3rd Q, Dillon added 67y sprint. Oregon (3-5), which had been highly regarded after 2 straight New Year's Day bowl games, lost its 5th conf game in row. Ducks tallied in last 2 mins of 1st H on banged-up TB Saladin McCullough's 1y plunge. Oregon managed only 103y rushing, but QB Tony Graziani passed 19-41/276y, 2 INTs and late-game TD pass to frosh WR Tony Hartley. Bad blood between teams continued to fester: Washington coach Jim Lambright, who year earlier had lobbied aggressively for his Huskies to go to Cotton Bowl over smaller-TV-market Ducks, said, "What felt wonderful was when the crowd started leaving early. There was a lot of them who didn't like me a whole lot when they came in."

USA Today Coaches Poll October 28

1	Florida (53)	1541	14	Brigham Young	733
2	Florida State (5)	1457	15	Penn State	585
3	Ohio State (4)	1455	16	Wyoming	566
4	Arizona State	1344	17	West Virginia	533
5	Nebraska	1308	18	Virginia	504
6	Tennessee	1242	19	Utah	379
7	Colorado	1144	20	Virginia Tech	375
8	North Carolina	1053	21	Notre Dame	350
9	Michigan	1001	22	Miami (Fla.)	276
10	Northwestern	913	23	Washington	225
11	Alabama	912	24	Southern Mississippi	140
12	Kansas State	805	25	Auburn	113
13	LSU	743			

November 2, 1996

Syracuse 30 WEST VIRGINIA 7: Fresh off its depressing last-min punt block defeat by Miami, still-staggering West Virginia (7-2) suffered 3 more special team nightmares. Syracuse (5-2) DB Phil Nash blocked 2 punts, and WR Deon Maddux sprinted 72y on punt TD RET. Mountaineers QBs were sacked 7 times, as team lost 10y rushing overall. WVU's run attack got minimal boost from star TB Amos Zereoue, who was limited to 15/17y. WVU scored late on sub QB Marc Bulger's TD pass.

Florida State 49 GEORGIA TECH 3: Looking for bowl bid, Georgia Tech (5-3) made mistake of irritating mighty Florida State (7-0) by scoring 1st against FSU's magnificent D. Georgia Tech quickly became just another ACC victim of Seminoles, their 37th of 38 since

joining conf. Yellow Jackets' K Brad Chambers booted 35y FG in otherwise scoreless 1st Q. Then, FSU picked just about every way to score in 2nd Q: LB Lamont Green's 56y INT RET, TB Rock Preston's 6y run, DB Shevin Smith's blocked punt REC in EZ, and QB Thad Busby's 38y TD pass to WR Andre Cooper. Seminoles TB Warrick Dunn rushed 13/121y, including 45y TD dash in 3rd Q. Georgia Tech had hefty time-of-possession advantage of 12 mins, but were held when it counted and totaled so-so 269y O.

CLEMSON 35 Maryland 3: Improving Clemson (5-3) donned lucky orange pants to trounce Maryland (4-5) by dominating both sides of ball. Happy coach Tommy West enjoyed discussing his team's devotion to brightly-colored britches, but realized that despite 30-6 all-time orange pants record, it was out of norm for post-game press conferences: "It sounds funny for a 42-year-old man to sit here and talk about a pair of pants." Terps managed wobbly 35y FG in 2nd Q by K Joe O'Donnell, and it represented 1st pts scored by Maryland on Clemson since 1992. Tigers D carried day as DE Trevor Pryce made 2 sacks of team's 8 and 3 tackles-for-losses of team's 15. Clemson DB Andy Ford ran back INT for 66y TD in 1st Q for 14-0 lead after Tigers FB Emory Smith scored 1st of his 2 TDs.

PENN STATE 34 Northwestern 9: After 4 frantic wins, Northwestern's bubble burst. Penn State (8-2) displayed rejuvenated D with 7 sacks and 5 TOs. S Kim Herring picked off 2 passes by Wildcats QB Steve Schnur (22-49/278y, TD, 3 INTs), caused FUM that led to TD. Lions' big plays in 27-3 1st H came on 39y TD run by now-healthy TB Curtis Enis (21/167y) and 63y TD reception by WR Joe Jurevicius from QB Wally Richardson (11-22/201y, 2 TDs, INT). Trailing 34-3 in 4th Q, Wildcats (7-2) broke loose star WR D'Wayne Bates—who had been completely shut down for 3 Qs—for 78y TD pass.

OHIO STATE 45 Minnesota 0: Buckeyes (8-0) offered indifferent 10-0 performance in 1st H as QB Stanley Jackson (8-15/93y, 2 INTs) threw INTs on each of their 1st 2 possessions and left game with sprained ankle. Still, Minnesota (3-5), owners of 1 of nation's better pass attacks, were held to 57y in air with 4 INTs and 104y overall. Gophers QB Cory Sauter (11-28/57y, 3 INTs) was sacked 4 times. Ohio State LB Andy Katzenmoyer ventured 42y on INT TD RET in 3rd Q for 24-0 lead, while Bucks TB Pepe Pearson rambled for 23/123y, 2 TDs.

MICHIGAN 45 Michigan State 29: Except for 2:01 span near end of 2nd Q, Michigan State (5-4) held its own against no. 9 Michigan (7-1). Spartans QB Todd Schultz (24-45/260y, 2 TDs, 4 INTs) provided hard-earned 10-7 2nd Q lead with 7y TD dart to WR Derrick Mason. Wolverines QB Scott Dreisbach (14-23/203y, 4 TDs) countered with TD pass for 14-10 lead with 2:09 left before H. After quick INT by Michigan and Spartans' immediate muff of KO, Dreisbach hit TE Jerame Tuman and WR-DB Charles Woodson with TDs, and Michigan led 28-10 at H.

Nebraska 73 OKLAHOMA 21: On-rolling Nebraska (7-1) juggernaut handed worst defeat ever to Oklahoma (2-6), building 52.2 scoring avg during 6 straight wins since being upset by Arizona State. Cornhuskers made 4 INTs, including 83y TD RET by frosh DB Ralph Brown. Dedicated and improving Huskers QB Scott Frost (10-22/163y, INT) threw 3 TD passes in 2nd H in building 52-0 lead. Sooners got all their pts against Huskers reserves in 4th Q on 34, 17, and 51y TD runs by frosh RB De'Mond Parker, 1st rushing scores vs. Nebraska in last 27 Qs.

RICE 51 Utah 10: Revived Rice (5-3) swept to 4th win in row and also enjoyed 4th straight game with 400y+ rushing attack. No. 20 Utah (7-2) sadly bid adieu to 7-game win skein. HB Michael Perry (6/108y) scored twice for Owls including 67y punt TD RET, HB Spencer George rambled 76y for TD, and DL Jason Winship rumbled 60y with INT TD RET. Utes had scored 1st on K Daniel Pulcipher's FG and added TD pass by QB Mike Fouts (13-24/138y, TD, INT) in 2nd Q.

Washington 21 SOUTHERN CALIFORNIA 10: Washington (6-2) TB Corey Dillon, late-bloomer who earned starting spot when Rashaan Shehee was injured, moved his season rush total to 1035y with execution of 37/128y, 2 TDs. Southern California (5-4) had led 10-3 at H, converting 2nd Q TOs into 15y TD pass from QB Brad Otton (13-29/138y) to FB Rodney Sermons and K Adam Abrams' 27y FG. Huskies QB Brock Huard (12-29/133y, INT) tossed TD pass in 3rd Q before Dillon bulled for 1 and 3y TDs.

CALIFORNIA 56 Arizona 55 (OT): Longest game to date in Div 1 history ended on Arizona's 2-pt try in 4th OT that surprised everyone but California (6-2) D. Each team scored 8 TDs with neither earning more than 2-TD lead. Arizona (4-4) gained 595y, and QB Keith Smith (25-35/418y, 5 TDs) threw 2 TDs in 4th Q to knot it at 35-35. Chance for OT was saved by Wildcats DB David Fipp's 2 FUM RECs at own 18 and 15YLs. Big part of Bears' 659y O came from QB Pat Barnes (35-46/503y), who threw school-record 8 TDs, including scores in 1st, 3rd, and 4th OTs. When Arizona got within 56-55 in 4th OT on TB Gary Taylor's short TD run, holder Ryan Hesson handed ball over his head to K Matt Peyton, whose 2-pt run was buried by California LB Andre Rhodes.

November 9, 1996

(Th) SAN DIEGO STATE 28 Wyoming 24: Late in 2nd Q, undefeated Wyoming (9-1) took 10-9 lead as TB Len Sexton wiggled away from tackler for 22y scoring reception from nation's leading TD thrower, QB Josh Wallwork (27-40/319y, 2 TDs). In seesaw 2nd H, Cowboys went 74y for 24-21 lead with 1:39 to play as sub TB Marques Brigham accounted for 44y including 2y TD run. San Diego State QB Billy Blanton (33-44/366y, 2 TDs, 2 INTs), who opened 2nd H by hitting 13 passes in row, quickly moved Aztecs (6-2) 72y, scoring on 11y draw off block by all-around standout WR LeAndrew Childs. Aztecs' win scrambled top of WAC Pacific Div.

Notre Dame 48 BOSTON COLLEGE 21: Emotional Boston College (4-6), hoping to erase tumult of 13 players suspended for gambling, took 10-7 lead early in 2nd Q on 7y TD run by RB Omari Walker (21/158y), then rallied in 3rd Q on Walker's 15y TD run and 2-pt pass by QB Matt Hasselbeck for 21-21 tie. Then, Eagles hit empty. Notre Dame (6-2), fresh from its triumph over Navy in Dublin, Ireland, exploded to TB Robert Farmer's 81y TD run and followed with 3 quick TDs.

ARMY 23 Air Force 7: Army (9-0), off to its best start since 1950, still was unknown quantity, having beaten 6 1-A teams with combined 18-34 record and 2 non-winning 1-AA teams. Cadets fell behind 7-3 as Air Force (5-4) FB Nakia Addison barreled 25y to score in 2nd Q. FB Joe Hewitt rushed 29/161y, 2 TDs as Army rallied for its 11th straight win, longest streak in nation. On Sunday, Cadets entered AP poll for 1st time since 1985.

Florida 28 VANDERBILT 21: No. 1 Gators (9-0) clinched SEC East title, and Alabama took inside track in SEC West with 26-0 whitewash at LSU. But, it hardly came easy for 43-pt favorite Florida as it was docked 147y in PENs. After 3 TDs by QB Danny Wuerffel (18-29/283y, 4 TDs, INT) made him 2nd player ever with more than 100 career TD passes, Florida overcame its 1st deficit of season to lead 21-3 at H. With score at 28-6, superb Vanderbilt (2-7) LB Jamie Duncan stripped ball from Wuerffel and ran 31y to TD. RB Jason Dunnavant raced 42y to score early in 4th Q, and Vandy trailed by slim TD. In last 6 mins, Commodores missed FG, failed on 4th down pass, and Gators got generous spot on 3rd down play to keep possession and end Dores' upset dream.

ARKANSAS 13 Mississippi 7: Rebels (4-4) held 7-3 lead on 12y TD run by TB John Avery (20/155y, TD) in 3rd Q, and they had chance to beef up lead after Avery sprinted 20y to Arkansas (3-5) 21YL midway in 3rd Q. On 2nd-and-2, game changed fortunes: Ole Miss QB Stewart Partridge (9-23/68y) tried swing pass that went behind intended target because Porkers LB Mark Smith blitzed quickly. Resultant lateral pass was recovered as FUM by Arkansas LB C.J. McLain at Hogs 29YL. Arkansas QB Pete Burks (10-17/123y, TD, INT) called timeout, 9 plays later, on 3rd-and-9 at Mississippi 12YL. It proved to be wise call as Razorbacks changed from option run play-call to Burks' TD pass to WR Anthony Eubanks, who beat coverage of LB Walker Jones for go-ahead TD at 10-7.

MEMPHIS 21 Tennessee 17: In 15 previous tries, Memphis (4-6) had never beaten its in-state tormentors. To look at stats, Tennessee (6-2) dominated as usual. Outgaining Tigers 381y to 153y, Vols ran 89 plays to 53 with 22-min possession advantage. With Vols up 7-0 and seeking another TD, Tigers DB Keith Spann set up tying TD run by QB Qadry Anderson with 77y INT RET. Tennessee QB Peyton Manning (23-40/296y, 2 INTs) tossed TD pass in 3rd Q, but Memphis DB Kevin Cobb was able to dash 95y with KO RET primarily because tacklers thought he was downed early in his run. (Video showed his elbow touched, which should have brought play-ending whistle.) Still, Vols led 17-14 until Tigers went 69y to nicked-up Anderson's winning 3y TD toss with 34 secs remaining.

PURDUE 9 Michigan 3: Frustrated Purdue (3-6) coach Jim Colletto started week by resigning effective at year's end, then capped it with emotional tribute to his Boilermakers' commitment to winning effort. TOs dearly cost no. 9 Michigan (7-2) as Wolverines lost 2 FUMs to Purdue LB Chris Koeppen, 1st stopped promising drive inside 5YL when DL-turned-RB Will Carr lost ball, 2nd led to game's only TD. Scrambling Purdue QB Rick Trefziger (20-30/170y) broke 3-3 tie with 5y TD flip to WR Brian Alford with 7:20 left in 4th Q.

COLORADO 49 Iowa State 42: In its 107 years of football, Colorado (8-1) never had won any game while it allowed 42 pts, and this verdict remained rather nervous for no. 7 Buffaloes until DB Ryan Sutter recovered Iowa State (2-7) on-side KO attempt with 26 secs to go. Bison QB Koy Detmer threw 27-47/401y, 5 TDs, INT, but Colorado hadn't secured lead until CB Toray Davis cut in front of receiver and returned INT to Iowa State 43YL to set up TB Herchell Troutman's 4y TD run 2 mins into 4th Q. Cyclone TB Troy Davis rushed for 35/228y to raise his season's total to 1822y and scored 2 TDs to provide Iowa State, 27-pt underdog, with 28-21 lead midway in 3rd Q. Trailing 49-28 after 42y TD catch by Buffs WR Rae Carruth (6/154y, 3 TDs) in 4th Q, Cyclones scored on TD pass and run by QB Todd Doxzon (16-27/153y, 2 TDs, 2 INTs) to trim deficit to 49-42 inside last half-min.

ARIZONA STATE 35 California 7: Just after 10th anniversary of Sun Devils' clinching of their only Rose Bowl trip, no. 4 Arizona State (10-0) joyfully wrapped up its 2nd appearance in Pasadena. Golden Bears (6-3) opened scoring on 2y run by TB Brandon Willis, but California finished with just 5y rushing against rugged Devils D. Emerging star TB Terry Battle ran 24/165y, scored game's next 4 TDs as ASU won going away.

November 16, 1996

(Th) MARYLAND 13 Georgia Tech 10: Struggling Georgia Tech (5-4) lost its 3rd of last 4 games as Maryland (5-5) win seemed to help beleaguered coach Mark Duffner. Terps QB Brian Cummings (21-29/192y, TD) set personal record for most completions in single game. FGs of 21 and 22y by K Joe O'Donnell in 1st and 3rd Qs respectively augmented Cummings' short TD pass to WR Geroy Simon in 2nd Q, so Terps owned 13-3 lead early in 3rd Q. Georgia Tech pulled closer with 11y TD pass from QB Joey Hamilton (20-37/228y, TD, 3 INTs) to WR Mike Sheridan. Any rally hope harbored by Yellow Jackets was doused by Maryland CB Orlando Strozier's 2 INTs in closing 2 mins, 1st coming on Hamilton's overthrow of Sheridan and 2nd coming after CB Lewis Sanders' midfield tip with 41 secs left. Veteran Strozier had suffered knee injury in frosh year, and he was happy to come through in his last home game: "To have my best game on Senior Day, with my mom here, it doesn't get any better than that."

Virginia Tech 21 MIAMI 7: When Miami (6-3) bungled scoring chance in last moment of 1st H with score at 7-7, Hurricanes were on their way to amazing 3rd straight home loss. Not since 1984 had Hurricanes lost 3 home games, even in full year. Go-ahead TD at 14-7 for Virginia Tech (8-1) came on QB Jim Druckenmiller's back-of-EZ 13y TD dart to WR Michael Stuewe in 3rd Q. Crusher for Canes came late in 4th Q when tying score seemed imminent: sub QB Scott Covington completed 2 3rd-and-long passes on 65y trip downfield to Tech 14YL. After Miami WR Tony Gaiter dropped likely TD pass on 2nd down, sub Hokies DB Keion Carpenter grabbed Covington's 4th down, underthrown slant pass at GL and cantered 100y for overwhelming 21-7 lead with 1:54 left.

VIRGINIA 20 North Carolina 17: Entering game, North Carolina (8-2) led nation in TO ratio, but critical INT of QB Chris Keldorf (19-39/154y, TD, 2 INTs) completely changed course of game. After 3-3 1st H, Tar Heels built 17-3 lead in 3rd Q on Keldorf's 7y TD pass to WR Octavus Barnes (7/66y, TD) at end of 80y drive and frosh DB Dre Bly's 51y INT TD RET. It was Bly's ACC-record 11th INT of season. Early in 4th Q, Heels LB Brian Simmons made INT and romped 57y to Virginia (7-3) 10YL. Keldorf went back to well once too often, passing over middle for Barnes (who lined up as SB), and Cavs DB Antwan Harris swiftly broke in front of Keldorf's pass and sprinted 95y for TD. Virginia QB Tim Sherman (10-24/136y, 2 INTs), benched earlier, twice converted 4th down plays on 52y drive and tied it 17-17 with 7y TD option run with 3:07 to play. Sherman hit WR Gremane Crowell with 41y pass and K Rafael Garcia kicked 32y FG with 39 secs left to end UNC's hope for at-large spot in Bowl Alliance. Cavs LBs Jamie Sharper (4 sacks) and James Farrior combined for 25 tackles and 5 sacks.

Florida 52 SOUTH CAROLINA 25: No. 1 Florida (10-0) played sloppy ball, and Heisman Trophy winner-in-waiting, QB Danny Wuerffel (11-34/290y, 2 TDs, 2 INTs), played his worst game since his frosh year. Still, Wuerffel pitched perfect TDs of 56y to WR Jacquez Green and 52y to WR Reidel Anthony. Gators TB Fred Taylor rushed 21/139y, 3 TDs, including 4th Q runs of 27 and 25y to put game away at 52-22. South Carolina (5-5) felt it played fairly well on D: "We played them as good as anyone and they scored 52 points," said impressed Gamecocks LB Shane Burnham. Carolina frosh TB Troy Hambrick rushed for 120y, becoming 1st back over 100y rushing all year against Florida, and had scored 2y TD late in 3rd Q to pull Cocks within 35-22.

Georgia 56 AUBURN 49 (OT): Clinging to flickering hope for SEC West title, Auburn (7-3) built 28-14 lead at H on 3 TD passes by QB Dameyune Craig (22-35/290y). After scoreless 3rd Q, versatile Bulldogs WR-RB Hines Ward (8/46y rushing and 9/175y receiving) took 67y TD pass early in 4th Q to trim Tigers' lead to 7 pts. With 1 sec left to play, Georgia (4-5) QB Mike Bobo (21-37/360y, 2 TDs) tossed high TD pass to WR Corey Allen to send game into OT. Bulldogs scored on each of their 4 OT possessions with sub TB Torin Kirtsey following starting TB Robert Edwards' 3 TD runs by sweeping left for TD that provided 56-49 lead. On Auburn's 4th OT possession, Tigers' Craig failed to convert 4th down run at Georgia 15YL.

MISSISSIPPI STATE 17 Alabama 16: Primed to clinch SEC West, Alabama (8-2) never got rolling against Mississippi State (4-5). Bulldogs built 14-7 lead in 2nd Q on 17y TD run by TB Robert Isaac and 12y TD pass by QB Derrick Taite. Budding frosh TB Shaun Alexander (15/106y), coming off Bama-record 291y and 4 TDs rushing against LSU, swept left to score in last 3 mins of 2nd Q. Conv kick by Bama K John Brock sailed wide left, so Mississippi State led 14-13. After K Brian Hazelwood's 39y FG gave Miss State 17-16 lead, Alabama faced 4th-and-3 with 38 secs left. QB Freddie Kitchens' pass went in and out of hands of WR Marcel West. Win was 1st career triumph in 8 tries for Bulldogs coach Jackie Sherrill against his alma mater.

Penn State 29 MICHIGAN 17: Nittany Lions (9-2) moved into Bowl Alliance contention, ending 8-game home win streak of TO-plagued Michigan (7-3). Penn State failed to make TDs on 2 early chances, but led 13-10 at H thanks to FB Aaron Harris' 1y blast in 2nd Q. Wolverines took 17-13 lead on their opening series of 3rd Q as TB Chris Howard (28/120y) charged 27y to score. Nittany Lions D next forced 5 TOs, including 2 INTs by DB Kim Hammond (10 tackles). Go-ahead TD came with 2:45 to go in 3rd Q as Penn State LB Aaron Collins carried blocked punt in from 2YL for 22-17 margin.

Ohio State 27 INDIANA 17: Resolute Hoosiers (2-8), playing hard for ousted coach Bill Mallory, had Buckeyes (10-0) on ropes at 10-7 entering 4th Q. After Ohio K Josh Jackson tied it early in 4th Q, Indiana QB Jay Rodgers (6-18/87y, INT), who had scored on 3rd Q TD run, scrambled to his left seeking 1st down near midfield. Ohio State's superb frosh LB Andy Katzenmoyer stripped ball, and DL Matt Finkes plucked ball off Rodgers' back, sprinted 45y to go-ahead TD in sudden and electrifying D gem. Bucks added DB Damon Moore's 28y INT TD RET for insurmountable 27-10 lead.

COLORADO 12 Kansas State 0: Determined to play better than its 49-42 escape against Iowa State on previous Saturday, Colorado (9-1) D held no. 9 Kansas State (8-2) to 228y and awaited November 29 showdown with Nebraska for Big 12 North title. Buffaloes TB Herchell Troutman rushed 28/112y and scored 1st Q TD on 27y sprint. Conv kick failed, but Colorado QB Koy Detmer sneaked over in 2nd Q and home team was ahead comfortably. When K-State's run attack sputtered with 65y, Wildcats QB Brian Kavanaugh (20-40/163y, 2 INTs) went to air with little success. Buffs DB Damen Wheeler made 2 INTs, and DT Ryan Olson came up with key sack on 4th down.

Wyoming 25 COLORADO STATE 24: Coupled with San Diego State's stunning 44-42 loss to UNLV, which ended Rebels' 12-game losing streak, come-from-behind win by Wyoming (10-1) put Cowboys in WAC title game. Wyoming enjoyed 13-0 H lead until Rams exploded for 24 pts in 3rd Q thanks to FB Calvin Branch's 3 TD runs. Although Cowboys gained but 77y rushing, they got pair of come-from-behind TD runs in 4th Q, including TB Marques Brigham's winning 6y dash with 1:48 to go.

USA Today Coaches Poll November 18

1	Florida (46)	1530	14	North Carolina	742
2	Ohio State (9)	1459	15	Washington	737
3	Florida State (7)	1453	16	Kansas State	693
4	Arizona State	1363	17	Syracuse	633
5	Nebraska	1323	18	LSU	522
6	Colorado	1233	19t	Wyoming	383
7	Brigham Young	1092	19t	Virginia	383
8	Penn State	1077	21	West Virginia	356
9	Virginia Tech	934	22	Michigan	262
10	Tennessee	921	23	Iowa	140
11	Northwestern	863	24	Clemson	109
12	Alabama	792	25	Miami (Fla.)	99
13	Notre Dame	768			

November 23, 1996

VIRGINIA TECH 31 West Virginia 14: Presence of nation's leading statistical D of West Virginia (8-3) inspired Virginia Tech (9-1) defenders. CB Loren Johnson said D "knew we would probably have to win the game." Leading big-play onslaught was quick Hokies DE Cornell Brown, who made 3 sacks and important FUM REC. QB Chad Johnston (20-51/209y, TD, INT) chucked 1y TD pass to WR David Saunders (9/87y, TD) late in 2nd Q to keep Mountaineers within hailing distance, down 10-7. But, Hokies used 2nd TD catch by WR Cornelius White (6/77y) from QB Jim Druckenmiller (16-28/238y, 2 TDs, INT) for 17-7 lead with 35 secs left in 1st H. After Virginia Tech gained only 24y rushing in 1st H, FB Ken Oxendine (19/104y, 2 TDs) broke 2 tackles for 39y TD early in 3rd Q. WVU responded with drive to Tech 25YL, but Brown totally ruined Johnston's pitchout on reverse run and gained possession for Hokies. Backup TB Alvin Swoope got Mountaineers back in it at 24-14 with 16y TD run with 11:40 to play in 4th Q, but ill-advised fake punt gave Va Tech field position for Oxendine's 2nd TD midway in 4th Q.

Navy 36 GEORGIA TECH 26: Navy (8-2) QB Chris McCoy returned to his native Georgia to haunt Yellow Jackets (5-5) with 3 TDs. McCoy scooted for scores of 8 and 4y to tie Joe Bellino's school single season record for TD runs of 15, and McCoy caught tricky 54y pass off handoff. Georgia Tech fought to gain 26-21 lead early in 4th Q when QB Joe Hamilton threw 19y TD pass to TB C.J. Williams. Midshipmen went 78y to McCoy's 4y TD run, and he added 2-pt pass to WR LeBron Butts. So, Navy led 29-26 with 8:02 left. Georgia Tech TB Charlie Rogers bolted 76y into Midshipmen territory with following KO, but Navy DB Gervy Alota made clutch INT of Hamilton at 12YL. Inside last 2 mins, Middies DB Rashad Smith returned INT for 54y TD.

TENNESSEE 56 Kentucky 10: Dismissed Kentucky (4-7) mentor Bill Curry experienced numb and sad farewell to coaching profession as Volunteers (8-2) ended 3-game Wildcats win streak and walloped them with 6 unanswered TDs after tight 1st Q. Tennessee QB Peyton Manning (16-23/317y, 3 TDs, INT) completed 3 long scoring passes: 80y and 59y to WR Peerless Price and 38y to WR Andy McCullough. Kentucky had scored 1st on FG and added QB Jack Haskins' 24y TD pass to trim deficit to 14-10 late in 1st Q. But, when Cats O couldn't create more than 154y, Vols' high-octane troops were able to romp. Curry's 1st road game as Georgia Tech C in 1960 had been at Tennessee's Neyland Stadium, prompting him to say, "To sort of start here and sort of finish here all seems to have gone so fast."

ALABAMA 24 Auburn 23: Crimson Tide (9-2) cruised to 17-0 edge in opening 11 mins as QB Freddie Kitchens (20-33/292y, 3 TDs, 3 INTs) pitched 2 TDs, including short flip turned into 64y score by TB Curtis Alexander. Auburn launched reversal in 2nd Q as QB Dameyune Craig (11-39/180y, 2 INTs) threw 57y TD, and frosh DB Brad Ware went 35y to INT TD RET. Auburn led 20-17 at H, extended it to 23-17, and generally frustrated Bama O. Crimson Tide woke up in time for 84y drive culminated by TB Dennis Riddle's elusive 7y TD catch with 26 secs left. Afterward, Bama coach Gene Stallings resigned after 7 years in Tuscaloosa.

PENN STATE 32 Michigan State 29: Potent Michigan State (6-5) dropped thriller. Penn State (10-2) held early 7-3 lead, then saw Spartans come to life in 2nd Q. Michigan State LB Courtney Ledyard blocked punt for safety, and TB Sedrick Irvin immediately pitched 56y TD pass to WR Nigea Carter after free-kick. Lions went 85y to 14-13 lead with WR Joe Jurevicius contributing 43y catch from QB Wally Richardson (21-31/281y, TD). Spartans regained 19-14 lead in 3rd Q on TB Duane Goulbourne's 34y TD run. Teams continued to trade scores, found it tied at 29-29 when Spartans K Chris Gardner—who had made 49y FG in 1st Q—hooked 33y try with 4:27 left. Penn State went 67y to K Brett Conway's winning 30y FG with 12 secs to play.

Michigan 13 OHIO STATE 9: Oh no, not 3rd time!? Thrice (1993, 1995, and now 1996) during coach John Cooper's 9 years, undefeated Ohio State (10-1) entered its annual bloodletting with Michigan (8-3) ranked in top-5 only to fail to beat its hated rival. After leading 9-0 in 1st H in which they squandered 3 TD chances, Buckeyes offered anemic 2nd H O which netted only 5y rushing. On 2nd play of 3rd Q, Wolverines QB Brian Griese (8-14/120y, TD), in for Scott Dreisbach who injured elbow in 1st H, caught Ohio State CB Shawn Springs in fall-down slip and threw slant-in that went for 68y TD to WR Tai Streets. Michigan took hard-earned 10-9 lead on K Remy Hamilton's FG on last play of 3rd Q. Late in 4th Q, Michigan TB Chris Howard rushed 9/57y on FG drive that consumed 5:33 against flagging Ohio State D.

Iowa 43 MINNESOTA 24: Hawkeyes (8-3) enjoyed 1st H scoring runs by TB Sedrick Shaw (27/108y, 2 TDs) and WR Tim Dwight. But, retiring Minnesota (4-7) coach Jim Wacker was brightened by Gophers' 17-pt rally to tie Iowa at 17-17 on 9y TD grab by WR Ryan Thelwell from QB Cory Sauter (17-47/235y, 2 TDs, 2 INTs) in last 10 secs of 2nd Q and Sauter's 1y TD run midway in 3rd Q. Then, roof of Humphrey Dome practically fell in on Gophers. In less than 2 mins of late 3rd Q, Hawkeyes racked up 16 pts: WR Richard Willock recovered EZ FUM, Minnesota punt snap flew through EZ for safety, and accurate QB Matt Sherman (17-21/226y, TD) launched 53y TD to Dwight. When Iowa added 10 pts in 1st 5 mins of 4th Q, score stood at bulging 43-17.

Brigham Young 37 UTAH 17: Was this really BYU (12-1), attempting only 12 passes and boasting pair of 100y rushers in wrapping up WAC Mountain Div title? Trying for 4th straight win over Cougars and share of Mountain Div crown, Utah (8-3) fell hopelessly behind 20-3 by H. Encouraged to stay on ground, BYU sprung RBs Brian McKenzie for 23/176y, TD, and Ronney Jenkins for 29/156y, 3 TDs. Utes got 2nd H TDs from massive FB Chris Faumatu-Ma'afala (18/87y) on 1y blast and QB Mike Fouts (14-31/179y, INT) on 19y toss to WR Kevin Dyson.

UCLA 48 Southern California 41 (OT): With frosh WR R. Jay Soward (6/260y, 3 TDs) setting school receiving y record, Southern California (5-6) enjoyed 17-0, 24-7, and 31-14 leads into late stages of 3rd Q. When Soward caught his last TD (78y from QB Matt Koffler, in for bruised Brad Otton), Trojans seemed to have salted it away at 38-21 with 11:06 to play. UCLA (5-6) trimmed it to 38-24 on K Bjorn Merten's 47y FG and 38-31 on TB Keith Brown's plunge, but only 2:49 remained as on-side KO went OB. But, Bruins LB Danjuan Magee created quick FUM, and QB Cade McNown (29-47/356y, TD, INT) hit 3 passes to poise TB Skip Hicks (20/116y) for tying TD with 39 secs left. After trade of OT FGs, Bruins sent inspired Hicks dashing to 25y TD and ended it on 4th down EZ INT by DB Anthony Cobbs.

Stanford 42 CALIFORNIA 21: Winning 4th game in row, TO-free Stanford (6-5) completed revitalization that earned invitation to Sun Bowl. Golden Bears (6-5) QB Pat Barnes (21-32/284y, 3 TDs, 2 INTs) had entered game with only 1 INT in last 272 pass tries, but he lofted 2nd Q screen pass that Card DE Kailee Wong quickly diagnosed. Wong took INT 53y to score for 17-0 lead. Cardinal QB Chad Hutchinson (16-25/184y, 3 TDs) threw short TD pass to FB Jon Ritchie and long TD pass to WR Troy Walters to highlight 1st H Stanford led 27-7. Stanford RB Mike Mitchell rushed 24/127y and caught TD pass. Cal's roughest play came afterward as unhappy fans attacked Stanford's silly mascot, The Tree. "They tore me limb from limb," cracked Chris Cary.

Washington 31 WASHINGTON STATE 24 (OT): It looked to be all over at 24-0 in favor of Washington (9-2) midway in 3rd Q. Huskies TB Corey Dillon (38/155y) had romped for 3 TDs, matching Pac-10 season rushing TD mark of 22, previously set by USC's O.J. Simpson (1968) and Marcus Allen (1981). After Cougars got K Tony Truant's short FG late in 3rd Q, they tied it with 3-TD splurge in 4th Q. QB Ryan Leaf (14-34/251y) ran for score, added TD pass, and RB Michael Black's 10y run knotted it with 1:18 to go in regulation time. Huskies QB Brock Huard found WR Jerome Pathon with winning TD pass in OT.

Arizona State 56 ARIZONA 14: Wanting to "rub it in their faces this year," according to TB Terry Battle, undefeated Arizona State (11-0) outgained bitter rival Arizona (5-6) 651y to 170y and allowed only 21y in 6 of last 7 Wildcats possessions of 2nd H. Sun Devils were bumbling along in mutually-belligerent 1st Q when they got inspiration from LB Derek Smith's vicious sack of Arizona QB Keith Smith (6-15/91y, INT). ASU then tallied 3 TDs in next 12 mins: Battle (23/143y, 3 TDs) scored his 1st TD, followed by DL Shawn Swayda's block of Wildcats QK to set up another Battle TD run, and WR Keith Poole snared 27y TD from QB Jake Plummer (10-19/201y, 3 TDs, 2 INTs). In middle of Devils' scoring surge, QB Smith wedged in Arizona's only TD in 28-7 1st H. Poole made brilliant 1-handed catch over middle in 3rd Q and quickly added leaping TD off fingertips of Wildcats DB Kelly Malveaux, making it 35-7. Arizona DB Mikal Smith authored meaningless 98y INT TD RET in 4th Q on which Cats DL Daniel Greer suffered severely injured ankle on hit by backup ASU G Glen Gable, who didn't even bother to pursue Smith.

USA Today Coaches Poll November 25

1	Florida (52)	1539	14	North Carolina	754
2	Florida State (7)	1480	15	Washington	751
3	Arizona State (3)	1429	16	Kansas State	663
4	Nebraska	1375	17	Syracuse	608
5	Colorado	1277	18	LSU	482
6	Ohio State	1182	19	Michigan	441
7	Brigham Young	1131	20	Wyoming	394
8	Penn State	1064	21	Virginia	363
9	Virginia Tech	971	22	Iowa	235
10	Tennessee	943	23	Miami (Fla.)	195
11	Northwestern	857	24	Army	113
12	Alabama	822	25	West Virginia	80
13	Notre Dame	809			

November 28-30, 1996

(Fri) VIRGINIA TECH 26 Virginia 9: In winning 20th of its last 21 games, Virginia Tech's surge swallowed no. 20 Virginia (7-4) as Hokies (10-1) triumphed going away. TB Tiki Barber (21/162y) went up middle on Cavaliers' 1st play for 80y run on his way to new Virginia career rushing y record. But for 1st of 3 times in 1st H, Cavs settled for K Rafael Garcia's FG. Trailing 9-7 at H, Virginia Tech D came up with big play that turned game: Hokiers DB Anthony Midget made FUM REC at Cavs 42YL after LB Myron Newsome slammed Barber. Hokies took 6 plays to take lead for good at 13-9 as QB Jim Druckenmiller (15-22/197y, 2 TDs) hit WR Michael Stuewe for 21y TD. Virginia disdained 1st down try on 4th-and-inches at Tech 22YL, and Garcia missed FG try. From there, Hokies iced it at 20-9 with Druckenmiller's 72y pass to WR Cornelius White (5/92y) that led to TB Marcus Parker's 9y TD jaunt. UVa D failed in bid to extend its NCAA-mark of INTs to 40 games.

(Fri) TEXAS 51 Texas A&M 15: Fast-improving Texas (7-4) earned surprise spot in Big 12 title game with easy win over disappointed Aggies (6-6), who completed their 1st non-winning year since 1983. Aggies hung within 17-9 at H thanks in part to 2y TD run by TB D'Andre Hardeman. Big play came early in 3rd Q as Longhorns stymied fake punt by A&M at Aggies 39YL. Texas QB James Brown (18-30/336y) quickly drilled his 2nd of 4 TD passes, and rout was on. Texas A&M TB Sirr Parker went 100y with 4th Q KO TD RET when it trailed 51-9.

(Fri) NEBRASKA 17 Colorado 12: Overcoming its decided inability to pass, Nebraska (10-1) let loose its ferocious D on Colorado (9-2). Huskers' pass rush forced Bison QB Koy Detmer into mediocre 11-39/226y slate. Detmer was picked off twice, including Cornhuskers LB Jay Foreman's 21y TD RET. Colorado had led 6-0, but could manage only 4 FGs by K Jeremy Aldrich by game's end. Nebraska IB DeAngelo Evans came off bench to rush for 123y and score TD for injured IB Ahman Green, who still went past 2000y career rushing mark.

Miami 38 SYRACUSE 31: Odd 2nd Q play helped Miami (8-3) end 8-game win streak of Syracuse (8-3): DB Nate Brooks was blocked into Orange punt returner, who lost FUM. Brooks recovered, and Canes soon led 14-3 on WR Yatil Green's TD catch. Miami WR Tony Gaiter made brilliant run after catch for 35y TD, but Syracuse answered when TB Malcolm Thomas (18/107y) burst 12, 11, 12 and 9y on consecutive runs to pull SU within 21-10. DB Tremain Mack immediately countered with 95y KO TD RET, so Miami led 28-10 at H. Syracuse rallied to 35-24 in 4th Q but lost FUM deep in Canes end to killits hope.

FLORIDA STATE 24 Florida 21: History's 30th meeting of top 2 teams went to no. 2 Seminoles (11-0) on massive pass rush (6 sacks) and TB Warrick Dunn's 24/185y rushing. FSU DE Peter Boulware blocked 1st Q punt, and DB Shevin Smith (10 tackles and EZ INT) got it at 2YL. FB Pooh Bear Williams quickly scored 1st of his 2 TDs for 10-0 Seminoles lead. WR Peter Warrick's 38y catch set up TE Melvin Pearsall's short TD catch, and FSU led 17-0 in 1st Q. Florida (10-1) made handsome comeback in 2nd Q as yellow flags rained on Florida State: QB Danny Wuerffel (23-48/362y, 3 TDs, 3 INTs) threw 2 TD passes to WR Jacquez Green. After both Ds dominated 3rd Q, Gators sought 17-17 tie, but K Bart Edmiston missed 41y FG. Seminoles went up 24-14 midway in 4th Q as Williams made TD run by twisting across GL. With 1:19 left, Florida WR Anthony Reidel (11/193y) went high for TD, but ensuing on-side KO failed.

SOUTHERN CALIFORNIA 27 Notre Dame 20 (OT): In Lou Holtz's last game as Notre Dame (8-3) coach, he lost for 1st time to Southern California (6-6). Loss knocked ND out of bowl picture which was stacked seriously against nation's few independent teams. Irish earned 7-6 H lead thanks to DB Benny Guilbeaux's EZ INT of USC QB Matt Koffler, playing because QB Brad Otton was injured on opening drive. Leading only 20-12 in 4th Q because of K Jim Sanson's hooked x-pt kick after TB Autry Denson's 9y TD run, ND allowed Trojans to tie it with 1:50 left on TB Delon Washington's 15y TD run and 2-pt run. In OT, revived Otton (13-25/183y, 2 TDs) pitched 3rd down 5y swing pass to FB Rodney Sermons for 1st Trojans win over Irish since 1982.

USA Today Coaches Poll December 2

1	Florida State (56)	1544	14	North Carolina	791
2	Arizona State (6)	1486	15	Kansas State	732
3	Nebraska	1418	16	LSU	596
4	Florida	1353	17	Michigan	506
5	Ohio State	1239	18	Notre Dame	461
6	Brigham Young	1166	19	Wyoming	443
7	Penn State	1112	20	Miami (Fla.)	401
8	Colorado	1084	21	Iowa	285
9	Virginia Tech	1080	22	Syracuse	255
10	Tennessee	987	23	Army	181
11	Alabama	890	24	West Virginia	126
12	Northwestern	885	25	Virginia	82
13	Washington	792			

December 7, 1996

Army 28 Navy 24 (Philadelphia): For 1st time in 33 years, both academies entered game with winning marks. Neither team in previous 96 games had come back from deficit as large as 18 pts built by Navy (8-3). Middies jumped to 3 quick TDs in 2nd Q for 21-3 edge as SB Patrick McGrew went 7y, and QB Chris McCoy threw 15y TD pass and followed 40 secs later with 2y TD run. Army (10-1) QB Ronnie McAda (5-10/116y, 15/134y rushing), who became all-time Cadets 3-game O leader vs. Navy, started rally with 44y TD option gallop bursting through arms of star Middies LB Clint Bruce. Cadets trimmed it to 21-13 at H and 21-19 early in 3rd Q on HB Bobby Williams' 81y TD sprint. After 75y TD march by Army, teams traded FGs, but Army's drive to 20y 3-pt boot by K J Parker ate 8:25 at beginning of 4th Q and provided 28-24 lead. Navy had 2 late chances to end 4-game series slide: McCoy's EZ pass bounced off receiver and sub QB Ben Fay's 4th down fling was picked off at GL by Cadets DB Garland Gay.

Texas 37 Nebraska 27 (St. Louis): Big 12's 1st title game turned into scenario Nebraska (10-2) coach Tom Osborne had warned against: highly-ranked team having its season upset by average foe from other division. Spicing proceedings was Texas (8-4) QB James Brown, who was goaded into prediction that 3-TD favorite Nebraska might lose by 3 TDs. Longhorns scored on opening drive, but it was matched by Huskers IB DeAngelo Evans' 3y TD run. TB Priest Holmes exploded up middle for 61y TD in 2nd Q to help Steers to 20-17 H lead. When Evans skirted RE for late 3rd Q TD, Huskers led 24-23. Midway in 4th Q, unsinkable Brown (19-28/353y, TD, 2 INTs) arched 66y TD pass to WR Wane McGarity for 30-27 lead. Nebraska, halted with less 4 mins left, punted to 7YL. Next came Texas coach John Mackovic's gamble of year: facing 4th-and-inches at own 29YL, Brown faked into line, rolled left. Huskers D sold out to stop run and left TE Derek Lewis wide open for floated pass he carried 61y. Holmes (9/120y) scored his 3rd TD on next play. Texas played its way into Alliance's Fiesta Bowl. Nebraska salvaged Alliance at-large bid to Orange Bowl.

Brigham Young 28 Wyoming 25 (Las Vegas): Despite 12 wins, no. 5 BYU (13-1) was unattractive Bowl Alliance at-large candidate because its fans were perceived as too thrifty to tunr heads of bowl-city merchants. In 1st-ever WAC title game, Cougars built 13-0 H lead on 2 FGs by K Ethan Pochman, and 72y drive capped by RB Brian McKenzie's TD run. Wyoming (10-2), also fighting bowl image problem, got ignited in 2nd H by its D. LB Jim Talich sacked Cougars QB Steve Sarkasian (26-37/250y, TD) early in 3rd Q, and LB Jay Jenkins scooped up FUM for 25y TD. Cowboys WR David Saraf made 2 TD catches in 4th Q, and K Cory Wedel threw 2-pt pass off botched kick snap for 25-20 lead. With 2:57 left, BYU failed to convert 4th down at Cowpokes 2YL. Soon forced to punt from own EZ, lame duck Wyoming coach Jim Tiller made interesting decision; he conceded safety to lead 25-22. But, free-kick was short, and BYU drove to 3YL only to nearly bungle its clock management. Pochman created OT with 20y FG with clock at 0:00. Cowboys failed on OT series, and Pochman won it with 32y FG. As it turned out, BYU was passed over by Alliance, while Wyoming went home empty.

Florida 45 Alabama 30 (Atlanta); When Gators players watched afternoon telecast of Texas' upset of Nebraska, they ran through hotel hallways "going crazy," according to LB James Bates. But sky-high Florida (11-1) stumbled briefly, allowing 36y TD on swing pass from Alabama (9-3) QB Freddie Kitchens (19-45/264y, 3 TDs, INT) to TB Dennis Riddle. Unflappable Gators QB Danny Wuerffel (20-35/401y, 6 TDs, 2 INTs) took command, pitching scores to WR Ike Hilliard, WR Reidel Anthony (11/171y, 3 TDs), and TB Elijah Williams. Trailing 24-7, Crimson Tide received late 2nd Q TD catch from WR Michael Vaughn, capitalized on botched punt snap in 3rd Q to close to 24-21. Wuerffel answered with TDs; best counterpunch was his 85y bomb to WR Jacquez Green after Vaughn caught 94y TD for Bama. Tide never got closer than 3 pts in 2nd H as Gators won 4th straight SEC title game and surprisingly leapt into rematch with Florida State for national title in Sugar Bowl.

USA Today Coaches Poll December 9

1	Florida State (57)	1545	14 Kansas State	727
2	Arizona State (5)	1491	15 Alabama	651
3	Florida	1410	16 LSU	615
4	Ohio State	1340	17 Michigan	529
5	Brigham Young	1235	18 Notre Dame	421
6	Nebraska	1185	19 Miami (Fla.)	408
7	Penn State	1162	20 Texas	324
8	Colorado	1106	21 Iowa	312
9	Virginia Tech	1098	22 Syracuse	251
10	Tennessee	989	23 Wyoming	246
11	Northwestern	889	24 Army	231
12	Washington	847	25 West Virginia	130
13	North Carolina	815		

1996 Conference Standings

Big East

Virginia Tech	6-1
Miami	6-1
Syracuse	6-1
West Virginia	4-3
Pittsburgh	3-4
Boston College	2-5
Rutgers	1-6
Temple	0-7

Atlantic Coast

Florida State	8-0
North Carolina	6-2
Clemson	6-2
Virginia	5-3
Georgia Tech	4-4
Maryland	3-5
North Carolina State	3-5
Wake Forest	1-7
Duke	0-8

Southeastern

EAST	
Florida	8-0
Tennessee	7-1
South Carolina	4-4
Georgia	3-5
Kentucky	3-5
Vanderbilt	0-8

WEST	
Alabama	6-2
Louisiana State	6-2
Auburn	4-4
Mississippi State	3-5
Mississippi	2-6
Arkansas	2-6

Conference USA

Southern Mississippi	4-1
Houston	4-1
Cincinnati	2-3
Louisville	2-3
Memphis	2-3
Tulane	1-4

Big Ten

Ohio State	7-1
Northwestern	7-1
Penn State	6-2
Iowa	6-2
Michigan	5-3
Michigan State	5-3
Wisconsin	3-5
Purdue	2-6
Minnesota	1-7
Indiana	1-7
Illinois	1-7

Mid-American

Ball State	7-1
Toledo	6-2
Miami (Ohio)	6-2
Ohio	5-3
Central Michigan	4-4
Akron	3-5
Bowling Green	3-5
Eastern Michigan	3-5
Western Michigan	2-6
Kent	1-7

Big Twelve

NORTH	
Nebraska	8-0
Colorado	7-1
Kansas State	6-2
Missouri	3-5
Kansas	2-6
Iowa State	1-7

SOUTH	
Texas	6-2
Texas Tech	5-3
Texas A&M	4-4
Oklahoma	3-5
Oklahoma State	2-6
Baylor	1-7

Pacific-10

Arizona State	8-0
Washington	7-1
Stanford	5-3
UCLA	4-4
California	3-5
Oregon	3-5
Southern California	3-5
Arizona	3-5
Washington State	3-5
Oregon State	1-7

Western Athletic

MOUNTAIN	
Brigham Young	8-0
Utah	6-2
Rice	6-2
Southern Methodist	4-4
New Mexico	3-5
Texas Christian	3-5
Tulsa	2-6
Texas-El Paso	0-8

PACIFIC	
Wyoming	7-1
San Diego State	6-2
Colorado State	6-2
Air Force	5-3
Fresno State	3-5
San Jose State	3-5
Hawaii	1-7
Nevada-Las Vegas	1-7

1996 Major Bowl Games

Aloha Bowl (Dec. 25): Navy 42 California 38

Setting tone for 1st H scoring spree was California (6-6) frosh TB Deltha O'Neal who scampered 100y with opening KO. Bears built 35-28 H lead as O'Neal (22/78y) added 31y TD dash and QB Pat Barnes (27-38/313y) flipped 3 TD passes. Meanwhile Navy (9-3) was on its way to building 646y in balanced attack, which included FB Omar Nelson's 119y rushing and QB Chris McCoy's 2 TD runs. Still, when K Ryan Longwell kicked 41y FG for 3rd Q's only score, Cal seemed in control at 38-28. Sr Middies QB Ben Fay was summoned from bench to spark 4th Q comeback, leading 80 and 84y marches. While Fay was in game as passing threat, he became Middie player who scored both TDs on runs of 2 and 10y. Winning tally came after Barnes lost FUM in Navy end and was scored with 1:21 left. Setting up game-winner was Fay's 52y pass to SB Cory Schemm (5/194y) with 2 mins to go.

Liberty Bowl (Dec. 27): Syracuse 30 Houston 17

In his last game for Syracuse (9-3), sr TB Malcolm Thomas (24/201y, TD) had his best career rushing effort, contributing long run on opening possession. With help of bad punt snap by Houston (7-5) for safety, but despite 0y passing, Orangemen enjoyed 16-7 lead with 1:15 left before H. Cougars crossed up preventative 6-DB setup with TB Antowain Smith's 53y run to set up 3y TD run by Smith (19/118y). Late in 3rd Q, Syracuse QB Donovan McNabb made brilliant 3rd down scramble and scored his 2nd TD early in 4th Q on 2y option run for 23-14 lead. WR Maurice Bryant made diving catch at Orange 9YL, but Houston had to settle for K Sebastian Villarreal's 23y FG. Syracuse answered with TD drive, aided by dominating O line, led by sub frosh C Cory Bowen, and expedient D-holding PEN on Houston DB William Fields.

Carquest Bowl (Dec. 27): Miami 31 Virginia 21

Looking for 1st bowl win since 1992 Orange Bowl, Miami (9-3) made big plays to secure and keep early lead. QB Ryan Clement (16-26/274y, TD, 2 INTs) arched 70y bomb to WR Yatil Green on Canes' 1st series. Virginia (7-5) was deflated when A-A TB Tiki Barber was felled by 1st Q hip-pointer. Barber's replacement, frosh TB Thomas Jones, lost FUM in Miami territory, and superb playmaker DB Tremain Mack scooped it up, racing 79y up sideline for TD. Cavs trimmed it to 14-7 when QB Aaron Brooks came off bench to toss 29y TD pass to leaping WR Germane Crowell. MVP Mack made other big play in 2nd Q for 24-7 lead: 42y INT TD RET. Virginia got spark early in 3rd Q on blocked punt by DB Anthony Poindexter. Brooks soon scored on sneak, and Cavs menaced again until ubiquitous Mack blocked FG, his 4th blocked placement or punt of year. Virginia made only 3 TDs in 11 trips into Hurricanes territory.

Copper Bowl (Dec. 27): Wisconsin 38 Utah 10

Battle of running back "Big Uns" never materialized as 275-lb Utah (8-4) FB Chris Famatu-Ma'afala limped off early with severe ankle sprain. Wisconsin (8-5) used its giant-sized TB Ron Dayne for 30/246y, 3 TDs. But 1st, QB Mike Samuel raced 38y to opening TD on 3rd down misdirection run around RE for 7-0 lead in 1st Q. Utes drew within 7-3 when QB Mike Fouts (27-49/327y, 4 INTs) pitched 20y pass to 22YL, then tossed 16y shovel pass to WR Kevin Dyson. K Daniel Pulsipher made FG. Dayne made it 14-3 with runs of 37 and 40y on consecutive plays to finish 1st Q with 100y rushing. Big play came deep in Badgers end in 2nd Q when Fouts tried angled pass to left flat. DE Tarek Saleh deflected it to outside where DB Cyrill Weems picked it off, went 82y to score for Wisconsin. Although Utah RB Juan Johnson scored in 3rd Q, Badgers FB Cecil Martin made fine GL blocks to spring Dayne for 2 short TD runs.

Peach Bowl (Dec. 28): Louisiana State 10 Clemson 7

LSU (10-2) coach Gerry DiNardo contended outcome would go to best passer. Thanks to soph QB Herbert Tyler (14-21/163y), it was LSU displaying its aerial skill. Oddly,

Clemson (7-5) QB Nealon Greene (6-20/66y) completed 22y flag pattern to WR Joe Woods on 1st series, but barely dented airways thereafter. Clemson scored 1st in dying moments of 1st Q. LB Trevor Pryce sacked Tyler, forced FUM REC by DB Harold Means at 10YL. Greene scored on 5y scramble for 7-0 edge. LSU answered with 80y TD march next time it had ball. Tyler contributed 13y run, hit FB Nicky Savoie at 7YL to set up TD run by TB Kevin Faulk. LSU went ahead 10-7 on K Wade Richey's 22y FG in 2nd Q after it bungled TD with false start on 4th down QB sneak. Despite rushing of Clemson TB Raymond Priester (25/151y), LSU menaced in 2nd H but abided TE David LeFleur's EZ pass drop, blocked FG. LSU came up with big D plays, stopping Clemson twice when it started drives in LSU end in 4th Q.

Alamo Bowl (Dec. 29): Iowa 27 Texas Tech 0

Iowa (9-3) coach Hayden Fry, who was born, played and once coached in Texas, had answer for Texas Tech (7-5) fans that preferred trip to Aloha Bowl: "It's difficult to drive a pickup truck from Lubbock to Hawaii." Hawkeyes D, led by DLs Jared DeVries and Jon LaFleur, also had answer for nation's 2nd leading rusher, Red Raiders TB Byron Hanspard, who gained only 18/64y. Meanwhile, Iowa TB Sedrick Shaw (20/113y) slipped out of backfield trap to sprint 24y behind block by T Ross Verba. QB Matt Sherman scored 2 plays later. Shaw made brilliant, spinning draw TD run of 20y in 2nd Q for 14-0 lead. Given 2nd chance by Texas Tech PEN, Hawks K Zach Bromert made 36y FG for 17-0 H lead. Iowa added another FG and TD by subs in 2nd H.

Holiday Bowl (Dec. 30): Colorado 33 Washington 21

Foes played typical Holiday Bowl barnburner in 24-21 1st H until Colorado (10-2) D wrestled control of Washington's balanced attack. Huskies (9-3) QB Brock Huard (21-37/203y, INT) opened with 8 straight completions. TB Corey Dillon (30/140y) gained 83y in 1st Q, tallied 2 TDs, 2nd behind block of pulling G Bob Sapp. Trailing 14-0, Buffs QB Koy Detmer arched 76y bomb to flying WR Rae Carruth. Colorado DE Nick Ziegler batted Huard's pass and plucked it out of air for TD RET and 14-14 tie. Washington WR Jerome Pathon answered with 86y KO TD RET. Back came Detmer (25-45/371y, 3 TDs) with TD pass to WR Darrin Chiaverini (7/94y). K Jeremy Aldrich put Buffs ahead for good at 24-21 with 43y FG late in 2nd Q. Colorado D dominated 2nd H as Aldrich added 36y FG, and Detmer tossed short TD pass.

Sun Bowl (Dec. 31): Stanford 38 Michigan State 0

Spartans (6-6) opened smartly, breaking TB Sedrick Irvin for nice runs before FUM ended early threat. On next possession, Michigan State QB Todd Schultz (8-21/68y, 2 INTs) hit 2 medium-range passes, but when he tried another, WR Derrick Mason slipped. Cardinal DB Josh Madsen made INT, raced to midfield, and flipped lateral to speedy DB Leroy Pruitt who completed 79y TD RET. That opened Cardinal (7-5) floodgates. QB Chad Hutchinson (22-28/226y, TD, INT) used his big league caliber pitcher's arm to hit FB John Ritchie with 8y score. Stanford FB Adam Salina went 1y for TD, Kevin Miller added FG, WR Damon Dunn scored on reverse and D blocked punt for TD. It was Stanford's 5th win in row.

Independence Bowl (Dec. 31): Auburn 32 Army 29

Auburn (8-4) QB Dameyune Craig was frightened twice: when Army (10-2) cheerleaders fired cannon to signify end of 1st Q and when he sprained his neck on 2nd Q sack. Otherwise, Craig was brilliant, passing 24-40/372y, 2 TDs, INT and rushing 13/75y, TD. Tigers opened in Shotgun set, freeing Craig to hit 4 quick passes, but Auburn settled for FG by K Jared Holmes. Craig threw TDs to WRs Tyrone Goodson and Willie Gosha for 20-7 H lead. Tigers appeared home free when Craig dodged blitz and raced down sideline for 33y TD in 3rd Q, and TB Rusty Williams ploughed over for 32-7 4th Q edge. Cadets suddenly came alive: FB Demetrius Perry blasted up middle for TD, DB Tom Mullins' long INT RET set up HB Bobby Williams' 2nd TD run, and QB Ronnie McAda hit sub WR Rod Richardson on 30y slant-in TD pass. All of sudden, Army trailed only 32-29. Cadets made successful onside-KO, followed by Williams' brilliant 28y catch as he was belted at Tigers 14YL by DB Brad Ware. On 3rd down with no timeouts left, Army looked for tying 27y FG. In came K J. Parker, who had 17 successful FG in row from inside 40YL, but he missed wide.

Orange Bowl (Dec. 31): Nebraska 41 Virginia Tech 21

Early going found both run-oriented teams vainly probing airlanes. Virginia Tech (10-2) scored late in 1st Q on 19y pass off fake screen from QB Jim Druckenmiller (16-33/214y, 3 TDs) to FB Marcus Parker. Nebraska (11-2) tallied game's next 17 pts including 31y FUM TD RET by DT Jason Peter as ball was knocked from Druckenmiller on option pitchout. Late in 2nd Q, Hokies WR Shawn Scales scored TD by yanking ball away from Huskers DB Octavious McFarlin, who appeared to have EZ INT. So, Virginia Tech trailed only 17-14 at H. It was Nebraska's 5th trip in 6 years to Orange Bowl, so perhaps familiarity with lengthy H show favored Huskers, who swamped Hokies by 24-7 in 2nd H. Nebraska scored on its 1st 4 possessions after 3rd Q KO: Huskers IB Damon Benning (15/95y) tallied on runs of 32 and 6y. Va Tech's sole answer was WR Cornelius White's long, blitz-beating TD catch.

Outback Bowl: Alabama 17 Michigan 14

Gene Stallings' last game as Alabama (10-2) coach turned out to have happy result, but as usual it took come-from-behind effort with Crimson Tide's D making big play. Alabama's pressure on Michigan P Paul Peristeris forced punt that failed by 2y of reaching line of scrimmage, and that gave Tide early FG. Having inherited Wolverines (8-4) QB job off his November performance vs. Ohio State, Brian Griese (21-37/287y, TD, INT) made some good early plays including 45y link with TB Clarence Williams and 18y run off fake FG. Michigan led 6-3 at H on 2 FGs by K Remy Hamilton and was driving to pad its lead in 4th Q. Griese was hit as he threw. Fluttering pass was picked off by Crimson Tide LB Dwayne Rudd, who rambled 88y to decisive score. TB Shaun Alexander raced 46y for TD on draw with 2:30 left for 17-6 Bama lead before Griese connected on late TD pass. Tide WR Chad Goss, 3rd Q goat for having made fair catch at own 1YL, preserved win by leaping to snare Michigan's late on-side KO attempt.

Gator Bowl: North Carolina 20 West Virginia 13

Playing without injured, all-ACC QB Chris Keldorf seemed to imperil North Carolina (10-2) as it faced nation's no. 1 D of West Virginia (8-4). Unheralded QB Oscar Davenport (14-26/175y, TD, and 14/31y, TD rushing) was called "America's best-kept secret" by teammate DE Russell Davis. Davenport gave Heels 17-3 jump in 2nd Q with 18y TD pass and 5y TD run. Mountaineers rushing game was held to 66y, so QB Chad Johnston (17-34/197y) got team back in game with early 3rd Q TD pass to WR David Saunders (9/130y). But UNC D, nation's best at takeaways, came up with 3 INTs, including frosh A-A DB Dre Bly's 12th and 13th pass thefts of year. Carolina D halted WVU on downs at own 24YL with 2 mins to go to salt away 1st 10-win season in 106-year history of North Carolina football.

Cotton Bowl: Brigham Young 19 Kansas State 15

Deep in its own end, Kansas State (9-3) suffered early safety when QB Brian Kavanaugh (14-23/233y, 2 TDs, 2 INTs) was sacked by Cougars LB Shay Muirbrook (4 sacks) on goofy EZ shovel pass. After poor free-kick, K-State fell behind 5-0, but on last play of 1st H, Kavanuagh lofted Hail Mary pass plucked for TD by WR Andre Anderson. TB Mike Lawrence added 2-pt run for 8-5 Cats' H advantage. Midway in 3rd Q, Kavanaugh found WR Kevin Lockett (7/135y) on short slant-in pass, and Lockett cruised away for 72y TD. Brigham Young (14-1) seemed to get boost when 2 straight apparent pass interferences went uncalled. Also helping BYU was 4th Q departure of best Wildcats CBs, Chris Canty and Joe Gordon, each of whom suffered leg cramps in late pinch. BYU QB Steve Sarkisian (21-36/291y, 2 TDs, INT) hit 3 passes in row, last of which was fine TD grab by WR James Dye. Sarkisian followed with late 28y TD pass to WR K.O. Kealaluhi, at which point Sarkisian wandered to Wildcats bench to ask (and receive 15y PEN) where mouthy Canty was sitting. DB Omarr Morgan locked up Cougars' NCAA-record 14th win of season with INT at 4YL with 1:17 to play.

Citrus Bowl: Tennessee 48 Northwestern 28

Volunteers (10-2) rolled to easy 21-0 1st Q lead as QB Peyton Manning bracketed own 10y bootleg TD run with TD passes to WRs Peerless Price (6/110y) and Joey Kent (5/122y). Flu-ridden Northwestern (9-3) rallied for 3 TDs within 5:18 span of 2nd Q. Wildcats' TD that made it 21-21, came on 28y counter-trey by TB Darnell Autry, whose 17/66y rushing was below his bodily temperature (101 degrees) and season's game avg (138.6y). It took only 29 secs for Tennessee to retake lead for good. Manning (27-39/408y, 4 TDs) beat safety blitz for 67y TD to Kent, and K Jeff Hall hit 19y FG just before H. Vols owned 2nd H as LB Tyrone Hines had 30y INT TD RET and Manning added his 4th TD pass. NW WRs D'Wayne Bates and Brian Musso each caught 10 passes and nabbed TD passes from QB Steve Schnur (25-45/228y, 2 TDs, 3 INTs).

GAME OF THE YEAR
Rose Bowl: Ohio State 20 Arizona State 17

In front of 1st bowl sellout of holiday season, undefeated Sun Devils (11-1) sought its shot at possible national title. Ohio State (11-1) held slim hope as well and built early 82y TD drive as QB Stanley Jackson scrambled 19y before finding WR David Boston at right pylon for 9y TD pass. Arizona State tied it at 7-7 in 2nd Q as WR Ricky Boyer made miraculous 25y TD catch above grass top, although replays showed ball hit ground. Devils opened 2nd H with drive that included effective reverse run by WR Keith Poole and QB Jake Plummer's 23y pass, but Ohio DB Damon Moore made big 3rd down stop at 19YL. So, Arizona State K Robert Nycz booted 37y FG for 10-7 lead. Buckeyes QB Joe Germaine (9-17/131y, 2 TDs), native of Mesa, Ariz., who once hoped to play for ASU, answered quickly by hitting 72y post-pattern TD pass to WR Dimitrious Stanley. But Germaine soon started firing blanks until being pulled for Jackson (6-14/59y, TD) midway in 4th Q. Jackson's 1st play came from own 3YL where Devils P Lance Anderson's 59y punt had been downed. Ohio TB Pepe Pearson (13/111y) broke behind OT Orlando Pace's pancake block for 62y gain. Devils D stiffened, so K Josh Jackson lined up for 38y FG that would extend Buckeyes lead to 7 pts with less than 6 mins to play. But, 6'8" DE Brent Burnstein made rare play, pushing through Pace to block kick, and DE Derrick Rodgers raced 50y to score. However, Rodgers had received lateral, which was ruled to have been forward. So, ball was moved back with Devils in possession at ASU 42YL. Poole caught his only pass early on drive, but ASU soon faced 4th-and-4 at Buckeyes 37YL. Calm QB Plummer (19-35/201y, TD, INT) tossed fade pass for 29y to WR Lenzie Jackson. After Ohio LB Greg Bellisari's sack, Jake "The Snake" dropped to pass, instead slithered away from pressure and avoided star frosh LB Andy Katzenmoyer to dive for EZ and 17-14 lead with 1:40 to play. "I thought I'd blown the game," said Katzenmoyer, but Germaine reentered to lead Buckeyes' winning 65y march. Germaine hit 4-9/41y on drive, including 11, 12, and 13y strikes to Stanley (5/124y). ASU DBs, under man-to-man pressure due to all-out blitz calls, twice were called for 15y interference PENs on drive. Germaine found Boston for 5y TD with 19 secs to go. Credit had to be given to Ohio State D, which limited Devils' rushing attack to 41/75y.

Fiesta Bowl: Penn State 38 Texas 15

Historically undefeated at 5-0 in Fiesta Bowl, Penn State (11-2) looked to stop Longhorns (8-5), who entered game hotter than Texas chili. Nittany Lions used early INT by DB Mark Tate to set up QB Wally Richardson's 4y TD swing pass to TB Curtis Enis. Texas quickly took O control, making long drives to perch K Phil Dawson in position for 2 FGs. RB Ricky Williams scored on 7y run after EZ interference PEN on Tate, so Longhorns earned 12-7 edge at H and seemed in complete command with 242y to 95y O advantage. But, Lions frosh WR Kenny Watson took 2nd H KO 81y to set up TD by FB Aaron Harris and 2-pt catch by Enis for 15-12 lead. Steers countered with pass off fake punt, but had to settle for Dawson's 48y FG and 15-15 knot. Sub TB Chafie Fields soon bolted 84y on reverse run to poise MVP Enis (16/95y) for his 2nd of

3 TDs. Penn State dominated 2nd H 31-3 and now sported strong scoring trend in its last 6 bowl games. It owned 131-40 2nd H scoring edge.

Sugar Bowl: Florida 52 Florida State 20

With Arizona State out of title picture, Bowl Alliance's championship game was for all marbles. Things that had gone wrong for Florida (12-1) in 1st meeting against FSU 32 days earlier were corrected in fine coaching job by Steve Spurrier. Pass protection, major pre-game issue as Spurrier complained loud and often about late hits by Seminoles in previous game, was significantly altered by putting QB Danny Wuerffel (18-34/306y, 3 TDs, INT) in Shotgun formation. Special teams, Gators nightmare on November 30, came through admirably, especially P Robby Stephenson, who had 48y avg and made critical 69y punt to 2YL when score was 24-20 in 3rd Q. Of course, Florida had been fortunate to be in position for national title shot since it required Ohio State's late-season tumble from no. 2 and Texas' upset of Nebraska to bar Huskers from Sugar Bowl. Gators took advantage, surprisingly pulling away in 2nd H. Florida State (11-1) had failed to convert 4th-and-2 inside Gators 20YL after 55y catch by WR Andre Cooper from QB Thad Busby (17-41/271y) on opening series. Wuerffel pitched 3 TD passes, and Gators led 24-10 late in 2nd Q. Seminoles collected only 15y rushing until TB Warrick Dunn, controlled nearly all night, used WR E.G. Green's fine crack-back block to slant for 12y TD run. FSU trailed 24-17 at H and got to 24-20 on K Scott Bentley's 45y FG early in 3rd Q. Next came Stephenson's killing punt, and resultant field position set up Florida for kill: Wuerffel threw slant-in TD to WR Ike Hilliard (7/150y), Wuerffel followed with 16y scramble run for TD, and TB Terry Jackson (12/118y, 2 TDs) raced 42y to 4th Q TD.

Final *USA Today* Coaches Poll January 3

1	Florida (58)	1546	14	Miami (Fla.)	636
2	Ohio State (4)	1466	15	Washington	622
3	Florida State	1408	16	Northwestern	594
4	Arizona State	1341	17	Kansas State	564
5	Brigham Young	1261	18	Iowa	549
6	Nebraska	1235	19	Syracuse	446
7	Penn State	1205	20	Michigan	390
8	Colorado	1128	21	Notre Dame	381
9	Tennessee	1077	22	Wyoming	259
10	North Carolina	971	23	Texas	141
11	Alabama	906	24	Army	106
12	Virginia Tech	791	25	Auburn	103
13	LSU	746			

Final AP Poll January 3

1	Florida (65.5)	1673.5	13	Virginia Tech	786
2	Ohio State (1.5)	1585.5	14	Miami	690
3	Florida State	1529	15	Northwestern	663
4	Arizona State	1486	16	Washington	643
5	Brigham Young	1360	17	Kansas State	625
6	Nebraska	1316	18	Iowa	535
7	Penn State	1293	19	Notre Dame	511
8	Colorado	1228	20	Michigan	466
9	Tennessee	1172	21	Syracuse	451
10	North Carolina	1070	22	Wyoming	314
11	Alabama	977	23	Texas	169
12	Louisiana State	849	24	Auburn	130
			25	Army	71

1996 Top Performance Formula

1	Florida	1.8018
2	Florida State	1.7634
3	Ohio State	1.7332
4	Arizona State	1.7048
5	Nebraska	1.6975
6	Brigham Young	1.6522
7	North Carolina	1.5638
8	Colorado	1.5402
9	Tennessee	1.5375
10	Penn State	1.5290
11	Virginia Tech	1.5265
12	Syracuse	1.4758
13	Washington	1.4740
14	Alabama	1.4505
15	Louisiana State	1.4384
16	Notre Dame	1.4300
17	Kansas State	1.4135
18	Miami	1.3821
19	Iowa	1.3654
20	Auburn	1.3611

1996 Top Opponent Records

1	Arkansas	.6410
2	Florida	.6380
3	Florida State	.6250
4	UCLA	.6154
5	Washington	.6124
6	Vanderbilt	.6121
7	Auburn	.6111
8	Nebraska	.6043
9	Ohio State	.6032
10	Colorado	.5969
11	Minnesota	.5966
12	Iowa State	.5933
13	Purdue	.5932
14	Alabama	.5882
15	Kansas State	.5860
16	Rutgers	.5831
17	Duke	.5812
18t	Arizona State	.578125
18t	Michigan	.578125
20t	Indiana	.577586
20t	Kentucky	.577586

1996 Out-of-Conference Records

	W-L	Percentage	Bowl W-L
Southeastern	30-9	.7692	5-0
Big Ten	30-12	.7143	4-3
Pacific-10	22-13	.6286	1-3
Big Twelve	22-17	.5641	2-3
Big East	18-16	.5294	2-2
Atlantic Coast	13-16	.4483	1-3
Western Athletic	23-30	.4340	1-1

1996 Individual Statistical Leaders

RUSHING YARDS	Attempts	Yards	Avg.
Troy Davis, Iowa State	402	2185	5.4
Byron Hanspard, Texas Tech	339	2084	6.1
Ron Dayne, Wisconsin	295	1863	6.3
Scott Harley, East Carolina	307	1745	5.7
Corey Dillon, Washington	271	1555	5.7
Silas Massey, Central Michigan	312	1544	4.9
David Thompson, Oklahoma State	293	1524	5.2
Beau Morgan, Air Force	225	1494	6.6
Darnell Autrey, Northwestern	263	1386	5.3
Pepe Pearson, Ohio State	286	1373	4.8

PASSING YARDS	Completions	Attempts	Yards	Pct.
Josh Wallwork, Wyoming	286	458	4090	62.5
Steve Sarkisian, Brigham Young	278	404	4027	68.8
Ryan Fien, Idaho	267	455	3674	58.7
Danny Wuerffel, Florida	207	360	3625	57.5
Pat Barnes, California	250	420	3499	59.5
Jason Martin, Louisiana Tech	247	415	3360	59.5
Peyton Manning, Tennessee	243	380	3287	64.0
Billy Blanton, San Diego State	227	344	3221	66.0
Koy Detmer, Colorado	208	363	3156	57.3
Moses Moreno, Colorado State	193	335	2921	57.6
Chad Darnell, Central Michigan	189	348	2921	54.3

RECEIVING YARDS	Catches	Yards
Marcus Harris, Wyoming	109	1650
Chad Mackey, Louisiana Tech	85	1466
Geoff Noisy, Nevada	98	1435
Nokia Jenkins, Utah State	82	1397
Reidel Anthony, Florida	72	1293
Brian Roberson, Fresno State	78	1248
Reggie Allen, Central Michigan	66	1229
Eugene Baker, Kent	69	1215
Antonio Wilson, Idaho	65	1203
Brandon Stokley, Southwest'n Louisiana	81	1160

1996 Consensus All-America Team

Offense

Wide Receiver:	Marcus Harris, Wyoming
	Ike Hilliard, Florida
	Reidel Anthony, Florida
Tight End:	Tony Gonzalez, California
Line:	Orlando Pace, Ohio State
	Juan Roque, Arizona State
	Chris Naeole, Colorado
	Dan Neil, Texas
	Benji Olson, Washington
Center:	Aaron Taylor, Nebraska
Quarterback:	Danny Wuerffel, Florida
Running Back:	Byron Hanspard, Texas Tech
	Troy Davis, Iowa State
Placekicker:	Marc Primanti, North Carolina State

Defense

Line:	Grant Wistrom, Nebraska
	Peter Boulware, Florida State
	Reinard Wilson, Florida State
	Derrick Rodgers, Arizona State
	Mike Vrabel, Ohio State
Linebacker:	Pat Fitzgerald, Northwestern
	Matt Russell, Colorado
	Jarrett Irons, Michigan
Backs:	Chris Canty, Kansas State
	Kevin Jackson, Alabama
	Dre Bly, North Carolina
	Shawn Springs, Ohio State
Punter:	Brad Maynard, Ball State

1996 Heisman Trophy Vote

Danny Wuerffel, senior quarterback, Florida	1,363
Troy Davis, junior tailback, Iowa State	1,174
Jake Plummer, senior quarterback, Arizona State	685
Orlando Pace, junior tackle, Ohio State	599
Warrick Dunn, senior tailback, Florida State	341

Other 1996 Major Awards

Maxwell (Player)	Danny Wuerffel, senior quarterback, Florida
Walter Camp (Player)	Danny Wuerffel, senior quarterback, Florida
Outland (Lineman)	Orlando Pace, junior tackle, Ohio State
Vince Lombardi (Lineman)	Orlando Pace, junior tackle, Ohio State
Doak Walker (Runner)	Byron Hanspard, junior tailback, Texas Tech
Davey O'Brien (Quarterback)	Danny Wuerffel, senior quarterback, Florida
Fred Biletnikoff (Receiver)	Marcus Harris, senior wide receiver, Wyoming
Jim Thorpe (Defensive Back)	Lawrence Wright, senior safety, Florida
Dick Butkus (Linebacker)	Matt Russell, senior linebacker, Colorado
Lou Groza (Placekicker)	Marc Primanti, senior kicker, North Carolina State
Johnny Unitas (Quarterback)	Danny Wuerffel, senior quarterback, Florida
Chuck Bednarik (Defender)	Pat Fitzgerald, senior linebacker, Northwestern
Bronko Nagurski (Defender)	Pat Fitzgerald, senior linebacker, Northwestern
AFCA Coach of the Year	Bruce Snyder, Arizona State

The Year of Return to Peyton Place, Nothing Wrong with Michigan, and Another Split Decision

An astounding 24 new coaches greeted their players for fall practice, but it was an incumbent who was happiest to see a familiar face. Phillip Fulmer welcomed back quarterback Peyton Manning, who surprised and delighted all of Tennessee (11-2) when he announced on March 5 that he would return to school and skip a likely no. 1 selection in the NFL draft. It also seemed likely that Manning was a shoo-in for the Heisman Trophy. Manning passed for 3,819 yards and 36 touchdowns, but Florida (10-2) beat the Volunteers, the fourth time that happened in Manning's tenure. At the same time, a bright Heisman star began rising at Ann Arbor, Michigan.

In its season preview magazine, *The Sporting News* ran a "What's wrong with Michigan?" story. The author, Michigan alum and free-lance writer Michael Bradley, called the Wolverines "a withering national power" and a school that looked "like a corporation that has just had a lucrative patent expire and is unprepared to handle the hungry competition banging on the market-place door."

The answer to *TSN's* question was that nothing was wrong with Michigan, though the disparaged Wolverines were coming off four straight years in which they lost four games in each season. Led by junior Charles Woodson's brilliant play in the defensive backfield and his touchdowns as a punt returner and an occasional wide receiver, Michigan (12-0) swept the Big 10 behind quarterback Brian Griese's sharp play and a truly superb defense. Michigan rallied to upend Cinderella Washington State (10-2) 21-16 in the Rose Bowl to earn the AP half of the national title. It was Michigan's first national championship since 1948. Perhaps, Mr. Bradley wished he had written his story earlier.

The Bowl Alliance, somewhat frail without Big 10 or Pac-10 endorsement, was supposed to provide the ultimate title bout in the Orange Bowl. With no. 1 Michigan playing in Pasadena, Big 12 champion and no. 2 Nebraska (13-0) pointed to and disassembled no. 3 Tennessee (11-2) 42-17 in Manning's swansong in Miami. The coaches' vote backed Nebraska as its top choice after the bowl results. Shortly before the Orange Bowl, Cornhusker coach Tom Osborne had announced the game would be his last before retirement. The number one ranking became a pleasant going away gift for Osborne as he left Lincoln with a 255-49-3 mark. That was good for a .836 winning percentage at the close of the 1997 season, sixth best among Division 1-A coaches all-time.

Split decisions in polls were nothing new, of course, although they carried a distinct air of dissatisfaction for many that were uncomfortable with multiple champions. The 1997 season was no exception.

The media, especially the ABC-ESPN axis that televised by far the most games, took delight in tagging various important game days with Armageddon-style names. September 20 was termed "Showdown Saturday" as Florida beat Tennessee and Nebraska went to Washington (8-4) to defeat the Huskies. October 18 became "Letdown Saturday" when five undefeated teams, Air Force (10-3), Auburn (10-3), Michigan State (7-5), New Mexico (9-4) and Texas A&M (9-4), lost for the first time. Top-ranked Penn State (9-3) slipped to no. 2 the same weekend when it nipped lowly Minnesota (3-9) by only 16-15 at home. November 8 was called "Judgment Day" as four top 5 teams tangled on the same weekend for the first time since 1971. On Thanksgiving, 1971, top-ranked Nebraska's late touchdown beat no. 2 Oklahoma 35-31 in what became known as "The Game of the Century" and no. 3 Alabama beat no. 5 Auburn, 31-7.

In 1997, no. 4 Michigan destroyed no. 2 Penn State 34-8 and no. 3 Florida State (11-1) cruised by no. 5 North Carolina 20-3. For good measure, Judgment Day saw no. 1 Nebraska require overtime to beat Missouri (7-5). The Huskers' tying touchdown on the last play of regulation was one of the most bizarre in football history: a Nebraska pass that was tipped and kicked before being caught at the grass top tied the game in miraculous fashion.

Defending national champion Florida had an up and down year with considerable and intentional upheaval at the quarterback position. After whipping Tennessee 33-20 in September, the Gators were surprised by Louisiana State (9-3) and Georgia (10-2). Coach Steve Spurrier briefly suspended quarterback Doug Johnson then successfully switched among Jesse Palmer, Noah Brindise, and Johnson to Florida's benefit.

New Mexico, Pittsburgh (6-6), Purdue (9-3) and Oklahoma State (8-4) all enjoyed surprising improvements and rare bowl trips, considering recent histories. Kansas State (11-1) and North Carolina (11-1) continued to advance in the rankings, although neither could displace their respective conference kingpin. The Wildcats won the Fiesta Bowl and finished eighth

in the AP poll. The Tar Heels was victorious in the Gator Bowl, but lost coach Mack Brown to Texas (4-7) shortly before its 42-3 win in Jacksonville over West Virginia (7-5). North Carolina finished sixth in the AP Poll.

Two schools made auspicious debuts in Division 1-A. Marshall (10-3) won the MAC championship behind the spectacular passing duo of quarterback Chad Pennington and receiver Randy Moss. Despite a tight loss in their season opener against in-state top dog West Virginia, the Thundering Herd came out of that trumpeted tilt to run off five wins in a row and produce one of the greatest 1-A debuts in history. Central Florida (5-6) faced a mountainous schedule, but beat a good team in Toledo (9-3), and dropped a considerable bit of fright on home-standing Nebraska at halftime before superior talent won out for the Huskers.

Milestones

⬤ Overtime rule was altered to require all conversion attempts in a third overtime period to be two-point runs or passes regardless of the score at the time of the conversion attempt. Rules committee also toughened crackback block and punt returner protection penalties.

⬤ Central Florida, Marshall and North Texas moved up to Division 1-A with Marshall being readmitted to its second stretch of membership in Mid-American Conference.

⬤ At last acknowledging its diverse membership that included three Virginia schools, 1-AA Yankee Conference changed its name to Atlantic-10 even though it had 12 members. Conference member Boston University soon made it an 11-team league when it announced in mid-season it would drop football after 91 years.

⬤ Don Hutson, All-America end at Alabama in 1934 and member of both college and pro Halls of Fame died at age 84. Aaron Brown, All-America end at Minnesota in 1965, was accidently killed by motorist less than week from his 54th birthday. Death visited two campuses: Mississippi State senior tailback Keffer McGee drowned in pool accident just before fall camp. Early in season, Brigham Young cornerback Terrence Harvey was killed in auto accident that injured two teammates.

⬤ Coaching Changes

	Incoming	Outgoing
Alabama	Mike DuBose	Gene Stallings
Arkansas State	Joe Hollis	John Bobo
Baylor	Dave Roberts	Chuck Reedy
Boise State	Houston Nutt	Pokey Allen
Boston College	Tom O'Brien	Dan Henning
California	Tom Holmoe	Steve Mariucci
Fresno State	Pat Hill	Jim Sweeney
Illinois	Ron Turner	Lou Tepper
Indiana	Cam Cameron	Bill Mallory
Kansas	Terry Allen	Glen Mason
Kentucky	Hal Mumme	Bill Curry
Maryland	Ron Vanderlinden	Mark Duffner
Minnesota	Glen Mason	Jim Wacker
New Mexico State	Tony Samuel	Jim Hess
Notre Dame	Bob Davie	Lou Holtz
Oregon State	Mike Riley	Jerry Pettibone
Pittsburgh	Walt Harris	Johnny Majors
Purdue	Joe Tiller	Jim Colletto
San Jose State	Dave Baldwin	John Ralston
Southern Methodist	Mike Cavan	Tom Rossley
Tulane	Tommy Bowden	Buddy Teevens
Vanderbilt	Woody Widenhofer	Rod Dowhower
Western Michigan	Gary Darnell	Al Molde
Wyoming	Dana Dimel	Joe Tiller

⬤ Longest winning streaks entering season:

Brigham Young 12	Penn State 5	Stanford 5

Preseason *USA Today* Coaches Poll

1	Florida (19)	1407	14	Miami (Fla.)	746
2	Penn State (9)	1335	15	Alabama	609
3	Washington (15)	1311	16	Syracuse	591
4	Florida State (3)	1298	17	Brigham Young	372
5	Tennessee (8)	1250	18	Stanford	370
6	Nebraska (4)	1240	19	Auburn	360
7	Colorado (3)	1153	20	Iowa	325
8	North Carolina (1)	1137	21	Clemson	318
9	Ohio State	1097	22	Southern California	272
10	Texas	973	23	Kansas State	238
11	LSU	874	24	Wisconsin	195
12	Notre Dame	780	25	Virginia Tech	180
13	Michigan	771			

August 23, 1997

Northwestern 24 Oklahoma 0 (Chicago): Underdog Oklahoma (0-1) saw Pigskin Classic chances fizzle on 2 missed FGs by K Jeremy Alexander, but crushing blow to Sooners came when QB Justin Fuente (11-22/149y, 2 INTs) threw INT from Wildcat 4YL while trailing only 6-0 early in 3rd Q. Northwestern (1-0) got spark from sub QB Chris Hamdorf (6-11/80y), who led 80y TD march, capped by sub TB Faraji Leary's 1y TD run. K Brian Gowins' 3rd FG soon created safe Wildcat margin at 17-0 in 3rd Q. (Sun) Syracuse 34

Wisconsin 0 (Meadowlands, N.J.): When WR Kevin Johnson charged 89y with opening KO, Syracuse (1-0) was off and winging. So were Orangemen QB Donovan McNabb (11-14/211y, TD passing, 5/27y rushing) and FB Rob Konrad, who powered for 8/76y rushing and threw block to spring McNabb on 21y TD run in 2nd Q. Ponderous Wisconsin (0-1) tried to blend newly-tooled pass attack into O, never advanced TB Ron Dayne (13/46y) with its young line, then lost Dayne to injury.

August 30, 1997

North Carolina State 32 SYRACUSE 31 (OT): Losers of 3 straight home openers, ambitious Orangemen (1-1) leapt to 14-0 edge in 1st Q. But as soph QB Jamie Barnette (18-29/279y, 3 TD, INT passing, 13/51y rushing) gained confidence, NC State (1-0) rallied to 17-17 tie in 3rd Q on Barnette's 2nd TD pass to WR Torry Holt. Syracuse WR Quinton Spotwood (6/155y, including 67y TD) scored on 72y punt RET midway in 4th Q, but Barnette matched it with TD pass for 24-24 knot. Spotwood made brilliant 52y catch between defenders at NC State 5YL with 1:07 to play in regulation, but coach Paul Pasqualoni nixed FG try. Instead, frosh TB Dee Brown lost FUM at GL. Orange scored 1st in OT on QB Donovan McNabb's 18y TD pass, but Wolfpack came right back to draw to within 31-30 on 1y TD run by TB Tremayne Stephens. While Pasqualoni screamed for timeout, Barnette tossed 2-pt pass to Holt for stunning win. Coach Mike O'Cain explained his 2-pt surprise: "...You need to choose your opportunity. Their defense was reeling and had lost its confidence."

WEST VIRGINIA 42 Marshall 31: Not since WVU's 81-0 win in 1923 had these in-state rivals met. Return to Div. 1-A opened darkly for Marshall (0-1) as Mountaineers (1-0) leapt to 28-3 lead late in 2nd Q. Herd thundered back as stellar WR Randy Moss caught 2 TD passes from QB Chad Pennington, his 2nd grab providing 31-28 lead late in 3rd Q. WVU DB Nate Terry made 2 vital 4th Q INTs to recharge Mountaineers. After Terry's 1st pickoff with 12:57 left to play, West Virginia took 4 plays to score from Herd 26YL as QB Marc Bulger hit TE Chad Wable with 15y TD pass. On next possession, Terry again made INT, this time at Marshall 35YL, and TB Amos Zereoue pounded across from 1YL. Zereoue totaled 174y rushing for Mountaineers, who were simply happy to survive. Afterward, veteran WVU coach Don Nehlen gushed, "I've never seen so much hype for a football game before."

KENTUCKY 38 Louisville 24: All-out aerial approach espoused by new coach Hal Mumme was embraced by ballyhooed QB Tim Couch (36-50/398y, 4 TDs, INT), who set Kentucky (1-0) single game records for completions and y. Louisville (0-1) QB Chris Redman (17-28/204y, 2 TDs, 2 INTs) hit TE Ibn Green with 17y TD pass to pull Cards within 21-17 late in 3rd Q. On game's next snap, Couch found WR Kio Sanford with short toss, and Sanford split two tacklers to roar 80y to TD and sizable 28-17 lead.

FLORIDA 21 Southern Mississippi 6: New Gator QB Doug Johnson (17-34/231y, 2 TDs, 3 INTs, and TD rushing) proved adequate if unspectacular as Florida (1-0) opened defense of its national title. Led by T Ed Chester, Gators D allowed only 26y rushing, forced 3 TOs, and spoiled every Southern Miss (0-1) opportunity until WR Todd Pinkston caught 13y TD pass from QB Lee Roberts (15-33/131y, 2 INTs) midway in 4th Q. Eagles made only 157y and were frustrated by being stopped by TOs and Florida D at 12, 10, 28, and 20YLs.

TENNESSEE 52 Texas Tech 17: Tennessee's Peyton Manning Love Fest got off to so-so start until QB Manning dealt brilliant and fortunate half-min late in 2nd Q. Red Raiders had just gotten on scoreboard as K Jaret Greaser nailed 38y FG to pull within 10-3 and start Neyland Stadium boobirds with 1:37 to go until H. Having already scored on QB Manning's 9y TD pass to WR Jermaine Copeland, no. 5 Volunteers (1-0) struck for 2 TDs within 13 secs. Key blunder: Texas Tech (0-1) was guilty of pass interference PEN on 3rd down incompletion to put Vols at Tech 23YL. Manning (26-38/30y, 5 TDs, INT) immediately hit WR Marcus Nash for TD, and when Red Raider TE Tim Winn bobbled fair catch of KO, Tennessee LB Raynoch Thompson recovered at Tech 28YL. Manning found Nash for 27y, and FB Mark Levine rammed over for 24-3 lead with :08 showing on H clock. Vols scored on their 1st 3 series of 2nd H, including WR Peerless Price's 5y catch of Manning's school-record tying 5th TD that lifted margin to 45-3 late in 3rd Q.

Miami 45 BAYLOR 14: When TB Dyral McMillan limped off with early hamstring strain, Miami (1-0) inserted star-in-waiting Edgerrin James (14/120y), who blistered overmatched Baylor (0-1) with TD runs of 23, 3, and 37y. Young Bears never wilted in blazing Texas sun, however, and clawed to within 31-14 in 4th Q as battered QB Jeff Watson threw TD pass and RB Jerod Douglas scored on 9y run. Hurricanes put it away on 72y fumble TD RET by DB Jeff Popovich and brilliant 85y punt TD RET by CB Duane Starks.

WASHINGTON STATE 37 Ucla 34: Frisky Cougars (1-0) O glided to 37-21 lead on QB Ryan Leaf's best career pass y to date: 17-32/381y, 3 TD. Leaf also ran for TD. UCLA (0-1) TB Skip Hicks keyed Bruins' comeback, rushing 27/190y, scoring 4 TDs. Bruins battled 93y in 13 plays to Washington State 1YL as clock ticked inside last 3 mins. With Hicks winded on sideline, UCLA coach Bob Toledo decided against FG that likely would have sent game to OT. Ball was handed to frosh TB Jermaine Lewis, but Cougars DL Leon Bender stuffed 4th down run with 2:48 to go.

September 6, 1997

(Th) Auburn 28 VIRGINIA 17: On game's 1st series, underdog Virginia (0-1) engineered blocked punt safety, then marched to Tiger GL only to lose pitchout FUM. Rebounding from bobble of opening snap for 15y loss, Auburn (1-0) QB Dameyune Craig scored at end of 98y march on 17y 2nd Q scramble. Game's key play opened 2nd H and gave Tigers 14-2 lead: LB Ryan Taylor stepped in front of flat pass by Cav QB Aaron Brooks (25-41/305y, 2TD, INT), dashed 25y for TD. After teams quickly traded long TD passes, Craig hit WR Karsten Bailey for 77y TD and 28-9 edge.

TEMPLE 28 Boston College 21: In their 40th Big East game, Owls (1-1) registered their 2nd win with 4th Q rally. Boston College (0-1) led 14-0 in 1st Q on TD run by FB Mike Hemmert and QB Matt Hasselbeck's TD pass. Temple rebounded on ensuing KO when RB Elmarko Jackson sprinted 95y for TD with :29 left in 1st Q. Temple WR Kevin Walker (6/138y, 2 TD) tied it at 21-21 in 4th Q on 34y catch from QB Pat Bonner (7-10/95y) With 1:18 to go, Owl RB Stacey Mack (16/121y) broke tackle and cut left for 27y TD run that shattered Temple's 11-game loss skein.

NOTRE DAME 17 Georgia Tech 13: Despite minor plumbing problem, Notre Dame's $50 million, 21,000-seat stadium improvement met approval of august New York Times: "...when the effort is made to maintain what is worth keeping and improve what requires fixing, the result is a merger of old and new." Fighting Irish (1-0) launched Bob Davie's coaching regime with come-from-behind win over D-minded Georgia Tech (0-1). Yellow Jackets built 13-10 4th Q lead, primarily on QB Joe Hamilton's 14y TD run in 2nd Q. Georgia Tech made 2 INTs of Irish QB Ron Powlus (18-29/217y, 2 INTs) in 4th Q, but K Dave Frakes missed 2 FGs that might have really mattered. Determined TB Autry Denson accounted for 44y of ND's winning 70y drive as game clock ticked down. Denson squeezed into EZ on run from 1YL with 2:37 to play.

COLORADO 31 Colorado State 21: Critical 3rd Q INTs by DBs Rashidi Barnes and Marcus Washington reversed fortunes for Colorado (1-0) over ambitious Colorado State (1-1). Rams led 14-7 at H on 2 TD passes in 2nd Q by QB Moses Moreno (14-22/215y, 2 TD, 2 INT). Barnes raced 20y to tying TD on his INT RET, and Washington set up 1st of 2 TD passes from QB John Hessler (18-28/223y, 2 TDs, INT) to WR Phil Savoy (5/73y). It was Buffs' 7th straight win in series.

Washington 42 BRIGHAM YOUNG 20: Year earlier, Huskies (1-0) TB Rashaan Shehee scored twice vs. BYU (0-1), then went on injured list. This time, Shehee scored twice, rushed 12/171y, including 75y sprint to set up TD that provided 28-7 lead in 3rd Q. Cougar sub QB Kevin Feterik lost FUM on next series, and Shehee caught 23y TD pass from QB Brock Huard (18-23/285y, 3 TDs). Feterik (13-20/216y, 2 TDs) threw 2 late scoring passes, but couldn't rally BYU to rescue its 12-game win streak.

Tennessee 30 UCLA 24: Returning to site of his collegiate debut in Pasadena, Volunteers (2-0) QB Peyton Manning threw 28-49/341y, 2 TDs, INT, but was outgained in air by UCLA (0-2) QB Cade McNown, who fired 27 completions/400y. DB Cory Gaines' 57y INT TD RET and Manning's 2 TD passes sparked Tennessee to easy 27-6 edge at end of 3rd Q. Then Bruins came to life, going 99y in 6 plays to TD by TB Skip Hicks (16/80y). Punt blunder in EZ led to UCLA safety, followed by Hicks' 50y TD with screen pass. FG drew UCLA within 27-24 midway in 4th Q, but Bruins failed to cash 2 late chances. However, what Bruins took out of their rally would become stepping stone to brilliance as season grew on.

Florida State 14 SOUTHERN CALIFORNIA 7: Sluggish no. 4 Seminoles (1-0) showed they might have O weak spots some predicted. Florida State took 7-0 lead in 1st Q on sub QB Dan Kendra's 1y TD run. It was matched by short 2nd Q TD run on 4th down by USC (0-1) QB John Fox (18-32/159y, INT). Meanwhile, FSU starting QB Thad Busby, was up-and-down in 19-39/276y, 2 INTs passing. With score at 7-7 in 4th Q, Busby came alive for 5-8/94y, including 46y strike to WR E.G. Green, as Seminoles went 97y to winning TD by TB Dee Feaster. Trojans DB Brian Kelly had certain TD INT slip through his hands early on FSU's winning drive. Victory was sealed when Seminoles DB Dexter Jackson made stopping, 4th down tackle at own 26YL with 2:20 left.

September 13, 1997

BOSTON COLLEGE 31 West Virginia 24: With Virginia Tech blasting Syracuse 31-3, unpredictable Boston College (1-1) scrambled Big East picture. Eagles overcame 17-3 H deficit, riding legs of sub TB Mike Cloud, who carried only once until TB Omari Walker (19/89y) left in 2nd Q with injured knee. Cloud rushed 24/211y, scored on runs of 11 and 66y that broke open 17-17 tie in 4th Q. Although West Virginia (2-1) TB Amos Zereoue was held to 19/68y rushing, he had 1y TD run in 1st Q. WVU QB Marc Bulger threw 2 TD passes among his 17-28/218y, INT.

Arizona State 23 MIAMI 12: Still smarting from snub by preseason polls, Arizona State (2-0) showed sparkling team speed, broke TBs Mike Martin, J.R. Redmond for combined 208y, 1st pair of RBs to each gain 100y vs. Miami (1-1) since Syracuse in 1979. Poised QB Ryan Kealy (18-26/239y, INT) threw tie-breaking TD pass to WR Ricky Boyer in 3rd Q.

Hurricanes trailed 16-6 midway in 4th Q when UM DB Nick Ward scampered 85y to score with FUM REC. This score briefly provided hope, even though Miami's sluggish O would finish with only 288y total O and only 68y rushing.

Clemson 19 NORTH CAROLINA STATE 17: Traditional ground power Clemson (2-0) unleashed potent air game for 2nd week in row. QB Nealon Green pitched 20-32/250y, but was at his best in last 9 min when he guided Tigers to 2 K Matt Padgett FGs by completing 7 of 10. Padgett's 20y chip shot winner came with 19 sec to play. NC State (2-1) struggled to 17-13 lead midway in 4th Q on TD pass from QB Jamie Barnette (14-28/204y) to WR Torry Holt (4/103y).

NORTH CAROLINA 28 Stanford 17: With starting QB Chris Keldorf stumbling, North Carolina (2-0) backup QB Oscar Davenport (12-14/116y, TD) provided spark with 9 straight completions while playing only 5 series. Stanford (1-1) QB Chad Hutchinson opened scoring with 11y TD pass to FB Jon Ritchie, then hit passes for 34y, then ran for 5y TD on 60y 3rd Q drive that tied it at 14-14. Ensuing KO was lost to Cardinal FB Greg Comella's REC, and K Kevin Miller's 27y FG gave Stanford 17-14 lead. Davenport's 15y TD pass to WR Octavus Barnes put UNC ahead for good with 12:15 left.

GEORGIA 31 South Carolina 15: Georgia (2-0) won its opening 2 tilts for 1st time since 1991. Essentially, it was over at H as Bulldogs built 31-6 score at midway. South Carolina (1-1) expected to have to stop run game, and Georgia QB Mike Bobo (19-33/285y, 2 TDs) took advantage by hitting TEs for 4/51y in 1st Q. With Gamecocks D often out of position, Bobo tossed screen and dump-off passes to WR Hines Ward (5/65y) and TBs Olandis Gary (17/96y, TDs running and receiving) and Patrick Pass for 199y. Carolina managed but 56y rushing, but QB Anthony Wright passed 21-40/275y, 2 TDs, 2 INTs.

MICHIGAN 27 Colorado 3: So shattering was Michigan's performance that Colorado (1-1) coach Rick Neuheisel said, "We have to rebuild ourselves emotionally." Game was tale of 2 QBs: Wolverines (1-0) sr Brian Griese had his best career day to date, throwing 21-28/258y, 2 TDs, INT. On other hand, Buffs QB John Hessler was blitzed by vet Wolverines D, finished day on bench after 15-40/141y, 4 INTs. Michigan TE Jerame Tuman (5/126y) caught 53y pass to set up TD after DB Charles Woodson's early INT. Reprising his 2-way stardom of 1996, Woodson caught 29y pass :06 before H to set up FG. Griese hit 6-7/70y to open 2nd H on 89y TD drive. Buffs' only score came late in 3rd Q on K Jason Lesley's 52y FG.

PURDUE 28 Notre Dame 17: New Notre Dame (1-1) coach Bob Davie wouldn't soon forget Purdue fans flooding field after sloppy Irish were upset, thanks in part to allowing 145y in screen pass plays. Inspired Boilermakers (1-1) were outstanding when they needed it. Purdue went 99y to opening TD, smash by TB Edwin Watson who later added another. With score at 14-10 in 4th Q, Purdue DL Roosevelt Colvin slapped ball from scrambling ND QB Ron Powlus (31-43/293y, all career highs in passing), and DB Adrian Beasley made FUM RET for TD and 21-10 lead. Frosh speedster WR Vinny Sutherland set up last Boilermakers TD with 40y advance with screen.

Ucla 66 TEXAS 3: After 2 frustrating, narrow defeats, Bruins (1-2) registered week's top "It's Not a Typo" win. Weak vs. passing to date, UCLA found no. 11 Texas (1-1) playing without injured QB James Brown. Game star was maligned QB Cade McNown, who tossed school-record 5 TDs among 15-23/202y in air. Bruins blew open 10-0 game early in 2nd Q when TB Skip Hicks (22/96y, 2 TD rushing) barreled over tacklers at end of 43y TD pass. McNown hit TE Mike Grieb 20 sec later for 1st of his 2 TD catches. Longhorns got 35y FG from Phil Dawson in 3rd Q, but suffered 8 TOs, 7 sacks in worst-ever home defeat, worst margin since 68-0 loss to Chicago in 1904, and worst loss by ranked team in 61-year history of AP polls.

Washington State 28 SOUTHERN CALIFORNIA 21: Cougars (2-0) fashioned 1st sweep of LA schools in its 103-year history. Trojans (0-2) bounced back from 21-6 H deficit as WR R. Jay Soward dashed 95y with 2nd H KO. Early in 4th Q, USC TB Lavelle Woods flipped 15y TD pass to WR Mike Bastianelli. QB John Fox then tossed 2-pt pass to WR Billy Miller (10/138y) to tie it at 21-21. After catching 31y pass on 3rd down, State WR Ryan McKenzie made 1-handed grab from QB Ryan Leaf (21-40/355y, 3 TD), got block from WR Shawn McWashington, went 51y to game-winning TD. Cougars D held Trojans to no 1st downs in last 2 possessions.

USA Today Coaches Poll September 15

1	Florida (25)	1451	14	Virginia Tech	705
2	Penn State (14)	1440	15	Clemson	543
3	Washington (12)	1430	16	Colorado	524
4	Tennessee (6)	1352	17	Arizona State	514
5	Florida State (2)	1316	18	Michigan State	490
6	Nebraska (1)	1195	19	Kansas State	458
7	North Carolina (1)	1177	20	Washington State	398
8	Ohio State (1)	1125	21	Miami (Fla.)	256
9	Michigan	1069	22	Texas A&M	206
10	LSU	1035	23	Stanford	175
11	Alabama	898	24	Texas	120
12	Auburn	782	25	Georgia	118
13	Iowa	777			

September 20, 1997

(Th) PITTSBURGH 21 Miami 17: Having lost 8 in row to Miami (1-2), Pittsburgh (3-1) used former South Florida HS QB Pete Gonzalez to spark fired-up O. But 1st, Hurricanes whirled to 7-0 edge on opening drive as QB Ryan Clement (17-38/ 250y, 2 INT) found FB Carlo Joseph with 57y TD pass. Gonzalez (19-33/187y) hit 2 TD passes for 14-7 lead, but Canes knotted it in 3rd Q when holder Jeff Popovich completed 15y TD off FG fake. Gonzalez scrambled 12y up middle for 21-14 edge after FUM by Miami TB Dyral McMillan. After late clinching INT by DB John Jenkins, happy Pitt fans stormed field.

North Carolina 40 MARYLAND 14: Tar Heels (3-0) coach Mack Brown kept team in suspense over which QB—Chris Keldorf or Oscar Davenport—would start. Jr Davenport (21-33/281y, 2 TDs) received his 2nd career start and was outstanding. His 3 perfect passes covered 96y in very quick fashion on drive capped by 19y TD reception by WR Jason Peace. Maryland (0-3) had opened scoring in 2nd Q on 86y march to 3y TD run by QB Brian Cummings (13-20/120y), but trailed 14-7 at H. After Keldorf (2-5/56y, TD) drove UNC 80y to its 14y TD pass to WR L.C. Stevens in 1 of his 3 series at Tar Heels helm, Terrapins DB Lewis Sanders bolted 90y to score with following KO.

Florida State 35 CLEMSON 28: Nimble WR Peter Warrick turned in spectacular act as Bobby Bowden won his 200th game as Florida State (3-0) coach. Warrick contributed 372y all-purpose, including 48y TD catch from QB Thad Busby (17-28/332y, 2 TD, INT) for 21-14 3rd Q lead and 80y TD bomb for 35-28 4th Q lead. In between, Warrick made over-shoulder punt catch, squirted right and broke away for 90y TD. New-found passing acumen served Clemson (2-1) well as QB Nealon Greene (14-28/213y, 2 INT) limped off bench with bad toe to fire 2 TD passes.

FLORIDA 33 Tennessee 20: Dark cloud over Vols QB Peyton Manning's 4-yr career continued to be tenacious Florida (3-0). Manning registered fine aerial numbers (29-51/353y, 3 TD), but 2 INTs killed Tennessee (2-1). Critical was Gators DB Tony George's 89y INT TD RET late in 1st Q that provided 14-0 lead. Florida QB Doug Johnson (14-32/261y, 2 INT) located 3 different receivers for scores that meant 7-0, 20-7, and 33-14 leads. Florida extended SEC win streak to 23 and endangered Volunteers hopes for winning SEC East title.

Auburn 31 LOUISIANA STATE 28: Nail-biting battle of Tigers went to Auburn (3-0) in last min when LSU (2-1) was flagged for 12-man PEN deep in own territory. TB Rusty Williams (14/47y) brought Auburn win by diving over for his 2nd TD with 30 secs left. LSU played without TB Kevin Faulk, but sub TB Cecil "The Diesel" Collins charged for 27/232y, 2 TDs, including 42y romp which gave LSU its 1st lead at 28-24 early in 4th Q. Auburn QB Dameyune Craig passed 23-45/342y, 2 TDs.

Michigan State 23 NOTRE DAME 7: Surprising Spartans (3-0) used big O line led by T Flozell Adams and G Scott Shaw to batter inexperienced Irish (1-2) D for 353y, balanced by 222y on ground. TBs Marc Renaud (22/112y), Sedrick Irvin (26/106y) led assault. ND gained only 23/61y on ground, got late 2nd Q TD from QB Ron Powlus (23-37/181y, INT) when LB Cory Minor's INT left Irish at Michigan State 29YL.

Brigham Young 13 ARIZONA STATE 10: During coach Lavelle Edwards era, Brigham Young (1-1) had 17-6 record after bye weeks. This win, 18th for Edwards after bye, was keyed on D that held Arizona State (2-1) to 35/92y rushing, including -36y in sacks. Cougar RB Brian McKenzie (23/112y) scored on 6y run, but Arizona State (2-1) went ahead 10-7 midway in 2nd Q on TB Mike Martin's 1y plunge. K Owen Pochman tied it 10-10 on 45y FG with 4:35 remaining in H after Sun Devil WR Ricky Boyer lost FUM on reverse run. At end of 77y drive in 4th Q, Pochman won it with 32y FG for 1st BYU win in Tempe since 1965.

Nebraska 27 WASHINGTON 14: Huskers (3-0) QB Scott Frost, booed at home during prior week's 38-24 win over Central Florida, scurried to TD runs of 34 and 30y, prompting Washington (2-1) LB Jason Chorak to say: "I don't see why there's any quarterback controversy in Nebraska." Behind 14-0 and losing battle of line of scrimmage, Huskies lost QB Brock Huard in 1st Q to ankle sprain on tackle by A-A DL Grant Wistrom. Frosh QB Marques Tuiasosopo, son of former UCLA star DL Manu, replaced Huard, passed 12-22/270y, 2 TDs. Tuiasosopo's 2nd score, 2y toss to sub TB Mike Reed, pulled Washington to within 21-14 late in 3rd Q. But on-side KO failed, and Huskers cruised away with ground attack (384y) and K Kris Brown's 2 FGs. Washington gained only 43y rushing in only its 6th loss in last 46 home games.

USA Today Coaches Poll September 22

1	Florida (43)	1517	14	Washington State	688
2	Penn State (14)	1478	15	LSU	674
3	Nebraska (3)	1407	16	Colorado	524
4	Florida State (1)	1372	17	Kansas State	474
5	North Carolina (1)	1285	18	Texas A&M	454
6	Michigan	1203	19	Alabama	380
7	Ohio State	1198	20	Georgia	366
8	Auburn	1036	21	Clemson	330
9	Iowa	987	22	Stanford	266
10	Tennessee	955	23	Arizona State	213
11	Washington	951	24	Brigham Young	162
12	Virginia Tech	851	25	Air Force	120
13	Michigan State	808			

September 27, 1997

(Th) WAKE FOREST 19 North Carolina State 18: In 2nd Q, NC State (3-2) QB Jamie Barnette turned hot, hitting 6th pass in row for TD to ace WR Torry Holt, then found speedy WR Alvis Whitted to set up FG for 10-3 H edge. Wake Forest (2-2) tied it 10-10 on WR Desmond Clark's TD catch, but Whitted answered with 69y KO RET that led to TB Tremayne Stephens' TD and holder Jason Biggs' 2-pt run off swinging gate play. Deacons went 90y to WR Thabiti Davis' TD catch, but tying 2-pt try failed. With 48 secs to play, Wake won on 37y FG by K Matthew Burdick, who had worked out anonymously with rivals while enrolled with his girlfriend in NC State summer school.

GEORGIA TECH 23 Clemson 20: Short 1st Q punt began Clemson (2-2) special teams woes, led to Georgia Tech (2-1) FG. When QB Joe Hamilton rolled right and found his cousin WR Harvey Middleton for TD, Georgia Tech led 10-0. After passing up FG early in 2nd Q, Tigers drew within 10-7 on FB Terry Witherspoon's short blast to cap 84y drive. But Engineers DB Jason Bostic blocked punt early in 3rd Q, and DB Travares Tillman raced to 17-7 lead. Trailing 20-14 in middle of 4th Q, Clemson TB Raymond Priester swept right behind block of TE Lamont Hall for 20-20 tie, but K Matt Padgett shanked x-pt. K Brad Chambers, in for injured David Frakes, booted FG in last 2 mins.

NORTH CAROLINA 48 Virginia 20: Jittery North Carolina (4-0) seemed jinxed again by Virginia (1-2) as Cavs took 20-3 lead in 2nd Q. DB Anthony Poindexter made brilliant punt block—slapping ball before it reached P's foot—and DB Dwayne Stukes raced 33y to Virginia TD. Cavs frosh TB Antwaine Womack ran for 72y on 88y TD drive. Tar Heels D prompted comeback after they within nipped within 20-13 early in 3rd Q,. DB Dre Bly, nation's 1996 INT leader, took pass from hip of Cavs WR Bryan Owens, raced to tying TD. After TE Alge Crumpler nabbed TD from trio of DBs, UNC opened floodgates with 21 pts.

IOWA 38 Illinois 10: On big Saturday for RBs—TB Ricky Williams of Texas raced for 259y in 38-31 win over Rice—Iowa (4-0) TB Tavian Banks, former HS soccer star with great vision of field, started demolition of hapless Illinois (0-4) with darting 76y run, finished with 25/191y, 2 TDs. Banks raised his nation's best rushing total to 835y, more than 92 teams. Illini hung close at 7-3 until Hawkeyes WR Tony Collins ignited 17-pt run with 61y punt TD RET with 8:08 left in H. RB Robert Holcombe rushed 32/157y as Illini became 1st team with more than 100y rushing vs. Hawkeyes in last 7 games.

MICHIGAN 21 Notre Dame 14: Not since end of Gerry Faust's 1985 season had Notre Dame (1-3) lost 3 games in row. Inspired Irish gained 14-7 H lead on TD pass by QB Ron Powlus (20-27/205y, TD, INT) and TD run by frosh TB Tony Driver. But Michigan (3-0) pounced for 2 TDs within opening 5:39 of 3rd Q. After TB Clarence Williams' 28y KO RET, QB Brian Griese (16-22/177y) pitched 41y TD to WR Tai Streets. Then FB Chris Floyd charged 14y to score. Down 21-14, ND wasted 3 golden opportunities in 4th Q; it got FUM RECs in UM territory each time. Irish outgained Wolverines 354 to 345y.

COLORADO 20 Wyoming 19: Using K Cory Wedel's 4 FGs as foundation, upset-bent Wyoming (3-2) appeared to seal win with RB Marques Brigham's 18y TD run with slightly more than 4 min to play. Trailing 19-10, slumbering Colorado (2-1) stunned Cowboys with frosh DB Ben Kelly's 99y TD RET on ensuing KO. Soon Brigham lost FUM while stretching for 1st down, and Buffs positioned K Jeremy Aldrich for short winning FG with 3 secs left.

AIR FORCE 24 San Diego State 18 (OT): Air Force (5-0), 1 of early season surprises that would fade in home stretch, won its 3rd straight OT game on clutch TD INT by DB Tim Curry. On 4th play of OT, San Diego State (1-3) QB Kevin McKechnie (15-33/114y, INT) threw fateful pass. Held to 154y (only 24y rushing), Aztecs turned around 12-0 deficit late in 3rd Q when LB Joseph Tuipala grabbed blocked punt, dashed 15y to pare it to 12-7. SDSU frosh K Nate Tandbeck sent it to OT with 49y FG with only 1 sec left in regulation.

USA Today Coaches Poll September 29

1	Florida (45)	1519	14	LSU	709
2	Penn State (13)	1471	15	Washington State	707
3	Nebraska (3)	1410	16	Kansas State	543
4	Florida State	1365	17	Texas A&M	489
5	North Carolina (1)	1262	18	Colorado	469
6	Michigan	1194	19	Georgia	416
7	Ohio State	1189	20	Alabama	411
8	Iowa	1048	21	Stanford	278
9	Auburn	1028	22	Arizona State	200
10	Tennessee	965	23	Air Force	190
11	Washington	918	24	Brigham Young	187
12	Virginia Tech	877	25	UCLA	117
13	Michigan State	822			

October 4, 1997

Miami (Ohio) 24 VIRGINIA TECH 17: No sooner had *The Sporting News* identified Virginia Tech's "road to perfection (as) the most uncluttered among the remaining unbeaten heavyweights," when Hokies (4-1) became rattled as if Miami of Ohio (4-1) was Miami of Florida of 1980s. RedHawks had 6 sacks and 2 blocked punts with 1 going for TD by LB Dustin Cohen. Hokies had opened with methodical TD drive and led 10-0 in 1st Q. After Miami's punt-block made it 10-7, RedHawks created trick-play TD. Prepped for long FG, holder Mike Bath instead went under C, slipped ball to RB Travis Prentice (21/82y, 2 TD) who faked block, then raced 32y to TD and 14-10 2nd Q lead. Although Virginia Tech regained 17-14 edge on RB Ken Oxendine's 2nd TD run, Miami rode passing of QB Sam Ricketts (13-24/190y) to dominance of 2nd H.

KENTUCKY 40 Alabama 34 (OT): After 6 lead changes, Wildcats (3-2) beat Crimson Tide (3-2) for 1st time in 75 years to improve mark vs. Alabama to 2-31-1. QB Tim Crouch hit 32-49/355y, 4 TD, 3 INT, broke Kentucky season completion mark. Among his scoring passes were 62y to RB Derek Homer and 26y to WR Craig Yeast for game-winner after Tide fumbled away its OT possession. Bama overcame 27-17 deficit, going ahead 31-27 early in 4th Q on TD pass by QB Freddie Kitchens (13-24/125y, 2 TD, INT). Kentucky DL Anwar Stewart rambled 68y with blocked FG for 34-31 lead with 6:54 left, but Tide K Brian Cunningham sent it to OT with his 2nd FG.

Louisiana State 7 VANDERBILT 6: Still smarting over nature of coach Gerry DiNardo's 1995 departure for LSU (4-1), Vanderbilt (2-3) was fired up for game DiNardo described afterward as bizarre. Tigers lost SEC's leading rusher TB Cecil "The Diesel" Collins to broken leg, but welcomed back TB Kevin Faulk who rushed 31/135y. QB Herb Tyler put Tigers on board at 7-0 with 3rd Q TD pass to WR Larry Foster. Consecutive delay PENs scotched Commodores coach Woody Widenhofer's plan for 2-pt conv after 12y TD catch by WR Tavarus Hogans came with :12 to play. When K John Markham tried 30y tying kick, it was blocked by LSU DB Kenny Mixon.

OHIO STATE 23 Iowa 7: Star Ohio State (5-0) LB Andy Katzenmoyer helped hold nation's leading rusher, TB Tavian Banks of Iowa (4-1), to 11/10y rushing in 1st H that was led 10-0 by Buckeyes. "He was probably in our backfield more than I was," said Banks, who finished with 22/84y. Katzenmoyer went on O late in 2nd Q for GL block to spring sub TB Michael Wiley (14/85y) for 1st of his 2 TD runs. Katzenmoyer had 11 tackles, INT that doomed Hawkeyes' flickering 4th Q hopes.

NEBRASKA 56 Kansas State 26: Nebraska (4-0) quickly dismissed 1 of its last conf roadblocks by squashing Kansas State (3-1) for 29th consecutive time. Huskers built 41-6 margin late in 3rd Q, limiting Wildcats at that point to 0y rushing, just 76y passing. Huskers IB Ahman Green tallied 4 TDs among his 20/193y rushing. K-State QB Michael Bishop (8-24/162y, 2 INTs) ran, threw for 4th Q window-dressing TDs.

Texas A&M 16 COLORADO 13: Aggies (4-0) were among group of undefeated teams (Iowa, Kansas State, New Mexico, and Oklahoma State) whose perception was clouded by level of opposition. Of these unknowns, Texas A&M proved its point, beating no. 16 Colorado (2-2) whose own value was flickering fast. Trailing 3-0, Texas A&M took lead for good on 2 FGs in 2nd Q by K Kyle Bryant. Aggies used array of TBs, led by Dante Hall (22/123y) and Sirr Parker (17/89y, TD), to compile 260y on ground. QB John Hessler pitched 15-27/194y, INT, but Buffs could manage only TB Herchell Troutman's 4th Q TD run despite 3 promising chances in late going.

OKLAHOMA STATE 42 Texas 16: Surprising Oklahoma State (5-0) built its 1st 2-0 conf record since 1972 by schooling its quick D to completely shut down Longhorns (2-2) TB Ricky Williams, who had rolled up 259y against Rice in previous week's game. Cowboys allowed Williams only 4y rushing in 1st H, and he finished with 16/79y. Texas was forced out of its run attack game plan when OSU scored 3 TDs in 1st Q. Frosh Cowboy QB Tony Lindsay scored 2 TDs rushing, and DB R.W. McQuarters raced 78y on punt TD RET late in opening Q. Sharp Lindsay rushed 19/126y on option runs, including 55y TD dash in 3rd Q, and passed 4-5/85y. Trailing 29-0, Texas QB James Brown (13-34/154y, TD, INT) finally put Steers on scoreboard with 2y pass to WR Courtney Epps.

NEW MEXICO 22 Southern Methodist 15: Opening year with 5 straight wins for 1st time since 1945, New Mexico (5-0) got 16 pts from K Colby Cason, who kicked FGs of 25, 25, 27, 28, and 36y. TB Che Johnson bolted to 9y TD run early in 4th Q for 16-7 lead, part of 227y run attack that moved Lobos to 5th in nation in rushing. SMU (1-4) jumped to 7-3 H lead on RB Donte Womack's 5y TD run, but its 212y O prevented it from scoring again until 1:03 was left. QB Chris Sanders tossed TD pass.

WASHINGTON 26 Arizona State 14: Sun Devil DL Albrey Battle stuffed reverse and created FUM at Washington (3-1) 20YL, both in active 2nd Q. Arizona State (3-2) soon had 7-6 lead on TB J.R. Redmond's slashing TD run behind block of FB Jeff "Jurassic" Paulk. But, soon Huskies began stuffing plays, compiling 9 sacks of frosh QB Ryan Kealy (13-20/180y, TD, INT). Game turned late in 2nd Q when Washington used 28y TD blast by sub TB Maurice Shaw (17/94y) for 13-7 lead just 1:37 before H. DB Nigel Burton picked off pass 9 sec later to poise leaping TD run by TB Rashaan Shehee (29/146y rushing, 3/70y receiving). Suddenly, Huskies led 19-7 at H.

USA Today Coaches Poll October 6

1	Florida (48)	1523	14	LSU	720
2	Penn State (11)	1469	15	Georgia	676
3	Nebraska (2)	1407	16	Iowa	664
4	Florida State	1374	17	Stanford	542
5	North Carolina (1)	1271	18	Air Force	397
6	Michigan	1245	19	UCLA	314
7	Ohio State	1216	20t	Oklahoma State	295
8	Auburn	1082	20t	Virginia Tech	295
9	Washington	983	22	Brigham Young	286
10	Tennessee	982	23	Kansas State	213
11	Michigan State	927	24	West Virginia	165
12	Washington State	844	25	Colorado	79
13	Texas A&M	721			

October 11, 1997

Air Force 10 NAVY 7: Alert DB Tim Curry was hero for undefeated Air Force (7-0), scoring TD by recovering punt blocked by teammate Charlie Jackson in 3rd Q. Curry also fell on FUM at own 42YL with 1:02 left when Navy (2-3) was driving for potential win. Earlier, Middies QB Chris McCoy (6-16/70y, INT, and 16/104y rushing) scored on 8y run before his late FUM to Curry sunk Navy.

Florida State 51 DUKE 27: Florida State (5-0) played well in spurts, prompting coach Bobby Bowden to say, "When you score over 50 points, you should be proud…Maybe by Wednesday I'll be proud." Duke (2-4) never quit despite a rash of injuries, and gained 246y at expense of nation's no. 1 D. Good beginning and end of 1st H gave Blue Devils 14 pts when QB Bobby Campbell plunged 1y for TD before being shelved with injured shoulder, and when 4th string QB Kevin Thompson (5-16/79y, 2 TDs, INT) arched 61y scoring toss to RB Scottie Montgomery (6/94y receiving). In between, Seminoles got 5 TDs, sparked by passing of QB Thad Busby (15-32/250y, TD), including 54y score on great catch and run by WR Peter Warrick (5/134y, TD). When FSU manufactured 2 quick TDs in 3rd Q on FUM RET and punt RET, Busby and starters were pulled. But, when Duke D stopped FSU O and Devils scored to cut deficit to 48-21, Bowden inserted his regulars. Duke's Montgomery excelled on KO RETs at pace of 5/146y.

TENNESSEE 38 Georgia 13: Bulldogs (4-1) entered game with SEC's top statistical D, but left with tail between legs having relinquished 628y. As usual, Tennessee (4-1) counted on QB Peyton Manning for prolific air game: 31-40/343y, 4 TDs. Vols also discovered TB Jamal Lewis, Georgia native, who rushed for school frosh record 232y on 22 tries. Georgia high moment came from TB Robert Edwards (17/131y), who ran for 49y TD in 2nd Q.

SOUTH CAROLINA 38 Kentucky 24: With "Don't panic!" support from coach Brad Scott, Gamecocks (3-3) rallied after Kentucky (3-3) vaulted to 14-0 lead in 1st Q. South Carolina found its running game as TB Boo Williams (24/93y) augmented QB draws of Anthony Wright (11/63y rushing). Wright's 1st draw dash went for 18y on 3rd down to keep alive march that netted sub TB Troy Hambrick's 17y tiptoe TD run down sideline. Wright threw 1st of his 3 TD passes to WR Kerry Hood midway in 2nd Q to knot it at 14-14. South Carolina S Arturo Freeman had pass by Wildcats QB Tim Couch land on his helmet and spun to make INT. Freeman followed legion of blockers to 47y TD RET and Carolina's 1st

lead at 21-14. Couch was on passing beam for 31-46/294y, 2 TDs, INT, and WR Craig Yeast returned punt 85y for TD that provided briefly encouraging 14-0 Kentucky lead in 1st Q. Couch and Yeast also whipped up 31y TD pass in 2nd Q.

LOUISIANA STATE 28 Florida 21: Inspired LSU (5-1) used Saturday night mystique of Death Valley to beat no. 1 team for 1st time in its history. Snapped were 2 long Florida (5-1) SEC streaks: 25 wins, 19 road wins. Rolling to 123y to 7y rush advantage in 1st H, LSU led 14-7. On opening snap of 3rd Q, Gator QB Doug Johnson (32-57/346y, 4 INTs) threw to TB Fred Taylor for 53y to set up 14-14 tie on Taylor's 2nd of 3 TD runs. But Florida's no. 1 rank evaporated in 1:33 span of 4th Q when Tigers DB Cedric Donaldson raced 31y to INT TD RET. Gators WR Bo Carroll dropped FUM on ensuing KO, and LSU QB Herb Tyler dashed 11y for 28-14 edge.

PENN STATE 31 Ohio State 27: As inspiration, Nittany Lions (5-0) TB Curtis Enis, Ohio native, saved hateful letter sent to him since trouncing by Ohio State (5-1) in 1996. Buckeyes QB Joe Germaine came off bench to throw 29-43/378y, 2 INTs and TDs that provided 10-10 tie and 20-17 lead. When Penn State fell behind 27-17 late in 3rd Q, emotional Enis joined revived O squad for 2-TD rally. Lions quickly sprung FB Aaron Harris on 51y TD jaunt and sent Enis (23/211y) for 26y TD at end of 86y march. Lions blockers, led by Gs Eric Cole and Phil Ostrowski and FB Harris, took on Ohio A-A LB Andy Katzenmoyer straight ahead all day and rolled to 41/316y rushing.

OKLAHOMA STATE 33 Colorado 29: For 1st time since 1945, Oklahoma State (6-0) opened with 6 wins. Cowboys led 19-14 at H, go-ahead TD coming on 40y TD RET by DB Kevin Williams of INT of Buff QB John Hessler (22-45/308y, TD, 2 INTs). But Hessler came back with 73y TD to TB Dwayne Cherrington that gave Colorado 29-26 with 9:46 to play. Buffs seemed home free after getting FUM at own 7YL with 3:52 left, but Cowboys DB Maurice Simpson picked off pass to set up winning 19y TD pass from frosh QB Tony Lindsay (5-12/105y, TD, INT) to TE Alonzo Mayes.

RICE 27 Brigham Young 14: Never trailing, resourceful Rice (4-2) snapped 11-game WAC win streak of BYU (3-2) by rushing 384y. FB Benji Wood slammed middle for 27/167y rushing, TDs of 1, 30y. QB Kevin Feterik (9-17/164y) kept Cougars close at 9-7 with 70y TD pass to WR Aaron Roderick in 1st Q. Leading 16-14 at H, Owls held BYU to 9y O in 2nd H; D scored when DL Judd Miller toppled 3rd string Cougar QB Drew Miller for safety with 3:21 left.

October 18, 1997

PENN STATE 16 Minnesota 15: Disagreeable Gophers (2-5) had no. 1 Penn State (6-0) on ropes, converting K Adam Bailey's 5 FGs, including 52 and 50y boots, for leads of 9-3 at H and 15-3 early in 4th Q. Lifeless Lions were ignited by 75y TD march at 15-10 as TB Curtis Enis (26/112y, 2 TDs) rushed 3/33y and drew dubious pass interference call at Gopher 6YL. Later, Minnesota stopped 4th down EZ pass with 5 mins left and set out to kill clock from own 6YL. But, RB Thomas Hamner (32/154y) peeked at hole, bobbled pitchout, and Lions DL Chris Snyder fell on FUM. Enis blasted 10y for TD with 3:59 left.

Florida 24 AUBURN 10: Playing without suspended QB Doug Johnson, Florida (6-1) knocked Auburn (6-1) from unbeaten ranks. Frosh James Palmer (8-14/92y, 2 INTs) and Sr Noah Brindise (5-11/69y, TD) filled in for Johnson, but star was WR Jacquez Green who accounted for TDs 3 different ways. Green threw his 1st career pass for 12y TD to WR Jamie Robinson in 1st Q, caught 10y TD from reliever Brindise in 3rd Q that broke 10-10 tie, ran for 5y TD late in 4th Q. Auburn (6-1) QB Dameyune Craig (18-34/187y) drew Tigers within 10-7 with 1st Q TD pass, but suffered 9 sacks/-80y, lost FUM, threw INT. Auburn's run game was 27/-28y.

Mississippi 36 LOUISIANA STATE 21: Ole Miss (4-2), so often at center of LSU's historical rollercoaster, sent Tigers (5-2) from penthouse to outhouse with win week after LSU's surprise of no. 1 Florida. Rebels TB John Avery rushed 26/128y, TDs of 13 and 5y, and QB Stewart Patridge (27-43/346y) passed for 2 TDs, including 60y to WR Grant Heard. LSU led 21-14 on 2 TDs by TB Kevin Faulk (25/172y), 72y TD dash by QB Herb Tyler (17/101y rushing despite 6 sacks), but were blanked in 2nd H.

Tennessee 38 ALABAMA 21: K Brian Cunningham put Crimson Tide (3-3) ahead 6-0 with 42 and 35y FGs on opening 2 series. During 15-min span launched in 1st Q, Tennessee (5-1) ran 36 plays to Bama's 7 and scored 3 TDs, including 2 runs by TB Shawn Bryson (6/33y). When QB Peyton Manning (23-37/304y) threw 2nd of 3 TD passes midway in 3rd Q, Vols led 28-6 on way to 3rd win in row in 80-year series.

MICHIGAN 28 Iowa 24: Undefeated Michigan (6-0) fell behind 21-7 at H as QB Brian Griese (15-26/165y, 2 TDs) suffered 3 INTs. Iowa (4-2) surged to 3 TDs in 2nd Q as TB Tavian Banks (held somewhat in check with 19/99y rushing) raced 53y to score and WR Tim Dwight sprinted 61y on punt TD RET on last play of 2nd Q. Wolverines opened 2nd H with 67y march ending in Griese TD pass, and tied it at 21-21 on Griese's 1y sneak. Dwight returned following KO to Michigan 26YL to set up FG by K Zach Bromert. Overcoming 3 2nd H sacks by DL Jared DeVries, Griese hit TE Jerame Tuman with

winning TD pass with 2:55 left. Dormant Hawkeyes air game came alive with 61y on late drive, but QB Matt Sherman (8-21/86y, 3 INTs) suffered INT by LB Sam Sword with :31 on clock.

Southern California 20 NOTRE DAME 17: Famous, but faded rivals each gained 315y in even match won by USC (3-3), inspired to "win one for the fat man," its beleaguered coach John Robinson. Notre Dame (2-5) got opening TD run from TB Autry Denson (30/133y) and led 17-14 on K Jim Sanson's late 2nd Q 27y FG. Trojans QB John Fox (11-21/115y, TD) pitched 2nd Q score to WR R. Jay Soward. K Adam Abrams tied it at 17-17 with FG midway in 3rd Q, and he won it with 37y boot with 1:05 to play in 4th Q.

KANSAS STATE 36 Texas A&M 17: While no. 2 Nebraska was blanking Texas Tech 29-0, fading Big 12 saw no. 20 Wildcats (5-1) wrench control from no. 14 Aggies (5-1) of dubious status as 2nd-best. Texas A&M TB Dante Hall limped off after game's 1st play, and Aggies run game fell apart with total of 17/-35y. K-State QB Michael Bishop (10-21/173y, INT) scored in 1st Q on 12y run, but hobbled off with ankle injury just before H. Bishop returned in 2nd H, turned to aerial game that produced 3 TD drives. Aggies managed only 4 1st downs and could score 2nd H TDs only because of DB Michael Williams' 27y blocked punt TD RET and his INT RET to Wildcats' 1YL.

Rice 35 NEW MEXICO 23: Roaring Rice (5-2) run game piled up 384y while its neglected air game went to 1 by QB Chad Nelson (17/109y rushing). Sub Owl FB Rodd Newhouse dashed 34y, HB Michael Perry (24/133y) tallied from 11y, and FB Benji Wood blasted 1y for 21-0 1st Q lead. New Mexico (6-1) QB Graham Leigh (21-36/317y, 3INT) pitched 3 TD passes to WR Pascal Volz (10/149y). Last of 3 TDs came early in 4th Q, but failed 2-pt pass left Lobos behind 28-23 until Perry put it away with his 2nd TD run.

WASHINGTON STATE 63 California 37: California (2-4) struck 1st as QB Justin Vedder (26-45/351y, 3 TDs, 2 INTs) launched 52y TD to WR Kofi Nartey. On way to 619y O, Washington State (6-0) countered with 8 unanswered TDs. TB Michael Black (9/86y) raced for 24 and 28y TDs, and QB Ryan Leaf (13-21/332y, 5TD) connected on 3 TDs. Then Leaf and Black collaborated on 55y TD. Cougars led 56-6 until TD and safety pulled Cal to 56-16 at end of 3rd Q. Vedder hit 2 TDs and LB Mawuko Tugbenyoh rambled 60y with FUM TD RET in 4th Q.

October 25, 1997

WEST VIRGINIA 30 Virginia Tech 17: Topsy-turvy, but somewhat weak Big East fell into grasp of West Virginia (6-1) when TB Amos Zereoue (29/153y, TD) piled up 102y rushing in 1st H to help build 27-7 lead. Key Mountaineer weapon in 24-pt 2nd Q was underrated QB Marc Bulger (15-25/217y, TD, INT), who contributed TDs passing and running. Virginia Tech (5-2) was limited to 195y O, but enjoyed 7-3 lead when QB Al Clark (14-34/129y, INT) completed 1st of his 2 TD passes.

Florida State 47 VIRGINIA 21: Returning to site of only ACC loss to date, Florida State (7-0) ended suspense early with 21-0 lead halfway through 1st Q on its way to 511y total O. Seminoles TB Travis Minor (17/159y, 2 TDs) roared 87y on 1st scrimmage play and later caught TD pass. Improving QB Thad Busby (18-39/285y, 3 TDs, INT) threw 38y TD to WR Peter Warrick, 74y TD to WR E.G. Green, and FSU had 3 TDs on its 1st 5 snaps. Virginia (4-3) TB Thomas Jones (19/32y) scored late in 1st Q, but Cavs didn't tally again until subs were playing late in 3rd Q. Seminole D registered -52y worth of sacks on UVa's 2 QBs, Aaron Brooks (6-16/136y, INT) and sub Dan Ellis (8-15/122y, TD). Ellis managed to score on sneak late in 3rd Q and toss 15y TD pass early in 4th Q. Minor scored his 3rd TD less than 3 mins later to break Virginia's 2-TD streak and lift margin to 44-21.

GEORGIA 23 Kentucky 13: Georgia (6-1) proved again to be different team with oft-injured TB Robert Edwards (19/186y) in lineup. Edwards roared 80y for 2nd Q TD, and DB Ronald Bailey zipped 37y for INT TD RET that put Bulldogs in front 14-7 just before H. Otherwise, unpredictable Kentucky (4-4) spent much of rainy day running up y. Wildcats had O edge of 436y to 275y, and QB Tim Couch set SEC completion record on 41-55/324y, 3 INTs passing, but his only TD didn't come until last 3 mins when WR Craig Yeast's 2y catch closed margin to 17-13 before Edwards' clinching 44y TD jaunt with 2:31 to go.

Michigan 23 MICHIGAN STATE 7: No. 15 Michigan State (5-2) sprung hideout play on 1st Q fake FG as sub QB Bill Burke hit TB Sedrick Irvin for 22y TD. That deceit was sufficient to rile up Michigan (7-0). But, UM trailed 7-3 with 5 mins left in 2nd Q and were backed into precarious corner at own 5YL. Wolverines proceeded to execute 11-play, turning point drive that ended in QB Brian Griese's 1y TD run. Michigan led 13-7 early in 4th Q when DB Charles Woodson made 1 of his 2 INTs, as Spartans threw 6 INTs. TB Chris Howard (21/110y) scored min later, so final result became doubtless. Michigan State QB Todd Schultz passed 16-30/130y, 5 INTs.

Missouri 51 OKLAHOMA STATE 50 (OT): Bubble burst for Oklahoma State (6-1), but not before Cowboys made remarkable comeback from 30-7 shortfall. Missouri (5-3) jumped to 23-pt edge early in 3rd Q after QB Corby Jones (13-25/231y, 4 TDs, INT) tossed 3 TD passes, ran 23y for another. Then, OSU held Tigers to 29y on next 5 series, came back with 4 unanswered TDs for 37-30 lead. QB Tony Lindsay (10-18/210y, 4 TDs, INT) threw

3 TDs, last to superb TE Alonzo Mayes (8/126y, 2 TDs) with 1:58 left. Missouri responded with tying 80y drive, capped by Jones' 38y TD pass to WR Ricky Ross with :18 left. Each team scored TDs in 1st 2 OT opportunities, but Cowboys tried 2-pt pass after Lindsay's 6y run on 4th down. On 2-pt conv, Lindsay looked for receivers, but was buried by host of Tigers on scramble run.

TEXAS TECH 16 Texas A&M 13: After riding bench for season-and-half, Texas Tech (4-3) K Tony Rogers was back in lineup for K Jaret Greaser, who broke leg in prior week's game. Rogers toed 3 FGs, including dramatic 47y boot that caromed off left upright to win game with 19 secs to play. Texas A&M (5-2) got 2 FGs in 1st H from K Kyle Bryant, tied game at 13-13 with 5:51 to go on QB Branndon Stewart's TD pass to WR Leroy Hodge.

WASHINGTON STATE 35 Arizona 34 (OT): QB Ryan Leaf threw for career best to date 384y on 23-46, 3 TDs, INT, but Washington State (7-0) found itself in catfight when it committed 14/112y PENs and Arizona (3-5) QB Ortege Jenkins (20-44/246y, 4 TDs plus TD rushing) came up big. "The better no. 16...was the one in white," said Leaf of Jenkins. Wildcats led 21-14 at H, Cougars tied it in 3rd Q on Leaf's TD pass to TB Michael Black. Jenkins' 34y TD pass in 3rd Q gave Arizona 7-pt lead, and WSU sent it to OT with sub TB DeJuan Gilmore's 4th QT TD run. Leaf's sneak put Cougars ahead in OT; then Wildcats fell into 4th-and-14 hole. But DB LeJuan Gibbons was called for pass interference which led to TD. Arizona went for 2-pt conv, and Gibbons led swarm to bury Jenkins, his former HS teammate, on rollout.

USA Today Coaches Poll October 27

1	Nebraska (37)	1507	14	LSU	673
2	Penn State (20)	1480	15	Georgia	672
3	Florida State (3)	1439	16	Iowa	625
4	Michigan (2)	1339	17	West Virginia	599
5	North Carolina	1331	18	Purdue	438
6	Florida	1223	19	Oklahoma State	432
7	Washington	1142	20	Michigan State	378
8	Tennessee	1111	21	Arizona State	316
9	Ohio State	1076	22	Virginia Tech	213
10	Washington State	995	23	Toledo	144
11	Auburn	903	24	Syracuse	101
12	Kansas State	802	25	Brigham Young	85
13	UCLA	708			

November 1, 1997

(Th) North Carolina 16 GEORGIA TECH 13: "I'm sure some of the kids looked beyond this one (to showdown with no. 3 Florida State)," said North Carolina (8-0) coach Mack Brown. "They're human beings." Carolina suffered 3 TOS in 1st H, but Georgia Tech (4-3) could convert them into only 3 pts in 6-6 battle of FGs. Tar Heels QB Oscar Davenport (26-41/360y, TD, 2 INTs) pitched precision pass 30y into left EZ corner to WR L.C. Stevens for 13-6 lead in 3rd Q. Georgia Tech QB Joey Hamilton (15-25/158y, TD, INT) overcame inoffensive 2nd H with 4y TD pass to TB Charlie Rogers with 1:10 left, but ensuing on-side KO failed. UNC outgained Yellow Jackets 521y to 186y as TB Jonathan Linton (28/138y and 6/137y receiving) became 1st Tar Heels ever to break century mark in rushing and receiving.

SYRACUSE 40 West Virginia 10: Hot Syracuse (6-3) dealt itself back into Big East race with big plays. After clutch WR Quinton Spotwood closed 1st H with last min TD catch for 13-10 lead, WR Jim Turner caught 50y TD from WR Kevin Johnson on reverse. After DB Jason Poles raced 96y to score with INT with 5:41 to go in 3rd Q, Orangemen led 26-10. West Virginia (6-2) TB Amos Zereoue, whose 100y rushing habit had guaranteed victory for 2 years, matched form and was held to 16/71y. Mountaineer QB Marc Bulger passed 19-32/209y, INT.

FLORIDA STATE 48 North Carolina State 35: Long, sloppy game saw some magnificent individual performances. Florida State (8-0) QB Thad Busby (26-36/career-high 463y, 5 TDs, INT) had great game and launched Seminoles to 27-0 1st Q cushion with 205y passing and 3 TDs. But, FSU was flagged 14 times, including 3 pass interference calls, had 2 TOs, and bobbled place kick snaps twice. Seminoles' proud D also allowed staggering 448y to North Carolina State (3-5) and couldn't cover crackling WR Torry Holt, who caught 12/168y, and 5 TDs. Wolfpack crawled back to within 41-28 early in 4th Q, but Busby threw his 5th D pass, to WR Jacquez Green, to scotch plans.

Mississippi State 20 AUBURN 0: No team fashioned winning mark more quietly than Mississippi State (6-2), but Bulldogs projected themselves into SEC West race with stunner over Auburn (7-2). Under severe blitz pressure, Tigers QB Dameyune Craig (20-54/270y) threw 4 INTs. Key pick came from DB Anthony Derricks who sprinted 90y to TD that provided 10-0 lead in 2nd Q. TB James Johnson (19/81y) raced 38y to close scoring in 4th Q and seal Auburn's 1st shutout loss in 55 games.

Georgia 37 Florida 17 (Jacksonville): After 7 losses in row in "World's Largest Outdoor Cocktail Party," Georgia (7-1) finally had chance to run victory lap. Florida (6-2) saw chance for 4th straight SEC crown snatched as Bulldogs TB Robert Edwards (26/124y) tied school record 4 TDs that provided 7-0, 14-3, 21-17, and 30-17 leads. Bulldogs WR Hines Ward caught 7/85y passes, contributed key all-around play with 1 completion, 5/21y rushing. Frustrated Gators coach Steve Spurrier yanked QB Doug Johnson after H, used 3 QBs in all—none to usual efficiency—as aerial game produced 19-44/212y, had 4 passes swiped. "We messed up thinking we can throw the ball the way we used to, and we can't do it," grumbled Spurrier.

IOWA 35 Purdue 17: Boilermakers (6-2), Big 10 leader in O, surged to 10-0, 17-7 leads on TD run, TD pass by QB Billy Dicken (14-35/269y, 2 INTs). Suddenly, Iowa (6-2) stiffened its D, blanked Purdue in 2nd H. QB Randy Reiners threw late 2nd TD pass to RB Rob Thein, his 2nd of 3 TDs, and TB Tavian Banks (24/126y) dashed 16y for go-ahead TD at 21-17 early in 3rd Q. Hawkeyes, who would go on to finish home season 6-0 with 286-43 scoring edge, held Purdue 156y under O avg.

NOTRE DAME 21 Navy 17: Navy (3-4) outgained Notre Dame (4-5) 399y to 283y, but couldn't stop 17-play, 93y TD drive in 4th Q that ended in TB Autry Denson's go-ahead 5y run with 5:48 left. Earlier, Middies QB Chris McCoy rushed 23/147y, scored on 9 and 2y runs, but suffered 2 INTs that were turned into TDs. On game's last play, McCoy launched Hail Mary pass tipped into hands of SB Pat McGrew who raced 69y before being bounced OB at 2YL by Irish DB Allen Rossum. Afterward, disappointed Navy sang school song, walked through ND band to kneel in prayer. "This is the first time we've been booed for praying," said coach Charlie Weatherbie.

TOLEDO 35 Miami (Ohio) 28: QB Chris Wallace, whose crippled legs in his youth were massaged into health by his prayerful mother, threw 24-36/364y, 4 TDs to spark undefeated Toledo (8-0). Trailing 27-7 early in 3rd Q, Miami (6-3) looked to QB Sam Ricketts (17-30/236y, 2 TD, INT), who sandwiched 2 TD passes around 61y TD run for stunning 21-pt turnaround for 28-27 lead. Clutch performer Wallace found lanky WR Brock Kreitzburg with winning 11y TD with 24 secs left to play.

Southern Mississippi 24 CINCINNATI 17: Liberty Bowl was ready to beckon Conf USA champion Southern Miss (6-2) as Eagles won for 1st time in 5 tries at Cincinnati (6-3). Bearcats gained 261y on ground, led 17-7 in 3rd Q on short FUM TD RET and 7y TD run by FB Landon Smith. Cincy QB Chad Plummer rushed 19/133y, but was 8-31/80y in air including 2 INTs. Last pickoff of Plummer came in EZ by DB Patrick Surtain as time ran out. Eagles QB Lee Roberts (15-31/148y) threw 2 TD passes to WR Sherrod Gideon, 2nd to break 17-17 tie with 5:55 left.

ARIZONA STATE 44 Washington State 31: Important Pac-10 game was played in three distinct segments. Sun Devils (6-2) controlled opening 22 min as QB Ryan Kealy (23-36/245y) threw 3 of his 4 TDs. Undefeated Toledo (7-1) overcame 24-0 margin to go ahead 25-24 early in 4th Q as QB Ryan Leaf (24-49/447y, 3 TDs, INT) threw 11y TD to WR Shawn McWashington (5/162y), then wedged for 2 pts. After Kealy drove Devils 80y to 30-25 edge with TD pass, DB Mitchell "Fright Night" Freedman keyed last segment with safety blitz. With 3 mins left, Freedman's blitz forced Leaf to FUM which standout D Hamilton Mee scooped up for 69y TD RET. DL Derrick Ford quickly followed with EZ REC of Leaf FUM for 44-25 ASU lead.

USA Today Coaches Poll November 3

1	Nebraska (50)	1526	14	Iowa	767
2	Florida State (2)	1449	15	Washington State	691
3	Penn State (8)	1438	16	Arizona State	635
4	Michigan (2)	1373	17	Auburn	476
5	North Carolina	1322	18	Virginia Tech	418
6	Washington	1198	19	Syracuse	334
7	Tennessee	1162	20	Toledo	302
8	Ohio State	1161	21	Texas A&M	275
9	Georgia	960	22	West Virginia	225
10	Kansas State	907	23	Oklahoma State	205
11	UCLA	898	24	Purdue	201
12	LSU	844	25	Southern Mississippi	126
13	Florida	790			

November 8, 1997

Florida State 20 NORTH CAROLINA 3: No. 5 North Carolina (8-1), superb on D all year, proved its O was not ready for prime time as Florida State (9-0) limited Tar Heels to 73y O. Seminoles D earned 9 sacks, 7 of Heels QB Oscar Davenport (4-10/50y, INT), who suffered broken ankle in 3rd Q. FSU QB Thad Busby (14-30/159y, 2 TDs, INT) threw pass to TE Melvin Pearsall for TD, and WR E.G. Green made brilliant 1-handed TD grab for 14-0 edge. TB Travis Minor chipped in with 30/128y rushing, and LB Brian Allen block Heels punt to set up FG for 17-0 lead just before H. Enjoying his 68th birthday, FSU coach Bobby Bowden was philosophical about Carolina's recent rise: "They haven't had enough 'Wide Rights' yet. You have to get kicked around enough in the big ones to learn how to win them."

Louisiana State 27 ALABAMA 0: Muddled, wide-open SEC West race came into greater focus as Arkansas was eliminated 19-9 by Ole Miss, and sinking Alabama (4-5) fell out of conf picture at 2-4. LSU (7-2) visited 1st shutout on Tide at home since 1990. Tiger DL Chuck Wiley disrupted play deep in Bama territory, scored 1st Q TD on FUM REC in EZ. LSU TB Kevin Faulk rushed 27/168y, 2 TD dashes of 5 and 53y. It was 2nd-largest Tigers win in 102-year history of series that still was led by Crimson Tide by 40-16-5.

Michigan 34 PENN STATE 8: Mighty Michigan (9-0) demolished undefeated Penn State (7-1), rolling to 10-0 lead in opening 2 possessions. Ominous 1st-play sack by DL Glen Steele sent Nittany Lions O reeling to afternoon of only 169y total O. Wolverines QB Brian Griese (14-22/151y, 2 TDs) dashed 40y as he faked going OB and continued on. Griese lofted 37y TD pass to wide-open DB-WR Charles Woodson for 17-0 edge 4 mins into 2nd Q. When Griese followed with 8y TD to TE Jerame Tuman, Wolverines had 24-0 H cushion, largest home H deficit ever faced by Joe Paterno-coached team. Penn State's solace was short 4th Q TD run by TB Curtis Enis (18/103y), only pts allowed all year by Michigan in any 4th Q.

BALL STATE 35 Toledo 3: Having clinched spot in conf title game, undefeated Toledo (8-1) saw dream season crash. Ball State (5-6) won its 4th straight, used clutch play of QB Jake Josetti, who threw 2 TD passes, ran for another, despite unimposing 6-11/131y air stats. Cards TB LeAndre Moore (16/110y, TD) helped build 28-0 lead. Rockets, 1st MAC team to crack AP rankings since 1975, gained only 218y (251y below avg), suffered 3 TOs, got only pts on on K Chris Merrick's 27y FG late in 3rd Q.

GAME OF YEAR
Nebraska 45 MISSOURI 38 (OT)

Nebraska (9-0) authored amazing "Immaculate Reception II" by frosh WR Matt Davison to tie game on last play of regulation. "Just one stinking play," according to Missouri coach Larry Smith, unfolded with 7 secs to go as excited Tigers fans waited to tear down

goalposts. Huskers QB Scott Frost fired over middle to WB Shevin Wiggins at GL, but ball was tipped toward ground. In falling backward, Wiggins kicked ball over his head into EZ—Wiggins later claimed it was intentional, therefore illegal—where Davison made diving, grass-top TD catch to tie and deflate Missouri (6-4). Then, Frost made sudden 12y TD option dash on OT's 3rd snap, and Huskers D ended it with 4th down sack of Tigers QB Corby Jones. Leading most of game, Tigers had gotten 3 TD passes from Jones (12-20/233y, INT) as RB Brock Olivo scored on 1y vault and 34y catch. Jones provided 38-31 lead with 4:39 to play when he hit WR Eddie Brooks with 15y TD. Frost (11-24/175y, TD, and 23/141y rushing) hit 5-10/67y on Nebraska's drive to miracle TD in last 1:02 of regulation.

Oregon 31 WASHINGTON 28: Nicked-up Huskies (7-2) played without 2 top O threats: QB Brock Huard, TB Rashaan Shehee. Up-and-down Oregon (5-4), just 34 pts from 6-0 Pac-10 mark, jumped to 1st H leads of 17-0 and 24-3 on way to ending Washington's 12-game conf win streak. Ducks got stellar game from TB Saladin McCullough (28/117y, TD), and when QB Akili Smith (15-25/193y, 3 TDs) hit TE Blake Spence with TD it was 24-3. Huskies clawed back as frosh QB Marques Tuiasosopo (15-30/261y, TD, INT) scored on 42y TD run and leapt ahead 28-24 on 41y TD pass from Tuiasosopo to frosh WR Ja'Warren Hooker with 8 min to go. Ducks countered with Smith's winning TD pass to WR Pat Johnson with 2:33 to play.

USA Today Coaches Poll November 10

1	Florida State (26)	1505	14	Washington	758
2	Michigan (20)	1493	15	Arizona State	723
3	Nebraska (16)	1459	16	Auburn	587
4	Ohio State	1312	17	Virginia Tech	486
5	Tennessee	1310	18	Texas A&M	405
6	Penn State	1130	19	Syracuse	372
7	Georgia	1069	20	Purdue	318
8	Kansas State	1066	21	Oklahoma State	305
9	North Carolina	1064	22	Iowa	291
10	UCLA	963	23	West Virginia	271
11	LSU	935	24	Wisconsin	206
12	Florida	869	25	Mississippi State	133
13	Washington State	828			

November 15, 1997

Syracuse 32 PITTSBURGH 27: Enroute to 7th straight win, Syracuse (8-3) got 2 TD runs from TB Dee Brown (38/154y) and TD pass from QB Donovan McNabb (20-31/263y, 2 TDs, INT), led 19-0 at end of 3rd Q. Pittsburgh QB Pete Gonzalez (20-37/274y, INT) threw 2 TD passes in 1st 5 mins of 4th Q, but Orangemen WR Kevin Johnson wedged 91y KO TD RET in between. But Pitt still was hot, sending forgotten TB Billy West over for 2 TDs, last coming with 2:12 left for 27-26 lead. Back came Syracuse as McNabb found WR Quinton Spotwood (8/109y) who barely outmaneuvered DB Hank Poteat for winning catch at left edge of EZ with :28 to go.

North Carolina 17 CLEMSON 10: D struggle was broken open by 3 long receptions by North Carolina (9-1) WR L.C. Stevens, who at 6'5" towered over willing, but outmanned Clemson (6-4) secondary. Stevens gathered in passes of 44, 67, 58y from QB Chris Keldorf (14-27/259y, TD, INT), and each set up Heels score. WR Na Brown's 5y TD catch with 5:40 to go in 2nd Q tied it at 7-7. Stevens' 2nd catch set up K Josh McGee's short FG with 5 sec before H. Tigers converted its 1st 3rd down at 6YL late in 3rd Q, but UNC D (132y allowed) stiffened to force K David Richardson's tying FG. Held to 40/68y rushing, Carolina still managed TB Jonathan Linton's winning 5y TD run early in 4th Q.

Auburn 45 GEORGIA 34: Left for dead after its November 1 blanking by Mississippi State, Auburn (8-2) used bye week to invigorate 109th-ranked rushing game. Led by frosh TB Demontray Carter (14/93y, TD) and FB Fred Beasley (16/62y, 2 TDs), Tigers totaled 159y on ground. Carter and Beasley each scored as Auburn jumped to 24-7 lead by succeeding on each of its 1st 4 possessions. Georgia (7-2) got within 24-14 on late 2nd Q TD from checked TB Robert Edwards (18/52y, 2 TDs) and marched to 21YL early in 3rd Q, only to miss FG. Auburn QB Dameyune Craig (12-19/231y) came right back with 76y TD pass to WR Karsten Bailey. Craig's TD run made it 38-14 late in 3rd Q before Bulldogs pass combo of QB Mike Bobo and WR Hines Ward combined on 2 TD passes for respectability at 38-28.

Mississippi State 32 ALABAMA 20: Legendary Alabama coach Bear Bryant was defeated only twice in 24 years at Bryant-Denny Stadium. In loss to Bulldogs (7-2), Crimson Tide (4-6) closed 1997 home slate with regrettable 0-4 mark, just 3rd time in history it went winless in Tuscaloosa. Mississippi State TB James Johnson, Bama fan as youth, charged 83 and 41y for TDs on way to 23/198y rushing. Alabama moved within 26-20 on trick pass with 6:14 left in 3rd Q: TB Dennis Riddle flipped 13y TD pass to QB Lance Tucker. But Bulldogs sunk teeth into SEC West crown by converting time-consuming 57 and 72y drives into clinching FGs by K Brian Hazelwood.

Notre Dame 24 LOUISIANA STATE 6: Improving Irish (5-5) won 3rd in row, eyed possible bowl bid after staging ground-oriented (260y) upset in Death Valley. Ace Irish RET artist DB Allen Rossum went 43y with opening KO to set up 6-play drive capped by TB Autry Denson's 9y TD run. Sub TB Clement Stokes (15/92y) scored late in 1st Q to make it 17-0 and added TD in 3rd Q for 24-0 ND margin. Down-trodden LSU (7-3) didn't penetrate Irish 20YL until last 8 mins when QB Herb Tyler (17-30/167y, 3 INTs) threw 26y pass to set up TD by TB Kevin Faulk (26/105y).

Michigan 26 WISCONSIN 16: Michigan, successfully defending its no. 1 ranking for 1st time in 7 years, gained 16-3 H lead, outgaining Badgers (8-3) 309y to 80y. Wolverines TB Chris Howard (26/100y) scored in 1st Q, and QB Brian Griese (19-26/254y) pitched 38y TD to WR Tai Streets in 2nd Q. Determined Wisconsin made it 16-10, going 80y, QB Mike Samuel's TD sneak was 11th play after 2nd H KO. Badgers LB Donnell Thompson dropped EZ INT early in 4th Q, allowing Michigan FG for 19-10 edge. When Howard scored his 2nd TD, Wolverines had safe 26-10 lead with 6:15 to go.

Texas Tech 27 OKLAHOMA STATE 3: Early in November, Texas Tech (6-4) announced it would skip any title playoff or bowl bid it earned because of pending investigation of violations. So Raiders players focused on dominant win over slumping Oklahoma State (7-3), which put Texas A&M, 51-7 winners over Oklahoma, in Big 12 title game. Game's y for O units was nearly even—Texas Tech had 295y to Cowboys' 289y—but Red Raiders D made 2 INTs, 5 sacks, and forced FUM. Little frosh TB Ricky Williams (21/91y) carried 6 times on 9-play, 56y 2nd Q Tech drive, scored from 2YL for 10-0 lead. Cowboys finally threatened early in 4th Q, but could only register K Tim Sydnes' 24y FG.

UCLA 52 Washington 28: Those clamoring for playoff system could likely count UCLA (8-2) among their partisans. Since 0-2 start, Bruins had battered foes by 359-133 margin. Latest victim, Washington (7-3), lost control of inside track to Rose Bowl. Huskies jumped to 7-0 lead in 1st Q as TB Maurice Shaw closed 80y drive with 47y TD run. Bruins took 28-20 H lead as TB Skip Hicks (25/147y, and 3/106y receiving) scored TDs by land, air, and QB Cade McNown did same, including 47y arrow to WR Jim McElroy. UCLA tallied 1st 24 pts of 2nd H as Hicks added 2 TDs. Hicks (who had gained only 24y in 3 prior games against Washington) made speech on Friday so emotional that fired up DL Trevor Turner vomited.

USA Today Coaches Poll November 17

1	Florida State (29)	1509	14	Georgia	689
2	Michigan (20)	1489	15	Virginia Tech	627
3	Nebraska (13)	1463	16	Texas A&M	611
4	Ohio State	1342	17	Syracuse	481
5	Tennessee	1235	18	LSU	427
6	Penn State	1203	19	Mississippi State	410
7	Kansas State	1119	20	Washington	405
8	North Carolina	1109	21	West Virginia	397
9	UCLA	1101	22	Colorado State	145
10	Florida	964	23	Missouri	140
11	Washington State	918	24	Wisconsin	137
12	Arizona State	859	25	Purdue	114
13	Auburn	797			

November 22, 1997

PITTSBURGH 30 Virginia Tech 23: Pesky Panthers (5-5) spoiled championship party for Virginia Tech (7-3) and put idle Syracuse in driver's seat for Big East crown. After 2 FGs by Hokies K Shayne Graham, Pitt QB Pete Gonzalez (15-24/314y, 4 TDs) brought Pitt back with TD passes in 2nd, 3rd Qs for 15-13 leading entering 4th Q. With most TD passes in single season since Dan Marino in 1981, 5th-year sr Gonzalez pitched 35y TD to TE Juan Williams and 56y TD to FB Kevan Barlow to put it away at 30-16.

MICHIGAN 20 Ohio State 14: Field position dominated 1st H just as if Bo Schembechler and Woody Hayes were calling shots. Game was busted open by Wolverines (11-0) DB-WR Charles Woodson, who caught crossing pass to set up 2nd Q TD, then burst 78y on punt TD RET. Even though conv was blocked after its 2nd score, Michigan led 13-0. Woodson made EZ INT to halt Ohio State (9-2) drive to open 2nd H. Before Woodson could count his Heisman votes, Buckeyes WR David Boston, who uttered midweek braggadocio, snuck behind Woodson for 56y TD catch. With Wolverines losing injured players throughout, their O stumbled, and QB Brian Griese (14-25/147y) lost FUM at 2YL on Buckeyes DB Gary Berry's 4th Q blitz. Ohio quickly made it 20-14, but Michigan D, led by pass rushing DE Glen Steele, clamped down on late Ohio drives.

FLORIDA 32 Florida State 29: Resilient Gators (9-2) ruined national title hopes of Florida State (10-1) in seesaw battle. Florida coach Steve Spurrier rotated QBs Noah Brindise and Doug Johnson on nearly every snap partly because of rumor FSU had stolen his sideline signals. "It gives you a chance to coach the quarterbacks between plays," he said. It was Johnson, checking off at scrimmage line at own 20YL while trailing 29-25, who fired big pass in last 2:38 to WR Jacquez Green (7/145y) for 63y. Pass set up 4th TD run by TB Fred Taylor (22/162y) for win. Taylor tore off RT for 61y in 3rd Q to lift Gators to 25-20 edge. Frosh TB Travis Minor (21/142y, TD) gave Seminoles 26-25 lead at end of 3rd Q when he dashed 18y.

AUBURN 18 Alabama 17: With Arkansas having upset Mississippi State 17-7 earlier in day, Auburn (9-2) was left with SEC West title fate in own hands. K-P Jaret Holmes' accurate punts and 2 FGs gave Tigers 6-0 lead in 1st Q. QB Freddie Kitchens (12-18/134y, TD) came off bench to spark Alabama (4-7) in 2nd Q, firing TD pass to WR Calvin Hall. Tide jumped to 17-6 margin in 3rd Q when FB Ed Scissum's block sprung TB Shaun Alexander (13/65y) for TD. QB Dameyne Craig (14-34/213y, 2 INTs) rallied Tigers with connections that led to FB Fred Beasley's soaring TD vault. After Holmes' 3rd FG (31y) trimmed Bama's lead to 17-15, Auburn chose to punt in Tide end with 3:06 left in 4th Q. Tigers were saved by Scissum's FUM at own 33YL on ill-advised 3rd down pass with barely more than min left. Holmes nailed 39y FG to win it with 15 secs left.

Colorado State 38 SAN DIEGO STATE 17: Rams (9-2) found San Diego State (5-7), winners of 4 of last 5, to be tough in early going. Trailing 3-0 and without 1st down 4 mins into 2nd Q, Colorado State QB Moses Moreno made quick work of Aztec secondary. In midst of 9 completions in row, Moreno pitched 3 straight passes for TDs to TE Eli Workman, WRs Frank Rice, and Darran Hall, and Rams led 21-3 at H. SDSU DL Kabeer Gbaja-Biamila made 4th down GL stop of Moreno to spark 2nd H hope for Aztecs. But, Rams opened 2nd H with K Derek Franz's FG and self-tipped INT TD RET by DL Jamie Bennett.

UCLA 31 Southern California 24: WR R. Jay Soward roared to 80y bomb, fulfilling hankering he'd had all season, to score on Trojans (6-5) 1st snap of game. Bruins (9-2) TB Skip Hicks broke Charles White's career Pac-10 TD record by scoring his 54th TD to break 7-7 tie. USC tied it 14-14 in 1st Q on 2nd TD pass by QB John Fox (14-34/258y, 2TDs, 2 INTs), then took 21-14 lead on speedy TB Chad Morton's 49y dash. But, Trojans didn't score again until last 2 mins of game on K Adam Abrams' 36y FG. Key UCLA drive came midway in 3rd Q to break 21-21 H tie with big plays coming on 36y scramble pass

by QB Cade McNown (15-24/213y, 3 TDs) and 24y run by Hicks. TE Mike Grieb broke 3 tackles on 38y TD catch, scoring his 2nd TD for 28-21 lead. Failed fake punt gave Bruins FG late in 3rd Q. It was Bruins 7th straight win in cross-town rivalry.

Washington State 41 WASHINGTON 35: After 67 years, Washington State (10-1) earned trip to Rose Bowl by winning 1st November road game during coach Mike Price's 9-year regime. After trailing 7-0 in opening Q on 1st of 4 TD passes by Huskies QB Brock Huard (18-36/283y, 5 INTs), Cougars tied it on 8y TD run by TB Michael Black (37/170y). Washington State QB Ryan Leaf (22-38/358y, 2 TDs, INT) hit WR Chris Jackson (8/185y) for 57y TD to help build handsome 24-7 margin midway in 3rd Q. Huard soon struck with 38y TD to WR Fred Coleman, and DB Tony Parrish raced to 32y TD with Leaf's wayward pass. WSU's Jackson made brilliant hurdling run with 50y TD pass, and when Leaf made TD REC of his own GL FUM, Cougars led 38-28 early in 4th Q. Washington State O was splendid in converting 13 of its 19 3rd down plays.

November 27-29, 1997

(Fri) Pittsburgh 41 WEST VIRGINIA 38 (OT): With chances for winning ledger and bowl invitation, improving Panthers (6-5) clawed to 21-10 H lead on 2 TD passes by QB Pete Gonzalez (22-34/273y, 5 TDs, 2 INTs). West Virginia (7-4) remembered its role in "Backyard Brawl" by charging out after H to 2nd of 3 TD runs by TB Amos Zereoue (41/151y). Still, Panthers led 35-25 with 10 min to go in 4th Q. Mountaineers sent it to OT on 53y TD pass from QB Marc Bulger (26-43/348y, TD, INT) to WR Pat Greene (12/205y) and 34y FG by K Jay Taylor with 1:18 left. Missed FGs and TOs spoiled 2 OTs, but Taylor nailed 52y FG after Pitt LB Rod Humphrey sacked Bulger. Down 38-35, Panthers faced do-or-die 4th-and-17, but Gonzalez zipped 20y pass over middle to WR Jake Hoffart (9/124y, TD), followed with game-winning 12y TD to WR Terry Murphy.

(Fri) Nebraska 27 COLORADO 24: QB Scott Frost scored on beautifully-blocked sprint up middle to give undefeated Nebraska (11-0) 10-3 H lead. IB Ahman Green propelled for 29/202y rushing, scored 2 TDs, and Cornhuskers were in comfortable position at 27-10. Using successful on-side KO, Colorado scored 14 pts in 39-sec span of 4th Q on TD catches by WRs Marcus Stiggers and Robert Toler, each launched by QB John Hessler (19-35/362y, 3 TDs, 2 INTs). Another on-side KO slipped through hands of DB Ben Kelly or Buffs would have had go-ahead chance with 2:30 left.

(Fri) TEXAS A&M 27 Texas 16: It had been water-logged year in Lone Star State, so, fittingly, season's big game was played in quagmire. Texas (4-7) RB Ricky Williams, nation's leading rusher, overcame ankle sprain to splash to 33/183y, 2 TDs to open scoring and draw Longhorns within 21-13 in 3rd Q. Hardly using passes, Texas A&M (9-2) sent FB D'Andre Hardeman (21/121y, TD), TBs Sirr Parker (2 TDs), Dante Hall (19/118y) barreling up middle. K Kyle Bryant's dual 4th Q FGs extended Aggies leads to 24-16 and 27-16 as R.C. Slocum won his 83rd, most by any Texas A&M coach in history.

(Fri) Arizona 28 ARIZONA STATE 16: It appeared so pat for Fiesta Bowl: extend bid to hometown Arizona State (8-3). But, rival Arizona (6-5) spoiled party by charging to 28-7 lead with help of odd plays. After QB Ortege Jenkins (7-19/194y, 3 TDs, 2 INTs) threw 37y TD pass to WR Rodney Williams, Wildcats used 2 QBs (Jenkins and Keith Smith) in same backfield with Smith taking pitchout, throwing 45y pass, then, with Jenkins in motion from under C, Smith tossed 8y TD to TE Paul Shields. Late in 2nd Q, blitzing Sun Devils S Mitchell Freedman went offside, bumped Wildcats C Rusty James trying to get back, and with stellar but stressed secondary standing around expecting whistle, Arizona WR Brad Brennan sprinted to EZ for unmolested 29y TD and 28-7 lead. ASU QB Ryan Kealy suffered knee injury, and sub Steve Campbell (7-23/122y, 2 INTs) managed 17y TD pass to WR Ricky Boyer in 2nd Q. Sun Devils got 9 pts in 3:49 span, but Arizona LB Chester Burnett made INT and picked up 1st down on unusual run with punt blocked by ASU LB Pat Tillman.

Syracuse 33 MIAMI 13: Syracuse (9-3) WR Jim Turner caught early TD pass, then when Miami (5-6) failed on fake punt run, he caught 49y TD bomb on next snap from QB Donovan McNabb. Rankled Hurricanes QB Ryan Clement fired 2nd Q TD to leaping WR Reggie Wayne, who became school's frosh reception king. McNabb tallied late in 3rd Q to make it 30-7 on wonderfully-devised 43y draw TD against blitz. Win clinched 1st unshared Big East title for Orange.

TENNESSEE 17 Vanderbilt 10: Vanderbilt (3-8) owned field position in scoreless 1st Q as it held Tennessee (10-1) QB Peyton Manning (12-27/159y, TD, INT) to 1-7 in air. Frosh K John Markham bombed 47y FG on 1st snap of 2nd Q for 3-0 Vandy lead. Manning beat blitz with 33y TD pass to WR Jeramine Copeland on way to 10-3 H edge. Manning's beautiful fake and bootleg left TD run provided 17-3 lead in 3rd Q. Commodores scored on RB Jared McGrath's 14y run late in 3rd Q, but dashes of Volunteers TB Jamal Lewis (36/196y) snuffed game clock.

Georgia 27 GEORGIA TECH 24: Bulldogs (9-2) took care of business, building 21-10 lead as WR Hines Ward opened scoring with 54y TD catch. Resurgent Georgia Tech (6-5) rode passing arm of hot QB Joe Hamilton (19-34/276y) to bring Georgia Tech back to 21-16. Yellow Jackets seemed intent on upset by fashioning late drive, going ahead

by 24-21 with 48 secs left on TD blast by FB Charles Wiley and 2-pt pass by Hamilton to WR Mike Sheridan. Georgia never quit, driving 65y in 4 plays. Pass interference PEN on Tech wiped out INT by DB Traveres Tillman with 14 secs left, and winning score came on next play: 8y pass from QB Mike Bobo (30-39/415y, 4 TDs, 2 INTs) to well-covered WR Corey Allen on left edge of EZ.

MICHIGAN STATE 49 Penn State 14: Up-and-down Michigan State (7-4) dominated Penn State (9-2) in 1st H, gaining 278y to 147y. But, Spartans led only 14-7 thanks to 2 missed FGs and 54y TD run by Lions TB Curtis Enis. Penn State quickly tied it in 3rd Q on WR Joe Jurevicius' 14y TD catch at pylon right after he made 47y grab of tipped pass. Michigan State countered on TD run by TB Sedrick Irvin, then got FUM REC at Lions 18YL on DE Robaire Smith's sack. QB Todd Schultz (stats) hit Irvin with 8y TD for 28-14 edge. Spartans continued onslaught with 3 TDs in 4th Q, finished with 452y on ground (most to-date vs. PSU) as T Flozell "The Hotel" Adams sparked dominating line play that resulted in 2 backs with 200y rushing: Irvin (28/238y) and sub TB Marc Renaud (21/203y).

December 6, 1997

(Fri) MARSHALL 34 Toledo 14: Playing MAC Championship game on home field in slippery snow, Marshall (10-2) started game with wrong shoes, switched to better gripping soles in 1st Q. Still, hopeful Toledo (9-3) led 7-3 at H as QB Chris Wallace pegged 56y TD pass to WR Ray Curry, and DB Clarence Love, using double-coverage help from LBs, held A-A WR Randy Moss in reasonable check. In 2nd H, Moss caught 4y TD from QB Chad Pennington on fade pattern and added brilliant 86y bomb. When Moss caught tipped 20y TD pass, he had NCAA record of 25 TD catches in season. Rockets TB Dwayne Harris rushed 30/106y.

Navy 39 Army 7 (East Rutherford, N.J.): After 5 straight narrow losses to Army (4-7), spirited Navy (7-4) sent QB Chris McCoy (31/205y rushing) to NCAA-record 20th TD run scored by QB in 1 season. Although it would gain but 13y later, Army had opened brilliantly: FB Joe Hewitt burst 36y on trap on game's 1st snap, and QB Johnny Goff raced 38y to score behind unbalanced line. Running effectively on draws, McCoy led Middies to K Tom Vanderhorst's 26y FG, and later slanted left for TD on 1st play of 2nd Q. McCoy ran 42y to set up TD by FB Tim Cannada (30/133y) for 17-7 lead. Cadets' FUMs, 1 on punt snap, led to another McCoy TD and Vanderhorst FG before H. It was over at 32-7 when McCoy opened 3rd Q with his 3rd TD on drive that consumed 7:25.

Tennessee 30 Auburn 29 (Atlanta): In stirring SEC championship affair, Tennessee (11-1) somehow overcame 6 TOs to rally for its 1st conf title since 1990. Vols QB Peyton Manning (25-43/373y, 4 TDs, 2 INTs) put Vols ahead 7-0 on 40y TD strike to WR Peerless Price (8/161y, 2 TDs). Auburn (9-3) quickly rebounded as DB Brad Ware raced 24y to TD with FUM by Vols WR Marcus Nash. K Jaret Holmes' 48y FG, his 12th straight, made it 13-7, and Tigers QB Dameyune Craig (14-34/262y, 2 TDs) connected on 51y TD bomb to WR Tyrone Goodson. Trailing 20-10 at H, capts Manning and LB Al Wilson made moving speeches, and back came Vols. DB Terry Fair, who had lost FUMs on previous 2 punt RETs, blazed 45y to Auburn 9YL early in 3rd Q as prelude to Manning's 5y TD pass to WR Jeremaine Copeland for 20-17 deficit. But with Vols apparently going in for lead, Copeland soon bobbled pass which went to Tigers DB Jason Bray, who raced 77y to Tennessee 19YL. Craig soon found FB Fred Beasley for TD and 27-17 lead. After Manning threw 3rd TD pass, K Jeff Hall's conv was blocked by Tigers DL Charles Dorsey and returned for 2 pts by LB Quinton Reese. Auburn led 29-23. Manning launched game-winner down right sideline to Nash (9/126y) for 73y midway in 4th Q. With feeble run game (21/-15y), Auburn was set to be victimized by pass rush led by Vols LB Leonard Little and DL Jonathon Brown.

Nebraska 54 Texas A&M 15 (San Antonio): Overmatched Texas A&M (9-3) paid for previous year's upset by Texas of Nebraska (12-0) in Big 12 title game as focused Cornhuskers roared to 37-3 H margin. , Huskers QB Scott Frost (12-18/210y) was stung by his selection as only 3rd team all-conf choice and passed for season-high 201y. Frost also scored 2 TDs on 15/79y rushing. IB Ahman Green ran for 179y, 3 TDs. On its way to its 4th perfect pre-bowl record in 5 years, Nebraska held Aggies to 23/13y rushing. Texas A&M QB Branndon Stewart (18-38/227y, TD, 2 INTs) hit TE Derrick Spiller for 63y gain that set up K Kyle Bryant's 32y FG in 2nd Q and later pitched TD to Spiller.

Colorado State 41 New Mexico 13 (Las Vegas): QB Graham Leigh (17-27/172y, INT) suffered early ankle injury which completely ruined option run attack of New Mexico (9-3). Lobos led early at 3-0 and 10-3, but Colorado State (10-2) broke TB Damon Washington for 51y TD run and 10-10 H tie. Sub TB Kevin McDougal (20/255y, 3 TDs) sparkled 2nd H surge, dashing 44y to give Rams their 1st lead at 17-10. K Colby Cason's 2nd FG trimmed it to 17-13 in 3rd Q, but 3 TOs on successive 4th Q possessions cost Lobos. CSU DB Eason Ramson's INT poised K Derek Franz's 2nd FG, Leigh's FUM led to McDougal's 42y TD run, and New Mexico TB Lennox Gordon's FUM on pass catch set up 18y option pass by Rams sub TB Corey McCoy.

1997 Conference Standings

Big East

Syracuse	6-1
Virginia Tech	5-2
West Virginia	4-3
Pittsburgh	4-3
Miami	3-4
Boston College	3-4
Temple	3-4
Rutgers	0-7

Atlantic Coast

Florida State	8-0
North Carolina	7-1
Virginia	5-3
Georgia Tech	5-3
Clemson	4-4
North Carolina State	3-5
Wake Forest	3-5
Maryland	1-7
Duke	0-8

Southeastern

EAST	
Tennessee	7-1
Florida	6-2
Georgia	6-2
South Carolina	3-5
Kentucky	2-6
Vanderbilt	0-8
WEST	
Auburn	6-2
Louisiana State	6-2
Mississippi	4-4
Mississippi State	4-4
Alabama	2-6
Arkansas	2-6

Conference USA

Southern Mississippi	6-0
Tulane	5-1
East Carolina	4-2
Cincinnati	2-4
Memphis	2-4
Houston	2-4
Louisville	0-6

Big Ten

Michigan	8-0
Ohio State	6-2
Penn State	6-2
Purdue	6-2
Wisconsin	5-3
Iowa	4-4
Michigan State	4-4
Northwestern	3-5
Minnesota	1-7
Indiana	1-7
Illinois	0-8

Mid-American

EAST	
Marshall	7-1
Miami (Ohio)	6-2
Ohio	6-2
Bowling Green	3-5
Kent	3-5
Akron	2-6
WEST	
Toledo	7-1
Western Michigan	6-2
Ball State	4-4
Eastern Michigan	3-5
Central Michigan	1-7
Northern Illinois	0-8

Big 12

NORTH	
Nebraska	8-0
Kansas State	7-1
Missouri	5-3
Colorado	3-5
Kansas	3-5
Iowa State	1-7
SOUTH	
Texas A&M	6-2
Oklahoma State	5-3
Texas Tech	5-3
Texas	2-6
Oklahoma	2-6
Baylor	1-7

Western Athletic

MOUNTAIN	
New Mexico	6-2
Rice	5-3
Southern Methodist	5-3
Utah	5-3
Brigham Young	4-4
Texas-El Paso	3-5
Tulsa	2-6
Texas Christian	1-7
PACIFIC	
Colorado State	7-1
Air Force	6-2
Fresno State	5-3
Wyoming	4-4
San Diego State	4-4
San Jose State	4-4
Nevada-Las Vegas	2-6
Hawaii	1-7

Pacific-10

Washington State	7-1
UCLA	7-1
Arizona State	6-2
Washington	5-3
Arizona	4-4
Southern California	4-4
Oregon	3-5
Stanford	3-5
California	1-7
Oregon State	0-8

1997 Major Bowl Games

Las Vegas Bowl (Dec. 20): Oregon 41 Air Force 13

Oregon (7-5), saddled with Pac-10's worst rushing D, did best thing to take Wishbone team—Air Force (10-3)—out of its run attack. Ducks scored 1st 2 times it snapped ball: Track star WR Pat Johnson (5/169y) caught 69y bomb from QB Akili Smith, then TB Saladin McCullough (17/150y) cut back behind G Stefan deVries' block, sprinted 76y to TD. Ducks frosh DB Garrett Sabol blocked punt for TD, and sub QB Jason Maas (9-15/188y, 2 TDs) and WR Tony Hartley hooked up on 1st of their 2 TD connections for 26-0 H lead. Falcons, stifled by deep thigh bruise to QB Blane Morgan, found bright spots in 2nd H as HB Jemal Singleton raced 51y to set up Morgan's TD sneak. Airmen DL Bryce Fisher scooped up FUM for 45y TD RET.

Aloha Bowl (Dec. 25): Washington 51 Michigan State 23

Matchup of up and down teams found Washington (8-4), heeled on O unit again, handing complete thrashing to Michigan State (7-5). Huskies TB Rashaan Sheehee raced for 29/193y and TDs of 33 and 10y for new Aloha Bowl rushing record, in his injury comeback. Husky QB Brock Huard, also recovered from injury, passed 18-30/179y, 2 TDs to WR Fred Coleman of 15, 22y. Huskies also made 3 killer plays: DB Tony Parrish raced 56y with INT TD RET for 31-10 H lead, sub TB Mike Reed roared 64y to 3rd Q TD off fake punt, and LB Lester Towns took look-what-I-found INT 66y for TD in 4th Q. Spartan QB Todd Schultz (14-24/220y, 3 INTs) threw 2 TDs to WR Gari Scott.

Motor City Bowl (Dec. 26): Mississippi 34 Marshall 31

Ole Miss (8-4), which quietly built inspiring comeback from scholarship limitations, hit Marshall (10-3) with 55y bomb to 1YL by QB Stewart Patridge (29-47/332y, 3 TDs, INT) on game's 1st scrimmage, and it led to HB John Avery's short TD plunge. Thundering Herd A-A WR Randy Moss (6/173y) punched right back with 80y TD bomb from QB Chad Pennington (23-45/337y, 3 TDs). When WR LaVorn Colclough caught 19y TD in 2nd Q, upstart Marshall led 17-7. Rebels went 87y at end of 2nd Q, only to die scoreless at 2YL. But, Ole Miss owned 3rd Q as Patridge threw for 104y and 2 TDs for 21-17 lead. Drained Herd summoned strength for pair of 80y drives in 4th Q, capped by TDs by TB Doug Chapman. Scores provided 31-27 lead. Ole Miss responded with WR Grant Heard's TD catch for 27-24 lead with less than 6 mins left, and sub TB Duce McAllister's clinching 1y TD leap with 30 secs left.

Insight.com Bowl (Copper) (Dec. 27): Arizona 20 New Mexico 14

Arizona (7-5) coach Dick Tomey honored 3rd string, 5th-yr sr QB Brady Batten with starting assignment because of his team loyalty. Batten (7-17/89y) was scheduled to go 2 to 3 series, instead played until dying moments of 3rd Q, and was steady. Wildcats D came up with 4 big INTs. Meanwhile, New Mexico (9-4) QB Graham Leigh was recovered ankle injury, accounting for 229y of team's 290y. Leigh passed 12-32/150y, TD, 4 INTs, tying it 7-7 in 2nd Q with TD pass to WR Milton Thomas. Leigh ran for 4y TD late in 3rd Q that trimmed it to 20-14. FB Kelvin Eafon scored twice for Arizona.

Independence Bowl (Dec. 28): Louisiana State 27 Notre Dame 9

LSU (9-3) coach Gerry DiNardo borrowed 20-year-old psych-up strategy from Notre Dame team. In 1977, coach Dan Devine fired up Irish by outfitting them in green jerseys for big upset over USC. Having been emotionally flat for November 15 loss to Notre Dame (7-6), Tigers this time trotted out 1st-time ever in white helmets and added gold jerseys, which had been used on occasion in previous years. Everything went swell for LSU until TB Kevin Faulk twisted his ankle in 1st Q. Things remained swell: In stepped 3rd team TB Rondell Mealey, who blasted for 34/222y and pair of 4th Q TDs on ground. After Fighting Irish led 6-3 at H on K Scott Cengia's 2 FGs, they were able to gain only 14y in 3rd Q. LSU K Wade Richey tied it with 42y FG midway in 3rd Q. Mealey contributed 26y on key blast late in 3rd Q, and frosh WR Abram Booty made his local Shreveport fans giddy with go-ahead 12y TD post-pattern TD catch from QB Herb Tyler (5-12/61y, TD). Tigers then led 13-6, and their D would seal win with 4 sacks of ND QB Ron Powlus, who closed his much-hyped career with 8-18/66y passing.

Holiday (Dec. 29): Colorado State 35 Missouri 24

Colorado State (11-2) took 6:04 off clock on powerful opening drive led by runs of TB Kevin McDougal (18/110y). WR Darran Hall finished off march with 14y reverse TD run. Missouri (7-5) QB Corby Jones (8-17/68y, INT, and 20/132y rushing) made 33y option run to set up K Scott Knickman's 32y FG. Tigers DL Donnell Jones made FUM REC at Rams 37YL in 2nd Q, and, using effective blocks of C Rob Riti and G Mike Morris, Mizzou roared to 10-7 lead. Jones zipped 20y, immense FB Ron Janes powered it close and threw lead block for Jones' 4y TD run. Teams traded TDs, so Missouri led 17-14 at H. Game's big play came early in 3rd Q: Colorado State's Hall zoomed untouched for 85y punt TD RET. Limping Rams QB Moses Moreno (18-24/206y, 2 TDs) launched 47y TD bomb to WR Dallas Davis for 28-17 lead in midway 3rd Q. WR Ricky Ross provided Mizzou's last gasp with 41y KO RET as Jones followed with 30y running to position TB Brock Olivo for TD run. Rams got 4th Q's only score on fake FG. Tigers accumulated 314y rushing.

Carquest Bowl (Dec. 29): Georgia Tech 35 West Virginia 30

Disintegrating turf had players stumbling all over Miami's Pro Player Park. Exciting Georgia Tech (7-5) QB Joe Hamilton kept his footing long enough to account for 356y. Teams traded early rushing TDs as Yellow Jackets frosh FB Ed Wilder scored from 1YL, and West Virginia (7-5) ace TB Amos Zereoue (17/84y, 2 TDs) rambled over from 14YL. Hamilton scrambled from Shotgun formation for 30y TD and pitched 3y TD pass to TE Mike Lillie for daunting 21-7 margin in 2nd Q. Hamilton reprised his Shotgun TD run with 27 secs left in H, and Tech led 28-14. Zereoue scored again in 3rd Q as Mountaineers trimmed deficit to 28-24. With 3:49 left in game, WVU QB Marc Bulger (25-40/353y, 2 TDs, INT) tossed 74y TD pass to WR Jerry Porter to get within

35-30, but Tech ran out clock. Oft-injured Tech WR Derrick Steagall caught passes for 7/112y.

Alamo Bowl (Dec. 30): Purdue 33 Oklahoma State 20

After fairly quiet 1st H led by Purdue (9-3) 10-6 thanks mostly to 18y TD pass flicked by QB Billy Dicken (18-34/325y, 2 TDs, 3 INTs) to WR Brian Alford, Boilermakers DB Adrian Beasley made his 2nd TD-building INT early in 3rd Q. Beasley returned INT to Oklahoma State (8-4) 6YL to put Dicken in position for 1y TD run. Cowboys countered quickly with TB Jamaal Fobbs' 21y TD run at end of 80y drive to pare deficit to 16-13. But, Boilers added 2 TDs before end of 3rd Q as Dicken hit TB Edwin Watson for 60y to set up WR Vinny Sutherland's 16y TD run. Then, Dicken threw Alamo Bowl-record 69y bomb to WR Chris Daniels, and Purdue led 30-13. Oklahoma State DB-WR R.W. McQuarters caught TD in last min.

Sun Bowl (Dec. 31): Arizona State 17 Iowa 7

Arizona State (9-3) became only underdog of entire 1997-98 bowl season to win its bowl contest. Sun Devils used smothering D to hold 424y-avg O of Iowa (7-5) to 19y rushing, and 209y total O. ASU blanked Hawkeyes until Iowa finally broke through on 26y TD pass by QB Randy Reiners (4-5/70y) in game's last min. Sun Devils QB Steve Campbell (5-11/109y, TD) played just well enough while in for injured Ryan Kealy. WR Lenzie Jackson made nice dodging run with 35y catch to score and put ASU ahead 7-0 midway in 2nd Q. K Robert Nycz's short FG as H clock expired provided 10-0 edge for Devils. ASU TB Mike Martin (27/169y) ran for TD late in 3rd Q for sufficient 17-0 lead.

Liberty Bowl (Dec. 31): Southern Mississippi 41 Pittsburgh 7

QB Lee Roberts and WR Sherrod Gideon collaborated on 3 TD passes for Southern Mississippi (9-3), 1st coming on game's 6th play. Eagles never trailed, but Pittsburgh (6-6) trimmed lead to 14-7 as QB Pete Gonzalez (13-29/172y, 2 INTs) hit WR Jake Hoffart along sideline for 89y TD 3 min before H. In 2nd H, alert SMU D came up with 3 TO TDs as DB Perry Phenix scored on FUM RET and DL Adalius Thomas and DB Terrence Parrish scored on INTs.

Fiesta Bowl (Dec. 31): Kansas State 35 Syracuse 18

Fiesta Bowl turned into personal battle between underrated Kansas State (11-1) QB Michael Bishop (14-23/317y, 4 TDs, INT, and 15/73y, TD rushing) and solid standby Syracuse (9-4) QB Donovan McNabb (16-39/271y, INT, and 16/81y rushing). Bishop made considerable impression with 2nd and 4th Q brilliance. After K Nathan Trout's 27y FG gave Orangemen 3-0 lead at end of 1st Q, Wildcats jumped to 21 straight pts as Bishop was magnificent. After DB Demetric Denmark and LB Travis Ochs (who later had INT and FUM REC at own 14YL) stopped fake FG by Syracuse, Bishop threw 2 TD passes, scrambled right out of pocket for 12y TD for 21-3 edge. Bishop's 28y TD pass to TE Justin Swift off clever misdirection screen to right flat was K-State's 3rd TD of 2nd Q, coming with 2:18 left before H. But, Syracuse owned last 2 mins of 2nd Q as WR Kevin Johnson made nice KO RET and TB Dee Brown followed with 24y TD run. Bishop mishandled Shotgun snap for safety, and Trout made 33y FG to turn 21-3 disadvantge to 21-15. But, Orangemen momentum evaporated in scoreless 3rd Q, and Bishop's 77y bomb to WR Darnell McDonald pushed Wildcats to 28-15 edge. Bishop and McDonald (7/school-record 206y) collaborated for their 3rd TD connection with 3:17 to go.

Outback Bowl: Georgia 33 Wisconsin 6

Overmatched Wisconsin (8-5) ended season just as it started it, being shut down early in bowl game by using its unpolished aerial game. Outweighed, but speedy Georgia (10-2) D handed gruesome stats to Badgers TB Ron Dayne, who found no holes, rushed for only 14/36y. Meanwhile, Bulldogs TB Robert Edwards (22/110y, 3 TDs) put game all but out of reach with TD runs of 2 and 40y in 12-0 1st Q. Georgia QB Mike Bobo had passing game of his life, hitting 26-28/267y. "I'm trying to figure out the two he missed. I can't believe it," said coach Jim Donnan of Bobo. Trailing 33-0 in 4th Q, Wisconsin finally scored on TE Dague Retzlaff's 12y catch with 4:04 left.

Gator Bowl: North Carolina 42 Virginia Tech 3

New North Carolina (11-1) head coach Carl Torbush took his accustomed seat in pressbox to direct storming Tar Heels D. So overwhelming were his men that Torbush, at urging of A-A DL Greg Ellis on headset, finished day on sideline and riding shoulders of his players. Carolina QB Chris Keldorf (17-28/290y, 3 TDs) threw long pass to WR Octavus Barnes for 62y TD 10-0 lead in 1st Q. Then, Tar Heels D took over: DB Dre Bly scored on TD RET of blocked punt, and Ellis pounced on EZ FUM created by blitzing LB Brian Simmons. Held to 185y, Virginia Tech (7-5) was hopelessly out of it all day, only score came on K Shayne Graham's 40y FG in 3rd Q.

Florida Citrus Bowl: Florida 21 Penn State 6

Penn State (9-3) arrived without 2 of its O stars who accounted for 30 of its 49 TDs during season. WR Joe Jurevicius was suspended for academic failure, and TB Curtis Enis was dismissed for illegal contact with sports agent, who bought suit for Enis' award show appearance. Game started just as Lions might have feared: Florida (10-2) scored 2 quick TDs for 14-0 lead as coach Steve Spurrier used alternating QBs Noah Brindise and Doug Johnson mostly to hand ball to TB Fred Taylor, who set Citrus Bowl records with 43/234y rushing. Brindise wedged over for opening TD, and Johnson hit WR Jacquez Green (2/72y) for 35y TD, which Green plucked off DB David Macklin's shoulder. After giving up 1st of 2 FGs by Lions K Travis Forney, Gators D made 2 GLSs late in 2nd Q as Nittany Lions tried to claw back. Johnson lost FUM at Florida 6YL, but Lions TB Chris Eberly (14/53y) was stuffed on 4th-and-1. Penn State soon reached 5YL on TB Kenny Watson's 52y punt RET only to have DB Mike Harris make EZ INT of QB Mike McQueary (10-332/92y, 3 INTs). Johnson sprained shoulder late in 3rd Q, and frosh Jesse Palmer was thrown into QB shuffle. Palmer completed his only pass for 37y TD to Green.

Cotton Bowl: UCLA 29 Texas A&M 23

UCLA (10-2) won its 10th straight but not without having to rally against fast-starting Texas Aggies (9-4) in 2nd-best Cotton Bowl comeback on record. Texas A&M K Kyle Bryant missed makeable early FG, and Bruins responded with long drive. Always tricky, UCLA tried rollout-throwback screen pass that star Texas A&M LB Dat Nguyen (20 tackles) leapt to grab at 16YL amid puzzled blockers. Nguyen raced upfield, was hemmed in, and pitched lateral to speedy DB Brandon Jennings who went last 64y for TD. Two possessions later, Bruins QB Cade McNown was tackled in EZ, and Aggies TB Dante Hall burst past blitzers for 74y TD run. So, Texas A&M led 16-0 late in 2nd Q. Key to Bruins hopes was last chance 1st H drive on which McNown (16-29/239y, 2 TDs, INT) hit WR Jim McElroy with 22y TD with 2 secs left. Although Aggies WR Chris Cole took 43y TD reverse pitchout to match McNown's 3rd Q TD pass to TB Skip Hicks, McNown scored on 20y run to pull Bruins within 23-21 as 3rd Q ended. Midway in 4th Q, surging UCLA scored on trick play it had practiced for month: TE Ryan Neufeld made 5y E-around TD run to cap 71y drive.

Rose Bowl: Michigan 21 Washington State 16

Washington State (10-2) air game turned out as good as advertised, taking 47y trip to QB Ryan Leaf's 15y TD to WR Kevin McKenzie. Early in 2nd Q, Cougars overcame dropped passes by "Fab Five" receivers to move to Wolverines 14YL. Under pressure, Leaf (17-35/331y, TD, INT) slightly overshot WR Shawn McWashington cutting across EZ. On next play, pass rush forced Leaf to make awkward throw, picked off in EZ by A-A DB Charles Woodson. Michigan (12-0) QB Brian Griese, out of character as long thrower, confidently pitched 1st of 2 TD bombs to WR Tai Streets to tie it 7-7 in 2nd Q. Washington State went 99y to 13-7 lead in 3rd Q as WR Shawn Tims swept right on 14y reverse run. But, Wolverines DL James Hall penetrated over C to block conv kick. Cougars led 13-7 until moments later when Griese and Streets connected for 58y bomb and 14-13 lead in 3rd Q. Powerful Michigan drive opened 4th Q as Griese used tried-and-true counter action pass for 23y TD to TE Jerame Tuman. K Rian Lindell countered with 48y FG, so Cougars trailed 21-16 with 7:25 to go. Michigan took nearly 6 mins off clock with ensuing march that ended with P Jay Feely's pooch to WSU 7YL out of FG formation. WR Nian Taylor pushed off Woodson for 46y catch as official pulled flag from pocket but didn't throw it. Hook-and-ladder pass went to Wolverines 26YL, but Leaf wasn't fast enough with ball spike with 2 secs on clock. Michigan clinched its 1st AP national title since 1948, but were denied in coaches' poll, thanks to next night's Orange bowl result.

Sugar Bowl: Florida State 31 Ohio State 14

With 1998 bringing birth of Super Alliance, theoretical assurance of no. 1 vs. no. 2 on an annual basis, observers were left to ponder situations like that of Florida State (11-1). Had Seminoles held on in late going of 3-pt loss to Florida on November 22, it would have left Florida State, Michigan, and Nebraska with legitimate, but imponderable arguments to fill 2 spots in upcoming season's Alliance showdown. Playing well early, no. 9 Ohio State (10-3) jumped to 3-0 lead on K Dan Stultz's 40y FG. Overcoming 2 early INTs, FSU QB Thad Busby (22-33/334y, TD, 2 INTs) pitched 27y TD to WR E.G. Green (7/176y) on last play of 1st Q. Ohio State TE John Lumpkin scored on fake FG pass in 2nd Q, but officials called PEN because Lumpkin slipped onto field illegally. Stultz then missed FG. Seminoles iced it with late surge in 2nd Q, starting with its D, led by DE Andre Wadsworth (2 sacks, INT), that sacked Buckeyes QB Stanley Jackson on 3 straight plays. Busby quickly hit Green with 46y pass and scored on 9y draw run. FSU DB Shevin Smith raced 51y with INT RET to poise frosh FB William McCray for 1y smash with 10 secs left in H. Ohio got FG and DL Winfield Garnett's safety sack of Busby to close within 21-8 at end of 3rd Q. Buckeyes finally reached EZ on fine juggling catch by Lumpkin, who made dive to EZ. Seminoles' 10 pts in 4th Q assured coach Bobby Bowden of 16-4-1 bowl record, just 2 wins off record.

Peach Bowl (Jan. 2): Auburn 21 Clemson 17

QB Dameyune Craig (15-45/258y) picked his last game for Auburn (10-3) to have perhaps his worst passing game, but he got lots of help from butterfingered receivers. Still, Auburn overcame rough moments with top D and hot 4th Q from Craig. Clemson (7-5) blocked 3 punts, 2 by LB Rahim Abdullah. Frosh DB Chad Speck scored 2nd Q TD on blocked punt for 7-3 Clemson edge, and FB Terry Witherspoon blasted over in 3rd Q from 2YL after another punt block. After K David Richardson's 48y FG, Clemson led 17-6 at end of 3rd Q. Craig scrambled for 22y TD, then lobbed 28y pass to WR Karsten Bailey to set up TB Rusty Williams' 7y TD run. Auburn built on 18-17 lead with K Jaret Holmes' 2nd FG with 4:11 to go.

Orange Bowl (Jan. 2): Nebraska 42 Tennessee 17

Orange Bowl became special as last game for graduating Tennessee (11-1) QB Peyton Manning and retiring Nebraska (13-0) coach Tom Osborne. Swift Volunteers D, keyed by LBs Raynoch Thompson and Leonard Little, DT Darwin Walker, and DE Jonathan Brown, was surprisingly good at holding Huskers run game to 69y in 1st H. But, Tennessee suffered 3 TOs in 10-min span of 1st H which set stage for 14-0 lead by Huskers. IB Ahman Green, who set Orange Bowl rush y record with 29/206y, scored on 1y run late in 1st Q after QB Scott Frost (9-12/125y) connected on passes of 25, 16, and 22y. WB Shevin Wiggins took rare run attempt to 10y TD in 2nd Q. Pressed into short passes, Manning (21-31/134y, TD, INT) positioned K Jeff Hall for 44y FG midway in 2nd Q. Determined Nebraska O-line came out for 2nd H with devastating 12-play drive and hammered away at wilting Vols D, opening holes for 227y in 3rd Q. Huskers tried just 1 pass in 3rd Q, cashed in Frost's 1 and 11y TD runs and Green's 22y tackle-breaking sprint off right side. Manning fit in 5y TD pass to WR Peerless Price in 3rd Q. Nebraska led 35-9. When sub Vols QB Tee Martin came in for 4-4/53y passing effort, including 3y TD to WR Andy McCullough, in closing mins, Manning's career was over. Osborne closed brilliant 25-year career with 255-49-3 record, including unprecedented (in modern age) 60-3 in last 5 years. When coaches' poll chose Nebraska over Michigan, it gave Osborne win or share of 3 titles in 5 years.

Final AP Poll January 3

1 Michigan (51.5)	1731.5	13 Louisiana State	856
2 Nebraska (18.5)	1698.5	14 Arizona State	773
3 Florida State	1599	15 Purdue	715
4 Florida	1455	16 Penn State	706
5 UCLA	1413	17 Colorado State	673
6 North Carolina	1397	18 Washington	617
7 Tennessee	1320	19 Southern Mississippi	490
8 Kansas State	1302	20 Texas A&M	421
9 Washington State	1259	21 Syracuse	331
10 Georgia	1121	22 Mississippi	255
11 Auburn	1025	23 Missouri	175
12 Ohio State	975	24 Oklahoma State	72
		25 Georgia Tech	64

Final *USA Today* Coaches Poll January 5

1 Nebraska (32)	1520	14 Arizona State	667
2 Michigan (30)	1516	15 Purdue	666
3 Florida State	1414	16 Colorado State	646
4 North Carolina	1292	17 Penn State	585
5 UCLA	1239	18 Washington	512
6 Florida	1209	19 Southern Mississippi	462
7 Kansas State	1192	20 Syracuse	380
8 Tennessee	1122	21 Texas A&M	359
9 Washington State	1076	22 Mississippi	188
10 Georgia	1007	23 Missouri	114
11 Auburn	854	24 Oklahoma State	103
12 Ohio State	826	25 Air Force	74
13 LSU	786		

1997 Top Performance Formula

1 Nebraska	1.8146
2 Florida State	1.7495
3 Michigan	1.7413
4 Florida	1.6500
5 Kansas State	1.6416
6 Tennessee	1.6389
7 Georgia	1.5940
8 North Carolina	1.5769
9 UCLA	1.5706
10 Auburn	1.5172
11 Washington State	1.5047
12 Ohio State	1.4853
13 Washington	1.4366
14 Louisiana State	1.4121
15 Penn State	1.3836
16 Arizona State	1.3730
17 Purdue	1.3573
18 Mississippi	1.3298
19 Syracuse	1.3259
20 Air Force	1.2892

1997 Top Opponent Records

1 Tennessee	.6835
2 Auburn	.6788
3 Colorado	.6721
4 Florida	.6667
5 Arkansas	.6581
6 Mississippi	.6406
7 Washington	.6357
8 Oregon	.6250
9 Georgia	.6124
10 Notre Dame	.6115
11 Florida State	.6111
12 Arizona	.6077
13t Alabama	.6068376
13t South Carolina	.6068376
15t Southern California	.601694
15t Stanford	.601694
17 Georgia Tech	.5827
18 UCLA	.5781
19 Virginia	.5778
20 California	.5690

1997 Out-of-Conference Records

	W-L	Percentage	Bowl W-L
Southeastern	37-5	.8810	5-1
Pacific-10	28-8	.7778	5-1
Atlantic Coast	20-9	.6897	3-1
Big Ten	27-16	.6279	2-5
Big Twelve	25-16	.6098	2-3
Western Athletic	19-32	.3725	1-2
Big East	13-24	.3514	0-4

1997 Individual Statistical Leaders

RUSHING YARDS

	Attempts	Yards	Avg.
Ricky Williams, Texas	279	1893	6.8
Ahman Green, Nebraska	278	1877	6.8
Tavian Banks, Iowa	246	1639	6.7
Travis Prentice, Miami (Ohio)	296	1549	5.2
Amos Zereoue, West Virginia	264	1505	5.7
Ron Dayne, Wisconsin	249	1421	5.7
Chris McCoy, Navy	246	1370	5.6
Jamal Lewis, Tennessee	232	1364	5.9
Curtis Enis, Penn State	228	1363	6.0
Fred Taylor, Florida	214	1292	6.0

PASSING YARDS

	Completions	Attempts	Yards	Pct.
Tim Rattay, Louisiana Tech	293	477	3881	61.4
Peyton Manning, Tennessee	287	477	3819	60.2
Ryan Leaf, Washington State	210	375	3637	56.0
John Dutton, Nevada	225	367	3526	61.3
Chad Pennington, Marshall	253	428	3480	59.1
Thad Busby, Florida State	235	390	3317	60.3
Daunte Culpepper, Central Florida	238	381	3086	62.5
Cade McNown, UCLA	173	283	2877	61.1
Mike Bobo, Georgia	199	306	2751	65.0
Pete Gonzalez, Pittsburgh	198	345	2657	57.4

RECEIVING YARDS

	Catches	Yards
Troy Edwards, Louisiana Tech	102	1707
Randy Moss, Marshall	90	1647
Eugene Baker, Kent	103	1549
Jerome Pathon, Washington	69	1245
Pascal Volz, New Mexico	69	1229
Troy Walters, Stanford	86	1206
Geoff Noisy, Nevada	86	1184
Brian Alford, Purdue	59	1167
Trevor Insley, Nevada	59	1151
Siaha Burley, Central Florida	77	1106"

1997 Consensus All-America

Offense

Wide Receiver	Jacquez Green, Florida
	Randy Moss, Marshall
Tight End	Alonzo Mayes, Oklahoma State
Line	Aaron Taylor, Nebraska
	Alan Faneca, Louisiana State
	Kyle Turley, San Diego State
	Chad Overhauser, UCLA
Center	Olin Kreutz, Washington
Quarterback	Peyton Manning, Tennessee
Running Back	Ricky Williams, Texas
	Curtis Enis, Penn State
Placekicker	Martin Gramatica, Kansas State
Kick Returner	Tim Dwight, Iowa

Defense

Line	Grant Wistrom, Nebraska
	Andre Wadsworth, Florida State
	Greg Ellis, North Carolina
	Jason Peter, Nebraska
Linebacker	Andy Katzenmoyer, Ohio State
	Sam Cowart, Florida State
	Anthony Simmons, Clemson
	Brian Simmons, North Carolina
Back	Charles Woodson, Michigan
	Dre Bly, North Carolina
	Fred Weary, Florida
	Brian Lee, Wyoming
Punter	Chad Kessler, Louisiana State

1997 Heisman Trophy Vote

Charles Woodson, junior cornerback-wide receiver, Michigan	1815
Peyton Manning, senior quarterback, Tennessee	1543
Ryan Leaf, junior quarterback, Washington State	861
Randy Moss, sophomore wide receiver, Marshall	253
Ricky Williams, junior tailback, Texas	135

Other Major Awards

Maxwell (Player)	Peyton Manning, senior quarterback, Tennessee
Walter Camp (Player)	Charles Woodson, junior cornerback-WR, Michigan
Outland (Lineman)	Aaron Taylor, senior guard, Nebraska
Vince Lombardi (Lineman)	Grant Wistrom, senior defensive end, Nebraska
Doak Walker (Running Back)	Ricky Williams, junior running back, Texas
Davey O'Brien (Quarterback)	Peyton Manning, senior quarterback, Tennessee
Fred Biletnikoff (Receiver)	Randy Moss, sophomore wide receiver, Marshall
Jim Thorpe (Defensive Back)	Charles Woodson, junior cornerback, Michigan
Dick Butkus (Linebacker)	Andy Katzenmoyer, sophomore LB, Ohio State
Lou Groza (Placekicker)	Martin Gramatica, junior kicker, Kansas State
Johnny Unitas (Quarterback)	Peyton Manning, senior quarterback, Tennessee
Chuck Bednarik (Defender)	Charles Woodson, junior cornerback, Michigan
Bronko Nagurski (Defender)	Charles Woodson, junior cornerback, Michigan
AFCA Coach of the Year	Lloyd Carr, Michigan

1998

The Year of the Bowl Championship Launch, Volunteer Triumph, and Bowdens in the News

At long last, a perfect college football title game was arranged as coming into being with the Bowl Championship Series, also known as the BCS. Or was it perfect? With the addition to the title pot of Big 10 and Pac-10 teams via BCS inclusion of the Rose Bowl, the criteria for matching the top two teams became far more complicated than it had been. The BCS employed a four-point plan: a combined tally of the Associated Press media poll with the ESPN/USA Today coaches polls, blend of computer rankings from Jeff Sagarin, The New York Times, and Seattle Times, strength of schedule ("Quartile") formula and a team's number of losses.

The BCS delivered nearly $117 million to the top conferences, so the question became: why jump for three- or four-tiered playoffs until the BCS was proven inadequate? The BCS came under immediate fire, however.

The flaw in the system was obvious. With no elimination tournament to be staged, only two teams were to be invited to the Tostitos Fiesta Bowl finale. What if more than two teams went unbeaten? What if there was only one?

For most of the season, four unbeaten teams were perched atop the polls: preseason no. 1 Ohio State (11-1), Tennessee (13-0), which finally beat Florida (10-2) in their annual early-season SEC showdown, Kansas State (11-2), which was devalued by its typically feeble non-conference slate, and UCLA (10-2), which saw its fabulous offense stressed week after week to overcome a young, easily-conquered defense.

Members of the media mostly ladled scorn upon the BCS. Chris Fowler of ESPN said that for each week that the top four stayed unbeaten "the closer we come to chaos." David Casstevens joked in the Arizona Republic: "The BCS is a complex statistical formula devised by the Internal Revenue Service and leaked by the White House to confuse the public and direct our attention away from the pending presidential impeachment hearings." (Pres. Bill Clinton faced perjury charges regarding sexual relations with White House intern Monica Lewinsky.)

As usual the season had to be played out, even though the media were already panicking. The most dominant of the four undefeated teams, Ohio State, was the first to fall, on November 7 to up-and-down Michigan State (6-6). Still, an unnerving and unwieldy three undefeated teams marched into the last day of the regular season. But, improving Miami (9-3) upset UCLA 49-45 in a thrilling makeup of a postponed September game. A few hours later, Texas A&M (11-3) came back from a 15-point deficit in the fourth quarter to win the Big 12 Championship over Kansas State in double overtime. Just minutes later, considerable underdog Mississippi State (8-5) went ahead of Tennessee 14-10 in the SEC Championship. Would all three undefeated teams fall? Reason finally prevailed: the Volunteers, destiny's darlings of 1998, rallied in the fourth quarter to secure a spot in the BCS title game.

Still, surprising Tulane (12-0), champions of the minor Conference USA, went unbeaten, and seven other hopefuls had only one loss after the dust settled in early December. Tulane's relatively low poll ranking understandably left it out in the cold with little protest. The two polls and the BCS, however, had no problem tapping Florida State (11-2) for the Fiesta Bowl, proving once again that if a team is to lose a game it should lose it early. FSU had been trounced 24-7 on September 12 by North Carolina State (7-5). In its first year, the BCS process was off the hook, for the time being.

Tennessee was a tempest in Tempe, winning a sloppy Fiesta Bowl 23-16 as quarterback Tee Martin, in the spotlight all year as heir to Peyton Manning's cherished spot, threw a pair of long passes to wide receiver Peerless Price, the second of which sealed the Volunteers' first national title in 47 years. Defense, Tennessee's hallmark all year, was the difference, but 12 Seminole penalties contributed as well. An unusually long layoff of 44 days and the emergency use of substitute quarterback Marcus Outzen (just 9 of 22 passing with two interceptions) seemed to insure Florida State's demise. Still, Ohio State, winner over Texas A&M in the Sugar Bowl, unlike bowl losers Kansas State and UCLA, was left to ponder what it might have achieved had it gotten the call against Tennessee in the Fiesta Bowl.

While Florida State coach Bobby Bowden failed to win his second national title, his family made big news. Son Tommy completed a miraculous turnaround at Tulane, but the school's marginal Conference USA schedule kept it out of a BCS bowl. Tommy was gone for Clemson (3-8) before Tulane's Liberty Bowl win. Older brother Terry came under fire at Auburn (3-8) which got off to its worst start in 52 years at 1-5. Terry, owner of a long but tenuous contract, was given no assurances that he would be allowed

back for 1999, so he resigned in midseason. Assistant Bill Oliver succeeded Terry, but was gone before Christmas in favor of Tommy Tuberville, who was recruited from Mississippi (7-5).

Milestones

⬤ Rules were changed to allow muffed lateral passes to be advanced by defensive players as if they were fumbles.

⬤ Death claimed two Hall of Famers Sid Luckman and Doak Walker. Luckman, All-America quarterback at Columbia in 1938, died at age 81 in July. Walker, unanimous All-America tailback and Heisman Trophy winner in 1948, died on September 27, 50 years to exact day from having appeared on cover of Life magazine in his Southern Methodist jersey and helmet, of complications from paralysis suffered in January skiing accident. Warren Woodson, head coach who had 203-95-14 record at several southwestern schools including Arizona (1952-56), died on February 22, 2 days short of his 95th birthday. Leon Bender, defensive tackle for Washington State's 1997 Pac-10 champions died of epileptic reaction several days after his selection by Oakland Raiders in NFL draft. While looking for golf balls, Mississippi tackle Joey Embry drowned in pond as result of diabetic seizure. Justin Brown, starting linebacker for Arkansas in 1996, died while awaiting heart transplant. Frank Hershey, who played for Penn State in 1962 Gator Bowl and was assistant coach at three small schools, died of cancer at 56. Jimmy Payne, All-America on Georgia's 1980 national champion, died of cancer at 38. Dave Huffman, All-America center at Notre Dame in 1978, died in car accident at age 41 on his way to Notre Dame-LSU game in November. Lamar McHan, 65, All-SWC tailback at Arkansas 1951-53 and top draft choice of Chicago Cardinals in 1954 died of heart attack. Lou Rymkus, Notre Dame tackle in 1940-42 and first coach of AFL's Houston Oilers in 1960, died in early November.

⬤ Former Notre Dame assistant coach Joe Moore, 68, won age discrimination suit, during which testimony revealed booster payments to players and that coach Bob Davie had questioned sanity of his predecessor Lou Holtz.

⬤ Coaching Changes

	Incoming	Outgoing
Arkansas	Houston Nutt	Danny Ford
Auburn	Bill Oliver (a)	Terry Bowden
Central Florida	Mike Kruczek	Gene McDowell
Kent	Dean Pees	Jim Corrigall
Louisville	John L. Smith	Ron Cooper
Nebraska	Frank Solich	Tom Osborne
New Mexico	Rocky Long	Dennis Franchione
North Carolina	Carl Torbush	Mack Brown
Southern California	Paul Hackett	John Robinson
Temple	Bobby Wallace	Ron Dickerson
Texas	Mack Brown	John Mackovic
Texas Christian	Dennis Franchione	Pat Sullivan

(a) Bill Oliver (2-3) replaced Terry Bowden (1-5) after Bowden resigned.

⬤ Longest winning streaks entering season:

Nebraska 13	Michigan 12	UCLA 10

Preseason USA Today Coaches Poll

1	Ohio State (31)	1465	14	Syracuse	662
2	Florida State (10)	1447	15	Texas A&M	600
3	Nebraska (12)	1372	16	Colorado State	543
4	Florida (1)	1346	17	Washington	506
5	Michigan (4)	1309	18	Georgia	448
6	Kansas State (1)	1205	19	Virginia	427
7	UCLA (3)	1139	20	Wisconsin	344
8	LSU	1062	21	Southern Mississippi	271
9	Arizona State	993	22	Auburn	222
10	Tennessee	934	23	Michigan State	211
11	North Carolina	778	24	Notre Dame	206
12	West Virginia	736	25	Arizona	180
13	Penn State	725			

August 29, 1998

Colorado State 23 MICHIGAN STATE 16: Employing cavorting D, Michigan State (0-1) took early control of Black Coaches Assn Classic. Spartan WR Plaxico Burress (7/55y) caught 2 passes to set up 1st Q FG by K Paul Edinger. QB Bill Burke (11-21/73y, TD, INT) and TE Brad Rainko connected on 4th down TD from 1YL in 2nd Q. MSU advanced to 16-0 when TB Sedrick Irvin (30/120y) used G Casey Jensen's block to slice 17y to score midway in 2nd Q. Then, teams reverted to 1997 habits. Spartans allowed big play, and Colorado State (1-0), nation's leader in '97 TDs longer than 30y, clicked on 57y TD bomb up left sideline as previously uncertain, new QB Ryan Eslinger (13-26/205y, TD, INT) hit WR Darren Hall for score. Trailing 16-9 in 3rd Q, CSU went 84y to tie it. After 18y burst, Ram TB Damon Washington saved poor-developing 4th down option pass by squirting for 3y TD. Ram FB Kevin McDougal scored 32y winning TD with 11:29 left behind block of G Anthony Cesario.

NEBRASKA 56 Louisiana Tech 27: Nebraska (1-0) exploded for 462y in coaching debut of Frank Solich. Huskers QB Bobby Newcombe, WB in 1997, clicked on year's 1st pass for 46y TD to TE Sheldon Jackson. Newcombe then ran for 2 TDs, pacing 35-6 H edge. Nebraska DB Joe Walker added 2nd Q KO TD RET of 99y. In 2nd H, Louisiana Tech (0-1) aerial duo of QB Tim Rattay (46-68/590y, 4 TDs, INT) and WR Troy Edwards wore Huskers to frazzle. Edwards set NCAA game record with 405y on 21 catches, scoring TDs of 52, 94, and 80y in 2nd H. Bulldogs racked up 569y.

(Sun) SOUTHERN CALIFORNIA 27 Purdue 17: Several L.A. Coliseum fans, including 91-year-old Giles Pellerin, who had attended every USC game since 1926, were treated for symptoms in 110-degree heat at Pigskin Classic. New USC (1-0) coach Paul Hackett accomplished what famous predecessors John McKay and John Robinson couldn't: he won his 1st game. For his trouble, Hackett ended up with QB controversy. Mike Van Raaphorst (11-22/89y, INT) started at QB, but was lifted with Trojans trailing 17-10 in 3rd Q. Frosh QB Carson Palmer (3-6/79y) sparked USC to 10 pts and 20-17 lead in 1st 2 series. Starting 7 newcomers, Purdue (0-1) dominated 1st H as QB Drew Brees (30-52/248y, 2 INT) pitched 2 TDs in 1st Q. In between, Trojan TB Chad Morton (15/53y) raced 98y untouched with KO RET. Morton tacked on 13y clinching TD run with 3:02 left.

(Mon) Florida State 23 Texas A&M 14 (East Rutherford, N.J.): QB Chris Weinke, relatively ancient 26-year-old new starter, guided Florida State (1-0) to 10-0 1st Q lead in Kickoff Classic. TB Travis Minor (34/146y) scored short TD run and K Sebastian Janikowski added 1st of 3 FGs. Texas A&M (0-1) came alive for 14-10 H lead when FB D'Andre Hardeman, who would be suspended later in season, plowed over from 1YL early in 2nd Q. LB Christian Rodriguez made blindside sack late in 2nd Q, and DB Jay Brooks scooped up FUM for 21y TD RET. Seminoles WR Peter Warrick (9/106y) made key 21y punt RET and made clever curl-back move to get loose for 9y TD catch and 20-14 lead with 5 secs left in 3rd Q.

September 5, 1998

(Th) Virginia 19 AUBURN 0: Most of 1st H was dominated by Ds, but Virginia (1-0) QB Aaron Brooks (16-28/220y, TD) avoided pressure to launch 61y TD to WR Kevin Coffey for 6-0 lead. Cavaliers held ball for 11:30 of 3rd Q, limited Auburn (0-1) to just 14y rushing, and added K Todd Braverman's 24y FG. Ahead 12-0 in 4th Q, Virginia lost FUM at own 42YL to Auburn LB Marcus Washington. But, Tigers, on way to 1st home opener blanking in 71 years, were halted on 4th down. Wahoo TB Thomas Jones (21/100y, TD) powered to TD with 2:09 left. Saddled with run O that made only 18y, new Auburn QB Ben Leard struggled and connected 11-25/146y, INT.

Tennessee 34 SYRACUSE 33: Thrilling "orange bowl" game saw Volunteers TB Jamal Lewis (20/141y) run 30y on his 1st carry and new QB Tee Martin (9-26/143y, 2 TDs) cap opening drive with 1st of 2 TD passes to WR Peerless Price. Syracuse (0-1) tied it in 2nd Q on TE Stephen Brominski's 10y TD catch. Tennessee (1-0) DB Fred White fell on FUM at Orangemen 14YL, leading to Martin's sneak in last min of 1st H. Vols led 14-10 at H and 24-13 at end of 3rd Q. Brilliant QB Donovan McNabb (22-28/300y, 2 TDs) threw TD pass and raced 6y for TD in opening 5 min of 4th Q, so Syracuse led 27-24. Martin answered with TD pass, but K Nathan Trout's 41y FG pulled Orangemen within 31-30 midway in 4th Q. On 3rd-and-8, McNabb wrestled off blitzing Vols LB Al Wilson to launch long completion that positioned Trout for 19y FG. But, Syracuse D, followed painfully familiar script in 5th straight home opener and allowed Tennessee to march back for K Jeff Hall's winning 27y FG as clock expired.

Ohio State 34 WEST VIRGINIA 17: No. 1 Ohio State (1-0) easily dismissed hopeful West Virginia (0-1) in what might have been dangerous trap for Buckeyes. Mountaineers opened scoring on K Jay Taylor's 47y FG in 1st 4 mins, but Ohio cruised to 20-3 lead on 18y TD run by TB Michael Wiley (17/140y), 14y TD pass by QB Joe Germaine (18-32/301y, 2 TDs) and K Dan Stultz's 2 FGs. WVU gained faith on TD pass late in 2nd Q by QB Marc Bulger (23-37/232y, 2 TDs, INT) to WR Shawn Foreman. That was quickly negated by Germaine's 39y TD to WR David Boston early in 3rd Q for 27-10 lead.

Miami (Ohio) 13 NORTH CAROLINA 10: High expectations of new, player-endorsed Tar Heels (0-1) coach Carl Torbush were quickly dashed by upstart Miami (1-0). Early knee injury to UNC QB Oscar Davenport sent touted frosh QB Ronald Curry (11-22/115y, TD) into game. Curry's 4y TD to TE Allen Mogridge highlighted 10-0 1st H margin. Red Hawks TB Travis Prentice (37/162y) powered for 119y on ground in 2nd H while scoring 4th Q TD and accumulating most run y vs. UNC since 1989. K John Scott booted 2 FGs in 2nd H as Red Hawks stunningly dominated 2nd H. Heels converted just 3 of 13 tries on 3rd down. UNC DB Dre Bly's 19th career INT tied him for most in ACC.

Boston College 41 GEORGIA TECH 31: Sr QB Scott Mutryn (16-26/220y, TD) added 2 running TDs to his sharp passing and TB Mike Cloud (34/200y) contributed pair of TDs rushing and caught 9y TD pass as Boston College (1-0) never trailed. Disappointed Georgia Tech (0-1) coach George O'Leary was troubled by "track meet" that led to 429y relinquished by his supposedly improved D. Favored Yellow Jackets depended on mastery of QB Joey Hamilton (15-29/227y, 2 TDs, INT) who added 8y TD run.

NOTRE DAME 36 Michigan 20: In 1st Q, key Fighting Irish (1-0) gain came on their 1st play as TB Autry Denson (24/162y, 2 TDs) raced 55y to set up K Jim Sanson's FG for 3-3 tie. Confident Michigan (0-1) ran 31 plays to Notre Dame's 6 in 1st Q, but poor GL decisions and 2 missed FGs left it tied. Wolverines WR Tai Street (8/101y) made 2 catches to help QB Tom Brady (23-36/267y) sneak over for 13-6 H lead. Notre Dame fashioned brilliant 3rd Q vs. stunned national champs. Irish opened with clever FG drive. FUM REC on following KO led to TD toss to TE Dan O'Leary for 16-13 lead. Irish QB Jarious Jackson (4-10/96y, 2 TDs, INT) nearly stumbled before launching 35y TD pass to wide open WR Raki Nelson. Denson scored early in 4th Q, added powerful 2y TD on 4th down to clinch it at 36-13 with 4:09 to play.

Colorado 42 Colorado State 14 (Denver): High-aspiring Rams (1-1) looked to vault up their program against in-state rival Colorado (1-0). While Buffs D held CSU to 17/1y rushing in 1st H, K Jeremy Aldrich booted 2 FGs in 1st Q, and JC transfer QB Mike Moschetti (21-32/257y, 3 TDs) fired 53y TD pass to WR Marcus Stiggers for 13-0 lead. CSU countered with 36y TD pass from QB Ryan Eslinger (13-28/124y, TD) to WR Frank Rice late in 2nd Q and Eslinger's TD plunge early in 3rd Q for 14-13 reversal. After Moschetti threw TD pass, frosh WR Cedric Cormier broke game open with 82y punt TD RET in 3rd Q. Colorado RB Dwayne Cherrington (25/100y) added 4th Q TD.

Washington 42 ARIZONA STATE 38: Washington's unknown band of receivers helped QB Brock Huard (27-47/318y, 4 TDs) surprise highly-regarded Arizona State (0-1) with 4- and 5-WR sets. Transfer WR and former basketball player Dane Looker, Huard's HS pal, broke 32-year-old Washington catching record with 11/108y, 2 TDs in his college debut. Sun Devils enjoyed 7-0, 14-7, 21-14, 28-14 leads in 1st H as QB Ryan Kealy (20-35/302y) threw 2 TD passes. Looker's 2 TDs earned 28-28 tie midway in 3rd Q. When WR Tariq McDonald caught short TD from Kealy with 2 min to play, ASU appeared in command at 38-35. But, with Huskies facing 4th-and-17 at own 47YL, sr TE Reggie Davis, former LB and DB, caught dramatic pass, broke tackles along right sideline and miraculously went 63y to winning TD in last 28 secs.

USA Today Coaches Poll September 8

1	Ohio State (38)	1512	14	Michigan	673
2	Florida State (12)	1471	15	Arizona State	524
3	Nebraska (8)	1388	16	Colorado	469
4	Florida (2)	1384	17	Wisconsin	428
5	Kansas State (1)	1289	18	Syracuse	383
6	UCLA (1)	1186	19	Texas A&M	349
7	Tennessee	1121	20	West Virginia	318
8	LSU	1084	21	Arizona	278
9	Penn State	1026	22	Texas	276
10	Washington	923	23	Southern California	274
11	Notre Dame	836	24	North Carolina	159
12	Virginia	774	25	Missouri	134
13	Georgia	766			

September 12, 1998

NORTH CAROLINA STATE 24 Florida State 7: Seminoles (1-1) QB Chris Weinke pitched 74y TD bomb to WR Peter Warrick on game's opening play. Then, mighty no. 2 Florida State completely unraveled. Weinke (9-32/243y, TD) suffered ACC-record 6 INTs, including pivotal pick by NC State (2-0) DB Jason Perry at Wolfpack 1YL in 1st Q. It was play that prevented possible 14-0 FSU lead. What happened next inflated NC State: its O cruised 99y to pull within 7-6. Then, brilliant WR Torry Holt raced 68y with punt RET for TD that put Wolfpack ahead for good at 13-7 later in 1st Q. Holt (9/135y), who scored 5 TDs vs FSU in 1997, added 63y TD catch from QB Jamie Barnette (17-32/287y, 2 TDs, INT) to ice it in 4th Q. It was just Florida State's 2nd ACC loss in 49 games to date.

Virginia Tech 37 CLEMSON 0: Virginia Tech (2-0) rained 31-pt storm on Clemson (1-1) in 2nd Q as long passes by Hokies QB Al Clark clawed Tigers. Oddly, Clark (7-26/171y, TD) completed just 4-20 in 1st H, but his avg was 38y per completion, including 56y score to WR Ricky Hall. Clemson went without 1st down in entire 2nd Q, and final score represented 1st home shutout of Tigers since 1979. Clemson O gained only 102y (31y rushing), and raw QB Brandon Streeter (6-23/64y) suffered 4 INTs when he failed to look off receivers as Hokies LB Lorenzo Ferguson (3 INTs) alleged in post-game interview. Virginia Tech K Shayne Graham booted 1st of his 3 FGs in 1st Q before Hokies administered their 2nd Q avalanche in which Clark scored on 1 and 10y runs.

Georgia 17 SOUTH CAROLINA 3: Frosh QB Quincy Carter (9-18/133y, INT) shook off rust of 2 years in minor league baseball and came alive in 2nd H to lead Georgia (2-0) to SEC win. South Carolina (1-1) started game just as rusty as Gamecocks committed 5 PENs around early INT of QB Anthony Wright (6-16/29y, 2 INTs). Pass was tipped by Bulldogs DE Antonio Cochran and picked off by LB Adrian Hollingshed, who landed in red zone at 19YL. Carter plunged over on 4th play for 7-0 Georgia edge. Carter suffered INT in 2nd Q as Carolina S Ray Green charged to Georgia 3YL, but Bulldogs held. K Courtney Leavitt's 24y FG pulled South Carolina to within 7-3 at H. Carter converted 2 passes on 3rd-and-long on 79y march to open 3rd Q and scored on 5y sprint around LE for 14-3 lead. Gamecocks succeeded twice on 4th down early in 4th Q, but Wright threw into double coverage from Bulldogs 37YL and was picked off at 1YL. Carter killed clock and led FG-drive spiced with 50y completion to exciting WR-DB Champ Bailey (3/74y).

PENN STATE 48 Bowling Green 3: After celebratory water bucket bath for his 300th career win, Penn State (2-0) coach Joe Paterno told sellout crowd of 96,291: "I've loved every moment of these 48 years. I love every one of you (fans) and it could not have been done without every single one of you." Nittany Lions WR Bruce Branch's 73y punt TD RET and LB LaVar Arrington's 16y INT TD RET launched rout. TB Cordell Mitchell (6/104y) scored on runs of 77, 16y. Bowling Green (0-2) managed only FG by K Jason Strasser in 2nd Q and was held to 3.7y per play on O. Paterno (300-77-3) became 1st major school coach to win 300 games at single school and was fastest to 300 victories.

Duke 44 NORTHWESTERN 10: Word out of Evanston was that Northwestern D might be 1 of Big 10's best. As counter, humble Duke (2-0) piled up 522y in 1st 3 Qs vs bigger Wildcats (1-1). WR Scottie Montgomery lost early FUM on backward pass to give NU opportunity at Blue Devil 28YL, but Duke allowed only K Brian Gowins' 25y FG for 3-0 deficit. Montgomery came back, gaining 60y on similar lateral-pass runs and scoring on same play from 37YL in 3rd Q. Duke finished with balanced attack of 272y rushing, 303y in air on QB Spencer Romine's 20-37, 3 TDs. Northwestern gained only 205y but got 36y TD run by TB Damien Anderson (12/67y).

Syracuse 38 MICHIGAN 28: Before football's largest to-date on-campus crowd, Michigan (0-2) became 1st defending national champion since Penn State in 1983 to open with 2 losses. Syracuse (1-1) QB Donovan McNabb was brilliant, hitting 21-27/233y, 3 TDs in air and running 19/60y including 17y TD that provided 24-0 lead midway in 2nd Q. Orangemen WR Kevin Johnson scored on 6y reverse 5 mins into game, and FB Rob Konrad hushed big crowd with 26y TD catch min-and-half later. McNabb put game in bag at 38-7 with 2 TD passes in 3rd Q. Wolverines tallied 21 pts in 4th Q as frosh QB Drew Henson mopped up with TD pass.

MICHIGAN STATE 45 Notre Dame 23: Earlier in week, ESPN questioned whether disappointed Michigan State (1-2) players had quit making effort for coach Nick Saban. Instead, DB capt Amp Campbell, who underwent serious neck surgery after previous week's 48-14 loss to Oregon, made inspiring coin toss appearance. Spartans demolished

Notre Dame (1-1) in 1st H, charging to miraculous 42-3 lead. Spartans blocked punt on 1st Irish possession, and DB Richard Newsome returned it for 25y TD. In 1st H, MSU QB Bill Burke (12-19/209y, 3 TDs) passed 7-9/181y, 2 TDs, including 86y TD to WR Plaxico Burress, longest-ever allowed by ND. Irish DB Deke Cooper's 96y FUM TD RET early in 4th Q prevented significant rout in Michigan State's 1st back-to-back wins over Irish since 1962-63.

Iowa State 27 IOWA 9: Since 1991, Iowa State's recent road record may have been 0-30-1, but fired-up Cyclones (1-1) ended their 15-game loss streak to Iowa (1-1). Cyclones TB Darren Davis rushed 37/244y and launched upset with early 1st Q TD after high snap allowed Iowa State WR Kevin Wilson to block Hawkeyes' punt at Iowa 12YL. Cyclones FB Joe Parmentier scored his 2nd TD which built 27-3 lead early in 3rd Q. Outrushed 254y to 42y, Hawkeyes managed 4y TD run in 3rd Q by TB Ladell Betts, who gained only 11/27y. Iowa State D had 5 sacks.

UCLA 49 Texas 31: Unlike 1997's "Rout 66," this game found UCLA (1-0) driving up and down field, instead of cashing easy TDs off Texas TOs. Bruins tallied on drives longer than 50y on 5 of 6 1st H possessions to create 35-3 H lead. Frosh WR Freddie Mitchell, who contributed 250y "variety pack" on 30y reverse run, 79y TD catch, 95y on RETs, and threw 34y TD off reverse to open scoring at 2:42 of 1st Q. Bruins TB Jermaine Lewis (22/113y) scored twice, and QB Cade McNown (20-30/339y, INT) tossed 3 TD passes. Texas (1-1) TB Ricky Williams rushed 29/160y and tallied 3 TDs in 4th Q to make final total look more respectable.

USA Today Coaches Poll September 14

1	Ohio State (52)	1537	14	Wisconsin	680
2	Florida (1)	1432	15	Colorado	661
3	Nebraska (7)	1425	16	Southern California	495
4	Kansas State (1)	1324	17	Arizona	490
5	UCLA (1)	1289	18	Texas A&M	424
6	Tennessee	1171	19	Missouri	342
7	LSU	1170	20	West Virginia	333
8	Penn State	1134	21	Virginia Tech	245
9	Washington	1020	22	Alabama	207
10	Virginia	952	23	Oregon	165
11	Florida State	901	24	North Carolina State	159
12	Georgia	879	25	Notre Dame	156
13	Syracuse	683			

September 19, 1998

(Th) AIR FORCE 30 Colorado State 27: LB Rick Crowell made FUM REC on game's opening play, and Colorado State (2-2) burst to 17-0 lead and seemed on its way to 6th straight win at Falcon Stadium. Rams QB Ryan Eslinger (18-26/193y, 3 INTs) hit early short passes, including TD to TE Derrek Uhl, and WR Darran Hall charged 77y on punt TD RET. But, diehard Air Force (3-0) QB Blane Morgan (8-16/141y, INT) pitched 2nd Q 40y pass to WR Matt Farmer to reinvigorate Falcons. Morgan also rushed 27/93y and scored 3 TDs. Air Force pounded 43y in 11 plays to kill 4th Q clock and position K Jackson Whiting's 40y FG that broke 27-27 tie with 11 secs left.

Virginia Tech 27 MIAMI 20 (OT): Miami (2-1) trotted out in green jerseys for 1st time since 1976, bolted to 13-3 edge as QB Scott Covington (13-28/282y, 3 TDs, INT) fired TD passes to WRs Santana Moss and Reggie Wayne. Virginia Tech (3-0) scored critical TD in last 30 secs of 1st H when QB Al Clark (14-26/153y, 2 TDs, INT) hit FB Cullen Hawkins for 14y TD. Hokies took lead at 17-13 as Clark sprinted 13y for TD midway in 3rd Q. Miami retook it at 20-17 on Covington's 84y TD to Wayne. Tech was halted at 1YL 6 mins into 4th Q, but K Shayne Graham tied it with FG. To start OT, Virginia Tech WR Ricky Hall, with 5" height edge, jumped over DB Nick Ward for EZ pass. Hurricanes went quietly: Covington was sacked twice and missed 4th down pass.

VIRGINIA 20 Clemson 18: No. 10 Cavaliers (3-0) got off to rousing start in 1st Q, which ended with Virginia ahead 17-3. Cavs DB Antwan Harris forced FUM on Clemson's opening series. TB Thomas Jones (24/118y, TD) scored on next play from 31y out, and QB Aaron Brooks (21-34/310y, TD) threw 20y TD pass to WR Kevin Coffey for 14-3 Virginia lead. "I don't know how it (momentum) got away from us," said Cavs coach George Welsh, but in 3rd Q, Tigers came alive. After Clemson (1-2) punt put UVa in hole at 2YL, Clemson DT Gary Childress broke through to nail Jones in EZ for safety. Cavs took FUM on free kick and drove 60y to 3YL. But, FUM by FB Tyree Foreman was turned into 95y TD RET by Tigers CB Antwan Edwards. Clemson grabbed 18-17 lead early in 4th Q on TD pass by QB Brandon Streeter (12-24/145y, TD, INT). It took 2 debatable PENs on 3rd down to sustain Virginia's winning march late in 4th Q. After D holding PEN at Cav 36YL, Brooks threw incomplete to Coffey from near midfield on 3rd-and-10. Coverage appeared to have been good, but interference was called. With 49 secs to go 6 plays later, K Todd Braverman nailed 30y FG as holder Will Thompson fielded low snap.

TENNESSEE 20 Florida 17 (OT): Volunteers (2-0) delivered much-anticipated win over Florida (2-1), their 1st in last 6 years. Gators outgained Tennessee 213y to 99y in 10-10 1st H, but lost 3 FUMs, all induced by Vols LB Al Wilson. TB Terry Jackson was headed into EZ on Florida's 1st possession when he lost FUM. Tennessee FB Shawn Bryson raced 57y to score in 1st Q. In 3rd Q, Vols WR Peerless Price made leaping TD catch for 17-10 lead. Gators tied it late in 3rd Q on QB Jesse Palmer's 70y TD to WR Travis McGriff (9/176y). In OT, K Jeff Hall's 41y FG gave Vols 20-17 edge. Florida, which lost 13y rushing all night, countered with 1st down at 15YL, but 3 misses by alternating QBs left K Collins Cooper with 32y FG try, which he hooked.

Louisiana State 31 AUBURN 19: On game's 1st play, LSU (2-0) DB Clarence LeBlanc started TO trend with 21y INT TD RET. On next Auburn (1-2) snap, TB Michael Burks lost FUM that led to 13-0 deficit on LSU QB Herb Tyler's diving 5y TD run. Auburn bounced back on 2 TD passes by QB Ben Leard (21-38/285y, 2 TDs, 3 INTs) and trailed 19-17 at H. LSU misfired on 2 excellent 3rd Q chances, but used Tyler's 29y TD to WR Larry Foster for 25-17 lead. Kick was blocked, returned for 2 pts by Auburn DB Brad Ware, but Tyler's 3rd TD pass clinched it in 4th Q.

Marshall 24 SOUTH CAROLINA 21: Sloppy Gamecocks (1-2) enjoyed 458y to 310y O, but committed 4 TOs, 2 inside Thundering Herd's 10YL. Upset-thrilled Marshall (3-0) made no such errors. "We should have had 14 more points in the first half," said South Carolina coach Brad Scott. USC led 10-7 at H, but 3rd Q's 1st play put Marshall back in contention: South Carolina QB Anthony Wright threw INT, and superb Herd QB Chad Pennington quickly produced TD for 14-10 lead. Astonishing TD came from Marshall midway in 3rd Q: On 2nd-and-goal at 7YL, Pennington faked handoff to SB LaVorn Colclough and deceptively placed ball between feet of TB Doug Chapman. Charging Gamecocks were allowed to rush by Chapman, who picked up ball and stepped untouched into EZ. Undaunted Carolina came back to tie it 21-21 and was moving in last 2 mins of 4th Q. Wright underthrew WR Zola Davis, and DB Daninelle Derricott made 30y INT RET to Gamecocks 20YL. K Billy Malashevich's 37y FG at 0:00 sent Herd players into wild celebration.

KANSAS STATE 48 Texas 7: Kansas State (3-0) took hiatus from creampuff non-conf slate, but blowout trend remained in place. Wildcats took 35-0 lead on 2nd Q explosion keyed by 93y punt TD RET by TB David Allen and 17y INT TD RET by LB Jeff Kelly. K-State WR Darnell McDonald caught 11/159y, 2 TDs from QB Michael Bishop (14-20/182y, 2 TDs). With starting QB Richard Walton sidelined, Texas (1-2) turned to frosh QB Major Applewhite (16-37/239y, 2 INTs) who managed 4th Q TD pass. Longhorns were limited to 53y rushing, including TB Ricky Williams' 25/43y.

BAYLOR 33 North Carolina State 30: Wolfpack (2-1) coach Mike O'Cain felt team was mentally ready after prior week's triumphant upset, but admitted "people were calling me right through Friday wanting to talk about Florida State." Unproven Baylor (1-1) jumped to stunning 26-0 lead by H. After K Matt Bryant's 1st Q FG, Bears overwhelmed NC State P Scott Earwood for safety on bobbled snap. Wolfpack moved to 4YL in 2nd Q, but QB Jamie Barnette (24-55/469y, 3 TDs) lost FUM on sack, and DB Kenyada Parker roared 82y to TD. Pack came back in 3rd Q with 23 pts, including 80, 11y TD catches by WR Torry Holt (11/255y). Bears QB Odell James squeezed in 4th Q TD run, and Baylor DB Gary Baxter blocked last play FG.

Ucla 42 HOUSTON 24: Little Bruins TB Jermaine Lewis (16/63y) had no runs more than 9y, but scored 4 TDs. UCLA (2-0) found itself in 21-14 H fight thanks primarily to 34y TD pass in 2nd Q by Houston (0-3) QB Jason McKinley (21-46/269y, 2 TDs, 3 INTs), but Lewis' 3rd score and DB Ryan Roques' 17y INT TD RET extended Bruin lead to 35-14. UCLA QB Cade McNown (17-32/315y, TD, INT) started slowly, but launched 61y TD to WR Brian Poli-Dixon early in 2nd Q.

USA Today Coaches Poll September 21

1	Ohio State (53)	1538	14	Wisconsin	719
2	Nebraska (7)	1451	15	Colorado	673
3	Kansas State (1)	1386	16	Arizona	558
4	Tennessee	1326	17	Southern California	549
5	UCLA (1)	1324	18	Texas A&M	491
6	LSU	1214	19	Virginia Tech	428
7	Penn State	1120	20	West Virginia	392
8	Washington	1069	21	Oregon	325
9	Florida	1041	22	Alabama	295
10	Virginia	960	23	Air Force	151
11	Florida State	915	24	Missouri	129
12	Georgia	840	25	Kentucky	96
13	Syracuse	798			

September 26, 1998

FLORIDA STATE 30 Southern California 10: With UCLA's game in Miami already postponed due to Hurricane Georges, USC (3-1) had reason to be nervous about its sojourn into Florida weather. Robyn Norwood's lead in *The Los Angeles Times* said it all: "It wasn't the heat, it was the humility." Trojans' miserable air attack was indeed humiliating: 3-19/23y, school's 2nd lowest pass ever. Aggressive Florida State (3-1) DB Mario Edwards held WR R. Jay Soward to only 1/5y receiving while other Trojans WR Billy Miller saw end of his 14-game catch streak. Florida State earned 13-3 H lead on K Sebastian Janikowski's 2 FGs and sub TB Jeff Chaney's 7y TD run at end of 54y march midway in 2nd Q. USC crossed midfield only once in 2nd H, that on out-of-blue 73y pitchout run by sub TB Frank Strong that set up TB Chad Morton's left-then-right 7y TD run that briefly brought Troy within 20-10 in 3rd Q.

ARKANSAS 42 Alabama 6: After falling behind 3-0, fabulous Razorbacks (3-0) D sent Alabama (2-1) O to sidelines 9 straight times after 3-and-out series. Arkansas run game, last in nation in 1997, charged for 206y vs. D that came in with 36y run avg. Arkansas balanced its attack with 239y in air on QB Clint Stoerner's 13-29 and 3 TDs. Scoring catches by WR Michael Snowden provided 7-3 and 21-6 leads for Hogs. Porkers TB Madre Hill, back after missing all of 1996-97, rushed 20/120y and added 4th Q TD. Crimson Tide TB Shaun Alexander, leading rusher in SEC, was held to 21/48y, and Bama was penalized 13/104y, all contributing to its worst defeat since 1957.

NOTRE DAME 31 Purdue 30: Notre Dame (2-1) DB Tony Driver, who briefly went home to ponder quitting after his switch from TB, turned into hero with 2 INTs in last 1:39. Driver's 1st INT set up K Jim Sanson's winning FG in last min, and 2nd preserved win. Purdue (2-2) had led for 59:03 as QB Drew Brees passed 24-36/261y, 2 TDs, 2 INTs. Boilermakers went up 14-0 in 1st Q on Brees' 13y TD to WR Randall Lane and 2y TD run. TB Autry Denson (31/143y, 2 TDs) scored his 1st TD and QB Jarious Jackson (13-24/199y, 2 TDs) threw his 1st TD pass in 2nd Q, but Irish trailed 24-14 at H. Jackson's 17y TD pass to TE Jabari Holloway pulled Notre Dame to within 30-28 with 3:36 to play.

NEBRASKA 55 Washington 7: Experts tabbed air game of Washington (2-1) as possible upset-maker, but Nebraska (4-0), with healthy backfield for change, rushed for 434y. Huskers built 35-0 lead by middle of 2nd Q in creating Huskies' worst loss since 1975. QB Bobby Newcombe (14/79y, 3 TDs rushing) scrambled 9, 13y to extricate Nebraska from early 2nd-and-20 at own 8YL on way to 82y TD march. IB DeAngelo Evans, out all of 1997, rushed 13/146y, scored on runs of 60, 14, and 19y. Doubt about Huskers pass D

was answered by heavy pressure on Huskies QB Brock Huard (18-32/160y, 2 INTs), who was sacked 3 times, lost 2 FUMs, but completed 6y TD pass to WR Joe Jarzynka late in 2nd Q.

TEXAS 59 Rice 21: Wondrous Texas (2-2) TB Ricky Williams rushed 30/318y, scored 6 TDs on runs of 31, 16, 17, 29, 27, and 41y. Williams moved into 2nd place in NCAA record book with 60 career TDs, 4 behind Indiana's Anthony Thompson (1986-89). Rice (1-3) briefly had tied it 7-7 on 1st Q TD run by FB Jamie Tyler (12/50y, 2 TDs).

TEXAS CHRISTIAN 35 Air Force 34: Falcon QB Blane Morgan (5-12/143y) threw 2 TD passes in 1st H, last of which came 39 secs before H to tie it 17-17. But, surprising TCU (2-1) got 49y FG from K Chris Kaylakie with 3 secs left in H. Morgan raced 14y to score early in 3rd Q, and Air Force (2-1) soon led 31-20. RB LaDainian Tomlinson (21/99y) scored his 2nd TD early in 4th Q to put Frogs ahead 35-31. Morgan missed all his late passes, and neither team could tally in last 10 mins.

USA Today Coaches Poll September 28

1	Ohio State (45)	1528	14	Arizona	693
2	Nebraska (15)	1491	15	Colorado	657
3	Kansas State (1)	1375	16	Virginia Tech	582
4	UCLA (1)	1342	17t	West Virginia	522
5	Tennessee	1341	17t	Oregon	522
6	LSU	1229	19	Texas A&M	491
7	Penn State	1121	20	Washington	407
8	Florida	1095	21	Missouri	200
9	Virginia	1018	22	Southern California	197
10	Florida State	980	23	Notre Dame	151
11	Syracuse	873	24	Arkansas	130
12	Georgia	864	25	Tulane	107
13	Wisconsin	777			

October 3, 1998

(Th) NORTH CAROLINA STATE 38 Syracuse 17: Looking for revenge from previous year's upset, Syracuse (2-2) opened with strong TD drive capped by QB Donovan McNabb's 2y TD sneak. NC State (3-1) QB Jamie Barnette (14-27/282y, TD) was under severe pressure much of game, but WR Torry Holt (6/132y) streaked 41y with 3rd down pass to launch 7y TD run by TB Rashon Spikes (17/96y) on option pitchout with 6:07 to go in 1st Q. On next series, DB Tony Scott made INT, nation-leading 11th for Wolfpack "Rough Riders" D backfield, to set up Barnette's TD run off right side. NC State was never headed on way to 28-10 H lead, but Syracuse seemed revived on FUM REC by DB Jason Poles with 6:31 left in 3rd Q. McNabb (17-32/170y, TD, 2 INTs) quickly sparked drive that led to 8y TD pass to TE Stephen Brominski. But, NC State DL Jeff Fisher's sack and 15y PEN put Orange in 3rd-and-39 hole from which they never climbed.

Tennessee 17 AUBURN 9: Tigers (1-3) surprised Vols (4-0) with early option run success, but DT Shaun Ellis stepped in to grab forward pitch by Auburn QB Ben Leard. Ellis rambled 90y TD. Tennessee TB Jamal Lewis (18/140y) roared 67y for quick TD, but was later lost for season with knee injury. After 2nd Q FG, Tigers had chance to get back in game with FUM REC at Vol 1YL. But Leard, 0-9 in air at this point, was on way for x-ray, and Auburn had to use frosh QB Gabe Gross on 1st 3 downs. Tennessee held, led 17-3 at H. Gross sparked Auburn in 2nd H by lighting fire under slumbering WR Karsten Bailey (2/33y). Their connections led to 2 FGs by K Robert Bironas. Tigers had 2 late chances, but suffered INT and tipped EZ pass with 2 secs left.

Georgia 28 LOUISIANA STATE 27: In his coming out party on ESPN, Georgia (4-0) frosh QB Quincy Carter (27-34/318y, 2 TDs) opened with superb 15-15/186y in air before 1st miss in 2nd Q. Bulldogs led 14-7 after 1st Q with all-around DB-WR star Champ Bailey catching TD pass. LSU (3-1) TE Kyle Kipps caught lob TD pass to tie it 14-14 early in 2nd Q. Throw-back pass from TB Patrick Pass to Carter clicked for 36y to poise another Bulldogs TD. Tigers QB Herb Tyler (16-26/205y, 2 TDs) tossed EZ pass that was knocked away by Bailey on 1 of his 96 plays. But ball deflected into arms of LSU WR Reggie Robinson for tying TD at 21-21 with 14 sec left before H. Midway in 3rd Q, Carter pitched 17y jump-ball TD to WR Tony Small. LSU could get no closer than K Christian Chauvin's 2 4th Q FGs.

OHIO STATE 28 Penn State 9: Young Nittany Lions (3-1) were up 3-0 in 2nd Q and deep in own end when wet ball slipped from passing hand of QB Kevin Thompson (11-20/106y, INT). Blitzing Buckeyes LB Jerry Rudzinski recovered for TD. Top-ranked Ohio State (4-0) sprung TB Michael Wiley over middle for 20y TD catch in last min of 2nd Q. Ohio DB Percy King blocked punt for TD and 21-3 lead early in 3rd Q. Lion WR Joe Nastasi jumped for 37y catch at 1YL to set up TD in 3rd Q, but 2-pt conv failed. Long pass by Ohio QB Joe Germaine (16-30/213y, TD, INT) led to TD blast by TB Joe Montgomery late in 3rd Q. Penn State was limited to 181y O.

Nebraska 24 Oklahoma State 17 (Kansas City): Crowding line of scrimmage, Oklahoma State (2-2) effectively halted Nebraska (5-0) run game in 3-3 1st H. In 4 min span of 3rd Q, Huskers tallied twice on QB Bobby Newcombe's 6y run and IB DeAngelo Evans' 1y blast on option pitchout. TB Jamaal Fobbs pulled Cowboys closer at 17-10 with short TD run late in 3rd Q. OSU QB Tony Lindsay (10-23/158y, INT) lobbed pass to wide-open WR Ethan Howell, who raced 67y to tie it 17-17. Nebraska DB Joe Walker answered with 73y TD sprint up middle with punt RET midway in 4th Q. Facing 4th-and-5 at Huskers 12YL with 14 secs left, Cowboys' Lindsay rolled out to find WR Sean Love, who nearly made it to EZ. Lindsay spiked ball to stop clock, then TB Nathan Simmons (26/116y) was stuffed at 1YL by Huskers line led by DL Mike Rucker. Afterward, OSU coach Bob Simmons admitted play failed in part because of formation confusion. Nebraska was held to 110y rushing.

Arizona 31 WASHINGTON 28: Surprisingly undefeated Arizona (5-0) continued to use QB tandem of Keith Smith (9-14/146y, TD) and Ortege Jenkins (10-19/111y, TD). Each threw TD pass in 1st H for 21-10 lead. Wildcats LB Marcus Bell was brilliant with 21 tackles, also blocked 3rd Q FG that would have given Washington (2-2) its 2nd lead. Still,

sub QB Marques Tuiasosopo (7-14/77y, INT, and 7/70y rushing) sparked Huskies with 15y TD pass to WR Chris Juergens and 2-pt run for 28-21 lead late in 3rd Q. With clock ticking down and Arizona trailing 28-24, Jenkins faced extinction as he dropped to pass from Washington 9YL. Jenkins scrambled up middle, leapt toward GL. Hit by LBs Lester Towns and Marques Hairston, DB Brendan Jones, Jenkins somersaulted for stunning winning TD with 4 secs left.

USA Today Coaches Poll October 5

1	Ohio State (54)	1538	14	Colorado	726
2	Nebraska (6)	1469	15	Virginia Tech	650
3	UCLA (1)	1392	16	Oregon	619
4	Kansas State (1)	1382	17	West Virginia	584
5	Tennessee	1333	18	Texas A&M	514
6	Florida	1165	19	Arkansas	346
7	Georgia	1149	20	Southern California	325
8	Virginia	1130	21	Missouri	250
9	Florida State	1066	22	Notre Dame	224
10	Wisconsin	885	23	North Carolina State	203
11	Arizona	845	24	Syracuse	181
12	LSU	821	25	Tulane	158
13	Penn State	758			

October 10, 1998

(Th) Virginia Tech 17 BOSTON COLLEGE 0: On rainy night when Boston College (3-2) retired Doug Flutie's no. 22 and Mike Ruth's no. 68, game became festival of TOs. DB Pierson Prioleau raced 85y to INT TD RET in 1st Q for Virginia Tech (5-0). Fabulous Hokie special teams blocked 2 punts, 2nd of which by WR Andre Davis set up TB Lamont Pegues' short TD run in 3rd Q for 14-0 lead. Eagles responded with 65y tackle-breaking run up middle by TB Mike Cloud (32/186y), but were turned back on 4 tries from inside Virginia Tech 1YL. BC outgained Hokies 295y to 236y.

Florida State 26 MIAMI 14: Although Florida State (5-1) never lost control of game, developing Miami (3-2) gained confidence by playing Seminoles tough. Improving FSU QB Chris Weinke (17-32/316y, 2 TDs) opened scoring with 62y TD pass to elusive WR Peter Warrick. Hurricanes came right back to tie it in 1st Q as QB Scott Covington (15-28/165y TD) tossed 9y TD to TE Daniel Franks. FSU's superb D shackled TB Edgerrin James, who rushed only 13/24y, and sub Seminoles FB William McCray scored key 3rd Q TD for 24-7 edge. Sub Miami QB Kenny Kelly pitched late 52y TD pass to WR Santana Moss.

Georgia Tech 47 NORTH CAROLINA STATE 24: Pivotal ACC tilt went to Georgia Tech (4-1) on strength of 28-pt explosion in 2nd Q. Yellow Jackets DB Jason Bostic broke open 5-3 contest with TD off blocked punt early in 2nd Q. After WR Torry Holt pitched 45y TD pass to pull NC State (3-2) to within 12-10, Tech scored TDs on pass by QB Joey Hamilton (15-22/236y, TD, INT) and run by TB Charles Wiley. Bostic capped big 2nd Q with 21y FUM TD RET, 4th of NCAA-record 5 straights games in which Engineer D would score TD on FUM RET. NC State WR Chris Coleman caught his 2nd TD pass in 4th Q in which each team scored 2 TDs.

Tennessee 22 GEORGIA 3: Vols (5-0), inspired by absence of injured TB Jamal Lewis, won 8th straight over Bulldogs (4-1) and opened door to SEC East throne room. "We're not supposed to be this good," gushed prideful Tennessee coach Phillip Fulmer. Georgia's superb frosh QB Quincy Carter (14-37/195y, 2 INTs passing, 7/-3y rushing) spent game running from Vols D, led by LB Al Wilson. K Hap Hines booted 48y FG late in 1st Q to earn 3-3 tie for Georgia, but Vols extended 9-3 H lead by scoring on opening 2 possessions of 3rd Q. After slow start, Vols QB Tee Martin (16-26/156y, 2 TDs, 2 INTs) set up own TD pass with 30y run early in 3rd Q.

FLORIDA 22 Louisiana State 10: On opening drive, LSU (3-2) held ball for more than 8 min, took 3-0 lead. Meanwhile, Florida (5-1) coach Steve Spurrier finally tapped QB Jesse Palmer as regular only to see Palmer and 2 other regulars go down with injury. But 1st, Palmer pitched 68y TD to WR Travis McGriff up right sideline when Tigers DB Chris Cummings gambled for INT. LSU regained H lead at 10-6 when QB Herb Tyler (15-31/234y, 2 INTs) pitched 50y TD bomb to WR Larry Foster. Florida took lead in error-filled 3rd Q on TD pass by QB Doug Johnson (13-22/156y) and FG after butchered drive. Key play of 2nd H gave Gators 22-10 lead: McGriff took long, wide lateral and tossed 49y TD to WR Travis Taylor. Halfway through 4th Q, Gators DL Derrick Chambers, LBs Mike Peterson, Keith Kelsey stopped LSU TB Kevin Faulk (19/77y) 3 times while Tigers needed 1y for 1st down at Gators 11YL.

WISCONSIN 31 Purdue 24: On his way to Big 10 season records in completions (336), pass y (3753y), Purdue (3-3) soph QB Drew Brees set 2 NCAA single game marks with 55-88 passing. Brees totaled 494y, but had 4 INTs. Wisconsin (6-0) DB Jamar Fletcher raced 52y with INT TD RET in 3rd Q that put Badgers ahead for good at 24-17. Badgers DB Mike Echols also made EZ INT. Wisconsin went up 31-17 on short TD blast by TB Ron Dayne (33/127y) midway in 4th Q. Boilermakers WR Chris Daniels (14/131y) caught his 2nd TD pass in game's last min.

TEXAS A&M 28 Nebraska 21: No. 2 Nebraska (5-1), which had won or shared 3 of last 4 national titles, experienced end of 19-game win skein and 40-game conf win streak. Boosted by thunderous crowd, Texas A&M (5-1) won vs. its highest-ranked foe ever. Previous best victim was no. 4 Tulane in 1939 Sugar Bowl when Aggies won national title. Members of that championship team were honored at H. Aggies QB Randy McCown completed only 2-8/93y, TD, INT, but opened with 81y TD to WR Chris Taylor. A&M rolled to 259y rushing with big play coming from frosh FB Ja'Mar Toombs, who dashed 71y to 1YL to set up TB Dante Hall's TD for 14-7 lead at H. Toombs made it 28-7 on 1st play of 4th Q. Huskers QB Bobby Newcombe (15-27/204y, INT, and 56y rushing) tallied on 11y run and sparked other TD drive. But, Newcombe was picked off by DB Sedric Curry near midfield in last min.

Kansas State 16 COLORADO 9: Kansas State (5-0) was getting heady feeling of top 5 ranking, but cautious coach Bill Snyder said afterward: "This is not a joyous locker room." Wildcats built 16-0 lead early in 4th Q on way to winning school record-tying 13th straight win. TB Eric Hickson rushed 29/137y, and K Martin Gramatica booted 3 FGs, but K-State couldn't get anywhere near its 60-pt scoring avg. Oft-injured Colorado (5-1) QB Mike "Paper" Moschetti, only hitting 7-18 passing through middle of 4th Q, came alive with 3 straight completions and found WR Marcus Stiggers for 5y TD with 5:42 to go. WR Darrin Chiaverini caught 3 straight Moschetti passes, but Wildcats stellar D forced Buffs into virtually useless FG with 1:46 left.

Ucla 52 ARIZONA 28: No. 10 Arizona (5-1) hit no. 3 UCLA (4-0) with its best tricks early, using P Ryan Springston's 35y pass from punt formation to set up RB Kelvin Eafon's 1st Q TD run. Wildcats enjoyed 3 leads of 7 pts until Bruins tied it at 21-21 at H on 2nd TD run by frosh TB DeShaun Foster (20/118y). Arizona WR Jeremy McDaniel (7/126y, 2 TDs) made 28y over-the-head TD catch from QB Ortege Jenkins (14-30/260y, TD, INT) for 28-24 edge. Trailing 31-28 early in 4th Q, Arizona opted for 49y FG try which went wide. "If somebody went to the bathroom (then), they would not have believed what happened when they came back," said Wildcats coach Dick Tomey. UCLA WR Danny Farmer ignited Bruins explosion, getting loose for 64y TD pass from QB Cade McNown (10-24/171y, 2 TDs). TB Keith Brown broke TD runs of 54 and 20y, and UCLA had 21 pts in 2:08 to seal it. Bruins outgained Wildcats 229y to 68y in 4th Q.

USA Today Coaches Poll October 12

1	Ohio State (59)	1547	14	Georgia	726
2	UCLA (1)	1452	15	West Virginia	650
3	Kansas State (2)	1410	16	Arkansas	565
4	Tennessee	1408	17	Arizona	542
5	Florida	1268	18	Colorado	409
6	Virginia	1193	19	Missouri	374
7	Florida State	1170	20	Notre Dame	367
8	Nebraska	1065	21	LSU	357
9	Wisconsin	1004	22	Syracuse	210
10	Virginia Tech	885	23	Texas Tech	209
11	Penn State	862	24	Tulane	183
12	Oregon	851	25	Georgia Tech	124
13	Texas A&M	849			

October 17, 1998

Temple 28 VIRGINIA TECH 24: For 2nd straight year, no. 14 Virginia Tech (5-1) was shocked on Homecoming. "We're the laughingstock of college football right now, and deservedly so," said DL Corey Moore. Hokies started well, building 17-0 lead as struggling 3rd string QB Nick Sorensen (14-24/143y, 2 INTs), in for injured Al Clark, tossed 2 TD passes. Hapless Temple (1-6), 0-26 all-time in Big East road games, faced its own O dilemma with its top 2 QBs on shelf. But frosh QB Devon Scott (4-9/155y, 2 TDs) enhanced effective run game with timely throws. Scott put Owls back in game late in 2nd Q when he threw screen to Slot-B Rahsaan Harrison, who used G Theo Ross' block to spring for 67y TD. Inspired Temple took lead on 2 TDs in 3rd Q, 2nd of which was Scott's 80y TD pass to WR Carlos Johnson. Virginia Tech TB Lamont Pegues (26/166y) scored early in 4th Q, but Scott countered with 1y TD run for 28-24 lead. Hokies went 85y to Owls 2YL, but WR Ricky Hall dropped EZ pass, and Pegues was stacked up by DB Jayson Thompson on final play.

Georgia Tech 41 VIRGINIA 38: Fired-up Georgia Tech (5-1) remained unbeaten in ACC with dramatic 24 unanswered pts during final 18 mins to shock unbeaten Virginia (5-1). On way to amassing 600y to 370y O advantage, Cavs seemed safe at 38-17 when TB Thomas Jones (27/207y, 2 TDs) raced 65y to score with 9:54 left in 3rd Q. But, Yellow Jackets DL Nate Stimson sacked and stripped Uva QB Aaron Brooks (19-32/312y, TD, 2 INTs), and LB DeLaunta Cameron scooped up ball for 34y FUM TD RET, NCAA record 5th straight game with FUM TD for Tech. Then, Jackets QB Joe Hamilton (11-23/288y, 3 TDs, 2 INTs) and WR Dez White (6/243y, 3 TDs) linked on 35y TD bomb. White later took flat pass, spun away from tackler, and cut across field for 54y TD that gave Georgia Tech its 1st lead at 41-38 with 4:40 left.

Kentucky 39 LOUISIANA STATE 36: Improving Kentucky (5-2) beat 1st ranked foe on road since 1977 on K Seth Hanson's last-play, 33y FG. LSU (3-3) never led, even with emotion on its side as 1958 national champs were honored. Tigers allowed HB Anthony White's 2 short TD runs, and saw deterioration of own kicking game. Tigers K Danny Boyd's 1st FG try hit upright, and when LSU QB Herb Tyler (15-26/268y, TD) scored in 2nd Q, bad snap allowed Kentucky DB Eric Kelly to tally 2 pts on RET of conv. Wildcats QB Tim Couch (37-50/391y, INT) threw 3 TD passes in 3rd Q for 36-22 lead, but Tyler's TD runs of 3 and 16y tied it with 5:35 to play. Facing 3rd-and-12 at own 24YL with 1:05 left, Kentucky seemed content to go to OT, but surprised LSU with 38y reverse by WR Quentin McCord, and 3 plays later, Hanson won it.

COLORADO 19 Texas Tech 17: Red Raiders (6-1) fell for 1st time thanks to TOs and late 91y drive by young Colorado (6-1) team without strong run attack (45/117y). Buffs led whole way, getting 1st of K Jeremy Aldrich's 4 FGs in 1st Q. Texas Tech QB Rob Peters (17-30/213y, INT) threw 25y TD to WR Darrell Jones early in 2nd Q, but Tech trailed 13-10 at H. Up 16-10, Buffs used 18 plays and 8:37 to go 91y to Aldrich FG which came with 2:50 to go. At beginning of march, Colorado QB Mike Moschetti appeared trapped for safety, but escaped for 1st down run. Among Raiders DL Montae Reagor's 9 tackles were 2 sacks, bringing his career total to 21.5.

UCLA 41 Oregon 38 (OT): In battle of Pac-10's unbeatens, UCLA (5-0) K Chris Sailer overcame nagging groin injury to kick 23y FG in OT to atone for short miss late in 4th Q. Bruins QB Cade McNown, in midst of mediocre spell, wasn't feeling well either. McNown led Bruins to 24-7 lead in 2nd Q on way to 20-36/395y, 3 TDs, 2 INTs for game, but after he vomited on field in 3rd Q, he closed with 9-13/202y, TD. Oregon (5-1) rallied to earn 31-31 tie as national pass efficiency leader QB Akili Smith (15-37/221y, INT) threw 3 TDs. Ducks TB Reuben Droughns rushed 25/172y, but fumbled 4 times, and was lost for season with multiple leg injuries. Droughns' last FUM came at UCLA 40YL, and McNown pitched 60y TD to WR Danny Farmer on next play for 38-31 lead with 2:36 left. Smith converted 4th-and-16 pass on 65y tying drive. But, UCLA came back on McNown's bomb before Sailer pulled 21y FG try at end. Bruins LB Brendan Ayanbadejo's 2 sacks ruined Oregon's OT series before Sailer got his 2nd chance after TB Keith Brown's key runs.

USA Today Coaches Poll October 19

1	Ohio State (58)	1545	14	Oregon	717
2	UCLA (1)	1452	15	Virginia	682
3	Kansas State (3)	1420	16	Arizona	602
4	Tennessee	1398	17	Colorado	545
5	Florida	1262	18	Missouri	444
6	Florida State	1227	19	Georgia Tech	420
7	Nebraska	1140	20	Notre Dame	391
8	Wisconsin	1111	21	Virginia Tech	355
9	Penn State	991	22	Syracuse	273
10	Texas A&M	986	23	Tulane	254
11	Georgia	838	24	Mississippi State	165
12	Arkansas	761	25	Texas Tech	89
13	West Virginia	729			

October 24, 1998

Miami 34 WEST VIRGINIA 31: Seesaw battle found West Virginia (4-2) leading 24-17 at H as QB Marc Bulger (32-43/380y, INT) threw 3 TD passes. Miami (4-2) TB Edgerrin James (31/162y) scored his 3rd TD in 10-pt 3rd Q as he caught 10y pass from QB Scott Covington (19-30/247y, 2 TDs, INT). WVU regained 31-27 lead in 4th Q on FB Anthony Green's short TD run. Miami pulled it out on Covington's 3y TD pass over middle to WR Daryl Jones. Mountaineers K Jay Taylor missed 53y tying FG at end.

Florida State 34 GEORGIA TECH 7: Hot Yellow Jackets (5-2) came out flying with 18-play, 80y TD march. TB Phillip Rogers capped drive by leaping to 2y TD. Florida State (7-1), looking to regain accustomed control of ACC race, used brilliant WR Peter Warrick for 44y TD catch to tie it. Seminoles D took control, allowing only 119y after 1st series, but FSU led only 10-7 entering 4th Q. Warrick (6/82y) keyed 24-pt blast with 8y TD catch, nifty 16y TD reverse run. Georgia Tech's flagging O was helpless with bruised QB Joey Hamilton (8-14/56y, INT) forced to sideline.

VIRGINIA 23 North Carolina State 13: Virginia (6-1) kept pace in ACC with Florida State, but 1st unpredictable NC State (4-3) broke TB Ray Robinson (27/202y) up middle for 88y TD sprint in early going. Wolfpack led 13-9 at H as they suffered 2nd Q punt block for safety. TB Thomas Jones (21/117y) powered over left side for 9y TD in 3rd Q, and Cavs led 16-13. Sub TB Antwoine Womack iced it with 21y TD run in 4th Q, but Virginia remained inept on 3rd down until late in 3rd Q.

Georgia 28 KENTUCKY 26: Wildcats QB Tim Couch threw 34-46/326y, 2 TDs, 2 INTs, but his Georgia (6-1) counterpart, QB Quincy Carter, supplied more balance. Carter also threw 2 TDs and rushed 14/114y, including 49y TD run that trimmed Kentucky's 10-0 lead in 2nd Q. Kentucky (5-3) led 17-14 at H, but Carter's 34, 8y TD passes in 3rd Q gave Bulldogs 28-20 edge. Wildcats led in O stats 530y to 332y but were penalized 75y on way to school record for season. Poor KO coverage allowed Bulldogs to start 2 drives near midfield. Additionally, Kentucky botched 2 big plays: 4th down run near Georgia GL and last play 49y FG try.

NOTRE DAME 20 Army 17: Big favorite Notre Dame (5-1) had week off to prepare for option O of Army (2-5). Still, Cadets rushed 49/218y and played their own inspired run D. Fighting Irish TB Autry Denson gained only 24/87y, but he and Cadets HB Bobby Williams (14/74y) traded TD runs in 10-10 1st H. Key TD was scored by Notre Dame in 3rd Q when WR Bobby Brown tried to finish 36y reception by stretching to EZ. Ball came loose, but was covered for TD by alert Irish WR Malcolm Johnson. Still, Army earned 17-17 tie in 4th Q on FB Craig Stucker's 19y blast up middle. Irish K Jim Sanson made up for 2 earlier misses by bombing winning, career-best 48y FG in last 1:06.

NEBRASKA 20 Missouri 13: Tigers (5-2) enjoyed 13-6 H edge on 41y FUM TD RET by DL Steve Erickson and short TD run by QB Corby Jones (8-20/89y). Nebraska (7-1) was bailed out in 2nd H by "The Count of Monte Christo." Oft-injured sr sub QB Monte Christo (20/67y rushing) stepped in for hurt Bobby Newcombe, made considerable run y after being hit and slammed for his 1st career TDs on 1 and 3y runs. Jones lofted unsuccessful EZ pass to WR John Dausman with 9 secs left, then was sacked at Huskers 34YL by LB Eric Johnson on last play.

TEXAS A&M 17 Texas Tech 10: Slow-starting Texas A&M (7-1) fell behind 3-0 as K Chris Birkholz belted 46y FG for Texas Tech (6-2), which was fired up for rivalry game. Aggies lined up for tying FG in 1st Q, but holder Shane Lechler rose up to find TE Daniel Campbell for surprise 8y TD pass in back of EZ. Red Raider TB Ricky Williams (21/94y) regained lead on 11y TD run in 2nd Q. TB Dante Hall made sharp broken field run with pass to set up own 1y TD run which gave A&M permanent lead at 14-10 in 2nd Q. Aggies D held Texas Tech to 205y O.

Ucla 28 CALIFORNIA 16: UCLA (6-0) WR Brian Poli-Dixon pulled in 17 and 35y TDs, 2nd of which was brilliant diving grab in EZ that provided 14-7 lead in 1st Q. California (4-3) LB Sekou Sanyika soon stuffed Bruin FB Durell Price for safety. Big play came at UCLA GL late in 2nd Q: Bruin LB Robert Thomas blasted Bears FB Josh White, and ball came loose. UCLA DB Larry Atkins scooped it, but coughed it up. Atkins was ruled down at own 1YL: UCLA led 21-9 at H. Bruins held again at GL in 3rd Q when frosh QB Sam Clemons entered game for ill-fated sneak. Bears QB Justin Vedder (13-22/109y, INT) threw 3rd Q TD to make it 21-16. UCLA QB Cade McNown (15-27/182y, 2 TDs) made beneficial runs for 57y, and TB Jermaine Lewis threw well-disguised 30y option TD pass to WR Jon Dubravac to ice it.

OREGON 17 Southern California 13: Cavorting USC (5-3) D shut down Oregon (6-1) run game in 1st H as Ducks lost 7y of O and lamented loss of 3 regulars. TB Chad Morton (20/104y) found hole at corner of Ducks D to sprint 70y to score with short pass from QB

Jeff Van Raaphorst (9-12/116y, TD, INT). Trojans led 10-3 at H. Oregon QB Akili Smith (15-28/231y, TD, INT) fired 55y TD to WR Tony Hartley (6/118y) to tie it in 3rd Q. Key play came in 4th Q as Smith slid left on option and used double-team block on USC LB Chris Claiborne to break 62y for TD and 17-10 edge. Frosh QB Carson Palmer (10-19/179y) guided Trojans to 7YL, but delay PEN forced K Adam Abrams' 2nd FG with 4:20 left. USC never saw ball again as Oregon padded its 170y 2nd H rushing total.

USA Today Coaches Poll October 26

1	Ohio State (55)	1543	14	Virginia	739
2	UCLA (1)	1453	15	Arizona	709
3	Kansas State (5)	1412	16	Notre Dame	521
4	Tennessee (1)	1402	17	Virginia Tech	471
5	Florida	1274	18	Tulane	451
6	Florida State	1233	19	Syracuse	424
7	Nebraska	1134	20	West Virginia	318
8	Wisconsin	1130	21	Missouri	302
9	Texas A&M	1018	22	Michigan	179
10	Penn State	1008	23	Air Force	170
11	Georgia	891	24	Georgia Tech	153
12	Arkansas	808	25	Colorado	143
13	Oregon	806			

Bowl Championship Series Rankings October 26

		Poll Avg.	Computer Avg.	Quartile Rank	Losses	Total
1	UCLA (6-0)	2.0	1.00	0.04	0	3.04
2	Ohio State (7-0)	1.0	2.67	0.64	0	4.31
3	Tennessee (6-0)	3.5	2.92	0.08	0	6.50
4	Kansas State (7-0)	3.5	3.33	1.96	0	8.79
5	Florida State (7-1)	5.5	6.33	0.56	1	13.39

October 31, 1998

VIRGINIA TECH 27 West Virginia 13: Hokies (7-1) welcomed back injured QB Al Clark, who passed 12-21/162y, 2 TDs, 2 INTs, but it was ferocious special teams that got them winging in 1st Q. WR Ricky Hall returned blocked punt 17y to score. When West Virginia (4-3) countered on short TD pass by QB Marc Bulger (26-43/240y, 4 INTs), Tech blocked kick of K Jay Taylor, who had made 96 straight. In 2 min span of 3rd Q, Hokies protected 17-13 lead by halting WVU after 1st-and-goal at Hokies 4YL and on EZ pickoff by DB Ike Charlton, 1 of his 3 INTs. Virginia Tech pulled away in 2nd H on Clark's 36y TD pass to Hall and K Shayne Graham's 41y FG.

Florida 38 Georgia 7 (Jacksonville): No. 6 Florida (7-1) opened with all its trump cards: running up 21-0 lead in opening 13 min as Gators outgained Bulldogs (6-2) 197y to 11y. Gators QB Doug Johnson tossed 2 TD passes of 25y each and scored on sneak. Georgia advanced inside Florida 30YL 4 times after 1st Q, but suffered FUM, missed FG, TO on downs, and INT. RB Ronnie Bradley scored only Bulldogs TD in 2nd Q. Florida coach Steve Spurrier, never reluctant to rub it in vs. biggest rival, called 2 late TD tricks: Johnson's 10y catch off WR pass by Travis McGriff and WR John Capel's 8y reverse run with 38 sec left.

Ohio State 38 INDIANA 7: Buckeyes QB Joe Germaine continued to build his fantastic weekly stats as he took what baffled Indiana (3-5) gave him and pitched 31-45/351y, his 4th straight 300y game. On other side, Ohio State (8-0) threw blanket over dangerous Hoosiers QB Antwaan Randle El (18/27y rushing), thanks to revitalized LB Andy Katzenmoyer (3 tackles for loss). Randle El lost FUM in 1st Q just when Indiana appeared ready to trim 14-0 deficit. Ohio WRs Dee Miller (11/159y) and David Boston (9/110y, 2 TD catches and 70y punt TD RET) had spectacular days.

Texas 20 NEBRASKA 16: Invincible facade of Nebraska (7-2) crumbled further as its 47-game home winning streak ended on 4th Q comeback by Texas (6-2). Longhorns sprung TB Ricky Williams for 37/150y rushing which helped set up 2 TD passes by QB Major Applewhite (14-26/269y, 2 TDs, INT). Longhorns led 10-3 at H, but Huskers rebounded for 13-10 lead on K Kris Brown's 47y FG and blistering 38y TD sprint by sub QB Eric Crouch. Texas held inside its 10YL on Crouch's FUM late in 3rd Q, but Nebraska broke 13-13 tie on Brown's 3rd FG with 8:33 to play. Applewhite found WR Wane McGarrity on winning 2y TD pass with 2:47 left.

UCLA 28 Stanford 24: Undefeated UCLA (7-0) avoided epic upset at hands of air-minded Stanford (1-7) when beleaguered Bruins D forced late-game FUM as it appeared ready to permit game-losing TD. Cardinal QB Todd Husak pitched for 3rd-most y in school history with 25-45/419y, TD, beating constant blitzes with quick, short throws. Card WR Troy Walters caught 10/192y. Stanford broke 14-14 tie with 10 pts in 3rd Q: K Kevin Miller's 36y FG and sub QB Randy Fasani's short TD pass. Bruins TBs Keith Brown (15/94y, 2 TDs) and gimpy DeShaun Foster scored 4th Q TDs for 28-24 lead. With less than 4 mins to go, Stanford WR Jeff Allen caught 26y pass over middle and appeared ready to score when UCLA DB Marques Anderson stripped ball from Allen's grasp. Bruins DB Larry Atkins fell on it in EZ for touchback.

ARIZONA 38 Oregon 3: With eyes on Rose Bowl, Wildcats (8-1) completely shut down 44-pt per game O of no. 12 Oregon (6-2). Without 3 top TBs, Ducks couldn't run (32/64y), and Arizona DB Chris McAlister blanketed WR Damon Griffin (1/13y). Arizona WR Brad Brennan spun out of tackle at Ducks 25YL to complete 48y TD pass in 1st Q. K Nathan Villegas booted FG in dying moments of 1st H for only Ducks pts. Wildcats TB Trung Canidate (17/180y) raced 71y to TD and 17-3 lead early in 3rd Q. Canidate also ran 61y in 4th Q to set up TB Kelvin Eafon's 3rd TD run.

USA Today Coaches Poll November 2

1	Ohio State (54)	1542	14	Virginia Tech	658
2	Kansas State (5)	1434	15	Nebraska	637
3	Tennessee (2)	1419	16	Tulane	545
4	UCLA (1)	1411	17	Syracuse	541
5	Florida	1291	18	Georgia	461
6	Florida State	1243	19	Missouri	422
7	Wisconsin	1168	20	Oregon	351
8	Texas A&M	1089	21	Air Force	318
9	Penn State	1056	22	Michigan	294
10	Arkansas	950	23	Texas	230
11	Arizona	907	24	Georgia Tech	215
12	Virginia	880	25	Colorado	156
13	Notre Dame	680			

Bowl Championship Series Rankings November 2

		Poll Avg.	Computer Avg.	Quartile Rank	Losses	Total
1	Ohio State (8-0)	1.0	1.75	0.96	0	3.71
2	Tennessee (7-0)	2.5	2.92	0.28	0	5.70
3	UCLA (7-0)	3.5	3.00	0.12	0	6.62
4	Kansas State (8-0)	3.0	2.33	2.72	0	8.05
5	Florida (7-1)	5.0	5.67	0.32	1	11.99

November 7, 1998

Notre Dame 31 BOSTON COLLEGE 26: Surprising Eagles (3-6) used TB Mike Cloud's 11y TD run and QB Scott Mutryn's 23y TD pass to build 17-14 H lead. TD pass late in 3rd Q by Notre Dame (7-1) QB Jarious Jackson (10-21/210y, 2 TDs) broke 17-17 deadlock, and 4th Q TD by TB Autry Denson (28/128y, 2 TDs) put Irish in control at 31-20. But, Mutryn threw TD pass to WR Anthony DiCosmo with 5:54 left and fashioned late, desperate BC drive. With 1:07 to play, Mutryn hit 26y pass to TE Rob Tardio, who advanced to ND 4YL. Cloud (28/141y), nation's 4th leading rusher, gained 2y on 2 tries and, on 3rd down, was stopped at GL by inside-charging LB Jimmy Friday when H-back chose to block outside tackler. With 11 sec left on 4th down, Cloud slanted left but was nailed inches short by Irish DB Deke Cooper.

WEST VIRGINIA 35 Syracuse 28: In 21-20 1st H led by Syracuse (5-3), each team scored on opening drive. Teams combined for 17 pts in last 2 min of H: West Virginia (5-3) TB Amos Zereoue (31/189y, 2 TDs) scored on beautiful 30y Statue of Liberty run. Orangemen countered on 2 passes from QB Donovan McNabb (16-29/281y, 3 TDs) to WR Kevin Johnson (11/196y, 2 TDs), 2nd of which went 7y to TD. K Jay Trout nailed 48y FG on last play of H for WVU. Johnson went uncovered on 22y TD catch to open 3rd Q for 28-20 Syracuse lead. Zereoue answered with short TD run late in 3rd Q, and WR Pat Greene caught 2-pt pass to tie it. K Nathan Trout of Syracuse missed 2 medium-length FGs in 4th Q before WVU WR David Saunders' 43y TD catch from QB Marc Bulger (15-31/257y, TD, INT) on rollout with 3:04 to go.

FLORIDA STATE 45 Virginia 14: After time-consuming, but empty opening drive by Virginia (7-2), Florida State (9-1) answered on next play: QB Chris Weinke (8-16/143y) launched 79y TD bomb to WR Peter Warrick. But, Cavs TB Thomas Jones (16/66y) dashed 37y to poise FB Anthony Southern's 2y TD blast. Jones' 8y TD catch late in 2nd Q pulled Virginia to within 21-14 at H. FSU QB Marcus Outzen (5-6/67y, INT) took over for out-for-season Weinke in 2nd H and rarely was in pressure situation. Seminoles DB Dexter Jackson's 2nd INT set up TD run by TB Travis Minor (28/130y), and LB Brian Allen blocked punt to set up K Sebastian Janikowski's FG for 31-14 lead in 4th Q. FSU subs added 2 TDs within 1:15 span of 4th Q.

ARKANSAS 34 Mississippi 0: In cold, pouring rain, undefeated Arkansas (8-0) poured it on Ole Miss (6-3). Early FUMs led to 2 TD passes from QB Clint Stoerner to WR Anthony Lucas (4/177y) that went 50 and 36y. In between, Rebels TB Deuce McAllister (17/63y) was belted by DL D. J. Cooper near Hogs GL, and Arkansas LB Harry Wilson fell on FUM. Razorbacks TB Madre Hill all but locked it up at 21-0 with 17y TD run in last 4 mins of 3rd Q. Mississippi was held to 33/84y rushing.

MICHIGAN 27 Penn State 0: Penn State (6-2) coach Joe Paterno was worried about his D's strength vs. power runs, but young Lions seemed ready to win big game. Michigan (7-2), winners of 6 straight but unimpressive on O, beat Penn State with its own D and sharp passing of QB Tom Brady (17-30/224y, 2 TDs, INT). Brady found FB Aaron Shea loose on right sideline for 26y TD pass on 1st Wolverine possession. Trailing 10-0 in 2nd Q, Penn State FB Aaron Harris was stopped on 4th down at Michigan GL. Brady added 2nd TD pass late in 2nd Q. Lions gained only 200y.

Michigan State 28 OHIO STATE 24: All started well for no. 1 Ohio State (8-1) as Buckeyes ran up 17-3 lead in 1st Q on 41y TD pass by QB Joe Germaine (16-34/239y, TD, INT) and short TD run by TB Michael Wiley (22/100y). From that moment, tenacious Michigan State (5-4), led by frosh LB Josh Thornhill's 15 tackles, slammed door, forced 4 FUMs. K Paul Edinger's 3rd of 5 FGs trimmed Spartan deficit to 17-9 at H. Ohio DB Damon Moore raced 73y to INT TD RET in 3rd Q, but his unnecessary plunge into EZ only seemed to fire up MSU. Spartans scored next 19 pts including 23y TD pass by QB Bill Burke (18-46/323y, TD, INT) for 28-24 lead. WR David Boston's 26y punt RET put Buckeyes at midfield with 1:39 to play. Germaine hit 16 and 20y passes to 15YL, but missed next 2 throws. Spartan DB Renaldo Hill batted down 3rd down pass in EZ, then, with aid of full blitz, picked off Germaine's underthrow for WR Dee Miller.

Ucla 41 OREGON STATE 34: With Beavers fans mockingly shouting, "Overrated!," at Bruins, Cardiac Kids of UCLA (8-0) scored 24 pts in last 16 mins to pull out another late win. Coming off 2 straight 1-pt losses, underrated Oregon State (4-6) mined 206y in KO RETs to come back from 10-0, 17-7, 31-24, and 34-31 shortfalls. Bruins led 17-10 at H as TB DeShaun Foster scored on 7y TD run, QB Cade McNown (23-37/377y, 4 TDs, INT) threw 28y TD pass to TE Ryan Neufeld. TB Jason Dandridge (16/130y, 3 TDs) scored his

2nd TD midway in 3rd Q to give Beavers 1st lead at 24-17. WR Danny Farmer caught 7, 43y TDs to regain lead for Bruins at 31-24. Beavers K Jose Cortez nailed 28y FG with 31 sec left to tie it 34-34, but his KO went OB at UCLA 41 to allow WR Brad Melsby to maneuver into clear for winning 61y TD catch from McNown with 21 sec to play.

1t	Kansas State (30)	1504	14	Tulane	683
1t	Tennessee (25)	1504	15	Missouri	576
3	UCLA (7)	1427	16	Michigan	564
4	Florida	1342	17	Penn State	531
5	Florida State	1306	18	Georgia	526
6	Wisconsin	1224	19	Oregon	427
7	Ohio State	1148	20	Air Force	382
8	Texas A&M	1131	21	Texas	373
9	Arkansas	1072	22	Virginia	359
10	Arizona	1012	23	Georgia Tech	249
11	Nebraska	785	24	Miami (Fla.)	115
12	Virginia Tech	766	25t	Wyoming	97
13	Notre Dame	762	25t	Syracuse	97

Bowl Championship Series Rankings November 9

	Poll Avg.	Computer Avg.	Quartile Rank	Losses	Total
1 Tennesse (8-0)	1.0	2.00	0.92	0	3.92
2 UCLA (8-0)	3.0	2.33	0.40	0	5.73
3 Kansas State (9-0)	1.5	2.33	3.16	0	6.99
4 Florida State (9-1)	5.0	3.67	0.20	1	9.87
5 Florida (8-1)	4.0	4.33	0.64	1	9.97

November 14, 1998

SYRACUSE 28 Virginia Tech 26: Highly-charged Virginia Tech (7-2) special teams blocked yet another kick for TD, had thrilling 2-pt RET, but lost to Syracuse (6-3) when QB Donovan McNabb (15-32/232y, 2 TDs, and 12/57y rushing) personally ran or passed on 12 of 14 plays in closing 83y TD drive. Hokies frosh FB Jarrett Ferguson raced 76y to TD at end of 1st Q. WR Ricky Hall soon added punt-block TD REC, and DB Loren Johnson sprinted 78y for FUM TD RET. Va Tech led 21-6 at H. McNabb threw TD pass early in 3rd Q, and FB Rob Konrad plunged for TD early in 4th Q for 22-21 Orange lead. Syracuse went for 2 pts, but Hokies DB Johnson picked off pass and raced to distant 10YL where he lost FUM. Hokies LB Jamel Smith made 2-pt REC in EZ for 23-22 lead. K Shayne Graham upped Tech lead to 36-22 with 49y FG with 4:42 to play. McNabb masterminded long drive capped by last-play TD pass to TE Stephen Brominski, play on which McNabb rolled right, threw crossfield to EZ. Tech made only 6 1st downs as QB Al Clark, off injured list, passed 4-12/35y, INT.

TENNESSEE 28 Arkansas 24: Great game turned on bizarre break with 1:54 left, and it gave Tennessee (9-0) chance to keep national title hopes alive. Leading 24-22 and looking for clinching 1st down, Arkansas (8-1) QB Clint Stoerner (17-34/274y, 3 TDs, INT) stumbled while pulling away from C on rollout pass. Stoerner accidentally left ball on ground as he tried to steady himself by leaning on throwing hand, and Vols DL Billy Ratliff fell on pigskin at Arkansas 43YL. Tennessee TB Travis Henry (32/197y) carried 5 straight plays, crashed over for game winner with 28 sec left. Stoerner's 3 TD throws had given Hogs 21-10 H lead, and K Todd Latourette's 33y FG early in 3rd Q boosted edge to 24-10 before Tennessee rallied. Vols QB Tee Martin (10-27/155y, INT) scored on 4y run, and K Jeff Hall kicked his 2nd FG in 3rd Q to trim it to 24-20. Latourette had 37y FG blocked with 6:29 to go in 4th Q, and Vols LB Al Wilson returned it 50y. Arkansas' gutty D held, but on next series Hogs painfully watched snap fly over head of P Chris Akin. Akin booted loose ball through EZ for safety to retain lead at 24-22. Razorbacks held after free kick, but lost Stoerner's FUM on next possession.

MICHIGAN 27 Wisconsin 10: While knocking Wisconsin (9-1) from unbeaten ranks, resilient Michigan (8-2) took command of Big 10 race. Badgers came in with nation's top run D but allowed 2 Wolverines to each rush for 100y in 257y team total: TBs Clarence Williams (22/121y) and Anthony Thomas (13/102y). Wisconsin QB Mike Samuel surprised Michigan with 80y TD pass to WR Chris Chambers in opening mins, but Thomas raced to 59, 15y TDs in 2nd Q for 21-7 H edge. Wolverines D held TB Ron Dayne to 16/53y and Badgers to 31/58y rushing.

KANSAS STATE 40 Nebraska 30: Not since 1968 had Kansas State (10-0) beaten Nebraska (8-3), and laconic coach Bill Snyder said, "I am happy...no matter what you may think." Meanwhile, K-State fans went crazy. In Sunday's ESPN/*USA Today* Coaches Poll, Wildcats advanced to no. 1, and Mike Francesa of WFAN (New York) radio called Snyder's elevation of K-State from worst pre-1990s win percentage in nation "the greatest coaching job in football history." QB Michael Bishop (19-33/306y, 2 TDs, INT passing, 25/140y rushing) gave Wildcats 1st lead at 21-17 with 17y TD pass to WR Darnell McDonald (12/183y) midway in 3rd Q, but lost 3 FUMs. QB Eric Crouch (10-21/139y, INT) threw his 3rd TD pass midway in 4th Q to put Huskers up 30-27 midway in 4th Q. Bishop's 2nd TD connection to McDonald with 5:25 left regained lead, and LB Jeff Kelly's 23y FUM TD RET iced it in last min. Nebraska's loss gave it 3 defeats in regular season for 1st time since 1977.

TEXAS A&M 17 Missouri 14: Fiercely-fought, rainy game was decided in late going and clinched Big 12 South title for Texas A&M (10-1). QB Corby Jones (18/85y rushing) sprinted 20y, then scored 10y TD for 7-3 Missouri (7-3) lead in 2nd Q. Shortly after K Shane Lechler's 69y punt died at Mizzou 2YL, Texas A&M (10-1) QB Randy McCown scored key TD early in 4th Q, then added 2-pt crossing pass to WR Leroy Hodge for 14-7 edge. Jones (7-19/78y, TD, INT) threw INT under pressure from 50YL, but Aggies DB Brandon Jennings was hit as he tried to lateral. Tigers G Jeff Hellerstedt fell on FUM, and 7 plays later Jones fired 9y TD pass to TE Dwayne Blakley to provide 14-14 tie in middle of 4th Q. With less than 6 min left, sr DB Randy Potter, who earlier erred on P Lechler's long

punt, bobbled another punt to position A&M at Missouri 30YL. Tigers threw Aggies WR Chris Taylor for 11y loss to 22YL, but with 1:30 to go K Russell Bynum smoothly booted his 3rd FG, 39y winner. Aggies LB Dat Nguyen was in on 17 tackles.

Air Force 10 WYOMING 3: Falcons (9-1) took control of WAC Mountain Div as their D limited Wyoming (8-2) to 33/28y rushing. Sacks of Cowboys QB Jay Stoner (11-18/174y) totaled 43y. After scoreless 1st H, Air Force QB Blane Morgan (5-11/91y, INT) tossed 18y TD pass to HB Qualario Brown 3:13 into 3rd Q. Wyoming trimmed margin to 7-3 late in 3rd Q on K Aaron Elling's 28y FG. Air Force rushed 58/228y.

Ucla 36 WASHINGTON 24: UCLA (9-0) clinched Pac-10 championship with win over fading Washington (5-5). DB Ryan Roques' 77y punt TD RET in last min of 1st H gave Bruins 20-10 lead. Little-used sub TB Braxton Cleman (16/100y) scored on 22, 1y runs for Huskies after he had made only 128y rushing all year. K Chris Sailer booted 5 FGs in building 36-17 UCLA lead before Husky QB Brock Huard (17-34/203y, INT) threw last min window-dressing TD pass.

1	Kansas State (36.5)	1521	14	Penn State	665
2	Tennessee (18.5)	1487	15	Georgia	652
3	UCLA (7)	1443	16	Oregon	589
4	Florida	1349	17	Air Force	495
5	Florida State	1304	18	Virginia	476
6	Ohio State	1202	19	Nebraska	473
7	Texas A&M	1191	20	Virginia Tech	356
8	Arizona	1109	21	Georgia Tech	315
9	Arkansas	928	22	Miami (Fla.)	269
10	Notre Dame	916	23	Missouri	267
11	Michigan	912	24	Syracuse	198
12	Wisconsin	830	25	Kentucky	70
13	Tulane	808			

Bowl Championship Series Rankings November 16

	Poll Avg.	Computer Avg.	Quartile Rank	Losses	Total
1 Tennessee (9-0)	1.5	1.75	0.52	0	3.77
2 UCLA (9-0)	3.0	2.33	0.48	0	5.81
3 Kansas State (10-0)	1.5	2.33	2.72	0	6.55
4 Florida State (10-1)	5.0	3.67	0.36	1	10.03
5 Florida (9-1)	4.0	5.00	1.56	1	11.56

November 21, 1998

FLORIDA STATE 23 Florida 12: Inexperienced Seminole QB Marcus Outzen (13-22/167y, TD) steadied himself after 2nd Q EZ FUM turned into controversial safety for Florida (9-2): FSU (11-1) T Ross Brannon made REC even though it appeared Gators DL Gerard Warren had control of ball for TD that would have provided 14-6 Gators lead. Instead, Florida led 12-6 at H, thanks to WR Travis McGriff speeding behind secondary for early 50y TD catch. Game's key play came early in 3rd Q as Outzen's pass went through grasp of Gators DB Marquand Manuel. Deflection went right to Seminoles WR Peter Warrick, who sped to 32y TD through dazed Florida secondary, depleted by absence of DB Tony George who was banished after massive on-field, pre-game fight. Warrick tossed his own TD pass in 4th Q, and Seminoles D dominated entire 2nd H, allowing only 64y and 2 1st downs. Elsewhere, Georgia Tech beat Wake Forest 63-35 to tie Florida State for ACC title.

TENNESSEE 59 Kentucky 21: While mourning truck crash deaths of transfer C Art Steinmetz, QB Tim Couch's best friend, Chris Brock, and injury to C Jason Watts in same crash, emotionally-drained Wildcats (7-4) turned out to be no match for no. 1 Tennessee (10-0). From 2nd series of 1st Q, Vols scored on 7 straight possessions in building 38-7 H lead. Vols FB Shawn Bryson tallied twice, including 58y burst, and QB Tee Martin (13-20/189y) threw TD pass. Couch (35-56/337y, INT) connected on 2 TD passes to WR Lance Mickelsen, and became 1st passer ever to make 400 completions in single season.

MISSISSIPPI STATE 22 Arkansas 21: Heady dream of Arkansas (8-2) took serious blow as Hogs lost 2nd straight heartbreaker. Mississippi State (7-3) took control of SEC West title chase. Lanky, frosh QB Wayne Madkin (16-31/224y, TD, 2 INTs) threw early TD pass to launch Bulldogs to 16-0 lead midway through 2nd Q. Razorbacks QB Clint Stoerner (14-23/213y, 3 TDs, 2 INTs) and WR Michael Williams sliced margin to 16-14 with pair of 2nd Q TD connections. Madkin was knocked woozy in late going, but returned to convert passes on 3rd-and-18 and 4th-and-15 to invigorate 44y drive that led to winning 27y FG by Mississippi State K Brian Hazelwood, his 5th of game.

OHIO STATE 31 Michigan 16: Overcoming recent Michigan (8-3) jinx, resolute Buckeyes (10-1) earned tie for Big 10 title as WR David Boston (10/217y) enjoyed career day. Boston caught 30 and 43y TD passes from QB Joe Germaine (16-28/330y, 3 TDs). Ohio got quick start as TB Michael Wiley (12/120y) streaked 53y to score early in 1st Q. Early in 2nd Q, Michigan K Jay Feely made 1st of 3 FGs, and QB Tom Brady (31-56/375y, 2 INTs) threw TD pass to give Wolverines hope at 21-10 at H. Bucks D permitted only 4y rushing.

WISCONSIN 24 Penn State 3: Wisconsin (10-1) all but clinched Rose Bowl trip with timely play. Seeking 1st big road win in several years, Nittany Lions (7-3) outgained Badgers in 1st H, but failed on 1st-and-goal at 4YL, and TOs delivered short end of 17-0 H score. Big play came late in 1st Q when Wisconsin RB Nick Davis broke away for 82y punt TD RET. After FUM REC, Badgers QB Mike Samuel slipped in 2nd Q 26y TD pass among his 4-13/69y. Penn State frosh TB Eric McCoo (22/91y) lost FUM that set up Badgers FG, but his runs led to Lions K Travis Forney's 3rd Q FG. Wisconsin TB Ron Dayne, hurt and used as decoy for much of 1st H, finished with 23/95y rushing.

Kansas State 31 MISSOURI 25: It proved difficult for Kansas State (11-0) to return to earth after its emotional win over Nebraska prior week, and tough Missouri (7-4) led its 4th top-10 foe at H. Tigers came back from 10-0 shortfall to lead 13-10 at H after QB

Corby Jones (14-30/249y, 2 TDs, INT passing, 19/54y rushing) ran for 5y TD, passed for 20y TD in 2nd Q. Wildcats ended 3rd Q with 24-16 edge after QB Michael Bishop (13-26/157y, TD, INT passing, 23/104y rushing) scored TD, led drive to TB Frank Murphy's 9y TD sweep left. Jones countered with 20y TD pass early in 4th Q to WR John Dausman, but Murphy recovered own FUM in EZ for 31-22 lead.

NOTRE DAME 39 Louisiana State 36: Having feasted recently, Fighting Irish (9-1) found themselves in fracas with speedy LSU (4-6). Star of largest ND comeback (34-20 in 3rd Q) since 1986 was QB Jarious Jackson (13-221/276y, 2 TDs, INT, 21/80y rushing). Jackson's 1st pass was picked off for 53y TD by Tigers DB Mark Roman. TB Kevin Faulk (31/108y) scored in 2nd Q for 13-7 LSU lead, but kick was missed, 1st of 4 such pratfalls in game. Faulk answered ND TD with 88y KO TD RET, so Tigers led 21-14 at H. LSU WR Abram Booty (8/153y) took 2 TD passes from QB Herb Tyler in 3rd Q. Irish LB Bobbie Howard ran back INT for 89y TD early in 4th Q, but conv was blocked, keeping LSU up 34-33. ND went 75y to Jackson's 10y TD pass to WR Raki Nelson with 1:27 left. With Tyler on bench with leg pull, Tigers sub QB Craig Nall barely missed EZ connection with Booty. In closing secs, Irish sent Jackson backpedaling into EZ to give safety to kill clock on 4th down. But, he suffered injured knee.

UCLA 34 Southern California 17: UCLA (10-0) used improved D to snare 7 TOs and create 6 sacks. Southern California's 4 lost FUMs in 23 min span killed whatever momentum it could have mustered to avoid its record 8th straight loss to Bruins. UCLA TB DeShaun Foster (15/109y) scored school record 4 TDs, including 65y run and 2 others on ground. Foster's 1st TD came on short pass from QB Cade McNown (12-20/146y, TD, 2 INTs) and provided 7-3 1st Q lead. Trojans (7-4) QB Carson Palmer (28-43/252y, TD, 2 INTs) threw 2nd Q TD pass, briefly pulling USC within 14-10.

OREGON STATE 44 Oregon 41 (OT): Beavers (5-6), coming off 35-34 and 20-19 losses to Washington and California that have ended 28 years of losing records, won notable "Civil War" game. QB Akili Smith (35-43/430y, 4 TDs) threw his 3rd TD pass with 2:34 to go in 4th Q to put Oregon (8-3) up 31-24. Oregon State required but 53 secs to send it to OT as QB Jonathan Smith (17-28/303y, TD) pitched 30y pass to WR Tim Alexander to set up 3rd TD run by frosh TB Ken Simonton (28/157y, 5 TDs). Simonton, 4th-ever 1000y Beaver rusher, scored 1st in OT on 1y sweep. Ducks then appeared to miss 4th down pass, so Beavers fans rushed field, not noticing flag against Oregon State for pass interference PEN. When order was restored, Ducks Smith hit TE Jed Weaver with tying TD pass. Oregon K Nathan Villegas made 26y FG for 41-38 lead in 2nd OT, but Simonson brought delirious fans back on field with winning 16y TD run.

USA Today Coaches Poll November 23
1	Kansas State (31.5)	1506	14	Air Force	644
2	Tennessee (22.5)	1501	15	Virginia	626
3	UCLA (7)	1449	16	Michigan	577
4	Florida State	1361	17	Nebraska	526
5	Ohio State (1)	1282	18	Georgia Tech	508
6	Texas A&M	1194	19	Virginia Tech	506
7	Arizona	1166	20	Miami (Fla.)	384
8	Florida	1059	21	Penn State	312
9	Wisconsin	1030	22	Syracuse	304
10	Notre Dame	1025	23	Oregon	229
11	Tulane	919	24	Mississippi State	131
12	Georgia	821	25	Missouri	116
13	Arkansas	648			

Bowl Championship Series Rankings

	Poll Avg.	Computer Avg.	Quartile Ranking	Losses	Total
1 Tennessee (10-0)	1.5	2.33	0.56	0	4.39
2 UCLA (10-0)	3.0	1.75	0.32	0	5.07
3 Kansas State (11-0)	1.5	2.33	2.45	0	6.31
4 Florida State (11-1)	4.0	3.00	0.20	1	8.20
5 Texas A&M (10-1)	6.0	5.00	0.52	1	12.52

November 26-28, 1998

(Th'g) TULANE 63 Louisiana Tech 30: Previous week's win over Houston clinched 1st conf title since 1949 for Tulane (11-0), and win over Louisiana Tech (6-6) gave Green Wave their 1st undefeated season since 1929. La Tech QB Tim Rattay (37-57/471y, 2 TDs, 2 INTs) hit WR James Jordan over middle for 69y TD, 7-0 1st Q lead. Then, Tulane QB Shaun King (19-26/330y, 3 TDs) and TB Toney Converse (24/182y, school record 4 TDs) went to work. King threw 63 and 59y TD passes to WR Kerwin Cook and became 1st 1-A player to throw for 3000y and rush for 500y in 11-game season.

(Th'g) Mississippi State 28 MISSISSIPPI 6: Late-closing Bulldogs (8-3) wrapped up SEC West title with well-balanced O vs Ole Miss (6-5), which was about to lose coach Tommy Tuberville to Auburn. With TB Deuce McAllister (40/177y) running for 39y, Rebels went 64y to gain 3-0 lead in 1st Q on 1st of 2 FGs by K Carlisle McGee. In pain with groin injury, Mississippi State TB James Johnson rushed 9/34y to take SEC rushing title, punched over from 2YL, then dived over from 1YL in 2nd Q, but separated his shoulder. Starting in place of injured Ole Miss QB Romaro Miller, frosh QB David Morris (8-24/75y) threw 3 INTs, last of which took odd deflection into hands of Bulldogs DB Tim Nelson. Nelson returned INT 30y for TD with 2:36 to play.

(Fri) TEXAS 26 Texas A&M 24: With NCAA career rushing record-holder Tony Dorsett watching on sideline, Texas (8-3) TB Ricky Williams burst behind blocks of FB Ricky Brown (at RG) and WR Wane McGarity (downfield) to race 60y to TD late in 1st Q and become all-time career rushing leader. But, Williams soon lost 1st of 2 FUMs that created TDs for Texas A&M (10-2). TE Derrick Spiller caught 19y TD pass to bring Aggies within 10-7. Superb Longhorns D-front held A&M to -5y rushing in 1st H, but their O couldn't punch it in EZ. Texas led 16-7 when Williams, who finished 44/259y for day, 2124y for season and 6279y for 4 years, ran 38y to set up QB Major Applewhite's 10y TD slant

pass to WR Kwame Cavil. Suddenly, Aggies came alive on FG after WR Chris Cole's 65y catch and Spiller's TD catch from QB Randy McCown (11-24/180y, 2 TDs) after Williams' FUM. Trailing 23-17, with 7 mins left, A&M DB Jason Webster raced 34y on punt RET to set up McCown's 4th down option TD run with 2:20 left. Down 24-23, Applewhite (24-35/232y, TS, INT) completed 6-7 short passes and hit Cavil for 25y to Aggies 19YL. Williams swept to 8YL, and K Kris Stockton nailed winning 24y FG with 4 secs left.

(Fri) ARIZONA 50 Arizona State 42: Desert shootout went to Arizona (11-1), thanks to superb game by TB Trung Canidate (18/288y, 3 TDs). After Arizona State (5-6) earned 15-7 lead on TDs by FB Jeff Paulk and WR Creig Spann, Wildcats went back ahead 19-15 when LB Scooter Sprotte picked up FUM and pranced into EZ. Gimpy Devils TB J.R. Redmond (15/71y) fired over to finish 68y TD march, but Canidate answered with 80y TD sprint behind massive cutback block of G Yusuf Scott. Wildcats opened 2nd H with punt block by DB Chris McAlister at ASU 24YL, and QB Ortege Jenkins burned Devils blitz with 13y TD run up middle to make it 33-22. Canidate burst 66y, again outran depleted ASU DBs for 43-28 edge. With 6 min left, ASU faced 4th down at Arizona 16YL, and QB Ryan Kealy (33-56/511y, 4 TDs, 2 INTs) lofted TD pass to TE Todd Heap to trim it to 43-35. Canidate struck again with 48y TD, but ASU rallied to 50-42 and Kealy's EZ pass fell incomplete at 0:00.

Georgia Tech 21 GEORGIA 19: Georgia Tech (9-2) broke 7-game losing streak to Georgia (8-3) as K Brad Chambers kicked 35y FG with 2 secs left. Bulldogs had gotten early jump when QB Quincy Carter (16-31/225y) pitched long lateral to WR Michael Greer who rifled long TD to wide-open TE Larry Brown for 68y. TB Olandis Gary's short TD run late in 3rd Q gave Georgia 19-7 lead, but 2-pt run failed. Georgia Tech QB Joey Hamilton (16-31/225y, TD, and 15/54y rushing) had thrown 55y TD pass in 2nd Q and led decisive 9-play, 52y drive to Chambers' winning FG in 4th Q.

SYRACUSE 66 Miami 13: Young Hurricanes (7-3) ran into indoor storm at Syracuse (8-3) as Orangemen built amazing 45-7 lead at H on way to capturing Big East title. Playing his last home game, stellar QB Donovan McNabb had 8/99y rushing, and 12-19/80y, 2 TDs passing. In 1st H, McNabb sneaked over twice, scrambled 51y to score and threw TD pass to WR Kevin Johnson. Miami briefly maneuvered into contention with late 1st Q TD plunge by TB Edgerrin James (18/115y) after James slashed 13y to 1YL. But, Johnson answered by racing 100y TD RET on ensuing KO. Syracuse LB Stan Gibbs had 2 sacks and INT, and K Nathan Trout booted 50y FG. It was most pts scored vs. Miami since Texas A&M won 70-14 in 1944.

Virginia 36 VIRGINIA TECH 32: Everything started wonderfully for Virginia Tech (8-3) as Hokies built quick 17-0 lead in 1st 9 mins as sub TB Shyrone Stith broke away for 51y TD run down left sideline. After Cavs scored TD, Hokies built 29-7 H lead. But, slumbering Virginia (9-2) used its D to make 2nd H comeback after coach George Welsh's angry H words. After Cavs QB Aaron Brooks (19-32/345y, 3 TDs, INT) hit 24y TD pass on his way to 2nd straight huge passing day vs. Virginia Tech, UVa LB Byron Thweatt made INT and raced down left sideline for 53y TD. Suddenly, Virginia trailed only 29-21 at end of 3rd Q. K Shayne Graham added 46y FG, his 4th, early in 4th Q for 32-21 lead for Hokies, but UVa TB Thomas Jones made brilliant diving 18y TD catch and WR Ahmad Hawkins got loose for 47y TD catch with 2:01 to go to complete Virginia's greatest comeback ever.

SOUTHERN CALIFORNIA 10 Notre Dame 0: Several mins into 3rd Q of 0-0 game, retiring ABC announcer Keith Jackson described tentative Os: "The way these two teams are playing is like walking out on a frozen lake and hearing it crack." Shortly thereafter, Southern California (8-4) finally sprung TB Chad Morton (27/128y) for 11, 21, and 5y runs. With 8:22 left in 3rd Q, USC scored on 2y naked bootleg run left by QB Carson Palmer. Trojans K Adam Abrams connected on 23y FG to end next possession. Without QB Jarious Jackson, Notre Dame (9-2) was significantly ineffective on O (217y O overall and 0y passing in 1st H) as young QBs Eric Chappell (0-3, 2 INTs) and Arnaz Battle (7-19/94y, 2 INTs) could do nothing other than Battle's controversial 2nd Q FUM inside USC 5YL after LB Kory Minor's INT carried to USC 14YL.

USA Today Coaches Poll November 30
1	Kansas State (30.5)	1506	14	Georgia Tech	702
2	Tennessee (24.5)	1503	15	Michigan	684
3	UCLA (6)	1447	16	Notre Dame	615
4	Florida State	1359	17	Nebraska	588
5	Ohio State (1)	1304	18	Syracuse	511
6	Arizona	1225	19	Georgia	426
7	Florida	1151	20	Penn State	392
8	Wisconsin	1110	21	Oregon	286
9	Tulane	1001	22	Mississippi State	281
10	Texas A&M	858	23	Texas	230
11	Arkansas	831	24	Virginia Tech	186
12	Virginia	799	25	West Virginia	137
13	Air Force	764			

Bowl Championship Series Rankings November 30

	Poll Avg.	Computer Avg.	Quartile Rank	Losses	Total
1 Tennessee (11-0)	1.5	2.33	1.16	0	4.99
2 UCLA (10-0)	3.0	1.75	0.28	0	5.03
3 Kansas State (11-0)	1.5	2.33	2.48	0	6.31
4 Florida State (11-1)	4.0	3.00	0.20	1	8.20
5 Ohio State (10-1)	5.0	5.33	1.00	1	12.33

December 5, 1998

Army 34 Navy 30 (Philadelphia): Highest-scoring Army-Navy game to date was marred by collapse of grandstand railing. Several Academy students, celebrating TD by Army (3-8) midway in 4th Q for 31-30 lead, were injured, some seriously, when they tumbled to artificial turf at Philadelphia's Veterans Stadium. Afternoon had started awfully for Army as QB Johnny Goff lost FUMs on each of 1st 2 series. Navy (3-8) went up 10-0 as result,

TD coming on 17y run by FB Irv Dingle (10/65y). Army QB Joe Gerena came off bench to sprint to 25 and 69y TDs for 13-10 1st Q lead. Middies WR Ryan Read (3/ 128y) caught TD passes of 49 and 69y from QB Brian Broadwater (7-17/188y, 2 TDs, INT) to put Navy back in front 24-19 at H. Read's receiving y set new Army-Navy record. Cadets finished with 401y, cinching national rushing leadership, and FBs Craig Stucker (7/106y) and Ty Amey (13/134y) raced for TDs of 71 and 70y. Amey's score provided Army with 31-30 lead after Navy lost FUM on touchback while appearing on its way to TD.

GAME OF THE YEAR
MIAMI 49 Ucla 45:

Embarrassed previous week by Syracuse and nearly out of this game in 2nd H, Miami (8-3) rallied to ruin national championship hopes of undefeated no. 3 UCLA (10-1). Collapse of Bruins' ever-bending D in "Hurricane Bowl"—game had been rescheduled from 10 weeks earlier thanks to Hurricane Georges—must have made Bruins wish they hadn't bothered to fulfill new date. Scoring on 1st 3 tries before intermission, Canes led 21-14 at H thanks to running of TB Edgerrin James (39/299y, 3 TDs), who broke countless tackles on way to 45 and 10y TDs. Meanwhile, Bruins QB Cade McNown had brilliant day, passing 26-35/513y with TDs of 77, 7, 14, 61, and 59y. WR Brad Melsby got free to catch McNown's last TD with 1:28 left in 3rd Q, and UCLA seemed safe with 38-21 lead. Miami went back to James for runs of 7, 14, and 36y to set up sub TB Najeh Davenport's 23y TD through more missed tackles near end of 3rd Q. UCLA then made 1st of 2 big mistakes, each was FUM by WR trying for extra y. After Hurricanes DB Al Blades fell on ball at own 13YL, WR Santana Moss ran corner route to catch 71y TD from QB Scott Covington (19-28/318y, 3 TDs). McNown answered with 1y TD sweep left, but Covington countered with 29y TD pass to TE Mondriel Fulcher less than min later. So, UCLA led 45-42 with 6:08 left. Melsby carried pass for 1st down at Canes 26YL, but officials ruled he lost debatable FUM with 3:25 to go. Covington was perfect 4-4 in air, and Davenport added runs of 17 and 9y before James powered left for winning 1y TD run. It was O field-day as Miami gained 689y and UCLA's O totaled 670y.

Texas A&M 36 Kansas State 33 (St. Louis) (OT): Announcement of Miami's upset of UCLA may not have been worst thing to happen to Kansas State (11-1), but it didn't help. Having just allowed Wildcats WR Darnell McDonald's 66y TD catch, Texas A&M (11-2) was on ropes at 17-3 in 2nd Q of Big 12 Championship when Miami result became known. It was 17-6 at H, but star A&M LB Dat Nguyen made 3rd Q INT to set up 57y TD march aided by 2 foul PENs—K-State lost 110y in PENs—and 24y pass by rusty sub QB Branndon Stewart (15-31/324y, 3 TDs, INT), who improved after 0-5, INT start. But, electric Wildcats QB Michael Bishop (19-28/341y, 2 TDs, INT passing, 28/101y rushing) slipped up middle for 5y TD draw run and 27-12 lead in last min of 3rd Q. Stewart, who passed 11-20/235y after start of 4th Q, tossed 13y TD to WR Leroy Hodge. K-State led 27-19 in last 4 mins and appeared to end it on LB Ben Leber's sack, DL Damion McIntosh's 4th down pass bat-down. But on 3rd down run with 2:26 to go, Bishop lost FUM at own 35YL on big hit by LB Warrick Holdman. WR Matt Bumgardner made diving 36y catch after PEN, and Stewart pitched 9y slant-in TD pass to TB-WR Sirr Parker. Motion-man Parker crossed to flat for tying 2-pt pass with 1:05 left. Teams traded FGs in 1st OT, and K-State's Martin Gramatica booted his 4th FG of game in 2nd OT. Aggies were nearly out of FG range, facing 3rd-and-17 on 32YL, when Parker went in motion right and took slant-in to beat DB Jerametrius Butler for TD, barely nudging pylon.

Tennessee 24 Mississippi State 14 (Atlanta): With UCLA and Kansas State losses already in books, Tennessee (12-0) had chance to secure Fiesta Bowl spot. But, Mississippi State (8-4) struck 1st as DB Robert Bean made over-the-head INT catch and weaved through Vols for 70y TD RET late in 1st Q. Tennessee countered with TB Travis Stephens' TD plunge and K Jeff Hall's 31y FG in 2nd Q. Bulldogs' small, but swift D continued good pressure on Vols QB Tee Martin (15-32/208y, 2 TDs, INT). Miss State took lead 6 mins into 4th Q when WR Kevin Prentiss tight-roped left sideline with 83y punt TD RET. Vols strongly replied with Martin's 2 quick TD passes: 41y to WR Peerless Price and 26y to WR Cedrick Wilson. Big TDs locked up 2nd SEC title in row for Volunteers.

Air Force 20 Brigham Young 13 (Las Vegas): Air Force (11-1) came from behind to take its 1st-ever undisputed WAC championship. Also, game was D struggle, unusual way for pts-happy WAC to end its 16-team existence. QB Kevin Feterik's 13y TD pass late in 2nd Q gave BYU (9-4) 7-0 H lead. Midway in 3rd Q, Falcons QB Blane Morgan limped off bench to slip into EZ on 2y TD run to tie it. K Owen Pochman's 2 FGs gave Cougars 13-7 lead midway in 4th Q. Shut down on ground all game, Air Force went to WR-screen pass to spring WR Matt Farmer for 59y TD pass and 14-13 edge. Airman FB Spanky Gilliam iced it with 29y TD burst in last 2 mins.

USA Today Coaches Poll December 7

1	Tennessee (60)	1548	14	Georgia Tech	749
2	Florida State (1)	1464	15	Michigan	674
3	Ohio State (1)	1405	16	Nebraska	590
4	Kansas State	1337	17	Syracuse	538
5	UCLA	1253	18	Notre Dame	522
6	Arizona	1244	19	Georgia	405
7	Florida	1156	20	Penn State	350
8	Wisconsin	1103	21	Oregon	270
9	Texas A&M	1092	22	Texas	253
10	Tulane	964	23	Mississippi State	205
11	Arkansas	820	24	Virginia Tech	189
12	Virginia	818	25	West Virginia	127
13	Air Force	799			

Bowl Championship Series Rankings

	Poll Avg.	Computer Avg.	Quartile Rank	Losses	Total
1 Tennessee (12-0)	1.0	1.67	.80	0	3.47
2 Florida State (11-1)	2.0	1.75	.16	1	4.91
3 Kansas State (11-1)	4.0	3.00	1.96	1	9.96
4 Ohio State (10-1)	3.0	5.25	5.25	1	10.37
5 UCLA (10-1)	5.5	4.08	.32	1	10.90

1998 Conference Standings

Big East

Syracuse	6-1
Virginia Tech	5-2
Miami	5-2
West Virginia	5-2
Boston College	3-4
Rutgers	2-5
Temple	2-5
Pittsburgh	0-7

Atlantic Coast

Florida State	7-1
Georgia Tech	7-1
Virginia	6-2
North Carolina State	5-3
North Carolina	5-3
Duke	2-6
Wake Forest	2-6
Clemson	1-7
Maryland	1-7

Southeastern

EAST	
Tennessee	8-0
Florida	7-1
Georgia	6-2
Kentucky	4-4
Vanderbilt	1-7
South Carolina	0-8
WEST	
Mississippi State	6-2
Arkansas	6-2
Alabama	4-4
Mississippi	3-5
Louisiana State	2-6
Auburn	1-7

Conference USA

Tulane	6-0
Southern Mississippi	5-1
Louisville	4-2
East Carolina	3-3
Army	2-4
Houston	2-4
Memphis	1-5
Cincinnati	1-5

Big Ten

Wisconsin	7-1
Ohio State	7-1
Michigan	7-1
Purdue	6-2
Penn State	5-3
Michigan State	4-4
Indiana	2-6
Illinois	2-6
Minnesota	2-6
Iowa	2-6
Northwestern	0-8

Mid-American

EAST	
Marshall	7-1
Miami (Ohio)	7-1
Bowling Green	5-3
Ohio	5-3
Akron	3-6
Kent	0-8
WEST	
Toledo	6-2
Central Michigan	5-3
Western Michigan	5-3
Eastern Michigan	3-6
Northern Illinois	2-6
Ball State	1-7

Big 12

NORTH	
Kansas State	8-0
Nebraska	5-3
Missouri	5-3
Colorado	4-4
Kansas	1-7
Iowa State	1-7
SOUTH	
Texas A&M	7-1
Texas	6-2
Texas Tech	4-4
Oklahoma State	3-5
Oklahoma	3-5
Baylor	1-7

Western Athletic

MOUNTAIN	
Air Force	7-1
Wyoming	6-2
Colorado State	5-3
Rice	5-3
Texas Christian	4-4
Southern Methodist	4-4
Tulsa	2-6
Nevada-Las Vegas	0-8
PACIFIC	
Brigham Young	7-1
San Diego State	7-1
Utah	5-3
Fresno State	5-3
Texas-El Paso	3-5
San Jose State	3-5
New Mexico	1-7
Hawaii	0-8

Pacific-10

UCLA	8-0
Arizona	7-1
Oregon	5-3
Southern California	5-3
Washington	4-4
Arizona State	4-4
California	3-5
Oregon State	2-6
Stanford	2-6
Washington State	0-8

1998 Bowl Games
Las Vegas Bowl (Dec. 19): North Carolina 20 San Diego State 13

With high winds and blowing sand, San Diego State (7-5) defied wind direction on game's 2nd play. WR Lonny Mitchell picked up FUM of teammate TB Jonas Lewis and raced 60y to score. But soon, short wind-blown punts by Aztecs P Don Copeland

(7/24.1y avg) helped North Carolina (7-5) to 2 FGs. On last play of 1st Q, Tar Heels sub QB Ronald Curry (10/93y rushing) scrambled 51y to TD behind block of FB Dion Dyer that eliminated 2 Aztecs. UNC made it 20-7 in 2nd Q as DB Quinton Savage blocked punt for TD REC by DB David Bomar. SDSU was boosted by playing scoreless 3rd Q against wind, but only could manage K Nate Tandberg's 2nd FG with 3:51 left in 4th Q. Aztecs LB Joseph Tuipala ran FUM to Heels 22YL with 1:29 left, but UNC LB Brandon Spoon tipped pass that LB Keith Newman picked off in EZ.

Aloha Bowl (Dec. 25): Colorado 51 Oregon 43

Coach Rick Neuheisel implored his hard-hitting Buffaloes (8-4) to wish Oregon (8-4) Merry Christmas "with your helmets." Colorado delivered 17-0 blow in 1st Q as DB Ben Kelly took opening KO 93y to TD. QB Akili Smith, 2nd in national pass efficiency, got off to slow 2-10 start, and Ducks suffered 6 TOs which led to 4 Buff scores. Oregon TB Derien Latimer (19/74y, 3 TDs) tallied twice in 2nd Q, trimming deficit to 27-14, but Smith (24-46/456y, 2 TDs, 2 INTs) threw EZ INT. Buffs quickly responded with 72y TD pass from QB Mike Moschetti (11-23/213y, Aloha-record 4 TDs) to WR Darrin Chiaverini (3/96y). DB Damon Wheeler stepped in front of Smith lateral throw, raced 52y for 44-14 Colorado edge in 3rd Q. Smith came alive with 2 TD passes, TD run, wrapped around Lattimer's 3rd TD run. Smith's 42y TD arrow to WR Donald Haynes and 2-pt pass pass came with 5:55 to go and pulled Ducks to within 51-43. In effort to keep his exhausted D on sideline, Neuheisel gambled on doomed 4th down fake-punt run with 3:11 left. Oregon took over on own 43YL, but Bison D held on 4 downs to seal highest-scoring Aloha Bowl to date. As opener of 1st-ever Bowl doubleheader, created by former broadcast ad salesman Lenny Klompus, game was played before sparse crowd, but blindly termed "sellout" by Westwood One Radio's Tony Roberts.

Oahu Bowl (Dec. 25): Air Force 45 Washington 25

In nightcap of Aloha Stadium doubleheader, Air Force (12-1) mixed QB Blane Morgan's superb 12-16/267y, 2 TDs passing with 234y option runs to trounce Washington (6-6). Falcons went 73, 83, and 74y to 1st H TDs, including 2 runs by HB Jemal Singleton. Huskies stayed close on passing of QB Brock Huard (23-32/267y, 3 INTs) and 2 TD runs by TB Braxton Cleman. But, Air Force surprised Huskies with 2-pt run by Morgan with 2:21 left in 2nd Q to advance to 22-7 lead. When WR Dane Looker took 36y pass from Huard to set up Cleman's 2nd TD, Huskies were forced to try failed 2-pt pass. Leading 22-13 at H, Falcons tallied 16 unanswered pts in 3rd Q to put verdict in bank at 38-13. Falcons K Jackson Whiting booted 42y FG, FB Spanky Gilliam went 4y up middle to TD, and Morgan arched 79y TD pass to WR Matt Farmer after Husky DB Toure Butler slipped twice in pass coverage.

Insight.com Bowl (Dec. 26): Missouri 34 West Virginia 31

Making his 1st career start in place of suspended DB Wade Perkins, Missouri (8-4) DB Julian Jones made big early plays to put Tigers in command. West Virginia (8-4) rode passing arm of QB Marc Bulger (34-50/429y, 4 TDs, 2 INTs) to nearly successful 2nd H comeback, but still lost NCAA-record 8th straight bowl game. Bulger hit his 1st 5 passes of game, but Mountaineers had FG blocked by Tigers DL Jeff Marriott. Mizzou DB Carlos Posey returned it 70y for 7-0 lead. Jones' INT poised 58y march capped by TD keeper by Mizzou QB Corby Jones (8-12/130y, and 18/51y, 3 TDs rushing). DB Jones blocked punt in 2nd Q for safety, then raced 39y with free-kick to set up QB Jones' powerful "loaf of bread" run and 2-pt pass. Tigers led 24-3 at H. WVU DB Boo Sensabaugh blocked punt at 10YL in 3rd Q to turn momentum. Bulger quickly hit WR David Saunders with TD pass, 1st of 4 in 2nd H. QB Jones scored his 3rd TD (11y run) for Missouri behind block of TE Jake Steuve to advance Tigers to 31-10. Methodical 4th Q drive by Tigers took 6:43 off clock and ended in 18y FG by K Brian Long and 34-24 lead with 3:44 left. Saunders caught TD with 2:11 to go, but on-side KO failed. WVU TB Amos Zereoue was held to 22/32y rushing, while Tigers TB Devon West pounded for 31/125y.

Music City Bowl (Dec. 29): Virginia Tech 38 Alabama 7

In Nashville's icy drizzle, Virginia Tech (9-3) was up to its usual tricks, disrupting punts and placekicks and playing pressure D. But 1st, Hokies QB Al Clark (7-14/71y, INT) broke out of pocket and sprinted 43y to score in 1st Q. Alabama (7-5) tied it at 7-7 in 2nd Q as QB Andrew Zow (19-35/224y, TD, 3 INTs) threw 5y TD to WR Michael Vaughn. From that point, Zow was under constant pressure (3 sacks) from Hokies D, led by DE Corey Moore, who made sack, blocked FG, and forced FUM. Virginia Tech DB Keion Carpenter blocked punt, and DB Anthony Midget raced 27y with it to 4th Q TD.

Micron PC (Blockbuster) Bowl (Dec. 29): Miami 46 N. Carolina State 23

Picking up where they left off vs. UCLA, Hurricanes (9-3) piled up 594y, scored school bowl-record 46 pts. Miami had long TD drives on 1st 3 possessions and built 20-7 advantage. QB Scott Covington (17-24/320y 2 TDs) completed 8-9/181y, 2 TDs during opening flurry. Including was 80y scoring hookup with WR Santana Moss. NC State (7-5) QB Jamie Barnette (22-41/201y, TD, 5 INTs) sparked several unproductive drives, K Danny Deskevich, perfect all season, missed FG, and Barnette suffered late 2nd Q INT when his pass bounced off umpire James Ina to Canes DL Matt Sweeeney. Miami turned 2nd H over to its dominant O-line which launched TBs Edgerrin James (20/156y, 2 TDs) and James Jackson (11/99y). Wolfpack WR Torry Holt was held to 52y on 7 catches, but TB Rashon Spikes rushed 24/176y.

Alamo Bowl (Dec. 29): Purdue 37 Kansas State 34

Sigmund Freud might have been useful coach for psychologically-fragile Kansas State (11-2). Upset on season's last day in Big 12 title game, Wildcats inexplicably tumbled out of BCS picture and ended up miffed to be in San Antonio. For its part, Purdue (9-4) showed up with just right kind of air attack to bother K-State, and jumpy Wildcats lost 7 TOs and suffered 14 PENs/125y. After scoreless 1st Q, Purdue QB Drew Brees (25-53/230y, 3 TDs, 3 INTs) threw 2 TD passes and DL Roosevelt Colvin's 2nd sack set up FG for 17-7 H edge. Teams traded 3rd Q TDs as bad Boilers' punt-snap was turned into score, but Cats FB Brian Goolsby's FUM was traded right back as TD REC in EZ by Purdue DL David Nugent. Trailing 30-20 with less than 7 min to play, K-State QB Michael Bishop (9-24/182y, 3 TDs, 4 INTs and only 20/7y rushing) struck with 88y TD to WR Darnell McDonald. Bishop appeared to pull it out at 34-30 when he pitched short TD pass to TE Justin Swift with 1:24 left, but Brees led dramatic 6-play, 80y drive to upset victory. Boilermakers WR Isaac Jones made brilliant 24y TD catch with :30 on clock.

Holiday Bowl (Dec. 30): Arizona 23 Nebraska 20

Ambitious Arizona (12-1) found Nebraska (9-4) in weakened state and sent Cornhuskers to 1st 4-loss season in 30 years. D battle was highlighted by Wildcats A-A DB Chris McAlister, who blocked FG and made 2 INTs. Ground-oriented Os were stymied: Nebraska rushed 87y, and Arizona made 107y. McAlister recovered punt FUM to set up 1st of K Mark McDonald's 3 FGs on way to 9-0 Wildcats lead. But, Arizona QB Ortege Jenkins lost 2nd Q FUM to set up K Kris Brown's 25y FG, and Huskers QB Eric Crouch quickly hit WR Shevin Wiggins with 25y TD pass. When Wildcats WR Dennis Northcutt was hammered by Huskers FB Billy Legate just after fielding punt, Brown followed with another FG, and Nebraska had 13 pts within 4:58 for 13-9 H edge. After scoreless 3rd Q, MVP Arizona QB Keith Smith (11-19/143y, TD) threw TD pass on 1st play of 4th Q that WR Brian Brennan caught at his fingertips. Huskers came back for 20-16 lead on Crouch's 2nd TD pass, but Smith scurried for runs of 20, 8, and 8y to set up Wildcats TB Kelvin Eafon's game-winning 1y TD plunge with 6:08 left. McAlister clinched it with INT at own 8YL in last 3 mins.

Liberty Bowl (Dec. 31): Tulane 41 Brigham Young 27

Surprising Tulane (12-0) finished 1st undefeated season since 1929, even with new coach Chris Scelfo standing in for departed (for Clemson) coach Tommy Bowden. Brigham Young (9-5) scored 1st on 11y pass from QB Kevin Feterik (27-44/267y, 2 TDs, INT) to WR Ben Horton (6/67y). Green Wave registered 34 unanswered pts as DB Michael Jordan sped 79y on INT TD RET in 1st Q. Tulane QB Shawn King (23-38/276y, 2 TDs) rushed for 3y TD in 2nd Q of his 16/109y rushing. King continued his season-long superb play with TD passes to WR Derwin Cook for 60y and to TB Jamaican Dartez for 13y.

Sun Bowl (Dec. 31): Texas Christian 28 Southern California 19

Texas Christian (7-5) was coming off 1-10 season in 1997 and had not won bowl game since 1957 Cotton Bowl. For its part, Southern California (8-5) had won 25 bowl games in its history. But, USC A-A LB Chris Claiborne noted Frogs had benefit of "small man's complex." In end, rush y indicated difference. Trojans tallied only 21/-23y rushing, including Frogs' 6 sacks/-47y of QB Carson Palmer (17-28/280y, TD passing). TCU's option attack sped for 61/314y. HB Basil Mitchell (19/186y) scored on runs of 3, 60y in 1st Q, and QB Patrick Batteaux scored on runs of 8 and 3y for 28-3 edge for TCU by middle of 3rd Q. Trojans converted 66 and 61y TD drives in 3rd Q as Palmer was able to click on 4th down passes each time.

Peach Bowl (Dec. 31): Georgia 35 Virginia 33

Virginia (9-3) walked out of Peach Bowl muttering about blown 21-0 lead that might have provided school's 2nd-ever 10-win season. Early on, Georgia (9-3) had terrible time keeping UVa DL Patrick Kerney out of its backfield, and Bulldogs QB Quincy Carter (18-33/222y, 2 TDs, 3 INTs) was picked off 3 times to set up 3 Cavaliers TDs, 2 coming on passes by QB Aaron Brooks (12-32/226y, 3 TDs, INT). Carter threw 2 of his own TDs, and TB Olandis Gary's 3rd Q TD run tied it 21-21 for Georgia. After WR Terrence Wilkins' 67y TD catch gave Cavs 27-21 lead in 3rd Q, K Todd Braverman flared vital conv off line. Carter's 1y sneak with 7:01 to go made it 35-27 for Bull-dogs. Brooks raced 30y to pull Cavs within 35-33, but his 2-pt pass failed. Using 2 Ks, Virginia recovered clever on-side KO, but running play losses forced Braverman into 48y FG try which he hooked wide with 19 secs left.

Independence Bowl (Dec. 31): Mississippi 35 Texas Tech 18

Leading up to bowl season, Ole Miss (7-5) saw QB Romaro Miller break collarbone, coach Tommy Tuberville skip out for Auburn, and new coach David Cutcliffe was hospitalized with inflamed pancreas. But time off after Thanksgiving loss to Mississippi State allowed Miller and Cutcliffe to heal. Cutcliffe, longtime Tennessee O coordinator, had no time to install new O, but Miller (14-23/216y, 3 TDs, 3 TDs, INT) sparked O to 355y vs. nation's 8th-ranked D of Texas Tech (7-5). Red Raiders enjoyed early 7-0 lead when WR Derek Dorris pulled in 22y TD from QB Rob Peters (5-11/69y, TD). Rebel TB Deuce McAllister (27/79y) scored 3 TDs, including nifty 32y swing pass to cap 79y drive that put Rebs ahead for good at 14-7. DL Kendrick Clancey led Rebels D that limited Tech's TB Ricky Williams (the other Big 12 star RB named Ricky Williams) to 85y rushing. But, Texas Tech trimmed deficit to 14-10 at H on 49y FG by Chris Birkholz. With Ole Miss leading 21-10 in 4th Q, game turned into scoring fest in last 3:28. Raiders sub QB Matt Tittle (11-19/134y, 2 INTs) threw INT, and McAllister soon ran in from 8YL. Texas Tech LB Kevin McCullar sprinted 14y to FUM TD RET, but McAllister scooped up subsequent on-side KO for 43y TD RET.

Outback Bowl: Penn State 26 Kentucky 14

Kentucky (7-5) was playing in its 1st New Year's Day bowl game since 1952 Cotton Bowl win over TCU, and aerial genius QB Tim Couch (30-48/336y, 2 TDs, 2 INTs) got Wildcats off to 14-3 start. Kentucky WR Lance Mickelsen caught 36y TD, and RB Anthony White nabbed 16y score in 1st Q. But, Nittany Lions D, led by ferocious rush of MVP DE Courtney Brown, pestered Couch, his future Cleveland Browns teammate, thereafter. Penn State (9-3) made 2 INTs and 6 sacks by mixing pass coverages and propelling LBs LaVar Arrington and Brandon Short on blitzes. Newly-healthy Lions WR Joe Nastasi caught 56y TD pass from QB Kevin Thompson (14-27/187y, TD) early in

2nd Q. K Travis Forney's 2nd of 4 FGs late in 2nd Q pulled Lions to within 14-13 at H. Forney added 2 FGs in 3rd Q.

Gator Bowl: Georgia Tech 35 Notre Dame 28

Georgia Tech (10-2) QB Joey Hamilton directed his O to vital scores every time his team needed them. For its part, Notre Dame (9-3) donned green jerseys for 1st time since 1995 Fiesta Bowl. Irish were hampered by tentative 1st H by nicked-up QB Jarious Jackson (13-24/150y). Hamilton caught his 1st career pass in 1st Q, 5y trick TD from TB Joe Burns. Yellow Jackets led 21-7 at H, but Irish scored on opening 2 possessions of 2nd H: TB Autry Denson (26/130y) scored his 2nd TD, and Jackson ran for 2y TD. But tying conv kick by K Jim Sanson was blocked. Hamilton answered with 44, 55y TD passes to Jacksonville native WR Dez White (4/129y). Winning verdict, Georgia Tech's 5th victory over ND in 32 tries and 1st since 1976, wasn't fully secured until DL Nate Stimson (2.5 sacks) sacked Jackson to force FUM to DL Jesse Tarplin with less than 2 mins to go.

Citrus Bowl: Michigan 45 Arkansas 31

Michigan (10-3) started well, endured 3rd Q lapse, and finished with 21-pt flurry in 4th Q to lock up win. Big 2nd Q highlighted by 2 TD runs by TB Anthony Thomas (21/132y, 3 TDs) and 46y INT TD RET by LB Ian Gold gave Wolverines 24-10 H margin. But, QB Tom Brady (14-27/209y, TD, 2 INTs) was plagued by pair of INTs in 3rd Q. Thus, Arkansas (9-3) rallied to within 31-24 lead early in 4th Q as QB Clint Stoerner (17-42/232y, 2 INTs) threw his 2nd TD. Brady fashioned reversal of fortune, leading 2 TD drives in final 6 mins with Thomas' tying TD coming after Brady's 4th down completion.

Cotton Bowl: Texas 38 Mississippi State 11

TB Ricky Williams rushed 30/203y, 2 TDs, and struck Heisman Trophy pose at end of 37y TD run in 3rd Q as Texas (9-3) easily won its 1st Cotton Bowl since 1982. It was future aerial style of their O that got Longhorns winging: QB Major Applewhite (15-26/225y 3 TDs) noticed that Bulldogs (8-5) moving up to crowd scrimmage line, so he tossed 59 and 52y TD passes to WR Wane McGarity (4/132y) for 14-3 H edge. Texas tallied 24 clinching pts in 3rd Q before Mississippi State QB Matt Wyatt pitched 5y TD pass.

Rose Bowl: Wisconsin 38 UCLA 31

When Big 10 tie-breaker rules prevented Ohio State from Pasadena trip, CBS' Craig James called tri-champion Wisconsin (11-1) "the worst team to ever play in the Rose Bowl." Regardless, Badgers were cheered on by huge red-clad throng, and they overpowered bickering Bruins (10-2) with strong running game. Huge Wisconsin TB Ron Dayne (27/246y) tallied 4 TDs to tie Rose Bowl record on runs of 54, 7, 10, and 22y. UCLA continued its Jekyll-and-Hyde performance that created late-season rift between its dynamic O and young, nicked-up D. Bruins were able to tie game at 7-7 in last min of 1st Q on TB Jermaine Lewis' 38y TD catch from QB Cade McNown (19-34/340y, 2 TDs, INT). In 2nd Q, Bruins earned 14-14 tie 50 secs after Dayne's 2nd TD when frosh WR Freddie Mitchell, back from broken leg, pitched 61y TD to FB Durrell Price. UCLA took lead at 21-14 with 5:15 left in 2nd Q as McNown hit WR Danny Farmer (7/142y) with 41y crossing pass. Dayne's 10y TD burst and K Matt Davenport's FG gave Badgers 24-21 edge at H. Bruins D improved in 2nd H allowing only Dayne's 4th TD, but 2 O plays doomed UCLA: TB DeShaun Foster lost FUM at Badgers 2YL in 3rd Q when din of Wisconsin partisans prevented frosh from hearing play check-off at scrimmage line. Secondly, McNown was jostled into early 4th Q INT which Wisconsin DB Jamar Fletcher returned for 46y TD to create 38-28 advantage. Frosh Badgers DT Wendell Bryant, outstanding all day as blockers concentrated on Wisconsin A-A DE Tom Burke, drove in final coffin nail with midfield sack of McNown with 1 min left.

Sugar Bowl: Ohio State 24 Texas A&M 14

Pressure was on Ohio State (11-1) to win, and win big, to maintain slim national championship hopes. Winning big looked easy after 1st Q, in which, after spotting Texas A&M (11-3) early TD by RB Dante Hall, Buckeyes scored 3 TDs over 6:23 span for 21-7 lead. Ohio QB Joe Germaine (21-38/222y, TD) pitched 28 and 17y passes to lead to his 18y TD pass to WR Reggie Germany. Stopping Texas A&M on downs, Buckeyes began from own 41YL and quickly used ground game for TD registered by sub TB Joe Montgomery (9/96y). Ohio State scored again on blocked punt by DB Derrick Ross. But, from 2nd Q on, Aggies D stiffened, and Ohio State weakened on 3rd down and also missed pair of 2nd H FGs. Texas A&M QB Branndon Stewart (22-39/187y, TD) threw 7y TD pass to WR Leroy Hodge in 4th Q as Aggies outgained Buckeyes 152y to 140y in 2nd H. Win gave Big 10 impressive 5-0 bowl mark for 1998-99 post-season.

Orange Bowl (Jan. 2): Florida 31 Syracuse 10

This bowl game was back in Miami's original Orange Bowl stadium because NFL Dolphins had 1st dibs on Pro Player Stadium. So smothering was D of Florida (10-2) that game was over almost at outset. Gators QB Doug Johnson (12-17/195y, 2 TDs) launched scoring passes to WR Travis Taylor (7/159y) of 51 and 26y. Orangemen (8-4) held ball for long period straddling 1st Q intermission, but managed only K Nathan Trout's 36y FG. Syracuse didn't score again until 3:33 remained in blowout: QB Donovan McNabb (14-30/192y, INT), playing last game of his fine career, pitched 62y TD to little WR Maurice Jackson. Gators Johnson broke his left leg in 2nd Q, but sub QB Jesse Palmer (110-14/113y) threw 4y TD on his 2nd snap and added 2y TD on unusual sneak. Palmer's TD succeeded despite his 1st lining up mistakenly in Shotgun formation, only to have intense coach Steve Spurrier frantically wave him into correct position. Otherwise, game lacked real intensity as had most of this year's major bowls that fell rung below championship Fiesta Bowl. In many ways, BCS made this Orange Bowl into lemon despite Florida making its 1st appearance in Miami since 1967.

Fiesta Bowl (Jan. 4): Tennessee 23 Florida State 16

Bowl Championship Series staged its 1st-ever title game in Tempe, Arizona, with no. 2 Florida State (11-2) entering as 5-pt favorite over no. 1 Tennessee (13-0). Teams were so rusty after long layoff that they played entertaining but somewhat sloppy game. Retiring (briefly) ABC announcer Keith Jackson said with less than 3 mins left: "We've had everything but beauty." FSU was penalized 12/110y, including roughing P on 1st series, which wiped out 29y RET by DB Reggie Durden. After nearly whole 1st Q of D slugging, Vols launched 76y bomb to WR Peerless Price (4/199y, TD) which carried to FSU 12YL. Tennessee K Jeff Hall made 24y FG early in 2nd Q, after missing from 33y out in 1st Q. Coach Phillip Fulmer chose to take those pts off board, and QB Tee Martin (11-18/278y, 2 TDs, 2 INTs) clicked on 2nd down, 4y play-action slant TD pass to FB Shawn Bryson. Seminoles QB Marcus Outzen (9-22/145y, 2 INTs), starting for injured Chris Weinke, soon looked to find ace WR Peter Warrick. But, Warrick's shadow, DB Dwayne Goodrich, stepped in front of square-out pass and went 54y on INT TD RET. Later in 2nd Q, Martin lost sight of Seminoles DB Derrick Gibson over middle, and Gibson made INT which he returned 44y to Vols 3YL. FB William McCray blasted from 1YL, barely reaching ball across GL before losing possession, to bring FSU back to within 14-6. Seminoles' bad snap allowed Tennessee to block K Sebastian Janikowski's conv kick. Janikowski came back with 34y FG with 1:17 left in 1st H, but not before PENs and Vols DL Corey Terry's sack damaged FSU's 1st-and-goal chance at 4YL. Scoreless 3rd Q was marked by partial punt block by Vols DB Tim Sewell and injuries that dwindled Tennessee's all-important secondary, including loss of Goodrich. Unable to get ball to Warrick, who only made 1/7y receiving and 1/11y rushing, but authored brilliant 51y punt RET, Outzen hit WR Ron Dugans (6/135y) for 29 and 16y passes to threaten in 3rd Q. But, holding PEN ruined Outzen's scramble for 1st down. DT Darwin Walker sacked FSU out of Tennessee territory early in 4th Q, and Martin arched killing 79y bomb to Price, who pulled in pass over tight outside coverage by DB Mario Edwards. Hall's conv was blocked to keep score at 20-9, but Outzen gave ball right back on FUM at FSU 28YL. Hall booted 23y FG after TB Travis Stephens ran 18y to 8YL. Outzen's scrambling rollout 39y pass to Dugans set up Outzen's 7y QB draw up middle for TD with 3:42 left. FSU succeeded on REC of Janikowski's on-side KO, but ball was ruled to have grazed Janikowski's hip before it went 10y. With 1:36 left, Martin lobbed short pass to Bryson on 4th down which carried to 11YL. Vols lost FUM on next play, but sr DB Steve Johnson came right back with INT to lock it up.

Final AP Poll January 5

1 Tennessee (70)	1750	13 Air Force	980
2 Ohio State	1673	14 Georgia	785
3 Florida State	1574	15 Texas	740
4 Arizona	1545	16 Arkansas	621
5 Florida	1463	17 Penn State	619
6 Wisconsin	1427	18 Virginia	544
7 Tulane	1252	19 Nebraska	454
8 UCLA	1123	20 Miami	426
9 Georgia Tech	1122	21 Missouri	335
10 Kansas State	1086	22 Notre Dame	315
11 Texas A&M	1071	23 Virginia Tech	256
12 Michigan	1052	24 Purdue	236
		25 Syracuse	161

Final *USA Today* Coaches Poll January 6

1 Tennessee (62)	1550	14 Georgia	677
2 Ohio State	1473	15 Penn State	640
3 Florida State	1376	16 Texas	577
4 Arizona	1347	17 Arkansas	566
5 Wisconsin	1289	18 Virginia	485
6 Florida	1282	19 Virginia Tech	471
7 Tulane	1117	20 Nebraska	321
8 UCLA	998	21 Miami (Fla.)	291
9 Kansas State	991	22 Notre Dame	256
10 Air Force	971	23 Purdue	233
11 Georgia Tech	932	24 Syracuse	192
12 Michigan	863	25 Missouri	171
13 Texas A&M	839		

1998 Top Performance Formula

1 Tennessee	1.7711
2 Ohio State	1.7269
3 Florida State	1.6821
4 Wisconsin	1.6309
5 Kansas State	1.6114
6 Air Force	1.5911
7 Arizona	1.5757
8 UCLA	1.5669
9 Florida	1.5339
10 Texas A&M	1.4971
11 Georgia Tech	1.4937
12 Nebraska	1.4574
13 Virginia Tech	1.4545
14 Penn State	1.4421
15 Michigan	1.4258
16 Texas	1.4144
17 Purdue	1.4076
18 Tulane	1.4005
19 Arkansas	1.3935
20 Virginia	1.3894

1998 Top Opponent Records

1	Auburn	.6860
2	Florida State	.6643
3	Missouri	.6313
4	Texas A&M	.6250
5	Washington	.6241
6	Alabama	.6212
7	UCLA	.6202
8	Louisiana State	.6198
9	Nebraska	.6197
10	Michigan State	.6077
11	Baylor	.6000
12	Syracuse	.5969
13	Southern California	.5929
14	Vanderbilt	.5917
15	Purdue	.5899
16	South Carolina	.5868
17	Army	.5862
18	Tennessee	.5857
19	Penn State	.5846
20t	Ohio State	.580153
20t	Texas	.580153

1998 Out-of-Conference Records

	W-L	Percentage	Bowl W-L
Big Ten	30-12	.7143	5-0
Big Twelve	31-13	.7045	3-4
Pacific-10	25-12	.6757	1-4
Southeastern	30-15	.6667	4-4
Atlantic Coast	17-12	.5862	2-3
Big East	16-17	.4848	2-2
Western Athletic	19-34	.3585	2-2

1998 Individual Statistical Leaders

RUSHING YARDS	Attempts	Yards	Avg.
Ricky Williams, Texas	361	2124	5.9
Travis Prentice, Miami (Ohio)	365	1787	4.9
Mike Cloud, Boston College	308	1726	5.6
Ricky Williams, Texas Tech	306	1582	5.2
Devin West, Missouri	283	1578	5.6
Denvis Manns, New Mexico State	269	1469	5.5
Amos Zereoue, West Virginia	261	1430	5.5
Edgerrin James, Miami	242	1416	5.9
James Johnson, Mississippi State	236	1383	5.9
Thomas Jones, Virginia	238	1303	5.5

PASSING YARDS	Completions	Attempts	Yards	Pct.
Tim Rattay, Louisiana Tech	380	559	4943	68.0
Tim Couch, Kentucky	400	553	4275	72.3
Chris Redman, Louisville	309	473	4042	65.3
Daunte Culpepper, Central Florida	296	402	3690	73.6
Akili Smith, Oregon	191	325	3307	58.8
Shaun King, Tulane	223	328	3232	68.0
Marc Bulger, West Virginia	240	369	3178	65.0
Cade McNown, UCLA	188	323	3130	58.2
Joe Germaine, Ohio State	209	346	3108	60.4
Michael Bishop, Kansas State	164	295	2844	55.6

RECEIVING YARDS	Catches	Yards
Troy Edwards, Louisiana Tech	140	1996
Torry Holt, North Carolina State	88	1604
Geoff Noisy, Nevada	94	1405
Travis McGriff, Florida	70	1357
David Boston, Ohio State	74	1330
Craig Yeast, Kentucky	85	1311
Trevor Insley, Nevada	69	1220
Sherrod Gideon, Southern Mississippi	66	1186
P.J. Franklin, Tulane	74	1174
Brandon Stokley, Southwestern Louisiana	65	1173

1998 Consensus All-America Team
Offense

Wide Receiver:	Torry Holt, North Carolina State
	Peter Warrick, Florida State
	Troy Edwards, Louisiana Tech
Tight End:	Rufus French, Mississippi
Offensive:	Kris Farris, UCLA
	Aaron Gibson, Wisconsin
	Matt Stinchcomb, Georgia
	Rob Murphy, Ohio State
Center:	Craig Page, Georgia Tech
Quarterback:	Cade McNown, UCLA
	Michael Bishop, Kansas State
	Tim Couch, Kentucky
Running Back:	Ricky Williams, Texas
	Mike Cloud, Boston College
Placekicker:	Sebastian Janikowski, Florida State
Kick Returner:	David Allen, Kansas State

Defense

Line:	Tom Burke, Wisconsin
	Montae Reagor, Texas Tech
	Jared DeVries, Iowa
Linebacker:	Chris Claiborne, Southern California
	Dat Nguyen, Texas A&M
	Jeff Kelly, Kansas State
	Al Wilson, Tennessee
Defensive Back:	Chris McAlister, Arizona
	Antoine Winfield, Ohio State
	Champ Bailey, Georgia
	Anthony Poindexter, Virginia
Punter:	Joe Kristosik, junior, UNLV

1998 Heisman Trophy Vote

Ricky Williams, senior tailback, Texas	2355
Michael Bishop, senior quarterback, Kansas State	792
Cade McNown, senior quarterback, UCLA	696
Tim Couch, junior quarterback, Kentucky	527
Donovan McNabb, senior quarterback, Syracuse	232

Other Major Awards

Maxwell (Player)	Ricky Williams, senior tailback, Texas
Walter Camp (Player)	Ricky Williams, senior tailback, Texas
Outland (Lineman)	Kris Farris, senior tackle, UCLA
Vince Lombardi (Lineman)	Dat Nguyen, senior linebacker, Texas A&M
Doak Walker (Running Back)	Ricky Williams, senior tailback, Texas
Davey O'Brien (Quarterback)	Michael Bishop, senior quarterback, Kansas State
Fred Biletnikoff (Receiver)	Troy Edwards, senior wide receiver, Louisiana Tech
Jim Thorpe (Defensive Back)	Antoine Winfield, senior cornerback, Ohio State
Dick Butkus (Linebacker)	Chris Claiborne, junior LB, Southern California
Lou Groza (Placekicker)	Sebastian Janikowski, sophomore K, Florida State
Johnny Unitas (Quarterback)	Cade McNown, senior quarterback, UCLA
Chuck Bednarik (Defender)	Dat Nguyen, senior linebacker, Texas A&M
AFCA Coach of the Year	Phillip Fulmer, Tennessee

1999

The Year of the Distracted Wire-to-Wire Win, the Magical Freshman, and November Nightmare

Since Associated Press started a preseason football poll in 1950 no team ever had gone wire-to-wire as no. 1. In 1999, Florida State (12-0) not only started the season as no. 1, but finished on top of the pigskin mountain in January. When the Seminoles defeated no. 2 Virginia Tech (11-1) 46-29 in the Sugar Bowl, it completed Bobby Bowden's first undefeated season after 34 years as a head coach. It was Bowden's second national title.

Getting there was no easy task because Florida State surely lived through one of the most widely publicized "distractions" in many years. In late September, star wide receiver Peter Warrick, whom many thought to be the front-runner for the Heisman Trophy, was arrested with teammate Laveranues Coles when a department store clerk accomplice sold them clothing at a deep discount. The felony was recorded on video and later seen on many television newscasts across the country. Warrick missed two games but returned when his crime was bargained down to a misdemeanor. Warrick had a superb Sugar Bowl, catching two touchdowns and returning a punt for a score.

The Hokies were a surprising entry into the Bowl Championship Series picture. The Hokies uncovered a magical freshman quarterback in Michael Vick, who was not only a lightning runner but a surprising sharp passer. As probably the most decorated newcomer in college history, Vick became the first freshman to lead the NCAA in passing since Travis Tidwell of Auburn in 1946.

Virginia Tech's relatively weak schedule nearly cost it an opportunity to challenge Florida State in the Sugar Bowl. Preseason no. 2 Tennessee (9-3) lost early to Florida 23-21, a seemingly annual event in the SEC, but turned hot in mid-season. The Volunteers beat Georgia (8-4), Alabama (10-3), and Notre Dame (5-7) and found themselves second in the BCS standings on November 8. Despite its one loss to Florida, Tennessee enjoyed a slim BCS lead over Virginia Tech, which had an 8-0 mark and no. 2 ranking in the AP Poll. Arkansas (8-4), which had lost a heartbreaker to Tennessee during the Vols' national title run in 1998, rallied from a 24-14 third quarter deficit to beat Tennessee 28-24 on November 13. And although Nebraska nipped at the Hokies heels, Virginia Tech qualified for the Sugar Bowl showdown with Florida State.

It turned out to be a magnificent showdown in New Orleans. The incomparable Vick led Virginia Tech to an early threat that was stopped. Florida State used two special teams touchdowns to gain a 28-7 lead in the second quarter, but suddenly the Hokies ran off 22 straight points to take a 29-28 lead entering the fourth quarter. Veteran Seminoles quarterback Chris Weinke came through as he had all season with clutch passing that provided the winning touchdown pass to Ron Dugans followed by a brilliant game-signature catch in the end zone by Warrick.

Penn State (10-3) was in the championship mix after trouncing preseason no. 4 Arizona (6-6) and opening with nine straight wins, but some victories were close shaves. On November 6, under-appreciated Minnesota (8-4) completed a miraculous fourth down pass to set up freshman Dan Nystrom's last-play field goal to stun Penn State 24-23. The Nittany Lions dropped subsequent games to Michigan (10-2) and Michigan State (10-2) and fell all the way from a potential national title shot to the Alamo Bowl. It truly was a November nightmare for coach Joe Paterno and his team, one that wouldn't go away. The Minnesota debacle started a two-year downward spiral in which Penn State lost 14 of 20 games. Thanks to the spark provided by freshman quarterback Zack Mills midway through the 2001 season, the Nittany Lions returned to their winning ways. They closed 2001 with a 5-2 mark, won nine games in 2002, but soon were losing again.

One of college football's most special traditions accidentally brought grief and sadness to the campus of Texas A&M (8-4). For decades, students and alumni built "the world's largest bonfire" as the sacred focal point for school spirit in preparation for the annual battle against rival Texas (9-5). In 1999, the Aggies hosted the game on Thanksgiving Friday, and Bonfire (with a capital B), a full seven stories high, was under construction the week prior. The stack of wood was being finished when it collapsed and killed 12 students and injured dozens more a week before its scheduled lighting. In grand Aggie spirit, more than 70,000 participated in "Yell Practice" the night before the game, which A&M won in emotional fashion.

Stanford (8-4) was the surprise champion of the Pacific-10. After being considerably trounced in its opener by Texas 69-17 and beaten by its pet peeve, San Jose State (3-7), Stanford was never ranked until it beat Notre Dame 40-37 in the regular season finale at Palo Alto. In between, the

Cardinal beat UCLA (4-7) and Southern California (6-6) as both traditional powers finished in the conference's second division. Stanford lost to second place Washington (7-5) and wasn't scheduled against Oregon (9-3), the other runner-up. In the Rose Bowl, Stanford was inspired by wide receiver Troy Walters, who despite an injured wrist, made key catches in the first half that the Cardinal led 9-3. But, Wisconsin (10-2) used its talented offensive line to batter holes for tailback and Heisman Trophy winner Ron Dayne to steamroller Stanford in the second half for a 17-9 win.

Baylor (1-10) lost an improbable 27-24 heartbreaker to UNLV (3-8). Needing only to take a knee with 20 seconds left for new coach Kevin Steele's first win, the Bears sent lightweight freshman tailback Darrell Bush for an eight-yard scoring blast. Rebel Kevin Thomas returned Bush's fumble for a 100-yard touchdown on the game's last play. Steele sought to build a killer instinct in his Bear players and looked at the attempt for an additional touchdown as symbolic of that attitude. Things went considerably downhill for Steele after that, and he was fired midway through 2002.

Milestones

● Bowl Championship Series formula was expanded with addition of five computer ratings, including 70-year-old Dunkel System. With input from seven computer services, ranking of each team was benefitted by dropping worst single computer rate.

● Change in Louisiana collegiate system found Northeast Louisiana changing its name to Louisiana-Monroe and Southwestern Louisiana to Louisiana-Lafayette.

● Brandon Burlsworth, 22, All-America guard of Arkansas in 1998, died in April auto accident only 11 days after his selection in NFL draft by Indianapolis Colts. Angelo Bertelli, 78, Notre Dame's Heisman Trophy winner of 1943, died of brain cancer on June 27. Matt Hartl, inspirational leader of Northwestern's 1996 Rose Bowl team, died after long battle with cancer. Former Notre Dame linebacker Demetrius DuBose, 28, was killed on July 24 by San Diego police in controversial shooting. Jaime Fields, 29, linebacker on Washington's 1991 national co-champions, was killed near Los Angeles in late August by motorist who ran red light. Georgia assistant coach Pat Watson died of heart attack on September 25 after Bulldogs' win over Central Florida. Oklahoma's three-time All-America (1972-74) linebacker Rod Shoate died at age 46. Death claimed Dave Whitsell, halfback at Indiana (1956-57) and 12-year NFL defensive back. On October 25, Robert Fraley, reserve quarterback at Alabama (1974-75) and agent to several athletes and NFL coaches, perished with golfer client Payne Stewart and four others when their private jet experienced sudden decompression and crashed after hours-long auto-pilot flight off course to South Dakota. Fran O'Brien, Michigan State tackle (1956-58) and Washington, D.C., area restaurateur, died of heart attack at 63 in late October. NFL's all-time leading rusher, Walter Payton, 1974 Little All-America at Jackson State and namesake of annual award (1987 to present) that honors Division 1-AA player of year, died at 45 on November 1 of bile duct cancer. Billy Pricer, starting fullback for many of Oklahoma's triumphs during its 47-game win streak, died at age 60. Lindsey Nelson, radio and TV voice of Cotton Bowl, died.

● Longest winning streaks entering season:
Tennessee, Tulane 13   Air Force 9

● Coaching Changes:

	Incoming	Outgoing
Auburn	Tommy Tuberville	Bill Oliver
Baylor	Kevin Steele	Dave Roberts
Clemson	Tommy Bowden	Tommy West
Colorado	Gary Barnett	Rick Neuheisel
Duke	Carl Franks	Fred Goldsmith
Hawaii	June Jones	Fred von Appen
Iowa	Kirk Ferentz	Hayden Fry
Louisiana Tech	Jack Bicknell, Jr.	Gary Crowton
Louisiana State	Hal Hunter (interim) (a)	Gerry DiNardo
Miami (Ohio)	Terry Hoeppner	Randy Walker
Michigan State	Bobby Williams (b)	Nick Saban
Mississippi	David Cutcliffe	Tommy Tuberville
Nevada-Las Vegas	John Robinson	Jeff Horton
Northwestern	Randy Walker	Gary Barnett
Oklahoma	Bobby Stoops	John Blake
Oregon State	Dennis Erickson	Mike Riley
South Carolina	Lou Holtz	Brad Scott
Tulane	Chris Scelfo	Tommy Bowden
Washington	Rick Neuheisel	Jim Lambright

(a) Hunter (1-0) replaced DiNardo in after DiNardo (2-8) was fired.
(b) Williams (1-0) replaced Saban (9-2) prior to Citrus Bowl, after Saban's acceptance of LSU offer.

Preseason USA Today Coaches Poll

1	Florida State (36)	1447	14	Virginia Tech	626
2	Tennessee (13)	1369	15	UCLA	596
3	Arizona (2)	1301	16	Texas	497
4	Penn State (8)	1267	17	Colorado	470
5	Florida	1113	18	Notre Dame	422
6	Nebraska	1095	19	Kansas State	379
7	Michigan	1094	20	Alabama	367
8	Texas A&M	1051	21	Southern California	360
9	Ohio State	1024	22	Arkansas	325
10	Wisconsin	902	23	Purdue	291
11	Georgia Tech	748	24	Virginia	191
12	Miami (Fla.)	704	25	Arizona State	167
13	Georgia	671			

August 28, 1999

PENN STATE 41 Arizona 7: No. 4 Arizona (0-1) came east for Pigskin Classic seeking notoriety, while no. 3 Penn State (1-0) looked to improve its O. On opening drive, Nittany Lions WR Chafie Fields raced 20y on reverse and broke tackle on 37y TD catch. Fields added 70y TD run on another reverse in 2nd Q as Lions built 31-0 H lead. Penn State D held Wildcats TB Trung Canidate to 10/31y rushing, had 5 sacks as lesser lights like DEs Justin Kurpeikis (2 sacks) and Jason Wallace amplified stars DE Courtney Brown (2 sacks) and LB LaVar Arrington (7 tackles). Arizona sub TB Leo Mills averted shutout with 1y TD run in game's last 47 secs. Penn State QBs Kevin Thompson (2 TD passes) and Rashard Casey (6-10/107y) led attack to 504y, but coach Joe Paterno said, "...I don't think this ballgame proves anything."

North Carolina State 23 TEXAS 20: Wolfpack (1-0) continued its recent trend of authoring early-season upsets as 3 blocked punts finally rattled no. 17 Texas (0-1) into late-game loss. NC State O gained meager 172y and made only 7 1st downs, but its special teams were special. Trailing 10-7 in 2nd Q, NC State TB Eric Leak blocked punt for safety, but Longhorns answered with 80y pass-and-run from QB Major Applewhite (2y TD run) to TB Victor Ike for 17-9 edge. With 12 mins left in 4th Q, Wolfpack DB Terrence Holt, kid brother of 1998 A-A WR Torry Holt, blocked punt for CB Tony Scott's 25y TD romp. K Kris Stockton responded with 26y FG and 20-15 lead after Texas answered with 64y march. Holt blocked another punt with 3:22 left and Leak took it 48y for decisive TD. "It had a magical ending," said NC State coach Mike O'Cain.

Miami 23 Ohio State 12 (E. Rutherford, NJ): Looking to reestablish its swagger lost in 1995 probation, Miami (1-0) tore into young Buckeyes (0-1) in Kickoff Classic. Hurricanes TB James Jackson (24/89y) broke down right sideline for 44y TD in 1st Q. Ohio State LB Na'il Diggs' blitz created FUM by Miami QB Kenny Kelly (17-25/245y, TD, 2 INTs), and Buckeyes soph QB Austin Moherman (10-22/107y, TD, 2 INTs) passed 6y over middle to TE Steve Wisniewski for TD and 9-7 lead. But, Hurricanes whirled to 16 pts in 2nd Q, capped by WR Santana Moss' spectacular adjustment to under-thrown long pass by Kelly. Moss caught it and blurred past 2 DBs for TD that provided 23-9 H lead for Miami.

September 4, 1999

(Th) MICHIGAN STATE 27 Oregon 20: Spartans DB Amp Campbell broke his neck against Oregon (0-1) in 1998, and he made his triumphant return in 1999 opener. Ducks picked on rusty Campbell for several 1st H completions by new QB A.J. Feeley (27-49/343y, 2 TDs, INT). Ducks led 17-7 early in 3rd Q when Feeley hit WR Tony Hartley with 18y TD pass. Michigan State (1-0) tied it on K Paul Edinger's 22y FG and QB Bill Burke's 2nd TD pass to WR Gari Scott. Then, with Ducks driving in 4th Q, Campbell fielded dribbling FUM and raced 85y for 24-17 lead.

BOSTON COLLEGE 30 Baylor 29 (OT): Game's stunning end propelled pair of young teams in different directions. Boston College (1-0), just 3 years removed from gambling scandal, would earn 1st bowl bid since 1994. Baylor (0-1) would reach low point in following week when it would blow sure win on way to 1-10 season. In Kevin Steele's coaching debut, Bears took 3-0 lead in middle of 1st Q after DB Samir Al-Amin blocked punt. Eagle TB Carlton Rowe slammed 1y for 7-3 Eagles lead late in 1st Q. Alert WR Lanny O'Steen gobbled up Bears EZ FUM for TD in 2nd Q edge. In last min of 2nd Q, Baylor LB McKinley Bowie raced 81y with INT TD RET, but K Kyle Atteberry's 35y PAT (after celebration PEN) was blocked by BC DL Chris Hovan. Eagles TB Cedric Washington rushed for 177y and 3 TDs, last of which, for 1y, provided 30-23 OT edge. Bears countered on its opening OT series with 1y TD sneak by QB Jermaine Alfred. But, Atteberry badly hooked tying kick for loss.

NORTH CAROLINA STATE 10 South Carolina 0: South Carolina's Lou Holtz returned to coaching after 2-year absence, but there to greet him at NC State (2-0), where he coached in 1972-75, was tropical storm Dennis that brought torrents of rain. Gamecocks outgained Wolfpack 232y to 96y, but lost 5 TOs. NC State K Kent Passingham booted 22y FG in 2nd Q for 3-0 lead. South Carolina dominated 3rd Q despite fighting stiff wind, but had punt blocked in 4th Q which WR Koren Robinson scooped up for 3y TD. Frosh TB Derek Watson rushed 15/118y for Gamecocks.

MICHIGAN 26 Notre Dame 22: Long-term bitter rivals staged another classic. Michigan (1-0) coach Lloyd Carr was irritated that Notre Dame (1-1) had scheduled 48-13 muscle-flexer over Kansas in Eddie Robinson Classic on August 28. Wolverines seemed on verge of running away with 1st H before college record crowd of 111,523, but had to settle for 3 FGs by K Jeff Del Verne. Irish led 14-9 at H on 4y reverse run by TB Joey Getherall and powerful, twisting 12y surge by QB Jarious Jackson (19-28/302y, TD). Each titan fought on in hard-hitting 2nd H until Fighting Irish went ahead 22-19 with 4:08 to play on Jackson's never-quit 20y TD pass to TE Jabari Holloway on 4th down. Celebration PEN was flagged against ND after Jackson's 2-pt pass, and after Michigan QB Tom Brady (17-24/197y, TD) executed 20y screen pass, 15y roughing call was tacked on against Irish DB Ron Israel. Wolverines TB Anthony Thomas (32/138y) powered for short winning TD on 3rd try from inside ND 5YL.

Nebraska 42 IOWA 7: Nebraska (1-0), determined to improve on 9-4 record of 1998, marched up and down Kinnick Stadium field to no avail in 1st Q and well into 2nd Q. Iowa (0-1) D bent but didn't break, thanks to heads-up play of DL Jerry Montgomery and DBs Matt Bowen and Matt Stockdale. Finally, sub Huskers QB Eric Crouch raced around LE for 28y TD in 2nd Q. In 2nd H, Hawkeyes D ran out of gas as Crouch scored 2 more TDs and starting QB Bobby Newcombe, who had 3 TOs in 1st H, scored twice. Iowa earned late TD on WR Tim Dodge's 10y scoop-and-run with blocked punt.

Colorado State 41 Colorado 14 (Denver): Colorado State (1-0) hadn't beaten Colorado (0-1) since 1986, but from opening mins Rams roared to 28-0 H lead. LB Rick Crowell picked off pass by Buffaloes QB Mike Moschetti (30-46/291y, 2 TDs, 3 INTs) and raced 54y to TD in 1st Q. It was followed by 59y burst by Rams FB Kevin McDougall (22/190y),

1st of his 2 TD runs. New CSU QB Matt Newton (10-18/109y, TD) sneaked over in 3rd Q for embarrassing 35-0 edge over Buffs. Down 41-0, Moschetti connected on TD passes to WRs Roman Hollowell and Javon Green.

(Mon) ARIZONA STATE 31 Texas Tech 13: Red Raiders' TB Ricky "The Other" Williams (13/33y), top returning rusher in Big 12, scored on short run in 1st Q for 7-0 Texas Tech (0-1) lead. But, Arizona State QB J.R. Redmond broke loose for 56y TD run in 2nd Q and went on to rush 20/157y, 2 TDs. Trailing 13-7 at H, Texas Tech was crushed by knee injury that sidelined Williams and 18 unanswered pts, including Sun Devil TB Delvon Flowers' 40y TD run. Raiders' DL Aaron Hunt made 53y fumble TD RET early in 4th Q.

September 11, 1999

(Th) BRIGHAM YOUNG 35 Washington 28: BYU (1-0) opened season with new blue jerseys with white bibs that oddly mimicked visiting shirts of Washington (0-1). Cougar QB Kevin Feterik passed 39-59/500y, 3 TDs, INT, including 38y TD pass over middle to WR Chris Hale with 1:16 remaining for winning score. Washington (0-1) lost debut of coach Rick Neuheisel, but by no fault of QB Marques Tuiasasopo (22-36/237y). In 3rd Q, Tuiasasopo passed 36y to WR Todd Elstrom for TD and then ran twice for scores that provided 28-27 lead with 5:04 to go in 4th Q. Tuiasasopo nearly pulled it out, but his last-play pass sailed through EZ. BYU frosh TB Luke Staley rushed for 39y, caught passes for 56y, and scored 2 TDs in 3rd Q.

CLEMSON 33 Virginia 14: Even though ex-coach Danny Ford received loudest cheer, Clemson (1-1), ground-based powerhouse in Ford's years (1978-89), on this day employed aerial game of new coach Tommy Bowden. Prime benefactor was Tiger QB Brandon Streeter, who passed for school record 342y on 24-32, INT. Streeter clicked for 2 TD passes in 1st Q to spark 20-0 H lead which grew to 33-0 in 3rd Q. Favored Virginia (1-1) scored 2 window-dressing TDs in 2nd H, including 3y run by TB Thomas Jones, who rushed 23/97y. By season's end, Jones set ACC rushing record of 1,798y, surpassing mark that North Carolina's Don McCauley posted in 1970.

FLORIDA STATE 41 Georgia Tech 35: Rousing O battle came to typify season of shootouts for no. 10 Georgia Tech (1-1). Mercurial Yellow Jacket QB Joe Hamilton (22-25/387y, 4 TDs) kept Tech competitive with 80, 56y TD passes and 19y TD run in 1st H. Florida State (2-0) never trailed, but was forced to go ahead for good at 28-21 with 1:08 to go in 2nd Q on QB Chris Weinke's 29y TD pass, his 2nd of 3 scoring tosses. Trumpeted Seminole WR Peter Warrick (8/142y) ran 17y, out of Shotgun, to score opening TD and caught TD pass for 35-21 lead early in 3rd Q.

PENN STATE 20 Pittsburgh 17: Pittsburgh (1-1), 5-TD underdog, bottled up run attack of Penn State (3-0) to tune of 41/65y and put terrible fright in old rival. Every time Nittany Lion air game (21-34/320y, TD, INT) set up go-ahead score, which it did at 7-0, 10-7, 17-10, Panthers retaliated with tying score. Pitt QB John Turman (19-35/316y, 2 TDs, INT) threw 16y TD to WR Antonio Bryant in 2nd Q and 42y TD to WR Julius Dixon with 4:34 left. Lion WR Eddie Drummond (4/155y) caught 51y pass to set up winning 24y FG by K Travis Forney with 1:20 to go, then made saving tackle at 50YL of DB Hank Poteat's potentially winning KO RET. Pitt made it to Penn State 25YL, but DL David Fleischhauer's sack and LB LaVar Arrington's FG block ended it.

PURDUE 28 Notre Dame 23: Boilermakers (1-0) and Fighting Irish (1-2) combined for 826y, but Purdue LB Mike Rose spilled ND QB Jarious Jackson (13/1y, 2 TDs rushing) for loss on 2nd-and-goal from 2YL as time expired. Confused Notre Dame O was late to get call from sideline. Purdue QB Drew Brees passed 24-40/317y, TD, INT, also dashed 9y to score in 1st Q. Less than famous as runner, Brees added 2-pt run for 22-16 3rd Q edge. Boilermakers K Travis Dorsch booted 2 FGs in 4th Q for 28-23 edge before Jackson (22-34/267y, INT) directed Irish to ill-fated last play.

OHIO STATE 42 Ucla 20: Alternating QB Drew Bennett (9-15/138y, INT) completed fluke, tipped 67y TD pass to FB Matt Stanley, which sent Bruins (1-1) to early 10-0 lead. Ohio State (1-1) ignited its O for 21 pts in 2nd Q as TB Michael Wiley (22/119y) tallied twice. Buckeye QB Steve Bellisari (11-16/159y) provided spark when he relieved QB Austin Moherman (10-19/107y, INT), threw 2 TD passes to WR Ken-Yon Rambo, 2nd of which clinched it at 35-17 early in 4th Q. TB DeShaun Foster (17/51y) scored in 3rd Q to pull UCLA within 20-17; Bruins scored fewer than 24 pts for 1st time in last 24 games.

September 18, 1999

(Th) BRIGHAM YOUNG 34 Colorado State 13: All 8 school mascots were on hand for 1st-ever Mountain West Conf game. Unlike old WAC shootouts, D was hallmark for winning Cougars (2-0). With star FB Kevin McDougall on sideline, normally run-powerful Colorado State (2-1) was limited to 17/28y on ground. Frosh TB Luke Staley scored 3 TDs as BYU built 31-0 lead by 3rd Q. Rams tallied on 1st play of 4th Q as QB Matt Newton (26-44/289y, 3 INTs) threw 1st of his 2 TD passes.

Michigan 18 SYRACUSE 13: You've got to hand it to Syracuse (2-1) for scheduling difficult non-conf games in Carrier Dome. In each of last 6 years, Orangemen lost September home game, but played Michigan (3-0) tough this time. Wolverine K Jeff Del Verne kicked 2 FGs 3 min apart in 2nd Q, and with UM D forcing Orange backward at -21y rate, rout seemed in offing for Michigan. But, Syracuse completed long march as WR Quinton Spotwood (4/59y) juked around in EZ for 6y TD from QB Madei Williams (7-12/128y, TD). Trailing 13-7, Orange opened 2nd H with 80y drive capped by HB James Mungro slipping out of Wishbone for unguarded 3y TD pass. But when K Nathan Trout attempted school record 73rd straight PAT, Wolverine DL James Hall blocked it to preserve 13-13 tie. Inside last 5 mins of 3rd Q, Syracuse frosh QB Troy Nunes scrambled into EZ and grounded pass for safety. Down 18-13 in dying moments, Syracuse faced 4th-and-4 at Michigan 9YL. Although partisans shouted for EZ interference on Wolverine DB James Whitley, Williams' passes landed incomplete.

FLORIDA 23 Tennessee 21: Entering SEC showdown, Gator D was under suspicion after allowing 784y in opening 2 wins. Florida (3-0) soph DL Alex Brown contributed game of his career with 5 sacks and INT of Tennessee (1-1) QB Tee Martin (16-39/192y, INT). Frustrated in air, Martin still managed 7y TD run for 7-3 edge early in 2nd Q. Gator QB Doug Johnson suffered 3 INTs, but threw 21-44/343y, 2 TDs. Johnson found WR Darrell Jackson for 11y TD and 16-7 lead in last min of 2nd Q. No. 2 Vols fought back from 23-7 deficit with 2 TD runs by TB Jamal Lewis (22/99y), but Tennessee was stuffed twice on late-game 4th down tries.

Louisiana Tech 29 ALABAMA 28: Thorny Louisiana Tech (2-2) took 6-0 and 12-3 leads on 1st H TD passes by topnotch QB Tim Rattay (27-50/368y, 3 TDs, INT). When K Kevin Pond bombed 42y FG, Bulldogs led 15-3 early in 3rd Q. Slumbering Alabama (2-1) was awakened by TB Shaun Alexander (30/173y, 2 TDs), who made 76y KO TD RET. Alexander raced 30y to score late in 3rd Q, and when WR Freddie Milons added 2-pt catch, Tide led 18-15. After trade of 4th Q TDs, K Chris Kemp booted 32y FG and Bama seemed safe at 28-22 with 2:36 to go. Rattay limped off with ankle injury, sub QB Brian Stallworth came off Bulldog bench to throw 28y TD pass to WR Sean Cangelosi, who went high among Tide DBs in EZ with :02 left.

Penn State 27 MIAMI 23: With Miami (2-1) O being held to -2y well into 2nd Q and QB Kenny Kelly (11-21/160y, TD, 4 INTs) suffering 2 INTs and FUM, Penn State (4-0) enjoyed 10-0 lead. Lion TD came on WR Chafie Fields getting loose in broken coverage for 49y TD pass from QB Rashard Casey (7-9/99y, TD, INT). Penn State seemed to have game well in hand at 17-3 early in 3rd Q after TE Tony Stewart's 2 receptions set up short TD run by TB Eric McCoo. Hurricane TB James Jackson (33/129y, 2 TDs) tallied on 18y TD run off right side. Poorly-thrown 40y lob by Kelly turned into tying TD when WR Santana Moss adjusted to whirling pass in EZ. Miami took its 1st lead at 23-20 when Jackson roared 39y behind block of RG Richard Mercier. Canes appeared ready to run out clock on flagging Lions, but 4th-and-2 run was stopped short of Penn State 20YL inside last 2 mins. Lion QB Kevin Thompson immediately launched bomb to Fields (5/177y, 2 TDs), who beat close coverage of DB Michael Rumph for winning 79y TD.

CINCINNATI 17 Wisconsin 12: In 1st-ever win over ranked opponent, Cincinnati (2-1) stunned no. 9 Wisconsin (2-1). Perhaps looking ahead to Michigan game and perhaps blinded by Bearcats' 31-24 loss to 1-AA Troy State week before, Wisconsin allowed Cincinnati TB Robert Cooper (20/143y) to burst 51y for 7-3 lead on 1st play of 2nd Q. Badgers trimmed H deficit to 7-6 on K Vitaly Pisetsky's 2nd FG. Wisconsin closed to 14-12 late in 3rd Q as TB Ron Dayne (28/231y), on his way to breaking Archie Griffin's Big 10 career rushing record, barreled 18y to score. In position to step up to take game, Badgers started bungling: Dayne dribbled FUM through Cincy EZ, WR Nick Davis dropped punt, which led to Bearcat K Jonathan Ruffin's 41y FG, and had game-winning TD pass called back by motion PEN.

NEBRASKA 20 Southern Mississippi 13: Cornhuskers (3-0) took field with redesigned backfield: TB DeAngelo Evans quit and QB Bobby Newcombe asked to be moved back to WB. Spark came from topnotch Husker D, which overcame team's sluggish O. LB Julius Jackson raced 16y with FUM for 1st TD, then put Nebraska ahead for good with 28y INT TD RET midway in 3rd Q. Southern Mississippi (2-1) outgained Huskers 293y to 185y and enjoyed 7-6, 13-12 leads on 1st, 3rd Q TD passes by QB Jeff Kelly (23-45/268y, 4 INTs). Eagles threatened late, but Nebraska DB Keyuo Craver's 2nd INT came at own 1YL with 1:17 left.

Air Force 31 WASHINGTON 21: Air Force (2-0) jumped to 14-6 lead in 2nd Q on TD runs by FB Jeremiah Laster and QB Cale Bonds. Washington (0-2) tied it with 2y TD run by TB Braxton Cleman, 2-pt pass by QB Marques Tuiasosopo (20-44/195y, 3 INTs). Turning pt came on partially blocked punt by Falcon LB Corey Nelson, HB Scott McKay (14/106y) quickly raced 39y to set up another Bonds TD. K Jackson Whiting made 44y FG early in 4th Q for 31-14 lead. INT by Falcon DB Tony Jones was returned to 1YL, setting up Bonds' 3rd score. Huskies answered with 100y KO TD RET by frosh TB Paul Arnold. It was coach Fisher DeBerry's 122nd win at Air Force, which broke Red Blaik's all-time military academy mark, set at West Point (1941-58).

New Mexico State 35 ARIZONA STATE 7: Incredible "Upset Saturday," day on which 8 Top 25 teams lost, became complete when late-night stunner from Tempe was revealed. Sun Devil D had been brilliant previous week, but lowly New Mexico State, which had been 0-14 vs. ranked foes since 1979, rushed 58/363y. Aggie QB K.C. Enzminger threw for career-best 205y on 10-20, 23y TD pass to TE Marcellus McCray. Enzminger pitched 9y TD pass for game's 1st score with 22 sec left before H, and it launched 21-pt 3rd Q explosion in 3rd Q. Arizona State gained only 234y, completed only 9-29 passes, but got 4th Q TD from TB J.R. Redmond (24/62y).

September 25, 1999

EAST CAROLINA 27 Miami 23 (Raleigh): Stranded from its campus for 2 weeks by devastating Hurricane Floyd, unsinkable East Carolina (4-0) used rival NC State's Carter-Finley Stadium, 85 miles west of Greenville. No. 9 Miami (2-2) dominated early, building 23-3 lead 3 min into 3rd Q. Hurricane sub TB Clinton Portis, in for 2 injured regulars, rushed 27/147y, tallied 2nd Q TD. FB Jamie Wilson (8/71y), whose 1st Q FUM set up TD catch by Miami WR Reggie Wayne (7/80y), scored on runs of 23, 18y to pull Pirates within 23-17 early in 4th Q. Trailing 23-20, Carolina went 79y to winning TD pass by QB David Garrard (30-46/328y, TD, INT) with 4:51 left. Wild celebration soon ensued, and at year's end Pirate team received Disney Spirit Award to commemorate emotional win that galvanized many communities in North Carolina.

WAKE FOREST 31 North Carolina State 7: Committed to improving ACC's worst rushing O (65y avg) of 1998, Wake Forest (2-1) rambled for 266y on ground vs. no. 25 North Carolina State (3-2). Up-and-down Wolfpack QB Jamie Barnette lost FUMs on 1st 2 possessions of game to set up TD run by Deacon TB Morgan Kane and TD catch by enormous TE Willie Lam. Barnette (16-29/129y) threw 19y TD pass late in 1st Q. Kane, ACC's leading rusher, gained 31/147y, added 2 more TD runs.

ALABAMA 35 Arkansas 28: Versatile WR Freddie Milons (7/109y) caught TD pass and threw clinching 66y TD pass in 4th Q as Alabama (3-1) snapped 2-game losing streak to Arkansas (2-1). Meanwhile, Razorback coach Houston Nutt was analytical afterward: "Any time the other team commits six turnovers, you should get the win." Indeed, Bama suffered 2 FUMs and 4 INTs, 3 picks against QB Andrew Zow (13-23/225y, 2 TDs). Tide overcame 7-0, 10-7 1st H deficits, then broke 21-21 tie late in 3rd Q on 12y TD run by TB Shaun Alexander (34/165y). QB Clint Stoerner had big day with 24-52/316y, TD passing, but no. 14 Razorbacks were limited to 20/64y rushing.

Mississippi 24 AUBURN 17 (OT): Rebel fans invaded enemy territory with unpleasant placards for Auburn (3-1) coach Tommy Tuberville, who left Ole Miss (3-1) near end of 1998 season. Rebels sneaked out of town with OT win when QB Romaro Miller (17-29/242y, 2 TDs, INT) connected with WR Cory Peterson on 23y TD pass and then halted 4 Tiger plays inside own 5YL. Frosh QB Jeff Klein (10-16/112y, 3rd Q TD) threw 23y pass on 1st play of Tiger OT possession, but was propelled backward by Rebel D. Earlier, Tigers blocked punt in OT and D which frosh DL Frank Walker recovered for TD to pull Auburn to within 14-10 at H.

Michigan 21 WISCONSIN 16: With coach Barry Alvarez infirmed in press box awaiting late-season knee-replacement surgery, Wisconsin (2-2) attempted to extend 8-game win streak at Camp Randall Stadium. Instead, no. 4 Michigan (4-0) won its 18th Big 10 opener in row when it held Badger TB Ron Dayne to 0y on 8 run tries in 2nd H. Wolverines gained only 94y on ground, but managed 2 scoring drives and got 45y reverse TD run from WR David Terrell (7/88y receiving) for 14-0 1st Q advantage. Dayne rambled 34y late in 2nd Q to pull Badgers to 14-9 at H. Michigan QB Tom Brady (17-27/217y, 2 TDs, INT) threw 23y TD in 3rd Q. Fueling critics of his big game play, Dayne was stopped on 2 critical tries for 1st downs in 2nd H.

Kansas State 35 IOWA STATE 28: Improved Iowa State (3-1) rolled to 332y to 102y H edge in O and led no. 15 Kansas State (3-0) 28-7 at intermission. Cyclone TB Darren Davis (26/152y) scored on runs of 26, 10y in 1st Q. "When you have them down, you've got to push them over the cliff," said Cyclone T Bill Marsau. K-State stayed on solid ground when sub QB Adam Helm relieved starter Jonathan Beasley (3-10/24y, INT) on 2nd series of 3rd Q. Helm (7-11/67y passing, 13/48y, 2 TDs rushing) led marches of 80, 75, 62y in biggest comeback of coach Bill Snyder's 11 years at K-State. Wildcat TB David Allen dashed 94y in 3rd Q, 6th punt TD RET of his career.

OREGON 33 Southern California 30 (2OT): Oregon (3-1) served notice it could be factor in wide-open PAC-10 race. After 10-10 tie in 1st H, Ducks used P Kurtis Doerr's 30y run on fake punt to set up K Nathan Villegas' short FG. Ducks followed with 69y TD drive after Trojan WR R. Jay Soward's FUM. Oregon rally was accomplished while Southern California (2-1) QB Carson Palmer stood on sideline, his throwing arm in sling. USC TB Chad Morton used GL blocks of 330-lb G Faasea Mailo, lined up at FB, to score 2 TDs in 4th Q. Trojans' 21st PEN cost them conv kick. Trailing 23-20, Ducks went 71y to Villegas' tying 26y FG with 33 sec left in regulation. But Villegas injured knee in celebration, and sub K Dan Katz badly missed 33y FG that would have won in 1st OT. After trade of TD passes in 2nd OT, K David Newbury of USC missed 37y FG, and 3rd string Duck K Josh Frankel won it with 27y FG.

STANFORD 42 Ucla 32: Pranksters took every opportunity to rub it in to UCLA (2-2) about its off-season handicapped parking scandal, and Stanford (3-1) O rubbed it in with 672y. Cardinal used flea-flicker to 95y TD drive in 1st Q, built 21-3 H and led 2 TD passes by sub QB Joe Borchard (15-19/207y, 5 TDs). Early in 3rd Q, Borchard teamed with WR Troy Walters (9/278y) for conf-record 98y TD pass. UCLA DB Lovell Houston immediately answered with 95y KO TD RET, which sparked Bruins to 2 TD runs by TB DeShaun Foster (19/100y) and TD run by QB Drew Bennett. Trailing 35-32 midway in 4th Q, UCLA was scorched by Borchard's 56y run on 3rd-and-15, which led to his clinching 13y TD pass to WR DeRonnie Pitts.

WASHINGTON 31 Colorado 24: When Rick Neuheisel left Boulder for Washington (1-2) he was lambasted for self-promotion and attempting to induce several Buffs (2-2) to transfer to Washington. Once game started, words stopped and teams settled into exciting struggle as each sought big win. Huskies scored 1st in 2nd Q when TB Willie Hurst (19/85y, 2 TDs) blasted over, but Buffalo DB Ben Kelly answered with 98y KO TD RET. With game tied 14-14 in 3rd Q, Kelly fielded FUM by QB Marques Tuiasosopo and raced 38y for TD. With score at 24-24, Husky WR Chris Juergens beat Kelly's coverage to spear Tuiasosopo's winning 9y TD pass with 3:17 to play. Colorado's gritty QB Mike Moschetti (19-34/167y, 2 INTs) withstood sprained knee to convert 2 4th down passes until throwing EZ INT to DB Anthony Vontoure 1:07 to go.

October 2, 1999

(Th) GEORGIA TECH 49 Maryland 31: At 3.3 pts/game, Maryland (3-1) brought in nation's best scoring D, but Georgia Tech (3-1) tallied on 2 straight snaps in 1st Q: Yellow Jacket TB Sean Gregory burst 48y up middle and WR Dez White made spinning move to cap 80y TD reception. Terrapin TB Lamont Jordan (27/79y) scored twice in 1st Q, and Maryland led 17-14 late in 2nd Q. But, Tech QB Joey Hamilton, on his way to 474y O, pitched 29 and 30y TDs in last 1:18 before H. Hamilton (19-31/ 387y, 3 TDs, 2 INTs) provided key TD—41y run off Shotgun sweep—that made it 35-24 with 5:37 left in 3rd Q.

Virginia Tech 31 VIRGINIA 7: Hokies' magical, frosh QB Michael Vick (7-9/222y, TD) opened scoring with 60y pass to WR Andre Davis, and TB Shyrone Stith (23/113y) tallied 1st of his 3 TD runs for 14-0 edge in 1st Q. Virginia Tech (4-0) outgained injury-riddled Virginia (3-2) 424y to 213y and divided y 202y rushing and 222y passing. Hokies notched win over 1 of few foes that appeared capable of overturning Hokies. Cavs briefly trimmed deficit to 14-7 in 2nd Q when QB Dan Ellis (16-26/162y, TD) tossed short TD pass to TE Billy Baber. Stith became 1st-ever Virginia Tech runner to open season with 4 consecutive 100y rushing games; he gained 85y in 2nd H as Hokies milked clock.

Alabama 40 FLORIDA 39 (OT): Seemingly on way out because of lies about extramarital affair (bad) and loss to Louisiana Tech (worse), Alabama (4-1) coach Mike DuBose launched new month with surprise win that ended 30-game Florida (4-1) win streak at "The Swamp." Crimson Tide led 13-7 at H, but DB Bennie Alexander's 42y INT TD RET gave Gators 14-13 lead in 3rd Q. Florida WR Darrell Jackson (6/127y) caught his 2nd TD from QB Doug Johnson (22-31/309y, 4 TDs) late in 3rd Q for 22-19 edge and his 3rd TD with 5:15 left in regulation for 33-26 lead. Alabama TB Shaun Alexander (28/106y) ran 13y to tie it 33-33 with 1:25 left. Tide held 42:47 to 17:13 time-of-possession edge. In OT, Gator K Jeff Chandler was wide right with conv kick, and Alexander of Bama tied it at 39-39 with 25y run. Amazingly, Tide K Chris Kemp also missed conv kick, but was given 2nd chance for winner when Florida jumped offside.

GEORGIA 23 Louisiana State 22: Undefeated Bulldogs (4-0) won by single pt for 2nd week in row, and beleaguered LSU (2-2) coach Gerry DiNardo was left to ponder his decision to ignore tie, that would have produced almost certain OT, and go for winning 2-pt conv with 18 secs to play. Battle of FGs, led by LSU 16-13 entering 4th Q was interrupted by 9y TD run by Tiger TB Rondell Mealey (18/25y), offset by 58y TD run by Georgia TB Patrick Pass (6/69y). Bulldogs took control 23-16 on QB Quincy Carter's 12y TD pass and K Hap Hines' 3rd FG. Tiger WR Reggie Robinson leapt to take QB Josh Booty's 4th down, 39y TD pass away from DBs, but, on fateful 2-pt try, Booty scrambled right, threw long cross-field pass that was batted away by Georgia LB Will Witherspoon.

MICHIGAN 38 Purdue 12: No. 11 Purdue (4-1) had case of drops in 1st H rain: several passes and lost Shotgun snap by QB Drew Brees (20-49/293y, TD, INT) at Wolverine 16YL. Boilers could manage only 2 FGs by K Travis Dorsch after FUM RECs deep in Michigan (5-0) territory. Meanwhile, Michigan QB Tom Brady (15-25/250y, 2TDs) hit 1st Q TD passes of 18y to WR David Terrell and 17y to WR Marcus Knight. Trailing 21-6 in 3rd Q, speedy Purdue WR Vinny Sutherland appeared ready to break away on 4th-and-2 reverse but slipped for no gain. Sutherland bounced right back with 66y TD catch, but Wolverines retorted with 75y TD drive for 28-12 lead. Powerful Michigan 4th Q iced end of nation's longest win streak at 10.

Wisconsin 42 OHIO STATE 17: On 9th play of 1st Ohio State (2-2) drive, TB Michael Wiley leapt at GL, but was nailed by Badger LB Chris Ghidorzi and lost EZ FUM. Wiley atoned with 17y option pass to TE Steve Wisniewski to set up his own slanting TD run. Buckeye WR Reggie Germany took long pass at GL away from DB Mike Echols for 41y TD. Down 17-0 midway in 2nd Q, Wisconsin (3-2) got 2 FGs from K Vitaly Pisetsky. Wiley lost another FUM on 2nd H KO, and Badger TB Ron Dayne (32/161y) blasted for TD behind lead block of FB Chad Kuhns. Dayne quickly added 11y TD blast off LT for 18-17 lead, grew stronger with 2 more TDs in 4th Q.

NOTRE DAME 34 Oklahoma 30: Notre Dame (2-3) scored early in 1st Q on QB Jarious Jackson's 10y TD run. Oklahoma (3-1) RB Brandon Daniels, Sooner GL in 1998, went 89y with KO to tie, part of his 4 KOs/229y. Although Jackson (15-21/276y, 2 TDs) inserted 58y TD pass to WR Joey Getherall, Sooners scored 23 pts over 17-min span for seemingly comfortable 30-14 edge. QB Josh Heupel (22-40/168y, INT) accounted for 3 TD tosses during Sooner spree. But, Jackson marshalled troops, pitching 15y TD pass to TE Jabari Holloway midway in 3rd Q. After DB Lee Lafayette's INT, ND went 56y to pull within 30-28. Early in 4th Q, Jackson's 23y scramble and 29y pass keyed winning 98y TD drive capped by TB Tony Driver's 2nd TD run.

Marshall 32 MIAMI (OHIO) 14: Confident Marshall (5-0) quickly obliterated any notion that Miami (3-2) would put up fight in MAC showdown. Herd thundered to 32-0 lead by midway in 4th Q as star QB Chad Pennington (18-35/294y) rifled 3 TD passes. Redhawk TB Travis Prentice (27/131y) was held to 13/18y rushing in 1st H, but gained 83y in late "garbage time." Prentice's performance prompted Marshall LB John Grace to sneer: "He had all the pretty yards in the fourth quarter so he could get his name in the paper tomorrow."

Kansas State 35 TEXAS 17: Kansas State (4-0) converted 3 INTs and 3 FUMs by Texas (4-2) QB Major Applewhite into 26 pts as Wildcats won with surprising ease. K Jamie Rheem kicked 2 of his school-record 5 FGs in 1st Q for 6-0 Kansas State lead, but TD pass by Applewhite (19-37/271y, TD, 3 INTs) and short TD run by FB Chris Robertson gave Longhorns 14-6 edge in 2nd Q. TB David Allen scored his NCAA record-tying 7th career punt TD RET (74y) to put Wildcats in front for good at 15-14 in 3rd Q. K-State A-A LB Mark Simoneau sprinted 37y for INT TD RET in 4th Q.

TEXAS TECH 21 Texas A&M 19: TB Sammy Morris (33/170y, TD) wasn't even mentioned during week as replacement for Texas Tech (2-2) star TB Ricky Williams, lost for year with knee injury. Aggie DB Jay Brooks blocked 1st Q punt for TD, but Red Raiders overcame 10-0 disadvantage with 3 TDs in 2nd Q, including 15y TD pass by QB Rob Peters (13-18/138y, INT). Texas A&M (3-1) depended on K Terence Kitchens' 4 FGs, last with 8:15 to go, inched Aggies within 21-19. A&M drove late, but suffered sack by LB Dorian Pitts and INT by DB Antwan Alexander in last 1:30.

WASHINGTON 34 Oregon 20: Huskies (2-2), fast learning to growl, opened Pac-10 slate with upset of Ducks (3-2). After 7 TOs in last 2 games, Washington QB Marques Tuiasosopo (17-21/211y, 3 TDs) was nearly perfect. Tuiasosopo's 24y TD pass to WR Gerald Harris on 1st play of 4th Q opened 27-13 edge. Oregon (3-2) lost 2nd time in last 6 matchups to Huskies, but received effective play from QB A.J. Feeley, who passed 24-32/371y, TD. Washington TB Willie Hurst rushed 30/161y, TD.

October 9, 1999

FLORIDA STATE 31 Miami 21: Banished by grand-theft arrest, Seminole WR and Heisman front-runner Peter Warrick was apologetic to ABC's sideline cameras. Meanwhile, Florida State (6-0) D was being lit up by hot-and-cold Miami (2-3) QB Kenny Kelly, who pitched 27-41/370y, 3 TDs, INT. Kelly connected with WR Reggie Wayne for 8y TD and WR Santana Moss for 80 and 14y TDs in 21-21 1st H led by Hurricanes. FSU D came alive in 2nd H, limited Hurricanes to 166y. Seminole QB Chris Weinke (23-34/332y, 2 TDs, INT) hit 11 different receivers, keyed clinching 97y drive with 54y toss to WR Ron Dugans that led to TB Travis Minor's 2y TD run with 9:55 left.

GEORGIA TECH 31 North Carolina 24 (OT): Only thing going right for North Carolina (1-4) was its 24-21 lead with 1:14 to play. With 4th down at Georgia Tech (4-1) 2YL, coach Carl Torbush aggressively chose to skip FG try and ram FB Deon Dyer because Tar Heels had rushed for season-high 276y. Gamble failed, and Yellow Jacket QB Joey Hamilton (14-26/273y, 2 TDs, 2 INTs) completed 31, 34y passes to WR Kelly Campbell (7/203y, 2 TDs in mid-game) to position K Luke Manget for tying 36y FG with :05 on clock. Hamilton scored on 6y draw in OT, and Tech D permitted 4y and forced 3 incompletions on UNC's OT possession. Earlier, Tar Heel QB Ronald Curry was lost with ruptured Achilles tendon, and stumbling UNC O earned just 3 pts during 3 trips inside Yellow Jacket 3YL.

TENNESSEE 37 Georgia 20: After 7-7 1st Q, Tennessee (4-1) QB Tee Martin (21-35/283y, TD, 2 INTs) ignited 21-pt 2nd Q with TD pass and scoring runs of 6, 1y. Georgia (4-1) trailed 30-7 when 2 quick TDs—including 2nd TD pass by QB Quincy Carter (20-34/228y)—pulled Dogs back into contest at 30-20 with 12:28 to go. But, Vol WR Leonard Scott, NCAA 60y indoor sprint champ, raced 100y with next KO.

Mississippi State 18 AUBURN 16: Late TD pass provided underappreciated Mississippi State (6-0) with miracle finish and Bulldogs stayed undefeated with best record in 55 years. Tigers (3-3) led 10-0 at H on frosh QB Jeff Klein's 64y TD pass to frosh WR Ronney Daniels. When another frosh, K Damon Duval, kicked his 2nd, 3rd FGs, Auburn led 16-0 midway in 3rd Q. State sr QB Matt Wyatt started 2nd H when QB Wayne Madkin couldn't continue due to injured finger. Wyatt pulled Bulldogs within 16-10 with 16y TD pass with only 2:28 left. Instead of punting in last min, P Duval conceded safety. Mississippi State DB Pig Prather raced 41y with free kick to set up Wyatt's 11y TD pass to WR Matt Butler with 19 sec to go.

Southern Mississippi 39 EAST CAROLINA 22: East Carolina (5-1), at home for 1st time since Hurricane Floyd floods of September, jumped to 15-3 1st Q lead on 2 TD passes by giant QB David Garrard (17-36/249y, 3 TDs, INT). Ridiculed Southern Miss (3-2) rush O, which was feeble in losses to Nebraska and Texas A&M, sprung TB Derrick Nix for 42/171y. Eagle QB Jeff Kelly threw 14-18/171y, 3 TDs. Meanwhile, Garrard's only INT went 60y for clinching TD RET by Eagle DB Leo Barnes in 4th Q.

MICHIGAN STATE 34 Michigan 31: For 1st time since 1961, both in-state rivals entered game undefeated. Confident Spartans (6-0) converted TDs on 3 straights possessions in 2nd H to build 34-17 lead in 4th Q. Michigan (5-1) coach Lloyd Carr had alternated QBs all season, and, although QB Drew Henson (6-12/111y, TD, INT) clicked on 81y score to WR Marcus Knight in 2nd Q, Carr turned to sr QB Tom Brady (30-41/285y, 2 TDs) who rallied Wolverines to 2 TDs and 34-31 deficit. Bungled on-side KO with 2:40 to play ended comeback hopes. State run D (21/42y) joined O stars WR Plaxico Burress (10/255y, TD) and QB Bill Burke (21-36/400y, 2 TDs), who gushed afterward: "One of my keys is to visualize playing a good game. I'm not sure I was thinking about 400 yards, though."

Texas 38 Oklahoma 28 (Dallas): Continuing its stunning departure from Sooner tradition, Oklahoma (3-2) used its new, all-out air game to fuel 17-0 1st Q lead. QB Josh Heupel (31-48/311y, 3 INTs) pitched 2 scoring passes. Sooner K Tim Duncan scored on fake-FG pass late in 3rd Q to pull Oklahoma within 31-28, but Texas (5-2) QB Major Applewhite (22-47/328y, 3 TDs) capped 99y 4th Q drive with his 3rd TD pass, 18y to WR Ryan Nunez, with 8:16 to play. That score clinched verdict at 38-28. Longhorn TB Hodges Mitchell rushed for 30/204y.

Washington 47 OREGON STATE 21: Improved Beavers (3-2) compiled 434y to 347y O advantage, but lost for 12th straight time to Washington (3-2) partly because INTs were returned for TDs by Husky DB Anthony Vontoure (44y) and LB Jamaun Willis (24y) in 45-0 1st H. Additional Oregon State insult came in 3rd Q when star TB Ken Simonton (24/106y, 2 TDs in 2:25 span of 2nd H) tripped in EZ for safety and 47-0 deficit. Washington O leaders were TB Willie Hurst (17/108y, 2 TDs) and QB Marques Tuiasosopo (11-16/93y, TD, INT passing and 9/49y rushing).

USA Today Coaches Poll October 11

1	Florida State (53)	1469	14	Georgia	648
2	Penn State (6)	1412	15	Syracuse	620
3	Nebraska	1334	16	Marshall	605
4	Virginia Tech	1271	17	Ohio State	525
5	Tennessee	1179	18	Wisconsin	472
6	Florida	1139	19	Texas	399
7	Michigan State	1128	20	Brigham Young	322
8	Kansas State	1072	21	Purdue	282
9	Georgia Tech	1047	22	Mississippi	244
10	Michigan	936	23	East Carolina	125
11	Texas A&M	862	24	Miami (Fla.)	93
12	Mississippi State	836	25	Air Force	71
13	Alabama	757			

October 16, 1999

VIRGINIA TECH 62 Syracuse 0: In its largest win since beating Catholic University in 1922, Virginia Tech (6-0) got 2 TDs from its D: DB Cory Bird's 26y FUM RET and backup DB Phillip Summers' 43y INT RET. Hokies limited Orangemen to 120y total O and only 3 1st downs until bench was cleared of Tech subs in late going. Sensational Hokies QB Michael Vick entered game with amazing stat: Vick had gone to air for more TD passes (5) than he had incompletions (3) during 2 most recent wins over Virginia by 31-7 and Rutgers by 58-20, but against Syracuse he passed economically: 8-16/135y, TD. Hokies TB Shyrone Stith rushed 22/140y, 2TDs to add to 411y attack. Crushing loss sent Syracuse (5-2) into spiral: 3 losses in next 4 games.

Alabama 30 MISSISSIPPI 24: TB Shaun Alexander rushed 36/214y, 3 short TDs as Crimson Tide (5-1) beat 3rd straight ranked SEC foe. Alabama cruised to 27-7 lead midway in 3rd Q before no. 22 Ole Miss (5-2) rallied. Rebel QB Romaro Miller (15-31/217y) passed 6y to WR Maurice Flournoy for 3rd Q TD, and TB Deuce McAllister (13/63y) scored his 2nd TD on 22y run in 4th Q to bring Rebels within 27-24.

PENN STATE 23 Ohio State 10: Penn State (7-0) dominated stats with 422y to 143y O edge. Lion TB Eric McCoo (22/211y) raced 53y on 1st series to set up QB Kevin Thompson's short TD pass. Ohio State (4-3) QB Steve Bellisari (7-21/78y, INT) ran for his life most of day, but managed 44y scramble to set up K Dan Stultz's 1st Q FG that pulled Buckeyes within 7-3. Late in 2nd Q, Ohio LB Na'il Diggs blitzed Thompson (6-10/67y, TD, INT) to loosen EZ FUM which DB Gary Berry grabbed for TD. Penn State led 13-10 at H but played thereafter without injured Thompson. Lions opened 2nd H with sub QB Rashard Casey's 5y TD sweep. Although he had 2 earlier FGs blocked, Penn State K Travis Forney booted his 3rd FG in 4th Q.

PURDUE 52 Michigan State 28: Unbeaten Spartans (6-1) rolled 91y on opening drive to WR Plaxico Burress' clever 18y TD catch for 6-0 lead. Purdue (5-2) quickly launched huge air game on way to ending 2-game losing streak: WR Chris Daniels, who set Big 10 receiving mark with 301y on 21 catches, beat limping DB Amp Campbell for 51y TD pass, followed late in 1st Q with 10y TD catch for 21-6 lead. Boilermaker QB Drew Brees threw brilliant 40-57/509y, 5 TDs, 4 INTs. Michigan State LB T.J. Turner picked off deflected Brees pass in 2nd Q and rumbled 88y to score. But Turner's TD was only nick in defiant Boilers' brilliant 2nd Q that ended with 35-14 H edge.

NOTRE DAME 25 Southern California 24: Fighting Irish (4-3) fashioned their biggest comeback since 1979 Cotton Bowl with 22 unanswered pts. Southern California (3-3) played nearly flawless 1st H, reviving its lost run attack for 113y. Trojans used big pass catch by frosh WR Kareen Kelly at end of 1st Q to set up TB Chad Morton (21/85y) for TD plunge and 14-0 lead. USC smoothly advanced to 21-3 by H. Then, sudden rain and wind, which switched against Trojan for both Qs of 2nd H, affected 2nd H play. In 3rd Q, ND QB Jarious Jackson (19-30/257y, TD, INT) rolled right, passed back left to TE Dan O'Leary for 7y TD. In 4th Q, Trojan QB Mike Van Raaphorst (23-41/298y, 2 TDs, INT) lost FUM on what he thought was incomplete pass. Irish quickly went 37y to TB Tony Driver's 2y TD run. USC DB Antuan Simmons blocked conv, so Trojans led 24-16. ND added FG thanks to USC's 11y punt, then went 74y to winning TD with 2:40 to play. Jackson scrambled 18y, lost FUM, but Irish TE Jabari Holloway fortuitously fell on it in EZ for TD that won it.

USA Today Coaches Poll October 18

1	Florida State (52)	1468	14	Georgia	715
2	Penn State (7)	1412	15	Marshall	625
3	Nebraska	1321	16	Wisconsin	618
4	Virginia Tech	1313	17	Purdue	514
5	Tennessee	1193	18	Texas	503
6	Florida	1179	19	Brigham Young	443
7	Kansas State	1127	20	East Carolina	250
8	Georgia Tech	1046	21	Southern Mississippi	176
9	Michigan	945	22	Ohio State	173
10	Texas A&M	926	23	Miami (Fla.)	130
11	Mississippi State	859	24	Syracuse	125
12	Alabama	847	25	Minnesota	120
13	Michigan State	744			

October 23, 1999

Miami 31 BOSTON COLLEGE 28: In small way, Miami (3-3) paid back BC for Doug Flutie's miracle pass of 1984 when it rallied from 28-0 deficit in last 17 mins. Boston College (5-2), which hadn't beaten Hurricanes since Flutie's 48y heave 15 years earlier, used TB Cedric Washington's 29/183y, TD rushing to set up 21-0 lead. Game seemed locked up when Washington tallied on 3y run with 6:18 left in 3rd Q. After mistake-riddled 1st H, Miami QB Kenny Kelly (20-36/218y, 3 TDs) led rally with TD passes to FB Will McPartland and TB James Jackson. TE Bubba Franks caught game-tying TD from Kelly with 3:51 left. At Eagles 35YL, Kelly faced 4th-and-17 with 14 secs left and hit WR Reggie Wayne with 22y pass at sideline. K Andy Crosland made 30y FG to win it with :03 on clock.

Florida State 17 CLEMSON 14: On big day for Bowden family, son Tommy, rookie coach for Clemson (3-4), cornered dad Bobby's no. 1 Seminoles (8-0) with 14-3 H disadvantage. FSU rallied in 2nd H for Bobby's 300th career win. Fake punt contributed to Tiger TD in 2nd Q when QB Woody Dantzler (9-24/102y, INT) passed 7y, ran 1y for TDs. K Sebastian Janikowski, who missed 2 FGs in 1st H, made his 2nd 33y FG in 3rd Q to bring FSU to within 14-6. Seminoles, who welcomed back suspended WR Peter Warrick (11/121y), tied it late in 3rd Q on TB Travis Minor's short TD run and FB Dan Kendra's 2-pt catch. Winning FG came after QB Chris Weinke (24-49/258y, INT) completed passes to WR Ron Dugans for 7, 7, and 22y.

Tennessee 21 ALABAMA 7: Perhaps hottest team in country was Tennessee (5-1) as it made easy work of Alabama (5-2) upon its 1st visit to Tuscaloosa in 69 years. "...I feel like we're coming together and peaking at just the right time," said Vol coach Phillip Fulmer, who had to marvel at clutch play of QB Tee Martin (11-17/147y, TD). Martin ran 6, 21y for TDs and lofted 43y scoring pass to WR David Martin. Crimson Tide scored on their 1st possession: QB Andrew Zow (19-37/168y) connected with TB Shaun Alexander for 26y TD. Alexander, who limped off field at end, was held to 20/98y rushing. Vols enjoyed post-game frolicking off field singing "we owe Alabama" to tune of Lynyrd Skynyrd's "Sweet Home, Alabama."

Penn State 31 PURDUE 25: Undefeated Penn State (8-0) survived raw-nerve finish as 4 passes by Purdue (5-3) QB Drew Brees (31-48/379y, 2 TDs, INT) fell incomplete from Lions 12YL in last 30 secs. Penn State's D created 2 TDs: In 2nd Q, LB LaVar Arrington sacked Brees and picked up FUM at 2YL which he toted over, and in 3rd Q, DL Courtney Brown made brilliant volleyball tip and catch of INT which he returned 25y for TD. After 14-14 H, QB Kevin Thompson (9-15/173y, 2 TDs) connected with WR Chafie Fields on 78y TD that Nittany Lions ahead for good. Down 28-14, Boilermakers pulled within 28-25 with flurry in last 7 mins of 3rd Q. K Travis Dorsch kicked 37y FG and LB Mike Rose recovered FUM by Lions QB Rashard Casey at Penn State 26YL to set up Brees' TD and 2-pt passes to WR Randall Lane. K Travis Forney's 24y FG for Lions was 4th Q's only score.

WISCONSIN 40 Michigan State 10: Led by TB Ron Dayne's 214y rushing, Wisconsin (6-2) sliced through nation's top run D for 301y. Entering contest, no. 11 Spartans (6-2) had allowed only 279y on ground (39.9y avg) in 7 games. Dayne scored on 1st H runs of 51, 15y as Badgers built 23-3 edge, then rested nearly all of 4th Q. Michigan State gained only 238y, got 55y FG from K Paul Edinger in 2nd Q and 53y TD run from TB T.J. Duckett (10/91y) in 4th Q. Coach Barry Alvarez continued to rest injured knee in press box and won his 67th game, most ever at Wisconsin.

TEXAS 24 Nebraska 20: Texas (6-2) beat no. 3 Nebraska (6-1) for 3rd straight time since creation of Big 12 in 1996, thus seriously damaging Husker hope for national title. Nebraska fashioned big 2nd Q with K Josh Brown's 2 FGs and IB Correll Buckhalter's 5y TD run for 13-3 H lead. Huskers never sacked Longhorn QB Major Applewhite (17-30/213y, 2 TDs), but permitted him to pass only 9-21/47y in 1st H. After H, Applewhite completed 8-9/166y, including 13y TD pitch to WR Kwame Cavil for 17-13 lead in 3rd Q. Husker QB Eric Crouch (204y passing, but only 35y rushing) scored on 9y run midway in 4th Q, but earlier TD was lost when Buckhalter lost FUM at Texas 1YL. Steers won game on 4-play drive culminated in TE Mike Jones' 17y TD catch on which he broke 3 tackles on way to left EZ pilon.

Stanford 35 SOUTHERN CALIFORNIA 31: Off to best Pac-10 start at 5-0 since 1970, Stanford (5-2) used 3-TD spree that provided 28-24 lead on DB Chris Johnson's 30y INT RET, 2:11 into 3rd Q. Game produced 1043y O as Trojan QB Mike Van Raaphorst threw school-record 415y on 25-51, 3 TDs, 3 INTs. But, USC (3-4) blew its 4th 2nd H lead so far. Trojans tallied on game's opening 3 possessions as Van Raaphorst threw 2 TDs. Cardinal QB Todd Husak (20-32/290y, 2 TDs, 3 INTs) ran for go-ahead TD at 35-31 on opening play of 4th Q.

USA Today Coaches Poll October 25

1	Florida State (41)	1456	14	Michigan	630
2	Penn State (16)	1427	15	Brigham Young	613
3	Virginia Tech (2)	1355	16	Alabama	539
4	Tennessee	1261	17	East Carolina	508
5	Florida	1232	18	Texas A&M	448
6	Kansas State	1199	19	Southern Mississippi	351
7	Georgia Tech	1114	20	Michigan State	332
8	Mississippi State	1022	21	Ohio State	323
9	Nebraska	1021	22	Purdue	245
10	Georgia	941	23	Miami (Fla.)	191
11	Wisconsin	862	24	Syracuse	147
12	Texas	786	25	Stanford	82
13	Marshall	729			

Bowl Championship Series Rankings October 25

	Poll Avg.	Computer Avg.	Schedule Strength	Losses	Total
1 Florida State (8-0)	1.0	1.71	0.84	0	3.55
2 Penn State (8-0)	2.0	3.43	0.32	0	5.75
3 Virginia Tech (6-0)	3.0	1.57	1.68	0	6.35
4 Tennessee (5-1)	4.0	4.57	0.16	1	9.73
5 Kansas State (7-0)	6.0	3.14	1.72	0	10.86

October 30, 1999

(Th) COLORADO STATE 31 Utah 24: WR Dallas Davis (214y punt RETs) saved game for Colorado State (5-3) with 2 punt TD RETs, last (56y) coming with 2:35 left in 4th Q to break 24-24 deadlock. Utah (6-2) D had allowed only 8 TDs in 1st 7 games, but Rams got 1y TD run from FB Kevin McDougall (28/115y) and Davis' 89y punt TD RET to build 24-3 H edge. Colorado State remained in command at 24-10 early in 4th Q when Utes became rejuvenated on FG block that DB Andre Dyson scooped and ran 47y to score. Rams lost ball on downs at Utah 41YL, and Utah sub QB T.D. Croshaw (18-29/241y, TD), in for ill QB Darnell Arceneaux, arched tying 59y TD pass to WR Stevonne Smith with 11:24 to play.

Boston College 24 SYRACUSE 23: Soaring Eagles (6-2) assured themselves of 1st winning seson since 1994 with come-from-behind upset of Syracuse (5-3). BC DB DuJuan Daniels opend game with 100y KO TD RET, but Orangemen earned 10-7 1st Q lead when sub QB Troy Nunes (7-9/61y, INT) ran 5y to score. Boston College snatched back lead at 21-17 in 3rd Q when TB Cedric Washington overcame being limited to 21y rushing to score from 1YL. K Nathan Trout kicked 31, 36y FGs for 23-21 Orange lead in 4th Q. K John Matich, mediocre 5-13 on FGs to date in 1999, split uprights with winning 34y FG with 2:53 on clock. BC LB Frank Chamberlain, who earned kudos with 24 tackles and 2 sacks, made open-field stop of Syracuse QB Madei Williams' 4th down scramble near midfield to end it.

Florida State 35 VIRGINIA 10: Florida State (9-0) juggernaut applied its now-familiar 2nd H power, but not before Virginia (4-4) took 7-0, 10-7 leads. Cavalier TB Thomas Jones rushed 26/164y, including 16y TD in 2nd Q. Seminole QB Chris Weinke (24-35/297y, 3 TDs, 3 INTs) tied it 7-7 on 4y TD pass to WR Marvin Minnis. Trailing 10-7 at H, FSU went to work on 20y TD catch by Minnis and 50y TD catch by WR Peter Warrick (6/81y).

Florida 30 Georgia 14 (Jacksonville): With Gator D controlling game, coach Steve Spurrier won his 100th game at Florida (7-1) by choosing to keep ball on ground in 2nd H. Gator pass O gained no y in 2nd H, but Bulldog QB Quincy Carter was limited to 6-23/76y, INT passing. Carter zipped for 3, 16y TD runs in 1st H for 14-10 lead. Georgia (6-2) twice was blanked after starting 2nd H drives inside Florida 40YL. At vital point in 2nd H, Florida LB Keith Kelsey forced Georgia TB Jasper Sanks to lose FUM at Gator 10YL. TB Bo Carroll (13/113y) quickly put Florida ahead 23-14 with 30y TD run in 4th Q. Gator DL Alex Brown, who later added INT, forced FUM at Georgia 2YL for QB Doug Johnson's clinching TD run.

Purdue 33 MINNESOTA 28: Golden Gophers coach Glen Mason, just weeks away from being named Football News Coach of the Year, still couldn't do right today. Minnesota (5-3) fans booed him twice: for conservatively running out clock in last 2 min of game when his team trailed 10-7 and for boldly trying on-side KO after Gophers' last TD with nearly 3 min to play. Purdue (6-3) QB Drew Brees (28-41/283y, 2 TDs) built 7-0 1st Q edge on 11y TD pass to TE Tim Stratton and wedged 8y TD pass to WR Randall Lane in middle of 4th Q rally by Gophers. Lane's TD catch provided 33-21 margin with 5:22 to play, but Minnesota QB Billy Cockerham (13-24/179y, TD, INT) accounted for his 2nd TD in 4th Q

with 12y pass to WR Ron Johnson aas prelude to Mason's on-side KO strategy. Purdue never again relinquished ball. Gopher TB Thomas Hamner (20/166y) earlier scored on runs of 9 and 60y.

Nebraska 24 KANSAS 17: Slumbering Nebraska (7-1), still shaking cobwebs left by previous week's upset loss to Texas, fell behind fired-up Kansas (3-6) by H. Jayhawk QB Dylan Smith (16-30/217y, 2 TDs) followed blocked punt safety by connecting on 22y TD to frosh TE David Hurst in 2nd Q. K Josh Brown, who missed 2 FGs to add to Husker woe of lost FUM at Kansas 1YL, finally put Nebraska on board at 9-3 with 31y FG 4 min into 3rd Q. WB Bobby Newcombe exploded for 86y punt TD RET and QB Eric Crouch (11-20/193y, TD) ran for TD, so Huskers seemed safe with 17-9 lead with 12 min to play. But, Smith quickly found WR Michael Chandler for 77y TD bomb, and they collaborated on 2-pt pass to tie it 17-all. With 3:24 left, Crouch and Newcombe combined on winning 49y TD connection.

Texas 44 IOWA STATE 41: After excitement of its Nebraska upset, Texas (7-2) had to struggle to beat thorny Iowa State (4-4) on last play. Cyclones led 20-17 in H as QB Sage Rosenfels (11-20/291y) threw 2 TD passes in 2nd Q. Longhorns built 41-27 lead as QB Major Applewhite (30-40/345y, 2 TDs) threw 4y TD pass to WR Montrell Flowers, and WR Beau Trahan scored 10 secs later on 5y FUM TD RET of KO. Iowa State rallied, tying it at 41-41 on TB Darren Davis' 1y TD run with 3:20 to go. After Applewhite's 38y pass, Texas TB Hodges Mitchell (33/158y) carried 7 straight plays to 1YL to set up K Kris Stockton for winning chipshot FG.

COLORADO 38 Oklahoma 24: Colorado (5-3) QB Mike Moschetti (22-31/382y, 4 TDs, INT), tough little guy with bounce-back tendencies, returned from missing previous week's game with concussion headaches to lead upset of no. 24 Oklahoma (4-3). WR Javon Green caught TD aerials of 49, 88y, 2nd of which iced game for Buffs in middle of 4th Q. Sooner QB Josh Heupel (26-58/328y, 4 INTs) threw 2 TD passes in 4th Q that narrowed score to 24-17 and 31-24. In addition to DB Ben Kelly's 2 INTs, Buffalo D sacked Heupel 3 times.

WASHINGTON 35 Stanford 30: Husky QB Marques Tuiasosopo had brilliant, record-setting day (19-32/302y, TD, 2 INTs passing and 22/207y, 2 TDs rushing) as he became 1st player ever to pass for 300y, rush for 200y. His total O of 509y was best of 4 players who exceeded 200y each on ground and in air. Tuiasosopo's 10y TD run with 9:54 left in 4th Q gave Washington (5-3) its 1st lead at 28-23. Amazingly, Tuiasosopo bruised hip on game's 2nd play and spent treatment time in locker room. Meanwhile, Stanford (5-3) temporarily lost inside track to Rose Bowl even though it led 7-0, 14-7 on WR Troy Walters' 49y TD catch, 17-12 at H, and 23-12 early in 3rd Q on WR DeRonnie Pitts' 26y TD reception. Card QB Todd Husak passed 22-41/300y, 3 TDs, 2 INTs.

USA Today Coaches Poll November 1

1	Florida State (44)	1456	14	Alabama	665
2	Penn State (13)	1424	15	Michigan	649
3	Virginia Tech (2)	1355	16	Georgia	620
4	Tennessee	1264	17	East Carolina	533
5	Florida	1242	18	Texas A&M	481
6	Kansas State	1196	19	Michigan State	400
7	Georgia Tech	1121	20	Ohio State	370
8	Mississippi State	1032	21	Purdue	341
9	Nebraska	1010	22	Miami (Fla.)	218
10	Wisconsin	932	23	Mississippi	146
11	Texas	849	24	Arkansas	124
12	Marshall	755	25	Southern Mississppi	109
13	Brigham Young	680			

Bowl Championship Series Standings November 1

	Poll Avg.	Computer Avg.	Schedule Strength	Losses	Total
1 Florida State (9-0)	1.0	1.43	0.68	0	3.11
2 Penn State (9-0)	2.0	3.00	0.48	0	5.48
3 Virginia Tech (7-0)	3.0	1.86	2.32	0	7.18
4 Florida (7-1)	5.0	4.29	0.24	1	10.53
5 Tennessee (6-1)	4.0	5.43	0.60	1	11.03

November 6, 1999

(Th) MISSISSIPPI STATE 23 Kentucky 22: Cardiac Kids of 1999, Mississippi State (8-0) overcame 143y PENs to pull out its 3rd straight win in last 2 mins of games when K Scott Westerfield made good on 2nd chance 45y FG with :05 to play. Despite gaining but 53y in opening H, opportunistic Kentucky (5-4) led 19-14 at H. Wildcat QB Dusty Bonner (28-44/189y, INT) registered TD pass, TD run in 12-7 1st Q. Wildcats opened 3rd Q with FG after TE James Whalen (11/99y) caught 2 passes toward season-total of 78, which broke NCAA TE record of Utah's Dennis Smith (73 in 1989). Bulldog QB Wayne Madkin injured ankle in 3rd Q, but sub QB Matt Wyatt (10-14/63y) passed 5-6/53y to position winning FG, after Westerfield missed from 46YL with 4:12 left.

Virginia Tech 22 WEST VIRGINIA 20: Hokies (8-0) seemed to have win well in hand at 19-7 after TB Shyrone Stith (21/84y) scored on 6y run with less than 5 min left in game. But, West Virginia (3-6) sub QB Brad Lewis (9-16/98y), in because QB Marc Bulger hurt his thumb, pitched TD passes to converted DB Jerry Porter (4y) and WR Khori Ivy (18y). Scoring passes by Lewis, who was felled for safety near end of 3rd Q, came with 3:15 and 1:15 left, so Mountaineers had stunning 20-19 lead. With no timeouts remaining, Tech QB Michael Vick (14-30/255y) directed magical 7-play, 58y drive, including his clutch scramble, with :23 on clock, down right sideline for 26y as he faked as if to run OB. K Shayne Graham kicked season-saving 44y FG as it ended.

TENNESSEE 38 Notre Dame 14: Volunteers (7-1) won 6th in row, and dominance of Notre Dame (5-4) proved they belonged back in national title hunt. It took mental mistake by Irish DL Lamont Bryant in 2nd Q to open floodgates. TB David Givens had just scored from 3YL to draw ND within 10-7, and Tennessee failed on 3rd down pass and prepared

to punt. But, Bryant had lined up off-side, so Vol QB Tee Martin (18-32/196y, 3 TDs) clicked on short TD pass to WR Eric Parker 9 sec before H for 17-7 edge. Martin pitched long TD to NCAA sprint champ, WR Leonard Scott, in 3rd Q, prompting Martin to say: "They really made a mistake not covering the fastest guy in America." Late in game, hungry Vols converted 4th-and-1 at ND 14YL which led to Martin's 13y bootleg TD run, icing meant to impress BCS computer rankings.

Minnesota 24 PENN STATE 23: Living on edge all season, Penn State (9-1) lost on last-play FG set up by miraculous, deflected pass. "We had them 4th-and-16 and then they make a miracle play," lamented coach Joe Paterno, who saw his Nittany Lions all but eliminated from national title chase. Plucky Minnesota (6-3) stayed close all game, trailing 7-3, 14-9, and 17-15 at ends of 1st 3 Qs, and outgaining Penn State 391y to 360y. Gophers TB Thomas Hamner (38/96y, 3/58y receiving) caught 49y TD pass from QB Billy Cockerham (14-24/277y, 2 TDs) for 21-20 lead with 11:25 left. Lions quickly went up 23-21 on K Travis Forney's 3rd FG. With 1:22 left, Cockerham's long 4th down pass was tipped out of hands of WR Ron Johnson's hands to WR Arland Bruce's diving, grasstop catch at Penn State 13YL. Frosh K Dan Nystrom made winning 32y FG 3 plays later.

Wisconsin 28 PURDUE 21: Badger TB Ron Dayne rushed 32/222y, including go-ahead 41y TD gallop in 4th Q. Wisconsin (8-2) led 14-7 at H as WR Nick Davis answered 1y TD run by Purdue (6-4) QB Drew Brees (36-64/350y, TD, 2 INTs) with 91y KO TD RET at 5:15 before H. Brees hit TE Tim Stratton with 11y TD pass to tie it 14-14 in 3rd Q, then, after Badger punt on next series, Brees connected on 6 throws to 19YL. On 2nd play of 4th Q, Boilermaker WR Vinny Sutherland ran misdirection and pitched pass picked off in EZ by DB Bobby Myers. Within 4 min, Dayne made his long run for 21-14 lead, and slippery Wisconsin DB Jamar Fletcher raced 34y for back-breaking INT TD RET with 4:43 to play.

KANSAS STATE 20 Colorado 14: With Nebraska visiting 1st shutout upon Texas A&M in 11 years, 37-0, Kansas State (9-0) was left to deal with up-and-down Colorado (5-4) before next week's Wildcat-Husker Big 12 North showdown. While quicksilver D blanketed Buffaloes, gigantic K-State TB Joe Hall (18/50y) polished off 14-0 1st H with 3y TD blast in last min of 2nd Q. K Jamie Rheem extended margin to 20-0 with short and long FGs in 3rd Q. In circumstances strangely similar to 1998's Big 12 title game collapse, K-State fans heard announcement of Penn State's loss just as they had learned, year earlier, of UCLA's upset. On cue, Colorado stormed back, placing nervous Cats on hot tin roof. Buff QB Mike Moschetti (11-25/187y, 2 TDs, 3 INTs)

passed 64y to WR Javon Green for TD, then, after K-State punt, Green broke several tackles to score on 70y pass play with 4:21 to play. Wildcat D, which allowed only 80y other than Green's long TDs, rose up to end it, stopping Moschetti's 4th down pass from Buff 38YL with 1:36 left.

Washington 33 ARIZONA 25: Egged on by Homecoming crowd, erratic Arizona (6-4) stifled Washington (6-3) in 1st Q, holding Huskies to 21y O and jumping to 3-0 lead. Bruised Husky QB Marques Tuiasosopo (16-28/208y, 2 TDs), helped by "adrenaline..best pain-killer," posted 19 pts in 2nd Q, including his TD pass to leaping WR Gerald Harris. Wildcats rallied behind QB Ortege Jenkins (12-18/198y, TD, INT) who found WR Marvin Brown alone behind secondary for 55y TD and 19-17 deficit in 3rd Q. TB Trung Canidate (11/105y, 74y TD run in 2nd Q) appeared to put Arizona ahead early in 4th Q, but his TD run was nullified by 1 of Cats' 10 PENs. Makeable FG was subsequently missed, and Washington stomped 80y on 17 plays for 26-17 lead, which was immediately followed by DB Anthony Voutore's 29y INT TD RET.

USA Today Coaches Poll November 8

1	Florida State (57)	1472	14	Georgia Tech	739
2	Virginia Tech (1)	1394	15	Michigan	684
3	Tennessee (1)	1333	16	Georgia	656
4	Florida	1282	17	Michigan State	563
5	Kansas State	1270	18	Mississippi	432
6	Nebraska	1120	19	Miami (Fla.)	379
7	Mississippi State	1115	20	Southern Mississippi	253
8	Penn State	1100	21	Minnesota	152
9	Wisconsin	1012	22	Washington	145
10	Texas	992	23	Texas A&M	141
11	Marshall	773	24	East Carolina	138
12	Brigham Young	766	25	Boston College	137
13	Alabama	764			

Bowl Championship Series Standings November 8

	Poll Avg.	Computer Avg.	Schedule Strength	Losses	Total
1 Florida State (9-0)	1.0	1.00	0.64	0	2.64
2 Tennessee (7-1)	3.0	2.71	0.36	1	7.07
3 Virginia Tech (8-0)	2.0	3.00	2.40	0	7.40
4 Florida (8-1)	4.0	4.57	0.32	1	9.89
5 Kansas State (9-0)	5.0	3.86	3.04	0	11.90

November 13, 1999

PITTSBURGH 37 Notre Dame 27: Soon to be demolished, 74-year-old Pitt Stadium, once a gem of collegiate stadiums but an exhausting uphill climb from campus, closed its doors forever in majestic style. Unpredictable Panthers (5-5) were fired up for reeling Notre Dame (5-5) as QB John Turman (10-27/231y, 2 TDs, 2 INTs) had eyes only for WRs Antonio Bryant (4/95y, 2 TDs) and Latif Grim (4/120y). Pitt TB Kevan Barlow (19/71y) also scored 2 TDs on ground. Irish QB Jarious Jackson (22-37/317y, 2 TDs) hit WR Joey Getherall for 5y TD with 1:32 left in 1st H for 10-10 tie, but Pitt took lead for good on K Nick Lotz's 33y FG late in 3rd Q at 20-17.

VIRGINIA TECH 43 Miami 10: Perhaps mesmerized by news of no. 3 Tennessse's earlier loss, jumpy Virginia Tech (9-0) was overwhelmed by Hurricanes (5-4), which scored 10 quick pts. Miami K Andy Crossland nailed 28y FG and QB Kenny Kelly (8-17/138y, 2

INTs) hit WR Andre King with 7y TD pass. Aided by Cane FUM at its 12YL and personal foul PEN, TB Shyrone Stith (16/78y) scored on 1y run, added 41y sprint for 14-10 Tech lead at H. "For a long time our defense kept us in the game, but they broke our backs with big plays," said Miami coach Butch Davis. Sure enough: Hokies blasted for 23 unanswered pts in 4th Q, keyed by 64y punt TD RET by WR Ricky Hall and 51y FUM TD RET by DB Ike Charlton.

ALABAMA 19 Mississippi State 7: Season's Cinderella team, Mississippi State (8-1), finally faced midnight. Red-hot Alabama (8-2) scored 1st on K Ryan Plugner's 40y FG. QB Wayne Madkin (14-21/168y, TD, 2 INTs) put Bulldogs ahead 7-3 in 2nd Q on 3y TD pass to FB Rod Gibson. After that Tide dominated, holding State to 22/24y rushing. TB Shaun Alexander rushed only 24/54y vs tough Bulldog run D, but scored go-ahead TD in 2nd Q. Alabama QB Andrew Zow (18-34/222y, INT) added 4th Q TD pass to WR Shamari Buchanan.

ARKANSAS 28 Tennessee 24: Just when red-hot Tennessee (7-2) appeared in position to wedge itself into national title race, it let 10-pt lead slip away in 2nd H. For Razorback (6-3) QB Clint Stoerner (18-28/228y, 3 TDs, INT), it was sweet revenge. Storener's 23y TD strike to WR Anthony Lucas with 3:44 left wiped out misery of his bizarre FUM that turned late 24-22 lead into loss to Vols in 1998. Tennessee QB Tee Martin (22-44/311y, INT) ran 19y to score midway in 2nd Q for 17-14 lead. Vol sub TB Travis Henry (12/79y) raced 28y to TD and 24-14 edge midway in 3rd Q before Stoerner exacted his revenge.

Michigan 31 PENN STATE 27: Damaged egos of Nittany Lions were bruised further when 2 TOs led to early 10-0 deficit. But, Penn State (9-2) was energized by WR Bruce Branch's 79y punt TD RET in 2nd Q. Lions took lead at 27-17 on 46y INT TD RET by DB Blawoh Jue with 9:44 left. But, Lions' touted D failed when it mattered. Michigan QB Tom Brady (17-36/259y, 2 TDs, 3 INTs) stout-heartedly directed 12-play, 81y drive that ended in his 5y scramble with 3:26 left. Trailing 27-24, Penn State was forced to punt because it ignored anemic run game of 20/7y. Brady pitched winning 11y TD to WR Marcus Knight with 1:46 left, and UM LB Ian Gold finished it by forcing FUM in last min by Lion QB Kevin Thompson (19-37/263y, TD).

WISCONSIN 41 Iowa 3: Brief holder of NCAA career rushing record, Ricky Williams admitted he would likely cast his Heisman vote for former Texas teammate, QB Major Applewhite. No matter that he dissed Ron Dayne. Low-key Wisconsin (9-2) TB Dayne (27/216y), who would lock up 1999 Heisman on this day, slammed off RG in 2nd Q and rambled 31y to break Williams' record set in 1998. Badgers led 27-3 at H as Dayne scored once and QB Brooks Bollinger (9-12/144y) threw 3 TDs. WR Chris Chambers made 24, 16y TD catches. Hawkeyes (1-9) dropped 7th straight, gained 247y, and reached 5YL in 2nd Q but had to settle for K Greg McLaughlin's 22y FG. Afterward, ever-humble Dayne told "5th Q" crowd: "Thank you so much for your support. I love you."

NEBRASKA 41 Kansas State 15: Vengeful Nebraska (9-1) turned tables on last year's loss to Kansas State (9-1). It was emotional for Huskers as described by LB Carlos Volk: "we knew they didn't fear Nebraska like they used to. We wanted to put that fear back into them." Huskers quickly jumped to 24-9 H lead as speedy QB Eric Crouch (27/158y rushing, 8-17/69y passing) raced for TD runs of 30, 18y in 1st Q. Whatever hope lingered for Wildcats at end of scoreless 3rd Q was dashed by 17-pt Husker blitz in 4th Q. Big TD came from frosh IB Dahrran Diedrick on 46y run.

UCLA 23 Washington 20 (OT): UCLA (4-6) O line, down to last 6 able-bodies, opened holes for 149y rushing after making fewer than that in last 3 games combined. Bruin D, which allowed 105 pts during 3 losses, limited Huskies (6-4) to 236y O and came up with big play in 2nd Q. DB Ricky Manning blitzed Washington QB Marques Tuiasosopo (12-25/134y, INT) who lost FUM at own 3YL. Bruin TB DeShaun Foster (24/69y, 2 TDs) quickly scored for 14-7 lead. K John Anderson of Huskies bombed 50y FG for 17-14 H lead and school-record 56y FG to tie it 20-20 with 2:34 left. In OT, UCLA DB Joey Strycula made leaping INT at own 4YL, then K Chris Griffith booted his 3rd FG (22y) to win it. Washington had been in control of its Rose Bowl destiny, but would have to hope for Stanford loss that never came.

USA Today Coaches Poll November 15

1	Florida State (58)	1474	14	Michigan State	753
2	Virginia Tech (1)	1410	15	Mississippi State	752
3	Florida	1347	16	Mississippi	547
4	Nebraska	1310	17	Southern Mississippi	423
5	Wisconsin	1218	18	Minnesota	407
6	Texas	1104	19	Brigham Young	372
7	Tennessee	1011	20	Texas A&M	345
8	Alabama	994	21	East Carolina	283
9	Kansas State	982	22	Boston College	260
10	Michigan	918	23	Georgia	241
11	Marshall	859	24	Arkansas	143
12	Georgia Tech	850	25	Purdue	108
13	Penn State	757			

Bowl Championship Series Standings November 15

	Poll Avg.	Computer Avg.	Schedule Strength	Losses	Total
1 Florida State (10-0)	1.0	1.00	0.64	0	2.64
2 Virginia Tech (9-0)	2.0	2.14	2.16	0	6.30
3 Nebraska (9-1)	4.0	2.86	0.84	1	8.70
4 Florida (9-1)	3.0	4.29	1.00	1	9.29
5 Tennessee (7-2)	7.0	6.50	0.24	2	15.74

November 20, 1999

Florida State 30 FLORIDA 23: No. 1 Seminoles (11-0) clinched spot in BCS title Sugar Bowl game with relative ease, considering Florida (9-2) had last-play Hail Mary pass try. Florida State fashioned 10-0 lead by 2nd Q, primarily on WR Peter Warrick's dazzling 4y TD run. FSU led 13-9 midway in 3rd Q when Gator DB Bennie Alexander made 43y INT

TD RET of QB Chris Weinke (24-36/263y, TD, INT). But resilient Weinke triggered 17 unanswered pts over next 18 min for 30-16 edge. Florida managed its only O TD—pass by QB Doug Johnson (20-36/214y, 2 INTs)—with 3:33 left, then got last chance from own 12YL in last min.

Alabama 28 AUBURN 17: Coming off decisive 38-21 win over Georgia, Auburn (5-6) jumped to 14-6 H lead on 2 TD passes by QB Ben Leard (26-39/237y, INT). In 3rd Q, Tigers' K Damon Duval hooked straight-on 22y FG, and Alabama (9-2) surged, mounting 16-play drive led by sub QB Tyler Watts. But, drive died at Auburn 4YL when Tide TB Shaun Alexander was stuffed by LB Kenny Kelly. On next snap with 42 sec left in 3rd Q, Bama DL Cornelius Griffin sacked Leard for safety. Tide WR Freddie Milons returned free kick 29y to midfield. Alexander (33/182y), who went on to break Bobby Humphreys' school career rushing record, took personal control of game. He scored 1st of his 3 TDs in 4th Q. Trailing 22-14, Auburn drove to 18YL with 2:58 left. Duval made 35y FG, but on-side KO failed which led to Alexander's clinching TD run.

MICHIGAN 24 Ohio State 17: It took 3 TDs in 2nd H and 2 late TD passes to rally Michigan (9-2) past Ohio State (6-6) and end Buckeyes' 1st non-bowl season since 1988. Ohio State QB Steve Bellisari completed just 8-20/84y, 2 INTs, but nailed 1st H TD passes to TE Kevin Houser, FB Jamar Martin. Trailing 14-7, Michigan made 1st of 2 INTs to set up K Hayden Epstein's 42y FG. Another INT led to Wolverine TD catch by TE Shawn Thompson that tied it 17-17 with 37 sec remaining in 3rd Q. Michigan frosh DB Cato June made FUM REC to start 77y winning drive, capped by TD pass by sturdy QB Tom Brady (17-27/150y, 2 TDs) with 5:01 to play.

MICHIGAN STATE 35 Penn State 28: Not since 1914 had Penn State (9-3) closed regular season with 3 losses in row, but Michigan State (9-2) rode strong back of frosh TB T.J. Duckett (22/159y, 4 TDs) to 28-7 H lead. Duckett blasted for TD runs of 20, 9, and 2y in 1st H. Nittany Lions rallied in 2nd H to tie it at 28-28. QB Kevin Thompson (17-35/185y, INT) threw 2nd H TD passes of 23, 12y to WR Eddie Drummond and added 2-pt pass to TB Eric McCoo. PSU's Travis Forney made FGs of 31, 30y, with 2nd coming midway in 4th Q for deadlock. But Penn State's November nightmare was sealed when TE John Gilmore lost FUM at own 39YL after catching pass for 1st down. On 8th play of drive, Duckett fittingly crashed 11y for game-winner with 2:30 to play.

TEXAS CHRISTIAN 52 Texas-El Paso 24: Little-known TCU (6-4) TB LaDainian Tomlinson overcame tender ankle from October 30 injury to set major college single game rushing record of 406y on 43 carries. While scoring Horned Frog record 6 TDs, Tomlinson broke 8-year-old Div1-A record of 396y by Tony Sands of Kansas. After 4th Q TD runs of 70 and 63y, he almost was pulled with TCU up 45-17, but coach Dennis Franchione said, "We just wanted to get him his 20 yards. If he's so close to something like that, you've got to let him finish it off." Tomlinson set record on 4y draw play with 5:30 left, added 9y on 2 more runs. After Tomlinson ran 13y for early-game TD, Frog LB Shannon Brazzell pounced on FUM at UTEP 9YL. Tomlinson quickly tallied again. Miners (5-7) rallied in 2nd Q for 17-17 H tie. UTEP QB Jay Stuckey passed 19-27/296y, 2 INTs and clicked on 47y TD to WR James Thompson (5/92y) in 2nd Q.

STANFORD 31 California 13: Stanford (7-3), preseason pick for at or near bottom of Pac-10, completed improbable run to conf title and Rose bowl berth, its 1st since 1971. This time, downtrodden Cardinal D (ranked next to last in national y avg) contributed mightily. California (4-7) gained only 130y with 5th-year sr QB Wes Dalton making his 1st career start. Bear A-A DB Deltha O'Neal offset 1st H TD runs by Stanford TB Brian Allen (22y) and FB Casey Moore (1y) by making thrilling TD RETs of 100y with KO and 58y with punt. After O'Neal's 2nd TD, Stanford DL Willie Howard, team's inspirational D leader, blocked conv to preserve 14-13 lead. Late in 2nd Q, Cardinal QB Todd Husak (11-27/216y, INT) provided breathing room with 36y TD pass to WR Dave Davis. Moore clinched it in 4th Q when he squirted through Cal's bunched DL and raced 94y to score.

HAWAII 48 Navy 41: Coming off 0-12 season of 1998, Hawaii (8-3) tied all-time most improved record. Mark was shared by 1940 Stanford (10-0 after 1-7-1) and 1943 Purdue (9-0 following 1-8). On November 27, Washington State beat Rainbows 22-14 to prevent all-time most improved record. Against Navy (4-7), Hawaii QB Dan Robinson (37-63/530y, 5 TDs, INT) set 4 school records (completions, attempts, y, TDs) to date. Middies used much of their 451y rushing to mount comeback from 41-27 4th Q obstacle. FB Raheem Lambert (18/120y) scored on 6y run with 8:27 to play and QB Brian Madden (29/150y) added 1y TD sneak 1:04 later to knot it at 41-41. Robinson's 5th TD pass to WR Dwight Carter (10/208y, 2 TDs) capped 7-play, 70y march with 5:21 left.

USA Today Coaches Poll November 22

1	Florida State (57)	1473	14	Minnesota	595
2	Virginia Tech (2)	1414	15	Penn State	479
3	Nebraska	1358	16	Georgia Tech	468
4	Wisconsin	1270	17	Texas A&M	455
5	Texas	1151	18	East Carolina	444
6	Florida	1139	19	Mississippi State	437
7	Tennessee	1109	20	Boston College	413
8	Kansas State	1067	21	Georgia	371
9	Alabama	1044	22	Arkansas	339
10	Michigan	987	23	Purdue	226
11	Michigan State	873	24	Mississippi	174
12	Marshall	854	25	Stanford	164
13	Southern Mississippi	602			

Bowl Championship Series Standings November 22

	Poll Avg.	Computer Avg.	Schedule Strength	Losses	Total
1 Florida State (11-0)	1.0	1.00	0.32	0	2.32
2 Virginia Tech (10-0)	2.0	2.14	2.64	0	6.78
3 Nebraska (9-1)	3.0	2.57	0.84	1	7.41
4 Tennessee (9-2)	6.5	5.14	0.24	2	13.88
5 Florida (9-2)	5.5	6.57	0.48	2	14.55

November 25-27, 1999

(Th'g) MISSISSIPPI STATE 23 Mississippi 20: Mississippi (7-4) held lead nearly all game as QB Romaro Miller (13-27/150y, 2 INTs) threw TD passes to WR Maurice Flournoy and TE Adam Bettis. Despite TB Dicenzo Miller's 29y TD run in 2nd Q, Mississippi State (9-2) trailed 20-6 going into 4th Q, its golden period all season. Bulldog QB Wayne Madkin (20-33/233y, 2 INTs) threw TD passes to TEs Donald Lee and C.J. Sirmones, latter after 88y drive with :27 left. Ole Miss coach David Cutcliffe chose to have Miller pass from own 24YL, and MSU DB Eugene Clinton made INT returned 27y to set up K Scott Westerfield's winning 44y FG with 4 sec to go.

(Fri) TEXAS A&M 20 Texas 16: With heavy hearts because of bonfire accident that killed 12 students previous week, Texas A&M (8-3) turned out 70,000 for Thursday's "Yell Practice." Emotional Aggie players would not be denied on Friday. Texas A&M WR Chris Cole made fine run after catch to set up TD blast by FB Ja'Mar Toombs (37/126y, 2 TDs) at end of 52y drive. But, K Shane Lechler tossed ill-advised pass on botched conv that was returned for 2 pts by Texas (9-3) DB Lee Jackson. Longhorn TB Hodges Mitchell (24/102y) made patient cutback for TD, and sub FB Chris Robertson powered over in 2nd Q for 16-6 margin at H. A&M QB Randy McCown (8-22/156y, TD), who missed 9 straight passes at one juncture, lobbed 30y pass to WR Bethel Johnson to set up Toombs' 9y TD run to pull Aggies within 16-13 with 4:47 left in 3rd Q. With 6:51 to play, Toombs converted 4th-and-1 at Texas 37YL. Cole caught 24y fade pass, and WR Matt Bumgardner caught another fade for TD. Aggies DB Jay Brooks sent 86,128, largest football crowd ever in state of Texas, home happy with forced FUM on sack of Texas QB Major Applewhite, who missed most of game with stomach flu.

(Fri) VIRGINIA TECH 38 Boston College 14: High-powered Hokies (11-0) completed 1st perfect season since 1918 and answered critics by walloping ranked teams by combined 178-31 score. Virginia Tech got rolling early as QB Michael Vick (11-13/290y, 3 TDs) made long dash on game's 1st play, later launched TD bombs of 69, 59y to WR Andre Davis on way to 24-0 H margin. Resilient no. 22 Boston College (8-3) came up with GLS late in 3rd Q, then clicked almost immediately on school-record 97y TD pass from QB Matt Hasselbeck (6-19/138y, TD) to WR Dedrick Dewalt. Vick refired Tech in 4th Q with TD pass and run before Eagle frosh TB William Green dashed 45y for last min score.

(Fri) Nebraska 33 COLORADO 30 (OT): Failed Colorado (6-5) on-side KO to start game left Nebraska (10-1) in position for IB Dan Alexander (17/180y, 3 TDs) to race 50y around RE for TD on game's 1st snap. Huskers rolled to 24-3 H edge, but Buff D stiffened in 2nd H, holding Huskers to single 1st down deep into 4th Q. Trailing 27-6 early in 4th Q, Colorado QB Mike Moschetti (21-41/317y, 3 TDs) found WR John Minardi in corner of EZ for 12y TD. After 80y drive, Moschetti completed 3y TD prayer of lob to TE Daniel Graham. Finally, WR Javon Green caught 21y TD pass from Moschetti in back of EZ to tie it with 2:54 left. Teams exchanged FUMs deep in Buff territory, but Minardi made brilliant adjustment on 22y pass to carry Colorado into FG range in last min. Buff K Jeremy Aldrich barely missed 34y FG on last play of regulation, but made 33y OT FG from nearly same spot. Alexander's powerful run to inside 1YL set up QB Eric Crouch's winning TD sneak.

GEORGIA TECH 51 Georgia 48 (OT): Seesaw game looked like classic whoever-has-ball-last thriller until officiating crew made FUM call so bad they ended up being suspended by SEC. Georgia Tech (8-3) built 41-24 lead late in 3rd Q as QB Joe Hamilton (22-32/341y, 4 TDs, INT) threw TD passes to WR Kelly Campbell, WR Dez White and TE Conrad Andrzejewski. But, Georgia (7-4) scored next 24 pts as QB Quincy Carter (29-55/345y, 2 TDs, 2 INTs) made 10y TD run, 30y TD pass to TE Jevaris Johnson. Trailing 48-41, Hamilton pitched tying, 4th TD pass with 2:37 left. Bulldogs drove right back and TB Jasper Sanks (17/81y, TD) rammed to 1YL with 13 sec left. Sanks was downed at 1YL again and ball came loose. Tech DB Chris Young picked it up, preventing Georgia's winning TD or FG. TV replays showed Sanks' knee clearly down. Amazingly, it was Georgia Tech's only 2nd FUM REC of year. In OT, Yellow Jackets played D with 12 men, but PEN was not called. Bulldogs drive ended with Tech DB Marvious Hester's EZ INT. Tech K Luke Manget had FG blocked on 3rd down, but holder George Godsey picked it up to save Manget's 2nd try: winning 38y FG.

STANFORD 40 Notre Dame 37: Winless November rung down coach Bob Davie's 3rd season at Notre Dame (5-7). Stanford (8-3) K Mike Biselli chipped 22y FG through uprights at end of 68y drive as time expired. WR Troy Walters (8/183y, 2 TDs) caught 62y TD pass from QB Todd Husak (24-34/334y, 2 TDs, INT) as Cardinal jumped to 17-0 lead until ND TB Tony Fisher (19/107y, 2 TDs) scored 1st of his 3 TDs late in 1st Q. When Fisher scored on 9y run, after his 42y scoring catch, Irish led 21-20, but Biselli (4 FGs) put Cardinal back up 23-21 on last play of 1st H. Notre Dame rallied for 37-37 tie when it ended 68y launched by LB Rocky Bolman's FUM REC. QB Jarious Jackson tossed 5y TD pass and followed with tying 2-pt pass to WR Joey Getherall with 1:32 left.

ARIZONA STATE 42 Arizona 27: Winner was set for Aloha Bowl, but loser was headed home. Bitter rivals racked up 1,026y. Arizona State (6-5) speedster WR Richard Williams took early pass from QB Ryan Kealy (14-22/287y, 2 TDs) and ran away from Arizona (6-6) DBs for 51y TD. Wildcat TB Trung Canidate, Pac-10's rushing leader, broke away for 80y TD which tied at 7-7 in 1st Q. It would set trend for Wildcats: WR Dennis Northcutt (8/127y) raced 80y with TD pass from QB Keith Smith (21-37/293y, TD) for 14-7 2nd Q edge and Northcutt pulled Wildcats within 28-20 in 3rd Q with dazzling 81 punt TD RET. Big 3rd Q play for Sun Devils came when Kealy rose up from fake FG and found TE Todd Heap uncovered for 28y TD pass. But, Kealy would soon tear up his knee for 2nd time in his career.

USA Today Coaches Poll November 29

1	Florida State (56)	1472	14	Texas A&M	626
2	Virginia Tech (3)	1416	15	Southern Mississippi	624
3	Nebraska	1346	16	Georgia Tech	605
4	Wisconsin	1274	17	Penn State	603
5	Florida	1196	18	Mississippi State	540
6	Tennessee	1166	19	East Carolina	486
7	Kansas State	1115	20	Purdue	314
8	Alabama	1076	21	Stanford	281
9	Michigan	1021	22	Boston College	145
10	Michigan State	937	23	Georgia	124
11	Marshall	832	24	Miami (Fla.)	120
12	Texas	759	25	Brigham Young	114
13	Minnesota	633			

Bowl Championship Series Standings November 29

	Poll Avg.	Computer Avg.	Schedule Strength	Losses	Total
1 Florida State (11-0)	1.0	1.00	0.24	0	2.24
2 Virginia Tech (11-0)	2.0	2.00	2.16	0	6.16
3 Nebraska (10-1)	3.0	2.86	0.84	1	7.70
4 Florida (9-2)	5.0	6.00	0.48	2	13.48
5 Tennessee (9-2)	6.0	5.57	0.56	2	14.13

December 4, 1999

(Fri) MARSHALL 34 Western Michigan 30: Already 31-17 winner over Western Michigan (7-5) in regular season, Marshall (12-0) surprisingly was bowled over by Broncos in 1st H. Western used good blocking to protect QB Tim Lester (27-41/282y, 2 TDs, 2 INTs), who threw 16y TD pass to WR Corey Alston in 1st Q. TB Robert Sanford (32/163y) added TD blast in 2nd Q as Broncos led 20-0 at H. Bronco TE Jake Moreland blocked and caught during FG drive that ate nearly half of 3rd Q. Trailing 23-0, Herd QB Chad Pennington (20-31/284y, 3 TDs, INT) finally brought crowd back to life with TD pass to WR Nate Poole. TB Doug Chapman made 24y TD run, and Pennington followed DB Maurice Hines' INT with fade route TD pass to WR James Williams. Suddenly, it was 23-20 at end of 3rd Q. Early in 4th Q, Chapman scored again for Marshall's 1st lead at 27-23. Western somehow mustered courage for TD drive to Moreland's TD catch and 30-27 lead with 7:20 left. Barely over min was left when Pennington converted 4th-and-6 pass, then scrambled 33y. With :04 to go, Pennington threw his 100th career TD, slant-out to RB Eric Pinkerton for winning TD. Herd won its 3rd MAC title in row.

Navy 19 Army 9 (Philadelphia): In 100th meeting of service academies, tenacious Navy (5-7) QB Brian Madden (41/177y rushing) refused to be brought down in his 5th straight game with 100y rushing. Although Army (3-8) played well on D (243y), it couldn't stop Madden's 2y TD run off left side late in 1st Q. K Tim Shubzda kicked 1st of his 4 FGs for 10-0 Middie lead after Cadet DB Imani Dupree muffed punt in 2nd Q. Navy DL Gino Marchetti created 1st of his 2 FUM RECs early in 3rd Q which led to 37y Shubzda FG and 16-3 edge. Army scored with 4:47 left when QB Joe Gerena (7-19/95y, INT) rolled right from Middie 2YL, threw back left to wide-open TE Shaun Castillo. Navy's 216y on ground gave it 1st-ever national rushing title with avg of 292.2y per game.

Alabama 34 Florida 7 (Atlanta): Crimson Tide (10-2) won their 1st SEC crown since 1992 with demolition of favored no. 5 Florida (9-3), which managed only 114y from its "Fun 'n' Gun" O as QB Jesse Palmer had off day (7-20/80y, 3 INTs). Gators, however, scored on their 1st possession when TB Earnest Graham started right from 3YL, stopped and fired TD pass to TE Erron Kinney. Alabama K Ryan Pflugner badly hooked his 1st FG try, but made 3 FGs, including beauties from 48 and 49y. His 1st long FG, with 2:03 left in H, pulled Tide within 7-6. Alabama overcame holding PEN to tally on WR Jason McAddley's 27y TD grab. Leading 15-7 and pinned at its 7YL early in 4th Q, Crimson Tide QB Tyler Watts scrambled for 1st down on 3rd-and-11 play. Then, WR Freddie Milons lined up as Shotgun QB, started left on option, then cut back right, and was sprung by block of Watts (at WR) and sprinted 77y to score. On Florida's 1st play after KO, Alabama DL Reggie Grimes took deflected INT 38y to TD to end it.

Nebraska 22 Texas 6 (San Antonio): In Big 12 title game, Nebraska (11-1) D crushed Texas (9-4), recent winners of 3 in row over Huskers. Nebraska D slammed Longhorn QB Major Applewhite (15-42/164y, 3 INTs) with 7 sacks, recovered FUM. After K Josh Brown's 42y FG, Husker QB Eric Crouch (23/72y rushing) made fake on 4th-and-1, slanted off RT nad made beautiful cut to 31y TD run. INT by LB Tony Ortiz set up another Brown FG, and bad Shotgun snap forced Applewhite to slap rolling ball through EZ for Big Red safety. Nebraska led 15-0 at H. Early in 3rd Q, Husker IB Correll Buckhalter (20/136y) sprinted 55y to Texas 4YL, and Crouch scored on option run for 22-0 edge. Huskers' season-long bugaboo, lost FUM, contributed to sole Longhorn score. Frosh IB Dahrran Diedrick lost ball in own territory, and Texas DB Ahmad Brooks ran it in 20y for 4th Q TD.

USA Today Coaches Poll December 6

1	Florida State (56)	1472	14	Southern Mississippi	653
2	Virginia Tech (3)	1415	15	Georgia Tech	616
3	Nebraska	1330	16	Mississippi State	590
4	Wisconsin	1276	17	Penn State	586
5	Tennessee	1187	18	Texas	563
6	Alabama	1183	19	East Carolina	473
7	Kansas State	1145	20	Purdue	347
8	Michigan	1065	21	Stanford	308
9	Michigan State	997	22	Boston College	181
10	Florida	898	23	Miami (Fla.)	153
11	Marshall	819	24	Georgia	147
12	Minnesota	715	25	Brigham Young	102
13	Texas A&M	701			

Bowl Championship Series Standings December 6

	Poll Avg.	Computer Avg.	Schedule Strength	Losses	Total
1 Florida State (11-0)	1.0	1.00	0.24	0	2.24
2 Virginia Tech (11-0)	2.0	2.00	2.12	0	6.12
3 Nebraska (11-1)	3.0	2.86	0.56	1	7.42
4 Alabama (10-2)	5.5	4.57	0.04	2	12.11
5 Tennessee (9-2)	5.5	5.57	0.64	2	13.71

Conference Standings

Big East

Virginia Tech	7-0
Miami	6-1
Boston College	4-3
Syracuse	3-4
West Virginia	3-4
Pittsburgh	2-5
Temple	2-5
Rutgers	1-6

Atlantic Coast

Florida State	8-0
Georgia Tech	5-3
Virginia	5-3
Clemson	5-3
Wake Forest	3-5
North Carolina State	3-5
Duke	3-5
Maryland	2-6
North Carolina	2-6

Southeastern

EAST	
Florida	7-1
Tennessee	6-2
Georgia	5-3
Kentucky	4-4
Vanderbilt	2-6
South Carolina	0-8
WEST	
Alabama	7-1
Mississippi State	6-2
Arkansas	4-4
Mississippi	4-4
Auburn	2-6
Louisiana State	1-7

Conference USA

Southern Mississippi	6-0
East Carolina	4-2
Louisville	4-2
Memphis	4-2
Alabama-Birmingham	4-2
Houston	3-3
Army	1-5
Tulane	1-5
Cincinnati	0-6

Big Ten

Wisconsin	7-1
Michigan State	6-2
Michigan	6-2
Penn State	5-3
Minnesota	5-3
Illinois	4-4
Purdue	4-4
Ohio State	3-5
Indiana	3-5
Northwestern	1-7
Iowa	0-8

Mid-American

EAST	
Marshall	8-0
Miami (Ohio)	6-2
Akron	5-3
Ohio	5-3
Bowling Green	3-5
Kent	2-6
Buffalo	0-8
WEST	
Western Michigan	6-2
Toledo	5-3
Northern Illinois	5-3
Eastern Michigan	4-4
Central Michigan	3-5
Ball State	0-8

Big Twelve

NORTH	
Nebraska	7-1
Kansas State	7-1
Colorado	5-3
Kansas	3-5
Iowa State	1-7
Missouri	1-7
SOUTH	
Texas	6-2
Texas Tech	5-3
Oklahoma	5-3
Texas A&M	5-3
Oklahoma State	3-5
Baylor	0-8

Mountain West

Brigham Young	5-2
Colorado State	5-2
Utah	5-2
Wyoming	4-3
San Diego State	3-4
New Mexico	3-4
Air Force	2-5
Nevada-Las Vegas	1-6

Western Athletic

Hawaii	5-2
Fresno State	5-2
Texas Christian	5-2
Rice	4-3
Southern Methodist	3-3
Texas-El Paso	3-4
San Jose State	1-5
Tulsa	1-6

Pacific-10

Stanford	7-1
Oregon	6-2
Washington	6-2
Arizona State	5-3
Oregon State	4-4
Arizona	3-5
Southern California	3-5
California	3-5
UCLA	2-6
Washington State	1-7

1999 Bowl Games
Mobile Alabama Bowl (Dec. 22): Texas Christian 28 East Carolina 14

In battle of purple-colored, future Conf USA rivals, East Carolina (9-3) got off to fast start on 58y TD pass from QB David Garrard (19-35/191y, INT) to WR Arnie Powell. TCU (8-4) answered on TB LaDainian Tomlinson's 2y TD run behind tenacious block of FB George Layne. Frogs pummeled Pirates with alternating QBs on option runs in 2nd Q and scored twice: QB Casey Printers (13-19/174y, INT) found WR Mike Scarborough roaming free at back of EZ and QB Patrick Batteaux's 35y option run set up another

TD by Tomlinson (36/124y). Pirates scored on FB Jamie Wilson's 13y run late in 3rd Q, then recovered on-side KO. TCU D, led by DL Aaron Schobel (3 sacks), remained strong (-16y rushing) and halted Carolina immediately, then followed with 32y INT TD RET by DB Russell Gary.

Aloha Bowl (Dec. 25): Wake Forest 23 Arizona State 3

With QB Ryan Kealy already out with knee injury, Arizona State (6-6) had 10 more players miss game with food poisoning. After 3-3 H, partially blocked punt by WR Marvin Chalmers put Wake Forest (7-5) in business at Sun Devils 37YL. But Chalmers dropped EZ pass, so Deacons had to settle for K Matthew Burdick's FG and 6-3 lead in 3rd Q. Sub WR Jimmy Caldwell, son of Wake coach Jim Caldwell, broke tackle over middle vs 9-up D for 56y TD catch from QB Ben Sankey (13-22/188y, INT) and 13-3 edge. Wake TB Morgan Kane (20/83y) made 2 runs totaling 32y to set up his 4th Q leaping 1y TD. Moribund Sun Devils crossed midfield only twice.

Oahu Bowl (Dec. 25): Hawaii 23 Oregon State 17

With local Rainbows (9-4) invited to Oahu Bowl, good crowd was on hand for matchup of coaches (Dennis Erickson of OSU and June Jones of Hawaii) who met in Seahawks-Chargers game 54 weeks earlier. Oregon State (7-5) took 7-0 lead as quick, little TB Ken Simonton (18/157y, 2 TDs) gained 40y, then scored from 1YL. Hawaii made 2 sacks to prevent subsequent TD and force Beaver K Ryan Cesca into 1st of 3 missed FGs of 1st H. Hawaii DL Tony Tuioti fell on FUM in 2nd Q to set up K Eric Hannum's 1st of 3 FGs. Rainbow WR Craig Stutzmann made effective run on 50y pass to set up QB Dan Robinson (23-40/266y, 2 TDs, INT) TD pass to WR Channon Harris. With score 10-10 in 3rd Q, Harris spun away from Beaver DB Terrance Carroll's 9YL tackle to finish 30y TD, his 3rd catch of 70y drive. With help of 6 sacks, Rainbows led 27-10 until Simonton scored on 13y run with 1:27 left. Oregon State's on-side KO worked, but Beavers were off-side and failed to recover ball on KO retry. Hawaii improved by 9 wins over 1998, new NCAA record including bowl games.

Motor City Bowl (Dec. 27): Marshall 21 Brigham Young 3

Undefeated Marshall (13-0), 35-4 since elevating to Div 1-A in 1997, made strong case for top-5 poll honors. Thundering Herd TB Doug Chapman (14/133y) scored in each of last 3 Qs. Chapman caught 30y TD pass from QB Chad Pennington (17-28/207y, TD, INT) in 2nd Q and got loose for 87y TD run in 3rd Q. Surprising was Marshall's D, which limited BYU (8-4) to -16y rushing, thanks to numerous sacks, and 220y in air. Game was supposed to feature Pennington versus Kevin Feterik air war, but Cougar QB Feterik (6-11/125y) left with shoulder injury in 3rd Q. BYU drew 1st blood: K Owen Pochman's 28y FG in 1st Q.

Alamo Bowl (Dec. 28): Penn State 24 Texas A&M 0

Vaunted Penn State (10-3) D gave last-game shutout gift to coordinator Jerry Sandusky, who was retiring after 32 years to become more involved in his charity for under-priviledged children. With Lion sub QB Rashard Casey in opening lineup but making slow start, it took D to initiate scoring. LB LaVar Arrington, recent Butkus Award winner, pressured passer, and DB Derek Fox made 30y INT TD RET in 1st Q. Texas A&M (8-4) WR Matt Bumgardner made good 17y catch to Penn State 31YL, but Arrington destroyed QB Randy McCown's option run on last play of 1st Q. K Shane Lechler then missed 44y FG. Casey (8-16/146y, TD, INT) came alive in 2nd Q with 17y scramble and immediate 45y fly-pattern TD pass to WR Eddie Drummond, who took pass in stride. Nittany Lions led 14-0 at H. With only 27y rushing in 1st H, Aggies opened 3rd Q with wider sets, rushed for more y on post-KO drive than what they earned in all of 1st H. A&M reached 12YL, but Arrington tipped pass that LB Ron Graham picked off. Casey beat Aggie blitz with 2 completions during 73y TD march.

Music City Bowl (Dec. 29): Syracuse 20 Kentucky 13

Wildcat record-setting TE James Whalen (4/79y) caught 2 passes, including 45y toss from QB Dusty Bonner (30-43/308y, INT) to set up RB Kendrick Shanklin's TD run on opening series. But, Whalen soon suffered badly dislocated elbow, and with him went Kentucky (6-6) O. Syracuse (7-5) O moved nicely early, but couldn't score vs Wildcat D, led by DL Dennis Johnson, who had sack and blocked FG, until sub TB James Mungro broke 86y run up middle to set up TD near end of 1st H. Kentucky led 10-7 at H. Orange opened 3rd Q with 13-play drive, but Cat LB Jamal White blocked another FG. Trailing 13-7 in 4th Q, veteran Orange O line sprung TB Dee Brown for 32y run which set up Mungro's 32y TD burst off LG to beat Kentucky blitz. With no timeouts remaining, Kentucky chose to concede 20y TD by Mungro (12/162y, 2 TDs), so to have 1 last chance to tie it. After Orange missed 2-pt run which would have put it beyond reach at 22-13, Cats faced 96y drive, but could not reach midfield in frantic close.

Holiday Bowl (Dec. 29): Kansas State 24 Washington 20

Fired-up Washington (7-5) took 3-0 led on K John Anderson's 39y FG to open game, but Kansas State (11-1), shunned for 2nd straight year by BCS, answered with QB Jonathan Beasley's 1y sneak for 7-3 lead. Key to TD was TB Frank Murphy, later injured, who made spinning catch at 22YL and broke 2 tackles on 4th-and-1 to run 12y to 1YL. But, Huskies wouldn't fold. WR Dane Looker slipped free for 42y crossing-pattern catch in 2nd Q to lead to FB Pat Conniff's 3y trap TD run and 13-10 H edge. Beasley (15-31/216y, INT) hit elusive WR Quincy Morgan for 38y pass and ran 3/32y on opening drive of 2nd H. TD came on Beasley's 11y QB draw, despite entire O looking confused as play-clock ticked down. Wildcats led 17-13 until Washington QB Marques Tuiasasopo (18-27/192y, INT) clicked on 6-6/66y and scrambled to 5YL to set up TB Maurice Shaw for TD that became 1st pts allowed in 3rd Q all year by K-State. Huskies came right back with 29y punt RET reverse by WR Todd Elstrom. But, on 1st play from Wildcat 33YL, DB Lamar Chapman made INT of Tuiasosopo in EZ which he returned to 8YL. Trailing 20-17, K-State fashioned dynamic 20-play, 92y TD march which bit 9:54 off clock. Beasley scored his 3rd TD on 1y option right run. Tuiasosopo was buried by DL Darren Howard (3 sacks) on 4th down run and later threw 4th down incompletion with 2:09 on clock.

Micronpc.com Bowl (Dec. 30): Illinois 63 Virginia 21

Young Fighting Illini (8-4), back from depths of 0-11 record of 1997, demolished Virginia (7-5) D through air and on ground. Illini TB Rockey Harvey sped 47y behind block of FB Elmer Hickman to unknot 7-7 1st Q tie after Cavs used FUM REC to set up 7y tying TD run by TB Thomas Jones (23/110y). Illinois eploded for 28 pts in 2nd Q, most-creative TD coming on reverse run by WR Brandon Lloyd, who stopped and threw cross-field to QB Kurt Kittner (14-24/254y, 2 TDs, INT), who ran in 30y TD pass. Illini FB Jamel Cook zipped 61y with TD pass, and blocked punts by WR Michael Dean, DB Ivory Lewis set up TDs. Virginia opened 2nd H with drive to WR Kevin Coffey's 5y TD catch, but could get no closer than 42-14. Illinois racked up 611y O.

Peach Bowl (Dec. 30): Mississippi State 17 Clemson 7

Scoreless 1st H was highlighted by big Mississippi State (10-2) plays on D: DBs Fred Smoot, Ashley Cooper made INTs inside own 20YLs and DB Robert Bean blocked 25y FG attempt. Clemson (6-6) LB Keith Adams completed dream season, leading ACC in tackles (176), tackle losses (33) and sacks (16); he also recovered 2nd Q FUM at Bulldog 28YL. MSU DB Pig Prather returned 2nd H KO 45y to set up K Scott Westerfield's 39y FG to break the scoring ice. Tigers ignored 30y FG opportunity to tie it and failed on 4th-and-7 when Bulldogs DL John Hilliard batted down his 3rd pass. Bulldog WR Kelvin Love came back from earlier hand fracture to catch 21y pass, that was followed by 2 pass interference calls. QB Wayne Madkin quickly evaded pass rush by squirming around LE for 2y TD run and 10-0 MSU edge early in 4th Q. Roughing P PEN (1 of Peach record 21 PENs on State) gave Clemson life at foe's 46YL, and QB Brandon Streeter (24-50/301y, 4 INTs) sneaked over with 8:15 to go. Any Tiger hopes quickly were dashed by MSU's TD drive, climaxed by TB Dontae Walker's 15y dash down left sideline with screen pass from Madkin (17-38/176y, TD)

Copper Bowl (Dec. 31): Colorado 62 Boston College 28

Rout by Colorado (7-5) occurred so quickly that Buffs tied largest 1st H margin in bowl history to date. Buffs led 45-7 at H break. Colorado TB Cortlen Johnson rushed 15/201y, scored twice. DB Ben Kelly, 1 of nation's most dangerous RET artists, went 88y to score with 2nd Q punt for Buffs. Boston College (8-4) QB Tim Hasselbeck (13-32/146y, TD) suffered 2 INTs in 1st H and both were returned for TDs: LB Jashon Sykes went 29y and DB Rashidi Barnes sped 21y within 6-min span. Colorado QB Mike Moschetti passed 14-24/149y, INT and scored on 2y draw. BC received 2 TDs from its D and special teams: DB George White's 78y INT TD RET for only score of 1st H and DB Doug Bessette's 9y RET of blocked punt in 4th Q.

Sun Bowl (Dec. 31): Oregon 24 Minnesota 20

Confident Oregon (9-3), best Pac-10 team in some eyes, set out to boost conf's miserable non-conf record over last 13 months. Minnesota (8-4) scored 1st in seesaw battle when QB Billy Cockerham (19-37/256y, 3 TDs, 2 INTs) tossed 1y fade TD pass to WR Ron Johnson. Ducks matched it by H when they cashed 66y march keyed by WR Tony Hartley's brilliant 38y catch, and QB Joey Harrington (20-43/232y, TD) scored on 5y option run left with 1:11 to go in 2nd Q. Cockerham hit 4-5 passes to open 3rd Q, and WR Arland Bruce carried tacklers across GL on 38y TD catch over middle. But, K Preston Gruening hooked x-pt, and Ducks earned 14-13 lead when Harrington sneaked 1y on 4th down in 3rd Q. Gophers took 20-17 lead when Johnson made TD catch at edge of right EZ sideline early in 4th Q. With oft-injured star TB Reuben Droughns (21/95y) suffering leg cramps, Oregon started winning drive from own 13YL. Hartley made 4th down grab at Gopher 21YL, his 2nd 1st down catch on drive, Droughns returned for 11y run, and WR Keenan Howry made sliding TD catch with 1:32 left.

Independence Bowl (Dec. 31): Mississippi 27 Oklahoma 25

In 1st-ever meeting between giants of 1950s, TB Deuce McAllister's big plays and 121y rushing spelled difference for Mississippi (8-4). Rebels built 21-3 H lead as McAllister scored on 25y pass from QB Romaro Miller (12-17/158y, 2 TDs, 2 INTs) and 80y sprint. McAllister also prevented Sooner TD (which turned into FG) by hauling down DL Cory Heinecke after 51y INT RET. Oklahoma (7-5) QB Josh Heupel (39-53/390y, all Independence Bowl records) created 3rd Q rally for 15 pts as he passed 10-12/109y on 2 scoring drives. Ole Miss went up 24-18 on K Les Binkley's 29y FG early in 4th Q, but Sooners took 25-24 edge on Heupel's 3rd TD pass with 2:17 to play. But, McAllister made 42y KO RET to launch winning drive capped by Binkley's 39y FG.

Outback Bowl: Georgia 28 Purdue 25 (OT)

Purdue (7-5) got off to glorious start, but before game was finished Georgia (8-4) had overcome biggest deficit at 25-0 in bowl history. Boilermaker QB Drew Brees (36-60/378y, 4 TDs, INT) hooked up with his favorite target, WR Chris Daniels (12/103y, 2 TDs) for 1st Q TD passes: 3y at left pilon and 11y crossing pattern. But, Purdue K Travis Dorsch missed 2nd PAT, and coach Jim Tiller foolishly started trying ill-fated 2-pt convs thereafter. Brees fired 21y TD pass to WR Vinny Sutherland for 19-0 lead in 1st Q. With 11 min to go in 2nd Q, PENs influenced Purdue to punt on 3 straight snaps. Flu-infected Bulldogs TB Patrick Pass made 2 RETs, but was too sick for 3rd. His replacement, WR Michael Greer, lost FUM, and Brees hit WR Chris James with 32y TD on next play. Desperate Georgia then resorted to trickery and it worked: frosh WR Terrence Edwards ran to 74y TD on reverse. K Hap Hines' line-drive FG pulled Bulldogs to within 25-10 at H. QB Quincy Carter (20-33/243y, TD) ran 8y to score late in 3rd Q and Pass added 2-pt run. Carter led 94y drive to tying TD with 1:19 in 4th Q: TE Randy McMichael took tipped 8y pass from 2 defenders. In OT, Georgia DL Josh Mallard sacked Brees, and Pass ran 10, 19y to set up Hines' winning 21y FG.

Cotton Bowl: Arkansas 27 Texas 6

Arkansas (8-4) ended 7-game bowl losing streak by overwhelming old SWC rival Texas (9-5). Longhorns were sacked 8 times and rushed for school low -27y. After 3-3 1st H, Arkansas took control after being pinned at own 3YL by punt. Texas nearly scored safeties on next 2 snaps, but Hog QB Clint Stoerner (12-23/194y, TD, 2 INTs) connected with 47y stop-and-go pass to WR Anthony Lucas, soon hit frosh TB Cedric Cobbs (15/98y, TD) with 30y TD pass. Now inspired, Razorbacks scored on next 3 drives, including Cobbs' 37y run and TB Michael Jenkins' 42y run. Texas, playing without suspended stars WR Kwame Cavil and DL Aaron Humphrey, lost 3rd straight to close season. Game's defining moment came in 3rd Q when Steers attained 1st down at Razorback 1YL but were held to K Kris Stockton's 2nd FG. Afterward, Arkansas coach Houston Nutt was in Hog Heaven: "To beat Texas in the Cotton Bowl is something our program and our fans will never forget."

Gator Bowl: Miami 28 Georgia Tech 13

Speedy Miami (9-4) D overwhelmed nation's top O of Georgia Tech (8-4), handing sad result to graduating star QB Joey Hamilton, who failed to complete TD pass for 1st time in 14 games. Hurricanes were efficient on opening drive, using DL Matt Sweeney's deflected INT to launch TB James Jackson (21/107y) for 50y in runs, capped by his 8y TD. On 1st play of 2nd Q, Cane WR Andre King caught 15y slant-in TD pass from QB Kenny Kelly. Yellow Jackets, under constant duress from MVP LB Nate Webster (14 tackles), let Dan Morgan and DL Michael Boireau, still managed TD in 2nd Q on Hamilton's 17y run. Miami frosh TB Clinton Portis (12/117y) bounced off 3 tacklers, raced 73y on draw run for 21-7 H edge. Georgia Tech trimmed it to 21-13 on 2 FGs in 3rd Q by K Luke Manget, but were left with season-lows in pts and y.

Citrus Bowl: Michigan State 37 Florida 34

Spartans (10-2) were fired up for new coach Bobby Williams, players' choice after Nick Saban abdicated in December for LSU. Florida (9-4) closed its season with coach Steve Spurrier's 1st 3-game losing streak in Gainesville. Gators DB Robert Cromartie, at 5'8", was at tremendous disadvantage vs 6'6" MSU WR Plaxico Burress, who caught 13/185y and 3 TDs from QB Bill Burke (21-35/257y, 3 TDs, 2 INTs). Florida O was sufficiently strong to create 3 lead changes. Michigan State was ahead 17-7 in 2nd Q after LB T.J. Turner made 24y FUM TD RET, but Gators answered with WR Travis Taylor's 8y TD catch, his 2nd of 3 TDs. Florida went ahead 21-20 at H on TD sneak by QB Doug Johnson (24-50/288y, 3 TDs). After 3rd TD snatch by Taylor (11/156y) gave Gators 27-26 lead, TB Robert Gillespie recovered own FUM in EZ early in 4th Q. But Burress' 3rd TD and WR Gari Scott's 2-pt catch tied it 34-34 with 10:46 to play. After exchanges of FUM, INT, and punt, Michigan State took over near midfield in last 2 mins. After Burress' 5y grab, TB Lloyd Clemons (20/105y) carried 4 times to Gator 22YL. K Paul Edinger nailed 39y FG on game's last play to win it. Coach Williams joined players in Spartan celebration.

Rose Bowl: Wisconsin 17 Stanford 9

Underdog Stanford (8-4) got early inspiration from 2 injured stars: WR Troy Walters (3/52y), who seemed certain to miss Rose Bowl with recently dislocated wrist, caught 2 passes in 1st Q, and DL Willie Howard shrugged off bad knee to make 2 tackles for losses. Walters' 2nd catch took Cardinal out of deep hole, and when FB Casey Moore made outstanding 23y grab, K Mike Biselli was set up for 28y FG. With gimpy coach Barry Alvarez on sideline for 1st time since September, Wisconsin (10-2) finally made its initial 1st down on 20y run by TB Ron Dayne (34/200y) 2 min into 2nd Q. WR Chris Chambers soon made diving 35y catch to set up tying 31y FG by K Vitaly Pisetsky. Walters made 19y reception to Badger 3YL to set up frosh RB Kerry Carter for slanting 1y TD run. Stanford botched PAT on bad snap, but led 9-3 at H. Wisconsin affected 2 major game-turners in 2nd H: Big O line, led by A-A T Chris McIntosh, broke holes for Dayne, who rambled 64y on 2nd snap of 3rd Q, and DB Jamar Fletcher shut down Walters. Dayne quickly followed his long run with 4y TD sweep for 10-9 edge. Stanford marched 62y to threaten lead, but on 1st-and-goal at 6YL, QB Todd Husak (17-34/258y) missed 2 passes and run was stopped for no gain. Another bad snap allowed Badgers to block 4th down FG try that would have given Cardinal 12-10 lead. Badgers QB Brooks Bollinger finished 4th Q drive with TD sneak, which was set up by juggling catch by TE John Sigmund.

GAME OF THE YEAR
Orange Bowl: Michigan 35 Alabama 34 (OT):

Considering large final score, opening Q was dominated by D. Alabama (10-3) gained 35y and had negative y on punt, while Michigan (10-2) advanced but 26y with best ground gain coming on LB Ian Gold's 6y run up middle on fake punt. Bama TB Shaun Alexander (25/161y, 3 TDs) turned things warm with runs of 33, 14y before QB Tyler Watts (6-6/35y passing, 4/15y rushing) scrambled 11, 16y to position Alexander for 4y TD run off right side. Wolverines were forced to punt for 5th time midway in 2nd Q, and WR Freddie Milons' 23y punt RET set up Alexander for easy 6y TD romp up middle. Michigan all but abandoned running game, which would finish with 23/37y, and QB Tom Brady clicked on his longest pass of 1st H, 27y post pattern TD to WR David Terrell. Wolverines trailed 14-7 at H. Brady and Terrell combined again early in 3rd Q as Terrell spun out of poor tackle by DB Milo Lewis and went 57y to tie it. Alexander powered through 3 tacklers, weaved away from Wolverine secondary for 50y TD and 21-14 Tide edge. Milons took Michigan's next punt, cut left, went 62y to score. But, Brady and Terrell connected 4 times on ensuing drive, last time for 20y TD. Then, before wild 3rd Q could end, Michigan FB Aaron Shea plowed through fading Bama tacklers for 24y to set up TB Anthony Thomas' 3y TD run that knotted it at 28-28. PENs ruined both team's O—Tide had 18 fouls in game—in 4th Q until Wolverines launched drive in last 2:05 against exhausted Bama D. Brady (34-60/369y, 4 TDs) hit WR Marquise Walker twice, then found TE Shawn Thompson for 16y TD on team's signature play: sprint draw, fake run and misdirection pass to crossing TE. With 2 secs to go, K Hayden Epstein lined up his potentially-winning 36y FG. But, Bama LB

Chris Horne blocked it. In OT, Wolverines had 1st chance and scored TD on 1st snap as Thompson took another signature pass to score. Trailing 35-28, Alabama tallied on its 2nd play as QB Andrew Zow fired over middle to wide-open frosh WR Antonio Carter. But, sr capt K Ryan Pflugner pushed conv kick wide right, and Michigan celebrated.

Fiesta Bowl (Jan 2): Nebraska 31 Tennessee 21

Powerful Nebraska (12-1) burst to 14-0 lead as QB Eric Crouch (9-15/148y, TD passing, 17/64y rushing) dashed 30y on option run in 1st Q to set up 7y TD slant by IB Dan Alexander (21/108y). Husker WB Bobby Newcombe soon used blocks by DBs Mike and Ralph Brown for 60y punt TD RET. Trailing 17-0 in 2nd Q, Tennessee (9-3) reinvigorated its run D and turned to its air game on O. Vol QB Tee Martin (19-34/223y, TD, 2 INTs) pitched 6-7/66y during 2nd Q advance and capped it with 8y slant-in pass to frosh WR Donte Stallworth. Huskers, prone to FUMs all season, lost their only TO early in 3rd Q, and TB Travis Henry (10/31y) quickly ran 4y TD trap up middle to pull Tennessee to within 17-14. After exchange of punts, Nebraska refocused its ground game, keyed by C Dominic Raiola and G Russ Hochstein, and fashioned 96, 99y TD marches on next 2 possessions. FB Willie Miller barreled 47y to set up Crouch's TD pass to TE Aaron Golliday in 3rd Q. Nebraska never left ground on 99y sortie, with key runs from sub IB Correll Buckhalter of 27, 11y before he slammed 2y to lift score to 31-14. Vols WR Sedrick Wilson, former HS QB, took long lateral pass from Martin and found wide-open Stallworth for TD. Tennessee never saw ball again as Huskers powered downfield, its last 23 plays being time-consuming runs for 156y.

Sugar Bowl (Jan 4): Florida State 46 Virginia Tech 29

BCS' 2nd championship found underdog Virginia Tech (11-1) driving on opening series, but being foiled on 4th down inside Seminoles 5YL by swift Florida State (12-0) D when short FG was eschewed. Seminoles star WR Peter Warrick (6/163y, 2 TDs), distinctly dismissed by Heisman and Biletnikoff Award voters due to his arrest earlier in season, got his just rewards by catching 64y TD bomb to open scoring in 1st Q and authoring 59y punt TD RET in 2nd Q. Earlier, LB Tommy Polley blocked punt, returned 6y for TD by sub TB Jeff Chaney. Trailing 28-7 late in 2nd Q, Virginia Tech D suddenly rose up and Seminoles virtually were blanked until 4th Q. Electric Hokies QB Michael Vick (15-29/225y, TD, and 23/97y rushing) scored late in 2nd Q. Va Tech ventured out from H break to own 3rd Q as DB Ike Charlton set up FG with 24y punt RET, later made another for 45y RET to poise sub TB Andre Kendrick for option, pitch left, 29y TD run. Va Tech DB Anthony Midget made INT, and dancing Vick to control by running for 15 and 22y gains before Kendrick scored again. Amazingly, Hokies led 29-28 at end of 3rd Q. But, FSU QB Chris Weinke (20-34/329y, 4 TDs, INT), who during his clutch 1999 season had passed for 77% while delivering 8 scores in 13 series that immediately followed FSU's foes having tied or overtaken Noles. This time, Weinke clicked on all but 1 pass of 85y drive. Biggest play of march, however, was TB in Travis Minor's 15y run (plus 15y roughing PEN) on 4th-and-1 near midfield. With both Hokies CBs out with injury, inexperienced DBs became confused on coverage, and Seminoles WR Ron Dugans was alone for winning 14y pass from Weinke. K Sebastian Janikowski followed with 32y FG for 39-29 FSU lead, and Warrick punctuated Seminoles' triumph with his 3rd TD: brilliant, juggling 43y TD catch as DB Ronyell Whitaker interfered with him in EZ.

Final AP Poll January 5

1 Florida State (70)	1750		13 Mississippi State	923
2 Virginia Tech	1647		14 Southern Mississippi	788
3 Nebraska	1634		15 Miami	678
4 Wisconsin	1519		16 Georgia	640
5 Michigan	1406		17 Arkansas	575
6 Kansas State	1402		18 Minnesota	452
7 Michigan State	1357		19 Oregon	358
8 Alabama	1236		20 Georgia Tech	345
9 Tennessee	1168		21 Texas	340
10 Marshall	1136		22 Mississippi	281
11 Penn State	1038		23 Texas A&M	272
12 Florida	941		24 Illinois	201
			25 Purdue	198

Final USA Today Coaches Poll January 6

1 Florida State (59)	1475		14 Florida	713
2 Nebraska	1390		15 Miami (Fla.)	605
3 Virginia Tech	1366		16 Georgia	505
4 Wisconsin	1283		17 Minnesota	395
5 Michigan	1189		18 Oregon	375
6 Kansas State	1188		19 Arkansas	357
7 Michigan State	1117		20 Texas A&M	344
8 Alabama	1042		21 Georgia Tech	337
9 Tennessee	985		22 Mississippi	231
10 Marshall	956		23 Texas	173
11 Penn State	840		24 Stanford	155
12 Mississippi State	810		25 Illinois	139
13 Southern Mississippi	763			

1999 Top Performance Formula

1	Florida State	1.8433
2	Nebraska	1.7193
3	Virginia Tech	1.6603
4	Kansas State	1.6336
5	Marshall	1.6168
6	Alabama	1.5419
7	Michigan State	1.5389
8	Penn State	1.5125
9	Tennessee	1.4881
10	Wisconsin	1.4824
11	Michigan	1.4710
12	Mississippi State	1.4079
13	Florida	1.4002
14	Miami	1.3894
15	Oregon	1.3466
16	Brigham Young	1.3161
17	Texas	1.3148
18	Minnesota	1.3131
19	Illinois	1.3061
20	Texas A&M	1.3042

1999 Top Opponent Records

1	Alabama	.6857
2	Florida State	.6308
3	Auburn	.6283
4	Michigan	.6260
5	Clemson	.6124
6t	Florida	.6071
6t	Penn State	.6071
8	South Carolina	.6033
9	Michigan State	.6031
10	Ohio State	.6000
11	Miami	.5986
12	Notre Dame	.5954
13	Texas	.5933
14	Missouri	.5932
15	Tennessee	.5923
16	Purdue	.5891
17	Iowa	.5882
18	Brigham Young	.5794
19	Louisiana State	.5763
20	UCLA	.5738

1999 Out-of-Conference Records

	W-L	Percentage	Bowl W-L
Big Ten	32-9	.7805	5-2
Southeastern	29-12	.7073	4-4
Big Twelve	28-14	.6667	3-3
Atlantic Coast	19-10	.6552	2-3
Mountain West	18-13	.5806	1-2
Pacific-10	19-18	.5135	1-4
Big East	16-18	.4706	2-2

1999 Individual Statistical Leaders

RUSHING YARDS

	Attempts	Yards	Avg.
LaDainian Tomlinson, Texas Christian	268	1850	6.9
Ron Dayne, Wisconsin	303	1834	6.1
Thomas Jones, Virginia	334	1798	5.4
Travis Prentice, Miami (Ohio)	354	1659	4.7
Lamont Jordan, Maryland	266	1632	6.1
Trung Canidate, Arizona	253	1602	6.3
Demario Brown, Utah State	279	1536	5.5
Darren Davis, Iowa State	287	1388	4.8
Shaun Alexander, Alabama	302	1383	4.6
Thomas Hamner, Minnesota	288	1362	4.7

PASSING YARDS

	Completions	Attempts	Yards	Pct.
Tim Rattay, Louisiana Tech	342	516	3922	66.3
Dan Robinson, Hawaii	288	556	3853	51.8
Chad Pennington, Marshall	275	405	3799	67.9
Chris Redman, Louisville	317	489	3647	64.8
Tim Lester, Western Michigan	282	470	3639	60.0
Kevin Feterick, Brigham Young	277	452	3554	61.3
Drew Brees, Purdue	301	494	3531	60.9
Josh Heupel, Oklahoma	310	500	3460	62.0
Patrick Ramsey, Tulane	310	513	3410	60.4
David Neill, Nevada	247	423	3402	58.4

RECEIVING YARDS

	Catches	Yards
Trevor Insley, Nevada	134	2060
Troy Walters, Stanford	74	1456
Dennis Northcutt, Arizona	88	1422
Dwight Carter, Hawaii	77	1253
Arnold Jackson, Louisville	101	1209
Drew Haddad, Buffalo	85	1158
Charles Lee, Central Florida	87	1133
Chris Daniels, Purdue	109	1133
Latef Grim, Pittsburgh	75	1106
Kelly Campbell, Georgia Tech	69	1105

1999 Consensus All-America Team
Offense

Wide Receiver:	Troy Walters, Stanford
	Peter Warrick, Florida State
Tight End:	Jim Whalen, Kentucky
Tackle/Guard:	Chris McIntosh, Wisconsin
	Chris Samuels, Alabama
	Cosey Coleman, Tennessee
	Jason Whitaker, Florida
Center:	Ben Hamilton, Minnesota
	Rob Riti, Missouri
Quarterback:	Joey Hamilton, Georgia Tech
Running Back:	Ron Dayne, Wisconsin
	Thomas Jones, Virginia
Placekicker:	Sebastian Janikowski, Florida State
All-Purpose:	Dennis Northcutt, Arizona

Defense

Line:	Courtney Brown, Penn State
	Corey Moore, Virginia Tech
	Corey Simon, Florida State
Linebacker:	LaVar Arrington, Penn State
	Mark Simoneau, Kansas State
	Brandon Short, Penn State
Back:	Tyrone Carter, Minnesota
	Brian Urlacher, New Mexico
	Ralph Brown, Nebraska
	Deon Grant, Tennessee
	Deltha O'Neal, California
Punter:	Andrew Bayes, East Carolina

1999 Heisman Trophy Vote

Ron Dayne, senior tailback, Wisconsin	2042
Joey Hamilton, senior quarterback, Georgia Tech	994
Michael Vick, freshman quarterback, Virginia Tech	319
Drew Brees, junior quarterback, Purdue	308
Chad Pennington, senior quarterback, Marshall	247

Other Major Awards

Maxwell (Player)	Ron Dayne, senior tailback, Wisconsin
Walter Camp (Player)	Ron Dayne, senior tailback, Wisconsin
Outland (Lineman)	Chris Samuels, senior tackle, Alabama
Vince Lombardi (Lineman)	Corey Moore, senior defensive end, Virginia Tech
Doak Walker (Running Back)	Ron Dayne, senior tailback, Wisconsin
Davey O'Brien (Quarterback)	Joe Hamilton, senior quarterback, Georgia Tech
Fred Biletnikoff (Receiver)	Troy Walters, senior wide receiver, Stanford
Jim Thorpe (Defensive Back)	Tyrone Carter, senior safety, Minnesota
Dick Butkus (Linebacker)	LaVar Arrington, junior linebacker, Penn State
Lou Groza (Kicker)	Sebastian Janikowski, junior kicker, Florida State
Johnny Unitas (Quarterback)	Chris Redman, senior quarterback, Louisville
Chuck Bednarik (Defender)	LaVar Arrington, junior linebacker, Penn State
AFCA Coach of the Year	Frank Beamer, Virginia Tech

2000

The Year of Oklahoma's New Millennium, Stupid Computer Picks, and Northwest Surprises

The new Millennium brought back a surprising old face. Entering October, tenth-ranked Oklahoma (13-0) still was a national afterthought. September wins over Texas-El Paso (8-4), Arkansas State (1-10), Rice (3-8), and Kansas (4-7) had earned the Sooners no special attention. Their pass-happy offense, so peculiar to their halcyon days of the run-oriented Wishbone, seemed too gimmicky for consistency, and while their defense earned kudos it could not be expected to handle a brutal October schedule of teams ranked no. 2 (Nebraska), no. 4 (Kansas State) and no. 11 (Texas). In one of the finest month-long performances in history, the Sooners not only beat those teams, they embarrassed them. Texas (9-3) was felled by a stunning 63-14 score, Kansas State (11-3), at home, trailed 38-14 in the second half before rallying to lose 41-31, and no. 1 Nebraska (10-2) allowed 31 straight points—24 in a wild second quarter alone—in losing 31-14. Oklahoma became no. 1 for first time since 1987. The Spread offense and quarterback Josh Heupel were now considered legitimate, and suddenly coach Bob Stoops was hailed as the next great coaching genius.

The Sooners cooled down greatly in November but finished as the nation's only undefeated team—it was their first unbeaten regular season since 1987—and was the easy leader in the Bowl Championship Series to determine combatants for the Orange Bowl. But whom would they play?

The "human" polls, and many of the country's fans, felt Miami (11-1) was the one. The BCS tapped Florida State (11-2), which lost to Miami 27-24 in October. With the coaches' poll poised to automatically name the Orange Bowl winner as national champion, the best the Hurricanes could hope for was the top spot in the AP Poll. Also, there was little trumpeting on behalf of Washington (11-1), eventual Rose Bowl champions and earlier victors over Miami. As Seminoles coach Bobby Bowden mockingly cracked, "I hope that stupid computer picks this thing, because it's dumb enough to pick us."

After Florida State's surprisingly quiet 13-2 losing performance in the Orange Bowl, Bowden agreed that, in retrospect, Miami should have received the BCS nod. The BCS saved face with Oklahoma's Orange Bowl performance, which was much more dominating than the 11-point margin would indicate. It was the Sooners' seventh title and first since 1985, while Florida State earned its 14th straight final ranking of no. 5 or better.

The Sooners were not the only surprise team of 2000. Except for Washington State (4-7), the Pacific Northwest absolutely sparkled, as Washington, Oregon State (11-1) and Oregon (10-2) built combined 32-4 records, while finishing in a three-way tie for the Pacific-10 title and nabbing third, fourth, and seventh respectively in the final AP Poll. It was thought that the rainy fall weather and the dazzle of nearby California were obstacles too large for the Northwest to overcome to produce many Top 10 squads, let alone three. The Huskies were no overnight sensation, of course, having won a national title in 1991 and six Rose Bowls while growing throughout the previous four decades, mostly under coach Don James. But, the cases of Oregon and Oregon State were somewhat amazing. For many years football in the state of Oregon was in a state of confusion, reaching its nadir in the 1970s and '80s when the Beavers won only 15 games in the 10 years from 1976-85. The Ducks were little better with 19 victories in the seven seasons spanning 1972-78.

Washington beat Purdue (8-4) in the Rose Bowl as the Boilermakers returned to Pasadena for the first time since 1966. Purdue QB Drew Brees became the Big Ten's all-time passing leader with 10,909 yards. He also was pitted in a battle for supremacy among college quarterbacks in the regular season with Florida State's Chris Weinke, who won the Heisman Trophy, and Heupel, who became the consensus All-America at the signal-caller spot. Still, Brees won the Maxwell Award.

The extremely gifted Virginia Tech (11-1) quarterback Michael Vick was an early phenomenon, but he suffered some September struggles and a mid-season ankle injury. Vick's injury knocked his team out of title contention as the Hokies fell from the no. 2 ranking when they lost to Miami 41-21 on November 4 with Vick only able to play a quarter of the action. Vick would leave Virginia Tech after two magical years that produced 22 wins.

With its win over the Hokies, Miami, previously wounded by recruiting restrictions in the 1990s, occupied the no. 2 spot in the AP poll, where it remained for the rest of the season. After entering the season with a miserable 0-10 record versus Florida State and league rival Virginia Tech, his two biggest annual hurdles, coach Butch Davis' reconstruction of the Hurricanes was complete.

While passing became the preferred attack choice of many teams, some running backs still earned headlines. Texas Christian (10-2) tailback LaDainian Tomlinson won the rushing title with the fourth-best total ever, 2,158 yards, and Virginia Tech tailback Lee Suggs emerged from Vick's shadow to rush for 1,207 yards and score 28 touchdowns.

Penn State (5-7) coach Joe Paterno needed seven wins for the lead in the all-time Division 1 coaching victories race. The leader, the late Paul Bryant (323 wins), who interestingly had gone 4-0 versus Paterno a generation earlier, hung on as Penn State suffered its worst record in Paterno's long tenure. Paterno (322 wins) passed Pop Warner (319), but Florida State's Bowden became a larger image in Paterno's rearview mirror. Bowden moved to 315 victories, even though the NCAA strangely and quietly continued to count the 31 wins Bowden earned at college-division Howard College early in his career.

Another major disappointment was Alabama (3-8), the pre-season no. 3 team before being swept by its non-conference foes, in this case, UCLA (6-6), Southern Mississippi (8-4), and Central Florida (7-4). Stressed coach Mike DuBose agreed to resign at season's end.

DuBose was joined on the sidelines after the season by a host of long-time members of the coaching fraternity. LaVell Edwards of Brigham Young (6-6), Don Nehlen of West Virginia (7-5), Dick Tomey of Arizona (5-6), and George Welsh of Virginia (6-6) all retired, while John Cooper of Ohio State (8-4) was fired as younger head coaches increasingly manned the sidelines. None of these respected men followed the lead of retired Tom Osborne, who won election to Nebraska's Third Congressional District.

The dangers of toppled goalposts became news, as every week fans around country seemed to over-celebrate football wins. Perhaps the last straw was not an injury to a fan—although there were plenty of those—but the exuberant destruction of the famous hedges at Georgia's Sanford Stadium on October 7 after a big win over Tennessee.

The sport proved itself dangerous with two accidents. On October 14, San Jose State (7-5) walk-on Neil Parry was injured in a loss to Texas-El Paso when a teammate fell on his right ankle, doing major damage to an artery and fracturing his leg. He later lost his foot and ankle when infection set in but courageously returned in 2003. Washington safety Curtis Williams was paralyzed on a tackle in an October 28 game against Stanford (5-6). The Huskies rallied around Williams, who made an emotional appearance at the Rose Bowl. He died from complications less than two years later.

Sometimes Mother Nature was the cause of alarm. A scary moment occurred when the Arizona State (6-6) airplane twice was hit by lightning on its return from a win at Washington State. The plane landed safely in Phoenix, but the jumpy Sun Devils lost their next three games.

NCAA football, not needing further watering down of its product, still stubbornly expanded by two an already excessive number of bowl games. The Silicon Valley Bowl could not find a sponsor—it was about five years too late for the Silicon Valley tech boom—and lowered its payout from $1.2 million to $750,000. Meanwhile, the Galleryfurniture.com bowl showcased a local Houston furniture store to a befuddled national TV audience.

An extended and divisive Presidential election took more than a week to sort out, and it eventually followed the results of the Harvard-Yale game as Yale's Republican George Bush (1968) nipped Harvard's Democratic Al Gore (1969), just as Old Blue's footballers defeated the Crimson by 34-24.

Milestones

■ Safety remained prime focus of rules committee as it limited ability of two blockers to engage single defender and continued to regulate crack-back blocks below waist by offensive players.

■ Nevada joined WAC and Connecticut moved up to Division 1-A status as independent.

■ Swarthmore College dropped football after 122 years.

■ Duke lost discrimination lawsuit to Heather Sue Mercer after she was allowed to try out for team as kicker and then dropped from squad in 1995. Mercer won $2 million in punitive damages, although amount was overturned on appeal.

■ Dave Rimington Center Trophy debuted, awarded by Boomer Esiason Foundation. Nebraska center Dominic Raiola won premier award.

■ Tom Fears, star two-way end for Santa Clara (1942) and UCLA (1947) before embarking on successful pro career with Los Angles Rams, died at age 76 on January 4. Fears led NFL in receiving in each of his first three years. Derrick Thomas, All-America linebacker at Alabama in 1988 before his nine-time all-pro career with NFL Kansas City Chiefs, died at age 33 from heart failure on February 8, 16 days after breaking his back in auto accident. One of best pass rushers in history, Thomas had 126.5 sacks in 11-year NFL career. Tom Landry, Texas halfback 1947-48, seven-year New York Giants defensive back, and longtime Dallas Cowboys coach, died of leukemia at 75 on February 12. Bob Blackman, who coached Dartmouth to seven of Ivy League's first 15 official championships, died on March 17 at age 81 after contracting bacterial infection. Employing innovative formations, Blackman's Big Green won 104 games from 1955-70, with three perfect seasons, and 1970 Lambert Trophy for team that was ranked no. 14 in AP Poll. He later coached Illinois and Cornell. Triple-threat HB Charlie O'Rourke, who led Boston College to 10-0 season in 1940 and 19-13 victory over Tennessee in Sugar Bowl, died at age 82 on April 14. Harry Newman, quarterback of Michigan's 8-0 national champions of 1932, died at 90 on May 2. Newman, consensus All-America and Helms Foundation Player of Year in 1932, sparked Wolverines to three Big 10 titles and 24-1-2 record. Winner of second Heisman Trophy in 1936, Yale end Larry Kelley died of self-inflicted gunshot wound at age 85 on June 27. Kelley had auctioned his Heisman Trophy in 1999, same year he suffered debilitating stroke. Hall of Fame coach Jerry Claiborne, who won 179 games and went to 11 bowls in 28-year career at Virginia Tech, Maryland and alma mater Kentucky, died on September 24 at 72. All-time iron man, tackle Leo Nomellini, died at age 76 on October 17. After World War II military service, Nomellini became four-year starter for Minnesota and was consensus All-America in 1948-49. Native of Italy, "Leo the Lion" also was collegiate wrestler, threw shot on track team, and amazingly anchored 440-relay team for Gophers before his 14-year NFL tour of duty with San Francisco 49ers, for which he played 176 straight games and made seven All-Pro teams. Chosen as all-time NFL player in 1970, Nomellini was also pro wrestler.

■ Yale became first program to win 800 games with 42-6 victory on September 16 over Dayton. Michigan joined Bulldogs on September 30, with 13-10 win over Wisconsin.

■ Silicon Valley and Galleryfurniture.com bowl games were added to schedule. NCAA announced limit of 26 bowl games, which included current 25 and New Orleans Bowl to start in 2001.

■ Longest winning streaks entering season:
Marshall 17   Florida State 12   Wisconsin 8

■ Coaching changes:

	Incoming	Outgoing
Army	Todd Berry	Bob Sutton
Central Michigan	Mike DeBord	Dick Flynn
Eastern Michigan	Jeff Woodruff	Rick Rasnick
Houston	Dana Dimel	Kim Helton
Idaho	Tom Cable	Chris Tormey
Louisiana State	Nick Saban	Gerry DiNardo
Michigan State	Bobby Williams	Nick Saban
Nevada	Chris Tormey	Jeff Tisdel
North Carolina State	Chuck Amato	Mike O'Cain
Texas Tech	Mike Leach	Spike Dykes
Tulsa	Keith Burns	Dave Rader
Utah State	Mick Dennehy	Dave Arslanian
Texas-El Paso	Gary Nord	Charlie Bailey
Wyoming	Vic Koenning	Dana Dimel

Preseason USA Today Coaches Poll

1	Nebraska (36)	1442	14	Washington	586
2	Florida State (21)	1426	15	Ohio State	543
3	Alabama (1)	1266	16	Southern California	530
4	Michigan	1196	17	Penn State	489
5	Wisconsin (1)	1192	18	Mississippi	376
6	Miami (Fla.)	1110	19	Clemson	340
7	Florida	1065	20	Oklahoma	283
8	Texas	997	21	Illinois	279
9	Kansas State	985	22	Michigan State	245
10	Virginia Tech	974	23	TCU	215
11	Georgia	933	24	Texas A&M	211
12	Tennessee	840	25	Southern Mississippi	197
13	Purdue	626			

August 26, 2000

FLORIDA STATE 29 Brigham Young 3 (Jacksonville): Florida State (1-0) built 22-0 H lead in spoiling final opener of Cougars long-time coach LaVell Edwards. Winning pts came early as QB Chris Weinke (32-50/318y, 2 TDs) lofted 19y TD pass to WR Javon Walker (8/70y) from QB was chased OB, running over unsuspecting coach Edwards. Seminoles D sacked BYU QBs Bret Engemann, brother-in-law of TV's Larry King, and Charlie Peterson 5 times and authored 3 INTs. Cougars (0-1) kept alive their streak of not being shutout at 314 games (Arizona State had been last to do trick in 1975.) with 42y FG by K Owen Pochman in 3rd Q. Game featured most-ever combined wins of opposing coaches contributing 304 and Edwards 251.

KANSAS STATE 27 Iowa 7 (Kansas City): Wildcats (1-0) took 17-0 H lead in easily pushing win streak to 53 regular season games against unranked opposition. Inconsistent performance by QB David Beasley was worry for Kansas State, as he threw for 250y and 2 TDs, but also had 3 costly TOs. Toting up 428y to 156y for Iowa, Wildcats led throughout. Hawkeyes (0-1) RB Ladell Betts rushed for 50y and caught 2/30y. Betts scored Iowa's sole TD on 1y run.

(Sun) Southern California 29 Penn State 5 (East Rutherford, NJ): While awaiting grand jury verdict concerning possible indictment on aggravated assault charges for incident on May 14, distracted Penn State (0-1) QB Rashard Casey was 7-24/106y with INT returned for TD before being benched in 2nd H. Nittany Lions' run game was no help, totaling only 6y. Southern California (1-0) TB Sultan McCullough rushed for 128y, igniting hopes of Trojans. QB Carson Palmer's return from injury was spotty at best (10-20/87y), but big production was unnecessary as USC built 20-3 lead on D and special teams masterpieces: S Troy Polamalu's 43y INT TD RET and WR Sandy Fletcher's 64y TD run with blocked punt. Crowd was largest in Kickoff Classic history.

1	Nebraska (40)	1446	14	Purdue	663
2	Florida State (17)	1416	15	Washington	606
3	Alabama (1)	1305	16	Ohio State	564
4	Michigan	1214	17	Mississippi	417
5	Wisconsin (1)	1211	18	Clemson	392
6	Miami (Fla.)	1112	19	Oklahoma	347
7	Florida	1088	20	Illinois	300
8	Texas	1040	21	TCU	250
9	Kansas State	989	22	Michigan State	225
10	Virginia Tech	955	23	Texas A&M	215
11	Georgia	924	24	Southern Mississippi	206
12	Tennessee	831	25	Colorado	154
13	Southern California	747			

September 2, 2000

WEST VIRGINIA 34 Boston College 14: Mountaineers (1-0) gave warning that last season's 4-7 record was aberration. WVU D scored twice, and HB Avon Cobourne easily won rushing duel with Boston College TB Cedric Washington, 132y to 31y. Converting TOs and riding Cobourne's swift feet, West Virginia opened with 17-0 lead before Eagles (0-1) scored twice to cut deficit to 17-14. Game was blown open in 4th Q as WVU S Shawn Hackett and LB Grant Wiley both returned INTs for TDs. Eagles QB Tim Hasselbeck threw for 119y and 4y TD to TE Robert Ellis, but he threw 3 key INTs.

RICE 30 Houston 27 (OT): With temperatures hovering near 100 degrees, Rice (1-0) frosh HB Robbie Beck was red-hot with 2 TDs, including 1y run in OT to win game. Houston (0-1) forced OT when QB Jason McKinley (32-47/339y) threw 2nd TD pass, 6y to WR Brian Robinson, with 33 secs left. Cougars could manage 37y FG by K Matt Clark in top of 1st OT. Owls had scored 2 TDs in 4th Q as Beck tied it at 17-17 on 1y TD run, and Rice took lead with blocked punt TD by another frosh, LB Jeff Vanover.

Colorado State 28 Colorado 24 (Denver): Buffs outgained rivals 532y to 392y but could not stop Colorado State (1-0) QB Matt Newton from throwing career-high 4 TD passes, 2 to WR Frank Rice (4/113y). Newton (19-30/327y, 2 INTs) got off to hot start, hitting 7-9 with 2 TDs in early stages. Buffaloes (0-1) roared back with 24 straight pts, with TDs on 5y run by frosh TB Marcus Houston, 15y reception by WR Javon Green, and 1y keeper by QB Bobby Pesavento (20-31/250y), subbing for injured QB Zac Colvin. Rams QB Newton was not done, leading pair of 2nd H TD drives for victory, with game-winner coming early in 4th Q on 30y TD pass to TE Jose Ochoa. "I guess there's a new sheriff in town," said Newton after game. TB Cortlen Johnson rushed for 121y to pace Buffs ground game.

UCLA 35 Alabama 24: Bruins (1-0) proved their mettle early after starting QB Cory Paus separated shoulder on 1st pass and special teams allowed 71y punt RET TD by WR Freddie Milons (189y total O). UCLA marched 64y behind TB DeShaun Foster (42/187y, 3 TDs), who scored on 1y run on 3rd successful 4th down conversion of drive. Bruins took lead on trick play, WR Freddie Mitchell's 31y TD toss to WR Brian Poli-Dixon. Later Alabama (0-1) regained edge at 24-21 on S Reggie Myles' 91y INT TD RET, but only for moment as reserve QB Ryan McCann (14-24/194y, TD, INT) soon found Mitchell for 46y scoring strike. Ball control was focus for UCLA, which held it for more than 37 mins as rugged Foster, who was measured as having gained 105y after taking initial hits, tied Karim Abdul-Jabbar's school record for game carries.

Stanford 24 WASHINGTON STATE 10: With Washington State (0-1) losing more y in 1st H on PENs (68y) than it gained on O (51y), season was off on wrong foot. Stanford (1-0) enjoyed 24-0 H lead thanks not only to Cougars' poor play, but to fine debut of QB Randy Fasani (16-25/250y), who threw for 220y in 1st H. Cardinal scored all of their pts in 2nd H as Fasani threw 8y TD to FB Casey Moore and hit screen pass that HB Kerry Carter took for 84y TD. QB Jason Gesser threw for 161y in defeat but could not get Wazzu into EZ as WR Josh Moen scored sole TD by pouncing on blocked punt.

1	Nebraska (43)	1456	14	Alabama	668
2	Florida State (15)	1422	15	Washington	631
3	Michigan	1303	16	Ohio State	627
4	Miami (Fla.)	1205	17	UCLA	491
5	Florida	1175	18	Mississippi	458
6	Wisconsin (1)	1131	19	Clemson	425
7	Kansas State	1037	20	Oklahoma	355
8	Texas	1036	21	Illinois	327
9	Virginia Tech	1022	22	TCU	234
10	Georgia	901	23	Michigan State	232
11	Tennessee	822	24	Southern Mississippi	117
12	Southern California	746	25	Notre Dame	115
13	Purdue	719			

September 9, 2000

North Carolina 35 WAKE FOREST 14: With its tough D wrecking havoc on pass rushes, North Carolina (2-0) needed little O to knock off Wake Forest (0-2). What UNC received was brilliant performance by WR Bosley Allen (2/114y), who scored on 60y reception and 78y punt RET. Tar Heels D meanwhile sacked Wake QB C.J. Leak (14-34/164y) 8 times, with 2 sacks by DE Julius Peppers who scored winning TD on 12y FUM RET in 3rd Q. Highlight for Wake was TD by DE Bryan Ray, who knocked ball away from QB Ronald Curry (6-12/143y) and fell on it in EZ for short-lived 14-10 lead in 2nd Q. Allen and Peppers led Carolina to 25 unanswered pts in 2nd H.

Florida State 26 GEORGIA TECH 21: Georgia Tech (1-1) proved pesky, but Seminoles (2-0) prevailed as QB Chris Weinke threw for career-high 443y and 2 TDs. Jackets QB George Godsey (18-32/189y) played well in defeat, completing 13 straight passes. He alternated QB duties with QB Jermaine Crenshaw on 63y trip in 3rd Q that posted TD

against confused FSU. That TD and subsequent 2-pt conv put Georgia Tech up 15-12, but Weinke's 30y TD strike to WR Robert Morgan returned lead to Florida State early in 4th Q. Florida State stretched its win streak to 14 games despite gaining paltry 93y rushing. Weinke's performance vaulted him past Gary Huff and Danny Kanell atop school's all-time passing y list with 6,433y. Amazingly, teams combined for 34 PENs.

SOUTH CAROLINA 21 Georgia 10: Even during disastrous, winless 1999 campaign, Gamecocks (2-0) played as well on D as could be expected. Now with some help from O and liberal use of zone blitzes, Carolina D held surprised Georgia (1-1) to 94y rushing and 108y passing. It crafted 5 INTs of UGa QB Quincy Carter, and Bulldogs were limited to 4 1st downs after their opening drive, which produced 5y TD run by RB Brett Millican. South Carolina TB Derek Watson rushed for 93y, scored 3 TDs, and added crucial 53y KO RET after Georgia's opening TD to set up his tying 5y TD run. Cocks soon broke deadlock to take control with great field position. South Carolina started 7 drives in Georgia territory. Gamecocks' win snapped 18-game SEC losing streak and victory was their 1st against Top 10 team since also beating Georgia in 1988.

Auburn 35 MISSISSIPPI 27: Bringing back memories of past Auburn (2-0) greats, transfer TB Rudi Johnson rushed for 165y and 2 TDs to help coach Tommy Tuberville beat his former team. Winning TD came on amazing play: Johnson bursting through bunched-up Rebels D for 42y TD run on 4th-and-2 early in 4th Q. Johnson's TD provided 28-27 lead, which grew when S Courtney Rice's INT was converted into QB Ben Leard's 1y scoring run. Mississippi (1-1) TB Duece McAllister dazzled in defeat, scoring 3 TDs on 257y total O, including 87y punt TD RET that gave Ole Miss 27-21 lead in 3rd Q. McAllister's scores came consecutively in wiping out Tigers' 21-7 advantage.

WISCONSIN 27 Oregon 23: Badgers TB Michael Bennett raced for 290y behind big O-Line, scoring on runs of 59y and 75y that showcased his sprinter speed. Teammate CB Jamar Fletcher dominated with 3 INTs, although other starting CB, suspended Mike Echols, was missed because replacement, B.J. Tucker, had difficulty covering Oregon WR Marshaun Tucker (6/196y). Ducks (1-1) QB Joey Harrington threw for 362y, helping build 23-20 lead after LB Matt Smith—yet another older player returning to gridiron after failed baseball career—scored on 47y INT RET. Bennett answered with 83y run to Ducks 1YL to set up TD keeper by QB Brooks Bollinger on next play for winning score. Win was not secured until Fletcher's INT at Wisconsin 11YL. Badgers were without 11 players (4 starters), who had been suspended over 4-game period.

Nebraska 27 NOTRE DAME 24 (OT): Nebraska fans took over Notre Dame Stadium, with vocal contingent of at least 30,000 that considerably eliminated home field edge. QB Eric Crouch's 7y dash gave Huskers (2-0) win in OT, although key play was pass that kept winning drive alive. After K Nicholas Setta kicked 29y FG for Irish (1-1) on opening OT possession, Crouch drove 25y to winning TD with his 9y pass to TE Tracey Wistrom on 3rd-and-9 sustaining drive. Crouch had scored twice earlier, including 62y scamper, as Nebraska opened 21-7 lead. Bruising Huskers IB Dan Alexander (24/112y) included 28y TD run that assisted 14-pt scoreboard jump. Fighting Irish used special teams to rally: TB Julius Jones took KO RET 100y to EZ and WR Joey Getherall went 83y with punt RET to tie game at 21-21. Crouch rushed for 80y and passed for 103y. Notre Dame QB Arnaz Battle rushed for 107y, but struggled with 3-15/40y passing; he broke his left wrist that ended his season.

WASHINGTON 34 Miami 29: QB Marques Tuiasosopo (18-31/223y, TD) soared in 1st H, throwing and rushing for TDs as Washington (2-0) built 21-3 H lead. But, Tuiasosopo relinquished 3 TOs in 2nd H as Huskies had to hold on for win. Hurricanes (1-1) twice cut deficit to 5 pts, but could get no closer. After Miami RB James Jackson's 2nd TD late in 4th Q, Canes O did not get ball back until only 20 secs remained. All QB Ken Dorsey (15-34/215y) could do was complete 42y pass to WR Reggie Wayne as time expired. After spraining ankle early in game, Miami WR Santana Moss had miserable afternoon. Moss caught only 1/7y, lost FUM that led to Washington pts, and made pass interference PEN in EZ that killed Miami scoring chance. Both teams displayed D stars as Hurricanes LB Dan Morgan made 20 tackles, while DT Larry Tripplett had 2 sacks, blocked FG, and recovered FUM for Huskies. It would be Miami's last loss until 2003.

September 16, 2000

PITTSBURGH 12 Penn State 0: QB John Turman threw for 272y and TD to lead Pittsburgh (3-0) to victory in last scheduled meeting of Keystone State rivals. Running game was nonexistent for Nittany Lions (1-3), who totaled only 33/64y. Most exciting play of game finished off Penn State as frosh multi-purpose QB-WR Rod Rutherford, who ran some option plays as backup QB, caught Turman's pass at midfield, ran to left sideline and then cut back to right to outrun Penn State secondary for game's only TD. K Nick Lotz added 2 FGs as Panthers won their 1st series tilt since 1988. After 96 games, Penn State held edge at 50-42-4.

Virginia 26 DUKE 10: Cavs (2-1) QB Dan Ellis was sharp, hitting 20-30/333y, 3 TDs. Blitzing Duke (0-3) D sent all but kitchen sink at Ellis, but he ignored hits to gain single coverage on WRs. This was especially true for favorite target, WR Billy McMullen, who caught 8/189y and TDs of 55y and 31y. Duke QB Spencer Romine (18-36/198y, INT) was unable to keep pace, but scored on 1y run to cut Virginia's lead to 20-10 in 3rd Q.

Florida 27 TENNESSEE 23: Game came down to final moments when, with 14 secs left, Florida QB Jesse Palmer (20-43/290y, INT) found WR Jabar Gaffney (6/91y) in EZ from 3y out for winning TD. Gaffney had ball only for split sec before being stripped by Tennessee (1-1) CB Willie Miles. Play was ruled TD, so Gators (3-0) won 7th of last 8 in heated rivalry. Winning drive traveled 91y and was source of redemption for Gaffney, who had been thrown off team in December of 1999 for theft but was reinstated in July, without scholarship. Volunteers blew opportunity for big margin by settling for 4 FGs in 1st H. Tennessee had penetrated Gators 20YL each time with 3 threats moving inside 6YL. Tennessee also gave away TD, as Gators CB Lito Sheppard enjoyed 19y INT TD RET. With redshirt frosh QB A.J. Suggs (17-29/140y, INT) and RB Travis Henry (37/175y, TD) leading way, Volunteers moved ball but could not crack Florida EZ sufficiently often to preserve their 23-game home win streak.

AUBURN 34 Louisiana State 17: With both teams vying to become SEC surprise team of year, Auburn (3-0) made pretenders out of Louisiana State (2-1) with easy victory. QB Ben Leard threw 2 TD passes as Auburn erased 10-pt deficit with 20 straight pts. Bayou Bengals QB Josh Booty connected with WR Josh Reed for 45y scoring pass play, their 2nd long TD hook-up of game, to bring LSU to within 20-17. LSU then kicked off to Auburn WR Tim Carter, who proceeded to race 100y to fire up home crowd. To help ice win, TB Rudi Johnson (36/139) rushed 19/59y in 4th Q.

NOTRE DAME 23 Purdue 21: K Nicholas Setta's 38y FG as time expired gave Fighting Irish (2-1) their 12th straight home win over in-state rival. Notre Dame had converted Purdue (2-1) mistakes to build 14-0 lead without so much as single 1st down: new starting QB Gary Godsey (14-25/158y, INT) ran in 9y TD moments after blocked punt, and CB Shane Walton returned INT 60y to paydirt. QB Drew Brees (13-22/221y) rallied Purdue, throwing 2 TDs to WR Vinnie Sutherland as visitors grabbed 21-20 lead. Godsey hit 3 passes on 3rd down on march to winning FG. Boilermakers beat ND in y battle by 398y to 236y, although Brees attempted fewest passes since he was frosh.

UCLA 23 Michigan 20: Beating team ranked no. 3 for 2nd time this season, UCLA (3-0) scored game's final 13 pts to pull out victory. Win was not ensured until Michigan (2-1) K Hayden Epstein missed from 24y out and then, on final drive, QB John Navarre (8-28/111y) threw INT to S Jason Stephens at Bruins 15YL. Navarre completed only 1-10/37y in 2nd H in relief of QB Drew Henson. QB Ryan McCann (21-40/236y) shook off sluggish 1st H to throw for 150y and 2 TDs in 2nd H to give Bruins their 1st lead with 6:30 left. He led 3 TD scoring drives of at least 80y, repeatedly finding WR Freddie Mitchell (10/137y) for big gains. Wolverines TB Anthony Thomas ran for 182y—68y on opening TD trip—while UCLA TB DeShaun Foster rushed for 83y of his 95y in 2nd H.

STANFORD 27 Texas 24: With Stanford (2-1) QB Randy Fasani suffering season-ending ACL injury in 1st Q, pressure fell on frosh QB Chris Lewis (12-33/214y, 3 TDs) to help team revenge 69-17 shellacking it took from Longhorns in 1999. Lewis' biggest completion was his last pass to WR DeRonnie Pitts, who broke tackle of Texas S Joe Walker en route to winning 15y TD. Pitts somersaulted into EZ on hit by CB Rod Babers. Texas (1-1) QB Major Applewhite shook off poor start to throw 2 TD passes—71y to WR B.J. Johnson and 38 to TB Victor Ike—to provide 24-20 lead with 5:44 left.

Washington 17 COLORADO 14: Washington coach Rick Neuheisel triumphantly returned to his old haunts in Boulder as no. 9 Huskies (3-0) erased 7-3 deficit in 4th Q with 2 TDs. Winning score came on 24y pass from QB Marques Tuiasosopo (15-29/200y, TD, 2 INTs) to WR Wilbur Hooks. Buffaloes (0-3) were clinging to lead despite anemic O that had not produced pts: 1st Colorado TD had come on CB Phil Jackson's 28y INT RET. Buffs closed scoring on 19y TD pass from QB Bobby Pesavento (15-27/174y, TD) to WR Javon Green. Huskies turned to their stars—TE Jerramy Stevens catching 7/102y and DT Larry Tripplett getting 3 sacks—to overcome 4 TOs.

September 23, 2000

SOUTH CAROLINA 23 Mississippi State 19: Replacing injured QB Phil Petty (19-40/305y, TD) on 4th-and-10 with less than 5 mins left, sub QB Erik Kimrey threw only 1 pass for Gamecocks (4-0), but it went 25y for winning TD to WR Jermale Kelly. Behind QB Wayne Madkin (17-36/224y, INT), Bulldogs (2-1) had taken 19-10 lead in 3rd Q on TDs by DE Mario Haggan on 27y FUM RET and RB Dicenzo Miller on 11y TD run. Gamecocks constructed 13 unanswered pts in 4th Q as K Reid Bethea's 2 FGs sandwiched Kelly's TD catch. Both teams' strong Ds were able to halt running attacks as South Carolina RB Derek Watson finished with -1y on ground, while Mississippi State RBs Dontae Walker and Miller rushed for 38y and 37y respectively.

Northwestern 47 WISCONSIN 44 (OT): Were Wildcats (3-1) for real? TB Damien Anderson's 12y TD run in 2nd OT provided winning pts as Wisconsin had settled for 39y FG by K Vitaly Pisetsky moments earlier. Badgers failed to extend 11-game win streak. Anderson rushed for 174y to lead Northwestern, who forced OT with K Tim Long's 46y FG at end of regulation. Wisconsin (3-1) TB Michael Bennett rushed 48/293y, but was forced to sideline with strained rib cage with score tied 31-31 with min left in 4th Q and Wisconsin facing 2nd-and-1 on Northwestern 29YL. Runs by TB Eddie Faulkner and QB Brooks Bollinger failed to convert 1st down, and Badgers settled for 47y FG. Wildcats flew downfield to tie game on Long's kick. To relief of coach Barry Alvarez, this contest marked last game that forced selected suspensions of Wisconsin players, with 6 missing action, including WR Chris Chambers and CB Jamar Fletcher.

Michigan 35 ILLINOIS 31: Controversial game featured 2 calls that went way of Wolverines (3-1) that were later deemed incorrect by conf officials. It was too late for Fighting Illini (3-1), who had to stomach Michigan TB Anthony Thomas' winning 3y TD run late in 4th Q that came secs after he lost FUM on play that officials ruled was down before ball came loose. Arguable play overshadowed Thomas' 228y rushing and 2 TDs, not to mention stellar performance of QB Drew Henson, who returned from broken foot to replace ineffectual QB John Navarre. QB Kurt Kittner (27-38/352y, 2 TDs, INT) propped up Illinois O, leading it to 21-7 and 31-21 margins in 2nd H.

OHIO STATE 45 Penn State 6: Penn State's dismal year took sad turn as frosh CB Adam Taliaferro injured spinal cord making tackle in worst defeat in coach Joe Paterno's 35 years in State College. (Taliaferro would make inspired recovery, but never played again.) Buckeyes (4-0) struck quickly with TDs on 1st 2 series. Nittany Lions (1-4) showed weak O, and starting QB Rashard Casey completed just 7-18/94y before being pulled. Penn State TB Eric McCoo rushed for 34y, 177y fewer than he gained versus Ohio State in 1999. When McCoo scored in 3rd Q on 2y run to cut deficit to 17-6, Ohio exploded for 21 pts before end of 3rd Q. Six Buckeyes scored TDs, while QB Steve Bellisari completed 10-17/203y. "I don't know what to do (to correct things) except for the way I have always done it," said Paterno.

OREGON 29 Ucla 10: In winning 17th straight home game, mighty Ducks (3-1) rolled behind balanced attack as TB Maurice Morris rushed for 139y and 2 TDs and QB Joey Harrington threw for 153y. Oregon D held UCLA (3-1) to 197y, including dismal -9y rushing. Lack of run game put pressure on QB Ryan McCann (13-33/152y), who lost 2 FUMs and threw INT. Sole Bruins TD came on trick 54y pass by WR Freddie Mitchell to WR Drew Bennett, which briefly tied it at 10-10 in 3rd Q. From then on it was all Oregon, who snapped 4-game series losing streak while extending UCLA's road losing string to 7. Ducks D coordinator Nick Aliotti gained revenge for having taken fall for UCLA's D collapses in losses to Miami and Wisconsin at end of 1998 season.

September 30, 2000

Virginia Tech 48 BOSTON COLLEGE 34: Perhaps 5-17/61y, INT was less than praiseworthy, but Virginia Tech (4-0) QB Michael Vick proved to be no normal QB. Rushing for 210y, 3 TDs with enough highlights for full season, Vick buried Eagles (2-2). Among examples: Vick withstood blitz on 3rd-and-12 from own 18YL by leaping over defender to race 82y for clinching TD. Vick also capped 59y drive earlier with 11y TD run that ended with him dragging 5 defenders over GL. Vick used catalogue of moves to spin away from would-be sackers throughout game. Hokies TB Lee Suggs rushed for 145y and 2 TDs, while TB William Green led Eagles with 117y and 2 TD runs.

MISSISSIPPI STATE 47 Florida 35: Bulldogs (3-1) stunned Gators by gaining 517y and snapping Florida's magnificent 72-game win streak against unranked opponents. RB Dicenzo Miller led charge with 172y rushing, while RB Dontae Walker chipped in with 156y as Bulldogs amassed most rushing (351y) by Gator opponent since 1982. Conversely, Florida (4-1) set school record with -78y rushing, victimized by multiple sacks of its QBs. QB Wayne Madkin directed Mississippi State attack with TD pass and 2 TD runs. Gators were stymied by 3 TOs, while 3 1st H drives ended on failed 4th-and-1 attempts. On 1 frustrating series, Gators went from 1st-and-10 near midfield to facing 3rd-and-57 at own 3YL due to 2 disastrous snaps.

LOUISIANA STATE 38 Tennessee 31 (OT): With excitement at Tiger Stadium at fever pitch, Louisiana State (3-2) QB Rohan Davey (23-35/318y, 4 TDs) fired 25y TD to TE Robert Royal on 1st play of OT that stood up for winning score. Volunteers (2-2) moved to LSU 3YL before LB Bradie Smith broke up 2 EZ passes as Tigers secured upset they thought they had at H by 24-6. Tennessee countered with 25 pts in 2nd H with QB A.J. Suggs (37-59/319y) tossing 3 TD passes to knot score at 31-31 with 1:30 left. Bengals had time to set up winning FG, but K John Corbello missed 46y boot. LSU had taken 1st H lead as Davey, despite injured ankle, threw 2 TDs and RB LaBrandon Toefield (15/120y) had 74y TD run. Tigers WR Josh Reed (7/146y) caught 3 TD passes.

ALABAMA 27 South Carolina 17: Surprising Gamecocks (4-1) were sent packing from list of unbeatens as Alabama (2-3) QB Andrew Zow (14-26/149y, INT) regained his starting job with inspired performance. His 8y TD run through host of South Carolina

---

defenders sealed deal with 4:57 left. Tide CB Milo Lewis set up score with 1st of his 2 4th Q pick-offs. After missing 1st H with ankle injury, Gamecocks QB Phil Petty hooked up with WR Jermale Kelly (6/107y) for 2 TDs. Overall South Carolina blew 4 drives that cracked 10YL of Crimson Tide, 2 on missed FGs by K Reid Bethea. Bama coach Mike DuBose had offered his resignation on prior Monday, but was rejected for time being.

Northwestern 37 MICHIGAN STATE 17: They did it again. For 2nd straight week, unpredictable Wildcats (4-1) upset ranked Big 10 rival on road. Elusive TB Damien Anderson sparkled, rushing for 219y and TDs of 32y and 41y. K Tim Long kicked 3 FGs as Northwestern built 23-10 H lead before running ball down Spartans' throat in 2nd H—Cats rushed for 201y in final 30 mins. As score mounted, Michigan State (3-1) RB T.J. Duckett (19/71y) was less of factor, while passing of QB Jeff Smoker (17-35/233y, TD, INT) could not keep pace with visitors.

MICHIGAN 13 Wisconsin 10: Michigan (4-1) WR David Terrell (5/96y) and Wisconsin CB Jamar Fletcher battled out on flank all game, with final victory going to Terrell on leaping catch in back of EZ of winning 15y pass. Wolverines QB Drew Henson and Terrell had clicked twice on winning drive with 3rd down completions of 21y and 20y before Henson pitched winner with 6:42 left. On TD throw, Henson (15-27/257y) was flushed from pocket and threw cross-field to closely-guarded Terrell. Badgers (3-2) marched into Wolverines territory, but lost chance to tie on missed 42y FG attempt by K Vitaly Pisetsky with 2:42 left. TB Michael Bennett led Wisconsin with 123y rushing.

MINNESOTA 44 Illinois 10: Illinois (3-2) clearly left something on field previous week vs Michigan as Gophers ran wild. Minnesota (3-2) RB Tellis Redmon rushed for 183y, including 50y on 2nd Q TD drive that featured him exclusively. Redmon's 6th carry went for 3y TD. He added 3 catches/116y. Gophers QB Travis Cole completed 8-13/170y and rushed for 82y, 2 TDs in 1st Q. DT Matt Anderle batted down 6 passes as D held Illini to 82y rushing and 178y passing. Illini QB Kurt Kittner completed 13-34/103y.

OREGON 23 Washington 16: Ducks (4-1) led throughout in taking key Pac 10 tilt. QB Joey Harrington's 13y TD pass to TE Justin Peelle midway through 1st Q capped 88y drive in giving Oregon lead for good. Ducks TB Maurice Morris helped keep it that way, rushing for 152y. After committing 3 TOs, Washington (3-1) rallied with 2 TDs in 4th Q as QB Marques Tuiasosopo threw and ran for TDs. Huskies were bounced from top 10 while Oregon entered AP pollsters' upper echelon for 1st time since 1964.

OREGON STATE 31 Southern California 21: Beavers (4-0) beat Southern California for 1st time since 1967, span of 26 defeats, as TB Ken Simonton raced for 234y and 3 TDs. Beavers took 14-0 lead before Trojans (3-1) rallied with 2 TDs to tie game at H, including 80y FUM RET by LB Zeke Moreno (11 tackles, 2 sacks). Game remained knotted until 4th Q, when 2y TD run by Simonton gave Beavers 21-14 lead. K Ryan Cesca's 42y FG proveded 24-14 lead, but Beavers later botched punt deep in own territory to set up 1y TD pass by QB Carson Palmer (19-38/282y, 2 TDs, 3 INTs) to FB Chad Pierson. Simonton soon broke away for 36y TD run that iced it with 1:18 to go.

October 7, 2000

MIAMI 27 Florida State 24: Oh no, not again. Wild ending featured 3 TDs and latest missed FG in rivalry. Florida State (5-1) QB Chris Weinke threw 2 TDs within 2 mins late in 4th Q—2y TD to WR Anquan Boldin and 29y TD pass to WR Atrews Bell (6/146y)—to rally Seminoles to 24-20 lead with 1:37 left. Miami (4-1) QB Ken Dorsey answered with 13y TD pass to TE Jeremy Shockey 51 secs later. More thrills were in offing as Weinke used remaining 46 secs to complete 4 straight passes to set up 49y FG attempt. K Matt Munyon brought back ghosts of past FSU nightmares by missing FG destined to be known as "Wide Right III." Miami had built 17-0 H lead behind Dorsey (27-42/328y, 2 TDs), O-Line that allowed no sacks, and D that held Seminoles scoreless at H for 1st time since 1988. Florida State continually stalled in good field position; it cracked Miami 30YL 4 times without scoring. FSU gained 565y as Weinke threw for career-high 496y, but whether it was INT, failed 4th down, or missed FG, Noles consistently misfired in red zone. Win was especially sweet for Miami srs, who ended 5-game series losing streak that included 47-0 defeat in 1997. Sr LB Dan Morgan had 17 tackles, forced FUM, and made INT at own 2YL, while classmate WR Santana Moss caught 7/115y. Loss snapped Florida State's 17-game win streak, marking 9th time since 1984 that Canes halted opponent's double-digit win streak.

CLEMSON 34 North Carolina State 27: Clemson (6-0) QB Woody Dantzler won dazzling duel with frosh QB Philip Rivers. Dantzler rushed for 103y and 2 TDs and threw for 220y and another TD. Rivers (21-48/370y, 3 TDs) answered with 3 long scoring passes to keep NC State (4-1) in contention. Wolfpack took 7-0 lead on 81y pass to TB Ray Robinson. Next, Clemson reeled off 20 straight pts. With Tigers D holding NC State to 32y rushing, Rivers sparkled with 2nd H TD passes of 52y to WR Bryan Peterson and 63y to WR Koren Robinson, but couldn't put Pack in EZ after leading them to Clemson 19YL late in 4th Q. Tigers RB Travis Zachery rushed for 147y.

GEORGIA 21 Tennessee 10: Scoring all 3 of their TDs on 1y runs, Bulldogs (4-1) beat Tennessee for 1st time since 1988 and ranked team at home for 1st time since 1991. Vols (2-3) took 10-7 lead in 3rd Q on RB Travis Stephens' 2y run. QB Quincy Carter (8-17/134y) then marched Bulldogs to 2 scores, winning 1y TD run by TB Jasper Sanks. Georgia TB Musa Smith's clinching TD plunge capped 99y drive that featured 47y catch by WR Terrence Edwards (4/109y). Georgia D stopped 2 drives on downs within own 10YL with each featuring stops of Vols TB Travis Henry for no gain on 4th-and-1. CB Tim Wansley had 2 INTs for winners, including 1 with 1:13 left to seal outcome. Tennessee QB A.J. Suggs started, but after 4 sacks and INT he gave way to QB Casey Clausen. Post-game celebration by fans trampled Sanford Stadium's famed hedges.

PURDUE 32 Michigan 31: With 2:11 left, Purdue (4-2) K Travis Dorsch missed 32y FG try, and he appeared to be measured for goat horns for 2nd straight week, following his late miss in 22-20 loss to Penn State. But, Purdue D forced punt, and QB Drew Brees went to work, passing Boilers to Dorsch's redemption. Dorsch kicked 33y FG and segued from goat to hero, obscene gesture he made to doubting crowd notwithstanding. Brees (32-44/286y, 2 TDs) was brilliant in earning his 1st victory against Big 10's big 3 (Michigan, Ohio State, Penn State). Brees upped his career TDs to 76 to break Big 10 mark of Iowa's Chuck Long and career y to 10,054y to break school record of Mark Herrmann. Game went way of Wolverines (4-2) early as they built 28-10 lead behind O provided by TB Anthony Thomas (21/120y, TD) and QB Drew Henson (26-35/256y, 3 TDs). But, Michigan could gain only 79y in 2nd H.

Oklahoma 63 Texas 14 (Dallas): Scoring TDs on its 1st 5 drives, Oklahoma (5-0) buried rivals en route to most pts scored in storied series. Sooners RB Quentin Griffin rushed for school-record 6 TDs—none longer than 8y—while QB Josh Heupel passed 17-27/275y. Sooners had 12 plays that gained 10y or more in 1st H in totaling 534y and converted 11-15 3rd downs. They had more TDs (6) in 1st H than Texas had 1st downs (5). Ravaged Longhorns (3-2) trailed 42-0 before scoring 1st TD as neither QB Chris Simms (11-23/63y, INT) nor QB Major Applewhite (9-18/98y, INT) was able to move O. With both teams ranked—1st time that had occurred since 1984—competitive match-up had been expected.

Nebraska 49 IOWA STATE 27: Nebraska (5-0) erupted for 36 pts in 2nd H—28 in 4th Q—to easily erase 1-pt H deficit. Ace Huskers QB Eric Crouch ran for 138y and TD, while passing for 164y to add another heroic chapter to his honor roll. Nebraska IB Correll Buckhalter powered for 3 TDs, 1 each in 2nd, 3rd, and 4th Qs. Improved Cyclones (4-1) were led by QB Sage Rosenfels' 346y, 2 TDs passing, that included 53y hook-up with WR Craig Campbell for 7-0 1st Q lead. Nebraska TE Tracey Wistrom (4/101y) was Crouch's favorite target, while Iowa State WR J.J. Moses hauled in 11/158y.

WASHINGTON 33 Oregon State 30: Unsung Beavers (4-1) had another upset in sights until K Ryan Césca missed 46y FG attempt with 14 secs left. Washington (4-1) QB Marques Tuiasosopo had 4y keeper for winning TD earlier in 4th Q; he also threw TD pass that had tied up seesaw battle in 1st Q. TBs Rich Alexis and Paul Arnold contributed 107y and 102y rushing to Huskies cause. Oregon State QB Jonathan Smith (13-25/314y, 3 TDs) followed Tuiasosopo's 4th Q score with 80y TD strike to WR Chad Johnson. Washington won 13th straight in series and gained 504y to 474y by Beavers.

USA Today Coaches October 9

1	Nebraska (53)	1468	14	Mississippi State	673
2	Virginia Tech (3)	1370	15	UCLA	643
3	Kansas State (3)	1358	16	Southern Mississippi	638
4	Clemson	1252	17	Michigan	627
5	Ohio State	1220	18	Northwestern	456
6	Miami (Fla.)	1205	19	Auburn	375
7	Florida State	1068	20	Oregon State	211
8	Oklahoma	1062	21	Purdue	191
9	Florida	1032	22	Arizona	189
10	Washington	847	23	Texas	155
11	TCU	830	24	South Carolina	124
12	Oregon	740	25	Mississippi	115
13	Georgia	679			

October 14, 2000

(Th) VIRGINIA TECH 48 West Virginia 20: After nightmarish 1st H, Virginia Tech (6-0) exploded with 27 pts in 3rd Q as WR Andre Davis (6/127y) excelled. Scoring TDs on 30y run on reverse, 64y bomb from QB Michael Vick (10-18/233y, 2 TDs), and 76y punt RET—all in span of 6:06—Davis finished off West Virginia (4-2). Mountaineers led 14-7 at H as Hokies self-destructed on virtually every series. Vick opened 3rd Q with 72y TD pass to TE Bob Slowikowski to pull Hokies within 14-13. Davis gave Tech lead, but West Virginia answered with long TD drive. Tech D made stop on 4th-and-3 that Vick turned into TD on 64y pass to Davis. Mountaineers had taken early lead on 22y TD run by TB Avon Cobourne and 4y TD pass from QB Brad Lewis to TE Sean Berton.

North Carolina State 38 NORTH CAROLINA 20: No matter what he tried, once again coach Mike O'Cain was on losing end of North Carolina-NC State rivalry. Ironically, Wolfpack (5-1) ended 7-game series losing streak, but O'Cain, their former head coach, was now O coordinator for Tar Heels. It was North Carolina D that could not stop State TB Cotra Jackson, who rushed for 94y and 2 TDs as replacement for injured TB Ray Robinson (23/110y). Tar Heels (3-3) had scored 13 straight pts on 6y TD run by QB Ronald Curry (11-24/114y, 57y rushing) and 2 FGs by K Jeff Reed to pull within 24-20. Although NC State QB Phillip Rivers threw for 202y, it was lowest output so far for frosh.

FLORIDA 38 Auburn 7: Florida (6-1) looked dominant as ever in whacking Tigers in "The Swamp." Frosh QB Rex Grossman (14-23/232y, 5 TDs) capped Gators' 1st 5 series with TD passes, 2 to WR Reche Caldwell in 1st Q and 3 to WR Jabar Gaffney

(4/101y) in 2nd Q, including 1 caught with spectacular leap in back of EZ. Gators D responded to media criticism by holding Tigers (5-2) to QB Ben Leard's 13y TD pass to WR Deandre Green. TB Rudi Johnson rushed for 133y to lead Tigers.

SOUTH CAROLINA 27 Arkansas 7: Sprite Gamecocks (6-1) became bowl eligible, taking control in 1st H when QB Phil Petty (12-21/170y, INT) clicked on pair of TD passes. Meanwhile, South Carolina D permitted only 89y in 1st H. Rushing TDs of 13y by TB Andrew Pinnock and 68y by TB Derek Watson (17/136y) in 3rd Q gave Gamecocks stranglehold at 27-0. Arkansas (4-2) finished with 251y O, its TD coming on RB Brandon Holmes' 9y run in 4th Q. "We're not in the driver's seat," said Carolina coach Lou Holtz in effort to calm his surprising team. "But at least we're in the car."

Purdue 41 NORTHWESTERN 28: Purdue (5-2) QB Drew Brees kept Boilermakers on path to Rose Bowl, throwing for 239y and 5 TDs. He even ran for 56y. Boilermakers RB Montrell Lowe also dazzled, rushing for 174y, while WRs Vinny Sutherland (2) and John Standeford (3) caught scoring passes. Northwestern (5-2) had scored TDs on opening 2 possessions and seemed in command, but Wildcats then were kept off scoreboard until 4th Q, but it came after Purdue blew it open with 20 pts in 3rd Q. NW QB Zak Kustok threw for 260y, but couldn't prevent Wildcats' 1st conf loss of 2000.

Minnesota 29 OHIO STATE 17: Minnesota (5-2) WR Ron Johnson (8/163y) was 1-man wrecking crew, making spectacular catch after spectacular catch in leading Gophers to 1st win over Ohio State (5-1) since 1981 and 1st in Columbus since 1949. Johnson's TD catch was twisting, turning effort around Ohio CB Nate Clements, while 3 scoring drives featured his highlight-reel catches. RB Tellis Redmon also delivered for Minnesota, rushing for 118y and scoring 20y clinching TD run in 4th Q. With rushing attack limited to 70y and QB Steve Bellisari completing 11-28/130y, only bright spot for Buckeyes was RET units, which totaled 222y. Gophers coach Glen Mason, Ohio State alumus and Bucks' O coordinator in 1981, particularly enjoyed Columbus homecoming.

Oklahoma 41 KANSAS STATE 31: Oklahoma (6-0) QB Josh Heupel vaulted into Heisman Trophy race with brilliant play in high profile game. Heupel completed 29-37/374y, 2 TDs to break national title hopes of Kansas State (6-1). After OU took 31-14 H lead, Heupel threw short pass to WR Antwone Savage, who eluded 5 tacklers to score on 74y TD early in 3rd that should have buried Cats. But, K-State rallied on K Jamie Rheem's 38y FG and 2 big-play TDs—QB Jonathan Beasley's 69y TD pass to WR Quincy Morgan and CB Terence Newman's 16y blocked punt RET—to cut deficit to 38-31. Oklahoma regrouped, going to K Tim Duncan's clinching 40y FG. K-State coach Bill Snyder's mark vs Top 10 teams fell to 1-18, while losing to coach by Bob Stoops, former Wildcats D coordinator (1989-95), snapped Cats' 25-game home win streak.

CALIFORNIA 46 Ucla 38 (OT): It took 3 extra sessions, but California (2-4) was willing to wait for upset. TB Joe Igber, who excelled as receiver with 5/126y, 2 TDs, ran 3y for winning score. After successful 2-pt conv, Bears sealed win with CB Jemeel Powell's INT, his 2nd of game. Bruins (4-2) had trailed by 14 pts entering 4th Q, but rallied as QB Cory Paus (20-39/309y, 4 TDs) converted 2 TOs into TD passes of 20y to TB Akil Harris and 35y to WR Freddie Mitchell (8/167y). Cal Bears QB Kyle Boller completed 16-34/252y, 3 TDs, while Bears P Nick Harris had another fine game, booting 7/44.1y avg. UCLA's loss was its 8th straight road defeat.

Oregon 28 SOUTHERN CALIFORNIA 17: Ducks (5-1) went to air often and QB Joey Harrington (28-42/382y) tossed TDs to 4 different receivers. Southern California focused its D on TB Maurice Morris (32/85y), which freed air lanes for Harrington and WRs, led by Keenan Howry (8/126y). Trojans (3-3) had opened scoring on 59y TD scamper by TB Sultan McCullough (23/152y), following key block by QB Carson Palmer (15-35/194y, TD, INT), who had inconsistent passing game, completing only 2-15 during middle of game. Loss was 3rd straight for reeling Trojans and 3rd straight in series, while Ducks defeated USC, UCLA, and Washington in same season for 1st time since 1948.

USA Today Coaches October 16

1	Nebraska (57)	1473	14	Mississippi State	731
2	Virginia Tech (1)	1412	15	Southern Mississippi	713
3	Clemson	1308	16	Michigan	621
4	Oklahoma	1276	17	Purdue	434
5	Miami (Fla.)	1262	18	Oregon State	433
6	Florida State	1166	19	South Carolina	362
7	Florida	1116	20	Arizona	346
8	Kansas State	943	21	Texas	193
9	Washington	934	22	Notre Dame	162
10	TCU	897	23	Minnesota	158
11	Oregon	894	24	UCLA	145
12	Georgia	794	25	North Carolina State	130
13	Ohio State	790			

October 21, 2000

Virginia Tech 22 SYRACUSE 14: With 5-game losing streak in Carrier Dome shadowing Virginia Tech (7-0) coach Frank Beamer, he had to be sweating it out as Hokies trailed 14-0 at H. His O had managed only 78y in 1st H, and his young secondary had allowed Syracuse (3-4) WR Maurice Jackson (4/155y) to beat it for 54y catch to set up TD and for 78y TD. Hokies stayed on course, however, scoring twice on short runs by TB Lee Suggs (21/91y) to take 15-14 lead, before QB Michael Vick iced things with 55y TD run late in 4th Q. Except for his TD, Vick (84y total O) was well-contained by Syracuse D that sacked him 8 times—with DE Dwight Freeney setting school and conf records with 4.5 sacks. Orangemen held nation's 7th-ranked O to 240y, 218y below its avg. Orangemen drew inspiration from 62-0 humiliation they had suffered in Tech in 1999, but did not have enough weapons. Virginia Tech S Willie Pile pulled down 3 INTs to tie Big East single-game mark and set up 2 scores.

LOUISIANA STATE 45 Mississippi State 38 (OT): Tigers brewed some magic as RB LaBrandon Toefield (26/119y) scored in OT from 13y out on toss sweep that worked all night. LSU D then held Bulldogs (4-2) as LBs Jeremy Lawrence and Teverance Faulk combined to tackle QB Wayne Madkins (12-26/215y, INT) on 4th-and-2. Madkins had opened scoring with 82y bomb to WR Terrell Grindle and sent game to OT after his 5y TD pass to RB Justin Griffith. Louisiana State ran for 220y against nation's top-rated rush D (24.2y per game), but displayed balance as QB Josh Booty threw 24-38/246y and 2 TDs, and both WR Josh Reed (10/113y) and WR Reggie Robinson (10/102y) sparkled. Bulldogs had blown 31-17 lead in 4th Q, allowing 21 straight pts.

INDIANA 51 Minnesota 43: To say that QB Antwaan Randle El did it all for Hoosiers (3-4) understated his value: he passed for 263y, 2 TDs, and rushed for 210y, 2 TDs. Randle El even recovered onside-KO with 1:34 left. Indiana RB Levron Williams added 3 TD rushes that averaged slightly less than 24y each. Gophers (5-3) fell behind 24-6 early, but rallied to take 29-24 lead, helped in large part by 100y KO TD RET by WR Jermaine Mays. Minnesota was helpless to prevent Randle El's career-high 473y total O but contributed to 1,100y gained by high-scoring combatants.

Oregon State 44 UCLA 38: Needing every 1 of 604y of O, Beavers (6-1) completed 1st-ever sweep of L.A. schools. Oregon State triumphed because of 9-min span in 4th Q that produced 23 pts in 3 FGs by K Ryan Cesca, 4y TD catch by TE Martin Maurer, and 66y TD run by TB Patrick McCall. Beavers QB Jonathan Smith (23-37/351y, INT) threw 3 TDs, while Bruin QB Cory Paus (19-33/363y) tossed pair of scores. Oregon State's 253y to 72y rushing advantage spelled difference: long drives wore down UCLA (4-3). Oregon State TB Ken Simonton (24/100y) left in 3rd Q with hamstring problems, so all back-up TB McCall did was rush for 146y and tally winning TD. Bruins scored late 18y TD pass to WR Jon Dubravac and then recovered onside-KO, but rally died on 4th down sack by Beavers DE LaDarius Jackson.

OREGON 14 Arizona 10: Oregon (6-1) D took center stage, dominating scrimmage line in chalking up 8 sacks and holding Arizona to 17y rushing. Although Ducks QB Joey Harrington somewhat was stymied in aerial attack with 9-22/104y, he still connected on pair of 1st H TD tosses to WR Marshaun Tucker. TB Maurice Morris helped Ducks win important field position battle with 114y rushing. Wildcats (5-2) drove late in game to Oregon 36YL as QB Ortege Jenkins (15-31/200y, INT) completed 3 passes to WR Brad Brennan for 44y, but 4 straight passes fell incomplete to preserve Oregon's outcome.

USA Today Coaches October 23

1	Nebraska (58)	1478	14	Southern Mississippi	709
2	Virginia Tech	1394	15	Michigan	678
3	Oklahoma (1)	1307	16	Purdue	541
4	Clemson	1306	17	Oregon State	526
5	Miami (Fla.)	1255	18	South Carolina	491
6	Florida State	1181	19	Notre Dame	333
7	Florida	1101	20	Texas	302
8	Kansas State	973	21	Mississippi State	300
9	Washington	950	22	North Carolina State	215
10	Oregon	936	23	Arizona	140
11	TCU	881	24	Colorado State	129
12	Georgia	809	25	Auburn	124
13	Ohio State	799			

Bowl Championship Series Standings October 23

	Poll Avg.	Computer Avg.	Schedule Ranking	Losses	Total
1 Nebraska (7-0)	1.0	1.57	1.04	0	3.61
2 Oklahoma (6-0)	3.0	1.71	0.72	0	5.43
3 Virginia Tech (7-0)	2.0	4.14	0.52	0	6.66
4 Miami (5-1)	4.5	4.14	0.12	1	9.76
5 Florida State (7-1)	6.0	4.14	1.00	1	12.14

October 28, 2000

VIRGINIA TECH 37 Pittsburgh 34: Shape of 2000 season for Virginia Tech (8-0) was greatly affected by ankle injury suffered by QB Michael Vick late in 2nd Q after sack by Pitt LBs Amir Purifoy and Gerald Hayes. It was up to backup QB Dave Meyer, with help from TB Lee Suggs (28/164y), to keep Virginia Tech undefeated. Meyer (7-13/114y) performed admirably, completing 3 straight passes/34y on winning 4th Q drive to K Carter Warley's 27y FG with 16 secs left. Pittsburgh (5-2) had run out of steam by then, despite fine passing of QB John Turman (17-26/311y, 4 TDs) to WRs Antonio Bryant (9/127, 3 TDs) and WR Latef Grim (3/106, TD).

Georgia Tech 31 CLEMSON 28: Georgia Tech went to air to pull upset of Tigers (8-1), caught looking ahead to Florida State. Yellow Jackets (6-2) QB George Godsey pitched 35-57/454y, 3 TDs, including 16y game-winner to WR Kerry Watkins with 7 secs left. Watkins' catch was highlight reel material, as he beat Tigers with 1-handed grab deep in EZ corner. Winning drive took 11 plays to traverse 80y in less than 2 mins. Godsey, who threw 57 passes without INT, set school records for game y and completions. WR Kelly Campbell had school-record-tying 14 receptions/209y. Clemson QB Woody Dantzler, who threw and ran for TDs, left at H with ankle injury, and QB Willie Simmons threw for 131y as replacement.

Florida 34 Georgia 23 (Jacksonville): Georgia (6-2) had chances, at least until Gators DEs Alex Brown and Clint Mitchell converged to sack QB Quincy Carter (20-39/240y, TD) and force FUM to set up RB Robert Gillespie's clinching 2y TD run. Play preceding TD was QB Rex Grossman's 27y arrow to WR Reche Caldwell. Florida (7-1) D picked off 3 passes, with CB Lito Shepherd's 61y INT RET setting up 1st H TD for 17-17 tie. Florida coach Steve Spurrier pulled Grossman (12-24/152y, TD, 3 INTs) after INTs on his 1st 2 passes, but reinserted him after QB Jesse Palmer (6-12/95y, TD) sprained his ankle in 3rd Q. Palmer had reeled off 18 straight pts from late in 1st H. WR

Jabar Gaffney (8/138y) was favorite target of both QBs. With RB Musa Smith rushing for 50y and 2 TDs 11 days after knee surgery, Bulldogs gained 413y to Gators' 306y, but still lost 10th of last 11 series games.

PURDUE 31 Ohio State 27: Sweep of Michigan and Ohio State propelled Purdue (7-2) into driver's seat for Rose Bowl. Boilermakers QB Drew Brees threw for 455y and 3 TDs, yet almost was goat as his 4th INT set-up RB Jerry Westbrooks' 2y TD run that gave Buckeyes (6-2) 27-24 lead with 2:16 left. There was more than enough time for Brees to redeem himself and on 2nd play after KO he connected with WR Seth Morales on 64y scoring pass for his 3rd TD of 4th Q. Brees looked off three covered receivers until finding Morales. Ohio State had taken 20-10 lead into 4th Q with help from CB Nate Clements, who returned punt 83y for TD. Purdue WR Vinny Sutherland caught 10/142y and 19y TD that put Purdue up 24-20 in seesaw contest.

Northwestern 41 MINNESOTA 35: Cinderella Wildcats (6-2) rallied from 21-pt deficit to win on amazing Hail Mary pass at game's end. QB Zak Kustok's 45y pass was deflected on purpose by WR Kunle Patrick—on play called "Victory Right" practiced every Thursday—to WR Sam Simmons (5/91y) for win. Northwestern registered game's last 27 pts as Kustok (18-32/209y) threw 2 TDs to Simmons and ran for 2 TDs. TB Damien Anderson led Northwestern run game with 230y and 2 TDs. Minnesota (5-4) had built 3-TD lead with big-play TDs of its own as QB Travis Cole (18-33/251y) tossed 32y TD to WR Ron Johnson (4/77y), P Preston Gruenning threw 45y TD pass to WR Elvin Jones on fake punt, and RB Tellis Redmon took punt RET 83y to EZ. Amazingly, Northwestern scored 4 of its TDs on 4th down plays.

NOTRE DAME 34 Air Force 31 (OT): Phrase "Luck of the Irish" had been rarely used during coach Bob Davie's time at Notre Dame (6-2), but magic was needed when Air Force K Dave Adams lined up 28y FG try at end of 4th Q. Falcons had rallied for 18 pts in 4th Q and were threatening to add FG before S Glenn Earl—who was supposed to hang back in case of fake—blocked Adams' kick to force OT. WR Joey Getherall (4/116y, 2 TDs) ran in 9y TD in OT to offset Adams' 26y FG and keep Irish in running for BCS bowl. During 4th Q rally, Air Force (5-3) enjoyed 265y to 30y O advantage behind QB Mike Thiessen (17-29/255y) who began rally with 30y TD pass to TE Chris Jessop. Notre Dame had taken lead with 3 TDs in 3rd Q as QB Matt LoVecchio hit Geatherall with TD passes of 28y and 68y, and WR David Givens raced 37y to EZ on reverse.

GAME OF THE YEAR
OKLAHOMA 31 Nebraska 14:

Both old foes entered game ranked in Top 5 for 1st time since 1987. Nebraska (7-1) raced to 14-0 lead, but Huskers had to play 2nd Q, and Oklahoma racked up 24 pts. Sooners gained 192y in 2nd Q, during which Nebraska had but 16y. Sooners QB Josh Heupel (20-34/300y) went to air for 7-10/149y and 34y TD to WR Curtis Fagan. Huskers still led, 14-7, when OU WR Andre Woolfolk made stunning catch of own tipped ball for 34y gain. Later on same march, Heupel found EZ on 3rd-and-14, backpedaling to buy time for Fagan to get open for his scoot into EZ. Oklahoma blocked punt, which was converted into 3-pt lead on K Tim Duncan's 19y FG. Sooners finished 1st H with E-around by WR Josh Norman for 8y TD. Oklahoma D broke Nebraska's heart on Huskers' 1st possession of 2nd H: it created 2 sacks by LB Torrance Marshall (12 tackles) and INT TD RET by CB Derrick Strait. Both Ds threw shutouts rest of way. Nebraska's opening 2 drives of 1st Q, which by game's end were mere memories, had concluded in 39y TD pass to WR Matt Davison, on play action that suckered Strait, and QB Eric Crouch's 37y run. Huskers ran 11 plays/167y on those marches, but gained only 161y over final 53:11. Crouch ran for 103y and passed 133y. Oklahoma was 3rd team ever to beat nos. 1 and 2 in consecutive weeks.

IOWA STATE 39 Missouri 20: Downed goalposts once meant something, but fans of improved Iowa State (6-2), tried to destroy uprights after rout of lowly Missouri (2-6). Even at that, Iowans failed to knock them down. After scoring 20 pts in 2nd Q for 26-14 lead, Iowa State never looked back. Cyclones TB Ennis Haywood rushed for 214y with TD runs of 14y and 4y. With dangerous QB Darius Outlaw throwing for 171y and rushing for 107y, Tigers were able to gain impressive 427y O.

TEXAS A&M 26 Kansas State 10: Texas A&M (6-2) played keep-away in ending Kansas State's string of 60 wins in row over unranked foes. Committing no TOs as they dominated time of possession, 36:18 to 23:42, Texas A&M grabbed 19-0 H lead and never let Wildcats (7-2) build any momentum. Big FB Ja'Mar Toombs rushed for 89y, 3 TDs to lead conservative, yet effective Aggies O. Erratic K-State QB Jonathan Beasley threw 14-39/227y, TD with WR Aaron Lockett (6/119y) serving as favorite target and nabbing 31y TD arrow. Texas A&M improved to 11-4 at home against ranked teams under quiet, confident coach R.C. Slocum.

Oregon 56 ARIZONA STATE 55 (OT): Ahead by 7 pts with time running out, Arizona State (5-3) coach Bruce Snyder elected to have frosh TB Mike Williams carry ball instead of having QB Jeff Krohn (21-34/432y, 5 TDs) take knee. Sadly, Williams lost FUM. Oregon (7-1) tied game moments later as QB Joey Harrington (26-43/434y) forced OT when he threw his 6th TD pass, 17y to TE Justin Peelle. Both teams scored TDs in 2nd OT, Oregon on 1y run by TB Allan Amundson and ASU pulling to within 56-55 after Krohn threw 21y to WR Richard Williams. Snyder passed up tying x-pt try and went for 2 pts on fake kick, play that failed as Krohn's pass to TE Todd Heap (6/98y) fell incomplete. Scorebook showed remarkable symmetry as each team scored 7 pts in 1st Q, 14 in 2nd Q, 7 in 3rd Q, and 21 in 4th Q, with ASU squandering leads in each Q. Sun Devils gained 667y against Oregon's 10th-ranked D, while Ducks maneuvered for 565y.

USA Today Coaches October 30

1	Oklahoma (55)	1470	14	Oregon State	646
2	Virginia Tech (4)	1403	15	Kansas State	590
3	Miami (Fla.)	1324	16	Notre Dame	489
4	Florida State	1289	17	Georgia	486
5	Florida	1217	18	Mississippi State	445
6	Nebraska	1180	19	Ohio State	444
7	Washington	1076	20	Texas	426
8	Oregon	1047	21	Colorado State	233
9	TCU	984	22	Auburn	222
10	Clemson	964	23	Northwestern	201
11	Southern Mississippi	805	24	South Carolina	184
12	Michigan	779	25	Texas A&M	151
13	Purdue	777			

Bowl Championship Series Standings October 30

	Poll Avg.	Computer Avg.	Schedule Ranking	Losses	Total
1 Oklahoma (7-0)	1.0	1.00	0.48	0	2.48
2 Virginia Tech (8-0)	2.0	4.43	0.72	0	7.15
3 Florida State (8-1)	4.0	2.29	0.64	1	7.93
4 Nebraska (7-1)	5.5	3.00	0.68	1	10.18
5 Miami (6-1)	3.0	5.57	0.80	1	10.37

November 4, 2000

MIAMI 41 Virginia Tech 21: With QB Michael Vick gamely playing about 15 mins of action, no. 2 Virginia Tech (8-1) was no match for high-flying no. 3 Miami (7-1). With Hokies trailing 14-0 late in 1st Q, Vick entered game, managing only 9y passing and 5y rushing, but also suffering FUM and INT. Vick departed for good with Hokies down 21-0. Highly-effective Miami QB Ken Dorsey completed 11-23/283y, 3 TDs, with WR Santana Moss (4/154y) scoring TDs of 42y and 80y. Canes RB James Jackson rushed for 145y and TD behind O-line that prevented any sacks in another big game. Miami S Al Blades had career-high 16 tackles. Hokies rode TB Lee Suggs, who rushed for 23/121y and scored 2 TDs. Hurricanes snapped 5-game series losing streak, while loss snapped Hokies' impressive 19-game regular season winning streak.

FLORIDA STATE 54 Clemson 7: After this whipping administered by Florida State (9-1), it seems like ancient history that Tigers (8-2) were ranked in top 5 as recently as October 22. FSU WR Snoop Minnis (4/164y) led charge by scoring on 98y TD reception in 1st Q on play that QB Chris Weinke was able to fool entire Clemson D. Standing in EZ for what seemed like eternity, ball on hip after faking Tigers front-7, Weinke patiently waited for Minnis to break open and hit him on stride at 35YL. FSU had another pair of wideouts top 100y in receiving: WR Atrews Bell (6/111y) and WR Javon Walker (6/109y). Weinke padded Heisman resume with 27-43/521y passing. With eyes firmly on BCS, Seminoles coach Bobby Bowden had Weinke directing attack until pt total reached 47. In wrapping up 9th straight ACC title, Seminoles gained 771y, most ever surrendered by any Clemson club.

NORTHWESTERN 54 Michigan 51: In amazing finish, Wildcats (7-2) pulled out victory as WR Sam Simmons (12/124y) caught 11y TD pass with 20 secs left against Wolverines D that was coming off 2 straight shutouts. Moments earlier, Michigan (6-3) was comfortably was running out clock when TB Anthony Thomas (37/199y, 3 TDs) lost FUM on play he had gained 1st down that should have ended matters. Ball was stripped by CB Sean Wieber and recovered by CB Raheem Covington. Northwestern TB Damien Anderson, who rushed for 268y and 2 TDs, had dropped 4th down pass in EZ less than min earlier that seemed to be final stake hammered into Wildcats' hope for victory. Wolverines had chance to tie at game's end on 57y FG attempt by K Hayden Epstein, who previously hit 52y FG. Snap went through hands of holder and Epstein was forced to fling desperation pass to FB Evan Coleman, who was tackled at 33YL. Michigan QB Drew Henson completed 23-35/312y and school-record tying 4 TDs, while Wildcats QB Zak Kustok completed 27-40/322y, 2 TDs, adding 55y and 2 TDs rushing as opponents combined for staggering 1189y total O. WR David Terrell (9/117y) caught 3 TDs for Michigan team that now had lost 3 road games by total of 7 pts. Anderson's 2 scores gave him 18 TDs for year, tying Darnell Autry's school record, while his rushing total was most ever surrendered by Michigan.

Texas 29 TEXAS TECH 17: Speedy Texas (7-2) TB Hodges Mitchell emerged from under spotlight trained on QB teammates to rush for 45/229y, more than doubling his season output. Mitchell also caught 6/38y and rushed for both Longhorn TDs. Texas game-plan turned to Mitchell from opening KO as he gained 114y in 1st Q and set up 1st of 5 FGs by K Kris Stockton, from 22y out, and his own 5y TD run. Lead increased to 16-0 before quick-striking Red Raiders (6-4) made 17 straight pts to take lead at 17-16. Stockton answered with another FG, and Texas failed to muster additional pts thanks to Texas' tough D and Raiders' 5 TOs. Rubber-armed Tech QB Kliff Kingsbury completed 29-49/282y, while Texas QB Major Applewhite threw for 164y before leaving in 3rd Q with recurrence of knee injury.

SAN JOSE STATE 27 Texas Christian 24: Spartans (7-3) broke open 17-17 deadlock with 10 pts and then withstood TCU's rally. On 4th-and-1 from midfield with 1:16 left, Horned Frogs (7-1) went to air. Pass fell incomplete, and rampant discussion of Horned Frogs' BCS merits went silent. TCU TB LaDainian Tomlinson rushed for 155y and 2 TDs in defeat. San Jose State was inspired by presence of special teamer Neil Parry, whose right foot and ankle had been amputated following injury in UTEP game October 14. San Jose State D, ranked last in nation, shut out Horned Frogs for more than 30 mins, allowing its O to score 24 straight pts for 27-17 lead. Spartans QB Marcus Arroyo threw for 237y and 2 TDs.

WASHINGTON 35 Arizona 32: Once again Washington (8-1) had to rally, needing QB Marques Tuiasosopo's 2y TD run with 1:10 left and CB Anthony Vontoure's block of 51y FG attempt as time expired. Perhaps caught up in emotion of pre-game ceremony

for injured DB Curtis Williams, Huskies surrendered 16 pts and 301y to Arizona (5-4) in 1st H. Wildcats RB Leo Mills excelled in 1st H, rushing for 119y of his eventual 185y and scoring on 10y TD run. Arizona stretched 16-10 H lead to 25-10 as WR Bobby Wade returned punt 60y for TD early in 3rd Q, and K Sean Keel booted his 2nd FG. Staying patient with option attack, Huskies exploded for 25 of game's final 32 pts. TB Willie Hurst (8/116y) broke off TD runs of 65y and 23y to spark Washington's comeback.

USA Today Coaches November 6

1	Oklahoma (58)	1474	14	Ohio State	604
2	Miami (Fla.) (1)	1403	15	Clemson	588
3	Florida State	1352	16	Mississippi State	579
4	Florida	1272	17	TCU	518
5	Nebraska	1265	18	Northwestern	470
6	Washington	1139	19	Texas	462
7	Oregon	1121	20	Colorado State	380
8	Virginia Tech	1081	21	Michigan	312
9	Purdue	935	22	Southern Mississippi	261
10	Oregon State	886	23	Auburn	252
11	Kansas State	807	24	Texas A&M	206
12	Notre Dame	655	25	South Carolina	199
13	Georgia	634			

Bowl Championship Series Standings November 6

	Poll Avg.	Computer Avg.	Schedule Ranking	Losses	Total
1 Oklahoma (8-0)	1.0	1.00	0.76	0	2.76
2 Florida State (9-1)	3.0	2.14	0.28	1	6.42
3 Miami (7-1)	2.0	3.57	0.24	1	6.81
4 Nebraska (8-1)	4.5	3.29	0.88	1	9.67
5 Florida (8-1)	4.5	5.00	0.68	1	11.18

November 11, 2000

MIAMI 35 Pittsburgh 7: It was record-setting day for Hurricanes (8-1), but they remained on outside of BCS title match. LB Dan Morgan totaled 13 tackles on way to Miami career mark (500), and WR Santana Moss (6/100y) had new pass receiving y (2462y). Panthers (5-4) WR Antonio Bryant received rude welcome home to Miami as he was held to 4/31y receiving. Hurricanes CB Phillip Buchanan helped contain Bryant and intercepted 2 passes, including 71y RET for game's opening TD. Miami defenders had returned 6 INTs for TDs, also school season record.

FLORIDA 41 South Carolina 21: In odd game, Florida (9-1) spotted Gamecocks (7-3) 18-pt lead, thanks to blocked punts returned for TDs by WR Carlos Spikes and RB Derek Watson within span of 7 plays. But, Gators exploded for 38 straight pts—including deflected pass TD by G Tommy Moody—to capture its 7th SEC East crown. P Alan Rhine sparked Gators by running around LE for 25y on fake punt. QB Jesse Palmer (15-27/250y) relieved QB Rex Grossman (12-19/106y) and threw pass bouncing off Carolina DB Sheldon Brown's helmet to WR Jabar Gaffney (7/168y) for 40y. It was followed by 6y TD pass to WR Reche Caldwell. Gaffney got his 13th TD of year on 72y catch. CB Lito Sheppard buried Carolina with 57y punt TD RET with 2 secs left in 1st H.

AUBURN 29 Georgia 26 (OT): After Georgia settled in OT for 25y FG by K Billy Bennett, Tigers (8-2) TB Rudi Johnson (34/152y) made 21y on 3 carries to set up QB Ben Leard's winning 1y keeper. With Johnson rushing for 104y, Auburn scored 23 consecutive pts from late in 2nd Q to early in 4th Q to take 23-13 edge. Leard (24-38/149y, 2 INTs) threw 2 TDs during that stretch. Bulldogs (6-3) scored 10 pts in 4th Q to send game into extra session on 16y pass from reserve QB Cory Phillips (23-35/164y, INT) to WR Terrence Edwards and 19y FG by Bennett.

MICHIGAN STATE 30 Purdue 10: Spartans (5-5) refused to let Purdue (7-3) clinch Rose Bowl berth on their watch, employing running of big TB T.J. Duckett (32/174y, TD) and passing D ranked 2nd in nation. Although QB Drew Brees threw for 279y, he was picked off 3 times, as Purdue was held to 24 pts lower than its season avg. Michigan State frosh QB Jeff Smoker completed 12-23/195y and TD, while also scrambling for valuable 1st downs 3 times. Early in 3rd Q, Brees threw his only TD pass, 68y to WR Vinny Sutherland, to cut deficit to 15-10. Spartans then scored on consecutive possessions, with help from CB Renaldo Hill's INT, to finish off Boilermakers.

IOWA 27 Northwestern 17: High-flying Northwestern (7-3) laid egg against Iowa (3-8) D in blowing opportunity to move into 1st place in Big Ten. Wildcats were held to 348y, 109y below their O avg, as slumbering Iowa awoke to win consecutive games for 1st time since 1997. QB Kyle McCann (17-27/250y) threw 2 TDs and ran in another to lead Hawkeyes. Northwestern TB Damien Anderson rushed for 132y, but was kept out of EZ, while QB Zak Kustok threw for 248y and had TDs passing and rushing. Rugged Iowa S Bob Sanders had 14 hard-hitting tackles to thwart Cats' no-huddle attack.

Oklahoma 35 TEXAS A&M 31: Oklahoma LB Torrance Marshall had moment of glory with winning TD on 41y INT RET with 7:18 remaining. It was Marshall's 1st-ever INT. Sooners (9-0) had just moved to within 3 pts on RB Quentin Griffin's 2y TD run. Aggies (7-3) had 1 more chance, beginning on Sooners 44YL, Texas A&M fell short after 4th down completion on 4th-and-goal was halted at OU 4YL. Oklahoma QB Josh Heupel finished with 28-42/263y, TD, 2 INTs against mobile Texas A&M D that was inspired by previous season's 51-6 defeat by Sooners. Play of year for Aggies in losing cause had occurred early in 4th Q when FB Ja'Mar Toombs (18/72y) carried 4 Oklahoma defenders into EZ on 4th down 27y TD rumble that gave encouraging 31-20 lead to Texas A&M.

KANSAS STATE 29 Nebraska 28: Wildcats (9-2) grabbed 1st place in Big 12 North with their 2nd win over Top 10 team in 20 tries during coach Bill Snyder's reign. Mixture of rain, sleet, snow, and Huskers D could not stay Kansas State WR Quincy Morgan from his swift rounds, as he turned in 7/199y and 2 TDs. Nebraska struggled on O through

3 Qs, gaining only 105y. IB Dan Alexander (19/130y) then took charge for Huskers, scoring on 19y TD run and then, on next scoring drive, gaining all 74y, on 5 carries as Nebraska (8-2) took 28-23 lead. Morgan was not done, catching 12y pass from QB Jonathan Beasley for winning TD with nearly 3 mins left. Nebraska hopes ended on 4th-and-5 incompletion—QB Eric Crouch hit only 2-14—that bounced off hands of WR Matt Davison. Win was only 2nd against Nebraska in 13 games for Snyder. Arousing game produced 24 PENs/197y; completely-spent Beasley broke down in tears after game.

Bowl Championship Series Standings November 13

	Poll Avg.	Computer Avg.	Schedule Ranking	Losses	Total
1 Oklahoma (9-0)	1.0	1.00	0.52	0	2.52
2 Miami (8-1)	2.0	3.14	0.20	1	6.34
3 Florida State (10-1)	3.0	2.14	0.68	1	6.82
4 Florida (9-1)	4.0	4.14	0.48	1	9.62
5 Washington (9-1)	5.5	6.86	0.08	1	13.44

November 18, 2000

Miami 26 SYRACUSE 0: While revenge for past blowouts by Orangemen was on Canes' mind, Miami (9-1) was more focused on BCS rankings. It took Hurricanes 20 mins to put away Syracuse (5-5), scoring all 3 of their TDs within 1st 5 mins of 2nd Q. Miami QB Ken Dorsey (16-28/263y) completed 5-6/119y on 1st 2 scoring drives, capping 2nd with 32y TD pass to WR Reggie Wayne. Hurricanes RB James Jackson scored 2 TDs and rushed for 101y. RB James Mungro eked out 50y rushing to lead Syracuse's meager O that totaled 166y, while Orange pass rush was limited by viral infection that kept DE Dwight Freeney on sideline.

FLORIDA STATE 30 Florida 7: Seminoles (11-1) regained 2nd place in BCS standings with convincing win. Fighting flu, Florida State QB Chris Weinke (23-44/353y, 2 INTs) led scoring drives of 77y and 84y, completing 8-10 to do so, as team forged 14-7 lead. For 2nd score, Weinke hit WR Atrews Bell with 42y completion just before 34y TD pass to WR Snoop Minnis (8/187y), who badly beat Florida (9-2) CB Bennie Alexander, in for injured H as Weinke offset Noles' 279y in 1st H with 2 INTs. Florida had no answer in 2nd H for Weinke and Minnis, however, as interference PEN on returning Sheppard set up FSU FB William McCray's 1y scoring plunge for 21-7 lead. Minnis later reeled in 51y TD pass to put game away. QB Jesse Palmer (17-30/180y, 2 INTs) got bulk of time for Gators. Winner would go on to play for national title for 6th time in last 8 seasons.

CLEMSON 16 South Carolina 14: Tigers (9-2) pulled victory out of thin air as tall WR Rod Gardner drifted down sideline for stunning 50y reception with 10 secs left. Clemson frosh K Aaron Hunt then booted 25y FG, his 3rd 3-pter of game, to pull out unlikely win. South Carolina (7-4) had just taken lead when TE Thomas Hill recovered RB Derek Watson's FUM in EZ with 59 ticks left. Trailing for 1st time, Clemson QB Woody Dantzler (14-28/185y) looked for Gardner (4/107y) on desperation pass that succeeded with help from some jostling of defenders by Gardner. Watson rushed for 150y, including long ramble off left side early in game. South Carolina QB Phil Petty threw for 200y with 3 INTs.

Arkansas 17 MISSISSIPPI STATE 10 (OT): After RB Brandon Holmes (16/95) scored on 7y run, Razorbacks (5-5) D thwarted Bulldogs' 4th-and-1 run to emerge victorious in extra session. Hogs LBs Quenton Caver and J.J. Jones combined to bring down Mississippi State (7-3) RB Dontae Walker as he swept left from 1YL. Mississippi State had converted 4th-and-21 to keep its OT drive alive, as QB Wayne Madkins found WR Terrell Grindle for required 21y. Bulldogs opened up with 10-pt 1st Q, but snoozed on O as Arkansas tied it. Bulldogs maneuvered for last-sec FG attempt by K Scott Westerfield, which was blocked to set up OT.

Michigan 38 OHIO STATE 26: Michigan (8-3) QB Drew Henson threw 3 TDs and ran for another as Wolverines erased early 9-0 deficit by scoring 31 of game's next 34 pts. Henson (14-25/303y, 3 TDs, INT) combined with TB Anthony Thomas on 70y TD pass play and then WR David Terrell on 21y scoring pass to give Michigan 14-9 lead. Ohio State (8-3) K Dan Stultz kicked 26y FG as 1st H elapsed to bring Buckeyes within 14-12. Michigan owned 3rd Q as Henson hooked up with Terrell for 32y score, K Hayden Epstein kicked 32y FG, and S Julius Curry authored 50y INT TD RET. Bucks showed some life, scoring twice to cut lead to 5 pts as TB Jonathan Wells ran for 2y TD, and QB Steve Bellisari hit WR Ken-Yon Rambo with 18y TD pass. All 3 of Wolverines' losses in 2000 had come when they led entering 4th Q, but Ohio could not rally as Wells was stopped on 4th-and-1 at his own 18YL with about 3 mins left. Henson added 1y TD run to seal it. Ohio State coach John Cooper's record against Michigan fell to 2-10-1.

OKLAHOMA 27 Texas Tech 13: Sooners (10-0) did not put away Texas Tech, coached by OU's former O coordinator Mike Leach, until 71y drive late in 4th Q. QB Josh Heupel (24-38/248y) hit 7-8/60y on drive, to set up 1y scoring run by RB Quentin

Griffin. Oklahoma O managed only 7 pts in 1st H, although Sooners led 14-3 because S J.T. Thatcher ran back INT 85y for opening score. Red Raiders (7-5) QB Kliff Kingsbury passed 41-61/295y and helped Texas Tech control large portions of game, but couldn't find EZ until midway through 4th Q on his 15y TD pass to WR Tim Baker. Sooners often struggled, suffering 2 INTs, 2 lost FUMs, and 11 PENs/124y.

TEXAS CHRISTIAN 47 Texas-El Paso 14: UTEP (8-3) held TCU (9-1) TB LaDainian Tomlinson to 101y fewer rushing y than he achieved prior year against Miners, but it is not good enough. Tomlinson gained "only" 305y with 3 TDs to lead rout of Miners, team he had burned for NCAA single-game rushing mark of 406y in 1999. Tomlinson's 1st 2 scores were breathtaking, rushing for 68y on 1st Q play in which he became all-time WAC rushing leader, and then adding 89y jaunt in 3rd Q. On 2nd long run, Tomlinson became 9th player to top 5000y in NCAA history. Horned Frogs QB Casey Printers (10-18/216y) added 2 TD passes. QB Rocky Perez (21-47/217y) led Texas-El Paso to 7-0 1st Q lead before Miners D allowed game's next 44 pts.

OREGON STATE 23 Oregon 13: Never before had state's "Civil War" meant so much nationally, pitting pair of Top 10 teams. Beavers (10-1) led throughout, picking off 5 passes in making their 1st Q lead of 14-0 hold up. Oregon State QB Jonathan Smith (14-27/246y, INT) threw 2 TD passes to WR Robert Prescott (6/109y) for that early edge. Beavers TB Ken Simonton (24/113y) added 20y TD run in 3rd Q for 23-7 lead. Led by QB Joey Harrington (24-46/333y), Ducks (9-2) gained more y and had more 1st downs, but could not overcome their 6 TOs. Harrington entered contest with 7 INTs on season and left with 12. Beavers S Jake Cookus nabbed 3 INTs. Result created 3-way tie for Pac-10 title among Oregon State, Oregon, and Washington, who whipped Washington State 51-3. Huskies slipped into Rose Bowl due to complex tiebreakers based on non-conf records.

Bowl Championship Series Standings November 20

	Poll Avg.	Computer Avg.	Schedule Ranking	Losses	Total
1 Oklahoma (10-0)	1.0	1.43	0.52	0	2.95
2 Florida State (11-1)	3.0	1.43	0.12	1	5.55
3 Miami (9-1)	2.0	2.86	0.20	1	6.06
4 Washington (10-1)	4.0	5.14	0.32	1	10.46
5 Oregon State (10-1)	5.5	5.71	1.12	1	13.33

November 23-25, 2000

(Th'g) MISSISSIPPI 45 Mississippi State 30: TB Deuce McAllister rushed for 121y and 3 TDs and threw another to lead Rebels (7-4) in game dedicated to his brother, who died earlier in month. Mississippi State (7-4) opened with 16-0 lead, scoring TDs on 39y catch by WR Terrell Grindle and 1y TD run by RB Dontae Walker (14/121y). With State QB Wayne Madkins soon knocked out with injury, Rebels scored 3 TDs in final 7:22 of 2nd Q. Rebs opened 2nd H with McAlister's 72y run for 28-16 lead. Bulldogs retaliated as Walker scored his 2nd and 3rd TDs for 30-28 lead. Ole Miss turned tricky to answer with winning TD: McAllister swept right and threw pass back to QB Romaro Miller for 20y TD. Rebels added 10 pts in 4th Q pts to make it highest-scoring Egg Bowl to date. Rebels D terrorized sub QB Kevin Fant, sacking him 7 times.

(Fri) TEXAS 43 Texas A&M 17: Texas (9-2) QB controversy continued to brew as QB Chris Simms (16-24/383y) completed all of his 8 pass attempts in 3rd Q for 234y and 3 TDs to quiet doubters—at least on this day. Simms' 3 targets for those scoring passes were all frosh WRs: Roy Williams (4/85y), B.J. Johnson (6/187y) and Sloan Thomas (2/74y). Williams also scored on 40y run on reverse. Aggies (7-4) were forced to throw and QB Mark Farris completed 25-43/290y, including 56y TD to WR Mickey Jones.

(Fri) NEBRASKA 34 Colorado 32: Huskers (9-2) needed 29y FG by K Josh Brown as time expired to pull out win. Colorado (3-8) QB Craig Ochs (25-41/254y) threw 15y TD throw to WR John Minardi (6/85y) with 47 secs remaining that looked like game-winner when Ochs added 2-pt conv throw to WR Javon Green for 32-31 lead. QB Eric Crouch, who threw for 139y and rushed for 125y, moved Nebraska 47y, completing 3-4 passes along way, including 17y throw to WR Bobby Newcombe with 10 secs left. Win was 9th straight in series for Nebraska, but avg margin of victory in last 5 victories was down to 3 pts. TB Cortlen Johnson led Buffs with 155y rushing and 3 TDs.

(Fri) Brigham Young 34 UTAH 27: "What a way to go out," Brigham Young (6-6) coach LaVell Edwards exclaimed after QB Brandon Doman rushed in winning 4y run with 23 secs left. "That was my best win ever!" Edwards' career-win no. 257 featured heroic final drive as Doman completed 4th-and-13 pass of 34y to WR Jonathan Pittman and hit him for 36y pass to set up TD. On play before 4th down conv, HB Luke Staley appeared to have lost FUM. Utah (4-7) scored 17 straight pts in 4th Q to stun Cougars, taking 27-26 lead with 2:16 left on 20y TD pass from QB Darnell Arceneaux to TE Matt Nickel.

(Fri) Arizona State 30 ARIZONA 17: Teams battled for bragging rights and bowl bid, while bidding farewell to both coaches. Arizona (5-6) coach Dick Tomey, who guided Wildcats for 14 seasons, retired to join fired counterpart Bruce Snyder, who had been in Tempe for 9 seasons. Sun Devils (6-5) made some big plays: REC of Arizona FUM in EZ by rampaging DE Terrell Suggs became 6 pts, as did 13y run off fake FG by K Mike Barth. Barth followed TOs by Wildcats with 2 of his 3 FGs. Arizona outgained Arizona State, 371y to 264y, but was ruined by 3 TOs. Wildcats QB Ortege Jenkins threw for 176y, including 14y TD pass to TE Brandon Manumaleuna for 17-13 lead in 3rd Q.

Georgia Tech 27 GEORGIA 15: Georgia Tech (9-2) raced out to 27-3 H lead and held off Bulldogs for 3rd straight series win. QB George Godsey (20-35/222y, 2 INTs) looked like predecessor, QB Joe Hamilton, on 33y TD run that opened scoring. He later threw 8y TD pass to WR Kerry Watkins and led drives to K Luke Manget's 3 FGs. LB Darryl Smith added 70y INT TD RET to seal Bulldogs' fate. Georgia (7-4) managed 2 TD passes by QB Corey Phillips (36-62/413y, 2 INTs) in 3rd Q, but stalled thereafter.

Oklahoma 12 OKLAHOMA STATE 7: Suddenly, Sooners (11-0) were playing shaky ball, but still completed 1st perfect regular season since 1987. Oklahoma D needed late 4th down tip in EZ by CB Derrick Strait on potential winning pass from QB Aso Pogi to TE Marcellus Rivers to hold off inspired Cowboys (3-8). Sooners O had to kill clock at game's end, and QB Josh Heupel (19-36/154y, 2 INTs) made pair of 1st downs, on 12y pass to WR Curtis Fagan on 3rd-and-11 and 4y run on 3rd-and-2 with 38 secs left. Game began well for Sooners on opening 99y drive that ended on Heupel's 3y TD pass to Fagan. Oklahoma O managed only 3 pts rest of way as Cowboys played tenaciously in final game for coach Bob Simmons, who resigned under pressure. Lone score for Oklahoma State came on 60y burst by TB Tatum Bell in 3rd Q.

Notre Dame 38 SOUTHERN CALIFORNIA 21: Notre Dame (9-2) converted 2 blocked punts into TDs and added scores after 2 INTs to win its 7th straight. Frosh QB Matt LoVecchio ran his starting record to 7-0 as he scored twice and led efficient O with 142y passing and 45y rushing, with 13y TD run in 2nd Q that put Irish up for good, 14-7. His mistake-free play had been demonstrated by having thrown only 1 INT in 7 starts. Trojans (5-7) QB Carson Palmer passed for 251y, 2 TDs, but had 2 INTs and FUM as Southern California finished with its 1st losing season since 1991. Win was worth $13.5 million as Irish earned BCS spot by finishing regular season in top 12 in polls.

USA Today Coaches November 27

1	Oklahoma (49)	1458	14	Purdue	675
2	Miami (Fla.) (5)	1410	15	TCU	620
3	Florida State (5)	1368	16	Michigan	610
4	Washington	1298	17	Auburn	564
5	Virginia Tech	1209	18	Georgia Tech	490
6	Oregon State	1181	19	Ohio State	392
7	Kansas State	1098	20	Northwestern	378
8	Florida	1026	21	Tennessee	281
9	Nebraska	1001	22	Colorado State	249
10	Notre Dame	871	23	Louisville	137
11	Oregon	869	24	Georgia	92
12	Texas	771	25	Toledo	61
13	Clemson	768			

Bowl Championship Series Standings November 27

	Poll Avg.	Computer Avg.	Schedule Ranking	Losses	Total
1 Oklahoma (11-0)	1.0	2.00	0.96	0	3.96
2 Florida State (11-1)	3.0	1.14	0.04	1	5.18
3 Miami (10-1)	2.0	2.71	0.08	1	5.79
4 Washington (10-1)	4.0	4.86	0.32	1	10.18
5 Virginia Tech (10-1)	5.5	5.29	0.52	1	12.31

December 2, 2000

Navy 30 Army 28 (Baltimore): Game ended in controversy as Army (1-10) rally ended with running-into-K PEN with 1:29 left. Cadets had narrowed 20-pt deficit to 30-28 and would be back on O after missed FG by Navy K David Hills. Instead PEN was called on CB Andrew Burke, who, after tripping over Navy player's leg, brushed Hills' back after kick. Navy (1-10) QB Brian Broadwater then took knee for 3 straight plays and game ended amid chorus of boos. Game had begun better for Army as RB Michael Wallace (19/159y) raced 65y to open scoring. Navy reeled off 27 straight pts as Broadwater (23/121y rushing) ran option to perfection, and Middies D forced 5 TOs. S Ben Woodruff recovered blocked punt for TD for Army's 1st scoring response. Then backup QB Curtis Zervic found WR Brian Breunton for 23y score on 4th-and-16, and, in 4th Q, Zervic followed up by hitting WR Anthony Miller for 21y score. Academies' combined 2-20 record was worst year-end W-L mark in history.

Florida 28 Auburn 6: In SEC Championship title game, Gators (10-2) manhandled Auburn for 2nd time in 2000 to win 6th conf title, 1st since 1996. Florida was unchallenged as QB Rex Grossman (17-26/238y, INT) enjoyed virtual full reign by throwing 4 TD passes. Florida RB Ernest Graham rushed for 169y. Auburn (9-3) lost FUM on 1st possession, which led to Grossman's needle-threading pass to WR Reche Caldwell for 10y TD. Caldwell scored again later in 1st Q as he took short pass and raced downfield for spectacular and backbreaking 66y TD. Auburn QB Ben Leard (17-30/158y, INT) tried to spark O that managed only 2 FGs by K Damon Duval.

MARSHALL 19 Western Michigan 14: Marshall (7-5), in midst of supposed rebuilding year, won MAC crown and trip to Motor City Bowl for 4th straight year. Despite blowout losses to Toledo and Western Michigan during regular season, Marshall won East Division on tiebreaker and hosted championship tilt. Thundering Herd QB Byron Leftwich (29-45/358y) was not to be denied as his 29y TD pass to WR John Cooper

midway through 4th Q was decisive. Marshall had squandered 13-0 lead as Broncos (9-3) QB Jeff Welsh (23-34/264y, INT) threw TDs of 22y to WR Steve Neal (10/93y) and 41y to WR Joshua Bush to put Western Michigan up by 14-13.

Oklahoma 27 Kansas State 24 (Kansas City): Oklahoma (12-0) swept past Wildcats in tight Big 12 title match as QB Josh Heupel (24-44/220y, 2 TDs) ran for TD. Game was tied at 10-10 at H and 17-17 after 3 Qs. Heupel's 2nd TD pass, 17y effort to WR Andre Woolfolk early in 4th Q, put Sooners up 24-17 and then K Tim Duncan's 46y FG with 1:25 to go provided winning pts. QB Jonathan Beasley whipped Kansas State (10-3) to 16y TD pass to WR Quincy Morgan, but Cats could not recover onside-KO at game's end. OU's clinching FG drive had featured only single pass and was set up by RB Quentin Griffin's 29y run. Griffin also had chipped in with 22y run on 4th down option pitchout to keep alive earlier trip for go-ahead TD. Kansas State WR Aaron Lockett returned punt 58y in 3rd Q for only game's big-play TD. After winning 8 games by 31-pt avg margin, OU won last 4 by grand total of 28 pts. It didn't help no. 1 Oklahoma's confidence any that Heupel threw 3 nerve-wracking INTs, giving him 9 in last 4 games.

USA Today Coaches December 4

1	Oklahoma (56)	1471	14	Purdue	686
2	Miami (Fla.) (2)	1400	15	Michigan	632
3	Florida State (1)	1366	16	TCU	628
4	Washington	1284	17	Georgia Tech	540
5	Virginia Tech	1200	18	Ohio State	427
6	Oregon State	1192	19	Northwestern	411
7	Florida	1119	20	Auburn	345
8	Nebraska	1005	21	Tennessee	304
9	Kansas State	938	22	Colorado State	267
10	Notre Dame	894	23	Louisville	159
11	Oregon	888	24	Georgia	90
12	Texas	822	25	Toledo	76
13	Clemson	708			

Bowl Championship Series Standings December 3

	Poll Avg.	Computer Avg.	Schedule Ranking	Losses	Total
1 Oklahoma (12-0)	1.0	1.86	0.44	0	3.30
2 Florida State (10-1)	3.0	1.29	0.08	1	5.37
3 Miami (10-1)	2.0	2.57	0.12	1	5.69
4 Washington (10-1)	4.0	5.43	0.24	1	10.67
5 Virginia Tech (10-1)	5.5	5.14	0.56	1	12.20

Conference Standings

Big East

Miami	7-0
Virginia Tech	6-1
Pittsburgh	4-3
Syracuse	4-3
West Virginia	3-4
Boston College	3-4
Temple	1-6
Rutgers	0-7

Atlantic Coast

Florida State	8-0
Clemson	6-2
Georgia Tech	6-2
Virginia	5-3
North Carolina State	4-4
North Carolina	3-5
Maryland	3-5
Wake Forest	1-7
Duke	0-8

Southeastern

EAST	
Florida	7-1
Tennessee	5-3
Georgia	5-3
South Carolina	5-3
Vanderbilt	1-7
Kentucky	0-8
WEST	
Auburn	6-2
Louisiana State	5-3
Mississippi	4-4
Mississippi State	4-4
Arkansas	3-5
Alabama	3-5

Conference USA

Louisville	6-1
Cincinnati	5-2
East Carolina	5-2
Southern Mississippi	4-3
Alabama-Birmingham	3-3
Tulane	3-4
Memphis	2-5
Houston	2-5
Army	1-6

Big Ten

Purdue	6-2
Michigan	6-2
Northwestern	6-2
Ohio State	5-3
Wisconsin	4-4
Minnesota	4-4
Penn State	4-4
Iowa	3-5
Illinois	2-6
Michigan State	2-6
Indiana	2-6

Mid-American

EAST	
Ohio	5-3
Akron	5-3
Marshall	5-3
Miami	5-3
Buffalo	3-5
Bowling Green	2-6
Kent	1-7
WEST	
Western Michigan	7-1
Toledo	6-1
Northern Illinois	4-3
Ball State	3-4
Eastern Michigan	2-5
Central Michigan	2-6

Big Twelve

NORTH

Kansas State	6-2
Nebraska	6-2
Iowa State	5-3
Colorado	3-5
Kansas	2-6
Missouri	2-6

SOUTH

Oklahoma	8-0
Texas	7-1
Texas A&M	5-3
Texas Tech	3-5
Oklahoma State	1-7
Baylor	0-8

Western Athletic

Texas Christian	7-1
Texas-El Paso	7-1
Fresno State	6-2
San Jose State	5-3
Tulsa	4-4
Rice	2-6
Hawaii	2-6
Southern Methodist	2-6
Nevada	1-7

Pacific Ten

Oregon State	7-1
Washington	7-1
Oregon	7-1
Stanford	4-4
UCLA	3-5
Arizona State	3-5
Arizona	3-5
Southern California	2-6
Washington State	2-6
California	2-6

Mountain West

Colorado State	6-1
Air Force	5-2
Nevada-Las Vegas	4-3
Brigham Young	4-3
New Mexico	3-4
Utah	3-4
San Diego State	3-4
Wyoming	0-7

2000 Major Bowl Games

Oahu Bowl (Dec. 24): Georgia 37 Virginia 14

Georgia (8-4) won school-record 4th straight bowl game as game MVP WR Terrence Edwards rushed for 5/97y and caught 8/79y. Bulldogs D added 2 TDs off FUM RECs. Chances for Cavs (6-6) took early hit: starting QB Dan Ellis left game on opening series with sprained ankle after hit by CB Jamie Henderson. With Ellis out, Georgia scored 17 pts over final 4:30 of 1st Q to put UVa in deep hole. K Billy Bennett put Georgia on scoreboard with 35y FG. Bulldogs then used fake punt to set up Edwards' 40y reverse TD for 10-0 lead. Only 21 secs later, Virginia RB Tyree Foreman lost FUM on own 8YL, recovered by Georgia S Kentrell Curry for TD. Cavs showed spirit by marching 97y behind frosh QB Bryson Spinner (13-21/153y, 2 INTs), who hooked up with WR Tavon Mason on 78y pass, to score on 14y run by WR Demetrius Dotson. Georgia answered momentum change by scoring 67 secs later on 3y TD run by RB Verron Haynes to go into H leading 24-7. Teams each scored on 2nd H FUM RETs as play turned sloppy. This was 3rd bowl match-up of schools in last 6 years (1996 and '99 Peach Bowls, which teams split). Bulldogs QB Cory Phillips threw for 22-35/213y.

Aloha Bowl (Dec. 25): Boston College 31 Arizona State 17

Boston College (7-5) broke open 10-10 tie with 2 long TD passes by QB Tim Hasselbeck (9-21/209y, INT) within 4-min spread of 3rd Q to spoil coach Bruce Snyder's final game in Arizona State (6-6). Hasselbeck connected with WR Dedrick Dewalt (2/88y) for 58y score for 17-10 lead and WR Ryan Read for 40y TD for bigger cushion. Eagles TB Cedric Washington (22/109y, 2 TDs), who returned to starting lineup with suspension of TB William Green, added late TD. TB Tom Pace led Sun Devils O with 139y rushing, but revolving door at QB and 5 TOs doomed them. QB Jeff Krohn (6-10/74y) started for ASU and led them on 46y TD drive on 1st possession, capped by Pace's 14y TD run. He later threw EZ INT before leaving in 2nd Q with dislocated right shoulder. Sub QB Griffin Goodman (9-19/73y, INT) lost FUM on BC 1YL that helped seal Devils' fate. Reserve QB Matt Cooper (2-5/73y) managed late 31y TD pass to WR Ryan Dennard. Eagles K Mike Sutphin had kicked career-long 50y FG in 1st Q.

Music City Bowl (Dec. 28): West Virginia 49 Mississippi 38

West Virginia (7-5) coach Don Nehlen ended career victoriously as QB Brad Lewis sparkled against SEC's best pass D. Recovered from knee and hand injuries, Lewis (15-21/318y) tossed 5 TDs—he threw only 8 TDs in season—to help build huge 49-9 lead. He was 7-7/216y and 4 TDs in 1st H as Mountaineers scored 5 TDs. WVU needed only 17 plays to produce its 35 pts. Amazingly West Virginia WR Shawn Terry returned opening KO of 3rd Q 99y to up lead to 42-9. Rebels (7-5), who finished with 484y, rallied behind backup QB Eli Manning for 29 straight pts over span of 8.5 mins, but Archie's son ran out of time. CB Lance Frazier's INT with 3 mins left sealed win. Manning (12-20/167y, 3 TDs, INT) and starter QB Romaro Miller (16-31/221y, INT) combined for 388y passing. West Virginia TB Avon Cobourne, like Lewis back from injuries that had limited him, ran for 125y, while WR Antonio Brown (6/156y, 2 TDs) burned Ole Miss' man-to-man D. Rebs TB Duece McAllister was held to 22y rushing. Nehlen's 202nd career win ended 8-game bowl losing streak; new West Virginia coach Rich Rodriguez played on last post-season winner (1984 Bluebonnet).

Micronpc.com Bowl (Dec. 28): North Carolina State 38 Minnesota 30

Having won 5 games with 4th Q comebacks, Wolfpack (8-4) remained confident when trailing 24-0 in 1st H. Gophers (6-6) built lead on running of workhorse RB Tellis Redmon (42/246y). With frosh QB Philip Rivers (24-39/310y, 2 INTs) at helm, NC State scored 8 pts at end of 2nd Q on 3y TD pass to TE Andy Vandeveer and 2-pt conv pass to TB Ray Robinson. Pack continued to roll after H, roaring for 17 straight pts in 3rd Q and 25-24 lead. Minnesota broke scoring string with K Dan Nystrom's 23y FG. But it took Rivers less than min for him to put NC State in front for good on 23y TD pass to favorite target WR Koren Robinson (7/157y), who started 2nd H scoring spree with 19y reverse run. After Nystrom booted another FG to pull Minnesota to within 31-30, Wolfpack D made huge play: DT Ricky Fowler stripped QB Travis Cole (16-29/202y) to be recovered by LB Corey Lyons deep in Gophers territory. Robinson ran in clinching

8y TD run 1 play later. Golden Gophers compiled whopping 502y; only Kansas State and Nebraska did better during bowl season.

Insight.com Bowl (Dec. 28): Iowa State 38 Pittsburgh 29

Sr QB Sage Rosenfels (23-34/308y, 2 TDs) engineered 1st bowl win in Iowa State (9-3) history. Panthers (7-5) had struck 1st as WR Antonio Bryant (5/155y) broke free for 72y TD on pass by QB John Turman. Aided by large contingent of fans, Cyclones then reeled off 27 straight pts with Rosenfels throwing 2 TD passes to WR Chris Anthony (5/71y). Panthers rallied in 2nd H but were stymied by 2 special teams plays, both featuring ISU S Doug Densmore. Down 27-20 in 3rd Q, Pittsburgh had to punt. With regular returner WR J.J. Moses woozy, frosh TB JaMaine Billups took his 1st-ever punt RET 72y for TD following Densmore's key block. Cyclones added 5 straight pts to trail 34-29 with 9:49 left in 4th Q when they forced Iowa State to punt. Densmore, while sprawled face down, downed punt with quick left hand at Pittsburgh 1YL. Facing 99y march to go-ahead TD, Panthers soon punted and Cyclones added 41y FG by K Carl Gomez to close scoring. Pitt RB Kevan Barlow gained 114y rushing and helped set up 2nd TD with 37y gain on shuffle pass, while Turman threw for 347y. Cyclones closed 1st 9-win season since 1906.

Sun Bowl (Dec. 29): Wisconsin 21 UCLA 20

Having labeled Bruins "soft" after Rose Bowl 2 years earlier, Wisconsin (9-4) CB Jamar Fletcher got last laugh with INT at midfield near game's end that sealed slim victory. Fletcher was target of pre-game scuffle, UCLA WR Freddie Mitchell's taunts at end of brilliant 64y TD reception, and head slap from Mitchell on next possession. All 3 incidents cost UCLA (6-6) 15y PENs, so Fletcher gained big y. Even with PENs, Mitchell had great game with 9 catches/game-record 180y despite Fletcher's close coverage. Mitchell's TD tied game 7-7 in 1st Q as Wisconsin had scored 1st on 54y TD catch by WR Lee Evans. Bruins increased lead to 20-7, but O sputtered once QB Cory Paus (8-15/147y) left with broken collarbone. Badgers kept hammering, turning to air game for QB Brooks Bollinger's 2nd TD throw, 4y pass to WR Chris Chambers, which was set up by TB Michael Bennett's 54y KO RET. Chambers made nifty catch, keeping 1 foot in-bounds by slim margin. Bennett later capped 12-play, 70y scoring drive with 6y TD run that put Wisconsin up 21-20 midway in 4th Q. Badgers' drive had been launched by failed fake FG that saw UCLA K Chris Griffith come up 1y short of 1st down. Bruins TB DeShaun Foster rushed for 107y, but could gain only 7y in 2nd H when UCLA managed only 3 pts.

Peach Bowl (Dec. 29): Louisiana State 28 Georgia Tech 14

It was tale of 2 Hs as each team alternated solid play with horrendous play, with Louisiana State (8-4) trumping Yellow Jackets in 2nd H. Georgia Tech (9-3) took 14-3 H lead on TD runs of 32y by RB Joe Burns (17/96y) and 9y by FB Jermaine Hatch. Tech's D stifled Tigers by surrendering only 117y. As 3rd Q opened, LSU coach Nick Saban replaced QB Josh Booty (8-19/110y) with QB Rohan Davey (17-25/174y, 3 TDs), out since Tennessee game. Saban also brought injured T Brandon Wiley—out with broken left hand and in street clothes during 1st H—into game as inspiration. With blocking tightened and Davey showing no signs of rust, Tigers romped for 25 unanswered pts in 2nd H. Davey hit 5-5 passing on opening 9-play, 70y drive that was capped by 1st of his pair of 3y TD passes to FB Tommy Banks. Georgia Tech still led 14-9 entering 4th Q, but tide had turned as indicated by Yellow Jackets' 13y total O in 3rd Q. LSU's next TD came on great catch by WR Josh Reed (9/96y, TD), who was just able to get left foot down in back of EZ. QB George Godsey (19-36/177y, 2 INTs) drove Georgia Tech to LSU 3YL in last-ditch, failed effort to rally before he was knocked out of game on hit by Bengals LB Trev Faulk. Suffering 6 TOs, after committing only 12 during season, Tech perhaps missed O-coordinator Ralph Friedgen, who left to take Maryland head coaching job.

Holiday Bowl (Dec. 29): Oregon 35 Texas 30

Frustrating season and bowl game for Longhorns (9-3) ended fittingly with 2 consecutive EZ drops by receivers. QB Joey Harrington (19-30/273y) did it all for Ducks (10-2), throwing TD pass, running for 2 others, and catching 4th. Oregon opened scoring with Harrington's 1y TD pass to TE Justin Peelle that capped 80y drive. Horns countered with long drive that ended with INT made by Ducks S Steve Smith at GL. Another Texas TO, WR B. J. Johnson's FUM after short pass, set up Oregon's creative TD: 18y pass on flea flicker from WR Bobby Howry to Harrington for 14-0 lead. Texas then began march to EZ, bravely converting 4th down at own 33YL en route to 3y TD run by TB Hodges Mitchell. TD was 1st of Texas' 3 straight to grab 21-14 H lead. Oregon TB Maurice Morris, team's leader in rushing with 82y and receiving with 104y, tied game with 55y TD catch-and-run. Neither team scored until Harrington made 9y TD run for 28-21 lead in 4th Q. On ensuing KO, Steers TB Victor Ike returned it 93y to re-knot matters. It was Ducks' turn, and Harrington drove them to game-winning 4y TD run by WR Jason Willis. QB Chris Simms (17-33/245y) had mixed results for Texas, throwing 4 INTs but putting Horns in position to tie at game's end until drops by Johnson and WR Roy Williams. Ducks completed 1st 10-win season in history.

Alamo Bowl (Dec. 30): Nebraska 66 Northwestern 17

Out of BCS spotlight, Cornhuskers (10-2) showcased talent and inherent strength of Big 12. Nebraska QB Eric Crouch ran for 2 TDs and threw 2 others, while IB Dan Alexander rushed for 240y, 2 TDs, as Nebraska O rumbled 636y, 476y on ground. Enjoying extra time to prepare for Northwestern's spread attack, Huskers D shook off its perceived vulnerability to passing and shut out Wildcats in 2nd H. Northwestern (8-4) gained only 151y through air as QB Zak Kustok spent more time being chased by DE Kyle Vanden Bosch and other Nebraska defenders than moving ball. Nebraska virtually scared purple pants off NW in 2nd Q, scoring 31 pts to forcefully grab 38-17 H lead. Wildcats briefly had held 10-7 edge after fake punt set up 10y TD pass to WR Teddy Johnson. After that, it was all Huskers as Crouch scored 20 secs later on 50y run. Alexander and IB Correll Buckhalter scored on short TD runs, and Brown kicked

51y FG. Wildcats had rallied all year and so when TB Damien Anderson (18/149y) raced 69y for TD that cut deficit to 31-17 with 70 secs left in 2nd Q, there still was hope. But not for long as Husker WR Bobby Newcombe's 58y TD on screen pass with H clock running out dashed hopes of Cardiac Cats.

Independence Bowl (Dec. 31): Mississippi State 43 Texas A&M 41 (OT)

In bizarre, snowy white-out, thrilling game ended with OT session that featured 2 TDs and RET of blocked x-pt. Moments after FB Ja'Mar Toombs (35/193y, 3 TDs), whose bulk was perfect for slippery conditions, opened extra session with 25y scoring run to put Aggies (7-5) up by 6 pts, Mississippi State DT Willie Blade blocked K Terence Kitchen's x-pt try. S Eugene Clinton grabbed loose ball, snow and all, and raced toward Texas A&M GL. Before being tackled at midfield, Clinton flipped ball back to CB Julius Griffith who ran untouched to EZ for 2 pts. Down 41-35 and needing TD to win, Mississippi State (8-4) moved quickly to 6YL, from where QB Wayne Madkins scored on keeper. To get to OT, Bulldogs had to overcome 14 pt deficit in 4th Q. S Marco Miner's INT of Texas A&M QB Mark Farris (9-11/133y) fired up Bulldogs as they scored on 32y run by RB Dontae Walker (16/143y, 3 TDs) and 3y catch by TE Donald Lee. Game had started inauspiciously for Madkins—playing his 1st game in snow—who lost FUM of 1st snap, recovered by A&M DE Ronald Flemons. Madkins and All-SEC C Michael Fair had snap problems throughout 1st H—they suffered 4 FUMs in 1st Q alone. Flemons' REC led to TB Richard Whitaker's 9y TD reception and 7-0 lead. Toombs scored from 4y out later in 1st Q for 14-0 lead. Walker answered with 40y jaunt up middle for TD that got State back in game. Bulldogs then partially blocked punt, taking over at A&M 21YL. After 2 runs, RB Dicenzo Miller scored on 4y screen pass to tie it late in 2nd Q. Aggies had little time before H, but Farris went deep for 42y bomb to WR Robert Ferguson for 6-pt lead. A&M scored twice inside 1st 6 mins of 4th Q, with Fariss throwing 35y TD to WR Bethel Johnson, and Toombs adding 13 TD run to take 35-21 lead.

Outback Bowl: South Carolina 24 Ohio State 7

Even for Hollywood, it would have been unbelievable. There was rags-to-riches story of team (South Carolina) bouncing back from 0-11 season to win 7 games for bowl bid. Game's star rose up as unheralded alternate, who despite lofty high school statistics (7,656y rushing) had been ignored by his fabled state university (Ohio State), yet played game of his life to lead stunning upset over same school. Amazing, yet true. Troy, Ohio, spawned South Carolina (8-4) TB Ryan Brewer, who was given chance to prove Buckeyes (8-4) recruiters wrong when he was moved from WR-WB to starting TB as replacement for suspended Carolina TB Derek Watson. Brewer responded with 219 all-purpose y and 3 TDs to win MVP award. He scored twice while rushing for 109y—43y more than he made all season—and caught 3/92y and another TD. Brewer scored untouched on 28y screen pass as Gamecocks cashed in QB Steve Bellisari's FUM for 17-7 lead early in 4th Q. It was 2nd time FUM by Bellisari led to TD by Brewer, other providing Gamecocks' 1st TD on 7y run. Things disintegrated for Buckeyes in 4th Q: O struggled, while D, unable to stop South Carolina, embarrassingly resorted to cheap shots against Brewer. Ohio State finished with only 85y rushing—South Carolina made 218y—while Bellisari threw for 14-25/157y. Ohio's sole TD was G Mike Gurr's EZ REC of TB Jonathan Wells' FUM. Drive featured WR Ken-Yon Rambo's 63y reception. Wells led Buckeyes in rushing with 52y, but he was stopped on 4th-and-1 at Gamecocks 20YL in 1st Q by LB Kenny Harney. Brewer received congratulations at game's end from Ohio State coach John Cooper, who acknowledged his recruiting mistake. Cooper was fired day later, although for far more than recruiting oversight.

Cotton Bowl: Kansas State 35 Tennessee 21

Kansas State O, which looked beautiful in victories and at times horrible in defeat, looked quite pretty indeed in fooling Tennessee's heralded D. QB Jonathan Beasley (13-27/210y) threw for 2 TDs and rushed for career-high 98y in leading Wildcats (11-3) to 4th straight 11-win season. At 1 point, Beasley even pooched QK to Vols 4YL. WR Quincy Morgan was on receiving end of 7/145y, 2 TDs, while RB Josh Scobey rushed for 147y, 2 TDs. Kansas State O-Line dominated in paving way for 297y rushing, most surrendered by Vols (8-4) all year, while allowing no sacks to D that made 50 during regular season. K-State totaled 507y, 2nd best of any bowl team. Cats D also excelled, limiting QB Casey Clausen—who entered game 6-0 as starter—to 7-25/120y passing, while 81y of RB Travis Henry's 180y rushing came on single scoring burst late in game. California native Clausen, who looked uncomfortable in snowy conditions, still crafted 7-7 tie with 17y pass to WR David Martin. Beasley and Morgan next scored twice as Kansas State began to take control, although Tennessee staunched its bleeding when CB Jabari Greer returned deflected pass 78y for TD that cut lead to 21-14 entering H. K-State improved record to 45-0 since 1990 when running for 200y.

Gator Bowl: Virginia Tech 41 Clemson 20

Miffed that they were closed out of BCS bowl berth, Hokies (11-1) took out frustration on Clemson (9-3). Virginia Tech QB Michael Vick proved his special talent when on healthy ankles, although he did most of his damage through air: 10-18/205y, TD. Vick's TD pass, which was set up by Tigers special teams miscue as P Jamie Somaini lost FUM after bounced snap at end of team's 1st series. Handed ball on Clemson 23YL, Vick wasted no time exploiting situation as he hit FB Jarrett Ferguson over middle for 23y TD pass. Vick added 6y TD run for 14-0 lead, and Hokies never trailed. Clemson was flagged for roughing P PEN that kept alive Va Tech's 1st drive of 2nd H with score standing at 21-10 for Hokies. Back on O, Vick connected with WR Andre Davis on 55y pass to set up 2nd TD run by scoring machine TB Lee Suggs (20/73y), from 1y out. Although inspired by match-up with Vick, Clemson QB Woody Dantzler (15-32/180, TD, INT) was at less than top condition with his own ankle injury. With Dantzler dinged and RB Travis Zachery knocked out of game with broken foot, Tigers found comeback chances greatly limited. Zachery injured himself in 2nd Q on Clemson's best play, his 23y TD reception. Tigers turned to team's relief pitcher, QB Willie Simmons, who promptly threw INT that set up Ferguson's TD run for 34-13 lead, but managed 14y TD pass to WR Rod Gardner (7/94y). Suggs—who scored 28 TDs on year—tallied his 3rd TD to close out Tigers and send them to 5th straight bowl loss.

Citrus Bowl: Michigan 31 Auburn 28

Game epitomized Wolverines (9-3) season as O had plenty of stars, but D allowed big play after big play to unheralded opponent. After blowing similar games during season, Michigan (9-3) won this time on 41y FG by K Hayden Epstein late in 3rd Q. QB Ben Leard led Auburn (9-4), completing 28-37/394y and 3 TDs. Despite Leard's heroics, he and Tigers could point to handful of crucial plays that prevented upset. First mistake occurred late in 2nd Q when INT deep in Michigan territory negated potential go-ahead score with game tied 14-14. Another happened early in 4th Q when Auburn WR Reggie Worthy dropped pass in EZ, forcing Tigers to try 40y FG attempt that was blocked. Later in 4th Q, Wolverines CB Jeremy LeSeur drilled Leard to force FUM that derailed Tigers. Auburn scored TD on next possession with Leard hitting WR Deandre Green for 21y pass that closed scoring. Michigan recovered onside-KO and ran out final 2 mins. In becoming Citrus Bowl's only 2-time MVP, Wolverines TB Anthony Thomas rushed 182y and 2 consecutive TDs for 28-14 lead early in 3rd Q. Michigan QB Drew Henson also had fine day, throwing 15-20/294y, 236y to starting WRs David Terrell (4/136y) and WR Marquise Walker (4/100y). Leard tossed scoring passes of 19y to WR Ronney Daniels (7/98y) and 20y to WR Clifton Robinson for short-lived 14-7 Auburn lead. Michigan won 4 straight bowl games for 1st time in school history.

Rose Bowl: Washington 34 Purdue 24

With paralyzed teammate Curtis Williams in attendance, inspired Huskies (11-1) laid claim to elite status with big win. QB Marques Tuiasosopo (16-22/138y) won MVP with gutsy performance as he returned from being sidelined for 3 plays with banged up right shoulder at start of 4th Q. Huskies were ahead 20-17 but faced 4th-and-1. Taking advantage of huge O-Line, TB Rich Alexis rushed for critical 3y. Washington converted 1st down into TD moments later, taking advantage of another size differential as Tuiasosopo lofted EZ pass to 6'3 WR Todd Elstrom, who was covered by 5'7 CB Chris Clopton. Elstrom's 8y TD catch put Huskies up by 27-17, permanent lead margin after foes traded TDs later in 4th Q. Purdue (8-4) had late chance after rare error by Tuiasosopo, when he elected, at midfield, to lateral on play on which he had already gained 1st down. Elstrom bobbled lateral away to Boilermakers, but Huskies D held Boilermakers to FG attempt that flew wide. Purdue QB Drew Brees completed 23-39/275y and 2 TDs to WR Vinny Sutherland (7/88y). After Huskies took 14-0 lead early, Brees knotted score 17-17 on 24y pass to Sutherland that was set up by Sutherland's 51y RET of 2nd H KO. Huskies pulled away from that point on, thanks to its run game advantage. Washington finished with 268y rushing, with 245y in 2nd H, while Boilermakers gained only 76y on ground. Win was 2nd for Pac 10 in last 9 Rose Bowls.

Fiesta Bowl: Oregon State 41 Notre Dame 9

Fiercely playing for respect, Oregon State (11-1) wanted to prove its tradition of losing was over. Fighting Irish (9-3) never had much chance as Oregon State was much too fast and aggressive for Notre Dame on both sides of ball. Beavers QB Jonathan Smith threw for 305y and 3 TDs—not bad for former walk-on coach Dennis Erickson had mistaken for team manager upon his arrival—while D held Notre Dame to 155y. Score at H was just 12-3, but Oregon State blew opportunities for more pts with early PENs, finishing with 18/174y, new school and Fiesta Bowl records. Beavers outgained Notre Dame by 110y to 8y in 1st Q but had only 3-0 lead to show for it. Biggest play for Irish D was S Ron Israel's 4th-and-goal tackle of TB Patrick McCall at 1YL. Smith finally got Beavers into EZ in 2nd Q on 74y pass to WR Chad Johnson, who taunted Irish defenders as he pulled away with relaxed dropping of ball. Problem was, he had yet to reach EZ and had, therefore, fumbled, something officials did not see. Struggle for pts ended in 3rd Q when Beavers put up 29, scoring 4 TDs within 8 mins. Smith threw 2 TDs during outburst, while TB Ken Simonton (18/85y) added final TD with 4y run. Notre Dame QB Matt LoVecchio completed 13-33/138y with 2 INTs, but was powerless to prevent Irish's 5th straight bowl loss.

Sugar Bowl (Jan. 2): Miami 37 Florida 20

As Miami scored its 37th pt on K Todd Sievers' x-pt from 50y—Hurricanes had been penalized twice including 1 on mascot Ibis—Florida coach Steve Spurrier must have thought to himself that his Gators never really had chance. On display for Hurricanes (11-1) was depth they stockpiled since probation was lifted. With leading rusher RB James Jackson knocked out after 62y in 1st H, and A-A WR Santana Moss (6/89y) hampered by back injury, Miami O still looked sharp as RB Clint Portis rushed for 97y off bench. Gators (10-3) put up fight, holding 17-13 lead early in 3rd Q on 36y TD run by RB Earnest Graham (15/136y), that featuring impressive stiff arms. Miami stormed back with dual 3rd Q TDs on passes by QB Ken Dorsey (22-40/270y, 3 TDs, 2 INTs) to FBs D.J. Williams for 19y and Najeh Davenport for 2y. Davenport's TD brought PEN-incurring congratulatory hug from mascot. Miami's Butkus-winning LB Dan Morgan had another huge game, totaling 12 tackles with preventive INT deep in Miami territory. Florida QB Rex Grossman threw for 252y in defeat, but completed only 18-41 with 6/110y going to WR Reche Caldwell. Amazingly Miami was able to sell less than 10,000 of 15,000 tickets allotted to it for what seemed like tempting match-up against in-state opponent who stopped playing Canes 13 years earlier. Despite that lack of support coach Butch Davis pushed his bowl record with Canes to 4-0. Spurrier was now 5-5 in post-season action with Gators.

Orange Bowl (Jan. 3): Oklahoma 13 Florida State 2

Seeming to fade after October peak, Sooners (13-0) had questions to answer prior to KO. How would they handle their lack of experience in national title tilts? What was wrong with QB Josh Heupel's arm? OU had limped into championship game with narrow wins over Texas A&M, Oklahoma State, and Kansas State, while Seminoles had won their final 6 games by 37-pt avg margin. When game was staged, any

concern over Oklahoma evaporated. Sooners blew away doubters with devastating performance that was not as close as final score. Oklahoma D was especially dominating, confusing Seminoles (11-2) with changing schemes while jarring them with big hits. Florida State opened with QB Chris Weinke's 35y completion to WR Atrews Bell (7/137), but it was all downhill from there. Oklahoma took away FSU run game, surrendering only 27y rushing with 4y coming in 2nd H. Florida State converted single 3rd down in 15 attempts. Although gaining fewer overall y (270y to FSU's 301y), Sooners ate more than 13 extra mins of possession time. Heupel completed 25-39/214y, so Oklahoma LB Torrance Marshall rightfully was named player of game, finishing with 11 tackles and INT that set up 1st score, 27y FG by K Tim Duncan. Still, Heisman Trophy runner-up Heupel bested winner, Weinke. Duncan added another FG, while Florida State missed another FG in huge game when K Brett Cimorelli hit low 30y attempt to right of posts just before H. OU hit H locker room with 6-0 lead. Sooners D finished off contest midway through 4th Q as LB Rocky Calmus stripped Weinke (25-51/274y), FUM REC made by S Roy Williams at FSU 15YL. Sooners scored 2 plays later as RB Quentin Griffin scored, untouched, on 10y run. Rest of game focused on whether Florida State could score at all—it last had been shut out by Miami in 1988—and it scored 2 pts with 55 secs remaining on bad OU punt snap. P Jeff Ferguson (41y avg with 3 punts inside 7YL) scooped up loose ball on 5YL and ran in EZ. Best starting field position for 2nd H drive for Noles was its 20YL. They were held to 301y, 248 less than yearly avg, while scoring 40.4 pts less than avg. Despite 2 losses in last 3 bowls—both deciding national title—Bowden remained with impressive 17-6-1 in post-season action. Half of his bowl losses had come at hands of Oklahoma.

Final AP Poll January 4

1	Oklahoma (71)	1775	14	Colorado State	640
2	Miami	1690	15	Notre Dame	611
3	Washington	1634	16	Clemson	563
4	Oregon State	1539	17	Georgia Tech	545
5	Florida State	1488	18	Auburn	498
6	Virginia Tech	1432	19	South Carolina	486
7	Oregon	1299	20	Georgia	430
8	Nebraska	1282	21	Texas Christian	406
9	Kansas State	1258	22	Louisiana State	340
10	Florida	1128	23	Wisconsin	208
11	Michigan	1061	24	Mississippi State	197
12	Texas	894	25	Iowa State	188
13	Purdue	765			

Final USA Today Coaches January 5

1	Oklahoma (59)	1475	14	Clemson	590
2	Miami (Fla.)	1404	15	Colorado State	587
3	Washington	1336	16	Notre Dame	457
4	Florida State	1253	17	Georgia	357
5	Oregon State	1245	18	TCU	341
6	Virginia Tech	1215	19	Georgia Tech	335
7	Nebraska	1099	20	Auburn	325
8	Kansas State	1077	21	South Carolina	314
9	Oregon	1009	22	Mississippi State	272
10	Michigan	901	23	Iowa State	225
11	Florida	899	24	Wisconsin	220
12	Texas	731			
13	Purdue	626			

2000 Top Performance Formula

1	Oklahoma	1.8104
2	Miami	1.7605
3	Florida State	1.7556
4	Virginia Tech	1.7182
5	Nebraska	1.6257
6	Washington	1.6107
7	Oregon State	1.5833
8	Florida	1.5626
9	Kansas State	1.5339
10	Oregon	1.4919
11	Texas Christian	1.4781
12	Georgia Tech	1.4096
13	Michigan	1.4079
14	Notre Dame	1.4076
15	Texas	1.3953
16	Clemson	1.3700
17	Ohio State	1.3156
18	Wisconsin	1.3152
19	Purdue	1.3139
20	Mississippi State	1.2905

2000 Top Opponent Records

1	Florida	.6549
2	Florida State	.6525
3	Miami	.6397
4	Virginia Tech	.6299
5	Colorado	.6167
6	West Virginia	.6142
7	UCLA	.6047
8	Oklahoma	.6042
9	Washington	.6032
10	Iowa	.5985
11	Stanford	.5932
12	Texas A&M	.5909
13	Alabama	.5882
14	Washington State	.5862
15	Notre Dame	.5859
16	Nebraska	.5833
17	Kansas State	.5789
18	Virginia	.57692
19	Kansas	.57685
20	Syracuse	.5763

2000 Out-of-Conference Records

	W-L	Percentage	Bowl W-L
Big Twelve	31-10	.7561	4-3
Big East	26-10	.7222	4-1
Pacific-10	25-10	.7143	3-2
Southeastern	28-14	.6667	4-5
Atlantic Coast	18-12	.6000	1-4
Big Ten	25-17	.5952	2-4
Mountain West	14-20	.4118	3-0

2000 Individual Statistical Leaders

RUSHING YARDS	Attempts	Yards	Avg.
LaDainian Tomlinson, Texas Christian	369	2158	5.9
Damien Anderson, Northwestern	293	1914	6.5
Michael Bennett, Wisconsin	294	1598	5.4
Deonce Whitaker, San Jose State	224	1577	5.4
Robert Sanford, Western Michigan	293	1571	4.8
Rudi Johnson, Auburn	324	1567	4.8
Anthony Thomas, Michigan	287	1551	5.4
Ken Simonton, Oregon State	266	1474	5.5
Chester Taylor, Toledo	250	1470	5.9
T.J. Duckett, Michigan State	240	1353	5.6

PASSING YARDS	Completions	Attempts	Yards	Pct.
Chris Weinke, Florida State	266	431	4167	61.7
Jared Lorenzen, Kentucky	321	559	3687	57.4
Kliff Kingsbury, Texas Tech	362	585	3618	61.9
Drew Brees, Purdue	286	473	3393	60.5
Josh Heupel, Oklahoma	280	433	3392	64.7
Bart Hendricks, Boise State	210	347	3364	60.5
Byron Leftwich, Marshall	279	457	3358	61.1
John Welsh, Idaho	251	399	3171	62.9
Philip Rivers, North Carolina State	237	441	3054	53.7
George Godsey, Georgia Tech	222	349	2906	63.6

RECEIVING YARDS	Catches	Yards
Marvin Minnis, Florida State	63	1340
Freddie Mitchell, UCLA	68	1314
Antonio Bryant, Pittsburgh	68	1302
Don Shoals, Tulsa	80	1195
Jabar Gaffney, Florida	71	1184
Justin McCareins, Northern Illinois	66	1168
Quincy Morgan, Kansas State	64	1166
Aaron Jones, Utah State	63	1159
Josh Reed, Louisiana State	65	1127
Ashley Lelie, Hawaii	74	1110

2000 Consensus All-America Team

Offense

Tight End:	Brian Natkin, Texas-El Paso
Wide Receiver:	Santana Moss, Miami
	Marvin Minnis, Florida State
Line:	Leonard Davis, Texas
	Steve Hutchinson, Michigan
	Chris Brown, Georgia Tech
	Ben Hamilton, Minnesota
	Dominic Raiola, Nebraska
Quarterback:	Josh Heupel, Oklahoma
Running Back:	LaDainian Tomlinson, Texas Christian
	Damien Anderson, Northwestern
Kicker:	Jonathan Ruffin, Cincinnati

Defense

Line:	Jamal Reynolds, Florida State
	Casey Hampton, Texas
	Richard Seymour, Georgia
	Andre Carter, California
Linebacker:	Keith Adams, Clemson
	Dan Morgan, Miami
	Rocky Calmus, Oklahoma
	Carlos Polk, Nebraska
Back:	Jamar Fletcher, Wisconsin
	Dwight Smith, Akron
	Fred Smoot, Mississippi State
Punter:	Nick Harris, California

2000 Heisman Trophy Vote

Chris Weinke, senior quarterback, Florida State	1628
Josh Heupel, senior quarterback, Oklahoma	1552
Drew Brees, senior quarterback, Purdue	619
LaDainian Tomlinson, senior tailback, Texas Christian	566

Other Major Awards

Maxwell (Player)	Drew Brees, senior quarterback, Purdue
Walter Camp (Player)	Josh Heupel, senior quarterback, Oklahoma
Outland (Lineman)	John Henderson, junior defensive tackle, Tennessee
Lombardi (Lineman)	Jamal Reynolds, senior defensive end, Florida State
Doak Walker (Running Back)	LaDainian Tomlinson, senior tailback, Texas Christian
Davey O'Brien (Quarterback)	Chris Weinke, senior quarterback, Florida State
Fred Biletnikoff (Receiver)	Antonio Bryant, sophomore wide receiver, Pittsburgh
Jim Thorpe (Defensive Back)	Jamar Fletcher, junior cornerback, Wisconsin
Dick Butkus (Linebacker)	Dan Morgan, senior linebacker, Miami
Lou Groza (Placekicker)	Jonathan Ruffin, sophomore kicker, Cincinnati
Chuck Bednarik (Defender)	Dan Morgan, senior linebacker, Miami
Bronko Nagurski (Defender)	Dan Morgan, senior linebacker, Miami
Ray Guy (Punter)	Kevin Stemke, senior punter, Wisconsin
John Mackey (Tight End)	Tim Stratton, junior tight end, Purdue
Johnny Unitas (Quarterback)	Chris Weinke, senior quarterback, Florida State
Mosi Tatupu (Special Teams)	J.T. Thatcher, senior defensive back, Oklahoma
Dave Rimington (Center)	Dominic Raiola, junior center, Nebraska
AFCA Coach of the Year	Bob Stoops, Oklahoma

2001

The Year of Helping to Heal a Nation, Cancellation in Pullman, and Return of Miami's Might

On September 11, a beautifully sunny Tuesday morning in the East, fundamental Islamic terrorists crashed hijacked U.S. airliners into each of New York City's World Trade Center towers and a third plane into the Pentagon building in Virginia. A fourth was headed for a target in Washington D.C. when courageous passengers—after hearing about the destruction in New York City via cell phones—fought back, and the plane crashed in western Pennsylvania. These events killed thousands and shocked a nation that soon went to war. The college football programs most affected by the attacks and the soon-to-be-initiated wars against the Taliban in Afghanistan and Al Qaeda and other terrorist groups throughout the world were those of the military academies. Former Navy tackle, Jonas Panik, died during the Pentagon bombing. Other players, current or former, would soon be heading off to war. "It's a possibility," said Navy linebacker Ryan Hamilton of wartime service. "But we're here to be a part of something that's bigger than ourselves."

As a nation mourned, the new college football season became an afterthought. The entire slate of games for September 15 was either postponed or, in some cases, cancelled when no future date could be secured. The same was true for pro sports leagues. Playing and viewing sporting events soon became an important way for a wounded nation to find succor, and the college football season was beneficial to all Americans, including those soon to be serving in Afghanistan.

By season's end, the schedule interruption, which had a profound impact on choosing teams for the Rose Bowl national title game, was overshadowed by media outrage over the Bowl Championship Series system. Undefeated Miami (12-0) was a clear-cut choice for one spot. With easy wins over Florida State (8-4), Syracuse (10-3), and Washington (8-4), Miami was a dynamic no. 1. Finding an opponent for a championship match was a challenge. Five teams blew chances to face Miami during a 16-day span. On November 23, undefeated Nebraska (11-2) had its plans blown up 62-36 by red-hot Colorado (10-3). Oklahoma (11-2) would have moved into the second spot in the BCS rankings, but the Sooners were upset the next day by Oklahoma State (4-7). The next week, new no. 2 Florida (10-2) was nipped 34-32 at home by Tennessee (11-2) and third-ranked Texas (11-2) lost 39-37 to Colorado in the Big 12 title game. Tennessee, which shot to the second spot, had left too much on the field at Gainesville to handle Louisiana State (10-3), which beat the Volunteers 31-20 in the SEC title game on December 8.

When the BCS smoke cleared, Nebraska edged Colorado and Oregon for second and earned a Rose Bowl berth opposite Miami. Mike Bellotti, coach of the Ducks, likened the BCS to "a bad disease, like cancer." His Ducks were hurt by the narrowness of their final 17-14 win over Oregon State (5-6), considered too close by voters and computers despite being played in a driving rainstorm, that it was a rivalry game, and that the talented, but struggling Beavers treated the in-state match-up as if it were a bowl game. What was hard to swallow was that the Cornhuskers did not win the North Division of the Big 12, and surrendered the most points in school history in the loss to Colorado. Despite the crushing defeat—and it was the margin that so troubled the critics of the BCS—Nebraska, with wins over Oklahoma and Kansas State (6-6), had an honest, if not overwhelming, argument for inclusion in the Rose Bowl.

The key to the season was the cancellation of a game way off in bucolic Pullman, Washington. No matter how the result may have turned out, Oregon and Colorado were done in by the inability of Washington State (10-2) to reschedule Colorado's September 15 visit to Pullman. Had the Buffaloes beaten the best Cougars team since 1997, it would have added a quality opponent to vault the Buffaloes past Nebraska in the BCS standings. Had Washington State prevailed over Colorado, Oregon, who beat the Cougars 24-17 in October, would have owned a sufficient opponents' record to overcome the Huskers.

Despite its season-ending destruction of contenders Nebraska and Texas, Colorado was left to lament coach Gary Barnett's decision to eschew a short field goal attempt in favor of a try for a third down touchdown pass late in an opening 24-22 loss to Fresno State (11-3). Quarterback Craig Ochs' end zone pass was intercepted. With a second loss from their regular season game with Texas, Colorado had the weakest argument of the three schools even though the Buffs may have been the hottest team at the time of the bowl games. One argument that supported Nebraska and Colorado

was the strength of the Big 12 as four teams (Texas, Oklahoma, Nebraska, and Colorado) finished in the AP's top nine.

Ironically the BCS formula was changed before the season to lessen the impact of margin of victory, while giving more credit to wins over top competition. The irony was that the biggest argument against Nebraska was its dreadful margin of defeat at the hands of Colorado. In altering the BCS, two of the original eight computer rankings refused to comply and were replaced, the long-standing Dunkel Index and *The New York Times*.

Once the game was played, the Miami Hurricanes made the discussion of their Rose Bowl opponent a moot story by easily beating Nebraska 37-14. The Pasadena match-up was the first since 1946 without the traditional Big Ten versus Pac 10 battle in what was the 100th anniversary of "The Granddaddy of Them All." Oregon finished second in the polls after shellacking no-longer-hot Colorado in the Fiesta Bowl.

Penn State may have been out of BCS mix, but supplied a big highlight. The Nittany Lions upset Ohio State 29-27 on October 27 for coach Joe Paterno's 324th win that passed Bear Bryant for the most victories for any Division 1-A coach. Penn State's 0-4 start, the events of September 11, and the reality that another coach was gaining on Paterno lessened the hoopla. Paterno finished the year with 327 wins, but Florida State coach Bobby Bowden ended the season with 323 wins. Neither the 74-year-old Paterno nor 72-year-old Bowden seemed ready for retirement with Paterno stating, "I hope I can go another five years."

Coaches remained in the news even after the season. In December, Notre Dame (5-6) fired coach Bob Davie, hired George O'Leary away from Georgia Tech (8-5), and quickly were embarrassed by news that O'Leary had lied years ago on his resume about his playing career and his education, adding football letters at the University of New Hampshire in the late 1960s and a graduate degree at the State University of New York in the 1970s. Unfortunately for O'Leary, he never rewrote his resume, and the truth now was out. The Fighting Irish waited out O'Leary's resignation five days later and hired Tyrone Willingham from Stanford (9-3). Willingham's hiring focused on the fact that he, one of only four African-American head coaches, would be the first black coach of any sport at Notre Dame.

The biggest fish to leave the college football coaching pond was Florida's dynamic Steve Spurrier, who departed for the riches of the NFL Washington Redskins after winning 122 games, six Southeastern Conference titles, and the 1996 national championship in 12 seasons in Gainesville. With a 56-23 handling of Maryland (10-2) in the Orange Bowl, Florida went out a winner for Spurrier, finishing third nationally. The 2001 season also was wonderful for assistants making their debuts as head coaches. Larry Coker of Miami won the national title after years of being an assistant. Despite losing in the Orange Bowl, Maryland coach Ralph Friedgen won the AFCA coach of the year for leading the Terrapins to the Atlantic Coast Conference title.

A changing of the guard occurred throughout the season beyond the improvements of weak sisters like Maryland, especially with programs from outside the BCS conferences. Fresno State (11-3) and Brigham Young (12-2) each cracked the Top 10 during the regular season, while Louisville (11-2) played TV games on Monday, Tuesday, Thursday, Friday, and Saturday to shine attention on its up-and-coming program.

Riding another successful debut of a first-year coach, BYU won 12 straight games under Gary Crowton before losing at Hawaii (9-3) in December. With the nation's leading rusher, tailback Luke Staley, pacing an explosive offense, the Cougars advanced their image as a wide-open team. Their defense left something to be desired, so BYU was left on the outside of the BCS even before they lost. Another western upstart flirting with BCS glory was Fresno State, which opened the season with wins over Colorado, Wisconsin (5-7), and Oregon State. The Bulldogs eventually reached no. 8 before losing in mid-season to Boise State (8-4).

As players at all levels prepared, mostly in the heat of summer, for the season, an alarming number collapsed and died. Florida State linebacker Devaughn Darling died at 18 of a heart attack following a February workout, and incoming Florida freshman Eraste Autin died in July from heat exhaustion. Darling's twin brother Devard, a Seminoles wide receiver, was present at the fatal workout, and Austin died during voluntary workouts that were hardly voluntary. Northwestern (4-7) safety Rashidi Wheeler died from an asthma attack on the same blistering August day that former star Ohio State tackle Korey Stringer died from multiple organ failure due to heat exhaustion at Minnesota Vikings camp. Heat was a factor in most of

the deaths that plagued the sport, while the use of supplements became a concern: there was such presence in the systems of Darling and Wheeler and in the locker of Stringer.

Milestones

■ New Orleans Bowl was added and Micron PC Bowl eliminated, replaced by return of Tangerine Bowl to boost Orlando's tourism. Hawaii's Aloha and Oahu Bowls moved to mainland (San Francisco and Seattle respectively) for 2002.

■ Florida State linebacker Devaughn Darling, 18, died after February workout. Brandon Cole Pittman, defensive tackle at Texas, died in car accident on February 26. Billy Ray Smith, Sr., standout Arkansas lineman from 1954-56 died of cancer on March 21, age 66. Smith played in the NFL for 14 seasons and appeared in two Super Bowls with the Baltimore Colts. Charley Pell, coach at Clemson, and Florida, died of lung cancer on May 29, age 59. Pell was All-SEC lineman at Alabama and coached 84 wins in 13 years, but became best known for winning obsession that resulted in probation at both Clemson and Florida. Pell later went public with 1994 suicide attempt and battle with clinical depression. John McKay, 77, coached Southern California to national championships in 1962, '67, '72, and '74 and nine Pac 8 titles, died of kidney failure on June 10. Known for his one-liners, McKay was innovative in developing I-formation offense and coached Heisman Trophy-winning tailbacks Mike Garrett and O.J. Simpson. After 127 wins in 16 seasons, McKay left USC to become first head coach of Tampa Bay Buccaneers. Northwestern defensive back Rashidi Wheeler suffered asthma attack and died after voluntary workout on August 3, and, on same day, former Ohio State tackle Korey Stringer, 27, collapsed and died at Minnesota Vikings camp. Billy Vessels, 70, Hall of Fame running back from Oklahoma and winner of the 1952 Heisman Trophy, died of congestive heart failure on November 17. Charlie McClendon, who won 137 games as LSU coach—most in history—from 1962-79, died on December 7 at age 78. Popular "Cholly Mac" played for and coached under Bear Bryant at Kentucky and was national coach of the year in 1970, when Tigers won SEC title. Billy Wells, who as Michigan State halfback starred in 1954 Rose Bowl, died at age 70 on December 25.

■ Big East ejected Temple, effective in 2002, for non-compliance of attendance requirements. Conference later extended timeline to 2004.

■ Big West conference dissolved after 32 years. Members Arkansas State, New Mexico State and North Texas moved to Sun Belt Conference, and Boise State joined WAC.

■ Longest winning streaks entering season:
Oklahoma 13   Miami 10   Washington 8

■ Coaching changes:

	Incoming	Outgoing
Alabama	Dennis Franchione	Mike DuBose
Arizona	John Mackovic	Dick Tomey
Arizona State	Dirk Koetter	Bruce Snyder
Boise State	Dan Hawkins	Dirk Koetter
Bowling Green	Urban Meyer	Gary Bleckney
BYU	Gary Crowton	LaVell Edwards
Buffalo	Jim Hofner	Craig Cirbus
Georgia	Mark Richt	Jim Donnan
Kentucky	Guy Morriss	Hal Mumme
Maryland	Ralph Friedgen	Ron Vanderlinden
Memphis	Tommy West	Rip Scherer
Miami	Larry Coker	Butch Davis
Missouri	Gary Pinkel	Larry Smith
North Carolina	John Bunting	Carl Torbush
Ohio	Brian Knorr	Jim Grobe
Ohio State	Jim Tressel	John Cooper
Oklahoma State	Les Miles	Bob Simmons
Rutgers	Greg Schiano	Terry Shea
San Jose State	Fitz Hill	Dave Baldwin
TCU	Gary Patterson	Dennis Franchione
Toledo	Tom Amstutz	Gary Pinkel
USC	Pete Carroll	Paul Hackett
Virginia	Al Groh	George Welsh
Wake Forest	Jim Grobe	Jim Caldwell
West Virginia	Rich Rodriguez	Don Nehlen

Preseason *USA Today* Coaches

1	Florida (25)	1401	14	Washington	652
2	Miami (Fla.) (15)	1349	15	UCLA	547
3	Oklahoma (8)	1314	16	Notre Dame	534
4	Nebraska (6)	1292	17	LSU	515
5	Florida State (1)	1249	18	Clemson	503
6	Texas (2)	1164	19	Mississippi State	481
7	Tennessee (1)	1042	20	Northwestern	366
8	Oregon (1)	1038	21	Ohio State	259
9	Virginia Tech	899	22	South Carolina	258
10	Michigan (1)	856	23	Wisconsin	204
11	Kansas State	844	24	Colorado State	168
12	Oregon State	796	25	Alabama	131
13	Georgia Tech	706			

August 25, 2001

WISCONSIN 26 Virginia 17: After struggling with new spread O in 1st H and losing QB Brooks Bollinger to contused liver, Badgers (1-0) went back to power football to finish off Virginia. Frosh TB Anthony Davis rushed for 147y in debut as featured Wisconsin back. Cavaliers (0-1) gave away 10 early pts as QB Matt Schaub threw INTs that NG Ben Herbert and LB Nick Greisen returned to UVA 18YL and 7YL to set up quick scores. Virginia had more 1st Q bad luck as RB Antoine Womack—ACC's leading rusher in 2000—had 74y TD on screen pass negated due to PEN and suffered badly sprained right ankle that knocked him out for several games. Backup QB Bryson Spinner threw for 154y and 2 TDs in relief of Schaub, but he could not completely rally Cavs. WR Lee Evans had 2 TD catches for Badgers.

NEBRASKA 21 Texas Christian 7: Nebraska (1-0) dominated Pigskin Classic as QB Eric Crouch threw for 151y and rushed for 69y, while Huskers D held TCU to 6 1st downs and 186y O, 65y in 2nd H when Frogs cracked 50YL once. TCU (0-1) scored TD on busted play as scrambling QB Casey Printers (10-21/122y) found TE Matt Schobel on short pass taken rest of way for 67y score and 7-7 1st Q tie. Crouch answered with 1y keeper 6 mins later, capping 55y drive that featured 41y pass to WB John Gibson. Crouch then led 98y drive—42y coming on QB keeper—at end of 3rd Q, with IB Thunder Collins rushing for 26y TD to end matters.

(Sun) Georgia Tech 13 Syracuse 7 (East Rutherford, NJ): Despite Kickoff Classic victory, Georgia Tech (1-0) had to feel disappointed. Expected to challenge for ACC title, Yellow Jackets looked lackluster and almost had game stolen from them. Tech QB George Godsey threw for 224y, with 10/193y to WR Kelly Campbell, and TB Joe Burns added 113y, TD rushing. QB Troy Nunes (19-32/183y) scored only Orangemen (0-1) TD on 1y keeper, and set up Georgia Tech TD with INT to CB Marvious Hester returned 10y to Syracuse 6YL. Yellow Jackets D sacked Nunes 3 times and twice knocked him out of game for short spells. K Luke Manget supplied margin of victory with 2 short FGs for Yellow Jackets.

(Sun) Fresno State 24 COLORADO 22: Sitting in short FG range with less than 4 mins to go, Buffaloes (0-1) had win all but secured until double coverage forced INT by QB Craig Ochs (31-51/346y, 2 TDs), picked off by Fresno State CB Devon Banks. Another INT ended late Colorado drive. Fresno State (1-0) had no TOs, while late INTs were 4th and 5th TOs for Colorado; 2 came on FUMs that Fresno converted into 14-0 lead. QB David Carr (21-36/198y, TD) opened scoring with 1y plunge after hitting all 5 passes on drive. WR Roman Hollowell put Buffs on scoreboard later in H with 77y punt TD RET. Carr answered with 80y drive, on which he hit 5-6 passes, including 21y TD to WR Marque Davis for 21-7 lead. Ochs led Buffs on quick drive at H's end, throwing for 55y and adding 16y run on 3rd-and-10. Following 8y TD pass to WR John Minardi, Buffs had x-pt blocked to trail 21-13 at H. Minardi's 2nd TD catch, of 16y, closed scoring as Ochs misfired on 2-pt conv pass.

USA Today Coaches August 27

1	Florida (28)	1429	14	Georgia Tech	658
2	Miami (Fla.) (16)	1379	15	UCLA	581
3	Oklahoma (10)	1348	16	LSU	549
4	Nebraska (2)	1255	17	Notre Dame	535
5	Florida State (1)	1251	18	Clemson	508
6	Texas (2)	1179	19	Mississippi State	470
7	Oregon (1)	1076	20	Northwestern	356
8	Tennessee	1071	21	Ohio State	260
9	Virginia Tech	969	22	South Carolina	236
10	Michigan	876	23	Wisconsin	224
11	Kansas State	852	24	Colorado State	146
12	Oregon State	828	25	Alabama	132
13	Washington	662			

September 1, 2001

BOSTON COLLEGE 34 West Virginia 10: Once Boston College (1-0) D adjusted to new no-huddle Mountaineers attack, game became showcase for TB William Green. Green exploited big holes to rush for 204y and 3 TDs as Eagles tipped 10-0 deficit. Green stepped up in 2nd H with 12/118y rushing in 3rd Q, including 67y scoring burst for 20-10 lead. No thanks to its hurry-up O that lost 5 TOs, West Virginia (0-1) D grew tired. WVU QB Brad Lewis threw for 183y, but had 2 INTs.

MARYLAND 23 North Carolina 7: It was new era at Maryland (1-0) under coach Ralph Friedgen as TB Bruce Perry rushed for 116y. Tar Heels (0-2) TB Willie Parker (13/102y) opened scoring with 77y TD gallop only secs into contest, but Terps tied it on QB Shaun Hill's 20y pass to WR Jafar Williams. Blitzing Terps S Tyrone Stewart nailed Parker for 2nd Q safety. Maryland put game away with 2 TDs in 4th Q, including Hill's 2nd TD pass, 5y to WR Scooter Monroe, and relied on P Brooks Barnard's 8/50.4y. UNC DE Julius Peppers had 3 sacks.

Ucla 20 ALABAMA 17: Losing 1st home opener since 1993, Crimson Tide slipped as UCLA (1-0) wiped out 10-0 edge with 20 straight pts. New Alabama (0-1) coach Dennis Franchione chose QB Tyler Watts (12-22/204y, INT) as starter and it paid off in 1st Q with 78y TD pass to WR Antonio Carter. Tide added 30y FG by K Neal Thomas, but then found pts hard to come by despite solid attack that outgained Bruins 459y to 291y. TB DeShaun Foster led Bruins with 110y rushing, while QB Cory Paus (8-22/123y) shook off sprained thumb to find WR Tab Perry (5/113y) for 53y TD pass as mistake-free UCLA grabbed 14-10 lead. Crimson Tide pulled to within 20-17 late on QB Andrew Zow's 71y strike to WR Freddie Milons (4/124y).

Miami 33 PENN STATE 7: Record crowd at expanded Beaver Stadium energized Penn State (0-1) as did presence of former DB Adam Taliaferro, recovering from crippling spinal injury suffered in 2000. Hurricanes (1-0) looked to win for new coach Larry Coker, who had 322 fewer wins than Lions' Joe Paterno. QB Ken Dorsey (20-27/344y, INT) threw 3 TDs and RB Clinton Portis ran for 164y for 30-0 H edge, Miami scoring on 6 of 1st 7 possessions. With K Todd Sievers chipping in 4 FGs, Canes totally outclassed Penn State, which failed to hit pass until game was 28 mins old. Nittany Lions, outgained 602y to 323y, scored late when QB Zack Mills (12-24/240y, 2 INTs) hit WR Bryant Johnson (6/149y) on 44y TD pass. Penn State had only 6 wins in last 17 games as it limped to Paterno's record for coaching wins.

COLORADO 41 Colorado State 14: After 2 straight series defeats, Colorado (1-1) regained some pride with decisive win. CB Donald Strickland and S Michael Lewis each returned INTs for TDs as Buffs D matched Rams (0-1) with 2 TDs. TB Bobby Purify rushed for 191y and TD, and TB Chris Brown rushed for 121y as Colorado deployed ball-control O behind QB Craig Ochs, who threw 15-18/95y. WR Pete Rebstock was bright spot for Colorado State, catching 6/103y.

Rice 21 HOUSTON 14: Mastering triple option, QB Kyle Herm successfully debuted at helm of Owls (1-0) O. Herm rushed for 108y as run game churned up 354y, 347y more than Cougars (0-1) gained on ground. Houston QB Kelly Robertson, also debuting as starter, threw for 192y but was sacked 6 times. Rice led 7-0 after outgaining Cougars 188y to 52y in 1st H. Lead was doubled on 25y run by HB Clint Hatfield before Robertson put Houston on board late in 3rd Q with 1st of his 2 TD passes, 13y to TE Grover Thompson. Rice drove to FB Ronnie Beck's 2y TD run midway through 4th Q to clinch Bayou Bucket trophy.

OREGON 31 Wisconsin 28: With game down to wire, wide-open Badgers (1-1) WR Nick Davis dropped 4th down pass in middle of field with 64 secs left. Winning 21st straight at home, Oregon (1-0) was led by QB Joey Harrington (22-47/277y, 2 INTs), 15-2 as starter, who capped 77y drive with winning 1y keeper 3 mins earlier for 8th 4th Q comeback of career. Harrington's TD provided 6th and final lead change in shootout-style 2nd H. Wisconsin QB Jim Sorgi (16-32/231y, INT) began pt explosion with 13y TD pass to WR Darrin Charles for 14-10 lead in 3rd Q. Harrington answered with 2nd TD pass to TE Justin Peelle, from 11y out. It was Wisconsin's turn: TB Anthony Davis (13/130y) broke free for 69y TD run. Ducks then scored on shovel pass to WR Jason Willis to close 3rd Q with 24-21 edge. Badgers had another TD in them: Sorgi's 1y keeper. Wisconsin WR Lee Evans (8/168y) nabbed half of Sorgi's completions, but, not enough on 3rd down where Badgers went 2-14.

(Sun) FRESNO STATE 44 Oregon State 24: As crowd chanted "Overrated!" in reference to Oregon State's no. 1 ranking in *Sports Illustrated*, Bulldogs (2-0) easily won 16th straight at home. Once again, QB David Carr (21-34/340y) was brilliant, throwing 4 TDs against Pac 10's best D of 2000. It was WR that won conf player of week, however, as WR Rodney Wright ripped up Beavers (0-1) secondary for 7/182y, 2 TDs. Wright's 70y romp with short pass gave Bulldogs 31-10 lead in 3rd Q and, after OSU rallied with 2 TDs including WR Seth Trimmer's 65y scoring catch, Wright caught 32y TD. Fresno D excelled, sacking QB Jonathan Smith (284y and 2 TDs passing) 6 times—3 by DT Alan Harper—and derailing TB Ken Simonton's Heisman campaign by holding him to 15/42y rushing.

September 8, 2001

South Florida 35 PITTSBURGH 26: Bulls (1-1), in only 5th year of football and 8th game ever against Div 1-A program, stunned Pittsburgh, who 1st played football 111 years ago, behind spread O that built 28-7 lead. QB Marquel Blackwell (37-65/343y, INT) threw 4 TDs and scored TD on 1y plunge after Panthers (1-1) rally pulled home team to within 28-26. WR DeAndrew Rubin was Blackwell's favorite target, catching 11/144y and 2 TDs. Pitt QB David Priestley (28-45/354y, 3 TDs, INT) threw 56y TD hook-up with WR Roosevelt Bynes and 71y TD pass to WR R.J. English (5/135y).

South Carolina 14 GEORGIA 9: Hard-fought game tilted to Gamecocks (2-0) on 16y TD pass from QB Phil Petty to WR Brian Scott that was wrestled away from CB Bruce Thornton with 1:22 left. South Carolina needed to convert trio of 3rd-and-10s during winning 62y drive. Georgia (1-1) settled for 3 FGs by K Billy Bennett, last with 3 mins had provided slim 9-7 lead. Bulldogs had 183y to 45y edge at H, but trailed 7-6 thanks to dropped pass in EZ by WR Terrence Edwards, blocked 37y FG, and INT by Gamecocks S Willie Offord at Carolina 3YL. Gamecocks FB Andrew Pinnock scored on 1y run, set up by 66y KO RET by TB Derek Watson.

Fresno State 32 WISCONSIN 20: Upstart Bulldogs (3-0) finished sweep of 3 BCS conf teams, utilizing 22-0 2nd H run that eliminated doubt of their place among nation's elite. WR Bernard Berrian's 96y KO TD RET to open 2nd H began surge; he finished with 300y all-purpose including 8/102y receiving. Fresno State CB Tierre Sams followed with INT that set up 31y drive, capped by QB David Carr's 16y TD pass to WR Rodney Wright and 2nd successful 2-pt conv for 26-20 lead. Despite play of WR Lee Evans, who caught 7/182y, Badgers (1-2) could not rally.

NEBRASKA 27 Notre Dame 10: Cornhuskers (3-0) jumped on visitors early, scoring 14 pts while Notre Dame O initiated only 1 play, which ended on lost FUM by TB Terrance Howard. After committing only 8 TOs in 2000, Notre Dame (0-1) had 3 in 1st H and quickly was in hole. Nebraska D dominated, holding Irish to 162y and TD. Sole Notre Dame score followed blocked punt that was recovered at Nebraska 4YL. ND switched from starting QB Matt LoVecchio (11-24/78y) to QB Carlyle Holiday (5-8/41y) and back again without success. Nebraska QB Eric Crouch threw for 108y, while IB Dahrran Diedrick rushed for 133y and 2 TDs.

KANSAS STATE 10 SOUTHERN CALIFORNIA 6: Wildcats (1-0) upped quality of maligned September competition and put 28-game regular season win streak against non-conf foes on line by traveling west. Kansas State run attack leaned on RB Josh Scobey rushed for 165y and QB Ell Roberson added 119y, while Cats D held USC (1-1) TB Sultan McCullough to 40y. Win, 100th for coach Bill Snyder, was saved when G Nick Leckey recovered Scobey's FUM in EZ for TD in 2nd Q. Scobey had raced 11y to Trojans 1YL where S Troy Polamalu stripped him and ball bounced into EZ. Kicking game also was crucial as K Jared Brite kicked 41y FG for K-State, while Troy K David

Davis missed 42y FG attempt and had x-pt kick blocked by Cats DT Tank Reese. Trojans marched to Kansas State 24YL on final drive, where USC QB Carson Palmer (16-36/197y) lost FUM to Cats DE Henry Bryant.

WASHINGTON 23 Michigan 18: Having specialized in 4th Q rallies to reach Rose Bowl in 2000, cardiac Huskies (1-0) turned game around midway through 4th Q on 2 huge plays within min by CB Omare Lowe. With Wolverines (1-1) aiming for 15-6 lead with 9:11 left, Lowe blocked K Hayden Epstein's FG attempt, with ball bouncing to CB Roc Alexander, who raced 77y for 13-12 lead. Two plays later, Lowe corralled pass tipped by TB Chris Perry at Michigan 21y and ran into EZ with INT for 20-12 lead. Lowe had had rough game covering WR Marquise Walker, who caught Michigan-record 15/159y and 2 TDs. In control most of way, Wolverines D allowed only 69y rushing and 3 FGs by Washington K John Anderson. Huskies frosh WR Reggie Williams debuted with 4/134y receiving, including 74y play.

September 15, 2001

No games were played due to September 11 terrorist attacks on United States.

September 22, 2001

(Th) South Carolina 16 MISSISSIPPI STATE 14: College football returned, and red-white-and-blue flag-waving crowd seemed glad for diversion. South Carolina (3-0) won 2nd straight on road as ground game earned 238y and D held Bulldogs (1-1) TBs Dontae Walker (10/50y, TD) and Dicenzo Miller (11/31y) in check. Mississippi State's best drive was its 1st: 77y to Walker's 2y TD run. Gamecocks FB Andrew Pinnock (12/97y) answered with 35y TD run to tie it 7-7. Teams slugged it out from then on, with Carolina building 9-pt lead on strength of 3 FGs by K Daniel Weaver. QB Wayne Madkin (27-46/261y, INT) threw 7y TD pass to WR Harold Lindsey in 4th Q, but it came too late for Bulldogs. As sign of new security procedures for large gatherings, even famed cowbells were banned from Scott Stadium.

NORTH CAROLINA 41 Florida State 9: After opening season with 3 straight losses by combined score of 108-48, Tar Heels (1-3) stunned Florida State with 34 pts in 2nd H. Seminoles (2-1) gift-wrapped 5 TOs and 14 PENs to hosts, while gaining only 11y in 3rd Q, 34y total in 2nd H. FSU trailed only 17-9 midway through 3rd Q when 84y TD pass to WR Javon Walker was called back for holding PEN. In 4th Q, Tar Heels scored 3 TDs, including 53y TD pass by QB Ronald Curry to WR Kory Bailey. Carolina DE Julius Peppers had 10 tackles, sack, and INT; his pressure forced costly 3rd Q PEN. Part-time Tar Heels QB Darian Durant (9-16/115y, 2 INTs) threw 2 TD passes. QB Chris Rix had poor game for Florida State, with INT, 2 FUMs, and 8-21/112y passing. Despite worst loss since 1985, Noles still owned gaudy 71-3 ACC record. North Carolina's 1st-ever win against Top-5 (Coaches poll) foe was revenge for 12 straight series losses, including 63-14 shellacking last year.

Virginia 26 CLEMSON 24: With Tigers not set on last-sec play, Virginia (2-1) secured upset on 1y TD pass from QB Bryson Spinner (15-25/186y) to WR Billy McMullen (8/88y, 2 TDs), who left CB Brian Mance on EZ floor. Tilt featured big swings in scoring as Cavs (2-1) opened with 10-0 lead before Cavs reeled off 20 straight pts as Spinner ran and threw for TDs. Tigers followed with pair of TDs as QB Woody Dantzler (24-34/251y, 2 INTs) completing 7-7 passes on 1st drive and producing 43y on 2nd drive of 59y to take 24-20 lead early in 4th Q. Clemson had opportunity to run out clock before Dantzler's FUM with less than 5 mins left. Teams then traded possessions before Spinner drove UVa 44y in final 1:43.

Michigan State 17 NOTRE DAME 10: WR Charles Rogers led Spartans (2-0) to 5th straight series win with play reminiscent of 2000's victory. Rogers (4/116y) caught quick pass over middle with Irish blitzing, broke tackle, and raced 47y for winning TD midway through 4th Q. Last season, Spartans won 27-21 on similar 68y scoring catch by WR Herb Haygood in game's final moments. Notre Dame (0-2) had 3 more possessions after Rogers' TD, but they ended on punt, failed fake FG, and INT by Michigan State CB Broderick Nelson off tipped pass. Spartans QB Ryan Van Dyke completed 9-15/149y, while Irish TB Tony Fisher rushed for 103y.

UCLA 13 Ohio State 6: Bruins (3-0), oft-reputed for O, showed D that seemed worthy of title aspirations. Buckeyes (1-1) managed 166y total O and 8 1st downs in game that was not as close as score indicated. Ohio State's lone TD was WR Ricky Bryant's REC of blocked punt in EZ. UCLA TB DeShaun Foster rushed for meager 66y and fumbled 4 times, but Buckeyes could not capitalize as QB Steve Bellisari completed only 5-23/45y with 2 INTs, and rush attack gained 121y. QB Cory Paus led Bruins O with 262y passing with 24y TD to WR Ryan Smith, while LB Robert Thomas sparked D with 9 tackles, 5 behind line of scrimmage.

OREGON 24 Southern California 22: After USC blocked FG attempt with shade less than 2 mins left, Ducks (3-0) needed stop from D and quick scoring drive to maintain home win streak, now at 22 games. They got both, regaining ball with 65 secs left and marching 61y to another FG try. This time, K Jared Siegel hit winning 32y 3-ptr to cap

drive that featured 2 22y completions from QB Joey Harrington to WR Kenan Howry. QB Carson Palmer threw for 411y in rallying Trojans (1-2) from 21-6 deficit to 22-21 4th Q lead by throwing 75y TD to TB Sultan McCullough and 93y TD to WR Kareem Kelly. Palmer suffered 3 INTs, all by Oregon CB Steve Smith who made 38y TD RET late in 1st H for 14-6 lead. Oregon's opening TD had come on 35y option pass from TB Onterrio Smith to TE Justin Peelle. USC K David Davis booted 3 FGs.

STANFORD 51 Arizona State 28: Crazy pt-scoring extravaganza saw both teams scoring quickly and often, with Stanford (2-0) scoring more quickly and more often. Game exploded when teams combined for 27 pts over final 4:14 of 1st Q as Stanford grabbing 20-7 lead. Spread was 30-13 by H as balanced Cardinal O set heady pace. Stanford O gained 548y as QB Randy Fasani threw for 295y with 4 TDs, RB Brian Allen rushed for 134y, TD, and WR Luke Powell had 6/134y. Sun Devils (1-1) QB Jeff Krohn threw for 366y and 3 TDs.

USA Today Coaches September 24

1	Miami (Fla.) (34)	1453	14	LSU	705
2	Florida (14)	1423	15	Florida State	679
3	Oklahoma (9)	1377	16	South Carolina	574
4	Nebraska (1)	1311	17	Michigan	564
5	Texas	1239	18	Northwestern	546
6	Oregon (1)	1120	19	Oregon State	338
7	Virginia Tech	1104	20	Brigham Young	267
8	Tennessee	1090	21	Purdue	252
9	Kansas State	980	22	Mississippi State	162
10	UCLA	914	23	Illinois	132
11	Georgia Tech	907	24	Michigan State	120
12	Washington	837	25	Clemson	98
13	Fresno State (1)	770			

September 29, 2001

Clemson 47 GEORGIA TECH 44 (OT): Clemson (3-1) QB Woody Dantzler wore jersey no. 1, and he played like top Tiger with amazing performance. Dantzler, who threw for 254y, 2 TDs and rushed for 164y, finally ended game that featured 7 lead changes in 2nd H by racing 11y up middle with winning TD in OT. Tigers RB Travis Zachery led scoring parade with 3 TDs. But, Clemson looked like loser with 2 mins left in regulation until Dantzler hooked up with WR J.J. McKelvey on 63y TD pass, on 4th-and-13, that gave Tigers 41-38 lead. QB George Godsey, who passed for 216y, 2 TDs, then drove Georgia Tech (3-1) 87y for tying FG with time elapsing. Teams combined for 29 pts in wild 4th Q. Yellow Jackets popped another FG by K Luke Manget, his 4th of game, in OT after Clemson D stopped RB Joe Burns (30/126y) for no gain on 3rd-and-1. Dantzler made them pay as Clemson snapped 4-game losing streak to Tech in 6th straight series game decided by 3 pts.

TENNESSEE 26 Louisiana State 18: WR Kelley Washington emerged as go-to guy in big way, catching 11/school-record 256y for Tennessee (3-0) team that scored on its opening 3 possessions of 2nd H. Go-ahead TD was scored on 3y run by QB Casey Clausen midway through 3rd Q. Clausen and Washington soon hooked up on 70y TD pass for 19-7 lead. Tigers (2-1) QB Rohan Davey, star of last year's thrilling OT win, threw for 356y and TDs of 67y in 1st Q to WR Michael Clayton and 30y to WR Josh Reed (7/125y) in 4th Q. Vols D held RB LaBrandon Toefield to 20y rushing with no TDs after he had scored 7 times in LSU's season-opening 2 wins.

MICHIGAN 45 Illinois 20: Illini (3-1), hoping for payback for last year's game that they felt was taken away by referees, were instead beaten by surprisingly tricky Michigan. After netting –4y on 1st 4 possessions, Wolverines (3-1) broke open game as dynamic WR Marquise Walker (6/108y) threw pass to backup QB Jermaine Gonzales for 51y gain and then caught 21y TD pass from RB Walter Cross. QB John Navarre (13-26/187y) and RB B.J. Askew (19/80y, 2 TDs) also contributed for Michigan. Wolverines D made big 4th-and-1 stop of QB Kurt Kittner (20-39/244y) when Illini gambled at their 33YL. Michigan quickly converted it into 33y TD pass to WR Ronald Bellamy for 21-10 lead.

NORTHWESTERN 27 Michigan State 26: Wild game ended when Northwestern (3-0) K David Wasielewski booted 47y FG moments after Michigan State K David Schaefer had x-pt blocked by Wildcats LB Napoleon Harris. Failed conv followed 84y KO RET by Spartans WR Herb Haygood with 18 secs left. With 4:42 left, WR Charlie Rogers had given Michigan State 20-17 lead on 64y punt TD RET. Wildcats QB Zak Kustok (23-40/231y, INT) then sparked drive—he hit 8-10/43y and rushed for 36y—that seemed to win game at 24-20 on 10y TD pass to WR Kunle Patrick with 29 secs left. But wait! Foes contributed for more 10 pts. Haygood's RET took 11 secs, giving Kustok time for "Victory Right" play that beat Minnesota last year; this time he threw 54y pass to WR Jon Schweighardt (6/101y) off designed tip by Patrick to give Cats 1st down on Spartans 33YL. Kustok gained 3y more—he rushed for 105y to top teammate RB Damien Anderson (28/75y) and Michigan State RB T.J. Duckett (22/104y)—before winning FG was launched. Ultimately, Spartans could fault their kicking game as Schaefer missed 3 FGs and they failed to convert 2 x-pts. Wildcats had opened 3-0 for 1st time since 1962.

OKLAHOMA 38 Kansas State 37: Winning 17th straight, Sooners (4-0) jumped out to 35-14 lead as WR Antwone Savage caught TD passes of 63y and 75y and threw 33y TD on fake punt to backup QB Hunter Wall. Also, S Roy Williams (9 tackles) returned FUM 18y for TD. Wildcats (2-1) rallied behind QB Ell Roberson, who rushed for 115y and threw for 257y while scoring on 3 runs. During late comeback, Roberson scored twice and added 57y scoring pass to WR Ricky Lloyd with 2 mins left. Coach Bill Snyder then curiously opted against trying onside-KO. KSU didn't see ball again until only 7 secs remained, which permitted time for incomplete Hail Mary pass. With rushing game held to 9y, QB Nate Hybl led Sooners O with 283y passing. Hybl also was picked off 3 times under heavy pressure. OU bogged down in 2nd H, gaining

only single 1st down during 1st 5 possessions of 2nd H before 71y drive produced K Tim Duncan's winning 33y FG. In dropping 3rd straight to Oklahoma, Wildcats lost 1st September game since 1991.

USA Today Coaches October 1

1	Miami (Fla.) (35)	1458	14	Florida State	690
2	Florida (16)	1436	15	Michigan	682
3	Oklahoma (8)	1370	16	Northwestern	674
4	Nebraska	1315	17	Georgia Tech	485
5	Texas	1263	18t	Brigham Young	395
6	Virginia Tech	1128	18t	Purdue	395
7	Tennessee	1119	20	LSU	339
8	Oregon	1108	21	Clemson	317
9	UCLA	1038	22	Texas A&M	245
10	Washington	924	23	Toledo	157
11	Fresno State (1)	821	24	Stanford	129
12	South Carolina	757	25	Maryland	105
13	Kansas State	746			

October 6, 2001

Georgia 26 TENNESSEE 24: Invoking memories of 1980 championship season, which was last time Bulldogs won at Neyland Stadium, Georgia (3-1) stunned Vols with last-sec win. Tennessee (3-1) dramatically had taken 24-20 lead with 44 secs left on 62y scoring romp on screen pass by TB Travis Stephens (176y rushing). Frosh QB David Greene (21-34/303y, INT), who would develop into amazing "Road Warrior," made his 1st away start memorable as he led Georgia on winning 59y drive, completing 4-5 with big gainer on 26y connection to TE Randy McMichael. Bulldogs FB Verron Haynes capped drive with 6y TD catch off play-action fake with 5 secs left. Vols QB Casey Clausen threw for 295y and 3 TDs in defeat. Bulldogs LB Tony Gilbert was in on 15 tackles, while WR Damien Gary contributed big 72y punt TD RET that pulled Georgia to within 14-10.

Florida 44 LOUISIANA STATE 15: At least LSU (2-2) kept Florida to fewer than 50 pts. Still, QB Rex Grossman threw for Florida-record 464y and 5 TDs—he had 320y and 4 TDs by H—as Gators topped 500y O. Grossman had exceeded 300y in each 2001 game. Florida (5-0) jumped out front to 21-3 lead in 1st Q as Grossman spread wealth, throwing scoring passes to WRs Jabar Gaffney (5/164y), Reche Caldwell (6/120y) and Taylor Jacobs (3/43y). Tigers found rallying difficult once QB Rohan Davey suffered knee injury; he had thrown for 154y by time he left in 2nd Q. LSU WR Josh Reed caught 6/123y. Florida DE Alex Brown authored 2 of his team's 5 sacks to become all-time school leader with 28.

OHIO STATE 38 Northwestern 20: Off to great 2001 start, Wildcats (3-1) seemed poised to end streak of 21 straight losses to Buckeyes. Instead, Ohio State (3-1) went to ground game as RB Jonathan Wells gained 179y of team's 287y rushing and added 3 TDs. Wells' big play was 71y jaunt on 2nd snap of game. Northwestern matched that with RB Damien Anderson's 8y TD run, but Bucks continued to score while Cats failed to keep pace. Turning point came late in 1st Q as Bucks S Mike Doss returned FUM by Anderson (21/80y) 30y for go-ahead score. Ohio D stymied Northwestern spread O until 4th Q when QB Zak Kustok (16-26/122y, TD, 2 INTs) led 2 TDs drives, resulting in his 2y run and 4y pass to WR Jon Schweighardt.

Oklahoma 14 Texas 3 (Dallas): Series of plays late in game doomed Longhorns (4-1). Nightmare ending began when Texas QB Chris Simms threw INT to CB Antonio Perkins in EZ. Sooners (5-0) soon faked FG and had K Tim Duncan pooch QK that was headed for EZ, until Longhorn S Nathan Vashar foolishly caught it at own 3YL. On next play, Oklahoma S Roy Williams blitzed, as both teams did all day, and his hit on Simms forced pass to pop into air. Alert OU LB Teddy Lehman caught it and ran 2y for clinching TD. Williams quickly followed his big rush with INT, giving harried Simms 3 pick-offs in as many attempts. In holding Texas to mere 3 pts, 42 fewer than avg, Oklahoma took away deadly Texas deep patterns and run game (27y). Simms manfully completed 24-42/198y, 4 INTs, but was sacked 5 times, 3 by DE Jimmy Wilkerson. OU lost QB Nate Hybl to injury, with backup QB Jason White (16-23/108y) finishing TD drive, which featured pitch to TB Quentin Griffin on 4th-and-2 that gained 17y. Sooners ran win streak to 18 games, including 8 straight vs. Top-10 teams. Horns coach Mack Brown fell to 3-8 vs. Top 10 teams.

Colorado 16 KANSAS STATE 6: Buffs (4-1) quietly rebuilt their season after falling off radar screen with opening loss to Fresno State. With its D posting shutout until midway through 4th Q, Colorado was back in Big 12 race. CU K Jeremy Flores booted 3 FGs, 3rd of which was set up by WR Roman Hollowell's 53y punt RET, and QB Craig Ochs hit TE Daniel Graham on 21y TD pass. Buffs TB Chris Brown led rushing attack with 114y. Meanwhile, Colorado D created 6 sacks and 2 INTs while dominating K-State O that had scored 37 pts against Oklahoma. Wildcats (2-2) were able to pull within TD on QB Ell Roberson's 2y run to cap drive that began after DE Henry Bryant's INT. Cats' kicking game went south, missing 2 FGs and x-pt, and watched P Travis Brown bobble snap to set up Flores' 1st FG for Colorado.

Oregon 63 ARIZONA 28: Oregon (5-0) QB Joey Harrington (15-24/279y, 3 TDs) seemed as large to Arizona as Times Square billboard in New York City that Ducks boosters had built to promote their QB for Heisman Trophy. In addition to throwing for 3 TDs, Harrington ran for 3 more scores. Ducks gained 607y with 2 rushers—TBs Maurice Morris (21/110y) and Onterrio Smith (15/131y)—topping 100y mark as they blew open 14-14 game with 7 straight TDs. Wildcats (0-2) were hampered by 5 TOs, all converted into TDs. Arizona TB Clarence Farmer rushed for 158y. "People were talking in the papers about how we didn't deserve to be ranked where we were (at no. 7)," said Harrington. "We just went out and had fun and put a game together."

October 13, 2001

(Th) Maryland 20 GEORGIA TECH 17 (OT): Despite having missed 7 of previous 11 FG attempts, K Nick Novak was needed to boot 46y effort to knot things up for Terps (6-0) and then kick 26y 3-ptr in OT. He made both FGs, and win was secured when Maryland S Randall Jones recovered Georgia Tech TB Joe Burns' OT FUM. Burns earlier lost FUM that was returned 36y for TD by LB E. J. Henderson (15 tackles), and late in game he needlessly ran OB when Jackets were trying to run out clock. After ensuing punt, QB Shaun Hill (20-39/206y, 2 INTs) moved Terps 51y, including 3rd-and-10 pass to WR Rich Parson for 17y with 15 secs left, to set up Novak's tying FG. Earlier, Yellow Jackets (4-2) had rallied with 17 straight pts behind QB George Godsey (26-45/320y, 2 TDs, 3 INTs) and WR Kelly Campbell (9/108y), who became school's all-time receptions leader.

VIRGINIA TECH 34 Boston College 20: Hokies (6-0) ended things early, building 21-0 lead after 1 Q as their D surrendered no 1st downs and held BC to −1y. Virginia Tech D scored TD for 4th straight game as S Kevin McCadam grabbed loose ball and returned it 9y for team's 3rd TD. Va Tech O had plenty of heroes too as QB Grant Noel hit 16-28/225y, 2 TDs, both to big-play WR Andre Davis (6/112y). Hokies TB Keith Burnell also rushed for 111y. Noel capped Hokies' 1st possession with 37y scoring pass to Davis and next went in from 1y out. Eagles (4-2) TB William Green was held to 74y after breaking 100y barrier in all 5 previous games. Boston College added 3 late TDs to make score respectable, including pair of 4th Q TD passes from QB Brian St. Pierre (13-26/180y) to WR Jamal Burke.

Miami 49 FLORIDA STATE 27: Miami's 5th-year srs got revenge for 47-0 pasting Florida State (3-2) administered back in 1997. In snapping FSU's 54-game home win streak, Hurricanes (5-0) were inspired by lean QB Ken Dorsey (14-27/249y). Dorsey threw 3 TD passes, leading 3rd Q explosion that produced 4 TDs. Dorsey's 3rd scoring pass, 18y to WR Andre Johnson (5/111y), gave Miami 28-13 lead early in 2nd H. Seminoles QB Chris Rix (13-30/222y) then lost ball controversially ruled FUM—his final TO tally was 4 INTs and lost 2 FUMs—that LB Jonathan Vilma returned 36y for TD. After Rix threw 57y TD pass to WR Talman Gardner to cut deficit to 35-20, Miami roared back with 2 TDs: 7y TD run by holder Freddie Capshaw during botched FG attempt and 8y TD run by RB Willis McGahee after INT by CB Phillip Buchanan. Miami botched another FG try in 4th Q, which led to 73y TD RET by FSU LB Michael Boulware that merely added respectability to score. Miami TB Clinton Portis rushed for 122y, while S Ed Reed—1 of those 5th year srs—had 2 INTs and blocked punt despite dislocating right shoulder in 1st H.

Wake Forest 42 DUKE 35: Struggling Blue Devils (0-6) had everything come together in 3rd Q when scoring 28 pts, but even that glorious surge was not enough to prevent 18th straight loss. Problem for Duke was that they trailed 28-0 at H, and Wake Forest (3-3) authored 2 more scores to hold off rally. Additionally, awakened Wake D prevented Devils from crossing midfield in game's final 7 mins. QB James MacPherson threw for 141y and RB Tarence Williams rushed for 121y to lead balanced Deamon Deacon attack that gained 409y. Duke's comeback came through air as QB D. Bryant, who rushed in 2 short TDs, threw for 251y and TD.

AUBURN 23 Florida 20: Tigers (5-1) had been expected to rebuild this season, reality they seemed to confirm with narrow win over Vanderbilt. Gators (5-1), meanwhile, arrived with 49.8 pts scoring avg in 5 games. Auburn D paid no heed, holding Florida to 328y O with 4 INTs off QB Rex Grossman (25-42/364y). Tigers QB Daniel Cobb came off bench to complete 11-23/152y and hit 7 of last 8 as Tigers scored 13 pts in 4th Q. Winning pts came on K Damon Duval's 44y FG with 10 secs left; Duval amazingly had kicked 3 straight late game-winners. Without injured RB Earnest Graham, Gators finished with −36y rushing. Florida WRs Reche Caldwell (9/128y) and Jabar Gaffney (4/110y) continued their big years, with each scoring TD, including Gaffney's 80y catch in 4th Q that tied game at 20-20.

MISSISSIPPI 27 Alabama 24: "We're starting a new tradition here," said winning QB Eli Manning after game, and, thanks to his heady play, Rebels (4-1) were doing just that. Mississippi scored 2 late TDs, including Manning's 3y pass to RB Joe Gunn with 46 secs left to beat Alabama (3-3) for 1st time in 13 years. Manning (22-41/325y, TD) began winning drive with 24y pass to WR Jamie Armstrong on 1st-and-20. Two plays later, he connected with FB Toward Sanford for 42y to bring Rebels to Alabama 4YL. Two plays after that, Gunn, who rushed for 78y and 25y TDs, caught swing pass at 5YL and ran through tackle at 2YL to score. Tide's last gasp ended with QB Tyler Watts' desperation pass picked off by Ole Miss LB Lanier Goethie. Watts was game's leading rusher with 110y, but hit only 7-24/136y in air.

ARKANSAS 10 South Carolina 7: With last-sec game-winning FGs all-the-rage in SEC, Hogs (3-3) DE Carlos Hall preserved win by blocking 32y FG attempt by Carolina K Daniel Weaver with 48 secs left. With its D dominant, Arkansas managed 3-0 lead at H on K Brennan O'Donohoe's 21y FG. South Carolina (5-1) gained only 65y in game's 1st H with QB Phil Petty throwing 2 INTs, his 1st of season. South Carolina coach

Lou Holtz called for reverse on 2nd H KO, and TB Derek Watson raced into Arkansas territory to set up 41y TD run by back-up QB Corey Jenkins for 7-3 lead. Razorbacks answered with 69y drive capped by QB Zak Clark's 10y TD pass to WR Richard Smith that went through hands of Gamecocks LB Kalimba Edwards. Carolina floundered until final drive, when Petty completed passes of 21y to Watson and 30y to WR Brian Scott (5/112y) to set up Weaver's FG try. Rushing for 111y, TB Fred Talley helped Hogs own almost 10 mins in possession advantage.

MICHIGAN 24 Purdue 10: As it had done all season, lackluster Wolverine O turned to WR Marquise Walker to lift it to victory. Trailing 7-0 early in 2nd Q, Michigan (5-1) got boost when Walker raced 42y with punt RET. He then caught 24y pass from QB John Navarre (21-27/233y) to set up 1st of FB B.J. Askew's 2 TDs, this from 3y out. With D beginning to handle Boilermakers (4-1), Walker next caught 43y TD pass for 14-7 lead. He finished with 7/112y receiving and 7/134y on punt RETs. Purdue had looked so sharp in moving 80y to TD on opening series, converting 4 3rd downs, that it was stunning that it finished with only 12 1st downs and 175y O. Boilermakers QB Brandon Hance (16-33/198y, TD) was sacked 7 times.

Wisconsin 20 OHIO STATE 17: Having lost week earlier 63-32 to Indiana, Badgers (4-3) would not have shocked if they had crumbled after falling behind 17-0 in Columbus, historical losing abyss for Wisconsin. Instead, Badgers rallied as QB Brooks Bollinger (12-22/202y, INT) led 4 scoring drives, including 53y trip to K Mark Neuser's winning 33y FG with 2:10 left. Comeback began late in 1st H when bad snap on Ohio State (3-2) punt led to 23y TD run by TB Anthony Davis (26/103y). On 1st possession of 2nd H, Bollinger avoided blitz to toss 42y TD pass to WR Nick Davis (6/90y). Next, Neuser booted 2 4th Q FGs. Ohio State had done all its scoring in game's opening 20 mins on TD runs by QB Steve Bellisari (10-21/132y, INT) and RB Lydell Ross, and 44y FG by K Josh Huston. Wisconsin D soon tightened, toting up 4 sacks and holding Ohio to −4y rushing in 2nd H.

COLORADO 31 Texas A&M 21: With Texas A&M (5-1) driving to tying FG or go-ahead TD, blitzing Buffs LB Kory Mossoni sacked QB Mark Farris and forced FUM that LB Joey Johnson returned 52y for TD with less than min to play. Farris (30-49/334y, 3 TDs, 2 INTs) had thrown 2 TDs to WR Jamaar Taylor (9/146y) and 36y arrow to WR Terrence Murphy (10/146y) to pull Aggies to within 24-21. Colorado (5-1) had scored 18 straight pts to build 24-14 4th Q lead as QB Craig Ochs (14-28/183y, INT) tied it 14-14 with 7y TD pass to WR Derek McCoy (5/113y). Buffs K Jeremy Flores soon added FG, and TB Cortlen Johnson made 2y TD run.

TEXAS TECH 38 Kansas State 19: Wild Texas Tech (3-2) O received credibility with 1st win over ranked team under coach Mike Leach. QB Kliff Kingsbury (32-47/409y, 3 INTs) threw 4 TDs, 2 to WR Wes Welker (6/102y). Hampered by absence of injured QB Ell Roberson, struggling Wildcats (2-3) lost 3rd straight in conf for 1st time since 1992 by not taking advantage of 343y O and 4 TOs tossed away by Red Raiders. K-State sub QB Marc Dunn threw for 197y, but was sacked 5 times and threw 2 INTs. Dunn's 47y TD pass to WR Brandon Clark gave Kansas State short-lived 7-0 lead in 1st Q, but Red Raiders ran off game's next 24 pts.

Iowa State 20 MISSOURI 14: Game came down to single play as S Adam Runk tipped away 4th down pass by Missouri QB Kirk Farmer to TE Dwayne Blakley with 3 secs left. Farmer had driven Tigers (2-3) 67y with 30y in scramble runs and 27y completion to diving WR Thomson Omboga. Margin of game proved to be pair of 4th FGs by Iowa State K Tony Yelk, who also averaged 6/49.5y punts. Missouri TB Zak Abron won battle of backs, rushing for 147y to 120y for Iowa State TB Ennis Haywood. Haywood, though, scored 2 TDs as Cyclones held on for win.

Fresno State 25 COLORADO STATE 22 (OT): Rams (2-4) had it all but won by grabbing 3-pt lead with 27 secs left on 21y TD pass by QB Bradlee Van Pelt to WR Pete Rebstock and 2-pt conv. Fresno State (6-0) QB David Carr (28-37/389y, 2 TDs), not wanting to let dream season die, completed 3 passes in frantic final 27 secs to set up K Asen Aparuhov's tying 48y FG. In OT, Bulldogs D stopped CSU on downs—Rams passed up FG—before Aparuhov booted winning 41y FG for Fresno State. Earlier, Van Pelt (13-24/116y, TD, and 148y rushing) seemed to upstage Carr with TD throw and 53y TD run in 3rd Q. Carr was not to be denied, however, and topped 300y passing for 4th time in 2001. Fresno TB Paris Gaines rushed for 111y, with 57y burst on team's 2nd play to set up TD.

UCLA 35 Washington 13: Facing D that had not surrendered rushing TD all year, Bruins (5-0) RB DeShaun Foster proved unstoppable as he rambled for 301y and 4 TDs. Foster's pair of 1st Q TDs were enough for resurgent UCLA D, led by LB Robert Thomas' 12 tackles. Bruins held Huskies by sacking QB Taylor Barton (22-44/316y, INT) 4 times and forcing him to cough up ball twice, while surrendering only 16y rushing. Barton's 4th down, 39y TD pass to WR Todd Elstrom (6/112y) with 20 secs left in 1st H was 1st TD allowed by Bruins' starting D in 11 Qs. At 21-6, Huskies were still in game until Foster scored twice more; his 92y jaunt for his 4th TD allowed him to break Theotis Brown's school mark of 274y, set in 1978. Bruins QB Cory Paus threw for 128y and stretched INT-free streak of passes to 175.

Washington State 45 STANFORD 39: Cougars (6-0) continued winning ways as QB Jason Gesser (15-28/178y, INT) hit WR Mike Bush with winning 11y TD pass midway through 4th Q. Teams combined for 35 pts in 1st Q, with Wazzu TD coming on WR Colin Henderson's 62y pass to Bush. Game was tied 21-21 in 2nd Q before Cougars scored twice before H on TDs coming from other than their O: S Jeremy Bohannon's 4y RET of blocked punt and S Billy Newman's 54y INT RET. Stanford (3-1) QB Randy Fasani was burned on Newman's TD RET, but threw for 202y and 2 TD passes to TE Darrin Naatjes, while RB Brian Allen rushed for 133y and 3 TDs.

October 20, 2001

(Tue) LOUISVILLE 24 Southern Mississippi 14: Rare Tuesday night spotlight showcased Conference-USA. As it did all season, Louisville capitalized on TOs, converting 4 by Eagles (3-2) into 21 pts. Cardinals (6-1) trailed 14-6 entering 4th Q, but were marching deep into enemy territory. But, Southern Miss halted threat on its 9YL, stuffing QB Dave Ragone on 4th down keeper. Eagles QB Jeff Kelly, who threw for 213y and TD, lost critical FUM to set up 9y TD pass from Ragone to TE Richard Owens. Ragone (17-32/186y) tied game 14-14 with 2-pt conv, improvising pass off busted play to WR J.R. Russell. Louisville D soon set up winning 36y FG by K Nathan Smith with S Anthony Floyd's INT and then forced TO to set up insurance TD as Kelly bobbled ball at own 35YL after big hit by Louisville LB Jeromy Freitag with less than 2 mins left. LB Chad Lee alertly returned Kelly's FUM 33y to 2YL, from where Cards RB Tony Stallings scored clincher.

(Th) Boise State 35 FRESNO STATE 30: Debate over Fresno State's inclusion in BCS final-6 ended with home loss. Broncos (4-3) posted 21 straight 2nd H pts as QB Ryan Dinwiddie (20-32/297y, 2 INTs) threw 2 of his 4 TDs to take 35-28 lead in 4th Q. Boise D stopped Fresno State (6-1) at game's end, doing so when LB Greg Sasser sacked QB David Carr (30-49/345y, INT) on 4th down at Boise 10YL with 51 secs left. Fresno had looked in control, leading 28-14, after marching 81y with 2nd H KO to score on Carr's 18y pass to WR Bernard Berrian (8/85y). Broncos answered with 81y drive of their own and tied it at 28-28 by converting Fresno TO into 33y TD drive. Boise took lead at on Dinwiddie's 54y TD pass to WR Jay Swillie, who absorbed big hit en route to EZ. Carr threw 3 TD passes included scoring grab by WR Rodney Wright (14/179y). Broncos' 1st-ever win over ranked opponent snapped Fresno's 17-game home win streak, 2nd longest in nation.

North Carolina 38 CLEMSON 3: Hot Tar Heels (5-3) won 5th in row behind ruling D that held QB Woody Dantzler to 118y total O, after his 467.5y avg in last 2 games. North Carolina sub QB Darian Durant (11-11/97y) threw TD and ran in 2 others, while QB Ronald Curry passed for 109y and rushed for 82y as Heels compiled 425y to 209y O margin. UNC DE Julius Peppers (5 tackles, sack) had another amazing INT, batting ball despite 2 blockers on him and catching it while falling to ground. Peppers' INT led to WR Bosley Allen's TD catch, 1st of his pair of 2nd Q scoring receptions. By managing only K Aaron Hunt's 38y FG, Tigers (4-2) dropped 2nd straight home game. North Carolina matched its biggest edge ever over Clemson, 1st achieved in 1970 when coach John Bunting starred at LB for Tar Heels.

Tennessee 35 ALABAMA 24: Despite big games by Tennessee (4-1) QB Casey Clausen (21-28/293y, 2 TDs) and RB Travis Stephens (33/162y), Alabama (3-4) held 4th Q lead as QB Tyler Watts threw 2 TDs to WR Sam Collins, TB Ahmaad Galloway ran for 4y TD, and K Neal Thomas kicked 25y FG. Clausen and Stephens—who had 60y TD romp in 2nd Q—each then scored 1y TD runs as Tide fell apart, allowing 156y in 4th Q while its O managed –3y. Bama TB Santonio Beard rushed 10/141y, setting up final TD with 69y jaunt that closed 3rd Q. Vols became 1st team ever to win 7 straight against Crimson Tide.

Penn State 38 NORTHWESTERN 35: After dropping all its games so far, Penn State (1-4) sprung surprise, going 69y, with WR Bryant Johnson (8/129y) nabbing 4/55y, in final 2 mins to win it. Calm frosh QB Zack Mills directed most of drive to 4y TD pass to RB Eric McCoo, coming in with 1:39 left for injured QB Matt Senneca (20-39/234y). Northwestern (4-2) had taken 35-31 lead moments earlier on QB Zak Kustok's 3rd rushing TD. Kustok gained 115y on ground and threw for 298y—including WR Sam Simmons' 7/168y—but could not overcome porous D that allowed Lions (501y O) to exceed 31 pts they had totaled in previous games.

MINNESOTA 28 Michigan State 19: Sealed off inside by Spartans D, Golden Gophers (2-4) rushing attack concentrated outside for 322y to control contest. Frosh TB Marion Barber III rushed for 158y, 2 TDs, and TB Tellis Redmon added 126y rushing with TD to pace Minnesota O. Redmon scored winning TD midway through 4th Q on 6y run that capped 75y drive in giving Gophers 21-17 lead. Michigan State (3-2) went to air for its success, passing for 351y, but being frustrated when confronted by field shortened in Minnesota red zone. Making things tougher for Michigan State were injuries suffered by top 2 QBs as starter Jeff Smoker (21-33/258y, 2 TDs, INT) left with sprained ankle only to return when sub Ryan Van Dyke (6-13/93y) was knocked out when sandwiched while hitting pass on drive that put MSU up 17-14. Van Dyke suffered broken jaw and concussion.

TEXAS 41 Colorado 7: Texas (6-1) QB Chris Simms exploited Buffs' secondary for 234y and 3 TD passes, while frosh TB Cedric Benson chipped in with 100y rushing and 2 scores as Longhorns snapped Colorado's 5-game win streak. Longhorns held 10-7 advantage in 2nd Q before erupting for 31 straight pts, including Benson's 2 TDs before H ended. WR Sloan Thomas added 2 receiving TDs for Longhorns. Colorado (5-2) contributed 4 TOs to Texas' cause, but QB Bobby Pesavento threw for 165y in defeat. Texas had tallied 40 or more pts in 11 straight home games.

BRIGHAM YOUNG 63 Air Force 33: Cougars (7-0) remained undefeated but had to deal with low ranking due to perceived easy schedule. Beating Air Force by 30 was impressive, however, as BYU received 338y and 4 TD passes from QB Brandon Doman and 134y rushing and 2 TDs from RB Luke Staley. TE Doug Jolley was receiving star as he corralled 10/conf-record 177y, 3 TDs. Cougars jumped out to early 21-7 lead after 1st Q, scoring on opening drive and recovering onside-KO to set up quick score, before adding 21 pts in each of following 2 Qs. Air Force (4-2) surrendered most pts in its history, but made score somewhat respectable with 20 pts in 4th Q, including TD on 46y run by HB Anthony Butler (8/120y).

Stanford 49 OREGON 42: With 1st BCS rankings only days away, unbeaten Oregon (6-1) seemed poised for top 5 spot. They spit bit, surrendering 21 straight pts in 4th Q to lose Top 10 spot and 23-game home win streak. Ahead 42-41, Ducks seemed to pull out win as DE Seth McEwen blocked x-pt following Stanford (4-1) TD with 5:32 left. Wishing to kill clock, Oregon faced 3rd-and-long; Cardinal S Tank Williams hit QB Joey Harrington as he attempted to pass with ball landing in hands of DE Marcus Hoover at Ducks 33YL. Stanford QB Chris Lewis carefully led drive that wiped out more than 4 mins and Oregon's lead: RB Kerry Carter ran in 3y TD for his 4th TD. Ducks built 42-28 lead as Harrington threw for 270y and 3 TDs and team tallied 2 special teams TDs: 96y KO RET by TB Onterrio Smith and 69y punt RET by WR Keenan Howry (9/152y). But Cardinal dominated 4th Q by converting blocked punt, recovered onside-KO, and Hoover's INT into TDs.

Bowl Championship Series Rankings October 22

	Poll Avg.	Computer Avg.	Schedule Rank	Losses	Total
1 Oklahoma (7-0)	2.0	1.50	0.56	0	3.06
2 Nebraska (8-0)	3.0	3.00	0.40	0	6.40
3 UCLA (6-0)	4.5	3.00	1.24	0	8.34
4 Miami (5-0)	1.0	7.33	3.68	0	12.01
5 Virginia Tech (6-0)	4.5	7.50	1.88	0	13.88

October 27, 2001

Syracuse 22 VIRGINIA TECH 14: Red-hot Orangemen (7-2) continued winning ways by chasing Virginia Tech (6-1) from ranks of unbeaten. Entering Lane Stadium with 41-3 avg loss margin in last 3 visits, Syracuse needed strong start. Syracuse D forced punt that WR Jamel Riddle took 51y for 7-0 lead early in 1st Q. Later in 1st Q, Syracuse D prompted FUM converted into 1y TD run by TB James Mungro (23/102y). Blocked punt added 3 pts late in H, and Syracuse was on way to 7th straight win with 17-0 lead. Virginia Tech pulled to 17-7 late in 3rd Q on 2y TD run by TB Keith Burnell and trailed 20-14 late in 4th Q after 17y TD pass by QB Grant Noel (15-32/162y). With 2:24 remaining, however, Syracuse DEs Dwight Freeney and Mark Holtzman sacked Noel for safety, team's 5th sack of game.

FLORIDA STATE 52 Maryland 31: Demise of Seminoles (5-2) was short-lived as QB Chris Rix (15-24/350y, INT) shook off effects of big hit by LB E.J. Henderson to throw 5 TD passes, trio to WR Talman Gardner (6/140y). Maryland (7-1) took 14-0 1st H lead as FB James Lynch rumbled 65y for TD, and TB Marc Riley made FSU pay for failed faked punt by capping ensuing 13-play drive with 1y TD run. Florida State scored quickly as pair of Gardner's TD catches were wrapped around FSU LB Michael Boulware's 23y INT TD RET. Those 21 pts and Maryland K Nick Novak's 51y FG were scored during final 6 mins of H. Despite 4 TOs, Terps were not done as they took 24-21 lead on 8y TD run by TB Bruce Perry and later tied game at 31-31 on 1y run by QB Shaun Hill (21-37/214y, 2 INTs). Rix came through with 3 TD passes during decisive 5-min span of 4th Q.

Florida 24 Georgia 10 (Jacksonville): Despite gaining 584y, their highest total in 78-game history of rivalry, Gators (6-1) struggled to put away Georgia. QB Rex Grossman threw for 407y, but tossed 2 INTs as Florida suffered 4 TOs and 106y in PENs. Gators D came through with 3 4th down stops in 2nd H and finally finished off Bulldogs (5-2) when S Marquand Manuel forced QB David Greene (25-42/258y, INT) into FUM. Grossman led 76y TD drive in 4th Q TD that he capped with 30y TD pass to WR Reche Caldwell for only pts of 2nd H. Florida WR Jabar Gaffney caught 9/143y, and TB Earnest Graham rushed for 131y, although he frustratingly lost FUM at Georgia 5YL in 3rd Q. Frosh WR Fred Gibson—who had once committed to play basketball for Florida—sparkled for Georgia with 7/131y receiving.

TENNESSEE 17 South Carolina 10: Tennessee (5-1) TB Travis Stephens kept up his ground assault with 120y and 2 TDs. His 2nd score, on 1y run with 7:08 remaining, answered 24y FG by South Carolina (6-2) K Daniel Weaver that had tied game at 10-10. On that drive, Carolina had moved to Vols 1YL before being stacked up twice and settling for 3 pts. Vols QB Casey Clausen (14-23/211y, INT) keyed winning drive, completing huge 32y pass to WR Bobby Graham on 3rd-and-21 to Gamecocks 4YL. Gamecocks fabricated late march to Tennessee 38YL, where ball was lost on downs with 54 secs left.

Mississippi 35 LOUISIANA STATE 24: QB Eli Manning led Rebels (6-1) to victory by throwing for 249y and 3 TDs. Win was jumpstarted by clutch 4th-and-10 completion by Manning, in teeth of safety blitz, for 27y gain to WR Bill Flowers. It set up 1y TD run by RB Joe Gunn for 14-10 lead in 2nd Q. Ole Miss special teams came through with blocked punt that set up Manning's 8y TD pass to WR Omar Rayford for 21-10 H lead. LSU (4-3) fought back with TDs on 71y punt RET by RB Domanick Davis and 39y catch by WR Michael Clayton for 24-21 lead. Manning sparked 2 scoring drives in final 7 mins, capping both with TD passes to TE Doug Zeigler.

ARKANSAS 42 Auburn 17: Hogs sent Auburn (6-2) to 1st SEC defeat behind 2-headed QB position and opportunistic D. QBs Zak Clark (10-13/128y) and Matt Jones each led TD drives as Arkansas (4-3) blew open tight game. Turning point came on INT thrown by Auburn QB Daniel Cobb (22-40/254y, 2 INTs) late in 1st H with Tigers trailing 14-10. LB Tony Bua's INT led to Clark's last-sec 16y TD pass to WR Richard Smith that featured Smith's nimble foot-down dance before falling backwards out of EZ. Smith had scored earlier on 21y pass on Jones' 1st-ever pass attempt. Hogs put game away in 4th Q with 3 TDs, crowned by LB Jermaine Petty's 88y INT TD RET. Auburn, led by RB Cadillac Williams' 177y rushing, earned 492y to 297y O advantage. Tigers WR Tim Carter caught 7/156y.

PENN STATE 29 Ohio State 27: Trailing 27-9 in 2nd H, improving Nittany Lions (2-4) rallied for coach Joe Paterno's record 324th coaching win. QB Zack Mills (17-32/280y, 3 INTs) shook off INT—on ball off hands of WR Eddie Drummond—that was returned 45y by Ohio CB Derek Ross for TD, to run, 2 plays later, to 69y TD. Mills added 2 TD throws; his 14y pass to TB Eric McCoo early in 4th Q capped 90y drive for winning margin. Ohio State (4-3) had chance to pull it out, but Penn State DT Jimmy Kennedy made clutch block of K Mike Nugent's late 34y FG try. Mills totaled school-record 418y O, passing for 280y and rushing for 138y. QB Steve Bellisari threw for 209y, with WR Michael Jenkins nabbing 4/172y, including 69y on Bucks 1st play from scrimmage for 7-0 lead. TB Jonathan Wells rushed for 143y, including 65y scoring run early in 3rd Q that put Buckeyes up 20-9.

Michigan 32 IOWA 26: Hawkeyes (4-3) led 26-21 and could smell upset. Driving for clinching score, Iowa was halted by Michigan S Cato June, who returned INT 30y to midfield. QB John Navarre converted this TO into 29-26 lead on 13y TD pass to TE Shawn Thompson. Iowa then was halted and Wolverines (6-1) closed scoring on K Hayden Epstein's 51y FG. Hawkeyes had opened with 10-0 1st H lead before Michigan blocked punt that LB Roy Manning recovered in EZ for TD. Hawkeyes answered in 3rd Q as WR C.J. Jones made 65y punt TD RET for 17-7 edge. Wolverines made 2 quick TDs late in 3rd Q, 2nd featuring WR Marquise Walker's nifty 1-handed catch for 21-20 lead. Soon after, Iowa S Bob Sanders forced FUM with jarring hit on WR Calvin Bell at UM 33YL, which led to TB Ladell Betts' 8y TD run for Hawkeyes' final lead. Iowa D, led by LB Roger Meyer's 15 tackles, played well, surrendering 63y rushing and only single drive longer than 50y.

NEBRASKA 20 Oklahoma 10: Huskers (9-0) turned to trickery to overturn Big 12. After multiple handoffs, former QB-turned-WR Mike Stuntz fired pass to QB Eric Crouch, who streaked down sideline for 63y TD to close scoring and finish off Sooners (7-1). Play was called "41 Flash Pass." Oklahoma had tried similar-looking trick play earlier, which failed when QB Nate Hybl, running in open, fell down. Hybl (17-36/184y, INT), former Oklahoma starter, replaced injured QB Jason White and led Sooners to 10 pts in 1st H before withering in 2nd H: OU gained only 10y total on last 2 drives. Nebraska thrived on balanced attack, with Crouch throwing for 102y and IB Dahrran Diedrick rushing for 90y, TD. In snapping Oklahoma's 20-game win streak, Huskers won their 8th of last 9 in series, while OU coach Bob Stoops lost for 1st time to Top 10 team after 8 wins.

STANFORD 38 Ucla 28: UCLA Bruins (6-1) became 3rd undefeated team to fall this Saturday as QB Chris Lewis (20-29/250y, 3 TDs, 3 INTs) led balanced Stanford attack that racked up 463y. Highlights were many as WR Teyo Johnson made amazing 1-handed catch for 3y TD and TB Brian Allen (16/87y) raced 35y for another. Cardinals (5-1) kept UCLA out of EZ until late in 3rd Q and held TB DeShaun Foster to 77y rushing. With QB Cory Paus injured in 1st Q, QB Scott McEwan (15-24/221y, 2 TDs, INT) rallied Bruins with 3 TD drives to cut deficit to 31-28. Late in 4th Q, UCLA took over on own 39YL after CB Matt Ware's 2nd INT, but drive stalled on downs—thanks in part to sack by Card DT Craig Albrecht. Stanford RB Kerry Carter (29/102y) iced cake with 27y TD run.

OREGON 24 Washington State 17: Unheralded Tennessee transfer TB Onterrio Smith—who had not even appeared in Ducks' starting lineup—rushed for school-record 285y, including winning 73y 4th Q run, as Oregon (7-1) gained 565y O. TB Maurice Morris rushed for 138y before leaving in 3rd Q with hamstring injury. No. 14 Cougars (7-1) rallied late, but their final drive ended on downs at Oregon 8YL. QB Jason Gesser (17-37/249y) had hit WR Jerome Riley with 15y TD pass to pull Washington State within 7 pts with 4:25 remaining. Ducks QB Joey Harrington threw for only 119y in taking backseat to run attack, while LB Wesley Mallard made 13 tackles, including 2 for losses. Smith broke Oregon's single-game mark of 249y, set by Bobby Moore (nee Ahmad Rashad) in 1971.

USA Today Coaches October 29

1	Miami (Fla.) (46)	1486	14 Florida State	704
2	Nebraska (14)	1454	15 Purdue	541
3	Florida	1308	16 Maryland	510
4	Oklahoma	1263	17 Texas A&M	411
5	Texas	1259	18 Illinois	402
6	Michigan	1186	19 Washington State	386
7	Tennessee	1112	20 South Carolina	360
8	Brigham Young	999	21 Georgia Tech	330
9	Oregon	963	22 Syracuse	286
10	Washington	953	23 Georgia	239
11	UCLA	936	24 Clemson	160
12	Virginia Tech	925	25 Colorado	145
13	Stanford	719		

Bowl Championship Series Rankings October 29

	Poll Avg.	Computer Avg.	Schedule Rank	Losses	Total
1 Nebraska (9-0)	2.0	1.00	0.32	0	2.02
2 Oklahoma (7-1)	3.5	3.83	0.36	1	7.59
3 Miami (6-0)	1.0	3.67	0.12	0	7.71
4 Michigan (5-1)	6.0	4.83	1.08	1	11.75
5 Texas (7-1)	5.0	7.17	0.04	1	14.25

November 3, 2001

(Th) GEORGIA TECH 28 North Carolina 21: There was no finger pointing at Georgia Tech RB Joe Burns this week, as he rushed for career-high 198y and 51y TD, while helping to run out clock at game's end after North Carolina (5-4) pulled within 28-21 on QB Darian Durant's 3rd TD pass with 5:29 left. By then Carolina D, on field for nearly 37 mins, was exhausted. Yellow Jackets powerful O-line was able to neutralize more-famous Tar Heels D-line en route to earning 26 1st downs. Georgia Tech QB George Godsey threw for 187y, with TDs both passing and rushing. Jackets D held Tar Heels to 13y rushing, although Durant threw for 22-37/286y, and WR Sam Aiken caught 2 TDs. Loss ended Heels' 5-game win streak.

(Th) Brigham Young 56 COLORADO STATE 34: Former Rams player, Gary Crowton, now coach at Brigham Young (9-0), had no mercy on alma mater in his return to Fort Collins. Cougars RB Luke Staley rushed for 196y, 5 TDs, while QB Brandon Doman threw for 284y, TD, and rushed for 165y, TD, as BYU compiled 698y on usually-rigid Rams D. Colorado State (4-5) got its ground attack fired up for 440y as QB Bradlee Van Pelt gained 184y while scoring twice. When Van Pelt took to air lanes, however, he was intercepted 3 times by nimble Cougars.

PITTSBURGH 38 Virginia Tech 7: Hokies' freefall continued as Pittsburgh (3-5), displaying wealth of young talent, outgained Virginia Tech 393y to 151y and forced 4 TOs. Panthers adjusted their O, and QB David Priestley (16-25/245y) threw 3 TD passes in 1st H, 2 to WR Antonio Bryant (5/93y). Up 24-7 at H, Pitt D finished off Hokies (6-2) as CB Shawntae Spencer took INT 68y for TD midway through 3rd Q. With Virginia Tech's O struggling to gain 1st downs—it finished with only 8—sole score came on staple of "(coach Frank) Beamer Ball:" CB Ronyell Whitaker's 71y RET of blocked FG.

Florida State 41 CLEMSON 27: Coach Bobby Bowden of Florida State (6-2) ran record to 3-0 versus son, coach Tommy Bowden of Clemson (5-3), as QB Chris Rix threw for 369y and 4 TD passes—2 each to WRs Javon Walker (6/162y) and Talman Gardner (6/112y). Key moment occurred in 2nd Q when 61y TD run on fake punt by Tigers RB Bernard Rambert was called back for illegal formation. TD would have cut Clemson's deficit to 17-14; instead FSU scored twice more before H for 27-7 lead. Clemson scored 13 of next 20 pts, but Noles TB Greg Jones (17/160y) squelched rally by racing 51y for clinching 4th Q TD. Clemson QB Woody Dantzler threw for 277y and added 59y rushing.

GAME OF THE YEAR
Arkansas 58 MISSISSIPPI 56 (OT):

This game had to end sometime, but before it was over, OT slugfest portrayed everything fans could ever want in NCAA's relatively new OT format. Longest game in Div 1 history finally ended in 7th OT as Ole Miss (6-2) failed on 2-pt conv because Arkansas LB Jermaine Petty tackled TE Doug Ziegler (5/102y)—who already had caught 2 TD passes in OT—before Ole Miss receiver could spin from 2YL into EZ. Teams were modestly tied 17-17 at end of regulation before exploding in extra periods for record 80 pts. Rebels QB Eli Manning (27-42/312y) threw 5 of his 6 TDs in OT sessions, and frosh QB Matt Jones of Arkansas (5-3) threw 2 extra period TDs and winning 2-pt conv to WR Decori Birmingham. Arkansas' winning conv pass followed FB Mark Pierce's 2nd 2y TD run. Jones also rushed for 110y, joining TBs Fred Talley (23/113y) and Cedric Cobbs (22/100y) in century club. Teams ran record 198 plays, producing 988y of O—531y for Razorbacks—as both easily surpassed previous high for pts scored by any Div 1-A team in OT. (Georgia had tallied 28 OT pts against Auburn in 1996.) Rebels, who tied record for most pts ever scored by losing team, had 5-game win streak snapped. "We expected them to go to the tight end. We knew it boiled down to that one play," said Petty. "We're just glad to win and glad it's over."

MICHIGAN STATE 26 Michigan 24: Post-game attention centered on slow-handed timekeeper and referees. Time ticked away too slowly at end of game to suit Wolverines (6-2) as Spartans (5-2) QB Jeff Smoker (15-35/183y, 2 TDs) assembled his troops at Michigan 2YL and miraculously got snap off and spiked ball to stop clock as it showed :01 in 4th Q. Smoker then threw to RB T.J. Duckett for TD: game over. Duckett had run for 211y against nation's top-ranked rush D to keep Spartans in game, but they trailed 24-20 with less than 5 mins left after Michigan QB John Navarre (14-27/195y, 2 INTs) threw 3rd TD pass, 20y effort to backup QB Jermaine Gonzales. Spartans went

44y in final 2:09, helped by Wolverine PENs, to game's 7th, and final, lead change. Michigan D did not stop Duckett, but sacked Smoker 12 times, 5 by DE Santee Orr to tie school record. Michigan WR Marquise Walker caught 9/150y, 2 TDs.

Illinois 38 PURDUE 13: Boilermakers (5-2) stormed to 13-0 lead behind QB Brandon Hance (15-29/132y, 2 INTs), who threw 8y TD pass to WR Seth Morales and led 2 drives that ended in FGs by K Travis Dorsch. Illini (7-1) QB Kurt Kittner shook off dreadful start to throw for 299y—including WR Brandon Lloyd's 6/112y—to lead comeback that swamped Purdue. Kittner suffered 4 INTs, but, as good gunslinger, he kept throwing until righting himself with 2 TD passes. DBs Bobby Jackson and Christian Morton chipped in with 83y and 62y INT TD RETs respectively for Illini D that held Purdue to 62y rushing and 178y passing.

Texas Tech 12 TEXAS A&M 0: Texas Tech (5-3) RB Ricky Williams scored game's sole TD on 6y run in 4th Q, and QB Kliff Kingsbury withstood 7 sacks to throw for 38-46/303y. Red Raiders D handed Texas A&M 1st shutout since 1983 as nothing went right for Aggies (7-2). They crossed midfield 6 times without scoring, including fake FG that went awry. Raiders also halted 10-13 3rd down plays and all 5 4th down attempts as unheralded D blanked A&M despite surrendering 372y. Aggies QB Mark Fariss completed 22-31/206y.

WASHINGTON 42 Stanford 28: Powered by new-found running game and timely passing, Huskies put upstart Stanford (5-2) back in place with 2 late TDs to snap 28-28 tie. Washington (7-1) TB Willie Hurst, who rushed for 108y and 3 TDs, scored on 2y run with 3:48 remaining after QB Cody Pickett (15-28/291y) set up winning TD with 2 completions to TE Kevin Ware. Hurst added 15y TD jaunt with 4 secs left after Huskies stopped Stanford on downs. Cardinal had rallied from 15 pts down in 2nd H on 2 TD runs by TB Brian Allen (23/138y), including 80y romp midway through 3rd Q.

WASHINGTON STATE 20 Ucla 14: S Lamont Thompson took it upon himself to discourage Bruins (6-2), picking off UCLA QB Cory Paus twice in game's final mins to finish with school-record 4 INTs. Cougars (6-1) LB Al Genatone scored game-winning TD with 73y RET of FUM by UCLA TB DeShaun Foster, who was game-high rusher with 102y. Bruins picked off 3 passes by Washington State QB Jason Gesser (16-36/187y, TD) and matched Wazzu's D TD with S Ben Emanuel's 29y INT TD RET. Combining for only 25 1st downs, each squad failed to reach 100y rushing or 200y passing.

USA Today Coaches November 5

1	Miami (Fla.) (41)	1479	14	Illinois	749
2	Nebraska (18)	1456	15	South Carolina	596
3	Florida (1)	1346	16	UCLA	570
4	Oklahoma	1330	17	Georgia Tech	513
5	Texas	1256	18	Syracuse	463
6	Tennessee	1173	19	Stanford	422
7	Oregon	1080	20	Colorado	317
8	Washington	1078	21	Georgia	303
9	Brigham Young	1074	22	Virginia Tech	286
10	Florida State	880	23	Michigan State	154
11	Maryland	767	24	Purdue	145
12	Washington State	758	25	Louisville	141
13	Michigan	755			

Bowl Championship Series Rankings November 5

	Poll Avg.	Computer Avg.	Schedule Rank	Losses	Total
1 Nebraska (10-0)	2.0	1.00	0.92	0	2.62
2 Miami (7-0)	1.0	2.83	2.88	0	6.61
3 Oklahoma (7-1)	3.5	3.67	0.76	1	7.83
4 Tennessee (6-1)	6.0	5.50	0.24	1	12.74
5 Texas (8-1)	5.0	6.33	1.60	1	13.93

November 10, 2001

Pittsburgh 42 RUTGERS 0: Panthers (4-5) finished off struggling Rutgers (2-7) with awesome 1st H performance, scoring 42 pts on 392y O while allowing scant 21y. While few fans remained for 2nd H, those who did witnessed Pitt mercifully run and run until final H was elapsed. QB David Priestley threw for 307y and 4 TDs, 3 to WR Antonio Bryant (5/107y). RB Ravon Anderson rushed for 40y and was leading gainer for Rutgers, which easily lost 14th straight in Big East play.

Miami 18 BOSTON COLLEGE 7: Stunning D play allowed top-ranked Miami (8-0) to narrowly escape at game's end. Boston College (6-3) played outstanding D to keep game close, picking off 4 passes by Miami QB Ken Dorsey (20-41/222y), doubling his season's total. Still, Hurricanes led 12-0 until frosh RB Frank Gore lost FUM as Canes tried to run out clock. QB Brian St. Pierre (12-29/162y, 2 INTs) moved Eagles 61y, last 21y coming on 4th-and-10 TD pass to WR Dedrick Dewalt. Eagles threatened again with 38 secs to go, but Miami DT Matt Walters caught St. Pierre's pass intended for WR Ryan Read. Ball bounced off CB Mike Rumph to Walters, who ran 10y before his teammate, S Ed Reed, pick-pocketed ball and raced extra 80y for clinching TD. Hurricanes K Todd Sievers had kicked 4 FGs and RB Clint Portis had rushed 160y as Miami won 12th straight in series—last time Canes lost was in 1984 on Doug Flutie's Hail Mary pass. BC was hampered by suspension of RB William Green; fill-in RB Derrick Knight rushed for 78y.

North Carolina State 34 FLORIDA STATE 28: Game represented pair of negative firsts for Florida State (6-3) coach Bobby Bowden. North Carolina State (6-3) coach Chuck Amato handed his former boss 1st-ever Homecoming Day loss after 25 wins and 1st-ever ACC home loss since joining conf in 1992. Wolfpack employed ball control, keeping it nearly 35 mins. NC State QB Philip Rivers threw for 245y and RB Ray Robinson rushed for 2 TDs, including 24y game-winner, as Wolfpack gained 463y and 26 1st downs. QB Chris Rix had put Seminoles up 14-7 in 1st Q with 2 TD passes. Rix

also threw another TD and ran for score to pull within 31-28 midway through 4th Q. NC State then held ball for nearly 8 mins on 17-play drive to K Adam Kiker's 32y FG with 2:11 left. Rix (20-35/302y, INT) marched FSU to NC State 14YL before 2 incompletions ended game, last tipped away in EZ by CB Brian Williams from WR Talman Gardner, who caught 2 TDs earlier.

Florida 54 SOUTH CAROLINA 17: Gators (8-1) scored on 1st 9 possessions to crush Carolina squad in front of largest home crowd (84,900) to date. Florida won 11th straight in series as QB Rex Grossman threw for 302y and 3 TD passes, while running for another score. Gamecocks (7-3) led 7-0 after RB Derek Watson scored on 7y run 1 play after Florida CB Lito Sheppard muffed punt. By managing only 57y passing and being unable to stop Gators' O, South Carolina stood little chance. Florida did not have to punt entire game and lost only Sheppard's FUM. Merciless Florida had QB Brock Berlin throw TD pass late in 4th Q with 47-17 lead.

Auburn 24 GEORGIA 17: Thriller was not decided until final moment: frustrated Bulldogs (5-3) went to Tigers 1YL as QB David Greene (15-32/294y, INT) hooked up with WR Terrence Edwards on 22y pass. After having sent FB Jasper Sanks into line for no gain, Georgia, without timeouts, was helpless to stop clock before game's end. Earlier in 4th Q, Bulldogs had seen their drive die on downs at 9YL, but their D quickly forced punt by stopping Auburn (7-2) frosh TB Carnell "Cadillac" Williams (41/167y, 2 TDs) on 3rd-and-1. Earlier, Williams had set up his own winning 1y TD run with 61y gain on screen pass. Both Bulldogs TDs had come on long 1st H passes: 67y to WR Fred Gibson and 56y to Edwards (6/124y).

NEBRASKA 31 Kansas State 21: Wildcats (4-5), hoping to salvage year, allowed 2 RET TDs and just enough O to lose. Nebraska (11-0) QB Eric Crouch, who rushed for 106y, and IB Dahrran Diedrick, who added 108y on ground, keyed 77y drive to open 3rd Q that Diedrick capped with 2y TD run for 24-21 lead. Soon after, Huskers CB DeJuan Groce went 60y with punt TD RET to clinch win. Earlier, S Willie Amos scored on 20y INT RET. Wildcats did their best work late in 1st H in scoring 2 TDs: CB Terence Newman blocked punt to put ball at Huskers 7YL for 5y TD run by QB Ell Roberson (16/119y) and WR Aaron Lockett's 32y scoring reception with 6 secs left in 2nd Q for 14-13 H lead. Passing was atrocious: Crouch, Roberson, and sub K-State QB Marc Dunn combined for 7-25/97y with 5 INTs.

OKLAHOMA 31 Texas A&M 10: Aggies (7-3) took 10-0 lead in effort to trump last season's near upset. Oklahoma (9-1) put pin in that balloon, exploding for 4 TDs and FG. Winning TD occurred in 3rd Q on fake FG as Sooners K Tim Duncan scored on 10y run, lunging in after being tripped up at 5YL. Oklahoma D by then was dominating, preventing Texas A&M from gaining any 1st downs in 2nd and 3rd Qs. Texas A&M was held to 132y total O and 5 1st downs—sole TD was scored on 18y FUM advancement by LB Brian Gamble after LB Everett Smith lost FUM on his INT RET—as struggling O failed to find EZ for 2nd straight game. Sooners QB Nate Hybl (25-38/195y) threw 2 TDs and ran for another.

TEXAS 59 Kansas 0: Gigantic difference in these 2 programs was on display as Longhorns (9-1) D held anemic Kansas O to 67y, while frosh TB Cedric Benson rushed for 213y to lead Texas O that gained 606y. Benson scored twice on rushes and once with 60y scamper on shovel pass by QB Chris Simms (16-24/284y, 2 TDs), who also hit WR Roy Williams (6/109y) on 68y scoring pass play. Committing only single PEN was only bright spot for Jayhawks (2-7).

Oregon 21 UCLA 20: For 9th time in his career, Oregon (9-1) QB Joey Harrington (13-23/195y) led 4th Q comeback as he capped 70y drive with 1y TD pass on 4th down to FB Josh Line. Harrington completed all 3 passes on drive for 52y. Ducks D held on over final 10 mins to preserve 500th victory in school history, with best UCLA chance to win ending on K Chris Griffith's missed FG attempt from 50y out as time expired. Bruins (6-3) ran ball 5 of last 6 plays before Griffith's kick. UCLA, without TB DeShaun Foster who was ineligible for benefits violation, went to air with mixed results as QB Cory Paus threw for 321y, with 2 INTs. His 53y pass to WR Craig Bragg on 3rd-and-17 set up UCLA TB Manuel White's 1y TD run early in 4th Q for 20-14 lead as coach Bob Toledo passed on 2-pt conv attempt. Bruins WR Brian Poli-Dixon returned from missing 3 games with injury to catch 6/149y. Ducks TB Maurice Morris rushed for 129y.

OREGON STATE 49 Washington 24: Once-hyped Beavers (4-5) had all but fallen off Pac-10 map. They earned back some pride by whipping Huskies (7-2) as QB Jonathan Smith (18-28/317y) threw 2 TD passes and TBs Steven Jackson (22/79y) and Ken Simonton (29/107y) each scored 3 times. Simonton nabbed 1st receiving TD of his career in 35-pt 1st H for Oregon State. There was no 2nd H rally for Washington, which gained only 6y in 3rd Q as aggressive Beavers D handled QB Cody Pickett (13-32/160y, INT). Win was Beavers' 1st over Huskies since 1985.

USA Today Coaches November 12

1	Nebraska (30)	1469	14	Washington	658
2	Miami (Fla.) (28)	1459	15	Stanford	639
3	Florida (2)	1350	16	Colorado	605
4	Oklahoma	1329	17	Virginia Tech	505
5	Texas	1261	18	Auburn	394
6	Tennessee	1183	19	Louisville	383
7	Oregon	1136	20	Florida State	361
8	Brigham Young	1055	21	UCLA	278
9	Maryland	956	22	South Carolina	251
10	Washington State	926	23	Georgia Tech	161
11	Michigan	902	24	Marshall	139
12	Illinois	860	25	Fresno State	74
13	Syracuse	703			

Bowl Championship Series Rankings November 12

	Poll Avg.	Computer Avg.	Schedule Rank	Losses	Total
1 Nebraska (11-0)	1.5	1.00	1.00	0	2.20
2 Miami (8-0)	1.5	3.17	2.64	0	7.31
3 Oklahoma (8-1)	3.5	3.67	0.72	1	7.89
4 Oregon (9-1)	7.0	4.17	0.60	1	11.97
5 Florida (8-1)	3.5	6.00	1.48	1	11.98

November 17, 2001

MIAMI 59 Syracuse 0: In whipping Syracuse and clinching Big East title, Hurricanes (9-0) eliminated lingering doubts over BCS worthiness. Miami enjoyed 566y to 185y advantage in advancing shutout streak against Syracuse to 10 Qs. Orangemen (8-3), whose hopes to continue 8-game win streak ended early, were held to only 12 1st downs. Each team forced other to pass, but with different results: Miami QB Ken Dorsey threw for 224y and 4 TDs, with no INTs, while 2 Syracuse QBs combined for meager 80y. Miami LT Bryant McKinnie won individual match-up with Orange DE Dwight Freeney, who set season record with 16 sacks, by not allowing Freeney to make even single tackle. Once Dorsey softened up Syracuse D, RB Clinton Portis was free to romp for 132y and RB Frank Gore for 153y as Canes gained 331y rushing. Miami D star was CB Phillip Buchanon, who returned INT 76y for TD, set up another TD with FUM REC, and added 59y punt RET and sack for good measure. Over past 3 seasons, Miami had built 130-13 pt advantage over Syracuse.

Maryland 23 NORTH CAROLINA STATE 19: Although end of Florida State's 9-year run atop ACC was overdue, Terrapins (10-1) didn't seem like team to do it. QB Shaun Hill (27-41/296y, 2 TDs, INT) marched Maryland 61y at game's end to pull out title-clinching win. Hill threw 8y TD to WR Guilian Gary with 41 secs left. Maryland's final TD marked game's 5th lead change of 2nd H. Terps had lost FUM on NC State 1YL with less than 3 mins left when WR Rich Parson was stripped at end of 64y pass play, but Maryland D held to provide last chance. Wolfpack (6-4) had taken 19-16 lead as QB Phillip Rivers (27-43/275y, INT) completed 8-9 on 80y drive, capped by 1y TD pass to FB Cotra Jackson. NC State K Adam Kiker booted 4 FGs, while WR Jerricho Cotchery caught 11/123y. Maryland won its 1st outright ACC title since 1985 and enjoyed 1st 10-win season since 1976.

FLORIDA 37 Florida State 13: Florida coach Steve Spurrier was not about to let Florida State (6-4) recover from its off-year against his Gators, who had lost 3 straight in series. RB Earnest Graham's 2y TD run midway through 1st Q—on drive that was keyed by WR Jabar Gaffney's 40y pass to Graham—gave Florida (9-1) lead at 7-0. Graham later left with knee injury on hit by FSU DT Darnell Dockett that angered Gators. Gaffney (4/65y) caught final TD with nifty grab of 28y pass from QB Rex Grossman (27-42/290y, INT). Seminoles QB Chris Rix threw for 26-39/229y, but could not prevent team from suffering most losses since 1986. Florida State, which rushed for only 40y, dropped out of Top 25 for 1st time since late September 1989, span of 210 weeks.

Alabama 31 AUBURN 7: With QB Andrew Zow starting for injured QB Tyler Watts, Crimson Tide threw more than usual in preventing Auburn (7-3) from clinching SEC West. Zow completed 22-29/221y, 2 TDs, in becoming Alabama's career passing leader. Another backup, RB Santonio Beard, enjoyed his 1st start by rushing for 199y and 2 TDs. Game was deadlocked 7-7 late in 1st H before Zow completed 45y scoring pass to WR Jason McAdley to break tie with 45 secs left in H. Beard then raced 47y to TD early in 3rd Q, as Alabama (5-5) had more than enough pts with D posting 2nd H shutout. Alabama rolled up 549y. Only bright spot for Tigers was play of QB Jason Campbell, who came off bench to complete 7-7/92y.

Georgia 35 MISSISSIPPI 15: Bulldogs (6-3) rode new-found ground attack as former walk-on TB Verron Haynes, who slid over from FB for game, rushed for 192y—22y more than he had all season—and 2 TDs. Ole Miss (6-3) dropped 5th straight in series despite 233y passing from QB Eli Manning, including 2 TDs. He also threw INT that Georgia S Jermaine Phillips returned 82y for key TD early in 4th Q. Bulldogs QB David Greene threw sparingly, hitting 8-14/93y, TD.

Illinois 34 OHIO STATE 22: With Buckeyes in bit of turmoil, Illinois (9-1) used 2nd H rally for 6th straight win. QB Kurt Kittner completed 18-28/274y, 2 TDs, at helm of Illini attack that took final lead at 28-22 on 1y TD run by FB Carey Davis. LB Ty Myers sealed win with 5y INT RET with 5:19 left. With starting QB Steve Bellisari suspended for DUI charges, QBs Scott McMullen (4-13/42y) and Craig Krenzel (11-23/164y, 2 INTs) led Ohio State (6-4). Buckeyes RB Jonathan Wells chipped in with 192y rushing, while WR Michael Jenkins corralled 10/155y.

Oklahoma 30 TEXAS TECH 13: Red Raiders (6-4) were meant to supply stern test, but O received failing grades against Oklahoma's fast D, managing 9 1st downs and -7y rushing. Sooners (10-1) QB Nate Hybl (33-55/274y, 3 TDs, 2 INTs) managed controlled attack for more than 40 mins possession to neutralize Texas Tech's normally-potent O. Highlight for Raiders was 40y hookup between QB Kliff Kingsbury and RB Ricky Williams, which narrowed H scored to 13-10. That was brief mirage as Oklahoma scored 17 unanswered 2nd H pts behind Hybl's pair of TD passes that included 48y scoring strike to WR Mark Clayton (6/103y). Kingsbury was held to season-low 224y passing, throwing 2 INTs and losing FUM.

BRIGHAM YOUNG 24 Utah 21: Cougars (11-0) needed late rally to claim MWC title. BYU erased 11-pt deficit as RB Luke Staley (17/169y) scored 2 TDs and added 2-pt conv in game's final 4 mins, including winning 30y run. After decades of aerial mastery, BYU interestingly turned to option run for big score: QB Brandon Doman (21-42/270y, 2 TDs, INT) faked and pitched out to Staley, who earlier in game had become BYU's season rush leader with 1,433y. Utes (7-3) soon returned to BYU 30YL, converting 4th-and-10 along way, before QB Lance Rice (15-31/173y, TD) threw INT to Cougars

CB Jernaro Gilford. BYU WR Reno Mahe (5/94y) scoffed at 6-day-old emergency appendectomy to score team's 1st TD on 23y pass. Utah RB Dameon Hunter rushed for 106y, with 15y on 3rd Q score for 14-3 lead.

SOUTHERN CALIFORNIA 27 Ucla 0: Once-promising UCLA season ended with thud as it dropped 4th straight. Southern California (6-5) QB Carson Palmer threw for 180y, with 66y pass to WR Kori Dickerson on game's 3rd play to set up 4y TD pass to WR Keary Colbert for 7-0 lead. CB Antuan Simmons doubled Troy's lead later in 1st Q when he returned INT 36y to TD. Trojans S Troy Polamalu crushed Bruins' hopes with blocked punt that led to 20y FG and INT that was converted into 34y TD run by TB Chris Howard. UCLA (6-4) was in trouble before opening KO, having lost TB DeShaun Foster in mid-season to suspension for driving illegally loaned Ford Expedition, was further distracted by QB Cory Paus' DUI arrest. Bruins gained only 114y, with Paus passing for 45y and 2 INTs.

WASHINGTON 26 Washington State 14: While Huskies (8-2) D stopped visitors 3 times deep within Washington territory, O had on display unstoppable QB Cody Pickett (25-38/371y, INT) to frosh WR Reggie Williams (11/203y) combination. D forced 4 TOs, with S Greg Carothers twice forcing FUMs in 3rd Q including hit on QB Jason Gesser that stopped Cougar drive on Washington 6YL. D also turned in GLS in 1st Q as Washington State RB Dave Minnich was halted on 4th-and-goal from 1YL. Huskies went other way as Pickett led 99y drive that RB Rich Alexis capped with 1y TD run. On drive Williams caught 3 passes for 59y and forced interference PEN. Gesser (22-34/227y) tied game up with 1st of 2 TD passes, 15y effort to WR Mike Bush, but then Cougars were kept off scoreboard until late in 4th Q.

Bowl Championship Series Rankings November 19

	Poll Avg.	Computer Avg.	Schedule Rank	Losses	Total
1 Nebraska (11-0)	2.0	1.17	1.00	0	2.87
2 Miami (9-0)	1.0	2.33	1.92	0	5.25
3 Oklahoma (9-1)	4.0	3.33	0.80	1	8.13
4 Florida (9-1)	3.0	4.83	1.12	1	9.95
5 Oregon (9-1)	6.5	5.00	0.92	1	13.22

November 22-24, 2001

(Th'g) ILLINOIS 34 Northwestern 28: Despite playing for Big 10 title, Illinois (10-1) played in front of half empty stadium because conf had virtually no Thanksgiving football tradition. Illini clinched at least share of league title, which they won outright with Michigan's subsequent loss on Saturday. QB Kurt Kittner was brilliant in completing 33-43/387y and 4 TDs as Illinois built commanding 34-13 lead in 4th Q. QB Zak Kustok (19-41/266y, INT) threw 2 TDs to rally Wildcats (4-7), who closed once-promising season with 6 straight losses. Illinois WR Brandon Lloyd caught 12/140y, 2 TDs, while WR Walter Young had 7 catches for 123y and TD.

(Fri) LOUISIANA STATE 41 Arkansas 38: LSU (7-3) overcame 5 TOs to remain in SEC West race because RB LaBrandon Toefield rushed for 173y and 3 TDs, including 62y romp that opened scoring, and WR Josh Reed had 183y receiving and 2 TDs. Three times Hogs (7-4) blew 2-pt conv tries and they also missed 43y FG. QB Zak Clark (10-22/137y) rallied Arkansas with pair of 4th Q TD passes, pulling within 3 after 15y TD pass to WR Sparky Hamilton with 2:27 left. Needing 1st down to clinch win, LSU QB Rohan Davey (19-33/359y, 4 INTs) threw 31y arrow to Reed on 3rd-and-13. Teams combined for 930y, with Tigers good for 518y.

(Fri) TEXAS CHRISTIAN 37 Louisville 22: Texas Christian's run to bowl berth continued with victory over Conf-USA champs. QB Casey Printers (13-24/256y, INT) threw 80y TD pass on game's 1st play to WR Adrian Madise (4/116y) and added 2 TD passes to TE Matt Schobel and TD run as Texas Christian (5-5) never trailed. After 1st TD, Horned Frogs pooched KO, recovering when no Cardinal fielded ball. Four plays later, Printers ran for 3y TD, and TCU owned 14-0 lead 2 mins into game. Louisville (10-2) never recovered despite 3 TD passes by QB Dave Ragone (32-50/359y) and WR Deion Branch's 7/133y receiving. TCU TB Ricky Madison led all rushers with 31/156y.

(Fri) COLORADO 62 Nebraska 36: Having lost last 5 series games by 15 total pts, Buffaloes (9-2) surreally exploded for most pts ever scored on Nebraska. When scoreboard read 35-3 early in 2nd Q it was clear undefeated Nebraska's D no longer would be ranked 6th in country. Colorado TB Chris Brown, running behind Buffs' huge and effective O-Line, rushed for 198y and 6 TDs, in 4th Q after Huskers (11-1) rallied to within 42-30. Amazingly, score was 21-3 before Brown ever reached EZ. On Brown's 2nd TD, G Andre Gurode rode defender through EZ and pinned him against back wall. Up by 42-30, Colorado went on 93y drive that ended with Brown's 4th TD. Starting TB Bobby Purifoy chipped in with 154y on ground as Buffs rushed for 380y, while QB Bobby Pesavento threw for 202y and scrambled for 1st down that kept that

long drive alive. QB Eric Crouch rushed for 168y and passed for 198y to set total O school record as Huskers gained 552y to Buffs' 582y. He threw pair of 4th Q INTs that were converted into Colorado's final TDs.

(Fri) Texas 21 TEXAS A&M 7: Longhorns (10-1) needed 2 TDs from RB Cedric Benson (27/79y) to cap short 4th Q drives. These advances, totaling only 54y, followed short punt into wind and INT by Texas LB Everick Rawls. Texas A&M (7-4) tied it 7-7 early in 2nd H on 4y TD run by TB Keith Joseph to cap short drive of their own (27y), which was set up by WR Mickey Jones' 37y punt RET. Texas QB Chris Simms threw for only 138y into wind gusts of up to 20 mph. Horns opened scoring in 1st Q as RB Tony Jeffrey scored on 23y RET of blocked punt by CB Rod Babers.

MIAMI 65 Washington 7: By scoring 30 pts in 2nd Q alone, Hurricanes (10-0) gained sharp-edged revenge for sole loss of 2000 and what they considered dirty play by Huskies. RB Clinton Portis scored 1st 3 TDs of game and QB Ken Dorsey (13-20/192y, INT) threw 3 TDs and to pace O, while DE Jerome McDougle's INT RET produced final score of explosive 2nd Q. With Miami scoring quickly, Washington (8-3) had more than 11-min advantage in time of possession and earned 1 more 1st down. But, Huskies also threw 6 INTs. Since final TD of Boston College game on November 10, Miami had toted up 109 straight pts against 3 foes before allowing Huskies TB Rich Alexis to score 5y TD run. Miami had now won 20 straight games since losing to Washington early last season.

SYRACUSE 39 Boston College 28: In battle for 2nd place in Big East, Orange (9-3) flexed O muscle in gaining 575y. QB R.J. Anderson (15-20/247y) and TB James Mungro (32/184y) led Orange team that never trailed. Mungro, who scored 2 1y TDs, rushed for 54y on opening 80y drive that was capped by 6y TD run by FB Kyle Johnson as Syracuse went up 7-0 en route to 28-14 H lead. Boston College (7-4) TB William Green rushed for 182y and TD runs of 40y and 62y, but could not prevent Eagles' winless streak versus Top 25 to reach 20 games. BC QB Brian St. Pierre (17-28/217y) threw TD passes of 68y and 15y to WR Dedrick Dewalt.

Georgia 31 GEORGIA TECH 17: At last, Georgia (7-3) srs tasted series win as K Billy Bennett kicked school-record 6 FGs and recent star, TB Verron Haynes, ran for 207y. Still, Bulldogs needed 28y INT TD RET by CB Tim Wansley in 4th Q to clinch 1st win over Yellow Jackets (7-4) since 1997. Bulldogs QB David Greene (11-24/210y) led 3 FG drives, ending in 9-0 lead in 2nd Q. Georgia Tech scored next 10 pts on QB George Godsey's 13y TD pass to WR Kelly Campbell and 28y FG by K Luke Manget. Georgia answered with another FG for 12-10 H lead. TB Joe Burns' dandy 37y TD run made it 17-15 in 3rd Q before Bulldogs ran off game's final 17 pts, with Hayes scoring winner on 3y plunge later in 3rd Q. "It's the most disappointed I've been all season," said coach George O'Leary after Tech's 3rd home loss.

Ohio State 26 MICHIGAN 20: Upon his hiring, coach Jim Tressel vowed that Ohio State (7-4) fans "would be proud of their team on November 24 in Ann Arbor." With Buckeyes earning 1st victory in Ann Arbor since 1987, Tressel owned his 1st win in rivalry as RB Jonathan Wells rushed for 129y and 3 TDs. Wells ran for 122y in 1st H when Bucks built 23-0 lead. Ohio held off Michigan rally thanks in large part to S Mike Doss' 2 INTs. Michigan (8-3) QB John Navarre threw 4 INTs while passing for 206y, 160y and 2 TDs going to WR Marquise Walker, whose 15 receptions tied his own school record and raised his career mark to 171 for Michigan record. New Buckeyes QB Craig Krenzel, in for QB Steve Bellisari who was suspended and benched following DUI arrest, completed 11-18/118y, INT.

Oklahoma State 16 OKLAHOMA 13: Struggling Cowboys (4-7) salvaged season with unlikely road upset 1 week after surrendering 517y to lowly Baylor. Frosh QB Josh Fields (19-38/231y, INT), who replaced QB Aso Pogi in 1st H, threw winning 14y TD pass to WR Rashaun Woods (8/129y) with 1:36 left, right after 3rd down 31y pass to WR T. D. Bryant. OSU D had 3 INTs and 7 sacks of QB Nate Hybl (22-48/220y, 3 INTs) in holding Oklahoma (10-2) to 0y touchdown. OU's sole TD, RB Quentin Griffin's 8y run, came after INT at State 14YL. Sooners tried to hold 13-6 lead with less than 9 mins left, but Cowboys K Luke Phillips booted his 2nd 52y FG, while D was forcing consecutive 3-and-outs. Oklahoma State began winning drive on own 35YL, using only 3 completions, 2 to Woods, to cover 65y. Late Oklahoma drives ended on downs and INT by CB Marcus Jones. "The bottom line is we just got outplayed today," said Sooners coach Bob Stoops.

IOWA STATE 17 Iowa 14: For 1st time in rivalry, Cyclones (7-4) owned 4 straight wins over Iowa, sealing result with S Adam Runk's INT with 1:37 left. QB Seneca Wallace was hot, completing 20-27/228y and 2y TD pass to WR Lane Danielson to open scoring in 1st Q. TB Ennis Haywood doubled State's lead with 7y TD run to open 2nd Q. Hawkeyes (6-5) answered with 2 TDs to tie it before H, both by RB Ladell Betts. Betts caught 14y TD pass to put Iowa on scoreboard and rambled for 42y of his game-high 150y to knot it at 14-14. Iowa State K Tony Yelk did all 2nd H scoring with game-winning 32y FG early in 4th Q. Game marked 1st time teams squared off in any season that both teams went to bowl games.

SOUTHERN METHODIST 37 Rice 20: Rallying from 13-pt deficit, Mustangs (4-6) won game for fired coach Mike Cavan with amazing 2nd H. QB Mike Page (16-30/245y, INT) was architect of comeback, throwing his 2nd and 3rd TDs and running in another as Mustangs scored 30 straight pts in 2nd H. SMU WR Chris Cunningham caught 5/109y and 3 TDs. Owls (8-4) opened with 7-0 lead as LB Dan Dawson returned INT 32y to TD in 1st Q. Rice tallied 13 2nd Q pts on 2 FGs by K Derek Crabtree and 30y TD pass by QB Kyle Herm to WR Gilbert Okoronkwo.

USA Today Coaches November 26

1	Miami (Fla.) (59)	1499	14 Washington State	699
2	Florida (1)	1432	15 South Carolina	596
3	Texas	1358	16 Michigan	553
4	Tennessee	1289	17 Syracuse	458
5	Oregon	1257	18 Marshall	425
6	Nebraska	1104	19 Georgia	420
7t	Brigham Young	1080	20 Washington	397
7t	Maryland	1080	21 Fresno State	334
9	Illinois	1065	22 Auburn	223
10	Colorado	991	23 Louisville	205
11	Oklahoma	915	24 LSU	164
12	Stanford	817	25 Ohio State	105
13	Virginia Tech	763		

Bowl Championship Series Rankings November 26

	Poll Avg.	Computer Avg.	Schedule Rank	Losses	Total
1 Miami (10-0)	1.0	1.00	1.12	0	2.92
2 Florida (9-1)	2.0	3.17	0.88	1	6.95
3 Texas (11-1)	3.0	3.83	1.84	1	8.77
4 Nebraska (11-1)	6.0	3.50	0.68	1	10.48
5 Oregon (9-1)	4.5	4.67	1.00	1	10.87

December 1, 2001

(Fri) TOLEDO 41 Marshall 36: Marshall's 4-year reign as MAC titlist came to fighting end. Thundering Herd (10-2) took quick 23-0 lead, but Rockets (9-2) QB Tavares Bolden hit 16-25/175y in air, while TB Chester Taylor rushed for 188y, 2 TDs. Toledo's rally began with 26y TD on screen pass to WR Carl Ford. After FUM on ensuing KO set up Toledo K Todd France's FG, Rockets had fought way back to trail 23-10 at H. Toledo romped in 3rd Q, adding 25 pts, including TD on France's 16y run off fake FG. Marshall countered with 3rd Q TD and regained 4th Q lead at 36-35 as QB Byron Leftwich (32-52/420y, 4 TDs, INT) threw TD to WR Denero Marriott. Herd bobbled punt FUM to set up winning TD, Taylor's 8y run.

Army 26 Navy 17 (Philadelphia): With American troops in Afghanistan less than 3 months since terrorist attacks, annual Army-Navy game held special significance. Army (3-8) led from get-go as TB Ardell Daniels rushed for 131y, including 60y TD run on draw on team's 2nd play from scrimmage. Any chance for Navy (0-10) rally ended with 2nd H KO, taken 96y by Cadets WR Omari Thompson for 23-3 lead. Midshipmen scored on 3 FGs by K David Hills and late 4y TD pass by QB Brian Madden to TE Steve Mercer, but could not prevent 1st winless season since going 0-8-1 in 1948. With security tight, President Bush attended game at Veterans Stadium, addressing both squads in locker rooms and tossing pre-game coin.

Miami 26 VIRGINIA TECH 24: All they had to do was win, something Hurricanes hadn't accomplished in Blacksburg since 1992. Miami (11-0) did just that, barely. Hurricanes stretched win streak to 21 games behind D that forced 5 TOs. Virginia Tech (8-3) rallied to within 26-24 with 6:03 left on LB Brandon Manning's 22y RET of CB Eric Green's punt block. Going for tie, Hokies went to air but wide-open WR Ernest Wilford dropped 2-pt conv pass. QB Grant Noel threw 2-pt pass well, but completed only 4-16/81y as he was sacked 5 times. QB Ken Dorsey hit 21-44/235y, TD, and RB Clinton Portis rushed for 124y, TD, as Canes carved 20-3 H lead. Va Tech's final 2 drives ended on S Ed Reed's INT—his 21st to become school's all-time leader—and on downs. Hokies TB Kevin Jones rushed 24/160y.

Tennessee 34 FLORIDA 32: Winning at Florida Field for 1st time since 1971, when present coach Phil Fulmer was starting lineman, Tennessee (10-1) scrambled BCS standings and vaulted themselves into BCS spot for Rose Bowl. QB Rex Grossman (33-51/362y, INT), who was sacked 4 times and had to hurry passes all day, led Florida (9-2) on late 77y drive to pull within 34-32. He then could not find anyone open for 2-pt conv. Vols TB Travis Stephens rambled for career-high 226y and 3 TDs, while QB Casey Clausen threw for 17-25/168y. Tennessee used passes to open things up for Stephens, and he broke runs of 49y, 35y for TD, 34y and 68y. His final 2 long runs came in 4th Q to set up short TDs by sub TB Jabari Davis. Key to game was Tennessee's ability to reach EZ: from late in 1st H through midway through 4th Q, each team scored 3 times but it came down to TDs for Vols and FGs for Gators. Earlier in week, Florida coach Steve Spurrier may have diverted team's focus by attacking Florida State for trying to cause injuries in game played 2 weeks earlier. Banged-up Florida RB Earnest Graham was missed as Gators rushed for only 36y.

LOUISIANA STATE 27 Auburn 14: To winner went SEC West crown, and QB Rohan Davey led balanced attack to send Louisiana State (8-3) to title game in Atlanta. Davey threw for 245y—10/186y of it to WR Josh Reed—and TD. In front of largest crowd, so far, in Tiger Stadium history (92,141), some Auburn (7-4) players jumped on LSU logo before game to earn 15y PEN. LSU WR Michael Clayton promptly pounced on onside-KO to lauch 36y TD drive as Bengals scored TD on 1st series for 4th straight game, all runs by RB LaBrandon Toefield. Toefield finished with 120y rushing as LSU won y battle by 431y to 293y. Auburn answered Toefield's TD on QB Jason Campbell's 72y connection to WR Tim Carter, but that was as close as it got as LSU stretched lead to 21-7 at H on 17y scoring reception by Reed and backup RB Domanick Davis' 7y TD run. LSU D kept Auburn off scoreboard until RB Chris Butler's late 13y TD run.

Colorado 39 Texas 37 (Irving, Texas): With Florida losing earlier in day, Texas (10-2) had Rose Bowl berth awaiting it in Big 12 championship should it defeat team it had beaten 41-7 earlier in year. Hot Buffaloes had other ideas as TB Chris Brown rushed for 182y and 3 TDs. Also, Texas QB Chris Simms committed 4 TOs in 1st H—all leading to pts for Colorado (10-2)—including 64y INT TD RET by Buffs S Medford Moorer for 29-10 lead. Longhorns turned to QB Major Applewhite—with Simms

suffering from dislocated finger—for immediate results. On Applewhite's 2nd play, he threw 79y TD pass to WR B.J. Johnson and soon led 2 drives that ended in FGs. When Longhorns CB Rod Babers intercepted pass on fake punt and returned 54y for TD, Colorado's lead dramatically was cut to 36-30. Buffs remained calm, marching 51y to K Jeremy Flores' clinching 43y FG. Drive was extended twice on 4th down, when Texas roughed P Flores and Buffaloes QB Bobby Pesavento gained 1st down on 1y dive. Applewhite (15-25/240y) quickly led TD drive, capped with 1y pass to Johnson, but Buffs recovered Horns' ensuing onside-KO try.

OREGON 17 Oregon State 14: WR Keenan Howry almost single-handedly kept Oregon's national title hopes alive with 70y punt TD RET for 10-6 lead early in 4th Q. After receiving subsequent punt, Ducks (10-1) marched 80y to TD with key play coming on 28y catch by Howry on 3rd-and-10. Oregon TB Maurice Morris rushed for 52y on clinching trip and finished drive with 8y scoring run by carrying 2 defenders into EZ. Oregon State (5-6) next went 69y in 11 plays—TD coming on QB Jonathan Smith's 24y pass to WR Josh Hawkins—but could not recover onside-KO. Game was not over just yet. Bizarrely, Oregon QB Joey Harrington (11-22/104y) lost FUM with 1:38 left. But, Ducks D refused to budge, and Smith (20-38/252y) threw INT to Ducks CB Rashad Bauman to end it. Beavers RB Ken Simonton finished with 84y rushing for 971y on season, falling short of bid to become 5th player in NCAA history to rush past 1,000y in each of 4 years. Oregon LB Kevin Mitchell had 17 tackles.

USA Today Coaches December 3

1	Miami (Fla.) (59)	1499	14	South Carolina	654
2	Tennessee	1419	15	Michigan	617
3	Oregon	1349	16	Virginia Tech	610
4	Nebraska	1267	17	Syracuse	526
5	Colorado	1212	18	Georgia	475
6	Florida	1132	19	Washington	401
7	Maryland	1126	20	LSU	358
8t	Brigham Young (1)	1094	21	Fresno State	345
8t	Illinois	1094	22	Louisville	208
10	Texas	1003	23	Ohio State	181
11	Oklahoma	902	24	Florida State	129
12	Stanford	852	25	Marshall	70
13	Washington State	742			

Bowl Championship Series Rankings December 3

	Poll Avg.	Computer Avg.	Schedule Rank	Losses	Total
1 Miami (11-0)	1.0	1.00	0.60	0	2.50
2 Tennessee (10-1)	2.0	2.83	0.16	1	4.79
3 Nebraska (11-1)	4.5	2.67	0.72	1	8.39
4 Colorado (9-2)	4.5	5.50	0.08	2	9.88
5 Oregon (10-1)	3.0	5.50	1.24	1	10.44

December 8, 2001

LOUISIANA STATE 31 Tennessee 20 (Atlanta): Result of SEC Championship made it seem as though no team really wanted to play Miami in Rose Bowl. This upset booted Tennessee out of BCS title game thanks to QB Matt Mauck, 22-year-old frosh who spent 3 years in Chicago Cubs organization and replaced injured QB Rohan Davey to rush for 2 TDs. Mauck led Tigers (9-3) to 1st SEC crown since 1988. Davey's injury ended up inspiring his mates because he was hurt on QB cheap shot to ribs by LB Keyon Whiteside. Davey returned later in 1st H but went out for good on another hit near end of 2nd Q. Despite modest 5-15/67y aerial numbers, Mauck, who hailed from Santa Claus, Indiana, had no Christmas presents for Vols, leading 6 scoring drives. Tennessee WR Kelly Washington, another minor leaguer, caught 9/140y including 31y catch for Vols' 1st TD and 47y reception that set up 3y TD for 17-7 lead on pass from QB Casey Clausen (27-43/332y, 2 TDs) to FB Troy Fleming. LSU D held Vols TB Travis Stephens to 37y rushing and forced him to lose FUM that set up Mauck's go-ahead TD run; Mauck went up middle for 13y TD and 24-17 lead for LSU. Bengals marched 65y, all gained on ground, to RB Domanick Davis' clinching 1y plunge on 4th down with 2:26 left. During that drive, S Julian Battle dropped sure INT that might have kept Vols in it.

USA Today Coaches December 10

1	Miami (Fla.) (60)	1500	14	South Carolina	660
2	Oregon	1398	15	Michigan	624
3	Colorado	1337	16	Virginia Tech	595
4	Nebraska	1334	17	Brigham Young	529
5	Florida	1184	18	Syracuse	492
6	Maryland	1167	19	Georgia	469
7	Illinois	1145	20	Washington	393
8	Tennessee	1105	21	Fresno State	323
9	Texas	1034	22	Louisville	221
10	Oklahoma	936	23	Ohio State	198
11	Stanford	889	24	Florida State	137
12	LSU	778	25	Marshall	59
13	Washington State	764			

Bowl Championship Series Rankings December 10

	Poll Avg.	Computer Avg.	Schedule Rank	Losses	Total
1 Miami (11-0)	1.0	1.00	0.72	0	2.62
2 Nebraska (11-1)	4.0	2.17	0.56	1	7.23
3 Colorado (9-2)	3.0	4.50	0.08	2	7.28
4 Oregon (10-1)	2.0	4.83	1.24	1	8.67
5 Florida (10-2)	5.0	5.83	0.76	2	13.09

Conference Standings

Big East

Miami	7-0
Syracuse	6-1
Virginia Tech	4-3
Boston College	4-3
Pittsburgh	4-3
Temple	2-5
West Virginia	1-6
Rutgers	0-7

Southeastern

EAST	
Tennessee	7-1
Florida	6-2
South Carolina	5-3
Georgia	5-3
Kentucky	1-7
Vanderbilt	0-8
WEST	
LSU	5-3
Auburn	5-3
Alabama	4-4
Arkansas	4-4
Mississippi	4-4
Mississippi State	2-6

Big Ten

Illinois	7-1
Michigan	6-2
Ohio State	5-3
Purdue	4-4
Iowa	4-4
Penn State	4-4
Indiana	4-4
Michigan State	3-5
Wisconsin	3-5
Minnesota	2-6
Northwestern	2-6

Big Twelve

NORTH	
Colorado	7-1
Nebraska	7-1
Iowa State	4-4
Kansas State	3-5
Missouri	3-5
Kansas	1-7
SOUTH	
Texas	7-1
Oklahoma	6-2
Texas A&M	4-4
Texas Tech	4-4
Oklahoma State	2-6
Baylor	0-8

Pacific Ten

Oregon	7-1
Washington State	6-2
Stanford	6-2
Washington	6-2
Southern California	5-3
UCLA	4-4
Oregon State	3-5
Arizona	2-6
Arizona State	1-7
California	0-8

Atlantic Coast

Maryland	7-1
Florida State	6-2
North Carolina	5-3
Georgia Tech	4-4
North Carolina State	4-4
Clemson	4-4
Wake Forest	3-5
Virginia	3-5
Duke	0-8

Conference USA

Louisville	6-1
Cincinnati	5-2
UAB	5-2
East Carolina	5-2
TCU	4-3
Southern Miss	4-3
Memphis	3-4
Army	2-5
Tulane	1-6
Houston	0-7

Mid-American

EAST	
Marshall	8-0
Miami of Ohio	6-2
Bowling Green	5-3
Kent State	5-3
Akron	4-4
Buffalo	1-7
Ohio	1-7
WEST	
Toledo	5-2
Northern Illinois	4-3
Ball State	4-3
Western Michigan	4-4
Central Michigan	2-6
Eastern Michigan	2-6

Mountain West

BYU	7-0
Colorado State	5-2
Utah	4-3
New Mexico	4-3
Air Force	3-4
UNLV	3-4
San Diego State	2-5
Wyoming	0-7

Western Athletic

Louisiana Tech	7-1
Fresno State	6-2
Boise State	6-2
Hawaii	5-3
Rice	5-3
SMU	4-4
Nevada	3-5
San Jose State	3-5
UTEP	1-7
Tulsa	0-7

2001 Major Bowl Games

Tangerine Bowl (Dec. 20): Pittsburgh 34 North Carolina State 19

Shaking off injured right ankle, WR Antonio Bryant (7/101y) burned NC State for 2 TD receptions to lead Pitt (7-5) to its 6th straight win. After teams traded 1st Q FGs, Bryant scored TDs on 15y and 2y catches, his 2nd followed his 49y catch-and-run, all from QB David Priestley (18-32/271y), who had thrown 13 TDs against single INT during Panthers' 5-game run to bowl bid. Panthers D, another key factor in team's surge to Tangerine Bowl with only 3 TDs allowed over final 5 games, also came up big: LB Lewis Moore sacked Wolfpack (7-5) QB Philip Rivers (26-40/189y, INT) to force FUM that DT Tyre Young returned 16y for clinching TD with 6:15 left. NC State D had been hampered by early loss of A-A LB Levar Fisher with broken arm as Pittsburgh drove 80, 98, and 70y to TDs on 1st 3 possessions following his injury. North Carolina State remained in game thanks to CB Greg Golden's 90y RET of KO for 2nd Q TD. Soon, Wolfpack aggressively went for punt block, but Pitt P Andy Lee was roughed by CB Lamont Reid. PEN kept alive Pittsburgh's drive that ended with back-up QB Rod Rutherford's 1y TD run at end of 1st H. Wolfpack rallied with 9 pts in 4th Q, including Rivers' 5y TD pass to WR Dovonte Edwards. "Thank goodness he had a bad ankle or

he (Bryant) really would have embarrassed us out there," said Wolfpack coach Chuck Amato facetiously.

Seattle Bowl (Dec. 27): Georgia Tech 24 Stanford 14

Wiping out negatives—disappointing record, departure of coach George O'Leary, and academic loss of TB Joe Burns—Yellow Jackets (8-5) played to potential that had earned them preseason accolades. Georgia Tech D had 4 sacks in holding Stanford (9-3) to season-low 125y rushing and stopped Cardinal 3 times at Tech 1YL on 1st possession of game, including LB Daryl Smith's tackle for loss of RB Kerry Carter on 4th down. Georgia Tech then marched 97y to take 7-0 lead on WR Will Glover's 5y run. Stanford again moved deep into Tech territory, settling for FG. Georgia Tech answered with 34y TD pass from QB George Godsey (23-37/266y) to WR Kelly Campbell (10/106y), so while each team had enjoyed 2 long drives, Tech led 14-3. Burns' sub, TB Sean Gregory (19/91y), burst 54y to set up FG at H's end. Late in 3rd Q Stanford blew another TD chance, earning 2nd-and-goal at Tech 2YL before settling for K Mike Biselli's 2nd FG, this of 26y. Backup QB Chris Lewis (6-13/110y) threw 4th Q TD pass to WR Teyo Johnson and 2-pt conv pass to WR Ryan Wells as Stanford pulled within 17-14 with less than 4 mins left. Campbell clinched it with 2y TD run after Jackets' 63y trip.

Independence Bowl (Dec. 27): Alabama 14 Iowa State 13

Playing hard on both sides of ball, Cyclones (7-5) were in position to beat another storied program in 2nd straight bowl. But poor special teams play reared its bumbling head in 4th Q as Iowa State missed 2 FGs and suffered punt block that was converted into Alabama TD. P Tony Yelk's punt was blocked by S Waine Bacon, and Alabama (7-5) QB Andrew Zow (11-19/119y) needed only 2 plays to score, tossing 27y pass to TE Terry Jones at 4:46 mark for what proved to be winning pts. K Yelk's last-sec FG attempt looked good as it sailed over right upright but was ruled wide right by inches as Crimson Tide held on. QB Seneca Wallace had led Iowa State attack with 25-42/284y passing, hitting 26y bullet to WR Jack Whitver on 2nd-and-25 during failed final FG drive. RB Ennis Hayward rushed for 125y as ISU outgained Tide 456y to 269y; Cyclones were now 12-1 when Hayward topped 100y. Cyclones built 10-0 lead in 1st H thanks to 1y TD run by FB Joe Woodley set up by 33y reverse by WR Lane Danielson. Tide answered with best drive of game as Zow capped 10-play, 80y march with 8y run. Alabama had now won 29 bowl games, most of any school, but 1st since 1997.

Galleryfurniture.com Bowl (Dec. 28): Texas A&M 28 TCU 9

Nostalgic reunion of old SWC foes took place in Houston as win was 24th straight by Texas A&M (8-4) over TCU and snapped A&M's 4-game bowl losing streak. Unheralded DB Byron Jones—one of 5 frosh in Aggies lineup—made his 1st-ever start memorable by intercepting 3 passes as part of pressure D. Horned Frogs (6-6) QB Casey Printers (15-30/144y, 4 INTs) also was sacked 6 times. After scoreless 1st Q and GLS by TCU D early in 2nd Q, Jones set up opening score with INT RET to Horned Frogs 1YL that set up TD keeper by QB Mark Fariss (9-19/191y). TCU tied up game with 89y FUM RET by S Charlie Owens, but could not keep up with its O struggling: Aggie D blanked TCU O and limited it to 118y. A&M FB Joe Weber ran for 2 TDs before WR Mickey Jones added late 82y TD reception, after yet another INT, to finish off Horned Frogs.

Music City Bowl (Dec. 28): Boston College 20 Georgia 16

Boston College (8-4) TB William Green (35/149y) romped 75y to set up TD, and his 7y TD run won it. Bulldogs (8-4) opened with KO reverse for 86y gain, WR Fred Gibson handing off to CB Decory Bryant. After Georgia was sacked on 1st play from scrimmage, Gibson (6/109y) caught pass behind line of scrimmage and ran for 15y TD with 55 secs elapsed in game. Bulldogs blew several chances to up lead before Eagles reaped 10 pts after pair of 1st H INTs: QB Brian St. Pierre hit WR Dedrick Dewalt with 10y TD pass on drive that featured Green's 70y run. Georgia grabbed 16-10 lead in 3rd Q as QB David Greene (22-38/288y) hit 5 throws on 69y trip TD by TB Verron Haynes (27/132y). Game turned on another Bulldogs TO—all 20 pts by BC tapped TOs—when Greene and TB Musa Smith fumbled in mid-4th Q. BC took over at UGa 37 YL, poised for Green's 7y TD run. With 1:32 left, Georgia coach Mark Richt took criticism for punting on 4th-and-17 from own 43YL; Bulldogs wouldn't see ball again until 14 secs were left.

Holiday Bowl (Dec. 28): Texas 47 Washington 43

After scoreless 1st Q, teams erupted. Texas (11-2) QB Major Applewhite (37-55/473y, 2 TDs) set personal bests for completions, attempts, and y in leading biggest rally in school history. Longhorns scored on 6 of last 7 series to pull out late win. It looked momentarily as if Huskies (8-4) had pulled it out themselves, as, after Texas took 40-36 lead on 4y TD pass to Bo Scaife, Washington QB Cody Pickett (27-54/293y) led 7-play, 80y drive that TB Willie Hurst (16/137y) capped with 34y run with 1:49 left. Applewhite ended his college career by hitting 4-5/75y to set up TB Ivan Williams' game-winning 3y TD run. Washington had built 13-0 lead on trio of 2nd Q INTs, including 38y TD RET by DE Terry Johnson. Longhorns settled down, marching 80y for TD on Applewhite's 43y pass to WR B.J. Johnson. Few mins later, he threw to other side of EZ to WR Roy Williams (11/134y) for 25y TD and 14-13 lead. Then it was Pickett's turn as he hit 6-7/72y, with 4y TD arrow to TE Joe Collier. Huskies led 23-14 at H after converting INT into FG. Washington, continuing its surge, embarked on 91y drive early in 3rd Q that ended with 17y TD grab by TE Jerramy Stevens (9/109y). Facing 19-pt deficit late in 3rd Q, Applewhite led 4 scoring drives to regain lead with 6 mins left.

Alamo Bowl (Dec. 29): Iowa 19 Texas Tech 16

Outstanding Iowa (7-5) K Nate Kaeding (4 FGs) equaled his longest 3-pter of season in booting winning 47y FG with 44 secs left. Less than 2 mins earlier Texas Tech (7-5) had tied game with 37y FG by K Robert Treece. QB Kyle McCann (19-26/161y) hit 12-13 in 1st H and TB Aaron Greveng rushed for 82y of game-high 115y as Hawkeyes had built 10-0 lead. QB Kliff Kingsbury (29-49/309y, 3 INTs) raced H clock to send Red Raiders upfield for 50y FG try by K Clinton Greathouse. Due to bad snap and late hold, Greathouse kicked low and wobbly, but still it went over crossbar to put Tech on scoreboard, down 10-3 at H. Raiders tied it 10-10 early in 3rd Q as Iowa's busted coverage allowed WR Wes Welker to get open in EZ for 20y TD reception. Later in 3rd Q, Kingsbury threw INT to Hawkeyes DT Derrick Pickens that was converted into Kaeding's FG and 13-10 lead. Red Raiders later faced 4th-and-1 deep at Iowa 20YL but elected to tie it with 37y FG. Hawkeyes D was able to frustrate Kingsbury most of game with 7- or 8-man deep zone coverage and great pass rush by nimble DL. After Kaeding's late heroics, Kingsbury moved Raiders 40y before Iowa S Bob Sanders (11 tackles) made INT of final heave in EZ.

Insight.com Bowl (Dec. 29): Syracuse 26 Kansas State 3

This was tale of teams that preferred running attacks. Syracuse (10-3) TB James Mungro rushed 19/112y, 3 TDs, against K-State's 3rd-ranked D, which had only allowed 6 ground-based TDs all season. Wildcats (6-6), meanwhile, went nowhere as they mustered only 34/33y rushing, 224y less than country's 5th-best season avg. Kansas State could not pass too well either, shuffling QBs Ell Roberson and Marc Dunn without much production. Mungro opened scoring when he took option pitch and raced down left sideline for 65y TD—although he seemed to step OB at midfield. KSU answered with 29y FG by K Joe Rheem after Roberson hit his only completion in 11 tries in 1st H: 50y pass to WR Aaron Lockett. Game then turned on Kansas State miscues, with 1st being botched catch of snap by P Mike Ronsik deep in own territory. Orange needed only 3y for TD, which came on Mungro's 1y plunge. Upon getting ball back quickly after 1st of 2 INTs by CB Willie Ford, Syracuse QB R.J. Anderson hit WR Johnnie Morant for 41y completion to set up another short TD run by Mungro. Trailing 19-3, Dunn moved K-State early in 3rd Q, before giving way to Roberson, who promptly fumbled ball back to Syracuse. Anderson and Morant hooked up again in 4th Q on 52y TD pass. LB Clifton Smith led Syracuse D with 14 tackles and 2 sacks.

Sun Bowl (Dec. 31): Washington State 33 Purdue 27

Washington State (10-2) D provided 4 INTs, while Boilermakers made 4 pickoffs as well, but fumbled INT back to Cougars and used another to set up aerial drive that ended with another INT. Wazzu CB Jason David opened scoring with 45y RET of errant pass by Purdue (6-6) QB Kyle Orton (38-74/419y). After same-play TO exchange, Washington State scored again on 46y TD pass by QB Jason Gesser (15-40/281y, 3 INTs) to WR Mike Bush. Purdue cut lead to 14-10 early in 2nd Q on RB Montrell Lowe's 1y TD run. WSU P Alan Cox improvised for 18y and 1st down after receiving low snap, and it led to 47y FG by K Drew Dunning, 1st of his quartet of 3-ptrs. Orton turned hot, hitting 9 passes in row in 2nd Q, with TD to WR Taylor Stubblefield. K Travis Dorsch gave Purdue 20-17 H lead with 50y FG. Cougars opened 2nd H with 13 pts in 3rd Q. Purdue CB Antwaun Rogers and Cougars S Lamont Thompson exchanged EZ INTs. Boilers made final chance for themselves, Orton hitting 51y TD to Stubblefield TD pass with 1:53 left and recovering onside-KO. They failed at WSU 22YL, with Cougars deflecting 3rd and 4th down passes. Despite Purdue's loss, WR John Standeford (12/103y) and TE Tim Stratton (12/86y) set game records for catches, while Stubblefield (9/196y) broke y mark.

Silicon Valley Classic (Dec. 31): Michigan State 44 Fresno State 35

After finishing tied for 8th in Big 10, Michigan State (7-5) earned measure of redemption with victory over Fresno that had flirted with BCS. For 10th time this year, Bulldogs (11-3) scored TD on opening series, racing 5 plays to QB David Carr's 5y pass to TE Stephen Spach. Spartans tied it on 72y bomb from QB Jeff Smoker (22-32/376y, INT) to WR Charles Rogers (10/270y). Carr (35-56/531y, 2 INTs) soon lost FUM, recovered in EZ by Michigan State LB Monquiz Wedlow. And so went 736y O show in 1st H with larger Spartans able to wear down Fresno State as huge TB T.J. Duckett (27/184y) rushed for 146y in 1st H with TD runs of 5y and 39y on way to 37-21 H lead. Blocked punt by Bulldogs S Bryce McGill was returned to 15YL by LB Maurice Rodriguez to get Fresno going late in 3rd Q. TB Paris Gaines soon took pass in right flat and scored to pull Fresno within 37-35. Spartans clinched it with 5y TD catch by TE Ivory McCoy with 2 mins left.

Peach Bowl (Dec. 31): North Carolina 16 Auburn 10

Tar Heels (8-5) completed turnaround from 0-3 start to season as they built 16-0 lead and held on. North Carolina struck 1st as CB Michael Waddell forced FUM by Tigers WR Tim Carter that DE Joey Evans returned to 9YL to set up TB Willie Parker's 10y TD run. Breaking tackle attempt by LB Karlos Dansby at Auburn 40YL, Heels QB Ronald Curry ended up-and-down career with 62y scramble for TD in 3rd Q that proved decisive. Auburn (7-5) rallied with 4th Q FG and 12y TD pass from QB Daniel Cobb to TE Lorenzo Diamond with 1:18 left. But, Tar Heels recovered onside-KO to seal win. Auburn A-A K-P Damon Duval sparkled as he booted 2 longest punts of year—61y and Peach Bowl-record 67y. Dansby authored amazing play late in 3rd Q that shifted momentum: LB who led SEC in INTs with 5, leapt over sideline to intercept pass and, before landing OB, tossed ball to LB Dontarrious Thomas. Tigers converted that INT into K Duval's 34y FG. Carolina DT Ryan Sims sacked QB Jason Campbell for -18y to kill rally, and Tigers could not score again until late in 4th Q.

Outback Bowl: South Carolina 31 Ohio State 28

For 2nd year in row, coach Lou Holtz's Gamecocks (9-3) upset Ohio State in Outback Bowl. Ohio State (7-5) had erased 28-pt lead and had ball deep in own territory following INT. With less than min left, Buckeyes QB Steve Bellisari (21-35/320y), who had come off bench to lead rally, threw deep INT to Gamecocks CB Sheldon Brown, who returned ball 37y to Ohio 29YL. Four plays later, South Carolina K Daniel Weaver dropped 42y FG over crossbar for last-sec victory. QB Phil Petty (19-37/227y), FB Andrew Pinnock (2 TDs), and WR Brian Scott (7/83y, TD) were O heroes as South Carolina built 28-0 lead by 3rd Q. Gamecocks, who dominated last year's Outback

Bowl, seemed to have easy victory in hand until sr Bellisari, making 1st appearance since November DUI arrest, began moving charges in his final game. Oft-criticized Bellisari was nothing short of spectacular on drive that knotted game 28-28 as he marched Ohio State from own 11YL with 3:56 left, completing all 6 passes/86y, including 9y TD pass to TE Darnell Sanders. Buckeyes soon were back on O as Petty threw pick to LB Cie Grant, although celebration PEN placed ball on Ohio 18YL. Buckeyes quickly paid on Brown's INT.

Cotton Bowl: Oklahoma 10 Arkansas 3

Oklahoma (11-2) put on devastating D show as good as in any bowl. Sooners sacked Arkansas' alternating QBs 9 times—twice on blitzes by S Roy Williams—en route to allowing only 2-13 passing, 6 1st downs (2 on PENs) and 50y total O. Hogs had paltry 0.9y avg on 55 snaps. Only 2 drives went more than 4 plays, and only 2 nosed into OU territory. Arkansas (7-5) cracked midfield once in 2nd H on 52y drive that produced K Brennan O'Donohoe's 52y FG. Oklahoma scored midway through 1st Q on 1y keeper by QB Nate Hybl (24-32/175y). Razorbacks laid on their share of big hits and hung in enough to be in position to launch last drive for tie or win after 49y FG miss by Oklahoma K Tim Duncan, who had hit 32y FG early in 3rd Q. Hogs' final drive ended with Sooners LB Teddy Lehman stripping backup Arkansas QB Matt Jones, FUM being recovered by LB Rocky Calmus (11 tackles).

Gator Bowl: Florida State 30 Virginia Tech 17

Reminiscent of Sugar Bowl game 2 years earlier, Virginia Tech entered 4th Q with lead before surrendering long TD passes. WR Javon Walker (4/195y) started scoring blitz, beating Hokies CB Ronyell Whitaker for 77y TD catch that provided winning pts and started 17-pt Florida State (8-4) blitz. After Seminoles D stopped TB Kevin Jones on 4th-and-1 at FSU 32YL, QB Chris Rix (12-25/326y, INT) and Walker connected on 51y pass play that set up K Xavier Beitia's FG. Rix and Walker also added 23y hookup. Virginia Tech D had played well for 3 Qs, stuffing Florida State on opening drive to control field position and launch FG drive. 'Sole Noles' TD in opening 3 Qs was not fault of Hokie D as punt block gave FSU 1st-and-goal at Va Tech 1YL. Rix scored on keeper for 7-3 lead. Florida State led 10-3 at H after 50y FG by Beitia. Recharged Hokies took opening possession of 2nd H to paydirt, scoring when Jones took pitch and danced in from 5YL. Florida State answered with Beitia's 47y FG before Va Tech regained 17-13 lead on 55y TD to WR Andre Davis (5/158y) as QB Grant Noel (15-27/269y) withstood blitz to deliver pass. Florida State TB Greg Jones rushed 23/120y.

Citrus Bowl: Tennessee 45 Michigan 17

Tennessee (11-2) unleashed host of weapons in handing Wolverines (8-4) worst bowl loss ever. QB Casey Clausen (26-35/393y, 3 TDs, 2 TDs rushing) and targets WR Donte' Stallworth (8/119y), WR Kelly Washington (6/70y), and TE Jason Witten (6/125y) were too much to handle as Vols gained 503y, most allowed by Michigan all season. Tennessee took opening drive into Michigan territory, with Washington even completing pass, before settling for 32y FG by K Alex Walls. Both Michigan QB John Navarre and FB B.J. Askew fumbled on same play, recovered by Vols DT John Henderson at UM 28YL to set up 3y TD catch by Washington for 10-0 lead. Next, Stallworth burned Michigan as he dove to catch 23y pass to set up Clausen's 1y keeper for 17-0 lead. Suffering 171y to 13y O differential, Michigan woke up in time to convert 4th down en route to 14y TD pass by Navarre (21-39/240y, INT) to Askew, but still trailed 24-10 at H. Clausen completed 10 straight tosses during middle of game, including 64y TD pass to Witten. WR Marquise Walker caught 5/100y, reaching century mark for Michigan-record 6th time during season.

Fiesta Bowl: Oregon 38 Colorado 16

Ducks (11-1) laid claim to honors despite BCS controversy by crushing Colorado (10-3) for 38 straight pts behind QB Joey Harrington (28-42/350y, 4 TDs, INT). Buffs got on scoreboard 1st as FB Brandon Drumm scored TD from 1y out, with drive's key play coming on 33y screen pass to TB Cortlen Johnson. Ducks answered quickly—all 5 of their TD drives lasted 2:38 or less—with Harrington throwing 28y TD pass to WR Keenan Howry. While Oregon's 81st-ranked D loaded scrimmage line and stuffed Buffs' celebrated run game, Ducks actually outrushed Colorado, which had gained more than 300y on ground in wins over Texas and Nebraska. Twice in 2nd Q, with outcome in doubt, Ducks stopped Buffs on 3rd-and-1 rushes. Play of game came from Oregon TB Maurice Morris, who made dazzling 49y scoring run, even though, despite appearances, his knee never touched because Colorado LB Joey Johnson was between him and turf. Morris (11/89y) spun until upright and raced to EZ. Oregon WR Samie Parker excelled with 9/162y, while CB Steve Smith turned in 3 INTs. Colorado A-A TE Daniel Graham caught 10/89y, but had crucial early drop.

Sugar Bowl: Louisiana State 47 Illinois 34

As they had done all year Illinois (10-2) dug themselves into hole. For brief moment in 4th Q, after WR Walter Young's amazing catch along sideline in EZ cut Illini deficit to 13, they had hope. But then LSU (10-3) turned to brilliant WR Josh Reed, who made 2 catches on ensuing Tiger drive to set up clinching TD. Reed ended up catching 14/239y for sweet Sugar Bowl marks. That drive ended on RB Dominick Davis' 4th running TD—yet another game record—and 47-28 lead for Tigers. Illini did get FUM that was converted into another nice TD catch by Young (6/178y), on 40y pass by WR Brandon Lloyd (5/56y, 2 TDs). That would end all scoring, and Tigers won 6th straight game of 2001, 5th straight bowl game, and 1st Sugar Bowl since 1968. LSU had marched to opening score behind QB Rohan Davey (31-53/444y), whose pass y also set Sugar Bowl record. He completed 4-4 on drive that ended when Davis crawled in from 4YL. With Illinois QB Kurt Kittner (14-35/262y, INT) starting slowly with 1-10/1y passing, Tigers stretched lead to 21-0 on runs by Davis (28/122y). Despite Kittner taking only 3 plays to travel 75y to TE Brian Hodges' 2y TD catch, Tigers never pushed

lead to 34-7 by H. LSU's win meant SEC had swept trio of January 1 match-ups with Big 10.

Orange Bowl: Florida 56 Maryland 23

Gators (10-2) made statement at expense of Maryland, rolling up record 659y in highest-scoring Orange Bowl ever. QB Rex Grossman (20-28/248, 4 TDs) came off bench in 2nd Q—he was not in starting lineup as he missed curfew—to lead TD drives 1st 6 times he had ball. WR Taylor Jacobs, who had Orange Bowl record 170y on 10 catches, gained 115y and TD receiving in 1st Q as Florida took 14-0 lead. On last play of 1st Q, Maryland (10-2) enjoyed its highlight: 64y scoring bomb from QB Shaun Hill (23-39/257y) to WR Jafar Williams (4/91y). Early in 2nd Q, Terps went to 3YL on INT RET by CB Dennard Wilson, and it set up K Nick Novak's 20y FG. Gators pushed lead to 28-10 with 2 more TDs, including 4y grab by WR Jabar Gaffney (7/118y) before 1st H ended. RB Robert Gillespie's nifty 11y TD run midway through 3rd Q put exclamation on Florida's victory.

Rose Bowl (Jan. 3): Miami 37 Nebraska 14

Sharp Miami (12-0) claimed national title with its 22nd straight win. Nebraska (11-2) had little margin for error as evidenced in 2 early, quick-striking plays: Huskers QB Eric Crouch lost FUM when stripped near midfield, and CB Keyuo Craver stumbled covering WR Andre Johnson (7/199y) on 49y scoring pass. Miami was soon back on O and Johnson caught 34y pass, followed by 39y TD run by RB Clinton Portis (20/104y). With game getting away from Huskers, Crouch overthrew TE Tracey Wistrom, and pass was picked off by Miami S James Lewis for 47y TD. Presto! Canes led 21-0. Miami soon moved TE Jeremy Shockey to FB as it again neared EZ, and Shockey capped 2-play drive by catching 21y TD pass for 27-0 lead. QB Ken Dorsey (22-35/362y, INT) added 8y TD pass to Johnson late in 2nd Q for Hurricanes that needed only 15 plays to score 4 TDs in 1st H. Star of 2nd H was Miami LB Jonathan Vilma, who had 2 big hits among his 8 tackles and forced FUM by WR Ben Zajicek. Nebraska CB DeJuan Groce chipped in with 71y punt TD RET, and Crouch rushed for 114y, but Huskers could get no closer than 20-pt margin. Dorsey set school bowl record for passing y, surpassing mark of 321y set by George Mira in 1962 Gotham Bowl, also against Nebraska. "I think anybody would have struggled with them if they're on top of their game the way they were tonight," said losing coach Frank Solich. By guiding Miami's 5th national title since 1983, but 1st since 1991, Larry Coker became 1st coach to win championship in 1st year as head coach since Bennie Osterbaan did it at Michigan in 1948.

Final *USA Today* Coaches January 4

1	Miami (Fla.) (60)	1500	14	Syracuse	736
2	Oregon	1434	15	Florida State	556
3	Florida	1351	16	Louisville	524
4	Tennessee	1284	17	Stanford	502
5	Texas	1207	18	Virginia Tech	394
6	Oklahoma	1141	19	Washington	369
7	Nebraska	1101	20	Michigan	363
8	Louisiana State	1099	21	Marshall	223
9	Colorado	1031	22	Toledo	188
10	Maryland	885	23	Boston College	174
11	Washington State	879	24	Brigham Young	172
12	Illinois	846	25	Georgia	163
13	South Carolina	837			

Final AP Poll January 4

1	Miami (72)	1800	14	Syracuse	856
2	Oregon	1726	15	Florida State	686
3	Florida	1611	16	Stanford	673
4	Tennessee	1581	17	Louisville	621
5	Texas	1374	18	Virginia Tech	437
6	Oklahoma	1373	19	Washington	414
7	Louisiana State	1350	20	Michigan	325
8	Nebraska	1348	21	Boston College	318
9	Colorado	1335	22	Georgia	277
10	Washington State	1074	23	Toledo	237
11	Maryland	1065	24	Georgia Tech	178
12	Illinois	1045	25	Brigham Young	144
13	South Carolina	975			

2001 Top Performance Formula

1	Miami	1.9071
2	Florida	1.7191
3	Nebraska	1.6423
4	Texas	1.6264
5	Oregon	1.6207
6	Tennessee	1.6016
7	Oklahoma	1.5563
8	Colorado	1.4898
9	Maryland	1.4832
10	Louisiana State	1.4783
11	Illinois	1.4677
12	Brigham Young	1.4547
13	Washington State	1.4538
14	Syracuse	1.4520
15	Stanford	1.3895
16	Florida State	1.3812
17	Virginia Tech	1.3579
18	South Carolina	1.3368
19	Michigan	1.3359
20	UCLA	1.2927

2001 Top Opponent Records

1	Colorado	.6483
2	Tennessee	.6408
3	Florida State	.6336
4	California	.6303
5	Miami	.6279
6	Mississippi State	.6250
7t	Nebraska	.6214285
7t	Louisiana State	.6214285
9	Kansas State	.6194
10	Florida	.6183
11	Arkansas	.6138
12	Auburn	.6031
13	Kentucky	.6050
14	Syracuse	.6028
15	Michigan	.6000
16	North Carolina	.5944
17	Wisconsin	.5939
18	Oklahoma State	.5934
19	Penn State	.5932
20	Kansas	.5917

2001 Out-of-Conference Records

	W-L	Percentage	Bowl W-L
Southeastern	31-10	.7561	5-3
Big Twelve	30-10	.7500	3-5
Pacific-10	24-10	.7059	2-3
Big East	25-12	.6757	4-1
Atlantic Coast	19-12	.6129	4-2
Big Ten	22-16	.5789	2-4
Mountain West	17-17	.5000	2-1

2001 Individual Statistical Leaders

RUSHING YARDS	Attempts	Yards	Avg.
Chance Kretschmer, Nevada	302	1732	5.7
Luke Staley, Brigham Young	196	1582	8.1
William Green, Boston College	265	1559	5.9
Larry Ned, San Diego State	311	1549	5.0
Anthony Davis, Wisconsin	291	1466	5.0
Travis Stephens, Tennessee	291	1464	5.0
Leonard Henry, East Carolina	184	1432	7.8
Chester Taylor, Toledo	268	1430	5.3
Mewelde Moore, Tulane	263	1421	5.4
Levron Williams, Indiana	212	1401	6.6

PASSING YARDS	Completions	Attempts	Yards	Pct.
David Carr, Fresno State	308	476	4299	64.7
Byron Leftwich, Marshall	315	470	4132	67.0
Rex Grossman, Florida	259	395	3896	65.6
Brandon Doman, Brigham Young	261	408	3542	64.0
Nick Rolovich, Hawaii	233	405	3361	57.5
Rohan Davey, Louisiana State	217	367	3347	59.1
Ben Roethlisberger, Miami (Ohio)	241	381	3105	63.3
George Godsey, Georgia Tech	249	384	3085	64.8
Dave Ragone, Louisville	231	383	3056	60.3
Casey Clausen, Tennessee	227	354	2969	64.1

RECEIVING YARDS	Catches	Yards
Josh Reed, Louisiana State	94	1740
Ashley Lelie, Hawaii	84	1713
Lee Evans, Wisconsin	75	1545
Kevin Curtis, Utah State	100	1531
Edell Shepherd, San Jose State	83	1500
Darius Watts, Marshall	91	1417
Rodney Wright, Fresno State	91	1331
Reno Mahe, Brigham Young	91	1211
Charles Rogers, Michigan State	57	1200
Jabar Gaffney, Florida	67	1191

2001 Consensus All-America
Offense

Wide Receiver:	Jabar Gaffney, Florida
	Josh Reed, LSU
Tight End:	Daniel Graham, Colorado
Linemen:	Bryant McKinnie, Miami
	Terrence Metcalf, Mississippi
	Mike Williams, Texas
	Toniu Fonoti, Nebraska
Center:	LeCharles Bentley, Ohio State
Quarterback:	Rex Grossman, Florida
Running Back:	Luke Staley, BYU
	William Green, Boston College
Kicker	David Duval, Auburn

Defense

Linemen:	Julius Peppers, North Carolina
	Dwight Freeney, Syracuse
	Alex Brown, Florida
	John Henderson, Tennessee
Linebacker:	Rocky Calmus, Oklahoma
	Robert Thomas, UCLA
	LeVar Fisher, N.C. State
	E.J. Henderson, Maryland
Back:	Quentin Jammer, Texas
	Edward Reed, Miami
	Roy Williams, Oklahoma
Punter:	Travis Dorsch, Purdue

2001 Heisman Trophy Vote

Eric Crouch, senior quarterback, Nebraska	770
Rex Grossman, sophomore, quarterback, Florida	708
Ken Dorsey, junior quarterback, Miami	638
Joey Harrington, senior quarterback, Oregon	364
David Carr, senior quarterback, Fresno State	280

Other Major Awards

Maxwell (Player)	Ken Dorsey, junior quarterback, Miami
Walter Camp (Player)	Eric Crouch, senior quarterback, Nebraska
Outland (Lineman)	Bryant McKinnie, senior tackle, Miami
Lombardi (Lineman)	Julius Peppers, junior defensive end, North Carolina
Doak Walker (Running Back)	Luke Staley, junior tailback, BYU
Davey O'Brien (Quarterback)	Eric Crouch, senior quarterback, Nebraska
Fred Biletnikoff (Receiver)	Josh Reed, junior wide receiver, LSU
Jim Thorpe (Defensive Back)	Roy Williams, junior safety, Oklahoma
Dick Butkus (Linebacker)	Rocky Calmus, senior linebacker, Oklahoma
Lou Groza (Placekicker)	Seth Marler, junior kicker, Tulane
Chuck Bednarik (Defender)	Julius Peppers, junior defensive end, North Carolina
Bronko Nagurski (Defender)	Roy Williams, junior safety, Oklahoma
Ray Guy (Punter)	Travis Dorsch, senior PK-P, Purdue
John Mackey (Tight End)	Daniel Graham, senior tight end, Colorado
Johnny Unitas (Sr. Quarterback)	David Carr, senior quarterback, Fresno State
Mosi Tatupu (Special Teams)	Kahlil Hill, senior WR-KR-PR, Iowa
Dave Rimington (Center)	LeCharles Bentley, senior center, Ohio State
AFCA Coach of the Year	Ralph Friedgen, Maryland

2002

The Year of the Twelfth Game, Irish Return to Glory, and Overtime Buckeyes

College football's 134th season was launched on August 22, the earliest starting date ever. The NCAA experimented with the scheduling of a 12th regular season game when the calendar had 14 Saturdays between Labor Day and the end of November. Some felt the extra game would serve only to create more once-beaten teams and complicate the villified Bowl Championship Series format. It didn't turn out that way.

Critics, who supported a playoff system, pointed out some teams, such as Nebraska (7-7), possibly could play as many as 15 games. The Huskers were scheduled for a preseason game, which, after 20 years since the christening of New Jersey's Kickoff Classic, were supposed to end after 2002. If Nebraska won the Big Twelve North, it would have a conference title game and a bowl game, or 15 games including its 13 regular season games. "If they can play 15 games, why can't we have a playoff?" wailed the naysayers.

Critics need not have worried about Nebraska, in particular, playing 15 games because its first non-winning season since 1961 was emblematic of a shift of power after the Huskers had played in the BCS title game the year before. Considerable pressure fell upon coach Frank Solich. The Huskers found themselves without great defensive speed and were green in the passing game with the graduation of 2001 Heisman-winning quarterback Eric Crouch. Nebraska was a sitting duck, especially in road games, and Texas (11-2) also ended the Huskers' 26-game winning streak in Lincoln.

Notre Dame (10-3), under new coach Tyrone Willingham, made a brilliant turnabout from its 5-7 mark of the previous fall. The difference-maker was the Fighting Irish's highly opportunistic defense, led by linebacker Courtney Watson and stellar cornerbacks Shane Walton and Vontez Duff. In fact, Willingham's "West Coast" offense, which was highly anticipated by Irish fans, never really clicked, finishing near the bottom in the nation in average yards gained per game. However, the ball-hawking defense, either scoring itself or gaining possession close to the foe's goal line, impacted positively on Notre Dame's low yardage ranking.

Bobby Bowden, 72-year-old coach of Florida State (9-5), expected his Seminoles to rebound from their mediocre 8-4 record of 2001. The experts agreed; the preseason AP Poll tabbed FSU for third. There was extensive talk that Florida State's relatively mild schedule might usher a trip to the BCS game in the Fiesta Bowl. But, the Seminoles squeaked through with a 38-31 win against Iowa State and were stunned by Louisville (7-6) for all the nation to see on an ESPN Thursday night cablecast, were nipped by no. 1 Miami (12-1) in a thriller, and were throttled at home by Notre Dame. To add to Bowden's woes, sophomore Adrian McPherson had no sooner won the quarterback job from Chris Rix in mid-season when he was suspended and investigated for theft and gambling. Even with four regular season losses, the Seminoles still eked out another ACC title, which placed them, somewhat embarrassingly, in a BCS bowl. Rix overslept and missed a final exam, so he was suspended for the Sugar Bowl. An outstanding Georgia (12-1) squad, under former FSU assistant Mark Richt beat Florida State and ended up third in national rankings.

Penn State (9-4) bounced back from two losing seasons. The defensive line, led by enormous tackle Jimmy Kennedy, pass-rushing end Michael Haynes, and honor student nose guard Anthony Adams, played very well. Sophomore quarterback Zack Mills led a new offense that ran a considerable number of plays out of Shotgun formation, something previously unheard of for the Nittany Lions. The offense involved a bevy of talented wide receivers, the establishment of 2,000-yard rusher Larry Johnson as the go-to back in his remarkable senior year, and use of second-string quarterback Michael Robinson to both run and pass.

Joe Paterno of Penn State and Bowden started the year with 327 and 323 victories respectively, the most for Division 1-A coaches. It was interesting to see the gap between the brilliant geezers stay exactly intact through mid-November, because, through some mystery of parallel circumstance, when Bowden lost to Louisville, Miami, and Notre Dame, Paterno would follow suit later in the same weekend—to Iowa (11-2), Michigan (10-3), and Ohio State (14-0). Paterno won out in November, and North Carolina State (11-3) beat Florida State on November 16 to keep the two coaches four wins apart. Auburn (9-4) edged Paterno in the Capital One Bowl, and Bowden, with a late-day opportunity, failed to capitalize in the Sugar Bowl.

Paterno screamed about Big Ten officiating and even chased down and yanked on the shirt of an official after an overtime loss to Iowa, the nation's

Cinderella team. Paterno, once mild mannered about bad calls, admitted to *Sports Illustrated* that his patience was growing thinner as he grew older.

Eight undefeated teams enjoyed the calendar's roll into November, and that represented the most in 31 years. All those unblemished records served as the virus for the media's annual case of BCS Fever. "What happens if there are three undefeated teams? What if Miami is undefeated as defending national champions and is left out of the championship game?" they railed. Note to members of the media: What if you simply let the games play out?

In November, the games played out. The results of November 2 went a long way in clearing the air. No. 3 Virginia Tech (10-3) led most of the game against physical Pittsburgh (9-4), but allowed three second-half touchdowns to lose 28-21. No. 4 Notre Dame donned their normally inspirational green jerseys against Boston College (9-4), but the Fighting Irish, who had lived by the turnover, died by the turnover, 14-7. No. 5 Georgia, finally in a position to overturn nemesis Florida (8-5), instead lost 20-13 in the "World's Largest Outdoor Cocktail Party." No. 10 North Carolina State, somewhat untested during its nine-game undefeated run, allowed injury-plagued Georgia Tech (7-6) to rally for a 24-17 win.

When the dust settled, only Miami, Oklahoma, Ohio State, and undervalued Mid-American Conference interloper Bowling Green (9-3) remained untouched by defeat. Even no. 1 Miami nearly caught upset fever on November's first Saturday. The Hurricanes trailed low-rated Rutgers (1-11) most of the day until awakening in the fourth quarter for a 42-17 win.

And then there were two: Oklahoma's difficulty defending deep throws by scrambling quarterbacks was exposed by Texas A&M (6-6) on November 9 and again at the end of the month by fast-closing Oklahoma State (8-5).

That left no. 1 Miami and no. 2 Ohio State to duke it out in the championship Tostitos Fiesta Bowl in Tempe, Arizona. Miami entered as nearly a two-TD favorite, but the Buckeyes hung close throughout a tremendous back-and-forth duel and prevailed in overtime.

It was a strange year for coaches. John Mackovic got in trouble for harsh verbal treatment of his Arizona players, who, if they thought Mackovic was tough, should have watched the legendary Bear Bryant portrayed in the ESPN film of "The Junction Boys." Miami of Ohio defensive coordinator Jon Wauford, flattened a taunting fan, who ran on the field after a last moment Marshall (11-3) win. Wauford had to resign in the midst of a court case, which eventually was dropped. Michigan State (4-8) had high hopes before the season, but fortunes skidded downhill, and coach Bobby Williams was bounced in early November after an embarrassing 49-3 trouncing by Michigan. Despite Alabama (10-3) facing hefty NCAA penalties, Dennis Franchione convinced every one of his players to stay for the good of the school, but amid rumors of more recruiting investigations, Franchione abandoned ship for Texas A&M right after the season.

Heisman candidate Larry Johnson had an incredible year running the ball for 2,087 yards for Penn State, but learned firsthand the downside to a new statistical rule that included bowl game results for the first time. Breaking the 2,000-yard barrier with a good team almost always seemed to be a sure-fire Heisman formula. Not this time; detractors pointed out Johnson failed to gain 100 yards in any of the Nittany Lions' three losses. Johnson set a new collegiate record of 8.03 yards per carry during the regular season only to be fairly well shut down by Auburn's great defense in the Capital One Bowl. So, in effect, Johnson had to give back his record because his post-bowl average of 7.70 yards per carry dropped him below the mark (7.81) set by Mike Rozier of Nebraska in 1983. This was similar to the fate of Dave Hampton, who reached the coveted 1,000-yard mark for the NFL's Atlanta Falcons in the 1972 season finale. The game was stopped and Hampton was awarded the ball. However, two more fourth quarter runs netted a loss of five yards, and Hampton finished the season with 995 yards.

Coming out of nowhere in his first full-time season was Iowa senior quarterback Brad Banks. The Hawkeyes, picked for the lower half of the Big Ten, stunned all with their first undefeated conference run since 1922, and the triggerman was Banks, who showed great skill behind a terrific offensive line.

Southern California fans impatiently waited for Carson Palmer to realize his vast quarterbacking potential since 1998. Finally working with the same offensive coordinator (Norm Chow) for two straight years seemed to do the trick, and Palmer was brilliant all season. His headline-making finale

in a 44-13 shellacking of Notre Dame was the difference in his winning the Heisman Trophy.

Milestones

■ Clock experiment was put in to help speed play: Offenses would have 25 seconds to snap ball after stopages for first down, out of bounds, change of possession, or penalty.

■ Roy Kramer, commissioner of SEC for 12 years, retired. Kramer created first conference championship game and was father of Bowl Championship Series.

■ Death claimed remarkable number of football luminaries: Active players Anthony Miller, 20, wide receiver of Army (undetermined illness), and Chris Campbell, linebacker for 2001 national champion Miami (car accident), died in February. Cornelius Patterson, 32, Texas A&M wide receiver (1987-90), died of infection while waiting for kidney transplant. Two former Big 10 quarterbacks died: Willie Thrower, part of Michigan State's 1952 national champion team and NFL's first African-American QB with Chicago Bears in 1953, at age 71, and John Borton, co-captain of Ohio State's 1954 national champions, at age 69. Byron "Whizzer" White, 84, died of pneumonia at nursing home on April 15. White was All-America halfback at Colorado in 1937 and member of both College and Pro Football Halls of Fame, and best known as Supreme Court Justice. He served from his appointment by Pres. John F. Kennedy in 1962 until retiring in 1993. Curtis Williams, 24, Washington Huskies DB paralyzed from neck down after injury in 2000 Stanford game, died of kidney failure in early May. Two-time Big 10 MVP and Major League Baseball pitcher Paul Giel of Minnesota died on May 22 at 70. Dan Devine, head coach at Arizona State, Missouri, and Notre Dame with record of 172-57-9 and during 22 seasons, died at 77 after long illness. Devine inserted quarterback Joe Montana in lineup for third game of 1977, and Montana led Notre Dame to national title. Coaches Bill Jennings of Nebraska from 1957-61, and Len Casanova, 97, of Oregon from 1951-66 also died. Jennings had 15-34-1 record that included 1959 upset of his alma mater, Oklahoma, that ended Sooners' 74-game Big 8 winning streak, and Casanova stepped up to Oregon athletic director as Ducks' winningest coach at 82-73-8. Fran Rogel, 74, Penn State fullback and leading ground gainer during 1947-49, died in Gibsonia, Pa., on June 3. Rogel, also solid runner for Pittsburgh Steelers, suffered from Parkinson's disease. Buck Martin, end on Georgia Tech's 1952 undefeated team died of cancer on June 19 at age 73. First recipient in 1935 of award that would become Heisman Trophy, University of Chicago halfback Jay Berwanger, 88, died of lung cancer on June 26. Kyle Rote, 73, great halfback at Southern Methodist in 1948-50, died August 15. Johnny Unitas, Louisville QB from 1951-54, considered one of greatest NFL signal-callers, died in September. Leon Hart, 73, twice consensus All-America end at Notre Dame (1946-49) as well as Heisman Trophy winner in 1949, also died in September. Hart played on undefeated teams throughout high school in Turtle Creek, Pa., and Notre Dame's record during Hart's years was 36-0-2 and included three national titles. Hart played on three NFL championship teams with Detroit Lions (1950-57). Terrorists bombed resort of Bali in Indonesia in October, killing 34-year-old attorney and All-America Nebraska (1988-89) center, Jake Young. Glenn Dobbs, star back in 1940s and later coach at Tulsa, died in November at age 82. Dying at 70 was TV sports innovator Roone Arledge, although more famous for his creative work with NFL and Olympics, still had great impact on college football coverage as ABC Sports president. On New Year's Eve, Jo Jo Heath, 45, defensive back on Pitt's 1976 national champions, was found murdered.

■ Longest Winning Streaks entering Season:

Miami 22	Louisiana State 6	Pittsburgh 6

■ Coaching Changes:

	Incoming	Outgoing
California	Jeff Tedford	Tom Holmoe
Florida	Ron Zook	Steve Spurrier
Georgia Tech	Chan Gailey	George O'Leary
Indiana	Gerry DiNardo	Cam Cameron
Kansas	Mark Mangino	Terry Allen
Navy	Paul Johnson	Charlie Weatherbie
Notre Dame	Tyrone Willingham	Bob Davie
San Diego State	Tom Craft	Ted Tollner
Southern Methodist	Phil Bennett	Mike Cavan
Stanford	Buddy Teevens	Tyrone Willingham
Vanderbilt	Bobby Johnson	Woody Widenhofer

Preseason *USA Today* Coaches

1	Miami (Fla.) (34)	1444	14	Washington State	748
2	Texas (9)	1399	15	Oregon	663
3	Oklahoma (11)	1397	16	Virginia Tech	550
4	Florida State (7)	1357	17	Louisville	378
5	Tennessee	1255	18	Michigan State	371
6	Colorado	1010	19	Southern California	349
7	Florida	972	20	Maryland	315
8	Nebraska	951	21	Marshall	280
9	Washington	914	22	South Carolina	213
10	Michigan	894	23	Wisconsin	210
11	Georgia	858	24	Penn State	206
12	Ohio State	761	25	North Carolina State	174
13	LSU	749			

August 24, 2002

(Th) Colorado State 35 VIRGINIA 29: Capacity crowd at Scott Stadium for Jim Thorpe Classic greeted earliest starting date in college football history. Virginia (0-1) coach Al Groh promised to play many of his elite freshmen, and he did. QB Marques Hagans (10-13/120y, and TD rushing) lifted Cavs, TB Wali Lundy (20/94y) showed running knack, and LB Darryl Blackstock had sack of Rams QB Bradlee Van Pelt (17-27/229y, TD). Colorado State (1-0) wilted from heat and humidity. In 2nd Q, Hagans took Cavs QB reins and made 12y pass and 19y run to set up his TD for 7-6 lead. Rams TB Cecil "The Diesel" Sapp (25/178y, 2TD), back after year on injury shelf, shrugged off tacklers at scrimmage and bolted for 72y TD that built 19-7 H edge. CSU led 22-21 after 3 Qs, but Hagans returned in 4th Q to lead 79y drive to 29-22 lead. Sapp scored again to tie it, and Rams took over at own 26YL midway through 4th Q. Rams faced 1st-and-32 at own 4YL but converted Van Pelt's 2 passes to WR Joey Cuppari. Soph K Jeff Babcock soon kicked winning 46y FG, 4th of his 5 FGs, with 4:07 to go.

(Fri) WISCONSIN 23 Fresno State 21: Top Fresno State (0-1) WR Bernard Berrian made 32y gain of 1st Q dump-off pass and followed on next play with 22y post-pattern TD catch for 7-0 lead. After Berrian limped off in 2nd Q, Bulldogs lost FUM at own 1YL to Wisconsin (1-0) DL Jake Sprague. Frosh FB Matt Bernstein blasted for 1st of his 2 TDs to tie it before K Matt Allen's FG gave Badgers 10-7 H lead. QB Jeff Grady (21-42/262y, 3 TDs, 2 INTs) put Fresno back in front 14-10 in 3rd Q with 8y TD pass to WR Adam Jennings. Trailing 20-14 in 4th Q, Bulldog DB Bryce McGill made hard tackle and FUM REC at Badger 25YL, and 2 plays later, Grady threw TD pass to TE Alec Greco for 21-20 edge. Allen missed 46 FG try, but Fresno DL Nick Burley, outstanding all night, jumped offside, and Allen made game-winner from 34YL with 2:05 on clock.

OHIO STATE 45 Texas Tech 21: Sharp Buckeyes (1-0) showed well-balanced O and ever-changing, quick D that blanketed sharp passing attack of Texas Tech (0-1) most of afternoon. TB Maurice Clarett (21/175y, 3 TDs) became only true frosh to start at TB in his 1st game for Ohio State and was brilliant. At 230 lbs, Clarett showed speed and power, charging for 59y TD run behind block of pulling LG Mike Stafford. Ohio led 21-7 at H after LBs Matt Wilhelm and Cie Grant stacked up TB Foy Munlin on 4th down at Buckeye 1YL near end of 2nd Q. Running same play as his 59y TD, Clarett burst 45y as score mounted to 38-7 at end of 3rd Q. Red Raiders QB Kliff Kingsbury (26-44/341y, 3 TDs, INT) inflated his passing numbers in superfluous 4th Q as he threw 2 TD passes to WR Wes Welker.

NEBRASKA 48 Arizona State 10: Husker fans were in tizzy over Nebraska's late 2001 meltdown and new QB Jammal Lord (5-13/33y, TD passing and 17/103y rushing), who took over for graduated Eric Crouch. Arizona State (0-1) hung close, trailing only 10-3 at H, but things quickly darkened on 2nd H KO as RB Hakim Hill was spilled at own 6YL. ASU QB Chad Christensen (6-16/77y) was sacked, and P Tim Parker's punt went OB at 20YL. Nebraska WR Wilson Thomas caught TD pass, and LB Demorrio Williams blocked Parker's next punt for LB Scott Shanle to take for 6y TD to launch rout.

Florida State 38 Iowa State 31 (Kansas City): No. 3 Florida State (1-0) coach Bobby Bowden passed Bear Bryant for 2nd on all-time win list with 324, but ended up saying, "I feel like we lost this game." Seminole DL Alonzo Jackson returned picked-off screen pass for 48y TD, and QB Chris Rix (17-25/210y, 2TDs, INT) flipped 2y TD pass to WR Anquan Boldin. So, FSU had tidy lead of 31-7 in last min of 1st H. But, sensational QB Seneca Wallace (22-33/313y, 2 TDs, INT) threw 29y TD to TE Kyle Knock to send Iowa State (0-1) to H trailing 31-14. After late 3rd Q FG, Wallace scored on 1y run early in 4th Q to pull Cyclones within 31-24. After Rix threw his 2nd TD pass, Wallace finished 91y drive with 39y TD pass to WR Jamaul Montgomery with 5:26 left. ISU forced punt and started at own 35YL, behind by 7 pts with 2:32 on clock. Wallace hit 5 passes and dashed 20y OB at FSU 1YL in closing sec, play some felt was TD. LBs Kendyll Pope and Jerel Hudson then stopped Wallace's option run inches short from potential tie.

USA Today Coaches August 16

1	Miami (Fla.) (42)	1466	14	LSU	751
2	Texas (10)	1424	15	Oregon	663
3	Oklahoma (7)	1400	16	Virginia Tech	644
4	Tennessee	1266	17	Michigan State	414
5	Florida State (2)	1216	18	Louisville	407
6	Colorado	1085	19	Southern California	359
7	Florida	1072	20	Maryland	340
8	Nebraska	1037	21	South Carolina	243
9	Washington	936	22	Marshall	240
10	Michigan	886	23	Penn State	181
11	Ohio State	878	24	North Carolina State	177
12	Georgia	858	25	Wisconsin	176
13	Washington State	756			

August 31, 2002

(Th) BRIGHAM YOUNG 42 Syracuse 21: BYU (1-0) QB Bret Engemann (35-64/386y, 3TDs, INT), sharp after missing nearly 2 years, picked giant TE Spencer Nead from bevy of receivers to build early 14-7 lead. Orangemen (0-1) got uncontested TD on option misdirection TD run by WR Jamel Riddle. In 2nd Q, Syracuse used tricky roll-right-throwback-left 4th-and-goal pass, but wide-open TE Lenny Cusumano dropped pass. Cougars directly answered with 99y TD drive, much of it on long run by RB Marcus Whalen behind block of LT Dustin Rykert. Syracuse tied it at 21-21 in 3rd Q, but Engemann sparked 92y TD drive finished with 3y TD scramble in 3rd Q. He followed with 50y TD pass to WR David Christensen early in 4th Q. Cougars gained 615y.

Notre Dame 22 Maryland 0 (E. Rutherford, NJ): Tyrone Willingham, 1st African-American coach in any sport at Notre Dame (1-0), had his players sharp for soldout 20th and final Kickoff Classic. DB Shane Walton made 3 INTs and in 3rd Q hustled across field to make block that sprung DB Vontez Duff for 76y punt RET, game's only TD. K Nicholas Setta walloped 5 FGs, including kicks of 51y to open scoring in 1st Q and 46y late in 3rd Q. ND QB Carlyle Holiday passed 17-27/226y. Maryland (0-1) played without star TB Bruce Perry, out with groin injury, and tried 2 QBs with little success: Scott McBrien (9-23/84y, 2INT) and Chris Kelley (3-9/33y, INT). Terps gained only 133y, their deepest penetration ending at ND 30YL when sub TB Mario Merrills was spilled for 3y loss on 4th down by Fighting Irish DB Gerome Sapp.

DUKE 23 East Carolina 16: Dark shadow of possible record-loss streak hovered over Duke (1-0), but Blue Devils ended 23-game loss string by snaring 20-0 lead in 1st H and allowing no y to East Carolina (0-1) after Pirates rallied to within 20-16 on 1st series of 3rd Q. LB Brendan Dewan ran 28y with INT RET to score 2nd Q TD for 20-0 Devil edge. Huge Duke FB Alex Wade slammed for 24/109y rushing, including 46y on march that netted K Brent Garber's 3rd and clinching FG with 2:57 to play. Garber's 2nd Q FG sailed 56y. ECU was limited to 155y O and lost 4 TOs. New Pirate QB Paul Troth (13-31/130y, TD, 3 INTs) was ineffective early, but settled down to lead 3 scoring drives.

GEORGIA TECH 45 Vanderbilt 3: Quiet Georgia Tech (1-0), barely mentioned in preseason, steamrolled Vanderbilt (0-1) for new coach Shan Gailey. Result spoiled Commodore coaching debut of Bobby Johnson. Gailey was booed by sellout crowd when he chose to punt on 4th-and-1 at Vandy 37YL in 1st Q, but it turned out as cool move when DB Dennis Davis downed punt at 1YL. Resultant field position created TD

on 1st play of 2nd Q when new QB A.J. Suggs flipped 2y pass to WR Will Glover. Tech scored on next 5 possessions for 38-0 lead early in 3rd Q. TB Tony Hollings (17/153y, 2 TDs), converted DB, became 1st Yellow Jacket ever to rush for 100y in his 1st game. Vandy, which had 225y O, averted shutout on K Greg Johnson's 37y FG with 3:26 left.

GEORGIA 31 Clemson 28: No. 8 Georgia (1-0) enjoyed 7-0 1st Q lead, and when Clemson (0-1) tied it less than 4 mins into 2nd Q on TB Bernard Rambert's 1y TD run, Bulldogs answered with WR Fred Gibson's 91y KO TD RET. Behind 21-7, Tigers clicked on 21y TD pass from QB Willie Simmons (17-37/165y, TD, INT) to WR Kevin Youngblood to beat H clock by 8 secs. Clemson owned 2nd Q as DL Bryant McNeal raced 55y to FUM TD RET and TB Yusef Kelly capped 76y drive w/ 1y TD run for 28-21 lead. Georgia comeback was sparked by sub QB D.J. Shockley, who passed 24y to WR Terrence Edwards to knot it at 28-28. K Billy Bennett made winning 43y FG with 5:19 to go, but Georgia had to weather near-miss 43y FG by K Aaron Hunt and convert 4th-and-1 run by TB Musa Smith (23/105y) at Clemson 38YL with 30 secs left.

MICHIGAN 31 Washington 29: Long TDs—67y run by TB Chris Perry (23/120y, 3TDs) and 45y pass from QB John Navarre (22-38/268y, TD, INT) to WR Braylon Edwards—gave Michigan (1-0) early 14-0 lead. Washington (0-1) stormed back to within 14-13 at H, and led after 1st series of 2nd H as WR Charles Frederick out-jumped double coverage for pass from QB Cody Pickett (28-45/318y, 2TDs, INT) that he toted 51y to score. Wolverines matched TD for 21-20 advantage and went to 28-23 lead early in 4th Q after 80y trip to Perry's 3rd TD. Huskies answered: Long dash up left sideline by TB Rich Alexis set up TD for 29-28 lead with less than 4 mins to go. Michigan faced 4th-and-2 with 36 sec left, and Navarre's pass went through Edwards' hands only to be recovered by Michigan WR Tyrece Butler. Officials ruled FUM REC, not incompletion: 1st down for Michigan. Navarre's 3rd down pass fell incomplete, but Huskies had 12 men on field. Resultant 15y PEN allowed 44y FG try, which previously unknown K Philip Brabbs kicked dead center, despite 2 misses earlier in game.

Missouri 33 Illinois 20 (St. Louis): Frosh QB Brad Smith passed 15-26/152y and ran 18/138y, including clinching 24y TD, as Missouri (1-0) gained 437y to surprise Big 10 champ Illinois (0-1). Tigers RB Zach Abron (26/116y) scored on short runs early in both 1st and 4th Qs, his 2nd TD providing 26-14 lead. Held to 67y rushing, Illini looked to ace WR Brandon Lloyd (8/137y, 2 TDs) for TD catch early in 3rd Q that tied game at 14-14.

Colorado State 19 Colorado 14 (Denver): No. 7 Colorado (0-1), team with high hopes after winning 2001 Big 12 title, lost its 4th opener in row under coach Gary Barnett. Raft of TOs ruined Buffs as 2nd TD run by Colorado State (2-0) TB Cecil Sapp (22/80y) with 3:52 left in 2nd Q provided 13-0 lead after Rams' FUM REC. Colorado greeted 2nd H with resolve: It racked up 1st downs on opening 4 plays. But, TB Chris Brown (22/93y) lost 2nd FUM, this at CSU 18YL. Later in 3rd Q, Brown and QB Craig Ochs (14-27/199y, INT) messed up handoff on 4th down at Rams 3YL. Frosh WR Jeremy Bloom ignited Buffs on 1st play of 4th Q as raced 75y on punt TD RET. On next drive, Colorado went 81y to Brown's short TD plunge. Trailing 14-13 and having accumulated only 43y O in 2nd H, Rams mustered 84y drive to go up 19-14. Twice converting 4th down runs by Brown and Ochs, Buffs rallied to 12YL, but Ochs' 4th down pass to GL was broken up.

(Sun) VIRGINIA TECH 26 Louisiana State 8: Happy Hokie fans shouted, "Overrated!" at defending SEC champ LSU (0-1) as clock ticked down in 4th Q. Virginia Tech (2-0) benched bum-kneed QB Grant Noel in favor of mistake-free soph QB Bryan Randall (5-9/47y) and used ground power to gain 14-0 H lead on matching scores by TBs Kevin Jones and Lee Suggs after short drives of 27 and 29y. Suggs' TD came after Tech frosh WR Justin Hamilton blocked Hokies' 91st kick in coach Frank Beamer's 176 games, in this case, punt by Tigers P Donnie Jones that came in midst of 4 straight 3-and-out series by LSU. Bengals rushed only 28/80y and were forced into many more-than-wished passes by QB Matt Mauck (15-35/134y, INT). Trailing 24-0 after Suggs' 2nd TD, LSU finally managed 82y drive in 4th Q that was ended by 1y smash by TB LaBrandon Toefield (10/46y, TD) and Mauck's 2-pt pass.

(Sun) Kentucky 22 LOUISVILLE 17: Big Louisville (0-1) QB Dave Ragone (14-39/193y, TD, INT) had to run for his life as new Cardinal OL was full of holes. "They beat him to a pulp," said Card coach John L. Smith, as his QB was sacked or slammed down more than 25 times by eager, young Wildcat D. Meanwhile, 300-lb Kentucky (1-0) QB Jared "The Hefty Lefty" Lorenzen (13-27/195y, TD) clicked on clutch plays all night, including blitz-beating dump-off pass to WR Ernest Simms, who zipped 64y for opening score and 2 QB-sneak 1st downs when clock needed to be killed in 4th Q. Ragone's 2nd Q FUM led to another Wildcat TD run for 16-0 lead. Exhausted Ragone ran or passed on team's final 15 plays of 2nd Q and pitched 2y TD to TE Ronnie Ghent. WR Broderick Clark swung momentum to Cardinals with blazing 100y TD RET of 2nd H KO, and FG briefly gave them 17-16 edge. Wildcats used 5 mins for answering FG drive.

(Mon) SOUTHERN CALIFORNIA 24 Auburn 17: TOs meant 4 TDs in 14-14 1st H as Southern California (1-0) LB Mike Pollard's early FUM REC sent QB Carson Palmer (23-32/302y, TD, 2 INTs) on 41y air mission, ended by 14y TD. Auburn (0-1), making its 2nd-ever California trip, unleashed its battling LBs. OLB Karlos Dansby made diving INT at USC 23YL, and TB Carnell "Cadillac" Williams (21/94y) drove for powerful TD on next play. Trojans DL Omar Nazel smartly dropped to flat for INT in 2nd Q that started 60y TD march. Tigers DB Junior Rosegreen dived for INT at own 9YL to launch tying drive. USC forced punt, but 12 Trojans participated, and PEN sustained Auburn drive, which ended on odd TD 11 sec before H. Auburn QB Daniel Cobb (10-21/132y, INT) dashed for EZ pylon, was met by DB DeShaun Hill, and ball popped backwards to Tiger TB Ronnie Brown who barely wedged into EZ pile. USC D owned 2nd H, holding leg-cramped Williams to −2y rushing and Tigers to 50y. Even though Auburn K Damon Duval's 39y FG tied it at 17-17 early in 4th Q, Palmer completed 13-15/147y in 2nd H and USC had ball for 21:35. Palmer sneaked for winning TD with 1:26 to go.

USA Today Coaches September 2

1	Miami (Fla.) (49)	1500	14	Washington	631
2	Texas (5)	1410	15	Michigan State	611
3	Oklahoma (4)	1372	16	Southern California	423
4	Tennessee	1318	17	Colorado	390
5	Florida State (2)	1249	18	Marshall	374
6	Florida	1207	19	South Carolina	320
7	Michigan	1087	20	Colorado State	264
8	Nebraska	1045	21	Wisconsin	258
9	Ohio State	965	22	North Carolina State	248
10	Virginia Tech	915	23	LSU	239
11	Georgia	891	24	Notre Dame	198
12	Washington State (1)	835	25	Penn State	195
13	Oregon	819			

September 7, 2002

BOSTON COLLEGE 34 Stanford 27: Eagles (2-0) needed entire game to rally as sub TB Derrick Knight (21/104y) scored winning 12y TD run with 36 secs left. Stanford (0-1) built 27-17 lead in coach Buddy Teevens' debut as frosh QB Kyle Matter threw for 244y and TD, with 6'7" WR Teyo Johnson gaining 117y, TD on catches. Cardinal D made 3 INTs, including LB Josh Ott's RET of FB Casey Moore's FUM at Stanford 10YL. Knight quickly scored his 1st TD, and K Sandro Sciortino then tied game at 27-27 with career-best 40y FG. Eagles QB Brian St. Pierre (22-36/260y) came back in game to engineer winning drive at game's end.

VIRGINIA 34 South Carolina 21: South Carolina (1-1) coach Lou Holtz's bad week continued as 7 TOs gift-wrapped win for Virginia (1-2). Amid talk of NCAA investigation, Holtz watched 6 lost FUMs and INT lead directly to Cavaliers TDs or spoil Carolina drives deep in Cavs territory. Virginia QB Matt Schaub (20-30/170y) threw 3 TD passes, hooking up with ace WR Billy McMullen (4/72y, 35y TD) on 3 conversions of 3rd down, including unbelievable one-arm-behind-back snare. In wildest turn of events, Cavs grabbed 20-14 2nd Q lead as Gamecocks TB Ryan Brewer fumbled KO following McMillan's TD, and ball popped into hands of Cavs DB Jermaine Hardy, who raced 17y to EZ. Holtz pulled Brewer from ensuing return and WR Matthew Thomas returned KO 95y for Carolina TD. That was Gamecocks' last highlight; Cavs converted 2 FUMs into 3rd Q TDs, including TE Heath Miller's 20y dipsy-doodle pass to TE Patrick Estes.

Miami 41 FLORIDA 16: Early edge swung back and forth until K Todd Sievers bombed 53 and 38y FGs for Miami (2-0). In 2nd Q, Florida (1-1) G Shannon Snell sprung TB Earnest Graham (20/89y) on spinning 18y TD run for 7-6 lead. Gators DB Todd Johnson blocked punt to Hurricanes 10YL, but Miami held after ruinous delay of game PEN by Gators who settled for FG and 10-6 edge. Miami answered right away with 80y TD drive on broad back of TB Willis McGahee (24/204y), capped by short out-pass from QB Ken Dorsey (16-32/202y, 4 TDs, 3 INTs) to WR Andre Johnson. Bobbled and lateralled punt snap put Florida in trouble as soph DB Antrel Rolle smothered it at 9YL. Dorsey quickly hit WR Ethenic Sands for slat-in TD for 20-10 lead. Soaring to 27-10 lead, Canes took 2nd H KO to 18y screen pass TD scored by TB Jason Geathers behind athletic blocking of G Chris Myers and C Brett Romberg. After LB Byron Hardmon's INT off stumbling Dorsey was returned for 25y TD, Gators threatened late in 3rd Q, but Miami DB Maurice Sikes slipped in front of receiver and raced 99y to INT TD RET.

OKLAHOMA 37 Alabama 27: Trailing 23-3 at H against 2nd-ranked Sooners (2-0), Crimson Tide had work cut out for them in 1st meeting of traditional powers in 22 years. Oklahoma WR Mark Clayton (4/129y) was 1st H star, catching TD passes from QBs Jason White, before White blew out his knee, and from sub Nate Hybl. Alabama (1-1) turned tables with 24 pts and 224y O in 2nd H, after gaining only 64y in 1st H. Alabama pulled within 23-17 on blocked punt TD RET—foes combined for 4 blocked punts and placekicks—and scored go-ahead TD on holder Lane Bearden's 4y run with fake FG. That gave Tide 27-23 lead late in 4th Q. After 4 disastrous 2nd H possessions produced -23y and single 1st down, Sooners marched 80y behind QB Hybl. Oklahoma RB Renaldo Works contributed mightily, racing 62y with shovel pass to set up RB Kejuan Jones' winning 8y run. Alabama QB Tyler Watts (16-32/185y) then lost ball on next possession for Tide, and it was scooped up by Sooner DB Eric Bassey for 45y TD RET.

UCLA 30 Colorado State 19: Rams (2-1) used 1st H avg field position of own 49YL to gain tidy 10-0 lead by 2nd Q. Colorado State DB Dexter Wynn's 55y punt RET set up TB Cecil Sapp's 7y TD pass to H-B Joel Dreesen. UCLA (1-0) quickly countered with WR Junior Taylor's reverse and cutback for 49y TD. NG Bryan Save blocked FG and Rams led 13-7 at H, advantage that had spelled 63-4 record for coach Sonny Lubick. Bruins took 14-13 lead early in 4th Q on 53y drive engineered by frosh QB Drew Olson. Game's biggest play came moments later as UCLA CB Ricky Manning caused FUM when he walloped Sapp on swing pass. TB Manuel White powered 15y for 21-13 Bruins' edge. Intense Rams QB Bradlee Van Pelt surged for 7y TD on 4th down, but needing 2-pt conv to tie it with 1:32 to play, Van Pelt made desperate pitchout in grasp of Bruins LB Brandon Chillar (INT) and DL Steve Morgan. UCLA DB Ben Emanuel picked up Van Pelt's mistake and went all the way to 2 pts for UCLA, now up 23-19.

September 14, 2002

(Th) VIRGINIA TECH 47 Marshall 21: Prior to game, Virginia Tech (3-0) retired no. 25 jersey of coach Frank Beamer (DB in 1966-68). Trailing early 3-0, Marshall (1-1) QB Byron Leftwich (31-49/406y, 3TDs, INT) got good protection and picked at Tech's pass D. But several dropped passes forced Herd into FG try, and sore-footed K Curtis Head kicked very low ball into back of his lineman. Hokies quickly went 90y in 9 runs, well-blocked surges shared by TBs Lee Suggs (24/153y, 2TDs) and Kevin Jones (24/171y, 3TDs), with Jones roaring 25y to score for 10-0 lead. Jones scored again on outside 15y sprint after LB Mikal Baaqee's INT. Another smashing drive of 85y in 3rd Q allowed Suggs to slam middle for TD on 4th-and-goal at 1YL. Behind 33-0 in 4th Q, Leftwich hit 6-6 passes on march, capped by slant-in TD to WR Darius Watts.

CLEMSON 24 Georgia Tech 19: Tigers QB Willie Simmons was great threat outside of pocket, passing for 111y and 2 TDs while on run. Clemson (2-1) D was dandy in 1st H, limiting Georgia Tech (2-1) to 48y on 27 plays, except for 72y TD sprint up left sideline by TB Tony Hollings. Tigers led 16-7 at H, thanks to 77y TD dash by WR Derrick Hamilton on inside handoff and Simmons' magical back-handed 2y TD flip to TE Bobby Williamson. Simmons rolled out for more conventional 44y TD pass to WR Tony Elliott for 24-6 edge. Yellow Jackets QB A.J. Suggs pitched 2 TD passes in 2nd H and passed to Tigers 29YL in closing mins, but LB Eric Sampson made INT to ice it.

Georgia 13 SOUTH CAROLINA 7: Tropical storm Hanna dropped heavy rain, delaying game's start. DL David Pollack made season's shortest INT for TD and earlier recovered FUM at own 3YL to help save Georgia (2-0). Bulldogs K Billy Bennett made early 22y FG that held up until unusual 4th Q. South Carolina (1-2) QB Corey Jenkins (14-24/180y, TD, INT and 17/101y rushing) dropped back to pass from EZ with 14 mins left. Officials ruled TD INT when ball slipped during Jenkins' throwing motion and tumbled down his body and into Pollack's hands. Min later, Gamecocks scored on RB Ryan Brewer's 25y TD catch to trim it to 10-7 and marched deep into Bulldogs end in last min. But, pitchout bounced off Carolina's TD specialist, RB Andrew Pinnock (11/27y), and Bulldog DB Thomas Davis fell on FUM at Georgia 2YL with :12 on clock.

PENN STATE 40 Nebraska 7: Opening Q was punt fest: Nebraska's P Kyle Larson toed punt OB at Penn State (2-0) 3YL, and Lions WR Tony Johnson downed punt at Huskers (3-1) 1YL. Nittany Lions went 80y in 2nd Q to score on TB Larry Johnson's 7y burst through 2 tacklers as QB Zack Mills (19-31/259y) threaded TD pitchout just out of reach. Nebraska quickly answered with tying 84y TD drive as QB Jammal Lord (8-16/76y, 3 INTs) clicked on 3-3/41y and mixed in 27y run. Penn State QB Michael Robinson entered game as RB-WR and ran 38y on reverse to set up 1st of K Robbie Gould's 2 FGs. Leading 13-7, Lions humbled Huskers with 20 pts in 3rd Q with Robinson running for 8 and 11y TDs and DB Richard Gardner racing 42y with INT TD RET.

OHIO STATE 25 Washington State 7: Cougars (2-1) scored 1st H's only TD as RB Jonathan Smith carried short pass 39y to set up QB Jason Gesser (25-44/247y, TD, 2 INTs) fade pass TD to WR Devard Darling. Ohio State (3-0) K Mike Nugent kicked pair of 1st H FGs, each at 43y. Washington State led 7-6 at H, but had dominant stretch from mid-2nd Q on. Cougars had 4 sacks, sr WR Collin Henderson completed pass for perfect 9-9 in career, and Gesser completed 23y toss to WR Scott Lunde on 3rd-and-21, but 27y FG attempt was foiled by early snap that bounced off holder Henderson's facemask. Buckeyes began rolling on 1st possession of 3rd Q, going 91y in 8 plays to take 13-7 lead. Ace frosh TB Maurice Clarett (31/230y, 2TDs) opened march with 44y run over left side and added 6 and 20y rushes before scoring from 3YL. Nugent's 3rd FG and bad punt snap safety through EZ provided 18-7 margin for OSU at end of 3rd Q. Ohio went 66y to eat up nearly 5 min of 4th Q, and Clarett's 1y TD slant iced it at 25-7.

California 46 MICHIGAN STATE 22: Golden Bears (3-0) QB Kyle Boller (19-33/231y, 2 TDs), finally living up to hype in his sr year, accounted for 4 TDs as slumbering Michigan State (2-1) woke up to find surprising Cal ahead 25-0 at H. In addition to his 2 TD throws, Boller caught late 2nd Q gadget pass from WR LaShaun Ward for TD and ran 2y TD keeper off RT in 3rd Q for 32-14 advantage. Spartans WR Charles Rogers caught 15y TD pass in 3rd Q, his 11th straight game with scoring reception.

NOTRE DAME 25 Michigan 23: Notre Dame (3-0), without TD on O so far, scored on opening march as FB Tom Lopienski threw thunderous blocks until TB Ryan Grant scored from 1YL. Irish were in control until late in 1st Q when their QB Carlyle Holiday erred by staring at out-breaking WR Arnaz Battle, and Michigan (2-1) DB Marlon Jackson stepped in, scoring untouched on 20y INT RET. After 2nd Q PEN pushed Wolverines back, OT Courtney Morgan was guilty of holding PEN in EZ for ND safety. Irish scored late in 2nd Q for 16-7 H edge as Holiday went in on 3y draw, even though ball appeared to come out before crossing GL plane. After only 8y rushing in 1st H, Michigan owned 3rd Q as QB John Navarre, TE Bennie Joppru, and TB Chris Perry (2y TD) came alive for 17-16 lead. Holiday sparked Irish on calm fake and 47y post-pass

to WR Omar Jenkins to 3YL. Grant scored, and when Nicholas Setta added FG, ND led 25-17. Navarre hit 5 passes on drive, including TD to Joppru with 2:53 left. Irish DB Shane Walton ruined 2-pt pass and iced it with INT in last 30 sec.

Iowa State 36 IOWA 31: Rally in 2nd H by Iowa State (3-1) seemed just another chapter in rivalry, but loss by Iowa (2-1) would have repercussions by season's end. Hawkeyes scored on their opening series as TB Fred Russell (16/139y) burst 46y for career-long to date TD run. Cyclones RB Hiawatha Rutland tied it 7-7 with 6y TD run at end of 80y march on which WR Lane Danielsen caught 60y sideline pass midway in 1st Q. Iowa flooded rival with 17 pts in 2nd Q. K Nate Kaeding booted his 9th straight FG (40y) and QB Brad Banks (12-21/178y, 2 TDs) threw deep down middle to WR Maurice Brown for 50y TD. Iowa CB Antwan Allen's FUM of his GL INT was advanced 32y by DB Bob Sanders to set up another TD by understudy TB Jermelle Lewis. Cyclones blew furiously with 23 unanswered pts in 3rd Q, including TD run and pass from QB Seneca Wallace (23-37/361y, TD, INT) and LB Jeremy Loyd's EZ tackle for safety. K Adam Beike's 2 FGs all but wrapped it up for Iowa State at 36-24 with 4 mins to play.

September 21, 2002

(Th) Auburn 42 MISSISSIPPI STATE 14: Tigers (3-1) QB Daniel Cobb (10-21/183y, 3 TDs) started with 1-9/14y passing in 1st Q, but with Auburn leading 14-7 late in 2nd Q, Cobb fooled everyone in stadium with his 3rd TD throw. Instead of positioning Auburn for anticipated FG try, Cobb launched 45y TD bomb to WR Ben Obomanu. Mississippi State (1-2) opened 3rd Q with tenacious 16-play TD drive as it thrice converted 3rd downs and overcame 15y PEN in red-zone to tally on TB Dontae Walker's 1y plunge, his 2nd score. Up by 21-14 early in 4th Q, Auburn went 67y to TB Cadillac Williams' 9y TD run, and when DE Reggie Torbor caused and recovered FUM by Bulldogs QB Kevin Fant (19-31/215y, INT) at 17YL, Williams scored in 3 rushes for 35-14 advantage.

MIAMI 38 Boston College 6: In stretching win streak to 26 games, Miami (4-0) scored 3 TDs within 3 mins during 4th Q onslaught. Hurricanes TB Willis McGahee rushed for 135y and caught 3 passes for 86y more, while QB Ken Dorsey (13-26/202y, 2 TDs) Balanced O and pressuring D allowed Boston College (2-1) to take 6-3 lead in 2nd Q on strength of 2 FGs by K Sandro Sciortino. McGahee then burst through 4 tacklers on 48y dash late in 1st H to set up own 1y TD run. H lead of 10-6 allowed Miami to avert H deficit, which would have been its 1st in 2 years. McGahee later added 32y run and 77y screen pass scamper to set up 2 more TDs, 2nd of which started Canes' 21-point avalanche. Up 24-6, Miami D made 2 FUM RECs, including LB Jonathan Vilma's 2y TD RET. Win was Miami's 13th straight over Eagles.

Florida 30 TENNESSEE 13: While Volunteers (2-1) had terrible time with C-QB exchange in heavy rain, efficient Florida (3-1) O ran up 418y. Big play came on Gators DT Ian Scott's block of Tennessee FG try in scoreless tie in 2nd Q. Gators QB Rex Grossman threw for 324y, 3 TDs. Grossman keyed decisive 2nd Q with 2 TD passes. He skipped away from pass rush to connect on 52y pass to WR Taylor Jacobs (9/141y) to set up TB Earnest Graham's controversial (Did he break GL plane?) 1y scoring plunge on 4th down. Grossman soon made Tennessee pay for 1 of its 8 FUMs (7 FUMs in 2nd Q) by tossing 28y scoring pass to WR Carlos Perez for 14-0 lead. Trailing 21-0, Tennessee rallied in 3rd Q as QB Casey Clausen (30-44/285y) threw 15y TD pass to TB Derrick Tinsley, and TB Jabari Davis added 1y TD run.

Ohio State 23 CINCINNATI 19: Looking for 1st win over Ohio State (4-0) since 1897, Bearcats (1-2) enjoyed 19-14 lead with 4th Q possession in Buckeyes territory. OSU DE Darrion Scott then sacked Cincinnati QB Gino Guidugli, forcing FUM that Buckeyes converted into clutch TD drive. QB Craig Krenzel (14-29/129y, 2 TDs) ran in winning TD from 6y out. Guidugli (26-52/324y) then marched Bearcats downfield before 2 dropped EZ passes ended Cincinnati's upset chances. With frosh sensation TB Maurice Clarett out after minor knee surgery, TB Lydell Ross led Buckeyes with 130y rushing. Bearcats outgained Buckeyes 415y to 292y. Cincinnati K Jonathan Ruffin kicked FGs of 44y and career-best 49y, but missed x-pt kick after making 65 straight.

Notre Dame 21 MICHIGAN STATE 17: Walk-on Notre Dame (4-0) QB Pat Dillingham relieved injured QB Carlyle Holiday and completed game-winning pass to WR Arnaz Battle, who raced 60y for TD with 1:15 remaining. ND built 14-3 lead in 1st H as former QB Battle set up 7y TD run by TB Ryan Grant on 30y pass to Holiday. Later, Holiday threw his 1st scoring pass of season, 15y to WR Maurice Stovall. In 4th Q, Irish surrendered 14 pts to Michigan State (2-2) and outstanding WR Charles Rogers (7-175y), who caught 2 TD passes, including amazing snare of 21y pass in back of EZ amidst 2 DBs for go-ahead score. That play, coming on 4th-and-11, ended 97y drive. Rogers tied NCAA record with TD receptions in 12 straight games. After Battle's TD put Irish back ahead, Spartans' last gasp ended when QB Jeff Smoker (19-34/281y) threw INT to DB Gerome Sapp. Irish win snapped 5-game series losing streak, and in post-game, Tyrone Willingham and Bobby Williams marked 1st time that opposing African-American coaches greeted each other after game that involved 2 major schools.

KANSAS STATE 27 Southern California 20: Kansas State (4-0) had to work for 1st-ever home win vs ranked non-conf foe. K-State surrendered 2 late TDs and allowed Trojans to march to KSU 33YL at game's end. From that spot, USC (2-1) QB Carson Palmer (18-47/186y) could not connect on 4th-and-15 pass, overthrowing WR Keary Colbert (11/125y). Wildcats built 27-6 lead as D shut down Trojans attack, and O used quickness of backup QB Eli Roberson to neutralize USC's excellent D line. Roberson (10-15/134y passing, 70y rushing) threw and ran for TDs. However, Roberson almost became goat, losing FUM into Trojan EZ late in 4th Q. Earlier, Roberson lost FUM in 2nd Q, and it was returned 3y by active NT Mike Patterson for Southern Cal's 1st TD.

Virginia Tech 13 TEXAS A&M 3: D struggle was won by Hokies (4-0), becoming 1st non-conf foe to win at Kyle Field since 1988. Trade of FGs represented 1st scores allowed by either team in 1st H all season. Ahead 6-3 in 4th Q, Virginia Tech O gained scoring cushion as WR Ernest Wilford's 52y run with short pass by QB Bryan Randall (10-11/119y) set up TB Lee Suggs' 1y clinching TD. Suggs (13/51y) scored TD in his 17th game in row. With Texas A&M (2-1) mustering only 156y against Tech D (2 INTs, FUM REC, 5 sacks), P Cody Scates (7/48.3y average) was big weapon. Aggies rushed for only 38y, marking 4th opponent (3 of them ranked) to be limited to less than 80y rushing by Virginia Tech. Speedy DE Nathaniel Adibi led Virginia Tech D with 3 sacks.

North Carolina State 51 TEXAS TECH 48 (OT): Wolfpack (5-0) frosh TB T.A. McLendon scored his 5th TD on 8y run in OT. Texas Tech (2-2) rallied from 38-10 3rd Q deficit behind QB Kliff Kingsbury's 3 TD passes, but K Robert Treece missed 39y FG try for game-winner in last min of regulation. Red Raiders could manage only Treece's 33y FG in OT. NC State then handed ball 4 times to McLendon to navigate winning 25y drive. State had blown game open in 3rd Q. After 59y drive established Wolfpack in 24-10 lead, Kingsbury (27-50/273y) then lost FUM, which was returned for TD by NC State DE Shawn Price. McLendon (32/150y), who tied school TD record, then capped 15y drive set up by WR Jerricho Cothery's 34y punt RET with his 3rd TD for 38-10 lead.

Colorado 31 UCLA 17: Buffs (2-2) dominated line of scrimmage, enjoying 325y to 62y run differential. TB Chris Brown tallied 188y rushing with 3 TDs as Colorado erased 7-0 deficit by scoring 31 of next 34 pts. While Colorado's new QB Robert Hodge (11-22/117y) improved his play, main duty was handoffs to Brown and sub TB Bobby Purifoy (14/87y). Bruins (2-1) could not answer until 5y TD pass by QB Cory Paus (21-35/189y) to WR Craig Bragg (7/70y) with less than 5 minutes left. Bragg scored early on 33y pass from WR Jon Dubravac.

Air Force 23 CALIFORNIA 21: Battle of early-season surprises ended with Air Force (3-0) DB Jeff Overstreet's deflection of California (3-1) QB Kyle Boller's 2-pt conversion pass with 31 secs left. QB Chance Harridge led Falcons attack, rushing for 124y and 3 TDs, including game-winner with 1:59 left. Boller immediately led 70y drive—despite 4 dropped passes by WR LaShaun Ward—which Boller capped with 17y TD pass to WR Jonathan Makonnen (5/92y). Boller finished with 13-37/216y, TD passing as dropped passes were game-long theme. Bears K Mark Jensen kicked school-record 5 FGs.

USA Today Coaches September 23

1	Miami (Fla.) (59)	1523	14	Michigan	703
2	Texas (2)	1436	15	North Carolina State	647
3	Oklahoma	1406	16	Wisconsin	559
4	Florida State	1343	17	Kansas State	513
5	Virginia Tech	1249	18	Washington State	481
6	Ohio State	1204	19	Nebraska	430
7	Georgia	1116	20	LSU	360
8	Oregon	1065	21	Iowa State	308
9	Florida	1047	22	Southern California	306
10	Notre Dame	958	23	Colorado State	187
11	Tennessee	866	24	Oregon State	177
12	Penn State	772	25	Auburn	79
13	Washington	771			

September 28, 2002

(Th) LOUISVILLE 26 Florida State 20 (OT): Monsoon conditions greeted Florida State (4-1), and QB Chris Rix (14-33/173y, 2 TDs, INT) had trouble gripping some of his throws. After teams traded 1st Q FGs, Louisville (3-2) squandered 1st-and-goal after special teamer James Green blocked Seminole punt, as FSU LB Jerel Hudson made 4th down INT to end threat. Rix, just 2-12 in 1st H, gripped ball well enough for 23y TD pass to WR Talman Gardner in 2nd Q for 10-3 H lead for Seminoles. Cardinals QB Dave Ragone (15-27/182y, 2 TDs, INT) and Rix traded 3rd Q TD passes, and with 11:37 left in 4th Q, Ragone tied it at 20-20 with his 2nd scoring pass, 1y to WR Damien Dorsey. OT required only 2 plays as ghost of Johnny Unitas, former Louisville QB who died on September 11, seemed to inspire Cards. DB Anthony Floyd made INT inside own 5YL as pass slipped away from Rix, and RB Henry Miller quickly surged 25y up middle for Louisville's winning TD.

Georgia Tech 21 NORTH CAROLINA 13: Having lost nation's leading rusher (TB Tony Hollings) and team's best defender (DL Greg Gathers) for season, Georgia Tech (4-1) carried on, beating North Carolina (1-3) for 5th straight time. Yellow Jackets led 14-13 at H as QBs Damarius Bilbo and A.J. Suggs (15-27/166y, TD, INT) completed TD passes to WRs Kerry Watkins and Will Glover respectively. Carolina QB Darian Durant (14-25/231y) threw TD pass early in 2nd Q and found giant TE Bobby Blizzard over middle on opening march of 3rd Q. Blizzard bounced off several tacklers and seemed headed to go-ahead 61y TD, but he was stripped of ball by Tech DB Rueben Houston at 2YL, and FUM was recovered in EZ by DB Jonathan Cox. Georgia Tech then used 8 min to go 80y to TD by frosh TB Ajenavi Eziemefe (32/136y) and 21-13 margin.

Virginia 38 WAKE FOREST 34: It was habit Virginia (3-2) would embrace often during season: falling well behind and rallying in 2nd H to win. Wake Forest (2-3) dominated 1st H as TB Chris Barclay, FB Ovie Mughelli, and TB Cornelius Birgs each scored TD for 27-10 edge. Cavaliers accurate QB Matt Schaub (22-27/312y, 3 TDs) tossed 2 TD passes in 2nd H, and frosh TB Wali Lundy showed his usefulness. Lundy was held to mere 17/25y rushing, but contributed 42y KO RET that started 2nd Q drive to FG, caught 9/62y, and threw 38y TD pass in 3rd Q. Sub QB Marques Hagans finished 10-play, 78y drive to Cavs' winning TD with 6:13 to go as he ran 13y on QB draw run to score.

FLORIDA 41 Kentucky 34: Special-teams play was bizarre in sloppy game. Florida (4-1) was carried by 2 TD runs by RB Ran Carthon in 2nd Q to 19-0 H lead, and rode passing arm of QB Rex Grossman (28-43/375y, 2 TDs to WR Taylor Jacobs) through tumultuous 3rd Q. Kentucky (4-1) WR Derek Abney took 14y TD pass from QB Jared Lorenzen (20-32/180y, 2 TDs, INT). Then, after Grossman's 1st TD pass, Abney raced 100y on KO TD RET, Wildcats blocked punt, and Lorenzen's 2nd TD pass after FUM by Gators RB Earnest Graham put Wildcats ahead 28-25 with 3:03 left in 3rd Q. DB Keiwan Ratliff raced 62y with INT TD RET to give Florida 39-28 4th Q edge, but Abney took punt back 49y to score with 5:24 to play. Lorenzen's 2-pt pass, that would have sliced UK deficit to 39-36, was picked off by Ratliff and returned for 2 pts.

Alabama 30 ARKANSAS 12: Fast-starting Alabama (4-1) won its 8th game in last 9 as it gained 218y in 1st Q, scoring on 1st snap as RB Shaud Williams burst 80y. Crimson Tide frosh QB Brodie Croyle made his initial start and passed 12-24/285y, 2 TDs. Croyle's 1st TD pass came on 2nd possession and went to WR Sam Collins. With less than 6 mins left in 1st H, Arkansas (2-1) QB Matt Jones (7-18/111y, 2 INTs) capped 76y drive with 7y TD run. Razorbacks cut lead to 17-10 on K Brennan O'Donohoe's 33y FG after WR DeCori Birmingham's 46y RET of 2nd H KO. It was all Alabama after that.

AUBURN 37 Syracuse 34 (3 OT): WR Jamel Riddle's 85y punt TD RET was key to 17-0 2nd Q lead built by Syracuse (1-3). Auburn (4-1) rallied with 24 unreciprocated pts, tying it at 17-17 and going ahead 24-17 on 2 TD passes by sub QB Jason Campbell (10-15/117y, 2 TDs, INT). Using its own backup QB, Troy Nunes, Orangemen moved back downfield to Nunes' tying 2y TD pass to WR David Tyree with 23 sec to play. In OT, Auburn TB "Cadillac' Williams (40/202y) traded TD runs with Syracuse TB Walter Reyes (19/111y, 2 TDs). After Collin Barber's 44y FG gave Orange 34-31 lead, Williams powered through wilted D for winning 7y TD run.

Iowa 42 PENN STATE 35 (OT): Dominant play by both its lines vaulted Iowa (4-1) to 17-0 1st Q advantage over Penn State (3-1), as QB Brad Banks (18-30/261y, 4 TDs, 2 INTs) augmented TB Fred Russell's darting runs of 35/142y. Hawkeyes WR Ed Hinkel made brilliant horizontal dive for 22y TD catch just inside 6 min to go in H, so Iowa led 23-0. Late in 2nd Q, QB Zack Mills (23-44/399y, 4 TDs, 2 INTs) rallied moribund Lions with 28y TD pass to WR Bryant Johnson (7/132y, 2 TDs), but Hawkeyes replied on K Nate Kaeding's 55y FG that banked off goalpost as H clock expired. Penn State pulled within 26-13 on its 2nd series of 3rd Q, but Iowa DB Derek Pagel (INT) blocked x-pt and DB D.J. Johnson went 99y to 2 pts. Having somehow survived Hinkel's 54y punt RET to its 8YL and DB Jevon Johnson's 33y INT RET to its 2YL with takeaway INT and FUM REC, Penn State was at its 8YL and trailed 35-13 with scant 9 mins to play. Mills caught fire, ending 92y drive with 36y TD pass to TB Larry Johnson. Short Iowa punt led to Mills' 44y TD pass to WR Tony Johnson and 2-pt run. Lions reclaimed ball at own 36YL with 2:23 to go. Mills hit 4-5 passes to tie it 35-35. In OT, Iowa scored on Banks' 6y TD pass to WR C.J. Jones, and State failed on 4th-and-4 screen pass at Iowa 5YL.

MICHIGAN STATE 39 Northwestern 24: In Big 10 opener, stretched D of Northwestern (2-3) managed respectable job on Spartans (3-2) star WR Charles Rogers, who caught 3 passes for only 53y. But Rogers went up over 2 defenders at left edge of EZ in 2nd Q to grab 21y TD pass from QB Jeff Smoker (15-24/263y, 2 TDs, 2 INTs); it was 13th straight game in which Rogers had caught scoring pass. Rogers broke NCAA record he shared with Marshall's Randy Moss, Michigan's Desmond Howard, and Pacific's Aaron Turner. MSU TB Dawan Moss (26/191y) carried on opening 6 plays of game, leading to 1st of 4 FGs by K Dave Rayner, and gained 53 of 82y TD drive early in 2nd Q before Rogers' catch put Spartans ahead 17-10. Wildcats DB Raheem Covington made 2 INTs. His 1st prevented extension of MSU's 20-17 3rd Q lead and his 2nd several mins later placed Wildcats in rally-mode. But NW was forced to punt, and WR Ziehl Kavanaght's 88y TD RET all but iced it for Spartans at 27-17 with 1:24 left in 3rd Q.

IOWA STATE 36 Nebraska 14: Dominating victory by ever-improving Iowa State (5-1) knocked Nebraska (3-2) out of national polls for 1st time since 1981. Trailing 10-0 early in 2nd Q, mostly-ineffective Huskers QB Jammal Lord (5-10/120y, TD, INT passing and 11/8y rushing) found wide-open frosh WR Ross Pilkington for 90y TD pass. Cyclones QB Seneca Wallace was at core of lead maintenance as he passed 19-32/220y, TD to WR Lane Danielson, and rushed 7/50y, 2 TDs. Iowa State led 26-7 in 3rd Q when Nebraska scored its 2nd TD, on FB Judd Davies' run after blocked punt went to 2YL. Rush of celebrators left ISU coach Dan McCarney with fat lip afterward, but he grinned, "I'll try to fight my way out of that danger any time!"

SOUTHERN CALIFORNIA 22 Oregon State 0: High-flying Beavers (4-1), averaging 47 pts and 500y per game, visited L.A. Coliseum where they hadn't won since 1960. Outstanding D line of Southern California (3-1), led by DTs Mike Patterson and Shaun Cody and DE Omar Nazel put great pass-rush pressure on Oregon State QB Derek Anderson (8-30/80y), who was sacked 5 times. USC QB Carson Palmer (23-41/231y, 2 TDs, INT) threw TDs to WR Mike Williams in middle Qs, admitted, "The defense won the game."

October 5, 2002

(Th) MINNESOTA 31 Illinois 10: Knocked from unbeaten ranks previous Saturday at Purdue, Minnesota (5-1) was forced to schedule into Thursday night to oblige Minnesota Twins' playoff game. Illinois (1-5) scored 1st when bad snap slipped by Gophers P Preston Gruening for safety. Minnesota went ahead 10-2 on TD pass by QB Asad Abdul-Khaliq (15-27/144y, TD, INT) and K Dan Nystrom's 23y FG. It was Nystrom's 58th career FG, Gopher record. Illinois tied it at 10-10 as QB Jon Beutjer (14-29/165y, TD) found WR Walter Young for 16y TD and 2-pt pass. Gophers made methodical late 2nd Q drive that featured 3 stop-clock spikes by Abdul-Khaliq, and 1y TD plunge by FB Thomas Tapeh (27/113y) on last play of 1st H. Minnesota dashed away in 2nd H with 2 TDs, including blocked punt for 3rd Q TD. Gophers TB Terry Jackson rushed 16/159y.

Wake Forest 24 GEORGIA TECH 21: Upset-minded Wake Forest (3-3) sported nation's 6th best rushing O upon its arrival, and won in Atlanta for 1st time since 1994 partly because it held ball for 38 mins. Georgia Tech (4-2) QB A.J. Suggs (15-24/178y, INT) threw 2 TD passes in 1st H as Tech led 14-10. K Matt Wisnosky kicked his 2nd FG of 2nd H early in 4th Q to give Demon Deacons 16-14 lead. Yellow Jackets countered quickly as backup QB Damarius Bilbo pitched 69y TD pass to WR Kerry Watkins (5/102y) with 10:04 left. Wake TB Tarance Williams (19/99y) ran 5/30y, including 10y score on 4th-and-2, on 65y drive to winning TD and 2-pt run with 5:29 left. Suggs, returning for Bilbo to chorus of home crowd boos, blundered 2 late chances on FUM and PEN.

Georgia 27 ALABAMA 25: Bulldogs (5-0), SEC's last unbeaten team, had manhood challenged in radio interview earlier in week by former Auburn coach (and Georgia All-America) Pat Dye. By game's end, Georgia ground out tough win. Bulldogs led 14-9 at H on 15y TD run by TB Musa Smith (21/126y) and brilliant 42y TD catch at pylon by WR Fred Gibson. Frosh Alabama (4-2) QB Brodie Croyle (16-29/197y, TD, INT) pulled Tide within 24-19 midway in 4th Q by leaping high over Bulldogs CB Bruce Thornton at GL to barely break plane for 1y TD sprint-out. Just 2 plays later, Georgia QB David Greene (15-27/224y, 2 TDs, 2 INTs) suffered odd INT as Gibson failed to hold pass in flat and bobbled ball into hands of Tide DB Charlie Peprah. Peprah stole away on 35y INT TD RET that suddenly gave Bama lead of 25-24. After sack by standout DL David Pollack (blocked FG), Georgia used WR Damian Gary's 15y punt RET to poise Smith to press through Bama's SEC-leading run D. K Billy Bennett nailed 32y FG with :38 on clock for 1st-ever Bulldogs win in Tuscaloosa.

MISSISSIPPI 17 Florida 14: It was clear from beginning that no. 6 Florida (4-2) was in for tussle even though it led 14-2 at H. Gators QB Rex Grossman (19-44/205y, 4 INTs) completed 2 TD passes in 1st H to WR Carlos Perez, 2nd coming at end of 98y drive late in 2nd Q, after Gators D stopped 4 runs inside own 2YL. In between his 2 scoring passes, Grossman was called for intentional grounding from EZ that resulted in safety for Mississippi (4-1). Rebels greeted 2nd H with D fire. DB Matt Grier picked off pass and returned it to Gators 18YL, and Rebels scored 4 plays later on RB Vashon Pearson's 4y run. QB Eli Manning (18-33/154y) pitched 2-pt pass to WR Jason Armstead to bring Ole Miss within 14-10. Midway in 3rd Q, Grier struck again, catching Grossman's pass into double coverage at Florida 24YL and returning INT for TD. Ole Miss D, which allowed 38pts to Vanderbilt 2 weeks earlier, clamped down rest of way.

Penn State 34 WISCONSIN 31: Penn State (4-1) jumped on slow-starting Wisconsin (5-1) for 10 quick pts and led 13-7 until DB B.J. Tucker grabbed INT and dashed 65y to give Wisconsin short-lived lead at 14-13. Lions TB Larry Johnson (14/114y) burst 24y to score and added 2-pt conv for 21-14 margin. Badgers QB Brooks Bollinger spotted WR Brandon Williams for 7y TD early in 4th Q, but PEN forced long and wide kick, so Lions held 28-20 edge. Midway in 4th Q, Penn State K Robbie Gould convinced coach Joe Paterno to try 51y FG, which he converted, and added another for 34-28 lead. Lions DE Michael Haynes and DT Jimmy Kennedy each had 3 sacks.

IOWA 31 Purdue 28: On Homecoming Saturday, Iowa (5-1) D allowed 507y and suffered 80y in PENs, but, thanks to great special teams play and late rally, Hawkeyes pulled out win in last min. Purdue (3-3) QB Kyle Orton (22-37/247y, TD) flipped late 1st Q crossing throw to WR John Standeford, who sped away for 61y TD. As Iowa O stalled, Boilermakers went up 14-3 on 71y TD march. Hawkeyes DB Bob Sanders blocked chip-shot FG, and DB Antwan Allen breezed down right sideline for 85y TD RET. Iowa DB Sean Considine blocked punt for TD early in 3rd Q, so Hawkeyes had 14 pts from special teams in less than 4 min and 17-14 lead. Iowa TE Dallas Clark added tackle-hurdling 95y run with TD pass, but when Orton went out with concussion, sub QB Brandon Kirsch devised TD drives of 89 and 67y. Having used all its TOs and forced punt, Iowa regained ball at own 13YL with 2:16 to play and trailed 28-24. QB Brad Banks stunned Purdue with 44y draw run and 20y pass to WR Maurice Brown. Banks found Clark 6 plays later on 7y delay pattern for winning TD with 1:07 left.

TEXAS 17 Oklahoma State 15: Perhaps No. 3 Longhorns (5-0) were looking ahead to Oklahoma showdown; they nearly bungled Big 12 opener to hot-and-cold Oklahoma State (2-3). Texas QB Chris Simms (24-46/267y, TD, INT) threw for TD and ran for TD in middle Qs, but it took DB Rod Baber's GL tackle in 4th Q on WR Rashaun Woods to stop 2-pt try that would have tied game. Cowboys took early 3-0 lead, 1st time Texas had trailed all season, then rallied from 17-3 deficit late in 3rd Q on TB Tatum Bell's 45y TD run and TD pass by QB Josh Fields (14-29/134y, TD, 2 INTs) with 4:04 to play.

COLORADO 35 Kansas State 31: Long gainers by both teams punctuated Colorado's opening defense of Big 12 title. Kansas State (4-1) scored on plays of 71 and 80y, while Buffaloes (3-2) tallied 94, 85, and 71y TDs. Buffs scored on their 1st 2 series, including 71y TD pass by previously ineffective QB Robert Hodge (13-20/289y, 3 TDs) on way to 28-14 H lead. Buffs' last 1st H TD came on 94y pass from Hodge to speedy frosh WR Jeremy Bloom. Trailing 35-14 midway in 3rd Q, Wildcats rallied on 2 TD runs by RB Darren Sproles (16/121y) set up by gains of QB Ell Roberson (21/178y rushing). But in late going, Colorado DL Sam Wilder sacked Roberson at Buffs 18YL, and K-State had to settle for FG that left them at 35-31. Pass interference PEN on Wildcats DB James Dunnigan with 1:24 left allowed Buffs to run out clock. Colorado TB Chris Brown rushed 26/167y and 2 TDs.

Oklahoma 31 MISSOURI 23: Missouri (3-2) frosh QB Brad Smith accounted for 391y and left big impression on no. 2 Oklahoma (5-0). Smith rushed 26/213y and pair of TDs of 25y each, while passing 19-39/178y, TD, 3 INTs. After Sooners TB Quentin Griffin (16/105y) scored on 53y run in middle of 3rd Q for 23-7 lead, Tigers responded with 24 unanswered pts on Smith's 23y scoring pass and his 2nd TD run in 4th Q. Trailing 24-23, Oklahoma DB Brandon Everage made INT at Missouri 16YL and coach Bob Stoops shunned FG on 4th-and-8 because K Trey DiCarlo had missed x-pt and 2 FGs. On FG fake, holder Matt McCoy tossed pass for frosh TE Chris Chester, who went high between 2 defenders to grasp winning TD with 6:33 to go.

Texas Tech 48 TEXAS A&M 47 (OT): Red Raiders (4-2) QB Kliff Kingsbury (48-58/468y, 5 TDs) threw 10y TD pass to WR Nehemiah Glover in OT and K Robert Treece followed his 42y game-tying FG with winning x-pt kick. Texas A&M (3-2) D was shredded by Kinsbury in O duel that also saw Aggies QB Dustin Long (21-37/367y) pitch 7 TD passes to break Kingsbury's week-old conf record. Texas Tech trailed 35-17 with 7 mins left in 3rd Q, but Kingsbury completed TD passes to WRs Wes Welker and Taurean Henderson, and Welker raced 88y to punt TD RET with 2:48 to play. That put Raiders ahead 38-35, but Long retaliated with 9y TD pass to WR Greg Porter. A&M K John Pierson missed kick and it allowed Treece's FG to tie it 41-41. Pierson also missed x-pt in Aggies' OT possession, and it kept Tech within range at 47-41.

California 34 WASHINGTON 27: It had been 26 long years, 19 losses since California (4-2) had beaten Washington (3-2). Bears sr QB Kyle Boller, consistent underachiever in prior seasons, was brilliant on 13-24/266y, 5 TDs in air. Boller matched Washington State's Jack Thompson (1976) and Illinois' Tom O'Connell (1952) as only QBs to ever toss 5 TDs vs. Huskies. Trailing 34-17, Washington nearly accomplished 4th comeback win in row vs. Cal. QB Cody Pickett (35-59/399y, 2 INTs) scored on option run with 4:03 to play, and K John Anderson added his 4th FG to slice it to 34-27. But, Cal WR Geoff McArthur recovered on-side KO with less than 2 mins left, and Bears killed clock.

WASHINGTON STATE 30 Southern California 27 (OT): Cougars (5-1) bruised QB Jason Gesser (23-44/315y, 2 TDs, INT) wore thick flak jacket to protect bad rib, still helped batter nation's top D as Southern California (3-2) relinquished 516y. Washington State led most of game as WRs Mike Bush (in 1st Q) and Devard Darling (early in 4th Q) caught short TD passes and RB Jermaine Green rocketed 75y for 3rd Q TD that provided 17-14 lead. Trojans rallied on 3y TD sprint to open left flank by QB Carson Palmer (32-50/381y, 2 TDs, INT) and 55y TD pass over middle to WR Mike Williams. But it was after Williams' catch with 4:10 to go that USC K Ryan Killeen missed x-pt, which allowed State K Drew Dunning to knot it at 27-27 with 1:50 left in regulation. Killeen missed 52y FG in OT; Dunning wrapped it up with 35y FG for Cougars.

October 12, 2002

(Th) Virginia Tech 28 BOSTON COLLEGE 23: Hokies (6-0) remained unbeaten behind stellar running of "The Untouchables:" TBs Lee Suggs (26/154y) and Kevin Jones (18/144y). Suggs set Big East record with 39th career TD that gave Hokies 14-0 advantage. Boston College (3-2) was blanked in 3 possessions inside Tech red zone in 1st H, but Eagles WR Jamal Burke sliced deficit to 14-7 late in 2nd Q with 84y punt TD RET. Tech O looked nearly perfect on 3rd Q, 74y drive ending with 4y TD run by Jones to take lead for good at 21-14. After BC responded with K Sando Sciortino's 49y FG, Suggs turned corner for 27y clinching 4th Q TD run. Eagles surprisingly gained whopping 298y on returns against Hokies' vaunted special teams.

MIAMI 28 Florida State 27: Ancient Orange Bowl hosted record crowd that watched Florida State (5-2), 2-TD underdog, build 27-14 lead on explosive run attack. Seminoles TB Greg Jones powered for 189y behind sparkling play of O-line. Backup

FSU TB Nick Maddox added 74y rushing, including 30y 2nd Q TD run that knotted score at 7-7. Miami (6-0) QB Ken Dorsey (20-45/362y) had tough day as he lost 3 TOs. But, Dorsey came through with 4th Q rally, which included 2y scoring pass to WR Kevin Beard and quick TD drive to go ahead 28-27. On latter move, Hurricanes TB Jason Geathers raced for 11y TD, just 1 play after TB Willis McGahee's 68y run with Dorsey's short pass. In dying mins, Miami sr P Freddie Capshaw tried to pin Seminoles deep, but sliced 3y punt OB, which launched FSU's final drive from own 46YL. FSU QB Chris Rix (8-19/83y) completed 2 passes to WR Talman Gardner for 23y to set up game-ending 43y FG attempt by K Xavier Beitia, 13 of 15 on season and good from 45y and 42y earlier. Rushed snap and hold were bad and 3-pt try sailed left of posts. Florida State now had lost 4 series games in 12 years on missing game-winning or game-tying FG on final play. Miami upped its win streak to 28 and stayed no. 1 in AP Poll for record 19th week in row, breaking Southern Cal's mark of 1972-73.

North Carolina State 34 NORTH CAROLINA 17: Wolfpack (7-0) used 27-pt explosion in 2nd H to avenge 2001 home loss to North Carolina (2-4). NC State frosh TB T.A. McLendon shook off broken right wrist to rush for 164y and score his 11th and 12th TDs of season. QB Philip Rivers, who threw for only 170y, spent 2nd H mostly handing off. Rivers threw only 5 passes in 2nd H, but completed all of them, including 13y TD pass to WR Bryan Peterson. After 2nd H KO, Tar Heels took 17-7 lead as 78y drive was finished by QB Darian Durant (18-36/266y, 2 TDs) throwing 5y TD to FB James Faison. NC State answered with 6 runs for 70y TD trip, capped by Rivers' keeper. Durant lost FUM, recovered by LB Dantonio Burnette, on UNC 4YL. McLendon scored on next play and 2nd H rout was on. Wolfpack D contributed 5 sacks, 3 by DE Drew Wimsatt. Coach Chuck Amato was LB on 1967 team, last Wolfpack squad to open season at 7-0.

GEORGIA 18 Tennessee 13: With Tennessee (4-2) QB Casey Clausen out with broken collarbone, ineffective frosh QB C.J. Leak was replaced in 1st H by frosh QB James Banks, who struggled himself until 2-TD spurt in 4th Q. Special teams of Bulldogs (6-0) set early tone: Blocked punt by WR Reggie Brown led to safety, and blocked FG by LB Boss Bailey was converted into 27y FG and 5-0 lead for Georgia. With neither team displaying much O, Georgia stretched lead to 18-0 in 2nd H as D held on 4th-and-1 on own 29YL and later forced FUM to start scoring drives led by QB David Greene (22-37/232y, TD, INT). Tennessee had only 32y passing through 3 Qs, when Banks finally sparked Vols to 2 TDs on 6-6/135y passing. With less than 2 mins left, Bulldogs went for 4th-and-2 on Vols 35YL, and TB Tony Milton clinched win with 25y run. Georgia WR Terrence Edwards (7/112y) was Greene's favorite target, while DE David Pollack and DT Shedrick Wynn had 2 sacks apiece.

Arkansas 38 AUBURN 17: Despite coming off 2nd longest game in NCAA history, Arkansas (3-2) overwhelmed Auburn (4-2) with 426y rushing and had sufficient 2nd H stamina to shut out home team, coming off bye last week. Teams traded early TDs:Arkansas TB De'Arrius Howard's 4y TD run followed Tiger FUM, and Auburn QB Daniel Cobb (13-23/225y) threw 65y scoring pass to WR Devin Aromashodu. Lead quickly was swapped 3 times. TB Cadillac Williams (24/99y) scored to put Tigers ahead, but Razorbacks took lead for good as TB Fred Talley raced for 80y TD, part of his 241y rushing total. Arkansas made 2 more long-distance runs to pull away in 2nd H: 44y by FB Mark Pierce and 70y by QB Matt Jones.

Louisiana State 36 FLORIDA 7: LSU proved it deserved status as top-rated statistical D in nation as Bengal Tigers (5-1) held Gators (4-3) to 237y and pressured QB Rex Grossman into 4 INTs. Tigers gained 402y as QB Matt Mauck (13- 20/153y),including 2 TD passes to WR Devery Henderson. Mauck, who rushed for 67y of team's 249y on ground, sparkled on LSU's 1st possession of 2nd H. Ahead 13-7, Mauck marched Tigers 80y, rushing for 16y asn 2 1st downs, and throwing for 48y and TD pass. LSU CB Corey Webster contributed 3 INTs, taking 1 back 45y for opening TD. K John Corbello added 3 FGs, while holder Blain Bech ran 35y with fake FG for TD that upped lead to 33-7 early in 4th Q. Feeling heat of Gainesville critics, Grossman (18-43/163y, 4 INTs) threw 16y TD to WR Taylor Jacobs for Florida's sole score.

NOTRE DAME 14 Pittsburgh 6: Fighting Irish (6-0) permitted 402y, but remained unbeaten as their D made 8 sacks and forced 2 huge 2nd H TOs. WR Arnaz Battle caught 10/101y for Notre Dame's imperfect O that produced only 185y. Battle's diving 2nd Q TD grab gave ND 7-3 lead and capped drive on which he contributed 23y and 22y receptions. QB Rod Rutherford (19-43/313y) continually moved Panthers (5-2) in middle of field, hooking up with WR Lamar Slade for 7/127y. Rutherford lost FUM on own 12YL after terrific hit by S Glenn Earl that set up 1y TD run by TB Ryan Grant and 14-6 lead. ND frosh CB Preston Jackson's INT with 1:05 remaining shut door on Panthers hope of fashioning comeback.

MICHIGAN 27 Penn State 24: Penn State (4-2) would score TD, and Michigan would answer with TD, scenario that would play out entire game until regulation time ended with 21-21 deadlock. Before OT, however, Penn State hoped to score with time running down. With 3rd down pass from QB Zack Mills (19-31/264y) to WR Tony Johnson at Michigan 23YL ruled OB despite contrary evidence, Nittany Lions had to settle for OT. In OT Penn State scored 1st on FG, thus leaving door ajar. Michigan (5-1) TB Chris Perry (25/80y) raced through that door for 3y TD run to win game. Wolverines were led by surprising performance of underrated QB John Navarre, who completed 27-41/244y with 2 TD passes to WR Braylon Edwards (7/66y). Navarre ran in another score, but most notably he passed 5-6 on crucial, late tying drive and in OT. Penn State WR Bryant Johnson (7/138y) had big game. Win was Michigan's 6th straight in series.

Oklahoma 35 Texas 24 (Dallas): With heroes aplenty for Oklahoma (6-0), it was easy to forget Longhorns actually owned 4th Q lead of 6 pts. Texas (5-1) took early 14-3 lead as QB Chris Simms (12-26/156y, 3 INTs) set up his 1y scoring keeper with 44y hook-up with WR Roy Williams, and soon CB Rod Babers took INT—1 of 4 for Texas D—73y for TD. Oklahoma WR Antwone Savage swung momentum back with 81y KO RET late in 1st H to set up score that cut Texas lead to 14-11: QB Nate Hybl (12-29/131y) hit TE Trent Smith for 3y TD pass and WR Curtis Fagan for 2-pt conversion. Darting, little TB Quentin Griffin knifed through Texas for 248y rushing, and Sooners D limited Steers to only 3 1st downs in 2nd H. After pushing lead to 17-11 on K Dusty Mangam's 37y FG, Longhorns collapsed, allowing 24 straight pts. Sooners took lead on unlikely TD: Griffin scooped up teammate WR Will Peoples' FUM at 2YL and zipping in for 1st of his 2 TDs in 4th Q. Griffin tallied 9 TDs against Texas in OU's 3 straight series wins.

Oregon 31 UCLA 30: QB Cory Paus (17-31/316y, TD) led Bruins (4-2) attack that totaled 477y, but was victimized by 3 INTs. For Oregon (6-0), K Jared Siegel provided spark on last play of 1st H as he bombed school-record 59y FG. UCLA WR Craig Bragg (9/230y) grabbed 3 TD passes, including 1-handed, 46y catch and dash to EZ for 30-24 lead in 3rd Q. But, Bruins K Chris Griffith's x-pt kick was blocked and it would haunt UCLA. Ducks QB Jason Fife (14-18/202y) scrambled and threw winning 74y TD pass to streaking WR Keenan Howry as 4th Q opened. With 61 points on board and 14:46 remaining, Oregon D had its work cut out for it. Griffith missed 46y FG with 1:54 remaining, so somewhat surprisingly Ducks D delivered 4th Q blanking of Bruins. Long-gainers formed game's theme: In addition to his winning catch, Howry also scored on 79y punt RET. UCLA's Bragg caught 71y scoring pass from Paus and added 53y TD on trick-play pass from WR John Dubravac.

USA Today Coaches October 14

1	Miami (Fla.) (58)	1522	14	Florida State	674
2	Oklahoma (3)	1457	15	Air Force	565
3	Virginia Tech	1386	16	Iowa	553
4	Ohio State	1320	17	Washington	531
5	Georgia	1286	18	Tennessee	528
6	Oregon	1203	19	Kansas State	453
7	Notre Dame	1164	20	Southern California	330
8	Texas	1062	21	Penn State	257
9	Michigan	993	22	Mississippi	165
10	North Carolina State	965	23	Bowling Green	155
11	Washington State	868	24	Florida	123
12	LSU	846	25	Colorado	92
13	Iowa State	836			

October 19, 2002

(Th) MARYLAND 34 Georgia Tech 10: Maryland (5-2) was out gained 241y to 141y during 1st H, but K Nick Novak made FGs of 35 and 27y for 6-0 Terps lead by midway in 2nd Q. Georgia Tech (4-3) QB A.J. Suggs (28-45/272y) clicked with 11y pass to WR Jonathan Smith and 15y to WR Kerry Watkins (9/127y) to set up 19y FG by K Luke Manget, but Tech blew 3rd-and-goal from 1YL opportunity. Terrapins were different team in 2nd H with altered blocking schemes and hard-running from TB Chris Downs, who rushed 26/212y after making only 7/29y on ground in 1st H. Downs scored on runs of 15, 1, and 64y to build 27-3 edge by middle of 4th Q.

WEST VIRGINIA 34 Syracuse 7: West Virginia (5-2) continued to fly under poll's radar, taking 2nd straight Big East win. Mountaineers QB Rasheed Marshall (8-16/108y, TD) scored 2 TDs in 1st H: 4y bootleg to right pylon and 14y middle scramble that ended in spectacular, double-hit whirlybird landing in EZ. Syracuse (1-6) lost 3 TOs in 1st H at own 35, 29, and 26YLs that led to pts for WVU's 20-0 lead. Orangemen rushed for only 72y, but capped 82y drive late in 3rd Q with FB Chris Davis' 2y plunge.

NORTH CAROLINA STATE 24 Duke 22: Wolfpack (8-0) tied school-best record to start season, matching 1967 squad's undefeated start. Nation's pass efficiency leader, NC State QB Philip Rivers (26-37/364y, 2 TDs) scored on 6y run and pitched WR screen TD pass that went 53y to lead Wolfpack to 17-3 H margin. After missing on all but 1 of 3 1st H trips inside State's 30YL, Duke (2-6) pulled within 17-12 late in 3rd Q. NC State seemed safe at 24-15 after Rivers fired 53y TD bomb to WR Jerricho Cotchery with 2:52 left in 4th Q. But Blue Devils soph QB Adam Smith (28-41/353y, TD) enjoyed his greatest game to-date by connecting on short passes until WR Khary Sharpe slipped behind secondary for spectacular 40y TD with :16 left. K Brent Garber's high-bounding on-side KO worked, but blitzes kept Duke out of long range of Garber, who earlier booted 47, 52, and 45y FGs.

Michigan 23 PURDUE 21: Maligned Michigan (6-1) QB John Navarre (17-35/271y TD, INT) followed his brilliant late-game passing prior week against Penn State with career-high aerial y and clutch throws to defeat desperate Purdue (3-5). Teams traded 2nd Q TDs as Wolverines FB B.J. Askew (16/42y) switched to his original TB spot to spell banged-up Chris Perry (16/74y) as he caught passes of 25 and 26y and scored from 1YL. Boilermakers answered with nimble frosh QB Brandon Kirsch (17-33/172y, TD) running for 31y, including 2y TD keeper, and passed 4-5/38y on 76y drive. After grabbing 10-7 lead on last play of 1st H, Michigan made it 17-7 on Navarre's 31y TD slant pass to WR Braylon Edwards. Kirsch completed 31y TD pass to WR John Standeford to cut lead to 17-14 late in 3rd Q. Navarre threw key block on 34y reverse TD run by WR Calvin Bell. Purdue switched to QB Kyle Orton, but he suffered 2 EZ INTs before final TD with 8 secs left came too late to matter.

Ohio State 19 WISCONSIN 14: Buckeyes (8-0) TB Maurice Clarett (30/133y) raced 25y on opening carry, but had to fight for every y thereafter vs. aroused Badgers (5-3). WR Michael Jenkins (5/114y) took short pass on Ohio State's opening series and raced 47y to score when DB missed INT. Wisconsin TB Anthony Davis (25/144y) sped 41y to 7-7 tie late in 1st Q. OSU pass rush sacked Badgers QB Brooks Bollinger 4 times in 1st H and sent him to sidelines with concussion. Sub QB Jim Sorgi (7-15/137y, TD, INT) sent tall frosh WR Jonathan Orr on long post-pattern in last 2 mins of H and hit Orr for 42y TD and 14-13 Wisconsin lead. Grim D battle marked 2nd H as Ohio State retook lead with 88y drive in 1st 5 mins of 4th Q. Critical to Ohio's advancement was Jenkins' leaping 45y catch on 3rd-and-6 from 16YL. "We had two guys (DBs B.J. Tucker and Brett Bell) in position; no one made a play on the ball," said downcast Badgers coach

Barry Alvarez afterward. Winning TD came on 3y slant pass from QB Craig Krenzel (12-19/204y, 2 TDs) to TE Ben Hartsock. OSU win was clinched when WR Chris Gamble was put at CB and made running and leaping INT at GL with 7 mins left.

Texas Christian 45 LOUISVILLE 31: TCU (6-1) won 6th straight with 1st H O explosion. Frogs frosh QB Tye Gunn (17-23/187y, 3 TDs) completed 10-13/125y and TD passes of 17, 20 and 27y to build 38-6 H margin. Pitching in as runners were TBs Ricky Madison with 23/137y, TD, and Lonta Hobbs with 22/106y, 2 TDs. Madison's 11y TD run came after Louisville (4-3) P Nate Smith fumbled snap in 2nd Q. Cardinals rallied for 18-pts in 3rd Q as QB Dave Ragone (18-34/309y, 3 TDs, INT) threw 6y TD pass and added 2-pt pass. Safety was credited to LB Jonathan Jackerson who blocked Louisville's nation-leading 6th punt of season. Comeback ended at 38-24 as Frogs DT John Turntine picked off deflected pass by Ragone, and Hobbs scored his 2nd TD from 1YL.

Texas 17 KANSAS STATE 14: Texas (6-1) won key game to keep alive its BCS hopes as K Dusty Mangum shook off recent slump to bore through 27y FG with 1:32 remaining to win it. With :07 showing, Kansas State (5-2) K Jared Brite had tying 36y FG swatted down by 6'4" DL Marcus Tubbs, inserted specifically to attempt to block FG try. Longhorns QB Chris Simms (13-24/184y, 2 TDs, INT) was effective if not brilliant in putting Longhorns ahead 7-0 and 14-6 with his TD passes to WR B.J. Johnson (4/132y) and TE David Thomas (4/132y). Wildcats scored after 4 mins of 4th Q on QB Ell Roberson (7-18/102y) scramble and 15y TD pass to TE Thomas Hill. RB Darren Sproles (20/136y) then ran right and slammed over for 2-pts to tie it 14-14.

OKLAHOMA 49 Iowa State 3: There was no post-Texas game hangover for Oklahoma (7-0) as some expected, and monstrous Sooners D focused on magical Iowa State (6-2) QB Seneca Wallace. Wallace was completely blanketed as he passed (4-22/43y, 3 INTs passing and 6/-28y rushing). "I don't give a hoot about the Heisman," said Wallace afterward. "If it (his performance) damages it, it damages it." Cyclones tallied 60y O, 4th lowest total in school history. Iowa State DB Anthony Forrest tried to knock spinning blocked punt out of EZ in game's 2nd min but he missed, and Oklahoma special teamer Terrance Sims dove on it for TD. Sooners slippery TB Quentin Griffin carried 23/111y, 2 TDs, including 15y run in 1st Q on which he squirted out of group of Cyclones.

OKLAHOMA STATE 24 Nebraska 21: Road woes continued for disappointing Nebraska (5-3) as it dropped 6th away game in row. Fired-up Oklahoma State (3-4) won for 1st time over Cornhuskers since 1961. IB Dahrran Diedrick scored from 2YL to give Huskers 7-3 H lead, but Cowboys QB Josh Fields (17-27/192y, 2 TDs) ran for TD and passed to elusive WR Rashaun Woods (11/134y) for 5y TD at pylon. Sub IB David Horne (24/125y) pulled Nebraska to within 17-14 midway in 4th Q, and after Fields' 2nd TD pass to WR John Lewis in deep right corner of EZ for 24-14 edge, Huskers QB Jammal Lord (18/73y rushing) ran for 1y TD with 2 mins left. Onside-KO went OB, so Cowboys killed clock before happy fans yanked down goalposts.

Notre Dame 21 AIR FORCE 14: Notre Dame's D, team's strength all season, executed its assignments beautifully in taking on option runs of undefeated Air Force (6-1). But difference in Fighting Irish (7-0) win came from O that finally came alive with 447y and 22 1st downs. TB Ryan Grant rushed 30/190y and scored on 18y run in 2nd Q. Irish erred early in 1st Q as QB Carlyle Holiday (8-15/112y passing and 9/86y, 2 TDs rushing) was blindsided by Falcons DL Jon Hicks, and DL Marchello Graddy raced 21y for FUM TD RET. Irish D applied heavy pressure to QB Chance Harridge, who had scored 15 TDs in Air Force's opening 6 wins, holding Harridge to 13/31y rusnning and 6-14/57y passing. CB Shane Walton of Notre Dame made his 6th INT of season in 3rd Q.

Arizona State 45 OREGON 42: Under-appreciated Arizona State (6-2) rallied from deficits of 21-0 in 2nd Q and 35-17 as late as 4 mins from end of 3rd Q. No. 7 Oregon (6-1) saw nation's 2nd-longest win streak die at 11 games. QB Jason Fife (21-32/288y 3 TDs, INT) and TB Onterrio Smith (27/172y, 3 TDs) seemed to place Ducks in comfortable waters. But Sun Devils scorched Ducks D for 590y. QB Andrew Walter (31-53/school record 536y, 4 TDs, 2 INTs) pitched 58y TD pass to WR Justin Taplin to take 39-35 lead early in 4th Q, and K Mike Barth extended edge to 42-35 with 44y FG. With 6:55 left, Oregon tied it 42-42 as Fife located WR Samie Parker (6/78y, 2 TDs) in EZ for 12y TD. Walter passed Arizona State into FG range, where Barth booted 29y FG with 1:58 to play. Ducks' final opportunity drowned when Devils DB Brett Hudson made INT of Fife, as Oregon QB was being buried by pass rush.

USA Today Coaches October 21

1	Miami (Fla.) (55)	1519	14	Iowa	724
2	Oklahoma (6)	1465	15	Tennessee	613
3	Virginia Tech	1393	16	Southern California	557
4	Ohio State	1319	17	Penn State	507
5	Georgia	1301	18	Iowa State	426
6	Notre Dame	1219	19	Air Force	373
7	Texas	1112	20	Colorado	267
8	Michigan	1070	21	Kansas State	221
9	North Carolina State	1014	22	Bowling Green	218
10	LSU	945	23	Florida	202
11	Washington State	933	24	Minnesota	194
12	Oregon	842	25	Arizona State	129
13	Florida State	799			

Bowl Championship Series Standings October 21

	Poll Avg.	Computer Avg.	Schedule Strength	Losses Wins	Quality	Total
1 Oklahoma (7-0)	2.0	1.50	.52	0	-0.10	2.62
2 Miami (6-0)	1.0	4.33	1.08	0		6.41
3 Notre Dame (7-0)	6.0	1.33	.04	0	-0.30	7.07
4 Virginia Tech (7-0)	3.0	4.83	1.00	0	-0.20	8.63
5 Georgia (7-0)	5.0	3.33	.36	0		8.69

(Th) North Carolina State 38 CLEMSON 6: Wolfpack (9-0) dominated slumping Tigers (4-4). TB T.A. McLendon rushed for 178y and 2 TDs to pace NC State O that enjoyed nearly 15-min possession edge, and D held Tigers to 229y total O and kept Clemson out of EZ. Tigers' 6 pts were surrendered by Wolfpack special teams on CB Justin Miller's 80y KO RET. Despite that gaffe, NC State special teams outscored Clemson as S Terrence Holt returned punt blocked by DE Manny Lawson 39y for opening score, and WR Jerricho Cotchery ended matters with 42y TD RET of onside KO.

Notre Dame 34 FLORIDA STATE 24: Knotted 10-10, D struggle was blown apart during 3-min stretch of 3rd Q as Irish (8-0) converted 3 Florida State (5-3) TOs into 17 points, needing only 34y of O to gain 27-10 lead. Notre Dame TB Ryan Grant rushed for 2 TDs and QB Carlyle Holiday threw 2 TDs, including 65y scoring pass to WR Arnaz Battle on 1st scrimmage play. FSU QB Chris Rix was hampered by dropped passes and TOs, while TB Greg Jones managed just 34y rushing as Seminoles (93y) became 6th ND victim to fail to reach 100y rushing. Irish upped pts off TOs to 95 for year. Record crowd of 84,104 at Doak Campbell Stadium watched Noles drop 7th of last 20 games.

AUBURN 31 Louisiana State 7: Auburn (5-3) forced 5 TOs and shackled young LSU QB Marcus Randall, who threw 4 INTs (3 of his 1st 5 passes were picked off). Contributing to win, LSU (6-2) INTs were converted into TD drives of 22y and 28y and FG. Auburn QB Jason Campbell (7-11/105, TD), starting for 1st time, threw no INTs, and TB Ronnie Brown, replacing injured TB Carnell Williams, rushed for 95y and 2 TDs. Bengals prevented being shutout on TB Joseph Addai's 8y TD run midway through 4th Q.

Alabama 34 TENNESSEE 14: With Tennessee (4-3) rushing for 59y and losing 6 TOs, Tide rode its D to easily snap 7-game series losing streak. Alabama grabbed early lead as CB Gerald Dixon raced 66y with FUM TD RET for 1st Q TD. Key TO, EZ INT by S Charles Jones, led to 80y Crimson Tide (6-2) TD drive in 2nd Q: TB Santonio Beard made it 14-0 on 10y TD run just after QB Brodie Croyle's 56y pass to WR Zach Fletcher. Both damaging TOs were dealt to Volunteers QB Casey Clausen, who was back from injury to throw 14-26/161y, 3 INTs and, significantly, no TDs. Vols DB Mark Jones followed Beard's TD with 87y KO TD RET to cut margin to 14-7 entering H.

Iowa 34 MICHIGAN 9: Dynamic Hawkeyes (8-1) rolled on, administering worst home defeat on Michigan since 1967. Iowa QB Brian Banks (18-29/222y) threw 3 TDs, 2 to WR C.J. Jones (8/81y), and backup TB Jermelle Lewis rushed for 109y and scored TDs both rushing and receiving. Wolverines (6-2) trailed 10-9 in 3rd Q and their D promisingly forced punt, which Michigan CB Markus Curry promptly fumbled away after crushing hit by S Bob Sanders. Hawks converted miscue into 16y TD drive, beginning of 21-pt surge that finished off UM. Sole Michigan TD, 1y run by TB Chris Perry, followed muffed Iowa punt catch at Hawks' 3YL. Hawkeyes enjoyed 399y to 171y O advantage to secure their 1st series win since 1990, when Iowa last won Big 10 title.

OHIO STATE 13 Penn State 7: Ohio State (9-0) WR-DB Chris Gamble, suddenly thrust into 2-way stardom, made memorable 1st start as CB. Gamble raced 40y with INT for eventual winning TD early in 3rd Q. Entire Buckeyes D excelled, holding Nittany Lions (5-3) to 179y and only 8 1st downs. Buckeyes O only managed 2 FGs as it blew its best TD opportunity on QB Craig Krenzel's 1st Q FUM at Lions 1YL. Penn State DB Anwar Phillips returned FUM 58y before Gamble, who participated in on 95 plays, caught him. Penn State did not convert then, but cashed in 80y drive later in 1st Q on TB Larry Johnson's 5y TD run. Johnson gained 45y on drive but finished with only 66y against OSU D that also had 3 INTs of QB Zack Mills. Buckeyes frosh TB Maurice Clarett left in 1st Q with shoulder injury after gaining 39y to top 1,000y for year.

TEXAS 21 Iowa State 10: Longhorns (7-1) rediscovered their buried ground game and overwhelmed Iowa State (6-3), piling up 245y and exhausting most of 4th Q on vital 80y TD drive. While frosh TB Selvin Young capped that trip with game-closing 2y TD run, it was 1st-team Texas TB Cedric Benson (30/199y, 2 TDs) who truly sparkled. Benson made 59y TD jaunt for 14-10 lead in 3rd Q. Magic-making Iowa State QB Seneca Wallace passed 18-39/226y, INT, and 16y TD that provided 10-7 H edge, but was lassoed by Texas D in 2nd H, as Cyclones were blanked and held to only 5 1st downs.

Southern California 44 OREGON 33: Oregon's passing D failed again as dynamic Trojan QB Carson Palmer threw for 31-42/448y, 5 TDs. Trojans (6-2) erased 19-14 H deficit with 20-0 3rd Q spurt as Palmer tossed 2 TDs and TB Justin Fargas (27/139y) tacked on 15y TD run. Frosh WR Mike Williams had another huge game for USC, catching 13/226y, 2 TDs. Oregon (6-2) QB Jason Fife managed sorry percentage at 20-45/336y, 2 TDs and was picked off twice. Ducks settled for K Jared Siegel's 4 FGs. Trojans snapped 4-game series losing streak.

USA Today Coaches October 28

1	Miami (Fla.) (53)	1517	14	Kansas State	639
2	Oklahoma (7)	1464	15	LSU	588
3	Virginia Tech	1371	16	Oregon	556
4	Ohio State	1311	17	Arizona State	472
5	Georgia	1300	18	Bowling Green	441
6	Notre Dame (1)	1264	19	Minnesota	426
7	Texas	1138	20	Florida State	344
8	North Carolina State	1105	21	Penn State	244
9	Washington State	1006	22	Florida	203
10	Iowa	975	23	Iowa State	198
11	Southern California	895	24	Colorado State	190
12	Colorado	686	25	Marshall	181
13	Michigan	680			

Bowl Championship Series Standings October 28

	Poll Avg.	Computer Avg.	Schedule Strength	Losses Wins	Quality	Total
1 Oklahoma (7-0)	2.0	1.17	.56	0	-0.40	3.33
2 Miami (7-0)	1.0	4.33	1.36	0		6.69
3 Notre Dame (8-0)	5.0	1.83	.16	0		6.99
4 Georgia (8-0)	5.0	3.00	.24	0		8.24
5 Ohio State (9-0)	5.0	3.83	.96	0	-0.30	9.49

November 2, 2002

(Wed) TEXAS CHRISTIAN 37 Southern Mississippi 7: Fantastic D of Horned Frogs (7-1) held Southern Miss (5-3) to 185y, made 9 sacks, and forced FUM and INT. TCU won 7th in row as frosh sub TB Lonta Hobbs rushed 15/123y, 3 TDs. Eagles rallied from 13-0 H discrepancy by opening 3rd Q with 48y TD pass. Frosh QB Dustin Almond (9-27/110y, TD, INT) dumped it to WR Marvin Young (5/91y), who slipped wide open into right flat and picked his way through mostly open field for score that tightened it at 13-7. But, TCU dropped 24-pt avalanche on Southerners before 3rd Q was over: K Nick Browne booted his national-best 19th FG, and DB Jared Smitherman picked off Almond's 1st pass after KO and raced 37y to score. After Eagles punt, Hobbs burst for 53y TD off RG on next play, then went 3y standing up to score in last min of Q.

Miami 42 RUTGERS 17: Etched against cool gray November sky rode mighty Scarlet Knights (1-8), and no. 1 Miami (8-0) bowed down as if lowly Rutgers was led by Four Horsemen. For awhile, anyway. Rutgers started frosh QB Ryan Hart (9-23/110y, 2 INTs) and he lofted early 40y pass to WR Aaron Martin to set up 1y TD run by TB Clarence Pittman. Hurricanes got 2 FGs from K Todd Sievers, and in 2nd Q Rutgers C Marty Pysczcymuka rolled Shotgun snap into EZ for safety. Miami led 8-7, but Knights DB Jason Nugent blocked punt of P Freddie Capshaw and DB Shawn Seabrooks gathered it in and stepped into EZ for 17-8 lead. In last min of H, Miami QB Ken Dorsey (16-32/191y, 2 TDs, INT) misread receiver's GL break, and Rutgers DB Nathan Jones made coast-to-coast INT RET. D holding PEN nullified TD, and Miami TB Willis McGahee (23/187y, 2 TDs) waltzed in for 2y TD. Thus, Rutgers led 17-14, but might have enjoyed 24-8 cushion. In 3rd Q, Canes DL Vince Wilfork stopped 3rd-and-1 run for loss at own 5YL, and Miami buried Knights' fake FG try. From there, Miami exploded with 4 TDs, including 2 TD passes by Dorsey to give him Big East career mark of 78.

Pittsburgh 28 VIRGINIA TECH 21: By Saturday night's KO, no. 3 Virginia Tech (8-1) should have known about upset fever that had swept top 10 teams. Hokies started well enough: Running combo of "The Untouchables" each scored early TD as TB Kevin Jones spun 3y on his 1st carry (only to pull hamstring on his 2nd carry) to open scoring midway in 1st Q and TB Lee Suggs pushed 1y for 14-0 lead. Special teams pressure on Pitt, including punt block by DL Nathaniel Adibi, made for short TD drives of 3 and 21y. Meanwhile, Panthers began assault on nation's best (40.8y avg) run D, which would eventually accumulate to 275y rushing. Trailing 21-7 after Suggs' explosive 59y TD run early in 3rd Q, Pitt QB Rod Rutherford (11-26/208y, 3 TDs, 2 INTs) threw TD passes to sensational frosh WR Larry Fitzgerald (5/105y, 3 TDs) who made brilliant ball adjustments in EZ. With 4:11 left, Pitt RB Brandon Miree (23/161y) burst up middle, slammed through tackle of Tech DB Willie Pyle and raced 53y to winning TD.

Georgia Tech 24 NORTH CAROLINA STATE 17: Schizophrenic Georgia Tech (6-3), battered by injuries to several top players during season, came up big against unbeaten NC State (9-1). Tech controlled ball for nearly 35 mins, just enough to keep its D fresh. Yellow Jackets led 9-3 in battle of FGs until late in 3rd Q when Wolfpack QB Philip Rivers (21-41/277y, INT) threw 19y TD to WR Jericho Cotchery. TB T.A. McLendon (17/49y) was held in check, but his 8y TD sprint early in 4th Q put NC State in command. Tech came from 17-9 deficit in 4th Q, tying game within 2 mins on short TD pass by QB A.J. Suggs (21-36/211y, TD) to TE John Paul Foschi and Suggs' 2-pt pass. After Tech DB Kelly Rhino's 26y punt RET to 22YL, TB Gordon Clinkscale (15/94y), sr who until recently had languished on bench for years, reversed field to score thrilling 14y TD run.

Florida 20 Georgia 13 (Jacksonville): No. 5 Georgia (8-1), losers of 11 of last 12 games to Gators (6-3), finally appeared to have Florida all but eliminated in SEC East race. But, unpredictable Florida stayed alive with come-from-behind win. Bulldogs scored in 1st Q on same deceptive 10y pass that beat Tennessee in 2001. FB J.T. Wall play-faked through line and drifted into vacated EZ for TD lob from QB David Greene (11-29/141y). In middle of 2nd Q, Gators missed x-pt after TD pass by QB Rex Grossman (36-46/339y, 2 TDs, 2 INTs), so they trailed 7-6. UGa sub QB D.J. Shockley threw over middle in 2nd Q; fast-closing Gators SS Guss Scott stepped in, his INT TD RET going 47y. Bulldogs retook H lead 13-12 on 2 FGs by reliable K Billy Bennett. But, Bennett missed 2 FGs in 3rd Q, and Bulldogs O was forced to punt 4 times as it gained only 127y in 2nd H. Florida traveled 89y early in 4th Q as Grossman, so sharp when protected, drilled 8-9/86y, including 10y TD to TE Ben Troupe. Grossman ran for 2 pts, and Gators stopped subsequent Bulldogs threats, including DL Marcus Oquendo-Johnson's 10y sack of Greene on game's last play at Georgia 30YL.

OHIO STATE 34 Minnesota 3: Minnesota (7-2) D, playing well early, blocked punt deep in Ohio State (10-0) end. But, Gophers could tally only K Dan Nystrom's 24y FG after 1st-and-goal at Ohio 8YL. Buckeyes O occasionally struggled without ace TB Maurice Clarett. Thanks to top-notch D, which limited Gophers' 271y-per-game run attack to 36/53y, Bucks began to roll: TB Lydell Ross rushed 20/89y, 2 TDs. Despite being sacked 5/-22y, QB Craig Krenzel passed 9-15/128y, including 30y TD to WR Chris Vance. Minnesota P Preston Gruening's punt was blocked by Ohio S Donnie Nickey and later dropped punt snap. His miscues led to 10 pts. Up by 10-3 at H, Buckeyes dominated 3rd Q with 17 unanswered pts; Minnesota lost 6y on 13 snaps in 3rd Q.

IOWA 20 Wisconsin 3: Unsinkable Hawkeyes (9-1), prone all year to periods of slumber, saw its O snoozing at start. Outstanding Iowa K Nate Kaeding kicked his 18th FG in 18 tries, and Wisconsin (6-4) K Mike Allen tied it 3-3 after Badgers sub TB Jerone Pettus dropped pass that he might have taken for TD. Then, Iowa QB Brad Banks caught fire, while Badgers secondary bungled coverages at critical times. WR Maurice Brown slipped through totally uncovered for TD from Banks, so Iowa led 10-3 at H. Wisconsin QB Jim Sorgi (8-17/84y, INT) replaced Brooks Bollinger (2-9/46y), who had his bell rung late in 2nd Q. Neither QB did well, because Badgers had difficulty running ball, despite notching its 10th straight year with 1000y rusher, mark attained by TB Anthony Davis (16/34y) early in 3rd Q. Iowa's gifted TE Dallas Clark broke up middle alone for 23y TD catch and 20-3 lead as Hawks faked "WR Jailbreak Screen." Big news: Kaeding actually was wide with late FG try, his only miss of season.

Boston College 14 NOTRE DAME 7: Notre Dame's 109th-ranked O had used 24 TOs, created by its D, to negotiate short fields for 95 pts so far in 2002. Fighting Irish (8-1) wore inspirational green jerseys, but Boston College (5-3) inspired itself by reversing trend and creating 5 critical TOs. Eagles TB Derrick Knight (26/129y) used powerful block of C Dan Koppen to go 3y to TD and 6-0 lead after LB Josh Ott recovered bobbled Irish handoff at ND 38YL in 1st Q. Notre Dame appeared to score on pass by QB Carlyle Holiday (16-32/198y, TD), but WR Omar Jenkins was ruled to have not held catch as he tumbled out of EZ. Holiday was knocked dizzy for much of 2nd Q, and sub QB Pat Dillingham drove Irish from BC 42YL after punt RET. In effort to dump pass while under pressure from DB Trevor White's outside blitz, Dillingham flipped ball back-handed. Ott was there to catch it and make 72y INT TD RET. QB Brian St. Pierre (9-20/77y, INT) completed 2-pt pass for 14-0 lead. ND made its 8th unsuccessful trip into BC territory early in 4th Q and had 1st-and-goal at 7YL. But 2 PENs forced Holiday's incompletions on 3rd and 4th downs. ND finally scored with 3:57 to go when scrambling Holiday found WR Maurice Stovall backing into EZ for 20y TD lob. Eagles were able to kill all but 22 secs of clock with their run game.

Texas 27 NEBRASKA 24: QB Chris Simms passed 29-47/school-record 419y, 2 TDs, INT as Texas (8-1) broke 26-game home win streak of Nebraska (6-4) and remained as only victor over Huskers in last 75 tilts at Lincoln. K Dusty Mangum gave Longhorns 6-3 H edge with FGs of 25, 41y. Texas WR Roy Williams (13/161y) caught 2 TDs from Simms in 3rd Q. After Huskers QB Jammal Lord (23/234y rushing) completed 60y TD pass to TE Matt Herion, Steers still led 20-17 and attempted to coddle lead. It appeared safe at 27-24 with 1:34 to go, but O interference PEN forced Texas to punt. Less than min remained as Nebraska DB DeJuan Groce zigzagged 44y on punt RET to Texas 16YL. Huskers coach Frank Solich eschewed tying FG, 3 plays later, because 2 earlier FG attempts had been bungled. Instead, Lord tried pass to EZ, but Texas DB Nathan Vasher made INT at 1YL in closing secs.

OKLAHOMA 27 Colorado 11: Magnificent D of Oklahoma (8-0) forced glut of mistakes in 1st H: Colorado (6-3), 8-0-1 vs Sooners since 1988, lost 2 FUMs, threw INT, muffed short KO, and allowed FG to be blocked. Miscues led to 17 pts of 20-3 H margin for Oklahoma. OU QB Nate Hybl (10-23/105y, 2 INTs) threw 3 TDs, as he guided marches of 39, 24 and 9y after Buff miscues. Sooner WR Mark Clayton (3/36y, 2 TDs) caught 17y TD midway in 2nd Q to build on WR Antwone Savage's early TD catch. Nation's leading rusher, TB Chris Brown of Colorado, was permitted grudging 25/103y on ground to become 1st 100y-rusher vs. Oklahoma in 4 years. But, Brown's 1st Q FUM led to Hybl's 1st TD pass. Sooner LB Teddy Lehman made 13 tackles and his 31y INT RET set up 3rd Q TD for 27-3 lead. Sub TB Bobby Purify scored on 12y run in 3rd Q, but after Buffs made 2-pt pass, they failed at OU 23, 8, and 10YLs in 4th Q. Outstanding effort lifted Oklahoma to top spot in AP Poll in wake of Miami's brief slumber at Rutgers.

WASHINGTON STATE 44 Arizona State 22: Locker room fight early in week broke cheekbone of Washington State (8-1) DB Jason David, Pac-10 leader in INTs, and LB Ira Davis, punch-thrower, was suspended. Depleted Cougars might have caved in, but D only bent before top-notch air game of Arizona State (7-3). ASU QB Andrew Walter (31-51/328y, 2 INTs) was pressured until tapping EZ with 2 TD passes in 4th Q. Sun Devils DE Terrell Suggs had broken single-season sack record previous week, but this time he got 1 sack, and DT Rien Long pressured Walter for 3 of 8 sacks by Wazzu D. Cougars scored on opening series as QB Jason Gesser (18-32/250y, 3 TDs, 2 INTs) hit WR Jerome Riley for TD, then followed 5 mins later with short TD pass to TE Troy Bienemann. Cougars led 17-3 at end of 1st Q, 27-6 at H. Leading team into 1st place in Pac-10, Gesser broke school career pass y record of Jack Thompson (1975-78).

USA Today Coaches November 4

1	Miami (Fla.) (47)	1511	14	LSU	702
2	Oklahoma (14)	1478	15	Oregon	653
3	Ohio State	1401	16	Bowling Green	503
4	Texas	1315	17	Florida	460
5	Washington State	1264	18	Florida State	444
6	Iowa	1210	19	Penn State	352
7	Virginia Tech	1047	20	Colorado State	339
8	Georgia	1036	21	Colorado	310
9	Southern California	1013	22	Iowa State	296
10	Notre Dame	972	23	Pittsburgh	249
11	Michigan	886	24	Arizona State	139
12	Kansas State	820	25	Maryland	138
13	North Carolina State	794			

Bowl Championship Series Standings November 4

	Poll Avg.	Computer Avg.	Schedule Ranking	Losses Wins	Quality	Total
1 Oklahoma (8-0)	1.5	1.00	0.24	0	-0.7	2.04
2 Ohio State (10-0)	3.0	2.33	0.84	0	-0.6	5.57
3 Miami (8-0)	1.5	2.67	0.16	0		6.01
4 Texas (8-1)	4.0	4.67	0.36	1		10.03
5 Washington State (8-1)	5.0	6.33	0.92	1	-0.2	13.05

November 9, 2002

SYRACUSE 50 Virginia Tech 42 (OT): Even in midst of its worst season since 1986, Syracuse (4-6) rallied from 14-3 1st Q deficit to upset no. 8 Virginia Tech (8-2). Sub frosh TB Damien Rhodes (17/67y, 2 TDs) raced around LE for 25y TD run on 1st play of 3rd OT. Orangemen clinched their 3rd straight win as DB Maurice McClain made EZ INT of Tech QB Bryan Randall (23-35/504y, 5 TDs, 3 INTs), who had his most prolific game of his short career. While Syracuse was able to limit Hokies to 55y rushing, WR Ernest Wilford caught 8/school record 279y, including TDs of 75, 34, 87, and 6y. Syracuse TB Walter Reyes (21/118y) registered 3 TDs. Rhodes forced OT when he tied it 35-35 in 4th Q on 3y TD run with 4:27 to go. In 1st OT, Tech K Carter Worley missed winning 36y FG after DB Garnell Wilds' EZ INT of QB Troy Nunes (24-40/403y, TD, 3 INTs).

PITTSBURGH 29 Temple 22: Letdown after their Virginia Tech upset previous week seemed natural for Panthers (8-2), and stubborn Temple (3-7) made Pitt sweat. Sr K Cap Poklemba set Big East record of 5 FGs, 3rd of which gave Owls 16-7 lead with 2:22 left in 1st H. Pitt QB Rod Rutherford (13-20/125y 2 TDs) hit 5 straight passes, including 4y TD to WR Larry Fitzgerald with 1:28 left in 2nd Q. Poklemba's 5th FG tied it at 22-22 in last min of 3rd Q. Temple QB Mike McGann was rushed fiercely and lost FUM, which Pitt DE Claude Harriott scooped and lumbered 11y to score winning TD early in 4th Q. Owls outgained Panthers 341y to 189y, but had 4 TOs and suffered blocked punt.

WEST VIRGINIA 24 Boston College 14: Letdown after Notre Dame upset previous week seemed natural for Eagles (5-4), and revved-up West Virginia (7-3) was happy to oblige. WVU's national-best rushing O gained 273y on ground as TB Avon Cobourne ran 25/138y, TD, and sub TB Quincy Wilson added 17/100y. Mountaineers jumped to 17-0 lead early in 2nd Q as QB Rasheed Marshall (12-18/124y) threw 2y TD pass to TE Tory Johnson, and Cobourne scored from 5YL. WVU P Mark Fazzalari toed 1st Q punts of only 21 and 23y, but LB James Davis, who had sack and forced INT, blocked FG tries each time. Held to 80y rushing, BC looked to QB Brian St. Pierre's 28-50/284y, 2 INTs passing that included 8y TD to WR Jamal Burke with 39 secs left in game.

MARYLAND 24 North Carolina State 21: Sizzling Terrapins (8-2) won 7th straight game to take 2nd place in ACC. NC State (9-2) lost 2nd in row, and its D forced Maryland into O adjustments after Wolfpack built 14-0 and 21-7 leads. In 1st Q, State QB Philip Rivers (24-40/297y, TD, 2 INTs) threw 32y TD pass to WR Jerrico Cotchery, who caught 12/144y. Swift Terps WR Steve Suter, who had already tallied on 4 punt TD RETs this year, sped 64y on reverse TD run in 2nd Q to pull within 14-7. Maryland TB Bruce Perry, out nearly all season, scored on 9y TD late in 3rd Q to make it 21-14. K Adam Kiker missed 28y FG that would have given 10-pt lead to Wolfpack with 11:20 left. Terps QB Scott McBrien (10-18/130y) tied it on 21y TD sprint after cool fake handoff. With 3:22 to go, McBrien got generous spot on 3rd down run, then pitched his only down-field completion, 36y to Suter, to position K Nick Novak for winning 26y FG with 34 secs left.

Louisiana State 33 KENTUCKY 30: Kentucky (6-4) K Taylor Begley made 29y FG with 11 secs left to break 27-27 deadlock after Wildcats QB Jared Lorenzen (12-26/210y, 4 TDs) hit WR Aaron Boone for 3 TDs and TB Artose Pinner rushed 27/143y. But, what goes around, comes around. Kentucky (6-4) coach Guy Morriss was Philadelphia Eagles center in 1978 when New York Giants QB Joe Pisarcik handed off to FB Larry Csonka when taking knee would have won game. Resultant FUM TD RET by Eagles DB Herman Edwards was precursor of this day's last-play TD pass by LSU (7-2). With 2 secs on clock, Tigers were at own 25YL, Morriss had already received water bucket splash, and Kentucky fans were attacking goalposts. LSU QB Marcus Randall (10-23/264y, 3 TDs) flung pass as far as he could; ball was deflected 3 times by Wildcats and landed in out-stretched hands of WR Devery Henderson (5/201y, 3 TDs) who dashed to EZ. Randall admitted Tigers practiced that play but it never worked before.

Florida 21 VANDERBILT 17: Gators (7-3) D was terrific when it needed to be. Florida DB Cory Bailey's 1st career INT was returned 24y to 1YL, and TB Earnest Graham (24/125y) scored on next play. Gators led 21-10 at H after sub TB Ran Carthan and QB Rex Grossman scored from 1YL. Vanderbilt (2-8) QB Jay Cutler's passing was limited to 10-26/94y with 2 INTs, but he scored rushing TD in 3rd Q to narrow deficit to 21-17. Vandy had ball in last 5 mins, but were stopped on 4th down at Gators 39YL.

Miami 26 TENNESSEE 3: Several experts gave home-standing, but injury-depleted Tennessee (5-4) good chance to upset Miami (9-0), but Canes dominated after several recent indifferent performance. Vols broke TB Cedric Houston (14/111y) for 74y gain on game's 2nd snap, had to settle for K Alex Walls' 21y FG, and managed only 142y rest of day. Hurricanes TB Willis McGahee rushed 30/154y, TD, while QB Ken Dorsey passed 18-35/245y, TD to TE Kellen Winslow. Miami K Todd Sievers nailed 4 FGs.

Ohio State 10 PURDUE 6: Undefeated no. 3 Ohio State (11-0) had not traveled well all season, and again Buckeyes had to fabricate late heroics to pull out win at Purdue (4-6). Hard-luck Boilermakers lost their 6th game by total of 26 pts. Buckeyes gained only 267y, were sacked 3 times, and barely got snap away in time for K Mike Nugent's 22y FG as H clock reached 0:00. That tied it at 3-3, but Purdue appeared to make key play on 59y crossing-pattern completion from QB Brandon Kirsch (9-11/116y) to WR Ray Williams in 4th Q. It set up K Berin Lacevic's 2nd FG for 6-3 margin. Facing 4th-and-1 at Boilers 37YL with 1:36 to play, Ohio QB Craig Krenzel (13-20/173y, INT) called pass at line of scrimmage. While pocket caved in, Krenzel stepped forward and lofted pass to EZ, where WR Michael Jenkins got away from tight coverage of DB Antwaun Rogers to make over-shoulder catch for winning TD that saved Buckeyes' national title hopes.

TEXAS A&M 30 Oklahoma 26: During week, no. 1 Oklahoma (8-1) was feeling similar to its 2000 championship run. "I like how it's setting up," said coach Bob Stoops. All started well as Sooners QB Nate Hybl (20-34/249y, 2 TDs, INT) flipped 6y TD pass to TB Quentin Griffin in 1st Q, and OU led 10-0 early in 2nd Q. Texas A&M (6-4) went to bench for frosh QB Reggie McNeal (8-13/191y, 4, INT) who, behind great protection,

turned game around with 4 TD passes, 3 on consecutive series in middle Qs. A&M WR Terrence Murphy (5/128y) caught 40y TD, his 2nd from McNeal to put Aggies ahead for good at 27-23 late in 3rd Q. It was A&M's 1st-ever win over top-ranked team.

WASHINGTON STATE 32 Oregon 21: Relentless no. 5 Cougars (9-1) shut down Oregon's banged-up running ace, TB Onterrio Smith (25/64y), and held high octane Ducks (7-3) O to 252y and lone TD in 2nd Q. Oregon QB Jason Fife (16-35/192y, INT) threw TD pass to WR Jason Willis for brief 14-10 lead. Other Oregon TDs came on DB Steven Moore's 12y FUM RET in 1st Q and LB Kevin Mitchell's 20y INT RET in 3rd Q. Washington State QB Jason Gesser and RB Jermaine Green were twin wrecking crew on O. Gesser passed 20-38/277y, 4 TDs, INT and Green rushed 25/180y.

Bowl Championship Series Standings November 11

	Poll Avg.	Computer Avg.	Schedule Rankings	Losses Wins	Quality	Total
1 Ohio State (11-0)	2.0	1.33	0.88	0		3.41
2 Miami (9-0)	1.0	1.50	1.60	0		4.10
3 Washington State (9-1)	3.5	3.67	0.80	1	-0.80	8.77
4 Oklahoma (8-1)	5.25	4.00	0.40	1	-0.20	10.05
5 Texas (9-1)	3.75	5.83	0.92	1	-0.60	11.50

November 16, 2002

Georgia 24 AUBURN 21: Resourceful Bulldogs (10-1), used "70-X-Takeoff" on 4th down with 85 seconds left to rally from 21-10 deficit. Georgia QB David Greene passed for 232y and connected with new starting WR Michael Johnson (13/141y), who leapt high to snag winning pass. Auburn's last-ditch rally quickly entered Georgia territory on 25y catch by TE Robert Johnson, but sack by UGa LB Boss Bailey and 2 PENs averted another 1st down. Tigers (7-4) enjoyed 14-3 H lead on 233y to 63y O advantage as D held Greene to 29y passing, and Auburn TB Ronnie Brown rushed for 103y, including 53y scoring romp for 7-0 edge. Although Auburn QB Jason Campbell had 21y TD run in 2nd H, Tigers stalled on 6 straight 3-and-out series, leading to Georgia's winning TD. Victory ensured SEC East title for Georgia, its 1st since conf split into divisions in 1992.

Alabama 31 LOUISIANA STATE 0: Crimson Tide (9-2) steamrolled Bengals by rushing 300y and controlling clock nearly 35 mins. Game was scoreless until late 2nd Q when Alabama TB Santonio Beard (18/109y, 2 TDs) ran for 6y TD. LSU (7-3) soon pinned Tide on its 4YL with less than 2 minutes left in H. Bama actualized amazing drive by using 7 rushes—mostly draws—to devour 96y for 14-0 H lead on QB Tyler Watts' 2y keeper. Alabama TB Shaud Williams (131y rushing) had 50y on 2 runs in drive. Bama got 17 pts in 4th Q, but not before Tigers menaced at outset of 2nd H, thanks to 29y run on fake punt by LB Brodie James (15 tackles). But, Alabama DE Antwan Odom, who had blocked LSU FG try in 1st Q, made FUM REC of QB Marcus Randall to halt threat. Tide's spectacular D allowed it to replace LSU atop NCAA D rankings.

Ohio State 23 ILLINOIS 16 (OT): Struggling even on road, no. 2 Ohio State (12-0) found itself in FG battle. Illinois (4-7) K John Gockman tied game at 16-16 with 48y FG at end of regulation. Gockman, who had only 3 prior attempts during season, matched Buckeyes K Mike Nugent with 3 FGs each. Each team in Illibuck Trophy battle earned its regulation TD through air. Illini QB Jon Beutjer (27-45/305y) threw 19y scoring pass to WR Walter Young (10/144y) for 10-6 lead early in 2nd H, and Ohio QB Craig Krenzel found WR Michael Jenkins (6/147y) for 50y TD moments later. Jenkins admitted afterward that he lost ball in lights but "it fell right in my hands." It had been that kind of season for Buckeyes, who used their clutch D to stop Illini on downs for OT win. Ohio State scored in 1st extra session on TB Maurice Hall's 8y run and then held off Illini as 3rd down EZ pass to Young was ruled incomplete and 4th down pass was batted down. Buckeyes DE David Thompson had 9 tackles, 3.5 sacks, including 1 in OT.

Iowa 45 MINNESOTA 21: Hawkeyes (11-1) completed their 1st undefeated conf season in 80 years with rout of reeling Minnesota (7-4). Iowa QB Brad Banks fueled surprising Heisman Trophy candidacy with 2 TDs running and 2 TDs passing. TB Fred Russell rushed 17/194y, TD, and backup TB Jermelle Lewis added 19/101y, TD. Gophers were competitive early, matching Iowa's opening TD as WR Antoine Burns bulled past 3 defenders to score with short pass at end of 70y march. Russell took next play from scrimmage 53y to set up Lewis' 6y go-ahead TD at 14-7 in 1st Q. Iowa D then forced 1st of 6 Minnesota TOs as DT Howard Hodges recovered FUM after he sacked QB Asad Abdul-Khaliq (18-30/205y, TD, 2 INTs) on Gophers 15YL. Banks soon went 11y with option keeper for 21-7 lead. Iowa's lead allowed it to neutralize Minnesota's top Big 10 run game at only 32/80y. Abdul-Khaliq was picked off twice, sacked 3 times. Banks passed 9-17/100y, with TDs to WRs Maurice Brown and Clinton Solomon.

KANSAS STATE 49 Nebraska 13: Wildcats (9-2) visited upon Nebraska (7-5) what Cornhuskers had delivered to others for years: superior athletes systemized to pour on pts. K-State QB Ell Roberson had 2nd highest rushing total in school history on 29/228y, 91y alone on 1st Q romp, and tallied 3 TDs. TB Darren Sproles added 21/155y, 3 TDs for K-State, which won O battle 507y to 231y. Kansas State bumped

its lead to 21-3 in 2nd Q when DB Jerad Johnson emerged in crowded Cornhuskers EZ with loose ball after RB Marcus Patton blocked punt. Cornhuskers rallied in 3rd Q as QB Jammal Lord (9-25/134y) followed Roberson FUM with 35y TD run that cut deficit to 21-13. Sproles then lost FUM on own 24YL, but Nebraska failed to convert as K Josh Brown hit right upright with FG attempt. K-State ran away with TDs on all 3 of its 4th Q possessions. K-State's most lopsided series win locked in Cornhuskers' 1st losing conf mark since 1968, and 1st 5-loss record since 1961.

TEXAS TECH 42 Texas 38: Woe to teams facing QB Kliff Kingsbury when he was hot. Kingsbury threw 38-60/473y, 6 TDs against nation's 5th-ranked D. Win by Texas Tech (8-4) dashed Texas' slim national title chances. Longhorns (9-2) QB Chris Simms threw 24-37/345y, 4 TDs, but tossed costly INT to Red Raiders S Ryan Aycock late in 4th Q. Texas built 14-0 1st Q advantage as TB Cedric Benson and WR Roy Williams (8/117y) each scored TDs. Kingsbury threw 3 TDs in 2nd Q, including 62y hookup with WR Nehemiah Glover, to close 1st H tied at 21-21. Texas Tech took its initial lead in 3rd Q on WR Wes Welker's 2nd TD reception. Welker (14/169y) made 1 clutch play after another, racking up 247y all-purpose y. Welker made huge FUM REC in 2nd H. Game was tied at 28-28 entering 4th Q before Texas sandwiched FG and Simms' 84y TD pass to WR B.J. Johnson around Kingsbury's 5th TD pass. Moving past QB Todd Santos of San Diego State (1984-87) for all-time NCAA career passing y, Kingsbury then hit RB Taurean Henderson with 25y scoring pass to win game.

Arizona 52 CALIFORNIA 41: After 40 Wildcats players met with AU pres Peter Likins to complain about coach John Mackovic's abrasiveness, Arizona (4-7) broke 6-game loss streak with inspired effort. Wildcats QB Jason Johnson threw for school-record 492y and 4 TDs, hitting WR Bobby Wade for 11/222y. TE Justin Levasseur, who got Mackovic's apology for being "disgrace to his family," caught 2 TD passes in front of his family members. California (6-5) stayed close—it was tied 31-31 after 3 Qs—thanks to WR LaShaun Ward's 94y KO TD RET and 60y blocked FG TD RET by CB James Bethea. Bears QB Kyle Boller (22-45/298y, 2 TDs) was picked off twice by LB Ray Wells, including 42y TD RET. Arizona's pt total was larger than last 4 games combined.

USA Today Coaches November 18

1	Miami (Fla.) (61)	1525	14	Florida State	719
2	Ohio State	1455	15	Colorado State	627
3	Washington State	1372	16	Penn State	624
4	Iowa	1336	17	Colorado	561
5	Oklahoma	1287	18	Maryland	518
6	Georgia	1193	19	Pittsburgh	473
7	Southern California	1133	20	LSU	314
8	Notre Dame	1070	21	Boise State	308
9	Michigan	1001	22	TCU	260
10	Kansas State	998	23	Texas Tech	136
11	Texas	939	24	UCLA	90
12	Virginia Tech	755	25	Hawaii	86
13	Florida	741			

Bowl Championship Series Standings November 18

	Poll Avg.	Computer Avg.	Schedule Rankings	Losses Wins	Quality	Total
1 Miami (9-0)	1.0	1.33	1.36	0		3.69
2 Ohio State (12-0)	2.0	1.50	1.00	0	-0.80	3.70
3 Washington State (9-1)	3.0	4.33	1.08	1	-0.30	9.11
4 Oklahoma (9-1)	4.5	4.67	0.88	1	-0.30	10.75
5 Georgia (10-1)	6.0	5.00	0.36	1	-0.20	12.16

November 23, 2002

(Wed) West Virginia 21 VIRGINIA TECH 18: With upset of fading Virginia Tech (8-3), West Virginia (8-3) sealed its turn-around season after 3-8 record in 2001. Hokies lost 3rd straight game for 1st time since 1992, but got on scoreboard 1st when TB Lee Suggs (15/71y) scored on 28y run in 1st Q. Suggs' score gave him TDs in 24 consecutive games, new NCAA record that toppled Arkansas' Bill Burnett's 47 TDs in 23 games, set in 1970. Suggs had 50 TDs over his span. WVU came right back on next 2 series, driving 80 and 70y to TDs by TB Avon Cobourne and QB Rasheed Marshall. Midway in 2nd Q, WR Ernest Wilford blocked punt, but Tech had to settle for K Carter Warley's 34y FG. Taking over on its 14YL in 3rd Q, WVU moved with help of interference PEN to Tech 42YL. Behind great right side blocking by G Ken Sandor and T Tim Brown, TB Quincy Wilson (11/125y) raced untouched for 42y TD and 21-10 lead. Hokies had 2nd-and-goal at 1YL in 4th Q, but WVU D, led by LB Grant Wiley, stopped 3 straight smashes. Hokies trailed only 21-18 after conceded safety, but QB Bryan Randall (18-30/168y, TD, INT and 18/125y rushing) suffered WVU DB Brian King's late EZ INT.

(Th) MIAMI 28 Pittsburgh 21: Hot Pittsburgh (8-3) had its 9-game Big East win streak snapped, but gave it every effort against no. 1 Miami (10-0). Panthers took 7-0 lead after 23y INT RET by LB Brian Beinecke set them up for sharp 5y fade pass to WR Larry Fitzgerald. Hurricanes needed 69y TD sprint by TB Willis McGahee (19/159y, 2 TDs) to tie it 14-14 just before H. After weak 5-15/13y, INT passing in 1st Q, Miami QB Ken Dorsey (14-26/163y, TD, INT) hit 3-3/58y and 30y TD to WR Andre Johnson on opening series of 3rd Q. McGahee leapt to 4y score in 4th Q and 28-14 lead. Pitt had late chance to tie it but wide-open WR Yogi Roth couldn't reach high pass at GL.

VIRGINIA 48 Maryland 13: Unpredictable Virginia (8-4) was furious over early-week words of Maryland coach Ralph Friedgen. "They compared us to Duke!," said Cavs LB Merrill Robertson, "That really ticked us off!" Virginia QB Matt Schaub (23-27/249y, 3 TDs) became UVa single season pass y leader (2751y with 26 TDs). Cavaliers TB Wali Lundy (19/84y, TD) caught 2 TD passes, and WR Billy McMullen threw 37y TD early in 3rd Q. Terps had opened game with 80y TD drive ended by 11y TD pass by QB

Scott McBrien (13-25/196y, TD, 2 INTs). Maryland threatened with 76y move on next series, but Virginia DE Chris Canty blocked K Nick Novak's FG try. Cavaliers scored next on next 4 custodies for 20-7 H margin and went 76 and 68y to TDs to begin 3rd Q.

NORTH CAROLINA STATE 17 Florida State 7: Despite 3-game slide, NC State (10-3) had 1 last great game in it to become school's 1st-ever team with 10 wins. But, when Virginia burned Maryland, Florida State (8-4) clinched its 10th ACC title in 11 years. Seminoles LB Michael Boulware made 1-handed pickup of Wolfpack's fumbled fake FG try and cruised 84y to TD for 7-3 lead in 2nd Q. Seminoles gained only 177y as all-out Wolfpack D threw blitzes from every angle. NC State TB T.A. McLendon (27/114y) scored vital TD late in 2nd Q for 10-7 H edge. Wolfpack earned 2 safeties in 4th Q on EZ holding call against Florida State and LB Manny Lawson's punt block through EZ.

Auburn 17 ALABAMA 7: Auburn (8-4) once complained that "neutral" site in Birmingham favored Alabama (9-3), so series was turned into home-and-home affair. Oddly enough, Tigers now owned wins in all 4 of games played in Tuscaloosa. Crimson Tide drove from its 20YL to Auburn 32YL on its 1st series, but RB Shaud Williams' 4th down catch was stopped short and OB by DB Junior Rosegreen. Auburn sent 4th-string TB Tre Smith (25/126y), in lineup due to injuries, galloping 51y to set up 14y TD catch by TE Robert Johnson from QB Jason Campbell (10-18/169y, 2 TDs, INT). DB Roderick Hood's 36y punt RET launched Tigers on 50y TD trip capped by another Campbell-to-Johnson TD pass. Auburn D allowed little from vaunted Tide run attack: over 34/111y and RB Santonio Beard's 1y TD run after DB Waine Bacon's INT at Auburn 46YL.

PENN STATE 61 Michigan State 7: After setting Nittany Lions single game rushing mark with 327y in previous week's win against Indiana, Penn State (9-3) sr TB Larry Johnson (19/279y, 4 TDs) needed 264y to become 9th runner in NCAA history to gain more than 2,000y. Johnson required only 28 mins to reach 2,015y. He scored on runs of 11, 78, 11, and threshold-breaking 38y. Penn State led 48-0 at H with TD run and pass from QB Zack Mills (5-10/94y, TD) and 81y punt TD RET and 41y pass TD reception by WR Bryant Johnson. Dispirited Michigan State (4-8) scored only on its opening series of 3rd Q as TB Jaren Hayes (23/113y) got 9y TD. Spartans gained 388y.

OHIO STATE 14 Michigan 9: Another classic between ancient rivals unfolded before record crowd of 105,539 fans huddled in "Horseshoe." Sparking Ohio State (13-0) was return of frosh TB Maurice Clarett, who shook off recurring shoulder injury to rush 20/119y and score on 2y sweep in 1st Q TD to put Buckeyes ahead 7-3. UM (9-3) controlled 1st H, never punted, but had to settle for 3 FGs by K Adam Finley. UM closed 2nd Q by consuming 8:24 on 19-play drive. Michigan took Finley's 22y FG because interference in EZ by WR Braylon Edwards (10/107y) wiped out his TD catch. Trailing 9-7, Buckeyes went ahead, traveling 57y as QB Craig Krenzel (10-14/124y) clicked on 4th down sneak at UM 32YL and pitched 26y toss to Clarett on newly-designed play. Ohio sub TB Maurice Hall took option-play pitchout for 3y TD around RE. Wolverines pressed twice more: QB John Navarre (23-46/247y, INT), who dinked short but effective passes all day, was hit by DT Darrion Scott and fumbled when hit by DE Will Smith at Ohio 30YL. Michigan came back to Bucks 24YL, but Navarre threw long in EZ for Edwards, and Ohio DB Will Allen soon stepped in front of pass at GL for INT on game's last play.

OKLAHOMA 60 Texas Tech 15: Texas Tech (8-5), America's upset-maker, couldn't manage another against as dominant D of Oklahoma (10-1) chased Red Raiders QB Kliff Kingsbury all game. "That's the best defense I've seen in four years," said Kingsbury, who threw for season-low 187y on 15-35. Sooners D contributed 2 safeties, had 2 INTs, and sacked Kingsbury 6 times. Tech entered Sooners territory only once in 1st H, outgained 263y to 64y. Oklahoma RB Quentin Griffin (31/207y) authored 62y TD run for 14-0 lead in 1st Q. By time Griffin scored his 3rd TD, Sooners led 46-0 in 3rd Q. Raiders DB Vincent Meeks scored on 98y KO RET, and Kingbury threw late TD pass.

Southern California 52 UCLA 21: Red-hot Southern California (9-2) won its 4th in row over crosstown rival UCLA (7-4). Trojans QB Carson Palmer, playing with abundant confidence under same O coordinator (Norm Chow) for 2nd straight year, passed 19-32/254y, 4 TDs. It was over almost before it began as Bruins WR Tab Perry lost FUM after his 30y RET of opening KO. Palmer arched 34y TD pass to WR Kareem Kelly on next play. USC went up 21-0 in 1st Q as it added TDs on its next 2 series: another Palmer TD pass and 1y run by TB Justin Fargas (16/41y). UCLA drove 89y to FB Manuel White's 7y TD run early in 2nd Q, but then allowed 31 straight pts. Bungling Bruins lost 4 FUMs, threw INT, suffered 5 sacks, and flew snap over P's head.

Washington 29 WASHINGTON STATE 26 (3 OT): Perhaps key moment of game came in 4th Q when Washington State (9-2) QB Jason Gesser (14-24/226y, TD, INT) was knocked from game with leg injury. To that moment, Cougars led 17-10 and went to 20-10 with 4:41 to play. "I don't get hurt, we would have won that game," said veteran QB. Indeed, insertion of sub QB Matt Kegel had State jumping on false-start PENs as it adjusted to his signal-calling. Next Washington (7-5) series went for TD that narrowed gap to 20-17 and was keyed by 4 completions by QB Cody Pickett (35-57/368y, TD), including 48y to WR Reggie Williams (12/169y). Cougars would have won by killing some of last 3:13, but Huskies DB Nate Robinson made INT of Kegel on 2nd play at Wazzu 35YL. K John Anderson, who had misfired on 4 earlier FG tries, nailed 27y FG to send it to OT. Anderson's 3rd OT FG provided 29-26 lead, and, soon, debatable play, forced by Huskies DL Kai Ellis, was ruled FUM and Husky REC to end game.

1	Miami (Fla.) (60)	1524	14	Michigan	741	
2	Ohio State (1)	1462	15	Colorado	698	
3	Iowa	1377	16	Boise State	499	
4	Oklahoma	1346	17	LSU	468	
5	Georgia	1253	18	Pittsburgh	406	
6	Southern California	1195	19	Virginia Tech	370	
7	Notre Dame	1146	20	North Carolina State	354	
8	Kansas State	1089	21	West Virginia	293	
9	Washington State	1025	22	Florida State	272	
10	Texas	991	23	Maryland	175	
11	Florida	865	24	Hawaii	157	
12	Penn State	784	25	Auburn	147	
13	Colorado State	760				

Bowl Championship Series Standings November 25

	Poll Avg.	Computer Avg.	Schedule Ranking	Losses Wins	Quality	Total
1 Miami (10-0)	1.0	1.17	0.72	0		2.89
2 Ohio State (13-0)	2.0	1.67	0.84	0	-0.30	4.21
3 Oklahoma (10-1)	3.5	3.83	0.96	1	-0.20	9.09
4 Georgia (10-1)	5.0	3.67	0.40	1		10.07
5 Iowa (11-1)	3.5	6.33	1.60	1		12.43

November 28-30, 2002

(Th'g) Mississippi 24 MISSISSIPPI STATE 12: Ole Miss (6-6) needed to win to become bowl-eligible and snap 5-game losing streak. Mississippi State (3-9) dominated early but held only 3-0 lead as Bulldogs lost Egg Bowl despite 419y to 297y advantage: QB Kevin Fant threw for 340y but was picked off 3 times. Rebels QB Eli Manning (16-29/207y, 2 TDs, 2 INTs) and WR Chris Collins (4/130y) connected twice for TDs. Winning TD was set up by S Von Hutchins' INT on Rebel 14YL, 3 plays before Manning completed 77y scoring pass to Collins midway through 3rd Q. Bulldogs pulled within 17-12 on 22y TD reception by WR Ray Ray Bivines (6/115y), but could get no closer. For State, rumors had it as coach Jackie Sherrill's last game, but instead he fired both O and D coordinators in wake of Bulldogs dropping all their SEC tilts in 2002.

(Fri) ARKANSAS 21 Louisiana State 20: Razorbacks (9-3) stunned LSU (8-4) with last-second 31y TD pass from QB Matt Jones to WR DeCori Birmingham to wrest SEC West crown from Bayou Bengals. Celebration PEN forced K David Carlton to kick x-pt from 35y out, which he barely made to clinch win. Arkansas had 34 seconds to move 81y; Jones, who was only 2-13 prior to drive, completed 50y pass to WR Richard Smith on 1st play, then found Birmingham in back of EZ. QB Marcus Randall threw for 203y to lead LSU, completing 67y TD pass to WR Skyler Green to open scoring and scrambling for 5y TD in 3rd Q, which provided Tigers with 17-7 lead. TB Fred Talley (15/118y) had been Hogs' best weapon until fateful final drive, scoring on 56y run.

(Fri) TEXAS 50 Texas A&M 20: Texas (10-2) QB Chris Simms threw for 278y and 3 TDs to win his 3rd straight over A&M, 1st Longhorns QB to do so since Bobby Layne won 4 straight in 1940s. Playing 4 days after death of frosh DT Brandon Fails and amidst rumors of coach R.C. Slocum's firing, Texas A&M (6-6) turned ball over on each of its 1st 3 possessions. Texas (10-2) converted each TO into FG by K Dusty Mangum to lead 9-0. Aggies QB Dustin Long threw 12y TD pass to WR Terrence Thomas to pull within 9-7. Simms then threw short passes to WRs B.J. Johnson and Roy Williams (6/149y), that each speedster converted into long scoring pass play for 23-7 lead. Aggies scored 1st in 2nd H to creep within 23-14 before Texas exploded for 27 straight pts to bury rivals and usher out Slocum after 14 years coaching in College Station.

West Virginia 24 PITTSBURGH 17: Mountaineers (9-3) secured 2nd place in Big East with Backyard Brawl win. Tied 10-10 in 2nd Q, West Virginia converted TOs on 3 straight Panthers (8-4) possessions and led 24-10. Eventual winning score was 79y TD pass to WR Phil Braxton from QB Rasheed Marshall, who also ran for TD and caught 25y pass to set up another. After Pitt QB Rod Rutherford threw 2 INTs and lost 2 FUMs, pulled Panthers within 24-17 on 25y TD pass to WR Larry Fitzgerald (11/159y, 2 TDs), Pittsburgh drove to West Virginia 11YL at game's end. Sack and 3 incomplete passes ended threat. Heinz Field crowd of 66,731 was 2nd largest in Panthers history, surpassed only by 1938 Fordham game that drew overflow 68,918 to old Pitt Stadium.

GEORGIA 51 Georgia Tech 7: Bulldogs (11-1) quickly extinguished Tech upset hopes, building 34-0 H lead enroute to scoring their most points to-date on in-state rivals. QB David Greene completed 10-14/205y and TB Musa Smith added 121y on ground as Bulldogs gained 552y and 24 1st downs. Georgia FB J.T. Wall chipped in with 2 TD runs. Yellow Jackets (7-5) finally doused shutout in 4th Q on QB A.J. Suggs' 4y TD pass to WR Jonathan Smith. Bulldogs DL David Jacobs, whose playing days were ended by stroke in 2001, sparked teammates by returning for pre-game roll call for sr players.

FLORIDA STATE 31 Florida 14: Florida State QB Chris Rix returned victoriously to lineup to replace QB Adrian McPherson, who was kicked off team earlier in week prior to being arrested on felony grand theft charges. Rix threw 2 TDs to WR Anquan Boldin as Seminoles (9-4) ended roller-coaster regular season on high note. Frosh TB Leon Washington rushed for 134y, and Rix added 83y on ground as Florida State enjoyed 225y to 83y rushing advantage. Gators (8-4), whose non-winning streak at Tallahassee now went back to 1986, were led by QB Rex Grossman's 303y passing. With game still in reach at 17-6 early in 3rd Q, Grossman threw pass that TE Aaron Walker tipped into hungry hands of FSU LB Kendyll Pope, whose RET went 13y to EZ for 24-6 lead. Undaunted, Grossman led 84y drive to pull within 24-14 before Rix answered with 19y TD pass to Boldin (8/101y) to close scoring. Rough game forced officials to stop play midway through 2nd Q to warn both teams about cheap shots.

OKLAHOMA STATE 39 Oklahoma 28: Perhaps Texas should have recruited soph QB Josh Fields (18-27/357y, 4 TDs), who ran his record against Oklahoma (10-2) to 2-0 with 2nd straight upset win. Fields and unstoppable WR Rashaun Woods (12/226y) teamed up for 3 TDs as Cowboys (7-5) beat Nebraska and Oklahoma in same season for 1st time ever. Early on, Cowboy TB Seymore Shaw raced 30y to 1YL, and WR teammate John Lewis alertly scooped up FUM and knifed into EZ. Cowboys pushed lead to 28-6 by H as Woods caught TDs of 41, 60, and 13y. QB Nate Hybl (25-38/211y) rallied Sooners with 3 late TD passes. All 6 Cowboy scoring drives began in own territory, so win was no fluke.

SOUTHERN CALIFORNIA 44 Notre Dame 13: Trojans (10-2) crushed longtime rival, making sound case for at-large BCS spot. QB Carson Palmer made equally strong Heisman bid as he completed 32-46/425y—most pass y ever allowed by ND—in leading O that compiled 610y, another record for ND opponent. Notre Dame (10-2) meanwhile was held to paltry 109y and 4 1st downs; Fighting Irish scored their sole TD on blocked punt by LB Carlos Pierre-Antoine. It gave Irish unlikely 13-10 lead late in 1st H, but it was wiped out in 62 secs by Trojans' 75y drive, capped by 2nd TD reception by frosh WR Mike Williams (10/169y). TB Justin Fargas led Troy's ground attack with 120y in Troy's 1st sweep of UCLA and Notre Dame in 21 years.

1	Miami (Fla.) (60)	1524	14	Virginia Tech	586	
2	Ohio State (1)	1463	15	Boise State	584	
3	Iowa	1388	16	West Virginia	555	
4	Georgia	1335	17	North Carolina State	491	
5	Southern California	1284	18	Florida State	490	
6	Kansas State	1194	19	Maryland	415	
7	Washington State	1113	20	Florida	367	
8	Texas	1059	21	Colorado State	316	
9	Oklahoma	1014	22	Arkansas	255	
10	Penn State	901	23	Auburn	228	
11	Michigan	885	24	Pittsburgh	194	
12	Colorado	852	25	LSU	125	
13	Notre Dame	851				

Bowl Championship Series Rankings December 2

	Poll Avg.	Computer Avg.	Schedule Ranking	Losses Wins	Quality	Total
1 Miami (11-0)	1.0	1.33	1.20	0		3.53
2 Ohio State (13-0)	2.0	1.67	0.84	0	-0.50	4.01
3 Georgia (11-1)	4.0	3.67	0.36	1		9.03
4 Southern Calif. (10-2)	5.0	3.00	0.04	2	-0.20	9.84
5 Iowa (11-1)	3.0	4.67	1.88	1		10.55

December 7, 2002

Navy 58 Army 12 (E. Rutherford, NJ): Adding his name to roll call of heroes, Navy QB Craig Candeto rushed for 6 TDs and threw for 7th in leading rout in 2nd biggest margin in series history. Middies (2-10) gained 508y and scored TDs on 1st 8 tries. Candeto, whose homer beat Army in previous spring's baseball game, rushed for 103y and hit 4-5/87y passing. Black Knights (1-11) scored sole TD in 4th Q as QB Reggie Nevels threw 36y TD pass to WR Aaron Alexander.

MIAMI 56 Virginia Tech 45: Thanks to late Virginia Tech (9-4) rally, Canes (12-0) needed each of TB Willis McGahee's 6 TD runs to finish undefeated. McGahee rushed 39/205y, and QB Ken Dorsey threw for 300y and 2 TDs. Foolish throw-back pass from TB Jarrett Payton for Dorsey near Tech EZ failed miserably as Hokies S Willie Pile went on 96y INT TD RET. Play ignited 18-pt Hokies surge to 49-37 at outset of 4th Q. Miami clinched it as McGahee carried 9 times/31y, and Dorsey hit TE Kellen Winslow, Jr. for 11y TD. Hokies QB Bryan Randall gained 297y in defeat, while TB Lee Suggs scored 3 TDs in stretching record streak to 26 games with TD. Win was 34th straight for Miami to tie Pennsylvania (1894-96) for 6th place on all-time list.

Georgia 30 Arkansas 3 (Atlanta): In SEC title game, dominant Georgia (12-1) captured its 1st crown since 1982, scoring 17 points before Arkansas earned positive y. Bulldogs CB Decory Bryant started onslaught early with blocked punt and recovered it on Porker 2YL. Bulldog TB Musa Smith (19/106y) rushed for TD on next play for 7-0 lead. Smith scored untouched on 17y run to close next series, while K Billy Bennett ended 3 1st H drives with FGs for 23-0 H lead. Arkansas (9-4) managed only 65y rushing—178y less than its conf-best avg—and 74y passing. Hog K David Carlton's 27y FG late in 3rd Q prevented shutout. Georgia totaled 381y and enjoyed 25 to 12 1st down advantage

MARSHALL 49 Toledo 45: In MAC Championship, QB Byron Leftwich hit WR Darius Watts (9/135y, 2 TDs) in stride for 40y TD pass with 49 seconds left as Marshall regained MAC title. Leftwich (32-42/402y, 4 TDs, 1 INT) opened scoring with 1st of 2 TD passes to WR Denero Marriott as Herd built 28-17 1st H lead. Marshall D scored team's 4th TD when LB Charlie Tynes forced FUM TD RET with sack of Toledo QB Brian Jones. Toledo RB Trinity Dawson (130y, 4 TDs) scored twice in 3rd Q as Rockets grabbed 32-28 lead. Teams traded TDs and lead rest of game with Toledo's final score, 1y keeper by Jones, coming with 3:35 left. Trailing by 3 pts, Herd went 73y for winning TD as Leftwich completed 4-5. Marshall coach Bob Pruett ran his home mark to 49-1.

Oklahoma 29 Colorado 7 (Houston): With Colorado (9-4) TB Chris Brown out of Big 12 Championship game with injury, Oklahoma (11-2) RB Quentin Griffin had stage to himself and he shone. Griffin, who finished with 2nd best single-season rushing total (1,740y) in Sooner history behind HB Billy Sims (1,762y) in '78, rushed for 188y and 2 TDs, scoring on runs of 36y and 27y after Buffs pulled within 6 at 13-7 on 80y PR TD by blistering-fast WR Jeremy Bloom. Sooner QB Nate Hybl threw 2 TD passes in 1st H that featured shutout by OU D with help from Colorado K Pat Brougham who missed 1 FG in each of 1st 3 Qs. Although Colorado TB Brian Calhoun rushed for 122y in relief of Brown, Buffs managed only 193y while surrendering 401y.

Washington State 48 UCLA 27: Needing win to take Pac 10 title, Washington State (10-2) turned to gimpy QB Jason Gesser. With braces on sprained right knee and ankle, Gesser threw 2 TDs and provided plenty of inspiration. Cougars had mistakes to overcome before securing win, surrendering INT RET TD by Bruin S Ben Emanuel, botching fake FG, setting up Bruin (7-5) TD with unwanted onside kick and having FG blocked. Onside-KO followed 80y TD run by TB Jermaine Green that put WSU up 31-14 with 48 seconds remaining in 1st H. Bruin QB Drew Olson made Cougars pay with 39y scoring pass to WR Junior Taylor. Cougar D surrendered only 1 TD rest of the way, matching that with S Erik Coleman's 4th Q 25y INT RET TD. Not only did each team have safeties score TDs, but UCLA WR Jon Dubravac and Cougar WR Collin Henderson each threw TDs in wild contest.

USA Today Coaches December 9

1	Miami (Fla.) (61)	1525	14	Colorado	641
2	Ohio State	1463	15	Boise State	588
3	Iowa	1381	16	Florida State	562
4	Georgia	1337	17	North Carolina State	555
5	Southern California	1283	18	Maryland	470
6	Kansas State	1187	19	Virginia Tech	457
7	Washington State	1141	20	Florida	364
8	Oklahoma	1088	21	Colorado State	337
9	Texas	1074	22	Auburn	263
10	Penn State	921	23	Pittsburgh	204
11	Michigan	917	24	Marshall	140
12	Notre Dame	844	25	LSU	114
13	West Virginia	651			

Bowl Championship Rankings December 8, 2002

	Poll Avg.	Computer Avg.	Schedule Ranking	Losses Wins	Quality	Total
1 Miami (12-0)	1.0	1.17	0.76	0		2.93
2 Ohio State (13-0)	2.0	1.67	0.80	0	-0.50	3.97
3 Georgia (12-1)	4.0	3.17	0.20	1		8.37
4 Southern Calif. (10-2)	5.0	3.67	0.04	2	-0.20	10.51
5 Iowa (11-1)	3.0	4.83	1.96	1		10.79

2002 Conference Standings

Big East

Miami	7-0
West Virginia	6-1
Pittsburgh	5-2
Virginia Tech	3-4
Boston College	3-4
Syracuse	2-5
Temple	2-5
Rutgers	0-7

Atlantic Coast

Florida State	7-1
Maryland	6-2
Virginia	6-2
North Carolina State	5-3
Georgia Tech	4-4
Clemson	4-4
Wake Forest	3-5
North Carolina	1-7
Duke	0-8

Southeastern

EAST	
Georgia	7-1
Florida	6-2
Tennessee	5-3
Kentucky	3-5
South Carolina	3-5
Vanderbilt	0-8
WEST	
Alabama (ineligible)	6-2
Arkansas	5-3
Louisiana State	5-3
Auburn	5-3
Mississippi	3-5
Mississippi State	0-8

Conference USA

Texas Christian	6-2
Cincinnati	6-2
Louisville	5-3
Southern Mississippi	5-3
East Carolina	4-4
Tulane	4-4
Alabama-Birmingham	4-4
Houston	3-5
Memphis	2-6
Army	1-7

Big Ten

Ohio State	8-0
Iowa	8-0
Michigan	6-2
Penn State	5-3
Purdue	4-4
Illinois	4-4
Minnesota	3-5
Wisconsin	2-6
Michigan State	2-6
Northwestern	1-7
Indiana	1-7

Mid-American

EAST	
Marshall	7-1
Central Florida	6-2
Miami (Ohio)	5-3
Ohio	4-4
Akron	3-5
Kent State	1-7
Buffalo	0-8
WEST	
Toledo	7-1
Northern Illinois	7-1
Bowling Green	6-2
Ball State	4-4
Western Michigan	3-5
Central Michigan	2-6
Eastern Michigan	1-7

Big 12

NORTH	
Colorado	7-1
Kansas State	6-2
Iowa State	4-4
Nebraska	3-5
Missouri	2-6
Kansas	0-8
SOUTH	
Oklahoma	6-2
Texas	6-2
Texas Tech	5-3
Oklahoma State	5-3
Texas A&M	3-5
Baylor	1-7

Western Athletic

Boise State	8-0
Hawaii	7-1
Fresno State	6-2
San Jose State	4-4
Nevada	4-4
Louisiana Tech	3-5
Rice	3-5
Southern Methodist	3-5
Texas-El Paso	1-7
Tulsa	1-7

Mountain West

Colorado State	6-1
New Mexico	5-2
Air Force	4-3
San Diego State	4-3
Utah	3-4
Nevada-Las Vegas	3-4
Brigham Young	2-5
Wyoming	1-6

Pacific-10

Washington State	7-1
Southern California	7-1
Arizona State	5-3
Oregon State	5-3
UCLA	4-4
California	4-4
Washington	4-4
Oregon	3-5
Arizona	1-7
Stanford	1-7

2002 Major Bowl Games

Las Vegas Bowl (Dec. 25): UCLA 27 New Mexico 13

Question prior to game was: How motivated could UCLA (8-5) be, playing without deposed head coach Bob Toledo? Sure enough, UCLA was lethargic on O, but tough on D in 1st H. Asst coaching staff developed game plan, and former asst Ed Kezirian led Bruins in his only head coaching assignment. Trailing 3-0 on K Nate Fikse's 49y FG for UCLA, New Mexico (7-7) DB Desmar Black stepped in front of out-route pass by Bruins QB Drew Olson and raced 55y for INT TD RET. Then, Lobos made history: K Katie Hnida, her blonde pony-tail hair partially obscuring her jersey name swatch, became 1st woman to play in Div. 1-A bowl game by placekicking x-pt. Unfortunately, Hnida's note in history turned awry; Bruins blocked her low kick in middle of line. Tied 6-6 early in 3rd Q, UCLA WR Craig Bragg took punt and was hit hard after short RET, but bounced outside and streamed downfield for 74y TD RET. On 2nd snap of 4th Q, Lobos QB Casey Kelly (18-32/237y, TD, INT) hurried pass toward TE Zach Cresap in left flat, but Cresap hadn't turned his head. Pass bounced off back of his left shoulder pad into arms of Bruins DB Jarrad Page, who returned 29y for TD. New Mexico fumbled on 1st play after KO as WR Joe Manning (late 4th Q TD catch) lost ball to UCLA LB Brandon Chillar at Lobos 31YL. TB Tyler Ebell's TD run gave Bruins 27-6 lead.

Insight.com Bowl (Dec. 27): Pittsburgh 38 Oregon State 13

Big receiving guns were fired early. Pittsburgh (9-4) frosh WR Larry Fitzgerald made marvelous diving, fingertip catch just over GL to crown opening drive for 7-0 lead. Oregon State (8-5) WR James Newson (10/165y) went high for catch, and, when Panthers DB Torrie Cox missed tackle, partly because of 3-man collision, Newson got away for 65y TD despite officials failing to see that his elbow touch ground. Beavers took 10-7 lead on K Kyle Ylinimi's 9th straight FG, good for 49y. OSU DL Bill Swancutt appeared to scuttle Pitt's late 2nd Q drive when he sacked QB Rod Rutherford (13-26/183y, TD) for 10y loss, but Panthers K David Abdul tallied tying 47y FG on last play of 1st H. Flea-flicker pass went awry for Beavers as Pitt DB Tez Morris made 35y INT RET, and Fitzgerald made sliding 22y catch at Oregon State 1YL. Rutherford quickly scored on keeper behind G Bryan Anderson. DB Shawn Robinson swung right to slip past wave of Beavers tacklers on 65y punt TD RET, and Pitt led 24-10. In 4th Q, State tried 4th-and-5 at midfield, only to receive 5y PEN. Still, coach Dennis Erickson persevered and 4th-and-10 was stopped. TB Brandon Miree (20/111y) soon scored on burst up middle from 7YL, and Panthers locked it up.

Independence Bowl (Dec. 27): Mississippi 27 Nebraska 23

Facing potential of its 1st non-winning season since 1961, Nebraska (7-7) sought to overpower Mississippi (7-6) with its traditional option run attack. It worked in 1st H as Huskers rushed for 207y. QB Jammal Lord (17/83y rushing) raced 47y on keeper to set up K Josh Brown's FG and hit TE Matt Herian with 41y TD pass off play action early in 2nd Q for 10-0 Nebraska lead. QB Eli Manning (25-44/313y, TD) put Rebels on scoreboard with 11y post-pattern TD pass to WR Kerry Johnson in 2nd Q. Stellar RET-specialist DB DeJuan Groce answered for Huskers with 60y punt TD RET, using blocks of DB Jerrell Pippens, DB Kevin Guse, and WR Kiffin Wigert. Manning hit 5 passes on clock-beating 88y drive just before H, so Ole Miss trailed only 17-14, even though it had −9y rushing. Rebels made significant 2nd H adjustment on D, while making considerable substitutions on D-line to keep fresh top DLs Jesse Mitchell and Josh Cooper. Huskers gained only 97y in 2nd H, and game got away while ahead 20-17 in middle of 3rd Q. On 4th down at own 35YL, Huskers inexplicably tried fake-punt: incomplete lob pass by FB Judd Davies gave Ole Miss chance for FB Toward Sanford's 2nd TD and its 1st lead at 24-20. Rebs made important stop after Huskers had 1st down at 10YL. Lord (7-16/93y, TD, 2 INTs) slipped on 2nd down and lost 4y, then threw incomplete on 3rd down. Nebraska settled for Brown's 3rd FG and never saw Ole Miss territory again.

Holiday Bowl (Dec. 27): Kansas State 34 Arizona State 27

Big underdog Arizona State (8-6) put up terrific fight, taking D control in 0-0 1st Q as collegiate sack leader, DE Terrell Suggs, twice spilled dynamic Kansas State (11-2) QB

Ell Roberson. Sun Devils built 20-14 lead entering 4th Q behind QB Andrew Walter, who threw for 293y, and D led by Suggs and LB Mason Unck (15 tackles). Roberson, held in check for 3 Qs, led Wildcats (11-2) to 20 late pts to cap another exciting contest in San Diego. Roberson rushed for 2 TDs before throwing 10y scoring pass to WR Derrick Evans to win game with 1:15 left. Evans' TD gave Wildcats their 1st lead of game. With 20-20 tie in 4th Q, Sun Devils regained lead on 10y pass from Walter to TB Mike Williams. But, Roberson wiped that out with brilliant 80y drive to his 3rd rushing TD, followed by 59y drive to winning TD. Cats' winning trip began with 34y punt RET by Thorpe Award-winning CB Terence Newman, who earlier went triple duty, catching 3/47y in his O debut. Newman finished with 10 tackles and 149y all-purpose.

Continental Tire Bowl (Dec. 28): Virginia 48 West Virginia 22

Teams traveled up and down gridiron at inaugural bowl at Charlotte's sold out Ericsson Stadium, including 6y TD run by West Virginia (9-4) TB Avon Cobourne (25/117y, 2 TDs) which gave Mountaineers 10-7 lead after 3 series of 1st Q. QB Marques Hagans roared up middle on 69y punt TD RET at midway in 2nd Q, providing turning point for Virginia (9-5) at 21-10. Cavs LB Darryl Blackstock's INT set up MVP TB Wali Lundy (22/127y, 2 TDs rushing and 5/76y, 2 TDs receiving) for 2nd of his 4 TDs, which came with 19 secs to go before H. Late in 3rd Q, WVU QB Rasheed Marshall (12-18/215y, INT) capped 80y drive with short TD run to trim deficit to 38-16, but K Todd James' conv was blocked to all but eliminate any comeback chance. West Virginia coach Rich Rodriguez called result "…bad way to end a good year." But, it was Rodriguez who probably inspired young Virginia players in pre-game buildup when he carped about his 2nd-place Big East team deserving much more prestigious New Year's Day bowl date.

Alamo Bowl (Dec. 28): Wisconsin 31 Colorado 28 (OT)

Big plays ruled day as Badgers (8-6) rallied for late TD and won in OT on K Mike Allen's 37y FG after Colorado (9-5) missed FG on its extra-time possession. TOs, 7 total, were catalystic in setting up most of game's scoring. Wisconsin went in early hole as 1st possession ended suddenly with INT that CB Donald Strickland returned 91y for 7-0 Colorado lead. Wisconsin then converted 3 INTs in its favor to forge 21-14 H lead on 4y TD run by TB Anthony Davis (25/99y) and 2 TD passes by QB Brooks Bollinger (163y passing and 82y rushing). Those 3 scoring drives averaged only 31y. Badgers DB Jim Leonhard, who made 1 of those INTs, returned favor to Colorado by losing FUM on punt RET that Buffs converted into TB Chris Brown's 4y TD. On 1st play from scrimmage following Brown TD, Davis lost FUM, which CU QB Zac Colvin turned into his 2nd TD pass, 11y effort to WR D.J. Hackett, for 28-21 lead. QB Bollinger needed 90 secs to lead wild 80y drive, featuring 2 conversions of 4th down, to tying 1y TD he ran in with 51 seconds remaining. Hampered by concussion suffered by Brown, who left after rushing 97y, Buffs had difficulty running out clock with 7-pt advantage. Badgers now sported 7-1 bowl record under coach Barry Alvarez.

Music City Bowl (Dec. 30): Minnesota 29 Arkansas 14

With wealth of O talent, Golden Gophers (8-5) outclassed Arkansas to post 1st bowl victory since 1985. Run-happy Hogs (9-5) surprised early by throwing for most of 74y drive to open scoring on 2y pass from QB Matt Jones to WR George Wilson (8/111y). Highlights were largely over for Arkansas as Minnesota reeled off 29 straight pts. Game became showcase for balanced Gophers attack and superb sr K Dan Nystrom, who kicked 5 FGs to boost career total to Big 10 record 69 FGs. Not relying totally on Nystrom, Minnesota QB Asad Abdul-Khaliq led 2nd H TD drives with oft-injured TE Ben Utecht catching 19y scoring pass and TB Thomas Tapeh (18/100y) knifing 33y through and around Hogs for another score. With Abdul-Khaliq throwing for 216y, Minnesota outgained Razorbacks 434y to 288y. Arkansas rated 11th in nation in both rushing and TO margin, but was soundly beaten in both as Minny rushed for 168y to 80y edge and forced 4 TOs and lost none. Gophers CB Michael Lehan had 2 INTs.

Seattle Bowl (Dec. 30): Wake Forest 38 Oregon 17

Nine years and 364 days earlier Demon Deacons rallied to beat Ducks in 1992's Independence Bowl in only meeting of schools. In new Seahawks Stadium, Wake Forest (7-6), ACC's 7th best team, stunned Oregon (7-6) again. Decidedly run-oriented, Wake ran and passed on 2 long drives in 1st Q. FB Ovie Mulghelli scored short TD after opening KO netted 65y drive, but was stopped on 4th down at 1YL at end of 72y drive. Ducks' weakness against long passes (most TD passes permitted in Div 1-A) was revealed again in 2nd Q on Deacons 57y post-pattern TD bomb from QB James MacPherson (9-16/241y, 2 TDs) to WR Jason Anderson. Oregon coach Mike Bellotti tapped frosh QB Kellen Clemens (19-31/161y, TD) when starter Jason Fife opened 1-7 passing. Fiery Clemens zipped 7y TD rocket to WR Samie Parker in last 30 secs of 1st H, but Wake still led 21-10. Deacons opened 2nd H with K Matt Wisnosky's 43y FG, but Oregon WR Kennan Howry personally set up TD that pulled Ducks within 24-17 midway in 3rd Q. Howry made 42y punt RET followed by 36y reverse run. But, Wake soon replied with long stop-and-go catch by Anderson for TD that lifted count to 31-17.

Sun Bowl (Dec. 31): Purdue 34 Washington 24

Washington Huskies (7-6) took advantage of myriad of Purdue (7-6) miscues in 1st Q to lead 17-0. Boilermakers P Brent Slaton allowed snap to slip away to set up Washington WR Patrick Reddick's 7y TD catch as he beat LB coverage. Purdue QB Kyle Orton (25-37/283y, 2 TDs) bobbled Shotgun snap, and Huskies LB Marquis Cooper barreled 25y for TD. RB Joey Harris (23/93y, TD) made 11y gain 7 mins into 2nd Q to finally pull Purdue up to 0y rushing, and with help of UW personal foul PENs, Boilers scored on Orton's 7y pass to WR Taylor Stubblefield with 5:09 to go in 2nd Q. After 3-and-out for Huskies, Purdue scored again on WR Ray Williams' EZ REC of FUM by RB Brandon Jones, who had caught Orton's pass. After WR Anthony Chambers returned 2nd H KO 51y, Boilers K Berin Lacevic tied it 17-17 with chip-shot FG. Washington's O was now going nowhere, and Purdue added 2 quick TDs late in 3rd Q for 31-17 lead. Harris burst through on trap as all 3 Huskies LBs adjusted in pre-snap to wrong side, and LB Gilbert Gardner stole ball as UW QB Cody Pickett (25-54/272y, 2 TDs, INT) cocked to throw. After Lacevic's 2nd FG made it 34-17, Huskies struck on Reddick's slant-in TD catch.

Liberty Bowl (Dec. 31): Texas Christian 17 Colorado State 3

TCU (10-2) secured 500th win in school history in grand fashion, playing brilliant D in swamping Colorado State (10-4). Rams looked like team to beat early as TB Cecil Sapp burst for 59y run during 1st series before stalling at Frogs 11YL. Fake FG went awry for State with dropped pass in EZ. Teams blundered through 1st H as Rams committed 4 TOs, while TCU showed little on O until late 15y TD pass from QB Sean Stilley to WR LaTarence Dunbar for 7-0 H lead. Horned Frogs D then dominated as Rams were held to 7y in 2nd H, while TCU TB Ricky Madison rushed for 107y of his 111y in rainy 2nd H. Sapp finished with 106y, but he had gained 84y on 2 runs in 1st Q before being shut down, while Rams QB Bradlee Van Pelt was held to 24y passing.

Peach Bowl (Dec. 31): Maryland 30 Tennessee 3

Maryland (11-3) won its 1st bowl game since defeating Syracuse in 1985 Cherry Bowl. On their 1st series, Terrapins went 62y on 13 plays, aided by roughing passer PEN and personal foul PEN on Vols DB Julian Battle. On 4th down from 1YL, QB Scott McBrien (11-19/120y) faked handoff and rolled left for easy TD. Early in 2nd Q, Tennessee (8-5) QB Casey Clausen (23-37/242y, INT) overthrew screen pass under pressure from Maryland LB Leon Joe, and DB Curome Cox picked it off and dashed crossfield to start 54y INT TD RET for 14-0 lead. Vols WR C.J. Fayton (5/68y) caught 3 passes from Clausen on next possession, but Terps A-A LB E.J. Henderson (12 tackles, 3 sacks, 4 tackles for loss, 4 pass breakups) blew up 3rd down sweep for 6y loss to force K Alex Walls into 38y FG. Maryland K Nick Novak kicked 1st of his 3 FGs for 48y in last min of 1st H to equal Peach Bowl distance record. Tennessee forced FUM and drove to 1st down at 12YL in 3rd Q only to have Henderson force FUM to DB Domonique Foxworth at 7YL. When Novak capped ensuing trip with 44y FG, it was 20-3.

San Francisco Bowl (Dec. 31): Virginia Tech 20 Air Force 13

Virginia Tech (10-4) TB Lee Suggs (19/70y, 2 TDs) finished his great career by running for 2 TDs, which gave him record 27 straight games in which he made TD. Hokies took their 1st lead on Suggs' 2 TDs as centerpiece of 17-pt burst late in 1st Q. Earlier, Air Force (8-5) QB Chance Harridge (4-19/91y, 2 INTs) hit WR Anthony Park with 47y arrow on game's 2nd snap, and it set up 15y TD reverse by HB Matt Ward on way to 10-0 lead. But, Harridge failed to complete another pass until last 90 secs of game. Trying to rally at end, Harridge finally clicked to Tech 10YL on 4th-and-10 completion to WR J.P. Waller with 17 secs to play. It was Falcons 4th conversion in 5 4th down tries. After 2 misses, Harridge scrambled for EZ, but was met by Hokies DB Ronyell Whitaker, and coughed up game-ending FUM at 4YL. "I don't think we lost the football game," mused Falcons coach Fisher DeBerry, "I think time ran out on us." With Air Force D holding Hokies to 140y rushing, Tech QB Bryan Randall led way with 18-23/177y passing.

Outback Bowl: Michigan 38 Florida 30

Back and forth both Os went as 2 legendary programs wrestled in 1st-ever meeting. In 1st Q, Florida (8-5) C Mike Degory whipped Shotgun snap over shoulder of QB Rex Grossman (20-41/323y, 2 TDs). Michigan (10-3) DE Alaine Kashama recovered at Gators 3YL, and TB Chris Perry (198y total O) dived for 1st of his 4 TDs. On initial play of 2nd Q, Grossman set up RB Earnest Graham's tying 3y TD with 51y strike over middle to RB Ran Carthon. Graham scored again after his 33y dash down left sideline, but Gators failed on x-pt run when their "Muddle Huddle" overload-left formation failed to surprise Wolverines. TE Bennie Joppru made 3 catches in 2nd part of 2nd Q to set up TDs by Perry and WR Ronald Bellamy on 8y pass from QB John Navarre. Trailing 21-16 at H, Florida retook lead at 23-21 on Grossman's 33y TD pass over middle. UM WR Braylon Edwards advanced short pass for 48y gain to poise Perry for TD no. 3, 7y slashing run up middle, and 28-23 edge. After Gators were forced to punt from own EZ, Michigan took over only 31y from GL late in 3rd Q. Edwards caught 17y out-pattern pass, and Perry used G David Baas' inside-pulling block to crash for 12y TD run up middle. Grossman's 3y TD pass over middle got Gators within 35-30, and when they gained ball, down 38-30 in last 2 mins, Grossman was roughed OB by Wolverine LB Victor Hobson. But, when WR Vernell Brown tried desperation rainbow fling off reverse run, Hobson was there to leap for INT that iced outcome.

Cotton Bowl: Texas 35 Louisiana State 20

Despite having elected to return in 2003 for his sr season, Texas (11-2) WR Roy Williams (4/142y, TD) treated LSU (8-5) as if it was 11 NFL scouts in putting on stirring display. Tigers started well, building 17-7 lead as QB Marcus Randall led 3 drives, while Texas D logged team's score on 46y FUM TD RET by LB Lee Jackson. Rallying Longhorns from their sluggish start, Williams caught TD pass of 51y, rushed for 39y TD on end around, and made 75y reception to set up winning 5y TD run by RB Cedric Benson. Texas erupted for 28 straight pts for dandy comeback. Win was 1st in 6 tries at Cotton Bowl stadium for Longhorns off-injured sr QB Chris Simms (15-28/269y, TD), who led Horns to their 2nd straight 11-win log. Once Texas took lead, 21-17 midway in 3rd Q, LSU (8-5) turned ball over on consecutive series that had moved across 50YL.

Gator Bowl: North Carolina State 28 Notre Dame 6

Outclassed for 2nd straight game this late season and dropping their 6th consecutive bowl tilt, Fighting Irish (10-3) saw dream season turn sour. Wolfpack (11-3) dominated as their QB Philip Rivers, who grew up Notre Dame fan, threw for 23-37/228y and 2 TDs, while NC State D finished season with 8 straight quarters without surrendering TD. Notre Dame moved downfield on its 2nd possession before stalling at State 1YL after losing QB Carlyle Holiday to injury on hit by Wolfpack LB Dantonio Burnette. Irish settled for 3 pts and had to go with inexperienced QB Pat Dillingham at helm. Wolfpack marched 96y to grab lead for good, scoring TD on 2y run by TB T.A.

McLendon (2 TDs). Rivers completed 6 straight passes on drive—2 to WR Jerricho Cotchery (10/127y, TD)—and 13 straight overall. Wolfpack added 3 2nd Q TDs, including trick play as Rivers took Shotgun snap and handed ball to McLendon, forward through his legs, with McLendon following blockers past bewildered defenders for 3y score. Sr S Rod Johnson, who entered game with 1 career INT, helped ruin any Irish comeback with 3 picks. WR Arnaz Battle caught 10/64y to set Irish bowl record for receptions.

Capital One Bowl (Citrus): Auburn 13 Penn State 9

Penn State (9-4) went looking for coach Joe Paterno's 21st bowl win and instead found Auburn (9-4) D that was so much more swift than those of Big 10. Nittany Lions DL Anthony Adams (9 tackles) forced early FUM which LB Derek Wake recovered at Tigers 15YL, but after making 1st-and-goal at 4YL, Lions had to settle for K Robbie Gould's 21y FG. It was sign of things to come. Superior speed of Auburn D influenced bad day for Penn State QB Zack Mills (8-24/67y, INT) and bottled up heretofore red-hot TB Larry Johnson (20/72y). LB Wake blocked Tigers' 34y FG try early in 2nd Q, his 4th block of season. Trailing 6-0 after 1st H in which it gained only 114y, Auburn stuck to ground for 13 straight plays to open 2nd H: TB Ronnie Brown (37/184y, TD) powered in from 1YL for 7-6 lead. After DT Jamie Kennedy stopped 4th down sneak in Penn State end, Lions sub QB Michael Robinson came on to pass 34y and scramble 20y. Johnson put Penn State at Tiger 11YL with 8y run, but Auburn D forced 2 negative plays, and Gould kicked his 3rd FG. P David Duval's punt dropped dead at Penn State 1YL past mid-4th Q mark, and, with answering punt out, Auburn found itself at Lions 40YL with 5:04 left. Brown lugged it 5 times in row, including 17y TD burst for win.

Rose Bowl: Oklahoma 34 Washington State 14

Washington State (10-3) QB Jason Gesser entered game with brace on knee and high right ankle sprain, neither of which felt better by game's end. Oklahoma (12-2) teed off on hobbled signal-caller, sacking him 6 times, hitting him many more times, and picking him off twice. Game was tight at 3-0 until late 1st H burst bumped OU's lead to 17-0. Down 3-0, Cougars failed on 4th down on Sooners 35YL with 3:38 remaining in 2nd Q. QB Nate Hybl (19-29/240y, TD) then drove Sooners downfield, completing 3 passes for 61y of drive's 65y, and throwing 12y TD to WR Antwone Savage. Sooners D held on next series, and DB Antonio Perkins took ensuing punt 51y for backbreaking score. Oklahoma upped lead to 27-0 in 4th Q before Cougars managed TD on Gesser's 37y scoring pass to WR Jerome Riley (9/139y, TD). After Sooners TB Quentin Griffin (30/144y), who enjoyed 10th straight 100y game, scored on 20y run to cap his great career, Cougars WR Sammy Moore took ensuing KO 89y to end scoring. DE Jonathan Jackson and LB Teddy Lehman each had 2 sacks for Sooners. Afterward, it was easy to forget that Wazzu at no. 7 had come to Pasadena ranked higher than Sooners at 8th.

Sugar Bowl: Georgia 26 Florida State 13

Up-and-down Florida State (9-5) was ACC champs, and therefore in BCS mix. FSU played without QB Chris Rix because he overslept on morning of final exam in December. In Rix's place was QB Fabian Walker (7-12/69y, TD, 2 INTs), who kept Seminoles competitive in early going, even throwing 2nd Q TD to WR Anquan Boldin for 7-3 lead. But, Walker soon forced pass into coverage, and CB Bruce Thornton went 71y to TD for lead for good at 10-7 for Bulldogs (13-1). TB Damian Gary authored 26y punt RET, and sub Georgia QB D.J. Shockley hit his only pass try for 37y TD to WR Terrence Edwards. Bulldogs turned to TB Musa Smith (23/145y) in 2nd H as Georgia threw season-low 15 passes, and K Billy Bennett kicked 4 FGs. Boldin got chance at QB for Seminoles and threw 40y TD pass to WR Craphonso Thorpe in 3rd Q.

Orange Bowl (Jan. 2): Southern California 38 Iowa 17

In battle of Heisman Trophy winner, Carson Palmer, against runner-up, Brad Banks, it was QB Palmer's Trojans (11-2) prevailing with long 2nd H drives. Iowa (11-2) got off winging on WR C.J. Jones' 100y TD RET of opening KO. USC answered quickly with 65y strike to WR Kareem Kelly by MVP Palmer (21-31/303y, TD). Troy's 4-play, 79y trip was ended with 4y TD run by TB Justin Fargas (20/122y, 2 TDs). Hawkeyes threatened twice more in 10-10 1st H: They settled for K Nate Kaeding's 35y FG after Troy DE Matt Grootegoed's sack of QB Banks (15-36/204y, TD, INT) spoiled 1st-and-goal at 2YL. Iowa also failed in last 10 secs of 1st H at 1YL on incomplete pass and blocked FG try. USC accepted 2nd H KO and went 80y, including dandy 18y catch by WR Mike Williams (6/99y, TD), who tied NCAA frosh record with his 14th TD. Iowa soon punted Trojans to 1YL. Palmer scrambled for 9y on 3rd down, and was short of 1st down until DB Bob Sanders (13 tackles) was called for late hit, 1 of 13 PENs against Iowa. Drive was sustained for Fargas' 50y TD sprint, which put USC comfortably ahead 24-10.

GAME OF THE YEAR
Fiesta Bowl (Jan 3): Ohio State 31 Miami 24 (OT)

BCS Championship Game turned out to be double OT masterpiece. Rarely has energy swung so often from 1 team to another as big plays by Miami (12-1) TE Kellen Winslow (11/122y, TD) and Ohio State (14-0) QB Craig Krenzel (19/81y, 2 TDs rushing) carried well into night. No. 1 Hurricanes, winners of 34 straight, broke on top on 1st Q TD pass by QB Ken Dorsey (28-43/296y, 2 TDs, 2 INTs), who would be harried all game by tough Buckeyes D. Krenzel and frosh TB Maurice Clarett scored in 2nd Q to forge 14-7 H bulge for Ohio. A-A TB Willis McGahee (20/67y) scored beautiful 9y TD run in 3rd Q to pull Miami within 17-14, but was lost with torn knee early in 4th Q. But, Canes rallied when WR Roscoe Parrish (25y TD in 1st Q) redeemed himself (4th Q FUM after 29y catch) by streaking 50y on punt RET to set up K Todd Sievers' tying 40y FG on last play of regulation. Winslow caught 4th down 7y TD pass from Dorsey early in OT. Krenzel converted 4th-and-14 pass on Bucks' 1st OT possession but soon faced another 4th down at Miami 5YL. Controversial pass interference was called on Miami DB Glenn Sharpe, and Krenzel quickly scored to tie it. Clarett, who earlier

saved Ohio by forcing FUM after INT, scored on spinning 5y run. Miami came back to 1YL, but Dorsey's 4th down pass was blitzed by Bucks LB Cie Grant, and DB Donnie Nickey batted it down.

Final AP Poll January 4

1	Ohio State (71)	1775	13	Maryland	844
2	Miami	1693	14	Auburn	821
3	Georgia	1593	15	Boise State	692
4	Southern California	1590	16	Penn State	675
5	Oklahoma	1476	17	Notre Dame	657
6	Texas	1363	18	Virginia Tech	544
7	Kansas State	1356	19	Pittsburgh	520
8	Iowa	1334	20	Colorado	307
9	Michigan	1182	21	Florida State	291
10	Washington State	1085	22	Virginia	250
11	Alabama	988	23	Texas Christian	231
12	North Carolina State	943	24	Marshall	201
			25	West Virginia	195

Final USA Today Coaches January 6

1	Ohio State (61)	1525	14	Virginia Tech	644
2	Miami (Fla.)	1451	15	Penn State	619
3	Georgia	1378	16	Auburn	579
4	Southern California	1362	17	Notre Dame	525
5	Oklahoma	1244	18	Pittsburgh	486
6	Kansas State	1230	19	Marshall	333
7	Texas	1140	20	West Virginia	297
8	Iowa	1105	21	Colorado	291
9	Michigan	1011	22	TCU	274
10	Washington State	932	23	Florida State	219
11	North Carolina State	876	24	Florida	145
12	Boise State	808	25	Virginia	141
13	Maryland	803			

2002 Top Performance Formula

1	Ohio State	1.7588
2	Miami	1.7189
3	Southern California	1.6967
4	Georgia	1.6720
5	Oklahoma	1.6493
6	Texas	1.6002
7	Kansas State	1.5888
8	Iowa	1.5613
9	Alabama	1.5131
10	Michigan	1.4725
11	Maryland	1.4569
12	Penn State	1.4275
13	Washington State	1.4242
14	Notre Dame	1.4147
15	Texas Christian	1.4128
16	North Carolina State	1.4019
17	Virginia Tech	1.3981
18	Florida State	1.3710
19	Pittsburgh	1.3408
20	Auburn	1.3329

2002 Top Opponent Records

1	Southern California	.6774
2	Florida State	.6374
3	Michigan	.6340
4	Iowa State	.6190
5t	Miami	.61818
5t	Wisconsin	.61818
7	Texas Tech	.6176
8	Alabama	.6154
9	Arkansas	.6149
10	Florida	.6118
11	Georgia	.6048
12	Colorado	.6047
13	Stanford	.6031
14	Ohio State	.5988
15	Notre Dame	.5909
16	Oklahoma	.5979
17	Texas	.5858
18	Virginia	.5858
19	Penn State	.5844
20	Washington State	.5819

2002 Out-of-Conference Records

	W-L	Percentage	Bowl W-L
Big Ten	36-15	.7059	5-2
Southeastern	35-16	.6863	3-4
Big Twelve	35-18	.6604	5-3
Pacific-10	27-14	.6585	2-5
Big East	26-15	.6341	3-2
Atlantic Coast	27-16	.6279	4-3
Mountain West	16-26	.3810	0-3

2002 Individual Statistical Leaders

RUSHING YARDS	Attempts	Yards	Avg.
Larry Johnson, Penn State	271	2087	7.7
Michael Turner, Northern Illinois	338	1915	5.7
Quentin Griffin, Oklahoma	287	1884	6.6
Chris Brown, Colorado	303	1841	6.1
Willis McGahee, Miami	282	1753	6.2
Avon Cobourne, West Virginia	335	1710	5.1
Steven Jackson, Oregon State	319	1690	5.3
Marcus Merriweather, Ball State	332	1618	4.9
Cecil Sapp, Colorado State	348	1594	4.6
Anthony Davis, Wisconsin	300	1555	5.2

PASSING YARDS	Completions	Attempts	Yards	Pct.
Kliff Kingsbury, Texas Tech	479	712	5017	67.3
Timmy Chang, Hawaii	349	624	4474	55.9
Cody Pickett, Washington	365	612	4461	59.6
Byron Leftwich, Marshall	331	491	4268	67.4
Carson Palmer, Southern California	309	489	3942	63.2
Andrew Walter, Arizona State	274	483	3877	56.7
Luke McCown, Louisiana Tech	296	505	3539	58.6
Jason Gesser, Washington State	236	402	3408	58.7
Rex Grossman, Florida	287	503	3402	57.1
Eli Manning, Mississippi	279	481	3401	58.0

RECEIVING YARDS	Catches	Yards
J.R. Tolver, San Diego State	128	1785
Rashaun Woods, Oklahoma State	107	1695
Nate Burleson, Nevada	138	1629
Kassim Osgood, San Diego State	108	1552
Reggie Williams, Washington	94	1455
Shaun McDonald, Arizona State	87	1405
Bobby Wade, Arizona	93	1389
Kevin Walter, Eastern Michigan	93	1368
Charles Rogers, Michigan State	68	1351
John Standeford, Purdue	75	1307

2002 Consensus All-America Team
Offense

Wide Receiver:	Charles Rogers, Michigan State
	Reggie Williams, Washington
	Rashaun Woods, Oklahoma State
Tight End:	Dallas Clark, Iowa
Line:	Shawn Andrews, Arkansas
	Eric Steinbach, Iowa
	Derrick Dockery, Texas
	Jordan Gross, Utah
Center:	Brett Romberg, Miami
Quarterback:	Carson Palmer, Southern California
Running Back:	Larry Johnson, Penn State
	Willis McGahee, Miami
Placekicker:	Mike Nugent, Ohio State
Kick Returner:	Derek Abney, Kentucky

Defense

Line:	Terrell Suggs, Arizona State
	David Pollack, Georgia
	Rien Long, Washington State
	Tommie Harris, Oklahoma
Linebacker:	E.J. Henderson, Maryland
	Teddy Lehman, Oklahoma
	Matt Wilhelm, Ohio State
Back:	Mike Doss, Ohio State
	Terence Newman, Kansas State
	Shane Walton, Notre Dame
	Troy Polamalu, Southern California
Punter:	Mark Mariscal, Colorado

2002 Heisman Trophy Vote

Carson Palmer, senior quarterback, Southern California	1328
Brad Banks, senior quarterback, Iowa	1095
Larry Johnson, senior tailback, Penn State	726
Willis McGahee, sophomore tailback, Miami	660
Ken Dorsey, senior quarterback, Miami	643

Other Major Awards

Maxwell (Player)	Larry Johnson, senior tailback, Penn State
Walter Camp (Player)	Larry Johnson, senior tailback, Penn State
Outland (Lineman)	Rien Long, junior defensive tackle, Washington State
Lombardi (Lineman)	Terrell Suggs, junior defensive end, Arizona State
Doak Walker (Running Back)	Larry Johnson, senior tailback, Penn State
Davey O'Brien (Quarterback)	Brad Banks, senior quarterback, Iowa
Fred Biletnikoff (Receiver)	Charles Rogers, junior wide receiver, Michigan State
Jim Thorpe (Defensive Back)	Terence Newman, senior cornerback, Kansas State
Dick Butkus (Linebacker)	E.J. Henderson, senior linebacker, Maryland
Lou Groza (Placekicker)	Nate Kaeding, senior kicker, Iowa
Chuck Bednarik (Defender)	E.J. Henderson, senior linebacker, Maryland
Ray Guy (Punter)	Mark Mariscal, senior punter, Colorado
Johnny Unitas (Sr. Quarterback)	Carson Palmer, senior QB, Southern California
John Mackey (Tight End)	Dallas Clark, senior tight end, Iowa
Dave Rimington (Center)	Brett Romberg, senior center, Miami
Ted Hendricks (Defensive End)	Terrell Suggs, junior defensive end, Arizona State
AFCA Coach of the Year	Jim Tressel, Ohio State

2003

The Year of Lack of Collegiality, Peasant's Revolt, and Three for Number One

While American forces went to war in Iraq, some football people figuratively must have felt they also were in combat. Two coaches self-destructed, star running back Maurice Clarett of Ohio State (11-2) got suspended, and the Big East and Atlantic Coast Conferences mounted a name-calling battle over the ACC's imperialistic design on four Big East schools.

Coach Mike Price of Alabama (4-9) was on the job at Tuscaloosa only a few months after 14 years at Washington State when he attended a spring golf tournament in Pensacola, Fla. Price acted like a fool at a topless bar, and, worse, one of the women from the bar ended up in Price's hotel room charging extravagant room service bills to Price's company credit card. Price was bounced in favor of Mike Shula, former Crimson Tide quarterback and son of NFL coaching great, Don Shula.

Like many Americans, Rick Neuheisel, football coach of Washington (6-6), enjoyed participating in a neighborhood pool when the annual NCAA basketball tournament ushered in "March Madness." This was considered harmless dollar-ante gambling in some circles. Trouble was, Neuheisel lived in a high-end neighborhood, and news broke that he had won several thousands of dollars by correctly picking Maryland in the 2002 hoop tournament. Neuheisel claimed he received written permission from the school to take part in the pool but was fired as football coach anyway. He received $4.5 million in 2005 as settlement of a wrongful dismissal suit.

Clarett, Ohio State's sensational sophomore-to-be tailback, was investigated for accepting unfair help in the form of an oral exam after he had walked out of a written final in the spring, and for exaggerating the value of items stolen from a car he was driving around Columbus during the summer. Clarett was suspended from playing and promptly sued Ohio State, the NFL for the right to enter the draft, and just about everyone except the Ohio governor, Earle Bruce, and Howard "Hopalong" Cassady.

The ACC announced its intention to invite the Big East's Miami of Florida to join its ranks as a 10th member in all sports. Then it dawned on the conference fathers that a two-division football platform, of six teams each, could make a lucrative playoff game for the ACC. So, two more schools, Boston College and Syracuse, were rumored as prime invitees. This news launched Big East commissioner Mike Tranghese into hysterics and accusations. Seven ACC votes were required to endorse expansion, and three of nine schools wavered. Virginia was under pressure from its state government to include Virginia Tech, a rival it didn't wish to help, and Duke and North Carolina vacillated early. Their athletic departments envisioned the elite Blue Devil and Tar Heel basketball teams, long legs dangling over chair arms, being stranded by a January blizzard at Syracuse Hancock Airport. In the end, invitations went to Miami, Virginia Tech, and, surprisingly, Boston College, to create a 12-member ACC to be completed by 2005. One ACC administrator shook her head over her group's piracy, regretting her conference's lack of "collegiality."

On the field, the supposed have-nots from the Mid-American Conference made headlines. Northern Illinois (10-2) opened the season by beating Maryland (10-3) and followed with wins at Alabama and against Iowa State (2-10). The MAC's Bowling Green (11-3) surprised Purdue (9-4) on the road in September, Marshall (8-4) also went on the road to stun Kansas State (11-4), a team that would surprise everyone later by knocking off top-ranked Oklahoma (12-2) in the Big Twelve title tilt, and Toledo (8-4) beat Pittsburgh (8-5) when the Panthers had high expectations. No one could recall a so-called minor conference ever winning so many games in one year against competition from top leagues.

Events late in the regular season considerably scrambled both polls and BCS computer calculations. At the core was Kansas State's 35-7 demolition of no. 1 Oklahoma at a time when *USA Today* and others were comparing the undefeated Sooners to the greatest teams ever. Along the way, BCS critics railed against the system's inability to tap a worthy foe for mighty Oklahoma. But with the Sooners' loss to the Wildcats, the BCS somehow had to fit three teams into a title game where only two would fit. The mess arose from the formula's selection of AP no. 3 Oklahoma and no. 2 LSU (13-1) for the BCS Sugar Bowl title game. Southern California (12-1), tapped no. 1 in both human polls in the last pre-bowl balloting, found itself in the unusual situation of winning the Rose Bowl convincingly over no. 4 Michigan (10-3) but still dropping out of the top spot in the coaches poll. In the Sugar Bowl, LSU handed Oklahoma its second straight loss to

cop the coaches' no. 1 spot. For the 11th time in history, the polls named different champions at season's end.

Was a split decision all that bad? Both Southern California and LSU teams were richly deserving, and each got to trumpet a national title. Both the Trojans and Tigers had rebounded after some lean years, and credit had to go to the dynamic recruiting success of their coaches, Pete Carroll of USC and Nick Saban of LSU. Had they met in some final playoff game, it would be difficult to speculate on a winner.

Milestones

■ New rules focused on safety by further restricting blocks below waist by flanked backs, but ended much-maligned "halo rule" that had protected punt receivers with two-yard safety zone.

■ Gene Calame, Oklahoma quarterback in 1953-54 who helped launch Sooners' record 47-game winning streak, died in January. George Conner, one of Notre Dame's all-time great tackles and first winner of Outland Trophy in 1946, died at age 78. Conner was twice consensus All-America and was named All-Pro in each of eight years with Chicago Bears (1948-55). Iowa State lost two of its top career runners in May: Dexter Green, tailback in 1976-78, died of cancer at 46, and Ennis Haywood, tailback in 1998-2001, died of unknown disease at 23. In June, Pittsburgh receiver Billy Gaines fell from high loft at church party and died of head injuries. Shea Fitzgerald, sophomore offensive tackle for Northern Illinois, was among 13 killed in collapse of apartment deck during party on Chicago's Southside on June 29. Former Texas Christian and Minnesota coach Jim Wacker, 66, lost long battle to cancer on August 26. Ron Burton, 67, All-America halfback for Northwestern in 1957-59, died in September. Otto Graham, 82, Northwestern tailback, who went on to play in 10 straight pro championship games as Cleveland Browns quarterback, died on December 17.

■ Coaching Changes

	Incoming	Outgoing
Alabama	Mike Price (a)	Dennis Franchione
Alabama	Mike Shula	Mike Price (a)
Arizona	Mike Hankwitz (b)	John Mackovic
Army	John Mumford (c)	Todd Berry
Ball State	Brady Hoke	Bill Lynch
Baylor	Guy Morriss	Kevin Steele
Bowling Green	Gregg Brandon	Urban Meyer
East Carolina	John Thompson	Steve Logan
Houston	Art Briles	Dana Dimel
Kentucky	Rich Brooks	Guy Morriss
Louisiana-Monroe	Charlie Weatherbie	Bobby Keasler
Louisville	Bobby Petino	John L. Smith
Michigan State	John L. Smith	Bobby Williams
Oregon State	Mike Riley	Dennis Erickson
Texas A&M	Dennis Franchione	R.C. Slocum
Tulsa	Steve Kragthorpe	Keith Burns
UCLA	Karl Dorrell	Bob Toledo
Utah	Urban Meyer	Ron McBride
Washington State	Bill Doba	Mike Price
Wyoming	Joe Glenn	Vic Koenning

(a) Price (0-0) replaced Franchione but was fired in spring. Shula coached entire 2003 season.
(b) Hankwitz (1-8) replaced Mackovic (1-4) on September 28.
(c) Mumford (0-7) replaced Berry (0-6) on October 12.

■ Longest Winning Streak Entering Season:

Ohio State 14	Boise State 11	Southern California 8

Preseason *USA Today* Coaches

1	Oklahoma (29)	1514	14	North Carolina State	682
2	Ohio State (28)	1495	15	LSU	662
3	Miami (Fla.) (5)	1448	16	Tennessee	658
4	Texas	1291	17	Virginia	526
5	Kansas State	1165	18	Notre Dame	515
6	Auburn (1)	1153	19	Washington	459
7	Michigan	1110	20	Wisconsin	348
8	Southern California	1075	21	Florida	312
9	Georgia	1030	22	Purdue	305
10	Virginia Tech	932	23	Arizona State	297
11	Pittsburgh	712	24	Oklahoma State	159
12	Florida State	711	25t	Penn State	143
13	Maryland	704	25t	Colorado State	143

August 23, 2003

Kansas State 42 California 28 (Kansas City): New season started with bang: Kansas State (1-0) SS Rashad Washington made ringing tackle on opening KO and would add several more big hits. But, Golden Bears (0-1) gained 440y against vaunted K-State D, including 478y in air. Wildcats ace TB Darren Sproles (22/175y, TD) quickly broke loose for long run to set up his 5y option-left TD run for 7-0 lead. Young California team was not about to roll over, scoring on WR Vincent Strang's diving TD reception and trailed only 10-7 as 1st Q ended. During Q break, Bears coaches talked about choices on 4th-and-ft less than 2 ft from K-State GL. On 2nd Q's opening snap, QB Reggie Robertson (16-29/257y, 3 TDs, INT) ran option play which was blown up by Wildcats sr LB Josh Buhl. Kansas State charged 98y to score on FB Travis Wilson's lonely 5y catch from QB Ell Roberson (9-18/205y, 3 TDs), who showed plenty to ESPN national TV audience with 18/145y, TD rushing for 350y of Cats' 535y total O.

USA Today Coaches August 24

1	Oklahoma (37)	1529	14	Maryland	718
2	Ohio State (23)	1477	15	LSU	679
3	Miami (Fla.) (2)	1471	16	Tennessee	617
4	Texas	1306	17	Virginia	542
5	Kansas State	1210	18	Notre Dame	498
6	Auburn (1)	1160	19	Washington	456
7	Michigan	1144	20	Wisconsin	342
8	Southern California	1090	21	Florida	310
9	Georgia	1057	22	Purdue	281
10	Virginia Tech	959	23	Arizona State	260
11	Florida State	761	24	Oklahoma State	160
12	Pittsburgh	743	25	Iowa	119
13	North Carolina State	721			

August 30, 2003

(Th) NORTHERN ILLINOIS 20 Maryland 13 (OT): Coach Ralph Friedgen feared it "would be a close game," and his no. 15 Terrapins (0-1) never ignited much O as sloppy Terps were outgained 325y to 222y. Northern Illinois (1-0) led 10-7 at H, on 5y TD pass by QB Joshua Haldi (21-35/266y, 2 TDs, INT) to WR P.J. Fleck (13/116y). K Mike Novak booted 46 and 50y FGs in 2nd H, so Maryland took 13-10 lead with 9:10 left. Highly-touted Huskies TB Michael Turner (30/90y) contributed 33y run to 18-play, 84y drive that tied it 13-13 on K Steve Azar's 2nd FG. NIU WR Dan Sheldon caught 20y TD pass on OT's 1st series. Then, Terps QB Scott McBrien (12-24/110y, INT) underthrew WR Latrez Harrison at GL, and pass caromed off DB Rob Lee's leg into arms of Huskies DB Randee Drew to start celebration by record crowd in DeKalb.

Wake Forest 32 BOSTON COLLEGE 28: New Boston College (0-1) QB Quinton Porter (22-39/243y, TD) threw 1st Q TD pass to TE Dave Kashetta (4/84y, TD), and led 14-0. Deacons (1-0) DB Warren Braxton raced 53y on FUM TD RET to beat H clock by 1:24. Wake Forest cut deficit to 14-12 early in 3rd Q when tiny frosh WR Willie Idlette made his 1st touch: he sprinted for 75y TD reverse run. Just 3 mins later, BC misfired on 3rd down pass from Deacons' 9YL, but pass interference moved ball to 2YL. Porter ran it in on next play for 21-12 edge. Wake took its 1st lead at 25-21 with 6:44 to play when QB Cory Randolph (13-23/149y, 2 TDs, 2 INTs) threw 4y TD to WR Jay Anderson. Eagles marched 89y to 28-25 lead on TD run by TB Derrick Knight (30/144y, TD). Randolph, in his 1st career start, overcame near INT by BC DB Jazzmen Williams to hit 4-5 on late winning drive that was finished by WR Chris Davis' 43y TD catch.

Georgia 30 CLEMSON 0: Many prognosticators gave Clemson (0-1) good chance of upsetting no. 11 Georgia (1-0). Instead, Bulldogs overcame long list of injured and suspended players to score on its 1st series as WR Fred Gibson (4/104y, TD) caught 56y TD in middle of field from hot-handed QB David Greene (12-17/203y, TD). K Billy Bennett added 3 FGs for 16-0 lead with 4:32 left in 3rd Q. Tigers tried tricky TB-to-QB pass on 4th-and-goal at Georgia 4YL midway in 2nd Q, but TB Duane Coleman's floater for QB Charlie Whitehurst (19-33/151y, INT) was broken up by UGa's retreating, 270-lb DL Robert Geathers. Another Bulldog DL, star David Pollack, picked off INT and made nimble but rumbling 24y RET to snuff Clemson's last chance in 4th Q.

Southern California 23 AUBURN 0: "Wild Bunch II," USC's remarkably quick and ferocious D, completely swamped Auburn (0-1), trendy pre-season no. 1 pick by *The Sporting News* and *ESPN, The Magazine*. DB Darnell Bing, wearing Trojan AD Mike Garrett's previously-retired no. 20, made INT of Tigers QB Jason Campbell (12-26/121y, INT) on game's 3rd play at Tigers 20YL. Trojans QB Matt Leinart (17-30/192y, TD, INT) flipped 5y TD pass to WR Mike Williams (8/104y, TD) in 1st 3 mins. TB Hershel Dennis (21/85y, TD) scored USC's put-away TD at 23-0 on 14y TD run early in 4th Q. Southern California D forced Campbell to fumble and crimped meager 68y rushing efforts by Tigers TBs "Cadillac" Williams (12/40y) and Ronnie Brown (8/28y).

Oregon 42 MISSISSIPPI STATE 34: Ducks (1-0) showed off new all bright yellow uniforms to mixed reviews. In his 1st start, Oregon QB Kellen Clemens (14-21/247y, 3 TDs) hit 7-8/183y and TDs of 55y to WR Samie Parker and 86y to WR Demetrius Williams in 28-0 1st Q. Mississippi State (0-1) QB Kevin Fant (23-40/285y, 3 TDs, INT) ran and passed Maroons to TDs in 2nd Q as they rallied within 28-21 in 3rd Q. After Clemens hit his 3rd TD and backup QB Jason Fife (8-8/111y) ran 6y option TD, Ducks had 42-21 lead that lasted until Fant's 1st of 2 TD passes midway in 4th Q.

OHIO STATE 28 Washington 9: Given ruckus over Buckeyes TB Maurice Clarett's investigation and Huskies coach Rick Neuheisel's firing, each team was anxious to put summer behind and play football. Bucks (1-0) QB Craig Krenzel (15-27/203y) nearly made home crowd forget Clarett as he showed outstanding new speed in scrambling to 2 TDs in 1st H on runs of 23 and 11y. Krenzel made 8/27y, 2 TDs rushing. Trailing 21-0 at H, Washington (0-1) took 2nd H KO and advanced 47y on 5 clicks by QB Cody Pickett (26-49/255y) to K Evan Knudson's 46y FG. TB Lydell Ross scored late in 3RD Q for 28-3 lead for Ohio, but Pickett ran for 2y TD to complete Huskies' best drive.

NEBRASKA 17 Oklahoma State 7: Wishing to forget miserable 2002 season and to harken back to grand tradition, Nebraska (1-0) returned to traditional red jerseys and invited back 800 lettermen for Memorial Stadium reunion. Scoring drives started on each team's opening possession until game settled into D battle. Huskers began with 54y drive to K Sandro DeAngelis' 28y FG. Oklahoma State (0-1) WR Rashaun Woods (5/47y, TD), who burned Nebraska with 11/134y receiving in last year's win, caught 2 passes from QB Josh Fields (13-28/97y, TD, 3 INTs) on ensuing 52y TD drive, but was kept in check for rest of game. Woods drove defender into EZ and hooked back for 4y TD catch and 7-3 Cowboy lead with 6:23 to go in 1st Q. Cornhuskers' famed Blackshirt D returned to old tricks: It held Oke State O to 183y and only 57y in 2nd H, while making 5 TOs. On Cowboys' 2nd series of 3rd Q, TB Tatum Bell (23/87y) lost FUM, and Nebraska LB Barrett Ruud scooped up ball for 15y TD RET. Fields attempted pass from own 23YL, 2 series later, and was sacked by blitzing Huskers DB Jerrell Pippens. Ball came loose, and was recovered by DL Ryon Bingham, and TB Judd Davies put Nebraska ahead 17-7 3 plays later.

Colorado 42 Colorado State 35 (Denver): Colorado State (0-1) QB Bradlee Van Pelt (18-38/339y, 3 TDs, INT) was most hated man in Boulder for his derogatory remarks against Buffaloes (1-0). Van Pelt backed up his mouth right away, leading Rams to 14-7 edge early in 2nd Q on 10y TD run and 32y TD pass to WR Chris Pittman (7/144y, 2 TDs). Former pro baseball washout, Colorado QB Joel Klatt (21-34/402y, 4 TDs) went vertical and suddenly Bisons had long passing game. Klatt hit TDs of 82, 10, and 45y TD throws in 2nd Q for 28-14 H lead. Competitive Van Pelt came back with 38y TD to Pittman early in 3rd Q, but Klatt found WR Derek McCoy (4/192y, 2 TDs) for 78y score on 78y reception while crossing left to right. Trailing 35-21, Van Pelt engineered 76y drive that ended on his TD pass. Rams DB Dexter Wynn foiled WR run and broke up Buff pass to force Colorado punt from CU 44YL. Wynn returned punt 40y to Buff 38YL. On 3rd down, Van Pelt ran option and ran through 2 tacklers to 30y TD that tied it 35-35 with 1:50 to play. Klatt completed 4 passes, including WR Jeremy Bloom's 33y catch OB at 4YL. CU TB Bobby Purify scored from 9YL after PEN with 40 secs left.

USA Today Coaches September 1

1	Oklahoma (32)	1530	14	Tennessee	714
2	Ohio State (26)	1498	15	Virginia	638
3	Miami (Fla.) (5)	1467	16	Notre Dame	568
4	Texas	1297	17	Wisconsin	502
5	Southern California	1291	18	Florida	500
6	Kansas State	1257	19	Auburn	485
7	Michigan	1200	20	Purdue	356
8	Georgia	1141	21	Arizona State	342
9	Virginia Tech	1033	22	Colorado	178
10	Florida State	947	23	Iowa	161
11	North Carolina State	823	24	Nebraska	152
12	Pittsburgh	783	25	Penn State	144
13	LSU	771			

September 6, 2003

MIAMI 38 Florida 33: Rallying from 23-pt deficit, Canes (2-0) made QB Brock Berlin (27-41/340y) winner versus former team. After slow start, featuring 2 INTs and FUM returned 34y by CB Keiwan Ratliff for TD, Berlin hit 12 straight completions in rally. He connected with WR Kevin Beard (7/164y) on 26y TD and 62y pass that set up another TD, threw 6y scoring pass to WR Ryan Moore and then led 89y drive for winning pts. Winning TD, 12y run by TB Frank Gore (24/127y), came 5 plays after Berlin rushed for 1st down on 4th-and-1 despite leg cramps. Gators (1-1) had 1 drive left, taking ball to Miami 20YL before frosh QB Chris Leak threw INT to CB Al Marshall. Florida used big plays to build 33-10 lead as WR Carlos Perez caught 50y TD pass and TB DeShawn Wynn went 65y with scoring run.

WAKE FOREST 38 North Carolina State 24: Break up those Deamon Deacs (2-0). Despite allowing 433y passing by QB Philip Rivers and 511y total—136y more than Deacons managed—Wake led throughout. QB Cory Randolph (8-10/131y) ran attack that did most damage on ground, with 202y rushing and 4 TDs, 2 by FB Nick Burney. Rivers threw for career-high y, but also 2 crucial INTs. NC State WR Jerricho Cotchery caught 9 passes for 173y and TD.

FLORIDA STATE 35 Maryland 10: Like death and taxes, nothing seemed more sure than Terps inability to beat Florida State (2-0). Seminoles upped series mark to 14-0 as TB Greg Jones rushed for 2 TDs, QB Chris Rix (16-29/228y, 1 INT) threw 2 TDs and D allowed less than 2 TDs. Terps (0-2) had 10-0 lead—7 pts on 58y INT RET by LB D'Qwell Jackson—but that just delayed inevitable. Noles settled down to 5 scoring drives, including 1 of 99y, to pull away. Terps managed only 197y, with QB Scott McBrien held to 61y on 6-18 passing.

GEORGIA TECH 17 Auburn 3: Auburn (0-2) freefall continued as team went 4 more Qs without TD. Frosh QB Reggie Ball (9-24/149y), who Auburn stopped recruiting, led upset, throwing 26y TD to WR Mark Logan and leading Yellow Jackets (1-1) to 2 other scores. TB P.J. Daniels tallied team's 2nd TD on 1y run 10 plays after S Chris Reis gained 1st down with 3y run on fake punt. Tech D sacked Tiger QB Randy Campbell (20-33/190y, 1 INT) 7 times, 3 by DE Eric Henderson. At final gun, crowd carried Ball away 3 hours too late for Tigers.

SOUTH CAROLINA 31 Virginia 7: Game turned quickly on incredible 99y TD pass from South Carolina (2-0) QB Dondrial Pinkins to WR Troy Williamson, who caught pass at own 15YL, broke tackle and was gone. USC now led 10-7 despite not gaining 1st down for 6 straight series. Gamecocks poured it on from there, with Pinkins adding 5y TD run and TB Daccus Turman rushing for 123y and score. Lack of depth limited Virginia (1-1) as frosh QB Anthony Martinez threw for 54y with 2 INTs as sub for injured starting QB Matt Schaub.

Oklahoma 20 ALABAMA 13: Oklahoma QB Jason White threw for 259y and 2 TD s as Sooners (2-0) won in dangerous confines of Bryant-Denny Stadium. White's 2nd scoring pass was set up by gutsy fake punt called with OU ahead 13-10 and facing 4th-and-11 on own 31YL. P Blake Ferguson threw pass that DB Michael Thompson took 22y, followed on next play by White's 47y TD pass to WR Brandon Jones. Sooner S Donte Nicholson picked off QB Brodie Coyle to end next Alabama (1-1) possession as momentum had swung completely. OU D had 5 sacks and 2 INTs. Hosting nation's top-ranked team for 1st time, Tide gained 303y with 91y rushing by TB Shaud Williams.

Boston College 27 PENN STATE 14: Eagles (1-1) jumped out to 21-0 1st Q lead and never looked back. With help from TB Derrick Knight (26/156y), QB Quinton Porter marched BC 80y with opening drive to 18y TD pass to WR Grant Adams. After Penn State (1-1) went 3-and-out, visitors doubled lead on 37y TD pass to WR Tony Gonzalez. Eagle DT Tom Martin then returned INT 25y to Penn State 1YL to set up

1y TD run by Penn State transfer TB Horace Dodd. Lions were limited by 4 BC sacks and 2 lost FUMs within BC 20YL. Lions QB Michael Robinson led late TD drive to 2y keeper that was too little, too late.

Bowling Green 27 PURDUE 26: Bowling Green (2-0) won 6th straight versus members of BCS confs as QB Josh Harris (22-40/357y, 1 INT) threw for 357y and 3 TDs against D returning 9 starters from Big 10-leading unit. Winning score came on 4th-and-14 as Harris avoided pressure to throw 32y pass to diving WR Charles Sharon with 2:08 left. QB Kyle Orton (26-42/255y, 3 TDs) drove Purdue (0-1) to Falcon 33YL before 4th down drop by WR Taylor Stubblefield (16/139y) ended chances. Last time Falcons defeated ranked team was 1972, when they beat Boilermakers 17-14.

NOTRE DAME 29 Washington State 26 (OT): After exploding in 4th Q for 20 pts and 181y, Irish (1-0) secured win on 5th FG by K Nick Setta, from 40y. WSU (1-1), which blew 19-0 lead, forced OT with 34y TD pass from QB Matt Kegel (22-39/274y, 1 INT) to WR Sammy Moore, tandem's 2nd scoring hook-up. Miss by Cougar K Drew Dunning from 34y set up Setta's heroics. Play of game was huge hit by ND CB Vontez Duff on Troy Bienemann to force FUM grabbed by S Glenn Earl on WSU 25YL. QB Carlyle Holiday (21-34/149y) then threw 11y TD to WR Rhema McKnight to cut deficit to 19-16. DE Isaac Brown helped Cougars build 19-0 lead by taking FUM 12y to EZ.

USA Today Coaches September 7

1	Oklahoma (41)	1543	14	Notre Dame	697
2	Miami (Fla.) (8)	1477	15	Wisconsin	674
3	Ohio State (13)	1429	16	Arizona State	491
4	Southern California (1)	1333	17	Colorado	480
5	Texas	1302	18	Nebraska	425
6	Kansas State	1257	19	Iowa	424
7	Michigan	1219	20	Florida	410
8	Georgia	1143	21	Wake Forest	230
9	Virginia Tech	1048	22	North Carolina State	221
10	Florida State	998	23	TCU	157
11	LSU	887	24	Washington	153
12	Pittsburgh	876	25	Texas A&M	120
13	Tennessee	830			

September 13, 2003

FLORIDA STATE 14 Georgia Tech 13: Florida State (3-0) rallied in 4th Q after facing prospect of 1st home shutout in coach Bobby Bowden's 28 years. Led by LBs Daryl Smith and Keyaron Fox, underappreciated Georgia Tech (1-2) dominated line of scrimmage in 1st H, allowing only 26y O, 16y of which came on reverse run on game's 1st snap by Seminole WR Craphanso Thorpe. Tech's D prowess and 42 to 15 snap advantage helped K Dan Burnett gave Yellow Jackets 6-0 H lead with 2nd Q FGs of 35 and 45y. CB Reuben Houston made EZ INT of Florida State QB Chris Rix (15-30/160y, TD, 2 INTs) early in 4th Q to launch Tech TB P.J. Daniels (19/113y, TD) to 47y TD run and 13-0 lead. Rix scored on 3y run with 7:09 to play and won game for Seminoles with 2:57 left on 5y TD pass to WR P.K. Sam.

Purdue 16 WAKE FOREST 10: Coming off 27-26 embarrassment to Bowling Green, Purdue (2-1) took on no. 20 Wake Forest (2-1), which was enjoying its 1st spot in AP Poll in 10 years. Boilermakers coach Joe Tiller frequently rotated his D, and Purdue D held good rushing team to 56y in 1st 3 Qs. Deacons coughed up INT by QB Cory Randolph (18-30/188y, INT) on game's 1st snap as S Stuart Schweigert made pick-off and returned 38y to Wake 28YL. Purdue K Ben Jones made 27y FG, 1st of his 3 FGs. Deacons immediately tied it on 60y drive as K Ryan Plackemeier hit 37y FG. After Boilers QB Kyle Orton (26-36/227y, TD) found WR Taylor Stubblefield (7/60y, TD) for 7y TD, Wake fashioned its last drive of 80y to tie it 10-10 in 2nd Q. Jones put Purdue ahead with 44y 3-ptr in last half-min of 1st H.

OHIO STATE 44 North Carolina State 38 (OT): Buckeyes (3-0) jumped to 14-0 edge in 1st Q as QB Craig Krenzel (26-36/273y, 4 TDs, 3 INTs) lofted 44y TD pass to WR Michael Jenkins (7/124y, 2 TDs). Although North Carolina State (1-2) QB Philip Rivers (36-52/315y, 4 TDs, 2 INTs) sifted in 11y TD pass to WR Jerricho Cotchery, Ohio built comfy 24-7 lead when Krenzel scored on 6y run with 11:25 to play in 4th Q. Rivers, who had 2 costly INTs earlier, rallied Wolfpack with another TD to Cotchery, and K Adam Kiker's 24y FG after CB A.J. Davis' INT RET to Bucks 12YL. Pack took over on its 14YL with 3:18 to play, and Rivers hit 6 straight passes to tie it 24-24 with :21 left. Teams traded pair of OT TDs to make it 38-38. Krenzel hit 7y slant pass to Jenkins for TD while score stayed at 44-38 when required 2-pt try was stopped by LB Pat Thomas. NC State earned 1st-and-goal at Ohio 4YL and emptied backfield with 4 WRs clustered left. With all LBs drawn wide by formation, Rivers checked off to QB sneaks on 1st and 3rd downs and could total only 3y. On 4th down, TB T.A. McLendon took pitchout, cut to GL, but was halted short by Ohio LB A.J. Hawk (12 tackles) and DB Will Allen.

MICHIGAN 38 Notre Dame 0: In front of collegiate-record 111,726 crowd, ambitious Michigan (3-0) overwhelmed Notre Dame (1-1) with its 1st blanking in series since 1902. It was Fighting Irish's worst defeat since Miami whipped them 58-7 in 1985. ND's O sputtered all day, never advancing past Michigan's 35YL and gaining only 140y. Irish QB Carlyle Holiday (5-14/55y, INT) was replaced by frosh QB Brady Quinn (3-10/36y, INT), who fared no better. Heisman talk began to surround UM TB Chris Perry (31/133y, 3 TDs), who added another TD on 9y pass from QB John Navarre (14-21/199y, TD) that raised score to 17-0 in 2nd Q. WR Steve Breaston made 4 punt RETs/105y, including 55 and 25y RETs that set up 10-0 lead early in 2nd Q.

Unlv 23 WISCONSIN 5: No. 14 Badgers (2-1) were stunned by Nevada-Las Vegas (2-1) SS Jamaal Brimmer, who had magnificent game in upset win. Brimmer returned FUM 55y for TD to extend Rebels' lead to 10-0 in 1st Q. Brimmer (11 tackles, including 2 sacks) made INTs in 2nd and 3rd Qs, which he returned for 65y, and each set up UNLV TD: 6 and 8y scoring catches by WR Earvin Johnson. Disappointed Wisconsin outgained Rebels 291y to 187y, but suffered 8 sacks and lost TB Anthony Davis to ankle sprain in rain. Badgers K Scott Campbell kicked 2nd Q FG to trim edge to 10-5.

Iowa 40 IOWA STATE 21: Hawkeyes (3-0) broke 5-year hex by in-state rival Cyclones (2-1), jumping to 10-0 lead in 1st Q and 33-7 by end of 3rd Q. Iowa K Nate Kaeding scored 16 pts to become school's all-time scoring leader. Kaeding kicked 4 FGs, including 42y boot that opened scoring and gave sr remarkable 21-26 career record on FGs from outside 40y. Iowa State QB Austin Flynn (24-41/239y, TD, INT), who would later run 25y for 1st Q TD, lost FUM 3 plays after Kaeding's 1st FG when hit by Hawk LB Abdul Hodge. Iowa QB Nathan Chandler (7-14/72y, TD) quickly hit 2 passes of 17y to WR Maurice Brown, 2nd of which went for TD. Leading 20-7 at H, Iowa stopped 1st series of 2nd H and FS Sean Considine blocked Iowa State P Troy Blankenship's boot, and DB Chris Smith fell on it in EZ for 27-7 Hawkeye advantage.

NEBRASKA 18 Penn State 10: Nebraska (3-0) spent extraordinary amount of 1st H in Penn State (1-2) territory. Nittany Lions D bent but didn't break in face of Huskers QB Jammal Lord's weak passing, allowing 3 FGs by K David Dyches. Meanwhile, Penn State's lethargic O got lift from WR Tony Johnson, who made brilliant 1-handed sideline grab, and TB Ricky Upton scored from 13YL on next play for 7-6 lead. Lions led 10-9 at H, but Nebraska came out at start of 3rd Q to completely disdain pass. TB Josh Davis (32/189y) ran ball down throat of Lions on 16-play, 80y drive that ate 8:12 and took Huskers to 15-10 lead. Penn State ran only 5 plays in 3rd Q as Nebraska snapped ball 29 times on 2 series until having FG blocked early in 4th Q. Rushing 20/100y, TD overall, Lord (4-6/60y, INT) threw only 1 pass in 2nd H.

Arkansas 38 TEXAS 28: Coach Houston Nutt seemed to always have Arkansas (2-0) peaked for special games, and Razorbacks' 60/265y running game was difference over old rival no. 6 Texas (1-1). Longhorns simply couldn't stop Hog runners, led by TB Cedric Cobbs (20/115y, TD) and QB Matt Jones (12/102y, TD). Jones' 3y TD run in 1st Q gave Arkansas lead for good at 14-7, and Cobbs busted up middle 3 mins into 3rd Q for 46y score that raised tally to 28-14. Texas WRs B.J. Johnson (6/123y, 2 TDs) and Roy Williams (10/117y) ran wild, but Johnson's 2 TDs from QB Chance Mock (21-40/264y, 3 TDs) could earn only 7-0 1st Q lead and pull Steers within 21-14 at H.

Washington State 47 COLORADO 26: Cougars (2-1) got off to 23-13 H lead on 74 and 77y TD passes by QB Matt Kegel (17-33/310y, 3 TDs, INT) to WR Sammy Moore and WR Scott Lunde respectively. After squandering 19-0 lead to Notre Dame week before, Washington State coach Bill Doba said, "All we preached was, finish!" Cougars finished by scoring 24 pts in 6:39 of 3rd Q, primarily on great work of Moore, who bobbled 2nd H KO and sprinted left for 97y KO TD RET, and RB Jonathan Smith 11/73y, TD), who broke 6 tackles on 26y TD run on next possession. Colorado (2-1) QB Joel Klatt was injured in 1st H after throwing short TD pass to TE Joe Klopfenstein (3/12y, 2 TDs), and left for good after being sacked in 3rd Q by Wazzu LB Don Jackson. Klatt's replacement, QB Erik Greenberg (19-30/199y, 3 TDs, 2 INTs) connected twice with WR Derek McCoy (11/131y, 2 TDs) for scores.

USA Today Coaches September 14

1	Oklahoma (46)	1551	14	Iowa	648
2	Miami (Fla.) (8)	1498	15	Nebraska	641
3	Southern California (1)	1397	16	Arizona State	637
4	Ohio State (7)	1366	17	Florida	587
5	Michigan (1)	1335	18	Arkansas	420
6	Kansas State	1265	19	TCU	298
7	Georgia	1217	20	Texas A&M	249
8	Virginia Tech	1123	21	Washington	204
9	Florida State	1031	22	Oregon	185
10	LSU	985	23	Notre Dame	140
11	Pittsburgh	933	24	Minnesota	122
12	Tennessee	892	25	Washington State	116
13	Texas	712			

September 20, 2003

(Th) VIRGINIA TECH 35 Texas A&M 19: Despite nasty effects of Hurricane Isabel, O was night's main feature as Virginia Tech TB Kevin Jones rushed for career-high 188y and 3 TDs, while Aggies QB Reggie McNeal toted up 47y rushing and 133y passing. Hokies (3-0) scored TDs on their 1st 2 possessions, but Aggies hung tough with 2 FGs before McNeal led 98y drive that cut deficit to 14-12 at H on 2y TD run by TB Courtney Lewis. Virginia Tech opened 2nd H with 76y drive for 21-12 lead on 2y TD run by Jones. Texas A&M (2-1) received special teams gift as Virginia Tech CB DeAngelo Hall muffed punt in wind on his own 24YL. McNeal faked run before throwing 15y TD pass to walk-on WR Tim Van Zant to pull within 21-19. Rally faded as A&M D wilted under weight of Hokies rush game that gained 273y and plowed on for 2 more TDs.

Miami 33 BOSTON COLLEGE 14: Miami's farewell tour to Big East began well as Hurricanes (4-0) built 33-0 lead by 3rd Q. WR Roscoe Parrish—yet another dynamic Miami returner—raced 92y to score on 1st Q punt RET, and S Sean Taylor went 67y with INT for TD as entire Miami team looked to score. Midway through 2nd Q, Canes had 21-0 lead even though they owned only trio of 1st downs. TB Derrick Knight led Eagles (2-2) with 83y rushing, but Eagles converted 2-16 3rd downs. Win was 14th straight in series for Miami that now had 7 TDs in 2003 from its D or special teams.

Tennessee 24 FLORIDA 10: Vols (3-0) converted fluke TD at end of 1st H and dominating line play to subdue Gators. Up 3-0, on own 20YL with 52 secs left in 2nd Q, Florida (2-2) inexplicably took timeouts in effort to move ball into FG range. Gators were forced to punt, and Tennessee got ball back with 20 secs left. After 13y gain on screen pass, Volunteers QB Casey Clausen threw desperation pass into EZ. Gators S Guss Scott and Vols WR Mark Jones each deflected ball off back of CB Keiwan Ratliff into hands of Tennessee WR James Banks. Unlikely 48y TD—on play called "Dancer All Go" that Banks said "never works" in practice—propelled Tennessee into lead it would not relinquish. After giving stirring H speech, Clausen, who finished with 12-23/235y, TD, INT, came up with 57y advance on 3rd Q pass to WR Bret Smith to set up 1y TD leap by TB Jabari Davis (20/78y, 2 TDs) for 17-3 lead. Florida managed 5y TD run by TB DeShawn Wynn, but could get no closer because of 5-min Vols TD drive.

LOUISIANA STATE 17 Georgia 10: LSU (4-0) QB Matt Mauck proved his mettle, ignoring pressure to throw 34y TD pass to WR Skylar Green with 1:22 left for win and redemption for both players. Green, who ran wrong route on winning play, earlier had dropped passes, while Mauck lost FUM on Georgia (3-1) 15YL with LSU ahead 10-3. After big hit by LB Odell Thurman caused Mauck to fumble, Bulldogs converted as TB Tyson Browning raced 93y with screen pass to tie game at 10-10. LSU WR Devery Henderson then set up Mauck's winning pass with 49y KO RET. Teams combined for 6 TOs with most important coming as LSU CB Corey Webster picked off QB David Greene to halt last-ditch Bulldogs drive. Injuries finally caught up with UGa, while healthy K Billy Bennett also hampered Georgia effort with 3 missed FGs in 1st H.

Northern Illinois 19 ALABAMA 16: Northern Illinois (3-0) upped its mark against ranked, BCS-conf teams to 2-0 with road win. TB Michael Turner rushed for 156y, and QB Josh Haldi threw for 2 TDs in 2nd H to pace Huskies attack. Ordinarily, Bama special teams sparkled, yet Northern Illinois owned category as K Steve Azar booted 51y FG, WR Kevin Woods took blocked x-pt back for 2 pts, and LB Jason Hawkins blocked punt. Sole Crimson Tide (2-2) highlight was 54y romp by TB Shaud Williams in 4th Q. Win propelled Huskies to their 1st-ever ranking at no. 20.

TOLEDO 35 Pittsburgh 31: Rockets (3-1) rallied for 2 late TDs, final coming with 43 secs left on 9y pass from Pittsburgh native QB Bruce Gradkowski to lunging WR Lance Moore in right corner of EZ. Gradkowski (49-62/461y,) marched Toledo 83y, converting 4th down with 13y pass to TE Andrew Clarke. At head of spread O that confused poor-tackling Panthers at times, Gradkowski set MAC record for single-game completions. Panthers (2-1) WR Larry Fitzgerald caught 12/201y and 9y TD near end of 1st H for what felt like comfy 24-14 lead at that time.

Marshall 27 KANSAS STATE 20: Wildcats (4-1) moved up in class from usual non-conf cupcakes and paid for it, losing 41-game home win streak against non-Big 12 foes. With each team starting reserve QB, Thundering Herd (2-2) backup QB Graham Gochneaur was hero by throwing 3y TD pass to TE Jason Rader late in 4th Q. S Chris Royal jump-started winning drive with 31y KO RET. Marshall also surprised K-State by running for 210y behind RB Butchie Wallace's 112y. Herd D contributed 2 GLSs and 4 forced TOs, including DE Jonathan Goddard's lumbering 84y RET of botched pitchout. Cats QB Jeff Schwinn threw for 241y, but suffered 3 TOs. Marshall D put wraps on K-State TB Darren Sproles (14/77y).

OKLAHOMA 59 Ucla 24: Refusing to change tactics and aim their punts elsewhere, Bruins (1-2) insisted on punting to Oklahoma DB Antonio Perkins, and he continued to kill UCLA with scoring RETs. Perkins ran back 7 punts for NCAA-record 277y, scoring thrice, new NCAA mark for punt RET TDs. Sooners (4-0) QB Jason White (17-25/243y) threw 2 TDs but suffered 2 INTs. UCLA TB Maurice Drew scored twice in 3rd Q, on 3y run and 91y KO RET. Bruins allowed most pts since 61-20 loss to Washington in 1970.

OREGON 31 Michigan 27: Energized by largest home crowd ever (59,023), spirited Ducks (4-0) pulled upset. Oregon focused on Michigan TB Chris Perry (11/26y) in holding Michigan O, averaging 307y on ground, to –3y rushing. Wolverines (3-1) went to air behind QB John Navarre, who threw for 360y and 3 TDs despite being held to 87y entering 4th Q. Navarre completed 9y TD pass to WR Steve Breaston to cut Oregon lead to 24-21 in 4th Q. Michigan soon got ball back to no avail. Ducks S Keith Lewis blocked P Adam Finley's punt, with Oregon S J.D. Nelson rumbling but fumbling at Wolverines 1YL, where it bounced into EZ to be recovered by WR Jordan Carey for clinching TD. Earlier CB Steven Moore returned punt 61y for Ducks TD.

USA Today Coaches September 21

1	Oklahoma (51)	1557	14	Arkansas	790
2	Miami (Fla.) (6)	1503	15	Oregon	780
3	Southern California (1)	1435	16	Kansas State	620
4	Ohio State (5)	1393	17	TCU	457
5	Virginia Tech	1294	18	Washington	356
6	Florida State	1251	19	Pittsburgh	340
7	LSU	1206	20	Minnesota	292
8	Tennessee	1139	21	Washington State	282
9	Iowa	964	22	Northern Illinois	238
10	Michigan	870	23	Missouri	164
11	Nebraska	808	24	Arizona State	157
12	Georgia	804	25	Florida	133
13	Texas	796			

September 27, 2003

VIRGINIA 27 Wake Forest 24: With game tied, Wake Forest (3-2) was determined to unravel 24-24 knot in regulation—which it did, but not to its favor. Demon Deacons QB Cory Randolph misfired to WR Jason Anderson, with pass being picked off by Virginia (3-1) CB Jamaine Winborne and returned to Wake 33YL. Cavaliers QB Matt Schaub (30-45/326y, 2 TDs, 3 INTs), who missed 2 previous games with shoulder injury, then completed 15y pass to TE Heath Miller (7/94y). Virginia K Connor Hughes, who had tied game with 53y FG less than 2 mins earlier, kicked winning 38y FG with 10 secs left. Schaub led O that amassed 487y, but had 5 TOs. Randolph (17-31/218y, 2 INTs) threw and ran for TDs as Deacs built 21-13 lead in 3rd Q. After Schaub tied game 21-21 with 5y TD pass to Miller at beginning of 4th Q, Wake drove 72y to go-ahead 25y FG by K Ryan Plackemeier. Cavs TB Wali Lundy rushed for 27/137y.

Arkansas 34 ALABAMA 31 (OT): After rallying from 21-pt deficit in 2nd H, Razorbacks (4-0) were in trouble in 1st OT after INT thrown by QB Matt Jones. Crimson Tide (2-3), however, was penalized 15y for excessively celebrating S Charles Jones' pick. Starting at Arkansas 40YL, Alabama could not cash in TO as K Brian Bostick missed 38y FG attempt. Razorbacks then showed how to convert OT TOs as S Jimarr Gallon's INT in 2nd OT set up game-winning 19y FG by Arkansas K Chris Balseiro. Game had been tied 10-10 at H, but Tide scored 3 TDs in less than 8 mins of 3rd Q on 80y run by TB Shaud Williams (19/135y) and TD passes of 71y and 12y from QB Brodie Croyle (12-25/204y, 3 TDs) to WR Dre Fulgham. Backup Hogs QB Ryan Sorahan led 2 TD drives, with help from RB Cedric Cobbs, who rushed 36/career-high 198y and 5y TD. Jones returned to throw tying TD on 3y pass to WR Richard Smith.

Texas Tech 49 MISSISSIPPI 45: Air show finally was won by Red Raiders (3-1) on 9y TD pass from QB B.J. Symons to WR Carlos Francis (9/184y) with 64 secs left. Symons threw for 44-64/661y, 6 TDs to break school and conf record he set prior week with 586y vs. NC State. QB Eli Manning's 409y passing had led Rebels (2-2) to 45-34 lead in 4th Q, but too many Mississippi scoring drives ended up as FGs—6 were booted by K Jonathan Nichols. Red Raiders S Ryan Aycock picked off Manning's final pass near Tech GL to kill comeback threat. Raiders WR Wes Welker caught 10/131y and TD, with 2 of his catches for 36y setting up Symons' winning pass.

Minnesota 20 PENN STATE 14: After sweeping through light non-conf schedule, Gophers (5-0) passed 1st test behind their deep squadron of rushers that gained 250y. Minnesota ran for 73y on 99y drive, that included consecutive gains of 13, 11, and 11y, late in 1st Q for 14-0 lead on frosh TB Laurence Maroney's 3y run. Penn State (2-3) backup QB Michael Robinson (16-27/178y)—in for QB Zack Mills, who sprained his knee—led 2 TD drives, capping 2nd with 10y scoring keeper, to cut deficit to 17-14 in 2nd Q. Lions would get no closer, thanks in part to 2 INTs. Gophers LB Terrance Campbell who appeared to trap ball, ended deep drive late in 1st H, and INT by S Justin Fraley, was converted into 30y FG by K Rhys Lloyd to close scoring. Penn State had last chance, which failed on downs after it reached Minnesota 13YL. RB Marion Barber III led Gophers with 23/134y, TD rushing.

Iowa 20 MICHIGAN STATE 10: With QB Jeff Smoker rewriting school record book, Spartans (4-1) jumped on Iowa with scoring passes on opening 2 possessions. Smoker (28-44/218y), who set school records for career pass attempts (818), TD passes (48), and completions (478), was perfect 7-7 on opening 80y drive that ended with his 17y TD pass to WR Ziehl Kavanaght. Hawkeyes (4-1) lost FUM on their 1st possession when WR Ramon Ochoa was stripped after reception, and bobble was recovered by Spartans S Jason Harmon on Iowa 41YL. Soon thereafter, MSU TE Eric Knott was in EZ with 7y TD catch for 14-0 lead. QB Nathan Chandler halved lead on 6y TD pass to cap 80y drive, but Hawks would get no closer despite RB Fred Russell's 122y rushing.

KANSAS 35 Missouri 14: Rebuilding Jayhawks (4-1) thrilled sellout crowd, contained Missouri (4-1) QB Brad Smith, and showcased own signal-caller. Kansas QB Bill Whittemore completed 14-22/111y and rushed 16/76y and 2 TDs. Kansas TB Clark Green (17/78y, 2 TDs) ran for 4y TD for 13-7 lead in 2nd Q, and his other TD came early in 4th Q on 6y run for 21-14 lead. Smith was held to 12-24/62y, TD passing and 17/33y rushing as Kansas D limited Tigers to 196y total O. But, Smith and Mizzou TB Zack Abron (17/112y) sparked 72y TD drive after 2nd H KO that was capped by WR Darius Outlaw's 9y TD grab. Game remained in doubt until 4th Q when Whittemore sparked 3 TD drives.

Air Force 24 BRIGHAM YOUNG 10: Falcons (5-0) finally won series road game for coach Fisher DeBerry, his 1st in Provo and Air Force's 1st since 1982, as QB Chance Harridge rushed for 2 TDs and threw for another. Cougars (2-3) QB John Beck (19-35/193y, TD) tied game at 10-10 in 3rd Q on 25y TD pass to TE Phillip Niu. Air Force then dominated scoring in 4th Q as Harridge threw 30y TD pass to WR J.P. Waller and scored on 1y keeper, while BYU lost ball on FUM and on downs. Falcons HB Darnell Stephens was game's leading rusher with 93y.

CALIFORNIA 34 Southern California 31 (OT): Unpredictable attack from underdog Bears (3-3) stunned Southern California when K Tyler Fredrickson booted 38y FG for game-winner in 3rd OT. After Trojans (3-1) wiped out 21-7 deficit in 2nd H, they got LB Lofa Tatupu's tying 27y INT TD RET in 3rd Q and DL Shaun Cody's block of 51y FG attempt late in 4th Q to stay alive. Troy began scoreless 1st OT in fine form with 20y run by TB Hershel Dennis, but Dennis lost FUM on next play, recovered by California LB Wendell Hunter. Cal TB Adimchinobe Echemandu (34/147y) raced 14y, but 29y FG attempt was blocked by Trojans TE Gregg Gunther. After trade of TD passes forced 3rd OT, Trojans K Ryan Killeen missed FG try to set up Fredrickson as game's hero. Cal QB Reggie Robertson came off bench to hit 9-12/109y, while starting QB Aaron Rodgers threw for 18-25/217y, 2 TDs, before leaving with injury. Trojans QB Matt Leinart completed 21-39/277y, 2 TDs, but was picked off 3 times.

Washington State 55 OREGON 16: Apparently Cougars (4-1) failed to note Oregon's press clippings from Michigan victory; they forced 9 TOs by Ducks in stunning rout that triggered 4 losses in 5 games. After not throwing single INT all season, Oregon (4-1) QBs Kellen Clemens and Jason Fife combined to pitch debilitating 7 pick-offs. Washington State QB Matt Kegel (13-33/242y) threw 3 TDs, while RB Jermaine Green added 2 rushing TDs. Cougars jumped to 38-2 lead at H after S Virgil Williams returned INT 40y for TD and S Jeremy Bohannon took blocked punt 4y for another score. Ducks WR Demetrius Williams caught 9/175y and 26y TD reception in 3rd Q.

USA Today Coaches September 28

1	Oklahoma (49)	1557	14	Kansas State	618
2	Miami (Fla.) (8)	1513	15	Washington State	546
3	Ohio State (6)	1433	16	Minnesota	504
4	Virginia Tech	1369	17	Washington	489
5	Florida State	1315	18	Pittsburgh	477
6	LSU	1260	19	Iowa	448
7	Tennessee	1193	20	Northern Illinois	413
8	Nebraska	988	21	TCU	404
9	Arkansas	969	22	Oregon	215
10	Southern California	953	23	Purdue	166
11	Michigan	950	24	Florida	133
12	Georgia	923	25	Air Force	132
13	Texas	892			

October 4, 2003

(Th) MIAMI 22 West Virginia 20: Maybe he talked too much, but Miami (5-0) TE Kellen Winslow could really play football. Winning play came on last-sec 23y FG by frosh K Jon Peattie, his school-record 5th of night, but Hurricanes season was salvaged earlier in drive on brilliant catch by Winslow (10/104y) on 4th-and-13 play. Overthrown pass forced 6'5" TE Winslow to leap and twist backward for 16y catch. QB Brock Berlin (37-54/352y, TD, 2 INTs) drove Canes 66y to winning FG after Mountaineers (1-4) scored on another brilliant play: TD run after catch by RB Quincy Wilson, like Winslow son of former NFLer (Chicago Bears' Otis Wilson). Wilson caught screen pass, eluded DT Vince Wilfork, and raced down sideline. He ran over Canes S Brandon Meriweather en route to 33y TD. Go-ahead TD was set up by lost FUM by Miami TB Jarrett Payton—yet another son of NFL great—who was subbing for TB Frank Gore, lost for season earlier in game with knee injury. Wilson led WVU with 99y rushing.

NAVY 28 Air Force 25: Improved Navy (3-2), which had not won Commander-in-Chief trophy since 1981, took step toward that goal with upset of Air Force (5-1). Midshipmen snapped 6-game series losing streak in process. Trailing 3-0 in 2nd Q, Navy scored 2 TDs in 48-sec span to grab lead it would never relinquish. Falcons cut deficit to 14-10 at H, but surrendered 82y drive that featured Navy QB Craig Candeto's 1st completion: 10y TD pass to SB Tony Lane. Air Force scored twice in 4th Q, including 2nd 1y TD run by QB Chance Harridge (21/129y) and EZ FUM recovered by T Brett Waller. Navy FB Kyle Eckel (33/176y) cemented upset by rushing for 55y of 71y drive to his clinching 4y TD run on 4th-and-1 with 7:35 left. Nation's top two rushing teams combined for 596y on ground with Navy notching 309y.

MARYLAND 21 Clemson 7: Terrapins (4-2) won 4th straight as QB Scott McBrien (14-27/204y) threw 3 TD passes, and D held Clemson to 10y rushing. McBrien hit WR Steve Suter for 25y TD on opening possession for lead Maryland would keep. After short Clemson punt, Maryland moved 44y to 10y TD pass to WR Rich Parson. Later in 1st H, Tigers (3-2) WR Derrick Hamilton (7/175y, TD) broke free for 70y TD catch to halve deficit. Clemson was done scoring, while Terps WR Derrick Fenner contributed to highlight reel, catching pass and racing across field to score on 69y play. Tigers QB Charlie Whitehurst threw for 320y, but was picked off twice.

Mississippi 20 FLORIDA 17: Rebels (3-2) suddenly owned 2-game win streak over Florida as QB Eli Manning (17-29/262y, INT) rallied his troops to victorious 50y TD drive at end of 4th Q. Manning had help from RB Vashon Pearson, who scored winning 1y TD run with 70 secs left. Florida (3-3) frosh QB Chris Leak (14-27/234y, 2 TDs, 3 INTs) threw TD passes of 18y to TE Ben Troupe and 4y to WR O.J. Small as Florida built 14-3 2nd Q lead. But, Rebels narrowed it to 17-10 at H, and Ole Miss D blanked Gators in 2nd H and picked off 3 of Leak's passes in 4th Q. Rebels RB Vashon Pearson scored short TD with 1:10 remaining for win, and S Eric Oliver's INT stopped last-gasp Florida drive. Mississippi gained 223y on ground as RB Ronald McClendon (8/107y, TD) sprinted 52y for 2nd Q score. Gators coach Ron Zook's early-career record dropped to 11-8, with half of his losses surprisingly coming at home in Gainesville.

AUBURN 28 Tennessee 21: Good run game could cure loads of ills. Auburn (3-2) dominated line of scrimmage as TB Carnell "Cadillac" Williams gained 185y of team's 264y rushing, while Vols managed but 4y on ground. Tennessee (4-1) found some success through air as QB Casey Claussen (30-47/355y, 2 TDs, INT) twice hit 4th Q TD passes, but they were not enough to prevent Claussen's 1st career SEC road loss after 11 wins. QB Jason Campbell threw 2 TDs on 157y passing to give Auburn terrific O balance. Tigers' early season struggles running ball now seemed to be history with their 3rd straight game that totaled more than 200y on ground.

IOWA 30 Michigan 27: Determined to avenge blowout loss of 2002, Wolverines (4-2) jumped to 14-0 lead behind QB John Navarre, who threw for 224y in 1st H. Iowa (5-1) rallied to tie 20-17 at H as QB Nathan Chandler (17-34/195y, INT), threw and ran for TDs. Hawkeyes D adjusted to hold Michigan to 5 1st downs in 2nd H, while O scored 20 straight pts for 30-20 lead. Iowa special teams led to go-ahead score: S Chris Smith blocked rugby-style punt on run by Wolverines P Garrett Rivas to set up 31y FG by K Nate Kaeding for 23-20 lead. Chandler's eventual winning TD: 31y pass to WR Ramon Ochoa. Leading O that totaled 463y—to 295y for Iowa—Navarre threw for school-record 389y, hitting WRs Jason Avant for 7/175y and Braylon Edwards for 7/114y, 2 TDs. Iowa RB Fred Russell was leading ground gainer with 110y rushing.

TEXAS 24 Kansas State 20: Practical elimination from BCS hovered over loser of this essential Big 12 tilt. Longhorns (4-1) dominated 1st H and trotted off with 17-3 edge. Texas WR Tony Jeffrey recovered blocked punt in EZ for 1st Q TD, and QB Chance Mock (7-16/88y, TD) lofted 51y TD pass to WR Sean Thomas who zipped down right sideline when K-State CB Randy Jordan fell. Kansas State (4-2) was revived for 2nd H, storming to 20-17 lead. Wildcats QB Ell Roberson (5-18/89y, 2 iNTs), back from hand injury, made fabulous pin-ball run for 27y TD 3 mins into 3rd Q. On Texas' next possession, K-State S Rashad Washington (9 tackles) blocked P Richmond McGee's punt, but ball took crazy sideways hop in EZ, and Cats, hankering for TD, had to settle for safety. In 1st min of 4th Q, Roberson gave Wildcats 20-17 lead with 1y TD run and 2-pt conv. Shortly thereafter, Longhorn DB Nathan Vasher, outstanding in pass coverage, fumbled punt at his 21YL, and K-State appeared ready to ice game. But, Roberson fumbled 2 plays later, and Texas began winning drive that was capped by 4th down TD sneak by frosh QB Vincent Young that came with 5:19 left.

TEXAS TECH 59 Texas A&M 28: Texas Tech (4-1) QB B.J. Symons' assault on record books continued as he threw conf-record 8 TD passes as Aggies permitted most pts in their long and proud history. Symons completed 34-46/505y in topping 500y for 3rd straight game. WR Nehemiah Glover caught 3 TDs, 2 coming in game's opening 6 mins, to lead wave of talented Red Raider wideouts. Texas A&M (2-3) QB Reggie McNeal threw for 251y. Previous Big 12 record for TDs thrown in game had been set in this matchup in 2002, when Aggies QB Dustin Long tossed 7 scores.

BAYLOR 42 Colorado 30: Golly! Break up Bears (3-2), winners of 3 straight games as stunning result was affected in Waco. Scoring 5 TDs in span of 17:15 allowed Baylor to win only its 5th Big 12 game after 52 losses. Baylor QB Aaron Karas threw 3 TDs and late-blooming sr TB Rashad Armstrong rushed for 166y, 2 TDs. Bears D came through with GLS early in 4th Q and TD on 7y FUM RET by LB Jamaal Harper. Harper's TD was set up by sack by LB Derrick Cash of Buffs QB Erik Greenberg and resultant FUM TD RET gave Baylor 28-23 lead. After teams traded TDs, Colorado (2-3) looked to regain lead after recovering FUM on Baylor 9YL. On 4th-and-goal from 1YL, LB John Garrett nailed Buffs TB Brian Calhoun to halt drive. Armstrong then burst free for 55y clinching TD run as centerpiece of 97y drive. Colorado's Greenberg threw for 346y, while WR Derek McCoy nabbed 6/171y and 2 TDs.

UCLA 46 Washington 16: It was difficult to remember Huskies had held 16-7 H lead after UCLA (3-2) permitted only 87y O in blitzing visitors 39-0 over final 30 mins. Washington (3-2) scored on its 1st 3 series, including short TD catch by WR Reggie Williams (10/105y). Huskies K Evan Knudson made his 3rd FG on last play of 1st H. UCLA souvenir program coverboy DE Dave Ball, who created 2 FUMs and 3 sacks, launched onslaught by forcing EZ FUM by Washington QB Cody Pickett (26-42/281y, TD, 2 INTs) recovered by DT Rodney Leisle for TD. Later in 3rd Q, RB Manuel White (19/83y) scored on 1y run as Bruins took their 1st lead at 21-16. Leisle, making up for lost time after suspension for game's 1st H, stopped Huskies drive at own 12YL with INT—DT would make 3 INTs by season's end—of pass that bounced off facemask of intended receiver, Huskies FB Zach Tuiasosopo. Bruins QB Drew Olson threw for 258y with WR Craig Bragg snaring 6/142y.

Oregon State 35 CALIFORNIA 21: California (3-4) D had to know Oregon State (5-1) TB Steven Jackson was going to carry ball over and over, but they were hard pressed in finding way to stop him. Jackson rushed 35/227y and 3 TDs as Beavers won 5th straight in series. Oregon State QB Derek Anderson turned in fine road performance, completing 18-27/224y, 2 TDs. Held to 52y passing when transfer QB sensation Aaron Rodgers struggled, Bears were forced to showcase TB Adimchinobe Echemandu (19/146y). Echemandu gained 142y of opening 178y O managed by Cal and scored 2 TDs as Bears fought to within 28-21 midway through 3rd Q. Jackson then raced 66y to set up his clinching 5y TD reception.

October 11, 2003

(Fri) Michigan 38 MINNESOTA 35: Billed as Minnesota's most important game since 1960, Gophers (6-1) got going fast as their nimble O-line, led by C Greg Eslinger, carved big holes for TBs Marion Barber (21/197y, TD) and Laurence Maroney (9/81y, 2 TDs). Minnesota rushed 53/423y, most all-time against Michigan (5-2) and went to 21-7 lead when Maroney scored his 2nd TD in middle of 3rd Q. Badly outplayed and trailing 28-7, Wolverines started 80y drive in last min of 3rd Q. Michigan TB Chris Perry (20/85y, TD) contributed 11/122y, TD receiving and scored on 10y pass on 5th play of 4th Q. Gophers QB Asad Abdul-Khaliq (8-18/71y, 2 INTs and 9/106y, TD rushing) erred by throwing off balance to right flat after spinning out of sack attempt. UM DB Jacob Stewart raced in front of receiver for easy 34y TD dash, and Wolverines were back in it at 28-21 with nearly 14 mins left. But, on 3rd-and-1, Abdul-Khaliq ran option off RG and burst through stacked D for 52y TD, so Minny was back up by 14 pts. Michigan QB John Navarre (33-47/353y, 2 TDs, INT) hit 15-20/195y, 52y TD to WR Braylon Edwards in 4th Q. After Perry tied it 35-35 with 10y run with 5:48 to play, Gophers had to punt, and UM K Garrett Rivas won it with 33y FG with 47 secs to play.

Notre Dame 20 PITTSBURGH 14: Pitt (3-2) had its RBs stuffed at scrimmage all night by aroused Notre Dame (2-3) D-front. Panthers ended with 8y rushing, while Fighting Irish used strong blocking by TE Anthony Fasano and constantly-pulling G Mark LeVoir to send TB Julius Jones, back from academic ineligibility this year, to school rushing mark of 24/262y, 2 TDs. ND turned Pitt CB Tutu Ferguson's early-game punt FUM into Jones' 25y TD run. Panthers packed virtually all its O into 2-min span of 1st and 2nd Qs. QB Rod Rutherford (12-30/167y, 2 TDs), who was sacked 8 times, finished 52y drive with 23y TD pass to WR Larry Fitzgerald (5/79y, 2 TDs) on last play of 1st Q, and, after Ferguson's 71y punt RET, Fitzgerald caught another TD pass. Irish led 17-14 at H and ate most of 4th Q with 8-min march that included Jones' 61y sprint.

CLEMSON 30 Virginia 27 (OT): Virginia (4-2) limped out of Palmetto State with its 2nd loss in 2003, having been whipped by South Carolina Gamecocks earlier. This time, Cavaliers arrived looking for 4-0 start in ACC and sporting best rushing attack in conf. But, Clemson (4-2) shut off run game at 53y level and jumped to 10-0 H edge on TD pass by QB Charlie Whitehurst (27-44/265y, 2 TDs). Virginia QB Matt Schaub (33-48/271y, 2 TDs, INT) threw 3rd Q TD passes to TEs Heath Miller and Patrick Estes and passed Cavs into position for TB Alvin Pearman's 1y TD run that tied it 24-24 in 4th Q. Tigers LB Leroy Hill stopped Pearman on 3rd-and-1 at 16YL in OT, so Cavs had to settle for FG. Clemson won it when Whitehurst lobbed 4y TD pass to big WR Kevin Youngblood (9/87y, TD) who muscled his way into catching position.

Miami 22 FLORIDA STATE 14: Deluge of rain helped obscure that Hurricanes (6-0) dominated play far greater than score indicated. Miami had 2 heroes. TB Jarrett Payton (26/97y), son of NFL great Walter, slept with his father's dark blue no. 34 Chicago Bears jersey on Friday night and caught 14y TD pass in 1st start of his injury-riddled 5-year career. Hurricanes S Sean Taylor made 2 INTs, including 50y TD RET late in 2nd Q for 19-0 lead. Meanwhile, Florida State (5-1) floundered, having punt blocked and watching Miami recover its own accidental onside-KO, with each leading to 1st Q FG by Canes K Jon Peattie (3 FGs). Seminoles lost 5 TOs during stretch of 7 series in mid-game. QB Chris Rix (20-42/235y, 2 TDs, 2 INTs), who had plenty of trouble until he adjusted to wet ball, finally was able to throw for 2 late scores.

Georgia 41 TENNESSEE 14: Georgia Bulldogs (5-1) took commanding role in SEC East even though they traded results of 2 odd and dramatic plays with Tennessee (4-2). Behind 10-0 early in 2nd Q after TD pass by UGa QB David Greene (22-27/228y, TD), Vols QB Casey Clausen (11-23/165y, TD, 2 INTs) launched long pass up left sideline. Bulldogs DB Decory Bryant went up for INT, but player he was covering, WR Mark Jones, snatched ball from over Bryant's back and cantered 90y for longest pass in UT history. Tennessee marched in last 3 mins of 2nd Q from its 5YL, with aid of 3 foul PENs, in attempt to take 14-13 H lead. With 7 secs to go at 1YL, Vols attempted TB dive off RG with FB as lead blocker. But, Clausen's handoff accidentally glanced off hip of FB, and Clausen's diving attempt for REC knocked ball back to 8YL where Georgia S Sean Jones scooped it for uncontested 92y TD RET and 20-7 H lead. That was all she wrote for Vols. Bulldogs iced it with 3 TDs in 3rd Q after 83y drive, LB Odell Thurman's 26y INT RET to 5YL, and DE Robert Geathers' INT at Vols 22YL.

Florida 19 LOUISIANA STATE 7: Mistake-prone Louisiana State (5-1) lost 3 TOs, committed 13/99y in PENs, and scored nary single pt on O. Florida (4-3), reeling under criticism aimed at coach Ron Zook, gladly got away from home and watched frosh QB Chris Leak blossom. Despite being sacked 6/-56y, Leak (18-30/229y, 2TDs) effectively located open targets in long-y situations all day. LSU got on scoreboard 1st as Gators punted on their 1st series: Bengals WR Skyler Green burst through tacklers for 80y punt TD RET. Leak brought Florida right back to tie it in 1st Q with 80y drive capped by his 22y TD arrow to RB Ran Carthon. LSU's D made some big plays to force K Matt Leach's 29y FG late in 1st Q, after DB Keiwan Ratliffe's 44y INT RET, and making REC of UF TB DeShawn Wynn's FUM as he leapt toward EZ from 1YL. However, Tigers gained only 103y in 1st H in which they trailed 13-7. Gators TB Ciatrick Fason (7/92y), listed deep down depth chart until injuries gave him chance to play, had 62y dash and caught 35y TD pass from Leak in 3rd Q.

Auburn 10 ARKANSAS 3: Auburn (4-2), all but written off after early losses, moved back into SEC West contention by dropping season's 1st loss on no. 7 Razorbacks (4-1). Tigers didn't exactly shut down Arkansas' most-prolific SEC rushing attack as Hogs gained 173y, led by TB Cedric Cobbs (16/78y). Arkansas DB Tony Bua halted early Auburn threat with INT at his 6YL. After Porkers K Chris Balseiro hooked 35y FG try, TB Carnell "Cadillac" Williams (35/150y, TD) scored game's only TD on 6y burst up middle with 29 secs left in 2nd Q. Late in 3rd Q, Arkansas QB Matt Jones (13-28/168y) converted testy 3rd-and-22 from his 46YL with 25y completion to WR DeCori Birmingham, but 1st-and-goal opportunity at 8YL was limited to Balseiro's successful 25y FG to trim deficit to 7-3. K John Vaughn made 34y FG in 4th Q for 10-3 Tigers advantage. Jones ran to Auburn 10YL with 6:30 left only to lose FUM at 8YL.

WISCONSIN 17 Ohio State 10: Ohio State's 19-game winning streak couldn't stand up to another nail-biter. Wisconsin (6-1) scored game-winning TD pass on 79y out-and-up fake by WR Lee Evans to beat stellar Buckeyes (5-1) CB Chris Gamble with 5:20 to play. Throwing long pass was Badgers backup QB Matt Schabert, who was in because starting QB Jim Sorgi (5-7/54y, INT) went out in 3rd Q with throat injury that was perpetrated by extracurricular choke at bottom of pile by Ohio LB Robert Reynolds (12 tackles). Wisconsin rushed for 141y against nation's top statistical run D (43.4y per game avg) as sub TB Booker Stanley (31/125y, TD) scored early in 2nd Q to lead Badgers to 7-3 H edge. Ohio State QB Craig Krenzel (14-26/202y, TD, INT) tied it 10-10 by finishing 75y march with 6y TD pass to WR Michael Jenkins with 6:09 to play. Just 3 plays later, Evans went long for perfect, in-stride TD catch.

MISSOURI 41 Nebraska 24: Mizzou Tigers (5-1) roared to finish line with 27 pts in 4th Q to beat Nebraska (5-1) for 1st time since 1978. Huskers, tops in nation on D with 219y avg, allowed 452y to Missouri. QB Brad Smith (13-27/180y, 2 INTs) gave up 1st pick-off in last 140 attempts until Huskers S Josh Bullocks made INT in 1st Q. It set up WR Mark LeFlore's 55y TD sprint on screen pass from QB Jammal Lord (12-18/146y, TD, INT). But, Bengals led 14-10 at H as Smith scored on tricky 47y pass from WR Darius Outlaw and RB Zack Abron scored his 34th career TD. Nebraska went up 24-14 as sub TB David Horne (26/119y, TD) went 5y and Lord (19/111y, TD rushing) dashed 35y to TDs. In 4th Q, masterful Smith scored on runs of 39, 1, and 9y to enhance fake FG 14y TD pass by holder and Tigers backup QB Santino Riccio.

Oklahoma 65 Texas 13 (Dallas): Jason White (17-21/290y, 4 TDs), Oklahoma's injury comeback QB, was model of precision as no. 1 Sooners (6-0) won by biggest margin and for 4th straight time over rival Texas (4-2) in Red River Shootout. Additionally, Oklahoma D forced 6 TOs, including DE Jonathan Jackson's 21y INT TD RET that popped into Jackson's hands after being blocked off throwing hand of Longhorns frosh QB Vincent Young (11-21/135y, INT, and 15/127y, TD rushing). Young, doing his best in tough situation, made 27y serpentine TD run in 2nd Q, but it elevated score only to 27-13. Sooners sent 7 different players into EZ, while RB Renaldo Works (15/112y, 2 TDs) scored on 6 and 54y runs. OU WR Mark Clayton caught 8/190y, TD.

USA Today Coaches October 12

1	Oklahoma (58)	1570	14	Nebraska	704
2	Miami (Fla.) (5)	1514	15	Purdue	699
3	Virginia Tech	1452	16	Northern Illinois	694
4	Southern California	1334	17	Michigan	675
5	Georgia	1333	18	Michigan State	581
6	Washington State	1108	19	Minnesota	369
7	Florida State	1086	20	Texas	293
8	Ohio State	1065	21	Oregon State	258
9	Iowa	981	22	Tennessee	249
10	LSU	938	23	Texas Tech	222
11	Arkansas	827	24	Oklahoma State	218
12	Wisconsin	733	25	Auburn	181
13	TCU	730			

October 18, 2003

Florida State 19 VIRGINIA 14: Bobby Bowden of Seminoles (6-1) tied Penn State's Joe Paterno atop Div1-A list of coaching victories with 338. Early on, Florida State WR Craphonso Thorpe (3/104y, TD) caught medium-distance pass, put on slight fake, and used his sprinter's speed for 79y untouched TD from QB Chris Rix (12-25/189y, TD). FSU cashed 1st Q tipped INT by FS B.J. Ward into 1st of 4 FGs by K Xavier Beitia. Trying to overcome poor punting and no running game (9/-5y), Cavaliers (4-3) pinned hopes on arm of QB Matt Schaub (39-53/326y, 2 TDs, INT). It was long O fight for Virginia, but Schaub finally fashioned 92y TD drive late in 2nd Q and just when ESPN analyst Mike Gottfried suggested he didn't have ponies to do so. TB Alvin Pearman, who set school reception mark with 16/134y, tallied on 21y TD pass. Trailing 16-7 at 3:43 mark of in 3rd Q, Cavs used frosh CB Tony Franklin's 39y KO RET to launch Schaub's 4 completions to Pearman that set up 8y TD catch by TE Heath Miller. Virginia drove near midfield, down 19-14, inside last 7 mins, but on 3rd-and-3, Schaub was directing his O when Shotgun snap flew past him unnoticed for 17y loss. Virginia had to punt and never regained possession.

Arizona State 33 NORTH CAROLINA 31: Struggles of Tar Heels continued as North Carolina (1-6) D surrendered 61y drive in game's final min, capped by Arizona State (4-3) QB Andrew Walter's winning 5y TD pass to WR Skyler Fulton (7/68y, 2 TDs). Drive began after failed 4th-and-1 run by Tar Heels TB Ronnie McGill on 3rd straight call of "45 Army" play that Sun Devils finally figured out. Biggest play of winning drive was 41y connection by Walter to WR Derek Hagan, who took short pass and broke tackles until finally being hailed at UNC 5YL. Hagan caught 11/185y, while Walter finished with 34-59/408y passing and RB Loren Wade rushed for 130y as Arizona State gained 598y. Devils gave chunks of that O back with 16 PENs/153y. QB Darian Durant led North Carolina with 167y passing and 1y TD pass to RB Jacque Lewis for 31-27 lead in 4th Q. Loss was 10th straight at home for beleagured Tar Heels.

Florida 33 ARKANSAS 28: With memory still fresh of Florida's collapse against Miami, Gators must have been edgy as no. 11 Arkansas rallied for 3 TDs in last 8:46 of game. Hogs were within official's decision of stopping Florida at midfield in last min, but suffered from crushing either-or personal foul PEN on S Tony Bua. But 1st, Arkansas TB Cedric Cobbs (14/88y, TD) gave his team 7-0 lead late in 1st Q with 7y TD run, only to see Florida QB Chris Leak (20-34/269y/TD, INT) gradually bloom into best day of his frosh season. Gators earned 13-7 H edge on TD pass and 2 FGs by K Matt Leach. RB Ciatrick Fason (11/98y, TD), who had scored on Leak's 33y pass in 2nd Q, bolted off RG Lance Butler's block on 1st snap of 2nd H and scorched 75y to score for 19-7 lead. When Gators DB Keiwan Ratliff tallied on 44y TD RET of his 3rd INT for 33-7 lead with 8:46 left, UF appeared home-free. Ratliff gleefully fired ball into stands after his TD, which brought 1st of several foolish Florida PENs. Normally better runner than thrower, Razorbacks QB Matt Jones (20-30/299y, 3 TDs, 2 INTs), suddenly got hot passing hand. Jones hit 8-11/142y, 3 TDs in last 8-and-half mins to pull Porkers within 33-28. On 3rd-and-5, Leak rolled out and foolishly lofted poor pass that was picked off near midfield. But, excited Bua made helmet-to-helmet contact on Leak in trying to knock him OB. Flag flew on close call, and Gators retained ball to run out clock.

OHIO STATE 19 Iowa 10: It would turn out to be rugged D skirmish, but Ohio State (6-1), coming off its 1st loss in nearly 2 years, scored 10 pts in less than 6 mins at outset. Buckeyes would win 3 games this season without scoring TD by its O. Outstanding K Mike Nugent bombed 53y FG. Hawkeyes (5-2) went 3-and-out, and Ohio WR Michael Jenkins raced 54y on punt TD RET. Iowa drove 51y before 1st Q ended, and K Nate Kaeding drilled 36y FG to make it 10-3. Score held until middle of 3rd Q when Hawks were halted twice on tackles by sub Bucks LB Mike D'Andrea and had to punt. Sub WR Roy Hall blocked Iowa P David Bradley's boot, and Ohio DB Donte Whitner recovered in EZ for TD. Hawkeyes got back in game on 2nd play of 4th Q when Kaeding took blind toss on fake FG and dashed 5y around RE for TD. But, Ohio D allowed only 9y rest of way and forced safety when Iowa C Eric Rothwell messed up Shotgun snap by sending it through EZ with 3:03 left to play.

Purdue 26 WISCONSIN 23: Evenly-matched Big 10 rivals squared off to keep pace with Michigan State and Michigan in conf derby. Purdue (6-1) QB Kyle Orton (38-55/411y, TD) took to air often for 15 completions in row and lifted Boilermakers to 14-0 lead after 1st Q TOs, including his 6y score to WR Taylor Stubblefield (16/130y, TD). Badgers (6-2) got 28y TD dash from TB Anthony Davis (18/96y, TD) late in 1st Q, but would end up with only 97y on ground. Wisconsin stayed competitive with LB Jeff Mack's 55y FUM TD RET in 2nd Q and S Jim Leonhard's 66y punt TD RET in 4th Q. Latter heroics lifted Badgers to 23-23 tie with 2:55 to go. Purdue took over at its 17YL, and Orton hit 5-7 throws on methodical trip to distant 1YL where K Ben Jones hit his 4th FG for win with :03 on clock. Boilers WR John Standeford made career-best 16/184y.

Michigan State 44 MINNESOTA 38: Golden Gophers (6-2) turned over opening KO to Spartans (7-1), and Michigan State RB Jaren Hayes quickly scored 2 TDs on way to 17-0 lead. Minnesota got on board early in 2nd Q as K Rhys Lloyd knocked through 23y FG, and QB Asad Abdul-Khaliq (27-40/377y, 4 TDs) threw TD pass to help

Gophers get within 24-17. But, Spartans DB DeAndra Cobb returned ensuing KO 100y for TD, and Minny TB Marion Barber fumbled—3rd lost FUM in 1st H by Gophers—to set up K Dave Rayner's 50y FG for 34-17 H lead. Abdul-Khaliq threw 3 TD passes in 2nd H, but Gophers had failed onside-KO after WR Aaron Hosack caught 8y score with 2:02 left. MSU QB Jeff Smoker passed 30-46/252y and scored on run.

Southern California 45 NOTRE DAME 14: "I loved our offense today," chirped USC (6-1) coach Pete Carroll over his team's 551y output. Young Trojans QB Matt Leinart (26-34/351y, 4 TDs) continued to grow as he got ample help from TB Reggie Bush (6/89y, TD) and WRs Keary Colbert (8/120y, TD) and Mike Williams (9/112y, TD). Notre Dame (2-4) was holding its own in 21-14 1st Q slugfest as TB Julius Jones (18/84y, TD) scored on 22y run and TE Anthony Fasano gathered in 2y TD pass from frosh QB Brady Quinn (15-34/168y, TD).

OKLAHOMA STATE 51 Texas Tech 49: All season, Texas Tech (5-2) QB B.J. Symons (42-67/552y, 5 TDs, 2 INTs) had piled up enormous aerial y by passing on virtually every down in coach Mike Leach's wide-open attack. This shootout was no different except that Red Raiders had to play from behind all afternoon. Oklahoma State (6-1) TB Tatum Bell (28/238y, 3 TDs) got Cowboys riding to 14-0 lead with 48y TD dash and broke away in 2nd Q for 95y scoring sprint for 28-14 edge. OSU led 34-14 at H when Bell added his 3rd TD. That's when Symons got cracking with 3 TD throws and scoring run. Momentum turned so decidedly in Raiders' direction that State coach Les Miles chose to try for 1st down on 4th down in 4th Q rather than punt away possession to dangerous Symons. Miles' strategy failed, but DB Jon Holland's INT with 1:05 affected end to Texas Tech's comeback bid from 27-pt deficit in 23 mins.

TEXAS CHRISTIAN 27 Alabama-Birmingham 24: It wasn't pretty but Texas Christian (7-0) remained in small class of 5 unbeaten Div 1-A teams. UAB QB Darrell Hackney (8-19/262y, TD, INT) clicked on aerial gains of 45, 44, 25, and 53y on his 1st 4 completions, last going for TD to WR Roddy White for 10-6 lead with 1:43 to go in 2nd Q. But, Purple Frogs landed like scene from film *Magnolia*: TB Lonta Hobbs (16/53y, 2 TDs) scored on 4y run, and Blazers lost FUM at their 15YL on ensuing KO. TCU K Nick Browne nailed 3rd of his 4 FGs for 16-10 H edge. UAB scored on 1st 2 drives of 3rd Q to vault to 24-16 lead, but clever Hackney, who tallied on 9y run at 2:06 of 3rd Q, was injured and with him went Blazers' O. TCU went ahead as Hobbs blasted 10y up middle early in 4th Q and sub QB Brandon Hassell, in for injured QB Tye Gunn (14-26/136y, INT), tacked on 2-pt pass.

UCLA 23 California 20 (OT): UCLA (5-2), darkest of darkhorses in Pac-10 race, remained unbeaten in conf play when K Justin Medlock's 41y FG in OT held up as California (3-5) K Tyler Frederickson's 50y tying attempt plunked off left upright. Long 3-ptr was necessitated when Cal RB Adimchinobe Echemandu (15/42y) was hemmed in for 9y loss on 3rd down dump-off pass. Bruins gained only 228y in net O for game, but had 14-3 lead in 2nd Q on 2 TD passes by QB Drew Olson (9-20/173y, 2 TDs). UCLA LB Spencer Havner twice blocked FG tries, and his OLB-mate, energetic Brandon Chillar, raced 65y with 2nd block for TD that put Bruins in 20-12 lead in 1st 2 mins of 4th Q. Unsinkable Bears started drive at their 32YL with 2:10 on clock, were flagged for 10y and allowed QB Aaron Rodgers (28-41/322y, TD) to be sacked back to 14YL by DE Dave Ball. Still, Rodgers hit 18, 21, and 12y passes until facing 4th down at UCLA 35YL. WR Burl Toler, grandson of U of San Francisco great, grabbed pass near 2YL and twisted through tackler for tying TD with 11 secs to play in regulation.

USA Today Coaches October 19

1	Oklahoma (57)	1569	14	Northern Illinois	760
2	Miami (Fla.) (6)	1516	15	Michigan	712
3	Virginia Tech	1450	16	Iowa	637
4	Southern California	1364	17	Wisconsin	438
5	Georgia	1327	18	Texas	426
6	Washington State	1183	19	Oklahoma State	410
7	Florida State	1171	20	Arkansas	404
8	Ohio State	1146	21	Auburn	350
9	LSU	1059	22	Tennessee	290
10	Purdue	898	23	Utah	158
11	Nebraska	855	24	Minnesota	120
12	Michigan State	786	25	Florida	95
13	TCU	781			

Bowl Championship Series Rankings

	Poll Avg.	Computer Avg.	Schedule Ranking	Losses Wins	Quality	Total
1 Oklahoma (7-0)	1.0	1.33	0.44	0		2.77
2 Miami (7-0)	2.0	1.50	1.20	0	-0.6	4.10
3 Virginia Tech (6-0)	3.0	4.83	2.40	0		10.23
4 Georgia (6-1)	4.5	6.17	1.32	1		12.99
5 Florida State (6-1)	6.75	4.67	0.72	1		13.14

October 25, 2003

(Wed) WEST VIRGINIA 28 Virginia Tech 7: Pepper spray was used to clear field of joyous Mountaineer fans, who took to dancing in streets of Morgantown until they set them on fire. Police estimated that fans ignited 90 fires, most of them destroyed dilapidated couches. RB Quincy Wilson sparked upset by rushing for 178y as West Virginia (3-4) controlled field position and prevented Virginia Tech (6-1) from crossing midfield during entire 2nd H. Leading O that gained 426y, West Virginia QB Rasheed Marshall was involved in both 2nd H TDs, hooking up with WR Travis Garvin on 93y scoring pass and reaching EZ on 4y run. Hokies QB Bryan Randall (14-22/146y) struggled with 3 INTs, bobbles that destroyed 3 plays, and lost FUM, while TB Kevin Jones was held to 57y rushing. Loss was compounded by sidelines slap to head by Virginia Tech coach Frank Beamer to WR Ernest Wilford.

(Th) GEORGIA TECH 7 Maryland 3: D players were in spotlight all night on ESPN. Game turned late in 3rd Q when Yellow Jackets (5-3) forced FUM deep in Maryland territory, recovered by CB Jonathan Cox to set up 4y scoring pass from QB Reggie Ball (12-28/98y, INT) to WR Jonathan Smith. FUM, caused by hit by LB Keyaron Fox on sub Terps QB Joel Statham, bounced in and out of hands of players on both sides until Cox scooped ball up on Maryland 35YL and returned it 17y. Terrapins (5-3) had entered game with 5-game win streak during which O averaged 37 pts per contest, but were hampered by loss of starting QB Scott McBrien to 2nd Q concussion. Maryland RB Bruce Perry was game's leading rusher with 75y.

PITTSBURGH 34 Syracuse 14: Continuing brilliant season, Pitt (5-2) WR Larry Fitzgerald caught 8/149y, 2 TDs, in stretching his streak of TD receptions to record-tying 13 consecutive games. In addition to tying mark set by Michigan State WR Charles Rogers in 2002, Fitzgerald already had set Big East mark for single-season scoring catches with 15, while cracking 1,000y barrier after only 7 games. QB Rod Rutherford (21-32/310y, INT) threw 3 TDs in leading Panthers to win. Syracuse (4-3) had taken 7-0 lead on CB Steve Gregory's 10y RET of FUM by Pitt P Andy Lee. After Fitzgerald tied game with 3y scoring catch, Orange took 14-7 margin on QB R.J. Anderson's 3y scoring keeper. Pitt D quickly tightened up as Syracuse O, averaging 407y, was held to 244y, and Panthers CB Josh Lay scored winning TD with 20y FUM TD RET late in 2nd Q.

FLORIDA STATE 48 Wake Forest 24: Florida State coach Bobby Bowden became all-time leader in Div 1-A coaching wins with 339, going ahead of Joe Paterno with Penn State's 26-14 loss to Iowa. With lot to play for—win also guaranteed share of ACC title—Seminoles (7-1) came out firing against Wake Forest (4-4) which had never beaten them in 12 tries. Embattled FSU QB Chris Rix threw for 22-34/339y with 2 TDs to WR Craphonso Thorpe, including 25y strike with 15 secs left in 1st H to push lead to 27-14. Wake Forest gained 230y rushing, despite 5 sacks, but its run attack was forced to play catch-up. Deacons QB Cory Randolph threw and ran for TDs which provided both his team's 1st H TDs, but passed for only 8-14/96y, TD.

Tennessee 51 ALABAMA 43 (OT): Small score stood at 6-3 in favor of Alabama (3-6) at H and 20-20 at end of regulation, but game would go down as shootout. Tennessee (5-2) QB Casey Clausen ended regulation with tying 1y TD pass to FB Troy Fleming before throwing TD passes in 3 OT periods and running in short game-winner in 5th extra session. Fresh-legged Vols backup RB Corey Larkins set up winning TD with 3/20y rushing. Becoming 1st visitor ever to win 3 straight at Bryant-Denny Stadium, Vols needed last D stand to win as Crimson Tide RB Shaud Williams (40/166y) was halted on 2nd-and-1 and 3rd-and-1 cracks before 4th down pass by QB Brodie Croyle (21-38/215y, 2 TDs, INT) was deflected in EZ by CB Jason Allen. Clausen had 283y passing, finding favorite target, WR James Banks, for 7/103y including 2 OT TDs.

MISSISSIPPI 19 Arkansas 7: Upstart Rebels (6-2) rolled into 1st place in SEC West as D held Arkansas to 82y rushing, 237y total. Mississippi QB Eli Manning threw for only 145y, but led 5 scoring drives, 4 capped by FGs by K Jonathan Nichols. Arkansas (4-3) was hampered by absence of its top 2 TBs and inability to exploit suspect Ole Miss aerial D behind run-oriented QB Matt Jones (12-29/140y, INT). Razorbacks could not gain single 1st down in 2nd H until less than 4 mins remained. By then they trailed 19-7. Nichols now had hit 22-23 FGs on season. Hogs WR George Wilson caught 6 /104y.

LOUISIANA STATE 31 Auburn 7: After lightning delayed KO for 19 mins, LSU (7-1) made up for late start by scoring 21 pts in 1st Q to end matters early. QB Matt Mauck (17-28/223y, 3 TDs, INT) set tone with 64y TD pass to WR Devery Henderson (6/101y, 2 TDs). Mauck and Henderson hooked up again on 17y scoring pass in 3rd Q, and by then score was 31-0. LSU frosh RB Josh Vincent ran for 127y as Tigers gained 381y to 193y. Auburn (5-3) struggled at line of scrimmage on O as TB Cadillac Williams was stuffed to tune of only 61y rushing. Auburn QB Jason Campbell (19-27/143y) was sacked 4 times, but pitched cosmetic 6y TD pass to WR Anthony Mix.

MICHIGAN 31 Purdue 3: Entering game with hopes of gaining 1st win in Ann Arbor since 1966, Boilermakers (6-2) became rudely aware of difficulty of that task. While QB Michigan (7-2) John Navarre (17-30/225y) hooked up with WR Braylon Edwards for 2 TD passes and threw key block on 21y scoring run by WR Steve Breaston on E-around, it was Wolverines D that truly dominated. Michigan held Purdue to 58y rushing with 7 sacks and scored TD on CB Markus Curry's 2y FUM RET for 28-3 lead in 4th Q. Wolverines frosh CB Leon Hall added EZ INTs and another deep in own territory to snuff Boilers' scoring chances. Harried Purdue QB Kyle Orton threw for 18-37/184y, but his 2 INTs doubled his season total to date.

NORTHWESTERN 16 Wisconsin 7: Ahead 9-7 in 3rd Q, Northwestern (4-4) lined up for 40y FG. RB Noah Herron, who led Wildcats with 104y rushing, took fake 20y to set up 1y TD run by RB Jason Wright (18/97y). Wright had scored earlier on 53y pass from QB Brett Basanez. Badgers (6-3) played entire game without injured QB Jim Sorgi and lost ace TB Anthony Davis to early ankle injury. QB Matt Schabert threw for 193y in relief of Sorgi and was Wisconsin's surprising rushing leader with 57y.

KANSAS STATE 42 Kansas 6: Wildcats' domination of Sunflower State rivalry continued as QB Ell Roberson rushed for 103y and 2 TDs, while passing for 138y and TD. Kansas State (6-3) RB Darren Sproles (19/98y) scored TDs on 7y rush and 63y punt RET and became school's all-time leading ground gainer with 2619y. Upset chances for Jayhawks (5-3) ended early with 1st Q shoulder injury to QB Bill Whittemore, who entered game 2nd in national passing efficiency. Without valuable Whittemore, Kansas was held to 89y on ground and 71y through air. Losing coach Mark Mangino was concerned about team spirit: "We lost our poise after the first quarter. We dressed 70 guys today. One guy goes down—we've got 69 others."

Texas Christian 62 HOUSTON 55: Score was sign of modern times as undefeated Horned Frogs (8-0) gained 782y in scoring 8 TDs. TCU opened with 21-3 lead after 1st Q, which was answered by 3-TD salvo by Cougars (5-3) in 2nd Q. Teams each scored 3 times in 3rd Q before Horned Frogs opened up 59-44 lead in mid-4th Q. QB Brandon

Hassell (17-27/375y) threw 4 TDs in leading TCU O that set single game school O record. TCU TB Robert Merrill rushed for 204y and 4y TD run to pace ground game that made 407y, while WR Cory Rodgers (6/171y) caught 2 TDs. Houston QB Kevin Kolb rushed for 144y, TD, and passed for 434y and 4 scores. WR Brandon Middleton caught 6/232y and 2 TDs as Kolb's favorite Cougars target.

New Mexico 47 UTAH 35: Lobos (5-3) chased Utah from top 25 ranking by compiling 633y while scoring on 5 straight possessions to flip 14-13 deficit into 36-14 lead. Utes (6-2) was able to gain 300y, but did most of their damage after game was decided, as 3 of Utah QB Alex Smith's 4 TD passes came after New Mexico had reached 36-pt total. Lobos QB Casey Kelly threw for 226y, 6y more than Smith, and rushed for 68y. Kelly's 57y TD pass to WR Adrien Boyd gave New Mexico 23-14 lead in 2nd Q. RB DonTrell Moore led New Mexico ground gainers with 119y and 2 TDs, while backup TB D.D. Cox added 106y and TD.

WASHINGTON STATE 36 Oregon State 30: Cougars (7-1) overcame mistake-filled performance to remain unbeaten in Pac 10 play as QB Matt Kegel suffered 3 TD passes, including 2 to WR Scott Lunde (8/110y) in decisive 4th Q. Kegel threw 5 INTs and lost 2 FUMs, however, as Washington State fell behind 25-14 at H. Beavers closed 1st H with 18-pt spurt during final 5:18, converting both of Kegel's FUMs into pts and scoring spectacularly on 66y bomb from QB Derek Anderson to handy WR Mike Hass. Unable to run consistently, Beavers netted 15y rushing with TB Steven Jackson held to 28/85y. In 2nd H, Oregon State added only FG by K Kirk Yliniemi and conceded safety on last play. Cougars rallied in 4th Q behind Kegel's pair of TD throws and RB Jonathan Smith's 22y scoring run. Oregon State S Mitch Meeuwsen ballhawked 3 INTs, taking back pick-off 45y for TD in 1st Q. Wazzu DB Erik Coleman contributed 11 tackles, INT, and stop for loss.

USA Today Coaches October 19

1	Oklahoma (58)	1570	14	Iowa	757
2	Miami (Fla.) (5)	1517	15	Oklahoma State	664
3	Southern California	1436	16	Texas	639
4	Georgia	1348	17	Purdue	499
5	Florida State	1265	18	Tennessee	457
6	Washington State	1237	19	Minnesota	375
7	Ohio State	1209	20	Bowling Green	310
8	LSU	1166	21	Florida	200
9	Nebraska	984	22	Northern Illinois	174
10	Michigan State	968	23	Pittsburgh	141
11	Virginia Tech	963	24	Missouri	140
12	Michigan	893	25	Louisville	136
13	TCU	816			

Bowl Championship Series Rankings

	Poll Avg.	Computer Avg.	Schedule Ranking	Losses Wins	Quality	Total
1 Oklahoma (8-0)	1.0	1.17	0.28	0		2.45
2 Miami (7-0)	2.0	1.67	1.00	0	-0.8	3.87
3 Florida State (7-1)	5.0	3.50	0.84	1		10.34
4 Southern California (7-1)	3.0	5.67	1.40	1		11.07
5 Georgia (7-1)	4.0	4.67	1.48	1		11.15

November 1, 2003

Pittsburgh 24 BOSTON COLLEGE 13: Trend continued of Big East regulars beating up on ACC defectors. No sooner had Boston College (5-4) been announced as 12th member of expanded ACC for 2005 that Panthers (6-2) clawed out come-from-behind victory. Pittsburgh built remarkable recent road record to 11-3, and it's overall 21-6 mark represented its best stretch since early 1980s days of Dan Marino and Hugh Green. Pitt TB Jawan Walker (9/36y, TD) broke 3-3 tie with 3y TD run in 2nd Q, but Eagles TB Horace Dodd scored on 1y run and K Sandro Sciortino's 2nd FG provided 13-10 BC edge at H. Early in 4th Q, Walker caught screen pass from QB Rod Rutherford (24-37/329y, TD, INT), charged up middle, and cut to sideline for 47y score for 17-13 lead. Eagles appeared to come back on 41y run by TB Derrick Knight (19/119y), but it was called back by PEN, and, when Pitt regained ball, Walker took handoff, faked sweep, and tossed pass to wide-open WR Larry Fitzgerald (7/156y, TD) who scored on 35y romp. Fitzgerald tied 1-year-old consecutive-game TD catch record of Michigan State's Charles Rogers and, with 28 TD grabs in less than 2 seasons, he broke frosh-soph TD receiving mark of Florida's Jabar Gaffney.

VIRGINIA TECH 31 Miami 7: Many called it greatest victory in Virginia Tech (7-1) history as Hokies knocked Hurricanes (7-1) from undefeated ranks. BCS bashers rejoiced as Tech opened national title door to bevy of 1-loss teams. Hokies built 31-0 lead with its opportunistic D to thunderous shouts of 65,115. Early in scoreless 2nd Q, Hurricanes ran WR Roscoe Parrish on reverse to left, and while he was tackled, Virginia Tech CB DeAngelo Hall stripped ball and grabbed pop-up REC. Hall raced 28y to score and, just before H, Hall set up FG with 10y punt RET on which 15y foul PEN against Canes was added. Nearly 5 mins into 3rd Q, Hokies' other CB, Eric Green, stepped in front of pass by ice-cold Miami QB Brock Berlin (16-25/164y, 2 INTs) and charged 51y to score for 17-0 lead. Another INT of beleagured Berlin brought ball inside Miami 10YL. Tech TB Kevin Jones (26/124y, TD) soon scored for 24-0 edge. It wasn't until this time that Hokies completed their 1st pass by job-sharing QB Marcus Vick (2-4/44y, TD), which lost 2y. Larry Coker, who would lose only his 2nd game in 33 as Miami coach, yanked Berlin for backup QB Derrick Crudup (13-21/97y, TD, INT) who clicked on 4th Q screen pass for team's only TD.

Florida 16 Georgia13 (Jacksonville): Young Gators (6-3) were maturing into 1 of hottest teams in country. After 1st Q filled with punts, perked up Florida (6-3) drew 1st blood on K Matt Leach's 24y FG that came at end of drive that reached Georgia (7-2) 2YL but then was thwarted by 5y PEN. Bulldogs tied it 3-3 on last play of 1st H as K Billy Bennett made 3-ptr from 21y after earlier miss. Gators QB Chris Leak (13-23/235y, TD) struck with 28 and 34y passes within 3 plays for TD, screen pass taken by WR Carlos Perez for 34y in middle of 3rd Q. Florida advanced its lead on another FG to 13-3 on 1st series of 4th Q, but Georgia countered with 84y drive to frosh TB Kregg Lumpkin's 1y TD off left side. After Bennett tied it with 3:49 to go, Gators rode Leak's 3 completions for 44y of 77y trip to winning 33y FG by Leach.

Arkansas 71 KENTUCKY 63 (OT): Score may have looked like SEC basketball tilt, but Arkansas (5-3), king of extra-long OT at 5-1, prevailed in record-tying 7-OT game. Razorbacks matched their 2001 mark of 7 OT periods in win over Mississippi and exceeded their 6-OT loss to Tennessee in 2002. Arkansas led 21-7 at H, its TDs included block punt REC by WR Tom Crowder. Kentucky (4-5) tied it 24-24 with 1:38 to go in 4th Q when QB Jared Lorenzen (28-49/326y, 2 TDs, INT) hit WR Chris Bernard with 13y TD pass. FB Alexis Bwenge (22/89y, 2 TDs) scored twice for Wildcats as teams traded TDs in 1st 2 OTs for 38-38 knot. Hogs led 41-38 when Kentucky had great chance to win on 4th down at 1YL in 3rd OT. But, Cats were flagged for illegal substitution and chose to tie it with K Taylor Begley's 24y FG. Lorenzen scored running TDs in next 3 OTs, and teams succeeded on required 2-pt convs in 4th and 6th OTs. TB DeCori Birmingham (40/196y, 2 TDs), 1-time WR moved to TB because of injuries, burst 25y to put Arkansas ahead 71-63. Hogs halted 4th down play at their 5YL when DB Vickiel Vaughn forced FUM by Lorenzen.

MISSISSIPPI 43 South Carolina 40: Rebels (7-2) QB Eli Manning (30-42/391y, 3 TDs, INT) had magnificent 1st H (20-26/260y, 3 TDs, INT) as Mississippi withstood 2nd H comeback by South Carolina (5-4) and moved to 5-0 in SEC for 1st time since its last title in 1963. Gamecocks QB Dondrial Pinkins (14-32/298y, 4 TDs) matched Manning in 1st Q with 2 scoring throws, but Ole Miss capped 16-pt 2nd Q with WR Kerry Johnson's 29y TD reception on which he barreled over tackler to score. TB Tremaine Turner (25/117y, 2 TDs) scored his 2nd TD with 3:28 left in 3rd Q so Rebs had seemingly safe 43-14 edge. But, Pinkins led 26-pt revival that included 98y TD connection with WR Matthew Thomas. Carolina's last KO went long, and Ole Miss made 1st down to kill clock.

Ohio State 21 PENN STATE 20: Ohio State's remarkable string of narrow victories, its hallmark for nearly 2 years, continued in last-min fashion as frustrated Penn State (2-7) "couldn't win a card game right now," according to Internet writer Dennis Dodd. On their opening possession, Buckeyes (8-1) marched straight downfield in small bites except for 31y burst up middle by TB Lydell Ross (24/110y, TD), who scored from 1YL. Nittany Lions answered with 80y voyage to FB Sean McHugh's TD pass from QB Zack Mills (27-42/253y, TD, INT), who showed his time out of lineup for leg injury might have healed his throwing arm. Bucks QB Craig Krenzel (5-12/36y, INT) was knocked out of game but not before Penn State CB Alan Zemaitis stepped in front of his pass and scurried 78y down sideline for TD. Lions led 17-7 at H after K David Kimball's 42y FG. Ohio opened 2nd H like it did 1st Q: It went 80y in 12 plays behind sub QB Scott McMullen (12-17/112y, 2 TDs), who threw 38y completion before hitting WR Michael Jenkins for TD. Down 20-14, Buckeyes took their 22nd win in last 23 games with 72y drive on last possession: Jenkins outfought Zemaitis for 5y TD toss with 1:35 left.

Michigan 27 MICHIGAN STATE 20: Wolverines (8-2) reverted to old school football, running 55 times among 86 O plays. Workhorse was TB Chris Perry (51/219y, TD), who got Michigan winging with short TD run early in 2nd Q on way to 13-3 H edge. No. 9 Michigan State (7-2) failed on fake punt at UM's 36YL in 3rd Q, and it launched 64y TD trip that consumed 5 plays. QB John Navarre (17-31/223y, 3 TDs, INT) threw 26y TD to TE Andy Mignery for 20-3 Wolverines lead. Although WR Agim Shabaj (4/106y, TD) was biggest offender among squadron of Spartans pass-droppers, he got loose when during Michigan secondary breakdown for 3rd Q 73y TD catch from QB Jeff Smoker (21-40/254y, TD, INT). Wolverines answered immediately with 2nd TD grab by WR Braylon Edwards for 27-10 lead early in 4th Q. State DE Clifford Dukes roared 65y to score with FUM RET after Navarre was blindsided by Spartans LB Robert Flagg. Now trailing only 27-20, MSU's last bit of fight expired on last play INT in EZ by Michigan LB Scott McClintock.

OKLAHOMA 52 Oklahoma State 9: Dynamic Oklahoma (9-0) had heard enough about 2 straight upsets at hands of Cowboys (7-2) and how it could happen again. "Sometimes it's good to be doubted," said Sooners coach Bob Stoops afterward. Sooners milked 10-0 lead until big TO came early in 2nd Q: Oklahoma State DB Darrent Williams dropped punt, picked it up, and lost it again to OU LB Russell Dennison at 50YL. RB Kejuan Jones (22/86y, 2 TDs) scored his 2nd TD for 17-0 lead 8 plays later as Oklahoma romped to 24-3 H lead. Difference was Sooners D that crimped State's powerful O: Pokes made 5 punts and only 3 1st downs in 1st H, and late in 3rd Q, they had more PEN y (58y) than total O (47y). Oklahoma QB Jason White (11-27/194y, 2 TDs, 2 INTs) passed 66y to WR Brandon Jones in 4th Q for 45-9 lead, and Stoops rubbed it with late-game reverse-run TD pass. OSU's only TD came on DB Williams' 11y INT TD RET to open 3rd Q.

TEXAS 31 Nebraska 7: QB Vincent Young (65y TD jaunt among his 14/163y rushing) and TB Cedric Benson (28/179y, 3 TDs) became 1st duo in Longhorns (7-2) history to each rush for 150y. Texas D was equally impressive, holding Nebraska (7-2) to 175y net y and 53y rushing, while cataloging 5 sacks. On strength of QB Jammal Lord's 42y pass to TE Matt Herian, Huskers advanced to Texas 4YL late in 2nd Q, but LB Brian Robison blocked FG to keep score at 7-0 for Steers. Young hit 15y pass and raced for his long TD to complete 2-play 80y trip to 14-0 lead. Nebraska trailed 17-0 in 4th Q when it finally scored: Lord (5-15/122y, TD, INT) launched 48y TD bomb to Herian.

SOUTHERN CALIFORNIA 43 Washington State 16: Mighty Trojans (8-1) took huge step toward Pac-10 title and seating themselves as potential BCS title pugilist. Southern California proved itself to be tops in Pac-10 by routing Cougars (7-2) after close 1st H. USC put considerable pressure on Washington State QB Matt Kegel (28-47/291y, TD, INT) by sacking him 5 times, and forcing game-end total of –25y rushing. Cougars also hurt their cause with 15 PENs/115y. Troy led only 15-10 at H as TB Hershel Dennis (7/53y, TD) scored on 24y sprint, while WR Devard Darling tallied

Washington State's 2nd Q TD on 5y reception for brief 7-3 lead. Southern California smoked Cougars for 4 TDs in 2nd H as QB Matt Leinart (17-31/191y, 3 TDs) pitched 3 scores and TB LenDale White (12/149y, TD) romped for gains of 49 and 66y in addition to scoring from close range. "All kinds of guys made special plays," said USC coach Pete Carroll. "It was really a fun night of football."

STANFORD 21 Ucla 14: UCLA (6-3) was hanging in, but with this defeat by improving Stanford (3-4), Bruins tumbled from top spot in conf. Win clearly was biggest in coach Buddy Teevens' short tenure at Palo Alto. Cardinal QB Chad Lewis (12-20/91y, TD, INT) passed and ran for TDs in building 21-7 lead late in 3rd Q. Lewis' 1y TD run came after punt bounced off leg of Bruins receiving player and was recovered by DB Marcus McCutcheon. UCLA, which out-totaled Cards 287y to 206y, got 2 TDs from frosh TB Maurice Drew (17/65y, 2 TDs) but QB Matt Moore (19-31/145y, INT) was blitzed to distraction by Stanford that had relinquished 35 pts previous week to Oregon.

USA Today Coaches November 2

1	Oklahoma (63)	1575	14	Purdue	667
2	Southern California	1502	15	Michigan State	645
3	Florida State	1412	16	Nebraska	558
4	LSU	1337	17	Tennessee	544
5	Virginia Tech	1281	18	Minnesota	490
6	Ohio State	1263	19	Florida	480
7	Miami (Fla.)	1208	20	Bowling Green	369
8	Michigan	1135	21	Pittsburgh	268
9	Georgia	951	22	Oklahoma State	240
10	Iowa	932	23	Northern Illinois	211
11	Texas	881	24	Mississippi	181
12	TCU	875	25	Louisville	155
13	Washington State	827			

Bowl Championship Series Rankings

	Poll Avg.	Computer Avg.	Schedule Ranking	Losses Wins	Quality	Total
1 Oklahoma (9-0)	1.0	1.00	0.24			2.24
2 Southern California (8-1)	2.0	3.50	0.52	1		7.02
3 Florida State (8-1)	3.0	4.00	1.52	1		9.52
4 Miami (7-1)	6.5	2.83	0.72	1	-0.8	10.25
5 Ohio State (8-1)	6.5	3.17	0.80	1		11.47

November 8, 2003

(Wed) TEXAS CHRISTIAN 31 Louisville 28: Horned Frogs' unlikely bid for BCS bowl remained alive as last-sec 44y FG attempt by Louisville (7-2) K Nate Smith bounced off crossbar. It was Smith's 3rd miss of game. QB Brandon Hassell threw for 251y and TD and ran for 61y and TD for Horned Frogs (9-0). Cardinals QB Stefan LeFors completed 31-46/459y in defeat, with RB Lionel Gates catching 9/134y. "The difference…was three inches (short on late FG)," said TCU coach Gary Patterson.

PITTSBURGH 31 Virginia Tech 28: Rarely had any competitive team defended runs so poorly as Pitt (7-2) had all year. Still, Panthers took sole occupancy of 1st place in Big East with late win, secured with 2y TD run by FB Lousaka Polite with 47 secs left. Polite's TD capped 70y drive featuring QB Rod Rutherford's 3 completions/49y to WR Larry Fitzgerald. Rutherford (24-31/303y, 2 TDs) riddled Hokies (7-2), who found it difficult to get fired back up after big Miami win. Va Tech TB Kevin Jones offered school record-setting 241y and 4 TDs rushing. Jones scored on 80y run late in 3rd Q to pull Hokies within 24-21, then scored go-ahead 13y TD in 4th Q. Fitzgerald finished with 8/108y and TD to stretch his NCAA-record 15 consecutive games with TD catch.

Tennessee 10 MIAMI 6: Freefall by Hurricanes (7-2) continued with ugly performance that lingered after game. Miami QB Brock Berlin (22-35/213y) threw 2 INTs and lost FUM, S Sean Taylor lost FUM on punt RET at game's end, and TE Kellen Winslow overshadowed his 7-catch performance with FUM, dropped pass in EZ and important PEN, 1 of Miami's dozen fouls. Afterward, Winslow threw embarrassing tirade about officiating and made insensitive comparisons between warfare to his standing over injured Tennessee S Corey Campbell. Becoming 1st team in 26 tries (since Penn State in 1999) to beat Miami in Orange Bowl, Volunteers (7-2) positioned themselves closer to SEC title game as BCS standings would help break potential tie with Georgia and Florida. Tennessee gaining only 170y, but rode 2y 4th-and-goal TD reverse run by WR Derrick Tinsley in 2nd Q. Last 2 times Miami players touched ball—Berlin threw INT to S Gibril Wilson on pass affected by blitzing S Mark Jones' hit and Taylor's FUM that was recovered by Tinsley—put stamp on disastrous fortnight for Canes.

DUKE 41 Georgia Tech 17: Blue Devils (3-7) snapped 30-game ACC losing streak as TB Chris Douglas ran wild, ripping through Georgia Tech's top-ranked ACC rush D for 218y. Douglas enjoyed his sr day, scoring on 2nd H runs of 12y and 27y. Duke D chipped in 3 INTs of QB Reggie Ball (27-47/247y), including 42y RET by LB Malcolm Ruff for insurance TD. Yellow Jackets (5-4) RB P.J. Daniels rushed for 108y. "It might not get any lower than this," summed up Georgia Tech WR Jonathan Smith (6/104y).

CLEMSON 26 Florida State 10: With vultures circling coach Tommy Bowden, Clemson (6-4) eliminated talk of coaching change. Holding Seminoles (8-2) to 11y rushing and twice intercepting QB Chris Rix (16-31/194y), Tigers snapped 11-game series losing streak. QB Charlie Whitehurst (17-27/272y, INT) threw and ran for TDs, and K Aaron Hunt booted 4 FGs as Clemson led throughout. Florida State's highlight was late 71y TD pass play from backup QB Fabian Walker to WR Chauncy Stovall. Tigers WR Derrick Hamilton caught 6/123y, including 58y TD in 3rd Q that provided commanding 23-3 lead. FSU coach Bobby Bowden's national title aspirations ended with on 74th birthday, but it prompted Clemson's contract extension for his son.

Mississippi 24 AUBURN 20: Delirious ride of Rebels (8-2) through SEC West continued as QB Eli Manning threw for 218y, 2 TDs. Auburn Tigers (6-4) had game literally fall through their fingers as WR Ben Obomanu dropped easy 3y TD pass in EZ on 3rd down with 37 secs left. Mississippi D snuffed out final Auburn play by pressuring QB Jason Campbell (14-26/231y), who threw hurried pass knocked down by S Eric Oliver. Obomanu (6/150y) would have been game's star had he nabbed critical catch since earlier he hauled in tipped pass for 68y scoring play for Auburn's 17-14 lead in 3rd Q. On their way to winning 80y TD drive, Rebels got big play from sub FB Lorenzo Townsend, who made 48y catch-and-run, 1 of 3 3rd-down convs on trip. RB Brandon Jacobs' 1y run served as Ole Miss' victory score.

OHIO STATE 33 Michigan State 23: Returning to starting lineup after missing game with concussion, QB Craig Krenzel (12-23/213y, INT) threw 3 TDs to lead Buckeyes (9-1). Krenzel shared heroics with TB Lydell Ross (24/125y), who topped 100y rushing for 3rd straight game, and K Mike Nugent, who booted 4 FGs. Game turned in 2nd Q with Ohio State ahead 10-7 and Spartans driving into Bucks territory: Ohio S Tyler Everett returned INT 66y to set up 17y TD catch by TE Ben Hartsock. Spartans (7-3) QB Jeff Smoker completed 35-55 (both school records)/351y, but was picked off twice and held to 86y in 2nd H. However, Michigan State enjoyed spectacular TD on TB DeAndra Cobb's 93y KO RET in 2nd H.

Purdue 27 IOWA 14: Boilermakers (8-2) moved into share of 1st place in Big 10 as their rushing attack pounded Iowa D that had allowed only 3 rushing TDs entering game. RB Jerod Void gained 120y and scored 2 TDs to lead Purdue O that built 27-0 lead by 3rd Q. Boilermakers QB Kyle Orton, an Iowa native, completed 13-20/167y with 45y TD pass to WR Anthony Chambers in 3rd Q. Hawkeyes (7-3) made score appear more respectable as QB Nathan Chandler (16-29/203y, INT) threw and ran for TDs. Purdue D held Hawkeyes RB Fred Russell to 35y rushing.

COLORADO 21 Missouri 16: Buffaloes (4-6) upset 22nd-ranked Missouri to halt 3-game losing streak as QB Joel Klatt (19-19-25/187y) threw 2 TDs. Tigers (6-3) outgained Colorado by 447y to 276y, but continually shot themselves in paw. Missouri entered game with 5 TOs, least TOs committed in nation, but star QB Brad Smith (278y, TD passing and 102y rushing) had 2 FUMs and threw 2 INTs. Game's key play was Smith's FUM at Colorado GL late in 1st H. Smith argued that he had scored TD, but Colorado S Brian Iwuh recovered ball in EZ. Scoring late on 48y pass play from Smith to TB Damien Nash, on which Nash broke tackle after tackle, gave Missouri hope, but Tigers' final drive was ended by Buffs S Dominique Brooks' INT.

Texas 55 OKLAHOMA STATE 16: Hitting on all cylinders, Longhorns (8-2) stunned Stillwater fans with awesome 2nd H feat. Trailing 16-14 at H, Texas marched 80y with opening possession of 2nd H to 1y TD run by outstanding TB Cedric Benson (27/180y). QB Vince Young, who hit WR Roy Williams (6/162y) with 67y TD pass in 2nd Q, added 23y scoring run later in 3rd Q as Texas began to pull away. Horns secondary fueled rout as S Michael Huff scored on 27y INT RET and S Matt Melton returned FUM 48y to score. Texas' dominance allowed it to build 502y to 309y O advantage. Cowboys (7-3) built 1st H lead on 3 FGs by K Luke Phillips—including 52 and 53y kicks—and 10y TD pass from QB Josh Fields to WR Rashaun Woods (4/43y). Blanketed by Texas CB Nathan Vasher, Woods was unable to catch single pass in 2nd H.

Washington State 31 UCLA 13: Each team had 7 TOs, while they combined for 21 PENs/189y as game looked like pre-season scrimmage. Washington State (8-2) could be excused once QB Matt Kegel left game in 1st Q with sprained right shoulder; frosh QB Josh Swogger hit 5-16/82y with 2 INTs in relief. Bruins' QB play was poor, as well, as QB Matt Moore (11-29/138y, TD, 2 INTs) was able to convert only 2 TOs into pts. Cougars were more efficient in building 28-6 H lead on 4 short drives that took only 7 plays in only 81 secs combined. Washington State RB Jonathan Smith rushed for 130y and 3 TDs, while Bruins TB Tyler Ebell gained 105y. "It was the ugliest football game I've ever been a part of," said Bruins (6-4) WR Ryan Smith. "It was a joke."

USA Today Coaches November 9

1	Oklahoma (63)	1575	14	Miami (Fla.)	806
2	Southern California	1508	15	Nebraska	680
3	LSU	1426	16	Pittsburgh	653
4	Ohio State	1397	17	Minnesota	612
5	Michigan	1286	18	Florida	548
6	Georgia	1154	19	Mississippi	488
7	Texas	1139	20	Iowa	435
8	Washington State	1008	21	Northern Illinois	298
9	TCU	965	22	Michigan State	269
10	Purdue	899	23	Boise State	194
11	Florida State	870	24	Miami (Ohio)	193
12	Virginia Tech	868	25	Kansas State	105
13	Tennessee	846			

Bowl Championship Series Rankings

	Poll Avg.	Computer Avg.	Schedule Ranking	Losses Wins	Quality	Total
1 Oklahoma (10-0)	1.0	1.00	0.28	0	-0.6	1.68
2 Southern California (8-1)	2.0	2.83	0.64	1	-0.2	6.27
3 Ohio State (9-1)	4.0	2.17	0.56	1		7.73
4 Louisiana State (8-1)	3.0	6.67	2.60	1	-0.1	13.27
5 Texas (8-2)	6.5	7.83	0.72	2		17.05

November 15, 2003

WEST VIRGINIA 52 Pittsburgh 31: Add West Virginia (6-4) RB Quincy Wilson to list of backs to run roughshod over pitiful Panthers rush D. Wilson rambled for 208y and 4 TDs as Mountaineers rolled into 3-way tie for 1st place in Big East with Miami and Pittsburgh (7-3). West Virginia QB Rasheed Marshall (14-23/216y, 2 TDs, INT) rushed for 3rd TD. Pitt went to air to match rivals in 1st H as QB Rod Rutherford (25-47/419y, 4 TDs, 3 INTs) threw 3 TDs, 2 to WR Larry Fitzgerald (9/185y), whose Heisman hopes

suffered with team's 3rd loss. With teams tied at 24-24 at H, West Virginia pulled away thanks to 2 INTs in 3rd Q, 2nd setting up 12y TD run by Marshall and 72y punt RET by CB Lance Frazier to set up Wilson's 1y TD run for 38-24 lead.

FLORIDA STATE 50 North Carolina State 44 (OT): In top half of 2nd OT, North Carolina State (7-4) coach Chuck Amato decided enough was enough; he eschewed 33y FG attempt and went for it on 4th-and-1. Pass, meant for WR Jerricho Cotchery (10/135y, 2 TDs) fell incomplete, and it allowed Florida State (9-2) TB Leon Washington (17/121y, TD) to romp untouched for 12y and winning TD that locked up Seminoles' 11th ACC title in 12 years. Wolfpack QB Philip Rivers passed 28-38/422y, 4 TDs and ran in score among NC State's 514y O. Noles gained 272y on ground, including 71y TD run by TB Lorenzo Booker that provided 27-23 lead with 4:18 left in 4th Q. Rivers' 3rd scoring throw, 44y caught by WR Tramain Hall (10/126y, 2 TDs), came with 4:06 left in 4th Q and tied it at 37-37. NC State T Derek Morris blocked FSU K Xavier Beitia's 32y FG try with 5 secs left to force OT.

WISCONSIN 56 Michigan State 21: Wisconsin (7-4) WR Lee Evans proved to be healthy while making secondary of Michigan State (7-4) look sick. Evans continued to rewrite Badgers record book, catching 10/school-record 258y and Big 10 record-tying 5 TDs. Badgers grabbed 21-0 lead in 2nd Q after S Jim Leonhard's 25y INT RET set up TD and Evans' 2nd TD catch, 75y bomb from QB Jim Sorgi (16-24/380y, 5 TDs). Spartans (7-4) finally scored TD after 59y KO RET by RB Chad Simon, which set up 21y scoring pass from QB Jeff Smoker to WR Kyle Brown. There would be no comeback however as Badgers TB Dwayne Smith—whose 21/207y, 3 TDs rushing were overshadowed by Evans' performance—raced 60y to set up Sorgi's 3rd TD pass to Evans (18y) for 28-7 H lead. Spartans may have been finished, but Evans was not. He took short pass and galloped 70y for his 4th score and soon made diving 18y TD catch only 7 plays later. Smoker threw for 16-31/207y, 2 TDs, but was picked off twice.

IOWA 40 Minnesota 22: Iowa's sensational sr K Nate Kaeding was emotional before his final home game, but he maintained his excellence by booting 4 FGs, including 55y 3-ptr, to lead scoring of Hawkeyes (8-3). Sr classmate, S Bob Sanders, made senior day special as well by forcing 3 FUMs and being in on 16 tackles for Iowa. Despite finishing game with 537y total O, Golden Gophers (9-3) lost 5 TOs which assisted Iowa in 37 straight pts through middle of game. Minnesota was hampered by injury to leading rusher, TB Marion Barber, in 1st H and shaky return from injury by QB Asad Abdul-Khaliq, who threw for 388y but lost 3 FUMs and threw INT. Iowa QB Nathan Chandler helmed his O unit by throwing for 210y with TDs rushing and passing.

OHIO STATE 16 Purdue 13 (OT): For 2nd straight year, Purdue (8-3) swallowed tough loss from Ohio State (10-1), failing to tie game in OT when K Ben Jones missed 36y FG. Moments earlier, Buckeyes K Mike Nugent had hit own 36y effort, despite ball being tipped by Boilers LB Bobby Iwuchukwu. For 3rd time this year, Ohio State played much-admired "Tressel Ball," winning without scoring TD on O. Buckeyes DE Mike Kudla scored team's only TD by grabbing FUM by Purdue QB Kyle Orton (27-47/249y) on 1YL and stepping into EZ early in 4th Q. Down 13-6, Orton then led 92y drive to tie game at 13-13, hitting 3 passes/58y and rushing for 18y, before handing off to RB Jeroid Void, who scored on 11y run. Orton's topsy-turvy 4th Q continued as he lost FUM in own territory late to set up Nugent's FG attempt that was blocked by Iwuchukwu to force extra session. Orton was lucky to not wear goat horns in OT too, throwing pass that Bucks CB Chris Gamble dropped 3 plays before Jones missed his tying FG. Ohio QB Craig Krenzel passed for 226y, with 6/123y caught by WR Michael Jenkins.

Kansas State 38 NEBRASKA 9: Scoring 31 pts in 2nd H, Wildcats (9-3) handed Nebraska worst home loss since Missouri won 31-0 in 1958. Kansas State QB Ell Roberson threw for 313y and 2 TDs to WR James Terry (6/175y) in 4th Q. It was K-State's 1st win in Lincoln since 1968. Huskers (8-3) tied game at 7-7 late in 2nd Q as 41y INT RET by S Josh Bullocks led to 6y TD pass from QB Jammal Lord to WR Mark LeFlore. Wildcats coach Bill Snyder painted it in purple: "Extremely important to me is the fact that long-suffering Kansas State football fans are happy this evening."

TEXAS 43 Texas Tech 40: Texas (9-2) coach Mack Brown took chance, and it paid off as former starting QB Chance Mock was inserted with just less than 2 mins left and led winning 86y drive. Mock, in relief of QB Vince Young (16-25/213y, 2 TDs, 2 INTs), completed 54y pass to WR Roy Williams (8/136y) to jumpstart Longhorns before tossing winning 9y TD pass to WR B.J. Johnson with 46 secs remaining. Texas Tech (7-4) had rallied from 35-21 deficit, scoring go-ahead TD on 11y run by RB Taurean Henderson, his 3rd of game, to convert FUM by Young. Once Texas regained lead, Red Raiders QB B.J. Symons (32-56/365y, 3 TDs) had time to drive his O unit to 48y FG attempt, which K Keith Toogood missed wide left as time ran out. Texas RB Cedric Benson rushed for 142y and 2 TDs.

Bowl Championship Series Rankings

	Poll Avg.	Computer Avg.	Schedule Ranking	Losses Wins	Quality	Total
1 Oklahoma (11-0)	1.0	1.00	0.40	0	-0.6	1.80
2 Ohio State (10-1)	4.0	2.00	0.52	1		7.52
3 Southern California (9-1)	2.0	3.33	1.48	1	-0.1	7.71
4 Louisiana State (9-1)	3.0	5.83	2.88	1	-0.5	12.21
5 Texas (9-2)	7.0	6.67	0.68	2		16.35

November 22, 2003

(Th) SOUTHERN MISSISSIPPI 40 Texas Christian 28: Unbeaten TCU (10-1) opened with 87y drive on 16 plays but had to settle for K Nick Browne's 21y FG. From that moment rugged D of Southern Miss (8-3) and inspired QB Dustin Almond (14-23/227y, 3 TDs, INT) seized control until near end. Almond found WR DaRon Lawrence all alone near right sideline for 50y TD when Horned Frogs DB fell down. Ahead 7-6 in 2nd Q, Eagles exploded to 17 pts as they gained short field possession 3 straight times. TD scorers were FB Anthony Harris and WR Antwon Courington on slant-in pass from Almond. Trailing 31-6, TCU rallied behind QB Brandon Hassell (18-31/260y, 2 INTs) and 2 onside-KOs for 3 TDs in span of 4:30 in 4th Q. Frog TDs came twice from FB Kenny Hayter and from Hassell and were enhanced by Hassell's 2-pt run and pass. USM added FG to build 34-28 lead, and CB Greg Brooks forced TCU's 4th and last TO. Eagles FB Anthony Harris scored clinching TD with 1:30 left. Southern Miss would go on to beat East Carolina for 8-0 mark for Conf USA title.

Maryland 26 NORTH CAROLINA STATE 24: Terrapins (8-3) rallied from 14-pt deficit in last 8:45 to swipe late win over Wolfpack (7-5). Sr QB Philip Rivers (16-30/276y, INT) had his no. 17 jersey retired by NC State, but loss closed highly disappointing year. TB T.A. McLendon (21/65y, 2 TDs) scored twice in 1st H and when TB Tremain Hall charged 83y on punt TD RET in 3rd Q and K Adam Kiker made 32y FG in 4th Q Wolfpack led 24-10. But, Maryland QB Scott McBrien (17-37/243y, 2 TDs, INT) pitched TD pass and ran 2y to score with 2:29 to play. Terps K Nick Novak missed tying x-pt to keep State ahead 24-23, but McLendon fumbled at his 46YL with 1:50 to go. Maryland gained 21y before Novak nailed 43y FG to win it with 23 secs on clock.

AUBURN 28 Alabama 23: TB Carnell "Cadillac" Williams (26/204y, 2 TDs) roared 80y on game's 1st snap to propel Auburn (7-5). Gaining early score was omen for Tigers as they won their 7th game when scoring 1st. Alabama (4-8) gained safety after Tide P Bo Freeland deadened punt at 1YL. Tigers QB Jason Campbell (18-27/270y, TD, 2 INTs) hooked up with WR Ben Obomanu for 64y TD and 15-2 lead after 2-pt run/pass. Auburn led 18-2 at H. WR Brandon Brooks took 2nd H KO 96y for Alabama TD, cutting deficit to 18-9 and igniting Bama. Crimson Tide soon went 83y to TB Shaud Williams' 6y TD run. Ahead now by only 18-16, Auburn countered with FG drive. Bama FS Charles Jones made EZ INT near pylon early in 4th Q, another play that seemed to prevent Tigers' wrap-up. Williams tallied short TD dive midway in 4th Q. But, Tide never quit: QB Brodie Croyle (13-29/180y, TD, 2 INTs) fired 14y pass that WR Triandos Luke couldn't hold, but ricochet was caught by WR Lance Taylor. Down 28-23, Bama couldn't recover onside-KO.

Louisiana State 17 MISSISSIPPI 14: It was 1st meeting of Deep South rivals since 1970 that found both teams ranked in AP Poll. Leading 7-3 on CB Travis Johnson's 6y INT TD RET, Rebels (8-3) employed solid D and effective punting by P Cody Ridgeway. But, LSU took 10-7 lead when WR Michael Clayton (9/83y, TD) grabbed flanking screen pass and waited for T Rodney Reed and G Stephen Peterman to charge wide to sweep away tacklers for 9y TD. LSU opened 4th Q with 53y TD bomb from QB Matt Mauck (16-29/189y, 2 TDs, 3 INTs) to WR Devery Henderson. Going nowhere against brilliant Bayou Bengals' D, Rebs' 4th Q drive was kept alive by D-holding PEN. Ole Miss QB Eli Manning (16-36/200y, TD, INT) then beat blitz with 43y pass to WR Bill Flowers, and FB Brandon Jacobs soon slipped up middle for 10y TD catch. Rebels got 2 more chances that went south: K Jonathan Nichols, amazingly accurate at 23-24 to-date in 2003, missed tying 36y FG, and Manning was stepped on by G Doug Buckles and fell on 4th down play near midfield with less than 2 mins left.

MICHIGAN 35 Ohio State 21: Collegiate record crowd of 112,118 at Ann Arbor's "Big House" watched 100th meeting of Big 10's most storied and competitive rivalry. Michigan (10-2) fashioned 18-play, 89y drive that ate much of 1st Q as TB Chris Perry (31/154y, 2 TDs and 5/55y receiving) converted 3rd-and-1 from Ohio State (10-2) 10YL. Then on 3rd down, frosh WR Steve Breaston went under C and scored on option run right. Early in 2nd Q, Wolverines QB John Navarre (21-32/278y, 2 TDs, INT) rifled slant-in pass to WR Braylon Edwards (7/130y, 2 TDs), who broke 2 tackles for 64y TD. Twice in 1st H, DB Dustin Fox nearly held INTs, but Fox was called for pass interference which led to Edwards' 2nd TD catch in 2nd Q. Resourceful Ohio State QB Craig Krenzel (20-33/221y, 2 TDs) hit 8-9/63y passes on late 2nd Q drive to TD pass to WR Santonio Holmes. Ahead 21-7 to start 3rd Q, Michigan sent Perry for 30y TD run with cut to left pylon. Bucks WR Michael Jenkins made 41y reception to help pin UM deep that led to Holmes' 2nd TD catch. P Adam Finley twice punted Ohio deep in their end, and, with Krenzel going out with left shoulder injury, sr QB Scott McMullen was left to rally Buckeyes. His high-lofted 40y pass to Holmes set up 2y TD by TB Lydell Ross. DB Chris Gamble picked off underthrown Navarre pass for 1st TO of game at Ohio 37YL, but UM held early in 4th Q. With 11 mins to go, Wolverines turned to their stalwarts. Navarre became 1st Michigander to exceed 3,000y passing in single season during drive to Perry's sprint-draw 15y TD run with 7:55 left. UM CB Markus Curry tipped pass into INT by S Ernest Shazor to clinch only 2nd loss for Ohio in last 2 years.

MICHIGAN STATE 41 Penn State 10: Nittany Lions (3-9), looking to build on previous week's O explosion against Indiana, went length of field early but had to settle for K Robbie Gould's angled 29y FG. That was about it for Penn State. Spartans (8-4) QB Jeff Smoker (29-50/357y, 4 TDs, INT) threw short out-pattern to WR Kyle Brown, and 2 awful tackle attempts allowed Brown to sprint down left sideline for 80y TD. Beautiful

execution of sprint draw turned into RB Tyrell Dortch's 14y TD run and 14-3 lead for Michigan State. Smoker added 2 more TD passes in 2nd H, and Penn State ended its worst-ever season despite TD pass in last 11 secs by QB-TB Michael Robinson.

Iowa 27 WISCONSIN 21: Coming off best 2-game passing numbers (39-58/685y, 9 TDs) in Wisconsin (7-5) history, QB Jim Sorgi (4-10/43y) looked for key win. Hawks (9-3) scored 1st when TB Fred Russell (18/137y, TD) ran 47y to set up WR Ramon Ochoa's 18y TD run. INTs by Badgers DBs Scott Starks (26y RET) and Kyle McCorison (33y RET) helped direct Wisconsin on top 21-7 in 2nd Q. But, Iowa DE Tyler Luebke's sack of Sorgi knocked sr QB from game, and in his place QB Matt Schabert threw 3 INTs. Each led to Iowa pts. CB Jovon Johnson made 2nd Q INT that led to Ochoa's 2nd TD, 6y catch from erratic QB Nathan Chandler (8-26/66y, TD, 2 INTs). Hawkeyes K Nate Kaeding made 1 of his long-range FGs (50y) just before H to trim it to 21-17. Iowa FS Sean Considine raced 24y on INT RET to Badgers 1YL late in 3rd Q to set up Russell's TD run, and, only 3 plays later, SS Bob Sanders went high for Schabert's poor-choice pass to set up Kaeding's 2nd FG. Wisconsin frosh QB John Stocco (5-9/84y) entered game with 11:53 to play and moved Badgers 44y to 4YL in dying secs, only to have 4th down EZ pass deflected by Considine.

KANSAS STATE 24 Missouri 14: TB Darren Sproles (43/school record 273y, 2 TDs) dominated 1st H with 186y rushing behind lead blocks of FB Victor Mann and went to wide run right for TD on Wildcats (9-3) 1st series. Sproles added TD run left in 2nd Q. With 5:45 left in 2nd Q, Tigers (7-4) TE Quincy Howard caught 2y crossing-pattern TD from QB Brad Smith (14-28/155y, TD, INT) to trim deficit to 14-7 after K-State QB Ell Roberson (7-16/70y, INT passing and 24/95y, TD rushing) bungled handoff at his own 2YL. But, Roberson sneaked over in last min of 1st H for 21-7 lead. Roberson overthrew 3rd Q pass, which was picked off by S Nino Williams and returned near midfield. Sticking mostly on ground, Mizzou moved into red zone only to have Cats CB Louis Lavender make EZ INT. Kansas State K Joe Rheem hit 30y FG into wind late in 3rd Q for 24-7 edge. Missouri RB Zack Abron powered 37y up middle for TD with 3:18 left, but Tigers failed on onside-KO. Win clinched Big 12 North for K-State.

Utah 3 BRIGHAM YOUNG 0: Not since September of 1975 had Brigham Young (4-8) been shut out, but mighty Utah (9-2) D, led by CB Eric Weddle's forced FUM and INT and SS Dave Revell's INT, strangled Cougars. Utes took Mountain West conf title and spot in Liberty Bowl on strength of K Bryan Borreson's 41y FG midway in 2nd Q. Once O geniuses of mountain region, BYU managed only 156y net while blustery winds and occasional snow hampered both Os. Cougars' aerial game was meager 4-14/41y, 2 INTs as backup QB Jackson Brown (3-9/36y, INT) had to take over for injured QB Matt Berry in 1st H. Utah QB Alex Smith rushed 23/55y and passed 11-19/113y, INT.

SOUTHERN CALIFORNIA 47 Ucla 22: Trojans received good news of Ohio State's loss just before they took field. Superb WR Mike Williams caught 11/181y, 2 TDs for Southern California (10-1) as Trojans rolled to 5th straight win over Bruins (6-6). Williams' 1st score came on high pass in EZ in face of UCLA DB Matt Clark, who was helpless in giving away 8" in height to Williams, who timed his leap perfectly. With QB Matt Leinart passing 23-32/289y, 2 TDs, USC scored 3 straight times to open game,

Bowl Championship Series Rankings

	Poll Avg.	Computer Avg.	Schedule Ranking	Losses Wins	Quality	Total
1 Oklahoma (12-0)	1.0	1.00	0.40	0	-0.5	1.90
2 Southern Calif. (10-1)	2.0	2.33	1.56	1		6.59
3 Louisiana State (10-1)	3.0	3.00	2.44	1	-0.4	8.04
4 Michigan (10-2)	4.0	4.33	0.52	2	-0.6	10.24
5 Ohio State (10-2)	7.5	4.83	0.24	2		14.57

November 27-29, 2003

(Th'g) Mississippi 31 MISSISSIPPI STATE 0: Jackie Sherrill suffered through rainy night in his retirement game as Bulldogs (2-10) coach and couldn't muster much from his downbeat athletes. Sherrill finished his 26-year career at Washington State, Pittsburgh, Texas A&M, and Mississippi State with 180-120-4 record. Within days, Sylvester Croom, 1-time Alabama A-A C and SEC's 1st African-American head coach filled Sherrill's spot. Mississippi (9-3) topped its SEC schedule with 7-1 record, but had to hope Arkansas could upset LSU next afternoon for chance at title game. Rebels QB Eli Manning passed 19-27/260y, 3 TDs. Manning got Rebels rolling on their 3rd series by firing 38y to WR Chris Collins (8/113y, TD) and spotting RB Treaiman Turner in back of EZ for 25y TD. Sub TE Lawrence Lilly made brilliant 11y TD reception from Manning that he tipped and collared in crowd. Bulldogs, who were outgained 359y to 192y, could look only to 2 forced FUMs in their own territory and passing of sr QB Kevin Fant, who threw 14-28/91y, INT.

(Fri) LOUSIANA STATE 55 Arkansas 24: Razorbacks (8-4) were giving all LSU (11-1) could handle, running well on back of TB Cedric Cobbs (21/170y, TD) in 17-17 tie early in 2nd Q. Hogs rushed for 201y against Bengals' run D that came in with nation's best

avg per game. But Arkansas lost 3 quick TOs, and Tigers QB Matt Mauck (12-19/186y, 4 TDs) exploded with scoring passes of 2y to WR Skyler Green, 22y to WR Devery Henderson, and 37y to TE David Jones. RB Justin Vincent (18/112y, 2 TDs) scored twice in waning mins of 3rd Q as LSU tallied 38 straight pts. Hogs had only themselves to blame in launching this avalanche; P Brennan O'Donohoe dropped snap in his end in 2nd Q, and QB Matt Jones (4-12/100y, 2 TDs, 2 INTs) threw foolish pass into intermediate range. It was picked off by Bayou DB Corey Webster (2 INTs).

(Fri) Nebraska 31 COLORADO 22: While wolves were howling for Nebraska (9-3) coach Frank Solich's job, Buffaloes (5-7) hoped to go bowling. Huskers twice failed on 4th down tries in Colorado territory in 1st Q, but QB Jammal Lord launched 58y TD pass to TE Matt Herian. Buffs came right back to tie it 7-7 on 80y drive to 33y TD by QB Joel Klatt (24-44/269y, 3 TDs, 2 INTs) and added 44y FG by K Mason Crosby. IB Josh Davies made 64y KO RET, and when face mask PEN was tacked on, Huskers had short field for Lord's 5y TD run for 14-10 lead in 2nd Q. Trailing 21-10, Bisons WR D.J. Hackett blocked punt and caught Klatt's 6y TD pass. Colorado WR Derek McCoy caught school career record-tying 20th TD pass in 3rd Q, but Buffs led only 22-21 because they had failed twice on ill-advised 2-pt tries. This allowed Nebraska to pull away with game's last 10 pts. It didn't help Solich, who despite 58-19 career record, was unable to live up to high expectations. He was fired before end of weekend.

(Fri) Texas 46 TEXAS A&M 15: Texas (10-2) thought it enhanced its chances for BCS at-large bowl bid with runaway decision over Aggies (4-8). Longhorns QB Vince Young (5-8/97y, TD passing, 90y rushing) passed sparingly but launched 60y TD to TE David Thomas on game's 2nd snap, and Texas A&M made game of it for awhile: It pulled within 10-9 early in 2nd Q as K Todd Pegram hit chip-shot FG, and QB Reggie McNeal (10-20/165y, INT) came off bench to score 1y TD after FUM REC at Longhorns 8YL. It was only 20-15 for Texas in 3rd Q when Horns TB Cedric Benson (35/283y, 4 TDs) took over. Benson scored his 2nd and 3rd rushing TDs before end of 3rd Q, on his way to his last score, 35y burst in 4th Q.

RUTGERS 24 Syracuse 7: Coach Greg Schiano's solid recruiting finally seemed to reap dividends for Rutgers (5-7). Orangemen (5-6) scored 1st when DB Steve Gregory returned punt blocked by DB Anthony Smith for 5y TD less than 2 mins into game. Wind and cold appeared to hamper both attacks until late in 2nd Q when Rutgers frosh DB Derek Roberson, who earlier blocked punt, recovered fumbled punt at Syracuse 42YL. Scarlet QB Ryan Hart (19-33/125y, TD, INT) then took command with 4-5/42y passing, including 19y TD to WR Tres Moses with 41 secs before H. Knights Eddie Grimes made 51y INT RET to 3YL in 3rd Q to set up Hart's go-ahead TD dive. FB Brian Leonard, who rushed for 37/138y, TD and caught 6/45y, plunged over to score after Rutgers recovered its own wind-blown KO after Hart's TD plunge.

Miami 28 PITTSBURGH 7: Pitt Panthers (8-4) ran ball straight at Miami (10-2) on opening 64y drive, used EZ pass interference PEN that prevented WR Larry Fitzgerald from TD, and scored on short rollout pass from QB Rod Rutherford (17-30/206y, 2 TDs, 3 INTs) to TE Kris Wilson. Hurricanes 3rd-unit TB Tyrone Moss zipped up middle to tie it 7-7. Moss supplied footwork for powerful 2nd Q 80y drive to 14-7 lead behind blocks to TE Kellen Winslow, T Eric Winston, and G Vernon Carey. QB Brock Berlin (12-17/195y, TD, INT) lobbed perfect screen pass to TB Jason Geathers for 78y to set up TB Jarrett Payton's 1y TD. Miami led 263y to 72y in 1st H as D shut down Fitz-gerald. Pitt's WR Greg Lee grabbed long pass to spark 1st drive of 2nd H; but Canes DB Sean Taylor made INT, his 8th of season, at 14YL. After pounding ball at Panthers, Berlin launched 45y TD pass to WR Roscoe Parrish for 28-7 lead. Fitzgerald extended his 18-game TD catching streak by nabbing 18y throw late in 4th Q.

Maryland 41 WAKE FOREST 28: Coach Jim Grobe challenged his Demon Deacons (5-7) to be more physical, and Wake Forest's O-line powered over Maryland (9-3) for 21-6 lead deep into 2nd Q. Deacs QB Cory Randolph scrambled 5y for TD, and TB Chris Barclay (28/243y, 3 TDs) capped 95y drive with TD that upped lead to 15 pts as H approached. But, Terrapins righted themselves before end of 2nd Q by switching to hurry-up O to go 77y to WR Dan Melendez's 14y TD catch from QB Scott McBrien (12-22/198y, 3 TDs). Terps TB Bruce Perry (25/237y, 3 TDs) took over in 2nd H as Maryland's power running dominated. Perry scored on runs of 49y and 80y to fuel 28-pt surge within 6:46 span in 3rd and 4th Qs. It was 5th time in NCAA history that opposing runners—Barclay and Perry—topped 200y each.

VIRGINIA 35 Virginia Tech 21: Virginia (7-5) got off to 7-0 lead on short score by TB Wali Lundy (24/89y, 3 TDs), but INT by Hokies (8-4) LB Vegas Robinson led to tying TD dive by TB Kevin Jones (25/75y, 2 TDs). QB Brian Randall (14-26/214y, TD, 2 INTs) pitched 43y TD to sub TB Mike Imoh for 14-7 Virginia Tech lead in 2nd Q. Virginia came out flying in 2nd H to end its 4-game losing skid to Tech. Twice UVa succeeded in 4th-and-goal at 1YL, Lundy taking TD pass from QB Matt Schaub (32-46/358y, 2 TDs, INT) 6 mins into 3rd Q and also plowing over on 1st play of 4th Q. In between, useful TB Alvin Pearman slipped outside backfield down right sideline to take 49y TD pass from Schaub that provided 21-14 edge for Cavaliers in 3rd Q. Hokies briefly got back into contention on Jones' 2nd TD with 7 mins to play, but Lundy countered with 19y TD run.

Georgia 34 GEORGIA TECH 17: Georgia Tech (6-6) failed on early 4th-and-2 slant-in pass by QB Reggie Ball (8-16/80y, INT) at Georgia 36YL, and on next play Bulldogs (10-2) QB David Greene (16-22/235y, TD) made brilliant fake and arched 46y pass to WR Fred Gibson. C Nick James soon fell on EZ FUM for TD after Greene lost ball on sweep left. WR Bryan McClendon blocked Jackets punt on next series, and TB Kregg Lumpkin charged left for 13y to TD on 1st play with 4:43 left in 1st Q. Tech came back with K Dan Burnett's 20y FG early in 2nd Q when TE John Paul Foschi made good grab and Ball lowered shoulder on DB Bruce Thornton on reversed-field scramble. After K Billy Bennett's 49y FG extended Georgia's lead to 17-3, Foschi accidentally derailed Tech drive by forcing mate Ball's FUM when he tried to peel back to block on scramble run. Down 20-3 at H, Jackets had to go without Ball, who had mild concussion. Sub QB A.J. Suggs (13-22/175y, 2 TDs, 2 INTs) threw INT that S Thomas Davis returned

to Georgia Tech 30YL. Greene's 26y pass to Gibson set up FB Jeremy Thomas' TD plunge for 27-3 edge. After 3rd Q TD catch by Georgia Tech WR Jonathan Smith (9/108y, TD), Greene and Suggs traded 4th Q TD passes.

Florida State 34 FLORIDA 31: K Matt Leach opened scoring for Florida (8-4) with 47y FG in 1st Q, but Gators were distracted by series of lost-possession calls, all going against them. It was clear that Seminoles (10-2) intended to run (atypical 43 tries against 19 passes), but QB Chris Rix (14-19/256y, 3 TDs) lofted 35y TD pass to WR Dominic Robinson (5/102y, TD) in 1st Q. FSU K Xavier Beitia and Leach traded 2nd Q FGs, so FSU led 10-6. TB Leon Washington's 77y RET of ensuing Florida KO set up Rix's 20y TD pass to TE Matt Henshaw. Gators surprised with WR Andre Caldwell's 30y pass-back to QB Chris Leak, followed by Leak's 25y TD arrow to TE Ben Troupe. Leak ran up middle for 2 pts to trail 17-14 just 1:35 into 3rd Q. Florida tied it 17-17 on their next chance halfway through 3rd Q. Florida State came back downfield, but UF S Guss Scott knocked ball away from Rix on rollout, and CB Keiwan Ratliff went 77y with FUM TD RET. Late in 3rd Q, Gators TB Ciatrick Faison fumbled, and S Pat Watkins scooped it for 25y TD RET, vital score that refired Seminoles. Tied 24-24, Leak hit Troupe to get out of 7YL hole to midfield. Leach's 4th FG gave Gators 27-24 lead with 8 mins to play, lead would change thrice more. Rix made 1y dive for 31-27 FSU lead, and Troupe nabbed 26y back-of-EZ catch to make it 34-31 for Florida with 2:50 to play. Finally, Rix converted 4th-and-14 pass before launching 52y bomb that WR P.K. Sam caught with twisting fall in EZ with :55 on clock. Emotions ran high as Gators and Seminoles brawled as FSU tried to celebrate on "F" logo at midfield.

Bowl Championship Series Rankings December 1

	Poll Avg.	Computer Avg.	Schedule Ranking	Losses Wins	Quality	Total
1 Oklahoma (12-0)	1.0	1.00	0.56	0	-0.5	2.06
2 Southern Calif. (10-1)	2.0	2.42	1.48	1		6.90
3 Louisiana State (11-1)	3.0	2.67	2.16	1	-0.4	8.43
4 Michigan (10-2)	4.0	4.42	0.40	2	-0.6	10.22
5 Ohio State (10-2)	7.5	5.17	0.16	2		14.83

December 6, 2003

(Th) Miami (Ohio) 49 BOWLING GREEN 27: Miami RedHawks (12-1) secured MAC title by riding QB Ben Roethlisberger's 440y passing to pull away from Bowling Green (10-3) in 2nd H. Roethlisberger (26-35/440y, 4 TDs) hit 4 different receivers—WR Ryne Robinson, TE Matt Brandt, WR Michael Larkin, and TB Cal Murray—for scores ranging from 16y to 55y. Falcons scored 1st at 4:14 of 1st Q as they went 33y to 6y TD dash by QB Josh Harris (30-49/260y, 2 TDs, INT). Harris pitched 7y TD to WR Charles Sharon early in 2nd Q for 14-7 lead, but Roethlisberger soon uncorked his 2nd and 3rd TD passes, and Miami led 21-17 at H. Roethlisberger's go-ahead rocket came after he sidestepped blitzing Bowling Green defender and picking out Larkin in back of EZ from 16YL. When TBs Murray and Mike Smith scored in 3rd Q, rout was on at 35-17.

SYRACUSE 38 Notre Dame 12: In 1st meeting since 1963, Syracuse (6-6) looked at this match as defacto bowl game. Orange DB Anthony Smith (2 INTs) made 1st Q INT deep in Notre Dame (5-7) end to set up 1st TD run by TB Walter Reyes (19/189y, 5 TDs). Although outgained, Syracuse led 10-3 at H, and swooped on fumbled snap by ND QB Brady Quinn (18-34/199y, TD, 2 INTs) to ignite Reyes for 3 TD bursts in 3rd Q, on his way to 38 running scores in his career. That beat Floyd Little's record from 1964-66. Late in 3rd Q, Irish LB Courtney Watson took advantage of pass miscommunication by Orangemen and lumbered 48y with INT RET. Quinn hit TE Anthony Fasano with 5y crossing TD pass. Reyes answered right back with 71y TD dash for his 4th score, so Syracuse led 31-12 at end of 3rd Q.

Navy 34 Army 6 (Philadelphia): SB Eric Roberts scored on outside run to cap competent 74y opening drive for Navy (8-4), but huge underdog Army (0-13) D began tackling sharply and made 3rd down sacks by DE Odene Brathwaite and LB Greg Washington to remain competitive through 2nd Q. And, Black Knights got within 7-6 on RB Carlton Jones' short TD run on pitchout early in 2nd Q. Ahead 13-6 after Navy K Eric Rolfs' 38 and 41y FGs, Midshipmen started 2nd H with 80y drive behind FB Kyle Eckel's power running and Roberts' 1-handed catch. Roberts scored on 2y wide run for 20-6 lead. Navy LB Bobby McClarin ended Cadets' counterpunch with INT inside his 5YL. Middies overpowered tiring Army D as Eckel (29/152y, 2 TDs) scored on 16 and 12y runs. Win gave Navy its 1st Commander-in-Chief trophy since 1981.

Louisiana State 34 Georgia 13 (Atlanta): In SEC title game, Bulldogs (10-3) made big play early when S Sean Jones leaped high to block punt, and LB Tony Taylor returned it to LSU (12-1) 31YL. But, Tigers' coverage fooled Georgia QB David Greene (17-41/199y, TD, 3 INTs) on next snap, and DB LaRon Landry made INT. Georgia was stopping LSU run attack when suddenly TE David Jones made kick-out block to spring TB Justin Vincent (18/201y, 2 TDs) for 87y TD run. X-pt hit upright, so Bengals led 6-0 in 1st Q. But, LSU quickly made it up with safety when UGa P Gordon Ely-Kelso dropped snap and was nailed by RB Alley Broussard. Tigers QB Matt Mauck (14-

22/151y, TD, INT) picked star WR Michael Clayton from among 3 open receivers for 43y TD pass and 14-0 lead. Trailing 17-3 at H, Georgia got 49y FG, halfway into 3rd Q, from K Billy Bennett, which tied Bennett with UCLA's John Lee (1983) for most season FGs with 29. LB Lionel Turner made INT, returning it 18y for LSU TD. Greene shook it off and responded with TD pass to TE Ben Watson. Trailing 31-13, Georgia faced 4th-and-2 at Bengals 6YL, but DT Chad Lavalais blew up pass-back play.

GAME OF THE YEAR

Kansas State 35 Oklahoma 7 (Kansas City): No. 1 Sooners (12-1) roared early on D, and TB Kejuan Jones used outstanding seal block from FB J.D. Runnels to burst 42y for TD around left side. Then, Kansas State (11-3) D began to jell in its "Purple on White" theme of pressuring QB Jason White, but its O stumbled until TB Darren Sproles (22/235y) slipped through T for 55y gain to Sooners 18YL early in 2nd Q. TE Brian Casey caught 3rd down pass over middle for 19y TD to tie it 7-7, and QB Ell Roberson (10-17/227y, 4 TDs) soon hit stop-and-go pass to WR James Terry for stunning 63y TD. Oklahoma QB White (27-50/298y, 2 INTs) dropped perfect 38y fade pass into hands of WR Mark Clayton, but S James McGill soon made EZ INT on 3rd down play in latter part of 2nd Q. Sproles caught short screen pass and rolled 60y to TD and 21-7 lead before H. Oklahoma fans were stunned. Sooners took nearly half of 3rd Q to drive downfield, but K Trey DiCarlo missed short FG. Wildcats responded with 80y trip, all on runs, except Roberson's 10y scoring pass to WR Antoine Polite. Kansas State LB Teddy Sims, who had made critical pass deflection that prevented early TD pass, made jumping 4th Q INT and returned it for TD. Big 12 title and trip to BCS Fiesta Bowl became Kansas State's prizes, and although Oklahoma would drop to no. 3 in both polls, mysteriously, it would retain its top spot in BCS rankings.

SOUTHERN CALIFORNIA 52 Oregon State 28: Confused USC pass coverage allowed Beavers (7-5) WR Mike Hass (8/208y) to get open for 90y gain to 1YL. Pac-10 rushing leader, TB Steven Jackson (22/62y, TD), rambled left for TD and 7-0 lead, but Southern California (11-1) calmly came back as majestic WR Mike Williams caught 3/33y, including 14y TD. When Trojans LB Lofa Tatupu caused FUM at Oregon State 30YL, QB Matt Leinart (22-38/278y, 5 TDs, 2 INTs) sent TB Reggie Bush long from wide left stance to grab 30y TD and 14-7 lead less than 5 mins into game. Troy DL Sean Cody broke through to block FG try, and it signaled that time was at hand for both Ds to establish themselves. Although Oregon State moved into USC territory, it was pressed into several TOs, and Beavers quickly improved their pass coverage. State QB Derek Anderson (34-60/485y, 2 TDs, 4 INTs) was picked off by Trojans CB Will Poole for 67y TD. Williams was brilliant, finger-tipped TD catch for 28-7 lead by Southern Cal. But, Oregon State zipped downfield to Anderson's 22y TD over middle to TE Tim Euhus (7/97y, TD) 6 secs before H. After Leinart and Williams collaborated on TD pass, Leinart was hit while throwing, and Beavers frosh DB Brandon Browner made 31y INT TD RET. When it seemed like Trojans were bogged down, WR Steve Smith took slant-in pass for 73y TD and 42-21 lead midway in 3rd Q. USC won going away to put itself in top spot in both polls, even though it gave up 543y total O.

Bowl Championship Series Rankings December 7

	Poll Avg.	Computer Avg.	Schedule Ranking	Losses Wins	Quality	Total
1 Oklahoma (12-1)	3.0	1.17	0.44	1	-0.5	5.11
2 Louisiana State (12-1)	2.0	1.83	1.16	1		5.99
3 Southern Calif. (11-1)	1.0	2.67	1.48	1		6.15
4 Michigan (10-2)	4.0	4.67	0.56	2	-0.6	10.63
5 Ohio State (10-2)	6.5	5.50	0.28	2		14.28

Conference Standings

Big East

Miami	6-1
West Virginia	6-1
Pittsburgh	5-2
Virginia Tech	4-3
Boston College	3-4
Syracuse	2-5
Rutgers	2-5
Temple	0-7

Atlantic Coast

Florida State	7-1
Maryland	6-2
Clemson	5-3
North Carolina State	4-4
Virginia	4-4
Georgia Tech	4-4
Wake Forest	3-5
Duke	2-6
North Carolina	1-7

Southeastern

EAST	
Georgia	6-2
Tennessee	6-2
Florida	6-2
South Carolina	2-6
Kentucky	1-7
Vanderbilt	1-7
WEST	
Louisiana State	7-1
Mississippi	7-1
Auburn	5-3
Arkansas	4-4
Alabama	2-6
Mississippi State	1-7

Big Ten

Michigan	7-1
Ohio State	6-2
Purdue	6-2
Iowa	5-3
Minnesota	5-3
Michigan State	5-3
Wisconsin	4-4
Northwestern	4-4
Penn State	1-7
Indiana	1-7
Illinois	0-8

Big 12

NORTH	
Kansas State	6-2
Nebraska	5-3
Missouri	4-4
Kansas	3-5
Colorado	3-5
Iowa State	0-8
SOUTH	
Oklahoma	8-0
Texas	7-1
Oklahoma State	5-3
Texas Tech	4-4
Texas A&M	2-6
Baylor	1-7

Western Athletic

Boise State	8-0
Tulsa	6-2
Fresno State	6-2
Hawaii	5-3
Rice	5-3
Nevada	4-4
Louisiana Tech	3-5
San Jose State	2-6
Texas-El Paso	1-7
Southern Methodist	0-8

Conference USA

Southern Mississippi	8-0
Texas Christian	7-1
Louisville	5-3
Memphis	5-3
South Florida	5-3
Houston	4-4
Alabama-Birmingham	4-4
Tulane	3-5
Cincinnati	2-6
East Carolina	1-7
Army	0-8

Mid-American

EAST	
Miami (Ohio)	8-0
Marshall	6-2
Akron	5-3
Kent State	4-4
Central Florida	2-6
Ohio University	1-7
Buffalo	1-7
WEST	
Bowling Green	7-1
Northern Illinois	6-2
Toledo	6-2
Western Michigan	4-4
Ball State	3-5
Eastern Michigan	2-6
Central Michigan	1-7

Mountain West

Utah	6-1
New Mexico	5-2
Colorado State	4-3
Air Force	3-4
San Diego State	3-4
Brigham Young	3-4
Nevada-LasVegas	2-5
Wyoming	2-5

Pacific-10

Southern California	7-1
Washington State	6-2
Oregon	5-3
California	5-3
Oregon State	4-4
UCLA	4-4
Washington	4-4
Arizona State	2-6
Stanford	2-6
Arizona	1-7

2003 Major Bowl Games

Tangerine Bowl (Dec. 22): North Carolina State 56 Kansas 26

Starting his NCAA-record 54th and final game, NC State (8-5) QB Philip Rivers (37-45/475y, 5 TDs), he of unorthodox shotput passing style, was brilliantly accurate. In 28-10 1st H led by Wolfpack, Rivers hit 21-24/268y, 3 TDs and ran for another score. Kansas (6-7) couldn't stop NC State O, but had solid moments with its own O, which rolled to 463y against young Wolfpack D. Jayhawks QB Bill Whittemore (20-41/243y, 2 TDs, 2 INTs) scrambled 21y to 1st down on 79y TD drive early in 3rd Q, then, under pass rush pressure, whipped terrific, long backhand pitch to RB Clark Green (14/87y), who carried it 11y to TD. NC State LB Manny Lawson blocked punt in 3rd Q to set up TD that built 42-20 lead as 4th Q opened. Whittemore scored on QB draw run early in 4th Q, but Rivers answered with his 5th TD pass, 21y to WR Jericho Cotchery for 49-26 edge. With 8 mins to go, Rivers (37-45/475y, 5 TDs) set new Tangerine Bowl passing y record and came out of game together with fellow star Cotchery (13/171y, TD).

Insight Bowl (Dec. 26): California 52 Virginia Tech 49

Spunky California (8-6), winners of 4 of last 5, took opening KO and waltzed to TD against Hokies (8-5), who finished their season being skewered by Thanksgiving arrows. Bears QB Aaron Rodgers, who threw for 394y, scrambled 8y inside 1YL before wedging for early TD. Virginia Tech QB Bryan Randall (24-34/398y, 4 TDs) rolled out late in 1st Q, and WR Chris Shreve slipped away for 53y catch to 3YL. TE Keith Willis caught 1st of his 2 TD passes, so Tech led 14-7. Late-hit PEN after Cal punt set up Randall's TD bomb to WR Marcus Vick in last min of 1st Q. Rodgers hit 2 TD passes in 2nd Q, so Bears trailed only 28-21 at H. When Hokies K Carter Warley badly hooked his 3rd FG try, Cal came right downfield for 80y voyage that tied it 28-28 on FB Chris Manderino's TD blast. Bears ignited for 21 pts in 3rd Q to lead 42-28. Tiny WR Vincent Strang ran TD reverse to end long Cal drive for 49-35 lead midway in 4th Q. Virginia Tech rallied for TD, and DB DeAngelo Hall made 3 tacklers miss on way to long, game-

tying punt TD RET down left sideline. California started from its 35YL with 3:11 to play because Hokies frustrated themselves by knocking KO OB for 3rd time. Bears carefully worked downfield to K Tyler Frederickson's 38y FG to win it.

Continental Tire Bowl (Dec. 27): Virginia 23 Pittsburgh 16

Dependable TE Heath Miller broke free for 52y post pattern TD pass from Cavaliers (8-5) QB and Game MVP Matt Schaub (20-31/244y, TD, INT) in 1st Q. After Panthers (8-5) tied it early in 2nd Q on similar TD pass by QB Rod Rutherford (18-26/246y, 2 TDs, INT), Miller went all way across field to snag throw at Pitt 5YL. On 4th-and-1, TB Wali Lundy battled through LG for TD and 14-7 lead. Panthers TB Brandon Miree (22/110y), back after missing several games with injury, took screen pass 17y to score as G Jon Schall and WR Princell Brockenbrough blocked effectively. K J.B. Gibboney tried to tie it with x-pt, but his kick hit right upright. Virginia added FGs late in 1st H and early in 3rd Q by K Connor Hughes for 20-13 edge. Pitt's record-setting WR Larry Fitzgerald (5/77y), who saw his 18-game TD catching streak end, had been largely ignored by Rutherford since Cav defenders started battering him in 1st H. But, Fitzgerald caught pass in middle of 3rd Q to set up Gibboney's FG in 3rd Q that pulled Pitt within 20-16. Pitt made 2 big D plays that could have turned tide: Late in 3rd Q, Panthers diagnosed 4th-and-1 pass from its 12YL and dumped UVa HB Alvin Pearman for loss, and early in 4th Q, DB Tutu Ferguson wrestled pass away from Miiller in EZ corner. But, Gibboney missed 36y FG try in middle of 4th Q, and Hughes made his 3rd 3-ptr for UVa on next series to extend lead to 23-16. Clinching play came in closing moments when Wahoos DL Brennan Schmidt delivered UVa's 5th sack of Rutherford.

Alamo Bowl (Dec. 29): Nebraska 17 Michigan State 3

Huskers (10-3) were having challenge locking up new coach for 2004 as several prospects were rumored to be on way or to have turned them down. Nebraska chancellor Harvey Perlman delivered good line to *Omaha World-Herald,* saying recently-resigned Washington Redskins (and former Florida Gators) coach "Steve Spurrier must own three houses in Lincoln already." Through it all, interim headman, D-coordinator Bo Pelini, had Nebraska ready to play hard against Spartans (8-5). Nebraska's feeble passing O, ranked 115th, met Michigan State's vacuous pass D (104th) with Huskers' air attack prevailing. Nebraska QB Jamaal Lord helped build 2-TD lead in 1st H by completing 7 passes/140y. During 2nd Q, run-conscious Huskers amazingly passed on 7 consecutive downs. Blackshirts' D held Spartans—who averaged 384y per game—to season-low 174y while picking off 3 passes of QB Jeff Smoker (21-39/156y). Huskers set tone immediately as DE Trevor Johnson sacked Smoker twice on 1st series for 2 of team's 5 sacks. Lord finished with career-high 160y passing, while IB Cory Ross (37/138y) lent to team's 229y rushing total and scored both TDs. Ross ran 22 times in 2nd H to kill clock behind dominating O-line. In his swansong, Smoker hit 21-39/156y, 3 INTs in losing cause.

Houston Bowl (Dec. 30): Texas Tech 38 Navy 14

Match-up of contrasting styles was won, as so many games of 2000s were, by team with best air attack. Texas Tech QB B.J. Symons (41-53/497y, 4 TDs, INT) completed most prolific year in college history before revealing he played 2nd H of season with torn ACL in left knee. After both teams blew early chances, Red Raiders (8-5) scored 2 TDs in 2nd Q—including 1 with 4 secs left—to pull away. Navy (8-5) was unable to keep up as Symons unleashed his myriad weapons: WR Wes Welker (7/107y), WR Nehemiah Glover (9/116y, TD), TE Mickey Peters (8/80y, 2 TDs), and WR Carlos Francis (6/90y). Navy QB Craig Candeto ran for 90y of team's 289y rushing and scored both TDs. With help from bruising FB Kyle Eckel (14/71y), Candeto led Navy on 79y drive with its 1st possession before losing controversial FUM on 1YL. Missed opportunity especially was damaging to Midshipmen, team ill-equipped to match high-powered Texas Tech score for score. Game ended in poor taste as some Red Raiders followed late TD with celebration simulated bomb explosion. Symons, who had 2 teeth chipped and sternum bruised on 2nd Q hit by CB Shalimar Brazier, admitted he injured his knee during EZ celebration in win against Iowa State on October 11.

Holiday Bowl (Dec. 30): Washington State 28 Texas 20

While Washington State QB Matt Kegel may have thrown for 203y and RB Jonathan Smith rushed for 110y, it was Cougars' hard-hitting D that toppled Texas (10-3). Wazzu (10-3) sacked Longhorns QBs 7 times, earned safety on UT holding penalty in EZ, and scored TD on CB Jason David's 18y FUM RET. Texas had late chance to tie after QB Chance Mock completed 45y pass to WR Roy Williams (9/97y) to 11YL. Blitzing LB Don Jackson then dashed those hopes by crashing into Mock to force FUM, recovered by LB Will Derting. Final Texas drive ended on 4th down sack by DE D.D. Acholonu, who came up with 3 sacks in game's final 2:16. Kegel and Smith's efforts enabled State to outscore Longhorns 19-0 in 3rd Q to forge 26-10 lead. Kegel and WR Sammy Moore had hooked up on their 2nd scoring pass (54y) to take 3-pt lead at 13-10. Smith scored next TD, taking Shotgun snap and scooting to EZ from 12YL to convert 51y punt return by Moore. David scored TD after S Erik Coleman jarred ball loose after reception by UT TE David Thomas. Mock, in relief of starting QB Vincent Young, stopped bleeding with 30y TD to Williams early in 4th Q. Cougars P Kyle Basler was named outstanding D player by dropping 4 punts within Texas 5YL.

Sun Bowl (Dec. 31): Minnesota 31 Oregon 30

Pressure? K Rhys Lloyd, native of Dover, England, had won Paul Bunyan Axe for Gophers (10-3) with last-sec FG against Wisconsin, so his 42y FG with 23 secs left to win Sun Bowl was piece of scone, err…cake. Despite being tipped by Oregon DT Junior Siavaii, Lloyd's 3-ptr was good to cap 55y winning drive led by QB Asad Abdul-Khaliq (12-21/172y). Ducks (8-5) had taken 30-28 lead on 47y FG by K Jared Siegel with 4:16 left as teams traded lead 5 times. Minnesota used its rushing superiority to fashion 241y to 77y edge on ground: TB Laurence Maroney gained 131y, TD, and FB Thomas Tapeh added 3 rushing TDs. Oregon used passing game to move ball behind QB Kellen Clemens, who threw for 363y with 200y going to WR Samie Parker's

16 catches. Parker hauled in 2 TDs. Clemens' last-gasp pass was intercepted by Minnesota CB Justin Isom, so Gophers were able to finish their season by winning 10 games for 1st time since 1905.

Music City Bowl (Dec. 31): Auburn 28 Wisconsin 14

For 1st time all season, Auburn (8-5) won when it gave up game's 1st score after having lost previous 5 such tilts. Wisconsin (7-6) K Mike Allen made 2 FGs in 2nd Q, but Tigers TB Ronnie Brown (13/62y), who would score twice, powered over from 1YL with 4:37 left in 2nd Q for 7-6 edge. In middle of 4th Q, Badgers QB Jim Sorgi (13-22/169y, TD, INT) lofted 12y pass on which WR Lee Evans (4/51y, TD) made brilliant catch over CB Carlos Rogers' back for TD that led to tying 2-pt pass. On Wisconsin's next possession, Rogers turned tables by deflecting long pass meant for Evans into hands of S Will Herring for INT. In barely over min, Auburn charged 87y for go-ahead TD as QB Jason Campbell (10-22/138y, INT) hit 51 and 28y passes to set up Brown's score for 21-14 lead. Tigers LB Karlos Dansby delivered finale by forcing FUM at 1YL that created TD for TB Carnell Williams (18/68y, 2 TDs) with 1:37 left.

Independence Bowl (Dec. 31): Arkansas 27 Missouri 14

Razorbacks (9-4) ran ball for 300y, and special teams of Missouri (8-5) failed it at 2 vital moments as Arkansas ended 3-game bowl losing streak and won for 2nd time in last 12 bowls. Hogs K Chris Balseiro made 4 of 4 FGs and TB Cedric Cobbs rushed 27/141y, including 41y scoring dash in 2nd Q that provided 21-7 H lead. Cobbs' backup, TB DeCori Birmingham ran 10/85y and QB Matt Jones added 7/74y, TD. Tigers, however, led 7-6 in 2nd Q on TD by TB Zack Abron (19/137y, TD) when snap sailed high over P Brock Harvey's head to his 3YL. Jones scored quickly and added 2-pt pass for 14-7 Arkansas lead. On last play of 2nd Q, Missouri tried fake FG which turned into INT by Hogs sr WR Tom Crowder, who also blocked 4th Q punt. QB Brad Smith accounted for 251y to top Mizzou career total y record in only his 2nd season.

San Francisco Bowl (Dec. 31): Boston College 35 Colorado State 21

There is something about throwing 5 INTs that makes it difficult for any team to win. Colorado State Rams (7-6) outgained BC 388y to 361y, but could not overcome their TOs and rushing of Eagle TB Derrick Knight. Knight (30/122y) ran for 3 TDs, including 2 in 1st Q that buried Colorado State at 21-0. CSU's change at QB, from backup QB Jesse Holland (8-12/79y, 2 INTs) to QB Bradlee Van Pelt (14-25/163y, TD, 3 INTs), who did not start due to broken bone in throwing hand, did little to help. QB Paul Peterson (16-25/224y, INT) tossed 2 TD passes for Boston College (8-5), both going to WR Larry Lester including 50y TD to cap 98y drive for BC's 2nd score. Entering game with only 1 career INT, Eagles S T.J. Stancil had 3 picks, while teammate CB Will Blackmon had INT and 59y punt RET that set up TD. Colorado State WR David Anderson caught 10/134y, including 40y TD. With Oklahoma's loss 5 days later, Boston College became nation's only school with 4 bowl wins in past 4 seasons.

Outback Bowl: Iowa 37 Florida 17

Hawkeyes (10-3) shook off opening score by Florida (8-5) to reel off 27 straight pts to win for 1st time in January since walloping California in 1959 Rose Bowl. TB Fred Russell (21/150y) led Hawkeyes rushing attack that gained 238y, while QB Nathan Chandler (13-25/170y) threw and ran for TDs. Florida opened scoring with 70y pass from QB Chris Leak (22-41/268y, 2 TDs, INT) to WR Kelvin Kight. Chandler tied things up less than 4 mins later with 3y scoring pass to WR Maurice Brown (6/96y). Nate Kaeding, playing his last game as 1 of college football's greatest Ks, began Iowa's 13-0 run in 2nd Q with 47y FG that provided 10-7 lead they would never relinquish. Ahead 20-7 entering 3rd Q, Iowa D immediately forced punt on Gators' 1st possession, and WR Matt Melloy ended Florida's hopes by blocking punt. Melloy recovered ball in EZ for TD, 3rd time this season Hawkeyes had scored on blocked punt. Iowa enjoyed consecutive double-digit win seasons for 1st time in its history.

Gator Bowl: Maryland 41 West Virginia 7

Fast-closing Maryland (10-3) won for 10th time in its last 11 outings and repeated its early-season destruction of Mountaineers (8-5). QB Scott McBrien, 1-time transfer from West Virginia, threw against many of his old pals for career-high 381y on 21-33, including 3 TDs. Terrapins WR Steve Suter, who played on gimpy knee, came up with 2 big plays. Suter collared punt at his 24YL early in 2nd Q and exploded for 76y TD RET as nary single Mountaineer touched him. That scamper built score to 17-0, by which time WVU had burned 2 timeouts and lost 2 FUMs before making its initial 1st down. Suter went high with West Virginia CB Lance Frazier for long pass in 3rd Q and came down with brilliant catch of tipped ball at 7YL. McBrien scored 3 plays later on 2y run for 31-0 edge. WVU scored with 6:10 to go in 3rd Q on QB Rasheed Marshall's 15y run. Stats for Mountaineer stars reflected rout: Marshall was 10-16/87y passing and TB Quincy Wilson rushed 12/49y as WVU gained fairly modest 241y on 48 plays. In coach Ralph Freidgen's 3 years, Terps earned status in small, elite group that had won 10 games each year. WVU lost its 10th bowl game in its last 11 tries.

Capital One Bowl: Georgia 34 Purdue 27 (OT)

Georgia (11-3) came sprinting into Orlando, bent on redeeming slightly disappointing year. So, Bulldogs jumped to 14-0 lead in 1st Q as QB David Greene (27-37/327y, 3 TDs) and WR Fred Gibson connected for 2 short scoring passes. Tally was upped to 24-0 in 2nd Q when Greene added his 3rd TD pass, but QB Kyle Orton (20-34/230y, TD, INT) rallied Purdue (9-4) with 10 quick pts near end of 2nd Q. After scoreless 3rd Q, Orton ran for his 2nd TD and hit WR Anthony Chambers with 3y TD pass to draw within 27-24 with 1:41 left. Boilers' onside-KO went OB, and that seemed to kill any comeback bid. But, in trying to kill clock, frosh Georgia TB Gregg Lumpkin (27/90y, TD) fumbled, and Purdue K Ben Jones sent it to OT on 44y FG with 49 secs to go. Lumpkin was disconsolate on sideline, but he was encouraged by coach Mark Richt and slipped into EZ on 4th down run on 1st OT possession. On Purdue's OT series, LB Tony Taylor made game-ending INT for Bulldogs.

Rose Bowl: Southern California 28 Michigan 14

Big 10 champion Michigan (10-3) had allowed only 5 TD passes in its previous 12 games, but fabulous scheme of O-coordinator Norm Chow of no. 1 Southern California (12-1) produced 4 TD passes. And, Wolverines QB John Navarre (27-46/271y, TD, INT) was presented with such pass pressure that he was sacked 9 times. Michigan took 6:15 off game-start clock with effective drive, but it was thwarted by Trojans on blitz by CB Will Poole and blocked FG by DT Shaun Cody. USC sr WR Keary Colbert (6/149y, 2 TDs), who would enjoy best game of his career, soon took 25y pass over middle for TD from soph QB Matt Leinart (23-34/327y, 3 TDs). Key TD for USC soon came on odd deflected pass: Michigan QB Navarre threw low 3rd down pass from deep in his end that bounced off heel of UM WR Braylon Edwards (10/107y) and was intercepted by Trojans LB Lofa Tatupu (12 tackles), who returned it to 3YL. TB Len Dale White scored on 3rd down pass at left flank with less than 5 mins to go in 2nd Q. Southern Cal, in hot pursuit of AP no. 1 spot, quickly jumped to 21-0 lead as 2nd H opened. Colbert made 1-handed TD pass catch as he was being grabbed by Michigan DB Jeremy LaSueur Wolverines came alive on next drive as Navarre made 1st down on 4th-and-3 scramble to USC 17YL. Navarre then hit backup TE Tim Massaquoi with short TD pass. But whatever comeback bid was left in Wolverines was nipped by big play by Trojans: Brilliant WR Mike Williams (8/88y) ran reverse and perfectly lofted short TD pass to QB Leinart for 28-7 edge with 3:44 left in 3rd Q.

Orange Bowl: Miami 16 Florida State 14

In winning 5th straight vs. Florida State, Hurricanes (11-2) did what usually has worked for them in this series: hold slim 4th Q lead and then watch Seminoles blow late FG attempt. K Xavier Beitia missed 39y effort, wide right, with 5:30 remaining that would have given Florida State (10-3) lead, marking 5th time Florida State missed decisive FG in game against Canes since 1991. Miami outgained Noles 375y to 206y with TB Jarrett Payton (22/131y) leading way, while its D clamped down on FSU's erratic QB Chris Rix (6-19/96y, INT) yet again. Rix completed only 2-12 for 18y in critical 2nd H. Still, Miami needed miss by Beitia and 3 FG connections from K Jon Peattie of 32, 44, and 51y to win. Peattie's 51y FG, which followed 5y FSU penalty on Miami punt, proved to be game-winner. Later in 4th Q, Canes used gutsy call to eat clock as LB D.J. Williams flashed his adept skills with 31y jaunt on fake punt from own 32YL. Brightest moments for Florida State came on consecutive 1st H TD drives as TB Lorenzo Booker scored on 9y run with direct snap and Rix threw 7y TD pass to TE Matt Henshaw. Miami P Brian Monroe's 8y punt and RB Greg Jones' brilliant 24y run around and over defenders set up Henshaw's score. Noles went scoreless in 2nd H.

Cotton Bowl (Jan. 2): Mississippi 31 Oklahoma State 28

Rebels (10-3) put stamp on 1 of school's finest seasons as QB Eli Manning delivered victory as much with his decision-making as his right arm. Manning (22-31/259y, 2 TDs, INT) dazzled with his play calling—SEC Player of Year was free to check D and call audibles, which he did on numerous occasions. He continually called for RB Tremaine Turner, who gained 133y on ground for team-high total for season. Final scoring drive for Rebels was thing of beauty: It totaled 97y with Manning passes twice converting 3rd-and-long situations and was capped by 1y QB keeper. Cowboys (9-4) fell behind 31-14 entering 4th Q, but had ace up sleeve in WR Rashaun Woods. Facing man-to-man coverage for 1st time since he burned SMU in midseason for NCAA-record 7 TDs, Woods (11/223y) caught 5/131y in 4th Q from QB Josh Fields (21-33/307y, TD). Woods began each of Oklahoma State's 4th Q TD drives with long reception: 44y to jump-start 72y drive and 42y to begin 78y drive he ended with 17y TD catch that pulled Cowpokes within 31-28 with 4:38 remaining. Ole Miss then ran out clock with help from pass interference PEN on OSU CB Darrent Williams (8 tackles). Fields' pass y and Woods' receptions and y all set new Cotton Bowl records.

Peach Bowl (Jan. 2): Clemson 27 Tennessee 14

Amid sea of bi-shaded orange-clad fans in Georgia Dome, Clemson's balanced attack did in Volunteers (10-3), who were outplayed by ACC opponent for 2nd straight Peach Bowl. QB Charlie Whitehurst threw for 246y and FB Chad Jasmin rushed for 130y and TD to pace Tigers (9-4), while Tennessee committed undisciplined 10 PENs/119y. Teams combined for 38 pts during wild 1st H that featured 5 TDs including rushing scores by 3 different Clemson backs. On 1 stupefying TD, Clemson lined up in old box formation: RB Kyle Browning was given football between his legs, paused while his teammates moved right to pull Vols defenders, and Browning went left to score untouched on 8y run. Down by 24-14 in 3rd Q, Tennessee marched 62y on 17 time-consuming plays before missing FG. With miss went Tennessee's momentum, and Vols never challenged again. QB Casey Clausen (31-55/384y) threw 2 TD passes in his final game for Tennessee, but too much was asked of him as Clemson D held Vols to meager and uncharacteristic 38y rushing.

Fiesta Bowl (Jan. 2): Ohio State 35 Kansas State 28

Kansas State (11-4), shaken by sexual assault accusations on New Years' Eve against QB Ell Roberson, seemed to start in mental fog, and Roberson was vexed by early ineffectiveness, hitting only 5-20 passes with disastrous INT in 1st H. Ohio State (11-2) QB Craig Krenzel (11-24/189y, 4 TDs, 2 INTs) won his 2nd straight Fiesta Bowl MVP. Buckeyes DB Harlen Jacobs blocked K-State punt in 1st Q, and WR John Hollins scored on 7y RET for 7-0 lead. Roberson (20-51/294y, INT) threw miscommunicated pass from deep in his end in 2nd Q, and star Ohio CB Chris Gamble picked it off at 17YL. Krenzel threw immediate TD pass to tall WR Michael Jenkins. Nation's leading rusher, Wildcats TB Darren Sproles (13/38y, TD), who was kept well-collared by Ohio State's fine LBs, A.J. Hawk, Robert Reynolds and Bobby Carpenter, finally gave his team hope with 6y TD run with 3 mins left in 1st H. K-State was far better O team in 2nd

H, but not before Bucks scored on 2 Krenzel passes in 3rd Q to build 35-14 lead. Cats got within 7 pts when Roberson scored his 2nd rushing TD with 2:47 to play.

Sugar Bowl (Jan. 4): Louisiana State 21 Oklahoma 14

After 43-year national title drought, Louisiana State (13-1) was happy to share split crown with Southern California, who, by virtue of its demonstrative win over no. 4 Michigan in Rose Bowl, was tapped as AP champions. In holding nation's highest scoring team to only 2 TDs, Tigers cuffed and pressured Oklahoma's Heisman-winning QB Jason White (13-37/102y, 2 INTs) on their way to *USA Today* coaches' poll title. Underdog Bayou Bengals set tone from get-go as frosh TB Justin Vincent (16/117y, TD) burned Sooners' blitz on game's 1st play with 64y run. Vincent's burst off right side was stopped short of TD, but it reopened wounds left in OU's once-proud run-D that had been sliced by Kansas State in Big 12 title game. Although Tigers lost FUM on Sooners 1YL, they soon regained ball on INT by CB Corey Webster, and it led to 24y scoring run by WR Skyler Green 3:22 into game. Oklahoma (12-2) stayed close without making any big-plays on O because it did not have to travel far. Sooners' 1st TD came on 2y drive after blocked punt, and 2nd score finished 31y trip that was set up by INT. Oklahoma tied game at 7-7 in 2nd Q after DB Brandon Shelby's blocked punt and 1y TD run by RB Kejuan Jones. Vincent put Tigers ahead to stay with 4:21 left in 1st H with 18y scoring run for 14-7 lead they held at H. LSU started 2nd H as it had opened game, with huge play: only 47 secs into 3rd Q, DE Marcus Spears cannily dropped into pass coverage on 2nd-and-13 and vaulted Tigers' lead to 21-7 when he took INT 20y to score. Sooners had time to rally, but only managed 7 pts on Jones' 2nd 1y TD run after INT by CB Brodney Poole early in 4th Q. Closest OU came to tying game was late drive to LSU 12YL, but S Jesse Daniels' pressure forced White's 3rd down pass, intended to wide-open Jones, to sail high. White's 4th down pass was tipped to ground. Bengals fittingly ending OU's chances with sack (team's 5th) by LB Lionel Turner late in 4th Q. LSU QB Matt Mauck (13-22/124y, 2 INTs) overcame early FUM and 2 INTs to move team to 312y to 154y total O edge by game's delirious end.

Final AP Poll

1 Southern Calif. (48)	1608	13 Mississippi		845
2 Louisiana State (17)	1576	14 Kansas State		833
3 Oklahoma	1476	15 Tennessee		695
4 Ohio State	1411	16 Boise State		645
5 Miami	1329	17 Maryland		564
6 Michigan	1281	18 Purdue		526
7 Georgia	1255	19 Nebraska		520
8 Iowa	1107	20 Minnesota		368
9 Washington State	1060	21 Utah		308
10 Miami (Ohio)	932	22 Clemson		230
11 Florida State	905	23 Bowling Green		189
12 Texas	887	24 Florida		165
		25 Texas Christian		126

Final *USA Today* Coaches January 4

1 LSU (60)	1572	14 Mississippi	730
2 Southern California (3)	1514	15 Boise State	704
3 Oklahoma	1429	16 Tennessee	684
4 Ohio State	1370	17 Minnesota	553
5 Miami (Fla.)	1306	18 Nebraska	532
6 Georgia	1183	19 Purdue	510
7 Michigan	1140	20 Maryland	462
8 Iowa	1119	21 Utah	327
9 Washington State	983	22 Clemson	219
10 Florida State	929	23 Bowling Green	170
11 Texas	894	24 TCU	145
12 Miami (Ohio)	800	25 Florida	124
13 Kansas State	746		

2003 Top Performance Formula

1 Southern California	1.7025
2 Oklahoma	1.6814
3 Louisiana State	1.6784
4 Miami	1.5426
5 Michigan	1.5331
6 Ohio State	1.5306
7 Texas	1.5167
8 Florida State	1.5137
9 Georgia	1.4996
10 Kansas State	1.4816
11 Maryland	1.4576
12 Iowa	1.4469
13 Miami (Ohio)	1.4330
14 Minnesota	1.4100
15 Washington State	1.4084
16 Nebraska	1.4052
17 Mississippi	1.4009
18 Tennessee	1.3995
19 Texas Christian	1.3960
20 Arkansas	1.3637

2003 Top Opponent Records

1 Alabama	.6774
2 Notre Dame	.6429
3 Florida	.6355
4 Texas A&M	.6268
5 Ohio State	.6129
6t Iowa State	.611111
6t Arizona	.611111
8 South Carolina	.6056
9 Kansas State	.6023
10 Florida State	.5960
11 Georgia	.5939
12 Colorado	.5931
13 Brigham Young	.5912
14 Oklahoma	.5893
15 Michigan	.5855
16 No. Carolina State	.5762
17t Texas	.5751633
17t Arkansas	.5751633
19 Mississippi State	.5734
20 Auburn	.5703

2003 Out-of-Conference Records

	W-L	Percentage	Bowl W-L
Southeastern	32-19	.6275	5-2
Atlantic Coast	23-14	.6216	5-1
Big Ten	31-19	.6200	3-5
Big Twelve	31-20	.6078	2-6
Pacific-10	26-17	.6047	4-2
Big East	26-17	.6047	2-3
Mountain West	17-18	.4857	1-2

2003 Individual Statistical Leaders

RUSHING YARDS	Attempts	Yards	Avg.
Darren Sproles, Kansas State	306	1986	6.5
Derrick Knight, Boston College	321	1721	5.4
Patrick Cobbs, North Texas	307	1680	5.5
Chris Perry, Michigan	338	1674	5.0
Michael Turner, Northern Illinois	310	1648	5.3
Kevin Jones, Virginia Tech	281	1647	5.9
Steven Jackson, Oregon State	350	1545	4.4
Anthony Sherrell, Eastern Michigan	338	1531	4.5
DonTrell Moore, New Mexico	276	1450	5.3
P.J. Daniels, Georgia Tech	283	1447	5.1

PASSING YARDS	Completions	Attempts	Yards	Pct.
B.J. Symons, Texas Tech	470	719	5833	65.4
Philip Rivers, North Carolina State	348	483	4491	72.0
Ben Roethlisberger, Miami (Ohio)	342	495	4486	69.1
Ryan Dinwiddie, Boise State	276	446	4356	61.9
Jason White, Oklahoma	278	451	3846	61.6
Josh Harris, Bowling Green	325	494	3813	65.8
Rod Rutherford, Pittsburgh	247	413	3679	59.8
Eli Manning, Mississippi	275	441	3600	62.4
Charlie Whitehurst, Clemson	288	465	3561	61.9
Matt Leinart, Southern California	255	402	3556	63.4

RECEIVING YARDS	Catches	Yards
Larry Fitzgerald, Pittsburgh	92	1672
Geoff McArthur, California	85	1504
Martin Nance, Miami (Ohio)	90	1498
Mark Clayton, Oklahoma	83	1425
Jerricho Cotchery, North Carolina State	86	1379
Rashaun Woods, Oklahoma State	77	1367
Mike Williams, Southern California	95	1314
James Newson, Oregon State	81	1306
David Anderson, Colorado State	72	1293
Brandon Middleton, Houston	55	1250.

2003 Consensus All-America
Offense

Wide Receiver:	Larry Fitzgerald, Pittsburgh
	Mike Williams, Southern California
Tight End:	Kellen Winslow II, Miami
Line:	Shawn Andrews, Arkansas
	Robert Gallery, Iowa
	Jacob Rogers, Southern California
	Alex Barron, Florida State
Center:	Jake Grove, Virginia Tech
Quarterback:	Jason White, Oklahoma
Running Back:	Chris Perry, Michigan
	Kevin Jones, Virginia Tech
Kicker:	Nate Kaeding, Iowa
	Nick Browne, Texas Christian
Kick Returner:	Antonio Perkins, Oklahoma

Defense

Line:
Dave Ball, UCLA
Tommie Harris, Oklahoma
Chad Lavalais, Louisiana State
Kenechi Udeze, Southern California

Linebacker:
Teddy Lehman, Oklahoma
Derrick Johnson, Texas
Grant Wiley, West Virginia

Back:
Derrick Strait, Oklahoma
Sean Taylor, Miami
Keiwan Ratliff, Florida
Will Allen, Ohio State

Punter:
Dustin Colquitt, Tennessee

2003 Heisman Trophy Vote

Jason White, junior quarterback, Oklahoma	1,481
Larry Fitzgerald, sophomore wide receiver, Pittsburgh	1,353
Eli Manning, senior quarterback, Mississippi	710
Chris Perry, senior tailback, Michigan	341
Darren Sproles, junior tailback, Kansa State	134

Other Major Award Winners

Maxwell (Player)	Eli Manning, senior quarterback, Mississippi
Walter Camp (Player)	Larry Fitzgerald, sophomore WR, Pittsburgh
John Outland (Lineman)	Robert Gallery, senior T, Iowa
Vince Lombardi (Lineman)	Tommie Harris, junior defensive tackle, Oklahoma
Doak Walker (Running Back)	Chris Perry, senior TB, Michigan
Davey O'Brien (Quarterback)	Jason White junior QB Oklahoma
Fred Biletnikoff (Receiver)	Larry Fitzgerald, sophomore WR, Pittsburgh
Jim Thorpe (Defensive Back)	Derrick Strait, senior cornerback, Oklahoma
Dick Butkus (Linebacker)	Teddy Lehman, senior linebacker, Oklahoma
Lou Groza (Placekicker)	Jonathan Nichols, junior kicker, Mississippi
Chuck Bednarik (Defender)	Teddy Lehman, senior linebacker, Oklahoma
Ray Guy (Punter)	B.J. Sander, senior punter, Ohio State
Johnny Unitas (Sr. Quarterback)	Eli Manning, senior quarterback, Mississippi
John Mackey (Tight End)	Kellen Winslow II, junior tight end, Miami
Dave Rimington (Center)	Jake Grove, senior center, Virginia Tech
Ted Hendricks (Defensive End)	David Pollack, junior defensive end, Georgia
AFCA Coach of the Year	Nick Saban, Louisiana State

2004

The Year of Finding a Quarterback, Sudden Fumble Reversal, and Auburn and AP Out of the BCS

A remarkable number of star quarterbacks were gone from top teams of 2003. So, it was the presence of USC's eventual Heisman Trophy-winning lefthander, Matt Leinart, Oklahoma's returning Heisman Trophy winner, Jason White, Georgia's David Greene, West Virginia's Rasheed Marshall, Florida's Chris Leak, California's Aaron Rodgers, Clemson's Charlie Whitehurst, and Purdue's Kyle Orton that prompted those schools to receive pre-season rankings and be considered contenders for national honors. How their rivals developed quarterbacks and offenses amid solid Division 1-A balance became a big story of 2004.

Michigan (9-3) threw poised freshman signal-caller Chad Henne into Big Ten action with championship success, Ohio State (8-4) took awhile finding Troy Smith but ended well, Wisconsin (9-3) sophomore quarterback John Stocco developed quickly but his late-season injuries contributed to the Badgers' inability to complete an undefeated season, Florida State (9-3) was a non-champion in the ACC for only the second time in 13 years in the conference partly because coach Bobby Bowden couldn't successfully count on unpredictable senior Chris Rix or sophomore Wyatt Sexton, Utah (12-0) became "America's Team" by displaying a magnificent offense and an undefeated season primarily because of the play of Alex Smith. Georgia (10-2) couldn't beat Tennessee (10-3) and its freshman quarterbacking duo of Brent Schaefer and Erik Ainge for the SEC East title, but not because of Greene, who broke the quarterback career record for wins, held by Tennessee's Peyton Manning, with 42. Iowa (10-2) had little semblance of a running game because the Hawkeyes lost a raft of running backs to injury. Still, Iowa earned a piece of the Big Ten title because new quarterback Drew Tate performed so well. Stefan LeFors of explosive Louisville (11-1) finished his season with a Liberty Bowl win and closed with a 73.54 completion percentage and 181.7 rating, both a smidgen from new records. Underappreciated senior Bryan Randall had a great season breaking in a bevy of freshmen receivers and led Virginia Tech (10-3) to a surprising championship in the Hokies' first season in the ACC. But, no quarterback improved with such great results as previously-maligned senior Jason Campbell of Auburn (13-0), who sparked his team to the SEC championship and an unbeaten season.

On the other hand, no quarterback experienced a more painful and sudden reversal from success than Orton of the Boilermakers. Orton opened the season magnificently and took the inside track to the Heisman Trophy by leading Purdue (7-5) to a 5-0 start and a fifth place ranking in the AP Poll. Orton rallied Purdue to 17 unanswered points for a lead against then-undefeated Wisconsin on October 16. But in trying to run for a first down to kill the clock in the last three minutes, Orton was tackled and cartwheeled into a sudden fumble that was returned 40 yards by Badgers cornerback Scott Starks for a 21-17 reversal. A week later, improving Michigan, with freshmen quarterback Henne and tailback Mike Hart leading the offense, edged the Boilermakers 16-14 when the Wolverines' standout safety Ernest Shazor walloped Purdue receiver Dorien Bryant, after a 25-yard pass-and-run from Orton, to cause a late fumble to decide the outcome. When Orton soon suffered injuries, Purdue's potentially great year was shot dead.

Balance from top to bottom of football was evident early in the season as the Western Athletic Conference, Conference-USA, and Mountain West Conference drilled several highly-regarded teams from BCS conferences. Fresno State (9-3) beat Washington (1-10) in the season opener and trounced Kansas State (4-7) 45-21 at Manhattan on September 11. Southern Mississippi (7-5) beat Nebraska (5-6) at Lincoln, and Louisville beat Kentucky (2-9) and North Carolina (6-6) and gave Miami (9-3) a mighty scare. Boise State (11-1) beat everybody on its schedule including Oregon State (7-5), surprising Texas-El Paso (8-4), and Brigham Young (5-6). Even the little Maine Black Bears of Division 1-AA went to Starkville, Miss., to surprise Mississippi State (3-8) and deliver a stunning defeat upon the proud Southeastern Conference.

Another stupefying trend was the sudden inability of placekickers to make critical kicks, including some crushing misses of seemingly automatic extra points. It all started on the first Saturday night of September: Oregon State freshman booter Alexis Serna missed three extra points, including the potential game-tying point in overtime, to ruin a likely victory over defending co-champion Louisiana State (9-3). Serna rallied to a superb season, never missing another conversion and making all but one field goal try. At mid-season, Notre Dame (6-6) hoped to sneak into the Bowl Championship fold, but eliminated itself by losing to Boston College (9-3) by 24-23 on October

23, thanks in part to a missed conversion kick. Oregon (5-6) had California (10-2) on the ropes at 27-14, but lost by a point because a conversion kick bounced off the upright.

The California Golden Bears played one of the year's thrillers, nearly beating no. 1 USC in the L.A. Coliseum on October 9. Cal quarterback Rodgers found his targets a remarkable 23 straight times on the way to a 29-34, 267-yard show. The outcome came down to the Bears' last chance, a first-and-goal from the Trojans' nine yard-line in the game's last minute. But, Rodgers missed three passes, including a fourth down slant-in to a stumbling receiver.

The Southeastern Conference had big Saturday showdowns in early October as Georgia and Auburn establishing themselves with wins over Louisiana State and Tennessee respectively on October 2. But, Tennessee rebounded to tip Georgia, and LSU came from behind to defeat Florida (7-5) a week later. Gators coach Ron Zook was shown the door at season's end because proud Florida was stunned by Mississippi State. The victory made a winner out of Sylvester Croom, the first-ever African-American to serve as an SEC head coach.

"Mischief Night" on Halloween Eve brought three big upsets. Undefeated Miami took a haymaker from North Carolina (6-6), which had never beaten a Top-5 team, Maryland (5-7), playing poorly on offense, turned matters around to surprise no. 5 Florida State for its first win over the Seminoles, and Baylor (3-8), without a win in the Big 12 Conference in its last 11 outings, knocked Texas A&M (7-5) out of a tie for the Big 12 South lead.

The BCS faced its seemingly annual firestorm. Not that the controversy wasn't warranted; Southern California and Oklahoma, the nation's no. 1 and 2 teams all season, naturally were matched in the championship Orange Bowl. But, Auburn, champions of the traditionally-tough Southeastern Conference, also remained undefeated and could boast a 4-0 record against three teams with at least nine wins. The pre-season poll, based completely on reputation and past and recent performances, came under fire. Because the Tigers, disappointing in 2003, started the season as 17th in the AP Poll, there was no chance to break into the top-2 so long as pre-season favorites USC and Oklahoma kept winning.

Meanwhile, the so-called human polls—writers voting in the AP Poll and a board of coaches, who controversially continued not to reveal their weekly votes in the USA Today-ESPN Poll—had been given more power in the championship selection process because, ironically, the media had castigated the exaggerated influence of computer input in recent years. Also, newspaper writers were beginning to grumble about making the news—that is, helping to decide which schools were to play in big money bowl games—instead of reporting the news. Just as the bowl season began, the Associated Press, purveyors of the writers poll since 1936, wrote a pointed cease-and-desist letter to the BCS that included the accusation that the BCS' use of the poll had been "unlawful." In 2005, AP lawyers wrote, the wire service would continue taking weekly votes—including the controversial pre-season poll—as it well pleased to promote newspaper sales and to crown a national champion. But, the AP wanted no part of participation in the BCS after 2004.

For once, though, a sense of humor was voiced about the BCS. Auburn coach Tommy Tuberville said he would accept any no. 1 votes after the Tigers squeaked by in the Sugar Bowl, even a no. 1 selection from "Golf Digest." Brian Murphy, writing for espn.com, suggested the cure for some NFC teams making the NFL playoffs with mediocre records was the BCS:

"That's right. The BCS. The (9-7) Seahawks? They'd be stripped of all championship gear and shipped out to the GMAC Bowl in Mobile, Ala. The (8-8) Rams? Mike Martz would never get sympathy in the coaches' poll, and St. Louis surely would find itself ranked behind the likes of Carolina and New Orleans. Meanwhile, anybody up for a Patriots-Steelers (match-up of the best regular season teams in the) Orange Bowl?"

College football put on a whale of a New Year's Day show as Georgia nipped Wisconsin in the Outback Bowl, Iowa magically beat LSU on a last-play pass in the Capital One Bowl, and Michigan and Texas staged a heavyweight slugfest in the Rose Bowl won by Texas 38-37.

Where the BCS would go possibly without either poll, or for that matter a much-discussed possible national playoff, was under speculation at the time that USC beat Oklahoma by 55-19 in Miami to be crowned Orange Bowl and national champions.

Milestones

■ Computer input to BCS rankings was reduced so that media and coaches polls supplied two-thirds of team point totals. Schedule quality factor and team losses were eliminated from formula completely.

■ Big Ten voted to experiment (successfully) with video replay to assist on-field officials. Press box official was assigned to make all reviewable decisions.

■ Expanded Atlantic Coast Conference played with 11 members as it welcomed Miami (Florida) and Virginia Tech, while awaiting 2005 arrival of 12th member Boston College.

■ Syracuse University changed its nickname from Orangemen to Orange.

■ In late summer, NCAA permanently suspended Colorado wide receiver-punt returner Jeremy Bloom, who had accepted endorsement money in defiance of NCAA to support his training for Olympic skiing. Also dismissed was Southern California wide receiver Mike Williams, who had left school in spring when court action, brought by former Ohio State back Maurice Clarett, opened NFL draft to those with less than three years of college. When NFL eventually won its legal appeal, Williams went undrafted and reenrolled in USC summer school to regain eligibility to no avail.

■ At end of regular season, Associated Press pulled its writers poll as of 2005 from use by Bowl Championship Series for determining teams for bowl games.

■ Dying at age 80 was Elroy "Crazy Legs" Hirsch, halfback at both Wisconsin (1942) and Michigan (1943) during World War II's less structured times and Los Angeles Rams (1949-57) receiving star who made 1,495 yards and 17 touchdowns with 1951 NFL champions. Hirsch earned his nickname by running in unusual squat in which he seemed to flail his legs. Hirsch served Wisconsin as athletic director for many years. On April 22, U.S. Army Ranger Pat Tillman, former linebacker at Arizona State and safety for NFL Arizona Cardinals, tragically died at age 27, killed by friendly fire in Afghanistan. Micah Harris, 21, Duke linebacker died in auto accident while exiting Route I-85 on June 11. On July 31, Edward Bock, College Football Hall of Famer and perhaps greatest-ever Iowa State two-way guard, died at age 88. U.S. Marine Corps First Lt. Ron Winchester, Navy offensive tackle in 1999-2000, died on September 3 while on patrol in Iraqi war zone. Ralph Hawkins, 69, Maryland back in 1956-57 and NFL assistant coach, died on September 9. Penn State end Bob Mitinger, two-way standout on consecutive bowl teams in 1959-61, died at 64 on September 26. Al Onofrio, Missouri coach in 1971-77 (38-41), died at 83 on November 5. Tom Haller, former Illinois quarterback best known for 12-year career as baseball catcher primarily with San Francisco Giants, died at 67 of viral infection on November 26. Pair of former Washington State coaches, Al Kircher (1952-55) and Bert Clark (1964-67), died on November 1 and December 13 respectively. Star Tennessee (1980-83) defensive lineman and 1983 SEC Player-of-the-Year Reggie White, 43, who went on to NFL greatness (198 career sacks) primarily with Philadelphia Eagles and Green Bay Packers, died of massive heart attack on December 26. Kwane Doster, Vanderbilt's leading rusher in 2002, was killed by random gunfire at age 21 in his native Tampa on December 26. Ohio State 1961 All-America fullback and Maxwell Award winner, Bob Ferguson, 64, died on New Year's Eve.

■ Longest Winning Streaks Entering Season:

Miami (Ohio) 13	Boise State 11	Southern California 9

■ Coaching Changes:

	Incoming	Outgoing
Akron	J.D. Brookhart	Lee Owens
Army	Bobby Ross	John Mumford (interim)
Arizona	Mike Stoops	Mike Hankwitz (interim)
Central Florida	George O'Leary	Mike Kruczek
Central Michigan	Brian Kelly	Mike DeBord
Cincinnati	Mark Dantonio	Rick Minter
Eastern Michigan	Jeff Genyk	Jeff Woodruff
Idaho	Nick Holt	Tom Cable
Kent State	Doug Martin	Dean Pees
Mississippi State	Sylvester Croom	Jackie Sherrill
Nebraska	Bill Callahan	Frank Solich
Nevada	Chris Ault	Chris Tormey
Texas-El Paso	Mike Price	Gary Nord

Preseason *USA Today* Coaches

1	Southern California (44)	1500	14	Tennessee	598
2	Oklahoma (12)	1426	15	California	566
3	LSU (5)	1387	16	Clemson	503
4	Georgia	1328	17	Missouri	502
5	Miami (Fla.)	1246	18	Auburn	473
6	Florida State	1177	19	Virginia	453
7	Michigan	1128	20	Maryland	443
8	Texas	1087	21	Utah	438
9	Ohio State	1030	22	Wisconsin	248
10	Florida	691	23t	Minnesota	187
11	West Virginia	684	23t	Purdue	187
12	Iowa	642	25	Oregon	175
13	Kansas State	639			

August 28, 2004

Southern California 24 Virginia Tech 13 (Landover, Md.): In defense of its AP national title, no. 1 Southern California (1-0) had 2 big plays: LB Lofa Tatupu's over-shoulder INT and 32y RET that set up 2nd Q TD catch by TB Reggie "President" Bush and another made by officials. Latter decision came in 3rd Q and turned momentum away from psyched-up Hokies (0-1): frosh WR Josh Hyman (1/12y, TD) was called for O pass interference on questionable push-off inside USC 15YL that wrecked potential decisive 94y drive. Virginia Tech was trying to add to its 10-7 H lead that had come on Hyman's 12y catch and wiggle into EZ. His PEN, followed by Tech punt, set Trojans on winning trail: Bush lined up at WR and roared by Hokies CB Jimmy Williams to haul in 53y TD pass from QB Matt Leinart (19-29/272y, 3 TDs), who trumped poor 1st H with sharp accuracy in 2nd H. Zipping from backfield to make mockery of LB-coverage in 4th Q, Bush took pass 29y to TD for insurmountable 21-13 edge with 5:35 left.

USA Today Coaches August 29

1	Southern California (43)	1495	14	California	622
2	Oklahoma (12)	1434	15	Tennessee	606
3	LSU (6)	1396	16	Clemson	555
4	Georgia	1341	17	Missouri	513
5	Miami (Fla.)	1248	18	Auburn	458
6	Florida State	1182	19	Utah	442
7	Michigan	1134	20	Virginia	435
8	Texas	1079	21	Maryland	418
9	Ohio State	1000	22	Wisconsin	258
10	Florida	747	23	Minnesota	191
11	West Virginia	719	24	Oregon	165
12	Kansas State	700	25	Purdue	161
13	Iowa	685			

September 4, 2004

(Th) UTAH 41 Texas A&M 21: Well-regarded Utes let ace QB Alex Smith (21-29/359y, 3 TDs, and 13/76y, 2 TDs rushing) do their talking as no. 20 Utah (1-0) exploded with 582y O. Meanwhile, Texas A&M (0-1), hoping for rebound in coach Dennis Franchione's 2nd season, were frequently helpless on D. Utah avenged its only non-conf loss of 2003 by jumping to 28-7 H on Smith's TD passes of 78 and 9y to WR Steve Savoy and 38y to WR John Madsen. Aggies' only 1st H respite came when harried QB Reggie McNeal (14-35/210y) found seam and scrambled 59y for TD with 3:02 left before H. Smith scored only TD of 3rd Q on 37y run to reestablish Utes' rout.

(Th) TEXAS CHRISTIAN 48 Northwestern 45 (OT): Wildcats (0-1) gained 637y and thrice rallied from 14-pt deficits to tie clash of purple teams in last 13 secs of regulation at Fort Worth: Northwestern QB Brett Basanez (39-62/513y, 4 TDs, INT) flipped his last scoring pass to WR Shaun Herbert from 8YL. Basanez, who set school single-game pass y record, completed 5 throws in row on tying march, including 4th down conversion of 20y to WR Ashton Aikens. Texas Christian (1-0) QB Tye Gunn (20-38/368y, 4 TDs, INT) also had career high in pass y. Now, if only each team's K could kick: NW K Brett Huffman missed 5-6 FG tries including both in OT, and TCU K Peter LoCoco overcame his low 25y 3-pt try that was blocked in 1st OT by making winning 47y FG. LB Andrew Ward participated in 12 tackles out of Horned Frogs' 4-2-5 D set.

(Fri) Washington State 21 NEW MEXICO 17: Favored Washington State (1-0) faced uphill battle, trailing 17-7 as of early in 4th Q. But, Cougars came up with 2 INTs and blocked punt in 4th Q to allow QB Josh Swogger (24-38/240y, 2 INTs) to throw his 2nd and 3rd TD passes: 13y to WR Trandon Harvey (6/46y) and 4y to TE Troy Bienemann in back of EZ for game-winner with 7:10 to play. Wazzu special teamer Omowale Dada blocked punt that was returned to 4YL to set up Bienemann's TD. Lobos (1-0) got 167y rushing from RB DonTrell Moore, including 61y TD burst for 14-7 lead midway through 3rd Q. New Mexico WR Hank Baskett (9/165y) made catches of 54y and 45y to set up FB Adrian Byrd's 3rd Q TD run and K Wes Zunker's 21y FG in 4th Q.

RUTGERS 19 Michigan State 14: Rutgers (1-0) FB Brian Leonard ran 57y on 1st snap of game, but Knights got iffy kicking after every 1st H possession went into Michigan State (0-1) territory. Frosh K Jeremy "Judge" Ito missed short and long FG tries, had another blocked, but made trio of short 3-ptrs for 9-7 lead by early 3rd Q. Spartans had scored on WR Matt Trannon's 9y reception from QB Damon Dowdell (22-39/270y, 2 TDs, INT). DE Ryan Neill, son of former Pitt star Bill Neill, made screen pass INT on Rutgers blitz and ran 31y for 16-7 lead. Ito added 4th FG late in 3rd Q. Early in 4th Q, Spartans TE Eric Knott snuck into flat for long run of 54y pass.

MISSISSIPPI STATE 28 Tulane 7: Former Alabama A-A Sylvester Croom, 1st African-American head coach in Deep South's SEC, won opening outing for Mississippi State (1-0). Bulldogs yelped and whooped around Croom, their helmets held high, as clock ticked down. Mississippi State RB Jerious Norwood rushed 20/112y, scored 9y TD for 7-0 lead early in 3rd Q, and dashed 43y to set up sub RB Fred Reid's 5y TD run to extend Bulldogs' lead to 21-7. Tulane (0-1) had trimmed deficit to 14-7 early in 4th Q when QB Lester Ricard (16-31/135y, TD, 2 INTs) found WR Chris Bush for 59y TD.

LOUISIANA STATE 22 Oregon State 21 (OT): Defending co-national titleist LSU (1-0) was shocked to gain only 93y in 1st H and trail 9-0 well into 3rd Q. Sub QB JaMarcus Russell (9-26/145y, TD), who started 2nd H, found WR Skyler Green over middle for 16y TD pass late in 3rd Q, but Oregon State (0-1) came right back with 65y drive to TD pass by QB Derek Anderson (26-47/231y, 3 TDs, INT) to frosh WR Anthony Wheat-Brown. When Wheat-Brown ran to sideline with ball, Beavers were levied 5y PEN which contributed to 2nd missed x-pt by frosh K Alexis Serna (40y FG). Still, Oregon State seemed to have verdict in hand at 15-7 when P Sam Paulescu nailed 54y punt to Tigers 36YL with 1:38 left in game. But, LSU WR Dwayne Bowe incredibly slipped behind exhausted Beavers secondary for 26 and 38y catches, latter for TD with 1:05 left. Russell scrambled and dived for tying 2-pt run. Tigers scored in 1st OT for 22-15 lead, but Anderson steadfastly pitched 19y TD over middle to TE Joe Newton on 4th down. Stunningly, K Serna missed his 3rd conv kick, this wide right by large margin.

MICHIGAN 43 Miami (Ohio) 10: Miami (1-1) was effective in 1st H, but TOs (7 by game's end) killed RedHawks as Wolverines (1-0) jumped to easy lead as frosh QB Chad Henne (14-24/142y, 2 TDs, INT) was surprise starter. Michigan TB David Underwood scored twice. Trailing 24-0, Miami finally touched scoreboard late in 3rd Q on FG by K Jared Parseghian, great-nephew of former Miami and Notre Dame coach Ara Parseghian. Quickly, RedHawks tallied for TD by RB Steve Smith after WR Ryne Robinson's 70y punt RET, and soon made big crowd squirm after Robinson's 46y punt RET as they threatened to move within 7 pts in 4th Q. But, Michigan S Ernest Shazor stepped in front of receiver, RB Luke Clemens, near right sideline and raced 89y to score for 30-10 edge. Wolverines added 2 more TDs in less than 3 mins, including brilliant catch, tipped to himself, by WR Braylon Edwards (6/91y, 2 TDs).

COLORADO 27 Colorado State 24: Wild conclusion at Colorado (1-0) GL underscored variety of decisions that went wrong for Rams (0-1). Colorado State reached 1YL with 30 secs left and no timeouts in its holster. After 1st down spike to stop clock, TB Marcus Houston (20/44y, TD) was stuffed for no gain, and instead of trying tying FG, Rams coach Sonny Lubick wanted another spike to set up 4th down try for win. Instead, backup TB Tristian Walker went wide left and was spilled by DB J.J. Billingsley and LB Lorenzo Sims as clock ran out. "It was a terrible way to lose a game," said QB Justin Holland (29-41/403y, 2 TDs, INT). Earlier, Buffaloes dominated for 17-0 lead as QB Joel Platt threw 13-25/117y, INT, and oft-injured TB Bobby Purify rushed 26/189y, TD. State rallied with 80y drive in last min of 1st H as Holland flipped 1y TD pass, and tied it early in 4th Q after Houston's short TD run and K Jeff Babcock's 26y FG. Buffs countered for 27-17 edge with K Mason Crosby's 55y 3-ptr and LB Brian Iwuh's nearly-immediate 37y INT TD RET.

(Sun) PURDUE 51 Syracuse 0: Workmanlike Purdue (1-0) carved 14-0 lead with early 75y TD bomb by QB Kyle Orton (16-30/278y, 4TDs). Boilermakers WR Taylor Stubblefield (5/111y, 2 TDs) made leaping, juggling catch in EZ for 20-0 edge in 2nd Q. Syracuse (0-1), led by smooth TB Walter Reyes (12/31y), used strong run game (10 runs in 12 plays) to 7YL, but holder Jared Jones threw INT after bad snap on FG try before H. Purdue killed 6:29 to start 2nd H, and on next snap after Orange punt, its O adjusted to blitz, and Stubblefield took slant-in pass 67y to TD. RB Brandon Jones made over-shoulder catch in traffic at pylon for TD and 34-0 Boilermakers lead in 3rd Q. When Reyes fumbled ensuing KO, K Ben Jones extended lead to 37-0 with FG.

USA Today Coaches September 7

1	Southern California (47)	1502	14	Kansas State	664
2	Oklahoma (10)	1452	15	Tennessee	623
3	Georgia (3)	1355	16	Utah	514
4	LSU (1)	1271	17	Missouri	503
5	Miami (Fla.)	1269	18	Clemson	501
6	Florida State	1206	19	Auburn	465
7	Michigan	1150	20	Virginia	417
8	Texas	1107	21	Maryland	302
9	Ohio State	1034	22	Wisconsin	297
10	West Virginia	767	23	Purdue	270
11	Florida	745	24	Minnesota	256
12	Iowa	698	25	Oregon	124
13	California	691			

September 11, 2004

(Fri) MIAMI 16 Florida State 10 (OT): Postponed 5 days by Hurricane Frances that wrecked havoc on most of Florida peninsula, rugged D match-up was rearranged to stay on ABC's primetime TV. Florida State (0-1), which gained only 165y total O, owned 10-0 lead for 3 Qs because of 2 TOs, including 61y FUM TD RET by CB Antonio Cromartie (INT) in 2nd Q. Miami (1-0) staved off defeat when it blocked Seminoles K Xavier Beitia's 34y FG try with 3:58 left that would have provided 13-3 lead. Instead, Hurricanes completed 10-pt 4th Q rally with 30y TD pass from QB Brock Berlin (20-36/255y, TD, 2 INTs) that sent it to OT. QB Chris Rix (12-28/108y, 2 INTs) lost Shotgun snap in OT that was recovered by Miami DE Thomas Carroll. RB Frank Gore (18/89y, TD) wriggled through line on Miami's 2nd OT play for 18y TD. Oft-criticized Rix became 1st college QB ever to lose 5 games in career to single foe.

BOSTON COLLEGE 21 Penn State 7: Eagles sr QB Paul Peterson (23-31/199y, 3 TDs) showed creativity in tight spots to surprise Penn State (1-1). Boston College (2-0), beneficiary of 2 PENs on game's opening drive, scored when hemmed-in Peterson lobbed 6y TD pass to TE David Kashetta. Trailing 14-0 at H thanks to crippling TOs, Nittany Lions fashioned 61y march from 2nd H KO to sr WR Ryan Scott's 1st-ever TD catch near edge of EZ. Peterson had clever, swift answer: 74y trip to his 2y TD pass. TB Andre Callender came off BC bench to rush for 27/114y. Penn State DB Andrew Guman made 14 tackles, LB Paul Posluszny 12.

Georgia Tech 28 CLEMSON 24: Wild finish, which saw 5 TDs tallied in last 8:19, turned out magically for underdog Georgia Tech (2-0). Yellow Jackets frosh WR Calvin Johnson (8/127y, 3 TDs) soared up over Tigers (1-1) DB Justin Miller to net QB Reggie Ball's 11y TD pass at edge of EZ with 11 secs left. Ball (20-36/251y, 4 TDs, INT) and Johnson had collaborated on 8y TD throw to pull within 24-21 with 1:50 remaining, but Georgia Tech couldn't come close to on-side KO REC. When Clemson QB Charlie Whitehurst (20-43/75y, TD, 2 INTs) gained 9y on 1st down all seemed lost for Jackets. But, Tech D jammed Tigers' next 2 runs up middle and forced punt. C Geoff Rigsby dribbled snap back that eluded P Cole Chasen, and Jackets swarmed over REC at 11YL. Clemson had appeared to have locked it up on 4th Q TD runs by sub TBs Reggie Merriweather and Kyle Browning of 62y and 54y respectively.

Georgia 20 SOUTH CAROLINA 16: Valiant Gamecocks (1-1) had it going their way early at home. South Carolina limited slow-starting Georgia (2-0) to 28y in 1st Q. Bruised Bulldogs frosh TB Danny Ware (8/41y) was knocked out but not before he was snowed under for safety midway through 1st Q. Carolina took advantage of missed FG try, and Gamecocks WR Troy Williamson spun away from 2 tacklers for 65y TD pass-run from QB Dondrial Pinkins (13-21/200y, TD, INT). Frosh DB Ko Simpson made it 16-0 for Gamecocks with 57y INT TD RET early in 2nd Q. Little TB Tyson Browning gave Georgia spark, and his 12y TD catch from QB David Greene, who threw for 19-38/213y, 2 TDs, INT, brought Bulldogs to within 16-13 after 73y march in 3rd Q. Georgia took lead for good on Greene's 2nd TD pass: 22y to WR Reggie Brown in 4th Q. Bulldogs advanced their road record under coach Mark Richt to 13-1.

NOTRE DAME 28 Michigan 20: Notre Dame's 1st play was wide pass by QB Brady Quinn picked off by Wolverines (1-1) CB Markus Curry, leading to 1st of K Garrett Rivas' 4 FGs. Sparked by frosh TB Darius Walker (31/115y, 2 TDs), Fighting Irish (1-1) got into Michigan end, but Wolverines halted TB Ryan Grant on 4th down at 1YL, and, just before H, QB Chad Henne hit 4 passes to provide another FG. Quinn got ND back in game at 9-7 with 46y TD bomb to WR Matt Shelton early in 3rd Q, but Rivas made career-long 47y FG late in 3rd Q. Walker skirted RE for 6y TD run behind block of TE Anthony Fasano for 14-12 lead for Irish early in 4th Q. Notre Dame blocked punt on next series, and Walker skirted LE for TD and 21-12 edge. Irish iced it on Quinn's 8y misdirection pass to FB Rashon Powers-Neal. WR Steve Breaston gave Michigan hope with TD and 2-pt catches, but Wolverines couldn't recover onside-KO.

OHIO STATE 24 Marshall 21: Buckeyes (2-0) WR Antonio Bryant had dazzling game with 10/208y and TD catches of 80y on opening snap and 47y, but green QB Justin Zwick (18-30/318y, 3 TDs) threw pair of costly INTs to Thundering Herd (1-1) S Chris Royal. Marshall rallied from 7-0, 14-7, and 21-14 deficits, and perhaps most notable was its 80y march to RB Earl Charles' 2y run that answered early 7-0 score. Herd DL Jonathan Goddard tallied important 2nd Q TD when he went 27y with unmolested FUM RET. QB Stan Hill displayed accurate throwing for Herd with 22-34/140y, and 23y TD pass to WR Brad Bates that knotted it in middle of 4th Q. Tied 21-21, Marshall K-P Ian O'Connor missed 35y FG with 3:17 to play and, in last 30 secs, hooked punt for only 26y. Brilliant Ohio State K Mike Nugent hit 55y FG at 0:00 to win it after Zwick wisely spiked ball and took 5y PEN even though his O-line wasn't set.

Arizona State 30 NORTHWESTERN 21: Arizona State (2-0), trying for rebound season, experienced some trying moments against Wildcats (0-2), but rode QB Andrew Walter's 3 TD passes to road win. Walter (19-36/292y, 3 TDs) started slowly; he hit 2-11, but Sun Devils led 3-0 at end of 1st Q on K Jesse Ainsworth's 20y FG. Northwestern rebounded, featuring RB Noah Herron (17/105y) on 80y TD trip ended with Herron's 22 and 9y runs. Devils took lead for good in 2nd Q as WR Derek Hagan (8/154y) got loose for TD catches of 47y and 41y. NW got back into it, trailing 24-21, when nation's leading passer, QB Brett Basanez (21-38/228y) scrambled 13y for TD late in 3rd Q. Down 27-21, Wildcats mounted effective 4th Q drive, but huge hit by S Riccardo Stewart jarred ball loose from NW RB Terrell Jordan. ASU knocked 6:23 off clock in marching 81y to Ainsworth's clinching 3rd FG.

Fresno State 45 KANSAS STATE 21: For years, Wildcats (1-1) had been criticized for cupcake non-conf slate of games, only to have trouble attracting tougher foes. Always courageous, hard-hitting Fresno State (2-0) had gained notoriety in 2001, knocking off BCS conf teams, and did it again in visit to "Little Apple" Manhattan. Kansas State struck 1st on DB Brett Jones' 1st of 2 INTs, that was returned 42y for TD, and hung close, down 17-14, when sub QB Dylan Meier (4-10/91y, TD, INT) launched 47y TD to WR Davin Dennis. But, Fresno QB Paul Pinegar (17-30/244y, 2 TDs, 3 INTs) soon threw and ran for TDs less than 4 mins apart for 31-14 H edge. Bulldogs RB Matt Rivera caught his 2nd scoring pass in 3rd Q, and rout was on. Fresno's eager defenders flooded gridiron to hold Cats to 180y O, make 2 sacks, author 7 plays that lost y, and keep home team out of red zone all but twice all day.

Southern Mississippi 21 NEBRASKA 17: QB Joe Dailey (22-42/202y, 2 TDs, 3 INTs), recruited to Nebraska (1-1) as option signal-caller, nearly made up for his 4 TOs with pair of late threats, but they fizzled. Dailey's pair of INTs in 1st Q led to 2 Southern Mississippi (1-0) FGs by K Darren McCaleb. Trailing 9-3 at H, Cornhuskers cashed their 1st opportunity of 3rd Q, going 73y, primarily on TB Cory Ross' 52y dash up middle, to Dailey's TD pass to WR Grant Mulkey. Dailey upped advantage to 17-9 with 13y TD toss to out-breaking TE Matt Herian (8/71y). Southern's big play came at end of 3rd Q: LB Naton Stewart picked off pass at scrimmage line and motored 49y for TD that moved Eagles within 17-15. Southern Miss QB Dustin Almond (12-28/142y, TD, INT) launched 46y TD bomb to WR Marvin Young on last snap of 3rd Q. Dailey lost FUM at Eagles 12YL and was forced OB on failed 4th down scramble at USM 7YL near game's end. Star LB Michael Boley participated in 19 stops for Eagles.

USA Today Coaches September 12

1	Southern California (47)	1505	14	Utah	651
2	Oklahoma (11)	1453	15	Auburn	643
3	Georgia (2)	1371	16	Virginia	634
4	LSU (1)	1315	17	Michigan	574
5	Miami (Fla.)	1312	18	Purdue	525
6	Texas	1209	19	Maryland	437
7	Ohio State	1058	20	Fresno State	408
8	West Virginia	975	21	Wisconsin	372
9	Florida	887	22	Minnesota	298
10	California	852	23	Boise State	272
11	Florida State	802	24	Louisville	128
12	Iowa	782	25	Clemson	111
13	Tennessee	717			

September 18, 2004

Nebraska 24 PITTSBURGH 17: Coming in, new Nebraska (2-1) coach Bill Callahan's new O was giving him indigestion as QB Joe Dailey had 7 INTs in 72 pass tries so far in 2004. But, it was Pitt's inexperienced O that handed out TOs: Cornhuskers led 10-0 after INTs by CB Fabian Washington and DE Wali Muhammad. Panthers (2-1) RB Marcus Furman returned KO 96y for TD, but Pitt bobbled away punt inside 10YL, and it led to slant-in TD pass to WR Ross Pinkington from Dailey (11-22/142y, TD, INT), who added 17y TD dash off fake and bootleg on 3rd-and-inches. Pitt owned field position in 2nd H, but couldn't score until WR Greg Lee's 34y catch from QB Tyler Palko (22-45/228y, TD, 3 INTs) with 4:45 left. Huskers had to sweat out late threat to their 14YL after Palko's completions of 21, 17, and 31y.

WEST VIRGINIA 19 Maryland 13 (OT): Mountaineers (3-0) looked for revenge against recent nemesis Maryland (2-1), which enjoyed 155- to 51-pt differential in 4 recent wins. West Virginia CB Adam "Pac-Man" Jones (2 INTs) made INT after opening game with 54y KO RET to set up TD run by TB Kay-Jay Harris (32/142y). WVU had many opportunities to put it away in 1st H thanks to Terps' 5 TOs, but Maryland survived WR Chris Henry's EZ INT and K Brad Cooper's missed FG in last 40 secs of 1st H it trailed 7-3. Cooper atoned with 45y FG, but 22y punt by West Virginia set up Terps

WR Derrick Fenner for 27y leaping TD catch that tie it at 10-10. Maryland went to its run game in 4th Q to take its 1st lead at 13-10 on K Nick Novak's 46y FG with 9:23 left. Cooper tied it with 13-13 with 37y FG, but had 39y FG blocked by DT Conrad Bolston with 5 secs to go. Novak made FG in OT, but WVU's Henry caught TD pass.

Ohio State 22 NORTH CAROLINA STATE 14: Magnificent K Mike Nugent blasted through school record-tying 5 FGs (Bob Atha in 1981) to keep Ohio State (3-0) just ahead of fast-closing NC State (1-1). Nugent hit 50 and 30y FGs in 1st H to augment short TD run by TB Lydell Ross (25/51y) that followed DB Donte Whitner's INT. Whitner's pick-off of inexperienced Wolfpack QB Jay Davis (12-24/99y, TD, 3 INTs) and 24y RET to 3YL spoiled last min of 2nd Q when Wolfpack appeared content to kill clock. Chuck Amato, coach of NC State, suggested Ohio D earned it: "They had a great defense; our quarterback was scratching his helmet." TOs continued to plague North Carolina State in 2nd H as TB T.A. McLendon (15/94y, TD), returned from injury list, dropped pitchout to position Nugent for his 3rd FG and 16-0 edge early in 3rd Q. Bucks LB A.J. Hawk (9 tackles) made INT to help Nugent extend lead to 19-7 early in 4th Q before Davis threw 26y TD pass with 1:28 on clock.

TENNESSEE 30 Florida 28: Volunteers (2-0) K James Wilhoit redeemed himself by blasting 50y FG with 6 secs to play after having blown game-tying x-pt less than 4 mins earlier. Unflappable Gators (1-1) QB Chris Leak (22-31/286y, INT) whipped 3 TD passes, last of which went for 81y to WR Chad Jackson and came midway in 4th Q to provide 28-21 lead. Frosh Tennessee QB Erik Ainge (16-24/192y, 3 TDs, INT), who as usual shared duties with fellow newcomer Brent Schaeffer (3-4/40y), led 80y drive to his 13y TD pass with 3:25 to play, but conv kick was missed to leave score at 28-27 for Florida. Gators were trying kill clock when WR Dallas Baker was goaded into retaliatory helmet slap and personal foul PEN, and it forced Florida to punt in last min. Ainge hit throws of 21 and 7y to WR Chris Hannon to set stage for Wilhoit's heroics.

AUBURN 10 Louisiana State 9: Auburn (3-0) coach Tommy Tuberville enjoyed his 50th birthday, but victory gift over defending national titleist LSU (2-1) from his Tigers was most nerve-wracking. LSU had led all game after QB Marcus Randall (4-9/45y, TD) got all his y on 80y opening drive and threw 9y TD pass to WR Dwayne Bowe before record crown at Auburn. But, margin stayed 6-0 because Bengals K Ryan Gaudet missed vital x-pt. Teams traded 1st H FGs, so LSU held 9-3 lead when Auburn launched late threat. Auburn QB Jason Campbell (16-27/170y, TD) beat 4th-and-12 blitz by rolling outside and zipping sidearm pass to sustain 59y march. WR Courtney Taylor hauled in 16y TD pass toss to tie it 9-9 with 1:14 to play. Bad snap ruined x-pt kick, but LSU DB Ronnie Prude was called for foul when he landed on Auburn lineman at end of his leap for kick-block try. Officials invoked new PEN that prevented defenders from taking 2 steps or more on attempts to block kicks and making contact with opponent. Auburn K John Vaughn nailed his 2nd try at winning pt.

Notre Dame 31 MICHIGAN STATE 24: Former Golden Gloves boxer, Notre Dame (2-1) S Tom Zbikowski, made 2 big plays in 1st Q: 1 from center of ring, when he returned INT 13y to set up 7-7 tie earned on sneak by QB Brady Quinn (11-24/215y, TD, INT), and another through in-fighting, when he went to the abdomen of Michigan State (1-2) TB Jason Teague to yank away FUM, which he returned 75y for unmolested TD. That gave Irish lead at 14-7, which they would not lose. Spartans had jumped on board 1st as special teamer Marshall Campbell blocked punt that WR Jerramy Scott recovered in EZ. Michigan State RB DeAndra Cobb (5/189y KO RETs) halved deficit to 28-14 with 89y KO TD RET in 3rd Q, and although Spartans scored 10 pts in 4th Q, Notre Dame salted it away with 10:36 of possession time in 4th Q.

OKLAHOMA 31 Oregon 7: Sensational Sooners (3-0) frosh RB Adrian Peterson (24/183y, 2 TDs) stepped in when RB Kejuan Jones was banged up and toted for his 3rd straight 100y rushing game. Peterson's 40y dash off LT down left sideline late in 3rd Q and 18y bouncing and spinning trip in 4th Q extended Oklahoma's 17-7 lead beyond flight of Ducks (0-2). Oregon had closed gap in 3rd Q when QB Kellen Clemens (24-35/179y, TD) lofted pass for 30y over-shoulder TD catch by FB Dante Rosario. Oregon K Jared Siegel hit kick to tie school scoring mark with 272 pts. OU WR Mark Clayton caught 6/91y from QB Jason White (17-23/213y, TD) to become all-time leading Sooners receiver with 173 receptions.

TEXAS A&M 27 Clemson 6: QB Reggie McNeal (14-26/178y) rushed 17/129y and totaled 307y O, and TB Courtney Lewis ran 28/165y of 324y gained rushing by Texas A&M (2-1). Lewis scored on 1y and 29y runs within 5-min duration of 2nd Q as Aggies jumped to 14-0 lead. Disappointing Clemson (1-2) scored late in 2nd Q on 15y TD pass to TE Ben Hall from QB Charlie Whitehurst (20-36/192y, TD, 3 INTs), but K Stephen Furr missed x-pt. Whitehurst was pressured all game by Aggies suddenly-aggressive D and thrown for losses 5 times. A&M went 99y on 9 plays on its 1st chance of 3rd Q to extend lead to 24-6: WR Jason Carter dashed over from 3YL on his only carry.

Ucla 37 WASHINGTON 31: Little Bruins (2-1) TB Maurice Drew became 75th ground-gainer to top 300y when he raced for 5 TDs enroute to all-time UCLA mark of 322y. Wild 1st Q saw Washington (0-2) cop 24-20 lead as QB Casey Paus (13-28/200y, 2 TDs) tossed scoring passes to WRs Anthony Russo and Charles Frederick (4/100y, TD). Drew countered with brilliant TD bursts of 47, 62, and 58y. UCLA led for good at 34-24 when Drew tallied from 15YL and 37YL to complete 65y and 80y drives in middle Qs. It came down to game's last play when Frederick caught 26y pass from Paus, spun away at Bruins 5YL, but was dropped at 1YL by UCLA CB Matthew Clark.

ARIZONA STATE 44 Iowa 7: Both teams sought to prove themselves before turning to conf title runs, but this win margin was surprising. Sharp Arizona State (3-0) QB Andrew Walter threw 31-43/428y, 5 TDs, INT, and broke Jake Plummer's team mark with his 66th career TD throw. Although opening KO was delayed 45 mins by lightning, Sun Devils were electrifying in scoring on 5 of its 6 possessions in 1st H for 27-0 edge. Walter tossed 3 TDs in 1st H, including 7y score to his "famous golfer" Walter-to-Hagan battery-mate, WR Derek Hagan (8/112y, 2 TDs). Stupefied Iowa (2-1) had single moment in 1st H: DB Antwan Allen made INT, but Devils LB Jamar Williams turned right

back with INT of Hawkeyes QB Drew Tate (8-19/44y, INT) and hustled it back to Iowa 13YL to set up 24-0 lead on Walter's 6y TD arrow to frosh TE Zach Miller (10/85y, 2 TDs). Hawks would have been blanked for 1st time since 2000 had DB Walter Bellous not made 83y punt TD RET with 18 secs to play.

Wisconsin 9 ARIZONA 7: Unusual desert drizzle turned into lightning-laced downpour and delayed 2nd Q for 88 mins. Wildcats (1-2), seeking improvement under new coach Mike Stoops, struck after delay when QB Kris Havener (9-15/103y, TD) pitched 44y TD strike to WR Mike Jefferson late in 2nd Q. Interestingly, 2nd H KO followed quickly thereafter as both coaches agreed to skip H intermission after long weather delay. Wisconsin (3-0) launched 56y drive that carried into 4th Q. It was capped by 7y TD run by TB Stanley Booker (30/135y), who substituted for injured ace, TB Anthony Davis. K Mike Allen missed x-pt, but after 72y drive, he booted 23y game-winning FG for Wisconsin with 3:47 to play.

September 25, 2004

(Fri) BOISE STATE 28 Brigham Young 27: Extending nation's longest win streak to 15, Broncos (4-0) jumped to 16-0 bulge in 1st Q as QB Jared "Z" Zabransky (20-28/302y, INT) threw 1st of his 2 TD passes. Back stormed BYU (1-3) with last 13 pts of 1st H as K Matt Payne booted 32 and 42y FGs. Boise made it 22-13 as K Tyler Jones made pair of FGs, including 47y screamer. Cougars rallied: QB John Beck (20-35/390y, 2 TDs) launched 79y TD missile to WR Todd Watkins (9/211y, TD), and, with 34 secs left in 3rd Q, hit another of 57y to WR Austin Collie (5/94y) for 27-22 lead. Boise went 57y in 3 plays to 44y scoring catch by WR T.J. Acree (7/133y, 2 TDs). Trailing 28-27, BYU was aided by late, disputed interference call, but Payne, who had been perfect on FGs all month, sailed 38y try wide with 19 secs left. Broncos coach Don Hawkins admitted his good fortune: "You give him (Payne) 100 of those kicks, and he makes 99 of them."

North Carolina State 17 VIRGINIA TECH 16: K Brandon Pace had made 32 and 37y FGs in 4th Q to pull Hokies (2-2) within 17-16, but missed 43y try as time expired. Virginia Tech's kicking game cost it victory: Pace missed 3-ptr from 33y in 1st Q, and P Vinnie Burns bobbled snap at Hokies 5YL for NC State (2-1) in 3rd Q. Wolfpack sub QB Marcus Stone rammed over to break 10-10 deadlock 3 plays later. NC State TB T.A. McLendon (24/93y, TD) had 6y TD run late in 2nd Q to tie it 10-10. Wolfpack D snarled at Tech QB Bryan Randall (11-25/156y, TD), sacking him 10 times.

WAKE FOREST 17 Boston College 14: For 2nd straight year, Wake Forest (3-1) surprised Eagles (3-1) with late lightning. This time, Deacons QB Cory Randolph (11-19/141y, TD) threw to WR Willie Idlette, who plucked pass from BC DB Ryan Glasper's diving INT attempt and raced 40y down left sideline for winning TD with 1:09 to play. Boston College QB Paul Peterson passed 21-38/for career-best 269y, and 2 TD, and led Eagles to 451y to 369y advantage in total O. But, frosh K Ryan Ohlinger missed 3 FG tries. Wake had scored on 53y trick pass on last play of 1st Q on way to 10-0 lead: WR Nate Morton tossed pass to WR Chris Davis (7/112y, TD). RB Chris Barclay (24/57y) made critical 2y gain on 4th-and-1 to keep alive late winning drive.

ARKANSAS 27 Alabama 10: Arkansas (3-1) blanked Alabama (3-1) in 2nd H and counted on QB Matt Jones (7-12/122y, TD, INT) for his usual big plays. Jones scrambled around RE for early TD to become Razorbacks all-time TD creator, but Hogs had to wait until their last drive of 1st H to go 84y to take 14-10 lead. Crimson Tide rushed for 176y in 1st H, but could get no closer than Hogs 39YL in last 30 mins. With less than 8 mins to play, Arkansas was clinging to 4-pt edge when Jones made 3rd down sortie to his right and blazed 50y to set up frosh RB Peyton Hillis' critical 7y TD spin up middle for 20-10 lead. TB Ray Hudson (20/170y, TD) led Crimson Tide by making 63y TD sprint for 7-3 lead in 2nd Q.

MICHIGAN 30 Iowa 17: Hawkeyes (2-2) had never won 3 straight from Wolverines (3-1), and TOs helped kill their 2-year reign over Michigan. After Iowa opened with WR Ed Hinkel's brilliant diving 1-handed TD catch, it started handing ball over to Michigan, nation's leader in gaining TOs. In all, Iowa suffered 3 FUMs and 2 INTs, and TOs resulted in 27 pts. Wolverines star WR Braylon Edwards (6/150y, TD) raced to 58y TD right after Hinkel's 2nd Q FUM, and Michigan quickly upped its margin to 16-7 after INT allowed Edwards' 39y reception and QB Chad Henne's TD sneak. Hawks were still in game at 16-10 when bungled handoff by QB Drew Tate (24-32/270y, 2 TDs, 2 INTs) gave Michigan another short field for emerging TB Michael Hart's 7y TD burst. Wolverines' magnificent D threw Iowa's injured running brigade for −15y net.

TEXAS TECH 31 Kansas 30: Jayhawks (2-2) ran wild in 1st H, building 30-5 edge late in 2nd Q: QB Adam Barmann (22-46/224y, 3 INTs) connected on 2 TD passes, and CB-turned-WR Charles Gordon threw and caught TDs. But, Texas Tech (3-1) QB Sonny Cumbie (28-52/356y, 2 TDs, 4 INTs) completed 6, 42, and 32y within 33 secs to spark Red Raiders just before H. In 2nd H, Texas Tech tallied 26 unanswered pts with FB Taurean Henderson (17/169y, 2 TDs) leading way. Henderson raced 70y for winning TD, his 2nd score, with 2:37 left, and CB Jabari Smith sealed it with INT.

SOUTHERN METHODIST 36 San Jose State 13: SMU's woe begotten program earned its 1st win since 2 victories closed 2002 season at 3-9. QB Tony Eckert (8-15/91y, TD), JC transfer, started for injured QB Chris Phillips and guided Mustangs (1-3) to TDs on opening pair of possessions, including his 5y TD flip to WR Chris Foster (5/76y, 2 TDs). QB Jerad Romo split time with Eckert and caught 14y TD pass from WR Matt Rushbrook and threw 34y TD pass to Foster. Other than K Jeff Carr's pair of 2nd Q FGs, San Jose (1-2) counted strictly on QB Dale Rogers (13-24/102y, TD), who threw 15y TD pass in last 3 mins and also was his Spartans' top rusher with 14/87y.

Southern California 31 STANFORD 28: USC (4-0) extended 13-game streak, but not without nervous moments. Stanford (2-1) hung within 10-7 on short TD pass late in 1st Q by QB Trent Edwards (23-35/183y, 2 TDs, INT). Cardinal exploded with 3 TDs in 2nd Q to take 28-17 H lead on strength of 291y O. Stanford gained style points as well: holder Kyle Matter ran untouched to 11y TD on fake FG, and RB J.R. Lemon (10/96y, TD) burst for 82y TD when content to run out 1st H clock. Trojans QB Matt Leinart (24-30/308y, TD) passed and ran for TDs, including his 1y TD run that pulled USC within 28-24 late in 3rd Q after 51y gain on pass to WR Steve Smith (8/153y, TD). TB Reggie Bush (16/95y, TD) contributed key 33y punt RET to start Troy in Cardinal territory, and big TB LenDale White dived for winning TD with 6:15 to play.

USA Today Coaches September 26

1	Southern California (45)	1508	14	Utah	729
2	Oklahoma (14)	1469	15	Purdue	681
3	Georgia	1379	16	Florida	526
4	Miami (Fla.) (2)	1352	17	Fresno State	517
5	Texas	1266	18	Michigan	484
6	Ohio State	1188	19	Minnesota	470
7	West Virginia	1055	20	Wisconsin	373
8	Tennessee	1005	21	Boise State	340
9	Auburn	972	22	Louisville	259
10	California	944	23	Maryland	223
11	Florida State	918	24	Oklahoma State	180
12	Virginia	817	25	Arizona State	113
13	LSU	785			

October 2, 2004

(Th) Navy 24 AIR FORCE 21: In game reminiscent of 1950s Split-T option action, service academy match-up had minimal possessions for each team. Air Force (2-3) owned 1st Q, gained 2 TOs and authored opening drive that consumed more than 8 mins to K Michael Greenaway's 1st of 2 FGs. Early in 2nd Q, Middies (5-0) made GLS that resulted in Falcons' FG, but Navy romped 80y to QB Aaron Polanco's 18y TD option run after FB Kyle Eckel (21/97y) softened up AFA with 37y rushing on drive. Ds took command in 2nd H until Air Force opened it up in 4th Q for 67y passing on 3 straight hits by QB Shaun Carney (17-21/221y, 2 TDs, 2 INTs), including brilliant 38y grab by WR J.P. Waller between 2 defenders and HB Darnell Stephens' 19y TD catch. Polanco countered with 66y aerial to WR Marco Nelson that led to Eckel's 3y TD run for 21-14 lead. Falcons came right back to Waller's 12y TD grab with 2:21 remaining. Middies K Geoff Blumenfeld nailed 30y FG to win it with 4 secs on clock.

VIRGINIA TECH 19 West Virginia 13: Just when murmurs of "running the table" were swirling around Mountaineers (4-1), they had much go wrong, including 11 PENs/119y, in combative game (25 PENs) at Blacksburg. Virginia Tech (3-2) led 6-0 in 2nd Q on pair of FGs by K Brandon Pace when it thrived on successive game-turning plays: West Virginia WR John Pennington dropped low 3rd down pass at Tech 1YL and Hokies DT Jim Davis blocked FG try, which S Vincent Fuller scooped up and dashed 74y to TD and 13-0 lead. Va Tech led 16-0 late in 3rd Q when scrambling QB Bryan Randall (16-34/142y, 2 INTs) made foolish cross-field pass which WVU S Eric Wicks intercepted for 34y TD. Mountaineers QB Rasheed Marshall (9-19/81y, INT) ran 46y draw play for 4th Q TD, but threw INT to Fuller to kill chances in dying secs.

NORTH CAROLINA STATE 27 Wake Forest 21 (OT): Wake Forest (3-2) took 14-0 lead to H on DB Marcus McGruder's 22y INT TD RET late in 1st Q to spring to 63y advance on next series to FB Micah Andrews' 1st of 2 short TD plunges. Deacons amassed 180y O in 1st H, 20y more than game avg allowed by NC State's D to date. At end of 3rd Q, Wake still had 180y O, and NC State (3-1) had stormed to 21-14 lead. Young QB Jay Davis (18-24/244y, TD) came alive in 2nd H with 57y TD pass to WR Sterling Hicks and 58y pass to set up TB T.A. McLendon's tying TD run. Wake, which rushed for 202y of its 263y total O, ran ball 10 plays in row to complete 80y drive to 21-21 tie early in 4th Q. In OT, Deacs K Matt Wisnosky hit upright with 34y FG try, and Wolfpack's McLendon barreled for gains of 11, 4, 2, and 8y, last to score winning TD.

Auburn 34 TENNESSEE 10: Auburn's fine D, led by DB Junior Rosegreen's 4 INTs that tied SEC record, exposed Volunteers' "7-10 Split" of QB job by frosh Brent Schaeffer (1-5/13y, INT) and Erick Ainge (17-35/173y, TD, 4 INTs), who wore jersey numbers 7 and 10 respectively. Tigers (5-0), on way to 1st Knoxville win since 1983, partially blocked Tennessee's 1st possession punt and took over at their 45YL. Tigers TB Ronnie Brown (13/57y, TD) caught passes of 8 and 10y before barreling 9y for TD. Vols (3-1) countered with K James Wilhoit's 41y FG, but Auburn stormed to 2 TD passes by QB Jason Campbell (16-23/252y, 2 TDs, INT) and 5y TD blast through Vols DB Jason Allen—2nd time that happened—by TB Cadillac Williams (24/95y). So, Tigers enjoyed 31-3 H edge, making final 30 mins academic.

GEORGIA 45 Louisiana State 16: QB David Greene hit modest 10-19/172y, but half went for Georgia (4-0) record 5 TDs. For 5th-ranked D of LSU (3-2), it was harsh medicine to have its touted secondary be burned by pair of TD receptions each by WRs Reggie Brown (5/110y, 2 TDs), who made 2 fine grabs at pylon, and Fred Gibson (3/56y, 2 TDs). Trailing 24-0, Bengals finally awakened with 10 pts in last half-min of 2nd Q, including QB JaMarcus Russel's 18y TD to WR Dwayne Bowe. When Greene hit TD passes to WRs Gibson and Sean Bailey in 3rd Q, verdict was over at 38-10.

FLORIDA 45 Arkansas 30: Much like same match-up in 2003, Arkansas (3-2) staged late comeback to fall short of victory. Florida (3-1) showed explosive O, jumping to 38-7 margin by 3rd Q. Gators TB Ciatrick Fason (2 TDs) found paydirt late in 1st Q after QB Chris Leak (23-38/career-high 322y, 3 TDs) connected on 39 and 12y passes. In 2nd Q, Florida WR Andre Caldwell raced 61y on reverse, and Leak hit 2 TD passes. Down 38-7, Razorbacks went 80y to RB DeCori Birmingham's 12y TD run in last min of 3rd Q to spark rally for 23 straight pts. QB Matt Jones (23-39/252y, TD, 3 INTs) got hot, leading Hogs to TDs on next 2 series, including his 25y TD romp and 2 passes for 2-pts convs. But, Gators LB Channing Crowder (11 tackles) made 22y INT RET of Jones' pass over middle to set up WR Dallas Baker's game-sealing TD catch.

NORTHWESTERN 33 Ohio State 27 (OT): Buckeyes (3-1) had won 24 series games in row and had not lost in Evanston since 1958. Wildcats (2-3) forced slow-starting attack of Ohio State to play from behind most of night. When Northwestern QB Brett Basanez (24-44/278y, 2 TDs, 2 INTs) whipped 27y TD arrow to WR Mark Philmore (11/134y, TD) early in 3rd Q and RB Noah Herron (33/113y, 2 TDs) went 1y to score on 1st play of 4th Q, Wildcats maintained leads of 20-10 and 27-17. But, Ohio soon rallied to NW 4YL, but was forced into K Mike Nugent's 29y FG, and, after Cats DB Jeff Backes picked off pass in EZ, WR Santonio Holmes (4/72y) tied it by hauling in 21y TD pass from QB Justin Zwick with 1:54 left in regulation. K Nugent, "Mr. Automatic," barely missed 40y FG in OT, opening door for Basanez to scramble 21y to set up Herron's 1y power run off left side for winning TD.

Purdue 41 NOTRE DAME 16: Not since 1974 and 13 losses had Purdue (4-0) won in South Bend. Boilermakers QB Kyle Orton (21-31/385y, 4 TDs) was outstanding from outset, but after trade of 1st Q FGs, sub RB Jerome Brooks spun out of tackle and sprinted 100y on KO TD RET for 10-3 lead. Notre Dame (3-2) trailed 13-3 in 2nd Q when Purdue offside PEN kept alive ND's drive near GL. TE Anthony Fasano (8/155y) made brilliant catch along way, but frosh TB Darius Walker was stripped by Purdue DE Anthony Spencer (2 sacks) while surging for EZ. Boilers DE Ron Ninkovich, in as TE in GL O, was wide open for short square-out TD catch for 20-3 H lead. Purdue was unstoppable in 3rd Q and WR Taylor Stubblefield (7/181y, 2 TDs) got behind secondary for 97y TD catch, longest scoring play ever against Fighting Irish. ND QB Brady Quinn (26-46/432y, TD) racked up most passing y ever in Notre Dame Stadium and hit WR Rhema McKnight with 40y crossing-pattern TD in 3rd Q. In their 4 wins, Boilermakers had scored 189 pts without single TO.

MISSOURI 17 Colorado 9: Tigers (3-1) took big step in wide-open race for Big 12 North by knocked Colorado (3-1) from unbeaten ranks. Missouri never fell behind, but had to surmount several costly PENs and 3 FG misses of 44, 42, and 39y by K Joe Tantarelli. Tigers went 80y after opening KO, riding 35y rushing by dependable QB Brad Smith (16-25/189y, TD, and 17/76y rushing) to 3y TD run by TB Damien Nash (25/102y). Buffs TB Bobby Purify (22/81y) scored on 4y run in 2nd Q, but Mizzou LB James Kinney blocked x-pt try by K Mason Crosby (21y FG) to keep 10-9 lead until Tigers WR Sean Coffey slipped through tackle to zip 51y for 3rd Q TD pass-run. Purify came up lame in 2nd H and gained only 8/6y. Colorado had chance after DE Alex Ligon's FUM REC at Missouri 36YL and advanced to 7YL. On 2nd down, Buffs QB Joel Platt (18-28/171y, 3 INTs) lofted pass to left edge of EZ, which WR Evan Judge appeared to catch until Tigers DB Shirdonya Mitchell plucked it from his grasp for INT.

California 49 OREGON STATE 7: Week away from Pac-10 showdown with USC, Cal Bears (3-0) played their 1st game in 21 days. California players felt time off did them good: DB Tim Mixon (INT) felt time off helped Bears focus on Oregon State. Frosh phenom TB Marshawn Lynch raced 69y with opening KO, and Bears quickly launched TD trip to 11y catch by WR Chase Lyman, who had his best game ever with 5/176y, 3 TDs. Beavers (1-4) quickly countered with TB Dwight Wright's 45y scoring romp, 5th play of 73y march. Lyman struck again just 18 secs later, catching 79y TD from Cal RB Terrell Williams. Bears forced 10 punts and made 2 INTs rest of way to uphold passing of QB Aaron Rodgers (12-16/140y, 3 TDs, 2 INTs).

USA Today Coaches October 3

1	Southern California (46)	1507	14	Michigan	644
2	Oklahoma (12)	1462	15	Ohio State	643
3	Georgia (1)	1398	16	Wisconsin	597
4	Miami (Fla.) (2)	1347	17	Tennessee	519
5	Texas	1283	18	West Virginia	497
6	Auburn	1189	19	Boise State	442
7	California	1116	20	Louisville	434
8	Florida State	1049	21	Oklahoma State	353
9	Virginia	966	22	Arizona State	314
10	Purdue	952	23	Maryland	307
11	Utah	876	24	LSU	232
12	Florida	731	25	North Carolina State	63
13	Minnesota	684			

October 9, 2004

(Th) VIRGINIA 30 Clemson 10: It took awhile, but Virginia (5-0) finally advanced to spot in AP Top 10 when sub TB Alvin Pearman (18/104y) left bench to score pair of 4th Q TDs to extend beyond 16-10 edge. Tigers (1-4), long-time nemesis of UVa, started hot, going 80y on opening series to TB Duane Coleman's 5y TD catch from QB Charlie Whitehurst (16-28/166y, TD, INT). Cavs remained behind through most of 1st H until QB Marquis Hagans' 3y TD pass to TE Heath Miller, who made marvelous stretch to touch ball to pylon. That broke 10-6 deficit in last 6 mins of 2nd Q. Virginia K Connor Hughes kicked 50y FG, his 3rd, late in 3rd Q for 16-10 edge.

ARMY 48 Cincinnati 29: After close call on prior Saturday against TCU, Black Knights (1-4) broke their 19-game losing skid by riding FB Tielo Robinson (16/82y, 3 TDs, 4/111y, 2 TDs receiving) to 5 TDs. Army marched to 554y total O, including FB Carlton Jones' 20/180y, TD, rushing. Cincinnati (2-4) started well as QB Gino Guidugli (25-39/350y, 4 TDs, INT) threw his 1st TD pass to TE Brent Celek. But, Robinson ran for

2 TDs and caught 2y scoring pass from QB Zac Dahman (13-21/270y, 2 TDs, INT) for 19-7 lead. Guidugli tossed trio of TD passes in 2nd Q, and Bearcats closed to within 32-29 by H. Down 35-29 in 3rd Q, Cincy advanced 57y but Guidugli lost FUM at Army 23YL. Key play came on dump-off pass to Robinson from deep in Cadets' territory in 4th Q: Robinson dodged and zipped to 93y score.

Tennessee 19 GEORGIA 14: No. 3 Bulldogs (4-1), fresh off their seemingly definitive win over LSU, had just about nothing go right. QB David Greene (15-34/163y), so effective with 5 TD throws week before, was inaccurate all day, including last-play toss to EZ. "I couldn't explain it last week, and I can't explain it today,' said Greene of his contrasting performances. Georgia also was flagged 12 times, including holding call that wiped out WR Bryan McClendon's KO RET to Tennessee (4-1) 2YL in 2nd Q. K Andy Bailey missed 29y FG in 3rd Q that could have pulled Bulldogs within 13-10. Vols, 2-TD underdog and on road for 1st time in 2004, jumped to efficient 10-0 lead on 22y TD pass by QB Erik Ainge (12-21/150y, 2 TDs) and K James Wilhoit's 1st of 2 FGs. Georgia rallied to within 10-7 as QB D.J. Shockley came off bench to flip 24y TD to WR Fred Gibson early in 2nd Q, but made it into UT territory only twice more before TB Danny Ware banged 1y for TD early in 4th Q. With wins over Florida and Georgia under their belt, Vols took inside track to SEC East title.

Louisiana State 24 FLORIDA 21: CBS announcer Todd Blackledge suggested Bayou Bengals (4-2) had made "every mistake in the book, but had to be happy to still be in it" after 1st H they trailed 21-14. Indeed, it proved true: LSU held Gators (3-2) to 110y O and forced punts on 5-6 possessions in 2nd H. Florida had taken advantage of 2 early miscues by Tigers QB JaMarcus Russell (6-10/56y, 2 TDs, sack) when CB Demetrice Webb returned INT 13y to 5YL and S Jarvis Herring stepped in front of another Russell throw and ran it to LSU 3YL. Gators TB Citarick Fason (21/92y, TD) scored 1st time, and QB Chris Leak (15-33/142y, 2 TDs) followed with 3y scoring pitch to TE Tate Casey. QB Marcus Randall (18-27/198y, 2 TDs, INT) came off Tigers bench when Russell was injured and rallied LSU 80y in 1:27 to beat H clock on his 15y TD pass. K Chris Jackson pulled LSU within 21-17 with 47y FG in 3rd Q before Randall capped 50y trip in game's last 27 secs by finding TB Joseph Addai for 10y TD pass.

Wisconsin 23 OHIO STATE 13: Badgers (6-0) TB Anthony Davis returned from injury list to run for 168y and score on 31y romp that launched Wisconsin's scoring in 2nd Q. Ohio State (3-2), winners of 18 straight in Columbus, had jumped to 10-0 lead, primarily on frosh DB Ted Ginn's 65y punt TD RET midway through 1st Q. Badgers' dandy D, tops in nation, kept Buckeyes O out of their EZ and limited Ohio to 49y on 22 snaps in 2nd H. Wisconsin took its 1st lead at 14-10 with 3:30 to go in 2nd Q when ever-improving QB John Stocco (15-24/160y, 2 TDs) hit 1st of his pair of scores. LB A.J. Hawk made 20 tackles and K Mike Nugent hit FGs of 42 and 55y for Ohio State.

MICHIGAN 27 Minnesota 24: Wolverines (5-1) started fast, going 65y to 8y burst up middle by TB Mike Hart (35/160y, TD) and 35y to K Garrett Rivas' 38y FG, his 1st of 2 FGs. Only 12 secs after Rivas' 3-ptr, Gophers were ignited by 80y TD sprint by TB Laurence Maroney (19/145y, TD). Confident Minnesota (5-1) strode to 2nd H leads of 21-17 and 24-17 on QB Bryan Cupito's 26y TD pass to WR Jared Ellerson and K Rhys Lloyd's 27y FG. Rivas' 2nd FG topped 68y drive with 9:36 to play, so Michigan pulled within 24-20. Wolverines stopped Minny's possession that began with 4:47 to play, and with help of 2 timeouts, started from their 13YL with 3:04 to go. Michigan QB Chad Henne (33-49/328y, 2 TDs, 2 INTs) hit WR Jason Avant (6/87y) twice totaling 37y, and, with 1:57 left, Henne found TE Tyler Ecker, who easily stepped through 2 tackles along left sideline when Gophers DBs took poor tackling angles. Ecker dashed 31y for winning TD. WR Braylon Edwards caught 10/98y, TD for Wolverines.

KANSAS 31 Kansas State 28: It had been 12 long years since hopeful Kansas (3-3) had won Sunflower State rivalry, but Jayhawks took 7-6 H lead, extended it to 17-6 in 3rd Q and held on through thrilling, but nerve-wracking 2nd H. But, Kansas State (2-3) slipped through to 21-17 lead early in 4th Q when Wildcats QB Dylan Meier (15-24/249y, 2 TDs) followed his 2y scoring keeper with 86y TD bomb to WR Tony Madison. Leading 10-6 in 3rd Q, Kansas scored on 24y hook-and-ladder TD: short toss by QB Adam Barmann (10-20/85y, 2 TDs) to WR Brandon Rideaau, who flipped pitchout to RB John Randle. WR Mark Simmons made outstanding 1-handed TD catch to put Jayhawks out in front at 24-21 with 5:28 left in 4th Q, and Randle raced 43y to score after short punt by Kansas State.

Oklahoma 12 Texas 0 (Dallas): Not in 282 games had Longhorns (4-1) been blanked, longest scoring streak in country. Not only did Texas not score, it barely threatened. Oklahoma (5-0) started quietly, using frosh sensation, TB Adrian Peterson (32/225y) sparingly. Eventually Peterson carried on 7 plays to K Trey DiCarlo's 22y FG late in 1st H. Peterson rambled for 44, 26, 19, 17, and 15y gains to prompt starting TB Kejuan Jones' 6y TD run with 8:07 to play in 4th Q. Sooners QB Jason White passed 14-26/113y, 2 INTs, including pickoff by Texas LB Derrick Johnson that stopped OU threat in 3rd Q. Texas QB Vince Young had tough day, passing 8-23/86y and 2 lost FUMs.

TEXAS TECH 70 Nebraska 10: Never in Nebraska's proud 114-year history had it lost by margin so large and allowed so many pts. Texas Tech (4-2) QB Sonny Cumbie pitched for 436y and 5 TDs, including 80y score along left sideline to WR Jarrett Hicks that built 21-3 late in 1st H. Huskers (3-2) QB Joe Dailey (14-34/187y, TD, INT) threw 74y TD pass to WR Mark LeFlore in 1st min of 3rd Q, but Nebraska QBs lost 5 INTs, several of which set up short Red Raiders TD thrusts.

SOUTHERN CALIFORNIA 23 California 17: Bears (3-1) QB Aaron Rodgers (29-34/267y, TD) threw underneath coverage with stunning accuracy. Rodgers connected on his 1st 23 passes to tie NCAA record held by Tennessee's Tee Martin (1998). When California earned 1st-and-goal at 9YL with 1:47 left, Rodgers was sacked by 5th different Trojans defender, DT Manuel Wright, then missed 3 throws, last because receiver stumbled. Southern California (5-0), outgained 424y to 205y, still came up with big plays when it needed them: REC of Cal's dropped punt snap in 1st Q that led to TD by TB LenDale White on 5y run, WR Dwayne Jarrett's 16y TD catch early in 3rd Q to provide 23-10 lead, and pass rush pressure on Rodgers' last min try. Troy K Ryan Killeen made 3 FGs in 1st H. Rodgers finished 14-14/133y 1st H performance with 20y TD to WR Geoff McArthur.

USA Today Coaches October 10

1	Southern California (45)	1509	14	Tennessee	732
2	Oklahoma (15)	1476	15	Oklahoma State	570
3	Miami (Fla.) (1)	1398	16	West Virginia	530
4	Auburn	1341	17	Louisville	512
5	Purdue	1160	18	Boise State	498
6	Virginia	1142	19	Arizona State	486
7	Florida State	1135	20	Minnesota	423
8	Georgia	978	21	LSU	405
9	California	942	22	Florida	299
10	Utah	931	23	Ohio State	157
11	Texas	911	24	Missouri	99
12	Wisconsin	881	25	Southern Mississippi	88
13	Michigan	862			

October 16, 2004

(Th) MIAMI 41 Louisville 38: Undefeated Louisville (4-1) arrived in south Florida with Miami-like swagger and stunned Orange Bowl stadium faithful with 24-7 H edge. QB Stefan LeFors (17-22/242y, 3 TDs) hit his 1st 9 pass attempts against puzzled Hurricanes (5-0), including TDs of 17y to RB Lionel Gates (13/109y, 2 TDs) and 12 and 22y to WR Tiger Jones, latter providing 31-14 lead just short of middle of 3rd Q. Much-maligned Miami (5-0) QB Brock Berlin (25-37/308y, 3 TDs, INT) sparked drives of 76, 66, 87, and 56y as Hurricanes scored on 6 straight possessions. Biggest TD was produced by rocket-fast Miami WR Devin Hester, who surged 78y on punt RET up middle to supply 34-31 lead with 8 mins left. Louisville rallied with 80y TD march, but Berlin converted on 4th-and-4 pass to 3YL, and TB Frank Gore scored from 1YL.

PITTSBURGH 20 Boston College 17 (OT): Big East banners fluttered, but BC's last-year went unrecognized on Heinz Field flagpoles. Panthers (4-2) made 2 big D stands and QB Tyler Palko passed 12-27/131y and scored on 3y run that provided 7-3 H edge. After RB Raymond Kirkley (21/88y, TD) lifted Pitt's lead to 14-3 with 2y run in 3rd Q, Boston College (4-2) QB Paul Peterson (32-53/367y, 2 TDs) passed for pair of 2nd H TDs, including game-tying score, 10y pass to WR Larry Lester, at end of 79y drive in 4th Q. In OT, K Josh Cummings gave Panthers 20-17 lead, and on Eagles' ill-fated series, Lester was knocked loose of ball on 3rd down reception by Pitt DB Mike Phillips.

Notre Dame 27 Navy 9 (East Rutherford, NJ): Navy (5-1) sought elusive win after 40 winless years in 78th meeting. But, speed and strength of Notre Dame (5-2) flattened Middies as TB Ryan Grant led trio of runners with 2 TDs among his 20/114y rushing. But, Navy (5-1) outrushed Irish 216y to 204y. Difference was QB Brady Quinn's 11-20/130y passing and Notre Dame D throwing Middies QB Aaron Polanco for 31y in losses. ND led 17-0 at H before Navy notched K Geoff Blumenfeld's FG in 3rd Q, but Grant thundered for TD for 24-3 edge. Big SB Frank Divis scored late 5y TD for Navy.

FLORIDA STATE 36 Virginia 3: Seminoles (5-1) appeared at risk against no. 6 Virginia (5-1), which had never won in 6 tries at Tallahassee. But, Florida State blocked punt for safety early on, added K Xavier Beitia's FG, and dominated all night. TB Lorenzo Booker ran for career-best 15/123y, 2 TDs, emerging QB Wyatt Sexton passed 20-26/275y, TD, and coach Bobby Bowden remarked that Sexton's performance was "too good to be true right now." No. 6 Virginia (5-1), in search of its 1st-ever road win over top 10 team, only made scoreboard on last play of 1st H as K Connor Hughes booted 23y FG. TE Heath Miller caught 9/110y for Cavaliers.

MICHIGAN STATE 51 Minnesota 17: For 12th straight year, Minnesota (5-2) followed up loss to Michigan with another defeat. Emerging Michigan State (4-3) QB Drew Stanton set school record with 410y total O, passing 20-31/308y, 3 TDs, 2 INTs. Gophers' big play came from speedy WR Ernie Wheelwright, who got behind Spartans' DBs for 58y TD catch from QB Bryan Cupito (11-33/211y, 2 TDs, 2 INTs), who was sacked thrice. MSU TE Eric Knott got loose for 25 and 36y TDs in 1st H led 31-10 by Spartans. RB Jason Teague sprinted through Minnesota for 43y TD run in 1st Q.

Wisconsin 20 PURDUE 17: It was all over in a flash: Purdue QB Kyle Orton (25-45/235y, TD, INT), trying to bootleg for 1st down to kill late-game clock, was upended and lost FUM, which Wisconsin (7-0) DB Scott Starks picked up and returned 40y for stunning TD with 2:36 to play. Boilermakers (5-1) had faced strong pass rush, led by Badgers DE Erasmus James, and was forced to throw shorter than desired. But, Orton, perceived Heisman Trophy front-runner with 18 TDs and 2 INTs passing coming into game, rallied his team after James and 2 other members of Wisconsin front-4 went out with injury. Badgers TB Anthony Davis (18/66y, TD) had been collared all game but slipped away for 33y dash to set up his short TD run for 7-0 lead late in 1st H. Orton hit TD pass to TE Charles Davis late in 3rd Q and scrambled to right pylon for 6y TD run with 8 mins to go in 4th Q for 17-7 edge. Wisconsin QB John Stocco (17-32/211y, TD, INT) was then up to occasion by hitting 6-7/73y, including sub TB Booker Stanley's ram into EZ with short toss for 7y TD that trimmed it to 17-14 with 5:29 to play. After his FUM, Orton had last chance: Purdue made it to 22YL, but, after LB Dontez Sanders' sack, Boilers K Ben Jones missed 42y FG try to right of upright.

TEXAS 28 Missouri 20: Preservation was hallmark for Texas (5-1) in key Big 12 match up. Longhorns jumped to 14-0 lead in 1st Q as DE Brian Robison swallowed INT off Missouri (4-2) QB Brad Smith and stepped mere 2y for TD. Tigers recovered in 2nd Q, going 66y to short TD pass by Smith (20-34/185y, TD, 2 INTs) and quickly came up with INT by CB Shird Mitchell which led to TB Damien Nash's tying 33y TD romp. Just as Missouri threatened again, Texas sub CB Aaron Ross returned INT 64y to Mizzou 12YL. TB Cedric Benson (28/150y, 2 TDs) quickly boosted Longhorns to 21-14 lead with TD run 2 plays later. Trailing 28-14, Tigers went 77y as Smith hit 6-6/69y and scored on 1y draw run. But winded Smith bobbled x-pt snap to keep Mizzou behind by 8 pts and was soon threw incomplete on 4th down with 1:33 left.

Texas A&M 36 OKLAHOMA STATE 20: QB Reggie McNeal (19-25/288y, 2 TDs) piled up 386y total O as Aggies (5-1) surprised undefeated Cowboys (5-1) for Texas A&M's 1st road win against ranked team since 1997. A&M jumped to 20-0 lead early in 2nd Q as nation's` leading rusher, Oklahoma State TB Vernand Morency (28/111y, TD) uncharacteristically bobbled away 2 FUMs. McNeal scored on 24 and 3y runs. Oke State countered with 80y march as QB Donovan Woods (15-26/202y, TD) hit 3 passes and scored on 2y run with 33 secs left in 1st H. But, McNeal lofted 55y "Hail Mary" TD to send Aggies off with 27-6 H edge. Cowboys trailed 36-6 before 4th Q when they added cosmetic scores on Morency's run and Woods' pass.

SOUTHERN CALIFORNIA 45 Arizona State 7: Trojans (6-0) crushed undefeated, upstart Arizona State (5-1), which had been unable to practice on its normal field because of ASU-hosted Presidential debate between George Bush and John Kerry. It was TB Reggie "Mr. President" Bush of USC who helped crush Sun Devils. Bush scored on 10y TD catch from QB Matt Leinart (13-24/224y, 4 TDs), who hit 11-16/193y and all of his TDs in 1st H. Trojans' touted WR Dwayne Jarrett (5/139y) caught 3 TDs, and TB LenDale White led rushers with 16/68y. Arizona State QB Ryan Walter (19-34/181y) came in with 15 TD passes and single INT, but was sacked 6 times and picked off twice. Walter's worst faux pas was his throw into triple coverage that was intercepted by Troy LB Matt Grootegard who returned it 41y to set up Leinart's 3rd TD pass for 21-0 lead early in 2nd Q. TB Hakim Hill made ASU's TD on 2y run in 2nd Q.

CALIFORNIA 45 Ucla 28: Cal's mighty O piled up 550y as QB Aaron Rodgers passed 19-29/260y, 4 TDs, and TB J.J. Arrington ran 29/205y, 2 TDs. UCLA (4-2) hung with Bears for awhile as QB Drew Olson (20-36/299y) hit 4 TDs, including pair in 2nd Q that briefly tied it 14-14. Bruins TB Maurice Drew tallied on 2 long runs after short passes, but was limited to 14/42y on ground. California WR Geoff McArthur (9/163y, 2 TDs) took on greater receiving role with season-ending knee injury to WR Chase Lyman.

USA Today Coaches October 17

1	Southern California (50)	1514	14	West Virginia	669
2	Oklahoma (10)	1470	15	Virginia	665
3	Miami (Fla.) (1)	1380	16	Boise State	557
4	Auburn	1359	17	LSU	489
5	Florida State	1234	18	Louisville	482
6	Georgia	1124	19	Florida	447
7	Wisconsin	1088	20	Texas A&M	404
8	California	1071	21	Oklahoma State	272
9	Texas	1026	22	Virginia Tech	253
10	Utah	1015	23	Arizona State	194
11	Michigan	943	24	Texas Tech	121
12	Purdue	832	25	Notre Dame	92
13	Tennessee	815			

Bowl Championship Series Rankings October 18

	AP Poll Pct.	USA Today/ESPN Poll Pct.	Computer Pct.	BCS Avg.
1 Southern California (6-0)	.991	.993	.990	.9912
2 Miami (5-0)	.891	.905	.960	.9187
3 Oklahoma (6-0)	.964	.964	.820	.9161
4 Auburn (7-0)	.910	.891	.910	.9036
5 Florida State (5-1)	.802	.809	.810	.8072

October 23, 2004

Florida State 20 WAKE FOREST 17: Deacons (3-4) may have been off to winless start in ACC, but it wasn't for lack of delivering anxiety to top teams. Wake Forest built 14-3 advantage in 1st H on TOs forced upon neophyte Seminoles (6-1) QB Wyatt Sexton (17-39/194y, 2 TDs, 2 INTs). Wake Forest DT Jerome Nichols deflected Sexton's pass in last min of 1st Q, and DE Matt Robinson picked it off for 19y INT TD RET. Wake CB Eric King burst in for sack of Sexton in 2nd Q, and FUM was returned 36y by LB Brad White for TD. Sexton hung in to finally put Florida State ahead 17-14 early in 4th Q on his 2nd TD pass: 46y to WR Dominic Robinson. Sexton's INT, however, set up Wake K Ryan Plackemeir's tying 41y FG. TB Lorenzo Booker scooted 46y on 3rd-and-10 to get FSU out of 18YL hole, and K Xavier Beitia made 22y FG.

Miami 45 NORTH CAROLINA STATE 31: Miami (6-0) arrived in Raleigh with attitude, and maligned QB Brock Berlin tied school record with 5 TD passes among his 15-30/265y, INT. North Carolina State (4-3), which came in with 204y per game D avg, allowed Hurricanes to roll up 416y total O. Miami WR Devin Hester took opening KO 5y deep in his EZ and sped up middle for 100y KO TD RET. Wolfpack took 17-14 lead in 2nd Q on 2nd TD pass by QB Jay Davis (20-38/260y, 4 TDs, INT) and hung close until Berlin followed his 10y TD pass to WR Sinorice Moss with 27y score to WR Roscoe Parrish just after NC State returner Bobby Washington fumbled KO.

TENNESSEE 17 Alabama 13: Both Ds turned in top-notch efforts, but in end, Tennessee (6-1) made key stops to enhance DE Parys Haralson's 18y FUM RET for TD on game's 2nd snap. Alabama (5-3) sported D that held its 3rd opponent to less than 200y as Vols managed only 1y in 1st Q and 195y total O. Tide tied it 7-7 on FB Tim Castille's short TD run in 1st Q after LB DeMeco Ryans' INT at Tennessee 44YL. QB Erik Ainge (10-22/132y, TD, 2 INTs) put Vols up 14-10 with 19y TD pass to WR Jayson Swain (5/80y) in 2nd Q, but threw costly INT to Bama LB Cornelius Wortham from Tide 4YL. Alabama, seemingly on its way to tying it at 17-17, had to settle for K Brian Bostick's 2nd FG in 4th Q. Vols DB Corey Campbell made INT at his 15YL to secure victory with 46 secs to play.

AUBURN 42 Kentucky 10: At season's start, Tigers (8-0) D was considered liability, but nation's no. 2 scoring D permitted only 110y O, including 36/37y on ground, to Wildcats (1-6), who lost their 5th straight game. Auburn TB Carnell Williams rushed for 149y

and scored on runs of 1 and 9y in 1st Q. Tigers led by 21-0. Kentucky frosh QB Andre Woodson (14-26/73y) made his 1st career start and lost 2 FUMs, including 4th Q TD RET by LB Kevis Burnam. Wildcats TB Rafael Little scored TD in 2nd Q, 1st rushing score allowed all season by Auburn D.

MISSISSIPPI STATE 38 Florida 31: Tale of 2 coaches: Bulldogs' Sylvester Croom, SEC's 1st African-American head coach, won his 1st conf game. Florida (4-3) coach Ron Zook was fired afterward, effective at season's end, because listless loss was humiliating to program usually on top. Mississippi State (2-5) RB Jerius Norwood rushed 29/174y and 2 TDs in 4th Q, including 37y burst through feeble tackling to win it with 32 secs to play. Norwood's 1st TD, short dive, had came with 9 mins left and had provided 31-24 lead. Gators QB Chris Leak (20-35/260y, 2 TDs) sparked 73y drive to tie it on his 1y keeper, but threw INT snatched by Bulldogs DB Jeramie Johnson to set up Norwood's winning run. MSU RB Jonathan Lowe had chipped in dazzling 73y punt TD RET for 24-17 lead in middle of 3rd Q. Florida TB Ciatrick Fason rushed for 143y and 55y TD that tied it 24-24 in 3rd Q. Gators LB Channing Crowder made 18 tackles.

Michigan 16 PURDUE 14: Precocious TB Mike Hart broke Rickey Powers' frosh rushing mark with 206y for on-charging Michigan (7-1), but it was Wolverines' superb secondary that made big play to stop late surge by Purdue (5-2). Soon after K Garrett Rivas' 3rd FG had give Michigan 16-14 lead with 2:45 to play, Boilermakers frosh WR Dorien Bryant swooped over middle to take 25y pass from QB Kyle Orton (14-30/213y, TD, INT), but slender receiver was hit low, and when S Ernest Shazor walloped him high, ball popped loose for Wolverines REC. Hart had caught 25y screen pass in 1st Q to tie it at 7-7 and contributed runs of 28, 33, 16, and 11y that led to 2 FGs. Orton had put Purdue ahead 14-10 early in 3rd Q when he threw 63y TD to RB Brandon Jones.

Oklahoma State 20 MISSOURI 17: With Nebraska's 45-21 loss to Kansas State, Missouri (4-3) hoped to gain stranglehold on Big 12 North, but blew 17-0 lead to Cowboys (6-1). Tigers saw 9-game home win streak evaporate, and defining moment came in last 54 secs of 1st H when Oklahoma State QB Donovan Woods (7-13/110y, TD, INT) hit his brother, WR D'Juan Woods, with 12y TD pass with 4 ticks left on H clock. It concluded 80y trip in 8 quick plays, featuring 21 and 19y dashes by TB Vernand Morency (31/173y). Drive frustrated Mizzou coach Gary Pinkel: "…all we had to do was tackle a guy inbounds one time (to stop it)." K Jason Ricks made 27y FG in 3rd Q, and QB Woods tied it 17-17 for Oklahoma State on 34y dash behind block of RT Kellen Davis with 11:36 to go in 4th Q. Missouri gained only 87y in 2nd H and permitted 78y drive to Ricks' winning 28y FG with 55 secs left. Tigers had owned most of 1st H: QB Brad Smith (18-29/96y, 2 TDs, INT) finished game with 154y, but sparked 83 and 41y TD drives that he capped with scoring passes.

TEXAS A&M 29 Colorado 26 (OT): QB Reggie McNeal (23-38/243y) set new Texas A&M (6-1) and Big 12 records by going 195 pass attempts without INT, but more importantly he accounted for 382 total y and rallied Aggies from 6-0, 19-7, and 26-23 deficits to force OT. Colorado (4-3) K Mason Crosby made 29 and 26y FGs in 1st Q, and QB Joel Klatt (23-42/346y, 2 TDs) hit WR Evan Judge for 2 TDs within 4:57 span that straddled 1st and 2nd Qs. That gave Buffaloes 19-7 lead, but they failed on questionable 2-pt try decision that would come back to vex coach Gary Barnett. Aggies took their 1st lead early in 4th Q when TB Courtney Lewis scored on 2y run for 20-19 advantage. Colorado went 82y for TD and 26-23 lead, sparked by WR Dusty Sprague's high-wire 34y catch. K Todd Pegram made 20y on last play of regulation to tie it and put A&M ahead in top half of OT with his 5th 3-ptr. Buffs TB Bobby Purify (20/130y, TD) quickly lost FUM to end it as Aggies LB Lee Foliaki picked Purify's pocket, clutching ball to his hip: "I had to get up and let (the officials) see the ball."

BOISE STATE 33 Fresno State 16: Playing on chilly night on its odd blue carpet, undefeated Boise State (7-0) extended nation's-longest win streak to 18 games. Broncos scored on their opening drive for 1st time in 2004 as sub frosh TB Calvin McCarty finished it off with 7y TD run. From there, Boise D took over, limiting Bulldogs' run attack (204y avg) to piddling 17y and Fresno State's whole O to only 191y. K Tyler Jones notched 3 of his 4 FGs for 16-3 H edge for Broncos, and they added TD sneak by QB Jared Zabransky (15-23/227y, TD). Fresno State (3-3) QB Paul Pinegar hit 17-30/174y, but was forced into 2 INTs, 2nd of which led to 20y move to clinching TD.

USA Today Coaches October 24

1	Southern California (49)	1513	14	Virginia	660
2	Oklahoma (11)	1469	15	Boise State	638
3	Miami (Fla.) (1)	1380	16	Louisville	582
4	Auburn	1358	17	Texas A&M	503
5	Florida State	1218	18	LSU	477
6	Wisconsin	1152	19	Purdue	457
7	Georgia	1127	20	Oklahoma State	415
8	California	1066	21	Arizona State	346
9	Texas	1032	22	Virginia Tech	338
10	Utah	1001	23	Minnesota	176
11	Michigan	970	24	Iowa	89
12	Tennessee	864	25	Southern Mississippi	52
13	West Virginia	738			

Bowl Championship Series Ranking October 25

	AP Poll Pct.	USA Today/ESPN Poll Pct.	Computer Pct.	BCS Avg.
1 Southern California (7-0)	.991	.992	.970	.9843
2 Oklahoma (7-0)	.964	.963	.870	.9325
3 Miami (6-0)	.887	.905	.980	.9239
4 Auburn (8-0)	.914	.890	.890	.8983
5 Florida State (6-1)	.779	.799	.750	.7759

October 30, 2004

MARYLAND 20 Florida State 17: O-challenged Terrapins (4-4) had scored only 17 pts in 3 losses in row, but charged downfield against nation's no. 8 D to K Nick Novak's 43y FG and never trailed. QB Joel Stratham (21-40/333y, TD, INT) managed 8 completions on 3rd down during game and by H led Maryland to 13-3 edge with 1y TD keeper. Foes traded spectacular 3rd Q TDs: Florida State (6-2) DB Antonio Cromartie angled in front of receiver to make 40y INT TD RET, but Terps countered quickly when TB Josh Allen zigzagged 72y for TD on screen pass. Seminoles sr QB Chris Rix (8-21/140y, TD) reclaimed his 1st-string QB job early in 4th Q, and, although he hit his 1st TD pass of season on fade route to WR Chauncey Stovall midway through 4th Q, he missed several important throws including 3 on last chance from own 27YL.

NORTH CAROLINA 31 Miami 28: Not since October 1978 had all major Florida-based teams lost on same date, but when Tar Heels (4-4) frosh K Conner Barth's nighttime, last-play, 42y FG flew true, undefeated Miami (6-1) joined Florida and Florida State in loss column. North Carolina stayed ahead most of game as 2 players had games of their careers: QB Darian Durant (21-29/266y, 2 TDs) accounted for 330y total O and TB Chad Scott overcame 3rd Q injury to rush for 175y and bullish 9y TD that provided 28-21 lead in 4th Q. QB Brock Berlin (20-35/338y, 2 TDs) rallied Canes for 89y drive in last 5 mins to tie it as WR-RB Devin Hester raced 4y on TD sweep. Durant countered with 4 pass darts and 5y run to set up Barth's FG at end of 65y trip.

Georgia 31 Florida 24 (Jacksonville): Even though Tennessee's 43-29 win over South Carolina gave it inside track to SEC East title, Georgia (7-1) gleefully beat Florida (4-4), which played hard for dethroned, lame duck coach Ron Zook. TE Leonard Pope (3/90y) nabbed 2 scoring throws from QB David Greene (15-23/255y, 3 TDs) in 1st Q, sandwiched around 80y TD trip by Gators to WR Jemalle Cornelius' 21y TD run out of curious spread that sent OTs out wide with WRs. Cornelius caught throw near right sideline and came crossfield in backfield to race to left pylon. Bulldogs were about to put Gators down by 3 TDs with 1st-and-goal at 1YL, but Greene lost handoff FUM, and Florida clawed back to within 24-21 as QB Chris Leak (22-34/247y, 2 TDs) hit 57 and 3y TD tosses. Georgia WR Fred Gibson, prone to dropped passes in 2 games against Florida, made beauty of fingertip TD grab on 3rd down slant-in for 31-21 edge on way for 1st win over Gators in 7 years.

MICHIGAN 45 Michigan State 37 (OT): Spartans (4-4) roared to leads of 17-7 and 27-10 as RB DeAndra Cobb (22/205y, 2 TDs) rocketed for TDs of 72 and 64y. Cobb's latter score came with 8:43 to play in 4th Q and appeared to seal Michigan's doom, even though State's ace QB Drew Stanton (10-13/95y, and 80y rushing) had gone down with 2nd Q shoulder injury. But, Wolverines (8-1) WR Braylon Edwards (11/189y, 3 TDs) made 46y catch to set up 24y FG by K Garrett Rivas and, after onside-KO, caught nearly identical 36 and 21y leaping TDs from QB Chad Henne (24-35/273y, 4 TDs) to knot it at 27-27 and force OT. After trade of FGs and TDs in 2 extra periods, Henne and Edwards hooked up for game-winner from 24YL.

Oklahoma 38 OKLAHOMA STATE 35: Sooners (8-0) WR Mark Bradley caught 3 TD passes in 1st H from QB Jason White (14-26/221y, 2TDs), including unusual grab across middle that he tipped high and far to himself. But, Oklahoma blundered twice in 1st H: WR Mark Clayton's muffed punt catch deep in his end and P Blake Ferguson's dropped snap, and Oklahoma State (6-2) capitalized respectively on QB Donovan Woods' misdirection rollout right for TD and special teamer Brent Jones' EZ REC. Clayton made up for his miscue by making daring punt catch and racing 50y to TD for 28-14 lead in 3rd Q. Cowboys WR Prentice Elliott caught under-thrown TD pass from Woods (8-20/207y, TD), but Sooners TB Adrian Peterson (33/249y, TD) spun out of tackle and raced 80y for TD just after ensuing KO. Cowpokes weren't through: WR D'Juan Woods caught 50y pass to set up TD by TB Vernand Morency (17y/93y, 2 TDs) to pull within 38-35, but K Jason Ricks' 49y FG try with 11 secs to play sailed wide left.

BAYLOR 35 Texas A&M 34 (OT): Perhaps looking ahead to Oklahoma, Texas A&M (6-2) found itself in dogfight with lowly Baylor (3-5), without single win in its last 11 Big 12 games. Aggies QB Reggie McNeal (20-31/268y, INT) threw 2 TD passes, but committed 1st pair of TOs all season; he was nation's only starting QB without INT to date. QB Shawn Bell (32-50/262y, 4 TDs), making his 1st start since end of 2003 season, rallied Bears from behind to win 4 times in 2nd H, including his 6y TD to WR Trent Shelton to send it to OT at 27-27. A&M RB Keith Joseph rambled for 16y TD in 1st OT possession, but Bell rolled right to hit WR Dominique Ziegler (12/121y, 2 TDs) with 12y scoring arrow. In a timeout huddle, Baylor coach Guy Morriss asked his players if they wanted to gamble, and Bell ran same play for surprise 2-pt pass.

CALIFORNIA 27 Arizona State 0: Pac-10's runner-up spot and possible Rose Bowl berth was dominated by D of Golden Bears (6-1), which forced 5 TOs. Cal fell on opening KO FUM at Arizona State (6-2) 24YL, and scored on next play as QB Aaron Rodgers (15-29/165y, TD) found frosh WR Robert Jordan (7/116y, TD) for score in Jordan's 2nd collegiate game. Bears CB Tim Mixon returned INT for 58y TD in 3rd Q as he stepped in front of pass by Sun Devils QB Andrew Walter (25-41/238y, INT), who failed to tie conf career TD pass record of 77, held by Stanford's John Elway. Cal TB J.J. Arrington rushed for 188y and short TD in 4th Q.

USA Today Coaches October 31

1	Southern California (52)	1516	15	Boise State	724
2	Oklahoma (8)	1459	16	Louisville	681
3	Auburn (1)	1409	17	LSU	576
4	Wisconsin	1262	18	Virginia Tech	503
5	Georgia	1221	19	Oklahoma State	352
6	California	1200	20	Iowa	341
7	Texas	1150	21	Southern Mississippi	239
8	Utah	1087	22	Texas A&M	151
9	Michigan	1025	23	Arizona State	144
10	Miami (Fla.)	979	24	Northern Illinois	110
11	Tennessee	931	25	Boston College	102
12	West Virginia	784			
13t	Florida State	743			
13t	Virginia	743			

Bowl Championship Series Ranking November 1

	AP Poll Pct.	USA Today/ESPN Poll Pct.	Computer Pct.	BCS Avg.
1 Southern California (8-0)	.9945	.9941	.980	.9895
2 Oklahoma (8-0)	.9575	.9567	.980	.9648
3 Auburn (9-0)	.9274	.9239	.920	.9238
4 California (6-1)	.8382	.7869	.790	.8050
5 Wisconsin (8-0)	.8363	.8275	.610	.7679

November 6, 2004

VIRGINIA 16 Maryland 0: Coupled with Virginia Tech's 27-24 win over North Carolina and Miami's upset loss, Virginia (7-1) kept itself in battle with Va Tech for ACC crown. Cavs' D came up big as Maryland (4-5) could rush for only 51y compared to Virginia's 295y. Cavaliers TB tandom of Alvin Pearman and Wali Lundy gained 170 and 107y respectively, with Lundy dashing for pair of TDs in 2nd Q. Pearman ran for 49y and zipped for 13y on swing pass to set up Lundy's 4y TD run. After Terps were stopped on 3 plays, Lundy then rambled for 47y of 59y trip to 13-0 lead. Maryland QB Joel Stratham (10-17/115y) was coming off 333y performance, but was picked off twice by Cavs LB Ahmad Brooks.

Clemson 24 MIAMI 17 (OT): Injured-prone TB Frank Gore (105y rushing) raced wide for 23y run to open scoring for Miami (6-2) and followed with 14y power trip off RT in dying moments of 1st H. That gave Canes 17-3 lead, and disappointing Clemson (5-4) was in position to fold its tent. But, Tigers used QB Charlie Whitehurst's 21-37/258y passing and 3 TD bursts posted by young TB Reggie Merriweather (20/114y). Clemson even dusted off fake FG that resulted in K Jad Dean's 6y run to set up tying TD early in 4th Q. Merriweather's 2y TD in OT provided Tigers' 1st lead, and Miami failed on 4th down when WR Lance Leggett appeared to be interfered with in EZ.

Notre Dame 17 TENNESSEE 13: Vols (7-2) led 10-7 as TB Cedric Houston roamed 56y on screen pass in 2nd Q, but QB Erik Ainge (11-18/149y, TD) suffered separated shoulder on last play of 1st H. With other frosh QB, Brent Schaeffer, already on sideline, Tennessee had to go with 3rd-string QB Rick Clausen (10-18/120y, INT). In middle of 3rd Q, pressured Clausen made terrible decision to unload pass over middle, and Notre Dame (6-3) LB Mike Goolsby (sack) grabbed it and headed 26y to EZ for go-ahead pts at 14-10. Irish TE Anthony Fasano had caught 8y TD pass at end of 80y drive in 1st Q from QB Brady Quinn (12-23/118y, TD).

WISCONSIN 38 Minnesota 14: Badgers (9-0) came out of open date ready to play and dominated possession time with 86 to 52 O-play advantage. Wisconsin traveled 80y after initial KO to 1y TD sneak by QB John Stocco (19-26/season-high 297y, TD). WR Jonathan Orr caught 17y TD and TB Anthony Davis (31/124y) followed with short TD runs as Badgers marched 66, 69, and 65y on next 3 possessions to 28-0 lead. Gophers (6-4) fell behind so quickly that they had to abandon their high-powered run attack, which was held to 18/73y. Minnesota QB Bryan Cupito (17-33/258y, TD) avoided shutout with 10y TD pass to WR Ernie Wheelwright late in 2nd Q, and TB Laurence Maroney (8/57y) scored on 31y run on opening series of 3rd Q.

IOWA STATE 34 Nebraska 27: How did Cyclones (5-4) sneak up on Big 12? By reversing 13-game conf losing streak with its 3rd straight win, Iowa State jumped to 10-7 lead in 1st Q enroute to win that tied it with Nebraska (5-4) atop North Div standings. Cyclones sealed it with 93y TD drive in 2nd Q as frosh QB Bret Meyer (17-38/season-best 345y, 3 TDs, INT) connected on passes of 12, 18, 12, 12, and 12y to set up TB Stevie Hicks' 12y TD run. WR Todd Blythe (8/188y) caught 17y TD late in 2nd Q for 24-7 lead for Iowa State. Trailing 34-14 in 4th Q, inconsistent Nebraska QB Joe Dailey (18-42/230y, TD, INT) got going with 46y pass that set up IB Brandon Jackson's 1st of 2 TDs, but last chance was snuffed by ISU LB Tim Dobbins' midfield 15y INT RET.

Oklahoma 42 TEXAS A&M 35: Snorting fire after 2003's 77-0 slaughter by Oklahoma (9-0), Aggies (6-3) smartly mixed their plays and took advantage of multiple talents of QB Reggie McNeal (11-24/213y, 2 TDs, INT), who passed and ran for scores that provided 14-0 and 21-7 leads for Texas A&M. Also, A&M coach Dennis Franchione employed fake punt in which P Jacob Young tossed wide pass to WR Earvin Taylor, who charged down right sideline for 71y TD that extended 2nd Q edge to 28-14. Back to receive 2nd H KO, Aggies WR Terrence Murphy lost ball in late afternoon sun and allowed KO to land at 10YL where Sooners gobbled it up. OU QB Jason White (19-35/292y, 5 TDs), looking every bit like defending Heisman Trophy winner, quickly found WR Mark Bradley for 11y TD that tied it 28-28 only 52 secs into 3rd Q. White hit TE Bubba Moses near left edge of EZ for 35-28 lead, but Aggie rallied to tie it on fake FG pass by holder Chad Schroeder and counted on former walk-on QB Ty Brandon, in for injured McNeal. But it was White who stepped up nimbly in pocket to whip laser throw over middle to Bradley, who spun away for winning 39y TD with 6:43 to play.

TEXAS 56 Oklahoma State 35: Cowpokes (6-3) led 35-7 in 2nd Q, only to have RB Cedric Benson lead Longhorns' largest comeback in history by scoring 5 TDs among his 31/141y rushing. Star Texas (8-1) LB Derrick Johnson (15 tackles) admitted his team made some early mistakes: TB Vernand Morency (20/100y, TD) raced 34y on 4th down pitchout to spark Cowboys' opening drive to TD and beautifully threaded his way for 68y TD on flat pass for 14-7 lead midway in 1st Q. Morency added 13y TD run, and Oklahoma State NG Clay Cole batted pass into LB Pagitte McGee's hands to set up 1y keeper for 28-7 lead by QB Donovan Woods (12-18/224y, TD, INT). Horns QB Vincent Young hit 7-8 passes on 80y drive to TE Bo Scaife's 5y TD grab that pulled Texas within 35-7 as teams headed to H. Benson notched 4 TDs as Texas scored on 6 series in row and its D kept OSU to 105y O in 2nd H.

CALIFORNIA 28 Oregon 27: WR Keith Allen's dropped 4th down pass with 1:38 to play inside Cal 25YL seemingly would have put Ducks (5-4) in winning FG position, so Golden Bears (7-1) survived scare at Berkeley. TB J.J. Arrington (26/188y, TD) got California rolling with 30y TD sprint in 1st Q, but red-hot Oregon QB Kellen Clemens (19-33/218y, 4 TDs) hit 1st of 2 TD throws to TE Tim Day to tie it 7-7 in 1st Q. Ducks FB Dante Rosario sneaked out of backfield to collar Clemens' 38y TD pass, and, when popup KO was mishandled by Cal, Ducks recovered to set up Day's 2nd TD catch on opening Q. But, K Jared Siegel hit right upright with conv kick, so Oregon led 20-14. Down 27-21 at H after Ducks gained 302y, Bears in 2nd H allowed 62y and made drives of 55, 42, 70, and 53y. They came away with WR Geoff McArthur's 2nd TD catch from QB Aaron Rodgers (21-32/275y, 3 TDs). McArthur caught 8/121y, 2 TDs.

Southern California 28 OREGON STATE 20: Beavers (4-5) emerged from chilly, pea-soup afternoon fog at Corvallis with 13-0 lead. Oregon State earned 6-0 lead in 1st Q on K Alexis Serna's FGs of 25 and 33y, 1st of which was mined from punt FUM by star Trojans TB Reggie Bush at USC 18YL. Beavers next went 65y to 1st of 2 TD passes by QB Derek Anderson (22-51/330y, 2 INTs). TE Dominique Byrd made brilliant 1-handed EZ grab late in 2nd Q to get Southern California (9-0) on board, and when Trojans kept possession for more than 11 mins in 3rd Q, it came back to pay in form of Byrd's 25y TD reception for 14-13 lead. Bush made amends with 65y punt TD RET for 21-13 lead that was extended later in 4th Q by TB LenDale White's 5y TD run.

UTAH 63 Colorado State 31: Utah (8-0) exceeded 50 pts for 3rd straight week, but when it dropped to 7th in Monday's BCS rankings—and thus likely to be denied big money BCS bowl—coach Urban Meyer told USA Today system was "officially a failure." Utes' scoring machine hardly failed: QB Alex Smith (21-26/291y) passed for 4 TDs, RB Marty Johnson rammed over for 3 short TDs, and DB Morgan Scalley returned FUM 88y to score in 1st Q. Utah led 42-10 at H and 56-10 at end of 3rd Q. Colorado State (3-6) Caleb Hanie (11-25/190y, 2 TDs, 3 INTs) passed 24y and ran 48y to lead cosmetic 21-pt outburst in 4th Q.

USA Today Coaches November 7

1	Southern California (50)	1514	14	Louisville	727
2	Oklahoma (10)	1452	15	LSU	649
3	Auburn (1)	1416	16	Virginia Tech	582
4	Wisconsin	1289	17	Miami (Fla.)	568
5	Georgia	1233	18	Tennessee	466
6	California	1203	19	Iowa	450
7	Texas	1169	20	Arizona State	331
8	Utah	1124	21	Boston College	244
9	Michigan	1060	22	Northern Illinois	205
10	West Virginia	886	23	Texas A&M	150
11	Virginia	877	24	Oklahoma State	138
12	Florida State	868	25	Texas Tech	112
13	Boise State	782			

Bowl Championship Series Rankings November 8

	AP Poll Pct.	USA Today/ESPN Poll Pct.	Computer Pct.	BCS Avg.
1 Southern California (9-0)	.9914	.9928	.970	.9847
2 Oklahoma (9-0)	.9569	.9521	.990	.9664
3 Auburn (9-0)	.9305	.9285	.870	.9097
4 California (7-1)	.8252	.7889	.860	.8247
5 Wisconsin (9-0)	.8517	.8452	.700	.7990

November 13, 2004

Boston College 36 WEST VIRGINIA 17: Mountaineers (8-2), all but handed Big East title in preseason, were handed comeuppance by unheralded Boston College (7-2). Special teams played big factor for Eagles as frosh DB DeJuan Tribble raced up to nab line drive punt and gallop 41y to TD that built 14-0 margin in 1st Q. DB Will Blackmon charged 71y with another punt TD RET in 4th Q for BC's last score. West Virginia QB Rasheed Marshall (21-35/224y, TD, INT) accounted for 324y total O and found WR Chris Henry (8/118y) for 3rd Q TD pass that pulled WVU to within 27-14 and gave Henry new school record with 12 TD catches in season. BC QB Paul Peterson passed 18-30/162y with TDs to RB L.V. Whitworth and TE David Kashetta in 1st H.

Miami 31 VIRGINIA 21: TB Frank Gore rushed 28/career-best 195y to lead Miami (7-2), including game's opening TD run. Cavaliers (7-2) star TE Heath Miller made 1-handed grab on EZ crossing pattern to tie it 7-7 in 2nd Q. Virginia TB Alvin Pearman earned another deadlock at 14-14 with 34y TD romp in 3rd Q, but Miami WR Roscoe Parrish wriggled away from tacklers to race 62y on punt TD RET for 24-14 edge midway in 4th Q. Still seeking defining victory in new ACC, 1st place Cavs rode QB Marques Hagans' 47y scramble to TB Wali Lundy's short TD blast with 3:19 to play. Virginia hopes were dashed when QB Brock Berlin (18-33/177y, 2 TDs) launched 44y strike on 3rd-and-5 from his 35YL on way to Parrish's 25y TD grab, on which he made tremendous adjustment while falling in EZ.

DUKE 16 Clemson 13: Rare incident of losing to Duke (2-8) after beating Miami befell up-and-down Clemson (5-5). K Michael Brooks bombed 53y FG as time expired to lift conf cellar-dwelling Blue Devils to triumph. Brooks, who earlier clicked on FGs of 21 and 27y, was put in position by Duke CB Deonto McCormick's midfield INT after Tigers WR Michael Collins fell down in pursuit of pass by QB Charlie Whitehurst (12-26/117y, 2 INTs). TB Reggie Merriweather had scored early in 4th Q to give Clemson 13-6 lead, but passing of Devils QB Mike Schneider (20-31/213y, TD) led way in last 5 mins.

AUBURN 24 Georgia 6: Auburn (10-0) dominated no. 5 Georgia (8-2) in season's most important matchup to date. When Sunday's AP Poll was released, Tigers had tied Oklahoma for no. 2 in poll, 1st such tie in history, but still trailed in BCS formula for all-important runner-up spot. Auburn's superb TB tandem, Cadillac Williams (19/101y, TD) and Ronnie Brown (7/88y, TD receiving), sparkled. Williams was on throwing end of surprise 2nd Q TD that built 14-0 lead: WR Anthony Mix filtered through maze at scrimmage line as would-be blocker and was all alone to haul in Williams' perfect 29y TD pass. Georgia QB David Greene (15-22/159y, TD, INT) broke shutout possibility with 6y score to TE Leonard Pope with 2:13 to play. Bulldogs were outgained 404y to 279y and suffered EZ INT by Tigers CB Carlos Rogers in 2nd Q.

MICHIGAN STATE 49 Wisconsin 14: Except for TB Anthony Davis' early 45y TD breakaway, things went badly for unbeaten Wisconsin (9-1), which had permitted only 9 TDs all season. Michigan State (5-5) exploded to 7 TDs, including blocked punt for 14-7 lead 6 mins from 1st Q's end. It really was last 7 mins of 2nd Q that projected Spartans past Badgers: Wisconsin DE Erasmus James seemed to explode Michigan State reverse, but somehow flat-footed QB Jason Teague flipped ball to WR Aaron Alexander and had sense to get up from James' tackle and sprint into open field to haul in Alexander's 30y TD pass. Still, Badgers had chance to tie it just before H, but Davis was stopped at GL, and Big 10 replay system failed to overturn what might have been score. Spartans romped to 4 TDs in 2nd H including TB DeAndra Cobb's 55y sprint.

Penn State 22 INDIANA 18: Indiana (3-7) used 26y TD dash by TB Courtney Roby and 46y INT TD RET by LB Kyle Killion (10 tackles, sack) to prompt 13-7 H edge. Penn State (3-7) had not won road game since its 2002 visit to Bloomington but won on 2 short TD runs by QB Zack Mills (11-19/169y, TD, INT) and TB Tony Hunt in 2nd H. But it was clutch GLS on heels of CB Anwar Phillips' saving tackle at 1YL that clinched beleaguered Joe Paterno's 342nd victory after 6 straight losses. Lions, 1 of only 3 Div 1-A teams whose D hadn't given up 3 TDs in any game, faced loss of that distinction as well as loss of game when Indiana, trailing 22-16, made 1st down at State 1YL in late going. Penn State stopped 4 cracks at line and conceded safety as clock expired.

Iowa 29 MINNESOTA 27: For 1st time in NCAA history, pair of backs—Gophers' Laurence Maroney and Marion Barber—rushed for 1,000y in second straight season. But, as Minnesota (6-5), which couldn't pass (9-17/73y, 3 INTs) appeared on its way to ground march to winning FG, Iowa (8-2) LB Chad Greenway (8 tackles, INT) shot into backfield to throw Barber for 4y loss with 56 sec left. Loss of y and high snap forced K Rhys Lloyd to hurry 51y FG attempt that missed. Earlier, Hawkeyes, who couldn't run (27/6y) because injuries left only 6th-string TB, owned 16-3 and 23-10 leads in 1st H thanks to 41 and 60y TD arrows by tenacious QB Drew Tate (24-39/333y, 2 TDs). But, Maroney (19/156y) scored on dashes of 79, 37, and 5y. His last TD came with 4:40 to play and pulled Gophers to within 29-27, but Greenway's big tackle thwarted plans.

Texas 27 KANSAS 23: No. 6 Longhorns (9-1) barely escaped trip to Lawrence, thanks in part to TB Cedric Benson's 161y rushing, including 16y TD sortie in 2nd Q. Still, tenacious Jayhawkers (3-7) led 9-7 at H on 3 medium-range FGs by K Johnny Beck. Trailing 13-9, Kansas used sub QB Brian Luke's 14-25/225y, TD passing to pair of 4th Q TDs and 23-13 edge with 7:41 to go. Texas went 87y behind QB Vince Young, who registered TD on 18y run. Kansas appeared to salt it away at 23-20 with WR Charles Gordon's catch, but O pass interference call reversed 1st down. Coach Mark Mangino complained bitterly afterward that officials wanted to enhance Texas' BCS chances, but soon apologized. Young scrambled for 1st down on 4th-and-18 and lofted 21y TD pass to WR Tony Jeffrey, who cut across EZ for winning catch.

Utah 45 WYOMING 28: Football's other "BCS-buster," Boise State, wished to impress Easterners on TV but had to struggle to beat San Jose State in double OT in earliest morning start in collegiate history. On other hand, unbeaten Utah (10-0) weathered hour-and-half power delay that sent its game deep into chilly Wyoming (6-4) night. Utes' O power never blacked out as QB Alex Smith (17-27/244y, 3 TDs) rushed for 14/90y, including 27y TD canter after LB Corey Dodds recovered FUM on game's 2nd play. Cowboys turned it over 3 of 1st 4 possessions, and Utah dashed to 31-7 H lead, surge interrupted only by Wyoming QB Corey Bramlet's 59y TD pass to WR Jovon Bouknight. Utes DB Morgan Scalley's 6th INT of season poised Smith's 1st TD pass.

USA Today Coaches November 14

1	Southern California (51)	1514	14	LSU	771
2	Oklahoma (6)	1435	15	Virginia Tech	688
3	Auburn (4)	1433	16	Tennessee	580
4	California	1311	17	Iowa	519
5	Texas	1222	18	Virginia	501
6	Utah	1203	19	Boston College	433
7	Michigan	1191	20	West Virginia	419
8	Florida State	999	21	Arizona State	411
9	Wisconsin	948	22	Texas A&M	272
10	Georgia	947	23	Oklahoma State	229
11	Louisville	880	24	Bowling Green	117
12	Boise State	827	25	Texas-El Paso	87
13	Miami (Fla.)	774			

	AP Poll Pct.	*USA Today*/ESPN Poll Pct.	Computer Pct.	BCS Avg.
1 Southern California (10-0)	.9895	.9928	.960	.9808
2 Oklahoma (10-0)	.9452	.9410	1.000	.9621
3 Auburn (10-0)	.9452	.9397	.920	.9350
4 California (8-1)	.8671	.8597	.830	.8522
5 Texas (9-1)	.8006	.8013	.840	.8140

November 20, 2004

Florida 20 FLORIDA STATE 13: While field at Doak Campbell Stadium was being named for beloved Florida State (8-3) coach Bobby Bowden, Gators' deposed mentor Ron Zook accomplished what his revered predecessor Steve Spurrier could not. Zook won at Seminoles' home field. Florida scored midway through 1st Q on QB Chris Leak's 13y arrow to WR Chad Jackson and never trailed. Down 10-0 with 17 secs before H, FSU got on board on K Gary Cismesia's 20y 3-ptr. After Gators made another FG for 13-3 lead early in 4th Q, Seminoles went 80y: Sr QB Chris Rix (9-16/150y, TD, INT) came off bench to captain 27y broken-play TD throw to WR Chauncey Stovall. Florida TB Ciatrick Fason (24/103y) burst for 8y TD, and S Jarvis Herring made late-game INT at Gators 8YL to halt FSU's rally.

Auburn 21 ALABAMA 13: Would Auburn's dreary 1st H, in which Alabama (6-5) took 6-0 lead on pair of FGs by K Brian Bostick, cost Tigers poll pts in wicked battle with Oklahoma for spot in BCS title game? Tigers (11-0) came through with 3 TDs in 2nd H as TBs Carnell Williams and Ronnie Brown scored 5 and 2y TDs respectively. In between, QB Jason Campbell (18-24/224y, TD, INT) whipped 32y TD to WR Courtney Taylor (4/89y) at end of 58y drive. Crimson Tide tested nation's best score-prevention D with 84y drive in dying moments. Bama scored on QB Spencer Pennington's 18y pass, but Taylor recovered onside-KO for Auburn in last 1:30.

OHIO STATE 37 Michigan 21: Scoring its most pts against Michigan (9-2) since 1968, Ohio State (7-4) upset its biggest rival. Key to victory was emergence of QB Troy Smith (13-24/241y), who threw for 2 TDs and scored once on ground among his 18/145y. After Smith's 68y TD pass opened scoring, Wolverines tallied on next 2 possessions on TD pass by QB Chad Henne (27-54/328y, 2 TDs, 2 INTs) and 1y TD smash off RT by TB Mike Hart. Game's signature play came on NCAA-record tying 4th punt TD RET by Buckeyes WR Ted Ginn, who raced 82y for 27-14 lead with 9:56 remaining in 3rd Q. WR Braylon Edwards caught 11/172y, TD to lead Michigan.

IOWA 30 Wisconsin 7: Results were in from Columbus, and Wisconsin (9-2) had Rose Bowl opportunity in its hands. After Iowa (9-2) QB Drew Tate (15-24/186y, 3 TDs, 3 INTs) pitched 1st Q score to WR Clinton Solomon (6/100y, 2 TDs), Badgers tied it at 7-7 early in 2nd Q as TB Stanley Booker plunged 4y. But, Hawkeyes scored within 5 plays with 1:00 on H clock as Solomon got loose deep over middle for 51y scoring strike from Tate. After another Tate TD pass in 3rd Q, K Kyle Schlicher hit 3 FGs. Wisconsin's loss sent Michigan to Pasadena and Iowa into Big 10 title tie.

Iowa State 37 KANSAS STATE 23: Unappreciated Iowa State (6-4) dropped stunning 3-TD avalanche on Kansas State (4-7) in game's last 3:24. While Wildcats finished worst season since 1992, Cyclones took step to Big 12 North title. Iowa State QB Bret Meyer (16-30/234y, TD) scored on keeper with less than 10 mins to play to pull within 23-16 and hit 51y pass to lead to his 3y TD toss to give ISU 23-23 tie with 3:24 to go. K-State had good field position after KO went OB, but QB Allen Webb (4-12/42y, INT) lost quick FUM, and Cyclones went ahead on 20y burst by TB Stevie Hicks (29/156y, TD). TB Darren Sproules rushed for 167y and scored TD in his last Cats game.

UTAH 52 Brigham Young 21: Utah (11-0) completed its 1st undefeated season since 1930 and all but wrapped up 1st-ever spot in BCS bowl for team outside major 6 confs. Utes QB Alex Smith hit 16-24/184y, TD, but threw 2 INTs to double his remarkable season's total to 4 pick-offs. Utes RB Quinton Ganther rushed 11/122y, but it was WR Steve Savoy who caught 20y TD pass and scored on 2 runs, including spectacular, weaving 92y tally on which he came in motion to take option pitchout from Smith. BYU (5-6) QB John Beck (17-32/213y, 2 TDs) threw short TD pass in 1st Q to tie game at 7-7, and RB Curtis Brown (18/84y) slipped 6y for 2nd Q TD that knotted it at 14-14.

TEXAS-EL PASO 57 Southern Methodist 27: Rejuvenated coach Mike Price blurted, "I've got my bowling shoes...I finally mentioned the 'B' word" as surprising Texas-El Paso (8-2) clinched bowl berth. SMU (3-8) had modest 2-game win streak snapped but not before jumping to 20-10 lead as QBs Tony Eckert (7-13/76y, INT) and Jerad Romo (14-20/158y) each tossed TD pass. UTEP rallied to take 24-20 H lead and scored 28 pts in 3rd Q. WR Johnnie Lee Higgins nabbed 5y TD pass from QB Jordan Palmer (20-27/career-high 339y, 5 TDs), and after successful onside-KO, Higgins caught quick 45y TD to raise score to 38-20.

USA Today Coaches November 21

1 Southern California (48)	1510	
2 Oklahoma (7)	1440	
3 Auburn (6)	1436	
4 California	1299	
5 Texas	1260	
6 Utah	1246	
7 Georgia	1092	
8 Louisville	1021	
9 Miami (Fla.)	950	
10 Boise State	887	
11 Virginia Tech	849	
12 LSU	841	
13 Michigan	813	
14 Iowa	704	
15 Tennessee	684	
16 Virginia	569	
17 Florida State	562	
18 Wisconsin	507	
19 Boston College	478	
20 Arizona State	421	
21 West Virginia	405	
22 Texas A&M	274	
23 Oklahoma State	230	
24 Bowling Green	141	
25 Texas-El Paso	104	

	AP Poll Pct.	*USA Today*/ESPN Poll Pct.	Computer Pct.	BCS Avg.
1 Southern California (10-0)	.9865	.9902	.960	.9789
2 Oklahoma (11-0)	.9483	.9443	1.000	.9642
3 Auburn (11-0)	.9452	.9416	.920	.9352
4 California (9-1)	.8695	.8518	.830	.8504
5 Texas (9-1)	.8142	.8262	.850	.8301

November 25-27, 2004

(Th'g) PITTSBURGH 16 West Virginia 13: Panthers (7-3) QB Tyler Palko (14-38/165y, INT) followed his 5-TD performance against Notre Dame by having dreary passing night until do-or-die 4th Q possession. West Virginia (8-3), hunting for Big East title, got off to 10-0 lead in 1st Q on TB Jason Colson's 6y TD sweep and K Brad Cooper's 26y FG. Pitt, stumbling on O despite TB Tim Murphy's career-high 106y rushing, could manage only K Josh Cummings' 37, 35, and 20y FGs to trail 13-9 through 3rd Q. Panthers gained possession at their 27YL with 10 mins left, and Palko hit 6 passes, including 3/38y by WR Greg Lee (8/124y). Palko rolled right for 2y TD keeper with 4 mins to go. WVU QB Rasheed Marshall (18/104y rushing) missed 4th down pass from Pitt 33YL after nearly catching TD on double reverse moments earlier.

(Fri) Colorado 26 NEBRASKA 20: After many ups and downs of off-season scandal and mid-season 1-4 slump, Buffaloes (7-4) stayed in contention for Big 12 North crown. QB Joel Klatt (18-29/222y, TD, INT) threaded 6y TD pass to WR Blake Mackey at right edge of EZ on Colorado's 1st possession. After K Mason Crosby booted 1st of his 4 FGs, Buffs sent TB Bobby Purify (22/130y) on beautifully blocked 9y TD run in 2nd Q after he swept right and reversed left. Nebraska (5-6) QB Joe Dailey (29-55/306y, 2 TDs, 4 INTs) had another shaky day but slithered to 2y TD scramble in 2nd Q to keep Huskers within 20-7 at H. Dailey hit 2 late TD passes, but they were not enough.

(Fri) TEXAS 26 Texas A&M 13: Teams traded 1st Q TDs with neither connecting on x-pt, so when Texas (10-1) threatened at Aggies (7-4) 1YL it was trying to unknot 6-6 tie. Longhorns QB Vince Young leapt to reach ball across GL, only to have it bound to Texas A&M CB Jonte Buhl, who cut left and charged 98y to TD and 13-6 lead with 10 secs before H. Despite this reversal, Texas was up to task as S Michael Griffin blocked punt early in 3rd Q for frosh S Bobby Tatum to run in for 10y TD. Due to bad snap, conv kick by K Dusty Mangum (2 FGs in 3rd Q) was drilled horribly low, but Horns tied it when Aggies recovered and fumbled into its EZ for rare 1-pt safety. Texas turned attack over to TB Cedric Benson, who rushed for 33/165y and clinching 1y TD run in 4th Q and Young (19/93y, TD rushing). LB Derrick Johnson led Longhorns D that sacked A&M QB Reggie McNeal (20-38/247yTD, INT) 8 times and held Aggies to 94y total O in 2nd H, when Texas came from behind for 3rd game in row.

(Fri) ARIZONA 34 Arizona State 27: Arizona (3-8) was scoring only 13 pts per game, but riled-up Cats were at their best. Frosh QB Richard Kovalcheck passed 17-31/239y, 3 TDs, INT to outduel Arizona State (8-3) QB Andrew Walter (23-38/320y, INT), who was knocked out in 4th Q. Wildcats led 20-17 at H as Kovalcheck pitched 54y TD to TE Steve Fleming as UA capitalized on 2 FUM RECs. ASU also profited with TOs, including DL Jimmy Verdon's 24y FUM TD RET. Sun Devils fought back and appeared poised to retake lead, but TB Hakim Hill (19/85y, TD) had FUM squirt into Cats' EZ for touchback. Arizona answered with 80y TD drive, sparked by TB Mike Bell's 57y run. Wildcats WR Mike Jefferson made fine adjustment to underthrown pass and scored on 47y play for 34-20 lead with 9:32 to go. ASU QB Sam Keller replaced Walter on 80y TD march, but his 4th down pass failed at Cats 10YL in last 2 mins.

Syracuse 43 BOSTON COLLEGE 17: With Big East title in their hands, Eagles (8-3) D, with good 114y rush avg, was burned in terrible 1st Q: Syracuse (6-5) sprung backup TB Damien Rhodes to career-best 69y TD romp on game's 1st series. When Rhodes joined starting TB Walter Reyes briefly on sideline, DB Diamond Ferri (28/141y, 2 TDs rushing, and 44y INT TD RET in 4th Q) went to TB and chipped in with brilliant 2-way play. Early in 2nd Q, Boston College, playing last conf game before going to ACC, failed to stop Ferri on 4th down TD run of 4y. Down 24-3 in last min of 1st H, Eagles frosh LB Brian Toal, who earlier committed 2 harmful PENs, blocked punt, and DB DeJuan Tribble scooted to TD RET. But, momentum failed to turn because Syracuse K Collin Barber kicked his 2nd and 3rd FGs for 30-10 lead until BC, struggling on O without injured QB Paul Peterson, finally got TD on TD pass by frosh QB Matt Ryan.

VIRGINIA TECH 24 Virginia 10: After scoreless 1st H, Cavaliers (8-3) wasted 78y dash by TB Alvin Pearman (28/147y) on lost FUM but still led 7-3 deep into 3rd Q on Pearman's subsequent leaping 32y TD catch. Playing his last home game, QB Bryan Randall (16-22/200y, 2 TDs) became all-time Hokies (9-2) pass y leader. He threw 45y TD bomb to WR Josh Hyman in 3rd Q, and combo clicked again on 32y TD for 17-10 lead in 4th Q. C Will Montgomery threw 2 blocks to spring TB Cedric Humes up middle for clinching 37y TD that lifted Va Tech's lead to 24-10 with 5 mins to go. Soon thereafter, DE Darryl Tapp fell on FUM to seal win and set up Miami showdown.

Missouri 17 IOWA STATE 14 (OT): Disappointing Missouri (5-6) showed up with strong D in chilly Ames and led 14-7 after QB Brad Smith (13-24/150y, INT) raced 36y for TD in 3rd Q. Cyclones (6-5) were able to tie it 14-14 midway in 4th Q when TB Stevie Hicks (24/49y) banged off right side for 2y TD. Iowa State S Steve Paris later picked up FUM and rambled 51y to Missouri 15YL. TD-saving tackle on Paris came from hustling Tigers QB Brad Smith (13-24/150y, INT). K Bret Culbertson missed badly to right on 24y FG try with 1:05 to go. After K Adam Crossert made FG on Missouri's OT possession, Iowa State frosh QB Bret Meyer (16-26/206y, INT) underthrew fade pass to EZ, and CB A.J. Kincade made INT. Cyclones' loss sent Colorado to Big 12 championship tilt and deprived ISU of chance at its 1st title since 1912.

SOUTHERN CALIFORNIA 41 Notre Dame 10: Rain in LA Coliseum arrived for USC game for 1st time since 1987. As with last 2 meetings, Fighting Irish (6-5) started well. Irish sprung heavy-duty TB Ryan Grant (15/94y) early, and QB Brady Quinn (15-29/105y, TD) hit passes to 6 different receivers before spotting TE Billy Palmer on crossing TD pass. Behind 10-3, no. 1 Southern California (11-0) finally exploded: QB Matt Leinart (24-34/400y, 5 TDs) looked left and threw right for TD to WR Dwayne Jarrett (2 TDs) to tie it 10-10 in 2nd Q. TB Reggie Bush scored tilt's signature TD by creating dazzling 69y run off short pass from Leinart that built 27-10 lead in 3rd Q. Comfortably ahead 34-10 in 4th Q, USC tried pass off fake-punt that produced 1st down when receiver was interfered with. Leinart followed with his 5th TD toss, 23y to sr WR Jason Mitchell. Defeat soon would cost ND coach Tyrone Willingham his job.

1	Southern California (48)	1509	14	Iowa	787
2	Oklahoma (6)	1442	15	Tennessee	706
3	Auburn (7)	1435	16	Florida State	606
4	California	1314	17	Wisconsin	568
5	Texas	1266	18	Virginia	411
6	Utah	1222	19	Florida	251
7	Georgia	1100	20	Texas Tech	208
8	Louisville	1038	21	Pittsburgh	193
9	Miami (Fla.)	983	22	Ohio State	172
10	Boise State	926	23	Arizona State	167
11	Virginia Tech	915	24	West Virginia	158
12	LSU	887	25	Texas A&M	152
13	Michigan	824			

Bowl Championship Series Rankings November 29

		AP Poll Pct.	*USA Today*/ESPN Poll Pct.	Computer Pct.	BCS Avg.
1	Southern California (11-0)	.9908	.9895	.970	.9813
2	Oklahoma (11-0)	.9477	.9456	.990	.9611
3	Auburn (11-0)	.9415	.9415	.920	.9342
4	California (9-1)	.8677	.8616	.800	.8431
5	Texas (10-1)	.8154	.8302	.880	.8418

December 4, 2004

Navy 42 Army 13 (Philadelphia): After scoreless 1st Q, Middies FB Kyle Eckel, who charged for career-best 179y rushing, scored 23y TD to create 14-0 lead. QB Aaron Polonco (7-11/100y, 2 TDs) also scored on run for Navy (9-2). Big play soon was made by Navy S Josh Smith, who jumped to snare INT of soft lob by Black Knights (2-9) QB Zac Dahman (20-39/163y, 2 TDs, INT) and ramble 67y to TD that built 21-0 lead in 2nd Q. Navy's victory, which knotted America's most competitive series at 49-49-7, was all but assured by its 28-7 H bulge. Army frosh WR Jeremy Trimble made nimble catch in back of EZ in last 22 secs of explosive 2nd Q.

Virginia Tech 16 MIAMI 10: Hokies (10-2), universal pre-season pick for 6th place in new ACC, won their 8th straight game to capture conf title. Hurricanes (8-3) were miffed that Virginia Tech had waved "ACC Champions" sign week before and blocked punt and x-pt, former led to 14y drive to TD run by TB Tyrone Moss for 7-7 tie. Game was knotted 10-10 when frosh WR Eddie Royal authored 18y punt RET to 39YL and caught TD pass on next play from QB Bryan Randall (11-18/148y, 2 TDs). Miami, attempting to secure 5th straight BCS berth, instead lost its home finale for only 2nd time since 1985. Canes saw it last possession die on downs in their territory as 3 passes by QB Brock Berlin (16-31/139y, INT) were tipped, 2 by Tech DT Jim Davis.

Auburn 38 Tennessee 28 (Atlanta): Auburn (12-0) scored on its opening 2 tries in SEC title game: TB Carnel Williams (19/100y) lost FUM into EZ for TD and soon slanted left behind kick-out block of LT Marcus McNeill. Volunteers (9-3) gained only 39y—to Auburn's 303y—in 1st H but had used dropped punt snap to take over at Tigers 14YL, and score in 4 plays. Tennessee trailed 21-7 at H but came up big in 2nd H. Early in 3rd Q, Vols were frustrated by PEN that ruined 70y TD run, but were right back at 14YL on FUM REC. WR Robert Meacham made diving TD grab to pull Tennessee within 21-14. TB Gerald Riggs (11/182y, 2 TDs) dashed 80y to tying TD in 3rd Q, but Vols continued to commit costly PENs. Auburn QB Jason Campbell (27-35/374y, 3 TDs, INT) wrapped up his greatest passing game with pair of TD bombs of 53y to WR Devin Aromashodu and 43y to WR Ben Obomanu, which reinvigorated flagging Tigers' D. Vols LB Omar Gaither made 18 tackles to help put lid on Tigers run attack (99y in 2nd H), while Vols rushed 233y total. Win clinched Auburn's 1st SEC crown since 1989, but narrow margin in no way advanced its BCS title game hopes.

Oklahoma 42 Colorado 3 (Kansas City): Big 12 championship game turned out as 1-sided as feared: Oklahoma (12-0) QB Jason White (22-29/254y, 3 TDs, 2 INTs) smartly clicked on 3 TD passes in opening 15:07 of 1st H on way to 28-0 lead. WR Mark Clayton made dandy fingertip catch early in 2nd Q. Sooners then turned matters over to TB Adrian Peterson, who scored 3 TDs among his 28/172y rushing. Meanwhile, Colorado (7-5) managed only single 1st down in 1st H, finishing with only 3 1st downs. Buffaloes roamed for meager 46y total O, but avoided shutout with stellar K Mason Crosby's 34y 3-ptr. TB Bobby Purify was held to 12/7y rushing for Buffs.

Southern California 29 UCLA 24: Trojans (12-0) blasted to quick 10-0 lead as superb TB Reggie Bush (15/204y and 334y all-purpose) broke away for 65y TD gallop on game's 2nd snap. UCLA (6-5) soon fired up its special teams: WR Craig Bragg roared up middle to set new school record with 96y punt TD RET, and when DB Chris Horton blocked punt on next USC possession, Bruins had 1st down deep in Troy end. But Trojans held and widened lead to 17-7 when Bush bolted 81y to score. On big call just before H, Bruins thought they had FUM RET for TD that would have tied it. Instead, USC K Ryan Killeen hit 1 of his 5 FGs for 20-10 lead. Big UCLA FB Manuel White blasted off right side for TD late in 3rd Q to pull within 23-17. Down 29-17, UCLA drove

to QB Drew Olson's 4th down lob TD pass to TE Marcedes Lewis. Bruins had last chance on FUM REC by LB Spencer Havner (6 tackles for 125 for season) but quickly turned it over on Olson's INT.

1	Southern California (35.33)	1490	14	Miami (Fla.)	738
2	Oklahoma (16.33)	1459	15	Florida State	643
3	Auburn (9.33)	1435	16	Wisconsin	599
4	California	1286	17	Tennessee	559
5	Texas	1281	18	Virginia	455
6	Utah	1215	19	Florida	324
7	Georgia	1117	20	Pittsburgh	318
8	Louisville	1066	21	Texas Tech	234
9	Virginia Tech	1037	22	Ohio State	181
10	Boise State	943	23	West Virginia	177
11	LSU	932	24	Arizona State	173
12	Michigan	874	25	Texas A&M	147
13	Iowa	812			

Bowl Championship Series Rankings December 5

		AP Poll Pct.	*USA Today*/ESPN Poll Pct.	Computer Pct.	BCS Avg.
1	Southern California (12-0)	.9840	.9770	.970	.9770
2	Oklahoma (12-0)	.9575	.9567	.990	.9681
3	Auburn (12-0)	.9385	.9410	.920	.9331
4	Texas (10-1)	.8228	.8400	.880	.8476
5	California (10-1)	.8609	.8433	.800	.8347

Conference Standings

Big East

Pittsburgh	4-2
Boston College	4-2
West Virginia	4-2
Syracuse	4-2
Connecticut	3-3
Rutgers	1-5
Temple	1-5

Atlantic Coast

Virginia Tech	7-1
Florida State	6-2
Miami	5-3
Virginia	5-3
North Carolina	5-3
Georgia Tech	4-4
Clemson	4-4
Maryland	3-5
North Carolina State	3-5
Wake Forest	1-7
Duke	1-7

Southeastern

EAST	
Tennessee	7-1
Georgia	6-2
Florida	4-4
South Carolina	4-4
Kentucky	1-7
Vanderbilt	1-7
WEST	
Auburn	8-0
Louisiana State	6-2
Alabama	3-5
Mississippi	3-5
Arkansas	3-5
Mississippi State	2-6

Conference USA

Louisville	8-0
Alabama-Birmingham	5-3
Southern Mississippi	5-3
Memphis	5-3
Cincinnati	5-3
Tulane	3-5
Houston	3-5
South Florida	3-5
Texas Christian	3-5
Army	2-6
East Carolina	2-6

Big Ten

Michigan	7-1
Iowa	7-1
Wisconsin	6-2
Northwestern	5-3
Purdue	4-4
Ohio State	4-4
Michigan State	4-4
Minnesota	3-5
Penn State	2-6
Illinois	1-7
Indiana	1-7

Mid-American

EAST	
Miami (Ohio)	7-1
Akron	6-2
Marshall	6-2
Kent State	4-4
Ohio University	2-6
Buffalo	2-6
Central Florida	0-8
WEST	
Toledo	7-1
Northern Illinois	7-1
Bowling Green	6-2
Eastern Michigan	4-4
Central Michigan	3-5
Ball State	2-6
Western Michigan	0-8

Big Twelve

NORTH	
Colorado	4-4
Iowa State	4-4
Nebraska	3-5
Missouri	3-5
Kansas	2-6
Kansas State	2-6
SOUTH	
Oklahoma	8-0
Texas	7-1
Texas A&M	5-3
Texas Tech	5-3
Oklahoma State	4-4
Baylor	1-7

Mountain West

Utah	7-0
New Mexico	5-2
Brigham Young	4-3
Wyoming	3-4
Air Force	3-4
Colorado State	3-4
San Diego State	2-5
Nevada-Las Vegas	1-6

Western Athletic		Pacific-10	
Boise State	8-0	Southern California	8-0
Texas-El Paso	6-2	California	7-1
Fresno State	5-3	Arizona State	5-3
Louisiana Tech	5-3	Oregon State	5-3
Hawaii	4-4	UCLA	4-4
Nevada	3-5	Oregon	4-4
Tulsa	3-5	Washington State	3-5
Southern Methodist	3-5	Stanford	2-6
Rice	2-6	Arizona	2-6
San Jose State	1-7	Washington	0-8

2004 Major Bowl Games

Champs Sports Bowl (Tangerine) (Dec. 21): Ga. Tech 51 Syracuse 14

Georgia Tech (7-5) arrived in Orlando with lowest scoring O among all bowl teams, but got immediate boost from D as LB Chris Reis trotted 20y from right flat with INT TD RET. After Syracuse (6-6) pulled within 7-6 as QB Perry Patterson cantered 21y for TD as part of option attack that Orange pinned their O plan on, Jackets WRs Calvin Johnson and Nate Curry scored 10y diving and 80y bomb TDs respectively from QB Reggie Ball (12-19/207y, 2 TDs, INT). Tech blew up Syracuse's "clothes-line" formation for punt block early in 2nd Q, and TB P.J. Daniels (17/119y, 2 TDs) caught screen pass to set up his short TD slam. Georgia Tech led 35-6 at H and upped it to 49-6 in 2nd H. Orange tacked on 4th Q TD pass by Patterson.

Las Vegas Bowl (Dec. 23): Wyoming 24 UCLA 21

UCLA (6-6) arrived with big size advantage on both lines, but didn't decide to steadily run ball until 3rd Q. Cowboys (7-5) started deep in their territory most of 1st Q but jumped to 10-0 lead: WR Jovon Bouknight (5/107y) got loose up left sideline for 56y catch from QB Corey Bramlet (20-34/307y, 2 TDs, INT) to set up FG, and Bramlet converted Bruins' FUM into 10y TD pass to WR Tyler Holden (4/115y, TD). UCLA, 12-pt favorite, finally awoke on well-covered WR Junior Taylor's leaping TD catch in middle of 2nd Q. Having trouble punting into stiff wind in 2nd Q, Wyoming left only 30y field for UCLA to traverse for 14-10 H lead, WR Craig Bragg catching 17y TD from QB David Koral (7-12/89y, 2 TDs), who replaced injured Drew Olson. Bragg caught 3rd Q TD at right edge of EZ for 21-10 lead at end of mostly land-bound 80y drive, sparked by 46y rushing by TB Maurice Drew (25/126y). But, it was Bragg's late 3rd Q punt FUM that got Cowpokes back in game. They moved to wobbly 22y TD pass by Bouknight, former HS QB. After Bruins missed FG, Wyoming battled 72y, including generously-spotted 4th down sneak by Bramlet, until TE John Wadkowski caught winning TD.

Hawaii Bowl (Dec. 24): Hawaii 59 Alabama-Birmingham 40

Someday there will be game ending at 100-99, and Honolulu foes tried to go that way early on. UAB (7-5) QB Darrell Hackney lofted 51y scoring pass to WR Roddy White on game's 1st series. Hawaii (8-5) WR Jason Rivers made jumping catch near sideline and blazed away for 74y TD and 7-6 lead. Blazers countered with 80y TD drive capped by RB Dan Burks' 4y run for 13-7 edge. Hawaii QB Timmy Chang (31-46/405y, 4 TDs) threw his 2nd TD pass to extend home team's lead to 21-13 at end of 1st Q. Birmingham scored 10 pts in last 6 mins of 2nd Q to narrow H disadvantage to 28-26. Chang found little WR Chad Owens for 15y TD early in 3rd Q, and Owens, 2004 Mosi Tatupu Special Teams Award winner and Warriors' career all-purpose y king (5461y), followed with quicksilver 59y punt TD RET for 42-26 lead. Chang threw another TD in 4th Q and finished his career with all-time record of 17,072y.

MPC Computers Bowl (Dec. 27): Fresno State 37 Virginia 34 (OT)

Fresno State (9-3), seemingly off with its recent level of play, was back knocking off prime competition. Bulldogs overcame deficits of 21-7 in 2nd Q and 31-24 in 4th Q on passing exploits of QB Paul Pinegar (23-36/235y, 5 TDs) to force OT, in which Pinegar pitched his 5th score. In building his team's early lead, Virginia (8-4) QB Marques Hagans (18-30/162y, TD) hit 7y TD pass in 1st Q and dashed 8y for 2nd Q TD. Fresno displayed strong run game in 2nd H and clawed back to 24-24 tie early in 4th Q on Pinegar's pair of 22y TD passes. UVa was in good shape after TB Wali Lundy followed his blockers for 20y TD stampede with 6:20 left. Pinegar used his run attack to work downfield for tying 4th down TD pass to WR Jaron Fairman. After Cavs made FG in OT, Pinegar hit TE Stephen Spach with 25y post-pattern TD throw.

Insight Bowl (Dec. 28): Oregon State 38 Notre Dame 21

Underappreciated Beavers (7-5) QB Derek Anderson (28-45/358y) rifled 4 TDs, including pair to TE Joe Newton (7/85y), to launch Oregon State past Notre Dame (6-6). With Tyrone Willingham having been fired, Fighting Irish vowed to win for their deposed coach while playing under interim coach Kent Baer, their D-coordinator. Still, ND lost its 7th straight bowl game. Oregon State jumped to 21-0 lead by early 2nd Q, having to travel only 26, 4, and 45y with key plays coming on WR Sammie Strougher's 52y punt RET and special teamer Derrick Doggett's punt block. Notre Dame QB Brady Quinn (17-29/214y, INT) hit his 2nd TD at end of 88y march to pull within 31-21 with just under 5 mins to play. Irish tried failed onside-KO which allowed Beavers to start at ND 28YL, and 3y TD run by TB Dwight Wright wrapped it up for Beavers, who after tough early-season slate rallied to won 6 of their last 7 tilts.

Houston Bowl (Dec. 29): Colorado 33 Texas-El Paso 28

Enhancing K Mason Crosby's 4 FGs, QB Joel Klatt (24-33/333y) pitched pair of TD passes in 4th Q to vault Colorado (8-5) past Texas-El Paso (8-4). Miners QB Jordan Palmer (22-42/328y, 2 TDs, 2 INTs) fashioned 80 and 67y marches in 1st Q for 14-3 lead and gave Texans 28-19 lead with short TD pass to WR Johnnie Lee Higgins early in 4th Q after driving team with 55y pass to WR Jayson Boyd. On next scrimmage play, Klatt tossed short pass to TE Joel Klopfenstein, who rumbled 78y for TD. Buffs

used fake punt from their own 35YL, and P John Torp galloped 22y around LE to prompt Klatt's 39y winning TD pass to wide-open WR Evan Judge.

Alamo Bowl (Dec. 29): Ohio State 33 Oklahoma State 7

Ohio State (8-4), in midst of money-to-players revelation which sent starting QB Troy Smith to sidelines, dusted off former starter, QB Justin Zwick (17-27/190y), who pitched 23y TD pass to WR Anthony Gonzalez in 1st Q. Behind 10-0, Oklahoma State (7-5) soon turned it over again on FUM, and Ohio K Mike Nugent booted 2nd of his 4 FGs. Bucks limited Cowboys to 286y and couldn't prevent cosmetic TD run by Oklahoma State FB Shawn Willis. Cowboys star RB Vernand Morency was held to 8/24y rushing.

Continental Tire Bowl (Dec. 30): Boston College 37 North Carolina 24

Faced with huge Charlotte fan support for nearby North Carolina (6-6), Eagles (9-3) buckled their chinstraps and looked to QB Paul Peterson (24-33/236y, 2 TDs), back from broken passing hand with 5 screws holding it together. Peterson threw pair of TD passes in 1st H, but Carolina QB Darian Durant (23-41/259y) hit 3 TDs, including brilliant leaping grab in EZ corner by WR Wallace Wright and 51y bomb to WR Derrele Mitchell. No sooner had BC CB Will Blackmon been beaten by Mitchell late in 2nd Q than Blackmon returned following KO past midfield. Peterson hit TE David Kashetta with 1y TD pass to tie it 21-21 at H. Fateful sequence occurred in opening 6 mins of 4th Q with Boston College ahead 27-21. Peterson, rolling left on 3rd down, briefly dribbled ball from his bad hand and was tackled by UNC DE Tommy Davis. Peterson had broken his left leg, but, while being wheeled off along sideline, he was able to cheer for stunning TD by Eagles: K Ryan Ohliger, who had missed x-pt and had FG blocked, already had lost his kicking job, but was sent in to line up as K and take handoff on fake FG, with which he blasted 21y for clinching TD. Sub RB Andre Callender contributed 174y rushing to BC's 5th bowl win in row.

Emerald Bowl (Dec. 30): Navy 34 New Mexico 19

After opening KO, New Mexico (7-5) marched nicely downfield with QB Kole McKamey (15-24/207y, TD, 2 INTs) throwing through wet conditions at San Francisco, including early TD. Lobos star RB DonTrell Moore injured his knee when he fumbled, and Midshipmen (10-2) QB Aaron Polanco scored his 2nd running TD for 14-7 edge in 1st Q. On opening play of 2nd Q, Polanco (234y total O) fired surprise 61y TD bomb to WR Corey Dryden. New Mexico came back on RB Rodney Ferguson's TD run after WR Hank Baskett's long run with flat pass. But, Navy led 24-19 at H and turned over 2nd H matters to Polanco for 27y TD romp and to its D that blanked Lobos thanks to GLS. After their GLS, Middies erased 14:26 of time on 26-play drive to FG.

Holiday Bowl (Dec. 30): Texas Tech 45 California 31

No. 4 Golden Bears had every reason to be disappointed in not making Rose Bowl, and it showed. On their 1st series, Red Raiders (8-4) surprisingly used runs to enhance their passes to score on reception by WR Jarrett Hicks. California (10-2) tied it late in 1st Q when TB J.J. Arrington (25/173y) barely broke GL plane for his 15th TD of season before ball was slapped away. Awakening Bears looked in control as Arrington steamed 34y, plus facemask PEN, to create 5y TD chance and 14-7 edge for his powerful backup, TB Marshawn Lynch. In 2nd Q, Texas Tech S Vincent Meeks turned things around by rambling 48y with deflected INT to Cal 22YL to set up Hicks' 2nd TD catch and 17-14 lead. Before H, Tech RB Taurean Henderson added TD run, 45th of his career. Team trailing at H had won 7 straight Holiday Bowls, but Cal's tottering D, down 24-14, allowed 60y TD bomb by QB Sonny Cumbie (39-60/520y, 3 TDs) to WR Joel Filani only 2 mins into 3rd Q. Raiders continued to pressure Cal QB Aaron Rodgers (24-42/246y, TD, INT). With most of their receivers out injured, Bears counted on Arrington, who exceeded 2,000y rushing mark for season in 3rd Q.

Music City Bowl (Dec. 31): Minnesota 20 Alabama 16

No runner had gained 100y against Alabama (6-6) all season, but Gophers (7-5) TB Marion Barber III (37/187y, TD) nicked Tide D for exactly 100y in 1st H, which was led by Minnesota 17-14. Gophers had scored go-ahead TD in 2nd Q by Barber after controversial non-call on fairly obvious FUM by TB Laurence Maroney (29/105y). Bama QB Spencer Pennington (22-36/243y, TD) hit 12 of his 13 passes in 1st H, including TD in game's 1st min. But, Alabama missed every 3rd down try on O and punted poorly. Minny added 3rd Q FG and turned it over to run attack. But, K Lloyd Rhys missed clinching FG with slightly more than 5 mins to play. Gophers surprisingly conceded safety on 4th down with 3:11 to go. Alabama WR Tyrone Prothro returned free-kick past midfield, but Pennington missed 4th down pass at 15YL.

Sun Bowl (Dec. 31): Arizona State 27 Purdue 23

Fired-up Sun Devils (9-3) were able to run ball against Purdue's 2nd-best Big 10 run D. Arizona State finished 1st Q with slim 3-0 lead but registered 9 1st downs to only 9y O for Boilermakers (7-5). Devils K Jesse Ainsworth missed 3 FGs, so Purdue remained competitive at 3-2 by H after safety on tackle by DL Brandon Villareal came on heels of P Dave Brytus' punt to 1YL. Teams traded TDs early in 3rd Q: Boilers struck for TD on 1 swift play, and Devils drove to WR Derek Hagan's 27y TD snatch. Early in 4th Q, WR Taylor Stubblefield, all-time NCAA reception king (325), grabbed 5y out-pattern TD from QB Kyle Orton (23-47/281y, 3 TDs). After FG pared margin to 16-13 with 10:33 left, Devils soon had perfect call against blitz, and RB Rudy Burgess (19/130y) dashed 41y on screen pass for TD and 20-16 lead. Purdue S Bernard Pollard blocked punt OB at ASU 37YL with less than 2 mins to go. Orton's scramble and arrow on post pattern to Stubblefield placed ball at 6YL. Orton lobbed high TD pass to TE Charles Davis for 23-20 lead with 1:14 on clock. ASU QB Sam Keller (25-45/370y, 3 TDs) hit 2 big throws and combined with Burgess on another TD screen pass against blitz with 43 secs to go. Game ended with Orton's Hail Mary being tipped OB.

Liberty Bowl (Dec. 31): Louisville 44 Boise State 40

Whole world expected high scoring shootout because both teams were among only 5 schools ever to score in excess of 55 pts in 4 or more straight games, and nobody watching was disappointed even though Broncos (11-1) were held to 284y. Boise State stayed competitive on LB Andy Avalos' 92y INT TD RET for new Liberty Bowl distance record. Broncos managed to score 24 straight pts from middle of 2nd Q through 5 mins into 3rd Q and led 34-21. Louisville (11-1) QB Stefan LeFors (18-26/193y, 2 TDs, INT, 12/76y rushing) came in with 74 percent passing mark and left with it nearly intact, and it was his 14y TD pass to WR J.R. Russell (6/59y) with 6 mins left in 3rd Q that got Cards back within 34-28. Boise went up 40-35 on 2y run by RB Jon Helmendollar in 1st 5 mins of 4th Q for 4th lead change of game. Boise had last chance after K Art Carmody's chip-shot FG upped Lousiville's lead to 44-40 with 1:19 to play. QB Jared Zabansky (14-29/199y, TD, INT) moved Broncos to UL 30YL, but his last-gasp pass was intercepted in EZ by Cardinals S Kerry Rhodes.

Peach Bowl (Dec. 31): Miami 27 Florida 10

Miami (9-3) made 2 big plays that turned decision in its direction: top return artist, DB Devin Hester (28y INT RET), stormed 78y for TD after DL Thomas Carroll blocked FG in middle of 1st Q, and WR Roscoe Parrish ripped off 72y punt TD RET in 2nd Q. Parrish's romp created 17-3 lead that Hurricanes D maintained despite permitting 406y to Gators (7-5). Florida QB Chris Leak passed for 262y (2 INTs), including 45y TD to WR Jemalle Cornelius late in 3rd Q, and rushed for 38y, while TB Citarick Fason ran for 17/94y. TB Frank Gore led Miami with 25/80y rushing, and QB Brock Berlin passed 13-23/171y, TD, in raising his mark against in-state rivals Florida and FSU to 5-0.

Outback Bowl: Georgia 24 Wisconsin 21

Red-helmeted Bulldogs (10-2) went right down field to FG, and along way QB David Greene (19-38/264y, 2 TDs, 2 INTs) bypassed Tennessee's Peyton Manning as SEC's all-time total O leader. Wisconsin (9-3) K Mike Allen tied it 3-3 later in 1st Q and added another FG, barely over crossbar from 44y, for 6-3 edge early in 2nd Q. Greene suffered only his 3rd INT of season, but bounced back with 19y crossing pass TD to WR Fred Gibson for 10-6 H edge. Georgia scored wild TD later in 3rd Q for 17-6 edge when tipped pass rocketed into unsuspecting FB Jeremy Thomas, who stumbled into TD. Badgers pulled within 24-13 and soon threatened deep in Bulldogs territory, but brilliant Georgia DE David Pollack (3 sacks) sacked and stripped Wisconsin QB John Stocco (12-27/170y, TD). Badgers LB Andy Crooks quickly shot through to steal Greene's screen pass and return INT for TD. After Wisconsin WR Jonathan Orr's 2-pt catch, UGa led 24-21 in last 2 mins but ran out clock on runs by TB Thomas Brown.

Cotton Bowl: Tennessee 38 Texas A&M 7

Tennessee (10-3) struck early as QB Rick Clausen (18-27/222y, 3 TDs) rifled 57y TD pass to WR C.J. Fayton. Clausen, 9-13 passing to start game, followed up with left-handed TD arrow to gigantic FB Cory Anderson late in 1st Q after FUM by Aggies (7-5) QB Reggie McNeal, who was woozy after that play. In middle of 2nd Q, Anderson, on only his 3rd carry of season, slammed downfield on effective run to set up Clausen's 3rd TD pass. Down 28-0 at H, Texas A&M looked for better things after 2nd H KO, and WR Terrence Thomas raced 54y to 15YL on misdirection sweep. But, Tennessee LB Jason Mitchell made terrific tackle to stop McNeal on 4th down run and Vols went back to piling up pts. Aggies tacked on 4th Q TD on McNeal's short pass.

Gator Bowl: Florida State 30 West Virginia 18

Even though underdog West Virginia (8-4) permitted longest run in Gator Bowl history in 1st min—Seminoles TB Leon Washington's 89y romp—it showed well in 1st H, gliding to 12-10 lead on TDs on 36 y catch-and-run and plunge by RB Kay-Jay Harris (25/134y, TD). WVU missed both conv kicks, so when short FG opportunity came up in 2nd Q, Mountaineers coach Rich Rodriguez opted for fake, which failed on S Pat Watkins' tackle. Florida State (9-3) jumped ahead by 16-12 on K Xavier Beitia's 2nd FG. Even though its kicking game looked awful, WVU opted for 44y FG which frosh K Andy Good made good to pull within 16-15. Seminoles overcame red zone holding PEN and went 90y to WR Craphonso Thorpe's jumping TD catch on 3rd down late in 3rd Q, which slightly improved FSU's national-worst 22 percent 3rd down conversion. Still, it was Noles up by 23-15, and they were on their way to another TD in 4th Q.

GAME OF THE YEAR
Capital One Bowl (Citrus): Iowa 30 Louisiana State 25

Iowa (10-2) scored early on bomb from QB Drew Tate (20-332/287y, 2 TDs, 2 INTs) to WR Clinton Solomon, but had to set its jaw in D battle with Louisiana State (9-3), which trimmed margin to 7-6 on 2 FGs. Hawkeyes, who would gain only 77y in 1st H, created big break with 1:04 left before H when S Miguel Merrick blocked punt and S Sean Considine returned it for 7y TD. When Tigers seemed content to go to H behind 14-6, big RB Alley Broussard veered right and outran Iowa's over-pursuing D. LSU K Chris Jackson missed x-pt after PEN on 2-pt try pushed LSU back. After Iowa made 3rd Q INT, Tate hit 4 sharp completions to WR Ed Hinkel to Bengals 8YL, but it had to settle for FG and 17-12 edge. LSU frosh holder Matt Flynn ran on FG fake and was stopped at Hawks 17YL. Iowa, last in nation in rushing, found decent run game as 3rd Q was dying and it led to 20y dump-off pass to TE Scott Chandler to 4YL. TB Marques Simmons went off LT on next snap for TD and 24-12 edge. QB JaMarcus Russell came off bench as 3rd passer used by LSU and hit 3 passes/56y including TD to WR Skyler Green. Hawkeyes had 8 mins to kill and couldn't do it. Russell passed Tigers and 25-24 lead with 46 secs left. Tate, Iowa's brilliant magician all season, found SB Warren Holloway behind slow-reacting LSU DBs for 56y TD as time expired.

Rose Bowl: Texas 38 Michigan 37

Pasadena's 91st Rose Bowl pitted Michigan (9-3) and Texas (11-1) for legendary programs' 1st-ever meeting. Longhorns coach Mack Brown successfully had politicked

---

to vault his team's BCS numbers past those of California, which had bombed 2 days earlier in Holiday Bowl. Nervous 1st Q was filled with yellow flags, but game-breakers soon took over as Texas QB Vince Young (16-28/180y, TD passing, 21/192y, 4 TDs rushing) sped between tacklers to 20y TD late in 1st Q. Wolverines WR Braylon Edwards (10/109y) made brilliant catch at edge of EZ to tie it 7-7, 1st of his Rose-record 3 TD catches. Longhorns went 68y to Young's play-action 3rd down TD pass to TE David Thomas for 14-7 lead. With 2:36 to go in 2nd Q, Michigan recovered punt FUM at UT 33YL, and tied it 14-14. Young made another spectacular free-wheeling TD run from 60y away in 3rd Q, but Michigan WR Steve Breaston, who chipped in several terrific KO RETs (6/221y), contributed another to midfield. Breaston soon caught 3rd down pass, and he broke away for tying 50y TD. Wolverines pulled away at 31-21, but Texas came back behind Young's brilliance: he scored on 10 and 23y runs. When K Garrett Rivas nailed his 3rd FG (42y), Michigan regained lead at 37-35 with 3:04 to play. Texas took over on its 34YL after KO and maneuvered to UM 19YL. Longhorns K Dusty Mangum, walk-on sr, was iced twice with timeouts but came through by barely lofting winning 37y FG over crossbar as time expired.

Fiesta Bowl: Utah 35 Pittsburgh 7

Lame duck coaches had done poorly during Bowl Week, but this game matched pair of head men each headed elsewhere in 2005: Utah's Urban Meyer to Florida and Pitt's Walt Harris to Stanford. Panthers (8-4) were biggest underdog of any bowl team, and fell irretrievably behind because QB Tyler Palko (22-40/251y, TD) was sacked 9 times. Utes (12-0), dubbed "America's Team" because they had busted into BCS' party from Mountain West Conf, went ahead 28-0 by middle of 3rd Q as QB Alex Smith (29-37/328y, 4 TDs) threw trio of scoring passes. Utah showed dizzying array of O plays, including TD off "hook-and-ladder" pass, shovel passes, and option runs. WR Paris Warren was everywhere in Pitt's secondary, catching 15/198y, 2 TDs. "It's going to be hard to say goodbye," said Meyer of his Utes, "but we're saying goodbye 12-0."

Sugar Bowl (Jan. 3): Auburn 16 Virginia Tech 13

Respective Ds showed well as each team threatened constantly in red zone with little to show for it. Auburn (13-0) came away with 3 short FGs by K John Vaughn for 9-0 H edge, even though Tigers snapped ball 7 times inside Virginia Tech (10-3) 10YL. Hokies QB Bryan Randall (21-38/299y, 2 TDs, 2 INTs) was off his passing game in 1st H, but his 9/45y running allowed him to scramble his way inside Auburn's 10YL 3 times. Virginia Tech made 2 major blunders: FB Jesse Allen dropped short 4th down EZ pass, which was slightly behind him, midway through 2nd Q. And, K Brandon Pace snap-hooked short FG early in 4th Q. Auburn's MVP QB Jason Campbell (11-16/189y, TD, INT) directed 78y drive right after 2nd H KO to his short TD pass and 16-0 lead. Shutout would have meant much to Tigers' cause with voters, but FUM led to Randall's 29y TD pass to WR Josh Morgan inside last 7 mins. Auburn D seemed completely asleep when Randall-to-Morgan struck again on 80y TD bomb.

Orange Bowl (Jan. 4): Southern California 55 Oklahoma 19

BCS title game in Orange Bowl matched pair of Heisman Trophy winners for 1st time in bowl game for national championship: Sooners' 2003 winner, QB Jason White, and USC's current king, QB Matt Leinart. Early on, it looked like White (24-36/244y, 2 TDs, 3 INTs) would sparkle as he directed Sooners (12-1) downfield on 92y drive in 12 plays to 5y TD pass to WR Travis Wilson. Soon, Leinart picked up Trojans (13-0) reins and it was soon lights out for Oklahoma's D. USC tied it in 6 plays as Leinart (18-35/332y, 5 TDs) whipped 33y TD to TE Dominique Byrd. Sooners WR Mark Bradley mistakenly fielded punt inside his 5YL and coughed up FUM at his 6YL. USC TE LenDale White (15/118y, 2 TDs) rumbled to TD on next snap. It was just beginning: Trojans tallied 38 pts in last 20 mins of 1st H for 38-10 H. They mastered 85y TD drive to start 3rd Q. In all, Oklahoma contributed 5 TOs to its downfall. USC gained 525y—more than 8y per play—while its D blanketed frosh sensation, TB Adrian Peterson (25/82y rushing).

Final USA Today Coaches January 5

1	Southern California (61)	1525	14	Florida State	776
2	Auburn	1460	15	Tennessee	771
3	Oklahoma	1366	16	LSU	693
4	Texas	1324	17	Texas Tech	478
5	Utah	1300	18	Wisconsin	449
6	Georgia	1191	19	Ohio State	430
7	Louisville	1166	20	Arizona State	377
8	Iowa	1022	21	Boston College	245
9	California	937	22	Fresno State	206
10	Virginia Tech	906	23	Virginia	157
11	Miami (Fla.)	903	24	Navy	129
12	Michigan	802	25	Florida	101
13	Boise State	792			

Final AP Poll January 5

1	Southern California (62)	1622	14	Michigan	842
2	Auburn (3)	1559	15	Florida State	754
3	Oklahoma	1454	16	Louisiana State	711
4	Utah	1438	17	Wisconsin	482
5	Texas	1391	18	Texas Tech	476
6	Louisville	1261	19	Arizona State	463
7	Georgia	1204	20	Ohio State	423
8	Iowa	1111	21	Boston College	314
9	California	1060	22	Fresno State	203
10	Virginia Tech	996	23	Virginia	157
11	Miami	917	24	Navy	126
12	Boise State	888	25	Pittsburgh	99
13	Tennessee	868			

2004 Top Performance Formula

1	Southern California	1.8345
2	Auburn	1.7923
3	Utah	1.7447
4	Oklahoma	1.7133
5	Texas	1.6868
6	Louisville	1.6857
7	California	1.5966
8	Iowa	1.5210
9	Georgia	1.5208
10	Miami	1.4982
11	Virginia Tech	1.4503
12	Arizona State	1.4312
13	Louisiana State	1.4265
14	Florida State	1.4121
15	Tennessee	1.4117
16	Michigan	1.4027
17	Virginia	1.3536
18	Texas Tech	1.3330
19	Ohio State	1.2995
20	Texas A&M	1.2976

2004 Top Opponent Records

1	Texas A&M	.6818
2	North Carolina	.6561
3	Arizona State	.6279
4	Notre Dame	.6260
5	Iowa	.6202
6	Oklahoma	.6187
7	Texas	.6176
8	Arkansas	.6172
9	Miami	.6124
10	Georgia	.6108
11	Oregon State	.6094
12	Arizona	.6051
13	Baylor	.5966
14	Kansas	.5950
15	Southern California	.5899
16	Brigham Young	.5897
17	Auburn	.5885
18	Oklahoma State	.5878
19	Colorado	.5870
20	Texas Tech	.5827

2004 Out-of-Conference Records

	W-L	Percentage	Bowl W-L
Big Twelve	29-11	.7250	4-3
Southeastern	24-13	.6486	3-3
Big Ten	25-14	.6410	3-3
Pacific-10	22-13	.6286	3-2
Atlantic Coast	22-14	.6111	3-3
Big East	19-15	.5588	2-3
Mountain West	14-17	.4516	2-1

2004 Individual Statistical Leaders

RUSHING YARDS	Attempts	Yards	Avg.
J.J. Arrington, California	289	2018	7.0
DeAngelo Williams, Memphis	313	1948	6.2
Adrian Peterson, Oklahoma	339	1925	5.7
Cedric Benson, Texas	326	1834	5.6
Ryan Moats, Louisiana Tech	288	1774	6.2
Garrett Wolfe, Northern Illinois	256	1656	6.5
Vernand Morency, Oklahoma State	258	1474	5.7
Michael Hart, Michigan	282	1455	5.2
Noah Herron, Northwestern	274	1381	5.0
Laurence Maroney, Minnesota	217	1348	6.2

PASSING YARDS	Completions	Attempts	Yards	Pct.
Sonny Cumbie, Texas Tech	421	642	4742	65.6
Timmy Chang, Hawaii	358	602	4258	59.5
Omar Jacobs, Bowling Green	309	462	4002	66.9
Derek Anderson, Oregon State	279	515	3615	54.2
Bruce Gradkowski, Toledo	280	399	3518	70.2
Dan Orlovski, Connecticut	288	457	3354	63.0
Matt Leinart, Southern California	269	412	3322	65.3
Jason White, Oklahoma	255	390	3205	65.4
Chris Leak, Florida	238	399	3197	59.7
Ryan Hart, Rutgers	295	453	3154	65.1

RECEIVING YARDS	Catches	Yards
Roddy White, Alabama-Birmingham	71	1452
Dante Ridgeway, Ball State	105	1399
Mike Hass, Oregon State	86	1379
Braylon Edwards, Michigan	97	1330
Greg Lee, Pittsburgh	68	1297
Chad Owens, Hawaii	102	1290
Eric Deslauriers, Eastern Michigan	84	1257
Derek Hagan, Arizona State	83	1248
Lance Moore, Toledo	90	1189
Jarrett Hicks, Texas Tech	76	1177

2004 Consensus All-America Team

Offense

Wide receiver:	Braylon Edwards, Michigan
	Taylor Stubblefield, Purdue
Tight End:	Heath Miller, Virginia
Linemen:	Jammal Brown, Oklahoma
	Elton Brown, Virginia
	David Baas, Michigan
	Alex Barron, Florida State
	Michael Munoz, Tennessee
Quarterback:	Matt Leinart, Southern California
Running Back:	Adrian Peterson, Oklahoma
	J.J. Arrington, California
Kick Returner:	Reggie Bush, Southern California
Kicker:	Mike Nugent, Ohio State

Defense

Linemen:	David Pollack, Georgia
	Erasmus James, Wisconsin
	Shaun Cody, Southern California
	Marcus Spears, Louisiana State
Linebacker:	Matt Groodegoed, Southern California
	Derrick Johnson, Texas
	A.J. Hawk, Ohio State
Backs:	Antrel Rolle, Miami
	Marlin Jackson, Michigan
	Carlos Rogers, Auburn
	Ernest Shazor, Michigan
	Thomas Davis, Georgia
Punter:	Brandon Fields, Michigan State

2004 Heisman Trophy Voting

Matt Leinart, junior quarterback, Southern California	1,325
Adrian Peterson, freshman tailback, Oklahoma	997
Jason White, senior quarterback, Oklahoma	957
Alex Smith, junior quarterback, Utah	635
Reggie Bush, sophomore tailback, Southern California	597

Other Major Awards

Maxwell (Player)	Jason White, senior quarterback, Oklahoma
Walter Camp (Player)	Matt Leinart, junior quarterback, Southern California
Outland (Lineman)	Jammal Brown, senior offensive tackle, Oklahoma
Vince Lombardi (Lineman)	David Pollack, senior defensive end, Georgia
Doak Walker (Running Back)	Cedric Benson, senior tailback, Texas
Davey O'Brien (Quarterback)	Jason White, senior quarterback, Oklahoma
Fred Biletnikoff (Receiver)	Braylon Edwards, senior wide receiver, Michigan
Jim Thorpe (Defensive Back)	Carlos Rogers, senior cornerback, Auburn
Dick Butkus (Linebacker)	Derrick Johnson, senior linebacker, Oklahoma
Lou Groza (Placekicker)	Mike Nugent, senior kicker, Ohio State
Chuck Bednarik (Defender)	David Pollack, senior defensive end, Georgia
Ray Guy (Punter)	Daniel Sepulveda, sophomore punter, Baylor
Johnny Unitas (Sr. Quarterback)	Jason White, senior quarterback, Oklahoma
Mosi Tatupu (Special Teams)	Chad Owens, senior punt returner, Hawaii
John Mackey (Tight End)	Heath Miller, junior tight end, Virginia
Dave Rimington (Center)	David Baas, senior center, Michigan, and Ben Wilkerson, senior center, Louisiana State
Ted Hendricks (Defensive End)	David Pollack, senior defensive end, Georgia
AFCA Coach of the Year	Tommy Tuberville, Auburn

2005

The Year of Trojans Try for Three, Austin City Elation, and Deep South's Hurricane Devastation

With a myriad of "best of" lists dominating sports coverage—with those lists stuffed full of contemporary players, teams and plays—it was easy for sports fans to become jaded about the truly exceptional. While this book presents a comprehensive approach to the modern history of college football, with respect bestowed on players, teams, and coaches from single-platoon football to the modern era, it must be stated that 2005 was one of the very best seasons in the history of college football. It also was one of the greatest seasons in any sport. Packed with thrilling games, all-time great players, and capped by an exciting Bowl Championship Series title game, the season confirmed that college football was immensely electrifying and deserved every bit of its popularity. And college football's popularity now ranked in practically every survey as neck-and-neck with NASCAR—and ahead of Major League Baseball—as America's second-most favorite sport behind the enormously successful National Football League.

The epicenter of attention was the University of Southern California (12-1) campus as the Trojans earned the right to be profiled incessantly due to their ability to win incessantly. By enjoying a perfect regular season in 2005 the Trojans stretched their overall winning streak to 34 games, tied for fourth all-time with Miami (2000-03), and trailing only Oklahoma (1953-57) with 47, Washington (1908-14) with 39 and Toledo (1969-71) with 35. With a shared national title in 2003 and an undisputed crown in 2004, USC was aiming for a so-called "three-peat," which happened at early times in college football history but never in the Associated Press Poll, which started in 1936. Four schools could claim at least three unofficial titles in a row when only a few dozen teams played before and just after the turn of the 20th century. Minnesota (1934-36) Army (1944-46), and Alabama (1964-66) could claim partial "three-peats," but earned one of its third championships through a minor selection service or historic throwback selection. The Minnesota Golden Gophers of the mid-1930s suffer only by way of timing since they were roundly considered the nation's best in the two years while waiting for the arrival of the AP poll which tapped the Gophers no. 1 in 1936. The school that came closest in recent times was Nebraska, which lost narrowly in a championship Orange Bowl match-up with Florida State in 1993 and then took the AP top spot after both the 1994 and 1995 seasons.

The 2005 edition of the Trojans won with offense, unleashing a collection of players who laid claim to many "best of" lists. At the helm of the attack, which averaged 50 points and 580 yards per game, was returning Heisman-Trophy-winning quarterback Matt Leinart, who surprised many by his reenrollment when the first round, and possibly the first overall pick, of the National Football League draft beckoned. That Leinart already had completed virtually all of his academic requirements bothered some people, especially in light of the single academic class the lefthanded quarterback and USC scholar chose to take. It was ballroom dancing. While much of the vitriol may have been little more than envy of Leinart's successes on and off the field, the fact remained that he was quickly placing himself among the most accomplished collegiate quarterbacks in history.

When Leinart dropped back to pass he had a wealth of talent to throw to, from the dynamic tailback Reggie Bush to wideouts Dwayne Jarrett and Steve Smith and tight end Dominique Byrd. When handing off he did so to Bush and bruising tailback LenDale White, who set a school record with 57 career touchdowns. Bush and White broke a sacred 59-year-old NCAA record for career touchdowns by teammates. They scored 99 times to pass the legendary Glenn Davis and Doc Blanchard of Army, who scored 97 touchdowns in 1943-46. Add a powerful line featuring four players who received All-America mention, plus wonderful offensive schemes, and there did not seem to be a flaw, even with the departure of heralded offensive coordinator Norm Chow to the professional ranks. The lowest number of points scored by USC during the regular season was 34, against Notre Dame (9-3). By season's end, the Trojans owned the first offense ever to feature a 3,000-yard passer (Leinart), two 1,000-yard rushers (Bush and White) and a 1,000-yard receiver (Jarrett). They were in the top five nationally in both rushing and receiving at end of regular season. "It's the best offense I've ever seen," said Oregon defensive coordinator Nick Allioti. "That thing is a juggernaut."

Almost as stunning was the presence of another long-time power who could claim superiority over the Trojans. Despite being compared to the best offenses of all-time—especially after scoring 70 against Arkansas (4-7) in September—Southern California did not even win the scoring title. Free from the intense national media scrutiny USC's success generated, Texas

(13-0) was quietly putting up similar offensive numbers and even outscored USC by nearly a point per game at 50.9. Texas' exciting 25-22 victory over Ohio State in Columbus—clearly the toughest opponent for either top team—against a squad loaded with future NFL draft picks was the only game in which Texas did not score at least 40 points. Armed with perhaps a better defense than the Trojans and blessed with a player, quarterback Vince Young, talented enough to threaten the stranglehold the Men of Troy had on the nation's list of exciting players, Texas became a figurative 1-A to Southern California's no. 1.

The two teams were ranked one and two for the whole season. Although USC remained number one in the AP Poll for the entire regular season—a spot they had held every week since December 8, 2003—Texas surpassed them for one week in the BCS standings. When the Longhorns walloped Colorado (7-6) in the Big 12 championship game they matched the 70 points Southern California had scored against Arkansas (4-7). And so for the first time in the seven-year history of the BCS, the two teams which were one-two in the opening poll played for the title. And what a game the Rose Bowl became, with its amazing ebbs and flows. There was an ill-advised lateral by Bush that probably cost USC a first-half touchdown, the controversy over Young's knee perhaps touching down before he made an important pitchout, Texas' fourth-down stop of big-back White to gain fourth quarter possession for the winning drive, and Young's amazingly calm final scamper to the end zone for victory near the game's end. It truly was one of the very best football games ever played, and might have been the greatest game ever played with the national championship on the line for both teams. With its 41-38 victory, Texas captured its first national title in 35 years.

Against Notre Dame in mid-season, Southern Calornia lived by a quarterback running the ball; at year's end they would die by a quarterback running the ball. If the Rose Bowl was the game of the year, then the 77th meeting of the Trojans and Fighting Irish would finish a very close second on any best-of-the-season list. It would also feature the best play of the year, or at least most famous, as the "Bush Push" entered college football lore with Billy Cannon's Halloween punt return and Doug Flutie's "Hail Mary" to just mention two from the pantheon. When USC coach Pete Carroll decided to go for the winning touchdown on the final play rather than a tying field goal, Leinart had to get into the end zone or USC would lose. Leinart got into the end zone to win 34-31.

The Notre Dame-USC game was just one of many memorable contests played on the same Saturday as Michigan (7-5) stunned unbeaten Penn State (11-1) with a last-second touchdown pass, Wisconsin (10-3) beat Minnesota (7-5) on a blocked punt, UCLA (10-2) rallied from 17 points down to beat Washington State (4-7), Louisiana State (11-2) bested Florida (9-3) in a battle of SEC powers, Alabama (10-2) rallied to prevent an upset loss to Mississippi (3-8), and West Virginia (11-1) outlasted Louisville (9-3) in three overtimes in the battle for Big East supremacy. There were more storylines in one day than most sports have in a whole season.

Notre Dame's near win over USC highlighted a resurgence of many traditionally powerful programs that had slipped a bit in recent times. Alabama, led by gutty quarterback Brodie Croyle, returned to the Top 10 after routing Florida on October 1. Penn State, 7-16 over the past two seasons that featured more focus on whether coach Joe Paterno should remain on the sidelines rather than anything the team did on the field, was suddenly back as a national championship contender and winners of their first Big Ten title since 1994. UCLA became wild "Cardiac Kids" by rallying four times when they trailed late enroute to an 8-0 start, only to run out of luck by season's end. Not one comeback team had been ranked in the AP preseason poll.

But then that preseason poll was already discredited by the end of the first week, when six of its teams lost, four to unranked teams including Oklahoma (8-4) to Texas Christian (11-1), which marked the first time since 1995—when Northwestern upset Notre Dame—that a Top 10 preseason team lost a home opener to an unranked team. The season remained topsy-turvy, despite the success of the top two teams in the nation. TCU followed its win over Oklahoma with a loss to middling Southern Methodist (5-6). Kansas (7-5) beat Nebraska (8-4) after 36 straight losses to the Huskers, and Vanderbilt (5-6) beat Tennessee (5-6) after 22 straight losses to the Volunteers to end the second and third longest such streaks. Navy (8-4), with 42 straight losses to Notre Dame, retained the unevable top spot. California-Davis (6-5)—yes the one and only UC Davis agriculture

school—won its first game of the season, after two losses in Division 1-AA competition, by beating Stanford (5-6). UCLA, living on the edge for much of the season, was trounced by 38 points by lowly Arizona (3-8).

With all of the craziness, one school, Notre Dame, became the one not only to challenge Southern California on the field but in terms of media coverage. The school's second choice as new coach, Charlie Weis, became a lightning rod for sound bites in the manner of his former mentor, Bill Parcells. He got his dream job only after Utah coach Urban Meyer spurned the Fighting Irish to accept the Florida job, just as notorious former Gators coach Steve Spurrier returned to the college ranks at South Carolina (7-5). Notre Dame opened with road upsets over two ranked opponents, including Michigan, while unveiling a dynamic attack that made a star out of quarterback Brady Quinn. Newspapers seemed compelled to remind fans almost daily, that Quinn happened to share a playbook with Tom Brady, Weis' charge with the New England Patriots. Readers even received reports on Quinn's sister Laura's love life; she was dating and later married A.J. Hawk, the 2005 Lombardi Trophy winner from Ohio State, who became the no. 1 draft choice of the Green Bay Packers.

Meanwhile, Notre Dame rallied against Michigan State (5-6) before losing in overtime and then beat Washington (2-9) in a match-up against Tyrone Willingham, Notre Dame's most recent coach. Need a cry? Weis let a dying boy, 10-year-old Montana Mazurkiewicz, call the first play ("pass right") of the Washington game. Young Mazurkiewicz, who was named after former Fighting Irish great Joe Montana, died the day before the game, the day before his play went for 13-yard completion to tight end Anthony Fasano. After routing Purdue (5-6), the Irish were primed to upset USC and put an end to another long winning streak. They came close.

The successes and honors earned by Bush, Leinart, Young, Weis, et al, became a secondary story for much of the first half of the season, due to a natural disaster that wrecked havoc on the gulf coast of Louisiana and Mississippi. With the season about to begin, Hurricane Katrina touched land on Monday morning, August 29. The strongest hurricane to hit the Gulf Coast since Camille in 1969, Katrina's damage was increased by a variety of human factors: levees being breached, poverty of area residents whose suspicions of government made them reluctant to heed evacuation orders, and finally a poor response by local, state, and federal officials. Although the storm affected millions of acres in multiple states, the city of New Orleans became the focal point of the disaster as the largest city hit and for the shockingly poor way supplies were brought in, people brought out, and order restored. By the end of the week when President Bush toured the area, 90% of the city was under water and the monetary damage was staggeringly high.

Although football was a tiny part of the story, teams from Tulane (2-9), Southern Mississippi (7-5) and Louisiana State were uprooted. Tulane's football team ended up sharing facilities with Louisiana Tech (7-4) and playing in 11 stadiums over the course of an exhausting year, while LSU risked its standing as a national championship contender by shifting a home game against Arizona State (7-5) to Sun Devil Stadium in Tempe because their Tiger Stadium was needed for relief efforts. That game proved to be a thriller with the Sun Devils jumping to a 17-7 lead entering the fourth quarter before surrendering touchdowns on both a blocked field goal and a blocked punt and finally a desperate 39-yard scoring pass from quarterback JaMarcus Russell to wide receiver Early Doucet. Russell's heroics on the field mirrored his performance off it for he had hosted eight storm refugees in his apartment including rock 'n roll legend Fats Domino, a family friend.

Representing the fortitude of all Louisianans, the Bayou Bengals reached the SEC title game. Tulane began its season on September 17, in an emotionally-charged contest versus Mississippi State (3-8). The Green Wave put up a fight but lost 21-14. Another storm, Hurricane Rita came through later in the fall, forcing postponement of the Navy-Rice and SMU-Houston games, while keeping area people on edge.

The typically rigid NCAA earned praise for relaxing rules governing gifts to help those athletes who now needed aid to live properly: clothing, housing, food, and medical care were now appropriate—even financial assistance—were provided to athletes put out by the storm. "Our number one priority is with the safety and well-being of student-athletes, their families, and the entire Gulf Coast population," said NCAA president Myles Brand.

The 2005 football season will forever be remembered as an amazing year.

Milestones

■ Boston College began play in new 12-member, two-division Atlantic Coast Conference. Domino effect throughout Division 1-A occurred with ACC's raid of Big East for Boston College and Miami and Virginia Tech, which had begun ACC play in 2004. To replace departees to ACC and Temple, booted for lack of competitiveness, Big East raided Conference USA for Louisville, Cincinnati and South Florida. Fearing weaker Conference USA, Texas Christian left for Mountain West. With Army already pulled out of Conference USA and returning to independent play, new teams Marshall and Central Florida were imported from Mid-America Conference and Rice, Southern Methodist, Tulsa, and Texas-El Paso were brought in from WAC. In turn, WAC recruited Utah State, New Mexico State, and Idaho.

■ Law professor Jill Gaulding started movement at University of Iowa to eliminate former coach Hayden Fry's dictum of painting Kinnick Stadium's visiting locker room pink on grounds that it was demeaning to women and gays.

■ Due to damage to Superdome, Sugar Bowl was moved outside of New Orleans for first time in history, taking place January 2, 2006 in Atlanta.

■ Longtime ABC broadcaster Keith Jackson, aged 77, retired (again) after broadcasting Rose Bowl. His final game, BCS championship that pitted Southern California and Texas, was watched on 21.7 percent of American TV sets. Ratings were astonishingly high for contemporary sports viewership and were highest for college football since 1987 Fiesta Bowl.

■ NCAA expanded use of video officiating review to all member conferences and instituted Academic Performance Rate program to measure success in graduating athletes. Programs unable to graduate 50 percent of their athletes now were open to penalties, including loss of scholarships.

■ Bill Snyder (136-68-1) and Barry Alvarez (118-73-7), who resurrected moribund programs at Kansas State and Wisconsin respectively, retired. Stadium at Kansas State was renamed Snyder Family Stadium at season's end, while Alvarez remained in Madison as athletic director.

■ Death claimed Bob Smith, Texas A&M All American halfback who rushed for school-record 297 yards versus SMU in 1950, in early January. Former Iowa star Reggie Roby, twice national punting leader in 1981, with then record 49.8 average, and 1982, died on February 22. Legendary Army halfback Glenn Davis, 80, died on March 9. Davis, "Mr. Outside" to teammate Doc Blanchard's "Mr. Inside," won 1946 Heisman Trophy and held NCAA record for career yards with 2,957, while still holding mark with 8.3 yards per carry career average. Fullback Prentice Gautt, who broke Oklahoma color barrier in 1957 and twice led Sooners in rushing, died on March 17 at age 67. Gautt served from 1979 as assistant and later associate Big 8 conference commissioner. Kurt Altenberg, UCLA end who caught touchdown pass that put Bruins into 1965 Rose Bowl, died of cancer at age 61 on April 4. Barney Poole, Hall of Fame end who played at Mississippi, North Carolina, and Army, died on April 12 at 81. Bob Ward, Maryland's All America "watcharm" guard in 1950-51 and coach in 1967-68, died on April 29. David Little, 46, former Florida linebacker suffered fatal cardiac flutter while weightlifting at home. Hall of Famer Banks McFadden, Clemson's 1939 All American halfback, died at age 88 on June 4. War hero, Hall of Famer, and Navy All America tackle in 1934, Slade Cutter, died at 93 on June 9. Cutter's field goal beat Army in 1934 for first Midshipmen victory over rivals in 13 years. Missouri linebacker Aaron O'Neal , 19, collapsed on field after conditioning drills. He was in full cardiac arrest by time help came and was pronounced dead at the hospital 90 minutes after the drill ended. Hall of Fame guard Jim Parker of Ohio State (1954-56) died at age 71 on July 18. Parker was two-time consensus All America who starred as sophomore for Buckeyes' undefeated 1955 Rose Bowl champions and later became eight-time All Pro with Baltimore Colts. Alvin Wistert, who served six years in U.S. Marine Corps during World War II before becoming 30-year-old freshman for Boston University and later All America tackle at Michigan died on October 3 at age 89. Wistert was last of three brothers to achieve All American status. Penn running back Kyle Ambrogi, age 21, committed suicide on October 10. Ambrogi had scored two touchdowns against Bucknell two days earlier. William "Barnacle Bill" Busik, All America Navy halfback who spearheaded 1941 upset of Army eight days before Pearl Harbor and who served decorously in World War II, died on October 16 at age 85. Busik served as Athletic Director at Navy from 1962-65.

■ Longest winning streaks entering the season:

Southern California 22	Utah 16	Auburn 15

■ Coaching Changes:

	Incoming	Outgoing
Brigham Young	Bronco Mendenhall	Gary Crowton
East Carolina	Skip Holtz	John Thompson
Florida	Urban Meyer	Ron Zook
Illinois	Ron Zook	Ron Turner
Indiana	Terry Hoeppner	Gerry DiNardo
Louisiana State	Les Miles	Nick Saban
Marshall	Mark Snyder	Bobby Pruett
Miami (Ohio)	Shane Montgomery	Terry Hoeppner
Mississippi	Ed Orgeron	David Cutcliffe
New Mexico State	Hal Mumme	Tony Samuel
Notre Dame	Charlie Weis	Tyrone Willingham
Ohio University	Frank Solich	Brian Knorr
Oklahoma State	Mike Gundy	Les Miles
Pittsburgh	Dave Wannstedt	Walt Harris
San Jose State	Dick Tomey	Fitz Hill
South Carolina	Steve Spurrier	Lou Holtz
Stanford	Walt Harris	Buddy Teevens
Syracuse	Greg Robinson	Paul Pasqualoni
UNLV	Mike Sanford	John Robinson
Utah	Kyle Whittingham	Urban Meyer
Utah State	Brent Guy	Mick Dennehy
Washington	Tyrone Willingham	Keith Gilbertson
Western Michigan	Bill Cubit	Gary Darnell

September 3, 2005

Maryland 23 Navy 20 (Baltimore): Playing for first time since 1965, in-state rivals put on good show for large audience (67,809) to suggest scheduling game with greater frequency. Maryland (1-0) QB Sam Hollenbach (19-30/217y) led winning 82y drive he capped with 11y TD pass to WR Drew Weatherly with 61 secs left, 1 play after TB Lance Ball raced 20y with short pass on 4th-and-8. Navy (0-1) had scored TDs on opening 2 drives, with Terps having managed FG in each of opening 2 Qs as Hollenbach threw 2 INTs. Maryland D settled down, with help from key injury. Navy QB Lamar Owens (5-11/97y, and 19/122y rushing) was lost midway through 3rd Q with hand injury and Midshipmen leading 14-6, 2 plays after their successful fake punt run by P Eric Shuey for 7y and 1st down near midfield. Navy O then stalled allowing Terps to rally with 3rd FG by K Dan Ennis, from 40y, and then in 4th Q with TD by TB Mario Merrills (30/149y) on 12y run. With Owens back, Navy traveled 80y to regain lead on FB Matt Hall's 2nd TD, on 6y run, setting up Hollenbach's heroics for Maryland.

CLEMSON 25 Texas A&M 24: Busy Clemson (1-0) K Jad Dean finished record-breaking evening with winning 42y FG with 2 secs remaining—his 6th successful 3-ptr of game. Although held without O TD, Tigers had just enough for win despite losing QB Charlie Whitehurst (14-19/185y) to dizziness after blow to head early in 4th Q. By that time frosh TB James Davis (19/101y) had emerged from Clemson's TB-by-committee, rushing on all 8 of team's plays on winning drive of 33y. QB Reggie McNeal carried Aggies (1-) O with 100y rushing and 110y passing, with 31y on TD pass to WR Chad Schroeder for 24-22 4th Q lead, but he did not reach his high standards from 2004 match-up when he produced 307y. WR Chansi Stuckey scored sole Clemson TD on 47y punt RET in 2nd Q.

Notre Dame 42 PITTSBURGH 21: Notre Dame (1-0) coach Charlie Weis decisively won match-up of former NFL coaches debuting as headmen at respective alma maters. QB Brady Quinn (18-27/227y, 2 TDs, INT) led visitors to TDs on 5 of its 1st 6 possessions, 502y total and whopping 33 1st downs. Irish D held coach Dave Wannstedt's Panthers (0-1) in check, limiting damage of Pitt passing attack while allowing only 103y rushing. Game started well for Pitt as QB Tyler Palko (20-35/220y, INT) drove O 73y in eight plays with opening possession, throwing 39y TD pass to WR Greg Lee (4/63y). After Notre Dame TB Darius Walker (20/100y) raced 51y to EZ with delayed screen to tie game 7-7, Panthers re-took lead later in Q on 49y FG by K Josh Cummings. Irish blew game open with 28 2nd Q pts, including 2 of FB Rashon Powers-Neal's 3 TDs and 18y scoring pass to heretofore unheralded (but not for long) WR Jeff Samardzija. Trailing 35-13 at H, Pitt failed to get up from canvas.

GEORGIA 48 Boise State 13: Ranked for 1st time ever in preseason, Boise State (0-1) picked wrong team to play in stepping up in class as Georgia had something to prove after graduation of heralded class of 2005. Bulldogs (1-0) enjoyed speed and huge size advantage. QB D.J. Shockley (16-24/289y), finally starter after 4 years of part-time duty, made up for lost time with 5 TD passes and TD run to lead rout, made easy by 6 1st H TOs by stunned Boise. Shockley even led Georgia in rushing with 85y. Broncos QB Jared Zabransky, who threw for 2927y in 2004, was held to 8-17/70y passing and lost 4 INTs and 2 FUMs before being pulled. Broncos did not score until 3y TD run by TB Lee Marks in 3rd Q after surrendering 38 straight pts. Georgia D had managed only 5 INTs in all of 2004.

Georgia Tech 23 AUBURN 14: It truly was new year for Tigers (0-1), who lost more games before Labor Day of 2005 than entire 2004 season. Georgia Tech (1-0) attacked inexperienced Auburn backfield, missing 3 players chosen in 1st round of April 2005 NFL draft, picking off QB Brandon Cox 4 times and allowing only 50y rushing. Cox did pass, however, for 342y and 2 TDs against numerous blitzes, but damage was limited to short passes. Still, game was not sealed until Georgia Tech LB Gerris Wilkinson returned INT 33y to set up 28y FG by K Travis Bell, his 3rd of game, with 1:28 left. Yellow Jackets relied on returning starters to power O as TB P.J. Daniels rushed for 111y and TD and QB Reggie Ball (17-36/174y, INT) threw 35y TD pass to WR Calvin Johnson (4/66y) that opened scoring in 1st Q. Loss snapped Tigers' 15-game win streak.

Texas Christian 17 OKLAHOMA 10: Horned Frogs (1-0) stunned nation—at least Sooner Nation--with demolition of Oklahoma (0-1) O, holding nation's 7th-ranked team to 225y with mere 63y gained on 22 carries by returning Heisman Trophy runner-up RB Adrian Peterson. Peterson was hampered by right ankle injury suffered in 3rd Q, although he had rushed for only 5y in 1st H. Petson's moment of brilliance occurred on opening drive of 2nd H when he rushed for 43y of 72y drive, including 11y TD scamper. TCU keyed on OU run game and still halted weak Sooners' passing attack as neither starting QB Paul Thompson (11-26/109y) nor reserve QB Rhett Bomar (2-5/19y) made Oklahoma fans forget departed QB Jason White. Thompson threw INT midway through 4th Q and lost FUM on 4th down with 1:03 left, while Bomar lost FUM on own 17YL early in 4th Q. Bomar's FUM, recovered by TCU LB David Hawthorne for his 2nd REC of day, set up winning 2y TD run by RB Robert Merrill. TCU did most of its damage through air as QB Tye Gunn passed for 226y with 16y TD pass to WR Derek

Moore. TD was first collegiate catch for soph walk-on Moore. Texas Christian last beat team ranked this high in 1961, when Frogs defeated no. 1 Texas. Sooners lost at home for 1st time since 2001 and in month of September for 1st time under coach Bob Stoops.

Air Force 20 WASHINGTON 17: Falcons (1-0) rallied with pair of 4th Q TDs to ruin debut of Washington coach Tyrone Willingham. Trying to entertain small Seattle crowd (26,482 was lowest attendance since 1950s), Huskies (0-1) built 17-6 lead as QB Isaiah Stanback (19-27/242y) dazzled in his second career start. Stanback's 27y TD pass to WR Cody Ellis capped 86y drive and gave Washington 11-pt lead with 10:50 left. Air Force WR Greg Kirkwood then fumbled ensuing KO RET OB at own 1YL. Huskies appeared to be in great shape but still needed lessons in putting away wins. Falcons surprisingly needed only 4 plays and 69 secs to score TD on stunning 84y pass from backup QB Adam Fitch to Kirkwood (6/134y). Stanback counter-moved Huskies to midfield when, on 3rd down, WR Corey Williams dropped pass. Starting QB Shaun Carney, who threw for 207y and rushed for 69y, marched Falcons 83y to winning TD, his own 1y keeper coming with 34 secs remaining. Huskies RB Louis Ruskin rushed for 112y.

(Sun) West Virginia 15 SYRACUSE 7: Charter Big East members opened 1st season of new-look conf with D-oriented struggle. Dominating Mountaineers (1-0) D allowed only 103y and 7 1st downs, while scoring TD on 31y INT RET by S Eric Wicks and safety when DT Ernest Hunter sacked QB Perry Patterson (15-31/85y, 2 INTs) in EZ. K Pat McAfee led West Virginia in scoring with 2 FGs, including 33y effort for 10-7 lead late in 3rd Q. After Mountaineers had squandered 2 1st Q scoring opportunities with lost FUMs—team had 5 TOs total including 3 FUMs by soon to be ex-starting TB Jason Colson—Syracuse (0-1) took 7-0 lead in 2nd Q on 5y run by TB Damien Rhodes. Wicks evened score soon after, and West Virginia controlled 2nd H by blanking Orange. In debut of new head coach Greg Robinson, most recently D coordinator at Texas, Orange allowed only 6 pts to Mountaineers O, but still lost 4th straight in series.

(Sun) Virginia Tech 20 NORTH CAROLINA STATE 16: With younger Vick brother at helm of O—and NFL-version Vick viewing from bench area—Virginia Tech (1-0) outlasted Wolfpack to avenge its sole ACC loss in 2004. With Atlanta Falcons QB Michael Vick watching, little brother, QB Marcus Vick (10-21/108y), threw 19y TD pass to WR David Clowney early in 4th Q for 20-13 lead and used timely runs to key victory. NC State (0-1) QB Jay Davis threw for 311y in leading pro-style O that bent Virginia Tech's D but could not break through for sufficient pts. NC State finished with 439y to 232y advantage, which was negated, in part, by 12 PENs/105y and 3 TOs.

(Sun) Louisville 31 KENTUCKY 24: To overlook Louisville (1-0) DE Elvis Dumervil because of his height (liberally listed at 5'11) was mistake no team would make again again in 2005. Dumervil had whopping 6 sacks and 2 forced FUMs in leading Cardinals to victory. RB Michael Bush, who at 6'3" had traditional DE-height that Dumervil lacked, paced O with 128y rushing, scored 2 TDs, and helped visitors run out clock with 1-TD lead. QB Brian Brohm (19-27/179y) rushed for 2 scores in his 1st start, but led Louisville to only 3 pts in 2nd H as squad almost wasted 28-7 H lead. Wildcats (0-1) QB Andre Woodson (17-27/278y) led rally with TD passes of 21y to WR Scott Mitchell and 15y to TE Jacob Tamme, but lost crucial FUM after hit by LB Brandon Johnson on Louisville 2YL with 6:41 remaining. Riding Bush, Cardinals converted 3 3rd downs on final drive to extinguish clock. Kentucky coach Rich Brooks was angry by lack of replay on Woodson FUM, wanting officials to make sure QB's knee was not down before ball came loose. "I don't understand why we have instant replay if we don't look at a pivotal play in the game like that," barked Brooks.

(Mon) FLORIDA STATE 10 Miami 7: This victory was long overdue. Not only did Florida State (1-0) beat Miami for 1st time since 1999, they were beneficiaries of botched Canes' FG attempt after years of missed FGs by Seminole Ks in closing moments of series match-ups. With less than 3 mins remaining, Miami K Jon Peattie hoped to tie game at 10-10 with 28y FG after 81y drive. Snap went awry, however, and Peattie—who earlier missed FG ATTs of 47y and 39y—was unable to launch his 3-pt try. Both teams featured inexperienced QBs, with Miami QB Kyle Wright (16-28/232y, TD, 2 INTs) getting better of stats vs. FSU QB Drew Weatherford (7-24/67y, INT), who was benched in 2nd H. Sacks wronged Wright as he suffered 9 times at hands of Florida State D. Incredibly, Seminoles sacked Wright on 4 straight plays during consecutive 3rd Q series. During 6-game series losing streak, FSU had sacked Miami QBs only 2 times total. Managing only 170y, Seminoles converted blocked punt and INT—both in Miami territory—into 2 1st Q scores, including 1y TD run by FB James Coleman. "We finally stole one from them like they've been stealing them from us," said winning coach Bobby Bowden, now 12-19 against rivals. "It's about time."

September 10, 2005

(Fr) OHIO UNIVERSITY 16 Pittsburgh 10 (OT): Bobcats CB Dion Bynum had exceptional game, scoring TDs twice on INT RETs—including winner in OT—as Ohio (1-1) stunned favored Panthers. Bynum took 1st Q INT 38y to pay-dirt and stunningly

won game by traveling 85y with INT in extra session. Neither team scored TD by its O unit as Pitt's sole 6-pter had come from 95y RET of opening KO by RB LaRod Stephens. Panthers QB Tyler Palko's success from 2004 seemed distant memory as he struggled with new O, throwing for 120y and 3 INTs. Win was sweet for head coach Frank Solich, entrusted with resurrection of lowly Bobcats program that had suffered 29 losing seasons in past 35 years. Counterpart Dave Wannstedt continued to struggle as Panthers fell to 0-2 for 1st time since 1984.

GEORGIA 17 South Carolina 15: With coach Steve Spurrier back on opposing sideline, Georgia had incentive to pay back past frustrations on underdog Gamecocks (1-1). But game turned out to be tight struggle, and Bulldogs (2-0) won with aid from South Carolina's missed FG, missed x-pt, and failed 2-pt try. Gamecocks held 9-7 H lead, scoring TD on 42y INT RET by CB Johnathan Joseph and 27y FG by K Josh Brown after PEN wiped out 19y TD pass by QB Blake Mitchell (22-34/236y, 2 INTs) to WR Sidney Rice. With QB D.J. Shockley (8-17/112y, 2 INTs) throwing poorly, Georgia rode its ground game to recovery; TB Thomas Brown rushed for 5y of his 144y total for what proved to be winning 4th Q TD. Gamecocks answered with drive, kept alive by Mitchell's 3rd-and-18 pass for 34y to WR Syvelle Newton, to Rice's 4y TD reception. Mitchell's 2-pt conv pass attempt was high and Bulldogs remained in front at 17-15. Georgia burned most of remaining 6:52, with Shockley contributing key 27y completion to WR Bryan McClendon on 3rd-and-22 from own 8YL. Gutty call by coach Mark Richt was more style of Spurrier, who had been bold Florida coach with 11-1 mark vs. UGa.

AUBURN 28 Mississippi State 0: With rebuilt O still finding its way, Auburn (1-1) D came to forefront as team earned 11th straight SEC win. Tigers stifled Mississippi State (1-1) TB Jerious Norwood (10/39y) and contained QB Omarr Conner (10-19/116y, INT) in keeping Bulldogs off scoreboard, while D scored itself when LB Will Herring recovered FUM by Bulldogs WR Tee Milons (4/54y) in Mississippi State EZ for 21-0 3rd Q lead. Although Auburn cut TOs from 5 to 1 from prior week and QB Brandon Cox (12-18/202y) showed great improvement, Tigers struggled on ground in gaining 118y against underrated Bulldogs D front-7. Cox's TD passes of 33y to TE Cole Bennett and 5y to WR Devin Aromashodu gave Tigers 14-0 H lead.

Notre Dame 17 MICHIGAN 10: When success reaches standards set by Knute Rockne, it was difficult for Notre Dame (2-0) coach Charlie Weis to stop hype machine. Weis became 1st coach at ND to open with 2 road wins since Rockne in 1918. In game dominated by crucial calls and non-calls by officials, including huge overruling by video replay in 4th Q, Irish won hard-hitting contest by outlasting Wolverines (1-1), who lost TB Mike Hart to injury in 1st H. QB Brady Quinn (19-30/140y) tossed pair of 1st H TDs, including 5y scoring pass to WR Rhema McKnight to cap impressive opening 76y drive—featuring Shotgun formation and empty backfield—that did not need 3rd down and gave lead for good to Irish. McKnight was later lost for season with knee injury. Irish TB Darius Walker added 104y rushing, while D made key plays when needed. These were highlighted by Irish S Chinedum Ndukwe's REC of 4th Q FUM by Michigan QB Chad Henne inside Notre Dame 1YL—which started as no-FUM call that was overturned—and S Tom Zbikowski's 3rd Q INT on ND 1YL. On series following Henne's FUM, Quinn was ruled to have lost FUM deep in own territory, which also was overturned in favor of Irish. Henne (19-44/223y) perservered to throw 25y TD pass to WR Mario Manningham on 4th-and-3 late in 4th Q, but could not prevent end of 16-game home win streak.

Texas 25 OHIO STATE 22: Ohio State (1-1) K Josh Huston kicked 5 FGs, but Bucks could have used at least 1 TD at right time. Still, Buckeyes led 16-13 at H as 2 FGs were set up by LB A.J. Hawk's FUM REC and INT. With Bucks QB Troy Smith returning from suspension, QB Justin Zwick (9-15/66y) started but left after 2 series. Smith (5-11/78y, TD) came in, and, after Texas TO set up Huston's 1st FG, he threw 36y TD pass to WR Santonio Holmes (4/73y). Doubts about Texas (2-0) coach Mack Brown's ability to win big games or QB Vince Young's ability to be more than running QB vanished with triumphant 72y drive in 4th Q that Young capped with 24y TD pass to WR Limas Sweed for 23-22 lead with 2:37 remaining. Young (18-29/270y, 2 TDs, 2 INTs, and 20/76y rushing) needed to be perfect on scoring pass as Sweed was double-covered by CB Ashton Youbuty and FS Nate Salley. What happened next in 1st-ever contest between storied programs seemed to seal Longhorns' win: Texas LB Drew Kelson forced FUM by alternating QB Zwick, recovered by DE Brian Robison. But, Ohio State made desperate GLS late in game to regain possession, but Texas DT Larry Dibbles sacked Ohio's other QB, Troy Smith in EZ for 2 pts.

IOWA STATE 23 Iowa 3: Sloppy play doomed Iowa as Hawkeyes (1-1) committed 5 TOs, each converted into pts by Iowa State (2-0) including TD when CB LaMarcus Hicks returned INT for 28y TD late in 2nd Q. Hicks' TD gave Iowa State 16-0 lead entering H, which was too much for Iowa without QB Drew Tate (5-11/57y). Tate left in 2nd Q after suffering concussion when tackling Iowa State FS Steve Paris after INT. In leading way to 6th win over Iowa in last 8 games, outgained Cyclones O tapped TB Stevie Hicks, who rushed for 118y, and QB Bret Meyer, who threw for 154y, including game-winning 12y TD pass to WR Austin Flynn in 1st Q. TB Albert Young paced Iowa attack with 140y rushing, while K Kyle Schlicher scored on 44y FG in 3rd Q. Iowa State beat top-10 opponent for 1st time since 1992 season's 19-10 win over no. 7 Nebraska.

SOUTHERN METHODIST 21 Texas Christian 10: Logic went out window. Providing ample proof that parity in college football, Mustangs (1-1) dealt with TCU as Horned Frogs (1-1) had treated Oklahoma week earlier. TCU's big win over Oklahoma meant nothing to SMU, rival thoroughly dominated by Frogs recently. Mustangs took control in 2nd Q, driving 79y to score on 9y run by RB Demyron Martin (26/118y) and later touring 71y to Martin's 22y TD reception. WR Cory Rodgers supplied some hope for TCU with 87y KO TD RET to open 2nd H, but SMU D continued to shine. Ponies were particularly hard on Horned Frogs QB Tye Gunn (16-36/134y), who threw 3 INTs including 2 near game's end. Martin added clincher with 2y TD run early in 4th Q.

SMU's win was its 1st over ranked foe since 1986, last season before application of famous NCAA "Death Penalty" that ruined Mustangs' program. "This just shows if you don't come to play every week, you will get beat," said losing coach Gary Patterson.

Louisiana State 35 ARIZONA STATE 31: First major game affected by Hurricane Katrina forced Louisiana State (1-0) to move home game against Arizona State west. In debut for new coach Les Miles, LSU wore home white against Sun Devils who were playing SEC opponent for first time in school history. Game featured stunning 4th Q in which teams traded lead 5 times before final Sun Devils possession ended on downs at LSU 28YL. ASU QB Sam Keller (35-56/461y, 4 TDs) had connected twice for 52y earlier in drive. Tigers had scored winning TD on desperate 4th-and-10 throw by QB JaMarcus Russell of 39y to WR Early Doucet with 1:13 left. Special teams squad turned in most of LSU's other heroics as DT Claude Wroten blocked FG attempt that CB Mario Stevenson returned 55y for TD that cut deficit to 17-14 early in 4th Q. ASU handed Tigers another TD as, on next possession, P Chris MacDonald took off on rugby-style running punt to see if he could make needed 4y for 1st down from own 40YL. He was soon engulfed by LSU players, who blocked his frantic attempt to kick ball away. LSU FB Kevin Steltz scooped it up at Sun Devils 29YL and ran it in for 4-pt lead. Keller soon regained lead with 26y TD pass to TE Jamaal Lewis as teams combined for 21 pts in 1st 5 mins of 4th Q. Tigers turned right around for new 28-24 lead on 5y TD run by TB Joseph Addai (16/109y, 2 TDs) before Keller put home team back in front again with 4y TD pass to WR Moey Mutz. Proceeds after expenses, much of which were underwritten by groups like Fiesta Bowl committee, went to Katrina Relief funds, raising more than $1 million.

September 17, 2005

(Fri) TEXAS-EL PASO 44 Houston 41 (OT): Wacky game finally ended in 2nd extra session when Houston (1-2) QB Kevin Kolb (32-50/331y) threw INT, his 5th of game, to Texas-El Paso FS Quintin Demps at GL. Miners (2-0) had gone ahead 44-41 on their 2nd OT series when K Reagan Schneider, who missed 27y 3-pt effort at end of regulation, booted 42y kick for eventual winning pts. Each team had scored TDs in 1st OT as Kolb threw his 5th TD of game, 14y to WR Jeron Harvey, and UCLA transfer RB Tyler Ebell (24/149y) scored for Miners on 2y run. Expected shootout between Kolb and UTEP QB Jordan Palmer (26-51/379y) lived up to hype as teams combined for 85 pts and 1067y. UTEP WR Johnnie Lee Higgins (6/156y) caught all 3 of Palmer's scoring passes, while Houston WR Donnie Avery (5/99y) had 2 scoring catches.

West Virginia 31 MARYLAND 19: Scoring 3 TDs in 4th Q, Mountaineers (3-0) posted 1st series road win since 1997. Highly-recruited West Virginia frosh TB Jason Gwaltney rushed twice for TDs, including 15y clincher with 5 mins remaining, while fellow frosh QB Pat White (3-5/29y, and 9/62y rushing) came off bench to lead O that gained 144y for 24 pts in final Q. Terrapins (1-2) QB Sam Hollenbach (20-31/291y) threw pair of TDs in wild 4th Q—including 73y connection with TE Vernon Davis (5/158y)—to make things interesting at 21-19 in favor of WVU, but White led Mountaineers 73y in 7 plays to Gwaltney's 2nd TD, and Hollenbach lost FUM to set up WVU's closing FG.

Florida State 28 BOSTON COLLEGE 17: ACC debut for Boston College (2-1) soured in 2nd H with loss of QB Quinton Porter (20-31/151y, TD) to ankle injury, with Eagles ahead 17-14. In 4th Q, Seminoles (3-0) QB Drew Weatherford (20-38/243y, 2 TDs, INT) threw 6y scoring pass to WR Greg Carr (3/34y, 2 TDs) and converted blocked punt by FSU S Darius McClure into 6 pts on 4y run by TB Lorenzo Booker. Seminoles LB A.J. Nicholson (19 tackles, 2 INTs) had welcomed Boston College into conf with INT on game's opening play, which he took 19y to TD. Eagles next countered with smash-mouth ball, controlling possession time by 15 mins on 48/140y rushing, while Seminoles made 13y rushing. Eagles drove deep in game's final moments before their PEN-aided 7 snaps all failed inside FSU 2YL.

Miami 36 CLEMSON 30 (OT): Facing its 1st 0-2 start in 27 years, Miami (1-1) pulled out thrilling game with INT by frosh S Kenny Phillips soon after TB Tyrone Moss scored winning 25y TD run. Finally showcasing his ability after years of injury, Moss rushed for 139y and 3 TDs. Hurricanes needed its ground game as Clemson (2-1) D harried QB Kyle Wright (16-26/152y, TD) all day, sacking him 5 times. QB Charlie Whitehurst (31-55/288y) threw for 2 TDs and ran 65y for another, but Tigers O failed to truly shine until late in game. Tigers had already rallied twice for victories in 2005, so they confidently wiped out 20-10 4th Q deficit with 2 scoring drives. With 19 secs left in regulation, Whitehurst had chance to win it but overthrew WR Chasi Stuckey in EZ.

FLORIDA 16 Tennessee 7: Gators (3-0) D has received little recognition since arrival of O-minded head coach Urban Meyer, but it had to occupy center stage after posting 2nd H shutout. Florida's victory, 1st at home over Tennessee (1-1) since 1999, made it team to beat in SEC East as its D dominated by holding Tennessee to only 66y rushing and 229y overall. Florida K Chris Hetland provided difference with trio of 2nd H FGs, each set up by special teams mishaps by Volunteers. QB Chris Leak (17-26/179y) paced

Gators O and threw key block on 18y TD reverse by roommate WR Andre Caldwell, who later would suffer broken leg. Vols QB Erik Ainge passed for 147y and TD before crowd of 90,716 that was largest in state of Florida to date.

VANDERBILT 31 Mississippi 23: It took little to please long-suffering Vanderbilt (3-0) fans, but their team's first 3-0 start since 1984 certainly qualified. QB Jay Cutler (24-41/314y) led O to 523y as Commodores ended five-game series losing streak. TB Jeff Jennings (24/103y) supplied 3 Vandy TDs, rushing for pair in 2nd Q. Mississippi (1-1) managed 400y but never rallied from 17-3 H deficit. Rebels pulled to within 24-23 on 51y PUNT TD RET by WR Mike Espy before Vanderbilt DT Ralph McKenzie blocked x-pt attempt to snap Ole Miss' NCAA-leading streak of 120 consecutive x-pts. Vanderbilt ate valuable time in marching 78y to missed FG and 64y to Jennings' 3rd TD. Vandy led 31-23 with 1:26 remaining. Rebs then drove to Vanderbilt 16YL before backup QB Robert Lane fumbled to LB Moses Osemwegie with 1 sec left. Ole Miss QB Micheal Spurlock had thrown for 257y, TD, but left final drive with finger injury.

Michigan State 44 NOTRE DAME 41 (OT): It seemed unlikely that Fighting Irish (2-1), in return to glory under coach Charlie Weis, could drop 5th straight at home to Michigan State (3-0). But Spartans scored TD in OT on 19y run by RB Jason Teague on option pitchout to overcome having squandered 21-pt lead in 2nd H. Notre Dame had settled for FG in top half of OT. Michigan State QB Drew Stanton threw himself into Heisman Trophy race, completing 16-27/327y, 3 TDs. WR Matt Trannon was Stanton's favorite target, catching 5/136y, 2 TDs, which included 65y catch-and-run for 38-17 lead in 3rd Q. Rallying Notre Dame with 3 straight TD drives, QB Brady Quinn (33-60/487y, INT) finished with school-record 5 TDs: trio to WR Jeff Samardzija (6/96y), another to WR Maurice Stovall (8/176y), and another to TB Darius Walker (116y rushing). Quinn's 487y was Irish's 2nd most O in game, after QB Joe Theismann's 526y vs. USC in 1970. Only other team to win 5 straight games at Notre Dame had been Purdue (1954-1962).

SOUTHERN CALIFORNIA 70 Arkansas 17: With host of weapons returning from nation's best O in 2004, defending national champion Trojans (2-0) lay claim to all-time best O by slaughtering Hogs. USC QB Matt Leinart(18-24/381y) threw 4 TDs and ran in another while TB Reggie Bush (8/125y) scored TDs on 1st 2 plays called for him, reaching EZ with 76y run on team's 3rd play and catching 29y TD less than 2 mins later. USC scored TDs on all 6 of its 1st H possessions to take 42-10 H lead. In 1st Q alone, Trojans took 28-7 lead despite having ball for only 1:32 to 13:28 for Razorbacks (1-2). Due to ever-increasing score deficit, Arkansas could not establish run, although RBs Darren McFadden (13/87y) and Felix Jones (11/75y) gave hint to good things to come. Southern California finished with 736y O. "I definitely think we're starting to send a message about this offense—that we've got a lot of weapons," said Bush. "For the teams that are going to be playing us, you just better be ready." After opening season with 63-17 demolition of Hawaii, monstrous Trojans had already surpassed 60-pt plateau twice on way to 7 games in 2005 with 50 pts or more.

UCLA 41 Oklahoma 24: Bruins (3-0) exploded for 21 pts in 4th Q to stun bumbling no. 21 Sooners and dash Oklahoma's hopes of 3rd straight BCS title game appearance. Sooners (1-2) fumbled 6 times—4 by QB Rhett Bomar (20-29/241y)—losing 3, which led to 17 pts for Bruins. QB Drew Olson (28-38/314y) threw 3 TDs at helm of UCLA attack, while Bruins D checked OU RB Adrian Peterson with 58y rushing. Peterson had bad week, being benched at beginning of game for missing classes. Peterson was met on several occasions by Bruins LB Spencer Havner (9 tackles), who scored team's 2nd TD on 13y FUM RET in 3rd Q. UCLA S Dennis Keyes forced 2 FUM RECs that were converted into 10 pts, including Havner's TD, to make up for missed tackle on Sooners' main highlight: 56y TD run on reverse by WR Travis Wilson in 1st H.

OREGON 37 Fresno State 34: Eugene was host to latest western shootout as Oregon (3-0) QB Kellen Clemens threw for 332y and 4 TDs in outscoring Bulldogs QB Paul Pinegar, who passed 33-43/418y, 3 TDs. Clemens' winning 42y TD pass was no deep spiral as TB Terrence Whitehead took short pass to EZ in spectacular fashion, bouncing through Fresno (1-1) defenders and leaping over sprawled blockers. TD put Ducks up 37-27 with little more than 4 mins left. But Pinegar quickly pulled Fresno within 3 pts on 14y scoring pass to RB Matt Rivera. Ducks sealed win by recovering Bulldogs' on-side KO attempt. Oregon WR Demetrius Williams (8/95y) had caught 2 2nd Q TD passes as Ducks rallied from 17-0 deficit to take 20-17 H lead. WR Paul Williams led Bulldogs receivers with 5/122y and 36y TD in 3rd Q. PENs totaling 155y helped to sink Bulldogs, who had won 3 straight vs. Pac 10 opposition.

USA Today Coaches September 18

1	Southern California (60)	1548	14	California	722
2	Texas (2)	1483	15	Georgia Tech	654
3	LSU	1364	16	Texas Tech	523
4	Virginia Tech	1350	17	Arizona State	395
5	Florida	1292	18	Notre Dame	385
6	Georgia	1240	19	Virginia	358
7	Florida State	1180	20	Alabama	340
8	Louisville	1035	21	Iowa	277
9	Ohio State	972	22	Michigan State	256
10	Purdue	909	23	UCLA	232
11	Tennessee	863	24	Wisconsin	205
12	Miami (Fla.)	852	25	Boston College	163
13	Michigan	736			

September 24, 2005

(Fri) Iowa State 28 ARMY 21: No. 22 Cyclones (3-0) needed 4th Q rally to put away stubborn Cadets on FB Ryan Kock's 2 short TD runs. Black Knights (0-3), gunning for 1st win over ranked opponent since beating Air Force 17-14 in 1972, had late chance. But, Army lost ball on downs in Iowa State territory with less than min left. Army had taken 21-14 3rd Q lead on 1y TD run by TB Scott Wesley, capping 40y drive begun after INT by Cadets S Caleb Campbell. Cyclones rallied thanks to their D recovering 2 Army FUMs and their special teams blocking punt. Iowa State QB Bret Meyer (18-26/158y, 2 TDs, 3 INTs) struggled at times, while QB Zac Dahman, who also tossed 2 TDs, threw for 233y to become all-time Army leader with 5655y. Dahman passed by Leamon Hall's 5502y (1974-1977). Army RB Carlton Jones made 34/122y rushing.

SOUTH FLORIDA 45 Louisville 14: Game was expected to be rout as 9th-ranked Louisville (2-1) needed to impress voters. But surprisingly, Bulls pulled off shocker in Big East debut for both teams. In only its 9th year of varsity play, South Florida (3-1) made bold statement behind series of trick plays, almost all revolving around WR Amarri Jackson. After catching 57y pass to set up team's opening score on 1y run by TB Andre Hall (22/83y), Jackson ran in pair of reverses for TDs and 21-0 lead. He followed up by throwing 11y TD pass to TE Derek Carter in 3rd Q for whopping 38-7 advantage. Jackson was remarkably efficient as he touched ball only 5 times. South Florida KR Chad Simpson had already dimmed Cardinals' comeback chances by returning 2nd H KO 94y for TD. Louisville, which had owned 9-game win streak and 13-game streak of scoring at least 30 pts, squandered 493y of O with 3 TOs, 4 sacks allowed, and 118y of PENs. Cardinals QB Brian Brohm threw for 389y, but no TDs. Win was 1st over ranked opponent in 6 tries for South Florida.

VIRGINIA TECH 51 Georgia Tech 7: Anticipated battle of Techs turned ugly fast as Hokies (4-0) scored in variety of ways. Virginia Tech QB Marcus Vick hit 13-18/223y, TD passing to lead O, while Hokies D and special teams combined to score 3 TDs. FS D.J. Parker scooped up blocked FG and raced 78y for TD that gave Hokies 14-0 lead in 1st Q, and LB Xavier Adibi and DE Chris Ellis scored on INT RETs of 25y and 29y respectively. They came 26 secs apart for 48-7 lead late in 3rd Q. Hokies TE Jeff King was surprise star player of 1st Q, catching 13y TD pass and blocking FG that led to Parker's TD. Yellow Jackets (3-1), hoping to start season 4-0 for 1st time since their 1990 national co-champions opened similarly, managed only 6 first downs and 217y O. Georgia Tech's sole TD was scored by WR Calvin Johnson (5/123y) on 11y pass from QB Reggie Ball (11-27/143y, TD, 2 INTs). Virginia Tech now had perpetrated remarkable 49 RET TDs since 1999. "I think that they're the best football team I've seen since I've been in the ACC," said Georgia Tech coach Chan Gailey.

ALABAMA 24 Arkansas 13: Rebirth of Crimson Tide (4-0) continued with conf win over Arkansas squad that salvaged some pride after huge loss to Southern California week prior. Alabama WR D.J. Hall caught 2 TD passes from QB Brodie Croyle (13-27/173y), including wide-open clinching 5y score with 2:22 left. Razorbacks (1-3) had rallied earlier in 4th Q, pulling to within 17-10 on 70y TD run by dynamic frosh TB Darren McFadden (8/95y) and converting blocked punt into 27y FG by K Chris Balseiro to trail by 17-13. Razorbacks D forced another punt but Arkansas QB Robert Johnson (11-26/81y) threw INT on ensuing drive. Alabama RB Ken Darby contributed 18/98y.

OHIO STATE 31 Iowa 6: Buckeyes (3-1) laid claim to Big 10 supremacy with surprisingly easy rout, more evocative of era when Ohio State picked on Big 10 have-not schools once known as "Little 8." Iowa (2-2) gained only 137y, with awful –9y rushing, thanks to 5 Ohio State sacks of Hawkeyes QB Drew Tate (22-39/146y, INT). Hawkeyes earned only 6 1st downs, converting 1-12 on 3rd downs. Ohio State gained 530y with QB Troy Smith (13-19/191y) throwing for 2 TDs—both to WR Anthony Gonzalez (6/90y)—and rushing for 127y and another TD. Buckeyes TB Antonio Pittman rushed for 171y of team's 314y. Iowa managed 2 FGs by K Kyle Schicher, including career-best 52y effort in 3rd Q.

WISCONSIN 23 Michigan 20: Winning with long-time staples of coach Barry Alvarez—power run game and hard-nosed D—Badgers (4-0) pulled out victory with 4y TD run by QB John Stocco (15-32/147y, INT) with 24 secs left. "I was a little surprised by the call, but it was unbelievable," said Stocco. His TD capped 17-pt surge in 4th Q for Badgers, who softened Wolverines (2-2) D with running of TB Brian Calhoun (35/155y), who made 6y TD run. Michigan did most of its damage through air as QB Chad Henne (16-34/258y, 2 TDs, INT) threw TD passes of 4y to WR Jason Avant (7/108y) and 49y to WR Mario Manningham (4/106y). Manningham's TD on flea-flicker play had reestablished Wolverines with lead at 23-16 with 9 mins left. Key D moment of game had been 1st H GLS at 1YL by Badgers to end 96y drive by Wolverines. With its 1st loss to Wisconsin since 1994, slumping Michigan dropped out of Top 25 for 1st time since October 1998, span of 114 weeks. Win was first for soon-to-retire coach Alvarez against Michigan coach Lloyd Carr after 6 losses.

Texas Christian 51 BRIGHAM YOUNG 50 (OT): Officials turned to TV replay to make big OT decision at GL, but replays proved inconclusive. So, Texas Christian WR Cory Rodgers, who had lost ball in pileup as he reached BYU (1-2) GL, was awarded TD after 3y E-around. At naked-eye speed, officials had ruled that ball crossed GL before it was stripped. Horned Frogs (3-1) K Chris Manfredini simply won game with x-pt kick because Cougars had missed x-pt with bad snap after their TD earlier in OT: QB John Beck had thrown 25y TD to WR Todd Watkins for that score. Horned Frogs had no answer for Beck as jr signal-caller threw for 30-51/517y, 5 TDs. Beck launched 3 TDs in 1st Q, 39y effort to Watkins (7/176y) and pair to WR Zac Collie. Rodgers had scored TCU's sole 1st Q TD on 100y KO RET. Frogs trailed 24-16 at H. Cougars ran off 1st 10 pts of 3rd Q, so Purple Frogs, now down 18 pts looked to sub QB Jeff Ballard (8-12/150y, 2 TDs). TCU's rally included expansion of Rodgers' resume as he scored on 2y run and 34y catch among his 9/137y receiving. That gave TCU 3-pt lead with 1:25 left, but Beck quickly moved Cougars to tying FG, from 39y by K Jared McLaughlin.

Southern California 45 OREGON 13: Ducks (3-1) played inspired ball for 25 mins, but that was not nearly enough to derail mighty USC. Southern California (3-0) QB Matt Leinart (23-39/315y) led rally from 13-0 2nd Q deficit with 3 TD passes as Trojans scored on 7 straight possessions to easily win 25th straight game for new Troy record. Trojans RB Reggie Bush (122y rushing, and 3/43y receiving) scored on 19y reception in 2nd Q and 11y run in 4th Q. "Once we got the train moving, there was no stopping it," said Bush. Oregon QB Kellen Clemens (15-30/168y) threw 36y TD pass to WR Demetrius Williams (5/83y), but ran out of gas in 2nd H under constant pressure from USC D. Trojans WR Dwayne Jarrett (8/94y) was his usual explosive self but caused INT for Leinart as pass slipped off Jarrett's hands at Oregon GL in 1st Q.

(Mon) Tennessee 30 LOUISIANA STATE 27 (OT): LSU transfer QB Rick Clausen (21-32/196y, TD, INT) accounted for air and ground scores for Tennessee (2-1) in haunting his hurricane-weary old mates. Vols rallied from 21-0 H deficit and scored 17 pts in 4th Q to stun faithful LSU fans who were glad to be back at Tiger Stadium. After LSU (1-1) settled for 31y FG by K Colt David with opening possession of OT, Tennessee went 25y to score winning 1y TD on persistent run by RB Gerald Riggs, Jr. (24/89y). Riggs gained every y of Vols' half of extra session with 10y catch and 4 rushes for 15 tough y. Tennessee had pulled Clausen off bench to replace QB Erik Ainge (7-19/54y), and Vols were able to tied it 24-24 with 2 mins left in regulation thanks to Clausen's 1y TD keeper, FS Jonathan Hefney's INT RET to LSU 2YL to set up 1y TD run by Riggs, and K James Wilhoit's 28y FG. No. 3 Tigers had built big 1st H lead with 70y drive to 1y TD run by QB JaMarcus Russell (14-28/158y, INT) and Ainge's FUM and INT set up 19y TD run by TB Joseph Addai (16/84y) and 3y INT TD RET by LB Kenneth Hollis. Game marked much-delayed home debut for new LSU coach Les Miles. Hurricane Katrina had postponed opener and moved Arizona State game. Friday's arrival of Hurricane Rita postponed this match-up from Saturday to Monday.

USA Today Coaches September 25

1	Southern California (60)	1547	14	Notre Dame	643
2	Texas (1)	1482	15	Arizona State	629
3	Virginia Tech (1)	1382	16	Alabama	609
4	LSU	1370	17	Wisconsin	489
5	Florida	1298	18	Virginia	484
6	Georgia	1239	19	Minnesota	396
7	Florida State	1196	20t	Purdue	360
8	Ohio State	1083	20t	UCLA	360
9	Tennessee	968	22	Louisville	308
10	Miami (Fla.)	945	23	Boston College	255
11	California	876	24t	Auburn	133
12	Michigan State	688	24t	Georgia Tech	133
13	Texas Tech	683			

October 1, 2005

(Fri) RUTGERS 37 Pittsburgh 29: Rutgers had not defeated Pittsburgh since 1998. So, Scarlet Knights (3-1) had to be riding high to have opened 2005 conf play with victory since they only owned 3 Big East wins in past 4 seasons. Rutgers built 27-0 H lead as QB Ryan Hart (12-25/207y, 2 INTs) threw 2 TD pass to FB Brian Leonard (18/68y, and 4/62y receiving), WR Willie Foster returned punt 71y for TD, and K Jeremy Ito booted 2 FGs. Panthers (1-4) flexed their muscles to open 2nd H: they earned pair of 3rd Q TDs on passes by QB Tyler Palko (35-58/371y, 2 TDs), to pull within 27-14. Having blown 20-pt 3rd Q lead to Illinois in season's 1st game, Rutgers D felt it had to respond, and it did as LB William Beckford stripped Palko for REC at Pitt 27YL. Hart quickly threw his 3rd TD pass for 25y to WR Tres Moses. Palko threw 2 more TD passes in 4th Q, but Pitt's final 2 possessions ended on fake punt incompletion and INT. Rutgers RB Ray Rice rushed 15/114y.

Virginia Tech 34 WEST VIRGINIA 17: Finale of 33-game series went way of Hokies (5-0) as QB Marcus Vick completed 15-17/177y, 2 TDs, while rushing for 74y. Mountaineers (4-1) hoped to repeat upset of 2003 when Virginia Tech was also undefeated and ranked 3rd before losing in Morgantown. That was not to be as Vick converted West Virginia's lost FUM into his 10y QB keeper for opening score and twice answering TD throws by WVU QB Pat White with TD passes of his own to keep Hokies in front. Vick's 3 TDs and K Brandon Pace's 35y FG kept Va Tech ahead 24-14 at H. Teams swapped FGs in 3rd Q before Virginia Tech clinched matters with 4y TD run by RB Cedric Humes (22/79y). Despite loss, Mountaineers discovered frosh O geniuses in White (9-11/85y, 2 TDs), in relief of injured QB Adam Bednarik, and whippet-fast TB Steve Slaton, who rushed 11/90y. White and Slaton would lead West Virginia to 7-0 mark rest of way.

WAKE FOREST 31 Clemson 27: Wild finish highlighted Deamon Deacons (2-3) upset, secured when officials ruled time had expired after Clemson (2-3) WR Curt Baham's 27y catch was halted on Wake 3YL. Wake Forest had just scored 33 secs earlier when QB Cory Randolph (20-25/222y, 2 TDs, INT) threw 6y TD pass to WR Kevin Marion to cap frantic 8-play, 66y drive. Despite gaining 454y for game, with QB Charlie Whitehurst throwing for 304y, Tigers (2-3) were unable to score more than 6 pts in 2nd H. Randolph was revelation, running for Deacs' 1st TD from 4y out and throwing 74y TD to WR Kenneth Moore and 34y TD to WR Nate Morton as they grabbed 21-7 lead in 2nd Q. Tigers had tied it 21-21 at H as TB James Davis notching his 2nd TD of game. Every Clemson game so far in 2005 had come down to nail-biting time.

ALABAMA 31 Florida 3: Match-up of early season unbeatens easily went way of Tide (5-0), who dominated every aspect of game. QB Brodie Croyle (14-17/283y) led resurgent Alabama with 3 TD passes, including 88y effort to WR Tyrone Prothro (5/134y) and 65y hook-up with WR Keith Brown in building 24-3 H lead. Alabama marched 80y with opening possession of 2nd H to score clinching TD on 15y pass to Protho. Not scoring TD for 1st time in game since 1992, Gators (4-1) suffered 1st loss because of pressure (4 sacks) by Bama that forced QB Chris Leak (16-37/187y) into throwing his 1st 2 INTs of season after 118 pass attempts. Gators WR Dallas Baker excelled on O, catching 6/119y. Croyle set team record with 36 career TD passes, surpassing mark jointly held by Andrew Zow and current Tide coach Mike Shula. Bad news for Tide was broken leg suffered by Prothro when attempting to catch 4th Q pass in EZ with game long having been decided.

PENN STATE 44 Minnesota 14: Run-conscious Golden Gophers went pretty much nowhere. While Penn State (5-0) D and big deficit against Minnesota (4-1) held TB Laurence Maroney to 48y rushing and team to 113y on ground. Meanwhile, Nittany Lions cruised to 364y rushing and 2 TDs apiece by WR Derrick Williams (4/32y, and 6/40y rushing) and Tony Hunt (21/114y). Penn State QB Michael Robinson (13-32/175y) chipped in with 112y rushing. Williams scored 1st 2 TDs by lining up in backfield for 13y run and taking E-around 5y for 17-0 2nd Q advantage. Minnesota QB

Bryan Cupito (16-28/174y, TD, INT) attempted to make game of it with 48y TD pass to WR Ernie Wheelwright late in 2nd Q, cutting deficit to 20-7, but Lions reeled off 17 straight pts in 3rd Q with Hunt scoring twice. Win seemed to indicate that Penn State was on long-awaited comeback since victory was 1st over ranked team since beating Wisconsin in 2002. "I don't want to get carried away here," said cautious coach Joe Paterno of Penn State's hot start. "We've got a long way to go."

Michigan 34 MICHIGAN STATE 31 (OT): Spartans (4-1) continued to struggle against in-state rivals, dropping 4th straight in series and 2nd consecutive in OT. Winning pts came courtesy of 35y FG by K Garrett Rivas, who earlier missed FG in final min of regulation. Michigan State K John Goss had missed 37y FG ATT with 1st possession of OT. Wolverines (3-2) TB Mike Hart rushed 36/218y to confirm his recovery from hamstring injury that plagued him at outset of season. Michigan QB Chad Henne (26-35/256y, INT) also threw 3 1st H TDs. Spartans QB Drew Stanton completed 20-30/282y with 61y TD pass to WR Kerry Reed that tied game 21-21 in 2nd Q. After active 1st H in which 44 pts had been scored, 2nd H yielded only Hart's 1y TD run 31-24 Michigan lead with 11:29 left. Spartans D tied it when DT Domata Peko scooped up FUM by Henne and rambled 74y for 31-31 deadlock.

TEXAS A&M 16 Baylor 13 (OT): Aggies (3-1) struggled, finally subduing stubborn and surprising Baylor (3-1) in overtime on 13y TD run by RB Courtney Lewis (16/58y) after Bears had settled for 21y OT FG by K Ryan Havens. Texas A&M was up against wall near end of regulation, needing to spend 17 plays to go 86y to tying 25y FG by K Todd Pegram with 1 min left. Baylor QB Shawn Bell (25-45/222y, TD) outpassed A&M QB Reggie McNeal (12-31/132y, 2 INTs), giving Bears 10-7 3rd Q lead on 3y scoring pass to WR Trent Shelton. Occasionally-electric McNeal rushed for 83y and played his best ball on drive to tying FG, twice converting 4th downs, including 13y completion to WR Chad Schroeder on 4th-and-7. Baylor twice had ball within Texas A&M 5YL in 1st H without scoring and continued its dreary 0-37 Big 12 mark on road. Bears RB Paul Mosley rushed for 133y.

Southern California 38 ARIZONA STATE 28: Arizona State (3-2) had upset in its grasp until 4th Q rally by Trojans, keyed by monstrous Cardinal and Gold running attack. Sun Devils WR Terry Richardson opened scoring with 84y punt RET TD, and Arizona State answered USC's FG with 2 TD drives in 2nd Q to take 21-3 H lead. Trojans (4-0) were in trouble but showed no panic. Instead, USC took advantage of ASU's exhausted defenders in 2nd H and rushed for game-total of 373y—behind TBs LenDale White (19/197y) and Reggie Bush (17/158y). It spelled USC's 26th straight win for new school and Pac-10 records. Once Trojans took 31-28 lead on 34y scoring romp by Bush with 3:44 left, pressure was back on ASU QB Sam Keller (26-45/347y, 2 TDs, 5 INTs), and Keller soon threw his 4th INT on pass to WR Derek Hagan (10/162y). In leaping to make catch, Hagan let ball bounce off him, and Trojans S Kevin Ellison made take-away catch. After White rumbled 46y to extend Trojans' lead to 38-28, Keller, who had confidently reached 213 straight passes without INT in 2nd Q, threw his 5th INT to end matters. It had taken Trojans until midway through 4th Q to cop 24-21 lead on 1y scoring keeper by QB Matt Leinart (23-39/258y). ASU regained lead on Keller's 1y TD pass to TE Lee Burghgraef, capping amazing drive that had overcome 1st-and-25 at own 15YL. Lead would be fleeting as Trojans needed only 5 plays to drive to Bush's TD. USC now had scored 140 2nd H pts during season, to 28 by foes.

USA Today Coaches October 2

1	Southern California (60)	1547	14	Wisconsin	737
2	Texas (1)	1483	15	Florida	717
3	Virginia Tech (1)	1425	16	UCLA	497
4	Georgia	1332	17	Boston College	449
5	Florida State	1287	18	Penn State	438
6	Ohio State	1169	19	Michigan State	418
7	Tennessee	1124	20	Arizona State	374
8	Miami (Fla.)	1081	21	Auburn	336
9	California	993	22	Louisville	326
10	Alabama	982	23	Georgia Tech	182
11	LSU	953	24	Michigan	175
12	Notre Dame	850	25	Virginia	111
13	Texas Tech	770			

October 8, 2005

(Th) North Carolina State 17 GEORGIA TECH 14: Sometimes tugging on Superman's cap actually works. With 33 secs left and 1st-and-goal at North Carolina State 2YL, Georgia Tech (3-2) looked to super WR Calvin Johnson (10/130y) for winning play. QB Reggie Ball (21-53/279y, 2 INTs, and 12/88y rushing) faked handoff and threw for Johnson, who leapt to get hands on ball as CB Marcus Hudson hit him. This sent ball airborne, and S Garland Heath picked it off and barely touched 2 feet down before tumbling out of back of EZ. WR Brian Clark was star on O for Wolfpack (2-2) as he caught 4/148y, 2 TDs, with 80y catch for winning 4th Q TD in which he outraced Tech secondary after catching short throw from QB Jay Davis (18-25/230y, TD, 2 INTs). Yellow Jackets had scored twice to take 14-10 lead on TDs by Johnson on 27y reception and TB P.J. Daniels (22/61y) on 12y run early in 4th Q. Pair of short FG misses by struggling K Travis Bell proved to be too much for Georgia tech to overcome. NC State snapped its 6-game conf losing streak and won in Atlanta for 1st time since 1988.

NAVY 27 Air Force 24: Midshipmen (2-2) needed 10-pt rally in final 2:22 to beat Air Force for 3rd straight season. Despite hurrying onto field and facing steady rain, Navy K Joey Bullen calmly nailed winning 46y FG with time elapsing. Navy had tied game on 40y scamper by SB Reggie Campbell, who set up TD by racing 29y with pass reception. On strength of 2 TD passes by QB Shaun Carvey (6-9/111y, INT), including 54y scoring pass to WR Greg Kirkwood, Falcons (2-4) had owned 17-7 advantage at H. Navy pulled to within 3 pts on 61y TD pass as QB Lamar Owens (8-12/171y, TD,

INT) teamed with WR Jason Tomlinson (4/114y). After Air Force regained 10-pt lead, Middies scored game's final 13 pts with help from their D that prevented AFA from earning more than single 1st down in 4th Q.

BOSTON COLLEGE 28 Virginia 17: Showing no effects from sprained ankle that sidelined him for 2 games, Boston College (5-1) QB Quinton Porter (25-37/301y, INT) threw 2 TD passes in leading charges to win. LB-RB Brian Toal,BC's short-y specialist, chipped in with dual TD runs to give him team-leading 5 for season. His 1st score, on 1y dive in 3rd Q for 21-14 lead came after blocked punt by SS Paul Anderson was recovered at 2YL. Cavaliers (3-2) QB Marques Hagans threw for 195y and 2 TDs. Eagles DE Mathias Kiwanuka was ejected in 3rd Q for punching Cavs T Bill Butler, who had earlier blocked Kiwanuka behind knees after whistle.

Georgia 27 TENNESSEE 14: Bulldogs (5-0) won their 3rd straight tilt in Knoxville as QB D.J. Shockley threw for 207y and rushed for 51y in helming Georgia O that generated 405y. Despite career-high 310y passing by QB Rick Clausen, Tennessee (3-2) trailed all game, due in part to 3 TOs and special teams advantage for Georgia. Bulldogs P Gordon Ely-Kelso continually pinned Tennessee deep in its territory, and Bulldogs CB Thomas Flowers contributed game-clincher with 54y punt TD RET midway through 4th Q. Down 13-0 in 3rd Q, Clausen scored Tennessee's 1st TD on keeper following 34y INT RET by CB Jonathan Wade to Georgia 1YL. Shockley next lost FUM in his territory, and momentum seemed to swing to desperate Vols. But, Tennessee returned favor when RB John Briscoe lost FUM to take air right out of Vols' balloon. After Ely-Kelso pinned UT to its 1YL with, Flowers countered with his TD RET on Vols' punt out with 8:50 remaining for 20-7 edge.

PENN STATE 17 Ohio State 10: Out of national spotlight for several years, Nittany Lions (6-0) finally roared again as legitimate conf and national honors contender. With LBs Paul Posluszny (14 tackles and sack) and Dan Connor (12 tackles and sack) proving that Penn State atill could be called "Linebacker U," Lions coach Joe Paterno captured his 349th win. Swift Penn State WR Derrick Williams scored game's 1st TD on 13y run early in 2nd Q for 7-3 lead. Less than 3 mins later, Penn State SS Calvin Lowry returned INT to Ohio 2YL, and QB Michael Robinson (11-20/78y, and 14/52y rushing) scored on short run. Ohio State (3-2) QB Troy Smith (13-25/19y, INT) added own 10y TD run later in 2nd Q. Nittany Lions added 41y FG by K Kevin Kelly on opening possession of 3rd Q, but that ended scoring. Smith was sacked in 4th Q by whirlwind DE Tamba Hali, and FUM REC was made by DT Scott Paxson. This clinched it as Penn State then ran out clock. Despite D reputations of both clubs, teams combined for 425y with Ohio State gaining 230y. Win vaulted Nittany Lions to 8th in AP poll, their highest since 1999, which was last season in which they beat team as highly ranked as no. 6 Buckeyes.

Minnesota 23 MICHIGAN 20: You could forgive visiting Minnesota (5-1) fans if they had forgotten what Little Brown Jug looked like, but their seemingly eternal wait for its return finally ended when K Jason Giannini booted 30y FG with 1 sec remaining. Gophers snapped 16-game series losing streak by dominating rushing category. Minneasota outgained Wolverines (3-3) on ground by 264y to 94y. TB Gary Russell (18/128y) gained 61y of that total on late dash to set up Giannini's heroics. Wolverines, off to their worst start since 1990, had 2 chances to break 20-20 tie but K Garrett Rivas missed FG attempts from 42y late in 3rd Q and 34y midway in 4th Q. Fact that Michigan had to settle for FGs instead of TDs was evident in its woeful 3 of 14 success rate on 3rd downs. Minnesota TB Laurence Maroney led all ground gainers with 36/129y, while Wolverines TB Mike Hart rushed 28/109y. Michigan's highlight came on 95y KO TD RET by WR Steve Breaston early in 3rd Q.

NORTHWESTERN 51 Wisconsin 48: Upset day in Big 10 continued with Wildcats winning shootout. Northwestern (3-2) gained 674y and scored on 7 straight possessions. But, Badgers (5-1) rallied with 21 pts in 4th Q, scoring final 2 TDs on passes of 13y and 21y from QB John Stocco to WR Jonathan Orr (5/87y), that combo's 3rd and 4th scoring hook-ups of day. Badgers next forced punt, but NW P Ryan Pederson pinned them on their 3YL. On next play, Cats FS Reggie McPherson sealed win with INT. Northwestern frosh RB Tyrell Sutton rushed for 244y and 3 TDs, including 62y jaunt in 4th Q for winning pts. QB Brett Basanez hit 26-36/361y, 3 TDs. Stocco threw for career-high 326y, but was picked off twice, while RB Brian Calhoun rushed for 122y and caught 11/128y. Teams combined for 72 pts in crazy 2nd H.

Texas 45 Oklahoma 12 (Dallas): Longhorns (5-0) put end to 5 years of frustrating series outcomes by pounding their Red River rivals. Texas QB Vince Young—year removed from being unable to score against Sooners—threw 3 TD passes. Oklahoma (2-3) earned just 12 1st downs on 77y rushing and 94y passing, with RB Adrian Peterson, who rushed for 225y vs. Texas in 2004, carrying only 3 times/10y due to continuing problems with his sprained ankle. Longhorns easily trumped those numbers by compiling 444y, with Young passing for 241y with 2 TDs to WR Billy Pittman. Leading 7-6, late in 1st Q after Oklahoma K Garrett Hartley booted FGs of 52y and 26y, frosh RB Jamaal Charles (9/116y) jump-started Texas to 31 straight pts with 80y scoring romp. "I'm excited about where we are and where I think we're going," said winning coach Mack Brown.

Texas Tech 34 NEBRASKA 31: Red Raiders (5-0) squandered 3-TD lead but kept their composure to win on 10y TD pass by QB Cody Hodges (34-45/368y, INT), his 4th score of game, to lunging WR Joel Filani (11/163y) with 12 secs remaining. Winning play occurred on 4th down and featured Hodges standing tall despite heavy pass rush. Cornhuskers (4-1), trying to avenge previous year's 70-10 debacle in Lubbock, seemed to have iced game when NG Le Kevin Smith picked off Hodges deep in Nebraska territory with 1:11 left, only to lose FUM on his unaccustomed RET that was recovered by Tech WR Danny Amendola. Nebraska QB Zac Taylor (21-35/229y, 2 INTs) threw 2 TD passes to WR Terrence Nunn as Huskers took 31-27 lead early in 4th Q. Red Raiders RB Taurean Henderson caught 6/ 51y and TD to tie Mark Templeton of Long Beach State (1983-86) for most career receptions by RB. Henderson would finish career with 303 catches, good for 3rd place all-time among all players. Nebraska had last lost on their Homecoming Saturday in 1968.

UCLA 47 California 40: Wild West Coast affair featured 5 TDs by Bruins (5-0) TB Maurice Drew (15/65y), including winning 28y reception with 95 secs left. Bears (5-1) lost despite making 545y and 26 1st downs. Cal had its share of O heroes: TB Justin Forsett (10/153y) and TB Marshawn Lynch (22/135y) each topped century mark and frosh WR DeSean Jackson caught 10/128y. Drew, who also had scored 5 TDs against Washington in 2004, enjoyed 299y all-purpose, with 162y on 3 punt RETs. Drew returned punt 81y on 3rd Q romp for 28-27 lead. He also converted late INT by CB Trey Brown, scoring on 2y run as time expired for final score. Bruins QB Drew Olson (17-33/225y, 2 TDs) engineered rally from 40-28 4th Q deficit in 4th Q, leading drives of 80y and 75y, latter to Drew's winning TD catch. Bears QB Joe Ayoob (18-35/215y, INT) threw 2 TD passes in defeat, including 35y effort to Jackson in 2nd Q.

Oregon 31 ARIZONA STATE 17: Once again Arizona State (3-3) blew lead to ranked team at home, but this time they spared fans 4th Q pain by surrendering 24 straight pts earlier in game. Sun Devils had taken 10-0 1st Q lead on 20y TD pass from QB Sam Keller (31-56/277y, 2 INTs) to WR Derek Hagan and 34y FG by K Jesse Ainsworth 4 plays after INT was returned to Oregon 8YL by LB Jamar Williams. Oregon (5-1) QB Kellen Clemens (20-39/278y, 2 INTs) shook off Williams' INT to lead visitors on 6 scoring drives, 2 he ended with TD passes and 3 backup K Matt Evensen ended with FGs, including 51y 3-ptr. Clemens' 2nd TD pass—34y to WR Demetrius Williams—provided dagger early in 4th Q, while Ducks D posted 4th Q shutout to hold off Sun Devils. Oregon RB Terrence Whitehead, who scored twice and led rushers with 122y, had 9 receptions/100y in becoming 2nd Duck player ever to reach 100y rushing and receiving in same game. HB Bobby Moore, nee Ahmad Rashad, did trick in 1970.

USA Today Coaches October 9

1	Southern California (57)	1544	14	Boston College	657
2	Texas (4)	1488	15	Ohio State	572
3	Virginia Tech (1)	1425	16	California	563
4	Georgia	1348	17	Michigan State	540
5	Florida State	1290	18	Tennessee	473
6	Miami (Fla.)	1187	19	Louisville	460
7	Alabama	1156	20	Auburn	444
8	LSU	1049	21	Oregon	311
9	Notre Dame	998	22	Minnesota	303
10	Penn State	942	23	Wisconsin	293
11	Texas Tech	918	24	Colorado	184
12	UCLA	862	25	West Virginia	91
13	Florida	840			

October 15, 2005

WEST VIRGINIA 46 Louisville 44 (OT): Unheralded West Virginia (6-1) TB Steve Slaton made national splash with 6 TDs—all after H with 3 in extra sessions—as Mountaineers became Big East team to beat. Slaton scored final TD on 1y run in 3rd OT, after which QB Pat White threw 2-pt conv pass to WR Dorrell Jalloh. Cardinals (4-2) then scored on RB Michael Bush's 4th TD, but QB Brian Brohm was tackled shy of EZ by S Eric Wicks to end game. Louisville had built 17-0 lead as D allowed only 56y in 1st H and O held close to 11-min advantage in time of possession. Cardinals D collapsed in 4th Q, however, surrendering 3 TD drives within 7-min span. Louisville O was unable to get 1st down holding 24-17 lead with 4 mins left. White, who entered game earlier in 4th Q after starter QB Adam Bednarik was injured, led drive to Slaton's tying 1y TD run. Slaton broke school record for 5 TDs in game, which had been held by Ira Errett Rodgers since 1919. Bush rushed 37/159y, while Brohm passed 31-49/277y, 2 TDs, INT.

VIRGINIA 26 Florida State 21: On 10th anniversary of Virginia handing Seminoles their 1st ACC loss, that band of 1995 Cavaliers was honored at H. That win had remained as only other for Cavaliers over Top 5 team, until this Saturday. Cavs (4-2) bounced no. 4 Florida State from unbeaten ranks as QB Marques Hagans hit 27-36/career-high 306y and pair of 1st H TD passes, both off scrambles. Cavaliers K Connor Hughes also booted 4 FGs, including 50y boot. Hagan escaped from defenders all game; his niftiest play may have been scrambling out of clutches of LB Ernie Sims to throw 18y completion that set up FG. "I've never seen a quarterback make as many one-man plays as he made tonight," said losing coach Bobby Bowden of Hagans. "We couldn't stop that dadgum number 18." Seminoles (5-1) QB Drew Weatherford (35-59/377y) led 4th Q rally from 26-10 deficit, throwing 22y TD pass to WR Chris Davis and leading 77y drive to 32y FG by K Gary Cismesia. Weatherford was undone by 3 INTs, however, 2 of which led to 10 pts by Virginia.

LOUISIANA STATE 21 Florida 17: Snapping 3-game home losing streak to Gators, Louisiana State (4-1) won despite making enough mistakes (5 TOs and 11 PENs) to keep that streak going. Tigers QB JaMarcus Russell (14-22/236y, 2 TDs, 2 INTs) shook off 5 sacks to throw pair of TD passes in 1st Q for 14-0 lead, while RB Joseph Addai rushed for 156y and TD. Although Florida (5-2) next wiped out deficit with 3 straight scores, including 32y TD run by RB Kestaun Moore, for 17-14 3rd Q lead. Tigers answered with 75y drive, capped on 12th play by Addai's 3y run for winning TD. Russell converted 4th-and-1 on drive with 4y run. Florida QB Chris Leak was held to 11-30/107y passing and was sacked 4 times.

MICHIGAN 27 Penn State 25: Penn State's unlikely unbeaten squad fell to Big 10 rivals on shocking final play as Wolverines (4-3) WR Mario Manningham secured winning 10y TD pass from QB Chad Henne (21-36/212y) with clock expired to cash in final frantic drive jump-started by 41y KO RET by WR Steve Breaston. Nittany Lions (6-1) had led 18-10 earlier in 4th Q after CB Alan Zemaitis scored on unusual 35y RET with ball snatched from Henne as QB made attempt to bowl over DB. Zemaitis got better of that encounter, and Lions luckily scored 2 pts after botched x-pt kick turned

into conv run by K Kevin Kelly. TD occurred 17 secs after Penn State had scored tying TD on 4y run by QB Michael Robinson (19-34/239y, and 17/67y rushing). Midway in 4th Q, Henne threw 33y TD pass to Manningham that, coupled with 2-pt conv run by TB Mike Hart (23/108y), tied game at 18-18. Michigan forced punt by Penn State and regained lead at 21-18 on 47y FG by K Garrett Rivas. Without timeouts, Robinson quickly moved Lions 81y to go-ahead TD he scored himself from 3y out with 53 secs left. Henne's final-play TD, which came on audible which sent Manningham slanting inside to beat Zemaitis, was fortunate even to have gotten off. Wolverines coach Lloyd Carr had to lobby with officials to get extra sec put back on clock during last drive. Penn State's loss, agonizing 7th straight to Michigan, proved additionally costly for frosh star WR Derrick Williams (6/59y) was knocked out for season with broken arm.

Wisconsin 38 MINNESOTA 34: Inside last 40 secs and leading 34-31, Golden Gophers (5-2) prepared to punt from deep in their territory. Wisconsin's crack special teams unit brought pressure as Minnesota P Justin Kucek stunningly dropped snap and attempted to run from pressure to get off rugby-style punt. Frosh LB Jonathan Casillas swooped in to block Kucek's feeble attempt toward EZ. Badgers CB Ben Strickland recovered hot potato for winning TD with 30 secs remaining as Wisconsin retained Paul Bunyan Axe trophy in memorable style. Loss overshadowed yeoman effort turned in by Gophers RB Laurence Maroney, who rushed 43/258y, including incredible 93y scoring jaunt early in 3rd Q. Wisconsin QB John Stocco (15-26/235y) had pulled Badgers to within 34-31 with 2:10 left on 21y TD pass to WR Brandon Williams (7/121y). Wisconsin TB Brian Calhoun chipped in with 96y of his 110y, 3 TDs rushing in 2nd H.

NORTHWESTERN 34 Purdue 29: Rallying from 28-9 H deficit, Boilermakers (2-4) marched 98y with determination to RB Brandon Jones' 2nd TD run to take 29-28 lead with 5:17 remaining. Now it was time for Northwestern O, which had dominated 1st H play, to regain its magic. QB Brett Basanez (37-55/463y) led 75y drive to game-winning score, RB Tyrell Sutton's 1y plunge on 4th down with 1:50 left. CB Marquice Cole then ended matters with INT of Purdue QB Brandon Kirsch (40-65/378y, 2 INTs). With both teams airing out ball, no lead was safe until game ended. Northwestern finished with 603y, topping 600y mark for 2nd straight week. WR Dorien Bryant caught 16 passes for 153y and jump-started Purdue rally with 95y KO RET TD to open 2nd H.

OHIO STATE 35 Michigan State 24: Using big plays, Ohio State (4-2) put away Spartans in emphatic fashion. QB Troy Smith pitched 3 long TD passes, CB Ashton Youboty returned blocked FG 72y for another score and LB Bobby Carpenter's 4 sacks sparked Buckeyes D to 12 sacks of Michigan State (4-2) QB Drew Stanton (26-36/340y, TD). Stanton led O that gained 456y, with 36y on TD pass to WR Jerramy Scott (7/129y) for 10-pt 2nd Q lead. Bonehead move of game that turned momentum occurred at end of 1st H when, with 24 secs left and ball on Ohio 17YL. Spartans, with had no timeouts and leading 17-7, should have spiked ball to stop clock. Instead FG unit hurried on—1 man short—which led to unblocked FS Nate Salley deflecting kick to Youboty who scored momentum-changing TD. Smith threw pair of 2nd H TD passes and ran in insurance score late in 4th Q to overcome Bucks' loss of 4 of 6 FUMs. With Michigan State's D surrendering big plays, Ohio State unusually never made nap in Spartans' territory until last 6 mins, and that play resulted in game-winning 46y TD pass caught by WR Santonio Holmes (5/150y). Buckeyes LB A.J. Hawk made 19 tackles.

Southern California 34 NOTRE DAME 31: Frantic last few moments saw officials make big mistake, and mighty Southern California (6-0) escaped thanks to dramatic 61y pass on 4th-and-9 that set up winning TD sneak by QB Matt Leinart (17-32/301y, 2 INTs) on game's last play. Leinart's controversial TD which allowed USC to extend its winning streak to 28 games became known as "The Bush Push." Game clock actually had reached 0:00 with Fighting Irish (4-2) ahead 31-28, but officials placed 7 secs on clock because it mistakenly had been allowed to run down even though Leinart had fumbled OB after brutal hit by LB Corey Mays. Refs were correct about restoring time but erred in placing ball inside ND 1YL because FUM had flown backwards closer to 5YL. Refs' decision was confusing, but if they were deciding Leinart had been stopped on forward progress at 1YL, clock would have properly expired. Compounding difficult situation, they allowed Leinart's twisting keeper to stand for winning pts, even though there clearly was illegal push from star TB Reggie Bush when QB's initial thrust was stopped by Irish's fast-penetrating D. ("Push" non-call was more difficult to criticize because any block by deep-back coming to line of scrimmage could be called push if block was intended to legally ply off tacklers from ball-carrier. Indeed, it happened frequently and was rarely called.) Bush, who rushed 15/160y with 3 TDs, shared spotlight with Leinart, who had engineered final, clutch 75y drive that featured 4th down 61y pass to WR Dwayne Jarrett (4/101y) on gutsy slant-and-go pattern. Jarrett caught ball despite close coverage by CB Ambrose Wooden and Jarrett's double vision, caused by earlier hit. Green-jersey-clad Irish had offset USC's star-studded O by controlling clock for 38:40, picking off Leinart twice, and scoring special-teams TD on nifty 60y punt RET by DB Tom Zbikowski. Notre Dame QB Brady Quinn had handled game's pressure brilliantly, passing for 265y and scoring go-ahead TD with 5y run that capped 87y drive with 2:04 left on clock. "It was just a great game and I'm still really speechless," said Leinart. "I would imagine this will go down as one of the greatest games ever played." Indeed, in normal year this would have qualified as game-of-the-year.

TEXAS 42 Colorado 17: As Texas (6-0) QB Vince Young continued to develop as signal-caller, Longhorns continued to develop into national title contender. Young cracked 300y passing for 1st time in his career with near-perfect performance, completing 25-29 for 336y and 2 TDs. Young also rushed 10/58y and 3 additional TDs. "Vince's performance was the best I've ever see him play," said impressed Texas coach Mack Brown. No. 24 Buffaloes (4-2) were stunned by Young's passing, which mocked their attempt to force Longhorns' O to beat them through air. Colorado QB Joel Klatt passed for 192y and 2 TDs, but in no way could maintain pace with his Texas counterpart.

Ucla 44 WASHINGTON STATE 41 (OT): Finding themselves down 38-21 entering 4th Q, undefeated Bruins (6-0) erupted for 2 TDs and FG to tie it in regulation time and answered Washington State's FG in extra session with winning TD run by RB Maurice Drew (29/109y). Game's star was UCLA QB Drew Olson (31-43/338y, 5 TDs, INT), who tied QB Cade McNown's school record for TD passes in single game. Loss snapped 4-games series win streak for Washington State (3-3), which featured RB Jerome Harrison's career-high 260y rushing on 34 carries to spark its O. Harrison scored twice in 1st H, on runs of 57y and 21y, as Cougars took 28-14 H lead. Olson and Drew hooked up on 45y scoring pass midway through 3rd Q to pull Bruins to within 28-21, but Cougars scored twice to go up 38-21. UCLA D suddenly stiffened and Olson turned hot with 13-16/132y passing hand in 4th Q. Olson had 2 more TD throws in him, tying game with 9y scoring pass to WR Marcus Everett. Drew ran on all 5 snaps of UCLA's half of OT, negotiaiting last y for game-winning TD.

Oregon State 23 CALIFORNIA 20: Oregon State (4-2) RB Yvensen Bernard carried pigskin 40 times for career-high 185y, with sweetest rush coming with 6:41 remaining when he scored winning 11y TD. California (5-2), which had won 10 in row at home, had last lost at home in 2003 to Beavers. Bears struggled on O against Beavers' D which emphasized stopping run. Forced to take O all in his hands, struggling Bears QB Joe Ayoob (13-39/219y, TD, 2 INTs) threw incomplete pass after incomplete pass and pair of INTs. Cal TB Marshawn Lynch (14/58y) was benched in 2nd H after losing 2 FUMs. However, Lynch and Ayoob shared highlight as Lynch had thrown 21y TD pass back to his QB as Bears took 7-6 lead in 2nd Q. Ayoob later threw for and ran in TDs, but those were offset by Beavers on pair of TD runs by Bernard while K Alexis Serna booted 3 FGs. Cal also lost T Ryan Callaghan to concussion in 1st H, making him 3rd O-line starter lost to injury. Sloppy game saw 9 TOs, 5 by California, and 15 PENs, 10 by Oregon State.

USA Today Coaches October 16

1	Southern California (54)	1540	14	Penn State	726
2	Texas (7)	1492	15	Auburn	655
3	Virginia Tech (1)	1428	16	Oregon	588
4	Georgia	1361	17	Wisconsin	553
5	Alabama	1255	18	Tennessee	543
6	Miami (Fla.)	1218	19	Florida	450
7	LSU	1154	20	West Virginia	405
8	Texas Tech	1079	21	TCU	221
9	UCLA	1053	22	Michigan State	190
10	Florida State	934	23	California	175
11	Boston College	859	24	Virginia	120
12	Notre Dame	846	25	Minnesota	90
13	Ohio State	742			

Bowl Championship Series Ranking October 17

	Harris Poll Pct.	*USA Today* Poll Pct.	Computer Pct.	BCS Avg.
1 Southern California (6-0)	.993	.994	.990	.9923
2 Texas (6-0)	.965	.963	.950	.9593
3 Virginia Tech (6-0)	.919	.921	.880	.9067
4 Georgia (6-0)	.882	.878	.920	.8933
5 Alabama (6-0)	.806	.810	.850	.8220

October 22, 2005

Rutgers 26 CONNECTICUT 24: Frosh RB Ray Rice shone for Rutgers (5-2), rushing for 217y as Scarlet Knights sharpened resume for rare post-season action. Game was tied at 17-17 early in 4th Q when Rutgers D provided lead for good. Playing in his 1st collegiate game due to injuries to Huskies' top 2 QBs, Connecticut (4-3) frosh QB Dennis Brown (18-35/196y, 2 TDs, INT), made fatal error. Brown mishandled snap deep in his territory which resulted in safety for Rutgers. QB Ryan Hart had come off bench to throw for 94y and 3 TDs, and he now led Rutgers 57y to pay-dirt after UConn's free-kick: Hart hit TD on 15y TD pass to TE Sam Johnson. Brown took 3 mins to bring score back to 26-24, throwing 15y TD pass to WR Jason Williams to cap 88y drive. But Huskies' 3-game series win streak soon was done.

ALABAMA 6 Tennessee 3: With score at 3-3 with little more than 5 mins remaining, Alabama (7-0) S Roman Harper needed to make big play with Vols RB Adrian Foster closing in on Tide EZ after catching swing pass. Harper made jarring hit, and ball popped loose and went through EZ for touchback. Instead of score for Tennessee (3-3) it was its 3rd lost FUM, including another earlier inside Alabama 10YL by RB Gerald Riggs, Jr. (18/68y). Alabama had 1st down possession at own 20YL, and that is how season would play out for both teams. QB Brodie Croyle (17-27/190y) then marched Crimson Tide 63y in 10 plays, hitting crucial 3rd-and-8 pass of 43y to WR D.J. Hall (10/139y), to set up 34y FG by K Jamie Christensen with 13 secs left. It was Christenson's 2nd straight game-winner this month and created Alabama's 2nd win over rival Vols in last 11 tries. Vols QB Rick Clausen threw for 144y.

LOUISIANA STATE 20 Auburn 17 (OT): After dropped pass by WR Early Doucet in EZ, Louisiana State (5-1) had to settle for 30y FG by K Chris Jackson on opening possession of OT. It was then up to its D to hold Auburn Tigers (5-2), and LSU's motivated defenders forced FG attempt by Auburn K John Vaughn. Vaughn's 39y 3-pt try hit left upright and bounded away for his 5th miss of game. End to 13-game SEC win streak had nothing to do with Auburn TB Kenny Irons, who carried ball to tune of 27/218y, with 74y on 3rd Q TD that had put Auburn ahead 10-7. LSU countered with 80y drive capped by QB JaMarcus Russell's 18y TD pass to WR Dwayne Bowe. LSU Bengals held 14-10 lead for close to 15 mins, until QB Brandon Cox (16-40/221y, TD) completed 87y drive with 5y scoring pass to WR Anthony Mix. Russell answered by maneuvering LSU into field position for K Jackson to tie it 17-17 with 44y FG. Auburn had chance to win at end of regulation, but Vaughn missed 3-pt try. Auburn special teams had permitted 66y PUNT TD RET by WR Skyler Green in 1st Q.

SOUTH CAROLINA 35 Vanderbilt 28: Gamecocks (4-3) won thriller as QB Blake Mitchell (15-27/221y) and WR Sidney Rice hooked up on their 2nd TD, this of 3y with 1:41 left, and then D held Commodores on downs after they reached USC 30YL. Vanderbilt (4-4) had rallied from 2-TD deficit in 4th Q as star QB Jay Cutler (27-49/339y, INT) threw 41y TD pass to WR Earl Bennett and TB Cassen Jackson-Garrison scored his 2nd TD to cap 87y drive. Mitchell next whipped Gamecocks 77y in 7 plays to game-winning TD. Soph WRs Rice and Bennett dominated game for their respective clubs: South Carolina's Rice nabbed 8/132y, 3 TDs—including scoring throw from QB-turned-RB Syvelle Newton (15/80y, TD)—and Vandy's Bennett came down with 16 catches/204y.

Michigan 23 IOWA 20 (OT): Whiff of desperation was in air for 2 unranked teams that had been expected at season's start to fight for national and Big 10 glory. Foes traded scores until 32y FG by Iowa (5-3) K Kyle Schlicher as time expired sent game to OT. Michigan (5-3) D, which had allowed TD drives on 2 of Iowa's 1st 3 possessions way back at game's beginning, continued to hold Hawkeyes. So, Schlicher hit another FG, this from 28y out. QB Chad Henne (14-21/207y, 2 TDs, INT) then negotiated 5 plays for 25y needed for winning TD on RB Jerome Jackson's 1y TD. Henne's 18y completion to WR Jason Avant (7/105y, TD) set up TD. Hawkeyes QB Drew Tate (27-39/288y, 2 TDs, INT) had thrown TD passes to WR Herb Grigsby (5/66y), and TB Albert Young had chipped in with 153y rushing. Henne's set of TD passes had included 52y connection with WR Steve Breaston on screen pass for 17-14 lead in 4th Q. Loss ended Iowa's 22-game home win streak, while Michigan won back-to-back games for 1st time all season, both on game's final play. Hawkeyes had entered game as least penalized team in college football but committed 11 PENs/94y.

Penn State 63 ILLINOIS 10: Seemingly insulted with FG earned by Illinois (2-5) on opening drive, Nittany Lions (7-1) answered with 63 straight pts. Scoring 28 pts in each Q of 1st H, Penn State wrapped it up quickly. QB Michael Robinson (11-18/194y) threw 4 TDs in opening Q, 2 to WR Deon Butler (4/95y), and ran for 2 more TDs in 2nd Q. Penn State D also outscored Illini as LB Dan Connor returned FUM 18y for 2nd Q TD and S Nolan McCready scored in 3rd Q with 77y INT RET. Reserve QB Chris Pazan threw 2y TD pass in 4th Q to RB Rashard Mendenhall for Illinois' sole TD. P Steve Weatherford was brilliant in defeat, punting 9/50.2y avg. Lions coach Joe Paterno marked his 350th career win.

MISSOURI 41 Nebraska 24: Missouri Tigers' most prolific O performer ever, QB Brad Smith, set another school record with 480y of total O as Missouri (5-2) beat Nebraska (5-2) for 2nd time in 3 years. Smith rushed 28/246y, 3 TDs, and hit 21-36/234y, TD passing to become 6th QB in NCAA history to reach both 200y passing and 200y rushing in same game. Making performance even more stunning was Nebraska's position atop national rush D rankings with 65y per game. Smith came out guns-ablazing as he threw and ran for TDs for quick 14-0 lead in 1st Q. After 32y FG by Huskers K Jordan Congdon, Smith raced 79y on next scrimmage for commanding 21-3 lead. QB Zac Taylor (22-43/281y, 2 TDs, 2 INTs) rallied Nebraska to 24-24 tie at end of 1st H by throwing for 2 TDs, including 34y effort to WR Todd Peterson. Prooving he wasn't perfect, Smith had suffered INT and FUM to aid Huskers' comeback but made amends with 45y scoring run in 3rd Q that gave Tigers lead for good. Nebraska WR Nate Swift had 9/135y, TD receiving.

COLORADO 44 Kansas 13: Colorado's recent dominance over Kansas (3-4) continued as QB Joel Klatt (16-27/193y) threw 4 TD passes to become school's all-time leader in that category with 42, and special teams contributed safety, blocked punt returned 28y for TD by SS Dominque Brooks, and 81y punt TD RET by WR Stephone Robinson. After Buffs (5-2) D halted 4th down play by Kansas in 1st Q with sack by LB Thaddeus Washington (10 tackles), Klatt needed 3 plays to score opening TD on 20y pass to TE Quinn Sypniewski. Although Colorado never relinquished lead, game was tight at H at 16-13 as Kansas scored on 2 FGs by K Scott Webb and 7y TD pass by QB Jason Swanson (26-50/291y, TD, 3 INTs) to WR Charles Gordon (8/85). Buffs pulled away in 3rd Q thanks to TDs by Brooks and Robinson, both of whom curiously had scored only once before, each against Kansas in 2004. Colorado TE Joe Klopfenstein caught 2 passes, both for TDs, including 40y effort in 2nd Q.

TEXAS 52 Texas Tech 17: Texas Tech's brief spell residing in nation's Top 10 was ended rudely as Texas won its 14th game in row with ease. Texas (7-0) D strategy was to surrender short passes but no big plays, forcing Raiders to play catch-up without benefit of long passes. Still, Red Raiders (6-1) QB Cory Hodges' numbers looked as goor as usual with exception of fair 5.14y per try. Hodges completed 42-64/369y and 2 TDs. Texas QB Vince Young shook off 2 early INTs to throw for 239y and 2 TDs, both to WR Billy Pittman (3/138y), including 75y score for 38-10 lead early in 2nd H. Consistant Longhorns scored TDs on 6 straight possessions during stretch in middle Qs. Precise Red Raiders WR Joel Filani worked his way open to catch 9/82y, TD. Texas Tech barely got to enjoy its 1st Top 10 ranking since 1977 as it dropped to no. 17 on Sunday. Win was 8th straight for Texas over ranked opponents.

USA Today Coaches October 23

1	Southern California (53)	1540	14	Oregon	712
2	Texas (8)	1493	15	Wisconsin	677
3	Virginia Tech (1)	1428	16	Texas Tech	603
4	Georgia	1357	17	West Virginia	539
5	Alabama	1277	18	Florida	513
6	Miami (Fla.)	1226	19	Auburn	427
7	LSU	1164	20	TCU	383
8	UCLA	1136	21	California	276
9	Florida State	1003	22	Minnesota	189
10	Notre Dame	934	23	Northwestern	179
11	Boston College	870	24	Fresno State	134
12	Penn State	835	25	Tennessee	133
13	Ohio State	803			

Bowl Championship Series Ranking October 24

	Harris Poll Pct.	*USA Today* Poll Pct.	Computer Pct.	BCS Avg.
1 Texas (7-0)	.966	.963	1.000	.9763
2 Southern California (7-0)	.993	.994	.940	.9757
3 Virginia Tech (7-0)	.918	.921	.910	.9163
4 Georgia (7-0)	.868	.876	.860	.8680
5 Alabama (7-0)	.830	.824	.900	.8513

October 29, 2005

(Th) VIRGINIA TECH 30 Boston College 10: Bringing this Big East rivalry to ACC was complete success for Virginia Tech (8-0), who enjoyed 492y to 183y advantage in unexpected laugher. Eagles (6-2) briefly owned 7-6 lead early in 2nd Q when QB Quinton Porter (13-24/139y) threw 29y TD pass to WR Will Blackmon to cap 80y drive. Hokies regained lead less than 5 mins later on 15y TD run by RB Eddie Royal and after Va Tech D forced 3-and-out, scored again on 3y pass by QB Marcus Vick to WR Josh Morgan before H for 20-7 lead. With Vick throwing 22-28/career-high 280y, rush attack (212y) also torching Eagles, who had come into game ranked 4th in rush D (78y avg). Eagles gained only 58y in 2nd H, so no rally ever materialized. Virginia Tech's opportunistic D scored in 2nd H as LB Vince Hall returned INT 13y for his 2nd TD of year. Hall's score was remarkable 100th non-O TD scored by Virginia Tech in 20 seasons under coach Frank Beamer.

MIAMI 34 North Carolina 16: Tar Heels (3-4) had no answer for Miami TB Tyrone Moss, who rushed for 195y and 4 TDs. Seeking redemption for 2004's upset loss at Chapel Hill, Hurricanes (6-1) nonetheless trailed 16-7 at H thanks to pair of TDs by North Carolina TB Ronnie McGill (66y rushing). Game turned when Moss scored TDs of 1, 4, and 15y after intermission, with help from struggling Tar Heels. North Carolina gained only 18y in 2nd H against blitzing Miami defenders, which provided excellent field position throughout 2nd H. In preparing Moss for 3 scores, Miami needed only to navigate 26, 4 and 41y after TOs by UNC. Canes also earned special teams TD when FB Quadtrine Hill recovered punt he blocked in EZ to give Miami 20-16 3rd Q lead.

Florida 14 Georgia 10 (Jacksonville): Playing without injured QB D.J. Shockley, Bulldogs (7-1) couldn't muster big effort against border rivals to remain undefeated. Georgia D allowed healthy Florida Gators (6-2) QB Chris Leak (15-20/108y)—enjoying slimmed-down playbook in Florida's complicated, new Spread O—to throw and run for TDs on opening 2 possessions that netted robust 121y. Georgia O, meanwhile, labored 13 mins to earn its opening 1st down. When Bulldogs finally got in gear to rally within 14-10 pts, Georgia K Brandon Coutu missed couple of wind-effected FG tries in 2nd H. On Bulldogs' final drive, Florida DE Jeremy Mincey, Georgia native not recruited by his home-state university, pressured QB Joe Tereshinski (8-21/100y, INT) into 4-and-out that sealed win. Tereshinski's highlight came in 3rd Q on handoff-and-go play as he caught 9y TD pass from TB Thomas Brown. Gators RB DeShawn Wynn rushed for 109y, although he lost FUM at Georgia 6YL with Florida hankering for 21-3 advantage late in 2nd Q. Win was Florid'as 14th in last 16 meetings with Georgia.

Ohio State 45 MINNESOTA 31: With attention lavished on Buckeyes (6-2) D, stars on O sometimes went unnoticed. Soph RB Antonio Pittman made splash in Metrodome, however, rushing 23/186y and 2 TDs as Ohio State ran away from Gophers (5-3). With Minnesota gaining 578y against OSU's highly-publicized D, 2nd most in Buckeyes history (Illinois gained 659y in 1980), Buckeyes O had to carry day. Pittman and QB Troy Smith (14-20/233y, 3 TDs) led way as visitors broke 17-17 H tie with 28 pts in 2nd H. Pittman started ball rolling in 3rd Q with 67y romp through middle for 24-17 lead. Ohio soon had ball back and Smith moved O 68y on 7 plays, closing with his 27y TD pass to WR Anthony Gonzalez. Ohio State WR Santonio Holmes (4/94y) had made TD catches of 41y and 30y and WR Ted Ginn returned KO 100y for 1st H TD. Minnesota QB Bryan Cupito hit 26-35/396y, with WR Jared Ellerson nabbing 5/113y and 5y TD. Minny TB Laurence Maroney rushed for 127y and TD.

Oklahoma 31 NEBRASKA 24: Slowly rounding into form after ankle injury robbed him of big chunk of season, Sooners (5-3) RB Adrian Peterson rushed for 146y and opening TDs as Oklahoma took early lead they would never relinquish. Peterson's 1st carry was beauty as he raced 36y for TD with CB Zackary Bowman along for ride for final 5y. Sooners enjoyed 21-3 lead at H, with CB Chijioke Onyenegecha returning INT 63y for 3rd TD, which they added to early in 3rd Q on 50y FG by K Garrett Hartley. Huskers, hoping to avoid 2 straight home losses, which had not happened since 1968, warmed up as QB Zac Taylor (25-45/249y, 2 TDs, 2 INTs) threw TD passes of 3y to WR Terrence Nunn and 25y to WR Nate Swift (9/116y). Teams next traded TDs, with Huskers scoring on IB Cory Ross' 18y pass to Swift, but Nebraska could get no closer than 7 pts. Sooners sacked Taylor 9 times, most ever in Nebraska history. Game marked 1st time in last 40 series games that both schools had arrived unranked.

Texas 47 OKLAHOMA STATE 28: For 3rd straight season Texas fell behind in game's first 30 mins to upstart Cowboys (3-5) before rallying with huge 2nd H. This season's deficit, as many as 19 pts, was more surprising as OSU had lost 4 straight in conf. Cowpokes were unable to keep Texas (8-0) QB Vince Young in check, especially once he tucked ball away. Young rushed for career-high 267y and 2 TDs while passing for 2 more to keep Steers undefeated. His 80y scoring romp at beginning of 2nd H ignited rally, 8y TD run continued it and 21y TD pass to TE Neale Tweedie gave Texas 34-28 3rd Q lead. Cowboys had built 28-9 1st H advantage behind 2 wild TD connections between QB Al Pena and WR D'Juan Woods. On 1st, Pena broke huddle early to catch Longhorns D napping, completing 49y TD pass to wide-open Woods. On 2nd, Woods caught deflection off of teammate WR Luke Frazier for 30y scoring play. Amazing numbers: At game's end Texas had outscored Oke State 118-0 in 2nd Hs of past 3 contests.

BRIGHAM YOUNG 62 Air Force 41: Cougars (4-4) romped, building 41-14 3rd Q lead and later took on task of limiting Air Force's rally. BYU QB John Beck (31-43/383y, 3 TDs, INT), orchestrated 683y of O; RB Curtis Brown rushed for career-best 219y and 4 TDs. Brown scored 3 times in 4th Q, capping 3 drives of 60y or more, to keep Falcons (3-6) at bay. Coming off bench in relief of injured starting QB Shaun Carney, QB Adam Fitch (13-24/265, 2 INTs) threw school-record 5 TDs. Falcons WR Jason Brown caught 9/156y and 2 TDs. Not only did Falcons struggle on D, but on O they suffered 5 TOs. Loss guaranteed 2nd straight losing season for declining Air Force program, whose heralded coach Fisher DeBerry called unwanted attention to himself earlier in week for comments made about recruiting and black athletes. He later apologized.

Ucla 30 STANFORD 27 (OT): Cardiac Bruins (8-0) maintained their perfect record with 3-TD rally over final 7 mins of contest, marking biggest comeback in school history. Rally forced OT where WR Brandon Breazell won game with 23y TD reception after Stanford (4-3) settled for FG. UCLA QB Drew Olson (24-35/293y,) led hurry-up O that jump-started rally, needing only 88 secs to move 65y for 1st TD, scored by RB Maurice Drew (16/82y) on 6y run after Olson went 5-5/59y. Forcing punt, Bruins D continued its turnaround: UCLA allowed 249y through 3 Qs, but only 11y thereafter in 4th Q and OT. This time Olson used but 34 secs to hit 3 passes for 72y including 31y TD to WR Joe Cowan (5/71y) to trail 24-17 with 4:43 left. Bruins D got ball right back for O. With help from 2 pass interference PENs and 4th-and-2 completion to Cowan, Drew scored tying TD from 1y out with 46 secs left. Deflated Cardinal had to settle for 42y FG by K Michael Sgroi to begin OT. Stanford QB Trent Edwards completed 18-25/189y and 2 TDs, both to TB J.R. Lemon, who rushed for 53y and caught 6/50y.

USA Today Coaches October 30

1	Southern California (56)	1544	14	Wisconsin	739
2	Texas (5)	1485	15	Florida	648
3	Virginia Tech (1)	1431	16	West Virginia	597
4	Alabama	1349	17	Texas Tech	596
5	Miami (Fla.)	1285	18	Auburn	514
6	LSU	1215	19	Boston College	445
7	UCLA	1200	20	TCU	398
8	Florida State	1060	21	California	327
9	Notre Dame	988	22	Fresno State	248
10	Georgia	966	23	Michigan	178
11	Penn State	927	24	Colorado	121
12	Ohio State	827	25	Louisville	113
13	Oregon	782			

Bowl Championship Series Ranking October 31

	Harris Poll Pct.	*USA Today* Poll Pct.	Computer Pct.	BCS Avg.
1 Southern California (8-0)	.994	.996	.940	.9767
2 Texas (8-0)	.961	.958	1.000	.9729
3 Virginia Tech (8-0)	.925	.923	.940	.9293
4 Alabama (8-0)	.868	.870	.870	.8693
5 UCLA (8-0)	.778	.774	.810	.7873

November 5, 2005

Miami 27 VIRGINIA TECH 7: Traditionally, Miami (7-1) has tended toward most-potent football when calendar turns to November, and this impressive road win did nothing to dispute history. Dominant performance by D centered on pressuring Virginia Tech (8-1) QB Marcus Vick (8-22/90y), who committed 6 TOs. Canes O converted those 6 TOs, including 4 lost FUMs, into 17 pts. Miami's most dramatic TD came from DT Kareem Brown having recovered ball in Hokies EZ late in 3rd Q for commanding 27-0 lead. Although missing most of 2nd Q after having his bell wrung, Miami QB Kyle Wright threw for 146y and 9y scoring pass to WR Darnell Jenkins. Vick prevented shutout with 2y scoring keeper in final Q.

NORTH CAROLINA 16 Boston College 14: Tar Heels (4-4) may have been struggling during coach JohnBunting's regime but continued to be tough at home. In beating 2nd straight ranked opponent in Kenan Stadium, North Carolina received all its scoring from special teams as K Connor Barth booted 3 FGs and WR Wallace Wright took opening KO 90y for TD. Best aspect of Tar Heels' O was passing combination of QB Matt Baker (20-32/211y, INT) and WR Jesse Holley, who caught 8/125y. Eagles (6-3) struggled with their running game, gaining only 100y, and were unable to mount more than 2 scoring drives. BC RB Andre Callender scored on 3y run for 7-7 tie early in 1st Q. Eagles never returned to scoring zone until near game's end when they closed scoring on 10y TD pass by backup QB Matt Ryan (10-14/93y) to WR Larry Lester.

North Carolina State 20 FLORIDA STATE 15: Seminoles (7-2) became 3rd ranked team from ACC to lose this Saturday. Defeat could be laid at feet of 3 issues: Florida State QB Drew Weatherford (19-38/181y) threw trio of INTs in 2nd H, Seminoles rushed for only 43y, and their D permitted North Carolina State (4-4) RB Andre Brown to gain 179y on ground. Brown opened scoring with 65y TD run on 2nd play of game. Seminoles reeled off 10 pts on 1st of 2 FGs by K Gary Cismesia and WR Chris Davis 33y TD reception midway through 2nd Q. But without injured TB Leon Washington and with WR Greg Carr, conf leader in TD catches, being held catch-less, Florida State's O staggered about. Weatherford hit only 5-17/55y in 2nd H; but backup QB Xavier Lee was worse with 1-7/3y. Brown continued doing his damage, and Wolfpack scored 13 straight pts on 2 FGs by K John Deraney and 4y TD pass from QB Marcus Stone (9-17/85y) to TE Anthony Hill. FSU special teams came through with pair of blocked punts late in 4th Q, including safety. But INTs by NC State CB A.J. Davis, his 2nd of game, and S Garland Heath saved Wolfpack. Despite its difficult day, FSU still clinched spot in ACC title thanks to Boston College's loss to North Carolina.

PENN STATE 35 Wisconsin 14: Penn State (9-1) showcased sr leaders on both sides of ball as DE Tamba Hali led D with 4 sacks and QB Michael Robinson (13-28/238y, 2 INTs) rushed for 125y and threw 2 TD passes. Not to be outdone, jr TB Tony Hunt

rushed for 151y and 2 TDs as Lions dominated battle for Big 10 supremacy. When not knocked to turf by Hali, Wisconsin (8-2) QB John Stocco threw for 313y and TD against D that successfully focused on stopping TB Brian Calhoun (20/38y, TD). Nittany Lions jumped to 7-0 lead when WR Deon Butler (5/125y) caught 43y TD pass less than 2 mins into game. Penn State scored twice more in 1st H for 21-0 H lead. After Calhoun rushed for short TD to cut Wisconsin's deficit to 21-7 early in 4th Q, Robinson and Butler struck again, this time on 47y connection.

NORTHWESTERN 28 Iowa 27: Cardiac Cats (6-3) did it again, pulling out another improbable late win. Northwestern scored 2 TDs during 88-sec span of game's final 3 mins to stun Hawkeyes (5-4). Comeback prospects seemed bleak when Iowa CB Adam Shada picked off QB Brett Basanez with 4:34 remaining and Hawkeyes up 27-14. Northwestern D forced punt and O took over at own 23YL. With new life, Basanez (31-51/338y, 2 TDs, 2 INTs) moved team 77y, with final y coming on TD plunge by RB Tyrell Sutton (17/65y, 2 TDs). Northwestern FS Reggie McPherson recovered ensuing onside-KO at Iowa 47YL. Basanez hit WR Mark Philmore (10/123y) for 16y. Officials tacked on 15y more for late hit, and soon thereafter WR Ross Lane was in EZ with ball, courtesy of 9y scoring pass with 42 secs left. Final, fleeting Iowa chance ended when Northwestern D halted them on downs just past midfield. Hawkeyes had dominated 1st H, scoring 24 pts with TD runs of 12y and 21y by RB Albert Young, who rushed 38/202y, and 10y by QB Drew Tate (21-35/273y).

NOTRE DAME 41 Tennessee 21: With programs going in different directions in 2005, Notre Dame (6-2) won as QB Brady Quinn (20-33/295y) continued to sparkle. After Quinn tossed 2 scoring passes within 1 min for 14-0 lead, CB Tom Zbikowski killed Vols with 2 daggers, returning punt 78y for 21-3 lead in 2nd Q and taking INT 33y to pay-dirt to close scoring in 4th Q. Zbikowski now had scored 4 TDs in past 3 games. Tennessee rallied to tie game at 21-21—scoring 18 straight pts on 3 drives that averaged only 46y—before Quinn gave Irish lead for good with 4y TD pass to WR Jeff Samardzija (7/127y), receiver's school-record 12th of season. Earlier on drive Samardzija took short pass 73y, with key block supplied by WR Maurice Stovall. Vols RB Adrian Foster rushed 28/125y, TD. Notre Dame's sharp O had scored at least 31 pts for 6th straight game.

KANSAS 40 Nebraska 15: Even with recent trend of fans over-celebrating even most mundane of wins, Kansas' 1st series win in 37 years deserved joyous celebration. Jayhawks were dominant on D, holding Huskers' West Coast O to 7 1st downs, 21y rushing and 117y passing. Kansas O displayed excellent balance, rushing for 213y and passing for 215y, in throttling visitors. RBs Jon Cornish (10/101y) and Clark Green (22/100y) shared rushing honors for Jayhawks, while QB Jason Swanson threw 2 TDs and teamed with WR Mark Simmons on 6/100y and 2 TDs. Nebraska QB Zac Taylor was held in check but managed 30y TD pass to WR Terrence Nunn in 2nd Q. Huskers pulled in within 17-15, on 3rd Q after RB Cory Ross converted Kansas TO with 1y TD run. Cornish answered 2 plays later with 72y TD romp as Jayhawks reeled off 23 straight pts. Kansas D fittingly scored final TD as LB Kevin Kane returned INT 40y for score. "I've got bruises from getting hit by (fans rushing field), not from getting hit in the game," said Kane. "It was great!"

COLORADO 41 Missouri 12: Having just lost FUM early in 3rd Q that was returned 12y for TD by Tigers (5-4) DT Jamar Smith to halve Buffs lead to 24-12, Colorado (7-2) QB Joel Klatt (23-31/253y) answered with 14-play, 80y drive to his 6y TD pass to TE Quinn Sypniewski that sapped life out of Missouri. Buffs D saw to it that Missouri could not rally, smothering Tigers QB Brad Smith, who threw for 160y and rushed for only 16y. Smith's 18y TD pass to WR Will Franklin in 1st Q provided Missouri's sole O TD. Colorado FB-turned-TB Lawrence Vickers rushed for 85y and 4 TDs, while Buffs K Mason Crosby booted 56y FG in 2nd Q that easily sailed through light mountain air and through uprights.

ARIZONA 52 Ucla 14: Arizona (3-6) built 52-7 lead entering 4th Q to see to it that there would be no late comeback by cardiac Bruins (8-1). UCLA had maintained perfect record with 4th Q rallies in 3 of 4 previous games, but 45 pt margin was another matter. Frosh QB Willie Tuitama (14-24/204y, 2TDs) led Arizona O that rolled up 519y, with TB Mike Bell contributing 153y rushing and TD, TB Gilbert Harris adding 116y on ground with TD, and WR Mike Thomas catching 5/104y and scoring rushing and receiving TDs. Bell's score, which put Cats up 38-7 in 3rd Q, featured nifty high jump over S Dennis Keyes. UCLA, who entered averaging 42-pts-per-contest, scored both its TDs on passes from QB Drew Olson (23-38/232y) to TE Marcedes Lewis (11/131y).

OREGON 27 California 20 (OT): Oregon's home magic vs. Bears (6-3) continued as QB Brady Leaf (9-13/93y) fired 15y TD pass to WR James Finley in 1st extra session, after Ducks D had allowed only 2y in 4 plays in top half of OT. California RB Marshawn Lynch (25/189y) had tied game 20-20 late in 3rd Q on 52y jaunt. Led by DT Haloti Ngata (11 tackles, 2 pass break-ups), Ducks D had stiffened at end of regulation after Bears drove to Oregon 33YL with game still tied 20-20: Cal ran 2 plays that lost 11y, forcing K Tim Schneider to try 53y FG try. He missed it short to bring about OT. Despite playing without injured QB Kellen Clemens, Oregon combined pair of QBs—Leaf and starter QB Dennis Dixon (15-26/139y, TD, INT)—for passing attack totaling 232y. Bears struggled with pass as QB Joe Ayoob (10-26/88y) threw 3 INTs, but led ground game that totaled 213y.

Bowl Championship Series Ranking November 7

	Harris Poll Pct.	USA Today Poll Pct.	Computer Pct.	BCS Avg.
1 Southern California (9-0)	.994	.996	.950	.9800
2 Texas (9-0)	.966	.964	1.000	.9767
3 Alabama (9-0)	.892	.902	.850	.8813
4 Miami (7-1)	.898	.894	.850	.8807
5 Penn State (9-1)	.776	.735	.930	.8137

November 12, 2005

(Th) FRESNO STATE 27 Boise State 7: After 4 years of frustrations, Fresno State (8-1) finally got best of Broncos and in doing so snapped Boise State's 31-game WAC conference win streak. QB Paul Pinegar (22-36/307y, INT) and WR Paul Williams (6/149y) connected on couple of 2nd Q TD passes, including stunning 98y play, as Bulldogs pulled away before H. On big play, Williams curled back for pass and shook off defenders enroute to longest scoring pass in Fresno history; he swatted away final would-be tackler, S Marty Tadman. With Bulldogs D holding Boise State to 294y—67y on TD run by RB Jeff Carpenter that had opened scoring—Broncos' 20-pt deficit was daunting. Fresno State finished game with 513y, which allowed them to keep possession for more than 40 mins. RB Wendell Mathis led that effort, rushing 25/121y and TD. QB Jared Zabransky threw for 190y with 2 INTs for Boise State. Pinegar's 1st TD pass to Williams, of 29y, set new Fresno State school-record of 71 TDs, breaking mark held by David Carr, currently of NFL's Houston Texans.

LOUISVILLE 56 Rutgers 5: Cardinals (7-2) made statement that, while they may not win Big East this year, they can still blow away 2nd-tier teams. Ahead 21-5 at H, Louisville scored 4 times in 3rd Q with 3 of 4 TDs scored on passes by QB Brian Brohm (22-30/315y). Best chance Rutgers (6-4) had to stay competitive ended late in 1st H, when it trailed 14-5 and QB Brian Teel threw INT to Louisville SS Jon Russell, who returned it 31y to Rutgers 4YL to set up TD run by RB Kolby Smith. Smith, part of committee of backs replacing injured RB Michael Bush, rushed for 55y and 3 TDs. With Cardinals, who reached 40-pt threshold for 6th game in row, scoring TDs on their 1st 5 possessions of 2nd H, even G Kurt Quarterman got into mix with 1y TD run late in 3rd Q. Rutgers won stat battle of 1st H by 130y to 128y, but finished with 500y to 187y disadvantage. Knights FB Brian Leonard rushed for 42y and caught 5/21y to lead O. Louisville WR Joshua Tinch caught 10/183y and TD.

BOSTON COLLEGE 30 North Carolina State 10: New Boston College (7-3) starting QB Matt Ryan (8-16/185y) enjoyed his new responsibilities, throwing 17y TD to TE Chris Miller late in 1st H for what proved to be winning score, and later rushing for pair of insurance TDs in 4th Q. Wolfpack (4-5) had jumped to 10-0 lead with help of long play: 96y TD pass from QB Marcus Stone to WR Brian Clark. Although Stone threw for 247y, North Carolina State run game garnered only 59y. Eagles, however, rushed for 150y with RB L.V. Whitworth gaining 26/119y 1y TD run for BC's 1st score. Eagles WR Will Blackmon caught 3/151y.

CLEMSON 35 Florida State 14: Clemson (6-4) QB Charlie Whitehurst may have had shoulder pain, but it would have been difficult to convince Florida State's D. Week after missing game to rest his injury, Whitehurst threw for 21-32/269y, 3 TDs to lead surprisingly easy victory. WR Chansi Stuckey caught 11/156y, 2 TDs from Whitehurst. Seminoles (7-3) continued to struggle on O, gaining only 226y total and not reaching EZ as LB Gene Hayes scored team's sole TD on blocked punt. Clemson D sacked 2 FSU QBs 6 times and grabbed 2 INTs, including S Michael Hamlin's INT TD RET that tied game 14-14 in 3rd Q. Tigers soon marched downfield to winning 32y scoring catch by Stuckey. For 1st time since joining ACC in 1992, Seminoles had dropped 3 conf games in 1 year. TB Lorenzo Booker was sole bright spot for Florida State with 112y rushing on 16 carries.

SOUTH CAROLINA 30 Florida 22: No matter how much he protested that game was same as any other, South Carolina (7-3) coach Steve Spurrier had to relish win over team he starred for as QB and took to new heights as coach. In snapping 14-game series losing streak—last Gamecocks win had occurred in 1939—Spurrier put stamp on his rebuilding effort in Columbia while bouncing Florida (7-3) from SEC East title race. South Carolina RB Mike Davis and FB Daccus Turman each rushed for 2 TDs, while WR Sidney Rice caught 5/112y of QB Blake Mitchell's 7 completions. Davis' 1st score converted INT returned 48y by NT Chris Tucker to Florida 5YL. After 1st of 2 FGs by Gators K Chris Hetland, Turman scored twice for Carolina's 20-3 lead in 2nd Q. Gators, however, blocked x-pt kick which was returned by Florida CB Dee Webb for 2 pts; it began 16-pt surge by Gators to pull within 20-19 in 3rd Q. Both TDs during Gators' momentum swing came courtesy of passes by QB Chris Leak (18-31/210y, 2 TDs). Moments later Cocks ace Rice raced 65y with short pass to set up Davis' 2nd TD, from 1y out, for 27-19 lead. "It's neat the way our guys are winning," said Spurrier of team's 5th straight SEC victory. "We are defying logic."

Louisiana State 16 ALABAMA 13 (OT): Bubble burst for Crimson Tide (9-1) in OT as Louisiana State scored winning TD on 11y reception by WR Dwayne Bowe (7/98y). Alabama D was tough until end as TD was scored on 3rd-and-6 play in which hard pass rush by Tide flushed QB JaMarcus Russell (16-30/229y) out of pocket. Alabama had grabbed 10-0 lead at H break after storming for 207y O in opening H. Bama's O tanked, however, as it had most of season, gaining only 4 1st downs in 2nd H. LSU (8-1) tied game with 1y 4th down TD run by TB Justin Vincent (20/56y) and 42y FG by K Chris Jackson. "Thirteen points is not going to win a football game against a top-5 team," surmised Alabama QB Brodie Croyle at game's end. Croyle threw for 187y and 8y TD to WR D. J. Hall, but fell victim to five sacks. Win propelled Tigers to top of SEC West standings

Arkansas 28 MISSISSIPPI 17: Razorbacks (3-6) had more staying power than Mississippi, outscoring Rebels 14-0 in 4th Q. Frosh QB Casey Dick (17-24/175y) threw 3 2nd H TDs, including pair of TDs to WR Marcus Monk (5/63y), as Arkansas rallied from 10-pt deficit. Surprisingly, neither team was able to run football effectively: Arkansas, ranked 5th nationally in ground gaining (252y avg) picked up only 89y against Mississippi (3-6) led by superb LB Patrick Willis, who made 9 tackles and gobbled up FUM REC. Ole Miss could manage meager 10y rushing. Rebels QB Ethan Flatt threw 20-37/309y, TD, 2 INTs in his 1st start of season, but he was sacked 4 times. Arkansas S Randy Kelly retuned INT for 42y TD in 1st Q. With leading rusher RB Mico McSwain knocked out of game in 1st Q with ankle injury, Rebels RB Larry Kendrick (23/48y) scored TD both rushing and receiving.

Auburn 31 GEORGIA 30: Georgia (7-2) dropped heartbreaker to another rival, allowing dramatic 62y completion from Auburn QB Brandon Cox (16-28/279y, INT) to WR Devin Aromashodu (4/135y) on 4th-and-10 that set up K John Vaughn 20y FG with 6 secs remaining. Aromashodu actually fumbled at end of his run with aerial, but Auburn (8-2) WR Courtney Taylor was in right place to recover ball, even though his advancement of ball registered as fumble in EZ. Tigers ran some time off clock before sending in Vaughn for winning FG. TB Kenny Irons was Tigers workhorse, carrying 37/179y and scoring 2 TDs. But, Irons lost FUM at Georgia 11YL early in 4th Q with Auburn trailing 27-21, so it appeared Irons had thrown away chance at victory. But, Bulldogs FB Brannan Southerland turned it right back with disastrous results: Auburn LB Karibi Dede raced 15y for FUM TD RET. With QB D.J. Shockley (20-36/304y, 2 TDs) back in after knee injury, Georgia had plenty of time to bounce back, which it did with K Brandon Coutu's 3rd FG (41y) for 30-28 lead with 3:25 left. "It will go down as a classic," said Auburn coach Tommy Tuberville of game that featured 8 lead changes.

OKLAHOMA STATE 24 Texas Tech 17: After withstanding Texas Tech's 17-pt rally that tied game, Cowboys (4-5) pulled out win on short TD run by reserve QB Al Pena with 23 secs left. Oklahoma State had taken 14-0 H lead on 83y TD run by RB Mike Hamilton (23/161y) and QB Bobby Reid's 17y scoring pass to WR D'Juan Woods. Teams traded FGs in 3rd Q before Red Raiders (8-2) scored quick, dual 4th Q TDs on 4y pass from QB Cody Hodges (29-42/308y, INT) to WR Jarrett Hicks and NT Chris Hudler's heads-up REC of Oke State's FUM in EZ. Teams next combined for 3 hot-potato TOs before Pena's TD. Cowboys rush attack gained 303y, while Texas Tech RB Taurean Henderson (-6y rushing and 23y receiving) was well-defensed. Still, Henderson reached impressive career milestone of becoming 3rd player all-time to both rush and receive 2,000y.

Southern California 35 CALIFORNIA 10: Toughest opponent for Trojans (10-0) during recent glory years and last team to beat them—in late September 2003—had been California. Usually taking backseat to Southern California O, Trojans D forced 6 TOs, picking off Bears (6-4) QB Joe Ayoob (9-19/98y) 4 times as USC won 32nd straight game. USC TB LenDale White (16/90y) rushed for 3 TDs, while QB Matt Leinart (20-32/246y, INT) rushed for 2 others. Cal managed to contain Trojans TB Reggie Bush (17/82y), but with plenty of O weapons in USC arsenal it was case of choosing its poison. Loss was 4th in last 5 games for struggling Bears, who were led on O by TB Marshawn Lynch's mild 82y rushing. "That's a great win for us against a team that we've struggled with for the last couple years," said Leinart. "We wanted to just leave a statement today that things are changing."

Bowl Championship Series Ranking November 14

	Harris Poll Pct.	USA Today Poll Pct.	Computer Pct.	BCS Avg.
1 Southern California (10-0)	.993	.996	.960	.9830
2 Texas (10-0)	.967	.965	1.000	.9773
3 Miami (8-1)	.915	.917	.840	.8907
4 Penn State (9-1)	.829	.807	.920	.8520
5 Louisiana State (8-1)	.868	.879	.720	.8223

November 19, 2005

Georgia Tech 14 MIAMI 10: Georgia Tech made wreck of Miami (8-2) QB Kyle Wright, harrying him from opening play and diffusing Hurricanes' conf title hopes. Yellow Jackets (7-3) finished with 7 sacks, while holding Canes to 1-14 3rd down conversions. Tech LB KaMichael Hall had 2 sacks and made 4th down tackle to halt Miami drive midway through 4th Q, and CB Dennis Davis ended matters with INT by on Miami's final possession. Miami D played well, but burned itself with crucial PENs on both of Georgia Tech's scoring drives. Pass interference on Canes CB Marcus Maxey eliminated INT in EZ, which was followed 3 plays later by Georgia Tech RB Tashard Choice's 2y TD run for 7-0 lead early in 1st Q. Excessive celebration PEN on LB Rocky McIntosh set up Jackets' winning TD, which was scored on 16y run by QB Reggie Ball (11-20/159y) in 3rd Q. Wright hit 14-31/207y and 19y TD pass to WR Sinorice Moss which had provided Miami with 10-7 lead in 2nd Q. Yellow Jackets ace WR Calvin Johnson caught 6/89y.

Virginia Tech 52 VIRGINIA 14: Maroon and orange Hokies (9-1) dominated in-state rivalry to keep alive ACC title and BCS bowl hopes. While Hokies O gained 503y, D held Cavaliers to 254y,, only 46y in decisive 1st H that had Virginia Tech bounding ahead by 24-0. Tech TB Cedric Humes (113y rushing) scored 3 TDs, RB Brandon Ore (115y rushing) scored twice, and QB Marcus Vick (15-21/170y, INT) tossed two scoring passes. Hokies S Aaron Rouse chipped in 2 INTs of Virginia (6-4) QB Marques Hagans, both of which were converted into TDs. Sr QB Hagans had to have been disappointed in his Cavaliers farewell as Hokies' D focus forced him into throwing for only 140y and tacking on only 19y rushing because of 3 sacks. Cavs RB Wali Lundy rushed for 67y and 2 TDs, his 49th and 50th career 6-ptrs.

Clemson 13 SOUTH CAROLINA 9: Gamecocks (7-4) could change from 1 big-name coach (Lou Holtz) to another (Steve Spurrier), but still failed to beat bitter in-state rivals. Clemson (7-4) won 4th straight in series, scoring game-winner with 6 mins to go on 2y TD run by frosh RB James Davis that capped 80y drive. Drive was keyed by clutch passing by Tigers QB Charlie Whitehurst (17-26/172y, 2 INTs), who completed 3 straight passes to get team out of 1st-and-35 hole on Tigers 22YL. Winner was game's 1st TD after 5 FGs, 3 by South Carolina K Josh Brown. K Jad Dean of Clemson made pair of FGs but saw his 3-ptr blocked by Cocks LB Orus Lambert in 4th Q. Gamecocks had late final chance, but pass by QB Blake Mitchell (16-29/180y, 3 INTs) was itipped and intercepted by DE Charles Bennett. Davis put his mark on rivalry with 145y rushing, while RB Mike Davis (21/111y) and WR Sidney Rice (7/122y) were O stars for South Carolina. Teams had met at midfield before game to shake hands, thus burying memory of brutal brawl of year ago.

Vanderbilt 28 TENNESSEE 24: Vanderbilt (5-6) QB Jay Cutler (27-39/315y) threw 5y scoring pass, his 3rd TD pass of game went to WR Earl Bennett (14/167y) with 71 secs left to lead Commodores (5-6) to their 1st win over in-state rivals since 1982. In throes of its most disappointing season since 1988, Volunteers (4-6) had taken 24-21 lead midway through 4th Q on 29y FG by K James Wilhoit. RB Adrian Foster keyed Tennessee's rally from 21-7 deficit, rushing 40/223y, scoring twice, and adding 4/45y receiving. Despite blowing 2-TD lead, Vanderbilt remained focused and, after exchange of punts, drove 63y to Bennett's game-winning TD. QB Rick Clausen (11-25/125y, TD) then frantically drove Vols to Vanderbilt 20YL before throwing his 2nd INT, which was picked off by Vandy CB Jared Fagan. LB Moses Osemwegie led Vandy with 16 tackles. "You see grown men crying and you realize how long it's been since we've won," said Cutler. "It tells you how much it means to this program."

AUBURN 28 Alabama 18: With Tigers (9-2) building 21-0 1st Q lead, they threw kitchen sink at rivals to prevent comeback and win 4th straight against Crimson Tide. Unremitting Auburn D sacked Alabama QB Brodie Croyle 11 times, holding Croyle to 107y passing and no. 8 Alabama (9-2) O to 188y. With its swift D causing havoc, Tigers O needed only to make their longest drive travel 61y, while all 4 of their TD trips averaged relatively easy 47y. Auburn WR Ben Obomanu scored twice, on 7y reception 5 mins into game and on back-breaking 45y run for 21-pt lead 6 mins later. Auburn QB Brandon Cox (14-21/118y) threw 2 TD passes and TB Kenny Irons rushed for 103y, TD. Crimson Tide sub QB John Parker Wilson got late chance to complete 36y pass to WR D.J. Hall to set up Wilson's 1y TD keeper that was followed by his 2-pt conv pass. Alabama RB Kenneth Darby rushed 18/89y. Tigers now had earned 6 wins in last 7 games against Top 10 opponents.

Ohio State 25 MICHIGAN 21: Ohio State coach Jim Tressel upped his career mark to 4-1 vs. Wolverines (7-4) but needed incredible game-ending 88y drive built on QB Troy Smith's 7-8/77y passing. Buckeyes (9-2) QB Smith delivered 27-37/career-high 300y, TD passing in continuing his mastery over Wolerines. Winning drive was capped by 3y TD run by RB Antonio Pittman (23/85y) with 24 secs remaining. Smith, who also rushed for 37y and scored 4y TD run in 1st Q, had thrown 26y TD pass to WR Santonio Holmes (6/72y) with 6:40 left to pull Buckeyes within 21-19. Wolverines took over and drove to Ohio 34YL before deciding to punt. Smith took over and twice eluded pass-rush to make completions, including 27y pass to WR Anthony Gonzalez, that brought ball to Wolverines 4YL. With meager running attack that gained only 32y, Michigan still was in position to win thanks to timely passes by QB Chad Henne (25-36/223y, TD) and its mistake-free play. Meanwhile, Buckeyes suffered 2 TOs, missed x-pt and FG, shanked punt, and mishandled punt RETs. Despite all of that, Buckeyes won thanks to Smith's heroics and clinched share of Big 10 title with Penn State. "There is nothing that can make you feel better after losing this game," said sad Michigan coach Lloyd Carr, now 6-5 in series.

Penn State 31 MICHIGAN STATE 22: Picked to finish in lower echelon of Big 10 rankings, Penn State (10-1) instead celebrated its 2nd Big 10 title and 1st berth in BCS with win over up-and-down Spartans (5-6). Nittany Lions were tied with Ohio State and owning tiebreaker to sit atop Big 10 standings. Lions QB Michael Robinson led way as he had done all season, rushing for 90y with 33y TD and passing for 105y and TD. Lions D held Spartans QB Drew Stanton in check, limit him to 233y passing with 4 INTs. Penn State CB Alan Zemaitis had 3 INTs, including 1 he returned 17y to MSU 4YL to set up 3y scoring reception by WR Deon Butler for 24-7 lead in 3rd Q. After falling behind 17-0 at H and 24-7 on Butler's TD, best Michigan State could muster was to pull back to within 9 pts with 53 secs left: Stanton's 15y TD pass to WR Kerry Reed and 2-pt score on QB keeper came as too-little-too-late.

KANSAS STATE 36 Missouri 28: After 17 mostly glorious seasons as head coach of Kansas State program he resurrected from near-extinction, Bill Snyder went out as winner. Scoring game's final 22 pts, Wildcats (5-6) stunned confident Missouri (6-5). Kansas State did most of its damage on ground as RB Thomas Clayton rushed for 102y and QB Allen Webb (10-14/93y) gained for 91y to lead 224y Purple ground game. Webb had come off bench to lead comeback, getting better of Missouri star QB Brad Smith (21-36/248y, 3 TDs), who rushed for 71y. Smith's final TD, 19y pass to WR Brad Ekwerekwu, had put Tigers up 28-14 early in 3rd Q. Smith's sole INT, thrown near midfield with team trailing 29-28 late in 4th Q, was death knell for Tigers as LB Brandon Archer returned it 45y for K-State's final TD. Mizzou TE Martin Rucker caught 8/102y with 16y TD that had opened scoring in 1st Q.

TEXAS TECH 23 Oklahoma 21: While Texas Tech (9-2) coach Mike Leach had rebuilt program to annually compete for rankings, he still hadn't beaten his former boss, Bob Stoops, after 5 losses in as many games. Here he was favored of all things, but facing desperate Oklahoma (6-4) club looking for strong close to season. Trailing 21-17 with time expiring, Red Raiders éschewed its pass-crazy bread-and-butter to hand ball to RB Taurean Henderson (16/109y). Sr back surprised Oklahoma with up middle surge to stretch out and barely crack GL—confirmed by replay—as clock showed 0:00. Henderson's TD sent Texas Tech to its 1st win over Sooners since 1999. QB Cory Hodges (24-37/232y, 2 INTs), who threw 2 TDs as Texas Tech took 17-7 lead early in 4th Q, led 65y drive to winning score as he hit 3 passes/ 51y. Sooners had rallied with 2 TDs scored in game's final 6 mins as QB Rhett Bomar (12-26/118y) threw 13y TD pass to WR Malcolm Kelly to cap 89y drive that pulled OU to within 17-14, and RB Adrian Peterson (29/108y) scored on 13y run with 1:33 left for Oklahoma's 1st lead since early in 2nd Q.

Utah 41 BRIGHAM YOUNG (OT) 34: Emergence of QB Brett Ratliff (17-32/240y) was key for Utes (6-5) as back-up enjoyed starting role with 4 TD passes and 112y rushing with another TD. After 5 plays in extra session, Utah was spinning its wheels on BYU 25YL, but from there Ratliff found WR Travis LaTendresse (6/88y) with winning TD strike. Utah, now winner of 4 straight over BYU, needed to stop Cougars (6-5), which it did on downs at Utah 6YL. QB John Beck (27-47/309y, 2 TDs) misfired on his final pass, as Utes received had receivers blanketed, but he had led BYU back from 24-3 H deficit. Each team received good games from RBs as Utah RB Quinton Ganther rushed for 131y, and BYU RB Curtis Brown (7/84y receiving) churned out 153y and 2 TDs, including 64y burst in 3rd Q.

OREGON 56 Oregon State 14: Jumping ahead 7-0 on 60y INT TD RET by CB Aaron Gipson 3 mins into game, Oregon (10-1) never let up in scoring most pts in 109 years of "Civil War". Avenging 50-21 loss in 2004, Ducks scored 2 TDs in each Q including 97y KO TD RET by RB Jonathan Stewart to open 2nd H that clinched matters. Ducks QB Dennis Dixon (12-17/204y) threw 3 TDs, including 66y effort to WR Jaison Williams midway through 4th Q. With RB Yvenson Bernard rushing for 128y, Beavers (5-6) vainly controlled ball for more than 36 mins. Oregon State could not overcome 5 TOs, including 4 INTs thrown by QB Ryan Gunderson (22-43/175y, TD). Former walk-on Beavers WR Mike Hass (10/107y) concluded his fine career that earned him A-A status and receipt of 2005 Biletnikoff Award.

SOUTHERN CALIFORNIA 50 Fresno State 42:With Fresno State (8-2) coach Pat Hill's willingness to play any team, anywhere to earn recognition for his Bulldogs, and wins against programs like Oregon State and Wisconsin, Fresno was getting invitations from nation's biggest fish, like USC and its 32-game win streak. Alas, Trojans (11-0) TB Reggie Bush was unstoppable, rushing for 294y and gaining 513y all-purpose, good for 2nd all-time behind Emmett White's 578y for Utah State vs. New Mexico State in 2000. S Darnell Bing finally ended matters with EZ INT with less than min left. As it had been all season, 3rd Q was charm for Trojans, who scored 28pts to obliterate 21-13 H deficit, with TD runs of 45y and 50y coming from Bush. Harried Bulldogs QB Paul Pinegar (27-45/317y, 4 TDs, 3 INTs) threw 3 of his INTs in 3rd Q, but he kept Fresno in game with key completions. His 4th TD pass of game, 6y to WR Joe Fernandez (7/75y) pulled Fresno to within 41-35. Ensuing KO proved Bush was mortal afterall: his FUM set up 18y TD run by Fresno State RB Wendell Mathis (23/109y) for Bulldogs' stunning 42-41 lead with 9:47 left. Trojans needed just 3:25 to regain its edge on 2y TD run by TB LenDale White. K Mario Danelo added 26y FG moments later, but Pinegar had time to march team 47y to USC 25YL before Bing's big INT. Trojans QB Matt Leinart hit 22-33/200y, TD.

USA Today Coaches November 20

1	Southern California (49)	1536	14	Alabama	727
2	Texas (13)	1501	15	TCU	704
3	LSU	1415	16	Fresno State	543
4	Penn State	1344	17	Texas Tech	525
5	Virginia Tech	1277	18	Louisville	520
6	Notre Dame	1185	19	Florida	383
7	Ohio State	1137	20	Boston College	345
8	Oregon	1102	21	Florida State	341
9	Auburn	1025	22	Wisconsin	218
10	Miami (Fla.)	990	23	Michigan	158
11	UCLA	970	24	Georgia Tech	149
12	West Virginia	881	25	Iowa State	135
13	Georgia	797			

Bowl Championship Series Ranking November 21

	Harris Poll Pct.	USA Today Poll Pct.	Computer Pct.	BCS Avg.
1 Southern Calif. (11-0)	.991	.991	.960	.9807
2 Texas (10-0)	.969	.968	1.000	.9790
3 Penn State (10-1)	.883	.867	.920	.8900
4 Louisiana State (9-1)	.899	.913	.700	.8373
5 Virginia Tech (9-1)	.794	.824	.870	.8293

November 24-26, 2005

(Th'g) WEST VIRGINIA 45 Pittsburgh 13: Despite icy conditions, West Virginia (9-1) continued hot play as QB Pat White rushed for 220y and 2 TDs to lead running attack that toted up 451y. TB Steve Slaton added 179y rushing with 2 TDs, while combining with White on 16y TD pass that had opened scoring in 1st Q. Pittsburgh (5-6) answered with 63y pass, which was 1st of 2 TD connections between QB Tyler Palko (24-43/308y, 2 INTs) and WR Greg Lee (6/142y). But, 5 TOs prevented Panthers from maintaining heady pace that followed. WVU S Jahmile Addae capped game by returning INT 40y for TD. White's rushing set school and Big East records for QBs.

(Fri) Texas 40 TEXAS A&M 29: For most of game best QB on field was not Texas QB Vince Young, nor even Texas A&M (5-6) starter QB Reggie McNeal, who was out with injury, but unsung Aggies backup QB Stephen McGee, who rushed for 108y and 2 TDs. A&M frosh RB Jorvorski Lane, weighing in neighborhood of 275 lbs, also made splash with 104y rushing and 35y TD pass to WR Jason Carter. Still, Texas (11-0) remained on pace for spot in BCS title game by taking lead for good midway through 3rd Q when Young led 80y drive to 2nd TD run by RB Ramonce Taylor (15/102y) for 28-22 lead. Texas forced punt and scored eventual winning pts when FS Michael Griffin blocked it, ball bouncing to CB Cedric Griffin for 11y TD RET. McGee answered with 65y drive to his 1y scoring keeper, but 34-29 deficit was as close as Texas A&M could come. Young threw for 162y, rushed for only 19y, and had 2 costly TOs. Win for Longhorns was 6th straight in series.

(Fri) Nebraska 30 COLORADO 3: New-fangled Nebraska (7-4) O seemed finally to be clicking as QB Zac Taylor tore apart Colorado, completing 27-43/392y and 2 TDs. Buffaloes (7-4) scored 1st on 33y FG by K Mason Crosby early in 1st Q, but struggled to keep up with suddenly high-flying Huskers. Huskers pulled away with 17-pt 2nd Q, as Taylor threw for 167y with 19y on TD pass to TB Cory Ross (9/129y receiving) and K Jordan Congdon booted 2nd of his 3 FGs. Nebraska totaled 497y to 212y for reeling Buffs. Colorado RB Hugh Charles rushed for 78y as game-high rusher, with 45y coming on single burst up middle on team's sole scoring drive.

RUTGERS 44 Cincinnati 9: Not leaving anything to chance, Rutgers (7-4) put on show for bowl scouts. Gaining 574y, Scarlet Knights showcased O in scoring every Q as RB Ray Rice rushed for 195y and 2 TDs, FB Brian Leonard rushed for 79y and 2 TDs, and QB Ryan Hart threw for 237y and TD. Rutgers D played just as well, sacking Cincinnati QB Dustin Grutza (15-24/169y) 9 times in holding Bearcats (4-7) to 146y. Cincinnati finally cracked Rutgers GL in 4th Q when Grutza threw 8y TD pass to TE Brent Celek, who led Bearcats with 5 catches/54y. Hoping for 1st bowl berth since 1978, nervous Rutgers needed Notre Dame to win, which it barely did over Stanford, so that Big East would not lose 1 of its 4 bowl spots.

FLORIDA 34 Florida State 7: Unusual year continued for Gators (8-3), who swept biggest rivals in Florida State, Tennessee, and Georgia for first time since their 1996 national championship season but managed to go 5-3 against rest of schedule. Florida QB Chris Leak (19-28/211y, 2 TDs, INT) sparked O that took advantage of huge advantage in field position. In throes of 3-game losing streak, Seminoles (7-4) stumbled on O, losing 4 TOs to negate their 334y to 284y advantage. Gators converted those TOs into 24 pts. Florida State also surrendered crucial special teams TD in 2nd Q when 45y FG attempt by K Gary Cismesia was blocked by NT Marcus Thomas and scooped up by CB Reggie Lewis for 52y RET for 14-0 lead. Florida WR Chad Jackson caught 9 passes/97y and game-opening 8y TD. Harassed by 5 sacks, FSU QB Drew Weatherford (24-42/285y, 2 INTs) prevented Seminoles from suffering shutout with 5y TD pass to WR De'Cody Fagg (5/68y).

Georgia 14 GEORGIA TECH 7: Playing aggressive D paid off for Bulldogs (9-2) in game's closing moments as CB Tim Jennings, knowing blitz was pressuring Georgia Tech QB Reggie Ball (18-35/155y, 2 INTs), jumped route to pick off pass thrown to WR Damarius Bilbo at own 5YL. Jennings raced 30y up sideline before being knocked OB, but not before he ended Tech's tying threat with 1:11 remaining. Winning TD had been scored 2 mins earlier when QB D.J. Shockley (15-34/198y) threw 19y pass to WR Bryan McClendon in EZ. UGa CB Thomas Flowers jump-started winning 39y drive with 33y punt RET. Yellow Jackets (7-4) had opened scoring when WR Calvin Johnson capped 78y drive with 2y scoring reception. Bulldogs answered with 80y drive to FB Brannan Southerland's 1y TD run and it appeared shootout was developing. But Yellow Jackets failed to sufficiently deliver ball to Johnson (2/14y) and suffered 3 TOs, while Georgia could only muster 68y rushing. Georgia Tech RB P.J. Daniels rushed 16/77y. Georgia coach Mark Richt had now lifted his record vs. Tech to 5-0.

KANSAS 24 Iowa State 21 (OT): Nightmare repeated itself for Cyclones (7-4), who lost final game in OT with berth in Big 12 championship game on line for 2nd straight season. Kansas (6-5) K Scott Webb booted winner from 34y out after Iowa State K Bret Culbertson missed from 41y out. Jayhawks sent game into OT on 15y TD pass from QB Brian Luke (9-12/82y), who played well off bench, to frosh WR Dexton Fields with 1:05 remaining to cap 4-play, 58y drive. Luke had scored earlier in 4th Q on 1y keeper on 4th-and-goal that was ruled as short by inches until overruled by TV replay. That TD tied game at 14-14, but Iowa State marched 87y on subsequent series for TD run by FB Ryan Kock. QB Bret Meyer (18-34/257y, 2 INTs) led Iowa State attack, with 5 completions to WR Austin Flynn for career-high 120y.

Notre Dame 38 STANFORD 31: With Notre Dame (9-2) playing for spot in BCS and Stanford (5-6) hoping for spot in any bowl, contest went down to wire. Irish did not score winning pts until 6y run by RB Darius Walker (37/191y) with 55 secs remaining. Notre Dame QB Brady Quinn threw for 432y and 3 TDs, but was picked off twice. Fighting Irish also struggled with their kicking game, missing 2 FGs and x-pt. None of that would have mattered if backup Cardinal QB T.C. Ostrander (11-11/197y) had not thrown 4y TD pass to TE Matt Traverso for 31-30 lead with 1:46 left; play was set up by 76y completion to WR Mark Bradford. Irish WR Jeff Samardzija continued his brilliant play, catching 9/career-high 191y and his 15th TD, which padded his single-season school record. Fellow WR Maurice Stovall (7/136y, TD) gave Notre Dame first pair of 1000y receivers, 4th such ND receiver all-time. Immediately after Stanford Stadium cleared out, $90 million construction effort began to refurbish 84-year-old facility.

USA Today Coaches November 27

1	Southern California (53)	1540	14	Alabama	731
2	Texas (9)	1497	15	TCU	705
3	LSU	1397	16	Texas Tech	605
4	Penn State	1369	17	Louisville	532
5	Virginia Tech	1290	18	Florida	506
6	Ohio State	1162	19	Boston College	436
7	Notre Dame	1153	20	Wisconsin	367
8	Oregon	1127	21	Michigan	250
9	Auburn	1049	22	Fresno State	186
10	Miami (Fla.)	990	23	Clemson	158
11	UCLA	946	24	Georgia Tech	80
12	West Virginia	883	25	Iowa	76
13	Georgia	827			

Bowl Championship Series Ranking November 28

	Harris Poll Pct.	USA Today Poll Pct.	Computer Pct.	BCS Avg.
1 Southern Calif. (11-0)	.995	.994	.970	.9863
2 Texas (11-0)	.965	.966	.990	.9737
3 Penn State (10-1)	.894	.883	.920	.8990
4 Louisiana State (10-1)	.885	.901	.760	.8487
5 Virginia Tech (10-1)	.818	.832	.850	.8333

December 3, 2005

Navy 42 Army 23 (Philadelphia): Recent Navy (7-4) domination of series continued as Midshipman pulled away by scoring 4 straight TDs over 16-min span covering end of 1st H through most of 3rd Q. Riding 4-game win streak, Army (4-7) hoped to snap 3-game series win drought and enjoyed fleeting 10-7 lead midway through 2nd Q. Eventually, force of Midshipmen rushing attack bore down on Black Knights D. Navy ran for 490y, led by FB Adam Ballard's 192y. Ballard scored twice, reaching EZ with 28y gallop in 3rd Q and clinching 67y romp in 4th Q. QB Lamar Owens (15/99y) added 3 TD runs for Middies. Army went to air to try to keep pace as QB Zac Dahman threw 23-35/255y, 3 TDs, 2 to WR Jeremy Trimble (6/81y). In his final game, Army TB Carlton Jones rushed for 80y to crack 1000y barrier for 2nd time and caught 18y TD. With its win, Navy now had earned marginal lead in overall series at 50-49-7.

West Virginia 28 SOUTH FLORIDA 13: Mountaineers (10-1) wrapped up perfect Big East season with rush attack that sliced up South Florida. WVU QB Patrick White led way with 11/177y rushing, including dazzling scoring runs of 65y in 3rd Q and 76y in 4th Q. White's 7y TD pass to WR Darius Reynaud in 2nd Q supplied winning pts as West Virginia took 14-3 H lead. South Florida's attack was more balanced, with 149y rushing and 221y passing, but Bulls could not penetrate West Virginia GL until 4th Q on 11y run by backup QB Carlton Hill. Hill, school's heralded recruit, threw for 98y and added 50y rushing off bench. White had rushed for 508y total in past 3 games.

Florida State 27 Virginia Tech 22 (Jacksonville): Given up for dead after losing final 3 regular season games, Seminoles (8-4) were suddenly ACC champs for 12th time in 14 years as conf title game gave them 2nd chance that they embraced. Everything came together for Florida State in 3rd Q as they shattered 3-3 H tie with 24 straight pts. FSU's 1st TD came courtesy of old scoring staple—special teams—as WR Willie Reid (5/79y), who gained 210y all-purpose, returned punt 83y for TD. Seminoles converted into 7 more pts as TB Leon Washington scored on 14y run, short punt into 3 pts on 41y FG by K Gary Cismesia, and Tech FUM into another TD on 6y pass from QB Drew Weatherford (21-35/225y) to WR Chris Davis. Hokies (10-2) rallied with 19 pts in 4th Q, as QB Marcus Vick (26-52/335y) threw 28y TD pass to WR Josh Morgan (7/128y) and ran in 2 others. Vick felt heat all game, however, and was sacked 6 times.

Georgia 34 Louisiana State 14 (Atlanta): LSU (10-2) woke up with outside chance for Rose Bowl berth. They went to sleep shutout of BCS bowls all together after being handled by Georgia (10-2) team that surprisingly won SEC championship. Bulldogs QB D.J. Shockley (6-12/112y) set tempo from game's start, throwing 45y TD pass to WR Sean Bailey on Bulldogs' opening play. Georgia D forced TO as CB DeMario Minter picked off LSU QB JaMarcus Russell (11-19/120y) near midfield. Soon after, Shockley and Bailey teamed up for 29y scoring pass for 14-0 lead. Russell next marched Tigers 80y to his 1y scoring keeper, but LSU's next possession ended with punt attempt from deep in own territory. WR Bryan McClendon blocked punt, giving Georgia 1st down at LSU 15YL. Shockley scored on 7y run 3 plays later for 21-7 lead. Tigers would have been hard-pressed to rally under normal conditions, but loss of Russell to separated shoulder on sack by DT Jeff Owens late in 3rd Q sealed Bayou Bengals' fate. QB Matt Flynn came off bench but was pressured into throwing INT returned 15y for crushing TD by Georgia CB Tim Jennings early in 4th Q for 34-7 lead. Flynn later threw 19y TD pass to WR Dwayne Bowe (5/74y).

Texas 70 Colorado 3 (Houston): While game was not expected to be close for programs headed in opposite directions, outrageous 67-pt differential put damper on Big 12 championship game. Fully aware that teams with national title aspirations have stumbled in this game before, Longhorns (12-0) took no chances with struggling Buffaloes (7-5) by scoring TDs on 6 1st H possessions. Playing little more than 1st H, QB Vince Young (14-17/193y, 3 TDs, INT) was near perfect passer, while also rushing for 57y and TD. Texas D allowed 191y and forced 4 TOs, while special teams blocked FG attempt, scored TD on blocked punt when ball was recovered in EZ by CB Brandon Foster, and answered Colorado's meager FG with 54y KO RET by RB Ramonce Taylor to set up TD. Colorado avoided shutout with 25y FG by K Mason Crosby in 2nd Q. Easy win wrapped up 1st Big 12 title for Longhorns since 1996 and they enter post-season with perfect record for 6th time since 1963.

SOUTHERN CALIFORNIA 66 Ucla 19: After more than 1 close call during season, top-ranked Trojans (12-0) wanted easy finish to their perfect regular season. Sporting 115th-ranked rush D, UCLA (9-2) had absolutely no answer for TB Reggie Bush, who torched them for 260y rushing and 2 TDs, or TB LenDale White, who rushed for 154y and 2 TDs. TB Matt Leinart played less than his best but managed 233y passing with 3 TDs at helm of O that gained 679y. In losing their 7th straight to rivals, Bruins could not crack USC GL until 4th Q on 15y TD run by TB Maurice Drew (14/84y). Win was 34th in row for Southern Cal, tying it with Miami from earlier this decade for 4th highest steak of all-time. Perhaps more impressive was USC's 16th straight win vs. ranked opponent.

USA Today Coaches December 4

1	Southern California (55)	1543	14	TCU		734
2	Texas (7)	1495	15	Texas Tech		636
3	Penn State	1424	16	Louisville		585
4	Ohio State	1300	17	UCLA		531
5	Oregon	1234	18	Florida		530
6	Notre Dame	1219	19	Boston College		427
7	Auburn	1141	20	Wisconsin		399
8	Georgia	1097	21	Michigan		274
9	Miami (Fla.)	1075	22	Florida State		256
10	LSU	1002	23	Clemson		191
11	West Virginia	959	24	Georgia Tech		114
12	Virginia Tech	955	25	Iowa		95
13	Alabama	787				

Bowl Championship Series Ranking December 5

	Harris Poll Pct.	*USA Today* Poll Pct.	Computer Pct.	BCS Avg.
1 Southern Calif. (12-0)	.995	.996	.970	.9870
2 Texas (12-0)	.965	.965	.990	.9733
3 Penn State (10-1)	.918	.919	.920	.9190
4 Ohio State (9-2)	.849	.839	.880	.8560
5 Oregon (10-1)	.781	.796	.820	.7990

Conference Standings
Big East

West Virginia	7-0
Louisville	5-2
Pittsburgh	4-3
Rutgers	4-3
South Florida	4-3
Cincinnati	2-5
Connecticut	2-5
Syracuse	0-7

Atlantic Coast

ATLANTIC

Florida State	5-3
Boston College	5-3
Clemson	4-4
Maryland	3-5
North Carolina State	3-5
Wake Forest	3-5

COASTAL

Virginia Tech	7-1
Miami	6-2
Georgia Tech	5-3
North Carolina	4-4
Virginia	3-5
Duke	0-8

Southeastern

EAST

Georgia	6-2
Florida	5-3
South Carolina	5-3
Tennessee	3-5
Vanderbilt	3-5
Kentucky	2-6

WEST

Auburn	7-1
Louisiana State	7-1
Alabama	6-2
Arkansas	2-6
Mississippi	1-7
Mississippi State	1-7

Conference USA

EAST

Central Florida	7-1
Memphis	5-2
Southern Mississippi	5-2
East Carolina	4-4
Marshall	3-5
Alabama-Birmingham	3-5

WEST

Tulsa	6-2
Texas-El Paso	5-3
Houston	4-4
Southern Methodist	4-4
Rice	1-7
Tulane	1-7

Big Ten

Penn State	7-1
Ohio State	7-1
Iowa	5-3
Michigan	5-3
Northwestern	5-3
Wisconsin	5-3
Minnesota	4-4
Purdue	3-5
Michigan State	2-6
Indiana	1-7
Illinois	0-8

Big Twelve

NORTH

Colorado	5-3
Iowa State	4-4
Nebraska	4-4
Missouri	4-4
Kansas	3-5
Kansas State	2-6

SOUTH

Texas	8-0
Texas Tech	6-2
Oklahoma	6-2
Texas A&M	3-5
Baylor	2-6
Oklahoma State	1-7

Western Athletic

Boise State	7-1
Nevada	7-1
Fresno State	6-2
Louisiana Tech	6-2
Hawaii	4-4
Idaho	2-6
San Jose State	2-6
Utah State	2-6
New Mexico State	0-8

Mid-American

EAST

Akron	5-3
Bowling Green	5-3
Miami (Ohio)	5-3
Ohio	3-5
Buffalo	1-7
Kent State	0-8

WEST

Northern Illinois	6-2
Toledo	6-2
Central Michigan	5-3
Western Michigan	5-3
Ball State	4-4
Eastern Michigan	3-5

Mountain West

Texas Christian	8-0
Brigham Young	5-3
Colorado State	5-3
New Mexico	4-4
Utah	4-4
San Diego State	4-4
Air Force	3-5
Wyoming	2-6
Nevada-Las Vegas	1-7

Pacific-10

Southern Cal	8-0
Oregon	7-1
UCLA	6-2
California	4-4
Arizona State	4-4
Stanford	4-4
Oregon State	3-5
Arizona	2-6
Washington State	1-7
Washington	1-7

2005 Major Bowl Games
Las Vegas Bowl (Dec. 22): California 35 Brigham Young 28

For 3 Qs, Las Vegas Bowl featured celebration of California O stars as Golden Bears (8-4) built 35-14 lead. BYU (6-6) QB John Beck (35-53/352y, 3 TDs, 2 INTs) led 4th Q rally that finally ended when Beck's arm was hit while passing by DE Philip Mbakogu, and pass was picked off by CB Daymeion Hughes. Cal then ran out clock. Bears had built big lead behind balanced O led by RB Marshawn Lynch's career-high 195y rushing with 3 TDs, including 23y scoring romp in 2nd Q without benefit of properly-tied shoelaces. QB Steve Levy, in only 2nd career start for QB, completed 16-28/228y, and another dynamic Bears underclassman, WR DeSean Jackson caught 6/130y. Frosh Jackson scored on receptions of 42y and 22y, diving for latter to close scoring for Bears. Cougars Beck threw TD passes of 7y to TE Jonny Harline and 9y to WR Todd Watkins, capping drives of 74y and 96y respectively. WR Nate Meikle was Beck's favorite target for game, catching 12/93y. Teams combined for 915y O.

Poinsettia Bowl (Dec. 22): Navy 51 Colorado State 30

In leading Navy (8-4) to bowl victory and 611y O, SB Reggie Campbell achieved rare milestone in scoring 5 TDs to become 5th player in bowl history to accomplish that feat. Campbell (16/116y), who compiled 290y all-purpose, scored on his only 2 receptions, of 55y and 34y, and reached end zone with rushes of 22, 2, and 21y. Colorado State (6-6) scored on its opening possession, driving 77y to short TD run by RB Kyle Bell (22/122y). Midshipmen and Campbell answered immediately as team's 1st play from scrimmage was his 55y scoring catch of pass by QB Lamar Owens. After 34y FG by CSU K Jason Smith, Navy pulled away with trio of 2nd Q TDs. Rams QB Justin Holland hit pair of TDs to WR Dustin Osborn in 2nd H and earned incredible statistics for QB of team losing by 3 TDs, completing 26-33/381y, 3 TDs, and no INTs. Navy FB Adam Ballard was game-high rusher with 15/129y.

Fort Worth Bowl (Dec. 23): Kansas 42 Houston 13

Kansas (7-5) celebrated rare bowl win with showcase of O firepower. QB Jason Swanson, whose return from injury jump-started Jayhawks' run to bowl bid, threw for 307y and 4 TDs to easily out-class Houston QB Kevin Kolb (20-44/214y). Normally unaccustomed to big-play O, Jayhawks gained 538y against blitzing Cougars (6-6). Houston hung tough, trailing 14-10 at H, but ran out of steam in surrendering game's final 21 pts. Kansas TB Jon Cornish rushed 16/101y and caught 2 shovel passes, converting them into TDs of 13y and 30y. WR Brian Murph also had Forth Worth Bowl to remember, scoring on 85y punt RET in 1st Q to give Jayhawks 7-0 lead and catching 48y TD pass in 4th Q that closed scoring. CB Theo Baines had 2 INTs for Kansas, while teammate DE Charlton Keith returned INT 14y for 4th Q TD. Houston gained only 244y—213y less than its avg—and scored only single TD, on Kolb's short keeper late in 2nd Q.

Champs Sports Bowl (Dec. 27): Clemson 19 Colorado 10

Frosh TB James Davis deservingly scored final, clinching TD for Clemson (8-4), reaching EZ after 6y run to cap 7-play, 61y drive against worn down Buffs. Davis rushed for career-high 150y on 28 carries to win game MVP honors. After surrendering 100 pts total for final 2 games of painful regular season, Colorado (7-6) D regained some pride in keeping game close. Buffs O barely registered, however, gaining 124y with just 17y on ground. Tigers O gained 365y as QB Charlie Whitehurst threw for 19-27/196y. His sole INT was costly as Colorado converted it into 36y FG by K Mason Crosby to tie game 3-3 early in 2nd Q. Weak answer for heavily-favored Clemson was 2nd FG by K Jad Dean, 9 mins later. Tigers opened 2nd H with 67y drive for what proved to be winning score as Whitehurst shook off LB Akarika Dawn at line of scrimmage before running for 5y TD. With starting QB Joel Klatt out and replacement QB James Cox (4-12/26y) struggling, Buffs moved ball best with 3rd-string QB Brian White (7-12/81y). White marched Colorado 69y to his 2y TD pass to TE Quinn Sypniewski with 5:45 remaining. Sypniewski's TD was team's 1st in 14 Qs.

Insight Bowl (Dec. 27): Arizona State 45 Rutgers 40

For lovers of O, Insight Bowl was delight as teams combined for 1210y—all-time record for any bowl game. Arizona State (7-5) gained 678y with QB Rudy Carpenter throwing for 467y. Carpenter also tossed 4 TDs, and each score was needed as Rutgers (7-5) provided better O competition than expected. In fact, upstart Scarlet Knights, double-digit underdog in only their 2nd bowl game ever, led 24-10 in 1st H and, after surrendering lead in 2nd H, regained it by 33-31 margin early in 4th Q. Carpenter put ASU into lead for good after connecting with WR Matt Miller (5/135y, 2 TDs) for 42y TD in 4th Q. Sun Devils added 4y TD run by TB Rudy Burgess (16/103y, 2 TDs) before Rutgers QB Ryan Hart (24-38/374y, 3 TDs, INT) completed last pass of his career for 29y TD to WR Tres Moses (7/113y). Frosh TB Ray Rice of Rutgers was game-high rusher with 20/108y, while K Jeremy Ito booted 4 FGs, including 52y effort. "That was a fun game to be part of," said winning coach Dirk Koetter. Previous record for y had been 1158y, amassed by Hawaii and Houston in 2003 Hawaii Bowl, and now had been broken twice in 1st week of 2005 season's bowl play as Navy and Colorado State had done so in Poinsettia Bowl.

MPC Computers Bowl (Dec. 28): Boston College 27 Boise State 21

When team plays "underdog card," it always has been best to keep quiet beforehand. That way favored opponent could be lulled into unfocused overconfidence due to perceived ease of effort needed to win game. Yet there was CEO of bowl sponsor Micron, Mike Atkins, making fun of Boston College (9-3) DE Mathias Kiwanuka's name at pre-game banquet that became defacto pep rally for hometown Broncos by town's mayor and other anything-but-impartial dignitaries. Fired up BC Eagles proceeded to torch Boise State (9-4) in 1st H, taking 24-0 lead. QB Matt Ryan (19-36/256y, INT), who threw for 178y in 1st H and led way with 3 TD passes including 35y arrow to WR Will Blackmon (5/144y) to lock up 1st H scoring. Blackmon just missed another TD as he caught 52y pass as time expired at end of 1st H; he was tackled at 1YL by Boise LB Colt Brooks. Broncos credited themselves by rallying to trio of 2nd H TDs before final drive ended with EZ INT by BC S Ryan Glasper with 37 secs left. Although thwarted on his final pass, QB Jared Zabransky threw for 279y in defeat with 53y on TD pass to WR Drisan James to put Boise on scoreboard late in 3rd Q. Zabransky later carried 2y for Broncos' 2nd tally, while CB Quinton Jones scored their final TD with 92y punt RET with 3:51 remaining. Boise State's 31-game home win streak ended, while inspired Eagles won 6th straight bowl game, currently longest in nation. "We go to a banquet that turns into a pep rally; I didn't have to say anything to this team. I ought to thank the mayor and the people of Boise for getting this team ready to play," summed up Eagles coach Tom O'Brien.

Alamo Bowl (Dec. 28): Nebraska 32 Michigan 28

Searching for return to glory days of past, Nebraska (8-4) took big step with comeback win over 1 of college football's big-name programs. Scoring final 15 pts of contest, Huskers stunned Woverines (7-5), who lost 5 games in single season for 1st time since 1984. RB Cory Ross rushed for 161y, including 31y TD that pulled Nebraska to within 28-25 midway through 4th Q. Huskers QB Zac Taylor added 167y passing, with 13y connection that became winning TD pass—his 3rd of game—to WR Terrence Nunn with 4:29 remaining. Taylor and Nunn had hooked up on 52y scoring connection in 1st Q and had 3y TD pass in 3rd Q overruled after replay. Michigan almost pulled off miracle win with 8 crazy laterals on final play before TE Tyler Ecker was driven OB at Cornhuskers 13YL: only piece missing on wild finale was premature on-field arrival of Stanford's band (see November 20, 1982). QB Chad Henne was main man for Michigan, completing 21-43/270y, 3 TDs while rushing for team's final TD early in 4th Q. However, Henne also threw INT and lost key FUM, which set up Nebraska's winning TD after DT Ola Dagundaro's RET carried to Wolverines 17YL.

Holiday Bowl (Dec. 29): Oklahoma 17 Oregon 14

Although not as high-scoring affair as typical Holiday Bowls have been, clash of Ducks (10-2) and Sooners (8-4) went down to wire in true spirit of San Diego's post-season history. With 33 secs left, Oklahoma LB Clint Ingram sealed victory with INT on own 10YL. Ingram was accidental hero as he was supposed to blitz on play, but instead positioned himself in front of WR Demetrius Williams to make leaping catch. Oregon, after struggling on O for most of 2nd H, had pulled to within 17-14 3 mins earlier on 3y TD pass from QB Brady Leaf (14-24/136y, INT) to TE Tim Day. It capped 78y drive. Next, Ducks D forced punt, with O taking over on its 22YL. Playing in city where brother Ryan failed miserably as Chargers pro QB, Leaf was lustily booed when entering game in relief of QB Dennis Dixon (11-19/107y). But, young Leaf made 2 big completions on final drive: 38y pass to RB Terrence Whitehead and, on 3rd-and-14, 19y throw to RB Jeremiah Johnson after being flushed out of pocket. Sooners RB Adrian Peterson rushed 23/84y, with 1 of his patented runs of 76y in 2nd H, while developing QB Rhett Bomar threw 17-30/229y with INT and 17y TD pass to FB J. D. Runnels for 10-7 lead in 3rd Q. Oklahoma RB KeJuan Jones capped ensuing 74y drive—which featured 3 runs by Peterson for 36y—with 8y TD run for what proved to be winning pts.

Emerald Bowl (Dec. 29): Utah 38 Georgia Tech 10

Showing glimpses of its 2004 unbeaten squad, Utah (7-5) routed Yellow Jackets behind O output of 550y. WR Travis LaTendresse seemed to gain 550y himself, catching 16 passes/214y and tying all-bowl record of 4 TDs. QB Brett Ratliff, making only his 2nd career start in relief of injured QB Brian Johnson, enjoyed bevy of open receivers with 30-41/381y passing, while RB Quinton Ganther rushed for 120y with 41y on 4th Q scoring burst. Georgia Tech (7-5) looked like team with no interest in playing in distant San Francisco. Yellow Jackets QB Reggie Ball managed 258y passing, with 31y on scoring pass to TE George Cooper, but was picked off twice and unable to get star WR Calvin Johnson (2/19y) going. Utah CB Eric Weddle had something to do with tight D that blanketed Johnson. Win was 5th straight in post-season for Utes.

Independence Bowl (Dec. 30): Missouri 38 South Carolina 31

Tigers (7-5) spotted Gamecocks 21-0 1st Q lead before rallying behind sr QB Brad Smith, whose final game was nothing short of tremendous. Smith threw for 282y and rushed for 150y and 3 TDs in leading Missouri's comeback. But 1st, South Carolina (7-5) dominated 1st H, gaining 312y and holding ball for more than 20 mins. Ahead 21-0 and marching toward potentially backbreaking 4th straight score to start Independence Bowl, Gamecocks instead allowed Tigers D to cut lead to 21-7 on tables-turning 99y INT TD RET by Mizzou CB Marcus King. QB Blake Mitchell (20-38/266y, 2 TDs, 3 INTs) shrugged it off and answered with 64y drive to regain Carolina's 21-pt lead on 2y scoring run by TB Mike Davis (18/125y). South Carolina D lost control of game in last 2 secs of 2nd Q: it allowed Tigers to drive 77y to Smith's 5y TD pass to TE Chase Coffman (8/99y). Smith's 31y TD run for game's sole score of 3rd Q pulled Missouri to within 28-21. Tigers converted another of Mitchell's 3 INTs to tie game early in 4th Q on Smith's 4y run. Teams next traded FGs, including 50y effort by K Adam Crossett for Missouri's 1st lead of game, before Smith's 3rd running TD served as game-clincher with 2:13 left. South Carolina WR Sidney Rice (12/191y) had opened game's scoring with 23y TD grab.

Sun Bowl (Dec. 30): UCLA 50 Northwestern 38

After dust in El Paso had settled on Sun Bowl with record 88 pts and 1037y, Northwestern's early 22-0 lead was as memorable as dust-in-the-wind. Wildcats (7-5) may have had early jump, but vivid Sun Bowl picture would be UCLA (10-2) WR Brandon Breazell scoring not once but *twice* on RETs of Northwestern on-side kicks late in 4th Q. After opening with dreadful 2-8/15y, 3 INTs passing and watching Wildcats DE Kevin Mims and LB Nick Roach both return INTs for TDs, Bruins QB Drew Olson (10-24/143y, 3 TDs) had led UCLA to 29 straight pts for 29-22 H lead. In 3rd Q, Bruins also converted Wildcats' TO into Olson's 5y TD pass to FB Michael Pitre for 36-22 lead. Northwestern continued to fling passes to try to regain momentum as QB Brett Basanez finished with 38-70/416y, 2 INTs, and he connected on pair of late TD passes to pull Cats briefly to within 36-30 and 43-38. But, Breazell returned failed short Kos each time for stunning TDs. Bruins sub TBs Chris Markey (24/161y) and Kahlil Bell (19/136y, 2 TDs) replaced TB Maurice Drew, who was injured in 1st H, to earn co-MVP honors. "I don't know if I've ever had a game quite like that one," said Northwestern coach Randy Walker of what would prove sadly to be his final game.

Music City Bowl (Dec. 30): Virginia 34 Minnesota 31

With 4 members of coaching staff off to new jobs elsewhere, resilient Virginia (7-5) squad had excuse if it had played poorly. But sr QB Marques Hagans was not going to let his final game get away, throwing for 25-32/career-high 358y in rallying Cavaliers from 14-pt deficit. Winning pts came courtesy of 39y FG by K Connor Hughes with 68 secs remaining, capping 75y drive keyed by two 19y completions by Hagans. Last gasp by Gophers (7-5), playing in Music City Bowl for 3rd time in 4 years, ended with EZ INT thrown by QB Bryan Cupito (18-28/263y) to Cavs CB Marcus Hamilton. Cupito had thrown 4 TDs including 44y delivery to WR Ernie Wheelwright (7/120y) as Gophers opened with 14-0 lead. Cupito also made 57y connection to WR Jared Ellerson (3/80y, 2 TDs) for 21-7 advantage in 2nd Q. Hagans constantly had 2nd H answers on O for Cavaliers, while Virginia D stonewalled Gophers' powerful rushing attack—led by TB Laurence Maroney's 109y—to tune of 74y in 2nd H when Minnesota would have liked to have killed clock with lots of possession time. Virginia TE Tom Santi worked his way open to catch 5 passes/128y.

Peach Bowl (Dec. 30): Louisiana State 40 Miami 3

With Miami (9-3) O utterly unable to penetrate Tigers' ferocious D—mustering only 6 1st downs and 153y for game—it was simply matter of time before Hurricanes' 3rd-ranked D would collapse. Foes were tied 3-3 entering 2nd Q, but from then on it was all Louisiana State (11-2). Consistently needing only single 1st down or 2 to reach Miami territory, Tigers took advantage of excellent field position to score on 8 straight possessions; Bayou Bengals' longest drive of night totaled only 68y. LSU sub QB Matt Flynn enjoyed his 1st start by throwing for 196y and 2 TDs, while TB Joseph Addai rushed for 130y and TD and added 4y scoring reception. Best play for folding Miami had occurred on opening possession when CB-turned-WR/TB Devin Hester raced 24y on run to set up 21y FG by K Jon Peattie. After game, fight broke out in tunnel heading to locker rooms. Miami players, so often in role of bullies over last 20 years of football history, became perturbed over 2 fake kicks employed by LSU in 2nd H when game was already out of hand.

Houston Bowl (Dec. 31): Texas Christian 27 Iowa State 24

Texas Christian (11-1) got its only pts of 2nd H, which were enough to secure victory, from unlikely source. K Peter LoCoco had been benched way back in September when his 3 missed FGs impacted Frogs' only defeat of season to lowly SMU. LoCoco reappeared in Houston Bowl to boot winning 44y FG with 5:25 left. Although Iowa

State (7-5) had spotted Horned Frogs 14-pt 1st Q lead, Cyclones stormed back to tie game 24-24 in 3rd Q on 22y TD pass from QB Bret Meyer (20-33/254y, 3 TDs, 2 INTs) to WR Todd Blythe (5/105y). Meyer and Blythe had launched Iowa State's rally in 2nd Q with 48y TD connection. Thanks in part to Iowa State's 4-TO generosity, TCU needed to drive length of field only once in 5 scoring drives. Horned Frogs scored on 84y pass from QB Jeff Ballard (21-33/275y, INT) to WR Michael DePriest and needed avg of only 31y on its other 3 scoring drives. With field position handicap Cyclones D often found itself, it did well to sack Ballard 6 times and force 3 TOs. RB Robert Merrill rushed for 109y and scored 20y TD for Purple Frogs, who won their 10th straight.

Capital One Bowl (Jan. 2): Wisconsin 24 Auburn 10

Inspired Badgers (10-3) desperately wanted to send retiring coach Barry Alvarez out as winner after he had spent 16 successful years resurrecting Wisconsin football. Wisconsin simply manhandled their 7th-ranked and favored SEC foe. Alvarez's chosen replacement Bret Bielema coached D to 1st H shutout of Auburn (9-3), and Badgers' O built 17-0 lead behind balanced attack that gained 311y of their final total of 548y against nation's 9th-best D (294y avg). Wisconsin TB Brian Calhoun finished with 213y rushing and 33y TD bolt. QB John Stocco threw for 301y including 6/173y to WR Brandon Williams. Stocco threw TD passes of 30y to Williams to open scoring in 1st Q and 13y to TE Owen Daniels to cap 86y drive in 2nd Q that took great deal of fight out of Tigers. Auburn woke up in 2nd H, scoring TD on 9y pass from QB Brandon Cox (15-33/137y, INT) to WR Courtney Taylor early in 4th Q. TB Kenny Irons, who had led SEC in rushing, managed 22/88y for Auburn. "This is Coach's day," said Stocco. "It just feels great to send him out of here like this." Alvarez finished with 8-3 bowl record (.727), 2nd to former Auburn and East Carolina coach Pat Dye's .750 percentage among coaches with at least 10 games.

Gator Bowl (Jan. 2): Virginia Tech 35 Louisville 24

As one of 3 new members of Big East Conf, invited in after departure of Boston College, Miami, and Virginia Tech to ACC, Louisville (9-3) had something to prove to departed Hokies and rest of country. Inspired Cardinals put on O show in 1st Q, driving 82y and 80y to TDs to grab 14-3 lead. Virginia Tech (11-2) hung in until 4th Q, when it reeled off 22 straight pts to rally spectacularly from 24-13 deficit. QB Marcus Vick led O in what proved to be final game of his troubled stay in Blacksburg, throwing for 204y and 2 TDs, including 5y scoring pass to TE Jeff King with 6:09 remaining. King's TD reception, which capped 53y drive begun with FUM REC by Va Tech LB James Anderson, gave Hokies 28-24 lead. Virginia Tech D clinched matters 1 min later when Anderson picked off pass from QB Hunter Cantwell—1 of 4 TOs for Louisville to 0 for Tech—and returned it 39y for TD. Frosh walk-on Cantwell, in his 2nd start in relief of injured QB Brian Brohm, threw for 216y and 3 TDs, but was sacked 4 times, picked off 3 times, and lost crucial FUM after strip by DE Chris Ellis. He also sported broken nose from big hit in 1st H of rugged game. Hokies RB Cedric Humes rushed for 112y with 24y TD in 4th Q. Game was marred by 2 unsportsmanlike incidents by Virginia Tech players: CB Jimmy Williams was ejected in 1st Q after bumping official and Vick drew flag for purposely stepping on Louisville A-A DE Elvis Dumervil late in 1st H.

Outback Bowl (Jan. 2): Florida 31 Iowa 24

Iowa's miracle comeback attempt—they had trailed 31-7 entering 4th Q—looked on track with Hawkeyes trailing by 7 pts and having possession after on-side KO was succesful with 90 secs remaining. But hold on, there was flag on play: offside call was controversial, and Gators (9-3) recovered next on-side KO try. Although Florida QB Chris Leak threw for 278y and TDs of 24y and 38y to WR Dallas Baker (10/147y), Gators went in front early on strength of 2 big non-O plays: blocked Iowa (7-5) punt recovered by CB Tremaine McCollum and returned 6y for score and CB Vernell Brown's 60y scoring RET of INT in 2nd Q. Brown heroically had returned from broken leg suffered against Vanderbilt on November 5. Hawkeyes scored game's 1st O TD on 20y TD pass from QB Drew Tate to WR Clinton Solomon in 2nd Q, but that just cut score to 17-7. Leak-to-Baker tandem then dominated scoreboard until final Q. In 2nd H, game became showcase for Tate, who threw 32-55/346y and 3 TDs. Hawkeyes WR Ed Hinkel was Tate's favorite target with 9 catches/87y and 2 short TDs.

Cotton Bowl (Jan. 2): Alabama 13 Texas Tech 10

Alabama (10-2) owned a rich post-season history with collegiate record 30 wins but had never won bowl game with last-sec FG. Bama won when K Jamie Christensen booted game-winner from 45y out. Christensen, who had beaten Mississippi and Tennessee on consecutive weeks earlier in season with late FGs, mis-hit his game-winner but its wobble proved to be nothing more than tease for Texas Tech (9-3). Real reason for victory was ball control, always goal of Red Raiders' opposition. QB Brodie Croyle (19-31/275y) led Tide attack that held ball for 2 secs shy of 39 mins, churning up 420y and gaining 21 1st downs. Despite that imbalance, and thanks partly to Christensen missing earlier FG attempt and having another blocked, Red Raiders needed only single TD to tie game late in 4th Q. QB Cory Hodges (15-32/196y), who left game earlier with knee injury, secured that TD with 12y pass to WR Jarrett Hicks with 2:56 left. Croyle then led his charges 58y to winning FG with 40y coming on completions of 17y to WR Matt Miller and 23 to WR Keith Brown. Brown contributed big game with 5 catches/141y, including 76y TD off screen pass early in 1st Q.

Sugar Bowl (Jan. 2): West Virginia 38 Georgia 35

West Virginia (11-1) had something to prove, while Georgia, playing virtual home game in Atlanta's Superdome, seemed to have its collective mind elsewhere. Combination proved truly potent as Bulldogs (10-3) found themselves behind 28-0 in 1st Sugar Bowl ever played outside of (hurricane damaged) New Orleans. Mountaineers showcased top-notch talent amid rumblings that depleted Big East no longer deserved automatic BCS bowl berth, scoring 3 TDs in opening Q to quiet partisan crowd. TB Steve Slaton dazzled for West Virginia, opening scoring with 52y TD run and adding 2 others—including another of 52y in 4th Q that provided winning pts—while finishing with 204y rushing. Slaton's rushing numbers were most in Sugar Bowl history, passing 202y mark set by Pittsburgh TB Tony Dorsett in 1977, also against Georgia. To UGa's credit it fought back, scoring 3 times in 2nd Q to go to H down 31-21. Bulldogs were able to pull within 3 pts twice in 2nd H. QB D.J. Shockley (20-33/277y) threw 3 TDs including 43y effort to WR Bryan McClendon that closed scoring with 5-and-half mins left. West Virginia surely felt pressure at this point, leading by 38-35. So, courageous Mountaineers opted for trickery to quell comeback, succeeding with fake punt from own 48YL with 1:38 remaining as P Phil Brady ran for 10y on 4th-and-6. WVU QB Pat White enjoyed 11-14/120y passing and 77y rushing output. Teams combined for 1003y with almost even break: West Virginia 502y and Georgia 501y. "I think we took to heart some of the criticism of our league and the fact that no one was predicting us to win," said winning coach Rich Rodriguez.

Fiesta Bowl (Jan. 2): Ohio State 34 Notre Dame 20

Buckeyes (10-2) unleashed year's worth of highlight-reel TD plays in subduing Notre Dame team that allowed 617y, most ever in Irish history. All-purpose Ohio State WR Ted Ginn, Jr (8/167y) answered an opening ND TD drive with 2 explosive 1st H scores: catching 56y bomb from QB Troy Smith and taking reverse 68y to EZ. Smith then launched Heisman trophy campaign for 2006 by completing 85y TD pass to WR Santonio Holmes (5/124y) late in 2nd Q. Challenged by excellent Buckeyes D, which kept Irish off scoreboard from early in 1st Q to late in 3rd, Notre Dame (9-3) QB Brady Quinn moved charges 71y late in 3rd Q to TB Darius Walker's 2nd scoring run, from 10y out to pull within 8 pts at 21-13. After Irish missed x-pt, Ohio State then moved 41y to 1st of 2 FGs by K Josh Huston. Crucial play of game occurred one play before Huston's kick as Notre Dame's big-play S Tom Zbikowski scooped up apparent FUM by Buckeyes WR Anthony Gonzalez and raced 87y to Buckeyes EZ. Using replay, officials negated FUM as Gonzalez was ruled to never make catch. After Huston's next FG, early in 4th Q, Irish trailed by 2 TDs again, but Quinn (29-45/286y), who rewrote school's bowl record book, revved up short passing game—he completed 14 straight passes at one point—to lead another long scoring drive capped by a Walker (16/90y) scoring run, from 3y out. But Irish O could not help Irish D stop speed on OSU O, which answered with explosive 60y TD run by RB Antonio Pittman (21/136y) that settled matters. Smith completed 19-28 for 342y and added 66y rushing to win game MVP. In final game, ND WR Maurice Stovall caught 9 passes for 126y.

Orange Bowl (Jan. 3): Penn State 26 Florida State 23 (OT)

All of vast experience that had gone into past wins of Penn State's Joe Paterno and Bobby Bowden of Florida State could not help either coach Orange Bowl win through 4 Qs and 2 OT sessions. In end it was frosh K Kevin Kelly, who missed 2 earlier FG attempts that would have won game, who supplied winning pts for Penn State (11-1) in longest BCS game to date. Kicking woes were storyline as Florida State (8-5) K Gary Cismesia missed 2 FG tries and x-pt. QB Michael Robinson threw for 253y for Nittany Lions, while RB Austin Scott led team in rushing with 110y as Tony Hunt left in 1st Q with injury. Scott put Nittany Lions on scoreboard 1st with 2y TD run that capped 85y 1st Q drive. Score might have stayed 7-0 at H but opponents exploded for 3 TDs within final 4:30 of 2nd Q as FSU WR Willie Reid returned punt 87y to tie score and TB Lorenzo Booker took pass 57y to EZ to give Seminoles 13-7 lead before WR Ethan Kilmer caught 24y TD pass from Robinson for 14-13 Penn State lead at H. Spurt was not rekindled in 2nd H as Penn State could only muster 2 pts on safety as DE Jim Shaw forced QB Drew Weatherford (24-43/258y, INT) into grounding from EZ and FSU managed only tying 48y FG by Cismesia with 4:08 left in 4th Q. Foes fought through 1st 2 OT sessions as each made FG in 1st inning and TD in 2nd. Cismesia missed FG attempt from 38y in 3rd OT, and Kelly converted from 29y out for win. Bowden, who had suffered through his worst season since 1981, now trailed by 1-7 head-up against fellow future Hall of Famer. Paterno pulled within 5 all-time wins of Bowden.

GAME OF THE YEAR

Rose Bowl (Jan. 4): Texas 41 Southern California 38

After great regular season, nothing but this classic seemed appropriate to close out mesmerizing 2005 season. Featuring undefeated editions of heralded college football programs, two Heisman Trophy winners and recent runner-up, host of other talent on both sides of ball, and coaches with lofty overall won-loss records, game was realization of ultimate BCS title game match-up. Yet, this match-up was not as highly anticipated as it should have been for one main reason: Southern California's recent dominance. Riding into Pasadena on throes of 34-game win streak, Trojans (12-1) were being compared to finest teams in history of sport. Toss in favorable nearby location of game and Texas (13-0) coach Mack Brown's spotty record in biggest games at both Texas (3-5 vs. Oklahoma) and North Carolina (0-6 vs. Florida State), and audience--outside of Texas anyway—could be forgiven for being confident that USC would win second outright title in row and unprecedented third straight, including 2003's split championship with LSU. But assuredness that Trojans would win was boon to Brown and his players, who were confident after wins against then-4th ranked Ohio State in September, Oklahoma, to snap 5-game series losing streak , in October and then Colorado in December to win Big 12 title—1st title of any kind for Brown. Southern California did nothing to dissipate confidence in their abilities early in game, scoring 7 pts with 5-play, 46y drive that ended with 4y TD run by TB LenDale White, who finished with 124y rushing with 3 TDs. Any chance that Trojans could pull away early ended quickly, with TB Reggie Bush (13/82y, and 9/95y receiving) making bonehead play of game with lateral to unsuspecting teammate, WR Brad Walker, after 37y run with screen pass that turned into lost FUM. Longhorns proceded to dominate most of 2nd Q behind QB Vince Young (30-40/267y), who began to put his stamp on game. Texas reeled off 16 straight pts on 46y FG by K David Pino and TD runs of 10y by RB Selvin Young and 30y by RB Ramonce Taylor. Selvin Young's TD featured controversial no-call as QB Vince Young's knee seemed to touch ground before pitchout on 12YL. Play could not be reviewed due to breakdown with monitor needed to supply different angles to replay crew. Game settled into nip and tuck fray; with

each side making statement plays and drives, only to have them answered by opposite 11. Trojans quickly raced to 43y FG by K Mario Danelo to close H, but still trailed 16-10, marking 5th time this season they trailed at H. Trojans scored 1st in 2nd H, on 3y run by White run to take lead at 17-16. Teams traded long TD scoring drives as Trojans led 24-23 entering 4th Q. USC looked ready to pull away after scoring 2 TDs as Bush reached EZ with scintillating 26y 4th Q TD run complete with somersault and QB Matt Leinart (29-40/365y) threw 22y TD pass to WR Dwayne Jarrett (10/121y) with 6:42 left that gave Trojans 38-26 lead. As comfortable as that lead may have seemed to USC, Texas was far from ordinary and needed only 2:39 to pull within 5 pts on Vince Young's 17y TD romp. With Young proving to be nearly unstoppable once he got into space against USC D—he finished with 19/200y rushing—Trojans O, which set Rose Bowl record with 574y, absolutely needed to keep ball away from Young at game's end. That thinking influenced coach Pete Carroll into decision that turned into memorable stand for Texas D: Trojans went for 4th-and-2 from their own 45YL. With Bush not even on field, White, who scored earlier on 4th-and-short, went for all but two inches of needed yardage, with key hit leveled by senior SS Michael Huff. Young quickly moved Longhorns downfield, but after short run and two incompletions, game came down to critical 4th-and-5 for Texas, on Southern California 8YL. Young had thrown for game-winner earlier in season against Ohio State, so USC D could not focus solely on his running ability. Young dropped back to pass, avoided blitz, and with receivers covered, took off toward right pylon and ever-lasting TD glory. Game was so tight that each team had same number of 1st downs (30), although USC needed 1 more to get into late FG position, which time prevented. Texas captured its 1st national title since 1970, while stretching its win streak to 20. "You couldn't ask for anything better," said Leinart after loss. "This was a great football game. We gave our hearts, they gave their hearts, and they came out on top."

Final *USA Today* Coaches January 4

1	Texas (62)	1550	14	Auburn	760
2	Southern California	1483	15	Wisconsin	739
3	Penn State	1421	16	Florida	718
4	Ohio State	1357	17	Boston College	584
5	LSU	1281	18	Miami (Fla.)	558
6	West Virginia	1235	19	Texas Tech	422
7	Virginia Tech	1176	20	Louisville	342
8	Alabama	1066	21	Clemson	310
9	TCU	914	22	Oklahoma	274
10	Georgia	900	23	Florida State	209
11	Notre Dame	866	24	Nebraska	109
12	Oregon	837	25	California	68
13	UCLA	774			

Final AP Poll January 5

1	Texas (65)	1625	14	Auburn	799
2	Southern California	1560	15	Wisconsin	786
3	Penn State	1484	16	UCLA	778
4	Ohio State	1428	17	Miami	589
5	West Virginia	1325	18	Boston College	545
6	Louisiana State	1314	19	Louisville	410
7	Virginia Tech	1197	20	Texas Tech	359
8	Alabama	1081	21	Clemson	339
9	Notre Dame	1019	22	Oklahoma	329
10	Georgia	994	23	Florida State	232
11	Texas Christian	937	24	Nebraska	128
12t	Florida	817	25	California	45
12t	Oregon	817			

2005 Top Performance Formula

1	Texas	1.9011
2	Southern California	1.7879
3	Penn State	1.6691
4	Virginia Tech	1.6490
5	Ohio State	1.6423
6	West Virginia	1.5817
7	Texas Christian	1.5559
8	Louisiana State	1.5336
9	Alabama	1.5127
10	Georgia	1.5123
11	Oregon	1.4604
12	Florida	1.4444
13	Auburn	1.4287
14	Boston College	1.4260
15	Miami	1.4197
16	Oklahoma	1.4128
17	Notre Dame	1.4114
18	Texas Tech	1.3996
19	UCLA	1.3985
20	Wisconsin	1.3808

2005 Top Opponent Records

1	Oklahoma	.7077
2	Michigan	.6462
3	Ohio State	.6357
4	North Carolina	.6281
5t	Texas	.6241
5t	Southern California	.6241
7	Northwestern	.6202
8	Tennessee	.6134
9	Georgia	.6115
10	Kansas	.6060
11	Colorado	.6056
12	Virginia Tech	.6043
13t	Geoegia Tech	.600000
13t	Maryland	.600000
13t	Minnesota	.600000
16	Florida	.5969
17	Arkansas	.5966
18	Texas A&M	.5917
19	Iowa	.5909
20	Washington State	.5898

2005 Out-of-Conference Records

	W-L	Percentage	Bowl W-L
Big Twelve	29-7	.8056	5-3
Big Ten	29-10	.7436	3-4
Atlantic Coast	29-12	.7073	5-3
Pacific-10	21-9	.7000	3-2
Southeastern	23-12	.6571	3-3
Big East	14-16	.4667	1-3
Mountain West	14-16	.4667	2-2

2005 Individual Statistical Leaders

RUSHING YARDS

	Attempts	Yards	Avg.
DeAngelo Williams, Memphis	310	1964	6.3
Jerome Harrison, Washington State	308	1900	6.2
Reggie Bush, Southern California	200	1740	8.7
Brian Calhoun, Wisconsin	348	1636	4.7
Garrett Wolfe, Northern Illinois	242	1580	6.5
Tyrell Sutton, Northwestern	250	1474	5.9
Laurence Maroney, Minnesota	281	1464	5.2
B.J. Mitchell, Nevada	261	1399	5.4
Andre Hall, South Florida	270	1374	5.1
Albert Young, Iowa	249	1334	5.4

PASSING YARDS

	Completions	Attempts	Yards	Pct.
Colt Brennan, Hawaii	350	515	4301	68.0
Cody Hodges, Texas Tech	353	531	4238	66.5
Brady Quinn, Notre Dame	292	450	3919	64.9
Matt Leinart, Southern California	283	431	3815	65.7
Brett Basanez, Northwestern	314	497	3622	63.2
Jordan Palmer, Texas-El Paso	258	434	3503	59.5
Paul Pinegar, Fresno State	265	416	3335	63.7
Kevin Kolb, Houston	254	420	3258	60.5
Drew Weatherford, Florida State	276	469	3208	58.9
Drew Olson, UCLA	242	378	3198	64.0

RECEIVING YARDS

	Catches	Yards
Mike Hass, Oregon State	90	1532
Dwayne Jarrett, Southern California	91	1274
Greg Jennings, Western Michigan	98	1259
Jeff Samardzija, Notre Dame	77	1249
Garrett Mills, Tulsa	87	1235
Ryan Grice-Mullen, Hawaii	85	1228
David Anderson, Colorado State	86	1221
Derek Hagan, Arizona State	77	1210
Brandon Marshall, Central Florida	74	1195
Maurice Stovall, Notre Dame	69	1149.

2005 Consensus All-America Team
Offense

Wide Receiver:	Dwayne Jarrett, Southern California
	Jeff Samardzija, Notre Dame
Tight End:	Marcedes Lewis, UCLA
Line:	Jonathan Scott, Texas
	Marcus McNeil, Auburn
	Max Jean-Gilles, Georgia
	Taitusi Lutui, Southern California
Center:	Greg Eslinger, Minnesota
Quarterback:	Vince Young, Texas
Runningback:	Reggie Bush, Southern California
	Jerome Harrison, Washington State
Placekicker:	Mason Crosby, Colorado
Kick Returner:	Maurice Drew, UCLA

Defense

Line: Elvis Dumervil, Louisville
                     Tamba Hali, Penn State
                     Haloti Ngata, Oregon
                     Rodrique Wright, Texas

Linebacker: A.J. Hawk, Ohio State
                     DeMeco Ryans, Alabama
                     Paul Posluszny, Penn State

Back: Jimmy Williams, Virginia Tech
                     Michael Huff, Texas
                     Greg Blue, Georgia
                     Tye Hill, Clemson

Punter: Ryan Plackemeier, Wake Forest

2005 Heisman Trophy vote

Reggie Bush, junior tailback, Southern California	2,541
Vince Young, junior quarterback, Texas	1,608
Matt Leinart, senior quarterback, Southern California	797
Brady Quinn, junior quarterback, Notre Dame	191
Michael Robinson, senior quarterback, Penn State	49

Other Major Awards

Maxwell (Player)	Vince Young, junior quarterback, Texas
Walter Camp Player)	Reggie Bush, junior tailback, Southern Cal
Outland (Lineman)	Greg Eslinger, senior center, Minnesota
Vince Lombardi (Lineman)	A.J. Hawk, senior LB, Ohio State
Doak Walker (Running Back)	Reggie Bush, junior tailback, Southern Cal
Davey O'Brien (Quarterback)	Vince Young, junior quarterback, Texas
Fred Biletnikoff (Receiver)	Mike Hass, senior wide receiver, Oregon State
Jim Thorpe (Defensive Back)	Michael Huff, senior safety, Texas
Dick Butkus (Linebacker)	Paul Posluszny, junior linebacker, Penn State
Lou Groza (Placekicker)	Alexis Serna, sophomore kicker, Oregon State
Chuck Bednarik (Defender)	Paul Posluszny, junior linebacker, Penn State
Ray Guy (Punter)	Ryan Plackemeier, senior punter, Wake Forest
Johnny Unitas (Sr. Quarterback)	Matt Leinart, senior quarterback, Southern Cal
John Mackey (Tight End)	Marcedes Lewis, senior tight end, UCLA
Dave Rimington (Center)	Greg Eslinger, senior center, Minnesota
Ted Hendricks (Defensive End)	Elvis Dumervil, senior defensive end, Louisville
AFCA Coach of the Year	Joe Paterno, Penn State

2006

The Year of the Colossal Clash of Columbus, Monstrous Months, and Redemption for the Big East

At no time in 40 years since the legendary 10-10 tie between Michigan State and Notre Dame in 1966 had one date on the college football regular season schedule prompted so many big circles on calendars. The Big Ten Conference's traditional season-ending bout, scheduled November 18 at Columbus, Ohio, captured the attention of the nation's football fans. In one corner stood the top-ranked Ohio State (12-1) Buckeyes; in the other corner ready to start swinging were the no. 2 Michigan (11-2) Wolverines.

As early as Michigan's mid-September whipping of then no. 2 Notre Dame (10-3), the thought of thrilling, unfinished business was in the air. For the first time since 1973—when the teams were under legendary coaches Woody Hayes and Bo Schembechler—the Buckeyes and Wolverines seemed certainly headed undefeated into their blood-letting at Ohio Stadium. Eagerness for the clash grew as the season progressed.

Ohio State reigned over the polls all season and was the more offensively explosive of the two teams. Michigan was considered more physical, especially its rampaging defense that had been revamped by new coordinator Ron English. The steady play of the Wolverines' offense and extreme defensive pressure, delivered by ends LaMarr Woodley and Rondell Biggs, tackle Alan Branch, and linebacker David Harris, helped Michigan rebound beautifully from its 7-5 disaster of 2005.

A sad note on the game's eve was the passing at age 77 of Schembechler, the boisterous coach with the most wins (194) in Michigan history who also had earned a masters degree from and served as an assistant coach at Ohio State.

Ohio State held on to defeat Michigan 42-39 in a surprising offensive shootout. Afterward there was strong conviction that the Wolverines remained the nation's second-best team. They had rallied in the second half to nearly overtake the Buckeyes, and another mitigating factor that went barely mentioned was Michigan's bad footing. Ohio Stadium's field had required re-sodding in late October with middling results, and it appeared Michigan might have employed the wrong length of cleats.

By virtue of victory over the second-ranked Wolverines, the Buckeyes clearly qualified for the BCS title game, played for the first time as an adjunct to the normal four participating BCS bowls. It was to take place a week after the Fiesta Bowl on January 8, in the new University of Phoenix Stadium in Glendale, Arizona, that had opened in September as home of the NFL Cardinals. What opponent would face Ohio State? Would there be or should there be a rematch of the colossal clash of Columbus?

Everyone knew the loser of the Michigan-Ohio State game would fall into a crowded category of one-loss teams. Excellent one-loss teams roamed the nation as several conferences boasted strong top-to-bottom balance—most notably the well-muscled Southeastern Conference, but also the Pac-10 and, interestingly, the Big East.

From the first appearance of the BCS rankings in mid-October, four teams maneuvered their way into one of the top-3 spots with Ohio State and Michigan. First it was Southern California (11-2), then West Virginia (11-2), Louisville (12-1), USC again, and finally Ohio State's ultimate BCS title opponent, the Florida Gators, champions of the SEC.

Ohio State was favored by a touchdown in the title game, but Florida (13-1) ran away by 41-14. It played ferociously fast defense in pressuring Troy Smith, the Buckeyes' Heisman-winning quarterback, and threw at Ohio State a blizzard of creative plays dreamed up by coach Urban Meyer and guided by once-maligned senior quarterback Chris Leak.

Florida's championship came as a surprise, especially its overwhelming margin over a team considered a dynamic best-in-the-nation. Interestingly, Florida became the first school ever to hold the collegiate football and basketball championships at the same time, the Gators having scored a similar upset in the NCAA Final Four in the spring of 2006.

The season's best three teams, excluding Michigan, had to overcome schedules that threw clusters of tough games at them, often wedging them into single months. Ohio State was tapped as preseason no. 1. Yet, the Buckeyes were diminished in some quarters for returning only two starters on defense. That tune changed quickly as the Buckeyes lay to waste three ranked opponents in September with big-play contributions from new starting linebacker James Laurinaitis, son of Joe, known as "The Animal" of pro wrestling's famed "Road Warriors" tag team. Ohio State trounced no. 2 Texas (10-3) on September 9, then whipped Big 10 foes, no. 24 Penn State (9-4), and no. 13 Iowa (6-7). Ohio State coach Jim Tressel noted the potential peril of his team's monstrous opening month: "That was something

we talked about, how brutal that September schedule is. We've played against some tough teams who brought all they could bring us."

Champion Florida was another that faced a monstrous month. The Gators lined up against SEC rivals Louisiana State (11-2), Auburn (11-2), and Georgia (9-4) on the first, second, and fourth Saturdays of October. The Gators couldn't quite overcome the trio of SEC powerhouses. They beat LSU, to move to no. 2 in the AP Poll, and Georgia, but in between Auburn defeated Florida 27-17 in a game tighter than the score would indicate.

November and the first Saturday in December looked formidable to Southern California as the Trojans had Oregon (7-6), California (10-3), Notre Dame, and UCLA (7-6) in their sights. Having rebounded from a mid-season upset at Oregon State (10-4), the Trojans rolled over the Ducks, Golden Bears, and Fighting Irish at home and were ready to clinch a spot in the BCS title game until the UCLA defense completely and stunningly stymied the mighty USC offense in a 13-9 upset.

Arkansas (10-4) with a big win over no. 2 Auburn was one of the surprise teams of the year after a 4-7 mark in 2005. Also pleasant among the surprises was a pair of teams that had a previous combined record of 50-88 in the first six years of the 2000s: Wake Forest (11-3) and Rutgers (11-2). October brought a heartbreaking defeat for Wake Forest. The Deacons lost a 17-3 quarter lead and victory momentum to Clemson (8-5) when a poorly spotted field goal attempt turned into a touchdown fumble return by the Tigers' magnificent defensive end Gaines Adams. But, Wake Forest won six of its last seven, including the ACC title game, to earn its first trip to a New Year's Day game, the Orange Bowl, since the 1946 Gator Bowl.

Rutgers rolled deep into November without defeat. In fact, as Halloween faded from memory the often disrespected Big East Conference boasted three of the nation's six undefeated Division 1-A teams. Redemption was at hand for the conference abandoned just two years earlier by Boston College (10-3), Miami (7-6), and Virginia Tech (10-3). No. 3 West Virginia and no. 5 Louisville, each with seven wins to open the season staged their an anticipated "Breeders' Cup" showdown in Louisville on the first Thursday night of November. The game was hyped to an extent as to over-shadow the annual high stakes horse racing epic that in 2006 was scheduled down the street and two days later at legendary Churchill Downs. Although the Mountaineers seemed the hotter of the two teams, Louisville won the biggest game in school history 44-34 with a third quarter burst fueled by linebacker Malik Jackson's fumble-return touchdown.

Louisville, however, had to face undefeated Rutgers on ESPN the following Thursday night. The Scarlet Knights barely had been noticed since hosting the very first collegiate game in 1869. For years, Rutgers played a minor schedule against Ivy League and low-level Eastern schools, followed by a brief 1970s renaissance, and mostly cellar-dwelling status since the Big East's inception in 1991. In good, old American underdog style, the Scarlet Knights came from a 25-7 deficit to beat third-ranked Louisville. Two days later on Veteran's Day, three Top 10 teams, Texas, Auburn, and California, all very hopeful with one loss apiece, were each upset. Also, Florida scraped by South Carolina (8-5) by one point.

Louisville ended up in the Orange Bowl as Big East champions because Rutgers was upset by Cincinnati (8-5) and lost the season finale in overtime to West Virginia. The Big East won all five of its bowl encounters.

Many players of Miami and Florida International got into an on-field fight during their game of October 14. The fracas quickly escalated into a riot of kicking, stomping, and swinging of helmets. The media lambasted the two schools, especially Miami which had an off-and-on history of extracurricular behavior. The two schools ultimately suspended a total of 31 players. Cynics mocked Miami because it punished most of its fight participants for only one game, against Duke (0-12), a rather easy opponent. The short-handed Hurricanes team traveled to Durham, N.C., and nearly were upset by Duke. Trailing only 20-15 and having thrown Miami runners for 19 yards in losses in the second half, the Blue Devils were six yards and a few seconds from their first win over a 1-A foe in two years. But, Miami defensive back Willie Cooper picked off Duke's slant-in pass at his goal-line and would have gone all the way had he not been tripped up by leg cramps on his lonely run for pay-dirt.

Miami's season hit rock-bottom on November 7. Senior defensive tackle Bryan Pata, considered a NFL draft prospect, was shot and killed in a parking lot near his off-campus apartment shortly after the day's practice session. Illustrating what 2006 was like for the Hurricanes, quarterback

Kirby Freeman said after a one-point loss to Maryland (9-4) four days after Pata's death: "Coach (Larry) Coker mentioned Bryan, and my throat clogged, and I wanted to cry. But I didn't have anything left."

Miami would spoil the ACC title hopes of Boston College late in the season and sneak into a bowl bid. The MPC Computers Bowl was the last game for the deposed Coker, who left with 2001 national title laurels, a good personal reputation, and an admirable 60-15 record.

Oklahoma (11-3) had quite an unusual season. The Sooners lost 34-33 at Oregon on September 16, the defeat riding on two egregious calls by officials late in the game. The most galling decision—which should have been reversed by TV replay—permitted the Ducks to recover an on-side kickoff prior to their winning score even though the ball had been touched illegally by Oregon, and Oklahoma actually came away with the recovery.

Still, coach Bob Stoops rallied his Sooners, even after a dislocated shoulder shelved star runner Adrian Peterson, and Oklahoma won the Big 12 championship. In the Fiesta Bowl, the Sooners were victimized by Cinderella Boise State (13-0), the nation's only undefeated team, which pulled off three miracle plays to win 43-42 in overtime. The Broncos used an amazing hook-and-ladder pass for the tying touchdown with seven seconds left, halfback pass for an overtime touchdown, and Statue of Liberty run off a pass fake for the winning two-point conversion.

Many media members claimed Boise State's Fiesta Bowl magic proved the need for a playoff, but as the *Arizona Republic* wondered: would new coach Chris Petersen have played with such entertaining abandon had Boise State been in a nail-biting position to advance in a bracketed playoff? Besides, the Broncos' schedule likely would have kept them out of a playoff smaller than 16 teams. They had met only one team from a BCS conference—Oregon State, which was trounced 42-14 at Boise on September 7—but otherwise met a raft of so-called mid-major opponents, most of which they swamped.

On the third Saturday of October, highly unpredictable Michigan State (4-8) trailed Northwestern (4-8) 38-3 at halftime. A blocked punt early in the fourth quarter sparked the Spartans, and they dramatically finished the largest comeback in 1-A history by rallying for 38 points and a completely improbable 41-38 victory. Earlier in the year, the Spartans had blown a 16-point fourth quarter lead over Notre Dame to lose 40-37 and a week later lost to lowly Illinois (2-10) 23-20. A week after their comeback, the Spartans were clobbered by Indiana (5-7) by 46-21 and lost all the rest of their games to send coach John L. Smith to the unemployment line.

Milestones

■ In effort to speed tempo of play and eradicate 4-hour college games, Rules Committee shortened games by starting clock at moment of kickoff not upon reception of kickoff and at ready-for-play signal after change of possession. Coaches complained about fewer plays but soon adapted their offenses for better readiness for change of possession. Another new rule permitted coaches one challenge per game of officials' decisions through use of TV replay, risking loss of time-out if challenge failed. In 2 previous experimental seasons, press-box-isolated replay officials generally had made quick judgments on every play (which remained core process), but new rule created delays that negated some gains earned through new clock procedures.

■ Western Michigan linebacker Ameer Ismail contributed six sacks and returned interception for touchdown in win 41-27 over Ball State on October 21.

■ In wake of recent pair of student deaths, City of Jacksonville officially requested media to refrain from referring to Florida-Georgia game as "The World's Largest Outdoor Cocktail Party."

■ Campaigning as Republican, former Southern California (1971-73) All-America and Pittsburgh Steelers Super Bowl MVP wide receiver Lynn Swann lost his bid, in significant landslide, to unseat Edward Rendell as Governor of Pennsylvania. Heath Shuler, former Tennessee (1991-93) quarterback, won seat in U.S. Congress as Democrat from North Carolina's 11th District.

■ Northern Colorado back-up punter Mitch Cozad was charged with attempted murder after his September 11 stabbing attack on kicking leg of starting punter Rafael Mendoza. Police believed Cozad attacked Mendoza in order to capture starting job.

■ NCAA relaxed its strict code for financial benefits given to athletes so that Clemson frosh corner back Ray Ray McElrathbey could become legal guardian for and support his 12-year-old brother Fahmarr. Ray Ray was permitted to accept donations from thousands of Americans and receive schooling assistance from Clemson officials for Fahmarr. McElrathbey brothers' parents had been rendered unfit by drug, alcohol, and gambling addiction.

■ College Football Hall of Fame lost several members: Lewis "Bud" McFadin, 77, All-America Texas guard, who nearly left school his freshman year because he missed his horse, grew up to become five-time NFL Pro Bowler, primarily with Los Angeles Rams, died February 13; Marshall Goldberg, 88, Pittsburgh halfback who was Heisman Trophy runner-up in 1938, died April 3; Bob Dove, 85, two-time All-America Notre Dame end, died April 19; Dick Wildung, 84, tackle for two-time national champion Minnesota, also died in April; John Kimbrough, 87, twice All-America fullback at Texas A&M and 1940 Heisman Trophy runner-up, died May 8; Jackie Parker, quarterback at Mississippi State in early 1950s and all-time Canadian Football League star, died in Canada on November 8; and on eve of Michigan-Ohio State game on November 17, Glenn "Bo" Schembechler, 77, died of heart failure. Schembechler was Michigan's all-time winningest coach with 194-48-5 record, who earned 13 Big 10 titles and 10 Rose Bowl trips in 21 years. Victim of heart attack at age 52 was Dave Brown, twice All-America defensive back at Michigan (1973-74). Craig "Ironhead" Heyward, bruising All-America tailback at Pittsburgh (1984, 86-87), died at age 39 of recurring brain tumor May 27. Tulane All-America guard Tony Sardisco, 73, died May 31. Joey Brodsky, Florida fullback in mid-1950s and later Miami assistant coach, died in May. Randy Walker, 52-year-old head coach of Northwestern and former running back at Miami (Ohio), died of sudden heart attack June 29. In July, death claimed Galen Fiss, 75, former Kansas center and defensive captain of 1964 NFL champion Cleveland Browns, as well as Texas' All-Southwest Conference defensive tackle (1970-71), Ray Dowdy, 56. Pete Harris, 49, 1978 Penn State All-America defensive back and younger brother of famed Franco Harris, died August 9. Former U.S. Congressman Bob Mathias, Stanford fullback in 1951-52 and twice Olympic decathlon champion (1948 in London and 1952 in Helsinki), died at 75 September 2. Erk Russell, 80, architect of Georgia's "Junkyard Dogs" defense in 1964-80 and later head coach who launched Div. 1-AA Georgia Southern program, died September 8. Death claimed Frank "Muddy" Waters, former Michigan State back and head coach, at age 83 September 20. Rice defensive back Dale Lloyd, 19, died September 25, day after collapsing during light workout. Inspired by Lloyd's memory five days later, Owls trounced favored Army 48-14 at West Point on way to school's 1st bowl appearance since 1961. On October 27, former Southern California All-America end Marlin McKeever died at 66 after injuring his head in fall at home. Bryan Pata, 22, senior defensive tackle for Miami (Florida) was shot and killed November 7. Dying November 24 was John Bridgers, 84, who had 49-53-1 coaching mark at Baylor (1959-68) and hired Bobby Bowden in 1976 to coach Florida State. Former Nebraska fullback (1977-80) Andra Franklin, 47, died of heart failure December 7. Charles "Mad Dog" Thornhill, leading tackler and middle linebacker for Michigan State's great defenses of 1965-66, died of heart failure at 62 December 22. U.S. President Gerald R. Ford, 93, captain and MVP center of Michigan's 1934 team, died peacefully at his California home December 26. Upon graduation, Ford turned down pro football offers in favor of Yale Law School. Starting in 1946, he was elected to 13 terms in Congress before being appointed Vice President and succeeding President Richard Nixon after Nixon's 1974 resignation.

■ Longest Winning Streaks Entering Season:

Texas 20	Texas Christian 10	Ohio State, West Virginia 7

■ Coaching Changes:

	Incoming	Outgoing
Boise State	Chris Petersen	Dan Hawkins
Colorado	Dan Hawkins	Gary Barnett
Buffalo	Turner Gill	Jim Hofher
Idaho	Dennis Erickson	Nick Holt
Kansas State	Ron Prince	Bill Snyder
Middle Tennessee	Rick Stockstill	Andy McCollum
Northwestern	Pat Fitzgerald	Randy Walker
Rice	Todd Graham	Ken Hatfield
San Diego State	Chuck Long	Tom Craft
Temple	Al Golden	Bobby Wallace
Wisconsin	Bret Bielema	Barry Alvarez

Preseason *USA Today* Coaches

1	Ohio State (28)	1487	14	Georgia	784
2	Texas (11)	1378	15	Michigan	778
3t	Southern California (1)	1348	16	Virginia Tech	591
3t	Notre Dame (9)	1348	17	Iowa	519
5	Oklahoma (13)	1320	18	Clemson	493
6	Auburn (1)	1206	19	Penn State	406
7	West Virginia	1202	20	Oregon	373
8	Florida	1054	21	TCU	270
9	LSU	1037	22	Nebraska	261
10	Florida State	874	23	Tennessee	216
11	Miami (Fla.)	839	24	Alabama	210
12	California	798	25	Texas Tech	198
13	Louisville	785			

September 2, 2006

(Th) South Carolina 15 MISSISSIPPI STATE 0: Swarming Gamecocks D handed coach Steve Spurrier his 150th career victory. Mississippi State (0-1) managed 240y total O, and Bulldogs threatened only on missed 38y FG after LB Quinton Culberson's INT in early going. Neither O could tally more than 4 1st downs in 1st H, led by Carolina 3-0 despite Gamecocks having gained no y rushing on 13 tries. South Carolina WR Syvelle Newton threw 54y TD pass to RB Cory Byrd early in 4th Q after Mississippi State failed on 4th-and-1 try. Carolina K-P Ryan Succop drilled 39, 35, and 47y FGs, while also punting 6/48.7y avg.

(Th) Northwestern 21 MIAMI (OHIO) 3: Each team wore tribute patches in memory of late Randy Walker, 52-year-old Northwestern (1-0) coach who had died in June, who also starred as Miami (Ohio) (0-1) HB during 1973-75. Pat Fitzgerald, youngest head coach in Div 1-A at age 31, won his 1st game after scoreless 1st H. Wildcats TE Erryn Cobb blocked punt early in 3rd Q and returned it 8y for TD. K Nathan Parseghian, great-grandnephew of former Miami, Northwestern, and Notre Dame coach Ara, scored RedHawks' pts on 22y FG midway in 3rd Q. Wildcats frosh QB Mike Kafka (13-17/106y) tossed 19y TD pass to TB Tyrell Sutton (13/69y) late in 3rd Q.

Rutgers 21 NORTH CAROLINA 16: Scarlet Knights (1-0) RB Ray Rice rushed for 201y and 3 TDs, and Rutgers held off late North Carolina (0-1) threat. Rutgers went 93y to Rice's 2y TD run in 1st Q, but Tar Heels responded with long drive to QB Joe Dailey's 4y bootleg TD run to tie it 7-7 on 1st play of 2nd Q. DB Manny Collins stopped another UNC drive and set up Rice's 2nd TD for 14-7 lead. Rutgers' 78y TD drive put it up 21-10 until Heels countered with closing drive that was stopped by another INT by Collins.

WAKE FOREST 20 Syracuse 10: Enhancing Demon Deacons' 245y ground attack, Wake Forest (1-0) QB Benjamin Mauk clicked on 14-21/105y, TD, INT passing before leaving with season-ending arm injury trying to recover FUM in 3rd Q. Shortly after Mauk's injury, K Sam Swank put Deacons ahead 13-10 with 40y FG. Syracuse (0-1) gained only 136y and lost its 10th game in row, but used 20y TD pass by QB Perry Patterson (5-18/45y) to tie it 7-7 late in 1st Q.

Notre Dame 14 GEORGIA TECH 10: Yellow Jackets (0-1) got off to excellent start as top weapon, tall and fast WR Calvin Johnson (7/111y, TD), rambled 29y with short pass, then nabbed 4y TD lob from QB Reggie Ball (12-24/140y, TD). Meanwhile, Notre Dame (1-0) displayed surprisingly tough D while its much-touted O struggled to make headway against Georgia Tech's strong D. Trailing 10-0 late in 2nd Q, Irish gambled against clock by sending QB Brady Quinn (23-38/246y) up middle on 5y TD draw just before H. Down 10-7, ND went 64y to 13y TD scamper by TB Darius Walker (22/99y, TD) on its opening possession of 3rd Q. Just prior, Tech appeared to have stopped 3rd down scramble by Quinn but was flagged for sideline personal foul against LB Philip Wheeler (13 tackles) inside Jackets 15YL. Irish D allowed only 66y in 2nd H.

TENNESSEE 35 California 18: Opener was perceived as pivotal game for both. Tennessee (1-0), coming off 5-6 season, could reclaim its swagger, while confident California (0-1), ranked highest (9th) in preseason since 1952, could prove it was ready for prime time. Vols quickly crushed Bear hopes as QB Eric Ainge (11-18/291y, INT) fired 4 TD passes to build 28-0 lead. Under tutelage of returning O-coordinator David Cutcliffe, Ainge went right to work, hitting WR Robert Meachem (5/182y, 2 TDs) with 41y pass and soon found TE Chris Brown for 12y TD. At start of 3rd Q, Meachem got loose for 80y TD, his 2nd long scoring reception. Golden Bears managed 2 long, but cosmetic TD drives in 2nd H, scoring on sub QB Joe Ayoob's 40y pass and 1y run. Tennessee LB Jerod Mayo had 3 sacks and pair of tackles for losses.

PENN STATE 34 Akron 16: On his 1st pass attempt, new Penn State (1-0) QB Anthony Morelli (16-32/206y 3 TDs) lofted 42y TD to WR Deon Butler, and Nittany Lions soon were off to 17-0 lead. Nittany Lions D permitted 225y, but Akron (0-1), week away from upsetting North Carolina State on road, managed 50y drive in 3rd Q to score on RB Dennis Kennedy's 4y TD run. Penn State came right back to lift its edge to 24-9 after frosh WR-DB A.J. Wallace raced 54y with ensuing KO to set up Morelli's 3rd TD: 20y throw to WR Derrick Williams.

MICHIGAN 27 Vanderbilt 7: Rock-solid Michigan D came up with 11 tackles for loss and forced 2 FUMs in defeat of Vanderbilt (0-1). Wolverines (1-0) DEs Rondell Biggs and LaMarr Woodley each chipped in 2 sacks of 6 registered against nimble Vandy QB Chris Nickson (11-25/99y), who still finished as Commodores' top rusher with 16/42y. TB Mike Hart rushed 31/146y to lead Michigan's 246y ground attack. Wolverines QB Chad Henne (10-22/135y) pitched pair of 2nd H TD passes. Vandy's score came on well-conceived WR pass by Earl Bennett for 30y to WR Marlon White which briefly and vainly narrowed margin to 10-7 in 2nd Q.

Southern California 50 ARKANSAS 14: Revenge for previous year's 70-17 pasting was on Razorback minds, but dynamic Trojans (1-0) replaced 2 departed Heisman Trophy winners (Matt Leinart and Reggie Bush) with relative ease. QB John David Booty (24-35/261y) threw 3 TD passes in 2nd H as Southern California's young O exceeded 2005 team's 49-pt avg. C.J. Gable (12/51y, TD) became USC's 1st-ever frosh starter at TB and scored Troy's 1st TD early in 2nd Q for 10-0 lead. Arkansas (0-1) soph TB Darren McFadden (9/42y) had dislocated big toe during summer bar fight, but was in lineup despite uncertainty. However, McFadden's TB-mate, Felix Jones (7/48y) lost 3 FUMs while Hogs were still competitive in 1st H. Trumpeted frosh QB Mitch Mustain (4-6/47y, INT) entered game for Arkansas in 2nd H to lead 80y drive to his 4y TD run.

(Mon) Florida State 13 MIAMI 10: Florida State (1-0) coach Bobby Bowden won his 360th collegiate game, heating up seat on which Miami (0-1) coach Larry Coker already resided. Offensively-challenged Hurricanes lost 10-3 H lead when it gained only 17y in 2nd H. Meanwhile, up-and-down Seminoles QB Drew Weatherford (16-32/175y, INT) succeeded on pair of 3rd down passing conversions good for 62y during Florida State's 67y drive for its only TD. FSU's march of 11 plays bridged 3rd and 4th Qs and tied it 10-10 before K Gary Cismesia accomplished what so many Seminole Ks had failed to do in recent past: beat Miami with 4th Q FG. Hurricanes played their best ball in 2nd Q, creating 51y and 48y drives to TB Charlie Jones' 4y TD and K Jon Peattie's 20y FG.

USA Today Coaches September 5

1	Ohio State (41)	1534	14	Virginia Tech	700
2	Texas (14)	1475	15	Iowa	647
3	Southern California (4)	1436	16	Miami (Fla.)	605
4	Auburn (2)	1272	17	Tennessee	579
5t	Notre Dame (2)	1248	18	Clemson	570
5t	West Virginia	1248	19	Penn State	459
7	Florida	1112	20	Oregon	458
8	LSU	1096	21	Nebraska	313
9	Florida State	1074	22	TCU	265
10	Oklahoma	1019	23	California	194
11	Georgia	899	24	Texas Tech	178
12	Louisville	820	25	Alabama	156
13	Michigan	786			

September 9, 2006

(Th) BOISE STATE 42 Oregon State 14: Win over BCS conf team like Oregon State (1-1) was exactly what Boise State (2-0) needed if it was to land among BCS elites at season's end. And, it was Broncos' 1st and last chance at such victory. Early on, Beavers stood toe-to-toe, earning 14-0 lead in 1st Q as QB Matt Moore (12-17/115y, INT) hit TE Joe Newton with short TD pass at end of 85y drive after opening KO and WR Sammie Stroughter charged 64y on punt TD RET. Then, RB Ian Johnson took over for Broncos. Johnson, new soph sensation, scored 3 TDs on runs of 59, 3, and 4y by middle of 2nd Q to fuel 28-14 turnaround. When Johnson added 19 and 50y TD runs in 2nd H he tied Boise record of 5 TDs in single game.

Iowa 20 SYRACUSE 13 (OT): Playing without injured QB Drew Tate, Iowa (2-0) found tough going against rebuilding Syracuse (0-2), which still lost its 11th straight when it failed to dent Hawkeyes D on 7 plays inside 2YL in 2nd OT. Iowa sub QB Jason Manson (16-32/202y, TD) found handy target in TE Scott Chandler (6/65y), who caught 2nd Q TD pass to tie it 7-7. Orange sent game into OT at 10-10 on K Patrick Shadle's 41y boot with 6 secs left. After trade of FGs in 1st OT, Iowa TB Albert Young (18/73y) scored on run off left side to put Hawks up 20-13. Iowa DB Marcus Paschal committed interference to prolong Syracuse's vain attempts to tie from close range.

BOSTON COLLEGE 34 Clemson 33 (OT): LB Jolonn Dunbar dramatically blocked x-pt in 2nd OT to position Boston College (2-0) for TB L.V. Whitworth's 6y TD run and K Ryan Ohliger's winning pt. No. 18 Clemson (1-1) had led 17-10 at H on wings of 2 TD passes by QB Will Proctor (25-40/343y, 2 TDs). Suddenly, little frosh RB Jeff Smith raced 96y with 2nd H KO to tie it for Eagles as his 213y in RETs would come within 1y of school record. After Tigers regained lead on 4th Q TD run by James Davis (24/93y, 2 TDs), BC sent game to OT on keeper by sore-ankle QB Matt Ryan (22-38/212y, TD). After exchange of OT FGs, Davis scored on 1y blast for Clemson, prior to blocked kick. In coach Tom O'Brien's 10 seasons, Eagles had not beaten ranked opponent at home.

TENNESSEE 31 Air Force 30: With 1:35 left to play, Falcons (0-1) seemed assured of forcing OT when FB Ryan Williams (16/98y, 2 TDs) scored his 2nd TD in barely more than min to pull Air Force to within 31-30. Veteran coach Fisher DeBerry chose to run HB Chad Hall (11/81y, TD) for 2-pt try which was smothered by Tennessee (2-0) DE Xavier Mitchell. Primarily on Hall's 5y TD run, Air Force led 10-3 well into 2nd Q. But, Volunteers QB Erik Ainge followed up his great game against California by ripping Falcons' pass D: Ainge hit 24-29/333y, 3 TDs, INT. Ainge's short scoring throws to WRs Robert Meachem and Jayson Swain put Tennessee on top 17-10 at H. Capping 99y drive that opened 3rd Q, TB Montario Hardesty (19/72y) put Vols up 24-10 with TD.

Georgia 18 SOUTH CAROLINA 0: Terrific Georgia (2-0) D visited 1st shutout on Steve Spurrier-coached O since 1987 as it held Gamecocks (1-1) to 35y rushing and 255y overall. With QB Joe Tereshinski going down early with injured ankle, Bulldogs got just enough from frosh QB Matthew Stafford (8-19/171y, 3 INTs) and 3 FGs by K Brandon Coutu. Stafford hit 10 and 19y passes on 72y drive in 2nd Q to TB Danny Ware's 9y TD run for 10-0 lead. Georgia slipped in 5 pts in last min of 1st H: DE Charles Johnson threw South Carolina TB Mike Davis for safety after Carolina DB Chris Hampton made INT and Coutu clicked on 46y FG as H clock expired after free-kick. On 4th down attempt for TD snaek, Cocks QB Blake Mitchell (16-22/156y) lost FUM that was punched through Bulldogs EZ for touchback.

NOTRE DAME 41 Penn State 17: Notre Dame's slumbering O returned to form as QB Brady Quinn (25-36/287y, 3 TDs) authored magnificent 2nd Q. Quinn hit 12-16/150y and connected for TDs to WRs Jeff Samardzija and Rhema McKnight in 2nd Q. Notre Dame (2-0) went off at H leading 20-0. Failure to get FG snap placed in 1st Q or to corral punt FUM in ND territory early in 2nd Q helped doom Penn State (1-1), which failed to finish off its few opportunities. Any hope for 2nd H comeback was quickly dashed when Irish S Tom Zbikowski returned FUM 25y for TD 1:02 into 3rd Q. Nittany Lions QB Anthony Morelli (21-33/189y, INT) threw TD pass to WR Deon Butler at end of 1st of 2 long, but superfluous scoring drives in last 6 mins of 4th Q.

MISSOURI 34 Mississippi 7: With 4-year star Brad Smith departed from Tigers' QB position, Missouri (2-0) looked to soph QB Chase Daniel (24-40/243y, TD) to carry load. Daniel delivered 322y total O, including all 80y of opening drive to his 3y TD run. Mizzou Tigers rolled to 17 pts in their 1st 3 possessions of 1st H and Daniel's 20y TD pass to WR Brad Ekwerekwu (8/95y). Meanwhile, Tigers D permitted only 162y and forced 3 INTs by Mississippi (1-1) QB Brent Schaefer (13-29/90y, TD), transfer from Tennessee. Schaefer clicked on Rebs' only TD, 30y pass to FB Marshay Green soon after S Charles Clark recovered punt FUM by Missouri RB Marcus Woods at 40YL.

OKLAHOMA 37 Washington 20: Coach Tyrone Willingham's improved Huskies (1-1) gave Oklahoma (2-0) brief scare, holding highly-favored Sooners to 13-13 deadlock at H. Washington scored on its 1st snap: sub RB Kenny James slipped through middle of line, broke tackle, and cruised 54y. Oklahoma retaliated when TB Allen Patrick downed P Mickey Cohen's punt at 1YL, and, on ensuing punt, DB Reggie Smith misplayed it, but returned 62y to Huskies 22YL. P Sean Douglas set UW school record with 82y boot on Smith's miscue and followed later with 81y punt. Paul Thompson (21-33/272y, 2 TDs, INT), back at Sooners QB spot after Rhett Bomar was scandalously dismissed during summer, quickly pitched 7y TD to WR Malcolm Kelly (6/121y) to tie it 7-7. Thompson and Kelly hooked up on 35y TD to launch 17-pt 3rd Q for OU. Sooners A-A TB Adrian Peterson (32/165y) came alive as well in 2nd H, rushing for 107y and pair of TDs. Huskies RB Louis Rankin rushed 17/112y.

Ohio State 24 TEXAS 7: Season's 1st big game unfolded in rematch that pitted no.1 vs. no. 2 in regular season for 1st time since 1996. Like 2005 game won by Texas in Columbus to launch its national title run, no. 1 Ohio State (2-0) looked to QB Troy Smith (17-26/269y, 2 TDs) to win on the road and keep it on top. Longhorns (1-1) came in with 21-game win streak and 12 games in row with 40+ pts scored. Longhorns opened quickly using frosh QB Colt McCoy (19-32/154y, TD, INT) on option runs, but WR Billy Pittman fumbled at Ohio 2YL. Buckeyes DB Donald Washington returned FUM to midfield to set up Smith's 14y TD pass to WR Anthony Gonzalez. With Texas keying on WR Ted Ginn, Gonzalez caught 8/142y, TD. Whipping up home crowd, McCoy bravely withstood 2 big hits on drive late in 2nd Q to tying TD: 7y TD arrow to Pittman. Ohio State answered right away: Smith hit Gonzalez and found explosive Ginn for 29y TD with 16 secs left in 2nd Q. On Texas' 1st series of 3rd Q, Buckeyes LB James Laurinaitis (13 tackles, 2 forced FUMs, tackle for loss) made 25y INT RET to position K Aaron Pettrey for 31y FG and insurmountable 17-7 advantage.

UCLA 26 Rice 16: Bruins (2-0) battered Rice (0-2) for 277y on ground as TBs Chris Markey (23/208y) and Kahlil Bell (19/102y) led way. Still, UCLA stalled sufficiently to require 4 FGs from K Justin Medlock, which prevented Bruins from landing knockout blow. After QB Ben Olson's TD pass to WR Brandon Breazell midway in 4th Q was ruled in-bounds in EZ for 26-10 Bruins lead, Owls responded as RB Quinton Smith (14/76y) dashed 48y down sideline for TD with 5:38 remaining. Although UCLA subsequently had to punt, DE Justin Hickman came through with 2 sacks.

USA Today Coaches September 10

1	Ohio State (59)	1571	14	Virginia Tech	770
2	Southern California (2)	1471	15	Miami (Fla.)	622
3	Notre Dame (1)	1391	16	Iowa	603
4	Auburn (1)	1369	17	Tennessee	600
5	West Virginia	1293	18	Oregon	529
6	Florida	1177	19	Nebraska	431
7	LSU	1159	20	TCU	333
8	Texas	1107	21	California	248
9	Georgia	997	22	Texas Tech	231
10	Florida State	977	23	Arizona State	159
11	Oklahoma	953	24	Alabama	150
12	Louisville	905	25	Boston College	146
13	Michigan	820			

September 16, 2006

(Th) WEST VIRGINIA 45 Maryland 24: No. 5 Mountaineers (3-0) took early 28-0 lead to send ESPN viewers channel-surfing. On its 1st series, West Virginia charged 69y, caped by RB Steve Slaton's 38y dash. Then, after FUM REC on ensuing KO, WVU cashed QB Pat White's 5y TD pass to WR Darius Reynaud in 3 plays. Slaton (21/195y, 2 TDs) soon roared 37y to end 96y trip, and when LB Jay Henry made INT of Maryland (2-1) QB Sam Hollenbach (24-45/211y, 2 TDs, 2 INTs), West Virginia was on way to 3rd straight win over Terps. WVU TE Brad Palmer recovered Slaton's forward EZ FUM for TD after speedy Slaton had rambled 52y to 2YL. With score at 31-10 in 2nd Q, Reynaud dropped ball on KO RET but picked it up and exploded for 96y TD RET. In Maryland's vane attempt at comeback, it totaled 333y O to come close to Mountaineers' 383y.

LOUISVILLE 31 Miami 7: Just before KO, Hurricanes stomped on Louisville Cardinals center-field logo but after pressuring Louisville (3-0) QB Brian Brohm (10-14/181y TD) early and scoring on 1y run by RB Tyrone Moss in middle of 1st Q, air went out of Miami's storm. With star RB Michael Bush out with broken leg from season opener, Cardinals also lost Brohm to dislocated throwing-hand thumb in 3rd Q. Still, Louisville took 10-7 H lead and was able to crush punchless Miami (1-2), which fell out of Top 25 for 1st time since 1999. "Well, it was pretty obvious today we were embarrassed," admitted Miami coach Larry Coker. Miami might have padded its early advantage, but RB Charlie Jones lost FUM at UL 8YL, and Cards responded with drive to FG. Brohm's 56y TD pass to WR Mario Urrutia (4/96y, TD) made it 10-7 in 2nd Q. QB Hunter Cantwell (3-4/113y, TD) replaced Brohm with Louisville on move in 3rd Q to 1st of pair of TD runs by RB Kolby Smith. Miami QB Kyle Wright passed 20-34/278y but spent much of 2nd H under heavy duress that yielded 4 sacks.

BOSTON COLLEGE 30 Brigham Young 23 (OT): Coach Tom O'Brien won his 69th game at Boston College (3-0) to set school record, but had to wait until officials verified through TV replay that S Jamie Silva had clinched win in 2nd OT with tipped, diving INT thrown by Cougars (1-2) QB John Beck (38-59/436y, TD, 2 INTs). BC earned 1st H TDs on short smash by LB-FB Brian Toal and on 18y pass from QB Matt Ryan (29-48/356y, 2 TDs, 2 INTs) to WR Tony Gonzalez, but trailed 13-12 because K Ryan Ohliger missed both x-pts. Teams traded long TD drives with Eagles making 2-pt pass by Ryan, and Ohliger made chip-shot FG in 4th Q for 23-20 lead. BYU K Jared McLaughlin tied it with his 3rd FG with 6:33 left in regulation. Cougars NG Russell Tialavea blocked Ohliger's FG in scoreless 1st OT. On 1st play of 2nd OT, Ryan fired 25y TD to Gonzalez to set stage for Silva's INT and long wait for video confirmation.

Clemson 27 FLORIDA STATE 20: Tigers (2-1) TB James Davis (19/87y, 2 TDs) made 47y dash to spice 67y he contributed to 87y drive to his winning 1y TD plunge with 8 secs remaining. Florida State (2-1) O struggled mightily, gaining only 204y. Seminoles received 2 big plays from "right place at the right time" CB Tony Carter: Carter scored 2 pts by returning blocked x-pt after Davis' 8y run had given Tigers 6-0 lead late in 1st Q, and he tallied TD for 9-6 edge when he raced 69y with blocked FG try in 2nd Q. QB Will Proctor (16-30/194y, TD) put Clemson back in front with 19y TD pass to WR Chansi Stuckey (3/34y, TD) in last 23 secs of 1st H and ran 20y for 20-9 edge early in 3rd Q. FSU tied it on K Gary Cismesia's FG and 53y drive to FB Joe Surratt's short TD run and 2-pt pass by QB Drew Weatherford (11-19/102y). Win was Clemson's 1st in Tallahassee since 1989.

Florida 21 TENNESSEE 20: "To get down 17-7 in that type of environment (Neyland Stadium) against that type of talent, and no one panicked," marveled coach Urban Meyer of his Florida Gators (3-0). Although Gators took early lead on QB Chris Leak's 21y pass to WR Jemalle Cornelius, Tennessee (2-1) tallied on 1st of 2 FGs by K James Wilhoit in 1st Q. In middle Qs, Volunteers mounted 64 and 61y drives to TDs with most exciting TD coming on handoff to WR Lucas Taylor, who arched pass to wide-open frosh TB LaMarcus Corker for 48y score. For all of Vols' success—and they were inspired by presence of star DT Justin Harrell, who played once more even though medics ruled him out for season—Florida D dominated most of contest. Tennessee lost 11y running, and QB Erik Ainge (17-32/183y, 2 INTs) was pressured continually and was sacked twice. Leak (15-25/199y, 2 TDs, INT) hit WR Dallas Baker for 4y TD at end of 72y trip late in 3rd Q. Trailing 20-14, Florida won on another Leak-Baker connection and S Reggie Nelson's INT when Tennessee went on 4th down from Gators 45YL.

AUBURN 7 Louisiana State 3: Brutal D war of Tiger teams went to Auburn (3-0) despite having gained only 182y. Louisiana State (2-1) took 3-0 lead at end of 55y march on 42y FG by K Colt David as 1st H expired. Auburn held Bayou Bengals runners to mere 42y, but LSU QB JaMarcus Russell put ball in air for 20-35/269y. Auburn took lead 7-3 with 75y drive late in 3rd Q. QB Brandon Cox scored on 1y keeper, 12th play of possession. Controversy shaped Russell's 4th down pass for WR Early Doucet with 2:43 to play: Inside Auburn 5YL, DB Zach Gilbert hauled down Doucet just as pass arrived and was flagged for interference. But, Auburn DB Eric Brock had angled his dive in front of Doucet-Gilbert and brilliantly tipped ball away. Officials overturned PEN call even though it appeared on replay that Brock's tip came instant after Gilbert's foul. Forcing 3-and-out, LSU had 1 more shot from its 20YL. Russell hit passes of 20, 21, and 21y. On game's last play, Russell went to WR Craig Davis who was dropped dead on 6YL by Brock's hard hit.

Michigan 47 NOTRE DAME 21: Michigan (3-0), its program dogged by some vocal doubters, put wood to Fighting Irish (2-1) from game's outset. Wolverines' 47 pts were most against Irish in Notre Dame Stadium since Purdue scored 51 in 1960. In game's 1st min, Michigan LB Preston Burgess intercepted ND QB Brady Quinn (24-48/234y, 3 TDs, 3 INTs) and returned it 31y for TD. Irish tied it briefly at 7-7 as Quinn found FB Ashley McConnell for 3y TD after S Chinedum Ndukwe raced 51y to 4YL with INT of Michigan QB Chad Henne (13-22/220y, 3 TDs, INT). Henne would soon pitch TDs of 69, 20, and 22y to WR Mario Manningham on way to 34-14 H lead.

Arizona State 21 COLORADO 3: Already having lost to Montana State in its opener, Colorado (0-3) had its work cut out in opposing hopeful Pacific-10 contender Arizona State (3-0). Buffaloes were suffering considerably on O as K Mason Crosby made 29y FG when O failed to make more than 5y after DT George Hypolite recovered FUM at ASU 17YL. TB Ryan Torain (18/80y), who shared time with TB Keegan Herring (9/82y), scored Sun Devils' 1st TD at end of 1st Q. Although Arizona State QB Rudy Carpenter (21-37/248y, 2 INTs) had so-so game, he completed 2nd H TD passes to WR Chris McGaha and TE Zach Miller (5/45y), latter of which set school record for career TDs (12) by TE. Devils entered with 13 sacks, most in nation, and added 5 more, all on 3rd down. Colorado QB Bernard Jackson (8-18/86y, INT) nearly scored in 2nd Q but had ball punched free by ASU S Zach Catanese just short of GL.

TEXAS A&M 28 Army 24 (San Antonio): Aggies (3-0) gained 262y on ground and scored on pair of 80y drives as QB Stephen McGee threw 7-11/102y, TD and rushed 11/142y. Gigantic Texas A&M TB Jorvorskie Lane (24/101y) blasted over for 3 short TD runs. Still, tenacious Army (1-2) stopped Aggies' gambling 4th-and-1 run with 2:55 left: Black Knights DE Cameron Craig threw Lane for 4y loss at A&M 26YL. Afterward Texas A&M coach Dennis Franchione admitted, "I had faith in our guys…When I look back at it with hindsight, I probably should have punted." With new life, Army drew pass interference PEN for 1st-and-goal at 2YL with 13 secs to play. LB Misi Tupe led band of Aggies tacklers to stop RB Tony Moore for loss as time expired. RB Wesley McMahand (14/68y) had scored earlier on 6 and 21y runs for Army.

SOUTHERN CALIFORNIA 28 Nebraska 10: Nebraska (2-1) fans had to wonder: For having endured growing pains associated with coach Bill Callahan's 3-year transition to passing attack, how was it Huskers built O game plan against no. 4 Trojans (2-0) around vanilla running plays? With Nebraska probing middle without success (36/68y rushing), USC moved efficiently. QB John David Booty passed 25-36/257y, 3 TDs, while WR Dwayne Jarrett set new USC career record for TD receptions in nabbing 11/136y, 2 TDs. Huskers showed some D spunk but allowed 2 critical Booty-Jarrett connections: In 2nd Q, Trojan duo converted 3rd-and-21 to set up Booty's TD to WR Steve Smith for 14-3 edge, and in 4th Q, Jarrett caught 19y pass on 2nd-and-20 to set up TB Chauncey Washington's 7y TD run for 28-10 lead. Nebraska QB Zac Taylor (8-16/115y) scored on 1y keeper at end of 74y trip early in 4th Q to move within 21-10.

OREGON 34 Oklahoma 33: Most controversial game in years unfolded before loud, record crowd in Eugene. As TV replays were shown all over America late on Saturday, it became apparent Oklahoma (2-1) was stiffed by replays misread by officiating crew at Autzen Stadium. Ducks (3-0) TB Jonathan Stewart (23/144y, TD) scored early TD and was head-and-shoulders ahead of rival TB Adrian Peterson (34/211y, TD) in early going, but magnificent Peterson made 145y in 4th Q and scored 17y TD that broke 20-20 tie with 12 mins left. When Sooners added FGs at end of 32 and 57y drives they led 33-20 with 3:12 on clock. Oregon QB Dennis Dixon (26-41/341y, 2 TDs, 2 INTs) scored on 1y dash with 1:12 left, and all reason broke loose on ensuing on-side KO by Ducks. Officials ruled Oregon REC even though TV evidence showed Ducks touching ball before required 10y advance, and that Oklahoma actually came away with possession. Soon, interference was called against Sooners although replays showed pass had been tipped. This foul helped Oregon go ahead 34-33 on Dixon's 23y pass and K Paul Martinez's kick. Oklahoma had last gasp chance at 44y FG but low boot was blocked. On Monday, Pac-10 Conf suspended entire officiating and replay crews for 1 week, and Sooners coach Bob Stoops railed at actions of officials as "absolutely inexcusable and unacceptable."

USA Today Coaches September 17

1	Ohio State (60)	1572	14	Iowa	781
2	Southern California (2)	1493	15	TCU	621
3	Auburn (1)	1432	16	Oklahoma	508
4	West Virginia	1359	17	Florida State	459
5	Florida	1282	18	Arizona State	397
6	Michigan	1181	19	Tennessee	376
7	Georgia	1178	20	California	366
8	Texas	1144	21	Boston College	348
9	Louisville	1106	22	Alabama	314
10	Virginia Tech	964	23	Clemson	283
11	LSU	911	24	Nebraska	167
12	Oregon	829	25	Boise State	139
13	Notre Dame	814			

September 23, 2006

NORTH CAROLINA STATE 17 Boston College 15: Seemingly on endangered list after losses to Akron and Southern Miss, Wolfpack (2-2) stunned to-date destiny's darlings, no. 20 Boston College (3-1), on desperate pass with 5 secs to play. In his 1st-ever start, soph QB Daniel Evans (15-31/179y TD, INT), son of NC State's 1974-77 QB Johnny Evans, lofted hopeful 34y pass, under D pressure, to WR John Dunlap, who bobbled before gripping it at back right corner of EZ. NC State's winning drive, executed with no timeouts left, took 38 secs after Wolfpack D stopped Eagles on 4th down at NC State 28YL. BC coach Tom O'Brien had chosen not to try 40+y FG because K Ryan Ohlinger had missed 1st Q x-pt. Eagles LB-FB Brian Toal, occasional short-y runner who had scored early in 4th Q for 15-10 lead, was tossed for loss on 4th down by Wolfpack LBs Lerue Rumph and Patrick Lowery. Earlier, in middle of 3rd Q, NC State had taken its 1st lead at 10-9 when RB Andre Brown raced 26y with pitchout.

ARKANSAS 24 Alabama 23 (OT): Arkansas Razorbacks (3-1) won 6th of their 7 all-time OT games in 2nd extra session, thanks to missed conv by Alabama (3-1) K Leigh Tiffin. Although Tiffin made 46y FG on last play of 1st H for 10-3 lead, he had awful day, missing 33, 30, and 37y FGs as well as vital OT x-pt. Hogs K Jeremy Davis also missed x-pt after 3y pitchout TD run by TB Darren McFadden (25/112y) in 3rd Q, but it was overcome when frosh QB Mitch Mustain (7-22/97y, TD, 3 INTs) threw 2-pt pass after S Randy Kelly ran 39y for FUM TD RET after DE Antwain Robinson sacked otherwise-effective Crimson Tide QB John Parker Wilson (16-20/243y, 3 TDs). Wilson's 14y TD pass at end of 75y march early in 4th Q knotted it 17-17, but Tiffin pushed wide-right 30y FG attempt with 3:06 remaining. Alabama made INT in 1st OT, but Tiffin again was wide right on 37y try for winning 3-ptr. Wilson threw his 3rd TD in 2nd OT, but Tiffin was wide right with his kick. Hogs relied on McFadden's 12y run to set up Mustain for TD pass to leaping TE Ben Cleveland. Davis nailed winning pt.

GEORGIA 14 Colorado 13: Feisty Buffaloes (0-4) put up real fight against highly-favored no. 9 Georgia (4-0). New Colorado coach Dan Hawkins said, "This loss tears your guts out...We came here to win." His team dominated 1st H at 10-0, but Buffs could have had more: K Mason Crosby had short FG try blocked by Bulldogs DT Dale Dixson, and they had to settle for Crosby's 26y FG when TD pass was called back. Colorado QB Bernard Jackson, who passed 14-26/140y, INT, and rushed 15/85y, sparked 63y TD trip in 2nd Q. He passed 16y, ran 28y, tossed 18y screen pass, before sneaking across. Frosh QB Joe Cox (10-13/154y, 2 TDs) rescued Georgia, taking over late in 3rd Q for ineffective classmate Matthew Stafford. Although Cox's 1st drive ended on failed 4th down run at Buffs 13YL, he pitched 23y TD pass to FB Brannan Southerland with 9:11 left. The next opportunity came on FUM REC at 50YL by Georgia DT Jeff Owens, but that try ended on deflected 4th down pass. Winning play eventually bloomed with 46 secs left on Cox's 20y pass toward EZ end-line that TE Martrez Milner snared by going high over defenders. K Brandon Coutu's kick won it.

OHIO STATE 28 Penn State 6: Counting on its fine D, young Nittany Lions (2-2) hung with no. 1 Buckeyes (4-0) in heavy rain despite coach Joe Paterno having to dash to locker room on several occasions to cope with flu symptoms. K Kevin Kelly gave Penn State 3-0 lead with 1st of 2 FGs on last play of 2nd Q. Superb Ohio State (4-0) QB Troy Smith (12-22/115y, TD, 2 INTs) hadn't suffered INT in 152 attempts, but his 2nd pick, taken by LB Dan Connor, put Lions in position to extend their lead in 3rd Q. Penn State failed to move, and Kelly missed 42y FG. From that moment, no. 1 Buckeyes took over, roaming 75y to 12y TD burst by TB Antonio Pittman. Early in 4th Q, Smith scrambled out of pocket and launched 37y TD pass to WR Brian Robiskie for 14-3 lead. Sniffing potential tying TD after Kelly made it 14-6, Penn State QB Anthony Morelli (16-25/106y, 3 INTs) suffered pair of INTs within span of 80 secs, and each was returned for TD by Buckeyes CBs Malcolm Jenkins and Antonio Smith.

Notre Dame 40 MICHIGAN STATE 37: Bad blood remained from Spartans' 2005 OT win when Michigan State players planted flag on Notre Dame Stadium's hallowed turf. In beginning of rematch in East Lansing, MSU looked like it was team affronted by past indignities. Spartans jumped to 17-0 lead in 1st Q, tallying TDs on 34y pass by QB Drew Stanton (10-22/114y, 2 TDs, 2 INTs) and 26y pass by WR Matt Trannon. After 2-8/6y disaster in 1st Q, Notre Dame QB Brady Quinn (20-36/319y, 5 TDs, INT) got untracked in 2nd Q, throwing TD passes to WRs Rhema McKnight (32y) and Jeff Samardzija (17y). But in between, DE Ervin Baldwin chugged 19y with INT TD RET, and Michigan State romped off leading 31-14 at H and 37-21 at end of 3rd Q. In 4th Q, Irish O began its comeback: Quinn found Samardzija (43y) and McKnight (14y) for another pair of TDs to cut margin to 37-34. "I Late in the game, I made some stupid mistakes," admitted Stanton as he was picked off twice by CB Terrail Lambert. Lambert returned 1st INT 19y for go-ahead TD with 2:53 on clock and later juggled and nabbed 2nd INT to seal victory.

Louisville 24 KANSAS STATE 6: Young Kansas State (3-1) D and possible letdown after big Miami win by no. 8 Louisville (4-0) conspired to diminish Cardinals' 50-pt-per-game O. Starting for injured star QB Brian Brohm, Louisville QB Hunter Cantwell (18-26/173y, TD, INT), sparked 97y drive from opening KO, finishing it off with 19y TD toss to WR Harry Douglas (6/81y). But as 1st H unwound at 10-0, explosive Cards had managed only 189y. Louisville earned early TDs in 3rd and 4th Qs on runs by TB George Stripling and FB Brock Bolen, but in between gave up pair of FUMs and Kansas State S Marcus Watts' INT. Watts returned Cantwell's underthrown INT 68y to 19YL, but Wildcats frosh QB Josh Freeman (3-10/18y), who replaced starter Dylan Meier (14-33/121y, INT), was sacked on 3rd down, and UL LB Malik Jackson then blocked FG try. K-State TB Thomas Clayton, who totaled 119y rushing, scored on 69y run in 4th Q.

TEXAS 37 Iowa State 14: Mighty Texas (3-1) won its 16th straight Big 12 game with rare interruptions coming from 1st H spurt by Iowa State (2-2) and at end of 3rd Q when lightning delayed play for 70 mins. Longhorns QB Colt McCoy (18-23/212y, 2 TDs, INT) engineered 2 quick 1st Q drives to scoring runs by TBs Jamaal Charles (17/78y) and Selvin Young (8/66y), while a bad punt snap by Cyclones provided safety in between. Iowa State QB Bret Meyer (24-43/274y, 2 INTs) was under immense pressure from Texas' pass rush (7 sacks) but managed to pull Cyclones to within 16-14. At end of 76y drive, Meyer was flushed from pocket but was able to shuffle 5y TD pass to TE Walter Nickel. After McCoy suffered INT by Cyclones CB Chris Singleton, Meyer and sure-handed WR Todd Blythe (6/68y) collaborated on 8y TD. McCoy came right back, connecting with WR Limas Sweed (7/107y) for 15y TD, and when mammoth 3rd-string TB Henry Melton banged over late in 2nd Q, Texas led 30-14 at H.

Army 27 BAYLOR 20 (OT): Week after near miss vs Texas A&M, Army (2-2) returned to Lone Star State to upset Baylor (1-3) in OT. Bears led 10-0 well into 2nd Q as QB Shawn Bell (26-35/241y, TD) threw 7y TD pass on his way to setting school career mark for completions. Black Knights got back into it in 3rd Q as WR Jeremy Trimble (7/63y) hustled for 59y punt TD RET for 10-10 tie. Trimble had to immediately sidestep defender as he took punt, completing his mission by faking out Baylor A-A P Daniel Sepulveda. Army took its 1st lead midway in 4th Q at 20-17 on K Austin Miller's 47y FG, but Bears went 73y to K Ryan Havens' tying 24y 3-ptr with 45 secs left. Army RB Tony Moore converted 4th-and-1 at Baylor 16 in top half of OT and soon scored winner on 4y run. Baylor then was halted without 1st down on its pale OT attempt.

CALIFORNIA 49 Arizona State 21: Cal Bears' season opening disaster at Tennessee was long forgotten now. California (3-1) demolished Arizona State (3-1) with array of might: QB Nate Longshore (18-26/270y, INT) threw 4 TD passes, TB Marshawn Lynch rushed 17/124y, WR DeSean Jackson caught TD pass and raced for 80y TD on punt RET, and CB Daymeion Hughes (10 tackles, 2 INTs) and LB Mickey Pimentel each returned INT for TD. With TB Keegan Herring going down with hamstring strain, TB Ryan Torain rushed 24/191y and TD for Sun Devils. Torain played early hero as ASU drove 76y in 12 plays after opening KO: Although QB Rudy Carpenter (16-36/177y, 2 TDs, 4 INTs, lost FUM) had terrible outing, he found Torain for early 9y TD pass and 7-0 lead. Longshore missed his 1st 2 passes but clicked on next 9-9/172y and 3 TDs.

WASHINGTON 29 Ucla 19: While Huskies (3-1) O got off to horrible start, not earning 1st down until last 3 mins of 1st H, UCLA scored on its 1st 4 series to cruise to 16-0 lead. But other than TB Chris Markey's TD run that was set up by Washington's mishandled punt snap at UW 6YL, Bruins settled for FGs—K Justin Medlock made 4 3-ptrs, including 51y boot—and UCLA O stalled thrice inside Washington 10YL in 1st H and again in late in 3rd Q when frosh WR Terrence Austin roared 79y on punt RET to 9YL. Washington's hurry-up O eventually confounded UCLA (2-1). At last in high gear, Huskies QB Isaiah Stanback (18-29/200y, 3 TDs, INT) hit WR Sonny Shackelford with 23 and 28y TD passes late in 2nd Q and early in 3rd Q. Stanback's 3rd TD throw provided Washington's 1st lead at 22-19 in 4th Q.

USA Today Coaches September 24

1	Ohio State (59)	1570	14	Notre Dame	758
2	Southern California (2)	1489	15	TCU	647
3	Auburn (2)	1441	16	Oklahoma	615
4	West Virginia	1357	17	Florida State	509
5	Florida	1294	18	Tennessee	504
6	Michigan	1239	19	Clemson	477
7	Texas	1155	20	California	452
8	Louisville	1105	21	Nebraska	289
9	Georgia	1079	22	Boise State	257
10t	Virginia Tech	963	23	Rutgers	124
10t	LSU	963	24	Texas Tech	81
12	Oregon	854	25	Boston College	78
13	Iowa	802			

September 30, 2006

(Th) Auburn 24 SOUTH CAROLINA 17: Big, bad no. 2 Auburn Tigers (5-0) came to Columbia, but it was improving South Carolina (3-2) that barely missed tying pass at game's end. TDs by TB Kenny Irons (27/117y, 2 TDs) and TE Tommy Trott (3/31y) on pass from QB Brandon Cox (13-19/180y, TD) kept Tigers in front by 14-10 at H. Then, Auburn dominated bizarre 3rd Q in which Gamecocks never took single snap. Cox, who completed 9 passes in 3rd period, hit pair to set up K John Vaughn's 24y FG for 17-10 edge. With Carolina retreating to set up KO RET blocking, Tigers executed flawless on-side KO. Cox hit 3 more passes, and Irons barged over GL on opening snap of 4th Q for 24-10 advantage. Gamecocks' rested O went to work, and QB Syvelle Newton (21-35/240y, 2 TDs, INT) found TE Jared Cook for 25y TD with 8:25 left. Carolina reached Auburn 6YL late in 4th Q, but CB Patrick Lee batted down pass.

(Fri) Rutgers 22 SOUTH FLORIDA 20: Last time no. 23 Rutgers (5-0) had been ranked in AP Poll on January 4, 1977, Jimmy Carter was President-elect and no. 1 song in nation was "You Don't have to be a Star," by Marilyn McCoo and Billy Davis, Jr. For its part, South Florida (3-2) lit fireworks in 2nd Q. After Scarlet Knights RB Ray Rice (35/202y, 2 TDs) capped 79y drive with 1st Q TD run, Bulls traveled 80 and 70y for TDs and 14-10 H lead with INT by CB Trae Williams serving as anchor moment. Bulls frosh QB Matt Grothe (16-25/241y, TD, 2 INTs) provided all 80y on 1st march and he scored on 1 and 22y runs. After Rutgers K Jeremy Ito made 2nd of 3 FGs in 3rd Q, Rice scored on 7y run to left pylon for 19-14 edge. Trailing 22-14 partly because of Grothe's subsequent INT and FUM, USF went 66y to Grothe's TD pass with 15 secs remaining. Grothe's tying 2-pt pass attempt was deflected away by Knights DB Jason McCourty.

MIAMI 14 Houston 13: Undefeated Cougars (4-1) arrived in Miami averaging 38 pts per game, but were outgained 420y to 276y as Hurricanes (2-2), trailing 13-7 late in 3rd Q, came up with big play to launch winning drive. Miami S Lovon Ponder slammed into Houston RB Jackie Battle (9/43y) at Canes 8YL to induce FUM REC by DB Chavez Grant. Leading 8-play, 84y drive to winning score, Miami QB Kyle Wright (16-27/190y, TD, 2 INTs) clicked on 27y pass to WR Lance Leggett before tossing 2y TD to new H-back James Bryant. RB Javarris James, nephew of Arizona Cardinals' Edgerrin James, set Canes' frosh single game rushing mark with 148y and had scored on 1y

run on Miami's opening 1st Q drive. Cougars QB Kevin Kolb (18-28/196y) tied it early in 2nd Q on 4y run after INT of Wright. Houston K Ben Bell followed with FGs in 2nd and 3rd Qs.

FLORIDA 28 Alabama 13: Clad in 1960s throw-back blue jerseys and white F-logoed helmets, Florida (5-0) honored greats Emmitt Smith, Steve Spurrier, Danny Wuerffel, and Jack Youngblood. Looking for big win to invigorate its season, Alabama (3-2) jumped to 10-0 edge on LB Prince Hall's 50y FUM TD RET and 1st of 2 FGs by K Jamie Christensen. Florida QB Chris Leak (14-20/174y, 2 TDs), who had lost Hall's scoring FUM, made up for it by scampering 45y to Tide 3YL late in 1st Q. Frosh QB Tim Tebow soon pushed over for 2y TD to complete 95y drive and pull Gators within 10-7 at H. Late in 3rd Q, Leak hit 22, 26, and 16y passes, last going to WR Andre Caldwell for TD. Leak's 2nd TD throw came with 6:47 to play and provided 21-13 lead. Triumph was wrapped up when Gators S Reggie Nelson picked off Alabama QB John Parker Wilson (21-40/240y, 3 INTs) and raced 70y for TD.

Illinois 23 MICHIGAN STATE 20: On heels of its collapse against Notre Dame, Michigan State (3-2) fell on its face against Illinois (2-3), which won its first Big 10 game since November 2004. Although frosh QB Isiah "Juice" Williams saw his 2nd career start marred by 62y INT TD RET by Spartans DB Demond Williams in 3rd Q, he completed 9-16/122y, TD, and INT, rushed 17/103y, and provided spark to Illini. Michigan State trailed 20-10 to begin 4th Q, but cut deficit to 3 pts after video replay changed FUM to incomplete pass by Michigan State QB Drew Stanton (15-24/144y). RB Jehuu Caulcrick then capped short drive with 1y TD run, and, 4 mins later with 2:46 left, Spartans K Brett Swenson tied it 20-20 with 27y FG. Illinois bounced back as Williams sparked 58y advance to K Jason Reda's 3rd FG, game-winner from 39y with 6 secs to play. At post-game press conference, Michigan State coach John L. Smith sarcastically slapped his own face while blaming himself and staff for poor preparation.

Ohio State 38 IOWA 17: Leading all night against fired-up Iowa, no. 1 Ohio State (5-0) proved its merit by crushing Hawkeyes. Thus, Buckeyes closed difficult early part of year undefeated. QB Troy Smith (16-25/186y) threw 4 TD passes, TB Antonio Pittman rushed 25/117y, TD, and WR Ted Ginn nabbed 7/69y to lead Buckeyes O, which led 21-10 at H. Iowa (4-1) lost for only 2nd time in last 27 games at Kinnick Stadium, and its all-time record against top-ranked teams dropped to 0-10-1. Hawkeyes lost O battle by 400y to 336y, but INTs by Ohio DB Brandon Mitchell and LB James Laurinaitis led to TDs as indications grew that Iowa star QB Drew Tate (19-41/249y, TD, 3 INTs) was having off year. Hawks TB Albert Young (11/48y) scored on 15y run in 2nd Q to trim deficit to 14-10, but Ohio answered with 89y march to WR Roy Hall's 6y TD grab.

MISSOURI 28 Colorado 13: Matching its best start in 25 years, Missouri (5-0) was beginning to look like legitimate contender in Big 12 North. Key to revitalized Tigers was play of new QB Chase Daniel (23-35/253y, 2 INTs), whose quartet of TD passes represented all of Mizzou's points. Tigers TE Chase Coffman (4/31y) caught pair of short scoring throws in 1st Q, leading to 21-6 edge at H. Colorado (0-5) QB Bernard Jackson (13-27/190y) collaborated with WR Dusty Sprague on 63y pass on opening snap of 3rd Q, and Jackson went over for 1y TD run 1 play later. Gambling Buffs failed to convert any of 4 attempts on 4th down, and especially frustrating was Jackson's miss of open receiver on 4th-and-goal from Tigers 4YL when Colorado trailed only 14-3 in 2nd Q.

NEBRASKA 39 Kansas 32 (OT): Nebraska Cornhuskers (4-1) jumped to 17-0 lead before defeating Kansas (3-2) in OT. Huskers QB Zac Taylor (15-33/395y, 4 TDs) launched 3 scoring passes of 75y or longer as WRs Terrence Nunn (3/98y, TD) and Frantz Hardy (3/159y, 2 TDs) caught long-distance 1st H passes to help Huskers to 24-10 advantage. Meanwhile, Jayhawks piled up 574y O on 94 plays by game's end but suffered 4 TOs in 1st H. Among Kansas' errors were pair of INTs by Nebraska S Andrew Shanle and another INT, in EZ to thwart KU threat, by frosh CB Andre Jones. Kansas QB Adam Barmann (27-54/405y, 2 TDs, 3 INTs) also lost FUM inside Huskers 5YL in 1st H. Kansas rolled to 9 pts in 3rd Q to narrow margin to 24-19 but bad snap cost x-pt that would matter later. Jayhawks went ahead 25-24 with 6:32 left on short TD pass by Barmann, but Nebraska DE Jay Moore sacked Barmann on 2-pt pass try. Less than 2 mins later, Taylor and Hardy, former JC teammates, struck again for 75y TD pass and 32-25 lead for Huskers. Barmann hit WR Brian Murph on 26y TD play to send it to OT at 32-32. Taylor pitched 21y pass to set up RB Cody Glenn for winning 1y TD run.

Texas Tech 31 TEXAS A&M 27: While Texas A&M (4-1) gained 250y rushing in trying to keep ball away from dynamic Texas Tech (4-1) aerial attack, it managed 4 possessions that ate 25 mins. But, Aggies' 127.5y per game air D was riddled for 392y by QB Graham Harrell, who hit 32-45 and 4 TDs. Texas Tech WR Joel Filani caught 54y TD pass in 1st Q among his 10/156y receiving. Texas A&M tried to kill clock with 15 runs leading up to K Layne Neumann's 32y FG that broke 24-24 tie with 2:12 remaining. Red Raiders WR Robert Johnson, who caught 3 TD passes from Harrell, hauled in 37y game-winner with 26 secs left. Aggies TB Jorvorskie Lane rushed 12/77y, TD, and WR Kerry Franks dashed 99y for KO TD RET.

Southern California 28 WASHINGTON STATE 22: Southern California's mighty Trojans (4-0) began nail-biting run of near-loss games that would eventually do them in. With USC star receiver Dwayne Jarrett out with bad shoulder, WR Steve Smith caught career-high 11 passes/186y with pair of TDs coming in 2nd H. Washington State (3-2) QB Alex Brink (26-46/287y, 2 TDs, INT) connected with WR Jason Hall (7/49y) for TD with 38 secs left in 1st H, but his poorly-aimed throw on 2-pt try kept Cougars behind at H by 14-12. Smith was magnificent on 99y 3rd Q drive that put USC up 21-12: he drew interference PEN on drive's opening play, threw block to spring TB Emmanuel Moody for 48y run, caught 12y pass on 4th-and-10, and, while navigating back-line of EZ, nabbed 7y TD from QB John David Booty (23-32/269y, 3 INTs, INT). Smith's 2nd TD catch with 5:52 left in 4th Q seemed to lock up matters at 28-15, but Washington State went 80y to Brink's 2nd TD pass and threatened at end until Brink suffered INT on desperation heave after reaching Southern California 38YL.

Oregon 48 ARIZONA STATE 13: Ducks (4-0) were flying all over Sun Devil Stadium, dropping 6 sacks on slumping Arizona State (3-2) QB Rudy Carpenter (6-19/33y, INT) and limiting Devils to 175y O. Oregon led 1st H 24-3 as QB Dennis Dixon (19-30/215y, 3 TDs) and WR Jaison Williams (10/137y, 2 TDs) connected for pair of TDs in 1st Q with Ducks CB Terrell Ward's EZ INT off Carpenter coming in between. In 3rd Q, Oregon sub RB Jeremiah Johnson scored on 4y TD run, set up by 63y burst up middle by Ducks RB Jonathan Stewart (12/142y). Next, Arizona State WR Terry Richardson fielded KO in EZ, faked handoff reverse right to RB Keegan Herring, and jetted 100y down left sideline for TD that trimmed score to 31-10.

October 7, 2006

(Th) NORTH CAROLINA STATE 24 Florida State 20: QB Daniel Evans (13-22/190y, 3 TDs) came up big in 4th Q again as Wolfpack (3-2) beat 2nd straight ranked opponent. Evans lobbed winning carbon-copy TD pass to WR John Dunlap at right side of EZ with 10:36 to play. Wolfpack DB DaJuan Morgan made INT to stall late drive by Florida State (3-2). No. 17 Seminoles had seemed to wrest control with GLS in 3rd Q, halting leap by NC State TB Toney Baker. FSU next rolled 99y to 12y TD pass by QB Drew Weatherford (16-29/249y, 2 TDs, INT) to TE Brandon Warren for 20-10 lead. Afterward, beleaguered Wolfpack coach Chuck Amato, who won his 3rd in 6 tries over his former boss, Bobby Bowden, wondered to ESPN interviewer, "What critics?" Unfortunately for Amato, his critics would get him fired after Wolfpack dropped their last 7 games of year.

Pittsburgh 21 SYRACUSE 11: Until RB LaRod Stephens-Howling bolted for 70y TD in 2nd Q, Panthers (5-1) struggled to get by improving Syracuse (3-3). Trailing 7-3 after Stephens-Howling's 40y run set up 1y TD run by QB Tyler Palko (20-24/177y, TD), Orange seemed poised to take lead. But, critical holding PEN against OT Eugene Newsome set back Syracuse, and Stephens-Howling (27/221y) made his long run on Pitt's 1st snap thereafter. Orange QB Perry Patterson (20-29/225y) pitched 29y TD and 2-pt passes to WR Mike Williams with 4:05 to go, but Pitt killed clock with 48y drive.

Clemson 27 WAKE FOREST 17: For 1st time in 54-year history of ACC, Wake Forest (5-1) arrived as conf's last undefeated team. Frosh QB Riley Skinner (18-23/169y, TD, INT) led Demon Deacons to 17-3 lead, throwing 6y TD pass to WR Willie Idlette and receiving 19y TD pass from WR Nate Morton. On 1st snap of 4th Q, Wake lined up for 42y FG that could have buried Tigers in 20-3 hole. Instead, holder John Temple mishandled placement of snap, was blasted by outstanding Clemson (5-1) DE Gaines Adams, and lost FUM. Adams grabbed pop-up FUM and rambled to 66y TD RET to pull within 17-10. Bursting Wake's bubble, Tigers charged to TDs on 20y pass by QB Will Proctor (20-30/214y, TD, 3 INTs) and dazzling 72y dash by TB C.J. Spiller (9/104y), who slipped tackle and raced down sideline for 24-17 lead.

Tennessee 51 GEORGIA 33: In its attempt to remain unbeaten, Georgia's O went back to banged-up vet QB Joe Tereshinski (12-20/164y, TD, 2 INTs) with pleasant results. Bulldogs (5-1) got off to 24-7 start by 2nd Q as Tereshinski sparked 80 and 81y drives and FB Brannan Southerland scored twice, while WR Mikey Henderson chipped in 86y punt TD RET. But, Georgia, nation's leader in scoring D with 6.8 avg, collapsed to 37-pt 2nd H comeback by Tennessee (5-1). Actually, Volunteers' rally began at end of 2nd Q as QB Erik Ainge (25-38/268y, 2 TDs) led 65y march with TB Arian Foster (3 TDs) diving across in last min of 2nd Q. Down 24-14, Tennessee's momentum carried to 2nd play of 3rd Q as S Antwan Stewart grabbed tipped pass for INT that led to Ainge's 1y TD keeper. Key to Vols' immense 2nd H—which launched them to 2nd-highest pt total ever against Georgia in Sanford Stadium—was tremendous protection O-line afforded Ainge. Vols' onslaught included go-ahead TD catch early in 4th Q by WR Robert Meachem (7/98y) and blocked punt for TD by DB Antonio Wardlow. It was interrupted by Bulldogs' 99y KO TD RET in 4th Q as seam was found by TB Thomas Brown.

FLORIDA 23 Louisiana State 10: Starting rough 3-game stretch vs. LSU, Auburn, and Georgia, Gators (6-0) capitalized on sloppiness of Bayou Bengals (4-2) and inspired play of sub frosh QB Tim Tebow. Florida DB Ryan Smith made 2 INTs as LSU turned ball over 5 times, including FUMs on punt and KO RETs, and discouragingly at Gators 1YL. Tigers had lost 5 TOs year earlier, but won. After LSU's 21-17 win over Florida in 2005, every team of 53 since then had lost if they suffered 5 or more TOs. Still, Tigers led 7-0 on short TD pass by QB JaMarcus Russell (24-41/228y, TD, 3 INTs), but LSU DB Chevis Jackson soon muffed punt at his 19YL. Florida tied it on Tebow's short run, but LSU answered with 75y trip to 1YL where C-QB exchange was bobbled away to Florida LB Brandon Siler. Gators took lead for good at 14-7 in 2nd Q with highly entertaining 1y pass: From Shotgun formation, running specialist Tebow faked inside run while TE Tate Casey, held up briefly, broke out of his blocking stance into EZ. Tebow stopped and lobbed high, double-clutch, jump pass for TD that looked much like basketball jump shot. When 2nd H KO was fumbled for safety, Florida enjoyed safe 16-7 lead. LSU S LaRon Landry had 12 tackles and blocked 4th Q punt.

Arkansas 27 AUBURN 10: In coach Houston Nutt's 9 years at helm of Razorbacks (4-1), no victory was sweeter than this big upset of no. 2 Auburn (5-1). Tigers had not permitted rushing TD during season, but Arkansas TB Darren McFadden (28/145y) exploded for 63y TD bolt. This score increased margin to 17-7 with 5 mins left in 2nd Q. Auburn had to defend from its 34YL after P Kody Bliss made 19y punt in 3rd Q. Arkansas soon sprung wonderful odd play: WR Reggie Fish, Hogs' shortest at 5'7", crab-walked out of the huddle and hid behind gigantic RG Zac Tubbs in position adjacent to QB Mitch Mustain. Fish took a quick handoff and ran left as the rest of Hogs' O went right. Fish's 25-yard run set up TD by backup TB Felix Jones (13/104y) that put Arkansas in front 24-10. Razorbacks DLs Jamaal Anderson and Keith Jackson combined for sack (Hogs made 5 sacks) of Tigers QB Brandon Cox (17-29/153y, TD) on 4th-and-9 on last play of 3rd Q, ending Auburn's last threat.

West Virginia 42 MISSISSIPPI STATE 14: RB Steve Slaton (26/185y, TD) led dynamic ground attack (314y) as Mountaineers won their season's highest profile non-conf game. West Virginia (5-0) scored on its opening series for 7th game in row as FB Owen Schmitt tallied after WR Darius Reynaud ran 25y reverse and caught 37y pass. Mississippi State (1-5) trimmed deficit to 14-7 at H. Bulldogs went 88y behind passing of QB Omarr Conner (10-19/135y), but score came on forward FUM REC in EZ by nimble WR Lance Long. Slaton scored in 3rd Q, and WVU QB Pat White (6-9/92y) authored brilliant 46y TD run to ignite 3-TD 4th Q romp.

MICHIGAN 31 Michigan State 13: In-state rivals met for 99th time, and no. 6 Michigan (6-0) dominated for its 5th straight series victory. Passing sparingly in 42-to-17 run-pass ratio, Wolverines QB Chad Henne (11-17/140y, 3 TDs) hit WR Adrian Arrington for 13y TD in back of EZ on team's 1st possession and provided 14-0 lead early in 2nd Q when he found WR Mario Manningham along right sideline for 47y score. Spartans (3-3) QB Drew Stanton (20-35/252y, 2 INTs) completed 5 passes/68y on 2nd Q drive which ended in frustration as K Brett Swenson's 33y FG attempt went left. Hungry Michigan answered right away with 73y trip to K Garrett Rivas' 24y FG for 17-0 H edge. On opening series of 3rd Q, Henne and Manningham collaborated on 27y TD, Manningham's 9th TD reception of season. Michigan State made final score look more respectable with short 2nd H TD runs by RB Jehuu Caulcrick (14/29y) and Stanton.

IOWA 47 Purdue 17: Rolling to 26th win in last 28 games at home and its 7th Homecoming win in row, Iowa (5-1) reaped season-highs in pts, total y (539y), and 1st downs (25). Hawkeyes TB Damian Sims rushed 20/155y, 2 TDs in relief of injured TB Albert Young. Starting with 52y throw on opening drive, Iowa QB Drew Tate passed 17-23/253y, 2 TDs. Trailing 20-3 at H, Purdue (4-2) stirred itself in 3rd Q by traveling 81 and 76y on consecutive series to TDs on 18y pass by QB Curtis Painter (22-46/249y, TD, 2 INTs) and 16y run by RB Jaycen Taylor (8/63y). But, Iowa matched those drives with its own pair of TDs to keep 34-17 edge. Hawkeyes CB Adam Shada returned INT for school-record 98y TD in middle of 4th Q to set, but it couldn't surpass Kinnick Stadium mark set by Purdue's Rod Woodson in 1986.

Texas 28 Oklahoma 10 (Dallas): Longhorns (5-1) reestablished their hopes to defend national title with relative cakewalk over no. 14 Oklahoma (3-2). But, Texas frosh QB Colt McCoy (11-18/108y, 2 TDs) lived through depressing 2nd Q in which his team gained only 1y to masterfully throw pair of TD passes in 3rd Q. Oklahoma (3-2) A-A TB Adrian Peterson (25/109y) roared to 29y TD run and K Garret Hartley booted 35y FG 4 secs before H for 10-7 Sooners' lead. McCoy opened Longhorns' 1st shot of 3rd Q with 17y pass and soon beat OU blitz with 33y TD throw to WR Limas Sweed (2/38y). When Texas reclaimed possession, McCoy found WR Jordan Shipley in back of EZ with 7y pass at end of 11 play, 79y march. Down 21-10, Oklahoma staged rally in 4th Q, but WR Juaquin Iglesias lost FUM at Horns 15YL. Sooners got ball back at their 17YL with less than 11 mins to go. Peterson dropped lateral pass which he failed to pursue under misconception it was ruled incomplete. However, DB Aaron Ross scooped it up to clinch Texas victory with 3y FUM TD RET, and later he made INT.

Navy 24 AIR FORCE17: Air Force Falcons (2-2) made valiant comeback from 17-pt deficit in 4th Q, and it took stiff Navy (5-1) D stand to take 1st rung to Commander-in-Chief Trophy. With Middies up 7-0, teams traded 80y drives in 2nd Q, only to poise 3rd Q as critical to Navy. Middies virtually salted away verdict at 24-7 with 2 time-consuming trips that ate more than 13 mins on way to 38y FG by K Matt Harmon and 2y TD run by QB Brian Hampton (22/105y, 2 TDs rushing). Air Force soared again in 4th Q for 65 and 80y drives as K Zach Sasser connected on 30y FG and QB Shaun Carney hit TE Travis Dekker with 5y TD pass with 3:06 left. AFA surprised Middies with fairly early, but successful on-side KO, but CB Rashawn King broke up Carney's 4th down pass from Navy 47YL. Navy FB Adam Ballard powered for 27/134y rushing.

CALIFORNIA 45 Oregon 24: Normally laid-back crowd in sold-out Memorial Stadium turned into rare, boisterous Strawberry Canyon mob when Cal Bears (5-1) trotted out in bright gold jerseys. Bears WR DeSean Jackson (2/77y) caught 36y TD pass for 14-3 lead late in 1st Q and "was following (only) yellow jerseys" on electric 65y punt TD RET in 2nd Q which put Cal ahead 28-3. Bears QB Nate Longshore (14-26/189y, INT) hit trio of TD passes and scored TD, and sub TB Justin Forsett (27/163y, TD) ran for 23y TD in relief of TB Marshawn Lynch, who reinjured balky ankle in 1st H. Oregon (4-1), normally bold in its variety of garish uniforms, had been sunk from game's outset: QB Dennis Dixon (20-35/263y, 2 late TDs, 3 INTs) threw off-balance INT to Bears S Brandon Hampton on Ducks' 1st snap. Longshore's 1y TD toss to TE Craig Stevens followed 4 plays later. Top Pac-10 runner, Oregon RB Jonathan Stewart, was limited to 18/25y on ground by fired-up Cal Bears D.

USA Today Coaches October 8

1	Ohio State (62)	1574	14	Georgia	661
2	Southern California	1461	15	Georgia Tech	592
3	Florida (1)	1412	16	LSU	565
4	West Virginia	1398	17	Virginia Tech	523
5	Michigan	1358	18	Oregon	510
6	Texas	1240	19	Boise State	472
7	Louisville	1207	20	Nebraska	460
8	Notre Dame	1044	21	Missouri	387
9	Tennessee	1031	22	Oklahoma	268
10	Auburn	958	23	Arkansas	264
11	California	911	24	Rutgers	261
12	Clemson	899	25	Boston College	108
13	Iowa	672			

October 14, 2006

(Th) BOSTON COLLEGE 22 Virginia Tech 3: ACC foes put up dismal O numbers through most of 1st H until Boston College (5-1) S Ryan Glasper made INT to launch 69y trip to 15y TD pass from QB Matt Ryan (16-29/174y, 2 TDs) to WR Kevin Challenger (3/45y, 2 TDs). Virginia Tech (4-2) countered with aerial excursion sparked by QB Sean Glennon (23-34/148y, 2 INTs) that ended with K Brandon Pace's 36y FG. Still, Hokies were frustrated by 1 of their 9 PENs that nullified TD pass by Glennon to WR David Clowney. BC went up 13-3 by adding pair of 3rd Q FGs by Cinderella K Steve Aponavicius, who had never played single game of organized football. In 4th Q, Ryan hit 4 passes on way to another TD throw to wide-open Challenger, play which left Va Tech DBs quarreling with each other. Under heavy pressure from Boston College DT B.J. Raji and LB Kevin Akins, dispirited Hokies earned only 33y O in 2nd H.

Wake Forest 25 NORTH CAROLINA STATE 23: Demon Deacons (6-1) surprised NC State (4-2), leaders of ACC's Atlantic Division. While spoiled FG had set in motion heartbreaking loss to Clemson prior week, this time K Sam Swank enhanced 7-0 lead with 51y FG early in 2nd Q and bombed 53y FG later in 2nd Q to pull Wake Forest within 14-13. Wolfpack had responded with short TDs on consecutive series in 2nd Q: TB Andre Brown (8/51y) went over from 1y out to close 76y march and TB Toney Baker (13/57y) scored 1st of his 2 TDs on 3y run. After Swank's 2nd FG, NC State's Brown set off flurry against his team by fumbling backwards on run from his 20YL. Mad scramble ensued at 5YL, and ball squirted into EZ where Wolfpack T James Newby recovered for Deacons safety. Min later, Wake WR Nate Morton spun free from pursuit to finish 57y TD pass play with QB Riley Skinner (9-14/124y, TD) and up lead to 22-14. Swank kicked 53y FG with 8 mins left, making him 5th collegian ever to click on trio of 50y+ FGs in single game. Wake Forest held 25-23 lead when NC State QB Daniel Evans (21-37/200y, INT) couldn't hit 2-pt pass with 5:06 to play and Evans was intercepted by S Josh Gattis in game's last min.

Vanderbilt 24 GEORGIA 22: Not since 1993 had Georgia (5-2) lost on Homecoming, and Vanderbilt (3-4) had managed that upset. Commodores' victory snapped their 53-game losing streak to ranked teams. K Bryant Hahnfeldt closed clutch drive from Vanderbilt's 20YL by kicking last-sec 33y FG right down middle in front of stunned Sanford Stadium crowd. Bulldogs owned 1st H, leading 13-7 on QB Joe Tereshinski's 23y TD pass to TE Martez Milner and pair of FGs by K Andy Bailey and nearly 200y O advantage. Vanderbilt QB Chris Nickson (15-29/190y, 2 TDs, 2 INTs) threw his 2nd TD pass late in 3rd Q for 21-13 lead. Bailey made another FG, and Georgia ball-hawking LB Tony Taylor dashed 24y with 4th Q INT TD RET—followed by 2-pt run by QB Matthew Stafford—to temporarily reestablish Bulldogs at 22-21 with 9:22 on clock.

AUBURN 27 Florida 17: Internecine SEC play was again on display as Auburn Tigers (6-1) rebounded from thrashing by Arkansas to hand Gators (6-1) damaging 1st loss. It was 4th time in 2006 that team ranked no. 2 in AP Poll lost, and it placed 4 SEC national crown suitors (also including Arkansas and Tennessee) in precarious 1-loss status. Florida took 17-11 H lead as QB Chris Leak (9-17/108y, TD, INT) hit WR Dallas Baker (4/62y, TD) with 15y TD for 10-pt edge early in 2nd Q, and sub QB Tim Tebow scored on 16y run at end of 80y drive in his only 1st H action. Tigers went without TD in 1st H as K John Vaughn made 3 FGs and they were awarded safety when Gators LG Jim Tartt was called for holding in EZ. Auburn coach Tommy Tuberville challenged his D at H, and they replied with spectacular effort (85y) even though Tigers O still failed to tally TD. Early in 3rd Q, Tigers special teamer Tre Smith returned blocked punt 15y for 18-17 edge. Early in 4th Q, Florida was on move when it gained 32y on catch by Baker and 27y on run by WR Andre Caldwell, but on 3rd down at 6YL, Leak tried to stop his throw but lost FUM to Auburn LB Tray Blackmon. It stayed as 1-pt game until Vaughn nailed FG with 32 secs left, and Gators' attempted lateral on desperate hook-and-ladder pass was returned for superfluous Auburn TD.

Michigan 17 PENN STATE 10: Mighty D of Michigan (7-0) kept Penn State (4-3) completely off balance and crashed through for 7 sacks in holding Lions to 186y O. Wolverines TB Mike Hart rambled for 26/112y and TD in 3rd Q. Michigan WR Adrian Arrington made fabulous impersonation of injured star WR Mario Manningham by logging 5/83y, TD receiving. In no way did it help Nittany Lions to lose their top 2 QBs to injury, but 3rd-string QB Paul Cianciolo flipped screen pass to TB Tony Hunt (13/33y), who slipped away for 43y TD with 3:18 left to trim deficit to 17-10. Although Wolverines had to punt with 1:44 to play, D easily finished its task to improve Michigan's all-time record at Penn State's Beaver Stadium to 5-1.

Ohio State 38 MICHIGAN STATE 7: History was on Michigan State's side; Spartans had upset Buckeyes last 2 times they played Ohio State (7-0) when Buckeyes were top-ranked (1974 and 1998). But this time, no. 1 Ohio State colossus rode into season's 2nd half, receiving little resistance from Spartans (3-4), who lost y on 2 of their 1st 4 series. Michigan State made early FUM REC of TB Chris Wells' bobble at Ohio 31YL, but PEN and sack ruined that chance. Spartans failed on 4th-and-2 draw run by QB Drew Stanton (8-16/54y, INT) in Buckeyes territory early in 2nd Q, and Stanton was knocked from game in 3rd Q as he hit his head against sideline Gatorade jug. With

Buckeyes leading 10-0, WR Ted Ginn went 60y to punt TD RET, 6th such TD in his career. Ohio QB Troy Smith (15-22/234y) followed with pair of TD passes on way to 38-0 lead before Spartans RB A.J. Jimerson finally tallied in last 1:07.

INDIANA 31 Iowa 28: Young Hoosiers (4-3) QB Kellen Lewis (19-25/255y, 3 TDs) found his lanky WR James Hardy for 3 TDs including game-winning 20y slant-in pass with 9:51 to play. No. 15 Iowa (5-2) had led from beginning, scoring in 1st Q on TB Damian Sims' short run and TE Scott Chandler's 19y post-pattern catch from QB Drew Tate (23-40/292y, TD, INT) on way to 21-17 H edge. Lewis had scrambled for 2y TD run late in 2nd Q, then sparked 50y advance with 4-5/37y passing to set up 46y FG by K Austin Starr to close 1st H. Hoosiers went 88y to Hardy's 2nd TD grab after LB Josh Bailey snatched Sims' FUM out of mid-air to halt Iowa's 82y maneuver on its opening try of 3rd Q. With 2:53 to go, S Will Meyers made diving INT to secure Indiana's biggest win in 19 years. Victory was especially gratifying since it came after coach Terry Hoeppner's 2nd brain surgery in 9 months and 2-game suspension of Hardy.

WISCONSIN 48 Minnesota 12: Hung over from prior Saturday's bad-call OT loss to Penn State, Minnesota (2-5) was no match for Wisconsin (6-1). Badgers DB Jack Ikegwuonu (3 pass break-ups) scooped up FUM for 50y TD RET, and frosh TB P.J. Hill (25/164y, 2 TDs) set up his own 5y TD blast for 14-0 lead with 28y romp around RE on 4th-and-1. K Jason Giannini chipped in with FG late in 1st Q to pull Gophers within 14-3, but pair of TD passes by Wisconsin QB John Stocco (12-19/193y, 4 TDs) in 2nd Q put game out of reach at 28-3. Stocco added another pair of TD passes in 2nd H. Minnesota managed 2 pts on LB Mario Reese's x-pt INT RET. Gophers TB Amir Pinnix (19/97y), who had lost big-play FUM to Ikegwuonu in 1st Q, scored on 2y run early in 4th Q. Badgers' 141 pts in 3 games were their most since 1915.

Oklahoma State 42 KANSAS 32: Thanks to pair of early FUMs lost by Oklahoma State (4-2) frosh RB Keith Toston (9/23y), Kansas (3-4) earned 17-0 lead nearly halfway into 3rd Q. Jayhawks frosh QB Kerry Meier (15-27/187y, 3 TDs, INT and 20/70y rushing) made his 1st start since suffering September shoulder injury and clicked on 1st H TD passes to WR Marcus Herford and TE Derek Fine after Toston's miscues provided field position at Oklahoma State 30 and 38YLs. But since Kansas entered contest ranked lowly 110th in national pass D, success would last only so long. Cowboys WR Adarius Bowman had spectacular afternoon, catching 13/300y and 4 TDs, while QB Bobby Reid (23-35/411y, INT) passed for 5 TDs, ran for another, and racked up 457y in total O to surpass coach Mike Gundy's school-record 434y against Kansas in 1989. Bowman took crossing-route pass and exploded for 54y TD that put Cowboys on scoreboard with 8:19 left in 3rd Q. Critical on-side KO led to Reid's 29y TD run. Bowman soon added 25y TD catch for Oklahoma State's 3rd TD in less than 4 mins and made fabulous 55 and 64y TD receptions in 4th Q.

COLORADO 30 Texas Tech 6: New coach Dan Hawkins grabbed his long-awaited 1st win at Colorado (1-6), and giddy Folsom Field fans carried QB Bernard Jackson (11-17/151y, 2 TDs) off on their shoulders. Buffaloes D did commendable job of nipping dynamic Texas Tech (4-3) passing attack: Red Raiders gained 245y in air on 29-45 for reasonable 5.4y per try avg. Colorado went 65 and 80y on pair of drives to early TD passes by Jackson, who felt "all game (that) they couldn't stop us." Buffs gained 380y and played PEN-free game. CU K Mason Crosby hit 56, 26, and 53y FGs in middle Qs for 23-0 lead. Texas Tech, which hadn't been blanked in 111 games, scored in 4th Q on TD pass to WR Danny Amendola (7/37y) by QB Graham Harrell (26-39/236y, TD, 3 INTs), who had been benched at start of 2nd H due to pair of INTs and lost FUM.

OKLAHOMA 34 Iowa State 9: Bittersweet day unfolded for Oklahoma (4-2) TB Adrian Peterson. His proud father Nelson, former prison inmate, was able to see his son play for 1st time in 12 years, but Peterson (26/183y, 2 TDs) broke his collarbone when diving into EZ at end of 53y scoring jaunt in 4th Q. Iowa State (3-4) briefly nudged itself back into contest at 14-7 on 31y TD pass from QB Bret Meyer (14-24/149y, 2 INTs) to WR Todd Blythe (3/60y). Sooners QB Paul Thompson (16-27/195y) connected twice for TDs to WR Malcolm Kelly (4/50y) in 1st H that Oklahoma led 24-7.

TEXAS A&M 25 Missouri 19: Missouri's dream of Big 12 supremacy began downward spiral as Tigers (6-1) dropped see-saw battle to Aggies (6-1). On game's 3rd snap, Missouri lost certain TD as WR Will Franklin sped toward GL until A&M DB Jordan Peterson punched ball out of Franklin's grasp for through-EZ touchback. Later in 1st Q, Texas A&M WR Chad Schroeder pitched 40y pass to WR Kerry Franks (3/115y) to set up K Layne Neumann's short FG that put Tigers behind for 1st time in 2006. RBs Tony Temple (13/37y) of Missouri and Jorvorski Lane (28/127y) of A&M traded 1st Q TDs. Temple fumbled, 1 of 4 in 1st H by Mizzou, that led to short TD pass by Aggies QB Stephen McGee (19-23/183y, TD), but Tigers tied it before H at 17-17. McGee hit 8 passes in row in 3rd Q to lead to winning TD, but, earlier on opening possession of 3rd Q, he fumbled snap that he fell on in EZ for safety that briefly put Tigers ahead 19-17. Pair of 4th Q stops and 41:30 in possession time served A&M well in protecting its lead.

SOUTHERN CALIFORNIA 28 Arizona State 21: TB Chauncey Washington (22/108y) carried 10/64y on 7-min, 74y drive as USC (6-0) battled back for winning TD with 4:29 left to play after having lost 3-TD lead to Arizona State (3-3), which itself battled for 21-21 deadlock. Southern California QB John David Booty (12-25/148y, 2 TDs, INT) threw early TD pass, and TB C.J. Gable followed with 2y TD run. Trojans' 2nd TD was made possible by bad-hop FUM off WR Terry Richardson, ASU's punt RET specialist. Behind 21-0, Sun Devils set up TB Ryan Torain (20/57y) for 39y screen pass, and Torain scored on 6y TD run before H. ASU LB Gerald Munns recovered Booty's FUM after sack at Troy 30YL in 3rd Q, and QB Rudy Carpenter (12-21/124y) fired 8y TD pass to TE Zach Miller. When Arizona State CB Keno Walter-White raced untouched for 37y INT TD RET late in 3rd Q, game was tied 21-21. Victory became no. 3 Trojans' 30th straight home win but this mid-season's 3rd win in row by TD or less.

OREGON 30 Ucla 20: Fast-starting Ducks (5-1) scored 3 TDs in as many possessions, including pair of scoring passes by QB Dennis Dixon (10-17/144y), for 20-3 lead in 1st Q. UCLA (4-2) entered game as nation's 2nd-best in run D (50y per game) but Oregon rushed for 256y, including 121y by TB Jonathan Stewart. Bruins soph QB Patrick Cowan (16-31/112y, INT) occasionally was sharp despite pressure from Ducks' good D-front, and UCLA managed pair of short 4th Q TD runs by back-up TB Kahlil Bell.

USA Today Coaches October 15

1	Ohio State (63)	1575	14	LSU	682
2	Southern California	1476	15	Oregon	660
3	Michigan	1430	16	Nebraska	596
4	West Virginia	1411	17	Boise State	575
5	Texas	1314	18	Arkansas	532
6	Louisville	1205	19	Rutgers	415
7	Auburn	1122	20	Oklahoma	354
8	Notre Dame	1068	21	Boston College	321
9	Tennessee	1060	22	Wisconsin	288
10	Florida	1045	23	Iowa	172
11	California	981	24	Georgia	139
12	Clemson	896	25	Texas A&M	111
13	Georgia Tech	703			

Bowl Championship Series Ranking October 15

	Harris Poll Pct.	*USA Today* Poll Pct.	Computer Pct.	BCS Avg.
1 Ohio State (7-0)	.999	1.000	.920	.9731
2 Southern California (6-0)	.931	.937	1.000	.9559
3 Michigan (7-0)	.934	.908	.960	.9341
4 Auburn (6-1)	.721	.712	.810	.7478
5 West Virginia (6-0)	.878	.896	.460	.7446

October 21, 2006

Rutgers 20 PITTSURGH 10: Rutgers (7-0), sporting nation's top scoring D, put clamps on Pittsburgh's 37.6-pts-per-game O avg. Scarlet Knights sacked Panthers (6-2) QB Tyler Palko, nation's pass efficiency leader, 4 times and permitted 67y rushing, Pitt's fewest ground y to date in 2006. Rutgers K Jeremy Ito made 2 of 3 FGs for 6-0 H lead. Pitt scored on K Conor Lee's 46y FG on opening series of 2nd H, and, after Knights QB Mike Teel (10-18/72y) threw short TD pass at end of 3rd Q, Panthers responded on next drive to WR Oderick Turner's 8y scoring pass from Palko (16-26/169y, TD) to pull within 13-10. After KO, Rutgers was pinned down at its 10YL. Knights turned to its star runner, TB Ray Rice (39/225y, TD), who roared up middle for 63y to set up his clinching TD run. Soph Rice passed 1000y for 2nd straight season.

CLEMSON 31 Georgia Tech 7: Uproarious crowd inspired all-purple-clad Tigers (7-1) to big win over Georgia Tech (5-2), leaders of Coastal Division, as Clemson went to 4-0 in Atlantic Division. Yellow Jackets' superb WR Calvin Johnson, ACC's leading receiver with 35/559y coming in, was blanked from stat sheet by Tigers' D that permitted only 205y. Clemson TB James Davis rammed for 216y, including 1st H's only score after gaining 66y on 71y TD drive. TB C.J. Spiller (16/116y, TD) raced 50y for 17-0 lead late in 3rd Q, but Georgia Tech answered on 35y TD pass by QB Reggie Ball (12-25/117y, TD, INT) early in 4th Q. Spiller made 2 magnificent fakes with swing pass in right flat to break free for 50y TD, game's signature play and clinching score.

TENNESSEE 16 Alabama 13: It wasn't pretty, but no. 7 Tennessee (6-1) prevailed on Third Saturday in October. Crimson Tide TB Kenneth Darby was held to 14/26y rushing, but Alabama (5-3) also put immense D pressure on Volunteers' 35.2 pts-per-game O. Big moment came as Tennessee QB Erik Ainge (28-46/302y, 3 INTs) made saving tackle on DB Simeon Castille's 2nd INT RET, forcing Castille OB at 8YL after 60y RET. Alabama had to settle for K Jamie Chistensen's 2nd FG for 6-3 H lead. Crimson Tide RB Tim Castille crashed over for 2y TD late in 3rd Q for 13-6 edge. After K James Wilhoit's 3rd FG pulled Vols to 13-9, Tennessee went 70y aided by pass interference PEN to 1y leap for TD by TB Arian Foster.

MICHIGAN 20 Iowa 6: Key sacks by both sides hallmarked rugged 1st H D battle, led 3-0 by Michigan (8-0): Wolverines LB Shawn Crable (3 sacks) nailed Iowa (5-3) QB Drew Tate (21-36/197y) on consecutive plays, 2nd time creating FUM recovered by DB Brandon Harrison at UM 41YL. Michigan QB Chad Henne (23-33/203y, INT) next hit WR Adrian Arrington (8/79y) 3/27y, but 2 sacks by Hawkeyes soon forced punt. Iowa tied it 3-3 in 3rd Q on K Kyle Schlicher's 34y FG, but Michigan WR Steve Breaston followed with 64y KO RET. Michigan turned things over to workhorse TB Mike Hart (31/126y), who scored 9y TD. Despite moving inside 10YL, Hawks had to settle for FG to trail 10-6. Hart added clinching 10y TD in 4th Q. Iowa rushed for only 41y; it was 6th time this season Michigan had held opponent to fewer than 50y on ground.

Michigan State 41 NORTHWESTERN 38: Michigan State's highly unusual season reached its peak as Spartans (4-4) surged to greatest comeback in college football history by scoring on 6 of last 7 possessions. After Michigan State led 3-0 in 1st Q, Northwestern (2-6) went ahead 24-3 by H as new starting QB C.J. Bacher (15-29/245y, 3 TDs, 2 INTs) sparked drives of 71, 74, and 88y resulting in his 5y TD pass and 2y TD run. When Bacher hit 3rd Q TD passes to WRs Ross Lane and Shaun Herbert—2nd TD catch for each—Wildcats led 38-3 with 24:54 left in game. Spartans QB Drew Stanton (27-37/294y, 2 TDs, INT) shook off varied injuries to lead TD drives of 65 and 53y before end of 3rd Q. Northwestern RB Tyrell Sutton (21/172y) raced 64y to MSU 11YL late in 3rd Q, which seemed to blunt Spartans' rally, but MLB Kaleb Thornhill made big INT of Bacher in EZ. Pair of MSU frosh made game's telling play next time Wildcats had ball early in 4th Q: WR Devin Thomas blocked punt, and DB Ashton Henderson returned it 33y for TD and 38-24 deficit. Stanton, who had missed previous series because of late hit, suddenly felt Spartans' energy, hitting 3 passes on 60y trip capped by his 12y TD run, then led 58y march, making his 6th straight connection work for tying TD to WR T.J. Williams with 3:43 left. On Wildcats' next snap, S Travis Key made INT RET to 30YL, and Spartans used 5 runs before K Brett Swenson's winning 28y FG.

NOTRE DAME 20 Ucla 17: In its storied history, Notre Dame (6-1), surprisingly, had only twice before scored TD in last 30 secs of game to win. This time, solid UCLA (4-3) D pressured Irish QB Brady Quinn (27-45/304y, 2 TDs) all afternoon, making 5 sacks, 3 by Bruins DE Justin Hickman. But at game's end, UCLA was incapable of stopping Quinn's passes of 21, 14, and finally 45y to WR Jeff Samardzija, who danced away from 2 tacklers to dash for winning score with 27 secs on clock. Setting up ND's last-chance success, that started with 1:02 to go, was judicious use of timeouts as UCLA tried to kill clock with conservative runs after having stopped Quinn on 4th down sneak at Bruins 35YL with 2:20 remaining. Fighting Irish had scored 1st as Samardzija caught short TD from Quinn. UCLA registered pair of long TD passes by QB Patrick Cowan (16-32/217y, 2 TDs, INT) while ND could only counter with 2 FGs by K Carl Gioia in middle Qs. Bruins K Justin Medlock had made 14 FGs in row but missed 47y 3-ptr after false-start PEN pushed him back, but made 29y FG for 17-13 lead in 4th Q.

Texas 22 NEBRASKA 20: In cold wind and late-game snow flurries of Lincoln, young Longhorns (7-1) QB Colt McCoy (25-39/220y, 2 TDs) faced his 1st rugged opponent outside of state of Texas. McCoy was highly poised when he needed to be, throwing TD pass of 6y to WR Quan Cosby and 55y to WR Limas Sweed in 2nd Q for 16-7 H lead. Nebraska (6-2) QB Zac Taylor (15-28/277y, 2 TDs, INT) threw 63y TD pass to WR Maurice Purify in 1st Q but turned it over on INT and FUM in 2nd Q during which Huskers made only 20y. IB Brandon Jackson (7/40y) took shovel pass and zipped though Texas line for 49y TD early in 4th Q which pulled Nebraska to within 16-14. K Greg Johnson hit 22y FG to put Texas up 19-14 but soon reported to coaches that his leg had stiffened. With less than 5 mins to play, Huskers IB Marlon Lucky threw surprise 25y TD pass to WR Nate Swift, but Taylor missed 2-pt pass. Holding 20-19 lead and its D forcing 3-and-out, Nebraska got ball back and appeared to earn clinching 1st down on 8y pass to WR Terrence Nunn. But, Nunn tried to turn upfield for extra y and had ball popped from his grasp by CB Aaron Ross. Texas S Marcus Griffin recovered at Huskers 44YL with 2:17 left. Nebraska coach Bill Callahan said, "Victory was more or less swept away on that third-down play." Longhorns got another break on winning series when G Kasey Studdard hustled to cop FUM lost by WR Jordan Shipley. With ball at 5YL, Texas coach Mack Brown sent soph walk-on K Ryan Bailey out for his 1st-ever FG try, which he made from 22y out with 23 secs to play.

CALIFORNIA 31 Washington 24 (OT): Presumably because of his painful ankles, California (7-1) TB Marshawn Lynch (21/150y, 2 TDs) celebrated OT victory by zipping left and right on borrowed cart, dodging excited fans and band members who had come on field. When game was on-the-line, Lynch made 2 great runs to pull Cal out of fire: he raced outside left for 17y TD run—and sub TB Justin Forsett added 2-pt run—in last 2 mins of regulation for 24-17 lead and dashed right for 22y TD on Cal's 2nd play of OT. Washington (4-4) had built 10-0 lead in 2nd Q as up-and-down QB Carl Bonnell (17-31/284y, 2 TDs, 5 INTs), in his 1st start for lost-for-season starting QB Isaiah Stanback, launched 49y TD pass to WR Anthony Russo. Bonnell's 7y TD run in 1st min of 4th Q reestablished Washington control at 17-13. Lynch's 4th Q TD appeared to save game for Cal, but Bonnell advanced Huskies 48y, and launched passing prayer from Bears 40YL with time expiring. While 2 Bears defenders, including LB Desmond Bishop (16 tackles), were in position to knock down Bonnell's flyball, they tipped it to UW WR Marlon Wood, who sprung into EZ with incredible tying TD. After Lynch's OT score, Huskies advance to 6YL, but Bishop picked off short pass and lit out 79y until exhaustion and giddy teammates ended his clinching INT RET.

WASHINGTON STATE 34 Oregon 23: Cougars (5-3) coaches retooled their O after 2 pitiful weeks with total of 16 pts scored, and QB Alex Brink (20-23/179y, 2 TDs, INT) and TE Jed Collins (3/57y, TD) were chief beneficiaries. Washington State duo combined on 8y TD pass to open scoring at 6-0 in 2nd Q, and, 5 mins into 3rd Q, Collins caught 32y pass, then scored on 1y trick-play run for 20-3 lead. When QB Dennis Dixon (12-20/105y, 2 INTs) was picked off 26 secs later for 24y TD RET by Cougars CB Tyron Blackenridge, it was time for QB change by coach Mike Bellotti of No. 16 Oregon (5-2). Bellotti didn't blame Dixon for TOs, but that "we just have to have a spark." Ducks backup QB Brady Leaf (16-27/262y) threw TD passes of 4 and 36y TD passes to WR Jordan Kent in latter half of 4th Q. WSU RB Dwight Tardy (20/147y) helped dissolve clock with 114y rushing in 4th Q, including 1y TD.

USA Today Coaches October 22

1	Ohio State (63)	1575	14	Arkansas	700
2	Southern California	1469	15	Boise State	667
3	Michigan	1454	16	Rutgers	557
4	West Virginia	1394	17	Boston College	530
5	Texas	1308	18	Wisconsin	525
6	Louisville	1205	19	Oklahoma	450
7	Auburn	1178	20	Nebraska	328
8	Florida	1051	21	Georgia Tech	264
9	Tennessee	1046	22	Texas A&M	263
10	Notre Dame	1019	23	Missouri	229
11	Clemson	962	24	Oregon	228
12	California	923	25	Georgia	163
13	LSU	720			

Bowl Championship Series Ranking October 22

	Harris Poll Pct.	*USA Today* Poll Pct.	Computer Pct.	BCS Avg.
1 Ohio State (8-0)	.999	1.000	.930	.9764
2 Michigan (8-0)	.942	.923	.970	.9451
3 Southern California (6-0)	.926	.933	.970	.9430
4 West Virginia (7-0)	.870	.885	.510	.7551
5 Auburn (7-1)	.742	.748	.750	.7466

October 28, 2006

(Th) VIRGINIA TECH 24 Clemson 7: Tigers (7-2), owners of nation's highest scoring O, went 77y to TB James Davis' banging 6y TD run off left side. But, fired-up Virginia Tech (6-2), looking to regain its form as "Kings of Thursday Night," allowing Clemson only 3 1st downs after 1st Q. Hokies led 10-7 at H after TB Branden Ore (37/203y, 2 TDs) raced for 40y gain before QB Sean Glennon wedged over for 1y TD in 1st Q, and K Brandon Pace added FG in 2nd Q. Virginia Tech LB Xavier Adibi's 3rd Q INT of Clemson QB Will Proctor (11-28/86y, INT) set up drive that was all power running by Ore, who roared up middle for 11y TD for 17-7 edge. Ore added another score later in 3rd Q and became 1st-ever Hokies runner to rush for 200y in consecutive games.

Wake Forest 24 NORTH CAROLINA 17: North Carolina (1-7) turned out inspired after announcement that beleaguered coach John Bunting would be fired at season's end. Despite allowing early TD on 16y blocked punt RET by Wake Forest (7-1) DB Alphonso Smith, Carolina took 17-14 lead on K Connor Barth's 35y FG 8 mins into 3rd Q. Deacons K Sam Swank tied it with 41y FG on 2nd play of 4th Q, and S Josh Gattis (13 tackles, INT) soon fell on FUM at UNC 39YL. On next play, Wake QB Riley Skinner (7-8/89y, TD) pitched winning 39y TD over middle to his favorite target, WR-RB Kenneth Moore (6/82y), who had scored on 34y run early in 2nd Q. Tar Heels battled back, twice converting 4th downs until reaching Wake 3YL with 41 secs left. But, Deacons outstanding LB Jon Abbate made EZ INT off QB Joe Dailey (13-19/156y, TD, 2 INTs) on last play.

GEORGIA TECH 30 Miami 23: Neither contender for ACC Coastal honors felt too secure off previous week: Yellow Jackets were blown out by Clemson and Hurricanes suffered through bad media and near-loss to lowly Duke. Things started horribly for Georgia Tech (6-2) as chronically-inconsistent sr QB Reggie Ball (11-27/188y, 2 TDs) was hammered by Miami (5-3) DE Calais Campbell, fumbled, and watched Canes LB Glenn Cook steam 19y for TD. "I was mad, hurt, and frustrated, but I've been down before," said Ball. Although Ball threw 46y TD pass to WR James Johnson in 2nd Q, he finished 1st H with pale 3-16 passing. Miami broke 13-13 tie with K Jon Peattie's 3rd FG after Canes consumed 7 mins late in 3rd Q. Meanwhile, Ball had stoked his game, hitting 8-11 in 2nd H. He tossed 1y TD pass to WR Calvin Johnson (5/68y). When Jackets D recovered FUM by Canes QB Kyle Wright (20-31/246y, TD, INT), TB Tashard Choice (26/107y) tore for 24y TD and 30-16 lead with 3:49 left to play.

Tennessee 31 SOUTH CAROLINA 24: Gamecocks (5-3), SEC's wild card, frightened another conf heavyweight. But not before South Carolina quickly was down 14-0: On 2nd play, Tennessee (7-1) LB Marvin Mitchell intercepted deflected pass and returned it 17y for TD, recently-anointed Carolina star QB Syvelle Newton (16-29/230y, 2 TDs, 3 INTs, 14/85y, TD rushing) led 74y drive only to be intercepted in EZ, and Volunteers went 80y to tipped 5y TD pass caught by WR Bret Smith (4/23y, 2 TDs) from hot-handed QB Eric Ainge (21-29/254y, 2 TDs). Back fought Gamecocks, taking lead late in 3rd Q after Newton had capped 80y trip in 2nd Q with 18y TD pass to WR Mike West and 73y drive in 3rd Q and 15y TD throw to WR Noah Whiteside. Tennessee answered with 79y trip to Smith's 2nd TD catch early in 4th Q. When Vols DB Jonathan Hefney streaked 65y with punt RET to 5YL, TB Arian Foster scored on next play for 28-17 lead. Newton tallied on 1y keeper at end of 95y drive, but it was not enough.

Florida 21 Georgia 14 (Jacksonville): Early in 1st Q, Gators (7-1) WR Andre Caldwell scored on 11y misdirection run for 7-0 lead. While Georgia (5-3) was going nowhere, its D stiffened until Caldwell got loose up middle for 40y scoring catch from QB Chris Leak (14-28/161y, TD, INT) in 2nd Q. Trailing 14-0, Bulldogs managed only 81y O in 1st H. Things went from bad to worse for Georgia on 1st snap of 3rd Q: simple run left was fumbled and run in for TD by Gators DE Ray McDonald. Down 21-0, Bulldogs finally got break as LB Tony Taylor made INT in zone coverage, and frosh QB Matthew Stafford (13-33/1511y, 2 INTs) sprinted 13y for TD on QB-draw. Bulldogs dropped several passes but recovered FUM by Gators QB Tim Tebow with less than 9 mins left. TB Kregg Lumpkin surged up middle for TD to trim it to 21-14, but Florida killed clock.

OHIO STATE 44 Minnesota 0: Golfing great Jack Nicklaus, Ohio State class of 1961, received thunderous cheers at H by "dotting the 'i 'in Ohio" during band's famed "Script Ohio" maneuver. No.1 Buckeyes (9-0) took care of business, scoring on their 1st 2 possessions and dropping slumping Minnesota (3-6) behind 17-0 by H. Winless in Big 10 play, Gophers had odd highlights: little CB Dominic Jones crushed OHio WR Roy Small for 3y loss just as 2nd Q swing pass arrived in Small's hands, and P Justin Kucek's 186y on 5 punts exceeded his teammates' total O by 4y. Buckeyes TB Antonio Pittman, perhaps nation's most underrated star, rushed for 21/116y, 2 TDs and caught 2/47y. QB Troy Smith, almost everybody's Heisman choice, passed 14-21/183y, 2 TDs and authored fabulous cutback 21y TD run. Ohio State D authored 3 INTs to stump Minnesota's O plans.

Oklahoma 26 MISSOURI 10: Long pass to little-used Missouri (7-2) WR Greg Bracey set up early FG. But, Oklahoma (6-2) INT by LB Zach Latimer off deflected pass thrown by Tigers QB Chase Daniel (23-44/284y, 3 INTs) soon put Sooners in good spot at 33YL, and QB Paul Thompson scored on option run. For rest of 1st H led by Oklahoma 16-3, Mizzou "beat itself," as coach Gary Pinkel told ABC: Tigers lost FUM, leading to Sooners TD, and had punt blocked by OU DB Jason Carter for safety. Missouri recovered FUM early in 3rd Q and it led to TD run by Daniel. Sooners went back on move midway in 3rd Q after iffy personal foul on punt sustained possession, and Thompson (11-19/127y, 2 TDs) threw TD to WR Quenton Chaney on slant pass for 23-10 lead. Missouri rallied to 1st down at 2YL, but Daniel was banged up on 1 of his pair of stonewalled Shotgun runs and his 4th down pass went awry. When Oklahoma State later beat Nebraska 41-23, Tiger hopes stayed alive in Big 12 North.

Brigham Young 33 AIR FORCE 14: In control of Mountain West Conf and quietly moving underneath national radar, Cougars (6-2) handed Air Force (3-4) defeat with stout D and balanced 411y attack. Worried about Falcons' option O consuming time, BYU kept ball for 7 mins on opening 81y drive to RB Fui Vakapuna's 6y TD run. Air

Force came right back but lost FUM to Cougars LB Cameron Jensen while trying 4th down run. BYU QB John Beck (23-31/258y, 3 TDs) flipped 8 and 1y TD passes in 2nd Q for 21-0 H edge. After Cougars K Jared McLaughlin bombed career-best-to-date 53y FG in 3rd Q, Air Force finally cranked up its O, marching 80y to QB Shaun Carney's TD sneak.

OREGON STATE 33 Southern California 31: Beavers (4-4) scored early TD, but Trojans (6-1) TB Chauncey Washington (18/81y, TD, 2 FUMs) powered to tying TD in 2nd Q. Ahead 10-7, Beavers recovered 2 FUMs in last 5 mins of 1st H, but had to settle for K Alexis Serna's FGs of 31 and 53y. Despite everything against it, USC trailed only 16-10 at H, but things quickly went downhill. Oregon State QB Matt Moore (21-32/262y, TD) threw TD pass to TE Joe Newton, and WR Sammie Stroughter raced 70y on punt TD RET for 30-10 edge in 3rd Q. Trojans' rally to try to keep alive string of 27 straight Pac-10 wins began late in 3rd Q with them down 33-10. Led by WR Steve Smith, who caught 11/258y, USC scored its 3rd straight TD—Smith's 2nd TD—with 7 secs left. But, Oregon State DE Jeff Van Orsow, rushing from right side, knocked down 2-pt pass by QB John David Booty (24-39/406y, 3 TDs, INT).

Bowl Championship Series Ranking October 29

November 4, 2006

(Th) LOUISVILLE 44 West Virginia 34: Big East battle of unbeatens was O parade. Both Ds were nearly invisible as West Virginia (7-1) won hollow triumph: 540y to 468y in O stat battle. Leading 16-14 at H but frustrated by its inability to cash TDs instead of K Art Carmody's 3 FGs, Louisville (8-0) seemed to come alive at same moment half of lights went out in Papa John Stadium. After exchange of TOs in semi-darkness of early 3rd Q, West Virginia started series at its 13YL, and on 1st play, star RB Steve Slaton (18/156y, TD) lost FUM. Cardinals LB Malik Jackson scooped it up for TD RET and 23-14 lead. Slaton went to sideline with limp left arm, and Mountaineers soon were forced to punt from own 6YL. Short punt was returned by streaking Cards WR Trent Guy for 40y TD. QB Pat White (13-20/222y and 23/125y, 4 TDs rushing) marshaled WVU for gutsy 92y TD march, mostly using his own runs, to 30-21 deficit. On 1st snap of 4th Q, however, Louisville QB Brian Brohm (19-26/354y, TD) tossed TD fade pass to 6'6" WR Mario Urrutia (6/113y). Slaton was back for WVU's next series that resulted in White's power-run TD that resembled 1950s Single Wing play. Cards quickly negated that score with another of their own. It came on 5y run from big frosh RB Anthony Allen (12/47y, 2 TDs) and provided 44-27 lead with 10:19 left.

WAKE FOREST 21 Boston College 14: Not since 1944 had Wake Forest (8-1) opened with 8 wins in 9 games. Afterward reserved coach Jim Grobe exclaimed, "They thought the party was going to be over tonight, but the Deacs move on. It's fun!" Using their speed, Demon Deacons got off to 7-0 lead in 1st Q on WR Willie Idlette's 9y E-around run and never trailed, although Boston College (7-2) tied on 1st snap of 2nd Q: short TD pass by QB Matt Ryan (40-57/402y, TD, INT), whose completions and pass y were career highs partly because BC was ineffective on ground. Ahead 14-7 early in 3rd Q, Wake again went to misdirection, QB Riley Skinner (15-23/120y, 2 INTs, and 46y TD pass in 2nd Q) handing to WR Kevin Marion, who faked handoff, and sprinted right where he received key block from WR-turned-RB (because of Wake injuries) Kenneth Moore to spring 81y TD romp. Ryan scored on 4th down, 2y scramble late in 3rd Q. Deacons got batch of 4th Q breaks: A. TV replay turned BC FUM REC at Wake 14YL into incomplete pass, B. Eagles RB J.V. Whitworth lost FUM to Wake DT Jyles Tucker (2 sacks) at Deacs 37YL, and C. in game's last min, Wake S Patrick Ghee went up for INT in EZ as Ryan overthrew his target 3 plays after converting 4th-and-10.

Maryland 13 CLEMSON 12: Terrapins (7-2) quietly had dealt themselves into ACC Atlantic Division race with 3 narrow wins in row over Virginia, NC State, and Florida State. Maryland scored game's only TD in 2nd Q as QB Sam Hollenbach (23-34/247y), in middle of stretch of 11 straight completions, fired 7y cross-field pass to WR Danny Oquendo at left pylon. Trouble in O red zone often thwarted Clemson (7-3), turning TDs into FGs. Maryland led 10-6 late in 3rd Q, and despite converting 4th-and-2 at Maryland 18YL, Tigers again had to settle for K Jad Dean's FG. Maryland had safety taken away by TV replay, which would have put Terps up 12-9, on odd play that saw ball stripped from Proctor at end of scramble to his own 10YL. Ball bounced to TB T.J. Spiller who recovered controversially at Tigers GL. Initially it was ruled 2 pts when Maryland LB David Holloway fell on Spiller as they rolled into EZ. Replay reversal seemed to rattle Maryland D, and Proctor fired pass over middle from his EZ which TE

Thomas Hunter carried 71y to Terps 28YL. PEN nullified Clemson TD, but Dean nailed his 4th FG, from 22y, for 12-10 lead with 2:25 left. Cool sr Hollenbach directed 54y drive, sneaking on 4th-and-inches, to K Dan Ellis' winning 31y FG as clock hit 0:00.

KENTUCKY 24 Georgia 20: This time, only 11th time in 60 meetings, Cats beat Dogs. Fresh legs of squat Kentucky (5-4) RB Tony Dixon allowed him to power through larger Georgia (6-4) defenders during winning drive he capped with 3y TD run with 1:21 to play. Bulldogs owned 14-10 lead in 2nd Q thanks to 92 and 1y drives, latter set up by DB Tra Battle's 32y INT RET. Foe's INT near end of 1st H ruined scoring bid for each team: Wildcats had their own INT RET, by LB Johnny Williams, that went deep to UGa 2YL. But, Kentucky QB Andre Woodson (23-32/204y, 2 TDs, 2 INTs) gave it right back on Bulldogs LB Tony Taylor's 5th INT of season. Taylor raced 52y to launch Bulldog drive to 2 that ended when QB Matthew Stafford (16-28/230y, TD, 3 INTs) threw his 2nd INT. TB Danny Ware put Georgia ahead 20-17 with 3y dash around LE with 4:37 left. Kentucky made its 3rd INT right after Dixon's winning score.

Louisiana State 28 TENNESSEE 24: Early in 1st Q, Louisiana State (7-2) QB JaMarcus Russell (24-36/247y, 3 TDs, 3 INTs, and 7/71y rushing) was banged up on sack, and Tigers were forced into long, unsuccessful FG try. Russell came back to pitch for 7-0 lead early in 2nd Q as he rifled 23y TD pass into middle of EZ to WR Craig Davis. Meanwhile with Volunteers (7-2) O at -5y on 1st 3 series, QB Erik Ainge (1-6/3y, sack) had to give in to his gimpy ankle, and in came frosh QB Jonathan Crompton (11-24/183y, 2 TDs, INT) as relief pitcher. When Tennessee went up 17-7 primarily on Crompton's 37y TD pass to WR Robert Meachem (5/121y, 2 TDs) and DB Demetrice Morley's 31y INT TD RET of Russell's overthrow early in 3rd Q, LSU seemed to have fallen into big trouble. But, Tigers tallied TDs for 21-17 edge after 77 and 52y 3rd Q drives. Opening of 4th Q turned wild as TOs ran rampant. With 7:29 to play, Crompton threaded rocket between defenders to Meachem for 54y score and 24-21 Tennessee lead. Russell exploited clock beautifully, once clicking on 4th down pass. Tigers' winning TD came with 9 secs to play as WR Early Doucet (8/73y, TD) turned to stab Russell's fastball in middle of EZ that had been ticketed for WR Dwayne Bowe in back of EZ. Vols' loss combined with Florida's 25-19 win over Vanderbilt put Gators in SEC title game.

Arkansas 26 SOUTH CAROLINA 20: Neither starting QB—Mitch Mustain for Arkansas (8-1) nor Syvelle Newton for South Carolina (5-4)—was around at end of contest. Hogs RB Darren McFadden (25/219y) scored on 43 and 14y runs, and QB Casey Dick (11-19/228y, TD, INT) hooked up with WR Marcus Monk (8/192y) on crazy 50y "Hail Mary" TD pass that was batted and bobbled by multiple Gamecocks defenders. It all provided Arkansas with 23-6 lead at H. QB Blake Mitchell (15-21/213y, INT) came off bench to relieve ineffective Newton and threw TDs to WR Kenny McKinley and brilliant toe-in-bounds EZ catch by WR Sidney Rice. Up 26-20, Arkansas took nearly 7 mins off clock in 4th Q, but came up empty as K Jeremy Davis missed 41y FG barely to right. Carolina took over with nearly 6 mins left, but Mitchell threw INT to CB Darius Vinnett at Arkansas 27YL. Pair of Dick-to-Monk passes helped kill clock.

Mississippi State 24 ALABAMA 16: Right off bat, Crimson Tide (6-4) continued its season-long red zone frustration. After taking opening KO, Alabama went 58y to Mississippi State (3-7) 2YL but had to settle for K Jamie Christensen's 19y FG. Tide made 3 more trips inside 20YL without TD as their only 6-ptr was scored on S Jeffrey Dukes' 24y INT RET in 2nd Q. Bulldogs, ranked 110th in national rushing, used effective runs of frosh TB Anthony Dixon (25/121y) to control much of 1st H they led 24-10 because they scored on 3 of their 1st 4 possessions. Crowning play for coach Sylvester Croom, who beat his alma mater for 1st time, was 51y INT TD RET by LB Quinton Culberson late in 1st H. Bama TB Kenneth Darby was held to 13/54y rushing.

Ohio State 17 ILLINOIS 10: Ohio State (10-0) and undefeated Michigan, having all its could handle in 34-26 win over lowly Ball State, both seemed distracted by countdown to their epic November 18 showdown in Columbus. Buckeyes got off to 17-0 H lead but when stats were tallied at game's end, they had gained only 224y in fairly listless style. TBs Chris Wells and Antonio Pittman (32/58y) scored TDs on 2 of 1st 3 possessions, but Ohio State earned only 20y O after making 2nd Q FG. Illinois (2-8) LB J Leman and rest of swift D had much to do with holding Pittman to 1.8y per carry; Leman made 19 tackles, including 3.5 tackles for loss, and sack of Smith. Fighting Illini fought back in 4th Q as K Jason Reda made 27y FG, and RB Rashard Mendenhall scored with 1:40 left at close of 80y drive on which QBs "Juice" Williams and Tim Brasic each hit 3 passes. Illinois' on-side KO failed, however, and Ohio State P A.J. Trapasso punted 55y to 2YL with 4 secs left.

WISCONSIN 13 Penn State 3: No. 17 Wisconsin (9-1), quiet 1-loss team with victories over only 2 winning Div 1-A teams, completely shut down anemic Penn State (6-4) O. With score tied at 3-3 and 23 secs left in 2nd Q, Badgers WR Paul Hubbard (5/77y, TD) made outstanding 14y TD catch from QB John Stocco (15-25/172y, TD) at back of EZ amid close coverage by 2 Lions defenders. Earlier, Lions LB Dan Connor (10 tackles, sack) forced FUM recovered by Penn State DE Sean Lee (13 tackles, 2 sacks, 2 FUM RECs) at 14YL. On next play, Wisconsin S Roderick Rogers nabbed twice-deflected INT of Lions QB Anthony Morelli (19-35/165y, INT). Pair of players rolled OB in EZ amid close coverage by 2 Lions defenders. Pair of players rolled OB in 4th Q, notably Penn State frosh TE Andrew Quarless after catching sideline pass, and banged hard into 79-year-old coach Joe Paterno. Lions mentor left on cart with fractured leg and knee injury and would miss his 1st game since 1977 on following Saturday. Penn State LB Paul Poluszny made 14 tackles and became career tackle leader at "Linebacker U" with 349.

Northwestern 21 IOWA 7: Northwestern (3-7) surprised fading Hawkeyes (6-4). Worst in Big 10 in many O categories, Wildcats scored 1st time they had ball, then threw balanced attack at Iowa that bagged 225y running and 218y passing. RB Tyrell Sutton (28/168y) scored on NW's 1st series after QB C.J. Bacher (19-29/218y, TD, 2 INTs) pitched 48y pass. Trailing 14-0 in 3rd Q, slumbering Hawks got boost from CB Charles Godfrey's midfield INT. Iowa WR Dominique Douglas (7/78y) made 24y catch, tapping

foot in-bounds at 3YL to send TB Damian Sims for TD run. Wildcats iced it with RB Terrell Jordan's TD run with 4:48 left, and followed with INT of Iowa QB Drew Tate (18-27/147y, 2 INTs).

NEBRASKA 34 Missouri 20: Playing on Homecoming in front of 281st straight sellout, Huskers (7-3) overloaded strong O formations to 1 side and pulled weak-side G for successful power runs by IB Brandon Jackson, who rushed for 111y. Still, it was 3 TD passes—2 by QB Zac Taylor (13-21/208y, 2 TDs) and another off E-around by WR Maurice Purify—that put Nebraska ahead 24-6 at H. But in last 2 weeks, Nebraska had had real trouble putting away Texas and Oklahoma State, both losses. Key 4th down play early in 3rd Q might have put nails in Missouri (7-3) coffin, but Huskers TE J.B. Phillips dropped wide open pass ticketed for 1st down deep in Mizzou end. While Tigers TE Martin Rucker caught 6y TD pass on slant-in screen, Nebraska answered early in 4th Q with Jackson's 2y TD run for 34-13 advantage. Missouri trimmed score to 34-20 but on Tigers' last 2 chances they missed 4th down pass and lost FUM to Huskers LB Bo Ruud. Nebraska DT Adam Carriker had big game, catching ricochet INT and causing FUM.

Oklahoma 17 TEXAS A&M 16: Leading 17-16, Oklahoma (7-2) gambled on 4th-and-inches at own 29YL with 1:29 to play. Sooners QB Paul Thompson's 2nd-effort earned winning 1st down, but it became moot when Texas A&M (8-2) was found to have 12 defenders on field. Oklahoma had gotten off to 14-3 lead in 1st Q as it reaped running TDs from TB Allen Patrick (32/173y), able replacement for injured TB Adrian Peterson, and Thompson, who chipped in only with 3-12/39y passing. TB Jorvorskie Lane (13/62y) powered for Aggies TD in 2nd Q, and K Layne Neumann added 3 FGs.

Arizona 27 WASHINGTON STATE 17: With new helmet that "felt like a pillow," QB Willie Tuitama was back in Arizona (4-5) lineup after missing month with his 2nd concussion, and RB Chris Henry regained his starting job. Together, 2 Wildcats accounted for 253y of team's 275y O. Tuitama launched 78y TD pass to WR Anthony Johnson on game's 3rd play, and Henry set school record with 35 carries/94y and TDs in 2nd and 4th Qs. Washington State (6-4), recent resident of 25th in AP Poll thanks to wins over Oregon and at UCLA, couldn't win its 3rd in row but was able to tie it midway in 1st Q on 91y TD pass from QB Alex Brink (18-33/265y, TD) to WR Brandon Gibson. Big play was turned in by Wildcats WR Syndric Steptoe (6/52y), who made spectacular 1-handed grab for 21y to set up Henry's 3rd Q TD that built 10-pt margin.

USA Today Coaches November 5

1	Ohio State (63)	1575	14	Rutgers	742
2	Michigan	1502	15	Tennessee	710
3	Texas	1397	16	Wisconsin	685
4	Louisville	1382	17	Oklahoma	597
5	Auburn	1309	18	Georgia Tech	480
6	Florida	1255	19	Wake Forest	448
7	Southern California	1148	20	Oregon	400
8	Notre Dame	1079	21	Virginia Tech	306
9	California	1048	22	Boston College	230
10	West Virginia	994	23	Texas A&M	121
11	Arkansas	946	24	Maryland	113
12	LSU	925	25	Nebraska	107
13	Boise State	769			

Bowl Championship Series Ranking November 5

	Harris Poll Pct.	*USA Today* Poll Pct.	Computer Pct.	BCS Avg.
1 Ohio State (10-0)	.999	1.000	.960	.9865
2 Michigan (10-0)	.958	.964	1.000	.9706
3 Louisville (8-0)	.885	.878	.910	.8907
4 Florida (8-1)	.798	.797	.810	.8017
5 Texas (9-1)	.883	.887	.630	.7998

November 11, 2006

(Th) RUTGERS 28 Louisville 25: Not since Rutgers (9-0) beat Princeton 6-4 in football's 1st game in 1869 had State University of New Jersey known moment so important in college history. In fact, Rutgers football history had been so bleak that never had no. 15 Rutgers ever met ranked opponent while ranked itself. No. 3 Louisville, in position to take grip on spot in BCS title game, scored 1st after 80y drive in 1st Q. Scarlet Knights tied it on 26y TD pass by QB Mike Teel (8-21/189y, TD, INT) after LB Devraun Thompson returned INT 32y. Cardinals DB JaJuan Spillman immediately raced 100y on KO TD RET, and Louisville jumped to 25-7 lead on next 2 possessions when QB Brian Brohm (13-27/163y, TD, INT) threw 5y TD pass to WR Jimmy Riley and K Art Carmody kicked 39y FG. Mixed in was fortunate 2-pt conv that saw Louisville have x-pt kick blocked, but 2 pts were tallied when RB Anthony Allen picked up spinning ball ignored by Rutgers D. But breaks went to Knights from then on. Rutgers WR Kenny Britt went high to spear pass in 3rd Q, raced 67y, only to fumble at 4YL. Britt somehow beat host of Cards for loose ball, and Knights TB Ray Rice (22/131y) quickly scored his 2nd TD. Teel's 2-pt pass pulled Rutgers within 25-22. With Rutgers D forcing 5th straight 3-and-out series (net 0y) upon Cards in 2nd H, its O moved 33y for K Jeremy Ito's 46y FG to tie it with 10:13 on 4th Q clock. Knights took over at their 9YL with 5:28 to play, and in 11 plays Rice ran 7/42y and FB Brian Leonard took flat-pass 26y to set up 33y FG attempt with 17 secs left. Normally-reliable Ito hooked FG wide left, but Louisville CB William Gay had jumped off-side with no effect on Ito's miss. Ito's 2nd try from 28y split uprights for 28-25 lead. Not out of woods yet, Rutgers chose to kick-off long, and Spillman dashed past several tacklers for 38y before Ito made firm tackle to save any possible UL heroics with 2 secs left.

MARYLAND 14 Miami 13: Playing with heavy hearts 4 days after death of DT Bryan Pata, Miami (5-5) lost 3rd game in row for 1st time since 1999. Maryland (8-2) won its 5th straight despite making only 6 1st downs and snapping ball only 37 times to Hurricanes' 74 O plays. Terrapins would make all pts they would need 2:02 into 2nd Q on pair of season's longest plays to-date. Maryland scored on TD passes of 65 and 96y from QB Sam Hollenbach (11-16/202y, 2 TDs) to quicksilver frosh WR Derrius Heyward-Bay (5/175y, TDs). Miami gained 320y with sub QB Kirby Freeman passing 14-27, TD, INT and rushing 9/51y. Freeman connected on 28y TD pass to WR Ryan Moore (5/50y) in 2nd Q, and K Jon Peattie nailed FGs of 32 and 25y. Maryland D was sparked by LBs Wesley Jefferson (14 tackles) and Erin Henderson (13 tackles), DB Josh Wilson (5 pass breakups), and DE Trey Covington, who made INT to snuff Canes' last series.

Georgia 37 AUBURN 15: In O coma for several weeks, especially in deflating losses to Vanderbilt and Kentucky, Bulldogs (7-4) exploded for 446y to 171y for no. 5 Auburn (9-2). Actually it was big-play D that played major role in Georgia piling up stunning 30-7 H advantage. Georgia D sacked Tigers QB Brandon Cox (4-12/35y, TD, 4 INTs) 4 times/-19y, and S Tra Battle picked off 3 passes including 30y TD RET that upped lead to 24-0 5 mins before H. Bulldogs frosh QB Matthew Stafford (14-20/219y), who tossed 14y TD pass to TB Kregg Lumpkin (21/105y, TD) to close 1st H, continually surprised Auburn with runs up middle, especially his waltz to 9y TD early in 4th Q. It snuffed Tigers' mini-rally that had pulled them to 30-15 late in 3rd Q: Auburn's Cox had followed WR Courtney Taylor's 31y E-around run with 34y TD to WR Rod Smith.

FLORIDA 17 South Carolina 16: While several other big-time, 1-loss contenders were splashed on this Saturday, Florida (9-1) escaped defeat in The Swamp by forcing South Carolina (5-5) K Ryan Succop to swim at his own risk. Gators DE Jarvis Moss used his 6'6" height to block Succop's last-play, 48y FG try, while earlier in 4th Q Moss' x-pt block kept Gamecocks from jumping to 17-10 lead with 8:13 left. Alternating QBs—Chris Leak (19-27/254y, TD, INT) and Tim Tebow (5/29y rushing)—sparked Gators to decisive drive to 17-16 lead with 3:03 on clock. Tebow converted 4th-and-1 run in Florida territory, Leak dashed 17 and 8y soon thereafter, and big Tebow roared 12y for TD that led to K Chris Hetland's winning kick. RB Mike Davis (16/94y) provided Carolina's only score 1st Q on 4y run, and he dashed for 14y TD in 4th Q that had appeared to place Gamecocks in driver's seat at 16-10, almost 17-10.

ARKANSAS 31 Tennessee 14: Dandy-looking Hogs (9-1) won 9th game in row as do-everything TB Darren McFadden rushed 30/181y, 2 TDs and threw 2nd Q 12y TD pass to WR Marcus Monk (8/137y, 2 TDs) on 3rd straight play of taking direct snap after runs of 9 and 10y. It provided 21-7 lead, and next time Arkansas got ball, McFadden scored his 2nd TD on 5y run for 28-7 H edge. Tennessee (7-3) had trimmed its deficit to 14-7 5 mins into 2nd Q as frosh QB Jonathan Crompton (16-34/174y, 2 TDs, INT), starting for injured QB Erik Ainge, sparked nation's 12th-best pass O. Crompton hit 11, 19, and 27y passes on 80y drive culminating in his TD to WR Robert Meachem (4/65y). But, Razorbacks sacked Crompton 4 times—3 by DE Jamaal Anderson—and made 10 tackles for losses. Arkansas soph QB Casey Dick chipped in with 10-15/154y, TD passing as he started his 2nd game in relief of frosh QB Mitch Mustain.

Wisconsin 24 IOWA 21: No. 16 Wisconsin (10-1) was perceived to have played soft schedule and was getting little credit for its fine record. It ended weekend at no. 12 in AP Poll, 2nd-lowest spot among 1-loss teams. On plus-side, Bret Bielema became 1st Big 10 coach ever to log 10 wins in his rookie season, getting win even though his Badgers had to go with backup QB Tyler Donovan (17-24/228y, 2 TDs). Iowa's once-promising season took another hit as Hawks dropped their 4th conf tilt in row. Still, Hawkeyes (6-5) were in position to spring upset, taking 14-10 lead on pair of TD passes by QB Drew Tate (10-31/170y, 3 TDs, INT) in 2nd Q and pulling within 24-21 with 10 mins to play. "I thought we came to life today…but we didn't get over the hump," said Iowa coach Kirk Ferentz. Hump that Iowa did stop was Big 10 rushing leader, TB P.J. Hill, who gained only 77y on 28 tries. However, Donovan rushed for 61y. He scrambled for pair of 1st downs on 73y drive that ended with his hitting WR Luke Swan for 42y TD that put Badgers ahead 17-14 in last 39 secs of 1st H. Hill scored early in 4th Q for 24-14 Wisconsin lead. Iowa got 2 opportunities to pull it out at end, but last bid died at it 35YL when wiry frosh WR Dominique Douglas dropped 4th down pass.

KANSAS STATE 45 Texas 42: Stream of purple-clad Kansas State (7-4) fans stormed field at end of tremendous upset of no. 4 Texas (9-2). Longhorns, looking to move up after West Virginia's Thursday loss, went ahead on 80y TD drive after opening KO on 1y sneak by QB Colt McCoy (4-4/51y). But, McCoy injured his throwing shoulder at bottom of GL pileup and had to be relieved by callow, fellow-frosh QB Jevan Snead (13-30/190y, TD). Snead trotted into what turned out to be big shootout. K-State got pair of TD passes from another frosh QB, Josh Freeman (19-31/269y, 3 TDs, INT), to lead 21-14 at H. On 1st series of 3rd Q, Steers S Michael Griffin blocked punt—2nd disastrous misadventure for K-State P Tim Reyer—and TB Selvin Young scored 5y TD on next play to tie it 21-21. However, Young and TB Jamaal Charles (16/87y, 2 TDs) would each lose 3rd Q FUM to DE Ian Campbell, and each would lead to TD by Wildcats, who scored 3 times in 3rd Q. Trailing 42-28 early in 4th Q, Snead whipped 33y TD to WR Limas Sweed 1 plays after Griffin's 12y INT RET set Texas up in K-State territory. Cats K Jeff Snodgrass bombed through 51y FG with 3:19 left to provide cushion against Longhorns' 84y TD drive that ended with 1:56 to play. K-State WR Jordy Nelson recovered Texas' onside-KO and caught clinching 6y pass for 1st down.

Nebraska 28 TEXAS A&M 27: With 21 secs left to play, QB Zac Taylor (21-35/267y, 2 TDs, INT) lofted 9y TD pass to left side of EZ that WR Maurice Purify soared over defender to catch, and Nebraska (8-3) clinched Big 12 North title. Huskers had gotten off to comfortable 21-7 lead as had been their mode in conf games all season: Cody Glenn, 1 of squadron of Nebraska IBs, had scored at end of 66 and 52y TD drives, and WR Todd Peterson had caught short pass from Taylor to build 2-TD lead in opening 19 mins. Texas A&M (8-3) rallied for 20 unanswered pts, starting with K Layne Neumann's 1st of 2 FGs from 37y with 16 secs left in 2nd Q. Aggies limited Huskers to 5 1st downs in 2nd H until Nebraska's late drive. A&M got 4th Q TDs by QB Stephen McGee (18-31/244y) on 57y run and TB Jorvorskie Lane on 1y smash for 27-21 lead with 7:28 left.

Aggies seemed to have clinched it on next series when LB Mark Dodge (17 tackles) made 16y INT RET to Huskers 29YL with 2:50 to play. But, Nebraska DE Barry Turner launched crowning 75y drive with clutch block of Neumann's FG attempt.

SOUTHERN CALIFORNIA 35 Oregon 10: Winning their 31st straight game at LA Coliseum, Trojans (8-1) marched back into national title hunt, thanks to cluster of weekend upsets. Oregon (7-3) arrived with 36.3 scoring avg, but use of 2 QBs—Dennis Dixon (15-23/130y, INT) and Brady Leaf (13-22/104y, TD)—couldn't get its O moving. Ducks failed on Dixon's 4th down run at USC 13YL on game's opening 17-play, 72y sequence and lost INT to Troy S Taylor Mays and FUM to S Dallas Sartz deep in own territory to set up pair of TD runs by Southern California TB Chauncey Washington (15/119y, 3 TDs) in 2nd and 3rd Qs. Trailing 28-3, Oregon went 80y to Leaf's 7y TD pass to RB Jonathan Stewart (14/42y) early in 4th Q. Play was endlessly reviewed, overturned, but finally called as TD. USC QB John David Booty passed 16-25/176y, TD, INT, while DE Lawrence Jackson was dazzling with 3 sacks.

Stanford 20 WASHINGTON 3: Washington's once-promising 4-1 beginning of year had disintegrated in outbreak of injuries. Huskies (4-7) lost their 6th straight, this to winless Stanford (1-9) that hadn't tallied O TD since October 7. Washington, seeking to win last 2 games for bowl-eligibility, scored early in 2nd Q on K Michael Braunstein's 28y FG for 3-0 lead but would gain only 17y until latter half of 4th Q. Cardinal D, ranked 113th in nation, permitted only 161y. UW gained only 97y after 1st Q when QB Carl Bonnell (10-25/118y, INT) had to leave for extended period. Stanford took lead for good in 3rd Q when Huskies sub QB Johnny DuRocher (1-9/4y, 2 INTs) overshot short receiver, and Cards S Bo McNally took INT 49y to TD. Early in 4th Q, WR Richard Sherman (6/177y) took jailbreak-screen pass from QB T.C. Ostrander (111-20/206y, TD) for 74y, untouched romp to Stanford TD to lock up win.

ARIZONA 24 California 20: In ruining national title hopes of Golden Bears (8-2), Arizona (5-5) rallied from 17-3 H deficit to stoke its unusual November record of having won 4 times over ranked foes in last 3 years. California WR DeSean Jackson fielded line-drive punt in 1st Q and raced 95y to TD, later hauled 2nd Q pass from QB Nate Longshore (17-36/250y, TD, 3 INTs) 62y for score. Wildcats WR Mike Thomas barely tiptoed in-bounds on 39y pass to Cal 5YL in 3rd Q to set up TB Chris Henry (25/57y) for 1st of 2 TD runs. Fate allowed Henry's 2nd TD in 3rd Q as Arizona QB Willie Tuitama (17-34/202y) twice threw INTs on 50y drive, but saw each nullified by Bears' PEN. Moments later, Cats CB Antoine Cason stepped in front of telegraphed flat pass and returned it 39y for TD and sudden lead for Arizona at 24-17. Longshore quickly hit wide open WR Lavelle Hawkins, who had easy path to TD except that he stumbled in making pass catch. In heroic effort to keep his footing, Hawkins finally tumbled at UA 1YL. Cal RB Marshawn Lynch (16/102y) was stuffed twice for losses, and when 3rd down pass was broken up by LB Dane Krogstad, Bears had to settle for FG. With 2:14 to play, California had last gasp: Jackson appeared to have scored on 63y pass catch-and-run along left sideline, but TV replay showed he stepped OB at Cats 41YL. Tipped pass landed in hands of Arizona LB Ronnie Palmer to end it 4 plays later.

USA Today Coaches Novenver 12

1	Ohio State (62)	1574	14	Wake Forest	724
2	Michigan (1)	1513	15	Auburn	721
3	Florida	1381	16	Oklahoma	711
4	Southern California	1373	17	California	580
5	Notre Dame	1273	18	Georgia Tech	566
6	Arkansas	1248	19	Virginia Tech	420
7	West Virginia	1113	20	Boston College	384
8	Rutgers	1082	21	Maryland	325
9	LSU	1054	22	Nebraska	228
10	Wisconsin	928	23	Tennessee	213
11	Texas	927	24	Brigham Young	116
12	Louisville	884	25	Clemson	94
13	Boise State	830			

Bowl Championship Series Ranking November 12

	Harris Poll Pct.	*USA Today* Poll Pct.	Computer Pct.	BCS Avg.
1 Ohio State (11-0)	1.000	.999	.930	.9765
2 Michigan (11-0)	.960	.961	1.000	.9735
3 Southern California (8-1)	.878	.872	.860	.8699
4 Florida (9-1)	.872	.877	.800	.8495
5 Notre Dame (9-1)	.810	.808	.840	.8193

November 18, 2006

(Th) West Virginia 45 PITTSBURGH 27: With Panthers (6-5) bottling up early runs of nation's 2nd-leading rusher RB Steve Slaton—except for his quick 15y TD burst up middle in 1st Q—West Virginia (9-1) QB Pat White (11-16/204y, 2 TDs) lofted perfect passes instead. White tossed 11y TD to Slaton (6/130y, 2 TDs receiving), for 14-7 lead on last play of 1st Q. Meanwhile, Pitt battled hard with QB Tyler Palko (28-37/341y) throwing 1st H scoring passes to high-jumping TE Nate Byham and EZ sideline-toeing WR Oderick Turner. Panthers seemed to grab late 2nd Q momentum, going ahead 24-17 on brilliant 73y punt TD RET by DB Darrelle Revis. Feinting and bobbing right to get outside hashmark, Revis set up crushing block by WR Derek Kinder that eliminated 2 Mountaineers. Revis broke tackles and spun down sideline for TD. Pitt would have been more comfortable had White and Slaton not whipped up tying 67y aerial TD collaboration right after Revis' TD RET, but Panthers still led 27-24 at H on late FG. Vaunted WVU ground attack made only 67y in 1st H with Slaton being held to 6/7y. Mountaineers returned to normalcy in 2nd H, rushing for 371y as Slaton (23/215y, 2 TDs), who roared to 55y TD, and White (22/220y, 2 TDs) became only 3rd pair of college teammates ever to surpass 200y rushing each in single game. Slaton became 1st Mountaineer to exceed 100y as both runner and receiver in single game.

CINCINNATI 30 Rutgers 11: This game appeared to be classic opportunity for Scarlet Knights (9-1) to employ coach Greg Schiano's "Keep Chopping" philosophy. Instead, Rutgers' inexperience was costly in "sandwich game" between meetings with Big East heavyweights Louisville and West Virginia. Dangerous Cincinnati (6-5), which had lost 4 times this year to Top 10 teams on road, enjoyed home advantage to go ahead 10-0 in 2nd Q as backup QB Nick Davila (11-15/277y, TD) celebrated his 1st start with short TD run. Bearcats D stacked line of scrimmage to successfully stop Knights star TB Ray Rice, who rushed only 18/54y and scored late, superfluous TD. Forced to carry Rutgers' O, QB Mike Teel (21-42/238y) was intercepted 4 times, including CB De-Angelo Smith's RET of Teel's weak sideline pass for 74y TD in 2nd Q for 17-0 lead.

BOSTON COLLEGE 38 Maryland 16: Needing to win and get help in Atlantic Division, Eagles (8-2) jumped all over Maryland (8-3) early. Before Boston College O even stepped on field, Eagles LB Jolonn Dunbar returned pair of FUMs for 14 and 38y TDs off bobbled Terps pitchouts. BC's O was less than overwhelming for awhile; perhaps it lost its edge after 8 mins of inactivity at game's start. Still, Eagles QB Matt Ryan (19-29/249y) threw pair of 2nd Q TD passes that launched 28-6 H edge. Maryland passing game suffered some weak moments as 3 passes were dropped in EZ and pair of WRs went out with injuries. Terps QB Sam Hollenbach (27-42/249y, 2 INTs) overthrew receiver in 3rd Q, and Eagles DB DeJuan Tribble made INT and went up right sideline for 42y TD and insurmountable 35-9 advantage.

Virginia Tech 27 WAKE FOREST 6: Boston College's help arrived in form of devastating D performance by Virginia Tech (9-2), which gave up 257y—only 62y rushing—on way to its 4th win in row. By virtue of its defeat, Wake Forest (9-2) fell into divisional tie with Maryland, next foe due on its schedule. Hokies QB Sean Glennon (14-21/252y) threw 2 long TD passes, including miraculous play by WR Josh Morgan. Morgan out-jumped 2 Deacons at sideline, spurted through 2 tacklers for 53y score. Most damaging blow to Deacons probably came when RB Kevin Harris fumbled when crushed on tackle by Tech S Aaron Rouse. After slight delay wondering whether whistle had blown, LB Xavier Adibi took FUM 35y for TD for 24-6 lead late in 3rd Q.

Auburn 22 ALABAMA 15: Auburn (10-2) sr CB David Irons happily said of his game-clinching INT with 1:17 to play: "My last name is Irons, and this is the Iron Bowl. I'll have that forever." Crimson Tide (6-6) lost its 5th straight to rival Tigers for 1st time since 1958, legendary coach Bear Bryant's 1st year at Tuscaloosa. After making 1st-and-goal at 3YL on early 74y drive, frustrated Alabama had to accept 3-0 lead on K Jamie Christensen's short 1st Q FG. After DE Quinton Groves made 2 clutch sacks that forced FUMs, Auburn struck for short-drive TDs on runs by sub TB Brad Lester and starting TB Kenny Irons (19/85y). Tide QB John Parker Wilson (18-33/252, 2 TDs, INT) hit wide open WR Nikita Stover for 52y TD on deep pass 1:23 before H. But, 2-pt pass failed, and Bama trailed 14-9 at H. Auburn QB Brandon Cox passed only 6-14/137y, but threw for 97y in 3rd Q. His 22y TD pass to WR Prechae Rodriguez propped up Auburn at 22-15 after Tide had taken 15-14 lead on Wilson's 2nd TD pass in middle of 3rd Q. With 5 mins to play, Wilson missed EZ pass on 4th down from 18YL, and on next series, he threw pass over middle that turned into Irons' crushing INT.

LOUISIANA STATE 23 Mississippi 20 (OT): For 1st time in history, LSU (9-2) completed 8-0 home slate, but Mississippi (3-8) overcame 7-0 deficit to dominate 1st H at 14-7. Ole Miss D held Louisiana State (9-2) to 97y in 1st H as Tigers damaged their attack by committing 55y PENs. QB Brent Schaeffer (6-14/72y) hit 22y TD in 2nd Q but passed sparingly as Rebs ran ball well in 1st H. K Joshua Shene booted pair of long FGs to build Rebels' edge to 20-7 entering 4th Q. Clutch QB JaMarcus Russell (20-36/223y, 3 TDs) led LSU to 59 and 58y drives and each time he hit short TD passes to WRs Early Doucet and Dwayne Bowe (7/64y, 2 TDs). Latter pass came with 14 secs to go, but Tigers K Colt David, who had made his 77th straight x-pt after Doucet's TD, had to face Ole Miss wild card sub. Rebs coach sent in 6'5" OL John Jerry, and Jerry dramatically blocked David's potential winning kick. Mississippi opened OT, but Schaeffer, forced into 3rd down pass, was blitzed into FUM by Tigers S Daniel Francis. On its OT try, LSU called on TB Jacob Hester for 5 runs to set up David's winning FG.

Arkansas 28 MISSISSIPPI STATE 14: SEC road games had been tough all year, and cellar-dwelling Mississippi State (3-8) proved to be difficult before Arkansas (10-1) won its 10th in row to clinch SEC West title. Hogs made big plays at right time: CB Chris Houston raced 87y for INT TD RET late in 1st Q, and, after Bulldogs frosh RB Anthony Dixon (17/89y) made his only big run of day for 65y TD, Razorbacks TB Darren McFadden surged 92y up crease on left side for KO TD RET. Mississippi State tied it at 14-14 on 22y TD pass by QB Mike Henig (9-25/123y, TD, INT) midway in 2nd Q. Again, Razorbacks responded, taking 21-14 edge to H on 29y TD pass to frosh WR Damian Williams by recently-tapped starting QB Casey Dick (8-17/112y, 2 TDs, INT).

GAME OF THE YEAR
OHIO STATE 42 Michigan 39:

Starting fast and trying to play with pride for former coach Bo Schembechler who died on Friday, Michigan (11-1) soared downfield on 3 catches by WR Mario Manningham to 1y TD dance to outside by TB Mike Hart (23/142y, 3 TDs). Ohio State (12-0) looked to star QB Troy Smith (29-41/316y, 4 TDs, INT), who immediately rallied Buckeyes for short, tying TD pass to WR Roy Hall and, in magnificent 1st H, added 2 more TD throws to WRs Ted Ginn and Anthony Gonzalez. Ohio led 28-14 at H. Wolverines made excellent H adjustments, gambling to put more pass pressure on Smith. For all of Smith's brilliant early throwing (21-26/241y, 3 TDs in 1st H), what hurt Michigan most were 2 long TD dashes up middle that caught S spots unprotected when middle DBs snuck up to scrimmage line: Frosh TB Chris Wells spun away from possible loss to go 52y to TD that put Ohio State ahead for good at 14-7 in 2nd Q. Later and just when Michigan appeared to gain control in 3rd Q with 10 pts to edge within 28-24, Buckeyes TB Antonio Pittman (18/139y) quickly broke away for 56y TD burst. These long-distance sprints came against D that had permitted only 329y rushing all year. Still, Wolverines fought back as giant DT Alan Branch followed his deflected INT in

early 3rd Q with FUM REC off bad Shotgun snap by Ohio C Doug Datish. Starting at Bucks 9YL, Michigan sent Hart over from 1YL for his 3rd TD 19 secs into 4th Q. Michigan gained another bad snap FUM, but had to punt. On Ohio State's next series, Wolverines appeared to make stop at their 38YL, but LB Shawn Crable made helmet-to-helmet hit at sideline on Smith as QB's 3rd down pass flew incomplete. With new life, Smith hit WR Brian Robiskie for 9 and 13y passes, latter for TD and 42-31 lead. Michigan QB Chad Henne (21-35/267y, 2 TDs) found TE Tyler Ecker for TD with 2:16 to play, but verdict soon was over as on-side KO failed. Michigan downplayed playing in Schembechler's memory. In no way did UM make excuses or did they reveal type of cleats worn, but Ohio Stadium's recently replaced grass surface sent many Wolverines slipping at wrong moment. Michigan's loss ended unbeaten season, 10th time in series that either Michigan or Ohio State had such season-long perfection ruined by its rival.

SOUTHERN CALIFORNIA 23 California 9: Hard-hitting 1st H had many missed chances and had California (8-3) in front 9-6. Each team lost 1st H TD: Procedure PEN doomed TD pass by Trojans (9-1) QB John David Booty (18-31/238y, 2 TDs), and replay ruling on USC WR Dwayne Jarrett's dropped catch scrubbed long FUM TD RET by Bears LB Mickey Pimentel. Long, punt-like INT thrown by Cal QB Nate Longshore (17-38/176y, TD, 2 INTs) to Southern California 3YL turned into safety when Bears DT Brandon Mebane nailed Troy TB C.J. Gable (19/91y) in EZ. Longshore clicked on 2 long passes before firing 6y TD to WR Lavelle Hawkins. Both teams' O snoozed through 3rd Q until Troy K David Buehler booted 49y FG through LA Coliseum fog to tie it 9-9. Jarrett and other Southern California WRs had been kept fairly quiet until early 4th Q when Jarrett made great catch of 25y TD just instant before being slammed by S Bernard Hicks. On 4th-and-2 in middle of 4th Q, Booty found WR Steve Smith all alone for 37y TD that put USC up 23-9. USC moved to 19-0 record in 6 Novembers under coach Pete Carroll.

Arizona 37 OREGON 10: Miraculous 3-win revival at Arizona (6-5) continued as it flourished in tough Autzen Stadium where Wildcats hadn't won in 20 years. TOs ruled outcome as they do so often. Wildcats fell behind 3-0 on K Paul Martinez's 27y FG at end of Ducks' 1st series, but Oregon (7-4) soon fumbled away 1st of 2 punt RETs it lost. On next play after REC by LB Spencer Larsen, Arizona TB Chris Henry (23/191y, 2 TDs) ducked outside for 15y TD run for 7-3 lead, 1st score of 5 that would follow Duck TOs. Oregon QB Dennis Dixon (14-22/88y) was intercepted 3 times and gave way in 4th Q to QB Brady Leaf (11-22/95y), who was intercepted by Larsen on his 2nd pass try upon his entrance. Arizona lost 2 of its O stalwarts to injury in 1st H in QB Willie Tuitama (8-9/120y, 2 TDs) and WR Syndric Steptoe. But, enjoying 24-10 H lead allowed Wildcats to not force their reentry.

USA Today Coaches Novemver 19

1	Ohio State (63)	1575	14	Oklahoma	795
2	Southern California	1444	15	Georgia Tech	655
3	Michigan	1428	16	Rutgers	641
4	Florida	1407	17	Virginia Tech	561
5	Arkansas	1302	18	Boston College	540
6	Notre Dame	1285	19	Nebraska	353
7	West Virginia	1151	20	Wake Forest	343
8	LSU	1081	21	Tennessee	326
9	Wisconsin	1053	22	California	265
10	Texas	994	23	Brigham Young	256
11	Louisville	944	24	Clemson	174
12	Boise State	862	25	Hawaii	97
13	Auburn	825			

Bowl Championship Series Ranking November 19

	Harris Poll Pct.	*USA Today* Poll Pct.	Computer Pct.	BCS Avg.
1 Ohio State (12-0)	1.000	1.000	1.000	1.0000
2 Michigan (11-1)	.912	.907	.960	.9263
3 Southern California (9-1)	.920	.917	.920	.9188
4 Florida (11-1)	.888	.893	.870	.8838
5 Notre Dame (10-1)	.824	.816	.820	.8198

November 23-25, 2006

(Th'g) MIAMI 17 Boston College 14: Before decidedly small turnout (23,308 in Orange Bowl represented smallest crowd since 1999) on Thanksgiving night, soon-to-be-fired coach Larry Coker led his last Miami (6-6) home game. His D came up with fantastic effort, holding Boston College (9-3) to 193y—24y rushing—and allowed single O TD by TB Andre Callender in 1st Q. Eagles' loss dashed their hopes of snatching ACC crown, but DB DeJuan Tribble was heroic with 3 INTs. Tribble was quick in stepping in front of Miami receiver in right flat in 2nd Q to snatch INT that he returned for 22y TD and 14-3 lead with 1:36 before H. Hurricanes quickly came up with big play they had needed for weeks: 49y pass from QB Kirby Freeman (13-26/181y, TD, 3 INTs) to WR Ryan Moore to set up 7y TD toss in EZ corner to WR Lance Leggett 10 secs before H. Miami went ahead in 3rd Q as TB Javarris James (20/45y) scored winning TD.

(Fri) Louisiana State 31 ARKANSAS 26: By game's end, it was LSU (10-2) cheering section not that of Arkansas that was screaming, "B-C-S!" Having little to play for, other than slender chance for BCS title game, SEC West champ Arkansas (10-2) showed up with gruesome aerial game. QB Casey Dick passed 3-17/29y, INT, although he managed 21y scoring pass to WR Marcus Monk to pull within 14-12 in middle of 2nd Q. Dick's INT was very costly as Tigers DB LaRon Landry's RET went 23y to 9YL to set up early 4th Q TD catch by WR Early Doucet from QB JaMarcus Russell (14-22/210y, 2 TDs). Hogs received another great effort from TB Darren McFadden (21/182y, 2 TDs), who bolted 80y for TD right after Doucet's 4th Q TD. No sooner had McFadden gotten Razorbacks back into it at 24-19, than LSU frosh TB Trindon Holliday raced to 92y TD with ensuing KO, game's 3rd TD in 45-sec span.

(Fri) NEBRASKA 37 Colorado 14: Nebraska (9-3) already owned spot in Big 12 title match, and Colorado (2-10) was out to enhance its continued improvement since September. Cornhuskers led at H by 14-7 while each team displayed effective D: Buffs permitted 156y, Huskers 101y in 1st 30 mins. DE Barry Turner played interesting special-teams role for Nebraska: Turner caught 29y TD pass from holder-QB Joe Ganz off 2nd Q fake FG that supplied 14-7 lead, and Turner downed punt at 1YL early in 4th Q. Colorado's next play resulted in safety as RB Mell Holliday was tackled in EZ by Nebraska DE Adam Carriker and LB Corey McKeon for Huskers' 23-14 edge. Holliday had rambled 45y for tying TD at 14-14 early in 3rd Q after LB Thad Washington (8 tackles) returned FUM 10y to own 29YL. QB Zac Taylor (119-28/249y, 2 TDs) tied Tommie Frazier for most career TD passes at Nebraska with 43, and IB Brandon Jackson rushed 34/142y, TD. Buffs LB Jordan Dizon made 17 stops, 2 for losses.

(Fri) Texas A&M 12 TEXAS 7: Season's Cardiac Kids, Texas A&M (9-3), played to game's last moment for 9th time in 2006 and came out on top thanks to jolting D and opportunistic O. Aggies jumped ahead 6-0 in 1st Q as frosh TB Mike Goodson (15/86y) exploded off right side and pulled away for 41y TD run. Unfortunately, A&M K Layne Neumann badly hooked x-pt, and it stayed at 6-0 until deep into 3rd Q. Texas (9-3) O took most of afternoon to get into gear and it's most disappointing moment came late in 2nd Q as A&M S Melvin Bullitt made INT at Aggies 1YL. Texas finally scored on RB Jamaal Charles' 6y run, and K Ryan Bailey converted for 7-6 lead with 4:20 left in 3rd Q. After exchange of punts, Texas A&M masterfully used option runs to travel 88y, eat nearly 9 mins off clock, and score on QB Stephen McGee's 8y run. Although 2-pt conv run failed, A&M led 12-7 with 2:32 left. Longhorns QB Colt McCoy (17-28/160y, 3 INTs) had arrived somewhat banged up from previous game when sneak against Kansas State left him with bad throwing shoulder. McCoy had several moments of erratic throwing, and problem rose to surface again at clutch moment. He underthrew INT picked off by Aggies LB Mark Dodge, then in last few secs was carted off with pinched nerve in previously-injured right shoulder. Texas' loss threw open Big 12 South conf title game berth.

(Fri) OREGON STATE 30 Oregon 28: With constant rain pouring down, Beavers (9-3) K Alexis Serna powered 40y FG through uprights with 1:12 remaining. When Oregon (7-5) K Matt Evensen tried 44y FG with 20 secs left, DT Ben Siegert rose up to knock it down so Oregon State came out winner, 10th straight time home team had won annual Civil War contest. It was Beavers' 6th win in their last 7 games since rough September. QB Brady Leaf (25-42/274y, TD, INT) made his 1st start for Ducks, and was intercepted by LB Derrick Doggett, who returned it 34y for TD that put Beavers ahead 17-7 in 2nd Q. In last min before H, Serna barely had enough to make 50y FG, which followed his 49y 3-ptr earlier in 2nd Q. Ducks RB Jonathan Stewart (17/94y) scored his 3rd running TD with 6 mins to play, and Oregon trailed 27-20 after K Paul Martinez's x-pt was blocked. After Ducks D forced 3-and-out, Leaf led 57y drive to his 26y TD pass to WR Jordan Kent, which he followed with 2-pt keeper for Ducks' 1st but short-lived lead.

South Florida 24 WEST VIRGINIA 19: Uncommon rash of TOs killed any chance West Virginia (9-2) would make BCS bowl. Mountaineers O had been among nation's most efficient all year with 41-pt avg and TDs on 77 percent of red zone possessions, but turned it over 4 times and on its 1st 3 series lost ball on downs at South Florida (8-4) 3YL and had to settle for 2 FGs by K Pat McAfee. Associated Press wrote WVU "looked listless." Bulls weren't any better early on: their 1st 4 possessions were halted by INTs and sacks. Trailing 6-0 midway in 2nd Q, USF LB Chris Robinson slammed Mountaineers QB Pat White (14-22/178y, 2 TDs, 2 INTs) on pass attempt, and DE George Selvie scooped up FUM and stepped into EZ for 9y TD RET. Bulls QB Matt Grothe (22-30/270y, TD, 2 INTs) completed 66y drive in last min of 1st H with 10y TD run for 14-6 lead. With his 330y run O stymied, White went to air for 1st of 2 TD passes to WR Brandon Myles in middle of 3rd Q, but 2-pt pass failed. USF answered with 70y trip to Grothe's 21y TD pass to WR Ean Randolph for 21-12 edge. Myles' 2nd TD catch (44y) came with 5 mins to play to pull Mountaineers within 5 pts, but White was intercepted on WVU's last chance.

Wake Forest 38 MARYLAND 24: With other ACC Atlantic suitors dropping by wayside, outcome decided championship between pair tabbed for bottom of division at season's start. Wake Forest (10-2) O gained 421y and had answer every time Maryland (8-4) came up with timely score. Terrapins stormed 70y downfield following opening KO with RB Keon Lattimore (23/119y) toting it 12y for TD. Deacons came right back with 69y drive as RB Kevin Harris scored 1st of his 2 TDs. INT RET by Wake CB Riley Swanson reached Maryland 16YL, but normally-efficient QB Riley Skinner (10-13/125y, TD) threw his only road-game INT of season, which Terps CB Isaiah Gardner imprudently ran out of his EZ only to 4YL. Short punt followed, and Wake quickly took lead for good on 19y TD run by RB Kenneth Moore (27/165y) early in 2nd Q. Maryland QB Sam Hollenbach (14-26/182y, TD, 3 INTs) was picked off on next 2 series, leading to Skinner's 49y TD pass to WR Willie Idlette. Deacons led 21-14 at H, and went 80y to Harris' TD to open 2nd H. Terrapins scored on K Dan Ennis' 3rd Q FG and Hollenbach's short 4th Q TD pass to WR Isaiah Williams, but Wake answered in kind each time. Deacons' win promoted them to 1st ACC team ever to go 6-0 on road.

South Carolina 31 CLEMSON 28: Sack by South Carolina LB Jasper Brinkley of Clemson (8-4) QB Will Proctor (13-19/191y, TD, INT) forced K Jad Dean into 39y FG try on last play. Palmetto State thriller was decided when Dean hooked it left. Clemson had led 21-14 at H thanks to 2 big plays: TB C.J. Spiller (10/155y) blazed to 80y score, and stampeding DT Jock McKissic went 82y with INT thrown by Gamecocks (7-5) QB Blake Mitchell (23-36/268y, 3 INTs) in last 8 secs of 2nd Q. After Tigers stopped 4th-and-2 play at Carolina 39YL early in 3rd Q, Spiller scored on 31y run for imposing 28-14 lead. Mitchell quickly turned around Gamecocks with his sharp passing: he hit 3-3/45y leading to 1y TD by RB Mike Davis (12/69y). After FUM REC by Cocks DE Jordin Lindsey at Tigers 34YL, Davis scored again in 3rd Q by soaring over 3 Clemson tacklers to tie it. Carolina survived mid-4th Q replay review—Mitchell's lateral throw was ruled incomplete pass rather than lost FUM—and 3 plays later K Ryan Succop made 35y FG for Carolina's 1st lead of game and ultimate winning

pts. Coach Steve Spurrier recognized Gamecocks fans had suffered during Tigers' 4 straight series wins, saying, "Hopefully, whatever bad things happened to South Carolina football may be erased today. Sometimes a game like this can do it."

GEORGIA 15 Georgia Tech 12: Riding its suffocating D but enduring its weak O, Georgia Tech (9-3) seemed so close to ending its frustration against rival Georgia (8-4). Having not defeated Bulldogs since 2000, Yellow Jackets this time had led 3-0 on 1st of 2 FGs by K Travis Bell and permitted only 156y O well into 3rd Q. That margin held up until strange FUM by sr QB Reggie Ball (6-22/42y, 2 INTs), who always seemed to save his worst for Georgia. Scrum for loose ball at Jackets 29YL—knocked from Ball as he scrambled on 3rd-and-15—appeared to be over as officials converged to un-pile players. But, no whistle had blown, and Georgia LB Tony Taylor kept yanking at back of pile until he dislodged ball. Taylor raced for TD with no one in pursuit. Bulldogs led 7-3, but Georgia Tech RB Jamaal Evans scooted 53y on following KO RET to Georgia 33YL. TB Tashard Choice (23/147y, TD) raced 25y to 4YL, but Tech had to settle for another FG to trail 7-6. Next time Jackets had ball, Choice ran for 39y on 56y drive to his 10y TD run. Ball's 2-pt run failed, so Tech led 12-7 with 8:50 to play. Georgia QB Matthew Stafford (16-29/171y, TD), who had been having tough time also, hit 4 passes on 64y drive to TD. WR Mohamed Massaquoi caught 4y TD and 2-pt conv from Stafford to grab victory for UGa. Georgia Tech hopes soon died on INT by Bulldogs CB Paul Oliver, who had done masterful coverage job on Jackets All-ACC WR Calvin Johnson (2/13y).

Florida 21 FLORIDA STATE 14: Oft-criticized sr Florida (11-1) QB Chris Leak (21-34/283y, 2 TDs) came through with 7-8/79y passing on game-winning drive early in 4th Q. Leak found WR Dallas Baker on 3rd down pass that carried 25y to Florida State (6-6) 26YL and, 2 plays later, hooked up again with Baker for 25y TD and 21-14 lead. In 1st Q, Gators WR Andre Caldwell (8/124y, TD) had raced 66y up right sideline to TD on short pass from Leak. Although versatile Florida RB-WR Percy Harvin was carted off with injury later, he had blazed to 41y TD on direct-snap in Shotgun TB position in 2nd Q. That provided 14-0 H edge. Seminoles fought back from 14-0 deficit, scoring on FB Joe Surratt's only carry of day: 1y smash in 3rd Q, right after TB Lorenzo Booker's 34y sprint. Early in 4th Q, Florida State QB Drew Weatherford (16-37/181y, 3 INTs) tied game at 14-14 by flipping 25y TD pass to WR Greg Carr, who soared over defenders near left edge of EZ. Seminoles nearly had immediate answer to Leak's 4th Q go-ahed TD pass with KO TD RET by DB Michael Ray Garvin. Replays showed Garvin barely touched right sideline at FSU 48YL on his apparent TD gallop. FSU failed on 4th down on each of its last 3 series.

Oklahoma 27 OKLAHOMA STATE 21: Sooners (10-2) survived against their Bedlam rivals to earn spot in Big 12 championship game. TB Allen Patrick rushed for 163y including 65y dash through right side of line on 1st play of 3rd Q. TD provided 20-7 lead for Oklahoma, which ran 47 times to only 11 passes. Only big pass by Sooners QB Paul Thompson (7-11/77y) was speared high in EZ by WR Juaquin Iglesias for 13y TD late in 2nd Q. Oklahoma State (6-6) QB Bobby Reid (8-12/82y, TD) scored 1y TD in 3rd Q and tossed short TD pass to WR D'Juan Woods (6/95y) in 4th Q but was in and out of lineup with banged up shoulder. In between, Oklahoma banged out 74y TD drive for 27-14 lead. Reid's replacement, QB Zac Robinson (8-17/149y), contributed some entertaining moments in 4th Q: Robinson was stacked up at GL on 4th down option run to left and fumbled into EZ. Whether FUM was purposeful or not, Sooners LB Demarrio Pleasant barely got it away from converging Cowboy. "That was the turning point of the game," declared Oklahoma DE C.J. Ah You. Later, after OU was forced into 3-and-out on its last 3 possessions, Robinson passed Cowboys to Sooners 25YL, but his last-play arrow for Woods was tad too high in back of EZ.

SOUTHERN CALIFORNIA 44 Notre Dame 24: Trojans (10-1) came out firing as QB John David Booty (17-28/265y, 3 TDs, 2 INTs) hit 6 of his 1st 7 passes. Southern California WR Dwayne Jarrett (7/132y, 3 TDs) made pair of TD grabs in EZ traffic, and Troy scored on its opening 3 series for 21-3 lead. Notre Dame (10-2) failed on 4th down attempt in USC territory on its 1st O opportunity, and its attack was stuck out of gear for awhile. But, ND QB Brady Quinn (22-45/274y, 3 TDs) found himself alone after dodging pass-rush and took off for 60y gain in 2nd Q. Although ND didn't score, it provided field position that led to blocked punt. TE Marcus Freeman soon caught 2y pass in last 2 mins of 1st H to rekindle Irish hopes at 21-10. Jarrett's brilliant 1-handed catch at right sideline set up TD on Trojans' opening possession of 3rd Q. After TB Chauncey Washington slammed across GL, USC was ahead 28-10. Inside last 2 mins of 3rd Q, Irish pulled within 28-17 on 4th down slant-in pass from Quinn to WR Rhema McKnight. Jarrett caught his 3rd TD midway in 4th Q, and USC scored on unusual 42y RET by LB Brian Cushing of Notre Dame's onside-KO after Irish had made it 37-24 on Quinn-to-WR Jeff Samardzija 2y TD pass with 3:39 left.

Brigham Young 33 UTAH 31: As clock hit 0:00, BYU (10-2) QB John Beck (28-43/375y, 4 TDs) seemed to scramble endlessly before he targeted TE Jonny Harline (7/118y, 3 TDs), who made EZ catch on his knees. Cougars had struck for TDs on each of their 1st 2 drives, and their 14-0 lead at end of 1st Q gave them unworldly 138-15 scoring edge in opening Qs during 2006. Utah (7-5), which lost to its in-state rival for 1st time since 2001, stormed back with trick plays to trigger 24 unanswered pts through end of 3rd Q: Utes P Louie Sakoda ran 18y on fake punt to set up DB Eric Widdle's entry at QB for 18y TD pass to WR Brent Casteel (5/100y, 2 TDs). With Utah ahead 24-14, it meant BYU trailed for 1st time in 34 Qs since September 16. After Beck and Harline collaborated on TD pass early in 4th Q, Beck and Utes QB Brett Ratliff (24-39/358y, 3 TDs) traded quick TD passes in 2-min span of last 3:23. Cougars negotiated 75y in 10 plays in last 1:19 for stunning victory.

USA Today Coaches Novemver 26

1	Ohio State (63)	1575	14	Virginia Tech	744
2	Southern California	1491	15	West Virginia	668
3	Michigan	1445	16	Wake Forest	607
4	Florida	1405	17	Texas	596
5	LSU	1255	18	Nebraska	523
6	Wisconsin	1221	19	Tennessee	434
7	Louisville	1169	20	California	343
8	Arkansas	1042	21	Brigham Young	339
9	Boise State	1018	22	Georgia Tech	259
10	Oklahoma	994	23	Hawaii	203
11	Auburn	985	24	Texas A&M	202
12	Notre Dame	928	25	Boston College	138
13	Rutgers	777			

Bowl Championship Series Ranking November 26

	Harris Poll Pct.	*USA Today* Poll Pct.	Computer Pct.	BCS Avg.
1 Ohio State (12-0)	1.000	1.000	1.000	1.0000
2 Southern California (10-1)	.951	.947	.940	.9460
3 Michigan (11-1)	.917	.918	.930	.9216
4 Florida (11-1)	.887	.892	.890	.8897
5 Louisiana State (10-2)	.805	.797	.830	.8106

December 2, 2006

Navy 26 Army 14: On game's opening series, Army (3-9) LB Barrett Scruggs stopped Midshipmen (9-3) FB Eric Kettani (15/67y)—who had to come in early for FB Adam Ballard, who broke his leg—on 4th-and-1 at Black Knights 32YL. Army WR Jeremy Trimble soon raced up sideline for 41y TD and 7-0 lead on deep reverse that nearly blew up in its backfield. Trimble's trip into EZ was aided by big downfield block by frosh QB Carson Williams (16-23/151y, TD, 2 INTs), who completed 2 passes on 5-play drive. Navy quickly came back to WB Reggie Campbell's 9y pitchout sweep for TD at end of 65y march. It stayed tied 7-7 until 6 mins into 3rd Q when Middies QB Kaipo-Noa Kaheaku-Enhada slipped up middle to convert 4th down before WB Jason Tomlinson took misdirection pitchout 33y for decisive TD and 14-7 edge. Army missed FG late in 3rd Q, and, after INT by S Jeff Deliz, Navy padded its lead to 17-7 in middle of 4th Q on 35y FG by K Matt Harmon. Then it fell apart for Black Knights as Navy DB Keenan Little ran back INT for 40y TD, and OLB Tyler Tidwell made pair of sacks, 2nd for safety and 26-7 lead.

WEST VIRGINIA 41 Rutgers 39 (OT): Big East battle waged deep into night as West Virginia (10-2) outlasted Rutgers (10-2) in 3 OTs. Failing to hold pair of difficult EZ catches in late going, Scarlet Knights lost opportunity to represent conf in BCS. Instead, Louisville, 48-17 winner over Connecticut much earlier in day, was tapped for Orange Bowl. Mountaineers star QB Pat White sat out with bad ankle, but his under-study, QB Jarrett Brown (14-29/244y, TD, INT), helmed O to 439y and chipped in with dazzling 40y TD run in 3rd Q that sent WVU to 20-10 lead. Knights frosh WR Tim Brown got loose for 72y TD catch from QB Mike Teel (19-26/278y) to shorten deficit to 20-17, and K Jeremy Ito hit 2 of his 4 FGs in 4th Q for 23-20 edge. WVU K Pat McAfee sent it to OT with 30y FG in last min of regulation. After trade of FGs and TD runs sent it to 3rd OT, Mountaineers WR Brandon Myles caught 22y TD over middle from QB Brown. Forced to try 2-pt play, WVU sent WR Dorrell Jalloh into EZ for catch in traffic and 41-33 edge. Rutgers RB Ray Rice was his usual outstanding self with 129y rushing, scoring TDs on game's opening drive for 7-0 lead and in 3rd OT to pull within 41-39. Rice got hand on Teel's 2-pt pass, but it was broken up by CB Vaughn Rivers.

Wake Forest 9 Georgia Tech 6 (Jacksonville): Football made inroads on hoop-crazed Tobacco Road: Wake Forest (11-2) showed video feed of ACC Championship Game to its campus auditorium prior to basketball game against Georgia. Indoor fans must have been happy because chilly rain fell in Jacksonville. Game was tied 3-3 at H as Georgia Tech (9-4) went 72y to K Travis Bell's 21y FG on game's 1st series, and Wake K Sam Swank matched it with 19y 3-ptr late in 2nd Q. LB Jon Abbate (15 tackles, sack) stopped Georgia Tech QB Reggie Ball (9-29/129y, 2 INTs) on 4th-and-1 run at 13YL early in 3rd Q. After Bell made 34y FG for Yellow Jackets' 6-3 lead, Deacons CB Riley Swanson made terrific tip-away INT from Tech's leaping ACC O Player-of-Year WR Calvin Johnson (8/117y). On subsequent 3rd-and-10, Wake TE John Tereshinski made 39y tight-rope run up right sideline to Tech 29YL, which led to Swank's tying 33y FG with 8:27 to play. Wake QB Riley Skinner (14-25/201y) launched 46y pass to WR Willie Idlette to Yellow Jackets 12YL with 5:15 left, and Swank made go-ahead 22y FG inside last 3 mins. On Jackets' next possession, Ball threw 2 incompletions and was sacked OB; Georgia Tech chose to punt with slightly more than 2 mins to play but never saw ball again. Victory secured Wake Forest's 1st conf title since 1970.

Florida 38 Arkansas 28 (Atlanta): SEC Championship Game offered BCS title shot if Gators (12-1) could defeat West champ Arkansas (10-3). Florida got off to fair start, scoring after 47y drive in 1st Q on K Chris Hetland's 33y FG, only his 4th success of 13 3-pt tries during season. It stayed 3-0 until last 9 mins of 2nd Q: Frosh WR Jarred Fayson blocked Hogs punt—Florida's new-record 9th blocked kick of season—and DB Tremaine McCollum recovered at Arkansas 9YL. Gators QB Chris Leak (16-30/189y, TD, 2 INTs) dove into EZ on 9y run to make it 10-0 and followed 4 mins later with 37y TD pass to WR Percy Harvin. Leak became Florida's all-time pass y leader on TD play. Razorbacks roared back before H: QB Casey Dick (10-22/148y, 2 INTs) pitched 48y scoring pass to WR Marcus Monk (3/69y). After INT by sub LB Weston Dacus, Arkansas started from Florida 32YL on its 1st shot in 2nd H. TB Darren McFadden (21/73y) tossed 2y TD pass to fellow-TB Felix Jones (13/57y). From this possession until Gators righted themselves with 4th Q flurry, Hogs outgained them 118y to 24y and returned INT by DE Antwain Robinson for 40y TD and 21-17 lead. Mistake by WR Reggie Fish late in 3rd Q sunk Arkansas: Trying to haul in punt over his shoulder inside 5YL, Fish bobbled catch, and Florida DB Wondy Pierre-Louis pounced on it in EZ for

TD. Gators' 24-21 lead was extended next time they saw ball as Harvin whipped away for 67y TD run. Hogs trimmed it to 3 pts again as Jones caught another TD pass, but Gators dusted off old WB pass out of simulated Single Wing: WR Andre Caldwell took handoff and swept right before tossing 5y TD pass to TE Tate Casey at end of 80y drive in middle of 4th Q.

Oklahoma 21 Nebraska 7 (Kansas City): On 1st scrimmage play of Big 12 Championship game, Nebraska (9-4) WR Maurice Purify caught pass at right sideline, and, in trying to shrug off tackler and stay in bounds at his 13YL, he briefly looked like 1-legged flamingo. Unfortunately, "Flamingo" Purify dropped ball, which was picked up by Oklahoma (11-2) S Reggie Smith, who scooted to 2YL. Smith's stunning FUM RET set up TD plunge by TB Allen Patrick (15/35y) only 48 secs into play. That was about last anyone saw of Sooners' run game—which totaled 42y on 28 carries—as QB Paul Thompson (19-34/265y, 2 TDs, INT) riddled Huskers' secondary all frigid night. Oklahoma's 2nd TD came later in 1st Q as WR Malcolm Kelly (10/142y, 2 TDs) hauled in Thompson's bomb in perfect stride for 66y TD and 14-0 edge. Nebraska had difficulty getting its receivers open, but scored in 2nd Q when QB Zac Taylor (23-50/282y, TD, 3 INTs) followed INT by Huskers S Andrew Shanle with 14y TD pass to back of EZ to TD specialist, TE Hunter Teafatiller. In 3rd Q, Huskers P Dan Titchener punted perfectly to within inches of OU GL, where DE Barry Turner downed it. Sooners had advanced nowhere in 2 downs, but Thompson faked handoff, dropped into EZ, and whipped 35y pass to frosh TE Jermaine Gresham. Thompson then smoothly hit 22, 9, 15, and 11y passes to 1st down at Nebraska 5YL. Kelly snared high toss 3 plays later for TD that was all Oklahoma would need. Huskers advanced past 50YL several times thereafter but lost it twice on downs and Taylor threw pair of INTs.

UCLA 13 Southern California 9: With BCS title game berth riding on outcome for determined no. 2 Southern California (10-2), Bruins (7-5), already inked in to Emerald Bowl, could play comfortably loose against their biggest rival. In 1st Q, UCLA went 91y in 12 plays to 1y TD run by QB Patrick Cowan (12-21/114y), who alertly picked up 55y on scrambles during sharp trip to paydirt. Magnificent back-spun and downed 46y punt by Trojans' P Greg Woidneck crammed Bruins within inches of their GL in 2nd Q. UCLA barely made it out of EZ on TB Chris Markey's 1st down run, so UCLA decided to pass. But, C Robert Chai was called for holding PEN in EZ against USC NG Sedrick Ellis. Resultant safety pulled Trojans within 7-2, and USC later moved 66y to 1y TD run by TB C.J. Gable for 9-7 lead at H. K Justin Medlock put Bruins ahead by single pt with 3rd Q FG. UCLA D-front, led by Es Bruce Davis and Justin Hickman, continued its ferocious pressure on USC QB John David Booty (23-39/274y, INT) and halted 4th down run early in 4th Q at Bruins 40YL. UCLA rambled to USC 2YL, but sack by LB Brian Cushing helped force Bruins to settle for Medlock's FG and 13-9 lead. With 4:31 to play, Trojans faced 4th-and-inches at own 39YL and made it on Booty's sneak. That kept alive drive on which Booty hit 6 passes until UCLA LB Eric McNeal jumped to deflect pass and twisted to make falling-down, upset-clinching INT at his own 20YL with 1:10 to play.

USA Today Coaches December 12

1	Ohio State (62)	1550	14	Virginia Tech	781
2	Florida	1470	15	Wake Forest	745
3	Michigan	1444	16	Texas	582
4	LSU	1299	17	Rutgers	567
5	Wisconsin	1263	18	Tennessee	500
6	Louisville	1223	19	California	436
7	Southern California	1173	20	Brigham Young	369
8	Oklahoma	1115	21	Texas A&M	303
9	Boise State	1053	22	Nebraska	242
10	Auburn	1000	23	Boston College	175
11	Notre Dame	923	24	TCU	95
12	West Virginia	800	25t	Oregon State	72
13	Arkansas	798	25t	Georgia Tech	72

Bowl Championship Series Ranking December 3

	Harris Poll Pct.	*USA Today* Poll Pct.	Computer Pct.	BCS Avg.
1 Ohio State (12-0)	.999	1.000	1.000	.9999
2 Florida (12-1)	.945	.948	.940	.9445
3 Michigan (11-1)	.932	.932	.940	.9344
4 Louisiana State (10-2)	.840	.838	.820	.8326
5 Southern California (10-2)	.769	.757	.860	.7953

2006 Conference Standings

Big East

Louisville	6-1
Rutgers	5-2
West Virginia	5-2
South Florida	4-3
Pittsburgh	2-5
Cincinnati	4-3
Connecticut	1-6
Syracuse	1-6

Atlantic Coast

ATLANTIC	
Wake Forest	6-2
Boston College	5-3
Clemson	5-3
Maryland	5-3
Florida State	3-5
North Carolina State	2-6
COASTAL	
Georgia Tech	7-1
Virginia Tech	6-2
Virginia	4-4
Miami	3-5
North Carolina	2-6
Duke	0-8

Southeastern

EAST	
Florida	7-1
Tennessee	5-3
Georgia	4-4
Kentucky	4-4
South Carolina	3-5
Vanderbilt	1-7
WEST	
Arkansas	7-1
Auburn	6-2
Louisiana State	6-2
Alabama	2-6
Mississippi	2-6
Mississippi State	1-7

Big Ten

Ohio State	8-0
Michigan	7-1
Wisconsin	7-1
Penn State	5-3
Purdue	5-3
Minnesota	3-5
Indiana	3-5
Iowa	2-6
Northwestern	2-6
Illinois	1-7
Michigan State	1-7

Big Twelve

NORTH	
Nebraska	6-2
Missouri	4-4
Kansas State	4-4
Kansas	3-5
Colorado	2-6
Iowa State	1-7
SOUTH	
Oklahoma	7-1
Texas	6-2
Texas A&M	5-3
Texas Tech	4-4
Oklahoma State	3-5
Baylor	3-5

Western Athletic

Boise State	8-0
Hawaii	7-1
Nevada	5-3
San Jose State	5-3
Fresno State	4-4
Idaho	3-5
New Mexico State	2-6
Louisiana Tech	1-7
Utah State	1-7

Conference USA

EAST	
Southern Mississippi	6-2
East Carolina	5-3
Marshall	4-4
Central Florida	3-5
Alabama-Birmingham	2-6
Memphis	1-7
WEST	
Houston	7-1
Rice	6-2
Tulsa	5-3
Southern Methodist	4-4
Texas-El Paso	3-5
Tulane	2-6

Mid-American

EAST	
Ohio University	7-1
Kent State	5-3
Akron	3-5
Bowling Green	3-5
Miami (Ohio)	2-6
Buffalo	1-7
WEST	
Central Michigan	7-1
Western Michigan	6-2
Northern Illinois	5-3
Ball State	5-3
Toledo	3-5
Eastern Michigan	1-7

Mountain West

Brigham Young	8-0
Texas Christian	6-2
Utah	5-3
Wyoming	5-3
New Mexico	4-4
Air Force	3-5
San Diego State	3-5
Colorado State	1-7
Nevada-Las Vegas	1-7

Pacific-10

Southern California	7-2
California	7-2
Oregon State	6-3
UCLA	5-4
Oregon	4-5
Arizona State	4-5
Washington State	4-5
Arizona	4-5
Washington	3-6
Stanford	1-8

2006 Major Bowl Games

Poinsettia Bowl (Dec. 19): Texas Christian 37 Northern Illinois 7

Texas Christian (11-2), which had dealt itself out of national picture by stumbling twice early in year, romped to 30-0 lead with its D, led by DE Tommy Blake, who made 2 of Horned Frogs' 5 sacks. TCU DB Brian Bonner contributed sparkling punt RETs that totaled 6/89y to set up pair of TDs, including early 4y run by TB Lonta Hobbs (18/109y). TCU QB Jeff Ballard (19-29/258y, TD) ran for 3 TDs and added another on 6y pass to TE Brent Hecht. Northern Illinois (7-6) had arrived with nation's top rusher in TB Garrett Wolfe (20/28y), but speed of Frogs' D so overwhelmed Huskies blockers that neither could Wolfe find running room nor could they protect their passer, QB Dan Nicholson (6-18/80y, INT). Huskies made only 60y O, and 2 of their 5 1st downs came on pass interference PENs. It took personal foul expulsion of Purple Frogs' only experienced long-snapper, Jared Retkofsky, for NIU to score TD in 4th Q: Huskies blocked punt after soft snap, and LB John Tranchitella returned it 32y for TD.

Las Vegas Bowl (Dec. 21): Brigham Young 38 Oregon 8

Cougars (11-2) sr John Beck (28-46/375y, 2 TDs, 2 INTs) displayed fine arm strength and sharp accuracy in breaking his own Las Vegas Bowl record for passing y. With BYU ahead 10-0 on strength of 6y TD run by RB Curtis Brown (17/120y, 2 TDs), Beck lofted perfect 41y pass to TE Jonny Harline (9/181y) up right sideline for TD just before H. Down 17-0 and floundering on O, Oregon (7-6) seemed to get spark midway in 3rd Q when DB Patrick Chung made 35y INT RET to near midfield. But struggling Ducks QB Brady Leaf (6-14/44y) gave it right back on 1st of 2 INTs by BYU CB Justin Robinson. Cougars tallied Brown's 2nd TD and went up 31-0 on Beck's 13y scramble to left pylon early in 4th Q. Oregon finally scored as QB Dennis Dixon (10-20/122y, INT) threw 47y pass to WR Spencer Paysinger, and RB Jeremiah Johnson followed with 2-pt run. BYU answered immediately on Beck's 2nd TD pass as Cougars clinched 10th straight win in 2006 but 1st bowl victory in 10 seasons.

New Orleans Bowl (Dec. 22): Troy 41 Rice 17

It had been since way back in 1961 that Rice Owls (7-6) had last qualified for bowl appearance. It had taken some good luck, namely pair of 1-pt wins and 3- and 4-pt victories among closing 6 wins. However, Owls were no match for speed of Troy (8-5) as bulky Trojans QB Omar Haugabook (14-28/217y, INT) ran for 1st Q TD and added 4 TD passes. Trojans led 21-7 at end of 1st Q, closing with Haugabook's 56y TD bomb. Troy intercepted Rice QB Joel Armstrong (35-54/305y, 2 TDs) 5 times and sacked him 4 times. Owls A-A WR Jarett Dillard (9/71y) went high for 1y TD catch in 4th Q to extend his streak of catching TD passes to 15 games.

Hawaii Bowl (Dec. 24): Hawaii 41 Arizona State 24

Keeping Hawaii's celebrated aerial attack in check, Arizona State (7-6) played sharp D in 1st H, which it led 10-3. After Sun Devils S Josh Barrett's leaping INT, QB Rudy Carpenter (13-26/191y, 2 TDs) had pitched 37y TD with 5:21 left to H. Warriors (11-3) QB Colt Brennan (33-42/559y, 5 TDs, INT) got hot in 3rd Q, pitching 3 TDs to zoom by Houston's David Klingler (1990) for most TD passes in single season. Brennan's TD passing mark reached 58. Carpenter's FUM led to Hawaii FG early in 4th Q, so Warriors led 27-10. ASU might have folded its tent in coach Dirk Koetter's swansong, but TB Ryan Torain (18/160y) rammed 64 and 12y, latter for TD. After Devils nabbed FUM at UH 27YL, Carpenter threw TD to trim deficit to 27-24. By this time, however, ASU's tiring D had lost both its top deep defenders—SS Barnett and FS Zach Catanese—to injury and was incapable of stopping hard-edged Hawaii and Brennan's 2 TD passes, including 79y sprint by WR Jason Rivers (14/308y, 2 TDs).

Emerald Bowl (Dec. 27): Florida State 44 UCLA 27

Everyone expected low-scoring outcome as each sported fine D. Instead, it became seesaw shootout that turned on big plays by Seminoles (7-6) and some odd blunders by UCLA (7-6). Bruins QB Patrick Cowan (15-36/240y, 2 TDs, 2 INTs) pitched 2 beautiful TDs in 1st H: WR Brandon Breazell took long pass in perfect stride and cantered 78y to 7-7 tie. Early in 2nd Q, UCLA WR Junior Taylor soared above pair of Florida State defenders to snare TD pass at back of EZ. Bruins led 20-13 at H. Seminoles bounced back nicely, profiting from Bruins' miscues. UCLA TB Chris Markey (19/144y) made 1st down on 4th down run near midfield in 3rd Q, but Bruins were flagged for illegal shift. Ensuing punt was blocked, which Florida State LB Lawrence Timmons returned for TD and 23-20 lead. Bruins countered to take back 27-23 lead, but FSU mounted 21-pt 4th Q. Seminoles went 90y to score when hitherto frustrated WR Greg Carr got loose for 30y TD on 4th-and-9 gamble. Florida State's next TD came from good field position gained when UCLA TB Derrick Williams foolishly pinned his team inside 3YL by tipping bounding KO that clearly was headed OB. FSU QB Drew Weatherford (21-43/325yTD, INT) overcame rough start, and TB Lorenzo Booker (22/91y, 2 TDs rushing and 117y receiving) had superior last game of his career.

Independence Bowl (Dec. 28): Oklahoma State 34 Alabama 31

Needing big effort for his 3rd straight 1000y rushing season, Alabama (6-7) TB Kenneth Darby (10/24y) lost FUM to set up opening TD for Oklahoma State (7-6), which came on short plunge by RB Dantrell Savage (19/116y, TD). In 2nd Q, Cowboys went ahead 14-7 on sub RB Keith Toston's blast, which was set up by punt downed on 1YL by Pokes DB Tommy Devereaux and assisted by Tide's personal foul PEN. Except for their 72y TD drive in 1st Q, Crimson Tide was completely stymied in 1st H until late 2nd Q drive of 80y resulted in TB Tim Castille's dive for TD that pulled Alabama within 17-14. But, Oklahoma State answered with TD in last min of 2nd Q because special teamer Grant Jones, nation's leading KO returner, made big RET, and Tide star LB Juwan Simpson sustained drive by foolishly trying to pick up FUM instead of safely falling on it. Although Cowboys hardly held ball in 3rd Q and gave up FG, they converted 4th down run by QB Bobby Reid (15-29/212y, TD, INT) on 1st snap of 4th Q and went on to WR Adarius Bowman's 10y TD catch at left pylon. Tide DB Javier Arenas spun away for 86y punt TD RET. It was now 31-24 for Cowboys, but they fumbled away ensuing KO. Alabama came up with great trick play as immense frosh LT Andre Smith stepped into backfield to catch overhand backward pass and carry it 2y for tying TD with 10 mins to go. OSU had 1 last surge left: Savage rolled 29y on screen pass on 3rd-and-9 to set up K Jason Ricks' 27y FG.

Holiday (Dec. 28): California 45 Texas A&M 10

Texas Aggies (9-4) got off to good start as WR Chad Schroeder got open for 19y TD pass from QB Stephen McGee (17-26/177y, TD). Motivation of California (10-3) had been questioned prior to Holiday Bowl, but Bears D, led by LB Desmond Bishop, walloped Aggies all over field. Cal used its powerful O-line to roll to 241y rushing as TBs Marshawn Lynch (20/111y, 2 TDs) and Justin Forsett (8/124y, TD) roared up middle. Bears quickly rode to answering 1st Q TD: sneak by QB Nate Longshore (19-24/235y, TD, INT). Lynch's 1st TD on direct snap sent Bears off at H leading 14-10. Texas A&M rightfully feared punt RETs of explosive Cal A-A WR DeSean Jackson, and P Justin Brantly had done good job of directional punts until his 1st try of 2nd H. Brantly badly shanked punt that barely made it to scrimmage line at A&M 41YL. Bears quickly roared downfield with Jackson making key catch at 2YL. Lynch soon vaulted over GL for 21-10 edge. Jackson rubbed off A&M SS Melvin Bullitt on 4th down pass to free WR Lavelle Hawkins for 4y TD catch which he took to right pylon. So, California led 28-10 with 2 mins left in 3rd Q. With 11:50 left, Bears held Aggies on downs at their 11YL, providing opportunity to pour it on with 17 pts on tiring A&M.

Texas Bowl (Dec. 28): Rutgers 37 Kansas State 10

Little-known Rutgers (11-2) frosh WR Tim Brown, all 150 lbs of him, made his presence known quickly. Brown sneaked outside to race 14y with swing pass to early TD, and on next series, Brown streaked downfield to haul in perfect 49y TD bomb from QB Mike Teel (16-28/268y, 2 TDs). Kansas State (7-6) came back to make it close before H. After K Jeff Snodgrass' 44y FG, WR Yamon Figurs fielded punt and charged 76y up middle for TD that sent Wildcats off at H trailing 17-10. On 1st snap of 3rd Q, Scarlet Knights LB Quintero Frierson made 1 of 2 INTs off K-State QB Josh Freeman (10-21/129y) and returned it 27y for TD and 24-10 lead. Rutgers pounded its running game in 2nd H as MVP RB Ray Rice ran 24/170y, including 46y TD gallop. Knights' victory was their 1st-ever bowl game win.

Music City Bowl (Dec. 29): Kentucky 28 Clemson 20

Without bowl win in 22 years, Kentucky Wildcats (8-5) roared to big early lead over disinterested Tigers (8-5), who ended up losing 4 of their last 5 games. Game MVP QB Andre Woodson passed 20-28/299y, 3 TDs to finish season with 31 scoring passes for Cats. Tigers missed x-pt kick after TD pass by QB Will Proctor (23-39/272y, 3 TDs, INT) and trailed 7-6 in middle of 2nd Q. Woodson connected with WR DeMoreo Ford on 70y TD with 2:14 left before H, so Wildcats led 14-6. WR Dickie Lyons, Jr. and TE Jacob Tamme nabbed 2nd H TD passes to put Kentucky up 28-6. Deficit, which coach Tommy Bowden blamed on frequent red zone TOs and PENs, forced Clemson to imbalance its play calling with 39 aerial ventures. Although Tigers rallied with pair of TD passes by Proctor in 4th Q, Kentucky's prevent D held on. Clemson's TB duo of James Davis and C.J. Spiller surprisingly were limited to 77y rushing by Wildcats' 116th-ranked defenders.

Sun Bowl (Dec. 29): Oregon State 39 Missouri 38

Oregon State coach Mike Riley figured he may as well play it "like in a card game at the end: we were all-in." With 22 secs remaining, courageous Beavers (10-4) surprised Missouri (8-5) with TB Yvenson Bernard's 2-pt wedge off LG to steal win as sun was setting on late afternoon in El Paso. Riley originally had decided to tie it with conv kick, but Tigers coach Gary Pinkel called timeout for TV review of possible EZ bobble by Beavers TE Joe Newton on his 14y TD catch that pulled Beavers to within 38-37. During that delay, Riley changed his mind in favor of 2-pt attempt. Missouri RB Tony Temple came up 4y short of Sun Bowl rushing record with 20/194y, while passing of QB Chase Daniel (16-29/330y, 2 TDs) fueled Tigers' 561y O. Temple made 7y TD run in 1st Q for 7-0 lead and raced 65y up left sideline in 3rd Q for 31-21 edge. Oregon State QB Matt Moore (31-54/356y, 4 TDs, INT) scored running TD in 1st Q for Beavers' 1st lead, extended his school record to 182 attempts without INT until Missouri S Brandon Massey picked him off in 3rd Q, and more importantly threw 2 TDs in 4th Q to help rally Beavers.

Liberty Bowl (Dec. 29): South Carolina 44 Houston 36

South Carolina (8-5) coach Steve Spurrier, long considered O wizard, enjoyed his D making big plays in 2nd H in Memphis. After trailing 28-27 at H, Gamecocks held Houston (10-4) to 63y in 3rd Q when Carolina took lead for good on K Ryan Succop's 45y FG. QB Blake Mitchell (19-29/323y, INT), who tied Liberty Bowl record with 4 TD passes, connected twice for 43y TDs with WR Kenny McKinley within 5-min span of 4th Q to launch South Carolina to 44-28 edge. Cougars sr QB Kevin Kolb made his 50th start and threw 26-39/386y, 3 TDs, INT, while RB Jackie Battle ran for 42 and 3y TDs.

Insight Bowl (Dec. 29): Texas Tech 44 Minnesota 41 (OT)

Texas Tech (8-5) came charging back from 38-7 deficit with 7:47 left in 3rd Q to fashion greatest comeback in bowl history. But, Minnesota (6-7), playing dominating football well into 3rd Q, had to examine its timid late play as reason for defeat. Golden Gophers soph TE Jack Simmons (7/134y, TD), in lineup for injured A-A TE Matt Spaeth, caught his 1st career TD pass to launch 14-0 advantage in 1st Q. Red Raiders, who failed on 4th down on their 1st series and suffered 3 TOs right off bat, lost FUM from Minny 9YL when Gophers DE Willie VanDeSteeg made sack to launch 87y TD drive for 21-0 edge. Texas Tech appeared to make break when CB Antonio Huffman intercepted Gophers QB Bryan Cupito (19-31/263y, 3 TDs, INT), but Huffman lost FUM into EZ as he spun from tackler in attempt to score. When Minnesota WR Logan Payne took diving TD catch away from 2 defenders 32 secs before H, Gophers went to dressing room with 35-7 lead. Minnesota kept ball for opening 7:13 of 3rd Q and appeared ready to lock it up with TD. But, Gophers were held at 3YL and had to settle for seemingly uneventful FG and 38-7 lead. WR Joel Filani (11/162y, TD) of nearby Paradise Valley, AZ, became Raiders' all-time receiving y leader and caught 1st of 2 TD passes by QB Graham Harrell (36-55/445y, 2 TDs, INT) with less than 5 mins left in 3rd Q. After Harrell's 2nd TD pass early in 4th Q, he scored on sneak with 7:49 to play. Gophers were drowning now, and Raiders RB Shannon Woods (19/109y) scored 2nd of his 3 TDs with 2:39 left. K Alex Trlica nailed 52y FG at end of regulation to knot wild game at 38-38. After Gophers made FG in top half of OT, Woods scored from 3YL for improbable victory that moved Tech coach Mike Leach nearly to tears. Minnesota hierarchy chose to fire Glen Mason, its only winning coach since Murray Warmath left Gophers program in 1971.

Champs Sports Bowl (Dec. 29): Maryland 24 Purdue 7

Effective passing and clock-eating ground game permitted Maryland (9-4) to play keep-away from Purdue's effective O. Terrapins gained 429y O while launching ground attack for 206y on 50 attempts. QB Sam Hollenbach passed 15-24/223y, 2 TDs to lead Maryland, while TBs Lance Ball (18/98y) and Keon Lattimore (20/85y) sparked ball control. Purdue (8-6) QB Curtis Painter (23-36/264y, INT) managed to throw 12y TD pass to WR Greg Orton in last 30 secs before H. Boilermakers could rush for only 21y by game's end, and while they nosed into Maryland territory 3 times in 2nd H, Boilers lost WR Dorien Bryant's FUM and Painter's INT by Terps CB Josh Wilson.

Meineke Car Care Bowl (Dec. 30): Boston College 25 Navy 24

After Middies (9-4) lost early FUM, Boston College (10-3) QB Matt Ryan (20-29/242y, TD, 2 INTs), bad foot and all, scrambled 2y up middle for TD followed by missed kick. Navy QB Kaipo-Noa Kaheaku-Enhada (4-6/77y, 2 TDs), who threw surprising number of passes in 1st H, connected twice on next possession: WR Jason Tomlinson's fine toe-in-bounds reception at right sideline and WR Tyree Barnes' 31y catch behind DBs in EZ. After old foes traded TDs, Tomlinson soared amid trio of BC defenders on

3rd-and-17 for another terrific catch: twice-gripped 24y TD. Eagles held at their 19YL in last min of 1st H and quickly crammed in FG as H clock reached 0:00 to trail 21-16. Navy added 3rd Q FG, but by 4th Q BC had solved Middies' option attack. Trailing 24-22 after Ryan's TD pass but failed 2-pt throw, Eagles fizzled on good field position series with 5 mins left. Navy's 2 1st downs appeared to have all but run out clock, but BC D forced errant lateral recovered by LB Jolonn Dunbar (14 tackles, 4 for loss) at Middies 40YL. On last play of game, Eagles K Steve Aponavicius nailed 37y FG.

Alamo Bowl (Dec. 30): Texas 26 Iowa 24

Fresh from rigorous pre-bowl training that Hawkeyes believed would mean dramatic turnaround from their 1-5 end to regular season, Iowa (6-7) roared 77y downfield after opening KO to 1y TD smash by TB Albert Young, who got scoring push from Academic A-A C Mike Elgin. When Hawks quickly regained ball, WR Andy Brodell (6/159y, 2 TDs) made spectacularly fast outside move on Thorpe-Award-winning Texas (10-3) CB Aaron Ross to race away to 63y TD pass and 14-0 lead. WR Quan Cosby's long ensuing KO RET set up Texas K Ryan Bailey's 27y FG. Game turned on Hawks' mental mistake late in 2nd Q: Iowa QB Drew Tate (15-25/274y, 2 TDs, INT), who was home in Texas for his last game, tossed misdirection pass to TE Scott Chandler for apparent TD. But, officials ruled Chandler was ineligible because he was covered outside by Iowa WR. Play that might have lifted Iowa to 21-3 was nullified. Texas' Ross made EZ INT 1 play later, and Longhorns QB Colt McCoy (26-40/308y, 2 TDs) turned it into WR Limas Sweed's TD pass for 14-10 deficit 45 secs before H. McCoy hit 72y TD in 3rd Q, which tied Nevada's David Neill's frosh record of 29 TD throws. Hawks battled back to take 21-20 edge late in 3rd Q as Brodell again raced away for 23y score. Early in 4th Q, Steers faced 4th-and-1 at Iowa 10YL. Instead of taking go-ahead FG, coach Mack Brown called rollout that McCoy took to 2YL to poise TB Selvin Young's 2y TD run for 26-21 lead. Up 26-24, Texas suffered 18y punt to its 48YL with less than 4 mins left. Iowa seemed in good shape, but strangely, pair of E-around razzle-dazzle plays would soon decide it. Iowa's turned into damaging 11y loss, and Texas' similar play by WR Billy Pittman, after it forced Hawkeyes' punt, gained 1st down that iced verdict.

Chick-Fil-A Peach Bowl (Dec. 30): Georgia 31 Virginia Tech 24

For 2nd straight season, Georgia (9-4) was playing virtual home bowl game in Atlanta's Georgia Dome. This time, game wasn't hurricane-displaced Sugar Bowl, but like previous year it looked for awhile as if Bulldogs would lay another egg. Fast-finishing Virginia Tech (10-3), winners of its last 6 regular season games in which it permitted only 29 pts, stepped out to 21-3 H lead. Hokies TB Brandon Ore (20/42y) was back from injured list, and while Ore may have shown his rustiness, he bumped over for 2 short TD runs in 2nd Q. WR Eddie Royal (4/45y) took long lateral and threw 53y TD pass to TE Sam Wheeler to put Virginia Tech ahead 21-3 with 4:36 before H. Meanwhile, Georgia had been held to K Brandon Coutu's 39y FG in 1st Q and demoralizing 47y O for 1st H, including -3y net in 2nd Q. Coutu booted 51y FG in 3rd Q, and K Brian Mimbs deftly recovered his own onside-KO to ignite Dogs to TD pass by QB Matthew Stafford (9-21/129y, TD, INT) which made it 21-13. Georgia forced TOs on 4 straight Hokies possessions, including LB Tony Taylor's pair of INTs. Within next 9 mins, Bulldogs rampaged with TB Kregg Lumpkin's TD run and Stafford's tying 2-pt pass, Coutu's 3rd FG, and FB Brannan Southerland's TD. Bulldogs' seesaw season ended with 3 wins in row over ranked foes, 1st time they had ever achieved such string.

MPC Computers Bowl (Dec. 31): Miami 21 Nevada 20

After his firing in November, Larry Coker coached his last game at Miami (7-6), finishing with 60-15 record. Coker's .800 winning percentage left him in top 30 all-time of coaches at any level. In wind-chill factor in upper teens, Hurricanes were decidedly out of their element in Boise, but QB Kirby Freeman (11-19/272y, INT) threw for TDs of 52 and 78y. Freeman's 2nd scoring pass went to frosh WR Sam Shields (4/101y) in last 6 mins of 3rd Q to gave Miami lead for good at 21-14. Nevada (8-5) had gained safety at end of 1st Q when Freeman was called for intentional grounding in EZ, but late in 2nd Q made unlucky chase for 2-pt conv after QB Jeff Rowe (20-31/192y, TD, INT) threw 27y TD pass to WR Marko Mitchell to go ahead 8-7. K Brett Jaekle kicked 4 FGs as Wolfpack crept within 21-20 in 4th Q. Nevada made 1st down at Canes 36YL in final min, but Miami DB Chavez Grant made diving INT with 18 secs left.

Outback Bowl: Penn State 20 Tennessee 10

While watching from coaching box and still recovering from broken leg, Nittany Lions (9-4) coach Joe Paterno won his 22nd bowl to extend his record number of post-season wins. With D-coordinator Tom Bradley leading sideline decisions, Penn State sloshed through rainy conditions to offer balanced attack and force 3 important TOs. Tennessee (9-4) scored 1st Q's only pts on K James Wilhoit's 44y FG. Lions QB Anthony Morelli (14-25/197y, TD), much improved since end of regular season, tossed 3y TD pass to frosh TE Andrew Quarless at end of 8-play, 92y drive in 2nd Q for 10-3 lead. Vols countered with drive that TB LaMarcus Coker completed by breaking through potential tackle-for-loss and romped to 42y TD with 1:15 before H. It sent teams to H knotted 10-10, which held up until 5 mins into 4th Q. After partially blocking FG try, Tennessee was poised for QB Erik Ainge (25-37/267y, INT) to launch 53y pass to normal short-range receiver, TE Chris Brown. Defending from its 14YL, Penn State quickly enjoyed LB Sean Lee's big play. Lee forced FUM by Vols rugged TB Arian Foster (12/65y), and Nittany Lions DB Tony Davis scooped up ball for 88y dash for go-ahead TD. On his way to ranking 2nd all-time on Penn State career rushing list, brawny TB Tony Hunt (31/158y) ground out 7/42y on final drive that led to K Kevin Kelly's clinching 22y FG with 3:29 left.

Cotton Bowl: Auburn 17 Nebraska 14

Except for 2 plays, Nebraska (9-5) seemed in good shape to win its 1st January Bowl since 2000 Fiesta Bowl. Pair of disastrous outcomes was enough to give coach Bill Callahan nightmares throughout long winter. Auburn (11-2), winners over BCS teams Florida and LSU, got TDs from powerful TB Carl Stewart only 2 times he touched ball to again "win ugly." "That's how this team as done it all year," said coach Tommy Tuberville. Huskers had marched 80y right down field to early 13y TD pass from QB Zac Taylor (14-26/126y, TD, INT) to WR Nate Swift. Nebraska was on move again later in 1st Q when 3rd down pass was deflected to Tigers LB Karibi Dede, who cantered 52y to Huskers 9YL. Stewart caught TD pass from QB Brandon Cox (10-21/111y, TD) 2 plays later. Big Red faced 4th-and-1 at own 29YL early in 2nd Q and mysteriously chose to run fake punt. Instead of running quick-hitting play, Nebraska went with reverse that blew up in backfield, resulting in FUM REC by Auburn S Tristan Davis at Huskers 14YL. Stewart scored from 1y out for 14-7 lead. Cornhuskers tied it on 20y run by IB Brandon Jackson (7/38y, TD) and left at H with 157y to 46y O advantage. Tigers salted away win with 2nd H's only score: K John Vaughn's 42y FG in 3rd Q. Nebraska, however, had late chance when LB Stewart Bradley (7 tackles) sacked Cox and recovered FUM at Tigers 42YL with 5:24 to play. Huskers reached Auburn's 27YL before losing ground to face 4th down at 30YL. Taylor was under strong pressure as his pass fell incomplete with 1:36 to go.

Capital One Bowl: Wisconsin 17 Arkansas 14

Wisconsin (12-1), miffed at constant reminders that it "hadn't played *anybody* this year," used slights for motivation. Despite being limited to -5y rushing, Badgers made big plays on D when needed. And big tackle was needed early: Dynamic but slightly hobbled Arkansas TB Darren McFadden (19/89y) streaked toward EZ on his 1st carry for 45y but was hauled down from behind by Badgers DB Jack Ikegwuonu at 9YL. When Hogs K Jeremy Davis missed 30y FG, Arkansas was frustrated and scoreless. "If Darren is 100 percent," said Razorbacks coach Houston Nutt, "I don't think anyone would have caught him." McFadden's fine back-up, TB Felix Jones (14/150y), put Arkansas up 7-3 on 76y TD bolt just after Wisconsin K Taylor Mehlhaff had made career-best 52y FG. Game MVP QB John Stocco (14-34/206y, 2 TDs, 2 INTs) chipped in pair of TD passes to give Wisconsin 17-7 H edge. Wisconsin P Ken DeBauche made odd but big play that cost Arkansas about 50y in field position: DeBauche's punt was blocked, but he was able to retrieve ball and successfully throw for 1st down. Ineligible receiver PEN spoiled DeBauche's impromptu effort but meant he could punt again with normally-expected result. Hogs played in Badgers territory most of 2nd H as their D built sack total to 6, but they committed 12 PENs/123y. Arkansas' only 2nd H score came early in 4th Q on another gallop by Jones. Razorbacks enjoyed 368y to 201y O advantage. Hogs' drives failed at Wisconsin 35, 34, 30, and 44YLs, mostly in 3rd Q.

Gator Bowl: West Virginia 38 Georgia Tech 35

When 4-year starting Georgia Tech (9-5) QB Reggie Ball was ruled academically ineligible, oddsmakers raised Tech's underdog status from 7 to 11 pts. But, Yellow Jackets soph QB Taylor Bennett (19-29/326y, 3 TDs, INT) made his 2nd career start and teamed with A-A WR Calvin Johnson (9/186y, 2 TDs) to riddle West Virginia's D in 1st H. Tech TB Tashard Choice also scored 1st H TD and finished with 27/169y rushing. Jackets led 28-17 at H. Meanwhile, Mountaineers (11-2) barely got any service out of RB Steve Slaton (3/11y), who was uncertain with bad charleyhorse. Filling in was RB Owen Schmitt (13/109y, 2 TDs), who kept West Virginia in game, scoring on 1 and 11y runs in 1st H. WVU QB Pat White wasn't feeling so hot himself, playing through hand, ankle, and neck injuries. But after Georgia Tech's Choice scored 1:12 into 3rd Q for 35-17 lead, White buckled down: "I was hurting a lot, but I had to block it out." White, who finished with 9-15/131y, 2 TDs passing and 22/145y, TD rushing, masterminded 21 pts for 38-35 lead before 3rd Q ended. White passed for 57 and 14y TDs and dashed 15y for another score with less than 6 mins to go in 3rd Q. Although 4th Q was scoreless, Jackets attempted potential tying 54y FG with 5 mins left. But, Tech K Travis Bell's boot fell well short.

Rose Bowl: Southern California 32 Michigan 18

Pair of heavyweights slugged it out to 3-3 1st H stalemate. Eye-popping stat from opening H was 5 sacks by Southern California (11-2) D. Trojans QB John David Booty (27-45/391y, 4 TDs) and WR Dwayne Jarrett (11/205y, 2 TDs) played brilliantly in 2nd H as USC rolled to 16 unanswered pts in 3rd Q and built 32-11 lead just past middle of 4th Q. Perhaps Michigan (11-2) felt it had received bad deal after being voted out of national title rematch with Ohio State, but its O never really clicked until it was too late. Michigan failed to penetrate USC 20YL until it was behind 19-3 early in 4th Q. Decisive 3rd Q began with Wolverines QB Chad Henne (26-41/309y, 2 TDs, INT) tossing pass into crowd and having Trojans DE Lawrence Jackson come away with INT. Booty soon hit his 1st TD pass, and on next possession he finished 70y drive with 22y TD arrow to Jarrett. Troy LB Brian Cushing soon sacked Henne, and Jackson fell on resultant FUM to lead to K Mario Danelo's FG. Michigan got close at 19-11 early in 4th Q on TD reception by WR Adrian Arrington and 2-pt run by TB Mike Hart (17/47y), but Jarrett soon got away for 62y TD by beating Wolverines A-A CB Leon Hall.

Fiesta Bowl: Boise State 43 Oklahoma 42 (OT)

Sounding clarion call for all schools left out of history's spotlight and prompting marriage proposal to boot, adventurous Boise State (13-0) authored 3 improbable and courageous plays to tie dramatic Fiesta Bowl in last 7 secs of regulation and steal thrilling OT win. Broncos jumped to early leads of 14-0, 14-7, and 21-10 through H as QB Jared Zabransky (19-29/262y, 3 TDs, INT) threw pair of scoring passes to WR Drisan James (3/96y, 2 TDs). Oklahoma (11-3) had tough time getting TB Adrian Peterson (20/77y,TD) going, but star runner, back from injury of October 14, scored on 8y TD run late in 3rd Q to cut deficit to 28-17. Nursing 28-20 lead in last 2 mins of regulation, Broncos gave up 77y in 6 plays as Sooners tied it on WR Quentin Chaney's 5y reception from QB Paul Thompson (19-32/233y, 2 TDs, 3 INTs) followed by Thompson's 2-pt pass to WR Juaquin Iglesias with 1:14 to play. No sooner had Broncos received KO that Zabransky threw out-pattern from far hashmark which Oklahoma CB Marcus Walker angled across to intercept and romp 33y for TD and

Sooners' 1st lead at 35-28. Boise soon faced dire 4th-and-18 at 50YL with 7 secs to play. Zabransky hit James on crossing pattern pass from left to center, and James flipped perfect hook-and-ladder toss to WR Jerard Rabb (4/79y, TD), crossing from right. Rabb dashed for left pylon and miraculously scored tying TD. In OT, Peterson took handoff on 1st snap and gave Oklahoma 42-35 lead by zooming for 25y TD. Boise came up with trick pass play on which Zabransky went in motion and snap went to WR Vinny Perretta who lobbed 5y TD to TE Derek Schouman (8/72y, TD) for TD. Everyone expected Broncos coach Chris Petersen to take x-pt kick and send it to 2nd OT. Instead, Boise flooded its formation strong-right, Zabransky took Shotgun snap, and turned right to throw empty-handed phantom pass. He finished his follow-through with ball in his left, non-throwing hand and slipped handoff to star RB Ian Johnson (23/101y, TD), who finished brilliant Statue of Liberty play by romping unmolested off LT for winning 2 pts. Minutes later, Johnson proposed to his girlfriend, Chrissy Popadics, Boise's head cheerleader. *Arizona Republic* headline decided that "Boise Belongs!"

Orange Bowl (Jan. 2): Louisville 24 Wake Forest 13

Nervous Wake Forest (11-3) stumbled frequently on 1st series and faced long y situations throughout 1st Q. Early Louisville (12-1) drive died with lost FUM, but its O appeared to be ticking time-bomb. Heavy pressure from Wake DB Alphonso Smith forced short punt OB at Cardinals 28YL late in 1st Q, but Deacons had to settle for K Sam Swank's 44y FG. Cards converted 4th-and-9 on way to K Art Carmody's tying 41y FG in middle of 2nd Q and clicked on 21y TD pass from WR (and former scout team QB) Patrick Carter, after long backward pass, to RB Anthony Allen. Wake appeared headed to tying TD but RB Kenneth Moore (12/76y) lost FUM inside Louisville 15YL on questionable replay call. Louisville led 10-3 at H. Wake struck quickly in 3rd Q to tie it on deep crossing-pattern pass from QB Riley Skinner (21-33/272y, TD, INT) to WR Nate Morton. As 4th Q opened, every Deacon player and thousands of their fans raised 5 fingers in on-going tribute to HS uniform number of Luke Abbate, late 16-year-old brother of Wake star LB Jon Abbate. Shortly thereafter, Swank booted 36y FG for 13-10 lead. Louisville answered with quick and highly efficient trip to Allen's wedge up middle for 17-13 edge. Cards' superiority began to show as 4th Q wore on, and FB Brock Bolen hammered 18y for TD in last 5 mins. MVP QB Brian Brohm passed 24-34/312y overall while sparking Louisville's decisive 81 and 71y drives on consecutive series. Cards WR Harry Douglas finished with 10/165y receiving.

Sugar Bowl (Jan. 3): Louisiana State 41 Notre Dame 14

Since 1994 Cotton Bowl, which was last bowl game won by Notre Dame (10-3), 87 other schools had won in post-season. Decisive Sugar Bowl defeat set new NCAA bowl streak of 9 losses, breaking ND's tie with South Carolina and West Virginia. Irish spun their wheels in 1st Q, including failed fake punt. Louisiana State (11-2) QB JaMarcus Russell (21-34/332y, 2 TDs, INT) immediately set out to carve up Irish's weak pass D. On LSU's 1st snap, Russell's 31y deep-out pass to WR Early Doucet to 3YL set up RB Keiland Williams' TD run, and Russell's 11y TD slant-in to WR Dwayne Bowe made short work to 14-0 in 1st Q. Notre Dame came back before 1st Q ended as QB Brady Quinn (15-35/148y, 2 TDs, 2 INTs) lofted 24y TD pass between 2 defenders to WR David Grimes. After having his soaring, tumbling 2nd Q INT at his 1YL called incomplete by TV replay, LSU DB Jonathan Zenon came right back to make real INT RET on errant 42YL few plays later. Irish RB Darius Walker (22/128y) ripped off 35y run behind pulling G Dan Santucci late in 2nd Q, which led to 10y TD pass to WR Jeff Samardzija (8/59y) who retaliated against Zenon's coverage. Russell, who had slumbered bit since early going, came alive with 58y rocket to Doucet to 5YL in last 2 mins of H and scrambled over for 21-14 lead 2 plays later. Snake-bitten Notre Dame CB Ambrose Wooden stole ball from Doucet at LSU 32YL in 1st min of 3rd Q, but replay reversal showed he couldn't control ball on his way OB. It allowed Tigers to begin 3rd Q possession domination and score on K Colt David's 2 FGs and Russell's 58y TD bomb to WR Brandon LaFell. LSU's big RB Williams was given job of killing clock by pounding ball at ND, and he responded with 14/107y and 20y TD in closing moments.

BCS Championship Bowl (Jan. 8): Florida 41 Ohio State 14

Tostitos BCS Championship Game opened explosively as quicksilver Ohio State (12-1) WR Ted Ginn took KO up middle, cut right, and flew 93y to TD. Florida (13-1) came right back to score on 46y drive, capped by 14y TD pass from QB Chris Leak (25-36/213y, TD) to WR Dallas Baker. Gators quickly got ball back 2nd time in Buckeyes' territory at 34YL as 2nd Buckeyes' personal foul PEN again assisted Florida. On 3rd down, Leak flipped 20y pass to TE Cornelius Ingram to 7YL, and WR-RB Percy Harvin soon scored on option run to left for 14-7 lead. Before 1st Q was over, Gators were well on way to disrupting Bucks' O (only 71y in 1st H) as Ginn limped to dressing room with debilitating instep strain: UF DE Derrick Harvey sacked Ohio State QB Troy Smith (4-14/35y, INT and 10/-29y rushing) 2nd of 3 times, and CB Reggie Lewis made diving INT. With Leak hitting his 1st 9 passes, Gators went 71y to RB DeShawn Wynn's short TD blast on 1st snap of 2nd Q. Heisman-winner Smith, who entered game with 25-2 career won-loss record, briefly got Buckeyes rolling again as TB Antonio Pittman (10/62y) rambled behind G Steve Rehring's block to 18y TD and manageable 21-14 deficit. K Chris Hetland, coming off bad year kicking FGs, put Florida up 24-14 with solid 42y 3-ptr inside 6 mins before H. Florida's dominant D-front forced next break: Ohio State foolishly went for and missed 4th-and-1 at own 30YL, which led to Hetland's 40y FG. Harvey next recovered Smith's FUM at Buckeyes 5YL on DE Jarvis Moss' sack with 1:27 to go in 1st H. Gators QB Tim Tebow pounded middle twice and rolled left to toss 1y TD pass to WR Andre Caldwell for stunning 34-14 lead. Scoreless 3rd Q was prelude to Florida clinching its 2nd national title in its 100th year of football: Gigantic Tebow (10/39y rushing) hammered over from 1YL on 4th down with 10:20 to play for 41-14 lead. Ohio State astoundingly totaled 82y O after posting 410y avg during year.

2006 Individual Statistical Leaders

RUSHING YARDS

	Attempts	Yards	Avg.
Garrett Wolfe, Northern Illinois	309	1928	6.2
Ray Rice, Rutgers	335	1794	5.4
Steve Slaton, West Virginia	248	1744	7.0
Ian Johnson, Boise State	276	1714	6.2
Darren McFadden, Arkansas	284	1647	5.8
P.J. Hill, Wisconsin	311	1569	5.1
Mike Hart, Michigan	318	1562	4.9
Ahmad Bradshaw, Marshall	249	1523	6.1
Tashard Choice, Georgia Tech	297	1473	5.0
Jon Cornish, Kansas	250	1457	5.8

PASSING YARDS

	Completions	Attempts	Yards	Pct.
Colt Brennan, Hawaii	406	559	5549	72.6
Chase Holbrook, New Mexico State	397	567	4619	70.0
Graham Harrell, Texas Tech	412	616	4555	66.9
John Beck, Brigham Young	289	417	3885	69.3
Kevin Kolb, Houston	292	432	3809	67.6
Jordan Palmer, Texas-El Paso	282	429	3595	65.7
Chase Daniel, Missouri	287	452	3527	63.5
Andre Woodson, Kentucky	264	419	3515	63.0
Brady Quinn, Notre Dame	289	467	3426	61.9
John David Booty, Southern California	269	436	3347	61.7

RECEIVING YARDS

	Catches	Yards
Chris Williams, New Mexico State	92	1415
Johnnie Lee Higgins, Texas-El Paso	82	1319
Joel Filani, Texas Tech	91	1300
Robert Meacham, Tennessee	71	1298
Sammie Stroughter, Oregon State	74	1293
Harry Douglas, Louisville	70	1265
Jarett Dillard, Rice	91	1247
Davone Bess, Hawaii	96	1220
Calvin Johnson, Georgia Tech	76	1202
Adarius Bowman, Oklahoma State	60	1181

2006 Consensus All-America Team
Offense

Wide Receiver:	Calvin Johnson, Georgia Tech
	Dwayne Jarrett, Southern California
Tight End:	Zach Miller, Arizona State
Linemen:	Joe Thomas, Wisconsin
	Sam Baker, Southern California
	Jake Long, Michigan
	Justin Blaylock, Texas
Center:	Dan Mozes, West Virginia
Quarterback:	Troy Smith, Ohio State
Running Back:	Darren McFadden, Arkansas
	Steve Slaton, West Virginia
Kick Returner:	DeSean Jackson, California
Kicker:	Justin Medlock, UCLA

Defense

Linemen:	Gaines Adams, Clemson
	Justin Hickman, UCLA
	Quinn Pitcock, Ohio State
	LaMarr Woodley, Michigan
Linebacker:	James Laurinaitis, Ohio State
	Patrick Willis, Mississippi
	Paul Posluszny, Penn State
Backs:	Leon Hall, Michigan
	Daymeion Hughes, California
	LaRon Landry, Louisiana State
	Reggie Nelson, Florida
	Eric Weddle, Utah
Punter:	Daniel Sepulveda, Baylor

2006 Heisman Trophy Vote

Troy Smith, senior quarterback, Ohio State	2540
Darren McFadden, sophomore tailback, Arkansas	878
Brady Quinn, senior quarterback, Notre Dame	782
Steve Slaton, sophomore running back, West Virginia	214
Mike Hart, junior tailback, Michigan	210

Other 2006 Major Awards

Maxwell (Player)	Brady Quinn, senior quarterback, Notre Dame
Walter Camp (Player)	Troy Smith, senior quarterback, Ohio State
Outland (Lineman)	Joe Thomas, senior offensive tackle, Wisconsin
Lombardi (Lineman)	LaMarr Woodley, senior defensive end, Michigan
Doak Walker (Running Back)	Darren McFadden, sophomore tailback, Arkansas
Davey O'Brien (Quarterback)	Troy Smith, senior quarterback, Ohio State
Fred Biletnikoff (Receiver)	Calvin Johnson, junior WR, Georgia Tech
Jim Thorpe (Defensive Back)	Aaron Ross, senior cornerback, Texas
Dick Butkus (Linebacker)	Patrick Willis, senior linebacker, Mississippi
Chuck Bednarik (Defender)	Paul Posluszny, senior linebacker, Penn State
Lou Groza (Placekicker)	Art Carmody, junior kicker, Louisville
Ray Guy (Punter)	Daniel Sepulveda, senior punter, Baylor
Johnny Unitas (Sr. Quarterback)	Brady Quinn, senior quarterback, Notre Dame
John Mackey (Tight End)	Matt Spaeth, senior tight end, Minnesota
Dave Rimington (Center)	Dan Mozes, senior center, West Virginia
Ted Hendricks (Defensive End)	LaMarr Woodley, senior defensive end, Michigan
AFCA Coach of the Year	Jim Grobe, Wake Forest

2007

The Year of Utter Disbelief, Wounded Quarterbacks, and Miraculous LSU, a Two-Loss Champion

It all began so innocently on a balmy Saturday afternoon in early September. Not a single Division 1-AA team—the group of second-tier programs that in 2007 was sporting the confounding new name of the Football Championship Subdivision—had ever defeated a Division 1-A (now were known as the Football Bowl Subdivision) team that was ranked in the top 25. And yet on Labor Day Saturday, a stunning result occurred when two-time defending 1-AA champion Appalachian State visited preseason no. 5 Michigan (9-4), the all-time collegiate victories leader starting the year with 860.

Appalachian's Spread Offense, all the rage in the mid-2000s as a great equalizing strategy against superior opposition, completely mystified the Wolverines' defense, and swift quarterback Armanti Edwards passed for three touchdowns and ran for another to prop up the Mountaineers to a 28-14 lead. But, it took Julian Rauch's 24-yard field goal with 26 seconds remaining to put Appalachian State ahead for good by 34-32. Michigan had a last-moment chance to pull it out with a 37-yard field goal, but defensive back Corey Lynch slipped through to block it to preserve the titanic upset. TV cameras covering the inaugural game of the new Big Ten Network picked up images of thousands of Michigan fans standing with their hands thrown to their heads in utter disbelief.

"We're still sort of shocked," Appalachian coach Jerry Moore admitted breathlessly moments afterward.

Oh Baby! It was only the beginning. An amazingly crazy season was launched with Appalachian State's win in front of more than 109,000 fans in Michigan's "Big House." The Wolverines became the first of a record 13 top-5 teams to be upset by an unranked opponent, eight of the surprise losers bowing at home. Additionally, top-10 teams lost 20 times to unranked teams. The AP's no. 2 spot became ominously perilous as the team a heartbeat from the top lost seven times.

The list of astounding upsets of top-5 teams of 2007 reads long and loud and does not include critical upsets authored by ranked teams:

- No. 5 Michigan was beaten by Appalachian State on September 1.
- No. 3 Oklahoma (11-3) was nipped on a late field goal at Colorado (6-7) on September 29.
- Also on September 29, Auburn (9-4) handed no. 4 Florida (9-4) a three-point loss on a last-play field goal in Gainesville.
- On October 6, much-improved Illinois (9-4) defeated no. 5 Wisconsin (9-4) 31-26.
- Late on October 6, no. 2 Southern California (11-2) was beaten at home by 41-point underdog Stanford (4-8).
- A week later, no. 2 California (7-6) lost to Oregon State (9-4) on Homecoming in Berkeley, falling short by three points.
- Rutgers (8-5) knocked Cinderella no. 2 South Florida (9-4) from the unbeaten ranks on October 18 in a Thursday night game.
- Fresh from a stirring comeback win at Virginia Tech (11-3), no. 2 Boston College (11-3) dropped its first game of the season to Florida State (7-6) on November 3 in Chestnut Hill, Mass.
- No. 1 Ohio State (11-2) won its first 10 games until running into Illinois, a 28-21 winner at Ohio Stadium on November 10.
- In a Thursday night game on November 15, no. 2 Oregon (9-4) lost at Arizona (5-7).
- The whirlwind passing attack of Texas Tech (9-4) fooled no. 3 Oklahoma by 34-27 on November 17.
- On November 23, Arkansas (8-5) went to Baton Rouge to knock off no. 1 Louisiana State (12-2) in triple overtime.
- On December 1, Pittsburgh (5-7) rode south to Morgantown to stun their biggest rival, no. 2 West Virginia (11-2).

With the plethora of upsets came some wonderful stories. Under new coach Jeff Jagodzinski, Boston College was projected anywhere but first in the ACC Atlantic Division. Sharp quarterbacking by Matt Ryan and an alert defense led the Eagles to eight straight wins to open the season and strong closing wins at Clemson (9-4) and Miami (5-7) to take the division crown. BC secured its eighth post-season win in a row in the Champs Sports Bowl and finished tied for 10th in the final poll.

Other coaches launched success in new surroundings. Brian Kelly of Cincinnati (10-3) built a turnover-creating defense that beat some good teams in Oregon State and Rutgers before being nipped 28-23 late in the season at West Virginia to cost the Bearcats a shot at the Big East title. Cincinnati finished 17th at season's end.

Dennis Erickson, somewhat of a controversial choice as new coach at Arizona State (10-3), took advantage of an amiable schedule and ripped off eight victories to start the year. A tougher defense and a better running game fueled the Sun Devils' rise to a share of the Pacific-10 title.

Missouri (12-2) opened unranked but quickly shot upward in the Big 12 North. The Tigers put on a terrific offensive show in their version of the Spread, but politics kept them out of a BCS Bowl. Missouri went to the Cotton Bowl where it thrashed Arkansas to finish no. 4 in the final poll.

Coach Ron Zook's excellent recruiting at Illinois (9-4) paid off as the Illini played in their first Rose Bowl since 1984 and authored big wins over Penn State (9-4), Wisconsin (9-4), and Ohio State.

Kansas (12-1) was picked universally near the bottom of the Big 12 North. But, coach Mark Mangino's young Jayhawks shored up their pass defense around a good rush and cornerback Aqib Talib and overcame their 2006 penchant for fourth quarter fold-ups with a sharp offense built around accurate sophomore quarterback Todd Reesing. Kansas crushed an easy early schedule and was undefeated entering the regular season finale against Missouri. The Jayhawks lost 36-28 at neutral site Kansas City but slipped into the Orange Bowl when Mizzou lost the Big 12 title game to Oklahoma. In Miami, Kansas surprised Virginia Tech 24-21 to cop AP's no. 7 spot in the January poll.

The Spread Offense was all the rage for teams with quick quarterbacks, and no school had a better one for most of the year than Oregon. In the season's second week the magic of Dennis Dixon, a swift runner-passer who also was an honor student, helped crush Michigan 39-7. After four straight wins, Oregon reached no. 11 in the AP Poll, lost a heartbreaker to California, but was able to defeat both eventual Pacific-10 co-champions USC and Arizona State on consecutive Saturdays and move back up to no. 2, where the season's upset bulls-eye seemed permanently attached. In a mid-November Thursday night game against Arizona, Dixon had the Ducks winging early until he badly twisted a previously-injured knee. The injury dismissed him from the Heisman Trophy race, eventually won by the very worthy Florida quarterback Tim Tebow. However, the fact that the Ducks folded with three losses in a row without Dixon pretty well proved how great their wounded quarterback really had been.

Oregon was one of several teams to see its season blow up because an indispensible quarterback went down. West Virginia lost only twice, and each time its star ball-handler, Patrick White, missed playing time with injuries. A chance at the national title evaporated in the tough late-season loss to Pitt, when the offense was ineffective without White. California opened with five straight wins and in mid-October was poised to become the new no. 1—thanks to an upset win by Kentucky (8-5) over top-ranked Louisiana State earlier that day—as Bears back-up freshman quarterback Kevin Riley, in for injured Nate Longshore, let his boyish exuberance get to him and tried to scramble for a last-moment winning touchdown against Oregon State. When Riley was tackled short of the end zone, the clock ran out to spoil a virtually-sure tying field goal and the opportunity of an overtime win. Longshore limped through the rest of the season but his ineffectiveness meant five more losses. USC's John David Booty broke a fingertip on his throwing hand, and a diminished, turnover-prone offense spelled the difference in Troy's losses to Stanford and Oregon. With Booty back in top form at season's end, many thought preseason no. 1 Southern California was the best team in the land.

Possibly the most injury-infected group was the quarterback stable at UCLA (6-7). The Bruins returned 19 starters from 2006, plus a pair of experienced quarterbacks in Ben Olson and Patrick Cowan, and were considered a darkhorse for national honors. But coach Karl Dorrell watched one passer after another fall by the wayside as Olson, Cowan, freshman McLeod Bethel-Thompson, and sophomore former receiver Osaar Rasshan swapped spots in and out of the lineup. UCLA's disappointing 6-6 regular season cost Dorrell his job, and defensive coordinator DeWayne Walker took over on an interim basis for the Las Vegas Bowl. Utah (9-4), a team the Bruins had beaten 27-17 earlier, nipped UCLA in the bowl when the Utes blocked a potentially-winning, chip-shot field goal on the game's last play. It was that kind of year for several teams that showed well enough to qualify for bowl games but miss expectations due to crippling injuries at quarterback.

As usual in the 2000s, the Southeastern Conference received well-earned but overwhelming publicity as the nation's best, so much so that wags had

to wonder if the 12 conference members might petition for entry into the NFL. And as usual, the SEC powerhouses failed to escape clean from their brutal internal schedules. Neither Georgia (11-2) nor defending national champion Florida could even qualify for the SEC title game. The Bulldogs closed with six wins, and at season's end, many thought Georgia was the best team in the land. The Bulldogs backed up those claims in some measure with a crushing Sugar Bowl win over the Cinderella of non-BCS conferences, the WAC's Hawaii (12-1), the only team in the FBS to escape undefeated from the 12-game regular season.

A unique experience for the SEC, or any conference for that matter, was that a pair of losses by its league champion—in the SEC's case it was LSU, a 21-14 winner over Tennessee (10-4) in the conference title tilt—didn't prevent it from qualifying for the BCS national title game in New Orleans on January 7. But in keeping with the crazy 2007 season, it took several amazing post-Thanksgiving events to send head coach Les Miles' Bengal Tigers to the title game.

First was the case of Ohio State, the national runner-up in 2006 which started out by rebuilding its offense from the previous year. So, Ohio State had begun the year at no. 11 in the AP Poll. Thanks to a soft early schedule, the Buckeyes really got rolling behind its great defense. They reached no. 1 on October 14 and followed with a trio of successive solid wins over Big Ten rivals Michigan State (7-6), Penn State, and Wisconsin. Ohio State maintained the AP top spot for four weeks, but, resurgent Illinois came to Columbus on the Big Ten's penultimate Saturday to surprise the Buckeyes 28-21. That danged Spread Offense, led by Illini whippet quarterback Isaiah "Juice" Williams, was the difference. Ohio State's loss meant that no undefeated team would make the BCS championship game. However, a week later, Ohio State beat Michigan 14-3 to stay alive in national contention with only one loss.

Up stepped Missouri and West Virginia to the top spots. But, on December 1, you guessed it, both stunningly lost. No. 1 Missouri, led by Spread Offense mastermind Chase Daniel, had reached its highest ranking since 1960 by beating upstart Kansas on Thanksgiving Saturday but couldn't get past speedy Oklahoma, which beat the Tigers in the Big 12 title outing, the second Sooners' win over the Tigers. As December's first Saturday developed around three league title games, the Big East's West Virginia appeared home-free as it faced disappointing Pittsburgh in a curtain-closer at Morgantown. The inspired Panthers ruined their rival's BCS title dreams with a tremendous defensive effort in a stunning 13-9 upset. The Mountaineers' star Spread Offense quarterback, Patrick White, missed much of the middle of the game with a bad thumb on his non-throwing hand to again spotlight 2007's common theme.

The door was reopened for Ohio State, which without worry of a Big Ten title match, jumped back to no. 1. A long list of two-loss teams panted eagerly off-stage, and the BCS formula anointed LSU as the Buckeyes' foe in the championship showdown. The Tigers, listed as no. 5 going into the December 1 weekend, leapfrogged idle no. 4 Georgia, which lost clout for its inability to catch Tennessee as SEC East champions. LSU came all the way from seventh in the BCS standings to second.

Georgia and Southern California stewed in the background parroting "What about us!" rhetoric but each would refocus to go on to win big verdicts in their major bowls, the Sugar and Rose respectively.

For its part, Ohio State looked for redemption as January began. In the previous year's BCS championship, the top-ranked Buckeyes had been embarrassed by the defensive speed of SEC champion Florida in a 41-14 loss. This time, determined Ohio State jumped to a 10-0 lead, but new SEC champion LSU's speed and size allowed it to deal 31 unanswered points on the way to a 38-24 BCS Championship victory.

The win closed a challenging season for LSU. Coach Miles often was forced to gamble with amazing results—including conversion on 12 of 15 fourth downs—in rallying his Tigers from behind in six of its 11 prior victories. They came from behind with back-up quarterback Ryan Perrilloux to win the SEC title game from Tennessee. Much-decorated defensive tackle Glenn Dorsey was the victim of an illegal chop block that damaged a knee, but still he fought on in the last five games through pain and frequent double-team blocks. The Tigers suffered a pair of three-overtime losses, and the 50-48 defeat to Arkansas on Thanksgiving Friday was a loss that temporarily ruined everything for LSU. To top it off, Miles was mentioned as the top candidate for the potential coaching opening at Michigan for about 50 straight days, until hours before the SEC title game when he held an intense press conference in which he flatly denied he would leave Baton Rouge for Ann Arbor.

Through it all, the miraculous Bengal Tigers became the first team with two losses ever to be crowned national champions at the close of the bowl season. LSU's championship was especially fantastic given that the Tigers lost as the no. 1 team in the last week of the regular season.

(In 1960, Minnesota became the only national champion ever to have two losses on its ledger. The undefeated Gophers beat no. 1 Iowa in early November but fell flat a week later against an average Purdue team to drop to no. 4. When Kansas upset the new no. 1, Missouri, Minnesota barely edged ahead of unbeaten, once-tied Mississippi, which suffered by not being scheduled against SEC powers Alabama, Auburn, Florida, and Georgia. The Gophers' eventual Rose Bowl loss to Washington lowered their mark to 8-2 and would have eliminated them in the current era. But in those days, electors voted in the final poll before bowl results were in.)

LSU quarterback Matt Flynn, who had struggled with a high ankle sprain suffered early in the year in a rout of eventual ACC champion Virginia Tech and a separated throwing shoulder that kept him out of the SEC title game, threw four touchdowns against Ohio State. Perhaps what lifted LSU from the rest of the pack in 2007 was that the Tigers somehow were able to survive the wounding of their quarterback.

Milestones

■ NCAA renamed top two football divisions: former top-tier Division 1-A became known as Football Bowl Subdivision (FBS), while former Division 1-AA kept its profile as championship playoff-decided group to be henceforth known as Football Championship Subdivision (FCS).

■ Rules committee restored 2005 clock procedures, thus again stopping clock on possession changes and starting clock when receiving team accepted kickoffs, not when kicker struck ball. Kickoff position was moved from kicking team's 35 yard-line to its 30 yard-line.

■ Southern California kicker and NCAA single season record holder for point-after-kicks (83 in 2005), Mario Danelo, 21, died just days after making pair of field goals in victorious Rose Bowl when he fell from high rocky cliff in Los Angeles on January 6. Lloyd Eaton, 88, winningest head coach in Wyoming history with 57-33-2 record from 1962-70, died on March 14. In late March, Oklahoma's Leon "Mule Train" Heath died at 78. Heath played fullback on Sooners' first national title team in 1950. After lengthy battle with Alzheimer's disease, Hall of Fame coach Eddie Robinson, 88, died on April 3 and lain in state at Louisiana's capitol rotunda in Baton Rouge. Robinson was head coach at Grambling for 55 years, won 408 career games (most ever at any single school), and was honored by National Football Foundation in 1992 with its Outstanding Contribution to Amateur Football Award. Darryl Stingley, 55, former wide receiver with Purdue and NFL's New England Patriots, died in early April. Stingley had been confined to wheelchair since tackle by Oakland Raiders' Jack Tatum in NFL preseason game caused spinal cord injury in 1978. George Webster, 61, Michigan State's two-time consensus All-America and innovator at roverback, died of heart failure on April 19. Webster was inducted into College Football Hall of Fame in 1987 and was one of only two Spartans to have uniform number (no. 90) retired. Bill Forester, 74, former Southern Methodist lineman and Green Bay Packers linebacking standout, passed away in Dallas in late April after battling Parkinson's disease. Hall of Famer Alex Agase, who played guard at both Purdue and Illinois during World War II and coached for four decades, died on May 3. Former Syracuse defensive lineman Kevin Mitchell (1990-93) died of a heart attack at 36 in early May. Tom Hutchinson, former record-setting, pass-catcher at Kentucky died on May 7 at 65. Charley Ane, 76, standout tackle for USC's Rose Bowl champions of January 1953 and center-tackle for Detroit Lions' NFL titleists in 1953 and '57, died of pneumonia on May 9 in Honolulu. Marquise Hill, 24, defensive end on Louisiana State's 2003 national champions, died in late May in a jet ski accident in Lake Pontchartrain near New Orleans. Terry Hoeppner, 59, head coach of Indiana, succumbed to complications from brain tumor after long and courageous fight on June 19. Bill Flemming, 80, former ABC college football announcer, died in late July. Bill Walsh, NFL Hall of Fame coach and two-time (1977-78 and 1992-94) head coach at Stanford (34-24-1, including three bowl wins) died of leukemia at age 75 on July 30. Walsh was considered one of game's great tactical minds in his role in development of short-passing attack that became known as West Coast Offense. Former Notre Dame place-kicker Harry Oliver, 47, whose 51-yard field goal against Michigan in 1980 provided Fighting Irish with last-play win, died on August 8 in Cincinnati. Max McGee, 75, halfback at Tulane (1951-1953) and surprise star of Super Bowl I in 1967 as wide receiver for Green Bay Packers, died after fall from roof of his house in Minneapolis on October 21. Former Notre Dame quarterback, Cleveland Browns back-up to Otto Graham, and network TV color analyst George Ratterman died in late October at 80. On November 11, Dick Nolan, former halfback on Maryland's 1953 national champions, died at 75. Nolan played defensive back in the NFL for New York Giants, Chicago Cardinals, Dallas Cowboys, and coached 11 pro seasons (69-82-5), including San Francisco 49ers to three straight division titles in early 1970s. John Ray, Kentucky coach (1969-72), passed away in his home in Granger, Ind., in mid-November at age 81. Jim Ringo, Pro Football Hall of Fame center for coach Vince Lombardi's Green Bay Packers NFL champions and Syracuse standout (1950-52), died at 75 on November 19. Sean Taylor, 24, former Miami Hurricanes All-America safety and on injury furlough from Washington Redskins, was shot in upper leg by intruders in his home on November 26. Killer's bullet hit Taylor's femoral artery, and he died next day from severe loss of blood. Robert Cade, University of Florida nephrologist and one of creators of Gatorade beverage in 1960s, died November 27 at 80. Bill Willis, Ohio State's first African-American All-America player, died at 86 on December 1. Willis' no. 99 had been retired month earlier, he being first Buckeyes' defensive player to have his number retired. Two-way tackle-guard in 1942-44, Willis was one of four players to reintegrate pro ball in 1946 as defensive star for Cleveland Browns and was elected to college and pro Halls of Fame. George Morris, 76, Georgia Tech Hall of Famer, died on December 10. Morris achieved All-America recognition in 1952 on basis of 114 unassisted tackles while captaining Georgia Tech to 12-0 record, including Sugar Bowl win over Mississippi. Morris was first in line of Yellow Jackets' All-America center-linebackers that included Larry Morris in 1953-54, Don Stephenson in 1956-57, and Maxie Baughan in 1959. Just before end of calendar year, Jim Cain, 94, Alabama star in 1934-36, died in Rancho Mirage, Calif. Cain was only man to both play and serve as official in Rose Bowl.

■ Bowl season was most successful ever with 2007-08 attendance reaching 1,733,499 for game average of 54,172. Of 64 teams competing, 28 sold out their ticket allotments, and 11 bowls sported record attendance. Eight bowls were proclaimed sellouts within 24 hours of their matchup announcements. Nearly129 million households tuned in to watch bowls on TV.

■ Longest winning streaks entering season:

Boise State 13	Brigham Young 10	Wisconsin 9

■ Coaching Changes:

	Incoming	Outgoing
Air Force	Troy Calhoun	Fischer DeBerry
Alabama	Nick Saban	Mike Shula
Alabama-Birmingham	Neil Callaway	Watson Brown
Arizona State	Dennis Erickson	Dirk Koetter
Arkansas	Reggie Herring (a)	Houston Nutt
Army	Stan Brock	Bobby Ross
Boston College	Jeff Jagodzinski	Tom O'Brien
Central Michigan	Butch Jones	Brian Kelly
Cincinnati	Brian Kelly	Mark Dantonio
Florida International	Mario Cristobal	Don Strock
Georgia Tech	Jon Tenuta (b)	Chan Gailey
Houston	Chris Thurmond (c)	Art Briles
Idaho	Robb Akey	Nick Holt
Indiana	Bill Lynch	Terry Hoeppner
Iowa State	Gene Chizik	Dan McCarney
Louisiana Tech	Derek Dooley	Jack Bicknell III
Louisville	Steve Kragthorpe	Bobby Petrino
Miami	Randy Shannon	Larry Coker
Michigan State	Mark Dantonio	John L. Smith
Minnesota	Tim Brewster	Glen Mason
Navy	Ken Niumatalolo (d)	Paul Johnson
North Carolina	Butch Davis	John Bunting
North Carolina State	Tom O'Brien	Chuck Amato
North Texas	Todd Dodge	Darrell Dickey
Rice	David Bailiff	Todd Graham
Stanford	Jim Harbaugh	Walt Harris
Texas A&M	Gary Darnell (e)	Dennis Franchione
Tulane	Bob Toledo	Chris Scelfo
Tulsa	Todd Graham	Steve Kragthorpe
UCLA	DeWayne Walker (f)	Karl Dorrell
West Virginia	Bill Stewart (g)	Rich Rodriguez

(a) Herring (0-1) replaced Nutt (8-4) fired prior to Cotton Bowl.
(b) Tenuta (0-1) replaced fired Gailey (7-5) prior to Humanitarian Bowl
(c) Thurmond (0-1) replaced Briles (8-4) prior to Texas Bowl
(d) Niumatalolo (0-1) replaced resigned Johnson (8-4) prior to Poinsettia Bowl
(e) Darnell (0-1) replaced fired Franchoine (7-5) prior to Alamo Bowl
(f) Walker (0-1) replaced fired Dorrell (6-6) prior to Las Vegas Bowl
(g) Stewart (1-0) replaced resigned Rodriguez (10-2) prior to Fiesta Bowl

Preseason *USA Today* Coaches

1	Southern California (45)	1481	14	Auburn	595
2	LSU (4)	1372	15	Tennessee	583
3	Florida (9)	1278	16	Rutgers	466
4	Texas	1231	17	UCLA	454
5	Michigan (2)	1218	18	Penn State	440
6	West Virginia	1205	19	Nebraska	388
7	Wisconsin	1114	20	Arkansas	360
8	Oklahoma	1026	21	Florida State	301
9	Virginia Tech	1005	22	TCU	233
10	Ohio State	919	23	Boise State	222
11	Louisville	836	24	Hawaii	214
12	California	763	25	Texas A&M	209
13	Georgia	604			

September 1, 2007

(Fri) Louisiana State 45 MISSISSIPPI STATE 0; Enormous skills on both sides of ball were on display for LSU (1-0) at Starkville, but interestingly, SEC's coach-on-a-hot-seat, Mississippi State's Sylvester Croom, came away with positive vibes from his Bulldogs (0-1) despite big final score margin. Bulldogs later would gain traction and qualify for their 1st bowl under Croom. Tigers reaped K Colt David's 27y FG in 1st Q, and RB Keiland Williams slammed over twice in 2nd Q for 17-0 lead. QB Matt Flynn (12-19/128y, 2 TDs) clicked on pair of 3rd Q TD passes to salt it away at 31-0. Mississippi State's quiet O suffered 4 sacks, which brought its rushing total down to 10y, but QB Michael Henig managed to complete passes of 45y to tall WR Tony Burks and 20y to RB Amil Stallworth. Bengals SS Craig Steltz forced FUM, broke up pass, and made 3 INTs, which he returned 100y.

VIRGINIA TECH 17 East Carolina 7: Back on chilly spring morning, Virginia Tech's Blacksburg campus had become scene of deadliest shooting rampage in American history as 32 students and faculty members were gunned down by insane, suicidal student gunman. Return of football to Lane Stadium had been looked upon as joyous step in Virginia Tech's healing process. Frank Beamer, 25 years as Hokies player and coach, said beforehand: "It's going to be a continuous process. As long as you're Virginia Tech, you're going to remember April 16th everyday." When Hokies (1-0) took field they carried heavy burden and gave up INT on 1st O play. East Carolina (0-1), opponent admired for its $100,000 contribution to Tech victims' memorial fund, jumped to 7-3 lead early in 2nd Q on RB Chris Johnson's 2y run. Pirates would end game with 142y to 33y rushing advantage. Hokies QB Sean Glennon said later that, "A loss just wouldn't have felt right." To rescue came CB Victor "Macho" Harris, who intercepted pass late in 2nd Q and charged 17y down right sideline to vault over right pylon for TD. Virginia Tech hung on with its tenacious D, and its struggling O finally added 21y TD pass in 4th Q from Glennon (22-33/142y, TD, INT) to TE Sam Wheeler. Afterward, most Hokies players admitted relief in having emotional opener behind them.

Central Florida 25 NORTH CAROLINA STATE 23: In his last 5 years as head coach at Boston College, Tom O'Brien averaged 9 wins. He faced rebuilding project with Wolfpack (0-1), stunned at home in O'Brien's debut by Central Florida Knights (1-0). North Carolina State fell behind for good on game's opening snap as UCF TB Kevin Smith raced 80y down right sideline for 7-0 lead. With Smith and mates dominating play, visitors built 25-3 H lead on nearly 200y O advantage. Sub QB Harrison Beck (17-28/207y), NC State's high profile transfer from Nebraska, led vain rally to UCF 41YL in final min before INT by Knights CB Joe Burnett sealed matters. Earlier, Beck managed 4th Q TD passes of 6y to FB Pat Bedics and 14y to WR Donald Bowen as Wolfpack dominated enough of 2nd H to finish game with 357y to 299y edge. Smith began campaign for national accolades with career-high 217y on 35 carries and 2 TDs. Win was 1st for Knights over BCS conf team in 7 years.

AUBURN 23 Kansas State 13: Loss snapped streak of 17 straight opening game wins for Kansas State (0-1), although road trip to Auburn (1-0) represented huge jump in class for Cats, who once feasted on home openers against weak out-of-conf foes. Neither team could run ball efficiently nor protect its QB—Tigers' rebuilt line allowed 5 sacks—which led to rush totals of 62y for Auburn and 27y for Wildcats. Tigers led 6-3 at H on strength of 2 FGs by K Wes Byrum. Kansas State turned game in its favor early in 3rd Q on TD drive set up by INT by S Marcus Watts at his 31YL. QB Josh Freeman (32-57/268y, 2 INTs) completed 4 straight passes to Auburn 21YL, where on 3rd-and-6 he tossed lateral to WR Jordy Nelson (9/90y), who pulled up and threw TD pass to RB Leon Patton in right side of EZ. Up 10-6, Wildcats used next series to register K Brooks Rossman's 2nd FG midway through 3rd Q. Auburn special teams propelled comeback late in 3rd Q as WR Robert Dunn returned punt 58y to set up 31y FG by Byrum. Auburn D held K-State to pair of 1st downs in 4th Q until its O could punch ball into EZ. Still, K-State retained 13-9 lead until 2:01 was left. Auburn QB Brandon Cox (17-30/229y, TD, 2 INTs) threw 3y TD pass to TE Gabe McKenzie to cap 57y drive. Tigers DE Antonio Coleman soon completed 17-pt rally with 34y FUM TD RET: DE Quentin Groves forced loose ball with sack of Freeman, who later threw INT on his 57th try to end K-State's final drive.

GEORGIA 35 Oklahoma State 14: Youthful Georgia Bulldogs (1-0) were considered potentially vulnerable, especially with 8 new D starters facing Oklahoma State's potent attack (35 pts-per-game in 2006). But Georgia D was aggressive all game, sacking Cowboys (0-1) QB Bobby Reid (16-30/191y, TD, INT) 5 times and swarming from start to finish. Youth was served on Georgia O side of ball too as soph QB Matt Stafford (18-24/234y) threw 2 TD passes, and frosh TB Knowshon Moreno came off bench for game-high 70y rushing and 51y on 2 screen passes. Bulldogs sr TB Thomas Brown (12/48y) scored 2 TDs including 14y TD run on Georgia's opening snap following FUM REC. Cowboys were in game early, tied at 7-7 in 1st Q and trailing 21-14 at H, but could not overcome porous D, 3-13 conversions on 3rd down, and 0-3 on 4th down. Bright spot for Pokes was Reid's 20y TD pass to WR Adarius Bowman (4/65y) to tie game midway through 1st Q.

GAME OF THE YEAR:
Appalachian State 34 MICHIGAN 32

Michigan Stadium crowd of 109,218 welcomed back trio of sr O stars—TB Mike Hart, QB Chad Henne, and T Jake Long—who forsook early-entry NFL pay to shoot for Big 10 and national glory in 2007. On other sideline was itty-bitty Appalachian State (1-0), winners of 14 straight games and most recent 2 Div 1-AA championships. Mountaineers were on their way to unprecedented 3rd straight such title but were expected to be opening-day cannon fodder for Michigan. As anticipated, Wolverines (0-1) took opening KO and glided to 1st of 3 TD runs by Hart (23/188y). But in less than 2 mins, Mountaineers QB Armanti Edwards (17-23/227y, 3 TDs, 2 INTs passing and 17/62y rushing) found WR Dexter Jackson (3/92y, 2 TDs), who streaked through UM's puzzled secondary for 68y TD. After Henne threw 10y TD pass to reestablish 14-7 lead for Michigan, Edwards fashioned brilliant 2nd Q. Using Spread O with great alacrity, Edwards threw pair of scoring passes and bolted 6y on TD run. Wolverines had all they could do manage short FG by K Jason Gingell to close 1st H with 28-17 deficit. After teams traded FGs, Hart scored on 4y run, and with 24 secs left in 3rd Q UM coach Lloyd Carr erred in trying for 2 failed pts which left Wolverines within 31-26. But Michigan's stars again took over as Hart bolted 54y for TD and 32-31 lead with 4:36 remaining in 4th Q. So, Michigan fans were highly relieved to have their team back in front, apparently for good, and seemed unmoved when their team missed another 2-pt try. Fans were cheering again when on 1st snap after Hart's go-ahead TD, S Brandent Englemon intercepted Edwards' errant pass. But, Wolverines couldn't lock it up and had their 1st of 2 FGs blocked. Appalachian State drove 69 yards without available timeout in 1:11 to set up K Julian Rauch's go-ahead 24y FG with 26 secs to play. But, Mountaineers' 34-32 lead still wasn't secure. Henne threw 46y pass to WR Mario Manningham, moving Michigan to Appalachian State 20YL with 6 secs left. DB Corey Lynch slipped through left side of UM line to block FG try and returned it toward other end. Lynch eventually was flagged down by pursuing tacklers, but final moments had ticked away on perhaps greatest-ever upset in football history.

Georgia Tech 33 NOTRE DAME 3: It was shocking how easily Georgia Tech (1-0) fired through O-line of Notre Dame (0-1). Fighting Irish's trio of young QBs was thrown for 72y in losses, and ND ended with -8y rushing. Irish's surprise starting QB Demetrious Jones, in for his ability to run, twice was stripped as he scrambled. Yellow Jackets converted both FUMs into FGs en route to 16-0 H lead. Jones, who finished with team-high 28y rushing, soon chose to leave program. Next-up QB Evan Sharpley ended up running for his life. Sharpley was sacked 7/-45y and threw for only 10-13/92y. Amazingly, 7 different Jackets took part in sacking of Sharpley, with LB Philip Wheeler earning 1.5 of them. Hotshot frosh QB Jimmy Clausen fared no better in his 2nd H debut, completing 4-6/34y on team's final possession before 3rd down sack by LB Anthony Barnes halted drive near midfield. In all, Irish finished with paltry 122y while Yellow Jackets D enjoyed 9 sacks. Georgia Tech TB Tashard Choice rushed for career-high 196y and 2 TDs. It was his 8th straight 100y game, breaking Eddie Lee Ivery's school record. Yellow Jackets gained 380y with K Travis Bell booting 4 FGs. Loss was Notre Dame's worst opener margin in history, topping 31-10 defeat to 1976 national champion Pittsburgh.

Missouri 40 Illinois 34 (St. Louis): Thrilling outcome heated up border war as both squads hoped for improvement in new season. It was heartbreaking loss for Illinois (0-1) as redshirt frosh QB Eddie McGee (17-31/257y, TD, 2 INTs), who replaced injured QB Juice Williams in 2nd Q, rallied his team from 24-pt shortfall late in 3rd Q, only to have Tigers (1-0) S Pig Brown make saving GL INT in final min. Missouri QB Chase

Daniel hit 37-54/359y passing, including TDs in each of 1st 3 Qs. Tigers frosh WR Jeremy Maclin pulled in 25y TD pass and returned punt 66y to score, both in 3rd Q. Maclin's punt RET upped margin to 37-13 with 6:11 to play in 3rd Q, just prior to Illini's comeback. On negative side for Illinois, McGee lost pair of FUMs, and Brown's 100y FUM TD RET proved very costly in 2nd Q as McGee had dashed to within inches of TD on QB Draw. Keeping his spirit up, McGee scored on 16y run with 4:08 left in 3rd Q, and, right after Mizzou WR Dana Alexander lost FUM on reverse, McGee fired 41y TD to WR Kyle Hudson. That pulled Illinois to within 37-27, and Daniel soon fumbled deep in his territory to set up Illini RB Rashard Mendenhall's 2nd TD run. Missouri extended its lead to 40-34 on K Jeff Wolfert's 32y FG nearly midway in 4th Q.

BRIGHAM YOUNG 20 Arizona 3: BYU (1-0) QB Max Hall, playing his 1st game in 4 years, hit 26-39/288y and 1st H TDs to stocky frosh RB Harvey Unga (15/67y rushing) of 27y and TE Dennis Pitta for 2y. Meanwhile, Arizona (0-1) gained only 41y and single 1st down in 1st H. "We never found a rhythm," said Arizona coach Mike Stoops of his team's new O. Wildcats finished game with 32y rushing, while QB Willie Tuitama passed 26-36/216y. Verdict was put out of reach at 20-0 by Unga's 11y TD run with 3:24 left. Arizona immediately launched its best move of game, traveling 80y to Tutitama's 7y TD pass to H-B Earl Mitchell. Big play on drive came on broken play: C snap eluded Tuitama who rolled right and found frosh WR Delashaun Dean (4/88y), who wrestled pass away from Cougars FS Quinn Gooch.

CALIFORNIA 45 Tennessee 31: Year earlier, optimistic California (1-0) was thrashed 35-18 by Tennessee (0-1) in Knoxville. Playing in Cal's scenic Strawberry Canyon this time around, Golden Bears responded with well-balanced attack and 2 non-O TDs. Physically-focused Bears blind-sided Vols QB Erik Ainge (32-47/271y, 3 TDs) on opening series, and LB Worrell Williams cantered 44y on FUM TD REC. Early in 2nd Q, Cal's magical WR DeSean Jackson danced 77y on punt TD RET. It was Jackson's 6th career punt RET for TD. But, Ainge answered each of those missteps with TD passes: Vols went 70y to Ainge's 12y TD to RB Arian Foster (13/89y rushing and 68y KO RET), and TE Chris Brown (7.54y, 2 TDs) nabbed 2y TD midway in 2nd Q. California QB Nate Longshore enjoyed 1 of his best outings, passing 19-28/241y, 2 TDs and scoring on 2y run in 1st Q. Longshore's TD pass to WR Robert Jordan, who leaped between defenders to land in EZ, broke 21-21 deadlock in 2nd Q. K Jordan Kay's 27y FG put Bears ahead 31-21 just 12 secs before H. Longshore and Ainge exchanged 3rd Q TD passes, and Cal RB Justin Forsett (26/156y) put it away with 13y TD run with 9:10 left in 4th Q. Tennessee WR Lucas Taylor led receivers with 6/103y.

(Mon) CLEMSON 24 Florida State 18: Florida State (0-1) had made wholesale offseason alterations to O coaching staff, highlighted by new O coordinator Jumbo Fisher. But, Seminoles opened new year by gaining 62y and single 1st down in 1st H versus revved-up Clemson (1-0). With their D dominating early going, Tigers O took advantage of fortuitous field position to carve TD drives of 57y, 24y, and 60y, and adding FG for 24-3 H lead. New starting QB Cullen Harper (14-24/160y) ended 2 of those drives with scoring passes, including 41y completion to WR Aaron Kelly (5/98y) on bubble screen early in 2nd Q. Clemson TB James Davis added 102y rushing, 29y scoring burst late in 1st Q. Seminoles QB Drew Weatherford (17-34/142y) managed pair of 2nd H TD drives, capping latter with 15y TD pass to WR Richard Goodman with 11:40 left. But FSU failed to score in final 3 series. On last drive, Seminoles made it to Clemson 31YL before 3 incompletions and sack by Tigers DE Philip Merling (9 tackles) ended it. "It looked like stage fright," said Florida State coach Bobby Bowden. "We were running a new offense, but I thought we grasped it better than that. We were bad." Bobby now had lost 3 straight and 4 of 5 "Bowden Bowls" to son Tommy of Clemson.

September 8, 2007

Nebraska 20 WAKE FOREST 17: D stands, something that would be in short supply as season progressed for Nebraska (2-0), won game for Cornhuskers. Grove Stadium at Wake Forest (0-2) had more than 10,000 red-clad Nebraska fans in attendance, and they cheered late EZ INT by Huskers CB Zackary Bowman, who jumped high to take away QB Brett Hodges' potential go-ahead pass with just more than 6 mins to play. In game's closing moments, NU "Blackshirts" D foiled 3rd and 4th down passes to snuff Wake's last try. Hodges (12-24/140y, 2 INTs), subbing for injured QB Riley Skinner, dived across GL with 5:13 left in 2nd Q to give Deacons 10-6 lead, but Nebraska QB Sam Keller (24-41/258y, TD, 2 INTs) mastered 2-min-drill that culminated in sr TE Sean Hill's 1st career reception and 25y TD with 16 secs to go before H. Wake Forest went to TD run by RB Kenneth Moore (8/116y) early in 3rd Q, but later in 3rd Q IB Marlon Lucky retook lead for Huskers at 20-17 with 22y runaway for TD. Nebraska DBs Bowman, Ben Eisenhart, and Cortney Grixby took over in late-going with critical pass D.

South Carolina 16 GEORGIA 12: After years of beating Georgia as coach of Florida (11-1 in annual rivalry), South Carolina (2-0) head man and respected O mind Steve Spurrier engineered upset of 11th-ranked Bulldogs (1-1) behind, of all things, his team's hard-hitting D. Gamecocks won battle in trenches, holding Georgia rush attack

to 128y, although stats were padded by 3 sacks of QB Matt Stafford (19-44/213y, INT). South Carolina D grew tough in red zone, holding Georgia to K Brandon Coutu 4 FGs. Cocks scored only single TD, but it was difference-making 9y run by RB Cory Boyd (14/76y) in 1st Q. After that, kicking contest rose up between Coutu and Gamecocks K Ryan Succop (3 FGs). Best chance for Bulldogs came on late drive that stalled when pass to frosh WR Tony Wilson bounced off his hands at GL. Win earned South Carolina QB Blake Mitchell (20-31/174y) measure of redemption after he was suspended for opening win over Louisiana-Lafayette for missing summer classes. Georgia bright spot was running of TB Knowshon Moreno (14/104y). At Carolina, Spurrier now stood at 1-2 vs. nearby Georgia.

South Florida 26 AUBURN 23 (OT): Going to Jordan-Hare Stadium to tangle with hard-nosed Auburn Tigers (1-1) was plenty intimidating no matter how promising South Florida (2-0) was considered. Yet, coach Jim Leavitt's naive Bulls jumped to 14-3 lead in 1st Q. South Florida frosh TB Mike Ford (21/74y, TD) set up opening score with 20y run, 2 plays before soph QB Matt Grothe's 1y TD keeper. After 49y FG by Auburn K Wes Byrum, Grothe sparked 69y drive that Ford capped with 2y TD run. On consecutive plays on drive, irrepressible Grothe had 23y completion to WR Taurus Johnson and 27y run to Tigers 4YL. Stunned, Auburn, which would end up losing TO to battle by 0-5, fought back with pair of 2nd Q TDs, QB Brandon Cox (16-35/165y, TD, 2 INTs) throwing 3y TD pass to TE Gabe McKenzie for 17-14 lead. South Florida K Delbert Alvarado missed 4 of 6 FG tries in 2nd H but came through with 18y chip-shot FG to create 20-20 tie and OT with 55 secs left. In 1st extra frame, Bulls held Auburn to 2y O, but Byrum booted 39y FG. It took Grothe (18-27/184y) 5 plays—including 3 solo runs for 1st down—to get ball into EZ, tallying winning TD on 14y pass to WR Jesse Hester (6/64y) in corner of EZ. With win, South Florida upped its OT record to 6-0.

LOUISIANA STATE 48 Virginia Tech 7: It was no surprise to see no. 2 Louisiana State (2-0) running up big score against out-of-conf opponent. This matchup was different, of course, as visiting Virginia Tech Hokies (1-1) had arrived in Bayou country with national title ambitions. In front of record crowd of 92,739 at Tiger Stadium, QB Matt Flynn (17-27/217y) drove LSU 87y and 85y to TDs on opening 2 possessions, capping 2nd with 7y scoring run. Tigers scored on 4 of 1st 5 tries, outgaining Virginia Tech 327y to 40y at H. Sharp LSU sub RB Keiland Williams came close to matching Hokies' final total of 149y O all by himself on 7/126y, 2 TDs. Williams' 67y scoring romp with option pitch from Flynn gave Tigers 24-0 lead they took to H. LSU's youthful depth dominated 2nd H as soph QB Ryan Perrilloux (5-5/84y) threw for pair of TDs, including 28y score to frosh WR Terrance Tolliver, and soph Williams added 32y TD run. LSU finished with 598y against Tech's respected D. Hokies reserve QB Tyrod Taylor scored sole TD on 1y run in 3rd Q. Taylor threw for 62y and rushed for team-high 44y. Loss was worst for coach Frank Beamer in his 21 years at Virginia Tech. "What a football team," said Beamer of rampaging Bengals. "They really took it to us."

PENN STATE 31 Notre Dame 10: Extent of rebuilding needed at Notre Dame (0-2) was evident in Irish's inability to protect frosh QB Jimmy Clausen (17-32/144y, INT), who was dumped for 6 losses/-50y. Penn State (2-0) D was cheered on by 110,000 clad almost entirely in white and led by LB Dan Connor, who supplied 12 tackles, crushing sack of Clausen, and 2 other tackles for loss. Fighting Irish gained 0y rushing and only 144y passing, yet got on scoreboard 1st when Nittany Lions QB Anthony Morelli (12-22/131y, TD, INT) suffered INT by ND CB Darrin Walls, who cruised down sideline for 73y TD in 1st Q. Penn State WR Derrick Williams soon tied it, snaring punt at his shoestrings and exploding for 78y TD RET. Morelli ended 51y drive in 2nd Q with 10y TD arrow to WR Jordan Norwood, and Lions led 14-7. Penn State DB A.J. Wallace returned 2nd H KO 68y to set up K Kevin Kelly's 37y FG for 17-7 lead. Notre Dame S Tom Zbikowski fired 47y through Lions' punt coverage team to 7YL. But, Penn State held Irish to K Brandon Walker's FG. Morelli's 51y pass set up TB Austin Scott's slam across GL for 24-10 edge. It was last scheduled match-up of long-time powers, and Penn State's victory knotted series at 9-9-1.

Oregon 39 MICHIGAN 7: Here arrived another Spread Offense QB to make Michigan (0-2) D look befuddled. QB Dennis Dixon (16-25/292y, 3 TDs) of Oregon (2-0) accounted for 368y and 4 TDs. Dixon's signature play was masterpiece of deception in 2nd Q: Taking long snap and faking handoff, Dixon slipped ball out of sight behind his back and hesitated as Wolverines chased flow to its right. He veered toward Michigan's left side and romped into EZ that built 25-7 lead. Michigan had owned brief 7-3 lead in 1st Q as QB Chad Henne (12-23/172y, TD, INT) tossed 7y TD to WR Adrian Arrington. In less than min, Dixon lofted 85y TD bomb to WR Brian Paysinger, 1st of his 3 TD throws. Henne suffered leg injury and missed 2nd H, but with Oregon leading 32-7 at H its win was foregone conclusion. Ducks TB Jonathan Stewart rushed 15/111y, TD. After Michigan's worst defeat since losing 50-14 to Ohio State in 1968, coach Lloyd Carr defined situation: "If losing doesn't make you hurt, you shouldn't be at Michigan."

OKLAHOMA 51 Miami 13: Largest-ever crowd for any sporting event in state history saw Sooners (2-0) gain some measure of revenge for 3-sweep by Miami (1-1) in 1980s. Intersectional series now stood at 3-3 after Oklahoma cruised away from 21-13 advantage in 3rd Q. Spectacular frosh QB Sam Bradford (19-25/205y, 5 TDs) tied Sooners school record with 5 scoring throws, 3 of which for 23, 24, and 30y were collared by WR Malcolm Kelly (4/102y). OU CB Reggie Smith added 61y FUM TD RET in 2nd Q. After settling for FG in their opening 7 possessions, Hurricanes turned to QB Kyle Wright (7-14/65y, TD), who promptly sparked 52y drive late in 2nd Q, kept alive by DE Calais Campbell's 5y reception on fake FG, to 6y TD pass to WR Ryan Hill. Oklahoma fumbled on its opening drive of 3rd Q, but Miami had to settle for FG that pulled it within 21-13. WR Juaquin Iglesius returned next KO 43y, Bradford hit his 3rd TD pass, and Sooners launched 30-pt ambush.

TEXAS 34 Texas Christian 13: In seeking to become this year's small-conf BCS Bowl breaker, TCU (1-1) had focused on early season visit to Austin against Longhorns (2-0), lords of Lone Star State. Purple "Beat Texas" T-shirts were in abundant supply and they appeared to be hot item when Horned Frogs moved to 10-0 H edge. CB Torrey Stewart went 45y to INT TD RET on 1 of pair of INTs thrown by Texas QB Colt McCoy (25-38/239y, TD, 2 INTs) in 1st H. Just 3 mins later, K Chris Manfredini closed 1st H with 19y FG for TCU's 10-0 lead. McCoy had faith he could come back: "...you're going to get tested. You get tested, then you're blessed." McCoy pitched 33y TD to WR Nate Jones (8/91y, TD) early in 3rd Q, and his 23y scramble set up RB Vondrell McGee's TD run that put Longhorns ahead 17-10 early in 4th Q. TCU earned only 17y and no 1st downs in 3rd Q as Horns D took command. DB Brandon Foster picked up fumbled snap by Frogs P Derek Walsh and went 20y for TD. Becoming late-game scourge, Texas RB Jamaal Charles added 39y TD run among his 22/134y on ground. Coach Gary Patterson lamented end of TCU's 5-game win streak over Big 12 foes: "This is not one of those games where you are happy you played well for a half. We came here to win."

BAYLOR 42 Rice 17: Old SWC rivals met for 1st time since 1995, and Baylor Bears (1-1) won its 4th straight over Rice (0-2). Soph QB Blake Szymanski (29-46/412y, 6 TDs) set Baylor record with 4 TD passes in 1st H led by Bears by 28-7. Owls were led by QB Chase Clement, who passed 20-25/207y, INT, scored on run in 1st H. RB James Casey scored from 2YL to pull Owls to within 28-17 in 3rd Q, but Szymanski struck for pair of aerial scores in less than 3 mins. WR Thomas White caught 20y TD, and CB Alton Widemon quickly nabbed INT. Szymanski and WR Ernest Smith failed on TD pass attempt late in 3rd Q, but came right back on same call on next play for 39y TD and 42-14 edge. Rice star WR Jarret Dillard (5/93y) failed to catch TD pass for 2nd time in 2007 after snatching scores in 15 games in row.

Air Force 20 UTAH 12: Picked universally for bottom of Mt West, Air Force (2-0) again was tough in league opener (8-1 to date) and upset Utah (0-2) with strong D. Falcons broke 3-3 H deadlock on 4y TD run by frosh TB Savier Stephens at end of 53y drive in 3rd Q. Air Force soon tried 4th-and-1 at Utah 47 and lost 1y, but Falcons S Chris Thomas got ball right back when he made diving INT. On 1st down, AFA QB Shaun Carney (16/113y rushing) broke option run for 53y, and TB Jim Ollis scored 2 plays later to give Falcons 17-6 lead with 12:52 left. After gaining only 162y in 3 Qs, Utes finally came alive in 4th Q. QB Tommy Grady (20-39/240y, TD, 2 INTs), making his 1st start, arched 34y TD pass to WR Derrek Richards (8/109y) but missed 2-pt pass to leave Utah down 17-12 with 6:24 to play. It was 1st TD permitted by Falcons after 7 Qs so far in 2007. Air Force built some breathing room at 20-12 on K Ryan Harrison's 2nd FG with 3:11 to go. Utah, which gained 151y in 4th Q, responded with 79y march that came up 6 inches short. ILB Drew Fowler, who would end year as Falcons' top tackler, stopped RB Darryl Poston on 4th down.

UCLA 27 Brigham Young 17: Prior to game, much was made of match-up of Cougars and Bruins QB Ben Olson, former Brigham Young (1-1) redshirt and church missionary, who transferred to UCLA (2-0) prior to 2006 season. Olson's passing was less than scintillating at 13-28/126y, but other forces built UCLA's 20-3 1st H lead as CB Trey Brown weaved 56y with INT TD RET and K Kai Forbath made 40y FG after Brown returned FUM 21y to BYU 41YL. In between, Bruins TB Kalil Bell (16/79y) lugged ball for 26 and 17y gains on his way to 4y TD blast. Down by 17 pts, Cougars started 2nd H with TD drives of 80 and 40y. QB Max Hall (30-52/391y, 2 TDs, INT) found WR Austin Collie for scores of 5 and 16y to trail 20-17. Bruins D bent under BYU's 2nd H rally but held off another scoring charge at its 19YL as DE Bruce Davis (2 sacks/-15y) sacked Hall, and DE Tom Blake recovered FUM. Finally, UCLA wrapped it up with 12-play, 45y drive in last 3 mins, capped by TB Chris Markey's short TD run.

ARIZONA STATE 33 Colorado 13: Critics of Dennis Erickson's intense coaching style could point to Arizona State's damaging 12/136y in PENs. New-found D prowess of Sun Devils (2-0) could be credited to intensity as personified by LB Robert James, who made 9 tackles, swooped in for 9y sack, and broke up passes on 2 straight plays. Erickson enjoyed his 150th career victory and comeback from 14-0 deficit in 2nd Q. Meanwhile, Colorado (1-1) frosh QB Cody Hawkins, son of Buffs coach Dan Hawkins, suffered end of his personal 60-game win streak that dated to 6th grade. Buffaloes got on scoreboard on game's 2nd snap as CB Terrence Wheatley intercepted Devils QB Rudy Carpenter (19-37/269y, 3 TDs, INT) for 35y TD. It was 14-0 for Colorado when WR Scotty McKnight caught 10y TD pass later in 1st Q after punt accidentally touched ASU WR Tyrice Thompson and roughing PEN on Buffs FG try provided young Hawkins with 2nd chance. Carpenter hit WR Michael Jones with 12y TD in 2nd Q, and James tipped pass to S Troy Nolan, who returned INT 26y to TD. Devils missed x-pt to trail 14-13, but WR Kyle Williams caught 22y TD from Carpenter for 19-14 lead with 14 secs before H. TB Ryan Torain (17/91y, TD) ran for TD and Carpenter added his 3rd TD pass as ASU pulled away with 14pts in 3rd Q. Buffs LB Jordan Dizon missed some time with cramps in 100-degree desert heat but still made 15 tackles, including 3/-14y.

USA Today Coaches September 9

1	Southern California (42)	1476	14	Nebraska	677
2	LSU (11)	1437	15	Georgia Tech	582
3	Florida (7)	1353	16	Arkansas	493
4	West Virginia	1269	17	Virginia Tech	371
5	Oklahoma	1264	18	Texas A&M	325
6	Texas	1156	19	Boston College	315
7	Wisconsin	1141	20	Clemson	311
8	California	1038	21	Oregon	309
9	Louisville	1020	22	Hawaii	308
10	Ohio State	972	23	South Carolina	294
11	UCLA	837	24	Tennessee	237
12	Penn State	804	25	Georgia	199
13	Rutgers	699			

September 15, 2007

(Th) West Virginia 31 MARYLAND 14: It would turn out to be injury-affected season for star TB Steve Slaton (137y rushing) of no. 4 West Virginia Mountaineers (3-0). But, against Terrapins (2-1), Slaton scored 3 TDs to move within 1 of school's all-time record of 42 career TDs. Yet talk after game centered on his frosh understudy, mercurial TB Noel Devine, team's highly-recruited speedster from Ft. Myers, Fla. After being worn down by Slaton and QB Patrick White (8-13/95y, and 22y TD run), Terps simply were unable to corral Devine, who rushed 5/136y. Having not carried ball in 1st H, fresh Devine raced 31y to Maryland 1YL early in 3rd Q to set up Slaton's 2nd TD run. Later in 3rd Q, Devine sliced through Maryland D for 76y romp, again reaching 1YL, to set up Slaton's 3rd scoring rush. With his 3rd carry of game, Devine went only 18y to set up 4th Q FG. Maryland TB Keon Lattimore rushed for 80y and TD, his 6th of young season, and QB Jordan Steffy (16-23/180y, 2 INTs) threw his 1st career scoring pass, but Terps were doomed to their 4th straight series loss because of stretch of 8 straight possessions without pts in middle of game.

(Th) AIR FORCE 20 Texas Christian 17 (OT): Remaining undefeated under new coach Troy Calhoun, Air Force (3-0) celebrated thrilling come-from-behind victory on K Ryan Harrison's 33y FG in 1st OT period. Texas Christian (1-2) built 10-3 H advantage on K Chris Manfredini's 39y FG—after blocked punt by S Stephen Hodges who charged through Falcons' "clothes-line" blocking protection—and short TD fade-route flip from frosh QB Andy Dalton (29-45/320y, 2 TDs, 2 INTs) to WR Ervin Dickerson (5/68y, TD). It was offset only by Falcons K Harrison's career-long 57y FG that came 1:31 before H. Frogs went up 18-3 early in 4th Q on Dalton's 11y pass to WR Walter Byant. But for several scoring blunders in 2nd H, TCU would have been on way home to Fort Worth when OT started. Manfredini's 20y chip-shot was blocked by SS Chris Thomas, Air Force's 100th blocked kick in 17 years, LB Drew Fowler's red-zone INT, and Dalton's underthrown INT in last min of regulation when Manfredini was well within range of game-winning FG at AF 22YL. Air Force began its 4th Q rally as QB Shaun Carney (17-28/193y, TD, INT) ripped 50y pass to TE Travis Dekker to set up his 9y TD pass to TE Keith Madsen. Falcons gambled on 4th-and-1 at their 29YL with 6 mins to go: Carney flipped option pitchout to TB Jim Ollis (16/138y, TD), who was home-free for tying TD sprint. In top half of OT, Manfredini hit left upright to open dor for Harrison to win it with 3-ptr.

Boston College 24 GEORGIA TECH 10: Boston College (3-0) maintained pace atop ACC Atlantic race with 3rd straight conf win, and much credit had to go to 1 of nation's top passers, QB Matt Ryan. Ryan was close to unstoppable, throwing for career-high 435y on 30-44. In fact, when stat dust settled, Georgia Tech (2-1), despite its strong D, had been outgained 527y to 267y. Ryan took over from opening series, which began on BC 5YL after excellent pooch punt by Georgia Tech P Durent Brooks (10/45.3y avg). Facing early 3rd-and-2, Ryan used play action to free TE Jon Loyte for 40y reception. Ryan then teamed up with WR Kevin Challenger (7/88y) for passes of 16y and 25y to set up 1y TD run by RB L. V. Whitworth. Early in 2nd Q, Ryan threw his only TD pass, 39y to WR Brandon Robinson (5/128y) that capped 79y drive. Eagles' 4th-ranked rush D stymied Jackets TB Tashard Choice, holding returning conf rush champ to meager 15/31y before he departed in 3rd Q with hamstring injury. By that point, BC had upped its lead to 21-0 on Whitworth's 2nd TD run (16y). With QB Taylor Bennett (20-34/209y) elevating his play in 2nd H, Yellow Jackets put 10 pts on scoreboard in 4th Q. But in waning moments, BC marched 71y to clinching 21y FG by K Steve Aponavicious.

Texas 35 CENTRAL FLORIDA 32: Fired-up Central Florida (1-1) opened it new on-campus stadium before packed house, while no. 6 Texas (3-0) was suffering delayed flights and bus breakdowns. "It was a trap game for us and a buzzsaw," said Longhorns coach Mack Brown. Still, Texas built 20-10 H lead in off-and-on heavy rain as CB Brandon Foster returned INT 33y for score and K Ryan Bailey beat H clock by 1 sec for his 2nd of 5 FGs. Trailing 23-10, Knights sent RB Kevin Smith (27/149y) to his 2nd TD run and QB Kyle Israel (9-26/134y, TD, INT) to TD sneak to take 24-23 lead early in 4th Q. Pair of FGs put Texas back in front 29-24, and CB Marcus Griffin recovered UCF FUM with less than 4 mins to go. Longhorns RB Jamaal Charles (22/153y) raced 46y to clinch it at 35-24 before Israel threw TD and 2-pt pass in last 35 secs to slice final margin.

VANDERBILT 31 Mississippi 17: Vanderbilt (2-1) improved its all-time record to 34-46-34-2 against Mississippi (1-2) as Rebs dropped their conf opener for 4th year in row. Vandy led 14-3 at H as sore-legged QB Chris Nickson (17-25/200y) hit his 1st 10 passes and scored on 2y run. RB Cassen Jackson-Garrison (23/119y, 3 TDs) scored on 8y run in 2nd Q. Ole Miss WR Mike Wallace (4/139y, 2 TDs) caught 36y TD from QB Seth Adams (10-17/154y, TD, INT) to trim 3rd Q mark to 14-10. After Jackson-Garrison's 2nd TD run 2 mins into 4th Q, Commodores were ahead 24-10, but Rebels QB Brent Schaeffer, in relief of banged-up Adams, completed his 1st attempt for 54y TD pass to Wallace. Ole Miss could get no closer as Schaeffer missed his last 4 pass tries. Vandy WR Earl Bennett caught 11/100y, his 9th career game with 100 or more receiving y. Commodores D permitted 262y, registered 6 sacks, and made their only takeaway on CB D.J. Moore's INT.

KENTUCKY 40 Louisville 34: Kentucky QB Andre Woodson upstaged counterpart Louisville QB Brian Brohm, his longtime rival, to propel Wildcats (3-0) to Blue Grass victory and national splash for both Cats and their ever-improving sr passer. As expected, both QBs had huge games as Brohm, who had never lost to Woodson dating back to HS, hit 28-43/366y, 2 TDs, while Woodson posted 4 TDs on 30-44/275y. With 74 pts on scoreboard, other players shone too: Wildcats RB Rafael Little rushing 27/151y and TD, and Cardinals WR Trent Guy scoring on 100y KO RET. Brohm led 83y TD drive, capped by 2y scoring run by RB Anthony Allen (18/96y, 2 TDs), to give Cards 34-33 lead with 1:45 left. Kentucky tallied game-winning TD on 57y strike from Woodson to WR Steve Johnson with 28 secs left. Johnson had gotten behind Louisville (2-1) secondary—as receivers would do all year—and hauled in scoring pass that chased humbled Cards out of nation's top 10. UK coaches had put image in their memory banks when Woodson overthrew Johnson on same 4-WR flood pattern at end

of 1st H. Brohm's final, desperate fling was caught by WR Harry Douglas (13/223y) off deflection at Kentucky 15YL. He got as far as 11YL before being tackled by Wildcats S Marcus McClinton with clock expired. Kentucky's win was its 1st over Louisville since 2002 and 1st over top-10 team since 1977.

FLORIDA 59 Tennessee 20: Gators (3-0) QB Tim Tebow's TD parade began reaching stratosphere as he ran and passed for 2 scores each and accounted for 366y. But 1st, it took little RB Brandon James to ignite Florida; he fielded punt less than 2 mins into game and flew 83y for TD. Later in 1st Q, Tennessee (1-2) frosh K Daniel Lincoln stayed perfect 6-6 in 2007 by hitting 1st of his 2 FGs. Tebow made his pair of TD throws before H as Florida led 28-13. Vols D played well in 3rd Q, pulling within 28-20 thanks to CB Eric Berry's 96y INT TD RET. But outcome turned for good after Florida punt when Tennessee RB Arian Foster (11/26y) lost FUM deep in his end, and Gators LB Dustin Doe collared loose ball for 18y TD for 35-20 lead. Florida was charging full steam now and racked up 24 unanswered pts in 4th Q. Vols QB Erik Ainge passed 26-41/249y, TD, INT, while Tebow countered with 14-19/299y, 2 TDs, INT.

Mississippi State 19 AUBURN 14: Bulldogs (2-1) crossed eastern state boundary and returned home upset winners for 2nd year in row. Last year's pelt was that of Alabama; this year they reversed 6-game series losing streak at hands of Auburn (1-2). Mississippi State needed late TD and even later D stand deep to pull out win. Choosing to run on all 10 downs of 44y drive, Bulldogs earned 4th Q winning TD set up by S Demario Bobo's 1st career INT. RBs Anthony Dixon (29/103y) and Christian Ducre (10/63y) hammered away until Ducre scored on 5y run with 5:27 left. Auburn QB Brandon Cox, benched in 1st H after throwing 2 INTs including 20y TD RET by S Derek Pegues, came back to lead Tigers' desperate late drive. Cox (4-10/42y) moved Auburn 67y, gaining 23y on pass to WR Rod Smith, before stalling on downs at Miss State 9YL. With DE Titus Brown bringing pressure, Cox's final pass fell short of Smith in EZ. Sub QBs Wesley Carroll (3-10/10y) and Josh Riddell (1-5/15y) engineered Bulldogs O but struck no fear in hearts of Auburn DBs. Auburn frosh QB Kodi Burns wiped out 13-0 2nd Q deficit with 2 TD drives, capping 2nd with 1y keeper for 14-13 lead, but was unable to sustain much O in 2nd H. Burns finished with 87y rushing, but only 8-12/65y through air.

ALABAMA 41 Arkansas 38: Alabama coach Nick Saban's return to college ranks continued its early success as his Crimson Tide (3-0) overcame spirited 4th Q comeback by Razorbacks to win in final moments. Falling behind 31-10 late in 3rd Q, Arkansas (1-1) rallied with 28 straight pts to take 38-31 lead on 7y TD pass by QB Casey Dick (11-23/145y, 3 TDs, INT) to FB Peyton Hillis. Alabama drove into Hogs territory before facing 4th-and-6 at 25YL. Saban opted for FG, which K Leigh Tiffin nailed from 42y out to pull within 38-34. Now it was up to Alabama D, which had blanched all game at sight of renowned Razorbacks TB Darren McFadden (33/195y). But McFadden, who rushed for 53y and 2 TDs in 4th Q, was forced to skip Arkansas' last series with slight concussion. Despite ending up with 301y rushing against it, Alabama D now delivered when it mattered, allowing 8y on 6 plays by Hogs. After punt, Alabama began final possession at own 27YL with 2:13 remaining. Tide QB John Parker Wilson (24-45/327y, 4 TDs, 2 INTs), whose FUM and INT each led to late Arkansas TD, stepped to up, hitting 7-8/56y of drive's 73y. Only 8 secs remained when Wilson hit sr WR Matt Caddell (9/91y) at left side of EZ with 4y TD pass. With WR D.J. Hall (6/172y, 2 TDs) serving as main focus of D, Caddell caught 4/41y on drive. Hall's 43y catch on game's 1st play had allowed him to break Ozzie Newsome's school career receiving y record.

MICHIGAN 38 Notre Dame 0: Slumping Michigan (1-2) was stirred by sr TB Mike Hart, who guaranteed victory by saying he'd have his teammates "ready" for this game. Hart provided enough O all by himself, rushing 35/187y and scoring 1st and 2nd Q TDs. Hart was hardly alone as frosh QB Ryan Mallett (7-15/90y, 3 TDs) spread trio of TD passes in middle Qs to 3 different receivers. Fighting Irish (0-3) was winless after 3 games for only 2nd time (2001) in school history. Michigan D, so overmatched in opening 2 losses, sacked Irish QB Jimmy Clausen (11-17/74y, INT) 7 times to drop ND's rushing total to 33/-6y. Happenstances were awful right from start for Notre Dame: Irish's 1st snap sailed over head of RB Armando Allen (9/24y), and ND lost 27y on its opening 2 possessions. After gaining 2 FUMs and INT, Michigan led 31-0 at H. Amazingly, it was 1st time since AP Poll started in 1936 that both super-powers entered weekend unranked.

MICHIGAN STATE 17 Pittsburgh 13: It was familiar turf for Michigan State (3-0): MSU earned its 3rd straight 3-0 start in as many years, and Spartans stayed undefeated all-time against Pittsburgh (2-1) at 6-0-1. After S Otis Wiley's 14y INT RET to Pitt 35YL late in 1st Q, Spartans QB Brian Hoyer (14-28/183y) hit top TE Kellen Davis with 32y pass. Huge TB Jehuu Caulcrick bulled over from 2YL early in 2nd Q. Panthers struck back quickly: star frosh TB LeSean McCoy (25/172y, TD) broke away for 64y TD gallop. Michigan State came back on Pitt's next possession: S Travis Key grabbed tipped screen pass and raced 31y untouched for 14-7 lead. In addition to blocking Spartans' 3-pt try in 3rd Q, Pitt got pair of FGs from K Conor Lee to pull within 14-13 midway in 4th Q. MSU K Brett Swenson was short with FG try with less than 3 mins to play, and Spartans had to survive 40y pass to EZ by Panthers QB Kevan Smith (9-18/95y, 2 INTs) on last play.

Southern California 49 NEBRASKA 31: TB Stafon Johnson, 1 of Southern California's large stable of running backs, gained career-high 144y and TD that provided Trojans (2-0) with 21-10 H lead. USC got off to ripping start on FB Stanley Havili's 50y run, followed by TB C.J. Gable's 40y sprint that led to Havili's 5y TD catch from QB John David Booty (19-30/144y, 2 TDs). Nebraska (2-1), playing before its 284th consecutive sellout at Memorial Stadium, clawed to 10-7 edge in 2nd Q. Huskers cashed RB Cody Glenn's 1st of pair of 1y TD runs and K Alex Henery's 37y FG halfway through 2nd Q. But, USC, which set Nebraska opponent's game record of 8.2y per carry, scored TDs on next 5 possessions for 42-10 lead in 3rd Q. Nebraska QB Sam Keller (36-54/389y, 2 TDs, 2 INTs) pitched pair of late TD passes to WR Todd Peterson (5/74y, 2 TDs).

Ohio State 33 WASHINGTON 14: Improved Washington (2-1) gave top-ranked D of Buckeyes (3-0) all it could handle, especially when QB Jake Locker (16-33/153y, TD, 3 INTs) handed ball to tune of 255y and took Huskies into enemy territory 6 times. Although INTs would hurt him, Locker pitched 23y TD on next to last play of 1st H to WR Anthony Russo, who made twisting grab at GL. Russo's TD was 1st permitted by Ohio State to date this year. Huskies looked to extend their 7-3 H edge on opening series of 3rd Q: Personal foul PEN gave UW 1st down at Ohio 19YL, but 3 plays lost y, including sack by Buckeyes LB James Laurinaitis (2 INTs) back to 29YL. Soph CB Kurt Coleman then blocked Washington's 46y FG attempt, and 2 plays later, Buckeyes QB Todd Boeckman (14-25/218y, 2 TDs) arched perfect 68y rainbow to WR Brian Robiskie (4/107y, TD) for TD that provided 10-7 lead. Washington frosh RB Curtis Shaw lost FUM on ensuing KO, and Ohio TB Chris Wells sprung 11 and 14y runs, latter through arm tackle for TD and 17-7 edge. Ohio State was rolling now as K Ryan Pretorius kicked his 2nd FG in 1st min of 4th Q and Boeckman added TD pass with 3:30 to go. Even though RB Louis Rankin (14/42y, TD) went 2y for Huskies' TD in last min, Bucks sent frosh TB Brandon Saine (9/83y, TD) on 37y TD run on last play. Wells rushed 24/135y of Ohio's 263y.

New Mexico 29 ARIZONA 27: Hopeful Wildcats (1-2) laid egg at home against New Mexico (2-1). Arizona failed to move on ground (21/38y), and, although QB Willie Tuitama (30-53/446y, 3 TDs, INT) was often effective in air, Cats bungled frequent chances. Lobos QB Donovan Porterie (29-41/327y, INT) zeroed in on 3 TDs: pair to WR Travis Brown (10/121y) of 6 and 38y and to WR Marcus Smith (11/164y) of 32y. Arizona's follies started with 1st down at Lobos 15YL in 1st Q that turned into missed 32y FG. Tuitama lost FUM inside New Mexico 5YL in 2nd Q. In 3rd Q, Tuitama was called for international grounding in his EZ for safety that lifted Lobos' lead to 19-13. Tuitama found WR Mike Thomas (7/137y, 2 TDs) for 12y TD early in 4th Q to pull Wildcats within 26-20, and duo soon hooked up for 48y gain. But, Cats RB Chris Jennings lost FUM to S O.J. Swift which led to K John Sullivan's clinching 44y FG.

UTAH 44 Ucla 6: Perhaps losing on road at Utah (1-2) wasn't biggest surprise, but Bruins' margin of defeat had to raise eyebrows. UCLA (2-1) lost 5 TOs, committed 10 PENs, and failed to score TD for 1st time in 4 years. Utes used plenty of new faces to dominate in 1st-ever win over Bruins after going 0-8 since 1933. This season's new signal-caller, QB Tommy Grady (17-30/246y, 3 TDs), pitched 53y TD to WR Marquis Wilson in 1st Q, RB Darrell Mack (19/101y, TD) made his 1st start memorable with 2 TD catches, and FS Robert Johnson made his maiden start impactful with 2 INTs, pass break-up, and forced FUM that opened floodgates for good in 3rd Q. After cashing pair of long FGs by K Kai Forbath, UCLA stayed within striking distance at 14-6 at H. Down 17-6, Bruins QB Ben Olson (20-40/290y, 3 INTs) sent WR Marcus Everett for apparent 52y TD. Everett stumbled and when he tried to extend ball over GL, Utah's Johnson was there to strip him: Everett's FUM bounded straight through EZ for touchback. Utah quickly cashed this exchange with TD pass by sub frosh QB Corbin Louks. K Louie Sakoda made 45 and 44y FGs, and Mack scored on pass from Grady and on 4y run to complete rout.

USA Today Coaches September 16

1	Southern California (44)	1478	14t	Clemson	595
2	LSU (8)	1438	14t	South Carolina	595
3	Florida (7)	1368	16	Texas A&M	530
4	Oklahoma (1)	1308	17	Virginia Tech	485
5	West Virginia	1244	18	Hawaii	404
6	Texas	1103	19	Louisville	383
7	Wisconsin	1098	20	Alabama	345
8	California	1093	21	Georgia	271
9	Ohio State	1062	22	Nebraska	228
10	Penn State	942	23	Kentucky	168
11	Rutgers	863	24	South Florida	165
12	Boston College	754	25	Missouri	145
13	Oregon	702			

September 22, 2007

(Th) MIAMI 34 Texas A&M 17: If only Hurricanes (3-1) could play every game on Thursday night at Orange Bowl as they ran record in such games to 10-0. Big moments would be few for Miami in 2007, but in this Thursday national TV game, Hurricanes owned night right from their early 18-play, clock-eating trip to 7y TD run on direct snap by RB Graig Cooper (7/50y, TD). Miami wedged 17 pts into last 5 mins of 2nd Q for 24-0 H lead: RB Javarris James (20/46y, TD) pounded over from 1YL, and, with 24 secs before H, Cooper caught 12y screen pass TD from QB Kyle Wright (21-26/275y, 2 TDs), who with this throw overtook George Mira (1961-63) for 10th on Canes' all-time passing TD list. Finally, when Texas A&M (3-1) C Cody Wallace bobbled away short KO, K Francesco Zampogna nailed 45y FG for 24-pt lead as H clock reached 0:00. To show it simply wasn't Aggies' night, Miami's 2nd TD was set up by pass that caromed off A&M LB Mark Dodge to Canes WR Darnell Jenkins, who made catch while lying on ground inside A&M 10YL. Aggies, whose nearly 300y per game rushing avg turned into modest 69y, earned measure of pride in 4th Q with 17 pts on K Matt Szymanski's 32y FG, QB Stephen McGee's 1y TD keeper, and TE Martell Bennett's 33y TD catch with 5 secs left.

Connecticut 34 PITTSBURGH 14: Beating Duke, Maine, and Temple to open season gave Connecticut (4-0) undefeated mark—its 1st to reach 4-0 since 1997—but did little to elevate its national profile. Road win at Pittsburgh (2-2) garnered some notice with tough UConn D keying win with 6 forced TOs. UConn went up 7-0 early as its drive to 1y scoring run by RB Lou Allen (2 TDs) required only to travel 7y, thanks to INT by UConn LB Danny Lansanah. Later, Huskies redshirt frosh LB Lawrence Wilson (11 tackles) returned INT 51y for TD early in 4th Q. Connecticut scored 4 more times in 1st H as QB Tyler Lorenzen (12-25/174y) paced 3 drives of 60y or more. Panthers' sole highlight in 1st H occurred on 62y scoring drive that pulled them within 10-7 in middle of 2nd Q when dynamic frosh RB LeSean McCoy (11/70y) completed 18y pass to TE Nate Byham to set up McCoy's 19y TD run. Another heralded Pittsburgh

recruit, QB Pat Bostick (27-41/230y, TD, 3 INTs), overcame his INTs to throw 21y TD to WR Oderick Turner late in game. Young Pitt O continued to fair badly on 3rd down, converting 4-17 and extending 3-game slump in which Panthers misfired on 22 straight 3rd downs.

Syracuse 38 LOUISVILLE 35: Suddenly, Louisville's aspirations were crashing as swiftly as opposing WRs could get wide open. On game's opening scrimmage play, Syracuse (1-3) WR Taj Smith (4/173y, 2 TDs) ran so uncovered at midfield that he was waving his arms before QB Andrew Robinson found him with 79y TD pass play. It got worse for Louisville (2-2) followers who dreamed of national contention. Instead it was lowly Orange, winners of only single Big East game in previous 2 seasons, who controlled pace with help from Cardinals' porous secondary that allowed Robinson to pass for 17-26/423y, 4 TDs. Louisville O lost 4 TOs, its KO defenders allowed 93y TD RET by S Max Suter when score was tied 7-7 early in 2nd Q, and team was flagged for 12 PENs/105y. Although slick O of Louisville never quite evaporated and rallied to within 3 pts at game's end, 5-TD favorite Cardinals never led. Cardinals star QB Brian Brohm had tremendous air game on 45-65/555y, 4 TDs, and his favorite target, WR Harry Douglas, caught 12/205y, TD.

Clemson 42 NORTH CAROLINA STATE 20: Clemson (4-0) looked very good indeed. Just ask Wolfpack (1-3), who dropped 4th straight "Textile Bowl" with little D resistance. Tigers gained whopping 608y as new QB Cullen Harper (25-39/268y, 2 TDs) was sharp in his 1st road test, and pair of outstanding runners each topped 100y mark. TB James Davis led way with 24/166y, with TDs both rushing and receiving, while alternate TB C.J. Spiller (21/141y, TD) opened scoring with 11y TD catch and contributed 44y scoring burst in 1st Q that gave Clemson 17-7 lead. WR Darrell Blackman scored 1st TD for Wolfpack when he interrupted Tigers' scoring parade with 99y KO RET, but early on, Tigers enjoyed mammoth 220y to 1y O advantage and 24-7 lead. Clemson K Mark Buchholz kicked 4 FGs. Wolfpack QB Daniel Evans (16-25/123y, TD, INT) played well in relief of injured starting QB Harrison Beck, still, North Carolina State had long way to go. "They could have done whatever they wanted to today. We couldn't stop them," said losing coach Tom O'Brien.

Georgia 26 ALABAMA 23 (OT): Bulldogs (3-1) soph QB Matt Stafford (19-35/224y, 2 TDs, 2 INTs) had answer for Georgia with game-winning toss in OT. After Georgia D held Crimson Tide (3-1) to 0y and 42y FG by K Leigh Tiffin on 1st series of extra session, Stafford produced victory on 1st snap when he perfectly placed 25y pass over shoulder of WR Mikey Henderson in left corner of EZ. Tide twice had rallied from 10-pt deficits, including 4th Q drives of 61y to Tiffin's FG and 88y to tie game with late TD. Bama QB John Parker Wilson (17-35/185y) ran for his 2nd TD of game—from 6y out—to knot it at 20-20. Wilson connected with WR Keith Brown on that drive's biggest play: 43y catch-and-run down sideline. Georgia coach Mark Richt continued his remarkable SEC road success, running his mark to 23-3.

LOUISIANA STATE 28 South Carolina 16: With play straight out of schoolyard playbook, Louisiana State Tigers (4-0) pulled away from Gamecocks (3-1) and established themselves as team with special daring. Leading 14-7 late in 2nd Q and lined up for 32y FG, LSU had holder Matt Flynn catch snap and casually flip ball over his head and behind him—without looking—to K Colt David, who sprinted wide. David caught ball in stride and waltzed 15y to EZ for TD against stunned South Carolina special teams unit lined up to block his FG try. Now needing to overcome 2-TD deficit against LSU's tough D, any South Carolina rally faced several tough factors: rainy conditions, tiring D that allowed 217y rushing in 1st H, and revolving door at QB. Most successful Gamecocks QB was Chris Smelley (12-26/174y, TD, INT), albeit after game was decided in 4th Q, as he led 2 scoring drives with 1y TD pass to WR Kenny McKinley. Starting QB Blake Mitchell's finest moment had come on 12-play, 67y drive in 1st Q that gave Carolina 7-0 lead on 1y TD run by RB Mike Davis. LSU needed only 4:22 to overcome its 1st deficit of season and tie game on nifty 33y TD run by TB Trinton Holliday. Tigers took lead for good early in 2nd Q on QB Flynn's 1y scoring pass to TE Richard Dickson. South Carolina coach Steve Spurrier's lifetime record versus LSU, built almost exclusively at Florida, fell to 11-2.

Florida 30 MISSISSIPPI 24: After his team edged rebuilding Rebels (1-3), Florida (4-0) coach Urban Meyer summed up his feelings after tough battle: "I'm just anxious to get on the plane and get the hell out of here." Florida QB Tim Tebow proved too tough for game Mississippi, passing for 261y and 2 TDs and rushing for 166y and 2 TDs. Tebow's rushing total set school record for QBs. With Rebels guarding against long passes, WR Percy Harvin sparkled underneath covereage with 11/121y and 19y TD catch. Ole Miss QB Seth Adams (18-31/302y), who was questionable with shoulder injury, played brilliantly by rallying Rebels from 27-9 deficit in 3rd Q with TD passes of 19y to WR Shay Hodge (7/81y) and 71y to WR Mike Wallace. After Adams completed 2-pt conv pass to WR Marshay Green, Rebs trailed by 27-24. After help from clocking-eating O, Florida S Tony Joiner picked off pass to set up 25y FG by Florida K Joey Ijjas. Gators DE Jermaine Cunningham stopped fake punt later in 4th Q, tackling TE Robert Lane short of 1st down, to end another drive by Ole Miss, which gained 390y against defending national champs.

Kentucky 42 ARKANSAS 29: After cracking AP Top 25 for 1st time since 1984, Wildcats (4-0) stunned Razorbacks (1-2) by closing game with 21-pt burst in final 8 mins. Arkansas had come out swinging with 58y drive to K Alex Tejada's 40y FG. Hogs DE Malcolm Sheppard quickly forced Kentucky QB Andre Woodson to FUM, returned 16y by DE Antwain Robinson for TD. Nonplussed, Woodson (21-39/265y, 2 TDs) answered with 5-play, 72y drive that ended on 14y TD run by RB Rafael Little. WR Steve Johnson (7/111y) caught 2/53y on drive. Arkansas' remarkable RB depth paid off in 2nd Q as TB Felix Jones (12/133y) raced 73y to set up FG and A-A TB Darren McFadden (29/173y) took direct snap 56y for TD and 20-7 lead. McFadden's speed and cutting ability were fully on display on his highlight-reel run. Razorbacks piled up fantastic 201y rushing in 2nd Q, but Wildcats got back into it with huge play right before H: CB Trevard Lindley recovered FUM by 3rd-string Arkansas TB Michael Smith at Kentucky 34YL, returning ball 66y to score TD that cut deficit to 20-14 with 26 secs left in 1st H. Having been outgained 373y to 131y, Kentucky opened 2nd H with 80y drive that Woodson finished with 15y TD pass to WR Keenan Burton for 21-20 lead. It took until 4th Q, but suddenly Arkansas shot back in front, 29-21: DT Fred Bledsoe sacked Woodson for safety, and Jones took ensuing free-kick 82y for TD. Next big break went to Cats as Hogs LB Ryan Powers roughed K Lones Seiber on missed 36y FG attempt, keeping drive alive that ended with 2y TD run by RB Derrick Locke. After punt, Woodson needed only 93 secs to move 68y to 35-29 lead with final 32y coming on Burton's brilliant TD catch. After Razorbacks failed again on downs—with QB Casey Dick (13-28/157y, 2 INTs) misfiring on 4th down pass—Woodson added TD run. It was fine day for Woodson as sr QB established new NCAA record for consecutive passes without INT at 296, breaking mark of 271 held by Trent Dilfer of Fresno State.

MICHIGAN 14 Penn State 9: It had been uproarious September in Ann Arbor so far, and Michigan (1-2) having to face No. 10 Penn State and its nationally top-rated run and sack-leading D looked to be difficult Big 10 opener. But last 2 Wolverine teams that opened 0-2 wound up with conf titles, and that became Michigan's new goal. When harried Penn State QB Anthony Morelli (15-31/169y) started game with lost FUM inside his own 10YL, Michigan struck for quick 10y TD run by frosh QB Ryan Mallett (16-29/170y, INT), who would pass enough to keep Lions D honest. UM maintained ball control game-plan, logging 34:52 of possession time, and making 10-18 3rd downs as TB Mike Hart (44/153y, TD) set new personal high for run attempts. Trailing 7-3 at H, Lions opened 3rd Q with WR Deon Butler's 19y catch and TB Austin Scott's 19y run. But, Scott soon fumbled at Michigan 11YL. Penn State fought back to Wolverines 2YL but had to settle for another of 3 FGs by K Kevin Kelly. Michigan made its only long drive count, going 77y on 15 plays in 4th Q. Hart wedged off right side for 1y TD that barely edged across GL for 14-6 lead.

Illinois 27 INDIANA 14: RB Rashard Mendenhall of Illinois made headlines with career-best 214y rushing, with TDs running and catching. But, Fighting Illini (3-1) also earned 4 TOs, registered 7 sacks, and blocked punt by CB Vontae Davis to spark opening win of Big 10 season. Meanwhile, improved Indiana (3-1) was having trouble getting its O going as quick QB Kellen Lewis was held to 17/35y rushing, his total highly affected by 7 sacks, 4 by Illinois DE Will Davis. Trailing 13-0 late in 2nd Q, Hoosiers went 80y to Lewis' 7y TD pass to star WR James Hardy. But, Illini QB Juice Williams had sufficient time to counter with 68y TD trip culminated in Mendenhall's flashy cut to EZ with 15y pass 44 secs before H. Mendenhall iced it at 27-7 with powerful 5y TD run with 12:45 left to play.

WISCONSIN 17 Iowa 13: Still looking for some traction in new season, Iowa (2-2) played excellent D as it went to last min of 1st H before allowing 1st TD of season, country's last such D unit to do so. On other hand, Hawkeyes struggled to run at all, notching 0y in 1st H and 59y by game's end. To earn its 13th win in row, Wisconsin (4-0) resorted to old-style ball control by TB P.J. Hill (29/113y, TD) to slam across decisive TD with 9:42 to play in 4th Q. Earlier, wild flurry in last 3 mins of 1st H turned scoreless chess match into 10-7 H lead for Hawkeyes. Iowa LB A.J. Edds picked off pass over middle by Badgers QB Tyler Donovan (12-23/138y, TD, INT) to lead to 41y FG by sub K Daniel Murray. Donovan quickly responded with 4 completions, and Hill broke loose for what appeared to be 20y TD gallop. But, squat Badger lost FUM near GL when hit by Edds, and wild scramble for loose ball ensued with it in various hands in and out of EZ. Wisconsin was awarded custody at 3YL, and Donovan and TE Travis Beckum collaborated on TD pass with 43 secs to go in 2nd Q. Iowa answered immediately with WR Derrell Johnson-Koulianos' dandy 1-handed 21y catch and tip-toe into EZ for 10-7 lead. Badgers ate nearly 6 mins of early 4th Q as workhorse Hill lugged ball on 10 of 11 plays to his 2y TD run for 14-10 lead. Murray kicked another FG for Iowa to slice it to 14-13, but Wisconsin answered with 47y drive to K Taylor Mehlhaff's clinching 40y FG with 2:02 to go, followed by more ball-control by Badgers on last series.

Purdue 45 MINNESOTA 31: In Big 10 opener for both clubs, Minnesota (1-3) had to play catch-up from 1st play: Purdue (4-0) back-up WR Desmond Tardy soared 95y with opening KO. In leading Boilermakers to 3rd straight game of 500y O (504y), QB Curtis Painter (33-48/338y, 3 TDs, INT) clicked on 16y TD pass in 1st Q to RB Kory Sheets (21/111y, TD, and 7/60y, TD receiving). DE Cliff Avril took INT 43y to TD in 2nd Q that built 24-3 H edge for Purdue. Gophers, on way to miserable 1-11 season under boisterous new coach Tim Brewster, found steady footing on opening series of 3rd Q: Minnesota advanced 66y to 4y TD run by frosh RB Duane Bennett (7/81y, TD). Young Gophers QB Adam Weber (23-44/237y, TD, INT) was active runner with 20/63y, TD and accounted for pair of scores in 4th Q. More typical of Gophers' bumbling play was Purdue FG blocked by FS Jamal Harris. Harris appeared headed to long TD RET until he simply bobbled away FUM to pursuing Purdue holder Jared Armstrong, 1 of 4 Gophers' TOs.

OKLAHOMA STATE 49 Texas Tech 45: Red Raiders (3-1), masters of aerial attack, piled up 718y O as QB Graham Harrell (46-67/646y, 5 TDs) set personal y high. Still, it came down to Oklahoma State (2-2) TE Brandon Pettigrew hauling in short pass from QB Zac Robinson (16-32/211y, 2 TDs, INT) that turned into 54y TD with 1:37 to play and superb Texas Tech frosh WR Michael Crabtree (14/237y, 3 TDs) failing to hold EZ pass with 11 secs remaining. With 100 passes filling air, it was amazing that only 1 was intercepted—Texas Tech CB Jamar Wall (11 tackles) in 2nd Q after Cowboys had scored on their 1st 4 possessions—but Cowpokes CB Ricky Price blocked Crabtree's vision just long enough to create vital, last moment EZ miss. Harrell threw 4 TDs and Crabtree caught 3 as Raiders led at H by 35-28. Robinson, who contributed 13/116y, 2 TDs rushing to Oklahoma State's 366y as 3 rushers exceeded 100y for 1st time in school history, scored to tie it 35-35 in 3rd Q. Cowboys came up with trick play—WR Seth Newton's 33y TD pass to WR Jeremy Broadway—for their 2nd lead of game at 42-35 early in 4th Q. Harrell's 5th TD throw, 41y to WR Danny Amendola (14/233y,

TD) quickly knotted it, and Raiders K Alex Trlica hit short FG for 3-pt lead with 4:49 to go. Tech couldn't kill clock with its short passes, and Oklahoma State scored Pettigrew's TD on 1st snap after taking over.

Oregon 55 STANFORD 31: No. 13 Oregon Ducks (4-0), Pac-10 scoring and total O leader, got off winging, then found themselves in shootout because Stanford (1-2) chalked up 28 straight pts while holding Ducks to 48y in 2nd Q. Oregon QB Dennis Dixon (27-36/367y, 4 TDs) fired 71y TD pass to WR Cameron Colvin (8/136y) only 15 secs into game to help put Ducks up 21-3 after 1st Q. Cardinal RB Anthony Kimble (16/119y) rushed for 115y in 1st H. Highlighting Kimble's day was 60y TD bolt, followed by 3y TD in 2nd Q. When QB T.C. Ostrander (25-44/262y, 2 TDs, INT) added pair of medium-range, 2nd Q scoring passes, Stanford led 31-21. But, Oregon got FG with 4 secs left in 1st H, and it launched Ducks to runaway 2nd H. Dixon found TE Ed Dickson along sideline for 33y TD 4 mins into 3rd Q, and Ducks piled up 31 unanswered pts, including 2 more TD passes by masterful Dixon, who received rushing support from RB Jonathan Stewart's 19/160y, TD.

ARIZONA STATE 44 Oregon State 32: As would be trademark of Arizona State (4-0) in 2007, Devils fell behind 19-0 in 1st Q, only to rally with 31 pts in 2nd H. Punt snap sailed over ASU P Jonathan Johnson in opening 2 mins for safety for Oegon State (2-2). Beavers RB Yvenson Bernard (24/128y, TD) bounced to right to smoke 41y to set up TD pass from QB Sean Canfield (28-48/324y, 2 TDs, 5 INTs), and CB Keenan Lewis intercepted Devils QB Rudy Carpenter (25-36/361y, 4 TDs, INT) to send Bernard across from close range. When K Alexis Serna powered through 47y FG, Oregon State led 19-0. In 2nd Q, Carpenter eluded pass-rush to launch 64y TD to WR Michael Jones (4/124y, 2 TDs). Frosh K Thomas Weber continued to be perfect in 4 games, hitting 1st and 2nd of 3 FGs, so ASU trailed 19-13 at H. Bernard keyed TD drive early in 3rd Q, but Carpenter went long for 43y TD to Jones on 1st snap after Beavers punt. Late in 3rd Q, Devils took their 1st lead at 27-26 as TB Ryan Torain (26/91y, TD rushing) hauled in 48y TD pass after S Troy Nolan picked off Canfield. Torain caught short TD pass and added 41y scoring run in 4th Q.

USA Today Coaches September 23

1	Southern California (44)	1481	14	Virginia Tech	585
2	LSU (8)	1438	15	Kentucky	545
3	Florida (4)	1347	16	Georgia	516
4	Oklahoma (4)	1336	17	Hawaii	479
5	West Virginia	1260	18	South Florida	451
6	California	1137	19	Penn State	397
7	Texas	1103	20	Missouri	369
8	Ohio State	1092	21	South Carolina	335
9	Wisconsin	1026	22	Nebraska	209
10	Rutgers	901	23	Michigan State	167
11	Boston College	881	24	Alabama	154
12	Oregon	878	25t	Arizona State	151
13	Clemson	767	25t	Purdue	151

September 29, 2007

(Fri) SOUTH FLORIDA 21 West Virginia 13: South Florida (4-0) officially had arrived. Bulls' program, which once had coaches working out of modest trailer instead of decorated offices, had reached such excellence that wins over teams like 5th-ranked West Virginia (4-1) no longer were stunning upsets. Abundance of TOs keyed sloppy game as Mountaineers finished with 6 costly miscues to 4 for Bulls, even though West Virginia enjoyed 437y to 274y O advantage. South Florida took lead for good at 7-0 in 1st Q on 26y INT TD RET by LB Ben Moffitt (2 INTs). DE Jarriett Buie caused INT with hit on WVU QB Patrick White (12-18/100y, INT) as ball was thrown. Bulls QB Matt Grothe (11-20/135y, TD, 2 INTs), who sparked 2006 upset over Mountaineers, contributed brilliant play to raise lead to 14-0 in scrambling away from pressure in 2nd Q before throwing 55y TD pass to WR Carlton Mitchell. Inability of bumbling WVU O to rally was hampered by injury to White, who suffered deep thigh bruise at end of 18y run late in 2nd Q. He did not return, so back-up QB Jarrett Brown (11-20/149y, TD) led Mountaineers to 10 pts in 2nd H, earning TD on 9y pass to WR Darius Reynaud, but misfiring on 4th down pass in dying moments. With White injured and TB Steve Slayton (13/54y, 2 FUMs) held in check, Brown finished as WVU's high rusher with 15/61y. Acknowledging big win, tired Bulls coach Jim Leavitt said, "Pretty neat stuff."

Maryland 34 RUTGERS 24: Maryland (3-2) had loomed as only hard shell on soft early schedule that appeared to set up Rutgers (3-1) for undefeated run until late October. Responding to H speech by coach Ralph Friedgen, Terps chased Rutgers (3-1) from ranks of Top 10 with 20 pts in 2nd H. With Friedgen exhorting players to "stop sulking" after blowing 14-3 lead during 1st H, Maryland scored 2 FGs in 3rd Q and 2 TDs in 4th Q. Backup QB Chris Turner (14-20/149y), who replaced injured QB Jordan Steffy (4-8/70y, TD) at end of 1st H, fired 28y pass to WR Isaiah Williams to set up 26y FG by K Obi Egekeze to tie game 17-17 midway through 3rd Q. On Terps' next chance, TB Lance Ball (12/90y, 2 TDs) chipped in big 32y run, and Turner hit WR Darrius Heyward-Bey for 18y before Egekeze provided go-ahead, 37y FG. Scarlet Knights O was stuck in neutral, gaining only single 1st down during their next 2 series and losing INTby QB Mike Teel (25-44/310y, 2 TDs). Turner and WR LaQuan Williams connected on 27y pass play on 3rd-and-12 to set up 2y TD run by TB Keon Lattimore (34/124y) that gave Maryland 27-17 lead. Later in 4th Q, after Rutgers pulled to within 27-24 on 1y TD run by RB Ray Rice (21/97y), Teel was sacked by DE Jeremy Navarre, and Ball added coup de grace on next play with 14y TD run through dispirited Knights D.

NAVY 31 Air Force 20: Trio of outstanding scoring plays by Naval Academy (3-2) QB Kaipo-Noa Kaheaku-Enhada (4-7/79y, and 15/101y, 2 TDs rushing) proved difference in Middies' highest pt total against Air Force (3-2) since scoring 37 in 1978. Just as Kaheaku-Enhada was belted on outside option run early in 2nd Q he pitched perfect toss to streaking SB Reggie Campbell (5/41y, TD), who charged 37y to score for 7-3 lead. Falcons moved ball effectively with perfect balance of 237y rushing and 237y passing. TB Chad Hall (6/29y) scored twice—16y run in 2nd Q and 5y in 3rd Q—for Air Force after long drives for 10-7 and 20-17 leads. Kaheahu-Enhada spun his magic twice in 4th Q to pull out victory in front of record crowd at Annapolis: He scored on 2y run early in 4th Q for 24-20 lead and followed with brilliant 78y dash nearly 4 mins later.

Auburn 20 FLORIDA 17: When Auburn K Wes Byrum's booming 43y FG soared through uprights with time expired, intense Auburn Tigers (3-2) upset Gators (4-1) for 2nd straight season, this time with their 1st series road win in 13 years. Tigers even posted 1st H shutout of Florida team that was averaging 49.2 pts per game. Auburn O drove 86y and 80y for pair of 1st H TDs, sandwiched around blocked FG that ended Gators' best drive of opening H. Facing little pressure behind maturing O-Line, Tigers QB Brandon Cox (17-26/227y) turned in fine performance. Most importantly, Cox minimized his mistakes and threw no INTs. Trailing by 17-3 entering 4th Q, Gators O and QB Tim Tebow (20-27/201y, TD, INT and 19/75y rushing, TD) finally put TDs on board. Converting CB Joe Haden's REC of FUM by Auburn TB Ben Tate (20/65y, TD) at Tigers 38YL, Tebow threw 6y TD pass to WR Cornelius Ingram 10 plays later. Florida now trailed 17-10 with 14:56 remaining. Beginning next possession at own 11YL, Tebow was magnificent, needing only 9 plays to march 89y to his 2y tying TD run. Drive's biggest play was 32y pass down sideline to WR Percy Harvin for 1st down at Tigers 6YL. Auburn soon punted with Florida taking over at own 42YL following 15y PEN on Tigers S Eric Brock for interfering with returner Brandon James. With 4:49 left, Auburn D needed to quell Gators' momentum, and DE Sen'Derrick Marks (blocked FG) nailed Harvin for 6y loss on swing pass. Florida P Chas Henry managed only 25y punt, so Auburn took over at own 39YL with 3:38 left. Cox used 9 time-consuming plays, including Tate's 7 runs/19y, to move to 26YL. It set up Byrum's heroics, which were delayed when cagey Gators coach Urban Meyer took Byrum's 1st 3-pt success off board by calling timeout as ball was snapped. When he made pressured FG again, giddy Byrum ran about "The Swamp" mocking Gator Chomp.

ILLINOIS 27 Penn State 20: Champaign's Memorial Stadium was sold out for 1st time in 6 years, and home crowd was delighted by 1st touch of game for Illini (4-1). Frosh WR Arrelious Benn's 90y KO TD RET came 13 secs after Penn State (3-2) completed 73y opening march to K Kevin Kelly's 26y FG. Teams traded TDs during remainder of 1st H: Illinois RB Rashard Mendenhall (18/76y) scored on 2y run on option pitchout late in 1st Q, but Nittany Lions answered in 3 plays as QB Anthony Morelli (21-38/298y, TD, 3 INTs) hit WR Jordan Norwood for 42y down sideline to set up 24y TD pass to WR Derrick Williams. After FUM by Lions TB Rodney Kinlaw (16/66y), Illinois QB Juice Williams (11-24/120y, TD, 2 INTs) threw slant pass to Benn (6/84y, TD), who broke 3 tackles on way to 29y TD. TB Austin Scott scored midway in 2nd Q to elevate Penn State to within 21-17 at H. In 2nd H, Penn State D permitted no pass completions but allowed 143 rushing, while its O started 4 possessions in Illini territory only to come away with only 3 pts. Illinois D capitalized on 3 INTs and FUM REC inside its 20YL. Biggest TO came with about 2 mins to go and Lions trailing by 7 pts: Morelli scrambled free on 4th-and-13 from Illini 22YL. In diving for 1st down, Morelli coughed up FUM as he was slammed hard from side by Illinois S Justin Harrison. Illinois moved to 2-0 in conf for 1st time since 1991, which was same year for last home victory over ranked conf foe (Ohio State).

WISCONSIN 37 Michigan State 34: Leading most of day, Wisconsin (5-0) padded nation's longest winning to 14 games when it rallied in 4th Q to K Taylor Mehlhaff's short, tie-breaking FG. Michigan State (4-1) TB Jehuu Caulcrick, 1 of nation's most powerful backs, slammed for 2 TD runs of 2y each, and Spartans led 14-7 in 1st Q. Badgers had power back of their own in TB P.J. Hill (34/155y), who scored twice. Michigan State TB Javon Ringer (14/145y, and 7/88y receiving) got loose for 70y dash on Spartans' 1st series of 3rd Q, but they had to settle for K Brett Swenson's 19y FG to stay within 27-24. Hill's 2nd TD with 9:13 left in 3rd Q provided 34-24 lead, but Michigan State rallied to tie on short TD pass by QB Brian Hoyer (22-30/323y, 2 TDs) to frosh WR Mark Dell and Swenson's 35y FG with 12 mins to play. Wisconsin went 64y to winning pts when Spartans committed 3 costly PENs, including D-holding in EZ. Hill couldn't punch it across from inside 1YL, so Mehlhaff booted 22y FG with 6:15 left.

Indiana 38 IOWA 20: Visiting Hoosiers (4-1) got off to 21-0 lead before mid-point of 2nd Q—their biggest Big 10 road lead in 3 years—on trio of TD passes by QB Kellen Lewis (19-26/322y,3 TDs, INT), soph passer who was enjoying his greatest day. Iowa (2-3) soph QB Jake Christiansen was busier and slightly less effective with 24-42/308y, 3 TDs, INT passing. Christiansen, who overcame 9 sacks, pitched 33y scoring pass to WR Trey Stross just as H arrived to pull Hawks within 21-7. Hawkeyes slipped to within 21-13 midway through 3rd Q when Christiansen clicked for another TD, this to TE Brandon Myers. But, K Austin Signor missed his kick. Indiana RB Josiah Sears rumbled for pair of TDs that more than offset Christiansen's 3rd TD pass. DEs Jammie Kirlew (3.5 sacks) and Greg Middleton (2.5 sacks) led Indiana's strong pass rush.

Kansas State 41 TEXAS 21: Former walk-on Kansas State (3-1) WR Jordy Nelson (12/116y, TD), sr who was on his way to unlikely consensus A-A recognition, authored 89y punt TD RET late in 3rd Q to all but ice upset of no. 7 Texas (4-1) at 34-21. Wildcats also enjoyed TD RETs that built 14-7 and 21-14 leads in 2nd Q: LB Ian Campbell scored on 41y INT RET with large escort, and, moments after Longhorns tied it 14-14 on 26y TD pass to WR Quan Cosby by QB Colt McCoy (19-39/200y, TD, 4 INTs), K-State RB James Johnson streaked 85y on KO RET. Texas permitted most pts in Austin since UCLA racked up 66 in 1997. Wildcats put extreme pressure on McCoy, sacking him once and forcing 4 INTs.

COLORADO 27 Oklahoma 24: In aftermath of Colorado (3-2) K Kevin Eberhart's 45y winning FG as time expired, ABC cameras caught little, toe-headed Sooners (4-1) fan with tear running down cheek right beside his OU face-paint decal. It would continue to be that kind of year in 2007: the upsets of top-rated teams would really, really hurt. Colorado coach Dan Hawkins admitted he expected victory: "Not because I'm 'The Swami.' I've done this for 25 years, and you just know. You know when your team's ready, you know when you're poised." It was Buffs' 1st win over Top-5 team since beating Texas in 2001 Big 12 title game, but it took comeback from 24-7 2nd H deficit.

No. 3 Oklahoma built 17-pt lead as S D.J. Wolfe's pair of INTs sparked WR Juaquin Iglesias' 13y TD catch in 1st Q and TB Allen Patrick's 17y TD burst in 3rd Q. But, Sooners would gain only 56y in 2nd H. Virtually flawless to this moment in season, OU frosh QB Sam Bradford (8-19/112y, TD, 2 INTs) suffered critical INT to Buffs FS Ryan Walters late in 3rd Q and was able to complete only 1-8 passes in 2nd H. Colorado QB Cody Hawkins (22-36/220y, 2 TDs, 2 INTs) flipped TD pass to TE Tyson DeVree on 1st play of 4th Q to narrow gap to 24-17. Hawkins tied it with another TD pass with 4:05 to go and brought Buffs downfield for Eberhart's winning FG, which touched off stampede of excited CU fans onto field.

California 31 OREGON 24: Showdown before full house in Eugene became Pac-10 classic decided by inches in last 16 secs, and only matter that kept this match-up from joining long list of Games-of-the-Year was late-season fold-up by both clubs. Everyone expected high-scoring shootout between undefeated foes, but until frenetic 4th Q, score stood at only 17-10 in favor of Oregon (4-1). Ducks led 10-3 at H, their only TD coming on 5y run by TB Jonathan Stewart (21/120y, TD). Bears (5-0) WR DeSean Jackson (11/161y, 2 TDs) came up with his greatest pass-catching game to date, including 25y TD grab in 3rd Q that tied it 10-10. Ducks QB Dennis Dixon (31-44/306y, TD) suffered 2 late-game INTs—his 1st INTs of season—but he untied it with 2:39 to go in 3rd Q with 42y scoring pass to WR Cameron Colvin (7/74y, TD). On 2nd snap of 4th Q, Cal RB Justin Forsett (23/101y, 2 TDs) slipped across GL to knot it again at 17-17, and QB Nate Longshore (28-43/285y, 2 TDs) found Jackson again for 31y TD, so Bears led for 1st time. Dixon took Oregon 91y in 10 pressurized plays, hitting 6 passes in row/73y and chipping in 10y run to 4YL. Dixon ran 1y TD keeper to deadlock it at 24-24 with 7:06 left. No sooner had Dixon become hero he threw INT to Bears LB Anthony Felder at Oregon 21YL with 4:23 to go. Forsett carried ball 3 times and went over for 31-24 lead with 3:11 left. Ducks took over for last time at their 23YL with 1:45 on clock. Dixon clicked on 6-8 passes to carry Oregon to 1st down at Cal 5YL. After timeout with 22 secs left and with stadium in pandemonium, Dixon calmly hit Colvin with crossing pattern pass, and Colvin surged toward GL as he was pursued angularly by Bears DB Marcus Ezeff. As he was hit hard by Ezeff, Colvin attempted to dive with outstretched ball at left pylon. FUM came loose, bounding into EZ and over sideline with 16 secs to play. With his right foot in bounds inside 2YL, Colvin was ruled to have lost possession prior to breaking GL plane. Game's outcome was up in air, so officials took long look at TV replay. But Cal coach Jeff Tedford was quickly happy, saying, "We knew when we saw it on the big board that there was no way it would be overturned."

Ucla 40 OREGON STATE 14: On tap for Beavers (2-3) was opportunity to propel their season and provide coach Mike Riley with his 1st win over UCLA (4-1), which had beaten Riley 4 times each as head man at Oregon State and USC as asst coach. Beavers had circumstances all their way as D stifled Bruins with 21y gained in opening 5 possessions, which included pair of lost FUMs by TB Kahlil Bell (24/80y, 2 TDs). FS Al Afalava scooped up Bell's FUM less than 4 mins into game and returned it 33y for TD, and Beavers went 63y at end of 1st Q to RB Yvenson Bernard (27/125y, TD) for 14-0 lead. Bell and QB Ben Olson (14-25/220y, 2 TDs, INT), back for UCLA after concussion suffered 2 weeks prior, finally cranked up Bruins for pair of FGs by K Kai Forbath. OSU still led 14-12—after Bell scored in 3rd Q—as game wore on in 4th Q, but CB Gerard Lawson contributed significantly to Beavers' gnawing meltdown over 7-min span that blew victory. Lawson was flagged for personal foul on sideline tackle, and Olson quickly followed with 69y TD bomb to WR Brandon Breazell (2/99y, 2 TDs) for UCLA's 1st lead with 9:12 to play. Lawson fumbled away next 2 KO RETs, and Bell, on run, and Breazell, on catch, scored quick TDs for Bruins' 33-14 lead. Oregon State recovered Lawson's 3rd straight KO FUM but had punt blocked to set up TB Chris Markey's 2y TD run for Bruins.

Southern California 27 WASHINGTON 24: Huskies (2-3) were decked out in throwback purple jerseys and plain gold helmets they wore on only occasion when they beat top-ranked team, 1961 Rose Bowl against Minnesota. Against no. 1 Southern California (4-0), Huskies lost their 3rd straight in September on way to 6 defeats in row. Energetic but erratic-throwing redshirt frosh QB Jake Locker (13-28/90y, INT, and 18/50y, 2 TDs rushing) got Washington on scoreboard with 10y run early in 2nd Q. USC QB John David Booty (20-37/236y, TD, 2 INTs) answered in less than 2 mins by finding WR Patrick Turner for 23y TD. Trojans took lead 6 mins later in 2nd Q on 8y run by soph TB Stafon Johnson (14/122y), another of USC's army of highly-recruited runners, many of whom were fighting for even smidgeon of playing time. Trojans K David Buehler avoided off-day by supplying chip-shot FG for permanent lead at 17-14 only 16 secs from H and eventual winning margin with 33y FG with 3:01 on clock in 4th Q. In between in 2nd Q, Washington S Mesphin Forrester (10 tackles) picked off INT thrown by frustrated Booty—that bounced off back of USC FB Stanley Havili—and cut cross-field for 54y TD RET and brief 14-14 tie. TB Chauncey Washington (21/106y, TD) made 3rd Q TD run. Trojans were sloppy, however, as they had 161y in PENs, 3 TOs, and suffered blocked punt that led to Locker's proximity TD in game's last min.

USA Today Coaches September 30

1	Southern California (45)	1483	14	Virginia Tech	661
2	LSU (14)	1454	15	Hawaii	585
3	California	1363	16	Texas	573
4	Ohio State (1)	1313	17	Missouri	532
5	Wisconsin	1251	18	South Carolina	529
6	Boston College	1138	19	Arizona State	466
7	Florida	1000	20	Purdue	423
8	Kentucky	971	21	Rutgers	347
9	South Florida	960	22	Clemson	278
10	Oklahoma	925	23	Nebraska	261
11	Georgia	758	24	Cincinnati	249
12	West Virginia	756	25	UCLA	79
13	Oregon	697			

October 6, 2007

Virginia Tech 41 CLEMSON 23: Allowing 3 RET TDs was no recipe for success, and Clemson (4-2) fell from rankings with thud. Virginia Tech (5-1), gold standard for special-teams skill and strategy under coach Frank Beamer, would enjoy its 1st-ever punt and KO RET TDs in same game, while also serving up additional INT TD RET by middle of 2nd Q in building 24-3 edge. Thereafter, Hokies, who managed only 219y O by game's end, played grind-it-out style in keeping Tigers no closer than 11 pts. S D.J. Parker got Va Tech rolling 2 mins into game with 32y INT TD RET. Later in 1st Q, Hokies K Jed Dunlevy booted 32y FG for 10-0 lead. Clemson had to punt moments later, and, having previously limbered up with 33y RET, WR Eddie Royal twisted and turned his way into clear for 82y TD RET. After Clemson cut deficit to 17-3 on 33y FG by K Mark Buchholz, Hokies CB Victor Harris broke game open with 100y KO RET. With Clemson O going 21 straight mins without 1st down, Virginia Tech was able to finish 1st H with commanding 31-8 lead, despite gaining only 98y O. Neutralized by both Hokies D and daunting scoreboard margin, Clemson's talented TB tandem of James Davis (6/9y) and C.J. Spiller (6/3y) were non-factors. Tigers QB Cullen Harper (38-66/372y, 2 TDs, 2 INTs), who set school records for single game completions and attempts, managed 2 TD throws in 4th Q. WR Aaron Kelly was Clemson's bright spot, catching 11/174y, TD.

LOUISIANA STATE 28 Florida 24: Buried in box score was verdict in nutshell: Logged on 7th line in LSU's stat column was 5-5 on 4th down. Gambling Tigers (6-0) nailed every daring 4th down try: 2 went directly for TDs and 2 propelled game-winning drive that culminated at 28-24 with 1:09 to play. Leading nearly all game, no. 9 Gators (4-2) opened scoring with 31y FG by K Joey Ijjas to cap 10-play drive on opening possession. After INT by Florida CB Joe Haden and exchange of punts, QB Tim Tebow (12-26/158y, 2 TDs, INT, and 16/67y, TD rushing) passed 4-4/52y to march Gators 77y to TD on his 2y pass to RB Kestahn Moore early in 2nd Q. Trailing 10-0, LSU answered with 80y drive, capped by 4th-and-goal 1y keeper by backup QB Ryan Perrilloux. Tebow needed only 3:45 to restore Florida's 10-pt lead with 9y TD run that capped 72y drive. Teams traded TDs in 3rd Q to maintain Florida's lead at 24-14. Tebow's costly INT early in 4th Q was snared by DE Kirston Pittman at Florida 27YL. LSU QB Matt Flynn (14-27/144y, TD, INT) needed 5 plays to pull Tigers within 24-21 on 4y TD pass to WR Demetrius Byrd, thrown on another 4th down. LSU D forced 3-and-out, which allowed LSU O to craft 15-play, 60y drive that ate 8:11 of remaining 9:20. On winning march, coach Les Miles passed up tying FG attempt on 4th down at Florida 6YL and sent FB Jacob Hester (23/106y) straight up middle for necessary 1y. Hester scored game-winning TD on 2y run 3 plays later to give Tigers their 1st lead. Earlier on drive, Hester had converted midfield 4th-and-1 with battering 2y run. With final possession, Gators were able to move into Tigers territory at 46YL before running out of time. Game was 1st since 1959 for LSU as AP no. 1, while Florida fell to 0-6 versus top-ranked teams in regular season (2-1 in bowl games).

Ohio State 23 PURDUE 7: No. 23 Purdue (5-1) had displayed O juggernaut (averaging 45 pts and 496y) against questionable Ds so far this season. Still, Boilermakers expected to make close game of it against no. 4 Ohio State (6-0). Instead, Buckeyes' magnificent D held foes to 272y total O, 17/4y rushing thanks to 3/-26y in sacks, and forced school record 12 punts by Purdue P Jared Armstrong. After its D halted game's opening series, Ohio State went 87y to WR Ray Small's 26y TD catch from QB Todd Boeckman (17-29/200y, 2 TDs, 3 TDs). Following 3-and-out and poor punt by Armstrong, Buckeyes took 5 plays to traverse 43y with Boeckman hitting short TD to WR Brian Hartline for 14-0 lead. Ohio K Ryan Pretorius made FGs in each of last 3 Qs while Boeckman's INTs—including failed chance at Buckeyes 2YL courtesy of Purdue CB David Pender's pick-off—stunted trio of Bucks' possessions. Still, Bucks' D slammed door on Boilers. Trailing 23-0 and mounting decent pass y against Buckeyes reserves, Purdue finally scored in last 10 secs on 1y reception by TE Jeff Lindsay from QB Curtis Painter (31-60/268y, TD). WR Greg Orton hauled in 10/91y receiving for Boilermakers.

ILLINOIS 31 Wisconsin 26: No. 5 Badgers' 14-game winning streak tumbled down as resurgent Fighting Illini (5-1) won 2nd straight game against ranked opponent. Illinois ran no-huddle, option-heavy O to ring up 17 unanswered pts midway into 2nd Q. RB Rashard Mendenhall (19/160y, 2 TDs) scored on run and pass in 1st H led by Illini 17-6 when Wisconsin (5-1) K Taylor Mehlhaff made 38 and 26y FGs in last 4 mins of 2nd Q. Wisconsin looked far better in 3rd Q as QB Tyler Donovan (27-49/392y, 2 TDs, 2 INTs), who would cough up pair of INTs in Illini territory, pitched 43y TD pass to frosh WR Kyle Jefferson (3/65y, TD). After Mendenhall scored his 2nd rushing TD for Illinois, Badgers traveled 78y to TB P.J. Hill's nudge into EZ late in 3rd Q to trim margin to 24-19. For 2nd week in row, Illini coach Ron Zook leaned on quick frosh QB Eddie McGee as reliever for QB Juice Williams (12-19/121y, TD), and McGee sparked time-consuming 71y drive to his 5y TD run for 31-19 lead.

Kansas 30 KANSAS STATE 24: Opening with all home games, Jayhawks (5-0) had pasted 4 patsies by combined 214-23 score behind soph QB Todd Reesing, but O got off to slow start in Big 12 opener at Manhattan. Reesing was intercepted twice in 1st H, including 1st play of game by Cats S Chris Carney. Kansas State (3-2) struck 2 possessions later on 68y TD connection between QB Josh Freeman (31-48/305y, TD, 3 INTs) and WR Jordy Nelson (10/137y, TD). Wildcats K Brooks Rossman, who would make 32y FG in 3rd Q, bounced 44y FG try off upright, and Kansas finally got going just before start of 2nd Q. Reesing (22-35/267y, 3 TDs, 3 INTs) led 86y march to RB Jake Sharp's 20y TD charge on which he bounced off stack of bodies and slipped down left sideline. K-State RB Leon Patton untied it with 7y run at end of 80y trip, but 11 secs before H, Kansas CB and occasional WR Aqib Talib soared high at left front corner of EZ for his 4th TD catch of season to send rivals to intermission knotted 14-14. Jayhawks were cruising in 2nd H after frosh WR Dezmon Briscoe (4/67y, TD) raced 28y with TD pass in middle of 3rd Q. But, pass soon caromed high off shoulder pad of Kansas WR Dexton Fields for Carney's 2nd INT at Kansas 16YL. Patton soon gave Kansas State lead of 24-21 with a gadget TD pass to WR Deon Murphy. Fields

made up for it with game-winning 30y TD catch as Jayhawks traversed 62y in only 1:05 and added K Scott Webb's 24y FG with 2:21 to go. Talib ended it with INT at his 37YL with min to play.

MISSOURI 41 Nebraska 6: Coming off nerve-racking home wins by 41-40 over Ball State and conf opener over Iowa State, in which Cyclones held ball for 40 mins, Nebraska (4-2) slipped into vortex of dreadful D that would destroy its season and send head coach Bill Callahan packing. Undefeated Missouri (5-0) rolled up 606y in O as QB Chase Daniel (33-47/401y, 2 TDs) threw for career high to date. Daniel selflessly talked about Mizzou's D: "If the defense plays like that week-in and week-out…the sky's the limit." Despite having won 8 in row over Big 12 North foes, Nebraska gained 297y, but was held to pair of medium-range FGs by K Alex Henery in 1st H. More than 70,000 gold-clad Tigers fans, most since 1984, packed Faurot Field and rejoiced in 3rd straight home win over Huskers, who had owned 24 game winning streak over Missouri in 1979-2002. TE Chase Coffman and WR Dana Alexander caught TD passes from Daniel, while TE Martin Rucker scored on 10y TD catch off in-your-eye fake FG early in 4th Q. Rucker's score established final score. Nebraska IB Marlon Lucky (17/67y) made 123y combined from rushing and receiving, and QB Sam Keller passed 25-43/223y, INT.

Oklahoma 28 Texas 21 (Dallas): After loss, Texas (4-2) amazingly stood 0-2 in conf play for 1st time since way back in 1956. Sooners (5-1) frosh QB Sam Bradford (21-32/244y, 3 TDs) showed his poise on OU's 3rd possession late in 1st Q when he checked off at scrimmage line on 3rd-and-14 at own 12YL and pitched 1st down pass. Before 84y TD drive was over Bradford hit 40 and 41y passes and flipped short TD to TE Jermaine Gresham for 7-0 lead. Longhorns forced 14-14 H knot because arm-bandaged QB Colt McCoy (19-26/324y, 2 TDs, INT) found TE Jermichael Finley (4/149y, TD) for long strikes of 55 and 58y they set up pair of 2nd Q scoring passes, including Finley's 22y catch that provided Texas' only lead at 14-7 just past midway in 2nd Q. Oklahoma RB DeMarco Murray (17/128y) went in for injured RB Allen Patrick and blazed to 65y TD run in 3rd Q for 21-14 lead. No sooner had Texas tied it again early in 4th Q than Bradford sparked winning 94y trip that was capped by his 35y TD laser into tight coverage to WR Malcolm Kelly (5/105y)

Notre Dame 20 UCLA 6: At long last, America's most famous football team secured its 1st victory of 2007. Notre Dame (1-5) hardly moved ball (140y O on 66 plays) but forced key turnovers to turn game its way. Irish never once gave ball away, while UCLA (4-2) coughed it up 7 times when it was forced to use highly-inexperienced frosh QB McLeod Bethel-Thompson (12-28/139y, 4 INTs) as replacement for injured QB Ben Olson (4-10/54y). Irish tied game 3-3 after S Tom Zbikowski sacked Olson, who twisted his left knee and fumbled on play late in 1st Q. Bruins K Kai Forbath made 29 and 49y FGs in 1st H that was led 6-3 by UCLA. Notre Dame tied it with 6:24 to go in 3rd Q when K Brandon Walker hit his 2nd FG, this from 48y out. In 50-sec span of late 3rd Q, ND scored 2 decisive TDs. Irish FS David Bruton returned INT 17y to UCLA 4YL, and QB Jimmy Clausen wedged over from 1YL on 3rd down. LB Maurice Crum, who became 1st-ever Golden-Domer to force and recover 2 FUMs in single game, scooped up his 2nd FUM REC and raced 34y for 20-6 edge with 1:03 in 3rd Q. Crum (7 tackles) made pair of INTs in 4th Q to help wrap it up.

Stanford 24 SOUTHERN CALIFORNIA 23: Unranked Stanford (2-3), 41-pt underdog to no. 2 Southern California (4-1), was quarterbacked by 2nd-string, soph QB Tavita Pritchard (11-30/149y, TD, INT), who was making his 1st start and had tried only 3 career passes to date. Trojans built 9-0 H lead, but after conv kick by K David Buehler (1st Q FG) was blocked, USC was thwarted at end of 1st H on 4th-and-goal at 1YL. Trojans heard some boos on their way off field for H intermission. Troy QB John David Booty (24-40/364y, 2 TDs, 4 INTs) broke middle finger on passing hand in 2nd Q but kept pitching. But, Booty was intercepted by Card SS Austin Yancy, who returned 31y to TD early in 3rd Q. Booty countered with 63y TD pass to TE Fred Davis (5/152y, TD) for 16-7 lead. On opening play of 4th Q, RB Anthony Kimble plunged for 1y TD, and Stanford pulled to within 16-14. Booty responded with 47y TD pass, and Cardinal countered with K Derek Belch's 26y FG for 23-17 deficit. Booty again was intercepted to start Stanford's winning 45y drive. Pritchard hit 4th-and-20 pass to WR Richard Sherman to keep drive alive until he lofted 4th down, 10y TD pass at left edge of EZ to WR Mark Bradford with 49 secs left. Belch's kick put Cardinal ahead by 24-23, DE Pannel Egboh and LB Clinton Snyder converged for sack, and S Bo McNally's INT at midfield soon iced it.

USA Today Coaches October 7

1	LSU (58)	1498	14	Florida	714
2	California	1416	15	Wisconsin	689
3	Ohio State (2)	1399	16	Hawaii	632
4	Boston College	1283	17	Cincinnati	578
5t	South Florida	1145	18	Kentucky	493
5t	Oklahoma	1145	19	Illinois	425
7	Southern California	1000	20	Kansas	390
8	Oregon	936	21	Florida State	213
9	West Virginia	931	22	Texas	195
10	Virginia Tech	913	23	Georgia	188
11	Missouri	897	24	Purdue	149
12	South Carolina	823	25	Auburn	143
13	Arizona State	763			

October 13, 2007

(Th) WAKE FOREST 24 Florida State 21: Demon Deacons (4-2) QB and Florida native Riley Skinner (19-27/215y, 2 INTs), who was not recruited by Florida State (4-2), sparked 395y of O and upped his series record to 2-0 as he threw pair of 2nd H TD passes, including 35y arrow to WR Kenneth Moore (3/74y, TD) midway through 4th Q for 21-14 lead. Drive of 82y featured 3 conversions of 3rd down with Skinner nimbly avoiding pass rush on last of them to find Moore at GL. S Chip Vaughn intercepted Florida State QB Xavier Lee (24-45/283y, 2 INTs) on next play. So, Wake was able to work 4:46 off clock before K Sam Swank booted clinching 48y FG. Deacs' highlight play had occurred in 1st Q when frosh RB Josh Adams (18/140y, TD) ripped 83y TD run for 7-0 lead. Looking to avenge 2006's embarrassing 30-0 home loss to Wake, Seminoles dominated rest of 1st Q as Lee tossed 2 TD passes for 14-7 lead. Lee worked receiver combinations on both drives, hitting WR Preston Parker (5/113y) with 58y pass to set up 6y TD connection to Parker for jr WR's 1st-ever TD, and connecting, 2 possessions later, with WR Greg Carr (8/108y) for 50y moments before Carr caught 4y TD pass. Finishing with 4 TOs, Wake Forest D settled down, especially in 2nd H when it forced 5 punts, picked off 2 passes, and held FSU to 105y O and TD. FSU gained 74y of that total on its final drive, which Lee capped with vain 17y TD run with 17 secs remaining.

(Fri) Hawaii 42 SAN JOSE STATE 35 (OT): Undefeated Hawaii (7-0) escaped with its 2nd WAC road victory in OT (45-44 at Louisiana Tech on September 8) when CB Myron Newberry intercepted San Jose State (3-4) QB Adam Tafralis (27-42/302y, 2 TDs, 3 INTs) in EZ after Warriors QB Colt Brennan (44-75/545y, 4 TDs, 4 INTs) had found WR Jason Rivers with TD pass in top half of 1st extra session. Hawaii had taken 14-0 lead on RB Kealoha Pilares' 6y TD run after LB Adam Leonard made 28y INT RET to Spartans 35YL and Brennan hit WR Ryan Grice-Mullen for 16y TD pass. Grice-Mullen would go on to set school record with 14 catches/175y. San Jose's superb sr CB Dwight Lowery had not scored TD in his A-A season of 2006, but on this night he tallied twice within 3 mins that spanned H: Lowery took punt late in 2nd Q, cut toward left sideline, and stormed away for 84y TD RET, and when Brennan tried to force out-pattern at sideline on 1st snap of 3rd Q, Lowery stepped in front of receiver to dance 24y for TD that tied it 14-14. Tafralis and WR Kevin Jurovich collaborated twice for scores in 3rd Q, and although Brennan slipped in another TD pass, SJSU went up 35-21 2:27 into 4th Q when FB James T. Callier (13/30y, TD) concluded 65y trip with 8y TD burst. Errors by Spartans late in regulation let Hawaii back into game: SJSU gifted 35y in PENs on 97y drive to Brennan's 3rd TD pass with 3:53 left, and Callier quickly lost FUM to provide start to tying drive at SJSU 45YL. Brennan ended trip with 2y TD run with 31 secs on clock.

Louisville 28 CINCINNATI 24: With loss by no. 1 LSU earlier in day, Cincinnati (6-1) enjoyed nation's longest win streak at 9—at least until beleaguered Louisville (4-3) D held firm during 4th Q. Cards TB Anthony Allen scored winning TD on 3y run early in 4th Q to cap quick 2-play drive, other being QB Brian Brohm's 51y pass to WR Harry Douglas (7/118y), who won fight for ball from CB DeAngelo Smith at Bearcats 3YL. Louisville D had just stopped Cincy QB Ben Mauk on 4th-and-1 keeper, with coach Brian Kelly rolling dice with score tied 21-21. Brohm was fantastic, completing 28-38/350y, 3 TDs. He threw no INTs against D that was leading nation in that category. Mauk (26-45/324y) also threw 3 TDs, but his INT thrown to CB Woodny Turenne during final, frantic moments ended Bearcats' chances. Overall, Louisville beat rival at their own game, committing 0 TOs to Cincinnati's 4, which included 2 lost FUMs inside Louisville red zone. Despite that ugly mark, Bearcats had chance to tie game midway through 4th Q when Mauk drove O to 1st-and-goal at Louisville 2YL. Cardinals D held Cincinnati to 23y FG by K Jake Rogers and posted shutout rest of way with help from gutsy decision by coach Steve Kragthorpe. Facing 4th-and-1 on own 29YL, Kragthorpe called for QB keeper, and Brohm, not known as runner, made it with inches to spare. Although Cincinnati program clearly was on upswing, it dropped 5th straight in border rivalry and 9th of last 10.

VIRGINIA 17 Connecticut 16: Hoping to remain undefeated, Connecticut (5-1) reached Virginia (6-1) 44YL late in contest after 19y FG by K Chris Gould had given 17-16 lead to Cavaliers. UConn needed about 15y to get into range for K Tony Ciaravino, who had already booted 3 FGs including 45y effort in 1st Q. Out of nowhere, Huskies looked more like also-ran of 2006 than Big East challenger of 2007 as ensuing snap went past QB Tyler Lorenzen (17-33/176y, TD) for loss of 21y. UConn got hit with false start PEN on next play, and Lorenzen lost FUM of following snap which was recovered by Virginia DE Jeff Fitzgerald. Huskies had rough time against UVa's charging D: they gaining only 254y, with 2 TOs and 9 PENs, while converting only single 3rd down in 13 tries. Virginia's O wasn't much better, but QB Jameel Sowell (14-24/149y, TD, 2 INTs) came through on winning 79y drive, completing 30y pass to WR Chris Gorham (3/76y). He was stopped short of GL after 6y run on 3rd down. Gould was summoned to hit chip-shot FG for winning pts. Cavaliers won their 4th game with margin of 5 pts or less. UConn LB Lawrence Wilson was in on 17 tackles, including 3 for loss.

KENTUCKY 43 Louisiana State 37 (OT): With top teams losing left and right it was matter of time before top-ranked Louisiana State (6-1) felt harsh sting of defeat in tough SEC. Wildcats (6-1) won game in 3rd OT as QB Andre Woodson (21-38/250y, 3 TDs, 2 INTs) threw 7y TD pass to WR Steve Johnson (7/134y) and Kentucky D stopped LSU on downs. Tigers, who rushed for 260y, ran ball 4 times during vital 3rd OT possession, falling short on 4th down when MLB Braxton Kelley stopped TB Charles Scott (7/94y, 2 TDs) 1y short of 1st down. "He came out of nowhere," said tearful Scott of Kelley. "I thought I was close." Indeed, Kentucky seemed to have come out of nowhere in past few seasons. Rebuilt by coach Rich Brooks, Wildcats reached zenith with this upset of Tigers. Wildcats had opened scoring in 1st Q on Woodson's 2y scoring pass to TE T.C. Drake. LSU answered with 3 straight scoring drives, Scott's 2 TD runs, followed by 31y FG by K Colt David to build 17-7 lead. Woodson hit 50y completion to Johnson and soon scored on 12y run late in 1st H to finish 78y drive that pulled Cats to within 17-14. LSU went for 3rd Q knockout with 10 straight pts, as RB Trinton Holliday set up 52y TD drive with 44y KO RET—with QB Matt Flynn tossing 4y TD pass to TE Richard Dickson—and frosh S Chad Jones picked off Woodson to set up 30y FG by David. Wildcats, however, scored final 13 pts of regulation to tie score at 27-27. Foes combined for 2 TDs and 2 FGs during opening pair of extra sessions before Tigers CB Jonathan Zenon fell down to allow Johnson to break open for winning TD catch.

Georgia 20 VANDERBILT 17: It was odd to see storied SEC opponent needing to feel defiant by dancing on Vandy's star logo at midfield. But, Georgia got worked up after near-loss at Vanderbilt (3-3) that some Bulldogs (5-2), happy to prevent 2nd straight upset loss to Vandy, demonstrated as soon as Georgia K Brandon Coutu hit game-winning 37y FG as time expired. Dawgs had marched 74y at end behind QB Matt Stafford (16-31/201y, TD), who hit 3-3/42y, and TB Knowshon Moreno (28/157y), who rushed 6/30y. Enjoying his 1st-ever start, Moreno ran for 123y in 2nd H as Georgia rallied from 17-7 H deficit. Bulldogs had opened scoring midway through 1st Q when Stafford connected with WR Sean Bailey on 32y TD pass. After driving late in 1st Q to 21y FG by K Bryant Hahnfeldt, Commodores dominated play in 2nd Q, taking 10-pt lead as WR Sean Walker capped 2 scoring drives with TDs. Walker ran reverse for final 15y of 80y drive for 10-7 lead and caught 16y TD pass from alternate QB Mackenzi Adams (7-10/125y) for 17-7 lead. Bulldogs came out fired up for 3rd Q and went 70y after KO to 1y TD run by FB Brannan Southerland. Moreno set up TD with 32y run. Adjusting to Commodores' trick plays, Georgia D posted shutout in 2nd H. After 1st FG by Coutu tied it 17-17 in 4th Q, Vandy managed 68y trip to 7YL before losing FUM by TB Cassen Jackson-Garrison on hit by LB Darryl Gamble. Georgia then embarked on 73y drive to winning FG.

Auburn 9 ARKANSAS 7: Red-hot D of Auburn (5-2) had its focus on none other than Razorbacks (3-3) A-A TB Darren McFadden, who was held to measly 17/43y rushing. Tigers won their 4th straight with outstanding D and continued clutch kicking. K Wes Byrum provided all pts Tigers would need with 3 FGs, including game-winner from 20y out with 21 secs left. Frosh Byrum now owned last-sec winning FGs against Florida and Arkansas in his 7-game career. QB Casey Dick (12-26/111y, TD, INT) nearly had won it for Arkansas, driving Hogs 71y to his 13y TD pitch to WR Lucas Miller with 1:36 remaining. Razorbacks found all sorts of pitchers in their lineup for desperate late drive: McFadden threw on opening play that earned 15y interference PEN, and WR Robert Johnson hit FB Peyton Hillis for 15y on next play. Play of game for Tigers O came 4 snaps after 22y RET of following KO by TB Brad Lester (21/89y) started Auburn on its 47YL: WR Robert Dunn caught short pass from QB Brandon Cox (13-23/101y) and raced to Arkansas 12YL. Byrum hit winning 3-ptr moments later, redeeming himself for 2 earlier misses. Auburn TBs Ben Tate (23/91y) and Lester both outgained McFadden as Arkansas finished with 67y rushing, 271y below season avg.

PENN STATE 38 Wisconsin 7: With legendary Franco Harris serving as grand marshal, Penn State (5-2) clearly was excited for Homecoming weekend. Nittany Lions took right to dominating no. 15 Wisconsin (5-2), winners of 14 of last 15 games. With their D creating 3 TOs in 1st H, Lions' O-line carved big holes for TBs Rodney Kinlaw (23/115y, TD) and Evan Royster (8/68y, TD). Penn State DE Josh Gaines forced FUM by Badgers TB P.J. Hill (19/75y, TD) on 1st play that LB Sean Lee returned to Wisconsin 12YL, and 9y pass by QB Anthony Morelli (16-28/216y, TD) set up vet FB Matt Hahn for 1y TD explosion. Next came 30y FG by Penn State K Kevin Kelly and Badgers' only sustained attack of afternoon: UW QB Tyler Donovan (16-29/220y, 2 INTs) authored 10y scramble and connections of 32 and 17y to set up Hill for powerful 1y TD run. Midfield INT by CB Lydell Sargeant paved way for Morelli's high TD arc to WR Deon Butler 2 mins into 2nd Q. Lions upped their margin to 24-7 at H when coach Joe Paterno used timeout to decide to skip FG try on 4th-and-1. LT Gerald Cadogan and FB Hahn sealed off left side to allow frosh rocket Royster to bounce outside for 19y TD dash. Wisconsin's inability to run—it was held to 34/87y rushing—forced Badgers into unaccustomed heavy reliance on air attack, and they had no chance to match Penn State's 2nd H TDs, scored by Kinlaw on 2y run and back-up QB Daryll Clark on 1y keeper after his 17y draw run.

NORTHWESTERN 49 Minnesota 48 (OT): Having beaten Michigan State on previous Saturday, Northwestern (4-3) was getting used to Big 10 wins in OT. Purple now was 7-1 in all OT contests and perfect 7-0 in conf extra innings. But, to get to extra session, Wildcats had to rally from 35-14 deficit in 2nd H and survive surprise 2-pt pass that fell incomplete after Minnesota's 2nd TD in OT. Gophers (1-6) trailed 7-0 in 2nd Q but scored on 21 and 26y TD passes by accurate QB Robin Weber (25-38/341y, 5 TDs, 2 INTs) and RB Amir Pinnix's 9y run. NW slipped in 1st of 4 TD throws by red-hot QB C.J. Bacher (41-58/470y) to get to H down by 21-14. Weber hit pair of TDs in 3rd Q, 2nd of which became 2nd scoring grab for WR Ernie Wheelwright (7/116y), and Minnesota led 35-14. Northwestern LB Malcolm Arrington turned momentum late in 3rd Q as he intercepted Weber and returned to Minny 8YL. Bacher, who would finish 2-game stretch with 990y passing, clicked on TD flip to WR Ross Lane on next play, and DE Corey Wootton made aother INT of Weber on next series to lead to Bacher's 6y TD run. Gophers missed possible clinching FG in closing mins, and WR Eric Peterman (12/114y) completed NW's stunning catch-up by nabbing tying TD only 8 secs before end of regulation. Each QB threw another TD in 1st OT, and Cats RB Brandon Roberson ran 6y for TD, followed by K Amando Villarreal's x-pt. Behind 49-42, Gophers advanced to Weber's 3y TD run but opted for failed 2-pt pass.

IOWA 10 Illinois 6: Losers of 8 straight Big 10 contests, Iowa (3-4) surprised Illinois (5-2) with late INT by S Brett Greenwood at Hawks GL with 1:12 to play. Illini sr K Jason Reda hit pair of FGs to make him 9-for-9 for season, while his 46y 3-ptr in 1st Q was his 5th in as many tries beyond 40y. Iowa QB Jake Christiansen (17-25/182y, TD) missed pair of passes from Illini 10YL late in 1st H, and Hawkeyes had to settle for K Daniel Murray's 28y FG to tie it 3-3 with 26 secs before H. Iowa, which ended up outgaining Illinois 323y to 287y, overcame frustration of several fruitless trips into enemy territory in 1st H. Trailing 6-3 late in 3rd Q, Hawkeyes were flagged for illegal formation on 3rd-and-2 when TB Albert Young (25/99y) was stopped short of 1st down. Christiansen used reprieve to fire 20y TD to TE Brandon Myers for Iowa's 1st lead at 10-6 with 6 secs left in 3rd Q. Illinois sub QB Eddie McGee (3-5/52y, INT) had 83y TD pass called back in 4th Q but rallied late in game to find WR Arrelious Benn for 28 and 24y receptions to Iowa 12YL. Under pass-rush pressure, McGee was picked off by Greenwood to seal Hawkeyes' 5th win in row over Illinois.

KANSAS STATE 47 Colorado 20: Drawn-out affair lasted to midnight and went Kansas State's way because it offered slightly more O from outset. Wildcats (4-2) outgained Buffaloes (4-3) 463y to 411y, scoring midway in 1st Q on 5y run by RB James Johnson (20/159y, 2 TDs) which was soon followed by 1st of 4 FGs by K Brooks Rossman. Before 1st Q ended, K-State WR Deon Murphy (4/47y, TD) scored on 20y misdirection run on pitchout from QB Josh Freeman (15-27/214y, TD) for 17-3 edge. Perhaps Rossman's most important boot was his longest: His 52y 3-ptr came as 2nd Q ended to up Kansas State's lead to 23-13. It came after Buffs failed on 4th-and-6 at Wildcats 46YL with 25 secs left in 2nd Q. Colorado got big game from RB Hugh Charles (22/171y, TD)—his 4th straight 100y game—but QB Cody Hawkins hit only 19-41/223y, TD in air, was sacked twice, and intercepted 3 times among CU's 4 TOs. Late in 3rd Q, Colorado P Matt DiLallo dropped snap near his GL, and WR Daniel Gonzalez blocked it for S Courtney Herndon to recover in EZ for Cats' TD and 40-20 advantage.

OKLAHOMA 41 Missouri 31: Oklahoma (6-1) would turn out to be only team Missouri (5-1) failed to solve in 2007. Even though no. 11 Tigers slugged it out and outgained no. 6 Sooners by 418y to 382y, this trip to Norman went down in flames. Foes would meet again in December's Big 12 Conf title game. Sooners' sharp redshirt frosh QB Sam Bradford (14-34/266y, 2 TDs) pitched TD passes to WR Juaquin Iglesias (7/77y, TD) and TE Jermaine Gresham in 1st H. But, Tigers K Jeff Wolfert booted 19y FG as H clock struck to slice margin to 17-10 for OU. Sooners scored 1st in 3rd Q, but x-pt was missed which allowed Missouri to take 24-23 lead to 4th Q after WR Jeremy Maclin scored his 2nd TD on E-around and RB Jimmy Jackson added another TD 3 mins later. Perhaps game's most important play came early in 4th Q in Mizzou EZ: Tigers SS Pig Brown let INT slip through his hands, and Oklahoma's Bradford regrouped to whip his team to go-ahead TD run by RB Chris Brown, his 2nd of 3 scores. Outstanding Missouri QB Chase Daniel (37-47/361y, TD, 2 INTs) and Maclin soon lost handoff exchange, which Oklahoma LB Curtis Lofton returned 12y for crushing TD and 35-24 lead for Sooners with 11:40 left. Although Daniel found TE Martin Rucker for short TD pass at end of 80y drive with 12 secs to play it was not enough.

HOUSTON 56 Rice 48: Houston (3-3) rode 4 school records by WR Donnie Avery, who notched 13/346y receiving—including 77 and 67y TDs—and 427y all-purpose. Cougars finished with 748y O and had quick 14-0 lead on way to 28-14 edge at end of 1st Q. But during next 26 mins, Houston suffered 5 TOs and relinquished 27 straight pts, capped by Rice Owls (1-5) QB Chase Clement's 3rd TD pass—15y to WR Tommy Henderson—nearly midway in 3rd Q. Cougars stormed back with 4 TDs in last 20 mins of play, including TD runs of 8, 33, and 50y by RB Anthony Alridge (24/215y, 4 TDs). Rice would persevere with sharp O that would average 31.2 pts per game by year's end. Yet, Rice's 48-35 lead early in 4th Q turned out to be insufficient despite Clement's career-high 355y passing on 24-44, 3 TDs, INT.

SOUTHERN CALIFORNIA 20 Arizona 13: Soph QB Mark Sanchez (19-31/130y, 2 INTs) was in for injured QB John David Booty for Southern California (5-1), and matters started well enough for Trojans. USC led 10-0 midway in 2nd Q, primarily on 18y TD run in 1st Q by TB Chauncey Washington (17/54y). But, rambunctious Arizona (2-5) tallied next 13 pts to grasp 3-pt lead by Wildcats' 1st series of 3rd Q. Teams settled into 2nd H D struggle until Trojans frosh TB Joe McKnight ignited 4th Q rally with 45y punt RET to set up Sanchez's 25y TD pass to TE Fred Davis on next play. McKnight (13/75y) zipped 59y late in game to set up K David Buehler for 23y FG which sealed USC's escape from potential 2nd straight home upset loss.

Oregon State 31 CALIFORNIA 28: Oregon State (4-3) was trouble from start, building 7-0, 10-7, and 20-14 leads at different moments of 1st 3 Qs in becoming 10th unranked team to upset top-10 foe so far in 2007. For its part, no. 2 California (5-1) was on verge of capturing its 1st no. 1 ranking since 1951, thanks to LSU's defeat by Kentucky earlier in day. Golden Bears QB Nate Longshore couldn't play because of badly sprained right ankle which would dog him remainder of season. QB Kevin Riley (20-34/294y, 2 TDs, INT) started for Cal and had some good moments even though he lacked consistency. Riley pitched 10y TD to WR Lavelle Hawkins (9/192y, 2 TDs) for 7-7 knot in 1st Q and launched 64y TD pass to Hawkins in 4th Q, which pulled Cal within 31-28 with 2:31 to play. QB Sean Canfield (18-33/186y) was consisitent, but Beavers' best weapon was RB Yvenson Bernard, who rushed 33/110y and scored TD in 3rd Q which provided 20-14 lead. Bernard also propelled himself over GL on 4th down from 1YL with 8:30 to pay in 4th Q. When Canfield followed with 2-pt pass, Oregon State led 28-21. Bears' fumbled KO led to K Alex Serna's 3rd FG, but Riley soon hit his long TD to Hawkins. Taking over at their 6YL with 1:27 on clock, Bears used Riley's passes of 18, 19, and 37y and pass interference foul for 1st down at 12YL with 14 secs to go. Even though Bears were without TO, tying FG seemed assured, so they chose to try 1 more pass for victory or throw it away to stop clock. Under moderate outside rush, Riley saw opening up middle, and his instincts mistakenly sent him goalward. Swift LB Joey LaRocque (9 tackles) of Beavers' nation-leading D closed in to knock Riley down at 10YL, and coach Jeff Tedford slammed down his clipboard in frustrated defeat. Tedford, however, absolved his frosh QB of blame: "He (Riley) played his heart out at the end to get us in that situation. We didn't lose the game because of that play."

USA Today Coaches October 14

1	Ohio State (56)	1495	14	Florida	726
2	Boston College (1)	1383	15	Kansas	705
3	South Florida (3)	1320	16	Hawaii	558
4	Oklahoma	1288	17	Missouri	519
5	LSU	1173	18	Texas	396
6	Oregon	1077	19	Auburn	372
7	West Virginia	1007	20	Georgia	282
8	South Carolina	997	21	Texas Tech	232
9t	California	983	22	Tennessee	193
9t	Southern California	983	23	Cincinnati	192
11	Virginia Tech	982	24	Virginia	184
12	Arizona State	936	25	Penn State	128
13	Kentucky	874			

Bowl Championship Series Ranking October 14

	Harris Poll Pct.	*USA Today* Poll Pct.	Computer Pct.	BCS Avg.
1 Ohio State (7-0)	.9982	.9967	.830	.9416
2 South Florida (6-0)	.8800	.8800	1.000	.9200
3 Boston College (7-0)	.9298	.9220	.820	.8906
4 Louisiana State (6-1)	.8081	.7820	.930	.8400
5 Oklahoma (6-1)	.8782	.8587	.550	.7623

October 20, 2007

(Th) RUTGERS 30 South Florida 27: Intense Scarlet Knights (5-2) coach Greg Schiano rarely had indicated he could be trickster, but on this night he pulled several fast ones on no. 2 South Florida (6-1). Big play came on fake FG, engineered by holder and backup QB Andrew DePaola, who rolled away from pressure and lofted 15y TD pass to TE Kevin Brock for 27-17 lead late in 3rd Q. Not always for better, Rutgers special teams earned almost all game's headlines, muffing 2 punts, 1 of which led to Bulls' TD, employing fake punt that led to FG, having FG blocked, but turning tables to block FG try by Bulls. Eventual winning pts came early in 4th Q on 51y FG by K Jeremy Ito, his career long and 3rd 3-ptr of game. Ito was up to mischief himself: it was his 36y pass to WR James Townsend on fake punt in 1st H that led to his FG. Knights TB Ray Rice rushed 39/181y and QB Mike Teel (11-29/179y) threw 2 TDs to WR Tiquan Underwood (5/114y) as Rutgers gained 400y. South Florida had not allowed rusher to crack 100y mark since Rice's 202y versus Bulls last season. Much of Bulls' burden fell on QB Matt Grothe (17-34/247y, TD, and 18/58y, TD rushing), and, with game on line in 2nd H, Grothe was sacked 5 times. Ahead 30-27 in 4th Q, Rutgers fired LB Brandon Renkart in to nail Grothe on 1st snap after Bulls recovered Rice's FUM near midfield. They eventually punted. When South Florida got ball back near midfield for final time, Rutgers frosh S Joe Lefeged blitzed and collared Grothe for 12y loss. Later, on 4th-and-37, Grothe threw INT to Knights S Zaire Kitchen. After incredible rise from unranked to no. 2 in nation, South Florida fell victim to Rutgers team finally playing up to its once-lofty expectations.

(Fri) CONNECTICUT 21 Louisville 17: Controversial non-call by officiating crew helped Connecticut (6-1) remain atop Big East as Huskies rallied with 2 TDs in 4th Q. Comeback would have been difficult without contentious TD that tied it 7-7 early in 2nd H: UConn WR Larry Taylor dashed 74y to punt TD RET. Problem was that Taylor appeared to call for fair catch—he was seen raising right hand although not waving it—which caused Cards special teamers to pull up. Play was not reviewable, although disgruntled Louisville (4-4) fans were able to view it over and over again all week. Still, Huskies trailed 17-7 after Louisville scored 10 pts within 1 min early in 4th Q as FUM by Connecticut TB Donald Brown popped to Cards DT Earl Heyman, who returned it 32y to EZ. UConn began its comeback with ensuing KO: Controversial Taylor returned KO 29y to midfield. Connecticut QB Tyler Lorenzen (9-18/130y) needed 5 plays to bank TD, earning final 7y on pass to WR D.J. Hernandez. Cards marched into UConn territory before stalling on downs with Huskies CB Tyvon Branch breaking up pass by QB Brian Brohm (29-41/228y, TD, 2 INTs). Lorenzen delivered game-winning 72y drive from there, hitting 3-3/40y. Soph TB Andre Dixon (22/115y), who had soared up Huskies depth chart this season, scored game-winning 5y TD run with bullish determination with 1:32 left.

Virginia 18 MARYLAND 17: Cardiac Cavaliers (7-1) won another nail-biter, scoring winning TD with 16 secs remaining when super sub TB Mikell Simpson dove into EZ from 1YL. Simpson was without ball when he landed, but officials ruled that he crossed GL plane. Virginia needed to go length of field to win, wiping out virtually all of remaining 7:42 in process. Simpson (16/119y, TD, and 13/152y receiving), who entered game with just 2 rushes for season but was elevated to first string with injury to TB Andrew Pearman, accounted for 92y of winning drive. Run-oriented Maryland (4-3) gained only 130y on ground, with most coming in 1st H in building 14-10 lead. Top TBs Lance Ball (17/72y) and Keon Lattimore (18/65y) each scored 1st H TD but were held in check in 2nd H. Virginia QB Jameel Sewell (22-35/243y) looked sharp, while DE Chris Long continued his terrific season with 10 tackles, 3.5 for loss, including 2 sacks, and 2 pass breakups. Long's sack of Maryland QB Chris Turner (13-19/105y) for safety on final scrimmage play of 3rd Q had pulled Cavs to within 17-12. Terps' Butkus Award semifinalist, LB Erin Henderson (18 tackles), also enjoyed huge game. Win was 7th in row—5th this year by 5 pts or less—and Cavs last won 7 straight in 1990.

VANDERBILT 17 South Carolina 6: Riled up over narrow loss to Georgia previous week, Vanderbilt (4-3) hosted invaders from Columbia, S.C., hometown of Vandy coach Bobby Johnson. Commodores owned 17-0 lead at end of 1st Q, which was enough since their D forced 4 TOs, allowed 26y rushing, and prevented no. 6 South Carolina (6-2) from crossing GL. Vanderbilt recorded 7 sacks by 7 different defenders. After CB D.J. Moore (8 tackles, 2 INTs) took opening KO to own 40YL, next 5 Vandy possessions began in Carolina territory, thanks often to TOs. Vanderbilt QB Mackenzi Adams (8-16/123y, 2 TDs, and 13/84y rushing) pitched 1st Q TD passes of 22y to WR George Smith (3/52y) and 20y to WR Justin Wheeler. Moore picked off pass in EZ to stop 3rd Q opportunity for Gamecocks, LB Patrick Benoist pressured backup Carolina QB Blake Mitchell (9-18/102y, INT) into horrible 4th down pass from Vandy 38YL, and LB Jonathan Goff later picked off pass on own 30YL to kill late threat in 4th Q. Gamecocks represented highest-ranked opponent beaten by Vanderbilt since 1937 when Vandy defeated no. 6 LSU.

LOUISIANA STATE 30 Auburn 24: LSU (7-1) pulled out fortunate victory as lunging WR Demetrius Byrd—tightly covered by Auburn CB Jerraud Powers—caught 22y fade-route pass gamble at back of EZ from QB Matt Flynn with 1 sec remaining. Coach Les Miles made gutsy call, leaving timeout in his quiver and going for EZ when likely FG would have clinched win. Flynn (22-34/319y, INT) threw 3 TDs, including 46y catch-and-run to TB Keiland Williams that tied score 7-7 in 1st Q. Auburn, which would end up being outgained 488y to 296y, retook lead midway through 2nd Q when FB Carl Stewart scored on 1y run after S Zac Etheridge forced backup LSU QB Ryan Perrilloux to lose FUM, returned 36y by CB Powers to LSU 3YL. After Auburn D forced punt, its O ran off 5:12 on 90y drive to 22y FG by K Wes Byrum that gave Auburn 17-7 H lead. From outset of 2nd H, Bayou Bengals growled on drives of 56, 60, 85, and 55y. They tallied TD and 3 FGs by K Colt David, with no series lasting longer than 3:39. RB Jacob Hester (9/50y) scored LSU's 2nd H TD on 5y reception, but it turned controversial after officials signaled they had flagged LSU for illegal formation. Flag was picked up—formation turned out to be okay—and TD awarded after refs also checked replay to see if Hester hit pylon. The officials checking for viability of PEN, then their altering different decision drew ire of Auburn coach Tommy Tuberville, who went berserk on sidelines. While it had dominated 2nd H so far, LSU led only 23-17 midway through 4th Q. Auburn QB Brandon Cox (18-28/199y, 2 TDs) delivered in clutch as he shook off effects of numerous hits from ferocious LSU D to deliver 82y drive he capped with 3y pass to WR Rodgeriqus Smith (6/56y). With Byrum's x-pt, Auburn took 1-pt lead in pursuit of 3rd straight SEC road win. Flynn made sure only streak to continue would be LSU's string of home wins which reached 18. LSU enjoyed return of WR Early Doucet (7/93y), after he had missed most of 1st H of season with groin injury, but saw standout DT Glenn Dorsey felled by chop-block.

ALABAMA 41 Tennessee 17: In 90th meeting of SEC rivals, passing battery of QB John Parker Wilson (32-46/363y, 3 TDs) and WR D.J. Hall (13/185y, 2 TDs) inspired Crimson Tide (6-2) with big game. Hall's 13 catches set new school mark. K Leigh Tiffin's 1st of 4 FGs opened scoring after Alabama employed surprise onside-KO to start game, and Wilson soon flipped 3y TD pass to frosh RB Terry Grant (26/204y, TD, and 6/31y, TD receiving) for 10-0 lead. Tennessee (4-3), however, rallied with 72 and 68y drives to short TDs by TB Arian Foster (13/91y, TD) on run and QB Erik Ainge (22-35/243y, TD, INT) on pass. Alabama went back up by 24-14 when Hall caught pair of scoring passes on consecutive long marches in middle of 2nd Q. Volunteers K Daniel Lincoln hit 45y as time ran out in 2nd Q. Down 24-17, Tennessee never sniffed EZ in 2nd H as Tide frosh CB Kareem Jackson (6 tackles) sparked D with 2 INTs and 2 pass breakups. Ainge was frustrated by Vols' 2nd H performance of 145y O as Tide was able to hog ball for nearly 20 mins: "...We'd have a bad snap or miscue to the receiver, or a bad throw. It was one little stupid thing after another in the second half." Grant scored on 8y run in 4th Q to set new Alabama frosh TD record. Interestingly, each team's fortunes would head in opposite direction: Tennessee would turn hot with 5 wins to end regular season, while Alabama would drop 4 straight.

OHIO STATE 24 Michigan State 17: Top-ranked Buckeyes (8-0) rolled to comfortable 24-0 lead deep into 3rd Q as QB Todd Boeckman (15-23/193y) hit on his opening 10 passes and threw 14y and 50y TD passes to TE Jake Ballard and WR Terry Robiskie, respectively. RB Chris "Beanie" Wells rushed for 221y and scored 5y TD in 2nd Q. Michigan State (5-3) was held to 185y by Ohio State's stingy D, but Spartans D came alive with pass-rush pressure in 3rd Q. In span of 4 plays, MSU narrowed gap to 24-14: S Otis Wiley intercepted Boeckman and charged 54y to TD. Soon after next KO, Boeckman was sacked by Spartans DE Jonal Saint-Dic, and LB SirDarean Adams scooped up FUM for 25y TD RET. Wells fumbled on 1st play after KO, and 2 Spartans had their hands on ball without coming up with it. Nervous coach Jim Tressel became so concerned over Buckeye butter-fingers that he ordered frosh RB Brandon Saine to take knee on KO RET after Michigan State pulled to within 24-17 on K Brett Swenson's FG with 3:42 left. Wells then calmly carried 7/36y to kill clock and keep Bucks undefeated.

Michigan 27 ILLINOIS 17: Seeking another win for bowl eligibility, Illinois (5-3) inspired its 3rd consecutive sellout crowd with 7-0 and 14-3 leads in 1st H. But, Illini were done in by their 10/107y in PENs, which kept alive 2 Michigan (6-2) scoring drives, and clutch performance by depleted Wolverines O, led by sore-handed QB Chad Henne (18-26/201y, 2 TDs, INT). Illini went up 7-0 on 26y TD pass by QB Juice Williams (8-14/70y, TD, INT) in opening min after CB Vontae Davis galloped 67y with KO. Illinois' short punt and pass interference PEN handed Wolverines 3 pts from K K.C. Lopata late in 1st Q. Illinois responded with its longest drive of season, going 90y on 13 plays to RB Daniel Defrene's 8y TD run. Michigan enjoyed its 1st lead at 17-14 in last min of 1st H as WR Adrian Arrington made diving grab of Henne's 14y TD pass. It culminated 80y trip that was launched by roughing-P PEN that followed pair of sacks of Henne. After Illinois K Jason Reda tied it 17-17 with 38y FG in 3rd Q, WR Kyle Hudson lost FUM on punt RET at his 13YL, and Michigan won it 2 plays later as WR Mario Manningham (9/109y, 2 TDs) caught TD pass from WR Arrington, who appeared poised to circle RE on E-around run.

Oklahoma 17 IOWA STATE 7: Cyclones (1-7), sporting worst D in Big 12, gave no. 4 Oklahoma (7-1) all it could handle in 1st H. "We were definitely fortunate to be down only 7-0," said Sooners QB Sam Bradford (16-28/183y, INT), who missed several open receivers due to an inability to adjust to 15 mph tail wind. Unable to throw TD pass for 1st time this season, Bradford also was sacked 3/-27y. Iowa State DE Rashawn Parker collected FUM by Sooners RB Allen Patrick (13/57y) at OU 35YL in middle of 1st Q, and Sooners committed pass interference PEN to assist RB Jason Scales' 2y

TD plunge. In 2nd Q, Iowa State CB Chris Singleton stopped Bradford's 4th down scramble, but K Bret Culbertson missed FG try. Cyclones CB Allen Bell made powerful 26y INT RET to Oklahoma 18YL, but Scales was squashed on 4th-and-1 at Oklahoma 9YL. Sooners RBs DeMarco Murray (9/59y) and Chris Brown (13/50y, 2 TDs) carried ball on 7 straight plays early in 3rd Q with Brown going last 8y for tying TD. TE Jermaine Gresham (3/62y) caught 30y screen pass on last play of 3rd Q, and Brown provided Oklahoma with its 1st lead at 14-7 on 4y run 1:10 into 4th Q. Poor punt gave Iowa State chance to tie it, and QB Bret Meyer (19-31/174y, INT) passed and ran—including 4th down dash to 6YL—but his tipped pass was intercepted by Sooners CB D.J. Wolfe in EZ to end threat. Bradford clicked on 14y pass to Gresham on 4th down to keep alive drive to clinching FG that consumed 5:20 of last 6:54.

MISSOURI 41 Texas Tech 10: Improving D of Tigers (6-1) struck for TD on 38y INT RET by DE Stryker Sulak in 1st Q and went on to take away 4 passes from Texas Tech (6-2) QB Graham Harrell (44-69/397y, TD). Harrell entered game with astounding 31-to-3 ratio of TDs-to-INTs but suffered from several bobbled passes and his pass y was his 2nd-lowest of season. However, Harrell connected on 68y TD pass to WR Edward Britton in 2nd Q. Meanwhile, Missouri surprisingly stuck to its ground game as it rushed 50 times (to gain 212y), and ace QB Chase Daniel passed effectively but infrequently at 14-19/210y, TD, INT. Daniel rifled 57y TD pass to WR Jeremy Maclin midway in 4th Q that upped lead to 38-10. Tigers had led 17-10 at H and owned 2nd H as RB Jimmy Jackson scored twice on short runs. Red Raiders WR Michael Crabtree (10/76y) didn't score but surpassed NCAA frosh single season receiving y mark set by Southern California's Mike Williams in 2002.

Texas A&M 36 NEBRASKA 14: Even contest that stood 16-14 in favor of Texas A&M (6-2) at H was turned into rout when Aggies consumed 34 plays in going 80, 80, and 76y to trio of short 2nd H TD runs by big TB Jorvorskie Lane (15/130y, 4 TDs). It was A&M's 1st-ever win in 6 visits to Lincoln. After Aggies QB Stephen McGee (13-22/100y, TD, and 35/167y rushing) flipped short TD pass in 1st Q, Nebraska (4-4) DT Ndamukong Suh blocked x-pt. So, Huskers took 7-6 led when frosh IB Quentin Castille (9/60y) scored on 3y run and K Alex Henery added kick. K Matt Szymanski kicked 39y FG late in 1st Q, and Lane soon tallied his 1st rushing TD for A&M. Trailing 16-7 late in 2nd Q, Nebraska went 79y in 9 plays to 10y TD pass from QB Sam Keller (26-44/275y, TD, INT) to WR Maurice Purify. When Huskers O was contained on opening series of 3rd Q, Aggies took control with its 344y ground attack. IB Marlon Lucky (8/23y) had spectacular afternoon catching 13/125y, records for Nebraska RBs in both receptions and y.

Kansas 19 COLORADO 14: For 1st time since 1995, Kansas (7-0) opened year with 7 wins as sharp-throwing QB Todd Reesing (20-29/153y, TD, and 7/84y rushing) guided 2nd H surge to 16 straight pts. Colorado (4-4) threatened late in 1st Q, advancing to 11YL where RB Hugh Charles (11/39y) lost FUM to Jayhawks DB Kendrick Harper. Reesing scampered 53y that keynoted 58y trip to K Scott Webb's 48y FG, only pts of 1st H. Buffaloes opened 2nd H with 80y TD drive finished by 27y TD pass from QB Cody Hawkins (27-44/287y, 2 TDs, 2 INTs) to TE Tyson DeVree (7/90y). Kansas recaptured lead quickly, going 58y in 5 plays as RB Jake Sharp finished with 2y TD run. After another FG by Webb made it 13-7, Jayhawkers fashioned their most impressive drive of 94y. Among 15 plays, Reesing hit 7-7/62y, including 4y TD to TE Derek Fine. It iced verdict at 19-7 with 10:23 to play.

UCLA 30 California 21: Down by 2 pts and threatening in UCLA (5-2) territory in last 2 mins, Golden Bears (5-2) stumbled in late going for 2nd straight week. From Bruins 30YL, California QB Nate Longshore (22-34/232y, 3 TDs, 3 INTs), who was back in lineup after ankle injury, threw pass picked off by UCLA CB Alterraun Verner, who coach Karl Dorrell felt was in right place because of extra week of preparation. Verner charged 76y to clinching TD with 1:31 to play. FS Dennis Keyes intercepted Longshore moments later to allow Bruins to run out clock. In UCLA's revolving QB situation, Patrick Cowan (18-27/161y, TD) was back from knee injury and threw 2nd Q TD pass to TE Logan Paulsen for 10-7 lead after TB Kahlil Bell (22/142y) cantered 64y up middle to Cal 2YL. But, 2 mins later, Cal WR DeSean Jackson (9/136y, 2 TDs) accentuated his big day with in-stride 39y TD catch over his left shoulder. Bears led 14-13 at H. Do-it-all Bruins WR Brandon Breazell (4/68y, and 3/21y rushing) pitched surprise 29y TD pass to WR Dominique Johnson early in 3rd Q, but California's Jackson came back with his 2nd scoring reception with 2:06 to go in 3rd Q for 21-20 lead. With 3:08 to play, Bruins K Kai Forbath provided 23-21 lead with 27y FG. After Bears RB Jahvid Best roared 54y to UCLA 35YL on following KO, stage was set for Verner's critical INT.

USA Today Coaches October 21

1	Ohio State (58)	1498	14	Hawaii	617
2	Boston College (2)	1412	15	Kentucky	604
3	LSU	1319	16	Texas	527
4	Oklahoma	1306	17	South Carolina	474
5	Oregon	1225	18	Virginia	466
6	West Virginia	1134	19	Georgia	402
7	Arizona State	1089	20	California	397
8	Southern California	1060	21	Michigan	325
9	Virginia Tech	1052	22	Penn State	294
10	Kansas	911	23	Auburn	179
11	Florida	906	24	Alabama	177
12	South Florida	813	25	Wisconsin	105
13	Missouri	790			

Bowl Championship Series Ranking October 21

	Harris Poll Pct.	*USA Today* Poll Pct.	Computer Pct.	BCS Avg.
1 Ohio State (8-0)	.9989	.9987	.930	.9759
2 Boston College (7-0)	.9389	.9413	.970	.9501
3 Louisiana State (7-1)	.8947	.8793	.960	.9114
4 Arizona State (7-0)	.7028	.7260	.860	.7629
5 Oregon (6-1)	.8004	.8167	.670	.7623

October 27, 2007

(Th) Boston College 14 VIRGINIA TECH 10: Boston College (8-0) QB Matt Ryan (25-52/285y, 2 TDs, 2 INTs) elevated himself in nation's eyes with brilliant end-of-game performance. Ryan not only rallied moribund BC with 2 stirring drives to his TD passes in final 4:16, he did so with winning TD so special it could be compared to 1980s magic of Doug Flutie. Ryan scrambled to his left to get away from defenders before throwing across field and across his body to TB Andre Callender in EZ. For 56 mins there was absolutely nothing memorable about Ryan's performance as Virginia Tech (6-2) D dominated in rainy, windy conditions. Led by DE Chris Ellis (4 tackles, 1.5 sacks, and 4 QB hurries), Hokies' pass rushers applied constant pressure, sacking Ryan 3 times and picking off 2 of his throws. Hokies struggled on O too, gaining 265y for game, but were able to piece together 91y drive in 2nd Q to 8y TD pass from QB Sean Glennon (15-25/149y, TD) to WR Eddie Royal (4/77y). K Jud Dunlevy's 44y FG in 3rd Q made it 10-0, which looked insurmountable with Boston College's struggles. It seemed nearly over when Eagles took over on own 8YL after 4th Q punt. Ryan, who had thrown INT on prior series, suddenly turned hot, hitting 23y and 22y passes to WR Brandon Robinson, completing 20y pass to TE Ryan Purvis, gaining 11y on run, and finding WR Rich Gunnell in EZ with 16y TD pass. With 2:11 remaining, BC recovered onside-KO as Virginia Tech WR Josh Morgan appeared certain to gain possession but somehow lost it to Eagles LB Tyronne Pruitt on BC 34YL. Ryan clicked on his 1st 3 pass attempts, and, needing only FG to tie, Eagles had 1st down at Va Tech 26YL. Ryan came out of timeout to find WR Kevin Challenger for 12y and another 1st down to stop clock. After misfire, Ryan hit Gunnell at GL but play was wiped out by holding PEN. After another incompletion, Ryan produced his magic, surprisingly throwing over heads of nearly every defender to right corner of EZ where Callender was open. Virginia Tech's excellent Thursday night record fell to 13-3 with all 3 losses having been delivered by BC.

TENNESSEE 27 South Carolina 24 (OT): Tennessee (5-3) won key game despite blowing 21-pt lead in 2nd H. After surrendering 24 straight pts to Gamecocks (6-3), Volunteers needed clutch 48y FG by K Daniel Lincoln, his career long, to tie it 24-24 with 5 secs left. Lincoln followed with 27y FG in 1st OT frame, which proved to be game-winner when, in bottom half of OT, South Carolina K Ryan Succop—who had gave Carolina its only lead with 49y FG with 1:24 left—flew 40y 3-pt try wide to right. Gamecocks dominated stats, racking up 501y with TB Cory Boyd rushing for 160y, QB Blake Mitchell throwing for 31-45/290y, and WR Kenny McKinley catching 14/151y. Some of that success was mitigated by 4 TOs with 2 bobbles coming near end of regulation. Tennessee managed 317y O, with only 70y coming in 2nd H. On way to 21-0 H lead, Tennessee twice had scored TDs thanks to heralded frosh S Eric Berry (12 tackles), whose 52y FUM RET and INT set up TD runs by TBs Arian Foster and Montario Hardesty. QB Erik Ainge (26-44/216y, TD, INT) capped Vols' longest scoring drive (72y) with 5y scoring pass to WR Josh Briscoe. "It was a good game for television, I guess, but it wasn't a very good game for us," said losing coach Steve Spurrier despite his team's 2nd H explosion.

Georgia 42 Florida 30 (Jacksonville): Mild-mannered Georgia coach Mark Richt turned extreme to fire up his Bulldogs (6-2), actually challenging them to be flagged for excessive celebration after team's 1st TD. When CB Asher Allen recovered early FUM at Florida (5-3) 39YL and, 9 plays later, TB Knowshon Moreno landed in EZ after 1y leap, entire Georgia bench raced to EZ to rejoice. They earned themselves not 1, but 2 PENs and soon kicked off from own 8YL. Florida coach Urban Meyer had his team jump up and down on their sideline to try to match Georgia's enthusiasm, and Gators quickly matched Moreno's TD when QB Tim Tebow (14-22/236y, TD) threw 40y TD pass to WR Louis Murphy. But, Georgia would prevail in battle of emotions. Bulldogs' 1-2 combination of Moreno, whose climb from frosh 3rd-stringer to star seemed complete with his 33/188y, 3 TDs rushing, and QB Matt Stafford (11-18/217y, INT), whose 3 TD passes quieted his critics, was too much for Florida's young D. Stafford trumped Tebow's scoring pass 2 plays later in connecting with WR Mohamed Massaquoi on 84y TD pass. Florida CB Woody Pierre-Louis' 25y INT TD RET 4 mins later did much to keep game close into 4th Q, but Georgia took lead for good at 21-17 with 1:48 left before H on Moreno's 10y TD run. Georgia's opening possession of 2nd H went 69y and mined FB Brannan Southerland's 1y scoring catch for 28-17 lead. Tebow would score twice on his patented short keepers, but his FUM of snap at UGa 11YL inside last 3 mins of 4th Q sealed Florida's fate. While Bulldogs O scored its most pts in series since 1982, Georgia D made sure right from DE Marcus Howard's pass-rush on game's 1st snap that Tebow's injured shoulder received no relief in sacking soph QB 6 times.

Mississippi State 31 KENTUCKY 14: Now 0-2 since upsetting LSU, Kentucky (6-3) never led but gave away game by committing whopping 6 TOs in 2nd H, including TB Alfonso Smith's FUM of 2nd H KO and P Tim Masthay's drop of high snap on own 26YL. Bulldogs (5-4) converted both miscues and FUM by Wildcats TE Jacob Tamme into scoring drives of 21y, 26y, and 40y to expand on their 14-7 H lead. Kentucky QB Andre Woodson (24-42/230y, 2 TDs, 3 INTs) fired 37y TD pass to WR Steve Johnson on 4th-and-8 that pulled Cats within 24-14 in 3rd Q. Johnson, who also caught UK's 1st TD on 18y reception in 1st Q, scaled over defenders to reel in pass. Mississippi State RB Christian Dulcre (19/career-high 119y) finished off Wildcats with 34y TD run

in middle of 4th Q, his runaway emphasizing D's exhaustion. Miss State frosh QB Wesley Carroll continued to improve, hitting 17-28/152y, 2 TDs and capping pair of 1st H drives of 80y with TD passes.

Ohio State 37 PENN STATE 17: Feeling as though they were under-respected, no. 1 Buckeyes (9-0) frayed Penn State's 7th-ranked D for 453y, scoring on 5 of their opening 7 possessions, and succeeding on 3rd down 7 times in 8 tries in 1st H. Enjoying his finest game to date, Ohio State QB Todd Boeckman (19-26/253y, 3 TDs, INT) quickly silenced loud, white-clad student section of Nittany Lions (6-3) with pair of long TD drives in 1st H. Ohio State WRs Brian Robiskie (4/59y) and Brian Hartline (4/69y) each caught TD pass in 1st H, which was dominated by Buckeyes by 17-7. Decisive score that lifted Ohio's edge to 24-7 was delivered on 87y voyage capped by TE Jake Ballard's 15y TD catch from Boeckman. TB Rodney Kinlaw (14/81y) had scored on 1st Q TD run for Nittany Lions, and DB A.J. Wallace sprinted 97y to superfluous KO TD RET late in 4th Q for Penn State.

TEXAS 28 Nebraska 25: Nebraska's criticized "Blackshirt" D responded with fine effort in Austin for 4 Qs, constantly belting Texas (7-2) QB Colt McCoy (12-28/181y, INT) and holding Longhorns to trio of FGs by K Ryan Bailey, who hit from fairly long distances of 38, 47, and 49y. But finally, Longhorns' "Scourge of the Fourth Quarter" took over: RB Jamaal Charles raced for 12/216y and TD runs of 25, 86, and 40y, all in game's closing 13:13. Charles' full-game run total of 290y set all-time Cornhuskers (4-5) opponent's single-game rushing record, eclipsing 247y of Oklahoma's Billy Sims in 1979. Trailing 3-0, Nebraska tied it in 2nd Q on K Alex Henery's 31y FG and beat H clock for 10-3 lead on 24y TD pass from QB Sam Keller (23-35/298y, 2 TDs) to WR Nate Swift (6/112y, 2 TDs). Same battery clicked early in 3rd Q, so Huskers led 17-9 entering 4th Q after Bailey chipped away with 2 FGs. Charles then exploded until Huskers QB Joe Ganz relieved injured Keller for last-moment drive to Ganz's short TD pass to WR Maurice Purify.

Kansas 19 TEXAS A&M 11: Normally dynamic passing attack of no. 12 Kansas (8-0) took backseat to Jayhawks' run O in holding off Texas A&M (6-3). Led by burly RB Brandon McAnderson's 21/183y, 2 TDs on ground, Kansas totaled 227y to 180y ground-to-air ratio. Scoreless 1st H saw A&M DE Chris Harrington block 27y FG attempt, and Jayhawks DT James McClinton and LB James Holt throw Aggies TB Jorvorskie Lane for 2y loss on 4th down at Kansas 9YL. Kansas scored on its opening 4 series of 2nd H: McAnderson's 6y TD run was bracketed by pair of FGs by K Scott Webb for 13-0 lead at end of 3rd Q. At beginning of 4th Q, KU DE John Larson recovered FUM at Aggies 43YL, and McAnderson slammed for 2y TD for 19-0 edge. Texas A&M vainly rallied, going 70y to K Matt Szymanski's 21y FG and 80y to 32y TD pass followed by 2-pt run by QB Stephen McGee (24-44/244y, TD).

Colorado 31 TEXAS TECH 26: Nation's leading tackler, Colorado (5-4) MLB Jordon Dizon (9 tackles), turned D ball-hawk to nab 1 of 4 INTs Buffs picked off from prolific Red Raiders (6-3) QB Graham Harrell (46-62/431y, 3 TDs) and returned 42y for TD that built 24-6 lead early in 3rd Q. Earlier in 2nd Q, Buffaloes QB Cody Hawkins (15-26/123y, 2 TDs) had followed 31y TD run by RB Hugh Charles (20/121y) with 1st of his 2 short scoring passes. Harrell finally got Texas Tech aerial game going in 3rd Q, hitting WR Eric Morris (10/125y) and Michael Crabtree (12/131y) for TDs. But, Colorado CB Terrence Wheatley made 3 INTs, 2 of which came in 4th Q on consecutive Tech possessions to preserve Buffs' 31-19 edge.

OREGON 24 Southern California 17: Although mighty O of no. 5 Oregon (7-1) was limited to moderate 339y—more than 200y less than its avg—Ducks' D forced trio of 2nd H TOs that proved poisonous to Southern California (6-2). Clad fully in green, Ducks were cheered by performance of QB Dennis Dixon, who passed 16-25/157y and ran 17/76y, including 3y TD burst up middle in 1st Q. Oregon led 10-3 at H, and RB Jonathan Stewart added 2nd H TDs of 16 and 1y among his 25/103y rushing to pave way to 24-10 lead early in 4th Q. Stewart's TDs came after FUM REC deep in USC territory and FS Matthew Harper's 26y INT RET to Oregon 41YL. Meanwhile, Trojans counted on sub QB Mark Sanchez (26-41/277y, 2 TDs, 2 INTs), who was staging his 3rd start for injured QB John David Booty. Sanchez took Troy 85y to 14y TD pass to WR David Ausberry with 4:44 to go. Trailing now by 24-17, Sanchez marched Trojans to Oregon 33YL, but Harper came through, intercepting 2nd by Sanchez. Oregon took inside track to Pac-10 title and possible claim to national championship, while USC's retention of conf crown now was in doubt.

ARIZONA STATE 31 California 20: Surprising Sun Devils (8-0) followed their usual script, spotting slumping Golden Bears (5-3) 13-pt lead in 1st Q and blanking Cal after H. In 8 wins, Arizona State has outscored its opponents 153-29 in 2nd H. Bears DE Rulon Davis sacked Devils QB Rudy Carpenter (17-29/219y, TD), and frosh DL Cameron Jordan, Arizonan from near-by Chandler, returned FUM 13y to TD. Up 10-0, California went 68y to 1st-and-goal at 5YL. But, ASU rose up to force K Jordan Kay's 2nd FG and on next possession traveled 59y to 1st of 3 TDs runs by TB Dimitri Nance (21/85y). Bears had something left, if only 1 TD: Cal's best drive (89y) came next, capped by 21y pass from QB Nate Longshore (18-36/261y, TD, 2 INTs) to mercurial WR DeShaun Jackson (5/88y) for 20-7 lead. Nance's 3rd TD came on 4th-and-1 at Bears 8YL in 1st 5 mins of 3rd Q and provided Arizona State with its 1st lead at 21-20. Devils had opened 2nd H by stopping Cal at midfield and going 91y in 9 plays. Scoring was finished midway through 4th Q when Carpenter hit WR Kyle Williams, son of Chicago White Sox GM Ken Williams, with 12y TD.

Bowl Championship Series Ranking October 28

	Harris Poll Pct.	USA Today Poll Pct.	Computer Pct.	BCS Avg.
1 Ohio State (9-0)	1.000	.9967	.930	.9756
2 Boston College (8-0)	.9351	.9427	.990	.9559
3 Louisiana State (7-1)	.9011	.8827	.880	.8879
4 Arizona State (8-0)	.8039	.8140	.930	.8493
5 Oregon (7-1)	.8537	.8533	.810	.8390

November 3, 2007

(Th) Virginia Tech 27 GEORGIA TECH 3: There were 2 QBs sporting Georgia Tech (5-4) jerseys, but only 1 QB had good game…and oddly, he played for Virginia Tech (7-2). With his own jersey among 5 Virginia Tech uniforms that turned up missing, Hokies QB Sean Glennon (22-32/296y, 2 TDs) was forced to wear Georgia Tech road white shirt. With his name printed in marker on back, "Yellow Jackets" blacked out across front, and Nike swoosh logo hand-drawn, Glennon, who almost attended Georgia Tech coming out of HS, threw 2 TD passes and ran for 3rd at helm of 481y O. Angry over his 4 INTs, Yellow Jackets QB Taylor Bennett wore his home gold far effectively, passing only 11-26/157y. With star TB Tashard Choice out with knee injury, Jackets were limited in ways to attack—other than WR James Johnson's 7/136y receiving—Virginia Tech's inspired D, led by LB Cam Martin (8 tackles, INT) and CB Victor Harris (2 INTs). Va Tech coach Frank Beamer made smart call when he went for onside-KO late in 1st Q after K Jud Dunlevy's 28y FG tied it 3-3. With Yellow Jackets caught off-guard, Dunlevy ran along side rolling ball for requisite 10y before jumping on it. Glennon quickly led 59y drive to his 2y TD keeper as Hokies took lead for good at 10-3 early in 2nd Q. Following Martin's INT, Glennon tossed 40y TD pass to WR Justin Harper later in 2nd Q for 17-3 lead at H. Georgia Tech coach Chan Gailey clearly was in trouble with Atlanta fans when his image was booed while delivering public service message on jumbo screen in 4th Q.

Cincinnati 38 SOUTH FLORIDA 33: Less than month after its AP no. 2 ranking, South Florida (6-3) lost 3rd straight and found itself last in Big East. Inexplicably, Bulls allowed 31 1st Q pts before rallying with 19 pts in 2nd H. Late-arriving fans missed 3 TDs—but never missed single scrimmage by South Florida—in opening 4:20 of wild 1st Q that ended with Cincinnati (7-2) ahead 31-14. Bearcats CB DeAngelo Smith took opening KO to So Florida 39YL. But, Bulls CB Trae Williams struck with 73y INT TD RET 3 downs later. Bearcats QB Ben Mauk (13-31/162y, 3 TDs, and 7/75y rushing) threw 63y TD pass to WR Antwuan Giddens on ensuing series, and USF answered immediately as CB Mike Jenkins returned KO for school-record 100y TD. Thanks to 4 scoring drives, none more than 56y, and D that posted 2nd H shutout, USF rallied despite its 8 TOs. After Bulls QB Matt Grothe (31-54/382y, 4 INTs, and 22/75y rushing, TD) threw 9y TD pass to WR Jesse Hester (3/52y) with 2:04 left, they trailed 38-33 and had their thinned-out crowd really jumping. Bearcats could not run out clock, and gave up ball on USF 38YL with 25 secs left. Grothe immediately hit 2 passes to Cincinnati 18YL with 8 secs left and got off 2 incompletions to EZ before time expired.

Florida State 27 BOSTON COLLEGE 17: Another 2nd-ranked school was chopped down as Eagles (8-1) became 4th such team to fall. Although BC never led, it trailed only 20-17 late in 4th game and looked for winning, last-sec TD for 2nd week in row. Florida State (6-3) LB Geno Hayes saw to it that Eagles QB Matt Ryan (26-53/415y, 2 TDs, 3 INTs) wouldn't play hero as he intercepted Ryan and returned 38y for back-breaking TD with 70 secs left. QB Drew Weatherford (29-45/354y, 2 TDs) led Florida State O to 452y, with no TOs, and opened scoring with 23y TD pass to WR Preston Parker (9/93y) late in 2nd Q. After Seminoles K Gary Cismesia hit 1st of pair of 2nd H FGs in 3rd Q, Ryan finally got BC on scoreboard with 30y pass to WR Brandon Robinson (7/163y). Weatherford's 42y TD pass to WR De'Cody Fagg (6/111y) with 8:11 left in game proved 20-10 lead. Exceeding 400y for 4th time in his career, Ryan tied Doug Flutie in BC annuls. Eagles S Jaime Silva continued his exemplary sr season with 18 tackles, sack, and forced FUM.

NORTH CAROLINA 16 Maryland 13: In late secs, win was possible for Maryland (4-5) as QB Chris Turner completed 4 passes in row to move to UNC 41YL with less than min left. But, Tar Heels (3-6) DT Kentwan Balmer pressured overthrown 4th down pass. Tar Heels had 16-3 lead at midway in 3rd Q on 3 FGs by K Connor Barth and 30y TD pass by frosh QB T.J. Yates (16-26/149y, TD, 2 INTs) to WR Hakeem Nicks (8/88y). After Nicks' TD, Carolina managed only 29y but killed clock over last 4 series. Maryland, meanwhile, went 80y as Turner hit 3-3/59y to set up TB Keon Lattimore's 5y TD run. Terps were within 16-10 and had 18 mins to come back, but all they could manage was K Obi Egekeze's 2nd FG. Lattimore (13/29y) and TB Lance Ball (15/69y) were held in check as Heels allowed only 93y rushing.

VIRGINIA 17 Wake Forest 16: Cavaliers (8-2) survived another heart-stopper, outlasting Wake Forest (6-3) to win by 1 pt for 3rd time in 4 games and by 2 or less for 5th time this season. Latter achievement gave Virginia new NCAA record previously

held by Columbia since 1971. Nip-and-tuck affair was secured with 2:18 to play when TB Mikell Simpson (16/35y, and 8/77y receiving) dived 1y for winning TD. Wake Forest made it downfield to attempt game-winning 47y FG, but 2006 All-ACC K Sam Swank missed with 2 secs left. Swank had hit 13 of his last 14 FGs before today. Continued emergence of soph QB Jameel Sewell keyed Cavs attack, with Sewell hitting 20-43/225y, TD. Sewell's 39y TD pass to WR Maurice Covington (4/76y) gave UVa 10-6 lead 10 secs before H. QB Riley Skinner (20-26/175y, INT), who had directed 6 straight wins, led Deacons to 16-10 lead in 2nd H, capping TD drive with 13y pass to WR Kenneth Moore (5/59y). Skinner hit 25y 3rd down pass to Moore and made runs of 2y on 4th-and-1 and 12y on 3rd-and-8, when he wasn't dodging disruptive UVa DE tandem of Jeffrey Fitzgerald (11 tackles, sack, forced FUM) and Chris Long (10 tackles, sack, 3 hurries). After Swank kicked 31y FG for 16-10 edge with 10:12 remaining, Wake was unable to add insurance pts. Sewell authored 56y winning drive which featured his 10y completion to Covington on 4th-and-2 and 19y run to set up Simpson's game-winner.

Louisiana State 41 ALABAMA 34: On 1 side, Alabama (6-3) coach Nick Saban was so close he could taste upset win over 3rd-ranked Tigers, his former team. On other side, LSU (8-1) QB Matt Flynn (24-44/353y, 3 TDs, 3 INTs) was driving his Tigers O, trying to overcome his 3 INTs on consecutive possessions that put his team in 34-27 predicament with 4:53 remaining. Taking over at his 16YL, ever-clutch Flynn completed 5-8/52y before facing 4th-and-4 at Alabama 32YL. Flynn, who had surprised Tide in 1st Q by catching 35y pass, dropped back and delivered dagger to hearts of Bama home crowd, throwing over middle to WR Early Doucet, speedy sr who took it 32y to EZ to tie game at 34-34 with 2:49 remaining. It was Flynn's 3rd TD pass. Despite pending possible OT, Crimson Tide stayed aggressive with their passing attack, but it cost them as blitzing LSU frosh S Chad Jones sacked Tide QB John Parker Wilson (14-40/234y, INT) on 3rd down on Alabama 14YL. Ball was stripped and bounced to S Curtis Taylor at 3YL with 1:39 left. It was 7th sack for Tigers. LSU scored winning TD 2 plays later on 1y run by FB Jacob Hester (16/47y, 2 TDs). Wilson had rallied Alabama from early 17-3 deficit with 3 TD passes, including 67y effort to WR D.J. Hall and pair to WR Keith Brown. Brown's 2nd TD grab (14y) gave Tide 27-17 lead late in 3rd Q. After Tigers were quick to tie it 27-27 on Flynn's 61y TD pass to WR Demetrius Byrd (6/144y) and K Colt David's 49y FG, Alabama regained lead, 34-27, on 61y punt RET TD by DB Javier Arenas. After its emotional win over former coach, LSU players presented game ball to coach Les Miles, while Saban turned fiery in news conference trying to deflect attention from his decision to return to college ranks at Alabama. No matter who was coaching whom, win was highlighted by yet another late bit of heroism by Tigers, who now had pulled out 3 late victories in last 4 games.

OHIO STATE 38 Wisconsin 17: By middle of 3rd Q, Ohio Stadium, once den of horrors in 19th and 20th centuries at 4-26-3 for Badgers (7-3), was beginning to look in like 21st century venue that might yield 4th straight win by Wisconsin in Columbus. While top-ranked Ohio State (10-0) jumped to 10-3 H lead thanks to WR Brian Robiskie's great spin-and-run to 30y TD with short pass from QB Todd Boeckman, its outstanding D was slugged twice by Wisconsin in 3rd Q. Badgers' comeback catalysts were gritty QB Tyler Donovan (17-29/238y, 2 TDs) and TE Travis Beckum (9/140y, TD). Duo hooked up on 46y pass to Buckeyes 13YL, and, after 15y PEN pushed UW back to 28YL, they got together on rocket connection to EZ that tied it 10-10. It was 1st TD allowed at home by Ohio State all season. Wisconsin quickly forced punt and went 62y to Donovan's 2y TD pass to sub TE Chris Pressley. "The season was on the line," said Buckeyes OT Kirk Barton, and they turned matters over to big TB Chris "Beanie" Wells (21/169y), who romped for 3 long TD runs in less than 15 mins. Wells tied it 17-17 by slashing to his left to cap 80y drive with 31y TD bolt. After Badgers punted, Wells ripped almost identical run for 30y TD early in 4th Q. Boeckman (17-28/166y, 2 TDs) and Robiskie (3/46y, 2 TDs) teamed up for another TD pass, and Wells rambled 23y for another score with 3:16 to play.

Iowa 28 NORTHWESTERN 17: Both teams hoped for 6 wins for bowl eligibility. Northwestern (5-5) had everything going its way in 1st Q, outgaining Iowa (5-5) 196y to 12y on way to slight game's end edge of 393y to 369y. Wildcats went to 14-0 on 2y run by RB Tyrell Sutton (23/116y), who was making his 1st start in nearly 2 months, followed at end of 1st Q by FB Mark Woodsum's 1st career TD on 2y pass from QB C.J. Bacher (27-54/264y, TD, 3 INTs). Iowa southpaw slinger, QB Jake Christiansen (21-36/299y, TD) was sharp after rough 1st Q, making smart decisions and spreading 10 of his passes among various receivers on Hawks' 4 TD drives. Hawkeyes cut margin to 14-7 in 2nd Q as Christiansen hit WR Derrell Johnson-Koulianos (8/119y) twice before finding WR Trey Stross for 20y TD. WR James Cleveland nabbed 26y pass to set up TB Albert Young (16/59y, TD) for 16y circle of RE for tying TD at 14-14. Wildcats took 17-14 lead to 4th Q as K Amado Villarreal knocked 42y 3-ptr through with 7 mins left in 3rd Q. Christiansen's 3rd connection of 85y drive—after Cats were halted after recovering FUM at Hawks 32YL—found Stross again for 53y to NW 7YL. Iowa TB Damian Sims went over from 2YL and added clinching 8y TD run with 3:47 to play.

Navy 46 NOTRE DAME 44 (OT): Eight U.S. Presidents had come and gone since Naval Academy (5-4) last defeated Notre Dame (1-8) in their annual tussle; famed QB Roger Staubach had led Midshipmen to their last series win (35-14) in 1963. RB Robert Hughes, whose brother had been fatally shot on Tuesday, emotionally scored Notre Dame's 1st Q TD, and teams began trading TDs. Midshipmen missed x-pt in 3rd Q to stay behind 21-20 but made up for it early in 4th Q when DE Chris Kuhar-Pitters (7 tackles, sack) returned FUM 16y to TD, and QB Kaipo-Noa Kaheaku-Enhada (6-8/81y, TD) ran for 2 pts. Notre Dame tied it 28-28 on TD run by RB Travis Thomas with 3:25 to go in 4th Q. Irish had chance to win it, but Kuhar-Pitters sacked ND QB Evan Sharpley (17-27/140y, TD) on 4th down. Contest stayed tied until 3rd OT, which was led off by Kaheaku-Enhada's 25y TD pass to SB Reggie Campbell, and duo repeated their connection on mandatory 2-pt try. Irish countered with Thomas' 3rd rushing TD. When pass interference gave ND 2nd chance on 2-pt try, Thomas' run was buried by Navy DE Michael Walsh and LB Irv Spencer.

KANSAS 76 Nebraska 39: Historians had to look way back to 1908 to find Kansas (9-0) undefeated after 9 games, and everyone had to scratch their heads over Jayhawks pasting 76 pts on dreadful D of once-proud Nebraska (4-6). Kansas was forced into 3-and-out on its 1st series, then proceeded to tally on 11 straight possessions. Still, Huskers had scored 1st on QB Joe Ganz's 3y run and led 14-7 after Ganz (25-50/405y, 4 TDs, 4 INTs) tossed pass with which IB Marlon Lucky (6/83y receiving) thundered 62y to score. Jayhawks RB Brandon McAnderson (25/119y) scored 4 TDs to tie school mark, while QB Todd Reesing (30-41/354y, 6 TDs) set new record in Lawrence with his 6 scoring throws. WRs Dezmon Briscoe caught 5/52y, 3 TDs, and WR Marcus Henry nabbed 6/101y, TD. WR Maurice Purify scored 3 TDs for Nebraska among his 7/158y receiving.

AIR FORCE 30 Army 10: JV QB 3 years earlier, sr TB Chad Hall set new Air Force (7-3) game record with 275y rushing. Hall's class secured its 1st academy home win, having lost to Navy in 2004 and '06 and Army in 2005. Black Knights (3-6) twice tied it in 1st H at 3-3 and 10-10. Army K Owen Tolson connected on 22y FG late in 1st Q, and, after LB Frank Scappaticci intercepted Falcons QB Shaun Carney (9-12/105y, TD, INT) and returned 21y to 3YL, QB Carson Williams (14-33/164y, TD) flipped 2y TD to TE Frank Bernal. Carney scored 5y TD in last min of 1st H and Hall raced 58y in 3rd Q to set up his 1y TD plunge for 24-10 lead.

SOUTHERN CALIFORNIA 24 Oregon State 3: Arriving with 3-game winning streak, Beavers (5-4) and their national-best rushing and sack D greeted largest crowd (85,713) ever to witness game in this Pac-10 series. Meanwhile, USC O had been somewhat off-kilter since September, but Trojans (7-2) welcomed back QB John David Booty (19-33/157y, 2 TDs) after 4-game absence. With Booty in control all was right with Troy attack, at least during efficient 1st H in which USC scored all its pts. After foes traded FGs by Southern California K David Buehler of 47y and Oregon State K Alexis Serna of 22y, Booty keyed 21-pt explosion in 7:28 spell of 2nd Q. Trojans TB Chauncey Washington (12/60y, TD) scored on 1y run on possession following Serna's FG, which had been set up by FUM REC by Beavers DE Victor Butler. In rapid sequence, Booty threw 2 TDs: Washington's 26y catch and WR Patrick Turner's 13y catch, latter after CB Terrell Thomas' 25y INT RET to 14YL. Troy D held Oregon State to only 50y and 3 1st downs in 1st H, and, although Beavers would gain 126y in 2nd H, they never saw scoreboard. Frosh DE Everson Griffen swooped in for 3 sacks to lead USC's charge to 9 sacks by game's end. But, Trojans gained only 287y themselves after quiet 2nd H on O.

OREGON 35 Arizona State 23: Resilient no. 6 Sun Devils (8-1) had rebounded from double-digit deficits on 4 occasions so far this season. But this time, any Arizona State comeback against no. 4 Oregon (8-1) was nixed by Ducks' 2nd H spurt. In 1st H, Oregon cruised to 21-3 lead on trio of TD passes on their 1st 3 series—each concluding long drive—by fabulous QB Dennis Dixon (13-22/189y 4 TDs). ASU rallied with 13 straight pts in middle Qs that included 2nd Q TD pass by QB Rudy Carpenter (22-36/379y, 2 TDs, INT). But, Ducks RB Jonathan Stewart (21/99y, TD) streamed 33y to TD in middle of 3rd Q, followed by Dixon's 4th TD pass on last play of 3rd Q for 35-16 lead. Devils sorely missed big, injured TB Ryan Torain twice: ASU had to settle for K Thomas Weber's chip-shot FG after having staked 1st-and-goal at 3YL on its opening possession, and Devils failed at critical moment in 3rd Q on 4th-and-2 at 37YL when TD could have brought them back to within 5 pts. Star frosh K Weber missed 1st FG try (32y) of his career at end of 1st H but came back to make 50y 3-ptr early in 3rd Q. That raised ASU to its closest margin at 21-16.

USA Today Coaches November 4

1	Ohio State (55)	1493	14	Texas	757
2	LSU (1)	1393	15	Southern California	706
3	Oregon (2)	1376	16	Connecticut	568
4	Oklahoma (2)	1330	17	Auburn	551
5	Kansas	1241	18	Florida	529
6	West Virginia	1222	19	Boise State	368
7	Missouri	1143	20	Clemson	318
8	Boston College	951	21	Virginia	259
9	Arizona State	946	22	Kentucky	197
10	Georgia	927	23	Alabama	174
11	Virginia Tech	829	24	Tennessee	114
12	Hawaii	807	25	Penn State	105
13	Michigan	770			

Bowl Championship Series Ranking November 4

	Harris Poll Pct.	*USA Today* Poll Pct.	Computer Pct.	BCS Avg.
1 Ohio State (10-0)	.9993	.9953	.990	.9949
2 Louisiana State (8-1)	.9345	.9287	.960	.9411
3 Oregon (8-1)	.9168	.9173	.920	.9180
4 Kansas (9-0)	.8219	.8273	.880	.8431
5 Oklahoma (8-1)	.8913	.8867	.740	.8393

November 10, 2007

(Th) BRIGHAM YOUNG 27 Texas Christian 22: BYU (7-2) had launched its 13-game Mt West Conf winning streak at TCU in September last season. With hard-fought victory, Cougars stayed unbeaten in conf, and, though they led from their opening series to touch off alternating scoring pattern, it was pair of late-game sacks by LBs David Nixon and Bryan Kehl that sealed fate of Horned Frogs (5-5). BYU RB Harvey Unga (16/64y, 2 TDs) zipped untouched to 15y TD after QB Max Hall (26-44/305y, TD, INT) scrambled 20y on 1st possession. TCU K Chris Manfredini knocked through 3 FGs in 1st H, but in between Hall completed 1y scoring pass to RB Joe Semanoff and K Mitch Payne made 1st of his 2 FGs. BYU led 17-9 at H. Cougars LB Kelly Poppinga's INT led off 3rd Q and prompted Unga's 2nd TD run. BYU's 24-9 edge was enough even when TCU scored its 2nd TD of 2nd H with 2:55 to go on pass by QB Andy Dalton (18-30/165y, TD, INT).

MARYLAND 42 Boston College 35: Reaching no. 2 in AP poll clearly had become poison: Like California and South Florida before them, BC Eagles (8-2) suffered unlikely loss. Boston College couldn't stop 472y O by middling Maryland (5-5), losers of 3 straight. Facing 42-21 deficit in 4th Q, Eagles QB Matt Ryan (33-56/421y, 2 INTs) was able to throw pair of 4th Q TD passes to TE Ryan Purvis (10/102y), but 2nd came too late with 52 secs left. Terps QB Chris Turner (21-27/337y, 3 TDs) had opened scoring with 10y TD pass to TE Jason Goode (6/56y, 2 TDs) and nailed 2 TDs, including screen that TB Da'Rel Scott toted 57y, to give Maryland 34-21 lead in 3rd Q. With their next possession, Terps put game out of reach with 68y drive capped by 37y TD reverse run by whippet-fast WR Darrius Heyward-Bey. With big lead, Terps were content to ride back of workhorse TB Lance Ball, who ran 32/109y and TD against nation's top-ranked rush D. Maryland LB Erin Henderson (13 tackles, sack) ignored back pain to turn in another superior effort.

VIRGINIA TECH 40 Florida State 21: Hokies (8-2) came up with frosh hero in alternate QB Tyrod Taylor and blew open tight game with 20 pts in 4th Q. Returning from ankle injury, Taylor (10-15/204y, 2 TDs, INT, and 92y, TD rushing) played every down after starting QB Sean Glennon got knocked out in 2nd Q. Denied his 300th win at Florida State (6-4), coach Bobby Bowden was impressed by Taylor: "I didn't expect to see the second coming of (Michael) Vick. We couldn't tackle that guy." Trailing 21-20 entering 4th Q, Taylor led Hokies on 53y drive that featured his 12y run, 45y completion to WR Justin Harper (5/167y, TD), and 1y draw run for TD. Taylor then hit WR Zach Luckett for 2-pt-conv to give Virginia Tech 28-21 lead with 10:10 to go. Seminoles (6-4) lost 3 TOs while playing without starting QB Drew Weatherford after 1st H injury. Backup QB Christian Ponder (8-18/105y, TD, 2 INTs) was solid in 3rd Q when Florida State scored 15 pts to take lead. In 4th Q, however, Ponder lost FUM that set up FG by Va Tech and threw INT to DE Chris Ellis that was returned 5y to TD for 38-21 lead with 5:13 remaining. FSU 3rd-string QB D'Vontrey Richardson was sacked in EZ for safety. FSU had reversed momentum in 3rd Q as K Gary Cismesia booted 50y FG, LB Dekoda Watson (6 tackles, sack) returned INT 40y for TD, and Ponder threw 8y TD pass to WR De'Cody Fagg (4/63y, TD). Win was coach Frank Beamer's 1st against Seminoles after 7 losses, while Bowden dropped his 1st game to Virginia Tech after 15 wins.

Virginia 48 MIAMI 0: Fond farewell to Orange Bowl stadium after 70 years of Miami football proved to be forgettable evening as Cavaliers (9-2) punished Hurricanes (5-5) for all beatings Miami had administered running up 318-143-7 mark in "Little Havana." With plenty of old Miami greats on hand for festivities, current Canes played nothing like glory teams, gaining 189y, earning only 9 1st downs, and committing 5 TOs. Miami trailed 14-0 after 1st Q and 31-0 at H. With sr QB Kyle Wright (9-23/94y) throwing 3 INTs in game's opening 16 mins, Hurricanes were as good as done. QB Jameel Sewell paced Virginia with 20-25/288y, TD, INT passing, while TB Mickell Simpson rushed for 93y and caught 3/54y. Virginia took right off, marching 96y with opening possession as Sewell hit 3-3/64y, including 29y TD pass to WR Maurice Covington. Cavs soon blocked punt to set up 5y run by TB Keith Payne. Miami surrendered final TD on 44y FUM RET by Virginia CB Chris Cook to set unfortunate record for most pts ever allowed by Miami in home shutout loss.

CLEMSON 44 Wake Forest 10: Trying to keep its ACC title hopes alive, Clemson (8-2) put pedal to metal in roaring away from Demon Deacons (6-4) with 27 pts in 1st H. Continuing his excellent season, QB Cullen Harper (27-35/266y) threw 3 TD passes including pair in 17-pt 2nd Q that upped Tigers lead to 27-7 by H. Harper now had thrown Clemson-record 26 TD passes to only 4 INTs. Wake Forest could only answer that surge with 52y FG by K Sam Swank midway through 3rd Q. Any hopes for Wake soon died as Tigers TB C.J. Spiller took ensuing KO 90y, his 9th TD longer than 50y in 23-game career. It gave Tigers 34-10 lead with 7:30 left in 3rd Q. Wake's sole TD came on 2y run by TB Josh Adams in 1st Q, capping 14-play, 72y drive. WR Aaron Kelly (10/93y) caught 2 TD passes to set Clemson single-season mark with 11; Derrick Hamilton caught 10 scores in 2003.

GEORGIA 45 Auburn 20: Auburn (7-4) arrived with 10 wins in last 12 trips to Sanford Stadium, so Bulldogs (8-2) coach Mark Richt succumbed to long-time desire of players and chose to dress his team in black jerseys. Richt had urged Georgia faithful to wear black, but fans had to wonder when Georgia warmed up in traditional red. When team finished pre-game prayer, noir-clad Bulldogs exploded from locker room to delight of excited crowd, and AC/DC's "Back in Black" blasting in background. Tigers made matters worse for themselves on opening play when QB Brandon Cox (14-30/133y, TD, 4 INTs) was picked off by UGa S Kelin Johnson to set up 32y FG by K Brandon Coutu. Cox would throw 4 INTs against Georgia for 2nd year in row. After Auburn tied game 3-3 on 22y FG by K Wes Byrum, Bulldogs QB Matt Stafford (11-19/237y, INT) pitched 2 TD passes: 58y to WR Mohamed Massaquoi and 13y to WR Sean Bailey (4/96y). Behind 17-3 in raucous stadium, Auburn manfully answered with 65y drive to TD on 7y run by TB Ben Tate (13/58y) with 6:13 left in 1st H. Tigers reeled off 1st 10 pts of 2nd H to snatch 20-17 lead. Bulldogs were not going to lose on this special night and answered loudly with 28 straight pts against SEC's top-rated D. TB Knowshon Moreno (22/101y), who topped 100y mark for 4th straight game, scored twice in 3rd Q. Bulldogs TB Thomas Brown (14/81y), returning from broken collarbone, raced 53y to set up FB Brannan Southerland's 1y run for 38-20 lead in 4th Q, and Brown scored own 1y TD plunge.

Illinois 28 OHIO STATE 21: Provided timeout by no. 1 Ohio State (10-1) to ponder 4th down run while leading 28-21 with 6:53 to play, Fighting Illini (8-3) coach Ron Zook pulled back his punt team from own 34YL. Instead, QB Juice Williams, who enjoyed his best game to date with 12-22/140y, 4 TDs passing and 70y rushing, sneaked required few inches, and Ohio State never owned ball during game's last 8:09. In icing its 1st win over any top-ranked team since beating Michigan State in 1956, Illinois counted on Williams to subsequently make trio of QB Draw runs on consecutive 3rd down conversions. Fireworks had erupted at game's beginning when Buckeyes scored in 2 plays after KO: TB Chris "Beanie" Wells (20/76y, 2 TDs) went 11y to 6 pts. Back-up RB Daniel Defrene charged 80y to set up Williams' 1st scoring pass, 3y lob to TE Michael Hoomanawanui, so Illini tied it up 7-7 with game only 1:12 old. Another trade of TDs marked balance of 1st Q, and Illinois took 21-14 H edge on frosh WR Brian Gamble's 8y catch 17 secs prior to H. Illini concentrated on running ball in 2nd H, in fact, Ohio State's 3rd-ranked rushing D became so run-conscious that Illinois WR Marques Wilkins popped wide open for 31y TD catch from Williams with 4 mins to go in 3rd Q. Now in trouble and down 28-14, Ohio State went 76y to Wells' 2nd TD run (17y) and was on move again in 4th Q when QB Todd Boeckman (13-23/156y, 3 INTs) threw into double coverage as Illinois frosh CB Marcus Thomas went high to stab INT from WR Brian Robiskie (4/31y) at Illini 24YL. Zook's up-and-coming Blue-and-Orange amazingly proceeded to hold ball for game's last 16 plays. Buckeyes' defeat marked end of conf-record 20 straight victories, which dated back to 2005.

Michigan State 48 PURDUE 31: Righting ship after 3 straight losses, Spartans (6-5) rode QB Brian Hoyer's 22-31/266y, 2 TDs passing, WR Devin Thomas' 10/116y receiving, and TB Jehuu Caulcrick's 19th and 20th rushing TDs of season. Purdue (7-4) piled up 517y O but suffered 3 costly TOs, including pair of INTs by Michigan State LB SirDarean Adams, which led to 10 pts. Boilermakers QB Curtis Painter passed 29-45/344y, TD, 2 INTs and scored pair of rushing TDs. With score at 21-21 in 2nd Q, Caulcrick tallied his 2nd TD with 1:13 left before H. Painter quickly was intercepted by Adams, and K Brett Swenson made 39y FG as H expired with MSU leading 31-21. Key score in 4th Q put Michigan State up 41-24 as S Otis Wiley hit Purdue WR Dorien Bryant to force FUM which S Travis Key returned 20y to score.

WISCONSIN 37 Michigan 21: Despite its loss, Michigan (8-3), winners of previous 8, still could pull out Big 10 title with closing win over Ohio State. Without stars QB Chad Henne (3-5/28y, INT), yanked early because of lingering shoulder injury, and TB Mike Hart, who didn't play at all, Wolverines were no match for inspired Wisconsin (8-3). Badgers looked to sr QB Tyler Donovan, who passed 14-27/245y, TD and used his quick feet to run 6/49y, TD in his last home game. Henne's early INT put Wisconsin in position near midfield for game's opening score: Donovan hit his favorite target, TE Travis Beckum (6/106y, TD), with 10y TD. Donovan scrambled for TD in 2nd Q, and Badgers left at H with 20-7 margin. Tall Michigan sub QB Ryan Mallett (11-36/245y, 3 TDs, 2 INTs) arched long TD pass to WR Mario Manningham (3/113y, 2 TDs) for 97y early in 4th Q and wraped up 86y march less than 6 mins later with 26y TD pass to WR Adrian Arrington (7/101y, TD). So, Wolverines had clawed back into contest, trailing 23-21, with half of 4th Q still to go. But, Mallett threw INT to Wisconsin DB Jack Ikegwuonu to set up clinching 6y TD run by frosh TB Zach Brown (27/108y, 2 TDs), who would add another score min later. Ikeguwuonu's key INT came at fortuitous moment with Donovan out with wrist injury. Afterward he was giddy about it: "I got Michigan helmet paint right here," he said to media, pointing to his throwing hand, "You should take a picture of that."

Kansas 43 OKLAHOMA STATE 28: Jayhawks' 1st win over Oklahoma State (5-5) in 12 years vaulted Kansas (10-0) to its best record since 1899. Kansas sr WR Marcus Henry hauled in 8/199y, 3 TDs, including 2 important scores. Ahead 20-14 at H, Jayhawks D made stop at beginning of 3rd Q, and QB Todd Reesing (27-40/318y, 3 TDs) lofted long pass for Henry, who took it near midfield and raced away for 82y TD. When RB Brandon McAnderson (25/142y, 2 TDs) zipped 12y for TD on Kansas's next series, Jayhawkers led 33-14. Cowboys still had their six-shooters poised as they tallied on 39y TD pass and 3y run by QB Zac Robinson (22-37/276y, 2 TDs, INT) at end of quick 82 and 89y drives. So, Oklahoma State trailed only 33-28 with most of 4th Q still ahead. Kansas answered with its own 89y trip that ended halfway through 4th Q: Decisive score came as Reesing scrambled to his right and found Henry racing across back of EZ for 4y TD.

MISSOURI 40 Texas A&M 26: Mizzou's sparkling frosh WR Jeremy Maclin (5/146y, 2 TDs) registered pair of critical scores that paved way for no. 7 Tigers (9-1) to stay in BCS Bowl contention. RB Tony Temple (22/141y, TD) scored on 44y gallop in 1st Q and QB Chase Daniel (27-35/352y, 3 TDs) hit TE Chase Coffman with 5y TD at end of 17-play march in 2nd Q, but Missouri couldn't quite shake Texas A&M (6-5), which trailed 17-9 just before H. Maclin caught simple pass at sideline and turned it up to sprint away for 82y TD. Texas A&M "battled hard" and "had a chance," according to stressed coach Dennis Franchione after 10-pt 3rd Q. Giant Aggies TB Jorvorskie Lane (12/50y) battered over GL early in 3rd Q to tie all-time career TD run mark in College Station at 44, and K Matt Szymanski made 22y FG late in 3rd Q. But, Szymanski missed 33y FG early in 4th Q that would have trimmed Tigers' lead to 24-22. Foes traded TDs in 1st half of 4th Q, and Maclin twisted through grasp of defender and reached ball over GL with 3:41 left to push Mizzou out of danger at 38-26. Moments later, NT Lorenzo Williams ended scoring with sack of A&M QB Stephen McGee (18-28/247y, 2 TDs, INT) in EZ.

TEXAS 59 Texas Tech 43: Fans had to wonder where D went as Big 12 South foes combined for 1,027y in total O and, after notably quiet 3rd Q, battered each EZ for combined 47 pts over game's last 12 mins. Longhorns (9-2) QB Colt McCoy (21-30/268y, INT) passed for 4 scores and ran for 2 more as Texas never trailed after breaking ice in 1st Q with McCoy's 18y TD pass to WR Jordan Shipley. As usual, Texas Tech (8-3) QB Graham Harrell (36-48/466y, 5 TDs, INT) was highly effective in air, but Red Raiders could gain only 10y rushing on absurdly-few 7 attempts. Longhorns were ahead 28-10 until Raiders made 10 pts in latter portion of 2nd Q, primarily on Harrell's 22y TD pass to WR Edward Britton. McCoy's 20y pass to WR Quan Cosby (8/94y, 2 TDs) earned only pts of 3rd Q, and Horns led 35-20. Tech twice pulled to 38-28 and 45-35 in wild 4th Q that saw teams alternate scoring every 2 or 3 mins. With 1:23 to play, Cosby caught his 2nd TD pass (14y) for 59-35 lead, but Tech frosh WR Michael Crabtree (9/195y, 2 TDs), nation's leading reciever took short pass from Harrell and swirled through tired D for 69y TD. Raiders' last bid was squashed as Texas quickly recoverd its 2nd onside-KO of 4th Q.

Bowl Championship Series Ranking November 11

November 17, 2007

(Th) ARIZONA 34 Oregon 24: If ever there was game that spotlighted importance QB position in 2000s, it was this contest in which no. 2 Oregon (8-2) experienced significant collapse as soon as superb QB Dennis Dixon left with season-ending knee injury with 6 mins to go in 1st Q. Without Dixon, Ducks would drop from 1st to 4th in Pac-10 standings, losing 3 in row to end year. Dixon scored untouched on 39y run in 1st Q and surprised Cats with 2-pt run. Arizona (5-6) quickly answered with 34y TD pass from QB Willie Tuitama (21-39/266y, 2 TDs, INT) to WR Mike Thomas (6/125y, 2 TDs) to trail 8-7. Oregon was leading 11-10 early in 2nd Q when back-up QB Brady Leaf (22-46/163y, 2 INTs) was picked off on wide pass by Wildcats CB Antoine Cason, who high-stepped 42y to TD and Arizona's 1st lead at 17-11. On his way to selection for Thorpe Award as nation's top DB, Cason also raced 56y on punt TD RET. Arizona led 31-14 at H. Oregon trimmed deficit to TD as sub RB Andre Crenshaw scored from 2YL in 4th Q. Wildcats RB Nicholas Grigsby (20/53y) lost FUM at Oregon 40YL with 4:33 to go, but TV replay overturned decision as QB Tuitama was shown to have had knee down before handoff. K Jason Bondzio's 46y FG padded Wildcats' lead to 34-24.

West Virginia 28 CINCINNATI 23: While Cincinnati may be baseball town, night's attention was centered on upstart Cincy Bearcats (8-3) and Nippert Stadium, where they hosted no. 5 ranked West Virginia (9-1). Until late rally perked it up, Bearcats crowd was witness to another scintillating performance by Mountaineers QB Patrick White (13-19/140y, INT), who rushed for 155y and 2 TDs to become 12th QB in history to top 3,000y rushing (3,129y to date). Having scored in 5 straight games, White had logged 37 career rushing TDs. Mountaineers gained 295y on ground and built 28-10 lead after TB Steve Slaton (23/103y) scored on 1y run early in 4th Q. Bearcats QB Ben Mauk (19-34/323y, 2 TDs) sparked comeback bid with 71y drive he capped with 13y TD pass to frosh WR Marcus Barnett (10/210y, including 70y TD in 1st Q) and, after 2nd lost FUM by White in 4th Q, 24y drive to 1y TD run by RB Bradley Glatthaar with 2:26 left. S Boogie Allen then recovered onside-KO for Mountaineers, who ran out clock as Slaton ran 3/22y and pair of 1st downs.

Boston College 20 CLEMSON 17: Frenetic finish followed familiar script as Eagles (9-2) ended Clemson's ACC Atlantic Div crown aspirations for 3rd seasons in row, each by 3 pts or fewer. QB Matt Ryan (31-47/315y, TD, INT) threw another dramatic TD pass, this time targeting wide-open WR Rich Gunnell, who caught 43y pass with 1:46 remaining to secure spot in ACC title game for Boston College. Ryan completed 5-6/68y of 71y drive to answer Clemson (8-3) QB Cullen Harper (26-40/226y, INT), who had scored go-ahead 4y TD run for 17-13 edge. Harper used last min to scare Eagles, just missing 45y scoring connection with WR Aaron Kelly, and K Mark Buchholz missed 54y FG attempt as time expired 7 plays later. BC D limited Clemson's dynamic TB tandem of James Davis (12/10y, TD) and C.J. Spiller (11/52y). After gaining 68y on opening drive of game, which ended on Davis's 1y TD run, Tigers O often stalled, gaining only 201y rest of way. Eagles gained 375y, with 182y coming on 4th Q drives to 17 pts. BC had trailed all game until FB James McCluskey tied it 10-10 with 2y TD run with 13:37 left in 4th Q.

GEORGIA 24 Kentucky 13: With their D taking center stage, hot Bulldogs (9-2) won 5th straight as they blanked Wildcats in 4th Q. With Kentucky (7-4) facing 3rd-and-4 at Georgia 15YL and trailing 21-13 with 10:20 left, Bulldogs DE Marcus Howard (2 sacks) dropped QB Andre Woodson (24-41/268y, TD, INT) for 18y loss. Wildcats K Lones Seiber then missed 51y FG try. On next Cats' next try deep in own end, UGa DT Geno Atkins threw TB Rafael Little for 2y loss on 3rd-and-1 to force punt inside 5-min mark. Georgia K Brandon Coutu soon clinched it with 46y FG with 2:09 left. DE Jeremy Lomax and Atkins put icing on cake with 4th down sack (5th of game) of Woodson after Kentucky drove to 20YL in closing moments. Wildcats had opened with 10-0 lead in 1st Q on Woodson's 36y TD pass to WR Keenan Burton and Seiber's 31y FG that converted INT, 1 of 4 TOs by Georgia. With QB Matthew Stafford (12-22/99y, 2 INTs) struggling, Bulldogs relied on 184y run game to take 21-10 lead by 3rd Q on TDs by TB Knowshon Moreno (22/124y), TB Thomas Brown (22/73y), and Stafford, who went 10y on naked rollout to right. Moreno became 1st Georgia back since Herschel Walker in 1982 to rush for 5 straight 100y games.

TENNESSEE 25 Vanderbilt 24: Losers of 22 of last 23 to in-state bullies, Vanderbilt (5-6) K Bryant Hahnfeldt's 49y FG try nicked upright to bounce away with 33 secs left. Down 24-9 in 4th Q, Tennessee (8-3) rallied to block Georgia from SEC East

title. Volunteers K Daniel Lincoln supplied game-winning pts with 33y FG with 2:46 remaining. Commodores QB Mackenzi Adams (14-26/139y, 3 TDs) had thrown pair of TDs during 17-pt run starting at end of 2nd Q. Vanderbilt struck for 10 pts in final 47 secs of 1st H: Adams threw 19y TD pass to TB Jeff Jennings, and Hahnfeldt kicked 33y FG after LB Patrick Benoist recovered Vols' FUM at Tennessee 16YL. Adams drove Vandy 75y at start of 2nd H to his short TD pass. In last 23 mins, Vols permitted only 38y to fuel their 2nd biggest 4th Q rally in history. Tennessee QB Erik Ainge (29-43/245y, 3 TDs) threw 2 TDs to pull Vols to within 24-22 with 7:14 left. However, they failed on tying 2-pt conv after Ainge's last TD pass, 5y to WR Austin Rogers (8/60y). After Tennessee D forced another 3-and-out, CB Dennis Rogan raced 45y on punt RET to Commodores 33YL. Lincoln booted game-winner 6 plays later. On ensuing KO, Vanderbilt CB D.J. Moore broke loose for 55y to Vols 42YL, but Dores barely advanced, and their long 3-pt try missed.

ARKANSAS 45 Mississippi State 31: Mississippi State (6-5) fell to 0-7-1 all-time in Arkansas as embattled Razorbacks (7-4) saw QB Casey Dick (14-17/199y, 4TDs) enjoy career day. Bulldogs QB Wesley Carroll (29-51/421y) threw 4 TD passes, but difference was Carroll's 4 INTs that helped Arkansas DE Antwain Robinson's RET for TD with 6:48 left to seal win at 45-24. Most impressive of his TD passes was 4th Q 80y bomb to WR Jamayel Smith (10/208y, 2 TDs). In what would be final home game for both jr TB Darren McFadden (28/88y) and coach Houston Nutt, Razorbacks went to air for 5 TDs. In addition to Dick's quartet of TDs, versatile McFadden threw 24y TD pass to WR Richard Johnson early in 4th Q. It was McFadden's 5th career TD throw. McFadden himself scored on 57y reception, catching short pass and outracing Miss State D. Bulldogs failed to overcome woeful 2nd Q when they surrendered 7-0 lead to barrage of 24 unanswered pts. Arkansas forced trio of 3-and-outs and Carroll's INT and scored TDs after 79, 35, and 55y trips. Miss State pulled to within 14 pts 3 times in 2nd H, but never closer.

Louisiana-Monroe 21 ALABAMA 14: Another upset victim was claimed as La-Monroe (5-6) won only its 3rd game in 33 tries vs. SEC. Loss prompted $4 million Alabama (6-5) coach Nick Saban to say afterward that he was "embarrassed for all our fans." ULM CB Quintez Secka (5 tackles, 2 INTs) made 38y INT RET to set up TB Calvin Dawson (33/91y) for 1y TD run in 2nd Q to earn 7-7 tie. Warhawks QB Kinsmon Lancaster (14-24/161y) threw winning 11y TD pass to WR Marty Humphrey late in 3rd Q. Tide committed 4 TOs, had FG try blocked, were shut out in 2nd H, and failed on 2 chances in 4th Q. With 4:46 left, Alabama killed its 69y drive when TB Jimmy Johns lost FUM to S James Truxillo at 13YL. Following 19y punt RET by TB Jonathan Lowe, Bama next faced 3rd-and-2 at 18YL and twice ran TB Terry Grant (21/96y), only to be stuffed for no gain. Tide took over at 37YL in last min, but QB John Parker Wilson (21-31/246y, TD, 2 INTs) missed 3 passes.

Ohio State 14 MICHIGAN 3: Jim Tressel became 1st Ohio State (11-1) coach ever to beat rival Michigan (8-4) 6 times in 7 seasons. On Monday it became official that Tressel would no longer face Lloyd Carr, who retired as Wolverines coach after 13 years. TB Beanie Wells rushed 39/222y, his career-high also set mark for Ohio State runners in storied series. Wells scored both big TDs: 1y run in 2nd Q, to eclipse 33y 1st Q FG by Wolverines K K.C. Lopata, and 62y sprint off LT on Ohio's 1st scrimmage play in 3rd Q. Against Buckeyes' tough D, injured-riddled Michigan O was 1-dimensional and remarkably ineffective with only 91y O. Sore-shouldered QB Chad Henne passed for miserable 11-34/68y, which allowed Ohio to stack its D against runs of TB Mike Hart, who managed only 44y on 18 tries.

MICHIGAN STATE 35 Penn State 31: Mighty comeback by Spartans (7-5) secured their 2nd straight win to close season and wrap up bowl invitation with upset of Nittany Lions (8-4), who finished few marquee victories. Although Michigan State scored 1st on WR Devin Thomas' 1st of 3 TD catches, Penn State cruised to 17-7 H lead on 37y pass from QB Anthony Morelli (16-37/188y, TD) to WR Deon Butler (3/68y, TD) and run by TB Rodney Kinlaw (28/125y, 2 TDs), latter coming 8 secs before H. Fake FG sent Lions K Kevin Kelly scooting for 5y TD, and it boosted Lions to 24-7 with 4:43 to go in 3rd Q. QB Brian Hoyer (16-21/257y, 4 TDs, 2 INTs) pitched pair of scores on Spartans' next 2 drives of 74 and 91y. Kinlaw scored again early in 4th Q to put Penn State up by 31-21. Thomas (7/139y) caught his school-record-tying 3rd TD, and Michigan State regained possession at its 20YL with 9:50 to go. Lions appeared to stop drive, but Spartans TB Jehuu Caulcrick (22/99y, TD) made 1st down in MSU territory on 4th down punt fake and went on to tally on 1y blast with 4:08 to go to extend his single-season school record to 126 pts.

INDIANA 27 Purdue 24: Before his untimely death during summer, admired Indiana (7-5) coach Terry Hoeppner urged Hoosiers to "Play 13," meaning to extend season to 13 games by qualifying for school's 1st bowl since 1993. Last-min victory over rival Purdue (7-5) gloriously locked up Insight Bowl. Playing in front of sellout crowd that included many members of 1967 team that played in school's only Rose Bowl, Hoosiers were decked out in throw-back uniforms that depicted that era. QB Kellen Lewis (23-39/216y, INT) mixed runs and passes in building 24-3 lead through Hoosiers' 1st possession of 2nd H. Lewis finished 95y drive with 9y scamper late in 1st Q, hit tall WR James Hardy (10/87y) for 8y TD in 2nd Q, and zipped 8y for score early in 3rd Q. TD catch was 36th career score for Hardy, Indiana's all-time receiving leader. Even though they were spilled for 12y in lost y in 1st H and held to 69y rushing by game's end, Boilermakers caught fire in 3rd Q. Purdue RB Kory Sheets twice barreled for 1y scores to cut margin to 24-17, and, with 4:18 to go, DE Cliff Avril forced FUM by Indiana RB Marcus Thigpen (19/140y) that recovered by DE Alex Magee at IU 36YL. After pass interference PEN, Purdue RB Jaycen Taylor (13/53y) zipped 16y and QB Curtis Painter (28-45/281y, TD, INT) found WR Jake Standeford all alone for tying 5y TD. Lewis hit 5 short passes to position Hoosiers for winning 49y FG by K Austin Starr with 30 secs to play.

TEXAS TECH 34 Oklahoma 27: No. 3 Oklahoma (9-2) was bounced from national title consideration when it ran into aerial buzzsaw and tough D concocted by Texas Tech (8-4) coach Mike Leach, former Sooners asst. QB Graham Harrell (47-72/420y, 2 TDs, 2 INTs) sparked Raiders O that rattled off 27 straight pts soon after opening KO. Before Harrell could riddle Sooners, CB Lendy Holmes picked off Harrell and returned INT 63y for TD. On OU's 1st snap, RB Allen Patrick bobbled FUM and Oklahoma QB Sam Bradford (2-3/11y) was injured trying to tackle Tech LB Marlon Williams who returned to OU 34YL. After another series, Bradford left for good with concussion. Except for pair of FGs in middle Qs by K Garrett Hartley, that was it for Sooners scoring until back-up QB Joey Halzle (21-41/291y, 2 TDs, INT) completed 2 TD passes late in game to make score look respectable. While trailing 7-6 in 1st Q, Harrell had rifled 60y pass to WR Michael Crabtree (12/154y, TD) to 1YL and scored for 13-7 lead on next play. Harrell hit pair of TDs within 3- min span of 2nd Q, and Texas Tech was on its way at 27-7.

WASHINGTON 37 California 23: While injuries had hampered Cal's O, opponents hastened 1-5 slump by Bears (6-5) by pounding ball up middle against smallish D-front. Washington (4-7) RB Louis Rankin (21/224y) missed last 20 mins but still rambled for his 2nd 200y game in 3 weeks, including opening-drive 5y TD run. Rankin's 46y run on Huskies' opening series of 3rd Q put him past 200y barrier and positioned K Ryan Perkins for 1st of 3 2nd H FGs, which provided 31-20 lead. Banged-up California QB Nate Longshore (20-28/236y, 3 TDs, INT) connected on 3 scoring passes in 1st H, but botched x-pt after TE Cameron Morrah's 19y TD catch in 1st Q kept Bears behind 21-20 late in 2nd Q. Next came 1st of 2 tough calls that went against Cal: Calling for fair catch of punt in last 35 secs of 2nd Q, Bears DB Brandon Hampton muffed it when Morrah was shoved into him. TV replay showed Hampton lost FUM before interference, and Washington was given possession at Cal 21YL. Huskies WR Marcus Reece cut inside for leaping 12y TD reception that made it 28-20 at H. With UW up 31-23 in 3rd Q, Bears LB Zack Follett's sack seemed to force FUM by Huskies QB Carl Bonnell (7-19/108y, TD). Ref's ruling was that Bonnell's pass—that landed behind QB—was intentional grounding PEN, not FUM. Bonnell then hit 51y aerial to WR Cody Ellis to set up Perkins' 29y FG.

Oregon State 52 WASHINGTON STATE 17: Fast-closing Oregon State (7-4) won its 5th game in last 6 behind 7 INTs and RB Yvenson Bernard's pair of TD runs to crush Cougars (4-7). Bernard rushed 17/74y and sat out 2nd H as precaution against minor knee injury; Beavers didn't need him as they already led 31-3. In his last home game, Washington State QB Alex Brink (21-45/314y, 6 INTs) was sacked once while suffering through half-dozen pickoffs, 2 by OSU LB Derrick Doggett, but Cougars still managed 397y O. Beavers took opening KO and went 78y to short TD keeper by QB Lyle Moevao (15-28/202y, TD). After Beavers S Daniel Drayton soon recovered FUM, Bernard dashed 18y to make it 14-0. RB Kevin McCall (14/62y) propped up Washington State with 19 and 1y TD runs in 2nd H.

USA Today Coaches November 18

1	LSU (51)	1483	14	Florida	736
2	Kansas (8)	1441	15	Virginia	626
3	West Virginia (1)	1345	16	Boston College	619
4	Missouri	1328	17	Boise State	593
5	Ohio State	1276	18	Illinois	485
6	Arizona State	1158	19	Tennessee	430
7	Georgia	1105	20	Wisconsin	343
8	Virginia Tech	1019	21	Connecticut	264
9	Oklahoma	931	22	Clemson	225
10	Oregon	890	23	Brigham Young	161
11	Texas	883	24	Texas Tech	80
12	Southern California	879	25	Auburn	65
13	Hawaii	828			

Bowl Championship Series Ranking November 18

	Harris Poll Pct.	*USA Today* Poll Pct.	Computer Pct.	BCS Avg.
1 Louisiana State (10-1)	.9926	.9887	.990	.9904
2 Kansas (11-0)	.9558	.9607	.930	.9488
3 West Virginia (9-1)	.8867	.8967	.880	.8878
4 Missouri (10-1)	.8867	.8853	.840	.8707
5 Ohio State (11-1)	.8499	.8507	.880	.8602

November 22-24, 2007

(Th'g) Southern California 44 ARIZONA STATE 24: If there was 1 statistic that told story it was USC's 133y rushing compared to Arizona State's 16y. Contributing to poor rush total of Sun Devils (9-2) was 6 sacks—4 by sr DE Lawrence Jackson—by Trojans (9-2). ASU was in habit of falling behind all season, and USC QB John David Booty (26-39/375y), who tied career-best with 4 TD passes, flipped 1st Q TDs of 4y to WR Vidal Hazelton and 5y to FB Stanley Havili. In between, Arizona State TB-WR Rudy Burgess stormed left on cut-back on 98y KO TD RET. Devils K Thomas Weber made short FG early in 2nd Q to knot it 17-17. ASU was within range of lead on long FG later in 2nd Q, but 4th down pass was crushed by Jackson's sack of Devils QB Rudy Carpenter (21-30/240y, TD). USC quickly registered K David Buehler's 20y FG and Booty's 1y keeper to go up 27-17 at H. Carpenter got bloody lip on opening snap of 3rd Q, and Booty's pair of TD throws in 3rd Q to frosh TB Joe McKnight and TE Fred Davis (5/119y, TD) pushe dit out of reach at 44-17.

(Fri) MISSISSIPPI STATE 17 Mississippi 14: It was sight to behold for Mississippi State (7-5) fans: stout coach Sylvester Croom running, perhaps plodding, around field with MSU flag in post-game jubilation. His Bulldogs, who turned season around by playing hard-nosed D and efficient O, had just stunned Rebels (3-9) with 17 pts in 4th Q to win Egg Bowl and likely bowl bid. Final 3 pts to secure victory and equal school-record for greatest 4th Q comeback came courtesy of career-long, 48y FG left by K Adam Carlson with 31 secs left. By rushing for 204y, behind TB Benjarvus Green-Ellis (29/117y), Rebs controlled tempo for 3 Qs. Until 4th Q, Ole Miss outgained Bulldogs 290y to 144y and enjoyed 20-4 advantage in 1st downs. Mississippi had scored TDs on 14y run by Green-Ellis in 1st Q and 13y pass from QB Brent Schaefer (10-30/115y) to WR Shay Hodge in 3rd Q and entered 4th Q with 14-0 lead. Rebels could blame themselves as tide turned on failed 4th down run in mid-4th Q when they could have punted from midfield: Green-Ellis was nailed for 3y loss by Bulldogs CB Jasper O'Quinn and S Keith Fitzhugh. Bulldogs scored TD 6 plays later on 4y pass from previously-cold QB Wesley Carroll (13-28/130y, TD, INT) to TB Anthony Dixon (11/26y, and 7/101y receiving). Forced to put, Ole Miss booted short to prevent long RET, but Miss State S Derek Pegues cheated up and caught ball on fly to charge for tying TD RET with 2:38 left. On Miss State's last chance, Carroll completed 2-3/23y and ran for 11y to set up Carlson's heroics.

(Fri) Arkansas 50 LOUISIANA STATE 48 (OT): Brilliant Arkansas (8-4) TB Darren McFadden rose to occasion against top competition, rushing 32/206y, 3 TDs, and throwing for TD as Hogs appeared to bounce top-ranked Tigers (10-2) out of national title hunt. For 2nd time in 2007, 3rd OT was no charm for LSU as QB Matt Flynn (22-47/209y, 3 TDs) had to force pass trying to tie game on 2-pt conv and threw INT on which CB Matterral Richardson made neat move to cut across bow of WR Demetrius Byrd near back of EZ. In gaining 513y against vaunted LSU D, Arkansas showed spectacular form expected by its fans all season. Arkansas led 7-6 at H and jumped to biggest lead either team would enjoy when McFadden raced 73y for TD and 14-6 edge midway through 3rd Q. It took less than 2 mins for LSU to tie it on 12y TD run by FB Jacob Hester (28/126y) and Flynn's 2-pt run. Foes traded pair of TDs by Razorbacks FB Peyton Hillis—65y run and 24y catch of McFadden's perfect pass over middle—for 2 TD receptions by Byrd (6/46y). Byrd's 2nd score from Flynn came in last min of regulation and tied it 28-28. Flynn ran in 12y TD on LSU's 1st OT try. QB Casey Dick (10-18/94y, TD) saved his sole TD pass for Arkansas' 1st OT as he found Hillis (11/89y, 2 TDs, and 5/62y, 2 TDs receiving) on 10y scoring pass after clicking with Hillis on 4th-and-10 pass. McFadden ran for 9y TD and Hester answered with 2y TD run to close 2nd OT. With Ds exhausted, ability to make mandatory 2-pt conv became imperative as Hillis scored his 4th TD on 3y run to open 3rd OT and TB Felix Jones (9/85y) succeeded on 2-pt run. Flynn threw 9y TD pass to WR Brandon LaFell, but Richardson's clutch INT sent Arkansas—mispronounced as "Ar-KAN-zuss" all week by Bengals coach Les Miles—into celebration while ending nation's longest home win streak at 19. "Hey, we were the best team in the country today," claimed besieged Hogs coach Houston Nutt. "To come down here to Baton Rouge and win is huge." Nutt's best decision was his frequent use of McFadden (3-6/34y, TD passing) at QB in "Wild Hog" formation. All 3 of McFadden's rushing TDs were scored on direct snaps, despite LSU deploying 2 defenders to shadow him. With McFadden leading way, Arkansas rushed for stunning 385y against disappointed D. Win was 1st for Razorbacks over nation's top-ranked team since beating Texas in 1981.

(Fri) COLORADO 65 Nebraska 51: Implosions on D side of ball continued to plague Nebraska (5-7), which had scored 163 pts in its last 3 games but had only 1 win to show for it because D permitted unworldly 172 pts. Huskers scored TDs on 4 of their last 5 possessions in 1st H to create 35-24 H edge. But, Colorado (6-6) was hungry for bowl bid and tallied 20 pts in 5:07 span of 3rd Q on its way to 34 unanswered pts in 2nd H. Big play that turned tide toward Buffs came with 10:26 to go in 3rd Q: Colorado CB Jimmy Smith nabbed INT by Nebraska QB Joe Ganz (31-58/484y, 4 TDs, 3 INTs) and returned it 31y for TD. Although it only narrowed CU's deficit to 35-31, it lit fuse that led to Huskers' demise. Ganz threw another INT on next series, and CU DE Alonzo Barrett blocked punt on subsequent series that was returned to 25YL by LB Jordan Dizon. RB Hugh Charles (33/169y, 3 TDs) rapidly scored on runs after each TO. Buffs opened 4th Q with completion of 84y drive as QB Cody Hawkins (17-29/241y, 2 TDs) hit WR Scotty McKnight with 10y TD arrow for 51-35 lead. Ganz tallied twice in 1st H on runs of 28 and 8y, and, WR Maurice Purify caught 11/136y, 3 TDs, in his last game for Nebraska.

(Fri) TEXAS A&M 38 Texas 30: Coach Dennis Franchione's controversial tenure at Texas A&M (7-5) ended with upset of biggest rival, Texas (9-3). "Been with him for five years and fought hard, and it's a hell of a way to go out," said Aggies sr C Cody Wallace. Longhorns fell behind on opening series as Aggies went 66y to 1st of 3 TD passes by A&M QB Stephen McGee, who posted career-high 362y in air on 25-36 and was his usual rambunctious self charging hard for 6y TD run in 3rd Q. After trailing 17-3 at H, Texas pulled within 7 pts twice in 3rd Q as RB Jamaal Charles (17/92y) ran 8y for score and WR Quan Cosby raced 91y on KO TD RET. But McGee hit pair of TD passes early in 4th Q to put it beyond reach at 38-17. Horns QB Colt McCoy (17-32/229y) passed for 4th Q TD but lost INT and 2 FUMs.

(Fri) HAWAII 39 Boise State 27: When prolific Warriors (11-0) QB Colt Brennan (40-53/495y, 5 TDs, 2 INTs) passed 6y to WR Ryan Grice-Mullen to tie game at 7-7 in 1st Q he surpassed NCAA record of Ty Detmer of BYU for career TD passes with 122. Brennan ran for TD in 2nd Q, and his subsequent scoring throws provided 19-14, 26-17, 32-27, and 39-27 bulges that insured Hawaii of its 1st-ever outright WAC title. Hawaii's biggest win ever over defending WAC champion Boise State (10-2) also had Island fans hungry for BCS bid. Broncos were denied 6th conf crown in row but didn't go quietly. RB Ian Johnson (22/86y) scored on 50 and 1y runs in 1st H but was limited to 11y rushing in 2nd H. Still, Boise rallied to take 27-26 edge in 3rd Q on QB Taylor Tharp's short TD pass and K Kyle Brontzman's 36y FG. Brennan finished up 3rd Q with pair of TD pitches to wrap it up.

WEST VIRGINIA 66 Connecticut 21: Looking like national title contenders, West Virginia (10-1) routed upstart Huskies (9-3) as QB Patrick White (9-13/107y, TD, INT) passed effectively and ran superbly at helm of attack that crushed Connecticut with 512y rushing. White ran for 186y and 2 TDs. UConn lost 3 FUMs, all leading to TDs, while allowing 624y. After Huskies opened scoring with WR Brad Kanuch's 6y TD reception to end opening series, White answered with 65y drive to his 3y scoring keeper. Huskies lost punt FUM 3 mins later, and White hit 14y TD pass to WR Darius Reynaud (5/76y, TD) on next play. Mountaineers TBs Steve Slaton (10/54y, 2 TDs)

and Noel Devine (11/118y, TD) also harmed Connecticut, which had harbored conf title dreams. Still, Huskies were alive at H as TB Donald Brown (22/129y) scored on 2y run to cap 77y drive at end of 2nd Q to pull within 24-14. WVU scored 6 TDs in 2nd H, including LB Reed Williams' REC of FUM in UConn EZ on 1 of 5 sacks of Huskies QB Tyler Lorenzen (14-28/151y, TD).

Virginia Tech 33 VIRGINIA 21: Plucky Virginia (9-3) was helpless to prevent ACC Coastal Div title going to rival Virginia Tech (10-2), which pulled away with dominant 4th Q performance. Hokies used QB tandem to full benefit to score clinching TD in 88th and perhaps most-important match-up of rivals: With Tech leading 23-21, starting QB Sean Glennon (13-19/260y, TD) began early 4th Q drive with 25y completion to WR Josh Morgan (4/75y). After TB Brandon Ore (31/147y) raced 25y to Virginia 16YL to help Hokies to 1st down at 5YL, speedy frosh sub QB Tyrod Taylor (4-6/39y) entered game to dodge into middle on draw run and bounce wide toward left pylon for 5y TD that gave Hokies 30-21 lead with 11:50 remaining. It was Taylor's 2nd TD dash of game, while Glennon earlier had thrown 39y scoring pass to WR Eddie Royal (6/147y, TD). Royal's TD pass came with 12 secs left in H for 20-14 lead. CB Brandon Flowers (7 tackles) set up score with INT that halted Virginia threat in Hokies territory. Although Virginia QB Jameel Sewell (15-24/121y, INT) threw costly INT to Flowers, he ran for 2 TDs, while TB Mikell Simpson led Cavs rushers with 16/81y, and 27y 1st Q TD. In 2nd H, Cavaliers could manage only Sewell's 2y TD run, which came as result of Taylor's FUM when sacked by UVa star DE Chris Long (6 tackles, 1.5 sacks) at Tech 28YL. Virginia Tech raised its ACC road game record to 15-1 since joining conf 4 years ago.

Clemson 23 SOUTH CAROLINA 21: Once ranked no. 6 earlier in season, South Carolina (6-6) had to accept its 5th straight defeat, longest losing streak in Steve Spurrier's college coaching career, when Clemson (9-3) K Mark Buchholz nailed 35y FG as clock hit 0:00. Mistakes ruined Carolina as it committed 3 TOs and had 1st Q blocked punt returned for 10y TD by Clemson WR La'Donte Harris. Despite all that, Gamecocks had chance to win as QB Blake Mitchell (18-31/284y, 3 TDs, 2 INTs) threw 4y TD pass to WR Dion Lecorn (5/65y) with 9 mins to go for their 1st lead at 21-20. With 1:40 left, Clemson QB Cullen Harper (28-38/229y, TD, INT) started 61y drive to Buchholz's 3rd and final 3-ptr, completing 12y pass to WR Aaron Kelly (9/134y) on 4th-and-4 along way and another 18y connection to Kelly, which led to centering run and timeout to bring on Buchholz with 3 secs left. South Carolina WR Kenny McKinley (8/125y) caught 2 TDs. Kelly (84) and McKinley (77) each became single-season reception leader for his school.

Tennessee 52 KENTUCKY 50 (OT): Needing victory to capture SEC East crown, Volunteers (9-3) slipped in 2nd H but finally won in 4th OT. New Tennessee record of 7 TD passes was set by QB Erik Ainge (28-45/397y, 3 INTs), who threw 3 of his TD passes in OT, while counterpart, QB Andre Woodson (39-62/430y, 2 INTs) of Kentucky (7-5), nearly matched him with 6 TD passes. But, Woodson came up short on game's final play, 2-pt conv attempt, that would have tied it. DE Antonio Reynolds made winning tackle to guarantee Tennessee's 23rd straight win over border rival. Tennessee opened game spectacularly as TB Arian Foster (27/118y, and 9/98y, TD receiving) caught screen pass on game's 1st play and raced 65y to EZ. Later in 1st Q, Ainge threw 18y TD pass to WR Lucas Taylor (6/103y) for 14-0 lead. After Woodson got Wildcats on board early in 2nd Q with 17y TD to WR Steve Johnson (6/86y), Ainge led Vols to 10 pts with 15y TD pass to WR Quinton Hancock. Down 24-7 at H, Cats drove 80y after 2nd H KO to score TD on Woodson's 3y pass to WR Dicky Lyons. Vols upped lead on another Ainge TD pass before Kentucky reverted to Spread for drives of 78, 66, and 90y to tie it 31-31. UK launched taxing 18-play trip before ultimately stalling at 1YL and settling for 20y tying FG by K Lones Seiber. After teams traded TDs in 1st OT, Kentucky LB Sam Maxwell picked off Ainge at GL in top of 2nd OT. Vols needed big play, and DT Dan Williams made game-saving block of 35y FG try by Seiber. Woodson and Ainge threw their 6th TD pass in 3rd OT, but each team missed 2-pt try. After 15y PEN against Vols, Ainge had to traverse 40y on TD hook-up with Hancock and then WR Austin Rogers in middle of EZ for 2 pts. Wildcats TB Derrick Locke scored on 2y TD run, but Woodson was unable to score tying conv as he tried too late to run.

AUBURN 17 Alabama 10: Auburn Tigers (8-4) won school-record 6th straight in famed series and won with usual punishing ground game and D. Tigers took 10-0 lead in 1st Q on 3y TD run by TB Ben Tate (11/77y) and 37y FG by K Wes Byrum. Cutting deficit to 10-7, Crimson Tide (6-6) QB John Parker Wilson (12-26/113y, INT) answered with 2y keeper at end of 53y drive as Tide drive used 6:35 and 4th down to score. Later in 2nd Q, Bama LB Rolando McClain (15 tackles) returned INT 23y to Auburn 19YL, but Auburn CB Jerraud Powers' deflected EZ INT ended threat right before H. Tigers used WR Robert Dunn's 31y punt RET to provide 1st down on Alabama 44YL with 9 mins left in 4th Q. With 3:58 to go, QB Brandon Cox (12-22/117y, INT) scored on 1y wedge to up margin to 17-7 and cap march boosted by 15y PEN on Tide LB Keith Saunders for hit OB. Alabama quickly got 3 pts back when K Leigh Tiffin booted 49y FG, but once Auburn TE Cole Bennett collared onside-KO with about 2 mins remaining, Tide faced its 4th loss in row. Auburn reached 4th-and-1 at Bama 30YL, but TB Brad Lester (22/98y) ran 12y to ice it.

Missouri 36 Kansas 28 (Kansas City): For 1st time since establishment of Big 12 in 1996, Tigers (11-1) snatched North crown by beating undefeated rival Kansas (11-1) at Arrowhead Stadium. And with LSU's loss on Friday, Missouri was ticketed, however briefly, for no. 1 in land. Missouri QB Chase Daniel (40-49/361y, 3 TDs) was magnificently sharp after slow start, hitting TE Martin Rucker for short TD for 7-0 lead in 1st Q. Incredibly accurate so far in 2007, Jayhawks QB Todd Reesing (28-49/349y, 2 TDs, 2 INTs) had dreadful 1st Q but zeroed in on WR Kerry Meier for 39y gain on opening play of 2nd Q to set new school mark with 213 throws without INT. But on next play, Tigers S William Moore changed course of game by intercepting Reesing at Mizzou 2YL. Kansas had avoided big PENs all season but was guilty of D-holding after stopping Missouri on 3rd-and-12 at 40YL. It kept 98y drive alive, and Daniel beat pressure to rifle 11y TD pass to WR Danario Alexander (8/117y, TD) for 14-0 H edge. Trailing 21-0 in 3rd Q, Kansas finally tallied on RB Brandon McAnderson's run. Daniel answered with is 3rd TD throw. Behind 28-7, Kansas came alive in 4th Q as Reesing tiptoed into EZ from 5y out and found WR Dexton Fields (8/116y, TD) for 10y score. Alexander made important 3rd down catch to set up K Jeff Wolfert's 2nd 43y FG of 4th Q to establish 34-21 lead for Tigers with 3:31 on clock. Reesing had another TD pass in his quiver with 2:03 left, and Mizzou RB Tony Temple (22/98y) was stopped on 3rd down run to force punt deep into KU territory. But, as he had 2 weeks earlier, Missouri NT Lorenzo Williams put cherry on top with sack for safety at game's end.

OKLAHOMA 49 Oklahoma State 17: QB Sam Bradford pitched 4 TD passes and RB Allen Patrick rushed for 29/202y, 2 TDs as Oklahoma (10-2) clinched Big 12 South in romp over rival Cowboys (6-6). Oklahoma State coach Mike Gundy agreed: "Their offensive line mashed us." Sooners scored on each of its 1st 4 series, going 50, 58, 68, and 87y. Patrick caught 11y pass from Bradford (11-15/150y, INT) for 1st Q TD and followed 4 mins later with 5y TD run for 14-0 lead for Sooners. Oklahoma State QB Zac Robinson 8-20/105y, TD) threw 16y TD pass to RB Dantrell Savage to trim it to 14-7 before end of 1st Q. Trailing 28-7, Cowpokes went 53y to K Dan Bailey's FG that came 4 secs before H. Cowboys CB Jacob Lacey made INT and returned 23y to OU 1YL in 3rd Q. Even though OSU was called for false start, Savage (19/108y) dashed for 6y TD to pull within 28-17. In only 8 plays, Oklahoma had another TD pass from Bradford to TE Joe Jon Finley.

Washington State 42 WASHINGTON 35: On fabulous throwing arm of QB Alex Brink, new Washington State career passing y leader, Cougars (5-7) came from behind in last min to defeat Washington (4-8) in 100th Apple Cup game. Brink (27-40/399y, 5 TDs, 2 INTs) became 1st Cougars QB to beat Huskies 3 times and set new record for passing y in Apple Cup. After RB Louis Rankin's 89y KO TD RET and QB Jake Locker's 23y TD run for Huskies, Cougars rallied from 10-0 and 17-7 deficits to grasp 21-20 H edge on TE Devin Frischknecht's 2nd TD reception 34 secs before intermission. Washington trailed 28-20 and its O was asleep with only 23y in its last 4 series when Cougars DB Alfonso Jackson (game-ending INT) roughed WR Marcel Reece with crown of his helmet to rile up UW. Reece broke into clear for 63y TD pass from Locker (12-35/224y, TD, 2 INTs), and Locker tied it 28-28 when he threw miraculous across-his-body 2-pt pass to Reece as he was hammered OB. Locker marshaled Huskies 73y and powered over RG on 4th down for TD and 35-28 lead early in 4th Q. D-holding PEN sparked WSU as WR Brandon Gibson (6/137y, 2 TDs) broke free for 40y TD catch from Brink midway in 4th Q. Brink and Gibson clicked again with 31 secs to play on winning 35y TD pass.

BRIGHAM YOUNG 17 Utah 10: BYU Cougars (9-2) earned outright Mt West title and undefeated conf record with last min victory over Utes (8-4). RB Harvey Unga ran 23/144y to become 1st BYU frosh to eclipse 1,000y mark. More importantly, Unga scored winning TD with 38 secs to play. Utah had been limited to 50y total O in 1st H it trailed 3-0 on 1st of trio of FGs by BYU K Mitch Payne. K Louis Sakoda tied it 3-3 with 35y FG in 3rd Q. Behind 9-3 as 4th Q was winding down, Utah took over at its 31YL, and Utes authored game's 1st TD march keyed on runs of QB Brian Johnson (17-29/129y, 2 INTs and 14/25y rushing). RB Darrell Mack surged for 3y TD with 1:34 to play to put Utes up 10-9. When BYU QB Max Hall (17-40/269y, INT) was sacked and missed 2 passes, things looked dark for Cougars. Hall, however, found WR WR Austin Collie (5/126y) for game-saving 49y connection on 4th-and-18. Unga scored on 11y run 3 plays later to wrap it up.

USA Today Coaches November 25

1	West Virginia (37)	1467	14	Illinois	674
2	Missouri (17)	1454	15	Tennessee	654
3	Ohio State (6)	1383	16	Wisconsin	493
4	Georgia	1232	17	Clemson	469
5t	Kansas	1161	18	Texas	417
5t	Virginia Tech	1161	19	Brigham Young	327
7	LSU	1134	20	Oregon	316
8	Oklahoma	1126	21t	Virginia	271
9	Southern California	1073	21t	Auburn	271
10	Hawaii	958	23	Boise State	247
11	Florida	898	24	Cincinnati	146
12	Boston College	861	25	Arkansas	145
13	Arizona State	756			

Bowl Championship Series Ranking November 25

	Harris Poll Pct.	*USA Today* Poll Pct.	Computer Pct.	BCS Avg.
1 Missouri (11-1)	.9751	.9693	.990	.9781
2 West Virginia (10-1)	.9660	.9780	.970	.9713
3 Ohio State (11-1)	.9256	.9220	.910	.9192
4 Georgia (10-2)	.8309	.8213	.830	.8274
5 Kansas (11-1)	.7614	.7740	.840	.7918

December 1, 2007

Navy 38 Army 3 (Baltimore): While overall record remained fairly close at 52-49-7 in favor of Navy, nation's most highly-combative, natural rivalry was beginning to get out of hand as Midshipmen (8-4) won their 6th straight over Army (3-9). It was longest-ever streak for either team. It would turn out to be coach Paul Johnson's last game for Annapolis, and he finished 6-0 against infantry brethren. SB Reggie Campbell (227y all-purpose) set new Navy record with 98y KO TD RET for 14-3 lead in 2nd Q and added 46y punt RET to set up K Joey Bullen's 51y FG for 24-3 H edge. Campbell (5/47y, TD rushing) added 12y TD run in 4th Q. Things had gone poorly for Army from beginning. After Black Knights pieced together good march from opening KO, WR Corey Anderson dropped 3rd down pass in EZ, and K Owen Tolson (28y FG in 2nd Q) missed chip-shot FG. Army also had punt blocked.

Pittsburgh 13 WEST VIRGINIA 9: Crazy season wound down in same way it had begun. Pittsburgh (5-7), in middle of disappointing year, rose up with fantastic D effort to stunningly knock no.2 West Virginia (10-2) from national title contention. "I thought we were ready," said Mountaineers coach Rich Rodriguez as he struggled through sad post-game press session, although he would be out door for Michigan within days. "We picked an awful time to have our worst offensive game in years." Of 100th Backyard Brawl, Rodriguez said: "The whole thing was a nightmare." Pittsburgh D was led by DE Joe Clermond, who made 8 tackles, 1.5 for losses, sack, and forced FUM to be named Big East D Player of Week. WVU had averaged 474.8y per game and was limited on this night to 183y. Mountaineers K Pat McAfee missed 19 and 32y FGs in 1st Q, but QB Jarrett Brown (4-6/29y), in for star QB Patrick White (5-10/50y, and 14/41y rushing) who missed considerable time in mid-game with dislocated non-throwing thumb, scored on 6y run for 7-0 lead 1:43 before H. Pitt used personal-foul PEN against WVU to position K Conor Lee for 48y FG just as H arrived. On 48y TD march after WVU CB Vauhn Rivers lost FUM on 2nd H KO, Panthers TB LeSean McCoy (38/148y), who had broken Tony Dorsett's 34-year-old school frosh TD record with 14, carried 5/19y, and QB Pat Bostick (10-19/67y, 2 INTs) hit WR Odreick Turner for 18y. Bostick slipped across GL from 1YL for 10-7 lead for Pitt. Trailing 13-7 after Lee's 2nd FG with 6:17 left, WVU hoped for spark as White returned, especially after RB Noel Devine raced 48y on KO RET. But, White couldn't get Mountaineers past 4th downs at Pitt 26 and 38YLs on his 2 series. Panthers P Dave Brytus conceded safety in EZ on last snap.

Virginia Tech 30 Boston College 16 (Jacksonville): This was rematch Hokies (11-2) desperately wanted after Boston College (10-3) QB Matt Ryan had thrown 2 late TDs to stun them in Blacksburg in mid-season. This time, Virginia Tech delivered as QB Sean Glennon (18-27/174y, INT) pitched 3 TDs, while Hokies' firm 2nd H D picked off Ryan (33-52/305y) twice in final 2 mins. It looked as if Ryan might pull off another miracle as Eagles, trailing 23-16 in 4th Q, drove 58y to Virginia Tech 13YL. In mid-drive, WR Kevin Challenger caught 19y slant-in pass and seemed in clear before S Kam Chancellor made TD-saving tackle. BC soon faced 4th-and-4, and LB Vince Hall (11 tackles) came up with INT of Ryan's pass over middle to dissolve threat. Virginia Tech had to punt, and Ryan was left with 34 secs to move BC from its 35YL. It was desperation time, and Ryan threw INT on 3rd down to LB Xavier Adibi (9 tackles), who returned 40y for clinching TD. Eagles A-A FS Jamie Silva (5 tackles, INT) had delivered opening score with 51y FUM TD RET late in 1st Q after stripping Va Tech QB Tyrod Taylor. Down 10-0, Glennon responded with 8-play, 77y drive he capped with 5y TD pass to WR Josh Morgan (8/55y) on fade rout. Big D play occurred after Ryan scrambled 14y to TD for 16-7 BC lead with 5:35 left in 2nd Q: Va Tech CB Brandon Flowers returned T Duane Brown's x-pt block for 2 pts for Hokies, so BC's lead was only 16-9. Glennon's 13y TD pass to WR Josh Hyman tied it 16-16 before H. Hokies D surrendered only 112y and 4 1st downs in 2nd H, so single TD was all Va Tech needed. Taylor's 31y run on QB Draw led to Glennon's 24y TD bullet to WR Eddie Royal (4/63y) to cap 84y march.

Louisiana State 21 Tennessee 14 (Atlanta): With rumors of coach Les Miles leaving to take over at Michigan—which he vehemently denied prior to game—LSU (11-2) could be excused for lack of focus for SEC Championship Game. But there was too much at stake for Tigers to fold. Wearing all orange uniforms for 1st time since 1999, Volunteers (9-4) saw to it that LSU would have to earn conf crown. Tennessee, in fact, drove 57y on opening series to take 7-0 lead on 11y TD pass by QB Erik Ainge (20-40/249y, 2 TDs, 2 INTs) to TE Chris Brown. With QB Matt Flynn out with shoulder injury, backup QB Ryan Perrilloux (20-30/243y, TD, INT) received his 2nd career start and soon led Tigers to pair of FGs by K Colt David. Despite cracking Tennessee 10YL thrice in 1st H, LSU managed only 6 pts. Meanwhile, after their sharp opening drive, Vols coped with just 31y on 4 more 1st H O series but still led 7-6 at H despite 271y to 93y disadvantage. Beginning of 2nd H found Perrilloux taking 6 plays to move Tigers 76y: his 48y completion to WR Brandon LaFell set up 27y TD pass to WR Demetrius Byrd. Tennessee regained 14-13 lead later in 3rd Q as Ainge hit 6y TD pass to WR Josh Briscoe (8/79y) at end of 69y voyage. D bailed out Tigers with huge 4th Q play: CB Jonathan Zenon stepped in front of WR Quinton Hancock to pick off Ainge's pass and dashed 18y for TD with 9:54 remaining. Interestingly, Zenon's TD was 1st scored by LSU's elite D all season. Perrilloux ran for 2-pt-conv, and LSU suddenly led 21-14. Tigers D delivered again when LB Darry Beckwith made INT at his 7YL with 2:42 left, 1 play after Ainge's 47y completion to TB Arian Foster (21/55y, and 2/40y receiving). Tigers tough FB Jacob Hester (23/120y) put his head down to slam 30y on 4 runs as LSU ran out clock to claim its 10th SEC title, its 1st since 2003. On flight home, pilot updated Tigers with scores of West Virginia-Pittsburgh and Missouri-Oklahoma games, and amazing results put LSU back in national title picture.

Oklahoma 38 Missouri 17 (San Antonio): Big 12 Title Game served as Lone Star State homecoming for 17 Tigers (11-2), notably QB Chase Daniel (23-39/219y, INT), from Southlake, Texas. But, Oklahoma (11-2) frustrated Missouri's efficient O on 3rd downs and in red zone to cop its 5th conf crown in last 8 years. Sooners clicked for TDs on 5 of its 6 trips inside Mizzou 20YL, while Tigers were limited to K Jeff Wolfert's 3 FGs—including 18y boot after O advanced to 1YL—and single successful 84y drive to TD. RB Chris Brown (23/71y) scored on 3 and 2y runs in 2nd Q, and OU led 14-6 late in 2nd Q. Daniel was masterful on 10-play, 84y drive that beat H clock by 14 secs. Daniel hit 5-6/53y and capped it with 4y burst up middle for TD. Missouri WR Jeremy Maclin (8/69y) caught pair of passes on TD trip and threw 2-pt reverse pass to TE Martin Rucker. It was 14-14 at H. Crucial sequence arrived early in 3rd Q: Tigers forced punt and snarled 68y to 1st down at Oklahoma 25YL. But, Sooners DE Jeremy Beal and LB Curtis Lofton threw Daniel for sack losses, and Tigers punted into EZ. OU RB Allen Patrick (13/88y, TD) raced 40y to Tigers 4YL and followed with TD run for 21-14 lead. QB Sam Bradford (18-26/209y, 2 TDs) added pair of TD passes in 7-min span, and Sooners won going away.

SOUTHERN CALIFORNIA 24 Ucla 7: Doubt that surrounded USC (10-2) in late October had been palpable. But, after another win over rival UCLA (6-6) clinched unprecedented 6th straight conf crown, coach Pete Carroll said, "I don't think anybody here was thinking we were going to be champions this year, but those guys (his players) knew they could be." Trojans' 4th win in row since losing to Oregon on October 27 wrapped up 4th Rose Bowl trip in 5 years. QB John David Booty (21-36/206y, TD, INT) led O that outgained Bruins by 437y to 168y and held ball for nearly 38 mins. Bruins S Dennis Keyes led D with 19 tackles, but as coach Karl Dorrell observed, "Our defense was playing well, but then, our defense was playing too many plays." Southern California led only 17-7 at H despite 142y discrepancy in y gained. TB Joe McKnight (13/89y, TD) scored on 5y run after LB Keith Rivers recovered FUM at UCLA 32YL, and Trojans went 79y early in 2nd Q to 10y TD run by TB Chauncey Washington (13/66y, TD). Down 17-0 and with single 1st down to their credit with less than 45 secs to go in 1st H, Bruins raced 65y in 5 plays behind QB Patrick Cowan (13-24/156y, TD) to his 9y TD pass to WR Dominique Johnson with 7 secs before H. Dorrell soon would be out at UCLA.

STANFORD 20 California 13: Never trailing, Stanford (4-8) won "Big Game" for 1st time since its last bowl team in 2001 and completed stunning 5-losses-in-6-games collapse by California (6-6), which had been ranked 2nd in nation back on October 7. Cardinal QBs T.C. Ostrander (16-23/151y, TD) and Tavita Pritchard (5-9/45y TD) alternated to lead balanced O that gained steady 316y. Ostrander's 28y TD pass to WR Mark Bradford (5/84y, TD) earned 7-0 lead right after LB Clinton Snyder sacked Bears QB Nate Longshore (22-47/252y, TD, 2 INTs) and made FUM REC at Cal 28YL 4 mins into game. Bears answered quickly, however, as Longshore launched 46y TD pass to WR Robert Jordan (4/99y, TD). K Derek Belch made pair of 2nd Q FGs to offset Cal K Jordan Kay's 3-ptr for 13-10 H lead for Stanford. Card CB Nick Sanchez grabbed pair of 4th Q INTs, his 2nd clinching victory with 1:55 left. Stanford RB Jeremy Stewart (24/70y) lost FUM, forced by LB Zack Follett, at Cal 36YL with 2:43 to play. Longshore hit Jordan for 31y gain, but, from Card 19YL, WR Lavelle Hawkins dropped certain TD. Sanchez made diving INT on next play at his 8YL.

ARIZONA STATE 20 Arizona 17: By winning Territorial Cup over Arizona (5-7) for 7th time in 9 tries, Sun Devils (10-2) wrapped up surprise Pac-10 co-championship with USC. Trojans' win over Arizona State on November 22 sent USC to Rose Bowl as conf's BCS representative. But, it remained possible for Devils to play in Tempe's Fiesta Bowl for 1st time since 1983. QBs Willie Tuitama (28-52/272y, 2 TDs, 2 INTs) of Arizona and Rudy Carpenter (20-37/247y, 2 TDs) of ASU traded TD passes in 1st H, led 10-7 by Devils. On opening snap of 2nd H, ASU CB Justin Tryon, assigned to Cats star WR Mike Thomas (9/98y), tipped ball to S Rodney Cox, who returned INT 37y to set up K Thomas Weber's 2nd short FG. Arizona CB Antoine Cason's 51y punt RET gave K Jason Bondzio chance at 47y FG halfway through 3rd Q, but Devils DT and honor student Michael Marquardt (1 tackle, FUM REC) blocked FG try. Thomas' falling 38y reception helped give Cats FG early in 4th Q to pull within 13-10. But, Arizona State iced it with 66y trip, enhanced by TE Brent Miller's 28y catch on 3rd-and-5. Carpenter's 20y TD pass to WR Michael Jones made it 20-10, which ASU maintained until permitting TD in last 26 secs.

HAWAII 35 Washington 28: While superb sr QB Colt Brennan (42-50/442y, 5 TDs) was having great game for Hawaii (12-0), Washington frosh QB Jake Locker (9-17/142y, INT, and 15/76y, TD rushing) sparked Huskies to 21-0 and 28-7 leads. Locker ran 8y for early TD, and FB Luke Kravitz scored twice on 1y smashes. Meanwhile, Brennan found WR Jason Rivers (14/167y) for 1st of 4 TDs early in 2nd Q. Warriors moved to 28-21 at H as Brennan and Rivers connected twice more after 75 and 80y drives. After scoreless 3rd Q, Hawaii knotted it 28-28 on Brennan's high-arched throw to Rivers. Washington suffered bad break with less than 5 mins to go when Locker seemed wrongly flagged for crossing line of scrimmage on pass deep into Hawaii's end. Warriors soon took at their 24YL and went distance in 8 plays: Brennan hit 6-6/70y, including 5y TD to WR Ryan Grace-Mullen (10/121y, TD) with 44 secs to play. Huskies weren't done as Locker hit 25 and 49y passes for 1st-and-goal at 4YL, but DB Ryan Mouton intercepted in EZ to clinch immense win that sent Hawaii to BCS bowl game. Warriors now had won 22 of last 23 games.

USA Today Coaches December 2

1	Ohio State (46)	1469	14	Boston College	617
2	LSU (11)	1418	15	Wisconsin	594
3	Oklahoma (2)	1331	16	Clemson	567
4	Georgia	1277	17	Texas	498
5	Virginia Tech	1242	18	Tennessee	480
6	Southern California	1227	19	Brigham Young	462
7	Missouri	1104	20	Virginia	332
8	Kansas	1099	21	Auburn	289
9	West Virginia	1010	22	Boise State	246
10	Hawaii (1)	994	23	Cincinnati	215
11	Arizona State	900	24	Arkansas	137
12	Florida	890	25	South Florida	115
13	Illinois	747			

Bowl Championship Series Ranking December 2

	Harris Poll Pct.	*USA Today* Poll Pct.	Computer Pct.	BCS Avg.
1 Ohio State (11-1)	.9870	.9793	.910	.9588
2 Louisiana State (11-2)	.9228	.9453	.950	.9394
3 Virginia Tech (11-2)	.8228	.8280	.960	.8703
4 Oklahoma (11-2)	.8842	.8873	.800	.8572
5 Georgia (10-2)	.8663	.8513	.800	.8392

2007 Conference Standings

Big East

West Virginia	5-2
Connecticut	5-2
Cincinnati	4-3
South Florida	4-3
Rutgers	3-4
Louisville	3-4
Pittsburgh	3-4
Syracuse	1-6

Atlantic Coast

ATLANTIC	
Boston College	6-2
Clemson	5-3
Wake Forest	5-3
Florida State	4-4
Maryland	3-5
North Carolina State	3-5

COASTAL	
Virginia Tech	7-1
Virginia	6-2
Georgia Tech	4-4
North Carolina	3-5
Miami	2-6
Duke	0-8

Southeastern

EAST	
Tennessee	6-2
Georgia	6-2
Florida	5-3
Kentucky	3-5
South Carolina	3-5
Vanderbilt	2-6

WEST	
Louisiana State	6-2
Auburn	5-3
Arkansas	4-4
Mississippi State	4-4
Alabama	4-4
Mississippi	0-8

Conference USA

EAST	
Central Florida	7-1
East Carolina	6-2
Memphis	6-2
Southern Mississippi	5-3
Marshall	3-5
Alabama-Birmingham	1-7

WEST	
Tulsa	6-2
Houston	6-2
Tulane	3-5
Rice	3-5
Texas-El Paso	2-6
Southern Methodist	0-8

Big Ten

Ohio State	7-1
Illinois	6-2
Michigan	6-2
Wisconsin	5-3
Penn State	4-4
Iowa	4-4
Indiana	3-5
Michigan State	3-5
Purdue	3-5
Northwestern	3-5
Minnesota	0-8

Mid-American

EAST	
Bowling Green	4-2
Miami (Ohio)	4-2
Buffalo	4-2
Ohio University	3-3
Temple	3-4
Akron	2-4
Kent State	1-5

WEST	
Central Michigan	4-1
Ball State	4-1
Eastern Michigan	3-2
Western Michigan	3-3
Toledo	2-3
Northern Illinois	0-5

Big Twelve

NORTH	
Missouri	7-1
Kansas	7-1
Colorado	4-4
Kansas State	3-5
Nebraska	2-6
Iowa State	2-6

SOUTH	
Oklahoma	6-2
Texas	5-3
Texas Tech	4-4
Texas A&M	4-4
Oklahoma State	4-4
Baylor	0-8

Mountain West

Brigham Young	8-0
Air Force	6-2
Utah	5-3
New Mexico	5-3
Texas Christian	4-4
San Diego State	3-5
Wyoming	2-6
Colorado State	2-6
Nevada-Las Vegas	1-7

Western Athletic

Hawaii	8-0
Boise State	7-1
Fresno State	6-2
Nevada	4-4
Louisiana Tech	4-4
San Jose State	4-4
Utah State	2-6
New Mexico State	1-7
Idaho	0-8

Pacific-10

Southern California	7-2
Arizona State	7-2
Oregon State	6-3
Oregon	5-4
UCLA	5-4
Arizona	4-5
California	3-6
Washington State	3-6
Stanford	3-6
Washington	2-7

2007 Major Bowl Games

Poinsettia Bowl (Dec. 20): Utah 35 Navy 32

Utah (9-4) notched its 7th straight post-season win, dating back to 1999, which had to be 1 of least-known successes in college football. Utes QB Brian Johnson (20-25/226y, TD, INT) pitched 40y TD pass to speedy, little WR Derrek Richards (4/61y, TD) late in 3rd Q—when Johnson hit 9-9/130y, TD—to provide permanent lead at 21-17 and soon followed with 19y TD scramble. Navy (8-5), which had built 17-7 lead early in 3rd Q, countered with 1st of 2 late TD passes by QB Kaipo-Noa Kaheaku-Enhada (7-14/122y, 2 TDs, INT) to pull within 28-25. Game's end turned wild: Middies were falsely denied touchback when Utah FUM dribbled OB after touching pylon at end of WR Jerome Brooks's 3y catch to Middies 1YL. Navy held on 4th down but soon gave up TD that made it 35-25 when it couldn't convert desperate 4th-and-2 from their 9YL

in last 2 mins. Kaheaku-Enhada launched 58y TD pass to SB Zerbin Singleton with 57 secs to go, and Singleton recovered onside-KO for another chance. But, Utah SS Joe Dale intercepted pass to lock up verdict.

Las Vegas Bowl (Dec. 22): Brigham Young 17 UCLA 16

Even though it lost on heartbreaking last play, UCLA (6-7) kept reasonable care of ball for change with 2 TOs even though Bruins were again down to their 4th-team QB, McLeod Bethel-Thompson (11-27/154y, TD, INT). Brigham Young (11-2), which was limited to season-low 265y O, clinched bowl win when DT Eathyn Manumaleuna extended fingertip to barely block chip-shot FG attempt by Bruins K Kai Forbath as clock ticked to 0:00. Cougars were under pressure from UCLA D all game, and BYU QB Max Hall (21-35/231y, 2 TDs) was sacked 3 times and lost FUM that set up 1st Q FG by Forbath for 3-0 lead. Hall hit pair of TDs in 2nd Q, so ahead 17-6, BYU appeared ready to run out H clock deep in own end. But, UCLA DT Brian Price stripped RB Harvey Unga, and Bethel-Thompson quickly hit 4y TD pass to WR Brandon Breazell (4/44y, TD). So, BYU was up 17-13 at H. Forbath nailed 50y FG 6:24 into 4th Q, and UCLA took over on own 2YL with 2:02 to go after Cougars P C.J. Santiago's punt was downed. Bethel-Thompson hit 3 clutch passes, including with 30 secs to play 3rd-and-9 pass from BYU 49YL to TE Logan Paulsen, who grabbed short throw and chugged 36y to 13YL. After 2y run and timeout, UCLA seemed perfectly positioned for Forbath's 4th FG from 28y out.

Holiday Bowl (Dec. 27): Texas 52 Arizona State 34

Surprise blowout win by slightly-favored Texas (10-3) over Sun Devils (10-3) might have caused yawns across America but for bizarre play early in 2nd Q which put Chris Jessie, stepson of Longhorns coach Mack Brown, squarely in media spotlight. With Texas ahead 21-0 on 3 lightning-quick drives in 1st Q, Arizona State fought back to drive to 14YL, where on 4th down, QB Rudy Carpenter (18-36/187y, 2 TDs, 2 INTs) was sacked by Horns LB Roddrick Muckelroy. Resultant FUM, which Jessie claimed he thought was incomplete pass, went backwards and toward Texas sideline. Jessie, member of Longhorns operations staff, stepped onto field to exhort pursuing Texas defenders, but in his excitement he appeared to touch live ball before DT Roy Miller slapped it away from sideline where Longhorns DE Aaron Lewis recovered and advanced into ASU territory. Jessie's unsportsmanlike PEN gave him cause to hide behind big orange-clad bodies on sideline and give ASU another chance at 7YL. Carpenter hit WR Chris McGaha (9/79y, TD) for TD. Texas QB Colt McCoy (21-31/174y, TD) came right back with 9y TD run, and Longhorns led 28-10 at H. Texas CB Brandon Foster was all over field with 2 INTs, tipped pass that turned into another INT, and FUM REC. It was curtains for Devils late in 3rd Q when Texas TE Jermichael Finley plopped on McCoy's FUM amid player pile in EZ for TD and 35-13 lead. Having won 10 games for 7th straight year, Longhorns now owned 3rd-best such streak in major college history.

Champs Bowl (Dec. 28): Boston College 24 Michigan State 21

Boston College (11-3) may have played on New Year's Day only twice since it last clinched 11-win season in 1941 Sugar Bowl, but Eagles still owned current-day, national-best 8 straight bowl victories when they held off Michigan State (7-6). All-ACC QB Matt Ryan (22-47/249y, INT) threw 3 TDs, including pair to WR Rich Gunnell (6/138y, 2 TDs). But BC D provided game MVP in FS Jamie Silva, who made 2 INTs, including 1st Q pick-off in EZ when Eagles trailed 7-0. Spartans were playing without 5 suspended players, including D stars DE Jonal Saint-Dic and LB SirDarean Adams, but were able to stuff Eagles' run attack (30/27y) by positioning extra defenders close to scrimmage line. Strategy let Gunnell get deep for 29 and 68y TD strikes, latter upping BC's lead to 24-13 almost 6 mins into 4th Q. Verdict seemed over, but Ryan was sacked by LB Greg Jones and lost FUM to DT Oren Wilson at BC 37YL. In middle of his worst game, Spartans QB Brian Hoyer (14-36/131y, 2 TDs, 4 INTs) still quickly hit WR Deon Cherry with 14y TD and TE Kellen Davis with 2-pt pass to pull within 24-21 with 6:04 left. Hoyer's 4th INT, however, was picked off by Eagles SS Paul Anderson to end it with 2:29 left.

Texas Bowl (Dec. 28): Texas Christian 20 Houston 13

Texas Christian (8-5) had been challenged all year to replace 2 star runners from 2006 and used slew of candidates during season. RB Justin Watts (12/46y, TD), who shared RB spot in Texas Bowl after starter Joseph Tunrer went down in 1st Q, hardly made Frogs fans forget Jim Swink or LaDanian Tomlinson but scored go-ahead 4th Q TD on 7y run. "I was pretty excited considering I hadn't scored since the first game," said happy Watts, "…it's like hitting a home run." Houston (8-5) QB Case Keenum (23-38/335y, TD) pitched 67y scoring pass in 1st Q for 7-0 lead but was pressured all game, especially by TCU DE Chase Ortiz, and sacked 5 times. TCU frosh QB Andy Dalton (21-30/249y, INT) tied it on 3y run in 2nd Q. Score was knotted 10-10 when Watts gave Frogs their 1st lead at 17-10 32 secs into 4th Q; TD drive stayed alive when TV replay allowed WR Jimmy Young's 15y catch from Dalton. Cougars nearly tied it near end when Keenum's pass slipped out of hands of WR Jeron Harvey in EZ. Houston lost its 8th bowl in row, tied for 2nd worst ever.

Emerald Bowl (Dec. 28): Oregon State 21 Maryland 14

Oregon State (9-4) was 1 of those teams that flew under radar for most of season. Beavers had dropped 3 of their opening 5 games while D improved and depth at TB came to fore. Latter feature allowed Beavers to spring pair of tough runners on Maryland (6-7): sr TB Yvenson Bernard (38/177y, TD) and frosh James Rodgers (10/115y, TD). Terrapins also had double-barrel run attack in TBs Keon Lattimore and Lance Ball, but Oregon State's rugged run D shut them down, limiting Terps to 2y on ground in 1st 3 Qs and 19y by game's finish. Maryland QB Chris Turner (17-29/205y,

2 TDs, 2 INTs) pitched scoring throws to WRs Isaiah Williams for 9y and Darrius Heyward-Bey for 63y in 1st Q. In between, Beavers' Rodgers romped to 14y TD on pass from QB Sean Canfield (8-14/68y, TD, INT), alternate signal-caller. Beavers tied it 14-14 on Bernard's 2y run only 16 secs before H. Winning TD came late in 3rd Q when both top backs were lined up for Oregon State at Maryland 1YL. Bernard fumbled short of GL, but alert Rodgers recovered it and stretched forward across GL. Steady rain fell on San Francisco crowd, and even Maryland's theoretically water-loving turtle mascot donned dry rain parka over his shell.

Meineke Car Care Bowl (Dec. 29): Wake Forest 24 Connecticut 10

Demon Deacons (9-4) WR Kenneth Moore (11/112y) broke ACC season mark with 98 receptions, and Wake Forest used rugged D to come from 10 pts behind to beat Conecticut (9-4). Former UConn QB and WR D.J. Hernandez threw crushing block to clear little WR Larry Taylor for 68y punt TD RET late in 1st Q. After RB Donald Brown (13/72y) broke away for 58y run in 2nd Q, K Tony Ciaravino kicked 29y FG for Huskies' 10-0 H edge. Wake came charging out in 2nd H, and after QB Riley Swanson (29-38/268y, TD, INT) hit 4 short passes, RB Josh Adams (19/66y, TD), who was otherwise collared by tough UConn D, raced 38y for TD. Skinner provided 1st lead at 14-10 for Deacons with 20y pass to TE John Tereshinski with 3:27 left in 3rd Q, and LB Stanley Arnoux keyed Wake D in 2nd H with INT and pair of 4th down stops. RB Micah Andrews, who had quiet sr year for Wake, polished off win with 9y TD run in last min. "You know 20 wins in two years for little ol' Wake Forest isn't too bad," said coach Jim Grobe, who had led Deacs to their best 2 years ever.

Liberty Bowl (Dec. 29): Mississippi State 10 Central Florida 3

Never mind that Barry Sanders had only 11 games in 1988 to set national collegiate single-season rushing record, Central Florida (10-4) A-A RB Kevin Smith was within hailing distance of Sanders' mark. With 13 games under his belt thanks to UCF's 44-25 win over Tulsa in Conf USA's Title Game, Smith started Liberty Bowl at attainable 181y behind former Oklahoma State star's total of 2,628y. But, inspired Mississippi State (8-5), enjoying its 1st winning season in 4 years under coach Sylvester Croom, forced Knights into low-scoring D struggle, and UCF threw more passes, to its detriment, than normal in much of 2nd H. Smith finished with 35/119y rushing, 62y short of Sanders' record. Knights broke onto scoreboard 1st in 2nd Q: Starting from Bulldogs 46YL, Central Florida advanced 18y to allow K Michael Torres to drop 45y FG just over crossbar. Game MVP, Mississippi State FS Derek Pegues (2 INTs/45y, 1 TFL, 1 pass break-up), returned INT 40y to 6YL 4 mins later, and K Adam Carlson knotted it 3-3 before H. Torres missed 32 and 37y FGs in 2nd H to sour UCF's brewing O. SS Keith Fitzhugh made MSU's 3rd and final pick-off of UCF QB Kyle Isreal (10-24/88y) at his 41YL with 5:47 to play. Employing mostly runs, Bulldogs used 10 plays to score on 1y push by RB Anthony Dixon (24/86y).

Alamo Bowl (Dec. 29): Penn State 24 Texas A&M 17

Head coach Joe Paterno enjoyed his 500th game with Nittany Lions (9-4), taking his 372nd victory as Penn State fashioned rally from 1st Q deficit and held off late attempt by Texas A&M (7-6) to tie it up. Paterno extended his all-time bowl marks with his record 23rd win in his record 34th appearance. Aggies struck for pair of TDs in lightning span of 12 secs late in 1st Q. After Lions missed early FG, Aggies traveled 70y to TB Mike Goodson's 1y TD run. Penn State CB A.J. Wallace immediately lost FUM on KO RET to fast-closing A&M special teamer Kenny Brown. Goodson circled LE on 1st play for 16y TD, and Texas A&M led 14-0. Event that turned momentum in Penn State's favor came early in 2nd Q: Lions had moved to A&M 30YL where they faced 4th-and-3, and WR Deon Butler (4/59y, TD) jammed his way through coverage and apparent pass interference to dive in EZ to barely get his fingertips under floating 30y TD pass from QB Anthony Morelli (15-31/143y, TD, INT). Wallace made up for his FUM by grabbing FUM coughed up by Goodson at Aggies 11YL after being hit by Penn State DE Maurice Evans. Lions surprised A&M by bringing in sub QB Daryll Clark (6/50y, TD rushing) as QB Morelli flanked wide. Clark took shotgun snap and charged up middle for 11y TD that tied it 14-14 with 9:02 to go in 2nd Q. Penn State's 78y drive to K Kevin Kelly's 25y FG provided 3-pt lead with :19 on H clock. Aggies devoured 8:45 of 3rd Q to go 78y to tie it on K Matt Szymanski's 38y FG. Lions used another 4th down success for TD near end of 3rd Q as frosh TB Evan Royster (9/65y, TD) used inside blocks of C A.J. Shipley and G Mike Lucien to squirt 38y through clustered Aggies D for 24-17 lead. Tough-minded A&M had another great drive in it: Aggies smashed 97y in 16 plays only to have 4th down option run strung out from Lions 1YL as QB Stephen McGee (19-31/164y, INT and 8/41y rushing), who accounted for 83y of long trip, ran out of options and was pinned for loss by sub LB Bani Gbadyu and LB Sean Lee (14 tackles).

Independence Bowl (Dec. 30): Alabama 30 Colorado 24

"We got off to a great start," said Alabama (7-6) coach Nick Saban, "which means we were well-prepared." And then some: Crimson Tide QB John Parker Wilson (19-32/256y, 3 TDs, INT) hit 13 of his 1st 15 throws and 3 went for scores. WRs Keith Brown, Matt Caddell, and Nikita Stover each nabbed TD, and Bama led 27-0 early in 2nd Q. Alabama piled up 170y in 1st Q and 285y by H, but added only 103y in 2nd H. Colorado (6-7) QB Cody Hawkins (24-39/322y, 3 TDs, 2 INTs) snuck in 2 TD passes in last 2:05 of 2nd Q, finishing 1st H with 9-10/87y, 2 TDs. So, Buffs had snuck back into it, down 27-14 at H. Gaining 10y or more on 9 plays in 3rd Q, Colorado had only FG to show for it and trailed 27-17 as 4th Q opened. Bama stiffened its D, permitting 19y in 2 series, and LB Darren Mustin's INT set up 3rd FG by K Leigh Tiffin, who set Tide single-season kick-scoring record with 111 pts.

Armed Forces Bowl (Dec. 31): California 42 Air Force 36

California (7-6) rose from its 2nd-half-of-season demise, and its O was led by 3 players who started game on sideline. WRs DeSean Jackson and Robert Jordan had been held out of 1st Q for disciplinary reasons, and frosh QB Kevin Riley (16-19/269y, 3 TDs) showed such hot hand when he got chance in 2nd Q that he stayed in to lead comeback from 21-0 deficit. Air Force (9-4) QB Shaun Carney (5-8/68y, TD and 15/108y rushing) scored on 1y run at end of 87y drive in 1st Q and flipped 8y TD pass to TE Travis Dekker early in 2nd Q. Right after ensuing KO, Jackson, Jordan, and Riley were scheduled to take field for Cal. But, Falcons' high KO into stiff wind caromed off back of Bears blocker, and S Aaron Kirchoff recovered for Air Force at Cal 40YL. TB Jim Ollis (16/101y, TD) carried it over on 8y run 5 plays later. Jackson made 3 catches on his 1st series in game, including brilliant backpedaling 40y TD catch from Riley. Cal went 70y for 2nd time in 2nd Q to go to H down 21-14 after Riley's 2nd TD throw. Ahead 24-21 and on their way to 11 possession mins in 3rd Q, Falcons threatened with 1st-and-goal at Bears 5YL after Carney's 17 and 20y passes. On 3rd down keeper, Carney, 4-year starter at QB, was hit by 3 defenders and badly damaged his right knee. With him seemed to go Falcons' spirit as they were forced into K Ryan Harrison's 19y FG, his 2nd of 3. RB Justin Forsett (23/140y, 2 TDs) scored on 1y run for Bears' 1st lead at 28-27 with 1:33 to go in 3rd Q and came back on next series with 21y TD gallop.

Sun Bowl (Dec. 31): Oregon 56 South Florida 21

Oregon's late-season meltdown could be laid at feet of its O, but, in month since their last game, Ducks (9-4) tapped redshirt frosh Justin Roper as starting QB. Roper (17-30/180y, 4 TDs) was very poised, but O star for Oregon turned out to be RB Jonathan Stewart, who set Sun Bowl record with 253y rushing. South Florida (9-4) played well in 1st H: After Roper threw 7y TD pass in 1st Q, followed by Oregon's surprise 2-pt run, teams traded FGs to lead to Bulls QB Matt Grothe (18-35/197y, TD, 2 INTs) hitting WR Taurus Johnson (4/51y, TD) with 21y TD and TE Cedric Hill for 2-pt pass and 11-11 deadlock. Stewart raced 71y, popping through cavern at LT to send Ducks off at H with 18-14 edge. Oregon scored Sun Bowl-record 28 pts in 3rd Q to fuel its record total of 56 pts. Roper hit pair of TD passes to open 3rd Q, and CB Walter Thurmond stepped in snatch INT by Grothe and speed to 25y TD RET. Oregon CB Jairus Byrd made 1st of his 2 INTs, and Stewart soon was on his way to 8y TD run to up margin to 46-14.

Music City (Dec. 31): Kentucky 35 Florida State 28

Incredibly depleted by injuries and large group of players suspended for cheating on—ironically in view of Music City Bowl invitation—music appreciation final exam, Florida State (7-6) shrugged off loss of 36 men and put up excellent fight against Kentucky (8-5). "I was worried about getting worn out," said Seminoles coach Bobby Bowden, who lost his 1st-ever December bowl game to run mark to 7-1-1. "We've always played a lot of people, and we simply couldn't play a lot of people in this ballgame." Wildcats QB Andre Woodson (32-50/358y, 4 TDs, INT) earned his 2nd straight Music City Bowl MVP by pitching scoring pass in each Q. Kentucky never went more than 7 pts ahead until 2 80y drives in 3rd Q gave it 28-14 lead. QB Drew Weatherford (22-48/276y, TD, 2 INTs) scored his 2nd running TD on bootleg early in 4th Q. That TD pulled Florida State back within 28-21, but Cats quickly answered when WR Steve Johnson took dump-off pass 38y to TD to make it 35-21.

Chick-Fil-A Bowl (Dec. 31): Auburn 23 Clemson 20 (OT)

Annual ACC-SEC battle in Chick-Fil-A (nee Peach) Bowl continued to stir southern fans, and this OT Tiger face-off was no exception. Auburn (9-4) frosh QB Kodi Burns (13/69y, TD rushing) shared snaps with starting QB Brandon Cox (25-39/211y, INT) in blue Tigers' new Spread O that wore down orange Tigers D with 90 fast-break plays out of no-huddle strategy. Burns produced 22y TD pass to WR Mario Fannan in 3rd Q for 10-7 lead, ran 15y to set up TB Ben Tate's tying 4th Q TD plunge, and dashed 7y for winning TD in bottom half of 1st OT period. Clemson (9-4) TB C.J. Spiller (8/112y, TD) raced 83y to TD that gave Clemson 7-3 lead in 2nd Q. TB James Davis (23/72y, TD) also scored to give Clemson 17-10 edge with 11:24 to go in 4th Q. Clemson chose not to blame minor shoulder surgery for so-so performance by QB Cullen Harper, who was ineffective with 14-33/104y passing.

Insight Bowl (Dec. 31): Oklahoma State 49 Indiana 33

With memory of their past coach Terry Hoeppner close to heart, Hoosiers (7-6) had fought so hard to qualify for their 1st bowl game in 14 years. Often when group achieves its quest—and subsequent bigger goal becomesavailable—they come up empty chasing final achievement. That truism and rough-riding O of Oklahoma State Cowboys (7-6) spelled trouble for Indiana, which seemed to have talked little about actually winning that quixotic post-season game. Cowpokes QB Zac Robinson (24-34/302y, 3 TDs, INT) accounted for 5 TDs as OSU rolled up 513y to Hoosiers' 399y. Contest was decided fairly early: After Indiana moved 52y from opening KO to K Austin Starr's 43y FG, Cowboys tallied TDs on their 1st 5 possessions to build 35-10 advantage by H. Oklahoma State RB Dantrell Savage (23/100y, TD) provided permanent lead with 3y TD run with 8:18 to go in 1st Q and, Robinson soon followed with pair of scoring passes. QB Kellen Lewis (22-43/204y, 2 TDs) ran for Indiana TD at end of 26y trip on heels of poor punt by OSU P Matt Fodge. But, Robinson countered with his 2nd TD pass to WR Dez Bryant (9/117y, 2 TDs). Indiana staged late flurry of 17 pts but never got closer than 42-27.

Outback Bowl: Tennessee 21 Wisconsin 17

Wisconsin (9-4) had opportunity to join Michigan (1998-2000 seasons) as only Big 10 teams to beat SEC foes in 3 straight bowl games, but it was Tennessee (10-4) D that pieced together clutch plays. Volunteers collected FUM at their 34YL to launch TD

drive in 1st Q, stopped 4th-and-2 pass from their 10YL with less than 6 mins to play, and S Antonio Wardlow picked off pass in own EZ in game's last min. Month from having served up TD INT that lost SEC championship game, sr Vols QB Erik Ainge passed 25-43/365y, 2 TDs to win MVP award in his last game. Ainge's 40y pass to frosh WR Denarius Moore set up frosh WR Gerald Jones to take direct snap for 3y TD run. Wisconsin came right back as Badgers unleashed their own frosh WR David Gilreath for 60y KO RET to Tennessee 22YL. Badgers QB Tyler Donovan (14-24/155y, TD, INT) took 6y dive for TD that tied it 7-7 but left him with severe headache. Ainge capped 59 and 51y 2nd Q drives with TD throws to WR Josh Briscoe—who took up slack after 1,000y receiver Lucas Taylor was declared academically ineligible—and TE Brad Cottam. Wisconsin trimmed H deficit to 21-14 as Donovan hit fellow-sr TE Andy Crooks for 4y score. Badgers K Taylor Mehlhaff made 27y FG with 9 secs left in 3rd Q, but Wisconsin suffered 2 misfires in 4th Q.

Capitol One Bowl: Michigan 41 Florida 35

Sr stars QB Chad Henne (25-39/373y, 3 TDs, 2 INTs) and TB Mike Hart (32/129y, 2 TDs) of Wolverines (9-4) were healthy again, and they bowed out with thrilling victory over Florida (9-4) that placed perfect cap on career of out-going coach Lloyd Carr. Michigan's sr players won their 1st bowl game and enjoyed dousing Carr with water and carrying him off on their shoulders. Still, Michigan lost 4 TOs, and fine performances by Heisman-winning QB Tim Tebow (17-33/154y, 3 TDs, and 16/57y, TD rushing) and RB Percy Harvin (13/165y, TD, and 9/77y, TD receiving) kept Gators close. Florida led 14-7 in 2nd Q after Tebow's 2nd TD pass and 35-31 in 4th Q after Harvin's 10y TD run. Down by 4 pts, Wolverines took over with 7 mins to play, and WR Adrian Arrington (9/153y, 2 TDs) caught 37 and 18y passes from Henne, latter good for TD that lifted UM to 38-35 lead. After desperate Florida could gain only 4y on 4 downs in next series, Wolverines K K.C. Lopata knocked through clinching 41y FG, his 2nd 3-ptr of 4th Q.

Cotton Bowl: Missouri 38 Arkansas 7

If Missouri (12-2) was disappointed to be demoted to Cotton Bowl, it didn't show. Led by several Texas-born-and-raised stars, Tigers put on great show on both sides of ball to dominate 71st football celebration of New Year's Day in Dallas. Coming off its huge Thanksgiving weekend upset of no. 1 LSU, Arkansas (8-5) looked flat under interim coach Reggie Herring, who replaced deposed head coach Houston Nutt. Herring's D strategy was to pack his lineup with DBs, so it wasn't normally-prolific passing of dynamic QB Chase Daniel (12-29/136y, INT) that won game for Missouri. Daniel handed ball 24 times to RB Tony Temple, and sr liked absence of Arkansas LBs enough to post brilliant 281y rushing and shatter Cotton Bowl record held since 1954 by Rice's Dicky Moegle (265y versus Alabama). Temple also set new Cotton record of 4 TDs on runs of 22, 4, 4, and 40y. Temple gained 159y in 1st H, led 14-0 by Mizzou, while cracking line of scrimmage for sprints of 22, 38, and 41y. Temple pulled hamstring in 3rd Q and missed some playing time. In 4th Q, coach Gary Pinkel learned Temple was near record at about same moment Temple's leg was worked back into shape. So, Temple ripped through Hogs on his best run, spinning and dodging to 40y TD on which he broke several tackles. It came with 8:33 to play and upped Tigers' lead to 38-7. TB Darren McFadden (21/105y) scored Razorbacks' only TD late in 3rd Q on 3y run. Jr McFadden sat out 4th Q and finished his career—he would soon declare for NFL draft—with 1,830y for season and 4,590y for his career. Both were school records and 2nd in SEC history to Georgia's Herschel Walker, who made 1,891y in 1981 and 5,259y in 1980-82.

Gator Bowl: Texas Tech 31 Virginia 28

Truly satisfying season for Virginia (9-4) was so close to being wrapped up with big bowl win as Cavaliers led 28-14 deep into 4th Q. QB Jameel Sewell (14-23/78y, TD) overcame modest passing numbers to flit to key gains in commanding Cavs O. Sewell twice darted for 1st downs on 3rd down on 1st Q TD drive that tied it 7-7 on his short TD pass. But, Sewell went out with tweaked leg early in 4th Q. Meanwhile, QB Graham Harrell (44-69/407y, 3 TDs), mastermind of nation's leading pass attack of Texas Tech (9-4), was frustrated by twice grounding passes in EZ for safeties. UVa NG Nate Collins and LB Clint Sintim put on pressure to be credited for 2 pts each to build 9-7 and 18-7 edges in 1st H. After Texas Tech started 2nd H with successful onside-KO, Harrell flipped 6y TD pass to WR Danny Amendola for 3rd Q's only score to stay close at 21-14. TB Mikell Simpson (20/170y, TD, and 5/36y, TD receiving) had superb game for Virginia, setting new bowl record with 96y TD run and catching 11y TD pass 3:24 into 4th Q to build 28-14 lead. Sub QB Peter Lalich threw scoring pass to Simpson but lost critical FUM at UVa 4YL right after Raiders WR Michael Crabtree (9/101y, TD) hauled in 20y TD pass with 3:31 to play. RB Aaron Crawford scored on next play to tie it 28-28. Following short punt by Virginia, K Alex Trlica nailed 41y FG with 2 secs remaining to win it for Texas Tech.

Rose Bowl: Southern California 49 Illinois 17

When Rose Bowl fathers lost their Big Ten champion, Ohio State, to BCS Title Game, they made somewhat controversial decision to preserve traditional Pac-10 vs. Big 10 match-up. Innkeepers in Phoenix were happy because surprise switches in bowl assignments took Fiesta Bowl off hook for having to invite local Arizona State Sun Devils so as to fill stadium with travelers spending plenty of money on hotel rooms. Unfortunately, Illinois (9-4) was no match for highly-focused Southern California (11-2), which felt it deserved shot at Ohio State in New Orleans. Much credit was due coach Pete Carroll when his Men of Troy showed up highly motivated. Trojans' D came up with 2 FUM RECs and INTs by LB Rey Maualuga (3 sacks) and CB Cary Harris, all of which set up TDs. USC QB John David Booty hit 25-37/255y, INT and TDs to TB Chauncey Washington (TD rushing), TE Fred Davis, and WR David Ausberry. Frosh TB Joe McKnight rushed 10/125y, TD and caught 6/45y, TD. Trailing 21-3 at H, Illinois broke loose TB Rashard Mendenhall (17/155y, TD), and he displayed speed and elusiveness on 79y TD gallop and, after Illini D held, Mendenhall slithered away for 55y on short pass. Sensing possible TD to move within 21-17, Illini WR Jacob Willis caught pass over middle but was stripped by Trojans LB Kaluka Maiava, and USC LB Brian Cushing fell on FUM. Odd but decisive play soon followed. McKnight missed swing pass from Booty, and whole stadium was unsure if it was incompletion; McKnight never hesitated, picked up lateral pass, and cruised 65y to Illinois 12YL. Davis' TD catch made it 28-10, and Rose Bowl decision was nailed down.

Sugar Bowl: Georgia 41 Hawaii 10

On heels of Boise State's fine performance in previous year's BCS Fiesta Bowl, Hawaii (12-1), nation's last undefeated major team, had reason to feel it could pull off Sugar Bowl upset. Many felt Georgia (11-2) was best team in nation at season's end, and Bulldogs set right out to prove it. When rout was over Dawgs did their share of whoofing: "We're supposed to be in the national championship game. The nation knows it, everyone knows it," proclaimed S Kelin Johnson. Bulldogs TB Knowshon Moreno zipped to 17 and 11y TD runs in 1st Q for 14-3 lead. Warriors QB Colt Brennan (22-38/169y, 3 INTs) was massacred by Georgia D-front, led by DE Marcus Howard (3 sacks, 2 forced FUMs), who recovered EZ FUM for TD. Brennan was sacked 8 times, smacked down several more, intercepted 3 times, and lost 2 FUMs, including Howard's 3rd Q TD. Brennan was so beat up he was out by time Hawaii finally got into EZ in 4th Q to cut margin to 41-10. Brennan decided Georgia was "probably the fastest team I've ever seen," demonstrated by Bulldogs' sharp open-field tackling as soon as Warriors' short passes hit their marks.

Fiesta Bowl (Jan. 2): West Virginia 48 Oklahoma 28

Another Fiesta Bowl disaster tacked unwanted reputation on Oklahoma (11-3), which seemed incapable of focusing on BCS games. Sooners now had lost 4 straight big bowls since winning 2003 Rose Bowl. West Virginia (11-2) CB Vaughn Rivers cruised 51y on 1st Q punt RET to set up 1st of 2 FGs by K Pat McAfee. Sooners TB Allen Patrick dashed 73y with ensuing KO, but QB Sam Bradford (21-33/242y, 2 TDs, INT) was picked off in EZ as Oklahoma finished 1st Q with only 1y O in 12 plays. WVU's intense FB Owen Schmitt barreled 57y for TD in 2nd Q, and QB Patrick White (10-19/176y, 2 TDs) found WR Darius Reynaud for 21y TD pass as Reynaud tied Chris Henry's school record with dozen TD catches in single season. Trailing 20-6, Sooners roared out for 2nd H and collected 1st 9 pts, primarily on RB Chris Brown's 1y run. But, Oklahoma bungled onside-KO which led to Mountaineers frosh RB Noel Devine's 17y TD run for 27-15 lead. Devine added 65y TD run in 4th Q as WVU held off Oklahoma in 13-13 standoff in last Q. White, frustrated in season's last game versus Pitt, sparkled by rushing 20/150y, which was especially helpful after prime RB Steve Slaton went down early with injury.

Orange Bowl (Jan. 3): Kansas 24 Virginia Tech 21

Oddsmakers continued to underestimate no. 8 Kansas (12-1), which was posted as more than 3-pt underdog. Known for their O, Jayhawks made some of their biggest plays on D against ACC champion Virginia Tech (11-3). Kansas picked off 3 passes, none more useful than 60y TD RET off Va Tech's early-relieving frosh QB Tyrod Taylor by bowl MVP, A-A CB Aqib Talib. It came with 5:15 to go in 1st Q. In 2nd Q, K Scott Webb was good with 32y FG after CB Chris Harris picked off Hokies vet starting QB Sean Glennon (13-28/160y, TD, 2 INTs) and returned to Tech 31YL. Kansas went 59y on 10 plays on its next try for 17-0 lead: QB Todd Reesing (20-37/227y, TD, INT) hit 5 passes, including 13y TD on slant-in to WR Marcus Henry. At this moment, KU had 135y to 64y O advantage, but Hokies awoke with 69y drive to 1y TD plunge by RB Brandon Ore (23/116y, TD). Virginia Tech sent its fans to their feet as WR Justin Harper took pitch from WR Eddie Royal to race 84y down sideline for punt RET TD that pulled Hokies to within 17-14 less than 4 mins into 3rd Q. Tech threatened again in 3rd Q after pass interference call on Harris and 4 runs by Ore, but Jayhawks LB Joe Mortensen blocked 25y FG try. It stayed as nail-biter until Kansas SS Justin Thornton grabbed INT 4 mins into 4th Q and returned it 30y to 2YL. Reesing scored on bootleg on 1st down for 24-14 lead. Hokies held on downs at their 21YL as 4th Q came within 6 mins of conclusion and answered with 78y drive to Glennon's 20y TD pass to Harper. Onside-KO failed with 3 mins to go, and KU RB Brandon McAnderson (15/75y) chipped in tough runs to kill clock.

BCS Championship Bowl (Jan. 7): Louisiana State 38 Ohio State 24

For 2nd season in row, Ohio State (11-2) arrived at national championship game ranked at top of BCS. Opposed to last year's 1-TD favorites, Buckeyes were 4-pt underdogs to LSU (12-2), which was playing virtual home game. Ohio State was looking for redemption after its trouncing by Florida in previous January's title game. Buckeyes turned up sharp, its O-line springing TB Chris "Beanie" Wells (20/146y, TD) for 65y TD gallop to start. Ohio State QB Todd Boeckman (15-26/206y, 2 TDs, 2 INTs) found swift frosh TB Brandon Saine (3/69y receiving) for 44y pass to set up K Ryan Pretorius' 25y FG for 10-0 lead before match had reached halfway through 1st Q. LSU K Colt David made FG late in 1st Q after Tigers succeeded 3-4 tries on 3rd down and would finish game with 11-18 such conversions. Early in 2nd Q, Buckeyes committed 2 uncharacteristic personal fouls to fuel LSU's tying 84y TD drive: TE Richard Dickson (4/44y, 2 TDs) slipped wide open to accept 13y TD pass from QB Matt Flynn (19-27/174y, 4 TDs, INT). On next possession, Ohio derailed its TD hopes with another personal foul PEN, and series ended with game's turning point: LSU DT Ricky Jean-Francois, who had been suspended nearly all season, jumped to get his right paw on Pretorius' 38y FG try. From that moment, Bayou Bengals took command. Flynn's perfect 10y TD toss to WR Brandon LaFell gave Tigers their 1st lead at 17-10, and CB Chevis Jackson sped 34y down LSU sideline with INT to set up 1y TD by FB Jacob Hester (21/86y, TD) for 24-10 H edge. After permitting 31 unanswered pts, Ohio

State regained some life late in 3rd Q when CB Malcolm Jenkins returned INT of Flynn to 11YL to set up Boeckman's 1st TD pass that trimmed deficit to 31-17. But LSU effectively killed clock, and Flynn added his 4th TD pass late in 4th Q. Ohio State's sad bowl record against SEC fell to 0-9.

Final *USA Today* Coaches January 7

1	Louisiana State (60)	1500	14t	Brigham Young	624
2	Southern California	1380	14t	Auburn	624
3	Georgia	1370	16	Florida	567
4	Ohio State	1287	17	Hawaii	427
5	Missouri	1241	18	Illinois	416
6	West Virginia	1239	19	Michigan	413
7	Kansas	1217	20	Cincinnati	376
8	Oklahoma	1016	21	Wisconsin	333
9	Virginia Tech	979	22	Clemson	319
10	Texas	924	23	Texas Tech	242
11	Boston College	898	24	Oregon	192
12	Tennessee	826	25	Penn State	127
13	Arizona State	635			

Final AP Poll January 8

1	Louisiana State (60)	1620	14	Brigham Young	654
2	Georgia (3)	1515	15	Auburn	648
3	Southern California (1)	1500	16	Arizona State	587
4	Missouri	1347	17	Cincinnati	566
5	Ohio State	1346	18	Michigan	508
6	West Virginia	1342	19	Hawaii	460
7	Kansas (1)	1303	20	Illinois	443
8	Oklahoma	1139	21	Clemson	353
9	Virginia Tech	1096	22	Texas Tech	308
10t	Boston College	962	23	Oregon	253
10t	Texas	962	24	Wisconsin	202
12	Tennessee	904	25	Oregon State	110
13	Florida	685			

2007 Top Performance Formula

1	Louisiana State	1.6496
2	West Virginia	1.6378
3	Kansas	1.6087
4	Missouri	1.5821
5	Oklahoma	1.5547
6	Ohio State	1.5402
7	Georgia	1.5335
8	Southern California	1.5130
9	Virginia Tech	1.4980
10	Florida	1.4786
11	Brigham Young	1.4532
12	Oregon	1.4343
13	Texas	1.4214
14	Arizona State	1.4083
15	Boston College	1.4027
16	Tennessee	1.3699
17	Clemson	1.3545
18	Penn State	1.3455
19	Michigan	1.3273
20	Auburn	1.3162

2007 Top Opponent Records

1	Texas A&M	.6289
2	Oklahoma State	.6238
3	Nebraska	.6224
4	Florida	.6209
5	Kentucky	.6185
6	Louisiana State	.6182
7	Virginia Tech	.6145
8	Tennessee	.6121
9	Mississippi	.6085
10	Washington	.6053
11	South Carolina	.6043
12	Oregon	.6013
13	UCLA	.5987
14t	Illinois	.5934
14t	Georgia	.5934
16	Missouri	.5914
17	Minnesota	.5857
18	Iowa State	.5830
19	Arizona	.5829
20	Auburn	.5816

2007 Out-of-Conference Records

	W-L	Percentage	Bowl W-L
Southeastern	38-10	.7917	6-2
Big Ten	34-14	.7083	3-5
Big Twelve	34-15	.6939	5-3
Big East	25-13	.6579	3-2
Pacific-10	23-12	.6571	4-2
Atlantic Coast	29-21	.5800	2-6
Mountain West	20-17	.5405	4-1

2007 Individual Statistical Leaders

RUSHING YARDS	Attempts	Yards	Avg.	
Kevin Smith, Central Florida	450	2567	5.7	
Matt Forte, Tulane	361	2127	5.9	
Ray Rice, Rutgers	380	2012	5.3	
Darren McFadden, Arkansas	325	1830	5.6	
Jonathan Stewart, Oregon	280	1722	6.2	
Rashard Mendenhall, Illinois	262	1681	6.4	
Eugene Jarvis, Kent State	279	1669	6.0	
Jamaal Charles, Texas	258	1619	6.3	
Chris Wells, Ohio State	274	1609	5.9	
Anthony Alridge, Houston	259	1597	6.2	

PASSING YARDS	Completions	Attempts	Yards	Pct.
Graham Harrell, Texas Tech	512	713	5705	71.8
Paul Smith, Tulsa	327	544	5065	60.1
Colt Brennan, Hawaii	359	510	4343	70.4
Chase Daniel, Missouri	384	563	4306	68.2
Brian Brohm, Louisville	308	473	4024	65.1
Andre Woodson, Kentucky	327	518	3709	63.1
Todd Reesing, Kansas	276	446	3486	61.9
Taylor Tharp, Boise State	289	423	3340	68.3
Colt McCoy, Texas	276	424	3303	65.1
Tim Tebow, Florida	237	350	3286	66.9

RECEIVING YARDS	Catches	Yards
Michael Crabtree, Texas Tech	134	1962
Jordy Nelson, Kansas State	122	1606
Donnie Avery, Houston	91	1456
Dante Love, Ball State	100	1398
Ryan Grace-Mullen, Hawaii	106	1372
Casey Fitzgerald, North Texas	111	1322
Davone Bess, Hawaii	108	1266
Danny Amendola, Texas Tech	109	1245
Kevin Jurovich, San Jose State	85	1183
Jason Rivers, Hawaii	92	1174

2007 Consensus All-America Team
Offense

Wide Receiver:	Michael Crabtree, Texas Tech
	Jordy Nelson, Kansas State
Tight End:	Martin Rucker, Missouri
Linemen:	Jake Long, Michigan
	Anthony Collins, Kansas
	George "Duke" Robinson, Oklahoma
	Ryan Clady, Boise State
Center:	Jonathan Luigs, Arkansas
Quarterback:	Tim Tebow, Florida
Running Back:	Darren McFadden, Arkansas
	Kevin Smith, Central Florida
Kick Returner:	Jeremy Maclin, Missouri
Kicker:	John Sullivan, New Mexico

Defense

Linemen:	Chris Long, Virginia
	George Selvis, South Florida
	Glenn Dorsey, Louisiana State
	Sedrick Ellis, Southern California
Linebacker:	James Laurinaitis, Ohio State
	Jordan Dizon, Colorado
	Dan Connor, Penn State
	J Leman, Illinois
	Curtis Lofton, Oklahoma
Backs:	Aqib Talib, Kansas
	Antoine Cason, Arizona
	Jamie Silva, Boston College
	Craig Steltz, Louisiana State
Punter:	Kevin Huber, Cincinnati

2007 Heisman Trophy Vote

Tim Tebow, sophomore quarterback, Florida	1957
Darren McFadden, junior tailback, Arkansas	1703
Colt Brennan, senior quarterback, Hawaii	632
Chase Daniel, junior quarterback, Missouri	425
Dennis Dixon, senior quarterback, Oregon	178

Other Major Awards

Maxwell (Player)	Tim Tebow, sophomore quarterback, Florida
Walter Camp (Player)	Darren McFadden, junior tailback, Arkansas
Outland (Lineman)	Glenn Dorsey, senior defensive tackle, LSU
Vince Lombardi (Lineman)	Glenn Dorsey, senior defensive tackle, LSU
Doak Walker (Running Back)	Darren McFadden, junior tailback, Arkansas
Davey O'Brien (Quarterback)	Tim Tebow, sophomore quarterback, Florida
Fred Biletnikoff (Receiver)	Michael Crabtree, freshman WR, Texas Tech
Jim Thorpe (Defensive Back)	Antoine Cason, senior cornerback, Arizona
Dick Butkus (Linebacker)	James Laurinaitis, jr. linebacker, Ohio State
Chuck Bednarik (Defender)	Dan Connor, senior linebacker, Penn State
Lou Groza (Plackicker)	Thomas Weber, freshman kicker, Arizona St.
Ray Guy (Punter)	Durant Brooks, senior punter, Georgia Tech
Johnny Unitas (Sr. Quarterback)	Matt Ryan, sr. quarterback, Boston College
John Mackey (Tight End)	Fred Davis, sr. tight end, Southern California
Dave Rimington (Center)	Jonathan Luigs, junior center, Arkansas
Ted Hendricks (Defensive End)	Chris Long, senior defensive end, Virginia
AFCA Coach of the Year	Mark Mangino, Kansas

Tim Tebow of Florida

2008

The Year of the SEC's Triad of Titleists, Jilted Longhorns, and Hootin' Utes

College football's 140th season started the same way most recent seasons had begun. The long-standing and presumptive kings of football, the Southeastern Conference, sat atop the college world. For instance, on September 14 the AP Poll had five teams from one conference in its top 10 for the first time ever. And they all hailed from the SEC: No. 3 Georgia (10-3), no. 4 Florida (13-1), defending national champion and no. 6 Louisiana State (8-5), no. 9 Alabama (12-2), and no. 10 Auburn (5-7).

By mid-season, however, the mantle of greatness had moved west. The spotlight focused on the Big 12 Conference and its remarkably high-scoring offenses found primarily in the South Division.

When it was all over, however, the SEC was back on top. Florida won its second national championship in three years to bookend LSU's 2007 crown and give the SEC its third consecutive BCS title. It only was the third time since 1936 that the Associated Press' season-end no. 1 spot had gone to teams from one league for three straight years. The Big Ten's Minnesota (1940 and '41) and Ohio State (1942) and the SEC's Alabama (1978 and '79) and Georgia (1980) were the previous triads of titleists.

But at times in 2008, it was easy to scoff at the SEC's depth of contenders. LSU and Auburn slipped substantially on offense with glaring problems at the quarterback position, and disappointing preseason no. 1 Georgia lost to fast-rising Alabama, Florida, and Georgia Tech (9-4) of the Atlantic Coast Conference. Big 12 teams, especially a trio from the South Division, played on an enormously higher offensive level than any other conference in the country. The attacks of Oklahoma (12-2), Texas (12-1), and Texas Tech (11-2) truly exemplified modern, wide-open, big-scoring football.

Heading Big 12 offensive juggernauts was a list of great quarterbacks, probably the finest group of signal-callers in any league in college history. Sam Bradford of Oklahoma, Graham Harrell of Texas Tech, and Colt McCoy of Texas all were serious Heisman Trophy candidates. Many of the conference's other passers—Chase Daniel, a 2007 Heisman finalist, of Missouri (10-4), Todd Reesing of Kansas (7-6), Joe Ganz of Nebraska (9-4), Zac Robinson of Oklahoma State (9-4), and freshman sensation Robert Griffin of Baylor (4-8)—were very efficient running their formidable attacks.

A question loomed, however, over the Big 12 as the season progressed into a BCS title match-up of Oklahoma and Florida. Was it the unprecedented greatness of Big 12 offenses or were its defenses less proficient than in the past? It was a true conundrum.

Still, there was no denying the offensive talent in the Big 12. Bradford, Harrell, and McCoy were tapped as the three national finalists for the Davey O'Brien quarterback award. The conference also boasted all three national finalists for the John Mackey tight end award: Chase Coffman of Missouri, Jermaine Gresham of Oklahoma, and Brandon Pettigrew of Oklahoma State. The three national finalists for the Fred Biletnikoff wide receiver award were Dez Bryant of Oklahoma State, Michael Crabtree of Texas Tech, and Jeremy Maclin of Missouri.

Bradford, who won the O'Brien Award, and McCoy, who won the Maxwell Award as the nation's best player, joined Tim Tebow of Florida, the 2007 Heisman Trophy honoree, at the Heisman award festivities in New York City. The Heisman went to Bradford, the second sophomore ever to win, but not without controversy blowing in from the Southwest region. Tebow earned the most first place votes (309) but finished third when 154 of 904 voters, many from Big 12 country, cast ballots that failed to name him at all.

All three were worthy candidates, parties to one of the closest-ever three-way votes. Bradford led Oklahoma to 50+ points nine times and a record 702 points during the regular season. Heisman runner-up McCoy, after two solid but injury-prone years, emerged as a chiseled, weight-lifting demon to earn respect as a "hard-nosed football player." Indeed, McCoy pounded his way to several key runs and scored 10 touchdowns on the ground. More importantly, he delivered a magnificent 76.5 passing percentage, the best in major college history, to top Central Florida's Daunte Culpepper, who had set the record in 1998 with 73.6 percent.

The Big 12 was fun all year. Prior to Texas Tech's monumental trip to Norman to play Oklahoma on November 22, Red Raiders offensive tackle Rylan Reed, a 6'7", former baseball pitcher, lent perspective to the pressure of playing big road games: "I think it's always good to beat someone at their own place…It reminds me of the old 'Thirsty Thursday' days in minor league baseball when you get beer thrown at you. I kind of enjoy it." Unfortunately for the traveling Red Raiders, Oklahoma dominated physically and

strategically in a 65-21 pasting, and thus the three Big 12 South giants soon would find themselves tied in the division with and 11-1 overall records.

On October 11, McCoy had rallied Texas past Oklahoma in an intense 45-35 shootout on a neutral field at Dallas' Cotton Bowl. The game began a remarkable stretch for the Longhorns in which for four straight weeks they faced conference rivals ranked no worse than 11th in the AP Poll. After outgunning the Sooners, Missouri by 56-31, and Oklahoma State by 28-24, Texas finally succumbed in Lubbock in the very last second to high-powered Texas Tech, which for the first time in coach Mike Leach's nine years boasted a decent running attack and defense. McCoy rallied the Longhorns to a 33-32 lead with a touchdown drive only 1:29 from the end, but Harrell whipped his Raiders goal-ward, and All-America wide receiver Crabtree ripped away from a sideline tackle to score the winner on a 28-yard reception. Had the tight-roping Crabtree stepped on the sideline, it was questionable whether Texas Tech could have gotten its field goal team on field in time since the Raiders were out of timeouts and a new 2008 rule would have started the clock upon the spot of the ball even with it going out of bounds. The other question for Leach would have been his choice of clutch placekicker between Donnie Carona, who had missed several extra points during the early season, and new recruit Matt Williams. Williams had been promoted to Raiders' extra-point kicker when the impulsive Leach watched the Tech student win a month's free rent by making a promotional field goal during a between-quarters stunt at Jones AT&T Stadium.

A week after their Texas Tech victory, the Sooners pulled away from Oklahoma State to win 61-41 and clinch the three-way deadlock atop the Big 12 South. Which team would play for the conference title?

The much-maligned BCS was called upon to unlock the tie; Big 12 rules called for the highest BCS ranked team, in this case Oklahoma, marginally ahead of Texas on the November 30 BCS list thanks to superior computer numbers, to play Missouri for the league championship. The jilted Longhorns were left to mutter that they already had beaten both finalists. Had the Big 12 employed the tiebreaker systems used by every one of the other two-division leagues in college football—the ACC, Conference USA, MAC and SEC—Texas would have been the team to advanced. "This was a perfect storm," said Big 12 Commissioner Dan Beebe. "You can't create a rule that accounts for every scenario."

Oklahoma scored 60 or more points in four straight games to close the regular season. Only five other schools ever had accomplished the feat and none since California in 1920. The Sooners topped 60 again in the Big 12 title game against Missouri and became the all-time scoring champion.

Non-BCS conferences offered two undefeated teams in the regular season. Boise State (12-1) of the Western Athletic Conference went to Eugene to make Oregon (10-3) its first-ever major conference victim in an enemy stadium. Undefeated Utah (13-0) of the deeper Mountain West Conference aced out the Broncos to earn a trip to the BCS Sugar Bowl. The Utes stunningly whipped Alabama, ranked no. 1 for all of November, by 31-17, by jumping to a 21-0 lead in the first quarter. By beating six bowl teams, Utah had swept a better schedule than other non-BCS teams of recent years. So there was substantial hooting on behalf of the Utes that as the only unbeaten FBS team and no playoff, they should be given the AP national championship vote. Coach Kyle Whittingham went against the rules of the USA Today Coaches Poll and cast a first-place vote for his Utes, but Florida, victorious over Oklahoma by 24-14 in the BCS Title Game, took the top spot in both polls. The Utes caught the eye of 16 media voters who voted them no. 1 on AP's post-season ballot. Those votes helped Utah earn AP's no. 2 spot. The final coaches' ballot placed Utah fourth behind Florida, Southern California (12-1), and Texas.

President-elect Barack Obama called for a college playoff and, in so doing, expressed the first serious form of college football policy offered by the Chief Executive since Richard Nixon anointed Texas as national champions in 1969. Although Congress seemed willing to listen to debate over the BCS, it was obvious when the 2009 session opened legislators had more pressing matters in front of them, primarily to consider legislation to attack a considerable downturn in the U.S. economy.

The Atlantic Coast Conference enjoyed an unusual season that could be described as either excitingly competitive or highly mediocre. Each of 12 conference members lost at least four games, but Jeff Sagarin, computer expert for USA Today, ranked the league as third-best behind only the SEC and Big 12. Both ACC division titles were up in the air until the last week as

no team seemed to want to take charge until Boston College (9-5) clinched the Atlantic and eventual league champion Virginia Tech (10-4) captured the Coastal. Form went out the window all season as ranked ACC teams, 5-3 outside the conference, fell to unranked conference opponents in 16 of 22 such matchups. Conference pride swelled on NFL Draft Day: four of the first nine selections—linebacker Aaron Curry of Wake Forest (8-5), receiver Darrius Heyward-Bey of Maryland (8-5), offensive tackle Eugene Monroe of Virginia (5-7), and defensive tackle B.J. Raji of Boston College—came from the ACC.

Pac-10 champion Southern California stirred itself into the national title mix for the seventh straight year. The Trojans, however, virtually were eliminated from title consideration by a glaring slip-up in late September at Oregon State (9-4). ESPN's Thursday night cameras caught the Beavers' little frosh running back Jacquizz Rodgers darting for 187 yards and two touchdowns in a 27-21 upset.

Still, the Trojans employed a magnificent defense during the season that ranked in the top-5 in every important category and led the nation in scoring with a meager 9.0 points per game, 2.3 points better than runner-up Texas Christian (11-2). USC's defensive stars included end Clay Matthews, tackle Fili Moala, linebackers Brian Cushing and Rey Maualuga, and defensive backs Kevin Ellison, Cary Harris, and Taylor Mays.

With Sylvester Croom of Mississippi State (4-8), Ron Prince of Kansas State (5-7), and Tyrone Willingham of Washington (0-12) forced out of their jobs by season's end, the number of African-American head coaches in the FBS dropped from six to three. Turner Gill, black third-year coach at Buffalo (8-6), miraculously won the Mid-American Conference East Division title after the Bulls had endured a 17-75 record in the first eight years of the 2000s. Charles Barkley, former Auburn basketball star, ripped his alma mater when it passed over Gill in early 2009 to hire white Gene Chizek, who had lost his last 10 games at Iowa State (2-10). However, new hires at the beginning of the off-season lifted the number of African-American head coaches in the FBS to seven.

Milestones

■ Rules Committee adopted new 40-second ready-for-play clock that mimicked NFL rule and had offenses adjusting to faster pace even after out-of-bounds plays, which no longer kept clock stopped until next snap. Also there was renewed effort to curb excessive player celebration, especially taunting of opponents and players acting in manner to bring attention to themselves.

■ Former University of Miami All-America halfback Jim Dooley, who played in 1949-51, died at 77 on January 8. Dooley, 1st round draft choice of Chicago Bears in 1952, spent nearly three decades with Chicago as wide receiver and head coach who succeeded George Halas from 1968-71, developed nickel-back defense, and later served as assistant under Mike Ditka. College Hall of Famer Mike Holovak, 88, died in Florida, late in January. Holovak starred as running back at Boston College under Hall of Fame coach Frank Leahy and as senior co-captain in 1942 he ranked second nationally in rushing to earn consensus All-America honors. He set records in 1943 Orange Bowl with 3 TDs and average yards per carry (15.0) against Alabama. Holovak returned to BC as head coach from 1951-59 with 49-23-3 record. He coached Boston Patriots of AFL from 1961-68. Larry Smith, former head coach (143-126-7) at Tulane, Arizona, Southern California, and Missouri, died of leukemia at 68 on January 28. Smith was best known to have begun 9-game unbeaten streak for Arizona over rival Arizona State and lead USC to Rose Bowl berths in his first 3 tries. Dying in February were Kenny Konz, 79, standout back for Louisiana State from 1948-50 and Cleveland Browns in 1950s, former All-Big 8 offensive tackle Byron Bigby of Oklahoma in 1967-69, Raleigh Blakely, 83, who played on SMU's 1948 and '49 Cotton Bowl teams, and Mississippi quarterback Herman "Eagle" Day, 75. Day led Ole Miss to 28-5-1 mark and two SEC championships in 1954-55 under Hall of Fame coach John Vaught. Houston Patton, 75, Day's back-up at Ole Miss, died in November. Pair of Hall of Famers, Buddy Dial, 71, of Rice, and Jerry Groom, 78, of Notre Dame each died on February 29. Dial was All-America end for Owls and member of Cotton Bowl All-Star team off his play in 1958 game against Navy. Groom was tapped as All-America center-linebacker during his Notre Dame career in 1948-50 and was named to 1954 Pro Bowl while playing for NFL's Chicago Cardinals. Otto Schnellbacher, 84, captain of Kansas' 1947 Orange Bowl squad and Jayhawks' career receiving leader for next 22 years with 58 catches for 1,069 yards, died on March 10. Bobby Luna, 74, died March 14. Luna played football and baseball from 1951-1954 at Alabama and later served as assistant coach under Paul "Bear" Bryant. Also dying on March 14 of heart attack was Mike Dawson, 54, 3-year starter (1973-75) at Arizona who was no. 1 draft pick of NFL's St. Louis Cardinals in 1976. Herb Rich, 79, 3-sport star at Vanderbilt, standout 2-way halfback for 12th-ranked Commodores in 1948, and NFL's leading punt returner in 1950 with Baltimore Colts, died March 28. Hal Wantland, versatile back who played several positions at Tennessee (1963-65) and served as captain of 1965 Volunteers, died at 63 on April 8. Hall of Famer Bob Pellegrini, 73, Maryland's unanimous All-America center and Knute Rockne Award and Jacobs Award winner in 1955, died on April 11. Pellegrini was top draft choice of Philadelphia Eagles and played for Eagles and Washington Redskins as linebacker in 1956 and 1958-65. Harry Ulinski, 83, center for Kentucky (1946-49) and Washington Redskins, died in late April. John H. McConnell, 84, former Michigan State guard, 1998 winner of National Football Foundation's Gold Medal, and steel industry titan, passed away April 25. McConnell, who started Worthington Industries in 1955 with his car as collateral, endowed NFF with $300,000 gift in 1999. Standout Oklahoma wishbone quarterback and former lieutenant governor of Oklahoma, Jack Mildren, 58, died on May 22 after long bout with stomach cancer. Mildren was first quarterback to run potent Wishbone attack under Sooners coach Barry Switzer, leading Oklahoma offense to still-standing NCAA major-division season mark of 472.4 rushing yards per game for 11-1 squad in 1971. Richard Evans, one of Iowa's "Ironmen" in 1939, died in late May at 93. Early June saw deaths of Tom Catlin, 76, 1952 all-America center and member of Oklahoma's 1950 national champions, Mitch Frerotte, 43, Penn State offensive guard in mid-1980s and three-time Super Bowler with Buffalo Bills, Ray Mallouf, 89, SMU's 1st All- America quarterback as member of 1940 Southwest Conference champions, and former Texas Tech quarterback Charles "Kenny" Napper, 58. John Pont, 80, who starred as halfback at Miami-Ohio (1949-51) and later coached his alma mater (1956-62), as well as Yale (1963-65), Indiana (1966-72), and Northwestern (1973-80), died on July 1 in Evanston, Ill. Texas A&M and 4-year San Diego Chargers defensive back Terrance Kiel, 27, was killed in San Diego car accident on July 4. Southern California's consensus All-America guard in 1952, Elmer Willhoite, 78, died August 19. Frank Cornish, UCLA's two-time All-America center during 1986-89 and who played on two Super Bowl-winning teams with Dallas Cowboys, died in his sleep at age 40 on August 22. Dick Enderle, former standout Minnesota guard in late 1960s, died at 60 on September 4. Also dying in early September were Colorado head coach (67-49-2 record in 1963-73) and AD, Eddie Crowder, 77, and Texas Christian guard and Kansas City Chiefs linebacker Sherrill Hendrick, who passed away at 71. Dying on September 23 at 66 was Wally Hilgenberg, standout Iowa guard-linebacker (1961-63) and 15-year NFL linebacker with Detroit Lions and Minnesota Vikings. On September 24, Dick Lynch, senior halfback who scored Notre Dame's winning TD to end Oklahoma's 47-game winning streak in 1957, died at age 72. Lynch went on to 9 years as pro cornerback with Washington Redskins (1958) and New York Giants (1959-66), where he twice led NFL in interceptions, and spent 41 years as Giants' radio broadcast analyst. Also on September 24, Charles "Cotton" Price, quarterback and captain of 1939 undefeated national champion Texas A&M, died at 90. Milt Davis, 79, former UCLA wingback (1952-53), twice Baltimore Colts All-Pro, and natural history professor at Los Angeles City College, died on October 1. Craig Fertig, 66, died of kidney failure on October 4. Fertig, former Southern California quarterback (1961-63) and head coach at Oregon State (1976-79), earned 3 national titles with USC, as sub quarterback in 1962 and as assistant coach in 1967 and '72. Chris Mims, 38, former defensive tackle-end at Tennessee (1990-91) and with San Diego Chargers, died in mid-October. Bob Jeter, 71, star halfback with Iowa, who raced 81 yards to TD and rushed for 194 yards in 1959 Rose Bowl and served as long-time cornerback star with Green Bay Packers, died in November. Hall of Famer "Slingin' Sammy Baugh, great passer for Texas Christian (1934-36) and Washington Redskins (1937-52), died on December 17. Baugh, All-America choice in 1935 and '36, helped revolutionize aerial game by throwing as many as 40 passes in single games during era when 10 passes was considered daring. Pete Case, 3-year starting tackle at Georgia in 1959-61 and 9-year NFL guard, died at 67 on December 18.

■ Coaching Changes:

	Incoming	Outgoing
Arkansas	Bobby Petrino	Houston Nutt
Baylor	Art Briles	Guy Morriss
Clemson	Dabo Swinney (a)	Tommy Bowden
Colorado State	Steve Fairchild	Sonny Lubick
Duke	David Cutcliffe	Ted Roof
Georgia Tech	Paul Johnson	Chan Gailey
Hawaii	Greg McMackin	June Jones
Houston	Kevin Sumlin	Art Briles
Michigan	Rich Rodriguez	Lloyd Carr
Mississippi	Houston Nutt	Ed Orgeron
Navy	Ken Niumatalolo	Paul Johnson
Nebraska	Bo Pelini	Bill Callahan
Northern Illinois	Jerry Kill	Joe Novak
Southern Methodist	June Jones	Phil Bennett
Southern Mississippi	Larry Fedora	Jeff Bower
Texas A&M	Mike Sherman	Dennis Franchione
UCLA	Rick Neuheisel	Karl Dorrell
Washington State	Paul Wulff	Bill Doba
West Virginia	Bill Stewart	Rich Rodriguez

a-Bowden (3-3) stepped down on October 13 and was replaced by Swinney (4-3).

Preseason *USA Today* Coaches Poll

1	Georgia (22)	1438	14	Texas Tech	644
2	Southern California (14)	1430	15	Virginia Tech	568
3	Ohio State (14)	1392	16	Arizona State	560
4	Oklahoma (3)	1329	17	Brigham Young	547
5	Florida (5)	1293	18	Tennessee	506
6	LSU (3)	1163	19	Illinois	422
7	Missouri	1143	20	Oregon	399
8	West Virginia	1008	21	South Florida	350
9	Clemson	999	22	Penn State	313
10	Texas	979	23	Wake Forest	203
11	Auburn	888	24	Michigan	112
12	Wisconsin	747	25	Fresno State	91
13	Kansas	714			

August 30, 2008

(Th) SOUTH CAROLINA 34 North Carolina State 0: Destruction of former ACC rival Wolfpack (0-1) was nice start for coach Steve Spurrier and his Gamecocks (1-0), who needed big win to eliminate bad taste from 5 straight losses that formed season-end collapse of 2007. Gamecocks D, under direction of new coordinator Ellis Johnson, dominated in posting South Carolina's 1st shutout since 2006 opener vs. Mississippi State. Defenders were especially impressive considering 4 INTs served up by 1st-time Gamecocks starter, QB Tommy Beecher (12-22/106y). With Beecher leaving game with 3rd Q head injury, Carolina fortunes turned on play of his replacement, former starting QB Chris Smelley (5-5/92y). Smelley, kept upright by line that allowed 5 sacks of Beecher, led 3 TD drives in 4th Q, capping 2 with scoring passes of 20y to WR Dion LeCorn and 13y to TE Jared Cook. Wolfpack had enjoyed moderate success in 1st H behind TB Andre Brown (21/101y) and trailed by only 3-0 at H. NC State QB Daniel Evans (4-12/37y) threw 2 INTs in 2nd H, including 2nd play of 3rd Q to Carolina CB Carlos Thomas. It occurred at Wolfpack 9YL and set up 1y TD run by Gamecocks RB Mike Davis (14/101y). Davis' TD gave Gamecocks 10-0 lead, which was more than enough for D that allowed only 138y O.

(Th) Wake Forest 41 BAYLOR 13: Precision field generalship of Wake Forest (1-0) QB Riley Skinner (27-36/220y, 3 TDs) prevailed as he became Deacons' all-time winning QB with 19. Thorough 1st H dominance by Wake D sent teams off at H at 20-6. But, Bears had gotten brief 2nd Q spark from frosh QB Robert Griffin (11-19/125y, and 11/29y, TD rushing) when he jitter-bugged 22y on sideline scamper before handing to big RB Jacoby Jones, who stormed 12y to TD on fine trap blocks by Baylor line. That pulled Bears to within 17-6, but when Skinner tossed pair of TD passes in 3rd Q, including 2nd scoring grab by WR Chip Brinkman, Deacons had iced it at 34-6.

(Th) STANFORD 36 Oregon State 28: As Oregon State (0-1) lost its 2nd late-game FUM in EZ, coaches had to wonder if it finally was time to start disciplining players who hopelessly tried to extend ball over GL, only to lose it. Beavers WR Darrell Catchings went airborne to try to stretch across GL with 47 secs left, and when S Taylor Skaufel knocked ball through EZ for touchback, Stanford (1-0) had earned its opening night upset. Cardinal, playing with considerably more aggression in coach Jim Harbaugh's

2nd season, sent bruising soph TB Toby Gerhart (19/147y) to 1y TD in 2nd Q, followed soon thereafter by Gerhart's smashing 46y TD run. Beavers, however, used perimeter passing of QB Lyle Moevao (34-54/404y, 3 TDs, 2 INTs) to knot it 17-17 as Moevao found WR Shane Morales with short TD pass 14 secs before intermission. With score tied 20-20 late in 3rd Q, game turned on odd bounce near Oregon State GL: Under blitz pressure from own 9YL, Moevao tried swing pass to frosh RB Ryan McCants. But, backward incompletion flew past EZ sideline after hitting at 1YL. Safety gave Stanford 22-20 lead, and after free kick, Cardinal converted on opening play of 4th Q when QB Tavita Pritchard (10-17/91y, TD) swung short pass to RB Anthony Kimble for 15y TD.

Bowling Green 27 PITTSBURGH 17: Season of promise began with thud for Pittsburgh (0-1), who wasted early 14-0 lead in losing at home to MAC team for 1st time after 24 wins. No. 25 Panthers lived up to press clippings in opening 20 mins, dominating with 137y to 6y O. But, Bowling Green (1-0) rally seemed inevitable after its D shackled Pitt star TB LeSean McCoy (23/71y, TD) and forced 4 TOs. Falcons FB Jimmy Scheidler contributed 2 TD receptions, including BG's 1st score on 5y pass by WR Freddie Barnes. Scheidler later rambled 22y with short pass from QB Tyler Sheehan (24-40/163y, TD, INT) to set up go-ahead TD late in 3rd Q on 8y run by TB Anthony Turner. Pittsburgh's next 2 series ended with FUMs, latter caused by CB Antonio Smith on Pitt QB Bill Stull (29-51/264y, TD, INT), snared by DE Angelo Mangone and returned 6y to Pitt 11YL. Sheehan scored 2 plays later for 20-17 lead. Panthers still had 3 possessions remaining in which to rally, and each reached Falcons territory only to fail.

Southern California 52 VIRGINIA 7: In disastrous 1st Q, Virginia (0-1) spent too much time standing in its decorative EZ, either catching long KOs or trying to punt out of trouble. Meanwhile, Southern California (1-0) QB Mark Sanchez (26-35/338y,3 TDs, INT) shrugged off dislocated kneecap of 3 weeks earlier and sparked Trojans to swift 21-0 lead on opening trio of possessions. TBs Stafon Johnson and C.J. Gable (9/73y, TD) tallied on short and long runs respectively, while in between Sanchez flipped short pass to another top TB, Joe McKnight (6/60y), who cruised 10y to score. Virginia went 62y on PEN-aided drive to TB Mikell Simpson's TD run late in 1st Q, but Cavs were dominated on O by wide margin at game's end: 558y to 187y. Sanchez threw 2 TD passes in 3rd Q to extend Troy's lead to 38-7. In all, 7 different Trojans reached EZ.

East Carolina 27 Virginia Tech 22 (Charlotte): East Carolina (1-0) beat Virginia Tech (0-1) at own special-teams game as WR T.J. Lee provided winning pts with stunning, late 27y TD RET of his punt-block. Lee came in unblocked to swat Va Tech P Brent Bowden's boot. There remained 1:52 on clock, but Hokies' final series could produce only 3y. Pirates outgained Hokies 369y to 243y as QB Patrick Pinkney (19-23/211y) was top O performer with TD both passing and running. His 3y scoring keeper with 4:05 remaining pulled underdog Pirates to within 22-20. Sr QB Sean Glennon (14-23/139y, 2 INTs) struggled with his passing, and Virginia Tech could gain only 35/104y rushing. Still, midway through 2nd Q, Va Tech had gained only 104y on 24 plays but enjoyed 14-0 lead: After Va Tech took 7-0 lead early in 2nd Q on CB Stephan Virgil's 30y FUM TD RET, Pirates muffed ensuing KO at their 25YL, and Hokies needed 6 plays to score on 6y run by RB Kenny Lewis (11/62y). With less than 4 mins remaining in 1st H, East Carolina LB Nick Johnson came up with 19y INT RET to 1YL, and RB Jonathan Williams scored to slice H deficit to 14-7. Pirates took 2nd H's opening possession 61y to Pinkney's 12y TD pass to WR Jamar Bryant. But, Hokies retained lead as Virgil returned blocked x-pt 98y for 16-13 lead. Loss snapped 17-game win streak for Hokies in games in which they blocked at least 1 kick or punt.

Alabama 34 Clemson 10 (Atlanta): As season started, no. 9 Clemson (0-1) was considered trendy pick for national title while experts seemed to agree no. 24 Alabama (1-0) was year away from greatness in coach Nick Saban's 2nd season. Tigers may have had O playmakers, but inexperienced line was unable to ignite attack: QB Cullen Harper (20-34/188y, INT), who threw for 2991y in 2007, was sacked 3 times and harried throughout; RBs James Davis (6/13y) and C.J. Spiller (2/7y), who combined for 1832y rushing in 2007, never found any openings; and WR Aaron Kelly (5/28y), who caught 88/1081y in 2007, was held well in check. "Obviously, we are not the ninth-ranked team in the country," grumbled losing coach Tommy Bowden. Holding ball for more than 41 mins, Alabama's unheralded O enjoyed whopping 80 to 48 play advantage, with 17 runs each called for RB Mark Ingram (96y rushing) and RB Glen Coffee (90y rushing). Crimson Tide finished with unbelievable 239y to 0y rushing edge. QB John Parker Wilson (22-30/180y) pitched 2 TDs and ran for another while becoming Bama's all-time leader in completions with 500. Wilson's 2nd TD pass went to heralded frosh WR Julio Jones (4/28y, TD). Tide K Leigh Tiffin made 4 FGs in 5 tries, including 54y boot for new career long. Spiller gave Clemson brief spark by authoring 96y KO TD RET to open 2nd H. Now trailing 23-10, Clemson could only produce 10y on next 2 possessions as Alabama D refused to budge. Win was Alabama's 12th straight over Clemson, although last had occurred in 1975.

Utah 25 MICHIGAN 23: Rich Rodriguez's debut was spoiled as he became only 2nd Wolverines (0-1) coach to drop his opener at home. Previous lid-lifter loser was Bump Elliott in 1959. Despite weak rushing attack, inexperienced Michigan led much of 1st H, scoring on 8y misdirection TD pass from QB Nick Sheridan (11-19/98y, TD, INT) to RB Michael Shaw and K K.C. Lopata's 50y FG. Utah (1-0) K Louie Sakoda (4 FGs) nailed trio of 2nd Q FGs, and cool QB Brian Johnson threw for 21-33/305y, including 19y TD to WR Bradon Godfrey, who back-peddled across GL with 13 secs left in 1st H for 22-10 edge. Trailing 25-10 after Sakoda's 53y FG in 3rd Q, Michigan blocked Sakoda's punt and rallied behind reserve QB Steven Threet (8-19/69y, TD), who lofted perfect 33y TD pass to WR Junior Hemingway in 4th Q. When Wolverines RB Sam McGuffie tallied on 3y run up middle with 6:26 to go, Threet's try for tying 2-pt pass play was too high for WR Tony Clemons in back of EZ.

NORTHWESTERN 30 Syracuse 10: Back after injury-riddled 2007 season, Northwestern (1-0) TB Tyrell Sutton (21/144y) overcame costly FUM early in 3rd Q to catch 12y go-ahead TD pass from QB C.J. Bacher (23-35/215y, 3 TDs, INT) while also racking up his 13th career 100y rushing game. Coming off 2-10 season in 2007, indoor-acclimated Syracuse (0-1) lost its 13th straight game on grass, but it scored 1st when it spent 10 plays to go 63y (including 36y of its 122y game-end rushing total) off opening KO to K Patrick Shadle's 36y FG. On 1st snap of 3rd Q, Sutton was thrown for 7y loss and coughed up FUM at his 9YL. Orange took 3 plays for RB Curtis Brinkley (9/49y, TD) to go across for 2y TD and 10-9 lead. After Sutton's TD catch on ensuing possession, Wildcats advanced to 23-10 lead later in 3rd Q when S Brandon Smith picked off Syracuse QB Andrew Robinson (14-28/103y, INT) and dashed 26y on INT TD RET. Northwestern gained 484y, while permitting only 68y in 2nd H.

Missouri 52 Illinois 42 (St. Louis): Despite flying somewhat below national radar, this compelling opener turned into another wild border duel between no. 6 Missouri (1-0) and no. 20 Illinois (0-1). Foes racked up 1081y in combined O, and Illini rallied from deficits of 31-10 at H and 45-20 in 3rd Q to pull within 45-35 in 4th Q on WR Will Judson's 65y TD catch from QB Juice Williams (26-42/451y, 5 TDs, 2 INTs). Missouri LB Sean Weatherspoon halted Illinois in 4th Q with INT at own 26YL and later tore pass from hands of Illini RB Daniel Dufrene (13/75y), returning it 35y for TD and 52-35 lead with 3:18 to play. As usual, Mizzou QB Chase Daniel served as O catalyst by passing 26-45/323y, 3 TDs, INT. Tigers WR Jeremy Maclin (234y all-purpose, including 45y punt RET) missed much of game with leg injury but returned KO for 99y TD in middle of 2nd Q which provided last lead change at 17-13. Illinois QB Williams was able to nearly double his career-best, single-game passing y of 227y.

OREGON 44 Washington 10: Oregon (1-0), which ended 2007 with QB injuries, experienced another setback as starting QB Justin Roper (7-11/114y, TD, INT) suffered concussion. In stepped JC transfer QB Jeremiah Masoli (9-17/126y), whose long TD passes to WRs Jaison Williams and Jeffrey Maehl fueled 23-pt 4th Q for Ducks. Trumpeted frosh RB Chris Polk was among 10 Huskies (0-1) underclassmen who started, even though Polk was limited to 14/19y rushing. Washington FB Paul Homer plunged over from 1YL late n 2nd Q to give Huskies life, trailing only 14-10. But, Ducks RB Jeremiah Johnson (15/124y, 2 TDs) scored his 2nd TD 4 mins into 3rd Q, and Ducks were on their way at 21-10 to series-record 5th win in row over UW.

(Mon) Fresno State 24 RUTGERS 7: It was nightmare holiday for Scarlet Knights (0-1), who labored fruitlessly in Fresno State (1-0) red zone in 1st H. At helm of O that gained 202y in 1st H, QB Mike Teel (20-39/263y, 2 INTs) had advanced Scarlet Knights into Fresno territory 6 times without pts. New K San San Te missed 2 FG tries in 1st H, including chip-shot 22y effort after bad snap. Later going 70y to 1st-and-goal at Fresno 10YL, Rutgers inexplicably called 4 running plays by back-up RB Mason Robinson (6/12y), who was stopped for 1y gain on quick-tempo 4th-and-4 play. Despite traveling cross-country for TV match-up, Bulldogs displayed their own 2nd H energy as they scored 24 pts in final 30 mins. Fresno QB Tom Brandstater (11-24/216y) threw for 163y in 2nd H with 139y coming on 3 game-breaking plays. Brandstater hit WR Devon Wiley with short pass which Wiley took 31y to set up 31y FG by K Kevin Goesslingfer for 3-0 lead in 3rd Q. On next Fresno series, Brandstater connected with WR Seyi Ajirotutu (3/116y) for 77y gain, and RB Ryan Mathews (26/163y) ran for 1st of his 3 TDs on next snap. In 4th Q, after Rutgers went 81y to pull to within 10-7 on 1y TD run by RB Kordell Young (26/94y), Brandstater and Ajirotutu converted 3rd-and-23 with 31y connection to 1YL. Mathews soon scored his 2nd TD. Giant-killer Fresno State logged its 13th win over BCS team since 2000.

(Mon) UCLA 27 Tennessee 24 (OT): Coach Rick Neuheisel's return to UCLA (1-0) became thrilling OT upset victory, made possible by D that he called "relentless" and remarkable 2nd H turnaround of transfer QB Kevin Craft (25-43/259y, TD, 4 INTs). Making poor decisions in 1st H when he threw 7-18/66y and 4 INTs, former 3rd-stringer Craft was new man in 2nd H. "It was just a matter of settling down," Craft said. "I wasn't nervous at all. I just wasn't in a good rhythm. In the second half, I found it." He led 80y drive to TB Raymond Carter's TD sweep to right pylon for 17-14 lead 8 mins into 4th Q. Tennessee (0-1) went back ahead 21-17 on TB Montario Hardesty's 20y TD romp with 1:54 to play. Craft answered by looking for key catches by WR Taylor Embree (4/53y) as he pitched 6-6/71y on trip to TE Ryan Moya's 3y TD catch over middle with 27 secs left. QB Jonathan Crompton (19-41/189y, INT) quickly brought Vols downfield for K Daniel Lincoln's tying 47y FG on last play of regulation. But, Lincoln missed his next 3-pt try after UCLA K Kai Forbath had nailed 42y FG in top half of OT. Late in 1st Q, pair of Bruins frosh had conspired on blocked punt for TD: LBs Akeem Ayers blocked it, which LB Sean Westgate carried for 17y TD. But, Vols went off at H ahead 14-7 when LB Nevin McKenzie raced 61y to score on INT of Craft late in 2nd Q.

USA Today Coaches Poll September 2

1	Southern California (23)	1462	14	Arizona State	679
2	Georgia (20)	1442	15	Brigham Young	629
3	Ohio State (10)	1385	16	Oregon	566
4	Oklahoma (2)	1344	17	Alabama	538
5	Florida (3)	1295	18	South Florida	480
6	LSU (3)	1202	19	Penn State	450
7	Missouri	1197	20	Wake Forest	388
8	West Virginia	1035	21	Fresno State	269
9	Texas	1030	22	Clemson	186
10	Auburn	962	23	Utah	158
11	Wisconsin	853	24	South Carolina	134
12	Kansas	820	25	Illinois	92
13	Texas Tech	732			

September 6, 2008

(Th) VANDERBILT 24 South Carolina 17: South Carolina (1-1) sought revenge against Commodores (2-0) for upset last October when Gamecocks were ranked no. 6. But Vanderbilt was motivated too: "They thought it was a fluke, and that motivated us," commented DE Steven Stone (6 tackles, sack). This was especially true in 2nd H when Vandy scored 3 straight TDs to convert 10-3 H deficit into 24-10 4th Q lead.

Despite losing stat battle 325y to 225y, Commodores played exceptional special teams and won TO battle 3 to 1. Vanderbilt produced 1st key play early in 3rd Q when S Ryan Hamilton recovered punt that brushed up against South Carolina blocker CB Addison Williams at Carolina 31YL. Commodores QB Chris Nickson (8-13/90y, TD) quickly tied it 10-10 with 31y TD pass to TE Branden Barden, who made impressive catch for his 1st-ever TD. Gamecocks QB Chris Smelley (23-39/233y, 2 TDs, 2 INTs) answered with 66y trip to Vandy 25YL, but Vandy special teams delivered again as DT Greg Billinger (6 tackles, 2 sacks) blocked FG try by K Ryan Stuccop. This time Nickson needed 5 plays to march now-potent Commodores O—held to only 50y in 1st H—to EZ, scoring on 1y keeper. After Carolina missed FG, Vandy went up 24-10 on 13y run by TB Jared Hawkins (17/84y). Down 2 TDs with 9:38 left, Cocks Smelley delivered 24y run with 4-4/41y passing, capped by 5y TD to WR Freddie Brown. With momentum swinging back to Carolina, its D forced 3-and-out and took over at Vanderbilt 48YL with 4:50 remaining. Smelley completed 2 quick passes to Vandy 34YL. Commodores Billinger and Stone responded with sacks on consecutive plays to force late punt, and Hawkins' 5/24y running clinched Vandy's 1st home win over ranked foe since 31-9 win over Mississippi in 1992.

Georgia Tech 19 BOSTON COLLEGE 16: With short gains and FG attempts dominating action, single O play proved difference: Georgia Tech (2-0) RB Jonathan Dwyer (18/108y) raced 43y with pitchout for winning TD midway through 4th Q. Yellow Jackets D stiffened on ensuing Boston College (1-1) drive once Eagles reached Tech 34YL. Facing 4th-and-5 with 4:20 remaining, Eagles lost ball on downs as QB Chris Crane threw 4th straight incompletion. Jackets QB Josh Nesbitt (6-13/73y, and 15/50y, TD rushing) then killed clock, gaining 1st downs on 30y run and 4th-and-1 conversion. Crane (18-35/142y, TD, 2 INTs), who threw 7y TD pass to WR Ifeanyi Momah late in 3rd Q to give BC 16-10 lead, struggled in 1st home start. Crane suffered sack for safety, lost FUM, and threw 2 INTs, all in 2nd H. In 1st H, BC had taken 9-7 lead to H after K Steve Aponavicius booted 3 FGs. Despite netting 3 FUM RECs in 1st H, Eagles squandered TD opportunities and Aponavicius also missed 30y FG try at end of 1st H.

WAKE FOREST 30 Mississippi 28: His smile said it all. Wake Forest (2-0) K Sam Swank, college football's active leader in FGs (62), trotted onto field with 3 secs remaining, Deacons trailing 28-27, sporting look of confident man. Swank calmly booted 41y FG for his 3rd successful 3-ptr of game as Wake Forest won 400th game in school history. "I was smiling because I knew I was going to make it," said Swank. "I was confident and that's how you have to be going out to kick a game-winning field goal." Wake QB Riley Skinner (32-43/267y, 2 TDs) led winning 56y drive, completing 5-8/41y with Rebels CB Marshay Green contributing 15y interference PEN. Mississippi (1-1) QB Jevan Snead (20-31/253y, 4 TDs, INT) had sparked 15-play, 80y drive to put Rebels ahead with 63 secs left on impromptu 5y TD pass to WR Cordera Eason on 4th-and-3: Snead raced right, and left, and back right again to escape Wake pass rush before releasing ball as he was hit by DT John Russell. Snead, Mississippi's much-ballyhooed transfer from Texas, needed to scramble for most of game, with his 3rd TD pass, 31y to WR Dexter McCluster (4/64y) for 21-20 lead early in 4th Q, also featured nifty bit of escape. Facing banged-up Rebels D, Skinner had more time in pocket and it showed, especially on final drive. Wake Forest sr WR D.J. Boldin caught 11/123y.

Northwestern 24 DUKE 20: Duke Blues Devils (1-1) outplayed Northwestern (2-0) much of game, enjoying 39 mins possession time and outgaining Wildcats 472y to 328y. Northwestern D, however, stopped several 4th down plays on Duke's last 2 drives, which upheld RB Omar Conteh's go-ahead TD run with 9 mins left. Devils QB Thaddeus Lewis (24-42/256y), who scored on 16y run early in 4th Q, apparently pulled out go-ahead 24y TD pass to RB Clifford Harris (18/86y, TD) on 4th down with less than 2 mins remaining, but top Duke LT Cameron Goldberg was called for holding PEN. Lewis then missed 4th down throw from 34YL for frosh WR Johnny Williams (11/135y). Earlier on 4th down in 4th Q, Lewis failed to hit Williams from 13YL. Cats RB Tyrell Sutton (16/66y, 2 TDs) had scored on 18 and 4y runs for 17-10 H lead.

EAST CAROLINA 24 West Virginia 3: East Carolina's momentum from upset of Virginia Tech continued; Pirates (2-0) scored TD on opening possession and never looked back against West Virginia (1-1), team that had beaten them 48-7 in 2007. Pirates rolled up 386y and 20 1st downs. With QB Pat White (11-18/72y, and 20/97y rushing) held somewhat in check, West Virginia could crack 30YL only once, producing 26y FG by K Pat McAfee late in 2nd Q. That made it 10-3 for ECU, and Pirates soon forced WVU FUM to set up quick 35y drive that featured hot QB Patrick Pinkney (22-28/236y, TD) connecting with jr WR Alex Taylor (3/41y) on passes of 22y and 13y to score TD for 17-3 H edge. East Carolina D took charge of 2nd H, holding Mountaineers to 120y (251y for game) with longest drive going 31y. Pirates' win was 1st over top-10 team since 1999 when ECU topped no. 9 Miami by 27-23.

FLORIDA 26 Miami 3: Florida (2-0) was big favorite to deliver Gators' 1st win since 1985 over young Miami (1-1) squad. Gators jumped out early with 7 pts on opening possession after Miami's 14y punt set them up at Hurricanes 35YL. QB Tim Tebow (21-35/256y, and 13/55y rushing) needed only 5 plays for 14y TD pass to TE Aaron Hernandez (5/58y, TD). Hurricanes avoided shutout in 2nd Q when soph K Matt Bosher booted 50y FG. Gators spent most of next 2 Qs on their side of 50YL until 17-pt 4th Q explosion finally put away determined Canes. Gators' most impressive advance was final 95y drive as Tebow hit 4 passes/95y with TD coming on 19y pitch to WR Louis Murphy (4/77y, TD). Florida D, led by dynamic LB Brandon Spikes (11 tackles), was in command all night, holding QB Robert Marve (10-18/69y) and Miami O to 140y. In snapping 6-game losing streak to Miami—once annual series had become sporadic—Florida coach Urban Meyer upped his 4-year record against fellow Sunshine State schools to 6-0.

PENN STATE 45 Oregon State 14: With pair of DL starters suspended over mid-week marijuana arrests, Lions (2-0) still mauled Beavers (0-2) from outset of game. Penn State QB Daryll Clark (14-23/215y, 2 TDs, and 5/61y, TD rushing) launched quick onslaught that built 28-0 lead less than 4 mins into 2nd Q. Nittany Lions TB Evan Royster (17/141y) scored on runs of 15, 28, and 4y to help boost H edge to 35-7. Oregon State's little frosh TB Jacquizz Rodgers (22/99y, 2 TDs) scored on 12y run in 2nd Q and added 4th Q TD run. Penn State TE Andrew Quarless also was to have been suspended, but suited up without playing when it was rumored he turned out to have not been involved in incident with his punished teammates. Afterward, coach Joe Paterno was asked about Quarless' status and feigned ignorance: "Was Quarless there? How did he look? Aw, I'm not going to talk about that stuff!"

OKLAHOMA 52 Cincinnati 26: QB Sam Bradford hit 5 TD passes among his 29-38/ career-best-to-date 395y effort as Oklahoma (2-0) won its 20th straight home game. Sooners TE Jermaine Gresham (7/93y) caught pair of TD passes, while much-awaited WR Ryan Broyles set OU frosh receiving y record on 7/141y, TD. Contest was in some doubt after Cincinnati (1-1) WR Mardy Gilyard (7/119y) raced 97y on KO TD RET in middle of 3rd Q to pull within 28-20 as Gilyard contributed school-record 365y all-purpose. Broyles soon made leaping 43y catch, and TB Demarco Murray (15/88y, TD) used trap block by pulling RG Brandon Walker to burst 11y up middle for TD that launched 24-pt run by Oklahoma. Bearcats QB Dustin Grutza (19-29/218y, TD, INT), who in 2nd Q scored on short sneak and threw 14y TD pass to WR Dominick Goodman (6/60y, TD), broke his right leg under avalanche of Sooners pass rushers in 4th Q.

OKLAHOMA STATE 56 Houston 37: All summer, billionaire Boone Pickens had run TV ads calling for wind and natural gas solutions to America's vexing energy issues. Oklahoma State (2-0) had easy football solution, claiming its 13th straight home-opener win in at newly-expanded Boone Pickens Stadium. Victory produced Cowboys' 1st-ever runner and receiver who each tallied 200y or more: RB Kendall Hunter rushed for 22/210y, 2 TDs and WR Dez Bryant caught 9/236y, 3 TDs. Yet, Houston (1-1) led 16-14 at H because Oklahoma State turned ball over 3 times that led to 2y TD run by RB Bryce Beall, 27y FG by K Ben Bell, and short TD throw to TE Mark Hafner by QB Case Keenum (35-61/387y, 4 TDs). Cougars S Ernest Miller returned INT 71y to Cowboys 5YL before Hafner caught 2nd Q TD pass. Oklahoma State took lead for good at 21-16 when RB Keith Toston went 28y to score 1:35 into 3rd Q. Cowpokes QB Zac Robinson passed sparingly but effectively with 14-21/320y, 3 TDs, 2 INTs.

Rice 42 MEMPHIS 35: With 11 secs left, Owls (2-0) frosh DB Chris Jammer raced 69y down left sideline for TD to break 35-35 deadlock after stepping in front of pass by Memphis (0-2) QB Arkelon Hall (29-38/373y, 3 TDs, 2 INTs). Just 1:04 earlier, Rice QB Chase Clement (26-44/318y, TD, 2 INTs, and 15/80y, 2 TDs rushing) had scrambled to 9y TD and followed with 2-pt bullet to TE James Casey (11/208y) to tie it. Hall and WR Maurice Jones (9/173y, 2 TDs) had collaborated for Tigers on 45 and 39y scores to build 7-3 lead in 2nd Q and 35-20 lead in 4th Q. Ace WR Jarrett Dillard (8/66y, TD) nabbed 5y TD from Clement with 6:28 to go to set stage for Rice's rally.

Brigham Young 28 WASHINGTON 27: Afterward, much was made of Huskies' excessive celebration PEN which set up victory-clinching x-pt block by BYU (2-0) DE Jan Jorgensen. Washington (1-1) QB Jake Locker (17-32/204y, TD, and 18/62y, 2 TDs rushing) had scrambled for 3y to tumble over GL to bring Huskies within 28-27 with 2 secs to play. In jumping up in celebration, Locker flipped ball over his head as he greeted his teammates. Ref Larry Farina claimed his crew made "no judgment call" as new 2008 rule specifically required 15y PEN, even if nearly everyone agreed Locker made no attempt to mock opponent nor to "bring attention to himself." After PEN walk-off, Huskies K Ryan Perkins faced 35y conv kick to send game to OT until Jorgensen and other Cougars penetrated middle to block kick. Cougars QB Max Hall (30-41/338y, INT) had pitched trio of TD passes, including 15y score over middle to star TE Dennis Pitta (10/148y, TD) to provide 28-21 edge with 3:31 remaining. Earlier in nail-biting affair, Hall had whipped 2 TD passes, and Locker ran for 14y score and fired 48y TD to frosh WR Jermaine Kearse in 14-14 1st H deadlock. Rugged FB Luke Kravitz blasted for TD to give Washington its only lead at 21-14 midway in 3rd Q, but BYU's comeback meant Cougars would extend nation's longest winning streak to 12 games.

USA Today Coaches Poll September 7

1	Southern California (34)	1481	14	Oregon	665
2	Georgia (18)	1454	15	Brigham Young	628
3	Oklahoma (3)	1370	16	Alabama	611
4	Florida (3)	1306	17	Penn State	547
5	Ohio State (1)	1289	18	South Florida	475
6	Missouri	1212	19	Wake Forest	419
7	LSU (2)	1198	20	East Carolina	375
8	Texas	1069	21	Fresno State	300
9	Auburn	1017	22	Utah	235
10	Wisconsin	946	23	Clemson	175
11	Kansas	854	24	West Virginia	145
12	Texas Tech	755	25	California	128
13	Arizona State	737			

September 13, 2008

(Fri) SOUTH FLORIDA 37 Kansas 34: Unknown South Florida (3-0) frosh K Maikon Bonani replaced struggling K Delbert Alvarado and stunned Kansas (2-1) with game-winning, 43y FG that snaked inside right upright as time expired. Moments earlier, Jayhawks QB Todd Reesing (34-51/373y, 3 TDs, INT) had thrown INT that Bulls S Nate Allen returned 40y to Kansas 27YL with 30 secs remaining. Reesing, now 14-2 as starter, had rallied Jayhawks to tie from 2-TD, 4th Q deficit with scoring passes of 18y to WR Jonathan Wilson (10/171y, 2 TDs) and 14y to RB Angus Quigley. Kansas D next forced punt. Reesing moved Jayhawks O from own 7YL to So Florida 40YL but needed 1 more completion to get into FG range. His pass instead found Allen. Firebrand Bulls QB Matt Grothe (32-45/338y, 2 TDs) had dominated middle of game when he rallied his team from 20-3 deficit with 31 straight pts from end of 2nd Q through early 4th Q. During 18-min span, Bulls outgained Kansas 346y to 15y. Grothe began scoring burst with 28y TD run to cap 4-play, 69y drive near end of 1st H that

breathed new life into Bulls. South Florida dominated 3rd Q with scoring drives of 76, 66, and 71y to 17 pts. After Grothe hit 37y TD pass to WR A.J. Love (5/83y) to build lead to 14 pts, Kansas answered with TD drives of 78 and 54y sandwiching 3-and-out by Bulls. Kansas had momentum but with time elapsing could not overcome final mistake.

MARYLAND 35 California 27: Slumbering Golden Bears (2-1), who entered game with 52-pt scoring avg, took long time to awaken in 2nd H. Still contest never was as close as final tally would indicate. Maryland (2-1), fresh off embarrassing 10-pt defeat by Middle Tennessee State, rattled California from onset of noon KO, which apparently was too early, too hot and humid for Cal. Terps virtually iced game with TDs on their 1st 3 possessions. With QB Chris Turner (15-19/156y, 2 TDs) providing improved QB play and RB Da'Rel Scott (19/87y) scoring twice, Maryland owned 21-3 lead in 2nd Q. Turner's 27y scoring pass to WR Darrius Heyward-Bey (2/59y) midway through 3rd Q boosted Terps to 28-6 lead. Bears QB Kevin Riley (33-58/423y, 3 TDs, INT) threw 3 TD passes within incredible 5-min span of 4th Q as Cal made it interesting at game's end. Final onside-KO went OB—Cal went 0-3 on onside-KO tries in 4th Q—and Maryland secured victory, 1st against Pacific Conf since 1955's win over UCLA.

VANDERBILT 38 Rice 21: Pair of "Brainiac" schools squared off, each with rare undefeated record. Superb Rice (2-1) WR Jarrett Dillard (7/105y, TD) opened 1st Q scoring with 26y reception from QB Chase Clement (25-39/299y, TD, INT, and TD rushing). WR James Casey gave Owls 21-14 lead late in 2nd Q on 2y TD run, but Vanderbilt (3-0) quickly rallied with 60y trip to tying 7y TD run by RB Jared Hawkins (20/107y, TD) in last 15 secs of 1st H. Commodores D blanked Rice in 2nd H, forcing 3 punts and stopping Owls' only serious advance on downs at Vandy 30YL. Vanderbilt CB D.J. Moore (31y INT RET) returned punt 67y to Owls 1YL in 4th Q to set up QB Chris Nickson (7-16/71y, and 13/85y rushing) for his 2nd rushing TD for 38-21 lead.

Georgia 14 SOUTH CAROLINA 7: Despite theories that former no. 1 Bulldogs (3-0) needed to rout South Carolina (1-2) to sway poll voters, this rivalry produced usual hard-fought game in oppressive heat. With less than 30 secs remaining, South Carolina O faced 2nd-and-20 on Georgia 27YL with QB Chris Smelley (23-39/271y, TD, INT) dropping back to pass. Georgia S Reshad Jones (6 tackles) stepped in for game-preserving INT at 3YL with 13 secs left. Bulldogs had not taken lead for good until 3rd Q when TB Knowshon Moreno (20/79y, TD), held in check by swarming Carolina D, scored on 4y run. QB Matt Stafford (15-25/146y), who had set up Moreno's TD with 30y run, quickly connected with WR Kris Durham for 2-pt conv and 14-7 lead. Bulldogs D preserved victory by slimmest of margins, forcing FUM by Gamecocks RB Mike Davis (12/22y) on Georgia 1YL midway through 4th Q. South Carolina managed 4th Q drives of 66y—before UGa LB Rennie Curran (6 tackles) forced Davis' FUM to CB Asher Allen (6 tackles) in EZ—58y, and 63y before Jones' INT. Gamecocks were forced deep by Georgia P Brian Mimbs (6 punts/49.8y avg), who boomed punts of 45, 77, and 50y in 4th Q. "My gut has churned more in this series, and on this field, than anywhere else at Georgia," said winning coach Mark Richt.

Oregon 32 PURDUE 26 (OT): Seemingly in control at 20-3 in 2nd Q, Boilermakers (1-1) counted on their aces to lead O that tallied on its opening 4 tries: QB Curtis Painter (26-50/207y, 2 INTs), who had up-and-down game, and RB Kory Sheets (29/180y, 2 TDs), who raced 80y for score on game's 2nd snap. Oregon (3-0), boasting nation's leading O, outscored Purdue 29-6 from K Matt Evensen's FG on last play of 1st H. CB Jairus Byrd got Ducks back in it at 20-13 when he cut right and sped 87y to TD on punt RET with 4:41 left in 3rd Q. RB LeGarrette Blount (12/132y, 2 TDs) followed his 72y burst with 5y TD run to knot it 20-20 late in 3rd Q. After trade of FGs, Purdue K Chris Summers (4 FGs) missed 44y 3-pt try on last play of regulation. Pair of opposing FGs in 1st OT, left Boilers with 1st chance in 2nd session, but Painter was sacked, and it forced another long miss by Summers. Oregon had lost QB Justin Roper (20-48/197y, 2 INTs) to twisted knee in 1st OT and turned to RBs Chris Harper, who made 19y in 2 tries in 2nd OT and Blount, who went off left side for winning 3y TD.

NOTRE DAME 35 Michigan 17: With help from bumbling visitors, Notre Dame (2-0) built 3-TD 1st Q lead that proved too difficult for struggling Wolverines (1-2). Committing 6 TOs, Michigan proved that switch to new head coach Rich Rodriguez's spread O was difficult. Notre Dame O was unspectacular with 260y, but benefitted from avg scoring-drive starting point at Michigan 44YL. Irish O-line perfectly protected QB Jimmy Clausen (10-21/147y, 2 TDs, 2 INTs) after allowing 8 sacks in Wolverines' 2007 romp over ND. Clausen's big moment occurred late in 1st Q on 48y scoring pass to emerging WR Golden Tate (4/127y) that bumped Irish lead to commanding 21-0. Notre Dame RB Robert Hughes (19/79y) added 2 rushing TDs. Frosh RB Sam McGuffie provided bright spot for Wolverines, rushing 25/131y and scoring TD on 40y reception from QB Steven Threet (16-23/175y, TD). Looking to rebound from disastrous 3-9 campaign in 2007, Irish coach Charlie Weis was upbeat despite having both MCL and ACL torn in left knee in 2nd Q when Notre Dame DE John Ryan was blocked OB into back of Weis' leg. "Tommy Brady's got nothing on me," joked Weis of his former protégé, New England Patriots injured QB.

SOUTHERN CALIFORNIA 35 Ohio State 3: Foot injury to Heisman-hopeful TB Beanie Wells and Buckeyes' considerable struggles in 26-14 win over Ohio U previous Saturday seemed to dampen this much-anticipated "Collision in the Coliseum." Prognosticators turned out to be correct as no. 1 USC (2-0) crushed no. 5 Ohio State (2-1). Buckeyes, however, scored 1st going 69y to K Ryan Pretorius' 29y FG. Trojans QB Mark Sanchez (17-28/172y, 4 TDs, INT) executed perfect wheel-pass with FB Stanley Havili (5/49y receiving) for 35y TD late in 1st Q for 7-3 lead and followed with 1y TD lob to frosh TE Blake Ayles off play-action fake in 2nd Q. Vital miscue by Ohio State came when holding PEN nullified TD pass by QB Todd Boeckman (14-21/84y, 2 INTs) on next possession of 2nd Q, and Pretorius missed long FG try. Troy's star LB Rey Maualuga cut across for INT and raced 48y down right sideline later in 2nd Q for intractable 21-3 edge. Sanchez added pair of TD throws in 3rd Q. Without Wells, Bucks could rush for only 71y; heralded frosh QB Tyrelle Pryor chipped in 11/40y.

Wisconsin 13 FRESNO STATE 10: Nail-biter turned out just as experts predicted: tough D battle between 2 hard-hitting, ranked foes. Visiting Wisconsin (3-0) led all way, having tipped 1st Q pass by Fresno State (2-1) QB Tom Brandstater (15-27/225y, TD, INT) that was intercepted by LB DeAndre Levy, who soared high for jump-ball at Bulldogs 27YL. Badgers TE Garrett Graham soon faked block and slipped into EZ to catch 2y TD pass from QB Allan Evridge (12-24/143y, TD) for 7-0 edge. Trailing 10-0 in 3rd Q, Brandstater flipped short pass to WR Devon Wylie, who slipped several tackles to romp 47y and bring Fresno within 10-7. But, Wisconsin D rose up when needed: its unit held after Badgers suffered blocked punt and forced FG that pulled Fresno within 13-10 after Bulldogs RB Ryan Mathews took screen pass 61y to 9YL late in 3rd Q. Bulldogs K Kevin Goessling missed 35y FG try early in 4th Q which would have tied it, and Badgers FB Bill Rentmeester carried tacklers for 8y and 1st down after Wisconsin had been punted back to its 1YL with less than 2 mins left.

BRIGHAM YOUNG 59 Ucla 0: It had been nearly 80 years since UCLA (1-1) had lost so badly: Southern California delivered 1929 crash by 76-0 score. QB Max Hall (27-35/271y, 7 TDs, INT) joined Marc Wilson and Jim McMahon in sharing BYU (2-0) record for 7 TD passes in game. Hall's brother-in-law, TE Dennis Pitta, caught pair of scores, as did WR Austin Collie (10/110y), and RB Harvey Unga. When Unga caught Hall's 7th TD pass midway in 3rd Q, Cougars enjoyed 49-0 lead and Hall headed to bench. Injury-riddled Bruins gained only 9y rushing and turned ball over 4 times, but QB Kevin Craft passed 23-39/230y, INT.

USA Today Coaches Poll September 14

1	Southern California (57)	1518	14	Ohio State	736
2	Oklahoma (1)	1423	15	Penn State	724
3	Georgia (2)	1393	16	South Florida	685
4	Florida (1)	1335	17	East Carolina	508
5	Missouri	1294	18	Wake Forest	498
6	LSU	1233	19	Kansas	416
7	Texas	1128	20	Utah	400
8	Wisconsin	1027	21	Clemson	233
9	Auburn	955	22	West Virginia	159
10	Texas Tech	887	23	Illinois	127
11	Brigham Young	846	24	Arizona State	113
12	Oregon	783	25	Florida State	110
13	Alabama	771			

September 20, 2008

(Th) COLORADO 17 West Virginia 14 (OT): Singer John Denver's voice was all over ESPN as "Rocky Mountain High" and "Take Me Home, Country Roads" were played alternately to exalt this matchup's respective home states. Early on, Golden Buffs (3-0), slight home underdog, filled thin air with passes by QB Cody Hawkins (22-33/179y, 2 TDs, INT), using fast-paced O to jump to 14-0 lead in 1st Q. Hawkins pitched pair of perfectly-placed TD passes to WR Josh Smith for 38y and TE Patrick Devenny for 13y. Calming hand for no. 21 West Virginia (1-2) came from star QB Patrick White (19/148y, 2 TDs rushing, and 10-14/43y), who delivered 44y option dash followed by 6y TD run on QB-draw. Then suddenly, D battle ensued until well into 2nd H. White had 4 completions in 6 passing tries with minus 2y to show for it until finally throwing downfield to WR Dorell Jalloh for 18y gain in 3rd Q. On next play, White faked pass and bolted 39y to tying TD at 14-14. Promising 4th Q drive from WVU 1YL was ruined by Mountaineers' pair of major PENs at midfield. Later, Mountaineers' trick-pass completely missed its mark as RB Jock Sanders ran all alone as receiver. It remained 14-14 in regulation. In 1st OT, WVU K Pat McAfee hit upright with short FG try, and transfer K Aric Goodman nailed 25y FG to win it for Colorado. Pinball frosh RB Rodney Stewart rushed 28/166y as vital cog in Buffs attack.

(Fri) CONNECTICUT 31 Baylor 28: Young and improved Baylor (2-2) went east looking for hard-to-earn win more than 1500 miles from home. Although spilled for 35y in losses, dangerous frosh QB Robert Griffin (14-25/208y) rushed for 46y, scored TD, and threw 3 TD passes to keep Bears in game all night. Mercurial Griffin sparked scoring drive in every Q, which traveled 67, 76, 72, and 70y respectively. Undefeated Connecticut (4-0) traded beefy blows with Baylor, relying on pair of TD runs each from national rushing leader, TB Donald Brown (34/150y), and QB Tyler Lorenzen (13-23/135y, 2 INTs). Bears TE Justin Akers (4/61y) caught 14 and 16y TDs from Griffin in 1st H that ended in 14-14 tie. Lorenzen scrambled 34y late in 3rd Q for 24-21 lead for Huskies. Baylor took 28-24 lead less than 4 mins into 4th Q when Griffin pitched 19y TD to frosh WR Kendall Wright (6/114y, TD). UConn answered after P Desi Cullen bombed 55y punt to pin Bears at their 7YL. After DE Julius Williams sacked Griffin, Baylor could manage only 35y punt, and when fair-catch interference was called, Huskies were in short range for Brown's winning 3y TD run with 6 mins left. Bears LB Joe Pawelek chipped in with 13 tackles and stopped Huskies' opening drive with 33y INT RET that launched Baylor's 1st scoring drive.

PITTSBURGH 21 Iowa 20: Pressure centered on sr P Dave Brytus (8/47.8y avg) when Pittsburgh (2-1) O was unable to gain single 1st down after taking 21-17 lead with 14 mins to go. With clock winding down and Pitt leading 21-20, Brytus boomed critical 57y punt downed at Iowa 1YL. Hawkeyes (3-1) began their last series with 2:19 left but it ended when QB Jake Christensen (12-24/124y) lost FUM at own 16YL, ball stripped away by DE Tony Tucker and recovered by DE Greg Romeus. Panthers had enjoyed early 14-3 lead: QB Bill Stull (11-25/129y, INT) hit 4-6/48y on 73y drive to backup QB Greg Cross' 17y TD run and traveled 54y to Stull's 6y TD run. Iowa trailed 14-10 at H when RB Shonn Greene (23/147y, TD) ran 6/62y to his 6y TD. On Iowa's 3rd Q scoring drive of 73y, Greene gained 4/40y. Meanwhile, Iowa D was holding Pitt to 5 consecutive 3-and-out possessions, and following series ended on INT by CB Amari Spievey (5 tackles, forced FUM, INT). Panthers TB LeSean McCoy (18/78y, TD), held to 18y rushing in 1st H with pair of FUMs, took 28y pass late in 3rd Q and scored TD on 27y run 5 plays later. Hawkeyes could add only 39y FG by K Trent Mossbrucker with 11 mins left.

Virginia Tech 20 NORTH CAROLINA 17: Tar Heels (2-1) D dominated early, surrendering only 66y in 1st H, as LB Mark Paschal would finish game with 12 tackles, including sack, and pass pick-off. Meanwhile, North Carolina QB T.J. Yates (11-18/181y, TD) threw effectively. So, everything appeared rosy for North Carolina after TB Greg Little (18/71y) raced 50y to score late in 3rd Q for 17-3 lead. But situation deteriorated rapidly as Yates left game with badly sprained ankle, that would cost him most of season, and Hokies (3-1) drove 89y to 10y TD run by frosh TB Darren Evans (14/61y). Little soon lost FUM at Tar Heels 30YL, recovered by Virginia Tech S Davon Morgan, and Hokies needed 5 plays to tie it 17-17 on 11y run by TB Kenny Lewis. With untested frosh QB Mike Paulus (3-8/23y, 2 INTs) now at helm of their O, Tar Heels needed to play smart ball. Instead their special teams suffered PENs on KO and on punt after they went 3-and-out. This helped set up Virginia Tech at UNC 29YL so that Hokies K Dustin Keys could boot 45y FG for 20-17 lead with 10:55 left. Carolina was able to drive to Hokies 23YL before CB Victor Harris picked off Paulus' pass at 3YL, and CB Stephan Virgil later sealed win with another INT.

Wake Forest 12 FLORIDA STATE 3: Having once lost 14 in row to former ACC bully Florida State (2-1), Demon Deacons (3-0) now had claimed 3 straight series wins against Seminoles, including 2 straight in Tallahassee. Stout Wake Forest D permitted only 220y O and forced whopping 7 TOs. Seminoles stayed in game thanks to their tenacious D that had to perform in constant trouble due to TOs. On 5 drives that began in FSU territory, Wake Forest could earn only 6 pts as it missed pair of FGs and lost FUM by QB Riley Skinner (17-29/217y) at Noles 2YL. Wake K Sam Swank managed 4 FGs, but 3 misses were his 1st of new season. Deacs' woes paled in comparison to those of Florida State as QB Christian Ponder (6-18/52y) threw 3 INTs, and his replacement, QB D'Vontrey Richardson (6-18/66y), surrendered 2 more. Able to rush for only 102y, Seminoles' longest drive went 35y to K Graham Gano's 37y FG, their only score. Florida State's 4 of last 5 series ended in TOs as Wake S Kevin Patterson (6 tackles, 2 INTs) forced FUM and INT 8 mins apart in 4th Q.

NORTH CAROLINA STATE 30 East Carolina 24 (OT): With no. 15 Pirates (3-1) serving as early-season darlings of non-BCS proponents, Wolfpack (2-2) found themselves as underdogs in intense local rivalry. Contest went to OT where Wolfpack DE Shea McKeen (7 tackles, sack) stripped East Carolina QB Patrick Pinkney (19-32/210y, TD, INT) right after Pirates had made first down at NC State 11YL, and DE Willie Young (8 tackles) recovered loose ball. NC State HB Andre Brown (12/73y, TD, and 4/35y, TD receiving) decided there was no better time to deliver upset. On 2nd down, Brown ripped off 16y run, and on next play, he scored on 10y run during which he bowled over Pirates DT Jay Ross to get close enough to stretch ball over GL. While Brown was brilliant on game's final 2 plays, QB Russell Wilson (21-31/210y) was key for Wolfpack attack as he threw 3 TD passes, including 5y score to frosh TE George Bryan (5/58y, TD) with 1:12 left to tie game at 24-24. East Carolina had scored all 3 of its TDs on big plays: S Van Eskridge (7 tackles, INT, forced FUM) made 23y INT TD RET to open scoring, TE Davon Drew caught 39y TD pass for 14-7 lead in 2nd Q, and sub RB Norman Whitley (9/83y) raced 42y for 21-14 advantage in 3rd Q.

Florida 30 TENNESSEE 6: Florida (3-0) coach Urban Meyer upped mark against Volunteers (1-2) to 4-0 with another laugher as QB Tim Tebow (8-15/96y) threw 2 TD passes, D forced 3 TOs, and RB Brandon James was brilliant on special teams. Gators took commanding 17-0 lead in 1st Q as James set up opening TD with 52y KO RET and scored his team's 2nd TD on 78y punt RET. Following James' opening KO RET, Tebow needed 8 plays to get Florida on scoreboard with 2y TD pass to TE Aaron Hernandez. Vols RB Montario Hardesty lost FUM on own 23YL which set up 39y FG by Florida K Jonathan Phillips. So, midway through 1st Q, Tennessee had run 3 plays/-5y and trailed 10-0. On next series, Vols gained 21y before punting, but James took Vols P Chad Cunningham's 36y effort and raced all way to EZ. Just when Tennessee appeared to get untracked by marching 71y to 2nd-and-goal at Florida 1YL, QB Jonathan Crompton (18-28/162y, INT) lost FUM, recovered by Gators DE Carlos Dunlap. From Vols 3YL, Tebow engineered 74y drive to another FG and 20-0 lead. Running out of time in 1st H, Crompton took Vols to Florida 1YL before throwing 4th down INT to frosh CB Janoris Jenkins with 2 secs to go. Gators secured victory on Tebow's 15y TD pass to RB Percy Harvin in 3rd Q. Crompton kept for 1y TD early in 4th Q to prevent shutout. Vols O edged Gators 258y to 243y yet lost to Florida for 17th time in past 23 meetings. "...That loss is on me," said embattled Tennessee coach Phillip Fulmer. "I've got big shoulders, and I take responsibility." Fulmer would resign at season's end with 151 victories at his alma mater.

Louisiana State 26 AUBURN 21: It would be difficult to have worse 1st H than that of LSU (3-0) alternating QB Jarrett Lee (11-22/182y, 2 TDs, INT), who pitched 0-5 including 24y INT TD RET by Auburn (3-1) DE Gabe McKenzie. But if LSU was going to win in Jordan-Hare Stadium, Lee would have to step up with co-starting QB Andrew Hatch knocked from game with concussion. Lee stepped up to throw for 182y in 2nd H, with 18y coming on winning TD pass to WR Brandon LaFell (4/92y) with 1:03 left. Lee hit 4-4/43y on winning 54y drive. Thanks in large part to Lee's turn-around, Louisiana State outscored Auburn 23-7 in 2nd H. Auburn's 2nd H TD, scored on 15y TD pass from QB Chris Todd (17-32/250y, TD, 2 INTs) to WR Robert Dunn (4/60y) with 6:40 to play, had provided 21-20 lead. Todd set up TD with 58y connection with WR Tim Hawthorne (2/87y). Last 5 meetings now had been decided by mere 19 pts between recent division title rivals. LSU snapped 8-game series win streak by home team and Auburn's 6-win string against Top 10 teams.

Alabama 49 ARKANSAS 14: SEC opener for both teams exploded in face of unbeaten, but struggling Razorbacks (2-1) as Crimson Tide RB Glen Coffee (10/162y, 2 TDs) exploded on simple dive play for 87y TD run in 1st Q. Before H had arrived with Alabama (4-0) ahead by 35-7, Tide D set single-game school mark by tallying on pair of INT TD RETs by CB Javier Arenas for 63y and SS Justin Woodall for 74y. QB Casey Dick (20-39/190y, TD, 3 INTs) briefly rallied Arkansas to within 21-7 by pitching 12y TD pass to TE Andrew Davie on 4th down early in 2nd Q. Bothering to pass infrequently, QB John Parker Wilson (6-14/74y, TD) still was able to answer Davie's TD by throwing his 42nd career TD pass to set new Alabama record. Long scoring romps by Coffee (31y) and sub RB Roy Upchurch (62y) highlighted Bama's 2nd H.

MICHIGAN STATE 23 Notre Dame 7: Bringing his entire O line to post-game media briefing, Michigan State (3-1) RB Javon Ringer credited them for his tremendous day in which he gained 201y on 39 carries and scored both Spartans TDs. Although Notre Dame (2-1) trailed whole way, Irish remained competitive until well into 4th Q. Without solid running attack (22/16y) to lean on, ND QB Jimmy Clausen (24-41/242y, TD, 2 INTs) was sacked twice. Even so, Clausen arched scoring pass to frosh WR Michael Floyd (7/86y, TD) to cap early 4th Q drive of 75y to trim deficit to 13-7. But overall, Irish turned ball over 3 times and missed 2 FGs. Spartans S Otis Wiley made pair of 1st H INTs, latter coming in 2nd Q at ND 22YL. It set up Ringer's 1y scoring wedge for 10-0 lead. Still, Michigan State didn't put verdict on ice until Ringer surged off LT and cruised 63y in last 5 mins to set up his 2nd 1y TD for 23-7 edge.

Miami 41 TEXAS A&M 23: Lightning TD strikes highlighted intersectional game as young passers earned spotlight. Tall Texas A&M (1-2) soph QB Jerrod Johnson (19-32/275y, 3 TDs, INT) was in for Stephen McGee, who was shelved by shoulder injury after 29 straight starts, and Miami (2-1) redshirt frosh Robert Marve (16-22/212y, 2 TDs, INT) received his 2nd career start. On game's opening scrimmage play, Aggies RB Mike Goodson took short pass from Johnson and broke multiple tackles on way to 62y TD. Marve quickly threw 29y pass, and RB Graig Cooper (16/128y, 2 TDs) scored on 19y run to tie it 7-7. Cooper tallied on 51y sprint 4 mins later for 14-7 edge, and swift Hurricanes had earned 121y on their 1st half-dozen snaps. Although Aggies pulled within 14-10 on 38y FG by K Richie Bean, Marve tossed TD pass in last 30 secs of 2nd Q for 24-10 H lead for Miami. Canes dashed any drama by striking for 17 pts in 1:09 span of 3rd Q: After K Matt Bosher's short FG, DE Eric Moncur speared 1-handed INT to set up Marve's 15y TD throw to WR Kayne Farquharson (5/67y, TD), and LB Glenn Cook knocked FUM away from A&M's Johnson on sack to trot 2y for TD.

Boise State 37 OREGON 32: Just when others like BYU and East Carolina were getting "BCS-Buster" props, good old Boise State Broncos (3-0) reared their heads to knock off no. 17 Oregon (3-1) for 1st-ever road win over BCS school. Ducks got on scoreboard 1st as they used virtually all-ground attack dominated by TBs Jeremiah Johnson (22/94y, TD) and LaGarrette Blount (18/99y, TD) to go 80y to Blount's 16y TD run off right side. Boise's lefty frosh QB Kellen Moore (24-36/386y, 3 TDs) lit up Ducks secondary for 3 TDs, including perfectly-lofted 73y score to WR Vinny Perretta (3/91y, TD) that built 31-13 lead 4:08 into 3rd Q. Meanwhile, injuries continued to deplete list of Ducks QBs: Jeremiah Masoli and frosh Chris Harper shared early duties—making only 3-6/27y, INT passing in 1st H—before Masoli went down with concussion. Oregon coach Mike Bellotti dipped down depth chart to his 4th QB—frosh Darron Thomas (13-25/210y, 3 TDs, INT)—who made Bellotti lament not reaching sooner. Thomas ignited rally that produced 19 pts in 4th Q, his last of 3 scoring passing going to TE Ed Dickson (7/103y, 2 TDs) with 2:07 to play. But, time ran out on Ducks.

Georgia 27 ARIZONA STATE 10: Much was made of no. 3 Georgia (4-0) venturing west of Mississippi River for its 1st regular season game since 1960. But, whatever hostility and jet-lag Bulldogs faced in Sonora Desert in Tempe was trumped by their superior talent. Georgia QB Matthew Stafford passed 16-28/career-high 285y, TD, but it was dominance on both sides of rushing attack that controlled outcome. RB Knowshon Moreno rushed 23/149y and pair of 2nd Q TDs that built 14-0 advantage as Bulldogs gained 176y on ground while yielding only 4y net to Arizona State (2-2). With TB Keegan Herring out with injury, starter Dimitri Nance could manage only 10/12y against Georgia's fierce front-4. Trailing 21-3, Sun Devils opened 2nd H by going 71y to short TD pass by QB Rudy Carpenter (23-36/208y, TD), but thereafter ASU punted 3 times and lost possession on downs at UGa 22YL when WR Kyle Williams couldn't quite reach stake on 4th down 9y reception. Bulldogs WR A.J. Green was Stafford's favorite target with 8/159y, TD receiving.

Utah 30 AIR FORCE 23: While Air Force (3-1) rediscovered its missing aerial game—Falcons failed to complete even 1 pass in previous week's 31-28 win over Houston—to tie Utah (4-0) 23-23 with 5:09 left, Utes stormed downfield to clinch win on 3rd TD run by TB Darrell Mack (18/101y). Utah led 9-0 in 1st Q on WR David Reed's 47y TD catch and safety picked up on EZ bobble by Air Force punter Ryan Harrison, but Falcons' pressure on Utes QB Brian Johnson (16-23/243y, TD, INT) resulted in 5 sacks, including tackle by DE Rick Ricketts that caused FUM returned for 25y TD by DE Jake Paulson. That provided Falcons with 16-9 H edge. Utah earned D edge by stuffing AFA's ground attack—which averaged 358y coming in—to tune of 42/53y. But, Air Force QB Shea Smith (7-13/138y, TD, 2 INTs) hit 42, 37, and 29y throws to set up pair of TDs that brought score to 23-23. Utes TB Matt Asiata (19/116y) shared running duties with Mack on closing 80y march to Mack's 9y winner with 58 secs left.

USA Today Coaches Poll September 21

1	Southern California (56)	1517	14	South Florida	721
2	Oklahoma (2)	1424	15	Wake Forest	678
3	Georgia (2)	1388	16	Auburn	650
4	Florida (1)	1345	17	Utah	528
5	Missouri	1284	18	Kansas	506
6	LSU	1247	19	Clemson	378
7	Texas	1143	20	Boise State	265
8	Wisconsin	1041	21	Illinois	233
9	Texas Tech	944	22	Oregon	174
10	Alabama	939	23	TCU	151
11	Brigham Young	931	24	Fresno State	117
12	Penn State	818	25	Vanderbilt	103
13	Ohio State	744			

September 27, 2008

(Th) OREGON STATE 27 Southern California 21: Beavers (2-2) had last knocked off top-ranked team in 1967 when they stopped USC and O.J. Simpson by 3-0 in Corvallis. No. 1 so far in 2008, Southern California (2-1) couldn't locate little Oregon State TB Jacquizz Rodgers behind his big lineman, and frosh darted for 187y and 2 TDs on 37 carries. Ahead 14-0 late in 2nd Q, Beavers seemed content to tack on FG, but frustrated USC D committed personal foul PEN to encourage 3rd down pass by Beavers QB Lyle Moevao (18-28/167y, 2 TDs). Trojans CB Kevin Thomas let EZ pass slip through his hands to Jacquizz's brother, James Rodgers (6/36y, 2 TDs), who made 3y TD catch for 21-0 H edge. USC was new team in 2nd H, gaining 238y to its 75y in 1st H. Troy QB Mark Sanchez (18-29/227y, 3 TDs, INT) threw 26 and 29y TD passes to WRs Ronald Johnson and Damian Williams in 3rd Q to pull within 21-14. However, Sanchez was forced into critical INT in last 3 mins of 4th Q as he overshot receiver from his 14YL, and Oregon State S Greg Laybourn returned it 28y to 2YL. Jacquizz Rodgers pierced through USC for his 2nd TD on next snap, but K Sean Sehnem hit upright with his x-pt kick for 27-14 lead. After USC's Johnson roared 50y on KO RET, Sanchez hit WR Patrick Turner with 14y TD pass with 1:19 to play. But, ecstatic Beavers were able to kill clock after Trojans' onside-KO attempt failed.

DUKE 31 Virginia 3: Blue Devils (3-1) crushed their 25-game ACC losing streak by routing hapless Virginia (1-3). It was Devils' 1st conf victory since beating Clemson 16-13 on November 13, 2004. Duke D forced 6 TOs in easily preventing Cavaliers from cracking GL: Virginia's deepest penetration ventured to 16YL. Thanks to its superb D, Blue Devils O needed only to travel avg of 34y on 4 scoring drives. Duke LB Michael Tauiliili made INT, forced FUM, recovered FUM, and was in on 16 tackles, while CB Jabari Marshall's 42y INT TD RET in 4th Q provided 24-3 lead. After 3-3 H tie, Duke QB Thaddeus Lewis (18-32/160y, 2 TDs, 2 INTs) took advantage of good field position to hit 9-10/87y and prompt pair of 3rd Q TD passes: 10y to RB Jay Hollingsworth and 30y to WR Eron Riley (3/36y). Despite his crafting 304y to 258y O advantage for UVa, Cavs QB Marc Verica (19-42/194y, 4 INTs) suffered 4 INTs in 2nd H.

Maryland 20 CLEMSON 17: Plucky Terrapins (4-1) shook off poor performance in opening H to rally to 4th straight win over ranked opponent. No. 20 Clemson (3-2) built 17-6 H lead as its D held Maryland to 99y, and Tigers' running tandem of RB James Davis (17/126y) and RB C.J. Spiller (14/98y) each scored TD as part of 204y ground attack in 1st H. Game turned early in 3rd Q when swift Terps WR Darrius Heyward-Bey raced 76y on reverse before being headed off at Tigers 4YL. Maryland QB Chris Turner (16-30/172y, TD) soon threw 6y TD pass to WR Torrey Smith to pull within 17-13. Maryland took lead early in 4th Q when Turner completed 3 passes to WR Danny Oquendo (4/49y) to set up 1y TD run by RB Da'Rel Scott (23/39y). From that moment on, Maryland D permitted only brief penetration of its territory: Spiller raced 17y with pass from QB Cullen Harper (15-22/151y, INT) to Terps 41YL, but Harper failed to advance on 4th down with 5:36 remaining. Scott, previously held in check, was able to assist in running out clock by rushing 6/30y. After earning 17 first downs in 1st H, Clemson managed only 2 in 2nd H. Visiting team had now won 4 straight in series.

North Carolina 28 MIAMI 24: With 10 mins remaining in what turned out to be wild 4th Q, Miami (2-2) looked to be in good shape as QB Robert Marve (18-27/135y, 3 TDs, 2 INTs) threw his 3rd TD pass, 4y to WR Aldarius Johnson for 24-14 lead. Miami D soon forced Tar Heels (3-1) into 3rd-and-10 deep in North Carolina territory, but that is when things began to unravel for Hurricanes. Tar Heels WR Hakeem Nicks (5/133y, TD) caught strike from QB Cam Sexton (11-19/242y, 2 TDs) at Miami 45YL and, with defender CB Bruce Johnson falling to turf, raced to EZ for stunning 74y TD and manageable 24-21 deficit. As game marched toward last min, Sexton, who had replaced QB Mike Paulus (1-4/10y) early on, completed 4-5/61y on late drive as WR Brooks Foster hauled in go-ahead 14y TD pass with 46 secs left. After Miami received KO, pass interference PEN against Heels moved ball to midfield, and from there Marve hit WR Kayne Farquharson (3/51y) with 31y pass to bring Miami to UNC 20YL. With 15 secs left, Farquharson, running post pattern to middle of EZ, got his hands on Marve's pass. For split sec Hurricanes looked like miraculous winner, but Carolina S Trimane Goddard snatched ball from Farquharson to sealed UNC's win with dramatic INT. Miami RB Graig Cooper rushed 19/110y and caught 3/29y and TD, while Tar Heels WR Brandon Tate set NCAA record for career RET y with 3549y, breaking mark of 3455y set by California CB Deltha O'Neal in 1999.

Navy 24 WAKE FOREST 17: "It's all on me," said glum Wake Forest (3-1) QB Riley Skinner (26-40/270y, TD) after game in which he lost FUM and threw 4 INTs, after pitching 133 straight passes without being picked off. While TOs clearly factored greatly in outcome, Navy (3-2) earned its 1st victory over ranked opponent in 23 years (Virginia in 1985) with full team effort as Middies O gained 343y and its D forced 6 TOs and held Deacons to 43y rushing. FB Eric Kettani paced Midshipmen with career-high 175y on 19 carries, and QB Kaipo-Noa Kaheaku-Enhada (2-3/58y, and 10/30y rushing) scored twice on early runs before departing in 2nd Q with hamstring injury. At time of Kaheaku-Enhada's injury Navy enjoyed 17-0 lead which it carried to H. Skinner rallied no. 16 Demon Deacons to 10 consecutive pts in 3rd Q. Looking to tie game with 6 mins left in 4th Q, Skinner drove Deacs into Navy territory before Middies S Emmett Merchant made 12y INT RET from his 25YL. On very next play, Kettani delivered back-breaker, bursting 57y to set up Navy at Wake 6YL. Two plays later, sub QB Jarod Bryant scored on 4y run with 3:45 left. Skinner was able to hit 8y TD pass to FB Mike Rinfrette, but Navy recovered onside-KO to clinch upset.

Alabama 41 GEORGIA 30: Crimson Tide (5-0) entered game wanting to prove their value and left as national championship contenders. They accomplished mission by totally outclassing Georgia Bulldogs (4-1), darlings of preseason prognosticators, as shocking 31-0 lead was built in 1st H. By utterly dominating line of scrimmage, Alabama scored on its 1st 5 possessions, setting tone with opening 80y drive to RB Mark Ingram's 7y TD run. Georgia QB Matt Stafford (24-42/274y, 2 TDs, INT) countered with 2 passes into Bama territory, but drive stalled there. Steady Alabama QB John Parker Wilson (13-16/205y, TD) answered with 3rd down conversions on 7y run and 14y pass to WR Nikita Stover to lead to K Leigh Tiffin's 23y FG by. Down 10-0 with 1st Q ending, Georgia P Brian Mimbs sliced 19y punt that didn't reach midfield. Wilson needed only 5 plays to negotiate 48y with RB Glen Coffee (23/86y, 2 TDs) running 4/17y—including 3y scoring run—and Wilson completing 31y pass to blossoming frosh WR Julio Jones (5/94y, TD). Early in 2nd Q, Tide LB Don't'a Hightower returned FUM by Bulldogs celebrated frosh WR A.J. Green (6/88y, TD) to Georgia 33YL and 2:48 later score mounted to 24-0 after RB Roy Upchurch scored on 3y run. Alabama scored again on 22y TD pass to Jones with less than 2 mins remaining in 1st H. Even with star TB Knowshon Moreno (9/34y, TD) negated by swarming Tide D, Bulldogs still rallied with 10 pts in 3rd Q pts to pull within 31-10. UGa CB Prince Miller roared 92y on punt RET TD to open 4th Q, and with score now at 31-17, hope lingered for those Georgia fans who had stuck around. But, Wilson engineered key drive to another FG by Tiffin to push Tide's advantage back to 34-17. Teams combined for 20 more pts, but Georgia never got as close as 11 pts until Green caught 21y TD pass from Stafford with 1:35 left. In 1st Qs of 5 games to date, Alabama had outscored opponents 74-0, and Wilson had now thrown for 6398y in his career, breaking Brodie Croyle's 3-year-old school record of 6382y.

Mississippi 31 FLORIDA 30: Florida's once reluctant recruit by way of Texas, Ole Miss (3-2) transfer QB Jevan Snead (9-20/185y, 2 TDs, INT) became player of game, throwing 2 TDs and running for another. Snead's finest moment came with 6 mins remaining in game when he hooked up with WR Shay Hodge (3/133y, TD) on 86y TD pass for 31-24 lead. Hodge was freed by play-action and zoomed past marginal coverage by Gators S Major Wright to finish longest pass in Rebels' history. Gators, ranked 4th in nation, were able to answer with quick 78y drive that ended on 15y TD run by dazzling RB-WR Percy Harvin (10/82y, TD rushing, and 13/186y, TD receiving). Harvin's score should have been knotted game at 31-31, but Ole Miss DE Kentrell Lockett jumped through gap in line to block x-pt kick. Florida D quickly held, and Gators O was back on field at own 22YL with 2:05 remaining. Florida QB Tim Tebow (24-38/319y, TD) completed 3 straight passes for 1st down at Rebels 41YL but then overthrew receivers on consecutive plays. RB Brandon James ran for 9y, which forced Gators coach Urban Meyer to decide between FG and 1st down attempt. Confident in Tebow, Meyer sought 1st down by calling off-T run. DE Greg Hardy (3 tackles, 1.5 sacks) led charge from outside, while interior of Mississippi's D-Line—led by NT Peria Jerry—stood up center of Florida's line. Result was no gain, and Mississippi clinched its 1st SEC win after 9 straight losses. Gators O converted only 1-11 3rd downs while losing 3 TOs, so it was frustrating afternoon for ringmaster Tebow. He lost FUM that led to Rebs' 2nd TD and threw only 1 TD pass, Harvin's incredible 43y catch in 2nd Q that could have been picked off by S Kendrick Lewis (9 tackles, FUM REC). Being driven person that he was, Tebow directed blame on himself in memorable post-game press conference remark that was replayed over and over during rest of season: "You have never seen any player in the entire country play as hard as I will play the rest of this season, and you'll never see someone push the rest of the team as hard as I will push everybody the rest of this season, and you'll never see a team play harder than we will the rest of this season," said emotional, determined QB. If Tebow believed in omens he must have been comforted by Mississippi's previous victory over top-5 team: In 1977, Rebels' victim (Notre Dame) went on to win national championship. As for Ole Miss, its 600th win in school history was extra special.

AUBURN 14 Tennessee 12: With its O struggling to get 1st downs, Tennessee (1-3) was in no position to give away any pts. Yet botched handoff midway through 2nd Q by Tennessee QB Jonathan Crompton to TB Arian Foster (8/30y) on 1st-and-10 from own 5YL produced FUM bounding into Volunteers EZ. Auburn (4-1) DE Jake Ricks pounced on ball for 14-6 lead, which would turn out to be enough for its ferocious D. From that moment on, Tennessee earned only 3 1st downs, 2 on short TD drive in 3rd Q and none in 4th Q. Vols required 9 plays to go 37y to TB Mario Hardesty's 2y TD run CB Dennis Rogan's INT, but were unable to convert tying 2-pt conv. Auburn was not much better on O but Tigers found themselves pinned within own 5YL on 3 occasions by excellent punts of Vols P Chad Cunningham (10/39.9y avg). But thanks to early 18y scoring pass from QB Chris Todd (14-23/93y, TD, INT) to WR Richard Dunn (6/54y) and Ricks' TD, Auburn beat Tennessee for 4th straight time. LB Josh Byrnes led Tigers with 11 tackles.

PENN STATE 38 Illinois 24: Nittany Lions (5-0) WR Derrick Williams (6/75y,TD, and 6/33y, TD rushing), exhorted by Joe Paterno to have "big game," broke open seesaw battle in Big 10 opener as he became 1st in Paterno's long coaching career to score TDs on run, reception, and KO RET in 1 game. Illinois (2-2) struck 1st as QB Juice Williams (13-24/183y, 2 TDs, INT) led 60y drive to frosh RB Jason Ford's 1y TD plunge, that quieted 109,626 Beaver Stadium "white-out" fans. Penn State QB Darryl Clark (14-20/181y, 2 TDs) wedged behind C A.Q. Shipley to tie it 7-7 at end of 73y trip. Illini's Williams set up his 33y TD pass to WR Arrelious Benn with 10y dash on 3rd-and-4 but before end of 1st Q was matched by Clark's 21y TD pitch to Penn State's Williams down right sideline. Lions led 21-14 at H as Williams circled LE for 5y on WB reverse. After trade of 3rd Q FGs in 3rd Q, WR Williams fielded bounded KO on opening play of 4th Q and burst 94y to TD for 31-17 lead that would be maintained after QBs traded TD throws.

MICHIGAN 27 Wisconsin 25: Coach Rich Rodriguez was prophetic earlier in week when talking about how young teams—like his Wolverines (2-2)—could improve dramatically in short period of time. Booed off Michigan Stadium turf after trailing 19-0 and having earned only 21y O at H, Michigan dramatically turned game around in 12 mins of 2nd H. Michigan QB Steven Threet (12-31/96y, TD, 2 INTs), who threw for -7y in 1st H, sparked 80y TD drive late in 3rd Q, capped by his 26y TD pass over middle to frosh TE Kevin Koger to pull within 19-7. RB Brandon Minor raced for 34y TD in 4th Q, and LB John Thompson almost immediately picked off pass by Wisconsin (3-1) QB Allen Evridge (20-37/226y, TD, 2 INTs) and followed convoy to 25y TD. Rodriguez mistakenly called for 2-pt try that failed to leave Wolverines ahead 20-19. Threet, not known for speed afoot, slipped away for 58y sprint up left side to set up frosh RB Sam McGuffie for TD that made it 27-19. With scant secs left, Evridge stood up to hard

pass rush to find WR David Gilreath for 22y TD. Badgers completed tying 2-pt pass to TE Travis Beckum, but Beckum had lined up illegally, so score was nullified. Another pass attempt by Evridge failed to collect tying pts.

Michigan State 42 INDIANA 29: Indiana (2-2) went toe-to-toe with Spartans (4-1) until gut-wrenching turn of events late in 3rd Q. Trailing 34-29, Hoosiers were given break on apparent safety after being punted to their 1YL by Michigan State P Aaron Bates. On 3rd down, sub QB Ben Chappell launched 97y TD strike to WR Terrance Turner, but G Cody Faulkner was called for safety when detected for holding PEN in EZ. Hoosiers never recovered from 9-pt swing. Earlier, Indiana RB Marcus Thigpen (9/113y) had scored on 1st H runs of 6 and 78y and caught 79y TD pass from QB Kellen Lewis (12-21/177y, 2 TDs, INT) in 3rd Q. S Jerimy Finch blocked his 2nd punt of season for safety to pull Hoosiers to within 20-16 in 2nd Q. This was balanced by Michigan State QB Brian Hoyer (14-26/261y, 2 TDs), who scored on sneak and threw pair of 2nd Q TD passes, including 82y connection with TE Charlie Gantt.

Northwestern 22 IOWA 17: QB C.J. Bacher (28-45/284y, INT) earned Big 10 O player of week with comeback pitching that garnered 3 TD passes and brought Northwestern (4-0) from 17-3 deficit on Homecoming Day in Iowa City. Hawkeyes (3-2) sent TB Shonn Greene (21/159y, TD) crashing through hole created by left side of their line for 18y TD at end of 90y drive for 10-0 lead in 2nd Q. Iowa WR Andy Brodell (8/126y, TD) took perfect over-shoulder 45y TD pass from new QB Ricky Stanzi (21-30/238y, TD, INT) for 17-3 lead, but Brodell bobbled punt just before H to give Northwestern WR Rasheed Ward (10/94y, TD) chance to nab 1y TD 17 secs before intermission. After 2nd H KO, Wildcats went 76y to pull within 17-16. Early in 4th Q, Cats knocked Greene from game when he was belted by S Brad Phillips; resultant FUM was recovered at Iowa 38YL. After Ward kept drive going with 1-handed 3rd down catch, WR Eric Peterman nabbed his 2nd TD pass from Bacher for Northwestern's 1st lead of game at 22-17. Stanzi's 6 completions led Iowa from its 28YL to NW 8YL, but DT John Gill knocked down 4th down pass with 1:08 left.

NOTRE DAME 38 Purdue 21: Displaying uncommon balance on O, Notre Dame (3-1) pulled away from mostly-lifeless Purdue (2-2) with 3 TDs in 3rd Q to help secure win that matched total from disastrous 2007 season. QB Jimmy Clausen (20-35/275y, 3 TDs) reached career-high in passing y, while RB Armando Allen rushed for career-best 134y as Irish topped 200y passing (275y) and rushing (201y). After 14-14 H tie, Irish went 81y on opening drive of 2nd H to Allen's 16y TD run, Allen concluding trip with 45y on 3 straight runs. Notre Dame soon was back on O, and Allen ran 3/48y to set up Clausen's 5y TD pass to TE Kyle Rudolph. With chances beginning to evaporate, Boilermakers QB Curtis Painter (29-55/359y, 2 TDs, INT) pulled Purdue within 28-21 on 54y TD pass to WR Desmond Tardy (10/175y). Allen halted any momentum swing with 36y KO RET which jump-started 54y drive to ND's clinching TD. It was scored on Clausen's 30y pass to WR David Grimes. Painter led Purdue to ND 13YL, before drive and Boilers' victory bid ended on 4 straight incompletions. Frosh WR Michael Floyd (6/100y) had his first 100y game for Irish.

Virginia Tech 35 NEBRASKA 30: Nebraska (4-1), off to good start on D against cupcakes so far in 2008, failed to corral speedy Virginia Tech (4-1) QB Tyrod Taylor (9-15/171y, and 15/87y, TD rushing), who made big plays to press Huskers into their red zone for much of night. Taylor hit 40 and 34y passes in 1st H and ran for 30y gain in 3rd Q before scoring clinching 2y TD with less than 3 mins to play. Early on, after punt block went for safety against Huskers, Hokies CB "Macho" Harris (21y punt RET) returned INT to Nebraska 5YL, and RB Darren Evans (21/72y) powered 3 times for 1st of his 2 TD runs for 9-0 lead. Nebraska QB Joe Ganz (17-26/278y, 2 TDs, INT) duped Hokies D with play-fake and found TE Mike McNeill for 32y TD that pulled Huskers to within 9-7 in 1st Q. Va Tech K Dustin Keyes hit his 4th FG early in 3rd Q for 21-10 lead. Big Red rallied from late in 3rd Q, using 88y TD punt RET by WR Nate Swift to pull within 28-23, but Taylor led 11-play, 80y drive to nail it down for Hokies.

OKLAHOMA 35 Texas Christian 10: On upset-alert after no. 1 USC's Thursday night disaster, Oklahoma (4-0) ignored Texas Christian's recent 13-5 record against BCS teams and rolled to early lead on way to capturing top spot in AP Poll on Sunday. It was 96th week—and 1st since 2003—Sooners had topped writers' weekly vote to break all-time (since 1936) tie they had shared with Notre Dame. OU QB Sam Bradford (19-34/411y, 4 TDs) looked to sr WR Manuel Johnson, whose spectacular receiving night set new school record for y with 5/206y, 3 TDs. Bradford hit WR Juaquin Iglesias with 24y score on opening possession, and while TCU (4-1) RB Aaron Brown raced 75y to Sooners 11YL with ensuing KO, Oklahoma D made stand to force FG by K Ross Evans. It was over when Bradford and Johnson collaborated on 76, 55, and 63y TDs through 3rd Q. Sooners won for 21st straight time at Owen Field with their last defeat coming at hands of Horned Frogs in 2005.

TEXAS 52 Arkansas 10: Delayed 2 weeks by Hurricane Ike, 77th meeting of former SWC rivals turned into breeze for Texas (4-0). Struggling Arkansas (2-2) was whipped by biggest margin in series since 1916 and prompted new coach Bobby Petrino to sigh in describing 101-24 margin in consecutive losses to Alabama and Texas: "Losing is hard. It takes a toll on you." Chief Longhorns culprit was QB Colt McCoy (17-19/185y, 3 TDs, and 9/84y 2 TDs rushing), who in far more chiseled condition in 2008, had turned into O dynamo. McCoy raced 35y down left sideline in 2nd Q to build 24-3 lead and added 5y TD run in last min of 1st H for 31-3 edge. McCoy lifted his season's passing stats to 80% on 80-100/1018y and his rating to phenomenal 209.7. Arkansas' O never registered TD as it allowed 81y INT TD RET by Texas CB Aaron Williams in 4th Q, and Hogs made their only TD on 80y FUM RET by DE Antwain Robinson.

October 4, 2008

(Th) Pittsburgh 26 SOUTH FLORIDA 21: Looking more like team that upset West Virginia at end of 2007 than squad that lost to Bowling Green to start 2008 season, suddenly-hot Panthers (4-1) freed heralded frosh WR Jonathan Baldwin to reel in 52y TD pass from QB Bill Stull (16-27/228y, TD) for Pittsburgh's opening score in 7-7 1st Q. After scoring only on DB Charlton Sinclair's 26y punt block RET in 1st H that it trailed 17-7, South Florida looked to RB Mike Ford (14/73y) to provide 10th-ranked Bulls with short-lived 21-20 lead in last 6 mins of 4th Q. Ford was featured on 9-play, 86y drive as he carried 7/53y to set up 22y TD pass to WR Jesse Hester (3/34y) from QB Matt Grothe (11-21/129y, TD, INT). Bulls could hold lead less than 2 mins, however, as Pitt soph superstar TB LeSean "Shady" McCoy (28/142y, 2 TDs) scored winning TD on 3y run with 4:38 left. McCoy's TD capped stunningly quick 60y drive on which he scampered 19y after Stull fired 38y to WR Oderick Turner (3/60y). Anxious to answer, Bulls went 3-and-out with 4 mins remaining as Grothe was called for intentional grounding on 3rd down. Panthers next killed sufficient time—with McCoy running for back-breaking 12y gain on 3rd-and-9—to hand ball back to Bulls with only 31 secs left. Grothe's final desperation pass was blocked, and USF's visit to nation's top 10 became as short-lived as it had in 2007.

Boston College 38 NORTH CAROLINA STATE 31: Behind brilliant play of big sr QB Chris Crane (34-51/428y, 2 TDs, INT), Eagles (4-1) built whopping 578y to 253y game-end O advantage only to blow 14-pt lead in 4th Q. But, Crane would not let Boston College lose, engineering winning 70y drive with 3-4/44y passing and 2/22y rushing and capping trip with 13y TD run, his 3rd scoring run, around LE with 23 secs remaining. Exciting frosh QB Russell Wilson (19-33/218y, TD) did his best to lead North Carolina State (2-4) to upset, throwing 61y TD to WR Owen Spencer (3/102y, TD) early in 4th Q and running for 2y keeper that tied it at 31-31 with 3:33 left. Wolfpack had stayed alive only because of BC's trio of TOs and 100y KO TD RET by NC State WR T.J. Graham late in 1st Q. Graham's TD put halt to potential blowout as Crane, pulled week prior for poor play against Rhode Island, led Eagles to 3 straight TD drives in 1st Q. BC WR Rich Gunnell (11/123y, TD) was game's top receiver, while DT B.J. Raji paced Eagles D with 3 sacks. Boston College's win ran its record to 2-0 versus former coach Tom O'Brien.

NORTH CAROLINA 38 Connecticut 12: While some experts were picking North Carolina and Connecticut to decide NCAA basketball title next spring, pair of rising football programs met at Kenan Stadium. North Carolina (4-1) topped ranked opponent for 1st time in 3 years in crazy game that featured 22-min stoppage due to lights going dark, vanquished Huskies (5-1) outgaining winners by 378y to 263y, 3 blocked punts by same player, and 100y rushing effort by former backup S. North Carolina LB Bruce Carter amazingly blocked 3 consecutive punts by Huskies P Desi Cullen, who admitted after game he took too long out of fear of Tar Heels' star returner Brandon Tate. S Matt Merletti fell on 3rd punt block in Connecticut EZ for TD and 17-3 lead in 2nd Q. Sloppy Huskies squandered their chances with 3 INTs and 11 PENs/97y to compound punt-block damage. UNC RB Shaun Draughn, listed in media guide as SS, rushed for 109y and scored on 39y TD run in 3rd Q that upped Tar Heels' lead to 24-6. QB Cam Sexton, 3rd on Carolina depth chart month earlier, passed 9-16/117y, TD, INT, and minimized his mistakes. Hampered by injury to QB Tyler Lorenzen, Connecticut hoped to ride RB Donald Brown, who ran for 161y and TD. But, UConn was forced to pass more than it liked: sub QB Zach Frazer (24-44/210y with trio of damaging INTs. Any doubt as to outcome ended late in 3rd Q on Frazer's 3rd INT, returned 23y for clinching TD at 31-6 by emerging soph DT Marvin Austin.

VANDERBILT 14 Auburn 13: Tigers (4-2), struggling to score so far in 2008, jumped to 13-0 lead on 1st Q slant-in TD passes to WRs Rodgeriqus Smith and Mario Fannin (3/56y, TD) by QB Chris Todd (8-16/70y, 2 TDs, INT). Scores came only 1 min apart as Auburn CB Jerraud Powers made diving INT off Vanderbilt (5-0) QB Chris Nickson on 1st snap after intermediate KO. But, K Wes Byrum missed kick after Fannin's TD, and it would weigh heavily on Auburn. Late in 2nd Q, Commodores QB Mackenzi Adams (13-23/153y, 2 TDs), in for injured Nickson, threw similar 15y slant-in to pull Vandy within 13-7. In middle of 3rd Q, Adams broke this pattern of TD passes by scrambling away from pressure to toss high 1y lob to frosh TE Brandon Barden in back of EZ. Vandy now led 14-13 and later sealed it with CB Myron Lewis' INT with barely more than 2 mins to play. Members of crowd displayed Biblical reference at game's end with placard that underscored Vanderbilt's reputation as SEC's most academically-oriented university: "The Geeks Shall Inherit the Turf." For heaven's sake, Vanderbilt's 5-0 beginning to 2008 matched its last undefeated 5-game beginning way back in 1943 season against likes of Tennessee Tech, Carson-Newman, and Milligan. All 5 wins this year had come in comeback form with Commodores' D blanking opponent to fuel resurgence in 2nd H.

Illinois 45 MICHIGAN 20: Like previous week's success, Michigan (2-3) played very effectively in single Q. Instead of finishing well, this time Wolverines started well: QB Steven Threet (18-35/250y, 2 TDs) led TD drives of 48 and 61y in 1st Q. Trailing 14-3, Illinois (3-2) QB Juice Williams (13-26/310y, 2 TDs, and 19/121y, 2 TDs rushing) went

to work for 431y O, new record for any player at Michigan Stadium. Williams sparked 45 pts, most Illini had tallied vs. Michigan since 39 they scored in legendary 1924 game in which Red Grange accounted for 5 TDs. With contest still in doubt, Williams authored pair of fabulous TD passes. Late in 2nd Q, Williams lofted perfect swing pass to RB Daniel Dufrene, who raced to 57y TD and Illini's 1st lead at 17-14. Early in 3rd Q, WR Jeff Cumberland made up for foolish PEN and made twisting adjustment to Williams' long toss and cantered away for 77y score. Illinois added 3 TDs in 4th Q.

Ohio State 20 WISCONSIN 17: Having won 16 straight tilts at Camp Randall Stadium, Wisconsin (3-2) fell behind 7-0 on 33y crash-and-sprint off left side by Buckeyes (5-1) TB Beanie Wells (22/168y, TD) on game's opening drive. Badgers QB Allan Evridge (13-25/147y, TD, INT) tied it in 2nd Q on 9y pass, and K Philip Welch put Wisconsin ahead 10-7 with short FG in last sec of 2nd Q. Ohio State tied it and took lead on pair of FGs by K Ryan Pretorius. After burly Wisconsin TB P.J. Hill (16/63y, TD) powered behind pulling LG Andy Kemp for 2y TD to make it 17-13 for Badgers, Buckeyes took over at their 20YL with 6:31 to play. QB Tyrelle Pryor hit passes of 19 and 27y, with nerve-wracking FUMs recovered by Ohio State until just more than 1 min was left. While Badgers LB corps scrambled to find their positions, Pryor ran left, faked pitchout, and cut sharply to dash into EZ for winning 11y TD. As last min ticked away, scrambling Evridge had to force pass over middle which was intercepted by Ohio State CB Malcolm Jenkins.

Kansas 35 IOWA STATE 33: There were 6 double-digit home underdogs this week in BCS conferences, and Iowa State (2-3), coming off bye-week that allowed young team time to improve, looked like it would break mold. Even though Jayhawks hadn't permitted single pt in any 1st H so far in 2008, Cyclones breezed to 14-0 edge in 1st Q as RB Alexander Robinson (10/51y) ran 16y for TD and QB Austen Arnaud (27-45/268y, 3 TDs, INT) hit WR Marquis Hamilton with 8y TD pass. Tally jumped to 20-0 at H as Kansas earned only 93y O in 1st H. But after coach Mark Mangino told his players they could still win if they stayed calm and poised, Jayhawks tallied 5 TDs and 343y O in 2nd H. Kansas scored on 3 straight possessions in 3rd Q: TB Jake Sharp (19/79y, TD and 3/107y, TD receiving) on 67y dash after hauling in pass in left flank from QB Todd Reesing (18-26/319y, 3 TDs, INT), TB Angus Quigley on short plunge after Sharp started drive with 42y run with shovel pass, and WR Kerry Meier (7/125y, 2 TDs) on 23y catch. Sharp seemed to crush Iowa State with short TD run early in 4th Q for 28-20 lead for Kansas, but Cyclones fought back and scored in last 1:15 to pull within 35-33 on Hamilton's 2nd TD grab. Iowa State recovered its on-side KO, but Arnaud was forced into 4 straight incompletions. Of 5 all-time-best Kansas comebacks, 3 now included rallies against Cyclones: from 26 pts behind in 1992, from 20 down in 2008, and 19 down in 1953.

Texas Tech 58 KANSAS STATE 28: QB Graham Harrell (38-51/454y, 6 TDs) led Red Raiders (5-0) to 626y O and established himself as Texas Tech's career pass y leader. Harrell moved past Cliff Kingsbury with 12,709y. Not punting until late in 4th Q, Tech scored 8 TDs and FG in 10 possessions, only failure coming on gamble turn-over on downs at own 29YL when RB Shannon Woods (18/70y) was stopped for no gain. Kansas State (3-2) QB Josh Freeman (13-28/170y, TD) had gone across on 1y TD run early in 2nd Q for 14-14 tie. It was 1st of 2 rushing scores for Freeman. Raiders WR Lyle Leong caught trio of Harrell's scoring throws, while soph WR Michael Crabtree (9/107y, 2 TDs) nabbed his 29th and 30th career TD catches.

Missouri 52 NEBRASKA 17: When one considers that Nebraska (3-2) went toe-to-toe with no. 4 Missouri (5-0) in 7-7 tie through much of 1st Q, it was stunning how Tigers simply bashed Cornhuskers with plenty of O thereafter. Missouri scored 1st 4 times it touched ball. First, WR Jeremy Maclin (5/89y, TD) simply sped away from Nebraska D to score on crossing pattern pass in opening min of game. Nebraska QB Joe Ganz (26-38/290y, 2 TDs, INT) matched it with 20y TD throw to WR Nate Swift. Mizzou QB Chase Daniel (18-23/253y) threw 3 TD passes, and RB Derrick Washington rushed for 139y, scoring twice on ground including 43y burst up middle, and catching TD pass. Crushing blow for Huskers came late in 2nd Q when Ganz rolled right under pressure and was picked off by MLB Brock Christopher who tight-roped left side for 17y TD and 31-7 lead. It was Mizzou's 1st win in Lincoln since 1978.

Texas 38 COLORADO 14: Pair of O stars combined to spark no. 5 Texas, especially on mind-blowing TD that opened scoring in game's 1st 2 mins. QB Colt McCoy (23-30/262y, 2 TDs, 2 INTs) was forced up in pass pocket and nearly reached scrimmage line when he pitched falling-forward, wide dump-off pass to RB Chris Ogbannaya (9/71y, TD, and 6/116y, TD receiving), who streaked 65y to score. Ogbonnaya, whose receiving y came within 4y of Terry Metcalf's RB record at Texas, saved TD late in 1st Q when he ran down Colorado (3-2) DB Kalil Brown's 56y INT RET and extended lead to 21-0 on powerful 13y run late in 2nd Q. Buffs, banged-up on O-line, could rush for no more than 49y and had trouble protecting QB Cody Hawkins (13-33/118y, TD), who managed short TD pass in 3rd Q finally to put Buffaloes on scoreboard, down 28-7.

SOUTHERN CALIFORNIA 44 Oregon 10: Ducks (4-2) marched right down field after opening KO, and all knowing critics who had decided USC couldn't stop good running attacks were nodding their heads. Oregon led 7-0 on handoff to RB Jeremiah Johnson for 1y option run to right. With score at 10-3 in 2nd Q, roof fell in on Ducks as Trojans (3-1) dropped 24 pts on Oregon in 7 and half mins. USC QB Mark Sanchez (19-28/332y, 3 TDs) hit wide-open WR Damian Williams for 34y TD, stepped up to fling long bomb to WR Ronald Johnson for 63y, and found WR Patrick Turner in tight coverage at GL for 11y score. Troy led 27-10 at H and was on its way to 598y O. "I guess they answered the wake-up call (Trojans' upset loss 9 days earlier) after Oregon State," said contrite Ducks coach Mike Bellotti.

CALIFORNIA 24 Arizona State 14: Veteran QB Nate Longshore (17-28/198y, 3 TDs, INT) returned to Golden Bears (4-1) starting lineup for 1st time this season and TB Shane Vereen (27/93y, and 5/51y receiving) chipped in good play in place of injured TB Jahvid Best, but still Cal misfired often after building 17-0 lead in 1st H. It was California D that significantly stifled sputtering Arizona State (2-3); in fact, Sun Devils virtually were given their 3rd Q TD when blocked FG by Cal was turned into 1st down at 13YL when 15y PEN was called against Bears for having assisted their effort by stepping onto linemen. TB Keegan Herring (14/37y, TD), himself just off ASU injury shelf, scored 8y TD 3 plays later to yank Devils within 24-14 in last min of 3rd Q. In 1st Q, Longshore had shrugged off his 3 incompletions and having settled for FG after 1st-and-goal at Arizona State 4YL when he hit WR LaReylle Cunningham for 19y TD and 10-0 lead. Sun Devils had earned only 16y before going 70y in 10 plays for their 1st TD in middle of 2nd Q: QB Rudy Carpenter (20-35/165y, TD, 2 INTs) found WR Kyle Williams for 30y score that temporarily got ASU in contention at 17-7.

USA Today Coaches Poll October 5

1	Oklahoma (60)	1524	14	Vanderbilt	704
2	Missouri	1404	15	Kansas	667
3	LSU (1)	1398	16	Boise State	624
4	Alabama	1339	17	Oklahoma State	523
5	Texas	1305	18	Virginia Tech	393
6	Penn State	1203	19	Michigan State	273
7	Texas Tech	1101	20	South Florida	267
8	Brigham Young	1086	21	Wake Forest	247
9	Southern California	1055	22	Northwestern	231
10	Georgia	937	23	Auburn	121
11	Ohio State	893	24	Wisconsin	105
12	Florida	883	25	California	98
13	Utah	793			

October 11, 2008

GEORGIA 26 Tennessee 14: Georgia (5-1) reversed its recent trend of poor play versus Tennessee (2-4) as QB Matthew Stafford (25-26/310y, TD, 2 INTs) threw for career-best y. Bulldogs dominated from opening KO, scoring on 4 of 5 1st H possessions with 5th ending on INT after going 67y to 13YL. Yet, Georgia settled for too many FGs—4 in all—and managed to allow Volunteers to stay within striking distance. When Tennessee QB Nick Stephens (13-30/208y, 2 TDs) threw 12y TD pass to WR Lucas Taylor (4/47y, TD) midway through 3rd Q, Vols trailed by only 20-14. But Stafford and RB Knowshon Moreno (27/101y) erased rest of 3rd Q on drive to K Blair Walsh's 41y FG and, after Dogs D forced 3-and-out series, wiped out whopping 11 mins of 4th Q. They used 17 plays to go 76y to 28y FG. On that amazing drive, Moreno rushed 5/27y and Stafford completed 2 passes to WR A.J. Green (7/53y) for 19y as Georgia moved to Tennessee 37YL. Backup RB Caleb King then took over, rushing for 23y on 4 straight plays as clock ticked ominously down. By time Vols regained possession, they faced 12-pt deficit with only 3 mins remaining. Stephens was able to complete 25y pass to WR Gerald Jones (4/68y) to midfield but hit only 2-10 passes rest of way. Held to 209y O and 10 1st downs, Tennessee fell to 0-3 in SEC for 1st time in 20 years.

FLORIDA 51 Louisiana State 21: After being derailed at home previous week by Mississippi, Florida Gators (5-1) righted ship by routing no. 4 Bengal Tigers (4-1). Game belonged to Gators QB Tim Tebow, who was center of attention before, during, and after game. Week before, Tebow challenged himself in post-game comments following loss to Rebels. Then on Monday, Tebow was challenged by LSU DT Ricky Jean-Francois, who said "If we get a good shot on (Tebow), we're going to try our best to take him out of the game." Jean-Francois ended up both amending his statement and (sheepishly) missing game due to injury. Duly inspired, Tebow sliced up Tigers D, completing 14-21/210y and leading Florida O to 475y. With game barely under way, Tebow connected with RB-WR Percy Harvin (6/112y, 2 TDs) on 70y TD pass despite ball being tipped by S Danny McCray. Florida scored twice more in 1st Q, including Harvin hauling in 7y TD pass, to build 17-0 lead. After LSU rallied to within 20-14 early in 3rd Q, Tebow took Gators 67y and set up his own 2y scoring run with 37y completion to WR Louis Murphy to LSU 2YL. Now leading 27-14, Gators D forced 3-and-out on next series. Rout soon was on when Florida RB Jeff Demps (10/129y) raced 42y for 34-14 lead. Florida LB Brandon Spikes (5 tackles, 2 INTs) added 52y INT TD RET to cap brilliant performance. LSU frosh QB Jarrett Lee (23-38/209y, 2 INTs) threw 2 TD passes but was unable to rally Tigers.

Arkansas 25 AUBURN 22: Razorbacks (3-3) faced plenty of challenges after consecutive routs at hands of powerhouses Alabama, Texas, and Florida. But, with Arkansas coach Bobby Petrino, former Tigers O coordinator, coming to town and 20th-ranked Auburn (4-2) stunningly firing its new O coordinator, Tony Franklin, earlier in week, Tigers seemed distracted and ripe for upset. Hogs unleashed latest in long line of top running backs: TB Michael Smith torched vaunted Tigers D for 176y rushing, with his thrilling 63y 4th Q romp accounting for winning score. Adding zest to 416y O, Arkansas QB Casey Dick (17-32/222y, 2 INTs) sparked 3 TD drives of 80y or more and scored on 1y run in 2nd Q and 6y reception in 3rd Q on trick pass from WR Joe Adams (4/60y). Special teams were needed to bail out Auburn's woeful O as RB Tristan Davis scored on 97y KO TD RET. Tigers needed to go only 24y to earn their 2nd TD, tallied on 3y run by QB Kodi Burns, when Arkansas TB Dennis Johnson lost FUM of 2nd H KO. Auburn's longest drive occurred in 4th Q, when trailing 25-20, as Burns (7-18/119y, 2 INTs) clicked on 4-5/65y passing to bring Auburn to 1st-and-goal at 5YL. Burns then ran for 1y before misfiring on 3 straight passes. "It's been a tough week," admitted losing coach Tommy Tuberville, "I put our guys in a tough situation."

Minnesota 27 ILLINOIS 20: Excitable Golden Gophers (6-1) coach Tim Brewster, former Illinois TE (1983 Rose Bowl team), made profitable return to Champaign as Minnesota led whole game and frustrated fine O of Illini (3-3). Especially perturbed was Illinois QB Juice Williams (26-41/462y, 2 TDs, INT), who was stopped inches short of GL on 4th down sweep late in 3rd Q, was sacked 5 times, and lost game-clinching INT at Minnesota 18YL when hit again. Game's biggest play came 5:24 from end: Williams' FUM was caused by DE Willie VanDeSteeg (3 sacks) and picked up by S Simoni Freeman (9 tackles), who carried it 9y for decisive TD that made it 27-13. Gophers WR Eric Decker (9/86y, TD), leading catcher in Big 10 with 50 coming in, had scored on opening drive when taking pass from QB Adam Weber (18-26/184y, TD) just

inside left pylon, and RB Deleon Eskridge (26/124y, 2 TDs) provided 20-6 lead early in 4th Q with 46y weaving, surging run. Frosh WR A.J. Jenkins (3/117y) kept Illini within reach at 20-13 and 27-20 in 4th Q with 54 and 35y TD receptions from Williams.

Penn State 48 WISCONSIN 7: With Nittany Lions D swarming Wisconsin's run-oriented attack, Penn State (7-0) took advantage of poor early punting. Penn State started at its 48 and 49YLs to tally 50y FG by K Kevin Kelly and 2y option pitchout run TD by TB Evan Royster (14/60y, TD). Five mins into 2nd Q, Lions WR Derrick Williams took low punt and exploded 63y for TD and 17-0 lead. Badgers (3-3) finally freed star TE Travis Beckham (5/79y) for 42y gain on crossing pattern pass from QB Allan Evridge (2-10/50y, INT) to Lions 35YL, and Evridge scrambled for 5y TD. When conservatism was needed late in 2nd Q, Wisconsin tried to pass from deep in its territory, and soph DE Aaron Maybin's stripping sack turned into LB Josh Hull's FUM REC for Penn State at 16YL. QB Daryll Clark (16-25/244y, TD, INT) scored 1st of his 2 TD runs on next play for 24-7 lead at H. Clark scored on run and threw 44y TD pass to WR Deon Butler on 1st 2 series after 2nd KO, and Penn State cruised to victory after authoring pair of 2nd H INTs.

Oklahoma State 28 MISSOURI 23: After Oklahoma State (6-0) LB Patrick Lavine (8 tackles) wedged himself into INT position in last 2 mins, ESPN's Bob Davie commented that we all had expected "Heisman Trophy kind of winning drive" by Missouri (6-1) QB Chase Daniel (39-52/390y, TD, 3 INTs). Instead, Lavine's big play stopped Heisman Trophy candidate Daniel, who had arrived with no INTs and nary single 3-and-out under his direction so far in 2008. Key to victory for Cowboys was pass-rush pressure, mixing up blitz and coverage looks delivered by D that had among nation's fewest sacks prior. Cowboys QB Zac Robinson (19-28/215y, 2 TDs, INT) accounted for 3 TDs, including TD run for 7-3 lead when he faked and kept ball on spread-option to kick 6y off LT. RB Derrick Washington's 5y TD run up middle in 2nd Q sent no. 3 Tigers off at H with 10-7 edge, but Washington would be held to 11y rushing. Cowpokes went ahead 14-10 when RB Kendall Hunter (24/154y) took pitchout and zoomed 68y for TD. After WR Damian Davis caught 40 and 31y TD passes from Robinson for Oklahoma State, Missouri clawed within 28-23 with 4:27 to play as WR Danario Alexander tip-toed right boundary of EZ to grab 7y TD pass from Daniel. But, Daniel suffered 3 INTs, all in 2nd H, to drop Tigers from undefeated rolls. Daniel would later call his trio of INTs "unacceptable."

Texas 45 Oklahoma 35 (Dallas): Each QB—Sam Bradford (28-39/387y, 5 TDs, 2 INTs) of no. 1 Sooners (5-1) and Colt McCoy (28-35/277y, TD) of no. 5 Longhorns (6-0) as well as their fabulous receivers—played superbly. Too bad officiating crew wasn't up to task. Several bizarre decisions contributed to outcome, including Oklahoma coach Bob Stoops' decision to fake punt while leading in 3rd Q, 2 roughing PENs at sideline against Sooners, well-acted roughing punter PEN against Texas, and clear EZ INT by OU DB Lamont Johnson that was ruled as non-catch. Oklahoma led most of way, scoring questionable TD on 3rd down catch on opening drive by WR Manuel Johnson, who appeared downed short of GL near left pylon. Sooners made it 14-3 in 2nd Q as TE Jermaine Grisham (5/90y, TD) bobbled pass inside 5YL, and ball popped right into hands of WR Ryan Broyles for TD. Texas fought immediately as WR Jordan Shipley (11/112y, TD) split middle and zoomed 96y for TD on KO RET. Horns trimmed H deficit to 21-20, and McCoy threw TD pass to Shipley to pull within 28-27 with 5:33 to go in 3rd Q. Holding 1-pt lead on next possession, Oklahoma coach Bob Stoops called fake-punt run by P Mike Knall on 4th-and-6 near midfield. Trying to block, Grisham got in Knall's way, and surprise run came up just short. This was chance Texas needed, and Horns went downfield to 30-28 lead on short FG, which was fortunate as McCoy forced 3rd down pass that DB Lamont Johnson cut across EZ to pick off, only to have his rolling catch be strangely judged as coming loose too soon. With 7:37 left, RB Cody Johnson provided 38-35 lead for Texas after Shipley took McCoy's 37y pass to within inches of GL. Neither team ran effectively—especially 1-dimensional OU which earned only 48y on ground—until about 5 mins remained when Longhorns RB Chris Ogbonnaya went wide right behind devastating blocks of pulling C Chris Hall and RG Cedric Dockery and raced 62y to 2YL. Johnson scored his 3rd short TD to wrap up Texas' upset of top-ranked Sooners.

TEXAS TECH 37 Nebraska 31 (OT): Running 80 plays, Nebraska (3-3) held ball all day, exceeding 40 mins in possession time, and racking up 471y O. Unfortunately, 3 big plays kept Cornhuskers from winning. First, Texas Tech (6-0) All-America WR Michael Crabtree took middle slant-in screen pass from QB Graham Harrell (20-25/284y, 2 TDs) against blitz and roared 35y to TD and 7-0 lead in 1st Q. With Red Raiders planning to try to draw Huskers off-side on 4th-and-5 at their 36YL, C Stephen Hamby surprisingly snapped ball with score tied 24-24 with 4:30 left in 4th Q. So Harrell lofted high pass downfield that Crabtree (5/89y, with 31st and 32nd career TD catches for school record) went high to catch for 47y gain. Harrell soon sneaked across for 31-24 lead. Undaunted, Nebraska QB Joe Ganz (36-44/369y, 2 TDs, INT) hit 6 straight passes, 3 to WR Todd Peterson, who slipped toward right pylon for tying TD at 31-31 with 29 secs left. It was 3rd TD of 4th Q for which Ganz accounted, including GL run that had pulled Huskers within 24-17 at 2:50. Final and 3rd decisive play came after Texas Tech WR Eric Morris scooted around RE for OT TD that put Raiders up 37-31, even though door remained open as Tech K Donnie Carona saw his x-pt partially blocked. Trying to scramble and throw ball away on 2nd down in Nebraska's half of OT, Ganz was being tackled when he tossed killing INT, of which Texas Tech CB Jamar Wall said, "He basically threw it right to me."

STANFORD 24 Arizona 23: Just when Arizona (4-2) appeared in position to make some noise in Pac-10, Stanford (4-3) rallied from 23-17 deficit in 4th Q despite being down to 3rd-string QB Alex Loukas (1-1/21y). Cardinal RB Anthony Kimble (10/110y, TD) overcame 3 TOs by 2nd-string QB Jason Forcier by sprinting 70y to Arizona 2YL in 3rd Q and plowing over 2 plays later to tie it 17-17. Wildcats had surged in 2nd Q as RB Nic Grigsby (15/66y, TD) scored on 25y run, and less than 3 mins later, S Nate Ness went 75y down sideline on INT TD RET. That made it 17-7 for Wildcats, who twice drove inside Stanford 5YL in 4th Q only to come away with K Jason Bondzio's 2nd and 3rd short FGs. Trailing 23-17 with 5:48 to play, Stanford went 60y as Loukas rushed for gains of 7, 6, 5, and 7y before big RB Toby Gerhart (24/116y, TD) plunged across for TD and K Aaron Zagory booted vital x-pt.

USA Today Coaches Poll October 12

1	Texas (44)	1505	14	LSU	776
2	Alabama (14)	1452	15	Kansas	676
3	Penn State (3)	1416	16	Boise State	648
4	Southern California	1198	17	Michigan State	468
5	Texas Tech	1195	18	Virginia Tech	467
6	Oklahoma	1147	19	Wake Forest	376
7	Florida	1145	20	South Florida	334
8	Brigham Young	1143	21	North Carolina	321
9	Georgia	1010	22	California	169
10	Oklahoma State	958	23	Vanderbilt	147
11	Ohio State	920	24	TCU	138
12	Missouri	886	25	Ball State	135
13	Utah	819			

October 18, 2008

(Th) TEXAS CHRISTIAN 32 Brigham Young 7: Extraordinarily swift D of Horned Frogs (7-1) devoured BYU's dynamic O to end nation's longest win streak at 16 games. TCU DE Jerry Hughes stormed in to sack Cougars (6-1) QB Max Hall (22-42/274y, 2 INTs) 4 times and create 2 FUMs, and DE Matt Panfil recovered FUM to position early TD. QB Andy Dalton, just off injury list, fired 25y to WR Jimmy Young on 1st scrimmage play by Frogs, and before end of 1st Q, CB Nick Sanders (2 INTs) picked off pass and returned it 29y to set up 2nd Q FG. Each TO helped TCU to 17-0 edge early in 2nd Q. In between, swift WR-turned-change-of-pace-QB Jeremy Kerley (9/77y) authored masterful 16y TD on QB-draw. Just before last min of 1st H, Dalton (12-19/170y, 2 TDs) lofted perfect fade route to WR Walter Bryant in EZ corner for 23-0 lead. Trailing 26-0 as 3rd Q marched on, BYU finally got ground game going after losing 1y in 1st H. On 4th and goal, Hall faked pass and dashed up middle for 2y TD to pull within 26-7, but Frogs RB Joseph Turner iced it with TD run late in 3rd Q.

BOSTON COLLEGE 28 Virginia Tech 23: Confident Boston College (5-1) started terribly in this key ACC tilt. On game's 3rd snap, Eagles QB Chris Crane (16-32/218y, TD, 3 INTs) threw INT which Hokies (5-2) LB Brett Warren returned 36y for TD. On ensuing KO, BC RB Jeff Smith lost FUM on own 28YL, and it set up 30y FG by Virginia Tech K Dustin Keys for quick 10-0 lead. Vaunted Hokies D couldn't hold it, however, and its 4 PENs on next possession allowed Eagles to score up-off-mat TD: 6y run by frosh RB Montel Harris (15/61y). BC roared to 3 TDs in 2nd Q to grip 28-17 edge at H. Eagles' biggest moment came on special teams: Despite being touched seemingly by entire Va Tech punt team, WR Rich Gunnell gave Eagles 14-10 lead with 65y punt RET TD. Also in 2nd Q, Crane threw TD for each side, his INT returned 55y for score by CB Victor "Macho" Harris for Hokies TD. Crane and WR Brandon Robinson (4/97y) connected on passes of 15y and 48y to set up FB James McCluskey's TD run late in 2nd Q. Boston College D dominated in 2nd H, surrendering only 6 pts and allowing no penetration of its red zone. Hokies QB Tyrod Taylor (12-27/90y, INT) struggled in pass game but rushed for 110y. Virginia Tech's 4-year ACC road-game record fell to 16-2, with former Big East rival Boston College administering both defeats.

VIRGINIA 16 North Carolina 13 (OT): After miserable 1-3 start to season, Cavaliers (4-3) coach Al Groh fashioned remarkable turn-around with 3rd straight win in upsetting no. 18 Tar Heels (5-2). Cavs TB Cedric Peerman (17/44y) ran for 2y TD to tie game with 47 secs left in regulation time and added another 2y TD run to win it in 1st extra session. Virginia QB Marc Verica (24-38/217y) was outstanding at game's end, completing 7-8/80y on tying 82y drive, and hitting TE John Phillips for 19y to set up winning score. North Carolina took game's opening possession 83y as bruising TB Ryan Houston scored from 1YL. Carolina's 10-play drive was so efficient, it needed to convert 3rd down only once, which QB Cam Sexton (16-25/166y, 2 INTs) did with 9y roll-out pass to WR Cooter Arnold, who was knocked OB just short of GL. From that moment on, UNC squandered chances—turning ball over 3 times—which allowed UVa O, that gained only 59y in 1st H it trailed 7-0, opportunity to overcome late 10-3 deficit. Tar Heels TB Shaun Draughn led all rushers with 30/138y, while Virginia LB Jon Copper was in on 16 tackles. In knocking off 18th-ranked Heels, Cavs had won 7 of last 8 in series and not lost to UNC in Charlottesville since 1981.

Georgia Tech 21 CLEMSON 17: Tears had been shed in Clemson (3-4) as coach Tommy Bowden was forced out early in week, replaced by asst Dabo Swinney. So, when emotional Tigers' early array of trickery—slow-developing misdirection pass by WR Tyler Grisham—went awry for 34y INT TD RET by Georgia Tech (6-1) FS Dominique Reese, it looked like thin-skinned Tigers might fold. Even though Clemson turned ball over 4 times in 1st H, its D played hard-nosed ball despite 21/109y rushing by Yellow Jackets FB Jonathan Dwyer and 26/77y, TD rushing by QB Josh Nesbitt. Tigers rallied in 3rd Q behind previously-benched QB Cullen Harper. ACC's preseason player of year, Harper relieved injured frosh QB Willy Korn, who had rough time with Tech's fine front-4. Trailing 14-3 at H, Harper (15-25/170y, 2 TDs, 2 INTs) hit pair of 3rd Q scoring passes of 32 and 31y to WR Aaron Kelly (7/122y). That tied Kelly with Glenn Smith (1948-51) for Tiger's record of18 career TD catches. But, with 5 mins to play Nesbitt lofted 24y TD pass to WR Demaryius Thomas (4/56y), who faked clear of defender to haul in winning score.

GEORGIA 24 Vanderbilt 14: Prior to season, no one had circled this SEC East contest. Yet there stood Vanderbilt (5-2) atop division. Entering game as most penalized team in nation, Bulldogs (6-1) couldn't match Commodores in disciplined play, but with talented individuals like frosh WR A.J. Green (7/132y, TD) and TB Knowshon Moreno (23/172y, TD) they did not have to. Georgia led throughout and enjoyed 425y to 245y advantage as Green opened scoring with 17y TD catch in 1st Q 2 plays after his nifty 49y grab, while Moreno rushed for season-high y and scored what proved to be winning TD on 11y run for 21-7 lead in 3rd Q. Vanderbilt tallied TD with help from 2

pass interference PENs and another after Vandy CB Myron Lewis intercepted QB Matt Stafford (13-23/194y, 2 TDs, 2 INTs) at Georgia 26YL. Both Commodores TDs came on short passes from QB Mackenzi Adams (16-32/131y, 2 TDs, 2 INTs) to frosh WR Jamie Graham (4/36y, 2 TDs), who twice went over UGa CB Bryan Evans. Bulldogs CB Asher Allen turned tables with preventive tackle of Graham on 4th-and-4 at Vandy 29YL, and it came moments before K Blair Walsh's clinching 39y FG with 17 secs left.

Louisiana State 24 SOUTH CAROLINA 17: Although 2 top 25 teams met in Columbia, game's signature play featured neither South Carolina (5-3) nor Louisiana State (5-1). Umpire Wilbur Hackett, former star LB at Kentucky in 1967-70, reflexively nailed Gamecocks QB Stephen Garcia (14-26/215y, TD, INT) after Garcia put his head down to charge forward from Tigers 8YL alte in 2nd Q. Oft-played TV replay showed Hackett, in proper position, raise his shoulder as he met Garcia, stunning QB who was then stopped by LSU S Curtis Taylor (7 tackles, INT, sack) after gain of 4y. After game, LSU coach Les Miles joked that "I want you to know that we were disappointed in his effort (to make tackle)." Play had nothing to do with outcome as TB Mike Davis (10/23y) scored on 1y TD run 3 plays later to give Gamecocks 17-10 H lead. Garcia was dominant figure of 2nd Q as he led South Carolina to 17 pts, throwing 12y pass to TE Jared Cook (5/74y) to set up FG, connecting with TE Weslye Saunders on 26y TD pass, and setting up Davis' TD with back-to-back runs of 7y to LSU 1YL. Hackett's odd hit may have inspired LSU D, which lived up to its reputation in 2nd H: Tigers blanked Gamecocks, made 3 sacks, and forced 2 TOs in surrendering only 42y. Gamecocks had -7y in 4th Q. Tigers tied it 17-17 late in 3rd Q on alternate QB Andrew Hatch's 7y TD pass to TE Richard Dickson and captured win with 83y TD drive in 4th Q capped by TB Charles Scott's 2nd TD run. QB Jarrett Lee (16-26/189y, INT) was 3-3/55y on winning drive with 36y completion to WR Demetrius Byrd (3/65y). Taylor sealed win with INT just after Scott's TD, and LSU eliminated final 4 mins by riding 7/37y running of TB Keiland Williams (15/72y).

ALABAMA 24 Mississippi 20: Mississippi (3-4) rallied from 24-3 H deficit with 17 straight pts and moved ball into Alabama (7-0) territory with chance to pull off 2nd trophy upset in 4 weeks. QB Jevan Snead (16-31/192y, TD, INT) led Rebels to Bama 43YL before his 4th down pass fell incomplete, and no. 2 Crimson Tide killed final min. Bama had enjoyed brilliant 17-min stretch from end of 1st Q into late 2nd Q when QB John Parker Wilson (16-25/219y, 2 TDs, INT) threw 2 TD passes on way to 24 straight pts. Rebels WR Mike Wallace got ball rolling Mississippi's way from opening of 3rd Q when he took KO 41y to near midfield. Mixing pass and run, Ole Miss marched inside Alabama 10YL, where it faced 4th down. Out came FG unit, but Rebs holder Rob Park flipped shuffle pass to streaking FB Jason Cook, who went 9y to EZ. Alabama answered with 40y catch by TE Nick Walker (5/65y) at Ole Miss 30YL, but S Kendrick Lewis soon made INT at his 2YL. At their 24YL in 3rd Q, Alabama DE Bobby Greenwood and LB Don't'a Hightower combined to halt 4th down run by Rebs RB Enrique Davis (11/70y). With 4th Q soon under way, Mississippi was running out of time, but Snead hit 17y scoring pass to WR Shay Hodge (4/64y) at pylon with 9:27 left. Alabama's once-fat lead had been trimmed to 24-17. Ole Miss K Joshua Shene booted 35y FG to narrow it to 4 pts, but when critical 4th down pass failed that was it.

PENN STATE 46 Michigan 17: Michigan (2-5), winners of 9 straight over Nittany Lions (8-0), came out hitting hard to frustrate no. 3 Penn State. Wolverines built 17-7 lead thanks mostly to power runs of little-used RB Brandon Minor (23/117y, 2 TDs). Lions' only score had come on 44y run in 1st Q by TB Evan Royster (18/174y, TD), who spun out of 2 tackle attempts in middle of line. QB Daryll Clark (18-31/171y, TD) got Penn State back in game, down 17-14, with 3y rifle pass to WR Jordan Norwood in last half-min of 2nd Q. Lions roared in 2nd H, with big play coming on safety that broke 17-17 deadlock late in 3rd Q. Penn State DT Jared Odrick caught up with Michigan sub QB Nick Sheridan in EZ. In quick succession, Penn State delivered Clark's 1y TD run after free-kick, partially blocked punt that led to FG, and sack-whiz DE Aaron Maybin's FUM-inducing hit on Wolverines QB Steven Threet (9-13/84y) that produced another TD run by Clark 5 snaps later. Michigan had gained 185y in 1st Q and was limited to 106y thereafter. Coach Joe Paterno, forced by leg and hip problems into watching his Lions from press box for 3rd straight week, joked about his bird's-nest view: "Am I starting to like it up there? I'll never like it. It doesn't mean that the team might be better off with me up there."

Ohio State 45 MICHIGAN STATE 7: Hopes were high in East Lansing as 2 of Big 10's 3 first-place teams met on heels of no. 12 Ohio State (7-1) having suffered through several poor O performances. While his veteran teammates wondered aloud about shared QB duties for sr Todd Boeckman, frosh QB Terrelle Pryor (7-11/116y, TD, and 12/72y, TD rushing) asked his coaches to bench him if he couldn't move team. To surprise of some, Pryor was terrific, looking like reincarnation of Vince Young, in scrambling left and cruising 18y to early TD. Pryor followed with 7y TD pass to WR Brian Robiskie, and Buckeyes jumped to 28-0 H lead when injury-recovered TB Beanie Wells (31/140y, 2 TDs) romped for 2 scores on his way to season-high in rush y. Michigan State (6-2) coach Mark Dantonio noticed change in Ohio's attack: "They (Pryor and Wells) came together today and had zero turnovers." Dantonio's Spartans lost primarily because of their 5 TOs—after losing only 6 TOs in 7 games—and their inability to deliver more than 52y rushing. Usually run-proficient Spartans could free star TB Javon Ringer only for 16/67y. Michigan State's only score came on opening drive of 3rd Q when back-up QB Kirk Cousins (18-25/161y, TD, INT) marched his unit 85y to his TD pass to TE Charlie Gantt. Buckeyes returned 2 FUMs for TDs in 4th Q.

OKLAHOMA 45 Kansas 31: While important Big 12 tilt may have turned out to be typical 2000s scoring shootout, it also was y bonanza in which school records fell. QB Sam Bradford set Sooners (6-1) mark with 468y on 36-53 passing and 3 TDs. Oklahoma WR Juaquin Iglesias set records for receptions and y on 12/191y. OU tallied 419y in 1st H on way to 674y. For its part, Kansas (5-2) went toe-to-toe and gained 491y with its records coming from WR Dezmon Briscoe, who hauled in 12/269y and both TDs thrown by QB Todd Reesing (24-41/342y, 2 TDs, 2 INTs). Kansas trailed 7-0, 14-7, 21-10, 24-17, and 31-17 and still kept coming back, pulling within 31-24 when TB Jake Sharp (12/103y, TD) tore up middle on 17y TD run less than 4 mins into 3rd Q. But, Sooners D finally got to Reesing, sacking him 3 times in next 4 possessions to force 4 punts. Before it was over, Jayhawks' taxed D had to stop nearly 100 plays by Oklahoma.

TEXAS 56 Missouri 31: There was no letdown for Longhorns (7-0) after big win over Oklahoma; new no. 1 Texas tallied TDs on each of its 1st H possessions. Texas jumped to 14-0 lead over Missouri (5-2) in 1st Q and extended it to 35-0 late in 2nd Q on WR Jordan Shipley's knifing run after pass catch. Texas QB Colt McCoy (29-32/337y, 2 TDs, and 11/23y, 2 TDs rushing) again outshone opponents' Heisman candidate as he hit school-record 17 straight completions, retrieved his own dribbled FUM only to pitch spectacular 23y pass, and scored pair of TDs running, often by powering his way through Tigers' D. Trailing 35-3 and showered with chants of "Overrated!" by giddy Austin crowd, Mizzou finally reached EZ twice in 3rd Q on 2y run by RB Derrick Washington and 13y pass by QB Chase Daniel (31-41/318y, 2 TDs, INT), who was under considerable pass-rush pressure all night.

UCLA 23 Stanford 20: Bruins (3-4) QB Kevin Craft (23-39/285y, 2 TDs, INT) was sacked 7 times but improvised on 2 TD passes in 2nd H, 2nd of which came with 10 secs left as he ran right to draw defenders away from TE Cory Harkey, who turned upfield all alone in EZ for winning 7y catch. Stanford Cardinal (4-4) had led most of way as RB Toby Gerhart (27/138y, 2 TDs) bashed for pair of short TD runs that provided 7-0 and 14-3 leads in 1st H. K Kai Forbath's 3rd FG on opening play of 4th Q gave UCLA its 1st lead at 16-14. But, Cardinal countered with 54y KO RET by frosh WR Chris Owusu that led to 40y FG by K Aaron Zagory. Gerhart carried 7/47y on 10-play trip to another FG by Zagory to make score 20-16. With 2:31 to go, UCLA took over at its 13YL before Craft hit 5-6/53y on way to winning throw off his deceitful dash.

ARIZONA 42 California 27: Hiding short frosh RBs behind big lines was becoming trend in topsy-turvy Pac-10 in 2008. After Arizona (5-2) bobble-prone starting RB Nic Grigsby fumbled on his 1st carry, 5'8" frosh RB Keola Antolin (21/149y, 3 TDs) was summoned to run wild through puzzled Golden Bears (4-2). "Number 2?" wondered Cal LB Anthony Felder, "We didn't see any of him on tape." Bears owned 7-0 lead in 1st Q on 1st of 2 TD throws by QB Nate Longshore (18-37/218y, INT) when little-used Antolin squirted up middle on 20 and 11y TD bursts on consecutive series in 2nd Q. Bears regained 24-14 H edge after RB Jahvid Best ran 67y to TD and TE Cameron Morrah went high in back of EZ for TD catch from Longshore. Although Antolin broke away for 59y gain before scoring from 1YL and Cats QB Willie Tuitama (16-27/225y, 2 TDs, INT) pitched 2 TDs, key score for Arizona among its 28 pts in 3rd Q was INT that CB Devon Ross wrestled away from receiver to barrel down right sideline for 21y TD.

USA Today Coaches Poll October 19

1	Texas (58)	1522	14	South Florida	643
2	Alabama (1)	1436	15	TCU	582
3	Penn State (2)	1413	16	Missouri	551
4	Southern California	1264	17	Brigham Young	464
5	Oklahoma	1218	18	Kansas	342
6	Texas Tech	1210	19	Tulsa	328
7	Florida	1184	20	Pittsburgh	292
8	Oklahoma State	1083	21	Georgia Tech	282
9	Georgia	1067	22	Ball State	274
10	Ohio State	995	23	Florida State	258
11	LSU	903	24	Northwestern	177
12	Utah	891	25	Minnesota	165
13	Boise State	786			

Bowl Championship Series Rankings October 19

	Harris Poll Avg.	*USA Today* Poll Avg.	Computer Pct.	BCS Avg.
1 Texas (7-0)	.9958	.9980	1.000	.9979
2 Alabama (7-0)	.9446	.9416	.960	.9487
3 Penn State (8-0)	.9232	.9266	.750	.8666
4 Oklahoma (6-1)	.8270	.7987	.870	.8319
5 Southern California (5-1)	.8165	.8289	.680	.7751

October 25, 2008

(Th) WEST VIRGINIA 34 Auburn 17: Tigers (4-4) arrived in Morgantown with stumbling O, but it seemed to find its legs in 2nd Q as QB Kodi Burns (13-21/111y, TD, INT, and 15/82y, TD rushing) tossed 16y TD screen pass to RB Brad Lester and 3 mins later—after 69y KO RET by RB Mario Fannin—scored at same EZ spot on 9y run. So, Auburn led 17-3 halfway through 2nd Q. But, West Virginia (5-2) QB Pat White (13-21/174y, 3 TDs, 2 INTs), who was playing his 1st full game in weeks because of head and hand injuries, shook off 2 early INTs to launch 44y TD pass to WR Alric Arnett. WVU went off at H trailing only 17-10. Mountaineers owned 2nd H as RB Noel Devine (17/207y, TD) turned game into track meet. Devine tore off runs of 13, 35, and 29y before closing night's scoring with 30y dash. Meanwhile, White's passes were picking apart Auburn D, which arrived as 9th-best in scoring avg but sometimes lost its desire to tackle. WR Dorrell Jolloh (4/53y, 2 TDs) yanked through several grabbing attempts to score decisive TD on 32y catch early in 4th Q. It put Mountaineers up by 27-17.

Rutgers 54 PITTSBURGH 34: Rutgers (3-5) was quietly putting back pieces to 2008 season after disastrous 1st half saw its record drop to 1-5. With rout of 17th-ranked Panthers, Scarlet Knights suddenly had turned loud. Resurrected Rutgers QB Mike Teel (14-21/361y, 6 TDs, INT) tore into Pittsburgh (5-2)—ranked 10th in nation in pass D—throwing school-record 6 TD passes, 5 in 1st H. Teel had entered contest with only 3 scoring passes all season. On team's 2nd play from scrimmage, Teel found WR Tim Brown (4/132y, 2 TDs) for 60y TD pass that tied game at 7-7. Later in 1st Q, Teel connected with WR Kenny Britt (5/143y, 3 TDs) on 79y scoring play for 14-7 lead. Rutgers never trailed again, although Panthers TB LeSean McCoy (26/146y, 4 TDs) and QB Bill Stull (17-23/283y) helped keep them close. With McCoy rushing for 3 TDs,

Pitt trailed 34-24 at H and took opening drive of 2nd H 59y to McCoy's 4th TD to trail by 34-31. But series of 3rd Q mishaps proved disastrous for Pitt as FUM of punt by CB Aaron Berry set up 36y TD pass from Teel to Brown, and, after Stull was knocked out of game, Rutgers LB Kevin Malast (8 tackles) returned INT of tipped pass by backup QB Pat Bostick (6-11/69y, INT) 74y to set up 8y TD run by RB Kordell Young (20/83y, 2 TDs). Suddenly deficit was up to 48-31, and Panthers were done. Road win was 1st for Rutgers over ranked foe since 1988 when Knights stunned no. 15 Penn State.

NORTH CAROLINA 45 Boston College 24: Winners of 4 straight games, BC Eagles (5-2) jumped to early 10-0 lead. Boston College's TD came when DT Ron Brace sacked North Carolina (6-2) QB Cam Sexton (19-30/238y, 3 TDs), and LB Kevin Akins gobbled up loose ball for 13y RET. That was it for Carolina TOs, however. With star WR-KR Brandon Tate lost for season with knee injury, Tar Heels WR Hakeem Nicks (8/139y, 3 TDs) stepped up as playmaking leader. On his way to 127y receiving in decisive 2nd Q, Nicks nabbed trio of TD passes from Sexton. Nicks' 1st TD featured 1-handed grab with nifty escape from tackle attempt by BC CB Roderick Rollins. Nicks' 3rd score broke 17-17 tie in final min of 1st H and featured his pull-away ability as he took short pass over middle for 43y TD. Carolina D, which entered game tied for national lead with 14 INTs, added 3 more with 2nd H picks by CB Kendric Burney (8 tackles, 2 INTs), who returned 37y to BC 1YL to set up TD run by TB Ryan Houston, and S Trimane Goddard, who delivered killer by racing 51y up middle to 4th Q TD. Hot and cold Eagles QB Chris Crane (28-42/204y, 3 INTs) managed 2 TD passes, but could not overcome his 3 INTs.

Virginia 24 GEORGIA TECH 17: As ordained minister and grad student, TB Cedric Peerman (25/118y, TD) was natural leader for Virginia (5-3). And it was Peerman's toughness that secured upset as he shrugged off knee pain to break multiple tackles throughout game and also scored winning TD with 3y race around RE that ended with stiff arm of Georgia Tech (6-2) CB Rashaad Reid that propelled Peerman through pylon for TD. "When a player sets a standard of laying it on the line like that, everybody follows," said admiring Virginia coach Al Groh. There were other stars for UVa O that gained 396y and needed to punt only once. QB Marc Verica (29-39/270y, 2 INTs) threw 2 TD passes, including 34y arrow to WR Maurice Covington (5/76y, TD) that gave Cavs 17-14 lead early in 3rd Q. Yellow Jackets had opened game in fine fashion, gaining 118y on pair of 1st Q TD drives as Georgia Tech built 14-3 lead. But Cavaliers D clamped down, allowing only 141y rest of game. Big play by Georgia Tech D permitted Jackets to tie it 17-17 midway through 4th Q: DE Michael Johnson forced FUM by Verica, recovered by DE Derrick Morgan at UVa 31YL to set up 39y FG by K Scott Blair. Peerman delivered 59y on 70y drive to winning TD as he rushed 5/46y and caught 13y pass. Virginia CB Vic Hall secured win with INT of Tech QB Josh Nesbit (7-15/103y) near midfield.

FLORIDA STATE 30 Virginia Tech 20: Since its disastrous O performance in 12-3 loss to Wake Forest on September 20, Florida State (6-1) had become scoring machine. Seminoles had won all 4 games since that loss, averaging 34 pts per game. But D served as catalyst for this win, FSU's defenders repeatedly gained good field position as 4 of 6 scoring drives began in Hokies territory. In holding Virginia Tech (5-3) to 243y with 2 TOs and 1-11 conversions on 3rd down, Seminoles D was flying all over field. Pair of Va Tech QBs were knocked out of game as starting QB Tyrod Taylor left after 1 play following hit by LB Toddrick Verdell, and former starting QB Sean Glennon (9-16/133y) left in 3rd Q after sack by LB Dekoda Watson. Both QBs suffered left ankle injuries. Hokies were forced to dust off QB Cory Holt (3-6/28y, TD), who played as well as could be expected, managing 4y TD pass to TE Andre Smith midway through 4th Q to pull Hokies to within 27-20. After QB Christian Ponder (11-19/159y, TD) led Florida State 40y to insurance 46y FG by K Graham Gano, Holt threw 3 straight incompletions. WR Greg Carr (3/100y) was Seminoles' best weapon as he collared passes of 48y and 39y that each set up 3rd Q TD.

Alabama 29 TENNESSEE 9: No. 2 Alabama (8-0) rolled over punchless Volunteers (3-5) who could gain only 173y O, with mere 36y from their once-proud rushing attack. Led by hard-hitting S Eric Berry, Tennessee's solid D limited Bama to 32y rushing in 1st H, but Vols simply couldn't dent Crimson Tide EZ until 10y TD pass by QB Nick Stephens (16-28/137y, TD), which came far too late in 4th Q. Tide K Leigh Tiffin tallied 2 of his 3 FGs in 1st Q, and Alabama's 1st TD, that provided 13-3 H lead, came on Bama's 5th conversion of 4th down in as many tries so far in 2008: RB Glen Coffee (19/78y, TD) bombed across from 3y out behind block of pulling LG Mike Johnson. Tennessee moved quickly late in 1st H to 14YL but PENs pushed Vols so far back that K Daniel Lincoln (31y FG in 1st Q) missed momentum-killing 43y FG try. Alabama QB John Parker Wilson (17-24/188y) capped 79y land-bound drive in 3rd Q with TD keeper that upped tally to 22-3.

Georgia 52 LOUISIANA STATE 38: What had happened to LSU's proud D? Tigers (5-2) allowed more than 50 pts for 2nd time in 3 weeks. It was fair to note that LB Darryl Gamble (13 tackles) scored Georgia's 1st and last TDs with INT RETs, bad trend beginning to dog LSU frosh QB Jarrett Lee (14-28/287y, 3 TDs, 3 INTs). Only 10 secs into contest, Gamble gave Bulldogs (7-1) 7-0 lead when he jumped route for 40y INT TD RET. Although Lee quickly answered with 10y TD pass to WR Brandon LaFell (3/62y, 2 TDs), Tigers D soon swooned with 443y against it. Bulldogs took control with consecutive 1st Q TD-scoring drives of 78y and 71y. UGa TB Knowshon Moreno (21/168y) ignited 2nd TD with 47y run left behind fine blocking. In 3rd Q, Moreno ran near-replica, dashing through left-side seam for 68y TD and 38-17 lead. Georgia QB Matthew Stafford (17-26/249y) threw 2 TD passes and ran for another, while WR A.J. Green (3/89y) caught beautifully-thrown 49y scoring pass and carried for 22y to set up 50y FG by K Blair Walsh late in 2nd Q. Although Tigers never led, they blocked well for RB Charles Scott, who gained 21/144y, 2 TDs. LSU finished with 469y but tallied 208y in frantic 4th Q. LSU K Colt David's 8 pts made him school's all-time scoring leader with 324 pts to date, breaking mark of 318 held by Kevin Faulk in 1995-98.

Duke 10 VANDERBILT 7: Hearkening back to simple, earlier time—halcyon days before World War II—when Duke (4-3) and Vanderbilt (5-3) match-up would have gotten national attention, Blue Devils and Commodores met with bowl implications surprisingly on line for both squads. Duke, who had not participated in bowl game since 1995, topped Vanderbilt, hoping for its 1st bowl invitation since 1982. Duke built 10-0 lead as QB Thaddeus Lewis (21-36/222y, TD) threw 22y TD pass to RB Tony Jackson in 2nd Q and K Nick Maggio booted 42y FG in 3rd Q. Frustrated by both Blue Devil D and series of O mistakes, including uncharacteristic 3 TOs, Vanderbilt had 1 moment to shine when QB Mackenzi Adams (14-31/210y, TD, 2 INTs) and WR Sean Walker (6/138y) hooked up on 79y TD pass down middle of field early in 4th Q. Commodores could get no closer than 10-7 as late-game threat was snuffed Duke reserve CB Chris Rwabukamba's 1st career INT on jump-ball with Walker at Duke 1YL with less than min remaining. Duke WR Eron Riley caught career-high 9 passes/83y, while star LB Michael Tauiliili paced D with 7 tackles, INT, and forced FUM. In on 16 tackles with sack and forced FUM, LB Chris Mavre was leader of Vandy D.

Penn State 13 OHIO STATE 6: Penn State (9-0) took over sole possession of 1st place in Big 10 in hard-hitting showdown with Buckeyes (7-2) in national telecast from Columbus. Nittany Lions D took away Ohio State's running attack, holding TB Beanie Wells to 22/55y and Scarlet-and-Gray to 61y on ground. Buckeyes QB Terrelle Pryor (16-25/226y, INT), Ohio's precocious frosh from Pennsylvania, was forced to throw more than coach Jim Tressel wanted but came up with some big plays. Pryor's 33y pass to WR Brian Robiskie (4/56y) allowed K Aaron Pettrey to boot 41y FG on last play of 1st H to knot score at 3-3. Lions opened 2nd H with power runs that took their toll on Buckeyes' D, but Pryor later hit RB Brandon Saine for 20y and Robiskie for 17y to set up Pettrey for FG late in 3rd Q for 6-3 edge. After Penn State K Kevin Kelly missed 45y FG early in 4th Q, Ohio moved to midfield and faced 3rd-and-1 at 50YL. Long-legged Pryor plunged ahead on sneak but saw opening to his right and slid down line for daylight. He was met hard by Lions S Mark Rubin (11 tackles), who admitted he accidentally poked in his left hand to pop ball backwards. At least 3 players were about to fall on bounding pigskin but each was knocked aside by diving opponent. Penn State LB Navorro Bowman (10 tackles) recovered FUM at Buckeyes 38YL. Inexperienced Lions QB Pat Devlin entered because QB Daryll Clark (12-20/121y), who had hit 49y rocket to WR Graham Zug to set up 2nd Q FG, stayed on sideline with head injury. Devlin threw only once, and WR Derrick Williams was interfered with to set up 1st down at 14YL. Devlin knifed across for TD sneak behind C A.Q. Shipley and LG Rich Ohrnberger for 10-6 lead 6 plays later. Trailing 13-6, Pryor had chance for last-play bomb, but CB Lydell Sargeant went high to intercept at front right EZ pylon. Penn State had lost 7 straight in Ohio Stadium since joining conf in 1993.

Texas Tech 63 KANSAS 21: To celebrate Halloween week, or every week for that matter, mammoth Texas Tech 6'7" 374-lb RG Brandon "Mankind" Carter showed up with bizarrely scary facial makeup. But horror laid upon Kansas (5-3) came from entire Red Raiders' O. QB Graham Harrell (34-42/386y 5 TDs), who moved past Philip Rivers of North Carolina State into 4th all-time in NCAA career passing y, found WR Edward Britton streaking on post-pattern for 55y TD in early mins. Texas Tech (8-0) WRs Eric Morris (7/39y) and Michael Crabtree (9/70y) each scored on 2 pass receptions, latter of Crabtree's coming on beautiful spin-away from tacklers for 16y. RB Shannon Woods (14/79y) also tallied twice. Although Jayhawks QB Todd Reesing (16-26/154y, 2 TDs) matched scoring passes in 14-14 1st Q, his uncharacteristic 3 INTs proved costly. Pair of INTs by Raiders FS Darcel McBath within 3 Kansas plays set up TDs in 3rd Q for 55-14 edge. K Matt Williams, Tech student who came out of the stands between Qs of September 20 game and won prize by making 30y FG, kicked all 9 Raiders x-pts. "I thought it was easy compared to the kick that got him free rent," Leach quipped. Regular Tech K Donnie Carona missed his only FG attempt.

TEXAS 28 Oklahoma State 24: Having played near-perfect ball for weeks, QB Colt McCoy (38-45/391y, 2 TDs, INT, and 10/41y, TD rushing) threw for career-high in y, but Longhorns (8-0) D had to bail him out after he threw INT in 3rd Q and lost FUM late in 4th Q. Oklahoma State (7-1) rallied from 14-0 and 21-7 deficits, but after CB Jacob Lacey made INT, State had to settle for K Dan Bailey's 39y FG which left Cowboys at 28-24 2 mins into 4th Q. Still alive with 5:27 to play, Cowpokes DT Jeray Chatham stripped McCoy at OSU 10YL but Cowboys couldn't advance beyond their 30YL on 4th down. Texas WR Jordan Shipley nabbed 15/168y and 14y TD that had provided 7-0 lead in 1st Q. McCoy threw 2nd Q TD pass to WR Quan Cosby and scored on 3y QB-Draw in 3rd Q that built 28-14 edge. Oklahoma State QB Zac Robinson passed 17-26/199y, TD, while RB Kendall Hunter rushed for 18/161y and 23y TD gallop in 2nd Q.

Southern California 17 ARIZONA 10: With both schools among 4 tied atop Pac-10 standings at 2-1, it was Southern California (6-1) D that took conf command to fuel close win in desert. USC TB Stafon Johnson (19/83y, TD) provided much of Trojans O, scoring on 2y blast from I-formation for 10-3 lead in 2nd Q. USC QB Mark Sanchez (21-36/216y, TD, INT) lost FUM in 3rd Q when Arizona (5-3) DE Brooks Reed looped deep on pass rush to sack Sanchez at Trojans 15YL. Arizona RB Nic Grigsby scored 4 plays later by knifing 5y off right side of line. Sensing upset of 7th ranked team in coach Mike Stoops' 5 seasons in Tucson, home crowd was silenced when Trojans went 80y for winning TD in 3rd Q. With big block, Johnson picked up blitz by former Pop Warner teammate, Arizona S Nate Ness, to allow Sanchez to loft 30y TD to uncovered FB Stanley Havili. Wildcats sr QB Willie Tuitama (14-30/88y, INT) had come in with 222y passing avg, but Trojans took away his downfield options with strong pass-rush pressure.

USA Today Coaches Poll October 26

1	Texas (58)	1522	14	Missouri	740
2	Alabama	1439	15	LSU	573
3	Penn State (3)	1414	16	Florida State	546
4	Oklahoma	1265	17	Brigham Young	545
5	Texas Tech	1246	18	Tulsa	524
6	Southern California	1228	19	Ball State	445
7	Florida	1199	20	Minnesota	403
8	Georgia	1137	21	Michigan State	292
9	Utah	987	22	North Carolina	232
10	Oklahoma State	972	23	South Florida	153
11	Boise State	894	24	Oregon	150
12	TCU	813	25	Maryland	71
13	Ohio State	752			

Bowl Championship Series Rankings October 26

	Harris Poll Avg.	*USA Today* Poll Avg.	Computer Pct.	BCS Avg.
1 Texas (8-0)	.9961	.9980	1.000	.9981
2 Alabama (8-0)	.9460	.9436	.960	.9499
3 Penn State (9-0)	.9298	.9272	.920	.9257
4 Oklahoma (7-1)	.8316	.8295	.820	.8270
5 Southern California (6-1)	.7912	.8052	.750	.7822

November 1, 2008

(Th) CINCINNATI 24 South Florida 10: Converted from TE prior to this season, Cincinnati (6-2) DE Connor Barwin had blossomed into star defender. Barwin, who had caught 31/399y in 2007, still remembered how to catch football and there he was lined up on O early in 4th Q with Cincinnati having 1st-and-goal at South Florida (6-3) 1YL. QB Tony Pike (20-28/281y, 2 TDs, INT), who ignored soft wrap on broken left forearm to play brilliantly, found Barwin in right side of EZ for 24-10 lead. Pain soon sent Pike to sideline, while Barwin (7 tackles, 2 passes defended) continued to harass Bulls QB Matt Grothe (13-31/174y, 3 INTs). Early in game, Barwin's pressure had forced Grothe out of pocket and into costly INT, returned 58y by Cincy CB Mike Mickens to set up opening 2y TD run by TB John Goebel (17/78y). Mickens' 13th career INT established him as school career leader. On next possession USF used 2 big plays—Grothe's 47y completion to WR Carlton Mitchell (4/77y) and RB Moise Plancher's 32y run—to tie game 7-7 on 1y run by Plancher (8/47y). His Bearcats ahead 10-7 in 2nd Q, Pike threw to WR Marshwan Gilyard (4/98y, TD) on bubble-screen for 26y TD. After Bulls LB Sabbath Joseph's 2nd Q 33y INT RET to Bearcats 43YL, Barwin made another key play, tipping pass by Grothe that was picked off by DE Lamonte Nelms. Twice cracking Cincinnati 10YL in 4th Q, frustrated South Florida saw both threats end on 4th down incompletions.

Air Force 16 ARMY 7: Early-striking Black Knights (3-6) clicked on opening series as WR Damion Hunter took flat-pass from QB Chip Bowden (3-11/64y, TD, INT) and nimbly stepped away from trio of Air Force (7-2) defenders on way to 47y TD. Army went on to outgain Air Force by 250y to 174y, but golden foot of K-P Ryan Harrison lifted Falcons to their 4th straight win. Replay reversal of FUM by workhorse Army FB Collin Mooney (22/92y) set up Harrison for 20y FG late in 1st Q. Air Force DB Reggie Rembert returned punt 35y to set up QB Tim Jefferson's 1y squeeze through line for TD and 10-7 H lead. Harrison, whose 8 punts totaled 328y to stymie Cadets all afternoon, made late 3rd Q FG of 29y and season-long of 48y to clinch it in last 2 mins. Thanks to good field position and tough Army D, Air Force's 4 scoring drives managed only 24, 34, 32, and 3y.

Florida 49 Georgia 10 (Jacksonville): Florida Gators (8-1), perhaps nation's hottest team now that November had arrived, had plotted entire year to avenge 2007 loss to Georgia (7-2), which had featured Bulldogs' much-publicized mass celebration after scoring early TD. Georgia outgained Florida by 398y to 373y this time, but Gators converted every mistake by Bulldogs. Despite his modest stats, Florida QB Tim Tebow (10-13/154y, 2 TDs, and 12/39y rushing) made his plays count for 5 TDs, including 3 rushing scores. In 3rd Q alone, when Gators padded their 14-3 advantage with 21 pts, Tebow ran for TDs of 1y and 8y and connected with WR Louis Murphy on 44y score. Gators forced TOs to bring about each of Tebow's 3rd Q TD runs: CB Joe Haden returned INT 88y to 1YL, and DT Terron Sanders advanced FUM by Georgia TB Knowshon Moreno 20y to 10YL. Moreno, who had torched Gators for 188y and 3 TDs in 2007, rushed for only 65y and was kept out of EZ. Georgia QB Matt Stafford (18-33/265y) fared as poorly, throwing 3 INTs without TD. "It's a weight off our shoulders," said S Ahmad Black, referring to photo of Georgia's 2007 celebration that had been posted for months in every Florida player's locker. "All we heard about was Georgia, Georgia, Georgia."

ARKANSAS 30 Tulsa 23: Arkansas (4-5) D may have surrendered 528y to unbeaten Tulsa (8-1) but ended up celebrating its 2nd H performance. After surrendering 20 1st H pts to 18th-ranked Golden Hurricane, Hogs made H adjustments to permit only 3 pts in 2nd H to team that had averaged 56 pts per game. Tulsa had scored in nation's-best 35 straight Qs until its 4th Q blanking. Tulsa K Jaron Tracy's 22y FG tied it 23-23 late in 3rd Q, and Razorbacks RB Dennis Johnson immediately delivered winning pts on ensuing 96y KO TD RET. Arkansas still had to weather late storm from Hurricane: At Hogs 7YL with 41 secs left, Tulsa QB David Johnson (17-31/322y, TD, INT) was unable to complete 4th down EZ pass to WR Trae Johnson (3/86y). Arkansas was unaccustomed to fast starts having totaled only 10 pts in opening Qs all season, but QB Casey Dick (25-38/385y, TD, INT), who threw for career-high y, led Razorbacks to 17-0 edge in 1st Q. Razorbacks promptly blew that lead as Tulsa rallied to 20-20 tie on pair of TDs by FB Charles Clay (7/117y, TD receiving): 28y run and 2y pass from Johnson. Dick's passes clicked for 4-8/46y as he sparked 55y drive to go-ahead 22y FG by K Alex Tejada at 23-20. Teams combined for more than 700y passing, and TE D. J. Williams (6/129y) and WR Jarius Wright (5/112y) had big games for Razorbacks.

MICHIGAN STATE 25 Wisconsin 24: Badgers (4-5) surprisingly outrushed TB Javon Ringer (21/season-low-to-date 54y, 2 TDs) and Michigan State (8-2) by 281y to 25y. Wisconsin QB Dustin Sherer (14-28/149y, TD) threw short 1st Q pass for only TD in 1st H led by Badgers 10-6. Badgers owned 24-13 lead nearly 6 mins into 4th Q as TB P.J. Hill (20/106y, TD) went 10y to score in 3rd Q and sub TB John Clay (14/111y, TD) burst off right side for 32y TD run. "We were flat, and I hate to say that," admitted MSU coach Mark Dantonio. But, Ringer capped 64y TD march, aided by 20y in Badgers' PENs, to pull within 24-19 in 4th Q. Spartans K Brett Swenson made 50y FG with 5:16 to play, and after Wisconsin PEN negated gain to MSU 4YL, Spartans took over at own 17YL with no timeouts left and 1:19 to go. Michigan State QB Brian Hoyer (19-44/252y) hit WR Blair White (7/164y) on 20 and 32y passes, and as Spartans kicking team dashed madly onto field, Wisconsin coach Brett Bielema inexplicably called timeout with 12 secs on clock, and used another, theoretically to unnerve Swenson. Swenson removed his helmet to laugh it off and drilled winning 44y 3-ptr with 7 secs to play. Afterward, he said, "The first timeout helped me out because it gave me a chance to relax after rushing on the field. The second timeout I thought was funny because he was trying to ice me and I knew that wouldn't work."

Northwestern 24 MINNESOTA 17: Okay, Northwestern students, let us study works of Kafka. Northwestern (7-2) QB Mike Kafka had been tapped as starter in 2006 but went to bench with hamstring injury after 4 games and barely resurfaced until hamstring injury ironically shelved Wildcats regular QB C.J. Bacher for this Homecoming Saturday at Minnesota (7-2). Kafka (12-16/143y, 2 TDs, 2 INTs) penned remarkable tale of ground assault: he rushed for school record for QBs of 217y. Enticing Minnesota (7-2) D to line of scrimmage with opening 11y run, Kafka soon found WR Jeremy Ebert for 36y TD pass. Kafka added runs of 53, 38, and 30y later in game. But he also was late with 2nd Q throw to outside, and Gophers CB Traye Simmons stepped in to pick it off and dash 23y to TD that gave 14-10 lead to Minnesota. With contest tied 17-17 in 3rd Q, Minny K Joel Monroe missed 20y FG from bad angle. It stayed deadlocked until late in 4th Q. Instead of playing for OT in last 30 secs, Minnesota QB Adam Weber (31-51/327y, TD, INT) fired pass for Big Ten's leading receiver, WR Eric Decker (7/62y, TD). Ball glanced off Decker's hands—"It was my fault," Decker said afterward—and was again deflected before Wildcats S Brendan Smith nabbed it before it hit turf. Smith weaved through stunned Gophers for winning 48y TD RET as clock ticked down to 12 secs.

Pittsburgh 36 NOTRE DAME 33 (OT): With last week's crushing loss to Rutgers still looming and trailing Notre Dame (5-3) 17-3 at H, Panthers (6-2) needed to prevent their season from possible evaporation. So, Pittsburgh opened 2nd H with 71y drive that sub TB Larod Stephens-Howling finished with 4y TD run. But, Pitt had gotten help from Fighting Irish: LB Harrison Smith's 15y personal foul PEN spoiled ND's 3rd-down stop early in possession. Pitt D, which had been burned by 2 TD passes from Irish QB Jimmy Clausen (23-44/271y, 3 TDs) to frosh WR Michael Floyd (10/100y, 2 TDs) in final 90 secs of 2nd Q, dominated 3rd Q by allowing only 7y on 10 ND plays. Panthers finally caught up at 17-17 early in 4th Q on 1y TD run by TB LeSean McCoy (32/169y), who carried on last 5 plays to chip in 37y of 70y drive. Notre Dame now needed to answer and did so with 75y TD drive that featured Clausen and WR Golden Tate (6/111y, TD) teaming for 3 completions/46y, capped by 6y TD pass. Next it was Panthers' turn, and QB Pat Bostick (14-27/164y TD, 3 INTs) knotted it 24-24 with 4th down 10y TD pass to WR Jonathan Baldwin on fade pattern to right side of EZ. Bostick had tried same play on 2nd and 3rd downs before finally hitting 6'5" frosh. Clock ticked down as Panthers stuffed Clausen's keeper on 4th-and-1 at midfield, but ND S David Bruton (16 tackles) quickly countered with INT at his 27YL with 22 secs left in regulation. Trade of FGs in 3 OT sessions brought mounting tension to 33-33 deadlock, and in 4th extra period, Irish K Brandon Walker missed 38y FG try. McCoy quickly raced 18y to 6YL to set up Panthers K Conor Lee for winning 22y FG.

GAME OF THE YEAR
TEXAS TECH 39 Texas 33:

Remarkable about nation's top conf was that no. 1 Texas (8-1) had to face its 4th Big 12 opponent in consecutive weeks that was ranked 11th or better. Longhorns had rolled up 129 pts on no. 1 Oklahoma, no. 11 Missouri, and no. 7 Oklahoma State when those teams had arrived with combined record of 17-1. Waiting in Lubbock, however, was O-fireworks of undefeated no. 6 Texas Tech (9-0). Red Raiders got winging fast, jumping to 19-0 lead by 2nd Q. Raiders NT Colby Whitlock spurted through to tackle Texas RB Chris Ogbonnaya in EZ for safety, K Matt Williams (2 FGs) made 29y FG, and RB Baron Batch scored 3y TD on last play of 1st Q for 12-0 lead. In 2nd Q, Texas Tech QB Graham Harrell (36-53/474y, 2 TDs) connected on 18y TD to WR Eric Morris, who slanted free toward left pylon. Trailing 22-6 early in 3rd Q, Texas P Justin Tucker booted 61y punt that was downed at 1YL. It set stage for clutch performer, WR Jordan Shipley (6/42y), to breathe life back into Horns: Shipley took punt near his right sideline and weaved cross-field for 45y TD RET to pull Texas within 22-13. Texas QB Colt McCoy (20-34/294y, 2 TDs, INT) made rare mistake 5 mins later when his pass was intercepted by Raiders S Daniel Charbonnet for 18y TD RET and 29-13 lead. WR Malcolm Williams (4/182y, 2 TDs) broke wide open for 91y TD pass down left sideline, his 2nd TD from McCoy, 4 mins into 4th Q. It lifted rallying Horns back to within 29-26. On next series, Texas Tech added 42y FG by K Donnie Carona, but McCoy led Longhorns downfield, starting with 5:45 left, by hitting 4-5 passes and running 11y. RB Vondrell McGee went 4y up middle for TD that put Texas ahead for 1st time at 33-32. Clock read 1:29 when Texas Tech took over after DB Jamar Wall's 38y KO RET. Harrell hit 4 straight passes to Longhorns 28YL with 15 secs to go. Harrell's next throw went high off receiver's hands, but frosh S Blake Gideon couldn't hold INT as ball bounced off his stomach inside 20YL. Would Tech coach Mike Leach call on long-range K Carona or inexperienced K Williams for 45y FG try with 8 secs left? No, Leach went for TD. Harrell threw into double coverage at right sideline where star WR Michael Crabtree (10/127y, TD) grabbed pass, shrugged off tackle by Texas CB Curtis Brown and slipped into EZ for winning TD with 1 sec to spare.

CALIFORNIA 26 Oregon 16: On stormy day in Berkeley best suited for water-loving Ducks (6-3), it was California (6-2) that overcame 5 TOs to knock Oregon from atop Pac-10. Oregon, clad all in white in 1 of its many uniform variations, had its share of murky blunders that put it behind after taking 6-0 lead as QB Jeremiah Masoli (7-21/44y, 2 INTs) faked option handoff and skirted RE for 17y TD after CB Spencer Paysinger launched Ducks' opening drive with INT at California 46YL. Oregon blunders included bobbled x-pt hold after Masoli's TD run, punt snap by C Zach Taylor that rocketed 38y through EZ for safety later in 1st Q, and pair of devastating INTs in 2nd Q. Cal DB Sean Cattouse picked off Masoli at GL early in 2nd Q to snuff threat, and LB Worrell Williams cruised 50y to 3YL in closing secs of 1st H to set up Bears QB Nate Longshore (13-27/136y, TD), who came in for injured QB Kevin Riley (7-12/80y, TD, INT), for 2y TD pass to WR Nyan Boateng. Boateng's slant-out TD catch gave Cal lead of 16-6 at H. After RB Jeremiah Johnson (20/117y, TD) slashed 17y for TD late in 3rd Q, Ducks trailed only by 19-16. But, Oregon CB Jairus Byrd muffed fair catch inside his 10YL with 10:07 to play, and Bears S Marcus Ezeff fell on it to set up RB Shane Vereen's clinching 2y TD run that went wide left around E.

OREGON STATE 27 Arizona State 25: Beavers (5-3) DE Victor Butler intercepted potential tying 2-pt pass by Arizona State (2-6) QB Rudy Carpenter (15-27/217y, TD) with 21 secs to play after Carpenter pulled Sun Devils to within 27-25 with 3y TD pass to TE Andrew Pettes at end of 72y TD march. It was only O TD scored by Arizona State in dropping its school-record 6th straight game. Oregon State QB Lyle Moevao threw 1st Q TD pass to WR Shane Morales but exited with bad shoulder in 2nd Q. On 1st series of 2nd H, Devils FS Troy Nolan intercepted Moevao's replacement, QB Sean Canfield (19-28/218y, 2 TDs, INT), and returned it 41y for TD that sent ASU up 13-7. Canfield soon countered with TD pass to Morales, but Devils K Thomas Weber hit 3rd of his 4 FGs from 44y for 16-14 edge with 5:17 to go in 3rd Q. In 4th Q, Canfield pitched TD pass, and K Justin Kahut (2 FGs) connected on 41y FG for 27-19 Beavers' lead.

USA Today Coaches Poll November 2

1	Alabama (40)	1498	14	Georgia	693
2	Penn State (14)	1437	15	LSU	683
3	Texas Tech (6)	1409	16	Brigham Young	591
4	Oklahoma (1)	1290	17	Michigan State	516
5	Florida	1268	18	Ball State	503
6	Southern California	1232	19	North Carolina	359
7	Texas	1227	20	Georgia Tech	289
8	Oklahoma State	1066	21	Maryland	243
9	Utah	1018	22	California	192
10	Boise State	958	23	West Virginia	172
11	TCU	862	24	Florida State	150
12	Ohio State	843	25	Northwestern	120
13	Missouri	794			

Bowl Championship Series Rankings November 2

	Harris Poll Avg.	*USA Today* Poll Avg.	Computer Pct.	BCS Avg.
1 Alabama (9-0)	.9818	.9823	.960	.9747
2 Texas Tech (9-0)	.9277	.9239	.960	.9372
3 Penn State (9-0)	.9435	.9423	.900	.9286
4 Texas (8-1)	.8147	.8046	.940	.8531
5 Florida (7-1)	.8389	.8315	.810	.8268

November 8, 2008

(Th) UTAH 13 Texas Christian 10: It was "Blackout Night" in Salt Lake City as fans donned ebony garb to match Utes' 1st-ever appearance in black. Horned Frogs (9-2) silenced crowd early by charging to 10-3 lead and 202y O in 1st Q. RB Ryan Christian scored TCU's TD on 3y run for 10-0 lead with 6 mins left in 1st Q. Utah (10-0) K-P Louie Sakoda kicked his 2nd FG in 2nd Q but spent most of 2nd H punting: 4 times on opening 4 possessions of 2nd H. TCU seemed set to jump to 17-6 lead in 3rd Q but WR Walter Bryant couldn't get foot in bounds for catch as he turned up-field for TD. On next play, Utah DE Paul Kruger sacked Frogs QB Andy Dalton (16-37/251y, 2 INTs) to push TCU out of FG range. As 4th Q wound down, Frogs K Ross Evans missed pair of FG tries, hitting upright from 26y and slipping wide from 35y. Utes took over after 2nd miss with 2:48 to play: On 80y drive, QB Brian Johnson (24-39/230y, TD) hit 6-8 passes, including 11y connection to WR Freddie Brown on 4th-and-5 at TCU 26YL. Johnson soon found Brown for winning 9y TD slant-in throw with 47 secs left.

Cincinnati 26 WEST VIRGINIA 23 (OT): Bearcats (7-2) knew road to Big East title would be bumpy on its way through Morgantown. Protecting 13-pt lead in 4th Q, Cincinnati D bowed its neck to stop not 1 but pair of 4th-and-goal plays by Mountaineers' potent O. So, Cincy appeared safe. However, like horror film monster that simply would not die, West Virginia (6-3) managed 3 scores in final 1:11 of regulation to tie it 20-20. Stunned Bearcats D regrouped to limit Mountaineers to FG in 1st OT as DT Terrill Byrd had huge sack of QB Pat White (20-38/219y, 2 TDs, INT, and 20/41y rushing) on 3rd-and-3 from Bearcats 7YL. Cincinnati QB Tony Pike closed it out in OT by throwing game-winning 2y misdirection TD pass to TE Kazeem Alli. Launched by WR Marshwan Gilyard's 100y TD RET of opening KO against WVU's 119th-ranked FBS school in KO y allowed, Bearcats went on to 20-7 H lead. Cincy converted West Virginia's lost FUM and bad punt into FGs and scored TD on Pike's 4y keeper that capped 77y drive during which he passed 7-7/75y. Both Ds enjoyed 3rd Q as neither team managed single 1st down until final secs when West Virginia RB Noel Devine (19/58y) raced 10y to Bearcats 39YL. That drive ended on downs at Cincy 3YL, and next WVU possession ended on 4th down INT by CB DeAngelo Smith at his 1YL. That's when fun began. Bearcats ran 3 plays and took safety to narrow their lead to 20-9 with 1:11 left. After free kick, White needed 53 secs to move 61y to his 3y TD pass to WR Dorrell Jalloh (4/54y). White went across for 2-pt conv to cut deficit to 20-17, and Mountaineers LB Mortty Ivy recovered ensuing onside-KO. White and Jalloh quickly hooked up on 21y pass to set up K Pat McAfee's tying 52y FG, longest of celebrated K's career. "It was just a great football game, one that we knew that we had to win if we wanted to talk about being a Big East contender," said Cincinnati coach Brian Kelly, whose growing team now shared 1st place in Big East with West Virginia and Pittsburgh.

NORTH CAROLINA 28 Georgia Tech 7: Inopportune FUMs by Georgia Tech (7-3) allowed Tar Heels (7-2) to inflate 7-0 lead with 3 TDs in 4th Q: pair of short TDs runs by TB Ryan Houston (13/74y, 2 TDs), followed by clinching 31y scoring reception by WR Hakeem Nicks (3/72y, TD). North Carolina pulled away as S Matt Merletti recovered fumbled punt late in 3rd Q by Yellow Jackets RB Roddy Jones at Georgia Tech 30YL. Tar Heels needed 6 plays to up their lead to 14-0 on 2y TD run by Houston. Carolina DE Robert Quinn soon stripped Ga Tech sub QB Jaybo Shaw, with FUM REC by LB Mark Paschal (10 tackles) at Jackets 32YL. Carolina drive needed only 5 plays—all runs by Houston—before he scored from 3y out. Later in 4th Q, RB Jonathan Dwyer (22/157y, TD) supplied only highlight for Yellow Jackets with blistering 85y TD run. After recovering Jackets' onside-KO attempt, UNC scored on 4th down pass by QB Cameron Sexton (7-16/100y, 2 TDs) to Nicks. With that catch, Nicks became school's career receiving leader with 2472y to top Corey Holliday (1989-93). Georgia Tech rushed for 326y, but as losing coach Paul Johnson lamented, "We fumble it away, then go back out there and lay it on the ground on the very next series: Lights out!"

FLORIDA STATE 41 Clemson 27: Florida State (7-2) fans serenaded coach Bobby Bowden on his 79th birthday moments after FSU O put finishing touches on win—Bowden's 380th—with 41y TD scamper around left side by TB Antone Smith (8/57y, 2 TDs). After spotting Clemson (4-5) early 10-pt lead, Seminoles snapped Tigers' 3-game winning streak in what was once called "Bowden Bowl." That nickname disappeared with firing of Clemson coach Tommy Bowden in October, but his father Bobby disclaimed verdict was any kind of family redemption. Tigers flew through 1st Q, building 132 to 0y O advantage after 2 scoring drives. Seminoles D then clamped down, holding Clemson to 184y rest of way and tying score at 10-10 later in 1st Q on 18y INT TD RET by DE Neefy Moffett. Seminoles D finished with 6 sacks—3 by DE Everette Brown—and held Tigers to 2-15 success on 3rd down. FSU O also woke up, torching Tigers for 419y behind QB Christian Ponder (16-27/153y, TD, INT) and 266y rush attack. Florida State TB Jermaine Thomas rushed 11/94y, while RB C.J. Spiller sparked Clemson with 13/66y, TD rushing and 3/55y, TD receiving. Seminoles K Graham Gano was 2-2 on FG tries, including 52y in 1st Q, to stretch his consecutive FG streak to 17. Amazingly, Gano had hit 5-5 from 50y+ during streak.

Georgia 42 KENTUCKY 38: Pushed to limit by Wildcats (6-4), Georgia (8-2) pulled out late win. Bulldogs QB Matthew Stafford (17-27/327y, 3 TDs), who passed for career-best y, threw winning 11y TD pass by racing to right under extreme pressure and throwing pass high and deep into EZ. Racing to back of EZ was 6'4" WR A.J. Green (2/53y, TD, and 1/28y rushing) who leapt to catch winning pass despite 3 snarling defenders. There was 1:54 remaining—enough time for Kentucky to threaten before another heroic play by Georgia. Since 2nd H had featured 6 lead changes, Commonwealth Stadium crowd was in no way surprised when Wildcats QB Randall Cobb (12-2/105y, INT) opened final drive with 29y pass to TE Maurice Grinter to Georgia 34YL. Next 4 plays produced only 8y, but Kentucky was saved by facemask PEN against Georgia frosh DB Nick Williams. On 1st down from Bulldogs 13YL, Cobb attempted middle screen pass, play that worked twice before for 24y. With 46 secs left, Georgia DE DeMarcus Dobbs rose into air and leaned backwards to snare INT before toss could reach TB Tony Dixon (18/61y). Bulldogs TB Knowshon Moreno (22/123y) and Cobb (18/82y) each rushed for 3 TDs, while UGa WR Mohamed Massaquoi (8/191y, TD) was top receiver. Despite losing pair of 4th Q FUMs, Massaquoi set up winning TD with 78y reception that featured his sprint down sideline after escaping from tackle. Kentucky rushed for 226y and scored its final TD in 4th Q on 1y keeper by Cobb after frosh S Winston Guy returned KO 96y to 4YL.

Alabama 27 LOUISIANA STATE 21 (OT): It was emotional, controversial, and, most importantly, victorious return of Alabama (10-0) coach Nick Saban to Baton Rouge where he coached Louisiana State (6-3) from 2000-04, including national championship season of 2003. Tigers put up great fight before record home crowd of 93,039, succumbing in extra session as LSU QB Jarrett Lee (13-34/181y, TD, 4 INTs) threw INT that Tide S Rashad Johnson took over his shoulder in EZ 3 plays before Bama QB John Parker Wilson (15-31/215y, INT) lunged over GL for winning TD from 1y out. Heroes for Alabama were plentiful as Wilson registered twice on TD runs, RB Glen Coffee rushed 26/126y and TD, WR Julio Jones caught 7/128y with sharp 24y OT catch that set up winning TD, and Johnson hauled in school-record-tying 3 INTs, including 54y TD RET in 2nd Q. Johnson set up earlier TD with 10y INT RET to LSU 15YL in 1st Q. Wilson converted that into 1y scoring keeper. By countering with 2 TDs within 24 secs later in 1st Q, Tigers owned 14-7 lead: Lee tied game 7-7 with 30y TD pass to WR Demetrius Byrd (4/51y) to cap 54y drive, and Alabama CB Javier Arenas fumbled ensuing KO to K Josh Jasper, which set up 30y TD run by Bengals RB Charles Scott (24/92y, 2 TDs) 2 plays later. Alabama had trailed for less than 2 mins entire season to date and needed close to 17 mins before Johnson knotted it at 14-14 with his INT TD RET. Teams traded 2nd H TDs before Tide drove 29y in waning secs before K Leigh Tiffin had 29y FG attempt blocked by LSU DT Ricky-Jean Francois to force OT. In its 1st game since 1980 as nation's no. 1 team, Alabama clinched its 1st SEC West title since 1999 while snapping 5-game series losing streak. Saban became 1st coach ever to win road game at school where he previously had won national title. Those who had failed previously were Jim Tatum, who lost at Maryland with North Carolina in 1957, Paul Dietzel, who lost at LSU with South Carolina in 1966, Howard Schnellenberger, who lost at Miami with Louisville in 1985, and Steve Spurrier, who to date had yet to win at Florida as coach of South Carolina.

IOWA 24 Penn State 23: Things started badly for no. 3 Penn State (9-1) as 3rd down sack and bobble by QB Daryll Clark (9-23/86y, INT) on opening series sent Nittany Lions back to own 1YL. Punting out of EZ against strong wind, Lions immediately

had to defend from their 25YL. Iowa (6-4) sent TB Shonn Greene (28/117y, 2 TDs) barreling on 11 and 14y runs, latter going for TD and 7-0 lead. From that point on, Penn State dominated 1st H, running 49 plays to Hawkeyes' 15 and outgaining Iowa by 203y to 70y. TB Evan Royster (26/90y, TD) pushed across for Penn State's only 1st H TD, but Lions uncharacteristically stumbled in red zone in face of Iowa's fine D-line play, led by DT Mitch King, and had to settle for pair of FGs by K Kevin Kelly to lead 13-7 at H. Hawks QB Ricky Stanzi (15-25/171y, TD, INT) got hot on 3rd Q drive against wind, hitting WR Derrell Johnson-Koulianos (7/89y, TD) with 9 and 11y strikes, followed by 27y TD. Penn State's lead, however, jumped to 23-14 late in 3rd Q when WR Derrick Williams (4/43y, and 12/53y, TD rushing) lined up at TB and dashed across for 9y TD. Ahead 23-21 after Greene narrowed margin on 6y run with 9:20 to go, Lions appeared ready to salt away verdict when they received fortunate roughing-P PEN to help drive to Hawkeyes 23YL with less than 5 mins left in 4th Q. Clark's pass into wind sailed high and was intercepted by S Tyler Sash. Iowa meticulously went 57y in 15 plays to K Daniel Murray's 31y FG with 1 sec left.

NEBRASKA 45 Kansas 35: Cornhuskers (6-4) bounced back from 62-28 shellacking at Oklahoma previous week to win their 20th straight over Jayhawks (6-4) in Lincoln. Kansas QB Todd Reesing (15-30/304y, 3 TDs, INT) pitched pair of 1st H TD passes, and when he found WR Dexton Fields for 11y TD in 3rd Q, Jayhawks enjoyed 21-17 lead. In 2nd H, RB Roy Helu, Jr. (16/115y, 2 TDs) emerged from trio of Nebraska runners to score pair of key TDs: Helu's 10y TD run late in 3rd Q put Huskers ahead for good at 24-21, and on next series, he took deceptive inside handoff to sprint 52y to score. Helu soon hurdled tackler to gain 23y to set up Nebraska's trickiest play: monstrous NT Ndamukong Suh (12 tackles) snuck out of backfield blocking spot to catch uncovered 2y TD from QB Joe Ganz (28-37/324y, 3 TDs, INT) for 38-28 lead with 5:58 left. DE Zach Potter intercepted Reesing on Kansas' next series, and after K Alex Henry ran 9y for 1st down on fake FG, Ganz hit WR Nate Swift for a 14y TD.

TEXAS TECH 56 Oklahoma State 20: No. 2 Texas Tech's well-oiled O machine sprung gasket in early going as QB Graham Harrell bobbled shotgun snap, and LB Patrick Lavine of no. 8 Oklahoma State (8-2) recovered at Red Raiders (10-0) 31YL. RB Kendall Hunter (17/112y, 2 TDs) soon dashed for 26y and plunged 2y for TD and 7-0 lead. Harrell (40-50/456y, 6 TDs) was quick to answer, hitting WRs Edward Britton and Eric Morris with TD passes after long 1st Q drives for 14-7 lead, and Texas Tech would score on 7 straight possessions. Raiders WR Michael Crabtree (8/89y, 3 TDs) caught pair of TDs on muscular slant-in moves in 2nd and 3rd Qs and added 1y fade-route score late in 3rd Q for 42-20 lead. It was 2nd straight win for Tech over top-10 foe.

SOUTHERN CALIFORNIA 17 California 3: For awhile, Golden Bears (6-3) D matched slug for slug with nation's top D of Southern California (8-1). With teams locked in 3-3 deadlock past middle of 2nd Q after K David Buehler of USC and Giorgio Tavecchio of Cal traded FGs, Trojans QB Mark Sanchez (18-29/238y, 2 TDs) hit TE Anthony McCoy with 20y pass and WR Damian Williams (4/67y) with 30y crossing-pattern throw. Sanchez soon followed with 19y TD on which WR Patrick Turner made diving catch in back of EZ. PENs vexed USC for most of night, and Trojans didn't lock it up until Sanchez tossed swing pass for 6y TD to WR Ronald Johnson with 3 mins to play. California seemed to have tied it 10-10 early in 3rd Q when RB Shane Vereen streaked out of backfield to catch 27y TD from QB Kevin Riley (4-16/29y, INT). But Bears were called for phantom ineligible-man-downfield PEN, and 5 plays later, Riley's pass was tipped and intercepted in EZ by USC CB Josh Pinkard. Cal could gain only 165y O, including miserable 26/27y rushing.

Bowl Championship Series Rankings November 9

November 15, 2008

(Th) MIAMI 16 Virginia Tech 14: It may not have been O masterpiece, but Miami still notched its 5th straight win. Dynamic player on each side returned from injury list to score TD in 7-7 1st H: Hurricanes RB Javarris James charged 3y up middle to cap 76y drive in 1st Q, and Hokies (6-4) QB Tyrod Taylor (6-12/75y, and 14/43y, 2 TDs rushing) zipped 14y on 2nd Q draw play. Miami dominated 3rd Q, outgaining Virginia Tech by 114y to -6y. But, Canes bogged down in red zone and settled for 21 and 31y FGs by K Matt Bosher in 3rd Q and his 23y FG early in 4th Q. Down 16-7, Virginia Tech managed 69y drive midway in 4th Q. Taylor capped it with 6y TD run to pull within 16-14. Hokies had 1 more chance from their 32YL, but Miami DE Allen Bailey sacked Taylor on 4th down with 1:56 on clock. Frosh LB Marcus Robinson contributed 3

sacks to Miami's mighty D, while frosh QB Robert Marve passed 7-16/121y and added 14/44y rushing. Match-up pitted dominant Thursday night TV teams as Miami ran its record to 13-1 while Virginia Tech dropped to excellent 15-4.

Notre Dame 27 NAVY 21: QB Casey Clausen passed 15-18/110y, 2 INTs and HB Armando Allen rushed for 60y and caught 7/60y as Notre Dame (6-4) enjoyed 27-7 lead as 4th Q clock wound down. But, it simply wasn't easy in 2008 for ND in trying to rebound from last year's dreadful 3-9 record and infamous 46-44 loss to Navy that snapped Irish's 43-year series win streak. With 1:43 left, Middies (6-4) RB Shun White scored what seemed to be meaningless 24y TD run. Navy LB Corey Johnson recovered ensuing onside-KO at Notre Dame 41YL, and QB Ricky Dobbs (2-8/54y) launched 40y pass to WR Tyree Barnes. Dobbs scored on 1y keeper 2 plays later with 1:21 remaining. Irish TE Kyle Rudolph was in position to snare next onside-KO try but was creamed before catching ball, clearing way for Johnson to again recover at ND 41YL. Dobbs ran twice for 10y to move chains, but Navy soon stalled, and 31YL was as close as Middies would come to another stunning victory. Before late-game craziness, Fighting Irish had dominated throughout. ND D held Navy to season-low 178y rushing, its O gained 340y with 24 1st downs, and its special teams had opened scoring on CB Mike Anello's blocked punt that LB Toryan Smith (10 tackles) returned 14y to score. Navy D forced 5 TOs and was led by S Jeff Deliz's 17 tackles.

MARYLAND 17 North Carolina 15: Running its 2008 record to 4-0 against ranked teams, Maryland (7-3) earned late victory over no. 16 North Carolina (7-3). QB Chris Turner (16-31/141y) engineered winning 19-play, 73y drive that K Obi Egekeze ended with 26y FG. Terps converted 3 straight 3rd downs before Turner ran 9y to Tar Heels 23YL on 4th-and-5. QB Cam Sexton (10-24/166y, TD, INT) came out throwing on final series, completing 10y pass to TB Shaun Draughn (13/46y) to gain 1st down at own 46YL. But 3 plays later, matters ended when Sexton threw INT deep over middle to CB Jamari McCollough. Sexton and Tar Heels O struggled all afternoon, gaining 285y and only 11 1st downs. UNC was particularly woeful on 3rd down, converting 1-11. Still, Carolina led into 4th Q after taking leads of 12-7 in 1st Q and 15-14 at H with its sole TD scored by WR Cooter Arnold (2/64y) on 59y pass play that featured his great cutback. RB Da'Rel Scott rushed 29/129y as Maryland earned 200th all-time win in ACC play, trailing only 225 of Clemson.

Boston College 27 FLORIDA STATE 17: Boston College (7-3) D continued to shine in holding Seminoles (7-3) to 285y O with only 73y rushing, 132y below Florida State's avg. Eagles D also led nation with 18 INTs coming in and forced FSU QB Christian Ponder (15-31/183y) into 3 errant throws, including 87y TD RET in 1st Q by S Marcellus Bowman and critical EZ INT, stolen by CB DeLeon Gause with 9:15 left in game when Seminoles trailed 24-17. Ponder was hampered by suspension of 5 reserve WRs for campus brawl. Seminoles P-K Graham Gano, who earlier had his 18-straight FG streak ended by 50y miss, kept late 3rd Q series alive with 24y run on fake punt until WR Preston Parker (6/53y) threw 29y trick TD to WR Greg Carr (2/40y, TD) on opening play of 4th Q that brought FSU to within 24-17. After Gause's INT, BC frosh TB Montel Harris (25/121y, TD) ran 9/26y and QB Chris Crane (14-26/181y, TD, INT) gained 6/21y on late 67y drive that killed 8:55 to 30y FG by K Steve Aponavicius. Homecoming game for Florida State was turned into trendy "blackout" as fans were invited to join team in wearing all black. BC spoiled things, becoming 4th straight road team to win in series. "They made a big deal about the blackout so we got all of our guys black shirts and said, 'Well, if we're not going to be invited we'll just crash the party,'" said Eagles coach Jeff Jagodzinski. "And that's what we did."

Vanderbilt 31 KENTUCKY 24: Coming off 4 straight losses after solid D had produced 5 opening wins, Commodores (6-4) received O spark from surprise source. CB D.J. Moore (3/51y, 2 TDs receiving), Vanderbilt's star KR and defender, came off bench to catch 1st Q TD passes of 18y and 24y from QB Chris Nickson (15-27/155y, 3 TDs, and 20/118y rushing). Kentucky (6-5) soon scored when CB David Jones returned blocked FG 57y for TD, but Moore returned on D to pick off 2nd Q pass by Wildcats QB Randall Cobb (11-26/144y, 2 INTs, and 15/72y rushing) at Kentucky 21YL. Nickson raced 20y on next snap before throwing 1y TD pass to TE Brandon Barden to rebuild lead to 21-7, before H. In 4th Q, after Cobb rushed for 10y TD on draw play to pull Kentucky within 31-24, Moore ended Cats rally with INT on own 17YL with 2:07 left. Cobb was multi-purpose star of game for Kentucky as team's leading passer and rusher, and he returned 2 punts/19y. With its win, Vanderbilt became bowl eligible for 1st time since 1982 and achieved 6 or more wins for only 4th time since 1955. Vanderbilt enjoyed relative O explosion with 368y and 21 1st downs, and its D permitted only single 1st down in 1st H, and it came on fake-punt run by P Tim Masthay.

FLORIDA 56 South Carolina 6: Never in Steve Spurrier's long playing and coaching career had his team lost by such large margin as South Carolina (7-4) did in Gainesville, site of many Spurrier conquests. For its role, Florida (9-1) became 1st SEC team to win 6 straight by more than 28 pts. Backbreakers in 1st Q for Gamecocks set dreadful tone: Under extreme pressure, QB Chris Smelley (13-24/92y, 2 INTs) lacked oomph on short pass which Gators LB Brandon Spikes leaped to stab and return for 12y TD; and cross-field pass on deceitful KO RET backfired at Carolina 1YL from which Gators QB Tim Tebow (13-20/173y, 2 TDs, and 14/39y, TD rushing) powered across for TD and 21-0 lead. RB Percy Harvin (8/167y, 2 TDs) scored on 26 and 80y runs during his greatest rushing game for Florida, and TE Aaron Hernandez made spectacular 1-handed TD catch from Tebow in 4th Q for 49-6 lead. K Ryan Succop kicked 41 and 44y FGs for Gamecocks' only scoring.

ALABAMA 32 Mississippi State 7: Special teams did much of damage as no. 1 Crimson Tide (11-0) advanced to 11-0 for 1st time since 1994. In 1st Q, Alabama CB Kareem Jackson sped in off left flank to block Mississippi State (3-7) P Blake McAdams' punt through EZ for safety. Trailing 5-0 in 2nd Q, Bulldogs QB Tyson Lee rolled right to launch 31y TD pas to WR Jamayel Smith in EZ. Bama DB Javier Arenas (6/school-record 153y punt RETs) went 46y to Miss State 2YL, and QB John Parker Wilson (10-17/148y) sneaked across for 12-7 H lead. Arenas, who set school record

153y on 6 punt RETs, dashed through perfect blocking for 80y TD early in 3rd Q to send Tide crashing for 20 unanswered pts in 2nd H. Held to 167y O, Bulldogs lost their 16th straight game to top-10 team.

Northwestern 21 MICHIGAN 14: Snow squalls punctuated history-making day in Ann Arbor. It was wrong sort of history for Michigan (3-8) which in falling to Northwestern (8-3) meant Wolverines had lost more games this year than in any of their mostly-glorious 129 years. In 1st Q, Wildcats 3rd string RB Stephen Simmons (22/56y, TD), playing because of injuries to RBs Tyrell Sutton and Omar Conteh, squirmed up middle on 3rd-and-18 for 21y TD run. Wolverines QB Nick Sheridan (8-29/61y) tied it on 3y run later in 1st Q, and Michigan went ahead when S Michael Williams blocked 2nd Q punt that WR Ricky Reyes took 3y to score for 14-7 lead. "All of a sudden you come out in the second half and it's snowing," gushed NW coach Pat Fitzgerald. "It's a beautiful Big Ten football weather day." Amidst 4 straight 3-and-outs forced by Wildcats D, Northwestern scored on its opening 2 series of 2nd H. Cats went 40y to WR Ross Lane's 17y EZ catch in traffic, and moments later, QB C.J. Bacher (17-29/198y, 2 TDs, 2 INTs) found WR Eric Peterman over middle for 53y TD and 21-14 lead. CB Jordan Mabin's diving INT in EZ in 4th Q helped clinch victory for Wildcats.

Texas 35 KANSAS 7: Efficient Texas (10-1) went to chilly, windy Lawrence to trounce fading Jayhawks (6-5), who lost their 4th Big 12 game in last 5. QB Colt McCoy (24-34/255y, 2 TDs) pitched pair of 3rd Q TD passes to lift his Longhorns record to 31 scoring throws in single season. "I was glad we got the wind in the third quarter. That really helped us," McCoy said, as Texas attached 3 TDs to its 14-7 H edge. Kansas QB Todd Reesing (25-50/258y, TD) notched 1 score against 3rd Q wind, hitting WR Dexton Fields with 7y TD pass. It was set up by miraculous catch made by WR Dezmon Briscoe against his helmet as he was smacked to turf after 25y catch on 4th down. With Texas battling Texas Tech and Oklahoma for Big 12 South supremacy, "style points" seemed to be important because BCS standing could affect which team was to make conf title game. So, Horns' regular defenders cheered on their subs as Reesing was sacked in last moments on 4th down pass attempt from Texas 2YL.

HOUSTON 70 Tulsa 30: No. 25 Golden Hurricane (8-2), FBS leader in both total O and scoring, dropped their 2nd straight game and fell into 3-way tie atop Conf-USA West with Rice and rampaging Houston (6-4), which won its 5th of last 6 games. Cougars QB Case Keenum (24-37/402y) pitched 6 scoring passes, and fleet, little WR Tyron Carrier (6/127y) caught pair of TD passes and returned KO for TD in last 9 secs of 1st H. Carrier's TD RET provided 42-17 H edge. With 52-pt avg in 9 games, Tulsa had scored in every 1st Q so far in 2008, but this time Hurricane failed on pair of 1st Q 4th down tries—including once at 1YL—and lost FUM to Cougars LB Cody Pree that led to 1st Q TD. Houston CB Loyce Means intercepted 3 passes, returning 3rd Q INT 69y for TD. Tulsa QB David Johnson passed 18-29/271y, 4 TDs, 2 INTs.

OREGON STATE 34 California 21: WR James Rodgers (6/50y, and 3/22y, TD) keyed terrific special teams play by Oregon State (7-3) that eliminated California (6-4) from Pac-10 championship contention. With Cal ahead 7-0 after early TD pass by Bears QB and Oregon native Kevin Riley (11-25/117y, TD, INT), Rodgers fielded KO at his 14YL and sprinted up right sideline for 86y TD RET. Late in 4th Q, WR Sammie Stroughter took punt down right sideline before cutting cross-field on 56y RET to Cal 2YL. RB Jacquizz Rodgers (27/144y, TD) quickly provided permanent lead for Beavers with 2y TD run. Cal scored pair of spectacular TDs—Riley passing laterally to WR Jeremy Ross who lofted 30y TD pass to WR Nyan Boateng in 2nd Q, and RB Jahvid Best (15/116y, TD) breaking away on 65y run—but it was not enough as WR James Rodgers ran 18y on his patented Fly Sweep for 27-14 lead midway in 3rd Q.

November 22, 2008

(Th) **GEORGIA TECH 41 Miami 23:** Youthful Hurricanes (7-4) entered contest on 5-game winning streak and appeared in AP Poll (no. 23) for 1st time in 2 years. Unfortunately, they joined long list of ranked ACC teams to lose to unranked conf foes in 2008; battle for division crowns had begun to resemble trench warfare. Miami had no D guns to stop triple-option O of Yellow Jackets (8-3) from overwhelming them with 472y rushing. Miami's O wasn't much better, struggling until 4th Q when sub QB Jacoby Harris (13-18/162y, 2 TDs, INT) finally rendered superfluous damage with 2 TD passes. Both Harris and starting QB Robert Marve (10-20/121y, TD, INT) suffered INTs, Marve's especially damaging since it was returned 26y for 1y by Tech DE Michael Johnson. Johnson's TD gave Yellow Jackets 10-0 lead, and FB Jonathan

Dwyer (10/128y, 2 TDs) ran for 2 more TDs before H, including 58y romp down right sideline. Despite not playing in 2nd H, Dwyer led contingent of Jackets who rushed for more than 75y, included FB Roddy Jones (7/97y), QB Josh Nesbitt (15/93y), and WB Lucas Cox (8/78y), as Georgia Tech counted 8 runs of 25y or more.

CINCINNATI 28 Pittsburgh 21: Cincinnati (9-2) QB Tony Pike barely had seen action in 2 years but emerged in his 3rd season only when drastic opportunities occurred. Oft-injured, Wake Forest transfer QB Ben Mauk, 2007 starter, lost his fight with NCAA for another year of eligibility. Then, new starting QB Dustin Grutza broke his leg in 2nd game of season. And when Pike himself broke his non-throwing arm, he had to play in pain upon his quick return because Bearcats O had struggled without him. In this battle for 1st place in Big East, arguably most important game in Cincy history, Pike (26-32/309y, 3 TDs) bested Pittsburgh (7-3) with brilliant performance. After throwing 2 scoring passes in 2nd Q to provide 14-7 H lead, Pike connected with WR Marshwan Gilyard (8/110y, TD) on 39y TD pass early in 3rd Q for 21-7 lead. Size of lead was crucial as it diminished number of carries for Panthers star TB LeSean McCoy (17/82y, 2 TDs), who had given Pitt 7-0 lead on 6y TD run in 1st Q. In 2nd H, McCoy was called upon to rush only 7/35y but did score on 16y run in 4th Q as Pitt rallied with pair of 4th Q TDs. Comeback fell short as Bearcats D contributed 4 of its 7 sacks of Panthers QB Bill Stull (18-28/229y, TD, INT) in 4th Q and ended 2 of Pitt's final possessions by forcing TOs. DE Connor Barwin led Bearcats D with 3 sacks, who formerly played WR. McKillop was in on 17 tackles. "River City Rivalry," as Ohio River match-up was now termed, went to Cincinnati for 1st time after 7 series defeats, and Bearcats had won 9 games in back-to-back seasons for 1st time in school history.

Mississippi 31 LOUISIANA STATE 13: Opponents in newly-minted "Magnolia Bowl" may have left Tiger Stadium sporting identical W-L records, but they seemed headed in different directions. Rising Rebels (7-4), winners of 4 consecutive games, feasted on struggling Louisiana State (7-4), which dropped its 3rd straight conf tilt and team home game this season. At helm of O that notched 409y, Mississippi QB Jevan Snead (16-25/274y, 2 TDs) led 4 TD drives of at least 72y. Rebels D dominated as well, holding Tigers ground attack to 37y and sacking LSU QBs 4 times. Rebs took control on opening possession as Snead sparked 76y trip with 34y TD pass on 3rd-and-17 to WR Mike Wallace (5/99y, 2 TDs). In 2nd Q, after Tigers had pulled to within 7-3 on K Colt David's 46y FG, Snead led Mississippi to TDs on consecutive possessions. On drive to RB Brandon Bolden's 3y TD run and 14-3 lead, Rebels converted fake punt from LSU 38YL with 33y pass by FB Jason Cook to S Kendrick Lewis (8 tackles, INT, forced FUM, sack), who formerly played WR. Bolden, taking direct snap, scored 3 plays later. After Ole Miss D forced 3-and-out, Snead marched Rebels 89y to another TD pass to Wallace. Situation for Tigers worsened as QB Jarrett Lee (4-12/49y, INT) was forced out with ankle injury late in 1st H. With backup QB Andrew Hatch already sidelined with concussion and leg injuries, Tigers turned to heralded, but unproven frosh QB Jordan Jefferson (10-20/129y, TD, INT). Jefferson, who entered game 1-6/5y passing on season, paid immediate dividends late in 2nd Q with 9y scoring pass to WR Terrance Tolliver (5/35y, TD) on his 4th play. Jefferson led Tigers to David's 52y FG early in 3rd Q, but LSU's comeback would get no closer than 21-13. Rebels sealed win that snapped 6-game series losing streak by scoring TD out of "Wild Rebel" formation—akin to ancient Single Wing—as WR Markeith Summers raced 13y to score on play similar to old WB-reverse. Victory marked 2nd straight upset at Baton Rouge for coach Houston Nutt, who led Arkansas to stunning upset last season.

PENN STATE 49 Michigan State 18: With long-time coach Joe Paterno still relegated to press box with hip that would require replacement surgery in subsequent days, Penn State (11-1) earned its 1st Rose Bowl trip since 1995. Lions QB Daryll Clark pitched career highs in TDs and y with 16-26/341y, 4 TDs. WR Deon Butler (3/133y, 3 TDs), Penn State's recently-crowned career receptions leader, broke loose for 70 and 59y scores. Lions WR Derrick Williams made nice catch on 32y slant-in TD pass by Clark in 2nd Q after S Anthony Scirrotto made 14y INT RET. Michigan State (9-3) TB Javon Ringer (17/42y, TD) was held in check but still scored his FBS-leading 21st TD late in 1st H to trim Spartans' deficit to 28-7. Penn State D pressured Spartans QB Brian Hoyer, who was able to pass 25-40/206y, but threw 2 INTs. Strong wind and temperature in 20s couldn't dampen celebration of Penn State's 800th all-time victory.

OHIO STATE 42 Michigan 7: For 1st time in 105-game series history, Ohio State (10-2) won its 5th straight over bitter rivals from Michigan (3-9). Except for 2 big plays permitted by UM in 1st H, Wolverines were fairly competitive. Pair of long Buckeyes' TDs came on 59y TD squirt up middle by TB Beanie Wells (15/134y, TD) in 1st Q and 53y post-pattern TD bomb from frosh-sensation QB Terrelle Pryor (5-13/120y, 2 TDs, INT) to WR Brian Hartline (2/71y, 2 TDs). Late in 2nd Q, Michigan pulled within 14-7 as RB Brandon Minor (14/67y, TD) powered through right side for 1y TD run on 4th down. Buckeyes exploded in 2nd H: sub TB Daniel Herron burst up middle for 49y TD romp, and Pryor connected for 8y TD to WR Brian Robiskie. With 2 more TDs in 4th Q, Ohio State won by rivalry's biggest margin since coach Woody Hayes guided 50-14 rout of Michigan in 1968, game in which he famously snarled that he went for late 2-pt conv "because I couldn't go for three!"

PURDUE 62 Indiana 10: Joe Tiller, most successful coach in Purdue (4-8) history with 87 wins in 12 seasons, went out with boisterous blast in Old Oaken Bucket rout. As late Pro Football Hall of Famer Hank Stram, 1-time Purdue asst coach, might have said, Boilermakers "matriculated the ball down the field" as sr QB Curtis Painter (38-54/448y, 5 TDs), healthy again, completed passes at will to spark scores on 10 straight drives. Painter hit WR Desmond Tardy in back of EZ on opening possession and WR Aaron Valentin on 79y TD bomb for 14-0 lead 6 mins into contest. When Indiana (3-9) mishandled bloop-kick on ensuing KO, Purdue was at it again, on its way to 41-3 H edge. Boilermakers RB Kory Sheets (15/61y, 3 TDs) scored twice in 2nd Q to exceed school record of 14 rushing TDs in single season, mark held jointly by Tony Butkovich (1943), Leroy Keyes (1968), and Mike Alstott (1994). Hoosiers managed their only TD

early in 4th Q as QB Kellen Lewis (13-25/92y, TD, 2 INTs) found WR Ray Fisher for 16y that made score 55-10. At end, Purdue band played "Happy Trails to You" as Tiller trudged off field for last time, with his family, headed for Wyoming.

NORTHWESTERN 27 Illinois 10: Wildcats (9-3) became only 5th team in Northwestern history to score at least 9 wins. Northwestern took control late in 1st Q, moving 76y to RB Stephen Simmons' short TD run. When Wildcats got ball back on their next try, QB C.J. Bacher (22-33/230y, 2 TDs, INT) scrambled right and threw cross-field to back of EZ where WR Ross Lane tapped his toes to stay inbounds for TD catch at end of 60y trip. Trailing 13-0, disappointed Illinois (5-7) surged after receiving 2nd H KO. On his way to setting new Illinois total O record for season, QB Juice Williams (20-36/212y, INT, and 25/94y rushing) threw 31y pass to WR Jeff Cumberland and scooted 16y to set up RB Jason Ford for 1y TD run. Ahead 16-10 in 4th Q after Fighting Illini K Matt Eller made 21y FG, Wildcats sprung S Brandon Smith for 51y punt RET to Illinois 20YL. On 2nd down, Bacher found WR Eric Peterman (8/111y, TD) for 18y TD and Simmons made 2-pt run for 24-10 lead with 9 mins to play.

Iowa 55 MINNESOTA 0: This was no way for Minnesota (7-5) to bid farewell to 27 years of playing at Hubert Humphrey Metrodome, that is, thousands of Iowa fans chanting for their team. Gophers, who were ready to move into new on-campus stadium in 2009, suffered their 2nd-biggest home loss in history (84-13 defeat by Nebraska in 1983). It was Minnesota's worst lopsided Big 10 loss and 4th straight after opening season at 7-1. Only 12 pts removed from undefeated year, Hawkeyes (8-4) improved by winning 5th of their last 6 season tilts. TB Shonn Greene (22/144y, 2 TDs) broke Iowa's single season rushing mark with 1729y, surpassing Tavian Banks' record set in 1997. Iowa QB Ricky Stanzi passed 15-28/255y and hit 3 TDs. CB Amari Spievey returned INT of Minnesota QB Adam Weber (14-28/127y, 2 INTs) 57y to score in 2nd Q. Gophers, limited to mere 51 plays, rushed for 7y rushing and 134y overall O.

Syracuse 24 NOTRE DAME 23: Thrilled to play in Notre Dame Stadium, Syracuse (3-8) sr QB Cameron Dantley (13-25/122y, TD), son of Fighting Irish basketball legend Adrian Dantley, threw 11y TD pass to WR Donte Davis in last 42 secs and K Patrick Shadle (48y FG) kicked x-pt to pull off upset win for 19-pt underdog Orange. His team pelted by snowballs thrown by disgruntled fans, Notre Dame (6-5) QB Jimmy Clausen (22-39/291y, 2 TDs) later was booed when he missed open receiver when verdict could have been clinched at 23-17. Still, Clausen and WR Golden Tate (7/146y, 2 TDs) had connected on 35 and 36y TD passes 3 mins apart around H to build 23-10 lead. Orange frosh RB Antwon Bailey (16/126y, TD) launched rally with 26y TD burst up middle 2:30 into 4th Q. Loss in nutshell: Irish came away with only 6 pts when starting 4 drives inside Syracuse 23YL.

OKLAHOMA 65 Texas Tech 21: And now there would be most-talked-about 3-way divisional tie in memory: Sooners (10-1) created round-robin deadlock in Big 12 South, crushing Texas Tech (10-1), which had beaten Texas, which had beaten Oklahoma. All of no. 2 Texas Tech's tough opponents in undefeated-to-date season had come at home until this disastrous trip to raucous and inhospitable Norman. Swift O of no. 5 Oklahoma surged to 299y rushing, while QB Sam Bradford bothered to pass only 19 times, hitting 14/304y and 4 TDs. Oklahoma scored on 6 of its 1st 7 possessions on way to 42-7 H edge. Sooners D clobbered Red Raiders QB Graham Harrell (33-55/361y, 3 TDs, INT) from beginning, and much of Harrell's pass y came in 4th Q when he cosmetically totaled 130y. Oklahoma RBs DeMarco Murray (18/125y, 2 TDs) and Chris Brown (21/108y, 3 TDs) each scored twice in 1st H, while WR Manuel Johnson contributed game's signature play with 1-handed stab of long pass by Bradford on way to 66y TD in 3rd Q. Raiders were held to only 45y rushing, and star WR Michael Crabtree, nation's leader with 18 TD catches, was kept out of EZ.

WASHINGTON STATE 16 Washington 13 (OT): Sorry state of football in state of Washington—where neither major school had beaten single FBS opponent all season—was best expressed by wags who referred 101st tussle as "The Apple Sauce Cup." It was 1st time 10-loss teams had ever faced each other in Pac-10 history. Winless Huskies (0-11), who would end season with their worst all-time record, jumped to 10-0 lead as frosh RB Willie Griffin rushed for 112y and 3y TD early in 2nd Q. Washington was able to control line of scrimmage, easily outgaining Cougars until late in 3rd Q when Washington State (2-10) broke frosh RB Logwone Mitz off RT for 57y TD sprint to make it 10-7. Cougars QB Kevin Lopina (17-29/167y, INT) struggled all day; then light popped on in last min of 4th Q. Lopina clicked on 3rd down pass to WR Brandon Gibson and twice went to Jared, frosh WR Jared Karstetter that is, for 48y bomb and 7y out-pattern to UW 11YL with 2 secs left. Wazzu K Nico Grasu made misstep in his approach but still came through with tying 28y FG as time expired in regulation. After trade of FGs in 1st OT, Washington K Ryan Perkins missed 37y 3-ptr, and Grasu came through with winning 37y FG.

Oregon State 19 ARIZONA 17: Oh, those kickers! While Oregon State (8-3) had its Pac-10 fate in its hands—wins on this night at Arizona (7-4) and against Oregon next Saturday would send Beavers to their 1st Rose Bowl since 1965—they had to put shaky faith in soph K Justin Kahut. Trailing 17-10 with 3:58 left to play, Oregon State QB Sean Canfield (20-32/224y, TD) hit WR Sammie Stroughter with 7y TD, but Kahut hooked potential tying x-pt wide to left. Behind by single pt, clutch Beavers D forced punt with 1:27 to go and took over on their 20YL. Canfield, 2nd-string passer who started because of QB Lyle Moevao's injury, found Stroughter, who inexplicably was allowed to slip past Wildcats secondary, for 47y pass to 7YL. After Oregon State positioned ball in center of field, coach Mike Riley called on Kahut again, who punched through winning 24y FG as time expired. Earlier, Arizona played physical football to tie it at 10-10 on TE Rob Gronkowski's 16y catch late in 3rd Q and to go ahead 17-10 on RB Keola Antolin's 9y TD run midway through 4th Q. Antolin's TD came after Wildcats D denied Oregon State on 4th-and-1 run near midfield.

TEXAS CHRISTIAN 44 Air Force 10: Coming off their only conf defeat of season to undefeated Utah, Horned Frogs (10-2) scored on their 1st possession on frosh RB Luke Shivers' 3y run and turned matters over to QB Andy Dalton (21-27/321y, 2 TDs). In middle Qs, Dalton wrapped 8 and 7y TD runs around his pair of TD passes to extend 10-0 lead to 37-3. Highlight for Air Force (8-4), which lost 11th straight time to ranked foe including all 4 of its losses this season, came in 4th Q as sub FB Jared Tew broke up middle for 57y TD run. Falcons arrived with 279.7y rushing avg—nation's 4th-best—but gained only 150y on ground, 111y of which came on Tew's TD and TB Asher Clark's 54y burst off pitchout which set up 2nd Q FG by K Ryan Harrison. TCU still had bowl game in offing but its sr class enjoyed its 40th victory, tying most in school history, record set in 1932-35 when "Slingin' Sammy" Baugh quarterbacked Frogs.

UTAH 48 Brigham Young 24: By forcing 6 TOs by Brigham Young (10-2) QB Max Hall (21-41/205y, 5 INTs) and pulling away with 3 TDs in 4th Q, unbeaten Utah (12-0) clinched BCS Bowl spot and dethroned 2-time Mountain West champion Cougars. QB Brian Johnson had brilliant passing night with 30-36/303y, 4 TDs as Utes jumped to 17-3 lead early in 2nd Q. Pair of PENs against Utah D led to 2 TD runs by BYU RB Harvey Unga (15/116y, 2 TDs) in 2nd Q that briefly tied it 17-17. Trailing 27-17 at H, Cougars managed only score of 3rd Q when Hall tallied on 11y run. BYU got ball right back, but Utah DE Paul Kruger recovered FUM knocked from Hall's passing hand at BYU 31YL with 8 secs to go in 3rd Q. Johnson hit WR Brent Casteel with 8y TD pass early in 4th Q, and conf championship soon belonged to Utah.

USA Today Coaches Poll November 23

1	Alabama (56)	1518	14	TCU	695
2	Oklahoma (4)	1412	15	Ball State	673
3	Florida (1)	1401	16	Cincinnati	572
4	Texas	1370	17	Oregon State	544
5	Southern California	1288	18	Oregon	397
6	Penn State	1157	19	Brigham Young	321
7	Utah	1153	20	Northwestern	310
8	Texas Tech	1073	21	Michigan State	296
9	Boise State	1033	22	Boston College	290
10	Ohio State	994	23	Georgia Tech	241
11	Missouri	896	24	Florida State	204
12	Oklahoma State	858	25	West Virginia	83
13	Georgia	842			

Bowl Championship Series Rankings November 23

	Harris Poll Avg.	*USA Today* Poll Avg.	Computer Pct.	BCS Avg.
1 Alabama (11-0)	.9961	.9954	.970	.9872
2 Texas (10-1)	.9042	.8984	.960	.9209
3 Oklahoma (10-1)	.9116	.9259	.900	.9125
4 Florida (10-1)	.9277	.9187	.780	.8755
5 Southern California (9-1)	.8375	.8446	.710	.7974

November 27-29, 2008

(Th'g) TEXAS 49 Texas A&M 9: Longhorns (11-1) were in precarious position, holding 2nd in BCS standings by only .0084 over Oklahoma, its October 11 victim in Red River Shootout. Since Oklahoma seemed likely to earn major road victory on Saturday at Oklahoma State, Texas needed at least to collect major "style points" against Texas A&M (4-8). Texas dominated from outset, jumping to 14-0 lead early in 2nd Q as QB Colt McCoy (23-28/311y, 2 TDs) charged up middle on 14y run for TD to end game's opening series and added 20y post-pattern TD pass to WR Brandon Collins. After Aggies K Randy Bullock made 37y FG in last 2 mins of 2nd Q, McCoy hit 6-7 passes just before H to fit in 9y scoring pass to WR Quan Cosby. McCoy duplicated his option TD in 3rd Q, this time for 16y and 28-3 lead. Texas sacked A&M QBs Stephen McGee (16-24/207y) and Jarrod Johnson (4-11/62y) 6 times to help pad its -24y D rushing stats. Johnson managed 33y pass for Aggies' only TD in 4th Q. By then, Longhorns coach Mack Brown had called off dogs by magnanimously pulling McCoy early in 4th Q.

(Fri) PITTSBURGH 19 West Virginia 15: Pitt Panthers (8-3) dealt West Virginia (7-4) costly loss for 2nd year in row in Backyard Brawl, rallying from 15-7 deficit as TB "Shady" McCoy (33/183y, 2 TDs) scored twice in 4th Q, including game-winner from 1y out with 52 secs left. Held in check for most of game, West Virginia QB Pat White (15-28/143y, 2 INTs, and 12/93y rushing, TD) led Mountaineers downfield in final moments before throwing incompletion on 4th-and-1 from Pitt 18YL as time elapsed. White's game highlight came on 54y TD run in 2nd Q. Panthers QB Bill Stull (12-23/156y, TD) also struggled, throwing 2 INTs and losing FUM. Pitt D, which throttled WVU's top RB Noel Devine (12/17y), jump-started 4th Q rally as CB Jovanni Chappel picked off White and returned it 14y to WVU 16YL. McCoy scored 2 plays later on 5y run, so, after failed 2-pt run by Stull, Pitt trailed 15-13 with 8 mins remaining. Panthers soon took over at own 41YL with 5:10 left, and McCoy was aimed right at West Virginia on winning 11-play drive as he gained 55y of 59y trip. McCoy's rushing total marked his career high, and he now boasted 331y in 2 career games versus rival Mountaineers. K-P Pat McAfee starred for WVU by going 3-3 on FGs and averaging 47.6y on 5 punts. West Virginia's loss clinched 1st-ever Big East title for Cincinnati, which would win its 5th straight game by beating Syracuse 30-3 on Saturday.

(Fri) ARKANSAS 31 Louisiana State 30: When Arkansas (5-7) WR London Crawford (3/34y, TD) came down in EZ corner with 24y TD pass with 22 secs remaining, it was reminiscent of 2002 game when Hogs WR Decori Birmingham caught similar late TD pass to propel Arkansas past LSU and into SEC title game. Losing 2nd straight in series, free-falling Tigers (7-5) dropped their 2nd straight home game to finish 6-game Tiger Stadium home-stand without single SEC victory. Winning pass was thrown by Razorbacks sr QB Casey Dick (18-29/197y, 2 TDs) in final game of his up-and-down career. Dick sparked 17-pt 2nd H rally, throwing 2 TD passes, including 46y pitch to WR Jarius Wright (3/63y, TD) after converting 4th-and-6 with 21y pass midway through 3rd Q. Dick had come off bench to relieve younger brother, frosh QB Nathan Dick (7-11/83y, TD, INT), who had led Arkansas to early 14-3 lead but had trouble in 2nd Q when LSU reeled off 20 pts. Tigers easily outgained Hogs 153y to 3y in 2nd Q, scoring

on RB Charles Scott's 5y TD run, QB Jordan Jefferson's 11y TD pass to TE Richard Dickson, and K Colt David's pair of FGs. Jefferson (9-21/143y, 2 TDs) added 32y TD pass to WR Brandon LaFell (2/49y, TD) in 3rd Q as LSU seemed in command at 30-14.

(Fri) NEBRASKA 40 Colorado 31: Cornhuskers (8-4) K Alex Henery (4 FGs) erred in 2nd Q when he prematurely tipped off fake FG play, which went other way for Colorado (5-7) TD and 24-24 H deadlock. But, with 1:43 to play when Nebraska found itself in big jam on 4th-and-25 while trailing 31-30, Henery bombed school-record 57y FG to secure winning pts at 33-31. Colorado had blasted from locker room in 1st Q to 14-0 lead as Buffaloes totaled 148y on their 2nd, 3rd, and 4th O plays. Buffs' early TDs came on 68y TD pass from QB Cody Hawkins (14-24/209y TD, 3 INTs) to TE Riar Geer and 36y TD run around LE by RB Demetrius Sumler (9/65y, 2 TDs). Nebraska battled back to tie it 14-14 on pair of TD passes by QB Joe Ganz (19-26/229y, 2 TDs), 2nd of which went 53y to TE Mike McNeill and gave Ganz school-record, single season pass y record. As clock moved toward last min of 1st H, credit was earned by Colorado coach Dan Hawkins, who had schooled his special teams to expect Nebraska's wild, blind toss from FG-holder Jake Wesch to K Henery not because Huskers had shown it but because LSU—whose D was coached last year by new Huskers head coach Bo Pelini—had used it during its national championship run in 2007. Buffs CB Jimmy Smith sped in and jumped to intercept trick over-head toss by Wesch and raced 58y to knot game 24-24. Sumler's 2nd TD run late in 3rd Q gave CU 31-27 lead. Henery added his 3rd FG from 37y out to pull within 31-30 before Huskers took over on their 36YL with 4:35 to play. IB Roy Helu (25/166y) ran for 16 and 25y gains to Buffs 25YL, but Ganz was unable to avoid 15y loss on sack by blitzing Buffaloes frosh S Patrick Mahnke. Stumped by play-call for necessary 25y, Pelini boldly summoned Henery, who nodded affirmatively and nailed his long FG. Moments later, 300-lb Nebraska DT Ndamukong Suh iced cake, running 30y for TD with pass, deflected into INT by DE Zach Potter.

BOSTON COLLEGE 28 Maryland 21: This Flutie magician had first name of Billy and was nephew of famed QB Doug, whose new statue stood outside Alumni Stadium. Midway through 3rd Q, Flutie, holder on FGs and backup QB-WR for no. 21 Boston College (9-3), threw 9y TD pass to TE Jordon McMichael off fake FG for 21-7 lead in game Eagles needed to clinch ACC Atlantic Div. McMichael caught ball at 6YL and rumbled in, leaving Maryland defender in his wake at GL. For season, it would be Flutie's sole completion in 2 tries and McMichael's only catch. Down 2 TDs, Terrapins (7-5) had to go almost exclusively to air rest of way because they had rushed 21/26y, losing 6y in 5 sacks. That strategy led to 3 scores—2 for Maryland and 1 for Eagles—as QB Chris Turner (33-57/360y, 2 TDs, 2 INTs) sandwiched his TD passes around 36y INT TD RET by BC LB Robert Francois (10 tackles, INT, sack) that served as clincher near end of game. It was Eagles' 7th straight game with TD from its D and/or special teams. Boston College's excellent D play amplified by strong 182y rushing attack led by RB Montel Harris' 25/116y, helped ease way for frosh QB Dominique Davis (12-24/134y, 2 TDs) in his 1st career start. WRs Danny Oquendo (9/111y, TD) and Torrey Smith (8/115y) were Terps' century-y receiving stars. Loss snapped several 2008 streaks for Maryland, which had been 7-0 in day games, 4-0 in games decided by 7 pts or less, and 4-0 versus ranked teams.

VIRGINIA TECH 17 Virginia 14: By beating rivals, Virginia Tech (8-4) wrapped up Coastal title for 3rd time in 4 years of ACC divisional play. Hokies QB Tyrod Taylor (12-18/137y, TD) showed uncanny balance with 137y both rushing and passing. Taylor tossed 3y TD pass to WR Jarrett Boykin (6/65y) in 1st Q and raced 73y early in 3rd Q to set up tying TD. That score came from "Wild Turkey" formation as 280-lb TE Greg Boone took direct snap and ran 4y up middle. In 4th Q, Taylor hit 3-3/30y on 40y drive to winning 28y FG by K Dustin Keys. Taylor now had rushed for 100y 4 times in his young career, matching his more heralded predecessor Michael Vick. Virginia (5-7) had built 14-7 H lead with surprise shakeup of starting lineup: 5'9" CB Vic Hall (16/109y rushing) opened at QB—his HS position—and ran for 40y and 16y TDs. Hall played D too, pitching in with 3 tackles and sack to earn true rarity: he both was sacked as QB, which happened once, and registered sack on D in same game. After Hall's mischief, Virginia Tech D settled down in 2nd H, permitting only 101y and posting shutout. With 2:15 left, Hokies S Dorian Porch sealed it with EZ INT of UVa sub QB Marc Verica (8-14/77y, INT). Cavs had driven to Va Tech 25YL before Verica overthrew WR Kevin Ogletree. Virginia Tech's narrow victory lowered its avg margin of decision to 7.3 pts, least in country, as all 12 games had been decided by 17 pts or less.

Georgia Tech 45 GEORGIA 42: There was talk when Paul Johnson took head coaching job at Georgia Tech (9-3) last offseason that his Triple Option O could not penetrate nation's best Ds: What worked at Navy would not work against bigger, more talented teams from top BCS confs. Was anyone talking now? After spotting Bulldogs (9-3) 28-12 H lead, Yellow Jackets laid 3rd Q whipping on their rival's SEC-tough D. Georgia Tech outscored Georgia by 26-0 and outrushed Bulldogs by 201y to 1y in decisive Q. RB Jonathan Dwyer (20/144y, 2 TDs) ignited rally by running right, breaking tackles, and racing 60y to TD on 1st scrimmage play of 2nd H. Dwyer immediately ran for 2-pt conv, and Jackets trailed 28-20. When Georgia gained only 2y before punting, Ga Tech was back on O and needed 10 plays this time to reach EZ on 8y run by SB Roddy Jones (13/214y, 2 TDs). QB Josh Nesbitt tallied on 2-pt run to tie game at 28-28. Bulldogs were sent reeling by RB Richard Samuel's FUM of ensuing KO, recovered by Georgia Tech RB Marcus Wright at Georgia 23YL. Once again, Yellow Jackets needed 1 play to score as Jones went 23y to pay-dirt for 35-28 lead. Georgia Tech DE Michael Johnson ended UGa's next possession with 3rd down sack of QB Matt Stafford (24-39/407y, 5 TDs, INT), and Jackets were back on O long enough to add 28y FG by K Scott Blair before 3rd Q ended. Georgia bounced back in 4th Q with pair of TDs, but could never regain lead thanks to 54y scoring romp by Jones down right sideline midway through 4th Q that gave Ga Tech 45-35 lead. Yellow Jackets' last possession erased game's final 3:53 and Georgia's 7-game series win streak. Bulldogs wasted Stafford's fine performance, which tied school single-game record for TD throws, multi-purpose effort by TB Knowshon Moreno (17/94y, TD, and 4/74y receiving), and brilliant play of WR Mohamed Massaquoi (11/180y, 3 TDs), which included slip through defenders on 49y TD sprint in 1st H. Georgia Tech S Morgan Burnett's 1st Q INT, which he returned 35y for TD, was his 7th of season, 2 more than entire team registered in 2007.

Florida 45 FLORIDA STATE 15: It was best never to rile up Florida (11-1) QB Tim Tebow (12-21/185y, 3 TDs, and 16/80y rushing, TD). With Gators in front 14-6 in 2nd Q, Seminoles (8-4) fans made mistake of cheering as dynamic Florida RB-WR Percy Harvin limped off field with ankle sprain. Incensed, Tebow bowled over multiple FSU defenders 2 plays later to score on 4y TD run. After Seminoles K Graham Gano kicked 32y FG to trim margin to 21-9 late in 2nd Q, Tebow led 76y drive in only 67 secs to put game away with 24y TD pass to TE Aaron Hernandez (4/61y, 2 TDs). Tebow completed 5-5/all 76y on drive. After LB Brandon Spikes made INT, Gators blew game open with 10 pts early in 3rd Q. Averaging 12.1y and 9.9y per carry respectively, RBs Chris Rainey (8/97y) and Jeff Demps (9/89y, TD) led Gators rushers. Outgained 502y to 242y while turning ball over 4 times, Florida State had few heroes, although Gano clicked on 3 FG tries to finish regular season with 24-26 FGs. It was Florida's 5th straight win and 2nd straight blowout in series that took legislative pressure to start 50 years ago. Despite heavy rain, Florida State coach Bobby Bowden had anticipated some home-field advantage: "I didn't think they would beat us like that here."

ALABAMA 36 Auburn 0: So complete was Alabama's win that it was hard to remember Auburn (5-7) had entered contest on 6-game series win streak. That was old news; Crimson Tide (12-0) won by controlling line of scrimmage, as it had all year. RB Mario Fannin (8/28y, and 3/44y receiving) led Auburn in both categories, but his stats proved Tigers' O struggles: 8 1st downs amid 170y, while losing 3 TOs. Bama rushed for 234y as RB Glen Coffee (20/144y, TD) launched scoring with 41y scamper down right sideline to provide 10-0 lead in 2nd Q. DE Bobby Greenwood ended Auburn's best chance to score by blocking 40y FG attempt by K Morgan Hull on final play of 1st H. Tigers D had hung tough in 1st H before series of mistakes by their O set up numerous Tide scoring chances in 3rd Q. Alabama pulled away with 19 pts as it required only 39, 45, and 50y to travel to its TDs; pair of Bama TDs followed FUMs by Tigers in their own territory. Tide's sr class had never beaten Auburn, so QB John Parker Wilson (8-16/134y, TD) was happy to note: "We don't have to hear about it anymore."

Kansas 40 Missouri 37 (Kansas City): Although Missouri (9-3) had already cinched spot in Big 12 title game in same stadium week hence, it was banged-up QB Todd Reesing (37-51/375y, 3 TDs, 2 INTs) who twice rallied injury-riddled Kansas (7-5) in 4th Q of 117th meeting between rivals. With steady rain at Arrowhead Stadium, Jayhawks kept Mizzou Tigers from any 1st downs until 2nd Q and went up 10-0 as Reesing flipped 9y flanker-screen to WR Dezmon Briscoe (9/115y, TD). Tigers QB Chase Daniel (25-41/288y, 4 TDs, 2 INTs) countered with short TD pass of his own to TE Chase Coffman, but Daniel soon was embroiled in biggest play of 1st H. Daniel was forced into intentional grounding PEN when rushed in EZ by Kansas DE Jake Laptad. Ensuing free-kick, returned by Briscoe 29y to his 44YL, set up WR Dexton Fields for 25y TD catch from Reesing. Trailing 26-10 in 3rd Q, Daniel rallied Missouri with 3 TD passes, starting with 26y strike to WR Jeremy Maclin (9/123y, TD), and Tigers eventually took 30-26 lead with 6:52 remaining to play. Reesing brought Kansas back downfield and retook lead at 33-30 when WR Kerry Meier, who caught school-record 14/106y, tapped his left foot inbounds at back of EZ on 8y TD catch. Mizzou came right back to RB Derrick Washington's 6y TD blast off right side. It came with 1:50 to go and gave Tigers 37-33 edge. Reesing hit 5 passes, including 4 in as many snaps to Meier, to reach MU 26YL. But, Kansas soon faced 4th down, and Reesing scrambled up into pocket to avoid pressure and found Meier breaking alone behind S Justin Garrett for winning TD with 27 secs left.

Oklahoma 61 OKLAHOMA STATE 41: To qualify for Big 12 title match, Oklahoma (11-1) needed not only to capture tough road win at Stillwater—Cowboys stood at 6-0 so far at T. Boone Pickens Stadium—but also make big statement to lift itself above Texas. Interestingly, it was not big jump with pollsters that made difference for Sooners, it was record 5th-straight 60-pt performance that bumped computer numbers sufficiently high to vault past Longhorns in BCS standings. QB Sam Bradford passed 30-44/370y, 4 TDs to pace OU to 557y. Despite banged-up non-throwing thumb, Bradford authored most memorable play. It came late in 3rd Q as he spun in head-over-heels somersault trying to dive for TD at right pylon. Bradford bobbled snap on next play—4th down at 2YL—but still wedged across to raise score to 37-26 for Sooners. Oklahoma State (9-3) had put up good battle, leading 10-7 early in 2nd Q after QB Zac Robinson (17-26/254y, 3 TDs, INT) hit RB Kendall Hunter (18/84y) with 23y TD pass. That score launched stretch where each team scored on 6 straight possessions except for single play Oklahoma State used to kill last 13 secs of 1st H. Even with its O proficiency, Oklahoma also got good bounces: Bradford's 3rd down pass in 3rd Q was tipped away from WR Manuel Johnson and flew over heads of 3 Cowboys defenders into arms of TE Jermaine Gresham (9/158y, TD), who raced 73y for TD. That gave Sooners 30-19 lead, but Cowpokes bounced back with Robinson's 3rd TD pass to open 4th Q to pull to 37-34 and 4th career KO TD RET by CB Perrish Cox for 90y that made it 44-41. WR Dez Bryant's 2 TD catches gave him school career record with 18. But Sooners' national-best scoring O persevered to tally last 17 pts of game as Bradford hit WR Juaquin Iglesias with 17y TD, and RB Chris Brown ripped 28y to score in last 28 secs.

TEXAS TECH 35 Baylor 28: Would former no. 2 Red Raiders (11-1) turn up flat after being thrashed by Oklahoma last week in its only loss of season? Answer came in 1 form: Texas Tech's dynamic O was held to fewer than 400y (365y) for 1st time all season. In toting up 320y of its own, young and dangerous Baylor (4-8), with nothing much to lose, led 21-14 at H and added another TD on their opening series of 2nd H for 28-14 lead. Baylor had taken lead in last sec of 1st H when star QB Robert Griffin (12-15/91y, TD, INT, and 18/99y, 2 TDs rushing) lobbed 1y TD pass to WR Ernest Smith after DE Leon Freeman slapped ball from passing hand of Texas Tech QB Graham Harrell (41-50/309y, 2 TDs, INT) for DT Vincent Rhodes to recover at Tech 16YL. "That first half was one to not be proud of, and the second half was one to be incredibly proud of," said Red Raiders coach Mike Leach. Even with ace WR Michael

Crabtree (9/63y) hobbled on sideline with ankle twist, Harrell rallied Raiders to TDs on 3 straight possessions, going 72, 90, and 38y to score. Harrell's winning 4y TD to WR Detron Lewis came with 6:14 to play.

Oregon 65 OREGON STATE 38: "Tonight, the bubble burst," lamented Oregon State (8-4) coach Mike Riley as rival Oregon (9-3) all but crushed Beavers' hopes of playing in their 1st Rose Bowl in 44 seasons. Sensationally-swift Ducks roared to 694y against nation's 13th-ranked D and gained 35y or more on 8 plays. Additionally, Ducks, who led 37-13 at H, returned pair of INTs for TDs: CB Walter Thurmond went 40y in 2nd Q and CB Spencer Paysinger traveled 70y for game's last TD in last 3 mins. Oregon RB Jeremiah Johnson rushed for 219y, scoring on 83y run, while his sub LeGarrette Blount rushed for 112y, scoring on 9y run. Ducks QB Jeremiah Masoli (11-17/274y) tossed 3 TD passes. After falling behind by 20 pts, Beavers battled back in 2nd H, thrice closing within 13 pts as QB Lyle Moevao (27-51/374y, 2 INTs) vainly threw 5 TDs. Loss ended Oregon State's 6-game winning streak and forced its fans to pin Pasadena hopes on unlikely upset of Southern California by UCLA next Saturday.

SOUTHERN CALIFORNIA 38 Notre Dame 3: So dominant was Southern California's best-in-nation D (now averaging 7.8 pts per game) that Fighting Irish (6-6) didn't earn their initial 1st down until last play of 3rd Q. Notre Dame gained only 91y by night's end. Trojans (10-1) TB Joe McKnight (4/63y, TD) cut behind block of FB Stanley Havili in 2nd Q and sped 55y on beautifully-fluid run to TD and 14-0 lead. Troy QB Mark Sanchez (22-31/267y, 2 TDs, 2 INTs) made it 21-0 less than 5 mins later when he found WR Damian Williams (7/86y, TD) cutting toward middle for 12y TD pass. Fighting Irish made its only pts on K Brandon Walker's 41y FG 3:15 into 4th Q when tally already was 31-0 against them. It was announced during following week that beleaguered ND coach Charlie Weis would be retained for 2009.

USA Today Coaches Poll November 30

1	Alabama (58)	1521	14	Oregon	658
2	Oklahoma (2)	1397	15	Oklahoma State	613
3	Texas	1396	16	Georgia Tech	590
4	Florida (1)	1385	17	Missouri	470
5	Southern California	1298	18	Brigham Young	461
6	Penn State	1176	19	Georgia	440
7	Utah	1153	20	Boston College	435
8	Texas Tech	1116	21	Michigan State	414
9	Boise State	1044	22	Northwestern	333
10	Ohio State	999	23	Pittsburgh	154
11	TCU	836	24	Oregon State	127
12	Cincinnati	770	25	Mississippi	126
13	Ball State	765			

Bowl Championship Series Rankings November 30

	Harris Poll Avg.	*USA Today* Poll Avg.	Computer Pct.	BCS Avg.
1 Alabama (12-0)	.9965	.9974	.920	.9713
2 Oklahoma (11-1)	.9094	.9161	.980	.9351
3 Texas (11-1)	.9115	.9154	.940	.9223
4 Florida (11-1)	.9271	.9082	.820	.8851
5 Southern California (10-1)	.8418	.8511	.730	.8076

December 6, 2008

(Fri) Buffalo 42 Ball State 24 (Detroit): No. 12 Ball State (12-1) had already turned down opportunity to go to Boise State's treacherous home field for Humanitarian Bowl showdown of undefeated stars outside BCS constellation. There is no way to know how Ball State administration's lack of confidence played on young minds. Meanwhile, Buffalo (8-5), more than 2-TD underdog, was surprise entry in MAC championship as coach Turner Gill delivered school's 1st winning season since program elevated to FBS in 1999. Bulls recovered 1st Q FUM at Cardinals 25YL and went ahead 7-0 as QB Drew Willy (19-28/206y, 3 TDs) lofted 2y TD pass to right corner of EZ to WR Naaman Roosevelt, MAC's leading receiver with 1196y on 86 catches. In 2nd Q, Cardinals answered with 9-play, 80y drive to RB MiQuale Lewis' 4y TD run off right side, and K Ian McGarvey pounded line-drive 47y FG on last snap of 2nd Q for 10-7 lead. No sooner had Buffalo drawn Ball State D off-side on 4th down in 3rd Q than Roosevelt (10/116y, 3 TDs) took swing pass behind clearing block at corner by WR Brett Hamlin to race down left sideline for 39y TD. Teams traded TDs including stunning 92y FUM RET by Bulls S Mike Newton after Lewis lost handle soaring toward GL, so Buffalo led 21-17 in last min of 3rd Q. Unaware Shotgun snap was coming, Cards QB Nate Davis (31-48/351y, TD, INT) lost another FUM which CB Sherrod Lott scooped up for 74y TD RET, 2nd long TD RET by Bulls D in less than 4 mins. Ahead 28-17, Buffalo added Roosevelt's 3rd TD catch for insurmountable 35-17 lead with 6:06 to play.

Navy 34 Army 0 (Philadelphia): What out-going Pres George W. Bush witnessed was rare display of overwhelmingly superior skill and speed of 1 team in classic academy rivalry. Navy (8-4) completely dominated Army (3-9) in 109th renewal. Swift SB Shun White (13/148y, TD rushing) raced 6y down right sideline to start scoring for Midshipmen. Later in 1st Q, Black Knights chose not to pressure Middies' punt and it cost them dearly: C snap flew way over head of Navy P Kyle Delahooke, but Delahooke was able to chase it down in his EZ and without anxiety boot safely out of trouble. Even though Army took over at midfield, its O went nowhere. RB Pat Mealy later returned KO 63y to Middies 27YL, but Army failed on fake-FG run. Ahead 10-0 in 2nd Q, Navy QB Kaipo-Noa Kaheaku-Enhada (3-10/62y, TD) found White alone in right flat and pitched pass which White took for 18y TD. Navy held ball for 8 mins to open 3rd Q, driving 72y in 14 plays to 5y TD run by FB Eric Kettani (24/125y, TD) for 24-0 edge. Army's only consolation—other than unveiling new camouflage helmets, pants, and numerals with its plain black jerseys—was FB Collin Mooney (17/54y) gaining 1y on game's last carry to exactly reach 54y needed 1338y to pass Mike Mayweather's 1990 school single-season rushing record. "It hurts too much losing to Navy. I didn't care about the record," Mooney said of his squad's 7th straight loss to rival.

Virginia Tech 30 Boston College 12 (Tampa): After odd but evenly-balanced season in ACC, it turned out that 2007's division champions repeated in 2008. History repeated itself as Virginia Tech (9-4) again avenged regular season loss to Boston College (9-4) by taking conf title rematch. Hokies QB Tyrod Taylor (11-19/84y, INT) used his feet to score twice in 1st H, which Virginia Tech led 14-7. Hokies K Dustin Keys boomed 50y FG in 3rd Q, and frosh TB Darren Evans (31/114y, TD) tallied on 10y run, set up by 36y INT RET by CB Stephan Virgil, 5 mins later for 24-7 lead. Evans' pounding effort materialized as difference against BC D that had limited its last 5 foes to 57y rushing avg per game. Va Tech totaled 150y on ground. Although he completed 16y TD pass to WR Rich Gunnell (7/114y, TD) late in 2nd Q, Eagles QB Dominique Davis (17-43/263y, TD, 2 INTs) showed his frosh greenness as he turned it over thrice, including 17y FUM TD RET by Hokies DE Orion Martin that clinched it 30-10 at in 4th Q.

Florida 31 Alabama 20 (Atlanta): As remarkable as it sounded, QB Tim Tebow had never rallied Florida from any 2nd H deficits in 5 tries during his fabulous career. Inspired by emotional Tebow (14-22/216y, 3 TDs, and 17/57y rushing), no. 2 Gators (12-1) dramatically surged from behind in 4th Q to win SEC championship game at Georgia Dome. It was 39th all-time meeting of AP Poll's top-rated twosome; No. 1 ranked teams still led 22-15 with 2 ties. Florida, 10-pt favorite, scored on its 1st possession on Tebow's low 3y bullet pass to sub WR Carl Moore, but top-ranked Alabama (12-1) stood toe-to-toe and eventually appeared to take control with strong 3rd Q. Trailing 17-10 at H with its only TD coming after WR Julio Jones' 64y reception set up RB Glen Coffee (21/112y, TD) to slash 18y off right side for 1st Q TD, Bama staged dominant 15-play drive to go 91y to TD in 3rd Q. Jones caught 3/38y from QB John Parker Wilson (12-25/187y, INT), and Coffee gained 31y before turning over TB duties to sub Mark Ingram who ripped 14y on 3 carries, last attempt going 2y into EZ behind block of LT Andre Smith. Outgaining Gators 156y to 49y in 3rd Q, Tide added K Leigh Tiffin's 27y FG for 20-17 lead. With star RB Percy Harvin sidelined by ankle injury, Tebow whipped Gators on TD drives of 62 and 65y that took up more than 10 mins of 4th Q. RB Jeffrey Demps, 1 of those filling in for Harvin, scored on 1y run, and Tebow threaded low 5y TD pass to WR Riley Cooper for clincher with 2:50 to play. Gators coach Urban Meyer raved about Tebow afterward: "Tim's got something special inside him…I'm talking about making everyone around him better. That fourth quarter was vintage Tim Tebow."

East Carolina 27 TULSA 24: After hot start tabbed East Carolina (9-4) as this year's BCS-buster, Pirates lost 3 in row, but in visiting Tulsa (10-3) Pirates copped Conf USA crown and Liberty Bowl berth. Hurricane QB David Johnson (23-42/195y, TD, 5 INTs) arrived as nation's top-rated passer but slipped up with 2 INTs in early going. QB Patrick Pinkney (10-24/122y, TD) threw TD pass after Johnson's 1st mistake, and CB Travis Simmons gathered in Johnson's boundary overthrow and galloped 72y for 14-0 lead. Tulsa rallied for 17-17 H deadlock as RB Tarrion Adams (28/120y, 2 TDs) scored pair of short TDs. Pirates RB Norman Whitley (14/104y, TD) burst through hole in 3rd Q and romped alone on 69y TD scamper for 24-17 edge. After Johnson's subsequent TD pass tied it, ECU K Ben Hartman kicked wining 36y FG with 1:43 to go.

Oklahoma 62 Missouri 21 (Kansas City): Texas Longhorns, winners over both Big 12 title combatants, felt highly disappointed at not being tapped for this conf playoff. But Oklahoma (12-1) was selected using Big 12's established, 3-way tie-breaker rule: Sooners stood 2nd, Texas 3rd, and Texas Tech 7th in BCS standings, method favored to insure conf winner would have best chance at national championship. Sooners fan held up poster-sized photo of young, teary-eyed woman in Texas cap with derisive caption: "But, but…We're Texas!" No team in college history had ever scored in excess of 60 pts in 5 straight games, and once this victory was secured by H on strength of 38-7 tally, 60-pt goal became Oklahoma's feverish focus. OU ran no-huddle O for significant periods of time after outcome was out of doubt. Early on, Sooners D had placed plenty of pressure on Missouri (9-4) QB Chase Daniel (27-43/255y, 3 TDs), who coughed up 2 INTs and FUM. Only 1 of Daniel's trio of TD passes really counted: his 27y arrow to WR Jeremy Maclin early in 2nd Q kept Tigers briefly competitive at 10-7. Sooners RB Chris Brown (27/122y, 3 TDs) moved up to top of depth chart when RB DeMarco Murray was injured on opening KO. Brown scored twice in 1st H, and QB Sam Bradford (34-49/384y, 2 TDs) hit WR Juaquin Igeslias (9/125y, 2 TDs) for TDs in almost same EZ spot 2 mins apart in 2nd Q. RB Mossis Madu (15/114y, 3 TDs) got his chance to shine, and Madu's 37y gallop with pitchout put Sooners over 60 pts late in 4th Q. It also gave Sooners 702 pts for season for new NCAA record. On Sunday, Oklahoma jumped to top of BCS standings to earn date with Florida in BCS Championship in Miami on January 8.

Southern California 28 UCLA 7: While Oklahoma was exceeding 700 pts, Southern California Trojans (11-1) were producing truly remarkable D stats. Not since Auburn's 1988 team allowed 7.2 pts per game had any D unit relinquished as few as 8 pts per game. By permitting only 7 pts to cross-town rival UCLA (4-8), Trojans finished regular season with 7.8 scoring avg. FBS schools in 2008 averaged 2 pts more per game than in 1988. Bruins took 7-0 lead in 1st Q as WR Dominique Johnson took wide backward pass in left flat and lofted 21y pass toward TB Kahlil Bell, who jumped up among 2 defenders to make terrific catch and tumble into EZ for TD. But, UCLA could cross midfield only once rest of day. Troy TB Joe McKnight (15/99y, TD) cruised around right edge for tying 12y TD run late in 1st Q, and WR Damian Williams (3/68y, TD) caught go-ahead TD pass from QB Mark Sanchez (18-33/269y, 2 TDs, INT) barely 2 mins later. Sanchez's 2nd TD pass, this for 18y to WR Patrick Turner (5/81y, TD), came in 3rd Q for 28-7 lead. USC gave up only 157y and gained 478y. Both teams looked cool wearing home jerseys for 1st time in 26 years: cardinal red for visiting Trojans and powder blue for Bruins. Such practice in this game had been traditional when both played home games at LA Coliseum. UCLA moved to Rose Bowl stadium in 1982, and NCAA soon passed rule that penalized teams 1 timeout if they didn't wear their proper home or road jerseys. Since 1983, visitors in this annual matchup wore white. Wanting to return to its red shirts, USC was penalized timeout after opening KO, and UCLA voluntarily took its 1st timeout immediately thereafter, as gracious coach Rick Neuheisel had promised to do.

1	Oklahoma (31)	1482	14	Oklahoma State	722
2	Florida (26)	1481	15	Georgia Tech	690
3	Texas (4)	1408	16	Brigham Young	541
4t	Alabama	1309	17	Georgia	537
4t	Southern California	1309	18	Michigan State	466
6	Penn State	1193	19	Virginia Tech	337
7	Utah	1134	20	Northwestern	334
8	Texas Tech	1132	21	Pittsburgh	316
9	Boise State	1034	22	Ball State	219
10	Ohio State	1004	23	Missouri	218
11	TCU	877	24	Mississippi	160
12	Cincinnati	830	25	Oregon State	131
13	Oregon	747			

Bowl Championship Series Rankings December 7

	Harris Poll Avg.	USA Today Poll Avg.	Computer Pct.	BCS Avg.
1 Oklahoma (12-1)	.9554	.9718	1.000	.9757
2 Florida (12-1)	.9827	.9711	.890	.9479
3 Texas (11-1)	.9260	.9233	.940	.9298
4 Alabama (12-1)	.8644	.8584	.810	.8443
5 Southern California (11-1)	.8542	.8584	.750	.8208

2008 Conference Standings

Big East

Cincinnati	6-1
Pittsburgh	5-2
West Virginia	5-2
Rutgers	5-2
Connecticut	3-4
South Florida	2-5
Syracuse	1-6
Louisville	1-6

Atlantic Coast

ATLANTIC

Boston College (a)	5-3
Florida State (a)	5-3
Maryland	4-4
Wake Forest	4-4
Clemson	4-4
North Carolina State	4-4

(a) Boston College won Atlantic Division by defeating Florida State 27-17 on Nov. 15.

COASTAL

Virginia Tech (b)	5-3
Georgia Tech (b)	5-3
North Carolina	4-4
Miami	4-4
Virginia	3-5
Duke	1-7

(b) Virginia Tech won Coastal Division by defeating Georgia Tech 20-17 on Sept. 13.

Southeastern

EAST

Florida	7-1
Georgia	6-2
Vanderbilt	4-4
South Carolina	4-4
Tennessee	3-5
Kentucky	2-6

WEST

Alabama	8-0
Mississippi	6-2
Louisiana State	3-5
Auburn	2-6
Arkansas	2-6
Mississippi State	2-6

(a)Tulsa won Western Division by defeating Rice 63-28 on October 4.

Conference USA

EAST

East Carolina	6-2
Memphis	4-4
Southern Mississippi	4-4
Alabama-Birmingham	3-5
Central Florida	3-5
Marshall	3-5

WEST

Tulsa (a)	7-1
Rice (a)	7-1
Houston	6-2
Texas-El Paso	4-4
Tulane	1-7
Southern Methodist	0-8

Big Ten

Penn State	7-1
Ohio State	7-1
Michigan State	6-2
Northwestern	5-3
Iowa	5-3
Wisconsin	3-5
Minnesota	3-5
Illinois	3-5
Purdue	2-6
Michigan	2-6
Indiana	1-7

Mid-American

EAST

Buffalo	5-3
Bowling Green	4-4
Temple	4-4
Ohio University	3-5
Akron	3-5
Kent State	3-5
Miami (Ohio)	1-7

WEST

Ball State	8-0
Central Michigan	6-2
Western Michigan	6-2
Northern Illinois	5-3
Toledo	2-6
Eastern Michigan	2-6

Big Twelve

NORTH

Missouri (a)	5-3
Nebraska (a)	5-3
Kansas	4-4
Colorado	2-6
Kansas State	2-6
Iowa State	0-8

SOUTH

Oklahoma (b)	7-1
Texas (b)	7-1
Texas Tech (b)	7-1
Oklahoma State	5-3
Baylor	2-6
Texas A&M	2-6

(a)Missouri won North Division by defeating Nebraska 52-17 on October 4.

(b) Oklahoma won three-way tiebreaker by virtue of highest rank in BCS Standings on November 30.

Western Athletic

Boise State	8-0
Hawaii	5-3
Nevada	5-3
Louisiana Tech	5-3
Fresno State	4-4
San Jose State	4-4
Utah State	3-5
Idaho	1-7
New Mexico State	1-7

Mountain West

Utah	8-0
Texas Christian	7-1
Brigham Young	6-2
Air Force	5-3
Colorado State	4-4
Nevada-Las Vegas	2-6
New Mexico	2-6
Wyoming	1-7
San Diego State	1-7

Pacific-10

Southern California	8-1
Oregon	7-2
Oregon State	7-2
California	6-3
Arizona	5-4
Arizona State	4-5
Stanford	4-5
UCLA	3-6
Washington State	1-8
Washington	0-9

2008-09 Major Bowl Games

Eagle Bank Bowl (Dec. 20): Wake Forest 29 Navy 19

Back on September 27, Wake Forest (8-5) QB Riley Skinner (11-11/166y, TD) shouldered blame for loss to Navy as he had lost 4 INTs and FUM. To make up for it, Skinner was amazingly perfect in air, only such occurrence in bowl history when more than 10 passes were tried. Georgia's Mike Bobo had owned best bowl passing percentage with .929 on 26-28 against Wisconsin in 1998 Outback Bowl. Before Deacons could take control, DB Rashawn King returned FUM 50y along right sideline for TD as Navy (8-5) jumped to 13-0 lead. Middies were driving for more in 2nd Q when QB Kaipo-Noa Kaheaku-Enhada (2-7/32y, INT, and 15/83y, TD rushing) overthrew his receiver near left GL pylon, and Wake A-A CB Alphonso Smith—who made up for his FUM on rare O appearance that turned into King's TD—picked off his 21st career INT, new ACC mark. Deacons responded on 98y drive, capped by RB Josh Adams' 4y TD run around LE with 36 secs remaining before H. Navy led 13-7 at intermission, but Adams went up middle in 3rd Q, again for 4y, so Deacs took their 1st lead at 14-13. Kaheaku-Enhada put Navy back in front at 19-14 with 2y keeper early in 4th Q. Skinner continued his aerial mastery, hitting 4-4/69y, including 8y TD to TE Ben Wooster at end of 80y drive. Trailing 22-19 with end closing in, Kaheaku-Enhada fumbled away Middies' last chance, and his TO led to last-min 35y TD run by Wake FB Rich Belton.

Las Vegas Bowl (Dec. 20): Arizona 31 Brigham Young 21

BYU Cougars (10-3) arrived with sharp record but had beaten only Air Force among FBS teams with winning records. Playing its 1st bowl game in 10 years, Arizona (8-5) and oft-criticized coach Mike Stoops was simply glad to be invited to Las Vegas. Sr QB Willie Tuitama (24-35/325y, 2 TDs), Wildcats all-time pass y leader, pitched 71y post-pattern pass to WR Terrell Turner, who was hauled down at 1YL. RB Nicholas Grigsby (20/87y, TD) soon plunged over for 7-0 lead in 1st Q. Arizona played pressure D throughout chilly night, forcing BYU QB Max Hall (30-46/328y, TD) into 2 lost FUMs and INT. Stymied by injury to his brother-in-law, topnotch TE Dennis Pitta (5/58y), Hall, however, did find another TE, Andrew George, in back of EZ for 1y TD pass early in 3rd Q. It gave Cougars their only lead at 14-10. Tuitama went right back to work with 40 and 65y drives to his TD passes to WR Delashaun Dean (7/88y, TD) and TE Chris Gronkowski. Cats built 31-14 lead when Tuitama scored on 6y run 6 mins into 4th Q. On game's last play, Arizona WR Mike Thomas (4/29y) caught 3y pass for his Pac-10 record 258th career reception. Afterward, Stoops described pressure Tuitama had felt: "Nobody has endured more—well, maybe me!—in the last four years."

Poinsettia Bowl (Dec. 23): Texas Christian 17 Boise State 16

Much hype surrounded normally-low-key Poinsettia Bowl as these foes joined unbeaten Utah as cream of crop of non-BCS schools. In no way did match-up disappoint, especially at outset when Boise State (12-1), famed for its trickery, used returner Ian Johnson to fall to turf on opening KO so that he could catch cross-field, lateral pass. Johnson took RET 34y to set up K Kyle Brotzman's 30y FG. Broncos soon led 10-0 as RB Johnson (7/28y, TD) dashed 20y, cutting around right side for 1st Q TD, Johnson's 58th rushing score for new WAC career record. Horned Frogs (11-2) were playing good D but looked lost on O. Midway in 2nd Q, Boise frosh DE Byron Hout intercepted short 3rd down pass by Frogs QB Andy Dalton (22-35/197y, INT) and spun away from tackler to charge 62y to TCU 10YL. Frogs WR Ryan Christian (6/53y) hustled back to wrestle down Hout and forced another FG. Christian's play barely was noticed but turned out to be vital. TCU's Dalton pulled himself together to hit 4 straight passes on 60y drive to 16y TD run by RB Aaron Brown (14/102y, TD) in last 24 secs of 1st H. So, Boise State led 13-7 at H. Using ground game that would total 278y, Horned Frogs kept ball for much of 2nd H and wore down Broncos D. TCU RB Joseph Turner (16/83y, TD) capped 80y drive in middle of 4th Q by breaking tackles on 16y TD

burst up middle. Trailing now 17-13, Broncos advanced to TCU 12YL, but sack by DE Jerry Hughes forced Brotzman's 3rd FG. On Boise's next possession, TCU S Stephen Hodge made INT of QB Kellen Moore (22-35/222y, INT) to all but end it.

Hawaii Bowl (Dec. 24): Notre Dame 49 Hawaii 21

Much had been made of Notre Dame's NCAA-record 9 straight bowl losses, while questions also had been raised over bowl worthiness of inconsistent Fighting Irish (7-6). Perhaps Irish's secret to explosive O came from head coach Charlie Weis calling plays from press box due to impending surgery on both knees. Previously inconsistent Notre Dame O exploded against hometown Hawaii Warriors (7-7), setting numerous school bowl records in 1st post-season win since beating Texas A&M in 1994 Cotton Bowl. QB Jimmy Clausen (22-26/401y/5 TDs) earned school bowl records for passing y, TDs and percentage (84.6), while favorite target WR Golden Tate (6/177y, 3 TDs), who shared MVP honors with Clausen, set marks for receiving y and TDs. Clausen threw for 300y before H break to top Brady Quinn's 2006 Fiesta Bowl high of 286y in 1 H. Clausen hit trio of 2nd Q TD passes: 14y to WR David Grimes and 69y and 18y to Tate. Irish tallied their most bowl pts and y (478y) and blew game open with 3 TDs scored in each of 2nd and 3rd Qs. Hawaii QB Greg Alexander (23-39/261y, 2 TDs, INT) threw 2 TD passes to WR Aaron Bain (8/109y) but was heavily blitzed to give 2 TOs and 8 sacks, 2 by Frosh DE Ethan Johnson. ND RB Armando Allen also returned KO 96y for TD to make it 49-14 following Bain's 2nd TD catch.

Meineke Bowl (Dec. 27): West Virginia 31 North Carolina 30

West Virginia (9-4) QB Pat White closed his record-breaking career with his most passing y in any game: 26-32/332y, 3 TDs, INT. North Carolina (8-5) WR Hakeem Nicks (8/217y, 3 TDs) also enjoyed brilliant afternoon in front of his hometown crowd in Charlotte. On his 1st spectacular TD, Nicks tied contest at 7-7 in 1st Q as he swiped potential INT from WVU CB Ellis Lankster and dragged helpless CB Keith Tandy nearly 15y on spinning surge to EZ. In 3rd Q, Nicks made absurdly brilliant catch as pass was behind him on crossing pattern and ball crawled across his back so that he cradled it in his right (opposite) hand while smoothly cutting away from defender. Ahead 21-14 in 2nd Q, Mountaineers allowed safety when UNC S Deunta Williams (INT) spilled WVU RB Noel Devine (13/61y, TD) in EZ. Nicks soon caught his 3rd TD pass to put UNC ahead by 23-21 at H. Late in 3rd Q, Tar Heels QB T.J. Yates (15-25/211y, 2 TDs, INT) scrambled 4y to right pylon for TD that put Tar Heels back in lead at 30-24. As 4th Q advanced, WVU chose to gamble with White's pass on 4th-and-1 from its 44YL, but North Carolina stopped it with converging sack at WVU 40YL with 8:45 to play. No sooner had Carolina O taken field, however, when RB Shaun Draughn (17/65y) lost FUM to West Virginia LB T.J. Thomas. White took command with 3 brilliant plays: He found WR Jock Sanders for 40y pass, ran 9y, and whipped 20y rocket TD pass to WR Alric Arnett (7/93y, 2 TDs) for 31-30 lead. In so doing, White, all-time NCAA career QB leader with 4480y rushing as he added 55y on this day, became 1st QB in college history to start and win 4 bowl games.

Champs Sports Bowl (Dec. 27): Florida State 42 Wisconsin 13

Hero of tight 1st H was Seminoles (9-4) P Graham Gano, who dropped 4 punts inside 10YL—3 of them stopping inside 3YL—to frustrate run-oriented Badgers. Rarely passing because of its revitalized O-line, Wisconsin (7-6) had QB Dustin Sherer (9-16/132y, TD) fire wide flank pass, which was ruled as live-ball lateral, in 2nd Q which was knocked down. Seminoles LB Derek Nicholson picked it up and rumbled 75y foor unmolested score and 7-0 lead. Badgers TB P.J. Hill (15/140y) soon broke away for 46y run to set up FG, but Wisconsin failed to effectively kill last moments of 1st H clock. It permitted Florida State QB Christian Ponder (18-31/199y, 2 TDs) to lob 26y swing pass to WR Louis Givens and 15y fade-route TD pass to tall WR Greg Carr with 7 secs left in 1st H. In 3rd Q, Seminoles exploded for TD runs by RB Antone Smith and frosh RB Carlton Jones for 28-6 lead. Early in 4th Q, Sherer was stripped on sack, and FSU LB Dekoda Watson scooped up FUM to race away for 51y TD RET. Wisconsin was able to fit in late TD pass by Sherer, but it was only matter of time before Seminoles coach Bobby Bowden wrapped up his 21st bowl victory.

Emerald Bowl (Dec. 27): California 24 Miami 17

Golden Bears (9-4) were playing 12 miles from home at San Francisco Giants' AT&T Ballpark, where gridiron was tight-fit on outfield grass. California WR Verran Tucker took early short pass and broke free for 74y gain, initially ruled TD. After video reversal placed ball at 2YL, RB Jahvid Best (20/186y, 2 TDs) looped around left side for TD 2 plays later. Best came right back with electrifying 42y TD sprint for 14-0 lead. After losing 4y on its early possessions, Miami (7-6) finally got its O going on 10-play drive that carried into 2nd Q: frosh QB frosh QB Jacory Harris (25-41/194y, 2 TDs, INT) lofted 9y TD pass to WR Laron Byrd. Suddenly, young Hurricanes became composed on both sides of ball as they got to H trailing 14-7 and tied it 14-14 midway in 3rd Q when Harris fired 6y TD slant-in pass to WR Thearon Collier on 3rd down. On next series, TE Tad Smith made block to spring Best for 25y gain on 4th-and-1 to Miami 30YL. Poor Cal QB Nate Longshore (10-21/121y, TD), target of boo-birds all night, was tripped by own lineman on 3rd down drop-back, so K Giorgio Tavecchio drilled FG for 17-14 lead with 27 secs left in 3rd Q. Miami K Matt Bosher's tying 22y FG in 4th Q was made possible by running-into-P PEN against Cal. With 3:28 to play, Harris tried to pass from deep in his territory but was overwhelmed by blitzing Bears LB Zack Follett (2 sacks). Harris fumbled, which was brought to 2YL by DE Cameron Jordan. On 2nd down, sr Longshore closed his up-and-down Bears career on uptick by rolling right and hitting little-used, frosh TE Anthony Miller for winning score.

Papajohns.com Bowl (Dec. 29): Rutgers 29 North Carolina State 23

Birmingham served as setting in which 1 bowl game came to epitomize each team's season. Rutgers (8-5), which had started 2008 with 1-5 record was plain lousy in 1st H but surged to 23 pts in 2nd H. When dazzling frosh QB Russell Wilson (11-23/186y, TD, and 8/46y rushing) was healthy during 2008, Wolfpack (6-7) showed to be up-and-coming outfit. Unfortunately, Wilson left with sprained knee after his 16y scramble late in 2nd Q led to RB Andre Brown's 5y TD run and 17-6 H lead. Rutgers CB Jason McCourty was relieved to no longer contend with Wilson: "You never know what would happen, but I'm kind of happy we didn't have to see him in the second half." Rutgers D, which forced 3 INTs in 2nd H, took advantage of Wilson's absence to hold NC State to 6 pts. Scarlet Knights reeled off 13 straight pts after H and took 19-17 edge early in 4th Q on 2nd of 3 FGs by K San San Te. Wolfpack QB Daniel Evans (5-12/82y, TD, 2 INTs), 3rd-stringer in his final game after 5 injury-plagued years, replaced QB Harrison Beck (0-4/0y, INT) and pitched 16y 4th Q TD to TE Anthony Hill under encouraging eye of his father, former QB Johnny Evans, who was calling game in Wolfpack radio booth. North Carolina State now led 23-19. Rutgers took lead for good on next possession when QB Mike Teel (22-37/319y, 2 TDs, INT) needed only 2 plays, hitting WR Dennis Campbell for 23y and WR Kenny Britt (6/119y, TD) for 42y TD pass for 26-23 lead with 8:30 left. Rutgers picked off Evans to halt final 2 NC State series, which sandwiched Knights' 61y drive that produced 3 pts and wiped out 7:43 of clock. In addition to Teel, who won his 3rd straight bowl by throwing for 204y in 2nd H, Rutgers had 2 sub stars: QB Rob Cervini provided 1st Q TD when, as holder, he raced to TD on fake FG and RB Joe Martinek (9/58y), who rushed 3/30y on 70y go-ahead FG drive in 4th Q.

Alamo Bowl (Dec. 29): Missouri 30 Northwestern 23 (OT)

Playing with passion, Northwestern (9-4), largest of all bowl underdogs this holiday season, looked to win its 1st post-season game since January 1, 1949. In 1st Q, Wildcats managed their 1st INT of Missouri (10-4) star QB Chase Daniel (27-44/200y, 2 TDs, 3 INTs), who suffered several puzzling moments before chipping in late-game heroics. WR Eric Peterman catalogued sharp cut inside ace Tigers S William Moore to snatch 35y TD arrow from Wildcats QB C.J. Bacher (27-43/304y, 3 TDs, INT) for 7-0 lead. As H clock ticked toward last min, Wildcats P Stefan Demos lost concentration on his strategic, low-bounding boots and lofted punt toward Mizzou WR Jeremy Maclin (7/39y, TD, and 5/43y rushing), nation's leader in all-purpose y. Maclin fired up middle and roared away to 75y TD RET that tied game at 10-10 and ignited listless Tigers. Still, Northwestern took advantage of Missouri's dreadful pass D as Bacher consistently hit 3rd down throws and lofted 3rd Q TD passes of 46y to WR Rasheed Ward (7/101y) and 23y to WR Ross Lane. Lane's TD came late in 3rd Q on diving EZ catch and put Wildcats ahead 23-20. Tigers knotted it 23-23 when Mizzou K Jeff Wolfert made 37y FG with 2:49 to play and tried to position Wolfert for last-play, winning 3-ptr. But, Missouri took strategic retreat just enough to force NCAA's all-time most-accurate K into 44y miss. But, there was no problem in OT: Daniel fired 7y slant-in TD to Maclin, and on NW's possession, fierce 3rd down pass rush against Bacher by Mizzou LB Sean Weatherspoon (17 tackles) resulted in huge loss that forced Cats into 4th-and-goal at 32YL which ended as failed prayer pass to EZ.

Humanitarian Bowl (Dec. 30): Maryland 42 Nevada 35

Quick glance at stat sheet might have easily overlooked Maryland (8-5) star TB Da'Rel Scott missing entire 1st H due to suspension, along with 6 others, for curfew violation. Fresh-legged Scott came off bench to dominate 2nd H, rushing 14/174y, 2 TDs. Scott's half-game set school record for most bowl rushing y and earned him game MVP honors. Scott's finest moment occurred early in 4th Q, with score tied at 28-28, when he raced 49y to give Terps lead for good. After Scott scored again in 4th Q on 2y run, Nevada Wolf Pack (7-6) QB Colin Kaepernick (24-47/370y, 3 TDs, 2 INTs), who set game record for passing y, closed scoring with 15y keeper. Terps recovered ensuing on-side KO with 2:19 left, and Scott rushed twice for 21y to end matters. With Scott and 5 other starters benched, Terrapins still were able to built 28-14 H lead as backups WR Adrian Cannon, WR Ronnie Tyler (5/55y, TD), and RB Morgan Green (10/72y, TD) all scored TDs. Green had not even single carry in his 8 prior games, and frosh Tyler's TD was his 1st. Also, Maryland WR Torrey Smith raced 99y for KO TD RET in 1st Q in becoming all-time ACC leader with 1089y on KO RETs. When Maryland's suspended players returned, it was Nevada, ironically, that regained momentum thanks to 2 big TOs. Maryland QB Chris Turner (13-27/198y, 2 TDs, INT) suffered INT by Nevada S Jonathon Amaya, who returned 33y to 22YL. Kaepernick soon pitched 17y pass to RB Vai Tuau (23/101y, TD). Wolf Pack tied it 28-28 early in 4th Q after Turner lost FUM in Nevada territory. Kaepernick crossed up D by ignoring workhorse WR Mike McCoy (13/172y) to throw 21y TD to WR Marko Mitchell. Win served as Maryland milestone as it reached 600-521-43 all-time record.

Holiday Bowl (Dec. 30): Oregon 42 Oklahoma State 31

San Diego's good old Holiday Bowl, which practically invented post-season shootouts, hosted another battle of O juggernauts. Oklahoma State (9-4) had its way in 1st H, led by Cowboys by 17-7, and was led by QB Zac Robinson, who passed 27-50/329y, TD, 2 INTs, and WR Dez Bryant, who, before going out early in 4th Q with knee injury, set Holiday Bowl records for catches and receiving y with 13/167y, TD. Cowboys' stellar battery collaborated on 33y TD pass in 1st Q for 10-0 edge. Oregon (10-3) struck right back, springing RB Jeremiah Johnson (12/119y, TD) up middle and surge to outside for 76y TD run, which broke game record for distance. Ducks turned physical with adjusted blocking patterns so that their run attack flourished in 2nd H. Cowpokes had no answer for inside bursts off option reads by Oregon QB Jeremiah Masoli (18-32/258y, TD, INT, and 16/106y, 3 TDs rushing), who scored on 1, 41 runs in 3rd Q for 21-17 lead. Oklahoma State RB Kendall Hunter (13/37y, 2 TDs) scored his 2nd TD to regain lead at 24-21, but Masoli added his 3rd TD (17y run) in 3rd Q for 28-24 edge for Ducks. Robinson, whose play suffered after taking couple of big hits, still wedged

across GL early in 4th Q for another Cowboys lead at 31-28. But, Ducks' Masoli found WR Jaison Williams at left side of EZ for 20y TD pass, and sub RB LeGarrette Blount (7/74y, TD) rammed 29y to clinching TD with 3:01 to play. Blount's TD pushed him over 1000y rushing for season to join Johnson (1201y) as 2nd pair in school history to top magic rushing number in 1 season.

Texas Bowl (Dec. 30): Rice 38 Western Michigan 14

Rice Owls (10-3) had quietly enjoyed terrific season, and their Texas Bowl romp over Western Michigan (9-4) provided only 2nd 10-win season in school history. Coach Jess Neely's 1949 Southwest Conf champions had earned 10-1 mark with Cotton Bowl win over North Carolina. Sr QB Chase Clement, who connected for only 42.7% for 1-10 Owls as frosh in 2005, passed 30-44/307y, 3 TDs, rushed 12/72y, including 26y TD run, and was voted game MVP. Rice WR James Casey (7/112y, TD) caught 45y TD pass from Clement late in 2nd Q for 24-0 edge. Owls WR Jarett Dillard (8/86y, TD) caught his NCAA-record 60th TD pass, and hooked up with Clement for Dillard's 1st career completion: 13y TD that built 31-0 lead in 3rd Q. On Broncos' 1st snap, WR Jamarko Simmons caught pass from QB Tim Hiller (19-42/198y, 2 TDs, 2 INTs) to set school season mark with 99 receptions, but slew of mistakes sunk Western Michigan from that point on: WR Juan Nunez dropped early apparent TD pass, S Louis Delmas' pass interference PEN set up Clement's 26y TD run for 7-0 deficit, S Mario Armstrong's helmet-to-helmet foul followed by pass interference by CB Londen Fryar put ball at 2YL for Clement's 1st TD pass, and INT by Rice S Andrew Sendejo poised Casey for his TD catch in 2nd Q. Hiller hit pair of 4th Q TD passes to get on scoreboard.

Music City Bowl (Dec. 31): Vanderbilt 16 Boston College 14

It was New Year's Eve 1955, and Tennessee Ernie Ford's single Sixteen Tons was no.1 on the pop music charts, the Mickey Mouse Club was hot new show for kids, and Oklahoma was can't-miss at movie theatres. And Vanderbilt beat Auburn, 25-13 to win Gator Bowl. After 53 years of waiting, Vanderbilt (7-6) finally won another bowl game this December 31. To achieve their 2nd-ever bowl victory, Commodores had to turn back Boston College (9-5) that arrived in Nashville with 8-year post-season win streak,2nd-best NCAA mark. Vandy outlasted Eagles when Nashville native, K Bryant Hahnfeldt (3 FGs), booted 45y FG with 3:26 remaining. QB Larry Smith (10-17/121y), making his 1st start, rushed twice for 13y and completed 15y pass to WR George Smith (no relation) to set up winning FG. Vandy D then twice halted Boston College in final mins to win, forcing punt and ending game with INT by CB Myron Lewis with 96 secs left. Lewis redeemed himself with INT for he had been beaten on 55y TD pass from QB Dominique Davis (15-36/190y, 2 TDs, 2 INTs) to WR Colin Larmond that gave Eagles 14-13 lead with 6:36 remaining. Commodores D had to overcome stale O which gained only 200y and converted only 1-15 3rd downs while failing to cross GL. Frosh S Sean Richardson earned Vanderbilt's sole TD when he fell on loose ball on Vandy punt that bounced off leg of Boston College S Paul Anderson into Eagles EZ early in 3rd Q. Remarkably, Commodores P Brett Upson was named game MVP, thanks to 42.6y avg on 9 punts, including 58y bomb midway through 4th Q. Boston College gained 331y but could not overcome vital fumbled punt. "I guess everyone can figure out we're pretty happy," said understated Vanderbilt coach Bobby Johnson.

Armed Forces Bowl (Dec. 31): Houston 34 Air Force 28

Garden State Bowl anyone? After bowl drought of 8 losses, devoted Cougars (8-5) fans had to recall their team's last bowl win had come in 1980, 35-0 over Navy in New Jersey's Garden State Bowl. With Notre Dame breaking its 9-game losing streak earlier this post-season, Houston entered Armed Forces Bowl with worst streak in country. Thanks to Cougars QB Case Keenum (22-33/252y, TD, INT), who ran for 2 TDs and threw another, and frosh RB Bryce Beall, who rushed for 134y and TD and caught 4/92y, inspired Houston never trailed. Of course, Air Force (8-5) did not simply roll over; Falcons tied game twice and pulled to within 31-28 on 2y TD run by FB Jared Tew (27/149y, 2 TDs) with 6 mins left. Tew enjoyed his 1st-ever start by coming within 30y of his entire regular season rushing total. But, Air Force never got airborne on it final desperate possession, gaining only 2y before 3 straight incomplete passes by QB Tim Jefferson (7-11/98y). Houston then ran out clock with Keenum flipping 21y pass to Beall to secure important 1st down. Keenum finished his soph season with 5020y passing to become 2nd Cougars passer ever to top 5000y: David Klingler had pitched 5140y in 1989. Bowl played at Fort Worth was rematch of regular season game played on September 13, won by Air Force 31-28, notable because it was moved from to nearby Dallas (from Houston) due to expected arrival of Hurricane Ike.

Sun Bowl (Dec. 31): Oregon State 3 Pittsburgh 0

Not since 1957 Gator Bowl when Tennessee beat Texas A&M by 3-0 had post-season game seen winning outcome so low. Coming off 65-pt nightmare against rival Oregon that cost Beavers trip to Rose Bowl, Oregon State (9-4) coach Mike Riley had to be happy about D that permitted only 178y O to Pittsburgh (9-4). K Justin Kahut's 44y FG with 2:18 remaining before H served as winning margin. Playing without star brothers, WR James and RB Jacquizz Rodgers, handicapped Beavers O nearly scored TD later in 2nd Q: TE John Reese was ruled OB on 9y EZ catch 10 secs before intermission. Pitt LB Scott McKillop, Big East D player-of-year, intercepted Oregon State QB Lyle Moevao (21-42/193y, 2 INTs) on next snap. Frustrated by their inability to spring star TB LeSean McCoy (24/85y), Panthers finally ignited on 36y punt RET by WR T.J. Porter to Oregon State 42YL early in 4th Q. But 3 plays later, Beavers DE Victor Butler (4 sacks) yanked down Pitt QB Bill Stull (7-24/52y, INT) and recovered FUM. Aided by wind, Panthers K Conor Lee's 58y FG try in closing mins still fell just short. Victory was Riley's 5th straight bowl win since his return as Oregon State coach in 2003.

Insight Bowl (Dec. 31): Kansas 42 Minnesota 21

Jayhawks' well-tooled O machine clicked off TD on its 1st try: After opening KO, highly-accurate Kansas (8-5) QB Todd Reesing (27-35/313y, 4 TDs, INT) rolled away from pass rushers to loft 60y scoring pass down left sideline to WR Dezmon Briscoe, who would go on to set Insight Bowl record with 14/201y, 3 TDs receiving. For its part, overmatched Minnesota (7-6), which arrived with 4 straight losses, took 14-7 lead in 1st Q. Gophers answered Kansas' early TD with 75y surprise: WR David Pittman, former JC QB, threw long pass to star WR Eric Decker (8/149y, TD), and soph RB Jon Hoese scored from 1y out on his 1st collegiate carry. Hoese scored again on short run more than 9 mins later. But, Kansas struck back with WR Kerry Meier (10/113y, TD) hauling in high 4y TD pass from Reesing late in 1st Q to tie it. Reesing added pair of TD passes in 2nd Q, and after FUM REC at Minny 32YL in 3rd Q, former-QB Meier immediately pitched TD pass to Briscoe for 35-14 lead. On next series Minnesota TE Jack Simmons caught 2 passes, and Gophers seemed poised to climb back in it with 1st-and-goal at KU 7YL. However, Jayhawks LBs Mike Rivera and Joe Mortensen (FUM REC) stacked up 4th down sneak by Gophers QB Adam Weber (19-34/176y TD).

Chick-fil-A Bowl (Dec. 31): Louisiana State 38 Georgia Tech 3

When Georgia Tech (9-4) coach Paul Johnson was hired prior to this season, questions were raised whether his unorthodox option O could work against top competition. Throughout 2008, Yellow Jackets proved it could, averaging 4th-best-in-nation 273.2y rushing per game. But in this outing, disappointing LSU (8-5) proved too way much, permitting Georgia Tech to gain 162y rushing. K Scott Blair's 24y FG late in 1st Q provided only pts for Jackets. Tigers RB Charles Scott (15/65y) scored 3 TDs on ground, 1st of which came on LSU's opening possession and last of which came halfway through 2nd Q for 21-3 lead. Soon after Scott's last TD, Georgia Tech gamble don 4th down fake punt, sending 270-lb DE Derrick Morgan running off left side. When Morgan was stopped after short gain, Tigers QB Jordan Jefferson (16-25/142y, TD) found TE Richard Dickson for 25y TD pass that upped edge to 28-3. Frosh Jefferson was making his 2nd start and clicked on his 1st 9 pass attempts in front of 12th straight sellout crowd at Peach/Chick-fil-A Bowl in Atlanta.

Outback Bowl: Iowa 31 South Carolina 10

Big 10 Conf would finish with dreadful 1-6 bowl record, but Iowa Hawkeyes (9-4), triumphant closers with 6 wins in last 7 games, dominated SEC foe throughout Tampa's Outback Bowl. Hawkeyes WR Trey Stross caught TD pass from QB Ricky Stanzi (13-19/147y, TD, 2 INTs) at left pylon midway through 1st Q, and star TB Shonn Greene (29/121y, 3 TDs) soon scored 1st of his pair of 1y TD runs. South Carolina (7-6) QB Stephan Garcia (9-18/79y, 3 INTs) turned ball over 4 times in 1st H, including overthrow that Iowa S Tyler Sash intercepted prior to Greene's 1st TD. Garcia gave way to QB Chris Smelley (16-31/179y, TD), who finally got Gamecocks on scoreboard early in 4th Q with 10y TD pass to TE Jared Cook. By then, South Carolina trailed 31-0 as Greene, who earned his 13th 100y-game of year and afterward announced he planned forego his sr year for NFL Draft, had tallied on 11y run for 31-0 edge.

Capital One Bowl: Georgia 24 Michigan State 12

Blitzing D of Spartans (9-4) kept Georgia (10-3) off balance throughout 1st H, which Michigan State led 6-3 on pair of FGs by K Brett Swenson. Bulldogs O made effective H adjustments that allowed QB Matthew Stafford (20-31/250y, 3 TDs, INT) to spark 96y TD drive in middle of 3rd Q. When Stafford hit WR Michael Moore with 32y TD pass, Bulldogs took lead for good at 10-6. Stafford, who succeeded on 14-17 2nd H passes, finished 3rd Q with another scoring pitch and 17-6 edge. Spartans TB Javon Ringer, held in check with 20/47y rushing, took handoff, read clogged middle and smartly skipped outside to right to score 1y TD. Ringer's score boosted Michigan State to 17-12, but Spartans missed 2-pt pass. With 3:43 to play, Stafford slipped sharp 21y TD throw to RB Knowshon Moreno, who himself was limited to 23/62y rushing.

Gator Bowl: Nebraska 26 Clemson 21

Clemson (7-6) came out snarling on D and earned 14-3 H edge by forcing big TOs: LB DeAndre McDaniel's 28y FUM TD RET and WR Aaron Kelly's 25y TD catch after CB Crezdon Butler's 59y INT RET. On other hand, Nebraska (9-4) sr QB Joe Ganz (19-36/236y, 2 TDs, INT) shook off slight-concussion cobwebs to have excellent 2nd H. His coach, Bo Pelini, said of Ganz: "You've got to be a pretty special guy to have a fumble returned for a touchdown, an interception returned for (set up to) a touchdown, and still be the MVP of a game." Indeed, Ganz hit 3rd Q TD passes to WRs Nate Swift and Todd Peterson (4/96y, TD) and positioned K Alex Henery for pair of 28y FGs. In between, Clemson WR Jacoby Ford (5/112y, TD) caught 2nd TD pass by QB Cullen Harper (17-37/206y, 2 TDs, 2 INTs). So, Huskers led 23-21 as 4th Q began. Quentin Castille (18/125y), Nebraska's 3rd string IB promoted by injuries, ran 41y to set up another FG by Henery with 5:20 left. Tigers made last bid as Harper hit 3 passes for 1st-and-goal at Huskers 10YL. CB Eric Hagg knocked down 1st down pass and blitzed Harper for -16y loss on 2nd down. Nebraska D forced 2 more incompletions, including FS Matt O'Hanlon's clutch EZ break-up, to ice it with 1:32 to play.

Rose Bowl: Southern California 38 Penn State 24

Pete Carroll became 1st coach and USC 1st school ever to win 3 straight Rose Bowl games as Southern California (12-1) romped to 24 pts in 2nd Q to all but wrap up verdict before H. Contest started quietly, but once Trojans QB Mark Sanchez (28-35/413y, 4 TDs) went to air, USC dramatically pulled away. Sanchez, enjoying his greatest game, hit WR Damian Williams (10/162y, TD) for 27y TD in 1st Q. It came 6 plays after sack and FUM REC by Penn State (11-2) was negated by DE Aaron Maybin having lined up offside, typical of frequent blunders by Nittany Lions. Penn

State was able to counter Williams' score immediately with 80y drive to pull into 7-7 tie on 9y draw run by QB Daryll Clark (21-36/273y, 2 TDs, 2 INTs), but Trojans soon were back exploiting large cracks in Lions' secondary. In 2nd Q, Sanchez scored on 6y QB draw run, hit 5 passes to set up K David Buehler's 30y FG, and found WR Ronald Johnson (4/82y, 2 TDs) for 19y TD. Trailing 24-7 with 1:24 to go before H, Lions sub TB Stephfon Green, in for TB Evan Royster who was hurt in 1st Q, took screen pass 30y but was stripped and lost FUM to USC DB Will Harris (INT) at midfield. Trojans TB C.J. Gable responded with 20y screen pass TD from Sanchez. Penn State began mild comeback in scoreless 3rd Q, but its 17 pts in 4th Q became mere window-dressing when Clark threw 2 late INTs that prevented any real hope. Lions' 4th Q TDs were tallied on short pass catches by WRs Derrick Williams and Jordan Norwood.

Orange Bowl: Virginia Tech 20 Cincinnati 7

Dolphins Stadium hosted 75th Orange Bowl, and festivities included donation of $2.5 million to City of Miami for new youth football stadium at Moore Park, site of 1933 Palm Festival game, which was precursor of Orange Bowl. All season, ACC and Big East had labored outside spotlight of national glare, and win in Orange Bowl was especially sweet for ACC, which had dropped 8 straight BCS bowls. Virginia Tech (10-4) delivered as frosh TB Darren Evans (28/153y, TD) emerged as future O star, and Hokies D snatched 4 INTs from Bearcats (11-3) QB Tony Pike (16-33/239y, TD, 4 INTs). Virginia Tech made 2 big plays on D in 4th Q to wrap it up: DE Orion Martin made diving INT on screen pass at Cincinnati 10YL to set up Evans for 6y TD run 3 plays later for 20-7 lead. In retaliation, Pike marched Bearcats to 4th-and-goal at 1YL before LB Barquell Rivers stuffed him on keeper. Cincinnati's only TD had been scored on opening possession as Pike found WR Mardy Gilyard (7/158y, TD, and 255y all-purpose), who barely dragged toe in EZ for 15y TD catch, 3 plays after duo combined on 38y pass. But, Bearcats could not get Virginia Tech off field for most of game as Hokies' 258y ground game allowed them to hold ball for nearly 40 mins. Hokies gradually took control as QB Tyrod Taylor (13-22/140y, INT and 15/47y, TD rushing) zigzagged 17y TD run to tie it 7-7 in 2nd Q, and K Dustin Keys split uprights with 43y FG as 1st H ended. Virginia Tech joined Southern California and Texas as only schools to win 10 games in each of past 5 seasons.

Cotton Bowl (Jan. 2): Mississippi 47 Texas Tech 34

Rebels (9-4) QB Jevan Snead (18-29/292y, 3 TDs, INT), 1 of nation's hottest throwers in November, was slow to warm up on bright afternoon as he was intercepted by Texas Tech (11-2) FS Darcel McBath, who retuned it 45y down left sideline for 14-0 edge in 1st Q. Snead rallied Mississippi to 24-21 H lead as he connected on TDs on 3 straight series: TE Gerald Harris twice and WR Mike Wallace's 41y TD in between. Wallace's score came on spectacular leap and cradle of pass between pair of defenders. Meanwhile, Texas Tech (11-2) QB Graham Harrell (36-58/Cotton Bowl record 364y, 4 TDs, 2 INTs) set new collegiate record with his 134th career TD pass. Record-breaking toss came from 2YL in 2nd Q to WR Michael Crabtree (4/30y, TD), who was ailing from bad ankle and also got poked in eye. Unusual sequence occurred in 3rd Q: When Crabtree slipped, little CB Marshay Green picked off pass by Harrell and returned it 65y for TD that boosted Ole Miss' lead to 31-21. Moments later, Green appeared to bolt 63y for TD on punt RET but was ruled to have stepped on sideline at 9YL. When Rebels K Joshua Shene missed short FG try, it looked as though door had reopened for Red Raiders, but on next series Harrell was stopped on gambling 4th down run from his 37YL. Ole Miss frosh RB Brandon Bolden (11/101y, TD) ran for 17y TD and 38-21 lead after RB Dexter McCluster (14/97y, TD) zipped 23y on 2 carries. With 2010 New Year's game moving to new Dallas Cowboys' suburban stadium, this exciting 73rd renewal in front of largest-ever crowd of 88,175 appropriately rang down curtain at venerable Cotton Bowl stadium on Dallas' Texas State Fairgrounds.

Liberty Bowl (Jan. 2): Kentucky 25 East Carolina 19

Kentucky (7-6) DE Ventrell Jenkins was unlikely hero, all 285 lbs of him. With score tied 19-19 late in 4th Q, and East Carolina (9-5) angling to get into range for potential winning score, Jenkins scooped up FUM and raced—it was relative term—down right sideline into Kentucky's bowl lore. "I saw the quarterback coming (to attempt tackle), and I knew I had to outrun him," said Jenkins. "I did two moves in one—a stiff arm and a high step—and the next thing I know I was lying in the end zone with my team on top of me." After Jenkins' exciting play, Pirates still had 3 mins remaining to potentially win game with TD after DE Linval Joseph blocked Kentucky's x-pt attempt for 2nd time. ECU's rally began poorly, however, when returner J.R. Rogers inadvertently ended ensuing KO RET at own 1YL by touching down his knee while collaring bouncing KO. East Carolina soon was forced to punt, and Wildcats ran out clock with 6 straight runs, including 2 that earned crucial 1st downs, by tireless TB Tony Dixon (28/89y). Most of damage by Pirates had come through air as QB Patrick Pinkney (18-36/296y, TD) connected with WR Darryl Freeney (5/112y, TD) for 80y TD pass in 2nd Q that provided 16-3 lead. Wildcats' strong 2nd H was jumpstarted dynamically by CB David Jones' 99y KO TD RET to open 3rd Q. It cut East Carolina's lead to 16-9. In poor field position after their 2nd straight 3-and-out of 3rd Q, Pirates punted, which was returned 14y by Cats WR Gene McCaskill to ECU 26YL. Kentucky QB Mike Hartline (19-31/204y, TD, INT) soon threw tying 16y scoring pass to WR Kyrus Lanxter (5/46y, TD) for soph Lanxter's 1st career TD. FGs were traded to knot it 19-19 for most of 4th Q. Wildcats now owned 3 straight bowl wins for 1st time in school history, while current streak of 4 consecutive non-losing seasons had not happened since 1953-56.

Sugar Bowl (Jan. 2): Utah 31 Alabama 17

Overwhelming performance in 75th Sugar Bowl by undefeated, but 10-pt underdog Utah (13-0) maintained Utes' status as only unbeaten team among 119 FBS schools. Perhaps this stunning verdict would change how lower half of division—shut out of BCS championship consideration—should be considered in future. Feeling disrespected by Alabama (12-2) coach Nick Saban's December remark that Tide was only "real BCS conference" team that had undefeated regular season, Utah roared to 21-0 lead in 1st Q. Star QB Brian Johnson (27-41/336y, 3 TDs) rifled 5 straight completions on Utah's opening series, last pass going 7y to WR Brent Casteel for TD. Utes' swift D, which completely outplayed Bama's large O-Line—which was shorthanded because of suspension of A-A LT Andre Smith—struck quickly as FS Robert Johnson converted pass-rush pressure into INT in Alabama territory. QB Johnson hit WR David Reed for 30y, and RB Matt Asiata went across GL for 2y of Utes' game-end total of 13y rushing for 14-0 lead. QB Johnson struck for another TD to WR Bradon Godfrey with 4 mins to go in 1st Q. Alabama staged protracted rally, starting with K Leigh Tiffin's 52y FG to open 2nd Q. Big play that seemed to turn tide in Tide's favor arrived 9-and-half mins into 2nd Q when DB Javier Arenas broke several tackles to bolt 73y to punt TD RET, longest in Sugar Bowl history. When Bama DE Bobby Greenwood recovered FUM by Johnson at Utah 30YL and QB John Parker Wilson (18-30/177y, TD, 2 INTs) rolled out for 4y TD pass to RB Glen Coffee (13/36y) in 3rd Q, Crimson Tide had pulled to within 21-17, and partisan crowd roared. Utah immediately silenced Superdome din as Johnson opened next series with 33y rifle-shot to WR Freddie Brown (12/125y) which led to WR David Reed's 28y TD catch for 28-17 lead. Tide answered with counter drive into Utah end, but RB Mark Ingram (8/26y) was stacked up on 3rd-and-2 at 32YL. Saban, who seemed to lose his composure several times on sideline, said afterward: "So if that (his perceived slight of Utah) is what gave them all their intensity, then I guess I'm responsible for the way they played and I'm responsible for the way we played." In end, it was sharp passing of Johnson and ferocious Utes' D that held Alabama, sporting 197y per-game rushing avg, to 31y, which included 8 sacks of Wilson.

International Bowl (Jan. 3): Connecticut 38 Buffalo 20

Few college football fans outside of Storrs may have realized it, but Connecticut (8-5) jr RB Donald Brown (29/261y, TD) ended up as national rushing leader with 2083y and anonymously became 15th FBS player to top 2000y in single season. Brown's dynamic display against Buffalo (8-6) in what would turn out to be his final college game, allowed Huskies to prevail over TO-conscious Bulls. En route to personal-best single-game rushing mark, Brown ran for 208y in 1st H alone as Connecticut did not bother to attempt single pass in opening 30 mins. Buffalo had become surprise MAC champion thanks to forced TOs—finishing 3rd in nation with +19 margin—and Bulls took 20-17 lead to H by snatching all their pts off 5 Connecticut miscues, including disastrous punt RET FUM into EZ by Huskies CB Jasper Howard that was recovered for TD by Bulls frosh LB Ray Anthony Long. By game's end, Bulls were limited to 237y O and 10 1st downs, their other 13 pts requiring only 24y O to rack up. While its D blanked Buffalo in 2nd H, UConn tightened its grip on ball, pulled away with 2 TDs, and clinched on dramatic 100y INT TD RET down left sideline by LB Dahna Deleston late in 4th Q. When Huskies QB Tyler Lorenzen (4-6/49y, TD) finally got around to trying his 1st pass—off play-action, of course—it found TE Steve Brouse for 4y TD and 24-20 lead in 3rd Q. Buffalo QB Drew Willy (29-43/213y, INT) led Bulls O that set school record with 404 pts during year. Game in Toronto marked bowl debut for Buffalo, which brought along members of 1958 team that had turned down Tangerine Bowl bid because Florida law at that time would have required Bulls' black players to stay home.

Fiesta Bowl (Jan. 5): Texas 24 Ohio State 21

Feeling they still had something to prove to year-end voters, Texas Longhorns (12-1) nonetheless were stymied in 1st H by hard-hitting D of Ohio State (10-3). Riding physical running of TB Beanie Wells (16/106y), Buckeyes generated pair of drives that ended in 51y FG tries by K Aaron Pettrey, 1 of which he made. Ohio State led 6-3 after its other K, Ryan Pretorius, untied 3-3 knot with 30y FG. Near end of 2nd Q, Longhorns QB Colt McCoy (41-59/414y, 2 TDs, INT) shook off some tough moments to hit 5 straight passes to Buckeyes 15YL. With time for 1 shot at EZ before FG try, McCoy put too little on his lob over middle, which Ohio State FS Anderson Russell intercepted inside his 1YL. Undaunted, McCoy opened 3rd Q by masterminding 15-play drive to go-ahead TD, scoring himself on 14y run behind sharp blocks of RB Chris Ogbonnaya (11/42y) and WR Quan Cosby to allow him to twirl across GL. Late in 3rd Q, McCoy found Cosby (14/171y, 2 TDs) cutting across EZ for 7y TD pass to lift Texas' lead to 17-6. Although they were soon to lose Wells to injury, Buckeyes pulled to within 17-9 on Pettrey's 44y FG. Ohio State frosh QB Terrelle Pryor (5-14/66y, and 15/78y rushing) effectively shared time with sr QB Todd Boeckman (5-11/110y, TD) and occasionally flanked wide in new look. Pryor ran for 16 and 25y out of Shotgun to set up Boeckman for tall fade pass to right corner of EZ, on which Pryor, now at WR, used his 6'6" height to haul in for TD. Buckeyes' 2-pt try failed, so they trailed 17-15. After its D forced 3-and-out, Ohio came back downfield as Boeckman hit WR Brian Robiskie for 22y, and sub TB Daniel "Boom" Herron boomed off left side for TD behind strong cave-in block by TE Jake Ballard. Again, 2-pt try missed, but revitalized Ohio State now led 21-17 with 2:05 to play. McCoy and Cosby, college's most prolific all-time passing battery, connected twice to open Longhorns' do-or-die drive, and McCoy hit slender WR Brandon Collins twice more until Texas faced 4th-and-3 at Ohio 43YL. WR James Kirkendoll took short out-pass and was spun backwards from 40YL by Bucks CB Chimdi Chekwa. Although 2 officials seemed to contradict each other on spot of ball—challenged by Ohio State coach Jim Tressel—TV replays confirmed 1st down was made by inches with less than 40 secs to play. Buckeyes needed to keep all plays in front of them since FG couldn't beat them, but from its 26YL, Ohio D surprisingly brought LBs up close, and Cosby slanted inside for pass to whirl away for winning TD against lone S, who failed on 1 of few tackles Buckeyes missed all night.

BCS Championship Bowl (Jan. 8): Florida 24 Oklahoma 14

Remarkably, BCS Title Game was 1st-ever meeting between 2 foundation programs of college football. Refreshingly, D battle broke out in lieu of expected scoring spree. After scoreless 1st Q in which Oklahoma (12-2) O hurt itself with PENs, Florida (13-1)

struck in 2nd Q as QB Tim Tebow (18-30/231y, 2 TDs, 2 INTs, and 22/109y rushing) scrambled and found WR Louis Murphy for 20y TD as Murphy spilled backwards to GL to extend ball with long right arm. Sooners briefly abandoned their out-sized passing attack in 2nd Q to insert TE Brody Eldridge at FB, spot where he had been All-Big 12 in 2007, and Eldridge opened big holes out of I-formation for RB Chris Brown (22/110y) to gain 16, 14, and 15y on consecutive runs before QB Sam Bradford (26-41/256y, 2 TDs, 2 INTs) tied it 7-7 on laser TD strike to TE Jermaine Gresham (8/62y, 2 TDs). Midway in 2nd Q, Oklahoma A-A DT Gerald McCoy dropped into zone blitz coverage for midfield INT, and Sooners quickly were near Gators 1YL for 3rd-and-goal try. But Florida, led by DT Torrey Davis, crushed pair of runs by Brown for no gain and loss of 2y. Shrugging off Florida WR-RB Percy Harvin's 45y run, Oklahoma forced punt and hurried to reach 6YL with 10 secs to go in 1st H. Heisman-winning Bradford fired to GL where his pass was turned into volleyball, bouncing off several Gators hands until FS Major Wright halted threat and 1st H with INT just outside his EZ. Tebow inspired Gators on 75y drive in 3rd Q, gaining 6/48y rushing until Harvin squirted over from 2YL for 14-7 lead. Sooners TE Gresham picked it up early in 4th Q, catching 2 passes on 77y drive, including tying 11y TD catch from Bradford. With 10:45 to play, Florida K Jonathan Phillips made 27y FG for 17-14 lead after Harvin (9/122y, TD rushing) had raced 52 and 12y. Oklahoma struggled back, but Gators S Ahmad Black soon snatched INT off hands of tumbling WR Juaquin Iglesias (5/58y) at UF 24YL. On ensuing possession, Tebow beat double coverage, throwing 29y rocket to WR David Nelson to OU 20YL. Gators converted 3rd-and-6 from Sooners 16YL with frequently-successful dual option on which Tebow faked wide pitchout and shoveled forward to TE Aaron Hernandez for 9y gain. Tebow put Gators ahead 24-14 with 4y fake-run, jump-pass to Nelson with 3:07 on clock. CB Joe Haden broke up 4th down pass by Bradford, and Florida took over to kill last 2:26.

Final USA Today Coaches Poll January 9

1	Florida (60)	1524	14	Virginia Tech	740
2	Southern California	1393	15	Mississippi	620
3	Texas	1389	16	Missouri	549
4	Utah (1)	1375	17	Cincinnati	493
5	Oklahoma	1333	18	Oklahoma State	480
6	Alabama	1157	19	Oregon State	407
7	TCU	1114	20	Iowa	250
8	Penn State	1091	21	Brigham Young	248
9	Oregon	1011	22	Georgia Tech	219
10	Georgia	904	23	Florida State	217
11	Ohio State	874	24	Michigan State	179
12	Texas Tech	867	25	California	116
13	Boise State	809			

Final AP Poll January 9

1	Florida (48)	1606	14	Mississippi	857
2	Utah (16)	1519	15	Virginia Tech	712
3	Southern California (3)	1481	16	Oklahoma State	534
4	Texas	1478	17	Cincinnati	506
5	Oklahoma	1391	18	Oregon State	467
6	Alabama	1264	19	Missouri	435
7	Texas Christian	1193	20	Iowa	317
8	Penn State	1153	21	Florida State	246
9	Ohio State	1013	22	Georgia Tech	223
10	Oregon	997	23	West Virginia	144
11	Boise State	938	24	Michigan State	138
12	Texas Tech	916	25	Brigham Young	137
13	Georgia	903			

2008 Top Performance Formula

1	Florida	1.8083
2	Texas	1.8017
3	Southern California	1.7263
4	Oklahoma	1.7161
5	Utah	1.6864
6	Alabama	1.6461
7	Penn State	1.5736
8	Texas Christian	1.5729
9	Texas Tech	1.5466
10	Ohio State	1.5025
11	Oregon	1.4244
12	Georgia	1.3836
13	Missouri	1.3781
14	Mississippi	1.3633
15	Pittsburgh	1.3575
16	Oregon State	1.3517
17	Iowa	1.3439
18	Rice	1.3411
19	California	1.3403
20	Oklahoma State	1.3368

2008 Top Opponent Records

1	Texas	.6471
2	Florida	.6371
3	Oklahoma	.6361
4	Arkansas	.6239
5	Virginia	.6135
6	Pittsburgh	.6090
7	Kansas	.6053
8	Oregon State	.598684
9	Ohio State	.598675
10	Mississippi	.5895
11	Virginia Tech	.5857
12	South Carolina	.5843
13	Baylor	.5818
14	Alabama	.5802
15	North Carolina	.5792
16	Michigan State	.57895
17	Syracuse	.57887
18	Georgia	.5759
19	Colorado	.5757
20	North Carolina State	.5755

2008 Out-of-Conference Records

	W-L	Percentage	Bowl W-L
Southeastern	34-13	.7234	6-2
Big Twelve	32-13	.7111	4-3
Mountain West	23-12	.6571	2-2
Big East	25-14	.6410	3-2
Atlantic Coast	27-17	.6136	4-6
Big Ten	24-18	.5714	1-6
Pacific-10	17-17	.5000	5-0

2008 Individual Statistical Leaders

RUSHING YARDS	Attempts	Yards	Average
Donald Brown, Connecticut	367	2083	5.7
Shonn Greene, Iowa	307	1850	6.0
MiQuale Lewis, Ball State	322	1736	5.4
Javon Ringer, Michigan State	390	1637	4.2
Jahvid Best, California	194	1580	8.1
Kendall Hunter, Oklahoma State	241	1555	6.5
Tarrian Adams, Tulsa	247	1523	6.2
Vai Taua, Nevada	236	1521	6.4
LeSean McCoy, Pittsburgh	308	1488	4.8
Gartrell Johnson, Colorado State	278	1476	5.3

PASSING YARDS	Completions	Attempts	Yards	Percentage
Graham Harrell, Texas Tech	442	626	5111	70.6
Case Keenum, Houston	397	589	5020	67.4
Sam Bradford, Oklahoma	328	483	4720	67.9
Chase Daniel, Missouri	385	528	4335	72.9
Chase Clement, Rice	326	490	4119	66.5
David Johnson, Tulsa	258	400	4095	64.5
Max Hall, Brigham Young	330	477	3957	69.2
Todd Reesing, Kansas	329	495	3888	66.5
Colt McCoy, Texas	332	433	3859	76.7
Tim Hiller, Western Michigan	339	522	3725	64.9

RECEIVING YARDS	Catches	Yards
Austin Collie, Brigham Young	106	1538
Dez Bryant, Oklahoma State	87	1480
Dezmon Briscoe, Kansas	92	1407
Naaman Roosevelt, Buffalo	104	1402
Kenny Britt, Rutgers	87	1371
James Casey, Rice	111	1329
Jarett Dillard, Rice	87	1310
Jamarko Simmons, Western Michigan	104	1276
Mardy Gilyard, Cincinnati	81	1276
Chris Williams, New Mexico State	86	1271

2008 Consensus All-America Team
Offense

Wide Receiver:	Michael Crabtree, Texas Tech
	Dez Bryant, Oklahoma State
Tight End:	Chase Coffman, Missouri
Line:	Michael Oher, Mississippi
	Andre Smith, Alabama
	George "Duke" Robinson, Oklahoma
	Brandon Carter, Texas Tech
	Herman Johnson, Louisiana State
Center:	Antoine Caldwell, Alabama
	A.Q. Shipley, Penn State
Quarterback:	Sam Bradford, Oklahoma
	Colt McCoy, Texas
Running Back:	Shonn Greene, Iowa
	Donald Brown, Connecticut
	Javon Ringer, Michigan State
Kicker:	Louis Sakoda, Utah
Kick Returner:	Percy Harvin, Florida
	Brandon James, Florida
	Jeremy Maclin, Missouri
	Derrick Williams, Penn State

Defense

Line:	Brian Orapko, Texas
	Jerry Hughes, Texas Christian
	Aaron Maybin, Penn State
	Nick Reed, Oregon
	George Selvie, South Florida
	Terrence Cody, Alabama
Linebacker:	James Laurinaitis, Ohio State
	Rey Maualuga, Southern California
	Scott McKillop, Pittsburgh
	Brandon Spikes, Florida
Back:	Malcolm Jenkins, Ohio State
	Alphonso Smith, Wake Forest
	Eric Berry, Tennessee
	Taylor Mays, Southern California
Punter:	Kevin Huber, Cincinnati

2008 Heisman Trophy Vote

Sam Bradford, sophomore quarterback, Oklahoma	1726
Colt McCoy, junior quarterback, Texas	1604
Tim Tebow, junior quarterback, Florida	1575
Graham Harrell, senior quarterback, Texas Tech	213
Michael Crabtree, sophomore wide receiver, Texas Tech	116

Other Major Awards

Maxwell (Player)	Tim Tebow, junior quarterback, Florida
Walter Camp (Player)	Colt McCoy, junior quarterback, Texas
Outland (Lineman)	Andre Smith, junior tackle, Alabama
Vince Lombardi (Lineman)	Brian Orakpo, senior defensive end, Texas
Doak Walker (Running Back)	Shonn Greene, junior tailback, Iowa
Davey O'Brien (Quarterback)	Sam Bradford, sophomore quarterback, Oklahoma
Fred Biletnikoff (Receiver)	Michael Crabtree, sophomore WR, Texas Tech
Jim Thorpe (Defensive Back)	Malcolm Jenkins, senior cornerback, Ohio State
Dick Butkus (Linebacker)	Aaron Curry, senior linebacker, Wake Forest
Chuck Bednarik (Defender)	Rey Maualuga, sr. linebacker, Southern California
Lou Groza (Placekicker)	Graham Gano, senior kicker, Florida State
Ray Guy (Punter)	Matt Fodge, senior punter, Oklahoma State
Johnny Unitas (Sr. Quarterback)	Graham Harrell, senior quarterback, Texas Tech
John Mackey (Tight End)	Chase Coffman, senior tight end, Missouri
Dave Rimington (Center)	A.Q. Shipley, senior center, Penn State
Ted Hendricks (Defensive End)	Brian Orakpo, senior defensive end, Texas
Bronko Nagurski (Defender)	Brian Orakpo, senior defensive end, Texas
AFCA Coach of the Year	Kyle Whittingham, Utah

2009

The Year of Subcommittee Hearings, Bizarre Coaching Behavior, and Sad Farewell to Bobby

Thanks to political lobbying by the Mountain West Conference, the Bowl Championship Series fur was flying during the off-season as the U.S. House of Representatives Energy and Commerce Committee held a hearing on the BCS in May. Utah's Orrin Hatch, the senior Republican in the U.S. Senate, launched an examination of the perceived bias of the BCS during Antitrust Subcommittee hearings in early July.

Prior to the Senate hearing, Hatch wrote in Sports Illustrated: "First and foremost there are serious questions regarding the legality of the BCS. The Sherman Antitrust Act prohibits contracts, combinations or conspiracies designed to reduce competition. I don't think a more accurate description of what the BCS does exists."

Hatch took his case to new U.S. President Barack Obama later that autumn, while the House of Representatives also sent a bill to committee that would make it illegal to promote anything called a championship if there were no playoff leading to it. With all the uproar, legislation still appeared unlikely at the close of calendar-year 2009.

Even if future action could be taken by a mostly reluctant national government, which had its hands full with a sagging economy and an unending debate over an overhaul of healthcare, destruction of the BCS would likely push major college football back to the same bowl game plan that predated the BCS. Such an arrangement would do little to salve the hurt feelings or fill the pocketbooks of teams like the Mountain West's Utah (10-3) and the Western Athletic Conference's Boise State (14-0), a pair of schools dreaming of breaking into national championship games rather than rest on recent successes in non-title BCS bowls. While it was terribly transparent of Hatch to be politicking for his own state university, the fact remained any team, even those like Utah and Boise State without automatic bids as received by the six BCS conferences, could certainly qualify for the title game if they finished in either of the top two spots in the final BCS standings. Truthfully, the quarrel wasn't so much with the BCS system as with the human and computer polls.

Mountain West officials reluctantly signed the new five-year BCS television agreement with ESPN just prior to a July 10 deadline. Conference directors really had no choice. To not sign would have meant banishment all together from BCS bowls, and it was that very inclusion that led to Boise State's thrilling win over Oklahoma in the 2007 Fiesta Bowl and Utah's decisive victory over Alabama in the 2009 Sugar Bowl. Those opportunistic wins had fueled the minor schools' claims for title equality in the first place.

Right on cue, not one but two teams outside the automatic BCS invitation list finished the regular season undefeated and were matched in the Fiesta Bowl. The Mountain West Conference's Texas Christian (12-1) was favored over Boise State, but the Broncos used a great run defense and a trick-play fourth down pass by punter Kyle Brotzman from their own territory to set up the winning fourth quarter touchdown for a 17-10 win.

A late-year public poll from Quinnipiac (Connecticut) University showed a 63 percent preference for abolishing the BCS. The BCS cartel had met the never-ending criticism by hiring a public relations firm headed by Ari Fleisher, former press secretary of the most recent President, George W. Bush. Fleisher's firm noted a Gallop poll that showed 85 percent favored a playoff three years earlier. So, fans could make their own deduction.

Media experts were certain the 2009 season would follow form. All three of the top 2008 Heisman Trophy finalists returned for another season, and Florida (13-1), the defending national champion, became the most endorsed preseason no. 1 in college history when 58 of 60 (96.67%) media members filled in the Gators at the top spot of their AP ballots. Fifty-three of 59 coaches voting in the USA TODAY poll also had the Gators on top in the summer. Florida stayed no. 1, but farther below the certainty evaporated. Before September ended, 18 teams from the preseason USA TODAY Coaches Top 25 had lost at least once. As usual preseason guesses were just that, amusing but useless speculation.

A new, short-lived sign of sportsmanship—a pre-game handshake between teams—was endorsed by the coaches association and seemed like a good idea until the season's very first night. Running back LaGarrette Blount was a greeter representing Oregon (10-3) before the game at Boise State, but he ended an awful night for the Ducks by punching Broncos defensive end Byron Hout in a post-game melee after Hout taunted him. Blount also had to be restrained from going after Broncos fans and was suspended for the season by new coach Chip Kelly. The handshake ritual, which had been questioned in some quarters because of a worldwide outbreak of H1N1, or so-called Swine Flu, appeared to be a lame politically-

correct gesture. Flu briefly would weaken returning Heisman finalists, Colt McCoy of Texas (13-1) and Tim Tebow of Florida.

Sucker-punches and flu symptoms weren't the only contributors to a sobering September. The Oklahoma (8-5) vs. Brigham Young (11-2) opener that helped christen Dallas NFL owner Jerry Jones' gigantic, new Cowboys Stadium in Arlington, Tex., turned against the Sooners. Before the first half was over, the returning Heisman Trophy winner, quarterback Sam Bradford, went down with an injured shoulder, and the Cougars prevailed 14-13. Bradford returned on October 10 but reinjured his shoulder a week later in a 16-13 rivalry loss to Texas. Surgery ended his season.

Joe Cox of Georgia (8-5) and Tebow each had to take a private plane to an away game so as not to infect teammates with the flu. Public opinion had been turned quite bitterly against corporate jets when earlier in the year the CEOs of the three major automakers each wastefully took his own private jet from Detroit to Washington, D.C., with hats in hand for government financial bailouts. Not a word of complaint was heard about SEC stars flying on private aircraft; it presumably proved the power and popularity of football despite government's apparent disdain for the BCS.

Tebow's air trip to play Kentucky (7-6) at Lexington was soured by a concussion he suffered when hitting his head during a third quarter sack. A story, apocryphal or not, made its way around the country and indicated so much about Tebow's upbeat personality. Supposedly, when coach Urban Meyer went on the field to check his quarterback's condition, the supine Tebow snapped awake and asked if he had maintained control of the ball. When Meyer assured Tebow he hadn't fumbled, the quarterback reportedly grinned and said, "It's great to be a Florida Gator!" But, he soon was in an ambulance headed for a night of hospital observation.

Tebow returned on October 10 for every offensive play as no. 1 Florida went on the road to beat no. 4 Louisiana State (9-4) 13-3 as the Gators defense owned the night in front of a record crowd at Tiger Stadium.

A Big Three stayed in the top spots in the polls virtually all year. Yet the gnawing feeling—accented by hackneyed media complaints of a dull season—persisted that each of Florida, Texas, and Alabama (14-0) was flawed, especially on offense, compared to the previous season. The Gators were missing home-run threat Percy Harvin, now an NFL professional, and the Florida line relinquished an alarming number of sacks. Texas couldn't get its running game going, and Alabama had trouble making touchdowns in the red zone.

Flawed or not, the three rolled through the regular season undefeated and on to simple resolution of the BCS title match-up. The winner of the SEC Championship Game—Alabama or Florida—would meet Texas in the title game. Everything went according to plan with the Crimson Tide winning the SEC convincingly, 32-13, and Texas barely taking the Big 12.

A last-second loss to Texas Tech had kept the Longhorns from a likely national title opportunity in 2008, and in 2009 they had to survive a 13-12 dogfight in the Big 12 Championship Game by kicking a last-play winning field goal against defense-mighty Nebraska (10-4) when McCoy nearly took too much time on a pass scramble to run the clock down to one second.

Texas was a small underdog to Alabama in the BCS Title Game at Pasadena and got off to a good start until McCoy was knocked out in the first quarter with a shoulder injury. Trailing 24-6 in the third quarter, the Longhorns rallied briefly to within 24-21 until the Crimson Tide's superiority finally sealed the championship in a 37-21 verdict.

Cincinnati (12-1) became the undefeated champion of the Big East but lost head coach Brian Kelly to Notre Dame (6-6) shortly after closing its season with a last-moment victory at Pittsburgh (10-3). The 45-44 win over the Panthers, which clinched the Bearcats' first unbeaten regular season since going 3-0-2 in 1918, moved them to third in the BCS ranking and on the doorstep of the BCS Title Game had Nebraska held on to beat Texas.

"Who knows what would have happened if Nebraska wins that game," Kelly told a Chicago radio station in mid-December. "I might not be here at Notre Dame because we don't know if they would have waited for me, because I was going to play in the national championship game."

Cincinnati, many of its players feeling betrayed by Kelly's defection, drew Florida in the Sugar Bowl, and a week before the game, Gators coach Meyer, owning a brilliant five-year record at Florida of 56-10 (.8485), shocked the world by resigning effective after the bowl game. Although not considered to be in a life-threatening health situation, Meyer had been treated for severe, stress-related chest pain after the SEC Championship Game loss. Strangely, Meyer announced a change of heart the next day: he wouldn't retire after all but take a leave-of-absence for an undetermined

length of time after the bowl game. He said he based his second decision on the spirit shown by his players at practice. However serious his decision about health had been, the reversal seemed bizarre.

Florida might have found itself in an unemotional bowl circumstance, having to face an undefeated foe while still reeling from a disheartening loss in the conference title game. After all, Alabama had been embarrassed by Utah in a similar scenario last season. Meyer's stunning announcements changed that. In Tebow's last game as a collegian, Florida trounced Cincinnati 51-24. Astoundingly, Tebow accounted for 533 yards.

Kelly and Meyer weren't alone in bizarre coaching behavior. Mark Mangino, national coach of the year just two years earlier, was bounced at Kansas (5-7) for extreme and personal abuse of his players. Mike Leach of Texas Tech (9-4) was suspended then fired for his unusual mistreatment of wide receiver Adam James, who suffered a mild concussion in preparation for the Alamo Bowl. Leach accused James—the son of former SMU star and current ESPN commentator Craig James—of being a pampered and lazy player and the school of wanting out of the big contract he had negotiated the previous winter. Finally, Jim Levitt, who had single-handedly launched the football program at South Florida (8-5) out of an office in a trailer in 1997, was fired for allegedly slapping a player's face.

Southern California (9-4) followed its familiar script by winning a big early game over Ohio State (11-2) only to lose for the fifth time in four years to an unranked Pac-10 team, in this case Washington (5-7), a team revived from its 0-12 mark of 2008 by former USC assistant coach Steve Sarkisian. The Trojans suffered an uncommon near-tragedy in September when senior running back Stafon Johnson, who had scored twice in the win over Ohio State, dropped a 275-lb. barbell on his throat during weight-lifting exercises. Johnson recovered after seven hours of larynx surgery, but doctors said he survived only because of his fine conditioning. Johnson's season was over, and, as seven-time conference champions, so was USC's.

Unlike recent years, Troy's once-mighty defense unraveled at mid-year and gave up a remarkable number of points. The Trojans lost a second conference game, a 47-20 thrashing at Oregon on October 31, and two weeks later the 55 points scored by Stanford (8-5) in a 34-point thrashing at the L.A. Coliseum were the most ever permitted by Southern California. Soon after an Emerald Bowl win, USC coach Pete Carroll surprisingly departed for a $35 million deal with the Seattle Seahawks of the NFL.

Oregon revived magnificently after its disastrous opener against Boise State. First-year head coach Chip Kelly, truly under the gun because he lost the opener and had to suspend Blount, rallied his players and kept Blount involved as the nation's best scout-team back. Oregon nipped Purdue (5-7), beat Utah's good team, and crushed its first five Pac-10 foes by an aggregate total of 208 to 58 to jump to a 7-1 record. But like several teams projected to "run the table" by an overly zealous, futures-oriented broadcast media, the Ducks were surprised along the way. Stanford beat Oregon in a 51-42 shootout on November 7. Oregon was fortunate to outlast Arizona (8-5) in overtime and ultimately clinch its first Rose Bowl trip in 15 years by edging Oregon State (8-5) in the regular season finale.

Blount, described as a model citizen since his suspension, was reinstated in mid-November but played little until contributing 51 yards rushing and an explosive touchdown at a critical moment against Oregon State. Blount scored a touchdown in Oregon's first Rose Bowl since 1995, but Ohio State flourished 26-17 behind the all-around skills of quarterback Terrelle Pryor.

Iowa (11-2) became the star-struck surprise of the Big Ten, but it was far from easy for coach Kirk Ferentz's squad. The Hawkeyes trailed in nearly every game they played, including the need to block field goal attempts on consecutive last-moment plays to beat Northern Iowa and to hit a touchdown pass as the clock ended another win over Michigan State (6-7). Sitting at 9-0 and 4th in BCS rankings after October 31, Iowa ran out of luck and lost 17-10 to Northwestern (8-5), when quarterback Ricky Stanzi hurt his ankle, and was nipped a week later in overtime by Ohio State. The Iowa win allowed the Buckeyes to make the Rose Bowl, their first trip to Pasadena—despite three recent BCS title appearances—since 1997.

At a time when Florida State (7-6) stood at 2-3 and a first-ever 0-2 start in ACC competition, beloved coach Bobby Bowden came under fire from Jim Smith, chairman of the university's board of trustees. In a rare and bold statement on athletic policy, Smith expressed the desire to "let the world know that this year will be the end of the Bowden era. I do appreciate what he's done for us, what he's done for the program, what he's done really for the state of Florida." Smith went on to say the program had been in decline recently and "we're paying for a quality program, and we're not getting that right now." A contributing factor to Smith's impatience was the commitment of $5 million to assistant and head-coach-in-waiting Jimbo Fisher should he not to be installed as Bowden's replacement by January 2011.

When Florida State was routed by rival Florida in the regular season finale, the Seminoles stood at 6-6, Bowden's worst record since his first season in Tallahassee, way back in 1976. After a Monday meeting with school officials where Bowden was offered a figurehead coaching position under Fisher for 2010, he chose to retire after the Gator Bowl, an emotional 33-21 win over West Virginia (9-4), the school he coached to 42 wins in 1970-75. Always a gentleman, Bowden chose the high road on the day of his announcement and remembered the good times: "Nothing lasts forever, does it? But I've had some wonderful years here at Florida State (where he won 316 of his 389 career victories), you know it? Hadn't done as good lately as I wish I could have, but I've had wonderful years, no regrets."

As the Gator Bowl ended, Bowden's players did the right thing. They hoisted him up for a brief ride to midfield to greet losing coach Bill Stewart, who had been a walk-on for Bowden's first West Virginia team in 1970. At least an old coach was able to skip the Gatorade bath and enjoy a traditional trip atop his players' shoulders.

The trip into Jacksonville Municipal Stadium had been longer. More than 350 of Bowden's former players, including Seminole greats Deion Sanders and Warrick Dunn, were there, and thousands of fans braved rain and chilly temperatures to line the route Bowden and his wife Ann would take into the stadium, followed by the rest of the current Seminoles team.

"That was the most emotional thing I have had," Bowden said. "I was determined, I ain't cryin'. But I tell you what, the closest I came is when I walked through them players and the fans. That was pretty tough."

Milestones

■ No major rules changes were enacted, but game officials were instructed to better protect "defenseless" players from helmet-to-helmet hits.

■ In its 2nd season of FBS competition after upgrade from FCS, Western Kentucky joined Sun Belt Conference as its 9th member.

■ John McGillicuddy, 78, player on Princeton's 1950-51 undefeated teams, died on January 3. McGillicuddy, retired chairman & CEO of Chemical Banking Corp., advised U.S. Presidents, Ronald Reagan and George H. W. Bush, and 3 governors on financial issues. On January 13, Eric Scoggins, linebacker for Southern California's 1978 national champions, died at 49 of Lou Gehrig Disease (ALS). Dante "Gluefingers" Lavelli, 85, member of Ohio State's 1942 national champions and Pro Football Hall of Fame offensive end for 11 years with Cleveland Browns team that sported 110-24-4 record in AAFC and NFL, died on January 20. Also dying on January 20 was Austin Denney, 65, former All-America tight end at Tennessee. Shane Dronnett, 38-year-old former defensive lineman for Texas (1989-90) and NFL's Denver Broncos and Atlanta Falcons, was found dead in his Atlanta-area home on January 21. Former Texas Tech tackle Bill Hershman (1954-55) died on January 22. John Gordy, 73, captain and All-SEC tackle for 1956 conference champion Tennessee, died on January 30 in California. Gordy played 10 years at offensive tackle for NFL's Detroit Lions, including 1957 league champions, while being chosen All-Pro 3 times. Jim Wilson, All-America tackle at Georgia in 1964, died of cancer in early February at age 67. Ken "Dude" McLean, 65, Texas A&M receiver of "Texas Special" 91-yard touchdown pass against Texas in 1965, and Pasquale "Pat" Bisceglia, 78, starting guard on Notre Dame's 1955 team, both died in mid-February. Michigan State's 3-sport star Brad Van Pelt, 57, died on his farm on February 17. Van Pelt won Maxwell Award in 1972 as Spartans defensive back and starred in NFL, primarily for New York Giants, for 14 years. George McAfee, 90, member of both College and Pro Football Halls of Fame, died March 4. Star in football, baseball, and track, McAfee played on Duke's 1937-39 teams that compiled 24-4-1 record. Lou Saban, 87, who in 52-year career coached 28 teams at various levels, including major college programs Northwestern (1955), Maryland (1966), Miami (1977-78), and Army (1979-80), as well as Boston Patriots, Buffalo Bills, and Denver Broncos pro teams, died on March 29. Passing away in early April were former defensive lineman Dwight Hood, 64, co-captain of 1966 Baylor team, former Arkansas defensive lineman in 1994-97, Ken Anderson, 33, and Texas Tech star linebacker Brad Hastings (1983-86), who died at 44. Former Tennessee offensive tackle Leslie Ratliffe, who started in 1993-94 for Vols died April 8 at 35. Bruce Snyder, head football coach at Utah State (32-32-2 record in 1976-81), California (29-24-1 in 1987-91), and Arizona State (58-47 in 1992-2000), passed away on April 13 after nearly year-long battle with cancer. Snyder, 69, was twice named Pac-10 coach of year and was AFCA national coach of year when he led Sun Devils to 11-1 mark, last-moment Rose Bowl loss, and 4th ranking in final poll. Former West Point fullback Felix "Doc" Blanchard, known as Army's "Mr. Inside" in tandem with Glenn Davis' "Mr. Outside," died on April 19 at 84. Blanchard was 1945 Heisman Trophy winner, played on 2 national champions in 1944-45, and helped Cadets to 27-0-1 record in 3 varsity seasons. Merle Harmon, 82, who was play-by-play voice for Super Bowls and hundreds of collegiate and pro games, died in mid-April. Bill Barnes, 91, head coach at UCLA from 1958-64, died in late April. Claude "Tee" Moorman, Duke All-America end on 1960 ACC champions and 1961 Cotton Bowl victors, died at 69 on April 28. Robert "Cotton" Letner, 72, who played end and placekicker for Tennessee from 1958-60, died in late May. Terry Barr, 73, former Michigan (1955-56) halfback and Detroit Lions (1957-65) wide receiver and defensive back, died May 28 after long battle with Alzheimer's disease. Dying at age 82 on June 6 was Jim Owens, former All-America end at Oklahoma (1946-49) and coach at Washington (1957-74). Owens' Huskies were 3-time Pac-8 champions and back-to-back Rose Bowl champions (1960-61), and he compiled 99-82-6 career mark. Former Tennessee Titans quarterback Steve McNair was killed by his girlfriend, Sahel Kazemi, in murder-suicide shooting on Fourth of July in Nashville. McNair, 36, had finished 3rd in 1994 Heisman Trophy vote despite playing for Div. 1-AA Alcorn State, and became first round draft pick of Houston Oilers, NFL team that moved to Tennessee in 1997. McNair joined Fran Tarkenton and Steve Young as only NFL players ever to gain 30,000 yards passing and 3,000 yards rushing. Oklahoma All-America (1982-83) defensive lineman Rick Bryan, 47, died on July 26 at his home in Coweta, Okla. Late August marked passing of 3 notables: Burl Toler, 82, first African-American official in NFL history in 1965 and standout back for 1948-51 University of San Francisco Dons; University of Houston and Miami Dolphins defensive tackle T.J. Turner at 46; and Jim Urbanek, 64, 3-time All-SEC and twice All-America defensive lineman during his 1965-67 career at Mississippi. NCAA president and former president of Indiana University Myles Brand, 67, died on September 16 after battling pancreatic cancer. Monte Clark, former Southern California tackle in 1956-58, 11-year NFL offensive tackle, and head coach of San Francisco 49ers (1976) and Detroit Lions (1978-84), died at 72 on September 16. Another USC star, end Leon Clarke, who played in 1955 Rose Bowl and made Pro Bowls appearances in his 1st 2 years (1956-57) as big wide receiver for Los Angeles Rams, died at 76 on October 7. Connecticut cornerback Jasper "Jazz" Howard, 20, fresh from big role in victory over Louisville, died early Sunday morning October 18, victim of stab wound after being attacked after on-campus dance. Forest Evashevski, 2000 College Football Hall of Fame inductee and former Iowa coach with 52-27-4 record and 3 Big Ten titles in 1956, '58, and '60 during his career from 1952 to '60, died October 30 at 91. Serfino "Foge" Fazio, 71, two-way center-linebacker in 1958-59 for Pittsburgh and also Panthers' head coach with 25-18-3 record in 1982-85, died on December 2 after battle with leukemia. Chris Henry, 26, outstanding but troubled receiver at West Virginia (2002-03) and NFL's Cincinnati Bengals, died of injuries on December 17, day after he fell from back of pickup truck driven by his fiancée in Charlotte. Jack Zilly, Notre Dame end on 1943 and '46 national title teams, died on December 18 at 88.

■ On September 26, Nebraska celebrated its 300th consecutive sellout, longest such streak in NCAA history, in front of record crowd of 86,304 at Memorial Stadium. Huskers beat Louisiana-Lafayette 55-0 while wearing special throwback uniforms to honor 1962 team that started sellout streak.

■ After conclusion of 2009 season, Colonial Athletic Association members Hofstra and Northeastern each ceased its FCS (I-AA) program.

■ Longest winning streaks entering season:
Utah 14 Florida, Southern California 10

■ Coaching Changes

	Incoming	Outgoing
Army	Rich Ellerson	Stan Brock
Auburn	Gene Chizik	Tommy Tuberville
Ball State	Stan Parrish	Brady Hoke
Boston College	Frank Spaziani	Jeff Jagodzinski
Bowling Green	Dave Clawson	Gregg Brandon
Cincinnati (a)	Jeff Quinn	Brian Kelly
Eastern Michigan	Ron English	Jeff Genyk
Iowa State	Paul Rhoades	Gene Chizik
Kansas State	Bill Snyder	Ron Prince
Miami (Ohio)	Mike Haywood	Shane Montgomery
Mississippi State	Dan Mullen	Sylvester Croom
New Mexico	Mike Locksley	Rocky Long
New Mexico State	DeWayne Walker	Hal Mumme
Oregon	Chip Kelly	Mike Bellotti
Purdue	Danny Hope	Joe Tiller
San Diego State	Brady Hoke	Chuck Long
Syracuse	Doug Marrone	Greg Robinson
Tennessee	Lane Kiffin	Phillip Fulmer
Texas Tech (b)	Ruffin McNeill	Mike Leach
Toledo	Tim Beckman	Tom Amstutz
Utah State	Gary Andersen	Brent Guy
Washington	Steve Sarkisian	Tyrone Willingham
Wyoming	Dave Christiansen	Joe Glenn

(a) Quinn (0-1) coached Sugar Bowl after Kelly (12-0) left for Notre Dame.
(b) McNeill (1-0) coached Alamo Bowl after Leach was suspended and subsequently fired.

Preseason USA TODAY Coaches Poll

1 Florida (53)	1466	14 Oregon	694
2 Texas (4)	1386	15 Georgia Tech	559
3 Oklahoma (1)	1358	16 Boise State	542
4 Southern California (1)	1321	17 Texas Christian	461
5 Alabama	1134	18 Utah	404
6 Ohio State	1126	19 Florida State	371
7 Virginia Tech	1020	20 North Carolina	293
8 Penn State	988	21 Iowa	257
9 Louisiana State	917	22 Nebraska	236
10 Mississippi	889	23 Notre Dame	194
11 Oklahoma State	861	24 Brigham Young	178
12 California	711	25 Oregon State	165
13 Georgia	707		

September 5, 2009

(Th) South Carolina 7 NORTH CAROLINA STATE 3: North Carolina State (0-1) RB Toney Baker, 1-time HS superstar, had missed nearly 2 years with knee injury, and on his 1st carry early in 1st Q, he lost FUM on hit by South Carolina (1-0) DE Devin Taylor. S Darian Stewart recovered at NC State 14YL, and Gamecocks sent TB Brian Maddox (23/66y, TD) slamming 4 straight plays for short TD. Cocks could have built sizable early lead as their D dominated, but push-off foul negated WR Tori Gurley's TD catch after Taylor blocked punt. South Carolina also blew 1st-and-goal opportunity in 2nd Q with bad snap on FG try, and K Spencer Lanning missed 27y FG try in 3rd Q. Wolfpack QB Russell Wilson (12-23/74y) was stymied by swift pass-rush, but after K Josh Czajkowski drilled 43y FG late in 3rd Q to pull Pack within 7-3, lofted pass that might have turned verdict. Wilson's pass slithered through hands of 2 defenders and glanced off fingertips of NC State WR Jay Smith as he tumbled in EZ.

(Th) BOISE STATE 19 Oregon 8: Determined no. 14 Oregon (0-1), 7th-best in total O during 2008 with 485y per game, sought to reverse previous year's chippy home loss to Broncos. Ducks O proved to be totally inept, gaining 14y in 1st H and not earning their initial 1st down until 54y TD drive well into 3rd Q. That Ducks' march led to 5y option TD run by QB Jeremiah Masoli (14-27/121y, INT) followed by 2-pt run by big RB LaGarrette Blount (8/-5y). By then, however, Boise State (1-0) led 19-0 despite its own slew of squandered chances. Broncos had managed 13-pt burst in 2nd Q as WR Austin Pettis slipped across Oregon's on-field-too-long D for 10y TD catch from QB Kellen Moore (19-29/197y, TD), and WR Michael Choate followed with uncontested 2-pt run out of bewildering, wide-flanked formation. Broncos soon made it 10-0 when Ducks tried option run across their EZ and Boise State DT Billy Wynn split blockers to spill Blount for safety. Broncos all but wrapped up their 65th win in last 67 home games with 64y mostly-ground trip to RB D.J. Harper's 1y TD run after 2nd H KO. Blount, who had been fairly mouthy leading up to game, became America's villain-for-the-week when he punched Boise DE Byron Hout in post-game melee after Hout taunted him. New Oregon coach Chip Kelly would quickly suspend Blount.

Minnesota 23 SYRACUSE 20 (OT): Return of prodigal star had everything but Hollywood ending. Syracuse (0-1) QB Greg Paulus, who transferred from Duke after 4 years of basketball, was big story prior to game, and for better or worse, during it. Attracting largest Carrier Dome crowd (48,617) since 2000, Paulus (19-31/167y, TD, INT), star athlete at Christian Brothers Academy in suburban Syracuse, had game's 1st snap sail over his head for FUM that led to Minnesota TD. He soon rallied Orange from 14-3 deficit with 3 scoring drives for 20-14 H lead. Paulus threw TD pass late in 1st Q, hooking up for 29y with WR Mike Williams (7/94y, TD), who set school record with 10 consecutive games with at least 1 TD reception. Gophers (1-0) K Eric Ellestad managed all of 2nd H scoring with 2 FGs, although his 47y effort was blocked early in 4th Q by Syracuse DT Anthony Perkins. Euphoria from 1st H rally petered out in 2nd H as Syracuse O managed only 48y against veteran Minnesota D, which returned 8 starters. On 1st OT possession, Syracuse gained 20y before Paulus threw pass picked off by LB Nate Triplett (9 tackles). Gophers ran three plays for 7y before Ellestad booted winning 35y FG that spoiled debut of Syracuse coach Doug Marrone. Minnesota WR Eric Decker was game's top weapon, catching 9/183y from QB Adam Weber (19-42/248y, TD, INT).

Baylor 24 WAKE FOREST 21: Dynamic Baylor (1-0) QB Robert Griffin (15-24/136y, TD) introduced himself to ACC fans by completing his 1st 8 passes in leading Bears to early 10-0 advantage. Griffin's 4th straight connection produced 8y TD to WR David Gettis (5/65y, TD) that capped opening series. Wake Forest (0-1) QB Riley Skinner (20-31/143y, 2 TDs, 3 INTs) came out as cold as Griffin was hot. Skinner had his 1st throw picked off by DT Phil Taylor midway through 1st Q. With Wake down by 10 pts, Skinner's 2nd pass fell incomplete to end drive early in 2nd Q. Demon Deacons got going later in 2nd Q when 15y pass interference PEN gave them 1st down at Baylor 35YL. Skinner converted 2y run on 4th down to Bears 24YL, then handed ball off 5 straight times to 3 backs who completed TD trip with 2y run by FB Mike Rinfrette. Wake's next 3 possessions ended in FUM, INT and 23y punt. Meanwhile, Baylor upped its lead to 24-7 with 2 trick TDs: WR Kendall Wright scored on 37y run after surprise pitch from Griffin, and WR Ernest Smith caught quick pass and pulled up to throw 33y TD to WR Lanear Sampson. Late in 3rd Q, Wake Forest O finally looked like veteran unit that returned 9 starters as Skinner hit 6-7/68y on 80y TD drive that ended with 19y TD pass to WR Devon Brown. Wake next converted Griffin's FUM deep in Baylor territory into 5y scoring catch by TE Andrew Parker in back of EZ. So, Wake trailed by only 3 pts with 4 mins remaining. Baylor wasted 2:46 on 39y drive before Skinner and mates took over on own 12YL with 1:11 left. Bears LB Antonio Jones (7 tackles) ended matters with sack after 3 misfired passes.

Alabama 34 Virginia Tech 24 (Atlanta): Shining like beacon in underwhelming lineup of opening week match-ups was this Top-10 battle. In 1st Q, Crimson Tide (1-0) K Leigh Tiffin booted 3 FGs, including 49y 3-ptr to open scoring. Tiffin's 9 pts offset TD by Virginia Tech (0-1) WR Dyrell Roberts on 98y KO RET. With Hokies up 10-9 lead on by K Matt Waldon's 28y FG, each team earned TD in final 4 mins of 1st H. Alabama marched 76y to RB Roy Upchurch's 19y TD run, with debuting QB Greg McElroy hitting 3-4/36y. Virginia Tech responded, thanks in large part to Tide largesse—trio of 15y personal fouls and pass interference—with 51y march to 1y TD run by frosh RB Ryan Williams (13/71y, 2 TDs), Va Tech's main replacement for RB Darren Evans, lost for season to August knee injury. Tide star LB Rolando McClain (5 tackles, 2 sacks) committed pair of major PENs on same play. Crimson Tide took lead for good early in 4th Q thanks to quick series of huge plays. Trailing 17-16, McElroy (15-30/230y, TD, INT) hooked up with WR Marquis Maze on 46y pass to set up 6y TD run by TB Mark Ingram (26/150y, TD). McElroy connected with TE Colin Peek on 2-pt pass for 24-17 lead. CB Chris Rogers forced and recovered FUM by Va Tech S Davon Morgan of ensuing KO at Hokies 21YL, and it led to Tiffin's 4th FG with 10:31 left. Williams scored on amazing 32y run to cut Hokies' deficit to 27-24. After Ingram rushed 3/47y to set up own 18y TD catch, Alabama D ended it pair of late 3-and-out stands. Alabama, now 11-1 all-time vs. Virginia Tech, finished with 498y to 155y O advantage, edge it nearly gave away with 2 TOs, Roberts' long RETs, and 10 PENs.

OHIO STATE 31 Navy 27: All week long former coach Lou Holtz wondered on ESPN why Ohio State Buckeyes (1-0) would schedule Navy (0-1) for opener when all their prep work for option runs would be wasted for rest of season. As it turned out, no. 6 Buckeyes seemed to have hardly prepped at all for Middies' clever attack and showed little to Southern California, next week's mighty visitor. However, Ohio State jumped to 7-0 lead on opening possession: QB Terrelle Pryor (14-21/174y, TD, INT) whipped 38y crossing-pattern TD pass to WR Dane Sanzenbacher (2/57y, TD). Star of game would turn out to be new Navy QB Ricky Dobbs (9-13/156y, 2 TDs, INT and 18/83y, 2 TDs rushing), and Dobbs brought Tars right back to tying TD on his 16y run. Pryor added TD sweep in 2nd Q, and Ohio State went off at H with 20-7 edge. Up 20-14 early in 4th Q, Ohio K Aaron Pettrey bombed 52y FG, his 3rd of game, but missed x-pt kick after TD run by RB Dan Herron (17/72y, TD). Now ahead 29-14 midway in 4th Q, Buckeyes ignored 4th down FG opportunity from Middies 15YL, and Navy LB Tyler Simmons made piercing stop. Never-say-die Dobbs rallied Navy on next snap: SB Marcus Curry (2/101y, 2 TDs) slipped over middle past Ohio FS Anderson Russell to snare Dobbs' 85y TD pass. S Emmett Merchant, son of former Georgia Tech WR of same name, quickly picked off Pryor, and 3 plays later Dobbs spurted 24y on draw run for TD. Stunningly, Navy trailed only 29-27 with 2:23 to play. Middies called 2-pt pass that blew up as Buckeyes D flooded middle of field, where LB Brian Rolle intercepted and dashed length of field down Navy's sideline for 2-pt reversal and 31-27 final score.

MICHIGAN 31 Western Michigan 7: While Detroit Free Press was investigating allegations of over-the-limit practice time and coach Rich Rodriguez was sued over condominium land deal, Michigan (1-0) looked ripe for upset. Instead, Wolverines roared to quick lead. Playing 4 QBs, Michigan found frosh QB Tate Forcier (13-20/179y, 3 TDs) most polished, but frosh QB Denard "Shoelaces" Robinson (2-4/18y, 11/74y, TD rushing) to be most exciting. Robinson, who earned his nickname in HS by fastening his shoes with Velcro as his laces flopped about, rocketed 43y to TD that gave UM 14-0 lead in 1st Q. Forcier returned in 2nd Q to throw his 2nd TD pass and add another to WR Junior Hemingway (5/103y, 2 TDs) to build 31-0 H edge. Coming off 2008's 9-4 record, Western Michigan (0-1) stumbled to only 15y on its opening 7 series but rallied with drives starting late in 2nd Q of 54, 80, 30, and 46y. Unfortunately, Michigan's alert D turned those sorties into missed FG try, stop on downs, INT, and FUM respectively. Finally in 4th Q, Broncos QB Tim Hiller (22-38/259y, TD, 2 INTs) connected with WR Juan Nunez for 73y TD.

Missouri 37 Illinois 9 (St. Louis): Standout Fighting Illini (0-1) WR Arrelious Benn went out early with ankle injury, joining top runners Jason Ford and Daniel Dufrene, and with him went Illinois' spirit. Wanting to repay recent shootout losses to border rival Mizzou

(1-0), Illinois quickly went down 10-0. For its part, graduation-depleted Missouri played as if it were irritated by widespread preseason underestimates. Tigers unveiled new QB Blaine Gabbert (25-33/319y, 3 TDs and 10/39y, TD rushing), who opened with 7-8/106y passing in 1st Q on his way to finest opening QB performance in coach Gary Pinkel's 9 years in Columbia. Gabbert hit new WR Wes Kemp with 49y TD arrow late in 1st Q. Illinois, however, fought back in 2nd Q while trailing 13-3 as it went 55y to 20YL. But on 4th-and-1, QB Juice Williams (18-28/179y, INT) tripped over lineman's foot and stumbled to 4y loss. When Gabbert struck for pair of 3rd Q TD passes, Missouri had clinched it at 37-9. Vet WR Danario Alexander caught 10/132y for Tigers.

IOWA 17 Northern Iowa 16: Iowa Hawkeyes (1-0), football big brothers of Hawkeye State, had to stage miraculous finish to hold off little brothers from Northern Iowa (0-1), national FCS power. Purple Panthers led most of way after 2nd Q 14y TD pass from QB Pat Grace (23-37/270y, TD) to TE Ryan Mahaffey, which provided 10-3 edge. Hawkeyes could gain only 87y rushing thanks to RB corps depleted by Shonn Greene's NFL defection and Jewel Hampton's injury, so vets QB Ricky Stanzi (22-34/242y, TD) and TE Tony Moeaki (10/83y, TD) fueled Iowa's comeback. After Hawkeyes frosh RB Adam Robinson tallied on 11y run in 3rd Q to pull within 13-10, Stanzi found Moeaki in corner of EZ early in 4th Q for Iowa's 1st lead at 17-13. Northern Iowa K Billy Hallgren booted his 3rd FG with 4:26 to play, and Panthers regained possession after punt to 8YL with 2:14 to play. Grace hit 6-7/61y, and with 7 secs left on 1st down, Hallgren lined up for 40y FG attempt. Iowa DE Broderick Binns blocked it, and even though LB Jeremiha Hunter easily could have fallen on spinning ball to end game, his Hawks teammates screamed at him to leave it alone, owing to standard coaching instruction that reasoned that FGs are attempted on 4th down. Mahaffey picked up loose ball—legally behind scrimmage line—and amazingly Panthers had earned another 3-pt chance. Hunter urged his teammates to stuff middle of line because Hallgren had kicked low all afternoon, and this time Hunter leaped to swat down Hallgren's FG attempt to clinch victory.

OKLAHOMA STATE 24 Georgia 10: It was difficult to know how much Georgia (0-1) QB Joe Cox (15-30/162y, TD, INT) was weakened by Swine Flu, but Bulldogs were plenty affected by stout D of Oklahoma State (1-0). Cowboys D, under new coordinator Bill Young, permitted only 177y after Georgia opened with 80y to Cox's 4y TD pass to WR Michael Moore. Pokes D also thrilled record crowd at renovated Boone Pickens Stadium with 2 key FUM RECs. SS Lucien Antoine forced FUM late in 2nd Q to set up K Dan Bailey's 28y FG for OSU's 10-7 H lead. Cowboys CB Perrish Cox returned Georgia's 2nd H KO 74y, and QB Zac Robinson (11-22/135y, 2 TDs) soon sneaked across for 17-7 lead. Cowboys DL Shane Jarka forced 4th Q bobble with sack of Cox, which led to 2nd TD catch by star WR Dez Bryant (3/77y, 2 TDs).

Brigham Young 14 Oklahoma 13 (Arlington, Tex.): Jerry Jones' new $1.2 billion Cowboys Stadium was opened to college ball, and no. 3 Sooners (0-1) wish they hadn't been invited. With only 1 starter back from its great O-line of 2008, Oklahoma never got rhythm going on O. Still, QB Sam Bradford (10-14/96y, TD) found WR Ryan Broyles for 8y TD pass in 2nd Q, but last year's Heisman Trophy winner faced considerable pass-rush pressure from BYU (1-0) when his line wasn't being called for 9 illegal procedure PENs. Cougars QB Max Hall (26-38/329y, 2 TDs, 2 INTs) pitched tying TD pass to TE Andrew George in 2nd Q. OU was moving late in 2nd Q when Bradford's 18y completion broke Jason White's school career passing y mark, but on next play from Cougars 18YL 12 secs before H BYU LB Coleby Clawson broke in free to dump Bradford with clean hit. Both players landed together on Bradford's throwing shoulder, and Bradford's arm had to go into sling with strained joint. On next play after injury, K Jimmy Stevens gave Oklahoma 10-7 lead with 35y FG. After both teams made less than 50y O in 3rd Q, PEN at 1YL forced Sooners to take Stevens' FG for 13-7 lead early in 4th Q. On next series, Hall hit 9 passes, including 4/62y to TE Dennis Pitta (7/90y). With Pitta attracting coverage near GL on 3rd-and-goal, Hall found WR McKay Jacobson in back of EZ for 14-13 edge. With 1:40 to go, Oklahoma tried desperate 54y FG by long-range K Tress Way, but it was short and left.

CALIFORNIA 52 Maryland 13: Tables were turned to counter last year's early day KO between these foes at College Park: It was nighttime on West Coast, and merciless California (1-0) was prime-time ready to roll for 542y O. Bears RB Jahvid Best (10/137y, 2 TDs) ran for pair of 1st Q TDs, including 73y gallop, while QB Kevin Riley (17-26/298y, 4 TDs) hit pair of TD passes in 2nd Q on way to Cal's 31-6 H lead. Maryland (0-1) WR Torrey Smith (1/29y) returned KO 48y late in 1st Q to launch Terps on trip to 4YL, and QB Chris Turner (17-30/167y) clicked on 5 completions during 2nd Q thrust to 22YL. But each time, Maryland had to settle for FGs by K Nick Ferrara. Cal opened 3rd Q with quick 54 and 53y TD drives, both taking less than 1:30, as sub RB Shane Vereen scored on run and WR Marvin Jones scored on reception from Riley. Terrapins RB Da'Rel Scott (13/90y, TD) went 39y to score in 3rd Q.

Louisiana State 31 WASHINGTON 23: Winless since November 2007, Washington (0-1) put up good fight for new coach Steve Sarkisian as Seattle crowd, several of whom wore "I Bark for Sark" purple t-shirts, was fired up for night opener against SEC power LSU Tigers (1-0). Barking Huskies outgained Bayou Bengals 478y to 321y as QB Jake Locker, back from 2008 injury list along with RB Chris Polk (21/90y), sparked several trips inside LSU 20YL. Locker (25-45/321y, 2 TDs, INT and 12/51y rushing) pitched 17y TD pass to frosh WR James Johnson to open scoring in 1st Q but didn't account for larruping LSU LB Jacob Cutrera, who sped to 29y TD RET after picking off INT late in 1st Q. While Washington trailed only 17-13 well into 3rd Q it had no answer for Tigers' speed as LSU WR Terrance Toliver (4/117y, 2 TDs) caught his 2nd long TD from QB Jordan Jefferson (11-19/172y, 3 TDs) for 24-13 lead. It was UW's 15th straight defeat, while LSU won its 20th in row against out-of-conf foes.

(Mon) Cincinnati 47 RUTGERS 15: Any notion that Cincinnati (1-0) would be unable to defend its Big East title due to graduation of 10 D starters went right out window with complete whipping of Scarlet Knights (0-1). Rutgers opened its renovated stadium in dreadful but appropriate fashion; stadium costs of $102 million were controversial in state hit hard by economic downturn. That was forgotten when it became clear Rutgers O needed to adjust to loss of school's all-time leading passer (Mike Teel) and receiver (Kenny Britt). Cincinnati had no such problem as QB Tony Pike (27-34/362y, 3 TDs, INT) and WR Mardy Gilyard (8/89y, TD) took seamlessly to strategic uptick in pacing of Cincy's O. Striking quickly, Cincinnati had 4 TD drives of 2:29 or less and Bearcats' longest drive took only 4:06. Win was so complete that Bearcats amassed 45 pts on 510y by end of 3rd Q, finishing with 564y to 293y disparity. Cincinnati D chased new Rutgers QB Dom Natale (8-12/108y, 3 INTs) in 1st H, including INT by sole returning starter, SS Aaron Webster (10 tackles, INT). Off bench, frosh QB Tom Savage showed better days lay ahead for Rutgers, completing 15-23/135y and 7y TD pass to TE Shamar Graves.

(Mon) Miami 38 FLORIDA STATE 34: While pregame talk focused on Bobby Bowden coaching his 34th season at Florida State (0-1), Miami (1-0) QB Jacory Harris (21-34/386y, 2 TDs, 2 INTs) was talk of postgame after his emergent performance. Harris, improving under tutelage of new O coordinator and former NFL QB coach, Mark Whipple, led Miami to 3 TDs in 4th Q to pull out win. Harris set up 1st of those scores, his own 1y TD run, with 29y completion to WR Travis Benjamin (4/128y, TD). Next, he drove Canes 73y to 31-31 tie, completing 4-6/70y, including 24y scoring pass to RB Graig Cooper. For 3rd TD, which overcame 34-31 deficit with less than 2 mins left, Harris completed 40y bomb to Benjamin down left sideline to set up Cooper's 3y TD run on next play. Harris was also key player in another 4th Q TD, but this 1 was for Seminoles as CB Greg Reid blitzed in untouched to nail Harris and force pop-up throw gathered in by DE Markus White for 31y TD RET that, with subsequent 2-pt conv, gave Noles short-lived 31-24 lead. And despite all of Harris' heroics, Florida State did have possession of ball last and marched deep into Miami territory behind QB Christian Ponder (24-41/294y, 2 TDs, INT). Ponder hit 2-2/16y and rushed 2/29y to spark Seminoles from Miami 49YL—following Reid's 20y RET of short KO—to Miami 2YL, where they faced 1st-and-goal in last 20 secs. But 3 straight missed throws to WR Jarmon Fortson ended matters, although Fortson came razor-close to scooping 3rd down pass off ground as game ended. For moment, Ponder even celebrated what he thought was TD. Instead Harris got final praise for best-ever pass y performance by any Hurricanes QB against FSU, topping mark of 370y set by QB Kenny Kelly in 1999.

USA TODAY Coaches Poll September 8, 2009

1 Florida (56)	1472	14 Oklahoma	682
2 Texas (2)	1407	15 Virginia Tech	633
3 Southern California (1)	1352	16 Texas Christian	543
4 Alabama	1299	17 Utah	503
5 Penn State	1145	18 Nebraska	360
6 Oklahoma State	1114	19 North Carolina	358
7 Ohio State	1106	20 Notre Dame	335
8 Mississippi	1006	21 Georgia	304
9 Louisiana State	977	22 Miami	276
10 California	935	23 Cincinnati	187
11 Boise State	803	24 Oregon State	169
12 Brigham Young	755	25 Kansas	139
13 Georgia Tech	685		

September 12, 2009

(Th) GEORGIA TECH 30 Clemson 27: Sometimes, too easy too early is bad. That was case for fast-starting Georgia Tech (2-0) which jumped to 24-0 1st H lead, only to watch Tigers (1-1) snarl back for 27 straight pts. Just as they had in opening win over Jacksonville State, Yellow Jackets sprung long run in early going: SB Anthony Allen (5/127y, TD) took pitchout behind great downfield blocking for 82y TD sprint. When Clemson tried to catch Jackets napping with fake-FG-punt, Georgia Tech DB Jerrard Tarrant sped up to catch pooch punt and roar 85y to TD. Georgia Tech built 21-0 lead before 1st Q ended with its own chicanery: Looking as though it might punt, Tech quickly sent FG unit on field as WR Demaryius Thomas (3/93y, TD) lingered illegally and uncovered near sideline. K Scott Blair lofted 34y TD to Thomas. With Tigers trailing 24-0 in 2nd Q, RB C.J. Spiller got Tigers going with 63y TD catch, his 14th career TD longer than 50y. As 3rd Q opened, Jackets O blocked ineffectively, and Tigers took command with 210y to 53y O advantage and pair of TD passes by frosh QB Kyle Parker (15-31/261y, 3 TDs, 2 INTs). When K Richard Jackson belted through 52y 3-ptr, Clemson took 27-24 lead with 11:33 to play. Jackets snapped back to life, fashioning 69 and 47y FG drives, capped by Blair's winning 36y FG with 57 secs left.

North Carolina 12 CONNECTICUT 10: Few finishes get odder than this: North Carolina (2-0) won with late safety earned when pass-blocking Huskies (1-1) LT Dan Ryan held—tackled was more like it—in-rushing Tar Heels DE Richard Quinn in EZ with 1:32 left. North Carolina had scored 10 straight 4th Q pts to knot game 10-10, and Connecticut was desperate for 1st down. Facing 3rd-and-22 deep in own territory after botched snap on 2nd down caused 12y loss, UConn QB Cody Endres (3-7/30y) dropped back to throw. Quinn beat Ryan with outside rush and had QB in sights until takedown, which occurred just within EZ. "I knew I beat him around the corner and it felt like I got pulled down…and then I saw the flag," said Quinn of winning play. Now trailing for 1st time, Huskies went for onside-KO which WR Alex Molina fell on for UConn at its 31YL. Endres, who entered game in 3rd Q when starting QB Zach Frazer (11-19/94y, INT) left with head injury, completed 2 passes to midfield for 2nd-and-6 with just 20y needed for FG range; soph K Dave Teggart had already booted career-long 47y FG in 2nd Q. But Carolina D saw to it that game ended right there by breaking up 2 passes and DE Quinton Coples (5 tackles, 2 sacks) sacking Endres on 4th down on Connecticut 44YL. Carolina QB T.J. Yates (23-32/233y, TD, 2 INTs) overcame costly INT to lead late rally, completing 5-7/67y on 78y drive to 22y FG by K Casey Barth and 6-7/55y on 76y drive that produced his tying 2y scoring pass to TE Zack Pianalto (7/87y). Yates had thrown INT to DT Twyon Martin at Heels 26YL, which set up 4y TD run by Huskies RB Jordon Todman (18/66y) late in 3rd Q for 10-0 lead.

WAKE FOREST 24 Stanford 17: After watching Stanford (1-1) frosh QB Andrew Luck (23-34/276y, 2 TDs, INT) have lots of fun through 3 Qs, veteran Wake Forest (1-1) QB Riley Skinner enjoyed last laugh by driving Deacons to pair of 4th Q TDs, including last-moment game-winner he capped with 1y TD run. Skinner (18-26/187y, TD), already winningest QB in school history, tied game 17-17 early in final Q by throwing 19y TD pass to WR Jordan Williams on 4th-and-4. Skinner faced serious pressure on TD pass before rolling right and hitting Williams in back of EZ. After both teams had drives stall in opposition territory, Deacons took over on own 9YL with 3:46 left. Skinner and Wake O were not to be denied, however: 3 different RBs produced 17y on opening 3 plays to provide some breathing room. After his 12y scramble for 1st down, Skinner hit WR Devon Brown with 20y pass to bring Wake into Stanford territory at 47YL. Two plays later, Skinner hit wide open RB Lovell Jackson in stride at Cardinal 5YL. Jackson fell, however, to give Wake 1st-and-goal at Stanford 2YL with 51 secs remaining. Jackson's fall proved to be blessing in disguise as Deacs were able to exhaust all but final 2 secs by using 3 plays to get Skinner's TD keeper. Stanford WR Ryan Whalen (9/123y, 2 TDs) had taken passes of 26 and 17y for TDs in 1st H, latter coming midway through 2nd Q for 14-3 lead. Cardinal RB Toby Gerhart rushed 17/82y for what would prove to be lowest total of year.

GEORGIA 41 South Carolina 37: Near-by rivals traditionally had played hard-hitting, D-dominated games. Not this Saturday as they combined for more pts (78) than SEC East series had seen in past 3 years combined (67). At 1 point in 1st H, Bulldogs (1-1) trailed 17-7 and had run only 2 plays from scrimmage as Gamecocks (1-1) converted FUM by Georgia WR A.J. Green (6/86y, TD) on game's 2nd snap into 32y trip to QB Stephen Garcia's 6y TD pass to WR Tori Gurley, trekked 77y to score 13y TD on pass by Garcia (31-53/313y, 2 TDs, INT) to TB Brian Maddox, and converted FUM by Georgia CB Branden Smith on next KO into 21y FG by K Spencer Lanning. Then again, Georgia had 21 pts on board after only 11 plays from scrimmage, thanks primarily to 100y KO TD RET by S Brandon Boykin. Itching to finally play some O, Georgia traveled 52y—after Boykin raced 48y with KO RET—on 7 plays to score TD on 1y run by RB Richard Samuel. It was that kind of game. Leading 31-23 at H, Bulldogs opened 2nd H with 80y drive that QB Joe Cox (17-24/201y, 2 TDs, INT) ended with 4y scoring pass to WR Michael Moore to go up 38-23. No lead was safe, and South Carolina S Chris Culliver raced 57y with KO—teams combined for 410y on 14 KO RETs—to set up FG. To add more excitement, UGa's punt snap flew over P Drew Butler's head and into EZ for safety. Down 38-28 as 4th Q began, Gamecocks got Lanning's 5th FG (34y), to tie school mark for most FGs in game. On next scrimmage play, Cox's pass was picked off by Cocks LB Eric Norwood and returned 34y to TD. Game hadn't yet seen blocked kick, so naturally Lanning's tying x-pt was swatted by DT DeAngelo Tyson to preserve Bulldogs' 1-pt edge. Georgia killed half of remaining 13 mins with 12-play drive to K Blair Walsh's 42y FG for 41-37 lead. Contest seemed to scream for final winning drive, and it appeared Garcia might deliver as he converted trio of 3rd downs to UGa 7YL, where Gamecocks faced 3rd-and-4 with 32 secs left.. But Garcia's final 2 throws, both intended for 6'5, 227-lb Gurley, could not find their target.

Ucla 19 TENNESSEE 15: Trailing 19-13 with little more than 2 mins left and facing 4th-and-goal at UCLA (2-0) 2YL, Tennessee (1-1) went at heart of Bruins D with rugged RB Montario Hardesty (26/89y, TD). But UCLA front-7 rose up and allowed Hardesty only 1y as LBs Kyle Bosworth (10 tackles) and Reggie Carter (14 tackles) combined for stop. UCLA soon designed time-killing play call it would regret: On 3rd down, QB Kevin Prince (11-23/101y, TD) rolled right in his EZ. UCLA's season and Prince's face were altered as Volunteers CB Dennis Rogan nailed Prince to not only score 2 pts but break QB's jaw. Tennessee had time to rally from its 40YL following RET of free-kick but floundering QB Jonathan Crompton (13-26/93y, 3 INTs) was sacked on 2nd down by DT Brian Price (2 sacks) and could complete none of 3 passes. Bruins O could gain only 186y in entire game and got 12 pts on 4 FGs by dependable K Kai Forbath. Bruins' TD created 2nd Q 10-10 deadlock on 12y pass from Prince to FB Chane Moline after Crompton lost FUM at his 36YL. Crompton's 4 TOs prompted finger pointing in Tennessee locker room after game. UCLA S Rahim Moore had 2 INTs. Back in LA on Sunday, Prince was operated upon and would miss next 2 games.

Southern California 18 OHIO STATE 15: Inspired by loud turnout at Ohio Stadium, Buckeyes (1-1) took advantage of good field-position, starting 5 drives in Southern California (2-0) territory. Ohio State overcame early 50y INT RET by USC LB Chris Galippo that led to short TD to gain 138y in 1st Q, but managed only 127y thereafter. Bucks played well behind QB Terrelle Pryor (11-25/177y, INT and 10/36y rushing). But, Ohio State twice bogged down in red zone to settle for short FGs by K Aaron Pettrey. Trojans tied it 10-10 on K Jordan Congdon's FG on last play of 1st H. Bad snap on 3rd Q punt flew through EZ for safety against Troy, and USC, while well-adjusted on D in 2nd H showed only 21y O through opening 23 mins of 2nd H. Trojans faced daunting task from own 14YL, down 15-10 with 7:29 to go. Trojans QB Matt Barkley (15-31/195y, INT), 19-year-old frosh who had played through bruised throwing shoulder from midway in 3rd Q, received great credit for orchestrating winning drive that followed, but RB Joe McKnight (16/60y) also sparked victory. On 3rd-and-8 from 16YL, McKnight wriggled away from coverage by LB Ross Homan to snare 21y pass from Barkley. Barkley then hit TE Anthony McCoy for 26y, and McKnight added 1, 4, 9, and 8y runs to Buckeyes 6YL. USC RB Stafon Johnson (11/50y, 2 TDs) skirted right side for 2y TD with 1:05 to play, and McKnight added 2-pt catch on swing pass to left.

MICHIGAN 38 Notre Dame 34: With both former powerhouses apparently back on track, this struggle turned into slugfest. Michigan (2-0) struck 1st on 2y power run up middle by RB Brandon Minor (16/106y, TD), set up by 40y soaring catch at sideline by WR Greg Mathews (5/68y, TD) from frosh QB Tate Forcier (23-33/240y, 2 TDs, INT and 13/70y, TD rushing). Down 7-0 due partly to early missed 28y FG try, Fighting Irish (1-1) had replay call go against them as RB Armando Allen (21/139y, TD) barely stepped on sideline at 22YL to kill his TD dash with screen pass. Notre Dame had to settle for frosh K Nick Tausch's 34y FG. Things got worse on next play: Michigan WR Darryl Stonum sped through crack at his 25YL and cut diagonally into clear for 94y KO TD RET. Rallying twice from 11-pt margins, ND QB Jimmy Clausen (25-42/336y, 3 TDs) hit star WRs Golden Tate (9/115y, 2 TDs) and Michael Floyd (7/131y, TD) for short scores and 17-14 lead. With Wolverines down 20-17 in 3rd Q, Forcier stamped his will on seesaw battle, hitting TE Kevin Koger with short TD pass and, on 4th-and-3, cutting sharply inside to spurt 31y to TD and 31-20 lead. Back surged Irish as Clausen hit Tate with 21y TD, and, with 5:13 to play, Allen ran for TD and added Statue of Liberty 2-pt run for 34-31 advantage. Needing to kill clock with 2:29 left, Notre Dame coach Charlie Weis drew criticism for calling 2nd and 3rd down passes which fell incomplete. Weis reasoned his run game would be contained because Allen had just twisted his ankle. After short Irish punt, Wolverines took over on their 42YL with 2:13 to go. According to coach Rich Rodriguez, Forcier was most calm when pressure reached its highest, and electric frosh clicked on 6-7/56y passing with his only miss coming on dropped EZ pass on 1st-and-goal. On next snap, Forcier sent Mathews in from left flank and back out for dramatic 5y TD pass at pylon with 11 secs left.

Central Michigan 29 MICHIGAN STATE 27: Michigan State (1-1) harbored high hopes, but lost to in-state, lesser-light Chippewas (1-1) when thrilling conclusion handed big win to Central Michigan. Never more than 7 pts ahead, Spartans led most of way: Frosh RB Caulton Ray (16/51y, TD) went for 1y TD run in 1st Q, and back-up QB Keith Nichol (3-8/51y, TD) found TE Charlie Gantt for 16y TD in 2nd Q for 17-13 H edge. CMU vet QB Dan LeFavour (33-46/328y, 3 TDs, INT) threw his 2nd TD pass early in 4th Q to knot it at 20-20, and in so doing passed Marshall's Byron Leftwich as MAC all-time total O leader. But, Michigan State QB Kirk Cousins (13-18/164y, TD) countered midway through 4th Q with his own TD toss. Back came LeFavour with 11y TD pass to little RB Paris Cotton with 32 secs on clock. LeFavour's 2-pt pass failed, so Chippewas trailed 27-26. K Andrew Aguila bounced perfect on-side KO over Spartans' heads to WR Bryan Anderson who collected it on CMU 47YL. With 8 secs left, Aguila missed 47y FG, but Michigan State was offside, and Aguila nailed winning 42y FG.

MINNESOTA 20 Air Force 13: Golden Gophers (2-0) donned all gold from shoulders to shoe-tops to celebrate opening of new on-campus stadium. More than 400 former players attended, including Bud Grant, star E from 1940s and beloved Minnesota Vikings coach. Before full house of 50,805 at TCF Bank Stadium, normally-impassive Grant openly cried at fan reception for current team and new facility. So, despite 10-3 lead enjoyed by Air Force (1-1) entering 4th Q, Minnesota simply would not accept defeat. Gophers LB Nate Triplett, 1-time Minnesota HS backfield star, made career-high 17 tackles and dashed 52y to go-ahead TD with FUM RET on aborted pitchout by Falcons QB Tim Jefferson (10-17/125y, TD). Triplett's TD gallop followed 4th Q 7y TD run by Minnesota RB DeLeon Eskridge (7/53y, TD) and provided 20-10 edge. With min to go, Air Force still needed 2 scores. So, Falcons eschewed TD try on 4th-and-3 at 13YL to accept K Erik Soderberg's 31y FG, but their on-side KO went to Minnesota. Gophers O was enhanced by their mainstays: QB Adam Weber hit 20-29/219y and WR Eric Decker nabbed 10/113y. "This place was magic tonight," Gophers coach Tim Brewster said. "We knew that it was our night and it was our house."

Houston 45 OKLAHOMA STATE 35: Houston's visit to Stillwater turned out as classic letdown for no. 6 Oklahoma State (1-1) after Cowboys' big win over Georgia. Or perhaps blame it on Sports Illustrated cover jinx. Cowboys WR Dez Bryant appeared on front of this week's issue. Cougars (2-0) received some lucky bounces but were sharp on O and determined to spring upset. Cougars QB Case Keenum (32-46/366y, 3 TDs, INT) scrambled 16y for TD and threw 3 TD passes, so Houston stunningly led 24-7 at H. Cowboys exploded for 3 unanswered TDs in 3rd Q, anchored by circling 82y punt TD RET by mercurial Bryant (5/85y) to swipe 28-24 edge. WR Josh Cooper gave Cowboys 35-31 with 11:22 to play with 22y TD pass from QB Zac Robinson (18-31/240y, TD, INT). Back came Houston as on 4th down Keenum scrambled and pitched arrow for EZ that Okla State LB Donald Booker tipped into 6y TD grab by Cougars RB Bryce Beall (2 TDs) for 38-35 lead with 6:42 to go. On next series, hard pass deflected off fingertips of Cowboys receiver to Houston CB Jamal Robinson, who returned it 26y for clinching TD. It was Cougars' 1st win over AP top-5 club since 1984.

OREGON 38 Purdue 36: After tough week in which star RB LaGarrette Blount was suspended, Oregon (1-1) seemed less excited for home opener than spirited crowd. Purdue (1-1) played inspired ball, sending tenacious RB Ralph Bolden (29/123y, 2 TDs) to 3 TDs. Boilermakers enjoyed leads of 7-3, 14-10, and 24-17, but Ducks' sleepy O was bailed out by pair of D TDs: CB Walter Thurmond returned INT 18y down sideline for 17-14 lead late in 2nd Q and S Javes Lewis returned FUM 28y for 24-24 deadlock late in 3rd Q. Oregon's frosh-dominated running brigade finally came to life on next possession as RB LaMichael James (9/56y) bolted for gains of 9, 7, and 27y. QB Jeremiah Masoli (11-21/163y and 14/84y, TD rushing) scored on 15y run to create 31-24 lead for Ducks with less than 2 mins to go in 3rd Q. Purdue bounced right back with 76y drive capped by Bolden slipping over middle for 22y TD catch from QB Joey Elliott (24-41/266y, TD, 2 INTs). But, Oregon DT Conrad Davis got his paw up to block x-pt kick, so Ducks led 31-30. After RB Kenjon Barner scored to put Oregon ahead 38-30, Purdue came back downfield to face 4th-and-11 at Ducks 14YL with barely min to play. Boilers WR Keith Smith looked like he was hemmed in on E-around but raised up to loft surprise TD pass to WR Aaron Valentin (8/82y, TD). Elliott's 2-pt pass was caught by TE Kyle Adams just over end-line, and Oregon survived.

USA TODAY Coaches Poll September 13, 2009

1 Florida (56)	1472	14 Virginia Tech	709
2 Texas	1399	15 Texas Christian	648
3 Southern California (3)	1368	16 Utah	533
4 Alabama	1277	17 Oklahoma State	485
5 Penn State	1216	18 Nebraska	471
6 Mississippi	1060	19 North Carolina	341
7tCalifornia	1051	20 Georgia	333
7tLouisiana State	1051	21 Cincinnati	328
9 Brigham Young	941	22 Miami	291
10 Boise State	913	23 Kansas	195
11 Ohio State	855	24 Oregon State	118
12 Oklahoma	794	25 Missouri	104
13 Georgia Tech	771		

September 19, 2009

(Th) MIAMI 33 Georgia Tech 17: Playing 3rd game in 12 days, weary Yellow Jackets (2-1) ran into superior Miami (2-0). Although Georgia Tech ran effectively to K Scott Blair's early 32y FG, it could block for its option O only well enough to earn 95y on ground after piling up 472y vs. Miami in 2008. Hurricanes scored on their 1st 3 series as cool QB Jacory Harris (20-25/270y, 3 TDs) riddled Jackets for 2 quick TD throws: 40y to WR LeRon Byrd and 13y to TE Dedrick Epps. Miami went off at H with 17-3 edge. When Hurricanes opened 2nd H by going 60y to RB Javarris James' TD run for 24-3 lead, Georgia Tech's 4-game win streak over Miami was all but over.

CLEMSON 25 Boston College 7: With Boston College (2-1) D holding Clemson (2-1) to 253y and single TD, chances seemed good for Eagles to stay unbeaten after road game twice stopped for rain and lightning. Instead, Eagles O managed pitiful 54y, special teams allowed 77y punt TD RET to Tigers RB C.J. Spiller, and Clemson K Richard Jackson squeezed off 6 FGs to tie school record. Was Eagles' playbook struck by lightning? Electrically-charged Spiller (17/77y), who left in 2nd H with foot injury, finished with 219y all-purpose and scored TD on his 1st-ever punt RET. Spiller, 1 of Clemson's all-time best players, now had produced TDs via rush, reception, KO RET, punt RET, and by throwing pass. This RET was sr Spiller's 15th career TD of 50y or more. No such heroics cropped up for Boston College, which finished 1st H with -2y O and single 1st down, which was earned via pass interference PEN. Early in 4th Q, BC managed to convert FUM REC into QB Justin Tuggle's 13y TD pass to WR Justin Jarvis to cut deficit to 19-7. After their TD, however, Eagles could add only 3y more, and Tuggle finished 4-20/23y with 3 INTs passing; while top runner, RB Montel Harris, limited to 12/13y. S DeAndre McDaniel (7 tackles, INT, sack) sparked D that allowed fewest y in any of more than 370 games in Clemson's 57 years of ACC play.

VIRGINIA TECH 16 Nebraska 15: Stalled all afternoon by tenacious Nebraska (2-1) D, Hokies (2-1) QB Tyrod Taylor (12-27/192y, TD) squirmed away from pressure in game's dying moments to find WR Danny Coale alone up right sideline, and Coale bolted for 81y to Huskers 3YL. Under more rush pressure, Taylor threaded winning TD pass 3 plays later to WR Dyrell Roberts with 21 secs left to play. Roberts had opened game with 76y KO RET that led to short TD run by RB Ryan Williams (21/107y, TD). Other than Williams' 46y run in 2nd Q that set up 39y FG by K Matt Waldron, Virginia Tech was stymied by Nebraska, led by DT Ndamukong Suh (8 tackles, 4 pass blocks, sack). After making 0y in 1st Q, Huskers outgained Hokies 343y to 278y—only 53y by Va Tech in 2nd H—until Coale's late, long reception. But, Nebraska constantly bumbled in red zone and settled for 5 FGs by K Alex Henery. Last 3-ptr by Henery came from 38y out with 4:33 to play and extended Huskers' lead to 15-10. Huskers IB Roy Helu rushed 28/169y, new career high.

FLORIDA 23 Tennessee 13: Pregame talk focused on extent of whipping top-ranked Florida (3-0) would administer to Tennessee (1-2) to punish mouthy new Vols coach Lane Kiffin, who since being hired in December had wrongly accused Florida of recruiting violations and had boasted of his plan to sing "Rocky Top" all night long after beating Gators. Well, Florida did win school-record 13th straight game and coach Urban Meyer did run his series record to 5-0, but anyone hoping for romp needed to look elsewhere. Tennessee's game-plan as 30-pt underdogs was to eat clock and keep Florida from big plays. Volunteers TB Mario Hardesty rushed 20/96y, TD, while Florida QB Tim Tebow (14-19/115y, INT and 24/76y rushing, TD) was prevented from anything longer than 18y screen pass to TE Aaron Hernandez in 2nd Q. Tennessee also snapped Tebow's 30-game TD-pass streak. After trade of FGs, Tebow scored sole TD of 1st H with 1y run that capped 72y drive in 2nd Q. On next possession, however, Tebow threw INT to S Eric Berry (11 tackles, INT), leader of Vols secondary, which set up 2nd FG by K Daniel Lincoln to pull Tennessee within 10-6. Gators owned slight 133y to 126y O advantage and 13-6 edge at H but reeled off 10 straight pts for 23-6 lead. Tebow lost FUM at Tennessee 2YL early in 4th Q, and Vols went distance to Hardesty's 17y TD run. Down 10 pts, Vols would not see ball again until 6 mins remained, and QB Jonathan Crompton (11-19/93y, 2 INTs) wasted more than 4 mins to travel 27y before throwing INT to S Ahmad Black (11 tackles) that sealed verdict.

Georgia 52 ARKANSAS 41: For 3 years, sr QB Joe Cox (18-26/375y, 5 TDs, INT) bided his time behind now-departed Matthew Stafford, patiently waiting his turn to become Georgia (2-1) starter. Cox's patience paid off in Fayetteville as he threw for 5 TDs to tie school record held by 3 others including Stafford. Arkansas (1-1) QB Ryan Mallett (21-39/408y, 5 TDs) pitched 5 record scores himself, while also setting new Razorbacks' mark for passing y. But, Hogs ran out of steam in crucial 4th Q—which opened with Arkansas behind 42-38—and could manage only K Alex Tejada's 2nd FG of 23y and gain only 52y of 485y total. Generally, each O had easy time as Bulldogs enjoyed 6 TD drives, trio of which required 3 plays or fewer. Of Hogs' 5 TDs, 2 were scored on 1st play of possession, while their longest scoring series required only 3:04 of time. Sophisticated attacks combined for 1011y, with 783y coming through aerial exploits of Cox and Mallett. Key play came on run, however: Georgia RB Richard Samuel (16/104y, TD) romped 80y in 2nd Q to spark 17-pt surge that retrieved Bulldogs from 21-10 hole. Bulldogs WR A.J. Green caught 7/137y with 2 TDs, while Arkansas WRs Greg Childs (5/140y, 2 TDs) and Jarius Wright (4/108y, TD) each topped 100y plateau. Georgia coach Mark Richt upped his remarkable SEC road record to 25-4.

KENTUCKY 31 Louisville 27: Exciting Governor's Cup battle featured 6 lead changes and down-to-wire finish. Louisville (1-1) grabbed 20-17 lead early in 4th Q on 5y TD pass from QB Justin Burke (15-28/245y, 2 TDs, INT) to TE Cameron Graham as Cardinals' 69y TD drive had started with 3rd TO of 2nd H by Wildcats (2-0). Trailing for 1st time since 1st Q, Kentucky chose ball-control and marched 73y on 12 plays to regain lead at 24-20 on 2y TD run by RB Derek Locke (15/72y, TD), who earned 310y all-purpose including 100y KO TD RET in 1st Q. Louisville WR Trent Guy (5/170y KO RETs) then took central role: Guy returned ensuing KO 30y and, on 2nd play of series, reeled in 66y TD pass for 27-24 advantage midway through 4th Q. Soon after, Guy disastrously benefited Kentucky by fumbling away punt at his 24YL, which UK FB A.J. Nance recovered. Wildcats QB Mike Hartline (20-27/178y, TD, INT) soon tossed 12y scoring pass to WR Randall Cobb (6/71y, TD) as Kentucky regained lead at 31-27. Determined Guy returned KO 28y to his 40YL, and Cardinals turned to runs of RB Victor Anderson (19/110y, TD), who gained 4 and 17y, around 15y facemask PEN on Cats LB Micah Johnson (12 tackles), to reach Kentucky 24YL. On 3rd down, Burke's pass was tipped by Wildcats DT Corey Peters and picked off by LB Sam Maxwell with 1:56 left. Cardinals got ball back with 50 secs left but Burke's final deep pass was broken up by Maxwell, who would end season as nation's top LB in passes defended.

California 35 MINNESOTA 21: Superb RB Jahvid Best (26/131y, 5 TDs) sparked Golden Bears (3-0), combining his speed and power to romp for 5 rushing TDs, which tied 88-year-old school mark. California, losers of 8 of its last 9 road games, never trailed, but after Golden Gophers (2-1) outgained Bears 104y to 22y in 3rd Q and deadlocked it 21-21 on TD pass tossed by Minnesota's own star, WR Eric Decker (8/119y, 2 TDs), Cal counted on Best for perhaps his most important if barely noticed play. With Minnesota crowd roaring, Cal faced 3rd-and-16 from its 22YL with less than 10 mins to play. Gophers blitzed, which Best picked up with stiff block, and WR Jeremy Ross, in for injured WR Nyan Boateng, nabbed 35y pass from Bears QB Kevin Riley (16-25/252y). "I'm almost glad that situation came up where they tied it up," said Riley. "Last year and the year before, when (other teams) came back and tied it up and took the lead, we didn't win those games." Riley soon found Ross again for 31y to 1YL, and Best rambled around RE for 2y TD. On Minny's next snap, Cal LB Michael Mohamed made 1st of 3 4th Q INTs off QB Adam Weber (21-32/226y, 2 TDs, 3 INTs) at Gophers 44YL to set up Best's clinching TD run. Minnesota had rallied in 2nd Q from 14-0 and 21-7 deficits as Weber hit Decker for pair of scores.

IOWA 27 Arizona 17: Hawkeyes' growing D prowess, which players had labeled "Six Seconds of Hell," showed itself in stopping Arizona (2-1), which arrived with nation's 5th-best rushing attack (305.5y/game) but made only 148y against Iowa (3-0). Pair of Hawkeyes frosh RBs—Adam Robinson (18/101y, 2 TDs) and Brandon Wegher—combined for 3 short TD dives, Robinson's 1st coming at end of 75y march to open game. With score tied 7-7 in 2nd Q after Wildcats CB Trevin Wade stepped in front of receiver and went 38y for INT TD RET, Arizona RB Nic Grigsby (11/75y) broke away for weaving 58y run to Iowa 1YL. But, Hawks D held, and Arizona had to settle for K Alex Zendejas' 20y FG. Robinson put Iowa ahead 14-10 before H, and Cats could make only 94y in 2nd H. Hawkeyes S Tyler Sash rambled 41y on INT RET to set up FG early in 4th Q, and Iowa soon kept possession for 14 plays and more than 8 mins before Wegher's TD made it 27-10 with 4:40 left.

NOTRE DAME 33 Michigan State 30: Fighting Irish's vaunted O lost star WR Michael Floyd (2/38y, TD) to broken collarbone, but QB Jimmy Clausen (22-31/300y, 2 TDs) and RB Armando Allen (23/115y, TD and 5y TD pass thrown) lifted Notre Dame (2-1) at vital moments as lead changed hands 5 times. Michigan State (1-2) trailed 13-3 early in 2nd Q, but WR Keshawn Martin, former HS QB, threw 30y TD pass and RB Larry Caper (12/51y, 2 TDs) scored his 1st TD late in 2nd Q for 17-16 H edge. QB Kirk Cousins (23-35/302y, TD, INT) rallied Spartans to 30-26 lead with 9:33 left in 4th Q with 17y TD pass to WR Blair White (6/75y, 2 TDs). Clausen in turn took ND downfield despite turf-toe injury and put Irish up 33-30 on 33y scoring toss to his other receiving star, WR Golden Tate (7/127y TD) with 5:18 to go. In closing secs, Cousins hit 7-8/62y and had chance from Irish 18YL to win or tie for Spartans. But Cousins missed on both opportunities: he misfired in EZ with Caper open for TD, and when FG could tie it, Cousins was intercepted at 4YL by clutch Notre Dame S Kyle McCarthy.

TEXAS 34 Texas Tech 24: QB Taylor Potts (46-62/420y, 3 TDs, INT) hit his 1st 6 passes and had Red Raiders (2-1) clicking efficiently on opening drive. But Texas Tech, which would suffer 14/108y in PENs, had to settle for 41y FG by K Matt Williams when stymied by 2 flags. Texas Tech's 3-0 edge would turn out to be last lead it would enjoy as Longhorns (3-0) counted on their sparkplug, WR Jordan Shipley (11/73y), to get them winging with 1st Q 46y punt TD RET, only TD of 1st H. As Shipley skidded through right corner of EZ, he came somewhat close to accidental goring by Texas' giant steer mascot, Bevo, who had just stood up to find out what shouting was all about. "Bevo surprised me. I looked up and there he was," Shipley laughed. "I'm going to try to avoid Bevo from now on." QB Colt McCoy (24-34/205y, TD, 2 INTs) was hit hard—as was Potts—and suffered lackluster passing day, but McCoy guided Texas to 17-3 and 24-10 leads in 3rd Q to overcome pair of scoring catches by Raiders WR Lyle Leong (6/80y, 2 TDs). McCoy, who had suffered from flu all week, provided bit of daylight with his short TD pass midway through 4th Q that built 31-17 lead.

COLORADO 24 Wyoming 0: Golden Buffaloes (1-2) had their backs to wall after pair of disheartening losses to Colorado State and Toledo: Even CU geology professor reputedly confronted sr LB Marcus Burton in class during prior week. Coach Dan Hawkins, who had talked boldly of 10 wins, had Colorado's running game rolling as little RB Rodney Stewart (32/127y, 2 TDs), back from hamstring injury, scored pair of TDs. Colorado D also sparkled as it permitted only 61y and 3 1st downs in 1st

H. Buffs doubled ground output by Wyoming (1-2) and enjoyed 35:08 in possession time. WR Scotty McKnight alertly scooped up FUM on Buffs opening series and scored 2y TD for 7-0 lead. Cowboys LB Brian Hendricks recovered bad shotgun snap at Colorado 18YL on CU's next possession. But, Wyoming went nowhere, and K Austin McCoy was wide with 35y FG try, 1st of 2 mid-range misses. Cowboys' best O performer was QB Austyn Carta-Samuels, who came off bench to pass 11-24/125y and rush 9/36y.

Florida State 54 BRIGHAM YOUNG 28: Coming off Seminoles' heart-breaking loss to Miami and near loss to lowly Jacksonville State, it was difficult to know what to expect from Florida State (2-1). That Seminoles delivered 26-pt victory—2000 miles from home and 4500 feet above sea level—over no. 9 BYU (2-1) seemed least likely of all expectations. Florida State QB Christian Ponder (21-26/195y, 2 TDs and 11/77y, TD rushing) accounted for 3 TDs, RB Ty Jones (12/108y, TD) scored 1st Q TD, frosh RB Lonnie Pryor scored pair of 2nd Q runs on his 1st 2 collegiate carries, and frosh CB Greg Reid returned INT for 63y TD in 3rd Q which built margin to 37-14. Reid's INT was 1 of 3 swiped from Cougars star QB Max Hall (20-31/306y, 2 TDs, 3 INTs). Hall's 2nd TD pass came in 3rd Q and went 80y to WR McKay Jacobson.

WASHINGTON 16 Southern California 13: USC had developed vexing habit: Trojans (2-1) held 24-2 record against ranked teams since 2002, but after this last-moment upset by Washington (2-1) Trojans now had suffered 5 defeats to unranked Pac-10 foes in that span. Still, Huskies' hidden advantages were abundant: Troy was coming off late-game road win over Ohio State, its QB (frosh Matt Barkley) and best defender (FS Taylor Mays) were both out with injury, and Huskies head coach (Steve Sarkisian) and D-coordinator (Nick Holt) were fresh off USC's staff. Matters started predictably as no. 3 USC cruised to 10-0 lead as RB Joe McKnight (11/100y, TD) scored on 10y run and K Jordan Congdon knocked through 42y FG. Trojans owned 133y to 15y O edge at this moment, but Washington countered behind star QB Jake Locker (21-35/237y), who tallied on 4y TD run late in 1st Q. USC suffered 75y in PENs and no 3rd down conversions, and as coach Pete Carroll admitted, "didn't throw the ball very well today" behind sub QB Aaron Corp (13-22/110y, INT). Trailing 13-10 midway in 4th Q, Trojans sprung McKnight for 34y sprint but had to settle for Congdon's tying 25y FG with 4:07 to go after Huskies LB Donald Butler (12 tackles, INT) made critical 3rd down stop. Locker hooked up with WR Jermaine Kearse on 21 and 19y passes and brought Washington to USC 8YL for K Erik Folk's winning 22y FG with 3 secs to play.

Cincinnati 28 OREGON STATE 18: Tall Bearcats (3-0) QB Tony Pike passed 31-49/332y, 2 TDs, INT and sparked 21-pt 2nd Q surge to end 26-game non-conf winning streak for Beavers (2-1) at Reser Stadium. In 2nd Q, Pike scored on 7y run and rifled 45y TD bomb to WR D.J. Woods (7/117y, TD) just before H for 21-8 lead. Oregon State RB Jacquizz Rodgers (20/73y TD), slowed in 1st H by tender ankle, opened 2nd H with 9y spurt to outside for TD. His brother, WR James Rodgers (11/90y) added 67y rushing, but it was not enough as Pike clinched it with 19y TD pass to WR Mardy Gilyard (9/65y, TD), which raised lead to 28-18 midway through 4th Q.

WASHINGTON STATE 30 Southern Methodist 27 (OT): Cougars (1-2) were outgained 504y to 276y but got pair of INT TD RETs—by LBs Alex Hoffman-Ellis (52y RET) and Myron Beck (67y RET)—in 2nd H and fashioned 80y TD drive in last 2 mins of regulation to turn 7-pt deficit into 27-27 deadlock. On tying TD drive, Wazzu QB Marshall Lobbestael (24-52/239y, 2 TDs, 2 INTs) took advantage of 4th down pass interference PEN called on Southern Methodist (2-1) DB Sterling Moore, who was trying to deal with Washington State WR Jared Karstetter (5/63y, TD), who had 6" height advantage. Karstetter soon caught tying 7y TD with 28 secs left. In OT, SMU QB Bo Levi Mitchell (40-57/424y, 2 TDs, 4 INTs) was picked off in EZ by Washington State S Chima Nwachukwu, and K Nico Grasu kicked winning FG moments later. Mustangs WR Emmanuel Sanders caught school-record 18/178y.

USA TODAY Coaches Poll September 20, 2009

1 Florida (59)	1475	14 Texas Christian	701
2 Texas	1412	15 Cincinnati	580
3 Alabama	1355	16 Oklahoma State	576
4 Penn State	1274	17 Georgia	457
5 Mississippi	1182	18 North Carolina	445
6 California	1149	19 Kansas	381
7 Louisiana State	1122	20 Brigham Young	279
8 Boise State	976	21 Missouri	214
9 Oklahoma	917	22 Michigan	205
10 Southern California	905	23 Houston	160
11 Ohio State	900	24 Nebraska	158
12 Virginia Tech	853	25 Florida State	154
13 Miami	724		

September 26, 2009

(Th) SOUTH CAROLINA 16 Mississippi 10: Give credit to South Carolina's fine D, but Ole Miss (2-1) QB Jevon Snead (7-21/107y, TD) in no way resembled sharp passer who closed 2008 season. Rebels gained only 118y O until well into 4th Q when they were energized on 83y TD trip by speedy little WR-RB Dexter McCluster (15/85y rushing). Snead capped that drive with 45y TD pitch up middle to WR Markeith Summers. That pulled Rebels within 16-10, but they failed on 4th-and-19 pass with 1:26 to play. Gamecocks (3-1) showed superiority going up and down field but had to settle for K Spencer Lanning's 3 FGs until DE Cliff Matthews (2 sacks) created sack and FUM by Snead at Mississippi 25YL in 3rd Q. It led to 2y TD pass from maturing QB Stephen Garcia (16-34/220y, TD) to FB Patrick DeMarco for 16-3 edge. Fine DE Eric Norwood authored pair of sacks for South Carolina career record and also partially blocked punt.

VIRGINIA TECH 31 Miami 7: Having vanquished Florida State and Georgia Tech in recent weeks, Miami (2-1) arrived in Blacksburg, Va., as national flavor-of-week, while soph QB Jacory Harris (9-25/150y, INT) was receiving early Heisman talk. Rough D of no. 12 Virginia Tech (3-1), playing with chip on its shoulder, would hear none of it: "We felt like we were being a little disrespected," said LB Cody Grimm (11 tackles), "we were defending ACC champs, and no one was talking about us having a chance in this game." Altering game on Miami's opening possession, Hokies D set early tone as rover Dorian Porch (9 tackles) sacked Harris to force FUM that Porch recovered on Miami 11YL. Virginia Tech needed 5 plays to punch across GL on 2y run by TB Ryan Williams (34/150y, 2TDs). Five mins later, QB Tyrod Taylor (4-9/98y, TD and 10/75y rushing) delivered next big play for Hokies as he threw 48y TD pass to WR Jarrett Boykin. Suddenly Canes trailed by 2 TDs, in driving rainstorm no less, and Hurricanes were struggling just to gain 1st downs. After Miami's 2nd 3-and-out series of 2nd Q, Va Tech CB Jacob Sykes blocked P Matt Bosher's boot from deep in Miami territory, scooped by S Matt Reidy on 1YL and taken for TD and commanding 21-0 lead. For moment in 3rd Q, Canes had momentum as Harris led 46y drive after KO to 1y TD run by RB Javarris James. Miami D quickly forced punt, but Canes cooled off after TE Jimmy Graham dropped 2 passes on next possession, which ended on downs at Hokies 33YL. Virginia Tech proceeded to drive to clinching 22y FG by K Matt Waldron.

South Florida 17 FLORIDA STATE 7: Game would be remembered by South Florida (4-0) fans for many years to come. After 12 years of steady building, Bulls finally beat 1 of state's big 3, and it came in 1st-ever meeting with Florida State (2-2). Amazingly, USF managed upset without Big East all-time total O leader, sr QB Matt Grothe, who was lost for season with knee injury during prior week's win over Charleston Southern. In Grothe's place emerged frosh QB B.J. Daniels (8-21/215y, 2 TDs, 1 INTs), native of Tallahassee, who ran 23/126y and threw 2 TD passes. Game may have been decided over course of 9 plays in 2nd Q. With no score, Florida State faced 1st-and-goal from South Florida 3YL. Noles were stopped in 4 plays, with Bulls LBs Sabbath Joseph and Sam Barrington stuffing TB Ty Jones (12/21y, TD) at 1YL on 4th down. Bulls O needed only 5 plays to score with Daniels delivering 77y pass to WR Theo Wilson and hitting TE Ben Busbee with 8y TD pass on next play. Daniels' stunning 73y scoring strike to WR Sterling Griffin doubled lead to 14-0 right before H. FSU QB Christian Ponder (25-37/269y) was able to move O between 20YLs but had little time to throw long against relentless USF pressure that sacked him 5 times. South Florida starting DEs George Selvie and newcomer Jason Pierre-Paul each had 4 tackles and 1 sack, while sub DE Craig Marshall added 2 sacks. Week after gaining 313y on ground against BYU, Seminoles rushed for meager 19y and also couldn't overcome 4 lost FUMs. Jones' TD run came early in 4th Q after CB Greg Reid returned punt 63y.

Texas Christian 14 CLEMSON 10: After earlier win at Virginia, Horned Frogs (3-0) upped 2009 road record against ACC to 2-0 as QB Andy Dalton (17-26/226y, 2 TDs and 19/86y rushing) threw pair of TD passes and TCU D blanked Clemson (2-2) in 2nd H. That was crucial because Tigers D played at high level too, and Horned Frogs trailed 10-7 entering 4th Q. But Dalton and WR Antoine Hicks hooked up on 25y TD pass early in 4th Q for 14-10 lead. On 1st possession after Hicks' stellar TD catch, Tigers dramatic RB C.J. Spiller (26/122y, TD and 3/79y receiving) carried 54y to help advance 59y to TCU 17YL. Drive stalled, however, and normally steady Clemson K Richard Jackson missed rainy 34y FG try. Jackson's 26y FG in 1st Q had been his 9th straight successful boot. When Clemson got ball back 3 mins later, hounded Spiller lost 4y on 4 runs. But, frosh QB Kyle Parker (17-37/192y) connected with Spiller for 15y and hit RB Jacoby Ford with 24y pass that, with corresponding TCU PEN, brought ball to Frogs 13YL. But 4 plays lost 3y, and threat died with 2 mins remaining. TCU's opening TD—Dalton's 1st Q 6y pass to WR Curtis Clay—had been set up by odd play: Facing 3rd-and-13 early in drive, Dalton threw pass tipped forward by Clemson DE Da'Quan Bowers into hands of RB Ed Wesley who raced 58y to 10YL. Dalton, who became school's 2nd all-time passer with 5159y, found Clay for TD 2 plays later. Tigers had regained lead late in 2nd Q when Spiller raced 60y with pass to 4YL to set up his 1y TD run moments later. Spiller became 2nd player after USC's Reggie Bush ever to gain 2500y rushing, 1000y receiving, 1500y on KO RETs, and 500y on punt RETs. TCU moved to 55-1 record under coach Gary Patterson when allowing 17 pts or fewer. Frogs now had won 13 of last 16 games against BCS conf teams dating back to 2002.

ALABAMA 35 Arkansas 7: Already blessed with outstanding run game, excellent D, and great special teams, Alabama's aerial attack surprisingly tore apart Arkansas' suspect secondary. Crimson Tide (4-0) QB Greg McElroy (17-24/291y, 3 TDs) easily outshined his Razorbacks (1-2) counterpart who led nation in pass efficiency, QB Ryan Mallett (12-35/160y, TD, INT), who had unfortunate task of facing Tide's pressuring D. With Tide ahead 7-0 on 52y TD run by RB Trent Richardson (9/65y, TD), McElroy threw his 1st TD pass midway through 2nd Q on trick play: RB Mark Ingram (17/50y, TD) took snap out of Wildcat formation, handed ball to RB Terry Grant, who tossed it to McElroy. By that point, WR Julio Jones was all alone downfield with time to stop and wait for McElroy's pass before scoring on 50y play. Hogs finally tallied early in 3rd Q on Mallett's 18y TD pass to WR Greg Childs. But any chance for Hogs' rally went out window 20 secs later when McElroy and WR Marquis Maze (2/88y, TD) connected on 80y TD. Soon after, Alabama DE Lorenzo Washington blocked Arkansas punt to set up 14y TD pass from McElroy to Ingram for 28-7 lead. Throughout game Tide used D-Line pressure and variety of blitzes to contain Mallett, with CB Javier Arenas contributing 1st 2-sack game of his storied career. Alabama won its 18th conf opener in row, longest such streak in school history.

Louisiana State 30 MISSISSIPPI STATE 26: It had to be agonizing for Mississippi State (2-2) to come so close after having lost 10 straight and 17 of last 18 to LSU (4-0). Trailing 30-24, Bulldogs drove 48y in game's final moments to 1st-and-goal at Tigers 2YL. RB Anthony Dixon (27/106y, 2 TDs) carried twice to within inches of GL. Mississippi State's surprise 3rd down jump-pass was broken up alertly by Tigers S Chad Jones, who earlier had scored on dazzling, tackle-breaking 93y punt RET, and QB Tyson Lee (15-38/172y, TD, 3 INTs) then went for Wishbone keeper on 4th down only to be stuffed by cadre of LSU defenders. Tigers' GLS underscored just how important each unit was to their win as, indeed, LSU scored TDs on O, D, and special teams. On O, QB Jordan Jefferson (15-28/233y, 2 TDs) and WR Brandon LaFell

(6/101y, 2 TDs) connected twice for scores, which offset LSU's paltry 30y rushing. On D, CB Patrick Peterson opened scoring with 37y INT TD RET early in 1st Q. And then there was Jones giving LSU 30-21 4th Q lead with his exhilarating punt RET. Featuring rugged Dixon, Mississippi State rushed for 151y and outgained LSU 374y to 263y. LSU's special teams gave away TD as punt snap went over P Derek Helton's head to 1YL to set up Dixon's TD run for 14-13 Bulldogs lead late in 1st Q.

GEORGIA 20 Arizona State 17: Unknown-quantity Arizona State (2-1) was competitive from outset, especially on D, but had no answer for Georgia star WR A.J. Green (8/153y, TD). Green opened scoring in 1st Q, going up for long pass from QB Joe Cox (17-31/242y, TD, 2 INTs) and eluding 2 defenders for 56y TD. After 43y FG by Sun Devils frosh K Bobby Wenzig, in for injured Groza Award winner of last year, Thomas Weber, Green got Georgia (3-1) moving with another catch on way to FB Fred Munzenmaier's 2y TD run late in 1st Q. Halfway through 3rd Q, Bulldogs clung to 14-3 lead, but RB Caleb King (11/55y) fumbled on his 37YL to ASU S Jarrell Holman. Arizona State QB Danny Sullivan (10-32/116y, TD, INT) soon flipped short TD pass into left flat to RB Dimitri Nance (25/92y), and Holman struck again with weaving 47y INT TD RET for 17-14 lead for Devils. Georgia tied it on FG by K Blair Walsh early in 4th Q after Devils D held near GL. Green went high to block ASU's potential go-ahead FG with 4:31 left and made 36y catch to set up Walsh's winning 37y FG as clock expired. Arizona State coach Dennis Erickson admitted, "Of all the games I've been involved in college football, this could be one of the hardest I've ever had to take."

Iowa 21 PENN STATE 10: Amazing sometimes how simple 2 pts can turn momentum. Ahead 10-0 thanks mostly to 79y TD bomb from QB Daryll Clark (12-32/198y, TD, 3 INTs) to WR Chaz Powell on Penn State's 1st play from scrimmage, no. 4 Nittany Lions (3-1) chose to pass on 3rd-and-13 from their 2YL in 2nd Q. Clark was sacked by Iowa (4-0) DE Broderick Binns as Clark's FUM turned into safety. Hawkeyes grabbed control from there, forcing negative y on each Lions' possession in rest of 1st H. Before 2nd Q ended, Iowa K Daniel Murray pulled Hawks to within 10-5 with 41y FG. Iowa built its momentum through scoreless 3rd Q, and Hawkeyes took their 1st lead early in 4th Q: DE Adrian Clayborn ignored his team's punt-RET strategy by going all out at Penn State P Jeremy Boone. Clayborn blocked punt and ball bounced perfectly into his hands for 53y TD RET for 11-10 lead. Now thriving, Iowa D forced 3 turnovers rest of way, which led to RB Adam Robinson's 18y TD charge around RE and Murray's 2nd FG. It was coach Kirk Ferentz's 7th win in last 8 games over Penn State's Joe Paterno.

MICHIGAN 36 Indiana 33: Indiana (3-1) had to settle for 4 FGs by K Nick Freeland on trips inside Wolverines (4-0) 20YL, and in end it cost Hoosiers dearly. In 1st Q, Michigan RB Carlos Brown 11/83y, TD) took short pass from QB Tate Forcier (11-21/184y, 2 TDs, INT) and raced 61y to score for 7-7 tie, and on next possession, Brown tallied on 41y run. Indiana was full of comebacks on this afternoon, however, snatching lead 4 times at 7-0, 17-14, 23-21, and 33-29. Hoosiers' last TD came in middle of 4th Q from RB Darius Willis (16/152y, 2 TDs), who roared 85y off left side. Just prior, Forcier had given Wolverines 29-26 edge with 7y leaping TD dash at right pylon followed by his 2-pt run. In last 5 mins, Forcier whipped his Wolveriens 52y to WR Martavious Odoms' 3rd down 26y post-pattern TD catch. Less than 2:30 remained on next scrimmage play after Odoms' TD, and Indiana WR Demarlo Belcher and Michigan DB Donovan Warren appeared to make simultaneous catch from QB Ben Cappell (21-38/270y, INT). Under rules, it might well have been decided as reception for Indiana. Although normally mind-mannered Hoosiers coach Bill Lynch went wild, Warren's INT was upheld by TV review to seal Wolverines' 24th straight Big 10 home opener win. Indiana outgained UM by 467y to 372y in attempt to win in Ann Arbor for 1st time since its legendary 1967 Cinderella team triumphed 27-20.

WISCONSIN 38 Michigan State 30: Wisconsin (4-0) might have been down in skill-position players in recent years, but QB Scott Tolzien (19-31/243y, 4 TDs) and RB John Clay (32/142y, TD) stepped up to log 5 TDs against disappointing Michigan State (1-3). Badgers TE Garrett Graham (5/58y, 3 TDs) snared TD passes of 15, 6, and 23y to set school TE career TD record with 13. Trying to overcome 4 TOs, Michigan State had nearly regained momentum in 3rd Q when QB Kirk Cousins (17-34/201y, 2 TDs, INT) hit WR B.J. Cunningham with 24y TD to clip deficit to 24-17. Wisconsin roared right back, however, as Tolzien hit passes of 45y to WR Isaac Anderson (3/66y) and 19y for TD to WR Nick Toon, son of former Badgers and New York Jets great Al Toon. Sub QB Keith Nicol (7-12/195y, 2 TDs, 2 INTs) came off bench to try to rally Spartans with pair of too-late TD passes to WR Keshawn Martin (4/139y, 2 TDs).

HOUSTON 29 Texas Tech 28: This big opportunity for hopeful Houston (3-0) was anticipated as aerial shootout. Neither Texas Tech (2-2) nor Cougars failed, combining for 105 pass attempts and 1063y O. What surprised observers was only 2 TD passes posted by Raiders QB Taylor Potts (30-45/321y, TD) and Cougars QB Case Keenum (38-58/435y, TD, INT). Keenum got his scoring throw—his school-record 19th straight game with TD pass—out of way early as WR James Cleveland (8/85y), former Iowa transfer, nabbed 6y TD less than 5 mins into game. Red Raiders RB Baron Batch (19/114y, 2 TDs) ran for pair of 1st H TDs, but Houston K Jordan Mannisto (3 FGs) nailed 50y FG as 2nd Q closed to narrow Texas Tech's H edge to 21-13. Raiders WR Tramain Swindall broke 3 tackles on his 24y TD catch from Potts—Texas Tech's only score of 2nd H—that built 28-20 edge with 4:19 left in 3rd Q. After another 3-ptr by Mannisto, Keenum capped winning 95y drive with his 4y QB Draw run for 29-28 lead with 49 secs to play and Houston's 2nd win in row over Big 12 opponent.

STANFORD 34 Washington 14: Positive carryover from Huskies' upset of USC and their 1st AP poll ranking since 2003 lasted as long as it took for opening KO to sail through air. Stanford (3-1) WR Chris Owusu fled 91y on KO TD RET, and while Washington (2-2) CB Justin Glenn tied it with 51y FUM TD RET, Cardinal's battering-ram TB Toby Gerhart (27/200y, TD) ran 60y for permanent lead at 14-7. QB Jake Locker (16-31/190y, TD, 2 INTs) pulled Washington within 17-14 with 2nd Q TD pass but turned it over thrice, including Stanford SS Delano Howell's pair of INTs. Passing sparingly, Cardinal QB Andrew Luck (7-14/103y) made 4th Q 9y TD keeper to cap scoring. Stanford opened Pac-10 play with consecutive wins for 1st time since 2001.

OREGON 42 California 3: Trashing about trying to settle their O after 3 relatively fruitless games under new coach Chip Kelly, Ducks (3-1) exploded for 524y as QB Jeremiah Masoli (21-25/253y, 3 TDs) admitted afterward, "These last couple of weeks we've been in a funk, but we moved past that." TE Ed Dickson (11/148y, 3 TDs) caught each of Masoli's 3 scoring throws, and frosh RB LaMichael James rushed 21/118y, TD. No. 6 California (3-1) recovered Oregon FUM on opening KO and took 3-0 lead on K Vince D'Amato's 47y FG but completely stalled thereafter as star RB Jahvid Best was limited to 16/55y rushing. Oregon's banished RB LaGarrette Blount was credited for excellent impersonation of Best for Ducks' scout team during week's practice sessions. Golden Bears, perhaps looking ahead to showdown with Southern California for conf supremacy, suffered their most-lopsided defeat in coach Jeff Tedford's 7+ seasons at Berkeley, where he had built 62-30 mark prior to this debacle. "The (overconfident) Bears showed up in Oregon to take a stroll," frustrated former Cal QB and coach Joe Kapp told The Wall Street Journal, "and they were on a freeway."

Arizona 37 OREGON STATE 32: Starting his 1st college game, Arizona (3-1) soph QB Nick Foles (25-34/254y, 3 TDs) calmly masterminded 388y attack and accounted for 3 TDs in 2nd H even though his top 2 RBs were out with injuries. In place of RBs Nic Grigsby (1/7y) and Keolo Antolin (12/46y), RB Greg Nwoko (9/44y, TD) ran for 19y TD and caught 52y pass to set up 3rd Q TD pass by Foles that upped Wildcats' lead to 28-17. Oregon State (2-2) led 17-14 at H on K Justin Kahut's last-play FG, and Beavers were sparked by QB Sean Canfield (31-47/303y, 2 TDs, 2 INTs) and RB Jacquizz Rodgers (16/85y, 2 TDs). Canfield hit WR Aaron Nichols with 13y TD pass to pull Beavers within 35-32 with 4:09 to play. Oregon State would have 3 tries to win it, but Arizona CB Devin Ross intercepted Canfield, and punt pinned Beavers at their 2YL. Canfield was sacked for safety on next snap. Oregon State recovered on-side free-kick, but Canfield was sacked twice more to end it.

USA TODAY Coaches Poll September 27, 2009

1 Florida (58)	1474	14 Georgia	616
2 Texas (1)	1410	15 Houston	539
3 Alabama	1364	16 Kansas	508
4 Louisiana State	1226	17 Iowa	462
5 Boise State	1144	18 Mississippi	424
6 Virginia Tech	1091	19 California	356
7 Southern California	1081	20 Michigan	304
8 Oklahoma	1055	21tBrigham Young	298
9 Ohio State	1036	21tMiami	298
10 Texas Christian	928	23 Missouri	295
11 Cincinnati	848	24 Nebraska	242
12 Oklahoma State	665	25 Oregon	198
13 Penn State	627		

October 3, 2009

(Th) WEST VIRGINIA 35 Colorado 24: While ace RB Noel Devine reached career-high in y with 22/220y rushing with 77y TD burst in 1st Q, West Virginia (3-1) didn't take command until efficient QB Jarrett Brown (12-19/148y, 2 TDs) threw TD passes late in 2nd Q and early in 3rd Q for 21-10 lead. Still, when Mountaineers were troubled by blitzes of Colorado (1-3), they turned to Devine to keep control in 2nd H. Buffaloes QB Cody Hawkins (27-52/292y, 2 TDs, 3 INTs) pitched pair of TD passes but his trio of INTs helped contribute to Colorado's failure to tally more than 3 pts on 4 other trips inside WVU 30YL. Buffs' other TD came in 1st Q for 7-7 tie when RB Rodney Stewart (21/105y, TD) dashed 36y to right pylon. Mountaineers overcame 4 FUMs in 1st H.

(Fri) Pittsburgh 35 LOUISVILLE 10: "Black Out" was called for night game at Louisville (1-3), with Cardinals wearing all black uniforms and many fans doing same. Positive effects lasted throughout 1st H as Louisville led 10-7 at break as FB Joe Tronzo scored on his only carry from 1YL in 1st Q. Sadly for its declining program, Louisville had to play 2nd H, and Panthers (4-0) laid waste to lowly Cardinals, black uniforms or no black uniforms. Pitt QB Bill Stull (16-23/242y, 3 TDs) threw pair of 3rd Q TD passes, while DE Greg Romeus (3.5 sacks) led ferocious pass rush that finished with 6 sacks including 4 in 2nd H and 3 during 4-play span midway through 2nd H. QB Adam Froman (18-30/166y) lost FUM at Pitt 29YL midway through 3rd Q; it was Cards' final gasp. Stull hit WR Jonathan Baldwin (4/105y, TD) on 71y TD bomb on next play for 21-10 lead as Baldwin beat double coverage over middle. RB Dion Lewis paced Panthers ground game with 21/87y, while TE Dorin Dickerson caught 3/50y, 2 TDs.

NAVY 16 Air Force 13 (OT): Winners of last 6 Commander-in-Chief Trophies, Navy (3-2) got 1st leg up toward another academy football title. Contest turned into D match, and although Air Force (3-2) outgained Middies 240y to 209y Falcons never found EZ with their O. After Navy QB Ricky Dobbs (3-4/36y, INT and 23/92y, TD rushing) tallied on 13y run in 1st Q, Falcons dramatically turned Dobbs' only incompletion into CB Anthony Wright's 67y INT TD RET in 2nd Q. Navy K Joe Buckley, who had lost his job earlier in season, hit 47 and 37y FGs for 13-10 lead in 4th Q. Air Force managed 13-play, 54y drive as clock ticked toward regulation's end, prolonged by roughing-passer PEN on Navy ILB Tony Haberer. Haberer's PEN negated Middies FS Wyatt Middleton's crushing INT of Falcons QB Tim Jefferson (6-14/57y, INT). Air Force K Eric Soderberg nailed 39y FG to tie it 13-13 just as clock reached 0:00. But Soderberg hooked FG try in OT to allow Buckley's 38y FG on Navy's 1st OT possession to win it.

MIAMI 21 Oklahoma 20: Was it Miami's tempting beaches full of bikinis? For whatever reason, Oklahoma (2-2) rarely played well in Miami. Since losing to Canes in Miami during 1986 regular season, Sooners stood at just 2-5 in "South Beach" and 0-3 vs. Miami Hurricanes (3-1). Miami rallied past Sooners, scoring 21 straight pts to turn 10-pt deficit into permanent lead. Hurricanes QB Jacory Harris (19-28/202y, 3 TDs, 2 INTs) overcame 2 early INTs to throw 3 TDs and RB Javarris James rushed for 150y.

Once settled down, Harris hit 3-3/40y with 18y TD pass to TE Jimmy Graham for his 1st TD, threw 11y TD pass to TE Dedrick Epps after OU lost FUM deep in own territory early in 3rd Q, and went 4-5/68y including 38y scoring pass to WR Travis Benjamin (3/61y, TD) later in 3rd Q for 21-10 edge. Playing once again in relief of injured Oklahoma QB Sam Bradford, young QB Landry Jones (18-30/188y, TD) was solid but held back by coaching staff that called for only 3 passes while its ship was sinking in 4th Q. Of those, Jones completed 2-3/6y. On Sooners final scoring drive, Oklahoma ran 6 straight times to set up 39y FG by K Jimmy Stephens. Harris responded with drive that wiped out final 4:18 on clock, throwing for 2 1st downs while James added 4/38y rushing. Game looked dead even on stat sheet: both teams earned 21 1st downs and Miami barely won y battle by 342y to 341y.

Auburn 26 TENNESSEE 22: Under-radar Auburn (5-0) remained unbeaten under new coach Gene Chizik and moved into national polls after 5th straight win over Tennessee (2-3). Tigers ripped through vaunted Vols D for 459y, passing for 235y and rushing for 224y while possessing ball for 34:46. "This was one of those old-school, physical SEC games," said Chizik, who had been controversial hire after posting 5-19 record at Iowa State. QB Chris Todd (19-32/218y, TD) and RB Ben Tate (25/128y, TD) continued to make Auburn's complicated new O look easy. Mistakes on O hurt Tennessee's worn-out D: QB Jonathan Crompton (20-43/259y, 2 TDs) missed open receivers while some well-thrown balls were dropped. Volunteers managed to rally from 23-6 4th Q deficit, scoring TD when RB Montario Hardesty (21/90y, TD and 3/56y, TD receiving) raced 31y with short pass. Ahead 23-16 with 4 and half mins remaining, Auburn RB Onterio McCalebb helped squash momentum swing by racing 52y with ensuing KO on way to K Wes Byrum's clinching 22y FG. Crompton padded his stats on meaningless final drive that produced 32y TD pass to WR Denarius Moore as time expired.

Mississippi 23 VANDERBILT 7: Rebels (3-1) bounced back from South Carolina loss by holding off struggling Vanderbilt (2-3). QB Jevan Snead (19-34/237y, 3 TDs, 3 INTs) led Ole Miss to commanding 23-0 lead on drives of 80, 71, and 63y, each ending with TD throw. Snead found WR Shay Hodge (8/122y, 2 TDs) twice for TDs but also suffered 3 INTs, including pair on consecutive 3rd Q possessions when conservatism seemed prudent. Snead's favorite target was CB Casey Heyward's 3rd Q INT set up Commodores' lone score when QB Larry Smith (10-27/69y, TD, INT) pitched 7y pass to WR Udom Umoh to complete 34y trip. Late in 3rd Q, Vandy drove 60y to Mississippi 5YL before Smith's pass was tipped and picked off by CB Marcus Temple in EZ. Another long Vanderbilt drive ended on downs at Rebs 12YL with 4:46 left, and Ole Miss ran out clock to avenge 2008 upset defeat.

Louisiana State 20 GEORGIA 13: Flawed as they appeared, Bayou Bengals (5-0) remained in contention in SEC West and national title races. Influence of officials prompted Bulldogs' 7-6 edge to evaporate in late scoring flurry. Georgia (3-2) had taken 1-pt lead early in 4th Q on 4th down TD pass by QB Joe Cox (18-34/229y, 2 TDs, INT). Back came LSU, and RB Charles Scott (19/95y, 2 TDs) scored 1st of his 2 TDs for 12-7 lead with 2:38 to play. It was followed by controversial call that came after Georgia took 13-12 lead with 69 secs remaining on WR A.J. Green's extraordinary 16y TD reception in which he soared over CB Chris Hawkins. Back judge Michael Watson called excessive celebration PEN on seemingly mild-mannered Green (5/99y, TD). Pushed back to 15YL, Bulldogs' KO went to Tigers swift WR Trindon Holliday at his 17YL and he scampered 40y to Georgia 43YL. After 5y PEN on Bulldogs, LSU had 1 min remaining with 1st down at 38YL. It took only 2 plays to score as RB Charles Scott ran for 5y, then raced 33y to Georgia EZ, pausing only to burst through 3 tacklers at scrimmage line. Scott also earned unsportsmanlike PEN, another mild offense which appeared to be make-up call that came too late to help Georgia. Tigers LB Perry Riley quickly ended matters with INT. Tigers could have avoided end-game predicament as they squandered chances in 1st H when they outgained Bulldogs 236y to 49y, yet led only 6-0. Game's tone clearly changed at outset of 2nd H as LSU QB Jordan Jefferson (18-27/212y, INT) was sacked all 3 downs of opening 3-and-out series. Bulldogs would thump Jefferson trying to pass 5 times in 2nd H. Green's PEN remained contentious point, and after reviewing CBS' tape, SEC director of officiating Rogers Redding said Monday: "We concluded the video did not support the call."

MICHIGAN STATE 26 Michigan 20 (OT): Undefeated Michigan (4-1) mounted furious 4th Q comeback from 20-6 deficit behind QB Tate Forcier (17-32/223y, 2 TDs, INT), who in last 5 mins found WR Darryl Stonum (5/97y, TD) on crossing pattern for 60y TD pass and capped 92y march with 9y TD arrow to WR Roy Roundtree with 2 secs left. Suddenly, Michigan State Spartans (2-3) must have felt 3-game losing streak closing in on them as teams headed to OT. But, Forcier made frosh mistake on 3rd down from 8YL, trying to force EZ throw to Roundtree: Deflected pass popped in air, and diving Spartans DB Chris L. Rucker snatched INT off grass-top. In FG range, Michigan State sent RB Larry Caper off RT on 3rd-and-9 and blocking was so effective Caper streamed 23y to winning TD. It was Spartans' 2nd straight win over their Ann Arbor rivals, marking 1st back-to-back wins over Michigan since taking 3 straight in 1965-67.

Northwestern 27 PURDUE 21: Purdue (1-4) QB Joey Elliott (20-28/313y, 3 TDs, INT) happily accepted 1st-play FUM by Wildcats (3-2) RB Arby Fields (18/43y, TD) on strip by DE Ryan Kerrigan and hit WR Keith Smith with 5y TD pass for 7-0 lead. Boilers led 21-13, when late in 1st H, miscues started going against them: RB Jaycen Taylor lost FUM, and, 9 secs from H, Northwestern K Stefan Demos booted 3rd of his 4 FGs to trim margin to 21-16. Northwestern trailed all game until QB Mike Kafka (28-44/224y and 18/39y, TD rushing) squirted up middle for 2y TD with 2:09 left to play. Kafka added 2-pt pass to WR Drake Dunsmore for Cats' 1st lead at 27-21. Purdue moved quickly from its 16YL, but on goal-to-go, Elliott, under pressure that forced him to roll right, overthrew WR Aaron Valentin in EZ on 4th down with scant secs left.

NOTRE DAME 37 Washington 30 (OT): Of all things, it took hard-hitting stop by Notre Dame's maligned D to finally secure OT win for Fighting Irish (4-1) as Ss Harrison Smith (6 tackles) and Kyle McCarthy (12 tackles) double-teamed Huskies (2-3) WR D'Andre Goodwin to prevent 4th down pass from being completed near Irish GL. ND had taken lead in opening extra session as RB Robert Hughes (8/70y, TD) ran TD in from 1y out. Despite allowing 457y, Notre Dame D made 2 clutch stops inside its 5YL in 2nd H. With Huskies winning 24-19 with 3rd down at Irish 1YL, Washington called on its meal ticket, QB Jake Locker (22-40/281y, TD), and twice he was halted on keepers. Midway through 4th Q, with Huskies ahead by 24-22, hard-charging TB Chris Polk (22/136y) appeared to score but was ruled down on 1YL. Washington chose FG attempt, but unusual PEN for roughing snapper on Notre Dame DT Ian Williams gave Huskies another 1st-and-goal from 1YL. They still couldn't earn TD as 2 runs—sandwiched around 5y PEN on Washington and 5y pass to FB Paul Homer—were stuffed. Finally, UW kicked FG, but huge opportunity was lost. Irish then raced 63y to go ahead 30-27 on 12y pass by QB Jimmy Clausen (23-31/422y, 2 TDs, INT) to TE Kyle Rudolph. Washington could have folded right then, but Locker answered with 70y drive in final min to tying 37y FG by K Eric Folk, his 3rd of game. Irish passing tandem of Clausen and WR Golden Tate (9/244y, TD), who connected on vital 22y completion in OT, each set personal y best as Irish gained 530y. Tate caught 67y TD pass in 2nd Q, and his 77y catch in 3rd Q set up 1 of K Nick Tausch's school-record tying 5 FGs.

Kansas State 24 Iowa State 23 (Kansas City): Miraculous chapter in coach Bill Snyder's 1st year back at helm of Kansas State (3-2) saw Wildcats pull out victory in last 32 secs when tall DB Emmanuel Lamur blocked x-pt try after Iowa State (3-2) QB Austen Arnaud (13-27/164y, 2 TDs and 16/84y, TD rushing) threw 23y TD pass to WR Jake Williams (5/61y, TD). Wildcats QB Grant Gregory (16-23/206y, 2 TDs, INT) had thrown his 2nd TD pass of 4th Q for 24-17 lead with 5:36 left. Gregory, South Florida transfer not even listed in pregame starting lineup, barely evaded big sack loss on his huge play to launch 54y TD pass to fleet WR Brandon Banks (4/66y, TD and 2/31y rushing), who week before had tied NCAA mark with pair of KO TD RETs vs. Tennessee Tech. Contributing to K-State's notable win was K Josh Cherry's wobbly 39y FG in last 5 secs before H. It came after pass interference PEN against Iowa State LB Fred Garrin prolonged Cats' possession.

Arkansas 49 Texas A&M 17 (Arlington, Tex.): Aerial D of undefeated Aggies (3-1) was slapped after slow start by Arkansas (2-2) QB Ryan Mallett (17-27/271y, 4 TDs, INT), who was blooming into 1 of nation's top passers. That is not to suggest that Texas A&M QB Jerrod Johnson didn't storm the airways as well. Johnson passed 30-58/345y, 2 TDs, but telling stat was Mallett's superior y per attempt at 10.0y to 5.7y. Aggies jumped to 10-0 1st Q lead as Johnson rolled left and launched off-balance rocket for 60y TD to frosh WR Brandal Jackson (4/118y, TD). Meanwhile, Mallett was suffering through 3 incompletions and pair of sacks, 1st of which was authored by national sack leader, swift A&M LB Von Miller. But, in less than 9 mins, Arkansas had struck on pair of TD passes by Mallett at end of 77 and 38y trips to paydirt. Latter march was set up by disastrous 5y punt to A&M 38YL. Texas A&M soon was knocking at GL, however, when Johnson lost FUM, which LB Jerry Franklin took 85y for TD and 21-10 Arkansas lead. Hogs led at H by 30-10.

TEXAS CHRISTIAN 39 Southern Methodist 14: SMU (2-2) RB Shawnbrey McNeal turned 2nd Q screen pass from QB Bo Levi Mitchell (17-38/240y, 2 TDs, 2 INTs) into 24y TD, and when 6'8" frosh DE Margus Hunt, world-class shotput-discus star, later blocked x-pt kick, Mustangs led 7-6. But, TCU (4-0) frosh LB Tanner Brock delivered block-heard-round-the-world. As Frogs WR Jeremy Kerley (4/48y) started up right sideline on punt RET from his 29YL, Brock leveled 2 SMU tacklers with his helmet flying. TCU DE Jerry Hughes whooped it up about Brock's play that sprung Kerley for 71y TD: "...it just kind of boosted everybody, got everybody amped up." Texas Christian upped its 12-7 lead to 25-7 with pair of 3rd Q TD runs, and WR Antoine Hicks (2 TDs) made spectacular catch from QB Andy Dalton (12-20/189y, 2 TDs, INT) in 4th Q. Sharp Mustangs O was limited to 224y, barely half of their 432y per game avg.

TEXAS-EL PASO 58 Houston 41: Ace QB Case Keenum (51-76/536y, 5 TDs) enjoyed career game, but Houston (3-1) still fell victim to over-hype. While pundits offered premature BCS-buster credentials to Cougars after wins over Big 12 South teams—Oklahoma State and Texas Tech—Houston ran smack into competent UTEP (2-3), conf rival playing at home and in need of saving its season. Game turned into O blizzard as UH outgained UTEP Miners by 664y to 581y. Keenum hit pair of TD throws in 1st H as Cougars jumped to 10-0 and 17-10 leads. Miners RB Jason Williams, back from last year's injury, tied it 17-17 3 mins before H. Starting UTEP RB Donald Buckram exploded in 2nd H, scoring on 4 runs and finishing with 32/262y on ground. Still, crushing blow came on Miners LB Roddray Walker's 70y FUM TD RET with 3:25 to play that built 58-34 lead. Cougars WR James Cleveland, 1-time Iowa Hawkeye, hauled in 14/147y, 2 TDs from Keenum. Joy in El Paso would be short-lived: Miners would go only 2-5 rest of way to drop to distant 3rd in Conf-USA West.

STANFORD 24 Ucla 16: TB Toby Gerhart, Stanford's downhill locomotive, rushed 29/134y, 3 TDs while displaying both power and nifty footwork. Gerhart upped his career rushing TD total to 24, 3rd-best in school history. Cardinal (4-1) stayed unbeaten in Pac-10 at 3-0 and moved into undisputed conf lead. Meanwhile, steady Stanford frosh QB Andrew Luck (14-20/198y), son of former West Virginia and Houston Oilers QB Oliver Luck, played his best game to date as he connected on 14 of his 1st 17 pass attempts. Much-maligned UCLA (3-1) QB Kevin Craft, playing only because QB Kevin Prince had suffered broken jaw at Tennessee, passed well enough at 22-34/202y but could nothing about Bruins' dreadful 2-10 3rd down conversion rate. UCLA settled for 3 mid-range FGs by star K Kai Forbath.

Southern California 30 CALIFORNIA 3: Trojans (4-1) was balanced on O and D and dropped 2nd nightmarish outcome upon once-optimistic California (3-2) in as many weeks of conf play. Southern California QB Matt Barkley struck for 20-35/283y, INT passing and TB Joe McKnight rushed 20/119y, 2 TDs as Trojans built 23-0 lead into 4th Q. California (3-2) Heisman candidate, RB Jahvid Best, was limited to 47y rushing, and QB Kevin Riley managed only 15-40/199y, INT in air. But Bears challenged off opening KO as Riley 22 and 21y passes, but on 3rd-and-goal from 6YL, Riley was picked off in EZ by USC FS Taylor Mays, who cut across backline. Pair of big plays

in 1st H put Troy on scoreboard: McKnight cut to his right and dived for pylon on 38y TD run for 7-0 lead, and WR Damian Williams streaked 66y early in 2nd Q on punt TD RET for 17-0 edge. Trojans RB Stafon Johnson, injured in freak weight-lifting accident, served as inspiration to his teammates from his hospital bed. "Stafon knew we were on a mission tonight," said Barkley.

USA TODAY Coaches Poll October 4, 2009

1 Florida (57)	1473	14 Iowa	655
2 Texas (1)	1408	15 Kansas	616
3 Alabama (1)	1366	16 Mississippi	460
4 Louisiana State	1273	17 Oregon	433
5 Virginia Tech	1141	18 Missouri	386
6 Boise State	1133	19 Auburn	369
7 Southern California	1123	20 Brigham Young	353
8 Ohio State	1072	21 Oklahoma	346
9 Texas Christian	965	22 Nebraska	329
10 Cincinnati	937	23 Georgia Tech	278
11 Miami	750	24 South Florida	220
12 Penn State	713	25 Wisconsin	156
13 Oklahoma State	702		

October 10, 2009

(Th) Nebraska 27 MISSOURI 12: It was raining cats and dogs and PEN flags at Memorial Stadium in Columbia. Each team was stymied by avalanche of PENs amid heavy rain. For much of game, Nebraska (4-1) was happy simply to execute punt play. Huskers endured several dangerous snaps and bobbled fair catches and trailed 2-0 when P Alex Henery was forced to throw away safety after having fielded bad snap in his EZ in 2nd Q. Although Tigers (4-1) held upper hand in O y, it took narrow replay decision on last play of 2nd Q to build 9-0 lead for Missouri: On 4th down from 1YL, QB Blaine Gabbert (17-43/134y, 2 INTs) barely nosed into EZ for TD before his knee touched. Trailing 12-0, Huskers were thoroughly inept on O, having gained only 103y, punted 10 times, and turned it over twice on 12 possessions through end of 3rd Q. Miraculously, Nebraska QB Zac Lee (14-33/158y, 3 TDs) mustered confidence to go deep on 3rd play of 4th Q. WR Niles Paul took long throw in stride and raced to 56y TD. Gabbert, who had suffered no INTs so far in his 1st season as starter, was picked off right after ensuing KO when brilliant Huskers DT Ndamukong Suh (sack, tfl, pass break-up, INT) went high at scrimmage line to come down with INT. Lee hit Paul for another TD 2 plays later and Big Red led 13-12. Gabbert was soon picked off again, this time by DB Dejon Gomes who returned 40y to Mizzou 10YL. On 3rd down, Huskers TE Mike McNeill blocked and spun off to catch beautifully-conceived TD pass over middle for 20-12 edge. IB Roy Helu (18/88y, TD) added last-min TD run.

ARMY 16 Vanderbilt 13: Pete Dawkins, West Point's 1958 Heisman Trophy winner, opened CBS College Sports' Armed Forces Appreciation Day TV tripleheader by enthusiastically waving American flag brought from overseas war zone. Army (3-3) K Alex Carlton, who missed potential game-winning FG previous week vs. Tulane, nailed 51y FG in 2nd Q, and contest was deadlocked 3-3 going into 4th Q. Black Knights frosh QB Trent Steelman (7-16/47y and 25/97y, TD rushing), his helmet flying off, surged across GL early in 4th Q for 2y TD, but RT Jason Johnson yanked off his own helmet to foolishly draw celebration PEN. Kicking off from its 15YL, Army was unable to prevent Vanderbilt (2-4) RB Warren Norman (15/62y) from storming down right sideline on 76y KO TD RET for 10-10 deadlock. Trailing 13-10, Commodores were in good shape to win it late in regulation, but Army D forced FG try, which K Ryan Fowler successfully banked off left upright from 41y away. In OT, Norman appeared on his way to TD for Vandy, but hustling Army LB Andrew Rodriguez stripped him just inches from GL. Ball dribbled through left side of EZ for touchback. Moments later, Carlton booted 42y FG, nearly identical to Fowler's tying 3-ptr, when he banked it off left upright to win it. Among celebrants was Gen. David H. Petraeus, leader of the U.S. Central Command, who was celebrating his 35th class reunion at West Point.

PITTSBURGH 24 Connecticut 21: Trailing 21-6 late in 3rd Q, Pittsburgh (5-1) desperately needed maturing QB Bill Stull (21-31/268y, 2 TDs, 2 INTs) to shake off pair of crucial INTs. TB Dion Lewis (24/158y) raced 32y on drive's 4th play, and Panthers drove from their 26YL until Stull fired 26y TD pass to WR Jonathan Baldwin (8/104y, TD) to pull within 21-13 with 12 secs left in 3rd Q. Thanks to sack by Pitt DE Greg Romeus on 2nd down, Connecticut (3-2) immediately failed at clock-wasting O. After punt, Stull went back to work from own 32YL, converting 3rd down with 2y run, gaining another 1st down with 21y pass to TE Nate Byham, and clicking on 4th-and-3 from Connecticut 34YL with 7y completion to Byham. On next play, Stull threw 27y TD pass to TE Dorin Dickerson. Stull then tied it 21-21 with 2-pt conv-earning pass to WR Cedric McGee. Panthers D forced 2nd 3-and-out of 4th Q with Romeus again applying pressure on QB Cody Endres (17-23/197y, TD) to force 3rd down incompletion. Pitt killed final 6:14 as it went 74y in 13 plays, with Stull completing 29y pass to WR Mike Shanahan, before K-P Dan Hutchins (3 FGs, 3/43y avg punting) booted game-winning FG on final play. Pair of big plays had given Huskies 14-3 lead by 3rd Q: Endres hit WR Marcus Easley (2/100y, TD) with 79y TD pass in 2nd Q, and S Robert Vaughn (10 tackles, 2 INTs) went 20y with INT TD RET in 3rd Q. In 2nd Q Vaughn had picked off Stull in EZ to stop Panthers' best TD chance of 1st H.

VIRGINIA TECH 48 Boston College 14: Strong D by Virginia Tech (5-1) helped vanquish recent regular-season nemesis, Boston College (4-2), winners of 3 straight in series. Scoring on its 1st 4 possessions, Virginia Tech built 34-0 lead by H on amazing 293y to 3y O edge. Eagles QB Dave Shinskie (1-12/4y, 2 INTs) must have longed for return to minor league baseball after bruising 1st H in which he threw 0-9, 2 INTs. In 2nd Q, Hokies CB Rashad Carmichael returned INT 22y for TD. Virginia Tech QB Tyrod Taylor threw 7-10/126y, 2 TDs, and TB Ryan Williams ran 18/149y with TD. Even when BC scored 4th Q TD, on 48y pass from sub QB Mike Marscovetra (10-16/114y, 2 TDs) to WR Colin Larmond, Hokies answered on next scrimmage play as back-up QB Ju-Ju Clayton and WR Marcus Davis hooked up on 80y TD pass for 41-7 lead. "We had some manners laid on us," summed up Boston College coach Frank Spaziani, who in 2nd Q benched his entire O unit to no avail as backups lost 15y in 3 plays. On next snap, Taylor threw 41y TD pass to WR Jarrett Boykin for 24-0 lead.

Georgia Tech 49 FLORIDA STATE 44: Heat had been turned up on long-time Florida State (2-4) coach Bobby Bowden earlier in week by chairman of university board of trustees, Jim Smith, who opined that Bowden should retire at season's end. Supportive crowd was at fever pitch, and Seminoles O played inspired ball in rolling up 382y in 1st H and scoring 35 pts. On 5 drives averaging 76y, Seminoles scored TDs on each of their 1st H possessions. Bad news was that it good enough only for 35-28 lead as FSU D could not contain Georgia Tech (5-1), which itself scored on 4 straight series. Stunning 73y TD catch by Yellow Jackets WR Demaryius Thomas (2/84y, TD) tied it 35-35 with early in 3rd Q. Jackets D tightened considerably in 2nd H, allowing 9 pts on 132y. Ga Tech QB Josh Nesbitt (4-8/131y, TD and 27/140y rushing, 3 TDs) did just about everything right, including huge 4th Q strip of Seminoles LB Nigel Carr, who was returning FUM by Ga Tech RB Roddy Jones. Nesbitt ripped ball from stunned Carr to give Jackets 1st down at FSU 25YL to set up Nesbitt's 22y run, which proved to be winning TD. Crazy game was tied 5 times before Georgia Tech scored 2 TDs to turn 38-35 3rd Q deficit into 49-38 4th Q lead. Florida State QB Christian Ponder (26-38/359y, 5 TDs) played about as well as losing QB could.

TENNESSEE 45 Georgia 19: Maligned Volunteers (3-3) QB Jonathan Crompton (20-27/310y, 4 TDs, INT) suddenly looked like star alum Peyton Manning as he enjoyed his finest game. Crompton threw for more than 300y for 1st time in his career and was especially brilliant in 1st H led 21-12 by Vols with 12-15/205y, 3 TDs in air. Tennessee D held Bulldogs (3-3) to 241y and permitted only 3 pts, coming on 52y FG by K Blair Walsh. All of Bulldogs' other pts came on 100y KO TD RET by CB Brandon Boykin, 28y INT TD RET by S Bacarri Rambo, and blocked-punt safety through EZ by S Zach Renner late in 1st H. After Rambo scored in 3rd Q, thoroughly-dominated Bulldogs remained alive, down only 24-19. But, Tennessee then went 80y to clinching TD, with TB Mario Hardesty (20/97y, TD) tallying on 39y run to boost lead to 31-19. QB Joe Cox (19-34/146y, 2 INTs) connected with WR A.J. Green for 8/60y, but Georgia fell to worst 6-game record in 9 years under coach Mark Richt.

Alabama 22 MISSISSIPPI 3: This SEC West clash was expected to impact national title race, but it ended as same old story for struggling Ole Miss (3-2). Alabama (6-0) extended its series lead to 46-9-2. Crimson Tide was excellence in every facet of game. RB Mark Ingram (28/173y, TD) was absolute beast for Tide O, scoring game's only TD on 36y run on 4th-and-1 late in 2nd Q. Four different players had INTs for Tide D, which held Mississippi to 19y and single 1st down in decisive 1st H. Alabama special teams sparkled as well: K Leigh Tiffen booted 5 FGs, and LB Cory Reamer set up FGs by blocking punt and forcing and recovering punt RET FUM by Ole Miss WR Dexter McCluster. Flashy McCluster was limited to 6/15y rushing, 3/22y receiving, and bobbled 9y punt RET. Battered by Tide pressure, Mississippi QB Jevan Snead (11-34/140y, 4 INTs) also had miserable day. Rebels only twice entered Alabama red zone, with 3rd Q drive capped by 25y FG by K Joshua Shene and other snuffed by Tide CB Kareem Jackson's INT at 5YL that he returned 79y early in 4th Q.

Florida 13 LOUISIANA STATE 3: Pregame hype centered on return of Florida (5-0) QB Tim Tebow (11-16/134y, TD, INT) after concussion suffered 2 games earlier. But, Gators D proved dominant storyline, and to deliver 15th straight victory it had to play at high level with team's O held to lowest pt total of coach Urban Meyer's 5-year run at Florida. Gators LB Brandon Spikes (11 tackles, 3 sacks) led aggressive unit that delivered 5 sacks of LSU (5-1) QB Jordan Jefferson (11-17/96y, INT). Tebow played conservatively in early moments, but unable to dodge defenders he started lowering his shoulder into LSU players by 2nd Q with kind of thud only he could deliver. On 80y drive to game's only TD late in 2nd Q, Tebow barreled into LB Harry Coleman for 8y on opening play, threw 20y to RB Brandon James, and rushed for 3y to convert 3rd-and-2 from LSU 27YL. On next play, he threw 24y TD pass to WR Riley Cooper as Florida took 10-3 lead. Gators CB Joe Haden ended LSU's next possession with INT, and Florida D prevented any Tiger prowls into its territory in 2nd H. LBs Kelvin Sheppard (13 tackles) and Perry Riley (12 tackles) paced Bengals D that had something to prove after last year's 51-21 loss in Gainesville. Still, it was not enough to extend LSU's 31-game win streak in Saturday night home games.

ARKANSAS 44 Auburn 23: Bubble burst in Fayetteville for surprising Auburn (5-1), which fell behind 34-3 in 3rd Q en route to its 1st loss. Arkansas (3-2) actually pulled away in 2nd Q thanks to 4-play sequence: Razorbacks TB Michael Smith (18/145y, TD) raced 25y around RE to score TD for 13-0 lead. CB Andru Stewart forced FUM by Tigers RB Mario Fannin on ensuing KO, recovered by S Jerell Norton at Auburn 34YL, and Razorbacks QB Ryan Mallett (24-37/274y, INT) needed just 2 passes for 20-0 lead: 18y to TE D.J. Williams (6/57y, TD) and 16y TD to WR Greg Childs (5/85y, TD). Down 27-3, Tigers came out fired up for 2nd H and forced 3-and-out before driving 67y to Arkansas 3YL. But, Hogs forced FUM by Auburn RB Ben Tate (22/184y, 2 TDs), recovered by DE Jake Bequette at 5YL, and Mallet sparked Arkansas 95y, completing 38y pass to Childs on 3rd-and-3 midway through possession, to score on 4y QB keeper off quick snap. Behind 34-3, Tigers made things interesting with 3 straight TDs over rest of 3rd Q, including dramatic 60y scoring romp by Tate. But Hogs RB Dennis Johnson raced 70y with KO RET following last of those scores to set up 3y TD run by RB Broderick Green for 41-23 rally-dampening lead. After Arkansas completed 4th Q shutout, coach Bobby Petrino lauded his D: "We came out and hit (Auburn) in the mouth early and didn't look back."

OHIO STATE 31 Wisconsin 13: Wisconsin (5-1) outgained Buckeyes (5-1) 368y to 184y and owned nearly 26 more possession mins but fell victim to Ohio State's trio of TD RETs. In 1st Q, SS Kurt Coleman snatched pass by Badgers QB Scott Tolzien (27-45/250y, 2 INTs), who would be sacked 6 times, and swerved to Ohio sideline to tight-rope 89y to TD. Badgers scurried into 10-7 lead in 2nd Q as holder Chris Maragos swept left for 9y TD run off fake FG play. Ohio State's only O TD came at

opportune time as QB Terrelle Pryor (5-13/87y, TD, INT and 10/35y rushing) connected on 32y TD to WR DeVier Posey 40 secs before H. LB Jermale Hines returned INT 32y for Buckeyes' 3rd Q TD for 21-10 edge. Wisconsin K Philip Welch soon kicked his 2nd long FG (50, 46y), but Ohio State WR Ray Small sailed up middle on ensuing KO for 96y TD and 28-13 lead. Losing coach Bret Bielema was unhappy: "I hate losing to these guys. Absolutely, it's something I can't stand, for whatever reason."

IOWA 30 Michigan 28: QB Ricky Stanzi (20-38/284y, 2 TDs, INT) overcame early 40y INT TD RET by Wolverines (4-2) CB Donovan Warren to lead Hawkeyes (6-0) to 10th straight victory, their longest streak since 20 games in 1920-23. Michigan RB Brandon Minor (22/95y, 2 TDs) tallied 1st rushing TDs vs. Hawkeyes in 33 Qs as he scored on short runs late in 1st Q for 14-10 lead and late in 3rd Q to pull within 23-21. Iowa was stopped on 4th-and-goal from 1YL early in 4th Q when LB Stevie Brown broke up pass. Iowa next forced punt, and TE Tony Moeaki (6/105y, 2 TDs) caught crossing-pattern pass from Stanzi for 32y TD that put Hawks up 30-21. Michigan coach Rich Rodriguez yanked QB Tate Forcier (8-19/94y, INT) in favor of fellow-frosh QB Denard Robinson (3-4/30y, INT and 9/49y, TD rushing), who scored up middle with 3:16 to play but later overshot his receiver on clinching INT by Hawkeyes FS Brett Greenwood.

Oregon 24 UCLA 10: Playing without injured QB Jeremiah Masoli, Ducks (5-1) were blanked 3-0 in 1st H by UCLA Bruins (3-2) when K Kai Forbath bombed 2nd Q 3-ptr 52y, his school-record 8th career FG of 50y or longer. Oregon, which made 135y O in 1st H, exploded in opening 4 mins of 3rd Q: RB Kenjon Barner ripped 100y for KO TD RET, CB Talmadge Jackson cut in front of wide pass by UCLA QB Kevin Prince (13-25/81y, INT) and went 32y for INT TD RET, and 8 plays after Prince's midfield FUM on next Bruins series, Ducks WR Jeff Maehl burst up middle on screen pass from QB Nate Costa (9-17/82y, TD, INT) for 20y TD and 21-3 lead. Before 3rd Q ended, UCLA LB Akeem Ayers made spectacular catch of INT, leaping to snare Costa's throw-away from Ducks' EZ and nimbly kept his feet inbounds as he fell for TD. Oregon, which closed game with 19 straight runs, got 152y rushing from RB LaMichael James.

WASHINGTON 36 Arizona 33: Once-in-a-million bounce off edge of Arizona (3-2) WR Delashaun Dean's shoe in last 3 mins provided 1 of wackiest finishes in many years. Huskies (3-3) LB Mason Foster (11 tackles) grabbed carom of low slant pass thrown by Wildcats QB Nick Foles (39-53/384y, TD, 2 TDs) and spun to dash untouched for 37y INT TD RET. It came moments after Washington QB Jake Locker (12-23/140y, 3 TDs, INT and 11/92y, TD rushing) had pitched 25y TD pass to TE Kavario Middleton in EZ corner to cut Wildcats' lead to 33-28 with 2:55 to play. Locker had run 56y to TD and tossed 1st of 2 TD passes to WR Devin Aguilar (3/43y, 2 TDs) to build 14-10 H edge for Washington. Thanks to pair of 3rd Q disasters that beset Huskies P Will Mahan—illegal kick PEN behind line of scrimmage and miss-hit 27y punt—Arizona had easy time rolling to 17 straight pts in 3rd Q. In advancing lead to 27-14, Foles passed for TD to WR David Roberts (12/138y, TD) and ran for score. Arizona led 33-21 with 4:22 to go when Huskies K Alex Zendejas booted his 4th FG. Despite their stunning loss, Cats vainly outgained Dogs 461y to 256y.

Texas Christian 20 AIR FORCE 17: Colorado Springs was icebox-cold for 3rd televised military academy contest of day. No. 9 Horned Frogs (5-0) earned 14-0 lead and never trailed as RB Joseph Turner (18/72y, TD) went over from 1YL and threw clearing block for 2y TD sweep by WR Jeremy Kerley (151y all-purpose). As 2nd Q clock wound down, Air Force (3-3) was stuck in its end with only 50y rushing to show for its 2nd-in-nation running attack. Finally, Falcons got ground game going, and, as TCU sought to adjust, HB Jonathan Warzeka surprisingly turned pitchout sweep into 16y TD pass to WR Kevin Fogler. Air Force trailed 14-7 at H. Frogs held ball for nearly 6 mins to open 3rd Q, but lost it at Falcons 6YL on 1 of their 3 TOs. After trade of 3rd Q FGs, TCU K Ross Evans made his 2nd 3-ptr for 20-10 lead early in 4th Q. Another TCU TO set up Air Force QB Connor Dietz (6-17/42y and 15/71y, TD rushing), who had only 5y passing in 1st 3 Qs, for 8y TD run in last min. TCU QB Andy Dalton managed to pass 16-28/198y, INT in miserable frozen drizzle.

USA TODAY Coaches Poll October 11, 2009

1 Florida (53)	1468	14 Oklahoma State	676
2 Texas (1)	1402	15 Kansas	640
3 Alabama (5)	1378	16 Oregon	620
4 Virginia Tech	1241	17 Nebraska	491
5 Southern California	1175	18 Oklahoma	447
6 Boise State	1170	19 Brigham Young	441
7 Ohio State	1122	20 Georgia Tech	420
8 Texas Christian	979	21 South Florida	305
9 Cincinnati	973	22 South Carolina	279
10 Louisiana State	944	23 Houston	96
11 Miami	847	24 Missouri	90
12 Iowa	785	25 Notre Dame	76
13 Penn State	782		

October 17, 2009

(Wed) Boise State 28 TULSA 21: Falling behind for 1st time in 2009, unbeaten Broncos (6-0) struggled to get by Tulsa (4-2) and with weak WAC schedule ahead had to answer new questions about margin of victory to justify their BCS bowl aspirations. After all, Oklahoma, with 2 losses, had pasted Tulsa 45-0 on September 19. Referring to his team's performance, coach Chris Petersen said, "It's usually never good enough for a lot of people, usually including us and our team." Hurricane struck for 1st Q TD on clever pitchback to WR A.J. Whitmore, who hurled 53y TD pass to wide-open WR Damaris Johnson. Tulsa QB G.J. Kinne (14-27/154y, 2 TDs) threw TD pass to WR Trae Johnson for 16-8 lead before end of 1st Q. Sharp QB Kellen Moore (22-32/187y, 3 TDs) hit his 2nd scoring pass in 2nd Q, and Boise State led for good at 15-14. RB Doug Martin 23/112y) gained 83y in 3rd Q as Broncos controlled ball for all but 2:48 of 3rd Q. Tulsa trimmed deficit to 28-21 when WR Slick Shelley (3/99y, TD) hauled in 55y TD pass from Kinne midway in 4th Q. But, late shot at GL failed for Hurricane.

(Th) Cincinnati 34 SOUTH FLORIDA 17: Enthusiastic Tampa crowd was ready to will no. 21 South Florida (5-1) to big win over no. 9 Cincinnati (6-0), and unbeaten Bulls answered Cincy's 1st Q FG with 28y TD pass over middle from QB B.J. Daniels (15-32/208y, TD, 2 INTs) to WR Jessie Hester (3/41y, TD). QB Tony Pike (12-25/140y, 2 TDs) struck for pair of TD passes in 2nd Q for Bearcats, but Pike reinjured his left, non-throwing arm before H which Cincinnati led 17-10. Pike had played brilliantly through much of 2008 with plate and 6 screws inserted in his arm. "The plate that's in there has shifted," said coach Brian Kelly afterward, but Kelly need not have worried about his O in 2nd H. Back-up Bearcats QB Zach Collaros (4-7/72y, INT and 10/132y, 2 TDs rushing) raced 75y for TD in 3rd Q on draw play. Collaros made INT mistake late in 3rd Q that led to Daniels' TD sneak but quickly countered it with 3y TD run at end of 70y drive that reestablished 2-TD lead at 31-17. Bearcats DB Aaron Webster had returned INT 83y in 2nd Q to set up Pike's 1st TD throw.

(Fri) Pittsburgh 24 RUTGERS 17: Short RB Dion Lewis (31/180y, 2 TDs) continued to spark Pittsburgh (6-1) as nation's most exciting frosh runner. Lewis scored TD in 2nd Q to put Panthers in lead to stay at 17-10 and on long burst in 3rd Q for 24-10 advantage. Scarlet Knights (4-2) had frosh standout of their own in QB Tom Savage (23-39/248y, TD, INT), who overcame 3 sacks to balance Rutgers' sparse rushing attack (20/38y). Knights took 1st Q lead of 7-0 after punt hit leg of Pitt CB Dom DeCicco and was recovered at 11YL. It set up QB Mohamed Sanu for quick TD off option run to right. Panthers responded with next 17 pts, including 7y slant-in TD pass to TE Dorin Dickerson by QB Bill Stull (16-24/153y, TD). Back-breaker for Rutgers came in 3rd Q as Lewis sifted through line and broke outside for 58y TD sprint, his 9th TD of year.

CONNECTICUT 38 Louisville 25: Connecticut's 3rd straight win over Louisville (2-4) would be overshadowed by tragedy on UConn (4-2) campus in overnight hours after game. CB Jasper "Jazz" Howard, leader of Huskies secondary, was fatally stabbed at on-campus party. Incident occurred at 12:30 a.m. outside Student Union building. Howard was airlifted to hospital in Hartford where he was pronounced dead from single wound to abdomen. Coach Randy Edsall, who recruited Howard from tough Miami neighborhood, identified body later that morning. "There's nothing written in the manual in how to deal with these situations," said Edsall. "But I know this: this is a strong team with strong leadership, and we'll get through it." Howard, whose girlfriend back home was expecting their 1st child, made career-high 11 tackles and critical forced FUM against Louisville. With score 21-13 in favor of Huskies early in 3rd Q, Howard ruined Cards' scoring opportunity by creating and recovering FUM by RB Bilal Powell (29/87y, 2 TDs) at UConn 4YL. Led by TB Andre Dixon (33/153y, 3 TDs) and QB Cody Endres (14-21/273y, TD, INT), Connecticut then reeled off 10 straight pts to seal win. Cardinals QB Adam Froman threw 24-31/295y with TD, but had 2 costly INTs.

CLEMSON 38 Wake Forest 3: Coming off 2 straight losses and bye week, Clemson (3-3) had spirited fortnight that featured players-only meeting and rumored shouting match between coaches. Tigers' intensity showed as they routed Wake Forest (4-3) behind 2 standards: aggressive D and multipurpose talents of RB C.J. Spiller (9/106y, 2 TDs). Spiller became 1st ACC player to reach 6000y all-purpose in dynamic fashion as he topped milestone with 66y TD run in 2nd Q; he now owned 60y+ play in each of 6 2009 games. Spiller's TD bumped Clemson's lead to 24-3, plenty as D logged 5 sacks in holding Wake to 178y. Deacons' longest drive went 45y to 28y FG by K Jimmy Newman. Wake had failed to execute onside-KO to open game: Tigers recovered at Deacs 46YL and rode perfect 4-4/43y passing of QB Kyle Parker (10-17/132y, TD) to his 1y TD pass to TE Michael Palmer. Thanks to INT later in 1st Q by S DeAndre McDaniel (5 INTs for season) they added 22y FG by K Richard Jackson and blew game open in 2nd Q as Parker hit 51y pass to WR Jacoby Ford to set up his 3y keeper for 17-0 lead. Spiller contributed his long TD on 1st snap after Newman's FG.

GEORGIA TECH 28 Virginia Tech 23: Georgia Tech (6-1) outlasted no. 4 Hokies (5-2) in game that brought back memories of coaching legend Bobby Dodd. On November 17, 1962, Dodd's Yellow Jackets upset top-ranked Alabama 7-6 for what would prove until today to be Jackets' last home upset of top-5 team in 17 tries. Win was forged on runs of QB Josh Nesbitt, who gained 23/122y with 3 TDs including 39y game-winner on 3rd-and-7 down left sideline with 3 mins left. That TD run gave Georgia Tech 28-16 lead which was just good enough even though Virginia Tech needed only 1:12 to score on 7y scoring pass to TB Ryan Williams from QB Tyrod Taylor (10-14/159y, TD, 2 INTs), who completed 4-4/59y on drive. But, Hokies were unable to recover ensuing onside-KO. Nesbitt completed only 1-7 passing, but his single success went 51y to WR Demaryius Thomas to 12YL that set up 1st H's only TD as Nesbitt needed 5 plays from there to score for 7-3 lead in 2nd Q. Georgia Tech, which rushed for only 37y in 1st H, made H adjustments and moved early in 2nd H: After RB Anthony Allen zipped for 16y, Nesbitt broke free on 31y scamper, and RB Jonathan Dwyer (20/82y) ran 3y to set up Nesbitt's 1y scoring keeper. Hokies WR Dyrell Roberts responded with 57y KO RET, only to see Va Tech lose it on downs at Ga Tech 17YL. Hokies S Dorian Porch picked off Nesbitt, however, and on very next play, Williams (14/100y, TD) went up gut and took off, racing 66y to TD that cut Hokies' deficit to 14-10. As 3rd Q was winding down, Yellow Jackets responded with 12-play, 86y drive that featured 5 different rushers until sub RB Marcus Wright took carry no. 12 into EZ from 13y out for 21-10 lead. With Georgia Tech driving, game was getting away from Hokies until errant pitchout by Nesbitt was scooped up by S Davon Morgan at his 23YL. Taylor needed 6 plays to set up his 22y TD run vainly to cut deficit to 21-16.

FLORIDA 23 Arkansas 20: Florida's goals for 2009 were quite straight forward. Gators (6-0) planned to win every contest including SEC and BCS title games to secure their 3rd national championship in 4 years with 1st undefeated record in that span. Yet, with 9:40 remaining, Arkansas (3-3), which would end up gaining 357y, was winning 20-13. Would this game mimic Florida's last loss, last season's upset in Gainesville by then-unheralded Ole Miss? Razorbacks had just stunned Florida with 75y TD pass from QB Ryan Mallett (12-27/224y, TD) to WR Greg Childs (4/135y, TD). Childs caught ball

on right sideline at UF 36YL and eluded entire star-studded Florida secondary—CB Janoris Jenkins twice—after working way to middle of field to outrace CB Joe Haden and S Major Wright to EZ. Ball came loose on Wright's strip, but Childs corralled it in back of EZ for TD. Gators answered quickly against Arkansas D, which had entered game as SEC's worst, needing only 5 plays to go 67y and tie it 20-20: RB Jeff Demps (9/54y, TD) raced for 10y TD. Now it was Arkansas's turn, and Mallett completed 3-3/48y as Razorbacks marched 51y to earn 1st down at 26YL. But, tackle for 1y loss by Gators DE Jermaine Cunningham soon forced 38y FG try, which Hogs K Alex Tejada missed wide left. Gators smelled blood and moved into Arkansas territory as Demps ran for 17y, and QB Tim Tebow (17-26/255y, TD and 27/69y rushing) hit WR Riley Cooper (6/58y) for 11, 7, and 12y for 1st down at Hogs 28YL. With clock to waste, it became "Tebow Time," and he pounded 5/18y to set up winning 27y FG by K Caleb Sturgis. "When it came down to it, you knew we were going to play with a little bit more heart, and our guys were going to dig a little bit deeper, and they did," said Tebow, who accounted for 324y of his team's 391y O. He also threw 77y TD pass to WR Delonte Thompson in 3rd Q that had given Gators their 1st lead. Despite its late heroics, Florida O was unimpressive in losing 4 FUMs and allowing 6 sacks. Still, Gators had now won 16 straight games. Razorbacks, without injured RB Michael Smith, saw sub RB Dennis Johnson gain 14/107y.

ALABAMA 20 South Carolina 6: While South Carolina's talented D permitted only 13 pts to O of undefeated Alabama (7-0), Gamecocks (5-2) couldn't stop punishing RB Mark Ingram (24/246y, TD), who enjoyed 3rd-best rushing game in Crimson Tide history. Ingram also tallied clinching TD on 4y run at end of 68y trip with 5 mins to play. Bama D came up with 5 sacks of Carolina QB Stephen Garcia (20-46/214y, INT) and scored early TD off Garcia's 1st pass. Alabama S Mark Barron knifed in front of pass in middle of field and returned it for 77y TD barely min into 1st Q. Tide also happily allowed pair of FGs by Carolina K Spencer Lanning when Garcia was forced into several EZ incompletions on promising drives into Tide territory in 2nd Q.

PENN STATE 20 Minnesota 0: Weather was frightful as State College, Pa., suffered through 3 days of wintery mix that featured earliest snowfall in recorded meteorological history of Penn State (6-1) campus. Counting on their Big 10-leading D that welcomed back injured LB Sean Lee, Nittany Lions rolled up 259y to 38y advantage in 1st H, which Penn State led 13-0. Highlight of 1st H came just before end of 2nd Q when Lions WR Derek Moye (6/120y, TD) stretched his tall frame far OB while dragging toe in EZ to snare 12y TD pass from QB Daryll Clark (21-32/287y, TD). Punchless Gophers (4-3) finally crossed midfield late in 3rd Q when WR Eric Decker (1/42y), Big 10 receiving leader, dived for long pass over middle from QB Adam Weber (10-22/101y, INT). But, Minnesota failed to score on this its only threat when Lions DE Jerome Hayes blew up 4th down sweep by RB Kevin Whaley (6/11y) and CB A.J. Wallace and LB Navorro Bowman (8 tackles) snowed Whaley under at 1YL. TB Evan Royster rushed 23/137y for Lions. LB Lee Campbell was in on 13 tackles for Minnesota.

PURDUE 26 Ohio State 18: Up-and-down Boilermakers (2-5) rose up to steal 5 TOs and snipe no. 7 Ohio State (5-2). Loss was 1st for Buckeyes since 2004 to opponent that wouldn't play in BCS Bowl and ended 16-game conf road winning streak. Purdue lost 5 TOs itself, but dominated opening 3 Qs. While QB Terrelle Pryor (17-31/221y, TD, 2 INTs) put Buckeyes ahead 7-3 with 1st Q TD run, Boilermakers were able to limit Ohio's run attack (66y by game's end), and Purdue K Carson Weggs blasted 55y FG, his 3rd, on last play of 1st H for 9-7 edge. Purdue QB Joey Elliott (31-50/281y, 2 TDs, INT) clicked twice on scoring passes at end of 67 and 47y marches in 3rd Q. Boilers led 26-10 with 10 mins left to play. Pryor rallied Buckeyes, firing 25y scoring pass to WR DeVier Posey (9/87y, TD) and running for 2 pts in middle of 4th Q. With 2:24 left, Purdue DE Ryan Kerrigan (9 tackles, 3 sacks, 2 forced FUMs, FUM REC), soon tapped as national defender of week, sacked Pryor on 3rd down to all but clinch it.

Iowa 20 WISCONSIN 10: Undefeated Hawkeyes (7-0) fell behind 10-0 in 1st H as Badgers (5-2) pounded TB John Clay (21/75y) to 58y in 10 carries. Clay hurt his leg, so it was back-up TB Montee Ball who powered around right side behind pulling LG John Moffitt for 10y TD 7 mins into 2nd Q. Iowa CB Amari Spievey (2 INTs) sparked 3rd Q comeback by picking off erratic Wisconsin QB Scott Tolzien (15-25/143y, 3 INTs). Iowa QB Ricky Stanzi (17-23/218y, TD) rolled away from pressure to loft 24y TD pass to TE Tony Moeaki, who went high in back right corner of EZ to beat tight coverage by CB Antonio Fenelus. Moeaki's TD catch deadlocked it 10-10 midway in 3rd Q. Early in 4th Q, Hawkeyes RB Adam Robinson (20/91y, TD) barreled 10y up middle for TD.

Southern California 34 NOTRE DAME 27: Fighting Irish was heading to same EZ made famous by "Bush Push" play of 2005 where Trojans had scored in last sec on QB Matt Leinart's "enhanced sneak" to beat Notre Dame in only competitive series game in recent memory—until today. Hoping to win its 4th nail-biter of season, Notre Dame (4-2) made it close with improbable 4th Q rally from 34-14 deficit. Miracle finish was not in cards as 3 final EZ throws came up empty: On 1st down, Irish QB Jimmy Clausen (24-43/260y, 2 TDs) went for fade pattern to tall TE Kyle Rudolph, but Rudolph's catch was just OB at sideline. On 2nd down, USC (5-1) CB Josh Pinkard knocked down pass. Officials restored 1 sec on clock, allowing Clausen, who had been sacked 5 times, to throw quickly to WR Duval Kumara, who slipped while cutting for open space. With neither D excelling, it had been close until midway through 2nd H when Trojans scored on consecutive series to increase 20-14 lead to 34-14. Troy QB Matt Barkley (19-29/380y, 2 TDs, INT) connected with TE Anthony McCoy (5/153y) for 60y to set up 3y TD run by TB Allen Bradford. On next drive, Barkley fired 28y to WR Damian Williams (4/108y, 2 TDs) and 25y to McCoy. Next play, which opened 4th Q, was TE Rhett Ellison's 12y catch that brought ball to ND 1YL. USC scored on run by TB Joe McKnight (19/79y, TD). Outcome seemed certain to all but "Cardiac Irish." Clausen quickly went 3-4/39y to set up his 2y TD run that cut deficit to 34-20. Irish secondary next forced mistake by Barkley as frosh QB threw INT to CB Gary Gray, who returned 30y to USC 13YL. Clausen found WR Golden Tate (8/117y, TD) for 15y TD pass, and Irish now trailed by 7 with 7:28 remaining. After USC killed more than 3 mins, Notre Dame took over on its 22YL. Fateful series ensued; it seemed destined to succeed with Notre Dame recovering its own FUM and gaining personal foul and roughing passer PENs along way. Still, Clausen's late trio of passes missed, and USC escaped with its 8th straight series win. "When you live on the edge like that, you're not always going to come out on the winning side," said Clausen.

Texas Tech 31 NEBRASKA 10: Having just had "Black Shirts" status reinstated by coach Bo Pelini, Nebraska (4-2) D gave up pair of 1st H TD drives to Red Raiders. Still, Huskers outgained Texas Tech by 285y to 259y by game's end. Texas Tech opened with 16y TD screen pass from QB Steven Sheffield (23-32/234y, TD), fresh from his 7-TD debut vs. Kansas State, to RB Baron Batch at end of 80y drive. Huskers appeared on their way to tying it when WR Niles Paul neglected lateral pass that Raiders DE Daniel Howard scooped up and rambled for 82y TD and 14-0 lead in 1st Q. Raiders failed on 4th down run near midfield in 2nd Q, but it was nullified because Pelini had called timeout just before snap. Texas Tech finished 65y trip to Sheffield's TD sneak and 21-0 lead. Trailing 24-3 because it gave up 2nd Q FG after 58y catch by Tech WR Detron Lewis (5/110y), Nebraska dominated 3rd Q, totaling 72y while thwarting Raiders with -3y, but failed to find EZ until backup frosh QB Cody Green (7-16/87y, TD) flipped 13y TD pass to WR Khiry Cooper with 8 mins left in game.

KANSAS STATE 62 Texas A&M 14: Nobody was prepared for this onslaught on both sides of ball by Kansas State (4-3), especially after being trounced 66-14 previous week by Texas Tech. RB Daniel Thomas (18/91y, 4 TDs) muscled his way for 4 TDs in 1st H, 2 of them coming on short drives after FUM by Texas A&M (3-3) RB Jamie McCoy and 24y punt RET plus facemask PEN on WR Brandon Banks (6/60y). Trailing 38-0 at H, Aggies kicked off to Banks, who sailed 97y behind great blocking for his 3rd KO TD RET in 2009. RB Keithen Valentine (10/61y, 2 TDs) scored twice in 3rd Q for 59-0 edge before Aggies QB Jerrod Johnson (21-45/314y, 2 TDs, 3 INTs) and WR Uzoma Nwachukwu (5/136y, 2 TDs) collaborated on 66 and 23y TD passes.

Texas 16 Oklahoma 13 (Dallas): Sooners (3-3) star QB Sam Bradford was back from injury of his throwing shoulder, giving it go against big rival Texas (6-0). But with OU up 3-0 in 1st Q, Bradford was spilled hard on same shoulder by Texas CB Aaron Williams (INT), who came clean on blitz off left edge. Bradford was done for season. Blitzes also confused Longhorns QB Colt McCoy (21-39/127y, TD, INT), who was suffering from nasal infection. Before record crowd of 96,009, contest went 8 mins into 3rd Q before either O could register TD. At that moment, it was tied 6-6 on FGs by Oklahoma K Jimmy Stevens (26, 37y) and Texas K Hunter Lawrence (both of 42y), with Lawrence's 2nd Q 3-ptr coming after muffed punt by Sooners CB Dominique Franks. Midway in 3rd Q, Steers frosh WR Marquise Goodwin (4/36y, TD) ducked under tackle and squirted into EZ on 14y TD pass from McCoy for 13-6 edge. Soon thereafter, OU WR Ryan Broyles tied it by similarly avoiding tackle on short pass from QB Landry Jones (24-43/250y, TD, 2 INTs) and sprinting down right sideline for 35y TD. After Lawrence's 3rd FG provided 16-13 lead to Texas 4 mins into 4th Q, Longhorns threatened after Williams' INT at Oklahoma 20YL. But, McCoy had to make game-saving tackle on 21y INT RET by Sooners CB Brian Jackson. Texas kept its 16-13 lead by countering with INT by S Earl Thomas after Jones threw into double coverage from his 45YL. Longhorns D limited Oklahoma to -16y rushing.

COLORADO 34 Kansas 30: Undefeated Kansas (5-1) hadn't played team with winning record, and that didn't change in visit to disappointing Colorado (2-4). What did change was starting QB for Buffaloes, as soph QB Tyler Hansen (14-25/175y, TD, INT) made his debut by running for TD in 24-pt 2nd Q and sparking 4th Q TD drive after Jayhawks rallied from 24-3 deficit to 30-27 lead early in 4th Q. Kansas QB Todd Reesing (30-51/401y, 2 TDs, INT) got Jayhawks in EZ late in 1st H as he found WR Kerry Meier (11/103y, TD) with short TD pass. After permitting Colorado K Aric Goodman's 2nd FG early in 3rd Q, Kansas scored next 20 pts, including 25y TD in 4th Q to WR Dezmon Briscoe (8/154y, TD), who became national BCS receiving y per game leader. Hansen moved Buffs 76y to winning score as RB Rodney Stewart (24/108y, 2 TDs) dragged tackler 5y on 13y TD burst. Reesing, who was sacked 6 times by CU, soon saw Buffs CB Jimmy Smith bat away 4th-and-goal pass from Briscoe, developed last chance by hitting Briscoe for 26y on way to 19YL. But, Colorado CBs Jalil Brown and Cha'pelle Brown tipped away last sec passes.

USA TODAY Coaches Poll October 18, 2009

1 Florida (49)	1464	14 Oregon	769
2 Alabama (9)	1398	15 Virginia Tech	672
3 Texas (1)	1386	16 Brigham Young	577
4 Southern California	1237	17 Ohio State	481
5 Boise State	1153	18 Houston	421
6 Cincinnati	1104	19 Pittsburgh	328
7 Texas Christian	1069	20 Utah	300
8 Iowa	1037	21 Kansas	222
9 Miami	998	22 West Virginia	188
10 Louisiana State	995	23 South Carolina	142
11 Penn State	894	24 Texas Tech	132
12 Oklahoma State	795	25 Mississippi	114
13 Georgia Tech	779		

Bowl Championship Series Rankings October 18, 2009

	Harris Poll Avg.	USA TODAY Poll Avg.	Computer Pct.	BCS Avg.
1 Florida (6-0)	.9832	.9925	.990	.9886
2 Alabama (7-0)	.9600	.9478	.950	.9526
3 Texas (6-0)	.9337	.9397	.800	.8911
4 Boise State (6-0)	.8032	.7817	.840	.8083
5 Cincinnati (6-0)	.7625	.7485	.850	.7870

October 24, 2009

(Th) Florida State 30 NORTH CAROLINA 27: Killing themselves with boatload of PENs (16/121y), Seminoles (3-4) were overrun by North Carolina's swarming D in 1st H. Tar Heels (4-3) built 17-6 H edge, including 13y TD pass from QB T.J. Yates (12-25/64y, TD, INT) to rarely-thrown-to TE Ed Barham. When Yates ran for 10y TD in 3rd Q, Heels led comfortably at 24-6. While Florida State had floundered with -14y rushing in 1st H, QB Christian Ponder (33-40/395y, 3 TDs) was ready for brilliant performance in closing 25 mins. North Carolina came into game as ACC's top team in defending passes, but Ponder burned Heels with pair of scoring flings within 2 mins, including school-record-tying 98y bomb to WR Rod Owens (9/199y, TD). Soon, Seminoles trailed only 24-23, and, Ponder found RB Beau Reliford swinging all alone up right sideline for 18y TD catch that snatched final lead change at 30-27 with 6:20 left. LB Kendall Smith sparked FSU D with 10 tackles, 3.5 tfls, and 2 sacks.

Clemson 40 MIAMI 37: Tigers (4-3) continued resurgent play with 1st win over ranked team in last 9 tries, winning on 26y TD pass by QB Kyle Parker (25-37/326y, 3 TDs, INT) to WR Jacoby Ford in 1st extra series after Hurricanes (5-2) settled for FG in OT. Clemson miraculously overcame its 7th deficit of game on Ford's improvised TD in which he curled over to middle to 5YL. RB C.J. Spiller (14/81y and 6/104y, TD receiving) was Clemson's O catalyst, gaining school-record 310y all-purpose. Spiller's 90y KO TD RET late in 2nd Q gave Clemson 14-10 lead and came somewhat by accident: Miami K Alex Uribe was ordered not to kick-off deep but did anyway with min left in 2nd Q. Spiller's 56y TD pass reception in 3rd Q was good for 21-17 advantage. Dangerous QB Jacory Harris (17-27/256y, 2 TDs, 3 INTs) continually put Hurricanes in lead but also gave away pts and field position with his 3 INTs. On consecutive 4th Q snaps, Harris allowed Clemson to take 31-27 lead when he threw INT returned 23y for TD by Tigers S DeAndre McDaniel but quickly connected with WR Travis Benjamin (3/82y, TD) on 69y TD pass for 34-31 lead. McDaniel chipped in with 2 INTs to take NCAA lead with 7 on season. Parker killed Tigers' 65y drive to Miami 4YL with INT by Canes S Randy Phillips with 5:37 remaining. But after Tigers forced punt, Parker redeemed himself with 3-3/28y passing on 48y trip to K Richard Jackson's tying 30y FG. On opening possession of OT, Canes reached Clemson 5YL before stalling and taking K Matt Bosher's 22y FG. Bosher kicked FGs of 51 and 49y earlier in game. In 3 games with Clemson since joining ACC, Miami had gone to OT each time.

ALABAMA 12 Tennessee 10: Alabama (8-0) NG Terrence Cody was immense at 354 lbs. No mere immovable object, "Mount Cody" could move well for his size and his gigantic wingspan was put to good use in stuffing Tennessee's last-sec threat for upset. Trailing 12-10 with time winding down, Volunteers (3-4) drove 31y to Alabama 28YL for K Daniel Lincoln to attempt game-winning 44y FG that would have squashed Alabama's undefeated season and no. 1 ranking. Cody, who had blocked 43y attempt earlier in 4th Q, batted down Lincoln's boot. While Cody's celebration would have gotten him bounced from ABC-TV's Dancing with the Star, jubilant crowd chanted his name. "It was just emotional, crazy," said Cody, who had never blocked any kicks prior to this game. Thanks to 4 FGs, including 50 and 49y 3-ptrs, by K Leigh Tiffin, Crimson Tide led 12-3 and were running out clock when RB Mark Ingram (18/99y) lost FUM on own 43YL after tackle by Vols S Eric Berry and CB Dennis Rogan. Berry recovered with 3:29 remaining. Ingram had never lost FUM in previous 322 career touches. On its way to 341y to 256y game-end advantage, Tennessee took 8 plays to score on 11y pass by QB Jonathan Crompton (21-36/265y, TD, INT) to WR Gerald Jones (7/72y, TD) for 1st TD allowed by Tide D in 11 Qs. Tennessee WR Denarius Moore then recovered onside-KO at Vols 41YL and in blink of eye Vols were sniffing major upset. Crompton completed 14y to Jones and 23y to TE Luke Stocker to Tide 27YL with 48 secs left. Tennessee then ran clock down questionably to set up long FG try: Lincoln had made 24y 3-ptr in 2nd Q before missing 47y FG at end of 1st H and having Cody block 43y effort 10 mins earlier. Alabama's undefeated season was preserved as soon as Cody lifted his mighty arms. "You talk about how fragile a season is," said Alabama coach Nick Saban. "You make one mistake and you have to go overcome it."

Florida 29 MISSISSIPPI STATE 19: Facing its former O coach and 1st-year Bulldogs (3-5) mentor Dan Mullen, slumbering Florida (7-0) O expected to be inspired. But Gators were unable to put it away until their brilliant D scored controversial TD on INT RET by LB Dustin Doe in 4th Q. Before largest crowd (57,178) in Davis Wade Stadium history, Bulldogs were fired up and aided greatly by 2 INTs by frosh S Johnthan Banks that were returned for TDs. Banks dashed 100y on INT TD RET at end of 1st H that pulled Mississippi State to within 13-10. Banks gained 120y in RETs, only 7y less than Florida gained passing. Bulldogs D forced 3-and-out on opening possession of 2nd H, which set up their 65y drive to tying 31y FG by K Derek DePasquale. Not much went right for Mississippi State after that, with Florida QB Tim Tebow (12-22/127y, 2 INTs and 22/88y, TD rushing) driving Gators 48y in 3rd Q to go-ahead-for-good 27y FG by K Caleb Sturgis. Early in 4th Q, Mullen opted for fake punt while needing 2y at own 26YL: Coming off E-around RB Robert Elliott stumbled after receiving handoff and lost 4y. It set up 8y TD run by Gators RB Chris Rainey (12/90y, TD) 6 plays later. Doe soon sealed win with 23y INT TD RET off tipped pass, although he appeared to have fumbled it away before reaching EZ when raising ball to celebrate. Highlight for Tebow occurred in 2nd Q when he raced 26y for TD that tied him with Georgia great Herschel Walker for most rushing TDs in SEC history with 49.

LOUISIANA STATE 31 Auburn 10: If rout of Auburn (5-3) was any indication, balance between LSU's attackers and its D, which in reality had been carrying its untried O for past 2 seasons, finally arrived in Baton Rouge. Tussle of Tigers went to Louisiana State (6-1) as it embarrassed Auburn's 8th-ranked O, while LSU QB Jordan Jefferson threw for 21-31/career-high 242y with 2 TDs. In 1st Q, Jefferson drove his O unit 83y to score on his 14y pass to WR Terrance Toliver (9/86y, TD). Later in 1st Q, LB Harry Coleman (9 tackles, 2 forced FUMs, 2 sacks) stripped Auburn QB Chris Todd (8-14/47y, INT) and resultant FUM was recovered by S Danny McCray at Auburn 16YL to set up Jefferson's 15y TD run for 14-0 lead. Auburn could gain only 42y in decisive 1st H and struggled to finish with 193y, 272y below its avg. Only once did Auburn reach LSU territory in 1st H, and on ensuing play Todd threw INT to Bayou Bengals CB Chris Hawkins. LSU's 3rd Q highlights included Jefferson's 17y TD pass to WR Brandon LaFell (6/67y, TD) and sub QB Russell Shepard's 69y scoring jaunt while lining up at RB. Auburn scored its sole TD with 3 secs left on sub QB Neil Caudle's 1y TD pitch to TE Philip Lutzenkirchen to cap 59y drive.

Penn State 35 MICHIGAN 10: Michigan (5-3) moved smartly downfield after opening KO for 70y in 11 plays to 1y TD plunge by RB Brandon Minor (12/48y, TD). Penn State (7-1) knotted it in less than 2 mins on QB Daryll Clark's 10y TD lob to WR Graham Zug (5/59y, 3 TDs). Fans were puzzled when Lions coach Joe Paterno ordered punt on 4th-and-3 from Michigan 33YL, but Wolverines self-destructed from their 8YL and suffered 3rd down safety when shotgun C snap flew past QB Tate Forcier (13-30/140y, INT). On next scrimmage play after Michigan's free-kick, Clark (16-27/230y, 4 TDs) lofted 60y TD to TE Andrew Quarless for 19-7 Penn State lead. Nittany Lions WR Chaz Powell raced 54y with 2nd H KO, and Zug caught Clark's 3rd TD pass for 25-10 edge. After FUM REC by S Nick Sukay, Clark and Zug collaborated again for TD and 32-10 lead midway in 3rd Q. Sharp Wolverines DE Brandon Graham blocked punt late in 3rd Q, but Michigan fumbled it right back to Penn State LB Navorro Bowman (11 tackles, sack, FUM REC, INT). Lions TB Evan Royster rushed 20/100y.

Iowa 15 MICHIGAN STATE 13: After Michigan State (4-4) had upper hand in 1st H, D struggle went well into 3rd Q tied 3-3. K Brett Swenson, who later put himself atop Spartans all-time scoring list, made chip-shot FG for 6-3 lead after Iowa (8-0) interior D mounted tremendous GLS. Spartans RB Edwin Baker (11/68y) had just broken loose around RE for 37y for 1st-and-goal at 1YL. Hawkeyes K Daniel Murray tied it again early in 4th Q, and Iowa appeared poised to lock up win that would provide its 1st 8-0 mark in history: QB Ricky Stanzi (11-27/138y, TD) found WR Derrell Johnson-Koulianos (3/59y) for soaring 32y catch at 8YL. Holding PEN forced Murray to kick 20y FG for 9-6 lead with 3 mins to go. Facing 3rd-and-18, Michigan State QB Kirk Cousins (16-32/225y, TD) fired "hook-and-ladder" pass to TE Brian Linthicum who tossed pitch to trailing WR Blair White (3/95y, TD) to Iowa 30YL. With pressure in his face, Cousins lofted 30y TD to White in middle of EZ for 13-9 lead with 1:37 to play. Stanzi calmly passed Iowa to Michigan State 15YL, but on 1st down, D-holding PEN sickened home crowd and wiped out INT by Spartans. After 3 nerve-racking pass misses by Stanzi, Iowa called its last TO with 2 secs left. Hawkeyes WR Marvin McNutt slanted in against CB Chris L. Rucker to grab Stanzi's last-play, game winning TD.

NOTRE DAME 20 Boston College 16: Lacking long tradition, this rivalry between last remaining Catholic football powers still could turn heated especially in light of recent series domination by Boston College (5-3), which owned 6-game win streak dating to 2001. And so at game's end there were O heroes for both teams, Eagles WR Rich Gunnell and Notre Dame (5-2) QB Jimmy Clausen (26-39/246y, 2 TDs) jawing at each other when handshakes were more fitting. Gunnell was definitely fired up for what would be one of his finest games as collegian, catching 10/179y, TD as cornerstone of nation's 106th-ranked passing O, which offered its best game of season against struggling Notre Dame secondary. At least until trio of 2nd H INTs did in Eagles QB Dave Shinskie (17-35/279y, TD, 3 INTs), who sealed BC's fate with his last INT to Irish LB Brian Smith on forced pass toward Gunnell with less than 2 mins remaining. When it counted Irish D played clutch ball near game's end, blanking Eagles in 4th Q as it forced pair of 3-and-outs on Boston College's opening possessions of 4th Q and ended last 2 with INTs, including ND S Kyle McCarthy's 2nd of game. Sandwiched in between was Notre Dame's winning 49y TD drive, which featured 2 runs by RB Armando Allen (21/98y) for 13y and 36y TD catch by WR Golden Tate (11/128y, 2 TDs). Budding star Tate, who had caught 11y TD pass at end of 1st H, continued his rise from HS runner into top-notch collegiate WR. On other side, Gunnell made name for himself with big catch after another, including 7y TD in 2nd Q. Thanks to struggles of BC passers to date, Gunnell had entered game with modest 22/253y receiving for season.

Texas 41 MISSOURI 7: After being sick and injured in opening half of season, Texas (7-0) QB Colt McCoy (26-31/269y, 3 TDs) returned to brilliant form as Longhorns roared to 35-7 H lead en route to crushing Missouri (4-3). McCoy clicked on his 1st 11 throws, including TD passes of 8y to WR Jordan Shipley (7/108y, 2 TDs) and 34y to WR John Chiles in 1st Q. After Tigers QB Blaine Gabbert (8-16/84y, TD) connected on 11y TD pass to WR Jared Perry in 2nd Q, McCoy and Shipley collaborated again on TD pass. Route was stamped in last min of 2nd Q when Texas CB Curtis Brown blocked EZ punt by Mizzou P Jake Harry, recovered for TD by WR Malcolm Williams.

Iowa State 9 NEBRASKA 7: Rarely had butter-fingered play so exasperated any 18-pt favorite as did Nebraska's 4 lost FUMs inside Iowa State Cyclones (5-3) 5 YL. Iowa State broke 15-game conf road losing streak despite playing without QB Austen Arnaud and RB Alexander Robinson, Big 12's leading rusher. Cyclones forced whopping 8 TOs, including FUM on 1st scrimmage by sore-shouldered Cornhuskers (4-3) IB Roy Helu (5/24y). Iowa State went nowhere but cashed 52y FG by K Grant Mahoney for 3-0 lead. Nebraska P Alex Henery later punted OB at 2YL, and resultant field position left Huskers only 42y to negotiate for 7-3 lead: After 17y pass from QB Zac Lee (20-37/248y, 3 INTs) to TE Mike McNeill, back-up IB Dontrayevous Robinson went over RT for TD with 3:26 to go in 1st Q. Lee's pass soon was tipped between both teams and intercepted by Iowa State S David Sims at 1YL, and Sims' 16y RET set up 83y TD march for 9-7 lead. It was keyed by 20y run off fake-punt from Iowa State 33YL by P Mike Brandtner and capped 1 play later by 47y TD pass from QB Jerome Tiller (9-19/102y, TD and 19/65y rushing) to WR Jake Williams. Later in 2nd Q, Nebraska WR Niles Paul got loose for 72y on long pass but bobbled ball into EZ after being knocked off balance at 7YL. On consecutive possessions in 3rd Q, Huskers watched in horror as Helu returned to action, only to fumble into EZ after 14y punch up middle, and Robinson carried on 5 straight plays for 36y only to fumble it away at 5YL. And so it went. Cyclones DT Nate Frere felt his team was blessed to come away with victory, saying, "Wacky game, but that's how it goes sometimes."

Oklahoma 35 KANSAS 13: Sooners (4-3) QB Landry Jones (26-38/252y, 2 TDs, INT) enjoyed his 1st big game as sub for injured QB Sam Bradford and got familiar with top target WR Ryan Broyles (11/121y) to riddle stunned D of no. 21 Kansas (5-2). Oklahoma D held Kansas' 2nd-best-in-nation O to 198y below its 503y avg. Rout was ignited early 2nd Q by CB Dominique Franks, who extended OU's 7-0 lead by jumping goal-to-go swing pass by Jayhawks QB Todd Reesing (22-42/224y, 3 INTs) and surging 85y on INT TD RET for 14-pt edge. Sooners went on to build 21-6 and 28-6 leads in 3rd Q when Jones hit pair of short TD throws to WR Adron Tennell (6/47y, TD) and RB Chris Brown (11/66y, 2 TDs). Calling it "rough day at the office," Reesing did his best to stoke his team's O after being picked off in each of Jayhawks' opening 3 possessions and tallied their only TD on 5y run with 4:27 to go. Coach Mark Mangino's career record vs. Big 12 South fell to 4-18.

Texas A&M 52 TEXAS TECH 30: Coming off 62-14 trouncing by Kansas State, which would beat Colorado 20-6 this Saturday, Texas A&M, losers of 3 straight games, put up tremendous, unforeseen O effort. Texas Tech (5-3) scored quickly to open game as QB Taylor Potts (25-35/310y, 2 TDs, 2 INTs) clicked on 56y TD pass, and things turned gloomy for Aggies when they quickly fumbled. But Texas A&M faced up to, according to coach Mike Sherman, "the turning point of the game." Trailing 14-7 after 1st Q, Aggies (4-3) fired up their running game, led by RBs Cyrus Gray (25/131y, 3 TDs and TD receiving) and Christine Michael (22/121y, 2 TDs), who raced for 44y TD to open 3rd Q. Also in 3rd Q, Texas A&M star LB Von Miller forced Potts into FUM, 3rd TO by Texas Tech QB, who soon would be yanked by coach Mike Leach. As 3rd Q was winding down, Aggies had tallied 31 pts in row for 38-14 lead. Red Raiders rallied for 2 TDs behind QB Seth Doege (18-25/146y) but were offset by 21y TD run by Aggies QB Jerrod Johnson (19-28/238y, TD and 10/71y, TD rushing). Leach said, "If it was easy anybody could do it. If it was easy, I'd be coaching the Swedish bikini team, and I'd have them coming out here to do all this (against Texas A&M)."

HOUSTON 38 Southern Methodist 15: Cougars' red-hot O received season-low passing y from QB Case Keenum (25-36/233y, TD), who despite only single TD pass still reached 10,000y career passing on game's last TD drive in 4th Q, which resulted in 6y TD run by frosh RB Charles Sims (15/105y, 2 TDs). Sims' 105y rushing represented career high. Southern Methodist (3-4) was behind whole way after permitting Sims' 20y TD run in 1st Q. Mustangs went 68y, mostly on ground, in 2nd Q but managed only 26y FG by K Matt Szymanski to trail 24-3 at H. When Cougars fast, little WR Tyron Carrier raced 2nd H KO back 92y for TD, verdict was sealed. Houston (6-1) LB C.J. Cavness was all over field, making 18 tackles, 1.5 sacks, and pair of FUM RECs. Cavness' RECs set up TD from 1YL and halted 3rd Q threat when SMU WR Darius Johnson took pass 28y to Cougars 2YL.

Texas Christian 38 BRIGHAM YOUNG 7: Provo fans fired up for upset victory by Brigham Young (6-2). But, powerful no. 7 Texas Christian (7-0) made it no contest by jumping to 21-0 lead 20 mins into game. Horned Frogs fired wide array of O weapons, led by QB Andy Dalton (13-24/241y, 3 TDs) who precisely hit RB Ed Wesley and speedy WR Jimmy Young with TD passes in 1st H. In 3rd Q, Dalton launched long TD pass to WR Antoine Hicks, which was lugged 75y for TD and 31-7 lead. Afterward Dalton commented on talents of Frogs: "We still haven't played our best game, but we played really well tonight." Cougars QB Max Hall (18-28/162y, TD, INT) remarked that TCU's D was best he had faced, saying: "We've been having fun all year. That wasn't very much fun." Frogs sacked Hall 5 times but allowed RB Harvey Unga to rush for 123y, while Unga scored BYU's only TD on short pass late in 2nd Q.

UTAH 23 Air Force 16 (OT): Utes (6-1) RB Eddie Wide (17/121y, 2 TDs) scored game's 1st TD, less than 3 mins into 1st Q, and last in OT to wrestle hard-fought outcome from Air Force (4-4). But it hardly was humdrum contest for Wide, who notched his 4th 100y rushing game since taking over for injured RB Matt Asiata: Wide's 45y TD run in 1st Q came after he scooped up FUM by Utah QB Terrance Cain (11-21/167y, TD) and he was bent backwards on tackle and had to convince trainers he could continue. In 3rd Q, Cain pitched slant pass to WR David Reed (7/149y, TD), who broke 2 tackles and sped 90y to TD that lifted Utes into 13-10 lead. Falcons QB Connor Dietz (28/98y rushing) consistently gored Utah for good y on option runs but while trailing 23-16 in OT finally was halted on 4th down at Utah 7YL by LB Stevenson Sylvester to clinch victory. Air Force had rallied in last 16 mins of regulation to force OT on FGs of 22 and 48y by K Erik Soderberg.

SOUTHERN CALIFORNIA 42 Oregon State 36: No. 4 Southern California Trojans (6-1) never trailed as QB Matt Barkley (15-202y, 2 TDs, 2 INTs) tossed pair of 1st H TD passes, his 1st score to TE Anthony McCoy coming after DE Everson Griffen returned FUM to Beavers 24YL. But storm clouds were brewing for USC D as Oregon State (4-3) rolled up 482y O and tacked on 27 pts in 2nd H. Beavers QB Sean Canfield (30-43/329y, 3 TDs) threw TD passes in 3rd Q to RB Jacquizz Rodgers (20/113y, TD) and WR Damola Adeniji to crawl within 21-16 and 28-23. Early in 4th Q, electric WR Damian Williams (6/58y) seemed to lift Trojans to safety when he veered to right sideline and went distance for 63y punt TD RET for 42-23 edge. "And then they (Beavers) went down and scored again like it was nothing," lamented Williams. Indeed, Oregon State rode DB Jordan Poyers' 70y KO RET to Canfield's 7y TD pass to WR James Rodgers. Relying on runs of TB Allen Bradford (15/career-high 147y, 2 TDs) and Barkley's 3-3/23y passing, USC was able to kill last 5:41.

STANFORD 33 Arizona State 14: It was crossroads tilt for both hopeful programs, especially Stanford (5-3), coming off 2 straight Pac-10 losses and facing tough closing slate. Sun Devils (4-3) struggled on O with only 4 1st downs in 1st H and continued to hurt themselves with 10/90y in PENs. Frosh sub WR Jamal-Rahad Patterson touched ball only once but tallied on 22y reverse TD run for game's opening pts as Cardinal cruised to 24-0 H lead behind balanced attack of 237y rushing and 236y passing. Stanford QB Andrew Luck passed 17-28/236y, while TB Toby Gerhart rushed 27/125y, TD. Arizona State QB Danny Sullivan (12-23/143y, 2 TDs) fairly pumped up 2nd H attack with TD passes to WR Chris McGaha (6/80y, TD) and T.J. Simpson (2/46y, TD). Devils D failed to earn INT, ending nation's longest such streak at 15 games.

Oregon 43 WASHINGTON 19: Oregon Ducks (6-1) blocked punt for TD by LB Tyrell Irvin and took 8-3 lead when Washington (3-5) was caught napping for holder Nate Costa to tack on 2-pt run. Still down by 5 pts and facing 4th-and-goal at 1YL in 2nd Q, Washington coach Steve Sarkisian eschewed virtually-certain FG, and QB Jake Locker (23-44/266y, TD, 2 INTs) forced throw that was intercepted in EZ by Ducks S Javes Lewis. Game's key TD followed at end of 80y trip on 1y run by QB Jeremiah Masoli (14-22/157y, TD and 11/54y, 2 TDs rushing) as Oregon went off at H leading 15-6. Ducks flew away in 2nd H, storming for 21 unanswered pts in 3rd Q as Masoli scored on 3y run and threw 16y TD pass. Ducks mercurial frosh RB LaMichael James (15/154y, 2 TDs) made it 36-6 with TD run late in 3rd Q and galloped to 56y TD in 4th Q.

USA TODAY Coaches Poll October 25, 2009

1 Florida (46)	1459	14 Virginia Tech	691
2 Alabama (9)	1399	15 Ohio State	569
3 Texas (4)	1390	16 Houston	544
4 Southern California	1244	17 Pittsburgh	542
5 Boise State	1152	18 Miami	433
6 Texas Christian	1131	19 Utah	403
7 Cincinnati	1126	20 West Virginia	365
8 Iowa	1086	21 South Carolina	279
9 Louisiana State	1037	22 Mississippi	223
10 Penn State	935	23 Oklahoma	168
11 Georgia Tech	865	24 Arizona	149
12 Oregon	839	25 Notre Dame	82
13 Oklahoma State	825		

Bowl Championship Series Rankings October 25, 2009

	Harris Poll Avg.	USA TODAY Poll Avg.	Computer Pct.	BCS Avg.
1 Florida (7-0)	.9788	.9892	.950	.9726
2 Alabama (8-0)	.9465	.9485	.940	.9450
3 Texas (7-0)	.9458	.9424	.790	.8927
4 Iowa (8-0)	.7384	.7363	1.000	.8249
5 Southern California (6-1)	.8198	.8434	.720	.7944

October 31, 2009

(Th) North Carolina 20 VIRGINIA TECH 17: Fine D of Tar Heels (5-3) managed to stifle elusive runs of Virginia Tech (5-3) frosh TB Ryan Williams, who gained 96y but lost crushing FUM in closing mins. K Casey Barth hit his 2nd short FG of 4th Q on game's last play to pull out road win for 2-TD underdog North Carolina. Heels' 105th-ranked passing O got boost from QB T.J. Yates (18-28/131y, 2 TDs, INT) whos hit TD passes in middle Qs, including WR Greg Little's fine 15y catch in corner of EZ in 3rd Q for 14-7 advantage. Early in 4th Q, Yates tried ill-advised swing pass to Little and was intercepted by Hokies CB Rashad Carmichael. Va Tech QB Tyrod Taylor (11-23/161y) soon scored his 2nd rushing TD by smashing off right side for 1y and 17-14 lead. After Yates hit Little over middle on 4th down, Barth tied it with 19y FG. On Hokies' next series and with 2 mins to play, Williams, inconsolable afterward, bobbled FUM to UNC S Deunta Williams from Va Tech 28YL. RB Ryan Houston ran on 6 plays in row to Hokies 4YL to set up Barth for game-winning 3-ptr.

(Fri) SOUTH FLORIDA 30 West Virginia 19: In recent years, South Florida (6-2) had started fast and fell on its face as Big East play got into full swing. This time, Bulls coach Jim Leavitt was determined to get his team on track, especially after pair of sub-par D performances in consecutive losses to Cincinnati and Pittsburgh. West Virginia (6-2) came in undefeated in conf play but couldn't spring speedy RB Noel Devine, who was limited to 17/42y rushing. Recent South Florida discovery, QB B.J. Daniels (13-26/232y, 3 TDs) sparked Bulls with 3 TD passes and 104y rushing. After Mountaineers QB Jarrett Brown (19-32/205y, INT) skirted RE for 3y TD early in 1st Q, Daniels threw for TDs as he went long down left sideline to WR Carlton Mitchell and scrambled to find lonely WR A.J. Love in right side of EZ. So, USF led 20-12 at H. Brown scored again on 11y run in 3rd Q to pull within 20-19, but Daniels struck back with 6y TD throw to frosh WR Sterling Griffin.

Rutgers 28 CONNECTICUT 24: While stunning, last-sec loss had to be devastating to Connecticut (4-4) program that honored slain CB Jasper "Jazz" Howard on this day, Rutgers' winning TD was appropriately scored by Howard's neighbor from Miami, Knights (6-2) WR Tim Brown (5/162y, 2 TDs). After Huskies excitingly scored TD on 2y run by RB Jordan Todman with 38 secs left for 24-21 lead, Rutgers needed only 1 play to turn cheers to stunned silence as speedy Brown caught over-middle throw from QB Tom Savage (13-24/236y, 3 TDs) near Rutgers 40YL and galloped to 81y TD with 22 secs left. "I just went out there and played that game for my friend," said Brown, who had "RIP" and "Jazz" written on his eye-black patches. Huskies QB Cody Endres was knocked out for season with shoulder injury in 1st Q, and rusty former starting QB Zach Frazer (21-46/333y, TD, 3 INTs) came off bench to see his 2nd and 6th passes picked off. Settled down by early in 4th Q, Frazer threw 32y TD pass to WR Marcus Easley (5/81y, TD) as UConn trimmed deficit to 21-17. Frazer was clutch on his team's would-be winning march, when he drove it 87y to Todman's TD, hitting 31y pass to WR Michael Smith to convert 3rd-and-10 and completing 32y pass to WR Kashif Moore with Huskies facing 4th-and-5 at Rutgers 39YL. Both teams had scored on KO RETs in 1st H: Rutgers CB Devin McCourty took opening KO 98y, and RB Robbie Frey returned favor in 2nd Q with 100y KO RET for UConn. Total of 13 pts would have reversed Connecticut's 4 to-date losses, all of which it had led in 2nd H.

Miami 28 WAKE FOREST 27: Cardiac Canes (6-2) were at it again, rallying with 2 TDs in 4th Q and scoring game-winner with 68 secs left as backpedaling QB Jacory Harris (22-43/330y, 3 TDs, INT) threw 13y pass to WR Travis Benjamin. Hoping to

snap 5-game series losing streak that went back 65 years, Wake Forest (4-5) had gained 555y in building 17-0 and 27-14 leads as QB Riley Skinner (29-43/349y, 2 TDs, INT) enjoyed his 4th career 300y game. Trying to protect 13-pt lead early in 4th Q, Deacons forced punt by K-P Matt Bosher that was boomed deep. With rain spraying his face, WR Devon Brown (12/101y) failed to catch wet ball over his left shoulder, and muff was recovered by Miami CB Sam Shields at Wake 2YL. On next play, Harris rolled out and hit TE Tervaris Johnson in back of EZ for TD. Soon facing 3rd-and-8, Skinner scrambled for 12y and 1st down but was met by 3 defenders who administered concussion-inducing tackle that ended Skinner's afternoon. Inexperienced Wake sr QB Ryan McManus (5-9/42y), 1-5/5y for his career, hit 2 passes in helping waste more than 5 mins, but Miami took over at 18YL with 2:40 to go. Harris found WR Thearon Collier for 29y on 3rd-and-10 and later converted 4th-and-16 with another 29y pass to leaping WR Aldarius Johnson at Wake 30YL. Harris connected with Benjamin on consecutive plays, including TD for 28-27 lead after Bosher converted kick. Now it was McManus' turn as he passed Deacs to Miami 43YL. But with only secs left, Wake had to try 60y FG by frosh K Jimmy Newman, which wasn't close.

TENNESSEE 31 South Carolina 13: Opting for black jerseys for 1st time in 87 years, Volunteers (4-4) opened up 14-0 lead in 1st 3 mins of Halloween. No. 21 South Carolina (6-3) helped by passing out FUMs like candy, losing ball on opening 2 possessions. Tennessee QB Jonathan Crompton (12-24/142y, 2 TDs) started scoring with 38y TD pass to FB Austin Johnson to cap quick 43y drive begun when NT Dan Williams fell on FUM. Vols RB Montario Hardesty (23/121y, 2 TDs) rushed 4 straight times/27y after Tennessee DT Wes Brown recovered FUM at Carolina 27YL with final 14y coming on TD run that featured brilliant spin to elude pair of South Carolinians. Tennessee increased its lead to 21-0 in 2nd Q—after 3rd lost FUM by Gamecocks at their 22YL—and to 28-6 in 3rd Q. Gamecocks tightened matters later in 3rd Q when QB Stephen Garcia (25-50/300y, TD, INT) threw 31y TD pass to WR Moe Brown to pull within 28-13. That was 1st TD surrendered by Tennessee D in last 10 Qs, and Vols would not allow Gamecocks past midfield for rest of game. Now 22-4-2 all-time in series, Tennessee had hoped to wear all black, but orange pants could not have been replaced in time. "It gave us some energy," said coach Lane Kiffin of black jerseys.

Florida 41 Georgia 17 (Jacksonville): There is nothing like matchup with Georgia (4-4) to bring out best in Gators (8-0). Running its series record over past 20 years to 17-3, Florida also added insult to injury as QB Tim Tebow (15-21/164y, 2 TDs and 18/85y, 2 TDs rushing) broke former Georgia star Herschel Walker's SEC record of 49 rushing TDs with his 50th going 23y late in 2nd Q for 24-10 lead. "Just to be mentioned in the same breath as Herschel Walker, it's extremely humbling and a little bit breathtaking because it's Herschel Walker," said Tebow. Fittingly Tebow's run provided winning pts while allowing him to set back record in his hometown of Jacksonville. Tebow also connected with WR Riley Cooper (4/78y, 2 TDs) on TD passes for 14-0 lead in 1st Q, and added 2nd rushing TD for 31-10 advantage in 3rd Q. Cooper's 2nd scoring catch was brilliant 1-handed snare in back corner of EZ. Bulldogs went for black helmets for 1st time in school history and black pants in effort to shake things up against rivals, but nothing short of playing extra men would have helped. Bulldogs managed to reel off 10 straight pts to open 2nd Q and pull within 14-10 but over-celebrated after QB Joe Cox (11-20/165y, 2 TDs, 3 INTs) threw 26y TD pass to TE Aron White. So, Gators ran off 17 straight pts, with 1st 3 tallied on K Caleb Sturgis's 56y FG, 2nd-longest in school history after Chris Perkins' 60y boot in 1984. Coach Urban Meyer ran his record against Gators' 3 biggest rivals, Georgia, Tennessee and Florida State, to 13-1.

AUBURN 33 Mississippi 20: Left for dead after 3 straight conf losses, Auburn (6-3) rose up to bring down erratic Ole Miss (5-3). Auburn coach Gene Chizik must have made some H speech as Tigers reeled off 21 straight 3rd Q pts, needing only 6 plays on O and 1 on D to do so. It stretched 10-7 H lead to 31-7. With 2nd possession of 3rd Q, Auburn raced 61y in 3 plays to score TD on 14y pass from WR-QB Kodi Burns to TE Tommy Trott. On next play from scrimmage, Auburn CB Walter McFadden picked off Rebels (5-3) QB Jevan Snead (16-35/175y, TD, 2 INTs), returning 29y to EZ for 24-7 edge. After Mississippi punted, Tigers scored when RB Ben Tate (25/144y, TD) raced 53y TD 3 plays later. Rout seemed to be full-fledged, at least until Auburn kicked off: Rebs CB Jesse Grandy returned KO 82y for TD. Rebels D forced 3-and-out, and RB Dexter McCluster (22/186y, TD) took off down left sideline 79y for TD to pull within 31-20. But Auburn halted surge on blocked x-pt by DE Antonio Coleman (5 tackles, 2 sacks, forced FUM) returned long-distance by CB Demond Washington for 2 pts. Tigers were not home free just yet as Rebels CB Marshay Green returned punt 29y to Auburn 46YL, but Rebs destructed on RB Brandon Bolden's FUM. All of this action came in 3rd Q, and Ole Miss only had to wait until early in 4th Q for another great opportunity on S Kendrick Lewis' sack of QB Chris Todd (12-22/212y, TD) to force FUM recovered by Rebels S Johnny Brown (10 tackles) at Auburn 24YL. But 3 plays each loss y, which coupled with holding PEN, forced Rebels to punt. With 5:21 left, Ole Miss surged again, but McFadden made his 2nd INT at Auburn 6YL.

IOWA 42 Indiana 24: Indiana Hoosiers (4-5), coming off disheartening 28-3 blown lead in 29-28 loss at Northwestern, scored on opening drive as RB Darius Willis (21/54y, TD) tallied on 4y run. QB Ben Chappell (23-41/227y, 2 TDs, 3 INTs) hit 2 TD passes in 2nd Q, latter coming in last 9 secs after star DE Jammie Kerlaw fell on punt FUM at Hawkeyes 12YL. In 3rd Q, Indiana was knocking on door to go up 28-7, but on bizarre play Iowa (9-0) S Tyler Sash, nation's INT leader, snatched blocked pass that caromed off 4 players in tight quarters and galloped away on 86y INT TD RET. In wild 3rd Q, Hoosiers lost pair of replay reversals on apparent TD passes by Chappell and missed chip-shot FG. Still, Hoosiers led 24-14 because they grabbed 4 INTs with wind at their back in 3rd Q. Having just thrown his 5th INT, Hawkeyes QB Ricky Stanzi (13-26/337y, 2 TDs, 5 INTs) rolled out early in 4th Q and shot pass to crossing WR Marvin McNutt (4/155y, TD), who pulled away for 92y TD. On Stanzi's next throw with 11:38 left, he hit streaking WR Derrell Johnson-Koulianos for 66y TD and Hawks' 1st back in at 28-24. After Iowa CB Shaun Prater made INT, frosh RB Brandon Wegher (25/118y, 3 TDs) burst up middle for 6y TD halfway through 4th Q and followed it up with 27y TD run.

Texas 41 OKLAHOMA STATE 14: Against Cowboys (6-2) who were unbeaten in Big 12 play, superb D keyed no. 3 Texas (8-0) to big 1st H lead as it forced 5 TOs, including career-worst 4 INTs thrown by Oklahoma State QB Zac Robinson (15-28/143y, TD, 4 INTs). Pair of Longhorns DBs—CB Curtis Brown (77y RET) and S Earl Thomas (31y RET)—each returned INT for TD. Also, Texas recovered FUM in 1st Q to set up its 1st TD, 1 of 2 short runs scored by big RB Cody Johnson (9/31y, 2 TDs). Behind 17-0, Cowboys traveled 84y as Robinson clicked on 3 passes and RB Keith Toston (19/70y) chipped in with 22y run to poise RB Beau Johnson for short TD run. Texas QB Colt McCoy (16-21/171y, TD) was at his best in leading 80y TD trip in 2:09 to beat H clock with his 100th career TD pass: WR Malcolm Williams neatly got toe down in back of EZ in last 9 secs for TD and 24-7 lead at intermission. When Steers rang up 17 pts—including Thomas' TD RET—in 3rd Q without response, they led 41-7.

TEXAS TECH 42 Kansas 21: Last week's upset loss to Texas A&M still had Texas Tech (6-3) coach Mike Leach perturbed. In quantifying his players' overconfidence, he said their "fat little girlfriends are telling them how great [they] are and how easy it's going to be." Leach must have felt sarcasm stirring over this week's effort until Red Raiders RB Byron Batch (17/123y, 4 TDs) scored 3 of his TDs during 28-pt spree in 4th Q. Tech's late 4-TD surge wiped out 21-14 lead Kansas (5-3) had snatched late in 3rd Q when WR Desmon Briscoe (9/110y, TD) capped 10-play, 81y drive with 6y TD catch from QB Todd Reesing (20-35/181y, TD). Frosh QB Seth Doege (14-28/159y, TD) made his 1st start for Raiders and coughed up pair of FUMs that led to Jayhawks' 1st 2 TDs. In 1st Q, Doege was sacked by DE Jeff Wheeler, and DE Maxwell Onyegbule picked up loose ball to step into EZ for TD and 7-0 lead. Late in 2nd Q, Doege lost FUM at his 2YL to set up TD plunge by Kansas RB Toben Opurum. In between, Doege launched 61y TD pass to WR Detron Lewis for 7-7 deadlock.

OREGON 47 Southern California 20: Of its remarkable 613y O, Oregon (7-1) powered and dodged for 391y rushing against USC's suddenly-vulnerable D as QB Jeremiah Masoli (19-31/222y, TD and 13/164y, TD rushing) playing masterful ringleader. Masoli scored early TD and scrambled 48y late in 2nd Q to set up his TD pass for 24-17 lead. Ducks frosh RB LaMichael James ripped Trojans for 24/183y on ground with vital 33y dash down right sideline to key drive to 2nd Q TD for 17-10 advantage and 3rd Q TD run that provided 34-20 lead. Southern California (6-2) hung close in 1st H, tying it 3 times, including squirming 2nd-effort plunge into EZ for 17-17 deadlock with 3:17 left in 2nd Q by WR Damian Williams (9/82y, TD) on 4y pass from QB Matt Barkley (21-38/187y, 2 TDs, INT). Ducks owned 2nd H, their 1st 3 drives going 62y to K Morgan Flint's 2nd of 4 FGs, 80y to James' 5y TD run, and 80y to another short TD run up middle by frosh RB Kenjon Barner. Oregon led 41-20 at end of 3rd Q. "It was intense," Oregon CB Talmadge Jackson said of raucous Autzen Stadium: "Halloween, USC, crazy night game, it was everything everyone expected it would be." "It was a real mess for us tonight," said Pete Carroll, who suffered his worst loss so far in 9 years as Troy coach.

November 7, 2009

CINCINNATI 47 Connecticut 45: Broken-hearted UConn Huskies (4-5), still mourning death of popular CB Jasper Howard, lost their 3rd straight nail-biter but gave undefeated no. 7 Bearcats (9-0) plenty of heart palpitations. Cincinnati was saved by super-sub QB Zach Collaros (29-37/480y, TD and 13/79y, 2 TDs rushing), throwing for 2nd-most y in school history in his 3rd replacement start for injured QB Tony Pike. Collaros passed for 447y through 3 Qs as Bearcats built 37-24 lead. Thereafter Huskies rallied to within 2 pts with 87y punt TD RET by CB Robert McClain and pair of TD runs by TB Jordan Todman (26/162y, 4 TDs). Collaros hit 4-4/33y on game clinching drive to 14y TD run on 4th-and-1 by RB Isaiah Pead (10/67y, 2 TDs) that gave Cincinnati 47-38 lead with less than 2 mins remaining. Huskies QB Zach Frazer (19-32/261y, TD) still had time for TD on his 9y pass to WR Marcus Easley (6/87y, TD), but ensuing on-side-KO failed. Frazer was 9-12/137y, TD in 4th Q. Cincinnati gained school-record 711y, with Collaros setting new mark with 559y combined rushing and passing. Having thrown 66-82/1028y in 3 starts, he would be cast to bench when Pike returned to health. WRs Mardy Gilyard (12/172y) and Armon Binns (5/108y, TD) made life easier for Collaros, while Gilyard added 144y on KO RETs.

NORTH CAROLINA 19 Duke 6: In 1st game in 15 years with both teams showing winning record, North Carolina (6-3) impressively allowed only 125y and 11 1st downs to resurgent Blue Devils (5-4), who entered game averaging 440y in 3 straight wins. Tied 6-6 at H as Duke K Nick Maggio and UNC K Casey Barth notched 2 FGs, Tar Heels edged ahead 9-6 on last play of 3rd Q as Barth booted 41y FG, set up by 54y

INT RET by CB Charles Brown. Thanks to sub TB Ryan Houston (37/164y), Carolina pulled away in 4th Q, as he ran for 55y on 12-play, 65y drive to 3y TD run by WR Jheranie Boyd that gave Heels 16-6 lead with 7 mins left. Houston, who came in early when TB Shaun Draughn was injured, threw key block to spring Boyd. QB Thaddeus Lewis (16-33/113y, INT), who emerged as Blue Devils' all-time pass y leader in his sr year, was unable to get anything going against UNC pressure: DE Robert Quinn paced Tar Heels D with 7 tackles, 3 sacks, 6 QB hurries, and forced FUM.

GEORGIA TECH 30 Wake Forest 27 (OT): After quartet of 4th down failures including gutsy midfield try in 4th Q, Georgia Tech (9-1) was overdue in OT. In extra session, after Demon Deacons (4-6) K Jimmy Newman (2 FGs) booted 34y FG, Georgia Tech drove to 5YL and faced 4th-and-inches. Confidently passing up tying FG, Yellow Jackets sent QB Josh Nesbitt (4-14/51y, INT and 21/54y, 2 TDs rushing) up middle for 2y and 1st down. Nesbitt's 3y TD run on next play won it. After RB Preston Lyons' 1st Q 31y TD run had made it 10-0, Yellow Jackets looked to pull away early, as they were outgaining Wake 135y to 4y by. But games go longer than 9 mins, and Deacs took over rest of 1st H by reeling off 17 pts with TDs by FB Kevin Harris and WR Devon Brown (7/62y, 2 TDs). QB Riley Skinner (26-40/263y, 2 TDs) was combined 11-12/105y on TD-producing drives. Jackets tied it 17-17 early in 3rd Q when RB Jonathan Dwyer (23/189y, TD) took pitch on team's opening snap of H and raced 59y to pay-dirt. With Tech D settled in, Wake earned only single 1st down in 3rd Q, while Jackets had multiple opportunities. But consecutive drives ended on 4th down in Wake territory, and Georgia Tech had to wait until middle of 4th Q to score, going 80y—avoiding 4th downs along way—to tally on 12y keeper by Nesbitt. Skinner answered with 11y TD pass to Brown. Facing late 50y FG try, coach Paul Johnson gambled again on 4th down, but Nesbitt was sacked by LB Hunter Haynes at Wake 41YL. Wake had min to score, but sack by Jackets DE Derrick Morgan ended threat. Wake Forest's season now had 5 losses by 3 pts or fewer.

ALABAMA 24 Louisiana State 15: With Bama's excellent play this year, it was easy to forget much was read into Tide's 2-game losing streak at end of 2008. No. 3 Crimson Tide (9-0) ground out tough win over LSU (7-2) with 14 pts in 4th Q to put it away. Win secured SEC West title and conf rematch with Florida with month to go. LSU controlled its destiny: victories today and in last 2 SEC games would have delivered West crown. Tigers played hard, building 15-10 4th Q lead that was difficult to protect given 3rd Q injuries to QB Jordan Jefferson (10-17/114y, TD) and RB Charles Scott (13/83y). Without its O leaders, LSU gained only 9y in 4th Q, with 2 punts and INT allowed by backup QB Jarrett Lee (4-10/44y, INT). Alabama, meanwhile, got 2 FGs from K Leigh Tiffin and 73y TD pass catch by WR Julio Jones (4/102y) and 2-pt conv run by RB Trent Richardson. Jones caught his scoring pass behind line of scrimmage, juked away from sub CB Brandon Taylor to race down left sideline. Tiffin's 2nd FG of 4th Q, which closed scoring, occurred because officials overruled Tigers CB Patrick Peterson's sideline INT due to foot on line. From start, LSU had loaded box to stop Tide TB Mark Ingram (22/144y), who was held to 38y in 1st H. Bama QB Greg McElroy (19-34/276y, 2 TDs, INT) was forced to throw 25 times in 1st H, not his strong suit, but Tigers D eventually was worn down as Ingram pounded for 106y in 2nd H. "It was a tough, physical game," said Alabama coach Nick Saban, who beat his former team for 2nd straight year. "Man, those games are fun to be a part of."

ARKANSAS 33 South Carolina 16: Game was tight—10-10 at H—until Arkansas (5-4) QB Ryan Mallett (23-27/329y) went nearly perfect in 2nd H by hitting 12-13/160y to spark game's final 23 pts. With Hogs trailing 16-10 in 3rd Q, Mallett scored on 1y keeper for go-ahead TD. He missed his 1st pass on that march, but then hit 2-2/44y. After Razorbacks CB Jerell Norton picked off EZ INT to halt next series by South Carolina (6-4), Mallett went 3-3/62y on 80y drive for 24-16 lead on RB Broderick Green's TD run. Mallett next went 3-3/26y but was unable to sustain drive because of 8y sack against him. After 38y punt RET by Norton set up Razorbacks at 37YL, Mallett hit 4-4/28y as Arkansas scored clincher on Green's 3y TD run. Gamecocks' sole 2nd H score had come early in 3rd Q on spectacular play: QB Stephen Garcia (20-34/327y, TD, INT) found WR Alshon Jeffery (5/116y, TD) over middle, and frosh outraced 3 defenders for 80y TD and 16-10 lead. Gamecocks missed x-pt kick, which served as omen: they had 4 failed possessions rest of 2nd H, including Garcia's errant EZ INT and snap flying over his head into EZ for safety. Loss was 2nd straight and 3rd in last 4 games for self-destructing South Carolina.

Ohio State 24 PENN STATE 7: Ohio State Buckeyes (8-2) suddenly had own fate in their hands as Iowa lost earlier in afternoon, and DE Cameron Heyward, son of Pittsburgh's former All-America "Ironhead" Heyward, sparked superior play by both Ohio State lines. Early in 1st Q, Buckeyes WR Ray Small took short punt for 41y RET to 9YL, and QB Terrelle Pryor (8-17/125y, 2 TDs) zoomed 7y for TD by squirting away from tackle by Penn State (8-2) LB Navorro Bowman. Nittany Lions fashioned smooth 71y march in 2nd Q, but it took QB Daryll Clark (12-28/125y, INT) barely nosing ball across GL on 4th down sneak to tie it 7-7. Buckeyes K Devin Barclay, 26-year-old former Columbus Crew MLS player, booted 37y FG for 10-7 lead at H. D slugfest marked 2nd H until Buckeyes took over with less than 2 mins to go in 3rd Q. On 1st down, Pryor launched bomb for his best receiver, WR DeVier Posey, who collected pass up left side for 62y TD and 17-7 edge. Small made 45y punt RET on last play of 3rd Q to set up Pryor's short TD pass to RB Brandon Saine. Quiet key to outcome: Penn State permitted 228y rushing, most against Lions D in more than 5 years.

Northwestern 17 IOWA 10: Sports Illustrated jinx struck once again after no. 6 Iowa (9-1) was trumpeted on magazine cover this week as "still undefeated." Jinxed or not, Hawkeyes smoothly moved to 10-0 lead as QB Ricky Stanzi (4-9/134y, TD, INT) pitched perfect 74y post-pattern to WR Marvin McNutt. But early in 2nd Q from his 6YL, Stanzi was hammered by twisting tackle by Northwestern (6-4) star DE Corey Wootton on ill-fated bootleg pass. Wildcats DT Marshall Thomas (2 FUM RECs) swooped in to fall on Stanzi's EZ FUM for TD, and Stanzi was knocked out with right ankle sprain. Frosh QB James Vandenberg (9-27/82y, INT) had to come on for Iowa with only 3 career pass attempts under his belt, immediately threw INT to set up Northwestern's go-ahead TD, and Hawkeyes could penetrate NW territory only once during last 3 Qs. It occurred when Vandenberg hit 3 passes, but K Daniel Murray, who made 39y FG in 1st Q, missed from 46y out. Northwestern also lost its starting QB Mike Kafka, whose normally fine running already was hamstrung by bad hamstring. With Kafka shelved, Wildcats backup QB Dan Persa (5-9/37y, TD, INT) tallied on short slant-in throw to WR Drake Dunsmore for 14-10 lead with 5:20 to go in 1st H. Iowa had trailed in 4th Q in 4 of its 9 wins, but it was out of miracles: only pts of 2nd H came early in 4th Q on FG by Cats K Stefan Demos which was plenty long enough from 47y away.

Wisconsin 31 INDIANA 28: All season Indiana (4-6) had been close, but not having quite enough. This time Hoosiers lost their 3rd Big 10 game by total of 7 pts. Meanwhile, no. 22 Badgers (7-2) pounded it on ground for another win. TB John Clay barreled for 15/134y and 2nd Q TD before concussion knocked him out for 2nd H. That turned battering duties over to back-up TB Montee Ball (27/115y, 2 TDs), who scored twice, including decisive 3y TD run with 8:18 to play. Ball gleefully said, "That's Wisconsin football: run the football and just beat your opponents up, and that's what we did." Hoosiers QB Ben Chappell kept pitching for 25-35/323y, 3 TDs, 2 INTs, and WR Tandon Doss (6/92y, 2 TDs) soared high to snatch 46y TD pass to pull Indiana within 17-14 with 2:32 to go before H. Badgers QB Scott Tolzien (11-20/194y, TD) threw it just enough, including 44y connection to WR Nick Toon that set up Ball's important 4th Q TD and 17y again to Toon to help extinguish game's last 4:01.

Navy 23 NOTRE DAME 21: Playing with poise, underrated Navy (7-3), fresh off upset loss to Temple, beat Notre Dame (6-3) and shoved Fighting Irish's Charlie Weis back on coaching hot seat. Win was 2nd straight at Notre Dame Stadium for Middies, who forced 3 TOs and enjoyed 4th down stop at their 3YL in 2nd Q. Navy DE Craig Schaefer (9 tackles) secured win with min remaining by sacking Notre Dame QB Jimmy Clausen (37-51/452y, 2 TDs, INT) for safety that lifted lead to 23-14. After Notre Dame WR Golden Tate (9/132y, TD) recovered ensuing onside free-kick, Clausen took 3 plays and 36 secs before finding Tate with 31y TD pass. But Irish could not recover onside-KO. QB Ricky Dobbs had another great game at helm of Navy's option attack, rushing 31/102y with opening 1y TD run and throwing 2-3/56y with stunning 52y TD pass to WR Greg Jones for 21-7 edge in 3rd Q. Clausen set career highs in pass y, attempts, and new school mark for completions. But, ND squandered it as K Nick Tausch missed pair of 1st H FGs, after having hit 14 in row, and Irish lost 2 TOs within Navy 10YL to spoil consecutive 2nd H drives. Navy FB Vince Murray (14/158y, TD) was game-high rusher, while LB Ram Vela had 9 tackles, FUM REC, and INT.

NEBRASKA 10 Oklahoma 3: No longer annual match of old Big 8 rivals, this was 1st visit by Sooners (5-4) to Lincoln since 2006. For its part, Cornhuskers (6-3) hadn't beaten Oklahoma since 2001. Outgained 325y to 180y, Nebraska overcame its remedial O and got 5 INTs—including trio by S Matt O'Hanlon—and rush D that averaged 2.8y per carry against it. Oklahoma QB Landry Jones (26-58/245y, 5 INTs) threw INT early in 2nd Q that Big Red CB Prince Amukamara returned 23y to 1YL. On next play, QB Zac Lee came off bench to loft 1y TD pass to TE Ryan Hill. Despite its O output, Sooners penetrated 20YL only once and it resulted in 24y FG by K Tress Way in 2nd Q. O'Hanlon returned 3rd Q INT 30y to set up K Alex Henery's 28y FG and went high in game's last 30 secs to snare clinching pick at his own 6YL.

COLORADO 35 Texas A&M 34: Even though Colorado (3-6) QB Tyler Hansen (21-32/271y, TD, INT) was sacked 8 times, he managed to overcome 2nd-and-25 predicament to lead 61y sortie to winning 7 pts late in 4th Q. Texas A&M (5-4) QB Jerrod Johnson (20-36/242y, TD, INT) passed and ran for TDs in 1st H and RB Cyrus Gray dashed 99y on KO TD RET in 2nd Q to boost Aggies to 21-10 H edge. Leading 31-28 with just more than 7 mins to play, A&M looked in good shape to clinch after Gray returned KO to near midfield and late hit OB was tacked on to Buffs 40YL. Drive stalled at 3YL, however, so Aggies K Randy Bullock knocked through 20y FG for 34-28 lead. Down 6 pts with 3:53 left, Colorado took over on its 39YL, but Buffs soon faced long odds after suffering procedure PEN and allowing Aggies LB Von Miller to earn his 2nd sack of game for 15.5, topping national list for season. After Hansen's shovel pass made 9y, he found WR Markques Simas (7/135y) for 45y and TE Patrick Devenny for 22y TD. K Aric Goodman put winning kick on board with 2:04 to go.

AIR FORCE 35 Army 7: Underdog Army (3-6) held on to 7-7 deadlock through 1st H as frosh QB Trent Steelman (18/102y, TD rushing) burst 42y for TD to match 88y punt TD RET by Falcons CB Anthony Wright. With Air Force (6-4) holding 14-7 lead late in 3rd Q and Black Knights playing 9-men-in-the-box to halt Falcons' running attack, tall Air Force WR Kevin Fogler broke loose for pass reception at midfield. Fogler deked single Army tackler and was away for 73y TD and 21-7 edge. Tiring Cadets could gain only 5 and 4y on their next 2 series, while they permitted 2 all-land assaults—except for 23y catch by Fogler—that netted TD run by Air Force QB Tim Jefferson (4-7/131y, TD) and 2nd scoring romp for RB Asher Clark (13/82y, 2 TDs).

Houston 46 TULSA 45: Tulsa (4-5), coming off 3 straight losses, struck 1st on 3y TD run by FB Charles Clay (4 TDs), and with game tied 14-14 in 2nd Q, Houston (8-1) got break on unusual reviewed play ruled as incomplete pass: QB Case Keenum (40-60/522y, 3 TDs) and RB Tyron Carrier (98y KO TD RET) lost handle on (forward) handoff that Carrier had to fall on in his EZ. Instead of Golden Hurricane taking 16-14 lead on safety and possession on free-kick, Cougars were able to move downfield to FG that provided 17-14 lead. Stubborn Hurricane built 38-34 lead as QB G.J. Kinne (19-25/339y, 3 TDs, 2 INTs and 16/100y rushing) tossed scoring pass in each of 1st 3 Qs, and Tulsa stopped Houston drive at their 1YL in 4th Q. In late going, Tulsa added Clay's 2nd TD run after Kinne scrambled twice for good gains. Trailing 45-37, Cougars started drive from own 39YL with 3:28 to play in 4th Q. Masterful Keenum clicked on 4th down pass near midfield on way to his 1y TD out-cut throw to WR James Cleveland (12/167y, 3 TDs). That pulled Cougars within 45-43 with 21 secs left. On 2-pt pass, Tulsa LB Tanner Antle blitzed off blind side and sacked Keenum without being touched

by blockers. That appeared to wrap it up for Hurricane until on-side KO bounced out of hands of Tulsa frosh DB Dexter McCoil to Houston WR Tim Monroe. Cool frosh K Matt Hogan, whose career-long FG was 34y since winning job just weeks earlier, nailed winning 51y 3-ptr. Inattentive officiating had marked closing mins as flags could easily have been thrown often: Tulsa D bought plenty of useless rest because players on several occasions appeared to fake injuries for clock stoppages, Houston OT Jarve Dean rose early out of his 2-pt stance just prior to snap on Keenum's last TD pass, and Cougars once broke huddle with 12 players on winning FG drive.

STANFORD 51 Oregon 42: Having rolled for 30-pt margins in 5 straight Pac-10 victories, Oregon (7-2) may have been nation's hottest team. But vastly-improved, home-standing Stanford (6-3) slugged it out to 10-0 lead midway in 1st Q on 1y TD run by TB Toby Gerhart (38/school-record 233y, 3 TDs) and never trailed despite 13 more scores in game. Tilt turned out as magnificent O show with Ducks flying to 570y and Cardinal to 505y. In 1st Q, RB LaMichael James (18/125y, TD) found enormous hole up middle and dashed 60y to TD that pulled Oregon within 10-7. Ducks QB Jeremiah Masoli (21-37/334y, 3 TDs and 10/55y, TD rushing) managed to slice deficits to 38-28 in 3rd Q on 3y TD run and to 48-42 with 2:38 to play on 21y TD pass to WR D.J. Davis. But, Cardinal recovered onside-KO and tacked on K Nate Whitaker's 48y FG—on bit of gamble by Stanford coach Jim Harbaugh—with 11 secs left. Victory promoted Stanford to bowl eligibility for 1st time since 2001.

SOUTHERN CALIFORNIA 14 Arizona State 9: Frustrated Sun Devils (4-5) gained 347y to 258y and outplayed long-time Pac-10 beast, USC (7-2), itself coming off ruinous D effort against Oregon. Arizona State took opening series to Trojans 12YL before fumbling, settled for K Thomas Weber's short FG in 2nd Q, and QB Danny Sullivan (12-23/113y, 2 INTs) threw ill-advised wide pass late in 2nd Q intercepted by Southern California LB Will Harris for easy 55y TD RET. USC made it 14-3 after 2nd H KO when QB Matt Barkley (7-22/112y, TD, INT) found WR Damian Johnson on right-to-left crossing pattern which Johnson carried 75y for TD. To great delight of perturbed ASU fans, coach Dennis Erickson opened 2nd H with frosh Brock Osweiler (11-27/123y, TD, INT) at QB. Osweiler brought fire to Devils O and enjoyed some good moments, especially when he hit 15 and 27y passes and ran 6y to set up his 23y TD lob to sprinting WR Chris McGaha late in 3rd Q. But from moment Trojans blocked x-pt, Devils faded as Osweiler hit only 1 of his next 11 pass tries and was sacked twice. ASU fizzled on 4th Q chance at USC 36YL after S Clint Floyd's much-deflected INT.

USA TODAY Coaches Poll November 8, 2009

1 Florida (48)	1460	14 Utah	688
2 Texas (4)	1399	15 Miami	685
3 Alabama (7)	1389	16 Oregon	665
4 Texas Christian	1262	17 Penn State	552
5 Cincinnati	1224	18 Oklahoma State	530
6 Boise State	1200	19 Arizona	472
7 Georgia Tech	1188	20 Wisconsin	341
8 Ohio State	944	21 Virginia Tech	268
9 Pittsburgh	940	22 Brigham Young	216
10 Southern California	847	23 West Virginia	121
11 Louisiana State	838	24 South Florida	106
12 Houston	766	25 Auburn	80
13 Iowa	757		

Bowl Championship Series Rankings November 8, 2009

	Harris Poll Avg.	USA TODAY Poll Avg.	Computer Pct.	BCS Avg.
1 Florida (9-0)	.9828	.9898	.980	.9842
2 Alabama (9-0)	.9432	.9417	.970	.9516
3 Texas (9-0)	.9516	.9585	.870	.9234
4 Texas Christian (9-0)	.8505	.8556	.880	.8620
5 Cincinnati (9-0)	.8340	.8298	.910	.8580

November 14, 2009

(Fri) CINCINNATI 24 West Virginia 21: Undefeated Bearcats (10-0) welcomed injured QB Tony Pike (2-4/16y 2 TDs) back as brief but effective contributor. He came in twice in scoring position to fire 10y and 6y TDs to WRs Armon Binns (5/62y, TD) and D.J. Woods respectively. Pike wasn't all that necessary as soph Zach Collaros (17-24/205y, INT) was efficient leading Cincy's solid O even if it was error-prone in 1st H. Bearcats lost their 1st FUM all season—and it led to tying 1st Q TD by West Virginia (7-3) QB Jarrett Brown (17-25/188y, TD) on scramble up middle—dropped pass in EZ, missed FG, and suffered Collaros' INT. WVU TB Ryan Clarke powered off LT out of I-formation on 3rd-and-2 to rumble 37y to TD for Mountaineers' only lead at 14-7 in middle of 2nd Q. Game's biggest play came from Cincy RB Isaiah Pead (18/175y, TD), who went airborne from WVU 3YL but lost ball at peak of his flight. TV replay appeared inconclusive, but officials decided Pead had broken GL plane for 14-14 deadlock at H. Pike's 2nd TD pass in 3rd Q and K Jake Rogers' 38y FG with 2:08 to go in 4th Q gave Cincinnati breathing room at 24-14, but Brown scrambled left to fire TD pass with 39 secs left to narrow it to 3 pts. Binns collected West Virginia's onside-KO attempt to keep Bearcats unbeaten. RB Noel Devine was held reasonably in check with 25/88y rushing but become 5th Mountaineers runner to top 3000y in career.

PITTSBURGH 27 Notre Dame 22: Notre Dame (6-4) authored familiar story, rallying late only to come up short at game's end. No. 9 Pittsburgh (9-1), continuing its climb up rankings, unleashed balanced attack (193y rushing and 236y passing) to build 27-9 lead before holding on with help of controversial call. After Notre Dame WR Golden Tate (9/113y, TD) scored twice within 2 mins of 4th Q on 18y catch and 87y punt RET, Irish had last chance to pull out late win, beginning at own 20YL with 3:39 remaining. But after QB Jimmy Clausen (27-42/283y, TD, INT) completed 3-3/22y, ND faced 2nd-and-16 and was ripe for Panthers' pass rushing specialist, DE Greg Romeus. His pressure forced Clausen to make weak throw-away. After review, FUM REC by Pitt DT Myles Caragein was ruled, and game essentially was over. "We got a little scare, but we always have confidence in our defense to make a big stop and they did," said TB Dion Lewis (21/152y, TD), whose 50y TD run closed scoring for Panthers early in 4th Q. Pittsburgh 6'5" WR Jonathan Baldwin (5/142y, TD) had 2 exceptional catches, including stretching 36y TD that gave Panthers 10-3 lead in 2nd Q. In 3rd Q, Baldwin leapt to haul in 51y pass from QB Bill Stull (15-27/236y, TD) that set up FG for 13-3 lead. Pitt TB Ray Graham made 53y run in 3rd Q that set up his own 2y TD run for 20-3 lead. Pitt improved to 9-1 for 1st time since 1982.

Georgia Tech 49 DUKE 10: It took most of 1st Q for Yellow Jackets (10-1) to get in gear, but once they did Georgia Tech put on 519y total-O clinic in subduing Duke (5-5) and wrapping up ACC Coastal crown. Georgia Tech gained only 18y on its 1st 11 snaps, but thanks to RB Orwin Smith's 84y KO RET followed by 2y TD keeper by QB Josh Nesbitt (6-10/195y, 2 TDs and 9/30y, TD rushing) it trailed only 10-7 late in 1st Q. On final play of 1st Q, RB Jonathan Dwyer (14/110y, 2 TDs) raced 46y and Tech finally was motoring. Game was getting away from Blue Devils, who were unable to garner single 1st down in decisive 2nd Q. Ga Tech RB Marcus Wright's 18y TD run was followed by Nesbitt's 37y completion to RB Embry Peeples to launch 66y drive for 21-10 lead on 2y TD run by Dwyer. Nesbitt gave Jackets 28-10 lead going into H break with 32y TD pass to WR Stephen Hill. Blue Devils continued to struggle in 2nd H as their longest drive went 46y and ended with 4th Q INT thrown by QB Thaddeus Lewis (22-35/212y, TD, INT) to CB Martin Frierson at Tech 22YL. Things had looked up for Dukies, searching for 1st bowl bid since 1994, on game's opening series when Lewis hit 5-5/54y with final 18y coming on TD pass to RB Re'quan Boyette. That 73y drive represented more than quarter of Duke's 281y game-long output.

Florida 24 SOUTH CAROLINA 14: Playing with torn biceps tendon, Florida (10-0) DE Justin Trattou helped deliver Gators' 20th straight victory by nabbing deflected pass by South Carolina (6-5) QB Stephen Garcia (17-32/186y, TD, 2 INTs) and racing 53y to set up 1y TD run by Florida QB Tim Tebow (14-25/199y, TD). It gave Gators 24-14 lead early in 4th Q and with D holding Gamecocks to 41y in 2nd H—with INT by CB Joe Haden (11 tackles, 2 forced FUMs, INT, sack) and 4 sacks in 4th Q—it proved enough to secure Florida's 1st perfect SEC regular season since 1996. Gamecocks trailed 17-14 when they managed only 1 good drive in 2nd H, on which Garcia converted 4th-and-2 with 6y run on way to to 22YL, but 2 plays later Garcia threw pass to WR Moe Brown deflected to Trattou. Florida's 2nd H D performance was in stark contrast to that of 1st H when South Carolina gained 206y and scored 14 pts. Tebow's TD run was his 53rd, tying him for tops in SEC history for overall TDs scored with former LSU's Kevin Faulk. Tebow also launched 68y TD pass to WR Riley Cooper (3/112y, TD). "We did not play perfect. I'm not sure we've played perfect in a while," said Florida coach Urban Meyer. "But that's 20 in a row and I'm awful proud of the guys in there." To honor injured military veterans, South Carolina wore black tops with words like "Courage" and "Integrity" on back in lieu of player names but had now lost 4 straight to Florida with former Gators player and coach Steve Spurrier at coaching helm.

MISSISSIPPI 42 Tennessee 17: All season long, fans of Ole Miss Rebels (7-3) had waited for O explosion. On this sunny day in Oxford, slender, fast Mississippi RB Dexter McCluster ran wild to school-record 282y rushing with TDs of 15, 23, 32, and 71y. Tennessee (5-5), having lost 3 frosh players earlier in week to armed robbery charges, looked flat, and although Vols tied it 7-7 and 14-14 on pair of 1st H TD passes by QB Jonathan Crompton (20-37/176y, 2 TDs) never seemed up to matching Ole Miss' energy. Tennessee's O couldn't match McCluster's numbers, gaining 275y with 99y rushing. McCluster's 32y TD run late in 2nd Q gave Rebels lead for good at 21-14, although Vols marched 49y after 2nd H KO to 28y FG by K Daniel Lincoln. By time Tennessee earned another 1st down early in 4th Q, score was at 35-17 as McCluster broke Vols' back with nifty 71y TD run. McCluster, who set record for most rushing y by Tennessee opponent, cracked Dou Innocent's 1995 single game rushing record, and his 324y broke Deuce McAllister's all-purpose school mark held since 1999. Win was Rebels' 1st over Volunteers since 1983, breaking 12-game losing streak.

OHIO STATE 27 Iowa 24 (OT): After its loss to Purdue, Ohio State (9-2) had appeared destined to miss out on its 5th straight solo or shared Big 10 title, but on heels of big win over Penn State, Buckeyes now held their destiny in own hands. Iowa (9-2), playing without QB Ricky Stanzi, got good performance from frosh QB James Vandenberg (20-33/233y, 2 TDs, 3 INTs), who directed late comeback to force OT. Buckeyes broke out of 10-10 tie at end of 3rd Q with pair of quick TDs: RB Daniel "Boom" Herron (32/97y, TD) took direct snap and went 11y to TD, and after Ohio State LB Russ Homan snatched INT, RB Brandon Saine (11/103y, 2 TDs) charged 49y down left sideline for 24-10 lead. Hawkeyes WR Derrell Johnson-Koulianos bounced wide with ensuing KO and went 99y to TD RET. Vandenberg hit WR Marvin McNutt (6/78y, TD) with tying TD with 2:42 left in regulation. In OT, Ohio State DT Doug Worthington sacked Iowa out of FG range, and Buckeyes K Devin Barclay, 26-year-old former Columbus Crew MLS soccer player, hit 39y FG to win it and clinch Rose Bowl bid.

Missouri 38 KANSAS STATE 12: Perhaps Kansas State (6-5) was looking ahead to Big 12 North showdown with Nebraska, 31-17 winner this week over Kansas. Holding half-game lead in North Division, Wildcats O fell on its face against up-and-down Missouri Tigers (6-4). Mizzou WR Danario Alexander (10/200y, 3 TDs), 1 of season's dynamic pass-catchers, caught long-range TDs of 54 and 80y from QB Blaine Gabbert (20-27/298y, 3 TDs), latter serving as killing tally in last min of 3rd Q that made it 24-12. Pair of 4th Q TOs by Wildcats led to 2 clinching TD runs by Missouri RB Derrick Washington (13/68y, 2 TDs). Kansas State saw its Big 12 leading rusher, RB Daniel Thomas, held to 23/79y on ground and was forced into 4 FGs by K Josh Cherry.

Texas 47 BAYLOR 14: QB Colt McCoy (23-34/181y, 2 TDs) lifted his Longhorns (10-0) career won-loss record to 42-7 to tie Georgia's David Greene (2001-04) for most wins in FBS history. WR Jordan Shipley (6/46y, 2 TDs) caught both of McCoy's TD passes. Yet, it was Texas' slumbering ground attack that awakened in easy rout of Baylor (4-6): RB Cody Johnson gained 109y and scored twice while RB Tre Newton sped 45y to TD among his 80y rushing. Mighty Longhorns D halted early threat in its EZ where

CB Aaron Williams made acrobatic INT and mystified Bears O by pushing them back -20y in 2nd Q. Texas extended its14-0 lead at end of 1st Q to 40-0 by H. Trailing 47-0, Baylor, which rushed only 28/6y, tallied 2 late TDs on short run by RB Terrance Ganaway and 19y TD pass by QB Nick Florence (28-45/240y, TD, 3 INTs).

TEXAS CHRISTIAN 55 Utah 28: No. 4 TCU (10-0) sported new-look, dark-silver helmets with thin red stripes arched back from crown to mimic blood spurt that real horned frog—not really frog at all but member of lizard family—oozes when riled up in its natural habitat. Riled up for this big tilt, Frogs romped 87y downfield on game's 1st possession to 41y TD burst up middle by RB Matthew Tucker (8/68y, 2 TDs). No. 14 Utah Utes (8-2), winners of 22 of their last 23 games and surprised to be 20-pt underdog, quickly exploited TCU's shanked 14y punt for 43y drive that tied it 7-7 as WR-turned-RB Shaky Smithson scored on draw run out of Wildcat formation, 1st of his pair of TD runs. Things soon went against Utes, however, as, on 3-and-out series, Horned Frogs star DE Jerry Hughes spilled runner for loss and sacked Utah frosh QB Jordan Wynn (16-32/219y, TD, INT). TCU LB Greg Burks immediately blocked punt at Utah 23YL, and WR Jeremy Kerley scored on sweep for 21-7 lead. Frogs dominated in building 38-14 H lead and crafted game-end total of 549y O. Key 1st H plays included Kerley's 39y punt RET and LB Tank Carder's 15y INT TD RET. Frogs QB Andy Dalton passed 17-29/207y, TD, INT and rushed 9/48y, while frosh RB Ed Wesley chipped in with 64y romp and ran for 137y and TD.

Stanford 55 SOUTHERN CALIFORNIA 21: Never had mighty Southern California (7-3) permitted so many pts in its proud history until dynamic Stanford (7-3) O arrived this Saturday. Cardinal gained 469y, including 325y rushing keyed by TB Toby Gerhart's 29/178y, 3 TDs. Stanford led only 28-21 at end of 3rd Q, as Trojans TB Joe McKnight (16/142y, TD) stormed 28y for score late in 3rd Q. But Cards romped to 27 unrequited 4th Q pts: QB Andrew Luck (12-22/144y, 2 TDs) found TE Coby Fleener with 24y TD pass and CB Richard Sherman, former WR, grabbed INT off USC QB Matt Barkley (21-31/196y, TD, 3 INTs) and galloped to 43y TD. Gerhart's 3rd TD run followed, and failed 2-pt run left Cardinal ahead 48-21 and Trojans coach Pete Carroll hot under collar for post-game handshake with Stanford's Jim Harbaugh.

CALIFORNIA 24 Arizona 16: Inspired by coin-toss participation by Jahvid Best, out with concussion, Golden Bears (7-3) rode back-up RB Shane Vereen's career-best 159y rushing and K Giorgio Tavecchio's lucky tackle after his go-ahead 4th FG with 4:46 to play. Arizona (6-3) WR Travis Cobb was bolting for good, perhaps great, KO RET when Tavacchio stuck out his leg. "Was that me?" he wondered, "I've never tackled anyone before." Wildcats still moved to 3rd-and-3 at Cal 25YL on 15 and 12y passes by QB Nick Foles (25-41/201y, TD, INT) with less than 2 mins to play. Foles had pass attempt swatted back in his hands and mistakenly fired another pass. Resulting spot-of-foul PEN left Arizona out of FG range. Upon taking over after 4th down incompletion, Cal sent Vereen speeding 61y to put game away at 24-16. Earlier in 4th Q, Foles had provided Cats with 16-15 lead with 8y TD pass to TE A.J. Simmons.

USA TODAY Coaches Poll November 15, 2009

1 Florida (48)	1460	14 Wisconsin	630
2 Texas (4)	1397	15 Iowa	584
3 Alabama (7)	1388	16 Virginia Tech	558
4 Texas Christian	1277	17 Stanford	516
5 Cincinnati	1219	18 Brigham Young	404
6 Boise State	1183	19 Clemson	274
7 Georgia Tech	1127	20 Oregon State	256
8 Ohio State	1019	21 Southern California	239
9 Pittsburgh	997	22 Houston	229
10 Louisiana State	956	23 Utah	212
11 Oregon	875	24 Miami	156
12 Penn State	772	25tNebraska	107
13 Oklahoma State	750	25tNorth Carolina	107

Bowl Championship Series Rankings November 15, 2009

	Harris Poll Avg.	USA TODAY Poll Avg.	Computer Pct.	BCS Avg.
1 Florida (10-0)	.9800	.9898	.980	.9833
2 Alabama (10-0)	.9453	.9410	.970	.9521
3 Texas (10-0)	.9512	.9471	.880	.9261
4 Texas Christian (10-0)	.8698	.8658	.870	.8685
5 Cincinnati (10-0)	.8242	.8264	.910	.8536

November 21, 2009

(Th) OKLAHOMA STATE 31 Colorado 28: Give credit to disappointing Colorado (3-8) for playing with pride. Cowboys (9-2) played mostly without their top 3 O performers when star QB Zac Robinson couldn't make go of it, joining suspended WR Dez Bryant and occasional participant, RB Kendall Hunter (11/47y). Oklahoma State struck 1st as CB Perrish Cox spun and weaved 67y to punt TD RET less than 3 mins into 1st Q. Buffaloes took 14-10 lead to H when QB Cody Hawkins (7-11/69y, TD) came off bench for QB Tyler Hansen (23-36/169y, 2 TDs) to engineer 7-play, 64y TD trip in 44 secs to TE Riar Geer's 5y scoring catch, while Cowpokes were struggling without single pass completion in 1st H. At H, Cowpokes coach Mike Gundy pulled 2nd-string QB Alex Cate (0-9, INT) in favor of QB Brandon Weeden (10-15/168y, 2 TDs), former New York Yankees minor league pitcher, who showed right stuff in 2nd H. Weeden's pitching overcame 21-10 deficit, and Oklahoma State took lead at 24-21 when he slipped short pass between pair of blitzers to RB Keith Toston (30/172y, TD and 2/45y, TD receiving), who raced 47y to TD. Although little RB Brian Lockridge put Colorado right back in front with 98y KO TD RET, Weeden tossed winning TD pass with 8:11 to play.

SYRACUSE 31 Rutgers 13: Ambitious Scarlet Knights (7-3) traveled to Big East cellar-dweller Syracuse (4-7) and laid egg. Blitzing Orange D sacked frosh QB Tom Savage (7-17/66y, 2 INTs) 9 times in allowing only 130y O, while Syracuse employed hurry-up tactics in gaining 424y O, 112y more than season avg. In decisive 1st H, Syracuse outscored Rutgers 24-10 while outgaining visitors 259y to 82y. Pair of Orange defenders sparkled: LB Doug Hogue forced FUM and recorded 7 tackles, including school-record 6.5 for loss with 3.5 sacks, while S Mike Holmes contributed 2 crucial INTs to stub Rutgers threats. On play right after Holmes' 2nd INT quelled last-gasp rally in 4th Q, Syracuse RB Averin Collier (6/66y, TD), who had gained 14y all season, closed scoring with 60y TD. QB Greg Paulus, enjoying his 2nd Senior Day after playing with Duke basketball team last winter, completed 13-16/142y with 2y TD pass to TE Carl Cutler for 21-2 lead in 2nd Q. On ensuing series, WR Tim Brown (4/67y, TD) scored Scarlet Knights' sole TD on 38y catch of pass from fellow WR Mohamed Sanu.

CLEMSON 34 Virginia 21: When North Carolina upset Boston College 31-13 earlier in day, Clemson (8-3), which gloomily stood at 2-3 in early October, could celebrate 6th straight win and 1st-ever trip to ACC title game. Dynamic RB C.J. Spiller (19/58y, TD), whose no. 28 was to be retired by Clemson, was serenaded near end of home finale as his 2066y set conf mark for single-season all-purpose y. With Virginia focused on Spiller, Clemson QB Kyle Parker (19-26/234y, 2 TDs) and sr WR Jacoby Ford (6/106y, TD) excelled. In looking to snap 4-game losing streak, Cavaliers (3-8) made things interesting in 1st H by scoring whopping—for them—21 pts to trail by 3. Virginia did some interesting things on O in 1st H, with QB-turned-WR Vic Hall's 30y TD pass to QB Jameel Sewell (11-17/160y, TD) off double reverse. Cavs reverted to form in 2nd H and were blanked while earning only 35y and 3 1st downs. Clemson coach Dabo Swinney received automatic $1 million raise for winning division title.

MISSISSIPPI 25 Louisiana State 23: Butchering game's final moments, Louisiana State (8-3) was scrambling about at Mississippi 6YL trying everything but potential winning FG. "I don't know what all happened down there at the end," said Rebels (8-3) coach Houston Nutt after his 4th straight coaching win over LSU, "I just know the scoreboard read: 25-23, Ole Miss Rebels." Rebels TB Dexter McCluster rushed 24/148y and threw 1st career pass for 27y TD to wide-open WR Shay Hodge (7/117y, TD) that provided 22-17 lead with 13:33 remaining. Mississippi later wasted more than 8 mins to drive 60y to 23y FG by K Joshua Shene to lift lead to 25-17. In last 2 mins, Tigers QB Jordan Jefferson (19-37/250y, 2 TDs, INT) delivered 25y TD pass to WR Reuben Randle. LSU went for tying 2 pts and had 2 cracks at it, thanks to PEN on Rebs CB Cassius Vaughn, but both pass tries failed. However, Tigers WR Brandon LaFell (5/75y) recovered onside-KO, and Tigers had last shot with 1:16 left. LaFell took short pass, broke 2 tackles, and raced 26y to Rebels 32YL, but LSU decided against calling runs to set up FG. On 2nd down Jefferson was sacked out of FG range by DE Emmanuel Stephens, his 2nd of game. Jefferson, who hit 8-15/120y in 4th Q, soon faced 4th-and-26 after another loss. LSU coaches called timeout to everyone but officials, so clocked ticked down to 9 secs before Jefferson threw desperate 42y pass to WR Terrance Toliver (5/107y) at 6YL. With clock stopped 1 sec to go and chain gang in confusion, LSU could have and should have used its last timeout because FG unit wasn't ready. Instead, Jefferson tried to spike ball, but clock expired.

Ohio State 21 MICHIGAN 10: Careful Buckeyes (10-2) seemed well aware of Michigan's past upsets in bitter Big 10 rivalry, such as 9-3 surprise in wicked blizzard that snatched Rose Bowl bid in 1950 and 24-12 upset that ended no. 1 Ohio State's 22-game winning streak in 1969. This time, Ohio State DE Cameron Heyward, son of late, former Pittsburgh All-America Craig Heyward, came up with big early play: Scrambling from pressure in his own EZ, Michigan (5-7) QB Tate Forcier (23-38/226y, TD, 4 INTs) dropped ball, and Heyward vacuumed it off GL and pulled it back into EZ for TD REC and 7-0 lead. That lead permitted coach Jim Tressel, now 8-1 in his Scarlet-and-Gray career versus Wolverines, to mine his rushing game, which outgained UM by 251y to 80y. For its part, Michigan was forced to pass so often that it coughed up 4 INTs in 4th Q—2 inside Buckeyes EZ and 10YL—to doom comeback bid. Ohio State received 29y TD run from RB Brandon Saine (12/84y, TD) in 2nd Q for 14-3 edge and 12y TD catch by RB Boom Herron (19/96y) of deft screen pass from QB Terrelle Pryor (9-17/67y, TD, INT and 19/74y rushing) late in 3rd Q for 21-10 lead. Buckeyes' 6th straight series win meant they had tied longest victory string in history—Michigan won 6 in row in 1922-27—and locked up undisputed Big 10 title.

NORTHWESTERN 33 Wisconsin 31: Wildcats (8-4), TD underdog, got off to good start at 10-0 and 17-14 as QB Mike Kafka (26-40/326y, 2 TDs) and WR Andrew Brewer (6/102y, 2 TDs) connected twice on TD passes, latter 12y diving slant-in grab in 2nd Q by Brewer. Northwestern got ball back 2 mins later, and WR Zeke Markshausen took wide, overhand lateral from Kafka and launched surprise 38y TD pass to WR Sidney Stewart. Wisconsin (8-3), trying to continue to balance its attack as it had successfully all season, had gotten TD run from big TB John Clay (23/100y, TD) and TD pass from QB Scott Tolzien (19-30/235y, 2 TDs, INT) early in 2nd Q. Down 27-17 midway in 3rd Q, Badgers WR David Gilreath took low punt, split tacklers, and was off on 68y TD RET, and Wisconsin was back in it at 27-24. After K Stefan Demos kicked his 3rd and 4th FGs, Northwestern led 33-24. Tolzien hit 4 passes in row to take Badgers 54y to TD catch by TE Garrett Graham. But when Tolzien overshot receiver in last min, Wildcats CB Jordan Mabin was there to catch it over his shoulder for clinching INT.

Connecticut 33 NOTRE DAME 30 (OT): "Jazz, this is for you, best win we have ever had," said Connecticut (5-5) coach Randy Edsall with tears in his eyes. Emotional rollercoaster after October death of Jasper "Jazz" Howard finally reached zenith as UConn players earned memorable win, in 2nd OT, after series of heartbreaking losses since Howard died. For Fighting Irish (6-5), loss was 3rd straight as once-promising season continued to fizzle. All of Notre Dame's 5 defeats had come by 7 pts or less. Huskies attacked Irish's run-D weakness as RB Jordan Todman (26/130y, TD) contributed 43y TD run in 2nd Q and 96y KO TD RET in 3rd Q, while RB Andre Dixon (20/114y, TD) scored winner on 4y TD run in 2nd OT. Todman's 2nd TD had tied it 17-17 before teams traded FGs in 4th Q. UConn QB Zach Frazer (12-25/141y, TD, INT) threw 11y TD pass to WR Kashif Moore in 1st OT, which gave Huskies their 1st lead of game at 27-20. It was matched by 4y TD pass by Notre Dame QB Jimmy Clausen (30-45/329y, 2 TDs) to WR Michael Floyd (8/104y, TD). Irish were held to 36y FG by K

David Ruffer in 2nd OT, which proved costly when Huskies ran 4 straight plays for win. WR Golden Tate (9/123y, TD) continued his magnificent jr season setting Irish records for catches (83) and yards (1295y) in single season.

NEBRASKA 17 Kansas State 3: As expected, Nebraska (8-3) snatched Big 12 North crown, thanks to its marvelous D. It was all or nothing for Kansas State (6-6), which owned only 4 victories over FBS teams, so this loss kept Cats home for holidays. But 1st, Wildcats took 3-0 lead on 44y FG by K Josh Cherry after 58y opening drive keyed by spurts of RB Daniel Thomas (19/99y). Huskers answered with own 56y march to K Alex Henery's 34y FG. K-State would outgain Huskers, 293y to 267y, but took costly PEN on Nebraska's go-ahead drive early in 2nd Q and squandered several trips into Huskers territory. Nebraska QB Zac Lee (13-19/166y, TD, INT) ran toward sideline at Wildcats 35YL, and MLB John Houlik was flagged for roughing to set up Lee's 17y TD pass to TE Mike McNeill, who broke wide open into EZ. Huskers IB Roy Helu (26/95y, TD), who had taken on greater role out of I-formation after recovering from mid-season shoulder injury, pounded for 14y TD run early in 3rd Q after Lee hit WR Niles Paul for 47y. Kansas State crossed midfield to 13, 15, 41, and 27YLs in 2nd H, and its biggest blunder came on RB Keithen Valentine's FUM after pass to 1YL in 3rd Q.

TEXAS 51 Kansas 20: With coach Mark Mangino under fire for alleged verbal mistreatment of his players, Kansas Jayhawks (5-6) were no match—despite 303y O and 98y KO TD RET in 4th Q by WR Dezmon Briscoe (5/101y)—for no. 2 Texas (11-0), which wrapped up Big 12 South title. Longhorns QB Colt McCoy passed 32-41/396y, 4 TDs, including long-range scores to WRs James Kirkendoll (8/86y, 2 TDs) for 41y, Jordan Shipley (10/108y, TD) for 38y, and Malcolm Williams (6/103y, TD) for 68y. Texas O posted impressive 10-17 on 3rd and 4th downs on its way to 532y. QB Todd Reesing (25-39/256y, INT) could get Kansas no closer than 27-13 in 3rd Q as demoralized Jayhawks dropped 6th straight contest. McCoy set new major college record for wins as starting QB; his 43 eclipsed Georgia's David Greene in 2001-04.

UCLA 23 Arizona State 13: Sun Devils' frustrations continued as they lost 6 TOs and failed to make much of dent in their 20-7 H shortfall. Arizona State (4-7) was starting its 3rd signal-caller in as many weeks as mobile QB Samson Szakaczy (15-22/197y, 2 TDs, INT) had predictable highs and lows for frosh. Outgained and without O TD, UCLA (6-5) still won its 3rd straight Pac-10 encounter thanks to opportunistic D. Big score came less than 4 mins into 1st Q when CB Alterraun Verner charged down left sideline on 68y INT TD RET. In 2nd Q that Bruins owned 13-0, Szakacsy was sacked by UCLA DT Brian Price for 11y loss, causing FUM scooped up by LB Akeem Ayers at Devils 9YL. In falling forward, Ayers stretched across GL with ball, pushing UCLA lead to 16-7. ASU WR Kyle Williams caught 6/128y, 2 TDs, including 70y tally in 4th Q. Loss insured back-to-back losing seasons for Arizona State, Devils' 1st consecutive-year failure since way back in 1946-47, 3rd-longest streak among major schools.

California 34 STANFORD 28: Try as they might, Cardinal (7-4) could not extend their heady 2-game victory strwak over Pac-10 kingpins Oregon and USC by winning Big Game against rival California (8-3). With star RB Jahvid Best on shelf, Golden Bears back-up RB Shane Vereen enjoyed his greatest moment. Vereen, who hadn't carried more than 30 times in single game, rushed 42/193y, 3 TDs, his 3 scores coming in span of 12 mins of 2nd and 3rd Qs to turn 14-3 deficit into 24-14 lead. Meanwhile, durable Stanford RB Toby Gerhart (20/136y, 4 TDs) kept Cardinal in game. Gerhart had launched scoring with 61y TD scamper in 1st Q and followed later in opening Q with short TD run for 14-0 edge. After Vereen's trio of TDs, Stanford was forced into catch-up mode and never quite made it. Gerhart tallied late in 3rd Q and again on 5y slanting run with 7 mins left in 4th Q to pull within 31-28. Down 34-28, Gerhart carried tacklers on 29y pass reception to 13YL with less than 2 mins to play. QB Andrew Luck (10-30/157y, INT) had his EZ toss barely tipped away on 1st down, and Cal LB Mike Muhamed went high to pick off Luck's next pass over middle to cinch upset win.

Oregon 44 ARIZONA 41 (OT): Each team arrived with their Rose Bowl destiny within control: win out and trip to Pasadena was theirs. Oregon (9-2) scored in 1st Q on 14y run by QB Jeremiah Masoli (26-47/284y, 3 TDs, INT and 16/61y, 3 TDs rushing). It was well-earned opening-possession TD by Masoli, but Ducks would benefit from very good fortune remainder of night. Ducks fumbled 5 mins into 2nd Q but recovered bobble to allow Masoli to make it 14-0 on 9y TD pass to outstanding WR Jeff Maehl (12/114y, 2 TDs), who wriggled neatly across GL. Later, Oregon K Morgan Flint pounded 43y line-drive that struck crossbar and crawled over to tie it 24-24 in 4th Q. Earlier, LB Sterling Lewis made deflected INT to help Arizona (6-4) to its 1st TD: high toss to left corner of EZ by QB Nick Foles (30-46/314y, 4 TDs, INT) to WR Juron Criner (5/93y, 3 TDs). Wildcats took their 1st lead in 3rd Q at 17-14 and extended it to 24-14 early in 4th Q. In 4th Q, Foles zipped bubble-screen to fleet Criner, who pulled away for 71y TD and 31-24 edge with 7:41 to play. Wildcats later tried to clinch it when conservatism might have helped kill late-game clock: With 3:11 left, Foles arched 40y pass to EZ on 3rd-and-16, but when ball was tipped sideways, Oregon DB Talmadge Jackson came away with auspicious INT. So, Ducks had 1 last chance to send it to OT. With thousands of U of A students prematurely ringing field and ready to celebrate, Masoli confidently hit Maehl with 4th down pass at 15YL and 2 plays later rifled 8y TD pass to sure-handed TE Ed Dickson (5/63y, TD) with 6 secs left in regulation time. Even Oregon's tying pt was fortunate: holder Nate Costa had to field low, inside snap at his shoes. After OT exchange of TD catches by Maehl and Criner, Cats were forced into FG in 2nd OT session that put them up 41-38. Masoli arched 22y pass to Dickson down left sideline to poise QB for winning TD run off LT.

USA TODAY Coaches Poll November 22, 2009

1 Florida (47)	1459	14 Virginia Tech	656
2 Texas (4)	1398	15 Brigham Young	510
3 Alabama (8)	1388	16 Clemson	467
4 Texas Christian	1279	17 Louisiana State	463
5 Cincinnati	1224	18 Oregon State	450
6 Boise State	1181	19 Utah	318
7 Georgia Tech	1125	20 Houston	305
8 Ohio State	1031	21 Miami	266
9 Pittsburgh	1021	22 Southern California	261
10 Oregon	941	23 Nebraska	191
11 Penn State	843	24 North Carolina	167
12 Oklahoma State	815	25 Mississippi	165
13 Iowa	714		

Bowl Championship Series Rankings November 22, 2009

	Harris Poll Avg.	USA TODAY Poll Avg.	Computer Pct.	BCS Avg.
1 Florida (11-0)	.9800	.9892	.930	.9664
2 Alabama (11-0)	.9432	.9410	1.000	.9614
3 Texas (11-0)	.9512	.9478	.880	.9263
4 Texas Christian (11-0)	.8726	.8671	.870	.8699
5 Cincinnati (10-0)	.8274	.8298	.920	.8591

November 26-28, 2009

(Th'g) Texas 49 TEXAS A&M 39: Perhaps Texas (12-0) showed some cracks in its pass D, but ace QB Colt McCoy (24-40/304y, 4 TDs) was brilliant in leading Steers O to 597y. McCoy became only 3rd NCAA player to exceed 300y passing and 150y rushing in 1 game. Early in 2nd Q, McCoy (18/175y, TD rushing) charged up middle on pass scramble and pulled away for 65y TD sprint. On other side, Texas A&M (6-6) QB Jerrod Johnson fired 4 TDs that kept Aggies in game: Johnson (26-33/342y, 4 TDs, INT) hit TDs for 7-0 lead and ties of 14-14 and 21-21 in 1st H. Speedy Johnson authored weaving 43y run to Horns 18YL in 3rd Q but soon was picked off in EZ by Texas SS Earl Thomas, his school-record 8th INT this year. Johnson's last scoring connection with WR Jeff Fuller (6/132y, 3 TDs) came with 7 mins to play and pulled A&M to within 42-39. No sooner had cheering at Kyle Field subsided when blazing fast Texas WR Marquise Goodwin tore downfield for clinching 95y KO TD RET. Game's 88 pts were most ever in 116 meetings of rivals.

(Fri) WEST VIRGINIA 19 Pittsburgh 16: Using last-play FG, West Virginia (8-3) turned tables on Panthers (9-2), who had staged ruinous "Backyard Brawl" upsets for 2 straight years. As time expired, frosh K Tyler Bitancurt (4 FGs) booted 43y 3-ptr. QB Jarrett Brown (19-31/164y) moved Mountaineers from own 32YL to Panthers 26YL to set up winner, rushing 3/21y and completing 11y pass to WR Alric Arnett (7/71y) along way. West Virginia FB Ryan Clarke converted 4th-and-1 by whisker at Pitt 36YL with 56 secs left. RB Noel Devine (17/134y, TD), who in 3rd Q dashed 88y for WVU's sole TD, ran 7y to put Bitancurt in range. Pitt had tied it at 16-16 less than 3 mins earlier as WR Jonathan Baldwin (8/127y, TD) made over-shoulder catch of 50y TD pass from QB Bill Stull (16-30/179y, TD, 2 INTs). Frosh TB Dion Lewis once again paced Panthers ground game with 26/155y. Although loss would knock Pittsburgh out of nation's top-10, Panthers remained alive for BCS berth. "We have high-character kids..." said Pittsburgh coach Dave Wannstedt. "We'll turn the page on this one in a hurry and get ready for Cincinnati." It was highest ranked Panthers team ever to lose to WVU.

(Fri) Alabama 26 AUBURN 21: Employing run-focused D, Auburn (7-5) made 2 huge O plays to put scare into Crimson Tide (12-0) before coming up short. Tigers built leads of 14-0 and 21-14 and did not fall behind until late in 4th Q. With Alabama's superb running attack limited to 73y on 35 carries—with star TB Mark Ingram managing only 16/30y—QB Greg McElroy (21-31/218y, 2 TDs) drove his charges 79y to game-winning TD on 4y play-action pass to RB Roy Upchurch. Catch was Upchurch's 1st TD reception in his 37th career game. With Tide trailing 21-20 with 8:34 remaining, McElroy performed brilliantly by completing 7-8/63y against D that had done great job all day. McElroy counted on WR Julio Jones (9/83y), who caught 4/33y on winning drive with 3 catches producing 1st downs. Auburn WR Terrell Zachery had scampered 67y to TD to open scoring in 1st Q. That TD marked largest deficit, 7 pts, Alabama faced all season, but that edge would quickly double. Pulling out all stops, Tigers K Wes Byrum recovered his own onside-KO at Auburn 42YL, and QB Chris Todd (15-25/181y, 2 TDs, INT) hit 22y pass to WR Darvin Adams (4/138y, TD) and scrambled 13y for 1st down to set up his 1y TD pass to RB Eric Smith. Tide bounced back in 2nd Q to knot it 14-14 as RB Trent Richardson ran for 2y TD and McElroy threw 33y scoring pass to TE Colin Peek. Auburn's 2nd big scoring play came early in 3rd Q: Todd's 72y TD pass to Adams. Best Alabama could manage over next 20 mins was pair of FGs by K Leigh Tiffin, which allowed him to set Alabama records for FGs in season (27) and career (80) and kicking pts in season (118).

(Fri) BOISE STATE 44 Nevada 33: Cold rain turned Boise's hideous blue carpet into synthetic plane of blotchy azure. Nevada (8-4), sporting unprecedented trio of 1000y rushers, arrived with high hopes and half-game WAC lead. But, no. 6 Boise State (12-0) got off to rip-roaring start, which forced Nevada somewhat out of its running strategy (44/242y), and finished off Wolf Pack with O flourishes every time Nevada threatened. Broncos WR Titus Young dropped opening KO, picked it up as wave of tacklers flew by, and scurried 95y for TD. Ace QB Kellen Moore (17-33/262y 5 TDs) and big WR-turned-FB Dan Paul collaborated on 3 TD passes, so Boise owned 27-3 lead 5 mins into 2nd Q. Nevada countered with pair of TD passes by QB Colin Kaepernick (12-22/141y, 3 TDs), so Pack was back in it at 27-16 at H. Moore was handy with 2nd H TD passes for leads of 34-19 and 44-26, and they blunted any comeback hopes despite 71y TD run in 3rd Q by Wolf Pack RB Vai Taua (24/160y, TD).

Virginia Tech 42 VIRGINIA 13: Hokies (9-3) won 6th straight Commonwealth Cup, pulling away with 28 pts in 2nd H. Virginia Tech frosh TB Ryan Williams rushed 24/183y and 4 TDs to lead 483y O production. Virginia (3-9) played inspired 1st H for

Al Groh, whose 9-year run as head coach neared its end. Cavaliers opened scoring with 15y TD run by QB Jameel Sewell (12-22/120y and 17/104y, TD rushing). K Robert Randolph added 2 FGs, and Virginia trailed only 14-13 at H. But Williams scored twice as Va Tech built 28-13 lead early in 4th Q. He later burst free for 51y that ended in FUM, recovered in EZ by WR Jarrett Boykin for Hokies TD. Cavs managed only 24/76y O in 2nd H, while losing pair of FUMs. With Cavaliers D focused on run D, Hokies QB Tyrod Taylor (8-15/185y, INT) and WR Danny Coale (6/135y) formed effective battery. Virginia Tech had now won 10 of 11 against rivals and ended Cavs' miserable season that began with loss to in-state FCS foe William & Mary.

Georgia 30 GEORGIA TECH 24: Tumultuous regular season for Bulldogs (7-5) ended on high note with upset of no. 7 Georgia Tech (10-2). Georgia's game-plan called for 10 straight runs on opening drive to 6y TD by RB Caleb King (18/166y, 2 TDs). With explosive Ga Tech attack held in check, Bulldogs stretched lead to 17-3 at H. Yellow Jackets finally cracked EZ on 76y pass from QB Josh Nesbitt (6-12/135y, TD and 19/41y, TD rushing) to WR Demaryius Thomas (5/127y, TD) early in 3rd Q, but King replied immediately, racing to 75y TD on next snap to up Georgia's advantage back to 24-10. Jackets RB Jonathan Dwyer (14/33y, TD) and Nesbitt each would score after 2 long drives but take too much time off clock considering UGa ran off extensive time on way to game-end 339y rushing and 2nd H FGs of 38 and 43y by K Blair Walsh. Georgia Tech had time for 1 last drive, but 4 straight incompletions from Bulldogs 46YL killed its hopes. Georgia improved to remarkable 11-3 on road against ranked opponents in 10 years under coach Mark Richt. English bulldog "Russ" debuted as temporary mascot after his half-brother, Uga VII, had died on November 19.

FLORIDA 37 Florida State 10: With venerable Florida State (6-6) coach Bobby Bowden's future to be announced on Tuesday, no. 1 Gators seemed like impossible foe for noble 80-year-old's likely last regular-season game. Gators (12-0) fans enjoyed their own nostalgia as 2007 Heisman-winning QB Tim Tebow (17-21/221y, 3 TDs and 15/90y, 2 TDs rushing) was brilliant in his last game at Florida Field. Florida increased its winning streak to 22 games and series win string to 6 as Gators secured their 1st-ever 12-0 regular season. Tebow now had 11,389y career total O to break school and SEC records held by former teammate Chris Leak. Gaining 545y, Gators led 7-0 after 1st Q, 24-0 at H, and 30-0 until late in 3rd Q when Seminoles finally tallied on 20y FG by K Dustin Hopkins. Late in 4th Q, Florida State QB E.J. Manuel (19-31/198y, TD, 2 INTs) threw 9y TD pass to WR Jarmon Fortson. Gators converted 10-13 3rd downs and scored perfect 4-4 in FSU red zone, which had been their bugaboo earlier in season. Not single Gators drive went 3-and-out; Florida State did so 3 times. "I want to coach next year, but let me say I want to go home and do some soul-searching," said Bowden after game. Problematic for Bowden had been 182-58 scoring discrepancy in Gators' favor since coach Urban Meyer took over in Gainesville in 2005.

SOUTH CAROLINA 34 Clemson 17: Putting damper on upcoming ACC title game, Atlantic Division winning Clemson (8-4) joined Coastal champ Georgia Tech as losers this Saturday as Gamecocks (7-5), who had lost 3 straight games themselves, used 223y rushing to set up passing of QB Stephen Garcia (10-21/126y, 3 TDs, INT). South Carolina focused on Tigers multi-purpose star RB C.J. Spiller (9/18y), who was brilliant nonetheless with 88y KO TD RET, his NCAA-record 7th career KO TD RET. Spiller also became 5th player in FBS history to surpass 7000y all-purpose. But Spiller was suffering from upset stomach and tweaked groin, so with him often neutralized Clemson managed only 260y O with 48y on ground. Garcia, meanwhile, threw 9y TD pass to TE Weslye Saunders (2/10y, 2 TDs) late in 1st Q to give Gamecocks their 1st lead at 14-7. He also pitched TD passes in 3rd and 4th Q as frosh RB Kenny Myles contributed 17/114y rushing. Clemson QB Kyle Parker (22-42/212y, TD, INT) did most of his damage to TE Michael Palmer (8/106y, TD), who not only caught 22y TD pass in 4th Q but became only 2nd TE in school history, and 1st since John McMakin way back in 1970, to earn 100y receiving in single game.

MISSISSIPPI STATE 41 Mississippi 27: Under 1st-year coach Dan Mullen, Bulldogs (5-7) stunningly nabbed Golden Egg Trophy as sub QB Chris Relf (3-5/43y, 2 TDs) rushed 15/131y, TD. Mississippi State blew open nail-biter by scoring 31 of 38 pts to convert 13-10 H deficit into 41-20 lead in 4th Q. Relf received great help from sr RB Anthony Dixon (29/133y, TD), who topped school single-season rushing mark with 1391y. Rebels (8-4), looking for back-to-back 9-win seasons for 1st time since 1961-62, contributed to own 2nd H demise as QB Jevan Snead (17-29/275y, 3 TDs, 3 INTs) relinquished 3 INTs, including 2 by Maroons S Charles Mitchell. Another INT was returned 64y for TD by CB Corey Broomfield that gave Bulldogs 41-20 lead with 5 mins left. Snead managed to connect on 4th Q TD passes of 48y to WR Markeith Summers and 52y to RB Dexter McCluster (16/82y and 5/63y, TD receiving). Bulldogs, which played with nation's toughest adjusted schedule in 2009, beat team led by Houston Nutt for 1st time since 1998. It ended span of 10 losses including 9 against Arkansas while Nutt was coach there. "This program is on the rise, maybe to the contrary of what some others are saying around the state," crowed happy Mullen.

LOUISIANA STATE 33 Arkansas 30 (OT): SEC thriller ended with anti-climatic 36y FG miss by Arkansas (7-5) K Alex Tejada at end of 1st OT. Louisiana State (9-3) K Josh Jasper, whose 41y boot sent game into extra session, had nailed 36y 3-ptr to end opening OT series. Tigers needed to drive 41y in final moments of regulation to tie it 30-30, and they learned from poor late-game management versus Mississippi week before. After allowing sack by Arkansas DE Jake Bequette on opening play of late-game series, Tigers transformed into O machine: QB Jordan Jefferson (17-25/179y, 2 TDs, INT) hit 4-5/38y as Tigers quickly moved into FG range. "We worked that situation a couple of times this week in practice and even in walkthroughs this morning," said LSU TE Richard Dickson. "We were not going to make the same mistake twice." Arkansas had taken 30-27 edge, its 1st lead since midway through 1st Q, with 1:18 remaining on 14y TD pass by QB Ryan Mallett (17-39/227y, TD, INT) that converted 4th-and-9. Rallying Hogs from 2-TD deficit, Mallett did his best work on late 75y drive, completing 18y pass to RB Dennis Johnson (9/78y rushing) on 3rd-and-10 and finding WR Greg Childs (5/124y) for 23y on 3rd-and-20 that gave Razorbacks 1st down at LSU 30YL. Arkansas had fallen behind 17-3 in 2nd Q on 87y punt TD RET by Tigers RB Trindon Holliday, who gained 212y all-purpose.

OKLAHOMA 27 Oklahoma State 0: Oklahoma State Cowboys (9-3) were still in BCS at-large nomination conversation until they ran smack into stonewall known as Oklahoma (7-5) D. Despite mounting injuries on both sides of ball, Sooners rose up to play spoiler to their in-state rival. Oklahoma State could barely move past its huddle, gaining only 109y. Back from injury, Cowboys QB Zac Robinson could pass only 9-21/44y, INT, while RB Keith Toston, soon to be named to All-Big12 1st team, could rush only 10/47y. Sooners RB DeMarco Murray scored 2 TDs while gaining 72y on ground. OU WR Ryan Broyles (9/103y) raced 87y for punt TD RET in 4th Q.

STANFORD 45 Notre Dame 38: With coach Charlie Weis' job up in air, Notre Dame (6-6) went to air to play inspired O and led 14-10,17-13, 24-13, 31-20, and 38-30. Fighting Irish QB Jimmy Clausen, soon to declare early for NFL draft, passed 23-30/340y, 5 TDs while WR Golden Tate, also headed to pro ball, scored thrice while catching 10/201y. In end, it was Stanford (8-4) Heisman candidate TB Toby Gerhart (29/205y, 3 TDs), who threw 18y TD pass to WR Ryan Whalen (6/75y, TD) on 4th-and-4 to tie it 38-38 6 mins into 4th Q and scored game-winning TD from 4YL in last min. It would turn out to be last ND game for Weis, who was fired 3 days later, and although eligible, Irish chose to skip any bowl invitations.

Arizona 20 ARIZONA STATE 17: Football can be so cruel sometimes: No sooner had Sun Devils (4-8) sr WR Kyle Williams (9/130y, 2 TDs, 200y all-purpose) shrugged off pass interference to make brilliant 14y diving catch in EZ to create 17-17 tie with 2:02 left to play, when he muffed Arizona (7-4) punt at his 22YL. REC by Wildcats DB Mike Turner set up K Alex Zendejas for winning 32y FG as clock struck 0:00. With prospects of OT looming and momentum decidedly against it, Arizona had faced possible bowl extinction, having lost heartbreaking Rose Bowl destiny game previous week and having USC on schedule next Saturday. Cats earned big win despite blowing 14-0 H edge, built on 67y TD burst up middle by RB Keola Antolin (7/78y, TD) in 1st Q and blocked punt for TD by LB Orlando Vargas. Maligned sr QB Danny Sullivan (14-28/168y, 2 TDs) had come off Arizona State bench in 2nd H to pitch 44y TD pass to Williams to pull Devils within 14-10 early in 4th Q.

BRIGHAM YOUNG 26 Utah 23 (OT): For 11th time in last 13 meetings in Beehive State rivalry, game was decided by TD or less. This time in OT, BYU (10-2) QB Max Hall (12-32/134y, 2 TDs) followed 5th FG of game by Utah (9-3) K Joe Phillips with pass dumped over middle to Cougars TE Andrew George, who ran unmolested to winning 25y TD. Afterward, Hall railed on about his hatred of everything about Utah, just sort of words to keep rivalry stoked high. Trailing 6-0, BYU had romped to 20 unanswered pts in middle Qs, including 2y TD run by RB Harvey Unga (23/116y, TD), slanting off left side in 2nd Q. Utes rallied in 4th Q on pair of FGs by Phillips, including tying 3-ptr with 29 secs left, sandwiched around 1y TD run by RB Eddie Wide (21/114y, TD) and QB Jordan Wynn's 2-pt pass. WR Shaky Smithson set up Utah's TD with 40y punt RET.

USA TODAY Coaches Poll November 29, 2009

1 Florida (53)	1468	14 Louisiana State	674
2 Texas (3)	1394	15 Pittsburgh	631
3 Alabama (3)	1380	16 Oregon State	607
4 Texas Christian	1285	17 Miami	509
5 Cincinnati	1231	18 Houston	473
6 Boise State	1197	19 Southern California	361
7 Ohio State	1104	20 Nebraska	335
8 Oregon	1061	21 Oklahoma State	309
9 Penn State	975	22 California	210
10 Iowa	889	23 West Virginia	163
11 Virginia Tech	831	24 Stanford	154
12 Georgia Tech	774	25 Utah	120
13 Brigham Young	680		

Bowl Championship Series Rankings November 29, 2009

	Harris Poll Avg.	USA TODAY Poll Avg.	Computer Pct.	BCS Avg.
1 Florida (12-0)	.9851	.9953	.980	.9868
2 Alabama (12-0)	.9384	.9356	.980	.9513
3 Texas (12-0)	.9494	.9451	.890	.9282
4 Texas Christian (12-0)	.8754	.8712	.860	.8689
5 Cincinnati (11-0)	.8294	.8346	.900	.8547

December 5, 2009

(Th) OREGON 37 Oregon State 33: Sign flashed by fan read: "Biggest Civil War since Gettysburg." Indeed, for 1st time, Rose Bowl bid was on line in State of Oregon's so-called Civil War. Oregon (10-2) QB Jeremiah Masoli (14-21/201y, TD, INT and 10/40y rushing) fired high early and was picked off, and Beavers (8-4) RB Jacquizz Rodgers (16/64y TD) wedged over on 4th down from 1YL. Ducks answered with quick drive, keyed by fine blocks by TE Ed Dickson, to short TD run by RB LaMichael James (25/166y, 3 TDs), and Oregon went ahead 14-10 on next opportunity when WR Jeff Maehl (6/138y, TD) zipped past bump-and-run coverage for 73y TD catch from Masoli. Oregon State notched pair of 2nd Q FGs by K Justin Kahut (4 FGs) for 16-14 lead after "Quiz" Rodgers took 2nd-and-25 screen pass 48y and DE Matt LaGrone recovered James' FUM in Ducks red-zone. Again, Oregon answered on James' 6y slicing run into EZ, but Beavers countered with game's next 14 pts for 30-21 3rd Q lead, including TD catch by WR James Rodgers (10/139y, TD). Off bench came once-suspended Oregon RB LeGarrette Blount (9/51y, TD) to dramatically power for his 1st carries since season opener. Blount blasted 12y for TD to pull within 30-28. Blount's presence gave James breather, so frosh speedster was fresh to roar 52y to go-ahead

TD at 34-33. Facing 2 4th downs in Beavers territory, Oregon converted each time to ice it with 47y possession that killed last 6:09. Oregon earned its 1st Rose Bowl trip since 1995.

(Fri) Central Michigan 20 Ohio University 10 (Detroit): Chippewas (11-2) QB Dan LeFevour (28-39/255y, 2 TDs, INT), O star hardly anybody ever heard of, pitched pair of TD passes in 1st H to put him atop all-time FBS career TD-responsibility list with 148. He broke deadlock at 146 with Texas Tech's Graham Harrell and Hawaii's Colt Brennan. Trailing 10-0 late in 1st Q, Ohio Bobcats (9-4) scored TD on 29y pass off reverse-pitch from WR Taylor Price to WR Terrence McCrae (7/141y, TD), who was Ohio's best weapon. After LeFevour's 2nd TD throw in 2nd Q on post-pattern to WR Bryan Anderson, Central Michigan led 17-7 at H. Try as they might, Bobcats never quite could get back into game, definitive late-game tackles coming from CMU DEs Frank Zombo on sack and Larry Knight on 4th down scramble by Ohio QB Theo Scott (10-23/308y and 9/36y rushing). MLB Noah Keller was in on 16 tackles for Ohio.

Cincinnati 45 PITTSBURGH 44: Pittsburgh (9-3) built 31-10 lead late in 2nd Q as frosh sensation TB Dion Lewis (47/194y, 3 TDs) ran wild, WR Jonathan Baldwin (6/113y, 2 TDs) caught 2 TD passes, and D forced Cincinnati (12-0) QB Tony Pike into 2 INTs in 1st H to snap his streak of 106 passes without INT. Bearcats' magical season was in trouble, so they turned to old favorites WR Mardy Gilyard (5/118y) and Pike (22-44/302y, 3 TDs, 3 INTs) to rally from 21 pts down. With H approaching, Gilyard returned KO 99y for TD that boosted Bearcats, who needed to win for 2nd straight Big East title. Pike and Gilyard produced another big play midway in 3rd Q, as Gilyard raced under Pike's pass and eluded Pitt defenders to score on 68y play to cut deficit to 31-24. Panthers WR Aaron Smith authored 18y punt RET to Cincinnati 32YL early in 4th Q, and Lewis' 15y TD run gave Panthers 38-24 lead. Gilyard (381y all-purpose) charged 49y on ensuing KO to Panthers 23YL to set up Pike's 8y TD pass to WR D.J. Woods (7/61y, TD), but x-pt was missed and Bearcats trailed 38-30. With 9 mins remaining, Pike competed 4-4/44y to position RB Isaiah Pead (9/76y, TD) for 1y TD run. Pike then tied it 38-38 with 2-pt conv pass to Gilyard in back of EZ. With clock winding down, Pitt rode hard-charging Lewis to his 5y TD run on 67y drive that featured 2 catches by Baldwin from QB Bill Stull (13-21/176y, 2 TDs, 2 INTs). But bobbled x-pt hold kept Panthers' lead at tenuous 6 pts with 1:36 remaining. Red-hot Pike again hit 4-4—he connected on his final 11 attempts of game—to drive Bearcats 61y with final 29y coming on his high TD lob down right sideline to lunging WR Armon Binns (5/104y, TD) with 33 secs remaining. K Jake Rogers booted x-pt, and Cincinnati remained undefeated by slimmest of margins. "When you imagine a championship game, the snow falling, and the stands packed, and two outstanding football teams just going after it, this game was it," said Cincy coach Brian Kelly.

Georgia Tech 39 Clemson 34 (Tampa): In just his 2nd year in charge, coach Paul Johnson led Georgia Tech (11-2) to its 1st outright ACC title in 19 years. Thanks to incredible conf title game act by Tigers (8-5) RB C.J. Spiller—even for his lofty ACC Player-of-Year standards—Yellow Jackets needed 86y TD march to pull out victory with 1:20 to play. Spiller rushed 20/233y, 4 TDs as he scored in each Q on runs of 3, 41, 36, and 9y. Spiller (301y all-purpose) had accounted for 20 TDs so far in 2009, 11 rushing scores, 4 via catches, and 5 on KO RETs. His 2nd-to-last carry went 54y down left sideline to set up 1y TD run by RB Andre Ellington 3 plays later for 34-33 lead with 6:11 remaining. Georgia Tech turned to RB Jonathan Dwyer (24/110y, 2 TDs) and QB Josh Nesbitt (9-16/136y, TD and 22/103y, TD rushing) to deliver winning pts: Nesbitt ran for 24y and hit 2-3/28y passing on ensuing 13-play, 86y drive to Dwyer's winning 15y TD run. Dwyer rushed 5/33y on drive. Nesbitt had given Ga Tech 30-20 lead in 3rd Q with 70y TD pass to long-range weapon, WR Demaryius Thomas, who made 4th reception of year of 70y or more. K Scott Blair, hero of Yellow Jackets' 3-pt win over Clemson earlier in season, kicked 4 FGs, including career-long efforts of 48y and 49y. Neither team punted as Georgia Tech had 10 possessions, with 4 TDs, 4 FGs, loss on downs, and taking knee to end 4th Q, while Clemson's 10 possessions featured 5 TDs, missed FG, 2 INTs, expiration of 1st H, and failure on downs late in 4th Q.

Alabama 32 Florida 13 (Atlanta): Alabama (13-0) arrived for SEC championship game with tremendous focus and excellent schemes on both sides of ball, rolling up 490y against Florida's national-best D, averaging 233y coming in. Crimson Tide staged 2 time-consuming drives, mixing runs by star TB Mark Ingram (28/113y, 3 TDs and 2/76y receiving) with passes by emerging QB Greg McElroy (12-18/239y, TD). Ingram scored on 7y burst up middle in 1st Q for 9-0 edge. Trailing 12-3 and having its running attack somewhat diminished, Gators (12-1) suddenly came to life in 2nd Q as QB Tim Tebow (20-35/247y, TD, INT) twice scrambled for good gains and found WR David Nelson at left pylon for TD pass. For all its dominance, Alabama now led only 12-10 but responded right away: Ingram took short pass from McElroy that beat Florida's CB-blitz, and Ingram sped 69y down sideline to 3YL before smashing off LT for TD on next snap. Bama led 19-13 at H. Tide TE and honor student Colin Peek, whose father played for Florida in 1960s, slanted left from right side of line to take 17y TD pass off misdirection midway in 3rd Q for 26-13 edge. Crimson Tide took 8:47 off clock on 88y TD drive that made it 32-13 early in 4th Q. As Tebow, under increasing rush pressure, attempted comeback, Bama DB Javier Arenas picked off pass in EZ when lofted throw might have gone for TD. It was rare moment of failure for Florida's brilliant sr QB, and in tears Tebow gave CBS' Tracy Wolfson post-game interview praising Crimson Tide. Bama was off to BCS title game, having bagged its 22nd SEC title, 1st since 1999.

GAME OF THE YEAR

Texas 13 Nebraska 12 (Arlington, Tex.): Despite its fine D and 2 losses by total of 3 pts, Nebraska Cornhuskers (9-4) arrived for Big 12 title game as 2-TD underdog to no. 2 Texas Longhorns (13-0). Following perfect script, Nebraska earned early INT when DE Pierre Allen tipped pass by Steers QB Colt McCoy (20-36/184y, 3 INTs), who would be sacked 9 times during game. After controversial 1st down spot went Nebraska's way, Texas' outstanding D held, and K Alex Henery booted 45y FG for 3-0 Huskers edge. After another INT, Henery's 52y FG made it 6-0, but Huskers squandered blocked punt in Texas territory in 2nd Q when long pass by QB Zac Lee (6-19/39y, 3 INTs) was intercepted in EZ by Texas CB Aaron Williams. As clock ticked toward H, McCoy clicked on 3rd down pass for 16y to WR Malcolm Williams to Huskers 15YL, and McCoy scored on 2y run up middle to cap 42y drive for 7-6 H lead. As Nebraska's D, led by star DT Ndamukong Suh (12 tackles, 4.5 sacks) continued to sparkle, pair of 3rd Q pooch-punts by McCoy pinned Huskers deep in their end until Texas K Hunter Lawrence finally turned good field position into 39y FG for 10-6 lead. WR Niles Paul's 43y punt RET to 10YL precluded another Nebraska O failure, so Henery made his 3rd FG. Texas appeared ready to extend 10-9 edge when Nebraska DB Dejon Gomes wrestled possession away from WR Dan Buckner for INT at Huskers 31YL with 4:56 left in 4th Q. Cornhuskers O, nearly comatose since 1st Q and 2-16 on 3rd downs by game's end, maneuvered for Henery's 4th FG, from 42y out, with 1:44 to play. Nebraska led 12-10. But, K Adi Kunalic, who had kicked-off well all night, hooked KO OB to allow Longhorns to start at their 40YL, and 15y PEN against Nebraska DB Larry Asante on 19y catch by Texas WR Jordan Shipley (7/71y) moved ball to NU 26YL. After 2 runs lost y, McCoy nearly blundered at game's end. He rolled right and lofted throw-away pass OB from 29YL, only to see clock reach 0:00. But, officials reviewed clock countdown on TV replay and restored 1 sec. Lawrence hit 46y FG to win it for Texas, relieved and excited to be bound for BCS title game.

Arizona 21 SOUTHERN CALIFORNIA 17: Already dethroned as conf champions, Southern California (8-4) seemed never to quite kick into emotional gear, and tasted home defeat for only 3rd time in last 50 games, 2nd time this season. Wildcats (8-4) scored early on WR Delashaun Dean's short TD catch from QB Nick Foles (22-40/239y, 2 TDs, INT and TD rushing) and led much of cloudy, cool afternoon. Trojans rallied from 14-7 deficit on 5y TD run by TB Allen Bradford (11/66y, TD) late in 3rd Q, and K Jordan Congdon made 37y FG halfway through 4th Q for 17-14 lead. Wildcats converted on 3 straight 3rd downs and went back in front 21-17 as WR Juron Criner (6/71y, TD) spun out of tackle and dived across GL to finish 36y TD pass play from Foles with 3:14 to play. Arizona quickly forced 3 incompletions by Trojans QB Matt Barkley (20-37/144y, TD, INT), including 4th down overshot to open WR Damian Williams. Cats had some nervous moments killing last secs but prevailed to knock Trojans to unthinkable tie for 5th place after having won 7 straight Pac-10 titles.

EAST CAROLINA 38 Houston 32: East Carolina Pirates (9-4) scored their 2nd consecutive Conf-USA championship despite being outgained 557y to 413y by pass-crazy Houston (10-3). QB Case Keenum (56-75/527y, 5 TDs, 3 INTs) threw trio of TD passes in seesaw 1st H, but because Cougars missed pair of x-pt kicks they led only 19-14. In 2nd H, East Carolina spurted to 3 straight scores as WR Dwayne Harris broke wide open down right sideline in 3rd Q for 22y TD catch from QB Patrick Pinkney (21-34/262y, TD) and 21-19 edge. Pirates S Van Eskridge returned INT 30y to set up 2nd TD run of RB Dominique Lindsay (25/75y, 2 TDs) that made it 31-19 early in 4th Q. After Keenum hit WR James Cleveland (19/247y, 3 TDs) with TD pass with 3:24 to play, Houston made 4th down run stop to get ball back to try to pull it out. Keenum lofted EZ pass for WR L.J. Castile, but ball bounced off Pirates CB Travis Simmons, and Eskridge, who had ended last year's conf title game with INT, did it again.

USA TODAY Coaches Poll December 6, 2009

1 Alabama (54)	1470	14 Brigham Young	702
2 Texas (4)	1409	15 Miami	611
3 Texas Christian	1336	16 Pittsburgh	506
4 Cincinnati	1280	17 West Virginia	429
5 Florida	1240	18 Oklahoma State	404
6 Boise State	1216	19 Nebraska	391
7 Oregon	1096	20 Oregon State	368
8 Ohio State	1077	21 Stanford	253
9 Penn State	950	22 Wisconsin	247
10 Georgia Tech	921	23 Arizona	237
11 Iowa	918	24 Utah	183
12 Virginia Tech	829	25 Houston	106
13 Louisiana State	718		

Bowl Championship Series Rankings December 6, 2009

	Harris Poll Avg.	USA TODAY Poll Avg.	Computer Pct.	BCS Avg.
1 Alabama (13-0)	.9968	.9966	1.000	.9978
2 Texas (13-0)	.9547	.9553	.920	.9433
3 Cincinnati (12-0)	.8656	.8678	.930	.8878
4 Texas Christian (12-0)	.9049	.9058	.840	.8836
5 Florida (12-1)	.8404	.8407	.910	.8637

December 12, 2009

Navy 17 Army 3 (Philadelphia): Trip to its 1st bowl game since 1996 awaited improved Army (5-7), but far bigger in this ultimate of rivalries was opportunity finally to upset Navy (9-4), winners of 7 straight over Black Knights. Throughout 1st H, Army mounted excellent D, led by DLs Victor Ugenyi and Mike Gann, which forced 2 TOs, including INT by S Steve Erzinger. Erzinger returned INT 26y to Navy 12YL and it set up FG by K Alex Carlton on last play of 1st Q. Black Knights led 3-0 at H, but Middies dominated 3rd Q, outgaining Army 123y to 11y, to capture 10-3 lead. Big play came on 25y TD pass from QB Ricky Dobbs (3-7/61y, TD, INT and 33/113y, TD rushing) to SB Marcus Curry. When Dobbs wedged over for 4th Q TD he became all-time NCAA single season TD scorer among QBs with 24.

2009 Conference Standings

Big East

Cincinnati	7-0
West Virginia	5-2
Pittsburgh	5-2
Rutgers	3-4
Connecticut	3-4
South Florida	3-4
Louisville	1-6
Syracuse	1-6

Atlantic Coast

ATLANTIC	
Clemson	6-2
Boston College	5-3
Florida State	4-4
Wake Forest	3-5
North Carolina State	2-6
Maryland	1-7
COASTAL	
Georgia Tech	7-1
Virginia Tech	6-2
Miami	5-3
North Carolina	4-4
Duke	3-5
Virginia	2-6

Southeastern

EAST	
Florida	8-0
Tennessee	4-4
Georgia	4-4
South Carolina	3-5
Kentucky	3-5
Vanderbilt	0-8
WEST	
Alabama	8-0
Louisiana State	5-3
Mississippi	4-4
Arkansas	3-5
Auburn	3-5
Mississippi State	3-5

Conference USA

EAST	
East Carolina	7-1
Central Florida	6-2
Southern Mississippi	5-3
Marshall	4-4
Alabama-Birmingham	4-4
Memphis	1-7
WEST	
Houston (a)	6-2
Southern Methodist (a)	6-2
Texas-El Paso	3-5
Tulsa	3-5
Rice	2-6
Tulane	1-7

(a)Houston won Western Division by defeating SMU 38-15 on October 24.

Big Ten

Ohio State	7-1
Iowa	6-2
Penn State	6-2
Northwestern	5-3
Wisconsin	5-3
Michigan State	4-4
Purdue	4-4
Minnesota	3-5
Illinois	2-6
Michigan	1-7
Indiana	1-7

Mid-American

EAST	
Ohio University (a)	7-1
Temple (a)	7-1
Bowling Green	6-2
Kent State	4-4
Buffalo	3-5
Akron	2-6
Miami (Ohio)	1-7
WEST	
Central Michigan	8-0
Northern Illinois	5-3
Western Michigan	4-4
Toledo	3-5
Ball State	2-6
Eastern Michigan	0-8

(a)Ohio won Eastern Division by defeating Temple 35-17 on November 27.

Big Twelve

NORTH	
Nebraska	6-2
Missouri	4-4
Kansas State	4-4
Iowa State	3-5
Colorado	2-6
Kansas	1-7
SOUTH	
Texas	8-0
Oklahoma State	6-2
Texas Tech	5-3
Oklahoma	5-3
Texas A&M	3-5
Baylor	1-7

Mountain West

Texas Christian	8-0
Brigham Young	7-1
Utah	6-2
Air Force	5-3
Wyoming	4-4
Nevada-Las Vegas	3-5
San Diego State	2-6
New Mexico	1-7
Colorado State	0-8

Western Athletic

Boise State	8-0
Nevada	7-1
Fresno State	6-2
Idaho	4-4
Hawaii	3-5
Utah State	3-5
Louisiana Tech	3-5
San Jose State	1-7
New Mexico State	1-7

Pacific-10

Oregon	8-1
Arizona	6-3
Oregon State	6-3
Stanford	6-3
California	5-4
Southern California	5-4
Washington	4-5
UCLA	3-6
Arizona State	2-7
Washington State	0-9

2009 Major Bowl Games

Las Vegas Bowl (Dec. 22): Brigham Young 44 Oregon State 20

On this odd night, what happened in Vegas practically blew out of Vegas, including punts, passes, showgirl costumes, and goalpost netting. Sr QB Max Hall (19-30/192y, 3 TDs) threw for trio of TDs and sr LB Matt Bauman, fresh from New York trip as National Football Foundation scholar-athlete nominee, returned 1st Q FUM for TD for 14-7 lead as they bid their farewell to Brigham Young (11-2). Bauman's REC, which put Cougars ahead to stay, came on swing pass dropped by Oregon State (8-5) RB Jacquizz Rodgers (18/63y, TD), amazingly, Rodgers' 1st lost FUM in 622 career touches. Hall adapted to cold and strong wind—gusts up to 50 mph—while his Beavers QB counterpart, Sean Canfield (19-40/168y, INT and TD rushing in 1st Q) had

terrible time passing in gusty conditions. In fact, wind seemed to bite Oregon State far more often than Cougars: Canfield hit only 4 throws in 1st H and P Johnny Hekker twice had punts fly back in his face for 6y each in 2nd Q. BYU RBs Harvey Unga (24/71y, TD) and Manase Tonga contributed 3 TDs, while A-A TE Dennis Pitta (5/45y, TD) nabbed 17y TD pass from Hall, his brother-in-law, for 30-7 3rd Q lead.

Poinsettia Bowl (Dec. 23): Utah 37 California 27

For 2nd straight night, ambitious Mountain West Conf team handed defeat to Pac-10 opponent. In 1st Q, emerging California (8-5) RB Shane Vereen (20/122y, 2 TDs), in for injured RB Jahvid Best, ran right and cut back to vacant backside where he steamed 36y to score. Slim secs later, Utes (10-3) QB Jordan Wynn (26-36/338y, 3 TDs, INT) never looked away from his slant-in target, and Golden Bears LB Eddie Young stepped in to take INT 31y to TD and quick 14-0 lead. So, frosh Wynn was in jeopardy of caving in front of his home-area San Diego fans. Instead, he bucked up to fire 3 TD passes before H for 24-14 lead. Still trailing by 10 pts late in 3rd Q, Cal Bears appeared to snatch momentum when they made 4th down stop at their 25YL. But, Cal QB Kevin Riley (20-36/214y, TD, 2 INTs) was quickly sacked and lost FUM to Utah LB Mike Wright, which led to FG by K Joe Phillips and 27-14 lead. After Riley hit 3-3/60y passing to set up Vereen's 2nd TD run, Utes countered with 10 quick pts to lock it up: Phillips' 3rd FG and LB Stevenson Sylvester's 27y INT TD RET.

Hawaii Bowl (Dec. 24): Southern Methodist 45 Nevada 10

Coach June Jones of SMU (8-5) returned to Aloha Stadium where he had earned 50-19 record with Hawaii in 1999-2007, and Mustangs returned to site of their last bowl game. It came way back in 1984, prior to NCAA death penalty that sentenced Mustangs to only 1 winning season in 20 years. SMU frosh QB Kyle Padron (32-41/460y, 2 TDs), mid-season injury replacement, set new school single-game passing y record, and he started early. Padron connected with WR Cole Beasley (TD catch) for 71y pass-and-run on game's 2nd snap, and it broke Doak Walker's mark of 53y in 1948 Cotton Bowl for SMU's longest bowl game pass. RB Shawnbrey McNeal (12/63y, 3 TDs) scored 1st of his 3 TD runs on next play. Mustangs WR Aldrick Robinson hauled in 9/176y, including 53y catch to set up TD run by RB Zach Line for 38-0 3rd Q lead. Nevada (8-5) had arrived with nation's best rushing attack at 362.3 avg, but 2 of its 1000y rushers, RBs Vai Taua and Luke Lippincott, were out. Taua was ruled academically ineligible and Lippincott was sidelined with toe injury. Wolf Pack's other 1000y rusher, QB Jason Kaepernick (15-29/177y, TD, INT), could gain only 23y on ground and didn't reach EZ until throwing TD pass with 1:04 left to play.

Meineke Car Care Bowl (Dec. 26): Pittsburgh 19 North Carolina 17

Pittsburgh (10-3) hadn't won 10 or more games since 1981, but Panthers used frosh running guile of TB Dion Lewis (28/159y, TD) and clutch kicking of K Dan Hutchins (4 FGs) to wrap up best results in 5 years under coach Dave Wannstedt. North Carolina Tar Heels (8-5) lost 2nd straight heartbreaking Meineke Bowl in home-away-from-home Charlotte. Heels scored in 1st Q for 7-0 lead as WR Greg Little (7/87y, 2 TDs) tallied 1st of his pair of TD catches on 15y grab from QB T.J. Yates (19-32/183y, 2 TDs, INT). Exuberant celebration PEN was called when Little happily punted ball into grandstand. Lewis soon passed legendary Tony Dorsett as Pitt's all-time frosh rusher, but on his 24y run to 2YL he fumbled forward and OB in EZ for touchback. Lewis came back in 2nd Q with 11y TD run, and Yates cost UNC at least 3 pts with GL INT. Hutchins ended 1st H with 31y FG for 13-10 H lead for Panthers. Carolina controlled Lewis in 3rd Q and took 17-16 lead late in 3rd Q when Little pulled in scoring pass, this time over middle and without PEN. With 9:39 to play, Pitt launched decisive 17-play, 79y trip to victory, using workhorse Lewis for 13/58y rushing. QB Bill Stull (17-24/163y) pushed for 3y on 4th-and-1 from Pitt 30YL, and Panthers again faced 4th down at Heels 30YL. With FG unit on field, Panthers used hard count to draw at least 2 DLs offside, and drive continued to 16YL where Hutchins booted winning 33y FG with 52 secs left.

Emerald Bowl (Dec. 26): Southern California 24 Boston College 13

There turned out to be no question about Trojans' desire, despite playing in their 1st non-BCS bowl since 2001. Southern California (9-4) frosh QB Matt Barkley (27-37/350y, 2 TDs, 2 INTs) started on fire, hitting 12-13 passes in opening 18 mins, including pair of TDs to FB Stanley Havili (6/83y, 2 TDs receiving). Havili burst through several tacklers for 53y TD saunter in 1st Q, and followed early in 2nd Q by sliding unseen across formation to nab 5y TD pass for 14-0 lead. Boston College (8-5) awoke on its next series as TB Montel Harris (23/102y, TD) surged for runs of 16, 11, and 14y, capped by 7y TD blast up middle. K Steve Aponavicius' x-pt was missed, however. USC A-A S Taylor Mays soon took terrible pursuit angle on Eagles WR Rich Gunnell (6/130y, TD), who galloped away for 61y TD to pull within 14-13 with 3:48 left in 1st H. Long play helped Gunnell become Eagles' all-time leader in career receiving y. Trojans held BC to 19y in 3rd Q, as DE Jurrell Casey came up with big FUM REC, and turned matters over to star WR Damian Williams (12/189y) in 4th Q. After Troy CB Shareese Wright's midfield INT, Williams soared high among 3 converging defenders to haul in 48y bomb at BC 1YL to set up Barkley for TD sneak and 24-13 edge. Later Williams would get USC out of hole with 23y catch as time soon ran out on BC.

Music City Bowl (Dec. 27): Clemson 21 Kentucky 13

Even though Wildcats failed to win their 4th straight bowl game, Kentucky (7-6) succeeded at its ball possession game plan and held it for 34:26. Unfortunately, Tigers (9-5) RB C.J. Spiller (15/67y, TD and 3/58y receiving) made his touches count, racking up 172y all-purpose for game MVP honors and becoming NCAA's 2nd highest y-maker in history. Late in 1st Q, Spiller's 42y catch launched 90y march to RB Jacoby Ford's 32y tying over-shoulder TD catch of pass from QB Kyle Parker (8-14/141y, TD).

Wildcats had led 7-0 after their opening drive when QB Morgan Newton (13-28/98y, TD) found WR Chris Matthews at left edge of EZ with 17y TD pass. Kentucky earned 10-7 lead on K Lones Seiber's 39y FG, but Clemson took 14-10 H advantage when Spiller's 30y KO RET ignited 60y trip to RB Jamie Harper's 1y TD run. After Tigers NG Jarvis Jenkins' FUM REC at UK 19YL, Spiller spurted 8y to outside for TD with 10 mins remaining in 4th Q. Newton led comeback to Clemson 32YL and scrambled for 7y on 4th down, only to get unhelpful spot just short of 1st down at 25YL.

Independence Bowl (Dec. 28): Georgia 44 Texas A&M 20

High scoring affair predicted by everybody took awhile getting started. With 2:33 left in 1st H, Texas A&M (6-7), which would outgain Georgia (8-5) 471y to 366y, broke scoreless tie as QB Jerrod Johnson (29-58/362y, 2 TDs, 2 INTs) hit TE Jamie McCoy with 15y TD pass. Bulldogs CB Brandon Boykin, who already had pair of TD RETs this season, raced up to field short ensuing KO and charged past great blocks for 81y TD romp to tie it 7-7. Less than min later, aptly-named Georgia special teamer Bacarri Rambo went on mission to block Aggies' punt to 2YL, and TB Caleb King (16/60y, 2 TDs) scored 1st of his 2 TD runs for 14-7 H edge. Texas A&M proved tenacious on opening drive of 3rd Q as RB Christine Michael (15/77y, TD) capped 73y drive by going wide for tying 14y TD romp. Leading 17-14 as middle of 3rd Q approached, Georgia's special teams struck again, recovering bad punt snap at A&M 24YL. On 3rd down, Bulldogs TE Aron White caught 24y TD pass from QB Joe Cox (15-28/158y, 2 TDs, INT) for 24-14 lead. Before 3rd Q ended, Georgia DBs Sanders Commings and Reshad Jones each intercepted pass by Johnson, Jones' setting up another TD catch by White early in 4th Q for 31-14 lead. UGa's ground power took it from there as Bulldogs won 7th of 9 bowl games under head coach Mark Richt.

Eagle Bank Bowl (Dec. 29): UCLA 30 Temple 21

This might have been called "No Jersey, No Coat Bowl." Bitter cold that froze patches of field at Washington's RFK Stadium were countered psychologically in pre-game "warm-up" by topless DT Brian Price of warm-weathered UCLA Bruins (7-6). Meanwhile, Temple (9-4) coach Al Golden manfully roamed sidelines only in white, long-sleeved dress shirt and tie. For Owls, contest came in 2 distinct parts: with and without frosh RB Bernard Pierce (12/53y, TD and 3/33y receiving), who left with injury late in 2nd Q. With Pierce in lineup, Temple led 21-7 in 2nd Q and had gained 224y, while without him Owls were blanked in 2nd H and earned only 58y. UCLA QB Kevin Prince (16-31/221y, 2 TDs, INT) threw quick out-pattern to WR Terrence Austin, who got sharp block on outside and zipped down sideline in 3rd Q for 32y TD that pulled Bruins within 21-17. After UCLA A-A K Kai Forbath made his 2nd long FG early in 4th Q to get within 21-20 key D play came on 3rd-and-20 at Owls 8YL: LB Akeem Ayers slipped on ice coming out of his stance and was out of sight for Temple QB Vaughn Charlton (13-23/159y, TD, 2 INTs). Ayers popped to his feet at right spot to snare INT at 2YL and step in EZ. Prince's 2-pt pass lifted Bruins into 28-21 lead with 6:01 left.

Champs Sports Bowl (Dec. 29): Wisconsin 20 Miami 14

Miami Hurricanes (9-4) shivered in chilly upstate Orlando, while Badgers (10-3) felt right at home as if it were October in Madison. But 1st, Hurricanes swept to early TD when RB Graig Cooper handed off to soaring WR Sam Shields for TD RET of opening KO, that is until unnecessary block-from-behind PEN as Shields crossed GL placed ball at Wisconsin 16YL. Cooper scored on next snap, and Miami led 7-0 after 23 secs. Undaunted, Badgers turned it over to their lines, OL carving holes for TBs John Clay (22/121y, 2 TDs) and Montee Ball (15/61y) and DL limiting Canes to 61y rushing. With pale run game, Miami QB Jacory Harris (16-29/188y, TD) was under constant pressure from Badgers DL, led by DEs O'Brien Schofield and J.J. Watt, which resulted in 5 sacks. Down 20-7 and time running out, Harris got hot after start of 7-16/109y passing. He hit 9-10/79y for TD to WR Thearon Collier with 1:22 left. Hurricanes recovered onside-KO but could go nowhere as UW made sack and forced 3 incompletions.

Holiday Bowl (Dec. 30): Nebraska 33 Arizona 0

Never in 31 Holiday Bowl games or in 45 bowl games in Nebraska (10-4) history had there been even 1 shutout posted. This blanking on rainy night in San Diego was highlighted by Cornhuskers D, sparked by its extraordinary DL led by sr DT Ndamukong Suh, which so dominated Arizona (8-5) that Wildcats didn't cross midfield until 2nd H and totaled only 109y O by game's end. Cats had barely surpassed 30y O until late 4th Q drive went 72y—thanks to 36y spurt by RB Keola Antolin—only to die on 4th down incompletion from Huskers 8YL. Nebraska had struck early as S Matt O'Hanlon returned INT 37y to Arizona 5YL. Huskers QB Zac Lee (13-23/173y, TD and 18/65y, TD rushing), who looked faster and stronger since end of regular season, skirted RE for TD and 7-0 lead. K Alex Henery mixed in 4 FGs, and late in 3rd Q Lee launched 74y TD bomb to WR Niles Paul (4/123y, TD) for 33-0 lead. Harried Wildcats QB Nick Foles, who arrived with 66.1% completion rate, could hit only 6-20/28y, INT.

Armed Forces Bowl (Dec. 31): Air Force 47 Houston 20

Air Force (8-5) was real force in air game with QB Tim Jefferson's 10-14/162y passing, much to surprise of aerial-minded Houston (10-4), which never got its O working smoothly. Falcons' best-in-nation pass D, picked off Cougars QB Case Keenum (24-41/222y, TD, 6 INTs) 6 times, including trio by CB Anthony Wright and pair by SS Chris Thomas (12 tackles). Air Force jumped to 14-0 lead in 1st Q and went on to possess ball for 41 mins, gaining 402y rushing as TB Asher Clark (17/126y, 2 TDs) and FB Jared Tew (27/175y, 2 TDs) each scored twice. Tew's 2nd TD was clinching 71y gallop up middle of Houston's tiring D for 47-20 lead with 3:32 to play. Big plays launched 2nd H: Houston WR Tyron Carrier weaved his way 79y for KO TD RET only to see Air Force RB Jonathan Warzeka break seemingly sure tackle at his 15YL and charge down right sideline for answering 100y KO TD RET and 31-13 lead.

Sun Bowl (Dec. 31): Oklahoma 31Stanford 27

Each team in hard-hitting game at El Paso offered up O star to pin their hopes upon. Sooners (8-5) came out on top because of record-setting performance of WR Ryan Broyles (13/156y 3 TDs), who set single-game school mark for receptions and Sun Bowl record for TD catches. Heisman Trophy runner-up TB Toby Gerhart (32/135y, 2 TDs) of Stanford (8-5) had to work awfully hard for his y against tough OU run-D to keep Cardinal in game. After S Bo McNally's 55y INT RET, Stanford called on FB Owen Marecic to plunge for 1y TD to knot it 7-7 in 1st Q. Gerhart tallied twice in 2nd Q, and Cards led 24-17 at H. Oklahoma tied it in 3rd Q on Broyles' 3rd TD catch from QB Landry Jones (30-51/418y, 3 TDs, INT), who came out from under Sam Bradford's big shadow in sparking Sooners' effective aerial attack. RB DeMarco Murray flipped over GL for wining pts after 42y punt RET by Broyles later in 3rd Q.

Texas Bowl (Dec. 31): Navy 35 Missouri 13

Nobody was more disappointed in Middies' surprising rout than Missouri's most-successful-ever sr class—with 38-16 record—that included bellwether WR Danario Alexander and LB Sean Weatherspoon. Alexander (6/137y, TD) caught swing pass from QB Blaine Gabbert (15-31/291y, TD, 2 INTs) on 2nd scrimmage play by Mizzou Tigers (8-5) and raced away for 58y TD. That was pretty well Missouri's last good moment as plucky Navy (10-4) used its effective option-run O to camp in Tigers territory for most of afternoon. Recent single season record setter for rushing TDs by QB, Midshipman QB Ricky Dobbs (9-14/130y, TD and 30/166y, 3 TDs rushing) added to his total by tallying twice for 14-7 lead by early in 2nd Q. Middies turned on D steam in 2nd H to close with 4 sacks of Gabbert as Dobbs threw and ran for TDs.

Insight Bowl (Dec. 31): Iowa State 14 Minnesota 13

Trying to avoid their 3rd Insight Bowl loss in 4 years, Golden Gophers (6-7) D made early 4th down stop to lead to 36y FG by K Eric Ellestad in 1st Q. Iowa State (7-6) leaned on its pair of O stars—QB Austen Arnaud (19-26/216y, TD, 2 INTs and 21/76y, TD rushing) and RB Alexander Robinson (22/137y)—to craft pair of long TD drives in 2nd Q. Arnaud ran for 9y TD and pitched 38y TD pass to WR Jake Williams, but Arnaud would turn ball over 4 times. In 2nd Q, Minnesota turned possession over on downs at 13YL and QB Adam Weber (18-32/261y, TD, INT) tossed INT by Cyclones SS David Sims in EZ. In 3rd Q, Gophers drove 69y to Weber's 23y TD pass to TE Nick Tow-Arnett. Minny trailed by only 1 pt when Ellestad kicked his 2nd FG late in 3rd Q. Gophers took over on their own 1YL after P Mike Brandtner's punt was downed by Cyclones with 7 mins left to play. Weber hit 3 passes/42y, and frosh QB MarQueis Gray chipped in with 28y run, but Gray lost FUM at Iowa State 17YL to kill victory chances. Paul Rhoads became ISU's 1st head coach since George Veenker in 1931 to post winning record in his debut season.

Chick-fil-A Bowl (Dec. 31): Virginia Tech 37 Tennessee 14

Time nearly had run out in 1st H, so Tennessee (7-6), which had just tied game at 14-14, expected Hokies to take knee to kill clock. Instead, Virginia Tech (10-3) QB Tyrod Taylor (10-17/209y, INT) arched 63y bomb to big-handed WR Jarrett Boykin (4/120y) inside 5YL; coach Frank Beamer quickly called timeout. Vols jogged off field but were called back, helpless to stop Va Tech K Matt Waldron from booting 1st of his 3 FGs on last play of 1st H. Virginia Tech, on way to its 5th straight victory since October, never again was in danger as frosh TB Ryan Williams (25/117y, 2TDs), who already had scored twice, came out for 3rd Q rampage on his way to school single-season rushing record of 1655y to best Kevin Jones' 1647y in 2003. Tennessee TB Montario Hardesty, who was limited to 18/39y rushing, scored on 4y run in 2nd Q, and QB Jonathan Crompton (15-26/235y, TD, INT) soon flipped short TD pass to WR Denarius Moore—who would drop almost sure long TD pass in 4th Q—to create deadlock with 18 secs left in 2nd Q. But, Vols could gain only 112y in 2nd H and were blanked.

Outback Bowl: Auburn 38 Northwestern 35 (OT)

Since introduction of OT in 1996, few OT games had turned out as wacky as Outback Bowl. When Northwestern (8-5) found it couldn't run other than on QB draws and scrambles, it simply stopped altogether and QB Mike Kafka set bundle of school passing records on 47-78/532y, 4 TDs, 5 INTs. Pair of INTs by Kafka put Wildcats in 14-0 hole as Auburn CB Walter McFadden picked off Kafka at NW 31YL to lead to 1y TD run by Tigers back-up QB Kodi Burns. When Wildcats responded with 17-play trip to 6YL, McFadden snatched INT at far left edge of EZ and steamed 100y down sideline for TD RET. Kafka bounced right back with 39y TD pass to WR Andrew Brewer (8/133y, 2 TDs). Auburn QB Chris Todd (20-31/235y, TD) pitched 46y TD to WR Quindarius Carr, WR Darvin Adams caught 12/142y, and RB Ben Tate (20/108y, 2 TDs) crashed for pair of 4th Q TD runs, but Kafka rallied Cats from deficits of 21-7 and 35-21. Kafka scored on 2y run with 3:20 left in 4th Q, but x-pt block by Tigers DE Antonio Coleman (4 tackles, sack) preserved 35-27 lead. Back came NW as Kafka hit WR Sidney Stewart with 18y TD pass. Wildcats ran trick play, and Brewer tossed 2-pt pass to WR Kevin Mitchell to send it to OT. Auburn K Wes Byrum made easy 21y FG in OT, and then fun began. NW WR Zeke Markshausen (12/84y) fumbled, but instead of game ending, Tigers DB Neiko Thorpe (14 tackles, INT) was penalized for illegally batting loose ball. Kafka was sacked and fumbled as he spun to unload pass. TV review ruled Kafka down on contact. K Stefan Demos, who barely missed winning FG at end of regulation, tried tying 37y FG only to bounce it off upright. Auburn celebrated for 3rd time in OT, but was penalized for roughing (and injuring) Demos. On 4th down at 5YL, frosh K Steve Flaherty was called on, but Northwestern coach Pat Fitzgerald, instead called fake with sweep by Markshausen, who was stopped by Thorpe.

Capital One Bowl: Penn State 19 Louisiana State 17

Thanks to pre-game rainstorm and Champs Sports Bowl staged 3 days earlier, Florida Citrus Bowl stadium's dreadful grass surface slowed teams as hundreds of massive divots were churned up. Muck quickly turned white of Tigers' jerseys and Lions' pants into dark gray. With coach Joe Paterno in search of his record 24th bowl victory, Penn State (11-2) somewhat dominated in gaining 16-3 lead by 3rd Q. However, LSU's resolve had kept Lions from cashing but 1 of 5 red zone trips into TD. K Collin Wagner's 4 FGs, kicked in tough conditions, were difference. Behind by 13 pts, LSU (9-4) struck swiftly on its last series of 3rd Q after short KO was returned to 47YL: QB Jordan Jefferson (13-24/202y, TD, INT) fired rocket to WR Brandon LaFell (5/87y, TD), who cut to center of field for 24y TD. On Tigers' next try launched by RB-WR Trinton Holliday's 37y punt RET, Jefferson hit WR Terrance Toliver with 39y pass to set up 1y TD plunge by RB Stevan Ridley. Suddenly, LSU led 17-16 early in 4th Q. With 6:54 to go, Penn State took over at its 31YL and pieced together determined drive as sr QB Daryll Clark (18-35/216y, TD), who had fired 37y TD to WR Derek Moye in 1st Q, hit 3-3/33y passing and C Stefen Wiesniewski threw block to spring RB Stephfon Green to 1st down at LSU 8YL. Wagner drilled winning 21y FG with 1:01 to play.

Gator Bowl: Florida State 33 West Virginia 21

All eyes were on Bobby Bowden as Florida State (7-6) rallied to send its 80-year-old coach to retirement with his 389th career win. Run attack of West Virginia (9-4) clicked early: QB Jarrett Brown got away for 32y TD run before being injured in 2nd Q, and RB Noel Devine (16/168y, TD) burst off right side and sped 70y before being knocked OB at 4YL. Devine scored 2 plays later. Trailing 14-3 in 2nd Q, Seminoles turned tide with INT of Brown by FS Jamie Robinson, which led to 1st of 2 TD runs by RB Jermaine Thomas (25/121y, 2 TDs). Florida State took its 1st lead at 16-14 on 3rd of 4 FGs by K Dustin Hopkins early in 3rd Q. Seminoles frosh QB E.J. Manuel passed 17-24/189y.

Sugar Bowl: Florida 51 Cincinnati 24

Playing his final collegiate game, Florida's brilliant QB Tim Tebow (31-35/482y, 3 TDs) went out with tremendous 533y total O. Tebow nearly passed for career-best y before H as he connected on his 1st 12 tries on his way to 20-23/320y, 3 TDs in 1st H. Tebow finished night with 14/51y rushing with 3rd Q TD in sparking Gators (13-1) to rout over previously-undefeated Bearcats (12-1). Gators TE Aaron Hernandez (9/111y, TD) caught early TD pass, and K Caleb Sturgis had his 1st x-pt blocked but hit 40y FG. In 2nd Q, Florida WR Deonte Thompson made great catch at right edge of EZ, and lead went to 23-0 as RB Emmanuel Moody (2 TDs rushing), something of disappointment since his transfer from USC, used seal block by LT Xavier Nixon to score 6y TD. Cincinnati finally hit scoreboard on 47y FG by K Jake Rogers, but on 1st snap after KO, Tebow launched perfect 80y TD bomb to WR Riley Cooper (7/181y, TD). When Tebow ran for his TD, score margin hit 44-10, and he had set new Sugar Bowl record with hand in 4 TDs. Cincinnati QB Tony Pike (27-45/170y, 3 TDs) kept pitching and completed 3 short scoring passes in 2nd H.

Rose Bowl: Ohio State 26 Oregon 17

America got to see best of heralded Ohio State (11-2) QB Terrelle Pryor (23-37/266y, 2 TDs, INT and 20/72y rushing), who definitely was given keys to Buckeyes passing game. Ohio State surprisingly opened with bundle of throws to weak perimeter of D of Oregon (10-3) and traveled 74y as Pryor hit 5-8/39y and scrambled 24y. RB Brandon Saine (14/45y and 2/59y, TD receiving) took pass and zipped along right sideline and ran over tackler at GL. Ohio K Devin Barclay added 19y FG for 10-0 lead. Ducks tied it on consecutive possessions once 2nd Q arrived: K Morgan Flint made 24y FG and big RB LaGarrette Blount smacked up middle for short TD run. Barclay made another FG 1:05 before H, and as Buckeyes DT Doug Worthington soon deflected pass by Ducks QB Jeremiah Masoli (9-20/81y, INT) LB Ross Homan intercepted. It poised long-range K Aaron Pettrey for 45y FG as H clock hit 0:00. Trailing 16-10, Oregon earned its only lead of 17-16 as RB Kenjon Barner returned 2nd H KO 39y and caught 14y flanker-screen pass from Masoli to set up Masoli's 1y TD keeper. Ohio answered on another FG by Barclay, and Pryor authored 81y TD drive in 4th Q. Pryor's key pass leading to 17y TD catch by Buckeyes WR DeVier Posey was bit of high-arched prayer. It came on 3rd down grab made by 6'6" TE Jake Ballard, who went high to haul in 24y pitch at Oregon 31YL. Secrets to Buckeyes securing Big 10's 1st Rose Bowl win since 2000 were their strong D and 41:37 of possession time.

Papajohns.com Bowl (Jan. 2): Connecticut 20 South Carolina 7

Excessive pass-rush pressure by Huskies (8-5) on Gamecocks (7-6) QB Stephen Garcia (16-38/129y, INT) and slew of dropped passes doomed South Carolina in what coach Steve Spurrier would call "sad, sad effort." While racing down sideline, Connecticut WR Kashif Moore made 1-handed spear of 37y TD pass from QB Zach Frazer (9-21/107y, TD) in 1st Q. After K Dave Teggart added pair of FGs, UConn led 13-0 at H. TB Andre Dixon (33/126y, TD) scored his 7th TD in 4 games for Huskies to build insurmountable lead to 20-0 early in 4th Q. Thick RB Brian Maddox went over from 2YL for late Carolina score. Remembering slain teammate Jasper Howard Huskies coach Randy Edsall said of his team: "I was a little worried that the season had been so long and so tough on them that I didn't see a whole lot of emotion from them. But I guess they were just saving it up for today."

Cotton Bowl (Jan. 2): Mississippi 21 Oklahoma State 7

With 7 losses between pair of clubs that each started season each ranked in AP Top 10, Cotton Bowl—making its 1st appearance in gigantic Cowboys Stadium—could have been dubbed "Disappointment Bowl." Mississippi (9-4) QB Jevon Snead (13-23/168y, 3 INTs), who had enjoyed brilliant performance in last year's Cotton Bowl victory, continued his mystifying inaccuracy of 2009 season. On Snead's 3rd INT, he was clobbered by blindside block on Oklahoma State (9-4) RET and was shelved until 2nd H. On Rebels sub QB Nathan Stanley's 1st play, star RB Dexter McCluster (34/182y, 2 TDs) took handoff and roared 86y to TD. Cowboys didn't tie it until midway in 3rd Q when Stanley was intercepted by OSU LB Andre Sexton and his RET to Rebs 12YL. On 3rd-and-goal at 1YL, Oklahoma State RB Keith Toston faked run out of Wildcat Formation and tossed jump-pass to TE Wilson Youman. Cowboys stunningly turned ball over on each of their 6 4th Q possessions, and Ole Miss finally cashed McCluster's 2y TD run for 14-7 lead. With barely more than 3 mins to play, Robinson hit WR Hubert Anyiam over middle, but catch was fumbled to Ole Miss LB Patrick Trahan (INT), who returned it 34y for clinching TD. McCluster became SEC's 1st player ever to exceed 1000y rushing and 500y receiving in single season.

Liberty Bowl (Jan. 2): Arkansas 20 East Carolina 17 (OT)

Fast-closing Conf USA champion East Carolina (9-5) sought its 7th win in last 8 games and went ahead 7-0 on 2nd Q TD run by RB Dominique Lindsay (33/151y, TD). But poor late-game FG kicking would kill Pirates. Razorbacks (8-5), who would end up being outgained 393y to 283y, were behind 10-3 in 3rd Q when FS Tramain Thomas ripped 37y up middle on INT TD RET to tie it. Late in 3rd Q, ECU QB Patrick Pinkney (17-33/209y, TD, 2 INTs) rebounded with TD pass, but moments later Arkansas QB Ryan Mallett (15-36/202y, TD) answered with his own scoring pitch to knot it 17-17. Pirates K Ben Hartman (2nd Q FG) missed twice late in 4th Q and again in OT. Poised Hogs K Alex Tejada, who had missed in upset try against Florida, won it with 37y FG.

Alamo Bowl (Jan. 2): Texas Tech 41 Michigan State 31

Plenty of drama dogged these bowl foes since November. Michigan State (6-7) coach Mark Dantonio suspended 14 team members, including much of his receiving corps, after dorm brawl. Texas Tech (9-4) was without its successful coach Mike Leach because school suspended, then fired Leach over allegations of mistreatment of injured WR Adam James. Taking Leach's place was his friend and D-coordinator Ruffin McNeill, who in relief afterward said, "It was the most difficult week of my life and the most rewarding night of my life." Spartans came to play hard, using 46y TD burst by frosh RB Edwin Baker in 1st Q and taking leads of 21-20, 28-27, 31-27 leads after K Brett Swenson (44y FG in 4th Q) dived onto Texas Tech's FUM of 2nd H KO at 26YL. MSU scored in creative fashion as backup QB-turned-WR Keith Nichol lined up in backfield and went up middle for 7y TD. After fake FG turned into 18y pass completion by holder-lined-up-as-K Aaron Bates, WR Blair White caught 8y TD pass from WR Keshawn Martin, who slipped into backfield lineup. Earlier, Texas Tech QB Taylor Potts (29-43/372y, 2 TDs, INT) had thrown 2 scoring passes, but he left before 4th Q to have his non-throwing hand x-rayed. Potts' x-ray was negative, but coaches decided to stick with sub QB Steven Scheffield, who arrived with hot hand in hitting 9-11/88y, TD, including 11y TD to WR Detron Lewis that provided last lead Tech needed at 34-31. RB Baron Batch wrapped it up at 41-31 with 13y TD burst with 2:08 left to go.

Fiesta Bowl (Jan. 4): Boise State 17 Texas Christian 10

Nothing went right for about 28 mins for undefeated Texas Christian (12-1). TCU played as if it had never seen big crowds (73,227 fans attended Fiesta Bowl) or heard loud crowd noise (roof to University of Phoenix Stadium was closed): Horned Frogs jumped prematurely on snap counts on both sides of ball, ran poor pass routes, couldn't get their ground game rolling, and for time couldn't communicate with their coaches upstairs. Still, despite QB Andy Dalton (25-44/272y, TD, 3 INTs) being picked off by Boise State (14-0) CB Brandyn Thompson for 51y TD in 1st Q, TCU trailed only 10-0 when it took over at its 38YL with 2:21 to go in 1st H. Dalton hit passes to WRs Antoine Hicks—who would drop potential TD pass in 4th Q—and Jimmy Young and launched 30y TD pass down left sideline that WR Curtis Clay hauled into EZ as he tumbled with Thompson in coverage. Frogs tied it in middle of 3rd Q on K Ross Evans' 29y FG after A-A DE Jerry Hughes, who struggled with double-team blocks all night, forced and recovered midfield FUM. Deadlocked 10-10 with about 10 mins to go in 4th Q, Broncos faced 4th-and-9 at their 33YL. Out of blue-and-orange bag of tricks came play called "Riddler," which permitted Frogs LB Tanner Brock to storm up middle of punt formation while TE Kyle Efaw slipped into Brock's vacated area as P Kyle Brotzman barely got his pass away. But it was right on money to Efaw for 29y gain, and RB Doug Martin scored 4 plays later to provide all pts Boise State would need to lock up modern college's 2nd 14-0 record in history. But 1st, Brotzman had to knock TCU WR Jeremy Kerley OB at Broncos 31YL when it looked as though Kerley might race down sideline to tying TD on punt RET. Brotzman also punted 55y to Frogs 1YL to hamper TCU's last series that ended with Thompson tipping pass for clinching INT by S Winston Venable (8 tackles, INT). Dalton leap-frogged Max Knake (1992-95) to become TCU's all-time career pass y leader, while Boise State QB Kellen Moore (23-39/211y) overcame weak 1st Q to maintain his fabulous FBS-record single season ratio of TDs-to-INTs of 39 to 3. In end, however, victory truly was secured by Boise's fine D, led by Thompson, Venable, CB Kyle Wilson, and frequent shifts by its front-7.

Orange Bowl (Jan. 5): Iowa 24 Georgia Tech 14

Given month to prepare, determined D unit of Iowa Hawkeyes (11-2) put net over sophisticated running attack of Georgia Tech (11-3). Coming in to coldest Orange Bowl on record, Yellow Jackets had fewest 3-and-out series (14) in nation but went without 1st down on their opening 4 O possessions. Thanks to Iowa's 1st H D, Georgia Tech managed meager 32y rushing and 0y passing. Sparkling on D was DE Adrian Clayborn, who bottled up outside runs with 9 tackles (2 tfls) and made 2 sacks. Meanwhile, Iowa QB Ricky Stanzi (17-29/231y, 2 TDs, INT) returned without any rust after missing nearly 3 games with ankle injury. Stanzi picked out right edge of EZ in 1st Q and pitched 3y TD lob in back corner to WR Marvin McNutt and 21y TD to WR Colin Sandeman. Tech CB Jerrard Tarrant had been victimized on both TDs, but before 1st Q could end, Tarrant turned tables by dashing 40y to TD with INT. Iowa led

14-7 at H. Jackets used more than 7 mins to open 3rd Q but missed FG try, and Iowa K Daniel Murray kicked FG for 17-7 lead. SB Anthony Allen, who had scored twice for Louisville in 2007 Orange Bowl, tallied for Jackets on pitchout run to right early in 4th Q. Hawks later tried tricky run off fake FG, but it didn't fool Jackets S Morgan Burnett, who smacked down Murray. On 1st snap, Iowa S Tyler Sash met Tech FB Jonathan Dwyer (14/49y) at scrimmage line. Dwyer reversed his path and swept into EZ, where it took missed tackles by 3 of Hawkeyes' best defenders—Clayborn, Sash, and LB A.J. Edds (INT)—to permit Dwyer to escape safety. After Jackets' punt, Hawks TB Brandon Wegher (16/113y, TD) powered off left side and broke free for clinching 32y TD sprint.

BCS Championship Bowl (Jan. 7): Alabama 37 Texas 21

After icy weather dominated bowl season, Pasadena's Rose Bowl Stadium was beautiful setting for 12th annual BCS Championship Game. Texas (13-1), 4-pt underdog, started well, sacking Alabama (14-0) QB Greg McElroy (6-11/58y) 3 times and taking 6-0 lead on pair of FGs by K Hunter Lawrence. But Longhorns' bubble already had burst less than 5 mins into contest when Crimson Tide DE Marcell Dareus made real tide-turner on his only tackle of game. His clean hit on Texas A-A QB Colt McCoy on run off left side sent star passer/runner to shelf with mild shoulder injury. "I would have given anything to be out there because it would have been different," vowed McCoy. Not only did Texas attack suffer with inexperienced frosh QB Garrett Gilbert (15-40/186y, 2 TDs, 4 INTs) at helm, but Horns D lost much of it edge for rest of 1st H. Alabama got its running game going as Heisman-winning RB Mark Ingram (22/116y, 2 TDs) pounded for TD on 2nd snap of 2nd Q that put Tide ahead for good at 7-6, and frosh RB Trent Richardson (19/109y, 2 TDs) burst up middle behind crushing block of A-A LG Mike Johnson for 49y TD, also in 2nd Q. With Bama ahead 17-6 in waning moments of 1st H, Texas coaches made disastrous decision. Facing 2nd-and-1 at their 37YL with only 15 secs remaining before H, Longhorns had choice to try long pass with unlikely hope of scoring or take knee to kill remaining time. Instead, they went with halfway measure: short shovel pass by Gilbert, which was batted about before landing in Dareus' hands for rumbling 28y INT TD RET. "I was thinking about grabbing the guy with the ball," recounted Dareus afterward. "But then I said, 'Let me just grab this football'...My legs were weak, my muscles were crazy, and I made it." With commanding 24-6 lead in 3rd Q and McElroy also banged up but playing, Alabama turned conservative while Gilbert turned hot for Texas. Gilbert pinpointed Steers' only O player who truly could hurt Bama: A-A WR Jordan Shipley (10/122y, 2 TDs) who broke clear for 44y TD catch on Gilbert's post-pattern pass late in 3rd Q and 28y TD catch against confused secondary 6 mins into 4th Q. When Texas took over at its 7YL down 24-21 with 3:14 to play, its O had makings of 1 of greatest Cinderella comebacks ever. But after D PEN moved ball out to 17YL, Crimson Tide LB Eryk Anders (7 tackles, sack) blew in untouched on 1st down blitz, and Gilbert lost FUM at his 3YL. Ingram scored TD 3 plays later, and, after INT by Crimson Tide CB Javier Arenas (5 tackles, 2 INTs, 1 pass break-up), Richardson tacked on another Bama TD with 2y run 47 secs from finish. Alabama had captured its 8th national title since AP Poll began in 1930s—its 1st since 1992—while practically mistake-free McElroy remained undefeated since 8th grade as QB starter. He also became Bama's all-time single-season leader with 2508y passing.

Final USA TODAY Coaches Poll January 8

1 Alabama (58)	1450	14 Nebraska	671
2 Texas	1360	15 Pittsburgh	667
3 Florida	1323	16 Wisconsin	587
4 Boise State	1312	17 Louisiana State	530
5 Ohio State	1190	18 Utah	466
6 Texas Christian	1104	19 Miami	336
7 Iowa	1087	20 Southern California	217
8 Penn State	1071	21 Mississippi	192
9 Cincinnati	943	22 West Virginia	159
10 Virginia Tech	940	23 Texas Tech	152
11 Oregon	846	24 Central Michigan	123
12 Brigham Young	814	25 Oklahoma State	92
13 Georgia Tech	741		

Final AP Poll January 8

1 Alabama (60)	1500	14 Nebraska	724
2 Texas	1399	15 Pittsburgh	697
3 Florida	1370	16 Wisconsin	571
4 Boise State	1366	17 Louisiana State	501
5 Ohio State	1224	18 Utah	491
6 Texas Christian	1163	19 Miami	310
7 Iowa	1126	20 Mississippi	296
8 Cincinnati	1060	21 Texas Tech	224
9 Penn State	1016	22 Southern California	216
10 Virginia Tech	953	23 Central Michigan	166
11 Oregon	886	24 Clemson	125
12 Brigham Young	806	25 West Virginia	91
13 Georgia Tech	768		

2009 Top Performance Formula

1 Alabama	1.8282
2 Texas	1.7483
3 Boise State	1.7216
4 Florida	1.7134
5 Texas Christian	1.6917
6 Ohio State	1.5991
7 Cincinnati	1.5911
8 Virginia Tech	1.5289
9 Penn State	1.5199
10 Oregon	1.5086
11 Iowa	1.4902
12 Brigham Young	1.4877
13 Pittsburgh	1.4523
14 Georgia Tech	1.4164
15 Nebraska	1.4143
16 Louisiana State	1.4109
17 Wisconsin	1.4001
18 Miami	1.3496
19 Texas Tech	1.3175
20 Oklahoma	1.3122

2009 Top Opponent Records

1 Mississippi State	.6611
2 Louisiana State	.63398
3 Alabama	.63393
4 Florida State	.6286
5 Oregon	.6209
6 Arkansas	.6168
7 Florida	.6134
8 Iowa	.6132
9 South Carolina	.6129
10 Virginia Tech	.6090
11 Miami	.6065
12 Texas	.6061
13 Oklahoma	.5961
14 Arizona	.5948
15 Syracuse	.5928
16 Ohio State	.5921
17 Clemson	.5915
18t Minnesota	.590789
18t West Virginia	.590789
20 Pittsburgh	.59067

2009 Out-of-Conference Records

	W-L	Percentage	Bowl W-L
Southeastern	38-9	.8085	6-4
Big East	26-10	.7222	4-2
Big Ten	27-15	.6429	4-3
Big Twelve	29-18	.6170	4-4
Pacific-10	19-14	.5758	2-5
Mountain West	19-16	.5429	4-1
Atlantic Coast	22-20	.5238	3-4

2009 Individual Statistical Leaders

RUSHING YARDS	Attempts	Yards	Average
Toby Gerhart, Stanford	343	1871	5.5
Ryan Mathews, Fresno State	276	1808	6.6
Dion Lewis, Pittsburgh	325	1799	5.5
Mark Ingram, Alabama	271	1658	6.1
Ryan Williams, Virginia Tech	293	1655	5.7
Donald Buckram, Texas-El Paso	259	1594	6.2
LaMichael James, Oregon	230	1546	6.7
John Clay, Wisconsin	287	1517	5.3
Noel Devine, West Virginia	241	1465	6.1
Montel Harris, Boston College	308	1457	4.7

PASSING YARDS	Completions	Attempts	Yards	Percentage
Case Keenum, Houston	492	700	5671	70.3
Tyler Sheehan, Bowling Green	373	575	4051	64.9
Jimmy Clausen, Notre Dame	289	425	3722	68.0
Ryan Mallett, Arkansas	225	403	3624	55.8
Todd Reesing, Kansas	313	496	3616	63.1
Blaine Gabbert, Missouri	262	445	3593	58.9
Jerrod Johnson, Texas A&M	296	497	3679	59.6
Max Hall, Brigham Young	275	409	3560	67.2
Kellen Moore, Boise State	277	431	3536	64.3
Colt McCoy, Texas	332	470	3521	70.6

RECEIVING YARDS	Catches	Yards
Danario Alexander, Missouri	113	1781
Freddie Barnes, Bowling Green	155	1770
Greg Salas, Hawaii	106	1590
Golden Tate, Notre Dame	93	1496
Jordan Shipley, Texas	116	1485
Emmanuel Sanders, SMU	98	1339
James Cleveland, Houston	104	1214
Mardy Gilyard, Cincinnati	87	1191
David Reed, Utah	81	1188
Demaryius Thomas, Georgia Tech	46	1154

2009 Consensus All-America Team
Offense

Wide Receiver:	Golden Tate, Notre Dame
	Jordan Shipley, Texas
Tight End:	Aaron Hernandez, Florida
	Dennis Pitta, Brigham Young
Line:	Russell Okung, Oklahoma State
	Trent Williams, Texas
	Mike Johnson, Alabama
	Mike Iupati, Idaho
Center:	Maurkice Pouncey, Florida
Quarterback:	Colt McCoy, Texas
Running Back:	Toby Gerhart, Stanford
	Mark Ingram, Alabama
Kicker:	Kai Forbath, UCLA
Kick Returner:	C.J. Spiller, Clemson

Defense

Line:	Jerry Hughes, Texas Christian
	Gerald McCoy, Oklahoma
	Ndamukong Suh, Nebraska
	Terrence Cody, Alabama
Linebacker:	Greg Jones, Michigan State
	Rolando McClain, Alabama
	Eric Norwood, South Carolina
	Brandon Spikes, Florida
Back:	Joe Haden, Florida
	Javier Arenas, Alabama
	Eric Berry, Tennessee
	Earl Thomas, Texas
Punter:	Drew Butler, Georgia

2009 Heisman Trophy Vote

Mark Ingram, sophomore running back, Alabama	1304
Toby Gerhart, senior tailback, Stanford	1276
Colt McCoy, senior quarterback, Texas	1145
Ndamukong Suh, senior defensive tackle, Nebraska	815
Tim Tebow, senior quarterback, Florida	390

Other 2009 Major Awards

Maxwell (Player)	Colt McCoy, senior quarterback, Texas
Walter Camp (Player)	Colt McCoy, senior quarterback, Texas
Outland (Lineman)	Ndamukong Suh, senior defensive tackle, Nebraska
Lombardi (Lineman)	Ndamukong Suh, senior defensive tackle, Nebraska
Doak Walker (Running Back)	Toby Gerhart, senior tailback, Stanford
Davey O'Brien (Quarterback)	Colt McCoy, senior quarterback, Texas
Fred Biletnikoff (Receiver)	Golden Tate, junior wide receiver, Notre Dame
Jim Thorpe (Defensive Back)	Eric Berry, junior safety, Tennessee
Dick Butkus (Linebacker)	Rolando McClain, junior linebacker, Alabama
Chuck Bednarik (Defender)	Ndamukong Suh, senior defensive tackle, Nebraska
Lou Groza (Placekicker)	Kai Forbath, junior kicker, UCLA
Ray Guy (Punter)	Drew Butler, sophomore punter, Georgia
Johnny Unitas (Sr. Quarterback)	Colt McCoy, senior quarterback, Texas
John Mackey (Tight End)	Aaron Hernandez, junior tight end, Florida
Dave Rimington (Center)	Maurkice Pouncey, junior center, Florida
Ted Hendricks (Defensive End)	Jerry Hughes, senior defensive end, TCU
Bronko Nagurski (Defender)	Ndamukong Suh, senior defensive tackle, Nebraska
AFCA Coach of the Year	Gary Patterson, Texas Christian

2010

The Year of Covetous Designs on the Big Twelve, the Un-whistled Run, and Disheartening News

In the spring of 2010 while the U.S. Census Bureau was busy counting Americans, it became quite difficult to count teams in college football's major conferences. The Big Ten and Pacific-10 both looked outside for new members to be able to split into divisions and promulgate conference title games. And each league had covetous designs on the Big Twelve.

It started in 2009 when Texas quietly floated the idea of going independent from the Big Twelve to develop its own television network, which would borrow from Notre Dame's home game arrangement with NBC and the new, quickly-profitable Big Ten Network, which beamed a full array of conference sports—with football as star attraction—to a national cable audience. Texas could do this because in recent years it built considerable fan following and the financial clout that came with the establishment of a national brand.

Texas' initiative served to weaken the Big Twelve and put the Longhorns and several other schools in play for the bold expansion plans of others. It was reported the Big Ten coveted the Big Twelve North's Nebraska and Missouri and the Big East's Rutgers and Connecticut. Notre Dame had rebuffed bids from the Big Ten in the past but this time was lured into talks, however unfulfilling, with its Midwestern neighbors.

The Pacific-10 had flirtations with the whole Big Twelve South, including Texas. Texas couldn't lose; it held all the trump cards in any Big Twelve maneuvers. In the end, the Longhorns rebuffed Pac-10 advances and saved most of the Big Twelve and with it the somewhat lesser football programs of Baylor, Iowa State, Kansas, and Kansas State. It was rumored that just to stay in place the other Big Twelve teams had to pay Texas reparations a departure would have cost the school. It still got its TV deal: in early 2011 an exclusive contract with ESPN was announced.

Meanwhile, Boise State, recent darling of the BCS-buster crowd, took a step up from the Western Athletic Conference by joining the Mountain West for 2011. When the Big Twelve changes finally reached fruition a few weeks later, Nebraska was headed to the Big Ten and Colorado to the Pac-10 in 2011. The Pac-10 added Utah from the Mountain West, and Brigham Young soon went independent from the same group. At year's end, TCU jumped all the way from the Mountain West to the Big East for 2012.

It all made for a scrambled off- and early-season in college football. Even new league names were up in the air as fans pondered a future in which the Big Ten would claim 12 members and the Big Twelve would have 10.

The final divisional split of the Big Ten received plenty of criticism. Many mocked the new division names—Legends and Leaders—and wondered how support had evaporated for naming them after coaching legends Woody Hayes and Bo Schembechler. Ohio State and Michigan were divided into separate groups but retained their rivalry season capper.

The Big Ten ignored the orderly set-up of the Southeastern Conference, which in 1992 had been split into logical east and west divisions. The Big Ten copied the hodgepodge of the Atlantic Coast Conference, which grouped its members in difficult-to-remember divisions.

In 2010, Boise State (12-1), defending Fiesta Bowl champions, returned 20 of 22 starters from 2009 and were tapped no. 3 in the AP preseason poll and no. 5 in the USA TODAY Coaches Poll. Traveling cross-country to take on Virginia Tech (11-3) in the opener at the Washington Redskins' Fed Ex Field, Boise State beat the Hokies in the last minute, 33-30. Virginia Tech lost at home a week later to James Madison of the FCS division. That ugly scar on the Hokies' record also briefly discredited Boise State; the Broncos didn't play that Saturday but still lost ground in perception. That was reversed when the Hokies righted the ship and ripped off 11 straight wins on their way to an ACC championship victory over Florida State (10-4) and Orange Bowl match against Stanford (12-1). On his way out the door to the San Francisco 49ers, Stanford coach Jim Harbaugh oversaw a tremendous second half effort in a 40-12 Orange Bowl victory.

Boise State rolled to a 10-0 record, crushing opponents by 38 points per game. But on November 26, when the Broncos stunningly fell in overtime at Nevada (13-1), thanks to a pair of missed short field goals, Boise fell all the way from a potential BCS title date to the middling Las Vegas Bowl.

A correction to a computer service contributing to the final BCS numbers elevated Boise State from 11th to 10th, which in no way changed the Broncos' bowl status but opened the door for university president Bob Kustra to rail further against the system.

"We allow the BCS to work its magic with no idea how accurate its rankings are on a week to week basis," fumed Kustra.

Kustra also had criticized the BCS in November, so Ohio State (12-1) president Gordon Gee disparaged the schedules of minor conference members like Boise State, saying, "We do not play the Little Sisters of the Poor." Gee had a point. While Boise State's 2010 victories over Virginia Tech and less-formidable-than-usual Oregon State (5-7) raised its six-year mark against BCS conference teams to 6-4, their 2010 WAC wins over Wyoming (3-9), New Mexico State (2-10), and San Jose State (1-12) were unimpressive next to a surge through a Big Ten, Big Twelve, or SEC slate.

Mountain West Conference champion Texas Christian (13-0), the other formidable non-automatic qualifier for BCS bowls, finished the regular season undefeated, but the Horned Frogs' only wins over BCS teams came against middling Oregon State and Baylor (7-6). TCU finished third in the BCS numbers and landed a plum spot in the Rose Bowl against Wisconsin (11-2). In a hard-fought game, the Horned Frogs edged Wisconsin 21-19 as TCU linebacker Tank Carder knocked down a two-point pass at the end.

The level of stress in the coaching profession went under the microscope in 2010. Mark Dantonio of Michigan State (11-2) got his Spartans off to an 8-0 start and earned his team's third victory in stunning fashion when he called a courageous overtime fake field goal while trailing Notre Dame (8-5) by three points. The pass worked magically for a 29-yard touchdown, but before the night's celebration was over Dantonio suffered a mild heart attack. Ball State coach Stan Parrish said, "He (Dantonio) had the happiest moment, probably of his career, and then a couple hours later he had a heart attack…Its why some of the guys walk away (from coaching)."

Les Miles of Louisiana State (11-2) seemed less stressed than lucky. On October 2, his no. 10 Tigers hosted Tennessee (6-7) and the Volunteers' new coach Derek Dooley. Tennessee, a young team trying to overcome the upheaval of three head coaches in three years—Lane Kiffin had caused uproar right after the 2009 season when he jilted Tennessee after one season to take the Southern California (8-5) job—built a 14-10 fourth quarter lead. With the clock ticking inside the last 10 seconds on third down at the Vols one yard-line, the Tigers, without a timeout, failed to spike the ball to stop the clock, choosing instead to make wholesale personnel changes at the line of scrimmage. In the loud confusion, the shotgun snap eluded quarterback Jordan Jefferson, and Tennessee seemingly clinched a win as the clock ran out. But, in its own confusion, Tennessee used 13 defenders, and the Tigers got a chance to send Stevan Ridley plunging for the winning touchdown to stay unbeaten. LSU survived its own clock mismanagement, while Dooley was left to wonder why his defense was cheated out of its right to substitute players in response to LSU's personnel changes. A similar last-moment fate awaited Tennessee in its Music City Bowl overtime loss to North Carolina (8-5). With too many men on-field for a clock-stopping spike, the Tar Heels might have been penalized 15 yards instead of the five that didn't bother kicker Casey Barth's 39-yard field goal.

Oregon (12-1) was without star quarterback Jeremiah Masoli, who was dismissed from the team after two brushes with the law. Masoli used a loophole in transfer rules to become eligible at Mississippi (4-8) but could do nothing to save the Rebels from a bleak year.

The slick Oregon Ducks, on the other hand, played at a breakneck offensive pace under second-year coach Chip Kelly and piled up a 49.3 points per game average in the regular season with new quarterback Darron Thomas and All-America running back LaMichael James on the way to an undefeated season and a trip to the BCS title game.

Oregon met Auburn (14-0), another offensive juggernaut at 42.7 points per game. All predicted a high scoring shootout, but instead, turnovers and solid defense held the combined points of the teams below 42. With the game tied 19-19 with about two minutes to play, Auburn freshman running back Michael Dyer gained six yards on a run where he was tackled, but his knee stayed just off the turf. Everyone stopped, including several Oregon tacklers who could have knocked down Dyer. The un-whistled run turned out to be critical. At the urging of his nearby bench, Dyer raced on for 37 yards to help position Wes Byrum for the championship-winning field goal. As great a game as the BCS Championship produced, it felt wrong that so spasmodic but technically-correct a play as Dyer's would so impact the outcome. After all, application of the age-old football rule of the "stop of forward progress" could easily be considered proper on a play when the runner and every defender thought the play was over.

It should have been of little surprise that Oregon's defense turned tentative at the wrong moment. All season, defenders were operating in an anxious

climate brought about by a multitude of penalties for tackling near sidelines and for helmet-to-helmet hits. Granted, the NFL was making more news about helmet-tackle fouls and resultant stiff fines from the commissioner, but a symptomatic wariness affected college defenders as well.

There was proper concern over helmet-to-helmet crashes, and a tremendous increase in penalties against defensive players resulted. But, everyone seemed to disregard the evidence that many so-called defenseless pass receivers ducked their own heads into harm's way through the natural defense of curling into a modified fetal position to absorb the blow of a violent tackle. All of football faced difficult future decisions in balancing the desire to best protect the players while not removing the toughness from a sport that has remained so incredibly popular.

Perhaps that was the least of the bad news in college football in 2010. In the spring, the NCAA slapped severe penalties on Southern California (8-5) over its inability to control money and other gratuities bestowed upon 2005 Heisman Trophy winner Reggie Bush by former convict and would-be professional agent Lloyd Lake. USC was docked 30 scholarships over the 2010-12 seasons, banned from bowl play for two years, and forced to forfeit 14 games, including the 2005 Orange Bowl that clinched the 2004 BCS national title. Then there was more bad news.

In mid-October, college football was discomforted by former sports agent Josh Luchs' revelations in Sports Illustrated that he gave cash to dozens of pro prospects while they were playing college ball. Some of those players, now long out of college, admitted to receiving money, and others denied it or refused comment. Few fans were naïve about star players, especially those from poor backgrounds, holding out their hands. Football news remained mostly bad the rest of the season.

The college game returned to Wrigley Field on November 20, but the Big Ten win by Illinois (7-6) over host Northwestern (7-6) was clouded by the necessity of an odd rule change enacted because of concerns over an end-line too close to the wall in right field. Officials decided to switch ends after each series so that all offensive plays would be directed only at the opposite end zone near the third base dugout. Then the news grew worse.

Late-season accusations developed around the transfer recruitment of Auburn star quarterback and soon-to-be Heisman Trophy-winning Cam Newton, who in his first year of full-time varsity play was leading the Tigers to the Southeastern Conference title and BCS national championship. Newton had left the Florida (8-5) program as a sophomore in 2008 for junior college in Texas. Newton's departure came under a cloud of accusations of dishonesty and misbehavior.

In 2010, Mississippi State (9-4) appeared to be the frontrunner in landing Newton because the youngster's former quarterback coach at Florida, Dan Mullen, now headed the Bulldogs' program. Newton ended up at Auburn, however, and it came out that Mississippi State had made a violations report accusing Newton's preacher father, Cecil, of extorting the school, through an intermediary, for $180,000 to land the services of his son.

Despite the release of such disheartening news in November, the brilliant Newton and the Tigers still plunged through the remainder of a difficult SEC schedule to finish undefeated behind a magnificent offense. The regular season highlight was a comeback from a 24-0 deficit at defending national champion Alabama (10-3) for a 28-27 victory. That late-season victory pushed the Auburn Tigers atop the BCS standings.

Auburn suspended Newton for a day, but the SEC reinstated him. Just before leading the Tigers to a 56-17 win in the conference title game over South Carolina (9-5), Newton was exonerated for having had no knowledge of his father's payment demand from suitor schools. However, ignorance should not have spared him from guilt, according to NCAA rules, specifically: "The solicitation of cash or benefits by either a potential student-athlete or another person on their behalf is not allowed under NCAA rules." The rules also define anyone who speaks for a student as an agent, i.e., "any individual who markets or promotes a student-athlete."

The NCAA investigation remained on-going, and important questions went unresolved after Auburn's victory in the BCS championship game:
• Would Auburn eventually have to vacate its national title just as Southern California had lost its 2004 title earlier in 2010?
• When Cecil Newton decided Cam wasn't going to attend college at his first choice, Mississippi State, didn't Cam ask his father, "Why not?" And how did Cecil answer his son?
• If the NCAA didn't punish Cam, how could there be any future deterrents to players who simply could claim ignorance of any relative and/or agent demanding pay-for-play?

The blow to the college game was in no way softened that Newton was runaway winner of the Heisman Trophy, with some suggesting he was the greatest college player in history. Would he eventually be ruled ineligible and have to vacate the Heisman as Reggie Bush had earlier this year?

Newton attracted the sixth-most first place votes ever, but 105 of 866 participants chose not to vote him at all among their three Heisman choices, a sign some were quite troubled by the controversy.

Several other schools made disheartening news, investigated for players having off-season contact with agents. Notable was North Carolina, which played reasonably well while many from one of the nation's top defenses couldn't suit up because of dragged-out investigations. Star receiver A.J. Green of Georgia (6-7) was forthcoming in his dealings with the NCAA but also sat out several games awaiting his fate over the sale of a jersey.

Before its Sugar Bowl trip, Ohio State found five juniors, including star quarterback Tyrelle Pryor, guilty of selling memorabilia awarded for their football excellence or trading them for tattoos. Each player played a prominent role in the Buckeyes' Sugar Bowl win over Arkansas (10-3) but would have to miss the first five games of the 2011 season. When it was learned coach Jim Tressel had early knowledge of the issue and failed to report it in a timely fashion, he too was docked five games to start 2011.

Paying players reemerged as a method to curb rule-breaking. Should pro prospects be allowed to receive loans or payments from prospective agents? Should all players be paid a stipend by their colleges?

The latter argument by people who saw only the figurative iceberg's lucrative tip was so complex it seemed impossible to resolve. Truth was the majority of football programs failed to make large profits, and those that did were forced to carry the financial burden of other varsity sports that never supported themselves. School athletic programs remained under pressure to maintain the male-female equality mandated by the U.S. government's Title IX law, even if few if any women's sports were capable of self-support. A school like Michigan (7-6) that sold out every football seat in excess of 110,000 per Saturday still operated its athletics department in the red.

If a school were to pay football players, could it lawfully choose not to pay female volleyball players? How were footballers to be paid: Academic class? Games started? Minutes played? Would quarterbacks earn more than guards or weak-side linebackers? There were more questions than answers hanging over an awfully dark year in college football.

Even misguided fans within a bitter rivalry darkened this season. A 62-two-year-old Alabama fan, Harvey Almorn Updyke Jr., was arrested in February 2011, accused of introducing a lethal dose of herbicide to the soil surrounding the 130-year-old oak trees at Toomer's Corner in Auburn, Ala. For about 50 years, Auburn students and fans had enjoyed tossing hundreds of rolls of toilet paper over tree branches to celebrate football victories. It was a silly tradition perhaps, but one that should not have been ruined by an angry opponent after the Tigers' championship season.

Milestones

■ Shifts in conference affiliation for future seasons were affected by Colorado and Utah going to Pacific-10, Nebraska to Big Ten, Boise State, Fresno State, and Nevada to Mountain West, and Texas Christian to Big East.

■ Brigham Young announced departure from Mountain West Conference for independence in 2011.

■ In June, NCAA completed its investigation of Southern California and running back Reggie Bush. USC forfeited 14 victories including its 2004 BCS title. USC, which also broke rules involving basketball star O.J. Mayo, was stripped of 30 football scholarships over three years and banned from bowl games after 2010 and 2011 seasons. Bush, who accepted luxury home for his parents and $300,000 in cash and automobile for himself, voluntarily returned his Heisman Trophy. New York Downtown Athletic Club's Heisman Trophy Trust chose to vacate 2005 award.

■ Dave Diles, 78, long-time host of ABC-TV's "Prudential College Football Scoreboard" show, died on January 2. Mike Weaver, lineman who selflessly switched from offense to defense and back again for Georgia teams that compiled 28-6-1 combined records in 1982-84, died in January. On January 17, recently-acquired, 26-year-old Chicago Bears defensive end Gaines Adams, ACC Defensive Player of Year at Clemson in 2006, died of heart attack in his home town of Greenwood, S.C. Adams was All-America in 2006 and 4th overall choice of Tampa Bay Buccaneers in 2007 NFL Draft. On January 22, former Mississippi guard-tackle (1957-58) Bull Churchwell died at 73. Late in January, University of Colorado and Philadelphia Eagles defensive back and long-time CBS NFL announcer Tom Brookshier died at 78. Walter Fondren, 73, Texas back in 1955-57, passed away in early February. "Bullet" Bill Dudley, 88, died February 4. Dudley, 1956 College Hall of Fame inductee, led nation in scoring with 134 points in 1941 and won Maxwell Trophy. Tennessee lost two footballers in mid-February: offensive tackle Daryle Smith, 46, of 1985 SEC and Sugar Bowl title team, and blocking back Joe Maiure, 80, of 1951 national titleists. Mosi Tatupu, 54, outstanding fullback with Southern California (1974-77) and Pro Bowl special-teamer with New England Patriots, died on February 23. Merlin Olsen, Utah State tackle and 1980 College Football Hall of Fame inductee, died March 11 at 69. Olsen was 1st player to be honored by National Football Foundation as both Hall of Famer and NFF National Scholar-Athlete. Olsen spent 15-year pro career with Los Angeles Rams, making Pro Football Hall of Fame in 1982, and starred on TV in "The Little House on the Prairie," "Father Murphy" and as a color commentator for NBC's pro football and Rose Bowl telecasts. Pair of West Coast stars both died on March 13: Cliff Livingston, 79, defensive end at UCLA in 1950-51 before his 12-year NFL career with New York Giants, Minnesota Vikings, and Los Angeles Rams, and Rich Koeper, 66, Oregon State tackle in 1962-64 and Green Bay Packers draft choice. Former Kansas State defensive end (1988-91) Elijah Alexander died at 39 in late March. Chris Limahelu, 59, kicker for Southern California's 1974 national champions, died April 7. Former Kansas State quarterback Dylan Meier died in mid-April at 26. Twice All-SEC fullback for Tennessee and long-time faculty member at UT, Dr. Andy Kozar, died on April 29 at 79. Kozar was national master's paddleball champion in 1972, and in 2002 he fulfilled his dream of documenting vast knowledge of his Hall of Fame coach: He authored book entitled Football as a War Game—The Annotated Journals of General R.R. Neyland. On May 21, former 2-way Maryland All-America tackle Stan Jones passed away at 78. Jones was member of 1953 national champions and earned Pro Football Hall of Fame induction after 12 years (1954-65) with Chicago Bears. Les Richter, 2-time All-American and 1982 College Hall of Fame inductee who played guard-linebacker for California from 1949-51, died on June 12 at 79. Richter played in 2 Rose Bowls and graduated as class valedictorian at Cal-Berkeley. After 9-year career (1954-62) as linebacker-kicker with Los Angeles Rams of NFL and as long-time auto racing track developer in southern California, NASCAR hired him in 1983. Richter was named NASCAR senior VP of operations in 1992. On June 12, Georgia Tech All-America tackle of late-1940s, Robert Davis, died at 83. Four Hall of Famers—Don Coryell, Gene Goodreault, Jack Tatum, and Bob Fenimore—died in July. Coryell, 85, coached at San Diego State (104-19-2) in 1961-72, innovatively tutored St. Louis Cardinals and San Diego Chargers offenses to great passing attacks in NFL. Goodreault, 92, was All-America end who played on Boston College's 1941 Sugar Bowl champions. Ohio State's 2-time All-America safety, Tatum, 61, anchored Buckeyes' defense in 1968-70, died of heart attack. Tatum, 2004 Hall of Fame inductee, was infamously remembered for his paralyzing tackle of New England Patriot Darryl Stingley when Tatum was All-Pro for Oakland Raiders. Fenimore, 1972 College Football Hall of Fame inductee and twice All-America halfback at Oklahoma A&M, died at 84. At Oklahoma A&M (now Oklahoma State), Fenimore led nation in 1944 in total offense and in rushing and total offense in 1945. Also dying in late July at age 45 was Harry Galbreath, All-America lineman at Tennessee. Another Tennessee line star, Steve DeLong, died at 67 on August 18. DeLong was named All-America in 1963 at guard and in 1964 at tackle and was first round choice of Chicago Bears in 1965 NFL Draft. Michigan's Ron Kramer, 1978 College Football Hall of Fame inductee, died September 11. Kramer, 75, was twice named All-America (1955-56) as two-way end and was one of all-time great Wolverines, starring on football, basketball, and track teams en route to 9 varsity letters. South Carolina's leading career receiver in catches and yardage, Kenny McKinley, on injured reserve list of NFL's Denver Broncos, took his own life on September 20 at age 23. LSU end Mickey Mangum, who caught pass for only touchdown of Sugar Bowl win over Clemson that closed Tigers' 1958 national championship season, died at age 71 in late September. George Blanda, 83, Kentucky and 26-year Pro Football Hall of Fame quarterback-kicker died September 27. South Carolina halfback Jim Hunter (1958-60) died at 71 on October 29. Hunter authored book on Gamecock football history and forged successful career in NASCAR. Michigan All-America tailback-fullback Rob Lytle, who finished his career in 1976 as Wolverines' top rusher with 3,317 yards, passed away at 56 in November. In early December, Hall of Famer Al Brosky, former Illinois halfback and member of Illini's 1952 Rose Bowl championship team, died at 82. Brosky grabbed 29 career interceptions, NCAA record that stood for 23 years. Don Meredith, 72, All-America quarterback at Southern Methodist in 1958-59 and 9-year "face" of Dallas Cowboys when they launched as NFL expansion team in 1960, died on December 6. Meredith won Emmy Awards as clever color announcer on ABC Monday Night Football from show's debut in 1970.

■ Coaching Changes:

	Incoming	Outgoing
Akron	Rob Ianello	J.D. Brookhart
Buffalo	Jeff Quinn	Turner Gill
Central Michigan	Dan Enos	Butch Jones
Cincinnati	Butch Jones	Brian Kelly
Colorado (a)	Brian Cabral	Dan Hawkins
East Carolina	Ruffin McNeill	Skip Holtz
Florida State	Jimbo Fisher	Bobby Bowden
Kansas	Turner Gill	Mark Mangino
Kentucky	Joker Phillips	Rich Brooks
Louisiana-Monroe	Todd Berry	Charlie Weatherbie
Louisiana Tech	Sonny Dykes	Derek Dooley
Louisville	Charlie Strong	Steve Kragthorpe
Marshall	Doc Holliday	Mark Snyder
Memphis	Larry Porter	Tommy West
Miami (b)	Jeff Stoutland	Randy Shannon
Minnesota (c)	Jeff Horton	Tim Brewster
Nevada-Las Vegas	Bobby Hauk	Mike Sanford
North Texas (d)	Mike Canales	Todd Dodge
Notre Dame	Brian Kelly	Charlie Weis
Pittsburgh (e)	Phil Bennett	Dave Wannstadt
San Jose State	Mike MacIntyre	Dick Tomey
South Florida	Skip Holtz	Jim Leavitt
Southern California	Lane Kiffin	Pete Carroll
Tennessee	Derek Dooley	Lane Kiffin
Texas Tech	Tommy Tuberville	Mike Leach
Vanderbilt	Robbie Caldwell	Bobby Johnson
Virginia	Mike London	Al Groh
Western Kentucky	Willie Taggart	David Elson

(a) Cabral (2-1) was named interim head coach when Hawkins (3-6) was dismissed on November 8.
(b) Stoutland (0-1) coached Sun Bowl after Shannon (7-5) was dismissed.
(c) Horton (2-3) was named interim head coach after Brewster (1-6) was dismissed on October 17.
(d) Canales (2-3) was named interim head coach after Dodge (1-6) was dismissed on October 20.
(e) Bennett (1-0) coached BBVA Compass Bowl after Wannstadt (7-5) resigned.

■ Longest winning streaks entering season:
Alabama 14 Boise State 14 Middle Tennessee 7

Preseason USA TODAY Coaches Poll

1 Alabama (55)	1469	14 Penn State	508
2 Ohio State (4)	1392	15 Pittsburgh	492
3 Florida	1245	16 Louisiana State	476
4 Texas	1240	17 Georgia Tech	455
5 Boise State	1215	18 North Carolina	445
6 Virginia Tech	1052	19 Arkansas	438
7 Texas Christian	1051	20 Florida State	374
8 Oklahoma	1035	21 Georgia	312
9 Nebraska	1001	22 Oregon State	263
10 Iowa	952	23 Auburn	260
11 Oregon	940	24tUtah	169
12 Wisconsin	778	24tWest Virginia	169
13 Miami	728		

September 4, 2010

(Th) UTAH 27 Pittsburgh 24 (OT): Vaunted rushing attack of Pittsburgh (0-1) had to endure learning curve of new QB, soph Tino Sunseri (16-28/184y, TD, INT) and couldn't deliver when it got close to Utah (1-0) GL. But, son of former Panthers A-A LB and asst coach Sal Sunseri looked good in 4th Q, passing for 127y, TD, and 2-pt conv. Trailing 17-10 and limited to 60y O in middle Qs, Panthers went 53y to K Dan Hutchins' FG early in 4th Q. When Utes QB Jordan Wynn (21-36/283y, 3 TDs, INT) continued his fine passing with 61y TD to WR DeVonte Christopher (8/155y, TD), they led 24-13. Sunseri cranked up his O unit and pitched 44y TD and 2-pt pass to WR Jon Baldwin to close within 3 pts. Hutchins made 3 tries at tying 30y FG with 3 secs left in regulation as Utah coach Kyle Whittingham called time out just before make and miss by Hutchins. His 3rd try tied it. In OT, Sunseri telegraphed rollout pass, picked off near sideline by Utah frosh S Brian Blechen, to allow K Joe Phillips to win it with short FG.

Louisiana State 30 North Carolina 24 (Atlanta): Story of Chick-fil-A Kickoff game was suspension of North Carolina's top 2 TBs and 7 starters on Tar Heels (0-1) D, including stars DE Robert Quinn and DT Marvin Austin, who had been expected to form backbone of 1 of nation's toughest Ds. Still, Carolina played inspired ball once it got over bundle of errors prior to 4th Q. No. 16 LSU (1-0) bolted to 30-10 lead by H, including trio of spectacular scores: 50y TD sweep by WR Russell Shepard, 87y punt TD RET by DB Patrick Peterson (7/257y, TD RET), and 51y TD pass by QB Jordan Jefferson (15-21/151y, 2 TDs, INT). Seemingly in control, Tigers let North Carolina WR Jheranie Boyd (6/221y, TD) get behind secondary, and tough QB T.J. Yates (28-46/412y, 3 TDs) rolled right in EZ to pitch 97y TD for longest score in school history. Yates added another TD pass, and UNC got ball back down only 30-24 with 1:08 to play. Yates hit 5 straight throws to 6YL, but TE Zack Pianalto couldn't quite haul in pair of EZ passes as he was closely guarded by LSU defenders in closing secs.

MICHIGAN 30 Connecticut 10: No Michigan (1-0) QB ever had exceeded 147y rushing in single game, but new starting QB Denard Robinson dashed for 197y, while passing 19-22/186y, TD. Amazingly-quick Robinson took off on 32y TD run late in 1st Q that provided 14-0 lead. Behind 21-0, Connecticut (0-1) crammed K Dave Teggart's 32y FG and 2y TD run by TB Jordan Todman (20/105y, TD) into last 4:21 of 2nd Q to trail 21-10 at H. "It was huge," according to Michigan coach Rich Rodriguez, when late in 3rd Q Huskies RB D.J. Shoemate fumbled to UM LB Obi Ezeh inside Wolverines 5YL with chance to pull UConn within TD. When Robinson pitched 4th Q TD pass to RB Vincent Smith, who also squirted for TD in 1st Q, Wolverines were home-free at 30-10.

Missouri 23 Illinois 13 (St. Louis): Illinois (0-1), losers 3 straight years to Missouri (1-0), effectively controlled 1st H possession for 18 mins behind runs of RB Mikel Leshoure (20/112y). Illini tallied 10 pts in last 2 mins for 13-3 H edge as new QB Nathan Scheelhaase (9-23/81y, TD, 3 INTs) pitched 13y TD to WR A.J. Jenkins (3/33y, TD) and K Derek Dimke nailed career-long 52y FG as H clock expired. Missouri QB Blaine Gabbert (34-48/281y, 2 TDs) launched 28 passes in 2nd H to spark Tigers to 17-13 lead after WR T.J. Moe (13/101y, TD) and TE Michael Egnew (10/60y, TD) snatched short scoring passes. Tigers CB Carl Gettis soon took 1-handed INT away from Jenkins early in 4th Q to all but end Illini hope. Mizzou K Grant Ressel made his 2nd and 3rd FGs in 4th Q to extend lead. Illinois was held to 85y O and 4 1st downs in 2nd H.

KANSAS STATE 31 Ucla 22: RB Daniel Thomas launched new season for Kansas State (1-0) by powering for 234y on 28 carries and 2 TDs, scoring early on short TD and clinching matters with 35y dash in last min. Thomas' 1st Q TD came after 4th down PEN spoiled GLS by Bruins D. UCLA (0-1), however, owned 2nd Q as it sacked Wildcats QB Carson Coffman (11-16/66y, TD) 4 times and P Jeff Locke's 60y punt set up LB Akeem Ayers' FUM REC at 11YL. QB Kevin Prince (9-26/120y, TD, 2 INTs) dashed around RE for TD on next snap, so UCLA led 10-7 at H. K Kai Forbath's 3rd FG pulled Bruins within 17-16 early in 4th Q, but with 2:03 to play Coffman's 5y TD pass to WR Broderick Smith extended Wildcats' edge to 24-16. UCLA came right back as frosh WR Ricky Marvray nabbed TD pass, but Prince's 2-pt pass fell incomplete.

Texas 34 RICE 17: Old SWC rivalry once was referenced by Pres John F. Kennedy in rationalizing United States' daunting exploration of outer space in early 1960s: "Why go to the moon? Why does Rice play Texas?" This daunting latter-day matchup was booked as Rice (0-1) home game at Houston Texans' Reliant Stadium, but Longhorns (1-0) enjoyed greater crowd support. Texas turned to its running attack with aerial star Colt McCoy gone to NFL, and RB Tre Newton (18/61y, 3 TDs) tallied thrice on ground. Longhorns DT Sam Acho sacked Owls frosh QB Taylor McHarque (6-11/90y, TD, INT) in 2nd Q to create FUM returned 10y for TD by LB Keenan Robinson for 17-3 lead. Rice's highlight came on bizarre TD just before H: McHarque found TE Vance McDonald over middle and ball deflected right to WR Randy Kitchens who dragged along Texas DB Christian Scott over last 10y to complete stunning 47y TD.

TEXAS CHRISTIAN 30 Oregon State 21: Frogs (1-0), tabbed by USA TODAY Poll at no. 7, played imperfect football but still beat ranked foe in no. 22 Beavers (0-1). TCU QB Andy Dalton (17-27/175y, TD, 2 INTs) suffered INTs to open each H, leading to Oregon State TDs by WR James Rodgers on 30y pass from QB Ryan Katz (9-25/159y, 2 TDs) and RB Jacquizz Rodgers (18/75y, TD) on 1y run. Dalton tied it at 7-7 with 6y TD scramble in 1st Q and provided winning pts at 28-21 in 3rd Q with another TD run on his way to eclipsing all-time great Sammy Baugh for most QB wins at TCU. Afterward, coach Gary Patterson said, "We just beat the 24th-ranked (AP) team that I think should be ranked higher." Surprisingly, win over what would turn out as weakest Oregon State team in several years would stand as TCU's emblematic triumph of undefeated regular season because Frogs' top Mountain West rivals would fade at midseason.

(Sun) TEXAS TECH 35 Southern Methodist 27: Sr WR Lyle Leong (11/142y, 3 TDs) enjoyed career day as Texas Tech (1-0) opened tenure of coach Tommy Tuberville with same dramatic aerial attack it had enjoyed for decade under former coach Mike Leach. Raiders QB Taylor Potts hit 34-53/359y and 4 TDs. Tuberville also brought some D fireworks as Raiders intercepted 3 passes and registered 5 sacks, including 3 by LB Brian Duncan. Held to 68y O until its 1st score late in 2nd Q, SMU (0-1) rallied from 35-14 3rd Q deficit. Mustangs K Matt Szymanski bombed 61y FG in 4th Q, and QB Kyle Patron (21-38/218y, 2 TDs, 3 INTs) hit TD pass midway through 4th Q.

(Mon) Maryland 17 Navy 14 (Baltimore): Infrequently-matched, in-state foes met for only 2nd time since 1965. Trying to rebound from dreadful 2-10 record of 2009, Maryland (1-0) heeded LB Alex Wujciak's direction: "Perseverance. That's all we've been preaching all summer." Terrapins tallied twice in 1st Q on 5y TD run by RB Da'rel Scott and 3y burst up middle by RB Davin Meggett (8/105y, TD). Meanwhile, Navy (0-1) was sailing up and down field, but star QB Ricky Dobbs (6-10/73y and 29/63y, TD rushing) twice lost FUMs at Maryland 1YL. "I can't remember a time when we rushed for 400 yards (412y, more accurately) and lost," Middies coach Ken Niumatalolo said. Dobbs' short TD run tied score 14-14 late in 3rd Q, until Maryland K Travis Baltz slipped short FG between uprights halfway through 4th Q for 17-14 edge. Navy immediately launched 15-play drive that reached 1YL with less than min to play. On 4th down, Navy eschewed tying FG, and both Terps Ss, Kenny Tate and Antwine Perez, combined to stuff Dobbs' wedge off left side of Middies line and complete dramatic GLS.

(Mon) Boise State 33 Virginia Tech 30 (Landover, Md.): Coming cross-country to play at neutral site at Washington Redskins' Fed Ex Field, Boise State (1-0) embraced big opportunity. Broncos roared to 17-0 lead in 1st Q: WR Austin Pettis (6/73y, 2 TDs) blocked punt and caught 8y TD pass from cool QB Kellen Moore (23-38/215y, 3 TDs), while TE Tommy Gallarda made brilliant diving TD catch. Back came Virginia Tech (0-1), and when Hokies cashed 3rd TD scored by TB Ryan Williams (21/44y, 2 TDs) 8-and-half mins into 3rd Q, they led 21-20. Advantage was short-lived when Broncos RB D.J. Harper burst 71y for TD less than min later. Before 3rd Q ended, Va Tech tried 4th-and-4 at Boise 28YL: QB Tyrod Taylor (15-22/186y, 2 TDs, and 16/73y rushing) fired wide to WR Jarrett Boykin, who slipped through tackle and glided to EZ to put Hokies up 27-26. Va Tech was unable to kill late-game clock, and Boise State took over at its 44YL after 25y punt RET by WR Mitch Burroughs. Hokies had 2 tough calls go against them: flag was picked up on potential illegal block on Burroughs RET, and subsequent tackle at sideline turned into roughing PEN on Hokies. With no TOs left, Moore calmly clicked on 4-5/43y on winning drive, capped by Pettis' 13y post-pattern catch with 1:09 to go. Week later, Broncos' big win was temporarily devalued when James Madison of FCS surprised fumbling, flat Hokies 21-16 at Blacksburg.

USA TODAY Coaches Poll September 7, 2010

1 Alabama (55)	1470	14 Penn State	655
2 Ohio State (4)	1397	15 Arkansas	531
3 Boise State	1304	16 Louisiana State	527
4 Texas	1264	17 Georgia Tech	519
5 Texas Christian	1144	18 Florida State	500
6 Florida	1130	19 Georgia	458
7 Nebraska	1085	20tAuburn	371
8 Oregon	1054	20tUtah	371
9 Iowa	1027	22 West Virginia	185
10 Oklahoma	969	23 Arizona	128
11 Wisconsin	821	24 Brigham Young	113
12 Miami	799	25 South Carolina	90
13 Virginia Tech	698		

September 11, 2010

(Th) Auburn 17 MISSISSIPPI STATE 14: JC transfer QB Cam Newton (11-19/136y, 2 TDs, INT, and 18/70y rushing) led Auburn (2-0) to hard-fought victory in SEC opener. Newton hit swing pass in early going that WR Emory Blake took 39y down left sideline for TD. Later in 1st Q after Tigers fumbled punt at their 20YL, Mississippi State (1-1) retaliated on play that looked every bit like old-fashioned, weak-side Single Wing power run from 2YL: Bulldogs QB Chris Relf (12-25/110y) blasted toward GL, lost ball, and pulling LG Gabe Jackson recovered FUM in EZ for tying TD. Trailing 17-7, Bulldogs opened 2nd H with 12-play, 63y drive to RB Vick Ballard's short TD run. They immediately struck with on-side KO, but Relf was forced into 3 straight missed passes. That was Mississippi State frustration added to others earlier: WR Leon Berry dropped pass in FG territory, and CB Corey Broomfield bobbled INT on certain TD RET. Bulldogs coach Dan Mullen said, "Every time we hit a high note…we would thud." Leading Auburn D was DT Nick Fairley, who exceeded his 2009 TFL total with 2.5 and equaled his 1.5 sack total while spending lots of time in Bulldogs' backfield.

WAKE FOREST 54 Duke 48: Final stats showed 987y O shared by in-state rivals, so it was unsurprising to have 35-35 tie at H or that Demon Deacons had to hold off Duke (1-1) in late going after Blue Devils QB Sean Renfree (28-44/358y, 4 TDs, 3 INTs) launched 51y TD bomb to WR Conner Vernon (8/181y, 2 TDs) with 1:39 to play. Backup Wake Forest (2-0) QB Tanner Price (12-19/190y, 3 TDs, INT) threw 3 TD passes and ran for another to help Deacs earn their 11th straight victory in series. Wake WR Chris Givins (4/159y, TD) scored on 13y RET of fumbled punt snap and was all alone to haul in 81y TD pass from WR Marshall Williams (2/51y, 2 TDs) on E-around, both in 2nd Q. Duke RB Desmond Scott (11/122y, TD) scored on 63y run.

SOUTH CAROLINA 17 Georgia 6: Workhorse Gamecocks (2-0) frosh RB Marcus Lattimore crashed for 182y on 37 carries, scored pair of 2y TDs, and summed up his game with: "I'm a little sore." Lattimore bulled his way to 16, 10, and 11y runs on game-opening TD drive that consumed 8 mins. Georgia (1-1) answered in kind, but dropped pass forced Bulldogs into K Blair Walsh's 27y FG. Lattimore keyed 62y TD march in 2nd Q and launched game-clinching 4th Q FG drive with 16y run. QB Aaron Murray (14-21/192y) led aerial surge that brought Bulldogs another FG to start 3rd Q.

Oregon 48 TENNESSEE 13: Underdog Tennessee (1-1) got off to good start, leading 13-3 early in 2nd Q as RB Tauren Poole (23/162y, TD) hammered over from 1y out, and presumptive heads began to nod: touted Pac-10 team comes east and can't handle SEC opponent. But, short punt by Volunteers late in 2nd Q set up Ducks at UT 38YL, allowing TE David Paulson to catch 2 passes from QB Darron Thomas (17-32/202y, 2 TDs), latter for 27y TD and 13-13 H tie. Then came 2nd H explosion: Ducks (2-0) swift RB LaMichael James (16/134y, TD), restricted to 27y in 1st H, seemed hemmed in for loss, slithered to his left and broke several tackles on brilliant 72y TD tour of left sideline. That score opened 5-TD floodgates, typified by Oregon CB Cliff Harris going 76y on INT TD RET and RB Kenjon Barner dashing 80y on punt TD RET.

ALABAMA 24 Penn State 3: D of defending national champion, no. 1 Crimson Tide (2-0) simply was too fast and too complex for Penn State (1-1) frosh QB Robert Bolden (13-29/144y, 2 INTs) and Lions' revamped O-line. Filling in for injured Heisman Trophy winning TB Mark Ingram, Alabama TB Trent Richardson (22/144y, TD) rushed for 102y in 1st H against Penn State D that hadn't allowed 100y rusher in almost 2 years. Tide QB Greg McElroy 16-24/229y, 2 TDs) tossed TD passes to WR Kevin Norwood and TE Preston Dial. With TB Evan Royster held to 32y rushing, Lions had trouble finishing drives, making 2 trips to red zone in 1st H but losing possession on INT and FUM. Alabama now owned 27-0 home record vs. ranked teams in last 15 years.

OHIO STATE 36 Miami 24: Familiar malady marked visit to "The Horseshoe" for Miami (1-1), that is, turnovers equaled defeat. Difference was 4 INTs permitted by Hurricanes QB Jacory Harris (22-39/232y, TD, 4 INTs) and his butter-fingered receivers. Ohio State (2-0) CB Chimdi Chekwa picked off 2 INTs. Buckeyes QB Tyrelle Pryor (12-27/233y, TD, and 20/113y, TD rushing) took perfect care of ball, although Miami helped by not holding 3 potential INTs. Pryor provided 18y TD pass to RB Brandon Saine, who slipped out of slot formation in 2nd Q, and Pryor scrambled 13y up middle and to left for 3rd Q TD. Miami's special teams kept them in ballgame: frosh RB Lamar Miller returned 1st Q KO 88y to TD that built brief 7-3 lead. Also, WR Travis Benjamin took back punt 79y for TD 3 mins before H. Benjamin's TD occurred just as Ohio State appeared in command at 20-10 after TD run by RB Dan Herron (14/66y, TD). K Devin Barclay made his 3rd and 4th of 5 FGs just before H to extend Bucks lead to 26-17. Canes took 2nd H KO and moved 70y to 1st down at 6YL. But on 3rd down, Ohio State DE Cameron Heyward dropped into coverage and made INT over middle. With wide-open field ahead, Heyward stampeded 80y. "I was trying to take it to the house," said 288-lb. Heyward, the son of former Pitt A-A back Craig "Ironhead" Heyward. "They caught me. That shows they didn't give up, and shows I'm not that fast."

IOWA 35 Iowa State 7: Scoring on 4 of its 1st 5 possessions, Iowa (2-0) took command from outset. QB Ricky Stanzi (11-18/204y, 2 TDs) tossed pair of scores and ran for another in 28-0 romp in 1st H over rival Cyclones (1-1). Hawkeyes enjoyed double-barrel running attack featuring TBs Adam Robinson (14/156y, TD) and Jewel Hampton (20/84y, TD) as Robinson rambled 39y to 3rd Q TD on power play off left side. Iowa State QB Austen Arnaud (20-44/197y, TD, 3 INTs) suffered INTs on 3 straight series in 3rd Q but managed 8y TD pass to WR Darius Darks late in 4th Q.

Michigan 28 NOTRE DAME 24: Lightning-fast Michigan (2-0) QB Denard Robinson (24-40/244y, TD and 28/258y, 2 TDs rushing) was talk of nation for his spectacular runs and improved passing. "Heisman frontrunner" was already being attached to Robinson's name, as for 2nd straight week, he set school total O and QB rushing records. After Notre Dame (1-1) Dayne Crist (13-25/277y, 2 TDs, INT) sparked 71y TD drive to open game, Robinson went to work. He hit 31y TD pass to WR Roy Roundtree after LB Jonas Mouton's INT, rifled another 31y throw to set up 1st Q go-ahead TD at 14-17, and magically raced 87y to score in 2nd Q. Crist, out much of 1st H with head injury as Irish O sputtered, came back to launch TD passes of 53y to WR T.J. Jones in 3rd Q and 95y to TE Kyle Rudolph (8/164y, TD) that stunningly put Irish in lead 24-21 with 3:41 left to play. Robinson directed clutch winning drive with 5-6/55y passing to his winning 2y TD run with 27 secs left.

KANSAS 28 Georgia Tech 25: Coming off disastrous 6-3 defeat at hands of North Dakota State of FCS, Kansas (1-1) rebounded nicely with new faces on O for coach Turner Gill's 1st win at Lawrence. Frosh QB Jordan Webb (18-29/179y, 3 TDs, INT) and RB James Sims (17/101y, TD) sparked Kansas' much-improved O. Georgia Tech (1-1) QB Joshua Nesbitt (5-15/116y, TD) scored twice in 1st H for 17-14 lead while presided over 291y rushing O. However, Yellow Jackets hurt themselves with poor tackling, 13y punt, roughing-passer PEN, and KO that went OB. Sims' short 3rd Q TD run gave Kansas 21-17 lead, and Jayhawkers DB-turned-WR Daymond Patterson tore through several weak tackles in 4th Q for 32y TD on flanker-screen pass.

OKLAHOMA 47 Florida State 17: Oklahoma's early dominance over no. 18 Florida State (1-1) came as surprise as Sooners (2-0) scored TDs on each of 4 opening series. OU QB Landry Jones (30-40/380y, 4 TDs) was razor sharp, hitting 7-9 throws on opening TD trip, clicking on 7 in row later in 1st Q, and 8 in row in 2nd Q. Oklahoma led 34-7 at H with Seminoles' only score coming on 1y run by RB Jermaine Thomas

(11/58y, TD) at end of 70y drive that briefly tied it 7-7 in 1st Q. Sooners coach Bob Stoops was less pleased than normal because his O carved up FSU D, coached by younger brother Mark, to tune of 487y.

Stanford 35 UCLA 0: It was expected Stanford (2-0) would be vcitrious on road in Pac-10 opener, but extent of win over Bruins (0-2) was remarkable. Cardinal QB Andrew Luck (11-24/151y, 2 TDs, and 7/63y rushing) was effective if not brilliant. Crushing moment for bumbling UCLA, which had 4 TOs, came late in 3rd Q when it allowed pair of TDs within 9 secs. FB-LB Owen Marecic, Stanford's 2-way star, pounded over for TD, and S Michael Thomas snatched FUM from hands of QB Kevin Prince (6-12/39y, INT) to whirl away for 21y TD RET and 28-0 lead. Luck, who found WR Ryan Whelan for 16y 1st Q TD, pitched 3y score to TE Coby Fleener in 4th Q.

AIR FORCE 35 Brigham Young 14: Undefeated Air Force (2-0) scored decisive win over BYU (1-1) on strength of 409y rushing to end 6-game skid to Cougars, who soon were departing Mountain West Conf. BYU scored twice in 1st Q on TD runs by RB J.J. DiLuigi (7/103y, TD) and QB Riley Nelson (8-19/73y). In between, Air Force's 3-play secret weapon, WR Mikel Hunter, scored on 37y pass from QB Tim Jefferson and would add 33y reverse run for 2nd Q TD. Air Force coach Troy Calhoun had trust in his D, led by CB Reggie Rembert (INT), so he chose to go on 4th-and-2 at Cougars 46YL while clinging to 21-14 lead late in 3rd Q. Falcons WR Jonathan Warzeka chose great time to break off career-long 46y TD run for 28-14 advantage.

USA TODAY Coaches Poll September 12, 2010

1	Alabama (55)	1470	14 Utah	625
2	Ohio State (4)	1410	15 Auburn	618
3	Boise State	1278	16 South Carolina	527
4	Texas	1262	17 Miami	417
5	Texas Christian	1168	18 Arizona	410
6	Oregon	1122	19 Stanford	338
7	Florida	1108	20 Penn State	296
8	Nebraska	1095	21 West Virginia	264
9	Oklahoma	1062	22 Michigan	254
10	Iowa	1050	23 Houston	220
11	Wisconsin	889	24 California	131
12	Louisiana State	740	25 Missouri	82
13	Arkansas	738		

September 18, 2010

WEST VIRGINIA 31 Maryland 17: West Virginia (3-0) came out in hurry-up O, and RB Noel Devine (27/131y) scampered 50y to set up TD pass by QB Geno Smith (19-29/268y, 4 TDs). Mountaineers had enjoyed little sharp passing in recent years, but Smith's career day included him hitting his 1st 10 throws on way to WVU's 28-0 lead early in 3rd Q. WRs Tavon Austin (7/106y, 2 TDs) and Stedman Bailey each caught pair of scores. Maryland (2-1) floundered in 1st H, outgained 359y to 53y, but briefly got back in it at 28-14 when QB Jamarr Robinson (13-24/227y, 2 TDs) launched 60 and 80y TDs to WR Torrey Smith (3/149y, 2 TDs) in 3rd Q.

Florida 31 TENNESSEE 17: Gators (3-0) O remained sluggish without departed great Tim Tebow but made enough plays behind QB John Brantley (14-23/167y, TD) to win 3rd straight in Knoxville for 1st time ever in 40-game rivalry. RB Mike Gillislee scored twice for Florida, including 2nd Q TD that provided 1st lead at 7-3, which carried to H. Tennessee (1-2) fought back to 10-10 deadlock in 3rd Q when QB Matt Simms (19-31/259y, 2 TDs, 2 INTs) clicked on 49y TD pass to WR Denarius Moore. Vols had Gators stopped on next possession, but coach Urban Meyer turned momentum toward Florida with successful fake-punt that led to Brantley's TD pass to WR Frankie Hammond. Gillislee's 2nd TD followed INT by CB Jeremy Brown and gave Gators all they needed at 24-10 late in 3rd Q.

Arkansas 31 GEORGIA 24: Tall QB Ryan Mallett (21-33/380y, 3 TDs) won his 1st road game as 16-game Arkansas (3-0) starter when with 15 secs left to play he hit WR Greg Childs (3/82y, TD), who cut inside Georgia (1-2) SS Shawn Williams to bolt 40y to winning TD. Bulldogs had trailed 24-10 in 4th Q but tied it on TD pass by QB Aaron Murray (15-27/253y, TD, INT, and 1y rollout TD run in 1st Q) and 3y run up middle by TB Washaun Ealey (18/87y, TD) with 3:55 to go. With 2:28 to play, Bulldogs had chance to break 24-24 tie, but Murray was sacked twice, including near beheading by Razorbacks DE Jake Bequette, and Ray Guy Award P Drew Butler hit poor 31y punt OB to launch Arkansas' winning bid from its 28YL with 47 secs left.

Vanderbilt 28 MISSISSIPPI 14: Commodores (1-2) RB Warren Norman (15/111y, TD) raced for decisive 80y TD right after Ole Miss (1-2) had tied it 14-14 in 3rd Q on 28y TD run by QB Jeremiah Masoli (19-35/190y, 2 INTs, and 19/104y, TD rushing). In coach Robbie Caldwell's 1st win, Vanderbilt played sharp football, while Rebels floundered with 3 TOs and 5-18 3rd down conversion rate. Vanderbilt RB Zac Stacy broke tackle for 35y TD after taking option handoff from Pistol formation to complete 94y drive in 1st Q. Dores CB Eddie Foster soon jumped route and sped 21y to INT TD RET in 1st Q, and finally, CB Casey Hayward iced it with 4th Q INT of high pass down left sideline.

AUBURN 27 Clemson 24 (OT): In 2nd Q, Clemson (2-1) RB Jamie Harper made 24y stretch-out diving TD catch from QB Kyle Parker (21-35/227y, 2 TDs) for 17-0 lead as Carolinians sought 1st win since 1951 in this occasional series. Down 17-3, Auburn (3-0) had big 3rd Q as RB Onterio McCalebb (10/81y, TD) tallied on 12y run and QB Cam Newton (7-14/203y, 2 TDs, 2 INTs) pitched 2 scores, including 78y pump-fake bomb to WR Terrell Zachery. Clemson tied it 24-24 early in 4th Q on TD run by RB Andre Ellington (22/140y, TD). In OT, K Wes Byrum put Auburn ahead with 39y FG. In bottom half of OT, banged-up Parker might have won game but was too wide with EZ pass that slipped off wide-open WR Jaron Brown's fingertips. Clemson K Chandler Catanzaro tied it with FG but had to try again when flag flew because of illegal double-clutch snap by C Matt Skinner. Catanzaro missed his retry for FG. Sometimes it takes such breaks to complete undefeated season, which Auburn would eventually achieve.

MICHIGAN STATE 34 Notre Dame 31 (OT): Spartans (3-0) were stunningly rescued by play named "Little Giants," and win sent celebrating fans to streets of East Lansing and, unfortunately, coach Mark Dantonio to hospital later that night with mild heart attack. While Irish stayed in air, Spartans stuck to ground with frosh RB Le'Veon Bell rushing for 114y, TD. Michigan State and Notre Dame (1-2) traded TDs all game: only 56y run by Spartans RB Edwin Baker (14/90y, TD), behind block of LG Joel Foreman, early in 3rd Q and 24y TD pass to WR Michael Floyd from Irish QB Dayne Crist (32-55/369y, 4 TDs, INT) stood as consecutive scores by same team. Baker's long TD up middle with cut to right sideline broke 7-7 H deadlock. Crist's 4th TD pitch 1:40 into 4th Q provided 28-21 edge. ND took 31-28 led in OT on K David Ruffer's 33y FG. MSU lined up for potential tying 46y 3-ptr, but holder Aaron Bates rose out of his stance and waited for TE Charlie Gantt to clear downfield for winning 29y TD pass. "That's the last thing anybody was expecting," said Bates. Actually, it appeared Irish was alert to fake, but several defenders unluckily got caught up in tangled bodies.

WISCONSIN 20 Arizona State 19: Genuine scare from undervalued Arizona State (2-1) came as utter shock to fans at Camp Randall Stadium, who hooted their shamed Badgers special teams throughout 2nd H. In fact, Sun Devils, preseason pick for 9th in Pac-10, would have beaten no. 11 Wisconsin (3-0) had it not been for frustrations like last play of 1st H when ASU RB Kyle Middlebrooks dashed 95y with KO only to be stopped at Wisconsin 1YL as clock expired and blocked x-pt by Badgers DB Jay Valai with 4 mins to go. Badgers TE Lance Kendricks (7/131y, TD) enjoyed big afternoon, including 14y TD catch from QB Scott Tolzien (19-25/246y, TD) 10 secs before H for 13-10 lead. It preceded Middlebrooks' near-score RET. Wisconsin broke 13-13 deadlock in 3rd Q by traveling 88y to 19y TD blast by TB John Clay (22/123y, TD). Arizona State expected to knot it when RB Cameron Marshall ran across late in 4th Q, but Valai squirted through right side of Devils line to block kick by K Thomas Weber.

Southern California 32 MINNESOTA 21: With cloud of bowl-ineligibility and Reggie Bush investigation hanging over their heads, PEN-infected Trojans (3-0) were playing just well enough to have defeated so-so opponents in Hawaii, Virginia, and Minnesota (1-2). With 5:47 left in 3rd Q, each team had 2 TDs, but because USC had failed on 2-pt attempt after WR Ronald Johnson's 53y TD grab in 2nd Q, Golden Gophers took 14-13 lead on TD pass by QB Adam Weber (15-29/224y, 2 TDs, 2 INTs). Frosh WR Robert Woods took ensuing KO and raced 97y for TD that turned game around for Troy. Within 12 mins, USC had 32-14 lead as struggling QB Matt Barkley (17-26/192y, 2 TDs, 2 INTs) pitched TD pass and TB Allen Bradford (12/131y, TD) raced 56y to TD.

OKLAHOMA 27 Air Force 24: Moral victory was no goal of Air Force (2-1), which outgained Oklahoma (3-0) by 458y to 367y and added pair of 4th Q TD runs to claw within 3 pts of Sooners. Falcons FB Jared Tew (21/93y, TD), who scored along with WR Kyle Halderman in 4th Q, said, "We don't come into any game just wanting to get close. Just because they're the No. 7 team (in AP Poll), we're not going to back down and just try to get close to the No. 7 team." Big guns on O for Oklahoma were QB Landry Jones (26-42/254y, TD), RB DeMarco Murray (26/110y, 2 TDs, and TD receiving), and WR Ryan Broyles (10/116y).

TEXAS CHRISTIAN 45 Baylor 10: Sharp QB Andy Dalton (21-23/267y, 2 TDs) connected on his 1st 11 passes as TCU (3-0) rolled to TDs on its opening 5 series. Frogs led 35-3 at H and finished with 558y total O. Frogs RB Ed Wesley also scored twice while rushing 19/165y. Disappointed Baylor (2-1) star QB Robert Griffin (16-28/164y, TD) finally led Bears to EZ in 3rd Q on 53y TD pass to WR Josh Gordon. TCU now owned 15 wins in its last 18 games vs. BCS conf teams, while this was 1st match-up of these former Southwest Conf rivals since league was folded up in 1994. Since that time, TCU had won or shared titles in three different leagues since being left out when Baylor, Texas, Texas A&M, and Texas Tech helped form Big 12 Conf.

Nebraska 56 WASHINGTON 21: Huskies (1-2) QB Jake Locker (4-20/71y, TD, 2 INTs) skipped NFL draft for this disaster? Electric Nebraska (3-0) frosh QB Taylor Martinez (7-11/150y, TD, and 19/137y, 3 TDs rushing) raced all over Husky Stadium in leading Huskers to 533y O. Locker and RB Chris Polk tallied TDs in 1st H, which Washington kept reasonably close, down 28-14. Early in 3rd Q, Martinez faked on option hadoff and dashed around LE for 80y TD. Nebraska had trio of 100y rushers, including RBs Roy Helu (10/110y, 2 TDs) and Rex Burkhead (13/104y, TD), each of whom scored in 2nd H. Huskers CB Alfonzo Dennard returned INT of Locker for 31y TD in 3rd Q.

ARIZONA 34 Iowa 27: Seemingly on its way to program-defining, easy win after leading 27-7 at H, Arizona (3-0) watched Iowa (2-1) rally on pair of TD passes by QB Ricky Stanzi (18-33/278y, 3 TDs, INT) and 20y INT TD RET by DE Broderick Binns on brilliant short-range pluck. Big 1st H plays had ignited fans at 83-year-old, desert-motif Arizona Stadium: Wildcats blocked punt to set up 1st Q TD pass by QB Nick Foles (28-39/303y, 2 TDs, INT), CB Trevin Wade ran back INT 85y for another TD, and WR Travis Cobb returned KO100y for TD. After Binns' INT TD, which came with 8:12 to go in 4th Q, Wildcats partially blocked x-pt, so it stayed tied 27-27. Arizona immediately awoke from its 2nd H slumber behind Foles, who overcame 2 negative plays to drive Cats 72y on his 5-6/76y passing and 4y TD toss to WR William "Bug" Wright. Arizona spilled Stanzi 3 times trying to pass to kill Iowa's last threat and defeated top-10, non-conf opponent at home for 1st time since 1989.

USA TODAY Coaches Poll September 19, 2010

1 Alabama (55)	1470	14 Auburn	655
2 Ohio State (3)	1410	15 South Carolina	612
3 Boise State	1291	16 Arizona	610
4 Texas	1251	17 Stanford	541
5 Texas Christian	1188	18 Iowa	463
6 Oregon	1181	19 Miami	418
7 Nebraska (1)	1135	20 Penn State	335
8 Florida	1092	21 West Virginia	315
9 Oklahoma	1060	22 Michigan	255
10 Wisconsin	884	23 Michigan State	125
11 Arkansas	846	24 Missouri	123
12 Louisiana State	801	25 Oklahoma State	103
13 Utah	693		

September 25, 2010

(Fri) Texas Christian 41 SOUTHERN METHODIST 24: High-flying Horned Frogs (4-0) briefly were brought down to earth by miscues, including INTs near end of 1st H and early in 3rd Q by normally-sharp QB Andy Dalton (14-26/174y, TD, 2 INTs). Dalton's 1st error led to FG which trimmed TCU's H lead to 14-10. Right after 2nd H KO, Southern Methodist (2-2) CB Sterling Moore dropped off his coverage to make 32y INT RET to 1YL. Mustangs QB Kyle Padron (14-35/169y, 2 TDs, INT) quickly tossed TD pass for 17-14 lead. Frogs WR Jeremy Kerley (4/33y and 5/172y KO RETs) next made game's biggest play, roaring 83y on KO RET. Suddenly, Dalton stepped out of his funk and led TD drives on next 3 possessions for 35-17 lead. His 49th career TD pass tied Max Knacke's school record. SMU RB Zach Line ran 17/139y, including 29y TD in 4th Q.

Virginia Tech 19 BOSTON COLLEGE 0: It had been rough year so far for Hokies (2-2). After losses to Boise State and James Madison of FCS, Virginia Tech had time outscoring East Carolina, 49-27, so D unit might face real test in ACC opener on road against Boston College (2-1). Hokies D more than returned to prominence but got help on 2 poor decisions by BC QB Dave Shinskie (11-25/130y, 2 INTs). After leading his O unit 63y on 1st Q drive, Shinskie forced pass to EZ where Hokies CB Jayron Hosley made INT. Va Tech QB Tyrod Taylor (16-21/237y, INT) soon hit TB Darren Evans for 30y catch, and Evans scored on 3y TD run. Just before H, Shinskie tried to run for left pylon but came up short as clock ran out. Hokies K Chris Hazley added 4 2nd H FGs. Eagles LB Mark Herzlich made INT after missing all of 2009 under cancer treatment.

North Carolina State 45 GEORGIA TECH 28: Surprising Wolfpack (4-0) rode star QB Russell Wilson (28-41/368y, 3 TDs, INT) to 31-14 lead at end of 3rd Q after Wilson's 6y TD run. Suddenly, Georgia Tech (2-2) struck for 2 TDs to claw within 31-28; key play came when Wilson, under heavy blitz pressure, threw up prayer picked off by Yellow Jackets CB Jerrard Tarrant, who maneuvered 33y for TD RET. Wilson, however, bounced back immediately with 74y drive, capped by his pump-fake right and 23y TD arrow over middle to WR T.J. Graham. NC State had scored in 1st Q when TE Asa Watson blocked punt that WR Jarvis Williams returned 1y for TD.

Army 35 DUKE 21: Converting 4 TOs into TDs, alert Army (3-1) built leads of 21-7 at H and 35-7 in 3rd Q. Black Knights QB Trent Steelman (4-6/85y, 2 TDs, and 18/62y, TD rushing) accounted for 3 scores, and SB Brian Cobbs also ran for 3 and 4y TDs. Struggling to overcome its miscues, Duke (1-3) barely possessed ball for 20 mins by game's end and didn't succeed in air until it was too late. Blue Devils QB Sean Renfree (17-30/261y, 2 TDs, 3 INTs), who came off bench last year to spark come-from-behind win over Army at West Point, connected with WR Conner Vernon (8/129y, TD) on 1st play of 4th Q for 58y TD and added another TD pass near end of 4th Q.

Alabama 24 ARKANSAS 20: Pair of young, new Alabama (4-0) DBs, S Robert Lester and CB Dre Kirkpatrick, came up with 4th Q INTs to launch winning 12y march and clinch verdict on road vs. nation's leading passer in Arkansas (3-1) QB Ryan Mallett (25-38/357y, TD, 3 INTs). Mallett enjoyed brilliant 1st H. While Tide had allowed only 5 plays longer than 20y in all of opening 3 games, Mallett hit passes of 31 and 43y to start game, latter going to RB Ronnie Wingo, who snuck out of backfield all alone for TD catch. Mallett brought Hogs 66y in last 2 mins of 2nd Q for 17-7 H lead with only blemish on Razorbacks ledger coming on 54y TD run by Tide TB Mark Ingram (24/157y, 2 TDs) in 1st Q. Trailing 20-7 late in 3rd Q, Alabama TB Trent Richardson took screen pass 20y for TD to initiate fight from behind. K Jeremy Shelley's 36y FG past middle of 4th Q cut Tide's deficit to 20-17. Next, Lester returned his 2nd INT of game 33y to Razorbacks 12YL, and Ingram pounded 3 straight times for winning TD.

AUBURN 35 South Carolina 27: For 2nd straight week, Auburn (4-0) overcame double-digit 1st H deficit to pull out win. Tigers QB Cam Newton (16-21/158y, 2 TDs, and 25/176y, 3 TDs) turned heads with spectacular performance. After Newton spun 54y through Gamecocks for early TD, South Carolina (3-1) jumped to 20-7 lead thanks to pair of TD passes between QB Stephen Garcia (15-21/235y, 3 TDs) and WR Alshon Jeffrey (8/192y, 2 TDs). Newton added another scoring run to pull Tigers within 20-14 at H. Garcia authored his 3rd TD pass in 3rd Q for 27-21 lead, but his 2 FUMs convinced coach Steve Spurrier to change to QB Connor Shaw, who threw 2 INTs. Garcia's FUM less than min into 4th Q saw Auburn set up shop at Gamecocks 26YL, and Tigers TE Philip Lutzenkirchen (3/22y, TD) slipped free into EZ for 7y TD flip from Newton, who hit another TD pass to extend advantage to 35-27 with 6:23 to play.

MISSISSIPPI STATE 24 Georgia 12: Coming in with 5-16 all-time mark against SEC's other Bulldogs (Georgia), Mississippi State Bulldogs (2-2) used fortuitous D to stifle Georgia (1-3), which was flagged 9/63y in PENs and struggled without its best weapon, WR A.J. Green, who missed his 4th game under suspension. Mississippi State's best weapon, QB Chris Relf (8-13/135y, TD, and 21/97y rushing), dashed 20y to set up RB Vick Ballard (14/77y, 2 TDs) for 13y TD run in 1st Q. UGa saw its 79y drive ruined when RB Washaun Ealey lost FUM inside 1YL, but K Blair Walsh made 2 FGs to pull within 7-6 by H. In 4th Q, Relf promoted 10-6 lead to 17-6 with 33y TD pass, and Ballard locked it up with TD with 3:15 to go. Georgia's improving QB, Aaron Murray (18-31/274y, TD), was able to fit in late 40y TD pass.

Stanford 37 NOTRE DAME 14: Winning at Notre Dame Stadium for 1st time since 1992 and for 1st time ever vs. Irish in successive years, Stanford Cardinal (4-0) paved way to victory with big 4th Q lift from 2-way battler, FB-LB Owen Marecic. Marecic bashed across GL for TD midway through last Q and successfully followed up 13 secs later when he intercepted Fighting Irish (1-3) QB Dayne Crist (25-44/304y, TD, INT) to ramble 20y on direct line to EZ for 34-6 lead. Crist came back with 20, 22, and 37y pass connections to set up his 3y TD throw to WR Theo Riddick (7/71y, TD). Stanford QB Andrew Luck hit 19-32/238y, TD, 2 INTs. Luck, who threw only 4 INTs in 2009, was picked off twice when looking for home-run-hitting WR Chris Owusu (2/23y).

Ucla 34 TEXAS 12: Nation was shocked by upset and extent of domination by UCLA (2-2) over no. 4 Longhorns (3-1), only 2nd defeat of Texas in last 21 games. Keys to victory were 264y rushing vs. nation's no. 2 run D and forcing of 4 TOs in 1st H that was led 13-3 by Bruins. Decisive drive went 80y to open 3rd Q as UCLA RB Johnathan Franklin (19/118y, TD) chipped in with 35y run before tallying on 11y sprint. After K Justin Tucker kicked his 2nd mid-range FG to pull Texas within 20-6, UCLA swept right back downfield to 38y TD dash around LE by QB Kevin Prince (5-8/27y, TD, and 13/50y, TD rushing) after deft fake handoff to left. Longhorns QB Garrett Gilbert (30-45/264y, TD, INT) was pressured all game but came up with 5y TD pass late in 4th Q.

Oregon 42 ARIZONA STATE 31: Arizona State (2-2) gained 597y O, more than it had in 10 years. ASU throttled swift Ducks (4-0) RB LaMichael James (28/94y, TD), who, except for early 40y TD burst that tied game at 7-7, was held to 2y-per-rush avg. Sun Devils frosh RB Deantre Lewis more than matched James with 11/127y rushing, with 53y stroke of TD lightning in 1st Q. What went wrong for ASU? It gave up staggering 7 TOs, including Oregon S John Boyett's 39y INT TD RET in 1st Q and LB Boseko Lokombo's 32y FUM TD RET in 3rd Q. Sun Devils had been able to lead 24-14 late in 2nd Q after 2nd TD pass by QB Steven Threet (30-53/387y, 3 TDs, 4 INTs). But, Ducks flew ahead 28-24 just before H as QB Darron Thomas (19-33/260y, 2 TDs, INT) went to air to negotiate not 1 but 2 80y TD drives totaling less than 2 mins. Oregon WR Josh Huff caught 54y TD off pump-fake by Thomas in 3rd Q, and Ducks were on their way to 42-24 lead until ASU WR Mike Willie nabbed his 2nd scoring pass with 2:25 left.

USA TODAY Coaches Poll September 26, 2010

1 Alabama (57)	1472	14 Arizona	689
2 Ohio State (2)	1412	15 Arkansas	576
3 Boise State	1312	16 Texas	563
4 Oregon	1243	17 Miami	517
5 Texas Christian	1221	18 Iowa	509
6 Nebraska	1164	19 Michigan	375
7 Florida	1154	20 Penn State	347
8 Oklahoma	1083	21 Michigan State	278
9 Wisconsin	989	22 South Carolina	272
10 Louisiana State	896	23 Missouri	182
11 Auburn	828	24 Oklahoma State	146
12 Utah	790	25 Nevada	102
13 Stanford	744		

October 2, 2010

(Th) Oklahoma State 38 TEXAS A&M 35: Rifle-armed QB Jerrod Johnson (40-62/409y, 5 TDs, 4 INTs) became Texas A&M (3-1) all-time career leader in pass y but his 5 TOs, including crushing FUM and INT in 4th Q, doomed his Aggies. Oklahoma State (4-0) had its share of miscues, 3, which contributed to Johnson's trio of 1st H TD passes and 21-7 advantage for A&M. Cowboys QB Brandon Weeden (28-42/284y, 2 TDs, 2 INTs) threw 29y TD pass to WR Justin Blackmon (10/127y, TD), and RB Kendall Hunter (22/101y, 2 TDs) scored twice in dynamic 3rd Q that pushed OSU ahead 28-21. Texas A&M were able to rally on Johnson's 2 TD passes to tie it 35-35 in strangely epic, but unfortunate 4th Q: Aggies held ball for 12:07 of last Q, converted 2 4th downs, and rolled up 278y O to 38y. But, Cowpokes LB James Thomas went 63y for TD with Johnson's FUM on sacvk, and LB Shaun Lewis returned Johnson's INT 28y in closing secs to set up K Dan Bailey's winning 40y FG, that was knocked true as time expired. "It was just a very emotional game that had a number of mistakes," said OSU coach Mike Gundy said, "and we were able to capitalize on the last one."

CONNECTICUT 40 Vanderbilt 21: Big East previously stood at 1-9 against BCS conf teams in 2010, but Connecticut (3-2) was able to pull away from Vanderbilt (1-3), weak sister of SEC, with 19 unanswered pts in 2nd H. Huskies RB Jordan Todman rushed 37/190y, and his 2 TD runs provided 14-0 lead 4 mins into 2nd Q. Then, Commodores RB Warren Norman, who would be held to 27y rushing, delivered thrilling 72y of his 162y in KO RETs. His long play sparked Vandy to 3 TDs in slightly more than 3-and-half mins: 2 TD passes by QB Larry Smith (15-25/157y, 2 TDs, 2 INTs) and 44y reverse TD run by frosh WR Jonathan Krause. UConn QB Cody Endres (21-30/179y, 2 TDs, INT) led quick 73y TD drive to his late 2nd Q tying TD pass. Little WR Nick Williams returned 2nd H KO 54y, Todman went for 25y, and Endres threw another TD pass to give UConn lead for good at 28-21 to start 3rd Q.

Miami 30 CLEMSON 21: Coming off surprisingly easy 31-3 win at Pittsburgh, Miami Hurricanes (3-1) closed tough 3-game road swing with big win in ACC opener. Miami QB Jacory Harris (13-33/205y, 4 TDs, 2 INTs) pitched 3 scoring passes in 2nd Q to overcome 14-7 lead held by Clemson (2-2). Sleek Canes WR Leonard Hankerson (7/147y, 3 TDs) got open for 22, 65, and 7y scoring catches in 1st H. Smooth Tigers RB Andre Ellington (17/107y, 3 TDs) kept his team competitive with 71, 14, and 3y TD runs. Harris still could be guilty of some frustrating plays: his 3rd Q intentional-

grounding PEN set up field position for Ellington's final TD that pulled Tigers dangerously close at 27-21, and Harris was bailed out early in 4th Q by teammate OT Seantrel Henderson's REC of his FUM at midfield.

ALABAMA 31 Florida 6: There was great anticipation for matchup of undefeated previous pair of national champions in Tuscaloosa. In strange way, it was last 2010 hurrah for both: this defeat launched 3-game losing streak for Florida (4-1), while Alabama (5-0) would be unable to get up for South Carolina week hence and would drop 2 SEC West tilts. Crimson Tide owned this contest with physical play in 1st H, running up 24-3 advantage as TB Mark Ingram (12/47y, 2 TDs) scored twice and WR Marquis Maze tossed TD pass out of Wildcat formation. Shortly after Gators K Chas Henry hit his 2nd FG in 3rd Q, Bama frosh LB C.J. Mosley dashed 35y on INT TD RET for 31-6 edge. Florida continued to alternate signal-callers as QB John Brantley passed 16-31/202y, 2 INTs and GL-specialist QB Trey Burton, coming off 6 TD runs vs. Kentucky previous Saturday, was picked off in EZ by Bama LB Nico Johnson when Burton tried Tim Tebow-like jump-pass off run fake on 4th-and-goal at 2YL in 1st Q.

LOUISIANA STATE 16 Tennessee 14: Bayou Bengals (5-0) coach Les "Mad Hatter" Miles was at it again, pulling out another game when late-game strategy seemingly was mangled. LSU rang up 434y O but was able to score its only pair of TDs on 1st and last snaps of game with QB Jordan Jefferson racing 83y to start day. Tennessee (2-3) matched Jefferson's TD that with short 1st Q TD dive by TB Tauren Poole (24/109y, TD). Outgained all day, Volunteers mustered 71y drive in 4th Q to 3y TD keeper by QB Matt Simms (12-23/121y) for 14-10 lead. Taking over with 5:41 to play, LSU sub QB Jarrett Lee (16-23/185y, INT) twice hit WR Terrence Toliver (3/52y) to convert 3rd-and-13 and 4th-and-14 downs, Toliver's latter catch finally making 1st-and-goal at Tennessee 2YL with less than min to play. After Lee threw incomplete, Jefferson was summoned and squeezed to 1YL. Confused and with no timeouts left, LSU watched 28 secs tick away without spiking ball, finally sending personnel changes racing on field. In bedlam, Shotgun snap eluded Jefferson as clock ran out, and Tennessee happily celebrated its presumed win. As LSU players flung helmets in frustration, officials flagged Vols for having 13 men on field. With no time on clock, Tigers RB Stevan Ridley (22/123y, TD) powered over left side for winning TD. That Vols were not permitted to match Tigers' personnel changes was never addressed, so LSU pulled win out of rabbit hat. Nearly out of breath at end, Miles huffed to CBS-TV: "We're a very talented team. I don't think we played near to our capacity. The series of downs on the back end of that game was embarrassing to me."

MICHIGAN STATE 34 Wisconsin 24: Playing their 2nd game without laid-up coach Mark Dantonio, Spartans (5-0) continued their gambling ways by twice converting 4th downs that led to key scores. Ahead 13-10 late in 2nd Q after WR Keshawn Martin's 74y punt TD RET, Michigan State RB Le'Veon Bell took pitchout on 4th-and-1 from Wisconsin 48YL and stormed 23y to set up 8y TD grab for 20-10 H edge by WR Mark Dell (6/91y, TD) from QB Kirk Cousins (20-29/269y, 3 TDs, 2 INTs). Badgers big TB John Clay rushed for 80y, which ended his 10-game streak of 100y or more. Swift frosh TB James White took over going for 98y and 2 TDs, including wide 34y TD dash in 3rd Q to cut Wisconsin's deficit to 20-17. TEs Charlie Gantt of MSU and Jacob Pedersen of Wisconsin traded TD catches until Spartans put it away with 84y TD drive that took nearly 8 mins off 4th Q clock. It was capped by 1y TD catch on 4th down by WR B.J. Cunningham, who had to fight his way through 2 defenders to catch clincher.

Ohio State 24 ILLINOIS 13: Just as if it were 1930s college movie, Ohio State (5-0) QB Terrelle Pryor (9-16/76y, 2 TDs, INT and 11/104y rushing) limped off to locker room in 2nd H as sub QB Joe Bauserman threw INT. Then Pryor gallantly returned to lead 2 drives that copped 10 pts to pull Buckeyes from behind in 4th Q. RB Dan Herron also contributed some tough running on 23/95y, including decisive TD at end of 53y trip with 1:49 to play. Illinois (2-2), pesky winners of 11 of last 25 from Buckeyes, had used trick pass play that had top receiver WR Jarred Fayson (8/83y) throwing to QB Nathan Scheelhaase (12-22/109y, INT) for 23y gain before Scheelhaase scored on 3y run for 7-0 lead in 1st Q. Pryor's pass to RB Brandon Saine tied it 2 mins later. Ohio State led 14-10 at H after Pryor's TD pass to WR Dane Sanzenbacher. Down 17-10, Illini marched inside Ohio State 15YL, and head coach Ron Zook made tough choice to kick FG on 4th-and-7 with 4:36 to play. It set stage for Herron's clinching score.

IOWA 24 Penn State 3: Steady sr QB Ricky Stanzi (16-22/227y, TD, INT) shook off 1st Q INT to bring Hawkeyes (4-1) to 10-0 lead on 9y TD pass, earned in part because WR Derrell Johnson-Koulianos created confusion in Penn State (3-2) secondary. Nittany Lions were happy to see 1st Q end as they suffered through 143y to 1y O discrepancy. Trailing 17-0 in last moments of 2nd Q, Lions WR Brett Brackett hauled in 49y pass from QB Robert Bolden (20-37/212y, INT) but was hauled down on TD-saving tackle by Iowa CB Shaun Prater at 2YL. Penn State had to settle for FG. Opening drive of 2nd H saw Penn State go 70y, but Bolden was stopped at 1YL on 4th down run. Prater tacked on late-game 33y INT TD RET.

Northwestern 29 MINNESOTA 28: Looking for their 10th road win in last 13 away-trips, undefeated Wildcats (5-0) took 14-7 lead in 1st Q behind fast-paced O directed by QB Dan Persa (23-30/309y, 2 TDs, INT, and 18/99y rushing). Minnesota Gophers (1-4), losers of 3 straight home games, fashioned excellent 2nd Q as they held Northwestern to 42y and scored 2 TDs. RB DeLeon Eskridge (22/119y, TD) slashed over for 4y TD run in last min of 2nd Q for 21-14 lead. Early in 4th Q, Minnesota TE Eric Lair (3/75y, 2 TDs) made nice out-fake and cut for post to snare 25y TD pass from QB Adam Weber (14-23/194y, 2 TDs, INT) for 28-20 lead. Wildcats WR Jeremy Ebert went high in EZ to catch 25y TD pass, but when 2-pt try failed NW still trailed 28-26 with 8:17 to play. Persa hit 15y pass to Ebert and ran 22 and 11y to set up winning 27y FG by K Stefan Demos, who made up for missed x-pt in 3rd Q.

IOWA STATE 52 Texas Tech 38: By time wild game was over, it was hard to believe 1st Q went by scoreless. QBs Austen Arnaud (20-28/190y, 4 TDs) of Iowa State (3-2) and Taylor Potts (42-62/377y, 5 TDs, INT) of Texas Tech (2-2) sold TDs like cheap potholders at flea-market. Cyclones jumped to 24-0 lead, only see Red Raiders score 2 TDs within 36 secs of last min of 2nd Q. When WR Lyle Leong (9/125y, 3 TDs) hauled in his 2nd TD pass with 5:25 left in 3rd Q, Texas Tech had knotted it 24-24. Iowa State went up 38-24, and with 1:30 left Leong nabbed his 3rd TD reception to pull within 45-38. Texas Tech tried on-side KO, but little Cyclones CB Jeremy Reeves fielded bounding ball and burst 42y for clinching TD, Iowa State's 1st KO TD RET since 1994.

Oklahoma 28 Texas 20 (Dallas): For floundering Longhorns (3-2), this Red River Rivalry game became bundle of self-inflicted errors: Texas D recovered FUM only to have lined up offside, extended several Oklahoma (5-0) possessions with PENs—including roughing when 3rd-and-29 pass fell incomplete—and finally lost muffed punt catch by CB Aaron Williams with min to play. It was 2nd such punt-muff late-stumbling Sooners—outscored 41-10 in 4th Qs so far in 2010—received to save their bacon in last 2 weeks. OU RB DeMarco Murray (25/115y, 2 TDs) used burst of speed and twinkle-toed move down sideline for his pair of TD runs: 18y when 1st Q was 4 mins old and 20y for 28-10 lead early in 4th Q. Sooners QB Landry Jones completed 24-39/236y, 2 TDs, while his Texas counterpart, QB Garrett Gilbert hit 27-41/266y, INT. Gilbert directed drives for 10 pts in 4th Q comeback bid on which he hit 5-8/105y.

COLORADO 29 Georgia 27: Landmark victory for Colorado (3-1) coach Dan Hawkins was clinched when Buffaloes LB B.J. Beatty caused late FUM to prevent Georgia Bulldogs (1-4) from trying winning FG. Georgia welcomed back star WR A.J. Green (7/119y, 2 TDs), who while suffering from leg cramps and adjustment to high altitude still made jumping, 1-handed 3y and 39y post-pattern TD catches in 2nd Q from QB Aaron Murray (16-27/221y, 3 TDs, INT). Green made 50y catch to set up 3rd Q TD that provided 24-14 edge to Bulldogs. But, Buffs battled back to take 29-24 lead late in 3rd Q when RB Rodney Stewart (19/149y, TD) took misdirection pitchout 11y to paydirt. Georgia K Blair Walsh (2 FGs) was warming up for 40+y 3-pt try in last 2 mins when Beatty blitzed and knocked FUM from Bulldogs RB Caleb King.

AIR FORCE 14 Navy 6: Falcons QB Tim Jefferson (5-7/83y, and 10/62y, 2 TDs rushing) was difference in breaking Navy's 7-game win streak over Air Force (4-2). Jefferson got loose on option run for 50y TD in 1st Q. After missing chip-shot 3-ptr in 1st Q, K Joe Buckley hit 25 and 32y FGs in middle Qs to bring Midshipmen (2-2) within 7-6. Early in 4th Q, frosh LB Jamil Cooks jumped over blocker to smother punt by Navy P Kyle Delahooke. Jefferson scored 4 plays later from 1YL. Navy drove to AFA 33YL before LB Jordan Waiwaiole intercepted pass by QB Ricky Dobbs (6-18/103y, 2 INTs, and 18/43y rushing) to seal victory with 25 secs left. "All of us seniors had lost to Navy every year we'd been here, and everyone comes up to us asking if we're going to beat

Navy this year," said FB Jared Tew (17/111y). "There was a lot riding on this game."

Washington 32 SOUTHERN CALIFORNIA 31: Washington (2-2) head coach Steve Sarkisian's Huskies were fired up for their 2nd straight upset of Troy as he returned to Los Angeles, where he had coached O of Southern California (4-1). UW QB Jake Locker (24-40/310y, TD, and 12/110y rushing) rebounded from terrible afternoon against Nebraska to lead O to 536y. "What a performance by No. 10 (Locker)," said Sarkisian, "He showed how big his heart is, that's for sure." USC had struck in 1st Q when G Khaled Holmes and T Tyron Smith collapsed Huskies D line on 37y TD run by TB Allen Bradford (21/223y, 2 TDs). When TB Marc Tyler (14/60y, 2 TDs) tallied twice in 2nd Q, Trojans led 21-17. Bradford's 16y TD run with 4:44 left in 3rd Q gave Trojans 28-23 edge, but Locker hit 3 passes and ran for 30y on 68y trip that bridged 3rd and 4th Q intermission. He ran for 1st down at USC 1YL on 2nd snap of 4th Q but was knocked woozy, so sub QB Keith Price came in to lob 1y TD pass to TE Chris Izbicki for 29-28 lead. Southern California K Joe Houston closed 49y drive with go-ahead 27y FG with 10 mins to play but hit right upright with his next FG try from 40y. Down by 2 pts, Washington took over with 2:34 left, and RB Chris Polk (13/92y, TD) ran for 26, 6, and 5y gains to position K Erik Folk's winning 32y FG, his 4th of game, as time expired.

OREGON 52 Stanford 31: With QB Andrew Luck (29-46/341y, 2 TDs, 2 INTs) passing and running for TDs and TB Stepfan Taylor (17/113y, TD) bolting 44y for score, no. 13 Stanford (4-1) popped to 21-3 lead at end of 1st Q. Calm Oregon (5-0) QB Darron Thomas (20-29/238y, 3 TDs, 2 INTs) hit pair of TD passes in 2nd Q, but Cardinal still led 31-24 at H. It was all Ducks in 2nd H as Thomas ran and passed for TDs and RB LaMichael James (31/257y, 3 TDs) capped 2nd-best rushing effort in Ducks history by dashing 76y to end night's scoring. It was 1st time 2 old rivals had ever met with both ranked. While Stanford had 2 recent upsets of Oregon when Ducks were ranked in top-10, Cardinal remained without win as AP top-10 team (no. 7 this week) since 1970.

USA TODAY Coaches Poll October 3, 2010

1 Alabama (57)	1449	14 Miami	679
2 Ohio State (1)	1377	15 Iowa	643
3 Oregon	1300	16 Michigan State	625
4 Boise State	1276	17 Michigan	541
5 Texas Christian	1187	18 Stanford	448
6 Nebraska	1176	19 Wisconsin	414
7 Oklahoma	1132	20 South Carolina	345
8 Auburn	988	21 Oklahoma State	299
9 Louisiana State	930	22 Missouri	271
10 Utah	868	23 Nevada	201
11 Arizona	835	24 Florida State	164
12 Florida	705	25 Northwestern	67
13 Arkansas	683		

October 9, 2010

(Fri) RUTGERS 27 Connecticut 24: Playing in place of injured QB Tom Savage, frosh QB Chas Dodd (18-29/322y, 2 TDs) rallied Rutgers (3-2) in closing mins with tying 52y TD pass to WR Mark Harrison and 45y connection to WR Jeremy Deering to set up K San San Te's winning 34y FG with 13 secs to go. Night's scoring had come in spurts as Dodd-to-Deering TD pass gave Scarlet Knights 7-0 with 8:49 left in 1st Q, but

UConn Huskies (3-3) WR Nick Williams answered immediately with 100y KO TD RET. Keyed by 66y TD run by TB Jordan Todman (24/123y, TD), Connecticut surged for 17 pts in last 6:36 of 2nd Q to lead 24-17 at H and well into 4th Q.

NORTH CAROLINA STATE 44 Boston College 17: Coach Tom O'Brien of North Carolina State (5-1) won for 1st time over Boston College (2-3), school he once led. After Wolfpack frosh DB D.J. Green recovered blocked punt for 10-0 lead in 1st Q, QB Russell Wilson (38-51/328y, 3 TDs, 2 INTs) pitched TDs to 3 different receivers. CB C.J. Wilson snatched underthrown pass and cantered 28y for TD in 3rd Q that lifted NC State's lead to 34-10. That poor pass by BC QB Dave Shinskie (7-24/89y, TD, 2 INTs) got him yanked in favor of soph QB Mike Marscovetra (4-8/84y, TD, INT), who launched 67y window-dressing TD bomb to frosh WR Alex Amidon with 5 mins left.

Florida State 45 MIAMI 17: Romp by Florida State (5-1) was keyed by RBs Jermaine Thomas (16/78y, 2 TDs), who scored 3 times, and Chris Thompson (14/158y, TD), whose 90y TD run in 4th Q was longest-ever allowed by Hurricanes (3-2). Sr QB Christian Ponder (12-21/173y, 2 TDs, INT) was left to happily ponder Seminoles' 3rd straight win against Canes in Miami. Largest crowd at Sun Life Stadium since Hurricanes left Orange Bowl turned to booing home team, which managed its TDs on runs by QB Jacory Harris (19-47/225y, INT) and RB Damien Berry (20/101y, TD).

Navy 28 WAKE FOREST 27: Coming off last-min 24-20 loss to Georgia Tech, Wake Forest's dandy throw-back gold jerseys still did nothing to stop trend. With 26 secs to play, Navy (4-2) QB Ricky Dobbs (8-19/94y, 2TDs, INT, and 22/100, 2 TDs rushing) tossed 6y TD pass at end of 64y march to WR Greg Jones in right corner of EZ. Demon Deacons (2-4) frosh QB Tanner Price (37-53/326y, 2 TDs) had scored running TD and pitched Wake to leads of 7-0, 17-14 at H, and 24-21 going into 4th Q.

Auburn 37 KENTUCKY 34: At end of 86y drive consuming final 7:22, steady Auburn (6-0) sr K Wes Byrum kicked 24y FG as time expired to win it. Kentucky (3-3) WR Randall Cobb (7/68y, TD, and 11/47y, 2 TDs rushing) had returned opening KO 36y past midfield, launching 49y march to his 2y TD run. Tigers QB Cam Newton (13-21/210y, INT, and 28/198y, 4 TDs rushing) scored on runs of 16, 8, 5, and 3y in 1st H, and Auburn led 31-17. After tossing 2nd Q TD on his only attempt, ubiquitous Cobb caught TD pass from Wildcats QB Mike Hartline (23-28/220y, TD) and also scored from 1YL in 3rd Q to knot contest at 31-31. With UK behind 34-31, Cobb kept 13-play drive alive by barely making 1st down on 3y run on 4th down to Auburn 15YL, but Kentucky had to settle for tying FG. That set stage for Auburn's winning FG trip on which Newton converted trio of 3rd downs with 2-3/20y passing and 10/48y rushing.

SOUTH CAROLINA 35 Alabama 21: Except for 2nd H down-spell triggered by strange safety, no. 20 South Carolina (4-1) dominated in winning for 1st time ever over any team ranked no. 1. Hard-hitting Gamecocks D stymied Alabama (5-1) running corps of TBs Mark Ingram and Trent Richardson, holding them to combined 17/64y. QB Stephen Garcia (17-20/201y, 3 TDs, INT) pitched 3 TDs in 1st H, led 21-9 by Carolina, but panicked early in 3rd Q and fired pass through his own EZ because he bobbled long snap. Safety fired up Tide, and they made 39y FG by K Jeremy Shelley and 51y TD connection between WR Darius Hanks and QB Greg McElroy (27-34/315y, 2 TDs) to move within 28-21 when 4th Q was 9 secs old. Moments later, Alabama DB Will Lowery nabbed INT when pass bounced off hands of Gamecocks star WR Alshon Jeffery (7/127y, 2 TDs). But, on 3rd down from Cocks 18YL, McElroy was sacked by CB Stephon Gilmore, and fake-FG pass completely blew up. Bruising Carolina RB Marcus Lattimore (23/93y, 2 TDs) proceeded to carry 5 times and scored his 2nd TD.

Louisiana State 33 FLORIDA 29: In SEC, victory often came down to plays decided by inches. On 4th down and trailing 29-26 with 35 secs to play, LSU Tigers (6-0) lined up for apparent tying 52y FG attempt. But LSU coach Les Miles dialed up his favorite gamble: holder Derek Helton tossing blind lateral over his head to K Josh Jasper for dash around RE. This time, toss arrived on bounce and dangerously close to forward, which would have created ruinous incomplete 4th down pass. But, Jasper ran for 1st down with 2y to spare. Bayou Bengals QB Jarrett Lee (9-11/124y, 2 TDs) tossed winning 3y TD pass to WR Terrence Toliver 3 plays later with 6 secs showing on clock. Gators (4-2) lost back-to-back games for only 2nd time in coach Urban Meyer's regime but thrillingly fought back from 26-14 deficit that was created when Tigers QB Jordan Jefferson ran in his 2nd TD on 3y keeper early in 4th Q. Right after Jefferson's scoring run, Florida RB Andre Debose cut to left sideline and went 88y on KO TD RET. Down 26-21, Gators stumbled on critical drive 11 mins later but were bailed out by 51y completion by hurting QB John Brantley (16-24/154y, INT) to set up RB Mike Gillislee's 5y TD run and Brantley's 2-pt pass for 29-26 lead. However, Gators couldn't halt LSU's nail-biting 62y drive, spiced by "Mad Hatter" Miles' risky FG ploy.

Illinois 33 PENN STATE 13: Homecoming Saturday in State College, Pa., was ruined for only 6th time in coach Joe Paterno's 45-year tenure by surging Illinois (3-2). It was Illini's 1st-ever win at Penn State (3-3), which saw its injury-riddled D fooled several times by sharp red zone tactics of Illinois: WR A.J. Jenkins was open over middle for 18y TD pass from QB Nathan Scheelhaase (15-19/151y, TD, and 8/61y rushing) in 2nd Q and pitchout to RB Jason Ford turned into surprise 4y TD toss to TE Evan Wilson in 3rd Q. In between, Nittany Lions frosh QB Robert Bolden (8-21/142y, TD, INT) was intercepted on wide pass by LB Nate Bussey for 16y TD RET for 2nd Q Illinois lead of 14-13. But, Bolden bounced right back after that error by launching 80y TD bomb to WR Derek Moye, who made excellent adjustment to ball flight.

Michigan State 34 MICHIGAN 17: Back in 2007, Michigan star Mike Hart referenced in-state rival Spartans (6-0) as "our Little Brother." Michigan State fans joyously left "Big House" this day chanting "Little Sister!" Neither Spartans football nor men's basketball team had lost to Wolverines since Hart's heartless remark. With Mark Dantonio coaching from press box as his convalescence continued, Spartans ran up 536y O and rolled 3-0 1st Q deficit into 17-10 H lead as RBs Edwin Baker (22/147y, TD) and Le'Veon Bell raced for 61 and 41y TDs respectively. Michigan (5-1) QB Denard

Robinson (17-29/215y, TD, 3 INTs), who had accounted for 1913y in 5 prior games, was held to season-low 86y rushing and his 3 INTs stunted consistency of Wolverines. MSU's 3rd straight win over its rivals marked 1st such occurrence since 1965-67.

Purdue 20 NORTHWESTERN 17: Highly-favored Northwestern (5-1) had to look all way back to coaching era of Ara Parseghian in 1962 for last 6-0 start, but such glory wasn't in cards for this season. Purdue Boilermakers (3-2) redshirt frosh QB Rob Henry (6-18/47y, INT) had rough time passing in his 1st start but rushed 16/132y, TD, including 67y dash on last play of 1st Q. Score was 10-10 at H and despite sharp passing of QB Dan Persa (30-41/305y), Wildcats were killed by own FG misadventures in 2nd H. But 1st, NW RB Jacob Schmidt caught 17y screen pass to set up Persa's 5yTD run to give the Wildcats 17-10 lead early in 3rd Q as drive was kept alive when Purdue CB Charlton Williams was called for D-holding when S Max Charlot intercepted Persa's pass in EZ. Block by Purdue WR O.J. Ross sprung RB Keith Carlos for a 51y run, but Boilers had to settle for K Carson Wiggs' 40y FG, making it 17-13. Still down 17-13 midway in 4th Q, Boilermakers tall DT Kawann Short blocked FG try by K Stefan Demos, which led to 75y march keyed by runs of Henry and RB Dan Dierking, who navigated last 7y for go-ahead TD. Demos missed tying 45y FG in last min.

NOTRE DAME 23 Pittsburgh 17: Fighting Irish (3-3) K David Ruffer kicked 3 FGs, including from 50y, to remain perfect in his career and set new Notre Dame record with 16 straight 3-ptrs. Effective at outset, QB Dayne Crist (24-39/242y TD) both threw and ran for 1st H TDs as Notre Dame opened 17-3 H lead. Meanwhile, Pittsburgh (2-3) moved inside red-zone thrice in 1st H but managed only single FG by K Dan Hutchins, who missed another and never got off 3rd attempt when hold was fumbled in closing moments before H. Panthers still threatened in 4th Q, as QB Tino Sunseri (27-39/272y, TD, INT) hit WR Jonathan Baldwin on 56y TD pass to pull within 23-17 with 7:23 left, but Pitt could do nothing with last 2 possessions that started at own 7 and 10YLs.

Arkansas 24 TEXAS A&M 17: QB Ryan Mallett (27-38/310y, 3 TDs, INT) started like house afire with 3 TD passes in 1st H, but Arkansas (4-1) squandered 3 FUM RECs inside 40YL of Texas A&M (3-2). Aggies continued to rack up good passing y, despite inconsistency of QB Jerrod Johnson (15-40/212y, TD, INT), who remained TO-prone. All Razorbacks could manage with their choice RECs was K Zach Hocker's 39y FG in 3rd Q. Aggies took over at own 20YL with 1:18 to play, and Johnson converted 4th-and-13 pass before Arkansas was called for interference PEN to its 39YL with 6 sec to go. Johnson launched prayer for EZ, but Hogs S Tramain Thomas intercepted to end it.

Mississippi State 47 HOUSTON 24: Making his 1st career start, Houston (3-2) frosh QB David Piland (30-57/301y, 2 TDs, 2 INTs) clicked on 5 passes on opening drive, including TD to WR Kierrie Johnson for 7-0 lead. Then, it was all downhill for Cougars as they permitted 142y rushing in 1st Q. Holding PEN caused safety, followed by sliced free-kick, and Piland had INT returned by Mississippi State (4-2) CB Corey Broomfield for 27y TD before 1st H was over. Bulldogs line paved big gaps for RB Vick Ballard, who gained 134y and scored 3 TDs, and QB Chris Relf tallied TD and ran for 96y before leaving in 3rd Q with injury. It was 40-10 for Bulldogs before Piland hit late 3rd Q TD pass to WR Patrick Edwards, whose punt FUM had set up Ballard's 1st TD in 1st Q.

STANFORD 37 Southern California 35: Epidemic of last-moment losses hit USC (4-2) for 2nd week in row as Stanford (5-1) responded with 62y drive in final 1:02 to K Nate Whitaker's 32y FG as clock expired. Trojans had tallied on their 1st series in 1st Q, and score was deadlocked 14-14 at H and 21-21 at end of 3rd Q. Tying late 3rd Q score came on 61y sprint down sideline by Southern California frosh WR Robert Woods (12/224y, 3 TDs), who became college football's 1st receiver in 2010 with 200+y and 3 TDs. Woods was broken loose by sharp downfield block by FB Stanley Havili, but it proved only small segment of 2-team O show that produced 5 TDs on 5 straight possessions. Stanford took 34-28 lead on 3rd TD pass by QB Andrew Luck (20-24/285y, 3 TDs), but Whitaker clanked his x-pt off left upright. Trojans QB Matt Barkley (28-45/390y, 3 TDs) was stopped by 4 incompletions from Cardinal 32YL with 6:54 to play, but Stanford RB Stephan Taylor (23/104y, TD) soon lost his 2nd FUM at midfield. USC rushed downfield on Barkley's 4 passes to TD run by TB Allen Bradford and 35-34 lead. Luck calmly hit 3 passes, and Taylor ran twice/21y to set up Whitaker's winning 3-ptr.

October 16, 2010

Pittsburgh 45 SYRACUSE 14: Panthers (3-3) had had bad time out of conf with losses to Utah, Miami, and Notre Dame but romped in Big East opener to possibly place them on predicted path to conf crown. But over-matched Syracuse (4-2) soon would turn in right direction under 2nd-year coach Doug Marrone, while Pitt would struggle. Panthers got off on right foot as WR Devin Street took screen pass and raced 79y to TD as young QB Tino Sunseri (17-24/266y, 4 TDs) enjoyed his best game to date.

When Orange was limited to only 77y rushing, QB Ryan Nassib (25-46/213y, TD, 2 INTs) wasn't up to task of carrying O. Behind 28-7 in 3rd Q, Nassib, under pressure, made under-throw to left flank, and Pitt CB Ricky Gary intercepted to roll 80y to TD.

Rutgers 23 Army 20 (OT) (Meadowlands, NJ): Subdued Rutgers (4-2) would be unable to return to its early-season triumphs after this rally to OT win in which DT Eric LeGrand suffered paralyzing injury on KO tackle. Army (4-3) had cruised to 17-3 H edge on TD runs by QB Trent Steelman (8-14/115y and 27/102y, TD rushing) and FB Jared Hassin (16/118y, TD). Army outgained Rutgers 404y to 250y but was called for 8/94y PENs, including major fouls that kept alive Scarlet Knights' 2 4th Q TD drives that sent contest to OT. Rutgers frosh QB Chas Dodd (18-30/251y, 2 TDs, INT), fresh from winning rally vs. Connecticut, overcame 8 sacks to pitch pair of TD passes in 4th Q: 3y to RB Kordell Young and 16y to WR Mark Harrison, latter set up by 53y completion to TE D.C. Jefferson. On opening OT possession, Steelman's run lost 1y on 3rd-and-3 at 7YL, and Cadets had to settle for FG. Dodd's 6y throw to WR Keith Stroud set up RB Joe Martinek's winning 1y TD dive. Rutgers would not win again in 2010.

Mississippi State 10 FLORIDA 7: For 1st time since 1965, Mississippi State Bulldogs (5-2) left Florida Field with victory, and slumping Gators (4-3) dropped 3rd straight regular season game for 1st time since 1988. "We're not very good right now," admitted Urban Meyer, coach of Florida's twice-in-4-years national champions. Bulldogs ran 49/212y in 58 O plays and got all their pts on consecutive 1st Q drives: K Sean Brauchle hit 31y FG after 54y trip, and QB Chris Relf (4-9/33y and 22/82y, TD rushing) faked pass to right and wedged left for 6y TD run after 64y march. Florida went 80y off 2nd H KO, and RB Omarius Hines (6/58y, TD) took option pitchout to 5y TD around right side. P-K Chas Henry, in to try 42y FG only because Florida K Caleb Sturgis was out injured, missed wide right in tying attempt on last play.

KENTUCKY 31 South Carolina 28: No more proof was needed as to brutality of SEC schedules than Gamecocks' failure to follow up their brilliant win prior Saturday over Alabama. However, there was no early hangover for no. 12 South Carolina (4-2) as RB Marcus Lattimore (15/79y, 2 TDs, and 4/133y, TD receiving) tallied on 30 and 10y runs and caught 47y TD pass from QB Stephen Garcia (20-32/382y, 2 TDs, 2 INTs). Gamecocks led 28-10 at H. In 2nd H, Wildcats (4-3) Mike Hartline went to work and he would finish with career-high 349y on 32-42 and 3 2nd H TDs. Kentucky flew 95 and 76y to Hartline TD passes, and with 7:31 left, Wildcats launched 68y trip capped by 24y TD catch by do-it-all WR-RB Randall Cobb on 4th-and-7 with 115 to play. Cobb followed with 2-pt run off LT, and CB Anthony Mosley soon ended it with EZ INT.

AUBURN 65 Arkansas 43: Highest-scoring non-OT game in SEC history folded into wild 4th Q when Auburn (7-0) crushed Razorbacks (4-2) with 4 TDs to end game. Arkansas opened relatively quiet 7-7 1st Q on TD pass by QB Ryan Mallett (10-15/96y, TD) before Mallett suffered head injury in 1st H. Sub QB Tyler Wilson (25-34/332y, 4 TDs, 2 INTs) stepped right in to keep pitching for Arkansas until he provided 43-37 lead with 23y TD pass and 2-pt pitch to WR Greg Childs (9/164y, 2 TDs) 3 plays into 4th Q. Tigers QB Cam Newton (10-14/140y, TD and 25/188y, 3 TDs rushing) next responded with 4 completions on 68y trip, including 15y TD to WR Emory Blake. Hogs were moving until RB Broderick Green fumbled, and Tigers FS Zac Etheridge returned FUM 47y for TD. Auburn LB Josh Bynes intercepted Wilson on consecutive series to set up TD runs by Newton of 3y and frosh RB Michael Dyer (6/53y, TD) of 38y.

WISCONSIN 31 Ohio State 18: Badgers (6-1) WR David Gilreath slipped up middle and dashed 97y to TD on opening KO, and using its imposing O-line, Wisconsin pounded 58y on its next try to 14-0 lead behind 51y rushing by TB John Clay (21/104y, 2 TDs). Clay rolled behind block of LT Gabe Carimi for 14y TD and added 1y TD dive over right side early in 2nd Q for 21-0 advantage. Down 21-3, Ohio State (6-1) RB Dan "Boom" Herron (19/91y, 2 TDs) boomed for 13y TD run in 3rd Q, and when Herron pushed across early in 4th Q and QB Terrelle Pryor (14-28/156y, INT) added 2-pt pass, Buckeyes were back in it within 21-18. Spurred on by boisterous home crowd, Wisconsin answered right away with 73y drive that included 20 and 9y passes from QB Scott Tolzien (13-16/153y, INT) to WR Nick Toon. TB James White put Badgers out of reach at 28-18 with swift, slicing 12y TD run off left side. It was 2nd straight week that nation's top-ranked team had fallen.

Texas 20 NEBRASKA 13: Perhaps 10 months of vengeful thinking after last year's 1-pt loss to Longhorns in Big 12 title game was too much for Nebraska (5-1). Just when Texas (4-2) was all but counted out in conf race, Longhorns came up with inspired effort at Lincoln. Texas QB Garrett Gilbert (4-16/62y and 11/71y, 2 TDs rushing) used his legs at opportune times to trick D of no. 4 Nebraska, dashing and sneaking for pair of 1st H scores to lead Horns to 209y rushing when they had been averaging 129.8y per game. On other hand, dynamic Huskers frosh QB Taylor Martinez, who arrived averaging nearly 11y per rush, was held to 13/21y rushing and was yanked in 3rd Q with his team trailing 20-3. Huskers had averaged 337.6y per game on ground, but Texas D held them to 125y. Nebraska dropped 3 potential TD passes and never threatened until DB Eric Hagg fielded pooch punt on hop with 3 mins to go and cut right to go 95y to TD. But it was not enough when Texas recovered on-side KO try.

Baylor 31 COLORADO 25: Brilliant Bears (5-2) QB Robert Griffin (22-27/234y, TD, INT, and 15/137y rushing) improved his 4th-best-in-nation total O avg, and RB Jay Finley rushed for career-best 149y and pair of TDs. Buffaloes (3-3) RB Rodney Stewart (30/125y, 2 TDs) ran for pair of 1st H TDs, but Baylor never looked back after Finley's 1st TD run late in 3rd Q supplied 21-15 lead. With 5:15 to play, Colorado QB Tyler Hansen (21-28/207y, TD, INT) found WR Scotty McKnight with short TD pass to pull within 28-25, but Bears K Aaron Jones added his 2nd FG, and CB Chance Casey knocked down Hansen's EZ pass for WR Toney Clemons in dying moments.

Missouri 30 Texas A&M 9: Missouri's underrated D sacked Aggies (3-3) QB Jerrod Johnson (27-48/322y, TD) 7 times. While Texas A&M didn't turned ball over as it had on 9 occasions in last 2 games, it still was blanked in weak 1st H as Johnson could complete only 7-21/63y. Meanwhile, Tigers (6-0) QB Blaine Gabbert (31-47/361y, 3 TDs) connected on trio of scoring passes to WRs Wes Kemp (10/89y, 2 TDs) and T.J. Moe (6/110y, TD), with Moe's TD catch toting up to 30-3 lead late in 3rd Q.

Oklahoma State 34 TEXAS TECH 17: Undefeated Cowboys (6-0) hadn't left Lubbock with victory in 66 years, but Oklahoma State put it away at 31-14 in 3rd Q when dynamic WR Justin Blackmon (10/207y, TD) got loose for 62y TD reception from QB Brandon Weeden (24-35/356y, TD, 2 INTs). Cowpokes RB Kendall Hunter (25/130y, TD) led early ground parade to his 15y TD to launch 21-pt outburst in 1st Q. Texas Tech (3-3) fought back to within 21-14 with 6 mins left in 2nd Q as QB Taylor Potts (28-43/226y, TD) clicked with WR Cornelius Douglas on 28y TD connection. But, Red Raiders failed to find EZ thereafter. Oklahoma State piled up 581y O.

RICE 34 Houston 31: Behind pair of TD passes by QB Nick Fanuzzi (14-21/206y, 3 TDs), Owls (2-5) flew to 27-7 lead with 6:23 left in 1st H. But, Houston (3-3) frosh QB David Piland (23-45/282y, 3 TDs, INT), in for injury dry-docked QB Case Keenum, led comeback with 2 long-range TD missiles to WR Patrick Edwards (9/169y, 3 TDs), and when K Matt Hogan made 37y FG with 8:55 to play, Cougars were ahead 31-27. Rice frosh WR Andy Erickson's 43y KO RET sparked drive to Fanuzzi's winning 6y TD pass to TE Vance McDonald. Houston launched another comeback try but Piland fumbled snap on 4th-and-1 at Rice 37YL with 1:37 to go.

USA TODAY Coaches Poll October 17, 2010

1 Oregon (42)	1452	14 Stanford	689
2 Boise State (11)	1385	15 Oklahoma State	659
3 Oklahoma (4)	1334	16 Missouri	640
4 Texas Christian (1)	1300	17 Florida State	608
5 Auburn (1)	1238	18 Arizona	494
6 Louisiana State	1132	19 West Virginia	323
7 Alabama	1085	20 South Carolina	284
8 Michigan State	1037	21 Arkansas	274
9 Utah	1004	22 Texas	256
10 Ohio State	936	23 Virginia Tech	165
11 Wisconsin	867	24 Mississippi State	133
12 Iowa	785	25 Miami	127
13 Nebraska	768		

Bowl Championship Series Rankings October 17, 2010

	Harris Poll Avg.	USA TODAY Poll Avg.	Computer Pct.	BCS Avg.
1 Oklahoma (6-0)	.8800	.9044	.980	.9215
2 Oregon (6-0)	.9819	.9844	.710	.8921
3 Boise State (6-0)	.9504	.9390	.780	.8898
4 Auburn (7-0)	.8531	.8393	.900	.8641
5 Texas Christian (7-0)	.8906	.8814	.800	.8573

October 23, 2010

(Th) OREGON 60 Ucla 13: Ducks (7-0) celebrated their 1st-ever no. 1 ranking by destroying UCLA (3-4) on national telecast. Swift Oregon RB LaMichael James (20/123y, 2 TDs) notched Pac-10 contest's 1st score by capping 90y advance with 9:15 remaining in 1st Q. James spent much of 1st H gimpy on sideline, but sub RB Ramene Alston (8/75y, 3 TDs) filled in admirably. Injuries continued to make Bruins QB post look like revolving committee: QB Kevin Prince was out in favor of soph QB Richard Brehaut, who passed 16-23/159y, INT. UCLA could not add to K Kai Forbath's 25 and 48y FGs until Brehaut sped to 6y TD in last 2 mins of game.

Navy 35 Notre Dame 17 (Meadowlands, NJ): Fighting Irish (4-4) D simply couldn't halt Navy (5-2) running attack as Middies' sharp option scheme totaled 367y on ground. Middies D halted 4th down run inside their own 1YL on opening series and soon set sail to quick TD. "We outman them by 70 pounds on average up front," Irish coach Brian Kelly complained. "If you can't get a foot on the one-half yard line, you get what you deserve." Deserved or not, ND soon gave up 54y sprint by Navy FB Alexander Teich (26/210y) on 3rd-and-1, followed quickly by Teich's 1-handed grab and 31y dash with screen pass for TD. It got easier for Navy thereafter on way to its 3rd win in last 4 meetings with Irish as QB Ricky Dobbs (2-2/71y, TD, and 20/90y, 2 TDs rushing) scored twice in 3rd Q to turn 21-10 lead into comfy 25-pt advantage. ND managed TB Cierre Wood's late TD run.

Syracuse 19 WEST VIRGINIA 14: Gone was 12-game home winning streak of West Virginia (5-2), and gone too was perception that Syracuse (5-2) football remained in depths of 5 straight years in Big East cellar. Mountaineers outgained Orange 284y to 246y as WVU QB Geno Smith (20-37/178y, TD, 3 INTs) overcame poor start to hit 5 passes in row to take early 7-3 edge. Orange passed for only 63y, but Syracuse QB Ryan Nassib (5-15/63y, TD) made 2 excellent hand-off fakes and found WR Van Chew for 17y gain and 29y TD in 1st Q for 10-7 lead. K Ross Krautman nailed 4 FGs for Orange as all of game's scoring came in 1st H.

CLEMSON 29 Georgia Tech 13: Clemson Tigers (4-3) soph RB Andre Ellington (20/166y, 2 TDs) cut through and around Georgia Tech (5-3) tacklers to score on 1st H runs of 55 and 42y. In 3rd Q, Ellington took 10y swing pass from QB Kyle Parker (17-27/167y, TD) for TD that pretty well put verdict out of reach at 24-6. Clemson D focused on QB Joshua Nesbitt and did excellent job stifling Yellow Jackets trigger-man by holding him to 15/2y rushing and 6-19/83y, TD, INT in air. Nesbitt managed 3rd Q TD pass to FB Anthony Allen (17/92y), but Clemson copied Ga Tech's normal strategic mode with 15-play FG drive lasting nearly 8 mins of 4th Q.

AUBURN 24 Louisiana State 17: No. 6 LSU's stingy D crimped aerial gymnastics of Auburn (8-0) QB Cam Newton (10-16/86y), who instead concentrated on his running ability to tune of 28/217y with scoring plays of 1 and 49y. His season rushing total of 1077y broke SEC QB record held since 1963 by Auburn's Jimmy Sidle. LSU (7-1) allowed 52/440y rushing, most y it had permitted in last 10 years. However, LSU twice

came from behind to tie it at 10-10 on 2y TD run by QB Jordan Jefferson (7-14/46y, INT, and 16/74y, TD rushing) right before H and 17-17 on 39y TD bomb pitched by RB Spencer Ware early in 4th Q. Ware's TD throw to WR Rueben Randle was only completion greater than 15y all game against riled-up Auburn D, which gave only 243y O and was sparked by DT Nick Fairley's 2.5 sacks and 3.5/-23y in TFLs. Game's big play came with slightly more than 5 mins left. Out of Shotgun formation, Newton handed to RB Onterrio McCalebb, streaking wide, who raced 70y to winning TD.

ARKANSAS 38 Mississippi 24: "Well, it took five hours, but we got the win," said Hogs coach Bobby Petrino of game in Fayetteville delayed several times by lightning. Injury lightning struck 2nd time to Razorbacks (5-2) QB Ryan Mallett (13-24/196y, TD, INT). He left in 3rd Q with bad shoulder after being concussed previous week against Auburn. By then, Arkansas led 24-3, thanks to 3 great efforts by WRs: Greg Childs made brilliant grass-top diving TD catch in 1st Q for 14-0 lead, and Joe Adams used devastating midfield block by Jarius Wright to speed 97y on punt TD RET in 2nd Q for 21-0 advantage. Mississippi (3-4) battled back as QB Jeremiah Masoli (21-36/321y, 3 TDs, and 15/98y rushing) threw 3 TD passes in less than 18 mins of 2nd H and pulled his Rebs within 24-17 and 31-24. After each of Ole Miss' pair of 4th Q TDs, emerging Hogs soph RB Knile Davis (22/176y, 3 TDs) tallied TDs, legging it 71 and 22y.

Michigan State 35 NORTHWESTERN 27: For 2nd straight week, undefeated Spartans (8-0) came up with 2nd H comeback after tallying final 23 pts in 26-6 win over Illinois. Trailing 17-7 at H in Evanston, Michigan State earned TDs after 48, 75, and 88y drives. It took 28-27 lead with 2 mins remaining on diving 1-handed EZ catch by WR B.J. Cunningham (8/113y, TD) of pass tipped by Northwestern (5-2) S Brian Peters. Cats QB Dan Persa completed 18-29/187y, INT, also tallied 3 TDs on 49y rushing. Persa scrambled 6y up middle late in 3rd Q for 24-14 edge. Spartans QB Kirk Cousins (29-43/329y, 3 TDs) responded next with 15y TD pass to WR Mark Dell (9/107, 2 TDs).

Wisconsin 31 IOWA 30: Backup TB Montee Ball lugged ball only 3 times for Badgers (7-1), but his replay-reviewed 8y TD run with 1:06 to go was margin of victory in vital Big 10 clash. TB Ball was going down just short of GL and reached ball out, only to have it bobble loose. Was runner down? Was it FUM REC by Iowa (5-2) in its EZ? Replay showed Ball barely kept his knee off ground and reached across GL to score. Another key play occurred way back in 1st Q when Hawkeyes had taken 6-3 lead on short TD run by TB Adam Robinson (23/114y, TD), but Wisconsin DE J.J. Watt blocked x-pt. TB John Clay scored twice in 3rd Q, so Wisconsin led 24-20. Iowa QB Ricky Stanzi (25-37/258y, 3 TDs) countered with his 3rd TD pass, and when K Michael Meyer added 40y FG, Iowa led 30-24. Badgers used 7:29 of clock on their last drive on which they converted twice on 4th down: P Brad Nortman ran 17y from his 26YL and Ball caught 7y pass from QB Scott Tolzien (20-26/205y, TD, INT) to Iowa 37YL.

MISSOURI 36 Oklahoma 27: Leader of season's 1st BCS rankings, Oklahoma (6-1) got ambushed in Columbia by undefeated Missouri (7-0), which opened 7-0 for 1st time since its 1960 Big 8 and Orange Bowl champions went on to finish 11-0. Tigers WR Gahn McGaffie took opening KO back 86y for TD, but Sooners QB Landry Jones (32-50/303y, 3 TDs, INT) clicked on pair of TD passes in 1st H led by Mizzou 17-14. TE James Hanna caught Jones' 3rd TD toss late in 3rd Q, and Oklahoma had its 1st lead at 21-20. Missouri soon went 72y as WR Jerrell Jackson (9/139y, TD) spun and bounced off tacklers on 38y TD pass from QB Blaine Gabbert (30-42/308y, TD). OU used less than min on its next 2 possessions as Jones threw out-pattern picked off by Tigers LB Zaviar Gooden and 2 incompletions later necessitated punt. Missouri turned those missteps into 10 pts and 36-21 lead with 6-and-half mins left.

Baylor 47 KANSAS STATE 42: Bears (6-2) became bowl-eligible for 1st time since formation of Big 12 Conf in 1996. Baylor's best O tandem in generation—QB Robert Griffin, who passed for career-high 404y, and RB Jay Finley, who rushed for school-record 250y—led way as Bears built 47-28 lead in 4th Q on 4th TD pass by Griffin (26-38/404y, 4 TDs, INT). Finley (26/250y, 2 TDs) tallied in 1st and 3rd Qs, helping his team to school-mark of 683y O. Kansas State (5-2) was led by RB Daniel Thomas (22/113y, 2 TDs) and got boost to within 34-28 in 3rd Q when RB William Powell went coast-to-coast on 100y KO TD RET.

Nebraska 51 OKLAHOMA STATE 41: Here at midseason, Nebraska (6-1) frosh QB Taylor Martinez mostly had been outstanding run threat, but in leading his end of bargain in Stillwater shootout, his passing prowess stunned undefeated no. 15 Cowboys (6-1) with. Martinez connected on 23-35/323y, 5 TDs, while adding 19/112y rushing. "He can hurt you with his feet. He can hurt you with his arm," said coach Bo Pelini of Martinez's growing aerial confidence. Along way, Huskers WR Niles Paul (9/131y) ran back KO 100y—Nebraska's 1st coast-to-coast KO TD RET since 1949—to provide 14-6 lead in 1st Q. Oklahoma State QB Brandon Weeden (18-235/283y, 2 TDs, INT) and WR Justin Blackmon (5/157y, 2 TDs) collaborated on 80y TD bomb on flea-flicker handoff and pass. It gave OSU its only lead at 27-24 with 6 mins left in 2nd Q. But before H, Martinez and WR Brandon Kinnie hooked up on Martinez's 3rd TD pass for 31-27 edge, and duo would combine again for TD in 4th Q for 51-34 lead.

TEXAS CHRISTIAN 38 Air Force 7: Coming off 31-3 trouncing of Brigham Young, no. 4 Texas Christian (8-0) made small error: it gave up its 1st TD in Mt West Conf play this year. Air Force (5-3) QB Tim Jefferson (3-7/47y, and 9/39y, TD rushing) climaxed 89y march by going 16y to knot game 7-7 in 1st Q, 1st TD allowed by Frogs in last 198 mins. Twice in 1st H, Falcons coach Troy Calhoun faced 4th-and-1 decisions near midfield, and each time he had Jefferson pooch-punt. Riding ripping runs of RB Ed Wesley (28/209y, 2 TDs), TCU turned Calhoun's cautious choices into K Ross Evans' 30y FG and WR Jeremy Kerley's 8y TD catch from QB Andy Dalton (11-20/185y, TD, INT, and TD rushing) for 17-7 lead. Workhorse Wesley tallied twice in 2nd H.

STANFORD 38 Washington State 28: Stanford (6-1) QB Andrew Luck passed 20-28/190y, 3 TDs, INT, and TB Stepfan Taylor rushed for 27/142y, 2 TDs, his 4th straight game with more than 100y on ground. Yet, Cardinal didn't feel as though they ever got into O groove. Washington State (1-7) QB Jeff Tuel (21-28/298y, 4 TDs, 2 INTs) enjoyed fine outing on rainy afternoon but coughed up INT early in 3rd Q after he drove Cougars 37y to 34YL, when TD would have made it more competitive. Instead, 3rd Q saw Stanford WR Doug Baldwin make jumping, twisting TD catch in back corner of EZ to make it 31-7. Tuel found range for trio of 4th Q scores, including 74y TD to WR Marquess Wilson in final min. Cougars dropped their 14th consecutive Pac-10 tilt.

ARIZONA 44 Washington 14: Visiting Washington (3-4) gobbled up CB Desmond Trufant's early FUM REC, and QB Jake Locker (17-29/183y, TD) soon rolled left and lofted pretty 36y TD pass to WR Jermaine Kearse. That was extent of Huskies' fun. Arizona (6-1) QB Matt Scott (18-22/233y, 2 TDs), in for injured QB Nick Foles, added running threat from his position and guided O to 467y. Wildcats RB Keola Antolin (14/114y, 2 TDs) enjoyed big 2nd Q with pair of TDs in barely more than 3 mins, including quick sprint up middle for 78y. Early in 3rd Q, Cats DE Ricky Elmore stripped Locker, and RB Nic Grigsby gave Arizona 37-14 lead with his 2nd TD of 4y.

USA TODAY Coaches Poll October 24, 2010

1 Oregon (50)	1463	14 Stanford	763
2 Boise State (5)	1383	15 Florida State	651
3 Auburn (3)	1350	16 Arizona	628
4 Texas Christian (1)	1308	17 South Carolina	431
5 Michigan State	1175	18 Arkansas	404
6 Alabama	1152	19 Iowa	401
7 Utah	1091	20 Oklahoma State	385
8 Missouri	1060	21 Virginia Tech	317
9 Wisconsin	973	22 Miami	260
10 Ohio State	966	23 Mississippi State	251
11 Oklahoma	871	24 Baylor	70
12 Nebraska	802	25 Michigan	50
13 Louisiana State	787		

Bowl Championship Series Rankings October 24, 2010

	Harris Poll Avg.	USA TODAY Poll Avg.	Computer Pct.	BCS Avg.
1 Auburn (8-0)	.9161	.9153	.980	.9371
2 Oregon (7-0)	.9888	.9919	.740	.9069
3 Boise State (6-0)	.9361	.9376	.780	.8846
4 Texas Christian (8-0)	.8930	.8868	.870	.8833
5 Michigan State (8-0)	.7895	.7966	.930	.8387

October 30, 2010

(Th) NORTH CAROLINA STATE 28 Florida State 24: Wolfpack (6-2) closed gap in ACC Atlantic Div while denying Florida State (6-2) possible 5-0 start in same group. FSU QB Christian Ponder (17-28/196y, TD) accounted for 105y O in 2nd Q, while passing for TD and running for 2 TDs, including beauty of wriggling stretch to right pylon. On other side, North Carolina State QB Russell Wilson (18-28/178y, TD, INT) had his own brilliant moments, running for 3 TDs, including 20y straining-for-GL scramble that built 21-21 tie midway in 3rd Q. After K Dustin Hopkins' 31y FG in 4th Q gave 3-pt lead back to FSU, Wilson rifled 1y TD pass to TE George Bryan on 4th down with 2:40 to play. On last drive, Ponder hit 3-6/50y and ran for 13y until his FUM on play-action fake from NC State 4YL was recovered by Wolfpack LB Nate Irving to doom Seminoles.

(Fri) CONNECTICUT 16 West Virginia 13 (OT): "You cannot win any games if you can't take care of the ball," said Mountaineers (5-3) coach Bill Stewart. Indeed, West Virginia lost 4 FUMs to Connecticut (4-4), including vital bobble on opening OT series. Carrying on 4th run in row on 1st down at UConn 1YL, WVU RB Ryan Clarke lost his 1st career FUM, fallen on by Huskies LB Lawrence Wilson. UConn TB Jordan Todman (33/113y,TD) lugged ball 4/16y, and K Dave Teggart split uprights with winning 27y FG. WVU had led 10-0 in 1st Q, thanks to 53y TD sprint around LE by WR Brad Starks. Todman, held in check in 1st H, broke up middle on 24y TD gallop in 3rd Q that tied it 10-10 before FGs were traded to send contest to OT. LB Sio Moore posted 17 tackles, 2 forced FUMs, and 2 FUM RECs in leading Huskies to 1st conf win of year.

BOSTON COLLEGE 16 Clemson 10: BC Eagles (3-5) ended 5-game skid and launched 5-game winning streak that would save their season. RB Montel Harris rushed 36/142y and caught 36y circle-route TD pass from QB Chase Rettig (9-16/136y, TD, INT) that furnished Boston College's 1st lead at 13-10 in middle of 2nd Q. Eagles K Nate Freese booted his 3rd FG to end 1st H. Clemson (4-4) DB Rashard Hall had picked off Rettig early in 1st Q and barreled 52y down left sideline for TD and 7-0 lead. In 2nd H, Tigers fell victim to missed FG, pass completion on 4th down that came up 1y short, and pair of INTs thrown by QB Kyle Parker (21-39/176y, 2 INTs), including BC LB Luke Kuechly's diving INT at sideline that all but sealed it late in 4th Q.

VIRGINIA 24 Miami 19: When victory was secure, rookie Virginia (4-4) coach Mike London fell to his knees in thanks, saying later, "I don't know how many other opportunities we are going to have to feel that before the season ends, but you have to start somewhere…" Virginia built 24-0 lead when enormous TB Keith Payne (17/81y, 2 TDs) battered for his 2nd TD 3 mins into 4th Q. Cavs DT John-Kevin Dolce had hammered Miami (5-3) QB Jacory Harris as 2nd Q pass—picked off by Virginia CB Chase Minnifield (2 INTs)—was released. Harris was knocked from game, and his substitutes were perfectly ineffective until frosh QB Stephen Morris (9-22/162y, 2 TDs, 2 INTs) managed long TD passes to WRs Leonard Hankerson and Travis Benjamin around his 9y TD run in 4th Q. Miami's ACC crown hopes were badly hampered.

Florida 34 Georgia 31 (Jacksonville) (OT): After 3 straight SEC defeats, Florida (5-3) was desperate for victory in FKAWLOCP (formerly known as "World's Largest Outdoor Cocktail Party") rivalry. For its part, rebounding Georgia (4-5) was coming off trio of conf wins after having dropped 4 games in row. Gators ignited their slumping O in 1st H, getting TD runs from RB Chris Rainey, who returned from suspension to gain 241y all-purpose, RB Jeffery Demps, and QB-RB Trey Burton (2-2/26y, 17/110y, 2 TDs

rushing, and 5/35y receiving) for 21-7 H lead. Bulldogs awoke in 2nd H, scoring on 4 straight possessions as QB Aaron Murray (18-37/313y, 3 TDs, 3 INTs) ran for 2 pts and completed pair of TD passes, last of which was grabbed by star WR A.J. Green for 15y in mob of Gators and sent contest to OT. Georgia had ball 1st and nearly blew it right away as Florida FS Will Hill intercepted Murray and returned it 89y before being spilled OB at 4YL. Starting at 25YL, Gators sent in K Chas Henry, who had struggled as replacement for injured K Caleb Sturgis, to split uprights with winning 37y FG.

PENN STATE 41 Michigan 31: With walk-on QB Matt McGloin (17-28/250y, TD) making 1st career start, Penn State (5-3) depended on TB Evan Royster (29/150y, 2 TDs) to carry O. Nicked up by injuries and extra lbs. in 2010, Royster scored twice on his way to breaking Lions' 28-year-old career rushing record held by Hall of Famer Curt Warner. After Michigan (5-3) K Seth Broeckhuisen's 37y FG cut Lions' edge to 14-10 in middle of 2nd Q, Penn State went 74y, with Royster gaining 5/33y to poise McGloin for TD keeper. Little RB Devon Smith's 22y punt RET soon set up McGloin for 20y TD pitch to WR Graham Zug and 28-10 H lead. Slick Wolverines QB Denard Robinson (11-23/190y, TD and 27/191y, 3 TDs rushing) made herculean 2nd H comeback attempt with 60y TD pass to TE Kevin Koger and his 2nd and 3rd TD runs, but K Collin Wagner's pair of FGs and FB Michael Zordich's 5y TD run kept Penn State in lead.

IOWA 37 Michigan State 6: Iowa Hawkeyes (6-2) mounted thorough dismantling of undefeated Michigan State (8-1) from early on. Iowa QB Ricky Stanzi (11-15/190y, 3 TDs) started with 80y drive to his short TD pass, and with score at 10-0 late in 1st Q, Iowa D made spectacular TD: S Tyler Sash intuitively stepped in front of receiver at Hawkeyes 28YL and made like option-QB by pitching out to CB Micah Hyde near right sideline. Hyde cut all way cross-field and dived for left pylon at end of 66y TD RET. "Did things snowball on us? I guess they did," admitted Spartans coach Mark Dantonio. When Iowa WR Marvin McNutt caught Stanzi's 3rd TD pass in 3rd Q, Hawks led 37-0. Spartans QB Kirk Cousins (21-29/198y, TD, 3 INTs), who had suffered only 4 INTs so far in 2010, finally found EZ with WR B.J. Cunningham early in 4th Q.

NEBRASKA 31 Missouri 17: For school known for traditionally great running game, perhaps it was surprising that Cornhuskers (7-1) single-game rushing record—held by Calvin Jones at 294y—had stood for 19 years. Behind brilliant blocking all afternoon, RB Roy Helu broke away on TD dashes of 66 (on 1st scrimmage play) 73, and 53y on his way to new mark of 307y on 28 carries. Nebraska led 24-0 after 1st Q as Helu's 66 and 73y TDs sandwiched K Alex Henery's 18th straight FG—another school mark—and 40y post-pattern TD pass to TE Kyler Reed from QB Taylor Martinez (6-9/115y, TD), before Martinez went out with injury. Missouri (7-1) QB Blaine Gabbert (18-42/199y, TD, INT) had terrible time with Huskers new-look 3-man D-front, being sacked 6 times, but managed 23y TD pass to WR T.J. Moe in 3rd Q to draw no. 8 Tigers within 24-14. But, Helu countered 3 plays later with his 3rd long TD, and Nebraska forced late 3rd Q FG after Missouri drove from its 20YL inside Huskers 1YL: K Grant Ressel booted 23y FG that wrapped up scoring.

Baylor 30 TEXAS 22: Not since 1997 had Baylor Bears (7-2) beaten Texas (4-4) and not since 1991 had Baylor won in Austin. It was heady time for Bears, but Big 12 South's iron (Oklahoma State, Texas A&M, and Oklahoma) lay in waiting, and 3 losses would ruin their title dreams. Dynamic QB Robert Griffin (16-24/219y, 2 TDs, INT) accounted for 3 TDs, and RB Jay Finley ran 15/116y, TD, including vital 69y TD sprint late in 3rd Q which pulled Baylor within 19-17. LB Antonio Johnson's 20y INT RET to Texas 11YL set up Griffin's short TD run early in 4th Q, and Griffin followed with 30y TD pass on next possession. K Justin Tucker's 4 FGs and 20y TD run by QB Garrett Gilbert (22-39/231y, INT) had given Longhorns 19-10 lead early in 3rd Q.

TEXAS A&M 45 Texas Tech 27: After 2-and-half seasons as solid WR, QB Ryan Tannehill (36-50/449y, 4 TDs, INT) set Texas Aggies (5-3) school record for passing y in his 1st career start. After his team took over on downs at midfield in 1st Q, Texas Tech (4-4) QB Taylor Potts (23-37/227y, TD) connected on 4 short passes to position RB Eric Stephens (10/47y, TD) for 1y TD run. Tannehill soon countered with TD passes at end of 70, 57, and 60y drives for 24-14 H edge for Texas A&M. WR Jeff Fuller caught 11/171y, 2 TDs, both of which came in big 2nd Q for Aggies. Fuller's 2nd TD catch came 9 secs before H as drive was helped by two personal fouls on Tech defenders for targeting defenseless receivers. When Aggies RB Christine Michael broke tibia in 3rd Q, RB Cyrus Gray (16/102y, TD) accepted rushing load, including 54y TD in 3rd Q. Red Raiders fumbled twice near Texas A&M GL, and Potts was replaced by QB Steven Sheffield in 4th Q. Sheffield hit 11-14/129y, 2 TDs, INT passing.

Oregon 53 SOUTHERN CALIFORNIA 32: Proverbial shoe was on other foot as top-rank-accustomed, but currently probationary USC Trojans (5-3) faced nation's no. 1 team in Oregon Ducks (8-0). Trojans DT Jurrell Casey picked off deflected pass early in 3rd Q, and QB Matt Barkley (26-49/264y, TD, 2 INTs) hit WR Ronald Johnson with short TD pass to climb within 29-24 of Oregon, which had enjoyed pair of TD catches by WR Jeff Maehl (8/145y, 3 TDs) in 1st H. Johnson soon made 51y punt RET, and Barkley put Trojans ahead 32-29 with 1y TD run and 2-pt pass to Johnson. "We have a tendency to wear people down," observed Ducks coach Chip Kelly of his racehorse O. Oregon did just that, tallying game's last 24 pts as Maehl nabbed his 3rd TD catch from QB Darron Thomas (19-32/288y, 4 TDs, INT), and nation's leading rusher, RB LaMichael James (36/239y, 3 TDs), scored twice on runs.

1 Oregon (51)	1464		14 Missouri	676
2 Auburn (4)	1384		15 Michigan State	652
3 Boise State (3)	1361		16 Iowa	647
4 Texas Christian (1)	1292		17 South Carolina	517
5 Alabama	1213		18 Oklahoma State	466
6 Utah	1141		19 Arkansas	446
7 Wisconsin	1100		20 Virginia Tech	379
8 Ohio State	1049		21 Mississippi State	320
9 Oklahoma	990		22 Baylor	250
10 Nebraska	961		23 Nevada	112
11 Louisiana State	861		24 Florida State	107
12 Stanford	846		25 North Carolina State	96
13 Arizona	704			

Bowl Championship Series Rankings October 31, 2010

	Harris Poll Avg.	USA TODAY Poll Avg.	Computer Pct.	BCS Avg.
1 Oregon (8-0)	.9905	.9925	.950	.9777
2 Auburn (9-0)	.9414	.9383	1.000	.9599
3 Texas Christian (9-0)	.8874	.9085	.950	.8911
4 Boise State (7-0)	.9246	.9227	.800	.8824
5 Utah (8-0)	.7618	.7736	.660	.7318

November 6, 2010

(Th) VIRGINIA TECH 28 Georgia Tech 21: Not long after Yellow Jackets (5-4) QB Joshua Nesbitt (6/86y, 2 TDs rushing) became all-time leading rusher among ACC QBs with 71y TD bolt that gave his team 14-0 lead in 1st Q, he threw INT at Virginia Tech (7-2) GL and broke his throwing arm trying to tackle S Davon Morgan. Still, Georgia Tech made it into 4th Q with 14-7 lead until speedy Hokies soph RB David Wilson tied it on 15y TD run. Hokies took their 1st lead with 6:34 to play when QB Tyrod Taylor (15-25/137y, TD, INT) pitched short TD pass after scrambling to his right. Jackets backup QB Tevin Washington quickly retaliated with 42y pass to WR Tyler Melton and called 8 straight runs to lock it at 21-21 on pitchout sweep by SB Orwin Smith. Wilson immediately unlocked it by bursting into clear on KO RET with only Georgia Tech K Scott Blair in his path. Year earlier, Blair tackled Wilson to save 28-23 win, but this time Wilson sped past for game-winning 90y TD RET with 2:23 to play. "When I saw green, I just cut the jets on," said Wilson, and Hokies owned their 7th win in row after 0-2 start this season.

LOUISVILLE 28 SYRACUSE 20: Had surprising Syracuse's bubble burst with Orange (6-2) as their Big East record dropped to 3-2? Louisville (5-4) sent LB Daniel Brown on 1st Q blitz to cause FUM converted into powerful 28y TD run by RB Jeremy Wright (19/98y, 2 TDs). Syracuse, however, led 17-14 at H after shuffle of TD passes by Orange QB Ryan Nassib (19-32/155y, TD) and Cardinals QB Justin Burke (13-25/143y, 2 TDs) and 8y scoring run by Syracuse RB Delone Carter (21/107y, TD). Louisville coach Charlie Strong gambled during 90y drive at beginning of 4th Q when he opted to go for it on 4th-and-4 at Syracuse 33YL. Decision paid off when Burke threw 12y pass for 1st down and then 21y TD to WR Josh Chichester for 28-20 edge.

CLEMSON 14 North Carolina State 13: While this game pitted pair of teams hoping to survive in ACC Atlantic Div, it also was battle of big-time baseball prospects: stat-battle between NC State (6-3) QB Russell Wilson (22-36/212y, TD, INT) and Clemson (5-4) QB Kyle Parker (20-29/214y, TD, INT) turned out as close as nail-biting final score. Wilson's 3y TD pass to RB Mustafa Greene fueled 10-0 Wolfpack lead, while Parker, yanked for mistake-strewn play, came back to pitch 12y TD pass to WR DeAndre Hopkins in 3rd Q. After Parker hit 4 passes, virus-stricken RB Jamie Harper scored Clemson's winning TD with 6:18 to play. On Wolfpack's next series, coach Tom O'Brien chose to punt from Tigers 43YL and it traveled only 4y. With less than 2 mins to go on 4th-and-10 in NC State territory, O'Brien had no choice but to go for it. Wilson, under heavy pressure from Clemson DE Da'Quan Bowers, rolled far right, threw way cross-field, and almost succeeded: WR T. J. Graham nearly came up with pass as CB Coty Sensabaugh defended closely.

North Carolina 37 FLORIDA STATE 35: Per normal in ACC divisional play, control by Florida State (6-3) would have to wait. North Carolina (6-3) rode momentous passing performance of QB T.J. Yates, who connected on 24-35/school-record 439y, 3 TDs. Yates launched 67y TD bomb to WR Dwight Jones (8/233y, TD) in 1st Q that broke 7-7 deadlock. QB Christian Ponder (24-34/264y, 3 TDs) countered with pair of 2nd Q TD passes, and Seminoles led 28-21 at H break. K Casey Barth hit 2 FGs and Yates another TD pass, so Tar Heels earned 34-28 advantage early in 4th Q. FSU went up 35-34 lead with 5:49 left on RB Lonnie Pryor's 2nd TD run, set up at 1YL by bad North Carolina snap over head of P C.J. Feagles. Yates and Jones hooked up for big 31y pass on 72y drive that positioned Barth for winning 22y FG with 55 secs on clock.

Arkansas 41 SOUTH CAROLINA 20: "The way we played, you wonder how we won six games already this year," lamented Gamecocks coach Steve Spurrier as South Carolina (6-3) was routed in worst home defeat in 5 years and only its 2nd loss in last 14 outings at Columbia. While ascending Arkansas Razorbacks (7-2) had no hope for SEC West crown they embraced possible BCS Bowl plans. Aided by Carolina's failed run on fake-punt in 2nd Q, Hogs scored on 4 of their 5 possessions in 1st H as RB Knile Davis (22/110y, 3 TDs) scored twice, including 22y tight-rope down right sideline, and QB Ryan Mallett (21-30/303y, TD, INT) accumulated 213y passing in 1st H. Arkansas led 41-10 after Mallett's short TD keeper early in 4th Q.

LOUISIANA STATE 24 Alabama 21: As vital SEC West match tumbled into decisive 4th Q, Alabama (7-2) led 14-10 on strength of TB Mark Ingram's 5y TD run late in 3rd Q that trumped 75y TD pass 6 mins earlier by Louisiana State (8-1) QB Jordan Jefferson (10-13/141y, TD) to WR Rueben Randle (3/125y, TD). On 2nd play of 4th Q, Tigers K Josh Jasper nailed 35y FG to pull LSU within 1 pt, and on next possession, Bayou

Bengals went 77y to take lead for good. On imperative drive, big LSU RB Steven Ridley banged for 7/47y and 1y TD run, but signature play came on another inspired 4th down play-call by coach Les "Mad Hatter" Miles. On 4th-and-1 at Bama 26YL, TE DeAngelo Peterson took E-around 23y to 3YL. After Randle's 2-pt catch and another FG by Jasper, Bayou Bengals led 24-14. Tide QB Greg McElroy (21-34/223y, 2 TDs, INT) responded with 6-8/62y, including 9y TD to WR Julio Jones. But, Tide fell short as Tigers QB Jarrett Lee found Randle for 47y gain to all but extinguish clock. At game's end, Jones out-fought LSU star CB Patrick Peterson in epic battle to tune of 10/89y, TD receiving.

PENN STATE 35 Northwestern 21: Tale of 2 Hs split Big 10 contest as if Dr. Jekyll and Mr. Hyde were coaching. Wildcats (6-3) stormed to 21-0 edge only to see Penn State (6-3) wedge in TD just before H and explode in 2nd H to deliver coach Joe Paterno his 400th career victory. No major-level coach had ever attained that plateau. Northwestern QB Dan Persa (16-25/201y, TD, and 25/109y, 2 TDs rushing) zipped for 6 and 4y TD runs and rifled 9y TD to SB Drake Dunsmore, who made extended 1-handed catch in back of EZ with 56 secs left before H. But, Nittany Lions responded by racing 91y in 9 plays as QB Matt McGloin (18-29/225y, 4 TDs) hit WR Brett Brackett with 7y TD pass. Penn State was all over NW in 2nd H as TBs Evan Royster (25/134y) and Silas Redd (11/131, TD) teamed for 168y rushing and McGloin added 3 TD throws, including 13y screen pass to Royster that clinched it at 35-21 with 11:38 left.

MICHIGAN 67 Illinois 65 (OT): Back on February 23, Michigan had hosted Illinois' basketball team and lost 51-44. So, it was hard to believe footballers could combine to outscore their hoop counterparts by astounding 37 pts. In 3rd OT of highest-scoring pigskin tilt in Big 10 history, ragged D of Wolverines (6-3) rose up to blitze Illinois (5-4) QB Nathan Steelhaase (14-25/211y, 3 TDs, and 21/101y, TD rushing) by preventing his tying 2-pt pass try to secure victory. Wild 2nd Q had seen 6 TDs and 2 FGs that turned Wolverines' 7-6 lead into 31-31 H deadlock. Michigan QB Denard Robinson (10-20/305y, 3 TDs, 2 INTs, and 19/62y rushing) was knocked dizzy in relatively tame, single-TD 3rd Q, so sub QB Tate Forcier (12-19/114y, 2 TDs) came off bench to toss tying TD with 1:47 left in regulation after Illini RB Mikel Leshoure (24/120y, 3 TDs, and 2/52y, 2 TDs receiving) had scored twice in 4th Q to build 45-38 lead. At beginning of 3rd OT, Forcier's 2-pt pass to WR Junior Hemingway put UM on top 67-59, enough to withstand Leshoure's 5th score. WR Roy Roundtree set Michigan receiving y record with 9/246y and 2 TDs.

KANSAS 52 Colorado 45: It was curtains for Dan Hawkins' coaching career at Colorado when Buffaloes (3-6) dropped their 5th game in row by blowing 45-17 lead. Up until their demise, Buffs rang up 432y O as RB Rodney Stewart (27/175y, 3 TDs) scored in 1st, 2nd, and 4th Qs, and QB Cody Hawkins (29-44/322y, 3 TDs, 2 INTs) twice connected for scores with WR Paul Richardson (11/1141y, 2 TDs). Down by 28 pts after 1st play of 4th Q, Jayhawks (3-6) went 66y to TD run by RB James Sims (20/123y, 4 TDs), who had scored his 1st TD late in 3rd Q. Kansas immediately took possession with on-side KO, and QB Quinn Mecham (23-28/252y, 2 TDs, 2 INTs) clicked on 38y TD pass to WR Johnathan Wilson. CB Tyler Patmon stepped up for Kansas with 28y FUM TD RET and INT that set up Sims' 6y TD run that knotted it 45-45 with 4:30 to play. After Colorado had to punt, Jayhawks went ahead on Sims' 28y TD gallop. Hawkins passed Buffaloes to 7YL but game ended with his 2 incompletions in EZ. Kansas' 35 pts represented 2nd-most scored in 4th Q to win in major college history.

Nebraska 31 IOWA STATE 30 (OT): Seeking 2nd straight upset over Cornhuskers, Iowa State (5-5) stood up to Big 12 North leader Nebraska (8-1), hoping to close its dreadful 17-85-2 history against Huskers on last-chance uptick. Keyed by 29y INT TD RET by DB Austin Cassidy, Nebraska enjoyed bug 3rd Q to turn 10-7 H deficit into 24-10 lead entering 4th Q. Less than 5 mins into 4th Q, Cyclones tied it with 2 TDs by QB Austen Arnaud (21-32/203y, 3 TDs, 2 INTs). After Cornhuskers RB Rex Burkhead (20/129y, 2 TDs) scored on 19y run behind 3 blocks by TE Mike McNeill to start OT, Iowa State coach Paul Rhoads called daring play after his team tallied on another pass by Arnaud. But, DB Eric Hagg clinched Nebraska's win by alertly intercepting soft, floating pass by Iowa State holder Daniel Kuehl on fake x-pt kick.

TEXAS TECH 24 Missouri 17: On game's 3rd snap, Missouri (7-2) RB Marcus Murphy galloped 69y for TD for his team's longest run of year, but fellow RB Kendial Lawrence (6/96y, TD) outdid him with 71y sprint to EZ for 14-0 lead later in 1st Q. For 1st time this season, Texas Tech (5-4) didn't start QB Taylor Potts (19-28/188y, 3 TDs, INT), but 23-year-old sr entered fray with 5:10 to go before H and hit his 1st 3 throws on way to 82y trip to 8y TD pass to WR Detron Lewis (8/64y, TD). That narrowed Raiders' deficit to 17-10. Potts sparked consecutive TD drives in 3rd Q, each culminating in TD throw to sure-handed WR Lyle Leong (9/123y, 2 TDs). Meanwhile, Mizzou QB Blaine Gabbert (12-30/95y) was suffering through quiet 2nd H with 6-17/45y passing.

TEXAS A&M 33 Oklahoma 19: Aggies (6-3) D brought back memories of 1980s-90s "Wrecking Crew" as Texas A&M permitted only 134y in 1st H shutout and stopped Oklahoma's only effective drive at 1YL. Sooners (7-2) suffered from start: On 1st play, snap eluded QB Landry Jones (36-59/290y, TD, INT) for safety, and A&M QB Ryan Tannehill (19-32/225y, 2 TDs, 2 INTs) dashed 48y and soon tossed 1y TD pass to TE Hutson Prioleau for 9-0 lead. When CB Coryell Judie took 2nd H KO 100y for TD, Aggies led 19-0. That awoke Oklahoma as in quick succession RB DeMarco Murray (25/80y, TD) scored TD, K Patrick O'hara booted FG, and Jones flipped TD pass to right edge of EZ to little WR Trey Franks. Ahead only 19-17 as 4th Q opened, A&M sent RB Cyrus Gray (21/122y, TD) on spinning 23y TD journey to 26-17 lead. Later, Tannehill found WR Ryan Swope breaking behind gambling secondary for 64y TD on 3rd-and-4 to make Aggies comfortable at 33-17.

STANFORD 42 Arizona 17: Almost throughout its history, Stanford (8-1) won when its O sparkled. In this 1st-ever meeting with Wildcats (7-2) when both were ranked, it hadn't much changed. Cardinal QB Andrew Luck passed 23-32/293y, 2 TDs and fleet WR Chris Owusu hauled in 9/165y, TD, but also in forefront was hard-hitting Stanford D that forced early mistakes that foiled Wildcats scoring chances and didn't allow TD until late in 3rd Q. Arizona QB Nick Foles (28-48/248y, TD, INT) returned nicely from injury list but in 1st Q was called for intentional grounding PEN and saw his pass dropped at 10YL. Cardinal RB Stepfan Taylor scored 4 TDs while rushing for 19/82y.

Texas Christian 47 UTAH 7: No. 6 Utes (8-1) had little chance against no. 4 Horned Frogs (10-0), who played their best game of year. It was 2nd-largest victory margin between BCS top-5 teams in 13 years of BCS history. Winning its 1st–ever game in Salt Lake City, TCU owned it from start. In 1st Q, Frogs QB Andy Dalton (21-26/355y, 3 TDs) launched scoring passes of 26 and 93y to WR Josh Boyce (3/126y, 2 TDs), and WR Jeremy Kerley found WR Bart Johnson for 26y TD pass. Dalton added another TD pass, and score rose to 40-0 before Utah RB Matt Asiata nabbed 19y TD pass from QB Jordan Wynn (16-35/148y, TD, 2 INTs) 4 mins into 4th Q.

BOISE STATE 42 Hawaii 7: Hawaii (7-3), winners of 6 games in row, including victory over previously unbeaten Nevada, had high hopes for its Mainland visit. Boise State (8-0) acted like poor northern hosts, dropping school-record 737y O on Rainbow Warriors. Canny Broncos QB Kellen Moore (30-37/507y, 3 TDs, 2 INTs) completed 19 straight passes during 1st H stretch, and only his 2 INTs suffered deep in Hawaii territory to S Mana Silva kept score from being much worse. Moore hit 3rd Q TDs to WRs Austin Pettis of 43y and Titus Young of 83y to lift lead to 35-0. Hawaii was limited to 196y, its lowest output in 12 years, and only late-game 54y TD burst up middle by RB Alex Green put Warriors in positive rushing column with 45y.

USA TODAY Coaches Poll November 7, 2010

1 Oregon (50)	1463	14 Arkansas	696
2 Auburn (4)	1389	15 Utah	659
3 Texas Christian (2)	1340	16 Oklahoma	569
4 Boise State (3)	1330	17 Virginia Tech	563
5 Wisconsin	1184	18 Mississippi State	477
6 Louisiana State	1153	19 Arizona	403
7 Ohio State	1123	20 Missouri	395
8 Nebraska	1067	21 Nevada	328
9 Stanford	1058	22 South Carolina	151
10 Michigan State	876	23 Central Florida	99
11 Oklahoma State	832	24 Florida	85
12 Alabama	791	25 Texas A&M	79
13 Iowa	779		

Bowl Championship Series Rankings November 7, 2010

	Harris Poll Avg.	USA TODAY Poll Avg.	Computer Pct.	BCS Avg.
1 Oregon (9-0)	.9895	.9919	.960	.9638
2 Auburn (10-0)	.9589	.9417	1.000	.9611
3 Texas Christian (10-0)	.9193	.9085	.950	.9259
4 Boise State (8-0)	.9070	.9017	.790	.8662
5 Louisiana State (8-1)	.7793	.7817	.890	.8170

November 13, 2010

(Th) CONNECTICUT 30 Pittsburgh 28: Pitt Panthers (5-4) arrived unbeaten with 2-game lead in Big East but were helpless to stop UConn Huskies (5-4) TB Jordan Todman (37/222y), who gained career-high y and converted big 4th down gamble in 4th Q. Intercepted flea-flicker pass on game's 1st play had led to Pitt RB Dion Lewis (13/77y, 2 TDs) to slip across GL from 4YL. Huskies answered on 36y TD pass by QB Zach Frazer (9-20/100y, 2 TDs, INT) to WR Kashif Moore and made it 13-7 in 3rd Q on K Dave Teggert's 2nd FG. Lewis and his backup, RB Ray Graham (16/75y, TD), next capped long 6-play drives with TD runs, so Pitt led 21-13 late in 3rd Q. Connecticut quickly trimmed it to 21-20 as WR Nick Williams went all way to 95y TD, his 2nd KO TD RET in 2010, and Teggert's 3rd FG 8 mins into 4th Q snatched 23-21 lead. With 2:33 to play and up 30-28, UConn coach Randy Edsall decided to roll dice on 4th-and-1 at own 19YL. Todman blasted for 4y, and UConn never again relinquished possession.

Syracuse 13 RUTGERS 10: Syracuse (7-3) remarkably won its 4th straight conf road game on K Ross Krautman's 24y FG with 1:07 to go after RB Antwon Bailey keyed 66y march with runs of 14 and 15y. Earlier, Bailey had tallied Orange's sole TD on slow-developing 4y swing pass from QB Ryan Nassib (16-31/214y, TD, INT) in 1st Q. WR Jeremy Deering (29/166y, TD rushing), who spent much of game in Wildcat formation, gave Rutgers (4-5) 10-7 lead early in 3rd Q when despite high snap he dashed 19y for TD. Krautman tied it for Syracuse 8 mins later on career-long 48y FG.

Virginia Tech 26 NORTH CAROLINA 10: Run-oriented O of Virginia Tech (8-2) unleashed QB Tyrod Taylor (13-28/249y, 2 TDs) at just right time in 17-pt 3rd Q to overcome stumbling 1st H in which it trailed 10-9. On 3rd-and-10 at Tar Heels 11YL in 3rd Q, Taylor pitched TD pass to WR Marcus Davis (4/81y, 2 TDs), and after K Chris Hazley's 4th FG, backpedaling Taylor lofted another TD pass to Davis for 26-10 lead. Hokies dominated 3rd Q with 141y O to Heels' 19y O. North Carolina (6-4) RB Anthony Elzy (17/82y, TD) had soared on 1st Q TD dive at end of 80y drive but would fumble into EZ in 4th Q when Tar Heels still harbored hope, while behind 26-10. UNC QB T.J. Yates (18-33/197y, 4 INTs) earlier had set school career completion record but was picked off 4th time at Virginia Tech 2YL in 4th Q.

TENNESSEE 52 Mississippi 14: Tennessee (4-6) never had gone without conf win in 78 seasons as charter member of SEC. After 0-5 start this season, determined Volunteers dominated in this momentum-changer, turning to 2nd-game-starter, QB Tyler Bray (18-34/323y, 3 TDs), for considerable aerial fireworks. Frosh Bray's 1st pass try was tipped into hands of WR Justin Hunter (3/114y, 2 TDs), who sped 80y to score. Vols also returned 2 INTs for TDs: CB Eric Gordon for 46y in 1st Q and S Prentiss Waggner for 10y in 3rd Q. Tennessee RB Tauren Poole rushed for 107y and

scored on 36 and 35y runs in 2nd H. Ole Miss (4-6) QB Jeremiah Masoli (7-18/80y, 3 INTs) was under fierce pressure, and Rebels got their only tallies from RB Brandon Bolden (12/113y, 2 TDs).

South Carolina 36 FLORIDA 14: Happiest man in Florida had to be coach Steve Spurrier, who returned to site of his greatest glory to snatch 1st win at Florida Field for South Carolina (7-3) in last 12 tries and 1st SEC East title since former independent school joined conf in 1992. Gators (6-4) WR Andre Debose was quickly inhospitable as he rocketed up middle for 99y TD RET of opening KO. Unfortunately, that was just about Florida's last moment of glee as South Carolina turned to RB Marcus Lattimore to pound for career-high 212y rushing and trio of TDs. Lattimore's 2nd score, 21y run, provided 22-7 advantage in 3rd Q. Gamecocks QB Stephen Garcia (15-22/156y) passed enough to be dangerous and added 4th Q TD run on 8y sneak.

AUBURN 49 Georgia 31: Per normal, Auburn (11-0) fell behind as Georgia (5-6) frosh QB Aaron Murray (15-28/273y, 3 TDs) connected on trio of 1st Q TD passes, including 31 and 40y to star WR A.J. Green (9/164y, 2 TDs). Behind 21-7, Tigers QB Cam Newton (12-15/148y, 2 TDs, INT and 30/151y, 2 TDs rushing) added to his slam-bang 31y TD run of 1st Q with pair of 2nd Q scoring passes to knot it 21-21 just before H. Leading 35-31 entering 4th Q, Auburn pulled away on Newton's 2nd TD pass to TE Philip Lutzenkirchen and his 1y TD leap with less than 3 mins to play. Victory by Tigers clinched SEC West crown and rematch with South Carolina in conf title tilt.

OHIO STATE 38 Penn State 14: Pair of TD passes by QB Matt McGloin (15-30/159y, 2 TDs, 2 INTs) had Penn State (6-4) ahead 14-3 after 67 and 82y drives and Ohio State (9-1) fans hooting their heroes as they trotted off for H. Buckeyes were backed up to their 4YL 3 mins into 3rd Q when they made determined ground march to TD run by RB Dan Herron (21/190y, TD). Just moments later, Ohio State CB Devon Torrence left his man to cut in front of Lions receiver in flat, tipped ball, and grabbed it for 34y INT TD RET and 17-14 lead. Early in 4th Q came crusher for Penn State: Bucks QB Terrelle Pryor (8-13/139y, 2 TDs, INT) lofted long, high pass to WR DeVier Posey, who as ball arrived was smacked hard by 2 Lions DBs only to have ball squirt to trailing WR Dane Sanzenbacher, who trotted for unmolested 58y TD and 24-14 advantage.

NORTHWESTERN 21 Iowa 17: Northwestern (7-3) QB Dan Persa (32-43/318y, 2 TDs, INT) threw across his body to WR Demetrius Fields for winning 20y TD pass with 1:22 left, but during his effort he went down for year with Achilles tear. With dynamic Persa would go much of Wildcats' spirit. Hawkeyes (7-3) dropped their 5th in last 6 tries against Wildcats despite 17-7 lead going into 4th Q on pair of TD passes in 3rd Q by QB Ricky Stanzi (23-41/270y, 2 TDs, INT). Hawks appeared ready to put it away early in 4th Q when INT by LB Jeremiha Hunter put Iowa at its 38YL, but 4 plays later Stanzi was picked off by Wildcats S Brian Peters at NW 5YL. "The interception cost us the game," Stanzi said later. Northwestern responded with 85y drive to Persa's 6y TD pass to WR Jeremy Ebert to pull within 17-14 and went 91y to Persa's winning pass.

WISCONSIN 83 Indiana 20: When enormous final score was posted, those not in attendance might be surprised to learn Indiana (4-6) actually had this contest tied 10-10 through early part of 2nd Q. But Hoosiers lost QB Ben Chappel (8-14/63y, TD) to hip injury in 1st H, and it was massive fall from there. Wisconsin (9-1) also played without star player, last year's Big 10 O Player of Year, TB John Clay. But backup TBs Montee Ball (22/167y, 3 TDs) and James White (19/144y, 2 TDs) ran through big holes carved by Badgers O-line, led by T Gabe Carimi and G John Moffitt. Wisconsin QB Scott Tolzien also was close to perfect with his strategic passing: 15-18/181y, 3 TDs. Wisconsin scored on all 12 of its possessions on way to 598y O, 338y rushing. It was Badgers' largest tally since beating Marquette 85-0 in 1915.

MISSOURI 38 Kansas State 28: QB Blaine Gabbert (17-25/208y, 2 TDs, INT) bounced back from his slump and righted Missouri (8-2) ship after 2 losses in row. Gabbert opened with 7 straight completions including 25y TD to WR T.J. Moe in 1st Q. Gabbert broke 7-7 tie in 2nd Q, weaving 32y on TD scramble behind great downfield blocking. Kansas State (6-4) back-up QB Collin Klein's effective running (141y) set up 2 TD runs by RB Daniel Thomas (12/66y, 2 TDs) in 2nd Q, but Wildcats QB Carson Coffman (11-19/170y, TD, INT) lost snap FUM to DE Jacquies Smith at Mizzou 1YL when Cats had chance to knot it late in 2nd Q. Smith scored important TD in 3rd Q when Tigers other DE, Aldon Smith, created-sack FUM that Jacquies lugged 53y to score for 28-14 margin. When Gabbert and Moe hooked up on another TD pass in 4th Q, Tigers had 38-14 lead, sufficient enough to withstand late TD tosses by Klein and Coffman.

Oklahoma State 33 TEXAS 16: It was difficult to figure badly-slumping Texas (4-6), on verge of losing 6th of last 7 games for 1st time since 1988, especially with its bevy of highly-regarded talent. Until now, Texas hadn't lost 4 in row at home in same season since way back in 1956. Oklahoma State (9-1) hadn't won in Austin since 1944 but was in command whole way as QB Brandon Weeden passed 29-43/409y, TD, INT, including 67y TD bomb to WR Justin Blackmon (9/145y, TD) in 2nd Q. When RB Kendall Hunter (23/116y, 2 TDs) scored his 2nd TD in 3rd Q, Cowpokes led 33-3. Even though they scored 2 TDs in 4th Q, Longhorns hadn't crossed midfield from late in 1st Q until late in 3rd Q against Cowboys so-so D that had permitted 28.4 pts per game avg.

Oregon 15 CALIFORNIA 13: Cal Bears (5-5) did wonderful job within and on fringe of rules to slow down no. 1 Oregon's racehorse O. Using slow-down tactics including too-pained-to-get-up tacklers, California D permitted sole TD on 29y catch by Ducks (10-0) WR Jeff Maehl (5/84y, TD) from QB Darron Thomas (15-29/155y, TD) early in 3rd Q. Otherwise, Oregon, averaging 54.7 pts per game in 9 previous starts, could tally only on DB Cliff Harris' 64y punt TD RET in 2nd Q, which furnished 8-7 lead when Ducks DE Dion Jordan scored 2 pts on trick conv run. RB Shane Vereen (26/112y, TD) closed out Cal's 1st series with 1y TD by carrying 5 straight plays but fumbled early in 3rd Q to set up Maehl's TD catch. Bears DT Derrick Hill forced Thomas to cough up FUM later in 3rd Q, which he recovered for TD that pulled Bears within 15-13. Cal K

Giorgio Tavecchio erased his 24y go-ahead FG early in 4th Q by making illegal-motion stutter-step just before snap, and he missed 29y do-over try on next play. By game's end, Oregon was slowing itself down, using 18 plays to kill last 9+ mins.

Washington State 31 OREGON STATE 14: Breaking 16-game Pac-10 losing streak, Washington State (2-9) went on road to surprise Beavers (4-5) for only its 2nd win in last 26 conf games. Cougars QB Jeff Tuel (10-15/157y, TD) used his mobility, weak point for Oregon State D all year, to rush 18/79y to help advance chains. Cougars gained 214y O in 1st H they led 14-0. When Tuel returned for 2nd H after brief injury respite, he led 94y march to his 33y TD pass to WR Marquess Wilson and 21-0 lead. Beavers could move no closer than 24-14 in 4th Q on 2nd TD connection between QB Ryan Katz (12-21/155y, 2 TDs, INT) and WR Markus Wheaton (6/97y, 2 TDs).

Stanford 17 ARIZONA STATE 13: Attendees at Sun Devil Stadium honored memory of fallen U.S. Army hero and former Arizona State LB Pat Tillman in celebration of his election to College Hall of Fame. Occasion seemed to inspire sometimes-brilliant D of Arizona State (4-6). Stanford (9-1) arrived with average of 38.1 pts scored per game and was on verge of from best 10-game start since 1951. WR Drew Terrell's 34y punt RET launched Stanford's 50y drive in 1st Q as FB Owen Marecic slammed over from 1YL. Sun Devils answered with sharp 74y drive, and QB Steven Threet (16-26/158y, TD, INT) optioned off left side for 4y TD run. Arizona State took 13-10 lead in 3rd Q when Threet hit 8y slant-in TD pass to WR Kerry Taylor (4/24y, TD), but x-pt was missed. Stanford started at its 15YL in 4th Q and was aided on 85y march to Marecic's 2nd TD dive by personal foul and unsportsmanlike conduct PENs for 30y on same play by MLB Vontaze Burfict, highly talented but most unpredictable member of stubborn Devils D. Cardinal O killed last 4 mins to finish with 42:25 in possession time. Stanford WR Doug Baldwin (10/122y) kept chains moving all night on catches from QB Andrew Luck (33-41/292y, INT), while ASU RB Cameron Marshall rushed for 92y.

Southern California 24 ARIZONA 21: TB Marc Tyler, bad ankle and all, transformed into workhorse for Trojans (7-3) with 31/160y, TD rushing. "I don't think I've ever carried the ball over 30 times," said son of former UCLA great Wendell Tyler, "(not) in high school, Pop Warner, nothing." USC never trailed as QB Matt Barkley (21-35/170y, TD, INT) sneaked and threw for 1st 3 TDs, and Trojans could brag once again they had beaten ranked team every year since 1997. Wildcats (7-3) WR David Douglas caught pair of TD passes from QB Nick Foles (32-48/353y, 3 TDs) but his costly 3rd Q FUM was lost at USC 15YL when Cats trailed only 21-14. K Joe Houston's 30y FG in 3rd Q lifted Troy's edge to 24-14 and proved to be winning margin.

November 20, 2010

Notre Dame 27 Army 3 (Yankee Stadium, Bronx, NY): Memories of epic Notre Dame-Army battles of yesteryear were revived as noble old foes renewed their House-that-Ruth-Built rivalry in Bronx's new Yankee Stadium. Teams had met 22 times in original Yankee Stadium, games that included Knute Rockne's legendary "Win One for the Gipper" speech in 1928 and Game of Century in 1946 that ended in 0-0 tie as 4 Heisman Trophy winners participated. Working on 13-game winning streak in on-and-off series with Cadets, present-day Notre Dame (6-5) dominated after Army (6-5) flourished early. Black Knights FS Donovan Travis halted opening 69y drive with INT in EZ. Then, only 1st H completion by Army QB Trent Steelman (2-7/39y, 2 INTs, and 14/41y rushing) went for 27y to WR Davyd Brooks to launch 77y march to ND 3YL. Irish D, which would permit only 97y thereafter, stacked up Steelman on 3rd down run from 3YL, and Army K Alex Carlton booted 20y FG for 3-0 lead. Army stalled on 3 straight 3-and-out possessions in 2nd Q as Notre Dame charged to 17 pts. ND TE Tyler Eikert (4/78y, TD) caught 35y pass to 1YL to set up RB Robert Hughes for TD run and reeled in 31y TD pass from young QB Tommy Rees (13-20/214y, TD, INT), who was privileged to dress at locker of Yankee shortstop Derek Jeter. Irish CB Darrin Walls wrapped up scoring with 42y INT TD RET early in 3rd Q.

Virginia Tech 31 MIAMI 17: What Hurricanes (7-4) once hoped would be home-field showdown for ACC Coastal title instead became coronation of Virginia Tech Hokies (9-2) as they finished 8-0 in conf play. While Hokies D relinquished 464y it intercepted Miami frosh QB Stephen Morris (15-33/202y, TD, 3 INTs) 3 times, all in last 9:01, decisive spell when they wrapped it up at 31-17 on 18y TD draw-run by QB Tyrod Taylor (7-14/94y, TD). Va Tech TB Ryan Williams (14/142y, 2 TDs) had broken 17-17 deadlock with 84y TD gallop early in 4th Q. WR Leonard Hankerson (6/79y, TD) had opened scoring with 9y TD reception, his 12th of year for new Miami record.

Florida State 30 MARYLAND 16: Florida State (8-3) visited College Park to administer its 19th defeat in 21 games to Maryland (7-4), yet with their conf slate complete at 6-2, Seminoles had to count on Terps to beat NC State next Saturday to clinch spot in ACC title game. Fans enjoyed back-and-forth 13-13 1st H as Seminoles speedster RB Chris Thompson (8/95y, TD) bolted 70y for TD in 1st Q, only to be matched by short TD pass by Maryland frosh QB Danny O'Brien (25-45/269y, TD, 2 INTs). Trailing 16-13 late in 3rd Q, FSU WR Bert Reed took pass from QB Christian Ponder (16-26/170y, TD, INT) and swivel-hipped his way through Terrapins D on 44y TD catch-and-run. Maryland threatened in game's final min, down 23-16, but Seminoles S Nick Moody took O'Brien's 4th down overthrow and took off on 96y INT TD RET.

LOUISIANA STATE 43 Mississippi 36: Suffering through difficult year, Ole Miss (4-7) rose up to challenge rival Louisiana State (10-1), thrice taking 1-pt leads during last 20 mins. Coach Houston Nutt had admiration for his Rebels: "You like the way they competed, and they left their heart out there. That's the thing that I'll go to sleep with tonight." For his part, coach Les Miles admitted that his Tigers had been 0-2 lately against Nutt and he "didn't see the significance of the Ole Miss rivalry" until former Arkansas coach arrived in Oxford in 2008. RB Brandon Bolden (18/91y, 2 TDs) scored his 2nd TD on 3y run with 4:34 left in 3rd Q for 24-23 edge for Rebels, and after he ran for 1st down in mid-4th Q to make Ole Miss 4-4 on 4th downs, QB Jeremiah Masoli (15-23/177y, TD, 2 INTs) slipped away for 22y TD run and 30-29 edge. Finally, Masoli pitched 65y TD pass to WR Markeith Summers (2/73y, TD), and again Ole Miss led 36-35 with 4:57 to go. LSU fought back, and although QB Jordan Jefferson enjoyed surprisingly effect passing effort with 13-17/254y, TD, INT, Tigers stuck completely to ground to advance 51y to winning TD run by RB Steven Ridley (18/89y, 3 TDs).

Ohio State 20 IOWA 17: Buckeyes (10-1) rallied on 76y march in last 6 mins, keyed by 14y run by QB Terrelle Pryor (18-33/195y, TD, 2 INTs, and 15/78y rushing) on vital 4th-and-10 play from midfield. "I was going to run the whole time," admitted Pryor. In 1st Q, Iowa (7-4) QB Ricky Stanzi (20-31/195y, TD) had beaten blitz with post-route TD pass to WR Marvin McNutt. Pryor answered with his own TD pass in 2nd Q. With score at 10-10 early in 4th Q, Pryor threw errantly over middle, ball being tipped and picked off by Hawkeyes CB Shaun Prater and returned to the Ohio State 27YL. TB Marcus Coker (9/70y, TD) followed his 26y run with short TD plunge to put Hawkeyes up 17-10 with 11:53 left. After K Devin Barclay's 2nd FG pulled Bucks to within 17-13, Ohio fashioned its winning drive in fits and starts to RB Dan Herron's 1y TD blast.

Wisconsin 48 MICHIGAN 28: Powerful Wisconsin (10-1) had starting TB John Clay unavailable so unleashed backups Montee Ball (29/173y, 4 TDs) and James White (23/181y, 2 TDs) to gallop to leads of 24-0 at H and 31-14 in 3rd Q. Michigan (7-4) QB Denard Robinson (16-25/239y, 2 TDs, INT, and 21/122y, 2 TDs rushing) set new FBS record for most rushing y in season by QB, overtaking 1496y of Beau Morgan of Air Force in 1996. Robinson threw for TD and ran for another to place Wolverines within 24-14 in 3rd Q, but their D couldn't slow Badgers' express train: White soon answered with 23y TD run, and Ball scored twice in 4th Q as Wisconsin piled up 357y rushing. Badgers QB Scott Tolzien (14-15/201y, INT) also was razor sharp, hitting his opening 13 passes to give him 24 straight connections over 2 games.

MICHIGAN STATE 35 Purdue 31: Comebacks were becoming 2nd nature for Michigan State (10-1), and this time Spartans overcame 28-13 deficit at end of 3rd Q after Purdue (4-7) QB Rob Henry (16-26/189y, 2 TDs, 2 INTs) had thrown his 2nd TD pass within 8:19 that overlapped H. Trailing 7-0 in 1st Q, Boilermakers RB Keith Carlos had slipped up middle and dashed 80y to TD, and moments later CB Ricardo Allen put Purdue up 14-7 with 35y INT TD RET. Banged-up Spartans QB Kirk Cousins (28-37/276y, 3 TDs, INT) heated up in 4th Q with 120y in air, hitting TD passes to WRs B.J. Cunningham and Mark Dell (8/108y, 2 TDs), plus 2-pt conv to Dell to pull within 31-28 with 6:54 to play. Purdue was stopped deep in its end, and MSU LB Denicos Allen blocked punt with his stomach for REC at 3YL. Cousins dived across GL 2 plays later, and Michigan State finally was ahead. LB Chris Norman's INT wrapped it up near end.

Illinois 48 Northwestern 27 (Wrigley Field, Chicago): Wrigley Field's 1st football game since Chicago Bears left in 1970 featured stadium marquee painted purple to pay tribute to Northwestern's home game against in-state rivals. Dampening glee was necessity that all O plays be directed at south EZ near 3rd base dugout. Friday's decision came about because Wrigley Field's right field wall jutted out too close to end-line and thus was considered unsafe. So, those with tickets in right field seemed destined to need binoculars for every TD of Big 10 battle. Not so: Northwestern (7-4) SS Brian Peters scored on 1st Q INT RET of 59y, which he ran into EZ right toward outfield protrusion but without pursuit or worry of collision with padded bricks. It pulled Wildcats within 14-7 even though their D was being torched by Illinois (6-5) RB Mikel Leshoure, who established school overland mark with 330y on 33 carries. Leshoure had scored 1st 2 TDs of game on way to 156y rushing in 1st Q alone. Illini led 21-7 late in 1st Q when NW RB Mike Trumpy (13/129y, 2 TDs) broke away for 80y TD run, and when Trumpy scored again late in 2nd Q Cats were back in game at 24-24. Illini posted next 17 pts, including 3rd Q TD pass by QB Nathan Scheelhaase (6-13/40y, TD, INT, and 19/97y rushing), who suggested Wrigley provided "a great atmosphere, something I'm always going to look back on."

TEXAS A&M 9 Nebraska 6: Workhorse RB Cyrus Gray (26/137y, and 9/65y receiving) grew stronger as tough D game wore on, sparking Aggies (8-3) to upset and 5th straight win. In 3 games since his sidekick, RB Christine Michael, broke leg, Gray had amassed 396y rushing, and he was 1st Texas A&M runner in 20 years to own 5 100+y games in row. No. 9 Nebraska (9-2) was penalized 16/145y, circumstance that had irate coach Bo Pelini screaming at officials for much of time. (Huskers fans also smelled rat: They were convinced Big 12 officials had it in for Nebraska, with its pending departure for Big 10 Conf.) Nebraska's hope dwindled when QB Taylor Martinez (11-17/107y, INT, and 11/17y rushing) had his sore right ankle accidentally squashed by foot of C Mike Caputo. Martinez missed about half of game and was noticeably slowed. Tied 3-3 after 3 Qs, Texas A&M SS Trent Hunter's 2nd INT set up K Randy Bullock (3 FGs) for 28y FG, but Huskers K Alex Henery tied it 6-6 with 29y 3-ptr. After Gray lugged ball 7/43y on 68y drive, Bullock won it from 19y with 3:02 to go.

USA TODAY Coaches Poll November 21, 2010

1 Oregon (48)	1459	14 Virginia Tech	723
2 Auburn (4)	1398	15 Nebraska	614
3 Boise State (5)	1341	16 Missouri	585
4 Texas Christian (2)	1300	17 South Carolina	577
5 Wisconsin	1211	18 Texas A&M	492
6 Louisiana State	1175	19 Nevada	456
7 Ohio State	1116	20 Arizona	279
8 Stanford	1112	21 Florida State	243
9 Oklahoma State	990	22 Utah	228
10 Michigan State	927	23 North Carolina State	208
11 Alabama	885	24 Iowa	74
12 Arkansas	784	25 Mississippi State	68
13 Oklahoma	733		

Bowl Championship Series Rankings November 21, 2010

	Harris Poll Avg.	USA TODAY Poll Avg.	Computer Pct.	BCS Avg.
1 Oregon (10-0)	.9800	.9892	.960	.9764
2 Auburn (11-0)	.9568	.9478	1.000	.9682
3 Texas Christian (11-0)	.8972	.8814	.920	.8995
4 Boise State (10-0)	.9189	.9092	.830	.8860
5 Louisiana State (10-1)	.7814	.7966	.880	.8193

November 25-27, 2010

(Th'g) Texas A&M 24 TEXAS 17: Only 1 year after playing in BCS title game, flabbergasted Texas (5-7) would be left out of this season's bowl picture. RB Cyrus Gray (27/223y, 2 TDs) legged out TD runs of 84 and 48y in middle Qs to propel Aggies (9-3) to 6th straight win in Big 12. Gray's latter score came with 4:34 left in 3rd Q and extended lead to 24-14. Texas got TD pass and run from QB Garrett Gilbert (20-37/219y, TD, 2 INTs), who at Aggies 8YL in 2nd Q botched handoff, 1 of 4 Texas TOs. After Longhorns drove 68y to A&M 12YL in closing 3 mins, Aggies star LB Von Miller made leaping INT of tipped pass off Gilbert.

(Fri) West Virginia 35 PITTSBURGH 10: On verge of taking control of Big East, Pittsburgh (6-5) showed up listless against its fiercest rival, and its poor performance assured end of coaching tenure of Dave Wannstedt, who soon resigned. Pitt lost 3 FUMs and QB Tino Sunseri (28-46/284y, TD, INT) served up INT to Mountaineers (8-3) CB Brandon Hogan that led to 1st of 2 short TD runs by RB Ryan Clarke (6/28y, 2 TDs). Hogan also recovered FUM by Panthers RB Ray Graham to position TD pass by QB Geno Smith (9-12/212y, 3 TDs) and 14-7 lead for West Virginia. Pitt led in O y at H by 205y to 75y, but when Smith connected with WR Tavin Austin on 71 and 12y TDs in 3rd Q it pretty well was over. Pitt's top runner, RB Dion Lewis, was held to 34y.

(Fri) Auburn 28 ALABAMA 27: In ordinary year, this incredible comeback for Auburn on road at Tuscaloosa, where Alabama owned 20-game win streak, would have been biggest game of season, but this outcome only paved way for Tigers (12-0) to win BCS title in thrilling fashion in January. Prideful Alabama (9-3) was determined to defend its turf and did magnificently for most of 1st H. Tide jumped to 24-0 lead on 9y run by TB Mark Ingram (10/36y, TD) and pair of TD passes by QB Greg McElroy (22-37/377y, 2 TDs). McElroy hit his 1st 12 passes on way to career high in aerial y and found WR Julio Jones (10/199y, TD) for 68y TD pass midway through 1st Q. It appeared Ingram might make it 28-0 when he caught a short pass and broke loose in 2nd Q. But Ingram was tripped up while trying to balance himself and had ball poked out by trailing Auburn DE Antoine Carter. FUM rolled nearly 30y to back of Tigers EZ, where DB Demond Washington fell on it for touchback. Bama came right back to 3YL, but RB Trent Richardson dropped certain TD pass, so K Jeremy Shelley's short FG raised Alabama's lead to 24-0 7 mins into 2nd Q. QB Cam Newton (13-20/216y, 3 TDs, only 22/39y rushing) rallied his Tigers with 78y drive to his 36y TD pass to WR Emory Blake to trail 24-7 at H. Next big play came just after 2nd H KO: Tide S Mark Barron appeared to have angle for INT but arrived split-sec too early, and Auburn WR Terrell Zachery was away for 70y TD, and Tigers hope was restored with deficit narrowed to 10 pts. Newton scored on 1y run at end of ground-oriented 75y trip in 3rd Q. Auburn trailed in 8 of 12 games so far in 2010, and while outgained 446y to 324y at game's end, Tigers freed TE Philip Lutzenkirchen for winning TD catch early in 4th Q. "That was a game that will certainly go down in history," Auburn coach Gene Chizik said.

(Fri) NEBRASKA 45 Colorado 17: Big story leading up to game was rebuke Nebraska (10-2) Bo Pelini had received from school chancellor Harvey Perlman for Pelini's sideline tirades previous week at Texas A&M. Meanwhile, Colorado (5-7) looked for 3rd straight win since interim coach Brian Cabral took over for deposed Dan Hawkins. RB Rex Burkhead (19/101y, TD) ran and passed for 2nd Q TDs, and Huskers led 17-3 at H. When Burkhead threw another TD pass out of Wildcat formation less than 5 mins into 3rd Q, verdict was all but sealed at 31-3. Buffs QB Cody Hawkins (10-26/163y, 2 TDs, 2 INTs) managed pair of 2nd H TD passes. Nebraska QB Cody Green, who played for injured QB Taylor Martinez, hit pair of TD passes and scored another on ground to clinch Big 12 North for Huskers.

(Fri) NEVADA 34 Boise State 31 (OT): Only impressive Nevada (11-1) stood between Boise State (10-1), winners of 24 games in row, and likely BCS Bowl. All seemed well when Broncos cruised to 24-7 H edge on pair of TD runs by RB Doug Martin (24/152y, 2 TDs) and TD pass by QB Kellen Moore (20-31/348y, 2 TDs). Wolf Pack snarled back in 2nd H behind its stiffened D and running attack, led by RB Vai Taua (32/131y, TD). Vital were 2 TDs by Nevada WR Rishard Matthews (10/172y, TD) on 44y misdirection run and 7y catch. QB Colin Kaepernick (19-35/259y, TD, INT) who made beautifully-desperate 18y TD run in 3rd Q, deadlocked it 31-31 with TD to Matthews with 13 secs

to go in regulation. Moore's long bomb gave dependable K Kyle Brotzman opportunity to win it for Boise with 26y FG with 2 secs left. But, Brotzman pushed his try to right, and soon hooked 29y FG try that could have won it in OT. Nevada frosh K Anthony Martinez nailed 34y FG to begin massive celebration in Reno.

MARYLAND 38 North Carolina State 31: QB Danny O'Brien threw for career-high 417y on 33-47, with 4 TDs to WR Torrey Smith (14/224y, 4 TDs), and Maryland (8-4) denied North Carolina State (8-4) spot in ACC title game next week. Instead, Florida State, easy 31-7 winners over out-of-conf rival Florida, was set to meet Virginia Tech, champs of Coastal Div. Do-all Wolfpack QB Russell Wilson (31-60/311y, 2 TDs, INT, and 17/53y, 2 TDs rushing) accounted for pair of early TDs for 14-0 lead. Maryland then went to work for 24-17 lead by end of 3rd Q, and led 31-17 as NC State advanced 80y to 4th-and-goal at 8YL midway through 4th Q. Terps DE Drew Glover sacked desperate Wilson for loss of 21y, and on next snap, O'Brien found Smith wide open down middle for 71y TD. It was not over at 38-17, however, because Wilson masterminded 2 quick TDs around successful on-side KO. After recovering Wolfpack's 2nd on-side KO try, Maryland sent squat RB D.J. Adams diving for 1st down on 4th-and-1 in last min. Generous spot by officials allowed Terps to hold on and kill clock.

North Carolina 24 DUKE 19: Duke (3-9) QB Sean Renfree (24-39/242y, TD, 2 INTs) threw 1st Q TD pass to WR Austin Kelly (7/67y, TD) to open scoring. But, QB T.J. Yates (28-35/264y, TD) led North Carolina (7-5) on 1st H scoring drives of 94 and 87y for 10-7 lead and along way hit diving WR Joshua Adams to lift his career passing y level to 9000y. When Yates and Adams connected for 5y TD throw at end of 80y trip to open 3rd Q, Tar Heels led 17-7. Verdict seemed sealed when UNC RB Shaun Draughn ended 81y drive with TD run early in 4th Q. Led by NG Charlie Hatcher, Devils D rose up to trap Draughn for safety, and, just to make it interesting after free-kick, Duke's big QB Brandon Connette made his 8th rushing TD of year on 2y keeper. But, Blue Devils had insufficient time when they finally got ball back.

South Carolina 29 CLEMSON 7: Hoping to cap his Clemson (6-6) career on high-note baseball prospect and QB Kyle Parker (7-17/117y, TD, INT) connected with frosh WR DeAndre Hopkins (7/124y, TD) on 45y scoring pass in 1st Q. Tigers O collapsed after that, and Parker was yanked in 2nd H after badly missing flat-receiver, and South Carolina (9-3) LB Antonio Allen legged INT 37y for TD. Before that, Gamecocks QB Stephen Garcia (14-30/227y, 2 TDs) had rolled out twice to throw 1st H TD passes: short (5y) to FB Patrick DiMarco and long (37y) to WR Alshon Jeffery (5/141y, TD).

GEORGIA 42 Georgia Tech 34: This season had not smiled on either Peach State school as Bulldogs (6-6) needed this win to ensure bowl eligibility and Georgia Tech (6-6), coming off ACC championship in 2009, was stuck in middle of conf. It was fitful contest full of blunders with total of 6 TOs, and each team lost FUM inside other's 10YL. Georgia QB Aaron Murray (15-19/271y, 3 TDs) broke David Greene's school passing y record for frosh, and his trio of TD passes formed backbone of 21-14 H edge. Yellow Jackets rushed for 411y and kept coming back, especially when they fell behind 35-21 late in 3rd Q as Georgia LB Justin Houston returned FUM 18y for TD. With just less than 5 mins to play, FB Anthony Allen (29/166y, TD) chugged up middle carrying several Bulldogs in his wake to pull Ga Tech within 35-34. But, dependable K Scott Blair pulled his x-pt wide left to end streak of 77 successes.

TENNESSEE 24 Kentucky 14: It had been year-long struggle for Tennessee (6-6) as coach Lane Kiffin left for Southern California and new leader Derek Dooley got late start, but this win made Volunteers eligible for bowl bid. Vols gangly, young QB Tyler Bray (20-38/354y, 2 TDs, 2 INTs) was still learning as he hit pair of TD passes in 2nd Q for 14-7 lead. WR Denarius Moore (7/205y, TD) became 1st Tennessee receiver to exceed 200+y twice in single season. Kentucky (6-6), bowl-eligible off November 13's 38-20 victory over Vanderbilt, managed 14-14 tie 5 mins into 3rd Q when QB Mike Hartline (31-44/272y, TD, INT) tossed 4th down, 2y TD pass to TE Tyler Robinson. Bray connected on 3-5/47y to lead to TB Tauren Poole's 2y run for decisive TD late in 3rd Q. Wildcats star WR Randall Cobb hauled in 13/116y receiving but failed to score TD for 1st time this year.

ARKANSAS 31 Louisiana State 23: Hogs' 6th straight win had them rooting about for BCS Bowl bid, and Arkansas (10-2) faithful could thank surprise bomb and 4th down gamble dialed up by coach Bobby Petrino at critical moments. Razorbacks QB Ryan Mallett (13-23/320y, 3 TDs, 2 INTs) hit pair of long TD passes to WR Cobi Hamilton (3/164y, 2 TDs) in 1st H to counter-balance 2 TD runs by Louisiana State (10-2) RB Stevan Ridley (17/75y, 2 TDs). Hamilton's 2nd TD went for 80y and came with 3 secs left in 2nd Q for 21-14 lead when whole world expected Mallett to take knee after LSU punt. "I would have liked to have had the (field goal) before the half, and who would have thought they would hit the long ball like they did for the score, certainly not I," LSU coach Les Miles said. Tigers K Josh Jasper hit pair of 3rd Q FGs to trim deficit to 21-20, so Arkansas was inclined to gamble on 4th-and-3 from LSU 39YL less than min into 4th Q: WR Joe Adams made stop-and-go move and was alone for TD pass from Mallett, more than enough as each team only could add FG each.

Mississippi State 31 MISSISSIPPI 23: While 2nd-year coach Dan Mullen was lifting his Bulldogs (8-4) to 3rd season of bowl eligibility since 2000, he also was adopting same non-deferential attitude Ohio State's Woody Hayes once used to describe Michigan. Mullen steadfastly limited his references to rival Mississippi (4-8) as "that school up north." Behind 6-0, Mississippi State exploded in 2nd Q by gaining 239y on only 18 plays. QB Chris Relf (13-20/288y, 3 TDs, INT, and 12/66y rushing) got things rolling with 71y run and followed with TD passes of 15, 33, and 36y. On receiving end of latter 2 scores was swift frosh RB LaDarius Perkins (13/98y, and 3/140y, 2 TDs receiving). Rebels trailed 31-9 when they finally came alive in 4th Q. His run attack all but shuttered, Ole Miss QB Jeremiah Masoli (24-44/261y, TD, INT) turned to air, and while he suffered INT in middle of 4th Q, he 1st hit 5-5/57y to set up RB Brandon Bolden for 10y TD run and later completed 5-8/65y, including 24y TD pass. Victory represented Bulldogs' 1st win in Oxford in 12 years.

Michigan State 28 PENN STATE 22: Michigan State (11-1) wrapped up regular season with share of its 1st Big 10 crown since 1990. Spartans won in Happy Valley for 1st time since 1965, year before Joe Paterno took over as Nittany Lions head coach. But, Penn State (7-5) put up fight in last season-ending Land Grant Trophy game, which had been established for nation's 2 original land-grant colleges when Lions joined Big 10 in 1993. Spartans built 21-3 lead by end of 3rd Q as RB Edwin Baker rushed for 188y and scored 1st Q TD at left pylon, and QB Kirk Cousins (17-22/152y, 2 TDs) hooked up with WR B.J. Cunningham for pair of TD passes in middle Qs. Penn State finally stopped taking uncharacteristic PENs long enough for QB Matt McGloin (23-43/312y, 2 TDs, INT) to click on TD passes to FB Joe Suhey and WR Derek Moye. In between, RB Evan Royster (14/85y, TD) ran for 10y TD, but it wasn't enough as Spartans TE Charlie Gantt also fit in his own 4th Q TD catch.

OHIO STATE 37 Michigan 7: Buckeyes (11-1) trotted out in scarlet helmets and jerseys with white swirl-shaped, drop-shadowed numerals to replicate 1942 national championship look. Ohio State didn't match 1942's 21-7 victory over Michigan; it more than doubled it in winning its 7th straight over rival Wolverines (7-5). After WR Dane Sanzenbacher caught short TD pass from QB Terrelle Pryor (18-27/220y, 2 TDs, INT) for 10-0 Buckeyes lead in 2nd Q, Michigan managed 80y trip to RB Michael Shaw's 1y TD run. Back in it at 10-7, Wolverines kicked off, only to see RB Jordan Hall roar 85y for TD, and WR DeVier Posey soon took crossing-pattern pass to 33y TD for 24-7 H lead to all but seal verdict for Ohio State. Bothered by injured non-throwing hand, Michigan QB Denard Robinson (8-18/107y) was held to 192y total O. Michigan's mode all year had been thrilling O, but in 2nd H, with little time from Robinson, it was limited to 93y O. Ohio State sub CB Travis Howard finished with INT and 2 FUM RECs.

Indiana 34 PURDUE 31 (OT): Behind record-setting show by QB Ben Chappell (31-50/330y, 3 TDs), Indiana (5-7) broke 12-game Big 10 losing streak and beat in-state rival Purdue (4-8) in West Lafayette for 1st time since 1996. Chappell broke school record for passing y in single season with 3295y and connected with WR Tandon Doss (8/64y, 3 TDs) for 3 scores. Chappell, however, missed 3rd down pass with 4:19 left, and Boilermakers appeared in position to force punt and hold on at 31-28. But on that play, Purdue was flagged for pass interference, and Chappell sparked 14-play drive capped by K Mitch Ewald's tying 26y FG with 9 secs left in regulation. Purdue QB Rob Henry (16-30/252y, 3 TDs, INT), whose scoring passes had built 7-0, 14-7, and 28-21 leads, was intercepted by Hoosiers LB Jeff Thomas in OT, and Ewald won it with 31y 3-ptr, even though Chappell and RB Trea Burgess nearly blew it by fumbling handoff.

MINNESOTA 27 Iowa 24: Tied for Big 10 lead just 3 weeks ago, fading Hawkeyes (7-5) dropped their 3rd straight contest, 5th occasion this season they permitted foe to score winning pts in last 5 mins of game. Golden Gophers (3-9), having upset Illinois 2 weeks prior, returned injured sr line-starters, LT Dominic Alford and RG Matt Carufel, in off-week and sprung surprising ground strength (216y) on Iowa's 6th-best national run D. Minnesota RB DeLeon Eskridge rushed for 95y and tallied 2nd Q TD that provided 17-7 edge. Iowa rallied before H to narrow it to 20-17, primarily because WR Derrell Johnson-Koulianos topped his short TD catch with 88y with KO TD RET. When QB Ricky Stanzi (10-22/127y, 2 TDs) hit WR Marvin McNutt with 18y TD pass with 11:35 to play, Hawks enjoyed their 1st lead at 24-20. Minnesota responded with winning TD run by RB Duane Bennett (11/63y, TD) on 3-min, 77y march that included 19y catch and 6y power run on 3rd-and-4 to Iowa 6YL by WR-RB-QB MarQueis Gray.

Oklahoma 47 OKLAHOMA STATE 41: Oklahoma State (10-2) and Texas A&M still held hope, but with Big 12 South pinning its title criteria on BCS standings for 2nd time in 3 years Oklahoma (10-2) would likely advance because it survived wild ending as teams combined for nearly 400y O and 40 pts in 4th Q that opened as 24-24 tie. OU QB Landry Jones (37-62/468y, 4 TDs, 3 INTs) pitched pair of clutch, long-distance TD passes 29 secs apart: WR Cameron Kenney went cross-field and down left sideline for 86y TD for 40-31 lead, and after Cowboys DB Justin Gilbert interjected 89y KO TD RET, TE James Hanna barreled 76y for Sooners TD and 47-38 edge. Oklahoma State QB Brandon Weeden (28-43/257y, 2 TDs, 3 INTs) had knotted it 24-24 with TD pass to SB Josh Cooper (10/84y, TD) early in 3rd Q and pulled Cowpokes within 33-31 with 4:06 to play when he found star WR Justin Blackmon (8/105y, TD) for 15y TD.

Washington 16 CALIFORNIA 13: Disappointing season ended for Cal Bears (5-7) as soon-to-be-renovated, 87-year-old Memorial Stadium would be closed until its reopening in 2012. Cold and dreary conditions seemed to suit chill-accustomed Washington (5-6) as heavy rain fell in 2nd H after dull 1st H saw myriad of miscues and only score coming on California K Giorgio Tavecchio's 53y FG as clock expired. Bears never did find EZ on own power: DE Cameron Jordan scooped up FUM by Huskies QB Jake Locker (17-27/237y, TD, INT) and hustled it 21y for TD that gave Cal 10-7 lead in 3rd Q. Huskies K Erik Folk tied it with FG 3 mins later, which enhanced Locker's 80y TD pass earlier in 3rd Q. Tavecchio might have won it 13-10 with 47y FG early in 4th Q, but Locker hit 46y pass to diving WR Jermaine Kearse on key play of late 79y TD trip. Locker was halted on pair of last-min sneaks, so UW had to call timeout with 2 secs to organize for winning 1y TD plunge by TB Chris Polk (18/86y, TD).

Notre Dame 20 SOUTHERN CALIFORNIA 16: Notre Dame Fighting Irish (7-5) slashed 7-game losing streak to Trojans (7-5) as true-frosh QB Tommy Rees (20-32/149y, 2 TDs, 3 INTs) stayed undefeated in his 3 starts to date. Southern California earned its 16 pts off TOs—all in ND end—by Rees, including 1y TD sneak in 3rd Q by QB Mitch Mustain (20-37/177y, INT), who was making his 1st start since 2006 when he led Arkansas to 8-0 record as highly-touted frosh. Mustain's 4th down score tied game at 13-13, and K Joe Houston gave Trojans 16-13 lead with 37y FG—his 3rd 3-ptr—with 6:25 to play after S Marshall Jones' INT of Rees at Notre Dame 38YL. Irish TB Cierre Wood's 26y run keyed 77y drive, with TB Robert Hughes powering up middle for go-ahead 5y TDrun with 2:23 left. USC's last chance was ruined by certain TD pass-drop by WR Ronald Johnson and game-saving INT at 1YL by ND S Harrison Smith, who read Mustain's eyes and dropped off coverage to make secure catch.

1 Oregon (46)	1459	14 Missouri	666
2 Auburn (10)	1419	15 Oklahoma State	661
3 Texas Christian (3)	1343	16 South Carolina	626
4 Wisconsin	1282	17 Nevada	621
5 Stanford	1233	18 Texas A&M	503
6 Ohio State	1213	19 Alabama	501
7 Michigan State	1083	20 Florida State	353
8 Arkansas	1012	21 Utah	291
9 Oklahoma	943	22 Mississippi State	223
10 Boise State	869	23 Northern Illinois	130
11 Virginia Tech	843	24 West Virginia	110
12 Louisiana State	796	25 Central Florida	62
13 Nebraska	773		

Bowl Championship Series Rankings November 28, 2010

	Harris Poll Avg.	USA TODAY Poll Avg.	Computer Pct.	BCS Avg.
1 Auburn (12-0)	.9716	.9620	1.000	.9779
2 Oregon (11-0)	.9839	.9892	.960	.9777
3 Texas Christian (12-0)	.9196	.9105	.920	.9167
4 Stanford (11-1)	.8481	.8359	.840	.8413
5 Wisconsin (11-1)	.8565	.8692	.730	.8185

December 4, 2010

(Th) Arizona State 30 ARIZONA 29 (OT): Arizona (7-5) failed not once but twice on most automatic play in football on cool, late desert night. Wildcats K Alex Zendejas couldn't launch his x-pts sufficiently high—including kick that would have won game—to avoid leaping blocks by 6'5" Sun Devils (6-6) DE James Brooks, who moved into MLB position to defend kicks. Thanks to WR Juron Criner's 2 long-range TD catches from QB Nick Foles (22-36/262y, 3 TDs), Wildcats enjoyed 14-6 lead going into 4th Q. Arizona State QB Brock Osweiler (22-49/267y, TD) led rally with passes for TD and 2-pt, and when scholar award-winning K Thomas Weber hit 40y 3-ptr, his 4th of 5 FGs, with 2:59 to go, ASU led 20-14. Foles quickly hit 7-9/60y to his 3rd TD pass, but x-pt was blocked by Brooks. Devils led 30-23 in 2nd OT after RB Cameron Marshall's TD run, but again Brooks spoiled what would have been Zendejas' tying kick. It had been frustrating season for Arizona State, and LB Brandon Magee summed it up well: "I'm not a sissy, but I'm not going to lie, I cried a little bit. It is the best feeling ever."

Connecticut 19 SOUTH FLORIDA 16: By virtue of its last-moment victory on wings of 52y FG by K Dave Teggart, Connecticut (8-4) clinched Big East tri-championship and, due to its wins over West Virginia and Pittsburgh, was headed to BCS bowl game. No sooner had UConn QB Zach Frazier (13-29/112y, INT) been picked off at midfield with 1:22 left in 2nd Q when South Florida (7-5) frosh QB Bobby Eveld (22-41/195y TD, 3 INTs) was intercepted by Huskies LB Lawrence Wilson, who raced 55y to score for 10-3 H edge. Teggart provided 16-6 lead early in 4th Q with 50y FG, but Huskies lost FUM at their 30YL with 9 mins to play. After Eveld's 28y TD pass and K Maiko Bonani's tying FG, UConn had 1:16 to position Teggart for his game-winner with 17 secs to go.

Virginia Tech 44 Florida State 33 (Charlotte): Not since Maryland in 1984 had ACC team lost its opening 2 games of season and come back to take conf crown. By winning ACC Championship Game, Virginia Tech (11-2) won its 11th straight and matched Maryland's 26-year-old achievement. Young Florida State (9-4) QB E.J. Manuel (23-31/288y, TD, 2 INTs), in for sore-elbowed vet QB Christian Ponder, had 1st Q pass tipped and LB Jeron Gouveia-Winslow take it 24y to TD and 7-3 edge for Hokies. Virginia Tech QB Tyrod Taylor (18-28/263y 3 TDs) hit trio of TDs in middle Qs, including 45y pick to quick WR Danny Coale (6/143y, TD), who streaked alone down left sideline. By time Taylor's nifty scramble produced 5y TD run, Hokies had built ample 41-24 lead early in 4th Q.

Auburn 56 South Carolina 17 (Atlanta): In no way did dynamic Auburn Tigers (13-0) suffer letdown in SEC championship game against team they had already defeated. Comeback-disposed Tigers stepped out of character by not permitting South Carolina (9-4) ever to own lead, although Gamecocks knotted it 7-7 in 1st Q when FB Patrick DiMarco caught 25y TD pass from QB Stephen Garcia (16-28/170y, 2 TDs, 2 INTs). Accounting for 6 of his Tigers' 8 TDs, superb QB Cam Newton (17-28/335y, 4 TDs, and 14/73y, 2 TDs rushing) led way and spoke to media afterward for 1st time in month. Stating he had done nothing wrong, Newton asked media not to ask about his father's attempt to get money for Cam's possible transfer from JC to Mississippi State. Auburn led 21-7 at end of 1st Q and 28-14 at H. It was locked up when heavily-pressured Garcia attempted to flip away screen pass, and it wound up in hands of Auburn CB T'Sharvan Bell, who made 10y TD RET for 42-14 lead midway through 3rd Q. After Newton's last run—defining effort in which he faked tackler and jumped over another—he flipped ball to official, inadvertently knocked off his cap. Smiling Newton scooped up hat, placed it on official's head and gave him pat on backside. Newton joined former Florida great Tim Tebow as only FBS players with 20+ rushing and 20+ passing TDs in same season, although Nevada's Colin Kaepernick would join their lofty ranks by scoring 3 TDs on this same Saturday in 35-17 win over Louisiana Tech.

Oklahoma 23 Nebraska 20 (Arlington, Tex.): Sooners (11-2) fashioned 2nd-largest comeback in Big 12 Championship Game history and sent Nebraska (10-3) off packing to Big 10 with bitter memories from this 86th and conceivably last confrontation between old rivals. RB Roy Helu (11/91y, TD) burst up middle for 66y TD run, A-A K Alex Henery toed 53y FG for Big 12 title game long-distance record, and RB Rex Burkhead (16/90y) flipped 5y TD pass to TE Kyler Reed out of Wildcat formation, so Cornhuskers enjoyed 17-0 lead early in 2nd Q. Oklahoma answered on 49y TD pitch from QB Landry Jones (23-41/342y, TD, INT) to WR Kenny Stills, and LB Travis Lewis came up with EZ INT to set up FG and soon scooped up Helu's FUM to set up Jones'

short TD run 58 secs apart. But, Henery's 42y FG in last min of 1st H put Nebraska up 20-17 at H. OU K Jimmy Stevens kicked FG in 3rd Q to knot it again at 20-20. When Burkhead and Helu disconnected on handoff early in 4th Q, Lewis came up with another big play: FUM REC at his 35YL. It set up Stevens' winning FG with 8:28 left.

Oregon 37 OREGON STATE 20: Winning its in-state Civil War for 3rd straight season, Oregon (12-0) made 2 rigid D stands, keyed by DT Brandon Bair and LB Casey Matthews, at its 2YL late in 3rd Q and its 5YL early in 4th Q. Even though Oregon State (5-7) K Justin Kahut kicked short FGs each time, Ducks were able to maintain control at 23-10 and 23-13 until RBs LaMichael James (28/134y, 2 TDs) and Kenjon Barner (15/133y, 2 TDs) each made their 2nd TD run to put it away at 37-13. Beavers had struck 1st on 6y TD reception by RB Jacquizz Rodgers (22/87y). Leading 16-7, Oregon gambled on 4th down deep in its territory as special-teamer Michael Clay, up-back in punt-formation, took snap and charged 64y up middle to set up 19y screen pass from QB Darron Thomas (14-24/145y, 2 TDs) to WR D.J. Davis.

1 Oregon (34)	1450	14 Missouri	712
2 Auburn (24)	1437	15 Nevada	640
3 Texas Christian (1)	1348	16 Nebraska	607
4 Wisconsin	1276	17 Texas A&M	542
5 Stanford	1239	18 Alabama	521
6 Ohio State	1200	19 Utah	375
7 Michigan State	1104	20 South Carolina	345
8t Arkansas	1008	21 West Virginia	261
8t Oklahoma	1008	22 Mississippi State	255
10 Boise State	914	23 Florida State	156
11 Virginia Tech	900	24 Central Florida	143
12 Louisiana State	826	25 Hawaii	98
13 Oklahoma State	718		

Bowl Championship Series Rankings December 5, 2010

	Harris Poll Avg.	USA TODAY Poll Avg.	Computer Pct.	BCS Avg.
1 Auburn (13-0)	.9856	.9742	1.000	.9866
2 Oregon (12-0)	.9730	.9831	.960	.9720
3 Texas Christian (12-0)	.9168	.9139	.900	.9102
4 Stanford (11-1)	.8495	.8400	.820	.8365
5 Wisconsin (11-1)	.8572	.8651	.690	.8041

December 11, 2010

Navy 31 Army 17 (Philadelphia): With Army Black Knights (6-6) D pressing line of scrimmage, Navy (9-3) QB Ricky Dobbs (6-11/186y, 2 TDs, INT, and 20/54y rushing) came out throwing, connecting on 31y pass to SB Aaron Santiago to set up early FG and TDs of 77y to SB John Howell and 32y to WR Brandon Turner by early in 2nd Q. Trailing 17-0 and without single 1st down so far, Army was boosted by FUM REC by DE Josh McNary at Middies 23YL midway in 2nd Q. Cadets QB Trent Steelman (11-20/123y, 2 TDs, and 19/74y rushing) tossed 5y TD to SB Malcolm Brown for Army's 1st TD vs. Navy since 2006. McNary soon forced another FUM at midfield, and Army with 1st-and-goal at 3YL appeared ready to cut deficit to 17-14. Steelman ran off right side, ball came loose, and rolled up his arm where Middies DB Wyatt Middleton snatched it and stunningly rambled 98y to TD and 24-7 H edge. SB Gee Gee Greene iced it at 31-10 with well-blocked 25y burst with less than 6 mins left. Fighting to end, Army nearly doubled Navy's O y in 2nd H to little avail.

2010 Conference Standings

Big East

Connecticut (a)	5-2
West Virginia (a)	5-2
Pittsburgh (a)	5-2
Syracuse	4-3
South Florida	3-4
Louisville	3-4
Cincinnati	2-5
Rutgers	1-6

Atlantic Coast

ATLANTIC	
Florida State	6-2
Maryland	5-3
North Carolina State	5-3
Boston College	4-4
Clemson	4-4
Wake Forest	1-7
COASTAL	
Virginia Tech	8-0
Miami	5-3
Georgia Tech	4-4
North Carolina	4-4
Duke	1-7
Virginia	1-7

(a)Connecticut was crowned Big East champion by virtue of victories over West Virginia and Pittsburgh.

Southeastern

EAST

South Carolina	5-3
Florida	4-4
Georgia	3-5
Tennessee	3-5
Kentucky	2-6
Vanderbilt	1-7

WEST

Auburn	8-0
Arkansas	6-2
Louisiana State	6-2
Alabama	5-3
Mississippi State	4-4
Mississippi	1-7

Conference USA

EAST

Central Florida	7-1
East Carolina	5-3
Southern Mississippi	5-3
Marshall	4-4
Alabama-Birmingham	3-5
Memphis	0-8

WEST

So. Methodist (a)	6-2
Tulsa (a)	6-2
Houston	4-4
Texas-El Paso	4-4
Rice	3-5
Tulane	2-6

(a) Southern Methodist advanced to Conference USA championship game by defeating Tulsa 21-18 on October 9.

Big Ten

Wisconsin	7-1
Ohio State	7-1
Michigan State	7-1
Iowa	4-4
Illinois	4-4
Penn State	4-4
Michigan	3-5
Northwestern	3-5
Purdue	2-6
Minnesota	2-6
Indiana	1-7

Mid-American

EAST

Miami (Ohio)	7-1
Ohio University	6-2
Temple	5-3
Kent State	4-4
Buffalo	1-7
Bowling Green	1-7
Akron	1-7

WEST

Northern Illinois	8-0
Toledo	7-1
Western Michigan	5-3
Ball State	3-5
Central Michigan	2-6
Eastern Michigan	2-6

Big Twelve

NORTH

Nebraska (a)	6-2
Missouri (a)	6-2
Kansas State	3-5
Iowa State	3-5
Colorado	2-6
Kansas	1-7

SOUTH

Oklahoma (b)	6-2
Oklahoma State (b)	6-2
Texas A&M (b)	6-2
Texas Tech	4-4
Baylor	4-4
Texas	2-6

(a) Nebraska advanced to Big 12 conference championship game by defeating Missouri 31-17 on October 30.
(b) Oklahoma advanced to Big 12 conference championship game by virtue of highest ranking in BCS Standing.

Mountain West

Texas Christian	8-0
Utah	7-1
San Diego State	5-3
Air Force	5-3
Brigham Young	5-3
Colorado State	2-6
Nevada-Las Vegas	2-6
New Mexico	1-7
Wyoming	1-7

Western Athletic

Nevada	7-1
Boise State	7-1
Hawaii	7-1
Fresno State	5-3
Louisiana Tech	4-4
Idaho	3-5
Utah State	2-6
New Mexico State	1-7
San Jose State	0-8

Pacific-10

Oregon	9-0
Stanford	8-1
Washington	5-4
Southern California	5-4
Oregon State	4-5
Arizona State	4-5
Arizona	4-5
California	3-6
UCLA	2-7
Washington State	1-8

2010 Major Bowl Games

Las Vegas Bowl (Dec. 22): Boise State 26 Utah 3

Utah's big D-line was having its way in early going against heavily-favored Boise State (12-1) as Broncos suffered pair of FUMs, INT, and surprise 4th down pass dropped by K Kyle Brotzman, whose short FG misses in November vs. Nevada cost his school likely BCS Bowl. Utah (10-3) could convert only K Joe Phillips' 44y FG late in 1st Q. Midway in 2nd Q, Boise burst out of its doldrums when RB Doug Martin (17/147y, TD) zipped 84y to score. Brotzman made 2nd Q FG to become all-time FBS career scoring leader with 435 pts. QB Kellen Moore, fresh from his trip to Heisman Trophy ceremony, settled down to pitch 28-38/339y, 2 TDs, INT and lead Broncos to 543y O. Utes were limited to 200y O as QB Terrance Cain could hit only 10-24/93y passing.

Independence Bowl (Dec. 27): Air Force 14 Georgia Tech 7

Pre-game demonstration went amiss, and Air Force Falcons (9-4) briefly lost their live mascot when bird-of-prey swooped out of stadium toward downtown Shreveport. Georgia Tech (6-7), trying to avoid 1st losing season since 1996, outgained stubborn Air Force but bobbled away 2nd H chances with 4 TOs in match-up of nation's pair of top rushing teams. FB Anthony Allen (23/91y, TD) burst up middle for 5y TD late in 1st Q to give Georgia Tech 7-3 lead. Air Force missed trio of 4th down attempts in 1st H, but back-up K Zack Bell made his 2nd FG on last play to pull Falcons within 7-6 at H. Subbing for injured star QB Joshua Nesbitt, QB Tevin Washington (5-13/41y, INT, and 28/131y rushing) sparked Yellow Jackets to 75y drive to open 2nd H but lost FUM at 5YL. On last play of 3rd Q, Georgia Tech WR Daniel McKayhan muffed punt at his 14YL to set up Falcons FB Jared Tew for go-ahead 3y TD run, followed by 2-pt conv. Washington rallied Georgia Tech in dying moments, but his pass for EZ was intercepted on great sideline catch by Air Force FS Jon Davis.

Champs Sports Bowl (Dec. 28): No. Carolina State 23 West Virginia 7

West Virginia (9-4) arrived with nation's 2nd-best scoring D but gave up most pts of its season when Mountaineers couldn't overcome 5 TOs. They also tallied their fewest pts since East Carolina held them to 3 pts early in 2008. North Carolina State (9-4) star QB Russell Wilson (28-45/275y, 2 TDs), who had to ponder pro baseball career in coming off-season, sparked unlikely 86y TD drive in 1st Q: WVU had allowed FBS-fewest 4 TD drives longer than 75y this season. Mountaineers briefly tied it 7-7 in 2nd Q when QB Geno Smith (22-39/196y, TD, INT) barely launched high 32y TD pass that WR Stedman Bailey soared over NC State DB David Amerson to snatch in EZ. K Josh Czajkowski kicked 3 medium-range FGs to put Wolfpack up by 16-7 by end of 3rd Q.

Insight Bowl (Dec. 28): Iowa 27 Missouri 24

In perhaps season's best bowl game, Hawkeyes (8-5), depleted by injuries and suspensions, steadily ground out early lead. On game's opening possession, sr QB Ricky Stanzi (11-21/200y, 2 INTs) hit WR Marvin McNutt for 49y to set up RB Marcus Coker (33/219y, 2 TDs), 4th string frosh at season's beginning, for short TD smash. Coker busted through big hole on right side and galloped 62y to TD early in 2nd Q, and Iowa soon led 17-3. Missouri Tigers (10-3) clawed back by having QB Blaine Gabbert (41-57/434y, TD, 2 INTs) pick apart Iowa D with endlessly successful crossing and dig routes. Gabbert, who hit 23-31/284y in 1st H, set up FG and RB Henry Josey's 10y TD run, so Mizzou trailed 20-10 at H. On consecutive marches of 77y and 57y in 3rd Q, Gabbert again picked apart Iowa secondary to lead to his 7y TD run and 3y TD pass to TE Michael Egnew. So, Tigers had their 1st lead at 24-20. With momentum on their side, they appeared ready to lock it up. But, Gabbert by his own admission "got greedy" with less than 6 mins to play: From Hawkeyes 29YL, he rolled left and tried to force short pass to WR Wes Kemp (7/61y). Iowa CB Micah Hyde was in way and took INT all way across field as 3 Tigers got paw on him and headed down left sideline for winning 72y TD RET. Missouri WR T.J. Moe caught 15/152y but his diving try couldn't hold last-gasp 4th down pass in Iowa territory in late going.

Texas Bowl (Dec. 29): Illinois 38 Baylor 14

MVP RB Mikel Leshoure (29/184y, 3 TDs) set Fighting Illini season records for rushing (1697y) and TDs (20). Baylor (7-6) QB Robert Griffin (30-41/306y, TD) fumbled in 1st Q, and Illinois (7-6) SS Travon Bellamy took it 44y to set up 1st of 3 straight FGs by K Derek Dimke. Leshoure's 1st score sent Illinois off at H up 16-0, and his next tally at end of 87y drive that opened 2nd H made it 24-0. Griffin hit 5 passes to poise RB Jay Finley for 5y TD sweep, and early in 4th Q, Griffin found WR Kendall Wright (12/127y, TD) for diving 39y grab at GL to trim Baylor's deficit to 24-14. That was as close as Bears could come: Leshoure scored again, and Illini QB Nathan Scheelhaase (18-23/242y) iced cake with 55y TD run for coach Ron Zook's 1st bowl win in 4 tries.

Alamo Bowl: Oklahoma State 36 Arizona 10

Oklahoma State (11-2), which set school mark for wins, scored TDs 1st 2 times it had ball, including 71y pass on which Biletnikoff Award-winning WR Justin Blackmon (9/117y, 2 TDs) somehow snuck 20y into clear. In between those scores, Arizona (7-6) wasted 64y KO RET by WR Travis Cobb by failing on 4th down at OSU 29YL. Wildcats worked its way into Cowboys territory 6 times in 1st H but resulted in just single TD: 5y TD pass from QB Nick Foles (32-50/280y, TD, 3 INTs), who was making homecoming to San Antonio, to WR Juron Criner. Oklahoma State DB Markelle Martin cut off Foles' out-pattern pass in 2nd Q and fled 62y down left sideline for 23-7 H edge. Blackmon would catch 3rd Q TD pass from QB Brandon Weeden (25-41/240y, 2 TDs) to clinch verdict at 30-10 and finish year tops in nation in 3 categories: 111 catches/1782y and 20 TDs. Arizona closed its season with 5 straight defeats.

Armed Forces Bowl (Dec. 30): Army 16 Southern Methodist 14

Army (7-6) hadn't won bowl game since 1985 and was without winning season since 1996. Black Knights started fast as LB Zach Watts forced FUM that sr DE Josh McNary picked up and scrambled 55y to TD. Army SB Malcolm Brown took pitchout for 13y TD run 8 mins later, but x-pt was blocked by 6-foot-8 SMU DE Margus Hunt, world-class shot put and discus thrower. Cadets K Alex Carlton added 44y FG in 2nd Q for 16-0 H lead. Mustangs (7-7) came out as new team in 2nd H as QB Kyle Patron (23-34/302y, 2 TDs, 2 INTs) pitched TDs to WR Aldrick Robinson and Darius Johnson. SMU K Matt Szymanski missed 47y FG with 4 mins left, and Army QB Trent Steelman converted pair of 3rd downs with run and pass to kill clock. Mustangs had inherited bowl game in own stadium when TCU's Carter Amon Field was undergoing renovation. SMU seemed oddly deferential, dressing out in black jerseys and encouraging its fans to wear black to honor Army and the U.S. military. Afterward coach June Jones talked about next year's "swagger" in his young team, while Army coach Rich Ellerson lauded his soldiers: "They've brought something back to West Point that has been absent. It will flourish there because of the culture these guys have created."

Pinstripe Bowl (Dec. 30): Syracuse 36 Kansas State 34

After blizzard 4 days earlier, massive piles of snow had to be removed from Yankee Stadium turf to prepare for inaugural New Era Pinstripe Bowl. Kansas State (7-6) star RB Daniel Thomas (22/90y, 3 TDs) roared for 51y TD run on game's 2nd snap, and trade of TDs was on. Underutilized-to-date Syracuse (8-5) WR Marcus Sales (5/172y, 3 TDs) exploded for 3 long TD catches, including flea-flicker with 3 mins left in 1st Q,

as QB Ryan Nassib (13-21/239y, 3 TDs) scrambled sufficiently to launch his bombs to Sales. Yet, Orange's O key was RB Delone Carter, who rambled for 198y on 27 carries and pair of TDs. When Thomas tallied his 3rd TD early in 4th Q, Wildcats took lead 28-27 because Syracuse K Ross Krautman had pushed x-pt wide late in 3rd Q. Sales hauled in his 3rd TD catch, and Krautman tacked on 39y FG for 36-28 Orange edge with 3:08 to go. K-State soon passed up FG try and was stopped on fake-FG run. Still, Cats WR Adrian Hilburn (5/84y, TD) broke tackle and sped down right sideline for 30y TD with 1:13 to play. In his excitement, Hilburn lifted his right hand and saluted crowd. His action was ruled excessive, even though other similar acts had been overlooked, and Kansas State's 2-pt pass for tie from 17YL flew too high.

Music City Bowl (Dec. 30): North Carolina 30 Tennessee 27 (OT)

Tennessee's young squad must have had its fill of premature victory celebrations this season. This was 2nd win snatched by fate from Volunteers (6-7) just when it seemed certain they had persevered at end. After frosh QB Tyler Bray (27-45/312y, 4 TDs, 3 INTs) threw his 3rd TD pass with 5:16 to play for 20-17 lead, Tennessee appeared to have won it, despite having had K Daniel Lincoln's x-pt blocked, when confused North Carolina (8-5) had several would-be FG-teamers rushing off field as QB T.J. Yates (23-39/234y, TD, INT) struggled to beat clock with spiked pass at end of regulation. Officials ruled game over, but when replay was reviewed, it was determined Yates had beaten clock by 1 sec. Carolina was assessed 5y PEN instead of possible 15y too-many-participants PEN. Tar Heels K Casey Barth tied it 20-20 with 39y FG, then won it in 2nd OT with 23y FG. "The referee says it's over, and they go back and review it, and it is not. It is tough to deal with," said Tennessee sr TE Luke Stocker, who had nabbed Bray's 4th TD pass in 1st OT to preserve 27-27 tie.

Holiday Bowl (Dec. 30): Washington 19 Nebraska 7

San Diego saw its coldest Bridgepoint Education Holiday Bowl ever at 48 degrees. Washington (7-6), 35-pt losers to Cornhuskers (10-4) back in September, had mental advantage over frustrated Nebraska, losers of 2 of last 3 games. "We whupped a team that didn't respect us," said Huskies TB Chris Polk, who was key to O with 34/177y rushing and 1st Q TD. QB Jake Locker (5-16/56y), who had dreadful passing day against Nebraska in early-season, wasn't much better but plowed through several tacklers for critical 25y TD run that provided 17-7 3rd Q lead. Locker, who returned for sr year for this very kind of program-reviving win, left game briefly in 1st H with head injury that turned out to be less serious than feared. With QB Taylor Martinez (7-9/53y, TD, INT) still hobbled by leg injuries, Nebraska failed to spark its run attack and was held to 189y total O. Huskers' only score came on TE Kyler Reed's 15y catch from Martinez in 2nd Q.

Car Care Bowl (Dec. 31): South Florida 31 Clemson 26

QB B.J. Daniels (20-27/189y, 2 TDs, INT) sparked South Florida (8-5) to 5th straight season of 8 or more wins by pitching 2 scores and tallying another on ground. Bulls WR Dontavia Bogan broke tackle to prance to 15y TD reception midway in 2nd Q for 17-3 lead. Striving for comeback in last min of 2nd Q, Clemson (6-7) saw its chances all but evaporate when QB Kyle Parker (11-21/134y, INT) had his ribs broken on option surge for EZ. Even though Tigers big TB Jamie Harper (20/34y, TD) scored on next play, Daniels' 8y TD run for Bulls early in 4th Q created 31-13 bulge that even Clemson sub QB Tajh Boyd's pair of late TD passes couldn't overcome.

Sun Bowl (Dec. 31): Notre Dame 33 Miami 17

In El Paso, there wasn't quite same frenzy of 1988's "Catholics vs. Convicts" win that vaulted Notre Dame (8-5) to that year's national title. Far less was on line in rematch of former titans. Fighting Irish started fast as QB Tommy Rees (15-29/201y, 2 TDs) twice hit WR Michael Floyd (6/109y, 2 TDs) for scores in 1st Q. Cold weather couldn't have helped tropical Hurricanes (7-6); many of taller Canes looked like giraffes with long-necked, white hoods tugged up into their helmets. Lanky Miami frosh QB Stephen Morris (22-33/282y, 2 TDs, INT) came off bench to connect on 4th Q TD passes to WRs Leonard Hankerson and Tommy Streeter. But it was too late as ND led 30-3 after 3 Qs.

Chick-fil-A Bowl (Dec. 31): Florida State 26 South Carolina 17

Pair of O stars went out as result of big hits: South Carolina RB Marcus Lattimore, who fumbled flank pass when walloped by CB Greg Reid and Seminoles (10-4) QB Christian Ponder (1-5/6y), who was plastered in trying for TD on 3rd down scramble, threw weak pass on 4th down to turn it over. Florida State RB Chris Thompson (25/147y, TD) highlighted 1st H with 27y TD run, but Gamecocks (9-5) rallied in late 3rd Q and early 4th Q with neat flanker-screen to WR Ace Sanders, who threw to right EZ corner for TD to QB Stephen Garcia (19-34/243y, 3 INTs), and TD run by RB Brian Maddox, who spelled Lattimore. In end, keys were Gamecocks' 5 TOs and Ponder's replacement, QB E.J. Manuel (11-15/84y, TD), who hit 7-7/50y on clinching 4th Q drive.

Outback Bowl: Florida 37 Penn State 24

Departing coach Urban Meyer retired from Florida (8-5) with his 65th victory in 6 seasons, thanks to 2nd H surge. Penn State (7-6) was competitive for most of game, leading 1st 3 Qs at 7-0, 17-14, and 24-20. Nittany Lions QB Matt McGloin (17-41/211y, TD, 5 INTs) turned early INT by CB D'Anton Lynn into 5y TD pass to WR Derek Moye (5/79y, TD) and scored on 2y sprint to right pylon in 3rd Q. But, McGloin's 5 INTs ended up killing Lions. INTs set up Gators WR Omarius Hines' 16y wide TD run in 2nd Q and RB Mike Gilleslee's 1y TD run early in 4th Q. Plus, Florida WR Solomon Patton

blocked punt that turned into 27y TD RET by DE Lerentee McCray in 2nd Q. With Penn State behind 30-24 and having moved 54y in closing mins, Florida SS Ahmad Black cut in front of receiver and took INT RET 80y down left sideline to clinching TD.

Capital One: Alabama 49 Michigan State 7

Crimson Tide (10-3) TB Mark Ingram helped crush Michigan State (11-2), his father's alma mater and team he cheered for as kid. Alabama tallied TDs on its 1st 5 possessions, leading 35-0 3 mins into 3rd Q. Ingram (12/59y, 2 TDs) scored on 1 and 6y runs in 1st H, QB Greg McElroy (13-17/220y, TD) pitched 37y TD pass to WR Marquis Maze, and back-up TB Eddie Lacy (5/86y, 2 TDs) sped 12 and 62y for 2nd H TDs. Michigan State fell to 0-4 in bowl games under coach Mark Dantonio and was held to 171y O. Spartans WR Bennie Folwer caught 45y TD pass from QB Keith Nicol.

TicketCity Dallas Classic Bowl: Texas Tech 45 Northwestern 38

Northwestern (7-6) had permitted 118 pts in its last 2 games, and Red Raiders (8-5) had scored 99 pts in its 2 closing wins, so it was unsurprisingly that shootout occurred in Dallas. Texas Tech started well, building H lead of 24-6 behind QB Taylor Potts (43-56/369y, 4 TDs, INT). When RB Eric Stephens (14/126y, TD) raced 86y up middle on fake flanker-screen in 3rd Q, Raiders led 31-9. Wildcats, playing without injured QB Dan Persa, alternated frosh QBs Evan Watkins (10-21/76y, TD, INT) and Kain Colter (18/105y, 2 TDs rushing) and even switched throughout game to option O. Aided by foolish on-side KO by Texas Tech, Northwestern fashioned comeback to 38-31. Texas Tech WR Lyle Leong (10/118y, 2 TDs) tagged left pylon with ball for 11y TD catch midway in 4th Q for 45-31 lead, and only 39y INT TD RET by Wildcats CB Jordan Maybin gave appearance of close final result.

Gator Bowl: Mississippi State 52 Michigan 14

Michigan's worst-ever bowl defeat hastened departure of coach Rich Rodriguez, who suffered through 3-year record of 15-22 which won no wins over Ohio State, Michigan State, or Penn State. Mississippi State (9-4), which just signed coach Dan Mullen to contract extension to shield him from Florida's job search, received top performance from QB Chris Relf (18-23/281y, 3 TDs, INT), who accounted for 4 TDs. Except for 2 punts and running out time at end of each H, Bulldogs scored on every possession against fading Michigan D. QB Denard Robinson (27-41/254y, 2 TDs, INT, and 11/59y rushing) started well, pacing Wolverines to 14-10 lead in 1st Q.

Rose Bowl: Texas Christian 21 Wisconsin 19

Heavy holiday rain in southern California cleared out in time for sunny New Year's in Pasadena. No. 4 Wisconsin (11-2), playing in front of smaller TV audience back home due to Rose Bowl being shown on ESPN cable instead of ABC network, got off to fine start. Badgers TB Montee Ball (22/132y, TD) rambled for 40y on game's 1st snap, and he followed with 9 and 5y runs before Wisconsin had to settle for 30y FG by K Philip Welch. No. 3 Texas Christian (13-0) QB Andy Dalton (15-23/219y, TD, and 9/28y, TD rushing), on way to his 3rd bowl MVP, hit 3 passes to WR Jimmy Young (5/57y) before finding WR Bart Johnson for 23y TD. Teams traded TDs on next 2 possessions as big Wisconsin TB John Clay blasted across from 1YL and Dalton skipped around E for 4y TD run. So, TCU led high-flying 1st Q by 14-10. Badgers took over with more than 6 mins left in 1st H and ran 14 plays, including 11y fake-punt 4th down run by P Brad Nortman, but without ever calling TO on threat that seemed to dwindle away. They had to settle for Welch's 2nd FG as H ended 14-13. TCU opened 3rd Q by going 71y, including Dalton's passes of 33 and 12y, to 1y TD wedge by FB Luke Shivers, who lined up as short-back. Trailing 21-13, Wisconsin sent Clay for 14 and 30y runs to start its last possession, and with 2 mins remaining, Ball powered off right side of Badgers big O-line for 4y TD. Wisconsin went for 2 pts, and TE Jacob Pederson was TE Jacob Pederson curled open at GL. But, TCU MLB Tank Carder, stopped effectively on blitz, ably jumped up to deflect pass by Wisconsin QB Scott Tolzien (12-21/159y). "We came up with a great tip, and it's like your life passes before your eyes," said happy Frogs coach Gary Patterson.

Fiesta Bowl: Oklahoma 48 Connecticut 20

Unranked Connecticut (8-5), which sold few tickets to Tostitos Fiesta Bowl 2600 miles from home, was in over its head against Oklahoma (12-2), team determined to make up for recent BCS bowl misadventures. Fast-paced Sooners O scored 1st on short pass from QB Landry Jones 34-49/429y, 3 TDs, INT) to TE James Hanna and added 1st Q 3y TD run by swiveling RB DeMarco Murray (25/93y, TD) just when he appeared hemmed in. Huskies depended on A-A RB Jordan Todman for 121y rushing and never gave up, scoring on their 5th INT TD RET of season: CB Dwayne Gratz's 46y RET in 2nd Q on overthrow by Jones. UConn trailed 20-10 at H but soon permitted Jones' 59y TD pass to WR Cameron Kenney and 55y INT TD RET by CB Jamell Fleming. Huskies answered with 95y TD KO RET by RB Robbie Frey, but it was over in 4th Q when OU WR Ryan Broyles (13/170y, TD) made it 41-20 with great TD catch.

Orange Bowl (Jan. 3): Stanford 40 Virginia Tech 12:

If any fans doubted NFL-ready skills of Stanford (12-1) QB Andrew Luck (18-23/287y, 4 TDs, INT), they got eyeful in Discover Orange Bowl. Luck decided few days later to return to Stanford for 2011 but 1st dismantled D of Virginia Tech (11-3) with 3 TD passes to TE Coby Fleener (6/173y, 3 TDs) in 27-pt 2nd H. It burst open 13-12 nail-biting lead after H. Remarkable about Stanford's play was its smash-mouth D, led by LBs Shayne Skov and Chase Thomas, as Hokies QB Tyrod Taylor (16-31/222y, TD, INT) was sacked 6 times. Taylor authored brilliant TD pass in 2nd Q when he rolled left, seemed to be cornered by LB Owen Marecic (TD run as FB), faked run, and twisted at sideline to square his feet for laser throw to left edge of EZ where RB David Wilson, suspended for 1st Q, made brilliant diving TD catch dragging toes at sideline.

Earlier, Hokies had earned safety when DT Antoine Hopkins swatted Luck's ill-advised pass backwards to where Cardinal OT Derek Hall caught it and was downed in his EZ. Cardinal sr RB Jeremy Stewart changed his injury-riddled season when he burst for 60y TD behind blocks of G David DeCastro and FB Marecic in 1st Q.

Sugar Bowl (Jan. 4): Ohio State 31 Arkansas 26

After disastrous New Year's Day when Big 10 teams went 0-5, conf hopes were pinned on Ohio State (12-1), which had its own issues. QB Terrelle Pryor (14-25/221y, 2 TDs, and 15/115y rushing) and 3 other O stars had been caught selling football awards and property. Instead of being suspended for Allstate Sugar Bowl, 5 tarnished jr Buckeyes had to commit to coach Jim Tressel to return for 2011 despite their looming suspension for opening 5 games. Most pundits figured Arkansas (10-3) might romp over gloomy Ohio, but instead inspired Buckeyes dominated 1st H, leading 28-10 and rolling up 338y O. Ohio State WR Dane Sanzenbacher (3/59y, TD) made hustling EZ FUM REC for TD and went low to catch TD from Pryor. Behind 31-13 late in 3rd Q, Razorbacks had backs to wall, but QB Ryan Mallett (24-47/244y, 2 TDs, INT) ignored half-dozen muffed passes by his receivers to drop perfect EZ pass into hands of WR Jarius Wright (4/70y, TD) and followed with 2-pt pass. From that moment, Ohio State did just about everything it could to blow its 31-21 lead: RB Boom Herron (24/87y, TD) was caught for safety making it 31-23, it permitted Hogs K Zach Hocher's 47y FG, Herron lost FUM which prevented his making 1st down on 4th-and-1 at Buckeyes 37YL, and allowed P Ben Buchanan's punt to be blocked at their 18YL with 1:09 to play. Soon on 2nd down, Ohio DE Solomon Thomas, 5th future suspended Buckeye, dropped into coverage and fooled Mallet into game-clinching INT. Ohio State DE Cameron Heyward played big role in disrupting Arkansas O to help end Buckeyes' 9-game bowl loss streak to SEC, but Hogs P Dylan Breeding was able to pin Ohio State 3 times inside its 5YL.

Cotton Bowl (Jan. 7): Louisiana State 41 Texas A&M 24

Unpredictable LSU (11-2) and QB Jordan Jefferson (10-19/158y, 3 TDs, INT) were like proverbial cute little girl; they were either very, very good or very, very bad. Hard-charging, confident Texas A&M (9-4) opened 75th AT&T Cotton Bowl with 69y KO RET by CB Coryell Judie, which led to 1st of 2 TD catches by WR Uzoma Nwachukwu. Judie soon made 1-handed INT near his GL to launch 76y drive to K Randy Bullock's FG, so Aggies led 10-0 in 50th meeting of old rivals. At this point, Jefferson turned very, very good and sparked Tigers to 4 TDs in next 5 possessions, so LSU led 28-17 at H. Texas A&M QB Ryan Tannehill (22-35/204y, 2 TDs, 3 INTs) had come in with 5-0 record after being switched from WR to QB in October to fuel Aggies' 6-game win streak to close regular season. After 127 attempts without INT, Tannehill's 3 INTs proved costly, especially Bengals S Eric Reid's pick-off, which he returned 34y to set up Jefferson's 2y TD pass 1:27 before H for 11-pt cushion. When LSU WR Terrence Toliver (5/112y, 3 TDs) hauled in his Cotton Bowl-record-tying 3rd TD catch in 3rd Q, Tigers had it all but wrapped up at 35-17, but consensus A-A K Josh Jasper tacked on 50y FG in 4th Q for Cotton-record for long distance.

BBVA Compass Bowl (Jan. 8): Pittsburgh 27 Kentucky 10

Coaching situation at Pitt was truly tumultuous. Dave Wannstadt had quit after disappointing regular season, and new head coach Mike Haywood barely had left Miami (Ohio) before being dumped after his arrest for domestic violence. So, D-coordinator Phil Bennett, on his way to new job at Baylor, was tapped to lead Panthers (8-5) in Birmingham. He enjoyed 13-3 1st H lead by Pitt after it fell behind 3-0 to 50y FG by Kentucky (6-7) K Craig McIntosh late in 1st Q. Panthers stopped 4th down play, recovered FUM by Wildcats QB Morgan Newton (21-36/211y), and, late in 2nd Q, S Andrew Taglianetti blocked punt that led to TD sneak by Pitt QB Tino Sunseri (9-19/96y, TD, INT, and 4/53y, TD rushing). Kentucky gambled in own territory early in 3rd Q and it backfired when Pitt S Kolby Gray sacked WR Matt Roark on fake-punt pass at 35YL. Sunseri found TE Brock DeCicco for 13y TD and 20-3 edge. Kentucky rallied late in 3rd Q as versatile WR Randall Cobb caught passes of 19, 5, and 8y and ran reverse 18y to set up short TD dive by FB Moncell Allen. Crushing blocks of Pitt FB Henry Hynoski led RB Dion Lewis (22/105y, TD) to clinching runs, including short TD, in 4th Q.

Game of the Year:
BCS National Championship (Jan. 10): Auburn 22 Oregon 19

Nervous start for both Os made for scoreless 1st Q, but Oregon Ducks (12-1) struck early in 2nd Q on 26y FG by K Rob Beard. That awoke QB Cam Newton (20-34/265y, 2 TDs, and 22/64y rushing), who whipped his Auburn Tigers (14-0) to 258y O in 2nd Q. Newton threw for TDs to WRs Kodi Burns for 35y and Emory Blake for 30y. In between, Ducks QB Darron Thomas (27-40/363y, 2 TDs, 2 INTs) launched long pass from his EZ, creating 81y gain with WR Jeff Maehl (9/133y) to Tigers 12YL. It led to Thomas' 8y misdirection TD pass to A-A RB LaMichael James (13/49y, and 4/39y, 2 TDs receiving). Auburn then launched 16-play drive that just missed another TD when Newton short-armed softly bounced pass to EZ on 4th down that looked like it might be easy score to open receiver. Oregon took over on downs at 1YL, but James was trapped for safety by DT Mike Blanc. That trimmed Tigers' deficit to 11-9. After free-kick, Tigers went 66y to Newton's 2nd TD throw. When Auburn opened 3rd Q with FG it led 19-11. Oregon P Jackson Rice shot-putted 4th down pass for 1st down at Tigers 46YL, and on next play TE Lavasier Tuinei speared 1-handed grab on crossing pattern, and he appeared gone for TD until DB Demetruce McNeal tripped him up at 3YL after 43y gain. Tackle saved TD because Auburn D-line, led by robust A-A DT Nick Fairley, held on 4th down at 1YL, so it remained 19-11. With 5 mins left, Oregon MLB Casey Matthews brilliantly swooped from behind to punch FUM away from Newton. Ducks covered 40y, Thomas converting 4th down pass to WR D.J. Davis for 29y until flipping 2y shovel pass to James for TD with 2:33 to play. Thomas made excellent catch of wide shotgun snap on vital 2-pt try, dashed to his right, and fired across his body to

Maehl, who cut left across back of EZ for catch that tied it 19-19. After Newton's 15y pass to Auburn 40YL, ball was given to frosh RB Michael Dyer (22/143y), who had been effective since entering game in 1st H. Dyer suddenly turned dynamic. Met and spun down after 6y gain, Dyer landed on tackler S Eddie Pleasant, his right knee coming within whisker of touching down. Everyone—including Dyer—stood around with no whistle being blown. Loudly urged to continue on by his nearby bench, Dyer lit out for 37y to Oregon 23YL. He nearly scored 3 plays later, dashing16y to within inches of GL with 10 secs to play. Sr K Wes Byrum split uprights with 6th winning FG of his career on game's last play. Critical to victory that ensured Auburn's 1st national championship since 1957, was run D, which limited Oregon to 75y after Ducks averaged 303.8y per game during 2010 regular season.

Final USA TODAY Coaches Poll, January 11, 2011

1 Auburn (56)	1424		14 Michigan State	676
2 Texas Christian (1)	1336		15 Virginia Tech	636
3 Oregon	1333		16 Florida State	506
4 Stanford	1254		17 Mississippi State	505
5 Ohio State	1197		18 Missouri	473
6 Oklahoma	1096		19 Nebraska	354
7 Boise State	1012		20 Central Florida	328
8 Louisiana State	1007		21 Texas A&M	277
8 Wisconsin	1007		22 South Carolina	181
10 Oklahoma State	883		23 Utah	156
11 Alabama	860		24 Maryland	111
12 Arkansas	818		25 North Carolina State	94
13 Nevada	734			

Final AP Poll, January 11, 2011

1 Auburn (56)	1472		14 Michigan State	696
2 Texas Christian (3)	1392		15 Mississippi State	578
3 Oregon	1379		16 Virginia Tech	577
4 Stanford	1300		17 Florida State	502
5 Ohio State	1220		18 Missouri	477
6 Oklahoma	1108		19 Texas A&M	359
7 Wisconsin	1055		20 Nebraska	334
8 Louisiana State	1051		21 Central Florida	225
9 Boise State	1031		22 South Carolina	169
10 Alabama	961		23 Maryland	144
11 Nevada	866		24 Tulsa	128
12 Arkansas	863		25 North Carolina State	119
13 Oklahoma State	833			

2010 Top Performance Formula

1 Auburn	1.7989
2 Texas Christian	1.7390
3 Ohio State	1.6989
4 Stanford	1.6586
5 Oregon	1.6412
6 Boise State	1.6336
7 Oklahoma	1.6222
8 Oklahoma State	1.5988
9 Louisiana State	1.5497
10 Alabama	1.5265
11 Arkansas	1.5025
12 Missouri	1.4809
13 Virginia Tech	1.4744
14 Wisconsin	1.4673
15 Michigan State	1.4368
16 Texas A&M	1.4317
17 Florida State	1.3828
18 West Virginia	1.3557
19 Nebraska	1.3484
20 North Carolina State	1.3287

2010 Top Opponents Records

1 Texas A&M	.6779
2 Notre Dame	.6429
3 Iowa State	.6352
4 Arkansas	.6340
5 South Carolina	.6310
6 Auburn	.6339
7 Louisiana State	.6289
8 Oregon State	.6286
9 Oklahoma	.6194
10 Missouri	.6078
11 Alabama	.6071
12 Minnesota	.6035
13 Illinois	.601316
14 Florida	.601266
15 Wake Forest	.6000
16 Miami	.5961
17 West Virginia	.593421
18 Michigan	.593377
19 Florida State	.5892
20 Washington	.5882

2010 Out-of-Conference Records

	W-L	Percentage	Bowl W-L
Southeastern	46-12	.7931	5-5
Big Twelve	43-13	.7679	3-5
Big Ten	38-14	.7308	3-5
Pacific-10	23-12	.6571	2-2
Big East	28-18	.6087	4-2
Atlantic Coast	34-23	.5965	4-5
Western Athletic	25-19	.5682	2-2
Mountain West	21-21	.5000	4-1

2010 Individual Statistical Leaders

RUSHING YARDS

	Attempts	Yards	Average
LaMichael James, Oregon	294	1731	5.9
Denard Robinson, Michigan	256	1702	6.6
Mikel Leshoure, Illinois	281	1697	6.0
Jordan Todman, Connecticut	334	1695	5.1
Vai Taua, Nevada	284	1610	5.7
Daniel Thomas, Kansas State	298	1585	5.3
Kendall Hunter, Oklahoma State	271	1548	5.7
Ronnie Tillman, San Diego State	262	1532	5.8
Zach Line, Southern Methodist	244	1494	6.1
Cam Newton, Auburn	264	1473	5.6

PASSING YARDS

	Completions	Attempts	Yards	Percentage
Bryant Moniz, Hawaii	361	555	5040	65.1
Landry Jones, Oklahoma	405	617	4718	65.6
Brandon Weeden, Oklahoma State	342	511	4277	66.9
Dominique Davis, East Carolina	393	609	3967	64.5
Ryan Mallett, Arkansas	266	411	3869	64.7
Kellen Moore, Boise State	273	383	3845	71.3
Ryan Lindley, San Diego State	243	421	3830	57.7
Kyle Patron, Southern Methodist	302	508	3828	59.5
Taylor Potts, Texas Tech	369	551	3726	67.0
G.J. Kinne, Tulsa	275	460	3650	59.8

RECEIVING YARDS

	Catches	Yards
Greg Salas, Hawaii	119	1889
Justin Blackmon, Oklahoma State	111	1782
Ryan Broyles, Oklahoma	131	1622
Alshon Jeffery, South Carolina	88	1517
Vincent Brown, San Diego State	69	1352
Kealoha Pilares, Hawaii	88	1306
Aldrick Robinson, Southern Methodist	65	1301
Juron Criner, Arizona	82	1233
DeMarco Sampson, San Diego State	67	1220
Titus Young, Boise State	71	1215

2010 Consensus All-America Team

Offense

Wide Receiver	Justin Blackmon, sophomore, Oklahoma State
	Ryan Broyles, junior, Oklahoma
Tight End:	Michael Egnew, junior, Missouri
	Lance Kendricks, senior, Wisconsin
Line:	Gabe Carimi, senior, Wisconsin
	Nate Solder, senior, Colorado
	Lee Ziemba, senior, Auburn
	Rodney Hudson, senior, Florida State
Center:	Chase Beeler, senior, Stanford
Quarterback:	Cam Newton, junior, Auburn
Running Back:	LaMichael James, sophomore, Oregon
	Kendall Hunter, junior, Oklahoma State
Kicker:	Josh Jasper, senior, Louisiana State
Kick Returner:	Cliff Harris, sophomore, Oregon
	Eric Page, sophomore, Toledo

Defense

Line:	Da'Quan Bowers, junior, Clemson
	Ryan Kerrigan, senior, Purdue
	Adrian Clayborn, senior, Iowa
	Nick Fairley, junior, Auburn
	Stephen Paea, senior, Oregon State
Linebacker:	Luke Kuechly, sophomore, Boston College
	Greg Jones, senior, Michigan State
	Von Miller, senior, Texas A&M
Back:	Prince Amukamara, senior, Nebraska
	Patrick Peterson, junior, Louisiana State
	Quinton Carter, senior, Oklahoma
	Tejay Johnson, senior, Texas Christian
Punter:	Chas Henry, senior, Florida

2010 Heisman Trophy Vote

Cam Newton, junior quarterback, Auburn	2263
Andrew Luck, junior quarterback, Stanford	1079
LaMichael James, sophomore running back, Oregon	916
Kellen Moore, junior quarterback, Boise State	635

Other Major Awards

Maxwell (Player)	Cam Newton, junior quarterback, Auburn
Walter Camp (Player)	Cam Newton, junior quarterback, Auburn
Outland (Lineman)	Gabe Carimi, senior offensive tackle, Wisconsin
Vince Lombardi (Lineman)	Nick Fairley, junior defensive tackle, Auburn
Doak Walker (Running Back)	LaMichael James, soph. running back, Oregon
Davey O'Brien (quarterback)	Cam Newton, junior quarterback, Auburn
Fred Biletnikoff (Receiver)	Justin Blackmon, soph. wide receiver, Oklahoma St.
Jim Thorpe (Defensive Back)	Patrick Peterson, junior cornerback, Louisiana State
Dick Butkus (Linebacker)	Von Miller, senior linebacker, Texas A&M
Chuck Bednarik (Defender)	Patrick Peterson, junior cornerback, Louisiana State
Lou Groza (Placekicker)	Dan Bailey, senior kicker, Oklahoma State
Ray Guy (Punter)	Chas Henry, senior punter, Florida
Johnny Unitas (Sr. Quarterback)	Scott Tolzien, senior quarterback, Wisconsin
John Mackey (Tight End)	D.J. Williams, senior tight end, Arkansas
Dave Rimington (Center)	Jake Kirkpatrick, senior center, Texas Christian
Ted Hendricks (Defensive End)	Da'Quan Bowers, junior defensive end, Clemson
Bronko Nagurski (Defender)	Da'Quan Bowers, junior defensive end, Clemson
Paul Hornung (Versatility)	Owen Marecic, senior fullback-linebacker, Stanford
AFCA Coach of the Year	Chip Kelly, Oregon

TEAM INFORMATION

In the following team information section, eight pages are devoted to each of 63 featured schools. The schools are arranged alphabetically.

ELEMENTS

- Basic School Information
- Career, Season, and Game Statistical Leaders
- Greatest Coach
- Greatest 55 Players
- Performance Formula: Top 10 Best Seasons
- Won-Loss, Polls, Conference Standing, Coaching, and Bowl Game Chart
- Annual Scores, Players Lineups, and Statistics

NOTE:

- Career, season, and game rushing, passing, and receiving statistics have been taken from updated information supplied on each school's athletic-team website. We tried to update the information through the end of the 2010 season even when the school failed to do so.

- Some seasonal won-loss records and career coaching records vary slightly from those officially listed by the schools. This almost always reflects changes eventually affected due to game result forfeitures. This often occurred when a school used an ineligible player. Frankly, we don't care about the occasional and accidental use of an ineligible player; one player, no matter how great, rarely impacts the outcome of a game. This book reflects the outcomes that occurred on the football field and credits victories to the teams and coaches that won on the field and demerits teams and coaches that lost on the field.
  If a team won or lost due to forfeit, it is noted in the annual list of game scores only. Forfeit wins are marked as (F-W), while such losses are noted as (F-L). Fortfeits are not applied to a team's or coach's seasonal or career records.

- During part of the 1960s, Associated Press did not publish top-20 or top-25 weekly poll lists. Instead the news service named top-10 teams, and, as a footnote, alphabetically listed other teams that received votes. To denote each "also-receiving-votes" team in this book, an "11+" is listed in the AP Poll column for such season-end achievement.

- At the bottom of each school chart (on the second page of the eight page sections) is a won-loss-tied total and winning percentage ranking in comparison to the other featured schools. These are not all-time records, but those records that have been earned since 1953. Ties are calculated as half-wins and half-losses.
  Since virtually every team played nearly or more than 600 games since 1953, there were sufficient data to allow no winning percentage ties among the 70 schools. With far fewer bowl game results credited to each school, there were several deadlocks among bowl winning percentages. The higher ranking spots among tied teams were given to the teams that had played more bowl games. Still, a few exact deadlocks existed. Those ties are duly noted.

- A team's 10 best seasons of College Football Performance Formula are included on the first page of each team's section. The Formula is a rating system developed exclusively by the authors of The USA Today College Football Encyclopedia. It is a three-point calculation of a team's seasonal winning percentage, opponents' winning percentage, and plus-minus scoring margin factored down to a maximum of 40-point outcomes.

ALABAMA

University of Alabama (Founded 1831)
Tuscaloosa, Alabama
Nickname: Crimson Tide
Color: Crimson
Stadiums: Bryant-Denny (1929) 92,138
Conference Affiliation: Southeastern
(Charter member 1933-present)

CAREER RUSHING YARDS	Attempts	Yards
Shaun Alexander (1996-99)	727	3565
Bobby Humphrey (1985-88)	615	3420
Kenneth Darby (2003-06)	702	3324
Mark Ingram (2008-10)	572	3261
Johnny Musso (1969-71)	574	2741
Dennis Riddle (1994-97)	612	2645
Bobby Marlow (1950-52)	408	2560
Johnny Davis (1974-77)	447	2519
Sherman Williams (1991-94)	535	2486
Shaud Williams (2002-03)	410	2288

CAREER PASSING YARDS	Comp.-Att.	Yards
John Parker Wilson (2005-08)	665-1175	7924
Brodie Croyle (2002-05)	488-869	6382
Andrew Zow (1998-2001)	459-852	5983
Greg McElroy (2007-10)	436-658	5691
Jay Barker (1991-94)	402-706	5689
Scott Hunter (1968-70)	382-672	4899
Freddie Kitchens (1993-97)	343-680	4668
Walter Lewis (1980-83)	286-504	4257
Mike Shula (1983-86)	313-578	4079
Gary Hollingsworth (1989-90)	345-621	3842

CAREER RECEIVING YARDS	Catches	Yards
D.J. Hall (2004-07)	194	2923
Julio Jones (2008-10)	179	2653
Ozzie Newsome (1974-77)	102	2070
Keith Brown (2004-07)	117	1863
Freddie Milons (1998-2001)	152	1859
David Bailey (1969-71)	132	1857
David Palmer (1991-93)	102	1611
Curtis Brown (1991-95)	106	1568
Dennis Homan (1965-67)	87	1495
Joey Jones (1980-83)	71	1386

SEASON RUSHING YARDS	Attempts	Yards
Mark Ingram (2009)	271	1658
Bobby Humphrey (1986)	236	1471
Glenn Coffee (2008)	233	1383
Shaun Alexander (1999)	302	1383
Shaud Williams (2003)	280	1367

SEASON PASSING YARDS	Comp.-Att.	Yards
Greg McElroy (2010)	222-313	2987
John Parker Wilson (2007)	255-372	2846
John Parker Wilson (2006)	216-379	2707
Greg McElroy (2009)	198-325	2508
Brodie Croyle (2005)	202-339	2499

SEASON RECEIVING YARDS	Catches	Yards
Julio Jones (2010)	78	1133
D.J. Hall (2006)	62	1056
D.J. Hall (2007)	67	1005
David Palmer (1993)	61	1000
Julio Jones (2008)	58	924

GAME RUSHING YARDS	Attempts	Yards
Shaun Williams (1996 vs. LSU)	20	291
Bobby Humphrey (1986 vs. Miss. State)	30	284
Mark Ingram (2009 vs. South Carolina)	24	246

GAME PASSING YARDS	Comp.-Att.	Yards
Scott Hunter (1969 vs. Auburn)	30-55	484
Jay Barker (1994 vs. Georgia)	26-34	396
Gary Hollingsworth (1989 vs. Tennessee)	32-46	379

GAME RECEIVING YARDS	Catches	Yards
Julio Jones (2010 vs. Tennessee)	12	221
David Palmer (1993 vs. Vanderbilt)	8	217
Julio Jones (2010 vs. Auburn)	10	199

GREATEST COACH:

When Paul "Bear" Bryant returned to Alabama in 1958 he said he was answering Mother's call and he always did what his mother told him to do. The rest is college football history.

Bryant spent 25 seasons at Alabama, and the Crimson Tide won 232 games, lost 46, and tied 9. They captured 13 Southeastern Conference championships, including eight of nine during the 1970s, a decade in which Alabama enjoyed 103 wins, 16 losses, and a single tie. Alabama's winning percentage of .863 for the 1970s is surpassed—since World War II—only by Oklahoma's 93-10-2 (.895) which was compiled while playing in a far less competitive conference in the 1950s.

Bryant won five national titles, and is the only coach to twice win back-to-back championships: 1964-65 and 1978-79.

Bryant had a surprisingly average bowl record of 12-10-2, owing mostly to a mysterious 0-7-1 streak starting with a 1968 Cotton Bowl upset loss to his former player and coach, Gene Stallings of Texas A&M. Losses in the 1972 Orange Bowl to Nebraska and the 1974 Sugar Bowl and 1975 Orange Bowl to Notre Dame were the only marks against Alabama teams in the entire seasons of 1971, '73, and '74.

Bryant captured his last game before retirement, an emotional 1982 Liberty Bowl over Illinois, and he sadly lived to nearly fulfill a joke he often told on himself: "If I ever quit coaching, I'd croak in a week." He was dead by January 26, 1983.

ALABAMA'S 55 GREATEST SINCE 1953

OFFENSE

WIDE RECEIVER: D.J. Hall, Dennis Homan, Freddie Milons, Ozzie Newsome
TIGHT END: Bart Krout, Lamonde Russell
TACKLE: Buddy Brown, Jim Bunch, Cecil Dowdy, Chris Samuels
GUARD: John Hannah, Billy Neighbors, Larry Rose
CENTER: Sylvester Croom, Dwight Stephenson
QUARTERBACK: Brodie Croyle, Walter Lewis, Joe Namath, Jeff Rutledge
RUNNING BACK: Shaun Alexander, Bobby Humphrey, Johnny Musso, Tony Nathan
FULLBACK: Steve Bowman, Johnny Davis

DEFENSE

END: Leroy Cook, Eric Curry, E.J. Junior, Mike Pitts
TACKLE: Bob Baumhower, Jackie Cline, Marty Lyons
NOSE GUARD: Robert Stewart
LINEBACKER: Cornelius Bennett, Thomas Boyd, Barry Krause, Dwayne Rudd, Derrick Thomas, Woodrow Lowe
CORNERBACK: Jeremiah Castille, Bobby Johns, Antonio Langham, Don McNeal, Mike Washington
SAFETY: Jim Bob Harris, Kevin Jackson, Tommy Wilcox

SPECIAL TEAMS

RETURN SPECIALISTS: Kerry Goode, Tyrone Prothro
PLACE KICKER: Philip Doyle
PUNTER: Greg Gantt

MULTIPLE POSITIONS

WIDE RECEIVER-QUARTERBACK-KICK RETURNER: David Palmer
RUNNING BACK-CORNERBACK-KICK RETURNER: Gene Jelks

TWO-WAY PLAYERS

CENTER-LINEBACKER: Lee Roy Jordan
CENTER-LINEBACKER: Paul Crane

PERFORMANCE FORMULA:
ALABAMA'S 10 BEST SEASONS

Year	Formula	Rank
2009	1.8282	1 of 71
1971	1.8025	2 of 70
1992	1.7679	1 of 70
1973	1.7572	4 of 70
1966	1.7346	2 of 70
1961	1.7292	1 of 71
1979	1.7239	1 of 70
1978	1.7150	2 of 70
1964	1.6937	2 of 70
1974	1.6889	2 of 71

ALABAMA CRIMSON TIDE

Year	W-L-T	AP Poll	Conference Standing	Toughest Regular Season Opponents	Coach (Record at School)	Bowl Games		
1953	6-3-3		1	Miss. So. 9-1, Georgia Tech 8-2-1, Maryland 10-0, Auburn 7-2-1	Harold "Red" Drew	Cotton	6 Rice	28
1954	4-5-2		8	Georgia 6-3-1, Georgia Tech 7-3, Miami 8-1, Auburn 7-3	Red Drew (54-28-7)			
1955	0-10		12	Vanderbilt 7-3, TCU 9-1, Georgia Tech 8-1-1, Miami 6-3, Auburn 8-1-1	J.B. "Ears" Whitworth			
1956	2-7-1		8t	TCU 7-3, Tennessee 10-0, Georgia Tech 9-1, Auburn 7-3	J.B. Whitworth			
1957	2-7-1		10	Tennessee 7-3, Mississippi State 6-2-1, Auburn 10-0	J.B. Whitworth (4-24-2)			
1958	5-4-1		6t	LSU 10-0, Georgia Tech 5-4-1, Auburn 9-0-1	Paul "Bear" Bryant			
1959	7-2-2	10	4	Georgia 9-1, Vanderbilt 5-3-2, Georgia Tech 6-4, Auburn 7-3	Bear Bryant	Liberty	0 Penn State	7
1960	8-1-2	9	3	Georgia 6-4, Tennessee 6-2-2, Auburn 8-2	Bear Bryant	Bluebonnet	3 Texas	3
1961	11-0	1	1	Tennessee 6-4, Georgia Tech 7-3, Auburn 6-4	Bear Bryant	Sugar	10 Arkansas	3
1962	10-1	5	2t	Miami 7-3, Georgia Tech 7-2-1, Auburn 6-3-1	Bear Bryant	Orange	17 Oklahoma	0
1963	9-2	8	3	Florida 6-3-1, Georgia Tech 7-3, Auburn 9-1	Bear Bryant	Sugar	12 Mississippi	7
1964	10-1	1	1	Georgia 6-3-1, Florida 7-3, LSU 7-2-1, Georgia Tech 7-3,	Bear Bryant	Orange	17 Texas	21
1965	9-1-1	1	1	Georgia 6-4, Mississippi 6-4, Tennessee 7-1-2, LSU 7-3	Bear Bryant	Orange	39 Nebraska	28
1966	11-0	3	1t	Mississippi 8-2, Clemson 6-4, Tennessee 7-3, LSU 5-4-1	Bear Bryant	Sugar	34 Nebraska	7
1967	8-2-1	8	2	Florida State 7-2-1, Mississippi 6-3-1, Tennessee 9-1, LSU 6-3-1	Bear Bryant	Cotton	16 Texas A&M	20
1968	8-3	17	3t	Mississippi 6-3-1, Tennessee 8-1-1, LSU 7-3, Auburn 6-4	Bear Bryant	Gator	10 Missouri	35
1969	6-5		8	Mississippi 7-3, Tennessee 9-1, LSU 9-1, Auburn 8-2	Bear Bryant	Liberty	33 Colorado	47
1970	6-5-1		7t	Mississippi 7-3, Tennessee 10-1, Houston 8-3, LSU 9-2, Auburn 8-2	Bear Bryant	Bluebonnet	24 Oklahoma	24
1971	11-1	4	1	Mississippi 9-2, Tennessee 9-2, Houston 9-2, LSU 8-3, Auburn 9-1	Bear Bryant	Orange	6 Nebraska	38
1972	10-2	7	1	Georgia 7-4, Tennessee 9-2, LSU 9-1-1, Auburn 9-1	Bear Bryant	Cotton	13 Texas	17
1973	11-1	4	1	Georgia 6-4-1, Florida 7-4, Tennessee 7-4, LSU 9-2	Bear Bryant	Sugar	23 Notre Dame	24
1974	11-1	5	1	Maryland 8-3, Mississippi State 8-3, Auburn 9-2	Bear Bryant	Orange	11 Notre Dame	13
1975	11-1	3	1	Missouri 6-5, Mississippi State 6-5, Tennessee 7-5	Bear Bryant	Sugar	13 Penn State	6
1976	9-3	11	2	Georgia 10-1, Mississippi State 9-2, LSU 6-4-1, Notre Dame 8-3	Bear Bryant	Liberty	36 UCLA	6
1977	11-1	2	1	Nebraska 8-3, Southern California 7-4, LSU 8-3	Bear Bryant	Sugar	35 Ohio State	6
1978	11-1	1	1	Nebraska 9-2, Southern California 11-1, Washington 7-4, LSU 8-3	Bear Bryant	Sugar	14 Penn State	7
1979	12-0	1	1	Baylor 7-4, Tennessee 7-4, Auburn 8-3	Bear Bryant	Sugar	24 Arkansas	9
1980	10-2	6	2t	Mississippi State 9-2, LSU 7-4, Notre Dame 9-1-1	Bear Bryant	Cotton	30 Baylor	2
1981	9-2-1	7	1t	Southern Miss 9-1-1, Tennessee 7-4, Miss. State 7-4, Penn State 9-2	Bear Bryant	Cotton	12 Texas	14
1982	8-4		6t	Vanderbilt 8-3, Penn State 10-1, LSU 8-2-1, Auburn 8-3	Bear Bryant (232-46-9)	Liberty	21 Illinois	15
1983	8-4	15	3t	Penn State 7-4-1, Boston College 9-2, Auburn 10-1	Ray Perkins	Sun	28 Southern Methodist	7
1984	5-6		7t	Boston Coll. 9-2, Georgia 8-3, Tennessee 7-3-1, LSU 8-2-1, Auburn 8-4	Ray Perkins			
1985	9-2-1	13	2t	Texas A&M 9-2, Penn State 11-0, LSU 9-1-1	Ray Perkins	Aloha	24 Southern California	3
1986	10-3	9	2t	Ohio State 9-3, Penn State 11-0, LSU 9-2, Auburn 9-2	Ray Perkins (32-15-1)	Sun	28 Washington	6
1987	7-5		4t	Penn St. 8-3, Tennessee 9-2-1, LSU 9-1-1, No. Dame 8-3, Auburn 9-1-1	Bill Curry	Hall of Fame	24 Michigan	28
1988	9-3	17	4t	LSU 8-3, Auburn 10-1	Bill Curry	Sun	29 Army	28
1989	10-2	9	1t	Tennessee 10-1, Penn State 7-3-1, Auburn 9-2	Bill Curry (26-10)	Sugar	25 Miami	33
1990	7-5		3t	Southern Miss 8-3, Tennessee 8-2-2, Penn State 9-2, Auburn 7-3-1	Gene Stallings	Fiesta	7 Louisville	34
1991	11-1	5	2	Florida 10-1, Georgia 8-3, Tennessee 9-2	Gene Stallings	Blockbuster	30 Colorado	25
1992	13-0	1	W1	Tennessee 8-3, Mississippi 8-3	Gene Stallings	Sugar	34 Miami	13
1993	9-3-1	14	W1	Tennessee 9-1-1, Mississippi 5-6, Auburn 11-0	Gene Stallings	Gator	24 North Carolina	10
1994	12-1	5	W1	Tennessee 7-4, Mississippi State 8-3, Auburn 9-1-1	Gene Stallings	Citrus	24 Ohio State	17
1995	8-3	21	W2t	Arkansas 7-4, Tennessee 10-1, Auburn 8-3	Gene Stallings			
1996	10-3	11	W1	Southern Miss 8-3, Tennessee 9-2, LSU 9-2, Auburn 7-4	Gene Stallings	Outback	17 Michigan	14
1997	4-7		W5t	Southern Miss 8-3, Tennessee 10-1, LSU 8-3, Auburn 9-2	Gene Stallings (74-23-1)			
1998	7-5		W3	BYU 9-3, Florida 9-2, Tennessee 11-0, Mississippi State 8-3	Mike DuBose	Music City	7 Virginia Tech	38
1999	10-3	8	W1	Florida 9-2, Tennessee 9-2, Mississippi State 9-2	Mike DuBose	Orange	34 Michigan	35
2000	3-8		W5t	South Carolina 7-4, Tennessee 8-3, LSU 7-4, Auburn 9-3	Mike DuBose (20-16)			
2001	7-5		W3t	South Carolina 8-3, Tennessee 10-1, LSU 8-3, Auburn 7-4	Dennis Franchione	Independence	14 Iowa State	13
2002	10-3	11	ineligible	Oklahoma 10-2, Arkansas 9-3, Georgia 11-1, LSU 8-4, Auburn 8-4	Dennis Franchione (17-8)			
2003	4-9		W5	Oklahoma 12-0, Georgia 10-2, Tennessee 10-2, LSU 11-1	Mike Shula			
2004	6-6		W3t	Tennessee 9-2, LSU 9-2, Auburn 11-0	Mike Shula	Music City	16 Minnesota	20
2005	10-2		W3	Florida 8-3, LSU 10-1, Auburn 9-2	Mike Shula	Cotton	13 Texas Tech	10
2006	6-7		W4t	Arkansas 10-2, Florida 11-1, Tennessee 9-3, LSU 10-2, Auburn 10-2	Mike Shula (26-23), Joe Kines [0-1]	Independence	31 Oklahoma State	34
2007	7-6		W3t	Arkansas 8-4, Georgia 10-2, Tennessee 9-3, LSU 10-2, Auburn 8-4	Nick Saban	Independence	30 Colorado	24
2008	12-2	6	W1	Georgia 9-3, Mississippi 8-4, Florida 12-1	Nick Saban	Sugar	17 Utah	31
2009	14-0	1	W1	Virginia Tech 9-3, Mississippi 8-4, LSU 9-3, Florida 12-1	Nick Saban	BCS Title	37 Texas	21
2010	10-3	10	W4	Arkansas 10-2, LSU 10-2, Mississippi State 8-4, Auburn 13-0	Nick Saban (43-10)	Capital One	49 Michigan State	7

TOTAL: 484-185-18 .7176 (5 of 70)   **Bowl Games since 1953:** 25-20-2 .5532 (24 of 70)

GREATEST TEAM SINCE 1953: Despite notching a Formula rating no better than seventh among Alabama's best, the 1979 Crimson Tide was Bear Bryant's only undefeated national champion. It gets a slight nod over Gene Stallings' undefeated 1992 champions and Nick Saban's undefeated 2009 champions.

1953 6-3-3
19	Miss. Southern	25	E Curtis Lynch / Bud Willis
7	LSU	7	T George Mason / Billy Shipp
21	Vanderbilt	12	G Harry Lee / Bob Wilga
41	Tulsa	13	C Ralph Carrigan
0	Tennessee	0	G Charles Eckerly / Jeff Moore
7	Mississippi St.	7	T Sid Youngelman / Ed Culpepper
33	Georgia	12	E Joe Cummings / Tommy Tillman
21	Chattanooga	14	QB Bart Starr / Albert Elmore
13	Georgia Tech	6	HB Bobby Luna / Cecil "Hootie" Ingram
0	Maryland	21	HB Corky Tharp / Bill Oliver
10	Auburn	7	FB Tommy Lewis / Bill "Rocky" Stone
6	Rice■	28	

RUSHING: Tharp 111/607y, Stone 73/336y, Luna 80/309y
PASSING: Starr 59-119/870y, 8TD, 49.6%
RECEIVING: Willis 11/191y, Tharp 11/129y, Luna 9/116y
SCORING: Luna (HB-K) 34pts, Tharp 30pts, Oliver 24pts

1954 4-5-2
2	Miss. Southern	7	E Nick Germanos
12	LSU	0	T George Mason / Ed Culpepper
28	Vanderbilt	14	G Harry Lee
40	Tulsa	0	C Knute Rockne Christian
27	Tennessee	0	G Charles Eckerly / Bo Collins
7	Mississippi St.	12	T Sid Youngelman / Doug Potts
0	Georgia	0	E Tommy Tillman / Curtis Lynch
0	Tulane	0	QB Bart Starr / Albert Elmore
0	Georgia Tech	20	HB Bobby Luna / Bill Hollis
7	Miami	23	HB Corky Tharp
0	Auburn	28	FB Rocky Stone / Hootie Ingram

RUSHING: Tharp 139/641y, Luna 75/310y, Stone 86/269y
PASSING: Elmore 39-74/499y, 7TD, 52.7%,
   Starr 24-41/276y, TD, 58.5%
RECEIVING: Luna 16/304y, Tharp 16/220y, Lynch 9/103y
SCORING: Tharp 36pts, Luna (HB-K) 29pts, Ingram (FB-K) 7pts

1955 0-10
0	Rice	20	E Nick Germanos / Billy Lumpkin
6	Vanderbilt	21	T Wes Thompson
0	TCU	21	G Max Kelly / Don Conner
0	Tennessee	20	C Knute Rockne Christian
7	Mississippi St.	26	G Doug Potts / Bo Collins
14	Georgia	35	T Curtis Lynch / Jim Cunningham
7	Tulane	27	E Tommy Tillman / Paul Donaldson
2	Georgia Tech	26	QB Bart Starr / Clay Walls
12	Miami	34	HB Bill Hollis /Jerry McBee /Marshall Brown
0	Auburn	26	HB Rocky Stone / Jimmy Bowdoin

RUSHING: Walls 49/164y, Stone 25/123y, Brown 26/111y
PASSING: Starr 55-96/587y, TD, 57.3%
RECEIVING: Brown 15/152y, Noojin Walker (FB) 14/154y,
   Germanos 13/106y
SCORING: Kinderknecht (FB-K) 15pts, 5 tied with 6pts

1956 2-7-1
13	Rice	20	E Charles Gray / Baxter Booth
7	Vanderbilt	32	T Wes Thompson / Sid Neighbors
6	TCU	23	G Don Holcomb / Phil Clark
0	Tennessee	24	C John Snoderly / Billy Brooks
13	Mississippi St.	12	G Doug Potts / Billy Rains
13	Georgia	16	T Jim Cunningham / Dave Sington
13	Tulane	7	E Don Owens / Willie Beck
0	Georgia Tech	27	QB Clay Walls / Bobby Smith
13	Miss. Southern	13	HB Jim Loftin
7	Auburn	34	HB Don Comstock / Jimmy Bowdoin
			FB Don Kinderknecht / Ed Pharo

RUSHING: Comstock 76/316y, Loftin 72/293y, Kelley 64/276y
PASSING: Smith 16-40/356y, 3 TD, 40.0%
RECEIVING: Gray 7/108y, Beck 7/93y, Ralph Blaylock (E) 5/72y
SCORING: Comstock 24pts, Walls & Loftin 12pts

1957 2-7-1
0	LSU	28	E Charles Gray
6	Vanderbilt	6	T Sid Neighbors
0	TCU	28	G Bill Hannah / Don Cochran
0	Tennessee	14	C Benny Dempsey
13	Mississippi St.	25	G Billy Rains
14	Georgia	13	T Dave Sington
0	Tulane	7	E Willie **Beck** / Ralph Blaylock
7	Georgia Tech	10	QB Bobby Smith / Bobby Skelton
29	Miss. Southern	2	HB Gary O'Steen / Marlin Dyess
0	Auburn	40	HB Clay Walls / Red Stickney
			FB Jim Loftin / Danny Wilbanks

RUSHING: Loftin 106/477y, Walls 60/198y, Wilbanks 47/155y
PASHING: Smith 32-83/377y, 2 TD, 38.6%
RECEIVING: Beck 9/126y, Gray 9/115y, Walls 6/66y
SCORING: Wilbanks 18pts, Dyess & Walls 12pts

1958 5-4-1
3	LSU	13	E Norbie Ronsonet / Jerry Brannen
0	Vanderbilt	0	T Carl Valletto
29	Furman	6	G Wayne Sims
7	Tennessee	14	C Kenneth Roberts
9	Mississippi St.	7	G Don Cochran
12	Georgia	0	T Dave Sington
7	Tulane	13	E Charles Gray / Baxter Booth
17	Georgia Tech	8	QB Bobby Jackson / Bobby Smith
14	Memphis State	0	HB Gary O'Steen / Marlin Dyess
8	Auburn	14	HB Duff Morrison / Mack Wise
			FB Milton Frank / Walter Sansing

RUSHING: Jackson 143/472y, O'Steen 79/284y, Morrison 49/151y
PASSING: Jackson 29-58/408y, 2 TD, 50.0%
RECEIVING: Dyess 12/204y, O'Steen 7/159y, Booth 3/34y
SCORING: Jackson 44pts, O'Steen 20pts, Dyess 12pts

1959 7-2-2
3	Georgia	17	E Bill Rice / Norbie Ronsonet
3	Houston	0	T Billy Neighbors
7	Vanderbilt	7	G Jimmy Sharp / Wayne Sims
13	Chattanooga	0	C John O'Linger / Jim Blevins
7	Tennessee	7	G Don Cochran / Bill Hannah
10	Miss State	0	T Fred Sington / Gary Phillips
19	Tulane	7	E Stanley Bell / Tommy Brooker
9	Georgia Tech	7	QB Bobby Skelton / Pat Trammell
14	Memphis State	7	HB Marlin Dyess / Leon Fuller
10	Auburn	0	HB Duff Morrison / Bill Richardson
0	Penn State■	7	FB Gary O'Steen / Tommy White

RUSHING: Trammell 156/525y, O'Steen 71/228y, White 46/169y
PASSING: Trammell 21-49/293y, TD, 42.9%,
   Skelton 13-30/189y, 4 TD, 43.3%
RECEIVING: Dyess 10/149y, Brooker 7/108y, Bell 6/100y
SCORING: Dyess 18pts, Sington (T-K) 17pts, 3 with 12pts

1960 8-1-2
21	Georgia	6	E Bill Battle / Jerry Spruiell
6	Tulane	6	T Bill Rice/ Charley Pell/Elbert Cook (LB)
21	Vanderbilt	0	G Gary Phillips / Jack Rutledge
7	Tennessee	20	C John O'Linger / Lee Roy Jordan
14	Houston	0	G Billy Neighbors / Darwin Holt (LB)
7	Mississippi St.	0	T Bobby Boylston / Richard O'Dell
51	Furman	0	E Tommy Brooker / Norbie Ronsonet
16	Georgia Tech	15	QB Pat Trammell / Bobby Skelton
34	Tampa	6	HB Leon Fuller / Bill Richardson
3	Auburn	0	HB Butch Wilson/Gary Wilson/Lrn. Stapp
3	Texas■	3	FB Tommy White / Mike Fracchia

RUSHING: Trammell 76/315y, Fracchia 68/290y, Stapp 66/229y
PASSING: Skelton 43-94/575y, 5 TD, 45.7%,
   Trammell 21-43/303y, 0 TD, 48.8%
RECEIVING: Wilson 13/204y, Fuller 6/84y, Spruiell 5/125y
SCORING: Trammell 28pts, Stapp 20pts, O'Dell (T-K) 13pts

1961 11-0
32	Georgia	6	E Bill Battle / Richard Williamson
9	Tulane	0	T Bill Rice / Charley Pell
21	Vanderbilt	0	G Jimmy Wilson / Al Lewis
26	N. Carolina St.	7	C Lee Roy Jordan / John O'Linger
34	Tennessee	3	G Jack Rutledge / Jimmy Sharpe
17	Houston	0	T Billy Neighbors / Darwin Holt (LB)
24	Mississippi St.	0	E Tommy Brooker / Butch Henry
66	Richmond	0	QB Pat Trammell / Ray Abruzzese (DB)
10	Georgia Tech	0	HB Cotton Clark / Bill Richardson
34	Auburn	0	HB Butch Wilson/Benny Nelson/Bill Oliver
10	Arkansas■	3	FB Mike Fracchia / Eddie Versprille

RUSHING: Fracchia 130/652y, Trammell 75/279y, Clark 34/149y
PASSING: Trammell 75-133/1035y, 8 TD, 56.4%
RECEIVING: Brooker 12/183y, Williamson 11/206y, Battle 11/168y
SCORING: Trammell 56pts

1962 10-1
35	Georgia	0	E Bill Battle / Richard Williamson
44	Tulane	6	T Charley Pell / Clark Boler
17	Vanderbilt	3	G Jimmy Sharpe / Steve Allen / Al Lewis
14	Houston	3	C Lee Roy Jordan
27	Tennessee	7	G Jimmy Wilson / Bob Pettee
35	Tulsa	6	T Dan Kearley / Steve Wright
20	Mississippi St.	0	E Richard O'Dell / Ray Ogden (WR)
36	Miami	3	QB Joe Namath / Jack Hurlbut
6	Georgia Tech	7	HB Butch Wilson / Hudson Harris
38	Auburn	0	HB Cotton Clark / Benny Nelson
17	Oklahoma■	0	FB Eddie Versprille

RUSHING: Versprille 76/373y, Namath 70/229y, Clark 61/211y
PASSING: Namath 76-146/1192y, 13 TD, 52.1%
RECEIVING: Williamson 24/492y, Clark 16/199y, Wilson 10/133y
SCORING: Clark 92pts, Tim Davis (K) 34pts, Battle 28pts

1963 9-2
32	Georgia	7	E Jimmy Dill
28	Tulane	0	T Ron Durby / Clark Boler
21	Vanderbilt	6	G Al Lewis / Steve Allen
6	Florida	10	C Paul Crane / Gaylon McCullough
35	Houston	0	G Wayne Freeman / Bill Wieseman
21	Houston	13	T Jim Simmons / Dan Kearley
20	Mississippi St.	19	E Charlie Stephens / Tommy Tolleson
27	Georgia Tech	11	QB Joe Namath / Steve Sloan
8	Auburn	10	HB Benny Nelson / Gary Martin (DB)
17	Miami	12	HB Hudson Harris / Ray Odgen (WR)
12	Mississippi■	7	FB Eddie Versprille / Steve Bowman

RUSHING: Nelson 97/612y, Harris 76/281y, Namath 76/201y
PASSING: Namath 63-128/765y, 7 TD, 49.2%
RECEIVING: Dill 19/316y, Tolleson 9/110y, Nelson 9/79y
SCORING: Nelson 62pts, Tim Davis (K) 35pts, Namath 34pts

1964 10-1
31	Georgia	3	E Tommy Tolleson / Ray Perkins
36	Tulane	6	T Ron Durby / Cecil Dowdy
24	Vanderbilt	0	G Jimmy Fuller / Ken Mitchell
21	N. Carolina St.	0	C Paul Crane / Gaylon McCullough
19	Tennessee	8	G Wayne Freeman / Creed Gilmer (DE)
17	Florida	14	T Dan Kearley / Jim Simmons
23	Mississippi St.	6	E Charlie Stephens / Wayne Cook
17	LSU	9	QB Joe Namath / Steve Sloan
24	Georgia Tech	7	HB Les Kelley / David Ray
21	Auburn	14	HB Hudson Harris / Ray Ogden (WR)
17	Texas■	21	FB Steve Bowman / Jackie Sherrill (LB)

RUSHING: Bowman 106/536y, Sloan 95/351y, Kelley 60/268y
PASSING: Namath 64-100/756y, 5 TD, 64.0%,
   Sloan 45-72/574y, TD, 62.5%
RECEIVING: Tolleson 22/248y, Ray 19/271y, Ogden 18/254y
SCORING: Ray (HB-K) 71pts, Bowman 54pts, Namath 36pts

1965 9-1-1
17	Georgia	■8	E Tommy Tolleson / Richard Brewer
27	Tulane	0	T Jerry Duncan / Byrd Williams (G)
17	Mississippi	16	G John Calvert
22	Vanderbilt	7	C Paul Crane (LB) / Terry Kilgore
7	Tennessee	7	G Bruce Stephens
21	Florida State	0	T Cecil Dowdy
10	Mississippi State	7	E Ray Perkins / Wayne Cook
31	LSU	7	QB Steve Sloan / Kenny Stabler
35	South Carolina	14	HB Les Kelley / Frank Canterbury
30	Auburn	3	WB David Ray / Dennis Homan
39	Nebraska■	28	FB Steve Bowman / Gene Raburn
			DL Lynn Strickland / Frank Whaley
			DL Jim Fuller / Richard Cole
			DL Tom Somerville / Allen "Bunk" Harpole
			DL Johnny Sullivan / Louis Thompson
			DL Creed Gilmer / Ben McLeod
			LB Tim Bates
			LB Stan Moss
			LB Jackie Sherrill
			DB Bobby Johns
			DB John Mosley
			DB Dicky Thompson / David Chatwood

RUSHING: Bowman 153/770y, Stabler 61/328y, Kelley 80/282y
PASSING: Sloan 97-160/1453y, 10 TD, 60.6%
RECEIVING: Tolleson 32/374y, Perkins 19/279y,
   Homan 10/298y
SCORING: Ray 50pts, Bowman & Sloan 36pts

1966 11-0

34 Louisiana Tech	0 WR Ray Perkins / Donnie Sutton
17 Mississippi	7 WR Dennis Homan / Richard Brewer
26 Clemson	0 T Cecil Dowdy
11 Tennessee	10 G John Calvert / Jim Fuller
42 Vanderbilt	6 C Jimmy Carroll
27 Mississippi St.	14 G Bruce Stephens / Billy Johnson
21 LSU	0 T Jerry Duncan / Byrd Williams
24 South Carolina	0 E Wayne Cook / Frank Whaley
34 Southern Miss.	0 QB Kenny Stabler / Wayne Trimble
34 Auburn	0 TB Les Kelley / Frank Canterbury
34 Nebraska■	7 FB David Chatwood / Gene Raburn
	DL Mike Ford
	DL Louis Thompson
	DL Bunk Harpole / Mike Reilly
	DL Richard Cole / Johnny Sullivan
	DL Charlie Harris / Wayne Stevens
	LB Stan Moss / Eddie Bo Rogers
	LB Mike Hall
	LB Bob Childs
	DB Bobby Johns / Eddie Propst
	DB Dicky Thompson / John Mosley
	DB Mike Sasser / Kent Busbee

RUSHING: Stabler 93/397y, Kelley 94/309y, Chatwood 74/271y
PASSING: Stabler 74-114/956y, 9 TD, 64.9%
RECEIVING: Perkins 33/490y, Homan 23/377y, Cook 14/115y
SCORING: Steve Davis (K) 55pts, Perkins 42pts, Homan 30pts

1967 8-2-1

37 Florida State	37 WR Dennis Homan / George Ranager
25 Southern Miss	3 WR Donnie Sutton / Richard Brewer
21 Mississippi	7 T John David Reitz
35 Vanderbilt	21 G Tom Somerville
13 Tennessee	24 C Billy Johnson
13 Clemson	24 G Bruce Stephens
13 Mississippi St.	0 T Nathan Rustin
7 LSU	6 TE Dennis Dixon / Danny Ford
17 South Carolina	0 QB Kenny Stabler
7 Auburn	3 TB Ed Morgan / Tommy Wade
16 Texas A&M■	20 FB Pete Jilleba / Kenny Martin
	DL Stan Moss
	DL Randy Barron
	DL Alvin Samples
	DL Mike Ford
	LB Mike Hall
	LB Wayne Owen
	LB Bob Childs
	DB Eddie Propst
	DB Bobby Johns
	DB Dicky Thompson
	DB Bob Higginbotham

RUSHING: Morgan 103/388y, Wade 55/165y, Martin 39/160y
PASSING: Stabler 103-178/1214y, 9 TD, 57.9%
RECEIVING: Homan 54/820y, Ford 10/122y, Brewer 6/90y
SCORING: Homan 54pts, Steve Davis (K) 42pts, Morgan 38pts

1968 8-3

14 Virginia Tech	7 WR Bobby Swafford / Donnie Sutton
17 Southern Miss	14 WR Griff Langston / George Ranager
8 Mississippi	10 T Danny Ford
31 Vanderbilt	7 G Charles Ferguson
9 Tennessee	10 C Richard Grammer
21 Clemson	14 G Alvin Samples (LB)
20 Mississippi St.	13 T Junior Davis
16 LSU	7 TE Hunter Husband
14 Miami	6 QB Scott Hunter
24 Auburn	16 TB Ed Morgan
10 Missouri■	35 FB Pete Jilleba / Pete Moore
	DL Bob Higginbotham
	DL Randy Barron
	DL Sam Gellerstedt
	DL Paul Boschung
	DL Mike Ford
	LB Bob Childs / Alvin Samples (G)
	LB Mike Hall
	DB Mike Dean
	DB Donnie Sutton
	DB Wayne Owen
	DB Tommy Wade

RUSHING: Morgan 134/450y, Moore 103/341y, Jilleba 68/248y
PASSING: Hunter 122-227/1471y, 10TD, 53.7%
RECEIVING: Ranager 31/499y, Jilleba 23/152y, Sutton 21/325y
SCORING: Dean (DB-K) 40pts, Morgan 30pts, Ranager & Sutton 24pts

1969 6-5

17 Virginia Tech	13 WR David Bailey
63 Southern Miss.	14 WR George Ranager
33 Mississippi	32 T Danny Ford
10 Vanderbilt	14 G Alvin Samples (LB) / Charles Ferguson
14 Tennessee	41 C Richard Grammer
38 Clemson	13 G Ried Drinkard / Mike Hand
23 Mississippi St.	19 T Ken Wilder
15 LSU	20 TE Hunter Husband
42 Miami	6 QB Scott Hunter
26 Auburn	49 TB Johnny Musso
33 Colorado■	47 FB Pete Jilleba
	DL Ken James
	DL Paul Boschung
	DL Terry Rowell / Don Harris
	DL Jim Duke
	DL Danny Gilbert / Robin Parkhouse
	LB Pete Moore
	LB Alvin Samples (G) / Woodie Husband
	DB Tommy Weigand / Danny Gilbert
	DB Steve Williams
	DB Mike Dean
	DB Bill Blair

RUSHING: Musso 157/516y, Jilleba 69/320y, Ranager 12/126y
PASSING: Hunter 157-266/2188y, 9TD, 58.6%
RECEIVING: Bailey 56/781y, Musso 26/321y, Husband 20/279y
SCORING: Musso 78pts, Ranager 48pts, Oran Buck (K) 22pts

1970 6-5-1

21 Southern Cal	42 WR David Bailey
51 Virginia Tech	18 WR Jerry Cash
46 Florida	15 T Jimmy Rosser
23 Mississippi	48 G Mike Hand
35 Vanderbilt	11 C Pat Raines
0 Tennessee	24 G Ried Drinkard
30 Houston	21 T John Hannah
35 Mississippi St.	6 TE Randy Moore
9 LSU	14 QB Scott Hunter / Neb Hayden
32 Miami	8 TB Johnny Musso / Buddy Seay
28 Auburn	33 FB Dave Brungard
24 Oklahoma■	24 DL Ed Hines
	DL Don Harris
	DL Terry Rowell
	DL Tom Lusk
	LB Jeff Rouzie
	LB Jim Krapf
	LB Danny Gilbert / Woodie Husband
	DB Steve Higginbotham
	DB Steve Williams
	DB Lanny Norris
	DB Tommy Wade

RUSHING: Musso 226/1137y, Brungard 73/418y, Seay 58/235y
PASSING: Hunter 103-179/1240y, 8TD, 57.6%
RECEIVING: Bailey 55/790y, Musso 30/160y, Brungard 20/201y
SCORING: Richard Ciemny (K) 56pts, Musso 54pts, Bailey 40pts

1971 11-1

17 Southern Cal	10 WR David Bailey / Wayne Wheeler
42 Southern Miss	6 T Jim Krapf
38 Florida	0 G Jimmy Rosser
40 Mississippi	6 C Jimmy Grammer / Pat Raines
42 Vanderbilt	0 G John Hannah
32 Tennessee	15 T Buddy Brown
34 Houston	20 TE Jim Simmons
41 Mississippi St.	10 QB Terry Davis
14 LSU	10 HB Johnny Musso
31 Miami	3 HB Joe LaBue
31 Auburn	7 FB Steve Bisceglia / Ellis Beck
6 Nebraska■	38 DL Robin Parkhouse
	DL Terry Rowell
	DL Jeff Beard
	DL John Mitchell
	LB Jeff Rouzie
	LB Chuck Strickland
	LB Tom Surlas
	DB Steve Higginbotham
	DB Steve Williams
	DB Steve Wade
	DB Lanny Norris / David McMakin

RUSHING: Musso 191/1088y, Beck 110/556y, Bisceglia 80/472y
PASSING: Davis 42-66/452y, 8TD, 63.6%
RECEIVING: Bailey 21/286y, Wheeler 6/143y, LaBue 5/43y
SCORING: Musso 100pts, Bill Davis (K) 75pts, T. Davis 40pts

1972 10-2

35 Duke	12 WR Wayne Wheeler / Dexter Wood
35 Kentucky	0 T Steve Sprayberry
48 Vanderbilt	21 G Greg Montgomery
25 Georgia	7 C Pat Raines
24 Florida	7 G John Hannah
17 Tennessee	10 T Jim Krapf
48 Southern Miss	11 TE Warren Dyar
58 Mississippi St.	14 QB Terry Davis
35 LSU	21 HB Wilbur Jackson
52 Virginia Tech	13 HB Joe LaBue
16 Auburn	17 FB Steve Bisceglia / Ellis Beck
13 Texas■	17 DL John Mitchell / David Watkins
	DL Skip Kubelius
	DL Mike Raines
	DL John Croyle
	LB Wayne Hall
	LB Mike Dubose
	LB Chuck Strickland
	DB Lanny Norris / Mike Washington
	DB Bobby McKinney
	DB David McMakin
	DB Steve Wade

RUSHING: Bisceglia 125/603y, Jackson 80/566y, LaBue 56/376y
PASSING: Davis 50-94/777y, 6TD, 53.2%
RECEIVING: Wheeler 30/573y, Wood 8/106y, LaBue 5/65y
SCORING: Bill Davis (K) 61pts, Bisceglia 60pts, T. Davis 54pts

1973 11-1

66 California	0 WR Wayne Wheeler
28 Kentucky	14 T Steve Sprayberry
44 Vanderbilt	0 G Morris Hunt / Larry Ruffin
28 Georgia	14 C Sylvester Croom
35 Florida	14 G John Rogers
42 Tennessee	21 T Buddy Brown
77 Virginia Tech	6 TE George Pugh / Warren Dyar
35 Mississippi St.	0 QB Gary Rutledge / Richard Todd
43 Miami	13 HB Wilbur Jackson
21 LSU	7 HB Randy Billingsley / Willie Shelby
35 Auburn	0 FB Ellis Beck / Paul Spivey
23 Notre Dame■	24 DL David Watkins / John Croyle
	DL Mike Raines
	DL Randy Hall / Skip Kubelius
	LB Mike DuBose / Dick Turpin
	LB Wayne Nall
	LB Chuck Strickland / Greg Montgomery
	LB Woodrow Lowe
	DB Mike Washington
	DB Tyrone King / Wayne Rhodes
	DB Ricky Davis
	DB David McMakin / Alan Pizzitola

RUSHING: Jackson 95/752y, Todd 88/560y, Billingsley 68/443y
PASSING: Rutledge 33-57/897y, 8 TD, 57.9%
RECEIVING: Wheeler 19/530y, Pugh 8/175y, Dyar 7/102y
SCORING: Bill Davis (K) 75pts, Jackson 50pts, Billingsley 48pts

1974 11-1

21 Maryland	16 WR Ozzie Newsome / Russ Schamun
52 Southern Miss	0 T Gerry Washco (DT)
23 Vanderbilt	10 G Larry Ruffin (T)
35 Mississippi	21 C Sylvester Croom
8 Florida State	7 G John Rogers / Steve Patterson
28 Tennessee	6 T Ray Maxwell (G) / Buddy Pope
41 TCU	3 TE Jerry Brown / George Pugh
35 Mississippi St.	0 QB Richard Todd / Robert Fraley
30 LSU	0 HB Willie Shelby
28 Miami	7 HB Randy Billingsley / Jimmy Taylor
17 Auburn	13 FB Calvin Culliver / Rick Watson
11 Notre Dame■	13 DL Mike DuBose
	DL Bob Baumhower / Charles Hannah
	DL Gus White / Greg Montgomery (LB)
	DL Randy Hall
	DL Leroy Cook
	LB Woodrow Lowe / Conley Duncan
	LB Ronny Robertson
	DB Mike Washington
	DB Wayne Rhodes
	DB Ricky Davis
	DB Alan Pizzitola

RUSHING: Culliver 116/708y, Shelby 84/541y, Billingsley 58/305y
PASSING: Todd 36-67/656y, 5 TD, 53.7%
RECEIVING: Newsome 20/374y, Pugh 9/178y, Brown 9/110y
SCORING: Culliver 48pts, Danny Ridgeway (K) 45pts, Shelby 36pts

1975 11-1

7	Missouri	20 WR Ozzie Newsome / Joe Dale Harris
56	Clemson	0 T David Hannah / K.J. Lazenby
40	Vanderbilt	7 G Larry Ruffin / Bob Cryder
32	Mississippi	6 C Terry Jones
52	Washington	0 G David Gersimchuk
30	Tennessee	7 T Ray Maxwell / Buddy Pope
45	TCU	0 TE Jerry Brown / George Pugh
21	Mississippi St.	10 QB Richard Todd
23	LSU	10 HB Willie Shelby
27	Southern Miss	6 HB Mike Stock
28	Auburn	0 FB Johnny Davis
13	Penn State■	6 DL Dick Turpin / Neil Calloway

DL Charles Hannah
DL Gus White / Colenzo Hubbard (LB)
DL Bob Baumhower
DL Leroy Cook
LB Conley Duncan / Greg Montgomery
LB Woodrow Lowe
DB Tyrone King
DB Wayne Rhodes
DB Roy Bolden
DB Alan Pizzitola / Mark Prudhomme

RUSHING: Davis 123/820y, Todd 113/429y, Shelby 81/315y
PASSING: Todd 47-89/661y, 7TD, 52.8%
RECEIVING: Newsome 21/363y, Harris 12/154y, Brown 8/122y
SCORING: Todd 54pts, Danny Ridgeway (K) 47pts, Davis 42pts

1976 9-3

7	Mississippi	10 WR Ozzie Newsome / Thad Flanagan
56	SMU	3 T K.J. Lazenby / David Hannah
42	Vanderbilt	14 G Louis Green
0	Georgia	21 C Terry Jones
24	Southern Miss	8 G David Gerosimchuk / Jim Bunch
20	Tennessee	13 T Tim Hurst / Bob Cryder
24	Louisville	3 TE Rick Neal / Tim Travis
34	Mississippi St.	17 QB Jeff Rutledge / Jack O'Rear
28	LSU	17 HB Calvin Culliver / John Crow
18	Notre Dame	21 HB Pete Cavan / Tony Nathan
38	Auburn	7 FB Johnny Davis
36	UCLA■	6 DL Bobby Mikel

DL Bob Baumhower / Marty Lyons
DL Gus White
DL Charley Hannah
DL Paul Harris
LB Colenzo Hubbard / Rich Wingo
LB Dewey Mitchell
DB Mike Kramer
DB Mike Tucker / Phil Allman
DB Les Fowler
DB Andy Gothard / Murray Legg

RUSHING: Davis 119/668y, Nathan 75/480y, O'Rear 95/467y
PASSING: Rutledge 62-109/979y, 8 TD, 56.9%
RECEIVING: Newsome 25/529y, Flanagan 19/304y, Culliver 7/78y
SCORING: Bucky Berrey (K) 53pts, Davis & Nathan 42pts

1977 11-1

34	Mississippi	13 WR Ozzie Newsome / Keith Pugh
24	Nebraska	31 T Chip Tillman
24	Vanderbilt	12 G Louis Green
18	Georgia	10 C Dwight Stephenson
21	Southern Cal	20 G Bob Cryder
24	Tennessee	10 T Jim Bunch
55	Louisville	10 TE Rick Neal
37	Mississippi St.	7 QB Jeff Rutledge / Jack O'Rear
24	LSU	3 HB Tony Nathan
36	Miami	0 HB John Crow / Major Ogilvie
48	Auburn	21 FB Johnny Davis
35	Ohio State■	6 DL Calvin Parker

DL Marty Lyons
DL Terry Jones
DL William Davis
DL John Knox
LB Barry Krauss
LB Rickey Gilliland
DB Phil Allman
DB Mike Tucker
DB Mike Kramer
DB Murray Legg

RUSHING: Davis 182/931y, Nathan 104/642y, Rutledge 109/311y
PASSING: Rutledge 64-107/1207y 8 TD, 59.8%
RECEIVING: Newsome 36/804y, Pugh 9/181y, Bruce Bolton (WR) 8/123y
SCORING: Nathan 92pts, Roger Chapman (K) 63pts, Davis 30pts

1978 11-1

20	Nebraska	3 WR Keith Pugh / Bruce Bolton
38	Missouri	20 T Buddy Aydelette
14	Southern Cal	24 G Mike Brock
51	Vanderbilt	28 C Dwight Stevenson
20	Washington	17 G Vince Boothe
23	Florida	12 T Jim Bunch
20	Tennessee	17 TE Rick Neal / Tim Travis
35	Virginia Tech	0 QB Jeff Rutledge
35	Mississippi St.	14 HB Tony Nathan
31	LSU	10 HB Major Ogilvie / Billy Jackson (FB)
34	Auburn	16 FB Steve Whitman
14	Penn State■	7 DL E.J. Junior

DL Byron Braggs / Curtis McGriff
DL Warren Lyles
DL Marty Lyons
DL Wayne Hamilton / Gary DeNiro
LB Barry Krause
LB Rickey Gilliland / Rich Wingo
DB Don McNeal
DB Ricky Tucker / Bobby Smith
DB Murray Legg / Jim Bob Harris
DB Allen Crumbley

RUSHING: Nathan 111/770y, Ogilvie 90/583y, Jackson 103/568y
PASSING: Rutledge 73-140/1078y, 13 TD, 52.1%
RECEIVING: Pugh 20/446y, Neal 17/268y, Bolton 15/270y
SCORING: Alan McElroy (K) 58pts, Ogilvie 54pts, Nathan 44pts

1979 12-0

30	Georgia Tech	6 WR Keith Pugh / Tim Clark
45	Baylor	0 T Buddy Aydelette
66	Vanderbilt	3 G Vince Boothe
38	Wichita State	0 C Dwight Stevenson
40	Florida	0 G Mike Brock / Scott Allison
27	Tennessee	17 T Jim Bunch
31	Virginia Tech	7 TE Tim Travis
24	Miss State	7 QB Steadman Sheely
3	LSU	0 HB Major Ogilvie
30	Miami	0 HB Billy Jackson / Mitch Ferguson
25	Auburn	18 FB Steve Whitman
24	Arkansas■	9 DL Wayne Hamilton / Gary DeNiro

DL Byron Braggs
DL Warren Lyles / Curtis McGriff
DL David Hannah
DL E.J. Junior
LB Randy Scott
LB Thomas Boyd
DB Don McNeal
DB Ricky Tucker
DB Jim Bob Harris
DB Tommy Wilcox

RUSHING: Shealy 152/791y, Whitman 126/653y, Ogilvie 97/512y
PASSING: Shealy 45-81/717y, 4 TD, 55.6%
RECEIVING: Pugh 25/433y, Travis 7/150y, Clark 5/79y
SCORING: Alan McElroy (K) 77pts, Shealy 68pts, Ogilvie 58pts

1980 10-2

26	Georgia Tech	3 WR Jesse Bendross / James Mallard
59	Mississippi	35 T Eddie McCombs
41	Vanderbilt	0 G Scott Allison
45	Kentucky	0 C Steve Mott
17	Rutgers	13 G Vince Cowell
27	Tennessee	0 T Bob Cayavec / Bill Searcey
42	Southern Miss	7 TE Bart Krout
3	Mississippi St.	6 QB Don Jacobs / Walter Lewis
28	LSU	7 HB Joe Jones / Linnie Patrick
0	Notre Dame	7 HB Major Ogilvie
34	Auburn	18 FB Billy Jackson / Charlie Williams
30	Baylor■	2 DL Gary DeNiro / Mike Pitts

DL Byron Braggs
DL Warren Lyles
DL Jackie Cline
DL E.J. Junior
LB Randy Scott / Eddie Lowe
LB Thomas Boyd
DB Ricky Tucker
DB Mike Clements
DB Jim Bob Harris / Jeremiah Castille
DB Tommy Wilcox

RUSHING: Jackson 111/606y, Ogilvie 78/439y, Patrick 50/361y
PASSING: Jacobs 32-76/531y, 4 TD, 42.1%
RECEIVING: Krout 16/218y, Bendross 11/169y, Mallard 5/142y
SCORING: Peter Kim (K) 71pts, Ogilvie 50pts, Jackson 30pts

1981 9-2-1

24	LSU	7 WR Jesse Bendross / Joey Jones
21	Georgia Tech	24 T Joe Beazley / Roy Rumbley
19	Kentucky	10 G Mike Adcock
28	Vanderbilt	7 C Steve Mott
38	Mississippi	7 G Doug Vickers / Gary Barmblett
13	Southern Miss	13 T Bob Cayavec / Mike McQueen
38	Tennessee	19 TE Bart Krout
31	Rutgers	7 QB Walter Lewis / Ken Coley / Alan Gray
13	Mississippi St.	10 HB Joe Carter / Paul Ott Carruth
31	Penn State	16 HB Jeff Fagan / Linnie Patrick
28	Auburn	17 FB Ricky Moore / Ken Simon
12	Texas■	14 DL Mike Pitts

DL Jackie Cline
DL Warren Lyles
DL Randy Edwards
DL Russ Wood
LB Robbie Jones
LB Thomas Boyd / Eddie Lowe
DB Jeremiah Castille
DB Benny Perrin / Jerrill Sprinkle
DB Jim Bob Harris / Al Blue
DB Tommy Wilcox

RUSHING: Moore 79/347y, Patrick 60/332y, Carter 59/331y
PASSING: Lewis 30-66/633y, 6 TD, 45.5%
RECEIVING: Bendross 13/256y, Jones 12/373y, Krout 8/125y
SCORING: Peter Kim (K) 70pts, Bendross & Patrick 30pts

1982 8-4

45	Georgia Tech	7 WR Joey Jones / Jesse Bendross
42	Mississippi	14 T Joe Beazley
24	Vanderbilt	21 G Mike Adcock
34	Arkansas St.	7 C Steve Mott
42	Penn State	21 G Gary Branmblett / Williard Sissum
28	Tennessee	35 T Doug Vickers
21	Cincinnati	3 TE Jay Grogan
20	Mississippi St.	12 QB Walter Lewis
10	LSU	20 HB Paul Ott Carruth / Joe Carter
29	Southern Miss	38 HB Jeff Fagan / Linnie Patrick
22	Auburn	23 FB Ricky Moore / Craig Turner
21	Illinois■	15 DL Mike Pitts

DL Jackie Cline
DL Mike Rodriguez / John Elias
DL Randy Edwards
DL Russ Wood
LB Robbie Jones / Steve Booker
LB Eddie Lowe
DB Jeremiah Castille
DB Stan Gay / Jerrill Sprinkle
DB Rocky Colburn / Al Blue
DB Tommy Wilcox

RUSHING: Moore 111/600y, Lewis 143/572y, Patrick 70/316y
PASSING: Lewis 102-164/1515y, 9 TD, 62.2%
RECEIVING: Jones 25/502y, Bendross 25/499y, Moore 19/166y
SCORING: Turner 72pts, Peter Kim (K) 66pts, Jones 36pts

1983 8-4

20	Georgia Tech	7 WR Joey Jones
40	Mississippi	0 WR Jesse Bendross
44	Vanderbilt	24 T Hardy Walker / Gary Otten
44	Memphis State	13 G Mike Adcock
28	Penn State	34 C Wes Neighbors / Mike White
34	Tennessee	41 G John McIntosh
35	Mississippi St.	18 T Doug Vickers
32	LSU	26 TE Preston Gothard / Thornton Chandler
28	Southern Miss	16 QB Walter Lewis
13	Boston College	20 HB Kerry Goode / Linnie Patrick
20	Auburn	23 FB Ricky Moore
28	SMU■	7 DL Jon Hand

DL Curt Jarvis / Mike Rodriguez
DL Randy Edwards
LB Emanuel King
LB Scott McRae
LB Venson Elder / Wayne Davis
LB Cornelius Bennett / Steve Booker
DB Stan Gay
DB Sammy Hood
DB Freddie Robinson / David Valletto
DB Ricky Thomas / Rocky Colburn

RUSHING: Moore 166/947y, Goode 103/693y, Patrick 85/454y
PASSING: Lewis 144-256/1991y, 14 TD, 56.3%
RECEIVING: Jones 31/468y, Bendross 27/435y, Gothard 24/294y
SCORING: Van Tiffin (K) 82pts, Moore 56pts, Carter, Jones, & Lewis 30pts

1984 5-6

31 Boston College	38 WR Clay Whitehurst
6 Georgia Tech	16 WR Greg Richardson
37 SW Louisiana	14 T Jim Ivey / David Johnson
21 Vanderbilt	24 G Mike White
14 Georgia	24 C Wes Neighbors
9 Penn State	0 G John McIntosh / Bill Condon
27 Tennessee	28 T Gary Otten
24 Mississippi St.	20 TE Preston Gothard
14 LSU	16 QB Vince Sutton / Mike Shula
29 Cincinnati	7 HB Paul Ott Carruth / Kerry Goode
17 Auburn	15 FB Ricky Moore / Don Horstead
	DL Brent Sowell / Larry Roberts
	DL Curt Jarvis
	DL Jon Hand
	LB Emanuel King
	LB Wayne Davis / Scott McRae
	LB Cornelius Bennett
	LB Randy Rockwell
	DB Freddie Robinson
	DB Vernon Wilkinson / Louis Dean
	DB Britton Cooper / Rory Turner
	DB Paul Tripoli / Ricky Thomas

RUSHING: Carruth 163/782y, Moore 113/376y,
Horstead 46/215y
PASSING: Sutton 60-135/662y, 4 TD, 44.4%
Shula 47-110/568y, 6 TD, 42.7%
RECEIVING: Richardson 22/357y, Moore 19/135y,
Carruth 18/224y
SCORING: Carruth & Van Tiffin (K) 68pts,
Goode & Richardson 18pts

1985 9-2-1

20 Georgia	16 WR Greg Richardson / Clay Whitehurst
23 Texas A&M	10 WR Al Bell
45 Cincinnati	10 T David "Hoss" Johnson
40 Vanderbilt	20 G David Gilmer
17 Penn State	19 C Wes Neighbors
14 Tennessee	16 G Bill Condon / John McIntosh
Memphis State	9 T Larry Rose
44 Mississippi St.	28 TE Thornton Chandler / Howard Cross
14 LSU	14 QB Mike Shula
24 Southern Miss	13 HB Bobby Humphrey / Kerry Goode
25 Auburn	23 FB Craig Turner / Mike Bobo
24 Southern Cal ■	3 DL Jon Hand
	DL Curt Jarvis
	DL Brent Sowell / Larry Roberts
	LB Cornelius Bennett / Derrick Thomas
	LB Wayne Davis / Desmond Holoman
	LB Joe Godwin / Todd Roper
	LB Randy Rockwell
	DB Freddie Robinson / Shannon Felder
	DB Britton Cooper / Vernon Wilkinson
	DB Rory Turner / Kermit Kendrick
	DB Ricky Thomas

RUSHING: Jelks 93/588y, Humphrey 99/502y, Turner 117/480y
PASSING: Shula 138-229/2009y 16 TD, 60.3%
RECEIVING: Bell 37/648y, Turner 25/224y, Chandler 16/244y
SCORING: Van Tiffin (K) 84pts, Bell 54pts, Humphrey 42pts

1986 10-3

16 Ohio State	10 WR Greg Richardson
42 Vanderbilt	10 WR Albert Bell
31 Southern Miss	17 T Hoss Johnson
21 Florida	7 G Larry Rose
28 Notre Dame	10 C Wes Neighbors
37 Memphis State	0 G Bill Condon
56 Tennessee	28 T Joe King
3 Penn State	23 TE Howard Cross
10 LSU	14 QB Mike Shula
24 Temple	14 TB Bobby Humphrey / Gene Jelks
17 Auburn	21 FB Doug Allen / Kerry Goode
28 Washington ■	6 DL Derrick Slaughter
	DL Curt Jarvis
	DL Cliff Thomas
	LB Cornelius Bennett
	LB Greg Gilbert / Vantriese Davis
	LB Wayne Davis
	LB Randy Rockwell / George Bethune
	DB Freddie Robinson
	DB Britton Cooper
	DB Kermit Kendrick
	DB Ricky Thomas

RUSHING: Humphrey 236/1471y, Jelks 84/509y, Allen 67/357y
PASSING: Shula 127-235/1486y 13TD, 54.0%
RECEIVING: Bell 26/315y, Richardson 23/393y, Humphrey 22/204y
SCORING: Humphrey 104pts, Van Tiffin (K) 78pts,
Jelks & Richardson 24pts

1987 7-5

38 Southern Miss	6 WR Clay Whitehurst / Angelo Stafford
24 Penn State	13 WR Marco Battle / Pierre Goode
14 Florida	23 T Jeff Bentley
30 Vanderbilt	23 G Larry Rose
38 SW Louisiana	10 C Mike Zuga / Roger Shultz
10 Memphis State	13 G Bill Condon
41 Tennessee	22 T Terrill Chatman
21 Mississippi St.	18 TE Howard Cross
22 LSU	10 QB David Smith / Vince Sutton / Jeff Dunn
0 Notre Dame	37 TB Bobby Humphrey / Kerry Goode
0 Auburn	10 FB Doug Allen / Bo Wright
24 Michigan ■	28 DL Tommy Cole / Thomas Rayam
	DL Willie Wyatt
	DL Phillip Brown / Anthony Smith
	LB Randy Rockwell
	LB Willie Shephard / Robert Stewart
	LB Greg Gilbert
	LB Derrick Thomas
	DB John Mangum
	DB Gene Jelks
	DB Kermit Kendrick
	DB Lee Ozmant

RUSHING: Humphrey 238/1255y, Goode 67/303y,
Wright 58/255y
PASSING: Dunn 36-87/484y, 3TD, 41.4%,
Smith 33-60/313y, 3TD, 55.0%,
Sutton 22-52/313y, 4TD, 42.3%
RECEIVING: Humphrey 22/170y, Whitehurst 18/278y,
Cross 17/158y
SCORING: Humphrey 78pts, Philip Doyle (K) 57pts, Wright 20pts

1988 9-3

37 Temple	0 WR Greg Payne
42 Vanderbilt	10 WR Marco Battle
31 Kentucky	27 T John Fruhmorgen (G) / Sam Atkins
12 Mississippi	22 G Chris Robinette
28 Tennessee	20 C Roger Shultz
8 Penn State	3 G Larry Rose
53 Mississippi St.	34 T Terrill Chatman
18 LSU	19 TE Howard Cross / Lamonde Russell
17 SW Louisiana	0 QB David Smith / Jeff Dunn
10 Auburn	15 TB Murry Hill / Bobby Humphrey
30 Texas A&M	10 FB Kevin Turner / William Kent
29 Army ■	28 DL George Bethune
	DL Willie Wyatt
	DL Tommy Cole
	LB Spencer Hammond
	LB Keith McCants / Vantriese Davis
	LB Greg Gilbert / Willie Shephard
	LB Derrick Thomas
	DB John Mangum / Kermit Kendrick
	DB Gene Jelks / Brian Stutson
	DB Lee Ozmint
	DB Charles Gardner

RUSHING: Hill 136/778y, Casteal 93/335y, Humphrey 42/192y
PASSING: Smith 135-223/1592y, 7TD, 60.5%
RECEIVING: Payne 33/442y, Russell 29/404y, Battle 28/367y
SCORING: Philip Doyle (K) 91pts, Casteal 36pts, Hill 32pts

1989 10-2

35 Memphis State	7 WR Craig Sanderson
15 Kentucky	3 WR Marco Battle
20 Vanderbilt	14 T Vince Strickland
62 Mississippi	27 G Chris Robinette
24 SW Louisiana	17 C Roger Shultz / Mike Zuga
47 Tennessee	30 G Trent Patterson
17 Penn State	16 T Terrill Chatman
23 Miss State	10 TE Lamonde Russell / Charlie Abrams
32 LSU	16 QB Gary Hollingsworth / Jeff Dunn
37 Southern Miss	13 TB Siran Stacy / Murry Hill
20 Auburn	30 FB Kevin Turner / Martin Houston
25 Miami ■	33 DL Steve Webb
	DL George Thornton
	DL Willie Wyatt
	DL Thomas Rayam
	LB Spencer Hammond
	LB Vantreise Davis / John Sullins
	LB Keith McCants
	DB John Mangum
	DB Efrum Thomas
	DB Lee Ozmint
	DB Charles Gardner

RUSHING: Stacy 216/1079y, Hill 81/417y, Houston 53/239y
PASSING: Hollingsworth 205-339/2379y, 14TD, 60.5%
RECEIVING: Russell 51/622y, Turner 48/465y, Stacy 36/371y
SCORING: Stacy 108pts, Philip Doyle (K) 100pts, Russell 30pts

1990 7-5

24 Southern Miss	27 WR Kevin Lee
13 Florida	17 WR David Palmer
16 Georgia	17 T Matt Hammond
59 Vanderbilt	28 G John Clay
25 SW Louisiana	6 C Tobie Sheils
9 Tennessee	6 G Jon Stevenson / Dennis Deason
0 Penn State	9 T Roosevelt Patterson
22 Mississippi St.	0 TE Tony Johnson
24 LSU	3 QB Jay Barker / Brian Burgdorf
45 Cincinnati	7 TB Sherman Williams / Chris Anderson
16 Auburn	7 FB Tarrant Lynch / Eric Turner
7 Louisville ■	34 DL Ozell Powell
	DL James Gregory / Shannon Brown
	DL Jeremy Nunley
	LB Will Brown / Andre Royal
	LB Michael Rogers
	LB John Walters / Mario Morris
	LB Lemanski Hall
	DB Antonio Langham
	DB Tommy Johnson
	DB Chris Donnelly / Willie Gaston
	DB Sam Shade

RUSHING: Williams 168/738y, Anderson 90/324y, Lynch 67/276y
PASSING: Barker 98-171/1525y, 4TD, 57.3%
RECEIVING: Palmer 61/1000y, Lee 26/510y, Lynch 19/171y
SCORING: Michael Proctor (K) 97pts, Williams 54pts,
Palmer 44pts

1991 11-1

41 Temple	3 WR Prince Wimbley / David Palmer
0 Florida	35 WR Donnie Finkley / Kevin Lee
10 Georgia	0 T Matt Hammond
48 Vanderbilt	17 G George Wilson
53 Tenn.-Chatt'ga	7 C Tobie Sheils
62 Tulane	0 G William Barger / John Clay
24 Tennessee	19 T Jon Stevenson
13 Mississippi St.	7 TE Derrick Warren / Steve Busky
20 LSU	17 QB Danny Woodson / Jay Barker
10 Memphis State	7 TB Siran Stacy / Derrick Lassic
13 Auburn	6 FB Kevin Turner
30 Colorado ■	25 DL John Copeland
	DL Robert Stewart
	DL Eric Curry
	LB Steve Webb
	LB John Sullins
	LB Derrick Oden / Michael Rogers
	LB Antonio London
	DB Antonio Langham
	DB George Teague
	DB Stacy Harrison
	DB Mark McMillian

RUSHING: Stacy 200/967y, Turner 73/430y, Lassic 70/368y
PASSING: Woodson 64-101/882y, 4TD, 63.4%
RECEIVING: Palmer 17/314y, Wimbley 14/174y, Stacy 13/178y
SCORING: Stacy 60pts, Palmer 42pts, Hamp Greene (K) 39pts

1992 13-0

25 Vanderbilt	8 WR Kevin Lee / Curtis Brown
17 Southern Miss	10 WR David Palmer / Prince Wimbley
38 Arkansas	11 T Matt Hammond
13 Louisiana Tech	0 G George Wilson
48 South Carolina	7 C Tobie Sheils
37 Tulane	0 G Jon Stevenson / William Barger
17 Tennessee	10 T Roosevelt Patterson / Joey Harville
31 Mississippi	10 TE Steve Busky / Tony Johnson
31 LSU	11 QB Jay Barker
30 Mississippi St.	21 TB Derrick Lassic / Chris Anderson
17 Auburn	0 FB Martin Houston / Tarrant Lynch
28 Florida □	21 DL John Copeland
34 Miami ■	13 DL James Gregory / Jeremy Nunley
	DL Eric Curry / Dameian Jeffries
	LB Antonio London
	LB Michael Rogers / Mario Morris
	LB Derrick Oden
	LB Lemanski Hall / Will Brown
	DB Antonio Langham / Tommy Johnson
	DB George Teague
	DB Chris Donnelly
	DB Sam Shade / Michael Ausmus

RUSHING: Lassic 178/905y, Anderson 94/573y,
Houston 103/457y
PASSING: Barker 132-243/1614y, 7TD, 54.3%
RECEIVING: Palmer 24/297y, Lee 21/286y, Wimbley 21/248y
SCORING: Michael Proctor (K) 94pts, Lassic 66pts,
Anderson & Sherman Williams (TB) 48pts

1993 9-3-1

31	Tulane	17	WR Kevin Lee / Curtis Brown
17	Vanderbilt	6	WR David Palmer / Toderick Malone
43	Arkansas	3	T Matt Hammond / Joey Harville
56	Louisiana Tech	3	G John Clay
17	South Carolina	6	C Tobie Sheils / John Causey
17	Tennessee	17	G Jon Stevenson
19	Mississippi	14	T Roosevelt Patterson
40	Southern Miss.	0	TE Tony Johnson
13	LSU	17	QB Jay Barker
36	Mississippi St.	25	TB Sherman Williams / Chris Anderson
14	Auburn	22	FB Tarrant Lynch
13	Florida □	28	DL Jeremy Nunley / Dameian Jeffries
24	North Carolina ■	10	DL James Gregory / Shannon Brown
			DL Elverett Brown
			LB Tyrell Buckner / Fernando Davis
			LB Michael Rogers
			LB Darrell Blackburn / John Walters
			LB Lemanski Hall
			DB Antonio Langham
			DB Tommy Johnson / Cedric Samuel
			DB Chris Donnelly / Willie Gaston
			DB Sam Shade

RUSHING: Williams 168/738y, Anderson 90/314y,
 Lynch 67/276y
PASSING: Barker 98-171/1524y, 4TD, 57.3%
RECEIVING: Palmer 61/1000y, Lee 26/510y, Lynch 19/171y
SCORING: Michael Proctor (K) 97pts, Williams 54pts,
 Palmer 44pts

1994 12-1

42	Tenn.-Chatt'ga	13	WR Curtis Brown
17	Vanderbilt	7	WR Toderick Malone / Chad Key
13	Arkansas	6	T Joey Harville
20	Tulane	10	G Maurice Belser
29	Georgia	28	C Jon Stevenson
14	Southern Miss	6	G Laron White
17	Tennessee	13	T Joel Holliday
21	Mississippi	10	TE Patrick Hape / Tony Johnson
35	LSU	17	QB Jay Barker / Brian Burgdorf
29	Mississippi St.	25	TB Sherman Williams / Dennis Riddle
21	Auburn	14	FB Tarrant Lynch
23	Florida □	24	DL Dameian Jeffries / Vann Bodden
24	Ohio State ■	17	DL Shannon Brown
			DL Matt Parker
			DL Darrell Blackburn
			LB Andre Royal / Ralph Staten
			LB Michael Rogers / Tyrell Buckner
			LB John Walters / Dwayne Rudd
			DB Deshea Townsend / Brad Ford
			DB Tommy Johnson
			DB Willie Gaston / Eric Turner
			DB Sam Shade / Cedric Samuel

RUSHING: Williams 291/1341y, Lynch 75/327y,
 Brian Steger (TB) 36/145y
PASSING: Barker 139-226/1996y, 14TD, 61.5%
RECEIVING: Brown 39/639y, Lynch 31/281y, Malone 26/459y
SCORING: Michael Proctor (K) 71pts, Williams 60pts,
 Brown 36pts

1995 8-3

33	Vanderbilt	25	WR Curtis Brown / Marcell West
24	Southern Miss	20	WR Toderick Malone / Michael Vaughn
19	Arkansas	20	T Joel Holliday
31	Georgia	0	G Will Friend
27	N. Carolina St.	11	C John Causey
14	Tennessee	41	G Laron White
23	Mississippi	9	T Pete DiMario / Sage Spree
38	North Texas	19	TE Tony Johnson / Patrick Hape
10	LSU	3	QB Brian Burgdorf / Freddie Kitchens
14	Mississippi St.	9	TB Dennis Riddle / Curtis Alexander
27	Auburn	31	FB Ed Scissum
			DL Kendrick Burton / Chris Hood
			DL Shannon Brown
			DL Matt Parker / Ozell Powell
			DL Darrell Blackburn / Kelvin Moore
			LB Ralph Staten
			LB John Walters / Tyrell Buckner
			LB Dwayne Rudd
			DB Deshea Townsend
			DB Fernando Bryant
			DB Cedric Samuel
			DB Kevin Jackson / Andre Short

RUSHING: Riddle 236/969y, Brian Steger (TB) 57/218y,
 Scissum 19/93y
PASSING: Burgdorf 96-162/1200y, 9TD, 59.3%
RECEIVING: Brown 43/557y, Malone 38/637y, Riddle 23/150y
SCORING: Michael Proctor (K) 64pts, Riddle 54pts,
 Malone 36pts

1996 10-3

21	Bowling Green	7	WR Calvin Hall / Shamari Buchanan
20	Southern Miss.	10	WR Michael Vaughn
36	Vanderbilt	26	T Chris Samuels
17	Arkansas	7	G Will Friend
35	Kentucky	24	C John Causey / Michael Ray
24	N. Carolina St.	19	G Laron White / Brenon Meadows
37	Mississippi	0	T Pete DiMario
13	Tennessee	20	TE Patrick Hape / Rod Rutleddge
26	LSU	0	QB Freddie Kitchens
16	Mississippi St.	17	TB Dennis Riddle / Shaun Alexander
24	Auburn	23	FB Ed Scissum
30	Florida □	45	DL Chris Hood / Reggie Grimes
17	Michigan ■	14	DL Michael Myers / Jamie Carter
			DL Kelvin Moore
			DL Ozell Powell / Edgar Walker
			LB Ralph Staten
			LB Tyrell Buckner / Paul Pickett
			LB Dwayne Rudd
			DB Deshea Townsend
			DB Fernando Bryant
			DB Cedric Samuel / Kelvin Sigler
			DB Kevin Jackson / Andre Short

RUSHING: Riddle 242/1079y, S. Alexander 77/589y,
 Curtis Alexander (TB) 61/240y
PASSING: Kitchens 152-302/2124y, 14 TD, 50.3%
RECEIVING: Vaughn 39/702y, Riddle 34/290y, Hall 16/313y
SCORING: Riddle 84pts, Brian Cunningham (K) 43pts,
 S. Alexander & Vaughn 36pts

1997 4-7

42	Houston	17	WR Calvin Hall / Shamari Buchanan
20	Vanderbilt	0	WR Chad Goss / Quincy Jackson
16	Arkansas	17	T Chris Samuels
27	Southern Miss	13	G Will Friend / Griff Redmill
34	Kentucky	40	C Paul Hogan / Brooks Brodie
21	Tennessee	38	G Brenon Meadows
29	Mississippi	20	T Michael Ray
20	Louisiana Tech	26	TE Rod Rutledge
0	LSU	27	QB Freddie Kitchens
20	Mississippi St.	32	TB Curtis Alexander / Shaun Alexander
17	Auburn	18	FB Ed Scissum / Dennis Riddle (TB)
			DL Chris Hood / Reggie Grimes
			DL Heath Panks
			DL Eric Kerley / Jamie Carter
			DL Kenny Smith
			LB Paul Pickett / Steve Harris
			LB Travis Carroll
			LB Steve Stanley
			DB Deshea Townsend / Kecalf Bailey
			DB Fernando Bryant / Michael Feagin
			DB Kelvin Sigler
			DB Andre Short / Tony Dixon

RUSHING: C. Alexander 155/729y, Riddle 97/454y,
 S. Alexander 90/415y
PASSING: Kitchens 121-237/1545y, 11TD, 51.1%
RECEIVING: Jackson 29/472y, Hall 19/301y, Goss 18/279y
SCORING: Brian Cunningham (K) 50pts, C. Alexander 48pts,
 Scissum 26pts

1998 7-5

38	BYU	31	WR Calvin Hall / Michael Vaughn
32	Vanderbilt	7	WR Quincy Jackson / Shamari Buchanan
6	Arkansas	42	T Chris Samuels
10	Florida	16	G Griff Redmill
20	Mississippi	17	C Paul Hogan
23	East Carolina	22	G Jason McDonald
18	Tennessee	35	T Will Cuthbert
30	Southern Miss	20	TE Terry Jones
22	LSU	16	QB Andrew Zow / John David Phillips
14	Mississippi St.	26	TB Shaun Alexander
31	Auburn	17	FB Dustin McClintock
7	Virginia Tech ■	38	DL Kindal Moorehead / Chris Hood
			DL Cornelius Griffin
			DL Jamie Carter
			DL Kenny Smith / Clint Waggoner
			LB Steve Harris / Canary Knight
			LB Travis Carroll / Chris Edwards
			LB Steve Stanley / Darius Gilbert
			DB Reggie Myles / Kecalf Bailey
			DB Fernando Bryant
			DB Tony Dixon
			DB Marcus Spencer

RUSHING: Alexander 258/1178y, Eric Locke (WR) 8/48y
PASSING: Zow 143-256/1969y, 11TD, 55.9%
RECEIVING: Jackson 48/621y, Vaughn 34/403y,
 Alexander 26/385y
SCORING: Alexander 102pts, Ryan Pflugner (K) 60pts

1999 10-3

28	Vanderbilt	17	WR Jason McAddley /Shamari Buchanan
37	Houston	10	WR Antonio Carter
28	Louisiana Tech	29	WR Dustin McClintock / Tim Bowens
35	Arkansas	28	T Chris Samuels
40	Florida	39	G Griff Redmill (C) / Marico Portis
30	Mississippi	24	C Paul Hogan
7	Tennessee	21	G Will Cuthbert
35	Southern Miss	14	T Justin Ellington
23	LSU	17	TE Terry Jones
19	Mississippi St.	7	QB Andrew Zow / Tyler Watts
28	Auburn	17	RB Shaun Alexander / Shawn Bohanon
34	Florida □	7	DL Kindal Moorehead
34	Michigan ■	35	DL Kenny Smith / Reggie Grimes
			DL Cornelius Griffin
			DL Kenny King
			LB Saleem Rasheed
			LB Marvin Constant
			LB Darius Gilbert / Miguel Merritt
			DB Milo Lewis
			DB Reggie Myles / Kecalf Bailey
			DB Tony Dixon / Gerald Dixon
			DB Marcus Spencer

RUSHING: Alexander 302/1383y, Bohanon 74/342y,
 Milons 15/178y
PASSING: Zow 148-264/1799y, 12TD, 56.1%,
 Watts 47-83/498y, 2TD, 56.6%
RECEIVING: Milons 65/733y, Carter 29/280y, Alexander 25/323y,
 McAddley 24/334y
SCORING: Alexander 144pts

2000 3-8

24	UCLA	35	WR Freddie Milons / Sam Collins
28	Vanderbilt	10	WR Antonio Carter
0	Southern Miss	21	WR Dustin McClintock / Jason McAddley
21	Arkansas	28	T Dante Ellington
27	South Carolina	17	G Griff Redmill
45	Mississippi	7	C Paul Hogan
10	Tennessee	20	G Will Cuthbert (T) / Alonzo Ephraim
38	C. Florida	40	T Dennis Alexander
28	LSU	30	TE Shawn Draper (T) / Terry Jones
7	Mississippi St.	29	QB Andrew Zow / Tyler Watts
0	Auburn	9	RB Ahmaad Galloway / Brandon Miree
			DL Jarret Johnson
			DL Kelvis White / Albert Means
			DL Kenny Smith / Brooks Daniels
			DL Kenny King / Aries Monroe
			LB Darius Gilbert / Adam Cox
			LB Victor Ellis
			LB Saleem Rasheed
			DB Milo Lewis
			DB Gerald Dixon / Kecalf Bailey
			DB Tony Dixon / Reggie Myles
			DB Marcus Spencer

RUSHING: Galloway 137/659y, Miree 94/426y, Watts 39/159y
PASSING: Zow 120-249/1561y, 6TD, 48.2%,
 Watts 31-56/303y, TD, 55.4%
RECEIVING: Carter 45/586y, Milons 32/287y, McAddley 27/413y
SCORING: Neal Thomas (K) 54pts, Galloway 42pts

2001 7-5

17	UCLA	20	WR Freddie Milons / Antonio Carter
12	Vanderbilt	9	WR Jason McAddley / Sam Collins
31	Arkansas	10	T Wesley Britt / Atlas Herrion
36	South Carolina	37	G Justin Smiley
56	Texas-El Paso	7	C Alonzo Ephraim
24	Mississippi	27	G Marico Portis
24	Tennessee	35	T Dante Ellington / Evan Mathis
21	LSU	35	TE Terry Jones / Theo Sanders
24	Mississippi St.	17	QB Andrew Zow / Tyler Watts
31	Auburn	7	TB Ahmaad Galloway / Santonio Beard
28	Southern Miss.	15	FB Donnie Lowe / Marvin Brown
14	Iowa State ■	13	DL Aries Monroe/Nautyn McK'y-Loescher
			DL Jarret Johnson
			DL Kenny King / Anthony Bryant
			DL Kindal Moorehead
			LB Cornelius Wortham / Victor Ellis
			LB Saleem Rasheed
			LB Brook Daniels
			DB Hirchel Bolden
			DB Gerald Dixon / Roberto McBride
			DB Reggie Myles / Charles Jones
			DB Waine Bacon / Shontua Ray

RUSHING: Galloway 174/881y, Beard 77/633y, Watts 111/564y
PASSING: Watts 94-172/1325y, 10TD, 54.7%,
 Zow 48-83/654y, 6TD, 57.8%
RECEIVING: Milons 36/627y, Carter 32/428y,
 McAddley 18/259y, Collins 18/252y
SCORING: Neal Thomas (K) 78pts, Galloway 36pts, Watts 30pts

2002 10-3

39	Middle Tenn.	34 WR Sam Collins / Zach Fletcher
27	Oklahoma	37 WR Dre Fulgham / Triandos Luke
33	North Texas	7 T Wesley Britt
20	Southern Miss	7 G Justin Smiley
30	Arkansas	12 C Alonzo Ephraim
25	Georgia	27 G Marico Portis
42	Mississippi	7 T Evan Mathis
34	Tennessee	14 TE Donald Clarke
30	Vanderbilt	8 QB Tyler Watts / Brodie Croyle
28	Mississippi St.	14 TB Santonio Beard / Shaud Williams
31	LSU	0 FB Greg McLain
7	Auburn	17 DL Nautyn McKay-Loescher
21	Hawaii	16 DL Jarret Johnson
		DL Kenny King / Anthony Bryant
		DL Kindal Moorehead / Antwan Odom
		LB Cornelius Wortham
		LB Freddie Roach
		DB Gerald Dixon
		DB Charlie Peprah
		DB Brooks Daniels
		DB Charles Jones / Derrick Pope
		DB Waine Bacon

RUSHING: Williams 130/921y
PASSING: Watts 112-181/1414y, 7TD, 61.9%
RECEIVING: Luke 41/482y
SCORING: Beard 72pts

2003 4-9

40	South Florida	17 WR Dre Fulgham / Zach Fletcher
13	Oklahoma	20 WR Triandos Luke / Brandon Greer
27	Kentucky	17 T Wesley Britt / Atlas Herrion
16	N. Illirios	19 G Justin Smiley
31	Arkansas	34 C J.B. Closner / Matt Lomax
23	Georgia	37 G Dennis Alexander / Danny Martz
17	Southern Miss	3 T Evan Mathis
28	Mississippi	43 TE David Cavan / Clint Johnston
43	Tennessee	51 QB Brodie Croyle
38	Mississippi St.	0 RB Shaud Williams / Ray Hudson
3	LSU	27 FB Tim Castille / Le'Ron McClain
23	Auburn	28 DL Nautyn McKay-Loescher
29	Hawaii	37 DL Anthony Bryant
		DL Ahmad Childress / Jeremy Clark
		DL Antwan Odom / Mark Anderson
		LB Derrick Pope
		LB Freddie Roach
		LB Demeco Ryans / Juwan Garth
		DB Charlie Peprah / Ramzee Robinson
		DB Anthony Madison
		DB Charles Jones
		DB Roman Harper / Carlos Andrews

RUSHING: Williams 280/1367y, Hudson 100/490y,
  Ken Darby (RB) 34/185y
PASSING: Croyle 182-341/2303y, 16 TD, 53.4%
RECEIVING: Luke 32/432y, Fulgham 30/475y, Williams 24/161y
SCORING: Williams 96pts, Brian Bostick (K) 81pts,
  Fulgham & Luke 24pts

2004 6-6

48	Utah State	17 WR D.J. Hall / Keith Brown
28	Mississippi	7 WR Matt Caddell / Tyrone Prothro
52	W. Carolina	0 T Wesley Britt
10	Arkansas	27 G Evan Mathis
3	South Carolina	20 C J.B. Closner
45	Kentucky	17 G Danny Martz
27	Southern Miss	3 T Kyle Tatum
13	Tennessee	17 TE Clint Johnst'n/Trent Davids'n/D.Cav'n
30	Mississippi St.	14 QB Spencer Pennington / Brodie Croyle
10	LSU	26 TB Kenneth Darby / Ray Hudson
13	Auburn	21 FB Tim Castille / Le'Ron McClain
16	Minnesota■	20 DL Todd Bates
		DL Rudy Griffin / Anthony Bryant
		DL Jeremy Clark / Justin Britt
		DL Mark Anderson
		LB DeMeco Ryans
		LB Cornelius Wortham
		LB Freddie Roach / Juwan Garth
		DB Ramzee Robinson / Simeon Castille
		DB Anthony Madison
		DB Roman Harper
		DB Cahrlei Peprah

RUSHING: Darby 219/1062y, Hudson 92/638y, Castille 62/247y
PASSING: Pennington 82-152/974y, 4TD, 53.9%,
  Croyle 44-66/534y, 6TD, 66.7%
RECEIVING: Prothro 25/347y, Caddell 17/331y, Brown 17/295y,
  Hall 17/186y
SCORING: Brian Bostick (K) 83pts, Darby 54pts, Castille 36pts

2005 10-2

26	Middle Tenn.	7 WR D.J. Hall / Tyrone Prothro
30	Southern Miss.	21 WR Keith Brown
37	South Carolina	14 T Chris Capps
24	Arkansas	13 G Antoine Caldwell (C) / Mark Sanders
31	Florida	3 C J.B. Closner / Taylor Britt
13	Mississippi	10 G B.J. Stabler / Marlon Davis
6	Tennessee	3 T Kyle Tatum
35	Utah State	3 TE Nick Walker / Travis McCall
17	Mississippi St.	0 QB Brodie Croyle
13	LSU	26 TB Kenneth Darby
18	Auburn	28 FB Le'Ron McClain / Tim Castille
13	Texas Tech■	10 DL Wallace Gilberty
		DL Jeremy Clark / Justin Bright
		DL Rudy Griffin / Dominic Lee
		DL Mark Anderson
		LB DeMeco Ryans / Terrence Jones
		LB Freddie Roach
		LB Duwan Simpson / Demarcus Waldrop
		DB Anthony Madison
		DB Ramzee Robinson / Simeon Castille
		DB Roman Harper / Jeffrey Dukes
		DB Charlie Peprah

RUSHING: Darby 239/1242y, Jimmy Johns (TB) 38/202y,
  Coffee 48/179y, T. Castille 45/124y
PASSING: Croyle 202-339/2499y, 14TD, 59.6%
RECEIVING: Hall 48/676y, Brown 34/642y, Prothro 17/325y
SCORING: Jamie Christensen (K) 73pts, T. Castille 42pts,
  Hall 32pts

2006 6-7

25	Hawaii	17 WR D.J. Hall
13	Vanderbilt	10 WR Keith Brown / Matt Caddell
41	La.-Monroe	7 T Andre Smith
23	Arkansas	24 G Justin Britt
13	Florida	28 C Antoine Caldwell
30	Duke	14 G B.J. Stbler / Marlon Davis
26	Mississippi	23 T Chris Capps
13	Tennessee	16 TE Travis McCall / Nick Walker
38	Florida Int'l	3 QB John Parker Wilson
16	Mississippi St,	24 TB Kenneth Darby / Jimmy Johns
14	LSU	28 FB Le'Ron McClain / Tim Castille
15	Auburn	22 DL Wallace Gilberty
31	Oklahoma St.■	34 DL Jeremy Clark
		DL Dominic Lee / J.P. Adams
		DL Bobby Greenwood
		LB Terrence Jones / Demarcus Waldrop
		LB Prince Hall / Matt Collins
		LB Duwan Simpson
		DB Simeon Castille / Lionel Mitchell
		DB Ramzee Robinson
		DB Marcus Carter / Rashad Johnson
		DB Jeffrey Dukes

RUSHING: Darby 210/835y, Johns 66/293y, T. Castille 46/129y
PASSING: Wilson 216-379/2707y, 17TD, 57.0%
RECEIVING: Hall 62/1056y, Brown 44/590y, Darby 23/130y
SCORING: Jamie Chrstensen (K) 56pts, Castille &
  Leigh Tiffin (K) 36pts

2007 7-6

52	W. Carolina	6 WR D.J. Hall
24	Vanderbilt	10 WR Mike McCoy
41	Arkansas	38 WR Matt Caddell / Keith Brown
23	Georgia	26 T Andre Smith
14	Florida State	21 G Justin Britt
30	Houston	24 C Antoine Caldwell (G) / Evan Cardwell
27	Mississippi	24 G Marlon Davis / B.J. Stabler
41	Tennessee	17 T Mike Johnson (G) / Chris Capps
34	LSU	41 TE Nick Walker / Travis McCall
12	Mississippi St.	17 QB John Parker Wilson
14	La.-Monroe	21 RB Terry Grant / Glenn Coffee
10	Auburn	17 DL Wallace Gilbey
30	Colorado■	24 DL Lorenzo Washington / Brian Motley
		DL Brandon Deaderick /Bobby Greenwood
		LB Ezekial Knight
		LB Rolando McClain / Prince Hall
		LB Darren Mustin
		LB Keith Saunders
		DB Simeon Castille / Javier Arenas
		DB Kareem Jackson / Lionell Mitchell
		DB Rashad Johnson
		DB Marcus Carter

RUSHING: Grant 180/891y, Coffee 129/545y,
  Roy Upchurch (RB) 50/237y
PASSING: Wilson 255-462/2846y, 18TD, 55.2%
RECEIVING: Hall 67/1005y, Caddell 40/475y, McCoy 28/207y
SCORING: Leigh Tiffin (K) 111pts, Grant 54pts, Hall 38pts

2008 12-2

34	Clemson	10 WR Mike McCoy / Marquis Maze
20	Tulane	6 WR Julio Jones
41	W. Kentucky	7 T Andre Smith
49	Arkansas	14 G Mike Johnson
41	Georgia	30 C Antoine Caldwell
17	Kentucky	14 G Marlon Davis
24	Mississippi	20 T Drew Davis
29	Tennessee	9 TE Travis McCall
35	Arkansas State	0 TE Nick Walker / Preston Dial
27	LSU	21 QB John Parker Wilson
32	Mississippi St.	7 TB Glenn Coffee / Mark Ingram
36	Auburn	0 DL Brandon Deaderick
20	Florida□	31 DL Terrence Cody
17	Utah■	30 DL Bobby Greenwood
		LB Don'ta Hightower
		LB Rolando McClain
		LB Cory Reamer / Courtney Upshaw
		LB Brandon Fanney / Eryck Anders
		DB Javier Arenas
		DB Kareem Jackson / Marquis Johnson
		DB Rashad Johnson / Ali Sharrief
		DB Justin Woodall

RUSHING: Coffee 233/1383y, Ingram 143/728y,
  Roy Upchurch (RB) 58/350y
PASSING: Wilson 187-323/2273y, 10TD, 57.9%
RECEIVING: Jones 58/924y, Walker 32/324y, McCoy 16/191y,
  Coffee 16/118y
SCORING: Leigh Tiffin (K) 106pts, Ingram 74pts, Coffee 66pts

2009 14-0

34	Virginia Tech	24 WR Marquis Maze / Darius Hanks
40	Florida Int'l	14 WR Julio Jones / Mike McCoy
53	North Texas	7 T James Carpenter
35	Arkansas	7 G Mike Johnson
38	Kentucky	20 C William Vlachos
22	Mississippi	9 G Barrett Jones
20	South Carolina	6 T Drew Davis
12	Tennessee	10 TE Preston Dial / Brad Smelley
24	LSU	15 TE Colin Peek / Michael Williams
31	Mississippi St.	3 QB Greg McElroy
32	Chattanooga	0 TB Mark Ingram / Trent Richardson
26	Auburn	21 DL Lorenzo Washington
32	Florida□	13 DL Terrence Cody
37	Texas■	21 DL Brandon Deadrick / Marcel Dareus
		LB Cory Reamer
		LB Rolando McClain
		LB Don't'a Hightower / Nico Johnson
		LB Eryk Anders / Courtney Upshaw
		DB Javier Arenas / Marquis Johnson
		DB Kareem Jackson / Robby Green
		DB Justin Woodall / Ali Sharrief
		DB Mark Barron / Tyrone King

RUSHING: Ingram 271/1658y, Richardson 137/751y,
  Roy Upchurch (RB) 48/313y
PASSING: McElroy 198-325/2508y, 17TD, 60.9%
RECEIVING: Jones 43/596y, Ingram 32/334y, Maze 31/523y,
  Peek 26/313y
SCORING: Leigh Tiffin (K) 132pts, Ingram 120pts, Richardson 50pts

2010 10-3

48	San Jose State	3 WR Julio Jones
24	Penn State	3 WR Darius Hanks
62	Duke	13 WR/TE Marquis Maze / Preston Dial
24	Arkansas	20 T James Carpenter
31	Florida	6 G Chance Warmack
21	South Carolina	35 C William Vlachos
23	Mississippi	10 G Barrett Jones / Anthony Steen
41	Tennessee	10 T D.J. Fluker / Alfred McCullough
21	LSU	24 TE Michael Williams
30	Mississippi State	10 QB Greg McElroy
63	Georgia State	7 TB Mark Ingrem / Trent Richardson
27	Auburn	28 DL Marcell Dareus / Damian Square
49	Michigan State■	7 DL Josh Chapman
		DL Kerry Murphy / Luther Davis
		LB Chavis Wilson / C.J. Mosley
		LB Nico Johnson / Jerrell Harris
		LB Dont'a Hightower / Alex Watkins
		LB Courtney Upshaw / Ed Stinson
		DB Dee Milliner / DeQuan Menzie
		DB Dre Kirkpatrick / Phelon Jones
		DB Robert Lester
		DB Mark Barron / Will Lowery

RUSHING: Ingram 158/875y, Richardson 112/700y,
  Eddie Lacy(TB) 56/406y
PASSING: McElroy 222-313/2987y, 20TD, 70.9%
RECEIVING: Jones 78/1133y, Maze 38/557y, Hanks 32/456y
SCORING: Jeremy Shelley (K) 86pts, Ingram 84pts,
  Richardson 66pts

ARIZONA

University of Arizona (Founded 1885)
Tucson, Arizona
Nickname: Wildcats
Colors: Cardinal Red and Navy Blue
Stadium: Arizona (1928) 57,803
Conference Affiliations: Border (Charter member, 1931-1960),
   Independent (1961), Western Athletic (1962-77),
   Pacific-10 (1978-present)

CAREER RUSHING YARDS	Attempts	Yards
Trung Canidate (1996-99)	604	3824
Ontiwaun Carter (1991-94)	805	3501
Art Luppino (1953-56)	513	3371
Hubert Oliver (1977-80)	649	3096
Nic Grigsby (2007-10)	572	2957
David Adams (1984-86)	600	2571
Clarence Farmer (2000-03)	521	2530
Jim Upchurch (1972-74)	488	2389
Bobby McCall (1970-72)	473	2074
Ken Cardella (1951-53)	336	2060

CAREER PASSING YARDS	Comp.-Att.	Yards
Willie Tuitama (2005-08)	786-1276	9211
Tom Tunnicliffe (1980-83)	574-1089	7618
Alfred Jenkins (1983-86)	456- 879	6016
Keith Smith (1996-99)	434- 726	5972
Jason Johnson (1999-2002)	413- 719	5749
Nick Foles (2007, 2009-10)	551- 843	5734
Dan White (1993-95)	446- 850	5723
Ortege Jenkins (1997-2000)	488- 717	5424
Bruce Hill (1973-75)	339- 680	5090
Jim Krohn (1976-79)	260- 513	3305

CAREER RECEIVING YARDS	Catches	Yards
Bobby Wade (1999-02)	230	3351
Dennis Northcutt (1996-99)	223	3252
Mike Thomas (2005-08)	258	3231
Theo "T" Bell (1972-75)	153	2509
Jon Horton (1983-86)	136	2415
Richard Dice (1993-96)	119	1957
Derek Hill (9185-88)	112	1925
Juron Criner (2008-10)	134	1903
Terry Vaughn (1990-93)	109	1884
Brad Anderson (1981-83)	97	1789

SEASON RUSHING	Attempts	Yards
Trung Canidate (1999)	253	1602
Art Luppino (1954)	179	1359
Art Luppino (1955)	209	1313
Clarence Farmer (2001)	209	1229
Trung Candidate (1998)	167	1220

SEASON PASSING YARDS	Comp-Att	Yards
Willie Tuitama (2007)	327-524	3683
Jason Johnson (2002)	239-410	3327
Nick Foles (2010)	286-426	3191
Willie Tuitama (2008)	259-399	3088
Tom Tunnicliffe (1982)	176-328	2520

SEASON RECEIVING YARDS	Catches	Yards
Dennis Northcutt (1999)	88	1422
Bobby Wade (2002)	93	1389
Juron Criner (2010)	82	1233
Keith Hartwig (1976)	54	1134
Mike Thomas (2007)	83	1038

GAME RUSHING YARDS	Attempts	Yards
Trung Canidate (1998 vs. Arizona State)	18	288
Jim Upchurch (1973 vs. Texas-El Paso)	27	232
Art Luppino (1954 vs. New Mexico St.)	6	228

GAME PASSING YARDS	Comp-Att	Yards
Willie Tuitama (2007 vs. Washington)	38-51	510
Jason Johnson (2002 vs. California)	31-45	492
Nick Foles (2010 vs. Oregon)	29-54	448

GAME RECEIVING YARDS	Catches	Yards
Jeremy McDaniel (1996 vs. California)	14	283
Dennis Northcutt (1999 vs. TCU)	10	257
Bobby Wade (2002 vs. California)	11	222

GREATEST COACH

Dick Tomey is far from a household name when it comes to the list of great coaches. But, fans ought to take a look at what he has accomplished in his coaching career. Not the least of his achievements is the 9-4 record he posted—including a bowl win—in 2006 at San Jose State. School officials were close to shutting down the San Jose program after an 8-25 record over the previous three years.

Tomey's winning percentage at Arizona is a modest .595, which is short of Hall of Famer Jim Young's .705 as well as Larry Smith's .627. But unlike Young, Tomey had to face the toughest teams of the Pacific-10 Conference at a time when several programs, including Washington, California, Oregon, and Oregon State were blooming into the best stretch those schools ever have had. Those teams joined the perennial tough Los Angeles schools (Southern California and UCLA) in a very deep league.

The highlights of Tomey's years in Tucson clearly are the 1993 team which went 10-2 and tied for the Pac-10 title with UCLA and the 1998 team that went 12-1. Tomey's Wildcats knocked off a pair of real powerhouses, Miami and Nebraska, in bowl games that followed those two seasons.

Tomey fashioned one of the greatest defenses of recent memory. His "Desert Swarm" unit keyed the 1993 team and featured stars Tedy Bruschi at end, Rob Waldrop at nose guard, Sean Harris at linebacker, and Tony Bouie and Brandon Sanders at safety.

ARIZONA'S 55 GREATEST SINCE 1953

OFFENSE

WIDE RECEIVER: Theo "T" Bell, Richard Dice, Troy Dickey, Bobby Wade
TIGHT END: Ron Beyer
TACKLE: John Fina, Makoa Freitas, Edwin Mulitalo, Glenn Parker
GUARD: Kevin Barry, Jeff Kiewel, Yusef Scott, Warner Smith
CENTER: Hicham El-Mashtoub, Joe Tofflemire
QUARTERBACK: Ortege Jenkins, Willie Tuitama, Tom Tunnicliffe
RUNNING BACK: Trung Canidate, Ontiwaun Carter, Art Luppino, Bobby McCall, Bobby Thompson
FULLBACK: Hubert Oliver, Jim Upchurch

DEFENSE

END: Tedy Bruschi, Chuck Osborne, Joe Tafoya
TACKLE: Cleveland Crosby, Joe Salave'a, Anthony Smith, Dana Wells
NOSE GUARD: Rob Waldrop
LINEBACKER: Marcus Bell, Byron Evans, Sean Harris, Ricky Hunley, Dane Krogstad, Spencer Larson, Chris Singleton
CORNERBACK: Antoine Cason, Darryl Lewis, Chris McAlister, Randy Robbins
SAFETY: Tony Bouie, Chuck Cecil, Dave Liggins, Brandon Sanders

SPECIAL TEAMS

RETURN SPECIALISTS: Chuck Levy, Dennis Northcutt
PLACE KICKER: Steve McLaughlin
PUNTER: Josh Miller

MULTIPLE POSITIONS

FULLBACK-LINEBACKER: Lance Briggs

TWO-WAY PLAYERS

GUARD-NOSE GUARD-LINEBACKER: Ed Brown
TACKLE-DEFENSIVE TACKLE: John Mellekas

PERFORMANCE FORMULA:
ARIZONA'S 10 BEST SEASONS

1998	1.5757	7 of 71
1993	1.4559	13 of 70
1961	1.4223	9 of 71
1986	1.3892	14 of 70
1954	1.3520	17 of 69
1988	1.3229	18 of 69
1983	1.3194	21 of 70
1989	1.2767	25 of 70
1960	1.2754	23 of 70
1973	1.2580	19 of 70

ARIZONA WILDCATS

Year	W-L-T	AP Poll	Conference Standing	Toughest Regular Season Opponents	Coach (Record at School)	Bowl Games		
1953	4-5-1		4	Utah 8-2, Colorado 6-4, Texas Tech 10-1, Kansas State 6-3-1	Warren Woodson			
1954	7-3		4	Colorado 7-2-1, Texas Tech 7-2-1, Texas Western 7-3	Warren Woodson			
1955	5-4-1		5	Colorado A&M 8-2, Texas Tech 7-2-1, Arizona State 8-2-1	Warren Woodson			
1956	4-6		4t	Wyoming 10-0, Texas Western 9-1, Arizona State 9-1, Colorado 7-2-1	Warren Woodson (26-22-2)			
1957	1-8-1		5t	Colorado 6-3-1, Texas Western 6-3, Arizona State 10-0	Ed Doherty			
1958	3-7		3	Tulsa 7-3, New Mexico 7-3, Colorado 6-4, Arizona State 7-3	Ed Doherty (4-15-1)			
1959	4-4-1		2	New Mexico 7-3, Colorado 5-5, Air Force 5-4-1, Arizona State 10-1	Jim LaRue			
1960	7-3		2	Utah 7-3, Wyoming 8-2, Arizona State 7-3	Jim LaRue			
1961	8-1-1			New Mexico 6-4, Wyoming 6-1-2, Arizona State 7-3	Jim LaRue			
1962	5-5		2t	Missouri 7-1-2, West Texas State 8-2, Arizona State 7-2-1	Jim LaRue			
1963	5-5		2	Utah State 8-2, Oregon 7-3, Arizona State 8-1	Jim LaRue			
1964	6-3-1		1t	New Mexico 9-2, Oregon 7-3, Arizona State 8-2	Jim LaRue			
1965	3-7		6	Washington State 7-3, Texas Western 7-3, Arizona State 6-4	Jim LaRue			
1966	3-7		5	Wyoming 9-1, BYU 8-2, Oregon State 7-3	Jim LaRue (41-37-2)			
1967	3-6-1		5	Wyoming 10-0, Ohio State 6-3, Missouri 7-3, Indiana 9-1, Arizona State 8-2	Darrell Mudra			
1968	8-3		2t	Indiana 6-4, Wyoming 7-3, Arizona State 8-2	Darrell Mudra (11-9-1)	Sun	10 Auburn	34
1969	3-7		5	Houston 8-2, Utah 8-2, Arizona State 8-2	Bob Weber			
1970	4-6		5	Michigan 9-1, Air Force 9-2, Arizona State 10-0	Bob Weber			
1971	5-6		3	New Mexico 6-3-2, Arizona State 10-1	Bob Weber			
1972	4-7		4	UCLA 8-3, Texas Tech 8-3, Arizona State 9-2	Bob Weber (16-26)			
1973	8-3		1t	Texas Tech 10-1, Arizona State 10-1	Jim Young			
1974	9-2		2	San Diego State 8-2-1, BYU 7-3-1	Jim Young			
1975	9-2	18	2	San Diego State 8-3, Arizona State 11-0	Jim Young			
1976	5-6		5t	UCLA 9-1-1, BYU 9-2, Wyoming 8-3	Jim Young (31-13)			
1977	5-7		5t	San Diego St. 10-1, BYU 9-2, Colorado St. 9-2-1, Arizona St. 9-2	Tony Mason			
1978	5-6		6t	Michigan 10-1, UCLA 8-3, Arizona State 8-3	Tony Mason			
1979	6-5-1		3t	Southern California 10-0-1, San Diego State 8-3	Tony Mason (16-18-1)	Fiesta	10 Pittsburgh	16
1980	5-6		5t	So. California 8-2-1, Notre Dame 9-1-1, UCLA 9-2, Washington 9-2	Larry Smith			
1981	6-5		6t	UCLA 7-3-1, Southern California 9-2, Arizona State 9-2	Larry Smith			
1982	6-4-1		5	Washington 9-2, UCLA 9-1-1, Southern California 8-3, Arizona St. 9-2	Larry Smith			
1983	7-3-1		5	Wash. St. 7-4, Washington 8-3, UCLA 6-4-1, Arizona St. 6-4-1	Larry Smith			
1984	7-4		3t	LSU 8-2-1, Southern Calif. 8-3, Washington 10-1	Larry Smith			
1985	8-3-1		2t	SMU 6-5, UCLA 8-2-1, Arizona State 8-3	Larry Smith	Sun	13 Georgia	13
1986	9-3	11	4	UCLA 7-3-1, So. California 7-4, Arizona State 9-1-1, Stanford 8-3	Larry Smith (48-28-3)	Aloha	30 North Carolina	21
1987	4-4-3		7	Iowa 9-3, UCLA 9-2, Southern California 8-3	Dick Tomey			
1988	7-4		3t	Oklahoma 9-2, Washington State 8-3, UCLA 9-2	Dick Tomey			
1989	8-4	25	2t	Texas Tech 8-3, Oklahoma 7-4, Washington 7-4, So. Calif. 8-2-1	Dick Tomey	Copper	17 North Carolina State	10
1990	7-5		5	Illinois 8-3, Oregon 8-3, So. California 8-3-1, Washington 9-2	Dick Tomey	Aloha	0 Syracuse	28
1991	4-7		6t	Ohio State 8-3, California 9-2, Washington 11-0, Miami 11-0	Dick Tomey			
1992	6-5-1		5	Miami 11-0, Stanford 9-3, Washington 9-2	Dick Tomey	John Hancock	15 Baylor	20
1993	10-2	10	1t	Southern California 7-5, UCLA 8-3, California 8-4	Dick Tomey	Fiesta	29 Miami	0
1994	8-4		2t	Colorado State 10-1, Oregon 9-3, Southern California 7-3-1	Dick Tomey	Freedom	13 Utah	16
1995	6-5		5t	Southern California 8-3-1, Washington 7-3-1, Oregon 9-2	Dick Tomey			
1996	5-6		5t	Iowa 8-3, Washington 9-2, Arizona State 11-0	Dick Tomey			
1997	7-5		5t	Ohio State 10-2, UCLA 9-2, Washington State 10-1	Dick Tomey	Insight.com	20 New Mexico	14
1998	12-1	4	2	UCLA 10-1, Oregon 8-3	Dick Tomey	Holiday	23 Nebraska	20
1999	6-6		6t	Penn State 9-3, TCU 7-4, Stanford 8-3, Oregon 8-3	Dick Tomey			
2000	5-6		5t	Ohio State 8-3, Oregon 9-2, Washington 10-1, Oregon State 10-1	Dick Tomey (95-64-4)			
2001	5-6		8	Washington State 9-2, Oregon 10-1, Stanford 9-2	John Mackovic			
2002	4-8		9t	Washington State 9-3, Oregon State 8-4, Arizona State 8-5	John Mackovic			
2003	2-10		10	LSU 12-1, Purdue 9-3, TCU 11-1, Southern California 11-1	John Mackovic (10-18), Mike Hankwitz [1-6]			
2004	3-8		8t	Utah 11-0, Wisconsin 9-2, California 10-1, Southern California 12-0	Mike Stoops			
2005	3-8		8	Southern California 12-0, Oregon 10-1, UCLA 9-2	Mike Stoops			
2006	6-6		5t	BYU 10-2, LSU 10-2, Southern California 10-2	Mike Stoops			
2007	5-7		6	BYU 10-2, Oregon State 8-4, So. California 10-2, Arizona St. 10-2	Mike Stoops			
2008	8-5		5	California 8-4, Southern California 11-1, Oregon 9-3	Mike Stoops	Las Vegas	31 Brigham Young	21
2009	8-5		2t	Iowa 10-2, California 8-4, Oregon 10-2, Southern California 8-4	Mike Stoops	Holiday	0 Nebraska	33
2010	7-6		5t	Stanford 11-1, Oregon 12-0	Mike Stoops (40-45)	Alamo	10 Oklahoma State	36

TOTAL:		**333-297-14 .5280 (39 of 70)**	**Bowl Games since 1953:**	**6-7-1 .4643 (44 of 70)**

GREATEST TEAM SINCE 1953: The 1998 Arizona Wildcats had a better record of 12-1 and better offensive skill players like Trung Canidate, Ortege Jenkins, Dennis Northcutt, and Keith Smith, but the "Desert Swarm" team of 1993 gains the nod for Arizona's greatest since 1953. Its magnificent defense was led by Tony Bouie, Tedy Bruschi, Sean Harris, Brandon Sanders, and Rob Waldrop and earned a smashing victory in the Fiesta Bowl over Miami of 29-0.

1953 4-5-1
7 Utah	28 E Bill Codd / Mark Owen
14 Colorado	20 T Buddy Lewis
46 New Mexico St.	7 G Phil Rutkowski / Nick Kondora
20 New Mexico	0 C Glenn Bowers
0 Marquette	14 G Alcide Webre / Carl Weller
39 West Texas St.	7 T John Mellekas / Ray Hannapel
27 Texas Tech	52 E Rollie Kuehl
20 Texas Western	28 QB Barry Bleakley / Marty Lang
26 Kansas State	26 TB Ken Cardella / Art Luppino
35 Arizona State	0 WB Wayne Mancuso / Bobby Fry
	FB Don Beasley / Carl Beard

RUSHING: Cardella 148/915y, Beasley 84/664y,
Luppino 59/372y
PASSING: Bleakley 30-68/419y, 3TD, 44.1%,
Fred Schuh (QB) 13-34/163y, 0TD, 38.2%
RECEIVING: Mancuso 17/199y, Kuehl 13/197y, Codd 8/96y
SCORING: Kuehl 18pts, Vaughn Corley (K) 15pts

1954 7-3
58 N. Mexico A&M	0 E Bill Codd / Don Bowerman
54 Utah	20 T Buddy Lewis
18 Colorado	40 G Alcide Webre / Nick Kondora
35 Idaho	13 C Paul Hatcher / Glenn Bowers
41 New Mexico	7 G Ed Brown
48 W. Texas State	12 T John Mellekas
14 Texas Tech	28 E Ham Vose / Gordon Phegley
21 Texas Western	41 QB Barry Bleakley / Fred Schuh
54 Arizona State	14 HB Art Luppino / Tommy Grimes
42 Wyoming	40 HB Bob Fry / Wayne Mancuso
	FB Ed McCluskey / Max Burnett

RUSHING: Luppino 179/1359y, McCluskey 67/473y,
Burnett 84/443y, Grimes 55/305y
PASSING: Bleakley 39-74/601y, 4TD, 52.7%,
Schuh 15-27/33y, 2TD, 55.5%,
Marty Lang 17-28/249y, 3TD, 60.7%
RECEIVING: Codd 17/275y, Phegley 16/146y, Mancuso 10/271y
SCORING: Luppino (HB-K) 166pts, Grimes 54pts,
Burnett & Mancuso 24pts

1955 5-4-1
20 Colorado State	7 E Bill Codd
0 Colorado	14 T Ev Nicholson / Jack Davis
47 Idaho	14 G Bob Griffis
20 West Texas	20 C Paul Hatcher / Doug Allred
0 Texas Western	29 G Ed Brown
27 Oregon	46 T John Mellekas / Clarence Anderson
7 Texas Tech	27 E Ed Sine / Ham Vose
29 Montana	0 QB Vaughn Corley / Ralph Hunsaker
27 New Mexico	6 TB Art Luppino / Gene Leek (WB-FB)
7 Arizona State	6 WB Pete Arrigoni / Gave Allen
	FB Ed McCluskey / Don Bowerman

RUSHING: Luppino 209/1313y, McCluskey 94/452y
PASSING: Corley 46-111/551y, 4 TD, 41.4%
RECEIVING: Codd 24/250y, Arrigoni 12/299y, Leek 10/166y
SCORING: Luppino 96pts, 3 with 18pts

1956 4-6
27 Montana	12 E Bob Whitlow / Gary Cropper
20 Wyoming	26 T Clarence Anderson / Doug Allred
60 So. Dakota St.	0 G Gary Slater / Marty Hurd
7 Utah State	12 C Paul Hatcher / Duane Foremaster
6 Texas Western	28 G Ed Brown
26 New Mexico	12 T Jack Davis / Alan Polley
7 Texas Tech	21 E Ed Sine / Willie Peete
20 West Texas	13 QB Ralph Hunsaker / Dalton Cole
0 Arizona State	20 TB Art Luppino / Sal Gonzalez
7 Colorado	38 WB Ray Martin / Gene Leek
	FB Don Beasley / Carl Hazlett

RUSHING: Gonzalez 70/337y, Luppino 66/327y, Martin 46/269y
PASSING: Hunsaker 75-148/823y, 4 TD, 50.7%
RECEIVING: Whitlow 17/157y, Sine 13/163y, Beasley 8/129y
SCORING: Luppino 41pts, Hazlett 24pts, Gonzalez 20pts

1957 1-8-1
14 BYU	14 E Gary Cropper / Norman Romero
13 Missouri	35 T Alan Polley / Bob Whitlow
14 Colorado	34 G Ed Brown
0 New Mexico	27 C Marty Hurd
6 Texas Tech	28 G Lyell Metcalf / Gary Slater
20 West Texas	21 T Jack Davis
20 Hardin-Simmons	28 E Joe Young / Billy Keasler
14 Texas Western	51 QB Ralph Hunsaker / Jim Mason
17 Marquette	14 HB Jim Tate / Tom Dunn
7 Arizona State	47 SB Gene Leek / Jack Redhair
	FB Sal Gonzales / Carl Hazlett

RUSHING: Dunn 67/341y, Tate 43/216y,
PASSING: Hunsaker 73-138/717y, 4TD, 52.9%,
RECEIVING: Leek 29/310y, Redhair 25/188y, Young 15/189y
SCORING: Tate 24pts, Hunsaker (QB-K) 20pts, Dunn 18pts

1958 3-7
7 Utah State	6 E Gene Bubala
0 Iowa State	14 T Tony Matz
0 Tulsa	34 G Marty Hurd
12 Colorado	65 C Ted Urness
13 New Mexico	33 G Mike Yeager / Joe Bognano
16 Idaho	24 T Mike Mullahey / Dennis Underwood
15 West Texas St.	8 E Billy Keasler / Pat Brown
6 Texas Tech	33 QB Ralph Hunsaker / Jim Geist /Dan Zion
14 Texas Western	12 HB Warren Livingston / Ray Martin
0 Arizona State	47 HB Dave Hibbert
	FB Jack Gillespie / Billy Overall

RUSHING: Overall 95/324, Livingston 63/187y, Gillespie 35/113y
PASSING: Hunsaker 106/191/1129y, 5TD, 55.5%
RECEIVING: Hibbert 61/606y, Livingston 18/183y, Overall 10/69y
SCORING: Hibbert 24pts, Overall 18pts, Hunsaker (QB-K) 14pts

1959 4-6
14 BYU	18 E Pat Brown / Larry Williams
7 West Texas St.	6 T Tony Matz
16 Idaho	14 G Ted Urness / Don Wild
7 New Mexico	28 C Marshall Pieczentkowski / Bob Garis
0 Colorado	18 G Chuck Raetzman
6 Utah	54 T Bill Ismay / Harold Tomlin
30 Texas Tech	26 E Gary Cropper / Willie Peete
15 Air Force	22 QB Jim Geist / Eddie Wilson
14 Texas Western	10 HB Warren Livingston / Minner Williams
9 Arizona State	15 HB Walter Mince / Francis Plinski
	FB Carl Hazlett / Jack Gillespie /Pat Foley

RUSHING: Livingston 57/380y, Mince 45/275y, Geist 82/238y
PASSING: Wilson 31-76/476y, 4TD, 40.8%
RECEIVING: Peete 10/173y, McCormick 7/159y
SCORING: Geist 34pts, Livingston 18pts, Wilson 14pts

1960 7-3
3 Utah	13 E Larry Williams / Don Wild
21 Wyoming	19 T Tony Matz / Carl Runk
16 Colorado	35 G Ted Urness
16 Tulsa	17 C Bob Garis
26 New Mexico	14 G John Smull / Craig Starkey
21 West Texas St.	14 T Bill Ismay
32 Idaho	3 E John Renner / Skip Townsend
28 Texas Western	14 QB Eddie Wilson / Jim Faulks
35 Kansas State	16 HB Bobby Thompson / Warren Livingston
35 Arizona State	7 HB Joe Hernandez / Minner Williams
	FB Jack Gillespie / Joe Carroll

RUSHING: Thompson 93/732y, Hernandez 74/406y,
Livingston 44/187y
PASSING: Wilson 62-116/1020y, 9 TD, 53.4%
RECEIVING: Hernandez 24/440y, Thompson 16/341y,
Livingston 10/93y
SCORING: Hernandez 76pts, Thompson 42pts

1961 8-1-1
28 Colorado State	6 E Ken Cook / Larry Williams
14 Nebraska	14 T Vern Alexander / Carl Runk
53 Hardin-Simmons	7 G Howard Breinig / Jim Osborne
15 Oregon	6 C Bob Garis
22 New Mexico	21 G John Smull / Virgil Grant
23 West Texas St.	27 T Dennis Underwood
20 Wyoming	15 E John Renner / Skip Townsend
43 Idaho	7 QB Eddie Wilson
48 Texas Western	15 HB Bobby Thompson / Jim Faulks
22 Arizona State	13 HB Joe Hernandez / Walt Mince
	FB Ted Christy / John Carney

RUSHING: Thompson 103/777y, Mince 53/332y,
Hernandez 55/282y
PASSING: Wilson 79-154/1294y, 10TD, 51.3%
RECEIVING: Hernandez 27/423y, Thompson 25/468y,
Mince 9/201y, Renner 9/104y
SCORING: Thompson 82pts, Wilson 54pts, Mince 44pts

1962 5-5
27 BYU	21 E Ken Cook / Mike O'Mahony
25 New Mexico	35 T Vern Alexander / Phil Wilson
7 Missouri	17 G Howard Breinig
6 Air Force	20 C Steve Kerr / Al Navarrete
8 Wyoming	31 G Craig Starkey / John Briscoe
8 West Texas St.	3 T Gerald Zeman / Ed Wimberly
12 Idaho	14 E Jim Singleton / John Fouse
14 Kansas State	13 QB Jim Faulks / Bill Brechler
7 Texas Western	0 HB Tom Kosser / Tom Phillips
20 Arizona State	17 HB Brian Hart
	FB Ted Christy / Dave Knott

RUSHING: Thompson 103/752y, Mince 53/328y,
Hernandez 55/278y
PASSING: Wilson 79-154/1294y, 10TD, 51.3%
RECEIVING: Hernandez 27/423y, Thompson 25/468y,
Mince 9/201y, John Renner (E) 9/104y
SCORING: Thompson 82pts, Wilson 54pts, Mince 44pts

1963 5-5
0 Utah State	43 E Mike O'Mahony / John Fouse
33 BYU	7 T Jim Pazerski / Casey Saloni
2 Washington St.	13 G Dave DeSonia / Don Kunitz
13 Texas Western	7 C John Briscoe / Steve Kerr
12 Oregon	28 G Jerry Davitch
6 West Texas St.	3 T Jerry Zeman / Ed Wimberly
15 Wyoming	9 E Jim Singleton
34 Idaho	7 QB Bill Brechler / Gene Dahlquist
6 Arizona State	35 HB Rickie Harris / Floyd Hudlow
15 New Mexico	22 HB Lou White /Brian Hart/L.Fairholm (DB)
	FB Jim Oliver / Ted Christy / Dave Knott

RUSHING: Oliver 49/214y, Harris 41/187y, Knott 42/179y
PASSING: Brechler 34-82/550y, 7 TD, 41.5%,
Dahlquist 20-48/252y, 3 TD, 41.7%
RECEIVING: Hudlow 13/167y, Fouse 9/162y, Oliver 9/111y
SCORING: Hudlow 24pts, Si Gimbel (FB) & Harris 18pts

1964 6-3-1
39 BYU	6 E Jeff Fries / John Woodall (DL)
28 Washington St.	12 T Jim Pazerski / Ollie Leviege (DL)
7 New Mexico	10 G Dave DeSonia / Don Kunitz (LB)
0 Oregon	21 C Ted Sweeting / John Briscoe (LB)
15 Wyoming	7 G Jerry Davitch / Joe Escalada
0 Air Force	7 T Roger Myers / Ray Wimberly (DL)
14 Idaho	7 E John Fouse / Tom Malloy (LB)
14 Texas Western	0 QB Lou White (HB) / Gene Dahlquist
0 Iowa State	0 HB Floyd Hudlow / Jim Oliver
30 Arizona State	6 HB Rickie Harris / Woody King (DB)
	FB Preston Davis / Tom Phillips (DB)

RUSHING: Hudlow 73/402y, Oliver 78/393y, Davis 110/375y
PASSING: Dahlquist 26-56/327y, TD, 46.4%,
White 25-67/419y, 2 TD, 37.3%
RECEIVING: Harris 28/391y, Fouse 10/235y, Hudlow 5/53y
SCORING: Hudlow 48pts, Davis 24pts, Oliver 22pts

1965 3-7
16 Utah	9 E Jeff Fries / Tim DeWan
23 Kansas	15 T Jim Pazerski
0 Wyoming	19 G Joe Escalada / Bob Beal
2 New Mexico	24 C Lee Rodgers
3 Washington St.	21 G Abe Johnson / Dominic Dellaccio
7 San Jose State	13 T Roger Myers
10 Texas Western	3 E Tim Plodinec / Joe Payton
7 Air Force	34 QB Phil Albert / Craig Liston
3 BYU	20 HB Brad Hubbert
6 Arizona State	14 WB Ray Homesley (DL) / Fro Brigham
	FB Rick Johnson
	DL Roger Calderwood / Ray Homesley
	DL Bill Lueck / Jerry Scelzi
	DL Ollie Leviege
	DL Jay Willett
	DL Steve Mass / Cliff Franzel
	DL Jim Douglas / Sam Castle
	LB Tom Malloy
	LB Mike Hawk / Larry Rogge
	DB Marty Hutchison / Jim White
	DB Wally Scott / Brian Acton
	DB Woody King

RUSHING: Hubbert 133/526y, Johnson 73/254y, Albert 111/103y
PASSING: Albert 58-123/559y, 2 TD, 47.2%
RECEIVING: Plodinec 20/191y, Hubbert 11/148y, Payton 9/92y,
Brigham 9/65y
SCORING: Jan Komorowski (K) 19pts, Thompson 12pts,
7 with 6pts

1966 3-7

20 Iowa	31 E Fritz Greenlee / Roger Brautigan (HB)
13 Kansas	35 T Bill Lueck
6 Wyoming	36 G Joe Escalada
36 New Mexico	15 C Bill Nemeth
19 Utah	24 G John Matishak
14 BYU	16 T Roger Myers / John Jones
12 Oregon State	31 E Ron Higuera / Tim DeWan
28 Washington St.	18 QB Marc Reed / Bobby Matthews
27 Iowa State	24 HB Brad Hubbert
17 Arizona State	20 WB Jim Greth / Tom Arboit
	FB Rick Johnson / Olden Lee
	DL Roger Calderwood
	DL Barnes Parker / Tom Brennan
	DL Mike Madeo / Jan Komorwski
	DL Tom Nelson
	DL Sam Castle
	LB Ray Homesley / Dan Frinfrock
	LB Abe Johnson / Larry Rogge
	DB Wally Scott / Marty Hutchison
	DB Brian Acton
	DB Phil Albert / Jim White
	DB Woody King

RUSHING: Hubbert 115/501y, Johnson 104/292y, Lee 15/52y
PASSING: Reed 193-365/2368y, 20 TD, 52.9%
RECEIVING: Greth 76/1003y, Greenlee 40/606y, DeWan 24/288y, Johnson 23/277y
SCORING: Greth 48pts, Greenlee 38pts, Hubbert & Reed 24pts

1967 3-6-1

17 Wyoming	36 E Roger Brautigan / Tim DeWan
14 Ohio State	7 T Mike Moody / Ron McElwee
3 Missouri	17 G Bill Lueck
9 Texas-El Paso	9 C Mike Aro / Bill Nemeth
29 Utah	33 G Bill Matishak
7 Indiana	42 T John Jones
48 New Mexico	13 E Ron Higuera / Jim Coddington
14 BYU	17 QB Marc Reed / Bruce Lee
14 Air Force	10 HB Wayne Edmonds / Noki Fuimaono
7 Arizona State	47 HB Paul Robinson / Wally Scott (DB)
	FB Dave Barajas
	DL Frank Jenkins
	DL Doug Klausen
	DL Olden Lee / Jim Farley
	DL Tom Nelson / Rex Macklin
	DL Gary Klahr
	LB Jerry Thompson
	LB Larry Rogge / Ray Homesley
	DB Bill Miller
	DB Wally Scott (HB) / Rich Moriarty
	DB Dennis Maley / Doug Schlueter
	DB Otis Comeaux / Ed Caruthers

RUSHING: Barajas 87/337y, Robinson 80/306y, Edmonds 80/271y
PASSING: Lee 57-137/635y, 5 TD, 41.6%, Reed 54-139/759y, 4 TD, 38.8%
RECEIVING: Scott 15/243y, Coddington 15/182y, Brautigan 14/247y, Edmonds 13/227y
SCORING: Barajas 30pts, Ken Sarnoski (K) 28pts, 3 with 12pts

1968 8-3

21 Iowa State	12 WR Mark Boche
19 New Mexico	8 WR Ron Gardin / Hal Arnason
25 Texas-El Paso	0 T Rich Crossman
19 BYU	3 G Kim Tompkins
13 Indiana	16 C Jim Sherman
28 Washington St.	14 G Mike Aro
14 Air Force	10 T John Matishak
16 Utah	15 TE Ted Sherwood
14 Wyoming	7 QB Mark Driscoll / Bruce Lee
7 Arizona State	30 TB Dan Hustead / Rick Stevenson
10 Auburn■	34 FB Noki Fuimaono / David Barajas
	DL Frank Jenkins
	DL Rex Macklin
	DL Tom Nelson
	DL Bill McKinley
	LB Charlie Duke
	LB Otis Comeaux
	LB Larry Rogge
	DB Jim White
	DB Bill Miller
	DB Doug Schlueter
	DB Rich Moriarty

RUSHING: Fuimaono 156/579y, Hustead 129/501y, Ed Mitchell (FB) 46/132y
PASSING: Driscoll 62-152/927y, 5TD, 40.8%, Lee 48-128/789y, 4TD, 37.5%
RECEIVING: Gardin 48/892y, Sherwood 21/347y, Boche 13/186y
SCORING: Steve Hurley (K) 38pts, Stevenson 36pts, Gardin 24pts

1969 3-7

7 Wyoming	23 WR Henry Harrison / Charles McKee
27 Kansas State	42 WR Hal Arnason/Mark Boche/Jack Ashby
19 Iowa	31 T Joe Hannasch
17 Houston	34 G Kim Tompkins / Larry McKee
26 Texas-El Paso	10 C Doug Rothery
52 New Mexico	28 G Jim Sherman
21 BYU	31 T Rich Crossman / Ron DaLee
0 Syracuse	23 TE Ted Sherwood / Clarence Fergerson
17 Utah	16 QB Brian Linstrom / Gary Paske
24 Arizona State	38 HB Ron Gardin / Don Reynolds
	FB Willie Lewis / Don Hustead
	DL Bill McKinley / John Naegle
	DL Rex Macklin (LB) / Tim Sheedy
	DL Jim Ventriglia / Doug Klausen
	DL Gary Klahr / Jerry Stump
	LB Charlie Duke
	LB Mark Arneson
	LB Tom Cooley / John Eggold
	DB Rick Stevenson
	DB Bill Miller
	DB Greg Woodward / Steve Wolfe
	DB John Black / Justin Lanne

RUSHING: Gardin 188/759y, Lewis 104/492y, Reynolds 34/152y
PASSING: Linstrom 119-258/1598y, 11TD, 46.1%
RECEIVING: Arnason 30/489y, Gardin 25/121y, Sherwood 23/261y
SCORING: Steve Hurley (K) 48pts, Gardin 42pts, McKee 36pts

1970 4-6

9 Michigan	20 WR Hal Arnason / Barry Dean
30 San Jose St.	29 WR Jack Ashby / Charlie McKee
17 Iowa	10 T Mike Treadwell / Jim Arneson
24 BYU	17 G Joe Hannasch
0 Utah	24 C Jim Sherman
20 Air Force	23 G Larry McKee / Kim Tompkins
7 New Mexico	35 T Doug Klausen / Ron DaLee
17 Texas-El Paso	33 TE Dennis Shields
38 Wyoming	12 QB Brian Linstrom / Bill Demory
6 Arizona State	10 HB Bobby McCall / Ceasar Pittman
	FB Willie Lewis
	DL Bob Crum / John Naegle
	DL Jim Johnson / Tim Sheedy
	DL Jim Ventriglia / Fernie Mendoza
	DL Bill McKinley
	LB Greg Boyd / Rich Dodson
	LB Mark Arneson / Jim Allison
	LB John Eggold
	DB John Black
	DB Ray Clarke
	DB Jackie Wallace / Greg Woodward
	DB Justin Lanne / Bob White

RUSHING: Lewis 163/665y, McCall 111/401y, Pittman 63/266y
PASSING: Linstrom 59-141/884y, 5TD, 42.0%, Demory 53-108/709y, 5 TD, 49.1%
RECEIVING: Arnason 35/569y, McKee 26/496y, Ashby 13/157y, Lewis 13/133y
SCORING: McKee 54pts, Al Mendoza (K) 22pts, Lewis 18pts

1971 5-6

39 Washington St.	28 WR Charlie McKee / Barry Dean
14 Texas-El Paso	6 WR Mark Neal / Chris Eddy
10 Texas Tech	13 T Mike Treadwell
3 Wyoming	14 G Dennis Shields / Lee Bolen
12 UCLA	28 C Jerry Stump / Lance Prickett
14 Utah	3 G Larry McKee / Chuck Brookfield
28 New Mexico	34 T Jim Arneson
34 Oregon State	22 TE Tom Camptell / Brian Linstrom (QB)
27 BYU	14 QB Bill Demory
10 San Diego St.	39 TB Joe Petroshus / Merle Gathers
0 Arizona State	31 FB Bobby McCall / Marty Shuford
	DL Bob Crum / Steve Lehmann
	DL Jim Johnson
	DL Jim Ventriglia
	DL Greg Poole / Ransom Terrell (LB)
	LB Rich Dodson
	LB Mark Arneson / Jim Allison
	LB Wally Brumfield / Kim Arnason
	DB Jackie Wallace
	DB Ray Clarke
	DB Bob White
	DB Greg Boyd

RUSHING: McCall 134/525y, Petroshus 121/474y, Shuford 86/329y
PASSING: Demory 91-199/1384y 10TD, 45.7%
RECEIVING: McKee 43/854y, Camptell 18/242y, Neal 15/247y
SCORING: McKee 30pts, Mike DeSylvia (K) 27pts, Petroshus & Wallace 24pts

1972 4-7

17 Colorado St.	0 WR Barry Dean
7 Oregon	34 WR Theo "T" Bell / Mark Neal
6 Washington St.	28 T Bill Irwin
31 UCLA	42 G Dennis Shields / John Bledsoe
27 New Mexico	15 C Bob Toon
10 Texas Tech	35 G Jim Arneson
45 Texas-El Paso	22 T Jim O'Connor / Ron DaLee
27 Utah	28 TE Rex Naumetz / John Muller
21 Brigham Young	7 QB Bill Demory / Jerry Davis
14 Wyoming	22 HB Bobby McCall / Jim Upchurch
21 Arizona State	38 FB Marty Shuford
	DL Bob Crum
	DL Glenn Gresham / Bill Adamson
	DL Steve Terrell / John D'Auria
	DL Greg Poole
	LB Rich Dodson
	LB Ransom Terrell
	LB Wally Brumfield / Leon Lawrence
	DB Jackie Wallace
	DB Roussell Williams
	DB Ray Clarke
	DB Bob White

RUSHING: McCall 228/1148y, Shuford 140/703y, Upchurch 62/187y
PASSING: Demory 76-174/1175y, 13TD, 43.6%
RECEIVING: Dean 22/418y, Bell 22/408y, Neal 18/249y
SCORING: Shuford & Charlie Gorham (K) 44pts, McCall 30pts

1973 8-3

31 Colorado	0 WR Mark Neal
21 Wyoming	7 WR "T" Bell
26 Indiana	10 T Brian Murray / Bill Irwin
23 Iowa	20 G Allyn Haynes
22 New Mexico	14 C Bob Windisch
17 Texas Tech	31 G John Bledsoe
42 Utah	21 T Jim O'Connor
35 Texas-El Paso	18 TE Tom Camptell / Dan Howard
24 BYU	10 QB Bruce Hill / Jerry Davis
26 Air Force	27 HB Willie Hamilton
19 Arizona State	55 FB Jim Upchurch
	DL Rex Naumetz
	DL Rich Hall
	DL Bill Adamson
	DL Mike Dawson
	DL Wally Brumfield / Willis Barrett
	LB Glenn Gresham / John Arce
	LB Ransom Terrell
	DB Wincent Phason / Joe Colace
	DB Roussell Williams
	DB Mike Battles / Greg Preston
	DB Leon Lawrence

RUSHING: Upchurch 210/1184y, Hamilton 109/737y, Davis 65/459y
PASSING: Hill 104-216/1529y, 9TD, 48.1%
RECEIVING: Bell 47/790y, Neal 23/393y, Camptell 18/162y
SCORING: Charlie Gorham (K) 64pts, Upchurch 60pts, Hill & Bell 42pts

1974 9-2

17 San Diego St.	10 WR Scott Piper
35 Indiana	20 WR "T" Bell
15 New Mexico	10 T Allyn Haynes
42 Texas-El Paso	13 G John Bledsoe
41 Utah	8 C Bob Windisch
8 Texas Tech	17 G Paul Schmidt / Greg Hodgeson
13 BYU	37 T Brian Murray
34 Colorado St.	21 TE Dan Howard
27 Air Force	24 QB Bruce Hill
21 Wyoming	14 HB Willie Hamilton
10 Arizona State	0 FB Jim Upchurch
	DL Rex Naumetz
	DL Mike Dawson
	DL Glenn Gresham / Jon Abbott
	DL Grant Swanson / Rich Hall
	DL Willis Barrett
	LB Obre Erby / Paul Cardoza
	LB Mark Jacobs
	DB Joe Colace / Greg Preston
	DB Roussell Williams
	DB Winsett Phason
	DB Dennis Anderson / Mike Battles

RUSHING: Upchurch 216/1004y, Hamilton 133/675y, Hill 135/304y
PASSING: Hill 133-249/1814y, 18TD, 53.4%
RECEIVING: Bell 53/700y, Piper 46/671y, Camptell 13/155y
SCORING: Bell 68pts, Lee Pistor (K) 51pts, Hamilton 42pts

1975 9-2

16	Pacific	0 WR Scott Piper / Keith Hartwig
14	Wyoming	0 WR "T" Bell / Charles Nash
41	Northwestern	6 T Brian Murray / Craig Irwin
36	Texas-El Paso	0 G Paul Schmidt / Bob Toon
32	Texas Tech	28 C Bob Windisch
34	New Mexico	44 G Greg Hodgeson
36	BYU	7 T Bill Segal
31	San Diego St.	24 TE Dan Howard
31	Colorado St.	9 QB Bruce Hill
38	Utah	14 RB Derral Davis / Tex Randolph
21	Arizona State	24 RB Dean Schock / Marvin Baker
		DL Gilbert Lewis
		DL Mike Dawson
		DL Jon Abbott
		DL Grant Swanson / Rich Hall
		DL Willis Barrett
		LB Obre Erby / John Arce
		LB Mark Jacobs / Larry Yena
		DB Mike Battles
		DB Van Cooper
		DB Greg Preston
		DB Dennis Anderson

RUSHING: Randolph 141/657y, Baker 78/464y, Davis 81/440y
PASSING: Hill 102-215/1747y, 18TD, 47.4%
RECEIVING: Piper 45/718y, Bell 31/611y, Hartwig 12/210y
SCORING: Lee Pistor (K) 80pts, Bell 56pts, Piper 42pts

1976 5-6

31	Auburn	19 WR Keith Hartwig
9	UCLA	37 WR Charles Nash / Harry Holt
16	BYU	23 T Craig Irwin (G) / John Schramm
27	Northwestern	15 G Neil Orr
62	Texas-El Paso	12 C Kirk Drummond
27	Texas Tech	52 G Greg Hodgeson
38	Utah	35 T Bill Segal
24	Wyoming	26 TE George Greathouse / Ron Beyer
23	Colorado St.	6 QB Marc Lunsford / Jim Krohn
15	New Mexico	21 TB Derriak Anderson / Harry Holt
10	Arizona State	27 FB Dean Schock / Allem Glasenapp
		DL Gilbert Lewis
		DL John Sanguinetti
		DL Jeff Hantla / Brian Wonderli
		DL Jon Abbott
		DL Ken Straw
		LB Obra Erby / Jeff Whitton
		LB Mark Jacobs / Larry Yena
		DB Van Cooper / Gary Harris
		DB Doug Henderson
		DB Greg Preston
		DB Ken Creviston

RUSHING: Anderson 114/506y, Glasenapp 81/454y,
Schock 82/334y
PASSING: Lunsford 70-132/1284y, 12TD, 53.0%,
Krohn 44-80/643y, 6 TD, 55.0%
RECEIVING: Hartwig 54/1134y, Nash 16/242y, Beyer 11/147y
SCORING: Lee Pistor (K) 69pts, Hartwig 62pts, Holt 36pts

1977 5-7

10	Auburn	21 WR Tim Haynes
14	San Diego St.	21 WR Harry Holt / Reed May
41	Iowa	7 T Ron Catlin / Chris Knudsen
12	Wyoming	13 G Neil Orr
26	Texas Tech	32 C Kirk Drummond
45	Utah	17 G John Schramm
14	BYU	34 T Bill Jensen / Neal Harris
14	Colorado State	35 TE Rick Beyer
15	New Mexico	13 QB Marc Lunsford / Jim Krohn
41	Texas-El Paso	24 TB Derriak Anderson
7	Arizona State	23 FB Hubert Oliver / Dean Schock
17	Hawaii	10 DL Gilbert Lewis / Chris Smith
		DL John Sanguinetti
		DL Jon Abbott / Darrell Solomon
		DL Jeff Whitton
		DL Ken Straw / Johnny Crawford
		LB Corky Ingraham
		LB Jack Housley / Sam Giangardella
		DB Van Cooper
		DB Doug Henderson / Gary Harris
		DB Tracy Converse / Dwayne Horton
		DB Darnell Wallace

RUSHING: Schock 131/563y, Oliver 96/519y,
Anderson 122/568y
PASSING: Lunsford 71-166/1344y, 6TD, 42.8%
RECEIVING: Holt 24/423y, Haynes 24/363y, Beyer 20/339y
SCORING: Anderson 48pts, Lee Pistor (K) 46pts, Holt 36pts

1978 5-6

31	Kansas State	0 WR Tim Holmes
21	Oregon State	7 WR Tim Haynes
26	Texas Tech	41 T Neal Harris / Ron Catlin
23	Iowa	3 G Neil Orr
17	Michigan	21 C Morman Katnik
20	California	33 G John Schramm / Ed Kybartas
14	UCLA	24 T Bill Jensen
21	Washington	31 TE Ron Beyer / Bill Nettling
24	Oregon	3 QB Jim Krohn
31	Washington St.	34 RB Larry Heater / Lynn Dickerson
17	Arizona State	18 RB Hubert Oliver
		DL Chris Smith
		DL Cleveland Crosby
		DL Jeff Whitton / Darrell Solomon
		DL Brian Wunderli
		DL Johnny Crawford
		LB Corky Ingraham / Frank Flournoy
		LB Sam Giangardella / Jack Housley
		DB Van Brandon / Mark Streeter
		DB Reggie Ware / Gary Harris
		DB Dave Liggins / Dwayne Horton
		DB Tracy Converse

RUSHING: Oliver 198/866y, Heater 159/793y, Krohn 141/335y
PASSING: Krohn 79-151/996y, 9TD, 52.3%
RECEIVING: Beyer 21/296y, Oliver 17/110y, Holmes 15/245y
SCORING: Bill Zivic (K) 49pts, Heater 48pts, Oliver 44pts

1979 6-5-1

33	Colorado State	17 WR Tim Holmes
22	Washington St.	7 WR Tim Haynes / Greg Jackson
7	California	10 T Ron Catlin
14	Texas Tech	14 G Guy Davis / Tom Manno
38	San Jose State	18 C Glenn Hutchinson / Morman Katnik
24	Oregon	13 G Ed Kybartas / Johnnye Wozniak
10	Stanford	30 T Bill Jensen
7	Southern Cal	34 TE Bill Nettling
10	San Diego St.	42 QB Jim Krohn
42	Oregon State	18 RB Larry Heater / Richard Hersey
27	Arizona State	24 RB Hubert Oliver
		DL Chris Smith
		DL Cleveland Crosby / Bob Cobb
		DL Jeff Whitton
		DL Mike Robinson / Chris Schultz
		DL Johnny Crawford / Gary Gibson
		LB Glenn Perkins
		LB Sam Giangardella / Jack Housley
		DB Reggie Ware
		DB Mark Streeter / Gary Harris
		DB Dave Liggins
		DB Marcellus Greene

RUSHING: Oliver 197/1021y, Heater 145/656y, Hersey 111/561y
PASSING: Krohn 93-175/1094y, 7TD, 53.1%
RECEIVING: Holmes 24/319y, Oliver 16/80y, Nettling 13/184y
SCORING: Bill Zivic (K) 55pts, Oliver 42pts, Heater 36pts

1980 4-7

13	Colorado State	15 WR Tim Holmes
31	California	24 WR Bob Carter / Alfondia Hill
5	Iowa	3 T Chris Knudsen / Neal Harris
10	Southern Cal.	27 G Frank Kalil / Guy Davis
14	Washington St.	38 C Glenn Hutchinson / Pete Mahoney
3	Notre Dame	20 G Jeff Kiewel (T) / Tom Manno
23	UCLA	17 T Bill Jensen
22	Washington	45 TE Bill Nettling
65	Pacific	35 QB Tom Tunnicliffe / Kevin Ward
24	Oregon St.	7 TB Brian Holland / Richard Hersey
7	Arizona State	44 FB Hubert Oliver / Rory Barnett
		DL Mike Robinson / Greg McElhannon
		DL Ivan Lesnik / Bob Cobb / Gary Shaw
		DL Chris Schultz / Mike Mosley
		LB Gary Gibson / Mike Meyer
		LB Jack Housley / John Pace
		LB Sam Giangardella / Ricky Hunley
		LB Kevin Hardcastle / Jerry Krohn
		DB Drew Hardville / Randy Robbins
		DB Marcellus Greene
		DB Dave Liggins
		DB Reggie Ware

RUSHING: Oliver 146/655y, Holland 110/590y, Hersey 56/252y
PASSING: Tunnicliffe 96-173/1204y, 8 TD, 55.5%
RECEIVING: Holmes 33/545y, Carter 23/427y, Holland 20/189y
SCORING: Brett Weber (K) 47pts, Hersey 36pts, Oliver 24pts

1981 6-5

18	UCLA	35 WR Kevin Ward / Brad Anderson
13	California	14 WR Bruce Bush / Bob Carter
37	Cal-Fullerton	16 T Neal Harris
17	Stanford	13 G Frank Kalil / Michael Freeman
13	Southern Cal	10 C Glenn McCormick / Brian Christiansen
18	Oregon	14 G Chris Knudsen / Gerald Roper
19	Washington St.	34 T Marsharne Graves / Jeff Kiewel (G)
48	Texas-El Paso	15 TE Mark Keel / Mark Gobel
40	Oregon State	7 QB Tom Tunnicliffe / Mark Fulcher
17	Fresno State	23 TB Vance Johnson / Brian Holland
13	Arizona State	24 FB Dearl Nelson/Wm. Redman/C. Brewer
		DL Ivan Lesnik
		DL Gary Shaw / Joe Drake
		DL Julius Holt / Chris Schultz
		LB Gary Gibson / Steve Boadway
		LB Ricky Hunley
		LB Glenn Perkins / John Pace
		LB Bob Gareeb / Frank Flournoy
		DB Randy Robbins / Ray Moret
		DB Jerome Crimes / Greg Turner
		DB Al Gross
		DB Tony Neely

RUSHING: Johnson 123/654y, Holland 126/577y,
Nelson 77/303y
PASSING: Tunnicliffe 117-217/1420y, 9TD, 53.9%,
Fulcher 53-116/674y, 4TD, 45.7%
RECEIVING: Keel 27/343y, Carter 25/427y, Ward 25/401y
SCORING: Brett Weber (K) 54pts, Johnson 48pts, Holland 44pts

1982 6-4-1

38	Oregon State	12 WR Brad Anderson / Phil Freeman
13	Washington	23 WR Kevin Ward / Jay Dobyns
14	Iowa	17 T Chris Schultz / Bryon Nelson
24	UCLA	24 G Michael Freeman
16	Notre Dame	13 C Glenn McCormick
55	Pacific	7 G Jeff Kiewel
34	Washington St.	17 T Marsharne Graves
41	Stanford	27 TE Mark Keel
41	Southern Cal	18 QB Tom Tunnicliffe
7	Oregon	13 TB Vance Johnson / Brian Holland
28	Arizona State	18 FB Courtney Griffin / Chris Brewer
		DL John Barthalt / Julius Holt
		DL Ivan Lesnik / Joe Drake
		DL David Wood
		LB Steve Boadway / Lamonte Hunley
		LB Ricky Hunley
		LB Glenn Perkins
		LB John Kaiser
		DB Randy Robbins / Greg Turner
		DB Ray Moret / Gordon Bunch
		DB Al Gross
		DB Tony Neely / Lynnden Brown

RUSHING: Johnson 111/443y, Griffin 91/392y, Holland 74/262y
PASSING: Tunnicliffe 176-328/2520y, 18TD, 53.7%
RECEIVING: Anderson 44/870y, Keel 32/513y, Johnson 25/186y
SCORING: Max Zendejas (K) 79pts, Johnson 42pts,
Holland 36pts

1983 7-3-1

50	Oregon State	6 WR Brad Anderson / Jon Horton
38	Utah	0 WR Jay Dobyns / Phil Freeman
45	Washington St.	6 T Bryon Nelson / Brian Denton
27	Cal-Fullerton	10 G Michael Freeman (C) / David Connor
33	California	33 C Nils Fox
52	Colorado State	21 G Charlie Dickey
10	Oregon	19 T Marsharne Graves
22	Stanford	31 TE Mark Walczak
22	Washington	23 QB Tom Tunnicliffe
27	UCLA	24 TB Vance Johnson / Courtney Griffin
17	Arizona State	15 FB Chris Brewer / William Redman
		DL David Wood
		DL Joe Drake
		DL John Barthalt / Ivan Lesnik
		LB Steve Boadway
		LB Ricky Hunley
		LB Lamonte Hunley / Cliff Thorpe
		LB John Kaiser / Craig Vesling
		DB Randy Robbins / Gordon Bunch
		DB Greg Turner / Bryan Evans
		DB Allan Durden
		DB Lynnden Brown / Don Be'Ans

RUSHING: Brewer 114/586y, Johnson 154/476y,
Redman 54/178y
PASSING: Tunnicliffe 185-351/2474y, 11 TD, 52.7%
RECEIVING: Dobyns 50/694y, Anderson 42/677y,
Johnson 31/264y
SCORING: Max Zendejas (K) 99pts, Johnson 78pts,
Brewer 42pts

1984 7-4

22 Fresno State	27 WR Jon Horton
23 California	13 WR Jay Dobyns
27 Oregon State	8 T John DuBose / Charlie Dickey (G)
26 LSU	9 G David Connor / Guy Collins
31 Long Beach St.	24 C Nils Fox / Jeff Jones
28 Oregon	14 G Val Bichekas / Curt DiGiamcomo
14 Southern Cal	17 T Brian Denton
12 Washington	28 TE Hugh Verbalaitis / Gary Parrish
45 Utah State	10 QB Alfred Jenkins / John Conner
28 Stanford	14 TB David Adams / Vance Johnson
16 Arizona State	10 FB Rory Barnett / Joe Prior
	DL David Wood
	DL Joe Drake
	DL John Barthalt / Jim Birmingham
	LB Steve Boadway
	LB Lamonte Hunley
	LB Byron Evans / Brent Wood
	LB Craig Vesling / Cliff Thorpe
	DB Gordon Bunch
	DB Greg Turner / Bryan Evans
	DB Allan Durden
	DB Lynnden Brown / Don Be'Ans

RUSHING: Adams 188/750y, Johnson 83/298y, Prior 42/167y
PASSING: Jenkins 156-312/2202y, 11TD, 50.0%
RECEIVING: Horton 45/880y, Dobyns 42/493y, Johnson 26/340y
SCORING: Max Zendejas (K) 86pts, Adams 42pts, Horton 36pts

1985 8-3-1

23 Toledo	10 WR Jon Horton / Derek Hill
12 Washington St.	7 WR Jeff Fairholm / Kip Lewis
23 California	17 T John DuBose / Frank Arriola
13 Colorado	14 G Curt DiGiancomo
28 SMU	6 C Jeff Jones / Joe Tofflemire
41 San Jose State	0 G Val Bichekas
17 Stanford	28 T Jeff Rinehart / Brian Denton
27 Oregon State	6 TE Hugh Verbalaitis / Gary Parrish
19 UCLA	24 QB Alfred Jenkins
20 Oregon	8 TB David Adams / Chuck Knox
16 Arizona State	13 FB Joe Prior / James DeBow
13 Georgia■	13 DL Dana Wells / Jim Birmingham
	DL Lee Brunelli
	DL George Hinkle / Stan Mataele
	LB Dan Lockett /Francis "Boomer" Gibson
	LB Byron Evans
	LB Brent Wood / Gallen Allen
	LB Craig Vesling / Cliff Thorpe
	DB Gordon Bunch
	DB Martin Rudolph / Don Be'Ans
	DB Allan Durden
	DB Chuck Cecil

RUSHING: Adams 138/511y, DeBow 84/330y, Prior 61/219y
PASSING: Jenkins 150-278/1767y, 7TD, 54.0%
RECEIVING: Horton 43/685y, Fairholm 22/340y, DeBow 15/117y
SCORING: Max Zendejas (K) 89pts, Horton & DeBow 18pts

1986 9-3

37 Houston	3 WR Jon Horton / Derek Hill
37 Colorado State	10 WR Jeff Fairholm / Kip Lewis
41 Oregon	17 T Jeff Rinehart / Hugh Verbalaitis
24 Colorado	21 G Frank Arriola
25 UCLA	32 C Joe Tofflemire
23 Oregon St.	12 G Val Bichekas
33 California	16 T Brian Denton
13 Southern Cal	20 TE Vince Lotti / Jim Hanawalt
31 Washington St.	6 QB Alfred Jenkins
34 Arizona State	17 TB David Adams / Art Greathouse
24 Stanford	29 FB Chris McLemore / Joe Prior
30 North Carolina■	21 DL George Hinkle / Reggie Gaddis
	DL Dana Wells
	DL Jim Birmingham / Stan Mataele
	LB Dan Lockett / Chris Singleton
	LB Byron Evans
	LB Brent Wood / Jerry Beasley
	LB Boomer Gibson / Kevin Singleton
	DB James DeBow / Durrell Jones
	DB Martin Rudolph / Randy Kindred
	DB Eugene Hardy / Troy Cephers
	DB Chuck Cecil

RUSHING: Adams 238/1175y, Greathouse 87/404y,
McLemore 58/238y
PASSING: Jenkins 118-232/1573y, 10 TD, 50.9%
RECEIVING: Hill 32/523y, Fairholm 24/382y, Horton 20/340y,
Adams 20/162y
SCORING: Gary Coston (K) 97pts, Adams 48pts,
Greathouse & Horton 24pts

1987 4-4-3

14 Iowa	15 WR Jeff Fairholm / Jon Horton
20 New Mexico	9 WR Derek Hill
24 UCLA	34 T Jeff Rinehart / Hugh Verbalaitis
45 Bowling Green	7 G John Brandom / Doug Penner
23 California	23 C Joe Tofflemire
31 Oregon State	17 G Rob Woods / Kevin McKinney
28 Washington St.	45 T Tom Lynch
23 Stanford	13 TE Vince Lotti
21 Washington	21 QB Richard Veal / Bobby Watters
10 Southern Cal	12 TB Art Greathouse / David Eldridge
24 Arizona State	24 FB Alonzo Washington / Reggie McGill
	DL Reggie Gaddis / George Hinkle
	DL Dana Wells
	DL Brad Henke / Keith Moody
	LB Chris Singleton / Kevin Singleton
	LB Gallen Allen / Darren Case
	LB Jerry Beasley / Blake Custer
	LB Boomer Gibson
	DB James DeBow / Randy Kindred
	DB Durrell Jones / Todd Burden
	DB Eugene Hardy / Troy Cephers
	DB Chuck Cecil

RUSHING: Veal 161/566y, Greathouse 77/435y,
Washington 62/316y
PASSING: Veal 75-153/1239y, 4 TD, 49.0%
RECEIVING: Hill 45/798y, Darryl Lewis (TB) 16/272y,
McGill 9/143y
SCORING: Gary Coston (K) 73pts, Veal 56pts,
Hill & Darryl Lewis (TB) 24pts

1988 7-4

24 Oregon St.	13 WR Kip Lewis / Melvin Smith
35 Texas Tech	19 WR Derek Hill / Kyle Jan
10 Oklahoma	28 T Rob Woods / Dave Roney
55 E. Michigan	0 G Doug Penner / Doug Pritchard
15 Southern Cal	38 C Joe Tofflemire
45 Washington St.	28 G John Brandom / Rob Flory
3 UCLA	24 T Glenn Parker / Paul Tofflemire
7 California	10 TE George Mihalopoulos
16 Washington	13 QB Ronald Veal / Bobby Watters
41 Oregon	27 HB Art Greathouse / David Eldridge
28 Arizona State	18 FB Alonzo Washington
	DL Brad Henke
	DL Dana Wells
	DL Ken Hakes / Reggie Johnson
	LB Chris Singleton / Arnulf Mobley
	LB Kevin Singleton
	LB Darren Case / Donnie Salum
	LB Zeno Alexander
	DB Darryl Lewis
	DB Todd Burden / Scott Geyer
	DB Jeff Hammerschmidt
	DB James DeBow / Chris Wright

RUSHING: Washington 113/651y, Eldridge 80/600y,
Greathouse 105/497y
PASSING: Veal 40-105/669y, 4 TD, 38.1%,
Watters 45-103/581y, 43.7%
RECEIVING: Hill 25/508y, Greathouse 12/150y,
Reggie McGill (HB) 11/107y
SCORING: Doug Pfaff (K) 58pts, Greathouse 36pts,
Eldridge, Hill & Veal 30pts

1989 8-4

19 Stanford	3 WR Kyle Jan / Kip Lewis
14 Texas Tech	24 T John Fina
6 Oklahoma	3 G Nick Fineanganofo / Dave Roney (T)
20 Washington	17 C Paul Tofflemire
10 Oregon	16 G John Brandom
42 UCLA	7 T Glenn Parker
23 Washington St.	21 TE Richard Griffith
38 Pacific	14 QB Ronald Veal / George Malauulu
28 California	29 HB Reggie McGill
3 Southern Cal	24 HB David Eldridge / Errol Sapp
28 Arizona State	10 FB Mario Hampton / Mike Streidnig
17 N. Carolina St.■	10 DL Reggie Johnson / Reggie Gaddis
	DL Ken Hakes
	DL Anthony Smith
	LB Chris Singleton
	LB Donnie Salum / Arnulf Mobley
	LB Darren Case
	LB Zeno Alexander
	DB Darryl Lewis
	DB Todd Burden / Richard Holt
	DB Jeff Hammerschmidt
	DB Scott Geyer / Chris Wright

RUSHING: Eldridge 143/788y, McGill 89/507y,
Hampton 103/424y
PASSING: Veal 46-117/517y, 2 TD, 39.3%,
Malauulu 19-35/381y, 4 TD, 54.3%
RECEIVING: McGill 11/170y, Hampton 10/90y, Lewis 9/140y
SCORING: Doug Pfaff (K) 62pts, Eldridge 48pts, Veal 30pts

1990 7-5

28 Illinois	16 WR Terry Vaughn / Kyle Jan
25 New Mexico	10 T John Fina
22 Oregon	17 G Rick Warren
25 California	30 C Paul Tofflemire
28 UCLA	21 G Nick Fineanganofo
21 Oregon State	35 T Rob Flory
35 Southern Cal	26 TE Richard Griffith
42 Washington St.	34 QB Ronald Veal / George Malauulu
10 Washington	54 RB Reggie McGill
10 Stanford	23 HB Art Greathouse
21 Arizona State	17 FB Mario Hampton / Mike Streidnig
0 Syracuse■	28 DL Reggie Johnson
	DL Rob Waldrop
	DL Ty Parten
	LB Jimmie Hopkins
	LB Marcel Wade / Richard Maddox
	LB Darren Case / Kevin Singleton
	LB Zeno Alexander / Gregg Shapiro
	DB Darryl Lewis
	DB Todd Burden
	DB Jeff Hammerschmidt
	DB Richard Holt / Bobby Roland

RUSHING: Greathouse 104/482y, Hampton 57/301y,
Veal 99/281y
PASSING: Malauulu 46-101/726y, TD, 45.5%,
Veal 36-66/446y, 3 TD, 54.5%
RECEIVING: Vaughn 22/431y, McGill 12/195y, Griffith 10/138y
SCORING: Gary Coston (K) 59pts, Veal 48pts,
Greathouse & Malauulu 30pts

1991 4-7

14 Ohio State	38 WR Lamar Lovett
28 Stanford	23 WR Terry Vaughn
21 California	23 T John Fina
45 Long Beach St.	21 G Nick Fineanganofo
0 Washington	54 C Mani Ott
14 UCLA	54 G Mike Heemsbergen / Paul Tofflemire
9 Miami	36 T Paul Stamer
45 Oregon State	21 TE Richard Griffith
27 Washington St.	40 QB George Malauulu
31 Southern Cal	14 TB Chuck Levy (QB) / Ontiwaun Carter
14 Arizona State	37 FB Billy Johnson
	DL Jimmie Hopkins
	DL Jim Hoffman / Pulu Poumele
	DL Rob Waldrop
	DL Ty Parten / Hicham El-Mashtoub
	LB Jamal Lee / Charlie Camp
	LB Sean Harris / Richard Maddox
	DB Darryl Morrison
	DB Richard Holt / Keshon Johnson
	DB Mike Scurlock
	DB Bobby Roland
	DB Tony Bouie / Heath Bray

RUSHING: Johnson 116/682y, Carter 113/606y, Levy 128/505y
PASSING: Malauulu 52-99/674y, 5TD, 52.5%,
Levy 26-52/315y, 2TD, 50.0%
RECEIVING: Vaughn 21/270y, Lovett 20/213y, Levy 19/289y
SCORING: Levy 60pts, Steve McLaughlin (K) 56pts

1992 6-5-1

49 Utah State	3 WR Terry Vaughn / Cary Taylor
20 Washington St.	23 WR Troy Dickey / Chris Corral
14 Oregon State	14 T Paul Stamer
8 Miami	8 G Eric Johnson / Vincent Smith
23 UCLA	3 C Hicham El-Mashtoub / Mu Tagoai
21 Stanford	6 G Warner Smith / Mike Ciasca
24 California	17 T Mike Heemsbergen
30 New Mexico St.	0 TE Richard Griffith / Rod Lewis
16 Washington	3 QB George Malauulu
7 Southern Cal.	14 TB Ontiwaun Carter / Chuck Levy
6 Arizona State	7 FB Billy Johnson / Lamont Lovett
15 Baylor■	20 DL Jim Hoffman / Ty Parten
	DL Rob Waldrop
	DL Jimmie Hopkins / Tedy Bruschi
	LB Richard Maddox
	LB Sean Harris
	LB Brant Boyer / Charlie Camp
	LB Jamal Lee / Shawn Jarrett
	DB Keshon Johnson
	DB Darryl Morrison / Jey Phillips
	DB Tony Bouie
	DB Brandon Saunders / Mike Scurlock

RUSHING: Carter 195/739y, Johnson 115/524y, Levy 104/421y
PASSING: Malauulu 97-198/1210y, 6 TD, 49.0%
RECEIVING: Dickey 28/395y, Vaughn 23/311y, Levy 19/103y
SCORING: Steve McLaughlin (K) 59pts

1993 10-2

24 Texas-El Paso	6 WR Troy Dickey / Richard Dice
16 Pacific	13 WR Terry Vaughn / Cary Taylor
16 Illinois	14 T Mu Tagoai / Paul Stamer
33 Oregon St.	0 G Pulu Poumele / Eric Johnson
38 Southern Cal	7 C Hicham El-Mashtoub / Mani Ott (G)
27 Stanford	24 G Warner Smith
9 Washington St.	6 T Joe Smigiel / Mike Ciasca
17 UCLA	37 TE Rod Lewis / Lamar Harris
31 Oregon	10 QB Dan White / Brady Batten
20 California	24 RB Billy Johnson / Lamar Lovett
34 Arizona State	20 RB Ontiwaun Carter / Chuck Levy (QB)
29 Miami■	0 DL Tedy Bruschi / Akil Jackson
	DL Jim Hoffman
	DL Rob Waldrop / Chuck Osborne
	DL Jimmie Hopkins
	LB Shawn Jarrett
	LB Sean Harris
	LB Brant Boyer / Chris Lopez
	DB Claudius Wright
	DB Jey Phillips / Mike Scurlock
	DB Tony Bouie
	DB Brandon Sanders / Spencer Wray

RUSHING: Carter 178/837y, Levy 126/567y, Johnson 100/454y
PASSING: White 103-207/1410y, 11TD, 49.8%
RECEIVING: Vaughn 36/474y, Dickey 27/381y, Taylor 13/260y, Dice 13/235y
SCORING: Steve McLaughlin (K) 66pts, Levy 60pts, Dickey 36pts

1994 8-4

19 Georgia Tech	14 WR Richard Dice / Jeff Chiasson
44 New Mexico St.	0 WR Lamar Lovett / Cary Taylor
34 Stanford	10 T Paul Stamer
30 Oregon State	10 G Pulu Poumele
16 Colorado State	21 C Hicham El-Mashtoub
10 Washington St.	7 G Warner Smith
34 UCLA	24 T Joe Smigiel
9 Oregon	10 TE Lamar Harris / Tim Thomas
13 California	6 QB Dan White
28 Southern Cal	45 FB Ontiwaun Carter / Gary Taylor
28 Arizona State	27 RB Jas'n Patterson/Kevin Schmidtke (TB)
13 Utah■	16 DL Tedy Bruschi / Jimmy Sprotte
	DL Joe Salave'a
	DL Chuck Osborne / Jim Hoffman
	DL Akil Jackson
	LB Chris Lopez / Thomas Demps
	LB Charlie Camp / Kevin Gosar
	LB Sean Harris
	DB Kelly Malveaux
	DB Mike Scurlock / Spencer Wray
	DB Tony Bouie
	DB Brandon Sanders

RUSHING: Carter 268/1163y, G. Taylor 72/307y, Schmidtke 48/191y
PASSING: White 169-296/2181y, 14TD, 57.1%
RECEIVING: Dice 56/969y, Lovett 26/299y, Carter 23/226y
SCORING: Steve McLaughlin (K) 95pts, Carter & Dice 48pts

1995 6-5

41 Pacific	9 WR Richard Dice / Rodney Williams
20 Georgia Tech	19 WR Cary Taylor / Ron Holmes
7 Illinois	9 T Ryan Turley / Willie Walker
10 Southern Cal	31 G Frank Middleton
20 California	15 C Wayne Wyatt
10 UCLA	17 G Mani Ott
17 Washington	31 T Ian McCutcheon
24 Washington St.	14 TE Mike Lucky / Mike Metzler
14 Oregon State	9 QB Dan White / Brady Batten
13 Oregon	17 TB Gary Taylor
31 Arizona State	28 FB Charles Myles / Kevin Schmidtke
	DL Tedy Bruschi
	DL Joe Salave'a / Daniel Greer
	DL Chuck Osborne / Van Tuinei
	LB Jimmy Sprotte
	LB Chester Burnett
	LB Charlie Camp / Mike Szlauko
	LB Thomas Demps / Armon Williams
	DB Kelly Malveaux
	DB Rashee Johnson
	DB Chuck Rich
	DB Brandon Sanders / Mikal Smith

RUSHING: Taylor 177/714y, Schmidtke 77/203y, Myles 49/180y
PASSING: Smith 150-297/1855y, 15TD, 50.5%
RECEIVING: Williams 46/587y, C. Taylor 33/290y, Dice 25/443y
SCORING: Dice 36pts, Williams 24pts

1996 5-6

23 Texas-El Paso	3 WR Richard Dice / Rodney Williams
20 Iowa	21 WR Jeremy McDaniel / Dennis Northcutt
41 Illinois	0 T Frank Middleton
17 Washington	31 G Willie Walker
34 Washington St.	26 C Wayne Wyatt / Rusty James
7 Southern Cal	14 G Ryan Turley / Yusef Scott
33 Oregon State	7 T Jose Portilla
55 California	56 TE Mike Lucky / Mike Metzler
31 Oregon	49 QB Keith Smith / Brady Batten
35 UCLA	17 TB Gary Taylor/Leon Callen/Tr. Canidate
14 Arizona State	56 FB Charles Myles / Kevin Schmidtke
	DL Van Tuinei / Tyrone Gunn
	DL Joe Salave'a / Chima Ugwu
	DL Daniel Greer / Steve Tafua
	LB Mike Szlauko
	LB Chester Burnett / Marcus Bell
	LB Jimmy Sprotte / DaShon Polk
	LB Armon Williams
	DB Kelly Malveaux
	DB Chris McAlister
	DB David Fipp
	DB Mikal Smith / Leland Gayles

RUSHING: Taylor 120/564y, Smith 136/546y, Callen 59/275y
PASSING: Smith 117-193/1450y, 11TD, 60.6%
RECEIVING: McDaniel 31/607y, Metzler 23/291y, Williams 23/275y
SCORING: Matt Peyton (K) 76pts, Smith 48pts, Taylor 24pts

1997 7-5

9 Oregon	16 WR Rodney Williams / Brad Brennan
24 Ala.-Birm'ham	10 WR Dennis Northcutt / Brandon Nash
20 Ohio State	28 T Edwin Mulitalo
27 UCLA	40 G Yusef Scott
31 San Diego State	28 C Rusty James / Bruce Wiggins
28 Stanford	22 G Ryan Turley
28 Washington	58 T Jose Portilla
34 Washington St.	35 TE Mike Lucky / Brandon Manumaleuna
7 Oregon State	7 QB Keith Smith / Ortege Jenkins
41 California	38 TB Trung Canidate / Leon Callen
28 Arizona State	16 FB Kelvin Eafon / William Blocker
20 New Mexico■	14 DL Mike Szlauka / Joe Tafoya
	DL Joe Salave'a / Anthony Thomas
	DL Daniel Greer
	LB DaShon Polk
	LB Chester Burnett
	LB Marcus Bell / Stadford Glover
	LB Jimmy Sprotte
	DB Kelly Malveaux / Leland Gayles
	DB Chris McAlister / Kelvin Hunter
	DB David Fipp / Rafell Jones
	DB Rashee Johnson / Scooter Sprotte

RUSHING: Canidate 116/742y, Eafon 117/396y, Jay Hinton (TB) 45/196y
PASSING: Jenkins 108-216/1475y, 16TD, 50.0%, Smith 60-118/691y, 6TD, 50.8%
RECEIVING: Northcutt 56/715y, Williams 40/572y, Brennan 30/508y
SCORING: T.J. Rodriguez (K) 57pts, Northcutt 48pts, Williams 36pts

1998 12-1

27 Hawaii	6 WR Jeremy McDaniel / Brad Brennan
31 Stanford	14 WR Dennis Northcutt
35 Iowa	11 T Edwin Mulitalo / Makoa Freitas
35 San Diego State	16 G Steven Grace
3 Washington	28 C Bruce Wiggins
28 UCLA	52 G Yusef Scott
28 Oregon State	7 T Manuela Savea / Ega Usa
45 NE Louisiana	7 TE Brandon Manumaleuna
38 Oregon	3 QB Keith Smith / Ortege Jenkins
41 Washington St.	7 TB Trung Canidate / Leon Callen
27 California	23 FB Kelvin Eafon
50 Arizona State	42 DL Eli Wnek / Mike Robertson
23 Nebraska■	20 DL Keoni Fraser
	DL Daniel Greer / Anthony Thomas
	DL Joe Tafoya / Idris Haroon
	LB DaShon Polk
	LB Marcus Bell
	LB Scooter Sprotte / Antonio Pierce
	DB Kelvin Hunter
	DB Chris McAlister / Leland Gayles
	DB Rafell Jones
	DB Greg Payne

RUSHING: Canidate 167/1220y, Eafon 145/532y, Callen 63/276y
PASSING: Smith 113-165/1732y, 13TD, 68.5%, Jenkins 70-142/1011y, 5TD, 49.3%
RECEIVING: Northcutt 63/922y, McDaniel 58/916y, Brennan 15/314y
SCORING: Eafon 96pts, Mark McDonald (K) 85pts, Canidate 60pts

1999 6-6

7 Penn State	41 WR Brad Brennan / Bobby Wade
35 TCU	31 WR Dennis Northcutt
34 Middle Tenn. St.	19 T Makoa Freitas
22 Stanford	50 G Steven Grace / Chris Redding
30 Washington St.	24 C Bruce Wiggins
31 Southern Cal	24 G Marques McFadden
34 Texas-El Paso	21 T Manu Savea / Ega Usu
41 Oregon	44 TE Brandon Manumaleuna / Eli Wnek
33 UCLA	7 QB Keith Smith / Ortege Jenkins
25 Washington	33 TB Trung Canidate / Leon Callen
20 Oregon State	28 FB Jim Wendler / Lance Briggs
27 Arizona State	42 DL Austin Uku / Alex Luna
	DL Keoni Fraser
	DL Joe Tafoya / J.J. Joppru
	DL Idris Haroon / Mike Robertson
	LB DaShon Polk
	LB Marcus Bell / Adrian Koch
	LB Antonio Pierce / Scooter Sprotte
	DB Leland Gayles / Anthony Banks
	DB Kelvin Hunter
	DB Rafell Jones / Jarvie Worcester
	DB Greg Payne

RUSHING: Canidate 253/1602y, Northcutt 14/200y, Callen 35/183y
PASSING: Smith 131-228/1903y, 10TD, 57.5%, Jenkins 79-131/1082y, 9TD, 60.3%
RECEIVING: Northcutt 88/1422y, Wade 30/454y, Canidate 30/253y
SCORING: Canidate 72pts, Northcutt 66pts, Jenkins 28pts

2000 5-6

17 Utah	3 WR Bobby Wade / Andrae Thurman
17 Ohio State	27 WR Malosi Leonard / Brad Brennan
17 San Diego State	3 T Makoa Freitas
27 Stanford	3 G Reggie Sampay / Steven Grace
31 Southern Cal	24 C Bruce Wiggins
53 Washington St.	47 G Kevin Barry
10 Oregon	14 T Darren Safranek
24 UCLA	27 TE Brandon Manumaleuna / James Hugo
32 Washington	35 QB Ortege Jenkins
9 Oregon State	33 TB Clarence Farmer / Leo Mills
17 Arizona State	30 FB Eli Wnek / Mike Detwiler
	DL Joe Tafoya / Alex Luna
	DL Keoni Fraser / Ben Alualu
	DL Anthony Thomas / Young Thompson
	DL Idris Haroon
	LB Shelton Ross / Stadford Glover
	LB Lance Briggs / Adrian Koch
	LB Antonio Pierce / Joe Siofele
	DB Michael Jolivette / Anthony Banks
	DB Jermaine Chatman /David Laudermilk
	DB Jarvie Worchester / Clay Hardt
	DB Brandon Nash / Zaharius Johnson

RUSHING: Farmer 138/666y, Mills 114/585y, Larry Croom (TB) 64/257y
PASSING: Jenkins 123-261/1647, 9TD, 47.1%
RECEIVING: Wade 45/626y, Brennan 15/299y, Thurman 14/145y
SCORING: Sean Keel (K) 64pts, Farmer & Jenkins 30pts

2001 5-6

23 San Diego State	10 WR Bobby Wade / Malosi Leonard
36 Idaho	29 WR Brandon Marshall / Andrae Thurman
38 UNLV	21 T Makoa Freitas
21 Washington St.	48 G Steven Grace / Reggie Sampay
28 Oregon	63 C Keoki Fraser
3 Oregon State	38 G Kevin Barry / Aaron Higginbotham
28 Washington	31 T Darren Safranek / Brandon Phillips
34 Southern Cal	41 TE Steve Fleming / James Hugo
38 California	24 QB Jason Johnson
37 Stanford	51 TB Clarence Farmer / Leo Mills
34 Arizona State	21 FB Mike Detwiler
	DL Alex Luna
	DL Anthony Thomas / Tony Thompson
	DL Young Thompson / Fata Avegalio
	DL Dusty Alexander
	LB Joe Siofele / Kirk Johnson
	LB Lance Briggs
	LB Ray Wells / Matt Molina
	DB Jermaine Chatman /David Laudermilk
	DB Michael Jolivette / Anthony Banks
	DB Jarvie Worchester
	DB Zaharius Johnson / Clay Hardt

RUSHING: Farmer 209/1229y, Tremaine Cox (TB) 44/230y, Mills 50/155y
PASSING: Johnson 169-298/2347y, 19TD, 56.7%
RECEIVING: Wade 62/882y, Leonard 43/582y, Thurman 30/470y
SCORING: Farmer 60pts, Wade 48pts

2002 4-8

37 N. Arizona	3 WR Bobby Wade
23 Utah	17 WR Andrae Thurman / Lance Relford
10 Wisconsin	31 T Chris Johnson / Makos Freitas
14 North Texas	9 G Reggie Sampay (C)
14 Oregon	31 C Keoki Fraser
28 Washington	32 G John Parada / Aaron Higginbotham
6 Stanford	16 T Brandon Phillips / Tanner Bell
13 Washington St.	21 TE James Hugo / Steve Fleming
3 Oregon State	38 QB Jason Johnson
7 UCLA	37 TB Clarence Farmer / Mike Bell
52 California	41 FB Sean Jones / Gilbert Harris
20 Arizona State	34 DL Carlos Williams / Fata Avagalio
	DL Vince Feula / Carl Tuitavuki
	DL Young Thompson / Brad Brittain
	LB Copeland Bryan / Matt Molina
	LB Joe Siofele
	LB Lance Briggs
	LB Ray Wells / Marcus Smith
	DB Gary Love / Luis Nunez
	DB Darrell Brooks / David Hinton
	DB Jarvie Worchester
	DB Clay Hardt / Tony Wingate

RUSHIING: Bell 106/341y, Farmer 84/309y,
Beau Carr (TB) 39/126y
PASSING: Johnson 239-410/3327y, 16TD, 58.3%
RECEIVING: Wade 93/1389y, Thurman 61/915y,
Relford 20/289y
SCORING: Wade 48pts, Bobby Gill (K) 38pts,
Sean Keel (K) 27pts

2003 2-10

42 Texas-El Paso	7 WR Lance Relford / Mike Jefferson
13 LSU	59 WR Biren Ealy / Ricky Williams
10 Oregon	48 T Chris Johnson / Tanner Bell
7 Purdue	59 G Reggie Sampay / Keith Jackson
10 TCU	13 C Keoki Fraser
7 Washington St.	30 G Kili Lefotu
21 UCLA	24 T John Abramo / Brandon Phillips
14 California	42 TE Steve Fleming / Matt Padron
23 Oregon State	52 QB Kris Heavner / Nic Costa
27 Washington	22 HB Mike Bell / Clarence Farmer
0 Southern Cal	45 FB Gilbert Harris / Clarence McRae (TE)
7 Arizona State	28 DL Copeland Bryan
	DL Carlos Williams / Paul Philipp
	DL Carl Tuitavuki / Clifton Stanford
	DL Matt Molina / Marcus Smith
	LB Clay Hardt / Marcus Hollingworth
	LB Joe Siofele
	LB Kirk Johnson / Patrick Howard
	DB Gary Love / Gary Sherman
	DB Michael Jolivette
	DB Darrell Brooks / Tony Wingate
	DB Lamon Means

RUSHING: Bell 168/920y, Farmer 90/326y, Costa 23/101y
PASSING: Heavner 121-237/1501y, 8TD, 51.1%
RECEIVING: Ealy 42/577y, Williams 36/563y, Fleming 24/222y
SCORING: Bell 36pts, Ealy 24pts, Bobby Gill (K) 22pts

2004 3-8

21 N. Arizona	3 WR Anthony Johnson / Biren Ealy
6 Utah	23 WR Mike Jefferson
7 Wisconsin	9 WR Syndric Steptoe / Ricky Williams
19 Washington St.	20 T Chris Johnson / Tanner Bell
17 UCLA	37 G John Abramo / Chris Johnson
14 Oregon	28 C Keoki Fraser
0 California	38 G Kili Lefouto / John Parada
14 Oregon State	28 T Peter Graniello (G) / Brandon Phillips
23 Washington	13 TE Steve Fleming / Clarence McRae
9 Southern Cal	49 QB Richard Kovalcheck / Kris Heavner
34 Arizona State	27 RB Mike Bell / Gilbert Harris
	DL Marcus Smith
	DL Carlos Williams
	DL Paul Philipp / Lionel Dotson
	DL Andre Torrey / Copeland Bryan
	LB Dane Krogstad
	LB Sean Jones / Randy Sims
	LB Patrick Howard / Kirk Johnson
	DB Wilrey Fontenot
	DB Antoine Cason
	DB Tony Wingate
	DB Lamon Means / Darrell Brooks

RUSHING: Bell 204/950y, Harris 67/285y,
Chris Henry (RB) 56/159y
PASSING: Heavner 84-143/837y, 4TD, 58.7%,
Kovalcheck 67-136/880y, 6TD, 49.3%
RECEIVING: Steptoe 30/446y, Fleming 23/332y,
Williams 22/264y
SCORING: Nick Folk (K) 42pts, Bell 30pts,
Jefferson & Steptoe 18pts

2005 3-8

24 Utah	27 WR Michael Thomas
31 N. Arizona	12 WR Anthony Johnson
24 Purdue	31 WR Syndric Steptoe
0 California	28 T Peter Graniello
21 Southern Cal	42 G John Abramo / Adam Hawes
16 Stanford	20 C Erick Levitre
21 Oregon	28 G Kili Lefotu / Joe Longacre
29 Oregon State	27 T Tanner Bell
52 UCLA	14 TE Brad Wood/Ryan Kilpatrick/Travis Bell
14 Washington	38 QB Willie Tiutama / Richard Kovalcheck
20 Arizona State	23 RB Mike Bell / Gilbert Harris / Chris Henry
	DL Copeland Bryan / Jason Parker
	DL Yaniv Barnett / Rickey Parker
	DL Paul Philipp / Lionel Dotson
	DL Johnathan Turner
	LB Dane Krogstad / McKinney
	LB Ronnie Palmer
	LB Spencer Larsen/Marcus Hollingsworth
	DB Antoine Cason
	DB Wilrey Fontenot
	DB Darrell Brooks
	DB Michael Johnson / Lamon Means

RUSHING: Bell 200/952y, Harris 79/284y, Henry 34/119y
PASSING: Kovalcheck 125-220/1351y, 10TDs, 56.8%,
Tiutama 82-142/1105y, 9TDs, 57.7%
RECEIVING: Thomas 52/771y, Steptoe 37/493y,
Johnson 32/419y
SCORING: Nick Folk (K) 52pts, Harris 42pts,
Wood & Thomas 36pts

2006 6-6

16 Brigham Young	13 WR Michael Thomas
3 LSU	45 WR Syndric Steptoe / Anthony Johnson
28 Stephen F. Austin	10 T Pete Graniello
3 Southern Cal	20 G Daniel Borg
10 Washington	21 C Blake Kerley
7 UCLA	27 G Joe Longacre / Bill Wacholz
20 Stanford	7 T Eben Britton / Tanner Bell
10 Oregon State	17 TE Brandyn McCall / Brad Wood
27 Washington St.	17 QB Willie Tuitama / Adam Austin
24 California	20 RB Chris Henry / Chris Jennings
37 Oregon	10 FB Earl Mitchell / Brandon Lopez
14 Arizona State	28 DL Louis Holmes / Marcus Smith
	DL Yaniv Barnett
	DL Lionel Dotson / Rickey Parker
	DL Johnathan Turner
	LB Dane Krogstad
	LB Ronnie Palmer / Adrian McCovey
	LB Spencer Larsen
	DB Antoine Cason
	DB Wilrey Fontenot
	DB Dominic Patrick
	DB Michael Johnson / Michael Klyce

RUSHING: Henry 165/581y, Jennings 105/451y,
Xavier Smith (RB) 23/120y
PASSING: Tuitama 118-211/1335y, 7TDs, 55.7%,
Austin 52-111/517y, 2TDs, 46.8%
RECEIVING: Steptoe 55/568y, Thomas 50/597y,
Johnson 26/312y
SCORING: Nick Folk (K) 67pts, Henry 48pts, 3 with 18pts

2007 5-7

3 BYU	20 WR Terrell Turner / Delashaun Dean
45 N. Arizona	24 WR Michael Thomas / Anthony Johnson
27 New Mexico	29 T Peter Graniello
27 California	45 G Colin Baxter / Daniel Borg
48 Washington St.	20 C Blake Kerley
16 Oregon State	31 G Joe Longacre
13 Southern Cal	20 T Eben Britton
20 Stanford	21 TE Rob Gronkowski
48 Washington	41 QB Willie Tuitama
34 UCLA	27 H-B Earl Mitchell
34 Oregon	24 RB Nic Grigsby / Chris Jennings
17 Arizona State	20 DL Louis Holmes
	DL Yaniv Barnett
	DL Lionel Dotson / Lolomana Mikaele
	DL Jason Parker / Johnathan Turner
	LB Dane Krogstad
	LB Ronnie Palmer
	LB Spencer Larsen
	DB Antoine Cason
	DB Wilrey Fontenot / Devon Ross
	DB Corey Hall / Dominic Patrick
	DB Cam Nelson /Nate Ness/Michael Klyce

RUSHING: Grigsby 161/704y, Thomas 10/173y,
Jennings 53/156y
PASSING: Tuitama 327-524/3683y, 28TD, 62.4%
RECEIVING: Thomas 83/1038y, Turner50/575y, Dean 37/418y,
Johnson 35/410y, Grigsby 35/200y
SCORING: Jason Bondzio (K) 100pts, Thomas 74pts,
Gronkowski 36pts

2008 8-5

70 Idaho	0 WR Mike Thomas / Juron Criner
41 Toledo	16 WR Terrell Turner / Delashaun Dean
28 New Mexico	36 T Eben Britton
31 UCLA	10 G Mike Diaz
48 Washington	14 C Colin Baxter
23 Stanford	24 G Joe Longacre
42 California	27 T James Tretheway / Adam Grant
10 Southern Cal	17 TE Rob Gronkowski
59 Washington St.	28 QB Willie Tuitama
45 Oregon	55 RB Nic Grigsby / Keola Antolin
17 Oregon State	19 H-B Chris Gronkowski
31 Arizona State	10 DL Ricky Elmore / D'Aundre Reed
31 BYU■	21 DL Kaniela Tuipulotu / Donald Horton
	DL Earl Mitchell
	DL Brooks Reed
	LB Adrian McCovy / Vuna Tuihalamaka
	LB Ronnie Palmer
	LB Xavier Kelley / Sterling Lewis
	DB Marquis Hundley / Corey Hall
	DB Devin Ross / Trevin Ross
	DB Nate Ness
	DB Cam Nelson / Joe Perkins

RUSHING: Grigsby 214/1153y, Antolin 117/525y,
Matt Scott (QB) 23/188y
PASSING: Tuitama 259-399/3088y, 23TD, 64.9%
RECEIVING: Thomas 74/825y, Dean 53/593y,
R. Gronkowski 47/672y
SCORING: Jason Bondzio (K) 97pts, Grigsby 78pts,
R. Gronkowski 62pts, Antolin 60pts

2009 8-5

19 C. Michigan	6 WR Terrell Turner / Juron Criner
34 N. Arizona	17 WR Delashaun Dean / David Roberts
10 Iowa	27 T Mike Diaz / Phillip Garcia
37 Oregon State	32 G Herman Hall (C) / Conan Amituanai
33 Washington	36 C Colin Baxter
43 Stanford	38 G Vaughn Dotsy
27 UCLA	13 T Adam Grant
48 Washington St.	24 TE A.J. Simmons / David Douglas
16 California	7 QB Nick Foles / Matt Scott
41 Oregon	44 RB Nic Grigsby / Keola Antolin
20 Arizona State	17 H-B Chris Gronkowski
21 Southern Cal	17 DL Ricky Elmore
0 Nebraska■	33 DL Donald Horton
	DL Earl Mitchell / Lolomana Mikaele
	DL Brooks Reed / D'Aundre Reed
	LB Sterling Lewis / Corey Hall
	LB Vuna Tuihalamaka
	LB Xavier Kelley
	DB Devin Ross
	DB Trevin Wade / Mike Turner
	DB Cam Nelson
	DB Robert Golden / Joe Perkins

RUSHING: Antolin 114/637y, Grigsby 79/567y, Scott 41/309y
PASSING: Foles 260-410/2486y, 19TD, 63.4%,
Scott 41-72/441y, 1TD, 56.9%
RECEIVING: Turner 48/458y, Criner 45/582y, Roberts 43/582y
Dean 42/396y
SCORING: Alex Zendejas (K) 89pts, Criner 54pts, Grigsby 30pts

2010 7-6

41 Toledo	2 WR David Douglas / David Roberts
52 The Citadel	6 WR Juron Criner / William Wright
34 Iowa	27 T Adam Grant
10 California	9 G Conan Amituanai
27 Oregon State	29 C Colin Baxter / Kyle Quinn
24 Washington St.	7 G Jovon Hayes / Vaughn Dotsy
44 Washington	14 T Phillip Garcia
29 UCLA	21 TE A.J. Simmons / Jack Baucus
17 Stanford	42 QB Nick Foles / Matt Scott
21 Southern Cal	24 RB Nic Grigsby/Keola Antolin/Greg Nwoko
29 Oregon	48 H-B/WR Taimi Tutogi / Terrence Miller
29 Arizona State	30 DL Ricky Elmore / D'Aundre Reed
10 Oklahoma State■	36 DL Justin Washington / Sione Tuihalamaka
	DL Lolomana Mikaele
	DL Brooks Reed
	LB Paul Vassallo
	LB Derek Earls
	LB/DB Jake Fischer / Adam Hall
	DB Robert Golden
	DB Trevin Wade
	DB Joseph Perkins
	DB Anthony Wilcox / Shaquille Richardson

RUSHING: Antolin 143/668y, Grigsby 118/533y, Nwoko 57/270
PASSING: Foles 286-426/3191y, 20TD, 67.1%,
Scott 66-93/776y, 4TD, 71%
RECEIVING: Criner 82/1233y, Douglas 52/515y, Roberts 44/487y
SCORING: Alex Zendejas (K) 83pts, Criner 66pts,
Antolin & Grigsby 54pts

ARIZONA STATE

Arizona State University (Founded 1885)
Tempe, Arizona
Nickname: Sun Devils
Colors: Maroon and Gold
Stadium: Frank Kush Field at Sun Devil Stadium (1958) 73,379
Conference Affiliations: Border (1931-61), Western Athletic
(1962-77), Pacific-10 (1978-present)

CAREER RUSHING YARDS	Attempts	Yards
Woody Green (1971-73)	675	4188
Freddie Williams (1973-76)	648	3424
J.R. Redmond (1996-99)	633	3299
Wilford White (1947-50)	505	3173
Leon Burton (1955-58)	373	2994
Darryl Clack (1982-85)	534	2737
Art Malone (1967-69)	565	2649
Keegan Herring (2005-08)	511	2635
Darryl Harris (1984-87)	571	2617
Ben Malone (1971-73)	385	2474

CAREER PASSING YARDS	Comp-Att.	Yards
Andrew Walter (2001-04)	777-1416	10,617
Rudy Carpenter (2005-08)	799- 1309	10,491
Jake Plummer (1993-96)	632-1142	8827
Ryan Kealy (1997-2000)	477- 859	6912
Danny White (1971-73)	387- 621	6717
Jeff Van Raaphorst (1984-86)	503- 868	6610
Dennis Sproul (1974-77)	379- 775	5914
Paul Justin (1987-90)	418- 753	5761
Mike Pagel (1978-81)	405- 786	5196
Joe Spagnola (1968-70)	282- 551	4396

CAREER RECEIVING YARDS	Catches	Yards
Derek Hagan (2002-05)	258	3939
John Jefferson (1974-77)	188	2993
Shaun McDonald (2000-02)	156	2867
Aaron Cox (1984-87)	136	2694
Keith Poole (1993-96)	140	2691
Eric Guliford (1989-92)	164	2408
Chris McGaha (2006-09)	168	2242
John Mistler (1977-80)	156	2149
Michael Jones (2005-08)	131	1853
Todd Heap (1998-2000)	115	1685

SEASON RUSHING YARDS	Attempts	Yards
Woody Green (1972)	233	1565
Wilford White (1950)	199	1502
Art Malone (1968)	235	1431
Freddie Williams (1975)	266	1427
Woody Green (1973)	209	1313

SEASON PASSING YARDS	Comp.-Att.	Yards
Andrew Walter (2002)	274-483	3877
Rudy Carpenter (2007)	246-398	3202
Andrew Walter (2204)	244-426	3150
Andrew Walter (2003)	221-421	3044
Danny White (1973)	160-284	2878

SEASON RECEIVING YARDS	Catches	Yards
Shaun McDonald (2002)	87	1405
Derek Hagan (2004)	83	1248
Derek Hagan (2005)	77	1210
Morris Owens (1973)	52	1144
Shaun McDonald (2001)	47	1104

GAME RUSHING YARDS	Attempts	Yards
Ben Malone (1973 vs. Oregon State)	24	250
Leon Burton (1955 vs. Hardin-Simmons)	5	243
Art Malone (1968 vs. New Mexico)	29	239

GAME PASSING YARDS	Comp.-Att.	Yards
Andrew Walter (2002 vs. Oregon)	31-53	536
Paul Justin (1989 vs. Washington St.)	33-47	534
Jeff Van Raaphorst (1984 vs. Florida St.)	38-58	532

GAME RECEIVING YARDS	Catches	Yards
Ron Fair (1989 vs. Washington State)	19	277
Eric Guliford (1990 vs. Houston)	12	232
Shaun McDonald (2002 vs. Stanford)	10	221

GREATEST COACH:

The field at Sun Devil Stadium is named for the greatest coach in Arizona State history and one of the most controversial in college football. That would be irascible Frank Kush, the coach with a 176-54-1 record, by far the most career victories at Arizona State.

Kush came from tough coal-mining country in western Pennsylvania to become a 170-lb All-America guard at Michigan State in the early 1950s. He never lost his brazen exterior, and it served him well, first as an assistant coach under Dan Devine and in whipping nine conference champions and 13 teams with eight or more victories as head coach in his 21 and a half seasons at Tempe.

Kush's toughness got him in trouble in the late 1970s when he allegedly slapped a player and tried to cover it up. This came at a time when his brand of coaching was losing its appeal everywhere in the country. And it came a scant five years after the Watergate cover-up scandal that forced President Richard Nixon from office. Those who supported Kush at the time were adamant about his devotion to his players. Still, Kush was fired in the middle of the 1979 season.

Like a lot of schools that stepped up in competition, Arizona State never has been as consistently competitive in the Pacific-10 as it had been under Kush in the Western Athletic Conference. Essentially, Kush lorded over the WAC with a .798 winning percentage in 16 years.

ARIZONA STATE'S 55 GREATEST PLAYERS SINCE 1953

OFFENSE

WIDE RECEIVER: Derek Hagan, J.D. Hill, John Jefferson, Keith Poole, Shaun McDonald
TIGHT END: Todd Heap, Zach Miller
TACKLE: Levi Jones, Juan Roque, Marvel Smith, Danny Villa
GUARD: John Houser, Victor Leyva, Randall McDaniel
CENTER: Dan Mackie, Grey Ruegamer
QUARTERBACK: Jake Plummer, Andrew Walter
RUNNING BACK: Leon Burton, Darryl Clack, Woody Green, Freddie Williams
FULLBACK: Art Malone, Ben Malone

DEFENSE

END: Junior Ah You, Shante Carver, Al Harris, Derrick Rodgers, Terrell Suggs
TACKLE: Jim Jeffcoat
NOSE GUARD: Curley Culp, Dan Saleaumua
LINEBACKER: Adam Archuleta, Bob Breunig, Vernon Maxwell, Ron Pritchard, Dale Robinson, Pat Tillman
CORNER BACK: Eric Allen, Mike Haynes, Courtney Jackson, Phillippi Sparks
SAFETY: Josh Barrett, Mitchell Friedman, David Fulcher, Nathan LaDuke, Mike Richardson

SPECIAL TEAMS

RETURN SPECIALISTS: Steve Holden, J.R. Redmond
PLACE KICKER: Luis Zendejas
PUNTER: Mike Black

MULTIPLE POSITIONS

QUARTERBACK-PUNTER: Danny White
WINGBACK-WIDE RECEIVER-SAFETY: Fair Hooker

TWO-WAY PLAYERS:

WINGBACK-CORNER BACK: Ben Hawkins
TACKLE-DEFENSIVE TACKLE: John Jankans

PERFORMANCE FORMULA:
ARIZONA STATE'S 10 BEST SEASONS

1970	1.7411	1 of 70
1996	1.7048	4 of 70
1971	1.6713	5 of 70
1975	1.6620	4 of 70
1973	1.6237	8 of 70
1986	1.5985	4 of 70
1957	1.5840	4 of 69
1963	1.5329	4 of 70
1981	1.5162	10 of 70
1982	1.4857	8 of 70

ARIZONA STATE SUN DEVILS

Year	W-L-T	AP Poll	Conference Standing	Toughest Regular Season Opponents	Coach (Record at School)	Bowl Games		
1953	4-5-1		5	Texas Western 7-2, Hardin-Simmons 6-5	Clyde Smith			
1954	5-5		2	Texas Western 7-3, San Jose St. 7-3, Cincinnati 8-2, Arizona 7-3	Clyde Smith (15-13-1)			
1955	8-2-1		2	Wichita 7-2-1, Texas Western 6-2-2, Hawaii 6-3	Dan Devine			
1956	9-1		2	North Texas State 7-2-1, Texas Western 9-1	Dan Devine			
1957	10-0	12	1	Texas Western 6-3, Montana State 8-2, Pacific 5-3-2	Dan Devine (27-3-1)			
1958	7-3		2	Pacific 6-4, Hardin-Simmons 6-4	Frank Kush			
1959	10-1		1	Colorado State 6-4, New Mexico State 7-3	Frank Kush			
1960	7-3		3	New Mexico State 10-0, NC State 6-3-1, Arizona 7-3	Frank Kush			
1961	7-3		1	Wichita 8-2, Utah 6-4, Arizona 8-1-1	Frank Kush			
1962	7-2-1		2t	Washington State 5-4-1, W. Texas State 8-2, Utah State 8-2	Frank Kush			
1963	8-1		ineligible	Wichita 7-2, Wyoming 6-4	Frank Kush			
1964	8-2		ineligible	Utah 8-2, Arizona 6-3-1	Frank Kush			
1965	6-4		2	Utah State 8-2, Texas Western 7-3, Washington State 7-3	Frank Kush			
1966	5-5		3	Wyoming 9-1, BYU 8-2, Oregon State 7-3	Frank Kush			
1967	8-2		2	Oregon State 7-2-1, Texas-El Paso 6-2-1, Wyoming 10-0	Frank Kush			
1968	8-2	23	2	Wyoming 7-3, Oregon State 7-3, Arizona 8-2	Frank Kush			
1969	8-2		1	Oregon State 6-4, BYU 6-4, Utah 8-2, Wyoming 6-4	Frank Kush			
1970	10-0	6	1	Kansas State 6-4, Utah 6-4, New Mexico 7-3	Frank Kush	Peach	48 North Carolina	26
1971	10-1	8	1	Houston 9-2, New Mexico 6-3-2, Air Force 6-4	Frank Kush	Fiesta	45 Florida State	38
1972	9-2	13	1	Houston 6-4-1, BYU 7-4, Air Force 6-4	Frank Kush	Fiesta	49 Missouri	35
1973	11-1	9	1t	Utah 7-5, Arizona 8-3	Frank Kush	Fiesta	28 Pittsburgh	7
1974	7-5		3	Houston 8-3, Missouri 7-4, BYU 7-3-1, NC State 9-2, Arizona 9-2	Frank Kush			
1975	12-0	2	1	Washington 6-5, BYU 6-5, Arizona 9-2	Frank Kush	Fiesta	17 Nebraska	14
1976	4-7		3	UCLA 9-1-1, Wyoming 8-3, Cincinnati 8-3, BYU 9-2	Frank Kush			
1977	9-3	18	1t	BYU 9-2, Colorado State 9-2-1	Frank Kush	Fiesta	30 Penn State	42
1978	9-3		4t	BYU 9-3, Southern California 11-1, Washington 7-4, Stanford 7-4	Frank Kush	Garden State	34 Rutgers	18
1979	6-6		7t	Florida State 11-0, Washington 8-3, Arizona 6-4-1	Frank Kush (176-54-1), Bob Owens [3-4]			
1980	7-4		4	Ohio State 9-2, Southern California 8-2-1, Washington 9-2, UCLA 9-2	Darryl Rogers			
1981	9-2	16	2t	Washington State 8-2-1, Washington 9-2, UCLA 7-3-1	Darryl Rogers			
1982	10-2	6	3t	California 7-4, Southern California 8-3, Washington 9-2	Darryl Rogers	Fiesta	32 Oklahoma	21
1983	6-4-1		6t	UCLA 6-4-1, Washington State 7-4, Florida St. 6-5, Arizona 7-3-1	Darryl Rogers			
1984	5-6		6	Okla. State 9-2, Southern Calif. 8-3, UCLA 8-3, Florida State 7-3-1	Darryl Rogers (37-18-1)			
1985	8-4		2t	Michigan State 7-4, UCLA 8-2-1, Washington 6-5, Arizona 8-3	John Cooper	Holiday	17 Arkansas	18
1986	10-1-1	4	1	UCLA 7-3-1, Southern Calif. 7-4, Washington 8-2-1, Arizona 8-3	John Cooper	Rose	22 Michigan	15
1987	7-4-1	20	4	Nebraska 10-1, Washington 6-4-1, UCLA 9-2	John Cooper (25-9-2)	Freedom	33 Air Force	28
1988	6-5		5	Nebraska 11-1, Washington State 8-3, Southern Calif. 10-1	Larry Marmie			
1989	6-4-1		5	Houston 9-2, Oregon 7-4, Washington 7-4, Arizona 7-4	Larry Marmie			
1990	4-7		8	Washington 9-2, Southern California 8-3-1, Houston 10-1-1	Larry Marmie			
1991	6-5		5	Nebraska 9-1-1, UCLA 8-3, Washington 11-0, California 9-2	Larry Marmie (22-21-1)			
1992	6-5		6t	Washington 9-2, Nebraska 9-2, Washington State 8-3	Bruce Snyder			
1993	6-5		5t	Washington 7-4, California 8-4, UCLA 8-3, Arizona 9-2	Bruce Snyder			
1994	3-8		7t	Miami 10-1, BYU 9-3, Oregon 9-3, Arizona 8-3	Bruce Snyder			
1995	6-5		5t	Washington 7-3-1, Nebraska 11-0, So. Calif. 8-2-1, Oregon 9-2	Bruce Snyder			
1996	11-1	4	1	Washington 9-2, Nebraska 10-1, Oregon 6-5, Stanford 6-5	Bruce Snyder	Rose	17 Ohio State	20
1997	9-3	14	3	Washington 7-4, So. Calif. 6-5, Wash. State 10-1, Arizona 11-1	Bruce Snyder	Sun	17 Iowa	7
1998	5-6		5t	BYU 9-3, So. Calif. 8-4, Notre Dame 9-2, Oregon 8-3, Arizona 11-1	Bruce Snyder	Aloha	3 Wake Forest	23
1999	6-6		4	Texas Tech 6-5, Washington 7-4, Oregon 8-3, Stanford 8-3	Bruce Snyder (58-47)	Aloha	17 Boston College	31
2000	6-6		5t	Colorado State 9-2, Washington 10-1, Oregon 9-2	Dirk Koetter			
2001	4-7		9	UCLA 7-4, Stanford 9-2, Oregon 10-1, Washington State 9-2	Dirk Koetter			
2002	8-6		3	Oregon State 8-4, Washington State 9-3, Southern Calif. 10-2	Dirk Koetter	Holiday	27 Kansas State	34
2003	5-7		8t	Iowa 10-3, Southern Calif. 11-1, Oregon 8-4, Wash. State 9-3	Dirk Koetter			
2004	9-3	19	3t	Iowa 9-2, Oregon State 6-5, Southern Calif. 12-0, California 10-1	Dirk Koetter	Sun	27 Purdue	23
2005	7-5		4t	LSU 10-1, Southern Calif. 12-0, Oregon 10-1, UCLA 9-2	Dirk Koetter	Insight	45 Rutgers	40
2006	7-6		5t	California 9-3, Southern Calif. 10-2, Oregon State 9-4	Dirk Koetter (40-34)	Hawaii	24 Hawaii	41
2007	10-3	16	1t	Oregon State 8-4, Oregon 8-4, Southern California 10-2	Dennis Erickson	Holiday	34 Texas	52
2008	5-7		6t	Georgia 9-3, California 8-4, Southern California 11-1, Oregon 9-3	Dennis Erickson			
2009	4-8		9	Stanford 8-4, California 8-4, Southern California 8-4, Oregon 10-2	Dennis Erickson			
2010	6-6		5t	Wisconsin 11-1, Oregon 12-0, Stanford 11-1	Dennis Erickson (25-24)			

TOTAL: 　　　　　　　　　　**422-222-7 .6536 (16 of 70)** 　　　　　　　**Bowl Games since 1953:** 　　**12-8 .6000 (16 of 70)**

GREATEST TEAM SINCE 1953: The 1996 Arizona State Sun Devils came within a matter of seconds of pulling out a win in the Rose bowl that would have given them an undefeated season and possibly a national championship. But, Frank Kush's terrific 1975 team stunned no. 6 Nebraska in the Fiesta Bowl to finish no. 2. The Sun Devils at 12-0 had a decent argument for the national title over no. 1 Oklahoma, which lost in early November.

1953 4-5-1

14 San Diego Navy	19 E John Allen
14 N. Texas State	0 T Tom Fallon / Norb Smorin
27 Texas Western	28 G John Jankans
35 San Jose State	20 C Nick Maucieri
39 West Texas St.	20 G Lyle Pierson / John Hickman
20 Houston	24 T Bob Luthcke / Lou Iani
20 Hardin-Simmons	27 E Jack Stovall / Al Derbis
26 BYU	18 QB Bob Hendricks / Dick Mackey
12 Midwestern St.	12 HB Dick Curran
0 Arizona	35 WB Dan Seivert / Jim Bilton
	FB Bob Sedlar / Bob Tarwater

RUSHING: Seivert 86/425y
PASSING: Hendricks 32-65/461y, 6TD, 49.2%
RECEIVING: Allen 30/505y
SCORING: Bilton 42pts

1954 5-5

28 Hawaii	14 E Charlie Mackey
28 BYU	19 T John Jankans / Frank Bell
34 Texas-Western	27 G Gus Poulos
12 San Jose State	19 C John Olenik / Fritz Province
7 Midwestern St.	14 G John Julian / John Hickman
21 West Texas St.	14 T Bob Luthcke
14 Hardin-Simmons	13 E Jack Stovall / Karl Grassl
7 Cincinnati	34 QB Dick Mackey / Dave Graybill
13 N. Texas State	20 HB Bobby Mulgado / Ruben Madril
14 Arizona	54 WB Jim Bilton
	FB Bob Sedlar / Jay Smith / Mike Coffinger

RUSHING: Bilton 104/557y
PASSING: D. Mackey 55-114/793y, 4TD, 48.2%
RECEIVING: C. Mackey 10/176y, Grassl 10/139y
SCORING: Bilton 42pts

1955 8-2-1

20 Wichita State	20 E Charlie Mackey
28 Midwestern St.	7 T John Jankans
42 San Diego Navy	0 G John Hickman
20 San Jose State	27 C Gino Della Libera / Jim Olenick
46 San Diego State	0 G Frank Bell
69 Hardin-Simmons	14 T Robert Noel / Ron Wunderly
27 West Texas St.	7 E Karl Grassl / Clancey Osborne
20 Texas Western	13 QB Dave Graybill
26 New Mexico St.	6 HB Bobby Mulgado / Leon Burton
6 Arizona	7 WB Gene Mitcham
39 Hawaii	6 FB Bob Sedlar

RUSHING: Burton 68/694, Mitcham 70/428y, Sedlar 74/384y
PASSING: Graybill 80-132/1079y, 60.6%
RECEIVING: Mackey 35/470y, Mitcham 27/552y, Graybill 11/123y
SCORING: Burton 60pts, Mitcham 48pts, Graybill 42pts

1956 9-1

37 Wichita State	9 E Charlie Mackey / Jack Stovall
27 North Texas St.	7 T Bart Jankans
28 New Mexico St.	7 G Ken Kerr
41 Idaho	0 C Gino Della Libera / Fritz Province
26 Hardin-Simmons	13 G Tom Ford
47 San Jose State	13 T Mike Stanoff / Bob Noel
61 San Diego State	0 E Clancey Osborne
0 Texas Western	28 QB Dave Graybill
20 Arizona	6 HB Leon Burton / Bobby Mulgado
19 Pacific	6 WB Gene Mitcham / Wayne Gedman
	FB Joe Belland / Mike Coffinger

RUSHING: Mulgado 107/721y
PASSING: Graybill 47-84/578y 5TD, 56%
RECEIVING: Mitcham 14/256y,
SCORING: Mulgado 55pts

1957 10-0

28 Wichita State	0 E Bill Spanko
19 Idaho	7 T Bart Jankans / Dan Napolitano
44 San Jose State	6 G Al Carr
35 Hardin-Simmons	26 C Dave Fonner
66 San Diego State	0 G Ken Kerr / Al Pagnetti
21 New Mexico St.	0 T Tom Ford
43 Texas Western	7 E Clancey Osborne / Karl Kiefer
53 Montana St.	13 QB John Hangartner
41 Pacific	0 HB Bobby Mulgado / George Greathouse
47 Arizona	7 WB Leon Burton
	FB Joe Belland / Ron Erhardt

RUSHING: Burton 117/1126y
PASSING: Hangartner 61-100/1203y, 14TD, 61%
RECEIVING: Osborne 20/351y
SCORING: Burton 96pts

1958 7-3

47 Hawaii	6 E Bill Spanko
16 Pacific	34 T Paul Widmer / Jesse Bradford
16 West Texas St.	13 G Mike Bartholomew / Al Carr
6 Hardin-Simmons	14 C Gino Della Libera / Dave Fonner
20 San Jose State	21 G Ken Kerr
27 Detroit	6 T Tom Ford / Charles Krofchik
23 New Mexico St.	19 E Karl Kiefer
27 Texas Western	0 QB John Hangartner
47 Arizona	0 HB Nolan Jones / Allen Benedict
42 Marquette	18 WB Leon Burton / Joe Drake
	FB Joe Belland / Ron Erhardt

RUSHING: Burton 108/642y, Belland 116/474y, Jones 88/440y
PASSING: Hangartner 67-121/1208y, 9TD, 55.4%
RECEIVING: Kiefer 22/324y, Spanko 21/463y, Jones 8/133y
SCORING: Burton 70pts, Belland 42pts, Spanko 34pts

1959 10-1

43 West Texas St.	22 E Bill Spanko
34 Utah State	12 T Bill Faust / Jesse Bradford
31 Montana St.	14 G Dick Locke / Mike Bartholomew
24 Colorado State	9 C Fred Rhoades / John Vucichevich
15 San Jose State	24 G Larry Reaves / Mike Cupchak
35 New Mexico St.	21 T George Flint / Charlie Krofchik
20 Texas Western	7 E Bob Rembert / Karl Kiefer
27 BYU	8 QB Joe Zuger / Fran Urban
14 Hardin-Simmons	8 HB Nolan Jones / Ray Young
15 Arizona	0 WB John McFalls / Joe Drake
14 Hawaii	6 FB Charley Jones / Clay Freney

RUSHING: N. Jones 143/689y, McFalls 103/569y, Young 54/306y
PASSING: Urban 40-73/536y, 5TD, 54.8%
RECEIVING: Rembert 15/232y, Spanko 15/231y, Jones 10/156y
SCORING: N. Jones 100pts, Young 30pts, McFalls 24pts

1960 7-3

39 Colorado State	0 E Tim Lee / Ron Jackson
14 West Texas St.	3 T Jesse Bradford
24 Washington St.	21 G Dick Locke
28 Hardin-Simmons	0 C John Vucichevich / Fred Rhoades
31 BYU	0 G Larry Reaves / Jim Lambeth
7 San Jose State	12 T Mike Cupchak / George Flint
24 New Mexico St.	27 E Bob Rembert
24 Texas Western	0 QB Ron Cosner / Joe Zuger
25 N. Carolina St.	22 HB Nolan Jones
7 Arizona	35 WB Clay Freney
	FB Joe Drake / Clay Freney

RUSHING: Jones 107/582y
PASSING: Cosner 25-56/422y, 4TD, 44.6%
RECEIVING: Rembert 11/178y, Lee 11/121y
SCORING: Jones 93pts,

1961 7-3

21 Wichita State	7 E Roger Locke / Tim Lee
14 Colorado State	6 T George Flint
26 Utah	28 G Dick Locke
28 West Texas St.	11 C Fred Rhoades / Steve Fedorchak
24 Oregon State	3 G Bob Widmer
47 Hardin-Simmons	0 T Larry Reaves
26 San Jose State	32 E Dale Keller / Herman Harrison
48 Texas Western	28 QB Joe Zuger / Ron Cosner
40 Detroit	6 HB Nolan Jones / Ozzie McCarty
13 Arizona	22 WB John McFalls / Charley Taylor
	FB Clay Freney / Dornel Nelson

RUSHING: Jones 85/411y, McFalls 66/387y, Taylor 57/277y
PASSING: Zuger 67-133/879y, 8TD, 50.4%
RECEIVING: Locke 14/222y, Harrison 14/175y, Taylor 13/235y
SCORING: Jones (K) 77pts, Taylor 56pts, McCarty 30pts

1962 7-2-1

21 Wichita State	10 E Dale Keller / Alonzo Hill
35 Colorado State	0 T Mike Krofchik
24 Washington St.	24 G Hase McKey / Joe Kush
14 West Texas St.	15 C Steve Fedorchak / Chris Stetzar
44 San Jose State	8 G Bob Widmer
35 Texas Western	7 T John Seedborg / Pat Appulese
34 Utah State	15 E Roger Locke / Herman Harrison
35 Utah	7 QB John Jacobs
45 New Mexico St.	20 HB Tony Lorick / Gene Foster
17 Arizona	20 WB Charley Taylor
	FB Mitch Siskowski / Dornel Nelson

RUSHING: Lorick 105/704y, Taylor 106/567y, Forster 55/238y
PASSING: Jacob 77-136/1263y, 14TD, 56.6%
RECEIVING: Keller 20/358y, Harrison 13/207y, Locke 12/215y
SCORING: Taylor 50pts, Lorick 48pts, Seedborg (K) 46pts

1963 8-1

13 Wichita State	33 E Alonzo Hill
14 New Mexico St.	13 T Sam Fanelli / Frank Mitacek
50 Colorado State	7 G Hase McKey / Bob Kec
24 West Texas St.	16 C Chris Stetzar
27 Texas Western	0 G Joe Kush
30 Utah	22 T John Seedborg
21 San Jose State	19 E Herman Harrison
35 Wyoming	6 QB John Jacobs / John Torak
35 Arizona	6 HB Ray Young / Gene Foster
	WB Charley Taylor
	FB Tony Lorick

RUSHING: Lorick 105/805y, Taylor 88/595y, Young 47/236y
PASSING: Torak 41-79/600y, 8TD, 51.9%
RECEIVING: Harrison 23/371y, Taylor 11/217y, Hill 10/91y
SCORING: Lorick 54pts, Taylor 48pts, Harrison 34pts

1964 8-2

24 Utah State	8 WR Ben Hawkins
34 West Texas St.	7 T Ray Shirey / Pat Appulese
24 Wichita State	18 G John Folmer
42 Texas Western	13 C Jim Murphy
3 Utah	16 G Bob Johnson
34 Colorado State	6 T Frank Mitacek / Joe McDonald
21 Kansas State	10 TE Jerry Smith
28 San Jose State	16 QB John Torok
14 Idaho	0 HB Gene Foster / Hal Lewis
6 Arizona	30 WB Larry Todd / Dewey Forrister
	FB Jesse Fleming / Jim Bramlet
	DL Darrell Hoover
	DL Ray Shirey / Pat Appulese
	DL Joe McDonald
	DL Sam Fanelli
	DL Don Switzenberg
	LB Bob Lueck / John Scarfo
	LB John Folmer
	DB John Goodman / Jerry Smith
	DB Ben Hawkins
	DB Hal Lewis
	DB Jesse Fleming / Larry Todd

RUSHING: Foster 82/311y, Fleming 75/276y, Lewis 60/276y
PASSING: Torok 139-251/2356y, 20TD, 55.4%
RECEIVING: Hawkins 42/719y, Smith 42/618y, Todd 35/633y
SCORING: Hawkins 44pts, Todd & Rick Davis (K) 36pts

1965 6-4

6 BYU	24 WR John Pitts
0 Utah State	13 T Ray Shirey
14 West Texas St.	22 G George Corneal
8 Wichita State	6 C Bob Lueck
14 San Jose State	21 G Charley Tribble / Obia Lowe
27 New Mexico	14 T Bobby Johnson
28 Texas Western	20 TE Dewey Forrister (DB) / Ken Dyer
7 Washington St.	6 QB John Goodman
14 Wyoming	10 HB Travis Williams
14 Arizona	6 WB Ben Hawkins (DB)
	FB Jim Bramlet / Max Anderson
	DL Jesse Fleming
	DL Bob Rokita
	DL Curley Culp
	DL Larry Hendershot / John Hanson
	DL Steve Timarac
	LB Leo Rossi
	LB John Folmer
	DB Ben Hawkins (WB)
	DB John Pitts / Dewey Forrister (TE)
	DB Darrell Hoover
	DB Ken Dyer / Reggie Jackson

RUSHING: Williams 130/523y, Bramlet 144/482y, Anderson 41/172y
PASSING: Goodman 96-175/1165y, 9TD, 54.9%
RECEIVING: Hawkins 36/504y, Dyer 20/215y, Pitts 19/156y
SCORING: Hawkins 38pts, Rick Davis (K) 18pts, 5 tied w/ 12pts

1966 5-5

30 Texas-El Paso	26 WR Ken Dyer (TE)
6 Wyoming	23 T Ray Shirey
20 West Texas St.	21 G Jim Kane
15 Washington St.	24 C George Hummer
10 BYU	7 G Obia Lowe
17 Oregon State	18 T Herman Serignese (G) / Larry Langford
6 Utah	21 TE Dewey Forrister
14 Oregon	10 QB John Goodman
28 New Mexico	7 HB Travis Williams / Wes Plummer (DB)
20 Arizona	17 WB Fair Hooker (WR-DB)
	FB Jim Bramlet / Max Anderson (WB)
	DL Jesse Fleming
	DL Bob Rokita / Nello Tomarelli
	DL Curley Culp
	DL Larry Hendershot
	DL Steve Timarac
	LB Dick Eglof / Tim Buchanan
	LB Ron Pritchard
	DB Ken Dyer
	DB John Pitts
	DB Phil Booker / Fair Hooker (WB)
	DB Wes Plummer / Chuck Hunt

RUSHING: Williams 137/557y, Anderson 121/392y, Bramlet 72/241y
PASSING: Goodman 90-168/1259y, 8 TD, 53.6%
RECEIVING: Dyer 29/496y, Hooker 25/322y, Plummer 14/205y
SCORING: Anderson & Rokita 30pts, Williams 24pts

1967 8-2

27 San Jose State	16 WR John Helton / Richard Mann
21 Oregon State	27 T Larry Langford
42 Wisconsin	16 G Jim Kane / Dan Grow
33 Texas-El Paso	32 C George Hummer
56 New Mexico	23 G Mike Chowaniec / Herman Serignese
31 Washington St.	20 T Nello Tomarelli
13 Wyoming	15 TE Ken Dyer
49 Utah	32 QB Ed Roseborough
31 BYU	22 HB Art Malone / Larry Walton
47 Arizona	7 WB J.D. Hill
	FB Max Anderson
	DL Dennis Farrell
	DL Bobby Johnson
	DL Curley Culp
	DL Bob Rokita
	DL Chuck Osborne / Richard Griffin
	LB Ron Pritchard
	LB Dick Egloff / Mike Kennedy
	DB Dickie Brown
	DB Rick Shaw
	DB Paul Ray Powell / Phil Booker
	DB Wes Plummer

RUSHING: Anderson 191/1188y, Malone 118/448y, Walton 70/225y
PASSING: Rosebrough 95-205/1494y, 12TD, 46.3%
RECEIVING: Dyer 39/654y, Hill 34/587y, Malone 10/139y
SCORING: Anderson 72pts, Hill 64pts, Rokita (LB-K) 45pts

1968 8-2

55 Wisconsin	7 WR Fair Hooker
31 Texas-El Paso	19 T Mike Chowaniec
13 Wyoming	27 G Jim Kane
41 Washington St.	14 C George Hummer
9 Oregon State	28 G Herman Serignese / Gary Venturo
63 New Mexico	28 T Nello Tomarelli
59 Utah	21 TE Richard Mann
47 BYU	12 QB Joe Spagnola / Ed Roseborough
66 San Jose State	0 HB Larry Walton / Dave Buchanan
30 Arizona	7 WB J.D. Hill / Mike Brunson
	FB Art Malone
	DL Chuck Osborne
	DL Bobby Johnson
	DL Ted Olivo
	DL John Helton
	DL Dennis Farrell / Richard Griffin
	LB Mike Kennedy
	LB Ron Pritchard
	DB Dickie Brown / J.D. Hill
	DB Tom Julian
	DB Paul Ray Powell
	DB Wes Plummer / Seth Miller

RUSHING: Malone 235/1431y, Walton 117/541y, Jim Shaughnessy (HB) 46/276y
PASSING: Spagnola 57-104/917y, 7TD, 54.8%
RECEIVING: Hooker 42/665y, Hill 23/391y, Mann 13/130y
SCORING: Malone 96pts Powell (DB-K) 77pts, Walton 54pts

1969 8-2

48 Minnesota	26 WR Calvin Demery
7 Oregon State	30 T Mike Tomco
23 BYU	7 G Gary Venturo
23 Utah	24 C Tom Delnoce
45 San Jose State	11 G Ken Coyle
30 Wyoming	14 T Ed Fisher
48 New Mexico	17 TE Ron Carothers
42 Texas-El Paso	19 QB Joe Spagnola
79 Colorado State	7 HB Dave Buchanan
38 Arizona	24 WB Mike Brunson
	FB Art Malone
	DL Junior Ah You / Joe Connolly
	DL Bob Davenport
	DL Ted Olivo
	DL Rich Gray
	DL Mike Fanucci
	LB Mike Mess / Prentice Williams
	LB Mike Kennedy
	DB Tom Julian
	DB Windlan Hall
	DB Seth Miller
	DB Mike Clupper

RUSHING: Buchanan 143/908y, Malone 212/770y, Spagnola 64/257y
PASSING: Spagnola 92-205/1488y, 10TD, 44.8%
RECEIVING: Demery 45/816y, Carothers 17/311y, Brunson 15/299y
SCORING: Buchanan 90pts, Ed Gallardo (K) 71pts, Malone 56pts

1970 11-0

38 Colorado State	9 WR J.D. Hill
35 Kansas State	13 T Ed Fisher
52 Wyoming	3 G Gary Venturo
37 Washington St.	30 C Mike Tomco
27 BYU	3 G Ken Coyle
42 Texas-El Paso	13 T Roger Davis
46 San Jose State	10 TE Joe Petty
37 Utah	14 QB Joe Spagnola
33 New Mexico	21 HB Monroe Eley / Dave Buchanan
10 Arizona	6 WB Steve Holden / Ed Beverly
48 North Carolina■	26 FB Bob Thomas / Brent McClanahan
	DL Mike Fanucci
	DL Bob Davenport
	DL Tim Hoban
	DL Rich Gray
	DL Junior Ah You
	LB Prentice Williams
	LB Mike Mess
	DB Windlan Hall
	DB Prentice McCray
	DB Mike Artozqui / Ron Lumpkin
	DB Mike Clupper

RUSHING: Thomas 165/900y, Eley 141/739y, McClanahan 85/470y
PASSING: Spagnola 133-242/1991y, 18TD, 55%
RECEIVING: Hill 58/908y, Beverly 24/402y, Petty 14/253y
SCORING: Hill 84pts, Don Ekstrand (K) 65pts, Thomas & Buchanan 42pts

1971 11-1

18 Houston	17 WR Calvin Demery / Ed Beverly
41 Utah	21 T Roger Davis
24 Texas-El Paso	7 G George Endres
42 Colorado State	0 C Mike Tomco
18 Oregon State	24 G Steve Matlock
60 New Mexico	28 T Ed Fisher
44 Air Force	28 TE Joe Petty
38 BYU	13 QB Danny White
52 Wyoming	19 HB Woody Green / Oscar Dragon
49 San Jose State	6 WB Steve Holden
31 Arizona	0 FB Ben Malone
45 Florida State■	38 DL Larry Shorty
	DL Rich Gray
	DL Ted Olivo
	DL Mike Shimkus
	DL Junior Ah You
	LB James Baker
	LB Larry Delbridge
	DB Windlan Hall
	DB Prentice McCray
	DB Ron Lumpkin
	DB Mike Clupper

RUSHING: Green 208/1209y, Malone 104/857y, Dragon 72/325y
PASSING: White 86-165/1393y, 15TD, 52.1%
RECEIVING: Demery 39/586y, Petty 36/577y, Holden 21/461y
SCORING: Don Ekstrand (K) 75pts, Green 72pts, Holden 70pts

1972 10-2

33 Houston	28 WR Ed Beverly / Greg Hudson
56 Kansas State	14 T Steve Gunther
43 Wyoming	45 G John Houser
38 Oregon State	7 C Ron Lou
59 Utah	48 G Steve Matlock
49 BYU	17 T Ed Fisher
31 Air Force	39 TE Joe Petty
55 Texas-El Paso	14 QB Danny White
60 New Mexico	7 HB Woody Green / Alonzo Emery
51 San Jose State	21 WB Steve Holden
38 Arizona	21 FB Ben Malone / Brent McClanahan
49 Missouri ■	35 DL Larry Shorty
	DL Deke Ballard
	DL Tim Hoban
	DL Neal Skarin
	DL Sam Johnson / Bruce Kilby
	LB Bob Breunig
	LB Larry Delbridge / James Baker
	DB Prentice McCray
	DB Reedy Hall
	DB Wayne Bradley
	DB Ron Lumpkin

RUSHING: Green 209/1363y, McClanahan 160/988y, Emery 57/401y
PASSING: White 113-219/1930y, 21TD, 51.6%
RECEIVING: Holden 38/848y, Petty 31/522y, Hudson 14/169y
SCORING: Green 90pts, Holden 84pts, McClanahan 80pts

1973 11-1

26 Oregon	20 WR Greg Hudson
20 Washington St.	9 T Steve Gunther
67 Colorado State	14 G John Houser
67 New Mexico	24 C Ed Kindig
28 San Jose State	3 G Randy Collett / George Endres
52 BYU	12 T Dave Orzall
44 Oregon State	14 TE Dave Grannell / Charley Hobbs
31 Utah	36 QB Danny White
47 Wyoming	0 HB Woody Green
54 Texas-El Paso	13 WB Morris Owens
55 Arizona	19 FB Ben Malone
28 Pittsburgh■	7 DL Larry Shorty
	DL Neal Skarin
	DL Sal Olivo
	DL Deke Ballard
	DL Sam Johnson
	LB Bob Breunig
	LB James Baker
	DB Mike Haynes
	DB Bo Warren
	DB Kory Schuknecht
	DB Reedy Hall / Alex Stencel

RUSHING: Green 184/1182y, Malone 176/1129y, Alonzo Emery (HB) 49/297y
PASSING: White 146-265/2609y, 23TD, 55.1%
RECEIVING: Hudson 54/788y, Owens 50/1076y, Green 22/328y
SCORING: Malone 90pts, Green 84pts, Dan Kush (K) 67pts

1974 7-5

30 Houston	9 WR Greg Hudson / John Jefferson
37 TCU	7 T Billy Joe Winchester / Scott Alden
0 Missouri	9 G John Houser
16 Wyoming	10 C Jim Helig
32 Utah	0 G Rick Torbert
41 New Mexico	7 T Dave Orzell
27 Texas-El Paso	31 TE Paul Ervin / Charley Hobbs
18 BYU	21 QB Dennis Sproul / Ray Alexander
14 N. Carolina St.	35 HB Freddie Williams
26 Colorado State	21 WB Morris Owens / Larry Mucker
0 Arizona	10 FB Mark Lovett
26 Hawaii	3 DL Clifton Alapa / Al Weigandt
	DL Chris Lorenzen / Tom Seiper
	DL Rocky Mataalii
	DL Randy Moore
	DL Ed Vaughn
	LB Bob Breunig
	LB Larry Gordon
	DB Mike Martinez
	DB Mike Haynes
	DB Kory Schuknecht
	DB Alex Stencel

RUSHING: Williams 249/1299y, Lovett 143/548y, Stan Robinson (HB) 46/210y
PASSING: Sproul 96-199/1438y, 10TD, 48.2%
RECEIVING: Jefferson 30/423y, Owens 28/560y, Williams 20/119y
SCORING: Dan Kush (K) 49pts, Williams & Owens 48pts

1975 12-0

35 Washington	12 WR John Jefferson
33 TCU	10 T Scott Alden / Bob Pfister
20 BYU	0 G George Fadok
29 Idaho	3 C Jim Helig
16 New Mexico	10 G Rick Torbert
33 Colorado State	3 T Steve Chambers
24 Texas-El Paso	6 TE Bruce Hardy / Kirk Carter
40 Utah	14 QB Dennis Sproul / Fred Mortensen
21 Wyoming	20 HB Freddie Williams / Ron Bonner
55 Pacific	14 WB Larry Mucker
24 Arizona	21 FB Mark Lovett
17 Nebraska■	14 DL Al Weigandt / Rob Peterson
	DL Chris Lorenzen
	DL Zack DiBrell
	DL Randy Moore
	DL Willie Scroggins
	LB Tim Petersen
	LB Larry Gordon
	DB Mike Martinez
	DB Mike Haynes
	DB John Harris
	DB Alex Stencel

RUSHING: Williams 248/1316y, Lovett 109/496y, Bonner 44/176y
PASSING: Mortensen 59-113/1058y, 4TD, 52.2%
RECEIVING: Jefferson 44/808y, Mucker 42/757y, Carter 15/162y
SCORING: Williams 54pts, Dan Kush (K) 52pts, Mortensen 42pts

1976 4-7

10 UCLA	28 WR John Jefferson
22 California	31 T Bob Pfister
10 Wyoming	13 G George Fadok
0 Cincinnati	14 C Norris Williams
23 Texas-El Paso	6 G Rick Torbert
31 New Mexico	15 T Steve Chambers
21 BYU	43 TE Bruce Hardy
30 Air Force	31 QB Fred Mortensen / Dennis Sproul
28 Utah	31 HB Freddie Williams / Arthur Lane
21 Colorado State	19 WB Larry Mucker
27 Arizona	10 FB Mark Lovett
	DL Al Harris / Rob Peterson
	DL Kit Lathrop
	DL Gary Padjen
	DL Robert Allison / Brad Kiburz
	DL Willie Scroggins
	LB Harry Garbarini /Bob Carl/Norm Ehasz
	LB Tim Petersen
	DB Mike Martinez
	DB Derrick Martin
	DB John Harris
	DB Raye Williams

RUSHING: Williams 102/516y, Lovett 110/437y, Lane 79/375y
PASSING: Sproul 111-243/1751y, 12TD, 45.7%
RECEIVING: Jefferson 48/681y, Mucker 40/835y, Hardy 18/223y
SCORING: Mucker 48pts, Dan Kush (K) 43pts, Jefferson 30pts

1977 9-3

35 Northwestern	3 WR John Jefferson
33 Oregon State	31 T Doug Dedrick
0 Missouri	15 G Greg Blakes
45 New Mexico	24 C Chris Mott
37 Air Force	14 G Rick Torbert
66 Texas-El Paso	3 T George Fadok
47 Utah	19 TE Bruce Hardy
45 Wyoming	0 QB Dennis Sproul
24 BYU	13 HB Arthur Lane
14 Colorado State	25 WB Chris DeFrance / Ron Washington
23 Arizona	7 FB Mike Harris / George Perry
30 Penn State■	42 DL Al Harris
	DL Kit Lathrop
	DL Gary Padjen
	DL Bob Pfister
	DL Bob Kohrs
	LB Tim Petersen
	LB Dave Barthel
	DB Raye Williams
	DB Carl Russell
	DB John Harris
	DB Darrell Gill

RUSHING: Harris 163/738y, Lane 167/648y, Perry 128/486y
PASSING: Sproul 113-220/1667y, 13TD, 51.4%
RECEIVING: Jefferson 53/912y, Hardy 19/299y, Washington 16/299y
SCORING: Steve Hicks (K) 67pts, Perry 66pts, Jefferson 54pts

1978 9-3

42 Pacific	7 WR John Mistler
24 BYU	17 T Steve Chambers
26 Washington St.	51 G Greg Blakes
27 Texas-El Paso	0 C Chris Mott
56 Northwestern	14 G Norris Williams
20 Southern Cal	7 T Kani Kauahi
7 Washington	41 TE Marshall Edwards
35 California	21 QB Mark Malone
14 Stanford	21 HB Robert Weathers / Alvin Moore
44 Oregon State	22 WB Chris DeFrance
18 Arizona	17 FB Gerald Riggs / Nate Williams
34 Rutgers■	18 DL Al Harris
	DL Joe Peters
	DL Tom Allen
	DL Bob Kohrs
	LB Ben Apuna
	LB Jeff McIntyre / Gary Padjen
	LB Bob Carl
	DB Raye Williams
	DB Mike Lee
	DB Kim Anderson
	DB Darrell Gill

RUSHING: Malone 143/705y, Williams 117/526y, Moore 94/448y
PASSING: Malone 93-205/1305y, 15TD, 45.4%
RECEIVING: DeFrance 31/617y, Edwards 21/289y, Mistler 20/310y
SCORING: Steve Hicks (K) 58pts, Malone 54pts, DeFrance & Mistler 36pts

1979 6-6

9 California	17 WR John Mistler
3 Florida State	31 T John Meyer / Kani Kauahi
49 Toledo (F-L)	0 G Daryl Mueske
45 Oregon St. (F-L)	0 C Dan Mackie
12 Washington (F-L)	7 G Norris Williams
28 Wash. St. (F-L)	17 T Tony Loia
28 Utah State (F-L)	14 TE Marshall Edwards / Bernard Henry
21 Stanford	28 QB Mark Malone
28 UCLA	31 HB Robert Weathers
42 West Virginia	7 WB Ron Washington / Melvin Hoover
24 Arizona	27 FB Gerald Riggs / Nate Williams
17 Hawaii	29 DL Bryan Caldwell
	DL Joe Peters
	DL Tim Allen
	DL Bob Kohrs
	LB Ben Apuna / Vernon Maxwell
	LB Gary Padjen
	LB Joey Lumpkin / Wayne Apuna
	DB Ralph Dixon
	DB Ron Brown / Mike Maloney
	DB Kendrall Williams
	DB Mike Richardson

RUSHING: Weathers 105/556y, Malone 132/471y, Williams 86/438y
PASSING: Malone 148-289/1886y, 10TD, 51.2%
RECEIVING: Mistler 36/498y, Washington 25/381y, Henry 27/301y
SCORING: Malone 72pts, Weathers 48pts, Scott Peterson (K) 41pts

1980 7-4

29 Houston	13 WR Ron Washington
42 Oregon State	14 WR John Mistler
21 Ohio State	38 T Tony Loia
21 Southern Cal	23 G Daryl Mueske / Rod Essley
27 Washington St.	21 C Dan Mackie
37 Pacific	9 G Bruce Branch
0 Washington	25 T John Meyer
34 California	6 TE Ron Wetzel / Jerry Bell
14 UCLA	23 QB Mike Pagel
42 Oregon	37 HB Willie Gittens / Robert Weathers
44 Arizona	7 FB Gerald Riggs
	DL Walt Bowyer
	DL Jim Jeffcoat
	DL Bryan Caldwell
	LB Darren Comeaux / Mark Hicks
	LB Joey Lumpkin
	LB John Sprein
	LB Vernon Maxwell
	DB Ron Brown
	DB Ralph Dixon
	DB Michael Lee / Mike Maloney
	DB Mike Richardson

RUSHING: Gittens 138/759y, Weathers 130/676y, Riggs 89/422y
PASSING: Pagel 184-334/2025y, 17TD, 55.7%
RECEIVING: Mistler 53/573y, Gittens 25/176y, Wetzel 22/272y
SCORING: Mistler 66pts, Scott Lewis (K) 66pts, Gittens 36pts

1981 9-2

52 Utah	10 WR Bernard Henry
33 Wichita State	21 WR Jerome Weatherspoon
21 Washington St.	24 T Tony Loia
26 Washington	7 G Bruce Branch
24 Oregon	0 C Dan Mackie
45 California	17 G Daryl Mueske
62 Stanford	36 T John Meyer
31 San Jose State	24 TE Jerry Bell / Ron Wetzel
24 UCLA	34 QB Mike Pagel
52 Colorado State	7 TB Robert Weathers / Willie Gittens
24 Arizona	13 FB Gerald Riggs
	DL Walt Bowyer
	DL Mike Langston
	DL Jim Jeffcoat
	LB Darren Comeaux
	LB John Sprein
	LB Joey Lumpkin
	LB Vernon Maxwell
	DB Duane Galloway
	DB Kendall Williams
	DB Mike Richardson
	DB Nate King / Paul Moyer

RUSHING: Riggs 148/891y, Weathers 122/711y, Gittens 73/374y
PASSING: Pagel 171-321/2484y, 29TD, 53.3%
RECEIVING: Henry 39/647y, Weatherspoon 23/444y, Bell 20/406y
SCORING: Luis Zendejas (K) 93pts, Henry 48pts, Riggs 36pts

1982 10-2

34 Oregon	3 WR Doug Allen
23 Utah	10 WR Jerome Weatherspoon
24 Houston	10 T Mike White
15 California	0 G Jim Hawn
30 Kansas State	7 C Mark Shupe / Dave Ohton
21 Stanford	17 G Ron Sowers
37 Texas-El Paso	6 T James Keyton
17 Southern Cal	10 TE Ron Wetzel / Don Kern
30 Oregon State	16 QB Todd Hons
13 Washington	17 TB Darryl Clack / Willie Gittens
18 Arizona	28 FB Dwaine Wright
32 Oklahoma■	21 DL Jim Jeffcoat
	DL Mitch Callahan / Mike Langston
	DL Bryan Caldwell
	LB Vernon Maxwell
	LB Jimmy Williams
	LB Greg Battle
	LB Mark Hicks
	DB Duane Galloway
	DB Mario Montgomery
	DB Mike Richardson
	DB Paul Moyer

RUSHING: Clack 111/606y, Gittens 99/487y, Wright 104/428y
PASSING: Hons 185-336/2338y, 9TD, 55.1%
RECEIVING: Allen 30/424y, Wetzel 28/365y, Wright 26/178y
SCORING: Luis Zendejas (K) 102pts, Clack 54pts, Wright 32pts

1983 6-4-1

39 Utah State	12 WR Doug Allen
26 UCLA	26 WR Paul Day
44 Wichita State	14 T Mike White
29 Stanford	11 G David Fonoti / Brian Lopker
34 Southern Cal	14 C Mark Shupe
21 Washington St.	31 G Dan Madden
26 Florida State	29 T James Keyton
24 California	26 TE Don Kern
38 Oregon State	3 QB Todd Hons
24 San Jose State	17 TB Darryl Clack / Mike Crawford
15 Arizona	17 FB Dwaine Wright
	DL Frank Rudolph / Taleni Wright
	DL Mitch Callahan / Dan Saleaumua
	DL Fred Gaddis
	LB Brian Noble
	LB Greg Battle / Willie Green
	LB Jimmy Williams
	LB Billy Robinson / Scott Stephen
	DB Mario Montgomery
	DB Bruce Hill
	DB David Fulcher
	DB Kevin Graven

RUSHING: Clack 184/932y, Crawford 133/547y, Wright 95/403y
PASSING: Hons 199-324/2394y, 14TD, 61.4%
RECEIVING: Kern 49/502y, Allen 31/472y, Wright 30/336y
SCORING: Luis Zendejas (K) 112pts, Clack 54pts, Allen 36pts

1984 5-6

3 Oklahoma State	45 WR Doug Allen
48 San Jose State	0 WR Aaron Cox / Paul Day
3 Southern Cal	6 T David Fonoti
28 Stanford	10 G Randall McDaniel / Brian Lopker
14 California	19 C Mark Shupe
45 Oregon State	10 G Kevin Thomas / Dan Madden
13 UCLA	21 T Tom Magazzeni
44 Florida State	52 TE Stein Koss / Jeff Gallimore
44 Oregon	10 QB Jeff Van Raaphorst / John Walker
45 Colorado State	14 TB Darryl Clack / Mike Crawford
10 Arizona	16 FB Vince Amoia / Channing Williams
	DL Frank Rudolph / Jim Reynosa
	DL Dan Saleaumua / Shawn Patterson
	DL Tom Gerber / Taleni Wright
	LB Brian Noble
	LB Greg Battle / Willie Green
	LB Pat Taylor / Jimmy Williams
	LB Scott Stephen / Stacy Harvey
	DB Anthony Parker / Vince Adams
	DB Jeff Joseph / Eric Allen
	DB Darren Willis / Steve Johnson
	DB David Fulcher

RUSHING: Clack 208/1052y, Crawford 109/469y
PASSING: Van Raaphorst 155-262/2062y, 17TD, 59.2%
RECEIVING: Allen 46/892y, Clack 32/385y, Koss 23/233y
SCORING: Allen 84pts, Luis Zendejas (K) 73pts, Clack 36pts

1985 8-4

3 Michigan State	12 WR Aaron Cox
27 Pacific	0 WR Paul Day / Bruce Hill
24 Southern Cal	0 T David Fonoti
17 UCLA	40 G Randall McDaniel
34 Utah	27 C Kevin Thomas
42 Utah State	10 G Todd Kalis
21 Washington St.	16 T Danny Villa
30 California	8 TE Jeff Gallimore
36 Washington	7 QB Jeff Van Raaphorst
21 Stanford	14 TB Mike Crawford / Darryl Harris
13 Arizona	16 FB Vince Amoia
17 Arkansas■	18 DL Skip McClendon
	DL Shawn Patterson
	DL Dan Saleaumua
	DL Jim Reynosa / Frank Rudolph
	LB Billy Robinson
	LB Greg Battle
	LB John Knight
	DB Eric Allen
	DB Anthony Parker
	DB David Fulcher
	DB Scott Stephen

RUSHING: Crawford 173/684y, Harris 106/442y, Amoia 70/401y
PASSING: Van Raaphorst 174-310/220y, 10TD, 56.1%
RECEIVING: Cox 40/788y, Day 24/348y, Crawford 20/169y
SCORING: Kent Bostrom (K) 74pts, Crawford 66pts, Harris & Cox 30pts

1986 10-1-1

20 Michigan State	17 WR Aaron Cox
30 SMU	0 WR Bruce Hill
21 Washington St.	21 T Danny Villa
16 UCLA	9 G Randall McDaniel
37 Oregon	17 C Kevin Thomas
29 Southern Cal	20 G Todd Kalis
52 Utah	7 T Jim Warne / Scott Kirby
34 Washington	21 TE Jeff Gallimore / Stein Koss
49 California	0 QB Jeff Van Raaphorst
52 Wichita State	6 TB Darryl Harris / Paul Day
17 Arizona	34 FB Channing Williams
22 Michigan■	15 DL Skip McClendon
	DL Shawn Patterson / Trace Armstrong
	DL Larry McGlothen / Dan Saleaumua
	DL Frank Rudolph / Jim Reynosa
	LB Greg Clark
	LB Stacy Harvey
	LB Scott Stephen
	DB Eric Allen
	DB Jeff Joseph / Anthony Parker
	DB Darren Willis
	DB Robby Boyd

RUSHING: Harris 228/1042y, Williams 147/609y, Day 93/447y
PASSING: Van Raaphorst 160-269/2181y, 17TD, 59.5%
RECEIVING: Cox 35/695y, Hill 32/562y, Gallimore 26/253y
SCORING: Kent Bostrom (K) 97pts, Hill 60pts, Harris & Williams 54pts

1987 7-4-1

21 Illinois	7 WR Aaron Cox
31 Pacific	12 WR Tony Johnson / Chris Garrett
28 Nebraska	35 T Fedel Underwood
35 Texas-El Paso	16 G Randall McDaniel
14 Washington	27 C Steve Spurling / Eddie Grant
38 Washington St.	7 G Todd Kalis
30 Oregon State	21 T Scott Kirby
23 UCLA	31 TE Gary Knudson / Scott Veach
37 Oregon	13 QB Daniel Ford
20 California	38 TB Darryl Harris
24 Arizona	24 FB Channing Williams / Kirk Wendorf
33 Air Force■	28 DL Trace Armstrong
	DL Shawn Patterson
	DL Mark Duckens / Saute Sapolu
	DL Pat Taylor
	LB Greg Clark / Stacy Harvey
	LB Drew Metcalf / Mark Tingstad
	LB Rodney Dillard
	DB Eric Allen
	DB Anthony Parker / Eric Crawford
	DB Jeff Mahlstede / Bernard Jones
	DB Robby Boyd / Nathan LaDuke

RUSHING: Harris 202/948y, Williams 131/763y, Wendorf 51/258y
PASSING: Ford 128-257/1756y, 12TD, 49.8%
RECEIVING: Cox 42/870y, Garrett 20/248y, Knudson 20/198y
SCORING: Alan Zendejas (K) 75pts, Williams 62pts, Harris 48pts

1988 6-5

21 Illinois	16 WR Leland Adams / Chris Garrett
28 Colorado State	17 WR Tony Johnson / Lynn James
16 Nebraska	47 T Fedel Underwood
24 Lamar	13 G Doug Larson / Eddie Grant
0 Washington	10 C Steve Spurling
3 Stanford	24 G Scott Claypoole
31 Washington St.	28 T Scott Kirby
21 Oregon	20 TE Gary Knudson / Ryan McReynolds
30 Oregon State	24 QB Paul Justin / Daniel Ford
0 Southern Cal	50 TB Bruce Perkins / David Winsley
18 Arizona	28 FB Kelvin Fisher / Kirk Wendorf
	DL Saute Sapolu / Tim Landers
	DL Shane Collins
	DL Israel Stanley / Don Chuhlantseff
	DL Greg Joelson / Bryan Hooks
	LB Mark Tingstad
	LB Drew Metcalf
	LB Rodney Dillard / Terence Johnson
	DB Eddie Stokes / Jeff Joseph
	DB Lawrence Hubley / Eric Crawford
	DB Nathan LaDuke / Jeff Mahlstede
	DB Robby Boyd

RUSHING: Perkins 118/446y, Winsley 74/35y, Fisher 80/327y
PASSING: Ford 85-165/1166y, 7TD, 51.5%
Justin 84-150/1063y, 5TD, 56%
RECEIVING: McReynolds 28/271y, Johnson 23/368y, Adams 22/420y
SCORING: Alan Zendejas (K) 40pts, McReynolds 30pts, Fisher 26pts

1989 6-4-1

31 Kansas State	0 WR Ron Fair
28 San Jose State	21 WR Lynn James
7 Houston	36 T Mark Hayes
19 Missouri	3 G Tony Sherman
14 UCLA	33 C Eddie Grant
17 Oregon State	17 G Fedel Underwood
7 Oregon	27 T Mike Ritter / Tim Kirby
44 Washington St.	39 TE Ryan McReynolds / Scott Veach
34 Washington	32 QB Paul Justin
30 Stanford	22 TB David Winsley / Bruce Perkins
10 Arizona	28 FB Kelvin Fisher / Jeff Simoneau
	DL Shane Collins
	DL Richard Davis
	DL Tim Landers
	LB Terence Johnson
	LB Mark Tingstad
	LB Drew Metcalf
	LB Darren Woodson
	DB Eddie Stokes
	DB Lawrence Hubley
	DB Nathan LaDuke
	DB Floyd Fields

RUSHING: Winsley 119/470y, Fisher 83/409y, Perkins 90/305y
PASSING: Justin 183-314/2591y, 17TD, 58.3%
RECEIVING: Fair 64/1082y, James 27/574y, Veach 26/318y
SCORING: Fisher 36pts, Mike Richey (K) 34pts, Veach & Simoneau 30pts

1990 4-7

34 Baylor	13 WR Eric Guliford
31 Colorado State	20 WR Kevin Snyder / Victor Cahoon
9 Missouri	30 T Mark Hayes
14 Washington	42 G Tim Kirby
24 California	31 C Toby Mills / Paul DeBono
7 Oregon	27 G Bob Robertson / Jeff White
6 Southern Cal	13 T Mike Ritter
34 Oregon State	9 TE Ryan McReynolds
51 Washington St.	26 QB Paul Justin
17 Arizona	21 TB Leonard Russell
45 Houston	62 FB Kelvin Fisher
	DL Israel Stanley (LB) / Arthur Paul
	DL Tim Landers
	DL Bryan Hooks / David Dixon
	LB Shante Carver
	LB Brett Wallerstedt
	LB Scott Woodford / David Tisdell
	LB Darren Woodson
	DB Phillippi Sparks
	DB Kevin Miniefield
	DB Nathan LaDuke
	DB Michael Williams / Floyd Fields

RUSHING: Russell 174/810y, Fisher 134/677y
PASSING: Justin 131-253/1876y, 10TD, 51.8%
RECEIVING: Guliford 48/837y, McReynolds 22/261y, Russell 22/257y
SCORING: Russell & Mike Richey (K) 60pts, Fisher 50pts

1991 6-5

30 Oklahoma State	3 WR Eric Guliford
32 Southern Cal	25 WR Kevin Snyder / Eric Moss
9 Nebraska	18 T Craig Ritter
21 Utah	15 G Tim Landers
24 Oregon State	7 C Toby Mills / Chad Ackerley
3 Washington St.	17 G Jeff White
16 UCLA	21 T Mike Ritter / Tim Kirby
16 Washington	44 TE Bob Brasher
24 Oregon	21 QB Bret Powers
6 California	25 TB George Montgomery / Mario Bates
37 Arizona	14 FB Kelvin Fisher / Parnell Charles
	DL Shane Collins / Greg Kordas
	DL David Dixon
	DL Arthur Paul
	LB Bryan Hooks / Shante Carver
	LB Brett Wallerstedt
	LB Justin Dragoo / Mike Fair
	LB Darren Woodson / Dereck Moore
	DB Phillippi Sparks / Lenny McGill
	DB Kevin Miniefield
	DB Adam Brass
	DB Michael Williams / Jean Boyd

RUSHING: Montgomery 113/475y, Bates 108/473y, Fisher 94/350y
PASSING: Powers 127-234/1500y, 8TD, 54.3%
RECEIVING: Guliford 55/801y, Brasher 22/282y, Moss 20/203y
SCORING: Mike Richey (K) 54pts, Fisher 36pts, Guliford & Montgomery 18pts

1992 6-5

7 Washington	31 WR Eric Guliford
19 Louisville	0 WR Clyde McCoy / Kevin Snyder
24 Nebraska	45 T Greg Thurston / DeMario Vaughn
20 Oregon	30 G Farrington Togiai
39 Pacific	5 C Toby Mills
40 Oregon State	13 G Craig Rittner
20 UCLA	0 T Jeff Kysar
13 Southern Cal	23 TE Bob Brasher / Brian Ryder
18 Washington St.	20 QB Grady Benton / Garrick McGee
28 California	12 TB Kevin Galbreath / Jerone Davison
7 Arizona	6 FB Gino Valpredo / George Montgomery
	DL Gavin Hill
	DL Bryan Hooks
	DL Israel Stanley
	DL Shante Carver
	LB Justin Dragoo / Mike Phair
	LB Brett Wallerstedt
	LB Dereck Moore / Mark Brown
	DB Kevin Miniefield / Marcus Soward
	DB Lenny McGill
	DB Adam Brass
	DB Kendall Rhyne / Jean Boyd

RUSHING: Davison 183/734y, Galbreath 142/553y, Mario Bates (TB) 66/441y
PASSING: Benton 149-225/1707y, 8TD, 66.2%
RECEIVING: Guliford 44/506y, Snyder 24/361y, Brasher 22/320y
SCORING: Mike Richey (K) 53pts, Davison 38pts, Guliford 30pts

1993 6-5

38 Utah	0 WR Johnny Thomas / Carlos Artis
17 Louisville	35 WR Clyde McCoy
12 Oklahoma State	10 T Jeff Kysar
14 Oregon State	30 G Taco Togiai / Joe Cajie
25 Washington St.	44 C Toby Mills
36 Oregon	45 G Chuck Underwood
38 Stanford	30 T DeMario Vaughn / Greg Thurston
32 Washington	17 TE Matt Nelson / Steve Bush
41 California	0 QB Jake Plummer / Grady Benton
9 UCLA	3 TB Mario Bates
20 Arizona	34 FB Barry Bacon / Parnell Charles
	DL Ken Talanoa / Brent Burnstein
	DL Larry Boyd
	DL Bryan Proby / Shawn Swayda
	DL Shante Carver
	LB Jason Kyle / Brian Easter
	LB Sam Santana / Dan Lucas
	LB Mark Brown
	DB Craig Newsome
	DB Lenny McGill
	DB Eddie Cade
	DB Jean Boyd / Harlen Rashada

RUSHING: Bates 246/1111y, George Montgomery (TB) 86/371y
PASSING: Plummer 102-199/1650y, 9TD, 51.3%
RECEIVING: Thomas 34/574y, McCoy 30/449y, Charles 26/291y
SCORING: Jon Baker (K) 80pts, Bates 50pts, Charles 44pts

1994 3-8

22 Oregon State	16 WR Clyde McCoy
10 Miami	47 WR Keith Poole
22 Louisville	25 T Jeff Kyser
21 California	25 G Juan Roque
36 Stanford	35 C Troy Martz
14 Washington	35 G Pat Thompson
21 Washington St.	28 T Demario Vaughn / Glen Gable
36 BYU	15 TE Matt Nelson
10 Oregon	34 QB Jake Plummer
23 UCLA	59 TB Chris Hopkins
27 Arizona	28 FB Parnell Charles
	DL Ken Talanoa
	DL Eric Schmidt
	DL Shawn Swayda
	DL Brent Burnstein / Mike Langridge
	LB Jason Kyle
	LB Dan Lucas
	LB Kendall Rhyne
	DB Craig Newsome
	DB Marcus Soward / Traivon Johnson
	DB Eddie Cade
	DB Harlen Rashada / Lee Cole

RUSHING: Hopkins 169/680y
PASSING: Plummer 159-284/2179y, 15TD, 54.1%
RECEIVING: McCoy 47/682y, Poole 14/360y
SCORING: Jon Baker (K) 74pts

1995 6-5

20 Washington	23 WR Keith Poole
45 Texas-El Paso	20 WR Kenny Mitchell / Isaiah Mustafa
28 Nebraska	77 T Juan Roque
20 Oregon State	11 G Kyle Murphy
0 Southern Cal	31 C Kirk Robertson
28 Stanford	30 G Pat Thompson
29 BYU	21 T Glen Gable
35 Oregon	24 TE Steve Bush
37 UCLA	33 QB Jake Plummer
38 California	29 TB Chris Hopkins / Michael Martin
28 Arizona	31 FB Ryan Wood
	DL Brent Burnstein
	DL Shawn Swayda
	DL Jason Reynolds
	DL Malchi Crawford / Mike Langridge
	LB Derek Smith
	LB Justin Dragoo
	LB Scott Von der Ahe
	DB Lee Cole
	DB Jason Simmons
	DB Mitchell Freedman
	DB Damien Richardson

RUSHING: Hopkins 130/646y
PASSING: Plummer 173-301/2222y, 17TD, 57.5%
RECEIVING: Poole 55/1036y
SCORING: Robert Nycz (K) 64pts,

1996 11-1

45 Washington	42 WR Lenzie Jackson
52 North Texas	7 WR Keith Poole
19 Nebraska	0 T Juan Roque
48 Oregon	27 G Kyle Murphy
56 Boise State	7 C Kirk Robertson
42 UCLA	34 G Pat Thompson / Glen Gable
48 Southern Cal	35 T Grey Ruegamer
41 Stanford	9 TE Steve Bush / Devin Kendall
29 Oregon State	14 QB Jake Plummer
35 California	7 TB Terry Battle / Michael Martin
56 Arizona	14 FB Ricky Boyer / Jeff Paulk
17 Ohio State■	20 DL Brent Burnstein
	DL Shawn Swayda
	DL Vince Amey / Albrey Battle
	DL Derrick Rodgers
	LB Pat Tillman
	LB Scott Von der Ahe
	LB Derek Smith
	DB Marcus Soward / Courtney Jackson
	DB Jason Simmons
	DB Mitchell Freedman /Thomas Simmons
	DB Damien Richardson

RUSHING: Battle 160/1043y, Martin 95/475y,
  Marlon Farlow (TB) 71/352y
PASSING: Plummer 179-313/2575y, 23TD, 57.2%
RECEIVING: Poole 46/857y, Jackson 36/505y, Bush 22/263y
SCORING: Battle 120pts, Robert Nycz (K) 93pts, Poole 72pts

1997 9-3

41 New Mexico St.	10 WR Lenzie Jackson
23 Miami	12 WR Kenny Mitchell / Ricky Boyle
10 BYU	13 T Marvel Smith
13 Oregon State	10 G Kyle Murphy
14 Washington	26 C Grey Ruegamer (T) / Randy Leaphart
35 Southern Cal	7 G Victor Leyva / Mike Barnes
31 Stanford	14 T Glen Gable / Troy Davis
44 Washington St.	31 TE Kendrick Bates
28 California	21 QB Ryan Kealy
52 Oregon	31 TB Michael Martin / J.R. Redmond
16 Arizona	28 FB Jeff Paulk
17 Iowa■	7 DL Vince Amey
	DL Albrey Battle
	DL Jeremy Staat
	DL Hamilton Mee
	LB Larry Johnson / Stephen Trejo
	LB Pat Tillman
	LB Paul Reynolds
	DB Jason Simmons
	DB Courtney Jackson
	DB Mitchell Freedman
	DB Damien Richardson

RUSHING: Redmond 142/865y, Martin 161/862y,
  Marlon Farlow (TB) 57/450y
PASSING: Kealy 162-297/2137y, 15TD, 54.5%
RECEIVING: Jackson 53/733y, Mitchell 29/429y, Bates 23/320y
SCORING: Robert Nycz (K) 81pts, Redmond 48pts, Martin & Jackson 30pts

1998 5-6

38 Washington	42 WR Lenzie Jackson
6 BYU	26 WR Tariq McDonald
34 North Texas	15 T Marvel Smith
24 Oregon State	3 G Scott Peters
24 Southern Cal	35 C Grey Ruegamer
9 Notre Dame	28 G Victor Leyva
44 Stanford	38 T Thomas Schmidt
38 Washington St.	28 TE Kendrick Bates
55 California	22 QB Ryan Kealy
19 Oregon	51 TB J.R. Redmond
42 Arizona	50 FB Jeff Paulk
	DL Albey Battle / Quincy Yancey
	DL Junior Ioane
	DL Ryan Reilly
	DL Erik Flowers
	LB Adam Archuleta
	LB Joe Cesta / Stephen Trejo
	LB Eric Fields
	DB Courtney Jackson
	DB J'Juan Cherry
	DB Mitchell Freedman
	DB Christon Rance

RUSHING: Redmond 166/883y
PASSING: Kealy 150-261/2161y, 19TD, 57.5%
RECEIVING: Jackson 41/568y
SCORING: Redmond 72pts

1999 6-6

31 Texas Tech	13 WR Richard Williams
7 New Mexico St.	35 WR Tariq McDonald
23 California	24 T Marvel Smith
28 UCLA	97 G Levi Jones
17 Notre Dame	48 C Kenneth Williamson
28 Washington	7 G Scott Peters (C) / Kyle Kosier
33 Washington St.	21 T Victor Leyva
17 Oregon	20 TE Todd Heap
26 Southern Cal	16 QB Ryan Kealy
30 Stanford	50 TB J.R. Redmond / Delvon Flowers
42 Arizona	27 FB Terrelle Smith
3 Wake Forest■	23 DL Quincy Yancy
	DL Junior Ioane / Che Britton
	DL Ryan Reilly
	DL Erik Flowers
	LB Mason Unck / Eric Fields
	LB Solomon Bates / Stephen Trejo
	LB Adam Archuleta
	DB Kareem Clark
	DB Courtney Jackson / Nijrell Edson
	DB Alfred Williams / Craig Koontz
	DB Willie Daniel

RUSHING: Redmond 241/1174y, Flowers 80/512y,
  Gerald Green (TB) 70/329y
PASSING: Kealy 148-267/1976y, 10TD, 55.4%
RECEIVING: Heap 55/832y, Williams 37/608y, McDonald 33/386y
SCORING: Redmond 80pts, Stephen Baker (K) 51pts,
  Flowers 36pts

2000 6-6

10 San Diego State	7 WR Richard Williams
13 Colorado State	10 WR Donnie O'Neal
44 Utah State	20 T Levi Jones
31 UCLA	38 G Marquise Muldrow/Kenn'th Williamson
30 California	10 C Scott Peters
15 Washington	21 G Kyle Kosier
23 Washington St.	20 T Victor Leyva
55 Oregon	56 TE Todd Heap
38 Southern Cal	44 QB Jeff Krohn / Griffin Goodman
7 Stanford	29 TB Tom Pace / Mike Williams
30 Arizona	17 FB Stephen Trejo
17 Boston College■	31 DL Terrell Suggs / Chad Howell
	DL Tommie Townsend / Danny Masaniai
	DL Kurt Wallin
	LB Quincy Yancy / Brian Montesanto
	LB Eric Fields
	LB Solomon Bates
	LB Adam Archuleta
	DB Kenny Williams / Machtier Clay
	DB Nijrell Eason
	DB Alfred Williams
	DB Willie Daniel

RUSHING: Pace 180/720y, Williams 121/514y,
  Davaren Hightower (TB) 43/164y
PASSING: Krohn 125-254/1751y, 12TD, 49.2%
RECEIVING: Heap 48/644y, Williams 44/744y, O'Neal 39/661y
SCORING: Mike Barth (K) 86pts, Pace 48pts, O'Neal 44pts

2001 4-7

38 San Diego State	7 WR Donnie O'Neal / Ryan Dennard
28 Stanford	51 WR Shaun McDonald
53 San Jose State	15 T Levi Jones
63 La.-Lafayette	27 G Marquise Muldrow
17 Southern Cal	48 C Scott Peters
41 Oregon State	24 G Regis Crawford
31 Washington	33 T Kyle Kosier
24 Oregon	42 TE Mike Pinkard / Frank Maddox
16 Washington St.	28 QB Jeff Krohn
21 Arizona	34 TB Delvon Flowers / Tom Pace
42 UCLA	52 FB Mike Karney
	DL Brian Monesanto
	DL Kurt Wallin
	DL Terrell Suggs
	DL Tommie Townsend
	LB Solomon Bates
	LB Mason Unck
	DB Lamar Baker / Emmanuel Franklin
	DB R.J. Oliver
	DB Willie Daniel
	DB Jason Shivers
	DB Alfred Williams

RUSHING: Flowers 188/1041y, Pace 72/438y,
  Mike Williams (TB) 38/188y
PASSING: Krohn 115-213/1942y 19TD, 54%
RECEIVING: McDonald 47/1104y, O'Neal 45/711y,
  Dennard 19/356y
SCORING: Mike Barth (K) 70pts, Flowers 66pts, McDonald 60pts

2002 8-6

10 Nebraska	48 WR Daryl Lightfoot
38 E. Washington	2 WR Shaun McDonald / Derek Hagan
46 Central Florida	13 T Regis Crawford
39 San Diego State	28 G Tim Fa'aita
65 Stanford	24 C Tony Aguilar
35 North Carolina	38 G Drew Hodgdon
13 Oregon State	9 T Chaz White
45 Oregon	42 TE Mike Pinkard
27 Washington	16 QB Andrew Walter
22 Washington St.	44 TB Mike Williams / Cornell Canidate
38 California	55 FB Mike Karney
13 Southern Cal	34 DL Jimmy Verdon
34 Arizona	20 DL Brian Montesanto
27 Kansas State■	34 DL Khoa Nguyen / Shane Jones
	DL Terrell Suggs
	LB Mason Unck
	LB Josh Amobi
	DB R.J. Oliver
	DB Riccardo Stewart
	DB Alfred Williams
	DB Jason Shivers
	DB Brett Hudson

RUSHING: Candidate 130/560y, M Williams 124/517y, Hakim Hill (TB) 104/374y
PASSING: Walter 274-483/3877y, 28TD, 56.7%
RECEIVING: McDonald 87/1405y, Lightfoot 40/552y, Hagan 32/405y
SCORING: Mike Barth (K) 118pts, McDonald 80pts, Hill 54 pts

2003 5-7

34 N. Arizona	14 WR Derek Hagan / Matt Miller
26 Utah State	16 WR Skyler Fulton
2 Iowa	21 T Andrew Carnahan
17 Oregon State	45 G Tim Fa'aita / Tony Aguilar
17 Southern Cal	37 C Drew Hodgdon
59 Oregon	14 G Regis Crawford
33 North Carolina	31 T Grayling Love
13 UCLA	20 TE Lee Burghgraef
23 California	51 QB Andrew Walter
27 Stanford	38 TB Loren Wade / Hakim Hill
19 Washington St.	34 FB Mike Karney
28 Arizona	7 DL Jimmy Verdon
	DL Brian Montesanto
	DL Shane Jones
	LB Ishmael Thrower
	LB Jamar Williams
	LB Justin Burks / Jordan Hill
	LB R.J. Oliver / Emmanuel Franklin
	DB Chris McKenzie / Josh Golden
	DB Riccardo Stewart / Matt Fawley
	DB Brett Hudson
	DB Jason Shivers

RUSHING: Wade 136/773y, H. Hill 115/452y, Randy Hill (TB) 47/228y
PASSING: Walter 221-421/3044y, 24TD, 52.5%
RECEIVING: Hagan 66/1076y, Fulton 62/901y, Miller 26/326y
SCORING: Fulton 60pts, Hagan 56pts, Jessie Ainsworth (K) 55pts

2004 9-3

41 Texas-El Paso	9 WR Derek Hagan
30 Northwestern	21 WR Terry Richardson / Matt Miller
44 Iowa	7 WR Moey Mutz / Jamaal Lewis
27 Oregon State	14 T Stephen Berg / Chaz White
28 Oregon	13 G Grayling Love
7 Southern Cal	45 C Drew Hodgdon
48 UCLA	42 G Zach Krula / Mike Pollak
0 California	27 T Andrew Carnahan
34 Stanford	31 TE Zach Miller / Lee Burghgraef
45 Washington St.	28 QB Ryan Walter / Sam Keller
27 Arizona	34 TB Hakim Hill/Rudy Burgess/Loren Wade
27 Purdue■	23 DL Jimmy Verdon
	DL Jordan Hill
	DL Kyle Caldwell / Gabe Reininger
	DL Ishmael Thrower
	LB Dale Robinson
	LB Justin Burks
	LB Jamar Williams / Lamar Baker
	DB Chris McKenzie
	DB Josh Golden
	DB Riccardo Stewart
	DB Emmanuel Franklin / Josh Barrett

RUSHING: H. Hill 122/566y, Burgess 77/404y, Wade 50/185y
PASSING: Walter 244-426/3150y, 30TD, 57.3%
RECEIVING: Hagan 83/1248y, Z. Miller 56/552y, Richardson 45/679y, Mutz 35/438y
SCORING: Jessie Ainsworth (K) 100pts, Hagan 60pts, Z. Miller & Richardson 36pts

2005 7-5

63 Temple	16 WR Terry Richardson / Matt Miller
31 LSU	35 WR Derek Hagan / Moey Mutz
52 Northwestern	21 T Brandon Rodd (G) / Chaz White
42 Oregon State	24 G Stephen Berg
28 Southern Cal	38 C Grayling Love / Mike Pollak (G)
17 Oregon	31 G Zach Krula / Leo Talavou
35 Stanford	45 T Andrew Carnahan
44 Washington	20 TE Zach Miller
27 Washington St.	24 QB Sam Keller / Rudy Carpenter
35 UCLA	45 TB Rudy Burgess / Keegan Herring
23 Arizona	20 H-B Jamal Lewis / Brent Miller
45 Rutgers■	40 DL Kyle Caldwell
	DL Jordan Hill / Quency Darley
	DL Willie Kofe / DeWayne Hollyfield
	DL Mike Talbot
	LB Robert James / Beau Manutai
	LB Dale Robinson
	LB Jamar Williams / Nick Clapp
	DB Mike Davis / R.J. Oliver
	DB Josh Golden
	DB Zach Catanese
	DB Maurice London / Josh Barrett

RUSHING: Herring 158/870y, Burgess 145/644y, Preston Jones (TB)
PASSING: Carpenter 156-228/2273y, 17TD, 68.4%, Keller 155-264/2165y, 20TD, 58.7%
RECEIVING: Hagan 77/1210y, Burgess 59/655y, Z. Miller 38/476y, Richardson 37/495y
SCORING: Jesse Ainsworth (K) 80pts, Burgess 60pts, Hagan 48pts

2006 7-6

35 N. Arizona	14 WR Nate Kimbrough / Michael Jones
52 Nevada	21 WR Rudy Burgess (DB) / Chris McGaha
21 Colorado	3 T Brandon Rodd / Julius Orieukwu
21 California	49 G Robert Gustavis
13 Oregon	48 C Mike Pollak
21 Southern Cal	28 G Paul Fanaika
38 Stanford	3 T Stephen Berg (G) / Andrew Carnahan
26 Washington	23 TE Zach Miller
10 Oregon State	44 QB Rudy Carpenter
47 Washington St.	14 TB Ryan Torain / Keegan Herring
12 UCLA	24 H-B Brent Miller
28 Arizona	14 DL Kyle Caldwell
24 Hawaii■	41 DL Michael Marquardt / Will Kofe
	DL Jordan Hill
	DL Dexter Davis
	LB Mike Nixon / Robert James
	LB Beau Manatai / Gerald Munns
	LB Derron Ware / Travis Goethel
	DB Keno Walter-White / Chris Baloney
	DB Justin Tryon / Rudy Burgess (WR)
	DB Zach Catanese
	DB Josh Barnett

RUSHING: Torain 223/1229y, Herring 94/549y, Dimitri Nance (TB) 56/229y
PASSING: Carpenter 184-332/2523y, 23 TDs, 55.4%
RECEIVING: Z. Miller 50/484y, Jones 20/318y, Torain 18/205y, McGaha 16/238y
SCORING: Jesse Ainsworth (K) 84pts, Torain 60pts, Herring 36pts

2007 10-3

45 San Jose St.	3 WR Michael Jones / Rudy Burgess
33 Colorado	13 WR Kyle Williams
34 San Diego St.	13 WR Chris McGaha
44 Oregon State	32 T Brandon Rodd
41 Stanford	3 G Shawn Lauvao / Robert Gustavis
23 Washington St.	20 C Mike Pollak
44 Washington	20 G Paul Fanaika
31 California	20 T Julius Orieukwu / Zach Krula
23 Oregon	35 TE Brent Miller / Brady Conrad
24 UCLA	20 QB Rudy Carpenter
24 Southern Cal	44 TB Ryan Torain / Keegan Herring
20 Arizona	17 DL Dexter Davis
34 Texas■	52 DL David Smith
	DL Michael Marquardt / Jon Hargis
	DL Luis Vasquez
	LB Travis Goethel / Mike Nixon
	LB Morris Wooten / Gerald Munns
	LB Robert James
	DB Justin Tryon
	DB Omar Bolden / Chris Baloney
	DB Troy Nolan / Rodney Cox
	DB Josh Barrett / Jeremy Payton

RUSHING: Herring 154/815y, Torain 110/553y, Nance 133/500y
PASSING: Carpenter 246-398/3202y, 25TD, 61.8%
RECEIVING: McGaha 61/830y, Jones 46/769y, Burgess 34/467y
SCORING: Thomas Weber (K) 198pts, Jones 60pts, Nance & Torain 42pts

2008 5-7

30 N. Arizona	13 WR Michael Jones
41 Stanford	17 WR Chris McGaha / Nate Kimbrough
20 UNLV	23 WR Kerry Taylor / Kyle Williams
10 Georgia	27 T Jon Hargis / Tom Njunge
14 California	24 G Shawn Lauvao
0 Southern Cal	28 C Thomas Altieri
20 Oregon	54 G Paul Fanaika
25 Oregon State	27 T Richard Tuitu'u / Adam Tello
39 Washington	19 TE Dane Guthrie / Andrew Pettes
31 Washington St.	0 QB Rudy Carpenter
34 UCLA	9 RB Dimitri Nance / Keegan Herring
10 Arizona	31 DL Dexter Davis
	DL Saia Falahola / Lawrence Guy
	DL David Smith / Jonathan English
	DL Luis Vasquez
	LB Travis Goethel / Shelly Lyons
	LB Morris Wooten / Gerald Munns
	LB Mike Nixon / Ryan McFoy
	DB Terell Carr / Pierre Singfield
	DB Omar Bolden
	DB Troy Nolan / Jeremy Payton
	DB Rodney Cox / Clint Floyd

RUSHING: Nance 105/410y, Herring 105/401y, Shaun DeWitty (RB) 62/270y
PASSING: Carpenter 213-351/2493y, 16TD, 60.7%
RECEIVING: Jones 61/744y, McGaha 35/501y, Taylor 27/405y, Pettes 21/151y
SCORING: Thomas Weber (K) 86pts, Jones & Williams 24pts

2009 4-8

50 Idaho State	3 WR Kyle Williams
38 La.-Monroe	14 WR Chris McGaha / T.J. Simpson
17 Georgia	20 WR Kerry Taylor / Gerrell Robinson
17 Oregon State	28 T Shawn Lauvao
27 Washington St.	14 G Jon Hargis
24 Washington	17 C Thomas Altieri
14 Stanford	33 G Garth Gerhart / Brent Good
21 California	23 T Tom Njunge (G) / Matt Hustad (G)
9 Southern Cal	14 TE Dan Knapp / Jovon Williams
21 Oregon	44 QB Danny Sullivan / Brock Osweiler
13 UCLA	23 RB Dimitri Nance / Cameron Marshall
17 Arizona	20 DL James Brooks / Dean DeLeone
	DL Lawrence Guy
	DL Saia Falahola / William Sutton
	DL Dexter Davis
	LB Travis Goethel / Shelly Lyons
	LB Vontaze Burfict / Gerald Munns
	LB Mike Nixon
	DB Pierre Singfield / Omar Bolden
	DB Terell Carr / Deveron Carr
	DB Jarrell Holman / Keelan Johnson
	DB Ryan McFoy / Clint Floyd

RUSHING: Nance 188/795y, Marshall 64/280y, Ryan Bass (RB) 29/173y
PASSING: Sullivan 168-312/1939y, 10TD, 53.8%, Samson Szakacsy (QB) 32-50/362y, 4TD, 64%, Osweiler 24-55/249y, 2TD, 45.6%
RECEIVING: K. Williams 57/815y, McGaha 56/673y, Nance 28/216y, Robinson 26/261y
SCORING: K. Williams 48pts, Thomas Weber (K) 43pts, Nance 42pts

2010 6-6

54 Portland State	9 WR Kerry Taylor / Aaron Pflugrad
41 N. Arizona	20 WR Mike Willie / George Bell
19 Wisconsin	20 WR T.J. Simpson / Gerell Robinson
31 Oregon	42 T Evan Finkenberg
28 Oregon State	31 G Mike Marcisz / Adam Tello
24 Washington	14 C Garth Gerhart
17 California	50 G Andrew Sampson / Brice Schwab
42 Washington St.	0 T Aderious Simmons / Dan Knapp
33 Southern Cal	34 TE/WR Trevor Kohl / Jamal Miles (TB)
13 Stanford	17 QB Steven Threet / Brock Osweiler
55 UCLA	34 TB Cameron Marshall / Deantre Lewis
30 Arizona	29 DL Jamaar Jarrett / Jamarr Robinson
	DL Lawrence Guy
	DL Saia Falahola / Bo Moos
	DL James Brooks / Junior Onyeali
	LB Vontaze Burfict / Oliver Aaron
	LB Brandon Magee / Gerald Munns
	LB Colin Parker / Shelly Lyons
	DB Omar Bolden
	DB Osahon Irabor / Deveron Carr
	DB Clint Floyd / Keelan Johnson
	DB Eddie Elder / Max Tabach

RUSHING: Marshall 150/787y, Lewis 92/539y, Osweiler 38/124y
PASSING: Threet 208-336/2534y, 18TD, 61.9%, Osweiler 62-109/797y, 5TD, 56.9%
RECEIVING: Taylor 54/699y, Willie 36/442y, Simpson 29/481y, Robinson 29/387y, Pflugrad 29/329y
SCORING: Thomas Weber (K) 93pts, Marshall 62pts, Miles 42pts

ARKANSAS

University of Arkansas (Founded 1871)
Fayetteville, Arkansas
Nickname: Razorbacks
Colors: Cardinal and White
Stadium: Donald W. Reynolds Razorback Stadium (1938) 76,000
War Memorial Stadium (1948) 53,727
Conference Affiliations: Southwest (1915-1991)
  Southeastern (1992-present)

CAREER RUSHING YARDS	Attempts	Yards
Darren McFadden (2005-07)	785	4590
Ben Cowins (1975-78)	635	3570
Dickey Morton (1971-73)	595	3317
Cedric Cobbs (1999-2003)	589	3018
Felix Jones (2005-07)	386	2956
James Rouse (1985-89)	559	2887
Fred Talley (1999-2002)	498	2661
Madre Hill (1994-98)	541	2407
Oscar Malone (1992-94, 1996)	471	2320
Bill Burnett (1968-70)	526	2204

CAREER PASSING YARDS	Comp.-Att.	Yards
Ryan Mallett (2009-10)	491-814	7493
Clint Stoerner (1996-99)	528-1023	7422
Matt Jones (2001-04)	417-755	5857
Casey Dick (2005-08)	473-850	5856
Barry Lunney (1992-95)	476-856	5782
Brad Taylor (1981-84)	333-644	4802
Bill Montgomery (1968-70)	337-602	4590
Quinn Grovey (1987-90)	292-526	4496
Joe Ferguson (1970-72)	327-611	4431
Tom Jones (1979-82)	238-432	2927

CAREER RECEIVING YARDS	Catches	Yards
Anthony Lucas (1995-99)	137	2879
Anthony Eubanks (1994-97)	153	2440
George Wilson (2000-03)	144	2151
Marcus Monk (2004-07)	138	2151
James Shibest (1983-86)	97	1920
Derek Russell (1987-90)	91	1874
Richard Smith (2000-03)	135	1858
D.J. Williams (2008-10)	152	1855
Chuck Dicus (1968-70)	118	1854
Greg Childs (2008-10)	112	1826

SEASON RUSHING YARDS	Attempts	Yards
Darren McFadden (2007)	325	1830
Darren McFadden (2006)	284	1647
Madre Hill (1995)	307	1387
Knile Davis (2010)	204	1322
Cedric Cobbs (2003)	227	1320

SEASON PASSING YARDS	Comp.-Att.	Yards
Ryan Mallett (2010)	266-411	3869
Ryan Mallett (2009)	225-403	3624
Clint Stoerner (1998)	167-312	2629
Casey Dick (2008)	205-357	2586
Clint Stoerner (1997)	173-357	2347

SEASON RECEIVING YARDS	Catches	Yards
Anthony Lucas (1998)	43	1004
Mike Reppond (1971)	56	986
Marcus Monk (2006)	50	962
James Shibest (1984)	51	907
George Wilson (2003)	50	900

GAME RUSHING YARDS	Attempts	Yards
Darren McFadden (2007 vs. So. Carolina)	34	321
Dickey Morton (1973 vs. Baylor)	28	271
Fred Talley (2002 vs. Auburn)	21	241

GAME PASSING YARDS	Comp.-Att.	Yards
Ryan Mallett (2010 vs. Vanderbilt)	27-44	409
Ryan Mallett (2009 vs. Georgia)	21-39	408
Ryan Mallett (2009 vs. Troy)	23-30	405

GAME RECEIVING YARDS	Catches	Yards
Mike Reppond (1971 vs. Rice)	12	204
Lucas Miller (2008 vs. Mississippi St.)	10	201
James Shibest (1984 vs. SMU)	13	199

GREATEST COACH:

Any discussion of Arkansas coaching begins and ends with Frank Broyles, who not only sculpted out a brilliant career as the head coach at Arkansas for 19 years beginning in 1958, but has had a role in the choosing and replacing—for better or worse—every coach since he stepped down to become the full-time athletic director. Unfortunately none live up to the high standards the boss set, still fresh in the minds of the baby boomer fans who grew up on some hugely successful Hog teams.

Broyles is so closely associated with the University of Arkansas that it is easy to forget his star turn as a Georgia Tech athlete. The SEC player of the year in 1944, Broyles owned the record for yards passing in the Orange Bowl with 304, set against Tulsa in January of 1945, until 2000 when it was broken by Tom Brady of Michigan. In addition to being the star quarterback for a Tech squad that went bowling and was ranked for each of the four years featuring Broyles at the helm of their offense, he was a three-time All-SEC basketball player.

After one season as head coach of Missouri at age of 32, Broyles was off to his Arkansas dream job to replace Jack Mitchell who had left for Kansas. As head coach Broyles led Arkansas to the national championship in 1964 and seven Southwest Conference titles. The totals would have been better if Broyles did not have to go head-to-head with Texas coach Darrell Royal. The two divvied up the SWC spoils with nary a crumb left for anyone else. Broyles won 144 games, to only 58 defeats.

Beginning in 1973 Broyles had tackled both the coaching and AD jobs, to the detriment of his coaching. Hiring Lou Holtz to run the football team, Broyles continued his administrative duties with an eye on top coaching talent and the best facilities, both of which should lead to championships. Broyles was correct on all fronts as Arkansas sports combined for 43 national championships, although ironically the football program rarely challenged for conference titles over the years, let alone national titles.

ARKANSAS' 55 GREATEST SINCE 1953

OFFENSE

WIDE RECEIVER: Chuck Dicus, Anthony Lucas, Marcus Monk
TIGHT END: Jerry Lamb, D.J. Williams
TACKLE: Shawn Andrews, Glen Ray Hines, Greg Kolenda, DeMarcus Love, Jim Mabry
GUARD: Jim Barnes, Brandon Burlsworth, Freddie Childress, Leotis Harris, Steve Korte, R.C. Thielemann
CENTER: Rodney Brand, Jonathan Luigs
QUARTERBACK: Matt Jones, Ryan Mallett, Bill Montgomery
RUNNING BACK: Lance Alworth, Ben Cowins, Darren McFadden, Dickey Morton
FULLBACK: Barry Foster

DEFENSE

END: Henry Ford, Bruce James, Billy Ray Smith, Jr.
TACKLE: Tony Cherico, Dan Hampton, Wayne Martin, Loyd Phillips, Jimmy Walker
LINEBACKER: Ronnie Caveness, Wayne Harris, Cliff Powell, Danny Rhodes, Dennis Winston
CORNERBACK: David Barrett, Ahmad Carroll, Ken Hatfield, Jerry Moore
SAFETY: Steve Atwater, Martine Bercher, Ken Hamlin, Kenoy Kennedy

SPECIAL TEAMS

RETURN SPECIALISTS: Bobby Joe Edmonds, Felix Jones
PLACE KICKER: Steve Little
PUNTER: Steve Cox

MULTIPLE POSITIONS

WIDE RECEIVER-TIGHT END: Bobby Crockett
RUNNING BACK-WIDE RECEIVER: Gary Anderson

TWO-WAY PLAYERS

GUARD-DEFENSIVE TACKLE: Bud Brooks
HALFBACK-DEFENSIVE BACK: Preston Carpenter

PERFORMANCE FORMULA:
ARKANSAS' 10 BEST SEASONS

1964	1.7149	1 of 70
1977	1.6703	4 of 70
1965	1.6415	2 of 70
1968	1.5920	4 of 70
1979	1.5520	9 of 70
1975	1.5515	6 of 70
1970	1.5287	9 of 70
1989	1.5140	14 of 70
2010	1.5025	11 of 71
1985	1.5001	12 of 70

ARKANSAS RAZORBACKS

Year	W-L-T	AP Poll	Conference Standing	Toughest Regular Season Opponents	Coach (Record at School)	Bowl Games		
1953	3-7		5	Rice 8-2, Mississippi 7-2-1, Texas 7-3, Baylor 7-3	Bowden Wyatt			
1954	8-3		1	Mississippi 9-1, Baylor 7-3, Rice 7-3	Bowden Wyatt (11-10)	Cotton	6 Georgia Tech	14
1955	5-4-1		4	TCU 9-1, Mississippi 9-1, Texas A&M 7-2-1	Jack Mitchell			
1956	6-4		4	Texas A&M 9-0-1, Baylor 8-2, Mississippi 7-3, TCU 7-3	Jack Mitchell			
1957	6-4		5	Mississippi 8-1-1, Texas A&M 8-2, Rice 7-3	Jack Mitchell (17-12-1)			
1958	4-6		6	Mississippi 8-2, TCU 8-2, Texas 7-3	Frank Broyles			
1959	9-2	9	1t	Mississippi 9-1, Texas 9-1, TCU 8-2	Frank Broyles	Gator	14 Georgia Tech	7
1960	8-3	7	1	Mississippi 9-0-1, Baylor 8-2, Rice 7-3, Texas 7-3	Frank Broyles	Cotton	6 Duke	7
1961	8-3	9	1t	Texas 9-1, Mississippi 9-1, Rice 7-3	Frank Broyles	Sugar	3 Alabama	10
1962	9-2	6	2	Texas 9-0-1, TCU 6-4	Frank Broyles	Sugar	13 Mississippi	17
1963	5-5		4	Texas 10-0, Missouri 7-3, Baylor 7-3	Frank Broyles			
1964	11-0	2	1	Texas 9-1, Tulsa 8-2, Texas Tech 6-3-1	Frank Broyles	Cotton	10 Nebraska	7
1965	10-1	3	1	Texas Tech 8-2, Tulsa 8-2, Texas 6-4, TCU 6-4	Frank Broyles	Cotton	7 LSU	14
1966	8-2	11	2	SMU 8-2, Texas 6-4, Tulsa 6-4	Frank Broyles			
1967	4-5-1		5	Texas 6-4, Texas A&M 6-4, Texas Tech 6-4, Tulsa 7-3	Frank Broyles			
1968	10-1	6	1t	Texas 8-1-1, SMU 7-3, North Texas 8-2	Frank Broyles	Sugar	16 Georgia	2
1969	9-2	7	2	Texas 10-0, Texas Tech 5-5, Oklahoma State 5-5	Frank Broyles	Sugar	22 Mississippi	27
1970	9-2	11	2	Texas 10-0, Stanford 8-3, Texas Tech 8-3	Frank Broyles			
1971	8-3-1	16	2	Texas 8-2, TCU 6-4-1, California 6-5	Frank Broyles	Liberty	13 Tennessee	14
1972	6-5		4	Southern California 11-0, Texas 9-1, Texas Tech 5-7, SMU 7-4	Frank Broyles			
1973	5-5-1		4	Southern California 9-1-1, Texas 8-2, Texas Tech 9-1	Frank Broyles			
1974	6-4-1		4	Southern California 9-1-1, Texas A&M 8-3, Texas 8-3, Baylor 8-3	Frank Broyles			
1975	10-2	7	1t	Texas A&M 10-1, Texas 9-2, Oklahoma State 7-4	Frank Broyles	Cotton	31 Georgia	10
1976	5-5-1		6	Texas Tech 10-1, Texas A&M 9-2, Houston 9-2, Oklahoma St. 8-3	Frank Broyles (144-58-5)			
1977	11-1	3	2	Texas 11-0, Texas A&M 8-3, Texas Tech 7-4	Lou Holtz	Orange	31 Oklahoma	6
1978	9-2-1	11	2t	Houston 9-2, Texas 8-3, Texas A&M 7-4	Lou Holtz	Fiesta	10 UCLA	10
1979	10-2	8	1t	Houston 10-1, Texas 9-2, Baylor 7-4	Lou Holtz	Sugar	9 Alabama	24
1980	7-5		6t	Baylor 10-1, SMU 8-3, Texas 7-4	Lou Holtz	Hall of Fame	34 Tulane	15
1981	8-4		4	SMU 10-1, Texas 9-1-1, Houston 7-3-1	Lou Holtz	Gator	27 North Carolina	31
1982	9-2-1	9	3	SMU 10-0-1, Texas 9-2, Navy 6-5	Lou Holtz	Bluebonnet	28 Florida	24
1983	6-5		5	Texas 11-0, SMU 10-1, Baylor 7-3-1	Lou Holtz (60-21-2)			
1984	7-4-1		3t	SMU 9-2, TCU 8-3, Texas 7-3-1, Houston 7-4	Ken Hatfield	Liberty	15 Auburn	21
1985	10-2	12	2t	Texas A&M 9-2, Texas 8-3, Baylor 8-3	Ken Hatfield	Holiday	18 Arizona State	17
1986	9-3	15	2t	Texas A&M 9-2, Baylor 8-3, Texas Tech 7-4	Ken Hatfield	Orange	8 Oklahoma	42
1987	9-4		2t	Miami 11-0, Texas A&M 9-2, Texas 6-5	Ken Hatfield	Liberty	17 Georgia	20
1988	10-2	12	1	Miami 10-1, Houston 9-2, Texas A&M 7-4	Ken Hatfield	Cotton	3 UCLA	17
1989	10-2	13	1	Houston 9-2, Texas A&M 8-3, Texas Tech 8-3, Mississippi 7-4	Ken Hatfield (55-17-1)	Cotton	27 Tennessee	31
1990	3-8		8	Texas 10-1, Texas A&M 8-3-1, Baylor 6-4-1	Jack Crowe			
1991	6-6		2t	Miami 11-0, Texas A&M 10-1, Baylor 8-3	Jack Crowe	Independence	15 Georgia	24
1992	3-7-1		W4	Alabama 11-0, Georgia 9-2, Tennessee 8-3, Mississippi 8-3	Jack Crowe [0-1], (9-15) Joe Kines (3-6-1)			
1993	5-5-1		W2	Auburn 11-0, Tennessee 9-2-1, Alabama 8-2-1	Danny Ford			
1994	4-7		W4t	Alabama 10-1, Auburn 9-1-1, Mississippi St. 8-3, Tennessee 7-4	Danny Ford			
1995	8-5		W1	Tennessee 10-1, Auburn 8-3, Alabama 8-3, LSU 6-4-1	Danny Ford	Carquest	10 North Carolina	20
1996	4-7		W5t	Florida 10-1, Alabama 9-2, Tennessee 9-2, LSU 9-2	Danny Ford			
1997	4-7		W5t	Tennessee 11-0, Auburn 9-2, Florida 9-2, LSU 8-3	Danny Ford (26-30-1)			
1998	9-3	16	W1t	Tennessee 11-0, Mississippi State 8-3, Kentucky 7-4, Alabama 7-4	Houston Nutt	Citrus	31 Michigan	45
1999	8-4	17	W3t	Tennessee 9-2, Alabama 9-2, Mississippi St. 9-2, Mississippi 7-4	Houston Nutt	Cotton	27 Texas	6
2000	6-6		W5t	Auburn 9-2, Tennessee 8-3, Georgia 7-4, LSU 7-4	Houston Nutt	Las Vegas	14 UNLV	31
2001	7-5		W3t	Tennessee 10-1, LSU 8-3, South Carolina 8-3, Georgia 8-3	Houston Nutt	Cotton	3 Oklahoma	10
2002	9-5		W1t	Tennessee 8-4, Auburn 8-4, LSU 8-4	Houston Nutt	Music City	14 Minnesota	29
2003	9-4		W3	LSU 11-1, Texas 10-2, Mississippi 9-3, Florida 8-4	Houston Nutt	Independence	27 Missouri	14
2004	5-6		W3t	Auburn 11-0, Texas 10-1, LSU 9-2, Florida 7-4	Houston Nutt			
2005	4-7		W4	Southern Cal 12-0, LSU 10-1, Auburn 9-2, Georgia 9-2, Alabama 9-2	Houston Nutt			
2006	10-4	15	W1	Southern California 10-2, LSU 10-2, Auburn 10-2, Tennessee 9-3	Houston Nutt	Capital One	14 Wisconsin	17
2007	8-5		W3t	Auburn 8-4, Tennessee 9-3, LSU 10-2	Houston Nutt (75-48) Reggie Herring [0-1]	Cotton	7 Missouri	38
2008	5-7		W4t	Alabama 12-1, Texas 11-1, Florida 12-1	Bobby Petrino			
2009	8-5		W4t	Alabama 13-0, Florida 12-1, Mississippi 8-4, LSU 9-3	Bobby Petrino	Liberty	20 East Carolina	17
2010	10-3	12	W2t	Alabama 9-3, Texas A&M 9-3, Auburn 13-0, LSU 10-2	Bobby Petrino (23-15)	Sugar	26 Ohio State	31

TOTAL: 423-233-10 .6426 (18 of 70)

Bowl Games since 1953: 11-23-1 .3286 (66 of 70)

GREATEST TEAM SINCE 1953: It was a glorious run for the Razorbacks in the mid 1960s. Winning 22 straight games, FWAA and Helms Foundation national championships for the 1964 season and two Southwest Conference titles, the 1964-5 Arkansas Hogs were the best team in school history with the nod going to the 1964 club for remaining unbeaten. Although a hard-fought 10-7 victory over Nebraska in the Cotton Bowl secured the 1964 national championship, the game of the year was versus Texas, the defending national champs, in mid-season when both schools were undefeated at 5-0. The play of the game was defensive back Kenny Hatfield's 81-yard scoring punt return, which keyed a thrilling 14-13 win.

1953 3-7

6	Oklahoma A&M	7 E Floyd Sagely / Edsel Nix
13	TCU	6 T Eddie Bradford / Bob Duncan
7	Baylor	14 G Harold Spain / Bobby Gilliam
7	Texas	16 C Charlie Ramsey / Jim Cauthron
0	Mississippi	28 G Bud Brooks
41	Texas A&M	14 T Jim Roth / Buster Graves
0	Rice	47 E Ron Forrester
7	SMU	13 BB Preston Carpenter / Joe Orr
8	LSU	9 TB Lamar McHan
27	Tulsa	7 WB Phil Reginelli / Joe Thomason
		FB Henry Moore

RUSHING: McHan 143/409Y, Moore 86/331y, Reginelli 27/106y
PASSING: McHan 78-150/1107y, 8TD, 52%
RECEIVING: Sagely 30/542y, Carpenter 18/185y, Thomason 11/189y

SCORING: McHan 32pts, Carpenter 24pts, Sagely & Moore 18pts

1954 8-3

41	Tulsa	0 E Walter Matthews / Teddy Souter
20	TCU	13 T Eddie Bradford / Billy Ray Smith
21	Baylor	20 G Wayland Roberts / Dick Hardwick
20	Texas	7 C Jerry Ford / Harold Steelman
6	Mississippi	0 G Bud Brooks
14	Texas A&M	7 T Jim Roth / Bill Fuller
28	Rice	15 E Jerry McFadden
14	SMU	21 BB Preston Carpenter / Bobby Proctor
6	LSU	7 TB George Walker / Buddy Benson
19	Houston	0 WB Joe Thomason / Ronnie Underwood
6	Georgia Tech■	14 FB Henry Moore

RUSHING: Moore 153/670y, Benson 80/349y, Walker 79/301y
PASSING: Walker 45-85/603y, 4TD, 52.9%
RECEIVING: Carpenter 21/234y, McFadden 9/108y

SCORING: Walker (TB-K) 51pts, Moore 48pts, Carpenter 21pts

1955 5-4-1

21	Tulsa	6 E Walter Matthews / Teddy Souter
21	Oklahoma A&M	0 T Jess Deason / Dick Bennett
0	TCU	26 G Wayland Roberts / Neil Martin
20	Baylor	25 C Jay Donathan / Harold Steelman
27	Texas	20 G Bobby Gilliam / Stuart Perry
7	Mississippi	17 T Bill Fuller / George Bequette
7	Texas A&M	7 E Jerry McFadden / Billy Lyons
10	Rice	0 QB George Walker / Don Christian
6	SMU	0 HB Ronnie Underwood / Buddy Benson
7	LSU	13 HB Preston Carpenter / Joe Thomason
		FB Henry Moore / Gerald Nesbitt

RUSHING: Moore 134/701y, Nesbitt 61/371y, Carpenter 57/257y
PASSING: Walker 22-47/347y, 2TD, 46.8%
RECEIVING: Carpenter 11/155y, Souter 6/94y, Underwood 6/93y
SCORING: Walker (QB-K) 41pts, Underwood 24pts, Moore 18pts

1956 6-4

21	Hardin Simmons	6 E Olan Burns / Bob Childress
19	Oklahoma A&M	7 T Billy Ray Smith
6	TCU	41 G Neil Martin
7	Baylor	14 C Jay Donathan / Jerry Ford
32	Texas	14 G Stuart Perry / Gerald Henderson
14	Mississippi	0 T George Bequette / Dick Bennett
0	Texas A&M	27 E Teddy Souter / Charlie Whitworth
27	Rice	12 QB Don Christian / James Monroe
27	SMU	13 HB Ronnie Underwood / Rogers Overbey
7	LSU	21 HB Donnie Stone / Don Ritschel
		FB Gerald Nesbitt

RUSHING: Nesbitt 129/663y, Christian 96/412y, Underwood 59/268y
PASSING: Christian 18-53/260y, 2TD, 34%
RECEIVING: Underwood 7/154y, Stone 4/85y, Burns 4/26y
SCORING: Nesbitt (FB-K) 49pts, Christian 30pts, Underwood 24pts

1957 6-4

12	Oklahoma State	0 E Bob Childress / Billy Tranum
41	Tulsa	14 T Rollie Luplow / Greg Pinkston
20	TCU	7 G Jerry Ford / Billy Gilbow
20	Baylor	17 C Jay Donathan
0	Texas	17 G Stuart Perry
12	Mississippi	6 T Dick Bennett / Billy Michael
6	Texas A&M	7 E Charlie Whitworth / Richard Bell
7	Rice	13 QB George Walker / Don Christian
22	SMU	27 HB Donnie Stone / Jim Mooty
47	Texas Tech	26 HB Don Horton / Billy Kyser
		FB Gerald Nesbitt / Jerry Ferguson

RUSHING: Nesbitt 145/624y, Stone 72/322y, Ferguson 35/216y
PASSING: Walker 35-63/587y, 4TD, 55.6%
RECEIVING: Kyser 10/179y, Stone 8/114y, Horton 8/99y
SCORING: Nesbitt (FB-K) 51pts, Stone, Kyser & Christian 24pts

1958 4-6

0	Baylor	12 E Billy Tranum / Les Letsinger
14	Tulsa	27 T Billy Michael / Jim Hollander
7	TCU	12 G Billy Gilbow / Barry Switzer (C)
0	Rice	24 C Wayne Harris / Gerald Gardner
6	Texas	24 G Jerry Green / Billy Luplow
12	Mississippi	14 T Marlin Epp / Paul Henderson
21	Texas A&M	8 E Richard Bell / Charlie Barnes
60	Hardin Simmons	15 QB Jim Monroe / Mike Cooney
13	SMU	6 HB Jim Mooty / Billy Kyser
14	Texas Tech	8 HB Don Horton / Don Ritschel
		FB Donnie Stone / Joe Paul Alberty

RUSHING: Mooty 71/395y, Stone 88/326y, Cooney 41/188y
PASSING: Monroe 41-96/512y, 3TD, 42.7%
RECEIVING: Barnes 15/175y, Bell 8/160y, Tranum 5/76y
SCORING: Stone 30pts, Mooty 26pts, Monroe 18pts

1959 9-2

28	Texas	0 E Steve Butler / Les Letsinger
13	Oklahoma State	7 T Marlin Epp / Paul Henderson
3	TCU	0 G Billy Luplow / Jerry Green
23	Baylor	7 C Wayne Harris / Barry Switzer
12	Texas	13 G Gerald Gardner
0	Mississippi	28 T Jim Hollander / Dean Garrett
12	Texas A&M	7 E Billy Tranum / Jimmy Collier
14	Rice	10 QB Jim Monroe / George McKinney
17	SMU	14 HB Jim Mooty / Fred Akers/ Darrell Williams
27	Texas Tech	8 HB Lance Alworth / Billy Kyser
14	Georgia Tech	7 FB Joe Paul Alberty /Paul Dudley / Curt Cox

RUSHING: Mooty 93/519y, Alworth 85/366y, Cox 63/245y
PASSING: Monroe 19-30/202y, 3TD, 63.3%
RECEIVING: Butler 9/107y, Alworth 7/82y, Letsinger 6/98y
SCORING: Mooty 30pts, Cox & Monroe 18pts

1960 8-3

9	Oklahoma State	0 E Steve Butler / James Gaston
48	Tulsa	7 T Marlin Epp / Jerry Mazzanti
7	TCU	0 G Dean Garrett / Ray Trail
14	Baylor	28 C Wayne Harris / Jerry Lineberger
24	Texas	23 G Johnny Fields / Danny Brabham
7	Mississippi	10 T Paul Henderson / John Childress
7	Texas A&M	3 E Jimmy Collier / Les Letsinger
3	Rice	0 QB George McKinney / Billy Moore
26	SMU	3 HB Lance Alworth / Jarrell Williams
34	Texas Tech	6 HB Darrel Williams / Harold Horton
6	Duke■	7 FB Curt Cox /Joe Paul Alberty / BJ Moody

RUSHING: Alworth 106/375y, Moore 57/215y, McKinney 84/193y
PASSING: McKinney 39-90/728y, 9TD, 43.3%
RECEIVING: Collier 17/356y, Alworth 12/243y, Gaston 6/84y
SCORING: Mickey Cissell (K) 27pts, Collier 24pts, Alworth & Moore 18pts

1961 8-3

0	Mississippi	16 E Tim Langston / Jim John
6	Tulsa	0 T Jerry Mazzanti
28	TCU	3 G Ray Trail
23	Baylor	13 C Danny Brabham (T) / Jerry Lineberger
7	Texas	33 G Dean Garrett / Tommy Brasher
42	NW Louisiana St.	7 T John Childress
15	Texas A&M	8 E Jimmy Collier
10	Rice	0 QB George McKinney / Billy Moore
21	SMU	7 HB Lance Alworth / Darrell Williams
28	Texas Tech	0 HB Paul Dudley / Harold Horton
3	Alabama■	10 FB Billy Joe Moody / Jesse Branch

RUSHING: Alworth 110/516y, Dudley 73/341y, Moody 81/298y
PASSING: McKinney 32-68/426y, 6TD, 47%
RECEIVING: Alworth 18/320y, Collier 10/139y, Dudley 7/121y
SCORING: Mickey Cissell (K) 33pts, Alworth 30pts, Dudley 26pts

1962 9-2

34	Oklahoma State	7 E Gary Howard (G) / Jim John / Jim Finch
42	Tulsa	14 T Jerry Mazzanti / Buddy Tackett (D)
42	TCU	14 G Tommy Brasher / Dave Walston
28	Baylor	21 C J. Lineberger/Ron Caveness/Tom Polk
3	Texas	7 G Ray Trail /Mike Hales (D)/Jim Johnson
49	Hardin Simmons	7 T Dave Adams / Wes Bryant (D)
17	Texas A&M	7 E Jerry Lamb / Jim Grizzle(D)
28	Rice	14 QB Billy Moore/Billy Gray/Ken Hatfield (D)
9	SMU	7 TB Jesse Branch / Jim Worthington
34	Texas Tech	0 WB George Rea Walker / Mike Parker (D)
13	Mississippi■	17 FB Danny Brabham / Billy Joe Moody

RUSHING: Moore 131/585y, Branch 102/480y, Brabham 128/466y
PASSING: Moore 51-91/673y, 5TD, 56%
RECEIVING: Lamb 23/378y, Finch 11/126y, Walker 10/143y
SCORING: Moore 84pts, Tom McKnelly (K) 42pts, Branch 30pts

1963 5-5

21	Oklahoma State	0 E Bobby Crockett / Jim John / Jim Finch
6	Missouri	7 T Wesley Bryant / Jerry Welch
18	TCU	3 G Ronnie Mac Smith / Gary Howard
10	Baylor	14 C Ronnie Caveness / Randy Stewart
13	Texas	17 G Jimmy Johnson / Jerry Jones
56	Tulsa	7 T Jerry Mazzanti/Dave Adams/G. R. Hines
21	Texas A&M	7 E Jerry Lamb / Jim Grizzle
0	Rice	7 QB Bill Gray / Fred Marshall
7	SMU	14 TB J. Brausell/Tommy Brasher/Tom Moore
27	Texas Tech	20 WB Jim Lindsey / Ken Hatfield
		FB Charles Daniel / Stan Sparks

RUSHING: Lindsey 130/444y, Brausell 56/253y, Marshall 44/143y
PASSING: Gray 34-79/483y, 4TD, 43%
RECEIVING: Lamb 16/240y, Brausell 15/159y, Crockett 9/156y
SCORING: Gray 30pts, Brausell 24pts, Tom McKnelly (K) 23pts

1964 11-0

14	Oklahoma State	10 E Bobby Crockett
31	Tulsa	22 T Glen Ray Hines
29	TCU	6 G Jerry Welch
17	Baylor	6 C Randy Stewart / Dick Hatfield
14	Texas	13 G Jerry Jones
17	Wichita State	0 T Mike Bender
17	Texas A&M	0 E Jerry Lamb
21	Rice	0 QB Fred Marshall / Billy Gray (DB)
44	SMU	0 TB Jack Brausell / Bobby Burnett
17	Texas Tech	0 WB Jim Lindsey
10	Nebraska■	7 FB Bobby Nix
		DL Jim Finch
		DL Loyd Phillips
		DL Jimmy Johnson
		DL Jim Williams
		DL Bobby Roper
		LB Ronnie Mac Smith
		LB Ronnie Cavness
		DB Billy Gray (QB)
		DB Ken Hatfield
		DB Harry Jones
		DB Charles Daniel

RUSHING: Brausell 173/542y, Lindsey 91/491y, Marshall 104/438y
PASSING: Marshall 50-94/656y, 4TD, 53.2%
RECEIVING: Lindsey 24/331y, Lamb 13/180y, Brausell 11/112y
SCORING: Tom McKnelly (K) 47pts, Burnett 42pts, Lindsey 30pts

1965 10-1

28	Oklahoma State	14 E Richard Trail / Tommy Burnett
20	Tulsa	12 T Glen Ray Hines
28	TCU	0 G Melvin Gibbs
38	Baylor	7 C Randy Stewart
27	Texas	24 E Mike Bender / Ernie Richardson
55	N. Texas State	20 T Dick Cunningham
31	Texas A&M	0 E Bobby Crockett
31	Rice	0 QB Jon Brittenum
24	SMU	3 WB Harry Jones / Jim Lindsey
42	Texas Tech	24 TB Bobby Burnett
7	LSU■	14 FB Bobby Nix
		DL Lee Johnson
		DL Loyd Phillips
		DL Guy Jones / Bill Douglass
		DL Jim Williams
		DL Bobby Roper
		LB Joe Black
		LB Buddy Sims
		DB Martine Bercher / Paul Conner
		DB Tommy Trantham
		DB Jack Brasuell
		DB Steven Hoehn

RUSHING: Burnett 232/947y, Jones 82/632y, Lindsey 55/242y
PASSING: Brittenum 75-149/1103y, 8TD, 50.3%
RECEIVING: Crockett 30/487y, Jones 16/297y, Lindsey 11/162y
SCORING: Burnett 96pts, Ronny South (K) 60pts, Jones 42pts

1966 8-2

14 Oklahoma State	10 E Richard Trail
27 Tulsa	8 T Ernest Ruple
21 TCU	0 G Travis Maudlin
0 Baylor	7 C Melvin Gibbs
12 Texas	7 G Jim Barnes
41 Wichita State	0 T Dick Cunningham
34 Texas A&M	0 E Tommy Burnett
31 Rice	20 QB Jon Brittenum
22 SMU	0 WB Harry Jones
16 Texas Tech	21 TB Bruce Maxwell / David Dickey
	FB Eddie Woodlee
	DL Hartford Hamilton
	DL Loyd Phillips
	DL David Cooper
	DL Terry Don Phillips / Don McElvogue
	DL Mickey Maroney
	LB Joe Black
	LB Lee Johnson / Alvin Jones
	DB Gary Adams
	DB Tommy Trantham
	DB Mike Jordan / Steve Hoehn
	DB Martine Bercher

RUSHING: Dickey 115/447y, Maxwell 105/376y, Jones 84/342y
PASSING: Brittenham 76-143/1103y, 7TD, 53.1%
RECEIVING: Burnett 29/401y, Jones 13/301y, Trail 10/145y
SCORING: Dickey 48pts, Bob White (K) 38pts,
 Jones & Maxwell 30pts

1967 4-5-1

6 Oklahoma State	7 E Mike Sigman
12 Tulsa	14 T Webb Hubbell
26 TCU	0 G Pat May / Jim Jordan / Jud Erwin
10 Baylor	10 C Rodney Brand
12 Texas	21 G Jim Barnes
28 Kansas State	7 T Ernest Ruple
21 Texas A&M	33 TE Max Peacock / Dennis Berner
23 Rice	9 QB Ronny South / John Eichler
35 SMU	17 WB David Dickey
27 Texas Tech	31 TB Russell Cody / Mike Hendren
	FB Glen Hockersmith
	DL Hartford Hamilton
	DL Jerry Dossey
	DL David Cooper
	DL Alvin Jones
	DL William Ketchner
	LB Lynn Garner
	LB Cliff Powell
	DB Gary Adams
	DB Tommy Trantham
	DB Steve Hoehn
	DB Terry Stewart

RUSHING: Cody 95/383y, Hendren 97/326y, Dickey 74/294y
PASSING: South 84-142/1159y, 11TD, 59.2%
RECEIVING: Peacock 30/468y, Dickey 27/431y, Sigman 17/239y
SCORING: Dickey 114pts, Peacock 30pts, Bob White (K) 26pts

1968 10-1

32 Oklahoma State	15 WR Max Peacock
56 Tulsa	13 WR Chuck Dicus
17 TCU	7 T Webb Hubbell / Ronnie Hammers
35 Baylor	19 G Jerry Dossey
29 Texas	39 C Rodney Brand
17 North Texas	15 G Jim Barnes
25 Texas A&M	22 T Bob Stankovich / Pat May
46 Rice	21 TE Mike Sigman
35 SMU	29 QB Bill Montgomery
42 Texas Tech	7 TB David Dickey / Bill Burnett
16 Georgia■	2 FB Bruce Maxwell / Glen Hockersmith
	DL Tommy Dew / Bruce James
	DL Terry Don Phillips
	DL Rick Kersey
	DL Gordon McNulty
	DL Lynn Garner
	LB Guy Parker / Mike Jacobs
	LB Cliff Powell
	DB Gary Adams
	DB Tommy Dixon
	DB Jerry Moore / Dennis Berner
	DB Terry Stewart

RUSHING: Burnett 207/859y, Maxwell 61/302y,
 Montgomery 116/239y
PASSING: Montgomery 134-234/1595y,10TD, 57.3%
RECEIVING: Peacock 39/497y, Dicus 38/589y, Sigman 19/233y
SCORING: Burnett 96pts, Dicus 48pts, Bob White (K) 48pts

1969 9-2

39 Oklahoma State	0 WR Chuck Dicus
55 Tulsa	0 WR John Rees / David Cox
24 TCU	6 T Mike Kelson
21 Baylor	7 G Jerry Dossey
52 Wichita State	14 C Rodney Brand / Terry Hopkins
35 Texas A&M	13 G Ronnie Hammers / Jim Mullins
30 Rice	6 T Bob Stankovich
28 SMU	15 TE Pat Morrison / Bobby Nichols
33 Texas Tech	0 QB Bill Montgomery
14 Texas	15 TB Bill Burnett / Russell Cody
22 Mississippi■	27 FB Bruce Maxwell / Russ Garber
	DL Bruce James
	DL Gordon McNulty / Roger Harnish
	DL Dick Bumpas
	DL Rick Kersey
	LB Lynn Garner / Richard Coleman
	LB Cliff Powell
	LB Mike Boschetti / Ronnie Jones
	DB Terry Stewart / Steve Walters
	DB Jerry Moore / David Hogue
	DB Dennis Berner
	DB Bobby Field / Steve Birdwell

RUSHING: Burnett 209/900y, Maxwell 106/582y, Garber 49/219y
PASSING: Montgomery 93-173/1333y, 9TD, 53.8%
RECEIVING: Dicus 42/688y, Rees 21/301y, Morrison 17/227y
SCORING: Burnett 120pts, Bill McClard (K) 61pts, Dicus 24pts

1970 9-2

28 Stanford	34 WR Chuck Dicus
23 Oklahoma State	7 WR Jim Hodge
49 Tulsa	7 T Mike Kelson
49 TCU	14 G Tom Reed
41 Baylor	7 C Terry Hopkins
62 Wichita State	0 G Ronnie Hammers
45 Texas A&M	6 T Tom Mabry
38 Rice	14 TE Pat Morrison
36 SMU	3 QB Bill Montgomery / Joe Ferguson
24 Texas Tech	10 TB Bill Burnett / Jon Richardson
7 Texas	42 FB Russ Garber
	DL Dave Reavis
	DL Rick Kersey
	DL Dick Bumpas
	DL Bruce James
	LB Guy Parker
	LB Ronnie Jones
	LB Mike Boschetti
	DB Jerry Moore
	DB Jack Morris / Dave Hogue
	DB Corkey Cordell / Steve Walters
	DB Bobby Field

RUSHING: Burnett 110/445y, Richardson 104/41y, Garber 81/409y
PASSING: Montgomery 110-195/1662y, 10TD, 56.4%
RECEIVING: Dicus 38/577y, Morrison 20/240y, Richardson 17/240y
SCORING: Bill McClard (K) 80pts, Burnett 78pts, Richardson 66pts

1971 8-3-1

51 California	20 WR Mike Reppond / Jack Ettinger
31 Oklahoma State	10 WR Jim Hodge
20 Tulsa	21 T Mike Kelson
49 TCU	15 G Tom Reed
35 Baylor	7 C Ron Revard
31 Texas	7 G Glen Lowe
60 NorthTexas	21 T Tom Mabry
9 Texas A&M	17 TE Bobby Nichols
24 Rice	24 QB Joe Ferguson
18 SMU	13 TB Dickey Morton / Jon Richardson
14 Texas Tech	0 FB Mike Saint / Russ Garber
13 Tennessee■	14 DL Les Williams
	DL Archie Bennett / Don Wunderly
	DL Dave Reavis
	DL Ronnie Jones
	LB Danny Rhodes
	LB Jim Benton
	LB Scott Binnion
	DB Jack Morris
	DB Louis Campbell
	DB Corky Cordell / Jim Taylor
	DB Clark Irwin

RUSHING: Morton 127/831y, Saint 101/501y, Richardson 104/483y
PASSING: Ferguson 160-271/2203y, 11TD, 59%
RECEIVING: Reppond 56/986y, Hodge 30/473y, Ettinger 16/226y
SCORING: Bill McClard (K) 71pts, Saint 48pts, Ferguson 38pts

1972 6-5

10 Southern Cal	31 WR Mike Reppond
24 Oklahoma State	23 WR Jim Hodge
21 Tulsa	20 T Mike Griffin
27 TCU	13 G Tom Reed
31 Baylor	20 C Stu Freeland
15 Texas	35 G Glen Lowe
42 N. Texas State	16 T Lee King / Ron Revard
7 Texas A&M	10 TE Steve Hedgepeth
20 Rice	23 QB Joe Ferguson
7 SMU	22 TB Dickey Morton / Jon Richardson
24 Texas Tech	14 FB Marsh White / Mike Saint
	DL Les Williams / Ivan Jordan
	DL Don Wunderly / Jon Rhiddlehoover
	DL Dave Reavis
	DL Doug Yoder / Roy Strain
	LB Danny Rhodes / Ed Rownd
	LB John Wheat / Jim Benton
	LB Scott Binnion / Billy Burns
	DB Mike Davis / Jim Irwin
	DB Louis Campbell / Freddie Douglas
	DB Tommy Harris
	DB Mark Hollingsworth / Clark Irwin

RUSHING: Morton 242/1188y, Richardson 97/313y, White 52/242y
PASSING: Ferguson 119-254/1484y, 9TD, 46.9%
RECEIVING: Reppond 36/475y, Hodge 27/449y,
 Hedgepeth 17/228y
SCORING: Mike Kirkland (K) 50pts, Richardson 42pts,
 Morton 36pts

1973 5-5-1

0 Southern Cal	17 WR Jack Ettinger
6 Oklahoma State	38 WB Kelvin O'Brien
21 Iowa State	19 T Gerald Skinner / Mike Parmer
13 TCU	5 G Russ Tribble
13 Baylor	7 C Stan Audas / Randy Drake
6 Texas	34 G R.C. Thielemann
20 Tulsa	6 T Lee King
14 Texas A&M	10 TE Nick Avlos / Matt Morrison
7 Rice	17 QB Mike Kirkland
7 SMU	7 TB Dickey Morton
17 Texas Tech	24 FB Alan Watson
	DL Ivan Jordan
	DL Brison Manor
	DL Harvey Hampton
	DL Jon Rhiddlehoover
	DL Dennis Winston / Danny Crawford
	LB Danny Rhodes
	LB Hal McAfee / Billy Burns
	DB Brad Thomas / Bruce Mitchell
	DB Rollen Smith
	DB Tommy Harris
	DB Bo Busby

RUSHING: Morton 226/1298y, Watson 69/296y, Kirkland 152/210y
PASSING: Kirkland 75-151/990y, 3TD, 50%
RECEIVING: Ettinger 28/411y, Douglas 14/158y, O'Brien 9/108y
SCORING: Mike Kirkland (QB-K) 34pts, Morton 30pts,
 Watson 18pts

1974 6-4-1

22 Southern Cal	7 WR Freddie Douglas
7 Oklahoma State	26 WB Barnabas White / Teddy Barnes
60 Tulsa	0 T Gerald Skinner
49 TCU	0 G Greg Koch
17 Baylor	21 C Richard LaFargue
7 Texas	38 G R.C. Thielemann
43 Colorado State	9 T Lee King
10 Texas A&M	20 TE Doug Yoder / Matt Morrison
25 Rice	6 QB Mark Miller / Scott Bull
24 SMU	24 RB Marsh White
21 Texas Tech	13 FB Ike Forte
	DL Ivan Jordan
	DL Brison Manor
	DL Mike Campbell
	DL Jon Rhiddlehoover
	DL Johnnie Meadors
	LB Dennis Winston
	LB Billy Burns / Hal McAfee
	DB Rollen Smith / Howard Sampson
	DB Brad Thomas
	DB Bo Busby / Tommy Harris
	DB Floyd Hogan

RUSHING: Forte 187/974y, White 76/354y, Miller 101/287y
PASSING: Miller 16-34/205y, 2TD, 47.1%
RECEIVING: Douglas 15/332y, Forte 6/21y, Morrison 5/76y
SCORING: Steve Little (K) 65pts, Forte 60pts, Miller 30pts

1975 10-2

35 Air Force	0 WR Freddie Douglas
13 Oklahoma State	20 WR Teddy Barnes
31 Tulsa	15 T Greg Koch
19 TCU	8 G R.C. Thielemann
41 Baylor	3 C Richard LaFargue
18 Texas	24 G Russ Tribble
31 Utah State	0 T Gerald Skinner
20 Rice	16 TE Doug Yoder
35 SMU	7 QB Scott Bull
31 Texas Tech	14 RB Jerry Eckwood / Rolland Fuchs
31 Texas A&M	6 FB Ike Forte
31 Georgia■	10 DL Jonnie Meadors / Ivan Jordan
	DL Mark Lewis
	DL Mike Campbell
	DL William Hampton
	DL Dennis Winston
	LB Curtis Townsend
	LB Hal McAfee / Reggie Freeman
	DB Brad Thomas
	DB Howard Sampson
	DB Bo Busby
	DB John Taylor / Tommy Harris

RUSHING: Forte 174/983y, Eckwood 104/792y, Fuchs 122/618y
PASSING: Bull 33-71/570y, 3TD, 46.5%
RECEIVING: Douglas 13/232y, Barnes 10/185y, Yoder 9/141y
SCORING: Steve Little (K) 65pts, Forte 60pts, Bull 50pts

1976 5-5-1

33 Utah State	16 WR Bruce Hay
16 Oklahoma State	10 WR Chris Warren
3 Tulsa	9 T Greg Koch
46 TCU	14 G Steve Heim
14 Houston	7 C R.C. Thielemann
41 Rice	16 G Leotis Harris
7 Baylor	7 T Gerald Skinner
10 Texas A&M	31 TE Charles Clay
31 SMU	35 QB Ron Calcagni / Houston Nutt
7 Texas Tech	30 RB Ben Cowins
12 Texas	29 FB Jerry Eckwood
	DL Johnnie Meadors
	DL Harvey Hampton
	DL Dale White
	DL Dan Hampton / Jimmy Walker
	DL Dennis Winston
	LB Larry Jackson / William Hampton
	LB Curtis Townsend
	DB Vaughn Lusby
	DB Patrick Martin
	DB Howard Sampson
	DB Bo Busby / Larry White

RUSHING: Cowins 183/1162y, Eckwood 122/494y,Forrest 77/354y
PASSING: Calcagni 17-57/366y, 2TD, 29.8%
RECEIVING: Clay 7/174y, Warren 7/113y, Hay 5/113y
SCORING: Steve Little (K) 56pts, Forrest 48pts, Cowins 42pts

1977 11-1

53 New Mexico St.	10 WR Robert Farrell / Bruce Hay
28 Oklahoma State	6 WR Danny Bobo
37 Tulsa	3 T Steve Heim
42 TCU	6 G Chuck Herman
9 Texas	13 C Rick Shumaker / Mike Burlingame
34 Houston	0 G Leotis Harris
30 Rice	7 T Greg Kolenda
35 Baylor	9 TE Charles Clay / Tim Adams
26 Texas A&M	20 QB Ron Calcagni
47 SMU	7 RB Ben Cowins
17 Texas Tech	14 FB Roland Sales / Micheal Forrest
31 Oklahoma■	6 DL Jim Howard / Marty Mitcham
	DL Jimmy Walker
	DL Reggie Freeman / Dale White
	DL Dan Hampton
	DL Jerry Saxton / Cornelius Smith
	LB Larry Jackson
	LB William Hampton
	DB Vaughn Lusby
	DB Patrick Martin
	DB Howard Sampson
	DB Brad Shoup

RUSHING: Cowins 220/1192y, Calcagni 125/546y, Sales 69/399y
PASSING: Calcagni 73-137/1147y, 10TD, 53.3%
RECEIVING: Bobo 22/454y, Farrell 13/241y, Hay 9/173y
SCORING: Steve Little (K) 94pts, Cowins 84pts, Bobo 36pts

1978 9-2-1

48 Vanderbilt	17 WR Robert Farrell
19 Oklahoma State	7 WR Donny Bobo
21 Tulsa	13 T Phil Moon
42 TCU	3 G George Stewart
21 Texas	28 C Rick Shumaker / Mike Burlingame
9 Houston	20 G Chuck Herman
37 Rice	7 T Greg Kolenda
27 Baylor	14 TE Charles Clay
26 Texas A&M	7 QB Ron Calcagni
27 SMU	14 RB Jerry Eckwood
49 Texas Tech	7 FB Ben Cowins
10 UCLA■	10 DL Jim Howard
	DL Jimmy Walker
	DL Dale White
	DL Dan Hampton
	DL Marty Mitcham
	LB Larry Jackson
	LB William Hampton
	DB Hugh Jernigan
	DB Vaughn Lusby
	DB Brad Shoup
	DB Kevin Evans

RUSHING: Cowins 188/1006y, Eckwood 110/596y,
Calcagni 153/448y
PASSING: Calcagni 62-103/807y, 4TD, 60.2%
RECEIVING: Farrell 13/229y, Eckwood 13/99y, Stiggers 10/218y
SCORING: Ish Ordonez (K) 78pts, Calcagni 66pts, Eckwood 42pts

1979 10-2

36 Colorado State	3 WR Robert Farrell
27 Oklahoma State	7 WR Gary Stiggers
33 Tulsa	8 T Phil Moon
16 TCU	13 G Chuck Herman
20 Texas Tech	6 C Mike Burlingame
17 Texas	14 G George Stewart
10 Houston	13 T Greg Kolenda
34 Rice	7 TE Steve Clyde / Darryl Mason
29 Baylor	20 QB Kevin Scanlon
22 Texas A&M	10 RB Gary Anderson / Darryl Bowles
31 SMU	7 FB Roland Sales
9 Alabama■	24 DL Jim Howard
	DL Billy Ray Smith / Danny Phillips
	DL Richard Richardson/Alfred Mohammed
	DL Jim Elliott
	DL Jeff Goff
	LB Mike Massey / Ozzie Riley
	LB Teddy Morris
	DB Hugh Jernigan / Kim Dameron
	DB Trent Bryant / Ron Matheney
	DB Randy Wessinger
	DB Kevin Evans

RUSHING: Sales 138/625y, Anderson 77/438y, Bowles 74/404y
PASSING: Scanlon 92-139/1212y, 9TD, 66.2%
RECEIVING: Stiggers 23/221y, Farrell 21/401y, Anderson 19/173y
SCORING: Ish Ordonez (K) 80pts, Scanlon 42pts, 3 tied w/ 18pts

1980 7-5

17 Texas	23 WR Bobby Duckworth
33 Oklahoma State	20 WR Gary Stiggers
13 Tulsa	10 T Phil Moon / Ronnie Trusty
44 TCU	7 G George Stewart / Daryal Pickett
27 Wichita State	7 C Keith Houfek
17 Houston	24 G Thurman Shaw / Jay Bequette
16 Rice	17 T Joe Shantz
15 Baylor	42 TE Darryl Mason
27 Texas A&M	24 QB Tom Jones
7 SMU	31 RB Gary Anderson
22 Texas Tech	16 FB James Tolbert / Darryl Bowles
34 Tulane■	15 DL Danny Phillips
	DL Billy Ray Smith
	DL Richard Richardson
	DL George Hall / Jim Elliott
	LB Jeff Goff / Bert Zinamon
	LB Teddy Morris
	LB Steve Douglas
	DB Trent Bryant / Kim Dameron
	DB Hugh Jernigan
	DB Keith Burns
	DB Kevin Evans

RUSHING: Tolbert 140/571y, Anderson 97/561y, Bowles 71/272y
PASSING: Jones 93-166/1161y, 6TD, 56%
RECEIVING: Anderson 23/153y, Duckworth 20/461y,
Stiggers 18/261y
SCORING: Ish Ordonez (K) 62pts, Bowles 36pts, Mason 20pts

1981 8-4

14 Tulsa	10 WR Gerald McMurray / Derek Holloway
38 Northwestern	7 WR John Mistler
27 Mississippi	13 T Ronnie Trusty
24 TCU	28 G Charles Ginn
26 Texas Tech	14 C Jay Bequette
42 Texas	11 G Steve Korte
17 Houston	20 T Alfred Mohammed
41 Rice	7 TE Darryl Mason
41 Baylor	39 QB Tom Jones / Brad Taylor
10 Texas A&M	7 RB Gary Anderson
18 SMU	18 TE Jessie Clark / Darryl Bowles
27 North Carolina■	31 DL Ron Faurot
	DL Richard Richardson
	DL Phil Boren
	DL Billy Ray Smith
	LB Teddy Morris
	LB Steve Douglas / Bert Zinamon
	LB Jeff Goff
	DB Danny Walters
	DB Kent Reber
	DB Keith Burns
	DB Kim Dameron

RUSHING: Anderson 121/616y, Clark 106/475y, Bowles 75/269y
PASSING: Jones 60-109/684y, 7TD, 55%
RECEIVING: Anderson 26/263y, Mason 23/285y,
Holloway 17/237y
SCORING: Bruce Lahay (K) 88pts, Clark 54pts, Anderson 24pts

1982 9-2-1

38 Tulsa	0 WR Derek Holloway
29 Navy	17 WR Kim Dameron / John Mistler
14 Mississippi	12 T Orson Weems / Marcus Elliott
35 TCU	0 G Charles Ginn
21 Texas Tech	3 C Jay Bequette
38 Houston	3 G Steve Korte
24 Rice	6 T Alfred Mohammed
17 Baylor	24 TE Eddie White
35 Texas A&M	0 QB Brad Taylor / Tom Jones
17 SMU	17 RB Gary Anderson (WR) / Daryl Bowles
7 Texas	33 FB Jessie Clark
28 Florida■	24 DL Billy Ray Smith
	DL Earl Buckingham
	DL Richard Richardson
	DL Ron Faurot
	LB Mark Lee
	LB Bert Zinamon
	LB Milton Fields
	DB Nathan Jones
	DB Danny Walters
	DB Keith Burns
	DB Greg Lasker

RUSHING: Bowles 155/619y, Clark 132/575y, Anderson 132/384y
PASSING: Taylor 59-141/1073y, 6TD, 41.8%
RECEIVING: Anderson 26/486y, Holloway 21/529y, Mistler 16/236y
SCORING: Anderson 54pts, Clark 42pts, Martin Smith (K) 31pts

1983 6-5

17 Tulsa	14 WR Keith Kidd / Donnie Centers
17 New Mexico	0 WR John Mistler
10 Mississippi	13 T Phil Boren
38 TCU	21 G Orson Weems
3 Texas	31 C Andy Upchurch
24 Houston	3 G Marcus Elliott
35 Rice	0 T Bob Wilcoxen
21 Baylor	24 TE Luther Franklin
23 Texas A&M	36 QB Brad Taylor
0 SMU	17 RB Bobby Joe Edmonds
16 Texas Tech	13 DL Carl Miller / Derrick Thomas
	DL Ron Faurot
	DL Bobby King
	DL Rodney Beachum
	DL Nick Miller
	LB Bert Zinamon
	LB Milton Fields
	LB Ravin Caldwell
	DB Kevin Wyatt
	DB Greg Gatson
	DB Greg Lasker
	DB Mark Lee

RUSHING: Thomas 117/432y, Miller 103/416y, Edmonds 69/212y
PASSING: Taylor 139-257/1837y, 9TD, 54.1%
RECEIVING: Mistler 33/401y, Edmonds 23/294y, Centers 22/206y
SCORING: Greg Horne (K) 58pts, Miller 32pts, Thomas 24pts

1984 7-4-1

14 Mississippi	14 WR James Shibest
18 Tulsa	9 WR Bobby Joe Edmonds (RB)
33 Navy	10 T Dave McGee
31 TCU	32 G Mike Ihrie
24 Texas Tech	0 C Andy Upchurch
18 Texas	24 G Marcus Elliott
17 Houston	3 T Dale Williams
28 Rice	6 TE Eddie White
14 Baylor	9 QB Brad Taylor
28 Texas A&M	0 RB Carl Miller
28 SMU	31 FB Marshall Foreman / Derrick Thomas
15 Auburn■	21 DL Ravin Caldwell
	DL Jeryl Jones
	DL Tony Cherico
	DL Rodney Beachum
	LB David Bazzel
	LB Nick Miller
	LB Mark Lee
	DB Kevin Wyatt
	DB Kevin Anderson / Greg Gatson
	DB Greg Lasker
	DB Nathan Jones

RUSHING: Foreman 183/804y, Thomas 83/401y, Edmonds 76/352y
PASSING: Taylor 82-147/1166y, 7TD, 55.8%
RECEIVING: Shibest 51/907y, Edmonds 31/284y, Miller 9/71y
SCORING: Greg Horne (K) 44pts, Foreman & Shibest 42pts

1985 10-2

24 Mississippi	19 WR Donnie Centers / James Shibest
24 Tulsa	0 WR Carl Miller
45 New Mexico St.	13 T Dave McGee
41 TCU	0 G Limbo Parks
30 Texas Tech	7 C Andy Upchurch
13 Texas	15 G Chris Bequette
57 Houston	27 T Dale Williams
30 Rice	15 TE Theo Young
20 Baylor	14 QB Greg Thomas / Mark Calcagni
6 Texas A&M	10 RB James Rouse / Bobby Joe Edmonds
15 SMU	9 FB Marshall Foreman / Derrick Thomas
18 Arizona State	17 DL Calvin Williams / Ravin Caldwell
	DL Rodney Beachum
	DL Tony Cherico
	DL Jeryl Jones
	LB David Dudley
	LB Nick Miller
	LB David Bazzel
	DB Kevin Wyatt
	DB Kevin Anderson
	DB Greg Lasker
	DB Odis Lloyd

RUSHING: Rouse 99/550y, Foreman 105/397y, Thomas 118/365y
PASSING: Thomas 33-72/554y, 4TD, 45.8%
RECEIVING: Shibest 20/446y, Centers 11/254y, Rouse 6/81y
SCORING: Rouse 56pts, Miller 36pts, Greg Horne (K) 35pts

1986 9-3

21 Mississippi	0 WR James Shibest / Donnie Centers
34 Tulsa	17 T David Smart
42 New Mexico St.	11 G Limbo Parks
34 TCU	17 C Bryan White
7 Texas Tech	17 G Freddie Childress
21 Texas	14 T Chris Bequette
30 Houston	13 TE Theo Young
45 Rice	14 QB Greg Thomas
14 Baylor	29 HB Joe Johnson
14 Texas A&M	10 HB Sammy Van Dyke
41 SMU	0 FB Derrick Thomas / Marshall Foreman
8 Oklahoma■	42 DL Wayne Martin
	DL Tony Cherico
	DL David Schell
	DL Carl Bradford / Kerry Owens
	LB David Dudley
	LB Albert Harris / Erik Whitted
	LB Rickey Williams
	DB Charles Washington
	DB Richard Brothers
	DB Steve Atwater
	DB Eric Bradford / Odis Lloyd

RUSHING: G. Thomas 141/461y, D. Thomas 104/456y, Foreman 96/387y
PASSING: G. Thomas 67-106/1032y, 6TD, 61.5%
RECEIVING: Shibest 22/473y, Johnson 11/85y, Centers 10/281y
SCORING: Kendall Trainor (K) 69pts, Johnson 66pts, G. Thomas 48pts

1987 9-4

31 Mississippi	10 WR Derek Russell
30 Tulsa	15 WR Joe Johnson
7 Miami	51 T Jim Mabry
20 TCU	10 G Freddie Childress
31 Texas Tech	0 C Bryan White
14 Texas	16 G John Stitten
21 Houston	17 T Chris Bequette
38 Rice	14 TE Billy Winston
10 Baylor	7 QB Greg Thomas / Quinn Grovey
0 Texas A&M	14 RB James Rouse / J.R. Brown
43 New Mexico	25 FB Barry Foster / Sammy Van Dyke
38 Hawaii	20 DL Wayne Martin
17 Georgia■	20 DL David Schell
	DL Tony Cherico
	DL Albert Harris
	LB Rickey Williams
	LB Erik Whitted
	LB Kerry Owens
	DB Anthoney Cooney
	DB Richard Brothers
	DB Steve Atwater
	DB Odis Lloyd

RUSHING: Rouse 182/1004y, Foster 89/484y, Johnson 98/411y
PASSING: Grovey 38-62/495y, 2TD, 61.3%
RECEIVING: Russell 16/297y, Rouse 12/121y, Brown 9/83y
SCORING: Rouse 102pts, Kendall Trainor (K) 71pts, Foster 24pts

1988 10-2

63 Pacific	14 WR Tim Horton / Derek Russell
30 Tulsa	26 WR Aaron Jackson
21 Mississippi	13 T Jim Mabry
53 TCU	10 G Freddie Childress
31 Texas Tech	10 C Elbert Crawford
27 Texas	24 G James Morris / Mark Henry
26 Houston	21 T Rick Apolskis
21 Rice	14 TE Billy Winston
33 Baylor	3 QB Quinn Grovey
25 Texas A&M	20 RB Joe Johnson / James Rouse
16 Miami	18 FB Barry Foster
3 UCLA■	17 DL Kerry Crawford / Chad Rolen
	DL Mike Shepherd
	DL Wayne Martin
	LB Odis Lloyd
	LB Kerry Owens
	LB LaSalle Harper
	LB Reggie Hall
	DB Anthoney Cooney
	DB Richard Brothers
	DB Steve Atwater
	DB Pat Williams

RUSHING: Foster 132/660y, Grovey 110/515y, Rouse 88/359y
PASSING: Grovey 62-98/966y, 4TD, 63.3%
RECEIVING: Horton 16/318y, Russell 15/396y, Jackson 12/189y
SCORING: Kendall Trainor (K) 102pts, Foster 66pts, Grovey 42pts

1989 10-2

26 Tulsa	7 WR Tim Horton
24 Mississippi	17 WR Derek Russell
39 UTEP	7 T Jim Mabry
41 TCU	19 G Todd Gifford
45 Texas Tech	13 C Elbert Crawford
20 Texas	24 G Mark Henry
45 Houston	39 T Rick Apolskis
38 Rice	17 TE Billy Winston
19 Baylor	10 QB Quinn Grovey
23 Texas A&M	22 RB James Rouse
38 SMU	24 FB Barry Foster
27 Tennessee■	31 DL Tony Ollison / Scott Long
	DL Chad Rolen
	DL Mike Shepherd
	LB Ken Benson
	LB Bubba Barrow / Mark Bell
	LB Mick Thomas
	LB Ty Mason
	DB Curtis Banks / Michael James
	DB Anthoney Cooney
	DB Aaron Jackson
	DB Pat Williams

RUSHING: Rouse 163/869y, Foster 154/833y, Grovey 120/565y
PASSING: Grovey 72-131/1149y, 5TD, 55%
RECEIVING: Horton 23/453y, Russell 17/284y, Winston 16/252y
SCORING: Todd Wright (K) 98pts, Grovey 48pts, Rouse 44pts

1990 3-8

28 Tulsa	3 WR Derek Russell
17 Mississippi	21 WR Tracy Caldwell
31 Colorado State	20 T Shon Flores
26 TCU	54 G Mark Henry (C) / Ray Straschinske
44 Texas Tech	49 C Eric Castillo
17 Texas	49 G Todd Gifford
28 Houston	62 T Pat Crocker / Chris Oliver
11 Rice	19 TE Lyndy Lindsey / Kirk Botkin
3 Baylor	34 QB Quinn Grovey
16 Texas A&M	20 RB Aaron Jackson / Ron Dickerson
42 SMU	29 FB E.D. Jackson
	DL Chad Rolen / Isaac Davis
	DL Owen Kelly / Henry Ford
	DL Scott Long
	DL Ken Benson
	LB Darwin Ireland
	LB Mick Thomas
	LB Ty Mason / Shannon Wright
	DB Michael James / Pat Burris
	DB Curtis Banks
	DB Richard David / Ben Floor
	DB Kirk Collins

RUSHING: E. Jackson 155/596y, A. Jackson 128/588y, Dickerson 83/362y
PASSING: Grovey 120-235/1886y, 18TD, 51.1%
RECEIVING: Russell 43/897y, Caldwell 25/429y, Lindsey 14/138y
SCORING: Todd Wright (K) 57pts, Russell 54pts, Grovey 34pts

1991 6-6

3 Miami	31 WR Tracy Caldwell
17 SMU	6 WR Ron Dickerson
9 SW Louisiana	7 T Cody Mosier
17 Mississippi	24 G Ray Straschinske
22 TCU	21 C Mark Henry
29 Houston	17 G Isaac Davis
14 Texas	13 T Chris Oliver
5 Baylor	9 TE Lyndy Lindsey / Kirk Botkin
21 Texas Tech	38 QB Jason Allen / Wade Hill / Gary Adams
3 Texas A&M	13 TB E.D. Jackson / Tony Jeffrey
20 Rice	0 FB Kerwin Price / Chris Kirby
15 Georgia■	24 DL Ray Lee Johnson / James Mallet
	DL MacKenzie Phillips / Scott Long
	DL Owen Kelly
	DL Henry Ford
	LB Darwin Ireland
	LB Mick Thomas / Ty Mason
	LB Tyrone Chatman
	DB Orlando Watters
	DB Michael James
	DB Kirk Collins
	DB Curtis Banks

RUSHING: Jackson 143/641y, Jeffrey 138/563y, Price 49/225y
PASSING: Allen 48-102/603y, 6TD, 47.1%
Hill 24-54/301y, 2TD, 44.4%
RECEIVING: Dickerson 25/372y, Caldwell 21/283y, Botkin 19/183y
SCORING: Todd Wright (K) 50pts, Dickerson 24pts, 3 tied w/ 12pts

1992 3-7-1

3 Citadel	10 WR Tracy Caldwell
45 South Carolina	7 WR Ron Dickerson
11 Alabama	38 T Chris Oliver
6 Memphis State	22 G Ray Straschinske
3 Georgia	27 C Earl Scott
25 Tennessee	24 G Isaac Davis
3 Mississippi	17 T Bryan Cornish
24 Auburn	24 TE Kirk Botkin
3 Mississippi St.	10 QB Barry Lunney, Jr. / Jason Allen
19 SMU	24 RB Oscar Malone / Jeff Savage
30 LSU	6 RB E.D. Jackson
	DL Ray Lee Johnson
	DL Scott Long / Vernon Wade
	DL Owen Kelly
	DL Henry Ford
	LB Tyrone Chatman
	LB Kevin Kempf
	LB Darwin Ireland
	DB Orlando Watters
	DB Dean Peevy
	DB Gary Adams
	DB Alfred Jackson

RUSHING: Jackson 118/466y, Malone 86/354y, Savage 61/259y
PASSING: Lunney 91-189/1015y, 4TD, 48.2%
Allen 55-108/511y, 2TD, 50.9%
RECEIVING: Botkin 33/257y, Dickerson 32/437y, Caldwell 30/381y
SCORING: Todd Wright (K) 62pts, Dickerson 26pts, Watters & Malone 18pts

1993 5-5-1

10 SMU	6 WR J.J. Meadors
18 South Carolina	17 WR Kotto Cotton / Tracy Caldwell
3 Alabama	43 T Chris Oliver
0 Memphis State	6 G Pat Baker
20 Georgia	10 C Don Struebing
14 Tennessee	28 G Isaac Davis
0 Mississippi	19 T Verl Mitchell
21 Auburn	31 TE Kirk Botkin
13 Mississippi St.	13 QB Barry Lunney, Jr.
24 Tulsa	11 TB Marius Johnson / Oscar Malone
42 LSU	24 FB Carlton Calvin / Oscar Gray
	DL Marcus Adair
	DL Vernon Wade
	DL Junior Soli
	DL Henry Ford
	LB Darwin Ireland
	LB Shannon Wright/Trent Knapp/MarkSmith
	LB Tyrone Chatman / Demetrius Smith
	DB Orlando Watters
	DB Dean Peevy / Tracy Cantlope
	DB Carl Kidd
	DB Alfred Jackson

RUSHING: Malone 89/555y, Johnson 116/554y, Calvin 76/350y
PASSING: Lunney 104-202/1241y, 6TD, 51.5%
RECEIVING: Meadors 28/429y, Botkin 23/257y, Gray 18/173y
SCORING: Malone 30pts, Johnson & Meadors 18pts

1994 4-7

34 SMU	14 WR Anthony Eubanks / Shannon Sidney
0 South Carolina	14 WR J.J. Meadors / James Perry
6 Alabama	13 T Carlos Showers / Scott Rivers
15 Memphis	16 G Tony Nagy / Tony Swartz
42 Vanderbilt	6 C Earl Scott
21 Tennessee	38 G Pat Baker
31 Mississippi	7 T Verl Mitchell
14 Auburn	31 TE Carl Johnson / Kevin Hile
7 Mississippi St.	17 QB Barry Lunney, Jr.
30 N. Illinois	27 TB Oscar Malone /M. Johnson /Madre Hill
12 LSU	30 FB Carlton Calvin / Oscar Gray
	DL Marcus Adair
	DL Geno Bell/Vernon Wade/Curtis Thomas
	DL Junior Soli
	DL Steven Conley / Waylon Wishon
	LB Willie Johnson / Vincent Bradford
	LB Trent Knapp / Don Bray
	LB Mark Smith
	DB Dean Peevy
	DB Tracy Cantlope / Spencer Brown
	DB Del Delco
	DB Carl Kidd / Mike Nunnerley

RUSHING: Malone 99/597y, Hill 74/351y, Johnson 76/290y
PASSING: Lunney 101-183/1345y, 11TD, 55.2%
RECEIVING: Meadors 43/613y, Perry 16/175y, Malone 16/106y
SCORING: Lance Ellison (K) 42pts, Meadors 30pts, Malone & Hill 24pts

1995 8-5

14 SMU	17 WR Anthony Eubanks
51 South Carolina	21 WR J.J. Meadors
20 Alabama	19 T Carlos Showers
27 Memphis	20 G Russ Brown
35 Vanderbilt	7 C Earl Scott
31 Tennessee	49 G Verl Mitchell
13 Mississippi	6 T Winston Alderson
30 Auburn	28 TE Mark Baker / Al Heringer
26 Mississippi St.	21 QB Barry Lunney, Jr.
24 SW Louisiana	13 TB Madre Hill
0 LSU	28 FB/WR Tyrone Henry / Anthony Lucas
3 Florida□	34 DL Marcus Adair
10 North Carolina■	20 DL Geno Bell
	DL Junior Soli
	DL David Sanders / Ken Anderson
	DL Steven Conley
	LB Vincent Bradford / Anthony Hicks
	LB Mark Smith
	DB Spencer Brown
	DB Tracy Cantlope
	DB Del Delco / Philip Hayes
	DB Mike Nunnerley

RUSHING: Hill 307/1387y, Marius Johnson (TB) 60/229y
PASSING: Lunney 180-292/2181y, 12TD, 61.6%
RECEIVING: Meadors 62/584y, Eubanks 43/596y, Lucas 27/526y
SCORING: Hill 96pts, Todd Latourette (K) 74pts, Eubanks & Lucas 24pts

1996 4-7

10 SMU	17 WR Michael Snowden / Emanuel Smith
7 Alabama	17 WR Anthony Eubanks
38 NE Louisiana	21 T Scott Rivers / Carlos Showers
7 Florida	42 G Russ Brown
38 Louisiana Tech	21 C Grant Garrett
17 South Carolina	23 G Brandon Burlsworth
7 Auburn	28 T Winston Alderson
13 Mississippi	7 TE Mark Baker / Joe Dean Davenport
14 Tennessee	55 QB Pete Burks
16 Mississippi St.	13 TB Oscar Malone / Chrys Chukwuma
7 LSU	17 FB Jesse Cornelius
	DL Ken Anderson / D.J. Cooper
	DL Melvin Bradley
	DL Ryan Hale / David Sanders
	LB Justin Brown / Vincent Bradford
	LB Mark Smith
	LB Anthony Hicks
	LB C.J. McLain / Norman Nero
	DB Marcus Campbell
	DB Zac Painter
	DB Kenoy Kennedy / Chris Akins
	DB Philip Hayes / Jeromy Flowers

RUSHING: Malone 197/814y, Chukwuma 139/590y
PASSING: Burks 115-224/1390y, 6TD, 51.3%
RECEIVING: Eubanks 51/809y, Smith 16/152y, Snowden 11/212y
SCORING: Todd Latourette (K) 45pts, Eubanks & Chukwuma 30pts

1997 4-7

28 NE Louisiana	16 WR Anthony Eubanks / Emanuel Smith
9 SMU	31 WR Anthony Lucas
17 Alabama	16 T Chad Abernathy
17 Louisiana Tech	13 G Russ Brown
7 Florida	56 C Grant Garrett
13 South Carolina	39 G Brandon Burlsworth
21 Auburn	28 T Bobbie Williams
9 Mississippi	19 TE J.D. Davenport / Al Heringer
22 Tennessee	30 QB Clint Stoerner
17 Mississippi St.	7 TB Rod Stinson / Eric Branch
21 LSU	31 FB Nathan Norman
	DL Ken Anderson / Geno Bell
	DL Melvin Bradley / D.J. Cooper
	DL Ryan Hale / David Sanders
	LB Randy Garner / J.J. Jones
	LB Jamel Harris / Quentin Caver
	LB Harry Wilson / Norman Nero
	LB Bryan Smith / C.J. McLain
	DB Marcus Campbell / David Barrett
	DB Zac Painter / Ontraia Moss
	DB Kenoy Kennedy / Jeremiah Harper
	DB Jeromy Flowers

RUSHING: Stinson 111/413y, Branch 91/251y, Chrys Chukwuma (TB) 35/186y
PASSING: Stoerner 173-357/2347y, 12TD, 48.5%
RECEIVING: Eubanks 51/870y, Smith 28/380y, Lucas 27/495y
SCORING: Todd Latourette (K) 41pts, Eubanks 30pts, Lucas 24pts

1998 9-3

38 La.-Lafayette	17 WR Anthony Lucas
44 SMU	17 WR Michael Williams / Emanuel Smith
42 Alabama	6 T Chad Abernathy
27 Kentucky	20 G Russ Brown
23 Memphis	9 C Grant Garrett
41 South Carolina	28 G Brandon Burlsworth
24 Auburn	21 T Bobbie Williams
34 Mississippi	0 TE Joe Dean Davenport
24 Tennessee	28 QB Clint Stoerner
21 Mississippi St.	22 TB Chrys Chukwuma / Madre Hill
41 LSU	14 FB Nathan Norman
31 Michigan■	45 DL Ryan Hale
	DL Melvin Bradley / Chris Brooks
	DL Carlos Hall / D.J. Cooper
	LB C.J. McClain
	LB Jamel Harris
	LB Jeromy Flowers / Harry Wilson
	LB Randy Garner / Quentin Caver
	DB David Barrett
	DB Orlando Green / Rossi Morreale
	DB Kenoy Kennedy
	DB Zac Painter

RUSHING: Chukwuma 149/870y
PASSING: Stoerner 167-312/2629y, 26TD, 53.5%
RECEIVING: Williams 44/560y, Lucas 43/1004y,
SCORING: Todd Latourette (K) 92pts, Lucas 60pts

1999 8-4

26 SMU	0 WR Anthony Lucas / Boo Williams
44 La.-Monroe	6 WR Michael Williams / Emanuel Smith
28 Alabama	35 T Shannon Money
20 Kentucky	31 G La'Zerius White
58 M. Tennessee	6 C Josh Melton
48 South Carolina	14 G Kenny Sandlin (C)/Jeremiah Washburn
34 Auburn	10 T Bobbie Williams
16 Mississippi	38 TE J.D. Davenport
28 Tennessee	24 QB Clint Stoerner
14 Mississippi St.	9 TB Chrys Chukwuma / Cedric Cobbs
10 LSU	35 FB Marvin Caston / Nathan Norman
27 Texas■	6 DL Randy Garner
	DL Curt Davis
	DL D.J. Cooper
	DL Carlos Hall / Sacha Lancaster
	LB Quentin Caver
	LB Jamel Harris
	LB Jeromy Flowers / Delancey Kent
	DB David Barrett
	DB Harold Harris / Orlando Green
	DB Kenoy Kennedy
	DB Ontraia Moss

RUSHING: Cobbs 116/668y, Chukwuma 127/522y, Mike Jenkins (TB) 33/224y
PASSING: Stoerner 177-317/2253y, 19TD, 55.8%
RECEIVING: Lucas 37/822y, Smith 32/331y, B. Williams 28/384y
SCORING: Tony Dodson (K) 67pts, Chukwuma 48pts, 3 tied w/30pts

2000 6-6

38 SW Missouri St.	0 WR Boo Williams / Sparky Hamilton
38 Boise State	31 WR Michael Snowden / Richard Smith
28 Alabama	21 T Shannon Money
7 Georgia	38 G La'Zerius White
52 La.-Monroe	6 C Josh Melton
7 South Carolina	27 G Kenny Sandlin
19 Auburn	21 T Gary Hobbs / Nathan Ball (TE)
24 Mississippi	38 TE Marcellus Poydras / Tim Craig
20 Tennessee	63 QB Robby Hampton / Zak Clark
17 Mississippi St.	10 TB Fred Talley/Brandon Holmes/C. Cobbs
14 LSU	3 FB Rod Stinson / Adam Daily
14 UNLV■	31 DL Randy Garner / Raymond House
	DL Sacha Lancaster / Jermaine Petty
	DL Curt Davis / Jermaine Brooks
	DL Carlos Hall
	LB J.J. Jones
	LB Quinton Caver
	LB Jeremiah Harper / Tony Bua
	DB D'Andre Berry
	DB Eddie Jackson / Orlando Green
	DB Ken Hamlin
	DB Corey G. Harris / Derrick Johnson

RUSHING: Talley 137/768y, Holmes 111/468y, Cobbs 70/291y
PASSING: Hampton 145-261/1548y, 13TD, 55.6%
RECEIVING: Williams 52/739y, Smith 33/320y, Snowden 18/156y
SCORING: Williams 44pts, Holmes 42pts, Brennan O'Donohoe (K) 32pts

2001 7-5

14 UNLV	10 WR George Wilson
3 Tennessee	13 WR Richard Smith / Gerald Howard
10 Alabama	31 T Shannon Money
23 Georgia	34 G La'Zerius White
42 Weber State	19 C Kenny Sandlin (G) / Josh Melton
10 South Carolina	7 G Mark Bokermann (T)
42 Auburn	17 T Shawn Andrews
58 Mississippi	56 TE Nathan Ball/M. Poydras/Jason Peters
27 Central Florida	20 QB Zak Clark /Ryan Sorahan /Matt Jones
24 Mississippi St.	21 TB Fred Talley / B. Holmes /Cedric Cobbs
38 LSU	41 FB Sacha Lancaster (DL) / Mark Pierce
3 Oklahoma■	10 DL Carlos Hall
	DL Jermaine Brooks
	DL Curt Davis
	DL Raymond House
	LB Caleb Miller
	LB Jermaine Petty
	LB Tony Bua
	DB Lawrence Richardson
	DB Eddie Jackson / Ahmad Carroll
	DB Corey G. Harris
	DB Ken Hamlin

RUSHING: Talley 164/774y, Jones 74/592y, Cobbs 102/340y
PASSING: Clark 88-179/1000y, 6TD, 49.2%, Sorahan 29-51/274y, 0TD, 56.9%
RECEIVING: Wilson 40/568y, Smith 38/383y, Pierce 8/75y
SCORING: Brennan O'Donohoe (K) 65pts, Cobbs 42pts, Jones & Smith 30pts

2002 9-5

41 Boise State	14 WR George Wilson
42 South Florida	3 WR Richard Smith/DeCori Birmingham
12 Alabama	30 T Bo Lacy
38 Tennessee	41 G Nathan Ball / Scott Davenport
38 Auburn	17 C Dan Doughty / Josh Melton
17 Kentucky	29 G Mark Bokermann / Jerry Reith
48 Mississippi	28 T Shawn Andrews
23 Troy State	0 TE Jason Peters / Marcellus Poydras
23 South Carolina	0 QB Matt Jones
24 La.-Lafayette	17 TB Fred Talley/Cedric Cobbs/D. Howard
26 Mississippi St.	19 FB Mark Pierce
21 LSU	20 DL Raymond House / Gavin Walls
3 Georgia□	30 DL Pervis Osborne
14 Minnesota■	29 DL Arrion Dixon / Jermaine Brooks
	DL Elliott Harris / Justin Scott
	LB Caleb Miller
	LB Clarke Moore / Jeb Huckeba
	LB Tony Bua / Jimarr Gallon
	DB Lawrence Richardson / Eddie Jackson
	DB Ahmad Carroll
	DB Ken Hamlin
	DB Jimmy Beasley

RUSHING: Talley 197/1119y, Jones 129/614y, Howard 131/595y
PASSING: Jones 122-234/1592y, 16TD, 52.1%
RECEIVING: Wilson 49/626y, Smith 34/582y, Birmingham 17/184y
SCORING: David Carlton (K) 64pts, Pierce 48pts, Wilson &
Howard 42pts

2003 9-4

45 Tulsa	13 WR George Wilson
38 Texas	28 WR Richard Smith / Stephen Harris
31 North Texas	7 T Bo Lacy / Caleb Perry
34 Alabama	31 G Jerry Reith
3 Auburn	10 C Dan Doughty
28 Florida	33 G Mark Bokermann
7 Mississippi	19 T Shawn Andrews
71 Kentucky	63 TE Jason Peters / Jared Hicks
28 South Carolina	6 QB Matt Jones
48 New Mexico St.	20 TB Cedric Cobbs/DeCori Birmingham (WR)
52 Mississippi St.	6 FB Mark Pierce
24 LSU	55 DL Jeb Huckeba / Brandon Holmes (TB)
27 Missouri■	14 DL Arrion Dixon
	DL Scott Davenport / Jeremy Harrell
	DL Justin Scott / Elliott Harris
	LB Jimarr Gallon / Desmond Sims
	LB Sam Olajubutu / Clarke Moore
	LB Caleb Miller
	DB Lawrence Richardson / Marvin Jackson
	DB Ahmad Carroll / Eddie Jackson
	DB Tony Bua
	DB Jimmy Beasley

RUSHING: Cobbs 227/1320y, Jones 96/707y,
Birmingham 88/549y
PASSING: Jones 131-229/1891y, 18TD, 57.2%
RECEIVING: Wilson 50/900y, Smith 30/573y, Peters 21/218y
SCORING: Chris Balseiro (K) 73pts, Cobbs 60pts, Jones 48pts

2004 5-6

63 New Mexico St.	13 WR Marcus Monk / Cedric Washington
20 Texas	22 WR Steven Harris / Carlos Ousley
49 La.-Monroe	20 T Tony Ugoh / Matt Gilbow
27 Alabama	10 G Stephen Parker
30 Florida	45 C Kyle Roper
20 Auburn	38 G Gene Perry
14 Georgia	20 T Robert Felton / Zac Tubbs
32 South Carolina	35 TE Jared Hicks / Mason Templeton
35 Mississippi	3 QB Matt Jones
24 Mississippi St.	21 TB DeCori Birmingham / De'Arrius Howard
14 LSU	43 FB Brandon Kennedy / Peyton Hillis
	DL Marcus Harrison / Elliott Harris
	DL Arrion Dixon / Keith Jackson
	DL Jeremy Harrell / Titus Peebles
	DL Jeb Huckeba
	LB John Jackson / Marcus Whitmore
	LB Sam Olajubutu / Clarke Moore
	LB Pierre Brown / Desmond Sims
	DB Michael Coe / Chris Houston
	DB Darius Vinnett / John Johnson
	DB Vickiel Vaughn
	DB Lerinezo Robinson / Randy Kelly

RUSHING: Jones 83/622y, Howard 124/529y,
Birmingham 111/456y
PASSING: Jones 151-264/2073y, 15TD, 57.2%
RECEIVING: Harris 37/617y, Monk 37/569y, Washington 17/284y
SCORING: Chris Balseiro (K) 52pts, Hillis 48pts, Monk 38pts

2005 4-7

49 Missouri State	17 WR Marcus Monk
24 Vanderbilt	28 WR Cedric Washington
17 Southern Cal	70 T Tony Ugoh
13 Alabama	24 G Stephen Parker / Chase Pressley
44 La-Monroe	15 C Kyle Roper (G)
17 Auburn	34 G Jonathan Luigs (C)/Jeremy Harrell
20 Georgia	23 T Robert Felton
10 South Carolina	14 TE Wes Murphy / Mason Templeton
28 Mississippi	17 QB Robert Johnson / Casey Dick
44 Mississippi St.	10 TB Darren McFadden / Felix Jones
17 LSU	19 FB Peyton Hillis / Brandon Kennedy
	DL Desmond Sims
	DL Marcus Harrison
	DL Keith Jackson
	DL Anthony Brown/Jamaal Anderson
	LB Sam Olajubutu
	LB Pierre Brown / Clarke Moore
	LB Freddie Fairchild / Weston Dacus
	DB Michael Coe / John Johnson
	DB Chris Houston / Darius Vinnett
	DB Vickiel Vaughn
	DB Randy Kelly/Matterral Richardson

RUSHING: McFadden 176/1113y, Jones 99/626y,
De'Arrius Howard (TB) 63/328y
PASSING: Johnson 89-158/876y, 5TD, 56.3%
Dick 53-99/584y, 7TD, 53.5%
RECEIVING: Hillis 38/402y, Monk 35/476y, Washington 27/365y
SCORING: Chris Balseiro (K) 70pts, McFadden 68pts, Monk
& Hillis 42pts

2006 10-4

14 Southern Cal	50 WR Marcus Monk
20 Utah State	0 WR Darien Williams/Felix Jones (TB)
21 Vanderbilt	19 T Tony Ugoh
24 Alabama	23 G Stephen Parker
27 Auburn	10 C Jonathan Luigs
63 SE Missouri	9 G Robert Felton
38 Mississippi	3 T Zac Tubbs
44 La-Monroe	10 TE Wes Murphy / Andrew Davie
26 South Carolina	20 QB Casey Dick / Mitch Mustain
31 Tennessee	14 TB Darren McFadden
28 Mississippi St.	14 FB Peyton Hillis / Farod Jackson
26 LSU	31 DL Jamaal Anderson
28 Florida□	38 DL Ernest Mitchell / Marcus Harrison
14 Wisconsin■	17 DL Keith Jackson / Cord Gray
	DL Antwain Robinson
	LB Sam Olajubutu
	LB Weston Dacus / Desmond Sims
	LB/DB Matt Hewitt/ Kevin Woods
	DB Chris Houston / John Johnson
	DB Matterral Richardson
	DB Michael Grant / Darius Vinnett
	DB Randy Kelly

RUSHING: McFadden 284/1647y, Jones 154/1168y
Michael Smith (TB) 35/247y
PASSING: Dick 65-132/991y, 9TD, 49.2%
Mustain 69-132/894y, 10TD, 52.3%
RECEIVING: Monk 50/962y, Williams 19/235y Hillis 19/159y,
SCORING: McFadden 98pts, Monk 66pts, Jeremy Davis (K) 64pts

2007 8-5

46 Troy	26 WR Marcus Monk / London Crawford
38 Alabama	41 WR Robert Johnson / Lucas Miller
29 Kentucky	42 T Jose Valdez
66 North Texas	7 G Mitch Petrus
34 Chattanooga	15 C Jonathan Luigs
7 Auburn	9 G Robert Felton (T)/DeMarcus Love
44 Mississippi	8 T Nate Garner
58 Fla. International	10 TE Andrew Davie
48 South Carolina	36 QB Casey Dick
13 Tennessee	34 RB Darren McFadden / Felix Jones (WR)
45 Mississippi St.	31 FB Peyton Hillis
50 LSU	48 DL Malcolm Sheppard / Chris Wade
7 Missouri■	38 DL Ernest Mitchell
	DL Marcus Harrison / Fred Bledsoe
	DL Adrian Davis / Antwain Robinson
	LB Weston Dacus / Ryan Powers
	LB Freddie Fairchild / Wendel Davis
	LB/DB Elston Forte / Jerell Norton
	DB Michael Grant
	DB Matterral Richardson / Jamar Love
	DB Kevin Woods / Rashaad Johnson
	DB Matt Hewitt

RUSHING: McFadden 325/1830y, Jones 133/1162y, Hillis 62/347y
PASSING: Dick 150-262/1695y, 18TD, 57.3%
McFadden 6-11/123y, 4TD, 54.5%
RECEIVING: Hillis 49/537y, McFadden 21/164y, Jones 16/176y
SCORING: Alex Tejada (K) 109pts, McFadden 102pts, Jones 80pts

2008 5-7

28 W. Illinois	24 WR Lucas Miller / Andrew Davie
28 La.-Monroe	40 WR London Crawford
14 Alabama	49 WR Jarius Wright / Joe Adams
10 Texas	52 T Ray Dominguez / Michael Aguirre
7 Florida	38 G Wade Grayson
25 Auburn	22 C Jonathan Luigs
20 Kentucky	21 G DeMarcus Love / Grant Cook
21 Mississippi	23 T Jose Valdez
30 Tulsa	23 TE D.J. Williams
21 South Carolina	34 QB Casey Dick / Nathan Dick
28 Mississippi State	31 RB Michael Smith / Dennis Johnson
31 LSU	30 DL Jake Bequette / Antwain Robinson
	DL Zach Stadther / Ernest Mitchell
	DL Malcolm Sheppard
	DL Adrian Davis / Damario Ambrose
	LB Freddy Burton / Jerico Nelson
	LB Jerry Franklin
	LB Wendel Davis / Elston Forte
	DB Ramon Broadway / Jamar Love
	DB Isaac Madison
	DB Elton Ford / Rashaad Johnson
	DB Dallas Washington / Matt Harris

RUSHING: Smith 207/1072y, Johnson 36/184y
PASSING: C. Dick 205-357/2586y, 13TD, 57.4%
N. Dick 36-62/454y, 4TD, 58.1%
RECEIVING: Williams 61/723y, Smith 32/298y, Adams 31/377y
SCORING: Smith 60pts, Alex Tejada (K) 32pts,
Shay Haddock (K) 25pts

2009 8-5

48 Missouri State	10 WR Jarius Wright / Cobi Hamilton
41 Georgia	52 WR Greg Childs / London Crawford
7 Alabama	35 WR Joe Adams / Lucas Miller
47 Texas A&M	19 T Ray Dominguez / Grant Freeman
44 Auburn	23 G Wade Grayson / Grant Cook
20 Florida	23 C Seth Oxner
17 Mississippi	30 G Mitch Petrus
63 E. Michigan	27 T DeMarcus Love
33 South Carolina	16 TE/FB D.J. Williams / Van Stumon
56 Troy	20 QB Ryan Mallett
42 Mississippi St.	21 RB Michael Smith / Broderick Green
30 LSU	33 DL Jake Bequette / Demario Ambrose
20 East Carolina■	17 DL Zach Stadther / DeQuinta Jones
	DL Malcolm Sheppard
	DL Adrian Davis / Tevarius Wright
	LB Jerry Franklin
	LB Wendel Davis
	LB Freddy Burton / Jerico Nelson
	DB Andru Stewart / Ramon Broadway
	DB Rudell Crim / David Gordon
	DB Elton Ford / Tramain Thomas
	DB Matt Harris / Anthony Leon

RUSHING: Green 104/442y, Smith 71/396y,
Dennis Johnson (RB) 57/342y, Ronnie Wingo (RB) 49/319y
PASSING: Mallett 225-403/3624y, 30TD, 55.8%
RECEIVING: Childs 48/894y, Wright 41/681y, Williams 32/411y,
Adams 29/568y
SCORING: Alex Tejada (K) 106pts, Green 72pts, Adams 48pts

2010 10-3

44 Tennessee Tech	3 WR Jarius Wright
31 La.-Monroe	7 WR Greg Childs / Cobi Hamilton
31 Georgia	24 WR/TE Joe Adams / Chris Gragg
20 Alabama	24 T DeMarcus Love
24 Texas A&M	17 G Wade Grayson
43 Auburn	65 C Travis Swanson
38 Mississippi	24 G Alvin Bailey
49 Vanderbilt	14 T Ray Dominguez
41 South Carolina	20 TE D.J. Williams / Ben Cleveland
59 Texas-El Paso	21 QB Ryan Mallett / Tyler Wilson
38 Mississippi State	31 RB Knile Davis/Ronnie Wingo/B. Green
31 LSU	23 DL Jake Bequette / Tenarius Wright
26 Ohio State■	31 DL Alfred Davis / Byran Jones
	DL DeQuinta Jones / Lavunce Askew
	DL Demario Ambrose
	LB Anthony Leon / Terrell Williams
	LB Jerry Franklin
	LB Jerico Nelson
	DB R. Broadway/ Greg Gatson/ F. Burton
	DB Isaac Madison / Darius Winston
	DB Rudell Crim / Elton Ford
	DB Tramain Thomas / Ross Rasner

RUSHING: Davis 204/1322y, Green 104/365y, Wingo 41/253y
PASSING: Mallett 266-411/3869y, 32TD, 64.7%
Wilson 34-51/453y, 4TD, 66.7%
RECEIVING: Williams 54/627y, Adams 50/813y, Childs 46/659y,
Wright 42/788y
SCORING: Zach Hooker (K) 104pts, Davis 84pts, Adams 42pts

AUBURN

Auburn University (Founded 1856)
Auburn, Alabama
Nicknames: Tigers, and formerly Plainsmen
Colors: Burnt Orange, Navy Blue
Stadium: Jordan-Hare Stadium (1939) 87,451
Affiliation: Charter Member, Southeastern Conference
(1933-present)

CAREER RUSHING YARDS	Attempts	Yards
Bo Jackson (1982-85)	650	4303
Carnell Williams (2001-04)	741	3831
James Brooks (1977-80)	621	3523
Joe Cribbs (1976-79)	657	3368
Ben Tate (2006-09)	678	3321
Stephen Davis (1993-95)	488	2811
Brent Fullwood (1983-86)	390	2789
Ronnie Brown (2000-04)	513	2707
Stacy Danley (1987-90)	526	2427
James Joseph (1986-90)	452	2264

CAREER PASSING YARDS	Comp.-Att.	Yards
Stan White (1990-93)	659-1231	8016
Jason Campbell (2001-04)	552- 854	7299
Brandon Cox (2004-07)	550- 927	6959
Pat Sullivan (1969-71)	452- 819	6284
Dameyune Craig (1994-97)	427- 782	6026
Patrick Nix (1992-95)	386- 656	4957
Reggie Slack (1986-89)	346- 585	4697
Ben Leard (1997-2000)	359- 592	4289
Jeff Burger (1984-87)	331- 538	4082
Chris Todd (2008-09)	284- 484	3515

CAREER RECEIVING YARDS	Catches	Yards
Terry Beasley (1969-71)	141	2507
Tyrone Goodson (1993-97)	136	2283
Karsten Bailey (1995-98)	150	2174
Courtney Taylor (2003-06)	153	2098
Frank Sanders (1991-94)	121	1998
Darvin Adams (2008-10)	115	1978
Freddy Weygand (1984-88)	99	1946
Lawyer Tillman (1985-88)	93	1808
Rodgeriqus Smith (2005-08)	114	1598
Byron Franklin (1977-80)	74	1573

SEASON RUSHING YARDS	Attempts	Yards
Bo Jackson (1985)	278	1786
Rudi Johnson (2000)	324	1567
Cam Newton (2010)	264	1473
Brent Fullwood (1986)	167	1391
Ben Tate (2009)	263	1362

SEASON PASSING YARDS	Comp.-Att.	Yards
Dameyune Craig (1997)	216-403	3277
Cam Newton (2010)	185-280	2854
Jason Campbell (2004)	188-270	2700
Chris Todd (2009)	198-328	2612
Pat Sullivan (1970)	167-281	2586

SEASON RECEIVING YARDS	Catches	Yards
Ronney Daniels (1999)	56	1068
Terry Beasley (1970)	52	1051
Darvin Adams (2009)	60	997
Darvin Adams (2010)	52	963
Frank Sanders (1994)	58	910

GAME RUSHING YARDS	Attempts	Yards
Curtis Kuykendall (1946 vs. Miami)	33	307
Bo Jackson (1985 vs. SW Louisiana)	23	290
Bo Jackson (1983 vs. Alabama)	20	256

GAME PASSING YARDS	Comp.-Att.	Yards
Ben Leard (1999 vs. Georgia)	24-32	416
Ben Leard (2001 vs. Michigan)	28-37	394
Dameyune Craig (1996 vs. Miss. State)	28-41	394

GAME RECEIVING YARDS	Catches	Yards
Alexander Wright (1989 vs. Pacific)	5	263
Ronney Daniels (1999 vs. Georgia)	9	249
Willie Gosha (1995 vs. Arkansas)	17	222

GREATEST COACH:

When Ralph "Shug" Jordan took over in 1951 as head coach at "The Loveliest Village on the Plain," the Auburn Tigers recently had suffered through 2-7, 1-8-1, 2-4-3, and 0-10 seasons. Auburn went 5-5- and 2-8 in his first two years. But, in 1953, the Tigers snapped Mississippi's 13-game winning streak in the Southeastern Conference early in the year and posted a 7-2-1 record.

Auburn headed to Jacksonville for the first of three straight Gator Bowls, the first post-season outing since the 1937 season. Jordan would take the Tigers to seven straight bowls starting in 1968.

In his 25 seasons at Auburn, Jordan won the 1957 national championship and the SEC title that same year with a 10-0 mark. He had only a 5-7 bowl record and finished only 9-16 against arch-rival Alabama. But, Jordan's record against Alabama should carry the consideration that for 18 years he went up against perhaps football's best-ever coach in Bear Bryant. His mark against Bryant was 5-13 for a .2778 winning percentage. That percentage looks poor until one realizes it is almost twice as good as what every other coach achieved against Bryant at Alabama, which was a .1394 winning percentage.

AUBURN'S 55 GREATEST SINCE 1953

OFFENSE

WIDE RECEIVER: Terry Beasley, Tyrone Goodson, Frank Sanders, Courtney Taylor, Lawyer Tillman
TIGHT END: Jimmy Phillips, Walter Reeves
TACKLE: Wayne Gandy, Marcus McNeill, Victor Riley, Stacy Searels, Steve Wallace
GUARD: Ed King, Keith Uecker
CENTER: Tom Banks, Ben Tamburello
QUARTERBACK: Jason Campbell, Cam Newton, Pat Sullivan
RUNNING BACK: James Brooks, Ronnie Brown, Brent Fullwood, Bo Jackson, Carnell Williams
FULLBACK: William Andrews, Joe Childress

DEFENSE

END: Jerry Elliott, Ron Stallworth, Jerry Wilson
TACKLE: Nick Fairley, Donnie Humphrey, Ken Rice, Tracy Rocker, Frank Warren
LINEBACKER: Aundray Bruce, Ken Bernich, Gregg Carr, Bill Cody, Karlos Dansby, Zeke Smith, Takeo Spikes
CORNERBACK: Tucker Frederickson, Carlos Rogers, Chris Shelling
SAFETY: Bob Harris, Buddy McClinton, Brian Robinson, Larry Willingham

SPECIAL TEAMS

RETURN SPECIALISTS: Thomas Bailey, Mike Fuller
PLACE KICKER: Damon Duval
PUNTER: Terry Daniel

MULTIPLE POSITIONS

CENTER-OFFENSIVE TACKLE: Bob Meeks

TWO-WAY PLAYERS

CENTER-LINEBACKER: Jackie Burkett
HALFBACK-CORNERBACK-PUNTER: Tommy Lorino

PERFORMANCE FORMULA:
AUBURN'S 10 BEST SEASONS

2010	1.7989	1 of 71
2004	1.7923	2 of 72
1957	1.7229	1 of 69
1983	1.7225	2 of 70
1993	1.6674	3 of 70
1972	1.6244	6 of 70
1970	1.5917	7 of 70
1988	1.5811	8 of 69
1987	1.5752	7 of 69
1958	1.5666	6 of 70

AUBURN TIGERS

Year	W-L-T	AP Poll	Conference Standing	Toughest Regular Season Opponents	Coach (Record at School)	Bowl Games			
1953	7-3-1	17	5	Mississippi 7-2-1, Georgia Tech 8-2-1-, Alabama 6-2-3	Ralph "Shug" Jordan	Gator	13	Texas Tech	35
1954	8-3	13	6t	Kentucky 7-3, Georgia Tech 7-3, Miami 8-1, Georgia 6-3-1	Shug Jordan	Gator	33	Baylor	13
1955	8-2-1	8	2	Kentucky 6-3-1, Georgia Tech 8-1-1, Clemson 7-3	Shug Jordan	Gator	13	Vanderbilt	25
1956	7-3		5	Tennessee 10-0, Georgia Tech 9-1, Houston 7-2-1, Florida 6-3-1	Shug Jordan				
1957	10-0	1	1	Tennessee 7-3, Florida 6-2-1, Mississippi State 6-2-1	Shug Jordan				
1958	9-0-1	4	2	Kentucky 5-4-1, Georgia Tech 5-4-1, Florida 6-3-1, Alabama 5-4-1	Shug Jordan				
1959	7-3		5	Georgia Tech 6-4, Miami 6-4, Georgia 9-1, Alabama 7-3	Shug Jordan				
1960	8-2	13	4	Tennessee 6-2-2, Florida 8-2, Alabama 8-1-1	Shug Jordan				
1961	6-4		7	Tennessee 6-4, Georgia Tech 7-3, Alabama 10-0	Shug Jordan				
1962	6-3-1		6	Georgia Tech 7-2-1, Florida 6-4, Alabama 9-1	Shug Jordan				
1963	9-2	5	2	Georgia Tech 7-3, Florida 6-3-1, Miss. State 6-2-2, Alabama 8-2	Shug Jordan	Orange	7	Nebraska	13
1964	6-4		6	Georgia Tech 7-3, Florida 7-3, Alabama 10-0	Shug Jordan				
1965	5-5-1		2	Tennessee 7-1-2, Southern Miss 7-2, Florida 7-3, Alabama 8-1-1	Shug Jordan	Liberty	7	Mississippi	13
1966	4-6		8	Georgia Tech 9-1, Florida 8-2, Georgia 9-1, Alabama 10-0	Shug Jordan				
1967	6-4		7	Tennessee 9-1, Miami 7-3, Georgia 7-3, Alabama 8-1-1	Shug Jordan				
1968	7-4	16	3	Florida 6-3-1, Tennessee 8-1-1, Georgia 8-0-2, Alabama 8-2	Shug Jordan	Sun	34	Arizona	10
1969	8-3	20	3	Tennessee 9-1, LSU 9-1, Florida 8-1-1, Alabama 6-4	Shug Jordan	Bluebonnet	7	Houston	36
1970	9-2	10	3	Tennessee 10-1, Georgia Tech 8-3, LSU 9-2	Shug Jordan	Gator	35	Mississippi	28
1971	9-2	12	2	Tennessee 9-2, Georgia 10-1, Alabama 11-0	Shug Jordan	Sugar	22	Oklahoma	40
1972	10-1	5	2	Tennessee 9-2, LSU 9-1-1, Georgia 7-4, Alabama 10-1	Shug Jordan	Gator	24	Colorado	3
1973	6-6		8	Tennessee 8-3, LSU 9-2, Houston 10-1, Alabama 11-0	Shug Jordan	Sun	17	Missouri	34
1974	10-2	8	2	Tennessee 6-3-2, Florida 8-3, Mississippi State 8-3, Alabama 11-0	Shug Jordan	Gator	27	Texas	3
1975	3-6-2		6	Georgia Tech 7-4, Florida 9-2, Georgia 9-2, Alabama 10-1	Shug Jordan (175-83-7)				
1976	3-8		6	Florida 8-3, Miss. State 9-2, Georgia 10-1, Alabama 8-3	Doug Barfield				
1977	5-6		3	NC State 7-4, Florida State 9-2, Florida 6-4-1, Alabama 10-1	Doug Barfield				
1978	6-4-1		3	Georgia Tech 7-4, Mississippi St. 6-5, Georgia 9-1-1, Alabama 10-1	Doug Barfield				
1979	8-3		3	Tennessee 7-4, Wake Forest 8-3, Georgia 6-5, Alabama 11-0	Doug Barfield				
1980	5-6		9	Mississippi State 9-2, Florida 7-4, Georgia 11-0, Alabama 9-2	Doug Barfield (27-27-1)				
1981	5-6		6	Tennessee 7-4, Nebraska 9-2, Georgia 10-1, Alabama 9-1-1	Pat Dye				
1982	9-3	14	3	Nebraska 11-1, Florida 8-3, Georgia 11-0, Alabama 7-4	Pat Dye	Tangerine	33	Boston College	26
1983	11-1	3	1	Texas 11-0, Tenn. 8-3, Florida 8-2-1, Georgia 9-1-1, Alabama 7-4	Pat Dye	Sugar	9	Michigan	7
1984	9-4	14	2	Miami 8-4, Texas 7-3-1, Florida State 7-3-1, Florida 9-1-1	Pat Dye	Liberty	21	Arkansas	15
1985	8-4		5	Tennessee 8-2-1, Florida State 8-3, Florida 9-1-1, Alabama 8-2-1	Pat Dye	Cotton	16	Texas A&M	36
1986	10-2	6	2t	Tennessee 6-5, Florida 6-5, Georgia 8-3, Alabama 9-3	Pat Dye	Citrus	16	Southern California	7
1987	9-1-2	7	1	Tennessee 9-2-1, Florida State 10-1, Georgia 8-3, Alabama 7-4	Pat Dye	Sugar	16	Syracuse	16
1988	10-2	8	1t	LSU 8-3, Southern Miss 9-2, Georgia 8-3, Alabama 8-3	Pat Dye	Sugar	7	Florida State	13
1989	10-2	6	1t	Tennessee 10-1, Florida State 9-2, Florida 7-4, Alabama 10-1	Pat Dye	Hall of Fame	31	Ohio State	14
1990	8-3-1	19	4	Mississippi 9-2, Tennessee 8-2-2, Florida State 9-2, Florida 9-2	Pat Dye	Peach	27	Indiana	23
1991	5-6		8	Tennessee 9-2, Florida 10-1, Georgia 8-3, Alabama 10-1	Pat Dye				
1992	5-5-1		W5	Mississippi 8-3, Florida 8-4, Georgia 9-2, Alabama 12-0	Pat Dye (99-39-4)				
1993	11-0	4	ineligible	Florida 9-2, Alabama 8-2-1	Terry Bowden				
1994	9-1-1	9	ineligible	Florida 10-1-1, Mississippi State 8-3, Georgia 6-4-1, Alabama 11-1	Terry Bowden				
1995	8-4	22	W2	LSU 6-4-1, Florida 12-0, Arkansas 8-4, Alabama 8-3	Terry Bowden	Outback	14	Penn State	43
1996	8-4	24	W3	LSU 9-2, Florida 11-1, Alabama 9-3	Terry Bowden	Independence	32	Army	29
1997	10-3	11	W1t	Virginia 7-4, LSU 8-3, Florida 9-2, Georgia 9-2, Tennessee 11-1	Terry Bowden	Peach	21	Clemson	17
1998	3-8		W6	Virginia 9-2, Tennessee 12-0, Florida 9-2, Arkansas 9-2	Terry Bowden (47-17-1), Bill Oliver [2-3]				
1999	5-6		W5	Tennessee 9-2, Mississippi State 9-2, Florida 9-3, Alabama 10-2	Tommy Tuberville				
2000	9-4		W1	LSU 7-4, Mississippi State 7-4, Florida 10-2, Georgia 7-4	Tommy Tuberville	Citrus	28	Michigan	31
2001	7-5		W2	Syracuse 9-3, Florida 9-2, Georgia 8-3, LSU 9-3	Tommy Tuberville	Peach	10	North Carolina	16
2002	9-4		W2t	So. Calif. 10-2, Arkansas 9-5, Florida 8-5, LSU 8-5, Alabama 10-3	Tommy Tuberville	Capital One	13	Penn State	9
2003	8-5		W3	So. Calif. 11-2, Tennessee 10-2, LSU 12-1, Georgia 10-3	Tommy Tuberville	Music City	28	Wisconsin	14
2004	13-0	2	W1	LSU 9-3, Tennessee 9-3, Georgia 9-2, Alabama 6-5	Tommy Tuberville	Sugar	16	Virginia Tech	13
2005	9-3		W1t	Georgia Tech 7-4, LSU 10-2, Georgia 10-2, Alabama 9-2	Tommy Tuberville	Capital One	10	Wisconsin	24
2006	11-2		W2t	LSU 10-2, Arkansas 10-2, Florida 12-1, Georgia 8-4	Tommy Tuberville	Cotton	17	Nebraska	14
2007	9-4	15	W2	So. Florida 9-3, Florida 9-3, LSU 10-2, Georgia 10-2	Tommy Tuberville	Chick-fil-A	23	Clemson	20
2008	5-7		W4t	West Virginia 8-4, Mississippi 8-4, Georgia 9-3, Alabama 12-1	Tommy Tuberville (85-40)				
2009	8-5		W4t	West Virginia 9-3, LSU 9-3, Mississippi 8-4, Alabama 13-0	Gene Chizik	Outback	38	Northwestern	35
2010	14-0	1	W1	Arkansas 10-2, LSU 10-2, Alabama 9-3	Gene Chizik (22-5)	BCS Title	22	Oregon	19

TOTAL: 453-199-12 .6913 (9 of 70)   **Bowl Games since 1953:** 20-13-1 .6029 (14 of 70)

GREATEST TEAM SINCE 1953: Despite the fact that the 1957 Auburn Tigers were selected as national champions, the undefeated 2004 team might have been superior. The 2004 Tigers were much better-rounded on offensive with a pair of All-America caliber running backs in Carnell Williams and Ronnie Brown and a quarterback in Jason Campbell who completed nearly 70 percent of his passes. Comparing eras, the 2004 defense (10.5 points per game average) was only a sliver behind the brilliant defense of the 1957 team that permitted a mere 2.8 points per game. The 2010 national champions deserve to be on a par with the 1957 and 2004 teams since it tops Auburn's greatest list as measured by the Performance Formula. The 2010 team was inferior on defense but sported quarterback Cam Newton, one of the Tigers all-time greats. This is a three-way toss-up.

1953 7-3-1

47	Stetson	0	E Jim Pyburn / Vince Nardone
13	Mississippi	0	T Frank D'Agostino / George Rogers
21	Mississippi St.	21	G George Atkins / Ed Duncan
6	Georgia Tech	36	C Jack Locklear / Ed Baker
34	Tulane	7	G Bob Scarbrough / Al Brame
16	Florida	7	T M.L. Brackett / Ted Neura
29	Miami	20	E Jimmy Long
39	Georgia	18	QB Vince Dooley / Bobby Freeman
45	Clemson	19	HB Fob James / Johnny Adams
7	Alabama	10	HB Bobby Duke / Dave Middleton
13	Texas Tech■	35	FB Charlie Hataway / Joe Childress

RUSHING: James 73/482y
PASSING: Freeman 42-85/603y, 4TD, 49.4%
RECEIVING: Pyburn 25/379y
SCORING: Freeman 54pts

1954 8-3

45	Chattanooga	0	E Jim Pyburn / Jerry Elliott
13	Florida	19	T Frank D'Agostino / George Rogers
14	Kentucky	21	G George Atkins / Ernest Danjean
7	Georgia Tech	14	C Jack Locklear / Frank Reeves
33	Florida State	0	G Bob Scarbrough / Al Brame
27	Tulane	0	T M.L. Brackett / Jim Warren
14	Miami	13	E Jimmy Long
35	Georgia	0	QB Bobby Freeman / Howell Tubbs
27	Clemson	6	HB Fob James / Johnny Adams
28	Alabama	0	HB Dave Middleton / Alton Shell
33	Baylor■	13	FB Joe Childress / Jim Walsh

RUSHING: Childress 148/836y, James 87/443y
PASSING: Freeman 54-96/865y, 6TD, 56.3%
RECEIVING: Pyburn 28/460y
SCORING: Childress (FB-K) 65pts

1955 8-2-1

15	Chattanooga	6	E Jerry Elliott / Booty Sansome
13	Florida	0	T Frank D'Agostino / Ben Preston
14	Kentucky	14	G Ernest Danjean
14	Georgia Tech	12	C Bob Scarbrough / Frank Reeves
52	Furman	0	G Chuck Maxime / Tim Baker
13	Tulane	27	T M.L. Brackett / Jim Warren
27	Mississippi St.	26	E Jimmy Phillips
16	Georgia	13	QB Howell Tubbs
21	Clemson	0	HB Fob James
26	Alabama	0	HB Bobby Hoppe / Alton Shell
13	Vanderbilt■	25	FB Joe Childress / Jim Walsh

RUSHING: James 123/879y
PASSING: Tubbs 28-49/471y, 5TD, 57.1%
RECEIVING: Phillips 14/272y
SCORING: N/A

1956 7-3

7	Tennesssee	35	E Jerry Elliott / Booty Sansom
41	Furman	0	T Ben Preston / Cleve Wester
13	Kentucky	0	G Ernest Danjean
7	Georgia Tech	28	C Frank Reeves
12	Houston	0	G Chuck Maxime / Tim Baker
0	Florida	20	T Paul Terry
27	Mississippi St.	20	E Jimmy Phillips / Jerry Wilson
20	Georgia	0	QB Howell Tubbs
13	Florida State	7	HB Tommy Lorino
34	Alabama	7	HB Bobby Hoppe
			FB Jim Walsh / Billy Atkins

RUSHING: Lorino 82/692y, Hoppe 83/542y, Walsh 109/537y
PASSING: Tubbs 34-61/514y, 5TD, 55.7%
RECEIVING: Phillips 23/383y, Sansom 13/183y, Elliott 13/183y
SCORING: Tubbs (QB-K) 39pts, Lorino & Phillips 24pts

1957 10-0

7	Tennessee	0	E Jerry Wilson / Mike Simmons
40	Chattanooga	7	T Ben Preston / Ted Foret
6	Kentucky	0	G Zeke Smith
3	Georgia Tech	0	C Jackie Burkett
48	Houston	7	G Tim Baker / Frank LaRussa
13	Florida	0	T Dan Presley / Cleve Wester
15	Mississippi St.	7	E Jimmy Phillips / John Whatley
6	Georgia	0	QB Lloyd Nix
29	Florida State	7	HB Tommy Lorino
40	Alabama	0	HB Bobby Hoppe / Lamar Rawson
			FB Billy Atkins

RUSHING: Lorino 78/445y, Atkins 90/359y, Hoppe 69/280y, Nix 82/261y
PASSING: Nix 33-60/542y, 4TD, 55.0%
RECEIVING: Phillips 15/357y, Wilson 8/97y, Lorino 8/58y
SCORING: Atkins (FB-K) 82pts, Phillips 30pts, 4 with 12pts

1958 9-0-1

13	Tennessee	0	E Jerry Wilson
30	Chattanooga	8	T Ted Foret / Jim Jeffrey
8	Kentucky	0	G Zeke Smith
7	Georgia Tech	7	C Jackie Burkett
20	Maryland	7	G Frank LaRussa / Don Braswell
6	Florida	5	T Cleve Wester / Ken Rice
33	Mississippi St.	14	E Mike Simmons / Lee Sexton
21	Georgia	6	QB Lloyd Nix / Richard Wood
21	Wake forest	7	HB Tommy Lorino
14	Alabama	8	HB Lamar Rawson / Jimmy Pettus
			FB Ed Dyas / Jimmy Reynolds

RUSHING: Lorino 67/349y, Dyas 76/343y, Nix 83/283y
PASSING: Nix 49-98/682y, 4TD, 50.0%
RECEIVING: Wilson 16/207y, Sexton 12/144y, Simmons 9/99y
SCORING: Dyas (FB-K) 28pts, Lorino 24pts, Pettus 24pts

1959 7-3

0	Tennessee	3	E Bobby Wasden / Joe Leichtnam
35	Hard-Simmons	12	T Ted Foret
33	Kentucky	0	G Zeke Smith
7	Georgia Tech	6	C Jackie Burkett / Wayne Frazier
21	Miami	6	G Jerry Gulledge / G.W. Clapp
6	Florida	0	T Ken Rice
31	Mississippi St.	0	E Dave Edwards / Leo Sexton
13	Georgia	14	QB Bobby Hunt / Richard Wood
28	Miss. Southern	7	HB Jimmy Pettus / Don Machen
0	Alabama	10	HB Lamar Rawson
			FB Ed Dyas / John McGeever

RUSHING: Hunt 98/552y, Dyas 96/504y, Rawson 60/332y
PASSING: Hunt 15-36/234y, TD, 41.7%,
Wood 11-38/170y, 3TD, 28.5%,
Bryant Harvard (QB) 11-33/94y, 0TD, 33.3%
RECEIVING: Sexton 8/75y, Wasden 6/76y, Leichtnam 4/82y
SCORING: Hunt & Dyas (FB-K) 44pts, Raws'n & McGeev'r 18pts

1960 8-2

3	Tennessee	10	E Joe Leichtnam
10	Kentucky	7	T Ken Rice / George Gross
10	Chattanooga	0	G Jimmy Putnam
9	Georgia Tech	7	C Jim Price / Wayne Frazier
20	Miami	9	G Jerry Gulledge
10	Florida	0	T Billy Wilson / Winkey Giddens
27	Mississippi St.	12	E Dave Edwards
9	Georgia	6	QB Bryant Harvard / Bobby Hunt
57	Florida State	21	HB Jimmy Burson
0	Alabama	3	HB Don Machen
			FB Ed Dyas

RUSHING: Dyas 89/451y, Burson 62/313y, Harvard 69/226y
PASSING: Harvard 36-59/494y, 2 TD, 61.1%
RECEIVING: Leichtnam 10/131y, Burson 6/88y, Edwards 6/74y
SCORING: Dyas (FB-K) 63pts, Burson, Harvard, & Machen 12pts

1961 6-4

24	Tennessee	21	E Bobby Foret / Reggie Allen
12	Kentucky	14	T George Gross
35	Chattanooga	7	G Jimmy Putnam
6	Georgia Tech	7	C Jim Price / Wayne Frazier
24	Clemson	14	G Joe Baughn
21	Wake Forest	7	T Billy Wilson / Winkey Giddens
10	Mississippi St.	11	E Dave Edwards
10	Georgia	7	QB Bobby Hunt / Mailon Kent
32	Florida	15	HB Jimmy Burson
0	Alabama	34	HB Don Machen / George Rose
			FB Larry Rawson / John McGeever

RUSHING: Rawson 121/448y, Hunt 101/347y, Machen 38/187y, Burson 44/187y
PASSING: Hunt 54-118/703y, 2TD, 45.8%
RECEIVING: Edwards 25/372y, Foret 10/131y, McGeever 7/64y
SCORING: Hunt & Woody Woodall (K) 36pts, 4 with 18pts

1962 6-3-1

22	Tennessee	21	E Howard Simpson
16	Kentucky	6	T Joe Baughn / Winkey Giddens
54	Chattanooga	6	G Herman Wilkes / Gary Price
17	Georgia Tech	14	C Jim Price / Mike Alford
17	Clemson	14	G Billy Van Dyke / Ernie Warren
3	Florida	22	T George Gross / Chuck Hurston
9	Mississippi St.	3	E Don Downs / Ronnie Baynes
21	Georgia	30	QB Jimmy Sidle / Mailon Kent
14	Florida State	14	HB Jimmy Burson / Larry Laster
0	Alabama	38	HB Tucker Frederickson/George Rose
			FB Larry Rawson / David Rawson

RUSHING: Sidle 61/394y, Laster 57/200y, Frederickson 54/192y
PASSING: Sidle 62-136/746y, 4TD, 45.6%,
Kent 59-121/748y, 2TD, 48.9%
RECEIVING: Simpson 24/301y, Downs 21/281y, D.Rawson 14/130y
SCORING: Woody Woodall (K) 41pts, Sidle 24pts, Laster 18pts

1963 9-2

21	Houston	14	E Howard Simpson / Jim Ingle
23	Tennessee	19	T Jack Thornton
14	Kentucky	13	G Don Heller / Gary Price
28	Chattanooga	0	C Mike Alford / Joe Miracle
29	Georgia Tech	21	G Billy Van Dyke / Ernie Warren
19	Florida	0	T Bobby Walton / Chuck Hurston
10	Mississippi St.	13	E Bucky Waid / Ronnie Baynes
14	Georgia	0	QB Jimmy Sidle / Bill Cody (LB)
21	Florida State	15	HB Tucker Frederickson
10	Alabama	8	HB George Rose / Doc Griffith
7	Nebraska■	13	FB Larry Rawson / David Rawson

RUSHING: Sidle 185/1006y, Frederickson 77/311y, L. Rawson 64/184y
PASSING: Sidle 53-136/706y, 5TD, 38.9%
RECEIVING: Rose 15/202y, Simpson 11/178y, Griffith 7/62y
SCORING: Sidle 60pts, Woody Woodall (K) 41pts, Rose 30pts

1964 6-4

30	Houston	0	E Scotty Long
3	Tennessee	0	T Chuck Hurston
0	Kentucky	20	G Mike Davis / Herman Burns
33	Chattanooga	12	C Mike Alford / Jerry Popwell
3	Georgia Tech	7	G Don Heller / Billy Edge
14	Southern Miss	7	T Bill Braswell / Steve Osborne
0	Florida	14	E Danny Fulford / Bucky Waid
12	Mississippi St.	3	QB Tom Bryan / Joe Campbell
14	Georgia	7	TB Jimmy Sidle (QB)
14	Alabama	21	WB Jim Partin
			FB Tucker Frederickson (DB)
			DL Ronnie Baynes
			DL Jack Thornton
			DL Larry Haynie / Ernie Warren
			DL John McAfee / Billy Van Dyke
			DL Bobby Walton / Alan Bohlert
			DL Bogue Miller / Jon Kilgore
			LB Bill Cody
			LB Doc Griffith / John Cochran
			DB Billy Edge / Bobby Beaird
			DB Mickey Sutton
			DB Tucker Frederickson (FB)

RUSHING: Frederickson 129/576y, Bryan 78/323y, Sidle 80/303y
PASSING: Campbell 30-53/424y, TD, 56.7%,
Sidle 24-60/262y, 40.0%
RECEIVING: Frederickson 14/101y, Long 11/149y, Partin 10/163y
SCORING: Frederickson 30pts, Don Lewis (K) 25pts

1965 5-5-1

8	Baylor	14	E Scotty Long / Freddie Hyatt
13	Tennessee	13	T Andy Gross
23	Kentucky	18	G Gusty Yearout / Mike Davis
30	Chattanooga	7	C Jerry Popwell / Forrest Blue
14	Georgia Tech	23	G Wayne Burns
0	Southern Miss	3	T Bruce Yates / Bill Braswell
28	Florida	17	E Danny Fulford
25	Mississippi St.	18	QB Alex Bowden
21	Georgia	19	TB Richard Plagge / Carl Hardy
3	Alabama	30	WB Jim Bouchillon / Mack Bell
7	Mississippi■	13	FB Tom Bryan (QB) / Mike Perillard
			DL Ronnie Baynes
			DL Jack Thornton / Charles Collins
			DL Larry Haynie
			DL John McAfee / Richard Wood
			DL Bobby Walton
			DL Marvin Tucker
			LB Bill Cody / Robert Margeson
			LB John Cochran
			DB Franklin Fuller / Jimmy Carter
			DB Robert Fulghum / Bucky Ayers
			DB Bobby Beaird

RUSHING: Bryan 133/561y
PASSING: Bowden 59-127/941y, 9 TD, 46.5%
RECEIVING: Hyatt 21/368y
SCORING: Bryan 32pts

1966 4-6

20 Chattanooga	6 WR Freddie Hyatt / Scotty Long
0 Tennessee	28 T Bill Braswell
7 Kentucky	17 G Mike Davis
14 Wake Forest	6 C Forrest Blue
3 Georgia Tech	17 G Ken Jones
7 Texas Christian	6 T Andy Gross / Charlie Glenn
27 Florida	30 TE Don Randolph / Hubert Comer
13 Mississippi St.	0 QB Loran Carter / Larry Blakeney
13 Georgia	21 TB Richard Plagge / Dwight Hurston
0 Alabama	31 WB Tim Christian
	FB Tom Bryan / Larry Ellis / Lee Kidd
	DL Tommy Groat
	DL Robert Miller
	DL Gusty Yearout
	DL Charles Collins / Ray Tatum
	DL Al Giffin
	LB Jim Bouchillon / Marvin Tucker
	LB Robert Margerson / Harrison McCraw
	LB Don McCay
	DB Robert Fulghum / Jimmy Carter
	DB Bobby Beaird / Bucky Ayers
	DB Tommy Lunceford / Bobby Wilson

RUSHING: Plagge 110/420y, Bryan 54/260y, Kidd 38/189y
PASSING: Blakeney 45-95/491y, 3 TD, 47.3%,
Carter 23-50/335y, 2 TD, 46.0%
RECEIVING: Hyatt 33/475y, Hurston 9/86y, Christian 7/90y
SCORING: Jimmy Jones (K) 32pts, Hyatt 24pts, 2 with 12pts

1967 6-4

40 Chattanooga	6 WR Freddie Hyatt / Mike Shows
13 Tennessee	27 T Bucky Howard
48 Kentucky	7 G Dick Pittman / Ken Jones
43 Clemson	21 C Tom Banks / Forrest Blue
28 Georgia Tech	10 G Charlie Glenn
0 Miami	7 T Jerry Gordon / Larry Hagan
26 Florida	21 TE Mike Perillard
36 Mississippi St.	0 QB Loran Carter
0 Georgia	17 TB Dwight Hurston / Richard Plagge
3 Alabama	7 WB Tim Christian / George Davison
	FB Al Giffin / Larry Ellis
	DL Jim Bouchillon / Harold Ham
	DL Charles Collins / Richard Wood
	DL Roy Tatum / David Campbell
	DL Bill James / Tommy Groat
	LB Gusty Yearout / Mike Kolen
	LB Robert Margerson / Mike Holtzclaw
	LB Don McCay / Ron Yarbrough
	DB Bucky Ayers
	DB Jimmy Carter / Don Webb
	DB Buddy McClinton / Robert Fulghum
	DB Marvin Tucker / Bobby Wilson

RUSHING: Giffin 121/392y, Hurston 81/307y, Plagge 52/201y
PASSING: Carter 86-178/1307y, 9 TD, 48.8%
RECEIVING: Hyatt 34/553y, Christian 25/413y, Hurston 16/203y
SCORING: John Riley (K) 43pts, Hyatt 36pts,
Giffin & Blakeney 30pts

1968 7-4

28 SMU	37 WR Tim Christian
26 Mississippi St.	0 T Richard Cheek
26 Kentucky	7 G John McDonald
21 Clemson	10 C Tom Banks
20 Georgia Tech	21 G Bucky Howard
3 Miami	6 T Jerry Gordon
24 Florida	13 TE Al Giffin
28 Tennessee	14 QB Loran Carter
3 Georgia	17 TB Dwight Hurston / Mike Currier
16 Alabama	24 WB Connie Frederick
34 Arizona■	10 FB Larry Ellis / Mickey Zofko
	DL Durwood Sauls
	DL David Campbell
	DL Jim Samford
	DL Bill James
	LB Mike Kolen
	LB Ron Yarbrough
	LB Bobby Strickland
	DB Don Webb
	DB Merrill Shirley
	DB Sonny Ferguson
	DB Buddy McClinton

RUSHING: Hurston 110/349y, Ellis 100/278y, Currier 76/211y
PASSING: Carter 112-248/1487y, 14 TD, 45.1%
RECEIVING: Christian 47/623y, Frederick 20/293y,
Hurston 15/228y
SCORING: John Riley (K) 61pts, Christian & Currier 42pts

1969 8-3

57 Wake Forest	0 WR Terry Beasley / Dick Schmatz
19 Tennessee	45 T Greg Robert
44 Kentucky	3 G Jimmy Speigner
51 Clemson	0 C Tom Banks / Bill McManus
17 Georgia Tech	14 G Johnny McDonald
20 LSU	21 T Richard Cheek
38 Florida	12 TE Ronnie Ross / Robby Robinet
52 Mississippi St.	13 QB Pat Sullivan
16 Georgia	3 TB Mickey Zofko / Mike Currier
49 Alabama	26 WB Connie Frederick
7 Houston■	36 FB Wallace Clark / Tommy Lowry
	DL Neal Dettmering
	DL David Campbell / Keith Green
	DL Don Bristow
	DL Bill James / Dick Ingwersen
	LB Bobby Strickland / Morrell Jenkins
	LB Bobby Woodruff
	LB Mike Kolen / John Hayworth
	DB Sonny Ferguson
	DB Don Webb
	DB Larry Willingham / Merrill Shirley
	DB Buddy McClinton

RUSHING: Zofko 119/565y, Clark 115/531y, Lowry 63/338y
PASSING: Sullivan 123-257/1686y, 16TD, 47.8%
RECEIVING: Beasley 34/610y, Frederick 32/515y, Ross 18/149y
SCORING: John Riley (K) 69pts, Sullivan & Zofko 42pts

1970 9-2

33 Southern Miss	14 WR Terry Beasley
36 Tennessee	23 T Danny Speigner
33 Kentucky	15 G Jimmy Speigner
44 Clemson	0 C Bill McManus
31 Georgia Tech	7 G Larry Hall
9 LSU	17 T Hal Hamrick
63 Florida	14 TE Ronnie Ross / Robby Robinett
56 Mississippi St.	0 QB Pat Sullivan
17 Georgia	31 TB Mickey Zofko
33 Alabama	28 WB Alvin Bresler
35 Mississippi■	28 FB Wallace Clark
	DL Neal Dettmering
	DL Keith Green
	DL Don Bristow
	DL Bob Brown
	LB Mike Neel / Morrell Jenkins
	LB Bobby Strickland
	LB Rick Chastain
	LB John Hayworth
	DB Dave Beck
	DB Larry Willingham
	DB Johnny Simmons

RUSHING: Clark 86/422y, Zofko 75/331y, Sullivan 52/270y
PASSING: Sullivan 167-281/2586y, 17TD, 59.0%
RECEIVING: Beasley 52/1051y, Zofko 34/443y, Bresler 23/530y
SCORING: Beasley 72pts, Gardner Jett (K) 71pts, Sullivan 54pts

1971 9-2

60 Chattanooga	7 WR Terry Beasley
10 Tennessee	9 T Danny Speigner
38 Kentucky	6 G Jay Casey
27 Southern Miss	14 C Bill McManus
31 Georgia Tech	14 G Larry Hill
35 Clemson	13 T Mac Lorendo
40 Florida	7 TE Robby Robinett
30 Mississippi St.	21 QB Pat Sullivan
35 Georgia	20 TB Terry Henley
7 Alabama	31 WB Dick Schmalz
22 Oklahoma ■	40 FB Tommy Lowry / Harry Unger
	DL Eddie Welch
	DL Benny Sivley
	DL Tommy Yearout
	DL Bob Brown
	LB Mike Flynn
	LB Mike Neel
	LB Bill Luka
	LB John Hayworth
	DB Dave Beck
	DB David Langner
	DB Johnny Simmons

RUSHING: Lowry 87/499y, Henley 87/427y, Unger 60/229y
PASSING: Sullivan 162-281/2012y, 20 TD, 57.6%
RECEIVING: Beasley 55/846y, Schmalz 44/647y,
Robinett 21/170y
SCORING: Beasley 72pts, Gardner Jett (K) 51pts,
Schmalz 42pts

1972 10-1

14 Mississippi St.	3 WR Sandy Cannon
14 Chattanooga	7 T Mac Lorendo
10 Tennessee	6 G Jay Casey
19 Mississippi	13 C Steve Taylor
7 LSU	35 G Bob Farrior
24 Georgia Tech	14 T Andy Steele
27 Florida State	14 TE Mike Gates / Rob Spivey
26 Florida	20 QB Randy Walls
27 Georgia	10 TB Terry Henley / Chris Linderman
17 Alabama	16 WB Mike Fuller / Thomas Gossom
24 Colorado■	3 FB Rusty Fuller / James Owens
	DL Danny Sanspree
	DL Benny Sivley
	DL Bob Newton
	DL Eddie Welch
	LB Bill Luka
	LB Ken Bernich
	LB Bill Newton
	LB Mike Neel / Steve Wilson
	DB David Langner
	DB Dave Beck
	DB Johnny Simmons

RUSHING: Henley 216/843y, Linderman 97/431y,
Walls 123/189y
PASSING: Walls 46-97/736y, 5TD, 47.4%
RECEIVING: Cannon 11/191y, Gossom 9/182y, Spivey 7/120y
SCORING: Henley 66pts, Gardner Jett (K) 46pts, Walls 24pts

1973 6-6

18 Oregon State	9 WR Rett Davis / Chris Vacarella (QB)
31 Chattanooga	0 T Dave Ostrowski
0 Tennessee	21 G Lee Gross
14 Mississippi	7 C Steve Taylor
6 LSU	20 G Bill Evans
24 Georgia Tech	10 T Chuck Fletcher
7 Houston	0 TE Rob Spivey
8 Florida	12 QB Wade Whatley / Randy Walls (DB)
31 Mississippi St.	17 TB Chris Linderman / Mitzi Jackson
14 Georgia	28 WB Ed Butler / Mike Gates
0 Alabama	35 FB Secdrick McIntyre
17 Missouri ■	34 DL Liston Eddins
	DL Bob Newton
	DL Benny Sivley
	DL Rusty Deen
	LB Bill Luka / Jimmy Sirmons
	LB Ken Bernich
	LB Bill Newton
	LB Mike Flynn
	DB Bruce Evans
	DB Mike Fuller / Randy Walls (QB)
	DB David Langner / Jim McKinney

RUSHING: McIntyre 64/315y, Linderman 84/259y,
Jackson 49/245y
PASSING: Whatley 29-52/340y, TD, 55.8%,
Walls 24-60/226y, TD, 40.0%
RECEIVING: Davis 12/112y, Spivey 9/147y, Butler 7/77y,
Gossom 7/48y
SCORING: Roger Pruett (K) 29pts, McIntyre 24pts,
Vacarella 18pts

1974 10-2

16 Louisville	3 WR Thomas Gossom / Jeff Gilligan
52 Chattanooga	0 T Dave Ostrowski
21 Tennessee	0 G Andy Steele
3 Miami	0 C Lee Gross
31 Kentucky	13 G Lynn Johnson / Ben Strickland
31 Georgia Tech	22 T Chuck Fletcher / Hamlin Caldwell
38 Florida State	6 TE Dan Nugent
14 Florida	25 QB Phil Gargis
24 Mississippi St.	20 TB Rick Neel / Mitzi Jackson
17 Georgia	13 WB Mike Gates
13 Alabama	17 FB Secdrick McIntyre
27 Texas ■	3 DL Rusty Deen
	DL Gaines Lanier
	DL Rick Telhiard
	DL Liston Eddins
	LB Carl Hubbard
	LB Ken Bernich
	LB Bobby Davis
	LB Mike Flynn
	DB Bruce Evans
	DB Mike Fuller
	DB Jim McKinney

RUSHING: McIntyre 170/839y, Gargis 151/687y,
Jackson 95/525y
PASSING: Gargis 35-81/518y, 5 TD, 43.2%
RECEIVING: Gossom 20/294y, Nugent 9/124y, Gilligan 6/119y
SCORING: Gargis & McIntyre 36pts, Wilson 28pts

1975 3-6-2

20 Memphis State	31 WR Chris Vacarella
10 Baylor	10 WR Jeff Gilligan / Billy Wood
17 Tennessee	21 T Dave Ostrowski / Arnoldo Abreu
16 Virginia Tech	23 G Lynn Johnson
15 Kentucky	9 C Ben Strickland / Marvin Trott
31 Georgia Tech	27 G Bill Evans
17 Florida State	14 T Chuck Fletcher / Lynn Johnson
14 Florida	31 TE Ed Butler / Rob Spivey
21 Mississippi St.	21 QB Phil Gargis / Clyde Baumgardner
13 Georgia	28 TB Mitzi Jackson / Mike Henley
0 Alabama	28 FB Kenny Burks / Secdrick McIntyre
	DL Liston Eddins
	DL Steve Stranaland / Jo Jo Eddins
	DL Rick Telhiard
	DL Jim Pitts / Jeff McCollum
	LB Pat Jones
	LB Carl Hubbard
	LB Ricky Sanders
	LB Kim Sellers / Raymond Phagan
	DB Rick Neel
	DB Lance Hill
	DB Bill Cunningham / Mike McCloud

RUSHING: Gargis 162/658y, Jackson 99/603y, Burks 75/471y
PASSING: Gargis 37-94/400y, 2 TD, 39.4%
RECEIVING: Gilligan 23/421y, Jackson 9/48y, Butler 6/75y
SCORING: Neil O'Donoghue (K) 49pts, Burks 24pts, McIntyre 24pts

1976 3-8

19 Arizona	31 WR Chris Vacarella / Ray Powell
14 Baylor	15 WR Terry Fuller
38 Tennessee	28 T Mike Burrow / Arnoldo Abreu
10 Mississippi	0 G Lynn Johnson / Bill Evans (DL)
27 Memphis State	28 C Marvin Trott / Mike Northrup
10 Georgia Tech	28 G Dave Ostrowski
31 Florida State	19 T Mike Skelton / Ronnie Jones
19 Florida	24 TE Reese McCall / Dick Hayley
19 Mississippi St.	28 QB Phil Gargis
0 Georgia	28 RB Bob Bradley / William Andrews
7 Alabama	38 RB Secdrick McIntyre / Forter Christy
	DL Lee Hanson
	DL Rodney Bellamy / Bert McGuffey
	DL Tony Long
	DL Anthony Jones / Bill Evans (G)
	DL Joe Shaw / Jeff McCollum
	LB Freddie Smith / Kim Sellers
	LB Tommy Hicks / Raymond Phagan
	DB James McKinney
	DB Alan Hardin / Jeff Gray
	DB Rick Freeman / Terry Fuller
	DB Bill Cunningham / Mike McCloud

RUSHING: Gargis 142/534y, McIntyre 114/393y, Bradley 92/386y
PASSING: Gargis 80-166/1118y, 7TD, 48.2%
RECEIVING: Vacarella 15/353y, Fuller 14/198y, Powell 12/1113y
SCORING: Gargis 56pts, Neil O'Donoghue (K) 52pts, Hayley 18pts

1977 5-6

21 Arizona	10 WR Rusty Byrd / Mark Robbins
13 Southern Miss	24 WR Byron Franklin
14 Tennessee	12 T Mike Burrow
21 Mississippi	15 G Lynn Johnson
15 N. Carolina St.	17 C Marvin Trott
21 Georgia Tech	38 G Marshall Riley
3 Florida State	24 T Mike Skelton
29 Florida	14 TE Reese McCall
13 Mississippi St.	27 QB Charlie Trotman / John Crane
33 Georgia	14 RB Joe Cribbs / James Brooks
21 Alabama	48 RB William Andrews
	DL Joe Shaw
	DL Rodney Bellamy
	DL Donnie Givens
	DL John Smith
	DL Bob Rhodes
	LB Freddie Smith
	LB Mike McQuaig
	DB Terry Fuller
	DB Alan Hardin
	DB James McKinney
	DB Rick Freeman

RUSHING: Cribbs 161/872y, Andrews 137/635y, Brooks 107/467y
PASSING: Crane 43-108/679y, 4TD, 39.8%
RECEIVING: Franklin 13/389y, Brooks 11/121y, Robbins 10/124y
SCORING: Jorge Portela (K) 64pts, Andrews 30pts, Cribbs 24pts

1978 6-4-1

45 Kansas State	32 WR Rusty Byrd / Byron Franklin
18 Virginia Tech	7 WR Mark Robbins
29 Tennessee	10 T Keith Uecker / Bard Everett
15 Miami	17 G George Stephenson
49 Vanderbilt	7 C Mark Clement
10 Georgia Tech	24 G Jim Skuthan
21 Wake Forest	7 T Mike Burrow
7 Florida	31 TE Dick Hayley
6 Mississippi St.	0 QB Charlie Trotman
22 Georgia	22 RB Joe Cribbs / James Brooks
16 Alabama	34 RB William Andrews
	DL Zac Hardy
	DL Frank Warren
	DL Marshall Riley
	DL Rodney Bellamy
	DL Bob Rhodes
	LB Donnie Givens
	LB Harris Rabren
	DB Jeff Gray
	DB Alan Hardin
	DB James McKinney
	DB Clifford Toney

RUSHING: Cribbs 253/1205y, Brooks 90/534y, Andrews 72/369y
PASSING: Trotman 53-111/760y, 3TD, 47.7%
RECEIVING: Byrd 14/220y, Robbins 13/259y, Franklin 10/213y
SCORING: Cribbs 98pts, Jorge Portela (K) 54pts, Brooks 24pts

1979 8-3

26 Kansas State	18 WR Rusty Byrd
31 Southern Miss	9 WR Mark Robbins / Byron Franklin
17 Tennessee	35 T George Stephenson
44 N. Carolina St.	31 G Jim Skuthan
52 Vanderbilt	35 C Mark Clement
38 Georgia Tech	14 G Bill Grisham
38 Wake Forest	42 T Claude Mathews
19 Florida	13 TE Mike Locklear
14 Mississippi St.	3 QB Charlie Trotman / Charlie Thomas
33 Georgia	13 RB James Brooks
18 Alabama	25 RB Joe Cribbs
	DL Zac Hardy
	DL Frank Warren
	DL Marvin Williams
	DL Edmund Nelson
	DL Ken Hardy
	LB Freddie Smith
	LB Harris Rabren
	DB Darryl Wilks
	DB Bob Harris
	DB Ken Luke
	DB Clifford Toney

RUSHING: Brooks 163/1208y, Cribbs 200/1120y, Thomas 56/326y
PASSING: Trotman 58-131/875y, 8TD, 44.2%
RECEIVING: Franklin 19/373y, Robbins 16/247y, Byrd 11/155y
SCORING: Cribbs 94pts, Brooks 72pts, Jorge Portela (K) 70pts

1980 5-6

10 TCU	7 WR Byron Franklin
35 Duke	28 WR Brian Atkins / Mike Edwards
0 Tennessee	42 T Keith Uecker
55 Richmond	16 G Phillip Hall
17 LSU	21 C Bishop Reeves
17 Georgia Tech	14 G Jim Skuthan
21 Mississippi St.	24 T George Stephenson
10 Florida	21 TE Bill Grisham
31 Southern Miss	0 QB Joe Sullivan / Charlie Thomas
21 Georgia	31 RB James Brooks
18 Alabama	34 RB George Peoples
	DL Edmund Nelson
	DL Frank Warren
	DL Marshall Riley
	DL Vernon Blackard
	LB Danny Skutack
	LB Ronny Bellow
	LB Christopher Martin
	DB Clifford Toney
	DB Jerry Beasley
	DB Bob Harris / Johnny Green
	DB Darryl Wilks

RUSHING: Brooks 261/1314y, Peoples 96/443y, Thomas 86/246y
PASSING: Sullivan 64-118/772y, 6TD, 54.2%
RECEIVING: Franklin 32/598y, Grisham 13/152y, Edwards 13/160y
SCORING: Brooks 66pts, Franklin 54pts, Al Del Greco (K) 51pts

1981 5-6

24 TCU	16 WR Chris Woods / Tommy Carroll
21 Wake Forest	24 T David Jordan
7 Tennessee	10 G Greg Zipp
3 Nebraska	17 C Bob Hix
19 LSU	7 G Keith Uecker
31 Georgia Tech	7 T Pat Arrington
17 Mississippi St.	21 TE Ed West
14 Florida	12 QB Joe Sullivan/Ken Hobby/C.Beauford
20 N. Texas State	0 HB Lionel James
13 Georgia	24 HB Mike Edwards
17 Alabama	28 FB George Peoples / Ron O'Neal
	DL Zac Hardy
	DL Edmund Nelson
	DL Dowe Aughtman
	DL Donnie Humphrey
	DL Jeff Jackson
	LB Christopher Martin
	LB Danny Skutack
	DB David King
	DB Tim Drinkard
	DB Mark Dorminey
	DB Bob Harris

RUSHING: James 111/561y, O'Neal 107/480y, Peoples 104/442y
PASSING: Sullivan 28-65/370y, 3TD, 43.0%
RECEIVING: Woods 13/213y, West 11/199y, Carroll 11/158y
SCORING: Al Del Greco (K) 47pts, O'Neal 30pts, Edwards 24pts

1982 9-3

28 Wake Forest	10 WR Mike Edwards / Chris Woods
21 Southern Miss	19 T Steve Wallace
24 Tennessee	14 G David Jordan
7 Nebraska	41 C Bishop Reeves
18 Kentucky	3 G Randy Stokes
24 Georgia Tech	0 T Pat Arrington
35 Mississippi St.	17 TE Ed West
17 Florida	19 QB Randy Campbell
30 Rutgers	7 HB Lionel James
14 Georgia	19 HB Bo Jackson
23 Alabama	22 FB Ron O'Neal
33 Boston College■	26 DL Scott Riley
	DL Doug Smith
	DL Dowe Aughtman
	DL Ben Thomas
	DL Jeff Jackson
	LB Gregg Carr
	LB Christopher Martin
	DB David King
	DB Tim Drinkard
	DB Dennis Collier / Mark Dorminmey
	DB Bob Harris

RUSHING: Jackson 127/829y, James 113/779y, O'Neal 90/371y
PASSING: Campbell 81-158/1061y, 7TD, 51.3%
RECEIVING: Woods 21/406y, Edwards 19/325y, James 15/56y
SCORING: Al Del Greco (K) 65pts, Jackson 56pts, James 42pts

1983 11-1

24 Southern Miss	3 WR Chris Woods / Trey Gainous
7 Texas	20 T Steve Wallace / Jay Jacobs
37 Tennessee	14 G David Jordan
27 Florida State	24 C Ben Tamburello / Yann Cowart
49 Kentucky	21 G Jeff Lott
31 Georgia Tech	13 T Pat Arrington
28 Mississippi St.	13 TE Ed West / Jeff Parks
28 Florida	21 QB Randy Campbell
35 Maryland	23 HB Lionel James
13 Georgia	7 HB Bo Jackson
23 Alabama	20 FB Tommie Agee
9 Michigan ■	7 DL Quency Williams / Gerald Robinson
	DL Doug Smith
	DL Dowe Aughtman
	DL Donnie Humphrey
	DL John Dailey
	LB Gregg Carr
	LB Jeff Jackson / Ben McCurdy
	DB David King
	DB Jimmie Warren
	DB Vic Beasley
	DB Tommy Powell

RUSHING: Jackson 158/1213y, James 124/728y, Agee 115/604y
PASSING: Campbell 78-142/873y, 7TD, 54.9%
RECEIVING: West 16/189y, Woods 15/227y, Jackson 13/73y
SCORING: Jackson 84pts, Al Del Greco (K) 72pts, Agee 32pts

1984 9-4

18 Miami	20 WR Clayton Beauford / Freddie Weygand
27 Texas	35 T Steve Wallace / Stacy Searels
35 Southern Miss	12 G Jeff Lott
28 Tennessee	10 C Ben Tamburello / Yann Cowart
17 Mississippi	13 G Randy Stokes
42 Florida State	41 T Rob Shuler
48 Georgia Tech	34 TE Jeff Parks
24 Mississippi St.	21 QB Pat Washington
3 Florida	24 HB Brent Fullwood / Collis Campbell
60 Cincinnati	0 HB Bo Jackson
21 Georgia	12 FB Tommie Agee
15 Alabama	17 DL Kevin Greene / Gerald Robinson
21 Arkansas ■	15 DL Gerald Williams
	DL Harold Hallman
	DL Ben Thomas
	DL John Dailey
	LB Gregg Carr
	LB Ben McCurdy / Jim Bone
	DB David King
	DB Alvin Briggs / Jonathan Robinson
	DB Arthur Johnson / Vic Beasley
	DB Tommy Powell

RUSHING: Fullwood 117/628y, Campbell 86/511y, Jackson 87/475y
PASSING: Washington 77-171/1202y, 4TD, 45.0%
RECEIVING: Weygand 32/796y, Beauford 19/316y, Trey Gainous (WR) 15/193y
SCORING: Robert McGinty (K) 67pts, Fullwood 48pts, Jackson 32pts

1985 8-4

49 SW Louisiana	7 WR Freddie Weygand / Scott Bolton
29 Southern Miss	18 WR Trey Gainous / Ron Middleton
20 Tennessee	38 T Steve Wallace
41 Mississippi	0 G Jeff Lott
59 Florida State	27 C Ben Tamburello
17 Georgia Tech	14 G Yann Cowart / Steve Wilson
21 Mississippi St.	9 T Stacy Searels
10 Florida	14 TE Jeff Parks
35 East Carolina	10 QB Pat Washington
24 Georgia	10 TB Bo Jackson / Brent Fullwood
23 Alabama	25 FB Tommie Agee
16 Texas A&M ■	36 DL Gerald Robinson
	DL Tracy Rocker
	DL Harold Halman
	DL Gerald Williams
	DL Gary Kelley
	LB Ben McCurdy / Edward Phillips
	LB Russ Carreker / Pat Thomas
	DB Kevin Porter
	DB Jimmie Warren
	DB Arthur Johnson
	DB Tommy Powell

RUSHING: Jackson 278/1786y, Fullwood 92/684y, Agee 81/402y
PASSING: Washington 56-122/772y, 2TD, 45.9%
RECEIVING: Weygand 19/367y, Gainous 16/251y, Bolton 11/139y, Parks 11/132y
SCORING: Jackson 102pts, Chris Johnson (K) 37pts, Fullwood 36pts

1986 10-2

42 Tenn-Chatt'ga	14 WR Lawyer Tillman
45 East Carolina	0 WR Trey Gainous
34 Tennessee	8 T Jim Thompson
55 W. Carolina	6 G Vincent Jones
31 Vanderbilt	9 C Ben Tamburello
31 Georgia Tech	10 G Yann Cowart
35 Mississippi St.	6 T Stacy Searels
17 Florida	18 TE Walter Reeves
52 Cincinnati	7 QB Jeff Burger
16 Georgia	20 TB Brent Fullwood / Tim Jessie
21 Alabama	17 FB Tommie Agee / Reggie Ware
16 Southern Cal ■	7 DL Ron Stallworth / Nate Hill
	DL Benji Roland
	DL Tracy Rocker
	LB Aundray Bruce
	LB Kurt Crain
	LB Edward Phillips
	LB Gary Kelley / Brian Smith
	DB Kevin Porter
	DB Chip Powell
	DB Arthur Johnson
	DB Tommy Powell / Shan Morris

RUSHING: Fullwood 167/1391, Jessie 61/282y, Agee 66/271y
PASSING: Burger 126-222/1671y, 9TD, 56.8%
RECEIVING: Tillman 35/730y, Gainous 19/207y, Agee 18/200y
SCORING: Knapp 79pts, Ware 66pts, Fullwood 60pts

1987 9-1-2

31 Texas	3 WR Lawyer Tillman / Alexander Wright
49 Kansas	0 WR Duke Donaldson/Freddy Weygand
20 Tennessee	20 T Eric Floyd
20 North Carolina	10 G Stacy Dunn
48 Vanderbilt	15 C John Hudson
20 Georgia Tech	10 G Rodney Garner / Brad Johnson
38 Mississippi St.	7 T Stacy Searels
29 Florida	6 TE Walter Reeves
6 Florida State	34 QB Jeff Burger
27 Georgia	11 TB Stacy Danley
10 Alabama	0 FB Reggie Ware / Vincent Harris
16 Syracuse ■	16 DL Nate Hill / Ron Stallworth
	DL Benji Roland
	DL Tracy Rocker
	LB Aundray Bruce
	LB Kurt Crain
	LB Edward Phillips
	LB Alvin Mitchell / Brian Smith
	DB Alvin Briggs
	DB Kevin Porter
	DB Carlo Cheattom
	DB Greg Staples

RUSHING: Danley 94/468y, Ware 104/322y, Harris 61/266y
PASSING: Burger 178-267/2066y, 13TD, 66.7%
RECEIVING: Donaldson 43/398y, Tillman 32/600y, Reeves 23/174y
SCORING: Win Lyle (K) 77pts, Tillman 36pts, Ware & Wright 30pts

1988 10-2

20 Kentucky	10 WR Lawyer Tillman / Greg Taylor
56 Kansas	7 WR Freddie Weygand
38 Tennessee	6 T Jim Thompson
47 North Carolina	21 G Ed King
6 LSU	7 C John Hudson
42 Akron	0 G Rodney Garner
33 Mississippi St.	0 T Rob Selby
16 Florida	0 TE Walter Reeves
38 Southern Miss	8 QB Reggie Slack
20 Georgia	10 TB Stacy Danley
15 Alabama	10 FB James Joseph (TB) / Vincent Harris
7 Florida State ■	13 DL Ron Stallworth
	DL Benji Roland
	DL Tracy Rocker
	LB Craig Ogletree
	LB Smokey Hodge / Steve Brown
	LB Quentin Riggins
	LB Brian Smith / Alvin Mitchell
	DB Carlo Cheattom
	DB Shan Morris / Frankie Stankunas
	DB John Wiley
	DB Greg Staples

RUSHING: Danley 179/877y, Joseph 108/668y, Love 65/287y
PASSING: Slack 168-279/2230y, 9TD, 60.2%
RECEIVING: Weygand 38/577y, Taylor 28/282y, Tillman 19/400y
SCORING: Win Lyle (K) 78pts, Danley 42pts, Joseph 36pts

1989 10-2

55 Pacific	0 WR Greg Taylor / Shane Wasden
24 Southern Miss	3 WR Alexander Wright
14 Tennessee	21 T Bob Meeks / Anthony Brown
24 Kentucky	12 G Ed King
10 LSU	6 C John Hudson
14 Florida State	22 G Mark Rose
14 Mississippi St.	0 T Rob Selby
10 Florida	7 TE Victor Hall
38 Louisiana Tech	23 QB Reggie Slack
20 Georgia	3 TB Stacy Danley / Darrell Williams
30 Alabama	20 FB James Joseph / Alex Strong
31 Ohio State ■	14 DL Fernando Horn / Jon Wilson
	DL Walter Tate / Richard Shea
	DL David Rocker
	LB Quentin Riggins
	LB Darrel Crawford
	LB Craig Ogletree
	LB Eltin Billingslea
	DB Eric Ramsey
	DB Corey Barlow
	DB John Wiley
	DB Frankie Stankunas / Dennis Wallace

RUSHING: Joseph 172/817y, Danley 150/652y, Williams 85/371y
PASSING: Slack 148-252/1996y, 11TD, 58.7%
RECEIVING: Wright 30/714y, Joseph 26/227y, Taylor 25/353y
SCORING: Win Lyle (K) 75pts, Wright 42pts, Williams 30pts

1990 8-3-1

38 Cal-Fullerton	17 WR Shayne Wasden / Herbert Casey
24 Mississippi	10 WR Greg Taylor / Dale Overton
26 Tennessee	26 T Rob Selby
16 Louisiana Tech	14 G Ed King
56 Vanderbilt	6 C Bob Meeks
20 Florida State	17 G Tim Tillman
17 Mississippi St.	16 T Chris Gray / Anthony Redmon
7 Florida	48 TE Victor Hall
12 Southern Miss	14 QB Stan White
33 Georgia	10 TB Stacy Danley / Darrell Williams
7 Alabama	16 FB James Joseph / Tony Richardson
27 Indiana ■	23 DL Lamar Rogers / Fernando Horn
	DL Walter Tate
	DL David Rocker
	LB Jason Merchant / Bennie Pierce
	LB Darrel Crawford
	LB Reggie Barlow / Ricky Sutton
	LB James Willis / Karekin Cunningham
	DB Eric Ramsey
	DB Corey Barlow
	DB John Wiley
	DB Dennis Wallace

RUSHING: Danley 103/430y, Joseph 94/413y, Williams 112/404y
PASSING: White 180-338/2242y, 14TD, 53.3%
RECEIVING: Taylor 46/650y, Casey 25/439y, Joseph 22/234y
SCORING: Jim Von Wyl (K) 78pts, Taylor 48pts, Richardson 24pts

1991 5-6

32 Ga. Southern	17 WR Thomas Bailey / Pedro Cherry
23 Mississippi	13 WR Herbert Casey / Dale Overton
14 Texas	10 T Wayne Gandy
21 Tennessee	30 G Tim Tillman
9 Southern Miss	10 C Bob Meeks
24 Vanderbilt	22 G Eddie Blake
17 Mississippi St.	24 T Chris Gray
10 Florida	31 TE Fred Baxter / Victor Hall
50 SW Louisiana	7 QB Stan White
27 Georgia	37 TB Joe Frazier / Alex Smith
6 Alabama	13 FB Reid McMilion
	DL Jon Wilson
	DL Tim Cromartie
	DL Richard Shea / Chuckie Johnson
	DL Ricky Sutton
	LB James Willis
	LB Darrel Crawford
	LB Bennie Pierce
	DB Corey Barlow
	DB Fred Smith
	DB Alex Thomas
	DB Frankie Stankunas / Mike Pina

RUSHING: Frazier 140/651y, Smith 60/348y, McMilion 59/304y
PASSING: White 158-317/1927y, 8 TD, 49.8%
RECEIVING: Baxter 28/391y, Casey 20/277y, Hall 19/211y
SCORING: Jim Von Wyl (K) 63pts, Frazier 32pts, White & McMilion 24pts

1992 5-5-1

21 Mississippi	45 WR Thomas Bailey / Frank Sanders
55 Samford	0 WR Orlando Parker / Melvin Hines
30 LSU	28 T Wayne Gandy
16 Southern Miss	8 G Jason Taylor / Shannon Robique
31 Vanderbilt	7 C Greg Thompson
7 Mississippi St.	14 G Anthony Redmon / Shane Keasler
9 Florida	24 T Chris Gray
25 SW Louisiana	24 TE Fred Baxter / Andy Fuller
24 Arkansas	24 QB Stan White
10 Georgia	14 TB James Bostic / Alex Smith
0 Alabama	17 FB Tony Richardson / Reid McMilion
	DL Willie Whitehead / Alonzo Etheridge
	DL Tim Cromartie
	DL Randy Hart / Damon Primus
	DL Ricky Sutton
	LB Karekin Cunningham
	LB James Willis
	LB Bennie Pierce / Anthony Harris
	DB Calvin Jackson
	DB Fred Smith
	DB Otis Mounds / Clarence Morton
	DB Chris Shelling

RUSHING: Bostic 186/819y, McMilion 43/215y, Smith 38/175y
PASSING: White 157-305/1790y, 5TD, 51.5%
RECEIVING: Parker 30/438y, Bailey 18/190y, Baxter 14/193y
SCORING: Scott Etheridge (K) 86pts, Bostic 30pts, Parker 20pts

1993 11-0

16 Mississippi	12 WR Thomas Bailey / Sean Carder
35 Samford	7 WR Frank Sanders
34 LSU	10 T Wayne Gandy
35 Southern Miss	24 G Jason Taylor
14 Vanderbilt	10 C Shannon Robique
31 Mississippi St.	17 G Todd Boland / Willie Anderson
38 Florida	35 T Anthony Redmon
31 Arkansas	21 TE Andy Fuller / Derrick Dorn
55 New Mexico St.	14 QB Stan White
42 Georgia	28 TB James Bostic / Stephen Davis
22 Alabama	14 FB Tony Richardson
	DL Willie Whitehead
	DL Damon Primus
	DL Randy Hart / Mike Pelton
	DL Alonzo Etheridge / Gary Walker
	LB Terry Solomon
	LB Jason Miska
	LB Anthony Harris
	DB Chris Shelling
	DB Calvin Jackson / Dell McGee
	DB Brian Robinson
	DB Otis Mounds

RUSHING: Bostic 199/1205y, Davis 87/480y,
Richardson 58/249y
PASSING: White 164-271/2057y, 13TD, 60.5%
RECEIVING: Sanders 48/842y, Richardson 28/273y,
Bailey 27/427y
SCORING: Scott Etheridge (K) 81pts, Bostic 78pts,
Sanders 42pts

1994 9-1-1

22 Mississippi	17 WR Thomas Bailey / Willie Gosha
44 NE Louisiana	12 WR Frank Sanders / Tyrone Goodson
30 LSU	26 T Victor Riley
38 E. Tenn. St.	0 G Jason Taylor
41 Kentucky	14 C Shannon Robique
42 Mississippi St.	18 G Leonard Thomas
36 Florida	33 T Willie Anderson
31 Arkansas	14 TE Andy Fuller
38 East Carolina	21 QB Patrick Nix / Daymeyune Craig
23 Georgia	23 TB Stephen Davis / Fred Beasley
14 Alabama	21 FB Joe Frazier / Harold Morrow
	DL Willie Whitehead / Bobby Daffin
	DL Gary Walker / Nate Smith
	DL Mike Pelton / Shannon Suttle
	DL Alonzo Etheridge
	LB Marcellus Mostella
	LB Jason Miska
	LB Anthony Harris / Ricky Neal
	DB Chris Shelling
	DB Dell McGee / Larry Melton
	DB Brian Robinson
	DB Ken Alvis

RUSHING: Davis 221/1263y, Beasley 47/223y, Frazier 38/139y
PASSING: Nix 201-331/2206y, 13TD, 56.5%
RECEIVING: Sanders 58/910y, Bailey 41/550y, Morrow 15/171y
SCORING: Matt Hawkins (K) 79pts, Davis 78pts

1995 8-4

46 Mississippi	13 WR Willie Gosha / Errick Lowe
76 Tenn-Chatt'ga	10 WR Tyrone Goodson / Robert Baker
6 LSU	12 T Victor Riley / Jim Roe
42 Kentucky	21 G Jason Taylor / Kevin Cummings
48 Mississippi St.	20 C Shannon Robique / James Kiger
38 Florida	49 G Leonard Thomas
34 W. Michigan	13 T Willie Anderson / DeMarcus Curry
28 Arkansas	30 TE Andy Fuller / Jesse McCorvey
38 NE Louisiana	14 QB Patrick Nix / Dameyune Craig
37 Georgia	31 TB Stephen Davis
31 Alabama	27 FB Fred Beasley / Kevin McLeod
14 Penn State■	43 DL Scott Stacey / Shannon Suttle
	DL Jimmy Brumbaugh
	DL Mark Smith / Nate Smith
	LB Marcellus Mostella / Bobby Daffin
	LB Takeo Spikes
	LB Jason Miska
	LB Anthony Harris / Terry Solomon
	DB Larry Melton / Tyreece Williams
	DB Dell McGee / Dan Evans
	DB Charles Rose / Liron Thomas
	DB Martavius Houston

RUSHING: Davis 180/1068y, Beasley 66/346y,
Eric Hines-Tucker (TB) 29/245y
PASSING: Nix 201-331/2574y, 15TD, 60.7%
RECEIVING: Gosha 58/668y, Goodson 37/597y,
Harold Morrow (TB-FB) 31/262y
SCORING: Davis 102pts

1996 8-4

29 Ala-Birm'ham	0 WR Karsten Bailey / Robert Baker
62 Fresno State	0 WR Tyrone Goodson / Errick Lowe
45 Mississippi	28 T Jim Roe
15 LSU	19 G Victor Riley / Kendell Mack
28 South Carolina	24 C James Kiger / Karl Lavine
49 Mississippi St.	15 G Leonard Thomas / T.J. Dunigan
10 Florida	51 T Jeno James / DeMarcus Curry
28 Arkansas	7 TE Jesse McCorvey / Tyrone Dillard
28 NE Louisiana	24 QB Dameyune Craig
49 Georgia	56 TB Rusty Williams / Markeith Cooper
23 Alabama	24 FB Kevin McLeod / Fred Beasley
32 Army■	29 DL Shannon Suttle / Ezell Powell
	DL Jimmy Brumbaugh
	DL Charles Dorsey / Leonardo Carson
	LB Marcellus Mostella / Bobby Daffin
	LB Takeo Spikes
	LB Ricky Neal / Marcus Camp
	LB Terry Solomon / Quinton Reese
	DB Larry Melton
	DB Jason Bray/Rodney Crayton/A. Nolan
	DB Brad Ware
	DB Martavius Houston

RUSHING: Williams 80/439y, Beasley 94/428y, Cooper 64/351y
PASSING: Craig 169-310/2296y, 16TD, 54.5%
RECEIVING: Bailey 45/592y, Goodson 36/642y, Baker 34/528y
SCORING: Jaret Holmes (K) 82pts, Craig 48pts

1997 10-3

28 Virginia	17 WR Karsten Bailey / Clifton Robinson
19 Mississippi	9 WR Tyrone Goodson / Errick Lowe
31 LSU	28 T Victor Riley / Colin Sears
41 C. Florida	14 G T.J. Meers / Kendall Simmons
23 South Carolina	6 C T.J. Dunigan
49 Louisiana Tech	13 G DeMarcus Curry
10 Florida	24 T Jeno James / Kendell Mack
26 Arkansas	21 TE Tyrone Dillard
0 Mississippi St.	20 QB Dameyune Craig / Ben Leard
45 Georgia	34 TB Rusty Williams / Markeith Cooper
18 Alabama	17 FB Fred Beasley / Tellie Embery
29 Tennessee □	30 DL Leonardo Carson / Jeff Dunlap
21 Clemson■	17 DL Jimmy Brumbaugh
	DL Charles Dorsey / Jermey Banks
	LB Ryan Taylor / Roderick Chambers
	LB Takeo Spikes / Haven Fields
	LB Ricky Neal / Nathan Gardner
	LB Quinton Reese / Marcus Washington
	DB Larry Casher
	DB Antwoine Nolan / Jason Bray
	DB Brad Ware
	DB Martavius Houston / Courtney Rose

RUSHING: Williams 97/277y, Beasley 75/244y,
Demontray Carter (TB) 56/233y
PASSING: Craig 216-403/3277y, 18TD, 53.6%
RECEIVING: Bailey 53/840y, Goodson 48/906y,
Hicks Poor (WR) 34/558y
SCORING: Jaret Holmes (K) 78pts, Bailey & Beasley 42pts

1998 3-8

0 Virginia	19 WR Karsten Bailey / Ronney Daniels
17 Mississippi	0 WR Clifton Robinson / Errick Lowe
19 LSU	31 T Jeno James
9 Tennessee	17 G Kendall Simmons
21 Mississippi St.	38 C Cole Cubelic / Ben Nowland
3 Florida	4 G Mike Pucillo / DeMarco Curry
32 Louisiana Tech	17 T Colin Sears / Kendell Mack
21 Arkansas	24 TE Reid Tankersley
10 C. Florida	6 QB Gabe Gross / Ben Leard
17 Georgia	28 TB Michael Burks / Demontray Carter
17 Alabama	31 FB Heath Evans
	DL Marcus Washington / Whit Smith
	DL Charles Dorsey / Jeff Dunlap
	DL Jimmy Brumbaugh
	DL Leonardo Carson / Jeremy Banks
	LB Quinton Reese / Marcus Washington
	LB Tavarreus Pounds / Haven Fields
	LB Ryan Taylor
	DB Larry Casher / Brandon Reed
	DB Antwoine Nolan / Jayson Bray
	DB Brad Ware
	DB Rob Pate / Courtney Rose

RUSHING: Burks 152/483y, Carter 109/406y, Gross 70/97y
PASSING: Gross 88-197/1222y, 7TD, 44.7%
RECEIVING: Bailey 43/651y, Robinson 42/672y, Lowe 10/90y
SCORING: Rob Birones (K) 54pts, Bailey 42pts

1999 5-6

22 Appalachian St.	15 WR Ronney Daniels / Travaris Robinson
30 Idaho	23 WR Reggie Worthy/Tim Carter/M'rc'l Wills
41 LSU	7 T Jeno James / Kendall Simmons (G)
17 Mississippi	24 G Hart McGarry
0 Tennessee	24 C Cole Cubelic / Ben Nowland
16 Mississippi St.	18 G Mike Pucillo
14 Florida	32 T Tim Castro / T.J. Meers
10 Arkansas	34 TE Lorenzo Diamond
28 C. Florida	10 QB Ben Leard / Jeff Klein
38 Georgia	21 TB Demontray Carter / Michael Owens
17 Alabama	28 FB Heath Evans
	DL Marcus Washington / Whit Smith
	DL Jeff Dunlap
	DL Quinton Reese / Josh Weldon
	DL Leonardo Carson
	LB Tavarreus Pounds/Dontarri's Thomas
	LB Alex Lincoln / James Callier
	LB Rob Pate
	DB Larry Casher / Antwoine Nolan
	DB Rodney Crayton / Brandon Reed
	DB Stanford Simmons / Adlai Trone
	DB Courtney Rose

RUSHING: Evans 93/357y, Williams 102/297y,
Clifton Robinson (WR) 91/227y
PASSING: Leard 111-157/1423y, 12TD, 70.7%,
Klein 85-169/1038y, 6TD, 50.3%
RECEIVING: Daniels 56/1068y, Markeith Cooper (TB) 36/365y,
Worthy 23/270y
SCORING: Damon Duval (K) 56pts, Daniels 54pts

2000 9-4

35 Wyoming	21 WR Ronney Daniels / Marcel Willis
35 Mississippi	27 WR Tim Carter / Deandre Green
34 LSU	17 T Kendall Simmons
31 N. Illinois	14 G Hart McGarry
33 Vanderbilt	0 C Ben Nowland
10 Mississippi St.	17 G Mike Pucillo
7 Florida	38 T Colin Sears / Mark Pera
38 Louisiana Tech	28 TE Robert Johnson / Lorenzo Diamond
21 Arkansas	19 QB Ben Leard
29 Georgia	26 TB Rudi Johnson
9 Alabama	0 FB Heath Evans
6 Florida □	28 DL Javor Mills
28 Michigan■	21 DL DeMarco McNeil
	DL Spencer Johnson
	DL Reggie Torbor / Alton Moore
	LB Dontarrious Thomas/Tavar'us Pounds
	LB Alex Lincoln / Mark Brown
	LB Rob Pate / Rashaud Walker
	DB Larry Casher / Travaris Robinson
	DB Rodney Crayton / Ronaldo Attimy
	DB Stanford Simmons
	DB Roderick Hood

RUSHING: Johnson 324/1567y, Evans 42/260y, Carter 15/116y
PASSING: Leard 193-319/2158y, 12TD, 60.5%
RECEIVING: Daniels 34/378y, Willis 27/352y, Worthy 23/282y,
Green 23/240y
SCORING: Johnson 78pts

2001 7-5

30 Ball State	0 WR Marcel Willis / Deandre Green
27 Mississippi	21 WR Tim Carter / Silas Daniels
14 Syracuse	31 WR Jeris McIntyre/Brandon Johnson (FB)
24 Vanderbilt	21 T Kendall Simmons
16 Mississippi St.	14 G Hart McGarry / Danny Lindsey
23 Florida	20 C Ben Nowland
48 Louisiana Tech	41 G Mike Pucillo
17 Arkansas	42 T Monreko Crittenden / Mark Pera
24 Georgia	17 TE Lorenzo Diamond
7 Alabama	31 QB Jason Campbell / Daniel Cobb
14 LSU	27 RB Carnell Williams / Ronnie Brown
10 North Carolina■	16 DL James Callier / Bret Eddins
	DL DeMarco McNeil
	DL Spencer Johnson / Dexter Murphy
	DL Javor Mills / Reggie Torbor
	LB Karlos Dansby
	LB Mark Brown
	LB Dontarrious Thomas / Derrick Graves
	DB Roderick Hood / Rashaud Walker
	DB Carlos Rogers
	DB Travaris Robinson / Donnay Young
	DB Junior Rosegreen / Roshard Gilyard

RUSHING: Williams 120/614y, Brown 84/330y
PASSING: Cobb 89-158/1165y, 7TD, 56.3%,
Campbell 89-142/1117y, 4TD, 62.7%
RECEIVING: Carter 35/570y
SCORING; Damon Duval (K) 76pts

2002 9-4

17 Southern Cal	24 WR Marcel Willis / Devin Aromashodu
56 W. Carolina	0 WR Ben Obomanu
31 Vanderbilt	6 WR Jeris McIntyre/Brandon Johnson (FB)
42 Mississippi St.	14 T Mark Pera
37 Syracuse	34 G Danny Lindsey / Troy Reddick
17 Arkansas	38 C Ben Nowland
23 Florida	30 G Monreko Crittenden
31 LSU	7 T Marcus McNeil
31 Mississippi	24 TE Lorenzo Diamond / Robert Johnson
52 La-Monroe	14 QB Daniel Cobb / Jason Campbell
21 Georgia	24 RB Ronnie Brown / Carnell Williams
17 Alabama	7 DL Jay Ratliff / Bret Eddins
13 Penn State■	9 DL DeMarco McNeil
	DL Spencer Johnson / Dexter Murphy
	DL Reggie Torbor
	LB Karlos Dansby
	LB Mark Brown
	LB Dontarrious Thomas / Travis Williams
	DB Roderick Hood
	DB Carlos Rogers
	DB Travaris Robinson / Donnay Young
	DB Junior Rosegreen / Roshard Gilyard

RUSHING: Brown 175/1008y, Williams 141/745y
PASSING: Campbell 94-149/1215y, 11TD, 63.1%
RECEIVING: Willis 31/417y, Aromashodu 18/304y, Obomanu 17/224y
SCORING: Brown 84pts

2003 8-5

0 Southern Cal	23 WR Courtney Taylor / Silas Daniels
3 Georgia Tech	17 WR Ben Obomanu / Devin Aromashodu
45 Vanderbilt	7 WR Jeris McIntyre / Jake Slaughter (FB)
48 W. Kentucky	3 T Mark Pera
28 Tennessee	21 G Troy Reddick
10 Arkansas	3 C Danny Lindsey
45 Mississippi St.	13 G Monreko Crittenden
7 LSU	31 T Marcus McNeil / Steven Ross
73 La.-Monroe	7 TE Cooper Wallace
20 Mississippi	24 QB Jason Campbell
7 Georgia	26 RB Carnell Williams / Ronnie Brown
28 Alabama	23 DL Bret Eddins
28 Wisconsin■	14 DL DeMarco McNeil
	DL Spencer Johnson / T.J. Jackson
	DL Reggie Torbor
	LB Travis Williams / Antarrious Williams
	LB Dontarrious Thomas
	LB Karlos Densby / Derrick Graves
	DB Carlos Rogers
	DB Kevin Hobbs / Montavis Pitts
	DB Will Herring / Karibi Dede
	DB Junior Rosegreen

RUSHING: Williams 241/1307y, Brandon Jacobs (RB) 72/446y, Brown 95/446y
PASSING: Campbell 181-293/2267y, 10TD, 61.8%
RECEIVING: McIntyre 41/621y, Taylor 34/379y, Daniels 23/284y
SCORING: Williams 102pts, Philip Yost (K) 31pts, Brown 30pts

2004 13-0

31 La.-Monroe	0 WR Courtney Taylor
43 Mississippi St.	14 WR Devin Aromashodu / Ben Obomanu
10 LSU	9 WR Anthony Mix / Jake Slaughter (FB)
33 Citadel	3 T Marcus McNeil
34 Tennessee	10 G Ben Grubbs
52 Louisiana Tech	7 C Jeremy Ingle
38 Arkansas	20 G Danny Lindsey
42 Kentucky	10 T Troy Riddick
35 Mississippi	14 TE Cooper Wallace / Cole Bennett
24 Georgia	6 QB Jason Campbell
21 Alabama	13 TB Carnell Williams / Ronnie Brown
38 Tennessee □	28 DL Doug Langenfeld / Stanley McClover
16 Virginia Tech■	13 DL Tommy Jackson
	DL Jay Ratliff
	DL Bret Eddins / Marquies Gunn
	LB Kevin Sears
	LB Travis Williams
	LB Derrick Graves / Antarrious Williams
	DB Carlos Rogers
	DB Montavis Pitts / Kevin Hobbs
	DB Will Herring
	DB Junior Rosegreen / Donnay Young

RUSHING: Williams 239/1165y, Brown 153/913y, Carl Stewart (TB) 39/184y
PASSING: Campbell 188-270/2700y, 20TD, 69.6%
RECEIVING: Taylor 43/737y, Brown 34/313y, Obomanu 25/359y, Aromashodu 24/513y
SCORING: John Vaughn (K) 87pts, Williams 78pts, Brown 54pts

2005 9-3

14 Georgia Tech	23 WR Anthony Mix / Courtney Taylor
28 Mississippi St.	0 WR Devin Aromashodu
63 Ball State	3 WR Ben Obomanu / Prechae Rodriguez
37 W. Kentucky	14 T Marcus McNeill
48 South Carolina	7 G Ben Grubbs
34 Arkansas	17 C Joe Cope / Steven Ross
17 LSU	20 G Tim Duckworth / Leon Hart
27 Mississippi	3 T Troy Reddick / Jonathan Palmer (G-C)
49 Kentucky	27 TE Cooper Wallace / Cole Bennett
31 Georgia	30 QB Brandon Cox
28 Alabama	18 TB Kenny Irons / Brad Lester
10 Wisconsin■	24 DL Marquies Gunn
	DL T.J. Jackson
	DL Wayne Dickens
	DL Stanley McGlover / Quentin Groves
	LB Karibi Dede / Kevin Sears
	LB Travis Williams
	LB Antarrious Williams
	DB Jonathan Wilhite / Montavis Pitts
	DB David Irons / Kevin Hobbs
	DB Will Herring
	DB Eric Brock / Steve Gandy

RUSHING: K. Irons 256/1293y, Lester 52/339y, Tre Smith 56/285y
PASSING: Cox 177-306/2324y, 15TD, 57.8%
RECEIVING: Obomanu 33/357y, Aromashodu 26/494y, Mix 23/288y, Taylor 22/278y, Wallace 20/195y
SCORING: John Vaughn (K) 86pts, K. Irons 78pts, Obomanu & Letser 42pts

2006 11-2

40 Washington St.	14 WR Courtney Taylor / Lee Guess
34 Mississippi St.	0 WR Rodgeriqus Smith/Pr'chae Rodriguez
7 LSU	3 T King Dunlap
38 Buffalo	7 G Ben Grubbs
24 South Carolina	17 C Joe Cope
10 Arkansas	27 G Tim Duckworth
27 Florida	17 T Jonathan Palmer
38 Tulane	13 TE Tommy Trott / Gabe McKenzie
23 Mississippi	17 QB Brandon Cox
27 Arkansas State	0 TB Kenny Irons / Brad Lester
15 Georgia	37 FB Carl Stewart
22 Alabama	15 DL Marquies Gunn
17 Nebraska■	14 DL Josh Thompson
	DL Sen'Derrick Marks /Chris'ph'r Browder
	DL Quentin Groves / Antonio Coleman
	LB Will Herring
	LB Karibi Dede
	LB Merrill Johnson / Tray Blackmon
	DB Jonathan Wilhite / Jerraud Powers
	DB David Irons / Patrick Lee
	DB Aairon Savage
	DB Eric Brock

RUSHING: K. Irons 198/893y, Lester 104/510y, Ben Tate (TB) 54/392y
PASSING: Cox 163-271/2198y 14TD, 60.1%
RECEIVING: Taylor 54/704y, Smith 26/452y, Rodriguez 14/168y, Stewart 13/239y, McKenzie 13/137y
SCORING: John Vaughn (K) 94pts, Lester 60pts, Stewart 30pts

2007 9-4

23 Kansas State	13 WR Rodgeriqus Smith / Robert Dunn
23 South Florida	26 WR Montez Billings / Prechae Rodriguez
14 Mississippi St.	19 T King Dunlap / Ryan Pugh
55 New Mexico St.	20 G Tyronne Green
20 Florida	17 C Jason Bosley
35 Vanderbilt	7 G Chaz Ramsey / Mike Berry
9 Arkansas	7 T Lee Ziemba
24 LSU	30 TE Cole Bennett
17 Mississippi	3 QB Brandon Cox / Kodi Burns
35 Tennessee Tech	3 TB Ben Tate / Brad Lester / Mario Fannin
20 Georgia	45 FB Carl Stewart / Tim Hawthorne (WR)
17 Alabama	10 DL Antonio Coleman / Quentin Groves
23 Clemson■	20 DL Josh Thompson
	DL Pat Sims
	DL Sen'Derrick Marks / Antoine Carter
	LB Craig Stevens
	LB Tray Blackmon / Bo Harris
	LB Chris Evans / Merrill Johnson
	DB Jerraud Powers
	DB Patrick Lee / Jonathan Wilhite
	DB Eric Brock / Aairon Savage
	DB Zac Etheridge / Mike McNeil

RUSHING: Tate 202/903y, Lester 125/530y, Fannin 84/448y
PASSING: Cox 188-316/2080y, 9TD, 59.5%
RECEIVING: Smith 52/705y, Billings 28/321y, Dunn 19/211y
SCORING: Wes Byrum (K) 84pts, Tate 48pts, Fannin 42pts

2008 5-7

34 La.-Monroe	0 WR Rodgeriqus Smith / Chris Slaughter
27 Southern Miss	13 WR Montez Billing / Mario Fannin (RB)
3 Mississippi St.	26 G Tyronne Green
21 LSU	12 C Ryan Pugh (T)
14 Tennessee	14 G Byron Isom / Mike Berry
13 Vanderbilt	25 T Jason Bosley (C)
22 Arkansas	34 TE Tommy Trott / Vance Smith
17 West Virginia	17 QB Kodi Burns / Chris Todd
7 Mississippi	20 RB Brad Lester / Ben Tate
37 Tenn.-Martin	17 RB Tristan Davis / Eric Smith
13 Georgia	36 DL Michael Goggans
0 Alabama	DL Mike Blanc / Tez Doolittle
	DL Sen'Derrick Marks / Zach Clayton
	DL Antonio Coleman / Antoine Carter
	LB Craig Stevens
	LB Tray Blackmon / Josh Bynes
	LB Merrill Johnson / Chris Evans
	DB Walter McFadden / D'Antoine Hood
	DB Jerraud Powers / Neiko Thorpe
	DB Zac Etheridge
	DB Mike McNeill

RUSHING: Tate 159/664y, Burns 98/411y, Lester 80/289y
PASSING: Burns 94-179/1050y, 2TD, 52.5%
Todd 86-156/903y, 5TD, 55.1%
RECEIVING: Smith 30/332y, Billings 24/277y, Fannin 20/223y, Trott 20/201y
SCORING: Wes Byrum (K) 55pts, Burns 30pts, 5 with 18pts

2009 8-5

37 Louisiana Tech	13 WR Darvin Adams / Jay Wisner
49 Mississippi St.	24 WR Terrell Zachery / Quindarius Carr
41 West Virginia	30 T Lee Ziemba
54 Ball State	30 G Mike Berry
26 Tennessee	22 C Ryan Pugh / Bart Eddins
23 Arkansas	44 G Byron Isom / John Sullen
14 Kentucky	21 T Andrew McCain
10 LSU	31 TE Tommy Trott / Philip Lutzenkirchen
33 Mississippi	20 QB Chris Todd / Kodi Burns
63 Furman	21 TB Ben Tate / Eric Smith
24 Georgia	31 FB Mario Fannin
21 Alabama	26 DL Antonio Coleman
38 Northwestern■	35 DL Mike Blanc / Nick Fairley
	DL Jake Ricks
	DL Michael Goggans / Antoine Carter
	LB Craig Stevens
	LB Josh Bynes / Adam Herring
	LB Eltoro Freeman / Jonathan Evans
	DB Walter McFadden
	DB Neiko Thorpe
	DB Zac Etheridge / Demond Washington
	DB Daren Bates / Mike Slade

RUSHING: Tate 263/1362y, Onterio McCalebb (TB) 105/565y, Fannin 34/285y, Zachery 9/214y
PASSING: Todd 198-328/2612y, 22TD, 60.4%
RECEIVING: Adams 60/997y, Fannin 42/413y, Zachery 26/477y
SCORING: Wes Bynum (K) 99pts, Adams & Tate 60pts

2010 14-0

52 Arkansas State	26 WR Kodi Burns
17 Mississippi State	14 WR Darvin Adams / Emory Blake
27 Clemson	24 WR/HB Terrell Zachery/Philip Lutzenkirchen
35 South Carolina	27 T Lee Ziemba
52 La. Monroe	3 G Mike Berry
37 Kentucky	34 C Ryan Pugh
65 Arkansas	43 G Byron Isom
24 LSU	17 T Brandon Mosley / A.J. Green
51 Mississippi	31 QB Cam Newton
62 Chattanooga	24 RB Michael Dyer / Onterrio McCalebb
49 Georgia	31 FB Eric Smith / Mario Fannin
28 Alabama	27 DL Antoine Carter / Corey Lemonier
56 South Carolina □	17 DL Zach Clayton / Mike Blanc
22 Oregon■	19 DL Nick Fairley
	DL Nosa Eguae / Michael Goggans
	LB Craig Stevens / Jonathan Evans
	LB Josh Bynes
	LB Daren Bates / Eltoro Freeman
	DB D. Washington / Demetruce McNeil
	DB Neiko Thorpe / T'Sharvan Bell
	DB Zac Etheridge
	DB Mike McNeil / Aairon Savage

RUSHING: Newton 264/1473y, Dyer 182/1093y, McCalebb 95/810y
PASSING: Newton 185-280/2854y, 30TD, 66.1%
RECEIVING: Adams 52/963y, Zachery 43/605y, Blake 33/554y
SCORING: Newton 126pts, Wes Byrum (K) 123pts, McCalebb 60pts

BAYLOR

Baylor University (Founded 1845)
Waco, Texas
Nickname: Bears
Colors: Green and Gold
Stadium: Floyd Casey Stadium (1950) 50,000
Conference Affiliations: Southwest (1914-95),
 Big Twelve South (1996-present)

CAREER RUSHING YARDS	Attempts	Yards
Walter Abercrombie (1978-81)	732	3665
Jerod Douglas (1994-97)	522	2811
Jay Finley (2007-10)	478	2660
Alfred Anderson (1980-83)	554	2424
Darrell Bush (1997-2000)	503	2249
Dennis Gentry (1977, 1979-81)	414	2231
David Mims (1989-92)	364	2060
Eldwin Raphel (1987-90)	435	1921
Robert Strait (1990-93)	428	1856
Rashad Armstrong (2002-03)	417	1721

CAREER PASSING YARDS	Comp.-Att.	Yards
Robert Griffin (2008-10)	509-790	6073
J.J. Joe (1990-93)	347-665	5995
Shawn Bell (2003-06)	559-914	5666
Jeff Watson (1994-97)	425-802	5531
Cody Carlson (1983-86)	366-705	5411
Brad Goebel (1987-90)	375-730	5026
Neal Jeffrey (1972-74)	321-603	4341
Blake Szymanski (2006-09)	387-678	4166
Terry Southall (1964-66)	328-629	4100
Jermaine Alfred (1995-99)	322-644	3968

CAREER RECEIVING YARDS	Catches	Yards
Gerald McNeil (1980-83)	163	2651
Reggie Newhouse (1999-02)	183	2552
Kendall Wright (2008-10)	194	2341
Lawrence Elkins (1962-64)	144	2094
Melvin Bonner (1989-92)	92	1984
Trent Shelton (2003-06)	155	1978
Dominique Ziegler (2003-06)	166	1923
David Gettis (2008-09)	116	1555
Matt Clark (1984-87)	81	1480
Robert Quiroga (2000-03)	131	1478

SEASON RUSHING YARDS	Attempts	Yards
Jay Finley (2010)	195	1218
Walter Abercrombie (1980)	229	1187
Jerod Douglas (1995)	211	1114
Cleveland Franklin (1975)	200	1112
Steve Beaird (1974)	267	1104

SEASON PASSING YARDS	Comp.-Att.	Yards
Robert Griffin (2010)	304-454	3501
Blake Szymanski (2007)	264-461	2844
Shawn Bell (2006)	241-383	2582
Cody Carlson (1986)	157-287	2284
Brad Goebel (1987)	158-305	2178

SEASON RECEIVING YARDS	Catches	Yards
Reggie Newhouse (2002)	75	1140
Gerald McNeil (1983)	62	1034
Kendall Wright (2010)	78	952
Charles Dancer (1973)	53	927
Lawrence Elkins (1963)	70	873

GAME RUSHING YARDS	Attempts	Yards
Jay Finley (2010 vs. Kansas State)	26	250
Robert Griffin (2008 vs. Washington State)	11	225
Jerod Douglas (1994 vs. Texas)	20	210

GAME PASSING YARDS	Comp.-Att.	Yards
Nick Florence (2009 vs. Missouri)	32-43	427
Blake Szymanski (2007 vs. Rice)	29-46	412
Blake Szymanski (2007 vs. Texas State)	31-51	411

GAME RECEIVING YARDS	Catches	Yards
Gerald McNeil (1981 vs. Arkansas)	10	197
Melvin Bonner (1992 vs. Georgia Tech)	5	174
Reggie Newhouse (2002 vs. Kansas State)	9	173
Charles Dancer (1973 vs. TCU)	7	173

GREATEST COACH:

Although it may not have seemed so fortuitous at the time, the best thing that Rudy Feldman could have done for the Baylor program upon being hired as its new head coach in 1972 was what he, indeed, did: resign after one day. The jilted Bears turned to a little-known Angelo State head coach named Grant Teaff to resurrect their dilapidated program, winners of a mere seven games over the most recent five years.

They scored a touchdown with their second choice. By 1974, Teaff had Baylor fans forgetting about both Feldman and their team's former losing ways. In that incredible season, the Bears won eight games, including a sweep of conference powers Arkansas and Texas, a feat they had not accomplished since 1956, to win the Southwest Conference and earn a Cotton Bowl bid. The season was dubbed the "Miracle on the Brazos."

But there was more. A Texan through and through, Teaff was content with the Baylor job, building the program into a second-tier power. He won 128 games, plus another SWC title, in 1980. The Bears went to bowl games eight times, winning four of them. He beat Texas 10 times, which made Baylor fans very happy. Included in that total was the 38-14 pasting of favored Longhorns in 1978 after Teaff gained some notoriety by eating a live worm as a motivational tool.

All-in-all, he did fine for a second choice.

BAYLOR'S 55 GREATEST SINCE 1953

OFFENSE

WIDE RECEIVER: Melvin Bonner, Lawrence Elkins, Gerald McNeil, Reggie Newhouse
TIGHT END: Ronnie Lee
TACKLE: Mark Adickes. Fred Miller, Joel Porter, Jason Smith, Danny Watkins
GUARD: Frank Ditta, Billy Glass, Monte Jones, Mark Kirchner
CENTER: John Adickes, Aubrey Schulz
QUARTERBACK: Cody Carlson, Robert Griffin, Neal Jeffrey, Don Trull
RUNNING BACK: Walter Abercrombie, Alfred Anderson, Jerod Douglas, Dennis Gentry
FULLBACK: Larry Hickman

DEFENSE

END: Charles Benson, Roger Goree, Donnie Laurence, Ervin Randle
TACKLE: Santana Dotson, Daryl Gardener, Gary Don Johnson, Greg Pipes
LINEBACKER: Ray Berry, James Francis, Derrell Luce, Bobby Maples, Le'Shai Matson,
 Mike Singletary
CORNERBACK: Gary Baxter, Ron Burns, Ron Francis, Gary Green
SAFETY: Robert Blackmon, Thomas Everett, Vann McElroy, Adrian Robinson

SPECIAL TEAMS

RETURN SPECIALISTS: Malcolm Frank, Kalief Muhammad
PLACE KICKER: Marty Jimmerson
PUNTER: Daniel Sepulveda

MULTIPLE POSITIONS

HALFBACK-FULLBACK: Ronnie Bull
CENTER-GUARD-TACKLE: Gary Gregory

TWO-WAY PLAYERS

CENTER-GUARD-TACKLE-DEFENSIVE TACKLE: Bill Glass
HALFBACK-DEFENSIVE BACK: Del Shofner

PERFORMANCE FORMULA:
BAYLOR'S 10 BEST SEASONS

1956	1.4684	8 of 69
1980	1.4581	14 of 70
1985	1.4347	17 of 70
1960	1.3483	18 of 70
1986	1.3237	21 of 70
1963	1.3192	17 of 70
1974	1.2675	21 of 71
1953	1.2576	26 of 69
1979	1.2448	23 of 70
1991	1.2357	26 of 71

BAYLOR BEARS

Year	W-L-T	AP Poll	Conference Standing	Toughest Regular Season Opponents	Coach (Record at School)	Bowl Games		
1953	7-3		3	Rice 8-2, Texas 7-3, SMU 5-5	George Sauer			
1954	7-4	18	3t	Arkansas 8-2, Miami 8-1, Rice 7-3, SMU 6-3-1	George Sauer	Gator	13 Auburn	33
1955	5-5		5t	Maryland 10-0, TCU 9-1, Texas A&M 7-2-1	George Sauer (38-21-3)			
1956	9-2	18	3	Texas A&M 9-0-1, TCU 7-3, Arkansas 6-4	Sam Boyd	Sugar	13 Tennessee	7
1957	3-6-1		7	Texas A&M 8-2, Rice 7-3, Texas 6-3-1, Arkansas 6-4	Sam Boyd			
1958	3-7		7	TCU 8-2, Texas 7-3, SMU 6-4	Sam Boyd (15-15-1)			
1959	4-6		5	LSU 9-1, Texas 9-1, Arkansas 8-2, Southern Cal 8-2, TCU 8-2	John Bridgers			
1960	8-3	12	2t	Arkansas 8-2, Texas 7-3, Rice 7-3, Colorado 6-4	John Bridgers	Gator	12 Florida	13
1961	6-5		6t	Texas 9-1, Arkansas 8-2, Rice 7-3	John Bridgers	Gotham	24 Utah State	9
1962	4-6		4t	Texas 9-0-1, Arkansas 9-1, TCU 6-4, Houston 6-4	John Bridgers			
1963	8-3		2	Texas 10-0, Rice 6-4	John Bridgers	Bluebonnet	14 LSU	7
1964	5-5		3	Arkansas 10-0, Texas 9-1, Oregon State 8-2, Texas Tech 6-3-1	John Bridgers			
1965	5-5		4t	Arkansas 10-0, Texas Tech 8-2, Texas 6-4, TCU 6-4	John Bridgers			
1966	5-5		5	Arkansas 8-2, Syracuse 8-2, SMU 8-2, Colorado 7-3	John Bridgers			
1967	1-8-1		8	Colorado 8-2, Syracuse 8-2, Texas A&M 6-4, TCU 6-4, Texas 6-4	John Bridgers			
1968	3-7		5	Arkansas 9-1, Texas 8-1-1, SMU 7-3, LSU 7-3	John Bridgers (49-53-1)			
1969	0-10		8	Texas 10-0, Arkansas 9-1, LSU 9-1	Bill Beall			
1970	2-9		7	Texas 10-0, Arkansas 9-2, LSU 9-2, Texas Tech 8-3	Bill Beall			
1971	1-9		8	Texas 8-2, Arkansas 8-2-1, TCU 6-4-1	Bill Beall (3-28)			
1972	5-6		4t	Texas 9-1, Texas Tech 8-3, SMU 7-4, Georgia 7-4	Grant Teaff			
1973	2-9		8	Texas 8-2, Texas Tech 10-1, Pitt 6-4-1	Grant Teaff			
1974	8-4	14	1	Texas 8-3, Texas A&M 8-3, Texas Tech 6-4-2	Grant Teaff	Cotton	20 Penn State	41
1975	3-6-2		5t	Texas A&M 10-1, Michigan 8-1-2, Arkansas 9-2, Texas 9-2	Grant Teaff			
1976	7-3-1		4	Houston 10-1, Texas Tech 10-1, Texas A&M 9-2	Grant Teaff			
1977	5-6		6	Texas 11-0, Arkansas 10-1, Kentucky 10-1, Texas A&M 8-3	Grant Teaff			
1978	3-8		6t	Georgia 9-1-1, Houston 9-2, Arkansas 9-2, Texas Tech 7-4	Grant Teaff			
1979	8-4	14	4	Alabama 11-0, Arkansas 10-1, Houston 10-1	Grant Teaff	Peach	24 Clemson	18
1980	10-2	14	1	SMU 8-3, Texas 7-4	Grant Teaff	Cotton	2 Alabama	30
1981	5-5		6	Texas 9-1-1, SMU 10-1	Grant Teaff			
1982	4-6-1		5	SMU 10-0-1, Texas 9-2, Ohio State 8-3	Grant Teaff			
1983	7-4-1		3t	Texas 11-0, SMU 10-1, BYU 10-1	Grant Teaff	Bluebonnet	14 Oklahoma State	24
1984	5-6		6	BYU, 12-0, SMU 9-2, Texas 7-3-1, Houston 7-4	Grant Teaff			
1985	9-3	17	2t	Texas A&M 9-2, Arkansas 9-2, Georgia 7-3-1	Grant Teaff	Liberty	21 LSU	7
1986	9-3	12	2t	Texas A&M 9-2, Arkansas 9-2, Texas Tech 7-4, Southern Cal 7-4	Grant Teaff	Bluebonnet	21 Colorado	9
1987	6-5		5t	Texas A&M 9-2, Arkansas 8-4	Grant Teaff			
1988	6-5		4t	Arkansas 10-1, Texas A&M 7-4	Grant Teaff			
1989	5-6		4t	Arkansas 10-1, Texas A&M 8-3, Texas Tech 8-3, Georgia 6-5	Grant Teaff			
1990	6-4-1		2t	Texas 10-1, Houston 10-1, Nebraska 9-2	Grant Teaff			
1991	8-4		2t	Texas A&M 10-1, Colorado 8-2-1, Arkansas 6-5, Texas Tech 6-5	Grant Teaff	Copper	0 Indiana	24
1992	7-5		2t	Texas A&M 12-0, Colorado 9-1-1	Grant Teaff (128-105-6)	Hancock	20 Arizona	15
1993	5-6		4t	Texas A&M 10-1, Colorado 7-3-1	Chuck Reedy			
1994	7-5		1t	Texas A&M 10-0-1, Texas 7-4, Washington St. 7-4, So. Cal 7-4	Chuck Reedy	Alamo	3 Washington State	10
1995	7-4		2t	Texas 9-2-1, Arkansas 8-3, Texas Tech 8-3, Miami 8-3	Chuck Reedy			
1996	4-7		S6	Nebraska 10-1, Texas 7-4, Texas Tech 7-4	Chuck Reedy (23-22)			
1997	2-9		S6	Michigan 11-0, Nebraska 11-0, Missouri 7-4	Dave Roberts			
1998	2-9		S6	Kansas St. 11-0, Texas A&M 10-2, Texas 8-3, Notre Dame 9-2	Dave Roberts (4-18)			
1999	1-10		S6	Kansas St. 10-1, Texas 9-3, Texas A&M 8-3, Boston College 8-3	Kevin Steele			
2000	2-9		S6	Oklahoma 11-0, Texas 9-2, Nebraska 9-2, Iowa State 8-3	Kevin Steele			
2001	3-8		S6	Texas 10-1, Nebraska 11-1, Oklahoma 10-2, Texas Tech 7-4	Kevin Steele			
2002	3-9		S6	Oklahoma 10-2, Texas 10-2, Kansas St. 10-2, Colorado 9-3	Kevin Steele (9-36)			
2003	3-9		S6	Oklahoma 12-0, Texas 10-2, Oklahoma State 9-3, Texas Tech 7-5	Guy Morriss			
2004	3-8		S6	Oklahoma 11-0, Texas 10-1, Texas A&M 7-4, Texas Tech 7-4	Guy Morriss			
2005	5-6		S5	Texas 11-0, Texas Tech 9-2, Oklahoma 7-4	Guy Morriss			
2006	4-8		S5t	Oklahoma 10-2, Texas 9-3, Texas Tech 7-5	Guy Morriss			
2007	3-9		S6	Kansas 11-1, Texas 9-3, Oklahoma 10-2	Guy Morriss (18-40)			
2008	4-8		S5t	Oklahoma 12-1, Oklahoma State 9-3, Missouri 9-4, Texas 11-1	Art Briles			
2009	4-8		S6	Oklahoma State 9-3, Nebraska 9-4, Texas 13-0	Art Briles			
2010	7-6		S4t	TCU 12-0, Oklahoma State 10-2, Oklahoma 11-2	Art Briles (15-22)	Texas	14 Illinois	38

| **TOTAL:** | | | **283-351-8 .4470 (55 of 70)** | | **Bowl Games since 1953:** | **7-8 .4667 (43 of 70)** | | |

GREATEST TEAM SINCE 1953: Although the surprise Southwest Conference champion Bears of 1974 may be the most special team in the hearts of fans, the best team was probably the 1980 edition. Sweeping their SWC competition, Baylor was led on defense by linebacker Mike Singletary, defensive end Charles Benson, and safety Vann McElroy. The offense did most of its damage on the ground behind Walter Abercrombie and Dennis Gentry. The Bears of 1980 finished with a national rank of 14th while posting Baylor's only 10-win season. Kudos also to the 1956 Bears, led by All-America guard Bill Glass and halfback Del Shofner, who stunned undefeated Tennessee in the Sugar Bowl.

1953 7-3
25 California	0 E Charlie Smith / Ron Black
21 Miami	13 T Jim Ray Smith / Bill Green
14 Arkansas	7 G Clarence Dierking / Jim Culvahouse
47 Vanderbilt	6 C Jim Taylor / Bill Barnard
14 Texas A&M	13 G Pete Erben / Bill Lucky
25 TCU	7 T Robert Knowles / Clyde Letbetter
20 Texas	21 E Wayne Hopkins / James Amyett
7 Houston	37 QB Fran Davidson / Billy Hooper
27 SMU	21 HB Jerry Coody
19 Rice	41 HB L.G. Dupre / Mickey Sullivan
	FB Allen Jones / Weldon Holley

RUSHING: Dupre 134/593y, Coody 113/514y, Jones 95/443y
PASSING: Davidson 74-156/1092y, 9TD, 47.4%
RECEIVING: Hopkins 21/351y, C. Smith 14/233y, Dupre 13/143y
SCORING: Dupre 50pts, Davidson 40pts, Coody 31pts

1954 7-4
53 Houston	13 E Charlie Smith
25 Vanderbilt	19 T Jim Ray Smith
13 Miami	19 G Clarence Dierking
20 Arkansas	21 C Bill Glass / Jim Taylor
34 Washington	7 G Dan Miller / Henry Rutherford
20 Texas A&M	7 T Dave Lunceford / Bill Green
12 TCU	7 E Henry Gremminger / James Amyett
13 Texas	7 QB Billy Hooper / Bobby Jones
33 SMU	21 HB Del Shofner / Ronnie Guess
14 Rice	20 HB L.G. Dupre / Weldon Holley
13 Auburn■	33 FB Allen Jones / Rueben Saage

RUSHING: Shofner 88/545y, Jones 68/382y, Dupre 97/377y
PASSING: Hooper 56-107/818y, 6TD, 52.3%
RECEIVING: Gremminger 18/323y, Smith 13/194y, Amyett 10/152y
SCORING: Shofner 43pts, Hooper 36pts, Dupre 30pts

1955 5-5
35 Hardin-Simmons	7 E Tony DeGrazier / Earl Miller
19 Villanova	2 T Bill Glass
6 Maryland	20 G Dan Miller / Henry Rutherford
25 Arkansas	20 C Lee Harrington / Jim Taylor
13 Washington	7 G Dugan Pearce
7 Texas A&M	19 T Dave Lunceford / Charley Bradshaw
6 TCU	28 E Henry Gremminger / Dick Baker
20 Texas	21 QB Bobby Jones / Doyle Traylor
0 SMU	12 HB Del Shofner
15 Rice	7 HB Weldon Holley / Bobby Peters
	FB Rueben Saage / Charley Dupre

RUSHING: Saage 87/380y, Shofner 62/352y, Holley 57/257y
PASSING: Jones 29-65/439y, 3TD, 44.6%
RECEIVING: Gremminger 15/181y, Miller 10/153y, Baker 8/100y
SCORING: Shofner 30pts, 4 tied w/ 18pts

1956 9-2
7 California	6 E Earl Miller / Tony DeGrazier
27 Texas Tech	0 T Bobby Jack Oliver / Charley Bradshaw
14 Maryland	0 G Bill Glass / Dugan Pearce
14 Arkansas	7 C Lee Harrington / Larry Cowart
13 Texas A&M	19 G Charles Horton / Clyde Letbetter
6 TCU	7 T Dave Lunceford / Bill Parsley
10 Texas	7 E Jerry Marcontell / J. Amyett/ B. Anderson
26 Nebraska	7 QB D. Traylor/Bob Jones/Buddy Humphrey
26 SMU	0 HB Del Shofner/Bob Morris/Farrell Fisher
46 Rice	13 HB Bobby Peters / Donnel Berry
13 Tennessee■	7 FB Rueben Saage / Larry Hickman

RUSHING: Shofner 70/449y, Hickman 92/431y, Peters 65/212y
PASSING: Traylor 15-27/209y, 2TD, 55.5%
RECEIVING: Shofner 14/249y, Marcontell 8/113y, Anderson 8/80y
SCORING: Shofner 60pts, Hickman, Peters & Fisher 18pts

1957 3-6-1
7 Villanova	0 E Earl Miller / Al Witcher / Gary Wisener
14 Houston	6 T Bobby Jack Oliver / Billy Joe Kelley
7 Miami	13 G Dick Pyburn / Willie Froebel
17 Arkansas	20 C Larry Cowart / Lee Harrington
15 Texas Tech	12 G Clyde Letbetter / Charles Horton
0 Texas A&M	14 T Charley Bradshaw / Paul Dickson
6 TCU	19 E Jerry Marcontell / Bill Anderson
7 Texas	7 QB Doyle Traylor / Buddy Humphrey
7 SMU	14 HB Farrell Fisher / Ronnie Guess
0 Rice	20 HB Bob Peters/Austin Gonsoulin/Art Beall
	FB Larry Hickman / Gaylen Crain

RUSHING: Hickman 145/612y, Beall 53/207y, Peters 42/187y
PASSING: Traylor 43-88/482y, 3TD, 48.9%
RECEIVING: Miller 16/249y, Anderson 16/181y, Wisener 15/161y
SCORING: Hickman 24pts, Beall (HB-K) 14pts, Miller 12pts

1958 3-7
12 Arkansas	0 E Austin Gonsoulin / Gary Wisener
14 Hardin-Simmons	7 T Billy Joe Kelly
8 Miami	14 G Buddy Burt
7 Duke	12 C Arlis James / Horace Dansby
26 Texas Tech	7 G Charley Horton
27 Texas A&M	33 T Paul Dickson
0 TCU	22 E Al Witcher / Gerry Moore
15 Texas	20 QB Buddy Humphrey / Bill McMillen
29 SMU	33 HB Billy Pavliska / Merton Fuquay
21 Rice	33 WB Art Beall / Farrell Fisher
	FB Larry Hickman / Gaylen Crain

RUSHING: Hickman 151/670y, Pavliska 99/395y, Crain 40/156y
PASSING: Humphrey 112-195/1316y, 7TD, 57.4%
RECEIVING: Moore 31/357y, Witcher 23/268y, Wisener 19/219y
SCORING: Hickman 42pts, Moore 17pts,
Pavliska & Gonsoulin 14pts

1959 4-6
15 Colorado	7 E Sonny Davis / Gary Wisener
0 LSU	22 T Buck McLeod
7 Arkansas	23 G Everett Frazier / Gayle Watkins
14 Texas Tech	7 C Bill Hicks
13 Texas A&M	0 G Herby Adkins
0 TCU	14 T Royce West
12 Texas	13 E Albert Witcher / Gerry Moore
8 Southern Cal	17 QB Ronnie Stanley
14 SMU	30 HB Austin Gonsoulin / Tommy Minter
23 Rice	21 HB Ronnie Bull
	Jim Evans

RUSHING: Bull 91/459y, Evans 63/206y, Minter 33/118y
PASSING: Stanley 83-145/800y, 4TD, 57.2%
RECEIVING: Bull 20/183y, Gonsoulin 18/235y, Moore 18/191y
SCORING: Bull 30pts, Davis & Gonsoulin 12pts

1960 8-3
26 Colorado	0 E Sonny Davis
7 LSU	3 T Buck McLeod / John Frongillo
28 Arkansas	14 G Everett Frazier
14 Texas Tech	7 C Bill Hicks
14 Texas A&M	0 G Herby Adkins
6 TCU	14 T Royce West
7 Texas	12 E Gerry Moore / Bobby Lane
35 Southern Cal	14 QB Ronnie Stanley / Bobby Ply
20 SMU	7 WB Ronnie Goodwin
12 Rice	7 HB Ronnie Bull
12 Florida■	13 FB Jim Evans / Robert Starr

RUSHING: Bull 113/454y, Goodwin 76/343y, Evans 37/148y
PASSING: Stanley 75-134/1151y, 5TD, 56%
RECEIVING: Goodwin 25/407y, Bull 20/254y, Lane 18/248y
SCORING: Bull 54pts, Goodwin 36pts, Starr 18pts

1961 6-5
31 Wake Forest	0 E Herbert Harlan / James Ingram
16 Pittsburgh	13 T John Frongillo
13 Arkansas	23 G Robert Burk
17 Texas Tech	19 C Bill Hicks / James Maples
0 Texas A&M	23 G Herby Adkins
28 TCU	14 T Pete Nicklas / John Markham
7 Texas	33 E Bobby Lane / Claude Pearson
7 Air Force	7 QB Ronnie Stanley / Bobby Ply
31 SMU	6 HB Tommy Minter / Elbert Whorton
14 Rice	26 HB Ron Goodwin / Don Adams /Ted Plumb
24 Utah State■	9 FB Ronnie Bull / Dalton Hoffman

RUSHING: Bull 91/441y, Adams 26/153y, Whorton 38/149y
PASSING: Stanley 44-84/451y, 4TD, 52.4%
Ply 39-86/468y, 6TD, 45.3%
RECEIVING: Bull 19/199y, Pearson 18/217y, Goodwin 14/188y
SCORING: Bull 48pts, Carl Choate (K) 38pts, Lane & Plumb 18pts

1962 4-6
0 Houston	19 E James Ingram / James Rust
14 Pittsburgh	24 T Bobby Crenshaw / Art Delgado
21 Arkansas	28 G Ron Rogers
28 Texas Tech	6 C Butch Maples
3 Texas A&M	6 G Robert Burk
26 TCU	28 T James Moore
12 Texas	27 E Claude Pearson / Ken Hodge
10 Air Force	3 QB Don Trull
17 SMU	13 HB Ronnie Goodwin
28 Rice	15 HB Al Tate / Lawrence Elkins / Don Adams
	FB Tom Davies / Dalton Hoffman

RUSHING: Davies 57/230y, Goodwin 41/227y, Hoffman 38/146y
PASSING: Trull 125-229/1627y, 11TD, 54.6%
RECEIVING: Goodwin 25/414y, Elkins 24/370y, Ingram 19/239y
SCORING: Elkins 30pts, Carl Choate (K) 25pts,
Goodwin & Trull 24pts

1963 8-3
27 Houston	0 E Ken Hodge / James Rust
15 Oregon State	22 T Bobby Crenshaw / Billy Allen
14 Arkansas	10 G Mike Bourland / Ron Rogers
21 Texas Tech	17 C Curtis Leggett / Ernie Erickson
34 Texas A&M	7 G Bill Ferguson / Stacy Mathis
32 TCU	13 T Billy Simpson / Art Delgado
0 Texas	7 E James Ingram / Bob Wolf
7 Kentucky	19 QB Don Trull / Donnie Laurence
21 Rice	12 HB Lawrence Elkins / Ed Whiddon
20 SMU	6 HB H. Pickett / Bob Christian / Roy Roberts
14 LSU■	7 FB Dalton Hoffman / Bobby Maples

RUSHING: Hoffman 98/458y, Pickett 36/181y, Roberts 49/162y
PASSING: Trull 174-308/2157y, 12TD, 56.5%
RECEIVING: Elkins 70/873y, Ingram 40/537y, Hodge 19/287y
SCORING: Trull 60pts, Elkins 50pts, Tom Davies (K) 27pts

1964 5-5
14 Washington	35 E Harlan Lane
6 Oregon State	13 T Tommy Schaffner
6 Arkansas	17 G Mike Bourland
28 Texas Tech	10 C Ernie Erickson / Cal Kirkham
20 Texas A&M	16 G James Miller
14 TCU	17 T Bill Ferguson
14 Texas	20 E Ken Hodge
17 Kentucky	15 QB Terry Southall
16 SMU	13 HB Lawrence Elkins
27 Rice	20 HB Henry Pickett / Richard Defee
	FB Tom Davies
	DL James Rust
	DL Jerry Lynn Haney / Mike Thomas
	DL Dwight Hood
	DL Art Delgado
	DL Mike Kennedy
	DL Willie Walker
	LB Jerry Ives
	LB Bobby Maples
	DB Donnie Laurence
	DB Bob Christian
	DB Ed Whiddon

RUSHING: Davies 94/401y, Defee 38/121y, Mitchell 35/116y
PASSING: Southall 118-225/1623y, 10TD, 52.4%
RECEIVING: Elkins 50/851y, Hodge 35/528y, Lane 32/393y
SCORING: Elkins 50pts, Tom Davies (FB-K) 46pts, Hodge 30pts

1965 5-5
14 Auburn	8 WR Tommy Smith / George Chesire
17 Washington	14 WR Harlan Lane
7 Florida State	9 T Tommy Schaffner
6 Arkansas	38 G Mike Bourland
31 Texas A&M	0 C Cal Kirkham
7 TCU	10 G Benny Brott
14 Texas	35 T Mike Jurecek
22 Texas Tech	34 TE Willie Walker / Bucky Bovenzi
20 SMU	10 QB Kenny Stockdale / Terry Southall
17 Rice	13 HB Richard Defee / Wayne Marshall
	FB Billy Gene Hayes
	DL Donnie Laurence
	DL Jerry Lynn Haney
	DL Greg Pipes
	DL Dwight Hood
	DL Bill Ferguson
	DL Dave Anderson
	LB Randy Behringer
	LB Billy Burk
	DB Rickey Head
	DB Ed Whiddon
	DB Joe Jones

RUSHING: Defee 86/429y, Marshall 77/321y, Hayes 93/290y
PASSING: Stockdale 89-177/978y, 5TD, 50.3%
RECEIVING: Lane 56/643y, Chesire 20/319y, Bovenzi 13/185y
SCORING: Charles Purvis (K) 36pts, Chesire & Hayes 24pts

1966 5-5

35 Syracuse	12 WR Tommy Smith
7 Colorado	13 WR Paul Becton, Jr. / George Chesire
20 Washington St.	14 T Mike Jurecek
7 Arkansas	0 G Tommy Schaffner
13 Texas A&M	17 C Cal Kirkham
0 TCU	16 G Bill May
14 Texas	26 T Gary Holliman
29 Texas Tech	14 TE John Eisenhart
22 SMU	24 QB Terry Southall
21 Rice	14 HB Richard Defee
	FB Charles Wilson / Pinkie Palmer
	DL David Anderson
	DL Jerry Lynn Haney
	DL Greg Pipes
	DL Dwight Hood
	DL Billy Burk
	DL Willie Walker
	LB Randy Behringer
	LB Raul Ortiz
	DB Billy Gene Hayes
	DB Ridley Gibson
	DB Jackie Allen / Steve Lane

RUSHING: Defee 80/332y, Palmer 98/299y, Wilson 63/211y
PASSING: Southall 173-337/1986y, 16TD, 51.3%
RECEIVING: Smith 41/483y, Becton 38/447y, Eisenhart 30/335y
SCORING: Defee 36pts, Smith 24pts, Charles Purvis (K) 24pts

1967 1-8-1

7 Colorado	27 WR Bob Green / Gary Alexander
0 Syracuse	7 WR George Chesire
10 Washington St.	7 T Gary Holliman / Calvin Hunt
10 Arkansas	10 G Joe Kelly / Tommy Denton
3 Texas A&M	21 C Danny Cantrell
7 TCU	29 G Richard Dennard / Ernie Stephenson
0 Texas	24 T Richard Stevens
29 Texas Tech	31 TE Ted Gillum
10 SMU	16 QB Alvin Flynn / Kenny Stockdale
25 Rice	27 HB Pinkie Palmer
	FB Charles Wilson / Brian Blessing
	DL David Anderson
	DL Greg Pipes
	DL Don Ellisor
	DL Ron Woodard / Earl Maxfield
	DL Joe Ward / Charles Russell
	DL Rich McFarland / Bill Dewald
	LB Randy Behringer
	LB Raul Ortiz / Dave Hupp
	DB Billy Gene Hayes
	DB Ridley Gibson
	DB Jackie Allen

RUSHING: Wilson 124/553y, Palmer 124/437y, Blessing 58/169y
PASSING: Flynn 63-144/924y, 4TD, 43.8%
RECEIVING: Chesire 37/475y, Green 29/419y, Gillum 13/164y
SCORING: Terry Cozby (K) 27pts, Chesire 24pts, Green 18pts

1968 3-7

36 Indiana	40 WR Mark Lewis / Don Huggins
10 Michigan	28 WR Jerry Smith
16 LSU	48 T Joe Kelly
19 Arkansas	35 G Ernie Stephenson
10 Texas A&M	9 C Calvin Hunt
14 TCU	47 G Richard Dennard
26 Texas	47 T Richard Stevens
42 Texas Tech	28 TE Ted Gillum
17 SMU	33 QB Steve Stuart / Alvin Flynn
16 Rice	7 HB Gene Rogers
	FB Pinky Palmer
	DL Roy McDearmon / Dennis Watson
	DL Walter Groth
	DL Bill Phipps
	DL Tommy Reaux
	DL David Jones
	LB Dave Blessing
	LB Randy Cooper
	LB Dennis Whitley / Steve Lane
	DB Ed Marsh
	DB Russell Serafin
	DB Jackie Allen

RUSHING: Palmer 222/818y, Rogers 160/763y
PASSING: Stuart 95-216/1320y, 7TD, 44%
RECEIVING: Smith 40/509y, Huggins 31/435y, Lewis 20/299y
SCORING: Rogers 38pts, Palmer 36pts, Terry Cozby (K) 33pts

1969 0-10

15 Kansas State	45 WR Derek Davis / Don Huggins
10 Georgia Tech	17 WR Jerry Smith
8 LSU	63 T Joe Kelly / Ron Evans
7 Arkansas	21 G Ernie Stephenson
0 Texas A&M	24 C Calvin Hunt
14 TCU	31 G Richard Dennard
14 Texas	56 T Richard Stevens
7 Texas Tech	41 TE Ted Gillum / Mark Lewis
6 SMU	12 QB Steve Stuart / Si Southall / Laney Cook
6 Rice	34 HB Gene Rogers / Gordon Utgard
	FB Randy Cooper
	DL Roy McDearmon
	DL Dennis Whitley / Gary Sutton
	DL Tommy Reaux
	DL David Jones
	DL Dennis Watson
	LB Dave Blessing
	LB Kyle Roberds
	LB Tommy Bambrick
	DB Russell Serafin
	DB John Miller
	DB Ed Marsh

RUSHING: Cooper 93/354y, Rogers 75/194y, Cook 63/141y
PASSING: Stuart 48-112/535y, 1TD, 42.9%
RECEIVING: Smith 31/373y, Davis 22/271y, Huggins 15/180y
SCORING: Utgard 24pts, Cook 18pts, Terry Cozby (K) 17pts

1970 2-9

0 Missouri	38 WR Derek Davis
10 Army	7 WR Terry Jackson / Don Huggins
10 Pittsburgh	15 T Joe Allbright
0 LSU	31 G Jerry Walters / Barry Morgan
7 Arkansas	41 C Mike Hale
29 Texas A&M	24 G Gil Beall
17 TCU	24 T Ron Evans
14 Texas	21 TE Rollin Hunter
3 Texas Tech	7 QB Si Southall / Delaney Cook
10 SMU	23 HB Matthew Williams
23 Rice	28 FB Randy Cooper
	DL Dennis Watson
	DL Gary Sutton
	DL Bob Henderson
	DL Trent Phipps / Glen Chmelar
	DL Roger Goree
	LB David Jones
	LB Harold Rodgers / Ed Taylor
	DB Ed Marsh
	DB William Stewart
	DB Phil Beall
	DB James Beane / Tommy Stewart

RUSHING: Williams 208/711y, Cook 108/296y, Cooper 68/253y
PASSING: Southall 56-160/905y, 5TD, 35%
RECEIVING: Davis 48/780y, Jackson 13/116y, Huggins 9/159y
SCORING: Mike Conradt (K) 37pts, Williams 36pts, Davis 24pts

1971 1-9

0 Kansas	22 WR Mike Chandler / Ron Henson
10 Indiana	0 WR Bill Cornelius
15 Miami	41 T Joe Allbright
7 Arkansas	35 G Jerry Walters
9 Texas A&M	10 C Mike Hale
27 TCU	34 G Lanus Treadwell
0 Texas	24 T Ron Evans
0 Texas Tech	27 TE Ken Townsend
6 SMU	20 QB Si Southall / Randy Cavender
0 Rice	23 HB Matthew Williams
	FB Godfrey White / Gene Wilson
	DL Roger Goree (LB) / Dwayne Trammell
	DL Gary Sutton
	DL Michail Wilder / Michael Morgan
	DL Rich Mason
	DL Jim Nunn
	LB Paul Savage / Tommy Lee Bambrick
	LB Walt Taylor
	LB Phil Beall
	DB William Stewart
	DB Ira Dean / Ricky Duff
	DB Tommy Stewart

RUSHING: Williams 131/469y, White 95/313y, Cavender 102/150y
PASSING: Southall 21-104/348y, 1TD, 20.2%
RECEIVING: Chandler 10/182y, Henson 8/186y, Townsend 4/64y
SCORING: White & Williams 18pts,
Cavender & Mike Conradt (K) 12pts

1972 5-6

14 Georgia	24 WR Charles Dancer
27 Missouri	0 T Rich Mason
10 Miami	3 G Tim Mills
20 Arkansas	31 C Cary Dorman
7 Oklahoma State	20 G Harold Rodgers
15 Texas A&M	13 T Walter Wright
42 TCU	9 TE Ken Townsend
3 Texas	17 QB Neal Jeffrey
7 Texas Tech	13 WB Brian Kilgore / Billy Wilson
7 SMU	12 HB Gary Lacy
28 Rice	14 FB Gene Wilson
	DL Roger Goree
	DL Joe Johnson
	DL Millard Neely
	DL Coy Zunker
	DL Mike Black
	LB Derrell Luce
	LB Paul Savage / Walt Taylor
	DB Tommy Stewart
	DB Ira Dean
	DB Tom Turnipseede
	DB Ricky Duff / Keith Stone

RUSHING: Lacy 168/669y, G. Wilson 65/316y, B. Wilson 83/264y
PASSING: Jeffrey 89-171/1030y, 5TD, 52%
RECEIVING: Dancer 34/463y, Kilgore 23/307y, Lacy 16/149y
SCORING: Mike Conradt (K) 44pts, Lacy 36pts, Townsend 18pts

1973 2-9

14 Oklahoma	42 WR Charles Dancer
20 Pittsburgh	14 T Mike Hughes
28 Colorado	52 G Rell Tipton / Tim Mills
21 Florida State	14 C Cary Dorman / Aubrey Schulz
7 Arkansas	13 G Allen Pittman / Gary Gregory
22 Texas A&M	28 T Rich Mason
28 TCU	34 TE Ken Townsend
6 Texas	42 QB Neal Jeffrey
24 Texas Tech	55 WB Brian Kilgore / Billy Wilson
22 SMU	38 HB Gary Lacy / Steve Beaird/Godfrey White
0 Rice	27 FB Pat McNeil
	DL Jim Arnold
	DL Coy Zunker
	DL Joe Johnson
	DL Phil Perry
	DL John Oliver / Mike Black
	LB Tim Black / Don Bockhorn
	LB Derrell Luce
	DB Les Ealey / Don Drake
	DB Gary Green
	DB Tom Turnipseede
	DB Keith Stone / Ken Quesenberry

RUSHING: Lacy 146/666y, White 66/320y, McNeil 54/250y
PASSING: Jeffrey 132-251/1897y, 5TD, 52.6%
RECEIVING: Dancer 53/927y, Wilson 17/233y, Lacy 17/105y
SCORING: Lacy 62pts, Dancer 44pts, Bubba Hicks (K) 17pts

1974 8-4

11 Oklahoma	28 WR Alcy Jackson / Ricky Thompson
21 Missouri	28 T Mike Hughes
31 Oklahoma State	14 G Rell Tipton
21 Florida State	17 C Aubrey Schulz
21 Arkansas	17 G Jon Kramer / Napoleon Tyler
0 Texas A&M	20 T Gary Gregory
21 TCU	7 TE Sam Harper
34 Texas	24 QB Neal Jeffrey
17 Texas Tech	10 WB Philip Kent
31 SMU	14 HB Steve Beaird
24 Rice	3 FB Pat McNeil
20 Penn State ■	41 DL Dennis DeLoach
	DL Joe Johnson
	DL Leslie Benson / John Oliver
	DL Wharton Foster
	DL Tim Black
	LB Derrell Luce
	LB Don Bockhorn
	DB Ron Burns
	DB Scooter Reed
	DB Tom Turnipseede
	DB Ken Quesenberry

RUSHING: Beaird 267/1104y, McNeil 93/459y, Kent 56/279y
PASSING: Jeffrey 100-181/1314y, 8TD, 55.2%
RECEIVING: Kent 24/406y, Jackson 22/436y, Beaird 22/223y
SCORING: Beaird 96pts, Bubba Hicks (K) 47pts, Kent 24pts

1975 3-6-2

20 Mississippi	10 WR Ricky Thompson
10 Auburn	10 T Mark Grayless / Billy Clements (C)
14 Michigan	14 G Rell Tipton
13 South Carolina	24 C Gary Gregory
3 Arkansas	41 G Jon Kramer / David Sledge
10 Texas A&M	19 T Mike Hughes
24 TCU	6 TE Ronnie Lee
21 Texas	37 QB Mark Jackson
10 Texas Tech	33 WB Alcy Jackson
31 SMU	34 HB Cleveland Franklin
25 Rice	7 FB Pat McNeil / Mike Ebow
	DL Keavin McDonald / Ricky Rand
	DL Wharton Foster / Gary Hutchison
	DL John Oliver / Gary Don Johnson
	DL Flynn Bucy / Leslie Benson
	DL Jim Arnold / Chris Quinn
	LB Shane Nelson
	LB Tim Black / Johnny Slaughter
	DB Gary Green
	DB Mike Nelms
	DB Ron Burns
	DB Ken Quesenberry

RUSHING: Franklin 200/1112y, McNeil 130/753y,
  M. Jackson 121/385y
PASSING: Jackson 70-151/1021y, 4TD, 46.4%
RECEIVING: Thompson 27/425y, Jackson 17/237y, Lee 10/208y
SCORING: Bubba Hicks (K) 57pts, Franklin 48pts,
  M. Jackson 18pts

1976 7-3-1

5 Houston	23 WR Tommy Davidson
15 Auburn	14 T Mark Grayless
34 Illinois	19 G Jon Kramer
18 South Carolina	17 C Billy Clements / Arland Thompson
27 SMU	20 G Rell Tipton
0 Texas A&M	24 T Gary Gregory
7 Arkansas	7 TE Ronnie Lee
38 Rice	6 QB Mark Jackson
20 Texas	10 WB Greg Hawthorne
24 TCU	19 HB Gary Blair / Cleveland Franklin
21 Texas Tech	24 FB Mike Ebow
	DL Chris Quinn
	DL Flynn Bucy
	DL Gary Don Johnson
	DL Gary Hutchison
	DL Keavin McDonald
	LB Tim Black
	LB Johnny Slaughter / Shane Nelson
	DB Scooter Reed
	DB Ron Burns / Tony Green
	DB Gary Green
	DB Mike Nelms

RUSHING: Blair 225/857y, Jackson 162/426y, Franklin 72/270y
PASSING: Jackson 105-211/1132y, 6TD, 49.8%
RECEIVING: Davidson 45/559y, Hawthorne 22/321y, Blair 16/121y
SCORING: Lester Belrose (K) 49pts, Blair 48pts, Franklin 24pts

1977 5-6

7 Texas Tech	17 WR Tommy Davidson
21 Kentucky	6 T Arland Thompson
10 Nebraska	31 G David Sledge
24 Houston	28 C Ron Barnes
9 SMU	6 G Jon Kramer
31 Texas A&M	38 T Billy Glass / Brent Jones
38 Air Force	7 TE Ronnie Lee
9 Arkansas	35 QB Steve Smith / Gene Wood
24 Rice	14 WB Bo Taylor
7 Texas	29 HB Greg Hawthorne / David Seaborn
48 TCU	9 FB Steve Howell / Gary Blair
	DL Gary Hutchison / Tom Caldwell
	DL James Rowell / Allen Stone
	DL Joe Campbell
	DL Ron Eickenberg / Lester Ward
	LB Doak Field / Paul Hurst
	LB Mike Singletary / Dennis Jiral
	LB Jerry Harrison
	DB Howard Fields
	DB Scooter Reed
	DB Ron Burns / Ken Griffin
	DB Tony Green

RUSHING: Hawthorne 132/670y, Seaborn 104/558y,
  Howell 54/387y
PASSING: Smith 46-91/484y, 2TD, 50.5%
RECEIVING: Davidson 34/419y, Lee 21/225y, Taylor 14/173y
SCORING: Robert Bledsoe (K) 57pts, Hawthorne & Blair 30pts

1978 3-8

14 Georgia	16 WR Gordon Marshall / Mike Fisher
21 Kentucky	25 T Arland Thompson
28 Ohio State	34 G David Sledge
18 Houston	20 C Keith Bishop
21 SMU	28 G Billy Glass
24 Texas A&M	6 T Ron Barnes
28 TCU	21 TE Ronnie Lee
9 Texas Tech	27 QB Steve Smith
14 Arkansas	27 WB Robert Holt / Bo Taylor
10 Rice	24 HB Greg Hawthorne / Walter Abercrombie
38 Texas	14 FB Frank Pollard / Steve Howell
	DL Andrew Melontree
	DL Gary Don Johnson
	DL Joe Campbell
	DL Thomas Brown
	LB Doak Field
	LB Mike Singletary
	LB Jerry Harrison / Lester Ward
	DB Howard Fields
	DB Stephen Brother / Benny Goodwin
	DB Tony Green
	DB Ken Griffin

RUSHING: Abercrombie 114/661y, Pollard 118/509y,
  Hawthorne 65/303y
PASSING: Smith 101-213/1387y, 11TD, 47.4%
RECEIVING: Holt 18/393y, Fisher 16/252y, Taylor 15/191y
SCORING: Robert Bledsoe (K) 31pts, Abercrombie & Fisher 24pts

1979 8-4

20 Lamar	7 WR Robert Mitchell / Gordon Marshall
17 Texas A&M	7 T Arland Thompson
0 Alabama	45 G Frank Ditta
27 Texas Tech	17 C Buzzy Nelson
10 Houston	13 G Billy Glass
24 SMU	21 T Ron Barnes
55 Army	0 TE Raymond Cockrell
16 TCU	3 QB Mike Brannan / Mickey Elam
20 Arkansas	29 WB Robert Holt / Bo Taylor
45 Rice	14 HB Walter Abercrombie
0 Texas	38 FB Dennis Gentry
24 Clemson ■	18 DL Thomas Brown
	DL Joe Campbell
	DL Gary Don Johnson
	DL Andrew Melontree
	LB Doak Field
	LB Mike Singletary
	LB Lester Ward
	DB Kirk Collins
	DB Howard Fields
	DB Ken Griffin
	DB Vann McElroy

RUSHING: Abercrombie 171/886y, Gentry 106/511y,
  Brannan 108/356y
PASSING: Brannan 31-90/604y, 2TD, 34.4%
RECEIVING: Mitchell 10/192y, Taylor 8/156y, Holt 8/152y
SCORING: Robert Bledsoe (K) 65pts, Abercrombie 42pts,
  Gentry 30pts

1980 10-2

42 Lamar	7 WR Mike Fisher / Robert Mitchell
43 W. Texas State	15 T Eddy Gregory
11 Texas State	3 G Frank Ditta
24 Houston	12 C Buzzy Nelson
32 SMU	28 G Mark Kirchner
46 Texas A&M	7 T Bobby Glass
21 TCU	6 TE Raymond Cockrell / Mike Lively
22 San Jose State	30 QB Jay Jeffrey
42 Arkansas	15 WB Robert Holt
16 Rice	6 HB Walter Abercrombie / Alfred Anderson
16 Texas	0 FB Dennis Gentry
2 Alabama ■	30 DL Charles Benson
	DL Tommy Tabor
	DL Joe Campbell
	DL Max McGeary
	LB Doak Field
	LB Mike Singletary
	LB Lester Ward
	DB Thomas Earl Young
	DB Cedric Mack / Vic Vines
	DB Vann McElroy
	DB Scott Smith

RUSHING: Abercrombie 229/1187y, Gentry 147/883y,
  Jeffrey 120/453y
PASSING: Jeffrey 72-162/1096y, 8TD, 44.4%
RECEIVING: Holt 29/464y, Fisher 22/494y, Mitchell 10/241y
SCORING: Abercrombie 60pts, Anderson 54pts,
  Robert Bledsoe (K) 51pts

1981 5-6

17 Lamar	18 WR Gerald McNeil
38 Bowling Green	0 T Mark Adickes
28 Louisiana Tech	21 G Mark Kirchner
28 Texas Tech	15 C Randy Grimes
3 Houston	24 G Mark Johnson
20 SMU	37 T Bobby Glass
19 Texas A&M	17 TE Mike Lively
34 TCU	21 QB Jay Jeffrey
39 Arkansas	41 WB Alfred Anderson
14 Rice	17 HB Walter Abercrombie
12 Texas	34 FB Dennis Gentry
	DL Charles Benson
	DL Tommy Tabor
	DL Paul Mergenhagen / Greg Bomkamp
	DL Travis Selph / Kent Townsend
	LB Keith Walters
	LB Geff Gandy
	LB John Breit / Ervin Randle
	DB Vic Vines
	DB Preston Davis / Cedric Mack
	DB Vann McElroy
	DB Scott Smith

RUSHING: Abercrombie 218/931y, Gentry 155/763y,
  Anderson 60/251y
PASSING: Jeffrey 111-198/1643y, 9TD, 56%
RECEIVING: McNeil 44/744y, Gentry 20/233y,
  Abercrombie 19/102y
SCORING: Marty Jimmerson (K) 68pts, Anderson 50pts,
  McNeil 38pts

1982 4-6-1

21 N. Texas State	17 WR Gerald McNeil
14 Ohio State	21 T Mark Adickes
24 Texas Tech	23 G Neal Donovan
21 Houston	21 C Randy Grimes
19 SMU	22 G Mark Kirchner
23 Texas A&M	28 T Mike Mackey
14 TCU	38 TE Sam Houston
15 Tulane	30 QB Mike Brannan
24 Arkansas	17 WB Bruce Davis
35 Rice	13 HB Alfred Anderson
23 Texas	31 FB Allen Rice
	DL Charles Benson
	DL Pat Coryatt
	DL Gregg Bomkamp
	DL Travis Selph
	LB Geff Gandy / John Breit
	LB Keith Walters
	LB Ervin Randle
	DB Cedric Mack
	DB Preston Davis / Ron Francis
	DB Bo Scott Metcalf
	DB Vic Vines

RUSHING: Anderson 201/837y, Rice 143/599y, Brannan 95/126y
PASSING: Brannan 100-204/1459y, 7TD, 49%
RECEIVING: McNeil 52/822y, Davis 20/340y, Anderson 17/206y
SCORING: Anderson 54pts, Rice 48pts,
  Marty Jimmerson (K) 30pts

1983 7-4-1

40 BYU	36 WR Gerald McNeil
20 UTEP	6 T Mark Adickes
11 Texas Tech	26 G Mark Johnson
42 Houston	21 C John Adickes
26 SMU	42 G Mark Cochran (T) / Mark Bates
13 Texas A&M	13 T Brian Camp
56 TCU	21 TE Joel Barrett
24 Tulane	18 QB Cody Carlson / Tom Muecke
24 Arkansas	21 WB Bruce Davis
48 Rice	14 TB Alfred Anderson
21 Texas	24 FB Allen Rice
14 Oklahoma St. ■	24 DL Ervin Randle
	DL Gregg Bomkamp / Paul Mergenhagen
	DL Pat Coryatt
	DL Kent Townsend
	LB Clark Hood / Steve Malpass
	LB Kevin Hancock
	LB Alan Jamison / Ray Berry
	DB Preston Davis
	DB Thomas Everett / Reyna Thompson
	DB Aaron Grant
	DB Jack Hurd / Johnny Subia

RUSHING: Anderson 231/1046y, Rice 95/412y,
  Ralph Stockemer (TB) 62/301y
PASSING: Carlson 98-180/1617y, 12TD, 54.4%
RECEIVING: McNeil 62/1034y, Davis 42/755y, Conrad 9/162y
SCORING: Anderson 62pts, Davis 56pts, Rice & McNeil 48pts

1984 5-6

13 BYU	47 WR Bobby Joe Conrad / Leland Douglas
15 Oklahoma	34 T Brian Camp / Jeff Palmer
18 Texas Tech	9 G Joel Porter
17 Houston	27 C John Adickes
20 SMU	24 G Mark Bates
20 Texas A&M	16 T Mark Cochran
28 TCU	38 TE Joel Barrett
38 New Mexico	2 QB Tom Muecke / Cody Carlson
9 Arkansas	14 WB Glenn Pruitt / Horace Ates
46 Rice	40 TB Ron Francis / Ralph Stockemer
24 Texas	10 FB Broderick Sargent
	DL Ervin Randle
	DL Paul Mergenhagen / Steve Grumbine
	DL Gregg Bomkamp / Pat Coryatt
	DL Derek Turner
	LB Ray Berry
	LB Kevin Hancock
	LB Robert Watters / Aaron Grant
	DB Johnny Thomas
	DB Anthony Coleman
	DB Thomas Everett
	DB Jack Hurd / Johnny Subia

RUSHING: Francis 127/558y, Stockemer 109/352y,
　Sargent 62/170y
PASSING: Muecke 97-213/1402y, 10TD, 45.5%
　Carlson 50-111/666y, 6TD, 45%
RECEIVING: Pruitt 32/586y, Ates 20/314y, Douglas 17/258y
SCORING: Marty Jimmerson (K) 52pts, Francis & Stockemer 42pts

1985 9-3

39 Wyoming	18 WR Matt Clark
14 Georgia	17 WR Glenn Pruitt / Leland Douglas
20 Southern Cal	13 T Mark Cochran
31 Texas Tech	0 G Mark Bates
24 Houston	21 C John Adickes
21 SMU	4 G Kyle Lane
20 Texas A&M	15 T Joel Porter
45 TCU	0 TE Kobe Fornes
14 Arkansas	20 QB Tom Muecke / Cody Carlson
34 Rice	10 RB Derrick McAdoo / Jackie Ball
10 Texas	17 RB Robert Williams / Ralph Stockemer
21 LSU■	7 DL Derek Turner
	DL Steve Grumbine
	DL Russell Sheffield
	DL Kevin Marsh
	LB Alan Jamison
	LB Ray Berry
	LB Aaron Grant / Robert Watters
	DB Ron Francis
	DB Jack Hurd
	DB Thomas Everett
	DB Anthony Coleman

RUSHING: McAdoo 76/369y, Ball 53/365y, Sargent 70/286y
PASSING: Muecke 86-156/1448y, 11TD, 55.1%
RECEIVING: Clark 29/540y, Douglas 17/267y, Williams 14/183y
SCORING: Terry Syler (K) 64pts, Stockemer 42pts, Muecke 30pts

1986 9-3

31 Wyoming	28 WR Matt Clark
38 Louisiana Tech	7 WR Leland Douglas / David Davis
14 Southern Cal	17 T Joel Porter
45 Texas Tech	14 G Kyle Lane
27 Houston	13 C John Adickes
21 SMU	27 G Mark Bates
30 Texas A&M	31 T Don Robinson
28 TCU	17 TE Kobe Fornes
29 Arkansas	14 QB Cody Carlson
23 Rice	17 TB Derrick McAdoo / Jeffrey Murray
18 Texas	13 FB Randy Rutledge / Charles Perry
21 Colorado■	9 DL Kevin Marsh / Eugene Hall
	DL Steve Grumbine
	DL Russell Sheffield
	DL James Lee
	LB Ray Berry
	LB Aaron Grant
	LB Robert Watters
	DB Ron Francis
	DB Anthony Coleman / Ray Crockett
	DB Johnny Thomas / Robert Blackmon
	DB Thomas Everett

RUSHING: Murray 106/459y, Carlson 103/356y, McAdoo 69/334y
PASSING: Carlson 157-287/2284y, 10TD, 54.7%
RECEIVING: Clark 23/418y, Davis 21/410y, Douglas 19/290y
SCORING: Terry Syler (K) 65pts, Clark 42pts, Perry 32pts

1987 6-5

13 Louisiana Tech	3 WR Matt Clark / Greg Anderson
18 Missouri	23 WR Ben Baker / Bobby Jack Goforth
21 UNLV	14 T Joel Porter
36 Texas Tech	22 G Jeff Palmer
30 Houston	18 C Mike Hensley
36 SW Texas State	15 G Errol Ware
10 Texas A&M	34 T Terry Hancock / Dennis Smith
0 TCU	24 TE Kobe Fornes
7 Arkansas	10 QB Brad Goebel
34 Rice	31 HB Eric Gilstrap / Jeffrey Murray
16 Texas	34 HB Charles Perry
	DL Eugene Hall / Reggie Howard
	DL Greg Oefinger / Henry Green
	DL Russell Sheffield / Vincent Carpenter
	DL Keith Rose / Sam Collins
	LB Gary Joe Kinne
	LB Gary Hays / John Godfrey
	LB James Francis
	DB Ray Crockett
	DB Norris Blount
	DB Mike Welch
	DB Robert Blackmon

RUSHING: Perry 156/ 494y, Gilstrap 65/237y, Murray 54/232y
PASSING: Goebel 158-305/2178y, 9TD, 51.8%
RECEIVING: Perry 25/242y, Anderson 21/294y, Clark 19/348y
SCORING: Terry Syler (K) 49pts, Perry 48pts, Jay Mapps (QB) &
　Gilstrap 18pts

1988 6-5

27 UNLV	3 WR Darnell Chase / Greg Anderson
27 Kansas	14 WR Bobby Jack Goforth
35 Iowa State	0 T Mark Bass
6 Texas Tech	36 G John Turnpaugh
24 Houston	27 C Bobby Sign / Scott McCool
45 SW Texas State	7 G Monte Jones / Terry Gray
14 Texas A&M	28 T Dennis Smith
14 TCU	24 TE David Bell
3 Arkansas	33 QB Brad Goebel
20 Rice	10 TB Eldwin Raphel / Anthony Ray
17 Texas	14 FB Charles Perry / Jeffrey Murray
	DL Eugene Hall / Reggie Howard
	DL Rod Duffie / Greg Oefinger
	DL Vincent Carpenter / Marcus Moore
	DL Sam Collins / Santana Dotson
	LB John Godfrey / Robin Jones
	LB Gary Joe Kinne
	LB James Francis
	DB Malcolm Frank / Charles Bell
	DB Norris Blount
	DB Ray Crockett
	DB Robert Blackmon / Daniel Morgan

RUSHING: Raphel 118/583y, Ray 67/311y, Perry 81/256y
PASSING: Goebel 117-237/1524y, 9TD, 49.4%
RECEIVING: Goforth 23/380y, Chase 21/307y, Bell 20/233y
SCORING: Terry Syler (K) 37pts, Perry 36pts, Ray 30pts

1989 5-6

7 Oklahoma	33 WR Greg Anderson
3 Georgia	15 WR David Frost / Reggie Miller
46 Kansas	3 T Terry Gray
29 Texas Tech	15 G John Turnpaugh
10 Houston	66 C Mark Bass / Scott McCool
49 SMU	3 G Monte Jones
11 Texas A&M	14 T Larry Vasbinder
27 TCU	9 TE Steve Stutsman / Alonzo Pierce
10 Arkansas	19 QB Brad Goebel
3 Rice	6 TB Eldwin Raphel / Lincoln Coleman
50 Texas	7 FB Jeffrey Murray / Eric Gilstrap
	DL Robin Jones / Darren Franklin
	DL Santana Dotson / Greg Oefinger
	DL Reggie Howard / Marcus Lowe
	DL John Godfrey / Yerritt Long
	LB James Francis
	LB Gary Joe Kinne
	LB Curtis Hafford / Daniel Morgan
	DB Charles Bell / Frankie Smith
	DB Malcolm Frank
	DB Mike Welch
	DB Robert Blackmon

RUSHING: Raphel 172/708y, Coleman 111/368y,
　David Mims (TB) 72/290y
PASSING: Goebel 95-175/1255y, 7TD, 54.3%
RECEIVING: Murray 37/321y, Anderson 22/357y, Miller 16/269y
SCORING: Jeff Ireland (K) 75pts, Raphel 24pts,
　Stutsman & Coleman 18pts

1990 6-4-1

0 Nebraska	13 WR Greg Anderson / Lee Miles
13 Arizona State	34 WR Melvin Bonner
13 Sam Houston St.	9 T Craig Bellamy
21 Texas Tech	15 G John Turnpaugh
15 Houston	31 C Scott Baehren / Mark Bass
52 SMU	17 G Monte Jones
20 Texas A&M	20 T Adam Arroyo
27 TCU	21 TE Mike McKenzie
34 Arkansas	3 QB J.J. Joe / Steve Needham
17 Rice	16 TB Eldwin Raphel / Carmichael Moore
13 Texas	23 FB Robert Strait
	DL Robin Jones
	DL Marcus Lowe
	DL Reggie Howard
	DL Santana Dotson
	LB Brian Hand
	LB Lee Bruderer
	LB Curtis Hafford
	DB Charles Bell
	DB Malcolm Frank
	DB Michael McFarland
	DB Mike Welch

RUSHING: Raphel 123/546y, Moore 114/532y, Strait 118/462y
PASSING: Joe 43-73/714y, 5TD, 58.9%
　Needham 31-73/323y, 2TD, 42.5%
RECEIVING: Anderson 24/288y, Bonner 11/227y, Miles 11/221y
SCORING: Jeff Ireland (K) 55pts, Strait 54pts,
　Moore & Bonner 24pts

1991 8-4

27 UTEP	7 WR Reggie Miller / Lee Miles
16 Colorado	14 WR Melvin Bonner
47 Missouri	21 T Adam Arroyo
45 SMU	7 G John Turnpaugh
38 Houston	21 C Scott Baehren
17 Rice	20 G Monte Jones
12 Texas A&M	34 T Craig Bellamy
26 TCU	9 TE Alonzo Pierce
34 Arkansas	3 QB J.J. Joe
24 Texas Tech	31 TB David Mims / John Henry
21 Texas	11 FB Robert Strait
0 Indiana■	24 DL Robin Jones
	DL Marcus Lowe
	DL Santana Dotson
	DL Teddy Patton
	LB Brian Hand
	LB Curtis Hafford
	LB Le' Shai Maston
	DB Frankie Smith
	DB Clifford Ellison / Farius Walker
	DB Michael McFarland
	DB Keith Caldwell

RUSHING: Mims 148/852y, Strait 99/551y, Henry 95/521y
PASSING: Joe 109-206/1853y, 7TD, 52.9%
RECEIVING: Bonner 34/836y, Miles 31/471y, Miller 15/150y
SCORING: Jeff Ireland (K) 64pts, Henry, Joe & Strait 36pts

1992 7-5

9 Louisiana Tech	10 WR Reggie Miller
38 Colorado	57 WR Melvin Bonner
45 Utah State	10 T Craig Bellamy
17 Texas Tech	36 G Will Davidson
49 SMU	7 C Chuck Pope
41 TCU	20 G David Leaks
29 Houston	23 T Fred Miller
13 Texas A&M	19 TE Mike McKenzie
31 Georgia Tech	27 QB J.J. Joe
24 Rice	31 TB David Mims / Kendrick Bell
21 Texas	20 FB Robert Strait / Bradford Lewis
20 Arizona■	15 DL Albert Fontenot
	DL Scotty Lewis
	DL Steve Strahan / Joe Isbell
	DL Matthew Pearson
	LB Robbie Birleson
	LB Shawn Cravens
	LB Le'Shai Maston
	DB Fred Robertson / Raynor Finley
	DB Keith Caldwell
	DB Chris Lewis
	DB Michael McFarland / Andrew Swasey

RUSHING: Mims 80/518y, Strait 126/496y, Lewis 56/402y
PASSING: Joe 88-189/1765y, 14TD, 46.6%
RECEIVING: Bonner 39/818y, Miller 25/484y, McKenzie 10/218y
SCORING: Bonner & Trey Weir (K) 66pts, Strait 50pts

1993 5-6

42 Fresno State	39 WR John Stanley / Pearce Pegross
21 Colorado	45 WR Marvin Callies / Ben Bronson
28 Utah State	24 T David Davis
28 Texas Tech	26 G Will Davidson
3 Houston	24 C Chuck Pope
31 SMU	12 G David Leaks
17 Texas A&M	34 T Fred Miller
13 TCU	38 TE Craig Bellamy
27 Georgia Tech	37 QB J.J. Joe
38 Rice	14 TB John Henry / Brandell Jackson
17 Texas	38 FB Bradford Lewis / Robert Strait
	DL Scotty Lewis
	DL Steve Strahan
	DL Charles Horton / Joseph Asbell
	DL Daryl Gardener
	LB Phillip Kent / Tony Tubbs
	LB Chris Dull
	LB LaCurtis Jones / Justin Still
	DB Kendrick Bell
	DB Tyrone Smith / George McCullough
	DB Chris Lewis
	DB Andrew Swasey / Adrian Robinson

RUSHING: Jackson 171/899y, Henry 117/592y, Lewis 89/387y
PASSING: Joe 107-197/1663y, 5TD, 54.3%
RECEIVING: Callies 22/435y, Bronson 15/281y, Jackson 15/91y
SCORING: Henry 60pts, Jarvis Van Dyke (K) 55pts, Strait 54pts

1994 7-5

44 Louisiana Tech	3 WR Ben Bronson / John Stanley
54 San Jose State	20 WR Dustin Dennard
14 Oklahoma State	10 T David Davis / Bruce Nowak
27 Southern Cal	37 G Jerome Jackson / Michael Johnson
42 TCU	18 C Marty Dunbar / John Turner
44 SMU	10 G Will Davidson / Curtis Draper
21 Texas A&M	41 T Fred Miller
7 Texas Tech	38 TE Damon Rhynes / Bradley Domel
52 Houston	13 QB Jeff Watson
19 Rice	14 TB Kalief Muhammad / Brandell Jackson
35 Texas	63 FB Bradford Lewis / Clifton Rubin
3 Washington St. ■	10 DL Scotty Lewis
	DL Steve Strahan / Roderick Kinney
	DL Daryl Gardener / Charles Horton
	LB Phillip Kent / Robert Mason
	LB Tony Tubbs / Chris Dull
	LB Gary Bandy / Glenn Coy
	LB LaCurtis Jones
	DB Joe Manor / Kendrick Bell
	DB Tyrone Smith / George McCullough
	DB Chris Lewis
	DB Adrian Robinson / Nikia Codie

RUSHING: Muhammad 97/529y, Jerod Douglas (TB) 63/473y, Jackson 86/446y
PASSING: Watson 102-201/1,615y, 10TD, 50.7%
RECEIVING: Bronson 33/571y, Stanley 26/466y, Dennard 15/251y
SCORING: Jarvis Van Dyke (K) 73pts, Rubin 54pts, Lewis 36pts

1995 7-4

37 Tulsa	5 WR Dustin Dennard / Pearce Pegross
21 Mississippi St.	30 T Fred Miller / Bruce Nowak
14 N. Carolina St.	0 G Anthony Williams / Danny Fletcher
9 Texas Tech	7 C John Turner
47 Houston	7 G Michael Johnson
9 Texas A&M	24 T David Davis
27 TCU	24 TE Bradley Domel
14 Miami	35 QB Jeff Watson / Jermaine Alfred
48 SMU	7 WB Kalief Muhammad
34 Rice	6 TB Jerod Douglas / Anthony Hodge
13 Texas	21 FB Shawn Washington
	DL Charles Horton / Donnie Embra
	DL Roderick Kinney / Derrick Fletcher
	DL Daryl Gardener / Sheldon Mallory
	LB LaCurtis Jones
	LB Gary Bandy / Glenn Coy
	LB Dean Jackson / Robert Mason
	LB Phillip Kent / Justin Still
	DB George McCullough / Raynor Finley
	DB Joe Manor / Tyrone Smith
	DB Michael Benjamin
	DB Adrian Robinson

RUSHING: Douglas 211/1114y, Hodge 89/402y, Washington 68/285y
PASSING: Watson 113-214/1508y, 5TD, 52.8%
RECEIVING: Muhammad 37/542y, Pegross 31/582y, Dennard 19/291y
SCORING: Jarvis Van Dyke (K) 69pts, Douglas 48pts, Washington 42pts

1996 4-7

24 Louisiana Tech	16 WR Pearce Pegross / Morris Anderson
14 Louisville	13 WR Kalief Muhammad
42 Oregon State	10 T Kelvin Garmon
24 Texas Tech	45 G Danny Fletcher / Chris Sampy
0 Nebraska	49 C Anthony Williams
24 Oklahoma	28 G Jerome Jackson
49 Iowa State	21 T Michael Johnson
23 Texas	28 TE Bradley Domel
7 Texas A&M	24 QB Jermaine Alfred / Jeff Watson
42 Missouri	49 TB Jerod Douglas / Elijah Burkins
17 Oklahoma State	37 FB Shawn Washington / Dexter Ford
	DL Sheldon Mallory / Dwight Johnson
	DL Derrick Fletcher / Roderick Kinney
	DL Donnie Embra / Justin Snow
	LB Clarence Cruse / Kenyada Parker
	LB Dean Jackson
	LB Glenn Coy / Malcolm Hamilton
	LB Robert Mason / Jason Jackson
	DB George McCullough / Matt Anderson
	DB Robert Neal
	DB Nikia Codie
	DB Rodney Atmore / Curtis Henderson

RUSHING: Douglas 117/667y, Burkins 82/393y, Ford 75.363y
PASSING: Alfred 90-184/1148y, 8TD, 48.9%
Watson 67-127/858y, 10TD, 52.8%
RECEIVING: Muhammad 39/479y, Pegross 25/474y, Anderson 13/163y
SCORING: Kyle Attebury (K) 50pts, Muhammad 42pts, Ford & Douglas 30pts

1997 2-9

14 Miami	45 WR Morris Anderson
37 Fresno State	35 WR Derrius Thompson
3 Michigan	38 T Michael Johnson
14 Texas Tech	35 G Derrick Fletcher
21 Nebraska	49 C Toby Summers / Anthony Williams
23 Oklahoma	24 G Kelvin Garmon
17 Iowa State	24 T David Davis
23 Texas	21 TE/WR Bradley Domel / Mark Cogdill
10 Texas A&M	38 QB Jeff Watson
24 Missouri	42 TB Jerod Douglas / Darrell Bush
14 Oklahoma State	24 FB Anthony Overstreet
	DL Glenn Coy
	DL Dwight Johnson / Rod Kinney
	DL Sheldon Mallory / Chris Sampy
	DL Charles Foster / Justin Snow
	LB Clarence Cruse
	LB Kris Micheaux / Jody Littleton
	LB Jason Jackson / Kenyada Parker
	DB Matt Anderson
	DB Robert Neal
	DB Nikia Codie / Samir Al-Amin
	DB Rodney Smith

RUSHING: Bush 103/693y, Douglas 131/557y, Elijah Burkins (TB) 50/218y
PASSING: Watson 143-260/1550y, 5TD, 55%
RECEIVING: Thompson 32/420y, Anderson 27/315y, Cogdill 16/179y
SCORING: Matt Bryant (K) 50pts, Douglas 30pts, Bush 24pts

1998 2-9

17 Oregon State	27 WR Morris Anderson
33 N. Carolina St.	30 WR Derrius Thompson
16 Colorado	18 T Greg Jerman
29 Texas Tech	31 G Kelvin Garmon / Chris Sampy
31 Kansas	24 C Joe Jackson / Toby Summers
14 Texas A&M	35 G Chris Watton / Scott Childress
20 Texas	30 T Derrick Fletcher
3 Notre Dame	27 TE Andrew Obriotti / Dan Arroyo
6 Kansas State	49 QB Jermaine Alfred / Odell James
16 Oklahoma	28 TB Darrell Bush / Elijah Burkins
10 Oklahoma State	24 FB Derek Lagway / Anthony Overstreet
	DL Eddrick Brooks / Clifton Rubin
	DL James Calvin
	DL Dwight Johnson / Ron Smith
	DL Justin Snow / Charles Foster
	LB McKinley Bowie / Kenyada Parker
	LB Kris Micheaux / Fred Rogers
	LB Jason Jackson
	DB Allen Pace / Robert Neal
	DB Gary Baxter
	DB Nikia Codie / Sean Armistead
	DB Rodney Smith

RUSHING: Bush 105/357y, Lagway 93/335y, Overstreet 63/330y
PASSING: Alfred 97-188/1268y, 2TD, 51.6%
RECEIVING: Anderson 37/639y, Lagway 37/266y, Thompson 33/478y
SCORING: Matt Bryant (K) 55pts, Burkins 30pts, 3 tied w/ 18pts

1999 1-10

29 Boston College	30 WR Mark Cogdill / Randy Davis
24 UNLV	27 WR Andra Fuller / Lanny O'Steen
10 Oklahoma	41 T Greg Jerman
0 Texas	62 G Ethan Kelley
23 North Texas	10 C Joe Jackson
13 Texas A&M	45 G Chris Watton
7 Texas Tech	35 T Tyshaun Whitson
7 Kansas State	48 TE Andrew Obriotti / Brandon Thompson
10 Kansas	45 QB Jermaine Alfred
0 Colorado	37 TB Darrell Bush
14 Oklahoma State	34 FB Derek Lagway / Melvin Barnett
	DL Justin Snow / Fred Rogers
	DL Dwight Johnson
	DL Ryan Gillenwater / Kevin Stevenson
	DL Eddrick Brooks
	LB Jason Jackson / Andre Taylor
	LB Kris Micheaux / Kelvin Chiasson
	LB Rodney Smith / McKinley Bowie
	DB Daniel Wilturner / Robert Neal
	DB Gary Baxter
	DB Sean Armistead
	DB Samir Al-Amin / Tommie Black

RUSHING: Bush 162/682y, Lagway 51/215y
PASSING: Alfred 111-228/1230y, 4TD, 48.7%
RECEIVING: Fuller 26/308y, O'Steen 16/158y, Davis 15/159y
SCORING: Kyle Atteberry (K) 41pts, Alfred 24pts, 4 tied w/ 12pts

2000 2-9

20 North Texas	7 WR Reggie Newhouse / Lanny O'Steen
9 Minnesota	34 WR Andra Fuller / Martin Dossett
28 South Florida	13 T Ethan Kelley (G)
17 Iowa State	31 G Greg Jerman (T) / Derrick Pearcy
0 Texas Tech	28 C Joe Jackson
0 Texas A&M	24 G Cedric Fields / Tyshaun Whitson
0 Nebraska	59 T Jon Erickson (G) / Derek Long
14 Texas	48 TE Andrew Obriotti
7 Oklahoma	56 QB Guy Tomcheck /J. Zachry / Kerry Dixon
22 Missouri	47 TB Darrell Bush / Chedrick Ricks
22 Oklahoma State	50 FB Melvin Barnett / Chris Schoessow
	DL Aaron Lard / Joe Simmons
	DL Ryan Gillenwater
	DL Kevin Stevenson / Travis Hicks
	DL Charles Mann / Eric Clay
	LB McKinley Bowie / Derrick Cash
	LB Kris Micheaux
	LB Anthony Simmons / John Garrett
	DB Gary Baxter / Eric Giddens
	DB Daniel Wilturner
	DB Matt Amendola / Odell James
	DB Samir Al-Amin / Kyle Staudt

RUSHING: Bush 133/517y, Ricks 38/122y
PASSING: Tomcheck 53-144/602y, 6TD, 36.8%
Zachry 34-66/428y, 4TD, 51.5%
RECEIVING: Newhouse 40/629y, O'Steen 21/279y, Robert Quiroga (WR) 17/199y
SCORING: Newhouse 24pts, Quiroga & Daniel Andino (K) 18pts

2001 3-8

24 Arkansas State	3 WR Reggie Newhouse
16 New Mexico	13 WR Andra Fuller
0 Iowa State	41 WR Robert Quiroga / John Martin
10 Texas A&M	16 T Jon Erickson / Quinton Outland
7 Nebraska	48 G Cedric Fields
17 Oklahoma	33 C Joe Jackson
19 Texas Tech	63 G Antoine Murphy / Derek Long
10 Texas	49 T Greg Jerman
24 Missouri	41 TE Andrew Obriotti
22 Oklahoma State	38 QB Greg Cicero
56 Southern Illinois	12 RB Anthony Krieg / Melvin Barnett
	DL Aaron Lard
	DL Ryan Gillenwater / Ethan Kelley
	DL Kevin Stevenson / Travis Hicks
	DL Charles Mann / A.C. Collier
	LB Greg Wade / Justin Crooks
	LB John Garrett / Mike Tolbert
	LB Stephen Sepulveda / Kelvin Chiasson
	DB Bobby Hart
	DB Randy Davis / Marcus Stenix
	DB Derrick Cash
	DB Samir Al-Amin

RUSHING: Krieg 70/245y, Barnett 63/218y, Jonathan Golden (RB) 75/215y
PASSING: Cicero 129-255/1239y, 6TD, 50.6%
RECEIVING: Newhouse 61/706y, Fuller 36/376y, Martin 32/345y
SCORING: Newhouse 48pts, Daniel Andino (K) 25pts, Adam Stiles (K) 21pts

2002 3-9

22 California	70 WR Reggie Newhouse / J.T. Thompson
50 Samford	12 WR Marques Roberts / John Martin
0 New Mexico	22 WR Robert Quiroga / Ray Harrington
37 Tulsa	25 T Quinton Outland
35 Kansas	32 G Derrick Pearcy
0 Texas A&M	41 C Cedric Fields
0 Colorado	34 G Antoine Murphy
10 Kansas State	44 T T.J. Helmcamp
11 Texas Tech	62 TE Chris DeLeenheer
0 Texas	41 QB Aaron Karas
9 Oklahoma	49 RB Rashad Armstrong / Jonathan Golden
28 Oklahoma State	63 DL Dominick Cravens / Joe Simmons
	DL Ethan Kelley
	DL Kevin Stevenson
	DL A.C. Collier / Khari Long
	LB Greg Wade / Justin Crooks
	LB John Garrett / Michael Tolbert
	LB Stephen Sepulveda / Kelvin Chiasson
	DB Bobby Hart / Matt Amendola
	DB Matt Johnson / Randy Davis
	DB Maurice Lane / Danielle McLean
	DB Derrick Cash

RUSHING: Armstrong 159/647y, Golden 112/392y
PASSING: Karas 150-251/1792y, 6TD, 59.8%
RECEIVING: Newhouse 75/1140y, Quiroga 49/556y, Thompson 16/133y
SCORING: Golden 54pts, Daniel Andino (K) 37pts, Armstrong 24pts

2003 3-9

19 UAB	24 WR Robert Quiroga
14 North Texas	52 WR Marquis Roberts / Trent Shelton
10 SMU	7 T Quinton Outland
27 Sam Houston St.	6 G Glenn Oskin / Joe DeWoody
42 Colorado	30 C Cedric Fields
10 Texas A&M	73 G LaQualan McDonald
21 Kansas	28 T Nick Pace
0 Texas	56 TE Shane Williams / Iris Williams
10 Kansas State	38 QB Aaron Karas / Shawn Bell
14 Texas Tech	62 TB Rashad Armstrong
3 Oklahoma	41 FB Jonathan Evans
21 Oklahoma State	38 DL Dominick Cravens
	DL Quincy Jenkins / Michael Gary
	DL M.T. Robinson
	DL Khari Long / Joe Simmons
	LB Stephen Sepulveda / John Garrett
	LB Justin Crooks
	DB James Todd / Tyson Hampton
	DB Matt Johnson / Anthony Arline
	DB Maurice Lane
	DB Willie Andrews
	DB Derrick Cash / Maurice Linquist

RUSHING: Armstrong 258/1074y, Anthony Krieg (TB) 56/222y
PASSING: Karas 135-239/1481y, 10TD, 56.5%
RECEIVING: Quiroga 42/490y, Shelton 25/298y, Roberts 25/224y
SCORING: Kenny Webb (K) 45pts, Armstrong 42pts, Quiroga 36pts

2004 3-8

14 UAB	56 WR Dominique Zeigler / Shaun Rochon
24 Texas State	17 WR Marques Roberts
37 North Texas	14 WR/FB Trent Shelton / Jonathan Evans
14 Texas	44 T Quintin Outland
10 Missouri	30 G Glen Oskin / Chad Smith
27 Nebraska	59 C Joseph DeWoody
25 Iowa State	26 G Lequalan McDonald
35 Texas A&M	34 T Evan Stone / Travis Farst
17 Texas Tech	42 TE Marcus Venus / Michael Miller
21 Oklahoma State	49 QB Dane King / Shawn Bell
0 Oklahoma	35 TB Anthony Krieg / Paul Mosley
	DL Khari Long / Corey Ford
	DL Klayton Shoals / Julian Hill
	DL Michael Gary / M.T. Robinson
	DL Montez Murphy / Marcus Foreman
	LB Michael Tolbert / Colin Allred
	LB Justin Crooks
	LB Maurice Linquist / Tyler Lindstrom
	DB James Todd / Braelon Davis
	DB Anthony Arline
	DB Maurice Lane
	DB Willie Andrews

RUSHING: Mosley 127/582y, Krieg 121/460y
PASSING: King 131-222/1370y, 9TD, 59%
Bell 68-113/544y, 9TD, 60.2%
RECEIVING: Zeigler 55/536y, Roberts 40/570y, Shelton 38/426y
SCORING: Kenny Webb (K) 58pts, Roberts 36pts, Zeigler 32pts

2005 5-6

28 SMU	23 WR Dominique Ziegler
48 Samford	14 WR Trent Shelton / Carl Sims
20 Army	10 WR Shaun Rochon / Mikail Baker
13 Texas A&M	16 TE/WR Jason Smith / Trey Payne
23 Iowa State	13 T Nick Pace
14 Nebraska	23 G Will Blaylock / Glen Oskin
30 Oklahoma	37 C Yancey Boatner / Chad Smith
0 Texas Tech	28 G Lequalan McDonald
0 Texas	62 T Evan Stone
16 Missouri	31 QB Shawn Bell / Terrance Parks
44 Oklahoma State	34 RB Paul Mosley / Brandon Whitaker
	DL Marcus Foreman
	DL M.T. Robinson / Vincent Rhodes
	DL Michael Gary / Quincy Jenkins
	DL Montez Murphy / Julian Hill
	LB Colin Allred / Nick Moore
	LB Jamaal Harper
	DB Anthony Arline / James Todd
	DB C. J. Wilson / Josh Bell
	DB Ty Lindstrom / Maurice Linquist
	DB Maurice Lane
	DB Willie Andrews

RUSHING: Mosley 180/657y, Whitaker 101/481y
PASSING: Bell 190-320/1964y, 12TD, 59.4%
RECEIVING: Ziegler 48/563y, Rochon 44/443y, Shelton 39/452y
SCORING: Ryan Havens (K) 70pts, Mosley 54pts, Rochon & Ziegler 30pts

2006 4-8

7 TCU	17 WR Dominique Ziegler
47 Northwestern St.	10 WR Trent Shelton / Carl Sims
15 Washington St.	17 WR Thomas White / Trey Payne
20 Army	27 WR Terrance Parks / Justin Fenty
17 Kansas State	3 T Travis Farst
34 Colorado	31 G Chad Smith
31 Texas	63 C Will Blaylock (G)/ Yancey Boatner
36 Kansas	35 G Dan Gay
21 Texas A&M	31 T Jason Smith
21 Texas Tech	55 QB Shawn Bell / Blake Szymanski
24 Oklahoma State	66 RB Paul Mosley / Brandon Whitaker
10 Oklahoma	36 DL Jason Lamb / Marcus Foreman
	DL Vincent Rhodes / Corey Ford
	DL M.T. Robinson / Klayton Shoals
	DL Geoff Nelson / Julian Hill
	LB Nick Moore
	LB Joe Pawelek / Antonio Jones
	DB Anthony Arline / James Todd
	DB C. J. Wilson
	DB Maurice Linquist
	DB Dwain Crawford / Alton Widemon
	DB Brandon Stiggers

RUSHING: Mosley 100/479y, Whitaker 41/158y
PASSING: Bell 241-383/2582y, 19TD, 62.9%
RECEIVING: Ziegler 54/741y, Shelton 53/802y, Whitaker 30/192y
SCORING: Ryan Havens (K) 65pts, Shelton 48pts, Mosley 42pts

2007 3-9

0 Texas Christian	27 WR David Gettis / Justin Fenty
42 Rice	17 WR Brad Taylor / Thomas White
34 Texas State	27 WR Justin Akers
34 Buffalo	21 WR Krys Buerck / Ernest Smith
10 Texas A&M	34 T Jason Smith / Jordan Hearvey
23 Colorado	43 G Chad Smith
10 Kansas	58 C J.D. Walton
10 Texas	31 G James Barnard
13 Kansas State	51 T Dan Gay
7 Texas Tech	38 QB Blake Szymanski / Michael Machen
21 Oklahoma	52 RB Brandon Whitaker / Jay Finley
14 Oklahoma State	45 DL Jason Lamb
	DL Vincent Rhodes
	DL Trey Bryant / Connor Redfearn
	DL Geoff Nelson / Damien Taylor
	LB Joe Pawelek
	LB Nick Moore / Leon Freeman
	DB Josh Bell
	DB Alton Widemon
	DB Jordan Lake
	DB Brandon Stiggers / Jeremy Williams
	DB Dwain Crawford / Jake La Mar

RUSHING: Whitaker 102/488y, Finley 55/207y, Jacoby Jones (RB) 49/192y
PASSING: Szymanski 264-461/2844y, 22TD, 57.3%
RECEIVING: Whitaker 58/425y, Akers 43/426y, Taylor 35/465y
SCORING: White 48pts, Whitaker 30pts, Shea Brewster (K) 26pts

2008 4-8

13 Wake Forest	41 WR Ernest Smith / Thomas White
51 Northwestern St.	6 WR Kendal Wright / Kyle Mitchell
45 Washington St.	17 WR David Gettis
28 Connecticut	31 T Jason Smith
17 Oklahoma	49 G Jordan Hearvey / Chad Griesenbeck
38 Iowa State	10 C J.D. Walton
6 Oklahoma State	34 G James Barnard
20 Nebraska	32 T Dan Gay
28 Missouri	31 TE Justin Akers / Brad Taylor
21 Texas	45 QB Robert Griffin
41 Texas A&M	21 RB Jay Finley / Larry Washington
28 Texas Tech	35 DL Leon Freeman / Zac Scotton
	DL Vincent Rhodes
	DL Trey Bryant
	DL Jason Lamb
	LB Antonio Jones / Earl Patin
	LB Joe Pawelek
	LB/DB Antonio Johnson / Tim Atchison
	DB Dwain Crawford / Trentson Hill
	DB Krys Buerck / Antareis Bryan
	DB Jordan Lake
	DB Jeremy Williams / Jake La Mar

RUSHING: Finley 149/865y, Griffin 173/843y, Jacoby Jones (RB) 52/203y
PASSING: Griffin 160-267/2091y, 15TD, 59.9%
RECEIVING: Wright 50/649y, White 35/385y, Gettis 29/391y
SCORING: Griffin 78pts, Ben Parks (K) 57pts, Finley 54pts

2009 4-8

24 Wake Forest	21 WR Lanear Sampson / Krys Buerck
22 Connecticut	30 WR Kendall Wright / Will Jefferson
68 Northwestern St.	13 WR David Gettis / Ernest Smith
31 Kent State	15 T Danny Watkins
7 Oklahoma	33 G Ivory Wade / John Jones
10 Iowa State	24 C J.D. Walton
7 Oklahoma State	34 G James Barnard / Cameron Kaufhold
10 Nebraska	20 T Philip Blake
40 Missouri	32 TE Justin Akers / Brad Taylor
14 Texas	47 QB Nick Florence / Robert Griffin
3 Texas A&M	38 RB Jay Finley / Jarred Salubi
13 Texas Tech	20 DL Tracy Robertson / Zac Scotton
	DL Phil Taylor
	DL Trey Bryant
	DL Jason Lamb
	LB Antonio Jones / Earl Patin
	LB Joe Pawelek / Chris Francis
	LB Antonio Johnson
	DB Tim Atchison
	DB Chance Casey / Clifton Odom
	DB Jordon Lake
	DB Jeremy Williams / Byron Landor

RUSHING: Finley 79/370y, Salubi 50/298y, Terran Ganaway (RB) 68/200y
PASSING: Florence 165-266/1786y, 6TD, 62%
Blake Szymanski (QB) 55-89/605y, TD, 61.8%
Griffin 45-69/481y, 4TDs, 65.2%
RECEIVING: Wright 66/740y, Gettis 52/675y, Smith 39/360y
Sampson 29/297y, Akers 27/249y
SCORING: Ganaway & Wright 30pts, Ben Parks (K) 29pts

2010 7-6

34 Sam Houston St.	3 WR Lanear Sampson / Josh Gordon
34 Buffalo	6 WR Kendall Wright / Krys Buerck
10 TCU	45 WR Terrance Williams / Tevin Reese
30 Rice	13 T Danny Watkins
55 Kansas	7 G Cameron Kaufhold
38 Texas Tech	45 C Philip Blake
31 Colorado	25 G R.T. Griffin / Cyril Richardson
47 Kansas State	42 T Ivory Wade
30 Texas	22 TE/FB Brad Taylor / Kaeron Johnson
28 Oklahoma State	55 QB Robert Griffin
30 Texas A&M	42 TB Jay Finley
24 Oklahoma	53 DL Gary Mason / Tevin Elliott
14 Illinois ■	38 DL Nic Jean-Baptiste
	DL Phil Taylor
	DL Tracy Robertson / Terrance Lloyd
	LB Elliot Coffey / Earl Patin
	LB Chris Francis / Chris McAllister
	LB Antonio Johnson / Rodney Chadwick
	DB Chance Casey / Clifton Odom
	DB Mikail Baker / Antareis Bryan
	DB Tim Atchison
	DB Byron Landor / Tyler Stephenson

RUSHING: Finley 195/1218y, Griffin 149/635y, Terrance Ganaway (TB) 46/295y
PASSING: Griffin 304-454/3501y, 22TD, 67%
RECEIVING: Wright 78/952y, Reese 45/401y, Williams 43/494y
Gordon 42/714y
SCORING: Aaron Jones (K) 103pts, Finley 72pts, Griffin 50pts

827

BOSTON COLLEGE

Boston College (Founded 1863)
Chestnut Hill, Massachusetts
Nickname: Eagles
Colors: Maroon and Gold
Stadium: Alumni Stadium (1957) 44,500
Conference Affiliations: Independent (1953-90), Big East (Charter member, 1991-04), Atlantic Coast Atlantic (2005-present)

CAREER RUSHING YARDS	Attempts	Yards
Derrick Knight (2000-03)	708	3725
Montel Harris (2008-10)	756	3600
Mike Cloud (1995-98)	614	3597
Troy Stradford (1982-86)	658	3504
William Green (1999-01)	501	2974
Andre Callender (2004-07)	637	2971
Mike Esposito (1972-74)	526	2759
L.V. Whitworth (2004-07)	588	2576
Keith Barnette (1973-75)	552	2500
Omari Walker (1994-97)	566	2471

CAREER PASSING YARDS	Comp.-Att.	Yards
Doug Flutie (1981-84)	677-1271	10579
Glenn Foley (1990-93)	703-1275	10039
Matt Ryan (2004-07)	807-1347	9313
Brian St. Pierre (1999-02)	457-803	5837
Shawn Halloran (1983-86)	416-723	5252
Frank Harris (1968-70)	366-655	4555
Matt Hasselbeck (1994-97)	390-701	4548
Tim Hasselbeck (1998-00)	278-501	3890
Mark Hartsell (1993-95)	349-608	3763
Paul Peterson (2003-04)	305-502	3718

CAREER RECEIVING YARDS	Catches	Yards
Rich Gunnell (2006-09)	181	2459
Pete Mitchell (1991-94)	190	2388
Kelvin Martin (1983-86)	133	2337
Brian Brennan (1980-83)	115	2180
Mark Chmura (1987-91)	164	2046
Grant Adams (2001-04)	137	2036
Brandon Robinson (2005-08)	141	2023
Darren Flutie (1984-87)	134	2000
Tom Waddle (1985-88)	139	1965
Dedrick Dewalt (1998-01)	126	1959

SEASON RUSHING YARDS	Attempts	Yards
Mike Cloud (1998)	308	1726
Derrick Knight (2003)	321	1721
William Green (2001)	265	1559
Montel Harris (2009)	308	1457
Derrick Knight (2002)	253	1432

SEASON PASSING YARDS	Comp.-Att.	Yards
Matt Ryan (2007)	388-654	4507
Doug Flutie (1984)	233-386	3454
Glenn Foley (1993)	222-363	3397
Brian St. Pierre (2002)	237-407	2983
Matt Ryan (2006)	263-427	2942

SEASON RECEIVING YARDS	Catches	Yards
Brian Brennan (1983)	66	1149
Kelvin Martin (1985)	49	958
Rich Gunnell (2007)	64	931
Tom Waddle (1988)	70	902
Rich Gunnell (2009)	60	880

GAME RUSHING YARDS	Attempts	Yards
Montel Harris (2009 vs. N. Carolina St.)	27	264
Phil Bennett (1972 vs. Temple)	36	253
Troy Stradford (1986 vs. Army)	34	240

GAME PASSING YARDS	Comp.-Att.	Yards
Doug Flutie (1982 vs. Penn State)	29-53	520
Doug Flutie (1984 vs. Miami)	34-46	472
Shawn Halloran (1985 vs. Syracuse)	34-57	453

GAME RECEIVING YARDS	Catches	Yards
Scott Nizolek (1982 vs. Penn State)	11	229
Gerard Phelan (1984 vs. Miami)	11	226
Brian Brennan (1983 vs. Temple)	10	185

GREATEST COACH:

Although after his recent departure for the head coaching ranks at North Carolina State, Tom O'Brien may not be overly popular in Massachusetts, he was overly consistent with winning football games as the head coach of Boston College. After opening his 10-year run with the Eagles with two 4-7 seasons, O'Brien led the Eagles to eight straight years of at least eight wins with a seven-game bowl win streak coming at the end of it all. They capped their Big East stay with a tie for first place in 2004's lame duck season.

The move to the ACC for the 2005 season did not slow him down; in fact, O'Brien seemed to have benefitted from the switch as the Eagles became a team to be reckoned with behind their tough Northeast style of play. After tying for first place in the Atlantic in 2005 with a 5-3 mark, the Eagles repeated that mark for a second place tie in 2006.

O'Brien came to Boston College from another ACC school, Virginia, where he was offensive coordinator for some of the most exciting units in Cavaliers history. Virginia topped 300 points in all six seasons with O'Brien as their offensive coordinator, including the 1995 unit that outscored Florida State in helping the Cavs win a share of the ACC title.

One other form of consistency for O'Brien has been with academic achievement as the discipline and hard work the former scholar-athlete from the Naval Academy preached for the football field he encouraged for the classroom. BC football players always ranked near the top of graduation rates during O'Brien's tenure.

BOSTON COLLEGE'S 55 GREATEST SINCE 1953

OFFENSE

WIDE RECEIVER: Brian Brennan, Artie Graham, Rich Gunnell, Kelvin Martin
TIGHT END: Mark Chmura, Pete Mitchell
TACKLE: Anthony Castonzo, Pete Kendall, Al Krevis, Dave Widell
GUARD: Doug Brzezinski, Gerry Raymond, Chris Snee, Joe Wolf
CENTER: Tom Nalen, Damien Woody
QUARTERBACK: Doug Flutie, Glenn Foley, Matt Ryan
RUNNING BACK: Mike Cloud, Mike Esposito, William Green, Derrick Knight, Troy Stradford
FULLBACK: Brendan McCarthy

DEFENSE

END: John Bosa, Byron Hemingway, Mathias Kiwanuka, Mike Mucci
TACKLE: Mike Hovan, Tim Morabito, Fred Smerlas
LINEBACKER: Stephen Boyd, Ivan Caesar, Steve DeOssie, Mark Herzlich, Tom McManus, Bill Romanowski
CORNERBACK: Kelly Elias, George Radachowsky, Mike Mayock, Jim McGowan
SAFETY: Charlie Brennan, Pedro Cirino, John Salmon, Tony Thurman

SPECIAL TEAMS

RETURN SPECIALISTS: Dave Bennett, Eddie Rideout
PLACE KICKER: Fred Steinfort
PUNTER: Jim Walton

MULTIPLE POSITIONS

CENTER-GUARD: Bob Hyland
DEFENSIVE TACKLE-LINEBACKER: Pete Cronan
NOSE GUARD-DEFENSIVE TACKLE: Mike Ruth

TWO-WAY PLAYERS

TACKLE-DEFENSIVE TACKLE: John Miller
WIDE RECEIVER-CORNERBACK: Will Blackmon

PERFORMANCE FORMULA:
BOSTON COLLEGE'S 10 BEST SEASONS

1984	1.4958	6 of 70
1993	1.4316	15 of 70
2005	1.4260	14 of 70
2006	1.4113	19 of 72
2007	1.4027	15 of 70
1962	1.3596	18 of 70
1986	1.3452	18 of 70
1954	1.3426	19 of 69
1957	1.3253	19 of 69
2002	1.3169	23 of 70

BOSTON COLLEGE EAGLES

Year	W-L-T	AP Poll	Conference Standing	Toughest Regular Season Opponents	Coach (Record at School)	Bowl Games		
1953	5-3-1			Louisiana State 5-3-3, Richmond 5-3-1	Mike Holovak			
1954	8-1			Boston University 7-2, VMI 4-6	Mike Holovak			
1955	5-2-1			Miami 7-2, Xavier 7-2	Mike Holovak			
1956	5-4			Miami 8-1-1, Holy Cross 5-3-1	Mike Holovak			
1957	7-2			Navy 8-1-1, Holy Cross 5-3-1	Mike Holovak			
1958	7-3			Syracuse 8-1, Clemson 8-2, Villanova 6-4	Mike Holovak			
1959	5-4			Pittsburgh 6-4, Navy 5-4-1, Army 4-4-1	Mike Holovak (49-29-3)			
1960	3-6-1			Navy 9-1, Army 6-3-1, Clemson 6-4	Ernie Hefferle			
1961	4-6			Syracuse 7-3, Holy Cross 7-3, Northwestern 4-5	Ernie Hefferle (7-12-1)			
1962	8-2			Syracuse 5-5, Houston 6-4, Villanova 7-2	Jim Miller			
1963	6-3			Syracuse 8-2, Air Force 7-3, Wichita 7-2	Jim Miller			
1964	6-3			Syracuse 7-3, Cincinnati 8-2, Villanova 6-2	Jim Miller			
1965	6-4			Syracuse 7-3, Miami 5-4-1, Penn State 5-5	Jim Miller			
1966	4-6			Syracuse 8-2, Penn State 5-5, Holy Cross 6-3-1	Jim Miller			
1967	4-6			Syracuse 8-2, Penn State 8-2, Army 8-2	Jim Miller (34-24)			
1968	6-3			Penn State 10-0, Army 7-3, Buffalo 7-3	Joe Yukica			
1969	5-4			Penn State 10-0, Syracuse 5-5, Villanova 6-3	Joe Yukica			
1970	8-2			Penn State 7-3, Air Force 9-2, Pittsburgh 5-5	Joe Yukica			
1971	9-2			West Virginia 7-4, Temple 6-2-1, Syracuse 5-5-1	Joe Yukica			
1972	4-7			Penn State 10-1, Georgia Tech 6-4-1, Air Force 6-4	Joe Yukica			
1973	7-4			Temple 9-1, Pittsburgh 6-4-1, Tulane 9-2, West Virginia 6-5	Joe Yukica			
1974	8-3			Texas 8-3, Pittsburgh 7-4, Temple 8-2	Joe Yukica			
1975	7-4			Notre Dame 8-3, West Virginia 8-3, Navy 7-4, Syracuse 6-5	Joe Yukica			
1976	8-3			Texas 5-5-1, Florida State 5-6	Joe Yukica			
1977	6-5			Texas 11-0, Pittsburgh 8-2-1, Syracuse 6-5	Joe Yukica (68-37)			
1978	0-11			Pittsburgh 8-3, Texas A&M 7-4, Navy 8-3	Ed Chlebek			
1979	5-6			Pittsburgh 10-1, Tennessee 7-4, Stanford 5-5-1, Syracuse 6-5	Ed Chlebek			
1980	7-4			Pittsburgh 10-1, Florida State 10-1, Navy 8-3	Ed Chlebek (12-21)			
1981	5-6			Penn State 9-2, Pittsburgh 10-1, North Carolina 9-2	Jack Bicknell			
1982	8-3-1			Penn State 10-1, Clemson 9-1-1, West Virginia 9-2	Jack Bicknell	Tangerine	26 Auburn	33
1983	9-3	19		Clemson 9-1-1, Alabama 7-4, West Virginia 8-3, Penn State 7-4-1	Jack Bicknell	Liberty	18 Notre Dame	19
1984	10-2	5		Miami 8-4, West Virginia 7-4, Army 7-3-1	Jack Bicknell	Cotton	45 Houston	28
1985	4-8			Penn State 11-0, Miami 10-1, BYU 11-2, Maryland 8-3, Army 8-3	Jack Bicknell			
1986	9-3	19		Penn State 11-0, SMU 6-5	Jack Bicknell	Hall of Fame	27 Georgia	24
1987	5-6			Syracuse 11-0, Notre Dame 8-3, Southern Cal 8-3, Penn State 8-3	Jack Bicknell			
1988	3-8			Southern Cal 10-1, West Virginia 11-0, Syracuse 9-2, Army 9-2	Jack Bicknell			
1989	2-9			Penn State 7-3-1, Ohio State 8-3, Pitt 7-3-1, West Virginia 8-2-1	Jack Bicknell			
1990	4-7			Penn State 9-2, Louisville 9-1-1, Ohio State 7-3-1, Syracuse 6-4-2	Jack Bicknell (59-55-1)			
1991	4-7			Miami 11-0, Michigan 10-1, Penn State 10-2, Syracuse 9-2	Tom Coughlin			
1992	8-3-1	21		Notre Dame 9-1-1, Syracuse 9-2, Penn State 7-4	Tom Coughlin	Hall of Fame	23 Tennessee	38
1993	9-3	13	3	Notre Dame 10-1, West Virginia 11-0, Miami 9-2, Virginia Tech 8-3	Tom Coughlin (21-13-1)	Carquest	31 Virginia	13
1994	7-4-1	23	5	Miami 10-1, Virginia Tech 8-3, Michigan 8-3	Dan Henning	Aloha	12 Kansas State	7
1995	4-8		4t	Ohio State 11-1, Virginia Tech 9-2, Notre Dame 9-2, Michigan 9-3	Dan Henning			
1996	5-7		6	Va. Tech 10-1, Miami 8-3, Notre Dame 8-3, Michigan 9-3	Dan Henning (16-19-1)			
1997	4-7		5t	Syracuse 9-3, Virginia Tech 7-4, Notre Dame 7-5, West Virginia 7-4	Tom O'Brien			
1998	4-7		5	Syracuse 8-3, Georgia Tech 9-2, Notre Dame 9-2, West Virginia 8-3	Tom O'Brien			
1999	8-4		3	Virginia Tech 11-0, Miami 8-4, Syracuse 6-5	Tom O'Brien	Insight	28 Colorado	62
2000	7-5		5t	Miami 10-1, Notre Dame 9-2, Virginia Tech 10-1, Pittsburgh 7-4	Tom O'Brien	Aloha	31 Arizona State	17
2001	8-4	23	3t	Miami 11-0, Virginia Tech 8-3, Syracuse 9-3, Stanford 9-2	Tom O'Brien	Music City	20 Georgia	16
2002	9-4		4t	Miami 12-0, Notre Dame 10-2, Virginia Tech 9-4, West Virginia 9-3	Tom O'Brien	Motor City	51 Toledo	25
2003	8-5		5	Miami 10-2, West Virginia 8-4, Pittsburgh 8-4, Virginia Tech 8-4	Tom O'Brien	San Fran.	35 Colorado State	21
2004	9-3	21	1t	West Virginia 8-3, Pittsburgh 8-3, Syracuse 6-5	Tom O'Brien	Continental Tire	37 North Carolina	24
2005	9-3	18	Atl1t	Virginia Tech 10-1, Florida State 7-4, Clemson 7-4	Tom O'Brien	MPC	27 Boise State	21
2006	10-3	20	Atl2t	Virginia Tech 10-2, Wake Forest 11-2, Clemson 8-4, BYU 10-2	Tom O'Brien (75-45) Frank Spaziani [1-0]	Meineke	25 Navy	22
2007	11-3	10t	Atl1	VirginiaTech 10-2, Clemson 9-3	Jeff Jagodzinski	ChampsSports	24 Michigan State	2
2008	9-5		Atl1t	Georgia Tech 9-3, Virginia Tech 9-4, Florida State 8-4	Jeff Jagodzinski (20-8)	Music City	14 Vanderbilt	16
2009	8-5		Atl2	Clemson 8-5, Virginia Tech 9-3, North Carolina 8-4	Frank Spaziani	Emerald	13 Southern California	24
2010	7-6		Atl4t	Virginia Tech 11-2, Florida State 9-4, Maryland 8-4	Frank Spaziani (16-11)	Kraft Hunger	13 Nevada	20

TOTAL:	370-264-6 .5828 (25 of 70)				**Bowl Games since 1953:**	12-7 .6316 (5 of 70)		

GREATEST TEAM SINCE 1953: Flutie! Flutie! Flutie! The 1984 team, with quarterback Doug Flutie at the helm, won 10 games for only second time in school history en route to a final spot of no. 5 in the AP Poll. In winning 10 games, the Eagles knocked off Alabama, North Carolina, a bowl-bound Army squad, Syracuse and...drum roll please... defending national champion Miami. They did so on Flutie's late-game heroics, a final pass forever destined to be associated with both the quarterback and program. Then after dispatching Holy Cross, Boston College trumped Houston in the Cotton Bowl.

1953 5-3-1

14	Clemson	14	E Tom Izbicki / John McDonnell
6	LSU	42	T Joe Hines / Frank Morze
7	Villanova	15	G Vin St. Pierre / Joe Mattaliano
20	Fordham	13	C Cliff Poirier
31	Xavier	14	G John Parker / Dick Myles
0	Richmond	14	T John Miller / Frank Furey
20	Wake Forest	7	E Emerson Dickie
33	Detroit	20	QB Jim Kane / Doc Mauro
6	Holy Cross	0	HB John Irwin / Dan Brosnahan
			HB Joe Johnson / Ed DeSilva
			FB Dick Zotti / Turk Petrarca

RUSHING: Johnson 126/510y
PASSING: Kane 25-64/414y, 3TD, 39.1%
RECEIVING: Brosnahan 5/102y
SCORING: Zotti 42pts

1954 8-1

12	Detroit	7	E Dick Lucas / Frank Furey
12	Temple	9	T Frank Morze / Tino Bertolini
44	VMI	0	G Joe Mattaliano / Vin St. Pierre
21	Fordham	7	C Cliff Poirier / Len Andrusaitis
42	Springfield	6	G Dick Myles
14	Xavier	19	T John Miller
13	Marquette	7	E Tom Izbicki / Emerson Dickie
7	Boston Univ.	6	QB Jimmy Kane / Billy Donlan
31	Holy Cross	13	HB Tom Magnarelli / Doc Mauro
			HB Eddie DeSilva / Bernie Teliszewski
			FB Turk Petrarca / Dick Gagliardi

RUSHING: DeSilva 99/635y, Petrarca 81/359y, Magnarelli 67/318y
PASSING: Kane 20-52/397y, 2TD, 38.5%
RECEIVING: Furey 5/107y, Gagliardi 5/68y, Lucas 4/93y,
SCORING: Magnarelli 36pts, Gagliardi 28pts, DeSilva 25pts

1955 5-2-1

27	Brandeis	0	E Dick Lucas
28	Villanova	14	T Frank Cousineau
23	Detroit	0	G Dick Myles / Tony Quintilliani
13	Marquette	13	C Len Andrusaitis
12	Xavier	19	G Tino Bertolini / Tom Meehan
7	Miami	14	T John Miller
40	Boston Univ.	12	E Emerson Dickie / Dick Gagliardi
26	Holy Cross	7	QB Billy Donlan / Henry Sullivan
			HB Tommy Joe Sullivan / Dorick Mauro
			HB Eddie DeSilva / Billy Alves
			FB Turk Petrarca / Larry Plenty

RUSHING: Petrarca 82/464y, DeSilva 86/401y, Plenty 42/236y
PASSING: Donlan 34-69/684y, 4TD, 49.3%
RECEIVING: Lucas 16/261y, Dickie 10/174y, Gagliardi 5/156y
SCORING: Donlan & Petrarca 36pts, DeSilva 25pts

1956 5-4

6	Miami	27	E Alex Kulevich / Fran Gallagher
26	Marquette	19	T Steve Bennett
32	Rutgers	0	G Tino Bertolini / Tony Quintilliani
7	Detroit	12	C George Larkin / Tony Folcarelli
7	Villanova	6	G Tom Meehan
6	Quantico	20	T Leon Bennett / Tom Lane
13	Boston Univ.	0	E Dick Reagan / John Flanagan
52	Brandeis	0	QB Billy Donlan / Don Allard
0	Holy Cross	7	HB Alan Miller / Tommy Joe Sullivan
			HB Henry Sullivan / Billy Alves
			FB Bernie Teliszewski / Larry Plenty

RUSHING: Miller 73/419y, Teliszewski 89/381y, Sullivan 37/254y
PASSING: Donlan 26-62/423y, 3TD, 4.9%
RECEIVING: Reagan 10/123y, Flanagan 8/116y, Gallagher 6/96y
SCORING: Teliszewski 36pts, Miller, Reagan & Sullivan 18pts

1957 7-2

6	Navy	46	E Don Tosi / Alex Kulevich
20	Florida State	7	T Jim O'Brien / Steve Bennett
13	Quantico	7	G Frank Casey / Tony Quintilliani
41	Dayton	14	C George Larkin
12	Villanova	9	G Tom Meehan / Ed McGraw
20	Detroit	16	T Leon Bennett / Tom Lane
27	Boston Univ.	2	E John Flanagan / Jim Cotter
19	Marquette	14	QB Don Allard
0	Holy Cross	14	HB Jim Colclough / Tommy Joe Sullivan
			HB Alan Miller / Vin Hogan / Robert Murphy
			FB Larry Plenty / Don Seagar

RUSHING: Miller 111/484y, Seagar 60/195y, Allard 86/129y
PASSING: Allard 53-121/910y, 8TD, 43.8%
RECEIVING: Colclough 12/254y, Flanagan 12/213y, Murphy 8/106y
SCORING: Colclough 42pts, Miller 30pts, Seagar 24pts

1958 7-3

48	Scranton	0	E John Flanagan / Don Tosi
14	Syracuse	24	T Jim O'Brien / Steve Bennett
19	Villanova	21	G Frank Casey / Frank Moretti
21	Marquette	13	C George Larkin / Terry Glynn
6	Miami	2	G Ed DeGraw / Don Gautreau
25	Pacific	12	T Leon Bennett / Harry Ball
40	Detroit	0	E Larry Eisenhauer / Jim Cotter
18	Boston Univ.	13	QB Don Allard / John Amabile
12	Clemson	34	HB Jim Colclough / Vin Hogan (FB)
26	Holy Cross	8	HB Alan Miller / Tom Casey
			FB James Duggan / Frank Robotti

RUSHING: Duggan 131/489y, Miller 89/421y, Hogan 64/322y
PASSING: Allard 43-90/691y, 7TD, 47.8%
RECEIVING: Colclough 24/462y, Flanagan 21/344y,
SCORING: Flanagan 36pts, Colclough 32pts, Miller 30pts

1959 5-4

8	Navy	24	E Don Tosi / Dick Gill / Joe Sikorski
8	Army	24	T Jim O'Brien / Dan Sullivan
39	Villanova	6	G Frank Casey / George McHugh
35	Dartmouth	12	C Terry Glynn / Tony Abraham
16	Marquette	0	G Bill Byrne
21	Detroit	9	T Harry Ball / Bob LaBlanc
14	Pittsburgh	22	E Larry Eisenhauer / Lou Kirouac
7	Boston Univ.	26	QB John Amabile / Ross O'Hanley
14	Holy Cross	0	HB Tom Casey / Bill Robinson
			HB Vin Hogan / Dyer / Ron Dyer
			FB Frank Robotti / Frank Moretti

RUSHING: Hogan 74/311y, Robotti 67/184y, Moretti 26/120y
PASSING: Amabile 85-159/1200y, 8TD, 53.4%
RECEIVING: Hogan 18/258y, Tosi 15/158y, Robinson 14/221y
SCORING: Hogan 40pts, Lou Kirovac (K) 33pts, Dyer 16pts

1960 3-6-1

7	Navy	22	E Artie Graham
7	Army	20	T Dan Sullivan
12	Marquette	13	G George McHugh
17	Detroit	19	C Terry Glynn / Tom Hall
14	VMI	14	G Bill Byrne / Don Gautreau
7	Miami	10	T Larry Eisenhauer / Don Antonellis
20	Villanova	6	E Joe Sikorski / Bob Perreault (HB)
23	Boston Univ.	14	QB John Amabile / George Van Cott
25	Clemson	14	HB John Janas / John McGann
12	Holy Cross	16	HB Dick Gill / Bill Robinson / Mike Tomeo
			FB Frank Robotti / Harry Crump

RUSHING: Crump 91/385y, Tomeo 43/268y, Janas 59/245y
PASSING: Amabile 53-123/726y, 2TD, 43.1%
RECEIVING: Sikorski 20/265y, Graham 14/221y, Perreault 8/126y
SCORING: Crump 24pts, Sikorski 18pts,
Van Cott & Lou Kirouac (K) 16pts

1961 4-6

23	Cincinnati	0	E Artie Graham
0	Northwestern	45	T Dan Sullivan / Gene Carrington
0	Houston	21	G Don Gautreau / Lou Cioci
3	Detroit	20	C Tom Hall / Joe Hutchinson
22	Villanova	6	G Bill Byrne / Dave Yelle
14	Iowa State	10	T Dave O'Brien / Don Antonellis
6	Texas Tech	14	E Joe Sikorski / Lou Kirouac
10	Boston Univ.	7	QB George Van Cott / Jack Concannon
13	Syracuse	28	HB J. McGann / John Barrett / Mike Tomeo
26	Holy Cross	38	HB Bill Flanagan / Pete Shaughnessy
			FB Harry Crump / John Sullivan

RUSHING: Crump 121/471y, Van Cott 82/198y, Tomeo 49/162y
PASSING: Van Cott 59-188/729y, 5TD, 31.4%
RECEIVING: Graham 15/255y, Sikorski 12/112y, Kirouac 11/112y
SCORING: Crump 30pts, Kirouac (E-K) 19pts, 4 tied w/ 12pts

1962 8-2

27	Detroit	0	E Artie Graham / Joe Lukis
28	Villanova	13	T John Frechette / Lou Cioci
18	VMI	0	G John McGourthy / Dave Yelle / Dick Cremin
0	Syracuse	12	C Tom Hall / Bart Connolly
6	Navy	26	G Frank DeFelice / John Sullivan
14	Houston	0	T Jay Donovan / Dave O'Brien
27	Vanderbilt	22	E Jim Whalen / Bob Smith
41	Texas Tech	13	QB Jack Concannon
41	Boston Univ.	25	HB Pete Shaughnessy / John Barrett
48	Holy Cross	12	HB Bob Shann / Jim McGowan
			FB Harry Crump

RUSHING: Crump 123/641y, Concannon 91/293y, Shann 35/187y
PASSING: Concannon 97-181/1450y, 6TD, 53.6%
RECEIVING: Graham 41/823y, Whalen 16/309y, Shann 10/72y
SCORING: Graham 50pts, Whalen 37pts, Concannon 36pts

1963 6-3

21	Syracuse	32	E Bill Cronin / Charlie Smith
22	Wichita	16	T Frank DeFelice / John Frechette
20	Detroit	12	G Dick Cremin / Bob Ryan
34	Villanova	0	C Bart Connelly / Frank Fitzgibbons
7	Air Force	34	G John Leone / Marty DiMezza
19	Vanderbilt	6	T Bill Schoelk / Jim Cheviolott
15	Buffalo	0	E Jim Whalen / Joe Lukis
30	Virginia	21	QB Jack Concannon
0	Holy Cross	9	HB John Barrett / Bob Shann
			HB Jim McGowan / Hank Blaha
			FB John Walsh / Don Moran

RUSHING: Concannon 94/281y, Walsh 54/225y, Moran 33/176y
PASSING: Concannon 85-192/1328y, 8TD, 44.3%
RECEIVING: Whalen 26/523y, Cronin 16/257y, McGowan 12/173y
SCORING: Concannon 40pts, McGowan 30pts, Barrett 14pts

1964 6-3

21	Syracuse	14	E Bill Cronin
13	Army	19	T John Frechette
14	Tennessee	16	G Dick Cremin / Bob Ryan
10	Cincinnati	0	C Bob Ryan
13	Air Force	7	G Marty DiMezza / John Leone
8	Villanova	7	T Emil Kleiner
4	Miami	30	E Jim Whalen
17	Detroit	9	QB Ed Foley / Larry Marzetti
10	Holy Cross	8	HB Jim McGowan
			HB Bobby Shann / Bob Budzinski
			FB Don Moran / John Walsh
			DL Charlie Smith
			DL Bill Schoeck / Bill Stetz
			DL Jim Chevillot / Bill Risio
			DL Bill Cronin / Frank Grywalski
			DL Dave Pesapane
			LB Marty DiMezza
			LB Frank DeFelice / John Walsh
			LB John Leone / Don Moran
			DB Jim McGowan / Bobby Shann
			DB Hank Blaha / Ron Gentili
			DB Larry Marzetti

RUSHING: Moran 100/385y, McGowan 22/165y, Walsh 34/149y
PASSING: Foley 72-144/947y, 4TD, 50%
RECEIVING: Whalen 31/398y, Cronin 19/389y, McGowan 6/30y
SCORING: Moran & Whalen 18pts, Shann & McGowan 12pts

1965 6-4

18	Buffalo	6	E Charlie Smith
28	Villanova	0	T Dick Powers
0	Army	10	G John Leone
0	Penn State	17	C Bob Hyland / Mike Evans
38	Richmond	9	G Marty DiMezza
41	VMI	12	T Jim Chevillot
6	Miami	27	E Joe Pryor / Gordie Kutz
30	William & Mary	17	QB Ed Foley / John Blair
13	Syracuse	21	HB Paul Della Villa / Terry Erwin
35	Holy Cross	0	HB Dick DeLeonardis / Bob Budzinski
			FB Brendan McCarthy
			DL Len Persin / Dick Capp
			DL Doug Shepard / Bill Risio
			DL Bill Stetz / Ed Lipson
			DL Tom Sarkisian
			DL Mike O'Neill
			LB John Leone
			LB Nick Franco / Marty DiMezza
			DB Dan Hostetter / Tom Carylon
			DB Hank Blaha
			DB Ron Gentili / Bob Budzinski
			DB Larry Marzetti

RUSHING: McCarthy 187/901y, Foley 79/266y,
DeLeonardis 67/180y
PASSING: Foley 57-120/979y, 5TD, 47.5%
RECEIVING: Smith 18/315y, Pryor 14/218y, Budzinski 11/200y
SCORING: Erwin 36pts, DeLeonardis 30pts, McCarthy 24pts

1966 4-6

7 Navy	27 E Jim Kavanagh / Barry Gallup
14 Ohio	23 T Kerry Horman / Jerry Ragosa
14 VMI	0 G Bob Hyland
30 Penn State	31 C Mike Evans
0 Syracuse	30 G Dick Collins
22 Buffalo	21 T Tom Sarkisian
15 William & Mary	13 E Mike O'Neill
0 Villanova	19 QB Joe Marzetti
14 Massachusetts	7 HB Paul Della Villa
26 Holy Cross	32 HB Dave Bennett
	FB Brendan McCarthy
	DL Barry Gallup / Len Persin
	DL Jerry Ragosa
	DL Bill Stetz
	DL Ron Persuitte / Doug Shepard
	DL Gordie Kutz
	LB Ed Lipson
	LB Gary Andrachik
	DB Al Giardi
	DB John Salmon
	DB Jim Grace / Harry Conners
	DB Tom Carlyon

RUSHING: McCarthy 139/585y, Marzetti 115/381y,
Della Villa 81/222y
PASSING: Marzetti 36-126/549y, 4TD, 28.6%
RECEIVING: Kavanagh 17/282y, DellaVilla 13/207y, Gallup 11/157y
SCORING: Della Villa 30pts, O'Neill 22pts, McCarthy 18pts

1967 4-6

27 Villanova	24 E Barry Gallup
10 Army	21 T Bob Bouley
28 Penn State	50 G Bud Kruger / Mike Nevard
14 Buffalo	26 C Al Borsari / Mike Evans
56 Maine	0 G Jim Garofalo / Chris Markey
21 Cincinnati	27 T Jerry Ragosa / Bill Ladewig
13 VMI	26 E Jim Kavanagh
20 Syracuse	32 QB Joe Divito / Mike Fallon
25 Massachusetts	0 HB Terry Erwin / Skip Coppola
13 Holy Cross	6 HB Dave Bennett
	FB Brendan McCarthy
	DL Carter Hunt
	DL John Fitzgerald
	DL Dick Kroner
	DL Ron Persuitte
	DL Ed McDonald
	LB Gary Andrachik / Mondell Davis
	LB Jim McCool / John O'Connell
	DB Harry Pierandri
	DB Gary Matz / Dan Zailskas
	DB Dave Thomas
	DB John Salmon

RUSHING: McCarthy 152/574y, Fallon 75/214y, Erwin 63/214y
PASSING: DiVito 69-159/964y, 5TD, 43.4%
RECEIVING: Gallup 28/414y, Kavanagh 27/488y, Erwin 19/218y
SCORING: Bennett & McCarthy 42pts, Gallivan (K) 31pts

1968 6-3

49 Navy	15 WR Barry Gallup
31 Buffalo	12 T Gary Guenther
28 Villanova	15 G Kerry Horman / Bernie Galeckas
14 Tulane	28 C John Egan
0 Penn State	29 G Mike Lardner / Walt Cullen
25 Army	58 T Bob Bouley
45 VMI	13 TE Steve Kives
21 Massachusetts	6 QB Frank Harris / Joe Marzetti
40 Holy Cross	20 HB Dave Bennett
	HB Jim Catone / Fred Willis
	FB Joe McDonald / Paul Della Villa
	DL Paul Cavanaugh
	DL John Fitzgerald
	DL Dick Kroner
	DL Jerry Ragosa / Jim Millham
	DL Jim O'Shea / Larry Daniels
	LB Jim King / Mondell Davis
	LB Jim McCool / Gary Andrachik
	DB Dave Thomas
	DB Jim Grace
	DB Gary Dancewicz
	DB John Salmon

RUSHING: Bennett 156/804y, Willis 68/498y, Catone 79/383y
PASSING: Harris 106-186/1398y, 13TD, 57%
RECEIVING: Gallup 46/735y, Kives 30/454y, Bennett 22/276y
SCORING: Bennett 96pts, Gallup 42pts, Gallivan (K) 41pts

1969 5-4

21 Navy	14 E Jim O'Shea
28 Tulane	24 T Bob Bouley
6 Villanova	24 G Walt Cullen
7 Army	38 C Mike Lardner
16 Penn State	38 G James Darcy
21 Buffalo	35 T Gary Guenther
49 VMI	32 TE John Bonistalli / George Gill
35 Massachusetts	30 QB Frank Harris
35 Syracuse	10 HB Jim Catone
	HB Fred Willis
	FB Joe McDonald / Bill Thomas
	DL Mike Mucci
	DL Jim Millham
	DL John Fitzgerald
	DL Joe McDonald
	LB Lucien Silva
	LB Jim McCool
	LB Kevin Clemente
	LB Edward Ransford
	DB Joe Coppola
	DB Gary Dancewicz
	DB Steve Kirchner

RUSHING: Willis 128/610y, Catone 104/434y, Thomas 60/214y
PASSING: Harris 121-228/1562y, 19TD, 53%
RECEIVING: Catone 28/281y, Bonistalli 27/473y, O'Shea 20/235y
SCORING: Willis 60pts, Bonistalli 50pts, Catone 48pts

1970 8-2

28 Villanova	21 WR John Bonistalli
28 Navy	14 WR Eddie Rideout / George Gill
56 VMI	3 T John Brennan
3 Penn State	28 G Gary Guenther
10 Air Force	35 C Kent Andiorio
21 Army	13 G Orrie Scarminach
65 Buffalo	12 T Ralph Angel
21 Pittsburgh	6 TE Jim O'Shea
21 Massachusetts	10 QB Frank Harris
54 Holy Cross	0 TB Fred Willis / Tom Bougus
	FB Gene Commella / Bill Thomas
	DL Mike Mucci
	DL Steve Cipot
	DL Jeff Yeates / Greg Fleck
	DL Greg Broskie
	LB Albert Dhembe / John Michaels
	LB Kevin Clemente
	LB Ed Ransford
	LB Lucien Silva
	DB Joe Coppola
	DB Gary Hudson / Gary Dancewicz
	DB Steve Kirchner

RUSHING: Willis 223/1007y, Commella 100/540y, Bougus 31/123y
PASSING: Harris 139-241/1595y, 13TD, 57.6%
RECEIVING: Bonistalli 35/455y, O'Shea 33/356y, Willis 27/222y
SCORING: Willis 95pts, Larry Berridge (K) 46pts, Bougus &
Gill 30pts

1971 9-2

14 West Virginia	45 WR Mel Briggs
17 Temple	3 WR Eddie Rideout
49 Navy	6 T Greg Aungst
24 Richmond	0 G Tom Condon / Steve Corbett
23 Villanova	7 C Kent Andiorio
6 Texas Tech	14 G Orrie Scarminach
40 Pittsburgh	22 T Al Krevis / Tom Szocik
10 Syracuse	3 TE Gordon Browne
20 N. Illinois	10 QB Ray Rippman
35 Massachusetts	0 TB Bill Thomas
21 Holy Cross	7 FB Tom Bougas
	DL Mike Mucci
	DL Jeff Yeates
	DL Greg Fleck / Steve Cipot
	DL Greg Broskie
	LB Dave Ellison
	LB Albert Dhembe
	LB Kevin Clemente
	LB Lucien Silva
	DB Gary Hudson
	DB Larry Molloy
	DB Steve Kirchner

RUSHING: Bougas 199/1058y, Thomas 119/598y,
Rideout 28/178y
PASSING: Rippman 88-192/1214y, 8TD, 45.8%
RECEIVING: Rideout 27/430y, Briggs 23/393y, Browne 18/226y
SCORING: Rideout 42pts, Bougas 36pts, Larry Berridge (K) 32pts

1972 4-7

0 Tulane	10 WR Mel Briggs
49 Temple	27 WR Dave Bucci
20 Navy	27 T Greg Aungst
21 Villanova	20 G Tom Condon
9 Air Force	13 C Chris Kete
20 Pittsburgh	35 G Steve Corbett
37 Syracuse	0 T Joe Sullivan
10 Georgia Tech	42 TE Bob Rush
26 Penn State	45 QB Gary Marangi
7 Massachusetts	28 TB Mike Esposito / Phil Bennett
	FB Frank Smith
	DL Pat Bentzel
	DL Jeff Yeates
	DL Brad Newman
	DL John Halcovich
	LB Dave Ellison
	LB Jim Combs
	LB John McElgunn
	LB John O'Hagan / Dennis McCleary
	DB Ken Ladd
	DB Tony Sukiennik
	DB Ned Guillet / Larry Molloy

RUSHING: Esposito 182/930y, Bennett 149/721y, Smith 92/306y
PASSING: Marangi 117-248/1381y, 11TD, 47.1%
RECEIVING: Briggs 42/620y, Bucci 17/183y, Esposito 16/165y
SCORING: Esposito 54pts, Briggs 48pts, Bennett 38pts

1973 7-4

45 Temple	0 WR Dave Zumbach
16 Tulane	21 WR Mel Briggs
32 Texas A&M	24 T Gordon Browne
44 Navy	7 G Tom Condon
10 Miami	15 C Steve Corbett
14 Pittsburgh	28 G Greg Brand
11 Villanova	7 T Gary O'Hagen / Al Krevis
25 West Virginia	13 TE Bob Rush
13 Syracuse	24 QB Gary Marangi
59 Massachusetts	14 TB Mike Esposito / Phil Bennett
42 Holy Cross	21 FB Keith Barnette / Frank Smith
	DL Byron Hemingway / Pat Bentzel
	DL Joe Sullivan / Pete Cronan
	DL Steve Turner / Mark Burlingame
	DL Paul Martin
	LB Bob Howatt (DL) / Bill Smith
	LB Brian Clemente
	LB Jim Combs
	LB Alex MacLellan
	DB Ken Ladd
	DB Steve Scialabba
	DB Ned Guillet

RUSHING: Esposito 254/1293y, Bennett 44/333y, Marangi 62/248y
PASSING: Marangi 102-169/1114y, 6TD, 60.4%
RECEIVING: Zumbach 41/509y, Briggs 23/388y, Esposito 18/136y
SCORING: Esposito 102pts, Fred Seinfort (K) 65pts, Bennett 42pts

1974 8-3

19 Texas	42 WR Dave Zumbach
7 Temple	34 WR Howie Richardson
37 Navy	0 T Tom Marinelli
31 William & Mary	16 G Jack Magee
11 Pittsburgh	35 C Don Macek
55 Villanova	7 G Steve Schindler
35 West Virginia	3 T Al Krevis
27 Tulane	3 TE Bob Watts / Don Petersen
35 Syracuse	0 QB Mike Kruczek
70 Massachusetts	8 TB Mike Esposito / Earl Strong
38 Holy Cross	6 FB Keith Barnette
	DL Joe Glandorf / Brian Murdock
	DL Pete Cronan
	DL Steve Turner
	DL Bob Moore / Byron Hemingway
	LB Bill Smith
	LB John Murphy / Brian Clemente
	LB Kevin Cunniff
	LB Alex MacLellan
	DB Ken Ladd
	DB Dave Almeida / Steve Scialabba
	DB John Petersen / Paul Murphy

RUSHING: Barnette 233/1097y, Strong 153/776y,
Esposito 90/540y
PASSING: Kruczek 104-151/1275y, 6TD, 68.9%
RECEIVING: Zumbach 43/557y, Richardson 25/289y, 2 tied w/ 12
SCORING: Barnette 134pts, Fred Seinfort (K) 71pts,
Zumbach 24pts

1975 7-4

3 Notre Dame	17 WR Dave Zumbach / Bill Paulsen
27 Temple	9 WR Mike Godbolt
18 West Virginia	35 T Tom Lynch
41 Villanova	12 G Steve Manni
7 Tulane	17 C Don Macek
17 Navy	3 G Steve Schindler
14 Syracuse	22 T John Maxwell
21 Miami	7 TE Don Petersen
31 Army	0 QB Mike Kruczek
24 Massachusetts	14 TB Glenn Capriola / Earl Strong
24 Holy Cross	10 FB Keith Barnette
	DL Byron Hemingway
	DL Pete Cronan
	DL Chuck Morris
	DL Bob Moore
	LB Joe Glandorf
	LB Rich Ramirez / Kevin Cunniff
	LB Rich Scudellari
	LB Bob Watts / Gene Brown
	DB Steve Scialabba / Kelly Elias
	DB Dave Almeida
	DB Paul Murphy

RUSHING: Barnette 199/958y, Capriola 184/846y, Strong 77/275y
PASSING: Kruczek 107-164/1132y, 6TD, 65.2%
RECEIVING: Godbolt 30/354y, Paulsen 22/264y, Petersen 14/172y
SCORING: Fred Seinfort (K) 51pts, Barnette & Capriola 48pts

1976 8-3

14 Texas	13 WR Dave Zumbach
27 Tulane	3 WR Paul McCarty
17 Navy	13 T Jim Rourke
9 Florida State	28 G Tom Lynch
14 West Virginia	3 C Joe Pendergast
27 Army	10 G Steve Schindler
3 Villanova	22 T John Maxwell
6 Miami	13 TE Don Petersen
28 Syracuse	14 QB Ken Smith / Joe O'Brien
35 Massachusetts	0 TB Glen Capriola
59 Holy Cross	6 FB Tony Melchiorre / Anthony Brown
	DL Byron Hemingway
	DL Bob Moore
	DL Fred Smerlas
	DL Bill Ohrenberger
	LB Rich Scudellari
	LB Pete Cronan
	LB Bob Watts
	DB Gene Brown
	DB Kelly Elias
	DB Paul Murphy / Mike Mayock
	DB Dave Almeida / Jeff Kaufman

RUSHING: Capriola 240/1003y, Melchiorre 110/491y, Brown 91/406y
PASSING: Smith 59-119/800y, 7TD, 49.6%
RECEIVING: Zumbach 24/354y, McCarty 14/254y, Melchiorre 6/159y
SCORING: Tim Moorman (K) 65pts, Capriola 42pts, McCarty 30pts

1977 6-5

0 Texas	44 WR Paul McCarty
18 Tennessee	24 WR Mike Godbolt / Pete LaBoy
49 Army	28 T Jim Rourke
7 Pittsburgh	45 G Greg Cantone
30 Tulane	28 C Bill Chaplick
28 West Virginia	24 G John Schmeding
17 Villanova	0 T Karl Swanke / Jerry Madden
36 Air Force	14 TE Mike Siegel/Steve Giordano/T. Sherwin
3 Syracuse	20 QB Ken Smith
34 Massachusetts	7 TB Joe O'Brien / Mike Curry
20 Holy Cross	35 FB Dan Conway / Anthony Brown
	DL Bob Moore
	DL Chuck Morris / Bill Ohrenberger
	DL Fred Smerlas
	DL Mike Gunn / Jack Kent
	LB Clint Gaffney / Al Haggen
	LB Jeff Dziama / Junior Hogan
	LB Rich Scudellari
	DB Doug Alston / Dave Johnson
	DB Kelly Elias
	DB Paul Murphy
	DB Jeff Kaufman / Jeff Ryan

RUSHING: Conway 137/613y, Curry 98/308y, O'Brien 101/299y
PASSING: Smith 149-257/2073y, 17TD, 58%
RECEIVING: Godbolt 34/711y, McCarty 27/514y, O'Brien 19/215y
SCORING: Conway 48pts, Godbolt & Tim Moorman (K) 42pts

1978 0-11

7 Air Force	18 WR Paul McCarty
2 Texas A&M	37 WR Jack O'Brien / Rob Rikard
8 Navy	19 T Greg Cantone / Matt Ciruolo
15 Pittsburgh	32 G Jim Rourke
3 Tulane	9 C Karl Swanke
16 Villanova	28 G Gerry Raymond / John Schmeding
26 Army	29 T Dan Cordeau / Steve Lively
23 Syracuse	37 TE Tim Sherwin
0 Massachusetts	27 QB Jay Palazola
29 Holy Cross	30 TB Anthony Brown
24 Temple	28 FB Dan Conway
	DL Jack Kent
	DL Mike Siegel / Joe Nash
	DL Bill Ohrenberger / Bill Stephanos
	DL Fred Smerlas
	DL Clint Gaffney / Greg Storr
	LB Jeff Dziama / Bob Walton
	LB Junior Hogan
	DB Jeff Ryan
	DB Rich Dyer / Dave Johnson
	DB Mike Mayock
	DB Doug Alston

RUSHING: Brown 162/748y, Conway 130/440y, Palazola 110/310y
PASSING: Palazola 71-152/926y, 4TD, 46.7%
RECEIVING: McCarty 36/531y, Sherwin 22/292y, Conway 15/101y
SCORING: Brown, Conway & McCarty 30pts

1979 5-6

16 Tennessee	28 WR Rob Rikard
34 Villanova	7 WR Jon Schoen / Kevin Dempsey
14 Stanford	33 T Karl Swanke
7 Pittsburgh	28 G Casey Muldoon / John Schmeding
18 West Virginia	20 C Bill Chaplick
8 Miami	19 G Gerry Raymond
29 Army	16 T Greg Cantone
8 Tulane	41 TE Tim Sherwin
27 Syracuse	10 QB Jay Palazola / John Loughery
41 Massachusetts	3 TB Shelby Gamble
27 Holy Cross	26 FB Dan Conway
	DL Jack Kent
	DL Bill Stephanos
	DL Joe Ferraro
	DL Joe Nash
	DL Clint Gaffney
	LB Jim Budness
	LB Jeff Dziama
	DB Mike Mayock / Jeff Ryan
	DB Jerry Stabile
	DB Doug Alston
	DB Rich Dyer

RUSHING: Conway 196/856y, Gamble 164/776y, Palazola 103/468y
PASSING: Palazola 55-144/747y, 2TD, 38.2%
RECEIVING: Rikard 24/603y, Sherwin 20/310y, Conway 15/98y
SCORING: Gamble 50pts, John Cooper (K) 39pts, Conway 36pts

1980 7-4

6 Pittsburgh	14 WR Jon Schoen
30 Stanford	13 WR Rob Rikard
9 Villanova	20 T Steve Lively
0 Navy	21 G Gerry Raymond
27 Yale	9 C Jack Belcher
7 Florida State	41 G Casey Muldoon / Bill Stephanos
30 Army	14 T Greg Michalec
23 Air Force	0 TE Tim Sherwin
27 Syracuse	16 QB John Loughery
13 Massachusetts	12 TB Shelby Gamble / Leo Smith
27 Holy Cross	26 FB Kevin Benjamin
	DL Russell Joyner
	DL Joe Nash
	DL Mark Roopenian
	DL Junior Poles / Joe Ferraro
	DL Greg Storr
	LB Bob Walton / Steve DeOssie
	LB Jim Budness
	DB Jerry Stabile
	DB Mike Mayock
	DB Rich Dyer
	DB Doug Alston

RUSHING: Gamble 181/702y, Benjamin 113/386y, Smith 56/214y
PASSING: Loughery 94-225/1519y, 6TD, 41.8%
RECEIVING: Sherwin 29/371y, Schoen 26/408y, Rikard 24/460y
SCORING: John Cooper (K) 67pts, Gamble 48pts, Loughery 18pts

1981 5-6

13 Texas A&M	12 WR Jon Schoen / Rob Rikard
14 North Carolina	56 WR Brian Brennan
10 West Virginia	38 T Steve Lively
7 Penn State	38 G Gerry Raymond
10 Navy	25 C Jack Belcher
41 Army	6 G Ed Broderick
24 Pittsburgh	29 T Dave Paulik
52 Massachusetts	22 TE Scott Nizolek
17 Syracuse	27 QB Doug Flutie / Dennis Scala
27 Rutgers	21 TB Leo Smith / Howie Brown / S. Strachan
28 Holy Cross	24 FB Bob Biestek
	DL Paul Shaw / Russ Joyner
	DL Rob Swanke
	DL Joe Nash / Scott Harrington
	DL Junior Poles / Joe Ferraro
	DL Greg Storr / Steve Lubischer
	LB Steve DeOssie
	LB Jim Budness
	DB Tony Thurman / Mike Sheppard
	DB George Radachowsky
	DB Vic Crawford / Todd Russell
	DB Rich Dyer

RUSHING: Smith 88/419y, Brown 67/332y, Strachan 64/294y
PASSING: Flutie 105-192/1652y, 10TD, 54.7%
RECEIVING: Brennan 37/726y, Nizolek 31/406y, Schoen 9/208y
SCORING: John Cooper (K) 55pts, Nizolek 26pts, 3 tied w/ 24pts

1982 8-3-1

38 Texas A&M	16 WR Jon Schoen
17 Clemson	17 WR Paul Zdanek / Brian Brennan
31 Navy	0 T Gary Kowalski
17 Temple	7 G Steve Lively
13 West Virginia	20 C Jack Belcher
14 Rutgers	13 G Glenn Reagan
32 Army	17 T Mark MacDonald
17 Penn State	52 TE Scott Nizolek
34 Massachusetts	21 QB Doug Flutie
20 Syracuse	13 TB Troy Stradford / Steve Strachan
35 Holy Cross	10 FB Bob Biestek
26 Auburn■	33 DL Paul Shaw
	DL Rob Swanke
	DL Scott Harrington / Mike Ruth
	DL Junior Poles
	LB Russ Joyner
	LB Steve DeOssie
	LB T. J. Fitzpatrick
	DB Vic Crawford
	DB George Radachowsky
	DB Tony Thurman
	DB Dave Pereira

RUSHING: Stradford 109/606y, Strachan 90/366y, Flutie 90/270y
PASSING: Flutie 162-348/2749y, 13TD, 46.7%
RECEIVING: Nizolek 39/658y, Zdanek 33/567y, Schoen 29/605y
SCORING: Kevin Snow (K) 62pts, Biestek 36pts, Stradford 30pts

1983 9-3

45 Morgan State	12 WR Gerard Phelan
31 Clemson	16 WR Brian Brennan
42 Rutgers	22 T Mark MacDonald
17 West Virginia	27 G Glenn Reagan
18 Temple	15 C Jack Bicknell
42 Yale	7 G Mark Bardwell
27 Penn State	17 T Shawn Regent
34 Army	14 TE Scott Gieselman
10 Syracuse	21 QB Doug Flutie
47 Holy Cross	7 TB Troy Stradford / Steve Strachan
20 Alabama	13 FB Jim Browne / Bob Biestek
18 Notre Dame■	19 DL David Thomas
	DL Scott Harrington
	DL Mike Ruth
	DL Rob Swanke
	LB Steve Lubischer / Paul Shaw
	LB Steve DeOssie
	LB Ted Gaffney
	DB George Radachowsky
	DB Todd Russell
	DB Dave Pereira
	DB Tony Thurman

RUSHING: Stradford 145/810y, Strachan 64/268y, Ken Bell (TB) 61/241y
PASSING: Flutie 177-345/2724y, 17TD, 51.3%
RECEIVING: Brennan 66/1149y, Gieselman 45/525y, Phelan 22/410y
SCORING: Brennan 50pts, Biestek & Stradford 48pts

1984 10-2

44 W. Carolina	24 WR Gerard Phelan
38 Alabama	31 WR Kelvin Martin
52 North Carolina	20 T Mark MacDonald
24 Temple	10 G Mark Bardwell / Darren Twombly
20 West Virginia	21 C Jack Bicknell / Mark Gowetski (G)
35 Rutgers	23 G Steve Trapilo
30 Penn State	37 T Shawn Regent
45 Army	31 TE Scott Gieselman / Peter Casparriello
24 Syracuse	16 QB Doug Flutie
47 Miami	45 TB Troy Stradford / Ken Bell
45 Holy Cross	10 FB Steve Strachan / Jim Browne
45 Houston■	28 DL David Thomas / Rick Nickeson
	DL Scott Harrington
	DL Mike Ruth
	DL John Bosa
	DL Chuck Gorecki
	LB Bill Romanowski / Andy Hemmer
	LB Ted Gaffney/Ed VonNessen/Pete Holey
	DB Todd Russell
	DB Neil Iton
	DB Dave Pereira
	DB Tony Thurman

RUSHING: Stradford 146/666y, Strachan 94/463y, Bell 77/346y
PASSING: Flutie 233-386/3454y, 27TD, 60.4%
RECEIVING: Phelan 64/971y, Martin 37/715y, Stradford 37/422y
SCORING: Kevin Snow (K) 82pts, Martin 72pts, Strachan & Stradford 60pts

1985 4-8

14 BYU	28 WR Darren Flutie
28 Temple	25 WR Kelvin Martin
13 Maryland	31 T Shawn Regent / Jeff Oliver
29 Pittsburgh	22 G Jim Ostrowski / Dave Widell
10 Miami	45 C Darren Twombly / Jack Bicknell, Jr.
20 Rutgers	10 G Joe Wolf
14 Army	45 T Steve Trapilo
6 West Virginia	13 TE Scott Gieselman / Peter Casparriello
17 Cincinnati	24 QB Shawn Halloran
12 Penn State	16 TB Troy Stradford / Tyrone Taylor
21 Syracuse	41 FB Ken Bell / John Mihalik
38 Holy Cross	7 DL Chuck Gorecki / Eric Lindstrom
	DL John Bosa
	DL Mike Ruth
	DL Mike Degnan / Tom Porell
	DL Bill Thompson
	LB Bill Romanowski
	LB Ted Gaffney / Andy Hemmer
	DB Gerrick McPhearson
	DB Neil Iton
	DB Carl Pellegate
	DB Karl Kreshpane

RUSHING: Bell 150/583y, Stradford 44/234y, Taylor 29/220y
PASSING: Halloran 234-423/2935y, 12TD, 55.3%
RECEIVING: Martin 49/958y, Flutie 42/469y, Gieselman 41/493y
SCORING: Martin 60pts, Mihalik & Bell 24pts

1986 9-3

9 Rutgers	11 WR Darren Flutie / Tom Waddle
21 California	15 WR Kelvin Martin
14 Penn State	26 T Jeff Oliver
29 SMU	31 G Joe Wolf
30 Maryland	25 C Darren Twombly
41 Louisville	7 G Steve Trapilo
19 West Virginia	10 T Dave Widell
27 Army	20 TE Peter Casparriello
38 Temple	29 QB Shawn Halloran
27 Syracuse	9 TB Troy Stradford
56 Holy Cross	26 FB Jim Turner / Jon Bronner
27 Georgia■	24 DL Eric Lindstrom
	DL John Bosa
	DL Dave Nugent / Tom Porell
	DL Mike Degnan
	DL Bill Thompson
	LB Ted Gaffney / John Galvin
	LB Bill Romanowski
	DB Gerrick McPhearson
	DB Vincent Munn / Steve Williams
	DB Carl Pellegata / Ed Duran
	DB Karl Kreshpane

RUSHING: Stradford 218/1188y, Bronner 80/313y, Jim Bell (TB) 69/307y
PASSING: Halloran 159-258/2090y, 17TD, 61.6%
RECEIVING: Martin 41/545y, Flutie 35/531y, Stradford 31/445y
SCORING: Brian Lowe (K) 81pts, Stradford 66pts, Martin 56pts

1987 5-6

38 TCU	20 WR Tom Waddle
28 Temple	7 WR Darren Flutie
17 Southern Cal	23 T Jeff Oliver
17 Penn State	27 G Mike Bumpus / Joe Wolf
13 Pittsburgh	10 C Brian Schoenle / Bill Scavone
29 Army	24 G Doug Widell
24 Rutgers	38 T Dave Widell
16 West Virginia	37 TE Pete Casparriello
20 Tennessee	18 QB Mike Power
25 Notre Dame	32 TB Jim Bell / Tim Frager
17 Syracuse	45 FB Jim Turner
	DL Peter Gray
	DL Dave Nugent
	DL Mark Murphy
	LB Kevin Pearson
	LB Bill Romanowski
	LB John Galvin
	LB Bill Thompson
	DB Steve Williams / Vincent Munn
	DB Gerrick McPhearson
	DB Ed Duran
	DB Rico Labbe / David Johnson

RUSHING: Bell 213/1015y, Frager 32/228y, Mike Sanders (TB) 45/203y
PASSING: Power 133-233/2071y, 10TD, 57.1%
RECEIVING: Flutie 48/786y, Waddle 43/781y, Bell 19/182y
SCORING: Brian Lowe (K) 57pts, Flutie 42pts, Power 32pts

1988 3-8

7 Southern Cal	34 WR Tom Waddle
41 Cincinnati	7 WR Marcus Cherry
20 Penn State	23 T Jim Kwitchoff / Mike Bumpas (G)
17 TCU	31 G Mark Anken
34 Pittsburgh	31 C Brian Schoenle / Bill Scavone
6 Rutgers	17 G Joe Wolf
19 West Virginia	59 T Doug Widell
7 Tennessee	10 TE Mark Chmura
20 Syracuse	45 QB Mark Kamphaus / Mike Power
38 Army	24 TB Jim Bell / Mike Sanders / Tim Frager
28 Temple	45 FB Ed Toner / Duke St. Pierre
	DL Mark Murphy / Jim Biestek
	DL Chris Gildea / Andy Klare
	DL Peter Gray / Dave Moore
	LB Ivan Caesar / Kevin Pearson
	LB Mike Saylor
	LB Matt Kelley
	LB Eric Lindstrom
	DB Brian Williams
	DB Steve Williams
	DB Rico Labbe
	DB Ed Duran

RUSHING: Sanders 81/424y, Bell 109/409y, Frager 57/303y
PASSING: Kamphaus 100-158/1323y, 7TD, 65.3%
RECEIVING: Waddle 70/902y, Cherry 37/717y, Chmura 27/377y
SCORING: Brian Lowe (K) 65pts, Toner 44pts, Cherry 32pts

1989 2-9

10 Pittsburgh	29 WR Marcus Cherry
7 Rutgers	9 WR Ray Hilvert
3 Penn State	7 T Mike Jovanovich
29 Ohio State	34 G Mike Bumphus
35 Temple	14 C Brian Schoenle
24 Navy	27 G Mark Anken
30 West Virginia	44 T Bill Scavone
11 Syracuse	23 TE Mark Chmura
24 Army	17 QB Willie Hicks / Mark Kamphaus
22 Louisville	36 TB Mike Sanders / Tim Frager
12 Georgia Tech	13 FB Ed Toner
	DL Jim Biestek
	DL Chris Gildea
	DL Peter Gray
	LB Matt Kelley
	LB Kevin Pearson
	LB Ivan Caesar
	LB Ron Perryman
	DB David Johnson
	DB Jeff Baker
	DB Rico Labbe
	DB Ed Duran

RUSHING: Sanders 153/707y, Frager 126/581y, Toner 67/178y
PASSING: Hicks 70-148/1219y, 7TD, 47.3%
Kamphaus 66-125/788y, TD, 52.8%
RECEIVING: Chmura 47/522y, Sanders 22/165y, Hilvert 20/335y
SCORING: Brian Lowe (K) 59pts, Toner 50pts, 3 tied w/ 18pts

1990 4-7

6 Pittsburgh	29 WR Andre Green
10 Ohio State	31 WR Ray Hilvert
28 Navy	17 T Matt Metz
19 Rutgers	14 G Mark Anken
41 Army	20 C Tom Nalen
21 Penn State	40 G Mike Bumphus
27 West Virginia	14 T Dan Britten / Mike Jovanovich
6 Syracuse	35 TE Mark Chmura
10 Louisville	17 QB Glenn Foley
12 Miami	42 TB Mike Sanders / Tim Frager
10 Temple	29 FB Ed Toner
	DL John Stolberg
	DL Mike Marinaro
	DL Ted Page
	LB Matt Kelley
	LB Jason Pohopek
	LB Ivan Caesar
	LB Kevin Pearson
	DB Brian Williams
	DB Chandler White
	DB David Johnson
	DB Charlie Brennan

RUSHING: Sanders 88/317y, Toner 83/273y, Frager 77/252y
PASSING: Foley 182-349/2189y, 11TD, 52.1%
RECEIVING: Chmura 47/560y, Hilvert 39/643y, Toner 36/263y
SCORING: Sean Wright (K) 49pts, Toner 36pts, Frager & Chmura 18pts

1991 4-7

13 Rutgers	20 WR Clarence Cannon
13 Michigan	35 WR Clint Kuboyama
14 Georgia Tech	30 T Dan Britten
21 Penn State	28 G Mark Kennedy
33 Louisville	31 C Tom Nalen
24 West Virginia	31 G Matt Metz
28 Army	17 T Mike Jovanovich / Kirk Ruoff
38 Pittsburgh	12 TE Mark Chmura / Pete Mitchell
33 Temple	13 QB Glenn Foley
16 Syracuse	38 TB Darnell Campbell / Chuckie Dukes
14 Miami	19 FB Dwight Shirley
	DL Mike Marinaro
	DL John Stolberg
	DL Ron Stone
	LB Jason Pohopek
	LB Tom McManus
	LB Stephen Boyd / Brian Howlett
	LB Dan Kerr / David Jones
	DB Mike Reed
	DB Joe Kamara
	DB Charlie Brennan
	DB Jay McGillis

RUSHING: Campbell 128/641y, Dukes 97/612y, Shirley 106/364y
PASSING: Foley 153-298/2222y, 21TD, 51.3%
RECEIVING: Chmura 43/587y, Mitchell 29/398y, Cannon 26/434y
SCORING: Sean Wright (K) 45pts, Chmura 38pts, Miller 30pts

1992 8-3-1

37 Rutgers	20 WR Clarence Cannon
49 Northwestern	0 WR Keith Miller
28 Navy	0 T Dan Britten
14 Michigan State	0 G Greg Landry
24 West Virginia	24 C Tom Nalen
35 Penn State	32 G Pete Kendall
17 Tulane	13 T Ron Stone
45 Temple	6 TE Pete Mitchell
7 Notre Dame	54 QB Glenn Foley
10 Syracuse	27 TB Chuckie Dukes
41 Army	24 FB Darnell Campbell / Dwight Shirley
23 Tennessee■	28 DL Mike Marinaro
	DL John Stolberg
	DL Chris Sullivan
	LB Dan Kerr / Russell Durham
	LB Tom McManus
	LB Stephen Boyd
	LB Jason Pohopek
	DB Michael Reed
	DB Joe Kamara / Clint Kuboyama
	DB Charlie Brennan
	DB Eric Shorter / Terence Wiggins

RUSHING: Dukes 238/1387y, Shirley 133/604y, Campbell 72/384y
PASSING: Foley 146-265/2231y, 15TD, 55.1%
RECEIVING: Mitchell 40/555y, Cannon 23/420y, Dukes 21/194y
SCORING: Dukes 60pts, Shirley 48pts, Sean Wright (K) 35pts

1993 9-3

7 Miami	23 WR Clarence Cannon
21 Northwestern	22 WR Keith Miller
66 Temple	14 T Pete Kendall
33 Syracuse	29 G Greg Landry
31 Rutgers	21 C Tom Nalen
41 Army	14 G Mark Borrelli
42 Tulane	14 T Ben Velishka / Dan Oriskovich
48 Virginia Tech	34 TE Pete Mitchell / Gordon Laro
33 Pittsburgh	0 QB Glenn Foley
41 Notre Dame	39 RB Anthony Comer / David Green
14 West Virginia	17 FB Darnell Campbell
31 Virginia■	13 DL Ted Page / Joe O'Brien
	DL Tim Morabito
	DL Chris Sullivan
	LB Mike Mamula
	LB Brian Howlett
	LB Stephen Boyd
	LB Dan Kerr
	DB Joe Kamara
	DB Michael Reed
	DB Terence Wiggins / Rob Clifford
	DB Eric Shorter

RUSHING: Campbell 221/1078y
PASSING: Foley 222-363/3397y, 25TD, 61.2%
RECEIVING: Mitchell 66/818y, Cannon 38/693y
SCORING: Campbell 126pts, David Gordon (K) 63pts, Mitchell 42pts

1994 7-4-1

26 Michigan	34 WR Kenyatta Watson
7 Virginia Tech	12 WR Greg Grice
21 Pittsburgh	9 T Pete Kendall
30 Notre Dame	11 G Greg Landry
45 Temple	28 C Tim O'Brien
7 Rutgers	7 G Mark Nori
30 Army	3 T Dan Oriskovich
35 Louisville	14 TE Pete Mitchell
31 Syracuse	0 TE Gordon Laro
20 West Virginia	21 QB Mark Hartsell / Scott Mutryn
7 Miami	23 RB David Green / Justice Smith
12 Kansas State■	7 DL Nick Gianacakos / Stalin Colinet
	DL Chris Sullivan
	DL Tim Morabito
	DL Mike Mamula / Joe O'Brien
	LB Matt Haff / Brian Maye
	LB Stephen Boyd
	LB Ed Sanabria
	DB Daryl Porter
	DB Michael Reed
	DB Terence Wiggins / Rob Clifford
	DB Eric Shorter

RUSHING: Green 199/1018y, Smith 146/708y
PASSING: Hartsell 159-257/1864y, 13TD, 61.9%
RECEIVING: Mitchell 55/617y, Watson 43/568y, Grice 30/462y
SCORING: David Gordon (K) 59pts

1995 4-8

6 Ohio State	38 WR Kenyatta Watson / Dennis Harding
20 Virginia Tech	14 WR Steve Everson/G. Grice/Brandon King
13 Michigan	23 T Pete Kendall
21 Michigan State	25 G Doug Brzezinski
17 Pittsburgh	0 C Tim O'Brien / Brian O'Connor
19 West Virginia	31 G Mark Nori
7 Army	49 T Dan Oriskovich
10 Notre Dame	20 TE Todd Pollack
10 Temple	9 TE Michael Hemmert
14 Miami	17 QB Mark Hartsell
29 Syracuse	58 RB Omari Walker/Justice Smith/Mike Cloud
41 Rutgers	38 DL Nick Gianacakos
	DL Tim Morabito / John Coleman
	DL Chris Sullivan
	DL Stalin Colinet
	LB Markell Blount / Erick Storz
	LB Bobby Edmonds / Brian Maye
	LB Matt Haff / Jermaine Monk
	DB Kiernan Speight
	DB Daryl Porter
	DB Rob Clifford
	DB Terence Wiggins / Billy Gustin

RUSHING: Cloud 102/626y, Walker 124/538y, Smith 102/336y
PASSING: Hartsell 189-349/1888y, 12TD, 54.2%
RECEIVING: Everson 42/557y, King 29/349y, Harding 28/263y
SCORING: Walker 36pts, Dan McGuire (K) 33pts, Pollack 30pts

1996 5-7

24 Hawaii	21 WR Dennis Harding / Kenyatta Watson
7 Virginia Tech	45 WR Anthony DiCosmo / Steve Everson
14 Michigan	20 T Dan Oriskovich / Andy Mitcham
43 Navy	38 G Doug Brzezinski
17 West Virginia	34 C Damien Woody / Brian O'Connor
24 Cincinnati	17 G Mark Nori
37 Rutgers	13 T Darnell Alford
17 Syracuse	45 TE Todd Pollack / Frank Chamberlin
13 Pittsburgh	20 TE Scott Dragos / Michael Hemmert
21 Notre Dame	48 QB Matt Hasselbeck / Scott Mutryn
21 Temple	20 RB Omari Walker / Mike Cloud
26 Miami	43 DL Erick Storz
	DL Nick Gianacackos / Mike Willetts
	DL Stalin Colinet / John Coleman
	DL Chris Hovan / Greg Bartlett
	LB Markell Blount
	LB Brian Maye / Rupert English
	LB Ryan Reckley / Jermaine Monk
	DB Tim Davis / Kiernan Speight
	DB Shalom Tolefree
	DB Daryl Porter
	DB Pedro Cirino / George White

RUSHING: Walker 261/1199y, Cloud 68/359y, Quinton Lee (RB) 34/149y
PASSING: Hasselbeck 171-330/1990y, 9TD, 51.8%
RECEIVING: Harding 42/444y, Di Cosmo 36/632y, Walker 32/187y
SCORING: Walker 80pts, John Matich (K) 67pts, Harding 18pts

1997 4-7

21 Temple	28 WR Dennis Harding
31 West Virginia	24 WR Anthony DiCosmo / Mike Guazzo
35 Rutgers	21 T Jon Miles
6 Cincinnati	24 G Doug Brzezinski
14 Georgia Tech	42 C Damien Woody
7 Virginia Tech	17 G Andy Mitcham
44 Miami	45 T Noah LaRose
20 Notre Dame	52 TE Todd Pollack
22 Pittsburgh	21 QB Matt Hasselbeck
13 Syracuse	20 HB Omari Walker / Mike Cloud
24 Army	20 FB Michael Hemmert
	DL Mike Willetts
	DL Chris Hovan
	DL Andrew Krauza
	LB Erick Storz
	LB Brooke Heald / Bobby Edmonds
	LB Markell Blount
	LB Greg Bartlett / Adam Newman
	DB Shalom Tolefree
	DB Carlton Rowe / D.J. Sutton
	DB Pedro Cirino
	DB George White

RUSHING: Cloud 136/886y, Walker 136/652y, Lee 49/313y
PASSING: Hasselbeck 188-305/2239y, 11TD, 61.6%
RECEIVING: Harding 29/432y, Pollack 28/296y, DiCosmo 24/362y
SCORING: Cloud 54pts, John Matich (K) 52pts, 3 tied w/ 24pts

1998 4-7

41 Georgia Tech	31 WR Anthony DiCosmo
41 Rutgers	14 WR Jermaine Walker / Dennis Harding
31 Temple	7 T Darnell Alford / Michael Cook
28 Louisville	52 G Doug Brzezinski
0 Virginia Tech	17 C Damien Woody
25 Syracuse	42 G Dan Collins
31 Navy	32 T Paul Zukauskas
17 Miami	35 TE Rob Tardio
26 Notre Dame	31 QB Scott Mutryn
23 Pittsburgh	15 HB Mike Cloud
10 West Virginia	35 FB Ryan Utzler
	DL Mike Willetts
	DL Chris Hovan
	DL Adam Grace
	LB Willie Wright
	LB Frank Chamberlin
	LB Brian Maye
	LB Adam Newman
	DB D.J. Sutton / RaMon Johnson
	DB Jonathan Ordway
	DB Pedro Cirino / Carlos Moore
	DB George White

RUSHING: Cloud 308/1726y, Cedric Washington (HB) 37/173y
PASSING: Mutryn 171-286/2218y, 12TD, 59.8%
RECEIVING: DiCosmo 47/804y, Tardio 33/332y, Cloud 24/198y
SCORING: Cloud 84pts, John Matich (K) 65pts, DiCosmo 42pts

1999 8-4

30 Baylor	29 WR Derrick Crittenden / Jamal Burke
14 Navy	10 WR Dedrick Dewalt
27 Rutgers	7 T Mike Cook
33 Northeastern	22 G Paul La Querre
14 Temple	24 C Butch Palaza
20 Pittsburgh	16 G Paul Zukauskas
28 Miami	31 T Darnell Alford
24 Syracuse	23 TE Bryan Arndt
34 West Virginia	17 QB Tim Hasselbeck
31 Notre Dame	29 TB Cedric Washington
14 Virginia Tech	38 FB Ryan Burch
28 Colorado■	62 DL Sean Guthrie / Antonio Garay
	DL Chris Hovan
	DL Mike Willetts
	DL Adam Newman
	LB Scott Bradley
	LB Frank Chamberlain
	LB Marco Williams / Jerome Ledbetter
	DB Jonathan Ordway
	DB RaMon Johnson
	DB Pedro Cirino
	DB George White

RUSHING: Washington 222/1122y, Carlton Rowe (TB) 73/262y, William Green (TB) 49/251y
PASSING: Hasselbeck 145-260/1940y, 11TD, 55.8%
RECEIVING: Dewalt 38/604y, Washington 29/178y, Arndt 27/340y
SCORING: John Matich (K) 59pts, Washington 42pts, 3 tied w/ 24pts

2000 7-5

14 West Virginia	34 WR Jamal Burke
55 Army	17 WR Dedrick Dewalt
48 Navy	7 T Mike Cook
34 Virginia Tech	48 G Paul La Querre / John Richardson
55 Connecticut	3 C Dan Koppen
20 Syracuse	13 G Paul Zukauskas
26 Pittsburgh	42 T Marc Colombo
42 Rutgers	13 TE Robert Ellis / Mike Guazzo
31 Temple	3 QB Tim Hasselbeck
16 Notre Dame	28 TB Cedric Washington / William Green
6 Miami	52 FB Ryan Utzler
31 Arizona State■	17 DL Sean Guthrie
	DL Tom Martin / Doug Goodwin
	DL Keith Leavitt
	DL Sean Ryan / Derric Rossy
	LB Curtis Bolden / Josh Ott
	LB Ryan Burch / Andy Romanowsky
	LB Marco Williams / Scott Bradley
	DB Willie Poole
	DB Lenny Walls / Jonathan Ordway
	DB Ralph Parent
	DB RaMon Johnson / Doug Dessette

RUSHING: Green 187/1164y, Washington 152/676y, Derrick Knight (TB) 52/235y
PASSING: Hasselbeck 124-229/1810y, 16TD, 54.1%
RECEIVING: Dewalt 38/676y, Burke 26/386y, Washington 16/193y
SCORING: Green 90pts, Mike Sutphin (K) 74pts, Dewalt 54pts

2001 8-4

34 West Virginia	10 WR Jamal Burke
22 Stanford	38 WR Dedrick Dewalt
38 Navy	21 T Leo Bell / Frank Wilpert
31 Army	10 G Chris Snee / Augie Hoffmann
33 Temple	10 C Dan Koppen
20 Virginia Tech	34 G Marc Parenteau / John Richardson
45 Pittsburgh	7 T Mark Colombo
21 Notre Dame	17 TE Sean Ryan / Frank Misurelli
7 Miami	18 QB Brian St. Pierre
38 Rutgers	9 TB William Green
28 Syracuse	39 FB J.P. Comella / Greg Toal
20 Georgia■	16 DL Sean Guthrie
	DL Tom Martin
	DL Douglas Goodwin
	DL Antonio Garay / Derric Rossy
	LB Scott Bradley
	LB Vinny Ciurciu
	LB Josh Ott / Andy Romanowsky
	DB Trevor White
	DB Lenny Walls / Peter Shean
	DB Ralph Parent
	DB Doug Bessette

RUSHING: Green 265/1559y, Derrick Knight (RB) 76/337y, St. Pierre 67/217y
PASSING: St. Pierre 149-279/2016y, 25TD, 53.4%
RECEIVING: Dewalt 37/539y, Burke 25/320y, Green 23/260y
SCORING: Green 102pts, Kevin McMyler (K) 50pts, Burke 48pts

2002 9-4

24 Connecticut	16 WR Jamal Burke / Grant Adams
34 Stanford	27 WR Keith Hemmings
6 Miami	38 T Leo Bell
43 Central Michigan	0 G Chris Snee
23 Virginia Tech	28 C Dan Koppen
46 Navy	21 G Augie Hoffmann
16 Pittsburgh	19 T Marc Parenteau
Notre Dame	7 TE Sean Ryan / Frank Misurelli
14 West Virginia	24 QB Brian St. Pierre
41 Syracuse	20 RB D.Knight/Horace Dodd/Brandon Brokaw
36 Temple	14 FB Greg Toal / J.P. Comella
44 Rutgers	14 DL Derric Rossy / Mathias Kiwanuka
51 Toledo■	25 DL Tim Bulman / Doug Goodwin
	DL Tom Martin
	DL Phil Mettling / Antonio Garay
	LB Brian Flores
	LB Vinny Ciurciu
	LB Josh Ott
	DB Larry Lester / Will Blackmon
	DB Trevor White
	DB Ralph Parent
	DB Doug Bessette / Paul Cook

RUSHING: Knight 259/1432y, Brokaw 96/334y, Dodd 51/141y
PASSING: St. Pierre 237-407/2983y, 18TD, 58.2%
RECEIVING: Hemmings 41/559y, Adams 37/542y, Knight 37/372y
SCORING: Sandro Sciortino (K) 92pts, Knight 78pts, Brokaw 54pts

2003 8-5

28 Wake Forest	32 WR Grant Adams
27 Penn State	14 WR Joel Hazard / Larry Lester
24 Connecticut	14 T Jeremy Trueblood
14 Miami	33 G Augie Hoffmann / Josh Beekman
53 Ball State	29 C Pat Ross
38 Temple	13 G Chris Snee
14 Syracuse	39 T Keith Leavitt
27 Notre Dame	25 TE Sean Ryan / David Kashetta
31 Pittsburgh	24 QB Quinton Porter / Paul Peterson
28 West Virginia	35 TB Derrick Knight / Horace Dodd
35 Rutgers	25 FB Greg Toal / Haven Perkins
34 Virginia Tech	27 DL Mathias Kiwanuka
35 Colorado State■	21 DL Tom Martin / Tim Bulman
	DL Doug Goodwin
	DL Phil Mettling
	LB Brian Flores / Ricky Brown
	LB Ray Henderson
	LB Josh Ott
	DB Will Blackmon
	DB Jazzmen Williams / Peter Shean
	DB T.J. Stancil
	DB Paul Cook / Ryan Glasper

RUSHING: Knight 321/1721y, Dodd 89/442y, Porter 78/159y
PASSING: Porter 140-250/1764y, 14TD, 56%
Peterson 84-147/1124y, 10TD, 57.1%
RECEIVING: Adams 46/720y, Ryan 35/447y, Hazard 32/401y
SCORING: Sandro Sciortino (K) 69pts, Knight 66pts, Dodd 60pts

2004 9-3

19 Ball State	11 WR Joel Hazard
21 Penn State	7 WR Grant Adams
27 Connecticut	7 T Jeremy Trueblood
14 Wake Forest	17 G James Marten
24 Massachusetts	7 C Pat Ross
17 Pittsburgh	20 G Josh Beekman
24 Notre Dame	23 T Gosder Cherilus
2 Rutgers	10 TE David Kashetta
36 West Virginia	17 QB Paul Peterson
34 Temple	17 TB Andre Callender / L.V Whitworth
17 Syracuse	43 FB Mark Palmer / Everett Lee
37 North Carolina■	24 DL Mathias Kiwanuka
	DL Al Washington
	DL Tim Bulman
	DL Phil Mettling / Nick Larkin
	LB Ricky Brown
	LB Ray Henderson
	LB Brian Toal / Jolonn Dunbar
	DB Peter Shean / Jazzmen Williams
	DB DeJuan Williams / DeJuan Tribble
	DB T.J. Stancil / Larry Anam
	DB Ryan Glasper / Jaime Silva

RUSHING: Callender138/637y, Whitworth 143/623y,
A.J. Brooks 57/319y
PASSING: Peterson 221-355/2594y, 18TD, 62.3%
RECEIVING: Adams 52/745y, Lester 35/515y, Hazard 34/413y
SCORING: Ryan Ohliger (K) 76pts, William Troost (K) 55pts,
Whitworth 36pts

2005 9-3

20 BYU	3 WR Will Blackmon / Tony Gonzalez
44 Army	7 WR Larry Lester / Kevin Challenger
17 Florida State	28 T Jeremy Trueblood
16 Clemson	13 G James Marten
38 Ball State	0 C Patrick Ross
28 Virginia	17 G Josh Beekman
35 Wake Forest	30 T Gosder Cherilus
10 Virginia Tech	30 TE Chris Miller
14 North Carolina	16 QB Matt Ryan / Quinton Porter
30 N. Carolina St.	10 HB L.V. Whitworth
31 Maryland	16 FB Mark Palmer / Paddy Lynch
27 Boise State■	21 DL Mathias Kiwanuka
	DL Al Washington
	DL B.J. Raji / Keith Willis
	DL Nick Larkin
	LB Brian Toal / Joloon Dunbar
	LB Ray Henderson
	LB Ricky Brown / Tyrone Pruitt
	DB Jazzmen Williams
	DB DeJuan Tribble
	DB Jamie Silva / Larry Anam
	DB Ryan Glasper

RUSHING: Whitworth 189/807y, Callender 142/708y
PASSING: Porter 136-214/1357y, 9TD, 63.6%
Ryan 121-195/1514y, 8TD, 62.1%
RECEIVING: Blackmon 51/763y, Lester 37/392y, Gonzalez 28/414y
SCORING: Ryan Ohliger (K) 46pts, Toal 36pts, 3 tied w/ 30pts

2006 10-3

31 C. Michigan	24 WR Kevin Challenger
34 Clemson	33 WR Tony Gonzalez / Brandon Robinson
30 BYU	23 T James Marten
15 N. Carolina St.	17 G Ryan Poles
22 Maine	0 C Kevin Sheridan / Tom Anevski
22 Virginia Tech	3 G Josh Beekman
24 Florida State	19 T Gosder Cherilus
41 Buffalo	0 TE Ryan Purvis / Ryan Thompson
14 Wake Forest	21 QB Matt Ryan
28 Duke	10 HB L.V. Whitworth / Andre Callender
38 Maryland	16 FB Mark Palmer
14 Miami	17 DL Nick Larkin
25 Navy■	24 DL B.J. Rali
	DL Ron Brace
	DL Austin Giles / Brady Smith
	LB Tyronne Pruitt / Kevin Akins
	LB Joloon Dunbar / Mark Herzlich
	LB Brian Toal / Robert Francois
	DB DeJuan Tribble
	DB Larry Anam / Taj Morris
	DB Jamie Silva
	DB Wes Davis / Paul Anderson

RUSHING: Whitworth 174/791y, Callender 146/633y
PASSING: Ryan 263-427/2942y, 15TD, 61.6%
RECEIVING: Challenger 47/543y, Gonzalez 43/491y,
Robinson 36/490y
SCORING: Steve Aponavicius (K) 48pts, Toal 36pts
Challenger & Ryan Ohliger (K) 32pts

2007 11-3

38 Wake Forest	28 WR Kevin Challenger/Clarence Megwa
37 N. Carolina St.	17 WR Brandon Robinson / Rich Gunnell
24 Georgia Tech	10 T Gosder Cherilus
37 Army	17 G Ryan Poles / Ty Hall
24 Massachusetts	14 C Matt Tennant
55 Bowling Green	24 G Clif Ramsey
27 Notre Dame	14 T Anthony Castonzo
14 Virginia Tech	10 TE Ryan Purvis / Ryan Thompson
17 Florida State	27 QB Matt Ryan
35 Maryland	42 TB Andre Callender / L.V. Whitworth
20 Clemson	17 FB James McCluskey/Jon Loyte
28 Miami	14 DL Alex Albright / Jim Ramella
16 Virginia Tech□	30 DL Ron Brace
24 Michigan State■	21 DL Brady Smith / Jerry Willette
	DL Nick Larkin / Austin Giles
	LB Tyronne Pruitt / Kevin Akins
	LB Jo-Lonn Dunbar/Mike McLaughlin
	LB Mark Herzlich / Robert Francois
	DB DeJuan Tribble / DeLeon Gause
	DB Taji Morris / Roderick Rollins
	DB Jamie Silva
	DB Paul Anderson

RUSHING: Callender 211/969y, Whitworth 82/355y
PASSING: Ryan 388-654/4507y, 31TD, 59.3%
RECEIVING: Callender 76/720y, Gunnell 64/931y,
Robinson 56/793y
SCORING: Steve Aponavicius (K) 82pts,
Callender 78pts, Gunnell 42pts

2008 9-5

21 Kent State	0 WR Rich Gunnell / Clarence Megwa
16 Georgia Tech	19 WR Brandon Robinson / Justin Jarvis
34 Central Florida	7 T Anthony Castonzo
42 Rhode Island	0 G Clif Ramsey
38 No. Carolina St.	31 C Matt Tennant
28 Virginia Tech	23 G Thomas Claiborne
24 North Carolina	45 T Rich Lapham
21 Clemson	27 TE Ryan Purvis
17 Notre Dame	0 QB Chris Crane / Dominique Davis
27 Florida State	17 TB Montel Harris / Josh Haden
24 Wake Forest	21 FB James McCluskey / Codi Boek
28 Maryland	21 DL Austin Giles / Alex Albright
12 Virginia Tech□	30 DL Ron Brace
14 Vanderbilt■	16 DL B.J. Raji
	DL Jim Ramella / Brad Newman
	LB Mark Herzlich
	LB Mike McLaughlin
	LB Brian Toal / Robert Francois
	DB DeLeon Gause / Donnie Fletcher
	DB Kevin Akins / Roderick Rollins
	DB Wes Davis / Marcellus Bowman
	DB Paul Anderson

RUSHING: Harris 179/900y, Haden 120/479y, Crane 82/219y
PASSING: Crane 169-307/1721y, 10TD, 56.1%
Davis 63-138/741y, 6TD, 45.7%
RECEIVING: Gunnell 49/551y, Robinson 42/646y, Jarvis 25/274y
SCORING: Steve Aponavicius (K) 83pts, Crane 42pts,
Harris 38pts

2009 8-5

54 Northeastern	0 WR Justin Jarvis / Colin Larmond
34 Kent State	7 WR Rich Gunnell
7 Clemson	25 T Anthony Castonzo
27 Wake Forest	24 G Nathan Richman / Emmett Cleary
28 Florida State	21 C Matt Tennant
14 Virginia Tech	48 G Thomas Claiborne
52 No. Carolina St.	20 T Rich Lapham
16 Notre Dame	10 TE Chris Pantale / Jordan McMichael
31 C. Michigan	10 QB Dave Shinskie / Justin Tuggle
14 Virginia	10 RB Montel Harris
13 North Carolina	31 FB Lars Anderson
19 Maryland	17 DL Alex Albright / Brad Newman
13 Southern Cal■	24 DL Austin Giles
	DL Damik Scafe / Kaleb Ramsey
	DL Jim Ramella
	LB Mike Morrissey / Dominick LeGrande
	LB Mike McLaughlin / Alexander DiSanzo
	LB Luke Kuechly
	DB DeLeon Gause / Donnie Fletcher
	DB Roderick Rollins / Isaac Johnson
	DB Wes Davis
	DB Marcellus Bowman

RUSHING: Harris 308/1457y, Josh Haden (RB) 58/213y
PASSING: Shinskie 149-288/2049y, 15TD, 51.7%
RECEIVING: Gunnell 60/880y, Larmond 29/596y, Pantale 25/223y
Jarvis 18/229y
SCORING: Harris 90pts, Steve Aponavicius (K) 77pts, Gunnell 48pts

2010 7-6

38 Weber State	20 WR Ifeanyi Momah
26 Kent State	13 WR Bobby Swigert / Clyde Lee
0 Virginia Tech	19 T Anthony Castonzo
13 Notre Dame	31 G Nathan Richman (C)
17 N. Carolina St.	44 C Mark Spinney (G)
19 Florida State	24 G Thomas Claiborne / Ian White
21 Maryland	24 T Emmett Cleary (G) / Rich Lapham
16 Clemson	10 TE Chris Pantale / Lars Anderson
23 Wake Forest	13 QB Chase Rettig / Dave Shinskie
7 Duke	16 RB Montel Harris / Andre Williams
17 Virginia	13 FB/WR J. McCluskey/Johnathan Coleman
16 Syracuse	7 DL Alex Albright / Max Holloway
13 Nevada■	20 DL Kaleb Ramsey / Dillon Quinn
	DL Damik Scafe / Conor O'Neal
	DL Brad Newman / Kasim Edebali
	LB Mark Herzlich
	LB Luke Kuechly
	LB Kevin Pierre-Louis / Steele Divitto
	DB Donnie Fletcher
	DB DeLeon Gause / Chris Fox
	DB Wes Davis / Okechukwu Okoroba
	DB Jim Noel / Dominick LeGrande

RUSHING: Harris 269/1243y, Williams 95/461y
PASSING: Rettig 100-195/1238y, 6TD, 51.3%
Shinskie 46-96/618y, 5TD, 47.9%
RECEIVING: Swigert 39/504y, Pantale 31/338y, Momah 19/296y
SCORING: Nate Freese (K) 90pts, Harris 54pts, Swigert 24pts

CALIFORNIA

University of California (1868)
Berkeley, California
Nickname: Golden Bears
Colors: Blue and Gold
Stadium: Memorial Stadium (1923) 72,516
Conference Affiliations: Pacific Coast (Charter Member, 1916-58),
   AAWU (1959-67), Pacific 8/10 (1968-present)

CAREER RUSHING YARDS	Attempts	Yards
Russell White (1990-92)	663	3367
Marshawn Lynch (2004-06)	490	3230
Justin Forsett (2004-07)	567	3220
Joe Igber (1999-2002)	678	3124
Chuck Muncie (1973-75)	549	3052
Paul Jones (1975, 1977-79)	715	2930
Shane Vereen (2008-10)	556	2834
Jahvid Best (2007-09)	364	2668
J.J. Arrington (2003-04)	396	2625
John Olszewski (1950-52)	416	2504

CAREER PASSING YARDS	Comp-Att	Yards
Troy Taylor (1986-89)	683-1162	8126
Kyle Boller (1999-2002)	622-1301	7980
Pat Barnes (1993-96)	549-950	7360
Rich Campbell (1977-80)	599-929	7174
Nate Longshore (2005-08)	558-936	6783
Gale Gilbert (1980-84)	548-984	6566
Dave Barr (1992-94)	502-791	6305
Kevin Riley (2007-10)	468-845	6182
Aaron Rodgers (2003-04)	424-665	5469
Mike Pawlawski (1988-91)	419-703	5181

CAREER RECEIVING YARDS	Catches	Yards
Geoff McArthur (2000-04)	202	3188
Bobby Shaw (1994-97)	180	2731
DeSean Jackson (2005-07)	162	2423
Dameane Douglas (1995-98)	195	2335
Brian Treggs (1988-91)	167	2335
Wesley Walker (1973-76)	86	2206
Na'il Benjamin (1993-96)	165	2196
Sean Dawkins (1990-92)	129	2124
Steve Rivera (1973-75)	138	2085
Robert Jordan (2004-07)	156	2047

SEASON RUSHING YARDS	Carries	Yards
J.J. Arrington (2004)	289	2018
Jahvid Best (2008)	194	1580
Justin Forsett (2007)	305	1546
Chuck Muncie (1975)	228	1460
Marshawn Lynch (2006)	223	1356

SEASON PASSING YARDS	Comp-Att	Yards
Pat Barnes (1996)	250-420	3499
Nate Longshore (2006)	227-377	3021
Aaron Rodgers (2003)	215-349	2903
Kevin Riley (2009)	209-382	2850
Kyle Boller (2002)	225-421	2815

SEASON RECEIVING YARDS	Catches	Yards
Geoff McArthur (2003)	85	1504
Dameane Douglas (1998)	100	1150
Bobby Shaw (1997)	75	1093
Sean Dawkins (1992)	65	1070
DeSean Jackson (2006)	59	1060

GAME RUSHING YARDS	Carries	Yards
Jahvid Best (2008 vs. Washington)	19	311
Jerry Drew (1954 vs. Oregon State)	11	283
John Olszewski (1951 vs. Washington State)	20	269

GAME PASSING YARDS	Comp-Att	Yards
Pat Barnes (1996 vs. Arizona)	35-46	503
Pat Barnes (1996 vs. UCLA)	26-57	435
Kevin Riley (2008 vs. Maryland)	33-58	423

GAME RECEIVING YARDS	Catches	Yards
Wesley Walker (1976 vs. San Jose State)	8	289
Geoff McArthur (2003 vs. Stanford)	16	245
Steve Riviera (1974 vs. Stanford)	9	205

GREATEST COACH:

Although he may not be keeping this spot for long, Pappy Waldorf remains the greatest Cal coach since 1953 even though his best work came in the 1940s. But, those good years were extremely good and we may never see California so dominant again. From 1947 through '56, Waldorf, a former Syracuse lineman, went 67-32-4 at the helm of the Cal Bears. From 1948-50, the Bears went 39-3-1 and reached three straight Rose Bowls. With losses coming unfortunately in post-season play, Cal still managed to win 38 straight regular season games.

Lynn Waldorf began coaching at Oklahoma A&M, where he won three Missouri Valley Conference championships in five seasons from 1929 to 1933. His 3-0-2 record versus Oklahoma opened eyes, including those of Kansas State administrators who offered him their job. He only lasted one year in Manhattan, but he did win the Big Six title for his third conference championship in a row after two straight MVC titles with Oklahoma A&M to close his run there.

He moved north to Northwestern for 12 seasons, with his most success in his second year when the Wildcats won the 1936 Big Ten championship. That would be four titles in five years with three different schools for Pappy.

Waldorf then went to Cal, a program that had not had a winning season since 1938. Pappy was an immediate hit, winning nine of ten games that opening year of 1947. With a star-studded lineup, which quickly became known as "Pappy's Boys," the Bears became a dominant force in college football.

After retirement from coaching, Waldorf headed the scouting and personnel department for the San Francisco 49ers of the NFL.

CALIFORNIA'S 55 GREATEST SINCE 1953

OFFENSE

WIDE RECEIVER: Sean Dawkins, Geoff McArthur, Steve Rivera, Bobby Shaw
TIGHT END: Tony Gonzalez, Jim Hanifan
TACKLE: Ted Albrecht, Troy Auzenne, Tarik Glenn, Harvey Salem, Todd Steussie
GUARD: John Garamendi, Duke Leffler, Chris Mackie
CENTER: Alex Mack, Jeremy Newberry
QUARTERBACK: Steve Bartkowski, Rich Campbell, Craig Morton, Mike Pawlawski
RUNNING BACK: J.J. Arrington, Marshawn Lynch, Chuck Muncie, Russell White
FULLBACK: Paul Jones

DEFENSE

END: Tully Banta-Cain, Andre Carter, Mike McCaffrey, Regan Upshaw
TACKLE: Rhett Hall, Brandon Mebane, Gary Plummer, Ed White, Sherman White, Brandon Whiting
LINEBACKER: Duane Clemons, Hardy Nickerson, David Ortega, Ron Rivera, Jerrott Willard
CORNERBACK: Daymeion Hughes, Deltha O'Neal, Ray Youngblood
SAFETY: Anthony Green, Donnie McCleskey, Ken Wiedemann, Eric Zomalt

SPECIAL TEAMS

RETURN SPECIALISTS: DeSean Jackson, Jemeel Powell
PLACE KICKER: Jim Breech
PUNTER: Nick Harris

MULTIPLE POSITIONS

WIDE RECEIVER-DEFENSIVE BACK: Wayne Stewart

TWO-WAY PLAYERS

CENTER-LINEBACKER: Matt Hazeltine
QUARTERBACK-DEFENSIVE BACK: Paul Larson
FULLBACK-LINEBACKER: Tom Relles

PERFORMANCE FORMULA:
CALIFORNIA'S 10 BEST SEASONS

2004	1.5966	7 of 72
1991	1.5369	10 of 71
2006	1.4688	14 of 72
1975	1.3725	18 of 70
2008	1.3403	19 of 71
1968	1.3348	19 of 70
1993	1.2732	24 of 71
1974	1.2526	24 of 71
1990	1.1969	29 of 70
2005	1.1968	28 of 70

CALIFORNIA GOLDEN BEARS

Year	W-L-T	AP Poll	Conference Standing	Toughest Regular Season Opponents	Coach (Record at School)	Bowl Games		
1953	4-4-2		4	UCLA 8-1, Baylor 7-3, USC 6-3-1, Stanford 6-3-1, Ohio State 6-3	Pappy Waldorf			
1954	5-5		4	Oklahoma 10-0, Ohio State 9-0, UCLA 9-0, Southern California 8-3	Pappy Waldorf			
1955	2-7-1		7t	UCLA 9-1, Stanford 6-3-1, Pitt 7-3, Oregon State 6-3	Pappy Waldorf			
1956	3-7		8	USC 8-2, Baylor 8-2, Pitt 7-2-1, UCLA 7-3, Baylor 7-2-1	Pappy Waldorf (67-32-4)			
1957	1-9		7t	UCLA 8-2, Oregon State 8-2, Michigan State 8-1, Navy 8-1-1	Pete Elliott			
1958	7-4	16	1	Washington State 7-3, Oregon State 6-4	Pete Elliott	Rose	12 Iowa	38
1959	2-8		4	Texas 9-1, Washington 9-1, Southern California 8-2, Oregon 8-2	Pete Elliott (10-21)			
1960	2-7-1		4	Washington 9-1, UCLA 7-2-1, Oregon 7-2-1, Oregon State 6-3-1	Marv Levy			
1961	1-8-1		4t	Texas 9-1, UCLA 7-3, Penn State 7-3, Missouri 7-2-1	Marv Levy			
1962	1-9		6	USC 10-0, Penn State 9-1, Washington 7-1-2, Missouri 7-1-2	Marv Levy			
1963	4-5-1		5	Pitt 9-1, Illinois 7-1-1, Southern California 7-3, Washington 6-4	Marv Levy (8-29-3)			
1964	3-7		8	Southern California 7-3, Illinois 6-3, Missouri 6-3-1, Utah 8-2	Ray Willsey			
1965	5-5		5t	UCLA 7-2-1, Notre Dame 7-2-1, Southern California 7-2-1, Stanford 6-3-1	Ray Willsey			
1966	3-7		5	UCLA 9-1, Army 8-2, Southern California 7-3, Michigan 6-4	Ray Willsey			
1967	5-5		6	Southern California 9-1, Notre Dame 8-2, UCLA 7-2-1, Syracuse 8-2	Ray Willsey			
1968	7-3-1		3t	Southern California 9-0-1, Michigan 8-2, Army 7-3	Ray Willsey			
1969	5-5		6	Texas 10-0, Southern California 9-0-1, UCLA 8-1-1, Stanford 7-2-1	Ray Willsey			
1970	6-5		2t	Texas 10-0, Stanford 8-3, Southern California 6-4-1, Washington 6-4	Ray Willsey			
1971	6-5		ineligible	Arkansas 8-2-1, Stanford 8-3, Washington 8-3, USC 6-4-1	Ray Willsey (40-42-1)			
1972	3-8		5	Southern California 11-0, Ohio State 9-1-1, UCLA 8-3, Washington 8-3	Mike White			
1973	4-7		5t	Alabama 11-0, Southern California 9-1-1, UCLA 9-2, Stanford 7-4	Mike White			
1974	7-3-1		3t	Southern California 9-1-1, Florida 7-3, UCLA 6-3-2	Mike White			
1975	8-3	14	1t	Colorado 9-2, UCLA 8-2-1, West Virginia 7-3, Southern California 7-4	Mike White			
1976	5-6		4t	Southern California 10-1, Georgia 10-1, UCLA 9-1-1, Oklahoma 8-2-1	Mike White			
1977	7-4		5t	Washington 7-4, Stanford 8-3, Southern California 7-4	Mike White (34-31-1)			
1978	6-5		6t	Southern California 10-1, Nebraska 9-2, UCLA 8-3, Stanford 7-4	Roger Theder			
1979	6-6		5	Southern California 10-0-1, Washington 9-2, Michigan 8-3, Arizona 6-3-1	Roger Theder	Garden State	17 Temple	28
1980	3-8		9	Michigan 9-2, Southern California 8-2-1, UCLA 8-2	Roger Theder			
1981	2-9		8	Georgia 10-1, USC 9-2, UCLA 7-3-1, Washington 9-2, Arizona State 9-2	Roger Theder (17-28)			
1982	7-4		6	UCLA 9-1-1, Arizona State 9-2, Washington 9-2, Southern California 8-3	Joe Kapp			
1983	5-5-1		8	Arizona State 7-3-1, UCLA 6-4-1, Washington State 7-4	Joe Kapp			
1984	2-9		10	Washington 10-1, UCLA 8-3, Southern California 8-3	Joe Kapp			
1985	4-7		10	UCLA 8-2-1, Arizona 8-3, Arizona State 8-3	Joe Kapp			
1986	2-9		9	ASU 9-1-1, Washington 8-3, Stanford 8-3, Boston Coll. 8-3, Arizona 8-3	Joe Kapp (20-34-1)			
1987	3-6-2		8	UCLA 9-2, Tennessee 9-2-1, Southern California 8-3, Arizona State 6-4-1	Bruce Snyder			
1988	5-5-1		10	Southern California 10-1, UCLA 9-2, Washington State 8-3	Bruce Snyder			
1989	4-7		10	Miami 10-1, Southern California 9-1-1, Arizona 7-4, Washington 7-4	Bruce Snyder			
1990	7-4-1		4	Miami 9-2, Washington 9-2, Oregon 8-3, Arizona 7-4	Bruce Snyder	Copper	17 Wyoming	15
1991	10-2	8	2t	Washington 11-0, UCLA 8-3, Stanford 8-3	Bruce Snyder (29-24-1)	Citrus	37 Clemson	13
1992	4-7		9	Washington 9-2, Stanford 9-3, Kansas 7-4	Keith Gilbertson			
1993	9-4	25	4t	Arizona 9-2, UCLA 8-3, Southern California 7-5	Keith Gilbertson	Alamo	37 Iowa	3
1994	4-7		5t	Oregon 9-3, Arizona 8-3, Southern California 7-3-1, Washington State 7-4	Keith Gilbertson			
1995	3-8		8t	Oregon 9-2, Southern California 8-2-1, Stanford 7-3-1, UCLA 7-4	Keith Gilbertson (20-26)			
1996	6-6		5t	Arizona State 11-0, Stanford 6-5	Steve Mariucci (6-6)	Aloha	38 Navy	42
1997	3-8		9	Washington St. 11-1, UCLA 9-2, Arizona State 8-3, Washington 7-4	Tom Holmoe			
1998	5-6		7	Arizona 11-1, UCLA 10-1, Southern California 8-4, Nebraska 9-3	Tom Holmoe			
1999	4-7		6t	Nebraska 11-1, Stanford 8-3, Oregon 8-3, BYU 8-3	Tom Holmoe			
2000	3-8		8t	Oregon State 10-1, Washington 10-1, Oregon 9-2	Tom Holmoe			
2001	1-10		10	Illinois 10-1, Oregon 10-1, Washington State 9-2, Stanford 9-2	Tom Holmoe (16-39)			
2002	7-5		4t	Southern California 10-2, Washington State 10-2, Oregon State 8-4	Jeff Tedford	Insight	52 Virginia Tech	49
2003	8-6		3t	Southern California 11-1, Kansas State 10-3, Oregon 8-4	Jeff Tedford	Holiday	31 Texas Tech	45
2004	10-2	9	2	Southern California 12-0, Arizona State 8-3, Oregon State 6-5	Jeff Tedford	Las Vegas	35 BYU	28
2005	7-4	25	4t	Southern California 12-0, Oregon 10-1, UCLA 9-2	Jeff Tedford	Holiday	45 Texas A&M	10
2006	9-3	14	1t	Southern California 10-2, Tennessee 9-3, Oregon State 9-4, Oregon 7-5	Jeff Tedford	Armed Forces	42 Air Force	36
2007	7-6		7t	Tennessee 9-3, Oregon 9-3, Arizona State 10-2, Southern California 10-2	Jeff Tedford	Emerald	24 Miami	17
2008	9-4		4	Michigan State 9-3, Oregon 9-3, Southern California 11-1	Jeff Tedford	Poinsettia	27 Utah	37
2009	8-5		5t	Oregon 10-2, Southern California 8-4, Oregon State 8-4	Jeff Tedford			
2010	5-7		8	Southern Cal 8-5, Oregon 12-0, Stanford 11-1	Jeff Tedford (70-42)			

TOTAL: 284-345-13 .4525 (54 of 70)   **Bowl Games since 1953:**   8-5 .6154 (10 of 70)

GREATEST TEAM SINCE 1953: Although they laid an egg in the post season, the 2004 Cal Bears were as good a team as there was in the country. Sure Southern California topped them 23-17 in October for their only regular season blemish, but the Bears did everything but win that road game against the nation's top team. Not only did they outgain the powerful Trojans offense 424 to 205 yards, but they reached the Trojans red zone at game's end before falling. Cal swept the rest of their regular season opposition, including rival Stanford 41-6, to climb all the way to no. 4 in the country before getting frozen out of a BCS bowl berth.

1953 4-4-2

0 Baylor	25 E Jim Carmichael / Joe Hibbs
26 Oregon State	0 T Jim Kotler / Mike Giddings
19 Ohio State	33 G Tom Dutton / George Gosling
40 Pennsylvania	0 C Matt Hazeltine / Lloyd Torchio
34 San Jose State	14 G Hal Norris / Dick Day
20 Southern Cal	32 T George Najarian / Tevis Martin
7 UCLA	20 E Jim Baxter / Jim Hanifan
53 Washington	25 QB Paul Larson / Mike Casey
0 Oregon	0 HB Al Talley / Jerry Drew
21 Stanford	21 HB Don Marks / John Wilson
	FB Steve Dimeff / Jim Dillon

RUSHING: Marks 71/469y, Talley 88/359y, Drew 23/180y
PASSING: Larson 85-171/1431y, 6TD, 49.7%
RECEIVING: Hanifan 19/247y, Carmichael 14/231y, Talley 13/269y
SCORING: Talley 66pts, Larson (QB-K) 50pts, Marks 30pts

1954 5-5

13 Oklahoma	27 E Jim Hanifan
45 San Jose State	0 T Bob Oliver / Cliff Wright
13 Ohio State	21 G Don Gilkey / Nick Poppin
27 Oregon	33 C Matt Hazeltine / Lloyd Torchio
17 Washington St.	7 G Mike Giddings / Joe Oliva
27 Southern Cal	29 T Harry Ghilarducci
6 UCLA	27 E Jim Carmichael / Norm Becker
27 Washington	6 QB Paul Larson
46 Oregon State	7 HB Hal Norris/Johnny Wilson/Sam Williams
28 Stanford	20 HB Sebastain Bordonaro / Ted Granger
	FB Jerry Drew / Tom Kramer

RUSHING: Drew 77/715y, Granger 43/172y, Norris 44/158y
PASSING: Larson 125-195/1537y, 10TD, 64.1%
RECEIVING: Hanifan 44/569y, Carmichael 33/420y,
  Williams 17/214y
SCORING: Larson (QB-K) 49pts, Hanifan 48pts, Drew 36pts

1955 2-7-1

7 Pittsburgh	27 E Jim Carmichael / Roger Ramseier
13 Illinois	20 T Bob Oliver / Walt Senior
27 Penn	7 G Don Gilkey / Bob Currie
20 Washington St.	20 C Don Mitchell
0 Oregon	21 G Joe Oliva / Remo Jacuzzi
6 Southern Cal	33 T Harry Ghilarducci / Don Tronstein
0 UCLA	47 E Ron Wheatcroft (T) / Bill Vallotton
20 Washington	6 QB Hugh Maguire / Gus Gianulias
14 Oregon State	16 HB Johnny Wilson / Herb Jackson
0 Stanford	19 HB Ted Granger / Sebastian Bordonaro
	FB Jerry Drew / Steve Dimeff

RUSHING: Granger 83/379y, Dimeff 96/352y, Wilson 43/153y
PASSING: Maguire 38-80/564y, 3TD, 47.5%
RECEIVING: Ramseier 17/209y, Carmichael 15/281y
SCORING: Wilson 30pts, Granger 24pts, 2 tied w/ 12pts

1956 3-7

6 Baylor	7 E Ron Wheatcroft / Roger Ramseier
20 Illinois	32 T Harley Martin / Proverb Jacobs
14 Pittsburgh	0 G Don Gilkey / Bob Currie
13 Oregon State	21 C Frank Mattarocci
20 UCLA	34 G Remo Jacuzzi
16 Washington	7 G Joe Oliva / Curtis Iaukea
6 Oregon	28 E Mike White / Norm Becker
7 Southern Cal	20 QB Joe Kapp / Joe Contestabile
13 Washington St.	14 HB Darrell Roberts / John Stewart
20 Stanford	18 HB Jack Hart / Nat Brazill
	FB Jerry Drew / Herb Jackson

RUSHING: Jackson 97/462y, Stewart 46/214y, Hart 50/205y
PASSING: Kapp 52-112/667y, 1TD, 46.4%
RECEIVING: Becker 22/313y, Ramseier 13/209y, Wheatcroft 11/123y
SCORING: Hart 36pts, Roberts (HB-K) 20pts, 2 tied w/18pts

1957 1-9

6 SMU	13 E Ron Wheatcroft / Roger Ramseier
7 Washington St.	13 T Harley Martin / Bob Currie
0 Michigan State	19 G Pat Newell / Charlie Johnson
6 Navy	21 C Bob Chiaponne / Terry Jones
12 Southern Cal	0 G Proverb Jacobs / Jim Green
6 Oregon	24 T Curt Iaukea / Charlie Holston
14 UCLA	16 E Mike White / Tom Rodger
19 Oregon State	21 QB Joe Kapp / Gabe Arrillaga
27 Washington	35 HB Darrell Roberts / Hank Olguin
12 Stanford	14 HB Jack Hart / John Stewart
	FB Art Forbes

RUSHING: Hart 101/396y, Olguin 67/227y, Roberts 68/203y
PASSING: Kapp 38-77/580y, 4TD, 49.4%
RECEIVING: Hart 13/276y, Olguin 10/194y, White 10/179y
SCORING: Hart 36pts, Roberts 28pts, Kapp 14pts

1958 7-4

20 Pacific	24 E Charlie Holston / Jerry Lundgren
12 Michigan State	32 T Pat Newell / Bill Streshly
34 Washington St.	14 G Pete Domoto / Jeff Snow
36 Utah	21 C Terry Jones / Frank Doretti
14 Southern Cal	12 G Don Piestrup / Jim Green
23 Oregon	6 T Frank Sally / John Michael
8 Oregon State	14 E Skip Huber / Tom Bates
20 UCLA	17 QB Joe Kapp
12 Washington	7 HB Wayne Crow / Grover Garvin /H. Olguin
16 Stanford	15 HB Jack Hart / Jack Yerman
12 Iowa ■	38 FB Bill Patton / Walt Arnold

RUSHING: Kapp 152/616y, Hart 127/487y, Patton 103/344y
PASSING: Kapp 64-114/775y, 56.1%
RECEIVING: Hart 32/395y, Olguin 9/84y, 3 tied with 6
SCORING: Hart (HB-K) 58pts, Patton 56pts, Kapp 32.pts

1959 2-8

20 Washington St.	6 E Dave George / Dave Maggard
12 Iowa	42 T Pat Newell / Roland Lasher
0 Texas	33 G Pete Domoto / Jim Green
6 Notre Dame	28 C Terry Jones / Andy Segale
12 UCLA	19 G Don Piestrup
20 Oregon State	24 T Frank Sally / Charlie Holston
7 Southern Cal	14 E Gael Barsotti / Tom Bates
18 Oregon	20 QB Wayne Crow / Larry Parque
0 Washington	20 HB Jerry Scattini / Jim Burress / G. Garvin
20 Stanford	17 HB Steve Bates / Bill Patton
	FB Walt Arnold / Bill Patton / G. Pierovich

RUSHING: Arnold 76/351y, Patton 90/338y, Bates 48/307y
PASSING: Crow 26-67/379y, 3TD, 38.8%
RECEIVING: Barsotti 6/111y, Wills 4/92y, Bates 4/68y
SCORING: Garvin 24pts, Arnold 18pts, Patton (FB-K) 17pts

1960 2-7-1

3 Tulane	7 E Dave George / Gael Barsotti
7 Notre Dame	21 T Ted Dinkler / John Bebelaar
10 Army	28 G Jerry Lundgren / Doug Graham
21 Washington St.	21 C Dick Carlsen / Roland Lasher
10 Southern Cal	27 G Roger Stull
0 Oregon	20 T Jeff Snow / Mel Piestrup
14 Oregon State	6 E Tom Bates / John Papini
0 UCLA	28 QB Randy Gold / Larry Balliet
7 Washington	27 HB Jerry Scattini / Bill Patton
21 Stanford	10 HB Steve Bates / Bob Wills
	FB George Pierovich / Walt Arnold

RUSHING: Bates 82/384y, Pierovich 90/330y, Scattini 66/289y
PASSING: Gold 65-117/696y, 2TD, 55.6%
RECEIVING: Pierovich 12/90y, George 10/128y, Papini 8/113y
SCORING: Pierovich 30pts, Bates 24pts, Jim Ferguson (K) 21pts

1961 1-8-1

3 Texas	28 E Ron Vaughn / Dave Muga
7 Iowa	28 T Andy Segale / Norm McLean
14 Missouri	14 G John Erby
21 Washington	14 C Tom Burke
14 Southern Cal	28 G Roger Stull
16 Penn State	33 T Larry Lowell / Lauren Bock
15 UCLA	35 E Bill Turner / Loren Hawley
14 Air Force	15 QB Randy Gold / Larry Balliett
7 Kansas	53 HB Jerry Scattini / Rudy Carvajal
7 Stanford	20 HB Alan Nelson / Bob Wills / Jim Burress
	FB George Pierovich / Jim Anderson

RUSHING: Nelson 59/331y, Carvajal 41/257y, Pierovich 80/238y
PASSING: Gold 41-81/403y, 4TD, 50.6%
RECEIVING: Wills 21/302y, Muga 10/98y, Vaughn 8/81y
SCORING: Gold 26pts, Wills 20pts, Jim Ferguson (K) 18pts

1962 1-9

10 Missouri	21 E Ron Vaughn / Bill Krum
25 San Jose State	8 T Ron Calegari / Jim Pinson
24 Pittsburgh	26 G John Erby / Jim Phillips
7 Duke	21 C Roger Stull
6 Southern Cal	32 G Dennis Abreu / Dave Urrea
21 Penn State	23 T Jim Anderson
16 UCLA	26 E Bill Turner
0 Washington	27 QB Craig Morton/Randy Gold/L. Balliett
21 Kansas	33 HB Tom Blanchfield / Rudy Carvajal
13 Stanford	30 HB Alan Nelson / Jim Blakeney
	FB Mike Epstein / Tom Lutes

RUSHING: Nelson 73/334y, Blanchfield 78/288y, Carvajal 40/138y
PASSING: Morton 69-126/905y, 9TD, 54.8%
RECEIVING: Turner 44/537y, Blanchfield 19/275y, Nelson 18/154y
SCORING: Turner 36pts, Nelson 34pts, Blanchfield (HB-K) 27pts

1963 4-5-1

15 Iowa State	8 E Steve Radich/Larry Lowell/Jack Schraub
0 Illinois	10 T Roger Foster / Tom Brown
15 Pittsburgh	35 G John Garamendi / Dave Urrea
22 Duke	22 C Jim Phillips
34 San Jose State	13 G Jim Norwood / Dennis Abreu
6 Southern Cal	36 T Jim Anderson / Jim Pinson
25 UCLA	0 E Bill Krum / Dick Williams
26 Washington	39 QB Craig Morton
35 Utah	22 HB Tom Blanchfield / Jim Blakeney
17 Stanford	28 HB Jerry Mosher / Loren Hawley
	FB Rudy Carajal / Tom Relles

RUSHING: Blanchfield 78/387y, Relles 51/298y, Blakeney 60/260y
PASSING: Morton 101-207/1475y, 14TD, 48.8%
RECEIVING: Schraub 30/467y, Hawley 25/305y, Mosher 18/245y
SCORING: Blanchfield (HB-K) 45pts, Schraub 32pts, Morton 24pts

1964 3-7

21 Missouri	14 E Mike Gridley / Dick Williams
14 Illinois	20 T John Rusev / Larry Lathrop
20 Minnesota	26 G John Garamendi
9 Miami	7 C Sam Hard / Jeff Palmer
27 Navy	13 G Dennis Abreu
21 Southern Cal	26 T Ron Calegari (G) / Jim Pinson
21 UCLA	25 E Jack Schraub
16 Washington	21 QB Craig Morton
0 Utah	14 HB Jerry Mosher / Jerry Bradley
3 Stanford	21 HB Tom Blanchfield / Jim Blakeney
	FB Tom Relles
	DL Stan Dzura / Jack Schraub
	DL John Cantlon
	DL John Schmidt
	DL Roger Foster / Larry Lathrop
	DL John Beasley
	LB Don Anderson
	LB Jeff Palmer
	LB Tom Relles
	DB Ken Moulton / Jim Blakeney
	DB Jerry Walter / Jim Hunt

RUSHING: Relles 145/519y, Blanchfield 91/293y,
  Blakeney 48/172y
PASSING: Morton 185-308/2121y, 13TD, 60.1%
RECEIVING: Schraub 52/633y, Mosher 37/427y, Relles 30/233y
SCORING: Blanchfield (HB-K) 52pts, Mosher 32pts, Bradley 24pts

1965 5-5

6 Notre Dame	48 E John Beasley
7 Michigan	10 T John Frantz / Dick Williams
17 Kansas	0 G John Garamendi
24 Air Force	7 C Jeff Palmer / John Salisbury
16 Washington	12 G Tom Brown
3 UCLA	56 T Roger Foster
21 Penn State	17 TE Jerry Bradley / Mike Gridley
0 Southern Cal	35 QB Dan Berry / Jim Hunt
24 Oregon	0 HB Tom Relles
7 Stanford	9 WB Lloyd Reist / Ted Parks
	FB Frank Lynch / Ron Minamide
	DL Sam Hard
	DL John Cantlon
	DL Mike Brown / John Schmidt
	DL Bobby Crittendon
	DL Dan Goich
	DL Larry Lathrop
	LB Greg Palamountain / Jim Fetherston
	LB Steve Radich
	DB Jerry Mosher
	DB Bobby Smith
	DB Ken Moulton / Don Guest

RUSHING: Relles 133/485y, Berry 81/285y, Reist 66/181y
PASSING: Berry 28-73/335y, 4TD, 38.4%
RECEIVING: Bradley 22/360y, Beasley 12/113y, Relles 7/93y
SCORING: Dan Sinclair (K) 29pts, Lynch 24pts, Relles &
  Bradley 18pts

1966 3-7

21 Washington St.	6 E Jerry Bradley
7 Michigan	17 T Duane Mayfield
30 Pittsburgh	15 G Brock Arner
0 San Jose State	24 C John Frantz
24 Washington	20 G John Schmidt
15 UCLA	28 T Greg Hatfield
15 Penn State	33 TE John Beasley
9 Southern Cal	35 QB Barry Bronk
3 Army	6 HB Dan Berry (QB) / Jim Sheridan
7 Stanford	13 WB George Gearhart / Lloyd Reist
	FB Frank Lynch / Rick Bennett
	DL Larry Reis / Mike McCaffrey
	DL Dan Goich
	DL Mike Brown
	DL Larry Lathrop / Sam Hard
	DL Bobby Crittenden / Rick Laven
	DL Jerry Woods
	LB Jim Fetherston
	LB Don Anderson
	DB Wayne Stewart
	DB Bobby Smith
	DB Don Guest

RUSHING: Bennett 96/319y, Berry 121/301y, Lynch 45/127y
PASSING: Bronk 84-183/965y, 7TD, 45.9%
RECEIVING: Bradley 32/473y, Beasley 19/214y, Berry 18/183y
SCORING: Bradley 42pts, Dan Sinclair (K) 20pts, 3 tied w/ 12pts

1967 5-5

21 Oregon	13 E Wayne Stewart
8 Notre Dame	41 T Mike Meers / Bill Laveroni
10 Michigan	9 G John Salisbury
14 Air Force	12 C John Frantz
14 UCLA	37 G Dan Ryan
14 Syracuse	20 T Jerome Champion (G) / DuaneMayfield
6 Washington	23 E Jim Calkins / Ned Anderson
12 Southern Cal	31 QB Barry Bronk / Randy Humphries
30 San Jose State	6 HB Troy Cox / Paul Williams / Gary Fowler
26 Stanford	3 WB George Gearhart
	FB John McGaffie
	DL Irby Augustine
	DL Mark Hultgren / Dennis Bugbee
	DL Ed White
	DL Bobby Crittendon
	DL Larry Reis
	DL Mike McCaffrey
	LB Jim Fetherston
	LB Dennis Pitta / Jerry Woods
	DB Jim Coleman / Paul Williams
	DB Bobby Smith
	DB Ken Wiedemann

RUSHING: Williams 116/432y, McGaffie 85/233y, Fowler 70/179y
PASSING: Bronk 65-146/708y, 2TD, 44.5%
RECEIVING: Stewart 45/503y, Gearhart 24/180y, Fowler 18/226y
SCORING: Ron Miller (K) 35pts, McGaffie & Fowler 18pts

1968 7-3-1

21 Michigan	7 WR Wayne Stewart
10 Colorado	0 T Mike Meers
46 San Jose State	0 G Gerald Borgia
7 Army	10 C Bill Laveroni
39 UCLA	15 G Jerome Champion
43 Syracuse	0 T Bob Richards
7 Washington	7 TE George Harris / John Phillips
17 Southern Cal	35 QB Randy Humphries
36 Oregon	8 TB Gary Fowler
0 Stanford	20 WB Paul Williams
17 Hawaii	12 FB John McGaffie / Bob Darby
	DL Irby Augustine
	DL Mark Hultgren
	DL Ed White
	DL Steve Schultz
	DL Larry Reis
	DL Mike McCaffrey
	LB Dennis Pitta
	LB Jerry Woods
	DB Jim Sheridan
	DB Eric Kastner
	DB Ken Wiedemann

RUSHING: Fowler 162/665y, Darby 117/386y, McGaffie 87/303y
PASSING: Humphries 98-207/1247y, 6TD, 47.3%
RECEIVING: Stewart 50/679y, Williams 26/418y, Fowler 12/108y
SCORING: Fowler 60pts, Ron Miller (K) 55pts, 3 tied w/ 24pts

1969 5-5

0 Texas	17 WR Geoff DeLapp / Ken Adams
17 Indiana	14 T Bob Richards / John Phillips
31 Rice	21 G Greg Hendren (C) / Steve Sawin
44 Washington	13 C Bill Laveroni
0 UCLA	32 G Gerald Borgia
17 Washington St.	0 T Mike Meers
9 Southern Cal	14 TE Jim Calkins
3 Oregon State	35 QB Dv. Penhall/Steve Curtis/R. Humphries
31 San Jose State	7 TB Gary Fowler
28 Stanford	29 WB Jim Fraser / Stan Murphy
	FB Bob Darby
	DL Irby Augustine / Dennis Acree
	DL Dave Seppi
	DL Dick Wagner / Sherman White
	DL Mark Hultgren / Andy Westfall
	DL Steve Schulz
	DL Steve Reece
	LB Phil Croyle
	LB Paul Martyr
	DB Ken Wiedemann
	DB Bernie Keeles / Ray Youngblood
	DB Joe Acker

RUSHING: Fowler 157/741y, Darby 118/532y, Murphy 37/172y
PASSING: Penhall 76-145/874y, 2TD, 52.4%
RECEIVING: DeLapp 25/261y, Fraser 23/335y, Murphy 15/178y
SCORING: Randy Wersching (K) 58pts, Fowler 32pts, Darby 24pts

1970 6-5

24 Oregon	31 WR Steve Sweeney / Ken Adams
15 Texas	56 WR Geoff DeLapp
56 Indiana	14 T Bob Richards
0 Rice	28 G Greg Hendren
31 Washington	28 C Rob Purnell / Skip Leonard
21 UCLA	24 G Eric Swanson
45 Washington St.	0 T Steve Sawin
13 Southern Cal	10 TE Brady
10 Oregon State	16 QB Dave Penhall
35 San Jose State	28 TB Stan Murphy / Isaac Curtis
22 Stanford	14 FB Tim Todd / Bob Darby
	DL Dennis Acree / Sam Garamendi
	DL Dave Seppi
	DL O.Z. White
	DL Dick Wagner
	DL Sherman White / Bob Rogers
	DL Steve Reece / Tom Grieb
	LB Phil Croyle
	LB Tom Hawkins
	DB Ray Youngblood
	DB Andy Anderson / Jerome Carter
	DB Joe Acker

RUSHING: Murphy 165/603y, Todd 123/587y, Curtis 103/427y
PASSING: Penhall 118-227/1785y, 10TD, 52%
RECEIVING: Sweeney 43/679y, DeLapp 27/451y, Curtis 17/217y
SCORING: Randy Wersching (K) 64pts, Todd 50pts, Penhall 36pts

1971 6-5

20 Arkansas	51 WR Geoff DeLapp
20 West Virginia	19 WR Steve Sweeney
34 San Jose State	10 T Bill Johnson
3 Ohio State	35 G Eric Swanson / Scott Hudgins
30 Oregon State	27 C Rob Purnell
24 Washington St.	23 G Ray Volker / Neil Agness
31 UCLA	24 T Mark Klink / Mike Vincent
0 Southern Cal	28 TE Bill Stowers / Larry Brumsey
7 Washington	30 QB Jay Cruze
17 Oregon	10 TB Isaac Curtis
0 Stanford	14 FB Steve Kemnitzer / Tim Todd
	DL Sherman White
	DL Bob Kampa
	DL O.Z. White / Mark Wendt
	DL Bill Backstrom / Bob Rogers
	LB Sam Garamendi
	LB Tom Hawkins
	LB Loren Toews / Don Alexander
	DB Clarence Duren
	DB Jerome Carter
	DB Joe Acker
	DB Ray Youngblood

RUSHING: Kemnitzer 157/686y, Curtis 110/475y, Todd 77/205y
PASSING: Cruze 119-242/1284y, 6TD, 49.2%
RECEIVING: DeLapp 48/464y, Sweeney 37/579y, Curtis 15/175y
SCORING: Kemnitzer 48pts, Ray Wersching
(K) 42pts, Sweeney & Curtis 20pts

1972 3-8

10 Colorado	20 WR Dave Bateman
37 Washington St.	23 WR Steve Sweeney
10 San Jose State	17 T Steve Lawrence
27 Missouri	34 G Ted Seifert / Ray Volker
18 Ohio State	35 C Randy Howard / Kevin O'Dorisio
14 Southern Cal	42 G Scott Hudgins / Kern Lawyer
13 UCLA	49 T Mark Klink
21 Washington	35 TE Randy Schmidt / Mike Shaughnessy
31 Oregon	12 QB J. Cruze / S. Bartkowski / V. Ferragamo
23 Oregon State	26 TB Steve Kemnitzer / Rick Jones
24 Stanford	21 FB Fred Leathers / Sylvester Youngblood
	DL Dave Gleason
	DL Bob Kampa / Chris Keyser
	DL Rob Swenson / Mark Wendt
	DL Fred Weber / Dave Frey
	LB Bill Johnson
	LB Bob Smith
	LB Loren Toews / Paul Giroday
	DB Robert Curry / Scott Stringer
	DB Paul James / Dave Lawson
	DB Jerry Jones
	DB Bill Armstrong / Clarence Duren

RUSHING: Kemnitzer 103/434y, Leathers 88/404y,
Youngblood 60/270y
PASSING: Bartkowski 70-165/944y, 4TD, 42.4%
Cruze 67-109/829y, 8TD, 61.5%
RECEIVING: Sweeney 52/785y, Leathers 29/429y,
Bateman 23/322y
SCORING: Sweeney 78pts, Ray Wersching (K) 38pts,
Leathers 36pts

1973 4-7

0 Alabama	66 WR Wesley Walker / Dave Bateman
7 Illinois	27 WR Steve Rivera / Fred Leathers
51 Army	6 T Steve Lawrence
54 Washington	49 G Chris Mackie / Setoga Setoga
10 Oregon	41 C Kevin O'Dorisio / Jack Harrison
24 Oregon State	14 G John Culpepper
21 UCLA	61 T Ted Seifert
14 Southern Cal	50 TE Randy Schmidt
19 San Jose State	9 QB Vince Ferragamo / Steve Bartkowski
28 Washington St.	31 TB Chuck Muncie / Mark Bailey
17 Stanford	26 FB Howard Strickland / Blane Warhurst
	DL Fred Weber / Dave Frey
	DL Rob Swenson
	DL Mark Wendt
	DL Jeff Sevy / Chuck Hextrum
	LB John Jackson / Phil Heck
	LB Ivan Weiss
	LB Kim Staskus / Dallas Hickman
	DB Steve Gritsch / Dwayne O'Steen
	DB Jerry Jones / Sam Williams
	DB Harold Fike
	DB Karl Crumpacker

RUSHING: Muncie 157/801y, Strickland 122/641y, Bailey 45/283y
PASSING: Ferragamo 82-170/1014y, 5TD, 48.2%
Bartkowski 61-129/910y, 4 TD, 47.3%
RECEIVING: Muncie 27/283y, Rivera 25/357y, Leathers 17/208y
SCORING: Muncie 72pts, Strickland 54pts,
Ron Vander Meer (K) 49pts

1974 7-3-1

17 Florida	21 WR Dave Bateman / Wesley Walker
17 San Jose State	16 WR Steve Rivera
27 Army	14 T Ted Albrecht
31 Illinois	14 G Chris Mackie
40 Oregon	10 C Jack Harrison / Whit Everett
17 Oregon State	14 G John Culpepper / Pat Micco
3 UCLA	28 T John Jackson / Joe de Rosa
15 Southern Cal	15 TE George Frietas
52 Washington	26 QB Steve Bartkowski
37 Washington St.	33 TB Chuck Muncie
20 Stanford	22 FB Howard Strickland / Mark Bailey
	DL Dave Hextrum
	DL Paul von der Mehden
	DL Dave Frey
	LB Robert Smith
	LB Ivan Weiss / Phil Heck
	LB Rob Swenson / Kim Staskus
	LB Blane Warhurst /Rick Booth /Rick Bailey
	DB Dwayne O'Steen / Steve Gritsch
	DB Herman Edwards
	DB Harold Fike
	DB Karl Crumpacker

RUSHING: Muncie 164/791y, Strickland 142/724y, Bailey 68/287y
PASSING: Bartkowski 182-325/2580y, 12TD, 57%
RECEIVING: Rivera 56/938y, Muncie 31/410y, Bailey 21/123y
SCORING: Muncie 68pts, Strickland 60pts, Jim Breech (K) 34pts

1975 8-3

27	Colorado	34 WR Wesley Walker
10	West Virginia	28 WR Steve Rivera
33	Washington St.	21 T Ted Albrecht
27	San Jose State	24 G Pat Micco / Ned Vessey
34	Oregon	7 C Duane Williams
51	Oregon State	24 G Jack Harrison
14	UCLA	28 T Joe de Rosa
28	Southern Cal	14 TE George Freitas
27	Washington	24 QB Joe Roth / Fred Besana
31	Air Force	14 TB Chuck Muncie
48	Stanford	15 FB Tom Newton / Paul Jones
		DL Bob Warner / Daryle Skaugstand
		DL Paul von der Mehden
		DL Chuck Hextrum /Sam Best /Greg Peters
		LB Jeff Barnes
		LB Larry Grady / Burl Toler / Pete Sitta
		LB Phil Heck / James Reed
		LB Greg Ricks
		DB Anthony Green / Jeff Moye
		DB Jack Holleman / Howard Fike
		DB Syd Lofton / Tim Mehan
		DB Steve Maehl / Tubby Harrell

RUSHING: Muncie 228/1460y, Newton 98/544y, Jones 65/302y
PASSING: Roth 126-226/1880y, 14TD, 55.8%
RECEIVING: Rivera 57/790y, Muncie 39/392y, Walker 36/839y
SCORING: Muncie 90pts, Jim Breech (K) 72pts, Walker 60pts

1976 5-6

24	Georgia	36 WR Wes Walker /Holden Smith/Ed Gillies
17	Oklahoma	26 WR Jesse Thompson
31	Arizona State	22 T Ted Albrecht
43	San Jose State	16 G Ned Vessey
27	Oregon	10 C Duane Williams
9	Oregon State	10 G Greg Peters
19	UCLA	35 T Leo Biedermann / Jack Clark
6	Southern Cal	20 TE George Freitas
7	Washington	0 QB Joe Roth / Fred Besana
23	Washington St.	22 TB Markey Crane / Oliver Hillman
24	Stanford	27 FB Tom Newton
		DL Burl Toler
		DL Craig Watkins / Ralph DeLoach
		DL Bob Warner
		DL Jeff Barnes
		DL Greg Ricks / Stanley Glenn
		LB James Reed / Phil Heck
		LB Pete Sitta
		DB Ken McAllister
		DB Jeff Moye
		DB Syd Lofton / Vern Smith
		DB Anthony Green

RUSHING: Newton 137/546y, Crane 110/451y, Hillmon 112/401y
PASSING: Roth 154-295/1789y, 7TD, 52.2%
RECEIVING: Thompson 37/411y, Frietas 34/327y, Gillies 24/389y
SCORING: Jim Breech (K) 72pts, Newton & Walker 36pts

1977 7-4

27	Tennessee	17 WR Jesse Thompson
24	Air Force	14 WR Dave Mogni / Floyd Eddings
28	Missouri	21 T Leo Biedermann / Bob Smiland
52	San Jose State	3 G Ernie Binggeli
10	Washington St.	17 C Rick Purnell
41	Oregon State	17 G Duke Leffler
19	UCLA	21 T Jack Clark
17	Southern Cal	14 TE George Freitas
31	Washington	50 QB Charlie Young
48	Oregon	16 TB Oliver Hillman / John Williams
3	Stanford	21 FB Paul Jones
		DL Ralph DeLoach
		DL Pat Graham / Bob Meredith
		DL Craig Watkins
		DL Don Alaman
		LB Burl Toler / John Harris
		LB David Shaw / Stan Glenn
		LB Greg Bracelin
		DB Anthony Washington / Wade Johnson
		DB Daryl Swanson
		DB Anthony Green
		DB Ken McAllister

RUSHING: Jones 189/805y, Williams 54/246y, Hillmon 88/232y
PASSING: Young 135-249/1875y, 12TD, 54.2%
RECEIVING: Thompson 51/797y, Freitas 50/673y,
Hillmon 24/315y
SCORING: Jim Breech (K) 82pts, Hillmon 48pts, Jones 42pts

1978 6-5

26	Nebraska	36 WR Holden Smith / Matt Bouza
34	Georgia Tech	22 WR Floyd Eddings / Michael Buggs
24	Pacific	6 T Craig Watkins / Mike Harmon
28	West Virginia	21 G Brian Bailey / Dave Heck
21	Oregon	18 C Dave Shaw
33	Arizona	20 G Duke Leffler
0	UCLA	45 T Kevin Uperesa
17	Southern Cal	42 TE Lamar Lundy / Ron Moffett
21	Arizona State	35 QB Rich Campbell
22	Washington St.	14 TB John Williams / Allen Blackmon
10	Stanford	30 FB Paul Jones / Mark Houghton
		DL Ralph DeLoach / Charles Glass
		DL Rich Miller / Pat Graham
		DL Daryle Skaugstad
		DL Bob Rozier
		LB Ron Hill
		LB David Shaw
		LB Stan Holloway / Rich Dixon
		DB Anthony Washington/Darnell Chapman
		DB Daryl Swanson
		DB Dwayne Wilkes / Timmy Washington
		DB Ron Coccimiglio

RUSHING: Jones 212/801y, Williams 53/236y, Houghton 40/192y
PASSING: Campbell 164-293/2287y, 14TD, 56%
RECEIVING: Smith 26/641y, Jones 25/189y, Moffett 22/337y
SCORING: Joe Cooper (K) 50pts, Jones 48pts, Smith 30pts

1979 6-6

17	Arizona State	9 WR Matt Bouza
10	Arizona	7 WR Michael Buggs
13	San Jose State	10 T Mike Harmon / Greg Woodard
10	Michigan	14 G Greg Stubblefield
14	Oregon	19 C Dave Heck / Bruce Sorenson
45	Oregon State	0 G Brian Bailey
27	UCLA	28 T Harvey Salem
14	Southern Cal	24 TE Joe Rose / Don Sprague
24	Washington	28 QB Rich Campbell
45	Washington St.	13 TB John Tuggle / Allen Blackmon
21	Stanford	14 FB Paul Jones
17	Temple■	28 DL Kirk Karacozoff
		DL Daryle Skaugstad / Dupre Marshall
		DL Pat Graham
		LB Ron Hill
		LB Stan Holloway
		LB Greg Bracelin / Ulysses Madison
		LB Rich Dixon
		DB Ahmad Anderson
		DB Fred Williams
		DB Ron Coccimiglio
		DB Darnell Chapman

RUSHING: Jones 230/937y, Tuggle 45/209y
PASSING: Campbell 241-360/2859y, 15TD, 66.9%
RECEIVING: Bouza 59/831y, Rose 49/567y, Jones 49/330y
SCORING: Mick Luckhurst (K) 60pts Jones 36pts, Bouza 30pts

1980 3-8

13	Florida	41 WR Matt Bouza
19	Army	26 WR Holden Smith/M. Buggs/TyronePortee
24	Arizona	31 T Brian Bailey
13	Michigan	38 G Jesse Covarrubias / Greg Stubblefield
31	Oregon	6 C Bruce Sorenson
27	Oregon State	6 G Tim Galas
9	UCLA	32 T Harvey Salem
7	Southern Cal	60 TE Don Sprague / David Lewis
6	Arizona State	34 QB Rich Campbell / J Torchio
17	Washington St.	31 TB John Tuggle / Terry Wiley
28	Stanford	23 FB David Palmer
		DL Pat Graham
		DL Rich Stachowski / Dupre Marshall
		DL Kirk Karacozoff
		LB Ulysses Madison
		LB Steve Cacciara
		LB Rich Dixon
		LB Paul Najarian
		DB John Sullivan / Ahmad Anderson
		DB Fred Williams / Mike Lozica
		DB Ron Coccimiglio
		DB Kevin Moen / Gregg Beagle

RUSHING: Tuggle 136/580y, Palmer 63/253y, Wiley 49/218y
PASSING: Campbell 193-273/2026y, 6TD, 70.7%
RECEIVING: Bouza 44/651y, Tuggle 36/332y, Wiley 33/254y
SCORING: Mick Luckhurst (K) 60pts, Tuggle 36pts,
Campbell 18pts

1981 2-9

28	Texas A&M	29 WR Tyran Wright
13	Georgia	27 WR Tyrone Portee / Mark Funderburk
14	Arizona	19 WR Mariet Ford
24	San Jose State	37 WR Floyd Eddings
26	Washington	27 T Harvey Salem
17	Arizona State	45 G Greg LoBerg
6	UCLA	34 C Pat Brady
45	Oregon State	3 G George Niualiku
3	Southern Cal	21 T Brian Bailey
0	Washington St.	19 QB J Torchio
21	Stanford	42 RB John Tuggle / Carl Montgomery
		DL Reggie Camp
		DL Gary Plummer / Dan Wetherell
		DL Rich Stachowski
		LB Eddie Walsh
		LB Chris Hampton / Steve Cacciari
		LB Tim Lucas
		LB Ron Rivera / Rich Dixon
		DB Fred Williams
		DB John Sullivan
		DB Clemont Williams / Kevin Moen
		DB Richard Rogers / Jimmy Stewart

RUSHING: Tuggle 110/486y, Montgomery 86/397y
PASSING: Torchio 155-363/2112y, 9TD, 42.7%
RECEIVING: Ford 45/600y, Funderburk 25/349y, Tuggle 20/190y
SCORING: Joe Cooper (K) 39pts, Montgomery 36pts,
Tuggle 30pts

1982 7-4

31	Colorado	17 WR Wes Howell
28	San Diego State	0 WR Mariet Ford
0	Arizona State	15 T Greg Loberg / Steve Shotwell
26	San Jose State	7 G George Niualiku
7	Washington	50 C Pat Brady
10	Oregon	3 G Tim Galas
31	UCLA	47 T Harvey Salem
28	Oregon State	14 TE David Lewis
0	Southern Cal	42 QB Gale Gilbert
34	Washington St.	14 TB Scott Smith / Ron Story
25	Stanford	20 FB John Tuggle
		DL Rich Stachowski
		DL Gary Plummer
		DL Reggie Camp
		DL Ron Rivera
		LB Tim Lucas / Rich Dixon
		LB Eddie Walsh
		LB Chris Hampton
		DB John Sullivan
		DB Fred Williams / Ahmad Anderson
		DB Richard Rodgers / Kevin Moen
		DB Clemont Williams

RUSHING: Tuggle 143/538y, Story 72/318y, Smith 54/167y
PASSING: Gilbert 147-270/1796y, 12TD, 54.4%
RECEIVING: Lewis 54/715y, Ford 42/568y, Howell 35/589y
SCORING: Joe Cooper (K) 56pts, Lewis & Tuggle 36pts

1983 5-5-1

19	Texas A&M	17 WR Rance McDougald
14	San Diego State	28 WR Andy Bark
30	San Jose State	9 T Greg Loberg
33	Arizona	33 G Mark Long / George Niualiku
17	Oregon	24 C Mike Reed
45	Oregon State	19 G Mark Stephens
16	UCLA	20 T Steve Shotwell
9	Southern Cal	19 TE Don Noble / David Lewis
26	Arizona State	24 QB Gale Gilbert
6	Washington St.	16 TB Dwight Garner / Mark Funderburk
27	Stanford	18 FB Ron Story / Scott Smith
		DL Don James
		DL John Haina
		DL Byron Smith / Mike Rusinek
		LB Chris Hampton / Steve Cacciari
		LB Eddie Walsh / Hardy Nickerson
		LB Paul Najarian / Miles Turpin
		LB Ron Rivera
		DB John Sullivan
		DB David Carter / Clemont Williams
		DB Richard Rodgers
		DB Ray Noble

RUSHING: Story 124/435y, Smith 68/233y, Garner 56/208y
PASSING: Gilbert 216-365/2769y, 13TD, 59.2%
RECEIVING: McDougald 46/797y, Bark 45/672y, Garner 39/291y
SCORING: Randy Pratt (K) 90pts, McDougald 30pts, Garner 24pts

1984 2-9

13 Arizona	23 WR Keith Cockett
28 Pacific	12 WR Rance McDougald
14 Oregon	21 T Keith Kartz
18 San Jose State	33 G Ron Zenker
19 Arizona State	14 C Mike Reed
6 Oregon State	9 G Mark Long
14 UCLA	17 T Mark Stephens
7 Southern Cal	31 TE Yancy Lindsey / Don Noble
14 Washington	44 QB Gale Gilbert
7 Washington St.	33 TB Dwight Garner / Mark Funderburk
10 Stanford	27 FB Ed Barbero / Scott Smith / Ron Story
	DL Doug Riesenberg
	DL Don James
	DL Mike Rusinek
	LB Pat McDonald / Marshall Hennington
	LB John Haina / John Johnson
	LB MilesTurpin
	LB Hardy Nickerson
	DB Ray Noble
	DB Ken Pettway
	DB Garey Williams
	DB Matt Grimes / David Carter

RUSHING: Barbero 120/554y, Garner 76/331y, Smith 47/188y
PASSING: Gilbert 166-306/1693y, 6TD, 53.9%
RECEIVING: Garner 46/376y, McDougald 31/473y, Cockett 29/386y
SCORING: Tom Gandsey (K) 42pts, Funderburk 30pts, McDougald 20pts

1985 4-7

48 San Jose State	21 WR Vincent Delgado
19 Washington St.	21 WR Keith Cockett / James Devers
20 Oregon State	23 T Keith Kartz
17 Arizona	23 G Blaise Smith
39 Missouri	32 C Brad Jackman / Chuck Steele
12 Washington	28 G Ron Zenker
27 Oregon	24 T Mark Stephens
7 UCLA	34 TE Don Noble / Darryl Ingram
8 Arizona State	30 QB Kevin Brown / Brian Bedford
14 Southern Cal	6 TB Marc Hicks / Dwight Garner
22 Stanford	24 FB Ed Barbaro
	DL Doug Riesenberg
	DL Majett Whiteside
	DL Marlin Wenstrom
	LB John Geringer
	LB Hardy Nickerson
	LB Mel McClanahan / John Johnson
	LB Brian Walgenbach
	DB Gary Hein
	DB Ken Pettway
	DB Darryl Stallworth / Garey Williams
	DB Matt Grimes

RUSHING: Barbaro 126/586y, Hicks 106/538y, Garner 96/407y
PASSING: Brown 122-227/1447y, 6TD, 53.7%
RECEIVING: Delgado 30/358y, Cockett 28/361y, Garner 28/282y
SCORING: Leland Rix (K) 45pts, Bedford 36pts, Hicks 30pts

1986 2-9

15 Boston College	21 WR Vincent Delgado / Wendell Peoples
31 Washington St.	21 WR James Devers
14 San Jose State	35 T Doug Riesenberg
18 Washington	50 G Steve Andersen
12 Oregon State	14 C Chuck Steele
10 UCLA	36 G Kam King
16 Arizona	33 T Dave Zawatson
9 Oregon	27 TE Don Noble
0 Arizona State	49 QB Troy Taylor/Kevin Brown/Brian Bedford
3 Southern Cal	28 TB Marc Hicks / Chris Richards
17 Stanford	11 FB Todd Powers / William Jackson
	DL Joe Nelms
	DL Majett Whiteside
	DL Natu Tuatagaloa
	LB John Geringer
	LB David Ortega
	LB Hardy Nickerson
	LB Ken Harvey
	DB Gary Hein
	DB Sidney Johnson
	DB Derek Taylor
	DB Darryl Stallworth

RUSHING: Hicks 98/357y, Richards 80/269y, Powers 66/249y
PASSING: Taylor 92-160/891y, 1TD, 57.5%
RECEIVING: Devers 40/582y, Hicks 34/345y, Richards 26/135y
SCORING: Leland Rix (K) 44pts, Bedford, Hicks & Jackson 18pts

1987 3-6-2

42 Pacific	0 WR Mike Ford
25 San Jose State	27 WR Michael Smith
23 Minnesota	32 T Stu McElderry
14 Southern Cal	31 G Tony Smith / Lou Sergeant
12 Tennessee	38 C Robert Dos Remedios
23 Arizona	23 G Kam King
18 UCLA	42 T Dave Zawatson
20 Oregon	6 TE Darryl Ingram / Brian Bedford
38 Arizona State	20 QB Troy Taylor
7 Stanford	31 TB Chris Richards / Tyrone Moore
17 Washington St.	17 FB Todd Powers
	DL Joe Nelms
	DL Majett Whiteside
	DL Natu Tuatagaloa
	LB David Ortega
	LB Steve Hendrickson
	LB Joel Dickson (DT) / DeWayne Odom
	LB Ken Harvey
	DB John Hardy
	DB Travis Oliver
	DB Jeff Ebert / Derek Taylor
	DB Darryl Stallworth

RUSHING: Richards 157/668y, Moore 69/362y, Powers 18/85y
PASSING: Taylor 169-278/2081y, 18TD, 60.8%
RECEIVING: Bedford 39/515y, Ford 33/479y, Powers 31/293y
SCORING: Richards 48pts, Robbie Keen (K) 45pts, Bedford 24pts

1988 5-5-1

30 Pacific	7 WR Mike Ford / Brian Treggs
16 Oregon State	17 WR Faasamala Tagaloa / Michael Smith
52 Kansas	14 T Troy Auzenne
21 San Jose State	14 G Steve Andersen
13 Washington St.	44 C Robert Dos Remedios
21 UCLA	38 G Tony Smith
31 Temple	14 T Dave Zawatson
10 Arizona	7 TE Darryl Ingram
3 Southern Cal	35 QB Troy Taylor
27 Washington	28 TB Chris Richards / Tim Jenkins
19 Stanford	19 FB Todd Powers
	DL Joe Nelms
	DL Majett Whiteside
	DL Natu Tuatagaloa
	LB Dan Slevin
	LB David Ortega
	LB Steve Hendrickson
	LB De Wayne Odom
	DB John Hardy
	DB Travis Oliver
	DB Derek Taylor
	DB Ron English / Darrin Greer

RUSHING: Richards 162/729y, Jenkins 75/289y, Powers 64/279y
PASSING: Taylor 202-330/2416y, 16TD, 61.2%
RECEIVING: Powers 45/378y, Ingram 37/513y, Tagaloa 29/362y
SCORING: Robbie Keen (K) 86pts, Ingram 36pts, Richards 30pts

1989 4-7

19 Oregon	35 WR Brian Treggs
3 Miami	31 WR Michael Smith
20 Wisconsin	14 T Troy Auzenne
6 UCLA	24 G James Richards
26 San Jose State	21 C Steve Gordon
15 Southern Cal	31 G Tony Smith
16 Washington	29 T Ernie Rogers
14 Oregon State	25 TE Brent Woodall / Faasamala Tagaloa
29 Arizona	28 QB Troy Taylor
38 Washington St.	26 TB Anthony Wallace
14 Stanford	26 FB Greg Zomalt
	DL Rhett Hall
	DL John Belli
	DL Chidi Ahanotu / Al Casner
	LB DeWayne Odom
	LB David Ortega
	LB Castle Redmond
	LB Dan Slevin
	DB David Wilson
	DB Doug Parrish
	DB Dwayne Jones / Ray Sanders
	DB Darrin Greer

RUSHING: Wallace 150/560y, Zomalt 84/308y
PASSING: Taylor 220-394/2738y, 16TD, 55.8%
RECEIVING: Treggs 54/746y, Zomalt 29/317y, Smith 28/439y
SCORING: Robbie Keen (K) 46pts, Zomalt 36pts, Tagaloa & Treggs 24pts

1990 7-4-1

28 Wisconsin	12 WR Brian Treggs
24 Miami	52 WR Sean Dawkins
31 Washington St.	41 T Troy Auzenne
30 Arizona	25 G James Richards
35 San Jose State	34 C Steve Gordon
31 Arizona State	24 G Todd Steussie
38 UCLA	31 T Ernie Rogers
7 Washington	46 TE Mike Caldwell / Brent Woodall
31 Southern Cal	31 QB Mike Pawlawski
28 Oregon	3 TB Anthony Wallace / Russell White
25 Stanford	27 FB Greg Zomalt
17 Wyoming■	15 DL Rhett Hall
	DL John Belli
	DL Joel Dickson
	LB Cornell Collier
	LB DeWayne Odom
	LB Castle Redmond
	LB Bill Ayer / Eric Zomalt
	DB John Hardy
	DB David Wilson / Chris Cannon
	DB Ray Sanders / Darryl Brown
	DB Ron English

RUSHING: Wallace 220/1002y, White 180/1000y, Zomalt 46/236y
PASSING: Pawlawski 179-299/2069y, 17TD, 59.9%
RECEIVING: Treggs 45/564y, Zomalt 30/318y, Caldwell 25/307y
SCORING: White 84pts, Robbie Keen (K) 62pts, Treggs 38pts

1991 10-2

86 Pacific	24 WR Brian Treggs
42 Purdue	18 WR Sean Dawkins
23 Arizona	21 T Troy Auzenne
27 UCLA	24 G Darryl Pessler
45 Oregon	7 C Steve Gordon
17 Washington	24 G Eric Mahlum
41 San Jose State	20 T Todd Steussie
52 Southern Cal	30 TE Mike Caldwell / Brent Woodall
27 Oregon State	14 QB Mike Pawlawski
25 Arizona State	6 TB Russell White / Lindsey Chapman
21 Stanford	38 FB Greg Zomalt
37 Clemson■	13 DL Jason Wilborn / Chidi Ahanotu
	DL Ryan Peery
	DL Mack Travis
	LB Cornell Collier
	LB Jason Wilborn
	LB Jerrott Willard
	LB Mick Barsala
	DB Chris Cannon
	DB Wolf Barber / Jody Graham
	DB David Wilson
	DB Eric Zomalt

RUSHING: White 241/1177y, Chapman 121/675y, Zomalt 39/243y
PASSING: Pawlawski 191-316/2517y, 21TD, 60.4%
RECEIVING: Treggs 43/643y, Dawkins 40/723y, Caldwell 27/342y
SCORING: White & Doug Brien (K) 98pts, Dawkins 66pts

1992 4-7

46 San Jose State	16 WR Sean Dawkins / Jeff Jones
14 Purdue	41 WR Mike Caldwell / Damien Semien
27 Kansas	23 T Todd Steussie
42 Oregon State	0 G Brian Thure
16 Washington	35 C Eric Mahlum
24 Southern Cal	27 G Todd Blackwell
17 Arizona	24 T Al Casner
48 UCLA	12 TE Steve Stafford / Chris Carpenter
17 Oregon	37 QB Dave Barr
12 Arizona State	28 TB Russell White / Lindsey Chapman
21 Stanford	41 FB Greg Zomalt
	DL Steve Roseman
	DL Mack Travis / Stafford Evans
	DL Chidi Ahanotu
	DL Brad Bowers
	LB Michael Davis
	LB Jerrott Willard
	LB Mick Barsala / Paul Joiner
	DB Issac Booth
	DB Wolf Barber
	DB Tyrone Edwards / Je'Rod Cherry
	DB Eric Zomalt

RUSHING: White 206/1069y, Chapman 87/264y, Zomalt 53/177y
PASSING: Barr 199-344/2343y, 19TD, 57.8%
RECEIVING: Dawkins 65/1070y, Zomalt 31/184y, Semien 24/262y
SCORING: Dawkins 84pts, Doug Brien (K) 76pts, White 54pts

1993 9-4

27 UCLA	25 WR Mike Caldwell
45 San Diego State	25 WR Damien Semien / Iheanyi Uwaezuoke
58 Temple	0 T Todd Steussie
46 San Jose State	13 G Frank Beede
42 Oregon	41 C Eric Mahlum
23 Washington	24 G Todd Blackwell / Ben Lynch
7 Washington St.	34 T Brian Thure
14 Southern Cal	42 TE Chris Carpenter / Matt Johnson
0 Arizona State	30 QB Dave Barr
24 Arizona	20 TB Lindsey Chapman / Reynard Rutherford
46 Stanford	17 FB Marty Holly / Tyrone Edwards
42 Hawaii	18 DL Brad Bowers / Duane Clemons
37 Iowa■	3 DL Bill Ayer
	DL Stafford Evans
	DL Regan Upshaw
	LB Paul Joiner / Maurice Johnson
	LB Jerrott Willard
	LB Michael Davis / James Stallworth
	DB Issac Booth / Kevin Devine
	DB Artis Houston / Ricky Spears
	DB Tim Manning / Je'Rod Cherry
	DB Eric Zomalt / Dante DePaola

RUSHING: Chapman 207/1037y, Rutherford 116/578y
PASSING: Barr 187-275/2619y, 21TD, 68%
RECEIVING: Caldwell 55/962y, Uwaezuoke 25/422y
SCORING: Chapman 102pts

1994 4-7

20 San Diego State	22 WR Na'il Benjamin
7 Hawaii	21 WR Iheanyi Uwaezuoke
25 Arizona State	21 T Brian Thure
55 San Jose State	0 G Todd Stewart (T) / Jeremy Becker
26 UCLA	7 C Ben Lynch
7 Oregon	23 G Frank Beede
0 Southern Cal	61 T Randy Nonhof
23 Washington St.	26 TE Sean Bullard / Tony Gonzalez
6 Arizona	13 QB Dave Barr/Pat Barnes/Kerry McGonigal
19 Washington	31 TB Reynard Rutherford
24 Stanford	23 FB Tyrone Edwards / Johnny Tavake
	DL Andy Jacobs
	DL Greg Webb
	DL Brandon Whiting
	DL Regan Upshaw
	LB Kevin Cunningham / Andre Rhodes
	LB Jerrott Willard
	LB James Stallworth
	DB Kevin Devine / Artis Houston
	DB Je'Rod Cherry
	DB Darrell Miles / Matt Clizbe
	DB Ricky Spears

RUSHING: Rutherford 163/713y, Edwards 110/521y
PASSING: Barr 95-144/1077y, 5TD, 66%
Barnes 65-97/738y, 3TD, 67%
RECEIVING: Uwaezuoke 56/716y, Benjamin 45/587y,
Rutherford 27/175y
SCORING: Ryan Longwell (K) 44pts, Edwards 38pts,
Uwaezuoke 30pts

1995 3-8

9 San Diego State	33 WR Na'il Benjamin
24 Fresno State	25 WR Iheanyi Uwaezuoke
40 San Jose State	7 T Tarik Glenn
15 Arizona	20 G Drake Porter / Jeremy Becker
16 Southern Cal	26 C Ben Lynch
30 Oregon	52 G Jeremy Newberry / Yauger Williams
13 Oregon State	12 T Todd Stewart
16 UCLA	33 TE Tony Gonzalez
27 Washington St.	11 QB Pat Barnes
29 Arizona State	38 TB Reynard Rutherford / Tarik Smith
24 Stanford	29 FB Johnny Tavake / Brent Malili
	DL Andy Jacobs
	DL Brandon Whiting / Evan Collins
	DL Brent Jones
	DL Regan Upshaw
	LB Duane Clemons / James Stallworth
	LB Marlon McWilson
	LB Andre Rhodes / Justin Flagg
	DB Kevin Devine
	DB Maurice Johnson / Marquise Smith
	DB Dante DePaola
	DB Je'Rod Cherry

RUSHING: Rutherford 191/868y, Smith 74/391y
PASSING: Barnes 197-362/2685y, 17TD, 54.4%
RECEIVING: Benjamin 52/594y, Shaw 38/658y, Gonzalez 37/541y
SCORING: Ryan Longwell (K) 57pts, Shaw, Rutherford &
Benjamin 36pts

1996 6-6

45 San Jose State	25 WR Na'il Benjamin / Dameane Douglas
42 San Diego State	37 WR Bobby Shaw
33 Nevada	15 T Tarik Glenn
48 Oregon State	42 G John Welbourn / Kursten Sheridan
22 Southern Cal	15 C Jeremy Newberry (G) / Caleb Brown
18 Washington St.	21 G Drake Parker / Brian Shields
29 UCLA	38 T Todd Stewart
56 Arizona	55 TE Tony Gonzalez
7 Arizona State	35 QB Pat Barnes
23 Oregon	40 TB Brandon Willis / Deltha O'Neal/ T. Smith
21 Stanford	42 FB Marc Vera / Brent Malili
38 Navy■	42 DL Jerry DeLoach / Chris Easley
	DL Brent Jones / Justin Flagg
	DL Brandon Whiting
	DL Andy Jacobs / Jeremiah Porter
	LB Nate Geldermann / Rasheed Hibler
	LB Matt Beck
	LB Andre Rhodes
	DB Kevin Devine
	DB Kato Serwanga / David Burnside
	DB Derrick Gardner / Pete DeStefano
	DB Marquise Smith / Don Lonon

RUSHING: Willis 187/701y, O'Neal 80/418y, Smith 56/400y
PASSING: Barnes 250-420/3499y, 31TD, 59.5%
RECEIVING: Shaw 58/888y, Benjamin 45/719y, Gonzalez 44/699y
SCORING: Ryan Longwell (K) 70pts, Shaw 54pts, Willis &
Benjamin 36pts

1997 3-8

35 Houston	3 WR Dameane Douglas
40 Oklahoma	36 WR Bobby Shaw
17 Southern Cal	27 T Todd Welbourn
34 Louisiana Tech	41 G Kevin Swillis / Kursten Sheridan
3 Washington	30 C Jeremy Newberry
37 Washington St.	63 G Yauger Williams / Drake Parker
17 UCLA	35 T Brian Shields
33 Oregon State	14 TE Brian Surgener / Reed Diehl
21 Arizona State	28 QB Justin Vedder
38 Arizona	41 TB Tarik Smith / Marcus Fields
20 Stanford	21 FB Joshua White / Marc Vera
	DL John McLaughlin / Mawuko Tugbenyoh
	DL Jerry DeLoach / Jeremiah Parker
	DL Brandon Whiting
	DL Andre Carter / James Gibson
	LB Albert Dorsey / Justin Flagg
	LB Matt Beck
	LB Sekou Sanyika
	DB Derrick Gardner
	DB Kato Serwanga / Chidi Iwuoma
	DB Pete DeStefano / David Burnside
	DB Marquise Smith

RUSHING: Smith 162/636y, Fields 98/419y, White 51/180y
PASSING: Vedder 221-390/2718y, 20TD, 56.7%
RECEIVING: Shaw 75/1093y, Douglas 53/610y, Vera 22/198y
SCORING: Shaw 60pts, Smith 44pts, Ignacio Brache (K) 36pts

1998 5-6

14 Houston	10 WR Joel Young / Bruce Pierre
3 Nebraska	24 WR Dameane Douglas
13 Oklahoma	12 T John Welbourn
24 Washington St.	14 G Kevin Swillis
32 Southern Cal	31 C John Romero
13 Washington	21 G Kevin Doherty / Brandon Ludwig
16 UCLA	28 T Langston Walker
20 Oregon State	19 TE A.J. Kunkle / Brian Surgener
22 Arizona State	55 QB Justin Vedder
23 Arizona	27 TB Marcus Fields
3 Stanford	10 FB Saleem Muhammed / Joshua White
	DL John McLaughlin / Mawuko Tugbenyoh
	DL Jacob Waasdorp
	DL Jerry DeLoach
	DL Andre Carter / Jeremiah Parker
	LB Albert Dorsey / Scott Fujita
	LB Matt Beck
	LB Sekou Sanyika
	DB Chidi Iwuoma / Mark Orr
	DB Derrick Gardner / Deltha O'Neal
	DB Pete DeStefano / Damien Marzet
	DB Marquise Smith

RUSHING: Fields 163/734y, Muhammed 36/128y
PASSING: Vedder 210-386/2322y, 11TD, 54.4%
RECEIVING: Douglas 100/1150y, Young 28/281y, Fields 19/232y
SCORING: Fields 36pts, Douglas 30pts, Ignacio Brache (K) 25pts

1999 4-7

21 Rutgers	7 WR Michael Ainsworth / Joel Young
0 Nebraska	45 WR Ronnie Davenport / Philip Pipersburg
24 Arizona St. (F-L)	23 T Reed Diehl
7 Washington St.	31 G Brandon Ludwig / Scott Tercero
28 BYU	38 C John Romero
17 UCLA	0 G Kevin Doherty
27 Washington	31 T Langston Walker
17 Southern Cal	7 TE Brian Surgener
7 Oregon State	17 QB Kyle Boller
19 Oregon	24 TB Joe Igber / Marcus Fields (WR)
13 Stanford	31 FB Saleem Muhammed / Joshua White
	DL Mawuko Tugbenyoh
	DL Jacob Waasdorp
	DL Jerry DeLoach / Daniel Nwangwu
	DL Andre Carter / Jeremiah Parker
	LB Keith Miller / Jamaal Cherry
	LB Matt Beck
	LB Sekou Sanyika / Scott Fujita
	DB Chidi Iwuoma
	DB Deltha O'Neal
	DB Pete DeStefano
	DB Damien Marzett / Dewey Hale

RUSHING: Igber 148/694y, Fields 98/368y, Muhammed 35/112y
PASSING: Boller 100-259/1303y, 9TD, 38.6%
RECEIVING: Ainsworth 34/499y, Davenport 15/211y,
Pipersburg 13/85y
SCORING: O'Neal 36pts, Mark Jensen (K) 24pts, 3 tied w/ 12pts

2000 3-8

24 Utah	21 WR Derek Swafford / Philip Pipersburg
15 Illinois	17 WR Geoff McArthur / Chase Lyman
3 Fresno State	17 T Langston Walker / Roy Jackson
17 Washington St.	21 G Brandon Ludwig
10 Arizona State	30 C Reed Diehl (T) / Nolan Bluntzer
46 UCLA	38 G Scott Tercero
24 Washington	36 T Mark Wilson
28 Southern Cal	16 TE Brian Surgener / Keala Keanaaina
32 Oregon State	32 QB Kyle Boller
17 Oregon	25 TB Joe Igber / Joseph Echema
30 Stanford	36 FB Ryan Stanger / Saleem Muhammad
	DL Tully Banta-Cain / Sean Paga
	DL Josh Beckham / Daniel Nwangwu
	DL Jacob Waasdorp
	DL Andre Carter
	LB Scott Fujita
	LB John Klotsche / Jason Smith
	LB Matt Nixon / Chris Ball
	DB Jemeel Powell / Harold Pearson
	DB Chidi Iwuoma
	DB Nnamdi Asomugha
	DB Dewey Hale / Bert Watts

RUSHING: Igber 195/901y, Muhammad 61/264y, Echema 58/215y
PASSING: Boller 163-349/2121y, 15TD, 46.7%
RECEIVING: Swafford 25/335y, Igber 23/229y, McArthur 20/336y
SCORING: Mark Jensen (K) 58pts, Igber 42pts, Echema 24pts

2001 1-10

17 Illinois	44 WR Charon Arnold / Burl Toler
16 BYU	44 WR LaShaun Ward (CB) / Sean Currin
20 Washington St.	51 T Langston Walker
28 Washington	31 G Brandon Ludwig (C) / Nolan Bluntzer (C)
7 Oregon	48 C Ryan Jones
17 UCLA	56 G Scott Tercero
10 Oregon State	19 T Mark Wilson
24 Arizona	38 TE Tom Swoboda / Jordon Hunter
14 Southern Cal	55 QB Kyle Boller / Reggie Robertson
28 Stanford	35 TB Joe Igber / Terrell Williams
20 Rutgers	10 FB Marcus Fields
	DL Tully Banta-Cain
	DL Daniel Nwangwu / Lorenzo Alexander
	DL Josh Beckham
	DL Tom Canada/Tosh Lupoi/J. Gustaveson
	LB Scott Fujita
	LB Matt Nixon
	LB John Klotsche
	DB Atari Callen / Ray Carmel
	DB James Bethea / Jameel Powell
	DB Nnamdi Asomugha
	DB Dewey Hale / Bert Watts

RUSHING: Williams 160/688y, Igber 94/399y
PASSING: Boller 133-271/1741y, 12TD, 49.1%
RECEIVING: Arnold 52/606y, Fields 26/301y, Ward 18/416y
SCORING: Mark Jensen (K) 55pts, Williams 30pts, Ward &
Igber 24pts

2002 7-5

70 Baylor	22 WR Geoff McArthur / LaShaun Ward
34 N. Mexico St.	13 WR Jonathan Makonnen
46 Michigan State	22 T Mark Wilson
21 Air Force	23 G Scott Tercero
38 Washington St.	48 C Ryan Jones
34 Washington	27 G Jonathan Giesel
28 Southern Cal	30 T Chris Murphy
17 UCLA	12 TE Tom Swoboda
13 Oregon State	24 QB Kyle Boller
55 Arizona State	38 TB Joe Igber
41 Arizona	52 FB/TE Manderino / Brandon Hall
30 Stanford	7 DL Tom Canada / Josh Gustaveson
	DL Daniel Nwangwu
	DL Lorenzo Alexander / Josh Beckham
	DL Tully Banta-Cain / Jamaal Cherry
	LB Matt Nixon / Wendell Hunter
	LB Marcus Daniels
	LB Paul Ugenti / Calvin Hosey
	DB Nnamdi Asomugha
	DB Jemeel Powell
	DB Bert Watts
	DB James Bethea / Donnie McCleskey

RUSHING: Igber 241/1130y. Terrell Williams (TB) 37/139y
PASSING: Boller 225-421/2815y, 28TD, 53.4%
RECEIVING: Makonnen 54/682y, Swoboda 42/451y, Ward 39/709y
SCORING: Mark Jensen (K) 107pts, Igber & Ward 60pts

2003 8-6

28 Kansas State	42 WR Geoff McArthur
34 Southern Miss	2 WR Burl Toler / Jonathan Makonnen
21 Colorado State	23 T Mark Wilson
24 Utah	31 G Jonathan Giesel / Aaron Merz
31 Illinois	24 C Nolan Bluntzer / Marvin Philip
34 Southern Cal	31 G Ryan O'Callaghan / David Hays
21 Oregon State	35 T Chris Murphy
20 UCLA	23 TE Brandon Hall / Garrett Cross
42 Arizona	14 QB Aaron Rodgers / Reggie Robertson
51 Arizona State	23 TB Adimchinobe Echemandu/J.J. Arrington
17 Oregon	21 FB/WR Chris Manderino / Chase Lyman
54 Washington	7 DL Monte Parson / Ryan Riddle
28 Stanford	16 DL Lorenzo Alexander
52 Virginia Tech■	49 DL Josh Beckham / Matt Malele
	DL Tosh Lupoi
	LB Wendell Hunter
	LB Joe Maningo/Brian Tremblay/Sid Slater
	LB Francis Blay-Miezah
	DB James Bethea / Daymeion Hughes
	DB Harrison Smith / Timothy Mixon
	DB Ryan Gutierrez / Matt Giordano
	DB Donnie McCleskey

RUSHING: Echemandu 238/1195y, Arrington 107/607y, Marcus O'Keith (TB) 40/230y
PASSING: Rodgers 215-349/2903y, 19TD, 61.6%
RECEIVING: McArthur 85/1504y, Toler 48/609y, Echemandu 22/185y
SCORING: Tyler Fredrickson (K) 99pts, Echemandu 80pts, McArthur 60pts

2004 10-2

56 Air Force	14 WR Geoff McArthur / Jonathan Makkonen
41 New Mexico St.	14 WR Robert Jordan/Chase Lyman/Burl Toler
49 Oregon State	7 T Andrew Cameron
17 Southern Cal	23 G Jonathan Giesel
45 UCLA	28 C Marvin Philip / Scott Smith
38 Arizona	0 G Aaron Merz
27 Arizona State	0 T Ryan O'Callaghan
28 Oregon	27 TE Garrett Cross / Craig Stevens
42 Washington	12 QB Aaron Rodgers
41 Stanford	6 TB J.J. Arrington / Marshawn Lynch
26 Southern Miss	16 FB Chris Manderino
31 Texas Tech■	45 DL Ryan Riddle
	DL Lorenzo Alexander
	DL Brandon Mebane
	DL Tom Sverchek
	LB Wendell Hunter
	LB Joe Maningo / Sid Slater
	LB Francis Blay-Miezah / Ryan Foltz
	DB Harrison Smith / Tim Mixon
	DB Daymeion Hughes
	DB Ryan Gutierrez
	DB Matt Giordano / Donnie McCleskey

RUSHING: Arrington 289/2018y, Lynch 71/628y, Rodgers 74/126y
PASSING: Rodgers 209-316/2566y, 24TD, 66.1%
RECEIVING: McArthur 57/862y, Jordan 29/332y, Cross 28/339y
SCORING: Arrington 90pts, Tom Schneider (K) 76pts, Lynch 60pts

2005 8-4

41 Sacramento St.	3 WR Robert Jordan
56 Washington	17 WR DeSean Jackson
35 Illinois	20 T Scott Smith / Andrew Cameron
41 New Mexico St.	13 G Erik Robertson / Noris Malele
28 Arizona	0 C Marvin Philip
40 UCLA	47 G Aaron Merz / Bryan Deemer
20 Oregon State	23 T Ryan O'Callaghan / Jon Murphy
42 Washington St.	38 TE Craig Stevens
20 Oregon	27 QB Joe Ayoob / Steve Levy
10 Southern Cal	35 TB Marshawn Lynch / Justin Forsett
27 Stanford	3 FB/WRC.Manderino/Lavelle Hawkins
35 BYU■	28 DL Phillip Mbakogu / Tosh Lupoi
	DL Matthew Malele / Abu Ma'afala
	DL Brandon Mebane
	DL Nu'u Tafisi
	LB Ryan Foltz / Mickey Pimentel
	LB Desmond Bishop
	LB Anthony Felder/Greg Van Hoesen
	DB Daymeion Hughes
	DB Tim Mixon
	DB Harrison Smith
	DB Donnie McCleskey

RUSHING: Lynch 196/1246y, Forsett 132/999y, Marcus O'Keith (RB) 22/243y
PASSING: Ayoob 125-254/1707y, 15TD, 49.2%, Levy 32-52/439y, 4TD, 61.5%
RECEIVING: Jackson 38/601y, Jordan 34/455y, Hawkins 18/171y
SCORING: Tom Schneider (K) 77pts, Lynch 60pts, Jackson 48pts

2006 10-3

18 Tennessee	35 WR Robert Jordan
42 Minnesota	17 WR DeSean Jackson
42 Portland State	16 T Andrew Cameron / Mike Tepper
49 Arizona State	21 G Erik Robertson
41 Oregon State	13 C Alex Mack
45 Oregon	24 G Noris Malele / Brian De La Puente
21 Washington St.	3 T John Gibson / Scott Smith
31 Washington	24 TE Craig Stevens / Eric Beegun
38 UCLA	24 QB Nate Longshore
20 Arizona	24 TB Marshawn Lynch / Justin Forsett
9 Southern Cal	23 FB/WR Byron Storer / L. Hawkins
26 Stanford	17 DL Abu Ma'afala
45 Texas A&M■	10 DL Brandon Mebane / Tyson Aluala
	DL Matthew Malele
	DL Nu'u Tafisi
	LB Mickey Pimentel / Justin Moye
	LB Desmond Bishop
	LB Worrell Williams / Zack Follett
	DB Daymeion Hughes
	DB Syd'Quan Thompson
	DB Bernard Hicks / Thomas DeCoud
	DB Brandon Hampton

RUSHING: Lynch 223/1356y, Forsett 119/626y, Marcus O'Keith (RB) 22/104y
PASSING: Longshore 227-377/3021y, 24TD, 60.2%
RECEIVING: Jackson 59/1060y, Hawkins 46/705y, Jordan 46/571y
SCORING: Tom Schneider (K) 97pts, Lynch 90pts, Jackson 76pts

2007 7-6

45 Tennessee	31 WR Robert Jordan / Lavelle Hawkins
34 Colorado State	28 WR DeSean Jackson
42 Louisiana Tech	12 T Mike Gibson
45 Arizona	27 G Brian De La Puente
31 Oregon	24 C Alex Mack
28 Oregon State	31 G Noris Malele
21 UCLA	30 T Mike Tepper
20 Arizona State	31 TE Craig Stevens
20 Washington St.	17 QB Nate Longshore / Kevin Riley
17 Southern Cal	24 TB Justin Forsett
23 Washington	37 FB/TE Will Ta'ufo'ou / Julian Arthur
13 Stanford	20 DL John Allen/Tad Smith/Rulon Davis
42 Air Force■	36 DL Cody Jones / Matt Malele
	DL Mika Kane / Derrick Hill
	DL Tyson Alualu / Cameron Jordan
	LB Zack Follett / Mike Mohamed
	LB Worrell Williams / Greg Van Hoesen
	LB Anthony Felder / Justin Moye
	DB Syd'Quan Thompson
	DB Brandon Hampton / Chris Conte
	DB Thomas DeCoud
	DB Bernard Hicks / Marcus Ezeff

RUSHING: Forsett 305/1546y, Jahvid Best (TB) 29/221y, James Montgomery (TB) 36/171y
PASSING: Longshore 230-384/2580y, 16TD, 59.9%, Riley 36-56/563y, 5TD, 64.3%
RECEIVING: Hawkins 72/872y, Jackson 65/762y, Jordan 47/689y
SCORING: Forsett 90pts, Jordan Kay (K) 87pts, Jackson 48pts

2008 9-4

38 Michigan State	31 WR Sean Young / Verran Tucker
66 Washington St.	3 WR LaReylle Cunningham/Nyan Boateng
27 Maryland	35 T Mark Boskovich / Chris Guarnero
42 Colorado State	7 G Mark Boskovich / Chris Guarnero
24 Arizona State	14 C Alex Mack
27 Arizona	42 G Noris Malele / Justin Cheadle
41 UCLA	20 T Chet Teofilo / Donovan Edwards
26 Oregon	16 TE Cameron Morrah
3 Southern Cal	10 QB Kevin Riley / Nate Longshore
21 Oregon State	34 TB Jahvid Best / Shane Vereen
37 Stanford	16 FB/WR Will Ta'ufo'ou / Jeremy Ross
48 Washington	7 DL Cameron Jordan / Rulon Davis
24 Miami■	17 DL Derrick Hill / Mika Kane
	DL Tyson Alualu
	LB Zack Follett
	LB Worrell Williams
	LB Anthony Felder
	LB Mike Mohamed / Eddie Young
	DB Syd'Quan Thompson
	DB Darian Hagan / Chris Conte
	DB Brett Johnson / Bernard Hicks
	DB Marcus Ezeff

RUSHING: Best 194/1580y, Vereen 142/715y
PASSING: Riley 112-221/1360y, 14TD, 50/7%, Longshore 93-164/1051y, 10TD, 56.7%
RECEIVING: Boateng 29/439y, Morrah 27/326y, Best 27/246y
SCORING: Best 96pts, Giorgio Tavecchio (K) 52pts, Morrah 48pts

2009 8-5

52 Maryland	13 WR Marvin Jones / Alex Lagemann
59 E. Washington	7 WR Jeremy Ross / Verran Tucker
35 Minnesota	21 T Mike Tepper
3 Oregon	42 G Matt Summers-Gavin / Mark Boskovich
3 Southern Cal	30 C Chris Guarnero
45 UCLA	26 G Justin Cheadle
49 Washington St.	17 T Mitchell Schwartz
23 Arizona State	21 TE Anthony Miller / Skylar Curran
14 Oregon State	31 QB Kevin Riley
24 Arizona	16 TB Jahvid Best / Shane Vereen
34 Stanford	28 FB/TB Brian Hoilley / Isi Sofel
10 Washington	42 DL Tyson Alualu
27 Utah■	37 DL Derrick Hill / Aaron Tipoti
	DL Cameron Jordan / Kendrick Payne
	LB Eddie Young
	LB Devin Bishop
	LB Mike Mohamed
	LB D.J. Holt / Michael Kendricks
	DB Syd'Quan Thompson / Darian Hagan
	DB Josh Hill / Bryant Nnabuife
	DB Marcus Ezeff / Sean Cattouse
	DB Brett Johnson / Chris Conte

RUSHING: Vereen 183/952y, Best 141/867y, Covaughn DeBoskie-Johnson (TB) 31/211y
PASSING: Riley 209-382/2850y, 18TD, 54.7%
RECEIVING: Jones 43/651y, Tucker 29/453y, Miller 26/357y, Vereen 25/244y, Ross 22/344y
SCORING: Best 96pts, Vereen 84pts, Vince D'Amato (K) 52pts

2010 5-7

52 Cal Davis	3 WR Marvin Jones / Jeremy Ross
52 Colorado	7 WR Keenan Allen / Michael Calvin
31 Nevada	52 T Mitch Schwartz
9 Arizona	10 G Brian Schwenke
35 UCLA	7 C Chris Guarnero / Dominic Galas
14 Southern Cal	48 G Justin Cheadle / Matt Summers-Gavin
50 Arizona State	17 T Donovan Edwards
7 Oregon State	35 TE Anthony Miller
20 Washington St.	13 TE/FB Spencer Ladner / Eric Stevens
13 Oregon	15 QB Kevin Riley / Brock Mansion
14 Stanford	48 TB Shane Vereen / Isi Sofele
13 Washington	16 DL Cameron Jordan
	DL Derrick Hill / Kendrick Payne
	DL Ernest Owusu / Trevor Guyton
	LB Mychal Kendricks
	LB D.J. Holt
	LB Mike Mohamed / D.J. Campbell
	LB Keith Browner
	DB Marc Anthony / Bryant Nnabuife
	DB Darian Hagan / Steve Williams
	DB Chris Conte
	DB Josh Hill / Sean Cattouse

RUSHING: Vereen 231/1167y, Sofele 69/338y, Allen 18/136y
PASSING: Riley 111-186/1409y, 60%, Mansion 67-136/646y, 2TD, 48.9%
RECEIVING: Jones 50/766y, Allen 46/490y, Vereen 22/209y
SCORING: Vereen 96pts, Giorgio Tavecchio (K) 70pts, Allen 36pts

CLEMSON

Clemson University (Founded 1889)
Clemson, South Carolina
Nickname: Tigers
Colors: Purple and Orange
Stadium: Frank Howard Field at Memorial Stadium (1942) 80,301
Conference Affiliations: Atlantic Coast (1953-present)

CAREER RUSHING YARDS	Attempts	Yards
Raymond Priester (1994-97)	805	3966
James Davis (2005-08)	753	3881
C.J. Spiller (2006-09)	606	3547
Travis Zachery (1998-2001)	691	3058
Kenny Flowers (1983-86)	590	2914
Terry Allen (1987-89)	523	2778
Woodrow Dantzler (1998-2001)	591	2761
Buddy Gore (1966-68)	600	2571
Ray Yauger (1968-70)	555	2439
Chuck McSwain (1979-82)	483	2320

CAREER PASSING YARDS	Comp.-Att.	Yards
Charlie Whitehurst (2002-05)	817-1368	9665
Woodrow Dantzler (1998-2001)	460-796	6037
Cullen Harper (2005-08)	518-815	5762
Nealon Greene (1994-97)	458-805	5719
Kyle Parker (2009-10)	401-710	4739
Rodney Williams (1985-88)	333-717	4647
Steve Fuller (1975-78)	287-554	4359
Tommy Kendrick (1969-71)	303-644	3893
Homer Jordan (1979-82)	250-479	3643
Brandon Streeter (1996-99)	294-519	3504

CAREER RECEIVING YARDS	Catches	Yards
Aaron Kelly (2005-08)	232	2733
Terry Smith (1990-93)	162	2681
Perry Tuttle (1978-81)	150	2534
Rod Gardner (1997-2000)	166	2498
Derrick Hamilton (2001-03)	167	2312
Jerry Butler (1975-78)	139	2223
Airese Currie (2001-04)	138	2030
Jacoby Ford (2006-09)	143	1986
Brian Wofford (1996-99)	138	1857
Chansi Stuckey (2003-06)	141	1760

SEASON RUSHING YARDS	Attempts	Yards
Raymond Priester (1996)	257	1345
Raymond Priester (1995)	238	1322
Terrence Flagler (1986)	192	1258
C.J. Spiller (2009)	216	1212
Kenny Flowers (1985)	227	1200

SEASON PASSING YARDS	Comp.-Att.	Yards
Charlie Whitehurst (2003)	288-465	3561
Cullen Harper (2007)	282-433	2991
Cullen Harper (2008)	221-360	2601
Woodrow Dantzler (2001)	203-334	2578
Kyle Parker (2009)	205-369	2526

SEASON RECEIVING YARDS	Catches	Yards
Rod Gardner (1999)	80	1084
Aaron Kelly (2007)	88	1081
Rod Gardner (2000)	58	1050
Derrick Hamilton (2003)	62	1026
Perry Tuttle (1980)	53	915

GAME RUSHING YARDS	Attempts	Yards
Raymond Priester (1995 vs. Duke)	32	263
Cliff Austin (1982 vs. Duke)	27	260
Don King (1952 vs. Fordham)	33	234

GAME PASSING YARDS	Comp.-Att.	Yards
Charlie Whitehurst (2002 vs. Duke)	34-52	420
Cullen Harper (2007 vs. Virginia Tech)	38-66	372
Brandon Streeter (1999 vs. Virginia)	24-32	343
Will Proctor (2006 vs. Boston College)	25-40	343

GAME RECEIVING YARDS	Catches	Yards
Rod Gardner (2000 vs. North Carolina)	7	182
Derrick Hamilton (2003 vs. Maryland)	7	175
Aaron Kelly (2007 vs. Virginia Tech)	11	174

GREATEST COACH:

There is no coach held in more loving esteem that the late, home-spun Frank Howard, who coached the Clemson Tigers from 1940 to 1969. Howard may not have fashioned football's most magnificent winning percentage at .580 on 165-118-12, but for every game he ever coached there came from his lips a great and witty observation that probably no one else would ever have thought of.

Howard signed a one-year contract in 1940, lost the paperwork, and never had another contract the rest of his career.

Howard won only three bowl games in six tries, but he coached five Atlantic Coast Conference titles. If he could look back today, Howard might thank his lucky stars for schedules that included Presbyterian College, The Citadel, and Furman, nearby schools against which Howard enjoyed a 38-1 career mark. Speaking of schedules, the Clemson slate in the mid- to late-1960s just about put Howard out of business because outside the Atlantic Coast Conference his Tigers were taking on Alabama, Auburn, Georgia, and Georgia Tech on an annual basis. He could have griped to the athletic director except Frank Howard was the athletic director.

Still today, Frank Howard is considered one of Clemson's most beloved figures.

CLEMSON'S 55 GREATEST SINCE 1953

OFFENSE

WIDE RECEIVER: Jerry Butler, Rod Gardner, Derrick Hamilton, Aaron Kelly, Perry Tuttle
TIGHT END: Gary Barnes, Bennie Cunningham
TACKLE: Jim Bundren, Lou Cordileone, Stacy Long, Lee Nanney
GUARD: Joe Bostic, Jeb Flesch, Harry Olszewski, John Phillips, Stacy Seegars
CENTER: Kyle Young
QUARTERBACK: Woodrow Danzler, Steve Fuller, Charlie Whitehurst
RUNNING BACK: Terry Allen, James Davis, Kenny Flowers, Raymond Priester, C.J. Spiller
FULLBACK: Ken Callicutt, Rudy Harris

DEFENSE

END: Gaines Adams, Jeff Bryant
TACKLE: Brentson Buckner, Chester McGlockton, Michael Dean Perry, Jim Stuckey
NOSE GUARD: Rob Bodine, William Perry
LINEBACKER: Keith Adams, Jeff Davis, Levon Kirkland, Ed McDaniel, Johnny Rembert, Anthony Simmons
CORNERBACK: Eddie Geathers, Dexter McCleon, Donnell Woolford
SAFETY: Robert Carswell, Brian Dawkins, Terry Kinard, Robert O'Neal, Rex Varn

SPECIAL TEAMS

RETURN SPECIALISTS: Justin Miller, Terrance Roulhac
PLACE KICKER: Chris Gardocki
PUNTER: Dale Hatcher

MULTIPLE POSITIONS

QUARTERBACK-STRONG SAFETY: Willie Jordan
QUARTERBACK-LINEBACKER: Patrick Sapp

PERFORMANCE FORMULA:
CLEMSON'S 10 BEST SEASONS

1981	1.7203	1 of 70
1978	1.5762	6 of 70
1989	1.5743	8 of 70
1988	1.5425	10 of 69
1990	1.5410	8 of 70
1983	1.5045	8 of 70
1982	1.4676	11 of 70
1987	1.4315	10 of 69
1991	1.4140	15 of 71
1959	1.4092	11 of 70

CLEMSON TIGERS

Year	W-L-T	AP Poll	Conference Standing	Toughest Regular Season Opponents	Coach (Record at School)	Bowl Games		
1953	3-5-1		6	Maryland 10-0, So. Carolina 7-3, Georgia Tech 8-2-1, Auburn 7-2-1	Frank Howard			
1954	5-5		5	Georgia 6-3-1, Virginia Tech 8-0-1 Maryland 7-2-1, Auburn 7-3	Frank Howard			
1955	7-3		3	Virginia Tech 6-3-1, Maryland 10-0, Auburn 8-1-1	Frank Howard			
1956	7-2-2	19	1	Florida 6-3-1, South Carolina 7-3, Virginia Tech 7-2-1, Miami 8-1-1	Frank Howard	Orange	21 Colorado	27
1957	7-3		3t	NC State 7-1-2, Rice 7-3, Duke 6-2-2	Frank Howard			
1958	8-3	12	1	North Carolina 6-4, South Carolina 6-4, Boston College 7-3	Frank Howard	Sugar	0 Louisiana State	7
1959	9-2	11	1	Georgia Tech 6-4, South Carolina 6-4, Wake Forest 6-4	Frank Howard	Bluebonnet	23 Texas Christian	7
1960	6-4		4	Virginia Tech 6-4, Maryland 6-4, Duke 7-3	Frank Howard			
1961	5-5		3t	Maryland 7-3, Duke 7-3, Auburn 6-4	Frank Howard			
1962	6-4		2	Georgia Tech 7-2-1, Duke 8-2, Auburn 6-3-1, Maryland 6-4	Frank Howard			
1963	5-4-1		3t	Oklahoma 8-2, Georgia Tech 7-3, NC State 8-2, No. Carolina 8-2	Frank Howard			
1964	3-7		7	NC State 5-5, Georgia Tech 7-3, Georgia 6-3-1	Frank Howard			
1965	5-5		3t	Georgia Tech 6-3-1, Georgia 6-4, Duke 6-4, TCU 6-4	Frank Howard			
1966	6-4		1	Georgia Tech 9-1, Alabama 10-0, Southern California 7-3	Frank Howard			
1967	6-4		1	Georgia 7-3, Auburn 6-4, Alabama 8-1-1, NC State 8-2	Frank Howard			
1968	4-5-1		2	Georgia 8-0-2, Auburn 6-4, Alabama 8-2, NC State 6-4	Frank Howard			
1969	4-6		3t	Georgia 5-4-1, Auburn 8-2, Alabama 6-4, South Carolina 7-3	Frank Howard (165-118-12)			
1970	3-8		6t	Georgia Tech 8-3, Auburn 8-2, North Carolina 8-3	Cecil "Hootie" Ingram			
1971	5-6		2	Georgia 10-1, Auburn 9-1, North Carolina 9-2	Hootie Ingram			
1972	4-7		5	Oklahoma 10-1, North Carolina 10-1, NC State 7-3-1	Hootie Ingram (12-21)			
1973	5-6		3	Georgia 6-4-1, NC State 8-3, Maryland 8-3, South Carolina 7-4	Red Parker			
1974	7-4		2t	Texas A&M 8-3, NC Stat 9-2, Maryland 8-3, Tennessee 6-3-2	Red Parker			
1975	2-9		5	Alabama 10-1, Georgia 9-2, Maryland 8-2-1, South Carolina 7-4	Red Parker			
1976	3-6-2		7	Georgia 10-1, North Carolina 9-2, Maryland 11-0	Red Parker (17-25-2)			
1977	8-3-1	19	2	Maryland 7-4, NC State 7-4, No. Carolina 8-2-1, Notre Dame 10-1-	Charley Pell	Gator	3 Pittsburgh	34
1978	11-1	6	1	Georgia 9-1-1, NC State 8-3, Maryland 9-2	Charley Pell (18-4-1), Danny Ford [1-0]	Gator	17 Ohio State	15
1979	8-4		2t	Wake For. 8-3, No. Carolina 7-3-1, No. Dame 7-4, So. Carolina 8-3	Danny Ford	Peach	18 Baylor	24
1980	6-5		4t	Georgia 11-0, Virginia Tech 8-3, North Carolina 10-1	Danny Ford			
1981	12-0	1	1	Georgia 10-1, Duke 6-5, North Carolina 9-2	Danny Ford	Orange	22 Nebraska	15
1982	9-1-1	8	1	Georgia 11-0, Boston College 8-2-1, Maryland 8-3	Danny Ford			
1983	9-1-1	11	ineligible	Boston College 9-2, Georgia 9-1-1, No. Carolina 8-3, Maryland 8-3	Danny Ford			
1984	7-4		ineligible	Virginia 7-2-2, Virginia Tech 8-3, Maryland 8-3, So. Carolina 10-1	Danny Ford			
1985	6-6		3t	Georgia 7-3-1, Georgia Tech 8-2-1, Maryland 8-3	Danny Ford	Independence	13 Minnesota	20
1986	8-2-2	17	1	Georgia 8-3, NC State 8-2-1, North Carolina 7-3-1	Danny Ford	Gator	27 Stanford	21
1987	10-2	12	1	Georgia 8-3, Virginia 7-4, Wake Forest 7-4, South Carolina 8-3	Danny Ford	Citrus	35 Penn State	10
1988	10-2	9	1	Florida State 10-1, Duke 7-3-1, NC State 7-3-1, South Carolina 8-3	Danny Ford	Citrus	13 Oklahoma	6
1989	10-2	12	3	Furman 10-1, Florida State 9-2, Duke 8-3, Virginia 10-2	Danny Ford (96-29-4)	Gator	27 West Virginia	7
1990	10-2	9	2t	Virginia 8-3, Georgia Tech 10-0-1, North Carolina 6-4-1	Ken Hatfield	Hall of Fame	30 Illinois	0
1991	9-2-1	18	1	Georgia 8-3, Virginia 8-2-1, NC State 9-2, North Carolina 7-4	Ken Hatfield	Citrus	13 California	37
1992	5-6		7	Florida State 10-1, Virginia 7-4, NC State 9-2-1, North Carolina 8-3	Ken Hatfield			
1993	9-3	23	3	Florida State 11-1, NC State 7-4, North Carolina 10-2, Virginia 7-4	Ken Hatfield (33-13-1), Tommy West [1-0]	Peach	14 Kentucky	13
1994	5-6		6	NC State 8-3, Virginia 8-3, Duke 8-3, Fla. St. 9-1-1, No. Carolina 8-3	Tommy West			
1995	8-4		3	Florida State 9-2, Virginia 8-4	Tommy West	Gator	0 Syracuse	41
1996	7-5		2t	North Carolina 9-2, Florida State 11-0, Virginia 7-4	Tommy West	Peach	7 Louisiana State	10
1997	7-5		5	Florida State 10-1, Virginia 7-4, North Carolina 10-1	Tommy West	Peach	17 Auburn	21
1998	3-8		8t	Virginia 9-2, Florida State 11-1, Georgia Tech 9-2	Tommy West (31-28)			
1999	6-6		2	Marshall 11-0, Virginia 7-4, Virginia Tech 11-0, Florida State 11-0	Tommy Bowden	Peach	7 Mississippi State	17
2000	9-3	16	2t	NC State 7-4, Ga. Tech 9-2, Florida State 11-1, So. Carolina 7-4	Tommy Bowden	Gator	20 Virginia Tech	41
2001	7-5		4t	NC State 7-4, Florida State 7-4, Maryland 10-1	Tommy Bowden	Humanitarian	49 Louisiana Tech	24
2002	7-6		5t	Georgia 11-1, Florida State 9-4, NC State 10-3, Maryland 10-3	Tommy Bowden	Tangerine	15 Texas Tech	55
2003	9-4	22	4	Georgia 10-2, Maryland 9-3, Florida State 10-2	Tommy Bowden	Peach	27 Tennessee	14
2004	6-5		6t	Texas A&M 7-4, Florida State 8-3, Virginia 8-3, Miami 8-3	Tommy Bowden			
2005	8-4	21	Atl3	Miami 9-2, Boston College 8-3, Georgia Tech 7-4, Fla. State 8-4	Tommy Bowden	Champs	19 Colorado	10
2006	8-5		Atl2t	Boston College 9-3, Wake Forest 10-2, Virginia Tech 10-2	Tommy Bowden	Music City	20 Kentucky	28
2007	9-4	21	Atl2t	Virginia Tech 10-2, Wake Forest 8-4, Boston College 10-2	Tommy Bowden	Chick-Fil A	20 Auburn	23
2008	7-6		Atl3t	Alabama 12-1, Georgia Tech 9-3, Boston College 9-4	Tommy Bowden (72-45), Dabo Swinney [4-3]	Gator	26 Nebraska	21
2009	9-5	24	Atl1	Georgia Tech 11-2, TCU 12-0, Miami 9-3	Dabo Swinney	Music City	21 Kentucky	13
2010	6-7		Atl4t	Auburn 13-0, Florida State 9-4, South Carolina 9-4	Dabo Swinney (19-15)	Meineke Care	26 South Florida	31

TOTAL: 393-251-13 .6081 (23 of 70)

Bowl Games since 1953: 13-16 .4483 (Tied 48 of 70)

GREATEST TEAM SINCE 1953: The 1981 national champion Clemson Tigers rebounded from a deceptively poor 6-5 mark in 1980 to sweep their schedule and win the Orange Bowl. Although unranked to begin the season, the Tigers shut down defending national champion Georgia in the third game of the year and were on their way.

1953 3-5-1

33 Presbyterian	7 E Dreher Gaskins
14 Boston College	14 T Clyde White
0 Maryland	20 G Mark Kane
7 Miami	39 C Bill McClellan / Avery Wingo
7 South Carolina	14 G Ormond Wild
18 Wake Forest	0 T Nathan Gressette
7 Georgia Tech	20 E Scott Jackson / Walt Laraway
34 Citadel	13 QB Don King
19 Auburn	45 HB Jimmy Wells
	HB Billy O'Dell / Ken Moore
	FB Red Whitten / Buck George

RUSHING: King 79/243y, Whitten 42/238y, O'Dell 42/233y
PASSING: King 46-98/706y, 5TD, 46.9%
RECEIVING: Gaskins 21/426y, Jackson 15/252y
SCORING: Gaskins 30pts, King & Jackson 18pts

1954 5-5

33 Presbyterian	0 E Walt Laraway / Dalton Rivers
7 Georgia	14 T Clyde White
7 Virginia Tech	18 G Mark Kane / Earle Greene
14 Florida	7 C Wingo Avery
8 South Carolina	13 G Buck Priester
32 Wake Forest	20 T Tommy Mattos / B.C. Inabinet
27 Furman	6 E Scott Jackson / Willie Smith
0 Maryland	16 QB Don King / Charlie Bussey
6 Auburn	27 HB Joel Wells / Joe Pagliei
59 Citadel	0 HB Ken Moore / Jim Coleman
	FB Billy O'Dell / Buck George

RUSHING: Wells 74/352y, O'Dell 77/292y, George 45/282y
PASSING: King 32-77/468y, 4TD, 44.4%
RECEIVING: Jackson 11/151y, Pagliei 7/202y, Laraway 7/112y
SCORING: Coleman (HB-K) 31pts, Pagliei (HB-K) 25pts,
  3 with 18pts

1955 7-3

33 Presbyterian	0 E Walt Laraway / Dalton Rivers
20 Virginia	7 T Dick Marazza
26 Georgia	7 G Earle Greene / Buck Priester
7 Rice	21 C Wingo Avery / Hampton Hunter
28 South Carolina	14 G John Grdijan / John Greene
19 Wake Forest	13 T B.C. Inabinet / Bill Hudson
21 Virginia Tech	16 E Willie Smith / Joe Bowen
12 Maryland	25 QB Don King / Charlie Bussey
0 Auburn	21 HB Joel Wells / Crimmins Hankinson
40 Furman	20 HB Joe Pagliei / Jim Coleman
	FB Billy O'Dell

RUSHING: Wells 135/ 782y, O'Dell 143/609y, Pagliei 80/476y
PASSING: King 33-79/586y, 3TD, 41.8%
RECEIVING: Pagliei 10/233y, Bowen 7/134y, Laraway 7/113y
SCORING: Pagliei (HB-K) 43pts, O'Dell 42pts, Wells 36pts

1956 7-2-2

27 Presbyterian	7 E Dalton Rivers / Ray Masneri
20 Florida	20 T Dick Marazza / Jim McCanless
13 N. Carolina St.	7 G Earle Greene Leon Kaltenbach
17 Wake Forest	0 C Donnie Bunton
7 South Carolina	0 G John Grdijan / H.B. Bruorton
21 Virginia Tech	6 T Bill Hudson / Jim Padgett
6 Maryland	6 E Willie Smith
0 Miami	21 QB Charlie Bussey
7 Virginia	0 HB Joel Wells
28 Furman	7 HB Jim Coleman / Charlie Horne
21 Colorado■	27 FB Rudy Hayes / Bob Spooner

RUSHING: Wells 174/803y, Hayes 98/384y, Coleman 67/290y
PASSING: Bussey 26-68/330y, 1TD, 38.2%
RECEIVING: Horne 6/84y, Rivers 5/76y, Smith 5/65y
SCORING: Wells 48pts, Spooner 30pts, Bussey (QB-K) 27pts

1957 7-3

66 Presbyterian	0 E Ray Masneri
0 North Carolina	26 T Jim Padgett
7 N. Carolina St.	13 G Jim Payne
20 Virginia	6 C Donnie Bunton / Bill Thomas
13 South Carolina	0 G John Grdijan
20 Rice	7 T Harold Olson
26 Maryland	7 E Bill Few / Whitey Jordan / Wyatt Cox
6 Duke	7 QB Bill Barbary / Harvey White
13 Wake Forest	6 HB George Usry / Bill Mathis
45 Furman	6 HB Charlie Horne / Sonny Quesenberry
	FB Rudy Hayes / Bob Spooner / Doug Cline

RUSHING: Spooner 88/358y, Horne 70/70/335y, Hayes 54/269y
PASSING: White 46-95/841y, 11TD, 48.4%
RECEIVING: Jordan 12/369y, Mathis 8/127y, Quesenberry 8/91y
SCORING: Spooner 30pts, Mathis 30 pts, Cline 24pts

1958 8-3

20 Virginia	15 E Ray Masneri
26 North Carolina	21 T Jim Padgett
8 Maryland	0 G Jim Payne
12 Vanderbilt	7 C Bill Thomas
6 South Carolina	26 G Dave Olson
14 Wake Forest	12 T Lou Cordileone
0 Georgia Tech	13 E Wyatt Cox / Jack Webb
13 N. Carolina St.	6 QB Harvey White
34 Boston College	12 HB George Usry / Bill Mathis
36 Furman	19 HB Charlie Horne
0 LSU■	7 FB Rudy Hayes / Doug Cline

RUSHING: Cline 103/450y, Usry 88/426y, Hayes 86/365y
PASSING: White 43-86/492y, 1TD, 49.4%
RECEIVING: Usry 18/171y, Cox 9/157y, Mathis 8/156y
SCORING: White 30pts, Usry 28pts, Mathis 26pts

1959 9-2

20 North Carolina	18 E Sam Anderson / Bob DeBardelaben
47 Virginia	0 T Lou Cordileone
6 Georgia Tech	16 G Sam Crout / Calvin West
23 N. Carolina St.	0 C Paul Snyder
27 South Carolina	0 G Dave Lynn / Dave Olson
19 Rice	0 T Harold Olson
6 Duke	0 E Gary Barnes / Ed Bost
25 Maryland	28 QB Harvey White / Lowndes Shingler
33 Wake Forest	31 HB Bill Mathis
56 Furman	0 HB George Usry / Doug Daigneault
23 TCU■	7 FB Doug Cline

RUSHING: Cline 119/485y, Mathis 104/445y, Usry 80/333y
PASSING: White 56-107/770y, 6TD, 52.3%
RECEIVING: Mathis 18/319y, Usry 13/147y, Anderson 13/135y
SCORING: Mathis 70pts, Usry 30pts, Daigneault 30pts

1960 6-4

28 Wake Forest	7 E Ed Bost / Sam Anderson
13 Virginia Tech	7 T Jimmy King
21 Virginia	7 G Calvin West
17 Maryland	19 C Ron Andreo
6 Duke	21 G Dave Lynn / Lon Armstrong
20 Vanderbilt	22 T Ronnie Osborne
24 North Carolina	0 E Gary Barnes
12 South Carolina	2 QB Lowndes Shingler
14 Boston College	25 HB Mack Matthews / Elmo Lam
42 Furman	14 HB Harry Pavilack
	FB Ron Scrudato / Bill McGuirt

RUSHING: McGuirt 99/320y, Shingler 71/274y, Scrudato 81/230y
PASSING: Shingler 61-145/790y, 1TD, 42.1%
RECEIVING: Pavilack 17/272y, Barnes 14/256y, Anderson 12/188y
SCORING: McGuirt 54pts, Armstrong 33pts

1961 5-5

17 Florida	21 E Coleman Glaze / Tommy King
21 Maryland	24 T Ronnie Osborne
27 North Carolina	0 G Calvin West
13 Wake Forest	17 C Jack Veronee
17 Duke	7 G Lon Armstrong
14 Auburn	24 T Dave Hynes
21 Tulane	6 E Bob Poole
14 South Carolina	21 QB Joe Anderson / Jim Parker
35 Furman	6 HB Wendall Black / Elmo Lam
20 N. Carolina St.	0 HB Gary Barnes
	FB Ron Scrudato / Bill McGuirt

RUSHING: Scrudato 99/341y, Anderson 97/310y, Lam 50/270y
PASSING: Parker 46-98/736y, 5TD, 46.9%
RECEIVING: Lam 17/237y, Barnes 16/247y, King 14/227y
SCORING: Scrudato 48pts, Armstrong 29pts

1962

9 Georgia Tech	26 E Coleman Glaze / Lou Fogle
7 N. Carolina St.	0 T Dave Hynes
24 Wake Forest	7 G Jack Aaron / Tracy Childers
16 Georgia	24 C Ted Bunton
0 Duke	16 G Walter Cox
14 Auburn	17 T Don Chuy
17 North Carolina	6 E Bob Poole/John'y Case/Oscar Thorsland
44 Furman	3 QB Joe Anderson / Jim Parker
17 Maryland	14 HB Hal Davis
20 South Carolina	17 HB Mack Matthews / Billy Ward
	FB Jimmy Howard/Pat Crain/Ch'rl's Dumas

RUSHING: Crain 94/348y, Davis 66/344y, Matthews 54/266y
PASSING: Parker 30-67/431y, 0TD, 44.8%
RECEIVING: Case 13/213y, Fogle 10/140y, Glaze 8/108y
SCORING: Rodney Rogers (K) 34pts, Dumas 32pts, Crain 24pts

1963 5-4-1

14 Oklahoma	31 E Lou Fogle / Charlie Meadowcroft
0 Georgia Tech	27 T Vic Aliffi / Ricky Johnson
3 N. Carolina St.	7 G Tracy Childers
7 Georgia	7 C Ted Bunton
30 Duke	35 G Billy Weaver / Walter Cox
35 Virginia	0 T Jack Aaron
36 Wake Forest	0 E Bob Poole / Johnny Case
11 North Carolina	7 QB Jim Parker / Thomas Ray
21 Maryland	6 HB Hugh Mauldin / Hal Davis
24 South Carolina	20 HB Mack Matthews / Billy Ward
	FB Pat Crain / Jimmy Howard / Bob Swift

RUSHING: Crain 137/513y, Matthews 67/321y, Swift 74/279y
PASSING: Parker 52-117/728y, 2TD, 44.4%
RECEIVING: Fogle 17/218y, Poole 11/220y, Davis 9/56y
SCORING: Frank Pearce (K) 33pts, Crain 24pts

1964 3-7

28 Virginia	0 E Wayne Bell / Charlie Meadowcroft
0 No. Carolina St.	9 T Johnny Boyette
7 Georgia Tech	14 G Joe Blackwell
7 Georgia	19 C Ted Bunton
21 Wake Forest	9 G Richard Cooper
10 TCU	14 T Butch Robbins
29 Virginia	7 E Hoss Hostetler
0 North Carolina	29 QB Jimmy Bell / Thomas Ray
0 Maryland	34 HB Hal Davis / Hugh Mauldin
3 South Carolina	7 WB Billy Ward / Phil Marion (DB)
	FB Pat Crain

RUSHING: Davis 87/533y, Crain 108/330y, Mauldin 57/270y
PASSING: Ray 21-59/253y, 1TD, 35.6%
RECEIVING: Hostetler 8/103y, Meadowcroft 7/77y, Mauldin 7/73y
SCORING: Davis 30pts, Frank Pearce (K) 19pts, Mauldin 18pts

1965 5-5

21 N. Carolina St.	7 WR Wayne Bell / Freddy Kelley
20 Virginia	14 T Johnny Boyette / Dave Burton
6 Georgia Tech	28 G Harry Olszewski
9 Georgia	23 C Randy Smith / Johnny Palmer
3 Duke	2 G Mike Facciolo
3 TCU	0 T Wayne Mass
26 Wake Forest	13 E Edgar McGee / Hoss Hostetler
13 North Carolina	17 QB Thomas Ray / Jimmy Addison
0 Maryland	6 HB Hugh Mauldin / Tom Duley
16 South Carolina	17 WB Phil Rogers
	FB Bo Ruffner
	DL Butch Sursavage
	DL Floyd Rogers
	DL Ricky Johnson
	DL Mac McElmurray / Wilson Childers
	DL Joey Branton / Ted Katana
	LB Joe Waldrep
	LB Bill Hecht / Ray Mullen
	DB Wayne Page
	DB Kit Jackson
	DB Phil Marion / Arthur Craig
	DB Jacky Jackson

RUSHING: Mauldin 194/664y, Ruffner 76/272y, Ray 74/146y
PASSING: Ray 74-175/1019y, 4TD, 42.3%
RECEIVING: Rogers 36/466y, Bell 25/377y, McGee 15/184y
SCORING: Mauldin 24pts, Ray 24pts, Frank Pearce (K) 21pts

1966 6-4

40 Virginia	35 WR Wayne Bell
12 Georgia Tech	13 WR Phil Rogers
0 Alabama	26 T Larry Keys
9 Duke	6 G Harry Olszewski
0 Southern Cal	30 C Wayne Mulligan
23 Wake Forest	21 G Mike Facciolo
27 North Carolina	3 T Wayne Mass
14 Maryland	10 TE Edgar McGee
14 N. Carolina St.	23 QB Jimmy Addison
35 South Carolina	10 TB Buddy Gore / Jacky Jackson

FB Jay Cooper / Charlie Hook
DL Butch Sursavage
DL Floyd Rogers
DL Mac McElmurray
DL Wilson Childers
DL Joey Branton
LB Billy Ware
LB Jimmy Catoe
DB Wayne Page
DB Arthur Craig / Frank Libertore
DB Phil Marion
DB Lee Rayburn

RUSHING: Gore 186/750y, Jackson 96/422y, Hook 28/121y
PASSING: Addison 103-186/1491y, 10TD, 55.4%
RECEIVING: Rogers 42/574y, McGee 25/312y, Bell 23/405y
SCORING: Jackson 48pts, Gore 24pts, Rogers & McGee 18pts

1967 6-4

23 Wake Forest	6 WR Jimmy Abrams
17 Georgia	24 WR Phil Rogers / Freddy Kelley
0 Georgia Tech	10 T Larry Keys
21 Auburn	43 G Harry Olszewski
13 Duke	7 C Wayne Mulligan
10 Alabama	13 G Gary Arthur
17 North Carolina	0 T Wayne Mass
28 Maryland	7 TE Edgar McGee / Hoss Hostetler
14 N. Carolina St.	6 QB Jimmy Addison
23 South Carolina	12 TB Buddy Gore / Jacky Jackson

FB Bo Ruffner / Charlie Tolley
DL Butch Sursavage / Joey Branton
DL Mike Locklair
DL Randy Harvey
DL John Cagle
DL Ronnie Ducworth
LB Jimmy Catoe
LB Billy Ware
DB Richie Luzzi
DB Frank Libertore
DB Kit Jackson
DB Lee Rayburn

RUSHING: Gore 230/1045y, Jackson 111/450y, Tolley 29/116y
PASSING: Addison 82-174/924y, 5TD, 47.2%
RECEIVING: Rogers 28/429y, Abrams 24/262y, Hostetler 12/113y
SCORING: Gore 54pts, Jackson 24pts

1968 4-5-1

20 Wake Forest	20 WR Jack Anderson / Ron Miller
13 Georgia	31 WR Charlie Waters
21 Georgia Tech	24 T Richard Garick
10 Auburn	21 G Grady Burgner
39 Duke	22 C Wayne Mulligan / Dave Thompson
14 Alabama	21 G Grady Burgner / Gary Arthur
24 N. Carolina St.	19 T Joe Lhotsky
16 Maryland	0 TE Jim Sursavage
24 North Carolina	14 QB Billy Ammons / Tom English
3 South Carolina	7 TB Buddy Gore / Ray Yauger

FB Benny Michael / Rick Medlin
DL Ivan Southerland
DL Mike Locklair / Randy Harvey
DL B.B. Elvinton
DL John Cagle / Ronnie Kitchens
DL Ronnie Ducworth / Fred Milton
LB Jimmy Catoe / Bill Depew
LB Billy Ware / George Burnett
DB Chuck Werner / John Fulmer
DB Gary Compton
DB Richie Luzzi / Bob Craig
DB Lee Rayburn / Sonny Cassady

RUSHING: Gore 185/776y, Yauger 149/760y, Michael 38/137y
PASSING: Ammons 74-162/1006y, 5TD, 45.7%
RECEIVING: Waters 22/411y, Anderson 22/344y, Miller 15/157y
SCORING: Yauger 42pts, Jimmy Barnette 27pts, Waters 24pts

1969 4-6

21 Virginia	14 WR Jim Sursavage
0 Georgia	30 WR Charlie Waters
21 Georgia Tech	10 T Jim Dorn
0 Auburn	51 G Grady Burgner
28 Wake Forest	14 C Dave Thompson
13 Alabama	38 G Jack King
40 Maryland	0 T Steve Lewter
27 Duke	34 TE John McMakin
15 North Carolina	32 QB Tommy Kendrick
13 South Carolina	27 TB Ray Yauger

FB Rick Medlin
DL Ivan Southerland
DL Ronnie Kitchens
DL B.B. Elvington
DL Waldo Watts
DL George Ducworth / Charlie Mayer
LB Larry Hefner
LB Bill Depew
DB Dale Henry
DB Bob Craig
DB Sonny Cassady
DB Don Kelley

RUSHING: Yauger 223/968y, Tolley 29/150y, Anderson 49/148y
PASSING: Kendrick 107-227/1457y, 10TD, 47.2%
RECEIVING: Waters 44/738y, McMakin 24/302y, Yauger 21/130y
SCORING: Yauger 68pts, Jimmy Barnette (K) 30pts, McMakin 26pts

1970 3-8

24 Citadel	0 WR Brad O'Neal
27 Virginia	17 WR Bobby Johnson / Don Kelley
0 Georgia	38 T Jim Dorn
7 Georgia Tech	28 G Buddy King
0 Auburn	44 C Dave Farnham
20 Wake Forest	36 G Dave Thompson
10 Duke	21 T Force Chamberlain
24 Maryland	11 TE John McMakin
13 Florida State	38 QB Tommy Kendrick
7 North Carolina	42 TB Ray Yauger / Chuck Huntley
32 South Carolina	38 FB Dick Bukowski

DL Wayne Baker
DL Ralph Daniel
DL Larry Hefner
DL B.B. Elvington
DL Charlie Mayer
LB Jim Sursavage
LB Ben Watson
DB Don Kelley
DB Jeff Siepe / Bobby Johnson
DB Rick Eyler / Dale Henry
DB Ben Anderson

RUSHING: Yauger 183/711y, Huntley 72/233y, Bukowsky 60/223y
PASSING: Kendrick 133-267/1407y, 8TD, 49.8%
RECEIVING: McMakin 40/532y, O'Neal 27/363y, Johnson 18/202y
SCORING: Eddie Seigler (K) 40pts, Yauger 30pts

1971 5-6

10 Kentucky	13 WR Gordie Bengel
0 Georgia	28 WR Don Kelley / Dennis Goss
14 Georgia Tech	24 T Jim Dorn
3 Duke	0 G Buddy King
32 Virginia	15 C Dave Farnham
13 Auburn	35 G Steve Lewter
10 Wake Forest	9 T Force Chamberlain
13 North Carolina	26 TE John McMakin
20 Maryland	14 QB Tommy Kendrick
23 N. Carolina St.	31 TB Ricky Gilstrap / Smiley Sanders
17 South Carolina	7 FB Heide Davis / Wade Hughes

DL Wayne Baker
DL Ralph Daniel
DL Larry Hefner
DL Frank Wirth
DL Charlie Mayer
LB John Bolubasz
LB John Rhodes
DB Jeff Siepe
DB Bobby Johnson
DB Dale Henry
DB Ben Anderson

RUSHING: Gilstrap 114/514y, Sanders 111/386y, Hughes 87/330y
PASSING: Kendrick 64-152/1040y, 6TD, 42.1%
RECEIVING: McMakin 29/421y, Kelley 18/505y, Goss 8/116y
SCORING: Eddie Seigler (K) 47pts, McMakin 30pts, Gilstrap 24pts

1972 4-7

13 Citadel	0 WR Gordie Bengel / David Sasser
10 Rice	29 WR Dennis Goss
3 Oklahoma	52 T Gary Gennerich
9 Georgia Tech	31 G Buddy King
0 Duke	7 C Ricky Harrell
37 Virginia	21 G Art Brisacher
31 Wake Forest	0 T Ken Peeples / Force Chamberlain
10 North Carolina	26 TE Karl Andreas
6 Maryland	31 QB Ken Pengitore
17 N. Carolina St.	42 RB Smiley Sanders / Jay Washington
7 South Carolina	6 RB Wade Hughes / Jerry Davis

DL Jeff Stocks
DL John Price
DL Willie Anderson
DL Frank Wirth
DL Mike Buckner
LB Jimmy Williamson
LB John Rhodes
DB Jeff Siepe
DB Ben Anderson
DB Jimmy Ness
DB Bobby Johnson

RUSHING: Hughes 177/761y, Sanders 117/398y, Washington 69/325y
PASSING: Pengitore 55-131/831y, 1TD, 42.0%
RECEIVING: Goss 21/385y, Bengel 12/187y, Sasser 10/142y
SCORING: Eddie Seigler (K) 47pts, Davis 30pts, Hughes 30pts

1973 5-6

14 Citadel	12 WR Gordie Bengel
14 Georgia	31 WR Jim Lanzendoen / Craig Brantley
21 Georgia Tech	29 T Maret Cobb / Al Murray
15 Texas A&M	30 G Curt Buttermore
32 Virginia	27 C John Bolubasz / Roland Bowlan
24 Duke	8 G Ken Peeples
6 N. Carolina St.	29 T Frank Bethea
35 Wake Forest	8 TE Bennie Cunningham / David Sasser
37 North Carolina	29 QB Ken Pengitore
13 Maryland	28 RB Smiley Sanders / Leon Hope
20 South Carolina	32 RB Jay Washington / Ken Callicutt

DL Jeff Stocks / Guy Gehret
DL Bruce Decock
DL Willie Anderson / Nelson Wallace
DL G.G. Galloway / Dan McBride
DL Bob Jones
LB Mike Buckner / Tim Stough
LB Frank Wise
DB Marion Reeves / Malcolm Marler
DB Jimmy Ness
DB Lynn Carson / Dennis Smith
DB Peanut Martin

RUSHING: Sanders 113/612y, Pengitore 182/571y, C'llic't 101/505y
PASSING: Pengitore 82-188/1370y, 8TD, 43.6%
RECEIVING: Cunningham 22/341y, Bengel 21/358y
SCORING: Sanders 60pts, Pengitore 36pts, Bob Burgess (K) 33pts

1974 7-4

0 Texas A&M	24 WR Steve Gibbs / Ricky Bustle
10 N. Carolina St.	31 WR Joey Walters
21 Georgia Tech	17 T Gary Alexander / Al Murray
28 Georgia	24 G Curt Buttermore
0 Maryland	41 C Maret Cobb / Roland Bowlan
17 Duke	13 G Ken Peeples
28 Tennessee	29 T Neal Jetton
21 Wake Forest	9 TE Bennie Cunningham
54 North Carolina	32 QB Mark Fellers
28 Virginia	9 RB Ken Callicutt / Leon Hope
39 South Carolina	21 RB Tony Mathews

DL Guy Gehret
DL Jeff Mills
DL Willie Anderson
DL Thad Allen / Nelson Wallace
DL Tom Boozer
LB Jimmy Williamson
LB Tim Stough
DB Mark Lee / Malcolm Marler
DB Billy Wingo
DB Dennis Smith
DB Jimmy Ness

RUSHING: Callicutt 161/809y, Mathews 117/567y, Fellers 145/444y
PASSING: Fellers 42-92/783y, 10TD, 45.7%
RECEIVING: Cunningham 24/391y, Bustle 9/152y
SCORING: Fellers 54pts, Cunningham 44pts, Bob Burgess 32pts

1975 2-9

13 Tulane	19 WR Joey Walters
0 Alabama	56 WR Craig Brantley / Ricky Bustle
28 Georgia Tech	33 T Neal Jetton
7 Georgia	35 G Lacy Brumley / Joe Bostic
16 Wake Forest	14 C Frank Beathea
21 Duke	25 G Jimmy Weeks
7 N. Carolina St.	45 T David LeBel
7 Florida State	43 TE Bennie Cunningham
38 North Carolina	35 QB Willie Jordan / Mike O'Cain
20 Maryland	22 RB Don Testerman / Harold Goggins
20 South Carolina	56 RB Ken Callicutt / Leon Hope
	DL Tim Stough
	DL G.G. Galloway
	DL Nelson Wallace
	DL Jeff Mills
	DL Frank Wise
	LB Ronnie Smith
	LB Jimmy Williamson
	DB Ogden Hansford
	DB Lynn Carson / Malcolm Marler
	DB Dennis Smith
	DB Peanut Martin

RUSHING: Callicutt 145/572y, Goggins 65/389y, O'Cain 98/246y
PASSING: O'Cain 48-84/697y, 2 TD, 57.1%
RECEIVING: Walters 26/394y,Brantley 22/475y,C'nin'h'm 18/312y
SCORING: Jordan 41pts, O'Cain 38pts, Callicutt 24pts

1976 3-6-2

10 Citadel	7 WR Jerry Butler / Dwight Clark
0 Georgia	41 WR Joey Walters / Rick Weddington
24 Georgia Tech	24 T Lacy Brumley
19 Tennessee	21 G Joe Bostic
14 Wake Forest	20 C Trav Webb / Danny Jaynes
18 Duke	18 G Steve Kenney / Bill Hudson
21 N. Carolina St.	38 T Jimmy Weeks / Thad Allen
15 Florida State	12 TE Harold Cain
23 North Carolina	27 QB Steve Fuller / Mike O'Cain
0 Maryland	20 TB Warren Ratchford / Lester Brown
28 South Carolina	9 FB Harold Goggins
	DL Jonathan Brooks / Gary Kesack
	DL Rich Tuten
	DL Nelson Wallace
	DL Toney Williams / Ken Weichel
	DL Mark Heniford
	LB Randy Scott / Ronnie Smith
	LB Bubba Brown / Bob Sharpe
	DB Malcolm Marler / Bill Wingo
	DB O.J. Tyler / Mike Cornell
	DB Rex Varn
	DB Willie Jordan / Gary Webb

RUSHING: Ratchford 119/676y,Goggins 140/591y,Fuller 157/503y
PASSING: Fuller 58-116/835y, 5TD, 50.0%
RECEIVING: Butler 33/484y, Walters 26/392y, Cain 9/99y
SCORING: Fuller 36pts, Butler 24pts, Jimmy Russell 24pts

1977 8-3-1

14 Maryland	21 WR Jerry Butler
7 Georgia	6 WR Dwight Clark
31 Georgia Tech	14 T Jimmy Weeks
31 Virginia Tech	13 G Steve Kenney
31 Virginia	0 C Jeff Bostic
17 Duke	11 G Joe Bostic
7 N. Carolina St.	3 T Lacy Brumley
26 Wake Forest	0 TE Anthony King / Rick Weddington
13 North Carolina	13 QB Steve Fuller
17 Notre Dame	21 TB Lester Brown / Warren Ratchford
31 South Carolina	27 FB Ken Callicutt
3 Pittsburgh■	34 DL Jonathan Brooks
	DL Jim Stuckey
	DL Rich Tuten
	DL Archie Reese
	DL Mark Heniford
	LB Randy Scott
	LB Bubba Brown
	DB Bubba Rollins
	DB Eddie Geathers / Ogden Hansford
	DB Rex Varn / Roy Eppes
	DB Steve Ryan

RUSHING: Ratchford 118/616y, Brown 108/416y, Fuller 165/403y
PASSING: Fuller 96-182/1497y, 8TD, 52.7%
RECEIVING: Butler 43/760y, Weddington 19/242y, Clark 17/265y
SCORING: Brown 54pts, Obed Ariri (K) 50pts, Fuller 36pts

1978 11-1

58 Citadel	3 WR Jerry Butler / Jerry Gaillard
0 Georgia	12 WR Dwight Clark / Perry Tuttle
31 Villanova	0 T Bill Hudson
38 Virginia Tech	7 G Chris Dolce
30 Virginia	14 C Jeff Bostic / Mark Thornton
28 Duke	8 G Joe Bostic
33 N. Carolina St.	10 T Steve Kenney / Lee Nanney
51 Wake Forest	6 TE Anthony King
13 North Carolina	9 QB Steve Fuller
28 Maryland	24 TB Lester Brown / Cliff Austin
41 South Carolina	23 FB Marvin Sims
17 Ohio State■	15 DL Jonathan Brooks
	DL Jim Stuckey
	DL Rich Tuten / Charlie Bauman
	DL Toney Williams / Steve Durham
	DL Steve Gibbs / David Reed
	LB Randy Scott
	LB Bubba Brown
	DB Willie Jordan / Eddie Geathers
	DB Steve Ryan
	DB Bubba Rollins / Jack Cain
	DB Rex Varn

RUSHING: Brown 196/1006y, Sims 124/651y, Fuller 136/611y
PASSING: Fuller 92-167/1392y, 7TD, 55.1%
RECEIVING: Butler 54/864y, Clark 10/179y, King 8/129y
SCORING: Brown 102pts, Obed Ariri (K) 81pts, Fuller 54pts

1979 8-4

21 Furman	0 WR Jerry Gaillard
0 Maryland	19 WR Perry Tuttle
12 Georgia	7 T Lee Nanney
17 Virginia	7 G Chris Dolce
21 Virginia Tech	0 C Mark Thornton
28 Duke	10 G Jeff Bostic
13 N. Carolina St.	16 T Gary Brown
31 Wake Forest	0 TE Mark Clifford
19 North Carolina	10 QB Bill Lott
16 Notre Dame	10 TB Lester Brown / Chuck McSwain
9 South Carolina	13 FB Marvin Sims / Tracy Perry
18 Baylor■	24 DL Bob Goldberg
	DL Jim Stuckey
	DL Charlie Bauman
	DL Steve Durham
	DL David Reed
	LB Jeff Davis / Chuck Rose
	LB Bubba Brown
	DB Eddie Geathers
	DB Rex Varn
	DB Jack Cain
	DB Willie Underwood

RUSHING: Sims 158/743y, Brown 156/605y, McSwain 94/443y
PASSING: Lott 90-174/1184y, 4TD, 51.7%
RECEIVING: Tuttle 36/544y, Gaillard 21/244y, Clifford 11/131y
SCORING: Obed Ariri (K) 62pts, Brown & McSwain 36pts

1980 6-5

19 Rice	3 WR Jerry Gaillard / Jeff Stockstill
16 Georgia	20 WR Perry Tuttle
17 W. Carolina	10 T Lee Nanney
13 Virginia Tech	10 G Brad Fisher
27 Virginia	24 C Tony Berryhill
17 Duke	34 G Brian Clark
20 N. Carolina St.	24 T Gary Brown
35 Wake Forest	33 TE Jeff Wells
19 North Carolina	24 QB Homer Jordan
7 Maryland	34 TB Chuck McSwain / Edgar Pickett
27 South Carolina	6 FB Jeff McCall
	DL Jeff Bryant
	DL Dan Benish
	DL Charlie Bauman
	DL Steve Durham
	DL Bill Smith
	LB Chuck Rose
	LB Jeff Davis
	DB Hollis Hall
	DB Eddie Geathers
	DB Terry Kinard
	DB Willie Underwood

RUSHING: McSwain 114/544y, Jordan 153/372y, Pickett 88/323y
PASSING: Jordan 85-172/1311y, 4TD, 49.4%
RECEIVING: Tuttle 53/915y, Gaillard 25/369y, Stockstill 10/123y
SCORING: Obed-Ariri (K) 87pts, Tuttle & Jordan 24pts

1981 12-0

45 Wofford	10 WR Jerry Gaillard / Frank Magwood
13 Tulane	5 WR Perry Tuttle
13 Georgia	3 T Brad Fisher
21 Kentucky	3 G James Farr
27 Virginia	0 C Tony Berryhill
38 Duke	10 G Brian Clark
17 N. Carolina St.	7 T Lee Nanney
82 Wake Forest	24 TE Bubba Diggs
10 North Carolina	8 QB Homer Jordan
21 Maryland	7 TB Cliff Austin / Chuck McSwain
29 South Carolina	13 FB Jeff McCall
22 Nebraska■	15 DL Bill Smith
	DL Dan Benish
	DL William Devane
	DL Jeff Bryant
	DL Andy Headen
	LB Danny Triplett
	LB Jeff Davis
	DB Hollis Hall
	DB Anthony Rose
	DB Terry Kinard
	DB Tim Childers

RUSHING: Austin 156/802y, McSwain 132/668y, Jordan 152/440y
PASSING: Jordan 96-174/1496y, 8TD, 55.2%
RECEIVING: Tuttle 47/827y, Magwood 16/303y, Gaillard 16/192y
SCORING: Austin 48pts, Bob Paulling (K) 45pts,
McSwain & Tuttle 42pts

1982 9-1-1

7 Georgia	13 WR Jeff Stockstill
17 Boston College	17 WR Frank Magwood
21 W. Carolina	10 T Gary Brown
24 Kentucky	6 G James Farr
48 Virginia	0 C Cary Massaro
49 Duke	6 G Brian Butcher
38 N. Carolina St.	29 T Bob Mayberry
16 North Carolina	13 TE K.D. Dunn / Kendall Alley
24 Maryland	22 QB Homer Jordan
24 South Carolina	6 TB Cliff Austin / Chuck McSwain
21 Wake Forest	17 FB Jeff McCall
	DL Edgar Pickett
	DL Dan Benish
	DL William Perry
	DL Jim Scott
	DL Andy Headen
	LB Otis Lindsey / Danny Triplett
	LB Johnny Rembert
	DB Ty Davis
	DB Reggie Pleasant
	DB Terry Kinard
	DB Tim Childers

RUSHING: Austin 197/1064y, McSwain 131/641y, McCall 79/333y
PASSING: Jordan 96-174/674y 2TD, 55.0%
RECEIVING: Stockstill 25/247y, Magwood 24/414y, Alley 9/143y
SCORING: Austin 84pts, Bob Paulling (K) 68pts, McSwain 42pts

1983 9-1-1

44 W. Carolina	10 WR Ray Williams
16 Boston College	31 WR Shelton Boyer / Terrance Roulhac
16 Georgia	16 T Reid Ingle
41 Georgia Tech	14 G James Farr
42 Virginia	21 C Dale Swing
38 Duke	31 G Steve Reese
27 N. Carolina St.	17 T Joe Ellis
24 Wake Forest	17 TE K.D. Dunn
16 North Carolina	3 QB Mike Eppley
52 Maryland	27 TB Stacey Driver / Kenny Flowers
22 South Carolina	13 FB Kevin Mack
	DL Edgar Pickett
	DL James Robinson
	DL William Devane
	DL Ray Brown
	DL Terence Mack
	LB Henry Walls
	LB Eldridge Milton
	DB Ty Davis
	DB Rod McSwain
	DB Ronald Watson
	DB Tim Childers

RUSHING: Mack 151/862y, Driver 146/774y, Flowers 127/557y
PASSING: Eppley 99-166/1410y, 13TD, 59.6%
RECEIVING: Williams 19/342y, Dunn 17/236y, Roulhac 15/214y
SCORING: Bob Paulling (K) 90pts, Flowers & Mack 48pts

1984 7-4

40	Appalachian St.	7	WR Richard Butler
55	Virginia	0	WR Terrance Roulhac
23	Georgia	26	T Reid Ingle
21	Georgia. Tech	28	G Steve Reese
20	North Carolina	12	C Dale Swing
54	Duke	21	G Andy Cheatham
35	N. Carolina St.	34	T Joe Ellis
37	Wake Forest	14	TE K.D. Dunn
17	Virginia Tech	10	QB Mike Eppley
23	Maryland	41	TB Stacey Driver / Steve Griffin
21	South Carolina	22	FB Kenny Flowers
			DL Jeff Wells
			DL Steve Berlin
			DL William Perry
			DL Michael Dean Perry
			DL Terence Mack
			LB Henry Walls
			LB Eldridge Milton
			DB Ty Davis
			DB Reggie Pleasant
			DB Ronald Watson
			DB Kenny Danforth

RUSHING: Driver 139/627y, Flowers 113/562y, Griffin 71/355y
PASSING: Eppley 116-213/1494y, 14TD, 54.5%
RECEIVING: Roulhac 26/512y, Williams 23/268y, Dunn 22/219y
SCORING: Donald Igwebuike (K) 89pts, Roulhac & Driver 48pts

1985 6-6

20	Virginia Tech	17	WR Ray Williams / Keith Jennings
13	Georgia	20	WR Terrance Roulhac / Gary Cooper
3	Georgia Tech	14	T John Watson
7	Kentucky	26	G Steve Reese
27	Virginia	24	C Jeff Lytton / Eric Nix
21	Duke	9	G John Phillips / Frank Deiulis
39	N. Carolina St.	10	T Wes Mann
26	Wake Forest	10	TE Jim Riggs
20	North Carolina	21	QB Rodney Williams / Randy Anderson
31	Maryland	34	TB Jackie Flowers/Stacey Driver/T. Flagler
24	South Carolina	17	FB Chris Lancaster / Richard Smith
13	Minnesota■	20	DL Michael Dean Perry
			DL Steve Berlin
			DL Brian Raber / Mark Drag
			DL Dwayne Meadows
			DL Terence Mack / Lawrence Brunson
			LB Henry Walls
			LB Keith Williams / James Earle
			DB Perry Williams
			DB Delton Hall / Donnell Woolford
			DB A.J. Johnson
			DB Kenny Danforth / Matt Riggs

RUSHING: Flowers 227/1200y
PASSING: Anderson 63-123/703y, 51.2%
RECEIVING: Roulhac 31/533y
SCORING: Flowers 78pts

1986 8-2-2

14	Virginia Tech	20	WR Ray Williams / Keith Jennings
31	Georgia	28	WR Terrance Roulhac
27	Georgia Tech	3	T Ty Granger
24	Citadel	0	G Pat Williams
31	Virginia	17	C Jeff Bak
35	Duke	3	G John Phillips
3	N. Carolina St.	27	T Frank Deiulis / Jeff Nunamacher
28	Wake Forest	20	TE Jim Riggs
38	North Carolina	10	QB Rodney Williams
17	Maryland	17	TB Terrance Flagler / Jackie Flowers
21	South Carolina	21	FB Chris Lancaster / Tracy Johnson
27	Stanford■	21	DL Raymond Chavous
			DL Tony Stephens / Brian Raber
			DL Dwayne Meadows
			DL Terrance Mack
			LB James Earle / Taylor Harps
			LB Henry Carter
			LB Norman Haynes / Dorian Mariable
			DB Donnell Woolford
			DB Delton Hall / Richard Smith
			DB James Lott / A.J. Johnson
			DB Gene Beasley / Matt Riggs

RUSHING: Flagler 192/1258y
PASSING: Rodney Williams 98-200/1245y, 49.0%
RECEIVING: Ray Williams 20/280y, Roulhac 20/228y
SCORING: Flagler 78pts

1987 10-2

43	W. Carolina	0	WR Ricardo Hooper
22	Virginia Tech	10	WR Keith Jennings
21	Georgia	20	T Ty Granger
33	Georgia Tech	12	G Eric Harmon
38	Virginia	21	C Jeff Bak
17	Duke	10	G John Phillips
28	N. Carolina St.	30	T Jeff Nunamacher
31	Wake Forest	17	TE Dan Pearman
13	North Carolina	10	QB Rodney Williams
45	Maryland	16	TB Wesley McFadden / Terry Allen
7	South Carolina	20	FB Tracy Johnson
35	Penn State■	10	DL Raymond Chavous
			DL Tony Stephens
			DL Michael Dean Perry
			DL Jesse Hatcher
			LB James Earle
			LB Norman Haynes
			LB Vince Taylor / Dorian Mariable
			DB Donnell Woolford
			DB James Lott
			DB Richard Smith
			DB Gene Beasley / Rusty Charpia

RUSHING: Allen 183/973y, McFadden 137/781y, Johnson 119/557y
PASSING: Williams 101-209/1486y, 6TD, 48.3%
RECEIVING: Cooper 34/618y, Jennings 31/475y, Hooper 13/153y
SCORING: David Treadwell (K) 82pts, Johnson 54pts, Allen 48pts

1988 10-2

40	Virginia Tech	7	WR Keith Jennings / Chip Davis
23	Furman	3	WR Ricardo Hooper / Gary Cooper
21	Florida State	24	T Frank Deiulis
30	Georgia Tech	13	G Jeb Flesch
10	Virginia	7	C Jeff Bak
49	Duke	17	G Eric Harmon
3	N. Carolina St.	10	T Jeff Nunamacher
38	Wake Forest	21	TE James Coley
37	North Carolina	14	QB Rodney Williams
49	Maryland	25	TB Terry Allen / Joe Henderson
29	South Carolina	10	FB Tracy Johnson / Tony Kennedy
13	Oklahoma■	6	DL Vance Hammond
			DL Mark Drag / David Davis
			DL Richard McCullough / Otis Moore
			DL Jesse Hatcher
			LB Levon Kirkland
			LB Ed McDaniel / Vince Taylor
			LB Doug Brewster / John Johnson
			DB Donnell Woolford / Tony Mauney
			DB Dexter Davis
			DB James Lott / Richard Smith
			DB Gene Beasley / Rusty Charpia

RUSHING: Allen 216/1192y, Henderson 110/538y, Johnson 113/441y
PASSING: Williams 78-186/1144y, 5TD, 41.9%
RECEIVING: Jennings 30/397y, Hooper 18/265y, Cooper 13/417y
SCORING: Allen 60pts, Chris Gardocki (K) 58pts, Johnson 50pts

1989 10-2

30	Furman	0	WR Rodney Fletcher
34	Florida State	23	WR Gary Cooper
27	Virginia Tech	7	T Stacy Long
31	Maryland	7	G Jeb Flesch
17	Duke	21	C Hank Phillips
34	Virginia	20	G Eric Harmon
14	Georgia Tech	30	T Bruce Bratton
30	N. Carolina St.	10	TE Stacy Fields
44	Wake Forest	10	QB Chris Morocco / DeChane Cameron
35	North Carolina	3	TB Joe Henderson / Terry Allen
45	South Carolina	0	FB Wesley McFadden
27	West Virginia■	7	DL Otis Moore
			DL Rob Bodine
			DL Vance Hammond
			DL John Johnson
			LB Levon Kirkland
			LB Vince Taylor
			LB Doug Brewster / Dorian Mariable
			DB Jerome Henderson
			DB Dexter Davis
			DB Arlington Nunn
			DB James Lott

RUSHING: Henderson 178/848y, Allen 124/613y, McFadden 112/452y
PASSING: Morocco 79-134/1131y, 6TD, 59.0%
RECEIVING: Fletcher 35/556y, Cooper 29/504y, Fields 12/101y
SCORING: Chris Gardocki (K) 107pts, Allen 60pts, Henderson 48pts

1990 10-2

59	Long Beach St.	0	WR Terry Smith
7	Virginia	20	WR Doug Thomas / Larry Ryans
18	Maryland	17	T Stacy Long / Kelvin Hankins
48	Appalachian St.	0	G Jeb Flesch / David Puckett
26	Duke	7	C Curtis Whitley / Mike Brown
34	Georgia	3	G Eric Harmon
19	Georgia Tech	21	T Bruce Bratton / Les Hall
24	N. Carolina St.	17	TE Stacy Fields
24	Wake Forest	6	QB DeChane Cameron
20	North Carolina	3	TB Ronald Williams / Derrick Witherspoon
24	South Carolina	15	FB Howard Hall / Rudy Harris
30	Illinois■	0	DL Chester McGlockton
			DL Rob Bodine / David Davis
			DL Vance Hammond / Al Richard
			LB Levon Kirkland
			LB Ed McDaniel
			LB Doug Brewster / Wayne Simmons
			LB John Johnson
			DB Jerome Henderson / Eric Geter
			DB Dexter Davis
			DB Robert O'Neal
			DB Arlington Nunn

RUSHING: Williams 178/941y, Harris 84/373y, Cameron 125/361y
PASSING: Cameron 98-194/1185y, 7TD, 50.5%
RECEIVING: Smith 34/480y, Thomas 21/309y, Fields 13/121y
SCORING: Chris Gardocki 96pts, Williams 50pts, Harris 30pts

1991 9-2-1

34	Appalachian St.	0	WR Terry Smith
37	Temple	7	WR Larry Ryans / Dwayne Bryant
9	Georgia Tech	7	T Bruce Bratton / Les Hall
12	Georgia	27	G Jeb Flesch / John Harris
20	Virginia	20	C Mike Brown / Curtis Whitley
29	N. Carolina St.	19	G Stacy Seegars
28	Wake Forest	10	T Kelvin Hankins
21	North Carolina	6	TE Ty Gibson
40	Maryland	7	QB DeChance Cameron
41	South Carolina	24	TB Rodney Blunt / Ronald Williams
33	Duke	21	FB Rudy Harris / Howard Hall /Paul Caputo
13	California■	37	DL Chester McGlockton / Al Richard
			DL Rob Bodine
			DL Brentson Buckner
			LB Levon Kirkland
			LB Kenzil Jackson / Chuck O'Brien
			LB Ed McDaniel
			LB Wayne Simmons / Ashley Sheppard
			DB Eric Geter
			DB Darnell Stephens / Tony Mauney
			DB Robert O'Neal / Norris Brown
			DB Tyrone Mouzon

RUSHING: Blunt 160/706y, Williams 82/585y, Harris 100/441y
PASSING: Cameron 111-193/1478y, 5TD, 57.5%
RECEIVING: Smith 45/758y, Ryans 20/273y, Blunt 17/150y
SCORING: Nelson Welch (K) 81pts, Harris 54pts, Smith 36pts

1992 5-6

24	Ball State	10	WR Terry Smith
20	Florida State	24	WR Larry Ryans / Dwayne Bryant
16	Georgia Tech	20	T Brent LeJeune
54	Tenn.-Chatt'ga	3	G Jeff Fortner
29	Virginia	28	C John Harris
21	Duke	6	G Stacy Seegars
6	N. Carolina St.	20	T Les Hall
15	Wake Forest	18	TE Ty Gibson
40	North Carolina	7	QB Richard Moncrief / Patrick Sapp
23	Maryland	53	TB Rodney Blunt
13	South Carolina	24	FB Rudy Harris
			DL Brentson Buckner
			DL Carlos Curry
			DL Warren Forney
			LB Tim Jones / Wardell Rouse
			LB Wayne Simmons
			LB Kenzil Jackson / Derek Burnette
			LB Ashley Sheppard
			DB Eric Geter / Andre Humphrey
			DB Norris Brown
			DB Robert O'Neal
			DB Darnell Stephens / Brian Dawkins

RUSHING: Blunt 149/812y
PASSING: Sapp 60-144/750y, 3TD, 41.7%
RECEIVING: Smith 38/596y
SCORING: Nelson Welch (K) 89pts

1993 9-3

24 UNLV	14 WR Terry Smith
0 Florida State	57 WR Jason Davis / Marcus Hinton
16 Georgia Tech	13 T Brent LeJeune
20 N. Carolina St.	14 G Will Young
13 Duke	10 C Bryce Nelson
16 Wake Forest	20 G Stacy Seegars
27 East Tenn. St.	0 T Robert Jackson
29 Maryland	0 TE Stephon Wynn
0 North Carolina	24 QB Patrick Sapp
23 Virginia	14 TB Rodney Blunt
16 South Carolina	13 FB Emory Smith
14 Kentucky■	13 DL Brentson Buckner
	DL Carlos Curry
	DL LaMarick Simpson
	LB Tim Jones
	LB Derek Burnette / Mike Barber
	LB Harom Pringle
	LB Wardell Rouse / Darnell Stephens
	DB Andre Humphrey / Dexter McCleon
	DB Peter Ford
	DB Leomont Evans
	DB Brian Dawkins

RUSHING: Smith 89/387y
PASSING: Sapp 66-133/1984y, 4TD, 49.6%
RECEIVING: Hinton 14/241y
SCORING: Nelson Welch (K) 62pts

1994 5-6

27 Furman	6 WR Kenya Crooks
12 N. Carolina St.	29 WR Marcus Hinton / Antwuan Wyatt
6 Virginia	9 T Jim Bundren
13 Maryland	0 G Glenn Rountree
14 Georgia	40 C Trevor Putnam
13 Duke	19 G Will Young
0 Florida State	17 T Dwayne Morgan / Robert Jackson
24 Wake Forest	8 TE Ed Glenn / Lamont Hall
28 North Carolina	17 QB Nealon Greene/Patrick Sapp
20 Georgia Tech	10 TB Lamont Pegues / Anthony Downs
7 South Carolina	33 FB Raymond Priester
	DL Marvin Cross / Warren Forney
	DL Carlos Curry / Raymond White
	DL LaMarick Simpson / Brett Williams
	LB Tim Jones
	LB Mike Barber / Chuck Winslow
	LB Wardell Rouse
	LB Darnell Stephens
	DB Andre Humphrey / Peter Ford
	DB Dexter McCleon
	DB Andre Carter
	DB Brian Dawkins

RUSHING: Pegues 92/390y, Priester 87/343y, L.Solomon 67/320y
PASSING: Greene 51-94/524y, 1TD, 54.3%
Sapp 39-88/444y, 2TD, 44.3%
RECEIVING: Wyatt 30/282y, Crooks 21/208y, Hinton 18/280y
SCORING: Nelson Welch (K) 62pts

1995 8-4

55 W. Carolina	9 WR Tony Horne / Kenya Crooks
26 Florida State	45 WR Joe Woods / Antwuan Wyatt
29 Wake Forest	14 T Jim Bundren
3 Virginia	22 G Glenn Rountree
43 N. Carolina St.	22 C Trevor Putnam / Jamie Trimble
17 Georgia	19 G Will Young
17 Maryland	0 T Robert Jackson / Holland Postell
24 Georgia Tech	3 TE Lamont Hall
17 North Carolina	10 QB Nealon Greene
34 Duke	17 TB Raymond Priester / Anthony Downs
38 South Carolina	17 FB Emory Smith
0 Syracuse■	41 DL Raymond White / Eric Bradford
	DL Carlos Curry
	DL LaMarick Simpson / Tony Plantin
	LB Brett Williams
	LB Andye McCrorey / Chris Jones
	LB Anthony Simmons / Mond Wilson
	LB Patrick Sapp
	DB Dexter McCleon / Peter Ford
	DB Andy Ford
	DB Leomont Evans / Antwan Edwards
	DB Brian Dawkins / Andre Carter

RUSHING: Priester 223/1286y, Smith 139/682y, Greene 94/343y
PASSING: Greene 107-183/1474y, 10TD, 58.5%
RECEIVING: Wyatt 42/662y, Horne 22/433y, Priester 10/58y
SCORING: Smith 90pts

1996 7-5

0 North Carolina	45 WR Kenya Crooks / Tony Horne
19 Furman	3 WR Joe Woods / Mal Lawyer
24 Missouri	38 T Jim Bundren
21 Wake Forest	10 G Glenn Rountree
3 Florida State	34 C Jamie Trimble / Ed Altman
13 Duke	6 G Matt Butler
28 Georgia Tech	25 T Holland Postell
35 Maryland	3 TE Lamont Hall / Wesley Ellis
24 Virginia	16 QB Nealon Greene
40 N. Carolina St.	17 TB Raymond Priester
31 South Carolina	34 FB Emory Smith / Kelton Dunnican
7 LSU■	10 DL Trevor Price / Donald Broomfield
	DL Raymond White
	DL Brett Williams / Lorenzo Bromell
	LB Adrian Dingle / O.J. Childress
	LB Mond Wilson / Chris Jones
	LB Anthony Simmons
	LB Howard Bartley / Rahim Abdullah
	DB Dexter McCleon
	DB Peter Ford
	DB Andy Ford / Michael Allen
	DB Antwan Edwards

RUSHING: Priester 257/1345y, Dunnican 74/374y, Smith 80/324y
PASSING: Greene 111-219/1446y, 8TD, 50.7%
RECEIVING: Crooks 30/444y, Woods 27/374y, Horne 20/339y
SCORING: Priester 44pts

1997 7-5

23 Appalachian St.	12 WR Tony Horne / Rob Gardner
19 N. Carolina St.	17 WR Brian Wofford / Mal Lawyer
28 Florida State	35 T Jim Bundren
20 Georgia Tech	23 G Glenn Rountree
39 Texas-El Paso	7 C Jason Gamble
7 Virginia	21 G Corey Hulsey / Brent Banasiewicz
20 Maryland	9 T Holland Postell / Matt Butler
33 Wake Forest	16 TE Lamont Hall / Wesley Ellis
29 Duke	20 QB Nealon Greene
10 North Carolina	17 TB Raymond Priester / Javis Austin
47 South Carolina	21 FB Terry Witherspoon / Travis Macklin
17 Auburn■	21 DL Adrian Dingle / Terry Bryant
	DL Raymond White / Terry Jolly
	DL Tony Plantin / Donald Broomfield
	DL Lorenzo Bromell
	LB Mond Wilson / Chris Jones
	LB Anthony Simmons
	LB Rahim Abdullah / O.J. Childress
	DB Michael Allen
	DB Antwan Edwards
	DB Robert Carswell / Chad Speck
	DB DoMarco Fox / Darrel Crutchfield

RUSHING: Priester 204/894y, Greene 111/352y, With'rsp'n 57/222y
PASSING: Greene 169-265/2126y, 16TD, 63.8%
RECEIVING: Horne 68/897y, Lawyer 27/378y, Wofford 26/383y
SCORING: David Richardson (K) 56pts

1998 3-8

33 Furman	0 WR Mal Lawyer / Rod Gardner
0 Virginia Tech	37 WR Brian Wofford
18 Virginia	20 T Matt Butler
19 Wake Forest	29 G Corey Hulsey
14 North Carolina	21 C Jason Gamble
23 Maryland	0 G Brent Banasiewicz
0 Florida State	48 T Holland Postell
23 Duke	28 TE Wesley Ellis
39 N. Carolina St.	46 QB Brandon Streeter
21 Georgia Tech	24 TB Travis Zachery / Javis Austin
28 South Carolina	19 FB Terry Witherspoon / Vince Ciurciu
	DL Gary Childress
	DL Terry Jolly/Jovon Bush/Jason Hollom'n
	DL Terry Bryant
	LB Rahim Abdullah
	LB Harold Means / Keith Adams
	LB Chris Jones
	LB Adrian Dingle
	DB Alex Ardley
	DB Antwan Edwards
	DB Robert Carswell / Chad Speck
	DB DoMarco Fox / Charles Hafley

RUSHING: Zachery 158/635y, Austin 72/279y, Witherspoon 56/157y
PASSING: Streeter 150-282/1948y, 13TD, 53.2%
RECEIVING: Wofford 35/535y, Lawyer 31/464y, Austin 24/159y
SCORING: David Richardson (K) 44pts

1999 6-6

10 Marshall	13 WR Rod Gardner
33 Virginia	14 WR Justin Watts
11 Virginia Tech	31 T Akil Smith
31 North Carolina	20 G T.J. Watkins / Will Merritt
31 N. Carolina St.	35 C Kyle Young
42 Maryland	30 G Theo Mougros
14 Florida State	17 T John McDermott
12 Wake Forest	3 TE Pat Cyrgalis / Jason LeMay
58 Duke	7 QB Woodrow Dantzler / Brandon Streeter
42 Georgia Tech	45 TB Travis Zachery
31 South Carolina	21 FB Terry Witherspoon
7 Mississippi St.■	17 DL Demonte McKenzie / Gary Childress
	DL Terry Jolly
	DL Jason Holloman
	DL Terry Bryant / Nick Eason
	LB Braxton Williams
	LB Chad Carson
	LB Keith Adams
	DB Alex Ardley
	DB Dextra Polite / Darrel Crutchfield
	DB Robert Carswell / Chad Speck
	DB DoMarco Fox / Charles Hafley

RUSHING: Zachery 184/827y, Dantzler 137/580y
PASSING: Dantzler 111-195/1501y, 9TD, 56.9%
Streeter 111-166/1165y, 4TD, 67.7%
RECEIVING: Gardner 73/1009y, Wofford 54/648y, Lawyer 34/350y
SCORING: Zachery 96pts

2000 9-3

38 Citadel	0 WR Rod Gardner / J.J. McKelvey
62 Missouri	9 WR Justin Watts / Matt Bailey
55 Wake Forest	7 T T.J. Watkins / Akil Smith
31 Virginia	10 G Will Merritt
52 Duke	22 C Kyle Young
34 N. Carolina St.	27 G Theo Mougros
35 Maryland	14 T John McDermott
38 North Carolina	24 WR Jackie Robinson / Kevin Youngblood
28 Georgia Tech	31 QB Woodrow Dantzler
7 Florida State	54 TB Travis Zachery / Bernard Rambert
16 South Carolina	14 FB Terry Witherspoon
20 Virginia Tech■	41 DL Nick Eason
	DL Terry Jolly
	DL Jovon Bush / Jason Holloman
	DL Terry Bryant
	LB Keith Adams / Altroy Bodrick
	LB Chad Carson
	LB Braxton Williams / Rodney Thomas
	DB Alex Ardley
	DB Darrel Crutchfield / Brian Mance
	DB Robert Carswell
	DB Charles Hafley / Eric Meekins

RUSHING: Zachery 201/1012y, Dantzler 172/947y, Kelly 47/240y
PASSING: Dantzler 122-212/1691y, 10TD, 57.5%
RECEIVING: Gardner 51/1009y, Zachery 27/648y
SCORING: Zachery 108pts

2001 7-5

21 Central Florida	13 WR J.J. McKelvey / Roscoe Crosby
38 Wofford	14 WR Derrick Hamilton / Airese Currie
24 Virginia	26 T Akil Smith / Gary Byrd
47 Georgia Tech	44 G T.J. Watkins
45 N. Carolina St.	37 C Kyle Young
3 North Carolina	38 G Will Merritt
21 Wake Forest	14 T Derrick Brantley
27 Florida State	41 TE Morgan Woodward / Ben Hall
20 Maryland	37 QB Woodrow Dantzler
15 South Carolina	20 TB Travis Zachery / Bernard Rambert
59 Duke	31 WR Jackie Robinson / Matt Bailey
49 La. Tech■	24 DL Bryant McNeal / J.J. Howard
	DL Nick Eason / Donnell Washington
	DL Jovon Bush / DeJuan Polk
	DL Khaleed Vaughn / Maurice Fountain
	LB Rodney Thomas / Rodney Feaster
	LB Chad Carson
	LB John Leake / Eric Sampson
	DB Brian Mance / Ryan Hemby
	DB Kevin Johnson / Toure Francis
	DB Charles Hafley / Braxton Williams
	DB Eric Meekins

RUSHING: Dantzler 221/1061y, Zachery 142/576y
PASSING: Dantzler 203-334/2578y, 21TD, 60.8%
RECEIVING: Hamilton 53/684y, Zachery 45/414y
SCORING: Aaron Hunt (K) 74pts, Zachery 66pts, Dantzler 60pts

2002 7-6

28 Georgia	31 WR Kevin Youngblood
33 Louisiana Tech	13 WR Derrick Hamilton / J.J. McKelvey
24 Georgia Tech	19 T Gary Byrd
30 Ball State	7 G Cedric Johnson
31 Florida State	48 C Jermyn Chester / Tommy Sharpe
17 Virginia	22 G Gregory Walker
31 Wake Forest	23 T William Henry
6 N. Carolina St.	38 TE Ben Hall / Bobby Williamson
34 Duke	31 QB Willie Simmons / Charlie Whitehurst
42 North Carolina	12 TB Bernard Rambert / Yusef Kelly
12 Maryland	30 WR Jackie Robinson / Airese Currie
27 South Carolina	20 DL Khaleed Vaughn / Maurice Fountain
15 Texas Tech■	55 DL Nick Eason / Eric Coleman
	DL Donnell Washington / DeJuan Polk
	DL Bryant McNeal / J.J. Howard
	LB John Leake / Brandon Jamison
	LB Rodney Thomas / Leroy Hill
	LB Eric Sampson / Rodney Feaster
	DB Brian Mance / Kevin Johnson
	DB Justin Miller
	DB Eric Meekins / Travis Pugh
	DB Altroy Bodrick / Kelvin Morris

RUSHING: Kelly 125/520y, Rambert 117/488y,
Tye Hill (TB) 42/225y, Hamilton 21/208y
PASSING: Simmons 142-244/1559y, 6TD, 58.2%,
Whitehurst 123-214/1554y, 10TD, 57.5%
RECEIVING: Youngblood 59/591y, McKelvey 52/785y,
Hamilton 52/602y
SCORING: Aaron Hunt (K) 88pts, Kelly 42pts, Rambert 36pts

2003 9-4

0 Georgia	30 WR Kevin Youngblood / Tony Elliott
28 Furman	17 WR Derrick Hamilton / Airese Currie
37 M. Tennessee	14 T William Henry
39 Georgia Tech	3 G Cedric Johnson / Roman Fry
7 Maryland	21 C Tommy Sharpe / Dustin Fry
30 Virginia	27 G Nathan Bennett / Chip Myrick
15 N. Carolina St.	17 T Gregory Walker
36 North Carolina	28 TE Bobby Williamson
17 Wake Forest	45 QB Charlie Whitehurst
26 Florida State	10 TB Duane Coleman / Kyle Browning
40 Duke	7 FB Chad Jasmin / Cliff Harrell / Yusef Kelly
63 South Carolina	17 DL Khaleed Vaughn / Vontrell Jamison
27 Tennessee■	14 DL Donnell Washington / Eric Coleman
	DL DeJuan Polk / Trey Tate
	DL Maurice Fountain / J.J. Howard
	LB John Leake
	LB Leroy Hill / Anthony Waters
	LB Eric Sampson / Lionel Richardson
	DB Tye Hill
	DB Justin Miller / Toure Francis
	DB Travis Pugh
	DB Jamaal Fudge

RUSHING: Coleman 133/615y, Jasmin 112/523y, Browning
PASSING: Whitehurst 288-465/3561y, 21TD, 61.9%
RECEIVING: Youngblood 70/897y, Hamilton 62/1026y,
Currie 43/560y
SCORING: Aaron Hunt (K) 92pts, Hamilton 66pts, Jasmin 54pts

2004 6-5

37 Wake Forest	30 WR Airese Currie
24 Georgia Tech	28 WR Chansi Stuckey / Michael Collins
6 Texas A&M	27 T Barry Richardson
22 Florida State	41 G Cedric Johnson
10 Virginia	30 C Tommy Sharpe
35 Utah State	6 G Nathan Bennett / Roman Fry
10 Maryland	7 T Marion Dukes
26 N. Carolina St.	20 TE Ben Hall
24 Miami	17 QB Charlie Whitehurst
13 Duke	16 TB Reggie Merriweather / Duane Coleman
29 South Carolina	7 WR Curtis Baham / Kelvin Grant
	DL Charles Bennett / Bobby Williamson
	DL Eric Coleman / Donnell Clark
	DL Trey Tate / Cory Groover
	DL Maurice Fountain / Gaines Adams
	LB Anthony Waters / Nick Watkins
	LB Leroy Hill / David Dunham
	LB Tremaine Billie / Eric Sampson
	DB Tye Hill / C.J. Gaddis
	DB Justin Miller
	DB Travis Pugh
	DB Jamaal Fudge

RUSHING: Merriweather 136/670y, Coleman 83/284y,
Yusef Kelly (TB) 38/109y, Kyle Browning (TB) 14/105y
PASSING: Whitehurst 177-349/2067y, 7TD, 50.7%
RECEIVING: Currie 61/868y, Stuckey 25/280y, Grant 23/274y
SCORING: Merriweather 66pts, Jad Dean (K) 53pts, J. Miller 18pts

2005 8-4

25 Texas A&M	24 WR Aaron Kelly / Kelvin Grant
28 Maryland	24 WR Chansi Stuckey
30 Miami	36 WR Curtis Baham / Rendrick Taylor
13 Boston College	16 T Barry Richardson
27 Wake Forest	31 G Roman Fry
31 N. Carolina St.	10 C Dustin Fry
37 Temple	7 G Nathan Bennett / Chip Myrick
9 Georgia Tech	10 T Marion Dukes
49 Duke	20 TE Bobby Williamson / Thomas Hunter
35 Florida State	14 QB Charlie Whitehurst
13 South Carolina	9 RB James Davis / Reggie Merriweather
19 Colorado■	10 DL Charles Bennett / Phillip Merling
	DL Donnell Clark / Cory Groover
	DL Tre Tate / Rashaad Jackson
	DL Gaines Adams
	LB Tramaine Billie
	LB Anthony Waters / Lionel Richardson
	LB Nick Watkins / David Dunham
	DB Tye Hill / Chris Clemons
	DB Duane Coleman / Sergio Gilliam
	DB Jamaal Fudge
	DB C.J. Gaddis / Michael Hamlin

RUSHING: Davis 165/879y, Merriweather 149/715y,
Kyle Browning 33/105y
PASSING: Whitehurst 229-340/2483y, 11TDs, 67.4%
RECEIVING: Stuckey 64/770y, Kelly 47/575y, Baham 32/500y
SCORING: Jad Dean (K) 106pts, Davis 54pts,
Merriweather 42pts

2006 8-5

54 Florida Atlantic	6 WR Aaron Kelly
33 Boston College	34 WR Chansi Stuckey
27 Florida State	20 WR Tyler Grisham / Jacoby Ford
52 North Carolina	7 T Barry Richardson
51 Louisiana Tech	0 G Roman Fry / Chris McDuffie
27 Wake Forest	17 C Dustin Fry
63 Temple	9 G Nathan Bennett
31 Georgia Tech	7 T Marion Dukes
7 Virginia Tech	24 TE Thomas Hunter / Akeem Robinson
12 Maryland	13 QB Will Proctor
20 N. Carolina St.	14 RB James Davis / C.J. Spiller
28 South Carolina	31 DL Phillip Merling / Brandon Cannon
20 Kentucky■	28 DL Jock McKissic / Rashaad Jackson
	DL Dorell Scott / Donnell Clark
	DL Gaines Adams
	LB Antonio Clay
	LB Maurice Nelson / Kavell Conner
	LB Nick Watkins
	DB Duane Coleman / Crezdon Butler
	DB C.J. Gaddis / Chris Chancellor
	DB Chris Clemons / Roy Walker
	DB Michael Hamlin

RUSHING: Davis 195/1134y, Spiller 124/914y,
Demerick Chancellor (RB) 45/276y
PASSING: Proctor160-265/2081y, 13TD, 60.4%
RECEIVING: Stuckey 45/607y, Kelly 24/289y, Grisham 20/215y
SCORING: Davis 102pts, Jad Dean (K) 91pts, Spiller 72pts

2007 9-4

24 Florida State	18 WR Aaron Kelly
49 La.-Monroe	26 WR Tyler Grisham
38 Furman	10 WR Jacoby Ford
42 N. Carolina St.	20 T Barry Richardson
3 Georgia Tech	33 G Chris McDuffie
23 Virginia Tech	41 C Thomas Austin (G)
70 C. Michigan	14 G Brandon Pilgrim / Barry Humphries (C)
30 Maryland	17 T Christian Capote
47 Duke	10 TE Michael Palmer / Brian Linthicum
44 Wake Forest	10 QB Cullen Harper
17 Boston College	20 RB James Davis / C.J. Spiller
23 South Carolina	21 DL Phillip Merling
20 Auburn■	23 DL Dorell Scott
	DL Rashaad Jackson / Jamie Cumbie
	DL Ricky Sapp / Kevin Alexander
	LB Tramaine Billie / Scotty Cooper
	LB Cortney Vincent / Antonio Clay
	LB Nick Watkins / Kavell Connor
	DB Chris Chancellor
	DB Crezdon Butler / Byron Maxwell
	DB Chris Clemons
	DB Michael Hamlin / DeAndre McDaniel

RUSHING: Davis 214/1064y, Spiller 145/768y, Ford 14/172y
PASSING: Harper 282-433/2991y, 27TD, 65.1%
RECEIVING: Kelly 88/1081y, Grisham 60/653y, Ford 17/310y
SCORING: Mark Buchholz (K) 106pts, Davis 72pts,
Ford & Grisham 24pts

2008 7-6

10 Alabama	34 WR Aaron Kelly
45 Citadel	17 WR Tyler Grisham
27 N. Carolina St.	9 WR Jacoby Ford / Xavier Dye
54 S. Carolina St.	0 T Chris Hairston
17 Maryland	20 G Thomas Austin (C) / David Smith
7 Wake Forest	12 C Bobby Hutchinson
17 Georgia Tech	21 G Mason Cloy / Barry Humphreys
27 Boston College	21 T Landon Walker / Cory Lambert
27 Florida State	41 TE Michael Palmer / Durrell Barry
31 Duke	7 QB Cullen Harper
13 Virginia	3 RB James Davis / C.J. Spiller
31 South Carolina	14 DL Da'Quan Bowers / Kourtnei Brown
21 Nebraska■	26 DL Dorell Scott / Brandon Thompson
	DL Jarvis Jenkins / Rashaad Jackson
	DL Ricky Sapp / Kevin Alexander
	LB DeAndre McDaniel / Jeremy Campbell
	LB Brandon Maye / Stanley Hunter
	LB Kavell Conner / Scotty Cooper
	DB Crezdon Butler / Byron Maxwell
	DB Chris Chancellor
	DB Chris Clemons
	DB Michael Hamlin / Marcus Gilchrist

RUSHING: Davis 171/751y, Spiller 116/629y,
Jamie Harper (RB) 34/133y
PASSING: C. Harper 221-360/2601y, 13TD, 61.4%
RECEIVING: Kelly 67/722y, Ford 55/710y, Grisham 37/372y
SCORING: Mark Buchholz (K) 85pts, Davis & Spiller 66pts

2009 9-5

37 Middle Tenn.	14 WR Xavier Dye / Chad Diehl
27 Georgia Tech	30 WR Terrance Ashe / Dwayen Allen
25 Boston College	7 WR Jacoby Ford / Marquan Jones
10 TCU	14 T Chris Hairston
21 Maryland	24 G Thomas Austin
38 Wake Forest	3 C Dalton Freeman / Mason Cloy
40 Miami	37 G Antoine McClain
49 Cstl. Carolina	3 T Landon Walker / Cory Lambert
40 Florida State	24 TE Michael Palmer / Durrell Barry
43 N. Carolina St.	23 QB Kyle Parker
34 Virginia	21 RB C.J. Spiller / Jamie Harper
17 South Carolina	34 DL Da'Quan Bowers / Andre Branch
34 Georgia Tech□	39 DL Jarvis Jenkins / Jamie Cumby
21 Kentucky■	13 DL Brandon Thompson / Miguel Chavis
	DL Ricky Sapp / Malliciah Goodman
	LB Kevin Alexander
	LB Brandon Moye
	LB Kavell Conner
	DB Crezdon Butler / Byron Maxwell
	DB Chris Chancellor
	DB Marcus Gilchrist / Rashard Hall
	DB DeAndre McDaniel / Sadat Chambers

RUSHING: Spiller 216/1212y, Andre Ellington (RB) 68/491y,
Harper 80/418y
PASSING: Parker 205-369/2526y, 20TD, 55.6%
RECEIVING: Ford 56/779y, Palmer 43/507y, Spiller 36/503y
SCORING: Spiller 128pts, Richard Jackson (K) 101pts, Ford 54pts

2010 6-7

35 North Texas	10 WR DeAndre Hopkins / Xavier Dye
58 Presbyterian	21 WR Jason Brown / Marquan Jones
24 Auburn	27 T Chris Hairston
21 Miami	30 G David Smith / Mason Cloy
16 North Carolina	21 C Dalton Freeman
31 Maryland	7 G Antoine McClain
27 Georgia Tech	13 T Landon Walker
10 Boston College	16 TE Dwayne Allen / Brandon Ford
14 N. Carolina St.	13 QB Kyle Parker
13 Florida State	16 RB Jamie Harper / Andre Ellington
30 Wake Forest	10 FB/WR Chad Diehl / Bryce McNeal
7 South Carolina	29 DL Da'Quan Bowers / Kourtnel Brown
26 South Florida■	31 DL Jarvis Jenkins / Rennie Moore
	DL Brandon Thompson / Miguel Chavis
	DL Andre Branch / Malliciah Goodman
	LB Brandon Maye / Jonathan Willard
	LB Corico Hawkins
	LB/DB Quandon Christian / Byron Maxwell
	DB Marcus Gilchrist
	DB Xavier Brewer / Coty Sensabaugh
	DB Rashard Hall / Jonathan Meeks
	DB DeAndre McDaniel

RUSHING: Harper 197/760y, Ellington 118/686y
PASSING: Parker 196-341/2213y, 12TD, 57.5%
RECEIVING: Hopkins 52/637y, Harper 35/328y, Allen 33/373y
Brown 32/405y
SCORING: Chandler Catanzaro (K), Ellington 72pts, Harper 60pts

COLORADO

University of Colorado (Founded 1876)
Boulder, Colorado
Nickname: Buffaloes
Colors: Silver, Gold and Black
Stadium: Folsom Field (1924) 53,750
Conference Affiliations: Big Seven (1948-59), Big Eight (1960-95),
  Big Twelve North (1996-2010), Pac 12 (2011-present)

CAREER RUSHING YARDS	Attempts	Yards
Eric Bieniemy (1987-90)	699	3940
Rashaan Salaam (1992-94)	486	3057
Bobby Purify (2000-04)	595	3016
Charlie Davis (1971-73)	538	2958
Rodney Stewart (2008-10)	620	2744
Chris Brown (2001-02)	465	2690
Hugh Charles (2004-07)	517	2659
James Mayberry (1975-78)	546	2544
Herchell Troutman (1994-97)	568	2487
Bob Anderson (1967-69)	568	2367

CAREER PASSING YARDS	Comp.-Att.	Yards
Cody Hawkins (2007-10)	691-1253	7733
Joel Klatt (2002-05)	666-1095	7375
Kordell Stewart (1991-94)	456-785	6481
Koy Detmer (1992-96)	350-594	5390
Mike Moschetti (1998-99)	366-607	4797
John Hessler (1994-97)	347-627	4788
Steve Vogel (1981-84)	309-688	3912
Darian Hagan (1988-91)	213-424	3801
Craig Ochs (2000-02)	265-453	3325
Gale Weidner (1959-61)	218-480	3033

CAREER RECEIVING YARDS	Catches	Yards
Michael Westbrook (1991-94)	167	2548
Rae Carruth (1992-96)	135	2540
Scotty McKnight (2007-10)	215	2521
Charles Johnson (1990-93)	127	2447
Phil Savoy (1994-97)	152	2176
Derek McCoy (2000-03)	134	2038
Javon Green (1997-00)	136	2031
Daniel Graham (1998-01)	106	1543
Monte Huber (1967-69)	111	1436
Dusty Sprague (2004-07)	103	1261

SEASON RUSHING YARDS	Attempts	Yards
Rashaan Salaam (1994)	298	2055
Chris Brown (2002)	275	1744
Eric Bieniemy (1990)	288	1628
Charles Davis (1971)	219	1386
Rodney Stewart (2010)	290	1318

SEASON PASSING YARDS	Comp.-Att.	Yards
Koy Detmer (1996)	208-363	3156
Cody Hawkins (2007)	263-463	3015
Joel Klatt (2005)	241-400	2696
Mike Moschetti (1999)	204-331	2693
Joel Klatt (2003)	233-358	2614

SEASON RECEIVING YARDS	Catches	Yards
Charles Johnson (1992)	57	1149
Rae Carruth (1996)	54	1116
Charles Johnson (1993)	57	1082
Michael Westbrook (1992)	76	1060
D.J. Hackett (2003)	78	1013

GAME RUSHING YARDS	Attempts	Yards
Charles Davis (1971 vs. Oklahoma State)	34	342
Rashaan Salaam (1994 vs. Texas)	35	317
Chris Brown (2002 vs. Kansas)	25	309

GAME PASSING YARDS	Comp.-Att.	Yards
Mike Moschetti (1999 vs. San Jose State)	25-32	465
Koy Detmer (1996 vs. Missouri)	19-33	457
Koy Detmer (1995 vs. NE Louisiana)	19-27	426

GAME RECEIVING YARDS	Catches	Yards
Walter Stanley (1981 vs. Texas Tech)	5	222
Rae Carruth (1996 vs. Missouri)	7	222
Derek McCoy (2003 vs. Colorado State)	4	192

GREATEST COACH:

Although inspiring mixed emotions from college football fans, Bill McCartney brought the Colorado football program to new heights during his 13 years in Boulder. The all-time leader in coaching wins in school history with 93, McCartney inherited a team that won just seven games the preceding three seasons. McCartney led the Buffaloes to that same number of wins for his first three seasons. A change was needed, and McCartney opted for a Wishbone offense. The move paid immediate dividends as the 1985 edition of the Buffaloes went 7-5 and earned a bowl bid for the first time since 1976, losing to Washington 20-17 in the Freedom Bowl.

But McCartney was not satisfied. Although dipping to 6-6 in 1986, the Buffs won six of seven down the stretch with a 20-10 victory over Nebraska that helped the program as much as anything. By 1989 they arrived as a national title contender, easily sweeping a tough out-of-conference schedule to vault into the no. 3 spot in the AP poll. Dedicating the season to quarterback Sal Aunese, who died September 23 from a rare form of stomach cancer, Colorado then ran through their Big Eight schedule unblemished, including back-to-back wins over Oklahoma and Nebraska. By season's end they were ranked no. 1 for the first time in school history, although they could not keep that spot after losing in the Orange Bowl to Notre Dame. But McCartney refused to let his program slip and Colorado repeated much of their success from 1989, sweeping the Big Eight schedule and finishing the season ranked first with a date with Notre Dame. The second time was the charm and despite a loss and a tie, Colorado earned its first-ever national championship with a capture of the AP Poll (Georgia Tech won the UPI poll by one vote).

McCartney had signed a 15-year after the success of 1989, but he would not make it more than five seasons. Although his final season produced an 11-1 record, 1994 would be the final year of coaching for McCartney who surprised his team and college football with his decision.

COLORADO'S 55 GREATEST SINCE 1953

OFFENSE

WIDE RECEIVER: Rae Carruth, Charles Johnson, Dave Logan, Michael Westbrook
TIGHT END: J.V. Cain, Daniel Graham
TACKLE: Stan Brock, Mark Koncar, Mike Montler, Mark Vander Poel
GUARD: Joe Garten, Andre Gurode, Chris Naeole, John Wooten
CENTER: Pete Brock, Jay Leeuwenburg
QUARTERBACK: Darian Hagan, Kordell Stewart
RUNNING BACK: Eric Bieniemy, Carroll Hardy, James Mayberry, Rashaan Salaam
FULLBACK: John Bayuk, Bo Matthews

DEFENSE

END: Bill Brundidge, Bill Fairband, Herb Orvis, Mike Schnitker
TACKLE: Troy Archer, Leonard Renfro, Laval Short, Joel Steed
LINEBACKER: Greg Biekert, Jordon Dizon, Ted Johnson, Kanavis McGhee, Joe Romig, Matt Russell, Alfred Williams
CORNERBACK: Deon Figures, Mark Haynes, Chris Hudson, Victor Scott
SAFETY: Dick Anderson, Cullen Bryant, Hale Irwin, Mickey Pruitt

SPECIAL TEAMS

RETURN SPECIALISTS: Cliff Branch, Ben Kelly
PLACE KICKER: Mason Crosby
PUNTER: Barry Helton

MULTIPLE POSITIONS

QUARTERBACK-TAILBACK: Bobby Anderson
MIDDLE GUARD-LINEBACKER: Bud Magrum
DEFENSIVE BACK-PUNTER: John Stearns

TWO-WAY PLAYERS

END-DEFENSIVE END: Jerry Hillebrand

PERFORMANCE FORMULA:
COLORADO'S 10 BEST SEASONS

1989	1.7289	3 of 70
1994	1.6642	4 of 71
1990	1.6452	3 of 70
1995	1.6163	4 of 70
1971	1.5969	7 of 70
1996	1.5402	8 of 70
2001	1.4898	8 of 70
1961	1.4603	7 of 71
1956	1.4345	12 of 69
1954	1.4094	15 of 69

COLORADO BUFFALOES

Year	W-L-T	AP Poll	Conference Standing	Toughest Regular Season Opponents	Coach (Record at School)	Bowl Games		
1953	6-4		4t	Oklahoma 8-1-1, Missouri 6-4, Kansas State 6-3-1	Dallas Ward			
1954	7-2-1		3t	Oklahoma 10-0, Nebraska 6-4, Kansas State 7-3	Dallas Ward			
1955	6-4		3t	Oklahoma 10-0, Nebraska 5-5, Colorado State 8-2	Dallas Ward			
1956	8-2-1	20	2	Oklahoma 10-0, Oregon 4-4-2, Missouri 4-5	Dallas Ward	Orange	27 Clemson	21
1957	6-3-1		3t	Oklahoma 9-1, Kansas 5-4-1, Missouri 5-4-1	Dallas Ward			
1958	6-4		3	Oklahoma 9-1, Missouri 5-4-1, Air Force 9-0-1	Dallas Ward (63-41-6)			
1959	5-5		3t	Washington 9-1, Oklahoma 7-3, Missouri 6-4	Sonny Grandelius			
1960	6-4		2	Missouri 9-1, Kansas 7-2-1, Baylor 7-3	Sonny Grandelius			
1961	9-2	7	1	Missouri 7-2-1, Kansas 6-3-1, Miami 7-3	Sonny Grandelius (20-11)	Orange	7 Louisiana State	25
1962	2-8		7	Oklahoma 8-2, Missouri 7-1-2, Nebraska 8-2	Bud Davis (2-8)			
1963	2-8		6	Nebraska 9-1, Oklahoma 8-2, Southern Cal 7-3	Eddie Crowder			
1964	2-8		7	Nebraska 9-1, Oregon State 8-2, Southern Cal 7-3	Eddie Crowder			
1965	6-2-2		3	Nebraska 10-0, Missouri 7-2-1, Iowa State 5-4-1	Eddie Crowder			
1966	7-3		2	Nebraska 9-1, Miami 7-2-1, Missouri 6-3-1	Eddie Crowder			
1967	9-2	14	2t	Oklahoma 9-1, Missouri 7-3, Nebraska 6-4	Eddie Crowder	Bluebonnet	31 Miami	21
1968	4-6		4t	Kansas 9-1, Missouri 7-3, Oklahoma 7-3	Eddie Crowder			
1969	8-3	16	3	Penn State 10-0, Missouri 9-1, Nebraska 8-2	Eddie Crowder	Liberty	47 Alabama	33
1970	6-5		4	Nebraska 10-0-1, Air Force 9-2, Oklahoma 7-4	Eddie Crowder	Liberty	3 Tulane	17
1971	10-2	3	3	Nebraska 12-0, Oklahoma 10-1, LSU 8-3	Eddie Crowder	Bluebonnet	29 Houston	17
1972	8-4	16	3t	Oklahoma 10-1, Nebraska 8-2-1, Oklahoma State 6-5	Eddie Crowder	Gator	3 Auburn	24
1973	5-6		6t	Oklahoma 10-0-1, Nebraska 8-2-1, LSU 9-2	Eddie Crowder (67-49-2)			
1974	5-6		5	Oklahoma 11-0, Michigan 10-1, Nebraska 8-3	Bill Mallory			
1975	9-3	16	3	Oklahoma 10-1, Nebraska 10-1, Kansas 7-4	Bill Mallory	Bluebonnet	21 Texas	38
1976	8-4	16	1t	Oklahoma 8-2-1, Nebraska 8-3-1, Texas Tech 10-1	Bill Mallory	Orange	10 Ohio State	27
1977	7-3-1		4	Oklahoma 10-1, Nebraska 8-3, Stanford 8-3	Bill Mallory			
1978	6-5		7	Oklahoma 10-1, Nebraska 9-2, Missouri 7-4	Bill Mallory (35-21-1)			
1979	3-8		5t	Oklahoma 10-1, Nebraska 10-1, LSU 6-5	Chuck Fairbanks			
1980	1-10		7t	Oklahoma 9-2, Nebraska 9-2, UCLA 9-2	Chuck Fairbanks			
1981	3-8		7	Nebraska 9-2, BYU 10-2, Missouri 7-4	Chuck Fairbanks (7-26)			
1982	2-8-1		6t	Nebraska 11-1, UCLA 9-1-1, Oklahoma 8-3	Bill McCartney			
1983	4-7		6t	Nebraska 12-0, Oklahoma 8-4, Missouri 7-4	Bill McCartney			
1984	1-10		7	Nebraska 9-2, Oklahoma 9-1-1, Oklahoma State 9-2	Bill McCartney			
1985	7-5		3t	Oklahoma 10-1, Nebraska 9-2, Ohio State 8-3	Bill McCartney	Freedom	17 Washington	20
1986	6-6		2	Oklahoma 10-1, Nebraska 9-2, Ohio State 9-3	Bill McCartney	Bluebonnet	9 Baylor	21
1987	7-4		4	Oklahoma 11-0, Nebraska 10-1, Oklahoma State 9-2	Bill McCartney			
1988	8-4		4	Nebraska 11-1, Oklahoma State 9-2, Oklahoma 9-2	Bill McCartney	Freedom	17 Brigham Young	20
1989	11-1	4	1	Nebraska 10-1, Illinois 9-2, Washington 7-4	Bill McCartney	Orange	6 Notre Dame	21
1990	11-1-1	1	1	Washington 9-2, Tennessee 8-2-2, Oklahoma 8-3	Bill McCartney	Orange	10 Notre Dame	9
1991	8-3-1	20	1t	Nebraska 9-1-1, Oklahoma 8-3, Stanford 8-3	Bill McCartney	Blockbuster	25 Alabama	30
1992	9-2-1	13	2	Nebraska 9-2, Kansas 7-4, Baylor 6-5	Bill McCartney	Fiesta	22 Syracuse	26
1993	8-3-1	16	2	Nebraska 11-0, Miami 9-2, Oklahoma 8-3	Bill McCartney	Aloha	41 Fresno State	30
1994	11-1	3	2	Nebraska 12-0, Michigan 7-4, Kansas State 8-3	Bill McCartney (93-55-5)	Fiesta	41 Notre Dame	24
1995	10-2	5	2t	Nebraska 11-0, Kansas State 9-2, Kansas 9-2	Rick Neuheisel	Cotton	38 Oregon	6
1996	10-2	8	N2	Nebraska 10-2, Kansas State 9-2, Michigan 8-3	Rick Neuheisel	Holiday	33 Washington	21
1997	5-6		N4t	Michigan 11-0, Nebraska 12-0, Kansas State 10-1	Rick Neuheisel			
1998	8-4		N4	Kansas State 11-1, Nebraska 9-3, Missouri 7-4	Rick Neuheisel (33-14)	Aloha	51 Oregon	43
1999	7-5		N3	Nebraska 11-1, Kansas State 10-1, Washington 7-4	Gary Barnett	Insight.com	62 Boston College	28
2000	3-8		N4	Washington 10-1, Nebraska 9-2, Kansas State 10-3	Gary Barnett			
2001	10-3	9	N1	Texas 10-2, Nebraska 11-1, Fresno State 11-2	Gary Barnett	Fiesta	16 Oregon	38
2002	9-5	20	N1	USC 10-2, Oklahoma 11-2, Kansas State 10-2	Gary Barnett	Alamo	28 Wisconsin	31
2003	5-7		N4t	Oklahoma 12-1, Florida State 10-2, Wash. St. 9-3	Gary Barnett			
2004	8-5		N1t	Texas 10-1, Texas A&M 7-4, Oklahoma State 7-4	Gary Barnett	Houston	33 UTEP	28
2005	7-6		N1	Texas 12-0, Miami 9-2, Nebraska 7-4	Gary Barnett (49-39)	Champs Sports	10 Clemson	19
2006	2-10		N5	Oklahoma 10-2, Georgia 8-4, Nebraska 9-3	Dan Hawkins			
2007	6-7		N3	Arizona State 10-2, Oklahoma 10-2, Kansas 11-1, Missourix 11-1	Dan Hawkins	Independence	24 Alabama	30
2008	5-7		N4t	Texas 11-1, Missouri 9-4, Oklahoma State 9-3	Dan Hawkins			
2009	3-9		N5	West Virginia 9-3, Texas 13-0, Oklahoma State 9-3, Nebraska 9-4	Dan Hawkins			
2010	5-7		N5	Missouri 10-2, Oklahoma 11-2, Nebraska 10-3	Dan Hawkins (19-39) Brian Cabral [2-1]			

TOTAL: **366-282-11 .5637 (30 of 70)**   **Bowl Games since 1953:**   **12-15 .4444 (50 of 70)**

GREATEST TEAM SINCE 1953: The 1990 (11-1-1) national champions, upset winner of the Orange Bowl over Notre Dame, capped a great two-year period in which Colorado finished the regular season ranked first in the country in both 1989 and 1990. With speed to burn throughout the line-up, the Buffs swept conference play for both seasons, losing only to Notre Dame in 1989 and to Illinois by one point in 1990.

1953 6-4

21	Washington	20	E Gary Knafelc
20	Arizona	14	T Lee Marshall / Ken Huffer (C)
16	Missouri	27	G Jim Stander
21	Kansas	27	C Dave Hill / Don Karnoscak
14	Kansas State	28	G Dick Knowlton
20	Oklahoma	27	T Bob Morton
41	Iowa State	34	E Alabama Glass
21	Utah	0	BB Roger Hunt (G) / Don Piper
14	Nebraska	10	HB Carroll Hardy / Ron Johnson
13	Colorado State	7	HB Frank Bernardi
			FB Emerson Wilson / Homer Jenkins

RUSHING: Wilson 118/591y, Bernardi 95/493y, Hardy 74/361y
PASSING: Bernardi 11-22/176y, 2TD, 50%
    Jenkins 9-26/163y, 3TD, 34.6%
RECEIVING: Knafelc 22/451y, Piper 6/65y, Bernardi 4/41y
SCORING: Knafelc 48pts, Wilson 36pts, Hunt (QB-K) 26pts

1954 7-2-1

61	Drake	0	E Lamar Meyer / Matt Balich
46	Colorado State	0	T Dick Golder / Bill Kucera
27	Kansas	0	G Dick Stapp / Harlan Branby
40	Arizona	18	C Don Karnoscak / Dick Freund
20	Iowa State	0	G Dave Jones / Jim Uhlir
6	Nebraska	20	T Sam Salerno / Harry Javernick
6	Oklahoma	13	E Wally Merz / Jerry Leahy / Les Lotz
19	Missouri	19	BB Sam Maphis / Bill Lamont
20	Utah	7	TB Carroll Hardy / Homer Jenkins
38	Kansas State	14	WB Frank Bernardi
			FB John Bayuk / Emerson Wilson

RUSHING: Bayuk 145/824y, Bernardi 75/668y, Hardy 70/642y
PASSING: Hardy 13-25/189y, 52%, 1 TD
RECEIVING: Bernardi 8/170y, Merz 5/49y, Lamont 5/28y

SCORING: Hardy 68pts, Bayuk 66pts, Bernardi 42pts

1955 6-4

14	Arizona	0	E Lamar Meyer / Jerry Leahy
12	Kansas	0	T Henry Smith / Arlin Hubka / Tom Giek
13	Oregon	6	G Dick Stapp / Bill Kucera
34	Kansas State	13	C Don Karnoscak / Jim Uhlir
21	Oklahoma	56	G Harlan Branby / Dave Jones
12	Missouri	20	T Sam Salerno / Dick Golder
37	Utah	7	E Wally Merz / Frank Clarke
20	Nebraska	37	BB Dick Hyson / Sam Maphis
40	Iowa State	0	TB Homer Jenkins / Bob Stransky
0	Colorado State	10	WB Emerson Wilson / Jack Becker
			FB John Bayuk / Jack Becker

RUSHING: Bayuk 95/460y, Becker 83/310y, Jenkins 60/293y
PASSING: Hyson 15-36/358y, 4TD, 41.7%
RECEIVING: Clarke 13/407y, Maphis 8/94y, 2 tied w/ 4

SCORING: Clarke 30pts, Stransky 27pts, Wilson 25pts

1956 8-2-1

0	Oregon	35	E Jerry Leahy / Gary Nady
34	Kansas State	0	T Dick Stapp / Bob Salerno
26	Kansas	25	G John Wooten / Tom Giek
47	Colorado State	7	C Jim Uhlir / Charlie Brown
52	Iowa State	0	G Dave Jones / Howard Vest / Bill Mondt
16	Nebraska	0	T Ken Schlagel / Dick Golder
19	Oklahoma	27	E Wally Merz / Frank Clarke
14	Missouri	14	BB Boyd Dowler / Dick Hyson
21	Utah	7	TB Bob Stransky / Howard Cook
38	Arizona	7	WB Eddie Dove / Gene Worden
27	Clemson■	21	FB John Bayuk / Leroy Clark

RUSHING: Bayuk 127/659y, Stransky 83/548y, Cook 90/396y
PASSING: Dowler 13-26/136y, 3TD, 50%
RECEIVING: Clarke 7/124y, Dowler 5/94y, Leahy 4/60y
SCORING: Bayuk 66pts, Stransky 34pts, Dove 24pts

1957 6-3-1

6	Washington	6	E Gary Nady / Bob Munson
30	Utah	24	T Bob Stapp / Jack Himelwright
34	Kansas	35	G John Wooten
34	Arizona	14	C Mel Warner / Charlie Brown
42	Kansas State	14	G Bill Mondt / Sherman Pruit
13	Oklahoma	14	T Jim Howell / Larry Call
6	Missouri	9	E Kirk Campbell / Ed Clark
20	Colorado State	0	BB Boyd Dowler
27	Nebraska	0	TB Bob Stransky / Howard Cook
38	Iowa State	21	WB Eddie Dove / Ray Engel
			FB George Adams / Gene Worden

RUSHING: Stransky 183/1097y, Dove 88/620y, Cook 91/442y
PASSING: Stransky 18-32/290y, 3TD, 56.3%
RECEIVING: Dowler 26/380y, Dove 6/168y, Nady 6/102y
SCORING: Stransky 77pts, Dove 54pts, 3 tied w/ 18pts

1958 6-4

13	Kansas State	3	E Bill Elkins
31	Kansas	0	T Bob Salerno
65	Arizona	12	G John Wooten
20	Iowa State	0	C Sherman Pruit / Terry Smotherman
27	Nebraska	16	G Bill Mondt
7	Oklahoma	23	T Jack Himelwright
9	Missouri	33	E Mel Semenko / Kirk Campbell
7	Utah	0	BB Boyd Dowler
14	Colorado State	15	TB Howard Cook
14	Air Force	20	WB Eddie Dove / Leroy Clark
			FB Chuck Weiss / George Adams

RUSHING: Cook 120/625y, Dove 108/618y, Weiss 78/452y
PASSING: Dowler 35-77/320y, 1TD, 45.5%
RECEIVING: Dowler 10/154y, Cook 9/71y, Adams 8/50y
SCORING: Cook 62pts, Weiss 36pts, Dowler 19pts

1959 5-5

12	Washington	21	E Bill Elkins / Chuck McBride
7	Baylor	15	T Bob McCullough / John Denvir
12	Oklahoma	42	G Ken Vardell
20	Kansas State	17	C Walt Klinker
0	Iowa State	27	G Joe Romig
18	Arizona	0	T Jim Perkins / Bill Eurich
21	Missouri	20	E Jerry Hillebrand / Mel Semenko
27	Kansas	14	QB Gale Weidner
12	Nebraska	14	HB Jerry Steffen / Don Maurer
15	Air Force	7	HB Dave Rife
			FB Chuck Weiss / Loren Schweninger

RUSHING: Rife 96/275y, Weiss 56/196y, Maurer 58/194y
PASSING: Weidner 100-207/1200y, 7TD, 48.3%
RECEIVING: McBride 16/189y, Steffen 14/119y, 2 tied w/ 12
SCORING: Weidner 36pts, Rife 14pts, 4 tied w/ 12pts

1960 6-4

0	Baylor	26	E Gary Henson / Bill Elkins / Ken Blair
27	Kansas State	7	T Chuck Pearson / John Denvir
35	Arizona	16	G Tom Wilscam / Ken Vardell
21	Iowa State	6	C Bill Scribner / Ralph Heck (G)
19	Nebraska	6	G Joe Romig
7	Oklahoma	0	T Bill Eurich
6	Missouri	16	E Jerry Hillebrand / Mel Semenko
6	Kansas (F-W)	34	QB Gale Weidner
13	Oklahoma State	6	HB Jerry Steffen / Ted Woods
6	Air Force	16	HB Ed Coleman /Dave Rife /Reed Johnson
			FB Chuck Weiss / Loren Scheninger

RUSHING: Weiss 108/391y, Steffen 63/256y, Coleman 48/245y
PASSING: Weidner 45-111/732y, 3TD, 40.5%
RECEIVING: Hillebrand 11/218y, Henson 8/206y, Coleman 6/67y
SCORING: Weiss 30pts, Woods 20pts, Weidner 18pts

1961 9-2

24	Oklahoma State	0	E Ken Blair / Chuck McBride
20	Kansas	19	T John Denvir
9	Miami	7	G Ralph Heck
13	Kansas State	0	C Walt Klinker
22	Oklahoma	14	G Joe Romig
7	Missouri	6	T Bill Frank / Jim Perkins
12	Utah	21	E Jerry Hillebrand / John Meadows
7	Nebraska	0	QB Gale Weidner
34	Iowa State	0	HB Ted Woods / Bill Harris
29	Air Force	12	HB Ed Coleman /L. Mavity / Ted Somerville
7	LSU■	25	FB Loren Schweninger

RUSHING: Woods107/525y, Schweninger122/512y, Harris 82/434y
PASSING: Weidner 73-162/1101y, 8TD, 45.1%
RECEIVING: Hillebrand 17/282y, Blair 10/200y, Somerville 8/78y
SCORING: Hillebrand (E-K) 49pts, Harris 36pts, Mavity 20pts

1962 2-8

21	Utah	37	E Stan Irvine
6	Kansas State	0	T Dan Grimm / Tom Lund
8	Kansas	35	G Tom Kresnak / Skip LaGuardia
16	Oklahoma State	36	C Dale Christensen
19	Iowa State	57	G Tom Monczka / Al Hollingsworth
6	Nebraska	31	T Bill Bearss
0	Oklahoma	62	E Ken Blair
0	Missouri	57	QB Frank Cesarek / Larry Etheridge
12	Texas Tech	21	HB Leon Mavity / Terry Locke
34	Air Force	10	HB John McGuire
			FB Bill Harris / Bill Symons

RUSHING: Harris 157/582y, Symons 98/391y, Mavity 73/279y
PASSING: Cesarek 78-167/786y, 5TD, 46.7%
RECEIVING: McGuire 36/376y, Blair 35/356y, Mavity 15/188y
SCORING: Cesarek (QB-K) 30pts, Symons 20pts, Blair &
  Mavity 14pts

1963 2-8

0	Southern Cal	14	E Dick Taylor
6	Oregon State	41	T Frank Van Valkenburg
21	Kansas State	7	G Tim Monczka / Jack Parmater
25	Oklahoma State	0	C Larry Ferraro / Steve Sidwell (LB)
7	Iowa State	19	G Tom Kresnak
6	Nebraska	41	T Stan Irvine / Jerry McClurg
0	Oklahoma	35	E Ben Howe / Ray LeMasters
7	Missouri	28	QB Frank Cesarek
14	Kansas	43	HB Bill Symons
14	Air Force	17	HB Bill Harris
			FB Noble Milton / Larry Portis

RUSHING: Milton 117/487y, Harris 70/470y, Portis 74/304y
PASSING: Cesarek 45-95/612y, 2TD, 47.4%
RECEIVING: Symons 14/197y, Harris 9/101y, 2 tied w/ 5
SCORING: Harris 42pts, Milton 18pts, Cesarek 12pts

1964 2-8

0	Southern Cal	21	WR Ray LeMasters
7	Oregon State	14	T Kirk Osborn / Tom Lund
14	Kansas State	16	G Tim Monczka
10	Oklahoma State	14	C Steve Sidwell
14	Iowa State	7	G Jack Parmater
3	Nebraska	21	T Stan Irvine
11	Oklahoma	14	TE Sam Harris
7	Missouri	16	QB Bernie McCall / Hale Irwin
7	Kansas	10	SB Bill Symons
28	Air Force	23	TB Robert Lee / Estes Banks
			FB Ben Howe
			DL Dick Taylor
			DL Bill Sabatino
			DL Jerry McClurg
			DL Bill Fairband
			LB Larry Ferraro / Steve Sidwell
			LB Bob Cortese
			LB Dick Mankowski
			DB Dave Peercy / Hale Irwin
			DB George Lewark
			DB Ted Somerville / John Marchiol
			DB Steve Graves / Ben Howe

RUSHING: Lee 89/310y, Banks 81/273y, McCall 114/223y
PASSING: McCall 48-87/569y, 1TD, 55.2%
RECEIVING: Symons 27/267y, Harris 12/134y, Fairband 8/104y
SCORING: Howe 24pts, Frank Rogers (K) 21pts, Lee 18pts

1965 6-2-2

0	Wisconsin	0	WR Frank Rogers / George Lewark
10	Fresno State	7	T Dick Taylor / Lee Hammett
36	Kansas State	0	G John Beard
34	Oklahoma State	11	C Larry Ferraro
0	Iowa State	10	G Kirk Tracy
13	Nebraska	38	T Frank Van Valkenburg
13	Oklahoma	0	TE Tad Polumbus
7	Missouri	20	QB Bernie McCall
21	Kansas	14	SB John Farler / Larry Fischer
19	Air Force	6	TB William Harris / Larry Plantz
			FB Estes Banks / Wilmer Cooks
			DL Sam Harris
			DL Bll Sabatino
			DL Ron Scott
			DL Frank Bosch
			DL Bill Fairband
			LB Kerry Mottl
			LB Steve Sidwell / Dennis Drummond
			DB Robert Lee / George Lewark
			DB Charles Greer
			DB Dick Anderson
			DB Hale Irwin

RUSHING: Harris 142/680y, Banks 114/317y, McCall 104/253y
PASSING: McCall 84-181/1175y, 2TD, 46.4%
RECEIVING: Farler 19/123y, Lewark 18/278y, Rogers 13/250y
SCORING: Frank Rogers (K) 61pts, Banks 30pts, Harris 18pts

1966 7-3

3 Miami	24 WR Larry Plantz
13 Baylor	7 T Mike Montler
10 Kansas State	0 G John Beard
10 Oklahoma State	11 C Bruce Heath
41 Iowa State	21 G Kirk Tracy
19 Nebraska	21 T Bill Csikos / Greg Springston
24 Oklahoma	21 TE Mike Martin
26 Missouri	0 QB Bernie McCall / Dan Kelly
35 Kansas	18 SB John Farler
10 Air Force	9 HB William Harris / Estes Banks
	FB Wilmer Cooks
	DL Sam Harris / Mike Schnitker
	DL Bill Sabatino / Larry Donley
	DL Ron Scott
	DL Frank Bosch
	DL Bill Fairband
	LB Kerry Mottl
	LB Dennis Drummond
	DB Charles Greer
	DB George Lewark / Isaac Howard
	DB Dick Anderson
	DB Hale Irwin

RUSHING: Cooks 159/594y, Harris 105/538y, Kelly 107/431y
PASSING: McCall 45-93/588y, 1TD, 48.4%
Kelly 27-65/353y, 2TD, 41.5%
RECEIVING: Platz 22/354y, Farler 13/177y, Cooks 10/75y
SCORING: Cooks 60pts, Farler (SB-K) 47pts, 3 tied w/ 18pts

1967 9-2

27 Baylor	7 WR Monte Huber
17 Oregon	13 T Mike Montler
34 Iowa State	0 G Bart Bortles
23 Missouri	9 C Bruce Heath
21 Nebraska	16 G Kirk Tracy
7 Oklahoma State	10 T Bill Csikos / Kile Morgan
0 Oklahoma	23 TE Mike Pruett
12 Kansas	8 QB Bobby Anderson / Dan Kelly
40 Kansas State	6 SB John Farler / Gary Kuxhaus
33 Air Force	0 TB William Harris / Larry Plantz (WR)
31 Miami■	21 FB Wilmer Cooks / Tom Nigbur
	DL Mike Schnitker
	DL Ron Scott / Bill Brundige
	DL Rocky Martin
	DL Frank Bosch
	DL Mike Veeder
	LB Dave Bartelt
	LB Kerry Mottl
	DB Charles Greer
	DB Isaac Howard
	DB Dick Anderson
	DB Mike Bynum

RUSHING: Anderson 166/625y, Harris 83/367y, Cooks 99/321y
PASSING: Anderson 63-110/733y, 57.3%
RECEIVING: Huber 45/486y, Pruett 7/131y, Plantz 7/57y
SCORING: Anderson 42pts, Cooks 36pts, Bartelt (LB-K) & Kelly 18pts

1968 4-6

28 Oregon	7 WR Monte Huber
0 California	10 T Mike Montler
28 Iowa State	18 G Dennis Havig / Ray Reuter
14 Missouri	27 C Don Popplewell
37 Kansas State	14 G Dick Melin
41 Oklahoma	27 T Kile Morgan
14 Kansas	27 TE Jim Cooch / Steve Dal Porto
17 Oklahoma State	34 QB Bobby Anderson
6 Nebraska	22 SB Mike Pruett
35 Air Force	58 TB Steve Engel
	FB Tom Nigbur / Ward Walsh
	DL Mike Schnitker
	DL Dave Capra / Dave Perini
	DL Bill Collins
	DL Bill Brundige
	DL Dave Bartelt / Tom Duncan
	LB Rocky Martin
	LB Phil Irwin / Bruce Smith
	DB Jeff Raymond
	DB Pat Murphy / Isaac Howard
	DB Steve Tracy
	DB Mike Bynum

RUSHING: Anderson 183/733y, Engel 110/491y, Nigbur 67/394y
PASSING: Anderson 112-222/1341y, 7TD, 50.5%
RECEIVING: Huber 38/462y, Pruett 22/281y, Walsh 14/136y
SCORING: Anderson 56pts, Nigbur & Walsh 36pts

1969 8-3

35 Tulsa	14 WR Monte Huber
3 Penn State	27 WR Bob Masten / Steve Dal Porto
30 Indiana	7 T Eddie Fusiek
14 Iowa State	0 G Dennis Havig
30 Oklahoma	42 C Don Popplewell
31 Missouri	24 G Dick Melin
7 Nebraska	20 T Jim Phillips
17 Kansas	14 TE Mike Pruett
17 Oklahoma State	14 QB Jimmy Bratten / Paul Arendt
45 Kansas State	32 TB Bobby Anderson (QB)
47 Alabama■	33 FB Ward Walsh
	DL Herb Orvis
	DL Rich Varriano / Dave Capra
	DL Bill Collins / Dave Perini
	DL Bill Brundige
	LB Bill Blanchard
	LB Phil Irwin
	LB Rick Ogle
	DB Eric Harris
	DB Jim Cooch
	DB Pete Jacobsen
	DB Pat Murphy

RUSHING: Anderson 219/954y, Walsh 114/502y, Bratten 92/234y
PASSING: Arendt 34-75/563y, 1TD, 45.3%
Bratten 34-80/539y, 3TD, 42.5%
RECEIVING: Huber 28/488y, Dal Porto 14/172y, Masten 11/177y
SCORING: Anderson 114pts, Dave Haney (K) 49pts, Arendt 24pts

1970 6-5

16 Indiana	9 WR Larry Brunson / Willie Nichols
41 Penn State	13 WR Steve Dal Porto / Cliff Branch
20 Kansas State	21 T Jim Phillips
61 Iowa State	10 G Dennis Havig / John Emmerling
15 Oklahoma	23 C Don Popplewell
16 Missouri	30 G Bill Kralicek
13 Nebraska	29 T Eddie Fusiek
45 Kansas	29 TE Bob Masten / Rick Kay
30 Oklahoma State	6 QB Jimmy Bratten / Paul Arendt
49 Air Force	19 TB John Tarver / Jon Keyworth*
3 Tulane■	17 FB Ward Walsh
	DL John Stavely
	DL Dave Capra / Carl Taibi
	DL Rich Varriano / Bruce Smith
	DL Herb Orvis
	LB Rick Ogle
	LB Phil Irwin
	LB Billie Drake / Chris Havens
	DB Jim Cooch
	DB Cullen Bryant / Brian Foster
	DB Pat Murphy
	DB John Stearns

RUSHING: Walsh 117/679y, Keyworth 125/667y, Tarver 137/623y
PASSING: Bratten 64-151/771y, 3TD, 42.4%
RECEIVING: Branch 23/335y, Brunson 14/295y, Dal Porto 13/153y
SCORING: Dave Haney (K) 70pts, Keyworth 54pts, Tarver 48pts

1971 10-2

31 LSU	21 WR Cliff Branch / Willie Nichols
56 Wyoming	13 T Greg Horton
20 Ohio State	14 G Chuck Mandrill
31 Kansas State	21 C Bill McDonald
24 Iowa State	14 G Bill Kralicek
17 Oklahoma	45 T Jake Zumbach
27 Missouri	7 TE Bob Masten / J.V. Cain
7 Nebraska	31 QB Ken Johnson / Joe Duenas
35 Kansas	14 SB Larry Brunson
40 Oklahoma State	6 TB Charlie Davis
53 Air Force	17 FB John Tarver / Bo Matthews
29 Houston■	17 DL Rick Kay
	DL Herb Orvis / Mark Cooney
	DL Carl Taibi
	DL Chris Havens / Stu Aldrich
	DL John Stavely
	LB Bud Magrum / Dave Orvis
	LB Billie Drake / Lenny Ciufo
	LB Randy Geist
	DB Cullen Bryant
	DB Brian Foster / Lorne Richardson
	DB John Stearns

RUSHING: Davis 219/1386y, Tarver 122/677y, Johnson 142/349y
PASSING: Johnson 64-163/1126y, 8TD, 39.3%
RECEIVING: Nichols 16/316y, Branch 13/330y, Masten 11/214y
SCORING: Branch 68pts, Davis 62pts, J.B. Dean (K) 55pts

1972 8-4

20 California	10 WR Steve Haggerty / Rick Ellwood
56 Cincinnati	14 T Jake Zumbach
38 Minnesota	6 G Chuck Mandrill
6 Oklahoma State	31 C Bill McDonald
38 Kansas State	17 G Greg Parr
34 Iowa State	22 T Greg Horton
10 Oklahoma	14 TE J.V. Cain
17 Missouri	20 QB Ken Johnson / Joe Duenas
10 Nebraska	33 WB Jon Keyworth
33 Kansas	8 TB Charlie Davis / Gary Campbell
38 Air Force	7 FB Bo Matthews
3 Auburn■	24 DL Rick Kay / Bill Donnell
	DL Stu Aldrich
	DL Mark Cooney
	DL Lennie Cuifo
	LB Bud Mangrum
	LB Randy Geist
	LB Jeff Geiser
	LB Billie Drake
	DB Cullen Bryant
	DB Lorne Richardson
	DB John Stearns

RUSHING: Davis 201/926y, Matthews 155/720y, Johnson 132/378y
PASSING: Johnson 83-182/1044y, 5TD, 45.6%
RECEIVING: Cain 30/407y, Keyworth 18/218y, Haggerty 11/178y
SCORING: Davis 84pts, Fred Lima (K) 80pts, Matthews 26pts

1973 5-6

6 LSU	17 WR J.B. Dean, Jr. / Steve Haggerty
28 Wisconsin	25 T Greg Horton
52 Baylor	28 G Harvey Goodman
38 Air Force	17 C Bill McDonald
23 Iowa State	16 G Doug Payton / Denis Cimmino
7 Oklahoma	34 T Mark Koncar / Wayne Mattingly
17 Missouri	13 TE J.V. Cain
16 Nebraska	28 QB Clyde Crutchmer / David Williams
15 Kansas	17 WB Dave Logan
24 Oklahoma State	38 TB Charlie Davis / Billy Waddy
14 Kansas State	17 FB Bo Matthews
	DL Bill Donnell / Lennie Ciufo
	DL Mark Cooney / Jeff Turcotte
	DL Steve Griffin
	DL Mark Sens
	DL John Stavely
	LB Jeff Geiser
	LB Rick Stearns / Ed Schoen
	DB Jerry Martinez / Jeff Kensinger
	DB Rick Cleveland / Rod Perry
	DB Rich Bland / Ozell Collier
	DB Randy Geist / Greg Westbrooks

RUSHING: Davis 118/646y, Waddy 101/551y, Matthews 97/488y
PASSING: Crutchmer 50-89/722y, 5TD, 56.2%
Williams 22-55/268y, 3TD, 40%
RECEIVING: Cain 23/293y, Logan 22/395y, Dean 8/131y
SCORING: Fred Lima (K) 42pts, Logan, Waddy & Matthews 30pts

1974 5-6

14 LSU	42 WR Larry Ferguson / Rick Ellwood
0 Michigan	31 T Mark Koncar
24 Wisconsin	21 G Leon White / Steve Stripling
28 Air Force	27 C Pete Brock
34 Iowa State	7 G Harvey Goodman
14 Oklahoma	49 T Steve Young / Doug Payton
24 Missouri	30 TE Don Hasselbeck
15 Nebraska	31 QB David Williams / Clyde Crutchmer
17 Kansas	16 WB Emery Moorehead / Dave Logan
37 Oklahoma State	20 TB Billy Waddy / Melvin Johnson
19 Kansas State	33 FB Terry Kunz
	DL Troy Archer
	DL Jeff Turcotte
	DL Steve Griffin / Tiloi Lolotai
	DL Tom Likovich / Bob Simpson
	DL Whitney Paul / Bill Donnell
	LB Jeff Geiser / Bobby Hunt
	LB Ed Shoen
	DB Rod Perry
	DB Mike McCoy / Jerry Martinez
	DB Tom Hilton / Tom Tesone
	DB Greg Westbrooks

RUSHING: Waddy 157/765y, Kunz 152/693y, Johnson 56/210y
PASSING: Williams 73-139/899y, 3TD, 52.5%
RECEIVING: Logan 21/273y, Ellwood 14/203y, Ferguson 13/184y
SCORING: Kunz 54pts, Tom Mackenzie (K) 40pts, Waddy 36pts

1975 9-3

34 California	27 WR Dave Logan
27 Wyoming	10 T Steve Young
52 Wichita State	0 G Leon White
20 Oklahoma	21 C Pete Brock
23 Miami	10 G Steve Stripling / Steve Hakes
31 Missouri	20 T Mark Koncar
21 Nebraska	63 TE Don Hasselbeck
28 Iowa State	27 QB David Williams
17 Oklahoma State	7 WB Emery Moorehead / Billy Waddy
24 Kansas	21 TB Tony Reed
33 Kansas State	7 FB Terry Kunz / Jim Kelleher
21 Texas■	38 DL Troy Archer
	DL Frank Patrick / Jackie Thornton
	DL Charlie Johnson
	DL Bob Simpson
	DL Whitney Paul / Dave Rice
	LB Brian Cabral / Tom Perry
	LB Gary Campbell / Bart Roth
	DB Mike Spivey
	DB Mike L. Davis
	DB Mike McCoy
	DB Tom Tesone / Chuck McCarter

RUSHING: Kunz 160/882y, Reed 157/722y, Williams 128/572y
PASSING: Williams 103-172/1282y, 7TD, 59.9%
RECEIVING: Logan 23/392y, Hasselbeck 23/235y,
 Moorehead 14/224y
SCORING: Kunz 66pts, Tom Mackenzie (K) 64pts, Williams 42pts

1976 8-4

7 Texas Tech	24 WR Steve Gaunty
21 Washington	7 T Matt Miller
33 Miami	3 G Steve Hakes
45 Drake	24 C Mike Tope / Willie Brock
12 Nebraska	24 G John Sutrina / Dave Griffin
20 Oklahoma State	10 T George Osborne
33 Iowa State	14 TE Don Hasselbeck
42 Oklahoma	31 QB Jeff Knapple / Jeff Austin
7 Missouri	16 WB Emery Moorehead / Billy Waddy
40 Kansas	17 TB Tony Reed
35 Kansas State	28 FB Jim Kelleher / James Mayberry
10 Ohio State ■	27 DL Stuart Walker
	DL Ruben Vaughn
	DL Charlie Johnson
	DL Laval Short
	DL Randy Westendorf
	LB Brian Cabral / Bart Roth
	LB Bill Muxlow / Tom Perry
	DB Odis McKinney
	DB Mike Spivey / Horace Perkins
	DB Mike L. Davis
	DB Mark Haynes

RUSHING: Reed 264/1210y, Kelleher 155/615y, Mayberry 54/258y
PASSING: Knapple 60-136/904y, 3TD, 44.1%
RECEIVING: Reed 19/128y, Moorehead 18/374y,
 Hasselbeck 14/214y
SCORING: Kelleher 90pts, Mark Zetterberg (K) 31pts, Reed 30pts

1977 7-3-1

27 Stanford	21 WR Steve Gaunty
42 Kent State	0 T Stan Brock
42 New Mexico	7 G Bruce Kirchner
31 Army	0 C Leon White
29 Oklahoma State	13 G Dave Griffin
17 Kansas	17 T Matt Miller
15 Nebraska	33 TE Bob Niziolek
14 Missouri	24 QB Jeff Knapple
12 Iowa State	7 WB Robert LaGarde
14 Oklahoma	52 TB Howard Ballage / Mike Kozlowski
23 Kansas State	0 FB James Mayberry / Mike Holmes
•	DL Stuart Walker
	DL Reuben Vaughn
	DL Laval Short
	DL Mike Hagan / Dan Kennelly
	DL Randy Westendorf
	LB Brian Cabral
	LB Tom Perry
	DB Odis McKinney
	DB Jesse Johnson
	DB Mark Haynes
	DB Tom Tesone

RUSHING: Mayberry 246/1299y, Ballage 87/462y,
 Kozlowski 61/239y
PASSING: Knapple 79-180/1203y, 4TD, 43.9%
RECEIVING: Niziolek 29/416y, Gaunty 13/370y, Mayberry 11/78y
SCORING: Mayberry 54pts, Pete Dadiotis (K) 54pts, Ballage 42pts

1978 6-5

24 Oregon	7 WR Kazell Pugh
17 Miami	7 WR Howard Ballage
22 San Jose State	7 T Stan Brock
55 Northwestern	7 G Brant Thurston
17 Kansas	7 C Bruce Kirchner
20 Oklahoma State	24 G Dave Griffin
14 Nebraska	52 T Matt Miller
28 Missouri	27 TE Greg Howard
7 Oklahoma	28 QB Bill Solomon
10 Kansas State	20 TB James Mayberry / Mike Kozlowski
16 Iowa State	20 FB Eddie Ford / Jeff Hornberger
	DL Stuart Walker
	DL Reuben Vaughn
	DL Laval Short
	DL George Visger
	DL Steve Doolittle
	LB Jeff Lee
	LB Bill Roe
	DB Jesse Johnson
	DB Mike E. Davis
	DB Mark Haynes
	DB Tim Roberts

RUSHING: Mayberry 230/920y, Solomon 189/484y,
 Hornberger 62/285y
PASSING: Solomon 77-158/944y, 3TD, 48.7%
RECEIVING: Howard 28/374y, Pugh 15/266y, Kozlowski 11/88y,
SCORING: Mayberry 78pts, Pete Dadiotis (K) 48pts,
 Solomon 42pts

1979 3-8

19 Oregon	33 WR Donnie Holmes
0 LSU	44 WR Kazell Pugh
9 Drake	13 T Stan Brock / Bob Sebro
17 Indiana	16 G Paul Butero / Bruce Campbell
24 Oklahoma	49 C Van Hammond / Roger Gunter / Joe Bell
7 Missouri	13 G Art Dale Johnson / Guy Thurston
10 Nebraska	38 T Brant Thurston / Karry Kelley
10 Iowa State	24 TE Greg Willet / Bob Niziolek
20 Oklahoma State	21 QB Bill Solomon
31 Kansas	17 TB Lance Olander / Lyndell Hawkins
21 Kansas State	6 FB Willie Beebe
	DL George Visger
	DL Laval Short
	DL Kevin Sazama
	LB Steve Doolittle
	LB Bob Humble / Brian McCabe
	LB Bill Roe
	LB Charlie Scott
	DB Mark Haynes
	DB Jesse Johnson / Tim Stampley
	DB Mike E. Davis
	DB Tim Roberts

RUSHING: Olander 88/440y, Beebe 101/408y, Hawkins 53/220y
PASSING: Solomon 91-184/1174y, 10TD, 49.5%
RECEIVING: Pugh 23/375y, Beebe 21/137y, Holmes 17/301y
SCORING: Tom Field (K) 48pts, 4 tied w/ 18pts

1980 1-10

14 UCLA	56 WR Ricky Ward / Reggie Harden
20 LSU	23 WR Lyndell Hawkins
7 Indiana	49 T Bruce Campbell / Bob Sebro
42 Oklahoma	82 G Doug Krahenbuhl
22 Drake	41 C Rich Umphrey
7 Missouri	45 G Joe Bell / Bo Halamandaris
7 Nebraska	45 T Roger Gunter / Art Dale Johnson
17 Iowa State	9 TE Bob Niziolek
7 Oklahoma State	42 QB Scott Kingdom / Randy Essington
3 Kansas	42 TB Lance Olander / Derek Singleton
14 Kansas State	17 FB Willie Beebe / Charlie Davis (QB)
	DL Graham Harrison
	DL Dan Ralph
	DL Pete Perry
	LB Rod Butler
	LB Steve Doolittle
	LB Bob Humble
	LB Kevin Hood / Scott Hardison
	DB Rickey Bynum
	DB Tim Stampley / Victor Scott
	DB Ellis Wood / Larry Lillo
	DB Brad Chace

RUSHING: Olander 130/611y, Davis 114/395y, Singleton 68/285y
PASSING: Essington 43-80/453y, 2TD, 53.8%
 Davis 33-74/430y, 4TD, 44.6%
 Kingdom 45-113/619y, 3TD, 39.8%
RECEIVING: Ward 25/428y, Hawkins 15/158y, 2 tied w/ 14
SCORING: Tom Field (K) 26pts, Olander 24pts, 3 tied w/ 18pts

1981 3-8

45 Texas Tech	27 WR Brad Parker / Ricky Ward
10 Washington St.	14 T Bob Sebro
20 BYU	41 G Doug Krahenbuhl
7 UCLA	27 C Rich Umphrey
0 Nebraska	59 G Vince Rafferty
11 Oklahoma State	10 T Bruce Alison / Mike Sylvester
10 Iowa State	17 TE Dave Hestera
0 Oklahoma	49 QB Randy Essington / Steve Vogel
14 Missouri	30 IB Lee Rouson / Richard Johnson
0 Kansas	27 HB Derek Singleton / Walter Stanley
24 Kansas State	21 FB Willie Beebe
	DL Mark Shoop
	DL Sandy Armstrong
	DL Pete Perry
	LB Dave Alderson
	LB Kevin Hood / Greg Willet
	LB Mark Remington
	LB Alan Chrite / Scott Hardison
	DB Victor Scott
	DB Clyde Riggins / Rickey Bynum
	DB Ellis Wood / Derek Hunter
	DB Jeff Donaldson

RUSHING: Rouson 159/656y, Beebe 70/266y, Johnson 57/231y
PASSING: Essington 95-197/1199y, 6TD, 48.2%
RECEIVING: Hestera 21/202y, Beebe 20/136y, Parker 19/204y
SCORING: Rouson 42pts, Jerry Hamilton 29pts, Stanley &
 Beebe 18pts

1982 2-8-1

17 California	31 WR Donnie Holmes
12 Washington St.	0 WR Brad Parker / Kent Davis
10 Wyoming	24 T Randy Hogbin / Derek Wiesner
6 UCLA	34 G Eric Coyle / Calvin Beaty
14 Nebraska	40 C Steve Heron
25 Oklahoma State	25 G Vince Rafferty
14 Iowa State	31 T John Firm
10 Oklahoma	45 TE Dave Hestera
14 Missouri	35 QB Randy Essington / Steve Vogel
28 Kansas	3 HB Lee Rouson / Richard Johnson
10 Kansas State	33 FB Chris McLemore / Guy Egging
	DL Mark Shoop / Joe O'Brien
	DL Don Muncie / George Smith
	DL Mark Washington / Mike Sylvester
	LB Kevin Hood
	LB Terry Irvin / Dave Alderson
	LB Ray Cone
	LB Alan Crite / Cleon Braun
	DB Clyde Riggins / Robert Johnson
	DB Victor Scott
	DB Ellis Wood/Steve Salvatore/Tony Rettig
	DB Jeff Donaldson

RUSHING: Johnson 117/584y, Rouson 103/421y,
 McLemore 41/142y
PASSING: Essington 109-219/1121y, 2TD, 49.8%
 Vogel 66-162/784y, 5TD, 40.7%
RECEIVING: Hestera 41/489y, McLemore 39/337y,
 Holmes 27/360y
SCORING: Johnson 60pts, Tom Field (K) 58pts, Scott 12pts

1983 4-7

17 Michigan State	23 WR Loy Alexander
31 Colorado State	3 T Mike Sylvester
38 Oregon State	14 G Junior Iii
3 Notre Dame	27 C Steve Heron
20 Missouri	59 G Shaun Beard / Derek Wiesner
10 Iowa State	22 T John Firm
19 Nebraska	69 TE Dave Hestera
14 Oklahoma State	40 QB Steve Vogel / Derek Marshall
34 Kansas	23 WB Ron Brown
28 Oklahoma	41 TB Lee Rouson / Darryl Johnson
38 Kansas State	21 FB Chris McLemore / Guy Egging
	DL Vince Rafferty / Randy Hogbin
	DL Don Muncie
	DL George Smith
	LB Sandy Armstrong
	LB Don Fairbanks / Barry Remington
	LB Terry Irvin
	LB Wayne Carroll / Dan McMillen
	DB Victor Scott
	DB Clyde Riggins
	DB Kent Davis
	DB Jeff Donaldson

RUSHING: Rouson 120/494y, McLemore 97/478y,
 Johnson 67/232y
PASSING: Vogel 110-236/1385y, 12TD, 46.6%
 Marshall 56-107/836y, 3TD, 52.3%
RECEIVING: Alexander 39/557y, Hestera 29/366y,
 Rouson 25/223y
SCORING: Tom Field (K) 58pts, McLemore 48pts,
 Alexander 36pts

1984 1-10

21 Michigan State	24 WR Loy Alexander
20 Oregon	27 T Pat Ryan / Jeff Glenn
14 Notre Dame	55 G Junior Iii
16 UCLA	33 C Eric Coyle / William Gulley
7 Missouri	52 G Shaun Beard
23 Iowa State	21 T Tim Harper / Jimmy Webb
7 Nebraska	24 TE Jon Embree / Ed Reinhardt
14 Oklahoma State	20 QB Steve Vogel / Craig Keenan
27 Kansas	28 WB Ron Brown
17 Oklahoma	42 TB Lee Rouson
6 Kansas State	38 FB Eric McCarty / Mark Hatcher
	DL Curt Koch / Calvin Beaty
	DL Don Muncie
	DL George Smith
	LB Dan McMillen
	LB Barry Remington / Miles Kusayanagi
	LB Alan Chrite / Don Fairbanks
	LB Darin Schubeck
	DB Lyle Pickens / Solomon Wilcots
	DB Tommy Streeter / Alvin Rubalcaba
	DB Kent Davis / John Nairn
	DB John Bennett / Mickey Pruitt

RUSHING: Rouson 199/725y, McCarty 53/190y
PASSING: Vogel 100-224/1432y, 9TD, 44.6%
Keenan 78-149/1012y, 3TD, 52.3%
RECEIVING: Embree 51/680y, Alexander 35/496y, Brown 29/673y
SCORING: Dave DeLine (K) 39pts, Brown & Rouson 30pts

1985 7-5

23 Colorado State	10 WR Loy Alexander
21 Oregon	17 T Pat Ryan
13 Ohio State	36 G Junior Iii
14 Arizona	13 C Eric Coyle
38 Missouri	7 G Chris Symington
40 Iowa State	6 T Jimmy Webb
7 Nebraska	17 TE Jon Embree
11 Oklahoma State	14 QB Mark Hatcher
14 Kansas	3 WB Ron Brown
0 Oklahoma	31 HB Sam Smith
30 Kansas State	0 FB Anthony Weatherspoon / Eric McCarty
17 Washington ■	20 DL Don Fairbanks
	DL Kyle Rappold
	DL Curt Koch
	LB Dan McMillen
	LB Don DeLuzio
	LB Barry Remington
	LB Darin Schubeck / Conley Smith
	DB Solomon Wilcots
	DB Rodney Rogers / John Nairn
	DB Mickey Pruitt

RUSHING: Weatherspoon 140/569y, Hatcher 125/539y,
Brown 90/524y
PASSING: Hatcher 16-51/325y, 1TD, 31.4%
RECEIVING: Embree 9/140y, 3 tied w/ 4 catches
SCORING: Hatcher 60pts, Larry Eckel (K) 45pts, Keenan &
Weatherspoon 14pts

1986 6-6

7 Colorado State	23 WR Drew Ferrando / Lance Carl
30 Oregon	32 T Joe McCreary
10 Ohio State	13 G Bob Lawrence / Darren Muilenburg
21 Arizona	24 C Eric Coyle
17 Missouri	12 G Bill Coleman
31 Iowa State	3 T Pat Ryan
20 Nebraska	10 TE Jon Embree
31 Oklahoma State	14 QB Mark Hatcher
17 Kansas	10 WB Mike Marquez
0 Oklahoma	28 HB O.C. Oliver / Sam Smith
49 Kansas State	3 FB Anthony Weatherspoon / Erich Kissick
9 Baylor ■	21 DL Jim Smith / Cole Hayes
	DL Kyle Rappold
	DL Curt Koch
	LB Tom Reinhardt / Tom Dunn
	LB Don DeLuzio / Eric McCarty
	LB Barry Remington
	LB Darin Schubeck
	DB David Tate
	DB Solomon Wilcots
	DB Rodney Rogers / John Nairn
	DB Mickey Pruitt

RUSHING: Oliver 136/668y, Weatherspoon 116/581y,
Hatcher 155/552y
PASSING: Hatcher 28-66/493y, 2TD, 42.4%
RECEIVING: Carl 9/171y, Embree 8/153y, Marquez 7/205y
SCORING: Dave DeLine (K) 52pts, Oliver 48pts, Hatcher &
Weatherspoon 24pts

1987 7-4

7 Oregon	10 WR Drew Ferrando / Lance Carl
31 Stanford	17 T Pat Ryan
26 Washington St.	17 G Joe Garten
29 Colorado State	16 C Erik Norgard
17 Oklahoma State	42 G Chris Symington
35 Kansas	10 T Darren Muilenburg
6 Oklahoma	24 TE George Hemingway / Troy Wolf
42 Iowa State	10 QB Sal Aunese / Mark Hatcher
27 Missouri	11 WB J.J. Flannigan
41 Kansas State	0 HB Eric Bieniemy
7 Nebraska	24 FB Erich Kissick / Michael Simmons
	DL Arthur Walker / Lee Brunelli
	DL Kyle Rappold
	DL Curt Koch
	LB Tom Reinhardt / Alfred Williams
	LB Michael Jones
	LB Eric McCarty
	LB Kanavis McGhee / Tom Stone
	DB David Tate
	DB John Nairn
	DB Rodney Rogers
	DB Mickey Pruitt

RUSHING: Aunese 122/612y, Kissick 97/584y, Bieniemy 104/508y
PASSING: Aunese 23-51/522y, 3TD, 45.1%
RECEIVING: Carl 15/270y, Bieniemy 10/186y, Ferrando 9/242y
SCORING: Aunese & Bieniemy 36pts, Eric Hannah (K) 28pts

1988 8-4

45 Fresno State	3 WR Jo Jo Collins / Jeff Campbell
24 Iowa	21 T Bill Coleman
28 Oregon State	21 G Joe Garten
27 Colorado State	23 C Erik Norgard
21 Oklahoma State	41 G Darren Muilenburg
21 Kansas	9 T Mark VanderPoel
14 Oklahoma	17 TE John Perak
24 Iowa State	12 QB Sal Aunese
45 Missouri	8 WB Mike Pritchard
0 Nebraska	7 HB Eric Bieniemy / J.J. Flannigan
56 Kansas State	14 FB Erich Kissick
17 BYU ■	20 DL Cole Hayes / Okland Salavea
	DL Tom Reinhardt / Brad Robinson
	DL Arthur Walker
	LB Alfred Williams
	LB Don DeLuzio
	LB Michael Jones
	LB Kanavis McGhee
	DB Deon Figures / Keith Pontiflet
	DB Dave McCloughan
	DB Bruce Young
	DB Tim James

RUSHING: Bieniemy 219/1243y, Flannigan 88/522y,
Aunese 113/397y
PASSING: Aunese 44-106/1004y, 2TD, 41.5%
RECEIVING: Campbell 15/466y, Collins 12/223y, 2 tied w/ 7
SCORING: Bieniemy 62pts, Aunese 48pts,
Ken Culbertson (K) 37pts

1989 11-1

27 Texas	6 WR Jeff Campbell / M.J. Nelson
45 Colorado State	20 T Bill Coleman
38 Illinois	7 G Joe Garten
45 Washington	28 C Jay Leeuwenburg
49 Missouri	3 G Darrin Muilenburg
52 Iowa State	17 T Mark VanderPoel
49 Kansas	17 TE John Perak
20 Oklahoma	3 QB Darian Hagan
27 Nebraska	8 WB Mike Pritchard
41 Oklahoma State	17 TB Eric Bieniemy / J.J. Flannigan
59 Kansas State	11 FB Erich Kissick
6 Notre Dame ■	21 DL Arthur Walker
	DL Joel Steed / Garry Howe
	DL Okland Salavea
	LB Alfred Williams
	LB Terry Johnson / Chad Brown
	LB Michael Jones
	LB Kanavis McGhee
	DB Dave McCloughan
	DB David Gibbs
	DB Tim James
	DB Bruce Young

RUSHING: Flannigan 164/1187y, Hagan 186/1004y,
Bieniemy 88/561y
PASSING: Hagan 48-85/1002y, 4TD, 56.5%
RECEIVING: Pritchard 12/292y, Campbell 10/286y, Nelson 9/266y
SCORING: Flannigan 108pts, Hagan 102pts,
Ken Culbertson (K) 98pts

1990 11-1-1

31 Tennessee	31 WR Mike Pritchard (WB) / Rico Smith
21 Stanford	17 T Ariel Solomon
22 Illinois	23 G Joe Garten
29 Texas	22 C Jay Leeuwenburg
20 Washington	14 G Russ Heasley / Bryan Campbell
33 Missouri	31 T Mark VanderPoel
28 Iowa State	12 TE Jon Boman / Sean Brown
41 Kansas	10 QB Darian Hagan / Charles Johnson
32 Oklahoma	23 WB Michael Simmons
27 Nebraska	12 TB Eric Bieniemy
41 Oklahoma State	22 FB George Hemingway
64 Kansas State	3 DL Leonard Renfro / Marcellous Elder
10 Notre Dame■	9 DL Joel Steed
	DL Garry Howe
	LB Alfred Williams
	LB Greg Biekert
	LB Chad Brown / Terry Johnson
	LB Kanavis McGhee
	DB Deon Figures
	DB Dave McCloughan
	DB Greg Thomas
	DB Tim James

RUSHING: Bieniemy 288/1628y, Pritchard 29/445y,
Hagan 138/442y
PASSING: Hagan 75-163/1538y, 11TD, 46%
RECEIVING: Pritchard 28/733y, Hemingway 14/217y,
Bieniemy 13/159y
SCORING: Bieniemy 102pts, Jim Harper (K) 83pts, Pritchard 66pts

1991 8-3-1

30 Wyoming	13 WR Rico Smith / Charles Johnson
14 Baylor	16 T Craig Anderson
58 Minnesota	0 G Clint Moore / Jason Perkins
21 Stanford	28 C Jay Leeuwenburg
55 Missouri	7 G Roger Ivey / Dolyn Jackson
34 Oklahoma	17 T Jim Hansen
10 Kansas State	0 TE Sean Brown / Sean Embree
19 Nebraska	19 QB Darian Hagan
16 Oklahoma State	12 WB Mark Henry / Michael Westbrook
30 Kansas	24 TB Lamont Warren / Kent Kahl
17 Iowa State	14 FB James Hill
25 Alabama ■	30 DL Leonard Renfro
	DL Joel Steed
	DL Brian Dyet / Marcellous Elder
	LB Ron Woolfork
	LB Greg Biekert
	LB Ted Johnson / Jon Knutson
	LB Chad Brown
	DB Deon Figures
	DB Ronnie Bradford
	DB Greg Thomas
	DB Eric Hamilton

RUSHING: Warren 157/830y, Hagan 133/386y, Hill 81/362y
PASSING: Hagan 88-170/1228y, 12TD, 51.8%
RECEIVING: Brown 24/300y, Westbrook 22/309y, Henry 13/292y
SCORING: Jim Harper (K) 54pts, Warren 42pts, Westbrook 30pts

1992 9-2-1

37 Colorado State	17 WR Charles Johnson
57 Baylor	38 WR T.J. Cunningham / Erick Mitchell
21 Minnesota	20 T Derek West
28 Iowa	12 G Roger Ivey / Clint Moore
6 Missouri	0 C Bryan Stoltenberg
24 Oklahoma	24 G Craig Anderson / Craig Hammond
54 Kansas State	7 T Jim Hansen
7 Nebraska	52 TE Christian Fauria
28 Oklahoma State	7 QB Kordell Stewart / Koy Detmer
25 Kansas	18 WB Michael Westbrook
31 Iowa State	10 TB Lamont Warren / James Hill
22 Syracuse■	26 DL Leonard Renfro
	DL Jeff Brunner/Darius Holland/S. Clavelle
	DL Marcellous Elder / Brian Dyet
	LB Ron Woolfork
	LB Greg Biekert
	LB Ted Johnson / John Katovsich
	LB Chad Brown
	DB Deon Figures
	DB Ronnie Bradford
	DB Chris Hudson
	DB Dwayne Davis

RUSHING: Warren 148/593y, Hill 107/428y,
Rashaan Salaam (TB) 27/158y
PASSING: Stewart 151-252/2109y,12TD, 59.9%
Detmer 67-117/962y, 8TD, 57.3 %
RECEIVING: Westbrook 76/1060y, Johnson 57/1149y,
Fauria 31/326y
SCORING: Westbrook 50pts, Warren 48 pts,
Pat Blottiaux (K) 46pts

1993 8-3-1

36 Texas	14 WR Charles Johnson
45 Baylor	21 WR Michael Westbrook
37 Stanford	41 T Tony Berti
29 Miami	35 G Heath Irwin / Chris Naeole
30 Missouri	18 C Bryan Stoltenberg
27 Oklahoma	10 G Chad Hammond / Craig Anderson
16 Kansas State	16 T Derek West
17 Nebraska	21 TE Christian Fauria
31 Oklahoma State	14 TE Sean Embree
38 Kansas	14 QB Kordell Stewart
21 Iowa State	16 TB Lamont Warren ./ Rashaan Salaam
41 Fresno State■	30 DL Shannon Clavelle
	DL Kerry Hicks
	DL Darius Holland / Brian Dyet
	LB Ron Woolfork
	LB Jon Knutson / Matt Russell
	LB Ted Johnson
	LB Sam Rogers
	DB Dalton Simmons
	DB Dennis Collier
	DB Chris Hudson
	DB Greg Lindsay / Dwayne Davis

RUSHING: Warren 183/900y, Salaam 161/844y, Stewart 102/524y
PASSING: Stewart 157-294/2299y, 11TD, 53.4%
RECEIVING: Johnson 57/1082y, Westbrook 33/490y,
  Fauria 30/351y
SCORING: Mitch Berger (K) 76pts, Johnson 60pts, Salaam &
  Warren 48pts

1994 11-1

48 NE Louisiana	13 WR Rae Carruth / Phil Savoy
55 Wisconsin	17 WR Michael Westbrook
27 Michigan	26 T Tony Berti
34 Texas	31 G Heath Irwin
38 Missouri	23 C Bryan Stoltenberg
45 Oklahoma	7 G Chris Naeole
35 Kansas State	21 T Derek West
7 Nebraska	24 TE Christian Fauria
17 Oklahoma State	3 TE Matt Lepsis / Desmond Dennis
51 Kansas	26 QB Kordell Stewart
41 Iowa State	20 TB Rashaan Salaam
41 Notre Dame■	24 DL Shannon Clavelle
	DL Kerry Hicks / Ryan Olson
	DL Darius Holland
	LB Greg Jones
	LB Matt Russell
	LB Ted Johnson
	LB Mike Phillips / Jon Knutson
	DB Chris Hudson
	DB Dalton Simmons
	DB Steve Rosga
	DB Donnell Leomiti

RUSHING: Salaam298/2055y, Stewart 122/639y,
  Herchell Troutman 49/244y
PASSING: Stewart 147-237/2071y, 10TD, 62%
RECEIVING: Westbrook 36/689y, Fauria 35/356y, Salaam 24/294y
SCORING: Salaam 144pts, Neil Voskeritchian (K) 80pts,
  Herchell Troutman (TB) 48pts

1995 10-2

43 Wisconsin	7 WR Rae Carruth
42 Colorado State	14 WR James Kidd / Chris Anderson
66 NE Louisiana	14 WR Phil Savoy
29 Texas A&M	21 T Kyle Smith
38 Oklahoma	17 G Heath Irwin
24 Kansas	40 C Bryan Stoltenberg
50 Iowa State	28 G Chris Naeole
21 Nebraska	44 T Melvin Thomas
45 Oklahoma State	32 TE Matt Lepsis / Tennyson McCarty
21 Missouri	0 QB Koy Detmer / John Hessler
27 Kansas State	17 TB Herchell Troutman / Lendon Henry
38 Oregon■	6 DL Greg Jones
	DL Ryan Olson
	DL Kerry Hicks
	DL Daryl Price
	LB Mike Phillips / Allen Wilbon
	LB Matt Russell
	LB Ron Merkerson
	DB Toray Davis / Kenny Wilkins
	DB T.J. Cunningham
	DB Steve Rosga
	DB Donnell Leomiti / Ryan Black

RUSHING: Troutman 171/826y, Henry 85/463y,
  Marlon Barnes (TB) 85/444
PASSING: Hessler 154-266/2136y, 20TD, 57.9%
RECEIVING: Carruth 53/1008y, Savoy 49/582y, Sepsis 25/341y
SCORING: Neil Voskeritchian (K) 81pts, Carruth 54pts,
  Troutman 50pts

1996 10-2

37 Washington St.	19 WR Phil Savoy / Chris Anderson
48 Colorado State	34 WR Rae Carruth
13 Michigan	20 WR/TE James Kidd / Brody Heffner
24 Texas A&M	10 T Andrew Welsh
35 Oklahoma State	13 G Kyle Smith
20 Kansas	7 C Adam Reed
28 Texas	24 G Chris Naeole
41 Missouri	13 T Melvin Thomas
49 Iowa State	42 TE Tennyson McCarty / Matt Lepsis
12 Kansas State	0 QB Koy Detmer
12 Nebraska	17 TB Herchell Troutman / Lendon Henry
33 Washington■	21 DL Greg Jones
	DL Ryan Olson
	DL Viliami Mauman
	DL Nick Ziegler / Terrell Cade
	LB Mike Phillips / Hannibal Navies
	LB Matt Russell
	LB/DB Ron Merkerson / Toray Davis
	DB Marcus Washington
	DB Dalton Simmons
	DB Steve Rogga
	DB Ryan Black

RUSHING: Troutman 193/804y, Henley 115/539y,
  Dwayne Cherrington (TB) 28/168y
PASSING: Detmer 208-363/3156y, 22TD, 57.3%
RECEIVING: Carruth 54/1116y, Savoy 43/652y, Anderson 21/344y
SCORING: Carruth 81pts, Jason Lesley (K) 55pts, Henry 42pts

1997 5-6

31 Colorado State	21 WR Phil Savoy
3 Michigan	27 WR Darrin Chiaverini
20 Wyoming	19 WR Marcus Stiggers / Chris Anderson
10 Texas A&M	16 T Andrew Welsh / Shane Cook
29 Oklahoma St	33 G Aaron Wade
42 Kansas	6 C Adam Reed
47 Texas	30 G Melvin Thomas
31 Missouri	41 T Ryan Johanningmeier
43 Iowa State	38 TE Tennyson McCarty / B. Heffner-Liddiard
20 Kansas State	37 QB John Hessler
24 Nebraska	27 TB Herchell Troutman/Dwayne Cherrington
	DL Terrell Cade
	DL Ryan Olson
	DL Viliami Maumau
	DL Nick Ziegler / Brady McDonnell
	LB Hannibal Navies
	LB Mike Phillips / Ty Gregorak
	LB Ron Merkerson / Brandon Southward
	DB Damen Wheeler
	DB Marcus Washington / Ben Kelly
	DB Ryan Sutter
	DB Ryan Black

RUSHING: Troutman 155/613y, Cherrington 57/356y,
  Marlon Barnes (TB) 63/320y
PASSING: Hessler 181-338/2478y, 14TD, 53.6%
RECEIVING: Savoy 43/659y, Chiaverini 35/461y, Stiggers 25/357y
SCORING: Jeremy Aldrich (K) 65pts, Cherrington 42pts,
  Hessler 34pts

1998 8-4

42 Colorado State	14 WR Darrin Chiaverini
29 Fresno State	21 WR Javon Green / Marcus Stiggers
25 Utah State	6 T Shane Cook
18 Baylor	16 G Brad Bedell
27 Oklahoma	25 G Ryan Johanningmeier (G)/Andre Gurode
9 Kansas State	16 G Chris Morgan / Ben Nichols
19 Texas Tech	17 T Victor Rogers
17 Kansas	33 TE Tom Ashworth
14 Missouri	38 QB Mike Moschetti
37 Iowa State	8 TB Marlon Barnes / Dwayne Cherrington
14 Nebraska	16 FB Marcques Spivey
51 Oregon■	43 DL Fred Jones / Ian Loper
	DL Aaron Marshall
	DL Justin Bannan / Jesse Warren
	DL Brady McDonnell / Terrell Cade
	LB Hannibal Navies
	LB Brandon Southward / Ty Gregorak
	LB Albus Brooks / Jashon Sykes
	DB Damen Wheeler
	DB Ben Kelly
	DB Rashidi Barnes / Marcus Washington
	DB John Sanders / Michael Lewis

RUSHING: Barnes 121/572y, Cherrington 103/350y,
  Damion Barton (TB) 61/195
PASSING: Moschetti 162-276/2104y, 15TD, 58.7%
RECEIVING: Chiaverini 52/630y, Green 39/539y, Stiggers 17/242y
SCORING: Jeremy Aldrich (K) 70pts, Chiaverini 30pts,
  Green 24pts

1999 7-5

14 Colorado State	41 WR Marcus Stiggers / Javon Green
63 San Jose State	35 WR Robert Toler / Eric McCready
51 Kansas	17 T Shane Cook
24 Washington	31 G Ryan Johanningmeier
46 Missouri	39 C Andre Gurode
10 Texas Tech	31 G Brad Bedell
16 Iowa State	12 T Victor Rogers / Justin Bates
38 Oklahoma	24 TE Daniel Graham / Brody Heffner-Liddiard
14 Kansas State	20 QB Mike Moschetti
37 Baylor	0 TB Cortlen Johnson / Dwayne Cherrington
30 Nebraska	33 FB/WR Brandon Drumm / John Minardi
62 Boston College■	28 DL Jesse Warren / Sean Jarne
	DL Justin Bannan
	DL Brady McDonnell / Robert Haas
	LB Fred Jones
	LB Ty Gregorak / Andy Peeke
	LB Jashon Sykes
	LB Drew Wahlroos
	DB Ben Kelly
	DB Damen Wheeler
	DB Rashidi Barnes
	DB Michael Lewis / Robbie Robinson

RUSHING: Johnson 172/835y, Cherrington 73/270y,
  Damion Barton (TB) 47/186y
PASSING: Moschetti 204-331/2693y, 18TD, 61.6%
RECEIVING: Green 40/663y, Stiggers 37/625y,
  Roman Hollowell (WR) 24/244y
SCORING: Jeremy Aldrich (K) 84pts, Johnson 48pts, Green 44pts

2000 3-8

24 Colorado State	28 WR John Minardi / Roman Hollowell
14 Southern Cal	17 WR Javon Green
14 Washington	17 T Tom Ashworth
21 Kansas State	44 G Justin Bates
26 Texas A&M	19 C Ryan Gray
14 Texas	28 G Andre Gurode (C) / Karl Allis
15 Kansas	23 T Victor Rogers
37 Oklahoma State	21 TE Daniel Graham
28 Missouri	18 QB Craig Ochs
27 Iowa State	35 TB Cortlen Johnson / Marcus Houston
32 Nebraska	34 FB Scott Nemeth
	DL Justin Bannan
	DL Sean Jarne
	DL Brady McDonnell / Tyler Brayton
	LB Anwawn Jones
	LB Andy Peeke
	LB Jashon Sykes
	LB Kory Mossoni / Drew Wahlroos
	DB Donald Strickland
	DB Phil Jackson
	DB Robbie Robinson
	DB Michael Lewis

RUSHING: Johnson 144/622y, Houston 66/332y,
  Bobby Purify (TB) 45/177y
PASSING: Ochs 145-245/1778y, 7TD, 59.2%
RECEIVING: Green 48/699y, Minardi 48/592y, Graham 33/443y
SCORING: Johnson 54pts, Mark Mariscal (K) 45pts, Ochs 32pts

2001 10-3

22 Fresno State	24 WR John Minardi / Cedric Cormier
41 Colorado State	47 WR Derek McCoy
51 San Jose State	15 T Justin Bates
27 Kansas	16 G Marwan Hage
16 Kansas State	6 C Wayne Lucier
31 Texas A&M	21 G Andre Gurode
7 Texas	41 T Victor Rogers
22 Colorado State	12 TE Daniel Graham
38 Missouri	24 QB Craig Ochs / Bobby Pesavento
40 Iowa State	27 TB Chris Brown/Bobby Purifoy/C. Johnson
62 Nebraska	36 FB Brandon Drumm
39 Texas□	37 DL Tyler Brayton
16 Oregon■	38 DL Justin Bannan
	DL Brandon Dahdoub / DeAndre Fluellen
	DL Marques Harris
	LB Sean Tufts
	LB Joey Johnson / Jashon Sykes
	LB Drew Wahlroos / Aaron Killion
	DB Donald Strickland
	DB Roderick Sneed / Phil Jackson
	DB Robbie Robinson
	DB Michael Lewis

RUSHING: Brown 190/946y, Purifoy 157/916y, Johnson 89/567y
PASSING: Pesavento 85-139/1234y, 8TD, 61.2%
  Ochs 99-166/1220y, 7TD, 59.6%
RECEIVING: Graham 51/753y, McCoy 30/512y, Johnson 24/382y
SCORING: Brown 96pts, Jeremy Flores (K) 94pts, Graham 36pts

2002 9-5

14 Colorado State	19 WR Derek McCoy
34 San Diego State	14 WR John Donahoe / Jeremy Bloom
3 Southern Cal	40 T Justin Bates
31 UCLA	17 G Marwan Hage
35 Kansas State	31 C Ryan Gray
53 Kansas	29 G Wayne Lucier
34 Baylor	0 T Josh Foster / Rawle King
37 Texas Tech	13 TE Beau Williams / Quinn Sypniewski
11 Oklahoma	27 QB Robert Hodge / Craig Ochs
42 Missouri	35 TB Chris Brown / Bobby Purify
41 Iowa State	27 FB Brandon Drumm
28 Nebraska	13 DL Gabe Nyenhuis / Dylan Bird
7 Oklahoma□	29 DL Tyler Brayton
28 Wisconsin■	31 DL Sam Wilder DeAndre Fluellen
	DL Marques Harris
	LB/DB Sean Tufts / Clyde Surrell
	LB Drew Wahlroos / Joey Johnson
	DB Donald Strickland
	DB Phil Jackson
	DB Roderick Sneed / Brian Iwuh
	DB Medford Moorer
	DB Kory Mossoni (LB) / J.J. Billingsley

RUSHING: Brown 275/1744y, Purify 132/739y,
Brian Calhoun 67/298y
PASSING: Hodge 131-245/1547y, 12TD, 53.5%
RECEIVING: McCoy 41/643y, Purify 21/224y, Drumm 18/145y
SCORING: Brown 108pts, Patrick Brougham (K) 73pts,
McCoy 46pts

2003 5-7

42 Colorado State	35 WR D.J. Hackett
16 UCLA	14 WR Derek McCoy / Jeremy Bloom
26 Washington St.	47 T Karl Allis
7 Florida State	47 G Brian Daniels / Clint O'Neal
30 Baylor	42 C Marwan Hage
50 Kansas	47 G Derek Stemrich / Gary Moore
20 Kansas State	49 T Sam Wilder
20 Oklahoma	34 TE Joe Klopfenstein / Jesse Wallace
21 Texas Tech	26 QB Joel Klatt / Erik Greenberg
21 Missouri	16 TB Brian Calhoun
44 Iowa State	10 FB Lawrence Vickers / Daniel Jolly
22 Nebraska	31 DL Gabe Nyenhuis
	DL Brandon Dabdoub / DeAndre Fluellen
	DL Matt McChesney / Vaka Manupunu
	DL James Garee / Alex Ligon
	LB Sean Tufts / Thaddeus Washington
	LB Akarika Dawn / Chris Hollis
	DB Sammy Joseph
	DB Phil Jackson / Terrence Wheatley
	DB Medford Moorer
	DB J.J. Billingsley / Dominique Brooks
	DB Clyde Surrell / Brian Iwuh

RUSHING: Calhoun 195/810y, Bobby Purify (TB) 52/167y,
Jolly 47/109y
PASSING: Klatt 233-358/2614y, 21TD, 65.1%
Greenberg 49-92/737y, 6TD, 53.3%
RECEIVING: Hackett 78/1013y, McCoy 63/883y, Calhoun 32/266y
SCORING: McCoy 66pts, Mason Crosby (K) 52pts, Hackett 44pts

2004 8-5

27 Colorado State	24 WR Ron Monteilh / Mike Duren
20 Washington St.	12 WR Evan Judge / Blake Mackey
52 North Texas	21 T Sam Wilder
9 Missouri	17 G Terrance Barreau
14 Oklahoma State	42 C Mark Fenton
10 Iowa State	14 G Brian Daniels
26 Texas A&M	29 T Clint O'Neal / Edwin Harrison
7 Texas	31 TE Joe Klopfenstein
30 Kansas	21 QB Joel Klatt
38 Kansas State	31 TB Bobby Purify
26 Nebraska	20 FB Lawrence Vickers
3 Oklahoma○	42 DL Abraham Wright / Alex Ligon
33 UTEP■	28 DL Vaka Manupunu / Brndon Dabdoub
	DL Matt McChesney
	DL James Goree
	LB Thaddueus Washington
	LB Jordon Dizon / Akarika Dawn
	LB Brian Iwuh
	DB Lorenzo Sims / Terrence Wheatley
	DB Gerett Burl
	DB Tom Hubbard
	DB Tyrone Henderson / Dominique Brooks

RUSHING: Purify 209/1017y, Vickers 60/248y
PASSING: Klatt 192-334/2065y, 9TD, 57.5%
RECEIVING: Judge 29/336y, Monteilh 28/314y,
Klopfenstein 28/284y
SCORING: Mason Crosby (K) 85pts, Purify 54pts, Klopfenstein 24pt

2005 7-6

31 Colorado State	28 WR Evan Judge / Patrick Williams
39 New Mexico St.	0 WR Dusty Sprague / Alvin Barnett
3 Miami	23 T Gary Moore / Tyler Polumbus
34 Oklahoma State	0 G Brian Daniels / Jack Tipton
41 Texas A&M	20 C Mark Fenton
17 Texas	42 G Daniel Sanders / Edwin Harrison
44 Kansas	13 T Clint O'Neil
23 Kansas State	20 TE Joe Klopfenstein
41 Missouri	12 QB Joel Klatt
16 Iowa State	30 TB Hugh Charles / Byron Ellis
3 Nebraska	30 FB/TE L. Vickers / Quinn Sypniewski
3 Texas□	70 DL Abraham Wright
10 Clemson■	19 DL Vaka Manupuna
	DL James Garee
	DL Maurice Lucas / Alex Ligon
	LB Thaddaeus Washington
	LB Jordan Dizon / Akarika Dawn
	LB Brian Iwuh
	DB Lorenzo Sims / Terry Washington
	DB Gerett Burl
	DB Tyrone Henderson
	DB J. J. Billingsley

RUSHING: Charles 176/842y, Vickers 67/243y, Ellis 75/216y
PASSING: Klatt 241-400/2696y, 14TD, 60.3%
RECEIVING: Sprague 43/468y, Judge 40/567y,
Klopfenstein 32/463y
SCORING: Mason Crosby (K) 94pts, Vickers 66pts, Charles 42pts

2006 2-10

10 Montana State	19 WR Patrick Williams / Cody Crawford
10 Colorado State	14 WR Alvin Barnett / Dusty Sprague
3 Arizona State	21 T Tyler Polumbus
13 Georgia	14 G Brian Daniels
3 Missouri	28 C Bryce MacMartin / Mark Fenton
31 Baylor	34 G Daniel Sanders
30 Texas Tech	6 T Edwin Harrison / Jack Tipton
3 Oklahoma	24 TE Riar Geer
15 Kansas	20 QB Bernard Jackson
21 Kansas State	34 TB Hugh Charles / Mell Holliday
33 Iowa State	16 FB Maurice Cantrell
14 Nebraska	37 DL Abraham Wright
	DL George Hypolite
	DL Brandon Nicolas
	DL Walter Boye-Doe
	LB Thaddeus Washington
	LB Jordan Dizon
	LB Brad Jones
	DB Terry Washington / Lorenzo Sims
	DB Terrence Wheatley
	DB Ryan Walters / Cha'pelle Brown
	DB J. J. Billingsley / Lionel Harris

RUSHING: Charles 139/779y, Jackson 155/677y,
Holliday 105/512y
PASSING: Jackson 108-219/1298y, 7TD, 49.3%
RECEIVING: Geer 24/261y, Barnett 21/232y,
Williams 19/242y
SCORING: Mason Crosby (K) 76pts, Jackson 42pts,
Geer 18pts

2007 6-7

31 Colorado State	28 WR Patrick Williams / Josh Smith
14 Arizona State	33 WR Scotty McKnight/Dusty Sprague
6 Florida State	16 T Tyler Polumbus
42 Miami (Ohio)	0 G Kai Maiava / Wes Palazzi
27 Oklahoma	24 C Daniel Sanders
43 Baylor	23 G Devin Head / Justin Drescher
20 Kansas State	47 T Edwin Harrison (G)/Ryan Miller (C)
14 Kansas	19 TE Riar Geer / Tyson DeVree
31 Texas Tech	26 QB Cody Hawkins
10 Missouri	55 TB Hugh Charles / Byron Ellis
28 Iowa State	31 FB/TE Jake Behrens / Nate Solder
65 Nebraska	51 DL Alonzo Barrett
24 Alabama■	30 DL George Hypolite
	DL Brandon Nicholas
	DL/DB Maurice Lucas/Cha'pelle Brown
	LB Jordon Dizon
	LB Jeff Smart
	LB Brad Jones
	DB Benjamin Burney
	DB Terrence Wheatley / Gardner McKay
	DB Ryan Walters / Lionel Harris
	DB Daniel Dykes

RUSHING: Charles 199/1058y, Demetrius Sumler (TB) 100/335y,
Brian Lockridge (TB) 40/215y
PASSING: Hawkins 263-463/3015y, 22TD, 56.8%
RECEIVING: McKnight 47/555y, DeVree 37/302y, Sprague 29/366y
SCORING: Kevin Eberhart (K) 83pts, Charles 54pts, DeVree 48pts

2008 5-7

38 Colorado State	17 WR Josh Smith / Cody Crawford
31 E. Washington	24 WR Patrick Williams / Scotty McKnight
17 West Virginia	14 T Nate Solder
21 Florida State	39 G Blake Behrens
14 Texas	38 C Daniel Sanders
14 Kansas	30 G Devin Head / Max Tuioti-Mariner
14 Kansas State	13 T Matthew Bahr / Ryan Miller
0 Missouri	58 TE Riar Geer / Patrick Devenny
17 Texas A&M	24 QB Cody Hawkins / Tyler Hansen
28 Iowa State	24 TB Rodney Stewart / Darrell Scott
17 Oklahoma State	30 FB Jake Behrens
31 Nebraska	40 DL Maurice Lucas
	DL George Hypolite
	DL Brandon Nicolas
	LB Jeff Smart
	LB Shaun Mohler
	LB Brad Jones
	DB Cha'pelle Brown
	DB Jimmy Smith / Gardner McKay
	DB Jahil Brown
	DB Ryan Walters
	DB D.J. Dykes / Anthony Perkins

RUSHING: Stewart 132/622y, Hansen 63/261y
PASSING: Hawkins 183-320/1892y, 17TD, 57.2%
Hansen 34-65/280y, 1TD, 52.3%
RECEIVING: McKnight 46/519y, Crawford 31/269y,
Williams 30/322y
SCORING: Aric Goodman (K) 45pts, McKnight 30pts,
Smith and Sumler 24pts

2009 3-9

17 Colorado State	23 WR Scotty McKnight
38 Toledo	54 WR Mark ues Simas / Will Jefferson
24 Wyoming	0 T Nate Solder
24 West Virginia	35 G Ethan Adkins / Blake Behrens
14 Texas	38 C Keenan Stevens / Mike Iltis
34 Kansas	30 G Ryan Miller (T) / Matthew Bahr
6 Kansas State	20 T Bryce Givens
17 Missouri	36 TE Riar Geer / Ryan Deehan (FB)
35 Texas A&M	34 QB Tyler Hansen / Cody Hawkins
10 Iowa State	17 TB Rodney Stewart / Demetrius Sumler
28 Oklahoma State	31 FB/WR Jake Behrens / Jason Espinoza
20 Nebraska	28 DL Marquez Herrod
	DL Curtis Cunningham
	DL Will Pericak / Nate Bonsu
	DL/DB Forrest Webb / Jalil Brown
	LB Marcus Burton / Michael Sipili
	LB Jeff Smart / Shaun Mohler
	LB B.J. Beatty / Tyler Ahles
	DB Cha'pelle Brown
	DB Jimmy Smith
	DB Anthony Perkins / Ray Polk
	DB Benjamin Burney

RUSHING: Stewart 198/804y, Sumler 36/128y
PASSING: Hansen 129-231/1440y, 8TD, 55.8%
Hawkins 121-239/1277y, 10TD, 50.6%
RECEIVING: McKnight 76/893y, Simas 43/585y, Geer 36/402y
SCORING: Aric Goodman (K) 61pts, Stewart 54pts, McKnight 42pts

2010 5-7

24 Colorado State	3 WR Toney Clemons / Will Jefferson (TB)
7 California	52 WR Paul Richardson / Travan Patterson
31 Hawaii	13 WR/FB Scotty McKnight / Matthew Bahr
29 Georgia	27 T Nate Solder
0 Missouri	26 G Ethan Adkins
25 Baylor	31 C Mike Iltis / Keenan Stevens
24 Texas Tech	27 G Ryan Miller
10 Oklahoma	43 T David Bakhtiar
45 Kansas	52 TE Ryan Deehan / Luke Walters
34 Iowa State	14 QB Cody Hawkins / Tyler Hansen
44 Kansas State	36 TB Rodney Stewart
17 Nebraska	45 DL Josh Hartigan / Forrest West
	DL Curtis Cunningham / Nick Kasa
	DL Will Pericak
	DL/DB Marquez Herrod/ Travis Sanderfield
	LB Michael Sipili / Patrick Mahnke
	LB Jon Major / Liloa Nobriga
	LB B.J. Beatty / Tyler Ahles
	DB Jalil Brown
	DB Jimmy Smith
	DB Ray Polk / Quentin Hildreth
	DB Terrel Smith / Anthony Perkins

RUSHING: Stewart 290/1318y, Brian Lockbridge (TB) 35/146y
PASSING: Hawkins 124-231/1547y, 14TD, 53.7%
Hansen 112-164/1102y, 6TD, 68.3%
RECEIVING: McKnight 50/621y, Clemons 43/482y,
Richardson 34/514y
SCORING: Aric Goodman (K) 62pts, Stewart 60pts, McKnight 42pts

DUKE

Duke University (Founded 1850)
Durham, North Carolina
Nickname: Blue Devils
Colors: Royal Blue and White
Stadium: Wallace Wade (1939) 33,941
Affiliation: Atlantic Coast Conference (1953-present)

CAREER RUSHING YARDS	Attempts	Yards
Chris Douglas (2000-03)	695	3122
Steve Jones (1970-72)	683	2951
Randy Cuthbert (1988-92)	577	2790
Mike Grayson (1980-83)	574	2441
Tony Benjamin (1973-76)	503	2251
Julius Grantham (1982-86)	475	1989
Mike Dunn (1975-78)	565	1939
Roger Boone (1986-89)	415	1900
Ace Parker (1934-36)	316	1856
Robert Baldwin (1991-94)	421	1848

CAREER PASSING YARDS	Comp.-Att.	Yards
Thaddeus Lewis (2006-09)	877-1510	10,065
Ben Bennett (1980-83)	820-1375	9614
Spence Fischer (1992-95)	786-1369	9019
Steve Slayden (1984-87)	699-1204	8004
Leo Hart (1968-70)	486-877	6116
Dave Brown (1989-91)	464-845	5717
Anthony Dilweg (1985-88)	342-594	4557
D. Bryant (2000-01)	316-642	3902
Spencer Romine (1997-2000)	281-571	3545
Mike Dunn (1975-78)	288-570	3511

CAREER RECEIVING YARDS	Catches	Yards
Clarkston Hines (1986-89)	189	3318
Eron Riley (2005-08)	144	2413
Wes Chesson (1968-70)	164	2399
Scottie Montgomery (1996-99)	171	2378
Corey Thomas (1994-97)	165	2297
Doug Green (1983-87)	142	2082
Walter Jones (1988-91)	119	1968
Cedric Jones (1978-81)	99	1732
Jomar Wright (2004-07)	122	1638
Stanley Dorsey (1990-93)	107	1507

SEASON RUSHING YARDS	Attempts	Yards
Steve Jones (1972)	287	1236
Robert Baldwin (1994)	276	1187
Chris Douglas (2003)	236	1136
Randy Cuthbert (1992)	227	1031
Randy Cuthbert (1989)	187	1023

SEASON PASSING YARDS	Comp.-Att.	Yards
Anthony Dilweg (1988)	287-484	3824
Thaddeus Lewis (2009)	274-449	3330
Ben Bennett (1983)	300-469	3086
Ben Bennett (1982)	236-374	3033
Steve Slayden (1987)	230-395	2924

SEASON RECEIVING YARDS	Catches	Yards
Clarkston Hines (1989)	61	1149
Clarkston Hines (1987)	57	1093
Wes Chasson (1970)	74	1080
Clarkston Hines (1988)	68	1067
Donovan Varner (2009)	65	1047

GAME RUSHING YARDS	Attempts	Yards
Robert Baldwin (1994 vs. Maryland)	33	238
Randy Cuthbert (1989 vs. Georgia Tech)	32	234
Chris Douglas (2003 vs. Georgia Tech)	30	218

GAME PASSING YARDS	Comp.-Att.	Yards
Dave Brown (1989 vs. North Carolina)	33-54	479
Anthony Dilweg (1988 vs. Wake Forest)	30-49	475
Ben Bennett (1980 vs. Wake Forest)	38-62	469

GAME RECEIVING YARDS	Catches	Yards
Chris Castor (1982 vs. Wake Forest)	11	283
Corey Thomas (1997 vs. Georgia Tech)	16	276
Clarkston Hines (1989 vs. Wake Forest)	6	251

GREATEST COACH

He wasn't the same person as "Saturday Night Live" and movie comedian Bill Murray, but the Duke Hall of Fame football coach by the same name bore a fascinating facial resemblance to the comic.

Football's Bill Murray arrived from the University of Delaware in 1951 to replace Duke's most respected coach, Wallace Wade, and stayed for 15 highly effective years. Students of today's football would not have recognized the Blue Devils of Bill Murray, who developed several All-America linemen who hit hard and fast. Murray coached the Blues to a 93-51-9 record. No Blue Devils coach has posted a winning record since, except for Steve Spurrier's brief stay in the late 1980s when he delivered a 20-13-1 mark.

Duke was a charter member of the Atlantic Coast Conference in 1953, and Murray led the Devils to titles in each of the league's first three seasons. In Murray's 13 years after the ACC was established, Duke ruled for seven championships. It has shared only one title (1989) since that time.

One great bit of trivia concerning Murray is that he is one of three consecutive coaches at Delaware (Murray, Dave Nelson, and Tubby Raymond) to subsequently be elected to the College Hall of Fame. No other school can make that claim.

DUKE'S 55 GREATEST SINCE 1953

OFFENSE

WIDE RECEIVER: Wes Chesson, Clarkston Hines, Cedric Jones, Tee Moorman
TIGHT END: Carl Franks, Bill Khayat
TACKLE: Dwight Bumgarner, Cameron Goldberg, Chris Port, Matt Williams
GUARD: Brian Baldinger, Jean Berry, Bobby Burrows, Roy Hord
CENTER: Bill Bryan, Phil Ebinger
QUARTERBACK: Ben Bennett, Anthony Dilweg, Spence Fischer
RUNNING BACK: Robert Baldwin, Wray Carlton, Randy Cuthbert, Chris Douglas, Bob Pascal
FULLBACK: Bryant Aldridge, Steve Jones, Hal McElhaney

DEFENSE

END: Ernie Clark, Jeff Green
TACKLE: Art Gregory, Ed Meadows, Ed Newman, Tom Topping
LINEBACKER: Dick Biddle, Mike Curtis, Mike Junkin, Bob Matheson, Mike McGee, Keith Stoneback
CORNERBACK: Quinton McCracken, Dennis Tabron, John Talley, Wyatt Smith
SAFETY: Jerry Barger, Ray Farmer, Erwin Sampson, Rich Searl

SPECIAL TEAMS

RETURN SPECIALISTS: Jabari Marshall
PLACE KICKER: Randy Gardner
PUNTER: Brian Morton

MULTIPLE POSITIONS

QUARTERBACK-FULLBACK-DEFENSIVE BACK-LINEBACKER: Worth Lutz
HALFBACK-END-CORNERBACK-DEFENSIVE END: Buddy Bass

TWO-WAY PLAYERS

END-DEFENSIVE END: Tracy Moon
QUARTERBACK-SAFETY: Sonny Jurgensen
HALFBACK-WIDE RECEIVER-DEFENSIVE BACK-KICK RETURNER: Jay Wilkinson

PERFORMANCE FORMULA: DUKE'S 10 BEST SEASONS

1954	1.4585	13 of 69
1955	1.4372	10 of 69
1962	1.3894	16 of 70
1953	1.3840	13 of 69
1960	1.3660	17 of 70
1961	1.3143	18 of 71
1994	1.2889	21 of 71
1957	1.2870	21 of 69
1989	1.2524	26 of 70
1956	1.2081	28 of 69

DUKE BLUE DEVILS

Year	W-L-T	AP Poll	Conference Standing	Toughest Regular Season Opponents	Coach (Record at School)	Bowl Games		
1953	7-2-1	18	1	South Carolina 7-3, Army 7-1-1, Georgia Tech 8-2-1	Bill Murray			
1954	8-2-1	14	1	Purdue 5-3-1, Army 7-2, Georgia The 7-3, Navy 7-2	Bill Murray	Orange	34 Nebraska	7
1955	7-2-1		1	Tennessee 6-3-1, Ohio State 7-2, Pittsburgh 7-3, Georgia Tech 8-1-1	Bill Murray			
1956	5-4-1		2	Tennessee 10-0, Pittsburgh 7-2-1, Georgia Tech 9-1, Navy 6-1-2	Bill Murray			
1957	6-3-2	16	2	Rice 7-3, NC State 7-1-2, Navy 8-1-1, Clemson 7-3	Bill Murray	Orange	21 Oklahoma	48
1958	5-5		3	South Carolina 6-4, Notre Dame 6-4, LSU 10-0, North Carolina 6-4	Bill Murray			
1959	4-6		6	South Carolina 6-4, Pittsburgh 6-4, Georgia Tech 6-4, Clemson 8-2	Bill Murray			
1960	8-3	10	1	NC State 6-3-1, Navy 9-1, UCLA 7-2-1	Bill Murray	Cotton	7 Arkansas	6
1961	7-3	20	1	Georgia Tech 7-3, Michigan 6-3, Navy 7-3	Bill Murray			
1962	8-2	11+	1	So. Calif. 10-0, Florida 6-4, Clemson 6-4, Ga. Tech 7-2-1, Maryland 6-4	Bill Murray			
1963	5-4-1		3	NC State 8-2, Georgia Tech 7-3, Navy 9-1	Bill Murray			
1964	4-5-1		2	Georgia Tech 7-3, Maryland 5-5, NC State 5-5, North Carolina 5-5	Bill Murray			
1965	6-4		1t	Illinois 6-4, Georgia Tech 6-3-1, NC State 6-4	Bill Murray (93-51-9)			
1966	5-5		6	Clemson 6-4, Georgia Tech 9-1, Notre Dame 9-0-1	Tom Harp			
1967	4-6		6	Army 8-2, Clemson 6-4, NC State 8-2, Navy 5-4-1	Tom Harp			
1968	4-6		5	Michigan 8-2, Virginia 7-2, Army 7-3, NC State 6-4	Tom Harp			
1969	3-6-1		3	South Carolina 7-3, Virginia Tech 4—5-1, North Carolina 5-5	Tom Harp			
1970	6-5		2	Florida 7-4, Ohio St. 9-0, West Va. 8-3, Ga. Tech 8-3, No. Carolina 8-3	Tom Harp (22-28-1)			
1971	6-5		3	Stanford 8-3, West Virginia 7-4, North Carolina 9-2	Mike McGee			
1972	5-6		4	Alabama 10-1, Washington 8-3, NC State 7-3-1, North Carolina 10-1	Mike McGee			
1973	2-8-1		5	Tennessee 8-3, Tualne 9-2, Maryland 8-3, NC State 8-31	Mike McGee			
1974	6-5		5	NC State 9-2, Florida 8-3, Maryland 8-3, North Carolina 7-4	Mike McGee			
1975	4-5-2		2	Southern Calif. 7-4, South Carolina 7-4, Florida 9-2, NC State 7-3-1	Mike McGee			
1976	5-5-1		4	Pittsburgh 11-0, Maryland 11-0, North Carolina 9-2	Mike McGee			
1977	5-6		5	Michigan 10-1, Clemson 8-2-1, North Carolina 8-2-1	Mike McGee			
1978	4-7		5	Michigan 10-1, Clemson 10-1, Maryland 9-2, NC State 8-3	Mike McGee (37-47-4)			
1979	2-8-1		7	South Carolina 8-3, Clemson 8-3, Wake Forest 8-3	Red Wilson			
1980	2-9		7	South Carolina 8-3, Maryland 8-3, North Carolina 10-1	Red Wilson			
1981	6-5		4	Ohio State 8-3, Clemson 11-0, North Carolina 9-2	Red Wilson			
1982	6-5		3t	Tennessee 6-4-1, Clemson 9-1-1, Maryland 8-3, North Carolina 7-4	Red Wilson (16-27-1)			
1983	3-8		4	Miami 10-1, Virginia Tech 9-2, Clemson 9-1-1, North Carolina 8-3	Steve Sloan			
1984	2-9		6t	South Carolina 10-1, Army 7-3-1, Virginia 7-2-2, Maryland 8-3	Steve Sloan			
1985	4-7		6t	West Virginia 7-3-1, Maryland 8-3, Georgia Tech 8-2-1	Steve Sloan			
1986	4-7		6	Georgia 8-3, Clemson 7-2-2, NC State 8-2-1, North Carolina 7-3-1	Steve Sloan (13-31)			
1987	5-6		7	Virginia 7-4, Clemson 9-2, Wake Forest 7-4	Steve Spurrier			
1988	7-3-1		6	Virginia 7-4, Clemson 9-2, NC State 7-3-1	Steve Spurrier			
1989	8-4		1t	Tennessee 10-1, Virginia 10-2, Clemson 9-2	Steve Spurrier (20-13-1)	All American	21 Texas Tech	49
1990	4-7		7	Virginia 8-3, Clemson 9-2, Georgia Tech 10-0-1	Barry Wilson			
1991	4-6-1		7t	Virginia 8-2-1, NC State 9-2, North Carolina 7-4, Clemson 9-1-1	Barry Wilson			
1992	2-9		9	Florida State 10-1, NC State 9-2-1, North Carolina 8-3	Barry Wilson			
1993	3-8		7	Florida St. 11-1, Tennessee 9-1-1, Clemson 8-3, North Carolina 10-2	Barry Wilson (13-30-1)			
1994	8-4		3t	Florida State 9-1-1, Virginia 8-3, NC State 8-3, North Carolina 8-3	Fred Goldsmith	Hall of Fame	20 Wisconsin	34
1995	3-8		8	Florida State 9-2, Virginia 8-4, Clemson 8-3	Fred Goldsmith			
1996	0-11		9	Florida State 11-0, Northwestern 9-2, Army 10-1, North Carolina 9-2	Fred Goldsmith			
1997	2-9		9	Florida State 10-1, Virginia 7-4, Clemson 7-4, North Carolina 10-1	Fred Goldsmith			
1998	4-7		6t	Florida State 11-1, Virginia 9-2, Georgia Tech 9-2	Fred Goldsmith (17-39)			
1999	3-8		5t	Florida State 11-0, Virginia 7-4, Georgia Tech 8-3	Carl Franks			
2000	0-11		9	Northwestern 8-3, Clemson 9-2, Florida State 11-1, Georgia Tech 9-2	Carl Franks			
2001	0-11		9	Florida State 7-4, Rice 8-4, Maryland 10-1, NC State 7-4	Carl Franks			
2002	2-10		9	Florida State 9-4, Virginia 8-5, NC State 10-3, Maryland 10-3	Carl Franks			
2003	4-8		8	Florida State 10-2, Maryland 9-3, Tennessee 10-2, Clemson 8-4	Carl Franks (7-45), Ted Roof [2-3]			
2004	2-9		10t	Navy 9-2, Virginia Tech 10-2, Virginia 8-3, Florida State 8-3	Ted Roof			
2005	1-10		Cst6	Virginia Tech 10-2, Miami 9-2, Florida State 8-4	Ted Roof			
2006	0-12		Cst6	Wake Forest 10-2, Virginia Tech 10-2, Navy 9-3, Boston College 9-3	Ted Roof			
2007	1-11		Cst6	Connecticut 9-3, Virginia 9-3, Virginia Tech 10-2, Clemson 9-3	Ted Roof (6-45)			
2008	4-8		Cst6	Northwestern 9-3, Georgia Tech 9-3, Virginia Tech 9-4	David Cutcliffe			
2009	5-7		Cst5	Richmond 10-1, Virginia Tech 9-3, Georgia Tech 11-2, Miami 9-3	David Cutcliffe			
2010	3-9		Cst5t	Alabama 9-3, Maryland 8-4, Virginia Tech 11-2	David Cutcliffe (12-24)			

TOTAL: 243-374-16 .3965 (65 of 70)   **Bowl Games since 1953:** 2-3 .4000 (58 of 70)

GREATEST TEAM SINCE 1953: The 1960 Blue Devils, coached by Bill Murray, won their last bowl game, defeating no. 7 Arkansas by 7-6 in the Cotton Bowl. The 1960 Duke team finished the regular season as ACC champions, having lost only to Michigan, rival North Carolina by a single point, and an underappreciated UCLA team on a trip all the way to Los Angeles at season's end. Duke finished 8-3 and was ranked no. 10 in the AP Poll. A close second was Murray's 1954 ACC champions that crushed Nebraska in the Orange Bowl.

1953 7-2-1

20	South Carolina	7	E Sonny Sorrell / Jerry Koucerek
19	Wake Forest	0	T Ed Meadows
21	Tennessee	7	G Bobby Burrows
20	Purdue	14	G Johnny Palmer / Doug Knotts
13	Army	14	G Ralph Tottance / Walter Smith
31	N. Carolina St.	0	T Jesse Birchfield
48	Virginia	6	E Howard Pitt / Tracy Moon
0	Navy	0	QB Jerry Barger / Worth Lutz
10	Georgia Tech	13	HB Lloyd Caudle / Bob Pascal
35	North Carolina	20	HB Red Smith
			FB Byrd Looper / Jack Kistler

RUSHING: Caudle 104/510y, Smith 65/372y, Kistler 64/222y
PASSING: Barger 21-38/353y,4TD, 55.3%,
Lutz 16-44/203y, 36.4%
RECEIVING: Pitt 14/189y, Smith 6/136y, Kocourek 4/45y
SCORING: Caudle 54pts, Smith 43pts, 3 with 18pts

1954 8-2-1

52	Pennsylvania	0	E Sonny Sorrell / Bob Benson
7	Tennessee	6	T Fred Campbell / Sid DeLoatch
13	Purdue	13	G Jesse Birchfield
14	Army	28	C Johnny Palmer / Ronnie Falls
21	N. Carolina St.	7	G Ralph Torrence / Jim Nelson
21	Georgia Tech	20	T Dan Cox / Doug Knotts
7	Navy	40	E Tracy Moon / Jerry Kocourek
28	Wake Foest	21	QB Jerry Barger / Worth Lutz (FB)
26	SouthCarolina	7	HB Bob Pascal / Ed Post
47	North Carolina	12	HB Buddy Bass / Bernie Blaney
34	Nebraska■		FB Bryant Aldridge

RUSHING: Pascal 98/470y, Aldridge 85/458y, Blaney 44/317y
PASSING: Barger 32-68/521y, 3TD, 47.1%
RECEIVING: Bass 9/147y, Post 8/203y, Pascal 7/58y
SCORING: Pascal 54pts, Aldridge (FB-K) 32pts,
Barger (QB-K) 25pts

1955 7-2-1

33	N. Carolina St.	7	E Sonny Sorrell / Bob Benson
21	Tennessee	0	T Sid Deloatch / Tom Topping
47	William & Mary	7	G Jesse Birchfield
20	Ohio State	14	C Ronnie Falls / Johnny Long
7	Pittsburgh	26	G Roy Hord / Jim Nelson
0	Georgia Tech	27	T Dan Cox / Doug Knotts
7	Navy	7	E Buddy Bass / Jerry Kocourek
41	South Carolina	7	QB Sonny Jurgensen
14	Wake Forest	0	HB Bob Pascal / Eddie Rushton
6	North Carolina	0	HB Ed Post / Bernie Blaney
			FB Bryant Aldridge / Hal McElhaney

RUSHING: Pascal 156/750y, Aldridge 92/404y, Blaney 49/236y
PASSING: Jurgensen 37-69/536y, 3TD, 53.6%
RECEIVING: Sorrell 12/153y, Pascal 9/124y, Blaney 8/169y
SCORING: Pascal 48pts, Blaney 30pts, Aldridge (FB-K) 24pts

1956 5-4-1

0	South Carolina	7	E Bob Benson/Leon'rd Black/Dave Hurm
40	Virginia	7	T Tom Topping / Milt Konicek
20	Tennessee	33	G Sid Deloatch
14	SMU	6	C Johnny Long / Wade Byrd
14	Pittsburgh	27	G Roy Hord / Jim Nelson
42	N. Carolina St.	0	T Dan Cox / Bill Recinella
0	Georgia Tech	7	E Buddy Bass / Bill Thompson
7	Navy	7	QB Sonny Jurgensen / Bob Brodhead
26	Wake Forest	0	HB Wray Carlton / Eddie Rushton
21	North Carolina	6	HB George Dutrow / Bernie Blaney
			FB Hal McElhaney

RUSHING: McElhaney 90/449y, Rushton 75/373y, Dutrow 54/340y
PASSING: Jurgensen 28-59/371y, 2TD, 47.5%
RECEIVING: Bass 9/136y, Thompson 7/96y, Hurm 5/58y
SCORING: Rushton 30pts, Blaney 28pts,
Carlton (HB-K) & Jurgensen 18pts

1957 6-3-2

26	South Carolina	14	E Dave Hurm / Bert Lattimore
40	Virginia	0	T Tom Topping
14	Maryland	0	G Roy Hord
7	Rice	6	C Wade Byrd / Bill Hoch
34	Wake Forest	7	G Buzz Guy / Mike McGee
14	N. Carolina St.	0	T Bill Recinella / John Kersey
0	Georgia Tech	13	E Bill Thompson / Doug Padgett
6	Navy	6	QB Bob Brodhaed
7	Clemson	6	HB Wray Carlton / Eddie Rushton
13	North Carolina	21	HB George Dutrow / John David Lee
21	Oklahoma■	48	FB Hal McElhaney / Phil Dupler

RUSHING: Carlton 143/749y, Dutrow 121/556y, Lee 48/261y
PASSING: Brodhead 26-56/354y, 4TD, 46.4%
RECEIVING: Dutrow 9/81y, Carlton 7/170y, Thompson 6/90y
SCORING: Carlton (HB-K) 71pts, Dutrow 24pts, 3 with 12pts

1958 5-5

0	South Carolina	8	E Bert Lattimore / Tee Moorman
12	Virginia	15	T Don Denne
15	Illinois	13	G Ron Bostian / Phil Scudieri
12	Baylor	7	C Wade Byrd / Ted Royall
7	Notre Dame	9	G Mike McGee
20	N. Carolina St.	13	T John Kersey / Jim Gardner
8	Georgia Tech	10	E Doug Padgett / Dwight Bumgarner
18	LSU	50	QB Bob Brodhead
29	Wake Forest	0	HB Wray Carlton
7	North Carolina	6	HB George Dutrow / John David Lee
			FB Butch Allie / Bob Cruikshank

RUSHING: Carlton 164/636y, Dutrow 112/442y, Lee 68/286y
PASSING: Brodhead 53-111/651y, 3TD, 47.7%
RECEIVING: Carlton 17/189y, Moorman 11/142y,Padgett 9/112y
SCORING: Carlton (HB-K) 56pts, Dutrow 14pts, Lee 12pts

1959 4-6

7	South Carolina	12	E Dwight Bumgarner / Tee Moorman
13	Ohio State	14	T Don Denne
24	Rice	7	G Art Browning / Ron Bostian
0	Pittsburgh	12	C Ted Royall / Butch Allie
6	Army	21	G Mike McGee
17	N. Carolina St.	15	T Jim Gardner / Dave Bosson
10	Georgia Tech	7	E Bob Spada
0	Clemson	6	QB George Harris / Don Altman
27	Wake Forest	15	HB Joel Arrington / Bunny Bell
0	North Carolina	50	HB John Wilson / John David Lee
			FB Bob Crummie / Jack Bush

RUSHING: Arrington 92/444y, Wilson 97/376y, Lee 48/173y
PASSING: Harris 27-65/381y, 2TD, 41.5%,
Altman 19-30/214y, TD, 63.3%
RECEIVING: Arrington 13/124y, Bumgarner 8/86y, Moorman 6/91y
SCORING: Wilson 24pts, Arrington 24pts, Browning 14pts

1960 8-3

31	South Carolina	0	E Tee Moorman / Pete Widener
20	Maryland	7	T Dwight Bumgarner
6	Michigan	31	G Art Browning / John Markas
17	N. Carolina St.	13	C Butch Allie / Paul Bengel
21	Clemson	6	G Jean Berry / Dick Havens
6	Georgia Tech	0	T Dave Bosson / Rod Kotchin
19	Navy	10	E Bob Spada / Dave Unser
34	Wake Forest	7	QB Don Altman / Walt Rappold
6	North Carolina	7	HB Joel Arrington / Dean Wright
6	UCLA■	27	HB Mark Leggett / John Wilson
7	Arkansas■	6	FB Red Burch / Jerry McGee

RUSHING: Leggett 87/436y, Wilson 75/335y, Wright 79/323y
PASSING: Altman 68-104/552y, 2TD, 46.2%,
Rappold 36-66/362y, 2TD, 54.5%
RECEIVING: Moorman 46/431y, Widener 13/126y
SCORING: Wright 34pts, Burch 30pts, Leggett 20pts

1961 7-3

7	South Carolina	6	WR Jay Wilkinson / Stan Crisson
42	Virginia	0	T Art Gregory / Dave Condon
23	Wake Forest	3	G John Markas / Dave Dalton
0	Georgia Tech	21	C Paul Bengel / Ken Williams
7	Clemson	17	G Jean Berry
17	N. Carolina St.	6	T Dick Havens / Fred McCollum
14	Michigan	28	E Pete Widener / Dave Unser
30	Navy	9	QB Walt Rappold / Gil Garner
6	North Carolina	3	HB Dean Wright / Joel Arrington
37	Notre Dame	13	HB Mark Leggett / Jack Wilson
			FB Red Burch / John Tinnell

RUSHING: Leggett 86/318y, Wright 68/251y, Burch 49/229y
PASSING: Garner 56-86/549y, 5 TD, 65.1%,
Rappold 54-96/657y, 7 TD, 56.3%
RECEIVING: Crisson 20/241y, Widener 17/182y, Wright 15/131y
SCORING: William Reynolds (K) 31pts, Wilkinson 24pts,
Leggett 22pts

1962 8-2

7	Southern Cal	14	WR Stan Crisson / Pete Widener
21	South Carolina	8	T Art Gregory
28	Florida	21	G John Markas / Dave Condon
21	California	7	C Paul Bengel / Ken Williams
16	Clemson	0	G Jean Berry / Jimmy Fuqua
21	N. Carolina St.	14	T Dick Havens / Fred McCollum
9	Georgia Tech	20	E Zo Potts / Dave Burdette
10	Maryland	7	QB Walt Rappold / Gil Garner
50	Wake Forest	0	HB Jay Wilkinson / Billy Futrell
16	North Carolina	14	HB Mark Leggett / Bobby Hawn
			FB Mike Curtis

RUSHING: Leggett 114/478y, Futrell 60/387y, Curtis 100/367y
PASSING: Rappold 57-113/696y 2 TD, 50.4%,
Garner 42-65/413y, 2 TD, 64.6%
RECEIVING: Crisson 30/307y, Widener 19/244y,Leggett 18/199y
SCORING: Curtis 50pts, Wm. Reynolds (K) 45pts, Futrell 36pts

1963 5-4-1

22	South Carolina	14	WR Stan Crisson / Chuck Drulis
30	Virginia	8	T Danny Lonon
30	Maryland	12	G Fred Cromartie / Jimmy Fuqua
22	California	22	C Bob Davis
35	Clemson	30	G Bob Johnson / Earl Yates
7	N. Carolina St.	21	T Danny Litaker / Don Lynch
6	Georgia Tech	30	E Dave Burdette
39	Wake Forest	7	QB Scotty Glacken
25	Navy	38	HB Billy Futrell / Billy Baird
14	North Carolina	16	HB Jay Wilkinson / Biff Bracy
			FB Mike Curtis

RUSHING: Wilkinson 117/631y, Futrell 54/220y, Bracy 26/174y
PASSING: Glacken 101-201/1265y, 12 TD, 50.2%
RECEIVING: Crisson 48/559y, Drulis 17/232y, Wilkinson 14/256y
SCORING: Wilkinson 72pts, Crisson 48pts, Curtis 35pts

1964 4-5-1

9	South Carolina	9	WR Chuck Drulis / Jim Scott
30	Virginia	0	T Danny Lonon / Bill Jones
24	Maryland	17	G Fred Cromartie / Earl Yates (DL)
35	N. Carolina St.	3	C Bob Davis / John Carlo (LB)
6	Army	0	G J.V. McCarthy / John McNabb
8	Georgia Tech	21	T Danny Litaker / Don Lynch
7	Wake Forest	20	TE Dave Burdette / Rod Stewart
14	Navy	27	QB Scotty Glacken / Mike Shasby (DB)
15	North Carolina	21	HB Bob Matheson / Bob Jamieson (DB)
9	Tulane	17	HB Sonny Odom
			FB Mike Curtis

RUSHING: Curtis 121/497y, Odom 88/375y, Matheson 62/247y
PASSING: Glacken 104-192/1178y, 7 TD, 54.2%
RECEIVING: Scott 29/388y, Drulis 20/193y, Odom 17/208y
SCORING: Curtis 24pts, Drulis 24pts, Mark Caldwell (K) 22pts

1965 6-4

21	Virginia	7	WR Chuck Drulis / Dave Dunaway
20	South Carolina	15	T Bill Jones
41	Rice	21	G Earl Yates / Jerry Barringer
21	Pittsburgh	13	C Mike Murphy / Don Ashby
2	Clemson	3	G John McNabb / Bob Astley
14	Illinois	28	T Don Lynch
23	Georgia Tech	35	TE Rod Stewart / Mike Swomley
0	N. Carolina St.	21	QB Scotty Glacken / Todd Orvald
40	Wake Forest	7	HB Ken Chatham / Jake Devonshire
34	North Carolina	7	HB Sonny Odom / Frank Ryan
			FB Jay Calabrese
			DL Roger Hayes
			DL Chuck Stavins / Bedford Cannon
			DL Bob Foyle
			DL Robin Bodkin
			DL Bruce Wiesley
			LB Rich Kraft / John Carlo
			LB Bob Matheson
			DB Art Vann
			DB John Gutekunst / Mark Telge
			DB Andy Beath
			DB Mike Shasby

RUSHING:Calabrese 154/658y,Odom 75/314y,Chatham 72/271y
PASSING: Orvald 63-105/850y, 7 TD, 60.0%,
Glacken 50-87/727y, 5 TD, 57.5%
RECEIVING: Drulis 39/390y, Dunaway 221/393y, Odom 12/201y
SCORING: Calabrese 54pts, Dunaway 30pts,
Mark Caldwell (K) 22pts

1966 5-5

34 West Virginia	15 WR Dave Dunaway
14 Pittsburgh	7 T Mike Renneker
27 Virginia	8 G Carl Gersbach / Jerry Barringer
19 Maryland	21 C Mike Murphy / Bucky Fondren
6 Clemson	9 G Rodger Parker / John Alexander
7 N. Carolina St.	33 T Malcolm Travelstead
7 Georgia Tech	48 TE Henley Carter
9 Navy	7 QB Al Woodall
0 Notre Dame	64 TB Jake Devonshire / Frank Ryan
41 North Carolina	25 WB Ed Hicklin
	FB Jay Calabrese
	DL Roger Hayes
	DL Bob Lasky
	DL Bob Foyle
	DL Robin Bodkin
	DL Bruce Wiesley
	LB Ed Newman
	LB Bob Matheson (TB)
	DB Andy Beath (WB)
	DB Art Vann / Don Brannon
	DB Mark Shasby
	DB Mark Telge / Larry Dempsey

RUSHING: Calabrese 175/580y, Devonshire 85/289y, Ryan 44/182y
PASSING: Woodall 39-71/482y, 2 TD, 54.9%
RECEIVING: Dunaway 43/614y, Hicklin 12/109y, Carter 9/131y
SCORING: Calabrese 60pts, Matheson 26pts, Dunaway 18pts

1967 4-6

31 Wake Forest	13 WR Jim Dearth / Ed Hicklin
7 Michigan	10 E Marcel Courtillet
17 South Carolina	21 T Mike Renneker / Ken Bombard
10 Army	7 G Herb Goins / Chuck Grace
13 Virginia	6 C Mike Murphy
7 Clemson	13 G J.B. Edwards / John Alexander
7 N. Carolina St.	28 T Malcolm Travelstead
7 Georgia Tech	19 TE Henley Carter / Jim Hysong
35 Navy	16 QB Al Woodall
9 North Carolina	20 TB Frank Ryan / Pete Schafer
	FB Jay Calabrese / Don Baglien
	DL Roger Hayes
	DL Fred Zirkle / Bob Lasky
	DL Bob Foyle / Frank Lilly
	DL Robin Bodkin
	DL George Joseph / Gene DeBolt
	LB Dick Biddle / Joe Compitello
	LB Ed Newman / Tom Hightower
	DB Andy Beath
	DB Don Brannon / Greg Wuerstle
	DB Larry Dempsey
	DB Art Vann

RUSHING: Calabrese 136/563y, Ryan 115/525y, Schafer 73/265y
PASSING: Woodall 79-150/1019y, 52.7%
RECEIVING: Dearth 20/284y, Carter 17/244y, Ryan 10/127y
SCORING: Calabrese 30pts, Mark Riesenfeld (K) 29pts, Ryan 24pts

1968 4-6

14 South Carolina	7 WR Wes Chesson / Marcel Courtillet
10 Michigan	31 WR Henley Carter
30 Maryland	28 T Ken Bombard (G) / Gene DeBolt
20 Virginia	50 G J.B. Edwards
22 Clemson	39 C Bob Morris
46 Georgia Tech	30 G Ken Homa
15 N. Carolina St.	17 T Guy Johnson / Mike Gartner
18 Wake Forest	3 TE Jim Dearth
14 North Carolina	25 QB Leo Hart / Dave Trice
	TB Phil Asack
	FB Dan Baglien
	DL George Joseph
	DL Fred Zirkle
	DL Frank Lilly
	DL Dan Rose
	LB Dick Biddle
	LB Joe Compitello / Mark Telge
	LB Ed Newman
	DB Ed Hicklin / John Cappellano
	DB Larry Davis / Bill McKee
	DB Larry Dempsey
	DB Phil Singer

RUSHING: Asack 168/690y
PASSING: Hart 162-301/2238y, 11 TD, 53.8%
RECEIVING: Carter 65/892y, Chesson 47/794y
SCORING: Asack 50pts

1969 3-6-1

20 South Carolina	27 WR Marcel Courtillet
0 Virginia	10 WR Wes Chesson / Bob Hepler
12 Pittsburgh	14 T Ken Bombard
27 Wake Forest	20 G Fred Rojas / Dan Phelan
7 Maryland	20 C Bob Morris
25 N. Carolina St.	25 G Mike Garner / John Dull
7 Georgia Tech	20 T Guy Johnson
34 Clemson	27 TE Jim Dearth / Bill Baker
12 Virginia Tech	48 QB Leo Hart
17 North Carolina	13 TB Bob Zwirko / John Cappellano
	FB Phil Asack (LB) / Don Baglien
	DL Gene DeBolt / Bob Bradley
	DL Curt Rawley
	DL Joe Sciulli
	DL Bob Shinn / Bruce Mills
	LB Lanny Murdock / John Kiefer
	LB Joe Compitello / Mike Fitzpatrick
	LB Paul Johnstone / Bob Wenzel
	DB Ernie Jackson
	DB Mike Davies
	DB Rich Searl
	DB Bill McKee / Dave Trice

RUSHING: Zwirko 94/504y, Cappellano 71/317y, Asack 66/229y
PASSING: Hart 145-268/1642y, 5 TD, 54.1%
RECEIVING: Courtillet 45/489y, Chesson 43/525y, Dearth 20/261y
SCORING: Hart 42pts, David Pugh (K) 27pts, Zwirko & Chesson 24pts

1970 6-5

19 Florida	21 WR Wes Chesson
13 Maryland	12 WR Brad Evans
17 Virginia	7 T Willie Clayton / Guy Guthrie
10 Ohio State	34 G Fred Rojas
21 West Virginia	13 C Dale Grimes
22 N. Carolina St.	6 G Bob Fitch / Tom Cain
21 Clemson	10 T Bob Parrish / John Dull
16 Georgia Tech	24 TE Bill Baker
14 Wake Forest	28 QB Leo Hart
42 South Carolina	38 TB Bill Thompson / Bob Zwirko
34 North Carolina	59 FB Steve Jones / Art Bosetti
	DL Bob Shinn
	DL Skeet Harris / Curt Rawley
	DL Bruce Mills
	DL Jerry Giffin / Jim Madden
	LB Lanny Murdock / Paul Johnstone
	LB Dick Biddle
	LB Phil Asack
	DB Ernie Jackson
	DB Mike Davies / Bob Lebby
	DB Rich Searl
	DB John Cappellano / Gary Rute

RUSHING: Jones 203/854y, Thompson 99/457y, Bosetti 61/221y
PASSING: Hart 180-308/2236y, 7 TD, 58.4%
RECEIVING: Chesson 74/1080y, Baker 27/294y, Jones 22/223y
SCORING: Jones 60pts, David Pugh (K) 36pts, Bosetti 24pts

1971 6-5

12 Florida	6 WR Dan Phelan / Rusty McDow
28 South Carolina	12 WR Brad Evans
28 Virginia	0 T John Dull
9 Stanford	3 G Willie Clayton / Tom Torrey
0 Clemson	3 C Dale Grimes
41 N. Carolina St.	13 G Gary Heady / Bob Fitch
14 Navy	15 T Joe Politan
0 Georgia Tech	21 TE Bill Baker
31 West Virginia	15 QB Dennis Satyshur
7 Wake Forest	23 TB Bill Thompson / Bob Zwirko
0 North Carolina	38 FB Steve Jones / Art Bosetti
	DL Melvin Parker
	DL Ed Newman / Jim Madden
	DL Bruce Mills / Bob Parrish
	DL Jerry Giffin
	LB Lanny Murdock
	LB Mike Peck
	LB Paul Johnstone
	DB Bill Hanenberg
	DB Ernie Jackson (TB)
	DB Rich Searl (QB)
	DB Mike Davies

RUSHING: Jones 193/861y, Jackson 65/360y, Thompson 67/341y
PASSING: Satyshur 41-84/631y, 2 TD, 48.8%
RECEIVING: Phelan 17/273y, Baker 17/238y, McDow 8/99y
SCORING: Jackson 48pts, David Wright (K) 38pts, Jones 36pts

1972 5-6

12 Alabama	35 WR Mark Landon
6 Washington	14 WR Tom Chambers
6 Stanford	10 T Willie Clayton
37 Virginia	13 G Gary Heady
0 N. Carolina St.	17 C Dale Grimes
7 Clemson	0 G Bruce Snider
20 Maryland	14 T Ted Hanenberg / Joe Politan
17 Navy	16 TE Rich Brienza
20 Georgia Tech	14 QB Mark Johnson / Bob Albright
7 Wake Forest	9 TB Steve Jones / Bill Thompson
0 North Carolina	14 FB Mike Bomgardner
	DL Melvin Parker
	DL Ed Newman
	DL Bob Parrish
	DL Ernie Clark
	LB Jim Horning
	LB Keith Stoneback / Mike Peck
	LB Winslow Stillman
	DB Bill Hanenberg
	DB Ronnie Hoots / Buck Bowers
	DB Buster Cox
	DB Ben Fordham

RUSHING: Jones 287/1236y, Johnson 114/462y, Bomgardner 67/296y
PASSING: Johnson 30-69/380y, TD, 43.5%, Albright 24-61/316y, 3 TD, 39.3%
RECEIVING: Landon 16/206y, Brienza 14/198y, Chambers 11/133y
SCORING: Jones 36pts, Johnson 26pts, Bomgardner 18pts

1973 2-8-1

17 Tennessee	21 WR Ben Fordham / Troy Slade
23 Washington	21 WR Randy Cobb
3 Virginia	7 T Gary Pellom / Ted Hanenberg
7 Purdue	27 G Jim Fehling
17 Tulane	24 C Dave Schmit / Bill Bryan
8 Clemson	24 G Bruce Snider
10 Maryland	30 T Robert Jackson
10 Georgia Tech	12 TE Rich Brienza / Mark Manuel
7 Wake Forest	7 QB Mark Johnson / Hal Spears
3 N. Carolina St.	21 TB Tony Benjamin / Mark Landon
27 North Carolina	10 FB Mike Bomgardner
	DL Ernie Clark
	DL Dennis Turner
	DL John Ricca
	DL Don Shannon
	LB Jim Horning / Craig Stephenson
	LB Keith Stoneback
	LB Dave Meier / Elmer Gilson
	DB Ronnie Hoots / Jeff Christopher
	DB Earl Cook / Buck Bowers
	DB Buster Cox
	DB David Dill

RUSHING: Benjamin 114/572y, Bomgardner 108/419y, Johnson 96/253y
PASSING: Johnson 38-91/497y, 3 TD, 41.8%, Spears 29-56/335y, 51.8%
RECEIVING: Fordham 30/438y, Cobb 13/203y, Slade 8/191y
SCORING: Dave Malechek (K) 34pts, Slade 18pts, 4 with 12pts

1974 6-5

21 N. Carolina St.	35 WR Troy Slade / Ben Fordham
20 South Carolina	14 WR Randy Cobb / Larry Upshaw
27 Virginia	7 T Gary Pellom
16 Purdue	14 G Ted Hanenberg
33 Army	14 C Bill Bryan
13 Clemson	17 G Bruce Snider
13 Florida	30 T Robert Jackson
9 Georgia Tech	0 TE Gene DeVine / Mark Manuel
23 Wake Forest	7 QB Hal Spears
13 Maryland	56 TB Art Gore / Larry Martinez
13 North Carolina	14 FB Tony Benjamin / Mike Bomgardner
	DL Mark Landon / Jeff Green
	DL Dennie Turner
	DL John Hill
	DL Dave Dusek / Elmer Gilson
	LB Dave Meier
	LB Keith Stoneback
	LB Craig Stephenson / Greg Gombar
	DB Ronnie Hoots
	DB Earl Cook / Bob Grupp
	DB Jeff Christopher
	DB Mark Johnson / Laniel Crawford

RUSHING: Gore 125/627y, Benjamin 107/381y, Martinez 80/354y
PASSING: Spears 79-141/1132y, 5 TD, 56.0%
RECEIVING: Slade 31/489y, Fordham 25/368y, Cobb 17/353y
SCORING: Martinez 48pts, Benjamin 32pts, Gore 24pts

1975 4-5-2

7 Southern Cal	35 WR Troy Slade / Ed Kornberger
16 South Carolina	24 T Gary Pellom
26 Virginia	11 G Terry Ketchel
0 Pittsburgh	14 C Bill Bryan
21 Army	10 G Tyrel Schneck
25 Clemson	24 T Jim Fehling
16 Florida	24 TE Larry Upshaw / Glenn Sandefur
6 Georgia Tech	21 QB Mike Dunn / Bob Corbett
42 Wake Forest	14 TB Mike Barney / Art Gore
21 N. Carolina St.	21 SB Chuck Williamson
17 North Carolina	17 FB Tony Benjamin
	DL Ernie Clark
	DL Steve Edwards
	DL Maurice Corders
	DL Dave Dusek / Jeff Green
	LB Carl McGee
	LB Dave Meieer
	LB Cary Rosoff
	DB Tom Knotts
	DB Bob Grupp
	DB Kirk May
	DB Laniel Crawford

RUSHING: Benjamin 136/674y, Barney 99/487y, Dunn 103/413y
PASSING: Corbett 81-131/1063y, 3 TD, 61.8%
RECEIVING: Slade 43/654y, Williamson 18/261y, Kornberger 18/254y
SCORING: Vince Fusco (K) 47pts, Benjamin & Martinez 36pts

1976 5-5-1

21 Tennessee	18 WR Tom Hall / Jeff Comer
6 South Carolina	24 T Frank DeStefano / Randy Bickel
21 Virginia	6 G Greg Mencio / Tom Luongo
31 Pittsburgh	44 C Bill Bryan
20 Miami	7 G Mike Sandusky
18 Clemson	18 T John Patterson
3 Maryland	30 TE Glenn Sandefur
31 Georgia Tech	7 QB Mike Dunn
17 Wake Forest	38 TB Art Gore / Mike Barney
28 N. Carolina St.	14 SB Chuck Williamson
38 North Carolina	39 FB Tony Benjamin
	DL Jeff Green / Willard Freeman
	DL Steve Edwards
	DL Lyman Smith
	DL Andy Schoenhoft / Jim McMahon
	LB Jim Reilly / Derrick Mashore
	LB Carl McGee
	LB Cary Rosoff / Derek Penn
	DB Bob Grupp / Earl Cook
	DB Dan Brooks / George Gawdun
	DB Kirk May / Tom Knotts
	DB Rick Sommers / Mike Mann

RUSHING: Dunn 176/757y, Gore 152/742y, Benjamin 156/624y
PASSING: Dunn 90-168/1078y, 2 TD, 53.6%
RECEIVING: Hall 44/594y, Sandefur 11/108y, Williamson 10/169y
SCORING: Dunn 80pts, Vince Fusco (K) 52pts, Gore 42pts

1977 5-6

16 East Carolina	17 WR Tom Hall
9 Michigan	21 WR Jeff Comer
31 Virginia	7 T Frank DeStefano
28 Navy	16 G Tom Luongo / Dennis Knox
25 South Carolina	21 C Kevin Kelly
11 Clemson	17 G Mike Sandusky / Tim Brazill
13 Maryland	31 T John Patterson
25 Georgia Tech	24 TE Joel Patten / Glenn Sandefur
38 Wake Forest	14 QB Mike Dunn
32 N. Carolina St.	37 TB Greg Rhett / Mike Addesa
3 North Carolina	16 FB Ned Gonet / Stanley Broadie
	DL Jeff Green
	DL Jack Algor / Tim Cadigan
	DL Andy Shoenhoft
	DL Lyman Smith
	DL Derrick Mashore / Jim McMahon
	LB Carl McGee
	LB Bill King / John McDonald
	DB Earl Cook
	DB George Gawdun / Craig Hoskins
	DB Dan Brooks / Larry Doby
	DB Rick Sommers

RUSHING: Broadie 132/579y, Dunn 161/576y, Gonet 70/312y
PASSING: Dunn 102-191/1239y, 7 TD, 53.4%
RECEIVING: Hall 33/418y, Sandefur 16/251y, Comer 15/264y
SCORING: Scott Wolcott (K) 49pts, Dunn 48pts, Broadie 36pts

1978 4-7

28 Georgia Tech	10 WR Derrick Lewis
16 South Carolina	12 WR Jeff Comer / Cedric Jones
0 Michigan	52 T Ken Staudinger
20 Virginia	13 G Bob Riordan / Jay Pelosky
8 Navy	31 C Kevin Kelly
8 Clemson	28 G Scott Hamilton
0 Maryland	27 T Tom Luongo / Greg Bamberger
0 Tennessee	34 TE Joel Patten / John Brinkman
3 Wake Forest	0 QB Mike Dunn
10 N. Carolina St.	24 RB Greg Rhett / Bobby Brower
15 North Carolina	16 RB Ned Gonet
	DL Jim McMahon / Charles Bowser
	DL Tim Cadigan / Paul Heinsohn
	DL Eric Drescher / Greg Pritchard
	DL Andy Schoenhoft
	DL Derrick Mashore
	LB Carl McGee
	LB Bill King / Gary Garstkiewicz
	DB Craig Hoskins
	DB George Gawdun / Dennis Tabron
	DB Dan Brooks / Larry Doby
	DB Rick Sommers

RUSHING: Rhett 85/412y, Gonet 91/362y, Brower 52/260y
PASSING: Dunn 65-144/668y, 2 TD, 45.1%
RECEIVING: Lewis 20/365y, Comer 16/227y, Jones 14/149y
SCORING: Rhett 30pts, Scott McKinney (K) 26pts, Jones 12pts

1979 2-8-1

28 East Carolina	14 WR Ron Frederick / Marvin Brown
0 South Carolina	35 WR Cedric Jones / Chris Castor
12 Virginia	30 T Jim Colantuoni
17 Army	17 G Bob Riordan
34 Richmond	7 C Kevin Kelly
10 Clemson	28 G ScottHamilton
0 Maryland	27 T Greg Bamberger
14 Georgia Tech	24 TE Joel Patten / John Brinkman
14 Wake Forest	17 QB Stanley Driskell
7 N. Carolina St.	28 TB Greg Rhett / Keith Crenshaw
16 North Carolina	37 FB Ned Gonet / Greg Boone
	DL Charles Bowser
	DL Paul Heinsohn
	DL Eric Drescher / Dan Yellott
	DL F.A. Martin / James McIvor
	DL Larry LeNoir / Glen Barner
	LB Jimmy Tyson / Dave Thielemann
	LB Craig Brown / Emmett Tilley
	DB Craig Hoskins
	DB Dennis Tabron / Paul Jenkins
	DB George Gawdun
	DB Greg Stroud / Eddie Brown

RUSHING: Rhett 121/412y, Crenshaw 67/264y,Driskell 111/190y
PASSING: Driskell 54-145/721y, 4TD, 37.2%
RECEIVING: Frederick 28/395y, Jones 18/382y, Brown 12/101y
SCORING: Scott McKinney (K) 38pts, Jones & Driskell 24pts

1980 2-9

10 East Carolina	35 WR Marvin Brown / Ron Frederick
28 Auburn	35 WR Chris Castor / Cedric Jones
17 Virginia	20 T Tim Bumgarner
21 Indiana	31 G Greg Bamberger / Jay Pelosky
7 South Carolina	20 C Tee Moorman III
34 Clemson	17 G Brian Baldinger
14 Maryland	17 T Robert Oxendine
17 Georgia Tech	12 TE John Brinkman
24 Wake Forest	27 QB Ben Bennett
21 N. Carolina St.	38 TB Bobby Brower / Mike Grayson
21 North Carolina	44 FB Greg Boone
	DL Charles Bowser
	DL Paul Heinsohn
	DL Dan Yellott
	DL F. A. Martin
	DL Larry LeNoir
	LB Jimmy Tyson / Dave Thielemann
	LB Emmett Tilley / Craig Brown
	DB Keith Crenshaw
	DB Dennis Tabron
	DB Gary Garstkiewicz
	DB Eddie Brown / Darrell Deaton

RUSHING: Boone 94/340y, Grayson 78/219y, Brower 51/212y
PASSING: Bennett 174-330/2050y, 11 TD, 52.7%
RECEIVING: Brown 34/451y, Brinkman 32/337y, Frederick 27/413y
SCORING: Scott McKinney (K) 46pts, Jones 36pts, Castor 24pts

1981 6-5

13 Ohio State	34 WR Ron Frederick
3 South Carolina	17 WR Cedric Jones
29 Virginia	24 T Tim Bumgarner
24 East Carolina	14 G Tee Moorman III
14 Virginia Tech	7 C Phil Ebinger
10 Clemson	38 G Brian Baldinger
21 Maryland	24 T Robert Oxendine
38 Georgia Tech	24 TE Carl Franks / Scott Russell
31 Wake Forest	10 QB Ben Bennett
17 N. Carolina St.	7 TB Mike Grayson / Joel Blunk
10 North Carolina	31 FB Greg Boone
	DL Charles Bowser
	DL Bill Smith
	DL Dan Yellott / Mark Higginbotham
	DL F. A. Martin
	DL Larry LeNoir
	LB Jimmy Tyson
	LB Emmett Tilley
	DB Keith Crenshaw / Johnny Hill
	DB Dennis Tabron
	DB Bill Obremskey / Aaron Stewart
	DB Mike Armstrong / Terron Teander

RUSHING: Grayson 179/744y, Boone 80/502y, Blunk 69/282y
PASSING: Bennett 110-202/1445y, 7 TD, 54.4%
RECEIVING: Jones 42/832y, Frederick 37/565y, Franks 21/235y, Grayson 21/156y
SCORING: Jones 60pts, Scott McKinney (K) 58pts

1982 6-5

25 Tennessee	24 WR Mark Militello
30 South Carolina	17 WR Chris Castor
51 Virginia	17 T Tim Bumgarner
21 Navy	27 G Tee Moorman III
21 Virginia Tech	22 C Phil Ebinger
14 Clemson	49 G Mark Milelr / Mike Higginbotham
22 Maryland	49 T Robert Oxendine
38 Georgia Tech	21 TE Carl Franks / Scott Russell
46 Wake Forest	26 QB Ben Bennett
16 N. Carolina St.	21 TB Mike Grayson / Joel Blunk
23 North Carolina	17 FB Greg Boone
	DL Greg Blackwell / Darryl Brunson
	DL Chris Arendt / Murray Youmans
	DL Bill Smith
	DL Rob Lenoir / Brian Walter
	DL Glen Barner / Mark Heninger
	LB Ralph Alderman
	LB Emmett Tilley / Nick Buoniconti
	DB Johnny Hill
	DB Darrell Deaton / Brick Johnstone
	DB Bill Obremskey
	DB Joby Branion

RUSHING: Grayson 136/693y, Boone 78/434y, Blunk 98/367y
PASSING: Bennett 236-374/3033y, 20 TD, 63.1%
RECEIVING: Militello 52/725y, Franks 49/446y, Castor 46/952y
SCORING: Castor 78pts, John Tolish (K) 53pts, Blunk 42pts

1983 3-8

30 Virginia	38 WR Mark Militello / Gary Frederick
10 Indiana	15 WR Chuck Herring / Glenn Tillery
24 South Carolina	31 T Justin Beckett / Ted Million
17 Miami	56 G Mike Higginbotham
14 Virginia Tech	27 C Phil Ebinger / Mark Higginbotham (G)
31 Clemson	38 G Mark Miller
3 Maryland	38 T Paul Burke / Dave Holler
32 Georgia Tech	26 TE Scott Russell
31 Wake Forest	21 QB Ben Bennett
27 N. Carolina St.	26 TB Mike Grayson / Julius Grantham
27 North Carolina	34 FB Joel Blunk / Scott Sime
	DL Mark Heninger
	DL Murray Youmans / Jerome Ley
	DL Bill Smith / Reggie Andrews
	DL Brian Walter
	DL Chip Anderson / Harry Ward
	LB Ralph Alderman / Nick Buoniconti
	LB Pete Stubbs / Marty Heninger
	DB Johnny Hill
	DB Mark Moseley / Brick Johnstone
	DB Darryl Brunson / Bill Obremskey
	DB Joby Branion

RUSHING:Grayson 181/785y,Grantham 101/556y,Blunk 40/109y
PASSING: Bennett 300-469/3086y, 17 TD, 64.0%
RECEIVING: Grayson 66/582y, Militello 63/682y,Russell 47/471y
SCORING: Grayson 60pts, Ken Harper (K) 56pts, Grantham 38pts

1984 2-9

31 Indiana	24 WR John Tolish / Greg Flanagan
0 South Carolina	21 WR Chuck Herring / Gary Frederick
9 Army	13 T Justin Beckett
10 Virginia	38 G Mike Higginbotham
0 Virginia Tech	27 C Paul Constantino
21 Clemson	54 G Mark Higginbotham / Paul Burke
7 Maryland	43 T Ted Million / Brian Walter
3 Georgia Tech	31 TE Scott Russell / Rick Reed
16 Wake Forest	20 QB Ron Sally / Steve Slayden
31 N. Carolina St.	13 TB Julius Grantham / Mike Peacock
15 North Carolina	17 FB Scott Sime / Stanley Monk
	DL Harry Ward / Ralph Alderman
	DL David Adams / Craig Owens
	DL Reggie Andrews
	DL Greg Blackwell / John El-Masry
	LB Pete Stubbs
	LB Mike Junkin / Bill Lucas
	LB Nick Buoniconti / Jim Godfrey
	DB Allen Scales
	DB Joby Branion
	DB Howard Woods / Pete Moore
	DB Johnny Hill

RUSHING: Grantham 110/395y, Peacock 99/373y, Monk 64/166y
PASSING: Slayden 113-202/1229y, 4TD, 55.9%
RECEIVING: Herring 37/627y, Russell 21/199y, Grantham 15/146y
SCORING: Ken Harper (K) 48pts, Grantham 18pts, 3 with 12pts

1985 4-7

40 Northwestern	17 WR Doug Green / Greg Flanagan
18 West Virginia	20 WR Chuck Herring
34 Ohio University	13 T Justin Beckett
14 Virginia	37 G Mike Higginbotham
5 South Carolina	28 C Paul Constantino
9 Clemson	21 G Ted Million / Paul Burke
10 Maryland	40 T Brian Walter / Roy Brabson
0 Georgia Tech	9 TE Jason Cooper / Rick Reed
7 Wake Forest	27 QB Steve Slayden
31 N. Carolina St.	19 TB Julius Grantham / Stanley Monk
23 North Carolina	21 FB Tracy Smith / Scott Sime
	DL Harry Ward / Dave Demore
	DL Craig Owens / David Adams
	DL Reggie Andrews / Murray Youmans
	DL John El-Masry / Jeff Patten
	LB Pete Stubbs / Nick Buoniconti
	LB Mike Junkin / Jim Godfrey
	LB Andy Andreasik
	DB Allen Scales
	DB Dewayne Terry / Mark Moseley
	DB Bob Calamari
	DB Terrence Laster

RUSHING: Smith 122/455y, Monk 102/431y, Grantham 90/301y
PASSING: Slayden 173-294/1937y, 10 TD, 58.8%
RECEIVING: Green 51/804y, Cooper 24/285y, Smith 24/179y
SCORING: Green 48pts, Ken Harper (K) 37pts, Smith 30pts

1986 4-7

17 Northwestern	6 WR Doug Green / Greg Flanagan
7 Georgia	31 WR Greg Downs / Clarkston Hines
22 Ohio University	7 T Chris Port / Brett Tulacro
20 Virginia	13 G Paul Burke / Jay Worley
18 Vanderbilt	24 C Paul Constantino / Carey Metts
3 Clemson	35 G Steve Ryan
19 Maryland	27 T Ted McNairy / Brad Paddock
6 Georgia Tech	34 TE Jason Cooper / Dave Colonna
38 Wake Forest	36 QB Steve Slayden
15 N. Carolina St.	29 TB Julius Grantham / Stanley Monk
35 North Carolina	42 FB Tracy Smith
	DL John El-Masry
	DL Murray Youmans
	DL Craig Owens / Brian Bernard
	DL Dave Demore / Jeff Patten
	LB Andy Andreasik
	LB Mike Junkin / Bill Lucas
	LB Jim Godfrey / George Edwards
	DB Mike Diminick / Rodney Dickerson
	DB Dewayne Terry / Steve Coyne
	DB Bob Calamari / Jim Bowker
	DB Fonda Williams

RUSHING: Grantham 158/677y, Smith 92/328y, Monk 26/165y
PASSING: Slayden 183-313/1914y, 14 TD, 58.5%
RECEIVING: Green 46/608y, Cooper 39/438y, Grantham 30/218y
SCORING: Doug Peterson (K) 44pts, Smith 40pts, Green 36pts

1987 5-6

41 Colgate	6 WR Doug Green / Greg Downs
31 Northwestern	16 WR Clarkston Hines
35 Vanderbilt	31 T Chris Port
17 Virginia	42 G Ted McNairy / Jay Worley
0 Rutgers	7 C Carey Metts
10 Clemson	17 G Steve Ryan
22 Maryland	23 T Brett Tulacro / John Beattie
48 Georgia Tech	14 TE Dave Colonna / Jason Cooper
27 Wake Forest	30 QB Steve Slayden
45 N. Carolina St.	47 TB Roger Boone / Wayne Charles
25 North Carolina	10 FB Stanley Monk
	DL Dave Demore
	DL Anthony Allen
	DL Brian Bernard
	DL Jeff Patten / Doug Atkinson
	LB Andy Andreasik / Reggie Gowdy
	LB Jim Godfrey
	LB George Edwards / John Howell
	DB Rodney Dickerson
	DB Eric Volk / Fonda Williams
	DB Bob Calamari
	DB Mike Diminick / John Intihar

RUSHING: Boone 137/550y, Monk 102/387y, Charles 29/142y
PASSING: Slayden 230-395/2924, 20TD, 58.2%
RECEIVING: Boone 62/587y, Hines 57/1093y, Green 31/410y
SCORING: Doug Peterson (K) 79pts, Hines 66pts, Monk 30pts

1988 7-3-1

31 Northwestern	21 WR Walter Jones / Keith Daniel
31 Tennessee	26 WR Clarkston Hines
41 Citadel	17 T Chris Port
38 Virginia	34 G Ted McNairy
17 Vanderbilt	15 C Carey Metts
17 Clemson	49 G Brett Tulacro
24 Maryland	34 T Chip Nitkowski
31 Georgia Tech	21 TE Dave Colonna / Bud Zuberer
16 Wake Forest	35 QB Anthony Dilweg
43 N. Carolina St.	43 TB Roger Boone / Randy Jones
35 North Carolina	29 FB John Rymiszewski / Randy Cuthbert
	DL John McDonald (LB)
	DL Anthony Allen / Kedrick Eily
	DL Doug Kley / Preston Anderson
	DL Jeff Patten / Tom Corpus
	LB John Howell
	LB Jim Worthington / Chris Rising
	LB Randy Sally / Mark Allen
	DB Wyatt Smith / Quinton McCracken
	DB Rodney Dickerson / Marc Mays
	DB Mike Diminick / Eric Volk
	DB Erwin Sampson

RUSHING: Boone 185/836y, R. Jones 97/388y, Cuthbert 8/63y
PASSING: Dilweg 287-484/3824y, 24 TD, 59.3%
RECEIVING: Boone 73/630y, Hines 68/1067y, W. Jones 36/578y
SCORING: Doug Peterson (K) 70pts, Hines 64pts, Boone 54pts

1989 8-4

21 South Carolina	27 WR Walter Jones / Darryl Clements
41 Northwestern	31 WR Clarkston Hines
6 Tennessee	28 T Chris Port
28 Virginia	49 G Pete Petroff
21 Clemson	17 C Carey Metts
35 Army	29 G Brett Tulacro
46 Maryland	25 T Chip Nitkowski
30 Georgia Tech	19 TE Dave Colonna
52 Wake Forest	35 QB Billy Ray / Dave Brown
35 N. Carolina St.	26 TB Randy Cuthbert / Roger Boone
41 North Carolina	0 FB Chris Brown / Randy Jones
21 Texas Tech ■	49 DL John McDonald
	DL Anthony Allen
	DL Doug Kley
	DL Preston Anderson / Tom Corpus
	LB John Howell / Mark Allen
	LB George Edwards / Darrell Spells
	LB Rodney Dickerson
	DB Wyatt Smith
	DB Quinton McCracken
	DB Derrick Jackson / Randy Sally
	DB Erwin Sampson / Fonda Williams (LB)

RUSHING: Cuthbert 187/1023y, Boone 93/514y, R. Jones 33/177y
PASSING: Ray 174-274/2035y, 15 TD, 63.5%, D. Brown 104-163/1479y, 14 TD, 63.8%
RECEIVING: Hines 61/1149y, Cuthbert 50/470y, Colonna 35/495y
SCORING: Hines 104pts, Randy Gardner (K) 63pts, Cuthbert 60pts

1990 4-7

10 South Carolina	21 WR Walter Jones / Brad Breedlove
27 Northwestern	24 WR Marc Mays / Darryl Clements
0 Virginia	59 T Al Hagaman / Brandon Moore
7 Clemson	26 G Pete Petroff
17 Army	16 C Stuart Albright
49 West'n Carolina	18 G Bobby Highsmith
20 Maryland	23 T Chip Nitowski
31 Georgia Tech	48 TE Aaron Shaw
57 Wake Forest	20 QB Dave Brown / Billy Ray
0 N. Carolina St.	16 TB Randy Cuthbert / Randy Jones
22 North Carolina	24 FB Chris Brown / Marcus Dyer
	DL Preston Anderson
	DL Scott Youmans
	DL Geoff Smith / Warren Scoville
	LB Duane Marks / Brad Sherrod
	LB Mark Allen
	LB Darrell Spells / Kurt Ligos
	LB Tom Corpus
	DB Wyatt Smith / Keith DuBose
	DB Quinton McCracken
	DB Derrick Jackson
	DB Erwin Sampson

RUSHING: Cuthbert 136/595y, C. Brown 48/207y, Ray 57/169y
PASSING: D. Brown 129-245/1444y, 8 TD, 52.7%, Ray 100-164/1247y, 8 TD, 61.0%
RECEIVING: Cuthbert 46/374y, Mays 35/457y, Shaw 35/383y
SCORING: Randy Gardner (K) 56pts, W. Jones 38pts, Cuthbert 30pts

1991 4-6-1

24 South Carolina	24 WR Walter Jones / Brad Breedlove
42 Rutgers	22 WR Keith Ewell/ Stan Dorsey / Marc Mays
42 Colgate	14 T Brandon Moore
3 Virginia	34 G Pete Petroff / Brian May
17 Vanderbilt	13 C Stuart Albright / Colin Mailloux
17 Maryland	13 G Steve Alderfer/P. J. Schunke
6 Georgia Tech	17 T Matt Williams / Richard Gulley
14 Wake Forest	48 TE Aaron Shaw / John Farquhar
31 N. Carolina St.	32 QB Dave Brown
14 North Carolina	47 TB Leroy Gallman / Ray Wright
21 Clemson	33 FB Chris Brown / Randy Cuthbert (TB)
	DL Preston Anderson
	DL Gregg McConnell / Scott Youmans
	DL Warren Scoville / Geoff Smith
	LB Duane Marks
	LB Mark Allen
	LB Darrell Spells / Scott Berdan
	LB Travis Pearson / Brad Sherrod
	DB Wyatt Smith
	DB Quinton McCracken / Keith DuBose
	DB Derrick Jackson
	DB Erwin Sampson

RUSHING: C. Brown 83/320y, Gallman 53/276y, Wright 61/177y
PASSING: D. Brown 230-437/2794y, 20TD, 52.6%
RECEIVING: C. Brown 38/302y, Jones 31/518y, Shaw 28/322y
SCORING: Randy Gardner (K) 49pts

1992 2-9

21 Florida State	48 WR Brad Breedlove / Ray Wright
37 Vanderbilt	42 WR Stanley Dorsey / Jon Jensen
17 Rice	12 T Brandon Moore / Drew MacFarlan
28 Virginia	55 G Steve Alderfer
45 East Carolina	14 C Jereon Egge
6 Clemson	21 G P. J. Schunke
25 Maryland	27 T Matt Williams / Jon Merrill
17 Georgia Tech	20 TE Dan Clark / Ray Farmer
14 Wake Forest	28 QB Spence Fischer
27 N. Carolina St.	45 TB Randy Cuthbert / Leroy Gallman
28 North Carolina	31 FB Robert Baldwin
	DL Travis Pearson / James Kirkland
	DL Scott Youmans / Warren Scoville
	DL David Wafle
	DL Duane Marks / Gil Winters
	LB Brad Sherrod
	LB Scott Berdan / P.J. Melnik
	LB Darrell Spells / Carlos Bagley
	DB Jamal Ellis / Sidney Wells
	DB Keith DuBose / Tee Edwards
	DB Derrick Jackson / Gavin Gray
	DB Sean Thomas

RUSHING: Cuthbert 227/1031y, Baldwin 73/312y
PASSING: Fischer 113-197/1505y, 10TD, 57.4%
RECEIVING: Cuthbert 37/345y, Breedlove 29/479y, Dorsey 23/291y
SCORING: Randy Gardner (K) 53pts

1993 3-8

7 Florida State	45 WR Brad Breedlove / Ray Wright
38 Rutgers	39 WR Stanley Dorsey / Jon Jensen
42 Army	21 T Clarence Collins / Geoff Smith
0 Virginia	35 G Steve Alderfer
19 Tennessee	52 C Jereon Egge
10 Clemson	13 G P.J. Schunke / Louis Clyburn
18 Maryland	26 T Matt Williams
21 Wake Forest	13 TE Dan Clark / John Farquhar
14 Georgia Tech	47 QB Spence Fischer / Joe Pickens
21 N. Carolina St.	20 TB David Lowman / Tijan Redmon
24 North Carolina	38 FB Robert Baldwin
	DL Travis Pearson
	DL Scott Youmans / Mike Stallmeyer
	DL David Wafle
	DL Duane Marks / James Kirkland
	LB Brad Sherrod / Carlos Bagley
	LB Scott Berdan / Billy Granville
	LB John Zuanich / David Hawkins
	DB Zaid Abdul-Aleem / Sidney Wells
	DB Sean Thomas
	DB Tee Edwards / Gavin Gray
	DB Ray Farmer

RUSHING: Lowman 110/439y, Baldwin 70/332y, Redmon 58/240y,
PASSING: Fischer 213-388/2563y, 12 TD, 54.9%, Pickens 35-87/413y, 2 TD, 40.2%
RECEIVING: Dorsey 44/678y, Breedlove 35/524y, Baldwin 29/268y
SCORING: Tom Cochran (K) 48pts, Lowman 30pts, Dorsey 26pts

1994 8-4

49 Maryland	16 WR Corey Thomas / Tijan Redmon
13 East Carolina	10 WR Jon Jensen
43 Army	7 T Jon Merrill
27 Georgia Tech	12 G Chad Melita / Clarence Collins
47 Navy	14 C Jereon Egge
19 Clemson	13 G Damon Wallace
51 Wake Forest	26 T Matt Williams / Phillip Chappell
20 Florida State	59 TE Bill Khayat / John Farquhar
28 Virginia	25 WR Ray Wright / Joel Nicholson
23 N. Carolina St.	24 QB Spence Fischer
40 North Carolina	41 RB Robert Baldwin / David Lowman
20 Wisconsin■	34 DL Mike Stallmeyer
	DL Bernard Holsey
	DL James Kirkland
	LB John Zuanich
	LB Carlos Bagley / LaVance McQueen
	LB Billy Granville
	LB David Hawkins
	DB Brandon Pollock
	DB Jamal Ellis / Sidney Wells
	DB Zaid Abdul-Aleem / Tee Edwards
	DB Ray Farmer

RUSHING: Baldwin 276/1187y
PASSING: Fischer 204-346/2285y, 16 TD, 59.0%
RECEIVING: Khayat 49/562y, Jensen 45/526y, Thomas 37/558y
SCORING: Baldwin 78pts, Tom Cochran (K) 44pts

1995 3-8

26 Florida State	70 WR Corey Thomas
24 Rutgers	14 WR Marc Wilson / Jeff Hodrick
23 Army	21 T Jon Merrill
28 Maryland	41 G Patrick Mannelly / Clarence Collins
9 Navy	30 C Jereon Egge
21 Georgia Tech	37 G Chad Melita
30 Virginia	44 T Phillip Chappell / Lennie Friedman
38 N. Carolina St.	41 TE Bill Khayat / Gerald Ford
42 Wake Forest	26 WR Joel Nicholson / Reco Owens
17 Clemson	34 QB Spence Fischer
24 North Carolina	28 RB Laymarr Marshall / Charles London
	DL Mike Stallmeyer
	DL Bernard Holsey / Eric Scanlon
	DL Orlando Adwaters / Brian McCormack
	LB James Kirkland / LaVance McQueen
	LB Carlos Bagley
	LB Chike Egbuniwe / Billy Granville
	LB John Zuanich
	DB Desi Thomas / Brandon Pollock
	DB Sidney Wells / Kenan Holley
	DB Tawambi Settles
	DB Ray Farmer

RUSHING: Marshall 188/708y, London 62/291y, Fischer 64/104y
PASSING: Fischer 256-438/2668y, 12TD, 58.4%
RECEIVING: Wilson 47/531y, Thomas 45/505y, Hodrick 34/396y
SCORING: Marshall 78pts, Tom Cochran (K) 74pts, Thomas 36pts

1996 0-11

7 Florida State	44 WR Corey Thomas
13 Northwestern	38 WR Reco Owens / Scottie Montgomery
17 Army	35 T Austin Smithwick / Patrick Mannelly
22 Georgia Tech	48 G Lennie Friedman
27 Navy	64 C John Gordon
6 Clemson	13 G Chad Melita
19 Maryland	22 T Gannon Shepherd
3 Virginia	27 TE Gerald Ford / Jeff Hodrick
22 N. Carolina St.	44 QB David Green / Matt Rader
16 Wake Forest	17 TB Letavious Wilks / Charles London
10 North Carolina	27 FB Laymarr Marshall / Dawud Rasheed
	DL Chris Ruzic / Mike Steinbaugh
	DL Eric Scanlan
	DL Chris Combs
	LB LaVance McQueen
	LB Chike Egbuniwe / Lyle Burdins
	LB Billy Granville
	LB Kevin Lewis / Brian McCormack
	DB Desi Thomas / Lamar Grant
	DB Alonzo Moyer
	DB Tawambi Settles
	DB Darius Clark

RUSHING: Wilks 116/554y, Marshall 115/390y, Rasheed 31/162y
PASSING: Green 88-165/958y, 4 TD, 53.3%, Rader 85-150/905y, 5 TD, 56.7%
RECEIVING: Thomas 38/527y, Hodrick 34/350y, Owens 23/194y
SCORING: Sims Lenhardt (K) 71pts, Thomas 24pts, Marshall 18pts

1997 2-9

14 N. Carolina St.	45 WR Corey Thomas
20 Northwestern	24 WR Scottie Montgomery / Reco Owens
20 Army	17 T Patrick Mannelly / Wes White
26 Navy	17 G Lennie Friedman / Robert Fleming
10 Maryland	16 C John Gordon
27 Florida State	51 G Chad Melita
10 Virginia	13 T Austin Smithwick / Benji Wallace
24 Wake Forest	38 TE Jeff Hodrick / Terrence Dupree
20 Clemson	29 QB Bobby Campbell / Spencer Romine
38 Georgia Tech	41 TB Letavious Wilks / Duane Epperson
14 North Carolina	50 FB Dawud Rasheed / Laymarr Marshall
	DL Chris Ruzic
	DL Eric Scanlan / Mike Steinbaugh
	DL Chris Combs / Gannon Shepherd
	LB Kendral Knight / Chris Norkus
	LB Chike Egbuniwe / Kyle Burdine
	LB Ryan Stallmeyer
	LB Kevin Lewis / Brian McCormack
	DB Tawambi Settles / Alonzo Moyer
	DB Lamar Grant / Kenan Holley
	DB Eric Jones
	DB Darius Clark

RUSHING: Marshall 70/359y, Wilks 79/305y
PASSING: Campbell 85-178/925y, 2 TD, 47.8%
RECEIVING: Montgomery 51/633y, Thomas 45/707y
SCORING: Sims Lenhardt (K) 70pts

1998 4-7

24 W. Carolina	10 WR Scottie Montgomery
44 Northwestern	10 WR Richmond Flowers
13 Florida State	62 T Wes White
0 Virginia	24 G Lennie Friedman
13 Georgia Tech	41 C Troy Andrew
19 Wake Forest	16 G Shawn Lynch
24 N. Carolina St.	27 T Austin Smithwick
28 Clemson	23 TE Terrence Dupree
33 Vanderbilt	36 QB Bobby Campbell / Spencer Romine
25 Maryland	42 TB B.J. Hill / Letavious Wilks
6 North Carolina	28 FB Dawud Rasheed
	DL Chris Combs / Nate Krill
	DL Eric Scanlan
	DL Gannon Shepherd
	LB Chris Norkus / Kendral Knight
	LB Todd DeLamielleure
	LB Ryan Stallmeyer
	LB Kevin Lewis
	DB Lamar Grant
	DB Ronnie Hamilton
	DB Eric Jones
	DB Darius Clark

RUSHING: Hill 192/798y, Wilks 109/362y
PASSING: Campbell 101-206/1199y, 6TD, 49.0%
RECEIVING: Montgomery 60/793y, Flowers 48/704y
SCORING: Sims Lenhardt (K) 69pts

1999 3-8

9 East Carolina	27 WR Scottie Montgomery / Kyle Moore
12 Northwestern	15 WR Richmond Flowers / Ben Erdeljac
14 Vanderbilt	31 T Wes White / Mike Alberto
23 Florida State	51 G Shawn Lynch / Greg Dufala
24 Virginia	17 C Troy Andrew
31 Georgia Tech	38 G John Miller
24 N. Carolina St.	31 T Austin Smithwick
25 Maryland	22 TE Terrence Dupree
7 Clemson	58 QB Spencer Romine
48 Wake Forest	35 TB Duane Epperson / Latavious Wilks
0 North Carolina	38 FB Devin Pierce
	DL Chris Combs
	DL Mike Steinbaugh / Troy Austin
	DL Gannon Shepherd / Nate Krill
	LB Kendral Knight
	LB Todd DeLamielleure / Randy Ament
	LB Ryan Stallmeyer
	LB Kevin Lewis (DB) / Brian McCormack
	DB Ronnie Hamilton
	DB Lamar Grant / Quentin Holley
	DB Eric Jones / Josh Kreider
	DB Darius Clark / Fred Harris

RUSHING: Wilks 95/334y, Epperson 107/324y, B.J. Hill (TB) 66/237y
PASSING: Romine 123-243/1638y, 6 TD, 50.6%
RECEIVING: Montgomery 51/819y, Flowers 42/649y, Erdeljac 19/268y
SCORING: Sims Lenhardt (K) 59pts, Montgomery 42pts, Flowers 32pts

2000 0-11

0 East Carolina	38 WR Nick Hartofilis / Kyle Moore
5 Northwestern	38 WR Ben Erdeljac / Reggie Love
10 Virginia	26 T Drew Strojny / Mike Alberto
7 Vanderbilt	26 G Daryl Lewis / Greg Dufala
22 Clemson	52 C Troy Andrew / Shawn Lynch
14 Florida State	63 G John Miller
10 Georgia Tech	45 T Wes White
9 Maryland	20 TE Mike Hart / Nick Brzezinski
26 Wake Forest	28 QB D. Bryant / Spencer Romine
31 N. Carolina St.	35 TB Duane Epperson / Chris Douglas
21 North Carolina	59 FB Devin Pierce / Alex Wade
	DL Troy Austin
	DL Tyran Grissom / Nick Wilkerson
	DL Shawn Johnson / Charles Porter
	LB Kendral Knight
	LB Todd DeLamielleure / Randy Ament
	LB Jamyon Small / Jason Davis
	LB Ryan Fowler / J.T. Cape
	DB Ronnie Hamilton / Terrell Smith
	DB Derrick Lee / Jeff Phillips
	DB Josh Kreider
	DB Fred Harris / Anthony Roberts

RUSHING: Douglas 110/503y, Epperson 111/400y, Wade 20/66y
PASSING: Bryant 129-258/1448y, 5 TD, 50.0%, Romine 53-118/613y, TD, 44.9%
RECEIVING: Hart 31/540y, Erdeljac 31/329y, Epperson 23/146y
SCORING: Douglas 42pts, Brent Garber (K) 37pts, Moore 18pts

2001 0-11

13 Florida State	55 WR Ben Erdeljac
13 Rice	15 WR Kyle Moore / Khari Sharpe
7 Northwestern	44 T Drew Strojny
10 Virginia	31 G Daryl Lewis
10 Georgia Tech	37 C Luke Bayer
35 Wake Forest	42 G John Miller / Rusty Wilson
17 Maryland	59 T Christian Mitchell
28 Vanderbilt	42 TE Mike Hart
31 N. Carolina St.	55 QB D. Bryant
17 North Carolina	52 TB Chris Douglas / Alex Wade (FB)
31 Clemson	59 FB Cedric Dargan / Zack Novak
	DL Shawn Johnson
	DL Tryan Grissom / Jeff Lonergan
	DL Matt Zielinski
	DL Charles Porter
	LB Jamyon Small
	LB Ryan Fowler / Nate Krill
	LB Jim Scharrer
	DB Ronnie Hamilton
	DB Jeff Phillips / Derrick Lee
	DB Anthony Roberts
	DB Terrell Smith / B.J. Hill

RUSHING: Douglas 218/841y, Wade 64/249y
PASSING: Bryant 187-384/2454y, 11TD, 48.7%
RECEIVING: Erdeljac 42/684y, Hart 30/476y
SCORING: Douglas & Brent Garber (K) 48pts

2002 2-10

23 East Carolina	16 WR Senterrio Landrum
3 Louisville	40 WR Khari Sharpe
21 Northwestern	26 WR Lance Johnson
17 Florida State	48 T Drew Strojny
43 Navy	17 G Daryl Lewis
22 Virginia	27 C Luke Bayer
10 Wake Forest	36 G Rusty Wilson
22 N. Carolina St.	24 T Christian Mitchell
12 Maryland	45 TE Calen Powell / Andy Roland
31 Clemson	34 QB Adam Smith
2 Georgia Tech	17 RB Chris Douglas / Alex Wade
21 North Carolina	23 DL Shawn Johnson
	DL Matt Zielinski
	DL Orrin Thompson
	DL Micah Harris
	LB Jamyon Small / Jim Scharrer
	LB Ryan Fowler
	LB Brendan Dewan
	DB Brian Greene / Temo George
	DB Kenneth Stanford
	DB Alex Green
	DB Terrell Smith

RUSHING: Wade 201/979y, Douglas 131/640y
PASSING: Smith 174-308/2031y, 12TD, 56.5%
RECEIVING: Sharpe 30/458y
SCORING: Brent Garber (K) 63pts

2003 4-8

0 Virginia	27 WR Senterrio Landrum / Khari Sharpe
29 W. Carolina	3 WR Lance Johnson
27 Rice	24 T Drew Strojny / Jim Moravchik
10 Northwestern	28 G Daryl Lewis
7 Florida State	56 C Luke Bayer
20 Maryland	33 G Rusty Wilson
13 Wake Forest	42 T Christian Mitchell
21 N. Carolina St.	28 TE Andy Roland / Calen Powell
6 Tennessee	23 QB Mike Schneider
41 Georgia Tech	17 TB Chris Douglas / Cedric Dargan
7 Clemson	40 FB Alex Wade
30 North Carolina	22 DL Phillip Alexander / Casey Camaro
	DL Matt Zielinski
	DL Orrin Thompson
	DL Micah Harris / Jim Scharrer
	LB Giuseppe Aguanno / Malcolm Ruff
	LB Ryan Fowler
	LB Brendan Dewan / DeAndre White
	DB Brian Greene / Temo George
	DB Kenneth Stanford / John Talley
	DB Alex Green
	DB Terrell Smith

RUSHING: Douglas 236/1138y, Dargan 69/264y, Wade 58/252y
PASSING: Schneider 97-208/1220y, 4 TD, 46.6%
RECEIVING: Love 27/290y, Johnson 23/247y, Sharpe 23/233y
SCORING: Douglas 36pts, Matt Brooks (K) 33pts, Dargan 30pts

2004 2-9

12 Navy	27 WR Ronnie Elliott / Jomar Wright
20 Connecticut	22 WR Corey Thompson / Senterrio Landrum
17 Virginia Tech	41 TE Ben Patrick / Calen Powell
21 Maryland	55 T Jim Moravchik
28 Citadel	10 G Chris Best (T) / Bob Benion
7 Georgia Tech	24 C Dan Mooney
6 Virginia	37 G Tyler Krieg
22 Wake Forest	24 T Christian Mitchell
7 Florida State	29 TE Andy Roland
16 Clemson	13 QB Mike Schneider / Chris Dapolito
17 North Carolina	40 RB Cedric Dargan / Justin Boyle
	DL Eli Nichols / Patrick Bailey
	DL Orrin Thompson
	DL Casey Camaro
	DL Justin Kitchen / Phillip Alexander
	LB Malcolm Ruff / Alex Williams
	LB Giuseppe Aguanno / Codey Lowe
	LB Brendon Dewan
	DB John Talley / Deonto McCormick
	DB Kenneth Stanford / Daniel Charbonnet
	DB Alex Green
	DB Brian Greene / C.J. Woodard

RUSHING: Dargan 125/462y, Boyle 50/241y, Ronnie Drummer (RB) 25/114y
PASSING: Schneider 150-253/1527y, 8TD, 59.3%
RECEIVING: Patrick 32/311y, Elliott 28/318y, Roland 20/257y
SCORING: Matt Brooks (K) 57pts, Roland 18pts, 4 with 12pts

2005 1-10

21 East Carolina	24 WR Eron Riley / Marcus Jones
0 Virginia Tech	45 WR Ronnie Elliott / Jomar Wright
40 VMI	14 T Lavdrim Bauta
7 Virginia	38 G Jim Moravchik
21 Navy	28 C Matt Rumsey / Paul Campitelli
7 Miami	52 G Tyler Krieg
10 Georgia Tech	35 T Demetrius Warrick
24 Florida State	55 TE Andy Roland / Ben Patrick
6 Wake Forest	44 QB Zack Asack / Mike Schneider
20 Clemson	49 TB Justin Boyle / Re'quan Boyette
21 North Carolina	24 FB Malcolm Ruff
	DL Eli Nichols / Justin Kitchen
	DL Casey Camero
	DL Brian Sallee
	DL Phillip Alexander
	LB Brendan Dewan / DeAndre White
	LB Mike Brown Tauiliili
	LB Patrick Bailey / Jeramy Edwards
	DB John Talley
	DB Deonton McCormick
	DB Brian Greene
	DB Chris Davis / Glenn Williams

RUSHING: Boyle 134/458y, Ronnie Drummer (TB) 33/337y, Boyette 60/252y
PASSING: Asack 90-180/966y, 5 TDs, 50.0%, Schneider 41-86/351y, 0 TDs, 47.7%
RECEIVING: Patrick 30/252y, Elliott 19/176y, Riley 11/247y, Jones 11/90y
SCORING: Boyle 54pts, Joe Surgan (K) 33pts, 4 with 12pts

2006 0-12

0 Richmond	13 WR Eron Riley
13 Wake Forest	14 WR Jomar Wright / Raphael Chestnut
0 Virginia Tech	36 T Cameron Goldberg / Garrett Mason
0 Virginia	37 G Zach Maurides
14 Alabama	30 C Matt Rumsey
24 Florida State	51 G Rob Schirmann
15 Miami	20 T Fred Rollins
28 Vanderbilt	45 TE Nick Stefanow
13 Navy	38 QB Thaddeus Lewis
7 Boston College	28 TB Justin Boyle / Re'quan Boyette
21 Georgia Tech	49 FB Tielor Robinson
44 North Carolina	45 DL Patrick Bailey / Greg Akinbiyi
	DL Ayango Okpokowuruk / Eli Nichols
	DL Casey Camero
	DL Vince Oghobaase
	LB Codey Lowe / Tim Ball
	LB Mike Brown Tauiliili
	LB Jeramy Edwards
	DB John Talley
	DB DeOnto McCormick / Leon Wright
	DB Chris Davis
	DB Adrian Aye-Darko / Glenn Williams

RUSHING: Boyette 87/388y, Boyle 91/358y, Clifford Harris (TB) 56/206y, Ronnie Drummer (TB) 29/148y
PASSING: Lewis 180-340/2134y, 11 TDs, 52.9%
RECEIVING: Wright 40/561y, Chestnut 39/375y, Riley 32/643y
SCORING: Boyle 30pts, Robinson 26pts, Riley & Joe Surgan (K) 18pts

2007 1-11

14 Connecticut	45 WR Jomar Wright / Raphael Chestnut
13 Virginia	24 WR Eron Riley / Austin Kelly / Sheldon Bell
20 Northwestern	14 T Cameron Goldberg
43 Navy	46 G Zach Maurides
14 Miami	24 C Matt Rumsey
36 Wake Forest	41 G Rob Schirmann
14 Virginia Tech	43 T Fred Roland / Bryan Morgan
6 Florida State	25 TE Nick Stefanow
10 Clemson	47 QB Thaddeus Lewis
24 Georgia Tech	41 RB Re'quan Boyette / Ronnie Drummer
7 Notre Dame	28 FB Clifford Harris / Brandon King
14 North Carolina	20 DL Patrick Bailey
	DL Ayanga Okpokowuruk / Kinney Rucker
	DL Vince Oghobaase
	DL Wesley Oglesby / Greg Akinbiyi
	LB Marcus Jones / Adam Banks
	LB Mike Tauiliili / Charles Robinson
	LB Vincent Rey / Tim Ball
	DB Leon Wright
	DB Glenn Williams / Jabari Marshall
	DB Chris Davis
	DB Adrian Aye-Darko / Catron Gainey

RUSHING: Boyette 104/432y, Justin Boyle (RB) 75/226y, Drummer 47/119y
PASSING: Lewis 199-360/2430y, 21TD, 55.3%
RECEIVING: J. Wright 56/599y, Riley 40/830y, Drummer 24/196y
SCORING: Riley 54pts, J. Wright 30pts, King 24pts

2008 4-8

31 James Madison	7 WR Eron Riley / Sheldon Bell
20 Northwestern	24 WR Johnny Williams / Donovan Varner
41 Navy	31 WR Austin Kelly / Raphael Chestnutt
31 Virginia	3 T Cameron Goldberg
0 Georgia Tech	27 G Kyle Hill
31 Miami	49 C Bryan Morgan
10 Vanderbilt	7 G Rob Schirmann
30 Wake Forest	33 T Fred Roland
17 N. Carolina St.	27 TE Tielor Robinson / Brett Huffman
7 Clemson	31 QB Thaddeus Lewis
3 Virginia Tech	14 RB Clifford Harris / Jay Hollingsworth
20 North Carolina	28 DL Ayanga Okpokowuruk / Wes Oglesby
	DL Clifford Repress / Kinney Rucker
	DL Vince Oghobbaase
	DL Greg Akinbiyi
	LB Marcus Jones
	LB Mike Tauiliili
	LB Vincent Rey
	DB Jabari Marshall / Lee Butler
	DB Glenn Williams / Leon Wright
	DB Catron Gainey / Chris Rwabukamba
	DB Adrian Aye-Darko / Matt Daniels

RUSHING: Hollingsworth 108/399y, Harris 98/345y, Tony Jackson (RB) 76/259y
PASSING: Lewis 224-361/2171y, 15TD, 62.0%
RECEIVING: Riley 61/693y, Williams 30/327y, Hollingsworth 25/188y, Varner 21/164y
SCORING: Nick Maggio (K) 61pts, Riley 48pts, Harris 36pts

2009 5-7

16 Richmond	24 WR Austin Kelly / Johnny Williams
35 Army	19 WR Donovan Varner
16 Kansas	44 WR Conner Vernon
49 N.C. Central	14 T Kyle Hill
26 Virginia Tech	34 G Brandon Harper / Mitchell Lederman
49 N. Carolina St.	28 C Bryan Morgan
17 Maryland	13 G Brian Moore
28 Virginia	17 T Jarrod Holt / Jon Needham
6 North Carolina	19 TE Brett Huffman
10 Georgia Tech	49 QB Thaddeus Lewis
16 Miami	34 RB Desmond Scott / Re'Quan Boyette
34 Wake Forest	45 DL Patrick Egboh / Wes Oglesby
	DL Charlie Hatcher
	DL Vince Oghobaase / Kinney Rucker
	DL Ayanga Okpokowuruk
	LB Adam Banks / Lee Butler
	LB Vincent Rey / Tyree Glover
	LB Damian Thornton / Abraham Kromah
	DB Leon Wright / Lee Butler
	DB Chris Rwabukamba
	DB Catron Gainey
	DB Matt Daniels / Jordan Byas

RUSHING: Scott 70/262y, Jay Hollingsworth (RB) 54/179y, Patrick Kurunwune (RB) 34/149y
PASSING: Lewis 274-449/3330y, 20TD, 61%
RECEIVING: Varner 65/1047y, Vernon 55/746y, Kelly 54/625y, Williams 31/385y
SCORING: Will Snyderwine (K) 75pts, Varner 48pts, Kelly & Lewis 24pts

2010 3-9

41 Elon	27 WR Austin Kelly / Tony Foster
48 Wake Forest	54 WR Donovan Varner / Brandon Braxton
13 Alabama	62 WR Conner Vernon
21 Army	35 T Kyle Hill
16 Maryland	21 G Brandon Harper / Dave Harding
13 Miami	28 C Bryan Morgan
7 Virginia Tech	44 G Brian Moore
34 Navy	31 T Perry Simmons
55 Virginia	48 TE Brandon King / Brett Huffman
16 Boston College	21 QB Sean Renfree / Brandon Connette
20 Georgia Tech	30 RB Desmond Scott / Josh Snead
19 North Carolina	24 DL Patrick Egboh / Justin Foxx
	DL Charlie Hatcher
	DL Sydney Sarmiento
	DL Wesley Oglesby / Kenny Anunike
	LB Abraham Kromah / Tyree Glover
	LB Kelby Brown / Austin Gamble
	LB/DB Damian Thornton / Walt Canty
	DB Ross Cockrell
	DB Chris Rwabukamba / August Campbell
	DB Lee Butler / Jordan Byas
	DB Matt Daniels

RUSHING: Scott 120/530y, Connette 78/321y, Snead 45/221y
PASSING: Renfree 285-464/3131y, 14TD, 61.4%, Connette 10-22/125y, 0TD, 45.5%
RECEIVING: Vernon 73/973y, Varner 60/736y, Kelly 47/486y
SCORING: Will Snyderwine (K) 95pts, Connette 50pts, 3 tied w/ 24pts

FLORIDA

University of Florida (Founded 1853)
Gainesville, Florida
Nickname: Gators
Colors: Royal Blue and Orange
Stadium: Ben Hill Griffin Stadium at Florida Field (1929) 88,548
Conference Affiliation: Southeastern (Charter member 1933-present)

CAREER RUSHING YARDS	Attempts	Yards
Errict Rhett (1990-93)	873	4163
Emmitt Smith (1987-89)	700	3928
Neal Anderson (1982-85)	639	3234
Fred Taylor (1994-97)	537	3075
Earnest Graham (1999-2002)	603	3065
Tim Tebow (2006-09)	692	2947
Tony Green (1974-77)	445	2590
John L. Williams (1982-85)	468	2409
Larry Smith (1966-68)	520	2186
Elijah Williams (1994-97)	343	2181

CAREER PASSING YARDS	Comp.-Att.	Yards
Chris Leak (2003-06)	895-1458	11,213
Danny Wuerffel (1993-96)	708-1170	10,875
Shane Matthews (1989-92)	722-1202	9287
Tim Tebow (2006-09)	661-995	9285
Rex Grossman (2000-02)	677-1110	9164
Kerwin Bell (1984-87)	549-949	7585
John Reaves (1969-71)	603-1128	7549
Wayne Peace (1980-83)	610-991	7206
Doug Johnson (1996-99)	504-907	7114
Steve Spurrier (1964-66)	392-692	4848

CAREER RECEIVING YARDS	Catches	Yards
Carlos Alvarez (1969-71)	172	2563
Jabar Gaffney (2000-01)	138	2375
Andre Caldwell (2003-07)	185	2349
Reidel Anthony (1994-96)	126	2274
Jack Jackson (1992-94)	143	2266
Dallas Baker (2003-06)	151	2236
Ike Hilliard (1994-96)	126	2214
Jacquez Green (1995-97)	113	2181
Willie Jackson (1990-93)	162	2172
Chris Doering (1992-95)	149	2107

SEASON RUSHING YARDS	Attempts	Yards
Emmitt Smith (1989)	284	1599
Emmitt Smith (1987)	229	1341
Jimmy DuBose (1975)	191	1307
Fred Taylor (1997)	214	1292
Errict Rhett (1993)	247	1289

SEASON PASSING YARDS	Comp.-Att.	Yards
Rex Grossman (2001)	259-395	3896
Danny Wuerffel (1996)	207-360	3625
Rex Grossman (2002)	287-503	3402
Tim Tebow (2007)	234-350	3286
Danny Wuerffel (1995)	210-325	3266

SEASON RECEIVING YARDS	Catches	Yards
Travis McGriff (1998)	70	1357
Carlos Alvarez (1969)	88	1329
Reidel Anthony (1996)	72	1293
Jabar Gaffney (2001)	67	1191
Jabar Gaffney (2000)	71	1184

GAME RUSHING YARDS	Attempts	Yards
Emmitt Smith (1989 vs. New Mexico)	31	316
Emmitt Smith (1987 vs. Alabama)	39	224
Red Bethea (1930 vs. Chicago)	N/A	218

GAME PASSING YARDS	Comp.-Att.	Yards
Tim Tebow (2009 vs. Cincinnati)	31-35	482
Rex Grossman (2001 vs. LSU)	22-32	464
Danny Wuerffel (1996 vs. Arkansas)	N/A	462

GAME RECEIVING YARDS	Catches	Yards
Taylor Jacobs (2002 vs. Ala.-Birmingham)	8	246
Carlos Alvarez (1969 vs. Miami)	15	237
Travis McGriff (1998 vs. So. Carolina)	13	222

GREATEST COACH

Florida's greatest coach could be none other than the fellow who likes to call himself "The Ol' Ball Coach." Steve Spurrier, the one-time Heisman Trophy winning quarterback at Florida returned to Gainesville to end many years of frustration Gator fans suffered while waiting for Florida to capture the elusive Southeastern Conference championship.

The University of Florida had been a charter member of the SEC when it started in 1933, yet it took until 1991 for a title to come to Gainesville. And then, Spurrier brought five more and the 1996 national championship to boot.

Spurrier holds the Florida record for most wins with 122, 40 percent more than his closest pursuer, Ray Graves. Spurrier's .817 winning percentage is among the greatest anywhere.

FLORIDA'S 55 GREATEST SINCE 1953

OFFENSE

WIDE RECEIVER: Carlos Alvarez, Reidel Anthony, Wes Chandler, Cris Collinsworth, Jabar Gaffney
TIGHT END: Charles Casey, Kirk Kilpatrick
TACKLE: Lomas Brown, Dan Fike, Vel Heckman, David Williams
GUARD: Larry Gagner, Burton Lawless, Jeff Zimmerman
CENTER: Mike Degory, Cal Dixon
QUARTERBACK: Rex Grossman, Chris Leak, Tim Tebow, Danny Wuerffel
RUNNING BACK: Neal Anderson, Errict Rhett, Emmitt Smith, Fred Taylor
FULLBACK: Larry Smith, John L. Williams

DEFENSE

END: Trace Armstrong, Alex Brown, Kevin Carter Jack Youngblood
TACKLE: Brad Culpepper, David Galloway, Ellis Johnson
NOSE GUARD: Robin Fisher
LINEBACKER: Ben Hanks, Alonzo Johnson, David Little, Wilber Marshall, Huey Richardson, Brandon Spikes
CORNERBACK: Richard Fain, Joe Haden, Steve Tannen, Fred Weary
SAFETY: Tony Lilly, Reggie Nelson, Will White, Jarvis Williams

SPECIAL TEAMS

RETURN SPECIALISTS: Willie Jackson, Sr., Brandon James
PLACE KICKER: Judd Davis
PUNTER: Bobby Joe Green

MULTIPLE POSITIONS

QUARTERBACK-PLACE KICKER-PUNTER: Steve Spurrier

TWO-WAY PLAYERS

FULLBACK-DEFENSIVE GUARD: Jimmy DuBose
HALFBACK-DEFENSIVE BACK: Jim Rountree

PERFORMANCE FORMULA:
FLORIDA'S 10 BEST SEASONS

2008	1.8083	1 of 71
1996	1.8018	1 of 70
2001	1.7191	2 of 70
2009	1.7134	4 of 72
2006	1.6968	2 of 72
1993	1.6803	2 of 70
1991	1.6688	3 of 71
1997	1.6500	4 of 70
1994	1.6405	5 of 71
1985	1.6270	4 of 70

Year	W-L-T	AP Poll	Conference Standing	Toughest Regular Season Opponents	Coach (Record at School)	Bowl Games		
1953	3-5-2		6	Rice 8-2, Georgia Tech 8-2-1, Kentucky 7-2-1, Auburn 7-2-1	Bob Woodruff			
1954	5-5		3t	Rice 7-3, Georgia Tech 7-3, Auburn 7-3, Kentucky 7-3, Miami 8-1	Bob Woodruff			
1955	4-6		8	Ga. Tech 8-1-1, Auburn 8-1-1, Tennessee 6-3-1, Vanderbilt 7-3	Bob Woodruff			
1956	6-3-1		3	Clemson 7-1-2, Auburn 7-3, Georgia Tech 9-1, Miami 8-1-1	Bob Woodruff			
1957	6-2-1	17	3t	Miss. State 6-2-1, Auburn 10-0, Vanderbilt 5-3-2, Miami 5-4-1	Bob Woodruff			
1958	6-4-1	14	7t	Vanderbilt 5-2-3, LSU 10-0, Auburn 9-0-1, Florida State 7-3	Bob Woodruff	Gator	3 Mississippi	7
1959	5-4-1	19	7	Vanderbilt 5-3-2, LSU 9-1, Auburn 7-3, Georgia 9-1, Miami 6-4	Bob Woodruff (53-42-6)			
1960	9-2	18	2	Rice 7-3, Auburn 8-2, Georgia 6-4, Miami 6-4	Ray Graves	Gator	13 Baylor	12
1961	4-5-1		5	Rice 7-3, LSU 9-1, Georgia Tech 7-3, Miami 7-3	Ray Graves			
1962	7-4		5	Georgia Tech 7-2-1, Duke 8-2, LSU 8-1-1, Auburn 6-3-1, Miami 7-3	Ray Graves	Gator	17 Penn State	7
1963	6-3-1		7	Georgia Tech 7-3, Alabama 8-2, LSU 7-3, Auburn 9-1	Ray Graves			
1964	7-3		2t	Alabama 10-0, Auburn 6-4, Florida State 8-1-1, LSU 7-2-1	Ray Graves			
1965	7-4		3	LSU 7-3, Mississippi 6-4, NC State 6-4, Georgia 6-4	Ray Graves	Sugar	18 Missouri	20
1966	9-2	11+	2	Florida State 6-4, LSU 5-4-1, Georgia 9-1, Miami 7-2-1	Ray Graves	Orange	27 Georgia Tech	12
1967	6-4		3t	LSU 6-3-1, Georgia 7-3, Florida State 7-2-1, Miami 7-3	Ray Graves			
1968	6-3-1		4t	Air Force 7-3, Florida State 8-2, Auburn 6-4, Georgia 8-0-2	Ray Graves			
1969	9-1-1	14	4	Houston 8-2, Florida State 6-3-1, Auburn 8-2	Ray Graves (70-31-4)	Gator	14 Tennessee	13
1970	7-4		5	Alabama 6-5, Florida State 7-4, Tennessee 10-1, Auburn 8-2	Doug Dickey			
1971	4-7		6t	Alabama 11-0, Tennessee 9-2, LSU 8-3, Auburn 9-1, Georgia 10-1	Doug Dickey			
1972	5-5-1		6	Alabama 10-1, Auburn 9-1, LSU 9-1-1, North Carolina 10-1	Doug Dickey			
1973	7-5		5t	LSU 9-2, Alabama 11-0, Georgia 6-4-1	Doug Dickey	Tangerine	7 Miami (Ohio)	16
1974	8-4	15	3t	California 7-3-1, Maryland 8-3, Mississippi State 8-3, Auburn 9-2	Doug Dickey	Sugar	10 Nebraska	13
1975	9-3		2t	NC State 7-3-1, Vanderbilt 7-4, Georgia 9-2	Doug Dickey	Gator	0 Maryland	13
1976	8-4		3	North Carolina 9-2, Houston 9-2, Miss. State 9-2, Georgia 10-1	Doug Dickey	Sun	14 Texas A&M	37
1977	6-4-1		5	LSU 8-3, Pittsburgh 8-2-1, Kentucky 10-1, Florida State 9-2	Doug Dickey			
1978	4-7		4t	LSU 8-3, Alabama 10-1, Georgia 9-1-1, Florida State 8-3	Doug Dickey (58-43-2)			
1979	0-10-1		9t	Houston 10-1, Alabama 11-0, Auburn 8-3, Florida State 11-0	Charley Pell			
1980	8-4		3t	Mississippi State 9-2, Georgia 11-0, Miami 8-3, Florida State 10-1	Charley Pell	Tangerine	35 Maryland	20
1981	7-5		3t	Miami 9-2, Mississippi State 7-4, Georgia 10-1	Charley Pell	Peach	6 West Virginia	26
1982	8-4		5t	Southern California 8-3, LSU 8-2-1, Auburn 8-3, Georgia 11-0	Charley Pell	Bluebonnet	24 Arkansas	28
1983	9-2-1	6	3t	Miami 10-1, Auburn 10-1, Georgia 9-1-1, Florida State 6-5	Charley Pell	Gator	14 Iowa	6
1984	9-1-1	3	ineligible	Miami 8-4, LSU 8-2-1, Tennessee 7-3-1, Auburn 8-4, Kentucky 8-3	Charley Pell (33-26-3), Galen Hall [8-0]			
1985	9-1-1	5	ineligible	Miami 10-1, LSU 9-1-1, Tennessee 8-2-1, Auburn 8-3, Fla. St. 8-3	Galen Hall			
1986	6-5		4t	Miami 11-0, Alabama 9-3, LSU 9-2, Auburn 9-2, Georgia 8-3	Galen Hall			
1987	6-6		5	Miami 11-0, LSU 9-1-1, Auburn 9-1-1, Georgia 8-3, Fla. St. 10-1	Galen Hall	Aloha	16 UCLA	20
1988	7-5		3t	LSU 8-3, Auburn 10-1, Georgia 8-3, Florida State 10-1	Galen Hall	All-American	14 Illinois	10
1989	7-5		2t	Auburn 9-2, Florida State 9-2	Galen Hall (40-18-1), Gary Darnell [3-4]	Freedom	7 Washington	34
1990	9-2	13	ineligible	Alabama 7-4, Tennessee 8-2-2, Auburn 7-3-1, Florida State 9-2	Steve Spurrier			
1991	10-2	7	1	Alabama 10-1, Syracuse 9-2, Tennessee 9-2, Florida State 10-2	Steve Spurrier			
1992	9-4	10	E1t	Tennessee 8-3, Mississippi State 7-4, Georgia 9-2, Fla. State 10-1	Steve Spurrier	Gator	27 North Carolina State	10
1993	11-2	5	E1	Tennessee 9-1-1, Auburn 11-0, Florida State 11-1	Steve Spurrier	Sugar	41 West Virginia	7
1994	10-2-1	7	E1	Tennessee 7-4, Auburn 9-1-1, Florida State 9-1-1	Steve Spurrier	Sugar	17 Florida State	23
1995	12-1	2	E1	Tennessee 10-1, Auburn 8-3, Florida State 9-2	Steve Spurrier	Fiesta	24 Nebraska	62
1996	12-1	1	E1	Tennessee 9-2, LSU 9-2, Auburn 7-4, Florida State 11-0	Steve Spurrier	Sugar	52 Florida State	20
1997	10-2	4	E2t	Tennessee 10-1, LSU 8-3, Auburn 9-2, Georgia 9-2, Fla. St. 10-1	Steve Spurrier	Citrus	21 Penn State	6
1998	10-2	5	E2	Tennessee 11-0, Alabama 7-4, Georgia 8-3, Florida State 11-1	Steve Spurrier	Orange	31 Syracuse	10
1999	9-4	12	E1	Tennessee 9-2, Alabama 9-2, Georgia 7-4, Florida State 11-0	Steve Spurrier	Citrus	34 Michigan State	37
2000	10-3	10	E1	Tennessee 8-3, LSU 7-4, Auburn 9-2, Georgia 7-4, Florida St. 11-1	Steve Spurrier	Sugar	20 Miami	37
2001	10-2	3	E2	Marshall 10-1, Tennessee 10-1, LSU 8-3, Georgia 8-3	Steve Spurrier (122-27-1)	Orange	56 Maryland	23
2002	8-5		E2	Miami 12-0, Georgia 11-1, Florida State 9-4	Ron Zook	Outback	30 Michigan	38
2003	8-5		E1t	Tennessee 10-2, LSU 11-1, Georgia 10-2, Florida State 10-2	Ron Zook	Outback	17 Iowa	37
2004	7-5		E3t	Tennessee 9-2, LSU 9-2, Georgia 9-2, Florida State 8-3	Ron Zook (23-14), Charlie Strong [0-1]	Peach	10 Miami	27
2005	9-3	12	E2t	Alabama 9-2, LSU 10-2, Georgia 10-2, Florida State 8-4	Urban Meyer	Outback	31 Iowa	24
2006	13-1	1	E1	Tennessee 9-3, LSU 10-2, Auburn 10-1, Georgia 8-4	Urban Meyer	BCS Title	41 Ohio State	14
2007	9-4	13	E3	Tennessee 9-3, Auburn 8-4, LSU 10-2, Georgia 10-2	Urban Meyer	Capital One	35 Michigan	41
2008	13-1	1	E1	Georgia 9-3, Florida State 8-4, Alabama 12-1	Urban Meyer	BCS Title	24 Oklahoma	12
2009	13-1	3	E1	LSU 9-3, Arkansas 7-5, Alabama 13-0	Urban Meyer	Sugar	51 Cincinnati	24
2010	8-5		E2	Alabama 9-3, LSU 10-2, South Carolina 9-4, Florida State 9-4	Urban Meyer (65-15)	Outback	37 Penn State	24

TOTAL: 449-208-17 .6788 (10 of 70)   **Bowl Games since 1953:**   18-18 .5000 (36 of 70)

GREATEST TEAM SINCE 1953: Florida's 1996 national champions came back from a late-season defeat by Florida State and crushed the Seminoles in a rematch in the Sugar Bowl. The school's other national champions, coach Urban Meyer's 2006 and 2008 teams were plenty impressive as well, blasting undefeated no. 1 Ohio State and no. 1 Oklahoma to win BCS titles

1953 3-5-2
16	Rice	20
0	Georgia Tech	0
13	Kentucky	26
45	Stetson	0
60	Citadel	0
21	LSU	21
7	Auburn	16
21	Georgia	7
7	Tennessee	9
10	Miami	14

E Jerry Bilyk / Welton Lockhart
T Howard Chapman / Jimmy Hatch
G Arthur Wright / Hubert Martin
C Steve De La Torre / Richard Martin
G Joe D'Agostino / Curt Haygood
T Dan Hunter
E Jack O'Brien / Ray Brown
QB Harry Speers / Doug Dickey
HB Larry Scott / Jackie Simpson
HB Bob Davis / John Burgess
FB Joe Brodsky / Rick Casares

RUSHING: N/A
PASSING: N/A
RECEIVING: N/A
SCORING: N/A

1954 5-5
14	Rice	34
13	Georgia Tech	12
19	Auburn	13
7	Clemson	14
21	Kentucky	7
7	LSU	20
7	Mississippi St.	0
13	Georgia	14
14	Tennessee	0
0	Miami	14

E Jerry Bilyk / Welton Lockhart
T Ross Winne / Don Hatch
G Curt Haygood / Hubert Martin
C Steve De La Torre / Jim Schwarzburg
G John Barrow / Bob Vosloh
T Buster Hill / Larry Wesley
E Ray Brown / Bobby Burford
QB Bobby Lance/D. Allen/Fred Robinson
HB Jackie Simpson / Don Chandler
HB Bob Davis / John Burgess /Bob Smith
FB Mal Hammack / Joe Brodsky

RUSHING: Brodsky 82/378y, Burgess 49/223y, Simpson 49/215y
PASSING: Dick Allen (QB) 26-63/353y, 4TD, 41.3%
RECEIVING: Burgess 14/147y, Smith 8/96y, Lockhart 8/74y
SCORING: N/A

1955 4-6
20	Mississippi St.	14
7	Georgia Tech	14
0	Auburn	13
28	Geo. Wash'gton	0
18	LSU	14
7	Kentucky	10
19	Georgia	13
0	Tebnnessee	20
6	Vanderbilt	21
6	Miami	7

E Welton Lockhart / Bobby Buford
T Charlie Mitchell / Hambone Hamilton
G Bob Vosloh / Hubert Martin
C Steve De La Torre / Bob Purcell
G John Barrow
T Buster Hill / Larry Wesley
E Ray Brown
QB Bobby Lance / Dick Allen
HB Jackie Simpson / Don Chandler
HB John Burgess / Jim Rountree
FB Joe Brodsky / Ed Sears

RUSHING: Simpson 65/422y, Rountree 47/385y, Sears 42/204y
PASSING: Allen 17-56/273y, 3TD, 30.4%
RECEIVING: Rountree 8/110y, Simpson 4/52y
SCORING: N/A

1956 6-3-1
26	Mississippi St.	0
20	Clemson	20
8	Kentucky	17
7	Rice	0
21	Vanderbilt	7
21	LSU	6
20	Auburn	0
28	Georgia	0
0	Georgia Tech	28
7	Miami	20

E Bobby Buford / Don Fleming
T Don Hicks / Vel Heckman
G Bob Vosloh / Howell Boney
C Bill Bolton / Joe Hergert
G John Barrow / Ray Midden
T Charlie Mitchell / Larry Wesley
E Jim Yeats / Dan Pelham
QB Jon May / Jimmy Dunn
HB Jackie Simpson / John Symank
HB Jim Rountree / Bernie Parrish
FB Joe Brodsky / Ed Sears

RUSHING: Sears 84/370y, Rountree 61/265y, Billy Booker (HB) 20/115y
PASSING: Dunn 15-34/268y, 4TD, 44.1%
RECEIVING: Rountree 9/176y, Parrish 7/93y, Yeats 4/67y
SCORING: N/A

1957 6-2-1
27	Wake Forest	0
14	Kentucky	7
20	Mississippi St.	29
22	LSU	14
0	Auburn	13
22	Georgia	0
14	Vanderbilt	7
0	Georgia Tech	0
14	Miami	0

E Don Fleming / Dan Edgington
T Vel Heckman / Don Hicks
G Howell Boney
C Joel Wahlberg / Joe Hergert
G Edwin Johns / Asa Cox
T Charlie Mitchell / Ray Midden
E Dan Pelham / Dave Hudson
QB Jimmy Dunn / Wayne Williamson
HB Jim Rountree / Billy Booker
HB Bernie Parrish / Bill Newbern
FB Ed Sears / Charlie Roberts

RUSHING: Rountree 91/411y, Sears N/A/394y, Parrish N/A/393y
PASSING: Dunn 14-32/187y, 2TD, 43.9%, Mickey Ellenburg (QB) 13-27/140y, 0TD, 48.1%
RECEIVING: Newbern 8/136y, Rountree 6/113y, Edgington 4/47y, Hudson 4/40y
SCORING: Parrish 44pts, Rountree 30pts

1958 6-4-1
34	Tulane	14
7	Mississippi St.	14
21	UCLA	14
6	Vanderbilt	6
7	LSU	10
5	Auburn	7
7	Georgia	6
51	Arkansas State	7
21	Florida State	7
12	Miami	9
3	Mississippi■	7

E Don Fleming / Pat Patchen
T Dick Brantley / Fred Schutz
G Asa Cox / Lawrin Giannamore
C Gene Graves / Joe Hergert
G Edwin Johns / Vic Miranda
T Vel Heckman
E Dave Hudson / Dan Edgington
QB Jimmy Dunn / Mickey Ellenburg
HB Don Deal / Billy Booker
HB Bill Newbern
FB Bob Milby / Jon MacBeth

RUSHING: Milby 53/288y, Deal 62/267y, MacBeth 56/201y
PASSING: Ellenburg 15-36/238y, 4TD, 41.7%
RECEIVING: Hudson 8/118y, Perry McGriff (E) 6/82y, Fleming 6/66y
SCORING: Dunn 26pts, Booker 22pts, Deal 18pts

1959 5-4-1
30	Tulane	0
14	Mississippi St.	13
55	Virginia	10
13	Rice	13
6	Vanderbilt	13
0	LSU	9
0	Auburn	6
10	Georgia	21
18	Florida State	8
23	Miami	14

E Dan Edgington / Pat Patchen
T Dick Brantley / Roger Seals
G Asa Cox
C Jim Young / Bill Hood
G Lawrin Giannamore
T Danny Royal / Jim Beaver
E Dave Hudson / Perry McGriff
QB Wayne Williamson / Dick Allen
HB Bobby Joe Green / Doug Partin
HB Don Deal / Don Goodman
FB Jon MacBeth / Bob Milby

RUSHING: MacBeth 59/257y, Partin 43/133y, Deal 38/116y
PASSING: Allen 31-80/613y, 5TD, 38.8%
RECEIVING: McGriff 14/360y, Nick Arafas (E) 9/138y, MacBeth 5/69y
SCORING: N/A

1960 9-2
30	Geo. Wash'gton	7
3	Florida State	0
18	Georgia Tech	17
0	Rice	10
12	Vanderbilt	0
13	LSU	10
7	Auburn	10
22	Georgia	14
21	Tulane	6
18	Miami	0
13	Baylor■	12

E Pat Patchen / Tommy Kelley
T Arthur Slack / Gerald Odom
G Ken Norris / Chester Collins
C Bob Wehking / Phil Culpepper
G Vic Miranda / Larry Travis
T Jim Beaver / Roger Seals
E Walter Holland / Nick Arafas
QB Larry Libertore / Bobby Dodd, Jr.
HB Don Deal / Lindy Infante
HB Bob Hoover / Bruce Starling
HB Bob Goodman / Jon MacBeth

RUSHING: Goodman 95/454y, Liberore 118/420y, Hoover 70/302y
PASSING: Dodd 30-55/448y, TD, 54.5%, Libertore 24-60/293y, 2TD, 40.0%
RECEIVING: Hoover 10/108y, Starling 6/136y, Infante 6/100y
SCORING: N/A

1961 4-5-1
21	Clemson	7
3	Florida State	3
14	Tulane	3
10	Rice	19
7	Vanderbilt	0
0	LSU	23
0	Georgia Tech	20
21	Georgia	14
15	Auburn	32
6	Miami	15

E Tom Smith / Russ Brown
T Fred Pearson
G Larry Travis
C Phil Culpepper / Bob Wehking
G Wade Entzminger
T Jim Beaver / Tony Peters
E Sam Holland / Bill Cash
QB Larry Libertore / Bobby Dodd Jr.
HB Lindy Infante / Bruce Starling
HB Bob Hoover / Hagood Clarke
FB Don Goodman

RUSHING: Goodman 111/413y, Infante 85/369y, Libertore 120/341y
PASSING: Tom Batten (QB) 30-67/460y, 3TD, 44.8%
RECEIVING: Brown 13/239y, Infante 11/129y, Hoover 9/213y
SCORING: Infante 42pts, Cash (E-K) 13pts, 6 with 6pts

1962 7-4
19	Mississippi St.	9
0	Georgia Tech	17
21	Duke	28
42	Texas A&M	6
42	Vanderbilt	7
0	LSU	23
22	Auburn	3
23	Georgia	15
20	Florida State	7
15	Miami	17
17	Penn State■	7

E Russ Brown / Tommy Kelley
T Gerald Odom (G) / Dennis Murphy
G Larry Travis
C Phil Culpepper / Roger Pettee
G Jack Katz
T Tony Peters / Frank Lasky
E Sam Holland / Tom Dean
QB Tom Shannon / Larry Libertore
HB Lindy Infante / Dick Skelly
HB Bob Hoover / Ron Stoner
FB Larry Dupree / Jim O'Donnell

RUSHING: Dupree 113/604y, O'Donnell 73/297y, Hoover 37/191y
PASSING: Shannon 56-100/551y, 2TD, 56.0%
RECEIVING: Brown 15/227y, Dean 10/144y, Stoner 9/121y
SCORING: Dupree 42pts, O'Donnell 24pts, Shannon 22pts

1963 6-3-1
0	Georgia Tech	9
9	Mississippi St.	9
35	Richmond	28
10	Alabama	6
21	Vanderbilt	0
0	LSU	14
0	Auburn	19
21	Georgia	14
27	Miami	21
7	Florida State	0

E Russ Brown / Lynn Matthews
T Dennis Murphy
G Gerald Odom / Larry Beckman
C Roger Pettee / Jimmy Morgan
G Jack Katz
T Frank Lasky / Sidney MacLean
E Barry Brown / Charles Casey
QB Tom Shannon / Bruce Bennett
HB Allen Trammell / Jack Harper
HB Alan Poe / Hagood Clarke
FB Larry Dupree / Jim O'Donnell

RUSHING: Dupree 189/745y, Harper 55/195y, Clarke 13/135y
PASSING: Shannon 84-158/9556y, 4TD, 54.5%
RECEIVING: R. Brown 12/113y, Clarke 10/118y, Casey 9/130y, Poe 9/75y
SCORING: Shannon 30pts, Dupree 24pts, Poe & Matthews 12pts

1964 7-3
24	SMU	8
16	Mississippi St.	13
30	Mississippi	14
37	South Carolina	0
14	Alabama	17
14	Auburn	0
7	Georgia	14
7	Florida State	16
12	Miami	10
20	LSU	6

E Gary Thomas
T Randy Jackson (E) / Jim Benson (DL)
G Larry Beckman / Ron Pursell
C Bill Carr / Gary Cliett
G Larry Gagner / Bill Richbourg (LB)
T John Whatley / John Preston
E Charles Casey / Barry Brown (DL)
QB Tom Shannon / Steve Spurrier
HB Jack Harper
HB Alan Poe / Don Knapp
FB Larry Dupree / John Feiber
DL Lynn Matthews / Don Barrett
DL Jim Benson / Ken McLean
DL Bill Richbourg (G)
DL Dennis Murphy / Gordon Colson
DL Barry Brown (E)
LB Roger Pettee / Jim Bernhardt
LB Jack Card / Steve Heidt
DB Dick Kirk / Stuart Grandy
DB Allen Trammell
DB Jerry Newcomer / Ken Russell
DB Bruce Bennett

RUSHING: Dupree 101/376y, Harper 43/191y, Feiber 62/184y
PASSING: Spurrier 65-114/943y, 6TD, 57.0%
RECEIVING: Casey 47/673y, Harper 12/210y, Dupree 6/62y
SCORING: Harper 42pts, Jim Hall (K) 25pts, Dupree & Casey 24pts

1965 7-4
24	Northwestern	14
13	Mississippi St.	18
14	LSU	7
17	Mississippi	0
28	N. Carolina St.	6
14	Auburn	28
14	Georgia	10
51	Tulane	13
13	Miami	16
30	Florida State	13
18	Missouri■	20

E Charles Casey
T John Whatley / John Preston
G Larry Beckman
C Bill Carr / Gary Cliett
G Jim Benson
T Randy Jackson / Gary Thomas
TE Barry Brown
QB Steve Spurrier
HB Alan Poe / Jack Harper
WB Richard Trapp / Paul Ewaldsen
FB John Feiber / Don Knapp
DL Lynn Matthews
DL Larry Gagner
DL Jerry "Red' Anderson
DL Gordon Colson / Doug Splane
DL Don Barrett / Frank Hoye
LB Jack Card / Wayne McCall
LB Ron Pursell / Steve Heidt
DB Dick Kirk
DB Allen Trammell / Dan Manry
DB Stuart Grandy / Tom Hungerbuhler
DB Bruce Bennett

RUSHING: Poe 83/366y, Harper 56/286y, Spurrier 125/230y
PASSING: Spurrier 148-287/1893y, 14TD, 57.0%
RECEIVING: Casey 58/809y, Brown 33/299y, Harper 28/403y
SCORING: Casey 48pts, Wayne Barfield (K) 44pts, Harper 36pts

1966 9-2

43 Northwestern	7 WR Richard Trapp / Tom Glenn
28 Mississippi St.	7 WR Paul Ewaldsen / Mike McCann
13 Vanderbilt	0 T John Preston
22 Florida State	19 G Jim Benson
17 N. Carolina St.	10 C Bill Carr
28 LSU	7 G Guy Dennis / Gary Duven
30 Auburn	27 T J.D. Pasteris / Terry Morris
10 Georgia	27 TE Jack Coons / Jim Yarbrough
31 Tulane	10 QB Steve Spurrier / Harmon Wages
16 Miami	21 TB Larry Smith / Don Knapp
27 Georgia Tech	12 FB Graham McKeel / Wayne Barfield
	DL Brian Jetter / Rex Von Rittgers
	DL Don Giordano / Paige Cutcliffe
	DL George Dean / Doug Splane
	DL Bill Dorsey
	DL Red Anderson / Eddie Foster
	DL Don Barrett
	LB Steve Heidt / Charles Pippin
	LB Jack Card / Wayne McCall
	DB Bobby Downs / Stuart Grandy
	DB Tom Hungerbuhler / Bobby Downs
	DB Larry Rentz

RUSHING: Smith 162/742y, McKeel 66/210y, Wages 18/82y
PASSING: Spurrier 179-291/2012y, 16TD, 61.5%
RECEIVING: Trapp 63/872y, Ewaldsen 41/427y, Coons 24/245y
SCORING: Smith 54pts, Trapp 44pts, Barfield (FB-K) 39pts

1967 6-4

14 Illinois	0 WR Richard Trapp / Paul Ewaldsen
24 Mississippi St.	7 WR Mike McCann / Guy McTheny
6 LSU	37 T Skip Amelung / J.D. Pasteris
35 Tulane	0 G Mac Steen
27 Vanderbilt	22 C Kim Helton
21 Auburn	26 G Guy Dennis
17 Georgia	16 T Terry Morris
28 Kentucky	12 TE Jim Yarbrough / Jack Coons
16 Florida State	21 QB Larry Rentz (WR) / Harmon Wages
13 Miami	20 TB Larry Smith
	FB Graham McKeel / Tom Christian
	DL Brian Jetter / David Ghesquiere
	DL Jim Hadley / Lloyd Turman
	DL Bill Dorsey / Mike Healey
	DL Don Giordano
	DL Britt Skrivanek / George Dean
	LB David Mann / Bill McBride
	LB Wayne McCall / Tom Abdelnour
	DB Steve Tannen
	DB Bill Gaisford / Tom Hungerbuhler
	DB Bobby Downs
	DB Paul Maliska

RUSHING: Smith 205/754y, McKeel 71/256y, Rentz 85/194y
PASSING: Rentz 80-140/1031y, 3TD, 57.1%,
   Wages 40-83/522y, 2TD, 48.2%,
   Jackie Eckdahl (QB) 22-52/343y, 2TD, 42.3%
RECEIVING: Trapp 58/708y, McCann 26/301y,
   Yarbrough 17/307y
SCORING: Smith 48pts, Wayne Barfield (K) 28pts, 3 with 18pts

1968 6-3-1

23 Air Force	20 WR Guy McTheny / Gene Peek
9 Florida State	3 WR Don Gramling / Ted Hager
31 Mississippi St.	14 T Skip Amelung / Terry Morris
24 Tulane	7 G Mac Steen / Donnie Williams
7 North Carolina	22 C Kim Helton
14 Vanderbilt	14 G Guy Dennis
13 Auburn	24 T Jim Kiley / Wayne Griffith
0 Georgia	51 TE Jim Yarbrough
16 Kentucky	14 QB Jackie Eckdahl / Larry Rentz
14 Miami	10 TB Tom Christian
	FB Larry Smith / Jerry Vinesett
	DL Mike Healey
	DL Bill Dorsey
	DL Jim Hadley / Jack Youngblood
	DL Britt Skrivanek / Bob Coleman
	LB David Ghesquiere / Brad Powell
	LB Tom Abdelnour
	LB David Mann / Mike Kelley
	DB Steve Tannen
	DB Ted Hager
	DB Mark Ely / Jack Burns
	DB Skip Albury

RUSHING: Smith 152/690y, Christian 112/509y, Vinesett 53/194y,
   Eckdahl 66/174y
PASSING: Eckdahl 56-125/572y, 2TD, 44.8%,
   Rentz 55-105/533y 0TD, 52.4%
RECEIVING: McTheny 34/347y, Yarbrough 24/275y, Smith 13/157y
SCORING: Smith 42pts, Youngblood (DT-K) 35pts, Christian 24pts

1969 9-1-1

59 Houston	34 WR Paul Maliska / Andy Cheney
47 Mississippi St.	35 WR Carlos Alvarez
21 Florida State	6 T Wayne Griffith
18 Tulane	17 G Donnie Williams
52 North Carolina	2 C Kim Helton
41 Vanderbilt	20 G Skip Amelung / Dale Hutcherson
12 Auburn	38 T Mac Steen / Jim Kiley
13 Georgia	13 TE Bill Dowdy / Jim Yancey
31 Kentucky	6 QB John Reaves
35 Miami	16 TB Tommy Durrence / Jerry Vinesett
14 Tennessee ■	13 FB Mike Rich / Garry Walker
	DL Jack Youngblood
	DL Robert Harrell / Alan Cole
	DL Robbie Rebol / Danny Williams
	DL Bob Coleman / Britt Skrivanek
	LB David Ghesquiere / Brad Powell
	LB Tom Abdelnour / Eric Taggert
	LB Mike Kelley
	DB Steve Tannen / Doug Sorensen
	DB Ted Hager / Harvin Clark
	DB Mark Ely / Jack Burns
	DB Skip Albury / Jimmy Barr

RUSHING: Durrance 189/731y, Rich 85/340y, Walker 46/167y
PASSING: Reaves 222-396/2896y, 24TD, 56.1%
RECEIVING: Alvarez 88/1329y, Cheney 37/518y, Dowdy 30/317y
SCORING: Durrance 110pts, Alvarez 76pts,
   Richard Franco (K) 51pts

1970 7-4

21 Duke	19 WR Willie Jackson / Jerry Vinesett
34 Mississippi St.	13 WR Carlos Alvarez / Andy Cheney
15 Alabama	6 T Bill Dowdy / David Peek
14 N. Carolina St.	6 G Dale Hutcherson
38 Florida State	27 C Richard Kensler
20 Richmond	0 G Donnie Williams
7 Tennessee	38 T Fred Abbott
14 Auburn	63 TE Jim Yancey / Jerry Coker
24 Georgia	17 QB John Reaves
24 Kentucky	13 TB Tommy Durrance
13 Miami	14 FB Duane Doel / Mike Rich / Garry Walker
	DL Jack Youngblood
	DL Alan Cole / Eddy Moore
	DL Danny Williams
	DL Robert Harrell
	LB Mike Kelley / Brad Powell
	LB Eric Taggert / Gary Petersen
	LB Richard Buchanan / Jim Kelly
	DB Harvin Clark
	DB John Faix
	DB John Clifford / Jack Burns
	DB Doug Sorensen / John Silman

RUSHING: Durrance 167/584y, Rich 79/326y, Doel 29/104y
PASSING: Reaves 188-376/2549y, 13TD, 50.0%
RECEIVING: Alvarez 44/717y, Yancy 40/550y, Jackson 25/439y
SCORING: Durrance & Alvarez 36pts, Richard Franco (K) 29pts

1971 4-7

6 Duke	12 WR Willie Jackson (TB) / Joel Parker
10 Mississippi St.	13 WR Carlos Alvarez / Hollis Boardman
0 Alabama	38 T David Peek / Tom Condon (C)
13 Tennessee	20 G Joe Sheppard / Bill Dowdy
7 LSU	48 C Mark King / Richard Kensler
17 Florida State	15 G Fred Abbott / Dale Hutcherson
27 Maryland	23 T Kris Anderson
7 Auburn	40 TE Jim Yancey / Hank Foldberg Jr.
7 Georgia	49 QB John Reaves
35 Kentucky	24 TB Tommy Durrence / Lenny Lucas
45 Miami	16 FB Mike Rich / Cary Geiger
	DL Richard Buchanan
	DL Eddy Moore / John Lacer
	DL David Hitchcock / Len Fuller
	DL Robert Harrell
	DL Mike Moore
	LB David Poff / Jan Gowland
	LB Ricky Browne
	DB Harvin Clark / Leonard George
	DB Doug Sorensen
	DB John Clifford / Jimmy Barr
	DB John Faix / John Silman

RUSHING: Rich 106/481y, Durrance 92/326y, Lucas 65/169y
PASSING: Reaves 193-356/2104y, 17TD, 54.2%
RECEIVING: Alvarez 40/517y, Durrance 39/366y, Jackson 27/331y
SCORING: Durrance 36pts, Richard Franco (K) 28pts, Yancey 18pts

1972 5-5-1

14 SMU	21 WR Joel Parker / Willie Jackson
28 Mississippi St.	13 WR Hollis Boardman / Lee McGriff
42 Florida State	13 T Paul Parker
7 Alabama	24 G Burton Lawless
16 Mississippi	0 C Jim Kynes
20 Auburn	26 G Mike Stanfield / Ron Iannarelli
7 Georgia	10 T Kris Anderson / Aubrey Padgett
40 Kentucky	0 TE Hank Foldberg Jr.
3 LSU	32 QB David Bowden / Chan Gailey
17 Miami	6 TB Nat Moore / Andy Summers
24 North Carolina	28 FB Vince Kendrick / Cary Geiger
	DL Ricky Browne / Jan Gowland
	DL David Starkey / John Lacer
	DL David Hitchcock
	DL Preston Kendrick / Mike Moore
	LB Ralph Ortega
	LB Fred Abbott
	LB David Poff / Glenn Cameron
	DB Tyson Sever
	DB Leonard George / Alvin Butler
	DB Jim Revels / John Clifford
	DB Wayne Fields / Robby Ball

RUSHING: Moore 145/845y, Kendrick 121/591y, Geiger 35/184y
PASSING: Bowden 108-229/1480y, 12TD, 47.2%
RECEIVING: Moore 25/351y, Jackson 23/397y, Parker 18/279y,
   Boardman 18/202y
SCORING: Moore 78pts, Clifton Aust (K) 27pts, Jackson 24pts

1973 7-5

21 Kansas State	10 WR Bill Nugent / Glenn Sever
14 Southern Miss.	13 WR Lee McGriff
12 Mississippi St.	33 T Mike Williams
3 LSU	24 G Gerald Loper / Kris Anderson
14 Alabama	35 C Jimmy Ray Stephens / Jimmy Kynes
10 Mississippi	13 G Burton Lawless
12 Auburn	8 T Aubrey Padgett / Mike Stanfield
11 Georgia	10 TE Hank Foldberg Jr. / Alvis Darby
20 Kentucky	18 QB David Bowden / Chan Gailey
14 Miami	7 TB Nat Moore / Jim Richards
49 Florida State	0 FB Vince Kendrick
7 Miami (Ohio) ■	16 DL Ricky Browne
	DL John Lacer / Clint Griffith
	DL David Hitchcock / Darrell Carpenter
	DL Preston Kendrick
	LB Ralph Ortega
	LB Glenn Cameron
	LB Joe Allen
	DB Tyson Sever
	DB Alvin Butler / Randy Talbot
	DB Jim Revels
	DB Wayne Fields / Robby Ball

RUSHING: Kendrick 127/516y, Moore 79/335y,
   Don Gaffney (QB) 68/151y
PASSING: Bowden 62-113/711y, 7TD, 54.9%,
   Don Gaffney 42-98/609y, 4TD, 42.9%
RECEIVING: McGriff 38/703y, Parker 15/233y, Kendrick 11/72y
SCORING: McGriff & Kendrick 30pts, John Williams (K) 23pts

1974 8-4

21 California	17 WR Lee McGriff / Wes Chandler
17 Maryland	10 T Mike Williams
29 Mississippi St.	13 G Burton Lawless
24 LSU	14 C Jim Kynes
10 Vanderbilt	24 G Mike Stanfield / Gerald Loper
24 Florida State	14 T Paul Parker / Bruce Mulliniks
30 Duke	13 TE Alvis Darby
25 Auburn	14 QB Don Gaffney / Jimmy Fisher
16 Georgia	17 TB Tony Green / Jim Richards
24 Kentucky	41 WB Larry Brinson
31 Miami	7 FB Jimmy DuBose
10 Nebraska ■	13 DL Preston Kendrick / Mike Smith
	DL Darrell Carpenter
	DL Sammy Green
	DL Clint Griffith
	DL Vern Barber / Joe Allen
	LB Ralph Ortega
	LB Glenn Cameron / Charlie Williams
	DB Tyson Sever
	DB Randy Talbot / Alvin Butler
	DB Alvin Cowans / Robby Ball
	DB Wayne Fields

RUSHING: Green 133/856y, DuBose 132/662y, Brinson 74/418y
PASSING: Gaffney 37-87/621y, 7TD, 42.5%,
   Fisher 25-46/445y, 5TD, 54.3%
RECEIVING: McGriff 36/698y, Green 9/96y, Darby 6/116y
SCORING: David Posey (K) 63pts, McGriff & Green 42pts

1975 9-3

40 SMU	14 WR Wes Chandler
7 N. Carolina St.	8 T Mike Williams
27 Mississippi St.	10 G Joe Pupello
34 LSU	6 C Robbie Moore
35 Vanderbilt	0 G Gerald Loper
34 Florida State	8 T Bruce Mulliniks
24 Duke	16 TE Alvis Darby / Jimmy Ray Stephens
31 Auburn	14 QB Don Gaffney / Jimmy Fisher
7 Georgia	10 HB Tony Green / Jim Richards
48 Kentucky	7 HB Larry Brinson
15 Miami	11 FB Jimmy DuBose
0 Maryland■	13 DL Mike Smith
	DL Darrell Carpenter
	DL Scott Hutchinson /Jimmy DuBose (FB)
	DL Joe Allen
	LB Jimmy Ray Stephens
	LB Charlie Williams
	LB Sammy Green / Kevin Logan
	DB Henry Davis
	DB Robby Ball
	DB Alvin Cowans
	DB Warren Gaffney / Vern Barber

RUSHING: DuBose 191/1307y, Green 103/471y, Brinson 72/315y
PASSING: Gaffney 42-90/755y, 8TD, 46.7%
RECEIVING: Chandler 20/457y, Brinson 7/88y, LeCount 6/200y, Green 6/79y
SCORING: David Posey (K) 64pts, DuBose, Brinson & Green 36pts

1976 8-4

21 North Carolina	24 WR Wes Chandler / Derrick Gaffney
49 Houston	14 T David Forrester
34 Mississippi St.	30 G Keith Tribble
28 LSU	23 C Robbie Moore
33 Florida State	26 G Joe Pupello
20 Tennessee	18 T Bruce Mulliniks
24 Auburn	19 TE Jimmy Ray Stephens
27 Georgia	41 QB Jimmy Fisher / Bill Kynes
9 Kentucky	28 HB Larry Brinson / Tony Green
50 Rice	22 HB Willie Wilder
19 Miami	10 FB Robert Morgan / Earl Carr
14 Texas A&M	37 DL Michael DuPree
	DL Darrell Carpenter
	DL Sylvester King / Ron Coleman
	DL Jeff Kanter / Richard Ruth
	LB Scot Brantley / Jimmy Ray Stephens
	LB Scott Hutchinson
	LB Charlie Williams
	DB Warren Gaffney
	DB Alvin Parrish / Chuck Hatch
	DB Tim Aydt
	DB Alvin Cowans / Steve Blair

RUSHING: Wilder 101/654y, Green 90/567y, Morgan 69/291y
PASSING: Fisher 83-146/1511y, 10TD, 56.8%
RECEIVING: Chandler 44/967y, Gaffney 16/279y, Stephens 15/198y
SCORING: David Posey (K) 64pts, Chandler & Wilder 60pts

1977 6-4-1

48 Rice	3 WR Wes Chandler / C. Collinsworth (QB)
24 Mississippi St.	22 T David Forrester
14 LSU	36 G Don Swafford / Bill Bennek
17 Pittsburgh	17 C Mark Totten
27 Tennessee	17 G Gary Lenard (T) / Mark Midden
14 Auburn	29 T Dennis Forrester
22 Georgia	17 TE Tony Stephens / Lewis Gilbert
7 Kentucky	14 QB Terry LeCount / John Brantley
38 Utah	29 HB Tony Green / David Johnson
31 Miami	14 HB Willie Wilder
9 Florida State	37 FB Earl Carr / Joe Portale
	DL Michael Dupree / Robert Adkins
	DL Melvin Flournoy / Dock Luckie
	DL Scott Hutchinson
	DL Sylvester King
	DL Richard Ruth / Jeff Kanter
	LB Scot Brantley / Bubba Pratt
	LB Charlie Williams / David Little
	DB Skipper Peek
	DB David Wright / Tim Aydt
	DB Chuck Hatch
	DB Vernon James / Derrick Burdgess

RUSHING: Green 119/696y, LeCount 130/628y, Wilder 87/495y
PASSING: LeCount 62-134/848y, 6TD, 46.2%
RECEIVING: Chandler 25/490y, Gaffney 14/319y, Stephens 12/187y
SCORING: Chandler 72pts, Berj Yepremian (K) 64pts, Wilder 24pts

1978 4-7

25 SMU	35 WR Tony Stephens / Johnny Gaffney
34 Mississippi St.	0 WR Cris Collinsworth
21 LSU	34 T Bill Bennek
12 Alabama	23 G Jim Subers / Jay Johnson
31 Army	7 C Doug Schroeder
13 Georgia Tech	17 G Harold Galloway / Mark Midden
31 Auburn	7 T Don Swafford
22 Georgia	24 TE Bill Bell / Ron Enclade
18 Auburn	16 QB John Brantley
21 Florida State	38 HB Terry Williams / Tony Waters
21 Miami	22 FB David Johnson / Calvin Davis
	DL David Galloway / Bubba Pratt
	DL Robin Fisher / Dozyier Hinton
	DL Dock Luckie / Wally Hough
	DL Mike DuPree
	LB David Little / Tim Golden
	LB Scot Brantley
	LB Yancey Sutton
	DB Bill Florillo / Kyle Coburn
	DB Warren Gaffney
	DB Juan Collins
	DB Chuck Hatch / Derrick Burdgess

RUSHING: Davis 126/497y, Williams 93/364y, Johnson 52/220y
PASSING: Brantley 85-170/1334y, 11TD, 50.0%
RECEIVING: Collinsworth 39/745y, Stephens 27/490y, Enclade 22/368y
SCORING: Berj Yepremian (K) 73pts, Collinsworth 62pts, Stephens & Johnson 24pts

1979 0-10-1

10 Houston	14 WR Darrell Jones / Spencer Jackson
7 Georgia Tech	7 WR Cris Collinsworth / Johnny Gaffney
10 Mississippi St.	24 T Bill Bennek / Vince Jones
3 LSU	20 G Jim Subers / Dan Plonk
0 Alabama	40 C Wally Hough /Phil Pharr/Ray Lawrence
10 Tulsa	20 G Harold Galloway
13 Auburn	19 T Joe Wickline
10 Georgia	33 TE James Jones / Chris Faulkner /Bill Bell
3 Kentucky	31 QB Larry Ochab /Ty Young /Tim Groves
16 Florida State	27 HB Johnell Brown / Gordon Pleasants
24 Miami	30 FB Terry Williams / John Whittaker
	DL Tim Golden
	DL David Galloway / Vince Jones
	DL Robin Fisher
	DL Dozyier Hinton / Dan Fike
	DL Bubba Pratt / Yancey Sutton
	LB David Little
	LB Scot Brantley / Jim Kreis
	DB Bill Florillo
	DB Derrick Burdgess / Kyle Coburn
	DB Juan Collins
	DB Chuck Hatch / Vernon James

RUSHING: Brown 104/306y, T. Williams 59/254y, Derald Williams (HB) 34/166y
PASSING: Ochab 98-185/1169y, 6TD, 52.9%
RECEIVING: Collinsworth 41/593y, Faulkner 22/246y
SCORING: Brian Clark (K) 40pts, Faulkner 24pts, Collinsworth 12pts

1980 8-4

41 California	13 WR Spencer Jackson / Tyrone Young
45 Georgia Tech	12 WR Cris Collinsworth
21 Mississippi St.	15 T Dan Fike
7 LSU	24 G Dan Plonk
15 Mississippi	3 C Doug Smith / John Redmond
13 Louisville	0 G Jim Subers
21 Auburn	10 T Joe Wickline
21 Georgia	26 TE Chris Faulkner
17 Kentucky	15 QB Wayne Peace / Bob Hewko
7 Miami	30 RB Johnell Brown / Doug Kellom
13 Florida State	17 FB James Jones / Terry Williams
35 Maryland■	20 DL Tim Golden / Rod Brooks
	DL David Galloway / Mike Clark
	DL Robin Fisher
	DL Dock Luckie / Ron Coleman
	DL Val Brown / Yancey Sutton
	LB Fernando Jackson
	LB David Little / Tom Weigman
	DB Vito McKeever / Sonny Gilliam
	DB Ivory Curry / Bruce Vaughan
	DB Tim Groves / Tony Lilly
	DB Kyle Knight

RUSHING: Jones 150/657y, Kellom 90/339y, Brown 39/153y
PASSING: Peace 91-180/1271y, 5TD, 50.6%, Hewko 47-83/529y, 5TD, 56.6%
RECEIVING: Collinsworth 40/599y, Young 24/468y, Faulkner 24/259y
SCORING: Brian Clark (K) 69pts, Jones 24pts, Young 20pts

1981 7-5

20 Miami	21 WR Tyrone Young / Broughton Lang
35 Furman	7 WR Dwayne Dixon / Spencer Jackson
27 Georgia Tech	6 T Dan Fike / Lomas Brown
7 Mississippi St.	28 G Ryan Fraser / Dan Plonk (T)
24 LSU	10 C John Redmond / Phil Bromley
15 Maryland	10 G Buddy Schultheis
49 Mississippi	3 T Russell Gallon
12 Auburn	14 TE Mike Mularkey / Chris Faulkner
21 Georgia	26 QB Wayne Peace / Bob Hewko
33 Kentucky	12 RB Johnell Brown / Calvin Davis
35 Florida State	3 FB James Jones / Lorenzo Hampton
6 West Virginia■	26 DL David Galloway
	DL Robin Fisher
	DL Roy Harris / John Whittaker
	LB Val Brown / Alonzo Johnson
	LB Fernando Jackson
	LB Tom Wiegmann
	LB Wilber Marshall
	DB Bruce Vaughan / Vito McKeever
	DB Ivory Curry
	DB Tony Lilly
	DB Kyle Knight / Sonny Gilliam

RUSHING: Jones 166/617y, Brown 56/249y, Hampton 43/171y
PASSING: Peace 159-273/1803y, 11TD, 58.2%
RECEIVING: Jackson 39/449y, Lang 29/426y, Dixon 28/315y
SCORING: Brian Clark (K) 82pts, Jones 56pts, Jackson 30pts

1982 8-4

17 Miami	14 WR Tyrone Young / Bee Lang
17 Southern Cal	9 WR Dwayne Dixon / Spencer Jackson
27 Mississippi St.	17 T Dan Fike
13 LSU	24 G John Hunt / Dwayne Hinson
29 Vanderbilt	31 C Phil Bromley
77 West Texas St.	14 G Buddy Schultheis
19 Auburn	17 T Lomas Brown / Russell Gallon
0 Georgia	44 TE Chris Faulkner / Mike Mularkey
39 Kentucky	13 QB Wayne Peace
21 Tulane	14 RB Neal Anderson / Lorenzo Hampton
13 Florida State	10 FB James Jones / John L. Williams
24 Arkansas■	28 DL John Whittaker
	DL Tim Newton
	DL Roy Harris
	LB Val Brown / Patrick Miller
	LB Fernando Jackson
	LB Tom Wiegmann / Fred McCallister
	LB Wilber Marshall
	DB Bruce Vaughan / Vito McKeever
	DB Ivory Curry/Ri'ky Easmon/Vernell Brown
	DB Tony Lilly / Roger Sibbald
	DB Randy Clark / Sonny Gilliam

RUSHING: Jones 150/752y, Hampton 128/664y, Anderson 82/449y
PASSING: Peace 174-246/2053y, 8TD, 70.7%
RECEIVING: Dixon 45/589y, Mularkey 29/356y, Jones 25/206y
SCORING: Jim Gainey (K) 60pts, Jones 54pts, Anderson & Hampton 36pts

1983 9-2-1

28 Miami	3 WR Gary Rolle
19 Southern Cal	19 WR Dwayne Dixon
17 Indiana State	13 T Lomas Brown
35 Mississippi St.	12 G Jeff Zimmerman / John Hunt
31 LSU	17 C Phil Bromley
29 Vanderbilt	10 G Buddy Schultheis / Dwayne Hinson
24 East Carolina	17 T Crawford Ker / Scott Trimble
21 Auburn	28 TE Tom Peddie / Walter Odom
9 Georgia	10 QB Wayne Peace
24 Kentucky	7 TB Neal Anderson / Lorenzo Hampton
53 Florida State	14 FB John L. Williams / Joe Henderson
14 Iowa■	6 DL Greg Cleveland / Alton Jones
	DL Tim Newton
	DL Roy Harris
	LB Alonzo Johnson / Patrick Miller
	LB Leon Pennington / Mark Korff
	LB Fred McCallister
	LB Wilber Marshall / Dean Drew
	DB Bruce Vaughan / Vito McKeever
	DB Vernell Brown / Ricky Easmon
	DB Tony Lilly / Roger Sibbald
	DB Randy Clark

RUSHING: Anderson 162/835y, Williams
PASSING: Peace 186-292/2079y, 10TD, 63.7%
RECEIVING: Dixon 47/596y, Lang 24/326y, Nattiel 22/307y, Hampton 22/238y
SCORING: Bobby Raymond (K) 89pts, Anderson 54pts, Williams 42pts

1984 9-1-1

20 Miami	32 WR Ray McDonald / Ricky Nattiel
21 LSU	21 WR Frankie Neal / Gary Rolle
63 Tulane	21 T Crawford Ker / Jack Gerzina
27 Mississippi St.	12 G Jeff Zimmerman
16 Syracuse	0 C Phil Bromley
43 Tennessee	30 G Dewayne Hinson / Jimmy Davis
48 Cincinnati	17 T Lomas Brown
24 Auburn	3 TE Walter Odom
27 Georgia	0 QB Kerwin Bell
25 Kentucky	17 TB Lorenzo Hampton
27 Florida State	17 FB Neal Anderson (TB) / John L. Williams
	DL Alonzo Mitz / Tommy Duhart
	DL Tim Newton
	DL Keith Williams / Sam Garland
	LB Alonzo Johnson
	LB Ron Moten / Leon Pennington
	LB Mark Korff / Scott Armstrong
	LB Patrick Miller
	DB Ricky Easmon / Curtis Stacey
	DB Jarvis Williams
	DB Roger Sibbald
	DB Vernell Brown / Adrian White

RUSHING: Anderson 157/916y, Williams 145/793y, Hampton 132/693y
PASSING: Bell 98-184/1514y, 16TD, 53.3%
RECEIVING: Williams 21/276y, Nattiel 20/447y, Neal 13/298y
SCORING: Bobby Raymond (K) 103pts, Anderson 48pts, Hampton 42pts

1985 9-1-1

35 Miami	23 WR Ray McDonald
28 Rutgers	28 WR Ricky Nattiel
36 Mississippi St.	22 T David Williams / Jack Gerzina
20 LSU	0 G Jeff Zimmerman
17 Tennessee	10 C Frank McCarthy
45 SW Louisiana	0 G Jimmy Davis / Kevin Sills
35 Virginia Tech	18 T Greg Cleveland / Earl Hiott
14 Auburn	10 TE Walter Odom / Rodney Jones
3 Georgia	24 QB Kerwin Bell
15 Kentucky	13 TB Neal Anderson
38 Florida State	14 FB John L. Williams
	DL Alonzo Mitz / Sam Garland
	DL Henry Brown / Jeff Roth
	DL Keith Williams
	LB Alonzo Johnson / Ron Moten
	LB Leon Pennington
	LB Arthur White / Scott Armstrong
	LB Patrick Miller
	DB Curtis Stacy / Ricky Mulberry
	DB Jarvis Williams
	DB Vernell Brown / Adrian White
	DB Ricky Knight

RUSHING: Anderson 238/1034y, J.L. Williams 160/659y, Wayne Williams (TB) 17/36y
PASSING: Bell 180-288/2687y, 21TD, 62.5%
RECEIVING: J.L. Williams 44/369y, Nattiel 31/653y, Anderson 25/349y
SCORING: Jeff Dawson (K) 78pts, Anderson 56pts, J.L. Williams 32pts

1986 6-5

38 Ga. Southern	14 WR Eric Hodges / Stacy Simmons
15 Miami	23 WR Ricky Nattiel / Tony Lomack
7 Alabama	21 T David Williams / John Durden
10 Mississippi St.	16 G Bob Sims
17 LSU	28 C Frank McCarthy
52 Kent State	9 G Jimmy Davis (T) / Charlie Wright
15 Rutgers	3 T Jeff Zimmerman
18 Auburn	17 TE Mark McGriff / Rodney Jones
31 Georgia	19 QB Kerwin Bell / Rodney Brewer
3 Kentucky	10 TB Octavius Gould / Wayne Williams
17 Florida State	13 FB Anthony Williams
	DL Keith Williams
	DL Jeff Roth
	DL Rhondy Weston
	LB Ron Moten / Steve Stipe
	LB Scott Armstrong
	LB Arthur White / Pat Moorer
	LB Clifford Charlton
	DB Ricky Mulberry / Richard Fain
	DB Jarvis Williams / Kerry Watkins
	DB Louis Oliver
	DB Adrian White

RUSHING: Gould 156/562y, W. Williams 79/340y
PASSING: Bell 131-242/1515y, 10TD, 54.1%
RECEIVING: Nattiel 44/679y, A. Williams 22/157y, Gould 21/235y
SCORING: Jeff Dawson (K) 61pts, Nattiel 54pts, Gould 24pts

1987 6-6

4 Miami	31 WR Stacy Simmons
52 Tulsa	0 WR Tony Lomack / Ernie Mills
23 Alabama	14 T David Williams
38 Mississippi St.	3 G Bob Sims
10 LSU	13 C Tracy Daniels / Chris Bromley
65 Cal-Fullerton	0 G Richard Starowesky / Charlie Wright
34 Temple	3 T Jimmy Davis
6 Auburn	29 TE Walter Odom / Mark McGriff
10 Georgia	23 QB Kerwin Bell
27 Kentucky	14 TB Emmitt Smith / Wayne Williams
14 Florida State	28 FB Anthony Williams / Cedric Smith
16 UCLA■	20 DL Henry Brown
	DL Jeff Roth
	DL Rhondy Weston / Glenn Neely
	LB Jason Lamberth / Huey Richardson
	LB Pat Moorer / Todd Gatlin
	LB Joe Nicoletto / Gerry Odom
	LB Clifford Charlton / Mark Murray
	DB Ricky Mulberry / Richard Fain
	DB Tony Jones / Kerry Watkins
	DB Louis Oliver
	DB Jarvis Williams

RUSHING: E. Smith 229/1341y, A. Williams 68/280y
PASSING: Bell 140-239/1769y, 9TD, 58.6%
RECEIVING: Simmons 25/392y, E. Smith 25/184y
SCORING: E. Smith 78pts, Robert McGinty (K) 72pts, Simmons 30pts

1988 7-5

69 Montana State	0 WR Stacy Simmons / Terence Barber
27 Mississippi	15 WR Tony Lomack / Ernie Mills
58 Indiana State	0 T David Williams
17 Mississippi St.	0 G Richard Starowesky
19 LSU	6 C Tracy Daniels / Cal Dixon
11 Memphis State	17 G Phil Bromley (C) / Hesham Ismail
9 Vanderbilt	24 T John Durden / Brad Hatcher
0 Auburn	16 TE Mark McGriff / Kirk Kirkpatrick
3 Georgia	26 QB Kyle Morris / Herbert Perry
24 Kentucky	19 TB Emmitt Smith / Willie McClendon
17 Florida State	52 FB Cedric Smith / William McGrady
14 Illinois■	10 DL Trace Armstrong
	DL Jeff Roth / Brad Culpepper
	DL Rhody Weston / Tony McCoy
	LB Huey Richardson
	LB Pat Moorer
	LB Jerry Odom / Joe Nicoletto
	LB Owen Bartruff / Ephesians Bartley
	DB Richard Fain / Tony Jones
	DB Kerry Watkins
	DB Louis Oliver / Bill Lang
	DB Adrian White

RUSHING: E. Smith 187/998y, McClendon 86/319y
PASSING: Morris 84-167/1217y, 3TD, 50.3%, Perry 50-103/488y, 0TD, 48.5%
RECEIVING: Lomack 22/276y, McGriff 20/253y
SCORING: John Francis (K) 77pts, E. Smith 54pts, McClendon 24pts

1989 7-5

19 Mississippi	24 WR Stacy Simmons / Terence Barber
34 Louisiana Tech	7 WR Ernie Mills / Tony Lomack
38 Memphis State	13 T John Durden
21 Mississippi St.	0 G Richard Starowesky
16 LSU	13 C Cal Dixon
34 Vanderbilt	11 G Chris Bromley
27 New Mexico	21 T Brad Hatcher
7 Auburn	10 TE Kirk Kirpatrick
10 Georgia	17 QB Kyle Morris / Donald Douglas
38 Kentucky	28 TB Emmitt Smith / Willie McClendon
17 Florida State	24 FB Cedric Smith / Dexter McNabb
7 Washington■	34 DL Tony McCoy
	DL Brad Culpepper / Mike Brandon
	DL Mark Murray / Glenn Neely
	LB Huey Richardson
	LB Pat Moorer
	LB Jerry Odom
	LB Tim Paulk / Monty Grow
	DB Richard Fain
	DB Kerry Watkins / Jimmy Spencer
	DB Will White
	DB Godfrey Myles / Ephesians Bartley

RUSHING: E. Smith 284/1599y, McClendon 97/510y, Douglas 53/226y
PASSING: Morris 65-131/1098y, 9TD, 49.6%
RECEIVING: Lomack 21/207y, Mills 19/404y, Kirkpatrick 18/245y
SCORING: E. Smith 90pts, John Francis (K) 44pts, Arden Czyzewski (K) 30pts

1990 9-2

50 Oklahoma State	7 WR Terence Barber / Tre Everett
17 Alabama	13 WR Ernie Mills / Harrison Houston
27 Furman	3 T Mark White
34 Mississippi St.	21 G Hesham Ismail
34 LSU	8 C Cal Dixon
3 Tennessee	45 G Chris Bromley / Jim Watson
59 Akron	0 T Tony Rowell
48 Auburn	7 TE Kirk Kirkpatrick / Greg Keller
38 Georgia	9 QB Shane Matthews
47 Kentucky	15 RB Errict Rhett / Willie McClendon
30 Florida State	45 FB Dexter McNabb
	DL Mike Brandon / Mark Murray
	DL Brad Culpepper / William Gaines
	DL Huey Richardson / Darren Mickell
	LB Tim Paulk
	LB Carlton Miles / Ed Robinson
	LB Jerry Odom
	LB Ephesians Bartley
	DB Richard Fain
	DB Jimmy Spencer / Del Speer
	DB Will White
	DB Godfrey Myles (LB) / Monty Grow

RUSHING: Rhett 148/845y, McClendon 127/631y
PASSING: Matthews 229-378/2952y, 23TD, 60.6%
RECEIVING: Kirkpatrick 55/770y, Mills 41/770y, Barber 35/431y
SCORING: Arden Czyzewski (K) 87pts, Mills 60pts, McClendon 48pts

1991 10-2

59 San Jose State	21 WR Harrison Houston / Tre Everett
35 Alabama	0 WR Alonzo Sullivan / Willie Jackson
21 Syracuse	38 T Mark White
29 Mississippi St.	7 G Hesham Ismail
16 LSU	0 C Cal Dixon
41 N. Illinois	18 G Jim Watson
31 Auburn	10 TE Terrell Jackson / Charlie Dean
35 Georgia	13 QB Shane Matthews
35 Kentucky	26 RB Errict Rhett / Willie McClendon
14 Florida State	9 FB Dexter McNabb
28 Notre Dame■	39 DL Harvey Thomas
	DL Brad Culpepper
	DL Tony McCoy / William Gaines
	DL Darren Mickell / Kevin Carter
	LB Tim Paulk / Ed Robinson
	LB Carlton Miles
	DB Larry Kennedy
	DB Del Speer / Lawrence Hatch
	DB Myrick Anderson / Marquette Oliver
	DB Will White
	DB Ephesians Bartley

RUSHING: Rhett 224/1109y, McNabb 49/257y, McClendon 48/213y
PASSING: Matthews 218-361/3130y, 28 TDs, 60.4%
RECEIVING: Jackson 51/725y, Rhett 40/361y, Houston 33/618y
SCORING: Arden Czyzewski (K) 77pts, Jackson & Rhett 60pts

1992 9-4

35 Kentucky	19 WR Houston Harrison / Jack Jackson
14 Tennessee	31 WR Willie Jackson / Tre Everett
6 Mississippi St.	30 T Jason Odom
28 LSU	21 G Dean Golden
24 Auburn	9 C Gantt Crouch
31 Louisville	17 G Jim Watson
26 Georgia	24 T Reggie Green / Ryan Taylor
24 Southern Miss	20 TE Greg Keller
5 South Carolina	9 QB Shane Matthews
41 Vanderbilt	21 RB Errict Rhett
24 Florida State	45 FB Kelvin Randolph
27 N. Carolina St.■	10 DL Johnnie Church / Harvey Thomas
	DL Henry McMillian / Ellis Johnson
	DL Bill Gunter / Mark Campbell
	DL Kevin Carter / Darren Mickell
	LB Ed Robinson / Ben Hanks
	LB Carlton Miles
	DB Larry Kennedy
	DB Del Speer
	DB Myrick Anderson
	DB Will White
	DB Monty Grow

RUSHING: Rhett 250/903y
PASSING: Matthews 275-463/3205y, 28TD, 59.4%
RECEIVING: Jackson 62/772y
SCORING: N/A

1993 11-2

44 Arkansas State	6 WR Harrison Houston / Chris Doering
24 Kentucky	20 WR Willie Jackson / Jack Jackson
41 Tennessee	34 T Jason Odom
38 Mississippi St.	24 G Dean Golden
58 LSU	3 C Gantt Crouch / David Swain
35 Auburn	38 G Jim Watson / Jeff Mitchell
33 Georgia	26 T Reggie Green
61 SW Louisiana	14 TE Charlie Dean / Shawn Nunn
37 South Carolina	26 QB Terry Dean / Danny Wuerffel
52 Vanderbilt	0 RB Errict Rhett
21 Florida State	33 FB Kelvin Randolph / Chris Bilkie
28 Alabama ☐	13 DL Mark Campbell
41 West Virginia	7 DL Ellis Johnson / Henry McMillian
	DL William Gaines / David Bernard
	DL Kevin Carter
	LB Dexter Daniels / James Bates
	LB Ed Robinson
	LB Ben Hanks
	DB Larry Kennedy
	DB Anthone Lott / Shea Showers
	DB Michael Gilmore / Lawrence Wright
	DB Monty Grow

RUSHING: Rhett 247/1289y
PASSING: Wuerffel 159-273/2230y, 22TD, 52.8%
RECEIVING: Jackson 51/949y
SCORING: N/A

1994 10-2-1

70 New Mexico St.	21 WR Jack Jackson / Reidel Anthony
73 Kentucky	7 WR Aubry Hill / Chris Doering / Ike Hilliard
31 Tennessee	0 T Jason Odom
38 Mississippi	14 G Donnie Young
42 LSU	18 C David Swain / Kevin Johnson
33 Auburn	36 G Jeff Mitchell / Reggie Green
52 Georgia	14 T Anthony Ingrassia
55 Southern Miss.	17 TE Shawn Nunn / Tremayne Allen
48 South Carolina	17 QB Danny Wuerffel / Terry Dean
24 Vanderbilt	7 RB Elijah Williams / Fred Taylor
31 Florida State	31 FB Chris Bilkie / Dwayne Mobley
24 Alabama ☐	23 DL Mark Campbell / Johnnie Church
17 Florida State■	23 DL Ellis Johnson / Keith Council
	DL Henry McMillian / David Bernard
	DL Kevin Carter
	LB Dexter Daniels / James Bates
	LB Kevin Freeman / Jason Bartley
	LB Ben Hanks
	DB Larry Kennedy / Fred Weary
	DB Anthone Lott / Shea Showers
	DB Michael Gilmore / Mike Harris
	DB Lawrence Wright

RUSHING: Taylor 171/873y, Williams 123/652y
PASSING: Wuerffel 132-212/1754y, 18TD, 62.3%,
Dean 109-180/1492y, 20TD, 60.6%
RECEIVING: Jackson 57/855y, Doering 35/496y, Hill 33/546y
SCORING: N/A

1995 12-1

45 Houston	21 WR Ike Hilliard / Jacquez Green
42 Kentucky	7 WR Chris Doering / Reidel Anthony
62 Tennessee	37 T Jason Odom
28 Mississippi	10 G Donnie Young
28 LSU	10 C Jeff Mitchell
49 Auburn	38 G Reggie Green
52 Georgia	17 T Mo Collins / Paul Browning
58 N. Illinois	20 TE Tremayne Allen / Shawn Nunn
63 South Carolina	7 QB Danny Wuerffel / Eric Kresser
38 Vanderbilt	7 RB Elijah Williams/Fred Taylor/T.Jackson
35 Florida State	24 FB Dwayne Mobley / Jerome Evans
34 Arkansas ☐	3 DL Mark Campbell / Tim Beauchamp
24 Nebraska■	62 DL Ed Chester / Keith Council
	DL David Bernard / Mike Moten
	DL Johnnie Church / Willie Cohens
	LB Dexter Daniels / Mike Peterson
	LB James Bates
	LB Ben Hanks / Johnny Rutledge
	DB Anthone Lott
	DB Fred Weary
	DB Teako Brown / Mike Harris
	DB Lawrence Wright / Demetric Jackson

RUSHING: Williams 114/858y, Jackson 122/780y, Tayor 48/281y
PASSING: Wuerffel 210-325/3266y, 35TD, 64.6%,
Kresser 65-112/992y, 12TD, 58.0%
RECEIVING: Doering 70/1045y, Hilliard 57/1008y,
Anthony 24/366y
SCORING: N/A

1996 12-1

55 SW Louisiana	21 WR Reidel Anthony / Jamie Richardson
62 Ga. Southern	14 WR Ike Hilliard / Jacquez Green
35 Tennessee	29 T Mo Collins
65 Kentucky	0 G Donnie Young
42 Arkansas	7 C Jeff Mitchell / Corey Yarbrough
56 LSU	13 G Ryan Kalich
51 Auburn	10 T Zach Piller / Cooper Carlisle
47 Georgia	7 TE Tremayne Allen / Erron Kinney
28 Vanderbilt	21 QB Danny Wuerffel
52 South Carolina	25 TB Fred Taylor / Elijah Williams
21 Florida State	24 FB Dwayne Mobley
45 Alabama ☐	30 DL Tim Beauchamp / Anthony Mitchell
52 Florida State■	20 DL Reggie McGrew / Keith Council
	DL Ed Chester
	DL Cameron Davis / Willie Cohens
	LB Johnny Rutledge / Dwayne Thomas
	LB James Bates / Keith Kelsey
	LB Mike Peterson / Jevon Kearse
	DB Fred Weary
	DB Anthone Lott / Elijah Williams
	DB Shea Showers / Mike Harris
	DB Lawrence Wright / Tony George

RUSHING: Williams 106/671y, Taylor 104/629y,
Terry Jackson (TB) 79/388y
PASSING: Wuerffel 207-360/3625y, 39TD, 57.5%
RECEIVING: Anthony 72/1293y, Hilliard 47/900y, Green 33/626y
SCORING: Anthony 108pts, Bart Edmiston (K) 91pts, Green 72pts

1997 10-2

21 Southern Miss	6 WR Jamie Richardson / Travis McGriff
82 C. Michigan	6 WR Jacquez Green / Travis Taylor
33 Tennessee	20 T Mo Collins
55 Kentucky	28 G Cheston Blackshear
56 Arkansas	7 C Wyley Ritch
21 LSU	28 G Ryan Kalich
24 Auburn	10 T Zach Piller
17 Georgia	37 TE Taras Ross / Erron Kinney
20 Vanderbilt	7 QB Doug Johnson / Jesse Palmer
48 South Carolina	21 TB Fred Taylor / Bo Carroll
32 Florida State	29 FB Rod Frazier / Eugene McCaslin
21 Penn State■	6 DL Tim Beauchamp
	DL Reggie McGrew / Mike Moten
	DL Ed Chester
	DL Willie Rodgers / Willie Cohens
	LB Johnny Rutledge
	LB Dwayne Thomas / Keith Kelsey
	LB Mike Peterson / Jevon Kearse
	DB Fred Weary
	DB Elijah Williams
	DB Teako Brown / Rod Graddy
	DB Tony George

RUSHING: Taylor 214/1292y, Carroll 42/317y, McCaslin 24/93y
PASSING: Johnson 148-269/2023y, 21TD, 55.0%
RECEIVING: Green 61/1024y, Richardson 27/408y,
McGriff 24/363y, Taylor 24/238y
SCORING: Green 84pts, Taylor 78pts, Collins Cooper (K) 74pts

1998 10-2

49 Citadel	10 WR Travis McGriff / Travis Taylor
42 NE Louisiana	10 WR Bo Carroll / Nafis Karim
17 Tennessee	20 T Cooper Carlisle
51 Kentucky	35 G Ryan Kalich
16 Alabama	10 C Zac Zedalis
22 LSU	10 G Cheston Blackshear
24 Auburn	3 T Kenyatta Walker
38 Georgia	7 TE Erron Kinney
45 Vanderbilt	13 QB Jesse Palmer / Doug Johnson
33 South Carolina	14 TB Terry Jackson / Eugene McCaslin
12 Florida State	23 FB Rod Frazier / Rob Roberts
31 Syracuse■	10 DL Tim Beauchamp / Derrick Chambers
	DL Reggie McGrew / Gerald Warren
	DL Ed Chester
	DL Willie Cohens
	LB Jevon Kearse
	LB Johnny Rutledge / Keith Kelsey
	LB Mike Peterson / Alex Brown
	DB Tony George
	DB Bennie Alexander / Robert Cromartie
	DB Teako Brown
	DB Rod Graddy

RUSHING: Jackson 105/587y, McCaslin 69/321y,
Robert Gillespie (TB) 71/310y
PASSING: Johnson 154-274/2346y, 19TD, 56.2%
Palmer 73-123/1246y, 14TD, 59.3%
RECEIVING: McGriff 70/1357y, Taylor 37/676y, Karim 34/552y
SCORING: Jeff Chandler (K) & McGriff 66pts, Taylor 54pts

1999 9-4

55 W. Michigan	26 WR Travis Taylor / Jabar Gaffney
58 C. Florida	27 WR Darrell Jackson / Taylor Jacobs
23 Tennessee	21 T Mike Pearson / Cooper Carlisle
38 Kentucky	10 G Ryan Kalich
31 LSU	40 C Zac Zeladis / David Jorgensen
32 Auburn	10 G Cheston Blackshear
30 Georgia	14 T Kenyatta Walker
13 Vanderbilt	14 TE Erron Kinney / Aaron Walker
20 South Carolina	6 QB Doug Johnson
23 Florida State	3 TB Earnest Graham / Robert Gillespie
7 Alabama ☐	30 FB Rob Roberts / Rod Frazier
34 Michigan State■	34 DL Tron LaFavor / Thaddeus Bullard
	37 DL Gerald Warren
	DL Buck Gurley
	DL Alex Brown/Marcus Oquendo-Johns'n
	LB Keith Kelsey / Mike Nattiel
	LB Andra Davis
	LB Eugene McCaslin
	DB Robert Cromartie
	DB Bennie Alexander / Lito Sheppard
	DB Daryl Dixon / Lester Norwood
	DB Marquand Manuel

RUSHING: Graham 117/654y, Bo Carroll (TB) 86/577y
PASSING: Johnson 190-337/2574y, 20TD, 56.4%
RECEIVING: Jackson 67/1156y,
SCORING: Jeff Chandler (K) 101pts,

2000 10-3

40 Ball State	19 WR Jabar Gaffney / Carlos Perez
55 Middle Tenn.	0 WR Reche Caldwell / Taylor Jacobs
27 Tennessee	23 T Mike Pearson
59 Kentucky	31 G Thomas Moody / Erik Strange
35 Mississippi St.	47 C David Jorgensen
41 LSU	9 G Leon Hires (T) / David Kearley
38 Auburn	7 T Kenyatta Walker / Max Starks
34 Georgia	23 TE Aaron Walker / Kirk Wells
43 Vanderbilt	20 QB Rex Grossman / Jesse Palmer
41 South Carolina	21 TB Robert Gillespie / Earnest Graham
7 Florida State	30 FB Rod Frazier / Rob Roberts
28 Auburn ☐	6 DL Clint Mitchell / Kinnard Ellis
20 Miami■	37 DL Gerald Warren
	DL Buck Gurley / Derrick Chambers
	DL Alex Brown
	LB Mike Nattiel / Daryl Owens
	LB Travis Carroll / Matt Farrior
	LB Byron Hardmon/Marc's Oq'do-J'hns'n
	DB Robert Cromartie / Bennie Alexander
	DB Lito Sheppard
	DB Todd Johnson / Lester Norwood
	DB Marquand Manuel

RUSHING: Gillespie 125/678y, Graham 121/676y,
Bo Carroll (TB) 14/66y
PASSING: Grossman 131-212/1866y, 21TD, 61.8%,
Palmer 116-223/1653y, 11TD, 52.0%
RECEIVING: Gaffney 71/1184y, Caldwell 49/760y,
Gillespie 26/218y
SCORING: Jeff Chandler (K) 97pts, Gaffney 84pts,
Graham 48pts

2001 10-2

49 Marshall	14 WR Jabar Gaffney / Taylor Jacobs
55 La.-Monroe	6 WR Reche Caldwell
44 Kentucky	10 WR Carlos Perez
52 Mississippi St.	0 T Mike Pearson
44 LSU	15 G Shannon Snell
20 Auburn	23 C Zac Zedelis / David Jorgensen
24 Georgia	10 G Thomas Moody / Jonathan Colon
71 Vanderbilt	13 T Max Starks
54 South Carolina	17 TE Aaron Walker / Ben Troupe
37 Florida State	13 QB Rex Grossman / Brock Berlin
32 Tennessee	34 TB Earnest Graham / Robert Gillespie
56 Maryland■	23 DL Kennard Ellis / Darrell Lee
	DL Tron LaFavor / Bryan Savelio
	DL Ian Scott
	DL Alex Brown / Bobby McCray
	LB Byron Hardmon
	LB Andra Davis / Travis Carroll
	LB Mike Nattiel / Matt Farrior
	DB Bennie Alexander
	DB Lito Sheppard
	DB Todd Johnson / Lester Norwood
	DB Marquand Manuel / Guss Scott

RUSHING: Graham 125/650y, Gillespie 94/395y,
Ran Carthon (TB) 36/162y
PASSING: Grossman 259-395/3896y, 34TD, 65.6%
RECEIVING: Gaffney 67/1191y, Caldwell 65/1059y,
Gillespie 41/445y
SCORING: Jeff Chandler (K) 103pts, Gaffney 78pts,
Graham 54pts

2002 8-5

51 Ala.-Birm'ham	3 WR Carlos Perez
16 Miami	41 WR Taylor Jacobs
34 Ohio	0 WR Kelvin Kight / Ray Snell (FB)
30 Tennessee	13 T Max Starks
41 Kentucky	34 G Shannon Snell
14 Mississippi	17 C Mike Degory
7 LSU	36 G Jonathan Colon
30 Auburn	23 T Mo Mitchell
20 Georgia	13 TE Ben Troupe / Aaron Walker
21 Vanderbilt	17 QB Rex Grossman
28 South Carolina	7 TB Earnest Graham / Ran Carthon
14 Florida State	31 DL Darrell Lee / Clint Mitchell
30 Michigan■	38 DL Tron LaFavor / Kenny Parker
	DL Ian Scott
	DL Bobby McCray / M. Oquendo-Johnson
	LB Mike Nattiel
	LB Matt Farrior / Reid Fleming
	LB Bam Hardmon / Todd McCullough
	DB Robert Cromartie
	DB Keiwan Ratliff
	DB Todd Johnson
	DB Guss Scott / Cory Bailey

RUSHING: Graham 240/1085y, Carthon 105/563y
PASSING: Grossman 287-503/3402y, 22TD, 57.1%
RECEIVING: Jacobs 71/1088y, Perez 58/591y, Kight 37/511y
SCORING: Graham 66pts, Matt Leach (K) 57pts, Jacobs 50pts

2003 8-5

65 San Jose State	3 WR Carlos Perez / O.J. Small
33 Miami	38 WR Kelvin Kight / Dallas Baker
65 Florida A&M	3 T Max Starks
10 Tennessee	24 G Shannon Snell
24 Kentucky	21 C Mike Degory
17 Mississippi	20 G Lance Butler
19 LSU	7 T Randy Hand
33 Arkansas	28 TE Ben Troupe
16 Georgia	13 QB Chris Leak / Ingle Martin
35 Vanderbilt	17 TB Ran Carthon / Ciatrick Fason
24 South Carolina	22 FB Billy Latsko
34 Florida State	38 DL Darrell Lee
17 Iowa■	37 DL Kenny Parker / Mo Mitchell
	DL Ray McDonald / Marcus Thomas
	DL Bobby McCray / Travis Harris
	LB Matt Farrior
	LB Reid Fleming
	LB Channing Crowder / Earl Everett
	DB Johnny Lamar
	DB Keiwan Ratliff
	DB Daryl Dixon / Jarvis Herring
	DB Guss Scott / Cory Bailey

RUSHING: Carthon 119/595y, Fason 84/583y,
DeShawn Wynn (TB) 115/540y
PASSING: Leak 190-320/2435y, 16 TDs, 59.4%
RECEIVING: Troupe 39/638y, Kight 39/591y, Perez 36/541y,
Small 35/379y
SCORING: Matt Leach (K) 104pts, Wynn 48pts, Carthon 42pts

2004 7-5

49 E. Michigan	10 WR O.J. Small / Reggie Lewis
28 Tennessee	30 WR Andre Caldwell / Chad Jackson
20 Kentucky	3 T Jonathan Colon
45 Arkansas	30 G Lance Butler
21 LSU	24 C Mike Degory
52 Middle Tenn.	16 G Mo Mitchell
31 Mississippi St.	38 T Randy Hand
24 Georgia	31 WR Dallas Baker / Jemalle Cornelius
34 Vanderbilt	17 QB Chris Leak
48 South Carolina	14 TB Ciatrick Fason / DeShawn Wynn
20 Florida State	13 FB Billy Latsko
10 Miami■	27 DL Steven Harris / Joe Cohen
	DL Marcus Thomas
	DL Ray McDonald
	DL Jeremy Mincey
	LB Earl Everett / Travis Harris
	LB Channing Crowder
	LB Brandon Siler / Todd McCullough
	DB Demetrice Webb
	DB Reynaldo Hill / Vernell Brown
	DB Jarvis Herring
	DB Cory Bailey / Terrence Holmes

RUSHING: Fason 222/1267y, Wynn 58/217y,
Skyler Thornton (TB) 55/230y
PASSING: Leak 238-399/3197y, 29TD, 59.6%
RECEIVING: Small 63/719y, Caldwell 43/689y, Fason 35/266y
SCORING: Matt Leach (K) 88pts, Fason 72pts, Jackson 36pts

2005 9-3

32 Wyoming	14 WR Chad Jackson / Billy Latsko (FB)
41 Louisiana Tech	3 WR Andre Caldwell
16 Tennessee	7 WR Dallas Baker / Jemalle Cornelius
49 Kentucky	28 T Randy Hand
3 Alabama	31 G Tavares Washington
35 Mississippi St.	9 C Mike Degory
17 LSU	21 G Drew Miller / Steve Rissler / Jim Tartt
14 Georgia	10 T Lance Butler
49 Vanderbilt	42 TE Tate Casey / Phil Trautwein
22 South Carolina	30 QB Chris Leak
34 Florida State	7 RB DeShawn Wynn / Markus Manson
31 Iowa■	24 DL Joe Cohen / Bryan Royal / Jarvis Moss
	DL Marcus Thomas
	DL Steven Harris
	DL Jeremy Mincey / Derrick Harvey
	LB Earl Everett / Brian Crum
	LB Brandon Siler
	LB Todd McCullough
	DB Demetrice Webb / Reggie Lewis
	DB Vernell Brown / Avery Atkins
	DB Reggie Nelson / Kyle Jackson
	DB Jarvis Herring / Tony Joiner

RUSHING: Wynn 130/621y, Manson 81/365y,
Kestahn Moore (RB) 48/277y
PASSING: Leak 235-374/2639y, 20TD, 62.8%
RECEIVING: Jackson 88/900y, Baker 52/697y,
Cornelius 29/383y
SCORING: Chris Hetland (K) 77pts, Jackson 66pts, Wynn 54pts

2006 13-1

34 Southern Miss	7 WR Andre Caldwell
42 Central Florida	0 WR Dallas Baker
21 Tennessee	20 WR Percy Harvin / Jemalle Cornelius
26 Kentucky	7 T Phil Trautwein
28 Alabama	13 G Jim Tartt
23 LSU	10 C Steve Rissler
17 Auburn	27 G Drew Miller
21 Georgia	14 T Carlton Medder
25 Vanderbilt	19 TE Tate Casey / Cornelius Ingram
17 South Carolina	16 QB Chris Leak / Tim Tebow
62 W. Carolina	0 RB DeShawn Wynn / Kestahn Moore
21 Florida State	14 DL Derrick Harvey
38 Arkansas □	28 DL Joe Cohen / Marcus Thomas
41 Ohio State■	14 DL Ray McDonald
	DL Jarvis Moss / Jermaine Cunningham
	LB Brian Crum
	LB Brandon Siler / Brandon Spikes
	LB Earl Everett
	DB Reggie Lewis
	DB Ryan Smith / Tremaine McCollum
	DB Reggie Nelson / Kyle Jackson
	DB Tony Joiner

RUSHING: Wynn 124/600y, Tebow 79/430y, Harvin 36/406y
PASSING: Leak 207-329/2729y, 22TD, 62.9%
RECEIVING: Baker 56/897y, Caldwell 55/571y,
Cornelius 29/473y
SCORING: Baker 54pts, Chris Hetland (K) 50pts, Tebow 42pts

2007 9-4

49 W. Kentucky	3 WR Andre Caldwell
59 Troy	31 WR Percy Harvin
59 Tennessee	20 WR Louis Murphy
30 Mississippi	24 T Jason Watkins
17 Auburn	20 G Jim Tartt
24 LSU	28 C Drew Miller
45 Kentucky	37 G Maurkice Pouncey
30 Georgia	42 T Carlton Medder / Marcus Gilbert
49 Vanderbilt	22 TE Cornelius Ingram / Aaron Hernandez
51 South Carolina	31 QB Tim Tebow
59 Florida Atlantic	20 RB Kestahn Moore
45 Florida State	12 DL Derrick Harvey
35 Michigan■	41 DL Javier Estopinan / Mike Pouncey
	DL Clint McMillan / Justin Trattou
	DL Jermaine Cunningham
	LB A.J. Jones / Brandon Hicks
	LB Brandon Spikes
	LB Dustin Doe / Ryan Stamper
	DB Joe Haden / Jacques Rickerson
	DB Wondy Pierre-Louis/Markihe Anderson
	DB Major Wright / K Kyle Jackson
	DB Tony Joiner / Dorian Munroe

RUSHING: Tebow 210/895y, Harvin 104/580y
PASSING: Tebow 234-350/3286y, 32TD, 66.9%
RECEIVING: Harvin 59/858y, Caldwell 56/761y, Murphy 37/548y,
Ingram 34/508y
SCORING: Tebow 138pts, Joey Ijjas (K) 102pts, Harvin 60pts,
Caldwell 48pts

2008 13-1

56 Hawaii	10 WR Louis Murphy / Deonte Thompson
26 Miami	3 WR David Nelson / Riley Cooper
30 Tennessee	6 WR Percy Harvin (RB)/Jeff'y Demps (RB)
30 Mississippi	31 T Phil Trautwein
38 Arkansas	7 G Carl Johnson
51 LSU	21 C Maurkice Pouncey
63 Kentucky	5 G Mike Pouncey
49 Georgia	10 T Jason Watkins
42 Vanderbilt	14 TE Aaron Hernandez / Tate Casey
56 South Carolina	6 QB Tim Tebow
70 Citadel	19 RB Chris Rainey / Emmanuel Moody
45 Florida State	15 DL Justin Trattou / Carlos Dunlap
31 Alabama□	20 DL Lawrence Marsh
24 Oklahoma■	14 DL Terron Sanders / Torrey Davis
	DL Jermaine Cunningham
	LB Brandon Hicks / A.J. Jones
	LB Brandon Spikes
	LB Ryan Stamper / Dustin Doe
	DB Joe Haden
	DB Janoris Jenkins
	DB Major Wright / Will Hill
	DB Ahmad Black

RUSHING: Tebow 176/673y, Harvin 70/660y, Rainey 84/652y,
Demps 78/605y, Moody 58/417y
PASSING: Tebow 192-298/2746y, 30TD, 64.4%
RECEIVING: Harvin 40/644y, Murphy 38/655y,
Hernandez 34/381y, Thompson 18/269y, Cooper 18/261y
SCORING: Jonathan Phillips (K) 114pts, Harvin 102pts,
Tebow 72pts, Demps 48pts

2009 13-1

62 Charleston So.	3 WR Deonte Thompson / Brandon James
56 Troy	6 WR Riley Cooper
23 Tennessee	13 WR David Nelson
41 Kentucky	7 T Xavier Nelson
13 LSU	3 G Carl Johnson (T) / Maurice Hurt
23 Arkansas	20 C Maurkice Pouncey
29 Mississippi St.	19 G Mike Pouncey / James Wilson
41 Georgia	17 T Marcus Gilbert
27 Vanderbilt	3 TE Aaron Hernandez
24 South Carolina	14 QB Tim Tebow
62 Florida Intern'l	3 RB Jeff Demps / Chris Rainey
37 Florida State	10 DL Carlos Dunlap
13 Alabama□	32 DL Justin Trattou / Jaye Howard
51 Cincinnati■	24 DL Terron Sanders / Omar Hunter
	DL Jermaine Cunningham
	LB A.J. Jones / Brandon Hicks
	LB Brandon Spikes
	LB Ryan Stamper / Dustin Doe
	DB Joe Haden
	DB Janoris Jenkins / Markihe Anderson
	DB Major Wright / Will Hill
	DB Ahmad Black

RUSHING: Tebow 217/910y, Demps 99/745y, Rainey 89/575y
Emmanuel Moody (RB) 58/378y
PASSING: Tebow 213-314/2895y, 21TD, 67.8%
RECEIVING: Hernandez 68/850y, Cooper 51/961y, Nelson 25/291y
Thompson 24/343y, James 24/215y
SCORING: Caleb Sturgis (K) 110pts, Tebow 84pts, Cooper 54pts

2010 8-5

34 Miami (Ohio)	12 WR Deonte Thompson
38 South Florida	14 WR Omarius Hines / Andre Debose
31 Tennessee	17 WR Carl Moore / Frankie Hammond
48 Kentucky	14 T Marcus Gilbert
6 Alabama	31 G Carl Johnson / James Wilson
29 LSU	33 C Mike Pouncey
7 Mississippi State	10 G John Halapio / Maurice Hurt (T)
34 Georgia	31 T Xaver Nixon / Jon Harrison
55 Vanderbilt	14 TE Trey Burton(FB-WR)/Jordan Reed (QB)
14 South Carolina	36 QB John Brantley
48 Appalachian St.	10 RB Chris Rainey / Jeff Demps / E. Moody
7 Florida State	31 DL Justin Trattou
37 Penn State■	24 DL Omar Hunter / Lawrence Marsh
	DL Terron Sanders / Sharrif Floyd
	DL Jaye Howard / Brandon Antwine
	LB Duke Lemmens (DL) / Brandon Hicks
	LB A.J. Jones
	LB Jonathan Bostic / Jelani Jenkins
	DB Janoris Jenkins / Cody Riggs
	DB Jeremy Brown / Moses Jenkins
	DB Will Hill / Josh Evans
	DB Ahmad Black / Matt Elam

RUSHING: Demps 92/551y, Rainey 51/366y, Burton 75/349y
PASSING: Brantley 200-329/2061y, 9TD, 60.8%
Reed 26-46/252y, 3TD, 56.5%
RECEIVING: Thompson 38/570y, Burton 32/210y, Moore 27/349y
SCORING: Burton 72pts, Chas Henry (K) 49pts,
Mike Gillislee (RB) 42pts

FLORIDA STATE

Florida State University (Founded 1857)
Tallahassee, Florida
Nickname: Seminoles
Colors: Garnet and Gold
Stadium: Bobby Bowden Field at Doak Campbell (1950) 82,300
Conference Affiliations: Independent (1947-1991), Atlantic Coast (1992-present)

CAREER RUSHING YARDS	Attempts	Yards
Warrick Dunn (1993-96)	575	3959
Greg Allen (1981-84)	624	3769
Travis Minor (1997-2000)	664	3218
Larry Key (1974-77)	625	2953
Sammie Smith (1985-88)	411	2539
Greg Jones (2000-03)	480	2535
Lorenzo Booker (2003-06)	477	2389
Antone Smith (2005-08)	493	2255
Mark Lyles (1976-79)	515	2218
Sean Jackson (1990-93)	347	2133

CAREER PASSING YARDS	Comp.-Att.	Yards
Chris Weinke (1997-2000)	650-1107	9839
Chris Rix (2001-04)	575-1042	8390
Drew Weatherford (2005-08)	644-1128	7567
Christian Ponder (2007-10)	596-965	6872
Gary Huff (1970-72)	436-796	6378
Danny Kanell (1992-95)	529-851	6372
Thad Busby (1994-97)	421-715	5916
Charlie Ward (1989-93)	473-759	5747
Bill Cappleman (1967-69)	349-636	4904
Casey Weldon (1988-91)	323-545	4628

CAREER RECEIVING YARDS	Catches	Yards
Ron Sellers (1966-68)	212	3598
Peter Warrick (1996-99)	207	3517
E.G. Green (1994-97)	166	2920
Kez McCorvey (1991-94)	189	2660
Greg Carr (2005-08)	148	2574
Barry Smith (1970-72)	119	2392
Mike Shumann (1973-75, 77)	134	2306
Craphonso Thorpe (2001-04)	123	2153
Lawrence Dawsey (1987-90)	128	2129
Jesse Hester (1981-84)	107	2100

SEASON RUSHING YARDS	Attempts	Yards
Warrick Dunn (1995)	166	1242
Sammie Smith (1987)	172	1230
Warrick Dunn (1996)	189	1180
Greg Allen (1983)	200	1134
Warrick Dunn (1994)	152	1026

SEASON PASSING YARDS	Att.-Comp.	Yards
Chris Weinke (2000)	266-431	4167
Thad Busby (1997)	235-390	3317
Drew Weatherford (2005)	276-469	3220
Peter Tom Willis (1989)	211-346	3124
Chris Rix (2003)	216-382	3107

SEASON RECEIVING YARDS	Catches	Yards
Ron Sellers (1968)	86	1496
Marvin "Snoop" Minnis (2000)	63	1340
Barry Smith (1972)	69	1243
Peter Warrick (1998)	61	1232
Ron Sellers (1967)	70	1228

GAME RUSHING YARDS	Attempts	Yards
Greg Allen (1981 vs. Western Carolina)	N/A	322
Sammie Smith (1987 vs. East Carolina)	N/A	244
Greg Allen (1984 vs. Arizona State)	22	223

GAME PASSING YARDS	Att.-Comp.	Yards
Chris Weinke (2000 vs. Duke)	37-N/A	536
Chris Weinke (2000 vs. Clemson)	27-43	521
Bill Cappleman (1969 vs. Memphis St.)	31-50	508

GAME RECEIVING YARDS	Catches	Yards
Ron Sellers (1968 vs. Wake Forest)	14	260
Ron Sellers (1968 vs. South Carolina)	16	259
Peter Warrick (1997 vs. Clemson)	N/A	249

GREATEST COACH

There can be only one greatest coach in Florida State history, and that would be Bobby Bowden. Sometime in 1975 or so, Bowden said to himself, "What's a southern boy like me doing wandering around in the snow in West Virginia." Bowden became coach of a slumbering football giant at Florida State to start the 1976 season.

What Bowden accomplished is remarkable. The Seminoles won the 1993 and 1999 national championships, 13 Atlantic Coast Conference titles (including 12 in a row), and attended bowl games for 27 straight seasons with 11 straight wins after the 1985-95 seasons. Perhaps the most remarkable achievement by Bowden was piloting the Seminoles to 14 straight seasons of a final rank of fifth or higher, from 1987 to 2000.

In 33 seasons in Tallahassee, Bowden has built a 309-91-4 record for a .7698 percentage.

FLORIDA STATE'S 55 GREATEST SINCE 1953

OFFENSE

WIDE RECEIVER: Fred Biletnikoff, Kez McCorvey, Marvin "Snoop" Minnis, Ron Sellers, Peter Warrick
TIGHT END: Zeke Mowatt, Tony Romeo
TACKLE: Alex Barron, Walter Jones, Ken Lanier, Tra Thomas, Del Williams
GUARD: Jamie Dukes, Jason Whitaker
CENTER: Clay Shiver, Michael Tanks
QUARTERBACK: Danny Kanell, Charlie Ward, Chris Weinke
RUNNING BACK: Greg Allen, Warrick Dunn, Sean Jackson
FULLBACK: William Floyd, Edgar Bennett

DEFENSE

END: Peter Boulware, Jamal Reynolds, Reinhard Wilson
TACKLE: Alphonso Carreker, Darnell Dockett, Corey Simon, Andre Wadsworth
NOSEGUARD: Ron Simmons
LINEBACKER: Derrick Brooks, Kirk Carruthers, Marvin Jones, Paul McGowan, Paul Piurowski, Tommy Polley, Ernie Sims
CORNERBACK: Clifton Abraham, Terrell Buckley, LeRoy Butler, Tay Cody, Deion Sanders, Corey Sawyer
SAFETY: Monk Bonasorte, Myron Rolle

SPECIAL TEAMS

RETURN SPECIALIST: Bobby Jackson, Tamarick Vanover
PLACE KICKER: Sebastian Janikowski
PUNTER: Rohn Stark

MULTIPLE POSITIONS

HALFBACK-QUARTERBACK-DEFENSIVE BACK: Lee Corso
WIDE RECEIVER-TAILBACK: Larry Key

TWO-WAY PLAYERS

END-DEFENSIVE END: Tom Feamster
END-DEFENSIVE END: Ronnie Schomburger

PERFORMANCE FORMULA:
FLORIDA STATE'S 10 BEST SEASONS

1993	1.8831	1 of 70
1999	1.8433	1 of 71
1987	1.7828	2 of 69
1996	1.7634	2 of 70
2000	1.7556	3 of 70
1997	1.7495	2 of 70
1980	1.7205	2 of 70
1992	1.7130	2 of 70
1994	1.7018	3 of 71
1988	1.6776	3 of 69

FLORIDA STATE SEMINOLES

Year	W-L-T	AP Poll	Conference Standing	Toughest Regular Season Opponents	Coach (Record at School)	Bowl Games			
1953	5-5			Miami 4-5, Mississippi Southern 9-1, Furman 7-2	Tom Nugent				
1954	8-4			Georgia 6-3-1, Auburn 7-3, Mississippi Southern 6-4	Tom Nugent	Sun	20	Texas Western	47
1955	5-5			Miami 6-3, Virginia Tech 6-3-1, Georgia Tech 8-1-1	Tom Nugent				
1956	5-4-1			Virginia Tech 7-2-1, Miami 8-1, Auburn 7-3	Tom Nugent				
1957	4-6			Boston College 7-2, NC State 7-1-2, Miami 5-4-1, Auburn 10-0	Tom Nugent				
1958	7-4			Georgia Tech 5-4-1, Virginia Tech 5-4-1, Florida 6-3-1	Tom Nugent (34-28-1)				
1959	4-6			Miami 6-4, Virginia Tech 6-4, Georgia 9-1	Perry Moss (4-6)				
1960	3-6-1			Florida 8-2, Miami 6-4, Auburn 8-2	Bill Peterson				
1961	4-5-1			Mississippi 9-1, Mississippi Southern 8-2	Bill Peterson				
1962	4-3-3			Miami 7-3, Georgia Tech 7-2-1, Auburn 6-3-1	Bill Peterson				
1963	4-5-1			Va. Tech 8-2, Ga. Tech 7-3, NC State 8-2, Auburn 9-1, Florida 6-3-1	Bill Peterson				
1964	9-1-1	11+		Georgia 6-3-1, Virginia Tech 6-4, Florida 7-3	Bill Peterson	Gator	36	Oklahoma	19
1965	4-5-1			Alabama 8-1-1, Virginia Tech 7-3, Florida 7-3	Bill Peterson				
1966	6-5			Miami 7-2-1, Florida 8-2, Virginia Tech 8-1-1, Syracuse 8-2	Bill Peterson	Sun	20	Wyoming	28
1967	7-2-2	11+		Alabama 8-1-1, NC State 8-2, Virginia Tech 7-3, Florida 6-4	Bill Peterson	Gator	17	Penn State	17
1968	8-3			Florida 6-3-1, Virginia Tech 7-3, Houston 6-2-2	Bill Peterson	Peach	27	Louisiana State	31
1969	6-3-1			Florida 8-1-1, South Carolina 7-3, Houston 8-2	Bill Peterson				
1970	7-4			Georgia Tech 8-3, Florida 7-4, Houston 8-3	Bill Peterson (62-42-11)				
1971	8-4			Florida 4-7, Houston 9-2, Georgia Tech 6-5	Larry Jones	Fiesta	38	Arizona State	45
1972	7-4			Virginia Tech 6-4-1, Auburn 9-1, Houston 6-4-1	Larry Jones				
1973	0-11			Kansas 7-3-1, San Diego State 9-1-1, Houston 10-1, Florida 7-4	Larry Jones (15-19)				
1974	1-10			Baylor 8-3, Alabama 11-0, Florida 8-3, Auburn 9-2, Houston 8-3	Darrell Mudra				
1975	3-8			Georgia Tech 7-4, Virginia Tech 8-3, Florida 9-2	Darrell Mudra (4-18)				
1976	5-6			Oklahoma 8-2-1, Boston College 8-3, Florida 8-3	Bobby Bowden				
1977	10-2	14		Auburn 6-5, San Diego State 10-1, Florida 6-4-1	Bobby Bowden	Tangerine	40	Texas Tech	17
1978	8-3			Miami 6-5, Houston 9-2, Pittsburgh 8-3, Navy 8-3	Bobby Bowden				
1979	11-1	6		Miami 5-6, LSU 6-5, South Carolina 8-3	Bobby Bowden	Orange	7	Oklahoma	24
1980	10-2	5		LSU 7-4, Miami 8-3, Nebraska 9-2, Pittsburgh 10-1, Virginia Tech 8-3	Bobby Bowden	Orange	17	Oklahoma	18
1981	6-5			Nebraska 9-2, Ohio State 8-3, Pittsburgh 10-1, Miami 9-2, Florida 7-4	Bobby Bowden				
1982	9-3	13		Pittsburgh 9-2, Ohio State 8-3, Miami 7-4, LSU 8-2-1, Florida 8-3	Bobby Bowden	Gator	31	West Virginia	12
1983	8-4			Auburn 11-1, Pittsburgh 8-2-1, Miami 10-1, Florida 8-2-1	Bobby Bowden	Peach	28	North Carolina	3
1984	7-3-2	17		Miami 8-4, Auburn 8-4, South Carolina 10-1, Florida 9-1-1	Bobby Bowden	Citrus	17	Georgia	17
1985	9-3	15		Nebraska 9-2, Auburn 8-3, Miami 10-1, Florida 9-1-1	Bobby Bowden	Gator	34	Oklahoma State	23
1986	7-4-1			Nebraska 9-2, Michigan 11-1, Miami 11-0	Bobby Bowden	All-American	27	Indiana	13
1987	11-1	2		Michigan State 8-2-1, Miami 11-0, Auburn 9-1-1	Bobby Bowden	Fiesta	31	Nebraska	28
1988	11-1	3		Miami 10-1, Clemson 9-2, South Carolina 8-3	Bobby Bowden	Sugar	13	Auburn	7
1989	10-2	3		Clemson 9-2, Auburn 9-2, Miami 10-1, Florida 7-4	Bobby Bowden	Fiesta	41	Nebraska	17
1990	10-2	4		Miami 9-2, Auburn 7-3-1, Florida 9-2	Bobby Bowden	Blockbuster	24	Penn State	17
1991	11-2	4		Michigan 10-1, Syracuse 9-2, Miami 11-0, Florida 10-1	Bobby Bowden	Cotton	10	Texas A&M	2
1992	11-1	2	1	NC State 9-2-1, Miami 11-0, North Carolina 8-3, Florida 8-4	Bobby Bowden	Orange	27	Nebraska	14
1993	12-1	1	1	North Carolina 10-2, Miami 9-2, Notre Dame 10-1, Florida 10-2	Bobby Bowden	Orange	18	Nebraska	16
1994	10-1-1	4	1	Virginia 8-3, North Carolina 8-3, Miami 10-1, Duke 8-3, Florida 10-1-1	Bobby Bowden	Sugar	23	Florida	17
1995	10-2	4	1t	Clemson 8-3, Miami 8-3, Florida 12-0	Bobby Bowden	Orange	31	Notre Dame	26
1996	11-1	3	1	North Carolina 9-2, Clemson 7-4, Miami 8-3, Virginia 7-4, Florida 11-1	Bobby Bowden	Sugar	20	Florida	52
1997	11-1	3	1	Clemson 7-4, Virginia 7-4, North Carolina 10-1, Florida 9-2	Bobby Bowden	Sugar	31	Ohio State	14
1998	11-2	3	1	Texas A&M 10-2, Miami 8-3, Ga. Tech 9-2, Virginia 9-2, Florida 9-2	Bobby Bowden	Fiesta	16	Tennessee	23
1999	12-0	1	1	Georgia Tech 8-3, Miami 8-4, Virginia 7-4, Florida 9-3	Bobby Bowden	Sugar	46	Virginia Tech	29
2000	11-2	5	1	Georgia Tech 9-2, Miami 10-1, Clemson 9-2, Florida 10-2	Bobby Bowden	Orange	2	Oklahoma	13
2001	8-4		15	1tMiami 11-0, Maryland 10-1, Florida 9-2	Bobby Bowden	Gator	30	Virginia Tech	17
2002	9-5	21	1	Maryland 10-3, Miami 12-0, Notre Dame 10-2, NC State 10-3	Bobby Bowden	Sugar	13	Georgia	26
2003	10-3	11	1	Maryland 9-2, Miami 10-2, Clemson 9-4, Florida 8-5	Bobby Bowden	Orange	14	Miami	16
2004	9-3	15	2	Miami 8-3, Virginia 8-3, Florida 7-4	Bobby Bowden	Gator	30	West Virginia	18
2005	8-5	23	Atl1t	Miami 9-2, Boston College 8-3, Florida 8-3, Virginia Tech 10-2	Bobby Bowden	Orange	23	Penn State	26
2006	7-6		Atl5	Boston College 9-3, Wake Forest 10-2, Florida 11-1	Bobby Bowden	Emerald	44	UCLA	27
2007	7-6		Atl4	Clemson 9-3, Boston College 10-2, Virginia Tech 10-2, Florida 9-3	Bobby Bowden	Music City	28	Kentucky	35
2008	9-4	21	Atl1t	Virginia Tech 9-4, Georgia Tech 9-3, Boston College 9-4, Florida 12-1	Bobby Bowden (316-97-4)	Gator	33	West Virginia	21
2009	7-6		Atl3	Miami 9-3, BYU 10-2, Georgia Tech 10-3, Florida 12-1	Bobby Bowden				
2010	10-4	17	Atl1	Oklahoma 11-2, Maryland 8-4, Virginia Tech 11-2	Jimbo Fisher (10-4)	Chick-fil-A	26	South Carolina	17

TOTAL: 445-216-16 .6691 (13 of 70)   Bowl Games since 1953:   23-14-2 .6154 (Tied 9 of 70)

GREATEST TEAM SINCE 1953: It is so difficult to choose just one great team from so many, but Bobby Bowden coached only one undefeated team, and that was the 1999 team. Those Seminoles were led by Ron Dugans, Travis Minor, Peter Warrick Chris Weinke, and Brett Williams on offense, and Tay Cody, Darnell Dockett, Tommy Polley, and Jamal Reynolds on defense.

1953 5-5

0	Miami	27	E Jimmy Lee Taylor
59	Louisville	0	T Don Powell / Al Makowiecki
7	Abilene Christ'n	20	G Jerry Jacobs
21	Louisiana Tech	32	C Bob Crenshaw / George Boyer
12	VMI	7	G Al Pacifico / Ray Staab
0	Miss. Southern	21	T Dwight Ochs / Jimmy Messinese
7	Furman	14	E Bud Leonard / Buddy Bryant
13	Stetson	6	QB Lee Corso / Harry Massey
23	N. Carolina St.	13	HB Bobby Fiveash / Buck Metts
41	Tampa	6	HB Billy Graham / Carl Green
			FB Eddie Johnson / Ronnie King

RUSHING: N/A
PASSING: N/A
RECEIVING: N/A
SCORING: N/A

1954 8-4

0	Georgia	14	E Jimmy Lee Taylor
0	Abilene Christian	13	T Al Makoweicki
47	Louisville	6	G Jerry Jacobs / Leo Baggett
52	Villanova	13	C Bob Crenshaw / Bud Leonard
13	N. Carolina St.	7	G Al Pacifico
0	Auburn	33	T Bob Barber / Don Powell
33	VMI	19	E Tom Feamster / Ronnie Schomberger
33	Furman	14	QB Harry Massey / Len Swantic
47	Stetson	6	HB Lee Corso / Buck Metts
19	Miss. Southern	18	HB Carl Green / Buddy Reynolds
13	Tampa	0	FB Joe Holt / John Griner
20	Tex. Western ■	47	

RUSHING: N/A
PASSING: N/A
RECEIVING: N/A
SCORING: N/A

1955 5-5

7	N. Carolina St.	0	E Ronnie Schomburger
0	Miami	34	T Don Powell / Bill Musselman
20	Virginia Tech	24	G Jerry Jacobs
14	Georgia	47	C Bob Crenshaw / Troy Barnes
0	Georgia Tech	34	G Vince Gibson / Al Pacifico
16	Villanova	13	T William Lee Proctor
19	Furman	6	E Tom Feamster / Hamilton Bisbee
39	Citadel	0	QB Len Swantic / Vic Prinzi
6	Miss. Southern	21	HB Lee Corso / Billy Odom
26	Tampa	7	HB Buck Metts / Gene Cox
			FB Joe Holt / John Griner

RUSHING: Corso 111/431y, Odom 60/294y, Metts 51/251y
PASSING: Swantic 37-73/576y, 2TD, 50.7 %
RECEIVING: Feamster 18/258y, Corso 13/123y, Metts 10/93y
SCORING: Swantic & Metts 24pts, Corso (HB-K) 19pts

1956 5-4-1

47	Ohio	7	E Ronnie Schomburger
0	Georgia	3	T Bill Musselman / Bob Thomas
7	Virginia Tech	20	G Leo Baggett / Robert Elliott
14	N. Carolina St.	0	C Troy Barnes / Bud Leonard
14	Wake Forest	14	G Al Pacifico
20	Villanova	13	T George Boyer / John Craig
7	Miami	20	E Bob Nellums / Bob Fountain
42	Furman	7	QB Lee Corso / Len Swantic / Vic Prinzi
20	Miss. Southern	19	HB Bobby Renn / Stan Dobosz
7	Auburn	13	HB Buck Metts / Billy Odom
			FB Joe Holt / Eddie Johnson

RUSHING: Renn 105/596y, Corso 88/356y
PASSING: Corso 32-59/369y, 5TD, 54.2%
RECEIVING: Holt 16/140y, Schomberger 16/140y
SCORING: N/A

1957 4-6

27	Furman	7	E Ronnie Schomburger / Bud Bagnell
7	Boston College	20	T Bill Musselman / John Craig
7	Villanova	21	G Al Ulmer / Bob Fountain
0	N. Carolina St.	7	C George Boyer
34	Abilene Christ'n	7	G Abner Bigbie / Joe McGee
20	Virginia Tech	7	T Jerry Graham / Troy Barnes
13	Miami	40	E John Spivey / Bill Kimber
0	Miss. Southern	20	QB Bobby Renn (HB) / Joe Majors
7	Auburn	29	HB Fred Pickard / Gerald Henderson
21	Tampa	7	HB Stan Dobosz / Billy Weaver
			FB Bob Nellums / Eddie Johnson

RUSHING: Pickard 86/463y, Renn 94/417y, Dobosz 75/255y
PASSING: Renn 23-54/263y, 2TD, 42.5%,
  Majors 20-49/206y, 2TD, 40.8%
RECEIVING: Nellums 21/217y, Schomberger 11/160y
SCORING: Nellums 32pts, Renn (QB-K) 25pts,
  Schomberger 18pts

1958 7-4

22	Tennessee Tech	7	E Pete Fleming / Bill Kimber
42	Furman	6	T Bob Swoszowski / John Craig
3	Georgia Tech	17	G Al Ulmer / Ray Lamb
27	Wake Forest	24	C Bo Davis / Ramon Rogers
13	Georgia	28	G Terry Moran / Jerry Graham
28	Virginia Tech	0	T John Spivey / Bud Bagnell
10	Tennessee	0	E Tony Romeo / Bob Fountain
43	Tampa	0	QB Vic Prinzi / Joe Majors
17	Miami	6	HB Bobby Renn / Bud Whitehead
7	Florida	21	HB Jack Espenship
6	Oklahoma St. ■	15	FB Fred Pickard

RUSHING: Pickard 122/602y, Renn 69/442y, Prinzi 54/117y
PASSING: Prinzi 40-71/480y, 7TD, 56.3%,
  Majors 26-71/380y, 3TD, 36.6%
RECEIVING: Espenship 18/200y, Romeo 14/274y, Renn 14/136y
SCORING: Renn 44pts, Pickard 30pts, John Sheppard (K) 28pts

1959 4-6

20	Wake Forest	22	E Jim Daniel / Ron Hinson
47	Citadel	6	T Steve Klesius / Bud Bagnell
6	Miami	7	G Al Ulmer / Abner Bigbie
7	Virginia Tech	6	C Ramon Rogers
6	Memphis State	16	G Terry Moran / Ray Lamb
22	Richmond	6	T John Spivey / Donald Donatelli
0	Georgia	42	E Tony Romeo / Fred Grimes
0	William & Mary	9	QB Joe Majors / Roy Bickford
8	Florida	18	HB Bud Whitehead
33	Tampa	0	HB Fred Pickard / Carl Meyer
			FB Jack Espenship / Paul Andrews

RUSHING: Pickard 131/481y
PASSING: Majors 90-168/1063y, 7TD, 53.6%
RECEIVING: Whitehead 31/320y
SCORING: Pickard 44pts

1960 3-6-1

28	Richmond	0	E Fred Grimes / Jim Daniel
0	Florida	3	T Steve Klesius / Bob Swoszowski
14	Wake Forest	6	G Abner Bigbie / Ray Lamb
0	Citadel	3	C Don Sellers / Jack Hardy
13	Miss. Southern	15	G Bruce Darsey / Gene McDowell (LB)
22	William & Mary	0	T Donald Donatelli / Marion Bronson
0	Kentucky	23	E Tony Romeo / John McConnaughhay
7	Miami	25	QB Eddie Feely / Ed Trancygier
6	Houston	7	HB Bud Whitehead / Roy Bickford (DB)
21	Auburn	57	HB Tom Hillabrand / Carl Meyer
			FB Paul Andews / Ed Parker

RUSHING: Whitehead 81/293y
PASSING: Trancygier 38-97/552y, 6TD, 39.2%
RECEIVING: Whitehead 23/212y
SCORING: Trancygier & Whitehead 18pts

1961 4-5-1

15	Geo. Wash'gton	7	E Jim Daniel / John McConnaughhay
3	Florida	3	T Jim Sims
0	Mississippi	33	G Gene McDowell / Jerry Bruner
3	Georgia	0	C Bruce Darsey
13	Richmond	7	G John Levings / Ferrell Henry
7	Virginia Tech	10	T Donald Donatelli / Tom Slicker
0	Kentucky	20	E Fred Grimes / Joe Verbinski
44	Citadel	8	QB Eddie Feely / Roy Bickford (DB)
0	Miss. Southern	12	HB Marion Roberts / Keith Kinderman
8	Houston	28	HB Tom Hillabrand / Jack Forehand
			FB Paul Andrews / Gene Roberts

RUSHING: G. Roberts 69/253y, Feely 98/251y,
  M. Roberts 49/159y
PASSING: Feely 48-83/471y, 4TD, 57.8%
RECEIVING: Daniel 10/113y, Hillabrand 10/66y
  McConnaughhay 9/102y
SCORING: Feely 18pts, M. Roberts & Andrews 12pts

1962 4-3-3

49	Citadel	0	E John McConnaughhay
0	Kentucky	0	T Tom Slicker
42	Furman	0	G Chuck Robinson / Ferrell Henry
6	Miami	7	C Bruce Darsey / Bill Daly
18	Georgia	0	G Gene McDowell
20	Virginia Tech	7	T Jim Sims
0	Houston	7	E Jim Causey / Donnie Floyd
14	Georgia Tech	14	QB Eddie Feely / Steve Tensi
7	Florida	20	HB Keith Kinderman / Phil Spooner
14	Auburn	14	HB Tom Hillabrand
			FB Marion Roberts / Gene Roberts

RUSHING: G. Roberts 75/299y
PASSING: Tensi 60-121/796y, 6TD, 49.6%
RECEIVING: Kinderman 21/275y
SCORING: Kinderman 30pts

1963 4-5-1

24	Miami	0	E Fred Biletnikoff / Max Wettstein
0	TCU	13	T Jerry Bruner
35	Wake Forest	0	G Chuck Robinson
0	Southern Miss.	0	C Bill Daly / Jack Edwards
23	Virginia Tech	31	G Dick Hermann / George D'Alessandro
49	Furman	6	T Avery Sumner
7	Georgia Tech	15	E Bill Dawson / Donnie Floyd
14	N. Carolina St.	0	QB Steve Tensi
15	Auburn	21	HB Dave Snyder / Phil Spooner
0	Florida	7	HB Winfred Bailey
			FB Larry Brinkley / Marion Roberts

RUSHING: Snyder 107/500y, Brinkley 69/370y,
  M. Roberts 47/140y
PASSING: Tensi 71-147/915y, 9TD, 48.3%
RECEIVING: Biletnikoff 24/358y, Dawson 19/231y,
  Wettstein 12/114y
SCORING: Brinkley 32pts, Biletnikoff 30pts,
  Doug Messer (K) 22pts

1964 9-1-1

14	Miami	0	E Donnie Floyd
10	TCU	0	T Del Williams
36	New Mexico St.	0	G Joe Avezzano
48	Kentucky	6	C Jack Edwards / John Stephens
17	Georgia	14	G Dale MacKenzie
11	Virginia Tech	20	T Tom West
34	Southern Miss.	0	TE Bill Dawson
13	Houston	13	QB Steve Tensi / Ed Pritchett
28	N. Carolina St.	6	HB Phil Spooner / Larry Green
16	Florida	7	WR Fred Biletnikoff
36	Oklahoma ■	19	FB Lee Narramore / Wayne Giardino
			DL George D'Alessandro
			DL Frank Pennie
			DL Jack Shinholser
			DL Avery Sumner
			DL Max Wettstein / Terry Garvin
			LB Bill McDowell
			LB Dick Herman / Howard Lurie
			DB Winfred Bailey
			DB Howard Ehler
			DB Maury Bibent / Pat Conway
			DB Jim Massey

RUSHING: Spooner 136/516y, Narramore 74/266y,
  Giardino 70/256y
PASSING: Tensi 121-204/1683y, 14TD, 59.1%
RECEIVING: Biletnikoff 57/987y, Floyd 41/556y,
  Dawson 12/148y
SCORING: Biletnikoff 68pts, Les Murdock (K) 49pts,
  Spooner 30pts

1965 4-5-1

3	TCU	7	E Jerry Jones / Buddy Blankenship
9	Baylor	7	T Del Williams
24	Kentucky	26	G Edwin Pope / Larry Williamson
10	Georgia	3	C John Stephens
0	Alabama	21	G Joe Avezzano / Larry Kissam
7	Virginia Tech	6	T Bob Mangan / David Braggins
35	Wake Forest	0	E Max Wettstein / Thurston Taylor
0	N. Carolina St.	3	QB Ed Prichett / Kim Hammond
16	Houston	16	HB Bill Moreman / Phil Spooner
17	Florida	30	WR T.K. Wetherell / Lane Fenner
			FB Jim Mankins / Wayne Giardino
			DL Terry Garvin / Stan Croley
			DL Charles Pennie / Jay Mac Matthews
			DL Jack Shinholser / Carlie McNeil
			DL Frank Pennie
			DL George D'Alessandro
			LB Bill McDowell
			LB Joe Parrish / Howard Lurie
			DB Maury Bibent / Bob Menendez
			DB Howard Ehler
			DB Bill Campbell / Butch Riser
			DB Pat Conway / Jim Massey

RUSHING: Mankins 85/336y, Spooner 76/323y,
  Moreman 49/249y
PASSING: Pritchett 110-247/1225y, 5TD, 44.6%
RECEIVING: Wettstein 24/365y, Wetherell 19/234y,
  Jones 19/223y
SCORING: Pete Roberts (K) 31pts, Wettstein 18pts, 4 with 12pts

1966 6-5
13 Houston	21 WR T.K. Wetherell / Lane Fenner
23 Miami	20 WR Ron Sellers / Bill Cox
19 Florida	22 T Jack Fenwick / Billy Rhodes
42 Texas Tech.	33 G Edwin Pope
10 Mississippi St.	0 C John Stephens
21 Virginia tech	23 G Del Williams / Ken Hart
32 South Carolina	10 T Larry Kissam / Frank Vohun
21 Syracuse	37 TE Thurston Taylor / Chip Glass
28 Wake Forest	0 QB Gary Pajcic / Kim Hammond
45 Maryland	21 HB Bill Moreman / Larry Green
20 Wyoming ■	28 FB Jim Mankins
	DL Wayne McDuffie / Jerry Jones
	DL Charles Pennie / David Braggins
	DL Larry Pendleton
	DL Jay Mac Matthews / Joe Kinnan
	DL Bob Menendez / Doug Gurr
	LB Wayne Giardino / Joe Benson
	LB Mike Blatt / Dale McCullers
	DB Walt Sumner / Butch Riser
	DB Bill Campbell
	DB Marty Kolbus / Howell Montgomery
	DB Chuck Eason / Pat Conway

RUSHING: Moreman 123/480y, Mankins 116/445y, Pajcic 57/145y
PASSING: Pajcic 125-233/1590y, 8TD, 53.6%
RECEIVING: Sellers 58/874y, Taylor 28/366y, Mankins 24/186y
SCORING: Mankins 10pts, Moreman 48pts, Green 30pts

1967 7-2-2
13 Houston	33 WR Lane Fenner / Bill Cox
37 Alabama	37 WR Ron Sellers
10 N. Carolina St.	20 T Jack Fenwick
19 Texas A&M	18 G Wayne McDuffie
17 South Carolina	0 C Ted Mosley / Ken Hart
28 Texas Tech	12 G Larry Pendleton / Stan Walker
24 Mississippi St.	12 T Billy Rhodes
26 Memphis State	7 TE Thurston Taylor / Chip Glass (LB)
38 Virginia Tech	15 QB Kim Hammond / Gary Pajcic
21 Florida	16 HB Larry Green / Bill Gunter
17 Penn State ■	17 FB Bill Moreman / John Pittman
	DL Floyd Ratliff
	DL Duke Johnston / Frank Vohun
	DL Joe Kinnan / Mike Bugar
	DL Randy Logan / Harvey Zion
	DL Bob Menendez / Doug Gurr
	LB Dale McCullers / Joe Benson
	LB Mike Blatt / Chuck Elliott
	DB Walt Sumner / Tommy Warren
	DB T.K. Wetherell / Mike Page
	DB John Crowe
	DB Chuck Eason / Clint Burton

RUSHING: Moreman 94/439y
PASSING: Hammond 140-241/1991y, 15TD, 58.1%
RECEIVING: Sellers 70/1228y
SCORING: Grant Guthrie (K) 53pts, Sellers 48pts

1968 8-3
24 Maryland	14 WR Bill Cox / Phillip Abraira
3 Florida	9 WR Ron Sellers
20 Texas A&M	14 T Jack Fenwick / Wayne Johnson
20 Memphis State	10 G Stan Walker / Ken Hart
35 South Carolina	28 C Ted Mosley
22 Virginia Tech	40 G Larry Pendleton
27 Mississippi St.	14 T Bill Rhodes / Jeff Curchin
48 N. Carolina St.	7 TE Chip Glass / Jim Tyson
42 Wake Forest	24 QB Bill Cappleman / Gary Pajcic
40 Houston	20 RB Tom Bailey / Bill Gunter
27 LSU ■	31 FB John Pittman / Brent Gillman
	DL Floyd Ratliff
	DL Duke Johnston
	DL Harvey Zion / Frank Vuhon
	DL Mike Bugar / Ronnie Wallace
	LB Chuck Elliott / Steve Gildea
	LB Dale McCullers / Bill Lohse
	LB Joe Benson / Bob Burt
	DB Walt Sumner
	DB Clint Burton / John Pell
	DB John Crowe / Howell Montgomery
	DB Chuck Eason

RUSHING: Bailey 116/570y, Gunter 136/465y, Pittman 66/277y
PASSING: Cappleman 162-287/2410y, 25TD, 56.4%
RECEIVING: Sellers 86/1496y, Cox 23/341y, Bailey 21/209y
SCORING: Sellers 72pts, Grant Guthrie (K) 55pts, Gunter 36pts

1969 6-3-1
24 Wichita State	0 WR Rhett Dawson / Kent Gaydos
16 Miami	14 WR Don Pederson
6 Florida	21 T Bill Rimby / Wayne Johnson
38 Tulsa	20 G Stan Walker
20 Mississippi St.	17 C Bill Hughes
34 South Carolina	9 G Jay Stokes / George Montgomery
10 Virginia Tech	10 T Jeff Curchin
26 Memphis State	28 TE Jim Tyson
33 N. Carolina St.	22 QB Bill Cappleman / Tommy Warren
13 Houston	41 TB Tom Bailey / Brett Gillman
	FB Paul Magalski / Mike Gray
	DL Randy Hall
	DL Robert McEachern
	DL Frank Vohun / Tom White
	DL Ronnie Wallace
	LB Barry Rice
	LB Bill Lohse
	LB Steve Gildea / Theron Bass
	DB John Montgomery / John Pell
	DB Bennie Rust / Danny Thomas
	DB Robert Ashmore
	DB John Lanahan / Phil Abraira

RUSHING: Bailey 144/630y
PASSING: Cappleman 183-344/2467y, 14TD, 53.2%
RECEIVING: Tyson 49/720y
SCORING: Grant Guthrie (K) 48pts

1970 7-4
9 Louisville	7 WR Kent Gaydos / Barry Smith
13 Georgia Tech	23 WR Rhett Dawson
19 Wake Forest	14 T Joe Strickler / Shane Gibbs
27 Florida	38 G J.W. McKinnie
12 Memphis State	16 C Allen Dees
21 South Carolina	13 G Bill Rimby / George Montgomery
27 Miami	3 T Roger Minor
38 Clemson	13 TE Jim Tyson
34 Virginia Tech	8 QB Frank Whigham / Tommy Warren
33 Kansas State	7 TB Tom Bailey / Paul Magalski
21 Houston	53 FB James Jarrett / John Lanahan
	DL Bill Shaw / Randy Hall
	DL Robert McEachern
	DL Richard Amman
	DL Ronnie Wallace / Beryl Rice
	LB Steve Gildea / Larry Strickland
	LB Bill Lohse
	LB Dan Whitehurst
	DB James Thomas / John Montgomery
	DB Benny Rust / Eddie McMillan
	DB David Snell / Robert Ashmore
	DB Buddy Gridley/G.Glisson/Clint Parker

RUSHING: Bailey 121/514y
PASSING: Warren 97-190/1594y, 11TD, 51.1%
RECEIVING: Dawson 54/946y
SCORING: Frank Fontes (K) 64pts,

1971 8-4
24 Southern Miss.	9 WR Rhett Dawson
20 Miami	17 WR Barry Smith / Kent Gaydos
30 Kansas	7 T Roger Minor / Don Sparkman
17 Virginia Tech	3 G J.W. McKinnie
27 Mississippi St.	9 C Allen Dees
15 Florida	17 G Phil Arnold
49 South Carolina	18 T Joe Strickler
7 Houston	14 TE Gary Parris
6 Georgia Tech	12 QB Gary Huff / Frank Whigham
45 Tulsa	10 TB Paul Magalski
31 Pittsburgh	13 FB James Jarrett / Art Munroe
38 Arizona State ■	45 DL Bill Shaw
	DL Bill Henson
	DL Richard Amman
	DL Charlie Hunt
	LB Clint Parker
	LB Larry Strickland
	LB Phil Arnold / Dan Whitehurst
	DB James Thomas / John Montgomery
	DB Eddie McMillan
	DB Robert Ashmore
	DB John Lanahan / Guy Glisson

RUSHING: Magalski 106/516y
PASSING: Huff 184-327/2736y, 23TD, 56.3%
RECEIVING: Dawson 62/817y
SCORING: Frank Fontes (K) 69pts, Dawson 42pts

1972 7-4
19 Pittsburgh	7 WR Barry Smith
37 Miami	14 WR Joe Goldsmith / Mike Allen
27 Virginia Tech	15 T Don Sparkman
44 Kansas	22 G Shane Gibbs / Bobby Anderson
13 Florida	42 C Allen Dees
25 Mississippi St.	21 G Bob Jones / Phil Arnold
37 Colorado State	0 T Mike Glass
14 Auburn	27 TE Gary Parris
27 Houston	31 QB Gary Huff
23 Tulsa	21 TB Hodges Mitchell / Mack Brown
21 South Carolina	24 FB Mike Davison / Fred Miller
	DL Bill Shaw
	DL Howard Jacobi
	DL Bob Anderson / Tom Prestwood
	DL Steve Bratton
	LB Phil Arnold
	LB Larry Strickland / Greg Pounds
	LB John Murphy
	DB James Thomas
	DB Eddie McMillan
	DB Ron Ratliff
	DB David Snell / Buzzy Lewis

RUSHING: Mitchell 192/944y, Davison 80/372y, Brown 31/98y
PASSING: Huff 206-385/2893y, 25TD, 53.5%
RECEIVING: Smith 69/1243y, Parris 49/629y, Davison 24/198y
SCORING: Smith 86pts, Ahmet Askin (K) 51pts, Davison 36pts

1973 0-11
7 Wake Forest	9 WR Joe Goldsmith / Joe Thomas
0 Kansas	28 WR Jim Everett / Mike Shumann
10 Miami	14 T Don Sparkman
14 Baylor	21 G Jeff Gardner / Bob Anderson
12 Mississippi St.	37 C Rocky Saldana
10 Memphis State	13 G Bob Jones
17 San Diego St.	38 T Smokey Ragins / Bobby Elam
3 Houston	34 TE Ed Davis / Rocky Blythe
13 Virginia Tech	36 QB Billy Sexton / Mark Orlando
12 South Carolina	52 TB Hodges Mitchell / Mike Davison
0 Florida	49 FB Bobby McKinnon
	DL Steve Bratton
	DL Tom Chandler
	DL John Malkiewicz
	DL Randy Coffield / Scott Meseroll
	LB Greg Pounds / Bruce Bell
	LB Phil Arnold
	LB John Murphy / Detroit Reynolds
	DB Chris Griffin / Andy Stockton
	DB Earl Humes
	DB Randy Kaiser
	DB Phil Cahoon / Buzzy Lewis

RUSHING: Mitchell 171/668y, McKinnon 57/224y, Davison 55/170y
PASSING: Orlando 71-153/709y, 4TD, 46.4%, Sexton 51-128/754y, 4TD, 40.0%
RECEIVING: Shumann 21/380y, Mike Allen (WR) 19/279y, Davison 15/75y
SCORING: Ahmet Askin (K) 20pts, 4 with 12pts

1974 1-10
6 Pittsburgh	9 WR Mike Allen
7 Colorado State	14 WR Mike Shumann / Roger Overby
9 Kansas	40 T Bruce Harrison / Wade Johnson
17 Baylor	21 G Jeff Gardner
7 Alabama	8 C Smokey Ragins
14 Florida	24 G Bob Jones
6 Auburn	38 T Billy McPhillips
14 Memphis State	42 TE Joe Goldsmith
21 Miami	14 QB Ron Coppess / Steve Mathieson
21 Virginia Tech	56 TB Larry Key / Rudy Thomas /Leon Bright
8 Houston	23 FB Fred Miller / Jimmy Heggins
	DL Randy Coffield / Dave Porter
	DL Phil Jones / Doug Dane
	DL Jon Thames
	DL Greg Johnson
	DL Detroit Reynolds / Rudy Maloy
	LB Bert Cooper
	LB Brian Schmidt / Aaron Carter
	DB Bobby Jackson
	DB Lee Nelson
	DB Joe Camps / Andy Stockton
	DB Aaron Carter / Jeff Ridings

RUSHING: Key 123/602y, Thomas 81/351y, Bright 61/296y
PASSING: Coppess 78-145/817y, 2TD, 53.8%, Mathieson 40-82/544y, 3TD, 48.8%
RECEIVING: Shumann 43/515y, Goldsmith 42/525y, R. Thomas 16/109y
SCORING: Ahmet Askin (K) 26pts, Bright 24pts, Shumann 20pts

1975 3-8

20 Texas Tech	31 WR Mike Shumann
17 Utah State	8 WR Larry Key (TB) / Roger Overby
6 Iowa State	10 T Tom Rushing
0 Georgia Tech	30 G Jeff Gardner
10 Virginia Tech	13 C Smokey Ragins / Bill Sawyer
8 Florida	34 G Tony Falvo / Wade Johnson
14 Auburn	17 T Bruce Harrison
43 Clemson	7 TE Billy McPhillips (DL) / Ed Beckman
14 Memphis State	17 QB Clyde Walker
22 Miami	24 TB Leon Bright / Rudy Thomas
33 Houston	22 FB Fred Miller / Jimmy Heggins
	DL Randy Coffield
	DL Greg Johnson
	DL Phil Jones / Jon Thames
	DL Louis Richardson
	DL Rudy Maloy / Willie Jones
	LB Brian Schmidt / Waldo Williams
	LB Detroit Reynolds
	DB Bobby Jackson
	DB Lee Nelson
	DB Gary Woolford / Aaron Carter (LB)
	DB Joe Camps

RUSHING: Bright 162/675y, Key 199/522y, Thomas 89/363y
PASSING: Walker 117-203/1619y, 10TD, 57.6%
RECEIVING: Shumann 38/730y, Beckman 20/283y, Key 20/212y
SCORING: Key & Thomas 36pts, Shumann 32pts

1976 5-6

12 Memphis State	21 WR Jackie Flowers / Mike Barnes
0 Miami	47 WR Kurt Unglaub
9 Oklahoma	24 T Jon Thames
20 Kansas State	10 G Mike Good / Mike Kissner
28 Boston College	9 C Bill Sawyer / Alan Risk
26 Florida	33 G Vic Rivas / Wade Johnson
19 Auburn	31 T Tom Rushing / Mark Meseroll
12 Clemson	15 TE Ed Beckman / Greg Lazzaro
30 Southern Miss.	27 QB Jimmy Black / Jimmy Jordan
21 N. Texas State	20 TB Larry Key / Rudy Thomas
28 Virginia Tech	21 FB Jeff Leggett / Mark Lyles
	DL Rudy Maloy
	DL Abe Smith / Walter Carter
	DL Jimmy Heggins
	DL Gary Rose
	DL Scott Warren / Willie Jones
	LB Aaron Carter
	LB Detroit Reynolds / Mike Stewart
	DB Bobby Jackson / Gary Woolford
	DB Ivory Lee Hunter / Mike Kincaid
	DB Jeff Ridings / Nat Terry
	DB Joe Joyner / Joe Camps

RUSHING: Key 144/712y, Black 129/347y, Leggett 66/312y
PASSING: Black 103-178/1506y, 9TD, 57.9%
RECEIVING: Beckman 37/521y, Unglaub 33/665y,
Thomas 15/233y, Key 15/91y
SCORING: Davy Cappelen (K) 43pts, Thomas & Key 30pts

1977 10-2

35 Southern Miss.	6 WR Roger Overby / Jackie Flowers
18 Kansas State	10 WR Mike Shumann / Kurt Unglaub
17 Miami	23 T Ken Lanier
25 Oklahoma State	17 G Mike Good (T) / Wade Johnson
14 Cincinnati	0 C Gil Wesley / Cedric Wyatt
24 Auburn	3 G Mark Meseroll / Bruce Harrison
35 N. Texas State	14 T Nate Henderson / Tom Rushing
23 Virginia Tech	21 TE Grady King / Greg Lazzaro
30 Memphis State	9 QB Wally Woodham / Jimmy Jordan
16 San Diego State	41 TB Larry Keys / Greg Ramsey
37 Florida	9 FB Mark Lyles
40 Texas Tech ■	17 DL Willie Jones
	DL Ed Richardson / Mark Macek
	DL Ron Simmons
	DL Walter Carter / Abe Smith
	DL Scott Warren
	LB Jimmy Heggins
	LB Aaron Carter / David Hanks
	DB Bobby Jackson
	DB Ivory Lee Hunter / Bobby Butler
	DB Nat Terry / Monk Bonasorte
	DB Mike Kincaid

RUSHING: Key 239/1117y, Lyles 70/298y, Ramsey 41/207y
PASSING: Woodham 94-154/1270y, 8TD, 61.0%,
Jordan 80-166/1139y, 10TD, 48.2%
RECEIVING: Overby 38/626y, Shumann 33/701y, Key 22/243y
SCORING: Davy Cappelen (K) 66pts, Shumann 38pts,
Woodham & Overby 30pts

1978 8-3

28 Syracuse	0 WR Jackie Flowers / Sam Platt
38 Oklahoma State	20 WR Kurt Unglaub / Phil Williams
31 Miami	21 T Ken Lanier
21 Houston	27 G Mike Good / Brent Brock
26 Cincinnati	21 C Gil Wesley
27 Mississippi St.	55 G Lee Adams / Greg Futch
3 Pittsburgh	7 T Nate Henderson
38 Southern Miss.	16 TE Grady King / Bill Keck
24 Virginia Tech	14 QB Wally Woodham / Jimmy Jordan
38 Navy	6 TB Mark Lyles / Homes Johnson
38 Florida	21 FB Ernie Sims
	DL Willie Jones / Jarvis Coursey
	DL Walter Carter / Ed Richardson
	DL Ron Simmons
	DL Jerry Mindlin / Mark Macek
	DL Scott Warren / Arthur Scott
	LB Reggie Herring
	LB David Hanks / Paul Piurowski
	DB Bobby Butler
	DB Mike Smith / Ozzie Harrell
	DB Monk Bonasorte / Gary Henry
	DB Mike Kincaid / Keith Jones

RUSHING: Johnson 183/817y, Lyles 148/641y, Sims 23/145y
PASSING: Jordan 108-199/1427y, 14TD, 54.3%,
Woodham 98-169/1322y, 9TD, 58.0%
RECEIVING: Flowers 43/757y, Lyles 35/364y,
Johnson 23/213y, King 23/212y
SCORING: Davy Cappelen (K) 60pts, Lyles 48pts,
Flowers & Platt 42pts

1979 11-1

17 Southern Miss.	14 WR Jackie Flowers / Hardis Johnson
31 Arizona State	3 WR Phil Williams / Kurt Unglaub
40 Miami	23 T Ken Lanier
17 Virginia Tech	10 G Mike Good
27 Louisville	0 C Gil Wesley / John Madden
17 Mississippi St.	6 G Greg Futch
24 LSU	19 T Tom Brannon
26 Cincinnati	21 TE Grady King / Sam Childers
27 South Carolina	7 QB Wally Woodham / Jimmy Jordan
66 Memphis State	17 TB Homes Johnson / Greg Ramsey
27 Florida	16 FB Mark Lyles / Mike Whiting
7 Oklahoma ■	24 DL Scott Warren / Jarvis Coursey
	DL Mark Macek / Walter Carter
	DL Ron Simmons / James Gilbert
	DL Jeremy Mindlin / Ed Richardson
	DL Arthur Scott
	LB Reggie Herring
	LB Paul Piurowski
	DB Bobby Butler
	DB Ivory Joe Hunter
	DB Monk Bonasorte
	DB Keith Jones / Gary Henry

RUSHING: Lyles 225/1011y, Whiting 109/522y, Ramsey 37/166y
PASSING: Jordan 87-180/1173y, 13TD, 48.3%,
Woodham 80-152/940y, 5TD, 73.5%
RECEIVING: Flowers 37/622y, Lyles 35/211y, King 23/246y
SCORING: Davy Cappelen (K) 70pts, Lyles 56pts, Flowers 44pts

1980 10-2

16 LSU	0 WR Hardis Johnson
52 Louisville	0 WR Dennis McKinnon / Phil Williams
63 East Carolina	7 T Ken Lanier
9 Miami	10 G Greg Futch
18 Nebraska	14 C John Madden
36 Pittsburgh	22 G Lee Adams
41 Boston College	7 T Tom Brannon / Eric Ryan
24 Memphis State	3 TE Sam Childers / Zeke Mowatt
45 Tulsa	2 QB Rick Stockstill
31 Virginia Tech	7 TB Sam Platt / Ricky Williams
17 Florida	13 FB Mike Whiting
17 Oklahoma ■	18 DL Scott McLean / Jarvis Coursey
	DL Mark Macek
	DL Ron Simmons / James Gilbert
	DL Garry Futch / Alphonso Carreker
	DL Arthur Scott
	LB Reggie Herring / Roger Brownlee
	LB Paul Piurowski / Ron Hester
	DB Bobby Butler
	DB James Harris / Harvey Clayton
	DB Monk Bonasorte
	DB Keith Jones / Gary Henry

RUSHING: Platt 224/983y, Whiting 133/500y, Williams 73/383y
PASSING: Stockstill 121-201/1377y, 15 TD, 60.0%
RECEIVING: Whiting 25/203y, Johnson 24/419y,
Childers 20/157y
SCORING: Bill Capece (K) 104pts, Johnson 54pts,
Platt & Whiting 36pts

1981 6-5

17 Louisville	0 WR Phil Williams / Tony Johnson
10 Memphis State	5 WR Dennis McKinnon / Jessie Hester
14 Nebraska	34 T Barry Voltapetti
36 Ohio State	27 G Tom Brannon / Ricky Render
19 Notre Dame	13 C Bob Merson / Tom McCormick
14 Pittsburgh	42 G Eric Ryan (T) / Redus Coggin
38 LSU	14 T Herbert Harp
56 W. Carolina	31 TE Zeke Mowatt / Sam Childers
19 Miami	27 QB Rick Stockstill / Blair Williams
14 Southern Miss.	58 TB Greg Allen / Ricky Williams
3 Florida	35 FB Mike Whiting
	DL Jarvis Coursey
	DL Alphonso Carreker
	DL James Gilbert / Lenny Chavers
	DL Garry Futch
	DL Allen Dale Campbell / Mike Rodrigue
	LB Tommy Young / Ken Roe
	LB Ron Hester / Henry Taylor
	DB Harvey Clayton / Eric Riley
	DB James Harris
	DB Larry Harris
	DB Gary Henry / Tracy Ashley

RUSHING: Allen 139/888y, Whiting 111/461y,
R. Williams 79/354y
PASSING: Stockstill 122-238/1356y, 11TD, 51.3%
RECEIVING: Whiting 29/211y, McKinnon 28/377y,
P. Williams 22/413y
SCORING: Mike Rendina (K) 52pts, Whiting 36pts,
Allen & McKinnon 24pts

1982 9-3

38 Cincinnati	31 WR Tony Johnson / Dennis McKinnon
17 Pittsburgh	37 WR Jessie Hester / Hassan Jones
24 Southern Miss.	17 T Jim Thompson / Eric Ryan
34 Ohio State	17 G Ricky Render / Herb Harp
59 S. Illinois	8 C Tom McCormick / Sam Restivo
56 East Carolina	17 G Jamie Dukes
24 Miami	7 T Terry Widner / John Ionata
56 South Carolina	26 TE Zeke Mowatt / Tom Wheeler
49 Louisville	14 QB Kelly Lowrey / Blair Williams
21 LSU	55 TB Ricky Williams/Greg Allen/Tony Smith
10 Florida	13 FB Ken Burnett / Darish Davis
31 West Virginia ■	12 DL John McLean / Brian Williams
	DL Alphonso Carreker
	DL David Ponder
	DL Brad Fojtik / Isaac Williams
	DL Allen Dale Campbell / Garth Jax
	LB Tommy Young
	LB Ken Roe / Henry Taylor
	DB Harvey Clayton
	DB Gary Henry / Kim Mack
	DB Brian McCrary
	DB Larry Harris / Tracy Ashley

RUSHING: Williams 134/857y, Allen 152/776y,
Smith 37/300y
PASSING: Lowrey 113-217/1671y, 11TD, 52.1%,
Williams 73-121/1084y, 9TD, 60.3%
RECEIVING: Johnson 30/500y, Hester 35/541y, Mowatt 22/209y
SCORING: Allen 126pts, P.M. Hall (K) 70pts,
Hester & Lowrey 30pts

1983 8-4

47 East Carolina	46 WR Jessie Hester / Hassan Jones
40 LSU	35 WR Tony Johnson / Weegie Thompson
28 Tulane	34 T Jim Thompson
24 Auburn	27 G Herb Harp / Ricky Render
16 Pittsburgh	17 C Tom McCormick / Sam Restivo
43 Cincinnati	17 G Jamie Dukes
51 Louisville	7 T John Ionato / Terry Widner
29 Arizona State	26 TE Pete Panton / Tom Wheeler
45 South Carolina	30 QB Kelly Lowrey / Bob Davis
16 Miami	17 TB Greg Allen / Cedric Jones
14 Florida	53 FB Roosevelt Snipes / Cletis Jones
28 North Carolina ■	3 DL Brian Williams
	DL Todd Stroud
	DL David Ponder / Brad Fojtik
	DL Alphonso Carreker
	DL John McLean / Garth Jax
	LB Prince Matt / Henry Taylor
	LB Ken Roe
	DB Billy Allen / Kim Mack
	DB Eric Riley
	DB Brian McCrary / Joe Wessel
	DB Tracy Ashley

RUSHING: Allen 200/1134y, Snipes 96/629y,
Ced. Jones 83/434y
PASSING: Lowrey 131-233/1720y, 12TD, 56.2%
RECEIVING: Hester 31/576y, Thompson 31/502y,
Jones 24/332y, Wheeler 24/235y
SCORING: Allen 80pts, P.M. Hall (K) 53pts, Lowrey 48pts

1984 7-3-2

47 East Carolina	17 WR Hassan Jones / Darrin Holloman
42 Kansas	16 WR Jessie Hester / Herb Gainer
38 Miami	3 T Jim Thompson / Pablo Lopez
44 Temple	27 G Dan Morris
17 Memphis State	17 C Parrish Barwick / Gerald Riopelle
41 Auburn	42 G Jamie Dukes
27 Tulane	6 T John Ionato
52 Arizona State	44 TE Pat Carter / Pete Panton
26 South Carolina	38 QB Eric Thomas / Kirk Coker
37 Tenn.-Chatt'ga	0 TB Greg Allen / Roosevelt Snipes
17 Florida	27 FB Cletis Jones / Cedric Jones
17 Georgia■	17 DL Isaac Williams / Jim Hendley
	DL Todd Stroud / Lenny Chavers
	DL Gerald Nichols
	LB Garth Jax / Jesse Solomon
	LB Fred Jones
	LB Henry Taylor / Paul McGowan
	LB Brian Williams / Darryl Gray
	DB Eric Williams / Kim Mack
	DB Eric Riley / Martin Mathew
	DB Brian McCrary / Joe Wessel
	DB Billy Allen / Anthony Smiley

RUSHING: Allen 133/971y, Snipes 118/756y,
Cle. Jones 120/631y
PASSING: Thomas 78-161/1218y, 14TD, 48.4%
RECEIVING: Hester 42/832y, Jones 28/501y, Carter 13/175y
SCORING: Derek Schmidt (K) 93pts, Hester 64pts, Allen 48pts

1985 9-3

38 Tulane	12 WR Hassan Jones / Phillip Bryant
17 Nebraska	13 WR Darrin Holloman
19 Memphis State	10 T Mark Salva / Pablo Lopez
24 Kansas	20 G Jamie Dukes
27 Auburn	59 C Jim Hendley / Parrish Barwick
76 Tulsa	14 G Pat Tomberlin
20 North Carolina	10 T John Ionato
27 Miami	35 TE Pat Carter / Tom O'Malley
56 South Carolina	14 QB Chip Ferguson / Danny McManus
50 W. Carolina	10 TB Tony Smith / Victor Floyd
14 Florida	38 FB Cletis Jones
34 Oklahoma St.■	23 DL Isaac Williams / Thomas Harp
	DL Lenny Chavers / Todd Stroud
	DL Gerald Nichols
	LB Garth Jax / Terry Warren
	LB Henry Taylor / Felton Hayes
	LB Fred Jones
	LB Paul McGowan / Darryl Gray
	DB Martin Mayhew / Deion Sanders
	DB Eric Williams
	DB Greg Newell
	DB Stan Shivers

RUSHING: Smith 111/678y, Floyd 90/619y, Jones 89/405y
PASSING: Ferguson 70-130/990y, 11TD, 53.8%,
McManus 40-69/513y, 3TD, 58.0%
RECEIVING: Jones 34/738y, Hollomon 20/323y, Bryant 17/ 360y
SCORING: Derek Schmidt (K) 98pts,
Bryant, Floyd, & Jones 30pts

1986 7-4-1

24 Toledo	0 WR Herb Gainer
17 Nebraska	34 WR Darrin Holloman
10 North Carolina	10 T Joey Ionata
18 Michigan	20 G Jason Kuipers
54 Tulane	21 C Jim Hendley / Parrish Barwick
59 Wichita State	3 G Mark Salva
54 Louisville	18 T Pat Tomberlin
23 Miami	41 TE Pat Carter / Tom O'Malley
45 South Carolina	28 QB Chip Ferguson / Danny McManus
49 Southern Miss.	13 TB Victor Floyd / Sammie Smith
13 Florida	17 FB Tanner Holloman / Dayne Williams
27 Indiana■	13 DL Steve Gabbard
	DL Thomas Harp / Odell Haggins
	DL Gerald Nichols / Eric Hayes
	LB Felton Hayes
	LB Fred Jones
	LB Paul McGowan
	LB Terry Warren / Kevin Grant
	DB Deion Sanders
	DB Eric Williams / Martin Mayhew
	DB Greg Newell / Dedrick Dodge
	DB Stanley Shiver

RUSHING: Floyd 129/654y, Smith 103/611y,
T. Hollomon 45/185y
PASSING: McManus 65-112/872y, 7TD, 58.0%,
Ferguson 63-128/807y, 4TD, 49.2%
RECEIVING: Gainer 27/441y, Floyd 21/231y, O'Malley 16/187y,
Carter 16/174y
SCORING: Derek Scmidt (K) 86pts, Floyd 48pts, Garner 32pts

1987 11-1

40 Texas Tech	16 WR Herb Gainer / Randy White
44 East Carolina	3 WR Ronnie Lewis / Lawrence Dawsey
41 Memphis State	24 T Pat Tomberlin
31 Michigan State	3 G Jason Kuipers
25 Miami	26 C Mark Salva
61 Southern Miss	10 G John Brown / Tony Yeomans
32 Louisville	9 T Joey Ionata
73 Tulane	14 TE Pat Carter / Tom O'Malley
34 Auburn	6 QB Danny McManus
41 Furman	10 TB Sammy Smith / Dexter Carter
28 Florida	14 FB Dayne Williams / Edgar Bennett
31 Nebraska■	28 DL Eric Hayes / Bart Schuchts
	DL Odell Haggins
	DL Steve Gabbard
	LB Shelton Thompson
	LB Paul McGowan
	LB David Palmer / Kelvin Smith
	LB Terry Warren / Kevin Grant
	DB Deion Sanders
	DB Martin Mayhew / Eric Williams
	DB Greg Newell / LeRoy Butler
	DB Stanley Shiver / Alphonso Williams

RUSHING: Smith 172/1230y, D. Carter 116/679y,
Bennett 58/276y
PASSING: McManus 138-264/1964y, 14 TD, 52.3%
RECEIVING: Gainer 30/478y, P. Carter 28/274y, Lewis 23/418y
SCORING: Derek Schmidt (K) 116pts, Williams 90pts,
Smith 54pts

1988 11-1

0 Miami	31 WR Terry Anthony / Bruce LaSane
49 Southern Miss.	13 WR Ronnie Lewis / Lawrence Dawsey
24 Clemson	21 T Pat Tomberlin
30 Michigan State	7 G Jason Kuipers
48 Tulane	28 C Michael Tanks
28 Ga. Southern	10 G Tony Yeomans / Mike Morris
45 East Carolina	21 T Joey Ionata
66 Louisiana Tech	3 TE Tom O'Malley / Reggie Johnson
59 South Carolina	0 QB Chip Ferguson / Peter Tom Willis
41 Virginia Tech	14 TB Sammie Smith / Dexter Carter
52 Florida	17 FB Dayne Williams
13 Auburn■	7 DL Eric Hayes
	DL Odell Haggins
	DL Steve Gabbard / Henry Ostaszewski
	LB Shelton Thompson
	LB Felton Hayes / Keith Carter
	LB Kelvin Smith
	LB John Hadley / Kevin Grant
	DB Deion Sanders / Corian Freeman
	DB Eric Williams / Tracy Sanders
	DB LeRoy Butler / Dedrick Dodge
	DB Stanley Shivers

RUSHING: Smith 108/577y, Chris Parker (TB) 71/391y,
Carter 58/330y
PASSING: Ferguson 122-194/1714y, 16TD, 62.9%,
Willis 48-85/637y, 9TD, 56.5%
RECEIVING: Anthony 32/550y, Lewis 27/484y, LaSane 22/406y
SCORING: Richie Andrews (K) 72pts, Dawsey 60pts,
Anthony 48pts

1989 10-2

26 Southern Miss.	30 WR Terry Anthony / Bruce LaSane
23 Clemson	34 WR Ronnie Lewis / Lawrence Dawsey
31 LSU	21 T Robert Stevenson
59 Tulane	9 G Hayward Haynes
41 Syracuse	10 C Michael Tanks
41 Virginia Tech	7 G Tony Yeomans / Mike Morris
22 Auburn	14 T John Brown / Kevin Mancini
24 Miami	10 TE Reggie Johnson
35 South Carolina	10 QB Peter Tom Willis / Casey Wheldon
57 Memphis State	20 TB Dexter Carter / Amp Lee
24 Florida	17 FB Edgar Bennett / Paul Moore
41 Nebraska■	17 DL Henry Ostaszewski
	DL Odell Haggins
	DL Eric Hayes
	LB Shelton Thompson / Anthony Moss
	LB Keith Carter / Kelvin Smith
	LB Kirk Carruthers
	LB Kevin Grant / Howard Dinkins
	DB Errol McCorvey
	DB LeRoy Butler / Terrell Buckley
	DB Dedrick Dodge / John Wyche
	DB Bill Ragans / Leon Fowler

RUSHING: Carter 131/684y, Lee 61/290y, Bennett 77/277y
PASSING: Willis 211-346/3124y, 20TD, 61.0%
RECEIVING: Dawsey 38/683y, Anthony 33/569y, Lewis 27/535y
SCORING: Richie Andrews (K) 58pts, Carter 54pts,
Anthony 48pts, Bill Mason (K) 37pts

1990 10-2

45 East Carolina	24 WR Shannon Baker / Matt Frier
48 Ga. Southern	6 WR Lawrence Dawsey / Kevin Knox
31 Tulane	13 T Robert Stevenson
39 Virginia Tech	28 G Reggie Dixon
22 Miami	31 C Robbie Baker
17 Auburn	20 G Mike Morris
42 LSU	3 T Kevin Mancini / Hayward Haynes
41 South Carolina	10 TE Reggie Johnson
70 Cincinnati	21 QB Casey Weldon / Brad Johnson
35 Memphis State	3 TB Amp Lee / Sean Jackson
45 Florida	30 FB Edgar Bennett / Paul Moore
24 Penn State■	17 DL Henry Ostaszewski / Todd McIntosh
	DL James Chaney / Joe Ostaszewski
	DL Carl Simpson / Troy Sanders
	LB Anthony Moss / Ken Alexander
	LB Marvin Jones / Bryce Abbott
	LB Kirk Carruthers
	LB Howard Dinkins / Reggie Freeman
	DB Errol McCorvey / Tommy Henry
	DB Terrell Buckley
	DB Leon Fowler / John Wyche
	DB Bill Ragans / John Davis

RUSHING: Lee 158/825y, Jackson 54/427y, Bennett 61/302y
PASSING: Weldon 112-182/1600y, 12TD, 61.5%,
Johnson 109-163/1136y, 8TD, 66.9%
RECEIVING: Dawsey 65/999y, Bennett 35/395y, Lee 34/360y
SCORING: Lee 108pts, Richie Andrews (K) 91pts, Bennett 54pts

1991 11-2

44 BYU	28 WR Kez McCorvey / Matt Frier
38 Tulane	11 WR Shannon Baker / Kevin Knox
58 W. Michigan	0 T Robert Stevenson
51 Michigan	31 G Reggie Dixon / Eric McGill
46 Syracuse	14 C Robbie Baker
33 Virginia Tech	20 G Mike Morris / Patrick McNeil
39 Middle Tenn. St.	10 T Kevin Mancini / John Flath
27 LSU	16 TE Lonnie Johnson
40 Louisville	15 QB Casey Weldon
38 South Carolina	10 TB Amp Lee / Sean Jackson
16 Miami	17 FB Edgar Bennett / William Floyd
9 Florida	14 DL Henry Ostaszewski / Dan Footman
10 Texas A&M■	2 DL James Chaney / Toddrick McIntosh
	DL Carl Simpson
	LB Sterling Palmer / Reggie Freeman
	LB Marvin Jones / Ken Alexander
	LB Kirk Carruthers / Kevin Adams
	LB Howard Dinkins / Derrick Brooks
	DB Errol McCorvey / Clifton Abraham
	DB Terrell Buckley / Corey Sawyer
	DB Leon Fowler
	DB John Davis

RUSHING: Lee 186/977y, Jackson 63/392y, Bennett 94/384y
PASSING: Weldon 189-313/2527y, 22TD, 60.4%
RECEIVING: Baker 30/451y, Bennett 29/345y, Lee 26/336y
SCORING: Lee 84pts, Gerry Thomas (K) 44pts,
Dan Mowrey (K) & Bennett 42pts

1992 11-1

48 Duke	21 WR Kez McCorvey / Matt Frier
24 Clemson	20 WR Tamarick Vanover / Kevin Knox
34 N. Carolina St.	13 T Robert Stevenson
35 Wake Forest	7 G Lewis Tyre
16 Miami	19 C Robbie Baker / Clay Shiver
36 North Carolina	13 G Patrick McNeil
29 Georgia Tech	24 T Marvin Ferrell
13 Virginia	3 TE Lonnie Johnson
69 Maryland	21 QB Charlie Ward / Danny Kanell
70 Tulane	7 TB Sean Jackson / Tiger McMillon
45 Florida	24 FB William Floyd / Zack Crockett
27 Nebraska■	14 DL Dan Footman / Derrick Alexander
	DL Toddrick McIntosh
	DL Carl Simpson
	LB Derrick Brooks
	LB Marvin Jones / Todd Rebol
	LB Ken Alexander / Chris Cowart
	LB Reggie Freeman / James Roberson
	DB Clifton Abraham / Corey Fuller
	DB Corey Sawyer
	DB Leon Fowler / Richard Coes
	DB John Davis / Devin Bush

RUSHING: McMillon 116/579y, Ward 100/504y, Jackson 96/489y
PASSING: Ward 204-365/2647y, 22TD, 55.9%
RECEIVING: Vanover 42/581y, Knox 35/396y,
McCorvey 34/521y
SCORING: Dan Mowrey (K) 81pts, Floyd 60pts, Vanover 42pts

1993 12-1

42	Kansas	0	WR Matt Frier / Kez McCorvey
45	Duke	7	WR Kevin Knox / Tamarick Vanover
57	Clemson	0	T Juan Laureano / Jesus Hernandez
33	North Carolina	7	G Lewis Tyre
51	Georgia Tech	0	C Clay Shiver
28	Miami	10	G Patrick McNeil
40	Virginia	14	T Marvin Ferrell / Forrest Conoly
54	Maryland	0	TE Lonnie Johnson / Billy Glenn
49	Maryland	20	QB Charlie Ward
24	Notre Dame	31	TB Sean Jackson / Warrick Dunn
62	N. Carolina St.	3	FB William Floyd / Pooh Bear Williams
33	Florida	21	DL James Roberson / Reinard Wilson
18	Nebraska ■	16	DL Toddrick McIntosh / Chris Cowart

DL Jon Nance
DL Derrick Alexander / Tyrant Marion
LB Derrick Brooks
LB Todd Rebol / Sam Cowart
LB Ken Alexander / Henri Crockett
DB Clifton Abraham / Byron Capers
DB Corey Sawyer / James Colzie
DB Richard Coes
DB Devin Bush

RUSHING: Jackson 134/825y, Dunn 65/511y, Ward 65/339y
PASSING: Ward 264-380/3032y, 27TD, 69.5%
RECEIVING: McCorvey 74/966y, Frier 45/598y, Vanover 45/542y
SCORING: Scott Bentley (K) 95pts, Dunn 60pts, Jackson 48pts

1994 10-1-1

41	Virginia	17	WR Kez McCorvey / E.G. Green
52	Maryland	20	WR 'Omar Ellison / Andre Cooper
56	Wake Forest	14	T Jesus Hernandez / Juan Laureano
31	North Carolina	18	G Lewis Tyre
20	Miami	34	C Clay Shiver
17	Clemson	0	G Patrick McNeil / Chad Bates
59	Duke	20	T Todd Fordham
41	Georgia Tech	10	TE Melvin Pearsall / Billy Glenn
23	Notre Dame	16	QB Danny Kanell
34	N. Carolina St.	3	TB Warrick Dunn / Rock Preston
31	Florida	31	FB Zack Crockett / Dennis Andrews
23	Florida ■	17	DL James Roberson / Reinard Wilson

DL Andre Wadsworth / Connell Spain
DL Orpheus Roye / Peter Boulware
DL Derrick Alexander / Tyrant Marion
LB Derrick Brooks / James Roberson
LB Daryl Bush
LB Todd Rebol / Sam Cowart
DB Clifton Abraham / James Colzie
DB Corey Fuller / Byron Capers
DB Sean Hamlet
DB Devin Bush / Robert Hammond

RUSHING: Dunn 152/1026y, Preston 68/587y, Crockett 83/341y
PASSING: Kanell 227-380/2781y, 17TD, 59.7%
RECEIVING: McCorvey 59/870y, Dunn 34/308y, Ellison 32/506y
SCORING: Crockett 66pts, Preston 56pts, Dunn 54pts

1995 10-2

70	Duke	26	WR E.G. Green
45	Clemson	26	WR Andre Cooper / Wayne Messam
77	N. Carolina St.	17	T Jesus Hernandez
46	C. Florida	14	G Lewis Tyre
41	Miami	17	C Clay Shiver / Kevin Long
72	Wake Forest	13	G Chad Bates / Marcus Long
42	Georgia Tech	10	T Todd Fordham / Tra Thomas
28	Virginia	33	TE Melvin Pearsall
28	North Carolina	12	QB Danny Kanell
59	Maryland	17	TB Warrick Dunn / Dee Feaster
24	Florida	35	FB Pooh Bear Williams / Rock Preston
31	Notre Dame ■	26	DL Reinard Wilson

DL Andre Wadsworth / Julian Pittman
DL Orpheus Roye / Connell Spain
DL Tyrant Marion / Peter Boulware
LB Sam Cowart / Henri Crockett
LB Daryl Bush
LB Todd Rebol / Lamont Green
DB Samari Rolle / James Colzie
DB Byron Capers
DB Sean Hamlet / Sean Kay
DB Robert Hammond / Dexter Jackson

RUSHING: Dunn 166/1242y, Preston 63/439y, Feaster 50/330y
PASSING: Kannell 257-402/2957y, 32TD, 63.9%
RECEIVING: Cooper 71/1002y, Green 60/1007y, Dunn 43/294y
SCORING: Dunn 96pts, Scott Bentley (K) 94pts, Cooper 90pts

1996 11-1

44	Duke	7	WR E.G. Green / Laveranues Coles
51	N. Carolina St.	0	WR Andre Cooper / Ron Dugans
13	North Carolina	0	T Walter Jones
34	Clemson	3	G Marcus Long / Jason Whitaker
34	Miami	16	C Kevin Long
31	Virginia	24	G Chad Bates
49	Georgia Tech	3	T Todd Fordham / Tra Thomas
44	Wake Forest	0	TE Melvin Pearsall
54	Southern Miss.	14	QB Thad Busby / Dan Kendra
48	Maryland	10	TB Warrick Dunn / Dee Feaster
24	Florida	21	FB Pooh Bear Williams / Rock Preston
20	Florida ■	52	DL Reinard Wilson / Greg Spires

DL Andre Wadsworth / Julian Pittman
DL Connell Spain / Jerry Johnson
DL Peter Boulware
LB Vernon Crawford / Lamont Green
LB Daryl Bush
LB Henri Crockett / Sam Cowart
DB Samari Rolle / James Colzie
DB Byron Capers / Mario Edwards
DB Sean Hamlet / Sean Key
DB Shevin Smith

RUSHING: Dunn 189/1180y, Preston 49/386y, Coles 14/91y
PASSING: Busby 134-243/1866y, 16TD, 55.1%,
  Kendra 46-89/665y, 9TD, 51.7%
RECEIVING: Green 34/662y, Dunn 30/355y, Cooper 26/338y
SCORING: Scott Bentley (K) 100pts, Dunn 84pts, Green 42pts

1997 11-1

14	Southern Cal	7	WR E.G. Green / Ron Dugans
50	Maryland	7	WR Peter Warrick / Laveranues Coles
35	Clemson	28	T Ross Brannon
47	Miami	0	G Jason Whitaker
51	Duke	27	C Kevin Long / Jared Moon
38	Georgia Tech	0	G Donald Heaven
47	Virginia	21	T Tra Thomas
48	N. Carolina St.	35	TE Melvin Pearsall / Myron Jackson
20	North Carolina	3	QB Thad Busby / Dan Kendra
58	Wake Forest	7	TB Travis Minor / Dee Feaster
29	Florida	32	FB Lamarr Glenn / William McCray
31	Ohio State ■	14	DL Andre Wadsworth / Jamal Reynolds

DL Jerry Johnson
DL Larry Smith / Corey Simon
DL Greg Spires / Tony Bryant
LB Sam Cowart / Deon Humphrey
LB Daryl Bush / Bobby Rhodes
LB Lamont Green / Brian Allen
DB Samari Rolle / Troy Saunders
DB Tay Cody
DB Dexter Jackson
DB Shevin Smith / Derrick Gibson

RUSHING: Minor 112/623y, Davy Ford (TB) 61/258y,
  Feaster 36/127y
PASSING: Busby 235-390/3317y, 25TD, 60.3%
RECEIVING: Green 54/1059y, Warrick 53/884y,
  Pearsall 31/326y
SCORING: Sebastian Janikowski (K) 85pts,
  Minor & Green 66pts

1998 11-2

23	Texas A&M	14	WR Ron Dugans / Laveranues Coles
7	N. Carolina St.	24	WR Peter Warrick / Marvin Minnis
62	Duke	13	T Ross Brannon
30	Southern Cal	10	G Jason Whitaker
24	Maryland	10	C Eric Thomas / Jarad Moon
26	Miami	14	G Jerry Carmichael
48	Clemson	0	T Tarlos Thomas
34	Georgia Tech	7	TE Myron Jackson
39	North Carolina	13	QB Chris Weinke / Marcus Outzen
45	Virginia	14	TB Travis Minor / Jeff Chaney
24	Wake Forest	7	FB Lamarr Glenn / William McCray
23	Florida	12	DL Jamal Reynolds / Tony Bryant
16	Tennessee ■	23	DL Jerry Johnson

DL Corey Simon / Larry Smith
DL Roland Seymour
LB Tommy Polley / Deon Humphrey
LB Demetro Stephens / Bobby Rhodes
LB Lamont Green / Brian Allen
DB Mario Edwards
DB Tay Cody
DB Dexter Jackson / Sean Key
DB Derrick Gibson

RUSHING: Minor 191/857y, Chaney 120/573y, Coles 15/128y
PASSING: Weinke 145-286/2487y, 19TD, 50.7%
RECEIVING: Warrick 61/1232y, Dugans 38/616y, Minnis 22/338y
SCORING: Sebastian Janikowski (K) 123pts, Warrick 78pts,
  Minor 48pts

1999 12-0

41	Louisiana Tech	7	WR Ron Dugans / Anquan Boldin
41	Georgia Tech	35	WR Peter Warrick / Marvin Minnis
42	N. Carolina St.	11	T Brett Williams
42	North Carolina	10	G Justin Amman
51	Duke	23	C Eric Thomas / Jarad Moon
31	Miami	21	G Jason Whitaker
33	Wake Forest	10	T Tarlos Thomas / Char-ron Dorsey
17	Clemson	14	TE Ryan Sprague / Patrick Hughes
35	Virginia	10	QB Chris Weinke
49	Maryland	10	TB Travis Minor/Jeff Chan'y/Nick Maddox
30	Florida	23	FB William McCray / Dan Kendra
46	Virginia Tech ■	29	DL Jamal Reynolds

DL Jerry Johnson
DL Corey Simon
DL Roland Seymour / David Warren
LB Tommy Polley
LB Bradley Jennings
LB Brian Allen
DB Clevan Thomas / Malcolm Tatum
DB Tay Cody
DB Sean Key / Chris Hope
DB Derrick Gibson

RUSHING: Minor 180/815y, Chaney 43/157y, Maddox 29/111y
PASSING: Weinke 232-377/3103y, 25TD, 61.5%
RECEIVING: Warrick 71/934y, Dugans 43/644y, Minnis 19/257y
SCORING: Sebastian Janikowski (K) 116pts, Warrick 72pts,
  Minor 42pts

2000 11-2

29	BYU	3	WR Anquan Boldin / Robert Morgan
26	Georgia Tech	21	WR Marvin Minnis / Atrews Bell
63	North Carolina	14	T Brett Williams / Todd Williams
31	Louisville	0	G Justin Amman
59	Maryland	7	C Jarad Moon
24	Miami	27	G Montrae Holland / Otis Duhart
63	Duke	14	T Tarlos Thomas / Char-ron Dorsey
37	Virginia	3	TE Ryan Sprague / Nick Franklin
58	N. Carolina St.	14	QB Chris Weinke
54	Clemson	7	TB Travis Minor / Davy Ford /Jeff Chaney
35	Wake Forest	6	FB William McCray
30	Florida	7	DL Jamal Reynolds / David Warren
2	Oklahoma ■	13	DL Darnell Dockett / Tony Benford

DL Jeff Womble / Kevin Emanuel
DL Roland Seymour / Alonzo Jackson
LB Tommy Polley / Kendyll Pope
LB Bradley Jennings / Jerel Hudson
LB Brian Allen
DB ClevanThomas
DB Tay Cody / Malcolm Tatum
DB Chris Hope
DB Derrick Gibson / Abdual Howard

RUSHING: Minor 181/923y, Chaney 71/346y,
  Greg Jones (TB) 41/266y
PASSING: Weinke 266-431/4167y, 33TD, 61.7%
RECEIVING: Minnis 63/1340y, Minor 42/333y, Boldin 41/664y
SCORING: Bell & Minnis 66pts, McCray 48pts

2001 8-4

55	Duke	13	WR Javon Walker / Anquan Boldin
29	Ala.-Birm'ham	7	WR Talman Gardner / Atrews Bell
9	North Carolina	41	T Brett Williams / Ray Willis
48	Wake Forest	24	G Montrae Holland
27	Miami	49	C Antoine Mirambeau
43	Virginia	7	G Milford Brown
52	Maryland	31	T Todd Williams
41	Clemson	27	TE Patrick Hughes
28	N. Carolina St.	34	QB Chris Rix
13	Florida	37	TB Greg Jones / Nick Maddox
28	Georgia Tech	17	FB William McCray / Chad Maeder
30	Virginia Tech ■	17	DL Alonzo Jackson

DL Darnell Dockett
DL Jeff Womble
DL Kevin Emanuel
LB Michael Boulware
LB Bradley Jennings / Jerel Hudson
LB Kendyll Pope / Allen Augustin
DB Rufus Brown / Malcolm Tatum
DB Stanford Samuels
DB Chris Hope / Gennaro Jackson
DB Abdual Howard

RUSHING: Jones 134/713y, Maddox 98/438y, Rix 99/389y
PASSING: Rix 165-286/2734y, 24TD, 57.7%
RECEIVING: Walker 45/944y, Gardner 33/649y, Bell 29/433y
SCORING: Xavier Beitia (K) 83pts, Gardner 66pts, Walker 42pts

2002 9-5

38 Iowa State	31 WR Anquan Boldin / Robert Morgan
40 Virginia	19 WR Talman Gardner / Craphonso Thorpe
37 Maryland	10 T Brett Williams
48 Duke	17 G Todd Williams / Milford Brown
20 Louisville	26 C Antoine Mirambeau
48 Clemson	31 G Montrae Holland
27 Miami	28 T Ray Willis
24 Notre Dame	34 TE Patrick Hughes
34 Wake Forest	21 QB Chris Rix / Adrian McPherson
21 Georgia Tech	13 TB Greg Jones / Nick Maddox
40 North Carolina	14 FB B.J. Dean
7 N. Carolina St.	17 DL Kevin Emanuel
31 Florida	14 DL Darnell Dockett
13 Georgia■	26 DL Travis Johnson / Jeff Womble
	DL Alonzo Jackson
	LB Michael Boulware
	LB Allen Augustin / Jerel Hudson
	LB Kendyll Pope
	DB Stanford Samuels
	DB Rufus Brown
	DB Kyler Hall / B.J. Ward
	DB Jerome Carter

RUSHING: Jones 161/938y, Maddox 106/602y, Rix 86/289y
PASSING: Rix 118-225/1684y, 13TD, 52.4%,
  McPherson 80-155/1017y, 12TD, 51.6%
RECEIVING: Boldin 65/1011y, Gardner 38/625y,
  Maddox 23/197y
SCORING: Xavier Beitia (K) 108pts, Boldin 78pts,
  Jones & Gardner 48pts

2003 10-3

37 North Carolina	0 WR P.K. Sam / Dominic Robinson
35 Maryland	10 WR Craphonso Thorpe/Chauncey Stovall
14 Georgia Tech	13 T Alex Barron
47 Colorado	7 G Matt Meinrod
56 Duke	7 C John Frady / Mario Henderson
14 Miami	22 G Bobby Meeks / Ron Lunford
19 Virginia	14 T Ray Willis
48 Wake Forest	24 TE Paul Irons / Matt Henshaw
37 Notre Dame	0 QB Chris Rix
10 Clemson	26 TB Greg Jones / Lorenzo Booker
50 N. Carolina St.	44 FB B.J. Dean / James Coleman
38 Florida	34 DL Kevin Emanuel
14 Miami■	16 DL Darnell Dockett / Charles Howard
	DL Travis Johnson / Jeff Wombley
	DL Chauncey Davis / Kamerion Wimbley
	LB Michael Boulware / Ray Piquion
	LB Allen Augustin
	LB Kendyll Pope
	DB Stanford Samuels / Leroy Smith
	DB Bryant McFadden / Rufus Brown
	DB B.J. Ward
	DB Jerome Carter / Cludius Osei

RUSHING: Jones 144/618y, Leon Washington (TB) 74/387y,
  Booker 62/334y
PASSING: Rix 216-382/3107y, 23TD, 56.5%
RECEIVING: Thorpe 51/994y, Sam 50/735y,
  Chris Davis (WR) 23/264y
SCORING: Xavier Beitia (K) 107pts, Thorpe 66pts, Jones 42pts

2004 9-3

10 Miami	16 WR Chauncey Stovall
34 Ala.-Birm'ham	7 WR Craph'nso Thorpe/Dominic Robinson
41 Clemson	22 T Alex Barron
38 North Carolina	16 G Cory Niblock / Matt Meinrod
17 Syracuse	13 C David Castillo / John Frady
36 Virginia	3 G Bobby Meeks / Ron Lunford
20 Wake Forest	17 T Ray Willis
17 Maryland	20 TE Paul Irons / Matt Henshaw
29 Duke	7 QB Wyatt Sexton / Chris Rix
17 N. Carolina St.	10 TB Leon Washington / Lorenzo Booker
13 Florida	20 FB B.J. Dean / James Coleman
30 West Virginia■	18 DL Chauncey Davis
	DL Brodrick Bunkley / Clifton Dickson
	DL Travis Johnson
	DL Eric Moore / Kamerion Wimbley
	LB Ernie Sims / Ray Piquon
	LB Buster Davis / Sam McGrew
	LB A.J. Nicholson
	DB Bryant McFadden
	DB Leroy Smith
	DB Pat Watkins
	DB Jerome Carter

RUSHING: Washington 138/951y, Booker 173/887y,
  Coleman 28/87y
PASSING: Sexton 139-252/1661y, 8TD, 55.2%,
  Rix 76-149/865y, 3TD, 51.0%
RECEIVING: Stovall 53/780y, Thorpe 40/496y, Booker 24/160y
SCORING: Xavier Beitia (K) 77pts, Washington 42pts,
  Stovall 36pts

2005 8-5

10 Miami	7 WR Chris Davis / Greg Carr
62 Citadel	10 WR Willie Reid / De'Cody Fagg
28 Boston College	17 T Cory Niblock / Mario Henderson
38 Syracuse	14 G Jackie Claude / Cornelius Lewis
41 Wake Forest	24 C David Castillo / John Frady (G)
21 Virginia	26 G Matt Meinrod / Ron Lunford
55 Duke	24 T David Overmyer
35 Maryland	27 TE Matt Henshaw / Donnie Carter
15 N. Carolina St.	20 QB Drew Weatherford / Xavier Lee
14 Clemson	35 TB Lorenzo Booker / Leon Washington
7 Florida	34 FB James Coleman / B.J. Dean
27 Virginia Tech □	22 DL Kamerion Wimbley / Willie Jones
23 Penn State■	26 DL Brodrick Bunkley
	DL Andre Fluellen
	DL Alex Boston / D.J. Norris
	LB Ernie Sims / Lawrence Timmons
	LB Buster Davis / Sam McGrew
	LB A.J. Nicholson / Marcello Church
	DB Tony Carter
	DB J.R. Bryant
	DB Pat Watkins / Roger Williams
	DB Kyler Hall

RUSHING: Booker 119/552y, Washington 97/430y,
  Antone Smith (TB) 36/188y
PASSING: Weatherford 276-469/3208y, 18TD, 58.8%
RECEIVING: Davis 51/666y, Reid 50/634y, Booker 38/329y,
  Fagg 35/404y, Carr 30/618y
SCORING: Gary Cismesia (K) 93pts, Carr 54pts, Booker 36pts

2006 7-6

13 Miami	10 WR De'Cody Fagg / Greg Carr
24 Troy	17 WR Chris Davis
20 Clemson	27 T Mario Henderson
55 Rice	7 G Jackie Claude
20 N. Carolina St.	24 C John Frady
51 Duke	24 G Cory Niblock / David Overmyer (T)
19 Boston College	24 T Shannon Boatman
24 Maryland	27 TE Brandon Warren / Caz Piurowski
33 Virginia	0 QB Drew Weatherford / Xavier Lee
0 Wake Forest	30 TB Lorenzo Booker / Antone Smith
28 W. Michigan	20 FB Joe Surratt
14 Florida	21 DL Neefy Moffett/Alex Boston/D.J. Norris
44 UCLA■	27 DL Andre Fluellen / Paul Griffin
	DL Letroy Guion / Budd Thacker
	DL Darrell Burston
	LB Lawrence Timmons
	LB Buster Davis
	LB Geno Hayes / Rodney Gallon
	DB Tony Carter / Michael Ray Garvin
	DB Jamie Robinson / J.R. Bryant
	DB Roger Williams
	DB Myron Rolle / Anthony Houllis

RUSHING: Booker 143/616y, Smith 88/456y, Lee 23/84y
PASSING: Weatherford 177-318/2155y, 12 TD, 55.7%,
  Lee 62-121/885y, 7TD, 51.2%
RECEIVING: Davis 49/684y, Fagg 37/439y, Carr 34/619y,
  Booker 33/420y, Warren 28/301y
SCORING: Gary Cismesia (K) 81pts, Carr 72pts, Surratt 36pts

2007 7-6

18 Clemson	24 WR De'Cody Fagg / Preston Parker
34 Ala.-Birm'ham	24 WR Greg Carr / Richard Goodman
16 Colorado	6 T Daron Rose / David Overmyer
21 Alabama	14 G Rodney Hudson
27 N. Carolina St.	10 C Ryan McMahon
21 Wake Forest	24 G Jacky Claude / Will Furlong
29 Miami	37 T Shannon Boatman (G)
25 Duke	6 TE Charlie Graham / Caz Piurowski
27 Boston College	17 QB Drew Weatherford / Xavier Lee
21 Virginia Tech	40 TB Antone Smith
24 Maryland	16 FB Seddrick Holloway / Marcus Sims
12 Florida	45 DL Everette Brown / Justin Mincey
28 Kentucky■	35 DL Budd Thacker / Kendrick Stewart
	DL Letroy Guion / Andre Fluellen
	DL Neefy Moffett / Alex Boston
	LB Dekoda Watson
	LB Derek Nicholson
	LB Geno Hayes
	DB Tony Carter
	DB Michael Ray Garvin / Patrick Robinson
	DB Roger Williams
	DB Myron Rolle

RUSHING: Smith 191/817y, Parker 52/270y, Holloway 26/129y
PASSING: Weatherford 181-318/2049y, 9TD, 56.9%,
  Lee 66-124/972y, 5TD, 53.2%
RECEIVING: Parker 62/791y, Fagg 54/758y, Carr 45/795y
SCRORING: Gary Cismesia (K) 109pts, Fagg & Parker 30pts

2008 9-4

69 W. Carolina	0 WR Greg Carr / Corey Surrency
46 Chattanooga	7 WR Preston Parker / Rod Owens
3 Wake Forest	12 WR Taiwan Easterling /Marcus Sims (FB)
39 Colorado	21 T Andrew Datko
41 Miami	39 G Rodney Hudson
26 N. Carolina St.	17 C Ryan McMahon
30 Virginia Tech	20 G David Spurlock / Will Furlong
28 Georgia Tech	31 T Zebrie Sanders / Antwane Greenlee
41 Clemson	27 TE Caz Piurowski / Joshua Dobbie
17 Boston College	27 QB Christian Ponder / Drew Weatherford
37 Maryland	3 TB Antone Smith / Jermaine Thomas
15 Florida	45 DL Neefy Moffett / Benjamin Lamkin
42 Wisconsin■	13 DL Budd Thacker / Moses McCray
	DL Kendrick Stewart / Justin Mincey
	DL Everette Brown
	LB Dakota Watson / Kendall Smith
	LB Derek Nicholson
	LB Toddrick Verdell / Nigel Bradham
	DB Tony Carter
	DB Patrick Robinson / Korey Mangum
	DB Darius McClure / Jamie Robinson
	DB Myron Rolle

RUSHING: Smith 177/792y, Thomas 69/482y, Ponder 119/423y
PASSING: Ponder 177-318/2006y, 14TD, 55.7%,
  D'Vontrey Richardson 23-44/315y, 3TD, 52.3%
  Weatherford 10-23/156y, 0TD, 43.5%
RECEIVING: Parker 40/372y, Carr 39/542y, Easterling 30/322y
SCORING: Graham Gano (K) 105pts, Smith 96pts, Carr 26pts

2009 7-6

34 Miami	38 WR/FB Rod Owens / Lonnie Pryor
19 Jacksonville St.	9 WR Jarmon Fortson / Richard Goodman
54 BYU	28 WR Taiwan Easterling / Bert Reed
0 South Florida	17 T Andrew Datko
21 Boston College	28 G Rodney Hudson
44 Georgia Tech	49 C Ryan McMahon
30 North Carolina	27 G David Spurlock
45 N. Carolina St.	42 T Zebrie Sanders
24 Clemson	40 TE Caz Piurowski / Bo Reliford
41 Wake Forest	28 QB Christian Ponder / E.J. Manuel
29 Maryland	26 TB Jermaine Thomas / Ty Jones
10 Florida	37 DL Kevin McNeil / Craig Yarborough
33 West Virginia■	21 DL Moses McCray / Budd Thacker
	DL Everett Dawkins / Kendrick Stewart
	DL Markus White / Jacobbi McDaniel
	LB Dakoda Watson / Nigel Carr
	LB Kendall Smith / Mister Alexander
	LB Nigel Bradham / Ricardo Wright
	DB Ochuko Jenije /Greg Reid /Dionte Allen
	DB Patrick Robinson / Nick Moody
	DB Jamie Robinson
	DB Korey Mangum

RUSHING: Smith 177/792y, Thomas 69/482y, Ponder 119/423y
PASSING: Ponder 177-318/2006y, 14TD, 55.7%
  D'Vontrey Richardson (QB) 23-44/315y, 3TD, 52.3%
RECEIVING: Parker 40/372y, Carr 39/542y, Easterling 30/322y
SCORING: Graham Gano (K) 105pts, Smith 96pts, Carr 26pts

2010 10-4

59 Samford	6 WR Bert Reed / Willie Haulstead
17 Oklahoma	47 WR Taiwan Easterling
34 BYU	10 WR/FB Rodney Smith / Lonnie Pryor
31 Wake Forest	0 T Andrew Datko / Henry Orelas (G)
34 Virginia	14 G Rodney Hudson / Rhonnie Sanderson
45 Miami	17 C Ryan McMahon
24 Boston College	19 G David Spurlock / Bryan Stork
24 N. Carolina St.	28 T Zebrie Sanders
35 North Carolina	37 TE Beau Reliford / Ja'Baris Little
16 Clemson	13 QB Christian Ponder / E.J. Manuel
30 Maryland	16 RB J. Thomas/ Chris Thompson / Ty Jones
31 Florida	7 DL Markus White / Bjoern Werner
33 Virginia Tech □	44 DL Jacobbi McDaniel / Anthony McCloud
26 South Carolina■	17 DL Everett Dawkins / Demonte McAllister
	DL Brandon Jenkins / Dan Hicks
	LB Mister Alexander / Christian Jones
	LB Kendall Smith / Vince Williams
	LB Nigel Bradham / Telvin Smith
	DB Xavier Rhodes / Lamarcus Joyner
	DB Greg Reid
	DB Nick Moody / Ochuko Jenije
	DB Terrance Parks / Mike Harris

RUSHING: Thompson 134/845y, Jones 87/527y, Thomas 86/490y
PASSING: Ponder 184-299/2044y, 20TD, 61.5%
  Manuel 65-93/861y, 4TD, 69.9%
RECEIVING: Reed 58/614y, Easterling 43/551y, Haulstead 38/587y
SCORING: Dustin Hopkins (K) 119pts, 3 tied w/ 42pts

GEORGIA

University of Georgia (Founded 1785)
Athens, Georgia
Nickname: Bulldogs, Dawgs
Colors: Red and Black
Stadium: Sanford Stadium (1929) 92,746
Affiliations: Southeastern (Charter Member, 1933-present)

CAREER RUSHING YARDS	Attempts	Yards
Herschel Walker (1980-82)	994	5259
Garrison Hearst (1990-92)	543	3232
Lars Tate (1984-87)	615	3017
Knowshon Moreno (2007-08)	498	2734
Rodney Hampton (1987-89)	472	2668
Thomas Brown (2004-07)	529	2646
Kevin McLee (1975-77)	562	2581
Frankie Sinkwich (1940-42)	447	2271
Willie McClendon (1976-78)	443	2228
Musa Smith (2000-02)	454	2202

CAREER PASSING YARDS	Comp.-Att.	Yards
David Greene (2001-04)	849-1440	11,528
Eric Zeier (1991-94)	838-1402	11,153
Matthew Stafford (2006-08)	564-987	7731
Quincy Carter (1998-2000)	483-853	6447
Mike Bobo (1994-97)	445-755	6334
Zeke Bratkowski (1951-53)	360-734	4836
Johnny Rauch (1945-48)	252-483	4044
Buck Belue (1978-81)	264-484	3864
D.J. Shockley (2002-05)	240-443	3555
James Jackson (1984-87)	223-439	3416

CAREER RECEIVING YARDS	Catches	Yards
Terrence Edwards (1999-2002)	204	3093
Fred Gibson (2001-04)	161	2884
A.J. Green (2008-10)	166	2620
Brice Hunter (1992-95)	182	2373
Mohamed Massaquoi (2005-08)	158	2282
Lindsay Scott (1978-81)	131	2098
Reggie Brown (2001-04)	144	2008
Juan Daniels (1993-97)	120	1975
Hines Ward (1994-97)	144	1965
Andre Hastings (1990-92)	124	1876

SEASON RUSHING YARDS	Attempts	Yards
Herschel Walker (1981)	385	1891
Herschel Walker (1982)	335	1752
Herschel Walker (1980)	274	1616
Garrison Hearst (1992)	228	1547
Knowshon Moreno (2008)	250	1400

SEASON PASSING YARDS	Comp.-Att.	Yards
Eric Zeier (1993)	269-425	3525
Matthew Stafford (2008)	235-383	3459
Eric Zeier (1994)	259-433	3396
David Greene (2003)	264-438	3307
Aaron Murray (2010)	209-342	3049

SEASON RECEIVING YARDS	Catches	Yards
Terrence Edwards (2002)	59	1004
Brice Hunter (1993)	76	970
Mohamed Massaquoi (2008)	58	920
Hines Ward (1996)	52	900
Hason Graham (1994)	46	881

GAME RUSHING YARDS	Attempts	Yards
Herschel Walker (1980 vs. Vanderbilt)	N/A	283
Herschel Walker (1981 vs. Mississippi)	41	265
Garrison Hearst (1992 vs. Vanderbilt)	21	246

GAME PASSING YARDS	Comp.-Att.	Yards
Eric Zeier (1993 vs. Southern Miss)	30-47	544
Eric Zeier (1994 vs. South Carolina)	31-51	485
Eric Zeier (1994 vs. Vanderbilt)	23-54	441

GAME RECEIVING YARDS	Catches	Yards
Fred Gibson (2001 vs. Kentucky)	9	201
Lamar Davis (1942 vs. Cincinnati)	10	198
Terrence Edwards (1999 vs. Utah State)	9	196

GREATEST COACH

The University of Georgia truly had its ups and downs until the arrival of coach Vince Dooley, a former Auburn quarterback, in 1964.

Dooley put the Bulldogs on the consistent winning path, claiming six SEC titles and the 1980 national championship. Although one could argue that Dooley's 1980 champions were carried by the incomparable Herschel Walker, his best teams were characterized by few great players but were charged by lots and lots of excellent team-oriented players. No memory gets Bulldog blood flowing faster than Dooley's "Junkyard Dawg" defenses.

GEORGIA'S 55 GREATEST SINCE 1953

OFFENSE

WIDE RECEIVER: Reggie Brown, Terrence Edwards, Fred Gibson, A.J. Green, Lindsay Scott
TIGHT END: Johnny Carson
TACKLE: Ray Rissmiller, Matt Stinchcomb, Bernard Williams, Jim Wilson, Mike "Moonpie" Wilson
GUARD: Edgar Chandler, Max Jean-Gilles, Joel Parrish
CENTER: Peter Anderson, Len Hauss
QUARTERBACK: Zeke Bratkowski, David Greene, Fran Tarkenton, Eric Zeier
RUNNING BACK: Rodney Hampton, Garrison Hearst, Knowshon Moreno, Herschel Walker
FULLBACK: Glynn Harrison, Ronnie Jenkins

DEFENSE

END: Freddie Gilbert, Bill Goldberg, David Pollack
TACKLE: George Patton, Jimmy Payne, Richard Seymour, Bill Stanfill
GUARD: Tim Crowe, Steve Greer
LINEBACKER: Boss Bailey, Knox Culpepper, Randall Godfrey, Nate Taylor, Ben Zambiasi
CORNERBACK: Champ Bailey, Scott Woerner
SAFETY: Thomas Davis, Terry Hoage, Lynn Hughes, Bill Krug, Jake Scott

SPECIAL TEAMS

RETURN SPECIALIST: Andre Hastings
PLACE KICKER: Kevin Butler, Rex Robinson
PUNTER: Bobby Walden

MULTIPLE POSITIONS

GUARD-TACKLE-DEFENSIVE GUARD: Mike Weaver
CORNERBACK-RUNNING BACK: Robert Edwards
QUARTERBACK-WIDE RECEIVER-RUNNING BACK: Hines Ward

TWO-WAY PLAYER

GUARD-LINEBACKER: Pat Dye

PERFORMANCE FORMULA:
GEORGIA'S 10 BEST SEASONS

2002	1.6720	4 of 70
1971	1.6517	6 of 70
1982	1.6457	3 of 70
1980	1.6161	5 of 70
1959	1.5987	3 of 70
1968	1.5974	3 of 70
1997	1.5940	7 of 70
1983	1.5787	6 of 70
1966	1.5721	4 of 70
1981	1.5696	4 of 70

GEORGIA BULLDOGS

Year	W-L-T	AP Poll	Conference Standing	Toughest Regular Season Opponents	Coach (Record at School)	Bowl Games		
1953	3-8		10t	Maryland 10-0, Alabama 6-2-3, Auburn 7-2-1, Georgia Tech 8-2-1	Wally Butts			
1954	6-3-1		5	Florida State 8-3, Auburn 7-3, Georgia Tech 7-3	Wally Butts			
1955	4-6		11	Mississippi 9-1, Vanderbilt 7-3, Auburn 8-1-1, Georgia Tech 8-1-1	Wally Butts			
1956	3-6-1		12	Miami 8-1-1, Florida 6-3-1, Auburn 7-3, Georgia Tech 9-1	Wally Butts			
1957	3-7		9	Texas 6-3-1, Navy 8-1-1, Florida 6-2-1, Auburn 10-0	Wally Butts			
1958	4-6		10	Texas 7-3, Florida 6-2-1, Auburn 9-0-1	Wally Butts			
1959	10-1	5	1	Alabama 7-1-2, Auburn 7-3, Georgia Tech 6-4	Wally Butts	Orange	14 Missouri	0
1960	6-4		6	Alabama 8-1-1, Florida 8-2, Auburn 8-2	Wally Butts (140-86-9)			
1961	3-7		9	Alabama 10-0, Miami 7-3, Georgia Tech 7-3	Johnny Griffith			
1962	3-4-3		7t	Alabama 9-1, Auburn 6-3-1, Georgia Tech 7-2-1	Johnny Griffith			
1963	4-5-1		9	Alabama 8-2, North Carolina 8-2, Auburn 9-1, Georgia Tech 7-3	Johnny Griffith (10-16-4)			
1964	7-3-1		2t	Alabama 10-0, Florida State 8-1-1, Florida 7-3, Georgia Tech 7-3	Vince Dooley	Sun	7 Texas Tech	0
1965	6-4		6t	Alabama 8-1-1, Florida 7-3, Georgia Tech 6-3-1	Vince Dooley			
1966	10-1	4	1t	Mississippi 8-2, Miami 7-2-1, Florida 8-2, Georgia Tech 9-1	Vince Dooley	Cotton	24 Southern Methodist	9
1967	7-4		5	Mississippi 6-3-1, Houston 7-3, Florida 6-4, Auburn 6-4	Vince Dooley	Liberty	7 North Carolina State	14
1968	8-1-2	8	1	Tennessee 8-1-1, Houston 6-2-2, Auburn 6-4	Vince Dooley	Sugar	2 Arkansas	16
1969	5-5-1		6	Tennessee 9-1, Florida 8-1-1, Auburn 8-2	Vince Dooley	Sun	6 Nebraska	45
1970	5-5		5t	Mississippi 7-3, Florida 7-4, Auburn 8-2, Georgia Tech 8-3	Vince Dooley			
1971	11-1	7	2t	Mississippi 9-2, Auburn 9-1	Vince Dooley	Gator	7 North Carolina	3
1972	7-4		5	NC State 7-3-1, Alabama 10-1, Tennessee 9-2, Auburn 9-1	Vince Dooley			
1973	7-4-1		5t	NC State 8-3, Alabama 11-0, Tennessee 8-3, Florida 7-4	Vince Dooley	Peach	17 Maryland	16
1974	6-6		2t	Mississippi State 8-3, Houston 8-3, Florida 8-3, Auburn 9-2	Vince Dooley	Tangerine	10 Miami (Ohio)	21
1975	9-3	19	2t	Pittsburgh 7-4, South Carolina 7-4, Florida 9-2, Georgia Tech 7-4	Vince Dooley	Cotton	10 Arkansas	31
1976	10-2	10	1	Alabama 8-3, Kentucky 7-4, Florida 8-3	Vince Dooley	Sugar	3 Pittsburgh	27
1977	5-6		7	Clemson 8-2-1, Alabama 10-1, Kentucky 10-1	Vince Dooley			
1978	9-2-1	16	2	Clemson 10-1, LSU 8-3, Auburn 6-4-1, Georgia Tech 7-4	Vince Dooley	Bluebonnet	22 Stanford	25
1979	6-5		2	Wake Forest 8-3, Clemson 8-3, South Carolina 8-3, Auburn 8-3	Vince Dooley			
1980	12-0	1	1	Clemson 6-5, South Carolina 8-3, Florida 7-4	Vince Dooley	Sugar	17 Notre Dame	10
1981	10-2	6	1	Tennessee 7-4, Clemson 11-0, Florida 7-4	Vince Dooley	Sugar	20 Pittsburgh	24
1982	11-1	4	1	Clemson 9-1-1, BYU 8-3, Vanderbilt 8-3, Florida 8-3, Auburn 8-3	Vince Dooley	Sugar	23 Penn State	27
1983	10-1-1	4	2	Clemson 9-1-1, Florida 8-2-1, Auburn 10-1	Vince Dooley	Cotton	10 Texas	9
1984	7-4-1		3t	South Carolina 10-1, Kentucky 8-3, Florida 9-1-1, Auburn 8-4	Vince Dooley	Citrus	17 Florida State	17
1985	7-3-2		4	Alabama 8-2-1, Baylor 8-3, Florida 9-1-1, Auburn 8-3	Vince Dooley	Sun	13 Arizona	13
1986	8-4		2t	Clemson 7-2-2, LSU 9-2, Auburn 9-2	Vince Dooley	Hall of Fame	24 Boston College	27
1987	9-3	13	4t	Clemson 9-2, South Carolina 8-3, LSU 9-1-1, Auburn 9-1-1	Vince Dooley	Liberty	20 Arkansas	17
1988	9-3	15	3	South Carolina 8-3, Florida 6-5, Auburn 10-1	Vince Dooley (201-77-10)	Gator	34 Michigan State	27
1989	6-6		4t	Tennessee 8-3, Florida 7-4, Auburn 9-2, Georgia Tech 7-4	Ray Goff	Peach	18 Syracuse	19
1990	4-7		7t	Clemson 9-2, Mississippi 9-2, Florida 9-2, Georgia Tech 10-0-1	Ray Goff			
1991	9-3	17	4t	Alabama 10-1, Clemson 9-1-1, Florida 10-1	Ray Goff	Independence	24 Arkansas	15
1992	10-2	8	E1t	Tennessee 8-3, Mississippi 8-3, Florida 8-4	Ray Goff	Citrus	21 Ohio State	14
1993	5-6		E4t	Tennessee 9-1-1, Florida 9-2, Auburn 11-0	Ray Goff			
1994	6-4-1		E4	Alabama 11-0, Florida 9-1-1, Auburn 9-1-1	Ray Goff			
1995	6-6		E3	Tennessee 10-1, Alabama 8-3, Clemson 8-3, Fla. 11-0, Auburn 8-3	Ray Goff (46-34-1)	Peach	27 Virginia	34
1996	5-6		E4	Tennessee 9-2, Florida 10-1, Auburn 7-4	Jim Donnan			
1997	10-2	10	E2t	Tennessee 10-1, Florida 9-2, Auburn 9-2	Jim Donnan	Outback	33 Wisconsin	6
1998	9-3	14	E3	Tennessee 11-0, Florida 9-2, Georgia Tech 9-2	Jim Donnan	Peach	35 Virginia	33
1999	8-4	16	E3	Tennessee 9-2, Florida 9-2, Georgia Tech 8-3	Jim Donnan	Outback	28 Purdue	25
2000	8-4	20	E2t	Tennessee 8-3, Florida 9-2, Auburn 9-2, Georgia Tech 9-2	Jim Donnan (40-19)	Oahu	37 Virginia	14
2001	8-4	22	E3t	South Carolina 8-3, Tennessee 10-1, Florida 9-2	Mark Richt	Music City	16 Boston College	20
2002	13-1	3	E1	Alabama 10-3, Tennessee 8-4, Florida 8-4, Auburn 8-4	Mark Richt	Sugar	26 Florida State	13
2003	11-3	7	E1t	Clemson 8-4, LSU 11-1, Tennessee 10-2, Florida 8-4	Mark Richt	Capital One	34 Purdue	27
2004	10-2	7	E2	LSU 9-2, Tennessee 9-2, Auburn 11-0	Mark Richt	Outback	24 Wisconsin	21
2005	10-3	10	E1	Boise State 9-4, Florida 8-3, Auburn 9-2, LSU 10-2	Mark Richt	Sugar	35 West Virginia	38
2006	9-4	23	E3t	Tennessee 9-3, Florida 11-1, Auburn 10-2, Georgia Tech 9-3	Mark Richt	Peach	31 Virginia Tech	24
2007	11-2	2	E1t	Tennessee 9-3, Florida 9-3, Auburn 8-4	Mark Richt	Sugar	41 Hawaii	10
2008	10-3	13	E2	Alabama 12-1, Florida 12-1, Georgia Tech 9-3	Mark Richt	Capital One	24 Michigan State	12
2009	8-5		E2t	Oklahoma State 9-3, LSU 9-3, Florida 12-1, Georgia Tech 11-2	Mark Richt	Independence	44 Texas A&M	20
2010	6-7		E3t	South Carolina 9-4, Arkansas 10-2, Mississippi State 8-4, Auburn 13-0	Mark Richt (96-34)	Liberty	6 Central Florida	10

TOTAL: 432-221-17 .6575 (14 of 70)   **Bowl Games since 1953:**   22-5-2 .5897 (Tied 18 of 70)

GREATEST TEAM SINCE 1953: The 1980 Georgia Bulldogs had not only the great Herschel Walker at tailback but a tremendous defense—led by Tim Crowe, Terry Hoage, Jimmy Payne, Nate Taylor, Eddie Weaver, and Scott Woerner—that paved the way to an undefeated season and a Sugar Bowl win over Notre Dame.

1953 3-8

32	Villanova	19
16	Tulane	14
12	Texas A&M	14
13	Maryland	40
6	LSU	14
27	North Carolina	14
12	Alabama	33
7	Florida	21
18	Auburn	39
0	Miss. Southern	14
12	Georgia Tech	28

E Johnny Carson
T Gerry Griffin / William Young
G Sam Mrvos / Bruce Wimberly
C Derwent Langley / Fred Nutt
G Don Shea / Bill Saye
T Pud Mosteller / Walter White
E Gene White / Joe O'Malley
QB Zeke Bratkowski
HB Jim Campagna / Bobby Garrard
HB Charlie Madison
FB Bob Clemens / Howard Kelly

RUSHING: Clemens 120/586y, Kelly 48/212y, Madison 54/146y
PASSING: Bratkowski 113-224/1461y, 6TD, 50.4%
RECEIVING: Carson 45/663y, Campagna 15/173y
SCORING: Clemens 36pts, Carson & Madison 24pts

1954 6-3-1

14	Florida State	0
14	Clemson	7
0	Texas A&M	6
21	North Carolina	7
16	Vanderbilt	14
7	Tulane	0
0	Alabama	0
14	Florida	13
0	Auburn	35
3	Georgia Tech	7

E Roy Wilkins / Laneair Roberts
T Walter White / John Luck
G Len Spadafino / Tony Cushenberry
C Bill Saye / Jimmy Brown
G Don Shea / Wayne Dye
T Pud Mosteller
E Joe O'Malley
QB Jimmy Harper / Dick Young
HB Charlie Madison / Charlie Harris
HB Bob Clemens / John Bell
FB Bobby Garrard / Howard Kelly

RUSHING: Garrard 93/442y, Madison 70/305, Clemens 50/251y, Bell 62/204y
PASSING: Harper 29-71/407y, 2TD, 40.8%
RECEIVING: Wilkins 6/70y, Madison 5/91y, Roberts 4/48y, O'Malley 4/37y
SCORING: Clemens 24pts, Madison (HB-K) 18pts, Harper 12pts

1955 4-6

13	Mississippi	26
14	Vanderbilt	13
7	Clemson	26
28	North Carolina	7
47	Florida State	14
0	Tulane	14
35	Alabama	14
13	Florida	19
13	Auburn	16
3	Georgia Tech	21

E Roy Wilkins
T John Luck / Walter White
G Tony Cushenberry / Len Spadafino
C Bill Saye / Jimmy Brown
G Don Shea / Wayne Dye
T Pud Mosteller / Gerry Griffin
E Laneair Roberts / Ken Cooper
QB Jimmy Harper / Dick Young
HB Charlie Madison / Henry Dukes
SB Jimmy Orr / Wendell Tarleton
FB Bobby Garrard / Knox Culpepper

RUSHING: Garrard 107/533y, Dukes 32/181y, Culpepper 42/173y
PASSING: Young 48-97/875y, 8TD, 49.5%
RECEIVING: Orr 24/443y, Roberts 11/225y, Wilkins 8/128y
SCORING: Garrard (FB-K) 26pts, Orr, Tarleton & Roberts 18pts

1956 3-6-1

0	Vanderbilt	14
3	Florida State	0
7	Mississippi St.	19
26	North Carolina	12
7	Miami	9
7	Kentucky	14
16	Alabama	13
0	Florida	28
0	Auburn	20
0	Georgia Tech	35

E Roy Wilkins / R.K. Brown
T Riley Gunnels / John Luck
G Tony Cushenberry
C Jimmy Brown / Hal Cook
G Wayne Dye
T Pud Mosteller / Mike Meathingham
E Laneair Roberts / Ken Cooper
QB Joe Comfort / Billy Hearn
HB J.B. Davis/C.Manning/George Whitton
SB Jimmy Orr/Henry Dukes/W.Tarleton
FB Knox Culpepper / Wilbur Lofton

RUSHING: Manning 83/348y, Lofton 71/269y, Whitton 65/219y
PASSING: Hearn 26-61/294y, 1TD, 42.6%
RECEIVING: Wilkins 9/116y, Manning 8/55y, Watkins 6/55y
SCORING: Whitton & Davis 12pts, Cooper (E-K) 10pts

1957 3-7

7	Texas	26
6	Vanderbilt	9
0	Michigan	26
13	Tulane	6
14	Navy	27
33	Kentucky	14
13	Alabama	14
0	Florida	22
0	Auburn	6
7	Georgia Tech	0

E Quint'n Smith/B'by Towns/B'll Watk'ns
T Riley Gunnels / George Hansen
G Cicero Lucas / Travis Vinesett
C Dave Lloyd
G Mike Anderson / Al Bishop
T Nat Dye / Mike Meathingham
E Ken Cooper / Gorden Kelley
QB Charlie Britt / Tommy Lewis
HB Gene Littleton / J.B. Davis
SB Jimmy Orr / Don Soberdash
FB Theron Sapp / Wilbur Lofton

RUSHING: Sapp 137/599y, Britt 83/202y, Orr 40/165y
PASSING: Britt 31-77/415y, 4 TD, 40.3%
RECEIVING: Orr 16/237y, Soberdash 6/30y, Towns 5/67y
SCORING: Sapp 30pts, Orr 18pts, Soberdash 12pts

1958 4-6

8	Texas	13
14	Vanderbilt	21
14	South Carolina	24
28	Florida State	13
28	Kentucky	0
0	Alabama	12
6	Florida	7
6	Auburn	21
76	Citadel	0
16	Georgia Tech	3

E Jimmy Vickers /Bill Herron /Norm King
T Riley Gunnels / Larry Lancaster
G Pat Dye
C Dave Lloyd / Phil Ashe
G Billy Roland / Mike Anderson
T Nat Dye / George Hansen
E Gorden Kelley / Gordon Kelley
QB Charlie Britt / Fran Tarkenton
HB Fred Brown / Carl Manning
HB Don Soberdash / Gene Littleton
FB Theron Sapp / Cicero Lucas

RUSHING: Sapp 114/635y, Brown 59/389y, Britt 86/211y
PASSING: Britt 31-75/535y, 3TD, 41.3%,
  Tarkenton 16-30/175y, 5TD, 53.3%
RECEIVING: King 8/138y, Soberdash 8/64y, Herron 7/85y, Kelley 7/77y
SCORING: Brown 24pts, Britt 18pts, Soberdash 16pts

1959 10-1

17	Alabama	3
21	Vanderbilt	6
14	South Carolina	30
35	Hardin-Simmons	6
14	Mississippi St.	0
14	Kentucky	0
42	Florida State	0
21	Florida	10
14	Auburn	13
21	Georgia Tech	14
14	Missouri	0

E Jimmy Vickers / Gorden Kelley
T Pete Case / Larry Lancaster
G Pat Dye
C Phil Ashe / Joe Thompson
G Billy Roland
T Fred Lawrence
E Aaron Box / Bill Herron
QB Charley Britt / Fran Tarkenton
HB Fred Brown / Bobby Walden
HB Bobby Towns / Bill McKenny
FB Don Soberdash / Bill Godfrey

RUSHING: Godfrey 79/319y, Brown 62/278y, Walden 53/197y
PASSING: Tarkenton 62-102/736y, 6TD, 60.8%
RECEIVING: Towns 18/263y, Walden 14/98y, Brown 13/188y
SCORING: Durward Pennington (K) 32pts, Britt 26pts, Tarkenton 24pts

1960 6-4

6	Alabama	21
18	Vanderbilt	7
38	South Carolina	6
3	Southern Cal	10
20	Mississippi St.	0
17	Kentucky	13
45	Tulsa	7
14	Florida	22
6	Auburn	9
7	Georgia Tech	6

E Ray Clark / Jackson Shamblin
T Pete Case / Leonard Vella
G Pat Dye
C Phil Ashe / Pat Smith
G Wally Williamson
T Fred Lawrence / Bobby Green
E Clyde Childers / John McEachern
QB Fran Tarkenton
HB Fred Brown / Billy Jackson
HB Bobby Walden / Bill McKenny
FB Bill Godfrey / Wayne Taylor

RUSHING: Brown 78/355y, Godfrey 67/227y, Taylor 56/179y
PASSING: Tarkenton 108-185/1189y, 7TD, 58.4%
RECEIVING:Brown 31/275y, McKenny 22/270y,Childers 17/202y
SCORING: Durward Pennington (K) 40pts, Brown 38pts

1961 3-7

6	Alabama	32
0	Vanderbilt	21
17	South Carolina	14
0	Florida State	3
10	Mississippi St.	7
16	Kentucky	15
7	Miami	32
14	Florida	21
7	Auburn	10
7	Georgia Tech	22

E Ray Clark / Clyde Childers
T Pete Case
G Wally Williamson
G Len Hauss
G Kenneth Vann / Terry Scott
T Paul Holmes / Bobby Green
E John Landry / Mickey Babb
QB Larry Rakestraw
HB Bill McKenny / Don Blackburn
HB Billy Knowles / Carlton Guthrie
FB Bill Godfrey / Wayne Taylor

RUSHING: McKenny 81/328y,Godfr'y 64/234y,Rak'str'w 83/131y
PASSING: Rakestraw 68-136/710y, 4TD, 50.0%
RECEIVING: McKenny 23/202y, Knowles 17/126y,
  Landry 11/191y, Clark 11/152y
SCORING: Durward Pennington (K) 18pts, 3 with 12pts

1962 3-4-3

0	Alabama	35
10	Vanderbilt	0
7	South Carolina	7
24	Clemson	16
0	Florida State	18
7	Kentucky	7
10	N. Carolina St.	10
15	Florida	23
30	Auburn	21
6	Georgia Tech	37

E Ray Crawford / Barry Wilson
T Ray Rissmiller
G Kenneth Vann / Terry Scott
C Len Hauss / Joel Darden
G Wally Williamson / Richard Kelly
T Paul Holmes
E Mickey Babb
QB Larry Rakestraw / Jake Saye
HB Don Porterfield / Frank Lankewicz
HB Billy Knowles / Carlton Guthrie
FB Leon Armbrester

RUSHING: Armbrester 64/266y, Rakestraw 115/222y
PASSING: Rakestraw 78-169/1135y, 8TD, 46.2%
RECEIVING: Babb 20/354y, Crawford 14/169y, Porterfield 9/161y
SCORING: Porterfield 30pts, Bill McCullough (K) 23pts, Guthrie 12pts

1963 4-5-1

7	Alabama	32
20	Vanderbilt	0
27	South Carolina	7
7	Clemson	7
31	Miami	14
17	Kentucky	14
7	North Carolina	28
14	Florida	21
0	Auburn	14
3	Georgia Tech	14

E Ray Crawford / Barry Wilson
T Ray Rissmiller
G Wayne Brantley
C Len Hauss
G Jim Smith / Vance Evans
T Jim Wilson / Benny Boyd
E Pat Hodgson / Mickey Babb
QB Larry Rakestraw
HB Bob Taylor / Fred Barber
HB Billy Knowles / Carlton Guthrie
FB Leon Armbrester / Frank Lankewicz

RUSHING: Rakestraw 102/170y, Taylor 49/160y, Armbrester 52/155y
PASSING: Rakestraw 103-209/1297y, 7TD, 49.3%
RECEIVING: Hodgson 24/375y, Babb 21/236y, Wilson 15/145y
SCORING: Bill McCullough (K) 31pts, Rakestraw & Taylor 24pts

1964 7-3-1

3	Alabama	31
7	Vanderbilt	0
7	South Carolina	9
19	Clemson	7
14	Florida State	17
21	Kentucky	7
24	North Carolina	8
14	Florida	7
7	Auburn	14
7	Georgia Tech	0
7	Texas Tech	0

E Pat Hodgson
T Ray Rissmiller / Ken Pillsbury
G Harold Steely
C Ken Davis
G Jimmy Denney
T Jim Wilson
E Frank Richter
QB Preston Ridlehuber / Lynn Hughes
TB Bob Taylor / Fred Barber
WB Don Porterfield
FB Frank Lankewicz / Leon Armbrester
DL Jerry Varnado
DL George Patton
DL Joel Darden
DL Dickie Phillips
DL Vance Evans
DL Barry Wilson
LB Leroy Dukes / Steve Neuhaus
LB John Glass
DB Wayne Swinford
DB Doug McFalls
DB Joe Burson

RUSHING: Ridlehuber 110/368y, Taylor 88/338y, Barber 87/311y
PASSING: Hughes 17-54/408y, TD, 31.5%
RECEIVING: Armbrester 7/104y, Porterfield 6/168y
SCORING: Ridlehuber 36pts, Bob Etter (K) 31pts, Taylor 18pts

1965 6-4

18	Alabama	17
24	Vanderbilt	10
15	Michigan	7
23	Clemson	9
3	Florida State	10
10	Kentucky	28
47	North Carolina	35
10	Florida	14
19	Auburn	21
17	Georgia Tech	7

E Frank Richter
T Ken Pillsbury
G Harold Steely / Wayne Brantley
C Ken Davis
G Jimmy Denney / John Kasay
T Edgar Chandler / Chuck Arkwright
E Pat Hogson / Wayne Ingle
QB Preston Ridlehuber / Kirby Moore
TB Bob Taylor / Randy Wheeler
WB Stu Mosher / Bill McWhorter
FB Ronnie Jenkins
DL Jerry Varnado / Marvin Tootle
DL George Patton / Terry Osbolt
DL Jimmy Cooley / Anthony Dennard
DL Dickie Phillips
DL Vance Evans / Bill Harber
DL Larry Kohn
LB John Glass / Tommy Lawhorne
LB Steve Neuhaus / Marvin Hurst
DB Joe Burson
DB Doug McFalls / Lynn Swinford
DB Lynn Hughes

RUSHING: Ridlehuber 142/401y,Jenkins 87/326y,Taylor 65/321y
PASSING: Moore 32-60/487y, 3TD, 53.3%,
  Ridlehuber 27-62/288y, 2TD, 45.5%
RECEIVING: Hodgson 25/312y, Wheeler 13/199y, Richter 12/150y
SCORING: Bob Etter (K) 46pts, Jenkins 36pts, Hodgson 20pts

1966 10-1

20	Mississippi St.	17 E Billy Payne / Sandy Johnson
43	VMI	7 T Edgar Chandler
7	South Carolina	0 G John Kasay
9	Mississippi	3 C Jack Davis
6	Miami	7 G Don Hayes
27	Kentucky	15 T Ken Pillsbury / Chuck Arkwright
28	North Carolina	3 E Frank Richter
27	Florida	10 QB Kirby Moore
21	Auburn	13 TB Kent Lawrence / Craig Elrod
23	Georgia Tech	14 WB Hardy King / Lynn Hughes

FB Ronnie Jenkins / Brad Johnson
DL Jerry Varnado
DL George Patton
DL Dickie Phillips / Bill McWhorter
DL Jimmy Cooley
DL Bill Stanfill
DL Larry Kohn
LB Tommy Lawhorne
LB Steve Neuhaus / Happy Dicks
DB Terry Sellers
DB Mark Holmes / David McKnight
DB Lynn Hughes / Jake Scott

RUSHING: Jenkins 171/669y, Moore 130/489y, Lawrence 69/304y
PASSING: Moore 36-80/524y, 4TD, 45.0%
RECEIVING: Payne 12/144y, Richter 10/177y, King 10/144y
SCORING: Bob Etter (K) 57pts, Moore, Jenkins & Lawrence 30pts

1967 7-4

30	Mississippi St.	0 E Billy Payne / Sandy Johnson
24	Clemson	17 T Edgar Chandler
21	South Carolina	0 G Pat Rodrigue / Bruce Yawn
20	Mississippi	29 C Ronnie Tidmore
56	VMI	6 G Don Hayes
31	Kentucky	7 T David Rholetter
16	Houston	15 E Dennis Hughes / Wayne Ingle
16	Florida	17 QB Kirby Moore
17	Auburn	0 TB Kent Lawrence
21	Georgia Tech	14 WB Hardy King / Steve Woodward
7	N. Carolina St.	14 FB Ronnie Jenkins / Brad Johnson

DL Gary Adams
DL Bill Stanfill
DL Hal Tarrer / Steve Greer
DL Tim Callaway / Terry Osbolt
DL Jiggy Smaha / Paul Handmacher
DL Larry Kohn
LB Happy Dicks
LB Tommy Lawhorne
DB Terry Sellers
DB Mark Holmes
DB Jake Scott

RUSHING: Jenkins 170/646y, Moore 124/507y, Lawrence 129/499y
PASSING: Moore 46-116/699y, 3TD, 39.7%
RECEIVING: Hughes 18/356y, Payne 10/144y, S. Johnson 9/97y
SCORING: Jim McCullough (K) 52pts, Moore & Jenkins 42pts

1968 8-1-2

17	Tennessee	17 WR Kent Lawrence / Charles Whittemore
31	Clemson	13 T David Rholetter / Curtis McGill
21	South Carolina	20 G Bruce Yawn / Jimmy Layfield
21	Mississippi	7 C Tommy Lyons / George White
32	Vanderbilt	6 G Pat Rodrigue
35	Kentucky	14 T Wayne Byrd
0	Houston	10 TE Dennis Hughes
51	Florida	0 QB Mike Cavan
17	Auburn	3 TB Steve Farnsworth / Bruce Kemp (FB)
47	Georgia Tech	8 WB Craig Elrod
2	Arkansas	16 FB Brad Johnson / Bruce Kent

DL Billy Payne
DL Bill Stanfill
DL Terry Osbolt / Tim Callaway
DL Steve Greer
DL Jiggy Smaha / Lee Daniel
DL David McKnight / Phillip Russell
LB Happy Dicks
LB Ronnie Huggins / Harold Tarrer
DB Mark Stewart
DB Penny Pennington / John Griffin
DB Jake Scott

RUSHING: Kemp 140/553y, Johnson 144/456y, Farnsworth 82/335y
PASSING: Cavan 116-207/1619y, 9TD, 56.0%
RECEIVING: Whittemore 40/608y, Lawrence 35/501y, Hughes 26/491y
SCORING: Jim McCullough (K) 52pts, Johnson 36pts, 5 with 24pts

1969 5-5-1

35	Tulane	0 WR Charles Whittemore
30	Clemson	0 T Tom Nash
41	South Carolina	16 G Mayo Tucker
17	Mississippi	25 C Tommy Lyons / Kendall Keith
40	Vanderbilt	8 G Royce Smith
30	Kentucky	0 T Wayne Byrd
3	Tennessee	17 TE Mike Greene
13	Florida	13 QB Mike Cavan
-3	Auburn	16 TB Steve Farnsworth / Craig Elrod
0	Georgia Tech	6 WB Dennis Hughes (TB)
6	Nebraska	45 FB Bruce Kemp / Julian Smiley

DL Chuck Heard
DL Larry Brasher / Jimmy Wood
DL Steve Greer
DL Tim Callaway / Dennis Watson
DL Lee Daniel
DL David McKnight / Phillip Russell
LB Chip Wisdom
LB Ronnie Huggins / Steve Kitchens
DB Billy Darby
DB Phil Sullivan
DB Buck Swindle

RUSHING: Smiley 124/481y, Kemp 129/439y, Elrod 54/274y
PASSING: Cavan 71-162/946y, 7TD, 43.8%
RECEIVING: Whittemore 28/452y, Hughes 22/360y, Greene 11/107y
SCORING: Jim McCullough (K) 46pts, Kemp 42pts

1970 5-5

14	Tulane	17 WR Charles Whittemore
38	Clemson	0 WR Rex Putnal / Jimmy Shirer
6	Mississippi St.	7 T Mike Lopatka / Mayo Tucker
21	Mississippi	31 G John Jennings
37	Vanderbilt	3 C Tommy Lyons
19	Kentucky	3 G Royce Smith
52	South Carolina	34 T Tom Nash
17	Florida	24 TE Billy Brice / Mike Greene
31	Auburn	17 QB Mike Cavan / Paul Gilbert
7	Georgia Tech	17 TB Ricky Lake / Jack Montgomery

FB Robert Honeycutt / Julian Smiley
DL Ken Shaw / Mixon Robinson (TE)
DL Jimmy Wood
DL Ronnie Rogers / David Saye
DL Dennis Watson
DL Larry Brasher
DL Phil Sullivan
LB Chip Wisdom
LB Steve Kitchens
DB Billy Darby
DB Buz Rosenberg
DB Buck Swindle

RUSHING: Lake 135/570y, Honeycutt 116/491y
PASSING: Cavan 42-79/651y, 4TD, 53.2%, Gilbert 44-82/624y, 2TD, 53.7%
RECEIVING: Whittemore 46/620y, Robinson 13/154y
SCORING: Kim Braswell (K) 61pts, Whittemore 32pts, Smiley 30pts

1971 11-1

56	Oregon State	25 WR Lynn Hunnicutt
17	Tulane	7 WR Jimmy Shirer
28	Clemson	0 T Paul Fersen / Jim Curington
35	Mississippi St.	7 G John Jennings
38	Mississippi	7 C Kendall Keith
24	Vanderbilt	0 G Royce Smith
34	Kentucky	0 T Tom Nash
24	South Carolina	0 TE Mike Greene / Billy Brice
49	Florida	7 QB Andy Johnson
20	Auburn	35 TB Jimmy Poulos
28	Georgia Tech	24 FB Robert Honeycutt
7	North Carolina	3 DL Mixon Robinson / Phil Robinson

DL Milton Brice
DL Paul McPipkin
DL Dennis Watson
DL Chuck Heard / Phil Sullivan
LB Chip Wisdom
LB Steve Kitchens
DB Gene Swinford
DB Buz Rosenberg
DB Jerome Jackson
DB Don Golden

RUSHING: Johnson 174/870y, Poulos 144/733y, Honeycutt 104/530y
PASSING: Johnson 33-77/341y, 1TD, 42.9%
RECEIVING: Hunnicutt 14/141y, Shirer 13/188y, Greene 10/144y
SCORING Johnson 78pts, Kim Braswell (K) 59pts, Poulos 58pts

1972 7-4

24	Baylor	14 WR Bobby Burns
13	Tulane	24 WR Rex Putnal
28	N. Carolina St.	22 T Jim Curington
7	Alabama	25 G Mac McWhorter
14	Mississippi	13 C Chris Hammond
28	Vanderbilt	3 G Buck Baker
13	Kentucky	7 T Paul Fersen
0	Tennessee	14 TE Lynn Hunnicutt
10	Florida	7 QB James Ray / Andy Johnson
10	Auburn	27 TB Jimmy Poulos / Hal Bissell
27	Georgia Tech	7 FB Robert Honeycutt

DL David McKnight
DL Jim Cagle
DL Danny Jones
DL Dan Spivey
DL Tommy Smoak / Lenny Ellspermann
LB Keith Harris
LB Steve Sleek
DB Buz Rosenberg / Larry West
DB Gene Swinford
DB Don Golden
DB Jerome Jackson / Dick Conn

RUSHING: Poulos 150/556y, Bissell 121/516y, Johnson 122/427y
PASSING: Ray 55-121/756y, 3TD, 45.5%, Johnson 41-89/671y, 2TD, 46.1%
RECEIVING: Burns 23/389y, Putnal 15/396y, King 13/134y
SCORING: Poulos 42pts, Kim Braswell (K) 42pts, Putnal 24pts

1973 7-4-1

7	Pittsburgh	7 WR Richard Appleby / Gordon Robbins
31	Clemson	14 T Barry Collier / Jim Curington
31	N. Carolina St.	12 G Mac McWhorter
14	Alabama	28 C Chris Hammond / Vern Smith
20	Mississippi	0 G Randy Johnson / Buck Baker
14	Vanderbilt	18 T Craig Hertwig / Steve Wilson
7	Kentucky	12 TE Les Stinson / John Gurley
35	Tennessee	31 QB Andy Johnson
10	Florida	11 TB Jimmy Poulos / Glynn Harrison
28	Auburn	14 WB Horace King / Kevin Hartman
10	Georgia Tech	3 FB Bob Burns / Mike Robinson
17	Maryland	16 DL David McKnight

DL Dan Spivey / Milton Bruce
DL Joe McPipken / Chuck Kinnebrew
DL Danny Jones / Dennis Hester
DL Jim Cagle
LB Clarence Pope / Sylvester Boler
LB Keith Harris
DB Steve Taylor
DB Dick Conn / Larry West
DB Jerome Jackson / Abb Ansley
DB Don Golden

RUSHING: Poulos 167/702y, King 113/515y, Johnson 135/502y
PASSING: Johnson 43-120/506y, 6TD, 35.8%
RECEIVING: Appleby 12/171y, Burns 11/119y, Hartman 7/94y
SCORING: Allan Leavitt (K) 49pts, Johnson 36pts, King 30pts

1974 6-6

48	Oregon State	35 WR Mark Wilson
14	Mississippi	38 WR Gene Washington
52	South Carolina	14 T Barry Collier
24	Clemson	28 G Steve Wilson
49	Mississippi	0 C Vern Smith
38	Vanderbilt	31 G Randy Johnson
24	Vanderbilt	20 T Craig Hertwig
24	Houston	31 TE Richard Appleby
17	Florida	16 QB Matt Robinson
13	Auburn	17 RB Horace King
14	Georgia Tech	34 RB Glynn Harrison / Andy Reid
10	Miami (Ohio)	21 DL David McKnight

DL Ric Reider
DL Mike Wilson
DL Chuck Kinnebrew
DL Rusty Russell
LB Sylvester Boler
LB Keith Harris
DB Steve Taylor
DB Larry West
DB Abb Ansley
DB Dave Schwak

RUSHING: Harrison 149/959y, King 133/590y, Reid 66/316y
PASSING: Robinson 60-121/1317y, 8TD, 49.6%
RECEIVING: Appleby 23/510y, Wilson 15/260y, Harrison 10/154y
SCORING: King 72pts, Allan Leavitt (K) 61pts, Robinson 42pts

1975 9-3

9 Pittsburgh	19 WR Mark Wilson
28 Mississippi St.	6 WR Gene Washington
28 South Carolina	20 T Mike Wilson
35 Clemson	7 G Hugh Hendrix
13 Mississippi	28 C Joe Tereshinski
47 Vanderbilt	3 G Randy Johnson
21 Kentucky	13 T Steve Wilson
28 Richmond	24 TE Richard Appleby
10 Florida	7 QB Ray Goff / Matt Robinson
28 Auburn	13 RB Kevin McLee
42 Georgia Tech	26 RB Glynn Harrison
10 Arkansas31	DL Lawrence Craft
	DL Brad Thompson
	DL Ronnie Swoopes
	DL Dicky Clark
	LB Rusty Russell
	LB Jim Griffith
	LB Ben Zambiasi
	DB Bobby Thompson
	DB David Schwak
	DB Johnny Henderson
	DB Bill Krug

RUSHING: Harrison 131/894y, McLee 166/806y, Goff 110/474y
PASSING: Robinson 29-72/369y, 2 TD, 40.3%, Goff 14-32/246y, 2 TD, 43.8%
RECEIVING: Appleby 13/221y, Washington 5/141y, Harrison 5/63y
SCORING: McLee 60pts, Harrison & Goff 30pts

1976 10-2

36 California	24 WR Mark Wilson / Steve Davis
41 Clemson	0 WR Gene Washington
20 South Carolina	12 T Mike Wilson
21 Alabama	0 G Joel Parrish
17 Mississippi	21 C Joe Tereshinski
45 Vanderbilt	0 G George Collins
31 Kentucky	7 T Steve Collier
31 Cincinnati	17 TE Wally Tereshinski / Mark Hodge
41 Florida	27 QB Ray Goff / Matt Robinson
28 Auburn	0 RB Kevin McLee / Rayfield Williams
13 Georgia Tech	10 RB Al Pollard / James Moreen
3 Pittsburgh27	DL Lawrence Craft
	DL Ronnie Swoopes / Paul Petrisko
	DL Jeff Sanders
	DL Dicky Clark
	LB Jeff Lewis / Ricky McBride
	LB Jim Griffith
	LB Ben Zambiasi
	DB Bobby Thompson / Robert Hope
	DB Johnny Henderson / Billy Woods
	DB Mark Mitchell
	DB Bill Krug

RUSHING: McLee 218/1058y, Goff 128/724y, Pollard 157/680y
PASSING: Robinson 36-81/609y, 7TD, 44.4%, Goff 18-29/322y, 4TD, 62.1%
RECEIVING: Washington 20/469y, Davis 15/235y, Norris 7/82y
SCORING: Allan Leavitt (K) 70pts, Goff 60pts, McLee 36pts

1977 5-6

27 Oregon	16 WR Mark Hodge
6 Clemson	7 WR Jesse Murray
15 South Carolina	13 T Mack Guest
10 Alabama	18 G Jim Milo
14 Mississippi	13 C Matt Braswell
24 Vanderbilt	13 G George Collins
0 Kentucky	33 T Steve Collier
23 Richmond	7 TE Ulysses Norris
17 Florida	22 QB Jeff Pyburn
14 Auburn	33 RB Kevin McLee
7 Georgia Tech	16 RB Willie McClendon
	DL Greg Williams
	DL Ronnie Swoopes
	DL Paul Petrisko
	DL Gordon Terry
	LB Jeff Lewis
	LB Jim Griffith
	LB Ben Zambiasi
	DB Bobby Thompson
	DB Billy Woods
	DB Johnny Henderson
	DB Bill Krug

RUSHING: McLee 178/717y, McClendon 116/705y, Pyburn 101/348y
PASSING: Pyburn 25-55/312y, 2TD, 45.5%
RECEIVING: Murray 13/216y, Hodge 11/133y, Norris 11/121y
SCORING: Rex Robinson (K) 45pts, McLee 30pts, Pyburn & McClendon 24pts

1978 9-2-1

16 Baylor	14 WR Lindsay Scott
12 Clemson	0 WR Carmon Prince
10 South Carolina	27 T Jim Milo
42 Mississippi	3 G Nat Hudson
24 LSU	17 C Ray Donaldson
31 Vanderbilt	10 G Matt Braswell
17 Kentucky	16 T Mack Guest
41 VMI	3 TE Ulysses Norris
24 Florida	22 QB Jeff Pyburn
22 Auburn	22 TB Willie McClendon
29 Georgia Tech	28 FB Jimmy Womack / Ronnie Stewart
22 Stanford25	DL Robert Goodwin
	DL Paul Petrisko
	DL Louis Freedman
	DL Gordon Terry
	LB Steve Dennis
	LB Danny Rodgers
	LB Ricky McBride
	DB Scott Woerner
	DB Robert Hope
	DB Bob Kelly
	DB Pat Collins

RUSHING: McClendon 287/1312y, Womack 98/395y, Stewart 51/252y
PASSING: Pyburn 72-133/878y, 6TD, 54.1%
RECEIVING: Scott 36/484y, Norris 11/123y, Hodge 11/115y
SCORING: McClendon 78pts, Rex Robinson (K) 74pts

1979 6-5

21 Wake Forest	22 WR Lindsay Scott
7 Clemson	12 WR Amp Arnold
20 South Carolina	27 T Matt Braswell
24 Mississippi	21 G Nat Hudson
21 LSU	14 C Ray Donaldson (G) / Hugh Nall
31 Vanderbilt	10 G Jeff Harper
20 Kentucky	6 T Tim Morrison
0 Virginia	31 TE Norris Brown
33 Florida	10 QB Buck Belue / Jeff Pyburn
13 Auburn	33 TB Matt Simon / Bob Kelly / Carnie Norris
16 Georgia Tech	3 FB Jimmy Womack
	DL Gordon Terry / Robert Miles
	DL Guy McIntyre / Jimmy Payne
	DL Eddie Weaver
	DL Tim Parks
	DL Pat McShea
	LB Nate Taylor
	LB Frank Ros
	DB Scott Woerner
	DB Dale Williams / Mike Fisher
	DB Jeff Hipp
	DB Pat Collins / Chris Welton

RUSHING: Simon 152/589y, Kelly 82/459y, Norris 82/279y
PASSING: Belue 59-112/719y, 8TD, 52.7%
RECEIVING: Scott 34/512y, Arnold 19/300y, Brown 11/153y
SCORING: Rex Robinson (K) 66pts, 4 with 18pts

1980 12-0

16 Tennessee	15 WR Lindsay Scott
42 Texas A&M	0 WR Chuck Jones / Amp Arnold
20 Clemson	16 T Jeff Harper
34 TCU	3 G Jim Blakewood
28 Mississippi	21 C Hugh Nall / Wayne Radloff
41 Vanderbilt	0 G Tim Morrison
27 Kentucky	0 T Nat Hudson / Tim Case
13 South Carolina	10 TE Norris Brown / Clarence Kay
26 Florida	21 QB Buck Belue
31 Auburn	21 TB Herschel Walker / Carnie Norris
38 Georgia Tech	20 FB Jimmy Womack / Ronnie Stewart
17 Notre Dame10	DL Robert Miles / Tim Bobo
	DL Jimmy Payne / Freddie Gilbert
	DL Eddie Weaver
	DL Tim Crowe / Tim Parks
	DL Ken McCranie / Pat McShea
	LB Nate Taylor / Bill Forts
	LB Frank Ros / Tommy Thurson
	DB Scott Woerner
	DB Mike Fisher / Terry Hoage
	DB Jeff Hipp / Dale Williams
	DB Chris Welton / Greg Bell

RUSHING: Walker 274/1616y, Norris 56/353y, Womack 49/209y
PASSING: Belue 77-156/1314y, 11 TD, 49.4%
RECEIVING: Arnold 20/357y, Scott 19/374y, Brown 12/253y
SCORING: Walker 90pts, Rex Robinson (K) 84pts, Belue 30pts

1981 10-2

44 Tennessee	0 WR Lindsay Scott
27 California	13 WR Lon Buckler
3 Clemson	13 T Warren Gray
24 South Carolina	0 G Wayne Radloff
37 Mississippi	7 C Joe Happe
53 Vanderbilt	21 G James Brown
21 Kentucky	0 T Jimmy Harper
49 Temple	3 TE Norris Brown / Clarence Kay
26 Florida	21 QB Buck Belue
24 Auburn	13 TB Herschel Walker / Carnie Norris
44 Georgia Tech	7 FB Ronnie Stewart
20 Pittsburgh24	DL Dale Carver
	DL Jimmy Payne
	DL Eddie Weaver / Kevin Jackson
	DL Tim Crowe
	DL Freddie Gilbert
	LB Nate Taylor
	LB Tommy Thurson
	DB Ronnie Harris / Darryl Jones
	DB Dale Williams
	DB Steve Kelly / Charlie Dean
	DB Tim Bobo

RUSHING: Walker 385/1891y, Stewart 66/385y, Norris 52/310y
PASSING: Belue 114-188/1603y, 12TD, 60.6%
RECEIVING: Scott 42/728y, Brown 18/380y, Kay 18/253y
SCORING: Walker 120pts, Kevin Butler (K) 94pts, Scott 36pts

1982 11-1

13 Clemson	7 WR Kevin Harris
17 BYU	14 WR Chuck Jones
34 South Carolina	18 T Jimmy Harper
29 Mississippi St.	22 G Mike Weaver / James Brown
33 Mississippi	10 C Wayne Radloff
27 Vanderbilt	13 G Warren Gray
27 Kentucky	14 T Guy McIntyre
34 Memphis State	3 TE Norris Brown / Clarence Kay
44 Florida	0 QB John Lastinger
19 Auburn	14 TB Herschel Walker
38 Georgia Tech	18 FB Chris McCarthy / Barry Young
23 Penn State27	DL Dale Carver / Carlyle Hewatt
	DL Jimmy Payne
	DL Kevin Jackson
	DL Tim Crowe
	DL Freddie Gilbert / Stan Dooley
	LB Nate Taylor
	LB Tommy Thurson / Knox Culpepper
	DB Ronnie Harris
	DB Tony Flack
	DB Jeff Sanchez
	DB Terry Hoage

RUSHING: Walker 335/1752y, Young 69/390y, McCarthy 58/322y
PASSING: Lastinger 62-148/907y, 8TD, 41.9%
RECEIVING: Kay 12/175y, Harris 10/166y, Simmons 9/118y
SCORING: Walker 104pts, Kevin Butler (K) 85pts, Lastinger 24pts

1983 10-1-1

19 UCLA	8 WR Kevin Harris / Jamie Wisham
16 Clemson	16 WR Herman Archie / Jimmy Hockaday
31 South Carolina	13 T Jimmy Harper
20 Mississippi St.	7 G Mike Weaver / James Brown
36 Mississippi	11 C Keith Johnson
20 Vanderbilt	13 G Warren Gray
47 Kentucky	21 T Guy McIntyre
31 Temple	14 TE Clarence Kay
10 Florida	9 QB John Lastinger
7 Auburn	13 TB Keith Montgomery
27 Georgia Tech	24 FB Barry Young
10 Texas 9	DL Calvin Ruff / Ed Moore
	DL Donald Chumley
	DL Mike Weaver
	DL Kenneth Sims
	DL Freddie Gilbert / Carlyle Hewatt
	LB Tommy Thurson
	LB Knox Culpepper
	DB Darryl Jones / Gary Moss
	DB Tony Flack
	DB Charlie Dean
	DB Terry Hoage

RUSHING: Montgomery 120/519y, Young 115/502y
PASSING: Lastinger 68-137/796y, 6TD, 49.6%
RECEIVING: Archie 31/355y, Kay/17/247y, Wisham 12/174y
SCORING: Kevin Butler (K) 82pts, Montgomery 48pts, McCluskey 30pts

SCORES, LINEUPS, AND STATISTICS

1984 7-4-1

26 Southern Miss.	19 WR Cassius Osborn / Herman Archie
26 Clemson	23 WR Jimmy Hockaday
10 South Carolina	17 T Victor Perry
24 Alabama	14 G Keith Johnson
18 Mississippi	12 C Peter Anderson
62 Vanderbilt	35 G Kim Stephens
37 Vanderbilt	7 T Mike Weaver
13 Memphis State	3 TE Scott Williams
0 Florida	27 QB Todd Williams / James Jackson
12 Auburn	21 TB Andre Smith / Lars Tate
18 Georgia Tech	35 FB David McCluskey
17 Florida State	17 DL Andy Loy
	DL Donald Chumley
	DL Jim Auer
	DL Kenneth Sims
	DL Carlyle Hewatt
	LB Knox Culpepper
	LB Bill Mitchell
	DB Tony Flack
	DB Kevin Harris
	DB Jeff Sanchez
	DB John Little

RUSHING: Smith 110/655y, Tate 114/421y, Jackson 51/313y
PASSING: T. Williams 64-130/620y, 4TD, 49.2%
RECEIVING: S. Williams 19/204y, Hockaday 14/143y, Archie 13/211y
SCORING: Kevin Butler (K) 92pts, Smith (K) 24pts, Archie & Tate 18pts

1985 7-3-2

16 Alabama	20 WR Jimmy Hockaday
17 Baylor	14 WR Fred Lane / Herman Archie
20 Clemson	13 T Victor Perry
35 South Carolina	21 G Mack Burroughs
49 Mississippi	21 C Peter Anderson
13 Vanderbilt	13 G Kim Stephens
26 Kentucky	6 T Wilbur Strozier
58 Tulane	3 TE Troy Sadowski
24 Florida	3 QB James Jackson
10 Auburn	24 TB Tim Worley / Lars Tate
16 Georgia Tech	20 FB Keith Henderson
13 Arizona	13 DL Calvin Ruff
	DL Henry Williams
	DL Henry Harris
	DL Jake Richardson
	DL Greg Waters
	LB Steve Boswell
	LB Bill Mitchell
	DB Gary Moss
	DB Greg Williams
	DB Tony Flack
	DB John Little

RUSHING: Henderson 108/731y, Worley 116/627y, Tate 105/626y
PASSING: Jackson 51-112/759y, 2TD, 45.5%
RECEIVING: Archie 10/116y, Lane 9/139y
SCORING: Jonathan Crumley (K) 65pts, Worley 60pts, Jackson 48pts

1986 8-4

31 Duke	7 WR John Thomas / Cassius Osborn
28 Clemson	31 WR Fred Lane
31 South Carolina	26 T Victor Perry
14 Mississippi	10 G Mack Burroughs
14 LSU	23 C Todd Wheeler
38 Vanderbilt	16 G Kim Stephens
31 Kentucky	9 T Wilbur Strozier
28 Richmond	13 TE Troy Sadowski
19 Florida	31 QB James Jackson
20 Auburn	16 TB Lars Tate
31 Georgia Tech	24 FB David McCluskey / Keith Henderson
24 Boston College	27 DL Wycliffe Lovelace / Tyrone McClendon
	DL Henry Harris
	DL Andy Dotson / Larry Brown
	DL Aaron Chubb
	LB Calvin Ruff
	LB John Brantley
	LB Steve Boswell
	DB Greg Williams
	DB Garry Moss
	DB John Little
	DB Will Jones / Mike Brown

RUSHING: Tate 188/954y, Henderson 96/523y, Jackson 108/410y
PASSING: Jackson 100-181/1475t, 9TD, 55.2%
RECEIVING: Tate 22/214y, Henderson 16/231y, Thomas 13/231y
SCORING: Tate 102pts, Jonathon Crumley (K) 75pts

1987 9-3

30 Virginia	22 WR John Thomas
41 Oregon State	7 WR Cassius Osborn
20 Clemson	21 T Scott Adams
13 South Carolina	6 G Matt Burroughs
31 Mississippi	14 C Todd Wheeler
23 LSU	26 G Kim Stephens
52 Vanderbilt	24 T Curt Mull
17 Kentucky	14 TE Troy Sadowski
23 Florida	10 QB James Jackson
11 Auburn	27 TB Lars Tate / Rodney Hampton
30 Georgia Tech	16 FB Alphonso Ellis
20 Arkansas	17 DL Tyrone McClendon
	DL Larry Brown
	DL Bill Goldberg
	DL Aaron Chubb
	LB Vince Guthrie
	LB John Brantley
	LB Terrie Webster
	DB Ben Smith
	DB Mark Vincent
	DB Rusty Beasley
	DB Will Jones

RUSHING: Tate 208/1016y, Hampton 126/890y, Jackson 113/519y
PASSING: Jackson 67-132/1026y, 7TD, 50.8%
RECEIVING: Thomas 25/391y, Osborn 15/301y, Tate 13/149y
SCORING: Tate 86pts, Jonathon Crumley (K) 60pts, Hampton 36pts

1988 9-3

28 Tennessee	17 WR John Thomas
38 TCU	10 WR Arthur Marshall
42 Mississippi St.	35 T Scott Adams (G) / Will Colley
10 South Carolina	23 G Shelly Anderson
36 Mississippi	12 C Todd Wheeler
41 Vanderbilt	22 G Lemonte Tellis
10 Kentucky	16 T Curt Mull
59 William & Mary	24 TE Troy Sadowski
26 Florida	3 QB Wayne Johnson
10 Auburn	20 TB Tim Worley / Rodney Hampton
24 Georgia Tech	3 FB Alphonso Ellis
34 Michigan State	27 DL Wycliffe Lovelace
	DL Bill Goldberg
	DL Paul Giles
	LB Mo Lewis
	LB Brent Collins / Demetrius Douglas
	LB Terrie Webster
	LB Richard Tardits
	DB Ben Smith
	DB David Hargett
	DB Rusty Beasley
	DB Vince Guthrie

RUSHING: Worley 191/1216y, Hampton 128/719y
PASSING: Johnson 66-122/945y, 4TD, 54.1%
RECEIVING: Thomas 23/354y, Henderson 20/297y
SCORING: Worley 108pts, John Kasay (K) 59pts, Hampton 42pts

1989 6-6

15 Baylor	3 WR Arthur Marshall
23 Mississippi St.	6 WR Sean Hummings
20 South Carolina	24 T Will Colley
14 Tennessee	17 G Haze Sadler
13 Mississippi	17 C Jack Swan
35 Vanderbilt	16 G Russell DeFoor
34 Vanderbilt	23 T Curt Mull
37 Temple	10 TE Kirk Warner
17 Florida	10 QB Greg Talley
3 Auburn	20 TB Rodney Hampton / Brian Cleveland
22 Georgia Tech	33 FB Tim Ware / Alphonso Ellis
18 Syracuse	19 DL Bill Goldberg
	DL Robert Bell
	DL Hiawatha Berry
	LB Morris Lewis
	LB Curt Douglas / Matt McCormick
	LB Demetrius Douglas
	LB Norman Cowins
	DB George Wynn
	DB Chris Wilson
	DB Ben Smith
	DB David Hargett / Mike Jones

RUSHING: Hampton 218/1059y, Ware 48/207y, Cleveland 36/129y
PASSING: Talley 92-174/1330y, 6TD, 52.9%
RECEIVING: Warner 30/404y, Hummings 26/429y, Hampton 26/219y
SCORING: John Kasay (K) 79pts, Hampton 72pts, Marshall 14pts

1990 4-7

13 LSU	18 WR Sean Hummings / Andre Hastings
18 Southern Miss.	17 WR Kevin Maxwell
17 Alabama	16 T Bill Rosenberg / Mike Fellows
19 East Carolina	15 G William Wynn / Haze Sadler
3 Clemson	34 C Jack Swan
12 Mississippi	28 G Russell DeFoor
39 Vanderbilt	28 T LeMonte Tellis
24 Kentucky	26 TE Chris Broom / Shannon Mitchell
7 Florida	38 QB Greg Talley / Preston Jones
10 Auburn	33 TB Garrison Hearst / Larry Ware
23 Georgia Tech	40 FB Mack Strong / Alphonzo Ellis
	DL Eric Coney
	DL Mike Steele / Willie Jennings
	DL Donnie Maib
	LB Morris Lewis
	LB Torrey Evans / John Allen
	LB Dwayne Simmons
	LB Greg Jackson / Mitch Davis
	DB George Wynn
	DB Al Jackson / Chuck Carswell
	DB Chris Wilson / Mike Jones
	DB David Hargett / Earl Fouch

RUSHING: Hearst 162/717y, Ware 119/534y, Dupree 51/186y
PASSING: Talley 72-123/871y, 4TD, 58.5%
RECEIVING: Hummings 25/376y, Hastings 24/333y
SCORING: John Kasay (K) 67pts, Hearst & Ware 30pts

1991 9-3

48 W. Carolina	0 WR Arthur Marshall / Damon Evans
31 LSU	10 WR Andre Hastings / Jeff Thomas
0 Alabama	10 T Bernard Williams
27 Cal-Fullerton	14 G Steve Roberts / Jack Sawn
27 Clemson	12 C Russell DeFoor
37 Mississippi	17 G LeMonte Tellis / Haze Sadler
25 Vanderbilt	27 T Alec Millen / Dan Rogers
49 Kentucky	27 TE Shannon Mitchell
13 Florida	35 QB Eric Zeier / Greg Talley
37 Auburn	27 TB Garrison Hearst / Larry Ware
18 Georgia Tech	15 FB Mack Strong
24 Arkansas	15 DL Curt Douglas
	DL Casey Barnum / Willie Jennings
	DL Donnie Maib
	LB Carlo Butler / Greg Jackson
	LB Mitch Davis
	LB John Allen / Maurice Harrell
	LB Dwayne Simmons
	DB George Wynn
	DB Chuck Carswell
	DB Ralph Thompson / Mike Jones
	DB David Hargett / Al Jackson

RUSHING: Hearst 153/968y, Ware 115/680y, Strong 67/254y
PASSING: Zeier 159-286/1984y, 7TD, 55.6%
RECEIVING: Hastings 48/683y, Marshall 39/524y, Mitchell 19/176y
SCORING: Hearst 56pts, Joe Peterson (K) 43pts, Strong 42pts

1992 10-2

28 South Carolina	6 WR Andre Hastings
31 Tennessee	34 WR Brian Bohannon / Brice Hunter
56 Cal-Fullerton	0 T Bernard Williams
37 Mississippi	11 G Steve Roberts
27 Arkansas	3 C Jack Swan / David Weeks
34 Ga. Southern	7 G Paul Taylor / Mike Fellows
30 Vanderbilt	20 T Alec Millen
40 Kentucky	7 TE Shannon Mitchell
24 Florida	26 QB Eric Zeier
14 Auburn	10 TB Garrison Hearst / Terrell Davis
31 Georgia Tech	17 FB Mack Strong / Frank Harvey
21 Ohio State	14 DL Tom Wallace / Phillip Daniels
	DL Casey Barnum / Travis Jones
	DL Greg Jackson
	LB Charlie Clemons / Damon Ward
	LB Mitch Davis
	LB Randall Godfrey
	LB Maurice Harrell / Carlo Butler
	DB Al Jackson / Charles Pledger
	DB Chris Wilson
	DB Greg Tremble
	DB Mike Jones / Buster Owens

RUSHING: Hearst 228/1547y
PASSING: Zeier 151-258/2248y, 12TD, 58.5%
RECEIVING: Hastings 52/860y
SCORING: Hearst 126pts

1993 5-6

21 South Carolina	23 WR Jeff Thomas / Hason Graham
6 Tennessee	38 WR Brice Hunter / Brian Bohannon
52 Texas Tech	37 T Bernard Williams
14 Mississippi	31 G Steve Roberts / Mike Fellows
10 Arkansas	20 C David Weeks / Scott Brownholtz
54 Southern Miss.	24 G Troy Stark / Chad Chosewood
41 Vanderbilt	3 T Adam Meadows / Paul Taylor
33 Kentucky	28 TE Shannon Mitchell / James Warner
26 Florida	33 QB Eric Zeier
28 Auburn	42 RB Terrell Davis / Bill Montgomery
43 Georgia Tech	10 RB Frank Harvey / Earl Fouch
	DL Matt Storm / Herman Bell
	DL Bill Rosenberg / Walter Rouse
	DL Phillip Daniels / Derrick Smith
	LB Mitch Davis
	LB Charlie Clemons
	LB Randall Godfrey
	LB Carlo Butler / Bryan Jones
	DB Charles Pledger / Carlos Yancy
	DB Greg Tremble / Chad Wilson
	DB Ralph Thompson
	DB Buster Owens / Will Muschamp

RUSHING: Davis 167/824y, Harvey 36/146y, Montg'm'ry 45/144y
PASSSING: Zeier 269-425/3525y, 24TD, 63.3%
RECEIVING: Hunter 76/970y, Mitchell 49/539y, Thomas 39/469y
SCORING: Kanon Parkman (K) 92pts, Hunter 56pts, Davis 48pts

1994 6-4-1

24 South Carolina	21 WR Hason Graham / Juan Daniels
23 Tennessee	41 WR Brice Hunter / Jeff Thomas
70 NE Louisiana	6 T Adam Meadows
17 Mississippi	14 G Steve Roberts
28 Alabama	29 C David Weeks
40 Clemson	14 G Resty Beadles
30 Vanderbilt	43 T Troy Stark
34 Kentucky	30 TE James Warner / Maurice Harrell
14 Florida	52 QB Eric Zeier
23 Auburn	23 RB Terrell Davis / Hines Ward
48 Georgia Tech	10 RB Larry Bowie / Bill Montgomery
	DL Matt Storm
	DL Travis Stroud / Walter Rouse
	DL Travis Jones / Deshay McKever
	LB Phillip Daniels / Derrick Smith
	LB Marcus Williams / Whit Marshall
	LB Randall Godfrey
	LB Greg Bright / Frank Watts
	DB Carlos Yancy
	DB Robert Edwards / Buster Owens
	DB Corey Johnson
	DB Will Muschamp

RUSHING: Davis 97/445y, Ward 77/425y, Montgomery 25/170y
PASSING: Zeier 259-433/3396y, 24TD, 59.8%
RECEIVING: Hunter 59/799y, Graham 46/881y, Daniels 37/586y
SCORING: Kanon Parkman (K) 91pts

1995 6-6

42 South Carolina	23 WR Juan Daniels / Matt Dickson
27 Tennessee	30 WR Brice Hunter / Chris McCranie
40 New Mexico St.	13 T Adam Meadows
10 Mississippi	18 G Paul Taylor / Matt Stinchcomb
0 Alabama	31 C David Weeks
19 Clemson	17 G Resty Beadles / Antonio Fleming
17 Vanderbilt	6 T Troy Stark
12 Kentucky	3 TE Larry Brown
17 Florida	52 QB Hines Ward / Mike Bobo / Brian Smith
31 Auburn	37 RB Torin Kirtsey / Robert Edwards
18 Georgia Tech	17 RB Selma Calloway / Odell Collins
27 Virginia34 DL Jason Ferguson / Derrick Byrd	
	DL Jermaine Smith / Travis Stroud
	DL Phillip Daniels / Chris Terry
	LB Brandon Tolbert / Marcus Williams
	LB Whit Marshall / D.J. Johnson
	LB Randall Godfrey
	LB Greg Bright
	DB Alandus Sims / Kirby Smart
	DB Buster Owens / Ronald Bailey
	DB Corey Johnson
	DB Armin Love

RUSHING: Kirtsey 134/603y, Edwards 45/325y, Ward 70/248y
PASSING: Ward 69-112/872y, 2TD, 61.6%,
  Smith 59-109/687y, 3TD, 54.1%
  Bobo 54-89/818y, 5TD, 60.7%
RECEIVING: Daniels 46/726y, Hunter 44/574y, Ward 18/249y
SCORING: Kanon Parkman (K) 62pts

1996 5-6

7 Southern Miss	11 WR Hines Ward / Corey Allen
14 South Carolina	23 WR Juan Daniels / Tony Small
15 Texas Tech	12 T Adam Meadows
38 Mississippi St.	19 G Antonio Fleming / Steve Herndon
17 Tennessee	29 C Brad Stafford
13 Vanderbilt	2 G Resty Beadles / Kenley Ingram
17 Kentucky	24 T Matt Stinchcomb
7 Florida	47 TE Larry Brown
56 Auburn	49 QB Mike Bobo
27 Mississippi	31 RB Robert Edwards / Robert Arnaud
19 Georgia Tech	10 RB Selma Calloway / Patrick Pass
	DL Derrick Byrd
	DL Jason Ferguson / Travis Stroud
	DL Jermaine Smith / Brandon Miller
	DL Paul Snellings / Chris Terry
	LB Brandon Tolbert
	LB Greg Bright / Orantes Grant
	LB Bryan Jones
	DB Champ Bailey
	DB Ronald Bailey / Glenn Ford
	DB Cor'y Johnson/K'rby Smart/L'rry Mann
	DB Alandus Sims / Trey Sipe

RUSHING: Edwards 184/800y, Pass 69/354y
PASSING: Bobo 175-344/2440y, 13TD, 50.9%
RECEIVING: Ward 52/900y, Daniels 37/663y, Allen 29/380y
SCORING: Edwards 60pts, Hines 42pts, Daniels 36pts

1997 10-2

38 Arkansas State	7 WR Hines Ward / Tony Small
31 South Carolina	15 WR Corey Allen / Michael Greer
42 NE Louisiana	3 T Matt Stinchcomb
47 Mississippi St.	0 G Antonio Fleming / Jonas Jennings
13 Tennessee	38 C Brad Stafford / Miles Luckie
34 Vanderbilt	13 G Kenley Ingram / Steve Herndon
23 Kentucky	13 T Chris Terry
37 Florida	17 TE Larry Brown / Jermaine Wiggins
34 Auburn	45 QB Mike Bobo
21 Mississippi	14 RB Robert Edwards / Patrick Pass
27 Georgia Tech	24 RB Olandis Gary
33 Wisconsin 6 DL Antonio Cochran / Brandon Miller	
	DL Travis Stroud
	DL Derrick Byrd / Richard Seymour
	DL Paul Snellings
	LB Brandon Tolbert
	LB Greg Bright / Mike Luckie
	LB Orantes Grant / Dustin Luckie
	DB Champ Bailey (WR)
	DB Ronald Bailey / Glenn Ford
	DB Kirby Smart / Larry Mann
	DB Trey Sipe / Earl Chambers

RUSHING: Edwards 165/908y, Gary 66/381y, Pass 64/232y
PASSING: Bobo 199-306/2751y, 19 TD, 65.0%
RECEIVING: Ward 55/715y, Allen 32/510y, Small 26/362y
SCORING: Edwards 78pts, Hap Hines (K) 51pts, Gary 48pts

1998 9-3

56 Kent State	3 WR Michael Greer
17 South Carolina	3 WR Tony Small / Thad Parker
16 Wyoming	9 T Matt Stinchcomb
28 LSU	27 G Steve Herndon / Brad Register
3 Tennessee	22 C Miles Luckie
31 Vanderbilt	6 G Jonas Jennings (C/T)
28 Kentucky	26 T Chris Terry
7 Florida	38 TE Larry Brown / Jermaine Wiggins
28 Auburn	17 QB Quincy Carter
24 Mississippi	17 RB Olandis Gary / Robert Arnaud
19 Georgia Tech	21 RB Patrick Pass / Nick Callaway
35 Virginia33 DL Dustin Luckie / Bruce Adrine	
	DL Richard Seymour / Josh Mallard
	DL Marcus Stroud
	DL Adrian Hollingshed
	LB Boss Bailey
	LB Kendrell Bell / Will Witherspoon
	LB Orantes Grant
	DB Champ Bailey (WR) / Cory Robinson
	DB Jeff Harris / Jamie Henderson
	DB Larry Mann
	DB Earl Chambers

RUSHING: Gary 143/698y, Carter 99/284y, Arnaud 24/161y
PASSING: Carter 176-290/2484y, 12TD, 60.7%
RECEIVING: Small 48/675y, Bailey 47/744y, Brown 31/431y
SCORING: Gary 60pts, Hap Hines 51pts, Bailey 30pts

1999 8-4

38 Utah State	7 WR Terrence Edwards / Jermaine Phillips
24 South Carolina	9 WR Michael Greer / Thad Parker
24 C. Florida	23 T Jonas Jennings
23 LSU	22 G Steve Herndon / Brad Register
20 Tennessee	37 C Miles Luckie
27 Vanderbilt	17 G Kevin Breedlove / Reggie Stargill
49 Kentucky	34 T Jon Stinchcomb
14 Florida	30 TE Jevaris Johnson / Randy McMichael
21 Auburn	38 QB Quincy Carter
20 Mississippi	17 RB Patrick Pass / Brett Millican
48 Georgia Tech	51 RB Jasper Sanks / Robert Arnaud
28 Purdue25 DL Charles Grant / David Jacobs	
	DL Marcus Stroud
	DL Richard Seymour
	DL Bruce Adrine / Josh Mallard
	LB Boss Bailey / Tony Gilbert
	LB Kendrell Bell
	LB Orantes Grant
	DB Tim Wansley / Cory Robinson
	DB Jamie Henderson / Jeff Harris
	DB Cap Burnett / Larry Mann
	DB Terreal Bierria / Earl Chambers

RUSHING: Sanks 177/896y, Pass 62/335y, Carter 102/255y
PASSING: Carter 216-380/2713y, 17TD, 56.8%
RECEIVING: Edwards 53/751y, McMichael 34/457y,
  Johnson 31/378y, Greer 31/332y
SCORING: Hap Hines 78pts, Edwards 54pts, Sanks 36pts

2000 8-4

29 Ga. Southern	6 WR Terrence Edwards
10 South Carolina	21 WR LaBrone Mitchell / Damien Gary
37 New Mexico St.	0 T Jonas Jennings
38 Arkansas	7 G Brady Pate
21 Tennessee	10 C Curt McGill
29 Vanderbilt	19 G Kevin Breedlove / Reggie Stargill
34 Kentucky	30 T Jon Stinchcomb
23 Florida	34 TE Randy McMichael / Jason Rader
26 Auburn	29 QB Quincy Carter / Cory Phillips
32 Mississippi	14 RB Brett Millican / Bruce Thornton
15 Georgia Tech	27 RB Jasper Sanks / Musa Smith
37 Virginia	14 DL Josh Mallard / Terin Smith
	DL Marcus Stroud / Johnathan Sullivan
	DL Richard Seymour
	DL Charles Grant / Bruce Adrine
	LB Will Witherspoon
	LB Kendrell Bell / Adrian Hollingshed
	LB Tony Gilbert
	DB Jamie Henderson
	DB Tim Wansley / Cory Robinson
	DB Jermaine Phillips / Cap Burnett
	DB Terreal Bierria

RUSHING: Millican 67/375y, Sanks 92/352y, M.Smith 75/330y
PASSING: Carter 91-183/1250y, 6TD, 49.7%,
  Phillips 89-158/1093y, 8TD, 56.3%
RECEIVING: Edwards 53/704y, Gary 36/552y,
  McMichael 32/475y
SCORING: Billy Bennett (K) 63pts, Gary, Sanks & M.Smith 30pts

2001 8-4

45 Arkansas State	17 WR Terrence Edwards / LaBrone Mitchell
9 South Carolina	14 WR Damien Gary / Fred Gibson
34.Arkansas	23 T George Foster / Clint Larkin
26 Tennessee	24 G Alex Jackson / Ian Knight
30 Vanderbilt	14 C Curt McGill
43 Kentucky	29 G Kevin Breedlove
10 Florida	24 T Jon Stinchcomb
17 Auburn	24 TE Randy McMichael / Ben Watson
35 Mississippi	15 QB David Greene
31 Georgia Tech	17 TB Musa Smith / Jasper Sanks
35 Houston	7 FB Verron Haynes / J.T. Wall
16 Boston College20 DL Johnathan Sullivan / Josh Mallard	
	DL David Pollack / Shedrick Wynn
	DL David Jacobs / Ken Veal
	DL Charles Grant
	LB Boss Bailey / Chris Clemons
	LB Tony Gilbert / Adrian Hollingshed
	LB Will Witherspoon
	DB Bruce Thornton
	DB Tim Wansley / Decory Bryant
	DB Terreal Bierria / Kentrell Curry
	DB Jermaine Phillips / Sean Jones

RUSHING: Haynes 126/691y, Smith 119/548y, Sanks 84/338y
PASSING: Greene 192-324/2789y, 17TD, 59.3%
RECEIVING: Edwards 39/613y, Gibson 33/772y, Gary 25/352y
SCORING: Billy Bennett (K) 85pts, Haynes 54pts,
  Smith, Gibson & Edwards 36pts

2002 13-1

31 Clemson	28 WR Terrence Edwards / Reggie Brown
13 South Carolina	7 WR Fred Gibson / Damien Gary
45 No'western St.	7 T John Stinchcomb / George Foster
41 New Mexico St.	10 G Alex Jackson / Josh Brock
27 Alabama	25 C Ian Knight
18 Tennessee	13 G Kevin Breedlove
48 Vanderbilt	17 T Kareen Marshall
52 Kentucky	24 TE Ben Watson
13 Florida	20 QB David Greene / D.J. Shockley
31 Mississippi	17 TB Musa Smith / Tony Milton
24 Auburn	21 FB J.T. Wall
51 Georgia Tech	7 DL Will Thompson / Robert Geathers
30 Arkansas	3 DL Johnathan Sullivan / Kedric Golston
26 Florida State 13	DL Ken Veal / Darrius Swain
	DL David Pollack
	LB Boss Bailey
	LB Tony Gilbert / Tony Taylor
	LB Chris Clemons
	DB Decory Bryant
	DB Bruce Thornton / Tim Jennings
	DB Sean Jones / Thomas Davis (LB)
	DB Kentrell Curry / Greg Blue

RUSHING: Smith 260/1324y, Milton 82/314y, Wall 30/149y
PASSING: Greene 218-379/2924y, 22TD, 57.5%
RECEIVING: Edwards 59/1004y, Gibson 43/758y, Watson 31/341y
SCORING: Billy Bennett (K) 130pts, Edwards 66pts, Smith 48pts

2003 11-3

30 Clemson	0 WR Reggie Brown / Michael Johnson
29 Middle Tenn. St.	10 WR Fred Gibson / Damien Gary
31 South Carolina	7 T Daniel Inman
10 LSU	17 G Josh Brock
37 Alabama	23 C Russ Tanner (G) / Nick Jones
41 Tennessee	14 G Bartley Miller
27 Vanderbilt	8 T Max Jean-Gilles
16 Ala.-Birm'ham	13 TE Ben Watson
13 Florida	16 QB David Greene
26 Auburn	7 TB Michael Cooper / Kregg Lumpkin
30 Kentucky	10 FB Jeremy Thomas
34 Georgia Tech	17 DL Robert Geathers
13 LSU	34 DL Ken Veal / Kedric Golston
34 Purdue 27	DL Gerald Anderson
	DL David Pollack
	LB Arnold Harrison
	LB Odell Thurman
	LB Tony Taylor / Derrick White
	DB Decory Bryant / Tim Jennings
	DB Bruce Thornton / DeMario Minter
	DB Thomas Davis
	DB Sean Jones

RUSHING: Cooper 156/673y, Lumpkin 112/523y, Tyson Browning (TB) 78/286y
PASSING: Greene 264-438/3307y, 13TD, 60.3%
RECEIVING: Brown 49/662y, Gary 43/494y, Gibson 36/553y
SCORING: Billy Bennett (K) 131pts, Cooper & Lumpkin 36pts

2004 10-2

48 Ga. Southern	28 WR Reggie Brown
20 South Carolina	16 WR Fred Gibson / Sean Bailey
13 Marshall	3 T Daniel Inman
45 LSU	16 G Nick Jones
14 Tennessee	19 C Russ Tanner / Ryan Schnetzer
33 Vanderbilt	3 G Max Jean-Gilles
20 Arkansas	14 T Dennis Roland
31 Florida	24 TE Leonard Pope
62 Kentucky	17 QB David Greene
6 Auburn	24 TB Thomas Brown / Danny Ware
19 Georgia Tech	13 FB Jeremy Thomas
24 Wisconsin 21	DL Will Thompson / Charles Johnson
	DL Gerald Anderson / Darrius Swain
	DL Kedric Golston / Quentin Moses
	DL David Pollack
	LB Derric White / Arnold Harrison
	LB Odell Thurman / Jarvis Jackson
	LB Danny Verdun Wheeler
	DB DeMario Minter / Thomas Flowers
	DB Tim Jennings
	DB Thomas Davis
	DB Greg Blue

RUSHING: T. Brown 172/875y, Ware 138/692y, Michael Cooper (TB) 29/125y
PASSING: Greene 175-299/2508y, 20TD, 58.5%
RECEIVING: R. Brown 53/860y, Gibson 49/801y, Pope 25/482y
SCORING: Andy Bailey (K) 78pts, T. Brown 48pts, Gibson 42pts

2005 10-3

48 Boise State	13 WR Bryan McClendon
17 South Carolina	15 WR Sean Bailey / Mohamed Massaquoi
44 La.-Monroe	7 T Dennis Roland
23 Mississippi St.	10 G Max Jean-Gilles
27 Tennessee	14 C Russ Tanner / Ryan Schnetzer
34 Vanderbilt	17 G Nick Jones
23 Arkansas	20 T Daniel Inman
10 Florida	14 TE Leonard Pope
30 Auburn	31 QB D.J. Shockley
45 Kentucky	13 TB Thomas Brown / Danny Ware
14 Georgia Tech	7 FB Brannan Southerland
34 LSU	14 DL Will Thompson / Charles Johnson
35 West Virginia 38	DL Kedric Golston / Jeff Owens
	DL Gerald Anderson / Ray Gant
	DL Quentin Moses / Marcus Howard
	LB Brandon Miller/Danny Verdun-Wheel'r
	LB Jarvis Jackson
	LB Tony Taylor / Dannell Ellerbe
	DB DeMario Minter / Paul Oliver
	DB Tim Jennings
	DB Greg Blue
	DB Tra Battle

RUSHING: Brown 147/736y, Wae 101/492y, Kregg Lumpkin (TB) 66/335, Shockley 78/322y
PASSING: Shockley 173-310/2588y, 24TDs, 55.8%
RECEIVING: Pope 39/541y, Massaquoi 38/505y, McClendon 35/529y
SCORING: Brandon Coutu (K) 114pts, McClendon 36pts, Southerland 30pts

2006 9-4

48 W. Kentucky	12 WR Mohamed Massaquoi / Mario Raley
18 South Carolina	0 WR A.J. Bryant / Kenneth Harris
34 Ala.-Birm'ham	0 T Ken Shackleford
14 Colorado	13 G Fernando Velasco
14 Mississippi	9 C Nick Jones
33 Tennessee	51 G Chester Adams
22 Vanderbilt	24 T Daniel Inman / Michael Turner (G)
27 Mississippi St.	24 TE Martrez Milner / Tripp Chandler
14 Florida	21 QB Matthew Stafford / Joe Tereshinski
20 Kentucky	24 TB Kregg Lumpkin / Thomas Brown
37 Auburn	15 FB Brannan Southerland
15 Georgia Tech	12 DL Charles Johnson
31 Virginia Tech 24	DL Jeff Owens
	DL Kade Weston / Ray Gant /Dale Dixson
	DL Quentin Moses
	LB Danny Verdun-Wheeler/Brand'n Miller
	LB Jarvis Jackson
	LB Tony Taylor
	DB Paul Oliver / Asher Allen
	DB Ramarcus Brown / Bryan Evans
	DB Kelin Johnson / C.J. Byrd
	DB Tra Battle

RUSHING: Lumpkin 162/798y, Danny Ware (TB) 81/326y, Brown 62/256y
PASSING: Stafford 135-256/1749y, 7 TDs, 52.7%
RECEIVING: Milner 30/425y, Massaquoi 30/366y, Lumpkin 17/116y
SCORING: Southerland 60pts, Brandon Coutu (K) 47pts, Lumpkin 42pts

2007 11-2

35 Oklahoma State	14 WR Sean Bailey / Mikey Henderson
12 South Carolina	16 WR Mohamed Massaquoi / Tony Wilson
45 W. Carolina	16 T Trinton Sturdivant
26 Alabama	23 G Chris Davis
45 Mississippi	17 C Fernando Velasco
14 Tennessee	35 G Clint Boling (T) / Scott Haverkamp
20 Vanderbilt	17 T Chester Adams
42 Florida	30 TE Tripp Chandler / Bruce Figgins
44 Troy	34 QB Matthew Stafford
45 Auburn	20 RB Thomas Brown / Knowshon Moreno
24 Kentucky	13 FB Brannan Southerland
31 Georgia Tech	17 DL Roderick Battle
41 Hawaii 10	DL Jeff Owens
	DL Geno Atkins / Kade Weston
	DL Marcus Howard
	LB Brandon Miller / Akeem Dent
	LB Dannell Ellerbe / Marcus Washington
	LB Darius Dewberry / Rennie Curran
	DB Asher Allen / Thomas Flowers
	DB Prince Miller / Bryan Evans
	DB C.J. Byrd / Reshad Jones
	DB Kelin Johnson

RUSHING: Moreno 248/1334y, Brown 148/779y, Kregg Lumpkin (RB)12/44y, Kalvin Daniels (RB) 8/44y
PASSING: Stafford194-348/2523y, 19TD, 55.7%
RECEIVING: Bailey 39/615y, Massaquoi 32/491y, Chandler 21/283y
SCORING: Brandon Coutu (K) 92pts, Moreno 84pts, Brown 72pts

2008 10-3

45 Ga. Southern	21 WR Mohamed Massaquoi / Kris Durham
56 C. Michigan	17 WR A.J. Green
14 South Carolina	7 T Clint Boling (G) / Kiante Tripp
27 Arizona State	10 G Cordy Glenn / Vince Vance (T)
30 Alabama	41 C Ben Jones
26 Tennessee	14 G Chris Davis (C)
24 Vanderbilt	14 T Justin Anderson / Josh Davis
52 LSU	38 TE Tripp Chandler / Bruce Figgins
10 Florida	49 QB Matthew Stafford
42 Kentucky	38 RB Knowshon Moreno / Caleb King
17 Auburn	13 FB Shaun Chapas / Brannan Southerland
42 Georgia Tech	45 DL Roderick Battle / Jermey Lomax
24 Michigan State	12 DL Corvey Irvin / Jeff Owens
	DL Geno Atkins
	DL Jarius Wynn / Demarcus Dobbs
	LB Akeem Dent / Darryl Gamble
	LB Dannell Ellerbe
	LB Rennie Curran
	DB Asher Allen
	DB Prince Miller / Bryan Evans
	DB Reshad Jones / John Knox
	DB C.J. Byrd

RUSHING: Moreno 250/1400y, King 61/247y, Richard Samuel (RB) 26/133y
PASSING: Stafford 235-383/3459y, 25TD, 61.4%
RECEIVING: Massaquoi 58/920y, Green 56/963y, Moreno 33/392y, Moore 29/451y
SCORING: Moreno 108pts, Blair Walsh (K) 95pts, Green & Massaquoi 48pts

2009 8-5

10 Oklahoma St.	24 WR Taverras King / Rantavious Wooten
41 South Carolina	37 WR A.J. Green / Michael Moore
52 Arkansas	41 T Clint Boling (G)
20 Arizona State	17 G Cordy Glenn (T)
13 LSU	20 C Ben Jones
19 Tennessee	45 G Chris Davis
34 Vanderbilt	10 T Josh Davis / Vince Vance
17 Florida	41 TE Orson Charles / Aron White
38 Tennessee Tech	9 QB Joe Cox
31 Auburn	24 RB Caleb King / Washaun Ealey
27 Kentucky	34 FB Shaun Chapas / Fred Munzenmaier
30 Georgia Tech	24 DL Justin Houston
44 Texas A&M	20 DL Jeff Owens
	DL Kade Weston / Geno Atkins
	DL Demarcus Dobbs
	LB Akeem Dent / Darius Dewberry
	LB Darryl Gamble / Marcus Dowtin
	LB Rennie Curran / Cornelius Washington
	DB Brandon Boykin / Vance Cuff
	DB Prince Miller
	DB Bryan Evans
	DB Reshad Jones / Baccari Rambo

RUSHING: Ealey 125/717y, C. King 61/247y, Richard Samuel (RB) 26/133y
PASSING: Cox 185-331/2584y, 24TD, 55.9%
RECEIVING: Green 53/808y, Moore 25/249y, Charles 23/374y, T. King 18/377y
SCORING: Blair Walsh (K) 102pts, King 48pts, Green 38pts

2010 6-7

55 Louisiana	7 WR/TE A.J. Green / Aron White
6 South Carolina	17 WR Kris Durham / Tavarres King
24 Arkansas	31 T Clint Boling (G) / Trinton Sturdivant
12 Mississippi State	24 G Cordy Glenn / Chris Davis (C)
27 Colorado	29 C Ben Jones
41 Tennessee	14 G Tanner Strickland / Kenarious Gates
43 Vanderbilt	0 T Josh Davis
44 Kentucky	31 TE Orson Charles / Bruce Figgins
31 Florida	34 QB Aaron Murray
55 Idaho State	7 TB Washaun Ealey / Caleb King
31 Auburn	49 FB Shaun Chapas / Fred Munzenmaier
42 Georgia Tech	34 DL Abry Jones / Brandon Wood
6 Central Florida	10 DL DeAngelo Tyson
	DL Demarcus Dobbs
	LB Cornelius Washington / Darryl Gamble
	LB Akeem Dent
	LB Christian Robinson / Marcus Dowtin
	LB Justin Houston
	DB Brandon Boykin / Branden Smith (WR)
	DB Sanders Commings / Vance Cuff
	DB Jakar Hamilton / Alec Ogletree (WR)
	DB Bacarri Rambo / Shawn Williams

RUSHING: Ealey 157/811y, King 80/430y, Carlton Thomas (TB) 64/272y
PASSING: Murray 209-342/3049y, 24TD, 61.1%
RECEIVING: Green 57/848y, Durham 32/659y, King 27/504y
SCORING: Blair Walsh (K) 106pts, Ealey 66pts, Green 54pts

GEORGIA TECH

Georgia Institute of Technology (Founded 1885)
Atlanta, Georgia
Nicknames: Yellow Jackets, Engineers, Rambling Wreck
Colors: Old Gold, White and Navy Blue
Stadium: Bobby Dodd Stadium at Grant Field (1913) 55,000
Affiliations: Southern Conf. (1902-32), Southeastern Conf. (1933-64),
Independent (1965-78), Atlantic Coast Conference (1983-present)

CAREER RUSHING YARDS	Attempts	Yards
Robert Lavette (1981-84)	914	4066
Jerry Mays (1985-89)	695	3699
Eddie Lee Ivery (1975-78)	609	3517
Tashard Choice (2005-07)	675	3365
P.J. Daniels (2002-05)	707	3346
Jonathan Dwyer (2007-09)	517	3226
Josh Nesbitt (2007-10)	655	2806
Joe Burns (1998-2001)	614	2634
C.J. Williams (1994-96)	539	2365
David Sims (1974-76)	379	2274

CAREER PASSING YARDS	Comps.-Att.	Yards
Joe Hamilton (1996-99)	629-1020	8882
Shawn Jones (1989-92)	652-1217	8441
Reggie Ball (2003-06)	662-1363	8128
George Godsey (1998-2001)	484-765	6137
Mike Kelley (1978-81)	391-785	5249
John Dewberry (1983-85)	310-533	4193
Eddie McAshan (1970-72)	360-698	4080
Josh Nesbitt (2007-10)	173-403	3276
Donnie Davis (1992-95)	270-478	3261
Taylor Bennett (2005-07)	211-422	2804

CAREER RECEIVING YARDS	Catches	Yards
Calvin Johnson (2004-06)	178	2927
Kelly Campbell (1998-2001)	195	2907
Kerry Watkins (1999-2002)	171	2680
Demaryius Thomas (2007-09)	120	2339
Harvey Middleton (1994-97)	165	2291
Jonathan Smith (2000-03)	174	2238
Dez White (1997-99)	90	1833
John Sias (1966-68)	110	1727
Bobby Rodriguez (1989-92)	115	1681
Derrick Steagall (1993-97)	99	1639

SEASON RUSHING YARDS	Attempts	Yards
Eddie Lee Ivery (1978)	267	1562
Tashard Choice (2006)	297	1473
P.J. Daniels (2003)	283	1447
Jonathan Dwyer (2008)	200	1395
Jonathan Dwyer (2009)	235	1395

SEASON PASSING YARDS	Comps.-Att.	Yards
George Godsey (2001)	249-384	3085
Joe Hamilton (1999)	203-305	3060
George Godsey (2000)	222-349	2906
Shawn Jones (1992)	190-362	2397
Joe Hamilton (1997)	173-268	2314

SEASON RECEIVING YARDS	Catches	Yards
Calvin Johnson (2006)	76	1202
Demaryius Thomas (2009)	46	1154
Jonathan Smith (2003)	78	1138
Kelly Campbell (1999)	69	1105
Kerry Watkins (2002)	71	1050

GAME RUSHING YARDS	Attempts	Yards
Eddie Lee Ivery (1978 vs. Air Force)	26	356
P.J. Daniels (2003 vs. Tulsa)	31	307
P.J. Daniels (2003 vs. North Carolina)	36	240

GAME PASSING YARDS	Comps.-Att.	Yards
George Godsey (2001 vs. Virginia)	39-55	486
George Godsey (2000 vs. Clemson)	35-57	454
Darrell Gast (1987 vs. Duke)	22-49	416

GAME RECEIVING YARDS	Catches	Yards
Dez White (1998 vs. Virginia)	6	243
Demaryius Thomas (2008 vs. Duke)	9	230
Derrick Steagall (1997 vs. Virginia)	7	223

GREATEST COACH

Georgia Tech's greatest coach may have been the man we all would have liked to have played for if rip-snorting practices and screaming intensity was not what we wanted out of football. Bobby Dodd, All-American quarterback at Tennessee and 22-year head coach at Georgia Tech, was a gentleman. He was the antithesis of Bear Bryant, and the two came to stand for two extremes in how the game was played. It was strong disagreement over a perceived dirty play in 1961 on Yellow Jacket halfback Chick Graning by Alabama's Darwin Holt—coached by Bryant—that precipitated Georgia Tech from withdrawing from the Southeastern Conference.

Dodd's teams were models of superb line play, especially personified by his quick-hitting linebackers, and they featured legions of swift little running backs. For many of his successful seasons in the 1950s, Georgia Tech ran exclusively "Belly Series" option plays out of a T-formation. Each play would start with the quarterback riding the fullback through one of the guard holes to read the first option of defensive reaction. Handoffs or wide pitchouts to darting halfbacks or running passes invariably came next. Combined with great defense, it was a great system.

Dodd never worked his players hard at bowl games; the team went to have a good time in its visits to New Orleans, Dallas, Miami, or Jacksonville. It was an idea that must have worked: Dodd won eight straight post-season games until his former assistant, Frank Broyles, coached Arkansas, a strong defensive team with darting halfbacks, to a 14-7 win over Tech in the Gator Bowl following the 1959 season.

Maybe Bryant's hard-nose style of football, which became fairly universal by the late 1950s, was the wave of the future. Although Dodd finished in 1966 with an overall record of 165-64-8, his bowl record slipped to 9-4, including an Orange Bowl loss to Florida in his swansong. Still, Dodd clearly was Georgia Tech's greatest, and with him went a certain grace.

GEORGIA TECH'S 55 GREATEST SINCE 1953

OFFENSE

WIDE RECEIVER: Kelly Campbell, Calvin Johnson, John Sias, Dez White
TIGHT END: Billy Martin
TACKLE: Nat Dorsey, Mike Mooney, Billy Shaw, Mike Taylor
GUARD: Allen Ecker, Rufus Guthrie, Dave Watson
CENTER: Jim Breland, John Davis, Craig Page, Don Stephenson
QUARTERBACK: Joe Hamilton, Shawn Jones
RUNNING BACK: William Bell, Tashard Choice, P.J. Daniels, Eddie Lee Ivery, Robert Lavette, Lenny Snow
FULLBACK: Ronnie Cone, Ken Owen

DEFENSE

END: Greg Gathers, Smylie Gebhart, Reggie Wilkes
TACKLE: Rock Perdoni, Coleman Rudolph, Larry Stallings
LINEBACKER: Maxie Baughan, Keith Brookings, Franklin Brooks, Marco Coleman, Larry Morris, Ted Roof, Lucius Sanford, Pat Swilling
CORNERBACK: Gerry Bussell, Willie Clay, Bill Eastman, Randy Rhino, Paul Rotenberry
SAFETY: Don Bessillieu, Wade Mitchell, Jeremy Muyres, Travares Tillman

SPECIAL TEAMS

RETURN SPECIALIST: Derrick Steagall
PLACE KICKER: Scott Sisson
PUNTER: Rodney Williams

MULTIPLE POSITIONS

FULLBACK-END-DEFENSIVE END-LINEBACKER: Taz Anderson
QUARTERBACK-SAFETY-PLACE KICKER-PUNTER: Billy Lothridge

TWO-WAY PLAYER

CENTER-LINEBACKER: Bill Curry

PERFORMANCE FORMULA:
GEORGIA TECH'S 10 BEST SEASONS

1956	1.6909	2 of 69
1990	1.6706	2 of 70
1955	1.6116	6 of 69
1966	1.5418	6 of 70
1998	1.4937	11 of 71
1953	1.4462	9 of 69
1954	1.4194	14 of 69
2009	1.4164	14 of 72
2000	1.4096	12 of 70
1970	1.3865	13 of 70

GEORGIA TECH YELLOW JACKETS

Year	W-L-T	AP Poll	Conference Standing	Toughest Regular Season Opponents	Coach (Record at School)	Bowl Games		
1953	9-2-1	8	2t	Auburn 7-2-1, Notre Dame 9-0-1, Alabama 6-2-3, Duke 7-2-1	Bobby Dodd	Sugar	42 West Virginia	19
1954	8-3		2	SMU 6-3-1, Auburn 7-3, Duke 7-2-1, Georgia 6-3-1	Bobby Dodd	Cotton	14 Arkansas	6
1955	9-1-1	7	3	Miami 6-3, Auburn 8-1-1, Duke 7-2-1, Tennessee 6-3-1	Bobby Dodd	Sugar	7 Pittsburgh	0
1956	10-1	4	2	Auburn 7-3, Tennessee 10-0, Florida 6-3-1	Bobby Dodd	Gator	21 Pittsburgh	14
1957	4-4-2		8	Auburn 10-0, Duke 6-2-2, Tennessee 7-2, Florida 6-2-1	Bobby Dodd			
1958	5-4-1		8t	Florida State 7-3, Auburn 9-0-1, Clemson 8-2, Alabama 5-4-1	Bobby Dodd	Gator	7 Arkansas	14
1959	6-5		7	Clemson 8-2, Auburn 7-3, Alabama 7-1-2, Georgia 9-1	Bobby Dodd			
1960	5-5		7	Rice 7-3, Florida 8-2, Auburn 8-2, Duke 7-3, Alabama 8-1-1	Bobby Dodd			
1961	7-4	13	4t	Rice 7-3, LSU 9-1, Duke 7-3, Alabama 10-0	Bobby Dodd	Gator	15 Penn State	30
1962	7-3-1		4	LSU 8-1-1, Auburn 6-3-1, Duke 8-2, Alabama 9-1	Bobby Dodd	Bluebonnet	10 Missouri	14
1963	7-3		6	Florida 6-3-1, LSU 7-3, Auburn 9-1, Alabama 8-2	Bobby Dodd			
1964	7-3			Auburn 6-4, Alabama 10-0, Georgia 6-3-1	Bobby Dodd			
1965	7-3-1			Duke 6-4, Tennessee 7-1-2, Georgia 6-4	Bobby Dodd	Gator	31 Texas Tech	21
1966	9-2	8		Clemson 6-4, Tennessee 7-3, Georgia 9-1	Bobby Dodd (165-64-8)	Orange	12 Florida	27
1967	4-6			Tennessee 9-1, Miami 7-3, Notre Dame 8-2, Georgia 7-3	Bud Carson			
1968	4-6			Tennessee 8-1-1, Auburn 6-4, Notre Dame 7-2-1, Georgia 8-0-2	Bud Carson			
1969	4-6			Tennessee 9-1-1, Auburn 8-2, Southern Calif. 9-0-1, Notre Dame 8-1-1	Bud Carson			
1970	9-3	13		Florida State 7-4, Tennessee 10-1, Auburn 8-2, Notre Dame 9-1	Bud Carson	Sun	17 Texas Tech	9
1971	6-6			Tennessee 9-2, Auburn 9-1, Florida State 8-3, Georgia 10-1	Bud Carson (27-27)	Peach	18 Mississippi	41
1972	7-4-1	20		Tennessee 9-2, Auburn 9-1, Georgia 7-4	Bill Fulcher	Liberty	31 Iowa State	30
1973	5-6			Southern California 9-1-1, Tennessee 8-3, Tulane 9-2	Bill Fulcher (12-10-1)			
1974	6-5			Notre Dame 9-2, Pitt 7-4, Clemson 7-4, North Carolina 7-4, Auburn 9-2	Pepper Rodgers			
1975	7-4			South Carolina 7-4, Notre Dame 8-3, Navy 7-4, Georgia 9-2	Pepper Rodgers			
1976	4-6-1			Pittsburgh 11-0, Notre Dame 8-3, Georgia 10-1	Pepper Rodgers			
1977	6-5			Clemson 8-2-1, Auburn 6-5, Notre Dame 10-1	Pepper Rodgers			
1978	7-5			Auburn 6-4-1, Notre Dame 8-3, Georgia 9-1-1	Pepper Rodgers	Peach	21 Purdue	41
1979	4-6-1			Alabama 11-0, Auburn 8-3, Tulane 9-2	Pepper Rodgers (34-31-2)			
1980	1-9-1		ineligible	Alabama 9-2, North Carolina 10-1, Notre Dame 9-1-1, Georgia 11-0	Bill Curry			
1981	1-10		ineligible	Alabama 9-1-1, North Carolina 9-2, Georgia 10-1	Bill Curry			
1982	6-5		ineligible	Alabama 7-4, Auburn 8-3, Tennessee 6-4-1, Georgia 11-0	Bill Curry			
1983	3-8		3	Clemson 9-1-1, Auburn 10-1, Georgia 9-1-1	Bill Curry			
1984	6-4-1		5	Virginia 7-2-2, Auburn 8-4, Tennessee 7-3-1, Georgia 7-4	Bill Curry	All-America	17 Michigan State	14
1985	9-2-1	19	2	Auburn 8-3, Tennessee 8-2-1, Georgia 7-3-1	Bill Curry (31-43-4)			
1986	5-5-1		4	Clemson 7-2-2, North Carolina 7-3-1, Auburn 9-2, Georgia 8-3	Bobby Ross			
1987	2-9		8	Clemson 9-2, Auburn 9-1-1, Tennessee 9-2-1, Georgia 8-3	Bobby Ross			
1988	3-8		8	Clemson 9-2, South Carolina 8-3, Georgia 8-3	Bobby Ross			
1989	7-4		4t	NC State 7-4, Virginia 10-2, Clemson 9-2, Duke 8-3	Bobby Ross			
1990	11-0-1	2	1	Clemson 9-2, North Carolina 6-4-1, Virginia 8-3	Bobby Ross (31-26-1)	Florida Citrus	45 Nebraska	21
1991	8-5		2t	Penn State 10-2, Virginia 8-2-1, Clemson 9-1-1, NC State 9-2	Bill Lewis	Aloha	18 Stanford	17
1992	5-6		4t	NC State 9-2-1, Florida State 10-1, North Carolina 8-3, Georgia 9-2	Bill Lewis			
1993	5-6		6	Clemson 8-3, Florida State 11-1, North Carolina 10-2	Bill Lewis (11-19),			
1994	1-10		9	Arizona 8-3, Duke 8-3, NC State 8-3, 8-3, North Carolina 8-3, Virginai 8-3, Florida State 9-1-1	George O'Leary [0-3]			
1995	6-5		4	Virginia 9-4, Florida State 9-2, Clemson 8-3	George O'Leary			
1996	5-6		5	North Carolina 9-2, Florida State 11-0, Navy 8-3	George O'Leary	Carquest	35 West Virginia	30
1997	7-5		3t	Florida State 10-1, North Carolina 10-1, Georgia 9-2	George O'Leary	Gator	35 Notre Dame	28
1998	10-2	9	1t	Virginia 9-2, Florida State 11-1, Georgia 8-3	George O'Leary	Gator	13 Miami	28
1999	8-4	20	2t	Florida State 11-0, Virginia 7-4, Georgia 7-4	George O'Leary	Peach	14 Louisiana State	28
2000	9-3	17	2t	Florida State 11-1, NC State 7-4, Clemson 9-2, Georgia 7-4	George O'Leary	Seattle	24 Stanford	14
2001	8-5	24	4t	Syracuse 9-3, Maryland 10-1, Georgia 8-3	George O'Leary (53-33)	Silicon	21 Fresno State	30
2002	7-6		5t	Maryland 10-3, NC State 10-3, Florida State 9-4, Georgia 12-1	Chan Gailey	Humanitarian	52 Tulsa	10
2003	7-6		4t	Florida State 10-2, Clemson 8-4, Maryland 9-3, Georgia 9-3	Chan Gailey	Champs	51 Syracuse	14
2004	7-5		6t	Miami 8-3, Virginia 8-3, Virginia Tech 10-2, Georgia 9-2	Chan Gailey	Emerald	10 Utah	38
2005	7-5		Cst3	Auburn 9-2, Virginia Tech 10-2, Georgia 10-2, Miami 9-2	Chan Gailey	Gator	35 West Virginia	38
2006	9-5		Cst1	Notre Dame 10-2, Va Tech 10-2, Maryland 8-4, Clemson 8-4, Georgia 8-4	Chan Gailey			
2007	7-6		Cst3	Boston College 10-2, Clemson 9-3, Virginia Tech 10-2, Georgia 10-2	Chan Gailey (44-33) Jon Tenuta [0-1]	Humanitarian	28 Fresno State	40
2008	9-4	22	Cst1t	Boston College 9-4, Virginia Tech 9-4, Florida State 8-4, Georgia 9-3	Paul Johnson	Chick-fil-A	3 Louisiana State	38
2009	11-3	13	Cst1	Clemson 8-5, Miami 9-3, Virginia Tech 9-3, Georgia 7-5	Paul Johnson	Orange	14 Iowa	24
2010	6-7		Cst3t	North Carolina State 8-4, Virginia Tech 11-2	Paul Johnson (26-14)	Independence	7 Air Force	14

TOTAL: 369-279-15 .5679 (27 of 70)

Bowl Games since 1953: 15-15 .5000 (37 of 70)

GREATEST TEAM SINCE 1953: It is a virtual toss-up between the 10-1 Engineers team of 1956 and the 10-0-1 national champions of 1990. The two teams played similar level of opponents, with the 1956 team holding a .5889 to .5818 edge in quality foes. The 1956 Georgia Tech team lost a heart-breaking 6-0 game to undefeated Tennessee but, unlike Tennessee, won its bowl game over a vengeful Pittsburgh Panthers, who had lost a tough outcome to Tech in the previous year's Sugar Bowl. Bobby Ross' 1990 team rebounded from two-, three- and seven-win seasons to go 10-0-1 to capture the coaches poll national title in 1990. Because the 1990 Yellow Jackets won big game after big game—several as underdogs—and got a raw deal from the AP voters, who went for a tainted Colorado team as champions, the nod here goes slightly to the 1990 Yellow Jackets.

1953 9-2-1

53 Davidson	0 E Sam Hensley / Jimmy Durham
0 Florida	0 T Roger Frey / Ben Daugherty
6 SMU	4 G Franklin Brooks / Ed Gossage
27 Tulane	13 C Larry Morris / Jimmy Morris
36 Auburn	6 G Orville Vereen / Jake Shoemaker
14 Notre Dame	27 T Bob Sherman
43 Vanderbilt	0 E Dave Davis / Henry Hair
20 Clemson	7 QB Pepper Rodgers / Wade Mitchell
6 Alabama	13 HB Leon Hardeman
13 Duke	10 HB Billy Teas / Joe Hall
28 Georgia	12 FB Glenn Turner / John Hunsinger
42 West Virginia■	19

RUSHING: Teas 111/554y, Hardeman 69/401y, Turner 91/374y
PASSING: Rodgers 51-85/643y, 7TD, 60.0%,
Mitchell 25-81/375y, 3TD, 30.9%
RECEIVING: Hair 16/187y, Hensley 15/244y, Davis 12/124y
SCORING: Rodgers (QB-K) 40pts, Hardeman 30pts, 3 with 24pts

1954 8-3

28 Tulane	0 E Jimmy Durham / Bill Sennett
12 Florida	13 T Carl Vereen / Ben Daugherty
10 SMU	7 G FranklinBrooks / Allen Ecker
30 LSU	20 C Larry Morris / Jimmy Morris
14 Auburn	7 G Bill Fulcher / Tommy Gossage
6 Kentucky	13 T Jake Shoemaker / Ormand Anderson
20 Duke	21 E Henry Hair / Don Ellis
28 Tennessee	7 QB Wade Mitchell / Bill Brigman
20 Alabama	0 HB BillyTeas/Paul Rotenb'ry/Geo. Volkert
7 Georgia	0 HB Johny Menger / Jimmy Thompson
14 Arkansas■	6 FB George Humphreys / John Hunsinger

RUSHING: Thompson 47/442y, Rotenberry 59/341y
PASSING: Brigman 39-77/573y, 4TD, 50.6%,
Mitchell 32-70/331y, 4TD, 45.7%
RECEIVING: Hair 24/270y
SCORING: Hair & Thompson 24pts

1955 9-1-1

14 Miami	6 E Tommy Rose / Jerry Nabors
14 Florida	7 T Carl Vereen / Frank Christy
20 SMU	7 G Franklin Brooks / Bill Fulcher
7 LSU	0 C Jimmy Morris / Don Stephenson
12 Auburn	14 G Allen Ecker / Jimmy Johnson
34 Florida State	7 T Ken Thrash / Ormand Anderson
27 Duke	0 E Don Ellis
7 Tennessee	7 QB Wade Mitchell / Toppy Vann
26 Alabama	2 HB Paul Rotenberry / Stan Flowers
21 Georgia	3 HB George Volkert / Jimmy Thompson
7 Pittsburgh■	0 FB Ken Owen / Dickie Mattison

RUSHING: Volkert 81/583y, Mattison 56/256y, Flowers 60/253y
PASSING: Vann 31-36/270y, 3TD, 86.1%,
Mitchell 18-43/221y, TD, 41.9%
RECEIVING: Volkert 8/171y, Thompson 7/51y, Ellis 6/78y
SCORING: Vann 37pts, Mitchell 34pts, Volkert 30pts

1956 10-1

14 Kentucky	6 E Tommy Rose / Jerry Nabors
9 SMU	7 T Carl Vereen / Frank Christy
39 LSU	7 G Jimmy Johnson / Don Miller
28 Auburn	7 C Don Stephenson
40 Tulane	0 G Allen Ecker / Leon Askew
7 Duke	0 T Ormand Anderson / Ken Thrash
0 Tennessee	6 E Don Ellis / Ted Smith
27 Alabama	0 QB Wade Mitchell / Toppy Vann
28 Florida	0 HB Paul Rotenberry / Stan Flowers
35 Georgia	0 HB George Volkert / Jimmy Thompson
21 Pittsburgh■	14 FB Ken Owen / Dickie Mattison

RUSHING:Owen 107/497y,Rotenberry 67/328y,Mattison 68/272y
PASSING: Vann 34-65/446y, 6TD, 52.3%,
Mitchell 10-32/106y, 0TD, 31.3%
RECEIVING: Flowers 10/141y, Rotenberry 7/65y, Nabors 6/80y
SCORING: Vann 39pts, Mitchell 36pts, 5 with 18pts

1957 4-4-2

13 Kentucky	0 .E Jerry Nabors / Jerome Green
0 SMU	0 T Urban Henry / Ted Thomas
13 LSU	20 G Dan Theodocion / Foster Watkins
0 Auburn	3 C Don Stephenson / Maxie Baughan
20 Tulane	13 G Leon Askew / John Neal Reed
13 Duke	0 T Rausey Mason
6 Tennessee	21 E Ted Smith / Jack Rudolph
10 Alabama	7 QB Fred Braselton
0 Florida	0 HB Stan Flowers / Floyd Faucetter
0 Georgia	7 HB Cal James / Joe DeLany /Jim Benson
	FB Lester Simerville / Larry Fonts

RUSHING: Simerville 86/275y, Flowers 55/228y, James 51/206y
PASSING: Braselton 56-107/486y, 4TD, 52.3%
RECEIVING: Green 9/86y, Smith 9/79y, Faucette 8/52y
SCORING: Braselton (QB-K) 15pts, Simerville & Benson 12pts

1958 5-4-1

0 Kentucky	13 E Jerome Green / Tommy Rose
17 Florida State	3 T Rausey Mason / Billy Shaw
14 Tulane	0 G Bob Stone / Foster Watkins
21 Tennessee	7 C Maxie Baughan
7 Auburn	7 G John Neal Reed / Buddy Pilgrim
0 SMU	20 T Ted Thomas / Toby Deese
10 Duke	8 E Ger'ld Burch/Jack Rud'lph/Fred M'rphy
13 Clemson	0 QB Fred Braselton
8 Alabama	17 HB Cal James
3 Georgia	16 HB Frank Nix / Joe DeLany
	FB Floyd Faucette / Lester Simerville

RUSHING: Faucette 83/473y, James 83/293y, Nix 45/144y
PASSING: Braselton 35-78/319y, 0TD, 44.9%
RECEIVING: Murphy 12/143y, Rudolph 9/87y, Burch 8/110y
SCORING: Tommy Wells (K) 19pts, Braselton 18pts, Nix 12pts

1959 6-5

14 Kentucky	12 E Gerald Burch / Belfield Carter
16 SMU	12 T Billy Shaw
16 Clemson	6 G Harold Ericksen / Bill McKinney
14 Tennessee	7 C Maxie Baughan / Willie McGaughey
6 Auburn	7 G John Neal Reed / Buddy Pilgrim
21 Tulane	13 T Toby Deese / Ed Nutting
7 Duke	10 E Jack Rudolph / Fred Murphy
14 Notre Dame	10 QB Fred Braselton / Marvin Tibbetts
7 Alabama	9 HB Floyd Faucette / Chick Graning
14 Georgia	21 HB Billy Williamson /Frank Nix/Cal James
7 Arkansas■	14 FB Taz Anderson / Lee Reid

RUSHING: Faucette 69/330y, Anderson 70/233y, Graning 40/129y
PASSING: Braselton 32-64/368y, 4TD, 50.0%,
Tibbetts 7-22/154y, 2TD, 31.8%
RECEIVING: Anderson 10/89y, Murphy 8/145y, Williamson 5/43y
SCORING: Tommy Wells (K) 21pts,
Faucette, Tibbetts, & Murphy 18pts

1960 5-5

23 Kentucky	13 E Gerald Burch / Bob Solomon
16 Rice	13 T Billy Shaw / Russ Foret
17 Florida	18 G Harold Ericksen
6 LSU	2 C Willie McGaughey / Bobby Caldwell
7 Auburn	9 G Rufus Guthrie / Dave Watson
14 Tulane	6 T Ed Nutting / Larry Stallings
0 Duke	6 E Taz Anderson / Belfield Carter
14 Tennessee	7 QB Marvin Tibbetts / Stan Gann
15 Alabama	16 HB Billy Williamson / Tom Winingder
6 Georgia	7 HB Chick Graning/Jimmy Nail/Zollie Sircy
	FB Lee Reid / Ben Smith

RUSHING: Graning 82/315y, Williamson 65/308y, Smith 56/181y
PASSING: Gann 43-96/523y, 3TD, 44.8%
RECEIVING: Graning 16/158y, Anderson 11/151y, Burch 9/118y
SCORING: Tommy Wells (K) 34pts, Graning 30pts,
Williamson 24pts

1961 7-4

27 Southern Cal	7 E Ted Davis / Frank Sexton
24 Rice	0 T Ed Griffin / Russ Foret
0 LSU	10 G Harold Ericksen / Rufus Guthrie
21 Duke	0 C Willie McGaughey / Bobby Caldwell
7 Auburn	6 G Dave Watson / Jack Moss
35 Tulane	0 T Larry Stallings
20 Florida	0 E Bob Solomon / Billy Martin
6 Tennessee	10 QB Stan Gann / Billy Lothridge
0 Alabama	10 HB Chick Graning / Tom Winingder
22 Georgia	7 HB Billy Williamson / Joe Auer
15 Penn State■	30 FB Mike McNames / Don Toner (LB)

RUSHING: McNames 94/350y, Williamson 63/331y
PASSING: Gann 43-79/450y, TD, 54.4%,
Lothridge 26-63/371y, 2TD, 41.3%
RECEIVING: Williamson 21/221y, Martin 16/233y, Auer 10/145y
SCORING: Lothridge 46pts, Gann 30pts, Williamson 24pts

1962 7-3-1

26 Clemson	9 E Ted Davis
17 Florida	0 T Ed Griffin
7 LSU	10 G Rufus Guthrie
17 Tennessee	0 C Bobby Caldwell / John Matlock
14 Auburn	17 G Dave Watson / Jack Moss
42 Tulane	12 T Larry Stallings
20 Duke	9 E Billy Martin
14 Florida State	14 QB Billy Lothridge
7 Alabama	6 HB Joe Auer / Tom Winingder
37 Georgia	6 HB Zollie Sircy / Gerry Bussell
10 Missouri■	14 FB Mike McNames / Don Toner (LB)

RUSHING: Lothridge 128/478y, McNames 81/305y, Sircy 41/182y
PASSING: Lothridge 83-156/1006y, 6TD, 53.2%
RECEIVING: Martin 21/323y, Auer 14/154y, Davis 11/149y
SCORING: Lothridge 89pts, Martin 24pts, McNames 24pts

1963 7-3

9 Florida	0 E Ted Davis
27 Clemson	0 T Joe Chapman
6 LSU	7 G Jimmy Seward
23 Tennessee	7 C Bill Curry / Dave Simmons
21 Auburn	29 G Brad Yates
17 Tulane	3 T Bill Farrington
30 Duke	6 E Billy Martin
15 Florida State	7 QB Billy Lothridge
11 Alabama	27 HB Joe Auer
14 Georgia	3 HB Johnny Gresham / Gerry Bussell
	FB Ray Mendheim / Ed Weinman (LB)

RUSHING: Mendheim 93/427y, Auer 59/257y,
Lothridge 117/223y
PASSING: Lothridge 76-153/1017y, 10TD, 49.7%
RECEIVING: Martin 19/221y, Auer 12/145y, Bussell 9/141y
SCORING: Lothridge 69pts, Mendheim 30pts, 3 with 12pts

1964 7-3

14 Vanderbilt	2 E Mike Fortier / George Morris
20 Miami	0 T Bill Moorer
14 Clemson	7 G Gary Lee / Joe Colvin
17 Navy	0 C W.J. Blane / Bill Curry (LB)
7 Auburn	3 G Bill Myddelton
7 Tulane	6 T Tom Ballard
21 Duke	8 E Gary Williams
14 Tennessee	22 QB Jerry Priestley / Bruce Fischer
7 Alabama	24 HB Terry Haddock / Craig Baynham
0 Georgia	7 HB Johnny Gresham / Giles Smith
	FB Jeff Davis
	DL Steve Copeland
	DL John Battle / Jimmy Seward
	DL Randy Watkins
	DL Billy Schroer / Mike Ashmore
	DL Dave Austin / Jim Trapnell
	LB Bill Curry (C)
	LB Dave Simmons
	DB Harry Cavan / Sammy Burke
	DB Tommy Jackson
	DB Gerry Bussell / Tommy Bleick
	DB Haven Kicklighter

RUSHING: Gresham 99/437y, Davis 97/332y, Haddock 49/196y
PASSING: Priestley 37-77/441y, 4TD, 48.1%,
Fischer 28-54/416y, 2TD, 51.9%
RECEIVING: Gresham 22/290y, Fortier 13/166y, Haddock 8/79y
SCORING: Gresham 24pts, Haddock 18pts,
Bunky Henry (K) 14pts

1965 7-3-1

10 Vanderbilt	10 E Mike Fortier / Tommy Elliott
10 Texas A&M	14 T Bill Moorer
38 Clemson	6 G Bill Myddelton / Rick Nelson
13 Tulane	10 C Jim Breland
23 Auburn	14 G Joe Colvin
37 Navy	16 T Lamar Wright / Jim Penley
35 Duke	23 TE Gary Williams / Steve Almond
7 Tennessee	21 QB Kim King
42 Virginia	19 TB Lenny Snow
7 Georgia	17 WB Craig Baynham / Don Foster
31 Texas Tech■	21 FB Tommy Carlisle / Giles Smith
	DL Steve Copeland / Alan Glisson
	DL Buddy McCoy / Mike Ashmore
	DL John Battle
	DL Bill Schroer / John Lagana
	DL Bill Ellis / Jim Trapnell
	LB Randall Edmunds
	LB W.J. Blane / Claude Shook
	DB Sammy Burke
	DB Bill Eastman / Dee Turner
	DB Tommy Bleick / Roy Jarrett
	DB Haven Kicklighter

RUSHING: Snow 125/597y, King 131/345y, Smith 46/187y
PASSING: King 112-191/1331y, 11TD, 58.6%
RECEIVING: Baynham 30/368y,Williams 24/338y,Fortier 22/260y
SCORING: Bunky Henry (K) 42pts, Baynham 42pts, Snow 30pts

1966 9-2

38 Texas A&M	3 WR Mike Fortier / Joel Stevenson
42 Vanderbilt	0 WR Craig Baynham / John Sias
13 Clemson	12 T Bill Moorer / Jim Penley
6 Tennessee	3 G Bill Myddelton (DL) / Rick Nelson
17 Auburn	3 C Jim Breland
35 Tulane	17 G Buddy McCoy
48 Duke	7 T Lamar Wright (G) / Terry Story
14 Virginia	13 TE Steve Almond / Lamar Melvin
21 Penn State	0 QB Kim King / Larry Good
14 Georgia	23 TB Lenny Snow
12 Florida■	27 FB Doc Harvin / John Weaver
	DL Tommy Carlisle / Danny Adams
	DL John Lagana
	DL Mike Ashmore
	DL Eric Wilcox / Alan Glisson
	LB Randall Edmunds
	LB W.J. Blane / Bob Hollender
	LB Billy Schroer / Claude Shook
	DB Havern Kicklighter
	DB Bill Eastman
	DB Sammy Burke / Roy Jarrett
	DB Giles Smith / David Barber

RUSHING: Snow 202/761y, Good 70/432y, Brown 66/198y
PASSING: King 64-124/690y, TD, 51.6%
RECEIVING: Almond 24/265y, Fortier 18/246y, Baynham 18/144y
SCORING: Snow 72pts, Bunky Henry (K) 47pts, Good & King 18pts

1967 4-6

17 Vanderbilt	10 WR Joel Stevenson / Jimmy Brown
24 TCU	7 WR John Sias
10 Clemson	0 T Rick Nelson / Terry Story
13 Tennessee	24 G Joe Vitunic / Tim Eubanks
10 Auburn	28 C Billy Kidd / John Collins
12 Tulane	23 G Lamar Melvin
19 Duke	7 T Jim Penley
7 Miami	49 TE Steve Almond / Al Gerhardt
3 Notre Dame	36 QB Kim King / Larry Good / Ken Bonifay
14 Georgia	21 TB Lenny Snow
	FB Doc Harvin / Bain Culton
	DL Tommy Carlisle
	DL John Lagana
	DL Mike Ashmore / Jim Taylor
	DL Chris Denney
	LB Claude Shook / Mike Bradley
	LB Randall Edmunds
	LB Eric Wilcox
	DB Joe Bill Faith / Doug Dale
	DB Bill Eastman (QB-TB) / Greg Wilkes
	DB Bill Kinard / Dee Turner
	DB David Barber

RUSHING: Snow 118/385y, Good 48/172y, Eastman 43/144y
PASSING: King 67-145/742y, 2TD, 46.2%
RECEIVING: Sias 42/671y, Almond 21/216y, Stevenson 16/201y
SCORING: Tommy Carmichael (K) 33pts, Sias 24pts, 5 with 12pts

1968 4-6

17 TCU	7 WR Tim Woodall
7 Miami	10 WR John Sias / Tom Chapman
24 Clemson	21 T Galin Mumford
7 Tennessee	24 G John Collins (C) / Mike Bradley
21 Auburn	20 C Billy Kidd
23 Tulane	19 G Todd Woodhull / Rick Evatt
30 Duke	46 T Terry Story / Sid Gunter
15 Navy	35 TE Joel Stevenson
6 Notre Dame	34 QB Larry Good
8 Georgia	47 TB Dennis James / Gene Spiotta
	FB Kenny Bounds / Steve Harkey
	DL Steve Foster / Joe Hardwick
	DL Bob Seamon / Richard Gardner
	DL Lou Santospago / Tim Eubanks
	DL Mike Glad
	LB Bill Flowers / Buck Shiver
	LB Eric Wilcox
	LB Steve Kramer / Steve DeBardelaben
	DB Mike Wysong
	DB Joe Bill Faith / Rich Cornwell
	DB Bill Kinard
	DB Tash Van Dora / Dave Polk

RUSHING: Bounds 56/188y, Harkey 62/178y, Spiotta 43/152y
PASSING: Good 97-191/1337y, 6TD, 50.8%
RECEIVING: Sias 61/902y, Stevenson 44/468y, Bounds 26/254y
SCORING: Bounds 28pts, Sias 24pts, Johnny Duncan (K) 22pts

1969 4-6

24 SMU	21 WR Larry Studdard / Chip Pallman
17 Baylor	10 WR Herman Lam / Percy Helmer
10 Clemson	21 T Allen Vezey / Pete Cordrey
8 Tennessee	26 G Joe Vitunic
14 Auburn	17 C Andy Mayton / John Callan
18 Southern Cal	29 G Mike Bradley
20 Duke	7 T Richard Gardner
7 Tulane	14 TE Steve Foster / Steve Norris
20 Notre Dame	38 QB Jack Williams / Charlie Dudish
6 Georgia	0 RB Brent Cunningham / Kenny Bounds
	RB Steve Harkey / Gene Spiotta
	DL Brad Bourne / Joe Hardwick
	DL Rock Perdoni
	DL Tim Broome / Wayne Laircey
	DL Smylie Gebhart / Randy Duckworth
	LB Stan Beavers
	LB Bill Flowers / Tash Van Dora
	LB Buck Shiver / John Riggle
	LB Bubba Hoats / Dave Beavin
	DB Rick Lewis / Dave Polk
	DB Jeff Ford / Greg Wilkes
	DB Mike Wysong / Joe Bill Faith

RUSHING: Cunningham 118/459y, Spiotta 85/248y, Harkey 58/226y
PASSING: Williams 30-59/358y, 2 TD, 50.8%
Dudish 33-65/290y, 3 TD, 50.8%
RECEIVING: Foster 19/200y, Lam 17/273y, Pallman 9/124y
SCORING: Jack Moore (K) 21pts, Ford 18pts, Harkey 18pts

1970 9-3

23 South Carolina	20 WR Larry Studdard / Herman Lam
23 Florida State	13 T Glenn Costello
31 Miami	21 G Richard Gardner
28 Clemson	7 C John Callan
6 Tennessee	17 G Scott Engel
7 Auburn	31 T Rick Lantz
20 Tulane	6 TE Steve Foster
24 Duke	16 QB Eddie McAshan / Jack Williams
30 Navy	8 HB Brent Cunningham / Bruce Southall
7 Notre Dame	10 HB Rob Healy
17 Georgia	7 FB Steve Harkey / Kevin McNamara
17 Texas Tech■	9 DL Rock Perdoni
	DL Brad Bourne
	DL Tim Broome / Randy Duckworth
	DL Smylie Gebhart
	LB Gary Carden
	LB Bill Flowers / John Riggle
	LB Buck Shiver
	LB Dave Beavin
	DB Rick Lewis
	DB Jeff Ford
	DB Bubba Hoats

RUSHING: Cunningham 144/740y, Healy 122/367y
PASSING: McAshan 110-223/1138y, 9TD, 49.3%
RECEIVING: Studdard 29/355y, Harkey 27/319y, Norris 21/220y
SCORING: Cunningham 42pts, Jack Moore (K) 34pts, Studdard 30pts

1971 6-6

7 South Carolina	24 WR Brent Cunningham (TB) / Jim Owings
10 Michigan State	0 WR Larry Studdard / Robert Stevenson
13 Army	16 T Al Hutko
24 Clemson	14 G Scott Engel / Vernon Jackson
6 Tennessee	10 C John Callan
14 Auburn	31 G Glenn Costello / Tommy Jones
24 Tulane	16 T Rick Lantz
21 Duke	0 TE Mike Oven / Mark Fields
34 Navy	21 QB Eddie McAshan
12 Florida State	6 TB Greg Horne / Tom Lang
24 Georgia	28 FB Rob Healy / Kevin McNamara
18 Mississippi■	41 DL Smylie Gebhart / Brad Bourne
	DL Joe Gaston / Tim Macy
	DL Randy Duckworth / Tommy Beck
	DL Brad Bourne / Bobby Daffer
	LB Stan Beavers / Witt Wisman
	LB Bruce Elliott
	LB Gary Carden / Proctor Allen
	LB Dave Beavin / Steve Putnal
	DB Mike McKenzie
	DB Jeff Ford
	DB Gary Faulkner

RUSHING: Horne 123/500y, Healy 96/395y, Cunningham 84/247y
PASSING: McAshan 125-234/1186y 7TD, 53.4%
RECEIVING: Oven 33/361y, Cunningham 22/172y, Studdard 19/236y
SCORING: Lang 32pts, Cam Bonifay (K) 27pts, Thigpen 20pts

1972 7-4-1

3 Tennessee	34 WR Jimmy Robinson
34 South Carolina	6 WR Billy Shields / Jim Owings
21 Michigan State	16 T Don Robinson
36 Rice	36 G John Sargent
31 Clemson	9 C Pete Geren / Rowland Bradford
14 Auburn	24 G Glenn Costello
21 Tulane	7 T Rick Lantz
14 Duke	20 TE Mike Oven / Mark Fields
42 Boston College	10 QB Eddie McAshan / Jim Stevens
30 Navy	7 TB Greg Horne / Tom Lang
7 Georgia	27 FB Rob Healy / Bruce Southall
31 Iowa State■	30 DL Beau Bruce / Bobby Daffer
	DL Joe Gaston
	DL Tim Macy / Tommy Beck
	DL Brad Bourne
	LB Witt Wisman / Steve Putnal
	LB Bruce Elliott
	LB Gary Carden
	LB Joe Harris
	DB Randy Rhino
	DB Mike McKenzie
	DB Scott Bridge / Gary Faulkner

RUSHING: Horne 139/558y, Southall 64/394y, Healy 62/226y
PASSING: McAshan 125-241/1756y, 16TD, 51.9%
RECEIVING: Robinson 48/812y, Oven 25/355y, Fields 19/318y
SCORING: Robinson 56pts, Thigpen 39pts, Owings 26pts

1973 5-6

28 South Carolina	41 WR Jimmy Robinson / Mike Mercer
6 Southern Cal	23 WR Jim Owings
29 Clemson	21 T Scott BeVier
14 Army	10 G Don Robinson / Mark Hunter
14 Tennessee	20 C Rowland Bradford
10 Auburn	24 G John Sargent / Tony Lubischer (DL)
14 Tulane	23 T Billy Shields
12 Duke	10 TE Mark Fields / Robert Stevenson
36 VMI	7 QB Jim Stevens
26 Navy	22 TB Cleo Johnson / Greg Horne
3 Georgia	10 FB Bruce Southall
	DL Bobby Daffer
	DL Beau Bruce / Rick Rawlins
	DL Rick Gibney
	LB Joe Harris / John Skalko
	LB Leavitt Sanders
	LB Don Shank / Bruce Elliott
	LB Witt Wisman / Steve Putnal
	DB Mike McKenzie
	DB Scott Bridge / Dennis Scully
	DB Mike McKenzie
	DB Randy Rhino

RUSHING: Johnson 92/451y, Horne 108/367y, Southall 85/316y
PASSING: Stevens 119-217/1481y, 4TD, 54.8%
RECEIVING: Robinson 34/597y, Fields 22/281y, Southall 21/201y
SCORING: Cam Bonifay 54pts, Hill 36pts, Horne 30pts

1974 6-5

7 Notre Dame	31 WR Jimmy Robinson
35 South Carolina	20 T Billy Shields
17 Pittsburgh	27 G Mark Hunter
17 Clemson	21 C Leo Tierney
28 Virginia	24 G Bill McLeod
29 North Carolina	28 T Jeff Urczyk
22 Auburn	31 TE Steve Raible
27 Tulane	7 QB Danny Myers / Rudy Allen
0 Duke	9 HB David Sims
22 Navy	0 HB Adrian Rucker
34 Georgia	14 FB Jimmy Murray / Pat Moriarty
	DL Bruce Elliott
	DL Rick Gibney
	DL Red McDaniel
	DL Tony Daykin
	LB Lucius Sanford
	LB Joe Harris
	LB Bob Bowen
	DB Randy Rhino
	DB Gil Kyle
	DB Danny Rhino
	DB Eddie Porter

RUSHING: Sims 144/881y, Myers 103/489y, Rucker 79/470y
PASSING: Allen 28-52/357y, 2TD, 53.8%
RECEIVING: Robinson 19/224y, Raible 8/150y, Moriarty 6/64y,
SCORING: Murry Smith (K) 45pts, Myers 42pts, Sims 36pts

1975 7-4

17 South Carolina	23 WR Steve Raible (TE) / Don Breece
38 Miami	23 T Jeff Urczyk
33 Clemson	28 G Mark Hunter
30 Florida State	0 C Leo Tierney / Charles Bloodworth
38 Va. Military	10 G Alex Bryan
27 Auburn	31 T Bob Curley
23 Tulane	0 TE Elliot Price
21 Duke	6 QB Danny Myers
3 Notre Dame	24 HB David Sims / Eddie Lee Ivery
14 Navy	13 HB Adrian Rucker / Tom Crowley
26 Georgia	42 FB Tony Head / Pat Moriarty
	DL Freeman Colbert
	DL Red McDaniel
	DL Rick Gibney
	DL Reggie Wilkes / Tony Daykin
	LB Lawton Hydrick / Don Shank
	LB Bob Bowen / Jimmy Coleman
	LB Lucius Sanford
	DB Gil Kyle
	DB Danny Rhino
	DB Eddie Porter / Don Bessillieu
	DB Harper Brown / Steve Crawford

RUSHING: Sims 72/590y, Moriarty 114/444y, Myers 98/432y
PASSING: Myers 16-27/272y, 3TD, 59.3%
RECEIVING: Raible 13/277y, Breece 6/59y, Sims 2/32y
SCORING: Myers 42pts, Bessillieu (DB-K) 37pts,
Sims & Raible 36pts

1976 4-6-1

17 South Carolina	27 WR Drew Hill / Don Breece / John Steele
14 Pittsburgh	42 T Roy Simmons
24 Clemson	24 G Randy Pass
35 Virginia	14 C Leo Tierney
7 Tennessee	42 G Elliott Price
28 Auburn	10 T Jay Garrett
28 Tulane	16 TE Bruce Yeager
7 Duke	31 QB Gary Lanier / Mike Jolly
23 Notre Dame	14 HB Eddie Lee Ivery
28 Navy	34 HB David Sims / Bucky Shamburger
10 Georgia	13 FB Adrian Rucker / Alan Bowen
	DL Freeman Colbert
	DL David Tedder
	DL Bob Bowen
	DL Mike Blanton
	DL Reggie Wilkes
	LB Lucius Sanford
	LB Mackel Harris
	DB Danny Rhino
	DB Tony Daykin / Gil Kyle
	DB Don Bessillieu
	DB Eddie Porter

RUSHING: Sims 163/803y, Ivery 146/754y, Shamburger 84/344y
PASSING: Jolly 20-50/274y, TD, 40.0%,
Lanier 16-33/290y, TD 48.5%
RECEIVING: Steele 14/233y, Hill 12/219y, Ivery 4/75y
SCORING: Sims 54pts, Murry Smith (K) 45pts, Ivery 36pts

1977 6-5

0 South Carolina	17 WR Drew Hill / John Steele
10 Miami	6 T Kent Hill
14 Clemson	31 G Scott Simons
30 Air Force	3 C Tom Daniel
24 Tennessee	8 G Terrell Osborne / Randy Pass
38 Auburn	21 T Mike Taylor
38 Tulane	14 TE Bruce Yeager
24 Duke	25 QB Gary Hardie / Gary Lanier
14 Notre Dame	69 HB Eddie lee Ivery
16 Navy	20 HB Bucky Shamburger
16 Georgia	7 FB Rodney Lee
	DL Freeman Colbert
	DL Mike Blanton
	DL Mike Cutting
	DL Roy Simmons
	DL Reggie Wilkes
	LB Lucius Sanford
	LB Mackel Harris
	DB Donald Patterson
	DB Jeff Shank
	DB Lawrence Lowe
	DB Don Bessillieu

RUSHING: Ivery 153/900y, Lee 138/780y, Hardie 72/429y
PASSING: Hardie 12-36/157y, 2TD, 33.3%
Lanier 10-26/182y, TD, 38.5%
RECEIVING: Hill 7/102y, Steele 4/79y, Ivery 3/93y
SCORING: Ivery 48pts, Johnny Smith (K) 46pts, Lee 42pts

1978 7-5

10 Duke	28 WR Drew Hill
22 California	34 T Kent Hill
27 Tulane	17 G Roy Simmons
28 Citadel	0 C Scott Simons
6 South Carolina	3 G Steve Walker
24 Miami	19 T Mike Taylor
24 Auburn	10 TE Donnie Sewell / George Moore
17 Florida	13 QB Mike Kelley / Gary Hardie
42 Air Force	21 TB Eddie Lee Ivery
21 Notre dame	38 WB Bucky Shamburger
28 Georgia	29 FB Rodney Lee / Ray Friday
21 Purdue■	41 DL Mark Bradley / Lynwood Volley
	DL Ivey Stokes
	DL Mike Blanton / Marvin Dyett
	LB Al Richardson
	LB Henry Johnson
	LB Mike Helm / John Kelley
	LB Mackel Harris
	DB Ken Taylor
	DB Donald Patterson
	DB Lawrence Lowe / Jeff Shank
	DB Don Bessillieu

RUSHING: Ivery 267/1562y, Lee 82/392y, Friday 8/122y
PASSING: Kelley 96-197/1479y, 7TD, 48.7%
RECEIVING: Hill 36/708y, Ivery 20/238y, Shamburger 14/208y,
SCORING: Ivery 68pts, Johnny Smith (K) 53pts, Hill 36pts

1979 4-6-1

6 Alabama	30 WR Kris Kentura / Marlon Heggs
7 Florida	7 WR Leon Chadwick
33 William & Mary	7 T David Lutz
13 Notre Dame	21 G Clint Momon
0 Tennessee	31 C Scott Simons
14 Auburn	38 G Ben Utt
7 Tulane	12 T Tom Daniel
24 Duke	14 TE George Moore
21 Air Force	0 QB Mike Kelley / Ted Peeples
24 Navy	14 TB Bo Thomas
3 Georgia	16 FB Ronnie Cone / Rodney Lee
	DL Rick Olive
	DL Ivey Stokes
	DL Lynwood Volley
	LB Al Richardson
	LB Henry Johnson
	LB Bill Haley
	LB Lance Skelton
	DB Kevin Schmidt
	DB Ken Taylor
	DB Mark Sheffield
	DB Lawrence Lowe

RUSHING: Cone 126/617y, Thomas 99/360y, Lee 25/78y
PASSING: Kelley 149-300/2051y, 10TD, 49.7%
RECEIVING: Kentera 25/526y, Heggs 25/397y, Chadwick 25/355y
SCORING: Johnny Smith (K) 38pts, Chadwick,
Cone & Kentura 24pts

1980 1-9-1

3 Alabama	26 WR Marlon Heggs / Kris Kentera
12 Florida	45 WR Leon Chadwick
17 Memphis State	8 T David Lutz
0 North Carolina	33 G Ben Utt
10 Tennessee	23 C Mark Schultz / Dean Waters
14 Auburn	17 G Ken Howell
14 Tulane	31 T Ellis Gardner
12 Duke	17 TE Glenn Etheridge / Ken Whisenhunt
3 Notre Dame	3 QB Mike Kelley / Ted Peeples
8 Navy	19 TB David Allen / Matt Bryant
20 Georgia	38 FB Ronnie Cone
	DL Mark Bradley / Rick Olive
	DL Marvin Dyett / Wally Cawthon
	DL Lynwood Volley / Sam Kelly
	LB Lance Skelton
	LB Duane Wood
	LB Steve Mooney
	LB Robert Jaracz
	DB Ted Thurson
	DB Ken Taylor
	DB Lawrence Lowe / Sammy Brown
	DB Mark Sheffield

RUSHING: Allen 134/466y, Cone 90/400y, Bryant 51/161y
PASSING: Kelley 68-137/832y, 3TD, 49.6%
Peoples 43-106/371y, TD, 40.6%
RECEIVING: Heggs 29/483y, Etheridge 21/207y,
Chadwick 17/171y
SCORING: Johnny Smith (K) 22pts, Chadwick 18pts,
Allen & Cone 12pts

1981 1-10

24 Alabama	21 WR Ken Thompson
6 Florida	27 WR Jeff Keisler
15 Memphis State	28 T Ellis Gardner
7 North Carolina	28 G Ken Howell
7 Tennessee	10 C Dean Waters
7 Auburn	31 G Mark Schultz / Derek Gwinn
10 Tulane	27 T David Lutz
24 Duke	38 TE Ken Whisenhunt / Glenn Etheridge
3 Notre Dame	35 QB Mike Kelley
14 Navy	20 TB Robert Lavette / David Allen
7 Georgia	44 FB Ronnie Cone
	DL Marvin Dyett
	DL Donnie Chisholm
	DL Mark Bradley
	LB Lance Skelton
	LB Duane Wood
	LB Rob Horton
	LB Robert Jaracz
	DB Ted Thurson
	DB Paul Menegazzi / Jack Westbrook
	DB Mark Sheffield / Ken Carney
	DB Sammy Brown

RUSHING: Lavette 188/866y, Cone 64/263y, Allen 25/110y
PASSING: Kelley 78-151/887y, 3TD, 51.7%
RECEIVING: Lavette 45/307y, Whisenhunt 22/295y,
Etheridge 17/177y
SCORING: Lavette 42pts, Ron Rice (K) 28pts, Cone 18pts

1982 6-5

7 Alabama	45 WR Mike Harrington / Darrell Norton
36 Citadel	7 WR Jeff Keisler / Kris Kentera
24 Memphis State	20 T Ellis Gardner
0 North Carolina	41 G Ken Howell
19 Tulane	13 C Dean Waters
0 Auburn	24 G Derek Gwinn
31 Tennessee	21 T David Lutz
21 Duke	38 TE Ken Whisenhunt / Gary Wilkins
38 Virginia	32 QB Jim Bob Taylor
45 Wake Forest	7 TB Robert Lavette / Cleve Pounds
18 Georgia	38 FB Eddie Fortier
	DL Marvin Dyett
	DL Donnie Chisholm
	DL Bobby Hodge
	LB Pat Swilling / Robert Jaracz
	LB Duane Wood
	LB Rob Horton / Ted Roof
	LB Dante Jones
	DB Ted Thurson
	DB Jack Westbrook / Paul Menegazzi
	DB Sammy Brown
	DB Mike Travis

RUSHING: Lavette 280/1208y, Fortier 79/353y, Pounds 42/244y
PASSING: Taylor 135-232/1839y, 3TD, 58.2%
RECEIVING: Lavette 25/286y, Fortier 24/196y, Wilkins 19/232y
SCORING: Lavette 114pts, Ron Rice 61pts (K), 3 with 12pts

1983 3-8

7 Alabama	20 WR Darrell Norton
14 Furman	17 WR Daryl Wise / Jeff Keisler
14 Clemson	41 T John Ivemeyer
21 North Carolina	38 G Derek Gwinn
20 N. Carolina St.	10 C Dean Waters
13 Auburn	31 G Tony Kepano
3 Tennessee	37 T John Davis
26 Duke	32 TE Ken Whisenhunt
31 Virginia	27 QB John Dewberry
49 Wake Forest	33 TB Robert Lavette / Cory Collier
24 Georgia	27 FB Ronnie Cone
	DL Ken Parker / Bobby Hodge
	DL Ivery Lee / Donnie Chisholm
	DL Glenn Spencer
	LB Pat Swilling
	LB Ted Roof
	LB Rob Horton
	LB Dante Jones
	DB Reginald Rutland
	DB Mike Travis
	DB Toby Lantz
	DB Jack Westbrook

RUSHING: Lavette 186/803y, Cone 101/497y, Collier 79/442
PASSING: Dewberry 74-134/790y, 6TD, 55.2%
RECEIVING: Lavette 21/123y, Cone 19/157y,
Whisenhunt 18/244y
SCORING: Ron Rice (K) 52pts, Lavette 36pts, Dewberry 30pts

1984 6-4-1

16 Alabama	6 WR Darrell Norton
48 Citadel	3 WR Gary Lee
28 Clemson	21 T John Ivemeyer
22 N. Carolina St.	27 G John Thomas
20 Virginia	20 C John Davis / Greg Hillmeyer
34 Auburn	48 G Tony Kepano
21 Tennessee	24 T Peter Blazek
31 Duke	3 TE Ken Whisenhunt
17 North Carolina	24 QB John Dewberry
24 Wake Forest	7 TB Robert Lavette / Cory Collier
35 Georgia	18 FB Keith Glanton/Dave Pas'n'lla/Mal King
	DL Pat Swilling
	DL Donnie Chisholm / Ivery Lee
	DL Glenn Spencer
	DL Ken Parker
	LB Ted Roof
	LB Jim Anderson
	LB Dante Jones
	DB Reginald Rutland
	DB Mike Travis
	DB Anthony Harrison
	DB Cleve Pounds

RUSHING: Lavette 260/1189y, King 54/377y, Dewberry 98/329y
PASSING: Dewberry 126-206/1846y, 11TD, 61.2%
RECEIVING: Whisenhunt 27/517y, Lavette 23/146y, Norton 19/265y
SCORING: Lavette 84pts, David Bell (K) 72pts, G. Lee 24pts

1985 9-2-1

28 N. Carolina St.	18 WR Gary Lee
13 Virginia	24 WR Toby Pearson
14 Clemson	3 T John Ivemeyer
31 North Carolina	0 G John Thomas
24 West'n Carolina	17 C Andy Hearn
14 Auburn	17 G Sam Bracken
6 Tennessee	6 T John Davis
9 Duke	0 TE Robert Massey / Tim Manion
35 Tenn-Chatt'ga	7 QB John Dewberry
41 Wake Forest	10 TB Cory Collier / Jerry Mays
20 Georgia	16 FB Malcolm King / Joel Carter
17 Michigan Staten	14 DL Pat Swilling
	DL Ken Parker
	DL Ivery Lee
	DL Mark Pike
	LB Ted Roof
	LB Jim Anderson
	LB Cleve Pounds
	DB Reginald Rutland
	DB Mike Travis
	DB Anthony Harrison
	DB Mark Hogan

RUSHING: Collier 139/606y, Mays 104/566y, King 112/441y
PASSING: Dewberry 110-193/1557y, 10TD, 57.0%
RECEIVING: Lee 29/645y, Manion 15/228y, King 13/93y
SCORING: Lee 42pts, David Bell (K) 36pts, King 30pts

1986 5-5-1

17 Furman	17 WR Gary Lee
28 Virginia	14 WR Toby Pearson / Richard Hills
3 Clemson	27 T Tyrone Sorrells
20 North Carolina	21 G Dean Weaver
59 N. Carolina St.	21 C John Davis
10 Auburn	31 G Eric Bearden
14 Tennessee	13 T Mitch Waters
34 Duke	6 TE Robert Massey / Tim Manion
52 VMI	6 QB Rick Strom
21 Wake Forest	24 TB Cory Collier / Jerry Mays
24 Georgia	31 FB Malcolm King / Nate Kelsey
	DL Paul Jurgensen
	DL Kyle Ambrose
	DL Travis Moody / Willie Burks
	DL Sean Smith
	LB Mark White / John Porter
	LB Rod Stephens / Eric Thomas
	LB Willis Crockett / Mike Rosamilia
	DB Reginald Rutland
	DB Cedric Stallworth / Don Wilson
	DB Andre Thomas
	DB Anthony Harrison / Riccardo Ingram

RUSHING: Mays 148/842y, Collier 103/443y, King 75/375y
PASSING: Strom 87-167/1011y, 5TD, 52.1%
RECEIVING: Lee 24/386y, Mays 23/161y, Collier 14/133y
SCORING: David Bell (K) 64pts, Mays 60pts, Lee 30pts

1987 2-9

51 Citadel	12 WR Steve Davenport / Terry Pattis
23 North Carolina	30 WR Greg Lester
12 Clemson	33 T Darryl Jenkins / Pat James
0 N. Carolina St.	17 G Dean Weaver / Scott Beavers
38 Indiana State	0 C Eric Bearden
10 Auburn	20 G Joe Siffri / Wayne Mote
15 Tennessee	29 T Jessie Marion
14 Duke	48 TE Robert Massey
14 Virginia	23 QB Rick Strom / Darrell Gast
6 Wake Forest	33 TB Richard Hills / Andre Thomas
16 Georgia	30 FB Malcolm King / Stefen Scotton
	DL Willie Burks
	DL Ivery Lee
	DL Sean Smith / Travis Moody
	LB Paul Jurgensen
	LB Eric Thomas / John Porter
	LB Mark White / Doug Sendobry
	LB Willis Crockett
	DB Sammy Lilly
	DB Cedric Stallworth
	DB Riccardo Ingram / Mike MacIntyre
	DB Jay Martin

RUSHING: King 89/383y, Hills 94/373y, Thomas 67/339y
PASSING: Strom 83-163/1066y, 6TD, 50.9%, Gast 80-179/1104y, 5TD, 44.7%
RECEIVING: Lester 33/593y, Davenport 29/524y, King 22/232y
SCORING: Thomas Palmer (K) 41pts, King 36pts, Lester & Davenport 30pts

1988 3-8

24 Tenn-Chatt'ga	10 WR Steve Davenport / David Stegall
16 Virginia	17 WR Greg Lester
13 Clemson	30 T Darryl Jenkins / Pat James
6 N. Carolina St.	14 G Scott Beavers
8 Maryland	13 C Eric Bearden
34 South Carolina	0 G Joe Siffri / Jim Lavin
17 North Carolina	20 T Jessie Marion
21 Duke	31 TE Alonzo Watson
34 VMI	7 QB Todd Rampley
24 Wake Forest	28 TB Jerry Mays / T.J. Edwards
3 Georgia	24 FB Nate Kelsey / Stefen Scotton
	DL Willie Burks
	DL Jeff Mathis
	DL Sean Smith
	LB Willis Crockett
	LB Rod Stephens
	LB Eric Thomas / Don Lear
	LB George Malone
	DB Kenneth Wilson / Gerald Chamblin
	DB Cedric Stallworth
	DB Andre Thomas (TB)
	DB Ken Swilling

RUSHING: Mays 194/942y, Edwards 58/214y, Thomas 39/193y
PASSING: Rampley 154-275/1579y, 6TD, 56.0%
RECEIVING: Mays 46/338y, Davenport 21/259y, Stegall 17/244y
SCORING: Thomas Palmer (K) 64pts, Edwards 42pts, Scotton 24pts

1989 7-4

28 N. Carolina St.	38 WR Emmett Merchant / David Stegall
10 Virginia	17 WR Scotty Barron / Bobby Rodriguez
10 South Carolina	21 T Darryl Jenkins
28 Maryland	24 G Joe Siffri
30 Clemson	14 C Billy Chubbs
17 North Carolina	14 G Jim Lavin / Scott Beavers
19 Duke	30 T Jessie Marion / Mike Mooney
34 W. Carolina	7 TE Tom Covington
43 Wake Forest	14 QB Shawn Jones
13 Boston College	12 TB Jerry Mays
33 Georgia	22 FB Stefen Scotton
	DL Willie Burks / Steve Mullen
	DL Jeff Mathis
	DL Sean Smith
	LB Kevin Salisbury / David Hicks
	LB Eric Thomas
	LB Jerrelle Williams
	LB Marco Coleman
	DB Willie Clay / Curley Day
	DB Kenneth Wilson
	DB Thomas Balkcom
	DB Ken Swilling

RUSHING: Mays 249/1349y, Jones 112/330y, Scotton 91/317y
PASSING: Jones 142-271/1748y, 12TD, 52.4%
RECEIVING: Mays 37/275y, Merchant 19/276y, Rodriguez 18/296y
SCORING: Scott Sisson (K) 75pts, Mays 72pts, Scotton 30pts

1990 11-0-1

21 N. Carolina St.	13 WR Emmett Merchant
44 Tenn-Chatt'ga	9 WR Bobby Rodriguez / Greg Lester
27 South Carolina	6 T Darryl Jenkins
31 Maryland	3 G Jim Lavin
21 Clemson	19 C Billy Chubbs / Veryl Miller
13 North Carolina	13 G Joe Siffri
48 Duke	31 T Mike Mooney
41 Virginia	38 TE Tom Covington / Anthony Rice
6 Virginia Tech	3 QB Shawn Jones
42 Wake Forest	7 TB William Bell / T.J. Edwards
40 Georgia	23 FB Stefen Scotton / Jeff Wright
45 Nebraska■	21 DL Coleman Rudolph
	DL Kevin Battle
	DL Jerimiah McClary / Richard Kimsey
	LB Marco Coleman
	LB Jerrelle Williams / Tom Johnson
	LB Calvin Tiggle
	LB Marlon Williams
	DB Curley Day / Keith Holmes
	DB Willie Clay
	DB Thomas Balkcom / Eric Bellamy
	DB Ken Swilling / Kevin Peoples

RUSHING: Bell 161/891y, Wright 89/395y, Jones 91/277y
PASSING: Jones 142-245/2008y, 13TD, 58.0%
RECEIVING: Merchant 29/489y, Rodriguez 27/493y, Lester 16/236y
SCORING: Scott Sisson (K) 84pts, Bell 42pts, Jones 38pts

1991 8-5

22 Penn State	34 WR Emmett Merchant / Jason McGill
30 Boston College	14 WR Bobby Rodriguez / Greg Lester
24 Virginia	21 T Mike Mooney
7 Clemson	9 G Kyle Frederick / John Lewis
21 N. Carolina St.	28 C Billy Chubbs
34 Maryland	10 G Scott Gold
14 South Carolina	23 T Russell Freeman
35 North Carolina	14 TE Tom Covington
17 Duke	6 QB Shawn Jones
19 Furman	17 TB Jimy Lincoln
27 Wake Forest	3 FB Michael Smith / Rodney Wilkerson
15 Georgia	18 DL Coleman Rudolph
18 Stanford■	17 DL Kevin Battle
	DL Richard Kimsey
	LB Marco Coleman
	LB Jerrelle Williams
	LB Tom Johnson / Erick Fry
	LB Marlon Williams / Jamal Cox
	DB Curley Day / Marcus Coleman
	DB Willie Clay
	DB Ken Swilling
	DB Kevin Peoples

RUSHING: Lincoln 199/913y, Smith 88/362y, Jones 114/361y
PASSING: Jones 178-339/2288y, 11TD, 52.5%
RECEIVING: Lester 35/676y, Smith 23/163y, Rodriguez 19/271y
SCORING: Scott Sisson (K) 63pts, Jones 42pts, Lester 30pts

1992 5-6

37 W. Carolina	19 WR Jason McGill / Keenan Walker
24 Virginia	55 WR Bobby Rodriguez
20 Clemson	16 T Jason Dukes
16 N. Carolina St.	13 G Woodie Milam / Brian Bravy
28 Maryland	26 C Michael Cheever
24 Florida State	29 G Gary Brown
14 North Carolina	26 T Jim Kushon
20 Duke	17 TE Jeff Papushak / Todd Vance
27 Baylor	31 QB Shawn Jones / Donnie Davis
10 Wake Forest	23 TB Jimy Lincoln / Dorsey Levens
17 Georgia	31 FB William Bell / Michael Smith
	DL Richard Kimsey / Elliott Fortune
	DL Kevin Battle / Bryan Baxter
	DL Coleman Rudolph
	LB Rodney Wilkerson
	LB Jamal Cox
	LB Tom Johnson
	LB Marlon Williams
	DB Curley Day
	DB Lethon Flowers / Marcus Coleman
	DB Mike Williams
	DB Kevin Peoples / David Hendrix

RUSHING: Smith 74/336y, Bell 74/281y, Lincoln 65/239y
PASSING: Jones 190-362/2397y, 15TD, 52.5%
RECEIVING: Rodriguez 51/621y
SCORING: Scott Sisson (K) 77pts

1993 5-6

37 Furman	3 WR Keenan Walker / Charlie Simmons
14 Virginia	35 WR Omar Cassidy / Derrick Steagall (TB)
13 Clemson	16 T Yoel Molina / Curtis McGee
0 Florida State	51 G Brian Bravy
38 Maryland	0 C Michael Cheever
3 North Carolina	41 G Chuck Vernau
23 N. Carolina St.	28 T Gary Brown
47 Duke	14 TE Jeff Papushak
37 Baylor	27 QB Donnie Davis
38 Wake Forest	28 TB William Bell / Dorsey Levens
10 Georgia	43 FB Jeff Wright
	DL Richard Kimsey / Elliott Fortune
	DL Bryan Baxter
	DL Bill Neuss
	LB Rodney Wilkerson
	LB Jamal Cox / Fred Coger
	LB Tom Johnson
	LB Marlon Williams / Don Hickson
	DB Mike Williams / Lethon Flowers
	DB Marcus Coleman / Nathan Perryman
	DB Mike Dee
	DB Ryan Stewart / Jimmy Clements (LB)

RUSHING: Levens 114/823y, Bell 166/752y,
Jimy Lincoln (TB) 71/344y, Davis 72/328y
PASSING: Davis 137-237/1739y, 12TD, 57.8%
RECEIVING: Cassidy 26/395y, Steagall 24/385y,
Simmons 17/311y
SCORING: Tyler Jarrett (K) & Levens 54pts, Bell 42pts

1994 1-10

14 Arizona	19 WR Charlie Simmons / Jason Bender
45 W. Carolina	26 WR Derrick Steagall / Cedric Zachery
12 Duke	27 T Curtis McGee
13 N. Carolina St.	21 G Brian Bravy
24 North Carolina	31 C Michael Cheever
7 Virginia	24 G Chuck Vernau / Ken Celaj
7 Maryland	42 T Jason Dukes / Yoel Molina
10 Florida State	41 TE Jeff Papushak / Grant Baynham
10 Clemson	20 QB Tommy Luginbill / Donnie Davis
13 Wake Forest	20 TB Jimy Lincoln / C.J. Williams
10 Georgia	48 FB Michael Smith / Mel Bowers
	DL Ralph Hughes
	DL Zach Piller
	DL Bill Neuss / Patrick Bradford
	LB Rodney Wilkerson
	LB Jamal Cox
	LB Ron Rogers
	LB Don Hickson / Freddie Coger
	DB Nate Perryman
	DB Lethon Flowers
	DB Mike Dee
	DB David Hendrix

RUSHING: Williams 120/564y, Smith 87/385y, Lincoln 45/105y
PASSING: Luginbill 182-327/2128y, 14 TDs, 55.7%
RECEIVING: Simmons 40/587y, Zachery 28/283y,
Bender 21/286y
SCORING: Chris Leone (K) 44pts

1995 6-5

51 Furman	7 WR Cedric Zachery
19 Arizona	20 WR Harvey Middleton / Derrick Steagall
14 Virginia	41 T Curtis McGee
31 Maryland	3 G Michael Minter
37 Duke	21 C Michael Cheever
27 North Carolina	25 G Ken Celaj
10 Florida State	42 T Jason Dukes / Steve Jackson
3 Clemson	24 TE Grant Baynham
24 Wake Forest	23 QB Donnie Davis / Brandon Shaw
27 N. Carolina St.	19 TB C.J. Williams / Phillip Rogers
17 Georgia	18 FB Charles Wiley
	DL Ralph Hughes / DeShaan Simmons
	DL Al Jackson / Patrick Bradford
	DL Derrick Shepherd / Dan Witherspoon
	DL Jermaine Miles
	LB Jimmy Clements / Jesse Tarplin
	LB Ron Rogers
	LB Keith Brookings
	DB Nathan Perryman / Kofi Smith
	DB Nick Ferguson / Jason Bostic
	DB Mike Dee / Brian Wilkins
	DB Ryan Stewart / Gary Joseph

RUSHING: Williams 245/1138y, Wiley 96/494y, Davis 96/390y
PASSING: Davis 124-223/1462y, 10TD, 55.6%
RECEIVING: Middleton 31/444y, Steagall 27/406y,
Williams 21/102y
SCORING: Williams 78pts, Dave Frakes (K) 46pts, Wiley 30pts

1996 5-6

28 N. Carolina St.	16 WR Harvey Middleton
30 Wake Forest	10 WR Mike Sheridan
0 North Carolina	16 T Curtis McGee
48 Duke	22 G Michael Minter / Jason Burks
13 Virginia	7 C Craig Page / Noah King
25 Clemson	28 G Kern Celaj
27 Central Florida	10 T Steve Jackson / Abe Frenandez
3 Florida State	49 TE Grant Baynham / Chris Myers
10 Maryland	13 QB Joe Hamilton / Brandon Shaw
26 Navy	36 TB C.J. Williams / Charles Rogers
10 Georgia	19 FB Charles Wiley / Virgil Johnson
	DL Ralph Hughes / DeShaan Simmons
	DL Derrick Shepherd / Dan Witherspoon
	DL Patrick Bradford
	DL Jermaine Miles / Jesse Tarplin
	LB Jimmy Clements / Delaunta Cameron
	LB Ron Rogers / Justin Robertson
	LB Keith Brookings / Chris Edwards
	DB Nathan Perryman / Kofi Smith
	DB Jason Bostic / Jerry Caldwell
	DB Brian Wilkins
	DB Mike Dee / Travares Tillman

RUSHING: Williams 174/663y, Rogers 115/551y,
Hamilton 95/248y
PASSING: Hamilton 108-188/1342y, 7TD, 57.4%,
Shaw 36-74/520y, 2TD, 48.6%
RECEIVING: Middleton 54/804y, Sheridan 28/461y,
Rogers 17/240y
SCORING: Williams 54pts, Brad Chambers (K) 49pts

1997 7-5

13 Notre Dame	17 WR Harvey Middleton / Mike Sheridan
28 Wake Forest	26 WR Derrick Steagall / David Powell
23 Clemson	20 T Ken Celaj
42 Boston College	14 G Jason Burks
27 N. Carolina St.	17 C Craig Page
0 Florida State	38 G Brent Kay / Bill Madigan
13 North Carolina	16 T Chris Brown / Jon Carman
31 Virginia	35 TE Mike Lillie / Chris Myers
41 Duke	38 QB Joe Hamilton
37 Maryland	18 TB Charles Wiley / Charlie Rogers
24 Georgia	27 FB Ed Wilder / Virgil Johnson
35 West Virginia■	30 DL Ralph Hughes / Felipe Claybrooks
	DL Derrick Shepherd / Ira Claxton
	DL Tony Robinson / Dan Witherspoon
	DL Jesse Tarplin / Chris Edwards
	LB Delaunta Cameron / Donte Booker
	LB Ron Rogers / Matt Miller
	LB Keith Brookings / Justin Robertson
	DB Jerry Caldwell
	DB Jason Bostic / Kofi Smith
	DB Brian Wilkins / Jon Muyres
	DB Travares Tillman / Troy Tolbert

RUSHING: Wiley 150/567y, Hamilton 140/478y, Rogers 58/297y
PASSING: Hamilton 173-268/2314y, 12TD, 64.6%
RECEIVING: Middleton 52/839y, Steagall 32/625y,
Sheridan 25/216y
SCORING: Dave Frakes (K) 61pts, Wiley 54pts,
Middleton 42pts

1998 10-2

31 Boston College	41 WR Dez White / Mike Sheridan
42 New Mexico St.	7 WR Charlie Rogers / Kelly Campbell
43 North Carolina	21 T Chris Brown
41 Duke	13 G Noah King
47 N. Carolina St.	24 C Craig Page / David Schmidgall
41 Virginia	38 G Brent Kay
7 Florida State	34 T Jon Carman
31 Maryland	14 TE Russell Matvay /Conrad Andrzejewski
24 Clemson	21 QB Joe Hamilton
63 Wake Forest	35 TB Phil Rogers /Joe Burns /Charles Wiley
21 Georgia	19 FB Ed Wilder
35 Notre Dame■	28 DL Nate Stimson / Felipe Claybrooks
	DL Merrix Watson / Bryan Corhen
	DL Tony Robinson / Guenter Kryszon
	DL Jesse Tarplin
	LB Delaunta Cameron
	LB Matt Miller
	LB Chris Edwards / Donte Booker
	DB Jamara Clark
	DB Jason Bostic
	DB Travares Tillman / Reggie Wilcox
	DB Jerry Caldwell

RUSHING: Burns 98/474y, P. Rogers 117/466y,
Charlie Rogers (TB) 47/439y, Hamilton 112/298y
PASSING: Hamilton 145-259/2166y, 17TD, 56.0%
RECEIVING: White 46/973y, C. Rogers 21/233y,
Sheridan 16/163y
SCORING: Brad Chambers (K) 82pts, White 54pts, Burns 30pts

1999 8-4

49 Navy	14 WR Dez White / Jon Muyres
35 Florida State	41 WR Kelly Campbell / Kerry Watkins
41 C. Florida	10 T Chris Brown
49 Maryland	31 G Jason Burks
31 North Carolina	24 C Noah King
38 Duke	31 G Brent Kay
48 N. Carolina St.	21 T Jon Carman
38 Virginia	45 TE Conrad Andrzejewski /Russell Matvay
45 Clemson	42 QB Joe Hamilton
23 Wake Forest	26 TB Sean Gregory/Joe Burns/Phil Rogers
51 Georgia	48 FB Ed Wilder
13 Miami■	28 DL Felipe Claybrooks / Nick Rogers
	DL Merrix Watson / Tony Robinson
	DL Guenter Kryszon
	DL Greg Gathers
	LB Recardo Wimbush
	LB Ross Mitchell / Matt Uremovich
	LB Chris Edwards / Matt Miller
	DB Jamara Clark / Marvious Hester
	DB Travares Tillman / Troy Tolbert
	DB Jeremy Muyres
	DB Chris Young

RUSHING: Gregory 172/837y, Hamilton 154/734y,
P. Rogers 72/310y
PASSING: Hamilton 203-305/3060y, 29TD, 66.6%
RECEIVING: Campbell 69/1105y, White 44/860y,
Watkins 33/476y
SCORING: Luke Manget (K) 86pts, Gregory 78pts,
Campbell 60pts

2000 9-3

21 C. Florida	17 WR Jon Muyres / Kerry Watkins
21 Florida State	26 WR Kelly Campbell / Will Glover
40 Navy	13 T Chris Brown
23 N. Carolina St.	30 G Raymond Roberts-Blake
42 North Carolina	28 C David Schmidgall
52 Wake Forest	20 G Brent Kay
45 Duke	10 T John Bennett
31 Clemson	28 TE Russell Matvay
35 Virginia	0 QB George Godsey
35 Maryland	22 TB Joe Burns / Sean Gregory
27 Georgia	15 FB Ed Wilder
14 LSU■	28 DL Nick Rogers
	DL Merrix Watson / Gary Johnson
	DL Tony Robinson
	DL Greg Gathers
	LB Recardo Wimbush / Keyaron Fox
	LB Daryl Smith / Matt Miler
	LB Ather Brown
	DB Jamara Clark / Marvious Hester
	DB Chris Young / Jonathan Cox
	DB Jeremy Muyres
	DB Cory Collins

RUSHING: Burn 220/942y, Gregory 63/300y,
Sidney Ford (TB) 49/260y
PASSING: Godsey 222-349/2906y, 23TD, 63.6%
RECEIVING: Campbell 59/963y, Glover 29/286y,
Watkins 26/480y, Burns 26/242y
SCORING: Burns 78pts, Luke Manget (K) 74pts, Campbell 60pts

2001 8-5

13 Syracuse	7 WR Kerry Watkins
35 Citadel	7 WR Jonathan Smith / Will Glover
70 Navy	7 WR Kelly Campbell
44 Clemson	47 T Nat Dorsey
37 Duke	10 G Raymond Roberts-Blake/Leon R'bins'n
17 Maryland	20 C David Schmidgall
27 N. Carolina St.	17 G Hugh Reilly
28 North Carolina	21 T John Bennett / Jason Kemble (G)
38 Virginia	39 TE Russell Matvay / Will Heller
38 Wake Forest	33 QB George Godsey
17 Georgia	31 TB Joe Burns /Sidney Ford/Sean Gregory
17 Florida State	28 DL Greg Gathers
24 Stanford■	21 DL Gary Johnson
	DL Merrix Watson / Alfred Malone
	DL Nick Rogers
	LB Recardo Wimbush
	LB Daryl Smith / Ross Micthell (FB)
	LB Keyaron Fox / Anthony Lawston
	DB Marvious Hester / Jonathan Cox
	DB Chris Young / Albert Poree
	DB Jeremy Muyres
	DB Cory Collins / Kelley Rhino

RUSHING: Burns 282/1165y, Ford 69/290y, Gregory 30/82y
PASSING: Godsey 249-384/3085y, 18TD, 64.8%
RECEIVING: Campbell 56/708y, J. Smith 53/590y,
Glover 42/546y, Watkins 41/674y
SCORING: Luke Manget (K) 97pts, Burns 92pts,
Watkins & J. Smith 30pts

2002 7-6

45 Vanderbilt	3 WR Kerry Watkins / Nate Curry
31 Connecticut	14 WR Will Glover / Jonathan Smith
19 Clemson	24 T Nat Dorsey
28 BYU	19 G Leon Robinson
21 North Carolina	13 C Hugh Reilly
21 Wake Forest	24 G Raymond Roberts-Blake
10 Maryland	34 T Kyle Wallace / Jeremy Phillips
23 Virginia	15 TE Will Heller / John Paul Foschi
24 N. Carolina St.	17 QB A.J. Suggs / Damarius Bilbo
13 Florida State	21 TB Tony Hollings / Gordon Clinkscale
17 Duke	2 FB Ajenavi Eziemefe (TB) / Jimmy Dixon
7 Georgia	51 DL Eric Henderson / Fred Wright
21 Fresno State ■	30 DL Travis Parker / Gary Johnson
	DL Alfred Malone
	DL Tony Hargrove
	LB Recardo Wimbush
	LB Daryl Smith / Matthew Etheridge
	LB Keyaron Fox / Ather Brown
	DB Marvious Hester / Reuben Houston
	DB Jonathan Cox
	DB Jeremy Muyres / Kelley Rhino
	DB Cory Collins / James Butler

RUSHING: Hollings 92/633y, Clinkscale 75/468y,
Eziemefe 70/282y
PASSING: Suggs 208-363/2242y, 12 TDs, 57.3%
RECEIVING: Watkins 71/1050y, Glover 47/434y, Smith 36/430y
SCORING: Hollings 66pts, Luke Manget (K) 65pts,
Watkins 30pts

2003 7-6

13 BYU	24 WR Nate Curry / Levon Thomas
17 Auburn	3 WR Jonathan Smith
13 Florida State	14 T Nat Dorsey
3 Clemson	39 G Andy Tidwell-Neal / Leon Robinson
24 Vanderbilt	17 C Hugh Reilly
29 N. Carolina St.	21 G Brad Honeycutt
24 Wake Forest	7 T Kyle Wallace
7 Maryland	3 TE John Paul Foschi
17 Duke	41 QB Reggie Ball
41 North Carolina	24 TB P.J. Daniels / Chris Woods
17 Virginia	29 FB Jimmy Dixon / Johnathan Jackson
17 Georgia	34 DL Eric Henderson
52 Tulsa ■	10 DL Travis Parker
	DL Mansfield Wrotto
	DL Gerris Wilkinson / Joe Anoai
	LB Keyaron Fox
	LB Daryl Smith
	LB Ather Brown
	DB Reuben Houston / Dennis Davis
	DB Jonathan Cox
	DB James Butler
	DB Dawan Landry

RUSHING: Daniels 283/1447y, Ball 139/384y, Woods 31/122y
PASSING: Ball 181-350/1996y, 10 TDs, 51.7%
RECEIVING: Smith 78/1138y,
SCORING: Dan Burnett (K) 79pts, Daniels 60pts, Smith 42pts

2004 7-5

28 Samford	7 WR Nate Curry
28 Clemson	24 WR Calvin Johnson / Levon Thomas
13 North Carolina	34 T Leon Robinson
3 Miami	27 G Matt Rhodes
20 Maryland	7 C Andy Tidwell-Neal
24 Duke	7 G Brad Honeycutt
20 Virginia Tech	34 T Kyle Wallace / Salih Besirevic
24 N. Carolina St.	14 TE Darrius Williams / Michael Matthews
30 Connecticut	10 QB Reggie Ball
10 Virginia	30 TB P.J. Daniels / Rashaun Grant
13 Georgia	19 FB Jimmy Dixon / Ajenavi Eziemefe
51 Syracuse ■	14 DL Eric Henderson
	DL Joe Anoai
	DL Mansfield Wrotto
	DL Travis Parker / Adamm Oliver
	LB Chris Reis
	LB Gerris Wilkinson / Tabugbo Anyansi
	LB KaMichael Hall
	DB Reuben Houston
	DB Kenny Scott
	DB James Butler / Nathan Burton
	DB Dawan Landry

RUSHING: Daniels 154/714y, Grant 94/425y, Ball 130/332y
PASSING: Ball 164-330/2147y, 16TD, 49.7%
RECEIVING: Johnson 48/837y, Thomas 31/480y, Curry 32/454y
SCORING: Travis Bell (K) 76pts, Daniels 54pts

2005 7-5

23 Auburn	14 WR Damarius Bilbo / James Johnson
27 North Caroiina	21 WR Calvin Johnson
28 Connecticut	13 T Andrew Gardner
7 Virginia Tech	51 G Matt Rhodes
14 N. Carolina St.	17 C Kevin Tuminello
35 Duke	10 G Nate McManus
10 Clemson	9 T Brad Honeycutt / Salih Besirevic
30 Wake Forest	17 TE George Cooper / Michael Matthews
17 Virginia	27 QB Reggie Ball
14 Miami	10 TB P.J. Daniels / Tashard Choice
7 Georgia	14 FB Mike Cox
10 Utah ■	38 DL Adamm Oliver
	DL Joe Anoai / Vance Walker
	DL Mansfield Wrotto / Darryl Richard
	DL Eric Henderson / Darrell Robertson
	LB KaMichael Hall
	LB Gerris Wilkinson / Gary Guyton
	LB Philip Wheeler
	DB Kenny Scott
	DB Dennis Davis / Rueben Houston
	DB Dawan Landry
	DB Chris Reis / Joe Gaston

RUSHING: Daniels 198/930y, Choice 117/513y, Ball 104/381y
PASSING: Ball 182-379/2165y, 11TD, 48.0%
RECEIVING: C. Johnson 54/888y, Bilbo 40/591y,
Daniels 21/174y
SCORING: Travis Bell (K) 60pts, C. Johnson & Choice 36pts

2006 9-5

10 Notre Dame	14 WR James Johnson / Chris Dunlap
38 Samford	6 WR Calvin Johnson
35 Troy	20 T Andrew Gardner
24 Virginia	7 G Matt Rhodes
38 Virginia Tech	27 C Kevin Tuminello
7 Clemson	23 G Nathan McManus
30 Miami	31 T Mansfield Wrotto
31 N. Carolina St.	23 TE George Cooper / Mike Matthews
7 North Carolina	23 QB Reggie Ball
49 Duke	0 TB Tashard Choice
12 Georgia	15 DL Darrell Robertson
6 Wake Forest □	9 DL Darryl Richard
35 West Virginia ■	38 DL Joe Anoai / Vance Walker
	DL Adamm Oliver / Michael Johnson
	LB Gary Guyton
	LB Philip Wheeler
	LB KaMichael hall / Sedric Griffin
	DB Avery Roberson / Jahi World-Daniels
	DB Kenny Scott / Pat Clark
	DB Djay Jones
	DB Jamal Lewis / Tony Clark

RUSHING: Choice 297/1473y, Ball 122/354y,
Jamaal Evans (TB) 41/215y
PASSING: Ball 135-304/1820y, 20TD, 44.4%,
Taylor Bennett (QB) 35-58/523y, 5TD, 60.3%
RECEIVING: C. Johnson 76/1202y, J. Johnson 39/608y,
Choice 12/98y, Dunlap 9/101y
SCORING: C. Johnson 90pts, Travis Bell (K) 79pts, Choice 72pts

2007 7-6

33 Notre Dame	3 WR James Johnson / Correy Earls
69 Samford	14 WR Greg Smith / Demaryius Thomas
10 Boston College	24 T Andrew Gardner / Jacob Lonowski
23 Virginia	28 G Dan Voss
13 Clemson	3 C Kevin Tuminello
26 Maryland	28 G Matt Rhodes / Nate McManus
17 Miami	14 T A.J. Smith / Cord Howard
34 Army	10 TE Colin Peek
3 Virginia Tech	27 QB Taylor Bennett / Josh Nesbitt
41 Duke	24 TB Tashard Choice / Jonathan Dwyer
27 North Carolina	25 FB Mike Cox
17 Georgia	31 DL Darrell Robertson
28 Fresno State ■	40 DL Darryl Richard
	DL Vance Walker
	DL Adamm Oliver / Michael Johnson
	LB Gary Guyton
	LB Philip Wheeler
	LB Shane Bowen / Anthony Barnes
	DB Avery Roberson / Morgan Burnett
	DB Jahi Word-Daniels / Dominique Reese
	DB Djay Jones
	DB Jamal Lewis

RUSHING: Choice 261/1379y, Dwyer 82/436y, Nesbitt 53/339y
PASSING: Bennett 162-327/2136y, 7TD, 49.5%
RECEIVING: Smith 37/588y, Thomas 35/558y, Johnson 25/447,
Peek 25/248y
SCORING: Travis Bell (K) 106pts, Choice 60pts, Dwyer 54pts

2008 9-4

41 Jacksonville St.	14 WR Tyler Melton / Correy Earls
19 Boston College	16 WR Demaryius Thomas
17 Virginia Tech	20 T Andrew Gardner / Nick Claytor
38 Mississippi St.	7 G Cord Howard / A.J. Smith
27 Duke	0 C Dan Voss
10 Gardner-Webb	9 G Joseph Gilbert
21 Clemson	17 T David Brown / Austin Barrick
17 Virginia	24 QB Josh Nesbitt / Jaybo Shaw
31 Florida State	28 SB Lucas Cox
7 North Carolina	28 SB Roddy Jones
41 Miami	23 FB Jonathan Dwyer
45 Georgia	42 DL Derrick Morgan
3 LSU ■	38 DL Vance Walker / Elris Anyaibe
	DL Darryl Richard
	DL Michael Johnson
	LB Tony Clark / Anthony Barnes
	LB Kyle Jackson / Travis Chambers
	LB Sedric Griffin / Brad Jefferson
	DB Mario Butler / Michael Peterson
	DB Jahi Word-Daniels / Rashaad Reid
	DB Dominique Reese / Cooper Taylor
	DB Morgan Burnett

RUSHING: Dwyer 200/1395y, Nesbitt 172/693y, Jones 81/690y
PASSING: Nesbitt 54-123/808y, 2TD, 43.9%,
Shaw 15-24/321y, 2TD, 62.5%
RECEIVING: Thomas 39/627y, Dwyer 8/209y, Jones 8/155y
SCORING: Dwyer 80pts, Scott Blair (K) 69pts, Nesbitt 44pts

2009 11-3

37 Jacksonville St.	17 WR Tyler Melton / Stephen Hill
30 Clemson	27 WR Demaryius Thomas / Kevin Cone
17 Miami	33 T Austin Barrick / Phil Smith
24 North Carolina	7 G Cord Howard
42 Mississippi St.	31 C Sean Bedford
49 Florida State	44 G Joseph Gilbert
28 Virginia Tech	23 T Brad Sellers
34 Virginia	9 QB Josh Nesbitt
56 Vanderbilt	33 SB Anthony Allen
30 Wake Forest	27 SB Roddy Jones / Embry Peeples
49 Duke	10 FB Jonathan Dwyer
24 Georgia	30 DL Derrick Morgan
39 Clemson □	34 DL Logan Walls / Jason Peters
14 Iowa ■	24 DL Ben Anderson / T.J. Walls
	DL Anthony Egbuniwe / Robert Hall
	LB Steven Sylvester / Julian Burnett
	LB Brad Jefferson
	LB Sedric Griffin / Anthony Barnes
	DB Mario Butler / Michael Peterson
	DB Jerrad Tarrant / Rashaad Reid
	DB Mario Edwards / Dominique Reese
	DB Morgan Burnett / Cooper Taylor

RUSHING: Dwyer 235/1395y, Nesbitt 279/1037y, Allen 64/618y
PASSING: Nesbitt 75-162/1701y, 10TD, 46.3%
RECEIVING: Thomas 46/1154y, Peeples 8/244y, Hill 6/137y
SCORING: Nesbitt 108pts, Scott Blair (K) 87pts, Dwyer 84pts

2010 6-7

41 So Carolina St.	10 WR Kevin Cone / Tyler Melton
25 Kansas	28 WR Stephen Hill / Correy Earls
30 North Carolina	24 T Nick Claytor
28 N. Carolina St.	45 G Will Jackson / Jay Finch
24 Wake Forest	20 C Sean Bedford
33 Virginia	21 G Omoregic Uzzi / Nick McRae
42 M. Tennessee St.	14 T Austin Barrick / Phil Smith
13 Clemson	27 QB Josh Nesbitt / Tevin Washington
21 Virginia Tech	28 SB Anthony Allen
10 Miami	35 SB Roddy Jones / Embry Peeples
30 Duke	20 FB Orwin Smith / Lucas Cox
34 Georgia	42 DL Izaan Cross
7 Air Force ■	14 DL Logan Walls / T.J. Barnes
	DL Jason Peters
	LB Steven Sylvester
	LB Brad Jefferson / Kyle Jackson
	LB Julian Burnett / Brandon Watts
	LB Anthony Egbuniwe
	DB Dominique Reese
	DB Mario Butler / Rod Sweeting
	DB Mario Edwards / Rashaad Reid
	DB Jerrard Tarrant / Isaiah Johnson

RUSHING: Allen 240/1316y, Nesbitt 166/737y, Smith 53/516y
Washington 116/514y
PASSING: Nesbitt 39-105/674y, 7TD, 37.1%
Washington 25-61/417y, 2TD, 41%
RECEIVING: Hill 15/291y, Smith 12/195y
SCORING: Scott Blair (K) 82pts, Nesbitt 62pts, Allen 48pts

ILLINOIS

University of Illinois (Founded 1867)
Urbana-Champaign, Illinois
Nickname: Fighting Illini
Colors: Orange and Blue
Stadium: Memorial Stadium (1924) 62,872
Conference Affiliation: Big Ten (charter member 1896-present)

CAREER RUSHING YARDS	Attempts	Yards
Robert Holcombe (1994-97)	943	4,105
Antoineo Harris (1999-2002)	676	2985
Thomas Rooks (1982-85)	560	2887
Jim Grabowski (1963-65)	579	2878
Rocky Harvey (1998-2001)	545	2711
Mikel Leshoure (2008-10)	424	2557
Juice Williams (2006-09)	637	2557
Pierre Thomas (2003-06)	453	2545
Rashard Mendenhall (2005-07)	388	2539
Howard Griffith (1988-90)	479	2485

CAREER PASSING YARDS	Comp.-Att.	Yards
Jack Trudeau (1981-85)	797-1245	8725
Kurt Kittner (1998-2001)	682-1264	8722
Juice Williams (2006-09)	606-1136	8037
Jason Verduzco (1989-92)	678-1083	7532
Tony Eason (1981-82)	561-911	7031
Johnny Johnson (1993-95)	432-819	5293
Jon Beutjer (2002-04)	462-772	5190
Jeff George (1988-89)	474-789	5189
Scott Weaver (1993-96)	306-565	3212
Dave Wilson (1980)	245-463	3154

CAREER RECEIVING YARDS	Catches	Yards
David Williams (1983-85)	262	3392
Brandon Lloyd (1999-2002)	160	2583
Walter Young (1998-2002)	147	2382
Mike Martin (1979-82)	143	2300
John Wright (1965-67)	159	2284
Arrelious Benn (2007-09)	159	2221
Jason Dulick (1993-96)	169	2004
Shawn Wax (1987-90)	97	1614
Greg Lewis (1999-2002)	103	1456
Mike Bellamy (1988-89)	95	1453

SEASON RUSHING YARDS	Attempts	Yards
Mikel Leshoure (2010)	281	1697
Rashard Mendenhall (2007)	262	1681
Antoineo Harris (2002)	278	1330
Robert Holcombe (1996)	260	1281
Jim Grabowski (1965)	252	1258

SEASON PASSING YARDS	Comp.-Att.	Yards
Tony Eason (1982)	313-505	3671
Tony Eason (1981)	248-406	3360
Jack Trudeau (1985)	322-501	3339
Kurt Kittner (2001)	221-409	3256
Juice Williams (2008)	219-381	3173

SEASON RECEIVING YARDS	Catches	Yards
David Williams (1984)	101	1278
David Williams (1985)	92	1156
Mike Martin (1982)	77	1068
Brandon Lloyd (2001)	65	1062
Arrelious Benn (2008)	67	1055

GAME RUSHING YARDS	Attempts	Yards
Mikel Leshoure (2010 vs. Northwestern)	33	330
Robert Holcombe (1996 vs. Minnesota)	43	315
Howard Griffith (1990 vs. Northwestern)	37	263

GAME PASSING YARDS	Comp.-Att.	Yards
Dave Wilson (1980 vs. Ohio State)	43-69	621
Tony Eason (1982 vs. Wisconsin)	37-51	479
Juice Williams (2008 vs. Minnesota)	25-41	462

GAME RECEIVING YARDS	Catches	Yards
David Williams (1984 vs. Northwestern)	11	208
Mike Sherrod (1980 vs. Indiana)	8	191
Rex Smith (1952 vs. Iowa)	11	188
David Williams (1983 vs. Minnesota)	11	188

GREATEST COACH:

A tackle at Illinois in the early 1930s, Ray Eliot returned to his alma mater in 1937 (an important year as he officially dropped his last name of Nusspickel that year) to become line coach under the master, Bob Zuppke. He stayed through 1959, becoming the head coach in 1942. "Mr. Illini" won 93 games and three Big Ten championships, crowning two of them with Rose Bowl wins. His 1946 squad crushed UCLA 45-14 en route to a fifth place finish in the final AP Poll and the 1951 team, whose sole blemish in a no. 4-ranked season was a 0-0 tie against Ohio State, routed Stanford 40-7.

Eliot passed up offers to depart Champaign for Southern California, Texas and Stanford in 1951. His successful run peaked however with 1953's 7-1-1 record and share of the conference title. With new coaches coming in at other Big Ten schools, his style of coaching, innovative in the 1940s, was suddenly surpassed by others. Announcing that 1959 would be his final year, the Illini fought to a 5-3-1 finish to finish tied for third in the conference and a final no. 13 ranking.

ILLINOIS' 55 GREATEST SINCE 1953

OFFENSE

WIDE RECEIVER: Brandon Lloyd, Mike Martin, David Williams, John Wright
TIGHT END: Cap Boso, Doug Dieken
TACKLE: Brad Hopkins, Jim Juriga, Tony Pashos
GUARD: Jon Asamoah, Ron Guenther, Kevin Pancratz, Revie Sorey, Tim Simpson
CENTER: Curt Lovelace, Larry McCarren
QUARTERBACK: Tony Eason, Kurt Kittner, Jack Trudeau
RUNNING BACK: J.C. Caroline, Robert Holcombe, Rashard Mendenhall
FULLBACK: Jim Grabowski, Howard Griffith

DEFENSE

END: Bo Batchelder, Scott Davis, Fred Wakefield
TACKLE: Mel Agee, Moe Gardner, Joe Rutgens, Archie Sutton, Don Thorp
LINEBACKER: Darrick Brownlow, Bill Burrell, Kevin Hardy, Dana Howard, J Leman, Simeon Rice, John Sullivan
CORNERBACK: Vontae Davie, Mike Gow, Henry Jones, Eugene Wilson
SAFETY: Ron Acks, Glenn Cobb, George Donnelly, Craig Swoope

SPECIAL TEAMS

RETURN SPECIALISTS: Mike Bellamy, Darryl Usher
PLACE KICKER: Mike Bass
PUNTER: Steve Fitts

MULTIPLE POSITIONS

END-DEFENSIVE END-GUARD: Gregg Schumacher

TWO-WAY PLAYERS

FULLBACK-LINEBACKER: Ray Nitschke
HALFBACK-DEFENSIVE BACK: Abe Woodson
CENTER-LINEBACKER: Dick Butkus

PERFORMANCE FORMULA:
ILLINOIS' 10 BEST SEASONS

1989	1.5295	13 of 70
1953	1.5064	7 of 69
2001	1.4677	11 of 70
1963	1.4534	9 of 70
1983	1.4370	12 of 70
2007	1.3157	21 of 70
1999	1.3061	19 of 71
1994	1.2716	24 of 71
1964	1.2601	18 of 70
1965	1.2429	18 of 70

ILLINOIS FIGHTING ILLINI

Year	W-L-T	AP Poll	Conference Standing	Toughest Regular Season Opponents	Coach (Record at School)	Bowl Games			
1953	7-1-1	7	1t	Wisconsin 6-2-1, Michigan 6-3, Ohio State 6-3	Ray Eliot				
1954	1-8		10	Ohio State 9-0, Wisconsin 7-2, Minnesota 7-2, Penn State 7-2	Ray Eliot				
1955	5-3-1		5	Michigan State 8-1, Ohio State 7-2, Michigan 7-2	Ray Eliot				
1956	2-5-2		7t	Michigan State 7-2, Minnesota 6-1-2, Michigan 7-2, Ohio State 6-3	Ray Eliot				
1957	4-5		7	Michigan State 8-1, Ohio State 8-1, UCLA 8-2	Ray Eliot				
1958	4-5		6	Wisconsin 7-1-1, Purdue 6-1-2, Ohio State 6-1-2	Ray Eliot				
1959	5-3-1	13	3t	Penn State 8-2, Northwestern 6-3, Wisconsin 7-2	Ray Eliot (83-73-11)				
1960	5-4		5t	Minnesota 8-1, Ohio State 7-2, Penn State 6-3	Pete Elliott				
1961	0-9		9t	Ohio State 8-0-1, Minnesota 7-2, Michigan State 7-2	Pete Elliott				
1962	2-7		8	Southern Cal 10-0, Wisconsin 8-1, Washington 7-1-2	Pete Elliott				
1963	8-1-1	3	1	Michigan State 6-2-1, Ohio State 5-3-1, Wisconsin 5-4	Pete Elliott	Rose	17	Washington	7
1964	6-3		4t	Michigan 8-1, Ohio State 7-2, Purdue 6-3	Pete Elliott				
1965	6-4		5	Michigan State 10-0, Ohio State 7-2, Purdue 7-2-1	Pete Elliott				
1966	4-6		3t	Michigan State 9-0-1, Purdue 8-2, SMU 8-2, Missouri 6-3-1	Pete Elliott (31-34-1)				
1967	4-6		5t	Indiana 9-1, Purdue 8-2, Minnesota 8-2, Notre Dame 8-2	Jim Valek				
1968	1-9		8t	Ohio State 9-0, Purdue 8-2, No. Dame 7-2-1, KU 9-1, Michigan 8-2	Jim Valek				
1969	0-10		10	Ohio State 8-1, Missouri 9-1, Michigan 8-2, Purdue 8-2	Jim Valek				
1970	3-7		9t	Ohio State 9-0, Michigan 9-1, Tulane 7-4, Northwestern 6-4	Jim Valek (8-32)				
1971	5-6		3t	Michigan 11-0, North Carolina 9-2, Washington 8-3	Bob Blackman				
1972	3-8		6t	Southern Cal 11-0, Penn State 10-1, Michigan 10-1, Ohio State 9-1	Bob Blackman				
1973	5-6		4t	Ohio State 9-0-1, Michigan 10-0-1, Minnesota 7-4, Stanford 7-4	Bob Blackman				
1974	6-4-1		5	Ohio State 10-1, Michigan 10-1, Cal 7-3-1, Wisconsin 7-4	Bob Blackman				
1975	5-6		3t	Ohio State 11-0, Michigan 8-1-2, Texas A&M 10-1, W. Virginia 7-3	Bob Blackman				
1976	5-6		3t	Michigan 10-1, Ohio State 8-2-1, Texas A&M 9-2	Bob Blackman (29-36-1)				
1977	3-8		8t	Michigan 10-1, Ohio State 9-2, Stanford 9-3, Minnesota 7-4	Gary Moeller				
1978	1-8-2		9	Michigan 10-1, Ohio State 7-3-1, Stanford 7-4, Purdue 7-2-1	Gary Moeller				
1979	2-8-1		9	Ohio State 11-0, Purdue 9-2, Michigan 8-3, Indiana 7-4	Gary Moeller (6-24-3)				
1980	3-7-1		6t	Michigan 9-2, Mississippi State 9-2, Ohio State 9-2, Purdue 8-3	Mike White				
1981	7-4		3t	Pittsburgh 10-1, Iowa 8-3, Michigan 8-3, Ohio State 8-3	Mike White				
1982	7-5		4	Michigan 8-3, Pittsburgh 9-2, Iowa 7-4, Ohio State 8-3	Mike White	Liberty	15	Alabama	21
1983	10-2	10	1	Michigan 9-2, Iowa 9-2, Ohio State 8-3, Missouri 7-4	Mike White	Rose	9	UCLA	45
1984	7-4		2t	Ohio State 9-2, Iowa 7-4-1, Wisconsin 7-3-1, Purdue 7-4	Mike White				
1985	6-5-1		3	Iowa 10-1, Michigan 9-1-1, Nebraska 9-2, Ohio State 8-3	Mike White	Peach	29	Army	31
1986	4-7		6t	Michigan 11-1, Nebraska 9-2, Ohio State 9-3, Iowa 8-3, USC 7-4	Mike White (47-41-3)				
1987	3-7-1		8	Michigan State 8-2-1, Indiana 8-3, Michigan 7-4	John Mackovic	All American	10	Florida	14
1988	6-5-1		3t	Michigan 8-2-1, Indiana 7-3-1, Washington State 8-3	John Mackovic	Citrus	31	Virginia	21
1989	10-2	10	2	Colorado 11-0, USC 8-2-1, Michigan 9-2, Michigan State 7-4	John Mackovic				
1990	8-4	25	1t	Colorado 10-0-1, Iowa 8-3, Michigan 8-3, Ohio State 7-3-1	John Mackovic	Hall of Fame	0	Clemson	30
1991	6-6		5	Michigan 10-1, Iowa 10-1, Ohio State 8-3	John Mackovic (30-16-1)	Hancock	3	UCLA	6
					Lou Tepper [0-1]				
1992	6-5-1		4	Michigan 8-0-3, Ohio State 8-2-1	Lou Tepper	Holiday	17	Hawaii	27
1993	5-6		4t	Wisconsin 9-1-1, Arizona 9-2, Ohio State 9-1-1, Michigan 8-3	Lou Tepper				
1994	7-5		5t	Penn State 11-0, Ohio State 8-3, Michigan 8-3, Washington St. 7-4	Lou Tepper	Liberty	30	East Carolina	0
1995	5-5-1		7t	Northwestern 10-1, Ohio State 11-1, Oregon 9-2, Michigan 9-3	Lou Tepper				
1996	2-9		9t	Ohio State 10-1, Northwestern 9-2, Michigan 8-3, Iowa 8-3	Lou Tepper (25-31-2)				
1997	0-11		11	Ohio State 10-2, Washington St. 10-1, Penn State 9-2, Purdue 8-3	Ron Turner				
1998	3-8		7	Ohio State 10-1, Wisconsin 10-1, Penn State 8-3, Purdue 8-4	Ron Turner				
1999	8-4	24	6t	Michigan 9-2, Michigan State 9-2, Penn State 9-3, Minnesota 8-3	Ron Turner	MicronPC	63	Virginia	21
2000	5-6		9t	Michigan 8-3, Ohio State 8-3, Northwestern 8-3	Ron Turner				
2001	10-2	12	1	Michigan 8-3, Louisville 10-2, Ohio State 7-4	Ron Turner	Sugar	33	LSU	47
2002	5-7		5t	Ohio State 13-0, Penn State 9-3, Michigan 9-3	Ron Turner				
2003	1-11		11	Michigan 10-2, Purdue 9-3, Iowa 9-3, Minnesota 9-3, MSU 8-4	Ron Turner				
2004	3-8		10t	Michigan 9-2, Iowa 9-2, Wisconsin 9-2, Purdue 7-4	Ron Turner (35-57)				
2005	2-9		11	Penn State 10-1, Ohio State 9-2, Wisconsin 9-3, California 7-4, Iowa 7-4	Ron Zook				
2006	2-10		10t	Ohio State 12-0, Wisconsin 11-1, Rutgers 10-2, Penn State 8-4	Ron Zook				
2007	9-4	20	2t	Missouri 11-1, Wisconsin 9-3, Ohio State 11-1	Ron Zook	Rose	17	Southern California	49
2008	5-7		6t	Missouri 9-4, Penn State 11-1, Ohio State 10-2	Ron Zook				
2009	3-9		6t	Central Michigan 11-2, Wisconsin 9-3, Iowa 10-2, Penn State 10-2	Ron Zook				
2010	7-6		4t	Missouri 10-2, Ohio State 11-1, Michigan State 11-1	Ron Zook (28-45)	Texas	38	Baylor	14

| TOTAL: | | 267-346-16 .4372 (57 of 70) | | | | Bowl Games since 1953: | | 5-9 .3571 (63 of 70) | |

GREATEST TEAM SINCE 1953: The 1963 edition of the Illini edge their 1983 brethren, due in part to their Rose Bowl victory over Washington 17-7. To secure the school's first Big 10 title in 13 years, Illinois had to finish strong after tying Ohio State and losing to Michigan earlier in the season. The Illini went to Madison and won 17-7 against a strong Badger 11 and then blanked powerful Michigan State 13-0 on Thanksgiving Day. That game was for the Roses and star center-linebacker Dick Butkus made sure that they would win, keying a defense that held the Spartans to 148 yards rushing. The Rose Bowl was more of the same, with fullback Jim Grabowski rushing for 125 yards and Butkus sealing the win with a late interception.

1953 7-1-1

21	Nebraska	21 E Clifford Waldbeser
33	Stanford	21 T Robert Lenzini
41	Ohio State	20 G Jan Smid
27	Minnesota	7 C Herbert Borman
20	Syracuse	13 G Don Tate / John Bauer
21	Purdue	0 T Don Ernst
19	Michigan	3 E Rocky Ryan
7	Wisconsin	34 QB Elry Falkenstein / Em Lindbeck
39	Northwestern	14 HB J.C. Caroline / Clarence DeMoss
		FB Ken Miller / Stan Wallace

RUSHING: Caroline 194/1256y
PASSING: Falkenstein 36-N/A/577y
RECEIVING: Ryan 16/308y
SCORING: Bates 66pts

1954 1-8

12	Penn State	14 E Steve Nosek / Herb Badal
2	Stanford	12 T Roger Wolf / Rudy Siegert
7	Ohio State	40 G Jan Smid
6	Minnesota	19 C Jack Chamblin
34	Syracuse	6 G Don Tate (T) / Wally Vernasco
14	Purdue	28 T Percy Oliver
7	Michigan	14 E Dean Renn / Charlie Butler
14	Wisconsin	27 QB Em Lindbeck / Hiles Stout
7	Northwestern	20 HB J.C. Caroline / Harry Jefferson
		HB Abe Woodson / Harry Jefferson
		FB Mickey Bates / Bob Wiman

RUSHING: Caroline 93/440y, Woodson 71/278y, Jefferson 55/198y
PASSING: Lindbeck 38-66/476y, 2TD, 57.6%
RECEIVING: Renn 17/246y, Woodson 10/155y, Jefferson 9/149y
SCORING: Woodson 42pts, Caroline 25pts, Jefferson 12pts

1955 5-3-1

20	Cal	13 E Rod Hanson / Gary Francis
40	Iowa State	0 T John Gremer
12	Ohio State	27 G George Walsh / Bob Baietto
21	Minnesota	13 C Jim Minor / Ron Yochem
7	Michigan State	21 G Percy Oliver
0	Purdue	13 T Rudy Siegert / Dick Nordmeyer
25	Michigan	6 E Bob DesEnfants / Dean Renn
17	Wisconsin	14 QB Em Lindbeck / Hiles Stout
7	Northwestern	7 HB Harry Jefferson / Abe Woodson
		HB Mickey Bates / Abe Woodson
		FB Ray Nitschke / Danny Wile

RUSHING: Jefferson 97/574y, Mitchell 61/504y, Woodson 59/399y
PASSING: Lindbeck 39-86/588y, 3TD, 45.3%
RECEIVING: DesEnfants 12/206y, Woodson 9/159y, Mitchell 7/110y
SCORING: Mitchell 30pts, Lindbeck 24pts, 2 tied w/ 18pts

1956 2-5-2

32	California	20 E Rod Hanson / Bob Delaney
13	Washington	28 T Dick Nordmeyer /Dick Miller/Paul Adams
6	Ohio State	26 G Dave Walker / Dick Perez
13	Minnesota	16 C Jim Minor
20	Michigan State	13 G Percy Oliver
7	Purdue	7 T Carl Johnson / Ron Nietupski
7	Michigan	17 E Gary Francis / Charlie Butler
13	Wisconsin	13 QB Hiles Stout/Tom Haller/Bill Offenbecher
13	Northwestern	14 HB Bobby Mitchell / Harry Jefferson
		HB Abe Woodson / Dale Smith
		FB Ray Nitschke / Jack Delveaux

RUSHING: Woodson 110/599y, Smith 90/509y, Jefferson 64/320y
PASSING: Stout 20-39/278y, 2TD, 51.3%
RECEIVING: Woodson 12/257y, Hanson 10/133y, Francis 7/92y
SCORING: Woodson 36pts, Jefferson 30pts, Smith 12pts

1957 4-5

6	UCLA	16 E Rod Hanson / Bob Delaney
40	Colgate	0 T Don Yeazel / Ron Nietupski
7	Ohio State	21 G Bill Burrell / Joe Bellephant / Dave Ash
34	Minnesota	3 C Gene Cherney / George Brokemond
14	Michigan State	19 G Bob Allen / Dick Nordmeyer
6	Purdue	21 T Carl Johnson / Paul Adams
20	Michigan	19 E Rich Krietling / Ron Hill
13	Wisconsin	24 QB Tom Haller/Bob Hickey /
	BillOffenbecher	
27	Northwestern	0 HB Bobby Mitchell / Don Grothe
		HB Dale Smith /Doug Wallace /L.T. Bonner
		FB Ray Nitschke / Jack Delveaux

RUSHING: Nitschke 79/514y, Mitchell 99/480y, Delveaux 64/280y
PASSING: Haller 51-100/675y, 5TD, 51%
RECEIVING: Kreitling 12/203y, Hanson 11/173y, Grothe 8/68y
SCORING: Nitschke 30pts, Mitchell & Delveaux 24pts

1958 4-5

14	UCLA	18 E Rich Krietling / Dave Stewart
13	Duke	15 T Don Yeazel / Ron Nietupski
13	Ohio State	19 G Bill Burrell / Dave Ash
20	Minnesota	8 C Gene Cherney / Bob Henderson
16	Michigan State	0 G Bob Allen
8	Purdue	31 T Joe Rutgens / Carl Johnson
21	Michigan	8 E Ron Hill / Bruce Beckman
12	Wisconsin	31 QB John Easterbrook / Bob Hickey
27	Northwestern	20 HB Don Grothe / DeJustice Coleman
		HB M. Starks / L.T. Bonner / Dick McDade
		FB Jack Delveaux /Jim Brown /Bill Brown

RUSHING: Starks 65/303y, B. Brown 51/234y, Delveaux 36/159y
PASSING: Easterbrook 34-66/656y, 5TD, 51.5%
RECEIVING: Kreitling 23/688y, Starks 5/97y, McDade 5/77y
SCORING: Kreitling 30pts, Bonner 18pts, Starks 16pts

1959 5-3-1

0	Indiana	20 E Ed O'Bradovich / Gary Hembrough
20	Army	14 T Cliff Roberts / Darrell Dedecker
9	Ohio State	0 G Bill Burrell / Pat Lennon
14	Minnesota	6 C Dave Ash / Tony Parilli
9	Penn State	20 G John Gremer / Gary Brown
7	Purdue	7 T Joe Rutgens / Don Yeazel
15	Michigan	20 E Jerry Patrick/Bruce Beckman/E.McMillan
9	Wisconsin	6 QB Mel Meyers / John Easterbrook
28	Northwestern	0 HB John Counts / D. Coleman / Gary Kolb
		HB Ethan Blackaby / Marshall Starks
		FB Bill Brown / Jim Brown

RUSHING: B. Brown 89/504y, Counts 30/416y, J. Brown 56/234y
PASSING: Meyers 32-63/495y, 2TD, 50.8%
RECEIVING: Counts 19/314y, Starks 10/167y, Blackaby 9/133y
SCORING: B. Brown 36pts, Counts 30pts, Gerald Wood (K) 13pts

1960 5-4

17	Indiana	6 E Ed O'Bradovich / Dick Newell
33	West Virginia	0 T Larry Lavery
7	Ohio State	34 G Tony Parilli / Pat Lennon
10	Minnesota	21 C John Kruze / Stan Yukevich
10	Penn State	8 G Joe Wendryhoski / Gary Brown
14	Purdue	12 T Joe Rutgens / Cliff Roberts
7	Michigan	8 E Ernie McMillan / Al Romani
35	Wisconsin	14 QB John Easterbrook / Mel Meyers
7	Northwestern	14 HB Joe Krakosi / Norm Willis
		HB Marshall Starks / Ethan Blackaby
		FB Bill Brown / Jim Brown

RUSHING: B. Brown 128/531y, Easterbrook 85/352y, Starks 64/239y
PASSING: Easterbrook 40-87/538y, 1TD, 46%
RECEIVING: O'Bradovich 21/233y, Sarks 9/124y, Newell 8/159y
SCORING: Starks 42pts, Gerald Wood (K)25pts, Easterbrook 24pts

1961 0-9

7	Washington	20 E Dick Newell / Bill Pasko
7	Northwestern	28 T Pat Murphy / Chuck Dickerson
0	Ohio State	44 G Tony Zeppetella / Tony Parilli
0	Minnesota	33 C Stan Yukevich / John Kruze
10	Southern Cal	14 G Dick Deller / Frank Lollino
9	Purdue	23 T Gary Brown / Bill Scharbert
6	Michigan	38 E Gary Hembrough / Thurman Walker
7	Wisconsin	55 QB Mel Romani /Ron Fearn /Dave McGann
7	Michigan State	34 HBTom McCullum/Cecil Young/Mike Dundy
		HB Ken Zimmerman / Glenn Glauser
		FB Al Wheatland/M. Summers/Denny Gould

RUSHING: Wheatland 73/230y, Fearn 55/219y, Zimmerman 50/185y
PASSING: McGann 27-49/269y, 0TD, 55.1%
RECEIVING: Newell 16/184y, Hembrough 16/170y, Walker 6/63y
SCORING: Jim Plankenhorn (K) 11pts, 7 tied w/ 6pts

1962 2-7

7	Washington	28 E Thurman Walker / Bill Pasko
0	Northwestern	45 T Bob Easter / Bill Minor
15	Ohio State	51 G Dick Deller / Ed Washington
0	Minnesota	17 C Dick Butkus / Bruce Capel
16	Southern Cal	28 G Archie Sutton / Frank Lollino
14	Purdue	10 T Bob Scharbert / Brian Dunicec
10	Michigan	14 E Lynn Stewart / Rich Callaghan
6	Wisconsin	35 QB Mike Taliaferro / Ron Fearn
7	Michigan State	6 HB Ken Zimmerman / Jim Warren
		HB Norm Willis / George Donnelly (DB)
		FB Dave Pike / Mike Summers

RUSHING: Zimmerman 55/225y, Summers 62/175y, Pike 43/157y
PASSING: Taliaferro 80-212/1139y, 5TD, 37.7%
RECEIVING: Warren 18/230y, Zimmerman 15/175y, Walker 14/240y
SCORING: Pike 12pts, Taliaferro 10pts, Jim Plankenhorn (K) 8pts

1963 8-1-1

10	California	0 E Dave Mueller / Gregg Schumacher (DE)
10	Northwestern	9 T Archie Sutton / Bob Easter
20	Ohio State	20 G Dick Deller / Wylie Fox
16	Minnesota	6 C Dick Butkus / Jim Plankenhorn
18	UCLA	12 G Ed Washington / Lynn Stewart
41	Purdue	21 T Bill Minor / Brian Dunicec
8	Michigan	14 E Rich Callaghan / Bill Pasko
17	Wisconsin	7 QB Mike Taliaferro / Fred Custrado
13	Michigan State	0 HB Sam Price / George Donnelly (DB)
17	Washington■	7 HB Jim Warren / Ron Acks (DB)
		FB Jim Grabowski / Don Hansen (LB)

RUSHING: Grabowski 118/616y, Price 88/326y, John Wheatland (FB) 82/283y
PASSING: Taliaferro 35-79/450y, 2TD, 44.3%
RECEIVING: Warren 10/121y, Price 10/98y, Pasko 9/131y
SCORING: Grabowski 42pts, Plankenhorn (C-K) 35pts

1964 6-3

20	California	14 E Dave Mueller
17	Northwestern	6 T Brian Dunice
0	Ohio State	26 G Dave Powless
14	Minnesota	0 C Bruce Capel / Dick Butkus
26	UCLA	7 G Gregg Schumacher / Ed Washington
14	Purdue	26 T Archie Sutton / Bill Minor
6	Michigan	21 TE Bob Trumpy
29	Wisconsin	0 QB Fred Custardo
16	Michigan State	0 HB Sam Price
		HB Ron Acks
		FB Jim Grabowski
		DL Ed Russell / Dave Mueller
		DL Gary Eickman
		DL Ed Washington / Archie Sutton
		DL Lynn Stewart / Wylie Fox
		DL Bill Minor / Gregg Schumacher
		DL Rich Callaghan
		LB Dick Butkus
		LB Don Hansen
		DB Dick Kee
		DB George Donnelly
		DB Wayne Paulson

RUSHING: Grabowski 186/1004y, Price 65/225y, Acks 49/158y
PASSING: Custardo 86-159/1012y, 3TD, 54.7%
RECEIVING: Trumpy 28/428y, Acks 24/198y, Grabowski 9/101y
SCORING: Grabowski 60pts, Custardo (QB-K) 42pts

1965 6-4

10	Oregon State	12 E John Wright
42	SMU	0 T Ed Russell
12	Michigan State	22 G Bill Allen
14	Ohio State	28 C Kai Anderson
34	Indiana	13 G Ron Guenther
28	Duke	14 T Willis Fields
21	Purdue	0 TE Craig Timko
3	Michigan	23 QB Fred Custardo
51	Wisconsin	0 HB Ron Bess / Cyril Pinder
20	Northwestern	6 HB Sam Price
		FB Jim Grabowski
		DL Ken Kmiec / Dick Tate
		DL Gary Eickman
		DL Al Waters
		DL Tom Smith / Fred Harms
		DL Dale Greco
		DL Bo Batchelder
		LB Don Hansen
		LB Bill Harder / Terry Miller
		DB Dick Kee
		DB Trent Jackson / Phil Knell
		DB Ron Acks

RUSHING: Grabowski 252/1258y, Pinder 56/287y, Price 46/178y
PASSING: Custardo 90-170/1124y, 12TD, 52.9%
RECEIVING: Wright 47/755y, Bess 16/138y, Timko 12/135y
SCORING: Custardo (QB-K) 43pts, Grabowski & Pinder 42pts

1966 4-6

7 SMU	26 WR John Wright
14 Missouri	21 T Willis Fields
10 Michigan State	26 G Ron Guenther
10 Ohio State	9 C Kai Anderson
24 Indiana	10 G Larry Jordan
3 Stanford	6 T Bob Robertson
21 Purdue	25 TE Craig Timko
28 Michigan	21 QB Bob Naponic / Dean Volkman
49 Wisconsin	14 HB Ron Bess
7 Northwestern	35 HB Bill Huston / Rich Johnson
	FB Carson Brooks / Doug Harford
	DL Ken Kmiec
	DL Tony Pleviak
	DL Fred Harms
	DL Tom Smith
	DL Al Waters / Joel Stellwagen
	DL Bo Batchelder / Dick Tate
	LB Terry Miller
	LB Dave Tomasula
	DB Mick Smith
	DB Phil Knell
	DB Bruce Sullivan

RUSHING: Huston 89/420y, Johnson 83/317y, Naponic 133/215y
PASSING: Naponic 70-162/998y, 4TD, 43.2%
RECEIVING: Wright 60/831y, Timko 17/252y, Bess 5/130y
SCORING: Naponic 36pts, Jim Stotz (K) 31pts, Wright 24pts

1967 4-6

0 Florida	14 WR John Wright
34 Pittsburgh	6 T Bob Robertson
7 Indiana	20 G Doug Redmann
7 Minnesota	10 C Bruce Erb
7 Notre Dame	47 G Steve Oman
17 Ohio State	13 T Willis Fields / Jerry Line
9 Purdue	42 TE Craig Timko / Len Wislow
14 Michigan	21 QB Dean Volkman
27 Northwestern	21 HB Carson Brooks
21 Iowa	19 HB Dave Jackson
	FB Rich Johnson
	DL Dick Tate
	DL Mickey Hogan
	DL Fritz Harms / Bill Nowak
	DL Larry Jordan / Mike McDonough
	DL Tony Pleviak
	DL Doug Whitman
	LB Dave Tomasula
	LB Terry Miller
	DB Ron Bess
	DB Ken Kmiec / Charlie Bareither
	DB Rich Erickson

RUSHING: Johnson 195/768y, Jackson 100/325y
PASSING: Volkman 77-183/1005y, 3TD, 42.1%
RECEIVING: Wright 52/698y, Timko 11/142y, Wislow 9/94y
SCORING: Johnson 36pts, Jackson 35pts, Wright 24pts

1968 1-9

7 Kansas	47 WR Doug Dieken
0 Missouri	44 T Bob Bieszczad / Jerry Piliath
14 Indiana	28 G Doug Redmann
10 Minnesota	17 C Jerry Rose
8 Notre Dame	58 G Steve Oman
24 Ohio State	31 T Tom Scott
17 Purdue	35 TE Len Wislow
0 Michigan	36 QB Bob Naponic
14 Northwestern	0 HB Bob Bess / Ken Bargo
13 Iowa	37 HB Tom Kmiec / Dave Jackson
	FB Rich Johnson
	DL Doug Whitman
	DL Tony Pleviak
	DL Bill Nowak / Tony Clements
	DL Carson Brooks
	DL Mickey Hogan
	DL John Mauzey
	LB Bruce Erb
	LB Jeff Trigger
	DB Ralph Waldron / Randy Rogers
	DB Fred Wolf / Mike Ryan
	DB Charlie Bareither

RUSHING: Johnson 243/973y, Bargo 76/297y, Naponic 147/171y
PASSING: Naponic 83-213/813y, 2TD, 38.9%
RECEIVING: Dieken 21/223y, Bess 17/170y, Johnson 10/68y
SCORING: Johnson 34pts, Naponic 32pts, Bess 14pts

1969 0-10

18 Washington St.	19 WR John Kaiser / Mike Pickering
6 Missouri	37 T Tom Scott
20 Iowa State	48 G Doug Redmann
6 Northwestern	10 C Julian Vyborny
20 Indiana	41 G Kirk McMillin (C) / Bob Bieszczad
0 Ohio State	41 T Jerry Cole / Dave Zochert vs osu
22 Purdue	49 TE Doug Dieken
0 Michigan	57 QB Steve Livas (S) / Gary Lange
14 Wisconsin	55 HB Dick Wright / Bob Bess
0 Iowa	40 HB Dave Jackson
	FB Darrell Robinson / Ken Bargo
	DL Willie Smith / Glenn Collier
	DL George Samojedny / Karl Pnazek
	DL Norris Coleman
	DL Tony Clements
	DL Bob Bucklin / John Mauzey
	LB Veto Santini
	LB Bruce Erb / Moe Kelly
	DB Tom Jones / Jaime Dufelmeier
	DB Tim McCarthy / Mike Ryan
	DB Steve Allen / John Spiller
	DB Bob Wintermute / Charlie Bareither

RUSHING: Jackson 118/465y, Robinson 112/446y, Bess 66/286y
PASSING: Livas 42-131/705y, 1TD, 32%
RECEIVING: Dieken 29/486y, Kaiser 8/149y, Pickering 8/125y
SCORING: Jackson, Livas, Dieken & Bess 18pts

1970 3-7

20 Oregon	16 WR John Kaiser
9 Tulane	23 WR Bob Burns / Willie Osley
27 Syracuse	0 T Larry McCarren
0 Northwestern	48 G Kirk McMillin
24 Indiana	30 C Julian Vyborny
29 Ohio State	48 G Rich Brennan
23 Purdue	21 T Tom Scott
0 Michigan	42 TE Doug Dieken
17 Wisconsin	29 QB Mike Wells
16 Iowa	22 TB Darrell Robinson
	FB Mike Navarro / Mike Walker
	DL Glenn Collier
	DL Tab Bennett
	DL Bob Bucklin
	DL Norm Cooper / Dan Rotzoll
	DL Jim Rucks / Alvin Keith
	LB Moe Kelly
	LB Dan Darlington
	DB John Graham / Jamie Dufelmeier
	DB Gary Windy
	DB Tom Baumgart
	DB Larry Huisinga / Tom Jones

RUSHING: Robinson 193/749y, Navarro 98/420y, Walker 53/204y
PASSING: Wells 71-170/906y, 8TD, 41.8%
RECEIVING: Dieken 39/537y, Kaiser 8/99y, Burns 7/75y
SCORING: Wells (QB-K) 57pts, Dieken 28pts, Robinson 24pts

1971 5-6

0 Michigan State	10 WR Garvin Roberson
0 North Carolina	27 T Bruce Dobson
0 Southern Cal	28 G John Gann
14 Washington	52 C Larry McCarren
10 Ohio State	24 G John Levanti
6 Michigan	35 T Gerry Sullivan
21 Purdue	7 TE John Bedalow / Jim Rucks
24 Northwestern	7 QB Mike Wells
22 Indiana	21 HB George Uremovich / Ed Jenkins
35 Wisconsin	27 HB John Wilson
31 Iowa	0 FB Mike Navarro
	DL Tab Bennett / Glenn Collier
	DL Dave Wright
	DL Willie Lee
	DL Bob Bucklin
	LB Larry Allen / Chuck Kolgut
	LB Moe Kelly / John Wiza
	LB Octavus Morgan
	DB Willie Osley
	DB John Graham
	DB Greg Colby
	DB Larry Huisinga

RUSHING: Wilson 115/543y, Navarro 107/542y, Uremovich 92/435y
PASSING: Wells 84-179/1007y, 7TD, 47%
RECEIVING: Roberson 28/372y, Wilson 10/114y, Jenkins 10/69y
SCORING: Wilson 42pts, Uremovich 36pts, Wells (QB-K) 31pts

1972 3-8

0 Michigan State	24 WR Garvin Roberson
20 Southern Cal	55 T Bruce Dobson
11 Washington	31 G John Gann
17 Penn State	35 C Larry McCarren
7 Ohio State	26 G John Levanti
7 Michigan	31 T Gerry Sullivan
14 Purdue	20 TE John Bedalow
43 Northwestern	13 QB Mike Wells
37 Indiana	20 HB George Uremovich
27 Wisconsin	7 HB Lonnie Perrin
14 Iowa	15 FB Mike Walker / Steve Greene
	DL Larry Allen
	DL Dave Wright
	DL Mick Heinrich / Mike Waller
	DL Tab Bennett
	LB John Wiza / Roy Robinson
	LB Ken Braid
	LB Chuck Kogut
	DB Bruce Beaman / Bill Uecker
	DB Mike Gow
	DB Greg Colby / Tom Hicks
	DB Larry Huisinga

RUSHING: Uremovich 152/611y, Perrin 106/466y, Wells 77/287y
PASSING: Wells 76-158/837y, 6TD, 48.1%
RECEIVING: Roberson 31/569y, Uremovich 21/219y, Perrin 16/142y
SCORING: Wells (QB-K) 51pts, Uremovich 42pts, Roberson 32pts

1973 5-6

28 Indiana	14 WR Garvin Roberson
27 California	7 T Bruce Dobson
10 West Virginia	17 G John Gann
0 Stanford	24 C Joe Hatfield
15 Purdue	13 G John Levanti
6 Michigan State	3 T Gerry Sullivan / Paul Yadron
50 Iowa	0 TE Tom Mullin / Doug Kleber
0 Ohio State	30 QB Jeff Hollenbach
6 Michigan	21 HB George Uremovich
16 Minnesota	19 HB Eddie Jenkins / Lonnie Perrin
6 Northwestern	9 FB Steve Greene
	DL Octavus Morgan
	DL Mick Heinrich
	DL Scott Studwell
	DL Mark Peterson
	LB Ty McMillin
	LB Tom Hicks
	LB Chuck Kogut
	DB Mike Gow
	DB Bruce Beamon
	DB Ken Braid
	DB Bill Kleckner

RUSHING: Uremovich 141/519y, Perrin 90/398y, Jenkins 93/379y
PASSING: Hollenbach 78-178/916y, 2TD, 45.1%
RECEIVING: Roberson 25/416y, Jenkins 19/198y, Uremovich 11/127y
SCORING: Dan Beaver (K) 50pts, Jenkins 24pts, 4 tied w/ 12pts

1974 6-4-1

16 Indiana	0 WR Jeff Chrystal / Frank Johnson
41 Stanford	7 T Doug Kleber
21 Washington St.	19 G Stu Levenick
14 Cal	31 C Joe Hatfield
27 Purdue	23 G Revie Sorey
21 Michigan State	21 T Paul Yadron / Phil McDonald
12 Iowa	14 TE Joe Smalzer
7 Ohio State	49 QB Jeff Hollenbach / Jim Kopatz
6 Michigan	14 SB Tracy Campbell / Mike Sullivan
17 Minnesota	14 TB Jim Phillips / Brian Ford
28 Northwestern	14 FB Larry Schulz
	DL Mark Peterson
	DL John DiFeliciantonio
	DL Mike Waller / Ed Murray
	DL Greg Williams / Dean March
	LB Tom Hicks
	LB Ty McMillin
	LB Roy Robinson
	DB Mike Gow
	DB Bruce Beamon
	DB Bill Kleckner
	DB Bill Uecker

RUSHING: Phillips 175/772y, Campbell 125/424y, Schulz 76/316y
PASSING: Hollenbach 64-131/1037y, 7TD, 49.4%
RECEIVING: Smalzer 29/525y, Chrystal 21/358y, Johnson 12/250y
SCORING: Phillips 56pts, Dan Beaver (K) 52pts, Johnson 30pts

1975 5-6

27 Iowa	12 WR Jeff Chrystal
20 Missouri	30 T Doug Kleber
13 Texas A&M	43 G Willie Gartrell
27 Washington St.	21 C Phil McDonald
42 Minnesota	23 G Kevin Pancratz / Jerry Finis
24 Purdue	26 T Stu Levenick
21 Michigan State	19 TE Joe Smalzer
9 Wisconsin	18 QB Kurt Steger / Jim Kopatz
3 Ohio State	40 SB Frank Johnson
15 Michigan	21 TB Lonnie Perrin / Chubby Phillips
28 Northwestern	7 FB Steve Greene
	DL Walter Graham
	DL John DiFeliciantonio
	DL Mike Waller
	DL Al Young / Dean March
	LB Scott Studwell
	LB John Sullivan
	LB Brian Ford (DB)
	DB Bill Cerney
	DB Bruce Beamon
	DB Jim Stauner
	DB Rick Williams (LB)

RUSHING: Perrin 171/907y, Phillips 117/483y, Greene 84/370y
PASSING: Steger 80-166/1136y, 8TD, 48.2%
RECEIVING: Chrystal 22/261y, Johnson 20/349y, Smalzer 18/241y
SCORING: Dan Beaver (K) 45pts, Perrin 42pts, Phillips 36pts

1976 5-6

24 Iowa	6 WR Eric Rouse
31 Missouri	6 WR Frank Johnson / Steve Gordon
19 Baylor	34 T Jerry Finis
7 Texas A&M	14 G Gary Jurczyk
14 Minnesota	29 C Phil McDonald
21 Purdue	17 G Kevin Pancratz
23 Michigan State	31 T Dan Melsek
31 Wisconsin	25 TE Marty Friel
10 Ohio State	42 QB Kurt Steger
7 Michigan	38 RB James Coleman / Chubby Phillips
48 Northwestern	6 FB Larry Schulz / Mike Collins
	DL Dean March
	DL John DiFeliciantonio
	DL Bruce Thornton / Walt Graham
	DL Chris Williams
	LB Mac McCracken
	LB Scott Studwell
	LB Paul Moore/Dominic Forte/John Sullivan
	DB Derwin Tucker / Jim Kirwan
	DB Jim Stauner
	DB Rickie Mitchem
	DB Dale Hardy / Bill Cerney

RUSHING: Coleman 170/687y, Phillips 154/651y, Schulz 59/226y
PASSING: Steger 87-187/1243y, 10TD, 46.5%
RECEIVING: Johnson 24/306y, Rouse 20/326y, Friel 18/321y
SCORING: Coleman 62pts, Dan Beaver (K) 51pts, Phillips 42pts

1977 3-8

9 Michigan	37 WR Eric Rouse
11 Missouri	7 WR Tom Schooley / Dan Bulow
24 Stanford	37 T Dennis Ashlock
20 Syracuse	30 G Gary Jurczyk
0 Wisconsin	26 C Randy Taylor
29 Purdue	22 G Kevin Pancratz
21 Indiana	7 T Rich Grimmett / Dan Melsek
20 Michigan State	49 TE Lee Boeke / Mike Sherrod
0 Ohio State	35 QB Kurt Steger / Mike McCray
0 Minnesota	21 RB James Coleman
7 Northwestern	21 FB Charlie Weber / Wayne Strader
	DL Ray Pavesic / Jim Kogut
	DL Brian Kingsbury / Stanley Ralph
	DL Bruce Thornton / John Thiede
	LB John Sullivan
	LB John Meyer / John Gillen
	LB Earnest Adams
	LB John Scott
	DB David Blakely
	DB Derwin Tucker
	DB Rickie Mitchem / Carooq Taylor
	DB Dale Hardy

RUSHING: Coleman 143/715y, Weber 87/369y, Strader 68/348y
PASSING: McCray 36-60/418y, 1TD, 60%
RECEIVING: Schooley 15/231y, Boeke 11/109y, Rouse 10/119y
SCORING: Dave Finzer (K) 25pts, McCray & Steger 24pts

1978 1-8-2

0 Northwestern	0 WR Jeff Barnes / Tom Schooley
0 Michigan	31 WR Eric Rouse / Lee Boeke (TE)
10 Stanford	35 T Tim Norman
28 Syracuse	14 G Mike Carrington / Bob McClure
3 Missouri	45 C Randy Taylor
20 Wisconsin	20 G Troy McMillin / Bob Noekle
0 Purdue	13 T Mike Priebe
10 Indiana	31 TE Doug Cozzen / Mike Sherrod
19 Michigan State	59 QB Rich Weiss / Lawrence McCullough
7 Ohio State	45 TB Larry Powell / Mark Dismuke
6 Minnesota	24 FB Wayne Strader / Charlie Weber
	DL Dennis Flynn
	DL Stanley Ralph / Kenny Durrell
	DL John Thiede / Bruce Thornton
	LB Earnest Adams
	LB Jerry Ramshaw / Tab Carmien
	LB John Gillen
	LB John Sullivan
	DB Derwin Tucker / Rick George
	DB Lloyd Levitt
	DB John Venegoni
	DB Dale Hardy / Dave Kelly

RUSHING: Strader 74/389y, Powell 97/325y, Weiss 154/297y
PASSING: Weiss 58-109/665y, 2TD, 53.2%
RECEIVING: Barnes 22/270y, Rouse 11/172y, Strader 10/109y
SCORING: Dave Finzer (K) 23pts, Powell 18pts, 3 tied w/ 12pts

1979 2-8-1

16 Michigan State	33 WR Larry Powell / John Lopez
6 Missouri	14 WR Greg Foster / Doug Cozen
27 Air Force	19 T John Mulchrone / Tom Coady
12 Navy	13 G Mike Carrington
7 Iowa	13 C Troy McMillin
14 Purdue	28 G Bob McClure / Bob Noelke
7 Michigan	27 T Mike Priebe
17 Minnesota	17 TE Lee Boeke / Mike Sherrod
7 Ohio State	44 QB Lawrence McCullough / Tim McAvoy
14 Indiana	45 RB Mike Holmes / Joe Curtis
29 Northwestern	13 FB Calvin Thomas / Wayne Strader
	DL Dave Dwyer
	DL Kenny Durrell / Scott Doney
	DL Stanley Ralph / Ken Gillen
	LB Earnest Adams
	LB Kelvin Atkins
	LB John Gillen
	LB Jack Squirek
	DB Rick George
	DB Lloyd Levitt / Sam Clear
	DB Bonji Bonner / Ken McDonald
	DB Dave Kelly

RUSHING: Holmes 147/792y, Thomas 122/469y
PASSING: McCullough 130-228/1254y, 7TD, 57%
RECEIVING: Holmes 25/127y, Strader 24/135y, Boeke 18/166y
SCORING: Holmes 38pts, Kirk Bostrom (K) 31pts, Boeke 30pts

1980 3-7-1

35 Northwestern	9 WR John Lopez
20 Michigan State	17 WR Greg Dentino / Mike Martin
7 Missouri	52 T John Mulchrone
20 Air Force	12 G Mike Carrington
21 Mississippi St.	28 C Greg Boeke
20 Iowa	14 G Marty Finis / Tom Coady
20 Purdue	45 T Tim Norman / Bob Stowe
14 Michigan	45 TE Mike Sherrod / Lee Boeke
18 Minnesota	21 QB Dave Wilson
42 Ohio State	49 TB Mike Holmes / Joe Curtis
24 Indiana	26 FB Calvin Thomas / Greg Foster
	DL Terry Cole / Don Thorp
	DL Mark Butkus / Ken Gillen
	DL Dave Dwyer
	DL Dan Gregus
	LB Kelvin Atkins / Tony Scarlelli
	LB John Gillen / Earnest Adams
	LB Jack Squirek
	DB David Edwards / Sam Clear
	DB Rick George
	DB Craig Zirbel / Joe Miles
	DB Carooq Taylor / Tyrone Worthy

RUSHING: Holmes 69/305y, Thomas 73/271y, Foster 32/164y
PASSING: Wilson 245-463/3154y, 19TD, 52.9%
RECEIVING: Dentino 40/512y, Lopez 32/448y, Martin 31/555y
SCORING: Mike Bass (K) 46pts, Dentino 36pts, Martin 30pts

1981 7-4

6 Pittsburgh	26 WR Mike Martin
27 Michigan State	17 WR Oliver Williams
17 Syracuse	14 T Bob Stowe
38 Minnesota	29 G Mike Carrington
20 Purdue	44 C Greg Boeke
27 Ohio State	34 G Troy McMillin
23 Wisconsin	21 T Dennis Flynn
24 Iowa	7 TE Miguel DeOliver / Lorenzo Siler
21 Michigan	70 QB Tony Eason
35 Indiana	14 TB Darrell Smith / Joe Curtis
49 Northwestern	12 FB Calvin Thomas / Mike Murphy
	DL Terry Cole / John Janata
	DL Mark Butkus / Dave Dwyer
	DL Don Thorp / Pete Mulchrone
	DL Dan Gregus / Willie Young
	LB Ron Ferrari / Darryl Byrd
	LB Jack Squirek
	LB Kelvin Atkins / John Venegoni
	DB Charles Armstead
	DB Dennis Bishop / Mike Heaven
	DB Rick George / Craig Zirbel
	DB Larry Mosley / Mark Jones

RUSHING: Thomas 110/390y, Curtis 69/312y, Smith 76/272y
PASSING: Eason 248-456/3360y, 20TD, 61.1%
RECEIVING: Smith 43/495y, Williams 38/760y, Curtis 35/259y
SCORING: Mike Bass (K) 63pts, Smith 42pts, Williams 36pts

1982 7-5

49 Northwestern	13 WR Mike Martin
23 Michigan State	16 WR Oliver Williams
47 Syracuse	10 T John Janata
3 Pittsburgh	20 G Rick Schulte / Chris Babyar
42 Minnesota	24 C Adam Lingner / Mark Helle
38 Purdue	34 G Bob Stowe
21 Ohio State	26 T Jim Juriga / Steve Collier
29 Wisconsin	28 TE Tim Brewster
13 Iowa	14 QB Tony Eason
10 Michigan	16 TB Joe Curtis /Dwight Beverly /M. Brookins
48 Indiana	7 FB Mike Murphy / Richard Ryles
15 Alabama■	21 DL Ken Gillen / Terry Cole
	DL Don Thorp / Mark Butkus
	DL Dan Gregus
	DL Nick Epps / Mike Johnson
	LB Clint Haynes / Pete Burgard
	LB Mike Weingrad
	LB Darryl Byrd / Archie Carter
	DB Charles Armstead
	DB Mike Heaven / Dennis Bishop
	DB Craig Swoope / Mark Jones
	DB Dave Edwards

RUSHING: Beverly 74/390y, Ryles 84/353y, Curtis 67/263y
PASSING: Eason 278-450/3248y, 17TD, 61.8%
RECEIVING: Martin 69/941y, Brewster 46/550y, Williams 35/573y
SCORING: Mike Bass (K) 101pts, Brookins 60pts, Williams 40pts

1983 10-2

18 Missouri	28 WR David Williams
17 Stanford	7 WR Cam Benson / Mitch Brookins
20 Michigan State	10 T Bob Stowe
33 Iowa	0 G Rick Schulte / Scott Kehoe
27 Wisconsin	15 C Bob Miller
17 Ohio State	13 G Chris Babvar
35 Purdue	21 T Jim Juriga
16 Michigan	6 TE Tim Brewster
50 Minnesota	23 QB Jack Trudeau
49 Indiana	21 TB Dwight Beverly / Ray Wilson
56 Northwestern	24 FB Thomas Rooks
9 UCLA■	45 DL Mike Johnson
	DL Don Thorp
	DL Mark Butkus
	DL Darryl Thompson / Terry Cole
	LB Archie Carter / Vince Osby
	LB Mike Weingrad / Ed Brady
	LB Clint Haynes
	DB Keith Taylor / John Ayres
	DB Mike Heaven
	DB Craig Swoope
	DB Dave Edwards

RUSHING: Rooks 156/842y, Beverly 157/685y, Wilson 63/295y
PASSING: Trudeau 203-324/2446y, 18TD, 63.7%
RECEIVING: Williams 59/870y, Brewster 59/628y, Rooks 25/178y
SCORING: Chris White (K) 78pts, Rooks 66pts, Beverly 54pts

1984 7-4

24 Northwestern	16 WR David Williams
30 Missouri	24 WR Randy Grant
19 Stanford	34 T Mark Dennis / Scott Kehoe
40 Michigan State	7 G Rick Schulte
16 Iowa	21 C Bob Miller
22 Wisconsin	6 G Chris Babvar
38 Ohio State	45 T Jim Juriga
34 Purdue	20 TE Cap Boso / Jerry Reese
18 Michigan	26 QB Jack Trudeau
48 Minnesota	3 TB Ray Wilson / Eric Wilson
34 Indiana	7 FB Thomas Rooks
	DL Dave Aina / Alec Gibson
	DL Guy Teafatiller
	DL Steve Nelson / Ron Bohm
	DL Curtis Clarke
	LB Bob Sebring
	LB Sam Ellsworth / Mark Tagart
	LB Rob Glielmi
	DB John Ayres / Todd Avery
	DB Mike Heaven
	DB Dave Edwards
	DB Craig Swoope / Ed White

RUSHING: Rooks 219/1056y, Wilson 75/302y
PASSING: Trudeau 247-378/2724y, 18TD, 65.3%
RECEIVING: Williams 101/1278y, Boso 44/363y, Grant 41/680y
SCORING: Chris White (K) 103pts, Williams & Grant 48pts

1985 6-5-1

10 Southern Cal	20 WR David Williams
28 S. Illinois	25 WR Stephen Pierce / David Boatright
25 Nebraska	52 T Scott Kehoe
31 Ohio State	28 G Jim Juriga
24 Purdue	30 C Mike Scully
30 Michigan State	17 G Mark Dennis
38 Wisconsin	25 T Brian Ward / Arael Doolittle
3 Michigan	3 TE Cap Boso
0 Iowa	59 QB Jack Trudeau
41 Indiana	24 TB Ray Wilson / Keith Jones
45 Northwestern	20 FB Thomas Rooks
29 Army■	31 DL Scott Davis / Curtis Gibson
	DL Guy Teafatiller
	DL Jim Blondell / Ron Bohm
	DL Alec Gibson
	LB Rob Glielmi
	LB Bob Sebring
	LB Mark Tagart / James Lynch
	DB Lance Harkey / Todd Avery
	DB Jackie Harkey
	DB Ed White / African Grant
	DB Craig Swoope

RUSHING: Rooks 143/753y, Wilson 118/479y, Jones 35/142y
PASSING: Trudeau 322-501/3339y, 18TD, 64.3%
RECEIVING: Williams 92/1156y, Rooks 59/372y, Pierce 55/706y
SCORING: Chris White (K) 78pts, Williams 64pts, Rooks 42pts

1986 4-7

23 Louisville	0 WR Stephen Pierce
16 Southern Cal	31 WR Darryl Usher / James Gordon
14 Nebraska	59 T Craig Schneider / Areal Doolittle
0 Ohio State	14 G Scott Kehoe
34 Purdue	27 C Dave Harbour
21 Michigan State	29 G Mark McGowan / Tom Schertz
9 Wisconsin	15 T Mark Dennis
13 Michigan	69 TE Anthony Williams / Jerry Reese
20 Iowa	16 QB Shane Lamb / Brian Menkhausen
21 Indiana	16 TB Keith Jones / Ray Wilson
18 Northwestern	23 FB Jeff Markland (LB) / Lynn McClellan
	DL Scott Davis / Ron Bohm
	DL Jim Blondell / Chris Carpenter
	DL Mike Piel / Shawn Jones
	LB Ray Hairston / Jason Guard
	LB James Finch / John Wachter
	LB Steve Glasson
	LB Sam Ellsworth / James Lynch
	DB Lance Harkey / Greg Boysaw
	DB African Grant / Keith Taylor
	DB Bobby Dawson
	DB Ed White

RUSHING: Jones 133/534y, Markland 49/189y, Wilson 51/174y
PASSING: Lamb 115-227/1414y, 7TD, 50.7%
  Menkausen 96-168/991y, 4TD, 57.1%
RECEIVING: Pierce 43/602y, Reese 37/468y, Williams 36/369y
SCORING: Chris Siambekos (K) 61pts, Jones 24pts,
  3 tied w/18pts

1987 3-7-1

14 North Carolina	34 WR Darryl Usher
7 Arizona State	21 WR James Gordon / Stan Fit
20 East Carolina	10 T C. Schneider / Tom Schertz /Brad James
6 Ohio State	10 G Mike Scully
3 Purdue	9 C Dave Harbour
16 Wisconsin	14 G Mark McGowan
14 Michigan State	14 T Areal Doolittle
27 Minnesota	17 TE Anthony Williams
22 Indiana	34 QB Scott Mohr / Brian Menkhausen
14 Michigan	17 TB K. Jones /Lynn McClellan /Ken Thomas
10 Northwestern	28 FB Jeff Markland / Greg Turner
	DL Mike Piel
	DL Moe Gardner / Jim Blondell
	DL Scott Davis
	LB Steve Glasson / Craig Moore
	LB Gabe de la Garza
	LB Sam Ellsworth / John Wachter
	LB Romero Brice / Jason Guard
	DB Keith Taylor
	DB Chris Green / Stephen Jordan
	DB Glenn Cobb
	DB Bobby Dawson

RUSHING: Jones 110/322y, Thomas 58/268y, McClellan 59/267y
PASSING: Mohr 106-212/1436y, 7TD, 50%
RECEIVING: Usher 43/723y, Williams 33/303y, Jones 21/213y
SCORING: Doug Higgins (K) 36pts, Usher 24pts, Turner &
  Gordon 18pts

1988 6-4-1

7 Washington St.	44 WR Mike Bellamy / Shawn Wax
16 Arizona	21 WR Steven Williams
35 Utah	24 T Craig Schneider
31 Ohio State	12 G Tim Simpson
20 Purdue	0 C Curt Lovelace
34 Wisconsin	6 G Joe Skubisz
21 Michigan State	28 T Mark McGowan
27 Minnesota	27 TE Jeff Finke
21 Indiana	20 QB Jeff George
9 Michigan	38 TB Keith Jones
14 Northwestern	9 FB Howard Griffith
	DL Mel Agee
	DL Moe Gardner
	DL John Wachter / Sean Streeter
	LB Greg Conradt / Shawn Turner
	LB Darrick Brownlow
	LB Steve Glasson
	LB Romero Brice
	DB Chris Green
	DB Stephen Jordan / Henry Jones
	DB Marlon Primous / Mark Kelly
	DB Glenn Cobb

RUSHING: Jones 206/1108y, Griffith 109/615y
PASSING: George 212-366/2257y, 9TD, 57.9%
RECEIVING: Jones 46/374y, Williams 38/523y, Bellamy 36/526y
SCORING: Jones 60pts, Doug Higgins (K) 57pts, Griffith 42pts

1989 10-2

14 Southern Cal	13 WR Mike Bellamy
7 Colorado	38 WR Steven Williams / Shawn Wax
41 Utah State	2 T Craig Schneider
34 Ohio State	14 G Tim Simpson
14 Purdue	2 C Curt Lovelace
14 Michigan State	10 G Cam Pepper
32 Wisconsin	9 T Tony Laster
31 Iowa	7 TE Frank Hartley / Jeff Finke
10 Michigan	24 QB Jeff George
41 Indiana	28 TB Wagner Lester / Steve Feagin
63 Northwestern	14 FB Howard Griffith
31 Virginia■	21 DL Mel Agee
	DL Moe Gardner
	DL Sean Streeter
	LB Romero Brice / Julyon Brown
	LB Darrick Brownlow
	LB Brian Williams / Jason Guard
	LB Steve Glasson
	DB Henry Jones
	DB Chris Green
	DB Marlon Primous / Mike Hopkins
	DB Quintin Parker

RUSHING: Griffith 164/747y, Lester 63/375y, Feagin 73/372y
PASSING: George 242-386/2738y, 22TD, 62.7%
RECEIVING: Bellamy 59/927y, Griffith 45/340y, Williams 34/458y
SCORING: Griffith 66pts, Doug Higgins (K) 56pts, Bellamy 54pts

1990 8-4

16 Arizona	28 WR Steve Mueller / Elbert Turner
23 Colorado	22 WR Shawn Wax
56 S. Illinois	21 T Brad Hopkins
31 Ohio State	20 G Tim Simpson
34 Purdue	0 C Curt Lovelace / Greg Engel
15 Michigan State	13 G Cam Pepper
21 Wisconsin	3 T Tony Laster
28 Iowa	54 TE Jeff Finke / Frank Hartley
17 Michigan	22 QB Jason Verduzco
24 Indiana	10 TB Wagner Lester / Steve Feagin
28 Northwestern	23 FB Howard Griffith
0 Clemson■	30 DL Mel Agee (LB) / Sean Streeter
	DL Moe Gardner / Mike Zitnik
	DL John Wachter
	LB Mike Poloskey (DL) / Jim Shaffer
	LB Darrick Brownlow
	LB Romero Brice
	LB Bill Henkel
	DB Henry Jones
	DB Jerry Hammer / Chris Green
	DB Marlon Primous
	DB Quintin Parker / Mike Hopkins

RUSHING: Griffith 186/1056y, Lester 64/251y, Feagin 51/204y
PASSING: Verduzco 213-330/2446y, 16TD, 64.5%
RECEIVING: Wax 54/786y, Mueller 29/420y, Lester 29/250y
SCORING: Griffith 90pts, Doug Higgins (K) 77pts, Wax 36pts

1991 6-5

38 East Carolina	31 WR Elbert Turner
19 Missouri	23 WR John Wright
51 Houston	10 T Brad Hopkins
24 Minnesota	3 G Tim Simpson
10 Ohio State	7 C Greg Engel / Pat Wendt
21 Iowa	24 G Jim Pesek / Jonathan Kerr
11 Northwestern	17 T Tony Laster
22 Wisconsin	6 TE Ken Dilger
41 Purdue	14 QB Jason Verduzco
0 Michigan	20 RB Steve Feagin / Clinton Lynch
24 Michigan State	27 FB Kameno Bell
	DL Sean Streeter
	DL Mark Zitnik / Erik Foggey
	DL Jon Gustafsson
	LB Mike Poloskey
	LB Julyon Brown
	LB Dana Howard
	LB Aaron Shelby / John Holecek
	DB Robert Crumpton / Fred Cox
	DB Filmel Johnson
	DB Marlon Primous
	DB Mike Hopkins

RUSHING: Bell 134/642y, Feagin 102/446y, Lynch 42/179y
PASSING: Verduzco 235-382/2825y, 15TD, 61.5%
RECEIVING: Bell 60/484y, Turner 42/646y, Wright 37/559y
SCORING: Chris Richardson (K) 65pts, Bell 48pts, Turner 38pts

1992 6-5-1

30 N. Illinois	14 WR Jim Klein / Scott Turner
24 Missouri	14 WR John Wright
13 Houston	31 T Brad Hopkins
17 Minnesota	18 G Jim Pesek
18 Ohio State	16 C Greg Engel
14 Iowa	24 G Jon Kerr
26 Northwestern	27 T Randy Bierman
13 Wisconsin	12 TE Dave Olson / Ken Dilger
20 Purdue	17 QB Jason Verduzco / Jeff Kinney
22 Michigan	22 RB Steve Feagin / Kevin Jackson
14 Michigan State	10 FB Darren Boyer
	DL Erik Foggey / Jeff Hasenstab
	DL Mike Cole
	DL Chad Copher
	LB Kevin Hardy
	LB John Holecek / Aaron Shelby
	LB Dana Howard
	LB Todd Leach / Simeon Rice
	DB Filmel Johnson
	DB Robert Crumpton / Rod Boykin
	DB Jeff Arneson / Antwaine Patton
	DB Tyrone Washington / Derrick Rucker

RUSHING: Boyer 157/593y, Jackson 87/481y, Feagin 111/437y
PASSING: Verduzco 184-282/1779y, 10TD, 65.2%
RECEIVING: Wright 47/508y, Boyer 29/260y, Klein 27/349y
SCORING: Chris Richardson (K) 58pts, Boyer 54pts, Verduzco &
  Wright 30pts

1993 5-6

3 Missouri	31 WR Jasper Strong / Shane Fisher
14 Arizona	16 WR Jason Dulick / Jim Klein
7 Oregon	13 T Phil Rathke/Mike Suarez/John Horn
28 Purdue	10 G Derek Allen
12 Ohio State	20 C Greg Engel
49 Iowa	3 G Jonathan Kerr
24 Michigan	21 T Randy Bierman
20 Northwestern	13 TE Dave Olson / Ken Dilger
23 Minnesota	20 QB Johnny Johnson / Scott Weaver
14 Penn State	28 RB Duane Lynch/ Damien Pratt/K. Jackson
10 Wisconsin	35 FB Ty Douthard
	DL Tim McCloud
	DL Mikki Johnson
	DL Chad Copher
	LB Simeon Rice
	LB Kevin Hardy
	LB John Holecek
	LB Dana Howard
	DB Robert Crumpton / Mike Russell
	DB Filmel Johnson. / Rod Boykin
	DB Antwoine Patton
	DB Tyrone Washington

RUSHING: Douthard 139/599y, Platt 54/337y
PASSING: Johnson 135-287/1688y, 11TD, 47%
RECEIVING: Ty Douthard 43/406y, Dulick 28/387y, Dilger 17/212y
SCORING: Chris Richardson (K) 60pts, Douthard 54pts,

1994 7-5

9 Washington St.	10 WR Jasper Strong
42 Missouri	0 WR Jason Dulick
34 N. Illinois	10 T Ken Blackman / Charles Edwards
16 Purdue	22 G Derek Allen
24 Ohio State	10 C Chris Koerwitz
47 Iowa	7 G Jonathan Kerr
14 Michigan	19 T Mike Suarez
28 Northwestern	7 TE Ken Dilger
21 Minnesota	17 QB Johnny Johnson / Scott Weaver
31 Penn State	35 RB Ty Douthard / Kevin Jackson
13 Wisconsin	19 FB/TE Robert Holcombe / Matt Cushing
30 East Carolina■	0 DL Jason Edwards
	DL Paul Marshall / Mikki Johnson
	DL Chad Copher
	LB Simeon Rice
	LB Kevin Hardy
	LB John Holecek
	LB Dana Howard
	DB Robert Crumpton / Rod Boykin
	DB E. Scott Turner
	DB Antwoine Patton
	DB Tyron Washington

RUSHING: Douthard 179/768y, Holcombe 125/520y, Jackson 106/105y
PASSING: Johnson 198-333/2495y, 19TD, 59.5% Weaver 37-65/463y, 4TD, 56.9%
RECEIVING: Dulick 52/550y, Dilger 48/607y, Strong 42/775y
SCORING: Chris Richardson (K) 73 pts, Douthard 66pts, Dilger & Dulick 36pts

1995 5-5-1

14 Michigan	38 WR Shane Fisher / Rob Majoy
31 Oregon	34 WR Jason Dulick
9 Arizona	7 T Ken Blackman
7 East Carolina	0 G Jay Kuchenbecker / Chico Brown
17 Indiana	10 C Chris Koerwitz (G) / Tom Schau
21 Michigan State	27 G Ryan Schau / Brent Taylor
14 Northwestern	17 T Chris Brown
26 Iowa	7 TE Matt Cushing
3 Ohio State	41 QB Johnny Johnson / Scott Weaver
48 Minnesota	14 RB Robert Holcombe
3 Wisconsin	3 RB Ty Douthard / Rodney Byrd
	DL Garrett Johnson / Cyron Brown
	DL Paul Marshall
	DL Tim McCloud
	LB Simeon Rice
	LB Kevin Hardy
	LB David James / Melvin Roberts
	LB Dennis Stallings
	DB Duane Lyle / James Williams
	DB Trevor Starghill
	DB Antwoine Patton
	DB Tyrone Washington

RUSHING: Holcombe 264/1051y, Douthard 70/232y
PASSING: Johnson 99-199/1110y, 5TD, 49.7%
RECEIVING: Dulick 36/453y, Douthard 27/253y, Fisher 17/181y
SCORING: Bret Scheuplein (K) 49pts, Holcombe & Douthard 30pts

1996 2-9

8 Michigan	20 WR Marquis Moseley
3 Southern Cal	55 WR Jason Dulick
0 Arizona	41 T Tom Schau / J.P. Machado
38 Akron	7 G Brent Taylor / Chris Koerwitz
46 Indiana	43 C Chris Brown
14 Michigan State	42 G Jay Kuchenbecker
24 Northwestern	27 T Ryan Schau
21 Iowa	31 TE Matt Cushing
0 Ohio State	48 QB Scott Weaver
21 Minnesota	23 RB Robert Holcombe
15 Wisconsin	35 RB Rodney Byrd / Ty Douthard
	DL Garrett Johnson / Tom Claussen
	DL Paul Marshall
	DL Rameel Connor
	LB Cyron Brown / Jeff Weisse
	LB Danny Clark
	LB Eric Guenther / David James
	LB Dennis Stallings
	DB James Williams
	DB Trevor Starghill
	DB Toriano Woods / Steve Willis
	DB Asim Pleas / Mike Gusich

RUSHING: Holcombe 260/1281y, Douthard 71/255y
PASSING: Weaver 176-314/1701y, 7TD, 56.1%
RECEIVING: Dulick 53/614y, Moseley 28/301y, Douthard 25/227y
SCORING: Holcombe 78pts, Dulick 26pts, Neil Rackers (K) & Douthard 24pts

1997 0-11

7 S. Mississippi	24 WR George McDonald / Michael Dean
14 Louisville	26 WR Lenny Willis
22 Washington St.	35 T Ryan Schau
10 Iowa	38 G Brent Taylor
6 Penn State	41 C Chris Brown (G) / Tom Schau
7 Wisconsin	31 G Ray Redziniak / J.P. Machado
3 Purdue	48 T Marques Sullivan
6 Indiana	23 TE Matt Cushing / Josh Whitman
21 Northwestern	34 QB Mark Hoekstra / Tim Lavery
6 Ohio State	41 HB Robert Holcombe
17 Michigan State	27 FB Eric Garrett / Steve Havard
	DL Ryan Murphy / Fred Wakefield
	DL Garrett Johnson
	DL Mike McGee / Joe Lauzen
	DL Karleton Thomas / Jeff Weisse
	LB Michael Young
	LB Danny Clark
	LB David James / Eric Guenther
	DB Trevor Starghill / Tony Francis
	DB Carlos McLaurin / James Williams
	DB Steve Willis / Mike Gusich
	DB Asim Pleas / Bobby Jackson

RUSHING: Holcombe 294/1253y, Steve Havard 13/58y
PASSING: Hoekstra 115-219/1029y, 5TD, 52.5% Lavery 62-158/623y, 2TD, 39.2%
RECEIVING: Holcombe 35/277y, Willis 33/354y, McDonald 27/330y
SCORING: Holcombe 38pts, Neil Rackers (K) 25pts, McDonald 18pts

1998 3-8

13 Washington St.	20 WR Larry Davis / Michael Dean
48 Mid. Tennessee	20 WR Lenny Willis / Rob Majoy
9 Louisville	35 T Ryan Schau
14 Iowa	37 G J.P. Machado
13 Northwestern	10 C Tom Schau
0 Ohio State	41 G Ray Redziniak
3 Wisconsin	37 T Marques Sullivan
9 Purdue	42 TE Brian Hodges / Josh Whitman
0 Penn State	27 QB Kurt Kittner /M. Hoekstra /Kirk Johnson
31 Indiana	16 HB Steve Havard / Rocky Harvey
9 Michigan State	41 FB Elmer Hickman / Chris Hoffman
	DL Jason Eberhart / Jeff Weisse
	DL Garrett Johnson
	DL Mike McGee / Karleton Thomas
	DL Rameel Connor / Fred Wakefield
	LB Mike Young / Eric Geunther
	LB Robert Franklin / Mon Long
	LB Danny Clark
	DB Tony Francis
	DB Asim Pleas
	DB Mike Gusich / Muhammad Abdullah
	DB Bobby Jackson

RUSHING: Harvey 134/634y, Havard 124/564y, Cook 48/190y
PASSING: Kittner 72-167/782y, 1TD, 44.4%
RECEIVING: Willis 26/301y, Majoy 22/202y, Hickman 19/158y
SCORING: Harvey 42pts, Havard 36pts, Neil Rackers (K) 35pts

1999 8-4

41 Arkansas State	3 WR Michael Dean
38 San Diego State	10 WR Brandon Lloyd / Greg Lewis
41 Louisville	36 T Marques Sullivan
10 Michigan State	27 G Jay Kulaga
31 Indiana	34 C Luke Butkus
7 Minnesota	37 G Ray Redziniak
35 Michigan	29 T Tony Pashos
7 Penn State	27 TE Josh Whitman
40 Iowa	24 QB Kurt Kittner
46 Ohio State	20 HB Steve Havard / Rocky Harvey
29 Northwestern	7 FB Jameel Cook / Elmer Hickman
63 Virginia■	21 DL Fred Wakefield
	DL Mike McGee / Jason Eberhart
	DL Brandon Moore
	DL Rameel Connor
	LB Eric Guenther / Robert Franklin
	LB Danny Clark
	LB Mike Young
	DB Tony Francis
	DB Johnny Rogers
	DB Muhammad Abdullah
	DB Asim Pleas

RUSHING: Havard 179/790y, Harvey 143/774y, Antoineo Harris (HB) 37/214y
PASSING: Kittner 216-396/2702y, 24TD, 54.5%
RECEIVING: Dean 45/608y, Hickman 34/243y, Lloyd 30/511y
SCORING: Neil Rackers (K) 110pts, Havard 60pts, Harvey 54pts

2000 5-6

35 Mid. Tennessee	6 WR Walter Young / Aaron Moorehead
49 San Diego State	13 WR Greg Lewis
17 California	15 T Marques Sullivan
31 Michigan	35 G Jay Kulaga
10 Minnesota	44 C Luke Butkus
31 Iowa	0 G Ray Redziniak
25 Penn State	39 T Tony Pashos
10 Michigan State	14 TE Josh Whitman
42 Indiana	35 QB Kurt Kittner
21 Ohio State	24 HB Rocky Harvey / Antoineo Harris
23 Northwestern	61 FB Jameel Cook
	DL Fred Wakefield
	DL Brandon Moore
	DL Jason Eberhart
	DL Terrell Washington
	LB Jerry Schumacher
	LB Robert Franklin
	LB Mike Young / Mondrian Long
	DB Trayvan Waller / Marc Jackson
	DB Eugene Wilson / Bobie Singleton
	DB Muhammad Abdullah
	DB Bobby Jackson

RUSHING: Harris 192/772y, Harvey 123/683y, Cook 49/215y
PASSING: Kittner 173-297/1982y, 18TD, 58.2%
RECEIVING: Lewis 40/544y, Cook 34/218y, Moorehead 30/520y
SCORING: Harris 42pts, Steve Fitts (K) 40pts, Lewis 36pts

2001 10-2

44 California	17 WR Walter Young / Dwayne Smith
17 N. Illinois	12 WR Brandon Lloyd
34 Louisville	10 T Sean Bubin
20 Michigan	45 G Jay Kulaga
25 Minnesota	14 C Luke Butkus
35 Indiana	14 G Bucky Babcock / David Diehl
42 Wisconsin	35 T Tony Pashos
38 Purdue	13 TE/WR Brian Hodges / Greg Lewis
33 Penn State	28 QB Kurt Kittner
34 Ohio State	22 HB Rock Harvey / Antoinoe Harris
34 Northwestern	28 FB Carey Davis
34 LSU■	47 DL Terrell Washington
	DL Brandon Moore
	DL Brett Kautter
	DL Mike O'Brien / Robby Long
	LB Ty Myers
	LB Jerry Schumacher
	LB Joe Bevis / Mario Ivy
	DB Eugene Wilson
	DB Christian Morton
	DB Muhammad Abdullah
	DB Bobby Jackson

RUSHING: Harris 169/629y, Harvey 145/620y, Davis 108/467
PASSING: Kittner 221-409/3256y, 27TD, 54%
RECEIVING: Lloyd 65/1062y, Young 50/890y, Davis 39/274y
SCORING: Peter Christofilakos (K) 65pts, Lloyd 60pts, Young 48pts

2002 5-7

20 Missouri	33 WR Walter Young / Aaron Moorehead
20 S. Mississippi	23 WR Brandon Lloyd / Greg Lewis
59 Arkansas State	7 T Sean Bubin
35 San Jose State	38 G David Diehl
28 Michigan	45 C Duke Preston
10 Minnesota	31 G Bucky Babcock
38 Purdue	31 T Tony Pashos
45 Indiana	14 TE Anthony McClellan
7 Penn State	18 QB Jon Beutjer / Dustin Ward
37 Wisconsin	20 HB Antoineo Harris
16 Ohio State	23 FB Carey Davis
31 Northwestern	24 DL Derrick Strong
	DL Jeff Ruffin / Jamie Hanton
	DL Brett Kautter
	DL Mike O'Brien / Brian Schaefering
	LB Matt Sinclair / Ty Myers
	LB Jerry Schumacher
	LB Joe Bevis / Winston Taylor
	DB Eugene Wilson
	DB Michael Hall / Christian Morton
	DB Marc Jackson
	DB Travis Williams / Taman Jordan

RUSHING: Harris 278/1330y, Davis 59/319y,
 Morris Virgil (HB) 28/216y
PASSING: Beutjer 193-327/2511y, 21TD, 59%
 Ward 65-126/877y, 5TD, 51.6%
RECEIVING: Lloyd 65/1010y, Young 56/822y, Lewis 38/538y
SCORING: Peter Christofilakos (K) 67pts, Lloyd 54pts,
 Harris 48pts

2003 1-11

15 Missouri	22 WR Lonnie Hurst / Ade Adeyemo
49 Illinois State	22 WR Kelvin Hayden / Mark Kornfield
3 UCLA	6 T Sean Bubin
24 California	31 G Bryan Koch / Dave Hilderbrand
20 Wisconsin	38 C Duke Preston
10 Purdue	43 G Matt Maddox
14 Michigan State	49 T Bucky Babcock
14 Michigan	56 TE Melvin Bryant / Anthony McClellan
10 Minnesota	36 QB Jon Beutjer / Dustin Ward /Chris Pazan
10 Iowa	41 HB E.B. Halsey/P. Thomas/ Marcus Mason
14 Indiana	17 FB Carey Davis / Jason Davis
20 Northwestern	37 DL Derrick Strong
	DL Ryan Matha / Jeff Ruffin
	DL Charles Gilstrap
	DL Scott Moss
	LB Winston Taylor
	LB Antonio Mason / Ty Myers / Joe Bevis
	LB Matt Sinclair
	DB Christian Morton / Alan Ball
	DB Sharriff Abdullah / Darnell Ray
	DB Travis Williams / Eric McGoey
	DB Marc Jackson

RUSHING: Halsey 140/525y, Thomas 43/233y, Mason 64/214y
PASSING: Beutjer 162-257/1597y, 10TD, 63%
 Ward 63-108/648y, 3TD, 58.3%
 Pazan 49-82/511y, 2TD, 59.8%
RECEIVING: Hayden 52/592y, Kornfield 44/527y,
 C. Davis 39/236y
SCORING: John Gockman (K) 63pts, Halsey 42pts, Hayden 20pts

2004 3-8

52 Florida A&M	13 WR Kendrick Jones
17 UCLA	35 WR Franklin Payne / Ade Adeyemo
30 W. Michigan	27 T J.J. Simmons
30 Purdue	38 G Martin O'Donnell / Bryan Koch
7 Wisconsin	24 C Duke Preston
25 Michigan State	38 G Matt Maddox
19 Michigan	30 T Bucky Babcock
0 Minnesota	45 TE Anthony McClellan / Melvin Bryant
13 Iowa	23 QB Jon Beutjer / Brad Bower
26 Indiana	22 HB E.B. Halsey / Pierre Thomas
21 Northwestern	28 FB Jason Davis
	DL Scott Moss / Xavier Fulton
	DL Ryan Matha / Brian Schaefering
	DL Chris Norwell
	DL Mike O'Brien
	LB Anthony Thornhill / J Leman
	LB Mike Gawelek / Joe Mele
	LB Matt Sinclair
	DB Alan Ball / James Cooper
	DB Kelvin Hayden
	DB Justin Harrison / Travis Williams
	DB Morris Virgil

RUSHING: Thomas 152/893y, Halsey 111/461y, Davis 49/230
PASSING: Beutjer 107-188/1082y, 8TD, 56.9%
 Bower 57-100/658y, 4TD, 57%
RECEIVING: Jones 47/687y, Davis 41/340y, Payne 25/214y
SCORING: Thomas 60pts, Jason Reda (K) 47pts, Halsey &
 Jones 30pts

2005 2-9

33 Rutgers	30 WR Kendrick Jones / Franklin Payne
40 San Jose State	19 WR Kyle Hudson / Jody Ellis
20 California	35 WR D. Warren / Derrick McPhearson
14 Michigan State	61 T J.J. Simmons / Charles Myles
7 Iowa	35 G Martin O'Donnell / Ben Amundsen
13 Indiana	36 C Matt Maddox
10 Penn State	63 G James Ryan
24 Wisconsin	41 T Ryan McDonald
2 Ohio State	40 TE/FB Melvin Bryant / Jason Davis
3 Purdue	37 QB Tim Brasic
21 Northwestern	38 RB E. B. Halsey / Pierre Thomas
	DL Derek Walker / Scott Moss
	DL Ryan Matha
	DL Chris Norwell
	DL Xavier Fulton / Sirod Williams
	LB J Leman / Sam Carson
	LB Anthony Thornhill / Remond Willis
	LB/DB Brit Miller / James Cooper
	DB Sharriff Abdullah
	DB Alan Ball / Charles Bailey
	DB Morris Virgil / Kyle Kleckner
	DB Kevin Mitchell / Justin Harrison

RUSHING: Thomas 127/664y, Brasic 151/420y, Halsey 84/349y
PASSING: Brasic 206-337/1979y, 11TD, 61.1%
RECEIVING: Halsey 38/185y, Hudson 31/469y, Thomas 28/225y
SCORING: Jason Reda (K) 59pts, Thomas 36pts

2006 2-10

42 E. Illinois	17 WR Kyle Hudson
0 Rutgers	33 WR Jody Ellis / DaJuan Warrren
21 Syracuse	31 WR Jacob Willis/Derrick McPhearson
7 Iowa	24 T Akim Millington / Jim LaBonte
23 Michigan State	20 G Martin O'Donnell /Brandon Jordan
32 Indiana	34 C Ryan McDonald
17 Ohio	20 G Matt Maddox
12 Penn State	26 T Charles Myles / Mike Ware
24 Wisconsin	30 TE Jeff Cumberland / Tom Sullivan
10 Ohio State	17 QB Isaiah "Juice" Williams / Tim Brasic
31 Purdue	42 RB P. Thomas / Rashard Mendenhall
16 Northwestern	27 DL Derek Walker / Will Davis
	DL Chris Norwell
	DL Josh Norris / David Lindquist
	DL Doug Pilcher
	LB Brit Miller / Anthony Thornhill
	LB J Leman
	LB Antonio Steele
	DB Alan Ball
	DB Vontae Davis
	DB Kevin Mitchell / Justin Sanders
	DB Justin Harrison

RUSHING: Thomas 131/755y, Mendenhall 78/640y,
 Williams 154/576y
PASSING: Williams 103-261/1489y, 9TD, 39.5%
 Brasic 35-66/346y, 0TD, 53%
RECEIVING: Hudson 30/403y, Willis 16/313y,
 Cumberland 16/232y
SCORING: Jason Reda (K) 69pts, Mendenhall &
 Thomas 36pts

2007 9-4

34 Missouri	40 WR Arrelious Benn
21 W. Illinois	0 WR Jacob Willis / Joe Morgan
41 Syracuse	20 WR Kyle Hudson
27 Indiana	14 T Xavier Fulton
27 Penn State	20 G Martin O'Donnell
31 Wisconsin	26 C Ryan McDonald
6 Iowa	10 G Jon Asamoah
17 Michigan	27 T Akim Millington
28 Ball State	17 TE Michael Hoomanawanui/J. Cumberland
44 Minnesota	17 QB Juice Williams
28 Ohio State	21 RB Rashard Mendenhall
41 Northwestern	22 FB/WR Russ Weil / Brian Gamble
17 Southern Cal■	49 DL Derek Walker / Martez Wilson
	DL Chris Norwell
	DL David Lindquist / Mike Ware
	DL Doug Pilcher / Will Davis
	LB Antonio Steele
	LB J Leman
	LB/DB Brit Miller / Justin Sanders
	DB Vontae Davis / Marcus Thames
	DB Dere Hicks
	DB Kevin Mitchell
	DB Justin Harrison

RUSHING: Mendenhall 262/1681y, Williams 165/755y
 Daniel Dufrene (RB) 47/294y
PASSING: Williams 153-267/1743y, 13TD, 57.3%
RECEIVING: Benn 54/676y, Mendenhall 34/318y, Willis 22/330y
SCORING: Mendenhall 119pts, Jason Reda (K) 92pts,
 Williams 42pts

2008 5-7

42 Missouri	52 WR Will Judson / Jeff Cumberland
47 E. Illinois	21 WR Arrelious Benn / A.J. Jenkins
20 La.-Lafayette	17 T Xavier Fulton
24 Penn State	38 G Eric Block
45 Michigan	20 C Ryan McDonald
55 Indiana	13 G Jon Asamoah
17 Wisconsin	27 T Jeff Allen / Ryan Palmer
27 Iowa	24 TE/WR M. Hoomanawanui / Fred Sykes
17 W. Michigan	23 QB Juice Williams
20 Ohio State	30 RB Daniel Dufrene / Jason Ford
10 Northwestern	27 FB/WR Rahkeem Smith / Chris Duvalt
	DL Derek Walker / Doug Pilcher
	DL David Lindquist / Corey Liuget
	DL Josh Brent
	DL Will Davis
	LB Martez Wilson / Sam Carson
	LB Brit Miller
	LB/DB Rodney Pittman / Garrett Edwards
	DB Dere Hicks
	DB Vontae Davis / Nate Bussey
	DB Travon Bellamy
	DB Donsay Hardeman / Bo Flowers

RUSHING: Williams 175/719y, Dufrene 117/663y, Ford 81/294y
PASSING: Williams 219-381/3173y, 22TD, 57.5%
RECEIVING: Benn 67/1055y, Dufrene 30/271y,
 Hoomanawanui 25/312y
SCORING: Matt Eller (K) 84pts, Ford 48pts,
 Benn & Williams 30pts

2009 3-9

9 Missouri	37 WR Chris Duvalt / A.J. Jenkins
45 Illinois State	17 WR Fred Sykes / Jarred Fayson
0 Ohio State	30 WR Arrelious Benn / Jeff Cumberland (TE)
17 Penn State	35 T Jeff Allen
14 Michigan State	24 G Randall Hunt
14 Indiana	27 C Eric Block
14 Purdue	24 G Jon Asamoah
38 Michigan	13 T Hugh Thornton / Ryan Palmer
35 Minnesota	32 TE/WR M. Hoomanawanui / Jack Ramsey
16 Northwestern	21 QB Juice Williams / Eddie McGee (WR)
36 Cincinnati	49 RB Mikel Leshoure/ D. Dufrene/Jason Ford
52 Fresno State	53 DL Doug Pilcher
	DL Sirod Williams / Corey Liuget
	DL Josh Brent
	DL Antonio James / Clay Nurse
	LB Ian Thomas
	LB Nate Bussey / Russell Ellington
	LB/DB Evan Frierson / Travon Bellamy
	DB Tavon Wilson
	DB Dere Hicks / Terry Hawthorne
	DB Donsay Hardeman / Walt Aikens
	DB Garrett Edwards

RUSHING: Leshoure 108/734y, Ford 97/588y, Williams 143/507y
 Dufrene 63/277y
PASSING: Williams 131-227/1632y, 12TD, 57.7%
 Jacob Charest (QB) 28-56/383y, 2TD, 50.0%
 McGee 25-47/303y, 1TD, 53.2%
RECEIVING: Benn 38/490y, Duvalt 23/361y, Fayson 16/218y
 Ramsey 16/182y
SCORING: Leshoure 42pts, Matt Eller (K) 35pts,
 Derek Dimke (K) 27pts

2010 7-6

13 Missouri	23 WR Eddie McGee / Jarred Fayson
35 So. Illinois	3 WR A.J. Jenkins / Darius Millines
28 No. Illinois	22 T Jeff Allen
13 Ohio State	24 G Jack Cornell / Hugh Thornton
33 Penn State	13 C Graham Pocic
6 Michigan State	26 G Randall Hunt
43 Indiana	13 T Ryan Palmer
44 Purdue	10 TE Evan Wilson
65 Michigan	67 QB Nathan Scheelhaasse
34 Minnesota	38 HB Mikel Leshoure
48 Northwestern	27 FB Jay Prosch / Jason Ford
23 Fresno State	25 DL Clay Nurse / Whitney Mercilus
38 Baylor■	14 DL Akeem Spence / Glenn Foster
	DL Corey Liuget
	DL Michael Buchanan / Justin Staples
	LB Ian Thomas / Jonathan Brown
	LB Martez Wilson
	LB Nate Bussey
	DB Travon Bellamy / Terry Hawthorne
	DB Justin Green
	DB Trulon Henry / Steve Hull
	DB Tavon Wilson / Ashante Williams

RUSHING: Leshoure 281/1697y, Scheelhaasse 185/868y,
 Ford 99/480y
PASSING: Scheelhaasse 155-264/1825y, 17TD, 58.7%
RECEIVING: Jenkins 56/746y, Fayson 38/355y, Leshoure 17/196y
SCORING: Leshoure 122pts, Derek Dimke (K) 115pts,
 Ford & Jenkins 42pts

INDIANA

Indiana University (Founded 1820)
Bloomington, Indiana
Nickname: Hoosiers
Colors: Cream and Crimson
Stadium: Memorial Stadium (1960) 53,500
Conference Affiliation: Big Ten (1899-present)

CAREER RUSHING YARDS	Attempts	Yards
Anthony Thompson (1986-89)	1161	5299
Antwaan Randle El (1998-01)	857	3895
Alex Smith (1994-96)	723	3492
Mike Harkrader (1976-80)	718	3257
Levron Williams (1998-01)	452	3095
Vaughn Dunbar (1990-91)	613	3029
Courtney Snyder (1973-76)	631	2789
John Isenbarger (1967-69)	487	2453
Lonnie Johnson (1977-80)	458	2228
Ric Enis (1974-77)	464	2096

CAREER PASSING YARDS	Comp.-Att.	Yards
Antwaan Randle El (1998-01)	528-1060	7469
Ben Chappell (2007-10)	651-1066	7251
Steve Bradley (1983-85)	532-1023	6579
Kellen Lewis (2006-08)	565-981	6395
Dave Schnell (1986-89)	406-722	5470
Trent Green (1989-92)	421-755	5400
Tim Clifford (1977-80)	333-631	4338
Babe Laufenberg (1981-82)	361-616	4256
Matt LoVecchio (2003-04)	308-562	3729
Harry Gonso (1967-69)	256-531	3446

CAREER RECEIVING YARDS	Catches	Yards
James Hardy (2005-07)	191	2740
Courtney Roby (2001-04)	170	2524
Ernie Jones (1984-87)	133	2361
Thomas Lewis (1991-93)	148	2324
Duane Gunn (1981-83)	116	2235
Damario Belcher (2008-10)	164	1939
Tandon Doss (2008-10)	154	1854
Jade Butcher (1967-69)	117	1810
Bill Malinchak (1963-65)	115	1686
Eddie Baety (1991-94)	132	1617

SEASON RUSHING YARDS	Attempts	Yards
Vaughn Dunbar (1991)	364	1805
Anthony Thompson (1989)	358	1793
Anthony Thompson (1988)	355	1686
Alex Smith (1994)	265	1475
Levron Williams (2001)	212	1401

SEASON PASSING YARDS	Comp.-Att.	Yards
Ben Chappell (2010)	302-483	3295
Kellen Lewis (2007)	265-442	3043
Ben Chappell (2009)	268-428	2941
Trent Green (1991)	200-339	2627
Steve Bradley (1984)	208-402	2544

SEASON RECEIVING YARDS	Catches	Yards
Ernie Jones (1987)	66	1265
James Hardy (2007)	79	1125
Thomas Lewis (1993)	55	1058
Courtney Roby (2002)	59	1039
Tandon Doss (2009)	77	962

GAME RUSHING YARDS	Attempts	Yards
Anthony Thompson (1989 vs. Wisconsin)	52	377
Levron Williams (2001 vs. Wisconsin)	20	280
Vaughn Dunbar (1991 vs. Missouri)	33	265

GAME PASSING YARDS	Comp.-Att.	Yards
Ben Chappell (2010 vs. Michigan)	45-64	480
Jay Rodgers (1997 vs. Ball State)	27-39	408
Babe Laufenberg (1982 vs. Iowa)	26-36	390

GAME RECEIVING YARDS	Catches	Yards
Thomas Lewis (1993 vs. Penn State)	12	285
Tyrone Browning (1998 vs. W. Michigan)	13	258
Nate Lundy (1980 vs. Colorado)	5	256

GREATEST COACH:

One of the more under-appreciated coaches in the modern era, Bill Mallory, won more games (69) at Indiana than any other coach, took the Hoosiers to more bowl games (6), had the team ranked in 1988 (no. 20), coached a Heisman Trophy candidate (Anthony Thompson) and won back-to-back Big Ten coach of the year awards (1986-87). Yet he was never truly accepted by the basketball-crazy fans at Indiana, nor by a national college football audience, as his teams were never quite flashy enough.

An old-fashioned coach from the Miami of Ohio pipeline, where he played under Bo Schembechler, Mallory began his head coaching career at his alma mater. By year five, in 1973, Miami was an 11-0 MAC champion, besting Florida in the Tangerine Bowl.

Next up was Colorado, and Mallory was able to win 35 games in five years and a share of the Big Eight title in 1976—impressive considering the peak form Oklahoma and Nebraska were in those days—but Colorado fans wanted flash and they paid dearly for it as replacement Chuck Fairbanks needed three seasons to win a total of seven games, which equaled Mallory's average for one year.

Mallory returned to the MAC and kept winning as he rebuilt Northern Illinois into a 10-win team by 1983. He returned to the bigger conferences with Indiana and by year three he had his Hoosiers poised for a post-season run of six bowls in eight years. But once his win totals began to shrank, IU fans wanted a bigger passing game. So in came Cam Cameron and out went any hopes of returning to post-season play; 13 years and counting until the 2007 Hoosiers made the Insight Bowl, inspired by the memory of their late coah, Terry Hoeppner.

INDIANA'S 55 GREATEST SINCE 1953

OFFENSE

WIDE RECEIVER: Duane Gunn, James Hardy, Ernie Jones, Thomas Lewis, Bill Malinchak
TIGHT END: Bob Stephenson
TACKLE: Charley Peal, Eric Moore, Rodger Saffold, Bob Skoronski
GUARD: Gary Cassells, Don Croftcheck, Tom Schuette, Don Shrader
CENTER: Mark Heidel, Ron Vargo
QUARTERBACK: Ben Chappell, Harry Gonso, Antwaan Randle El
RUNNING BACK: Vaughn Dunbar, John Isenbarger, Alex Smith, Anthony Thompson, Levron Williams
FULLBACK: Ric Enis

DEFENSE

END: Ted Aucreman, Nathan Davis, Earl Faison, Ed McGuire, Adewale Ogunleye
TACKLE: Carl Barzilaukas, Hurvin McCormack
LINEBACKER: Joe Fitzgerald, Ken Kaczmarek, Joe Norman, Jim Sniadecki, Donnie Thomas, Van Waiters
CORNERBACK: Dave Abrams, Eric Allen, Nate Cunningham, Tim Wilbur
SAFETY: Lance Brown, Quinn Buckner, Mike Dumas, Dale Keneipp

SPECIAL TEAMS

RETURN SPECIALISTS: Derin Graham, Steve Porter
PLACE KICKER: Pete Stoyanovich
PUNTER: Alan Sutkowski

MULTIPLE POSITIONS

TACKLE-DEFENSIVE TACKLE: Doug Crusan
GUARD-TACKLE-DEFENSIVE TACKLE-LINEBACKER: Mike Rabold

TWO-WAY PLAYERS

END-DEFENSIVE END: Brad Bomba
RUNNING BACK-DEFENSIVE BACK: Marv Woodson
FULLBACK-LINEBACKER-KICKER: Tom Nowatzke

PERFORMANCE FORMULA:
INDIANA'S 10 BEST SEASONS

1967	1.3278	18 of 71
1988	1.2907	23 of 69
1993	1.2616	25 of 70
1987	1.2439	25 of 69
1979	1.2192	27 of 70
1991	1.2123	27 of 71
1994	1.1447	34 of 71
1968	1.1206	34 of 70
1958	1.1122	35 of 70
1976	1.0760	32 of 70

INDIANA HOOSIERS

Year	W-L-T	AP Poll	Conference Standing	Toughest Regular Season Opponents	Coach (Record at School)	Bowl Games		
1953	2-7		9	Michigan State 8-1, Ohio State 6-3, Southern Cal 6-3-1, Iowa 5-3-1	Bernie Crimmins			
1954	3-6		7	Ohio State 9-0, Miami (Ohio) 8-1, Michigan 6-3	Bernie Crimmins			
1955	3-6		9	Michigan State 8-1, Notre Dame 8-2, Ohio State 7-2, Michigan 7-2	Bennie Crimmins			
1956	3-6		10	Iowa 8-1, Michigan State 7-2, Michigan 7-2	Bennie Crimmins (13-32)			
1957	1-8		9t	Michigan State 8-1, Ohio State 8-1, Iowa 7-1-1, Notre Dame 7-3	Bob Hicks (1-8)			
1958	5-3-1		5	Iowa 7-1-1, Purdue 6-1-2, Ohio State 6-1-2	Phil Dickens			
1959	4-4-1		8t	Purdue 5-2-2, Northwestern 6-3, Illinois 5-3-1	Phil Dickens			
1960	1-8		ineligible	Minnesota 8-1, Ohio State 7-2, Michigan State 6-2-1	Phil Dickens			
1961	2-7		9t	Ohio State 8-0-1, Michigan State 7-2, Purdue 6-3, Wisconsin 6-3	Phil Dickens			
1962	3-6		9	Wisconsin 8-1, Northwestern 7-2, Ohio State 6-3	Phil Dickens			
1963	3-6		10	Michigan State 6-2-1, Oregon 7-3, Ohio State 5-3-1	Phil Dickens			
1964	2-7		9t	Ohio State 7-2, Oregon State 8-2, Oregon 7-2-1, Purdue 6-3	Phil Dickens (20-41-2)			
1965	2-8		9	Michigan State 10-0, Ohio State 7-2, Purdue 7-2-1	John Pont			
1966	1-8-1		9	Michigan State 9-0-1, Purdue 8-2, Miami 7-2-1, Texas 6-4	John Pont			
1967	9-2	4	1t	Purdue 8-2, Minnesota 8-2	John Pont	Rose	3 Southern Cal	14
1968	6-4		5t	Michigan 8-2, Purdue 8-2, Kansas 7-1, Minnesota 6-4	John Pont			
1969	4-6		5t	Purdue 8-2, Colorado 7-3, Iowa 5-5	John Pont			
1970	1-9		9t	West Virginia 8-3, Colorado 6-4, Northwestern 6-4	John Pont			
1971	3-8		9	Michigan 11-0, Northwestern 7-4, Ohio State 6-4	John Pont			
1972	5-6		6t	Michigan 10-1, Ohio State 9-1, Purdue 6-5	John Pont (31-51-1)			
1973	2-9		9t	Ohio State 9-0-1, Michigan 9-0-1, Arizona 8-3, Minnesota 7-4	Lee Corso			
1974	1-10		10	Ohio State 10-1, Michigan 10-1, Arizona 9-2, Wisconsin 7-4	Lee Corso			
1975	2-8-1		10	Ohio State 11-0, Nebraska 10-1, Michigan 8-1-2, NC State 7-1-2	Lee Corso			
1976	5-6		3t	Michigan 10-1, Ohio State 8-2-1, Nebraska 8-2-1	Lee Corso			
1977	5-5-1		4	Ohio State 9-2, Nebraska 8-3, LSU 8-3, Minnesota 7-4	Lee Corso			
1978	4-7		7	Nebraska 9-2, Ohio State 7-3-1, Purdue 7-2-1, MSU 8-3, LSU 8-3	Lee Corso			
1979	8-4	19	4	Ohio State 11-0, Purdue 9-2, Michigan 8-3	Lee Corso	Holiday	38 Brigham Young	37
1980	6-5		6	Michigan 9-2, Ohio State 9-2, Purdue 8-3	Lee Corso			
1981	3-8		8	USC 9-2, Iowa 8-3, Michigan 8-3, Ohio State 8-3, Wisconsin 7-4	Lee Corso			
1982	5-6		6	Michigan 8-3, Ohio State 8-3, USC 8-3, Illinois 7-4, Iowa 7-4	Lee Corso (41-68-2)			
1983	3-8		8t	Illinois 10-1, Michigan 9-2, Iowa 9-2, Ohio State 8-3	Sam Wyche (3-8)			
1984	0-11		10	Ohio State 9-2, Iowa 7-4, Wisconsin 7-3-1, Purdue 7-4, Illinois 7-4	Bill Mallory			
1985	4-7		9t	Michigan 9-1-1, Ohio State 8-3, Michigan State 7-4, Illinois 6-4-1	Bill Mallory			
1986	6-6		6t	Michigan 11-1, Ohio State 9-3, Minnesota 6-5	Bill Mallory	All-American	13 Florida State	27
1987	8-4		2t	Michigan State 8-2-1, Iowa 8-3, Michigan 7-4	Bill Mallory	Peach	22 Tennessee	27
1988	8-3-1	20	5	Michigan 8-2-1, Iowa 6-3-3, Illinois 6-4-1, Michigan State 6-4-1	Bill Mallory	Liberty	34 South Carolina	10
1989	5-6		6t	Michigan 9-2, Illinois 9-2, Michigan State 7-4	Bill Mallory			
1990	6-5-1		7	Michigan 8-3, Illinois 8-3, Ohio State 7-3-1	Bill Mallory	Peach	23 Auburn	27
1991	7-4-1		3t	Michigan 10-1, Iowa 10-1, Notre Dame 9-3, Ohio State 8-3	Bill Mallory	Copper	24 Baylor	0
1992	5-6		6t	Michigan 8-0-3, Ohio State 8-2-1, Michigan State 5-6	Bill Mallory			
1993	8-4		4t	Wisconsin 9-1-1, Ohio State 9-1-1, Penn State 9-2, Kentucky 7-4	Bill Mallory	Independence	20 Virginia Tech	45
1994	7-4		6t	Penn State 11-0, Ohio State 9-3	Bill Mallory			
1995	2-9		11	Northwestern 10-1, Ohio State 11-1, Michigan 9-3, Penn State 8-3	Bill Mallory			
1996	3-8		9t	Ohio St. 10-1, PSU 10-2, Northwestern 9-2, Michigan 8-3, Iowa 8-3	Bill Mallory (69-77-3)			
1997	2-9		9t	Michigan 11-0, UNC 10-1, Ohio St 10-2, Wisconsin 8-4, Purdue 8-3	Cam Cameron			
1998	4-7		7t	Ohio State 10-1, Wisconsin 10-1, Michigan 9-3, Purdue 8-4	Cam Cameron			
1999	4-7		8t	Michigan 9-2, Wisconsin 9-2, Penn State 8-3, Minnesota 8-3	Cam Cameron			
2000	3-8		9t	Michigan 8-3, Northwestern 8-3, Purdue 8-3, Wisconsin 8-4	Cam Cameron			
2001	5-6		4t	Illinois 10-1, Ohio State 7-4, Iowa 6-5	Cam Cameron (18-37)			
2002	3-9		10t	Ohio State 13-0, Iowa 11-1, Penn State 9-3	Gerry DiNardo			
2003	2-10		9t	Michigan 10-2, Purdue 9-3, Ohio State 10-2, Minnesota 9-3	Gerry DiNardo			
2004	3-8		10t	Michigan 9-2, Ohio State 7-4, Purdue 7-4	Gerry DiNardo (8-27)			
2005	4-7		10	Ohio St. 9-2, Wisconsin 9-3, Michigan 7-4, Minnesota 7-4, Iowa 7-4	Terry Hoeppner			
2006	5-7		6t	Ohio State 12-0, Wisconsin 11-1, Michigan 11-1	Terry Hoeppner (9-14)			
2007	7-6		7t	Illinois 9-3, Penn State 8-4, Wisconsin 9-3	Bill Lynch	Insight	33 Oklahoma State	49
2008	3-9		11	Ball State 12-1, Michigan State 9-3, Northwestern 9-3, Penn State 11-1	Bill Lynch			
2009	4-8		10t	Ohio State 10-2, Iowa 10-2, Wisconsin 9-3, Penn State 10-2	Bill Lynch			
2010	5-7		11	Ohio State 11-1, Wisconsin 11-1, Penn state 7-5	Bill Lynch (19-30)			

| **TOTAL:** | **230-386-8 .3750 (66 of 70)** | | | | **Bowl Games since 1953:** | **3-6 .3333 (64 of 70)** | | |

GREATEST TEAM SINCE 1953: Can there be any other? Fresh off of a 1-8-1 season in 1966, the 1967 Indiana Hoosiers achieved something no other team in school history achieved: a trip to the Rose Bowl. Needing a huge upset over no. 3 Purdue in the regular season finale, the Hoosiers knocked off their upstate rivals by a 19-14 score. One of three teams tied atop the conference, IU secured the Rose Bowl bid and traveled west to face big, bad USC. The "Cardiac Kids" played the national champions tough, but lost a hard-fought battle. Names like quarterback Harry Gonso, halfback John Isenbarger, and linebacker Ken Kaczmarek are still treated with reverence among followers of Indiana football.

1953 2-7

12	Ohio State	36 E Pat Fellinger / John Zuger
14	Southern Cal	27 T Conney Kimbo / John Connors
21	Marquette	20 G Tom Dailey / Tommy Hall
18	Michigan State	47 C Wayne Ethridge / Jim Vesel razmic
13	Iowa	19 G Ted Karras / Ed Slosky
7	Missouri	14 T Harry Jagielski
20	Minnesota	28 E Nate Borden
14	Northwestern	6 QB Florian Helinski
0	Purdue	30 HB Bill Holzbach / Bob Robertson
		HB Jerry Ellis / Dave Rogers
		FB Lester Kun / John Bartkiewicz

RUSHING: Ellis 69/264y, Bartkiewicz 44/226y, Kun 55/207y
PASSING: Helinski 59-146/879y, 4TD, 40.4%
RECEIVING: Bartkiewicz 13/150y, Borden 11/214y, Ellis 11/146y
SCORING: Rogers 30pts, Helinski 28pts, Ellis 24pts

1954 3-6

0	Ohio State	28 E Brad Bomba
34	Pacific	6 T Nate Borden / Ron Rauchmiller
14	Michigan State	21 G Tom Dailey / Tommy Hall
14	Missouri	20 C Jim Vesel
14	Iowa	27 G Ted Karras
13	Michigan	9 T Bob Skoronski / Bob Sobczak
0	Miami (Ohio)	6 E Tony Aloisio / Bob Fee (HB)
14	Northwestern	13 QB Florian Helinski
7	Purdue	13 HB Jim Stone / Don Domenic
		HB Milt Campbell / George Bell
		FB John Bartkiewicz

RUSHING: Bartkiewicz 103/430y, Campbell67/345y, Domenic47/163y
PASSING: Helinski 46-115/797y, 4TD, 40%
RECEIVING: Bomba 11/221y, Domenic 9/133y, Stone 7/113y
SCORING: Helinski 31pts, Campbell 24pts, Bartkiewicz 18pts

1955 3-6

13	Michigan State	20 E Pat Fellinger
0	Notre Dame	19 T Ron Rauchmiller
6	Iowa	20 G Tommy Hall
14	Villanova	7 C Joe Amstutz (T) / Ed Wietecha
20	Northwestern	14 G Ted Karras
21	Ohio	14 T Bob Skoronski
13	Ohio State	20 E Brad Bomba / Bob Fee
0	Michigan	30 QB Gene Cichowski
4	Purdue	6 HB Barry Johnson / Dick Klim
26	Wyoming	14 HB Milt Campbell
		FB John Bartkiewicz

RUSHING: Bartkiewicz 114/456y, Campbell 86/327y,
PASSING: Cichowski 50-102/654y, 3TD, 49%
RECEIVING: Bomba 13/171y, Johnson 11/155y, Campbell 10/132y
SCORING: Campbell 24pts, Cichowski 19pts, Bartkiewicz 12pts

1956 3-6

0	Iowa	27 E Brad Bomba
6	Notre Dame	20 T Mike Rabold / Ted Ross
6	Michigan State	53 G Don Howell / Tom Cousineau
19	Nebraska	14 C Joe Amstutz/Arnie Steeves/Ed Wietecha
19	Northwestern	13 G John Gentile / Pete Piccirillo
19	Marquette	13 T Bob Sobczak / Conney Kimbo
14	Ohio State	35 E Tony Aloisio / Norm Craft / Delnor Gales
26	Michigan McDonald	49 BB SteveFilipowski/T. Kendrick/T.
20	Purdue	39 TB Gene Cichowski/Will Jones /Ted Smith
		WB Dave Whitsell / Barry Johnson
		FB Bob Fee / Jim Yore

RUSHING: Fee 134/621y, Whitsell 58/240y, Yore 54/230y
PASSING: Filipowski 32-63/391y, 2TD, 50.8%
RECEIVING: Bomba 31/407y, Whitsell 9/72y, Craft 8/157y
SCORING: Fee 36pts, Whitsell 30pts, Yore 24pts

1957 1-8

0	Michigan State	54 E Norm Craft / Joe Aveni
0	Notre Dame	26 T Mike Rabold
7	Iowa	47 G Don Howell / Tom Cousineau
0	Ohio State	56 C John Razmic
14	Villanova	7 G Don Noone / Elvin Caldwell
0	Minnesota	34 T Bob DeMarco
0	Cincinnati	21 E Tony Aloisio / Delnor Gales
13	Michigan	27 BB Tommy McDonald
13	Purdue	35 TB Tom Kendrick / Vic Jones
		WB Dave Whitsell / Jim Yore
		FB John Meegan / Ken Hubbart

RUSHING: Meegan 43/114y, Kendrick 52/106y, Yore 31/101y
PASSING: McDonald 43-123/544y, 1TD, 35%
RECEIVING: Whitsell 14/290y, Aloisio 14/138y, Aveni 10/89y
SCORING: Whitsell 12pts, Yore (WB-K) 7pts, Norm Mackin (TB-K) 6pts

1958 5-3-1

0	Notre Dame	18 E Ted Aucreman / Norm Craft
13	West Virginia	12 T Pete Piccirillo / Joe Moore
13	Iowa	34 G Mike Rabold / Elvin Caldwell
8	Ohio State	49 C Tony Aloisio
12	Miami (Ohio)	7 G Don Noone / Bill Kerr
6	Minnesota	0 T Bob Corrigan / Sam Congie
6	Michigan State	0 E Earl Faison (T) / Jon Aveni
8	Michigan	6 BB T. McDonald /Ken Hubbart /Eddie Fritz
15	Purdue	15 TB Ted Smith/Tom Kendrick/Tom Campbell
		WB Wil Scott / Richie Bradford
		FB Vic Jones / Randolph Williams

RUSHING: Smith 89/452y, Jones 128/421y, McDonald 102/309y
PASSING: McDonald 15-42/201y, 2TD, 35.7%
RECEIVING: Faison 6/76y, Aveni 6/50y, Aucreman 4/63y
SCORING: Smith 26pts, Faison 14pts, Jones 12pts

1959 4-4-1

20	Illinois	0 E Ted Aucreman
14	Minnesota	24 T Charley Leo / Joe Moore / Moses Gray
33	Marquette	13 G Elvin Caldwell / Bob Battaglia
23	Nebraska	7 C Fred Lauter / Jim Miller
6	Michigan State	14 G Don Noone / Bob Boak
13	Northwestern	30 T Bob Corrigan
0	Ohio State	0 E Earl Faison
26	Michigan	7 BB Wil Scott / Eddie Fritz
7	Purdue	10 TB Ted Smith / John Jackson
		WB Richie Bradford / Willie Hunter
		FB Vic Jones / Don Cromer

RUSHING: Smith 111/439y, Jones 124/386y, Jackson 80/187y
PASSING: Jackson 24-55/478y, 6TD, 43.6%
RECEIVING: Aucreman 13/260y, Faison 13/192y
SCORING: Faison 20pts, 4 tied w/ 18pts

1960 1-8

6	Illinois	17 E Roy Pratt / Tony Rocco
0	Minnesota	42 T Jim Haas / Charles Campbell
6	Oregon State	20 G Dave Martin / Ken Ellis
34	Marquette	8 C Fred Lautar / Jim Miller
0	Michigan State	35 G Mike Wasdovich / John Giangiacomo
3	Northwestern	21 T Moses Gray / Jeff Slabaugh
7	Ohio State	36 E Earl Faison / Bill Olsavsky
7	Michigan	29 QB Frank Hunter / Woody Moore
6	Purdue	35 HB Don Cromer / Joe Maroon
		WB Rich Bradford/Nate Ramsey/Mike Lopa
		FB Wil Scott / Jack Holder

RUSHING: Maroon 66/348y, Cromer 35/141y, Ramsey 28/123y
PASSING: Moore 13-51/228y, 3TD, 25.5%
RECEIVING: Faison 7/154y, Olsavsky 6/84y, Ramsey 4/83y
SCORING: Faison, Maroon & Ramsey 12pts

1961 2-7

8	Kansas State	14 E Bill Quinter / Tony Rocco
3	Wisconsin	6 T Ralph Poehls / Jeff Slabaugh
8	Iowa	27 G Bob Vecchio / Mike Wasdovich
33	Washington St.	7 C Jack Holder
0	Michigan State	35 G Ken Ellis
8	Northwestern	14 T Gregg Orth / Jim Haas
7	Ohio State	16 E Bill Olsavsky / Dave Martin
17	West Virginia	9 QB Byron Broome / Woody Moore
12	Purdue	34 HB Marv Woodson / Jim Helminiak
		WB Nate Ramsey / Mike Lopa
		FB Don Cromer / Jim Bailey

RUSHING: Woodson 115/425y, Ramsey 71/300y, Cromer 59/260y
PASSING: Broome 60-117/627y, 3TD, 51.3%
RECEIVING: Olsavsky 17/237y, Quinter 12/129y, Woodson 6/37y
SCORING: Woodson (HB-K) 36pts, Moore 14pts, Olsavsky 12pts

1962 3-6

21	Kansas State	0 E Bob DeStefano / Dick Wervey
26	Cincinnati	6 T John Johnson / Ralph Poehls
6	Wisconsin	30 G Mike Wasdovich / Don Croftcheck
10	Iowa	14 C Jack Holder
15	Washington St.	21 G Larry Coleman
8	Michigan State	26 T Jeff Slabaugh
21	Northwestern	26 E Rudy Kuechenberg / Paul Kuchuris
7	Ohio State	10 QB Woody Moore
12	Purdue	7 HB Marv Woodson / Jim Helminiak
		WB Nate Ramsey / Mike Lopa
		FB Jim Bailey / Tom Nowatzke

RUSHING: Woodson 136/540y, Ramsey 70/314y, Bailey 66/288y
PASSING: Moore 57-109/770y, 3TD, 52.3%
RECEIVING: Woodson 15/200y, Ramsey 10/149y, Kuechenberg 10/115y
SCORING: Woodson 36pts, Moore 24pts, Ramsey 18pts

1963 3-6

21	Northwestern	36 E Dick Wervey / Bob DeStefano
0	Ohio State	21 T Ralph Poehls / Ken Hollister
26	Iowa	37 G Don Croftcheck
3	Michigan State	20 C Ted Worcester / Joe Grubish
20	Cincinnati	6 G Mel Branch / Dennis DeBlasis
24	Minnesota	6 T Randy Beisler / Bob Gergeley
20	Oregon State	15 E Rudy Kuechenberg / Bill Malinchak
22	Oregon	28 QB Rich Badar / Dave Mayoras
15	Purdue	21 HB Trent Walters / Bruce Ellwanger
		WB Don Dilly / Doug Spicer / Fred Lussow
		FB Tom Nowatzke

RUSHING: Nowatzke 160/756y, Walters 61/239y, Dilly 29/181y
PASSING: Badar 55-94/679y, 2TD, 58.5%
RECEIVING: Malinchak 25/353y, Lussow 9/46y, Wervey 8/101y
SCORING: Nowatzke (FB-K) 58pts, Badar 36pts, Dilly 12pts

1964 2-7

13	Northwestern	14 E Bill Malinchak
9	Ohio State	17 T Randy Beisler
20	Iowa	21 G Don Croftcheck
27	Michigan State	20 C Joe Tate / Bob Van Pelt / Ted Worcester
28	Miami	14 G Mel Branch / Dennis DeBlasis
0	Minnesota	21 T Ken Hollister
14	Oregon State	24 TE Rudy Kuechenberg
21	Oregon	29 QB Rich Badar
22	Purdue	28 HB John Ginter / Trent Walters
		WB Don Dilly / Fred Lussow
		FB Tom Nowatzke
		DL Bob DeStefano
		DL Joe Sutor / Ken Hollister
		DL Joe Tate / Jim Rapp
		DL Don Croftcheck / Dennis BeBlassis
		DL Brendan Moriarty
		DL Rudy Kuechenberg / Bill Malinchak
		LB Tom Nowatzke / Gil Frisbie
		LB Kevin Duffy / Dick Coachys
		DB Bruce Ellwanger / Bart Moore
		DB Doug Spicer / Fred Lussow
		DB Dave Mayoras / Gary Tofil

RUSHING: Nowatzke 150/545y, Ginter 57/236y, Walters 47/130y
PASSING: Badar 121-245/1571y, 9TD, 49.4%
RECEIVING: Malinchak 46/634y, Nowatzke 16/172y, Lussow 15/146y
SCORING: Nowatzke (FB-K) 73pts, Malinchak 32pts, Badar 18pts

1965 2-8

19	Kansas State	7 E Bill Malinchak
0	Northwestern	20 T Doug Crusan
12	Texas	27 G Bob Russell
18	Minnesota	42 C Joe Tate
13	Illinois	34 G Tom Schuette / Joe Sutor
7	Washington St.	8 T Mike Field / Lorenzo Ashley
21	Iowa	17 TE Rick Spickard / Ed Kalupa
10	Ohio State	17 QB Frank Stavroff
13	Michigan State	27 HB John Ginter / Reggie Woods
21	Purdue	26 HB Terry Cole
		FB Jim Smith
		DL Alan Myszewski
		DL Tom Gallagher
		DL Randy Beisler
		DL John Jones
		DL Ken Hollister
		DL Al Voorhis
		LB Cordell Gill
		LB Glenn Holubar / Bill Huff
		DB Dave Kornowa / Trent Walters
		DB John Durkott
		DB Dave Mayoras

RUSHING: Cole 91/286y, Ginter 69/243y, Smith 61/233y
PASSING: Stavroff 74-159/1045y, 8TD, 46.5%
RECEIVING: Malinchak 44/699y, Kalupa 13/178y
SCORING: Malinchak 42pts, Ginter 30pts, Stavroff 19pts

1966 1-8-1

10 Miami (Ohio)	20 E Bill Couch
26 Northwestern	14 T Doug Crusan
0 Texas	35 G Tom Schuette
7 Minnesota	7 C Bob Van Pelt
10 Illinois	24 G Bob Russell / Gary Cassells
7 Miami	14 T Rick Zoll
19 Iowa	20 TE Al Gage / Al Kamradt
0 Ohio State	7 QB Frank Stavroff
19 Michigan State	37 WB John Ginter / Ray Terry
6 Purdue	51 HB Terry Cole
	FB Mike Krivoshia
	DL Brown Marks
	DL Cordell Gill
	DL Jerry Grecco / Cal Snowden
	DL Bill Bergman
	DL Jim Sniadecki
	LB Kevin Duffy
	LB Ken Kaczmarek
	LB Bob Moynihan
	DB Nate Cunningham
	DB Cal Wilson
	DB Gary Tofil

RUSHING: Krivoshia 179/675y, Cole 84/256y, Ginter 60/197y
PASSING: Stavroff 119-224/1406y, 7TD, 53.1%
RECEIVING: Couch 45/546y, Ginter 21/172y, Terry 18/219y
SCORING: Krivoshia 18pts, Cole 14pts, Dave Kornowa (K) 13pts

1967 9-2

12 Kentucky	10 WR Eric Stolberg / Ben Norman
18 Kansas	15 WR Jade Butcher
20 Illinois	7 T Bob Kirk / Al Schmidt
21 Iowa	17 G Gary Cassells
27 Michigan	20 C Harold Mauro
42 Arizona	7 G Bob Russell
14 Wisconsin	9 T Rick Spickard
14 Michigan State	13 TE Al Gage
7 Minnesota	33 QB Harry Gonso
19 Purdue	14 HB John Isenbarger / Mike Krivoshia
3 Southern Cal	14 FB Terry Cole
	DL Tom Bilunas
	DL Doug Crusan
	DL Bill Wolfe / Jerry Grecco
	DL Cal Snowden
	LB Kevin Duffy / Karl Pankratz
	LB Ken Kaczmarek
	LB Jim Sniadecki
	LB Brown Marks
	DB Nate Cunningham
	DB Dave Kornowa
	DB Mike Baughmann

RUSHING: Isenbarger 120/579y, Cole 109/517y, Gonso 168/512y
PASSING: Gonso 76-143/931y, 9TD, 46.9%
RECEIVING: Butcher 38/654y, Gage 21/343y, Isenbarger 6/103y
SCORING: Butcher 60pts, Isenbarger 32pts, Gonso 18pts

1968 6-4

40 Baylor	36 WR Eric Stolberg
20 Kansas	38 WR Jade Butcher
28 Illinois	14 T John Andrews
38 Iowa	34 G Don DeSalle
22 Michigan	27 C Steve Applegate
16 Arizona	13 G Bill Wood / Chris Morris
21 Wisconsin	20 T Rick Spickard
24 Michigan State	22 TE Al Gage
6 Minnesota	20 QB Harry Gonso
35 Purdue	38 HB John Isenbarger / Bob Pernell
	FB Hank Pogue / Tom Fleming
	DL Tom Bilanus / Clarence Price
	DL Bill Wolfe / Bob White
	DL Jerry Grecco
	DL Cal Snowden
	LB Karl Pankratz
	LB Jim Sniadecki / Bob Moynihan
	LB Mike Adams / Rene Banks
	LB Dan Silas
	DB Nate Cunningham
	DB Benny Norman
	DB Mike Baughman / Jay Mathias

RUSHING: Isenbarger 130/669y, Pernell 98/606y, Rick Thompson (HB) 77/371y
PASSING: Gonso 76-163/1109y, 12TD, 46.6%
RECEIVING: Butcher 44/713y, Gage 23/286y, Stolberg 16/276y
SCORING: Butcher 60pts, Isenbarger 36pts, Don Warner (K) 32pts

1969 4-6

58 Kentucky	30 WR Eric Stolberg / James O'Hara
14 California	17 WR Jade Butcher
7 Colorado	30 T Chris Morris
17 Minnesota	7 G E.G. White
41 Illinois	20 C Steve Applegate
34 Wisconsin	36 G Don DeSalle
16 Michigan State	0 T Steve Brown / Doug Bailey
17 Iowa	28 TE John Andrews
27 Northwestern	30 QB Harry Gonso
21 Purdue	44 HB John Isenbarger
	FB Hank Pogue
	DL Ed Maguire
	DL Bob White
	DL Bob Jones / Tom Kruyer
	DL Larry Morwick
	LB Mike Adams
	LB Karl Pankratz
	LB Bob Nichols
	DB Chuck Thomson / Vic Malinovsky
	DB Mike Deal
	DB Steve Porter
	DB Jay Mathias

RUSHING: Isenbarger 233/1217y, Pogue 88/417y, Gonso 154/237y
PASSING: Gonso 107-207/1336y, 11TD, 51.7%
RECEIVING: Butcher 37/532y, Andrews 36/417y, Isenbarger 13/147y
SCORING: Butcher 60pts, Don Warner (K) 40pts, Isenbarger 32pts

1970 1-9

9 Colorado	16 WR Charley Byrnes
14 California	56 WR Glen Scolnik
10 West Virginia	16 T Chris Morris
0 Minnesota	23 G Tom Kruyer
30 Illinois	24 C E.G. White
12 Wisconsin	30 G Keith Morran
7 Michigan State	32 T Tom Bove
13 Iowa	42 TE John Andrews
7 Northwestern	21 QB Ted McNulty
0 Purdue	40 TB John Motil / Rick Thompson
	FB Greg Harvey
	DL Ed Maguire
	DL Bob Jones
	DL John Debbout
	DL Bob White / Jerry Wiseman
	LB Tom Fleming
	LB Chuck Thomson
	LB Mike Fulk
	LB Jerry Johnson
	DB Dan Lintner
	DB Mark Findley
	DB Steve Porter

RUSHING: Motil 101/358y, Thompson 58/295y, Harvey 72/276y
PASSING: McNulty 55-126/488y, 1TD, 43.7%
RECEIVING: Andrews 29/268y, Scolnik 14/291y, Byrnes 12/136y
SCORING: Thompson 20pts, Dan Grossman (K) 18pts, Chris Gartner (K) 14pts

1971 3-8

0 Minnesota	28 WR Charley Byrnes
26 Kentucky	8 WR Alan Dick
0 Baylor	10 T Dave Spungen
0 Syracuse	7 G Tom Kruyer
29 Wisconsin	35 C Chuck Sukurs
7 Ohio State	27 G Dean Shumaker / Gordon May
10 Northwestern	24 T Tom Bove
7 Michigan	61 TE Keith Morran
21 Illinois	22 QB Ted McNulty
14 Iowa	7 TB Ken Starling / Rick Hoffman
38 Purdue	31 FB Ken St. Pierre
	DL Marshall McCullough
	DL Joe Dawlitsch
	DL Carl Barzilauskas / John Debbout
	DL Bill Pipp
	LB Rob Spicer
	LB Mike Fulk
	LB Chuck Thomson
	LB Jerry Johnson
	DB Dan Lintner
	DB Mark Findley
	DB Larry Wright / Mike Heizman

RUSHING: St. Pierre 181/760y, Starling 110/529y, Hoffman 43/162y
PASSING: McNulty 95-201/1140y, 6TD, 47.3%
RECEIVING: Dick 25/312y, Byrnes 24/332y, St. Pierre 22/166y
SCORING: Chris Gartner (K) 38pts, Dick & St. Pierre 30pts

1972 5-6

27 Minnesota	23 WR Charley Brynes / Mike Flanagan
28 TCU	31 WR Glenn Scolnik
35 Kentucky	34 T Greg McGuire
10 Syracuse	2 G Dan Boarman
33 Wisconsin	7 C Chuck Sukurs
7 Ohio State	44 G Dean Shumaker
14 Northwestern	23 T Dave Spungen
7 Michigan	21 TE Steve Mastin
20 Illinois	37 QB Ted McNulty
16 Iowa	8 TB Ken Starling
7 Purdue	42 FB Ken St. Pierre
	DL Bill Pipp
	DL Carl Barzilaukas
	DL Joe Pawlitsch
	DL Marshall McCullough
	LB Mike Fulk
	LB Dan Grossman
	LB Jerry Johnson
	LB Rob Spicer
	DB Dan Lintner
	DB Mark Findley
	DB Quinn Buckner

RUSHING: Starling 196/781y, St. Pierre 129/490y, Dennis Cremeens (FB) 66/313y
PASSING: McNulty 74-132/906y, 7TD, 56.1%
RECEIVING: Scolnik 53/727y, St. Pierre 17/102y, Mastin 16/183y
SCORING: Chris Gartner (K) 62pts, Starling 50pts, Scolnik 38pts

1973 2-9

14 Illinois	28 WR Mike Flanagan
10 Arizona	26 WR Rodney Harris / Bill Armstrong
17 Kentucky	3 T Bill Sparhawk
28 West Virginia	14 G Dan Boarman
3 Minnesota	24 C Chuck Shukurs / John Babcock
7 Ohio State	37 G Dean Shumaker
7 Wisconsin	31 T Larry Jameson (DL) / Elmer Burton (DL)
13 Michigan	49 TE Trent Smock / Steve Mastin
20 Northwestern	21 QB Willie Jones / Mike Glazier
9 Michigan State	10 TB Ken Starling
23 Purdue	28 FB Courtney Snyder / Dennis Cremeens
	DL Stu O'Dell / Mark DiSalvo
	DL Carl Barzilaukas
	DL John Jordan
	DL Mike Winslow
	LB Mark Deming / Steve Sanders
	LB Tom Buck
	LB Donnie Thomas
	DB Marc Bailey / Bill Atkinson
	DB Gary Powell / Kirk Edwards
	DB Rod Lawson
	DB Quinn Buckner

RUSHING: Starling 180/676y, Snyder 87/424y, Cremeens 100/355y
PASSING: Jones 76-135/881y, 5TD, 56.3%
RECEIVING: Smock 36/305y, Flanagan 33/416y, Mastin 7/66y
SCORING: Cremeens 36pts, Smock 30pts, Frank Stavroff (K)27pts

1974 1-10

0 Illinois	16 WR Mike Flanagan
20 Arizona	35 WR Keith Calvin
22 Kentucky	28 T Greg McGuire
0 West Virginia	24 G Joe Doggett
34 Minnesota	3 C Jim Shuck
9 Ohio State	49 G Tim Mills
25 Wisconsin	35 T Bill Sparhawk
7 Michigan	21 TE Trent Smock
22 Northwestern	24 QB Terry Jones
10 Michigan State	19 TB Courtney Snyder
17 Purdue	38 FB Dennis Cremeens / Reggie Holmes
	DL Mike Winslow
	DL Jack Hoffman
	DL Don Schanz / Derek Foree
	DL Larry Jameson
	DL Mark Miklozek / Carl Smith
	LB Craig Brinkman
	LB Donnie Thomas
	DB Harold Waterhouse / Doug Gordon
	DB Bill Atkinson
	DB Rod Lawson / Willie Jones
	DB Willie Wilson / Rodney Harris

RUSHING: Snyder 291/1254y, Cremeens 60/347y, Calvin 28/102y
PASSING: Jones 129-220/1347y, 11TD, 58.6%
RECEIVING: Smock 31/549y, Calvin 29/367y, Flanagan 21/262y
SCORING: Smock 42pts, Snyder 26pts, Frank Stavroff (K) 22pts

1975 2-8-1

20 Minnesota	14 WR Trent Smock
0 Nebraska	45 WR Keith Calvin
31 Utah	7 T Greg McGuire (DL) / Jim O'Rourke
0 N. Carolina St.	27 G Russ Compton (DL)/Mike Eikenberry (T)
0 Northwestern	30 C Jim Shuck
10 Iowa	20 G Joe Doggett / Terry Colby
7 Michigan	55 T Charles Peal / Dave Knowles
14 Ohio State	24 TE George Edgar / Mark Miklozek
6 Michigan State	14 QB Terry Jones / Dobby Grossman
9 Wisconsin	9 TB Courtney Snyder
7 Purdue	9 FB Ric Enis
	DL Greg McIntosh / Derek Foree
	DL Clifton Payne / Marlon Flemming
	DL Don Schanz / Jack Hoffman
	DL Carl Smith / Mark Deming
	LB Craig Brinkman
	LB Tom Buck
	LB Donnie Thomas
	DB Harold Waterhouse / Walter Booth
	DB Willie Wilson
	DB Tim McVay
	DB Dan Zarlingo / Kevin Grump

RUSHING: Snyder 248/1103y Enis 105/427y,
Darrick Burnett (TB) 34/157y
PASSING: Jones 65-135/787y, 3TD, 48.1%
RECEIVING: Smock 25/427y, Calvin 25/309y, Edgar 10/129y
SCORING: Frank Stavroff (K) 24pts, Snyder 20pts, Smock 18pts

1976 5-6

13 Minnesota	32 WR Don Burrell / Mark Fishel
13 Nebraska	45 WR Keith Calvin
20 Washington	13 T Charles Peal
21 N. Carolina St.	24 G Doug Peacock / Angelo Burrelli
7 Northwestern	0 C Mark Heidel
14 Iowa	7 G Joe Doggett
0 Michigan	35 T Dave Knowles
7 Ohio State	47 TE Kevin Westover / George Edgar
0 Michigan State	23 QB Scott Arnett
15 Wisconsin	14 TB Mike Harkrader
20 Purdue	14 FB Ric Enis
	DL Greg McIntosh
	DL Danny Marr
	DL Marlon Flemming / Steve Weissert
	DL Craig Marks
	DL Carl Smith
	LB Joe Norman
	LB Steve Sanders
	DB Walter Booth
	DB Harold Waterhouse
	DB Tim McKay
	DB Dale Keneipp

RUSHING: Harkrader 192/1003y, Enis 157/ 675y,
Darrick Burnett (TB) 50/192y
PASSING: Arnett 42-93/398y, 3TD, 45.2%
RECEIVING: Calvin 26/319y, Westover 13/121y, Edgar 9/109y
SCORING: Enis 30pts, David Freud (K) 17pts, 4 tied w/ 12pts

1977 5-5-1

14 Wisconsin	30 WR Keith Calvin
24 LSU	21 WR Markus Hardy
20 Miami (Ohio)	21 T Charley Peal
13 Nebraska	31 G Jeff Phipps / Terry Colby
28 Northwestern	3 C Mark Heidel / Bob O'Keefe
13 Michigan State	13 G Gary Autry
7 Illinois	21 T Doug Peacock
34 Minnesota	22 TE Dave Harangody
24 Iowa	21 QB Scott Arnett
7 Ohio State	35 TB Ric Enis / Darrick Burnett
21 Purdue	10 FB Tony D'Orazio
	DL George Doehla
	DL Al Leake
	DL Russ Compton
	DL Craig Marks
	DL Paul Yarian
	LB Doug Sybert
	LB Joe Norman
	DB Willie Wilson
	DB Dave Abrams
	DB Dale Keneipp
	DB Tim McVay

RUSHING: Enis 199/978y, Burnett 157/774y, D'Orazio 112/491y
PASSING: Arnett 73-151/796y, 5TD, 48.3%
RECEIVING: Calvin 41/604y, Harangody 11/127y, D'Orazio 9/75y
SCORING: David Freud (K) 55pts, Arnett 36pts, Burnett 30pts

1978 4-7

17 LSU	24 WR Mark Fishel
14 Washington	7 WR Mike Friede
17 Nebraska	69 T Gerhard Ahting
7 Wisconsin	34 G Jeff Phipps
38 Northwestern	10 C Mark Heidel
14 Michigan State	49 G Mark Johnson
31 Illinois	10 T Doug Peacock
31 Minnesota	32 TE Dan Powers
34 Iowa	14 QB Scott Arnett / Tim Clifford
18 Ohio State	21 TB Mike Harkrader / Darrick Burnett
7 Purdue	20 FB Lonnie Johnson
	DL George Doehla
	DL Al Leake
	DL Terry Tallen / Randy Willhite
	DL Brent Tisdale
	DL Carl Smith / Greg McIntosh
	LB Doug Sybert
	LB Joe Norman
	DB John Swinehart
	DB Tim Wilbur
	DB Dave Abrams
	DB Dale Keneipp

RUSHING: Harkrader 198/880y, Burnett 135/473y,
Johnson 81/421y
PASSING: Clifford 60-130/726y, 4TD, 46.2%
RECEIVING: Friede 17/412y, Johnson 14/103y, Powers 12/136y
SCORING: David Freud (K) 52pts, Harkrader 42pts, Burnett 30pts

1979 8-4

30 Iowa	26 WR Mike Friede / Al Darring
44 Vanderbilt	13 WR Nate Lundy / Steve Corso
18 Kentucky	10 T Marlon Flemming / Mark Johnson
16 Colorado	17 G Jeff Phipps
3 Wisconsin	0 C Lucky Wallace / Kevin Speer
6 Ohio State	47 G Jeff Goldin
30 Northwestern	0 T Gerhard Ahting
21 Michigan	27 TE Bob Stephenson
42 Minnesota	24 QB Tim Clifford
45 Illinois	14 TB Lonnie Johnson / Mike Harkrader
21 Purdue	37 FB Tony D'Orazio
38 BYU37	DL Brent Tisdale
	DL Mark Rodriguez / Martin Young
	DL Terry Tallen / Robert Iatarola
	DL Ken Ball / Rodney Walden
	DL Eric DeBord / David Stewart
	LB Craig Walls
	LB Randy Willhite
	DB Tim Wilbur
	DB Stoner Gray / Marc Longshore
	DB Chuck Alexander
	DB Dart Ramsey / Steve Mitchell

RUSHING: Harkrader 210/807y, Johnson 172/708y,
D'Orazio 70/281y
PASSING: Clifford 160-288/2078y, 13TD, 55.6
RECEIVING: Stephenson 49/564y, Friede 19/346y,
Johnson 17/202y
SCORING: Johnson 54pts, Clifford 48pts, Harkrader 42pts

1980 6-5

7 Iowa	16 WR Steve Corso
38 Kentucky	30 WR Nate Lundy
49 Colorado	7 T Gerald Michko / Mark Rodriguez
31 Duke	21 G Jeff Goldin
24 Wisconsin	0 C Lucky Wallace / Kevin Speer
17 Ohio State	27 G Chuck Gannon / John Taylor
35 Northwestern	20 T Gerhard Ahting
0 Michigan	35 TE Bob Stephenson / Dave Harangody
7 Minnesota	31 QB Tim Clifford / Chad Huck
26 Illinois	24 TB Lonnie Johnson / Mike Harkrader
23 Purdue	24 FB Jerry Bowers / John Mineo
	DL Jimmy Hunter / Steve Rohe
	DL Greg Brown / Brent Tisdale
	DL Denver Smith / Ken Ball
	DL Rod Walden / Mark Smythe
	DL Craig Kumerow / Lou Cristofoli
	LB Craig Walls / Kevin Kenley
	LB Marlin Evans / Terry Tallen
	DB Tim Wilbur
	DB Mike Pendleton / Dave Weir
	DB Steve Mitchell
	DB Dart Ramsey / Chuck Alexander

RUSHING: Johnson 200/1075y, Harkrader 118/567y,
Bowers 40/211y
PASSING: Clifford 105-198/1391y, 13TD, 53%
RECEIVING: Stephenson 26/337y, Corso 22/362y, Lundy 19/459y
SCORING: Johnson 66pts, Kevin Kellogg (K) 47pts, Lundy 24pts

1981 3-8

21 Northwestern	20 WR Todd Shroyer
0 Southern Cal	21 WR Duane Gunn
7 Syracuse	21 T Chuck Gannon
17 Michigan	38 G Jim Sakanich
28 Iowa	42 C Jeff Wiebell
17 Minnesota	16 G Mark Filburn
10 Ohio State	29 T Mark Rodriguez
3 Michigan State	26 TE Bob Stephenson
7 Wisconsin	28 QB Babe Laufenberg
14 Illinois	35 TB John Roggeman / Tim Hines
20 Purdue	17 FB John Mingo / Jack Walsh
	DL Craig Kumerow
	DL Greg Brown
	DL Marty Young
	DL Rod Walden
	DL Jimmy Hunter
	LB Craig Walls
	LB Ralph Caldwell / Mark Weiler
	DB Marc Longshore
	DB Mike Pendleton
	DB Steve Mitchell
	DB Dart Ramsey

RUSHING: Hines 67/271y, Roggeman 88/268y, Walsh 50/209y
PASSING: Laufenberg 144-252/1788y, 8 TD, 57.1%
RECEIVING: Stephenson 32/280y, Gunn 31/656y,
Roggeman 20/228y
SCORING: Gunn 30pts, Mike Greenstein (K), Doug Smith (K)
& Laufenberg 18pts

1982 5-6

30 Northwestern	0 WR Duane Gunn
7 Southern Cal	28 WR John Boyd / Terry Smith
17 Syracuse	10 T Kevin Allen / Chuck Gannon
10 Michigan	24 G Mark Filburn / Tom Van Dyck
20 Iowa	24 C Dennis Mills / Jeff Wiebell
40 Minnesota	21 G Jim Sakanich
25 Ohio State	49 T Mark Rodriguez
14 Michigan State	22 TE Scot McNabb / Chris Cook
20 Wisconsin	17 QB Babe Laufenberg
7 Illinois	48 TB Orlando Brown / Bobby Howard
13 Purdue	7 FB Jack Walsh / Johnnie Salters
	DL Jimmy Hunter
	DL Steve Moorman
	DL Denver Smith
	DL Mark Smythe
	DL Kevin King / Dennis Edwards
	LB Marlin Evans / Ralph Caldwell
	LB Mark Weiler
	DB Marc Longshore / Jeff McBain
	DB Tim Wilbur / Jeff Gedman
	DB Mark Sutor
	DB Tom Hendrickson / Chris Sigler

RUSHING: Brown 136/580y, Walsh 71/297y, Howard 57/199y
PASSING: Laufenberg 217-364/2468y, 11 TD, 59.6%
RECEIVING: Gunn 136/764y, McNabb 33/361y, Brown 33/238y
SCORING: Brown 48pts, Doug Smith (K) 43pts, Gunn 38pts

1983 3-8

15 Duke	10 WR Duane Gunn
13 Kentucky	24 WR Len Kenebrew / Stephan Benson
8 Northwestern	10 T Kevin Allen
18 Michigan	43 G Mark Filburn
38 Minnesota	31 C Tom Van Dyck / Mike Anderson
24 Michigan State	12 G Jim Sakanich
14 Wisconsin	45 T George Gianakopoulos / Bob Sikora
3 Iowa	49 TE Scot McNabb
17 Ohio State	56 QB Steve Bradley
21 Illinois	49 TB Bobby Howard / Orlando Brown
30 Purdue	31 FB Jack Walsh / Johnnie Salters
	DL Mark Smythe
	DL Dave Zyzda / Vince Fisher
	DL Rob Schmit / Steve May / Tim Eckert
	LB Dennis Edwards / Mark Claahsen
	LB Lou Cristofoli / Van Waiters
	LB Leonard Bell / Dave Kinniry
	LB Joe Fitzgerald
	DB Nate Borders
	DB Jeff McBain
	DB Tom Hendrickson
	DB Chris Sigler

RUSHING: Brown 72/312y, Howard 85/ 309y, Salters 37/151y
PASSING: Bradley 182-355/2298y, 14TD, 51.3%
RECEIVING: Gunn 50/815y, Kenebrew 47/687y, McNabb 23/201y
SCORING: Doug Smith (K) 43pts, Gunn 40pts, Kenebrew 36pts

1984 0-11

24 Duke	31 WR Ernie Jones / Terry Smith
14 Kentucky	48 WR Len Kenebrew
37 Northwestern	40 T Kevin Allen
6 Michigan	14 G Jerry Paige
24 Minnesota	33 C Tom Van Dyck
6 Michigan State	13 G Jeff Lemirande
16 Wisconsin	20 T Bob Riley
20 Iowa	24 TE Dave Lilja / Chris Cook
7 Ohio State	50 QB Steve Bradley
7 Illinois	34 TB Bobby Howard / Alex Green
24 Purdue	31 FB Jack Walsh / Tom Polce
	DL Rob Schmit
	DL Vince Fisher
	DL Tom Weidenbenner
	LB Lou Cristofoli
	LB Charles Mallory
	LB Mark Weiler
	LB Joe Fitzgerald
	DB Nate Borders
	DB Mike Pendleton
	DB Chris Sigler
	DB Leonard Bell

RUSHING: Howard 78/268y, Orlando Brown (TB) 42/176y, Green 68/168y
PASSING: Bradley 208-402/2544y, 10TD, 51.7%
RECEIVING: Kenebrew 41/750y, Jones 26/408y, Smith 25/317y
SCORING: Mark Rogers (K) 37pts, Orlando Brown (TB) 24pts, Lilja 18pts

1985 4-7

41 Louisville	28 WR Kenny Allen
38 Navy	35 WR Stacy Dawsey / Ernie Jones
36 Missouri	17 T Bob Riley
26 Northwestern	7 G Tim Radtke
7 Ohio State	48 C Dave Kinniry
7 Minnesota	22 G Don Schrader / Jeff Lemirande
15 Michigan	42 T Eric Moore
20 Wisconsin	31 TE Dave Lilja
16 Michigan State	35 QB Steve Bradley / Dave Kramme
24 Illinois	41 TB Bobby Howard / Damon Sweazy
21 Purdue	34 FB Tom Polce
	DL Rob Schmit / Dan Bauer
	DL Vince Fisher / Mike McCurry
	DL Tom Weidenbenner
	LB Joe Ford / Van Waiters
	LB Brad Mitchell / Tom Houts
	LB Willie Bates / Brad Money
	LB Steve May
	DB Erick Coleman / Efren Edwards
	DB Alex Green / Rob VanVliet
	DB Leonard Bell
	DB Jeff Wade

RUSHING: Howard 194/967y, Sweazy 109/421y, Polce 67/337y
PASSING: Bradley 142-266/1737y, 11TD, 53.4%
RECEIVING: Allen 55/929y, Lilja 43/540y, Howard 25/169y
SCORING: Howard 42pts, Seazy 36pts, Pete Stoyanovich (K) 30pts

1986 6-6

21 Louisville	0 WR Tony Buford / Kenny Allen
52 Navy	29 WR Stacy Dawsey / Ernie Jones
41 Missouri	24 T Eric Moore
24 Northwestern	7 G Don Schrader / Joe Dedic
22 Ohio State	24 C Dave Kinniry
17 Minnesota	19 G Tim Radtke / Brian Finney
14 Michigan	38 T Bob Riley
21 Wisconsin	7 TE Dave Lilja
17 Michigan State	14 QB Brian Dewitz / Dave Kramme
16 Illinois	21 TB Anthony Thompson / Damon Sweazy
15 Purdue	17 FB Tom Polce
13 Florida State	27 DL Dan Bauer
	DL Larry Luther
	DL Doug Schlereth / Walt Harris
	LB Joe Huff
	LB Brad Mitchell
	LB Willie Bates
	LB Van Walters
	DB Eric Hickerson
	DB Erick Coleman
	DB Leonard Bell
	DB Alex Green

RUSHING: Thompson 191/806y, Sweazy 116/545y, Spud Washington (TB) 41/204y
PASSING: Kramme 98-180/1334y, 6TD, 54.4%
RECEIVING: Buford 26/416y, Jones 25/483y, Dawsey 22/469y
SCORING: Pete Stoyanovich (K) 63pts, Sweazy 36pts, Dewitz 30pts

1987 8-4

35 Rice	13 WR Ernie Jones
15 Kentucky	34 WR Kenny Allen
20 Missouri	17 T Eric Moore
35 Northwestern	18 G Tim Radtke
31 Ohio State	10 C Brian Finney
18 Minnesota	17 G Don Shrader
14 Michigan	10 T Chris Simons
21 Iowa	29 TE Tim Jorden
34 Illinois	22 QB Dave Schnell
3 Michigan State	27 TB Anthony Thompson
35 Purdue	14 FB Tom Polce
22 Tennessee	27 DL Walt Harris / Nolan Harrison
	DL Dan Bauer / Jim Sams
	DL Doug Schlereth
	LB Joe Huff
	LB Darren Bush / Brad Money
	LB Willie Bates
	LB Van Walters
	DB Joe Ziegler
	DB Eric Hickerson
	DB Marc Ferry / Andre Hall
	DB Brian Dewitz

RUSHING: Thompson 257/1014y, Polce 40/184y
PASSING: Schnell 121-207/1707y, 13TD, 58.5%
RECEIVING: Jones 66/1265y, Jorden 31/351y, Thompson 26/242y
SCORING: Jones 78pts, Thompson 72pts, Pete Stoyanovich (K) 59pts

1988 8-3-1

41 Rice	14 WR Tony Buford
36 Kentucky	15 WR Rob Turner / Gary Gooden
28 Missouri	28 T Jeff Fryar / Phil Trinter
48 Northwestern	17 G Tim Radtke
41 Ohio State	7 C Ron Vargo
33 Minnesota	13 G Don Shrader
6 Michigan	31 T Chris Simons
45 Iowa	34 TE Tim Jorden
20 Illinois	21 QB Dave Schnell
12 Michigan State	38 TB Anthony Thompson
52 Purdue	7 FB Cal Miller / Gene Boyd
34 South Carolina	10 DL Walt Harris
	DL Dan Bauer / Jim Sams
	DL Doug Schlereth
	LB Joe Huff
	LB Willie Bates
	LB Brad Money / Paul Williams
	LB Terry Saunders
	DB Erick Coleman / Andre Hall
	DB Mike Dumas
	DB Marc Ferry
	DB Brian Dewitz

RUSHING: Thompson 355/1686y, Schnell 83/307y, Miller 50/277y
PASSING: Schnell 119-225/1877y, 9TD, 52.9%
RECEIVING: Turner 36/814y, Buford 30/564y, Jorden 25/298y
SCORING: Thompson 156pts, Pete Stoyanovich (K) 96pts, Turner 48pts

1989 5-6

14 Kentucky	17 WR Eddie Thomas
24 Missouri	7 WR Scott McGowan / Todd Walker
32 Toledo	12 T Randy Schneider / Phil Trinter
43 Northwestern	11 G Jeff Marx / Jack Francis
31 Ohio State	35 C Ron Vargo
28 Minnesota	18 G Ian Beckles
10 Michigan	38 T Todd Oberdorf
20 Michigan State	51 TE Terry Saunders
45 Wisconsin	17 QB Dave Schnell
28 Illinois	41 TB Anthony Thompson
14 Purdue	15 FB Cal Miller
	DL Nolan Harrison
	DL Larry McDaniel / Jason Mack
	DL Brian Hunnicut
	LB Greg Farrall
	LB Paul Williams / Gene Boyd
	LB Mark Hagen
	LB Troy Mason
	DB Mike Middleton
	DB Mike Dumas
	DB Dave Ane
	DB Joe Ziegler / Mark Newell

RUSHING: Thompson 358/1793y, Miller 44/221y, Schnell 94/188y
PASSING: Schnell 146-258/1608y, 4TD, 56.6%
RECEIVING: Thomas 38/559y, Thompson 35/201y, McGowan 15/284y
SCORING: Thompson 154pts, Scott Bonnell (K) 61pts, Schnell 24pts

1990 6-5-1

45 Kentucky	24 WR Rob Turner
58 Missouri	7 WR Scott McGowan / Eddie Thomas
37 E. Michigan	6 T Randy Schneider
42 Northwestern	0 G Todd Smith / Jim Hannon
27 Ohio State	27 C Jason Mack / Scott Boatman
0 Minnesota	12 G Troy Newton / Steve Fiacable
19 Michigan	45 T Shawn Harper / Phil Trinter
20 Michigan State	45 TE Todd Walker
20 Wisconsin	7 QB Trent Green / Chris Dyer
10 Illinois	24 TB Vaughn Dunbar
28 Purdue	14 FB Cal Miller / Ernie Thompson
23 Auburn	27 DL Brian Hunnicut
	DL Larry McDaniel
	DL Chris McCoy
	LB Charles Beauchamp / Troy Mason
	LB Mark Hagen
	LB John Miller / Matt Egenolf
	LB Greg Farrall
	DB Mike Middleton
	DB Mose Richardson
	DB Mike Dumas
	DB Dave Ane / Jim Summerall

RUSHING: Dunbar 250/1224y, Thompson 73/323y, Miller 66/304y
PASSING: Green 60-128/934y, 4TD, 46.9%
Dyer 51-102/701y, 3TD, 50%
RECEIVING: Turner 33/717y, Thomas 18/285y, McGowan 16/228y
SCORING: Dunbar 78pts, Scott Bonnell (K) 74pts, Turner 48pts

1991 7-4-1

27 Notre Dame	49 WR Scott McGowan / Eddie Baety
13 Kentucky	10 WR Thomas Lewis / Eddie Thomas
27 Missouri	27 T Shawn Harper
31 Michigan State	0 G Jim Hannon / Todd Smith
44 Northwestern	6 C Jason Mack
16 Michigan	24 G Troy Newton
28 Wisconsin	20 T Randy Schneider
34 Minnesota	8 TE Rod Coleman
21 Iowa	38 QB Trent Green
16 Ohio State	20 TB Vaughn Dunbar
24 Purdue	22 FB Todd Walker / Corey Taylor
24 Baylor	0 DL Charles Beauchamp
	DL Larry McDaniel
	DL Hurvin McCormack / Matt Bomba
	DL Greg Farrall / Troy Mason
	LB Mark Hagen
	LB Paul Williams
	LB John Miller
	DB Mike Middleton
	DB Mose Richardson
	DB Damon Watts
	DB Jim Summerall

RUSHING: Dunbar 364/1805y, Green 115/202y, Brett Law (TB) 36/169y
PASSING: Green 200-339/2627y, 12TD, 59%
RECEIVING: Thomas 54/687y, Lewis 39/581y, Coleman 33/412y
SCORING: Green 78pts, Dunbar 72pts, Scott Bonnell (K) 71pts

1992 5-6

16 Miami (Ohio)	0 WR Scott McGowan
25 Kentucky	37 WR Thomas Lewis
20 Missouri	10 T Chris Smith
31 Michigan State	42 G Todd Smith
28 Northwestern	3 C Josh DeWitt / Rod Carey
3 Michigan	31 G Jim Hannon / Andrew Greene
10 Wisconsin	3 T Tom McKinnon
24 Minnesota	17 TE Ross Hales
0 Iowa	14 QB Trent Green
10 Ohio State	27 TB Brett Law / Emmett Pride / Michael Batts
10 Purdue	13 FB Louis Pinnock / Tobi Kerns / Eddie Baety
	DL Lamar Mills / Charles Beauchamp
	DL Larry McDaniel / Matt Bomba
	DL Hurvin McCormack
	DL Bernard Whittington
	LB John Miller / Steve Perkins
	LB Alfonzo Thurman
	LB Jay Davis
	DB Mose Richardson / Jason Orton
	DB Mike Middleton
	DB Damon Watts
	DB Chris Dyer / Lance Brown

RUSHING: Law 130/541y, Pride 58/254y, Chaney 67/204y
PASSING: Green 154-278/1780y, 7TD, 55.4%
RECEIVING: Lewis 54/685y, Baety 39/398y, Hales 34/375y
SCORING: Scott Bonnell (K) 55pts, Lewis 36pts, Law 18pts

1993 8-4

27	Toledo	0	WR	Eddie Baety / Greg Hobbs
28	Northern Illinois	10	WR	Thomas Lewis
24	Kentucky	8	T	Tom McKinnon / Chris Smith
15	Wisconsin	27	G	Todd Smith / Tom Lukawski
23	Minnesota	19	C	Rod Carey
16	Iowa	10	G	Andrew Greene
24	Northwestern	0	T	Clay Williams
10	Michigan State	0	TE	Ross Hales / Dan Thompson
31	Penn State	38	QB	John Paci
17	Ohio State	23	TB	Jermaine Chaney / Brett Law
24	Purdue	17	FB	Sean Glover
20	Virginia Tech	45	DL	Bernard Whittington

DL Troy Drake
DL Hurvin McCormack / John Hammerstein
DL Lamar Mills
LB Charles Beauchamp
LB Alfonzo Thurman
LB Jay Davis / Trevor Wilmot
DB Mose Richardson
DB Jason Orton / Damon Watts
DB Lance Brown / Steve Perkins
DB Chris Dyer

RUSHING: Chaney 186/716y, Michael Batts (TB) 56/246y, Law 53/205y
PASSING: Paci 133-258/1796y, 8TD, 51.6%
RECEIVING: Lewis 55/1058y, Glover 27/186y, Baety 26/348y
SCORING: Bill Manolopoulos (K) 77pts, Lewis 48pts, Chaney 36pts

1994 7-4

28	Cincinnati	3	WR	Eddie Baety
35	Miami (Ohio)	14	WR	Eric Matthews
59	Kentucky	29	T	Chris Smith
13	Wisconsin	62	G	Tom Lukawski
27	Minnesota	20	C	Jay Seib
27	Iowa	20	G	Andrew Greene
7	Northwestern	20	T	Clay Williams / Chris Liwienski
21	Mich. St (F-W)	27	TE/WR	Tom McKinnon / Ajamu Stoner
29	Penn State	35	QB	John Paci / Chris Dittoe
17	Ohio State	32	TB	Alex Smith
33	Purdue	29	FB	Steve Lee

DL Louis Pinnock
DL John Hammerstein
DL Troy Drake
DL Nathan Davis
LB Trevor Wilmot / Jaime Baisley
LB Derrick Terrell
LB Alfonzo Thurman
DB Kris Mucci
DB Eric Smedley
DB Lance Brown
DB Aaron Warnecke

RUSHING: Smith 265/1475y, Jermaine Chaney (TB) 49/330y, Brett Law (TB) 39/219y
PASSING: Paci 96-176/996y, 6TD, 54.5%
RECEIVING: Baety 45/559y, Stoner 29/409y, Smith 17/115y
SCORING: Smith 60pts, Bill Manolopoulos (K) & Paci 50pts

1995 2-9

24	W. Michigan	10	WR	Ajamu Stoner
10	Kentucky	17	WR	Eric Matthews / Dorian Wilkerson
27	S. Mississippi	26	T	Chris Liwienski / Greg Jenkins
7	Northwestern	31	G	Tom Lukawski
10	Illinois	17	C	Jay Seib
13	Iowa	22	G	Mike Mihelic / George Batalis
17	Michigan	34	T	Clay Williams
21	Penn State	45	TE	Darin Ward / Ben Klusmeyer
13	Michigan State	31	QB	Chris Dittoe / Adam Greenlee
3	Ohio State	42	TB	Alex Smith / Sean Glover
14	Purdue	51	FB	Steve Lee

DL Louis Pinnock
DL John Hammerstein / Jason Kaylor
DL Victor Allotey / Eli Rasheed
DL Nathan Davis
LB Jabar Robinson / Jon Pilch
LB Jamie Baisley / Saute Dean
LB Matt Surface
DB Eric Allen / Joe King
DB Joey Eloms
DB Eric Smedley
DB Aaron Warnecke

RUSHING: Smith 166/769y, Glover 120/395y, Michael Batts (TB) 49/163y
PASSING: Dittoe 102-196/1214y, 3TD, 52%
RECEIVING: Glover 33/239y, Stoner 29/412y, Matthews 29/371y
SCORING: Bill Manolopoulos (K) 37pts, Dittoe 24pts, Glover & Smith 18pts

1996 3-8

40	Toledo	6	WR	Ajamu Stoner / Craig Goode
21	Miami (Ohio)	14	WR	Darian Wilkerson / Darin Ward
0	Kentucky	3	T	Khalfani Banks / Greg Jenkins
17	Northwestern	35	G	Tom Lukawski
43	Illinois	46	C	Jay Seib
10	Iowa	31	G	George Batalis
20	Michigan	27	T	Chris Liwienski
26	Penn State	48	TE	Ben Klusmeyer / Randy Maxwell
15	Michigan State	38	QB	Chris Dittoe / Jay Rodgers
17	Ohio State	27	TB	Alex Smith / John Spear
33	Purdue	16	FB	Steve Lee

DL Adewale Ogunleye / Aaron Williams
DL Benyard Jones
DL Damien Gregory
DL Nathan Davis
LB Matt Surface
LB Jaime Baisley
LB Jabar Robinson
DB Joe King
DB Pat Shaw / Joey Eloms
DB Eric Allen / Kywin Supernaw
DB Aaron Warnecke

RUSHING: Smith 292/1248y, Spear 59/226y
PASSING: Dittoe 83-159/1035y, 3TD, 52.2%
RECEIVING: Wilkerson 40/490y, Stoner 33/417y, Ward 23/205y
SCORING: Bill Manolopoulos (K) 62pts, Smith 48pts, Rodgers & Spear 24pts

1997 2-9

6	North Carolina	23	WR	O.J. Conner
33	Ball State	6	WR	Tyrone Browning / Dorian Wilkerson
7	Kentucky	49	T	Chris Liwienski
26	Wisconsin	27	G	Victor Allotey
0	Michigan	37	C	Chris Lee
6	Michigan State	38	G	Khalfani Banks
0	Ohio State	31	T	Craig Robeen
0	Iowa	62	TE	Randy Maxwell / Ben Klusmeyer
23	Illinois	6	QB	Jay Rodgers
12	Minnesota	24	TB	De'Wayne Hogan / Jason Spear
7	Purdue	56	FB	Chris Gall

DL Adewale Ogunleye
DL Benyard Jones
DL Damien Gregory
DL Aaron Williams
LB Jason Czap / James Lamar
LB Jabar Robinson
LB Aaron Warnecke / Joslin Goodman
DB Joey Eloms
DB Joe King
DB Kywin Supernaw
DB Curtis Randle El / Pat Shaw

RUSHING: Hogan 148/503y, Spear 103/338y, Glynn Johnson (TB) 37/162y
PASSING: Rodgers 192-330/2156y, 6TD, 58.2%
RECEIVING: Gall 54/422y, Spear 33/289y, Conner 28/520y
SCORING: Andy Payne (K) 53pts, Hogan 24pts, Gall & Conner 12pts

1998 4-7

45	W. Michigan	10	WR	Versie Gaddis / Levron Williams
27	Kentucky	31	WR	Tyrone Browning
48	Cincinnati	14	T	Pita Elisara
20	Wisconsin	24	G	Matt Snyder
31	Michigan State	38	C	Chad Miller
14	Iowa	7	G	James Broyles
10	Michigan	21	T	Craig Robeen
7	Ohio State	38	TE	C. Osika/Bryan Bobay/Sterling Mintzer
16	Illinois	31	QB	Antwaan Randle El
20	Minnesota	19	TB	Marcus Floyd / Frankie Franklin
7	Purdue	52	FB	Chris Gall

DL Adewale Ogunleye
DL Damien Gregory / Paul Mandina
DL Jason Czap
DL Aaron Williams
LB Tony Brown / Devan Schaffer
LB Jabar Robinson
LB/DB Brad Gecina / Maurice Tucker
DB O.J. Spencer / Sharrod Wallace
DB Curtis Randle El
DB Michael McGrath
DB Justin Smith / Greg Yeldell

RUSHING: Randle El 227/873y, Franklin 69/386y, Gall 74/329y
PASSING: Randle El 127-273/1745y, 6TD, 46.5%
RECEIVING: Browning 47/764y, Gall 30/243y, Williams 15/323y
SCORING: Randle El 66pts, Andy Payne (K) 57pts, Gall 48pts

1999 4-7

21	Ball State	9	WR	Jerry Dorsey / Derin Graham
30	North Carolina	42	WR	Versie Gaddis
35	Kentucky	44	T	Craig Robeen
24	Penn State	45	G	Enoch DeMar
34	Illinois	31	C	Matt Snyder / Chad Miller
34	Northwestern	17	G	Jamarkus Gorman / James Broyles
0	Wisconsin	59	T	Craig Robeen
38	Iowa	31	TE	Craig Osika
31	Michigan	34	QB	Antwaan Randle El
20	Minnesota	44	TB	Levron Williams / Frankie Franklin
24	Purdue	30	FB	De'Wayne Hogan / Jeremi Johnson

DL Adewale Ogunleye / Sean Nelson
DL Paul Mandina
DL Jason Czap
DL Kemp Rasmussen
LB/DB Joslin Goodman / John Anderson
LB Devan Schaffer / Herman Fowler
LB Justin Smith
DB Maurice Tucker / O.J. Spencer
DB Sharrod Wallace / Curtis Randle El
DB Michael McGrath
DB Greg Yeldell

RUSHING: Williams 118/817y, Randle El 224/788y, Johnson 69/282y
PASSING: Randle El 150-279/2277y, 17TD, 53.8%
RECEIVING: Gaddis 35/633y, Williams 33/360y, Dorsey 31/602y
SCORING: Randle El 78pts, Andy Payne (K) 63pts, Williams 42pts

2000 3-8

38	N. Carolina St.	41	WR	Jerry Dorsey
34	Kentucky	41	WR	Versie Gaddis
42	Cincinnati	6	T	A. C. Myler
45	Iowa	33	G	Anthony Oakley
33	Northwestern	52	C	Craig Osika
0	Michigan	58	G	Sione Ohuafi
51	Minnesota	43	T	Enoch DeMar
24	Penn State	27	TE	Bobby Brandt
35	Illinois	42	QB	Antwaan Randle El
22	Wisconsin	43	TB	Levron Williams / Brian Lewis
13	Purdue	41	FB	De'Wayne Hogan

DL Derek Bryant
DL Paul Mandina
DL Dominique Smith / Jamil Frink
DL Kemp Rasmussen
LB Justin Smith
LB Joslin Goodman / Scott Genord
LB Devan Schaffer
DB Duane Stone / Marcus Floyd
DB Sharrod Wallace / Joe Gnzalez
DB Ron Bethel
DB Johnny Anderson

RUSHING: Randle El 218/1270y, Williams 116/821y, Lewis 67/373y
PASSING: Randle El 133-277/1783y, 10TD, 48%
RECEIVING: Gaddis 29/554y, Dorsey 27/514y, Williams 20/116y
SCORING: Randle El 78pts, Andy Payne (K) 65pts, Williams 60pts

2001 5-6

14	N. Carolina St.	35	WR	Glenn Johnson / Courtney Roby
26	Utah	28	WR	Travis Haney / Henry Frazier
14	Ohio State	27	T	A.C. Myler
63	Wisconsin	32	G	Anthony Oakley
14	Illinois	35	C	Craig Osika
28	Iowa	42	G	Enoch DeMar
56	Northwestern	21	T	Bobby Brandt
37	Michigan State	28	TE	Kris Dielman / Aaron Halterman
14	Penn State	28	QB	Antwaan Randle El (WR) / Tom Jones
13	Purdue	7	RB	Levron Williams
26	Kentucky	15	FB	Jeremi Johnson

DL Kemp Rasmussen
DL Dominique Smith
DL Colin Christopher / Jamil Frink
DL Derek Barnett
LB Justin Smith
LB Devin Schaffer / Herana-Daze Jones
LB Ron Bethel/Brandonn Baker/Rob Brown
DB Michael Hanley / Marcus Floyd
DB Sharrod Wallace
DB Ron Bethel / A.C. Carter
DB Joe Gonzalez

RUSHING: Williams 212/1,401y, Randle El 188/964y, Johnson 95/546y
PASSING: Randle El 118-231/1664y, 9TD, 51.1%
RECEIVING: Williams 26/289y, Johnson 21/229y, Frazier 16/271y
SCORING: Williams 114pts, Johnson & Randle El 48pts

2002 3-9

25 William & Mary
13 Utah
17 Kentucky
39 C. Michigan
17 Ohio State
32 Wisconsin
8 Iowa
14 Illinois
17 Northwestern
21 Michigan State
25 Penn State
10 Purdue

17 WR Glenn Johnson
40 WR Courtney Ray
27 T Enoch DeMar
29 G A.C. Myler / Anthony Oakley (C)
45 C Chris Jahnke
29 G Adam Hines
24 T Bobby Brandt
45 TE Aaron Halterman
41 QB Gibran Hamdan / Tommy Jones
56 RB Yamar Washington / Brian Lewis
58 FB/TE John Pannozzo / Stephen Anthony
34 DL Victory Adeyanju / Derek Barnett
DL Kris Dielman
DL Russ Richardson / Colin Christopher
DL Jodie Clemons
LB Herana-Daze Jones / Ron Bethel
LB John Kerr
LB Kevin Smith / Kyle Killion
DB Damien Jones / Duane Stone
DB Antonio Watson
DB Buster Larkins / Joe Gonzalez
DB A.C. Carter

RUSHING: Washington 174/688y, Lewis 104/458y,
Chris Taylor (RB) 48/229y
PASSING: Hamdan 152-293/2115y, 9TD, 51.9%
RECEIVING: Roby 59/1039y, Johnson 53/837y,
Halterman 27/292y
SCORING: Washington 54pts, Bryan Robertson (K) 50pts,
Johnson 30pts

2003 2-10

10 Connecticut
13 Washington
33 Indiana State
17 Kentucky
17 Michigan
3 Michigan State
31 Northwestern
6 Ohio State
7 Minnesota
17 Illinois
7 Penn State
16 Purdue

34 WR Glenn Johnson
38 WR Courtney Roby
3 T Isaac Sowells
34 G Adam Hines
31 C Chris Mangiero / Brandon Hatcher
31 G Chris Jahnke
37 T Justin Frye
35 TE Aaron Halterman / Chris Rudanovic
55 QB Matt LoVecchio
14 RB Brian Lewis/Chris Taylor/B. Green-Ellis
52 FB John Pannozzo
24 DL Victor Adeyanju
DL Martin Lapostolle / Courtney Young
DL Jodie Clemons
DL Kenny Kendal
LB Josh Moore / Jake Powers
LB Kyle Killion
LB/DB Kevin Smith / Buster Larkins
DB Duane Stone
DB Cedric Henry / Leonard Bryant
DB Joe Gonzalez / Will Lumpkin
DB Herana-Daze Jones / Will Meyers

RUSHING: Green-Ellis 225/938y, Taylor 116/464y, Lewis 90/398y
PASSING: LoVecchio 155-291/1778y, 3TD, 53.3%
RECEIVING: Roby 45/504y, Johnson 36/436y, Halterman 23/230y
SCORING: Bryan Robertson (K) 55pts, Green-Ellis 48pts,
Taylor 24pts

2004 3-8

41 C. Michigan
30 Oregon
32 Kentucky
20 Michigan State
14 Michigan
24 Northwestern
7 Ohio State
30 Minnesota
22 Illinois
18 Penn State
24 Purdue

10 WR Travis Haney
24 WR Courtney Roby
51 T Adam Hines (G) / Isaac Sowells
30 G Chris Voltattorni
35 C Brandon Hatcher / Chris Mangiero
31 G Chris Jahnke
30 T Justin Frye
21 TE Aaron Halterman / Chris Rudanovic
26 QB Matt LoVecchio
22 RB BenJarvus Green-Ellis / Chris Taylor
63 FB/WR John Pannozzo / David Lewis
DL Victor Adeyanju
DL Jodie Clemons
DL Russ Richardson / Martin LaPostolle
DL Kenny Kendal
LB Paul Szczesny
LB Kyle Killion
LB Jake Powers
DB Buster Larkins
DB Leslie Majors / Tracy Porter
DB Herana-Daze Jones
DB Will Meyers/ W. Lumpkin/Aaron Mitchell

RUSHING: Green-Ellis 231/794y, Taylor 82/329y
PASSING: LoVecchio 153-271/1951y, 13TD, 56.5%
RECEIVING: Roby 55/810y, Gilmore 23/308y, Lewis 17/183y
SCORING: Roby 54pts, Bryan Robertson (K) 48pts,
Green-Ellis 32pts

2005 4-7

20 C. Michigan
35 Nicholls State
38 Kentucky
24 Wisconsin
36 Illinois
21 Iowa
10 Ohio State
15 Michigan State
21 Minnesota
14 Michigan
14 Purdue

13 WR Jahkeen Gilmore / James Bailey
31 WR James Hardy / B. Walker-Roby
14 WR Marcus Thigpen
41 T Isaac Sowells
13 G Adam Hines
38 C Chris Mangiero
41 G Brandon Hatcher
46 T Justin Frye (G) / Scott Anderson
42 TE Matt O'Neal
41 QB Blake Powers
41 RB Chris Taylor / Yamar Washington
DL Victor Adeyanju
DL Russ Richardson / Joe Kremer
DL Charlie Emerson / Greg Brown
DL Ben Ishola / Kenny Kendal
LB Geno Johnson / Josh Moore
LB John Pannozzo / Jake Powers
LB Kyle Killion
DB Leslie Majors
DB Tracy Porter
DB Troy Grosfield / Will Lumpkin
DB Will Meyers (LB) / Aaron Mitchell

RUSHING: Taylor 156/740y, Washington 127/443y,
Powers 100/121y
PASSING: Powers 212-376/2305y, 22TD, 56.4%
RECEIVING: Hardy 61/893y, Thigpen 32/432y, Gilmore 30/383y
SCORING: Hardy 60pts, Joe Kleinsmith (K) 40pts, Powers
& Taylor 24pts

2006 5-7

39 W. Michigan
24 Ball State
28 S. Illinois
7 Connecticut
17 Wisconsin
34 Illinois
31 Iowa
3 Ohio State
46 Michigan State
26 Minnesota
3 Michigan
19 Purdue

20 WR Jahkeen Gilmore / Ray Fisher
23 WR J. Hardy / Brandon Walker-Roby
35 WR Nick Polk / James Bailey
14 T Rodger Saffold / Scott Anderson
52 G Kyle Thomas / Pete Saxon
32 C Justin Frye (T) / Chris Mangiero
28 G John Sandberg
44 T Charlie Emerson
21 TE/WR Matt O'Neal / Andrew Means
63 QB Kellen Lewis / Blake Powers
34 RB M. Thigpen / Demetrius McCray
28 DL Jammie Kirlew / Brian Faires
DL Joe Kremer / Todd Newman
DL Greg Brown
DL Kenny Kendal / Keith Burrus
LB Geno Johnson
LB Adam McClurg / Jake Powers
LB Josh Bailey / William Patterson
DB Chris Phillips / Leslie Majors
DB Tracy Porter
DB Will Meyers
DB Troy Grosfield / Austin Thomas

RUSHING: Lewis 124/441y, Thigpen 98/387y, McCray 88/320y
PASSING: Lewis 190-346/2221y, 14TD, 54.9%
RECEIVING: Hardy 61/772y, Bailey 40/401y, Polk 32/326y
SCORING: Austin Starr (K) 64pts, Hardy 60pts,
Thigpen 42pts

2007 7-6

55 Indiana State
37 W. Michigan
41 Akron
14 Illinois
38 Iowa
40 Minnesota
27 Michigan State
31 Penn State
3 Wisconsin
38 Ball State
28 Northwestern
27 Purdue
33 Oklahoma St.

7 WR James Hardy
27 WR Andrew Means
24 WR Ray Fisher / James Bailey
27 T Rodger Saffold
20 G Pete Saxon
20 C Ben Wyss
52 G John Sandberg (C)
36 T Charlie Emerson (G)/Mike Stark
33 TE/WR Nick Sexton/Terrance Turner
20 QB Kellen Lewis
31 RB Marcus Thigpen / Bryan Payton
24 DL Jammie Kirlew / Brian Faires
49 DL Joe Kremer / Kevin Burrus
DL Greg Brown / Keith Burrus
DL Greg Middleton
LB Will Patterson
LB Adam McClurg / Matt Mayberry
LB Geno Johnson / Justin Carrington
DB Leslie Majors / Chris Phillips
DB Tracy Porter / Joe Kleinsmith
DB Nick Polk
DB Austin Thomas / Mitchell Evans

RUSHING: Lewis 147/736y, Thigpen 138/568y, Payton 90/381y
PASSING: Lewis 265-462/3043y, 28TD, 60%
RECEIVING: Hardy 79/1125y, Fisher 52/482y, Means 48/559y
SCORING: Austin Starr (K) 111pts, Hardy 96pts, Lewis 60pts

2008 3-9

31 W. Kentucky
45 Murray State
20 Ball State
29 Michigan State
7 Minnesota
9 Iowa
13 Illinois
21 Northwestern
34 C. Michigan
20 Wisconsin
7 Penn State
10 Purdue

13 WR Terrance Turner / Damario Belcher
3 WR Andr. Means / Brandon Walker-Roby
42 WR Ray Fisher
42 T Rodger Saffold / Justin Pagan
16 G Pete Saxon (C) / Andrew McDonald
45 C Alex Perry (G) / Mike Reiter
55 G Cody Faulkner
19 T Mike Stark
37 TE Troy Wagner / Max Dedmond
55 QB Kellen Lewis / Ben Chappell
34 RB Marcus Thigpen / Bryan Payton
62 DL Jammie Kirlew
DL Deonte Mack / Keith Burrus
DL Greg Brown
DL Ryan Marando / Greg Middleton
LB Will Patterson / Tyler Replogle
LB Matt Mayberry
LB Geno Johnson
DB Richard Council / Christopher Phillips
DB Chris Adkins / Donnell Jones
DB Nick Polk / Brandon Mosley
DB Austin Thomas / Joe Kleinsmith

RUSHING: Thigpen 94/631y, Lewis 93/500y, Payton 79/339y
PASSING: Lewis 110-193/1131y, 6TD, 57%
Chappell 80-153/1001y, 4TD, 52.3%
RECEIVING: Fisher 42/373y, Means 34/450y, Turner 29/289y
SCORING: Austin Starr (K) 57pts, Thigpen 54pts, Fisher 30pts

2009 4-8

19 E. Kentucky
23 W. Michigan
38 Akron
33 Michigan
14 Ohio State
7 Virginia
27 Illinois
28 Northwestern
24 Iowa
28 Wisconsin
20 Penn State
21 Purdue

13 WR Terrance Turner
19 WR Tandon Doss / Mitchell Evans
21 T Rodger Saffold
36 G Justin Pagan
33 C Will Matte
47 G Pete Saxon / Mike Reiter
14 T James Brewer
29 TE Troy Wagner / Brian Zematis
42 TE/WR Max Dedmond / Demarlo Belcher
31 QB Ben Chappell
31 RB Darius Willis / Demetrius McCray
38 DL Greg Middleton
DL Adam Replogle
DL Larry Black
DL Jammie Kirlew
LB Will Patterson / Justin Carrington
LB Matt Mayberry
LB/DB Tyler Replogle / Collin Taylor
DB Richard Council / Adam Burks
DB Ray Fisher / Donnell Jones
DB Nick Polk
DB Austin Thomas

RUSHING: Willis 123/607y, McCray 60/290y,
Bryan Payton (RB) 40/290y
PASSING: Chappell 268-428/2941y, 17TD, 62.6%
RECEIVING: Doss 77/962y, Belcher 61/770y, Turner 46/443y,
Evans 33/366y
SCORING: Nick Freeland (K) 76pts, Willis & Doss 36pts

2010 5-7

51 Towson
38 W. Kentucky
35 Akron
35 Michigan
10 Ohio State
36 Arkansas State
13 Illinois
17 Northwestern
13 Iowa
20 Wisconsin
24 Penn State
34 Purdue

17 WR Terrance Turner
21 WR Tandon Doss / Duwyce Wilson
20 WR Demario Belcher
42 T Andrew McDonald
38 G Aaron Price / Marc Damisch (T)
34 C Will Matte
43 G Justin Pagan / Jordan Marquette
20 T James Brewer / Josh Hager
18 TE Ted Bolser / Max Dedmond
83 QB Ben Chappell
41 RB Trea Burgess / Darius Willis
31 DL Darius Johnson
DL Adam Replogle / Larry Black
DL Mick Mentzler / Nicholas Sliger
DL Terrance Thomas
LB Leon Beckum
LB Jeff Thomas / Chad Sherer
LB Tyler Replogle
DB Matt Ernest / Richard Council
DB Greg Heban / Adrian Burks
DB Donnell Jones
DB Mitchell Evans

RUSHING: Burgess 104/352y, Willis 64/278y, Doss 28/163y
PASSING: Chappell 302-483/3295y, 24TD, 62.5%
RECEIVING: Belcher 78/832y, Turner 67/681y, Doss 63/706y
SCORING: Mitch Ewald (K) 81pts, Doss 48pts, Willis & Bolser 30pts

IOWA

University of Iowa (Founded 1847)
Iowa City, Iowa
Nickname: Hawkeyes
Colors: Old Gold and Black
Stadium: Kinnick Stadium (1929) 70,585
Conference Affiliation: Big Ten (1899-present)

CAREER RUSHING YARDS	Attempts	Yards
Sedrick Shaw (1993-96)	837	4156
Ladell Betts (1998-01)	831	3686
Albert Young (2005-07)	660	3173
Tavian Banks (1994-97)	505	2977
Fred Russell (2001-03)	523	2760
Tony Stewart (1987-90)	532	2562
Owen Gill (1981-84)	489	2556
Ronnie Harmon (1982-85)	443	2271
Shonn Greene (2005-06, 2008)	376	2228
Eddie Phillips (19080-83)	465	2177

CAREER PASSING YARDS	Comp.-Att.	Yards
Chuck Long (1981-85)	782-1203	10461
Drew Tate (2003-06)	565-1090	8292
Ricky Stanzi (2007-10)	542-907	7377
Chuck Hartlieb (1986-88)	512-802	6934
Matt Rodgers (1988-91)	550-905	6725
Matt Sherman (1994-97)	448-776	6399
Kyle McCann (1998-01)	357-603	4349
Gary Snook (1963-65)	280-631	3738
Brad Banks (2001-02)	213-362	3155
Larry Lawrence (1968-69)	201-395	2987

CAREER RECEIVING YARDS	Catches	Yards
Derrell Johnson-Koulianos (2007-10)	173	2616
Tim Dwight (1994-97)	139	2271
Danan Hughes (1989-92)	146	2216
Ronnie Harmon (1982-85)	146	2045
Kevin Kasper (1997-00)	157	1974
Dave Moritz (1980-83)	109	1912
Kahlil Hill (1998-01)	152	1892
Clinton Solomon (2002-05)	118	1864
Harold Jasper (1991-94)	107	1863
Quinn Early (1984-87)	106	1845

SEASON RUSHING YARDS	Attempts	Yard
Shonn Greene (2008)	307	1850
Tavian Banks (1997)	260	1691
Sedrick Shaw (1995)	316	1477
Fred Russell (2003)	282	1355
Albert Young (2005)	249	1334

SEASON PASSING YARDS	Comp.-Att.	Yards
Chuck Hartlieb (1988)	288-460	3738
Chuck Long (1985)	260-388	3297
Chuck Hartlieb (1987)	217-334	3092
Ricky Stanzi (2010)	221-345	3004
Chuck Long (1984)	216-322	2871

SEASON RECEIVING YARDS	Catches	Yards
Keith Chappelle (1980)	64	1037
Kevin Kasper (2000)	82	1010
Quinn Early (1987)	63	1004
Maurice Brown (2002)	48	966
Karl Noonan (1964)	59	933

GAME RUSHING YARDS	Attempts	Yards
Tavian Banks (1997 vs. Tulsa)	29	314
Ed Podolak (1968 vs. Northwestern)	17	286
Sedrick Shaw (1995 vs. Michigan State)	42	250

GAME PASSING YARDS	Comp.-Att.	Yards
Chuck Hartlieb (1988 vs. Indiana)	44-60	558
Chuck Hartlieb (1987 vs. Northwestern)	25-32	471
Scott Mullen (1999 vs. Indiana)	36-60	426

GAME RECEIVING YARDS	Catches	Yards
Quinn Early (1987 vs. Northwestern)	10	256
Deven Harberts (1988 vs. Indiana)	11	233
Bill Happel (1985 vs. N. Illinois)	9	207

GREATEST COACH:

Hayden Fry was Texan through and through. In fact, Fry's great-great-grandfather fought alongside Sam Houston in the war against Mexico.

But Fry was also an adopted son of the Hawkeye State. Winning three Big Ten championships and 143 games for a program once given up for dead could have had keys to every city in the state (except perhaps Ames). So, although Fry was a high school football star for Odessa High, and played for Baylor, and taught Roy Orbison when he, Fry, was a young history teacher, and coached the defensive backs at Baylor, and was head coach at SMU and North Texas for 11 years, he was most associated with his adopted state.

Hired to rescue Iowa football in 1978—the program's last winning season came in 1960—Fry touched Iowa soil for the first time upon arriving for his interview. Fry immediately changed the attitude in Iowa City, making it clear that losing was not an option. Although many of his moves seemed cosmetic: the changing of the uniforms to look like the Pittsburgh Steelers, then the dominant professional team, or the famous painting of the visitors' locker room pink in an effort to relax, if not distract, the opposition, Fry was creating a new mindset.

Fry also knew that he needed a lot of help to turn this program around and with a sharp eye for talent he assembled a remarkable staff, including two other men who make our list of best coaches from featured schools: Bill Snyder and Barry Alvarez.

Fry's most important decision may have been in his choice of offense. Deciding that beating Michigan and Ohio State at their own power run game would be futile, Fry opted for an explosive passing attack for which the rest of the Big Ten would be unprepared. Adding in trick plays and trick formations, the Hawkeyes were also fun to watch and the rabid faithful began to appreciate their team again. Everything paid off in 1981 with an unlikely Rose Bowl berth. By 1985, Fry had established Iowa as one of the nation's best programs. They were ranked no. 1 during that season for five weeks and produced a near Heisman Trophy winner in quarterback Chuck Long.

The winning, for the most part, continued for Fry until his retirement after 1998 season.

IOWA'S 55 GREATEST SINCE 1953

OFFENSE

WIDE RECEIVER: Jim Gibbons, Kevin Kasper, Quinn Early, Karl Noonan
TIGHT END: Dallas Clark, Marv Cook
TACKLE: John Alt, Bryan Bulaga, Dave Croston, Robert Gallery, Ross Verba
GUARD: Joe Devlin, Bob Kratch, John Niland, Eric Steinbach
CENTER: Joel Hilgenberg, Bruce Nelson
QUARTERBACK: Randy Duncan, Chuck Long
RUNNING BACK: Tavian Banks, Shonn Greene, Ronnie Harmon, Ed Podolak, Sedrick Shaw
FULLBACK: Owen Gill

DEFENSE

END: Adrian Clayborn, Frank Gilliam, Joe Mott, Matt Roth, Leroy Smith, Andre Tippett
TACKLE: Mark Bortz, Jared DeVries, Dave Haight, Alex Karras, Mitch King
LINEBACKER: Chad Greenway, Wally Hilgenberg, Abdul Hodge, Andre Jackson, Brad Quast, Larry Station
CORNERBACK: Craig Clemons, Merton Hanks, Bob Jeter
SAFETY: Devon Mitchell, Kenny Ploen, Bob Sanders, Mike Stoops

SPECIAL TEAMS

RETURN SPECIALISTS: Earl Douthitt, Tim Dwight
PLACE KICKER: Nate Kaeding
PUNTER: Reggie Roby

TWO-WAY PLAYERS

GUARD-LINEBACKER: Calvin Jones
HALFBACK-WINGBACK-WIDE RECEIVER-DEFENSIVE BACK-RETURNMAN: Paul Krause

PERFORMANCE FORMULA:
IOWA'S 10 BEST SEASONS

1960	1.6846	2 of 70
1958	1.6484	5 of 70
1956	1.6059	5 of 69
2002	1.5613	8 of 70
1985	1.5390	9 of 70
2004	1.5210	8 of 72
1957	1.5030	7 of 69
1991	1.4961	12 of 71
2009	1.4902	11 of 72
2003	1.4469	12 of 71

IOWA HAWKEYES

Year	W-L-T	AP Poll	Conference Standing	Toughest Regular Season Opponents	Coach (Record at School)	Bowl Games		
1953	5-3-1		5t	Notre Dame 9-0-1, Michigan St. 8-1, Wisconsin 6-2-1, Michigan 6-3	Forest Evashevski			
1954	5-4		5	Ohio State 9-0, Notre Dame 9-1, Minnesota 7-2, Wisconsin 7-2	Forest Evashevski			
1955	3-5-1		7	UCLA 9-1, Notre Dame 8-2, Ohio State 7-2, Michigan 7-2	Forest Evashevski			
1956	9-1	3	1	Minnesota 6-1-2, Michigan 7-2, Ohio State 6-3	Forest Evashevski	Rose	35 Oregon State	19
1957	7-1-1	6	3	Ohio State 8-1, Notre Dame 7-3, Wisconsin 6-3	Forest Evashevski			
1958	8-1-1	2	1	Air Force 9-0-1, TCU 8-2, Wisconsin 7-1-1, Ohio State 6-1-2	Forest Evashevski	Rose	38 California	12
1959	5-4		6	Wisconsin 7-2, Northwestern 6-3, Purdue 5-2-2	Forest Evashevski			
1960	8-1	3	1	Minnesota 8-1, Michigan State 6-2-1, Ohio State 7-2, Kansas 7-2-1	Forest Evashevski (52-27-4)			
1961	5-4		7	Ohio State 8-0-1, Minnesota 7-2, Michigan 6-3, Wisconsin 6-3	Jerry Burns			
1962	4-5		5t	Wisconsin 8-1, Minnesota 6-2-1, Ohio State 6-3	Jerry Burns			
1963	3-3-2		8	Washington 6-4, Ohio State 5-3-1	Jerry Burns			
1964	3-6		9	Notre Dame 9-1, Michigan 8-1, Ohio State 7-2, Purdue 6-3	Jerry Burns			
1965	1-9		10	Michigan St. 10-0, Ohio State 7-2, Purdue 7-2-1, Washington St. 7-3	Jerry Burns (16-27-2)			
1966	2-8		10	Michigan State 9-0-1, Purdue 8-2, Miami 7-2-1	Ray Nagel			
1967	1-8-1		9t	Indiana 9-1, Notre Dame 8-2, Minnesota 8-2, Purdue 8-2	Ray Nagel			
1968	5-5		5t	Ohio State 9-0, Purdue 8-2, Notre Dame 7-2-1	Ray Nagel			
1969	5-5		5t	Michigan 8-2, Purdue 8-2, Oregon State 6-4	Ray Nagel			
1970	3-6-1		4	Michigan 9-1, Southern California 6-4-1, Oregon State 6-5	Ray Nagel (16-32-2)			
1971	1-10		10	Michigan 11-0, Penn State 10-1, Northwestern 7-4	Frank Lauterbur			
1972	3-7-1		8t	Michigan 10-1, Penn State 10-1, Ohio State 9-1	Frank Lauterbur			
1973	0-11		9t	Penn State 11-0, Ohio State 9-0-1, Michigan 10-0-1, UCLA 9-2	Frank Lauterbur (4-28-1)			
1974	3-8		7t	Ohio State 10-1, Michigan 10-1, USC 9-1-1, Penn State 9-2	Bob Commings			
1975	3-8		7t	Ohio State 10-1, Penn State 9-2, Michigan State 7-4, USC 7-4	Bob Commings			
1976	5-6		7t	Southern California 10-1, Ohio State 8-2-1, Penn State 7-4	Bob Commings			
1977	5-6		6t	Michigan 10-1, Ohio State 9-2, Iowa State 8-3, Minnesota 7-4	Bob Commings			
1978	2-9		8	Michigan 10-1, Purdue 7-2-1, Ohio State 7-3-1, Michigan State 8-3	Bob Commings (17-38)			
1979	5-6		5	Ohio State 11-0, Nebraska 10-1, Oklahoma 10-1, Purdue 9-2	Hayden Fry			
1980	4-7		4	Ohio State 9-2, Nebraska 9-2, Purdue 8-3	Hayden Fry			
1981	8-4	18	1t	Nebraska 9-2, Michigan 8-3, UCLA 7-3-1, Illinois 7-4	Hayden Fry	Rose	0 Washington	28
1982	8-4		3	Nebraska 11-1, Michigan 8-3, Illinois 7-4	Hayden Fry	Peach	28 Tennessee	22
1983	9-3	14	3	Illinois 10-1, Michigan 9-2, Ohio State 8-3, Penn State 6-4-1	Hayden Fry	Gator	6 Florida	14
1984	8-4-1	16	4t	Ohio State 9-2, Purdue 7-4, Wisconsin 7-3-1	Hayden Fry	Freedom	55 Texas	17
1985	10-2	10	1	Michigan 9-1-1, Ohio State 8-3, Michigan State 7-4, Illinois 6-4-1	Hayden Fry	Rose	28 UCLA	45
1986	9-3	16	3t	Michigan 11-1, Ohio State 9-3	Hayden Fry	Holiday	39 San Diego State	38
1987	10-3	16	2t	Indiana 7-3-1, Michigan 7-4	Hayden Fry	Holiday	20 Wyoming	19
1988	6-4-3		3t	Michigan 8-2-1, Colorado 8-3, Indiana 7-3-1	Hayden Fry	Peach	23 North Carolina State	28
1989	5-6		6t	Michigan 10-1, Illinois 9-2, Oregon 7-4, Michigan State 7-4	Hayden Fry			
1990	8-4	18	1t	Miami 9-2, Ohio State 7-3-1, Illinois 8-3, Michigan 8-3	Hayden Fry	Rose	34 Washington	46
1991	10-1-1	10	2	Michigan 10-1, Ohio State 8-3	Hayden Fry	Holiday	13 BYU	13
1992	5-7		5	Miami 11-0, Michigan 8-0-3, Ohio State 8-2-1, NC State 9-2-1	Hayden Fry			
1993	6-6		8	Penn State 9-2, Indiana 8-3, Michigan 7-4	Hayden Fry	Alamo	3 California	37
1994	5-5-1		7	Penn State 11-0. Michigan 8-3, Oregon 8-3	Hayden Fry			
1995	8-4	25	6	Ohio State 11-1, Northwestern 10-1, Penn State 8-3	Hayden Fry	Sun	38 Washington	18
1996	9-3	18	3t	Ohio State 10-1, Penn State 10-2, Northwestern 9-2	Hayden Fry	Alamo	27 Texas Tech	0
1997	7-5		6t	Michigan 11-0, Ohio State 10-2, Purdue 8-3, Wisconsin 8-4	Hayden Fry	Sun	7 Arizona State	17
1998	3-8		7t	Ohio State 10-1, Wisconsin 10-1, Michigan 9-3, Purdue 8-4	Hayden Fry (143-89-6)			
1999	1-10		11	Nebraska 11-1, Wisconsin 9-2, Michigan State 9-2, Penn State 9-3	Kirk Ferentz			
2000	3-9		8	Kansas State 10-2, Nebraska 9-2, Ohio State 8-3, Wisconsin 8-4	Kirk Ferentz			
2001	7-5		4t	Michigan 8-3, Iowa State 7-4	Kirk Ferentz	Alamo	19 Texas Tech	16
2002	11-2	8	1t	Michigan 9-3, Penn State 8-4, Minnesota 7-5	Kirk Ferentz	Orange	17 Southern California	38
2003	10-3	8	4t	Ohio State 10-2, Michigan 10-2, Purdue 9-3, Minnesota 9-3	Kirk Ferentz	Outback	37 Florida	17
2004	10-2	8	1t	Michigan 9-2, Wisconsin 9-2, Arizona State 8-3, Ohio State 7-4	Kirk Ferentz	Capital One	30 Louisiana State	25
2005	7-5		3t	Ohio State 9-2, Wisconsin 9-3, Michigan 7-4, Northwestern 7-4	Kirk Ferentz	Outback	24 Florida	31
2006	6-7		8t	Ohio State 12-0, Michigan 11-1, Wisconsin 11-1, Purdue 8-5	Kirk Ferentz	Alamo	24 Texas	26
2007	6-6		5t	Wisconsin 8-3, Penn State 8-4, Illinos 9-3	Kirk Ferentz			
2008	9-4	20	4t	Northwestern 9-3, Michigan State 9-3, Penn State 11-1	Kirk Ferentz	Outback	31 South Carolina	10
2009	11-2	7	2t	Arizona 8-4, Penn State 10-2, Wisconsin 9-3, Ohio State 10-2	Kirk Ferentz	Orange	24 Georgia Tech	14
2010	8-5		4t	Wisconsin 11-1, Michigan State 11-1, Ohio State 11-1	Kirk Ferentz (89-60)	Insight	27 Missouri	24

TOTAL: 339-293-15 .5355 (35 of 70)   **Bowl Games since 1953:**   14-10-1 .5800 (22 of 70)

GREATEST TEAM SINCE 1953: The 1956 squad edges other Iowa teams coached by Forest Evashevski and the best Hawkeyes squads led by Hayden Fry and Kirk Ferentz. With quarterback-defensive back Kenny Ploen pacing the offense and Alex Karras, Bob Commings, and Frank Gilliam dominating the line of scrimmage, the Hawkeyes were balanced and tough. Better known for a defense that posted four shutouts, the Hawkeyes offense ended the season with 48 points scored against Notre Dame and 35 in a Rose Bowl win over Oregon State.

1953 5-3-1

7 Michigan State	21 E Frank Gilliam
54 Washington St.	12 T Andrew Hough / John Hall
13 Michigan	14 G Don Chelf / George Kress
21 Wyoming	7 C Jerry Hilgenberg
19 Indiana	13 G Calvin Jones
6 Wisconsin	10 T Jerry Clark / Cameron Cummins
26 Purdue	0 E Bill Fenton
27 Minnesota	0 QB Lou Matykiewicz / Jerry Reichow
14 Notre Dame	14 HB Dusty Rice /Bobby Stearns/Earl Smith
	HB Eddie Vincent
	FB Binkey Broeder / Roger Wiegman

RUSHING: Broeder 96/410y, Rice 71/391y, Vincent 59/374y
PASSING: Matykiewicz 18-44/234y, 2TD, 40.9%
RECEIVING: Gilliam 12/71y, Fenton 7/54y, Rice 6/199y
SCORING: Rice 60pts, Broeder & Smith 18pts

1954 5-4

14 Michigan State	10 E Frank Gilliam / Lou Matykiewicz
48 Montana	6 T Rodger Swedberg
13 Michigan	14 G John Hall / Boyd Green
14 Ohio State	20 C Bud Lawson / Don Suchy / Norm Six
27 Indiana	14 G Calvin Jones
13 Wisconsin	7 T Cameron Cummins / Terry Shuck
25 Purdue	14 E Jim Freeman / Ken Meek
20 Minnesota	22 QB Jerry Reichow / Ken Ploen
18 Notre Dame	34 HB Earl Smith / Bobby Stearnes
	HB Eddie Vincent / Eldean Matheson
	FB George Broeder / Roger Weigmann

RUSHING: Vincent 95/618y, Smith 54/385y, Reichow 99/327y
PASSING: Reichow 34-73/386y, 1TD, 46.5%
RECEIVING: Gilliam 15/223y, Smith 7/149y, Matykiewicz 5/69y
SCORING: Smith 66pts, Reichow, Vincent & Stearnes 30pts

1955 3-5-1

28 Kansas State	7 E Jim Gibbons
14 Wisconsin	37 T Frank Bloomquist
20 Indiana	6 G Dick Deasy / John Burroughs
20 Purdue	20 C Don Suchy / Bill Van Buren
13 UCLA	33 G Calvin Jones
21 Michigan	33 T Rodger Swedberg / Don Bowen
26 Minnesota	0 E Jim Freeman
10 Ohio State	20 QB Jerry Reichow / Ken Ploen
14 Notre Dame	17 HB Earl Smith / Don Dobrino
	HB Eddie Vincent / Collins Hagler
	FB Roger Weigmann / Fred Harris

RUSHING: Vincent 73/381y, Reichow 88/369y, Wiegmann 84/320y
PASSING: Reichow 48-88/722y, 4TD, 54.5%
RECEIVING: Gibbons 16/257y, Freeman 8/85y, Dobrino 7/132y
SCORING: Vincent 30pts, Freeman (E-K) 27pts, Dobrino 24pts

1956 9-1

27 Indiana	0 E Jim Gibbons / Ken Meek
14 Oregon State	13 T Alex Karras / John Burroughs
13 Wisconsin	7 G Frank Bloomquist / Dick Deasy
34 Hawaii	0 C Don Suchy / Bill Van Buren
21 Purdue	20 G Bob Commings / Hugh Drake
14 Michigan	17 T Dick Klein / Frank Rigney
7 Minnesota	0 E Frank Gilliam /Bob Prescott /Tony Hatch
6 Ohio State	0 QB Ken Ploen / Randy Duncan
48 Notre Dame	8 HB Don Dobrino / Bill Gravel
35 Oregon State	19 HB Bill Happel / Collins Hagler
	FB Fred Harris / John Nocera

RUSHING: Ploen 86/487y, Dobrino 87/437y, Happel 103/430y
PASSING: Ploen 33-64/386y, 5TD, 51.5%
RECEIVING: Gibbons 17/255y, Harris 8/88y, Gilliam 7/94y
SCORING: Ploen 38pts, Hagler 36pts, Prescott (E-K) 30pts

1957 7-1-1

70 Utah State	14 E Jim Gibbons / Curt Merz
20 Washington St.	13 T Alex Karras / Dick Theer
47 Indiana	7 G Frank Bloomquist / Gary Grouwinkel
21 Wisconsin	7 C Mac Lewis / Bill Lapham
6 Northwestern	0 G Bob Commings / Hugh Drake
21 Michigan	21 T Dick Klein / Frank Rigney
44 Minnesota	20 E Don Norton / Bob Prescott
13 Ohio State	17 QB Randy Duncan / Olen Treadway
21 Notre Dame	13 HB Bill Gravel / Bob Jeter
	HB Collins Hagler /Bill Happel /Ray Jauch
	FB John Nocera / Fred Harris / Don Horn

RUSHING: Hagler 67/456y, Happel 57/365y, Nocera 48/314y
PASSING: Duncan 70-119/1124y, 10TD, 58.8%
RECEIVING: Gibbons 36/587y, Norton 8/154y, Horn 8/92y
SCORING: Prescott 42pts, Duncan 30pts, Gibbons & Happel 24pts

1958 8-1-1

17 TCU	0 E Curt Merz / Jeff Langston
13 Air Force	13 T John Burroughs / Charles Lee
34 Indiana	13 G Gary Grouwinkel / Jerry Novack
20 Wisconsin	9 C Bill Lapham / Lloyd Humphreys
26 Northwestern	20 G Hugh Drake / Dick Shipanik
37 Michigan	14 T Mac Lewis / John Sawin
28 Minnesota	6 E Don Norton / Bob Prescott
28 Ohio State	38 QB Randy Duncan
31 Notre Dame	21 HB Bob Jeter / Kevin Furlong
38 California	12 WB Willie Fleming / Ray Jauch
	FB John Nocera / Don Horn

RUSHING: Jauch 76/524y, Fleming 71/505y, Jeter 65/469y
PASSING: Duncan 106-179/1397y, 12TD, 59.7%
RECEIVING: Norton 25/374y, Merz 25/354y, Furlong 13/111y
SCORING: Fleming 66pts, Jeter 36pts, Duncan 30pts

1959 5-4

42 California	12 E Curt Merz / Jeff Langston
10 Northwestern	14 T Charles Lee
37 Michigan State	8 G Sherwyn Thorson
16 Wisconsin	25 C Bill Lapham / Lloyd Humphreys
7 Purdue	14 G Mark Manders / Don Shipanik
53 Kansas State	0 T John Sawin / Al Hinton
33 Minnesota	0 E Don Norton / Al Miller
16 Ohio State	7 QB Olen Treadway / Wilburn Hollis
19 Notre Dame	20 HB Bob Jeter / Jerry Mauren
	WB Ray Jauch / Bernie Wyatt
	FB Don Horn / Gene Mosley

RUSHING: Jeter 108/609y, Jauch 74/335y, Mauren 51/313y
PASSING: Treadway 86-147/1014y, 6TD, 58.5%
RECEIVING: Norton 30/428y, Langston 17/224y, Jeter 10/94y
SCORING: Horn 42pts, Norton 34pts, Jeter 24pts

1960 8-1

22 Oregon State	12 E Felton Rogers / Jim Winston
42 Northwestern	0 T Charles Lee / Chester Williams
27 Michigan State	15 G Sherwyn Thorson / Bill DeCindio
28 Wisconsin	21 C Bill Van Buren / Lloyd Humphreys
21 Purdue	14 G Mark Manders
21 Kansas	7 T Al Hinton / Earl McQuiston
10 Minnesota	27 E Bill Whisler / Bill Perkins
35 Ohio State	12 QB Wilburn Hollis / Matt Szykowny
28 Notre Dame	0 HB Larry Ferguson / Sammie Harris
	WB Jerry Mauren / Bernie Wyatt
	FB Joe Williams / Eugene Mosley (QB)

RUSHING: Ferguson 90/665y, Hollis 107/477y, Williams 70/393y
PASSING: Hollis 22-62/289y, 3TD, 35.5%
RECEIVING: Rogers 8/96y, Whisler 6/104y, Perkins 5/72y
SCORING: Hollis 68pts, Ferguson 36pts, Tom Moore (K) 32pts

1961 5-4

28 California	7 E Felton Rogers
35 Southern Cal	34 T Gus Kasapis
27 Indiana	8 G Sherwyn Thorson / Bill DiCindio
47 Wisconsin	15 C Bill Van Buren
0 Purdue	9 G Earl McQuiston / Wally Hilgenberg
13 Ohio State	29 T Al Hinton
9 Minnesota	16 E Cloyd Webb / Bill Whisler
14 Michigan	23 QB Matt Szykowny / Wilburn Hollis
42 Notre Dame	21 HB Joe Williams (FB) / Paul Krause
	WB Bernie Wyatt / Sammie Harris
	FB Bill Perkins

RUSHING: Perkins 62/380y, Williams 64/297y, Harris 76/267y
PASSING: Szykowny 79-120/1078y, 7TD, 56.1%
RECEIVING: Webb 25/425y, Whisler 18/244y, Rogers 12/171y
SCORING: Williams 54pts, Szykowny (QB-K) 46pts, Webb 24pts

1962 4-5

28 Oregon State	8 WR Paul Krause
0 Southern Cal	7 E/T Tony Giacobazzi / Gus Kasapis
14 Indiana	10 G Wally Hilgenberg / Mike Reilly
14 Wisconsin	42 C Gary Fletcher / Jim Robshaw
3 Purdue	26 G Earl McQuiston
28 Ohio State	14 T George Latta / Phil Deutsch
0 Minnesota	10 E Cloyd Webb / Lou Williams
28 Michigan	14 QB Matt Szykowny / Bob Wallace
12 Notre Dame	35 HB Larry Ferguson
	WB Bobby Grier / Lonnie Rogers
	FB Bill Perkins / Vic Davis

RUSHING: Ferguson 113/547y, Grier 77/331y, Perkins 48/237y
PASSING: Szykowny 59-115/737y, 6TD, 51.2%
RECEIVING: Krause 16/214y, Ferguson 13/180y, Webb 12/179y
SCORING: Ferguson 18pts, Jay Roberts (K) 15pts, 2 tied w/ 14pts

1963 3-3-2

14 Washington St.	14 WR Cloyd Webb / Lou Williams (D)
17 Washington	7 T Leo Miller / George Latta
37 Indiana	26 G Wally Hilgenberg
7 Wisconsin	10 C Gary Fletcher / Dave Recher
0 Purdue	14 G Mike Reilly
3 Ohio State	7 T Gus Kasapis / John Niland
27 Minnesota	13 E Tony Giacobazzi / Bill Niedbala
21 Michigan	21 QB Fred Riddle / Gary Snook
	HB Bob Sherman / Lonnie Rogers
	WB Paul Krause
	FB Bobby Grier

RUSHING: Grier 98/406y, Rogers 83/356y, Snook 44/82y
PASSING: Snook 34-90/667y, 5TD, 37.8%
RECEIVING: Webb 24/424y, Krause 19/442y, Grier 7/33y
SCORING: Krause 36pts, Webb 26pts, Jay Roberts (K) 22pts

1964 3-6

34 Idaho	24 WR Rich O'Hara
28 Washington	18 WR Karl Noonan
21 Indiana	20 T Bob Ziolkowski
21 Wisconsin	31 G John Niland
14 Purdue	19 C Dave Recher
19 Ohio State	21 G Bernie Budzik
13 Minnesota	14 T Leo Miller
20 Michigan	34 TE Tony Giacobazzi
0 Notre Dame	28 QB Gary Snook
	HB Dalton Kimble / Craig Nourse
	HB Karlin Ryan (DB) / Gary Simpson
	DL Dave Long
	DL Bob Mitchell
	DL Steve Hodoway / John Niland
	DL Phil Deutsch
	DL Bill Briggs
	DL Cliff Wilder / Terry Mulligan
	LB Delbert Gehrke
	LB Dan Hilsabeck
	DB Dave Moreland / Bob Sorenson
	DB Ivory McDowell
	DB Al Randolph

RUSHING: Kimble 68/284y, Nourse 63/232y, Ryan 31/133y
PASSING: Snook 151-311/2062y, 11TD, 48.5%
RECEIVING: Noonan 59/933y, O'Hara 32/469y, Giacobazzi 29/363y
SCORING: Kimble 48pts, Noonan, O'Hara & Snook 24pts

1965 1-9

0 Washington St.	7 WR Rich O'Hara
27 Oregon State	7 WR Karl Noonan
13 Wisconsin	16 T John Hendricks
14 Purdue	17 G John Niland
3 Minnesota	14 C John Ficeli / James Cmejrek
0 Northwestern	9 G John Diehl
17 Indiana	21 T Roger Lamont
0 Michigan State	35 TE Cliff Wilder / Paul Usinowicz
0 Ohio State	38 QB Gary Snook
20 N. Carolina St.	28 HB Jerry O'Donnell / Dalton Kimble
	FB Silas McKinnie / Gary Simpson
	DL Dave Long
	DL Bill Briggs
	DL Leo Miller
	DL Bill Restelli
	DL Terry Mulligan
	LB Dan Hilsabeck / Tom Knutson
	LB Terry Huff / Richard Hendryx
	DB Terry Ferry
	DB Alvin Randolph
	DB Dick Gibbs
	DB Tony Williams

RUSHING: McKinnie 89/286y, O'Donnell 80/228y, Kimble 38/98y
PASSING: Snook 95-230/1009y, 4TD, 41.3%
RECEIVING: Noonan 43/545y, Wilder 23/231y, O'Hara 21/230y
SCORING: Bob Anderson (K) 28pts, Snook, Kimble & Wilder 12pts

1966 2-8

31 Arizona	20 WR Al Bream/Gary Larson/ Larry McDowell
3 Oregon State	17 T Roger Lamont / Mike Lavery
0 Wisconsin	7 G Phil Major
0 Purdue	35 C John Ficeli
0 Minnesota	17 G Jeff Newland
15 Northwestern	24 T Bill Smith
20 Indiana	19 TE Paul Usinowicz (T) / John Hayes
7 Michigan State	56 QB Ed Podolak
10 Ohio State	14 HB Tony Williams
0 Miami	44 HB Barry Crees / Rick Thiele
	FB Silas McKinnie
	DL Andrew Jackson
	DL Terry Mulligan
	DL Richard Somodi / Steve Hodoway
	DL John Hendricks
	DL John Evenden
	DL Scott Miller
	LB Dan Hilsabeck
	LB Dave Moreland
	DB Guy Bilek
	DB Bill McCutchen
	DB Dick Gibbs

RUSHING: McKinnie 124/516y, Pdlk 141/450y, Williams 88/299y
PASSING: Podolak 77-191/1041y, 3TD, 40.3%
RECEIVING: Bream 30/418y, Williams 14/220y, Crees 12/149y
SCORING: Bob Anderson (K) 24pts, Podolak 20pts, Crees & Williams 12pts

1967 1-8-1

24 TCU	9 WR Al Bream
18 Oregon State	38 T Melvin Morris / Mike Lavery
6 Notre Dame	56 G Larry Ely
17 Indiana	21 C Paul Usinowicz
21 Wisconsin	21 G Jon Meskimen / Jeff Newland
22 Purdue	41 T Mike Phillips / Bill Smith
0 Minnesota	10 TE Paul Laaveg
24 Northwestern	39 QB Ed Podolak / Mike Cilek
10 Ohio State	21 WB Barry Crees
19 Illinois	21 TB Silas McKinnie
	FB Tim Sullivan / Cornelius Patterson
	DL Peter Paquette
	DL Rich Stepanek / Bill Bevill
	DL John Hendricks
	DL Greg Allison
	DL Duane Grant / John Diehl
	DL Scott Miller
	LB Rod Barnhart
	LB Don Sibery / Terry Huff
	DB Tony Williams
	DB Guy Bilek
	DB Steve Wilson

RUSHING: McKinnie 166/588y, Sullivan 79/323y, Podolak 112/323y
PASSING: Podolak 79-162/1014y, 5TD, 48.9%
RECEIVING: Bream 55/703y, Crees 32/520y, McKinnie 18/157y
SCORING: McKinnie 56pts, Bream 32pts, Bob Anderson (K) 25pts

1968 5-5

21 Oregon State	20 WR Al Bream
17 TCU	28 T Jim Miller / Paul Laaveg
28 Notre Dame	51 G Chuck Legler
34 Indiana	38 C Greg McManus
41 Wisconsin	0 G Jon Meskimen
14 Purdue	44 T Mel Morris
35 Minnesota	28 TE Ray Manning
68 Northwestern	34 QB Larry Lawrence / Mike Cilek
27 Ohio State	33 WB Barry Crees / Dennis Green
37 Illinois	13 TB Ed Podolak
	FB Tim Sullivan
	DL Bill Bevill / Ken Price
	DL Layne McDowell
	DL Greg Allison / Mike Edwards
	DL Rich Stepanek
	DL Dan McDonald
	LB Larry Ely
	LB Mike Phillips / Rod Barnhart
	DB Ray Churchill
	DB Ray Cavole
	DB Coleman Lane
	DB Charles Bolden / Steve Wilson

RUSHING: Podolak 154/937y, Sullivan 131/682y, Green 48/279y
PASSING: Lawrence 88-156/1307y, 7TD, 56.4%
RECEIVING: Manning 35/426y, Bream 29/518y, Crees 22/400y
SCORING: Lawrence 60pts, Podolak 54pts, Sullivan 48pts

1969 5-5

14 Oregon State	42 WR Don Osby / Dave Krull
61 Washington St.	35 T Paul Laaveg / Jim Miller
31 Arizona	19 G Geoff Mickelson
17 Wisconsin	23 C Alan Cassady
31 Purdue	35 G Jon Meskimen
19 Michigan State	18 T Mel Morris
8 Minnesota	35 TE Ray Manning
28 Indiana	17 QB Larry Lawrence
6 Michigan	51 WB Kerry Reardon
40 Illinois	0 TB Dennis Green / Levi Mitchell
	FB Steve Penney / Tom Smith
	DL Bill Bevill
	DL Layne McDowell
	DL Jerry Nelson
	DL Bill Windauer / Rich Stepanek
	DL Dan McDonald
	LB Dave Brooks
	LB Larry Ely / Rod Barnhart
	DB Ray Cavole / Tom Hayes
	DB Craig Clemons
	DB Jerry Johnson
	DB Chris Hamilton

RUSHING: Penney 102/484y, Lawrence 108/406y, Mitchell 71/404y
PASSING: Lawrence 113-239/1680y, 10TD, 47.3%
RECEIVING: Reardon 43/738y, Manning 28/361y, Osby 19/276y
SCORING: Alan Schuette (K) 45pts, Green 42pts, Reardon & Mitchell 36pts

1970 3-6-1

14 Oregon State	21 WR Kerry Reardon
0 Southern Cal	48 T Jim Miller
10 Arizona	17 G Geoff Mickelson
24 Wisconsin	14 C Alan Cassady
3 Purdue	24 G Chuck Legler / Lorin Lynch
0 Michigan State	37 T John Muller
14 Minnesota	14 TE Ray Manning
42 Indiana	13 QB Roy Bash / Kyle Skogman
0 Michigan	55 WB Dennis Green
22 Illinois	16 TB Levi Mitchell
	FB Tim Sullivan
	DL Layne McDowell
	DL Bill Windauer / Wendell Bell
	DL Charles Podolak
	DL Jerry Nelson / Mike Dillner
	LB Dan McDonald
	LB Dave Brooks
	LB Dave Clement
	DB Craig Clemons
	DB Rich Solomon
	DB Jerry Johnson
	DB Tom Hayes

RUSHING: Mitchell 205/900y, Sullivan 147/579y, Steve Penney (FB) 36/151y
PASSING: Bash 32-70/473y, 3TD, 45.7%
RECEIVING: Reardon 27/438y, Sullivan 12/94y, Manning 9/113y
SCORING: Sullivan 36pts, Marcos Melendez (K) 21pts, Bash & Mitchell 20pts

1971 1-10

21 Ohio State	52 WR Dave Triplett / Brian Rollins
19 Oregon State	33 WR Jerry Reardon
14 Penn State	44 T Craig Darling
13 Purdue	45 G Geoff Mickelson / John Farrell
3 Northwestern	28 C Joe Ritchie
14 Minnesota	19 G Kelly Disser
3 Michigan State	34 T Wendell Bell / Jim Kaiser
20 Wisconsin	16 TE Don Osby / Tom Cabalka
7 Michigan	63 QB Frank Sunderman / Rob Fick
7 Indiana	14 TB Levi Mitchell / Craig Johnson
0 Illinois	31 FB Steve Penney / Frank Holmes
	DL Larry Horton / Dan Dickel
	DL Charlie Podolak
	DL Rich Lutz
	DL Jim Waschek / Ernie Roberson
	DL Ike White
	LB Dave Simms
	LB Harry Young / Rich Byard
	DB Craig Clemons
	DB Rich Solomon
	DB Mike Wendling
	DB Charlie Cross / Bill Schoonover

RUSHING: Mitchell 149/623y, Johnson 66/235y, Holmes 54/118y
PASSING: Sunderman 109-235/1297y, 9TD, 46.3%
RECEIVING: Triplett 28/426y, Mitchell 22/263y, Reardon 15/192y
SCORING: Harry Kokolus (K) 25pts, Mitchell 24pts, Triplett & Cabalka 18pts

1972 3-7-1

0 Ohio State	21 WR Brian Rollins
19 Oregon State	11 T Rod Walters / Jim Waschek
10 Penn State	14 G Ernie Robertson
0 Purdue	24 C Jock Michelosen / Johnny Campbell
23 Northwestern	12 G Craig Darling
14 Minnesota	43 T John Muller
6 Michigan State	6 TE Ike White / Brandt Yocom
14 Wisconsin	16 QB Butch Caldwell/K. Skogman/BobOusley
0 Michigan	31 SB Bob Sims
8 Indiana	16 TB Dave Harris
15 Illinois	14 FB Frank Holmes
	DL Lynn Heil / Romero Hawthorne
	DL Bill Windauer
	DL Jerry Nelson
	DL Les Washington / Tyrone Dye
	DL Dan Dickel
	LB Dave Simms
	LB Andre Jackson
	DB Earl Douthitt
	DB Sid Thomas / Jerry Reardon
	DB Charlie Cross
	DB Rick Penney

RUSHING: Harris 136/621y, Holmes 141/500y, Sims 54/218y
PASSING: Skogman 24-57/356y, 1TD, 42.1%
RECEIVING: Rollins 29/378y, Harris 13/160y, Yocom 9/102y
SCORING: Harris & Holmes 24pts, Harry Kokolus (K) 21pts

1973 0-11

7 Michigan	31 WR Brian Rollins
18 UCLA	55 T Jim Waschek
8 Penn State	27 G Joe Devlin
20 Arizona	23 C Jock Michelosen / Ed Myers
15 Northwestern	31 G Rod Walters
23 Minnesota	31 T Ernie Roberson
0 Illinois	50 TE Ike White / Tom Cabalka
23 Purdue	48 QB Butch Caldwell / Kyle Skogman
7 Wisconsin	35 HB Bill Schultz
13 Ohio State	55 HB Mark Fetter
6 Michigan State	15 FB Jim Jensen
	DL Nate Washington / Lynn Heil
	DL Les Washington
	DL Dave Bryant / Mark Essy
	DL Tyrone Dye
	DL Dan Dickel
	LB Dan LaFleur
	LB Andre Jackson / John Campbell
	DB Jim Caldwell
	DB Earl Douthitt
	DB Rick Penney / Ed Donovan
	DB Bob Salter

RUSHING: Jensen 111/509y, Caldwell 91/312y, Fetter 73/263y
PASSING: Caldwell 36-99/549y, 2TD, 36.4%
RECEIVING: Rollins 33/408y, Schultz 14/314y, Cabalka 7/69y
SCORING: Jensen 40pts, Caldwell 26pts, Harry Kokolus (K) 22pts

1974 3-8

7 Michigan	24 WR Bill Schultz
21 UCLA	10 T Rod Walters
0 Penn State	27 G Joe Devlin
3 Southern Cal	41 C Ed Myers
35 Northwestern	10 G Dan McCarney
17 Minnesota	23 T Jock Michelosen
14 Illinois	12 TE Brandt Yocom
14 Purdue	38 QB Rob Fick
15 Wisconsin	28 HB Jim Jensen
10 Ohio State	35 HB Rod Wellington
21 Michigan State	60 FB Bobby Holmes / Mark Fetter
	DL Lynn Heil
	DL Mike Lopos / Steve Wojan
	DL Dave Bryant / Dennis Armington
	DL Les Washington / Tyrone Dye
	DL Dave Wagner
	LB Dan LaFleur / John Campbell
	LB Andre Jackson
	DB Earl Douthitt
	DB Shanty Burks
	DB Bob Elliott
	DB Jim Caldwell

RUSHING: Jensen 163/659y, Wellington 125/472y, Holmes 96/377y
PASSING: Fick 79-165/1059y, 6TD, 47.9%
RECEIVING: Schultz 25/432y, Yocom 18/248y, Fetter 10/63y
SCORING: Wellington 30pts, Nick Quartaro (K) 27pts, Fetter 24pts

1975 3-8

12 Illinois	27 WR Bill Schultz
7 Syracuse	10 T Rod Walters
10 Penn State	30 G Joe Devlin
16 Southern Cal	27 C Jim Hilgenberg
0 Ohio State	49 G Dave Butler / Bruce Davis
20 Indiana	10 T Gary Ladick
7 Minnesota	31 TE Brandt Yocum
24 Northwestern	21 QB Tom McLaughlin / Butch Caldwell
45 Wisconsin	28 HB Dave Schick / Rod Wellington
18 Purdue	19 HB Jim Jensen / Ed Donovan
23 Michigan State	27 FB Mark Fetter / Bobby Holmes
	DL Mark Phillips / Dean Moore
	DL Rick Marsh
	DL Dave Bryant
	DL Doug Benschoter
	DL Nate Washington
	LB Andre Jackson
	LB Denny Armington
	DB Bob Elliott
	DB Roger Stech
	DB Shanty Burks
	DB Rick Penney

RUSHING: Schick 90/492y, Jensen 81/473y, Fetter 83/395y
PASSING: McLaughlin 23-87/358y, 1TD, 26.4%
RECEIVING: Schultz 8/238y, Wellington 8/160y, Yocom 7/75y
SCORING: Nick Quartaro (K) 40pts, Holmes 24pts, Schick 20pts

1976 5-6

6 Illinois	24 WR Jim McNulty / Bill Schultz
41 Syracuse	3 T Barry Tomasetti
7 Penn State	6 G Gary Evans
0 Southern Cal	55 C Mike Mayer
14 Ohio State	34 G Bruce Davis / Rich Cunningham
7 Indiana	14 T Steve Wojan
22 Minnesota	12 TE Tom Grine
13 Northwestern	10 QB Butch Caldwell / Tom McLaughlin
21 Wisconsin	38 WB Mike Brady
0 Purdue	21 TB Tom Renn / Ernie Sheeler
30 Michigan State	17 FB Jon Lazar / Nate Winston
	DL Doug Benschoter / Nate Washington
	DL Joe Hufford
	DL Dan Schultz
	DL Steve Vasquez
	LB Dean Moore
	LB Tom Rusk
	LB Kerry Feuerbach / Leven Weiss
	DB Rod Sears / Dave Becker
	DB Jim Caldwell
	DB Cedric Shaw
	DB Chuck Danzy

RUSHING: Lazar 95/392y, Caldwell 125/389y, Sheeler 85/362y
PASSING: Caldwell 37-101/616y, 3TD, 36.6%
RECEIVING: Grine 12/195y, Schultz 10/288y, Brady 9/154y
SCORING: Nick Quartaro (K) 39pts, Schultz & Caldwell 24pts

1977 5-6

24 Northwestern	0 WR Mike Brady
12 Iowa State	10 T Barry Tomasetti
7 Arizona	41 G Mike Mayer
16 UCLA (W-F)	34 C Jim Hilgenberg
18 Minnesota	6 G Rich Cunningham
6 Ohio State	27 T Sam Palladino
21 Purdue	34 TE Jim Swift
6 Michigan	23 QB Tom McLaughlin
21 Indiana	24 WB Jim Frazier / Jesse Cook
24 Wisconsin	8 TB Dennis Mosley / Rod Morton
16 Michigan State	22 FB Jon Lazar
	DL Darrell Hobbs
	DL Mark Mahmens / Joe Hufford
	DL John Harty
	DL Steve Vazquez / Jim Molini
	LB Leven Weiss / Mike Jackson
	LB Tom Rusk
	LB Dean Moore
	DB Cedric Shaw / Charles Danzy
	DB Rod Sears
	DB Shanty Burks
	DB Dave Becker

RUSHING: Lazar 100/411y, Mosley 59/327y, Morton 61/259y
PASSING: McLaughlin 78-152/1081y, 4TD, 51.3%
RECEIVING: Brady 26/357y, Lazar 19/225y, Frazier 12/126y
SCORING: Dave Holsclaw (K) 39pts, Lazar 30pts, Morton 24pts

1978 2-9

20 Northwestern	3 WR Brad Reid
0 Iowa State	31 T Mike Mayer / Matt Petrzecka
3 Arizona	23 G Don Willey
9 Utah	13 C Jay Hilgenberg
20 Minnesota	22 G Greg Gilbaugh
7 Ohio State	31 T Sam Palladino
7 Purdue	34 TE Jim Swift
0 Michigan	34 QB Jeff Green
14 Indiana	34 WB Rod Morton
38 Wisconsin	24 TB Kenny Burke / Dennis Mosley
7 Michigan State	42 FB Jon Lazar
	DL Darrell Hobbs / Pat Dean
	DL John Harty / Joe Hufford
	DL Doug Benschoter
	DL Steve Vazquez
	LB Leven Weiss / Jim Molini
	LB Tom Rusk
	LB Tim Gutshall
	DB Mike Steverson / Cedric Shaw
	DB Mario Pace
	DB Dave Becker
	DB Charles Danzy

RUSHING: Lazar 108/423y, Burke 76/293y, Mosley 96/292y
PASSING: Green 41-103/556y, 3TD, 39.8%
RECEIVING: Lazar 18/72y, Reid 14/322y, Swift 12/211y
SCORING: Reid 36pts, Scott Schilling (K) 27pts, 3 tied w/ 12pts

1979 5-6

26 Indiana	30 WR Mike Brady / Keith Chappelle
6 Oklahoma	21 T Matt Petrzecka
21 Nebraska	24 G Lemuel Grayson / Greg Gilbaugh
30 Iowa State	14 C Jay Hilgenberg
13 Illinois	7 G Dave Mayhan
58 Northwestern	6 T Sam Palladino
7 Minnesota	24 TE Jim Swift
24 Wisconsin	13 QB Phil Suess
14 Purdue	20 WB Brad Reid
7 Ohio State	34 TB Dennis Mosley
33 Michigan State	23 FB Dean McKillip
	DL Jim Molini
	DL Don Willey / Mark Bortz
	DL Pat Dean / Mark Mahmens
	DL John Harty
	DL Bryan Skradis
	LB Leven Weiss
	LB Todd Simonsen
	DB Cedric Shaw
	DB Mario Pace
	DB Bobby Stoops
	DB Kent Ellis / Mike Jackson

RUSHING: Mosley 270/1267y, McKillip 95/407y
PASSING: Suess 88-159/1165y, 6TD, 55.3%
RECEIVING: Reid 25/290y, Chappelle 22/340y, Mosley 21/235y
SCORING: Mosley 96pts, McKillip 42pts, Reggie Roby (K) 37pts

1980 4-7

16 Indiana	7 WR Keith Chappelle
0 Nebraska	57 T Matt Petrzelka
7 Iowa State	10 G Greg Gilbaugh / Lemuel Grayson
3 Arizona	5 C Jay Hilgenberg / Dave Oakes
14 Illinois	20 G Paul Postler / Dave Mayhan
25 Northwestern	3 T Raul Ibanez / Herlyn Harrington
6 Minnesota	24 TE Lon Olejniczak
22 Wisconsin	13 QB Phil Suess / Pete Gales
13 Purdue	58 WB Nate Person / Doug Dunham
7 Ohio State	41 TB Jeff Brown / Phil Blatcher
41 Michigan State	0 FB Dean McKillip
	DL Andre Tippett
	DL Mark Bortz
	DL Pat Dean
	DL John Harty
	DL Brad Webb
	LB Todd Simonsen
	LB Mel Cole
	DB Kevin Ellis
	DB Tracy Crocker
	DB Bobby Stoops
	DB Kent Ellis

RUSHING: Brown 132/673y, McKillip 81/289y, Blatcher 41/198y
PASSING: Suess 87-166/1031y, 6TD, 52.4%
Gales 66-152/882y, 6TD, 43.4%
RECEIVING: Chappelle 64/1037y, Brown 22/129y, Dunham 17/209y
SCORING: Chappelle 36pts, McKillip & Reggie Roby (K) 24pts

1981 8-4

10 Nebraska	7 WR Jeff Brown / Dave Moritz
12 Iowa State	23 WR Ivory Webb
20 UCLA	7 T Dave Mayhan
64 Northwestern	0 G Joe Levelis
42 Indiana	28 C Bill Bailey
9 Michigan	7 G Ron Hallstrom
10 Minnesota	12 T Paul Postler
7 Illinois	24 TE John Alt
33 Purdue	7 QB Gordy Bohannon / Pete Gales
17 Wisconsin	7 TB Paul Blatcher / Eddie Phillips
36 Michigan State	7 FB Norm Granger
0 Washington	28 DL Andre Tippett
	DL Mark Bortz
	DL Pat Dean
	DL Jim Pekar
	DL Brad Webb
	LB Mel Cole
	LB Todd Simonsen
	DB Lou King
	DB Tracy Crocker
	DB Jim Frazier
	DB Bobby Stoops

RUSHING: Blatcher 145/708y, Phillips 121/543y,
Bohannon 81/304y
PASSING: Bohannon 72-142/999y, 7TD, 50.7%
RECEIVING: Brown 20/301y, Moritz 17/390y, Webb 16/170y
SCORING: Tom Nichol (K) 59pts, Blatcher 48pts, Phillips 30pts

1982 8-4

7 Nebraska	42 WR Dave Moritz
7 Iowa State	19 T John Alt
17 Arizona	14 G Jon Roehlk / Joe Levelis
45 Northwestern	7 C Joel Hilgenberg
24 Indiana	20 G Loren Gerleman
7 Michigan	29 T Brett Miller
21 Minnesota	16 TE Mike Hufford
14 Illinois	13 QB Chuck Long
7 Purdue	16 WB Ronnie Harmon / J.C. Love-Jordan
28 Wisconsin	14 TB Eddie Phillips / Owen Gill
24 Michigan State	18 FB Norm Granger
28 Tennessee	22 DL Tony Wancket
	DL Mark Bortz
	DL Dave Browne
	DL Clay Uhlenhake
	DL Dave Strobel
	LB James Erb / Larry Station
	LB Mike Yacullo
	DB Keith Hunter / Devon Mitchell
	DB Zane Corbin / Nate Creer
	DB Bobby Stoops
	DB Ron Hawley

RUSHING: Phillips 166/806y, Gill 136/683y, Granger 67/356y
PASSING: Long 148-227/1678y, 11TD, 65.2%
RECEIVING: Moritz 41/605y, Phillips 26/200y, Granger 25/260y
SCORING: Tom Nichol (K) 43pts, Gill 42pts, Phillips 36pts

1983 9-3

51 Iowa State	10 WR Dave Moritz
42 Penn State	34 T John Alt
20 Ohio State	14 G Tim Hanna
0 Illinois	33 C Joel Hilgenberg
61 Northwestern	21 G Jon Roehlk
31 Purdue	14 T Joe Levelis
13 Michigan	16 TE Mike Hufford / Jonathan Hayes
49 Indiana	3 QB Chuck Long
34 Wisconsin	14 WB Ronnie Harmon / Bill Broghamer
12 Michigan State	6 TB Owen Gill / Eddie Phillips
61 Minnesota	10 FB Norm Granger
6 Florida	14 DL Tony Wancket
	DL Paul Hufford
	DL Hap Peterson
	DL George Little
	DL Mike Hooks
	LB Kevin Spitzig / George Davis
	LB Larry Station
	DB Keith Hunter / Ken Sims
	DB Nate Creer
	DB Mike Stoops
	DB Devon Mitchell / Ron Hawley

RUSHING: Gill 129/798y, Phillips 162/773y, Granger 71/466y
PASSING: Long 157-265/2601y, 14TD, 59.2%
RECEIVING: Moritz 50/912y, Harmon 35/729y, Broghamer 15/204y
SCORING: Tom Nichol (K) 86pts, Gill 60pts, Phillips 54pts

1984 8-4-1

59 Iowa State	21 WR Bill Happel
17 Penn State	20 T Herb Wester / Dave Croston
26 Ohio State	45 G Bill Glass
21 Illinois	16 C Mark Sindlinger
31 Northwestern	3 G Kelly O'Brien
40 Purdue	3 T Mike Haight
26 Michigan	0 TE Jonathan Hayes / Mike Flagg
24 Indiana	20 QB Chuck Long
10 Wisconsin	10 WB Robert Smith / Scott Helverson
16 Michigan State	17 TB Ronnie Harmon
17 Minnesota	23 FB Owen Gill
17 Hawaii	6 DL Mike Hooks
55 Texas	17 DL Paul Hufford
	DL Jeff Drost
	DL George Little
	DL Dave Strobel / Bruce Gear
	LB Kevin Spitzig / George Davis
	LB Larry Station
	DB Keith Hunter
	DB Nate Creer
	DB Mike Stoops
	DB Devon Mitchell

RUSHING: Gill 199/920y, Harmon 190/907y
PASSING: Long 216-322/2871y, 22TD, 67.1%
RECEIVING: Happel 47/632y, Hayes 42/512y, Harmon 32/318y
SCORING: Tom Nichol (K) 89pts, Harmon 72pts, Hayes 36pts

1985 10-2

58 Drake	0 WR Bill Happel
48 N. Illinois	20 WR Scott Helverson / Robert Smith
57 Iowa State	3 T Mike Haight
35 Michigan State	31 G Tom Humphrey
23 Wisconsin	13 C Mark Sindlinger
12 Michigan	10 G Bob Kratch / Kelly O'Brien
49 Northwestern	10 T Dave Croston
13 Ohio State	22 TE Mike Flagg
59 Illinois	0 QB Chuck Long
27 Purdue	24 TB Ronnie Harmon
31 Minnesota	9 FB David Hudson
28 UCLA	45 DL Richard Pryor
	DL Jeff Drost
	DL Hap Peterson
	DL Jon Vrieze
	DL George Millett / Bruce Gear
	LB George Davis
	LB Larry Station
	DB Ken Sims
	DB Nate Creer
	DB Devon Mitchell
	DB Jay Norvell

RUSHING: Harmon 223/1166y, Hudson 77/362y, Kevin Harmon (TB) 37/188y
PASSING: Long 260-388/3297y, 27TD, 67%
RECEIVING: Harmon 60/699y, Happel 56/901y, Helverson 54/703y
SCORING: Rob Houghtlin (K) 105pts, Harmon 60pts, Happel 48pts

1986 9-3

43 Iowa State	7 WR Jim Mauro
57 N. Illinois	3 WR Quinn Early
69 UTEP	7 T Dave Croston
24 Michigan State	21 G Chris Gambol
17 Wisconsin	6 C Mark Sindlinger
17 Michigan	20 G Herb Wester
27 Northwestern	20 T Bob Kratch
0 Ohio State	31 TE Mike Flagg
16 Illinois	20 QB Mark Vlasic
42 Purdue	14 TB Rick Bayless
30 Minnesota	27 FB Richard Bass / David Hudson
39 San Diego St.	38 DL Joe Mott
	DL Jeff Drost / Myron Keppy
	DL Dave Haight
	DL Jon Vrieze
	DL Bruce Gear
	LB Brad Quast
	LB George Davis
	DB Kyle Crowe
	DB Ken Sims
	DB Keaton Smiley
	DB Kerry Burt

RUSHING: Bayless 216/1150y, Hudson 73/511y, Bass 81/355y
PASSING: Vlasic 108-180/1456y, 11TD, 60%
RECEIVING: Mauro 30/600y, Bayless 30/209y, Early 22/490y
SCORING: Rob Houghtlin (K) 81pts, Bayless 66pts, Hudson 44pts

1987 10-3

22 Tennessee	23 WR Travis Watkins
15 Arizona	14 T Bob Kratch
48 Iowa State	9 G Bob Schmitt
38 Kansas State	13 C Bill Anderson
14 Michigan State	19 G Dave Alexander (T) / Greg Divis
31 Wisconsin	10 T Herb Wester
10 Michigan	37 TE Marv Cook
38 Purdue	14 QB Chuck Hartlieb
29 Indiana	21 WB Quinn Early
52 Northwestern	24 TB Kevin Harmon / Tony Stewart
29 Ohio State	27 FB David Hudson
34 Minnesota	20 DL Joe Mott
20 Wyoming	19 DL Myron Keppy / Steve Thomas
	DL Dave Haight
	DL Joe Schuster
	DL Mike Burke
	LB J.J. Puk
	LB Brad Quast
	DB Merton Hanks
	DB Greg Brown
	DB Kerry Burt
	DB Dwight Sistrunk

RUSHING: Harmon 151/715y, Hudson 113/464y, Stewart 68/326y
PASSING: Hartlieb 217-334/3092y, 19TD, 65%
RECEIVING: Early 63/1004y, Cook 49/803y, Watkins 33/534y
SCORING: Rob Houghtlin (K) 104pts, Early 60pts, Hudson 48pts

1988 6-4-3

24 Hawaii	27 WR Deven Harberts / Jon Filloon
45 Kansas State	10 T Bob Kratch
21 Colorado	24 G Bob Schmitt / Jim Poynton
10 Iowa State	3 C Bill Anderson
10 Michigan State	10 G Greg Divis
31 Wisconsin	6 T Jeff Croston / Rob Baxley
17 Michigan	17 TE Marv Cook
31 Purdue	7 QB Chuck Hartlieb
34 Indiana	45 WB Travis Watkins / Sean Smith
35 Northwestern	10 TB Tony Stewart
24 Ohio State	24 FB David Hudson / Richard Bass
31 Minnesota	22 DL Mike Burke / Tyrone Berrie
23 N. Carolina St.	28 DL Dave Haight
	DL Jeff Koeppel
	DL Jim Johnson
	DL Joe Mott
	LB Brad Quast
	LB Jim Reilly
	DB Keaton Smiley / Anthony Wright
	DB Merton Hanks
	DB Brian Wise / Mark Stoops
	DB Greg Brown / Gary Clark

RUSHING: Stewart 215/1036y, Hudson 77/292y, Mike Saunders (TB) 56/285y
PASSING: Hartlieb 288-460/3738y, 17TD, 62.6%
RECEIVING: Cook 63/767y, Harberts 53/880y, Watkins 35/552y
SCORING: Jeff Skillett (K) 64pts, Stewart 54pts, Harberts 38pts

1989 5-6

6 Oregon	44 WR Travis Watkins
31 Iowa State	21 T Rob Baxley / Mike Miller
30 Tulsa	22 G Bill Anderson
14 Michigan State	17 C Mike Devin
31 Wisconsin	24 G Scott Davis / Jim Poynton
12 Michigan	26 T George Hawthorne
35 Northwestern	22 TE John Palmer / Michael Titley
7 Illinois	31 QB Matt Rodgers
0 Ohio State	28 WB Danan Hughes / Mike Saunders
24 Purdue	0 TB Nick Bell / Tony Stewart
7 Minnesota	43 FB Richard Bass
	DL Larry Blue / Moses Santos
	DL Matt Ruhland / Rod Davis
	DL Jeff Koeppel
	DL Jim Johnson
	DL Jason Dumont / Leroy Smith
	LB Melvin Foster
	LB Brad Quast / John Derby
	DB Merton Hanks
	DB Anthony Wright / Greg Brown
	DB Brian Wise / Mark Stoops
	DB Eddie Polly / Tork Hook

RUSHING: Bell 117/603y, Stewart 92/356y, Bass 54/211y
PASSING: Rodgers 178-312/2222y, 12TD, 57.1%
RECEIVING: Watkins 36/583y, Hughes 28/471y, Saunders 28/343y
SCORING: George Murphy (K) 35pts, Bell 30pts, 3 tied w/ 24pts

1990 8-4

63 Cincinnati	10 WR Sean Smith/Mike Saunders/Jon Filloon
45 Iowa State	35 T Scott Davis
21 Miami	48 G Greg Aegerter
12 Michigan State	7 C Mike Devlin
30 Wisconsin	10 G Ted Velicer / Mike Miller
24 Michigan	23 T Rob Baxley
56 Northwestern	14 TE Michael Titley
54 Illinois	28 QB Matt Rodgers
26 Ohio State	27 WB Danan Hughes
38 Purdue	9 RB Nick Bell / Tony Stewart
24 Minnesota	31 FB Lew Montgomery / Paul Kujawa
34 Washington	46 DL Moses Santos / Jason Dumont
	DL Matt Ruhland
	DL Rod Davis / Mike Wells
	DL Jim Johnson / Jeff Nelson
	DL Leroy Smith
	LB John Derby
	LB Melvin Foster
	DB Eddie Polly / Scott Plate
	DB Merton Hanks
	DB Doug Buch / Gary Clark
	DB Brian Wise / Jason Olejniczak

RUSHING: Bell 166/1009y, Stewart 157/844y, Montgomery50/221y
PASSING: Rodgers 187-310/2228y, 15TD, 60.3%
RECEIVING: Hughes 29/410y, Titley 29/280y, Smith 24/361y
SCORING: Bell 84pts, Jeff Skillett (K) 82pts, Rodgers 56pts

1991 10-1-1

53 Hawaii	10 WR Jon Filloon
29 Iowa State	10 WR Danan Hughes
58 N. Illinois	7 T Scott Davis
24 Michigan	43 G Ted Velicer
10 Wisconsin	6 C Mike Devlin
24 Illinois	21 G Mike Ferroni / Dave Turner
31 Purdue	21 T Rob Baxley
16 Ohio State	9 TE Alan Cross
38 Indiana	21 QB Matt Rodgers
24 Northwestern	10 RB Mike Saunders
23 Minnesota	8 FB Lew Montgomery
13 BYU	13 DL Larry Blue
	DL Ron Geater / Jason Dumont
	DL Bret Bielema / Rod Davis /Maurea Crain
	DL Mike Wells / Jeff Nelson
	DL Leroy Smith
	LB Teddy Jo Faley / Matt Hilliard
	LB John Derby
	DB Scott Plate / Carlos James
	DB Eddie Polly
	DB Gary Clark
	DB Brian Wise / Jason Olejniczak

RUSHING: Saunders 216/1022y, Montgomery 121/220y, Marvin Lampkin (RB) 40/220y
PASSING: Rodgers 185-283/2275y, 14TD, 65.4%
RECEIVING: Hughes 43/757y, Filloon 36/451y, Montgomery 35/271y
SCORING: Saunders 78pts, Jeff Skillett (K) 67pts, Hughes & Montgomery 48pts

1992 5-7

14 N. Carolina St.	24 WR Harold Jasper / Jeff Anttila
7 Miami	24 WR Danan Hughes
21 Iowa State	7 T Scott Davis / Bill Lange
12 Colorado	28 G Ted Velicer / Matt Purdy
28 Michigan	52 C Mike Devlin
23 Wisconsin	22 G Mike Ferrani
24 Illinois	14 T Bob Rees / Hal Mady
16 Purdue	27 TE Alan Cross
15 Ohio State	38 QB Jim Hartlieb / Paul Burmeister
14 Indiana	0 RB Marvin Lampkin / Ryan Terry
56 Northwestern	14 FB Lew Montgomery
13 Minnesota	28 DL Larry Blue
	DL Jeff Nelson / Jason Dumont
	DL Maurea Crain / Bret Bielema
	DL Mike Wells
	DL John Hartlieb
	LB Matt Hilliard / Bobby Diaro
	LB Mike Dailey/ / Tyrone Boudreaux
	DB Scott Plate
	DB Carlos James
	DB Jason Olejniczak
	DB Doug Buch

RUSHING: Lampkin 171/653y, Terry 75/429y, Montgomery 86/358y
PASSING: Hartlieb 144-226/1579y, 12TD, 63.7%
RECEIVING: Cross 55/600y, Hughes 46/578y, Jasper 28/469y
SCORING: Hughes 38pts, Cross 34pts, Terry 30pts

1993 6-6

26 Tulsa	25 WR Harold Jasper
31 Iowa State	28 WR Anthony Dean
0 Penn State	31 T Bill Lange
7 Michigan	24 G Fritz Fequiere / Matt Quest
10 Indiana	16 C Casey Wiegmann / Hal Mady
3 Illinois	49 G Matt Purdy
10 Michigan State	24 T Ross Verba / Aaron Kooiker
26 Purdue	17 TE Scott Slutzker
54 Northern Illinois	20 QB Paul Burmeister
23 Northwestern	19 RB Ryan Terry / Sedrick Shaw
21 Minnesota	3 FB Cliff King
3 California	37 DL Larry Blue
	DL Chris Webb
	DL Maurea Crain / Scott Sether
	DL Mike Wells
	DL Parker Wildeman / Tony Bates
	LB Matt Hilliard / John Hartlieb
	LB Mike Dailey
	DB Damien Robinson / Tom Knight
	DB Scott Plate
	DB Jason Olejniczak
	DB Marquis Porter / Chris Jackson

RUSHING: Terry 157/664y, Shaw 127/561y, King 47/200y
PASSING: Burmeister 184-309/2152y, 10TD, 59.6%
RECEIVING: Jasper 38/641y, Dean 29/408y, Slutzker 29/307y
SCORING: Todd Romano (K) 49pts, Terry 42pts, King 24pts

1994 5-5-1

52 C. Michigan	21 WR Harold Jasper
37 Iowa State	9 WR Anthony Dean
21 Penn State	61 T Brian McCollouch
18 Oregon	40 G Fritz Fequiere
14 Michigan	29 C Casey Wiegmann / Hal Mady
20 Indiana	27 G Matt Purdy
7 Illinois	47 T Ross Verba
19 Michigan State	14 TE Mark Roussell / Scott Slutzker
21 Purdue	21 QB Ryan Driscoll / Matt Sherman
49 Northwestern	13 RB Sedrick Shaw / Ryan Terry
49 Minnesota	42 FB Kent Kahl
	DL Bill Ennis-Inge / Hausia Fuahala
	DL Jon LaFleur / Lloyd Bickham
	DL Parker Wildeman
	DL Chris Webb / Jeremy McKinney
	LB John Hartlieb / Brett Chambers
	LB Bobby Diaco
	LB George Bennett / Jason Henlon
	DB Damien Robinson / Billy Coats
	DB Tom Knight / Plez Atkins / Kerry Cooks
	DB Bo Porter
	DB Chris Jackson / Pat Boone

RUSHING: Shaw 170/1002y, Kahl 114/624y, Terry 61/350y
PASSING: Driscoll 78-154/1018y, 3TD, 50.7%
Sherman 42-59/736y, 6TD, 71.2%
RECEIVING: Jasper 33/621y, Slutzker 27/379y, Dean 21/271y
SCORING: Kahl 54pts, Shaw 50pts, Tavian Banks (RB) 30pts

1995 8-4

34 Northern Iowa	13 WR Demo Odems / Willie Guy
27 Iowa State	10 WR Tim Dwight
59 New Mexico St.	21 T Ross Verba
31 Michigan State	9 G Matt Purdy
22 Indiana	13 C Casey Wiegmann
27 Penn State	41 G Mike Goff
35 Ohio State	56 T Aaron Kooiker
7 Illinois	26 TE Scott Slutzker
20 Northwestern	31 QB Matt Sherman
33 Wisconsin	20 RB Sedrick Shaw / Tavian Banks
45 Minnesota	3 FB Rodney Filer / Michael Burger
38 Washington	18 DL George Bennett
	DL Jared DeVries
	DL Lloyd Bickham
	DL Jon LaFleur
	DL Bill Ennis-Inge
	LB Bobby Diaco
	LB Vernon Rollins
	DB Tom Knight
	DB Plez Atkins
	DB Damien Robinson / Kerry Cooks
	DB Chris Jackson

RUSHING: Shaw 316/1477y
PASSING: Sherman 170-295/2546y, 14TD, 57.6%
RECEIVING: Dwight 46/816y
SCORING: Shaw 92pts, Zach Bromert (K) 56pts, Dwight 54pts

1996 9-3

21 Arizona	20 WR Demo Odems
38 Iowa State	13 WR Tim Dwight
20 Tulsa	27 T Ross Verba
37 Michigan State	30 G Matt Reischl
31 Indiana	10 C Bill Reardon
21 Penn State	20 G Derek Rose
26 Ohio State	38 T Jeremy McKinney
31 Illinois	21 TE Chris Knipper / Zeron Flemister
13 Northwestern	40 QB Matt Sherman
31 Wisconsin	0 RB Sedrick Shaw / Tavian Banks
43 Minnesota	24 FB Michael Burger
27 Texas Tech 0	DL Brett Chambers
	DL Jared DeVries
	DL Aron Klein
	DL Jon LaFleur / Jon Ortlieb
	DL Bill Ennis-Inge / Jason House
	LB Vernon Rollins
	LB Matt Hughes
	DB Tom Knight
	DB Plez Atkins
	DB Damien Robinson
	DB Kerry Cooks

RUSHING: Shaw 224/1116y, Banks 144/629y, Burger 50/269y
PASSING: Sherman 154-264/1918y, 12TD, 58.3%
RECEIVING: Dwight 51/751y, Banks 21/137y, Odems 18/262y
SCORING: Banks 62pts, Shaw & Zach Bromert (K) 60pts

1997 7-5

66 Northern Iowa	0 WR Damon Gibson
54 Tulsa	16 WR Tim Dwight
63 Iowa State	20 T Chad Deal
38 Illinois	10 G Matt Reischl
7 Ohio State	23 C Derek Rose
24 Michigan	28 G Mike Goff
62 Indiana	0 T Jeremy McKinney
35 Purdue	17 TE Chris Knipper
10 Wisconsin	13 QB Matt Sherman / Randy Reiners
14 Northwestern	15 RB Tavian Banks
31 Minnesota	0 FB Michael Burger
7 Arizona State	17 DL Jason House / Tariq Peterson
	DL Jared DeVries
	DL Aron Klein
	DL Jon LaFleur / Epenesa Epenesa
	DL Jeff Kramer / Ryan Loftin
	LB Matt Hughes
	LB Raj Clark / Vernon Rollins
	DB Ed Gibson
	DB Plez Atkins / Tariq Holman
	DB Eric Thigpen
	DB Kerry Cooks

RUSHING: Banks 260/1691y, Rob Thien (RB) 78/382y,
Doug Miller (RB) 28/175y
PASSING: Sherman 82-158/1199y, 11TD, 51.8%
Reiners 54-100/907y, 12TD, 54%
RECEIVING: Dwight 42/704y, Gibson 26/595y, Banks 20/212y
SCORING: Banks 114pts, Zach Bromert (K) 72pts, Dwight 66pts

1998 3-8

38 C. Michigan	0 WR Bashir Yamini
9 Iowa State	27 WR Kahlil Hill
11 Arizona	35 T Ben Sobieski
37 Illinois	14 G Chad Deal / Travis Raitt
9 Michigan	12 C Derek Rose
26 Northwestern	24 G Matt Reischl
7 Indiana	14 T Alonzo Cunningham / Matt Rogers
0 Wisconsin	31 TE Jed Dull / Zeron Flemister
14 Purdue	36 QB Kyle McCann / Randy Reiners
14 Ohio State	45 RB Ladell Betts / Rob Thein
7 Minnesota	49 FB Trevor Bollers
	DL Ryan Loftin
	DL Jared DeVries
	DL Aron Klein
	DL Ed Saidat / Anthony Herron
	DL Jeff Kramer
	LB Matt Hughes / Travis Senters
	LB Roger Meyer/Raj Clark/AaronKampman
	DB Joe Slattery
	DB Tariq Holman / D.J. Johnson
	DB Eric Thigpen / Matt Stockdale
	DB Matt Bowen

RUSHING: Betts 188/679y, Thein 45/163y
PASSING: McCann 86-159/1179y, 2TD, 54.1%
RECEIVING: Hill 35/432y, Yamini 31/317y, Betts 20/259y
SCORING: Hill, Betts & Zach Bromert (K) 30pts

1999 1-10

7 Nebraska	42 WR Bashir Yamini
10 Iowa State	17 WR Kevin Kasper / Chris Oliver
24 Northern Illinois	0 T Bruce Nelson
3 Michigan	49 G Eric Steinbach / Jay Bickford
7 Penn State	31 C Chad Deal / A.J. Blazek
21 Northwestern	23 G B.J. Van Briesen / Andy Lightfoot
31 Indiana	38 T Alonzo Cunningham
11 Ohio State	41 TE Zeron Flemister / Austin Wheatley
24 Illinois	40 QB Scott Mullen / Randy Reiners
3 Wisconsin	41 TB Ladell Betts
21 Minnesota	25 FB Randy Thein
	DL Anthony Herron
	DL Corey Brown
	DL Jerry Montgomery / Colin Cole
	DL Scott Pospisil / Ed Saidat
	DL LeVar Woods / Mike Dolezal
	LB Aaron Kampman
	LB Fred Barr / Derrick Davison
	DB Tariq Holman
	DB Joe Slattery / D.J. Johnson
	DB Shane Hall / Matt Stockdale
	DB Matt Bowen

RUSHING: Betts 189/857y, Mullen 48/114y
PASSING: Mullen 126-226/1415y, 5TD, 55.8%
RECEIVING: Kasper 60/664y, Yamini 26/348y, Oliver 26/309y
SCORING: Tim Douglas (K) 37pts, Betts 36pts, Mullen 24pts

2000 3-9

7 Kansas State	27 WR Kahlil Hill / Ryan Barton
21 W. Michigan	27 WR Kevin Kasper
14 Iowa State	24 T Alonzo Cunningham
13 Nebraska	42 G Bruce Nelson
33 Indiana	45 C A.J. Blazek
21 Michigan State	16 G E.Steinbach/Pete Traynor/Andy Lightfoot
0 Illinois	31 T Robert Gallery (TE) / Sam Aiello
10 Ohio State	38 TE Kyle Trippeer
7 Wisconsin	13 QB Scott Mullen/Jon Beutjer/ Kyle McCann
26 Penn State	23 RB Ladell Betts
27 Northwestern	17 FB Jeremy Allen / Jonathan Babineaux
24 Minnesota	27 DL Anthony Herron
	DL Derrick Pickens
	DL Jerry Montgomery
	DL Aaron Kampman / Colin Cole
	LB LeVar Woods
	LB Roger Meyer / Mike Dolezal
	LB Fred Barr / Derrick Davison
	DB Tim Dodge / Matt Stockdale
	DB Benny Sapp / Cameron Smith
	DB Ryan Hansen / Chris Smith
	DB Robbertto Rickards

RUSHING: Betts 232/1090y, Allen 34/135y
PASSING: Mullen 74-141/877y, 5TD, 52.5%
Beutjer 77-125/841y, 61.6%
McCann 79-136/862y, 5TD, 58.1%
RECEIVING: Kasper 82/1010y, Hill 58/619y, Trippeer 19/188y
SCORING: Nate Kaeding (K) 62pts, Kasper 42pts, Betts 30pts

2001 7-5

51 Kent State	0 WR Khalil Hill / C.J. Jones
44 Miami (Ohio)	19 WR Chris Oliver / Tim Dodge
24 Penn State	18 T Robert Gallery
14 Purdue	23 G Eric Steinbach / Kory Borchers
28 Michigan State	31 C Bruce Nelson
42 Indiana	28 G A. Lightfoot/A. Cunningham/ Sam Aiello
26 Michigan	32 T David Porter
28 Wisconsin	34 TE Dallas Clark / Erik Jensen
59 Northwestern	16 QB Kyle McCann / Brad Banks
42 Minnesota	24 RB Ladell Betts / Aaron Greving
14 Iowa State	17 FB Jeremy Allen
19 Texas Tech 16	DL Colin Cole
	DL Derrick Pickens
	DL Jerry Montgomery / Jared Clauss
	DL Aaron Kampman
	LB Grant Steen
	LB Roger Meyer / Mike Dolezal
	LB Fred Barr
	DB Matt Stockdale / D.J. Johnson
	DB Benny Sapp
	DB Derek Pagel / Shane Hall
	DB Bob Sanders

RUSHING: Betts 222/1060y, Greving 60/333y, Allen 52/242y
PASSING: McCann 167-253/2028y, 17TD, 66%
RECEIVING: Hill 59/841y, Clark 38/539y, Jones 34/434y
SCORING: Nate Kaeding (K) 85pts, Betts 66pts, Hill & Allen 48pts

2002 11-2

57	Akron	21 WR Ed Hinkel / Clinton Solomon
29	Miami (Ohio)	24 WR C.J. Jones / Maurice Brown
31	Iowa State	36 T Robert Gallery
48	Utah State	7 G Eric Steinbach
42	Penn State	35 C Bruce Nelson
31	Purdue	28 G Andy Lightfoot / Ben Sobieski
44	Michigan State	16 T David Porter
24	Indiana	8 TE Dallas Clark
34	Michigan	9 QB Brad Banks
20	Wisconsin	3 RB Fred Russell / Jermelle Lewis
62	Northwestern	10 FB Edgar Cervantes
45	Minnesota	21 DL Howard Hodges
17	Southern Cal38 DL Jared Clauss	
		DL Colin Cole
		DL Jonathan Babineaux / Matt Roth
		LB Grant Steen
		LB Fred Barr
		LB Kevin Worthy
		DB D.J. Johnson / Jovon Johnson
		DB Antwan Allen
		DB Derek Pagel
		DB Bob Sanders / Scott Boleyn

RUSHING: Russell 220/1264y, Lewis 123/709y, Banks 81/423y
PASSING: Banks 170-294/2573y, 26TD, 57.8%
RECEIVING: Brown 48/966y, Clark 43/742y, Jones 38/468y
SCORING: Nate Kaeding (K) 120pts, Brown 66pts, Jones & Lewis 60pts

2003 10-3

21	Miami (Ohio)	3 WR Ramon Ochoa / Ed Hinkel
56	Buffalo	7 WR Maurice Brown / Calvin Davis
40	Iowa State	21 T Robert Gallery
21	Arizona State	2 G Mike Jones / Brian Ferentz
10	Michigan State	20 C Eric Rothwell
30	Purdue	27 G Peter McMahon / David Walker
10	Ohio State	19 T Sam Aiello
26	Penn State	14 TE Erik Jensen / Mike Follett
41	Illinois	10 QB Nathan Chandler
14	Purdue	27 RB Fred Russell
40	Minnesota	22 FB Edgar Cervantes
27	Wisconsin	21 DL Howard Hodges / Derreck Robinson
37	Florida	17 DL Jared Clauss / Tyler Luebke
		DL Jonathan Babineaux / Matt Neubauer
		DL Matt Roth
		LB Grant Steen / George Lewis
		LB Abdul Hodge
		LB Chad Greenway
		DB Jovon Johnson
		DB Antwan Allen
		DB Sean Considine / Miguel Merrick
		DB Bob Sanders / Chris Smith

RUSHING: Russell 282/1355y, Jermelle Lewis (RB) 46/241y, Schnoor 29/163y
PASSING: Chandler 165-307/2040y, 18TD, 53.7%
RECEIVING: Brown 33/507y, Ochoa 34/477y, Davis 23/330y
SCORING: Nate Kaeding (K) 106pts, Ochoa 48pts, Russell 42pts

2004 10-2

39	Kent State	7 WR Ed Hinkel / Scott Chandler
17	Iowa State	10 WR Warren Holloway / Clinton Solomon
7	Arizona State	44 T Lee Gray
17	Michigan	30 G Mike Jones
38	Michigan State	16 C Mike Elgin / Ben Cronin
33	Ohio State	7 G Brian Ferentz / Ben Gates
6	Penn State	4 T Peter McMahon
23	Illinois	13 TE Tony Jackson
23	Purdue	21 QB Drew Tate
29	Minnesota	27 RB Sam Brownlee / Jermelle Lewis
30	Wisconsin	7 FB Aaron Mickens / Tom Busch
30	LSU	25 DL Derreck Robinson
		DL Tyler Luebke
		DL Jonathan Babineaux
		DL Matt Roth
		LB George Lewis / Edmond Miles
		LB Abdul Hodge
		LB Chad Greenway
		DB Jovon Johnson
		DB Antwan Allen
		DB Sean Considine
		DB Marcus Paschal / Miguel Merrick

RUSHING: Brownlee 94/227y, Lewis 57/200y, Marques Simmons (RB) 51/194y
PASSING: Tate 233-375/2786y, 20TD, 62.1%
RECEIVING: Hinkel 63/744y, Soloman 58/905y, Holloway 29/283y
SCORING: Kyle Schlicher (K) 92pts, Hinkel 42pts, Solomon 36pts

2005 7-5

56	Ball State	0 WR Clinton Solomon / Andy Brodell
3	Iowa State	23 WR Ed Hinkel / Herb Grigsby
45	N. Iowa	21 T Ben Gates / Seth Olsen
6	Ohio State	31 G Mike Jones
35	Illinois	7 C Brian Ferentz
34	Purdue	16 G Mike Elgin
38	Indiana	21 T Marshall Yanda
20	Michigan	23 TE Scott Chandler / Ed Majerus
27	Northwestern	28 QB Drew Tate / Jason Manson
20	Wisconsin	10 RB Albert Young
52	Minnesota	28 FB Tom Busch
24	Florida31 DL Ken Iwebema	
		DL Matt Kroul / Ryan Bain
		DL Mitch King / Alex Willcox
		DL Bryan Mattison / Mike Follett
		LB Edmond Miles / Mike Humpal
		LB Abdul Hodge
		LB Chad Greenway
		DB Jovon Johnson
		DB Antwan Allen / Adam Shada
		DB Marcus Paschal
		DB Miguel Merrick / Charles Godfrey

RUSHING: Young 249/1334y, Damian Sims (RB) 30/296y, Shonn Greene (RB) 37/173y
PASSING: Tate 219-352/2828y, 22TD, 62.2%
  Manson 24-48/230y, 0TD, 50%
RECEIVING: Chandler 47/552y, Solomon 46/800y, Hinkel 40/518y
SCORING: Kyle Schlicher (K) 94pts, Hinkel & Young 48pts

2006 6-7

41	Montana	7 WR Dominique Douglas/Andy Brodell
20	Syracuse	13 WR Herb Grigsby / Trey Stess
27	Iowa State	17 T Dace Richardson / Seth Olsen (G)
24	Illinois	7 G Mike Jones
17	Ohio State	38 C Rafael Eubanks
47	Purdue	17 G Mike Elgin (C)
28	Indiana	31 T Marshall Yanda
6	Michigan	20 TE Scott Chandler / Tony Moeaki
24	N. Illinois	21 QB Drew Tate / Jason Manson (WR)
7	Northwestern	21 RB Albert Young / Damian Sims
21	Wisconsin	24 FB Tom Busch
24	Minnesota	34 DL Ken Iwebema / Alex Kanellis
24	Texas	26 DL Matt Kroul
		DL Mitch King / Ryan Bain
		DL Bryan Mattison
		LB Mike Humpal
		LB Mike Klinkenborg
		LB Edmond Miles
		DB Adam Shada / Bradley Fletcher
		DB Charles Godfrey
		DB Marcus Paschal / Marcus Wilson
		DB Miguel Merrick

RUSHING: Young 178/779y, Sims 132/664y, Shonn Greene (RB) 32/205y
PASSING: Tate 207-352/2623y, 18TD, 58.8%
RECEIVING: Douglas 49/654y, Chandler 46/591y, Brodell 39/724y
SCORING: Kyle Schlicher (K) 71pts, Young 48pts, Chandler & Sims 36pts

2007 6-6

16	N. Illinois	3 WR James Cleveland/Paul Chaney
35	Syracuse	0 WR Derrell Johnson-Koulianos/Andy Brodell
13	Iowa State	15 T Kyle Calloway / Dace Richardson
13	Wisconsin	17 G Travis Meade / Bryan Bulaga
20	Indiana	38 C Rafael Eubanks
7	Penn State	27 G Julian Vandervelde / Dan Doering
10	Illinois	6 T Seth Olsen
6	Purdue	31 TE Brandon Myers / Tony Moeaki
34	Michigan State	27 QB Jake Christensen
28	Northwestern	17 RB Albert Young / Damian Sims
21	Minnesota	16 FB/WR Tom Busch / Trey Stross
19	W. Michigan	28 DL Ken Iwebema / Adrian Clayborn
		DL Matt Kroul
		DL Mitch King
		DL Bryan Mattison / Chad Geary
		LB A.J. Edds / Jacody Coleman
		LB Mike Klinkenborg / Bryon Gattas
		LB Mike Humpal
		DB Adam Shada / Bradley Fletcher
		DB Charles Godfrey
		DB Brett Greenwood / Devan Moylan
		DB Harold Dalton

RUSHING: Young 206/968y, Sims 100/499y
PASSING: Christensen 198-370/2269y, 17TD, 53.5%
RECEIVING: Johnson-Koulianos 38/482y, Cleveland 36/464y, Young 23/212y
SCORING: Young 42pts, Daniel Murray (K) 37pts, Myers 30pts

2008 9-4

46	Maine	3 WR Derrell Johnson-Koulianos
42	Fla. International	0 WR Andy Brodell / Trey Stross
17	Iowa State	5 T Bryan Bulaga
20	Pittsburgh	21 G Julian Vandervelde / Rafael Eubanks
17	Northwestern	22 C Rob Bruggeman
13	Michigan State	16 G Seth Olsen / Andy Kuempel
45	Indiana	9 T Kyle Calloway
38	Wisconsin	16 TE Brandon Myers / Tony Moeaki
24	Illinois	27 QB Ricky Stanzi / Jake Christensen
24	Penn State	23 RB Shonn Greene
22	Purdue	17 FB Brett Morse / Wade Leppert
55	Minnesota	0 DL Adrian Clayborn / Chad Geary
31	South Carolina10 DL Matt Kroul	
		DL Mitch King
		DL Christian Ballard / Broderick Bunns
		LB A.J. Edds
		LB Pat Angerer / Jacody Coleman
		LB Jeremiha Hunter
		DB Bradley Fletcher
		DB Amari Spievey
		DB Brett Greenwood
		DB Tyler Sash / Harold Dalton

RUSHING: Greene 307/1850y, Jewel Hampton (RB) 91/463y
PASSING: Stanzi 150-254/1956y, 14TD, 59.1%
  Christensen 36-63/396y, 2TD, 57.1%
RECEIVING: Johnson-Kouliano 44/639y, Brodell 36/533y, Myers 34/441y
SCORING: Greene 110pts, Trent Mossbrucker (K) 70pts, Jewel Hampton (RB) 42pts

2009 11-2

17	N. Iowa	16 WR D. Johnson-Koulianos / Marvin McNutt
35	Iowa State	3 WR Trey Stross / Colin Sandeman
27	Arizona	17 T Bryan Bulaga
21	Penn State	10 G Riley Reiff (T)
24	Arkansas State	21 C Rafael Eubanks
30	Michigan	28 G Julian Vandervelde / Dace Richardson
20	Wisconsin	10 T Kyle Calloway
15	Michigan State	13 TE Tony Moeaki / Allen Reisner
42	Indiana	24 QB Ricky Stanzi / James Vandenberg
10	Northwestern	17 RB Adam Robinson / Brandon Wegher
24	Ohio State	27 FB Brett Morse
12	Minnesota	0 DL Adrian Clayborn
24	Georgia Tech	14 DL Karl Klug
		DL Christian Ballard
		DL Broderick Binns
		LB A.J. Edds
		LB Pat Angerer
		LB Jeremiha Hunter / Troy Johnson
		DB Shaun Prater / William Lowe
		DB Amari Spievey
		DB Brett Greenwood
		DB Tyler Sash

RUSHING: Robinson 181/834y, Wegher 162/641y
PASSING: Stanzi 171-304/2417y, 17TD, 56.2%
  Vandenberg 42-87/470y, 2TD, 48.3%
RECEIVING: Johnson-Koulianos45/750y, McNutt 34/674y, Stross 31/414, Moeaki 30/387y
SCORING: Daniel Murray (K) 89pts, McNutt & Wegher 48pts

2010 8-5

37	E. Illinois	7 WR D.Johnson-Koulianos/Colin Sandeman
35	Iowa State	9 WR Marvin McNutt / Brad Herman
27	Arizona	34 T Riley Reiff
45	Ball State	0 G Julian Vandervelde / Adam Gettis
24	Penn State	3 C James Ferentz
38	Michigan	28 G Nolan MacMillan / Josh Koeppel
30	Wisconsin	31 T Markus Zusevics
37	Michigan State	6 TE Allen Reisner
18	Indiana	13 QB Ricky Stanzi
17	Northwestern	21 RB Adam Robinson / Adam Coker
7	Ohio State	20 FB Brett Morse / Brad Rogers
24	Minnesota	27 DL Adrian Clayborn
27	Missouri	24 DL Karl Klug
		DL Mike Daniels / Broderick Binns
		DL Christian Ballard
		LB Tyler Nielsen / Troy Johnson
		LB James Morris / Jeff Tarpinian
		LB Jeremiha Hunter / Shane DiBona
		DB Shaun Prater / Greg Castillo
		DB Micah Hyde
		DB Brett Greenwood
		DB Tyler Sash

RUSHING: Robinson 203/941y, Coker 114/622y
PASSING: Stanzi 221-345/3004y, 25TD, 64.1%
RECEIVING: McNutt 53/861y, Johnson-Koulianos 46/745y, Reisner 42/460y
SCORING: Mike Meyer (K) 73pts, Robinson & Johnson-Koulianos 66pts

IOWA STATE

Iowa State University (Founded 1858)
Ames, Iowa
Nickname: Cyclones
Colors: Cardinal and Gold
Stadium: Jack Trice Stadium (55,000)
Conference Affiliations: Big Seven (1948-59), Big Eight (1960-95),
Big Twelve North (1996-present)

CAREER RUSHING YARDS	Attempts	Yards
Troy Davis (1994-96)	782	4382
Darren Davis (1996-99)	823	3763
Dexter Green (1975-78)	738	3437
Alexander Robinson (2007-10)	705	3309
Mike Strachan (1972-74)	728	3010
Ennis Haywood (1998-01)	572	2862
Joe Henderson (1985-88)	627	2715
Stevie Hicks (2003-06)	649	2601
Dave Hoppmann (1960-62)	588	2562
Dwayne Crutchfield (1980-81)	591	2501

CAREER PASSING YARDS	Comp.-Att.	Yards
Bret Meyer (2004-07)	820-1414	9499
Austin Arnaud (2007-10)	616-1031	6777
Alex Espinoza (1984-86)	454-891	5307
Seneca Wallace (2001-02)	411-712	5289
Todd Bandhauer (1995-98)	404-826	5235
Sage Rosenfels (1997-00)	306-587	4164
David Archer (1982-83)	359-647	4104
Bret Oberg (1988-89)	251-424	3602
Tim Van Galder (1964-66)	259-578	3417
Todd Doxzon (1993-96)	244-443	3158

CAREER RECEIVING YARDS	Catches	Yards
Todd Blythe (2004-07)	176	3096
Lane Danielson (2000-03)	163	2690
Tracy Henderson (1982-84)	150	2048
Ed Williams (1994-97)	132	1850
R.J. Sumrall (2005-08)	156	1805
Otto Stowe (1968-70)	132	1751
Dennis Ross (1985-88)	118	1529
Marquis Hamilton (2006-09)	127	1509
Jon Davis (2003-06)	126	1445
Jim Doran (1948-50)	79	1410

SEASON RUSHING YARDS	Attempts	Yards
Troy Davis (1996)	402	2185
Troy Davis (1995)	345	2010
Blaise Bryant (1989)	299	1516
Darren Davis (1999)	287	1388
Dwayne Crutchfield (1980)	284	1312

SEASON PASSING YARDS	Comp.-Att.	Yards
Seneca Wallace (2002)	244-443	3245
Bret Meyer (2005)	227-368	2876
Austin Arnaud (2008)	247-401	2792
David Archer (1983)	234-403	2639
Bret Meyer (2006)	211-374	2546

SEASON RECEIVING YARDS	Catches	Yards
Lane Danielson (2002)	63	1073
Tracy Henderson (1983)	81	1051
Todd Blythe (2005)	51	1000
Tracy Henderson (1984)	64	941
Todd Blythe (2004)	39	833

GAME RUSHING YARDS	Attempts	Yards
Troy Davis (1996 vs. Missouri)	41	378
Troy Davis (1995 vs. UNLV)	38	302
Troy Davis (1995 vs. Ohio)	40	291

GAME PASSING YARDS	Comp.-Att.	Yards
Austin Arnaud (2008 vs. Kansas State)	31-45	440
Todd Bandhauer (1998 vs. Texas)	30-62	437
Seneca Wallace (2002 vs. Missouri)	31-47	425

GAME RECEIVING YARDS	Catches	Yards
Tracy Henderson (1984 vs. Texas A&M)	11	217
Todd Blythe (2005 vs. Texas A&M)	8	214
Steve Lester (1989 vs. Oklahoma)	13	203
Jim Doran (1949 vs. Oklahoma)	8	203

GREATEST COACH:

Although head men Clay Stapleton, Johnny Majors, and Dan McCarney all produced some good Iowa State teams, there is only one man who has coached in Ames during the past 55 seasons with an overall winning record: Hall of Famer Earle Bruce. That fact may be the main reason Bruce is enshrined in South Bend.

Bruce applied classic winning-with-a-secondary-program technique. Playing a lot of kids early on, then adding a great recruiting class, Bruce finally had a team combined with experienced veterans and talented youngsters. It took three straight 4-7 teams coming out of the chute, but there is patience in places like Ames. In 1976 everything came together when Bruce's Cyclones won 8 games, including a stunning 37-28 upset over Nebraska. It was ISU's first win over the Huskers since 1960. The season ended with disappointment when no bowl invitations came their way.

Bruce did it again the following season, winning 8 of 11 regular season games with another upset of Nebraska. The Cyclones did earn a bowl bid, losing to North Carolina State in the Peach Bowl, 24-14. 1978 was more of the same: 8 wins (but this time Nebraska won 23-0) and a bowl loss. But, Iowa State never won 24 games over a three-year period, not before Bruce's arrival nor after.

Of course, for programs like Iowa State all good things must come to an end. The winning senior class had graduated and Bruce moved on to Columbus, Ohio, to inherit Woody Hayes's Ohio State program. While the Cyclones dipped down to 3 wins in 1979, Bruce's Buckeyes won all 11 regular season contests to enter the bowl season with a no. 1 ranking. They fell to Southern California in the Rose Bowl by one point, 17-16, however, to lose out on a national championship. Bruce then reeled off six straight 9-3 seasons, which would have permanently endeared him to the Iowa State faithful but angered the Ohio State fans. After winning 10 games in 1986, the Buckeyes slipped to 6-4-1 in 1987 and Bruce was gone. Ironically he was replaced by John Cooper, a member of the "Dirty Thirty" 1959 Iowa State team that surprisingly went 7-3.

IOWA STATE'S 55 GREATEST SINCE 1953

OFFENSE

WIDE RECEIVER: Eppie Barney, Lane Danielson, Tracy Henderson, Otto Stowe
TIGHT END: Mike Busch, Keith Krepfle
TACKLE: Aaron Brant, Karl Nelson, John Van Sicklen, Doug Skartvedt
GUARD: Dan Celoni, Geary Murdock, Bruce Reimers, Reggie Stephens, Gene Williams
CENTER: Ben Bruns, Arden Esslinger
QUARTERBACK: George Amundson, Bret Meyer, Seneca Wallace
RUNNING BACK: Troy Davis, Dexter Green, Ennis Haywood, Dave Hoppmann, Mike Strachan
FULLBACK: Tom Watkins

DEFENSE

END: Merv Krakau, Kenny Neil, Rick White
TACKLE: Jordan Carstens, George Dimitri, Tom Randall, James Reed, Mike Stensrud
LINEBACKER: Tom Boskey, Dennis Gibson, Keith Schroeder, Mike Shane, Brad Storm, Chris Washington
CORNERBACK: Joe Brown, Tony Hawkins, Marcus Robertson
SAFETY: Matt Blair, Mark DouBrava, Barry Hill, Mike Schwartz, Tony Washington

SPECIAL TEAMS

RETURN SPECIALISTS: Luther Blue, James McMillion
PLACE KICKER: Jeff Shudak
PUNTER: Marc Harris

MULTIPLE POSITIONS

NOSE GUARD-LINEBACKER: Larry Hunt

TWO-WAY PLAYERS

HALFBACK-DEFENSIVE BACK-KICK RETURNER: Dwight Nichols
FULLBACK-DEFENSIVE BACK-KICK RETURNER: Tom Vaughn

PERFORMANCE FORMULA:
IOWA STATE'S 10 BEST SEASONS

1976	1.3972	17 of 70
1971	1.3476	18 of 70
2000	1.2764	23 of 70
1960	1.2131	26 of 70
1977	1.1990	27 of 70
1959	1.1864	31 of 70
2005	1.1857	30 of 70
1978	1.1602	29 of 70
2001	1.0974	40 of 70
1962	1.0837	39 of 70

IOWA STATE CYCLONES

Year	W-L-T	AP Poll	Conference Standing	Toughest Regular Season Opponents	Coach (Record at School)	Bowl Games		
1953	2-7		7	Oklahoma 8-1-1, Kansas State 6-3-1, Missouri 6-4	Abe Stuber (24-38-3)			
1954	3-6		6	Oklahoma 10-0, Colorado 7-2-1, Nebraska 6-4, Kansas State 7-3	Vince DiFrancesca			
1955	1-7-1		5t	Oklahoma 10-0, Colorado 6-4, Denver 8-2	Vince DiFrancesca			
1956	2-8		7	Oklahoma 10-0, Colorado 7-2-1,	Vince DiFrancesca (6-21-1)			
1957	4-5-1		5t	Oklahoma 9-1, Colorado 6-3-1, Darkae 7-1	J.A. Myers (4-5-1)			
1958	4-6		7	Oklahoma 9-1, Colorado 6-4, Missouri 5-4-1	Clay Stapleton			
1959	7-3		3t	Oklahoma 7-3, Missouri 6-4	Clay Stapleton			
1960	7-3		4	Missouri 9-1, Kansas 7-2-1, Colorado 6-4	Clay Stapleton			
1961	5-5		5	Colorado 9-1, Missouri 7-2-1, Kansas 6-3-1	Clay Stapleton			
1962	5-5		5	Nebraska 8-2, Oklahoma 8-2, Missouri 7-1-2, Oregon State 8-2	Clay Stapleton			
1963	4-5		4t	Nebraska 9-1, Oklahoma 8-2, Missouri 7-3	Clay Stapleton			
1964	1-8-1		8	Nebraska 9-1, Oklahoma 6-3-1, Missouri 6-3-1, Arizona 6-3-1	Clay Stapleton			
1965	5-4-1		4	Nebraska 10-0, Missouri 7-2-1, Colorado 6-2-2	Clay Stapleton			
1966	2-6-2		6	Nebraska 9-1, Colorado 7-3, Missouri 6-3-1, Colorado State 7-3	Clay Stapleton			
1967	2-8		7	Oklahoma 9-1, Colorado 8-2, Missouri 7-3, Nebraska 6-4	Clay Stapleton (42-53-4)			
1968	3-7		8	Kansas 9-1, Oklahoma 7-3, Arizona 8-2, Missouri 7-3	John Majors			
1969	3-7		7	Missouri 9-1, Nebraska 8-2, Colorado 7-3	John Majors			
1970	5-6		8	Nebraska 10-0-1, Oklahoma 7-4, New Mexico 7-3, Colorado 6-4	John Majors			
1971	8-4		4	Nebraska 12-0, Oklahoma 10-1, Colorado 9-2, Idaho 8-3	John Majors	Sun	15 LSU	33
1972	5-6-1		6	Oklahoma 10-1, Nebraska 8-2-1, Colorado 8-3, San Diego St. 10-1	John Majors (24-30-1)	Liberty	30 Georgia Tech	31
1973	4-7		6t	Oklahoma 10-0, Nebraska 8-2-1, Kansas 7-3-1, Missouri 7-4	Earle Bruce			
1974	4-7		6	Oklahoma 11-0, Nebraska 8-3, BYU 7-3-1, Missouri 7-4	Earle Bruce			
1975	4-7		7	Oklahoma 10-1, Nebraska 10-1, UCLA 8-2-1, Missouri 6-5	Earle Bruce			
1976	8-3	19	4t	Oklahoma 8-2-1, Colorado 8-3, Missouri 6-5	Earle Bruce			
1977	8-4		2t	Oklahoma 10-1, Nebraska 8-3	Earle Bruce	Peach	14 North Carolina St.	24
1978	8-4		3t	Oklahoma 10-1, Nebraska 9-2, Missouri 7-4	Earle Bruce (36-32)	Hall of Fame	12 Texas A&M	28
1979	3-8		5	Oklahoma 10-1, Nebraska 10-1, Texas 9-2	Donnie Duncan			
1980	6-5		6	Oklahoma 9-2, Nebraska 9-2, Missouri 8-3	Donnie Duncan			
1981	5-5-1		6	Nebraska 9-2, Iowa 8-3, Oklahoma 6-4-1, Missouri 7-4	Donnie Duncan			
1982	4-6-1		6t	Nebraska 11-1, Oklahoma 8-3, Iowa 7-4, Missouri 5-4-2	Donnie Duncan (18-24-2)			
1983	4-7		4t	Nebraska 11-0, Iowa 9-2, Oklahoma State 7-4, Missouri 7-4	Jim Criner			
1984	2-7-2		8	Oklahoma 9-1-1, Nebraska 9-2, Oklahoma St. 9-2, Iowa 7-4-1	Jim Criner			
1985	5-6		5	Iowa 10-1, Oklahoma 10-1, Nebraska 9-2, Oklahoma State 8-3	Jim Criner			
1986	6-5		5	Oklahoma 10-1, Nebraska 9-2, Iowa 8-3, Colorado 6-5	Jim Criner (16-24-2), Chuck Banker [1-1]			
1987	3-8		6	Oklahoma 11-0, Nebraska 10-1, Oklahoma State 9-2, Iowa 9-3	Jim Walden			
1988	5-6		5	Nebraska 11-1, Oklahoma 9-2, Oklahoma St. 9-2	Jim Walden			
1989	6-5		4	Colorado 11-0, Nebraska 10-1, Minnesota 6-5	Jim Walden			
1990	4-6-1		4t	Colorado 10-1-1, Nebraska 9-2, Oklahoma 8-3, Iowa 8-3	Jim Walden			
1991	3-7-1		6	Iowa 10-1, Nebraska 9-1-1, Colorado 8-2-1, Oklahoma 8-3	Jim Walden			
1992	4-7		6t	Colorado 9-1-1, Nebraska 9-2	Jim Walden			
1993	3-8		6t	Nebraska 11-0, Wisconsin 9-1-1, Kansas St. 8-2-1, Oklahoma 8-3	Jim Walden			
1994	0-10-1		7t	Nebraska 12-0, Colorado 10-1, Kansas State 9-2	Jim Walden (28-57-3)			
1995	3-8		7t	Nebraska 11-0, Colorado 9-2, Kansas State 9-2, Iowa 7-5	Dan McCarney			
1996	2-9		N6	Nebraska 10-1, Colorado 9-2, Kansas State 9-2, Iowa 8-3	Dan McCarney			
1997	1-10		N6	Nebraska 11-0, Kansas State 10-1, Texas A&M 9-2, Iowa 7-4	Dan McCarney			
1998	3-8		N5t	Kansas St. 11-0, Nebraska 9-3, Texas 8-3, Missouri 7-4	Dan McCarney			
1999	4-7		N5t	Nebraska 10-1, Kansas State 10-1, Texas 9-3, Oklahoma 7-4	Dan McCarney			
2000	9-3	25	N3	Kansas State 10-2, Nebraska 9-2, Texas A&M 7-4	Dan McCarney	Insight.com	37 Pittsburgh	29
2001	7-5		N3	Colorado 9-2, Nebraska 11-1, Texas A&M 7-4	Dan McCarney	Independence	13 Alabama	14
2002	7-7		N3	Iowa 11-1, Kansas State 10-2, OU 10-2, Texas 10-2, Colorado 9-3	Dan McCarney	Humanitarian	16 Boise State	34
2003	2-10		N6	OU 12-0, Texas 10-2, Kansas State 10-3, Nebraska 9-3, Iowa 9-3	Dan McCarney			
2004	7-5		N1t	Iowa 9-2, Texas A&M 7-4, Colorado 7-4	Dan McCarney	Independence	17 Miami (Ohio)	13
2005	7-5		N2t	Iowa 7-4, Colorado 7-4, Nebraska 7-4	Dan McCarney	Houston	24 TCU	27
2006	4-8		N6	Oklahoma 10-2, Nebraska 9-3, Missouri 8-4	Dan McCarney (56-85)			
2007	3-9		N5t	Texas 9-3, Oklahoma 10-2, Missouri 11-1, Kansas 11-1	Gene Chizik			
2008	2-10		N6	Iowa 8-4, Oklahoma State 9-3, Missouri 9-4	Gene Chizik (5-19)			
2009	7-6		N4	Iowa 10-2, Nebraska 9-4, Oklahoma State 9-3	Paul Rhoads	Insight	14 Minnesota	13
2010	5-7		N3t	Utah 10-2, Oklahoma 11-2, Nebraska 10-3, Missouri 10-2	Paul Rhoads (12-13)			

TOTAL: 250-371-14 .4047 (64 of 70)   **Bowl Games since 1953:**   3-7 .3000 (68 of 70)

GREATEST TEAM SINCE 1953: With all due respects to the heroic effort of the "Dirty Thirty" squad from 1959, the 1978 team was arguably the most talented squad as yet assembled by Iowa State. Ranked for half the year, the 1978 team won eight games for the third season in a row before falling to Texas A&M in the Hall of Fame Bowl.

1953 2-7

35	South Dakota	0	E Barney Allemon / Bob Clark
0	Northwestern	35	T Ralph Brown / Ron Thompson
0	Kansas	23	G Bill Wilson / Wayne Horras
12	Kansas State	20	C Jim Rawley
13	Missouri	6	G Gean Kowalski / Erhard Moosman
7	Drake	12	T Jack Lessin / Chuck Coey
34	Colorado	41	E Kim Tidd / Bob Rohwedder
19	Nebraska	27	QB Bill Plantan / Daryl Hobbs
0	Oklahoma	47	HB Dan Rice / Gary Lutz
			HB Dick Cox
			FB Max Burkett / Hank Philmon

RUSHING: Burkett 109/342y
PASSING: Plantan 57-100/723y, 4TD, 57%
RECEIVING: Lutz 15/249y
SCORING: Plantan (QB-K) 41pts

1954 3-6

34	So. Dakota St.	6	E Barney Allemon / Mell Wostoupal
14	Northwestern	27	T Ray Tweeten / Ralph Brown
14	Nebraska	39	G Wayne Horras / Herb McDermott
33	Kansas	6	C Elmer May / Dick Wager
0	Colorado	20	G Weldon Thalacker / Jim Lyons
14	Missouri	32	T Jim McCaulley / Oliver Sparks
35	Drake	0	E Harold Potts / Kim Tidd
0	Oklahoma	40	QB John Breckenridge / Jerry Finley
7	Kansas	12	HB Gary Lutz / Hank Philmon
			HB Bruce Alexander / Fred Rippel
			FB Max Burkett / Donn Lorenzen

RUSHING: Burkett 97/528y, Philmon 42/238y, Alexander 43/187y
PASSING: Breckenridge 35-76/236y, 2TD, 46.1%
RECEIVING: Wostoupal 12/151y, Alleman 10/103y, Philmon 9/51y
SCORING: Burkett 30pts, Alexander 26pts, Lorenzen 24pts

1955 1-7-1

7	Denver	19	E Jerry Bartell / Jim Stuelke
0	Illinois	40	T Ray Tweeten / Dick Callahan
7	Kansas	7	G Bob Bird
20	Missouri	14	C Jack Falter / Grant Blaney
7	Kansas State	9	G Jim Lyons / Ron Bredeson
21	Drake	27	T Jim McCaulley / Oliver Sparks
7	Nebraska	10	E Harold Potts / Mell Wostoupal
0	Oklahoma	52	QB John Breckenridge / Al Rickert
0	Colorado	40	HB Gary Lutz /Hank Philmon /Jack Hansen
			HB Bruce Alexander / Fred Rippel
			FB Donn Lorenzen/Bill Jensen/Marv Walter

RUSHING: Lorenzen 32/179y, Alexander 55/142y, Rippel 12/122y
PASSING: Breckenridge 36-89/354y, 4TD, 40.4%
RECEIVING: Potts 14/173y, Alexander 8/47y, Philmon 6/85y
SCORING: Potts 18pts, Hansen 12pts, Callahan 9pts

1956 2-8

13	Denver	10	E Brian Dennis / Jerry Donohue
13	Northwestern	14	T Andris Poncius
7	Nebraska	9	G Howie Heinrich / Ron Bredeson
14	Kansas	25	C Grant Blaney /Jack Falter / Frank Powell
0	Colorado	52	G Chuck Muelhaupt / Ralph Losee
0	Missouri	34	T Oliver Sparks
39	Drake	14	E John Scheldrup / Gale Gibson
0	Oklahoma	40	QB Terry Ingram / Charley Martin / Phil Hill
6	Kansas State	32	HB Fred Rippel / Jack Hansen
0	Villanova	26	HB Bob Harden / Jim Lary / Paul Shupe
			FB Marv Walter

RUSHING: Harden 70/244y, Rippel 50/229y, Walter 56/183y
PASSING: Hill 14-38/205y, 3TD, 28.2%
RECEIVING: Scheldrup 6/140y, Harden 5/63y, Rippel 4/61y
SCORING: Harden 24pts, Latting 18pts, Hansen & Walter 12pts

1957 4-5-1

10	Denver	0	E Brian Dennis / Bob Anderson
7	Syracuse	7	T Andris Poncius / Lyle Carlson
14	Oklahoma	40	G Bob Bird / Ralph Losee
21	Kansas	6	C Jack Falter / Frank Powell
13	Missouri	35	G Dave Munger / Jack Tilles
10	Kansas State	14	T Don Metcalf
0	Drake	20	E Gale Gibson / Jim Stuelke
13	Nebraska	0	BB Marv Walter / Terry Ingram
33	So. Dakota	0	TB Dwight Nichols / Pete Goeser
21	Colorado	38	WB Jim Lary / Roger Spaulding
			FB Bob Harden / Ron Pohl

RUSHING: Nichols 211/668y, Goeser 69/232y, Harden 55/193y
PASSING: Nichols 50-99/51y, 7TD, 50%
RECEIVING: Dennis 15/256y, Stuelke 15/226y, Gibson 10/138y
SCORING: Nichols & Ingram 24pts, Dennis & Carlson 18pts

1958 4-6

33	Drake	0	E Bob Anderson / Gerald Winstead
14	Arizona	0	T Larry Van Der Heyden
6	Nebraska	7	G Dave Munger/Ray Fauser/Tom Ferrebee
0	Kansas	7	C Arden Esslinger
0	Colorado	20	G Jerry Schoenfelder/ Astleford Donohue
6	Missouri	14	T Charlie Martin / Ralph Losee
53	South Dakota	0	E Gale Gibson
0	Oklahoma	20	BB Ron Pohl / Cliff Rick / Phil Hill
6	Kansas State	14	TB Dwight Nichols/Don Webb/Terry Ingram
9	San Jose State	6	WB Tom Watkins/Mike Fitzgerald/P Goeser
			FB Bob Harden / Chuck Lamson

RUSHING: Nichols 220/815y, Harden 90/354y, Lamson 52/262y
PASSING: Nichols 26-55/357y, 0TD, 47.3%,
RECEIVING: Gibson 9/148y, Fitzgerald 6/156y, Watkins 4/88y
SCORING: Harden 42pts, Nichols & Fitzgerald 18pts

1959 7-3

41	Drake	0	E Bob Anderson / Lou Gartner
28	Denver	12	T Jerry Schoenfelder / Tom Graham
0	Missouri	14	G Tom Ferrebee / Dick Scesniak
41	South Dakota	6	C Arden Esslinger / Jon Spelman
27	Colorado	0	G Dan Celoni /Alex Perez /Hank Vogelman
26	Kansas State	0	T Larry Van Der Heyden / Ron Walter
0	Kansas	6	E Don Webb / Leo Marshall
18	Nebraska	6	BB Cliff Rick / John Cooper / Jim Stehbens
55	San Jose State	0	TB Dwight Nichols
12	Oklahoma	35	WB Mickey Fitzgerald / Steve Sturek
			FB Tom Watkins / Paul Sullivan

RUSHING: Watkins 161/843y, Nichols 207/749y, Fitzgerald 53/374y
PASSING: Nichols 43-80/609y, 8TD, 53.7%
RECEIVING: Webb 24/309y, Fitzgerald 9/179y, Anderson 5/77y,
SCORING: Nichols & Watkins 54pts, Fitzgerald 42pts

1960 7-3

46	Drake	0	E Larry Montre/L Gartner/Duane Marcellus
44	Detroit	21	T Gary Astleford / Ron Walter
10	Nebraska	8	G Dick Scesniak / Carl Proto
14	Kansas	28	C Arden Esslinger
6	Colorado	21	G Dan Celoni
8	Missouri	34	T Larry Van Der Heyden
13	Oklahoma State	9	E Don Webb
10	Oklahoma	6	BB Cliff Rick / John Cooper
20	Kansas State	7	TB Dave Hoppmann / Mickey Fitzgerald
14	Pacific	6	WB Dave Clayberg / J.W. Burden
			FB Tom Watkins

RUSHING: Hoppmann 161/844y, Watkins 163/688y
PASSING: Hoppmann 17-40/214y, 3TD, 42.5%
RECEIVING: Webb 13/203y, Fitzgerald 5/92y, Montre 4/57y
SCORING: Watkins 60pts, Hoppmann 30pts, Fitzgerald 16pts

1961 5-5

21	Drake	0	E Larry Schreiber / Larry Montre
14	Oklahoma State	7	T Tom Graham / Don Anderson
21	Oklahoma	15	G Dan Celoni
7	Kansas	21	C Jon Spelman
7	Missouri	13	G Carl Proto
31	Kansas State	7	T Dick Walton
10	Boston College	14	E Steve Sturek / Larry Hannahs
13	Nebraska	16	BB Paul Sullivan / Jim Clapper
27	Tulsa	6	WB J.W. Burden / Dick Limerick
0	Colorado	34	TB Dave Hoppmann
			FB Dave Clayberg

RUSHING: Hoppmann 229/920y, Hoover 79/327y, Burden 37/169y
PASSING: Hoppmann 41-91/718y, 7TD, 45.1%
RECEIVING: Limerick 21/402y, Montre 10/210y, Burden 7/84y
SCORING: Hoppmann 30pts, Montre, Limerick & Hoover 24pts

1962 5-5

14	Drake	7	E Larry Schreiber / Larry Hannahs
35	Oregon State	39	T John Van Sicklen / Don Anderson
22	Nebraska	36	G Tim Brown / Carl Proto
8	Kansas	29	C Ray Steffy / Jim Clapper
57	Colorado	19	G Dick Walton
6	Missouri	21	T Norm Taylor / Chuck Steimle
34	Oklahoma State	7	E Larry Montre / John McGonegle
0	Oklahoma	41	QB Dave Hoppmann (HB) / Larry Switzer
28	Kansas State	14	HB Dick Limerick
31	Ohio	22	HB Dave Hoover / Otis Williams
			FB Tom Vaughn

RUSHING: Hoppmann 198/798y, Vaughn 190/597y, Hoover 46/233y
PASSING: Hoppmann 40-89/679y, 6TD, 44.9%
RECEIVING: Limerick 17/296y, Montre 10/105y, Schreiber 8/167y
SCORING: Hoppmann 66pts, Vaughn 60pts, Schreiber 33pts

1963 4-5

8	California	15	E Larry Hannahs
21	VMI	6	T Norm Taylor
7	Nebraska	21	G Chuck Steimle
17	Kansas	14	C John Berrington
19	Colorado	9	T Tim Brown
0	Missouri	7	T John Van Sicklen
33	Oklahoma State	28	E Randy Kidd
14	Oklahoma	24	QB Ken Bunte
10	Kansas State	21	HB Dave Hoover / Ozzie Clay
Drake cancelled			HB Dick Limerick / Otis Williams
			FB Tom Vaughn

RUSHING: Vaughn 190/795y, Hoover 43/253y, Williams 57/185y
PASSING: Bunte 26-70/347y, 2TD, 37.1%
RECEIVING: Limerick 24/339y, 5 tied w/ 2
SCORING: Limerick 59pts, Vaughn 54pts, Hoover 12pts

1964 1-8-1

25	Drake	0	E Ernie Kun / Eppie Barney (DB)
14	Oklahoma State	29	T Norm Taylor
7	Nebraska	14	G Wayne Lueders
6	Kansas	42	C John Berrington
7	Colorado	14	G Sam Ramenofsky
0	Missouri	10	T John Van Sicklen
0	Army	9	E Denny Alitz
20	Oklahoma	30	QB Tim Van Galder / Ken Bunte
6	Kansas State	7	HB Ernie Kennedy / Larry Carwell
0	Arizona	0	HB Tom Vaughn
			FB Mike Cox / Tony Baker
			DL Ken Pigott
			DL Bill Allen
			DL Ed Kimbrough
			DL Lynn Kettleson
			DL Bob Evans
			DL George Maurer
			LB Jim Wipert
			LB Cal Lewis / Harry Alley
			DB Eppie Barney (E)
			DB Joe Beauchamp
			DB Kip Koski

RUSHING: Vaughn 129/497y, Baker 99/403y, Cox 27/112y
PASSING: Van Galder 35-105/354y, 0TD, 33.3%
RECEIVING: Baker 6/76y, Carwell 6/73y, Barney 6/73y
SCORING: Vaughn 25pts, Baker 18pts, Halda 7pts

1965 5-4-1

21	Drake	0	E Eppie Barney
38	Pacific	13	T John Chism
0	Nebraska	44	G Dennis Storey
21	Kansas	7	C Dick Kasperek
10	Colorado	10	G Rich Burchett / Bill Brooks
7	Missouri	23	T Larry Brazon
14	Oklahoma State	10	E George Maurer
20	Oklahoma	24	QB Tim Van Galder
38	Kansas State	6	HB Tom Busch
9	New Mexico	10	HB Les Webster
			FB Willie Robinson / Tony Baker
			DL Dennis Esselmann
			DL Wayne Lueders
			DL Bob Evans
			DL Frank Belichick
			DL Sam Ramenofsky
			DL Ernie Kennedy
			LB Ron Halda
			LB Jim Wipert
			DB Doug Robinson
			DB Larry Carwell
			DB Cal Lewis

RUSHING: Webster 137/498y, Robinson 100/366y, Baker 64/278y
PASSING: Van Galder 100-228/1418y, 6TD, 43.8%
RECEIVING: Barney 35/495y, Busch 28/443y, Maurer 19/221y
SCORING: Steve Balkovec (K) 34pts, Webster & Robinson 30pts

1966 2-6-2

10 Wisconsin	20 E Eppie Barney
11 Oklahoma	29 T Dick Schafroth
6 Nebraska	12 G Dennis Storey
24 Kansas	7 C Don Stanley
21 Colorado	41 G Bill Brooks / Rick Burchett
10 Missouri	10 T Ted Tuinstra
14 Oklahoma State	14 TE George Maurer
30 Kansas State	13 QB Tim Van Galder
24 Arizona	27 WB Tom Busch
10 Colorado State	34 TB Les Webster
	FB Willie Robinson / Ben King
	DL Sam Campbell
	DL Willie Muldrew
	DL Bob Evans
	DL Ted Hall / George Dimitri
	DL Dennis Esselmann
	DL Don Graves
	LB Dave Mayberry / Alan Staidl
	LB Terry Voy / Jon Soucek
	DB Doug Robinson / Jeff Simonds
	DB Larry Carwell
	DB Cal Lewis

RUSHING: Webster 149/572y, Robinson 82/305y, Busch 20/144y
PASSING: Van Galder 124-245/1645y, 6TD, 50.6%
RECEIVING: Barney 56/782y, Maurer 30/320y, Busch 21/423y
SCORING: Busch 52pts, Webster 36pts, Van Galder 30pts

1967 2-8

3 South Carolina	34 WR Greg Dukstein
0 Texas Tech	52 T Dan Robinson
17 New Mexico	12 G Dennis Storey
0 Colorado	34 C Don Stanley
17 Kansas State	0 G Rick Burchett
7 Missouri	23 T Ken Bixby
14 Kansas	28 TE Brian Feikema
0 Nebraska	12 QB John Warder
14 Oklahoma	52 WB Tom Busch
14 Oklahoma State	28 HB Les Webster
	HB Ben King
	DL Sam Campbell / Mike Kirar
	DL George Dimitri / Craig Boller
	DL Willie Muldrew
	DL Roger Ashland
	DL Dennis Esselmann / Ted Reimer
	LB Dave Mayberry
	LB Don Graves
	DB Doug Robinson
	DB/LB Larry Holton / Lon Snook
	DB Jerry Fiat
	DB Jeff Simonds

RUSHING: King 110/388y, Webster 109/322y, Warder 181/271y
PASSING: Warder 80-196/949y, 3TD, 40.8%
RECEIVING: Busch 33/429y, Feikema 18/194y, Dukstein 10/138y
SCORING: Vern Skripsky (K) 20pts, Warder 18pts, Webster & Busch 12pts

1968 3-7

28 Buffalo	0 WR Tom Lorenz / Sam Campbell
12 Arizona	21 T Jerry Berna / Tom Barnes
28 BYU	20 G Mike Bliss
18 Colorado	28 C Wayne Beske
23 Kansas State	14 G Bill Easter
7 Oklahoma	42 T Tim Jeffries
25 Kansas	46 TE Otto Stowe
13 Nebraska	24 QB John Warder
7 Missouri	42 HB Jeff Allen
17 Oklahoma State	26 HB Jock Johnson / Roger Guge
	FB Ben King
	DL Tom Potter / Chuck Wilkinson
	DL George Dimitri
	DL John Griglione
	DL Andy Waller / Fred Jones
	DL Ted Reimer
	LB Jerry Fiat / Mark Withrow
	LB Steve Powers
	DB Tom Elliott
	DB Tom Hilden
	DB Bob Williams / Roy Snell
	DB Tony Washington

RUSHING: King 124/437y, Warder 151/355y, Allen 57/309y
PASSING: Warder 89-201/1184y, 7TD, 44.3%
RECEIVING: Stowe 34/421y, Campbell 21/372y, Allen 17/277y
SCORING: Allen 30pts, Campbell 24pts, Warder 20pts

1969 3-7

13 Syracuse	14 WR Otto Stowe
10 BYU	0 T Tom Barnes / Ray Harm
48 Illinois	20 G Mike Bliss
0 Colorado	14 C Wayne Beske
7 Kansas State	34 G Jerry Berna
44 Kansas	20 T Tim Jeffries
14 Oklahoma	37 TE Tom Lorenz / Greg Dukstein
3 Nebraska	17 QB Obert Tisdale
13 Missouri	40 WB Jeff Allen
0 Oklahoma State	35 TB Mike Palmer (TE)
	FB Jock Johnson / Dennis McDonald (TB)
	DL Tom Potter / Mike Kirar
	DL John Griglione
	DL Fred Jones
	DL Andy Waller / Jerry Boyington
	LB Keith Schroeder / Steve Powers
	LB Mark Withrow
	LB Jerry Fiat
	DB Bob Williams
	DB Tom Elliott
	DB Larry Holton
	DB Tony Washington

RUSHING: Johnson 98/427y, Palmer 63/210y, McDonald 75/201y
PASSING: Tisdale 79-189/896y, 5TD, 41.2%
RECEIVING: Stowe 39/508y, Allen 18/168y, Palmer 15/191y
SCORING: Vern Skripskey (K) 32pts, Tisdale & Stowe 24pts

1970 5-6

32 New Mexico	3 WR Otto Stowe
37 Colorado State	6 WR Dave McCurry
16 Utah	13 T Joe Marconi
10 Colorado	61 G Ray Harm
0 Kansas State	17 C Dave Pittman
10 Kansas	24 G Mike Terrizzi / Jerry Berna
28 Oklahoma	29 T Geary Murdock
29 Nebraska	54 TE Tom Lorenz
31 Missouri	19 QB Dean Carlson / George Amundson
27 Oklahoma State	36 TB Jock Johnson
28 San Diego State	22 FB Dennis McDonald / Mike Palmer
	DL Therman Couch
	DL John Griglione
	DL Harold Bassett / Bob Matey
	DL Chuck Wilkinson
	LB Mark Withrow
	LB Keith Schroeder
	LB Ken Caratelli
	DB John Schweizer / Steve Wardlaw
	DB Jeff Allen
	DB Obert Tisdale
	DB Tony Washington

RUSHING: Amundson 111/440y, Johnson 122/434y, McDonald 60/239y
PASSING: Carlson 105-220/1391y, 11TD, 47.7%
RECEIVING: Stowe 59/822y, Lorenzen 32/443y, McCurry 18/268y
SCORING: Reggie Shoemake (K) 60pts, Amundson 42pts, Stowe 38pts

1971 8-4

24 Idaho	7 WR Ike Harris
44 New Mexico	20 WR Willie Jones
17 Kent State	14 T Geary Murdock
14 Colorado	24 G Ray Harm
24 Kansas State	0 C Dave Pittman
40 Kansas	24 G Mike Terrizzi / Bob Belluz
12 Oklahoma	43 T Joe Marconi
0 Nebraska	37 TE Keith Krepfle
45 Missouri	17 QB Dean Carlson
54 Oklahoma State	0 TB George Amundson
48 San Diego State	31 FB Dennis McDonald / Larry Marquardt
15 LSU 33	DL Harold Bassett
	DL Larry Hunt
	DL Bob Matey
	DL Merv Krakau
	LB Ted Jornov / Steve Burns
	LB Keith Schroeder
	LB Ken Caratelli
	DB John Schweizer
	DB George Campbell
	DB Matt Blair
	DB Dave McCurry

RUSHING: Amundson 287/1361y, McDonald 130/566y, Marquardt 45/230y
PASSING: Carlson 141-285/1867y, 14TD, 49.4%
RECEIVING: Krepfle 40/570y, Harris 32/529y, Jones 22/428y
SCORING: Amundson 90pts, Reggie Shoemake (K) 56pts, Carlson & Krepfle 42pts

1972 5-6-1

41 Colorado State	0 WR Ike Harris
44 Utah	22 WR Willie Jones
31 New Mexico	0 T Dan Kneller
22 Colorado	34 G Sherman Miller
55 Kansas State	22 C Dave Pittman
34 Kansas	8 G Geary Murdock
6 Oklahoma	20 T Willie Gillis
23 Nebraska	23 TE Keith Krepfle
5 Missouri	6 QB George Amundson
14 Oklahoma State	45 TB Mike Strachan
14 San Diego State	27 FB Moses Moore / Larry Marquardt
30 Georgia Tech 31	DL Doug Wilke
	DL Tom Karr
	DL Larry Hunt
	DL Merv Krakau
	LB Brad Storm
	LB Ken Caratelli / John McKillop
	LB Ted Jornov
	DB George Campbell
	DB Barry Hill
	DB John Schweizer / Matt Blair
	DB Dave McCurry / Randy Bozich

RUSHING: Strachan 268/1261y, Amundson 134/508y, Moore 68/283y
PASSING: Amundson 155-332/2110y, 17TD, 46.6%
RECEIVING: Jones 36/671y, Krepfle 30/450y, Harris 30/446y
SCORING: Tom Goedjen (K) 69pts, Amundson 54pts, Strachan 48pts

1973 4-7

48 Idaho	0 WR Ike Harris
19 Arkansas	21 WR Willie Jones
16 Colorado	23 T Willie Gillis
26 BYU	24 G Dan Kneller/Jeff Jones/Jack Thomas
19 Kansas State	21 C Chuck Blaskovich
20 Kansas	22 G Bob Bos / Sherman Miller
17 Oklahoma	34 T Henry Lewis
7 Nebraska	34 TE Keith Krepfle
17 Missouri	7 QB Wayne Stanley / Buddy Hardeman
28 Oklahoma State	12 TB Mike Strachan
28 San Diego State	41 FB Phil Danowsky
	DL Andre Roundtree
	DL Tom Karr / Ron McFarland
	DL Rick Howe
	DL Lon Coleman / Ray King
	LB Ted Jornov
	LB Larry Hunt
	LB Brad Storm / Gerry Forge
	DB Barry Hill
	DB Randy Bozich
	DB Bruce Fling / Ramsey Jay
	DB Matt Blair

RUSHING: Strachan 272/1103y, Hardeman 89/468y, Mike Tyson (TB) 67/316y
PASSING: Stanley 49-116/723y, 8TD, 42.2%
RECEIVING: Krepfle 30/436y, Jones 20/293y, Harris 14/251y
SCORING: Tom Goedjen (K) 70pts, Krepfle 30pts, Strachan & Danowsky 24pts

1974 4-7

3 Texas Tech	24 WR Luther Blue / Jerry Moses
28 Washington	31 WR Forry Smith
34 BYU	7 T Arlen Ciechanowski
27 New Mexico	3 G Bob Bos
7 Colorado	34 C Jeff Jones
23 Kansas State	18 G Jack Thomas
22 Kansas	6 T Randy Young
10 Oklahoma	28 TE Dave Greenwood / Al Dixon
13 Nebraska	23 QB Wayne Stanley / Buddy Hardeman
7 Missouri	10 TB Mike Strachan / Mike Williams
12 Oklahoma State	14 FB Phil Danowsky
	DL Ray King
	DL Mike Stensrud
	DL Jimmy Potter
	DL Rick Howe / Ron McFarland
	DL Andre Roundtree
	LB Brad Storm
	LB Gerry Forge
	DB Tony Hawkins
	DB Ramsey Jay / Jerry Jaksich
	DB Barry Hill
	DB Sy Bassett

RUSHING: Strachan 189/647y, Williams 98/464y, Danowsky 113/379y
PASSING: Stanley 58-121/842y, 6TD, 47.9%
RECEIVING: Blue 26/450y, Dixon 11/149y, Smith 11/143y
SCORING: Tom Goedjen (K) 60pts, Danowsky 42pts, Blue 30pts

1975 4-7

21 UCLA	39 WR Forry Smith / Ray Hardee
17 Air Force	12 WR Luther Blue
10 Florida State	6 T Pierre Gelinas
31 Utah	3 G Bob Bos
17 Kansas State	7 C Jeff Jones
10 Kansas	21 G Rob Stoffel
7 Oklahoma	39 T Kevin Cunningham / Randy Young
27 Colorado	28 TE D. Greenwood/ Guy Preston/ G. Rogers
14 Missouri	44 QB Tom Mason / Buddy Hardeman
0 Nebraska	52 TB Jim Wingender
7 Oklahoma State	14 FB Mike Williams
	DL Otis Rodgers
	DL Tom Randall / Mike Larson
	DL Maynard Stensrud
	DL Ron McFarland
	DL Ray King
	LB Mark Benda
	LB Greg Pittman
	DB Tony Hawkins
	DB Jim Randolph / Jerry Jaksich
	DB Bill Larkin
	DB Sy Bassett

RUSHING: Wingender 195/1070y, Williams 165/781y, Hardeman 80/395y
PASSING: Mason 42-128/725y, 4TD, 32.8%
RECEIVING: Smith 31/493y, Blue 10/179y, Hardee 7/127y,
SCORING: Williams 36pts, Hardeman 30pts, Doug Lenth (K) 20pts

1976 8-3

58 Drake	14 WR Luther Blue
41 Air Force	6 WR Ray Hardee
47 Kent State	7 T Kevin Cunningham
10 Oklahoma	24 G Rob Stoffel
44 Utah	14 C Mark Boehm / Denny Engel
21 Missouri	17 G Dave Greenwood
14 Colorado	33 T Gerry Petsch / Al Grissinger
45 Kansas State	14 TE Al Dixon / Glover Rogers
31 Kansas	17 QB Wayne Stanley / Buddy Hardeman
37 Nebraska	28 TB Dexter Green
21 Oklahoma State	42 FB Cal Cummins
	DL Otis Rodgers
	DL Tom Randall
	DL Maynard Stensrud (LB) / Dick Cuvelier
	DL Mike Stensrud
	DL Lenzy Perine / Craig Volkens
	LB Tom Boskey
	LB Mark Benda
	DB Mike Clemons / Kevin Hart
	DB Jerry Jaksich
	DB Mark Williams
	DB Tony Hawkins

RUSHING: Green 208/1074y, Hardeman 100/583y, Cummins 100/397y
PASSING: Stanley 70-146/1084y, 11TD, 47.9%
RECEIVING: Blue 33/644y, Dixon 25/336y, Green 19/240y
SCORING: Scott Kollman (K) 75pts, Green 60pts, 3 tied w/ 36pts

1977 8-4

35 Wichita State	9 WR Ray Hardee
10 Iowa	12 WR John Solomon / Stan Hixon
35 Bowling Green	21 T Dick Cuvelier
17 Dayton	13 G Al Grissinger
7 Missouri	0 C Mark Boehm
24 Nebraska	21 G Brian Neal
16 Oklahoma	35 T Kevin Cunningham
41 Kansas	3 TE Guy Preston
7 Colorado	12 QB Terry Rubley
22 Kansas State	15 TB Dexter Green
21 Oklahoma State	13 FB Cal Cummins
14 N. Carolina St.24	DL Rick White
	DL Mike Stensrud
	DL Ron McFarland / Greg Rensink
	DL Tom Randall
	DL Craig Volkens
	LB Tom Boskey
	LB Mark Settle
	DB Kevin Hart
	DB Jerry Washington / Mike Clemons
	DB Tom Perticone
	DB Mike Schwartz

RUSHING: Green 300/1412y, Cummins 130/539y, Pat Kennedy (TB) 39/158y
PASSING: Rubley 83-142/1037y, 4TD, 58.4%
RECEIVING: Green 25/203y, Hixon 22/334y, Hardee 19/183y
SCORING: Green 90pts, Scott Kollman (K) 43pts, Cummins & Jeff Curry (TB) 18pts

1978 8-4

23 Rice	19 WR Ray Hardee
14 San Diego State	13 WR Stan Hixon
31 Iowa	0 T Brian Neal
35 Drake	7 G Al Grissinger / Tom Stonerook
0 Nebraska	23 C Ron Bockhaus
13 Missouri	26 G Jim Wilson / Tim Stonerook
6 Oklahoma	34 T Dick Cuvelier
13 Kansas	7 TE Guy Preston
24 Kansas State	0 QB Walter Grant / Terry Rubley
28 Oklahoma State	15 TB Dexter Green
20 Colorado	16 FB Tom Roach / Jack Seabrooke
12 Texas A&M28	DL Rick White
	DL Mike Stensrud
	DL Chris Boskey / John Meis
	DL Kenny Neil / Greg Rensink
	DL Steve Weidemann
	LB John Less / Mike Leaders
	LB Tom Boskey / Scott Cole
	DB Jerry Washington
	DB Larry Crawford / Mike Clemons
	DB Tom Perticone
	DB Mike Schwartz

RUSHING: Green 251/1139y, Victor Mack (TB) 74/319y, Grant 119/263y
PASSING: Grant 66-154/992y, 6TD, 42.8%
RECEIVING: Hixon 26/474y, Preston 25/296y, Hardee 14/281y
SCORING: Green 78pts, Brian Johnson (K) 37pts, Hardee 24pts

1979 3-8

38 Bowling Green	10 WR Jim Knuth
9 Texas	17 WR Greg Smith / Lamar Summers
14 Iowa	30 T Tim Stonerook
7 Pacific	24 G Ted Clapper
7 Kansas State	3 C Ron Bockhaus
7 Kansas	24 G Dick Cuvelier
9 Oklahoma	38 T Karl Nelson
24 Colorado	10 TE Mickey Leafblad / Al Moton
9 Missouri	18 QB Terry Rubley / Walter Grant
3 Nebraska	34 TB Dan Goodwin / Mike Payne
10 Oklahoma State	13 FB Jack Seabrooke
	DL Kenny Neil
	DL Chris Boskey / Lloyd Studniarz
	DL Shamus McDonough / Marc Butts
	LB Joel Jenson
	LB Bill Herren
	LB Mike Leaders
	LB Lou Vieceli
	DB Joe Brown
	DB Larry Crawford
	DB Jeff Stallworth
	DB Mike Schwartz

RUSHING: Seabrooke 105/441y, Payne 108/331y, Goodwin 91/316y
PASSING: Rubley 71-132/716y, 1TD, 53.8%
RECEIVING: Leafblad 18/168y, Knuth 15/212y, Smith 14/213y
SCORING: Alex Giffords (K) 41pts, Rocky Gillis (TB) & Payne 18pts

1980 6-5

42 NE Louisiana	7 WR Jim Knuth
27 San Jose State	6 WR Jerry Lorenzen / Vinny Cerrato
10 Iowa	7 T Tim Stonerook
69 Colorado State	0 G Ted Clapper
31 Kansas State	7 C Jim Meyer
17 Kansas (F-W)	28 G Brian Neal
7 Oklahoma	42 T Karl Nelson
9 Colorado	17 TE Dan Johnson
10 Missouri	14 QB John Quinn / David Worsham
0 Nebraska	35 TB Dwayne Crutchfield
23 Oklahoma State	21 FB Jack Seabrooke
	DL Kenny Neil
	DL Shamus McDonough
	DL Marc Butts / Cal Jacobs
	DL James Ransom
	LB George Jessen / John Less
	LB Mark Carlson
	LB Joel Jensen
	DB Larry Crawford
	DB Joe Brown
	DB John Arnaud
	DB Ronnie Osborne

RUSHING: Crutchfield 284/1312y, Rocky Gillis (TB) 71/378y, Quinn 100/272y
PASSING: Quinn 69-153/835y, 4TD, 45.1%
RECEIVING: Lorenzen 15/203y, Gillis 12/103y, Cerrato 10/144y
SCORING: Crutchfield 66pts, Alex Giffords (K) 59pts, Seabrooke 18pts

1981 5-5-1

17 W. Texas St.	13 WR Michael Wade / Frankie Leaks
23 Iowa	12 WR Vinny Cerrato / Rocky Gillis
28 Kent State	19 T Brian Neal
7 Oklahoma	7 G Bruce Reimers
31 San Diego State	52 C Jim Meyer / Chuck Meyers
34 Missouri	13 G Ted Clapper
17 Colorado	10 T Karl Nelson
7 Kansas State	10 TE Dan Johnson
11 Kansas	24 QB John Quinn
7 Nebraska	31 TB Dwayne Crutchfield
7 Oklahoma State	27 FB Jerry Lorenzen
	DL James Ransom
	DL Shamus McDonough
	DL Marc Butts
	DL Rodney Hutchins / Chris Boskey
	LB George Jessen
	LB Chris Washington
	LB Doug Fischer
	DB Joe Brown
	DB Darren Longshore
	DB Ronnie Osborne
	DB John Arnaud / Kevin Coughlin

RUSHING: Crutchfield 307/1189y, Lorenzen 54/298y
PASSING: Quinn 140-251/1576y, 3TD, 55.8%
RECEIVING: Wade 27/343y, Crutchfield 24/154y,Johnson 21/290y
SCORING: Crutchfield 104pts, Alex Giffords (K) 45pts,Quinn 14pts

1982 4-6-1

21 Tennessee	23 WR Michael Wade / Rocky Gillis
19 Iowa	7 WR Frankie Leaks
35 Drake	10 T Benn Musgrave
3 Oklahoma	13 G Ted Clapper
44 Kent State	7 C Jim Meyer
17 Missouri	17 G Bruce Reimers
31 Colorado	14 T Karl Nelson
3 Kansas State	9 TE Doran Geise
13 Kansas	24 QB David Archer
10 Nebraska	48 TB Tommy Davis / Harold Brown
13 Oklahoma State	49 FB Jason Jacobs / Jerry Lorenzen
	DL James Ransom
	DL Shamus McDonough
	DL Chris Boskey
	DL Lester Williams
	LB George Jessen
	LB Chris Washington
	LB Mark Carlson
	DB Alvin Baker
	DB John Arnaud
	DB Ronnie Osborne
	DB George Walker

RUSHING: Davis 193/832y, Brown 114/622y, Jacobs 99/483y
PASSING: Archer 125-244/1465y, 5TD, 51.2%
RECEIVING: Leaks 25/427y, Jacobs 20/123y, Geise 17/221y
SCORING: Giffords 69pts, Brown 48pts, Davis 18pts

1983 4-7

10 Iowa	51 WR Robbie Minor
26 Vanderbilt	29 WR Tracy Henderson
21 Colorado State	17 T Benn Musgrave
17 New Mexico St.	24 G Bruce Reimers
38 Kansas	35 C Chuck Meyers
22 Colorado	10 G Scott Nelson
18 Missouri	41 T Dan Martin
11 Oklahoma	49 TE Dave Smoldt
29 Nebraska	72 QB David Archer
49 Kansas State	27 TB Tommy Davis
7 Oklahoma State	30 FB Jason Jacobs
	DL Greg Liter / Roger Youngblut
	DL Barry Moore
	DL Rodney Hutchins / Steve Little
	DL Doug Fischer / Jim Luebbers
	LB Dwayne Gilyard
	LB Chris Washington
	LB Lester Williams
	DB Billy McCue / Joe Jackson
	DB Kevin Williams / Anthony Davis
	DB Alvin Baker
	DB George Walker / Sam Clear

RUSHING: Jacobs 99/490y, Davis 156/396y
PASSING: Archer 234-403/2639y, 18TD, 58.1%
RECEIVING: Henderson 81/1051y, Jacobs 64/584y,Davis 24/155y
SCORING: Henderson 52pts, Marc Bachrodt (K) 42pts, Jacobs 40pts

1984 2-7-2
21 Iowa — 59 WR Tracy Henderson
21 Drake — 17 WR Robbie Minor
17 Texas A&M — 38 T Kevin Eggleston
14 W. Texas State — 0 G Eric Huhndorf
14 Kansas — 33 C Channon Mawdsley
21 Colorado — 23 G Vince Jasper
10 Oklahoma — 12 T Bruce Westemeyer
14 Missouri — 14 TE Dave Smoldt
0 Nebraska — 44 QB Alex Espinoza
7 Kansas State — 7 TB Richard Hanson
10 Oklahoma State — 16 FB Tommy Davis
DL Lester Williams
DL Steve Little
DL Barry Moore
DL Jim Luebbers
LB Dennis Gibson
LB Jeff Braswell
LB Tim Iversen
DB Terrence Anthony / Joe Jackson
DB Kevin Williams
DB Anthony Mayze
DB Anthony Davis
RUSHING: Hanson 155/507y, Davis 71/304y
PASSING: Espinoza 143-262/1580y, 10TD, 54.6%
RECEIVING: Henderson 64/941y, Hanson 29/244y, Davis 29/213y
SCORING: Marc Bachrodt (K) 37pts, Henderson 36pts, Hanson 18pts

1985 5-6
10 Utah State — 3 WR Hughes Suffren
20 Vanderbilt — 17 WR Danny Gantt
3 Iowa — 57 T Keith Sims / Bruce Westemeyer
17 Drake — 20 G Eric Huhndorf
22 Kansas — 21 C Channon Mawdsley
6 Colorado — 40 G Vince Jasper
14 Oklahoma — 59 T Brett Lawrence / Kevin Eggleston
27 Missouri — 28 TE Jeff Wodka
0 Nebraska — 49 QB Alex Espinoza
21 Kansas State — 14 TB Andrew Jackson / Matt Rodgers
15 Oklahoma State — 10 FB Kirk Thomas
DL Lester Williams
DL Greg Liter
DL Bill Berthusen / Perry Laures
DL Jim Luebbers
LB Tim Iversen / Randy Richards
LB Jeff Braswell
LB Dennis Gibson
DB Terrence Anthony
DB Milon Pitts / Aaron Manning
DB Anthony Mayze
DB Brian Reffner / Kevin Colon
RUSHING: Jackson 113/415y, Thomas 103/326y, Rodgers 94/323y
PASSING: Espinoza 159-330/1704y, 8TD, 48.2%
RECEIVING: Wodka 35/390y, Suffren 31/433y, Jackson 29/254y
SCORING: Rick Frank (K) 47pts, Suffren 24pts, Jackson & Don Poprilo (TB) 18pts

1986 6-5
7 Iowa — 43 WR Robbie Minor
64 Indiana State — 9 WR Dennis Ross / Tom Schulting
36 Wichita State — 14 T Keith Sims
21 Wyoming — 10 G Eric Huhndorf
13 Kansas — 10 C Channon Mawdsley
3 Colorado — 31 G Vince Jasper
0 Oklahoma — 38 T Brett Lawrence
37 Missouri — 14 TE Tom Stawniak
14 Nebraska — 35 QB Alex Espinoza
48 Kansas State — 19 TB Andrew Jackson
14 Oklahoma State — 21 FB Joe Henderson
DL Scott Benson / John Cinefro
DL Greg Liter
DL Bill Berthusen
DL Robert Dabney
LB Dennis Gibson
LB Chris Moore
LB Darrin Trieb
DB Terrence Anthony / Terry Sheffey
DB Aaron Manning
DB Brian Reffner
DB Milon Pitts / Kevin Colon
RUSHING: Jackson 143/455y, Henderson 122/436y, Curtis Warren (TB) 30/148y
PASSING: Espinoza 153-299/2023y, 15TD, 51.2%
RECEIVING: Minor 35/592y, Ross 23/312y, Jackson 21/97y
SCORING: Rick Frank (K) 63pts, Henderson 42pts, Minor 24pts

1987 3-8
12 Tulane — 25 WR Dennis Ross
9 Iowa — 48 WR Tom Schulting / Eddie Bridges
17 Wyoming — 34 T Ben Mitchell
3 Oklahoma — 56 G Trent Van Hoosen / Rick Wells
39 No. Iowa — 38 C David Heyn / Chris Mussman
17 Missouri — 42 G Rich Moore
42 Kansas — 28 T Gene Williams
10 Colorado — 42 TE Mike Busch
3 Nebraska — 42 QB Brett Sadek
16 Kansas State — 14 TB Edwin Jones
27 Oklahoma State — 48 FB Joe Henderson
DL Don Edwards / Tom Stawniak
DL Alan Patten / Scott Benson
DL Randy Bern
DL Robert Dabney
LB Anthony Hoskins
LB Chris Moore / Mike Shane
LB Randy Richards / Charles Vondra
DB Ray Carreathers
DB Lopey Williams / Marcus Robertson
DB Tim Baker / Chad Welding
DB Jeff Dole
RUSHING: Henderson 262/1232y, Jones 50/166y,
PASSING: Sadek 117-229/1443y, 7TD, 51.1%
RECEIVING: Ross 53/673y, Schulting 31/443y, Bridges 26/324y
SCORING: Jeff Shudak (K) 77pts, Henderson 30pts, Ross 26pts

1988 5-6
30 Tulane — 13 WR Dennis Ross
0 Baylor — 35 WR Eddie Brown
3 Iowa — 10 T Ben Mitchell / Rich Moore
7 Oklahoma — 35 G Trent Van Hoosen / Rick Wells
20 No. Iowa — 17 C David Heyn
21 Missouri — 3 G Keith Sims
42 Kansas — 14 T Gene Williams
12 Colorado — 24 TE Mike Busch
16 Nebraska — 51 QB Bret Oberg / Derek DeGennaro
16 Kansas State — 7 TB Curtis Warren / Edwin Jones
28 Oklahoma State — 49 FB Joe Henderson
DL Randy Bern
DL Alan Patten
DL Don Edwards / Matthew Rehberg
DL Mark Foley
LB Anthony Hoskins
LB Mike Shane / Tyrone Davis
LB Robert Lendino / John Cinefro
DB Ray Carreathers
DB Marcus Robertson
DB Tim Baker / Adam Beck
DB Jeff Dole
RUSHING: Henderson 242/1040y, Warren 93/387y,
PASSING: Oberg 99-179/1360y, 6TD, 55.3%
RECEIVING: Ross 39/506y, Busch 27/343y, Brown 18/403y
SCORING: Henderson 62pts, Jeff Shudak (K) 55pts, Warren & Ross 18pts

1989 6-5
28 Ohio University — 3 WR Steve Lester / Tyrone Williams
20 Minnesota — 30 WR John Glotfelty / Troy Moore
21 Iowa — 31 T Dave Benoit
25 Tulane — 24 G Trent Van Hoosen
24 Kansas — 20 C George Tsiotsias / Rick Wells
17 Colorado — 52 G Keith Sims
40 Oklahoma — 43 T Gene Williams
17 Nebraska — 49 TE Mike Busch
36 Kansas State — 11 QB Bret Oberg
35 Missouri — 21 TB Blaise Bryant
31 Oklahoma State — 21 FB Ron Wilkinson
DL Matt Rehberg
DL Travis Block
DL Don Edwards / Matt Grubb
DL Dean Ahlers / Randy Bern
LB Larry Ratigan
LB Phil Navarro
LB Mike Shane / Charles Vondra
DB Marcus Robertson
DB Andrew Buggs / Dave Eder
DB Tim Baker
DB Jeff Bauer / Mark DouBrava
RUSHING: Bryant 299/1516y, Wilkinson 51/293y, Oberg 110/273y
PASSING: Oberg 152-245/2242y, 9TD, 62.0%
RECEIVING: Lester 46/612y, Busch 23/375y, Glotfelty 22/394y
SCORING: Bryant 120pts, Jeff Shudak (K) 50pts, Oberg 32pts

1990 4-6-1
35 No. Iowa — 6 WR Chris Spencer
16 Minnesota — 20 WR John Glotfelty
35 Iowa — 45 T Chris Mussman
34 W. Michigan — 20 G Scott Armbrust
34 Kansas — 34 C George Tsiotsias
12 Colorado — 28 G Doug Skartvedt
33 Oklahoma — 31 T Gene Williams
13 Nebraska — 45 TE Craig Mahoney
14 Kansas State — 28 QB Chris Pedersen
27 Missouri — 25 TB Blaise Bryant / Sherman Williams
17 Oklahoma State — 25 FB Sundiata Patterson
DL Matt Rehberg
DL Travis Block
DL Matt Grubb
DL Mark Dunn
LB Larry Ratigan
LB Dan Milner
LB Dan Watkins / Jim Doran
DB Marcus Robertson / Andrew Buggs
DB Shawn Walker
DB Kevin Lazard / Jeff Bauer
DB Mark DouBrava
RUSHING: Bryant 187/753y, Pedersen 130/570y, Williams 92/309y
PASSING: Pedersen 114-206/1601y, 6TD, 55.3%
RECEIVING: Spencer 31/485y, Glotfelty 30/455y, Bryant 18/210y
SCORING: Jeff Shudak (K) 84pts, Bryant 78pts, Patterson & Glotfelty 24pts

1991 3-7-1
42 E. Illinois — 13 WR Chris Spencer
10 Iowa — 29 WR Lamont Hill / Brandon Hughes
6 Wisconsin — 7 T Doug Skartvedt / Lance Keller
28 Rice — 27 G Lawrence Roberts
8 Oklahoma — 29 C Scott Armbrust
0 Kansas — 41 G Tony Booth
6 Oklahoma State — 6 T Todd McClish
23 Missouri — 22 TE Paul Schulte / Scott English
7 Kansas State — 37 QB Chris Pedersen / Kevin Caldwell
13 Nebraska — 38 TB Jim Knott / Sherman Williams
14 Colorado — 17 FB Sundiatta Patterson
DL Matt Grubb
DL Matt Rehberg
DL Travis Block
DL Mark Dunn / Dan Watkins (LB)
LB Larry Ratigan / Malcolm Goodwin
LB Dan Milner
LB Matt Nitchie
DB Andrew Buggs / Kevin Lazard
DB Shawn Walker
DB Mark DouBrava
DB Kevin Fulton
RUSHING: Patterson 100/467y, Caldwell 156/428y, Knott 45/223y
PASSING: Pedersen 46-90/598y, 2TD, 51.1%
RECEIVING: Spencer 25/356y, Hill 22/316y, Schulte 15/189y
SCORING: Ty Stewart (K) 51pts, Patterson 30pts, Knott & Caldwell 18pts

1992 4-7
35 Ohio University — 9 WR Chris Spencer
7 Iowa — 21 WR Brandon Hughes / James Brooks
38 Tulane — 14 T Doug Skartvedt
10 No. Iowa — 27 G Tony Booth (T) / Jim Thompson
3 Oklahoma — 17 C Scott Armbrust
47 Kansas — 50 G Mark Konopka
21 Oklahoma St. — 27 T Todd McClish
28 Missouri — 14 TE Dan Dostal
13 Kansas State — 22 QB Bob Utter / Marv Seiler
19 Nebraska — 10 TB Jim Knott/Sherm Williams/Jim McMillion
10 Colorado — 33 FB Chris Ulrich / Sundiata Patterson
DL Shane Dunlevy
DL Troy Petersen
DL Todd Miller
DL Dan Watkins
LB Marcus Allen / Jeff Cole
LB Malcolm Goodwin
LB Dan Milner
DB Andrew Buggs / Matt Goodwin
DB Shawn Walker
DB Mark DouBrava
DB Kevin Fulton
RUSHING: Ulrich 103/474y, Patterson 85/386y, Seiler 74/269y
PASSING: Utter 50-86/712y, 2TD, 58.1%
RECEIVING: Spencer 26/437y, Knott 11/164y, Patterson 9/54y
SCORING: Ty Stewart (K) 57pts, McMillion 30pts, Williams 24pts

1993 3-8

54 Northern Illinois	10 WR Lamont Hill / Mike Horacek
28 Iowa	31 T Doug Skartvedt
7 Wisconsin	28 G Jim Thompson
21 Rice	49 C Tony Booth
7 Oklahoma	24 G Mark Konopka
20 Kansas	35 T Brian Wilkinson
20 Oklahoma State	17 TE Dan Dostal
34 Missouri	37 QB Bob Utter / Todd Doxzon
27 Kansas State	23 HB Jim Knott / Artis Garris
17 Nebraska	49 HB Calvin Branch / James McMillion
16 Colorado	21 FB Chris Ulrich / Rodney Guggenheim
	DL Todd Miller / Scott Schulz
	DL Sheldon Napastuk
	DL Troy Peterson
	DL Anthony Scott
	LB Matt Nitchie / Marc Lillibridge
	LB Jeff Cole
	LB Marcus Allen / Tim Sanders
	DB Weylan Harding
	DB Kevin Lazard
	DB Cedric Linwood
	DB Kevin Fulton

RUSHING: Branch 84/478y, Doxzon 327y, Guggenheim 282y
PASSING: Utter 60-105/893y, 6TD, 57.1%
RECEIVING: Branch 16/350y,
SCORING: Ty Stewart (K) 53pts, Branch 36pts

1994 0-10-1

14 Northern Iowa	28 WR Mike Horacek / Ed Williams
9 Iowa	37 T Tim Kohn
19 W. Michigan	23 G Doug Ragaller / Matt Rahfeldt
18 Rice	28 C Tony Booth
6 Oklahoma	34 G Jim Thompson
23 Kansas	41 T Brian Wilkinson
31 Oklahoma State	31 TE Dan Dostal
20 Missouri	34 QB Todd Doxzon / Jeff St. Clair
20 Kansas State	38 HB Calvin Branch
12 Nebraska	28 HB Geoff Turner
20 Colorado	41 FB Jim Knott / Rodney Guggenheim
	DL Nick Clausen / Sheldon Napastuk
	DL Troy Petersen
	DL Anthony Scott / B.J. Spyksma
	LB Marcus Allen
	LB Tim Sanders
	LB Matt Nitchie
	LB Marc Lillibridge / Michael Cooper
	DB Russell Johnson / Daryl Hall
	DB Jason Brown
	DB Matt Straight
	DB Cedric Linwood

RUSHING: Doxzon 148/375y, Guggenheim 72/330y
PASSING: Doxzon 51-90/745y, 3TD, 56.7%
RECEIVING: Horacek 22/368y, Turner 20/230y, Branch 19/370y,
SCORING: Ty Stewart (K) 48pts, Doxzon 24pts

1995 3-8

36 Ohio Univ.	21 WR Mike Horacek
10 TCU	27 WR Ed Williams
10 Iowa	27 T Tim Kohn
57 UNLV	30 G Mark Konopka
26 Oklahoma	39 C Pat Augafa
7 Kansas	34 G Doug Easley / Matt Rahfaldt
28 Colorado	50 T Byron Heitz
38 Oklahoma State	14 TE Dennis DiBiase
14 Nebraska	73 QB Todd Doxzon / Todd Bandhauer
7 Kansas State	49 TB Troy Davis
31 Missouri	45 FB Rodney Guggenheim
	DL Jason Putz / B.J.Spyksma
	DL Greg Schoon / Sheldon Napastuk
	DL Kevin Fleecs / ChinAchebe
	LB Angelo Provenza
	LB Tim Sanders
	LB Michael Cooper
	LB Rudy Ruffolo
	DB Dawan Anderson
	DB Kevin Hudson
	DB Mike Lincavage / Jason Brown
	DB Matt Straight

RUSHING: Davis 345/2010y, Graston Norris (TB) 40/233y
PASSING: Doxzon 58-100/730y, 4TD, 5%
Bandhauer 42-90/501y, 5TD, 46.7%
RECEIVING: Williams 46/639y, Horacek 31/353y, Davis 14/159y
SCORING: Davis 96pts, Jamie Kohl (K) 56pts, Williams 44pts

1996 2-9

38 Wyoming	41 WR Ed Williams / Daman Green
13 Iowa	38 WR Tyrone Watley
42 Northern Iowa	23 T Tim Kohn
45 Missouri	31 G Matt Rahfaldt
21 Texas A&M	24 C Pat Augafa
27 Oklahoma State	28 G Doug Easley
21 Baylor	49 T Kurt Levetzow / Chris Brunsvold
31 Kansas	34 TE Dennis DiBiase
42 Colorado	49 QB Todd Doxzon
14 Nebraska	49 TB Troy Davis
20 Kansas State	35 FB Joe Parmentier
	DL Bill Marsau
	DL Greg Schoon
	DL Rudy Ruffolo
	LB Michael Cooper
	LB Dave Brca
	LB Derrick Clark
	LB James Elmore / Chin Achebe
	DB Dawan Anderson
	DB Kevin Hudson
	DB Jason Brown / Tracy Williams
	DB Mike Lincavage

RUSHING: Davis 402/2185y, Doxzon 86/223y,
Darren Davis (TB) 30/204y
PASSING: Doxzon 124-231/1498y, 12TD, 53.7%
RECEIVING: Williams 34/491y, Watley 27/419y, Green 22/222y
SCORING: Davis 126pts, Jamie Kohl (K) 60pts, Doxzon 28pts

1997 1-10

14 Oklahoma State	21 WR Ty Watley
10 Wyoming	56 WR Ed Williams / Daman Green
29 Minnesota	53 T Oliver Ross
10 Iowa	63 G Matt Rahfaldt
21 Missouri	45 C Charley Bogwill
17 Texas A&M	56 G Ben Beaudet
24 Baylor	17 T Kurt Levetzow
24 Kansas	34 TE Damian Gibson / Andy Stensrud
38 Colorado	43 QB Todd Bandauer
14 Nebraska	77 TB Darren Davis / James O'Neal
3 Kansas State	28 FB Joe Parmentier
	DL Antonio Mays
	DL James Reed
	DL Greg Schoon
	DL Chin Achebe
	LB James Elmore / Jim Morse
	LB Dave Brca
	LB Michael Cooper
	DB Dawan Anderson
	DB Breon Ansley
	DB Kevin Hudson
	DB Dustin Avey / Kemp Knighten

RUSHING: Davis 212/1005y, O'Neal 58/220y,
Jerome Heavens (TB) 27/94y
PASSING: Bandauer 180-374/2514y, 20TD, 48.1%
RECEIVING: Watley 50/827y, Williams 39/534y, Green 21/366y
SCORING: Jamie Kohl (K) 50pts, Watley 48pts, Williams 32pts

1998 3-8

21 TCU	31 WR Chris Anthony
27 Iowa	9 WR Damien Groce
38 Ball State	0 T Bill Marsau
24 Texas Tech	31 G Eugene Bernal / Ryan Gerke
33 Texas	54 C Charley Bogwill
19 Missouri	35 G Ben Bruns
7 Kansas State	52 T Ben Beaudet
14 Oklahoma	17 TE Damian Gibson
7 Nebraska	42 QB Todd Bandauer
8 Colorado	37 TB Darren Davis
23 Kansas	20 FB Joe Parmentier
	DL Reggie Hayward
	DL James Reed
	DL Ryan Harklau
	DL Chin Achebe
	LB Ab Turner
	LB Kip King
	LB Jesse Beckom
	DB Jamarcus Powers
	DB Breon Ansley / Javon Daniels
	DB Jeff Waters
	DB Dustin Avey

RUSHING: Davis 294/1166y
PASSING: Bandauer 179-355/2206y, 14TD, 50.4%
RECEIVING: Groce 47/640y, Anthony 42/490y, Stensrud 25/421y
SCORING: Davis 54pts, Jamie Kohl (K) 51pts, Groce 42pts

1999 4-7

33 Indiana State	7 WR Chris Anthony
17 Iowa	10 WR J.J. Moses / Michael Brantley
24 UNLV	0 T Bill Marsau / Cory Hannen
28 Kansas State	35 G Ben Beaudet (T) / Scott Rickard
14 Nebraska	49 C Ben Bruns / Zach Butler
24 Missouri	21 G Ryan Gerke
12 Colorado	16 T Marcel Howard
41 Texas	44 TE Michael Banks
16 Texas Tech	28 QB Sage Rosenfels
10 Oklahoma	31 TB Darren Davis
28 Kansas	31 FB Hez Jackson
	DL Robert Brannon / Kevin DeRonde
	DL Ryan Harklau / Nigel Tharpe
	DL James Reed
	DL Reggie Hayward
	LB Eric Weiford / Ab Turner
	LB Dave Brcka / Chris Whitaker
	LB Jesse Beckom / James Elmore
	DB Atif Austin / Adam Runk
	DB Ryan Sloth
	DB Dustin Avey
	DB Jeff Waters

RUSHING: Davis 287/1388y, Ennis Haywood (TB) 55/278y,
Rosenfels 80/225y
PASSING: Rosenfels 127-235/1781y, 10TD, 54%
RECEIVING: Anthony 37/432y, Davis 21/160y, Moses 18/296y
SCORING: Davis 96pts, Mike McKnight (K) 47pts, Rosenfels 24pts

2000 9-3

25 Ohio Univ.	15 WR Chris Anthony
37 UNLV	22 WR J.J. Moses / Craig Campbell
24 Iowa	14 T Marcel Howard
31 Baylor	17 G Ben Beaudet
27 Nebraska	49 C Ben Bruns
33 Oklahoma State	26 G Lorenzo White
7 Texas A&M	30 T Andy Stensrud
39 Missouri	20 TE Mike Banks
10 Kansas State	56 QB Sage Rosenfels
35 Colorado	27 TB Ennis Haywood / Michael Wagner
38 Kansas	17 FB Joe Woodley
37 Pittsburgh	29 DL Reggie Hayward
	DL James Reed / Jordan Carstens
	DL Ryan Harklau
	DL Kevin DeRonde / Nigel Tharpe
	LB Derrick Walker
	LB Matt Word / Chris Whitaker
	LB Ab Turner / Justin Eilers
	DB Atif Austin
	DB Jamarcus Powers
	DB Dustin Avey / Marc Timmons
	DB Doug Densmore / Adam Runk

RUSHING: Haywood 229/1237y, Wagner 85/396y,
Rosenfels 78/381y
PASSING: Rosenfels 172-333/2298y, 8TD, 51.7%
RECEIVING: Moses 53/775y, Anthony 35/449y, Banks 27/273y
SCORING: Rosenfels 60pts, Haywood 50pts,
Mike McKnight (K) 37pts

2001 7-5

45 No. Iowa	0 WR Lane Danielsen
31 Ohio	28 WR Craig Campbell / Jamaul Montgomery
41 Baylor	0 WR/TE Jack Whitver / Kyle Knock
14 Nebraska	48 T Marcel Howard
20 Missouri	14 G Bob Montgomery
28 Oklahoma State	14 C Zach Butler
21 Texas A&M	24 G Lorenzo White
3 Kansas State	42 T Cory Hannen
27 Colorado	40 TE Mike Banks
49 Kansas	7 QB Seneca Wallace
17 Iowa	14 TB Ennis Haywood
13 Alabama14	DL Tyson Smith / Beau Coleman
	DL Jordan Carstens
	DL Willie Judd
	DL Kevin DeRonde
	LB Jeremy Loyd
	LB Matt Word
	LB Justin Eilers
	DB Harold Clewis / Johnny Smith
	DB Atif Austin / DeAndre Phillips
	DB Marc Timmons
	DB Adam Runk / Anthony Forrest

RUSHING: Haywood 258/1169y, Wallace 114/475y
PASSING: Wallace 167-269/2044y, 11TD, 62.1%
RECEIVING: Danielsen 49/694y, Campbell 31/486y,
Banks 23/212y
SCORING: Haywood 84pts, Tony Yelk (K) 62pts, Wallace 42pts

2002 7-7

31 Florida State	38 WR Lane Danielsen
45 Kansas	3 WR Jamaul Montgomery
58 Tennessee Tech	6 WR Jack Whitver / Lance Young
36 Iowa	31 T Casey Shelton
42 Troy State	12 G Bob Montgomery
36 Nebraska	14 C Zach Butler
31 Texas Tech	17 G Dwayne Johnson / Collin Menard
3 Oklahoma	49 T Cale Stubbe
10 Texas	21 TE Kyle Knock
42 Missouri	35 QB Seneca Wallace
7 Kansas State	58 TB Michael Wagner / Hiawatha Rutland
27 Colorado	41 DL Tyson Smith
20 Connecticut	37 DL Jordan Carstens / Tim TeBrink
16 Boise State	34 DL Nick Leaders
	DL Beau Coleman
	LB Brandon Brown
	LB Matt Word
	LB Jeremy Loyd
	DB Atif Austin / Anthony Forrest
	DB Ellis Hobbs
	DB Marc Timmons
	DB JaMaine Billups

RUSHING: Rutland 160/614y, Wagner 153/542y, Wallace 123/437y
PASSING: Wallace 244-443/3245y, 15TD, 55.1%
RECEIVING: Danielsen 63/1073y, Whitver 52/685y, Young 43/704y
SCORING: Adam Benike (K) 97pts, Wallace 50pts, Wagner 42pts

2003 2-10

17 Northern Iowa	10 WR Lane Danielsen
48 Ohio University	20 WR Lance Young / Jamaul Montgomery
21 Iowa	40 T Casey Shelton
16 N. Illinois	24 G Bob Montgomery / Seth Zehr (C)
7 Oklahoma	53 C Luke Vander Sanden / Mott Bockes
21 Texas Tech	52 G Aaron Brant
19 Texas	40 T Cale Stubbe
0 Nebraska	28 TE James Wright / Tim TeBrink
0 Kansas State	45 QB Austin Flynn / Waye Terry
10 Colorado	44 TB Michael Wagner / Stevie Hicks
7 Kansas	36 FB/WR Ryan Kock / Jack Whitver
7 Missouri	45 DL Jason Berryman
	DL Jordan Carstens
	DL Nick Leaders
	DL Cephus Johnson / Brent Curvey
	LB Nik Moser / Erik Anderson
	LB Brandon Brown
	LB Joe Woodley / Jamarr Buchanan
	DB Ellis Hobbs
	DB Harold Clewis / DeAndre Jackson
	DB Marc Timmons
	DB JaMaine Billups

RUSHING: Hicks 123/471y, Wagner 96/420y, Flynn 124/396y
PASSING: Flynn 99-212/1238y, 5TD, 46.7%
Terry 42-96/415y, 2TD, 43.8%
RECEIVING: Danielsen 46/772y, Young 32/467y, Montgomery 24/239y
SCORING: Adam Benike (K) 37pts, Danielsen 36pts, Wagner & Rutland 18pts

2004 7-5

23 Northern Iowa	0 WR Todd Blythe
10 Iowa	17 WR Jon Davis / Todd Miller
48 N. Illinois	41 T Cale Stubbe
7 Oklahoma State	36 G Kory Pence
3 Texas A&M	34 C Luke Vander Sanden
14 Colorado	19 G Seth Zehr
26 Baylor	25 T Aaron Brant
13 Kansas	7 TE Brett Kellogg / Ben Barkema
34 Nebraska	27 TE/FB James Wright / Ryan Kock
37 Kansas State	23 QB Bret Meyer
14 Missouri	17 TB Stevie Hicks
17 Miami (Ohio)	13 DL Tyson Smith
	DL Brent Curvey
	DL Nick Leaders
	DL Shawn Moorehead / Cephus Johnson
	LB/DB Erik Anderson / LaMarcus Hicks
	LB Tim Dobbins
	LB Brandon Brown / Jamarr Buchanan
	DB DeAndre Jackson
	DB Ellis Hobbs
	DB Steve Paris
	DB Nik Moser

RUSHING: Hicks 270/1062y, Meyer 144/331y, Davis 9/103y
PASSING: Meyer 149-290/1926y, 10TD, 51.4%
RECEIVING: Davis 48/614y, Blythe 39/833y, Miller 31/341y
SCORING: Blythe 54pts, Bret Culbertson (K) 40pts, Hicks 30pts

2005 7-5

32 Illinois State	21 WR Todd Blythe
23 Iowa	3 WR Jon Davis / R. J. Sumrall
28 Army	21 WR/HB Austin Flynn / Walter Nickel
20 Nebraska	27 T Johannes Egbers / Scott Fisher
13 Baylor	23 G Kory Pence
24 Missouri	27 C Scott Stephenson
37 Oklahoma State	10 G Seth Zehr
42 Texas A&M	14 T Aaron Brant
45 Kansas State	17 TE Ben Barkema
30 Colorado	16 QB Bret Meyer
21 Kansas	24 RB Stevie Hicks/Greg Coleman/Ryan Kock
24 TCU 27	DL Shawn Moorehead/Cephus Johnson
	DL Brent Curvey
	DL Nick Leaders
	DL Jason Berryman
	LB Matt Robertson / Alvin Bowen
	LB Tim Dobbins
	LB Jamarr Buchanan / Adam Carper
	DB DeAndre Jackson
	DB LaMarcus Hicks
	DB Steve Paris
	DB Nik Moser

RUSHING: Hicks 149/545y, Coleman 116/419y
PASSING: Meyer 227-368/2876y, 19TD, 61.7%
RECEIVING: Flynn 56/624y, Blythe 51/1000y, Davis 41/319y
SCORING: Kock 78pts, Bret Culbertson (K) 70pts, Blythe 54pts

2006 4-8

45 Toledo	43 WR Todd Blythe / Milan Moses
16 UNLV	10 WR Jon Davis / R. J. Sumrall
17 Iowa	27 WR/TE Austin Flynn / Walter Nickel
14 Texas	37 T Scott Fisher
28 N. Iowa	27 G Seth Zehr
14 Nebraska	28 C Scott Stephenson
9 Oklahoma	34 G Tom Schmeling / Reggie Stephens
26 Texas Tech	42 T Aaron Brant
10 Kansas State	31 TE Ben Barkema
10 Kansas	41 QB Bret Meyer
16 Colorado	33 RB Stevie Hicks / Ryan Kock
21 Missouri	16 DL Bryce Braaksma/Rashawn Parker
	DL Ahtyba Rubin / Nate Frere
	DL Brent Curvey
	DL Shawn Moorehead
	LB Alvin Bowen
	LB Tyrone McKenzie
	LB Jon Banks (DB) / Adam Carper
	DB DeAndre Jackson / Drenar Williams
	DB Chris Singleton
	DB Jason Harris / Steve Johnson
	DB Caleb Berg

RUSHING: Hicks 107/523y, Kock 74/332y, Meyer 137/177y
PASSING: Meyer 211-374/2546y, 12TD, 56.4%
RECEIVING: Flynn 41/470y, Davis 36/508y, Blythe 34/484y
SCORING: Bret Culbertson (K) & Blythe 48pts, Meyer 38pts

2007 3-9

14 Kent State	23 WR Todd Blythe
13 Northern Iowa	24 WR Marquis Hamilton
15 Iowa	13 T Doug Dedrick
35 Toledo	36 G Reggie Stephens
17 Nebraska	35 C Brandon Johnson
17 Texas Tech	42 G Tom Schmeling / Lee Tibbs
3 Texas	56 T Ben Lamaak
7 Oklahoma	17 TE Ben Barkema
28 Missouri	42 QB Bret Meyer
31 Kansas State	20 RB Alexander Robinson / J.J. Bass
31 Colorado	28 FB/WR Derrick Catlett / R.J. Sumrall
7 Kansas	45 DL Rashawn Parker
	DL Bryce Braaksma
	DL Ahtyba Rubin
	DL Kurtis Taylor
	LB Jon Banks
	LB Jesse Smith
	LB Alvin Bowen
	DB Allen Bell
	DB Chris Singleton
	DB James Smith / Caleb Berg
	DB Chris Brown / Steve Johnson

RUSHING: Robinson 118/465y, Bass 123/462y, Jason Scales (RB) 99/333y
PASSING: Meyer 233-382/2151y, 9TD, 61%
RECEIVING: Sumrall 54/434y, Blythe 52/779y, Hamilton 45/534y
SCORING: Bret Culbertson (K) 56pts, Robinson 36pts, Blythe 30pts

2008 2-10

44 San Diego State	17 WR R.J. Sumrall
48 Kent State	28 WR Houston Jones / Marquis Hamilton
5 Iowa	17 T Doug Dedrick
31 UNLV	34 G Reggie Stephens
33 Kansas	35 C Alex Alvarez / Mike Knapp
10 Baylor	38 G Ben Lamaak
7 Nebraska	35 T Matt Hulbert / Scott Haughton
35 Texas A&M	49 TE Derrick Catlett / Collin Franklin
17 Oklahoma State	59 QB Austen Arnaud
24 Colorado	28 RB Alexander Robinson / Jason Scales
20 Missouri	52 FB/WR Taylor Mansfield / Darius Darks
30 Kansas State	38 DL Rashawn Parker
	DL Michael Tate
	DL Nate Frere
	DL Kurtis Taylor
	LB Michael Bibbs / Cameron Bell
	LB Jesse Smith / Christopher Lyle
	LB Fred Garrin / Josh Raven
	DB Leonard Johnson / Ter'ran Benton
	DB Chris Singleton / Devin McDowell
	DB James Smith
	DB Brandon Hunley / Kennard Banks

RUSHING: Robinson 153/703y, Arnaud 109/401y, Scales 60/185y
PASSING: Arnaud 247-401/2792y, 15TD, 61.6%
RECEIVING: Sumrall 57/750y, Darks 49/477y, Jones 32/384y
SCORING: Grant Mahoney (K) 84pts, Sumrall 42pts, Robinson 36pts

2009 7-6

34 N. Dakota St.	17 WR Marquis Hamilton / Darius Reynolds
3 Iowa	35 WR Jake Williams / Sedrick Johnson
34 Kent State	14 WR Darius Darks / Josh Lenz
31 Army	10 T Kelechi Osemele / Brayden Burris
23 Kansas State	24 G Abe Alvarez
36 Kansas	41 C Reggie Stephens
24 Baylor	10 G Ben Lamaak
9 Nebraska	7 T Scott Haughton
10 Texas A&M	35 TE Derrick Catlett / Collin Franklin
8 Oklahoma State	34 QB Austen Arnaud / Jerome Tiller
17 Colorado	10 RB Alexander Robinson / Jeremi Schwartz
24 Missouri	34 DL Patrick Neal / Rashawn Parker
14 Minnesota	13 DL Nate Frere / Stephen Ruempolhamer
	DL Bailey Johnson / Austin Alburtis
	DL Christopher Lyle
	LB Fred Garrin
	LB Jesse Smith
	LB/DB Josh Raven / Ter'ran Benton
	DB Kennard Banks
	DB Leonard Johnson
	DB James Smith / Michael O'Connell
	DB David Sims

RUSHING: Robinson 232/1195y, Arnaud 147/561y, Schwartz 71/264y, Tiller 44/216y
PASSING: Arnaud 178-303/2015y, 14TD, 58.7%
Tiller 41-73/376y, 1TD, 56.2%
RECEIVING: Hamilton 50/606y, Williams 36/403y, Catlett 29/301y, Darks 28/303y, Lenz 20/186y
SCORING: Grant Mahoney (K) 65pts, Robinson 54pts, Arnaud 48pts

2010 5-7

27 No. Illinois	10 WR Darius Reynolds / Sedrick Johnson
7 Iowa	35 WR Jake Williams
20 Kansas State	27 WR/RB Darius Darks / Shontre Johnson
27 No. Iowa	0 T Kelechi Osemele
52 Texas Tech	38 G Alex Alvarez / Sean Smith
27 Utah	68 C Ben Lamaak
0 Oklahoma	52 G Hayworth Hicks
28 Texas	21 T Brayden Burris
28 Kansas	16 TE Collin Franklin
30 Nebraska	31 QB Austen Arnaud / Jerome Tiller
14 Colorado	34 RB Alexander Robinson / Jeff Woody
0 Missouri	14 DL Patrick Neal / Jacob Lattimer
	DL Bailey Johnson / Jake McDonough
	DL S. Ruempolhamer / Taylor Mansfield
	DL Rashawn Parker / Roosevelt Maggitt
	LB A.J. Klein / Matt Tau'fo'ou
	LB Jake Knott
	LB/DB Matt Morton / Ter'ran Benton
	DB Leonard Johnson / Anthony Young
	DB Jeremy Reeves
	DB Michael O'Connell / Zac Sandvig
	DB David Sims

RUSHING: Robinson 202/946y, Arnaud 103/287y, Johnson 35/218y
PASSING: Arnaud 171-290/1703y, 13TD, 59%
RECEIVING: Franklin 54/530y, Williams 35/404y, Darks 29/355y
SCORING: Robinson 60pts, Grant Mahoney (K) 56pts, Williams 24pts

KANSAS

University of Kansas (Founded 1866)
Lawrence, Kansas
Nickname: Jayhawks
Colors: Crimson and Blue
Stadium: Memorial Stadium (1921) 50,250
Conference Affiliations: Big Seven (Charter member, 1948-56),
    Big Eight (1957-95), Big Twelve North (1996-present)

CAREER RUSHING YARDS	Attempts	Yards
June Henley (1993-96)	823	3841
Tony Sands (1988-91)	778	3788
Laverne Smith (1973-76)	472	3074
Clark Green (2002-05)	641	2754
Gale Sayers (1962-64)	412	2675
John Riggins (1968-70)	518	2659
David Winbush (1997-00)	565	2608
L.T. Levine (1992-95)	422	2248
Jon Cornish (2003-06)	387	2245
Jake Sharp (2006-09)	456	2239

CAREER PASSING YARDS	Comp.-Att.	Yards
Todd Reesing (2006-09)	932-1461	11,194
Frank Seurer (1980-83)	467-934	6410
Kelly Donohoe (1986-89)	392-745	5382
David Jaynes (1971-73)	389-754	5132
Mike Norseth (1984-85)	363-647	4677
Chip Hilleary (1989-92)	335-636	4598
Bill Whittemore (2002-03)	310-568	4051
Dylen Smith (1999-00)	275-569	3562
Adam Barmann (2003-06)	296-527	3020
Bobby Douglass (1966-68)	183-379	2817

CAREER RECEIVING YARDS	Catches	Yards
Dezmon Briscoe (2007-09)	219	3240
Kerry Meier (2006-09)	226	2309
Willie Vaughn (1985-88)	133	2266
Mark Simmons (2002-05)	155	2161
Richard Estell (1982-85)	117	1997
Emmett Edwards (1972-74)	105	1808
Bob Johnson (1981-83)	87	1779
Brandon Rideau (2001-04)	131	1636
Marcus Henry (2004-07)	104	1599
Termaine Fulton (1997-01)	88	1565

SEASON RUSHING YARDS	Attempts	Yards
Jon Cornish (2006)	250	1457
Tony Sands (1991)	272	1442
June Henley (1996)	302	1349
Laverne Smith (1974)	176	1181
John Riggins (1970)	209	1131

SEASON PASSING YARDS	Comp.-Att.	Yards
Todd Reesing (2008)	329-495	3888
Todd Reesing (2009)	313-496	3616
Todd Reesing (2007)	276-446	3486
Mike Norseth (1985)	227-408	2995
Frank Seurer (1983)	187-353	2789

SEASON RECEIVING YARDS	Catches	Yards
Dezmon Briscoe (2008)	92	1407
Dezmon Briscoe (2009)	84	1337
Bob Johnson (1983)	58	1144
Richard Estell (1985)	70	1109
Kerry Meier (2008)	97	1045

GAME RUSHING YARDS	Attempts	Yards
Tony Sands (1991 vs. Missouri)	58	396
Nolan Cromwell (1975 vs. Oregon State)	28	294
Gale Sayers (1962 vs. Oklahoma State)	22	283

GAME PASSING YARDS	Comp.-Att.	Yards
Todd Reesing (2009 vs. Missouri)	37-55	498
Mike Norseth (1985 vs. Vanderbilt)	24-38	480
Todd Reesing (2009 vs. Iowa State)	37-49	442

GAME RECEIVING YARDS	Catches	Yards
Dezmon Briscoe (2008 vs. Oklahoma)	12	269
Dezmon Briscoe (2009 vs. Missouri)	14	242
Quintin Smith (1989 vs. Louisville)	11	221

GREATEST COACH:

Many of the fondest memories for Kansas fans stem from the Jack Mitchell years, when Kansas was a threat to anyone in football and attracted a host of star players. A native of Arkansas City, Kansas, Mitchell, who starred at Oklahoma and coached Wichita and Arkansas, returned home in 1958 to become the Jayhawks coach and immediately began the recruiting efforts that attracted future star players to Lawrence. In 1960, Kansas knocked off no. 1 ranked Missouri en route to a 7-2-1 record and conference title that was later rescinded due to the use of an ineligible player, halfback Bert Coan. In 1961 they won seven games again, including the Bluebonnet Bowl.

The Jack Mitchell era is more defined by the many all-time Jayhawk players he coached, from quarterback John Hadl and halfback Curtis McClinton of the 1960-61 teams to the dynamic Gale Sayers, who played from 1962-64. Five players made All American lists in Mitchell's nine years, while the core of the great 1968 team, coached by Pepper Rodgers, was recruited by Mitchell including an athletic quarterback much like himself in Bobby Douglass.

KANSAS' 55 GREATEST SINCE 1953

OFFENSE

WIDE RECEIVER: Dezmon Briscoe, Emmett Edwards, Willie Vaughn, David Verser
TIGHT END: Jim Letcavits, John Mosier
TACKLE: Keith Christensen, Anthony Collins, Chris Perez, Brian Schweda
GUARD: John Greene, Hessley Hempstead, Bob Whitaker
CENTER: Dale Evans, Fred Hageman
QUARTERBACK: Bobby Douglass, David Jaynes, Todd Reesing
RUNNING BACK: June Henley, Tony Sands, Gale Sayers, Laverne Smith
FULLBACK: John Riggins

DEFENSE

END: Mike Shinn, Dana Stubblefield, Dean Zook, John Zook
TACKLE: Eldridge Avery, Mike Butler, Nate Dwyer, James McClinton
LINEBACKER: Terry Beeson, Emery Hicks, Kenny Page, Willie Pless, Nick Reid, Mike Sweatman, Steve Towle
CORNERBACK: Milt Garner, LeRoy Irvin, Aqib Talib
SAFETY: Gary Adams, Tony Blevins, Chris Golub, Kurt Knoff, Kwamie Lassiter

SPECIAL TEAMS

RETURN SPECIALISTS: Marcus Herford, Donnie Shanklin
PLACE KICKER: Bruce Kallmeyer
PUNTER: Bucky Scribner

MULTIPLE POSITIONS

KICKER-PUNTER: Dan Eichloff
QUARTERBACK-WIDE RECEIVER: Kerry Meier

TWO-WAY PLAYERS

QUARTERBACK-HALFBACK-DEFENSIVE BACK-RETURNMAN-PUNTER: John Hadl
GUARD-LINEBACKER: Elvin Basham
QUARTERBACK-SAFETY: Nolan Cromwell

PERFORMANCE FORMULA:
KANSAS' 10 BEST SEASONS

2007	1.6087	3 of 70
1968	1.4846	7 of 70
1960	1.4633	8 of 70
1995	1.4513	11 of 70
1961	1.3690	13 of 71
2008	1.2583	27 of 71
1973	1.2372	20 of 70
1992	1.2306	22 of 70
1962	1.2100	27 of 70
2005	1.1702	34 of 70

KANSAS JAYHAWKS

Year	W-L-T	AP Poll	Conference Standing	Toughest Regular Season Opponents	Coach (Record at School)	Bowl Games			
1953	2-8		4t	UCLA 8-1, Oklahoma 8-1-1, Kansas State 6-3-1, Missouri 6-4	J.V. Sikes (35-25)				
1954	0-10		7	Oklahoma 10-0, UCLA 8-0, Colorado 7-2-1, Kansas State 7-3	Chuck Mather				
1955	3-6-1		5t	Oklahoma 10-0, TCU 9-1, Colorado 6-4	Chuck Mather				
1956	3-6-1		5t	Oklahoma 10-0, UCLA 7-3, TCU 7-3, Colorado 7-2-1	Chuck Mather				
1957	5-4-1	2		Oklahoma 9-1, Oregon St. 8-2, Colorado 6-3-1, Oklahoma St. 6-3-1	Chuck Mather (11-26-3)				
1958	4-5-1		4	Oklahoma 9-1, TCU 8-2, Oklahoma State 7-3	Jack Mitchell				
1959	5-5		3t	Syracuse 10-0, TCU 8-2, Oklahoma 7-3, Iowa State 7-3	Jack Mitchell				
1960	7-2-1	11	3	Missouri 9-1, Iowa 8-1, Syracuse 7-2, Iowa State 7-3	Jack Mitchell				
1961	7-3-1		2t	Colorado 9-1, Missouri 7-2-1, Wyoming 6-1-2	Jack Mitchell	Bluebonnet	33	Rice	7
1962	6-3-1		4	Missouri 7-1-2, Oklahoma 8-2, Nebraska 8-2, TCU 6-4	Jack Mitchell				
1963	5-5		4t	Nebraska 9-1, Syracuse 8-2, Oklahoma 8-2	Jack Mitchell				
1964	6-4		3	Nebraska 9-1, Syracuse 7-3, Missouri 6-3-1, Oklahoma 6-3-1	Jack Mitchell				
1965	2-8		5t	Nebraska 10-0, Texas Tech 8-2, Missouri 7-2-1, Colorado 6-2-2	Jack Mitchell				
1966	2-7-1		7t	Nebraska 9-1, Colorado 7-3, Missouri 6-3-1, Oklahoma 6-4	Jack Mitchell (44-42-5)				
1967	5-5		2t	Oklahoma 9-1, Indiana 9-1, Colorado 8-2, Missouri 7-3	Pepper Rodgers				
1968	9-2	7	1t	Oklahoma 7-3, Missouri 7-3, Nebraska 6-4	Pepper Rodgers	Orange	14	Penn State	15
1969	1-9		8	Missouri 9-1, Nebraska 8-2, Colorado 7-3	Pepper Rodgers				
1970	5-6		6t	Nebraska 10-0-1, Texas Tech 8-3, Oklahoma 7-4, New Mexico 7-3	Pepper Rodgers (20-22)				
1971	4-7		5t	Nebraska 12-0, , Oklahoma 10-1, Colorado 9-2, Iowa State 8-3	Don Fambrough				
1972	4-7		7	Oklahoma 10-1, Nebraska 8-2-1, Colorado 8-3	Don Fambrough				
1973	7-4-1	18	2t	Oklahoma 10-0, Nebraska 8-2-1, Tennessee 8-3, Missouri 7-4	Don Fambrough {see below}	Liberty	18	North Carolina State	31
1974	4-7		7t	Oklahoma 11-0, Nebraska 8-3, Texas A&M 8-3, Missouri 7-4	Bud Moore				
1975	7-5		4	Oklahoma 10-1, Nebraska 10-1	Bud Moore	Sun	19	Pittsburgh	33
1976	6-5		7	Oklahoma 8-2-1, Colorado 8-3, Kentucky 7-4	Bud Moore				
1977	3-7-1		6	Oklahoma 10-1, Nebraska 8-3, Iowa State 8-3, Texas A&M 8-3	Bud Moore (17-27-1)				
1978	1-10		8	Oklahoma 10-1, Nebraska 9-2, UCLA 8-3, Missouri 7-4	Don Fambrough				
1979	3-8		5t	Nebraska 10-1, Oklahoma 10-1, Pitt 9-1, Michigan 8-3	Don Fambrough				
1980	4-5-2		4	Pitt 10-1, Oklahoma 9-2, Nebraska 9-2, Missouri 8-3	Don Fambrough				
1981	8-4		3t	Nebraska 9-2, Missouri 7-4, Oklahoma 6-4-1	Don Fambrough	Hall of Fame	0	Mississippi State	10
1982	2-7-2		6t	Nebraska 11-1, Oklahoma 8-3	Don Fambrough (36-49-5)				
1983	4-6-1		6t	Nebraska 11-0, Oklahoma State 7-4, Missouri 7-4	Mike Gottfried				
1984	5-6		4	Oklahoma 9-1-1, Nebraska 9-2, Oklahoma State 9-2, FSU 7-2-2	Mike Gottfried				
1985	6-6		6	Oklahoma 10-1, Nebraska 9-2, Oklahoma State 8-3, FSU 8-3	Mike Gottfried (15-18-1)				
1986	3-8		8	Oklahoma 10-1, Nebraska 9-2, North Carolina 7-3-1	Bob Valesente				
1987	1-9-1		7t	Oklahoma 11-0, Nebraska 10-1, Oklahoma State 9-2, Auburn 9-2	Bob Valesente (4-17-1)				
1988	1-10		7	Nebraska 11-1, Auburn 10-1, Oklahoma 9-2, Oklahoma State 9-2	Glen Mason				
1989	4-7		6	Colorado 11-0, Nebraska 10-1	Glen Mason				
1990	3-7-1		4t	Colorado 10-1-1, Miami 9-2, Nebraska 9-2, Oklahoma 8-3, UVA 8-3	Glen Mason				
1991	6-5		5	Nebraska 9-1-1, Colorado 8-2-1, Oklahoma 8-3, UVA 8-2-1	Glen Mason				
1992	8-4	22	3	Colorado 9-1-1, Nebraska 9-2	Glen Mason	Aloha	23	BYU	10
1993	5-7		5	Florida State 11-1, Nebraska 11-0, Kansas St. 8-2-1, Oklahoma 8-3	Glen Mason				
1994	6-5		5	Nebraska 12-0, Colorado 10-1, Kansas State 9-2, TCU 7-4	Glen Mason				
1995	10-2	9	2t	Nebraska 11-0, Colorado 9-2, Kansas State 9-2	Glen Mason	Aloha	51	UCLA	30
1996	4-7		N5t	Nebraska 10-1, Colorado 9-2, Kansas State 9-2, Utah 8-3	Glen Mason (47-54-1)				
1997	5-6		N5	Nebraska 11-0, Kansas State 10-1, Missouri 7-4	Terry Allen				
1998	4-7		N5	Kansas State 11-0, Nebraska 9-3, Texas A&M 10-2, Missouri 7-4	Terry Allen				
1999	5-7		N4t	Nebraska 11-1, Kansas State 10-1, Texas A&M 8-3	Terry Allen				
2000	4-7		N5	Oklahoma 11-0, Kansas State 10-2, Nebraska 9-2, Texas 9-2	Terry Allen				
2001	3-8		N6	Nebraska 11-1, Texas 10-1, OU 10-2, Colorado 9-2, Iowa State 7-4	Terry Allen (20-33)				
2002	2-10		N6	Kansas State 10-2, Colorado 9-3	Mark Mangino				
2003	6-7		N4t	Kansas State 10-3, Nebraska 9-3, Missouri 8-4, Oklahoma St. 9-3	Mark Mangino	Tangerine	26	North Carolina State	56
2004	4-7		N5t	Texas 10-1, Texas Tech 7-4, Colorado 7-4	Mark Mangino				
2005	7-5		N5	Texas 11-0, Texas Tech 9-2, Nebraska 7-4, ISU 7-4, Oklahoma 7-4	Mark Mangino	Fort Worth	42	Houston	13
2006	6-6		N4	Nebraska 9-3, Texas A&M 9-3, Missouri 8-4, South Florida 8-4	Mark Mangino				
2007	12-1	7	N1t	Colorado 6-6, Texas A&M 7-5, Missouri 11-1	Mark Mangino	Orange	24	Virginia Tech	21
2008	8-5		N3	Oklahoma 12-1, Texas Tech 11-1, Texas 11-1, Missouri 9-4	Mark Mangino	Insight	42	Minnesota	21
2009	5-7		N6	Oklahoma 7-5, Texas Tech 8-4, Nebraska 9-4, Texas 13-0	Mark Mangino (50-48)				
2010	3-9		N6t	Texas A&M 9-3, Nebraska 10-3, Oklahoma State 10-2, Missouri 10-2	Turner Gill (3-9)				

TOTAL: 268-357-17 .4307 (59 of 70)   **Bowl Games since 1953:**   6-5 .5455 (27 of 70)

GREATEST TEAM SINCE 1953: The 2007 edition of the Jayhawks was a wonderful story, but the nod here goes to the a team from an earlier era. 1968's Jayhawks were led by a memorable group of players: quarterback Bobby Douglass, fullback John Riggins, and defensive end John Zook. They beat Nebraska, Missouri, and Kansas State, while only dropping one regular season game (27-23, Oklahoma). They then dropped a tough 15-14 Orange Bowl to Penn State, in which they led by a touchdown with time elapsing only to lose on a late two-point conversion play after a controversial, but correct, twelve-man penalty against Kansas.

1953 2-8

0	TCU	13	E Morris Kay / Jerry Taylor
7	UCLA	19	T Joe Lundy / Gene Vignatelli
23	Iowa State	0	G Joe Fink / Bob Hubbard
27	Colorado	21	C Merle Hodges / Don Aungst
0	Oklahoma	45	G Bob Hantla
6	SMU	14	T Lester Bixler / Richard Knowles
0	Nebraska	9	E Don Bracelin / Harold Patterson
0	Kansas State	15	QB John McFarland
14	Oklahoma A&M	41	HB Don Hess / Robert Conn
6	Missouri	10	HB R. Moody/Charles Forsyth/John Handley
		41	FB Frank Sabatini / Bob Allison

RUSHING: Hess 83/369y
PASSING: McFarland 28-79/343y, 1TD, 35.4%
RECEIVING: Patterson 10/179y
SCORING: Hess 20pts

1954 0-10

6	TCU	27	E Don Martin / Joe Held
7	UCLA	32	T Gene Vignatelli / John Drake
0	Colorado	27	G Dud Budrich / Don Pfutzenreuter
6	Iowa State	33	C Dick Reich / Frank Black
0	Oklahoma	65	G Bob Hubbard / Bob Preston
18	SMU	36	T Dick Knowles / Gene Blasi
6	Kansas State	28	E John Anderson / Bill Bell
20	Nebraska	41	QB Bev Buller / John McFarland
12	Oklahoma A&M	47	HB Ralph Moody / Terry McIntosh
18	Missouri	41	HB Dick Blowey / Rex Sullivan
			FB Bud Laughlin

RUSHING: Laughlin 94/339y, Anderson 31/225y, Moody 43/193y
PASSING: Buller 18-51/303y, 35.3%
RECEIVING: Martin 7/87y, Bell 6/74y, Moody 6/50y
SCORING: Anderson, Held, McIntosh & Moody 12pts

1955 3-6-1

14	TCU	47	E Lynn McCarthy / Don Martin
13	Washington St.	0	T Frank Gibson / John Drake
0	Colorado	12	G Bob Kraus / Don Pfutzenreuter
7	Iowa State	7	C Frank Black / Galen Wahlmeier
6	Oklahoma	44	G George Remsburg / Dud Budrich
14	SMU	33	T Gene Blasi / Jim Hull
14	Nebraska	19	E Jim Letcavits / Paul Smith
0	Kansas State	46	QB Wally Strauch / Bev Buller
12	Oklahoma A&M	7	HB John Francisco / Ralph Moody
13	Missouri	7	HB Dick Blowey / Jim Traylor
			FB Dick Reich / Joe Held

RUSHING: Francisco 107/459y, Reich 63/231y, Blowey 46/182y
PASSING: Strauch 28-76/498y, 3TD, 36.8%
RECEIVING: Letcavits 9/169y, Smith 7/118y, McCarthy 7/95y
SCORING: Francisco 24pts, Reich & Letcavits 12pts

1956 3-6-1

0	TCU	32	E Don Martin / Lynn McCarthy
27	Pacific	27	T Frank Gibson
25	Colorado	26	G Bob Kraus / Bob Lewis
25	Iowa State	14	C Frank Black / Galen Wahlmeier
12	Oklahoma	34	G Don Pfutzenreuter / Paul Swoboda
21	Oklahoma A&M	13	T Jim Hull / Ed Prelock
20	Kansas State	15	E Jim Letcavits
20	Nebraska	26	QB Wally Strauch / Dave Preston
0	UCLA	13	HB Charlie McCue / John Francisco
13	Missouri	15	HB Bobby Robinson / Bob Marshall
			FB Homer Floyd / Jerry Baker

RUSHING: Floyd 134/638y, McCue 100/453y, Francisco 77/263y
PASSING: Strauch 32-80/596y, 5TD, 40%
RECEIVING: Letcavits 14/246y, McCue 6/98y, Floyd 4/71y
SCORING: McCue 48pts, Floyd 36pts, Marshall & Strauch 19pts

1957 5-4-1

13	TCU	13	E John Peppercorn / H.C. Palmer
6	Oregon State	34	T Frank Gibson / Jim Hull
35	Colorado	34	G Tom Russell / Paul Swoboda
6	Iowa State	21	C Chet Vanatta (G) / Bill Burnison
0	Oklahoma	47	G Bob Kraus / Dewitt Lewis
6	Miami (Fla.)	48	T Ed Prelock / Ron Claiborne
14	Nebraska	12	E Jim Letcavits / Dale Remsberg
13	Kansas State	7	QB Wally Strauch / Duane Morris
13	Oklahoma State	7	HB Don Feller / John Francisco
9	Missouri	7	HB Charlie McCue / Larry Carrier
			FB Homer Floyd

RUSHING: Floyd 127/505y, Feller 49/217y, Francisco 50/206y
PASSING: Strauch 26-43/320y, 3TD, 60.5%
RECEIVING: Letcavits 10/176y, Floyd 9/189y, Remsberg 6/90y
SCORING: Floyd 30pts, Strauch 16pts, 3 tied w/ 12pts

1958 4-5-1

0	TCU	42	E John Lewis / Dale Remsberg
0	Oregon State	12	T John Peppercorn / Stan Kirshman
0	Colorado	31	G Ken Fitch / Dick Rohlf
7	Iowa State	0	C Chet Vanatta / John Wertzberger
0	Oklahoma	43	G Tom Russell / Gary Clothier
14	Tulane	9	T Bill Blasi / H.C. Palmer
21	Kansas State	12	E Sam Simpson / Jim Hill
29	Nebraska	7	QB Larry McKnown / Bill Crank
3	Oklahoma State	6	HB Bob Marshall / Duane Morris
13	Missouri	13	HB Homer Floyd / Charles Lukinac
			FB Doyle Schick/Norm Mailen/Fred Bukaty

RUSHING: Floyd 103/391y, Crank 82/375y, Marshall 75/276y
PASSING: McKnown 10-23/219y, 2TD, 43.5%
RECEIVING: Floyd 15/307y, Morris 5/74y, Lukinac 4/29y
SCORING: Floyd 26pts, Crank 24pts, Marshall 12pts

1959 5-5

7	TCU	14	E John Peppercorn
21	Syracuse	35	T Ken Fitch / Larry Lousch
28	Boston Univ.	7	G Benny Boydston / Jim Mills
10	Nebraska	3	C Fred Hageman / Kent Staab
33	Kansas State	14	G Dick Rohlf / Elvin Basham
6	Oklahoma	7	T DeWitt Lewis / Dick Davis
7	Iowa State	0	E Dale Remsberg / Sam Simpson
14	Colorado	27	QB Duane Morris / Lee Flachsbarth
28	Oklahoma State	14	HB John Hadl / Dave Harris
9	Missouri	13	HB Curtis McClinton / Jim Jarrett
			FB Doyle Schick / Norm Mailen

RUSHING: McClinton 91/472y, Hadl 68/348y, Schick 64/306y
PASSING: Flachsbarth 14-27/345y, 2TD, 51.9%
RECEIVING: Hadl 7/126y, Peppercorn 7/53y, McClinton 6/87y
SCORING: Hadl 48pts, McClinton 40pts, Suder 19pts

1960 7-2-1

21	TCU	7	E Larry Allen / Andy Graham
41	Kansas State	0	T Larry Lousch / Dick Davis
7	Syracuse	14	G Elvin Basham / Jim Mills
28	Iowa State	14	C Fred Hageman
13	Oklahoma	13	G Benny Boydston / Duke Collins
14	Oklahoma State	7	T Stan Kirshman / Mike Fisher
7	Iowa	21	E Sam Simpson / Mike Deer
31	Nebraska	0	QB John Hadl / Rodger McFarland (DB)
34	Colorado (F-L)	6	HB Bert Coan / Roger Hill (DB)
23	Missouri (F-L)	7	HB Curtis McClinton
			FB Doyle Schick / Jim Jarrett

RUSHING: Coan 73/488y, McClinton 86/389y, Hadl 108/375y
PASSING: Hadl 43-87/566y, 3TD, 49.4%
RECEIVING: McClinton 11/184y, Coan 9/133y, Graham 7/81y
SCORING: Coan 54pts, Hadl 42pts, Suder 36pts

1961 7-3-1

16	TCU	17	E Larry Allen
6	Wyoming	6	T Dick Davis / Larry Lousch
19	Colorado	20	G Elvin Basham
21	Iowa State	7	C Kent Staab / Kent Converse
10	Oklahoma	0	G Benny Boydston (E) / Jim Mills
42	Oklahoma State	8	T Stan Kirshman
28	Nebraska	6	E Mike Deer
34	Kansas State	0	QB John Hadl / Leland Flachsbarth
53	California	7	HB Rodger McFarland (QB) / Tony Leiker
7	Missouri	10	HB Curtis McClinton
33	Rice■	7	FB Ken Coleman

RUSHING: Coleman 130/656y, McClinton 135/553y, McFarland 65/334y
PASSING: Hadl 51-103/729y, 7TD, 49.5%
RECEIVING: McClinton 10/166y, McFarland 9/155y
SCORING: McClinton 60pts, Coleman & McFarland 42pts

1962 6-3-1

3	TCU	6	E Pack St. Clair / Mike Shinn
14	Boston Univ.	0	T Fred Eiseman / Tommy Thompson
35	Colorado	8	G Mickie Walker / Duke Collins
29	Iowa State	8	C Pete Quatrochi / Kent Converse
7	Oklahoma	13	G Ken Tiger / Ron Marsh
36	Oklahoma State	17	T Marv Clothier / Brian Schweda
38	Kansas State	0	E Jay Roberts / Bob Robben
16	Nebraska	40	QB Rodger McFarland
33	California	21	SB Tony Leiker / Phil Doughty (DB)
3	Missouri	3	HB Gale Sayers
			FB Ken Coleman / Armand Baughman

RUSHING: Sayers 158/1125y, Baughman 88/409y, McFarland 123/352y
PASSING: McFarland 28-66/366y, 3TD, 42.4%
RECEIVING: Roberts 8/108y, Leiker 7/93y, Sayers 7/61y
SCORING: Sayers 42pts, Baughman 36pts, Leiker 30pts

1963 5-5

6	TCU	10	E Mike Shinn
10	Syracuse	0	T Karl Satore
25	Wyoming	21	G Larry Ledford
14	Iowa State	17	C Pete Quatrochi
18	Oklahoma	21	G Harley Catlin
41	Oklahoma State	7	T Brian Schweda
34	Kansas State	0	E Jay Roberts
9	Nebraska	23	QB Steve Renko
43	Colorado	14	SB Ron Oelschlager / Tony Leiker
7	Missouri	9	HB Gale Sayers
			FB Wes Baughman / Ken Coleman

RUSHING: Sayers 132/917y, Coleman 93/397y, Baughman 94/323y
PASSING: Renko 31-86/505y, 3TD, 36%
RECEIVING: Sayers 11/155y, Oelschlager 6/117y, Roberts 5/112y
SCORING: Sayers 50pts, Coleman 30pts, Baughman 24pts

1964 6-4

7	TCU	3	E Sandy Buda
6	Syracuse	38	T Greg Roth
14	Wyoming	17	G George Harvey
42	Iowa	6	C George Hornung (E)
15	Oklahoma	14	G Dick Pratt
14	Oklahoma State	13	T Brian Schweda
7	Kansas State	0	E Mike Shinn / Robert Robben
7	Nebraska	14	QB Bobby Skahan / Steve Renko
10	Colorado	7	HB Mike Johnson / Gary Duff
14	Missouri	34	HB Gale Sayers
			FB Ron Oelschlager / Bill Gerhards
			DL Bill Walters
			DL Mike Shinn
			DL George Hornung
			DL Brian Schweda
			DL George Harvey
			DL John Garber
			LB Greg Roth
			LB Richard Brewster
			DB Charles Hess / Lloyd Buzzi
			DB Gary Duff / David Crandall
			DB Halley Kampschroeder / Steve Renko

RUSHING: Sayers 122/633y, O'lschlager 95/431y, Skahan 82/276y
PASSING: Skahan 41-78/550y, 2TD, 52.6%
RECEIVING: Sayers 17/182y, Hornung 9/141y, Johnson 9/117y
SCORING: Sayers 30pts, Duff 20pts, Oelschlager & Skahan 18pts

1965 2-8

7	Texas Tech	26	E Sandy Buda
15	Arizona	23	T Harold Montgomery
0	California	17	G George Harvey
7	Iowa State	21	C Bob Kreutzer
7	Oklahoma	21	G Dick Pratt
9	Oklahoma State	0	T Larry Dercher
34	Kansas State	0	E Willie Smith
6	Nebraska	42	QB Bobby Skahan / Bill Fenton
14	Colorado	21	HB Dan Miller / Mike Johnson
20	Missouri	44	HB Richard Abernathy / Sim Stokes
			FB Rich Bacon / Bill Gerhards
			DL Thurm Edwards
			DL Mike Shinn
			DL Bill Walters
			DL Bill Wohlford
			DL Jerry Barnett
			DL George Hornung
			LB Mike Sweatman
			LB Greg Roth / John Greene
			DB J.C. Hixon
			DB Dave Waxse
			DB Dave Hess / Ward Coleman

RUSHING: Miller 66/356y, Abernathy 38/226y, Fenton 97/214y
PASSING: Fenton 35-104/500y, 2TD, 33.7%, Skahan 33-76/324y, TD, 43.4%
RECEIVING: Stokes 25/271y, Johnson 10/94y, Abernathy 10/66y
SCORING: Abernathy 24pts, Fenton 24pts, Buda 15pts

1966 2-7-1

7 Texas Tech	23 E Halley Kampschroeder
35 Arizona	13 T Keith Christensen
16 Minnesota	14 G Bill Perry / Larry White
7 Iowa State	24 C Bob Kreutzer / Bill Wohlford
0 Oklahoma	35 G John Greene
7 Oklahoma State	10 T Harold Montgomery
3 Kansas State	3 E Sandy Buda / Jeff Elias
13 Nebraska	24 QB Bobby Skahan / Bill Fenton
18 Colorado	35 HB Donnie Shanklin / Thermus Butler
0 Missouri	7 HB John Jackson / Junior Riggins
	FB Dick Bacon
	DL Dave Peterson
	DL Jerry Barnett
	DL Bill Wohlford
	DL Larry Dercher
	DL John Zook
	LB George Harvey
	LB Mike Sweatman
	DB Bill Lynch / Dave Morgan
	DB J.C. Hixon
	DB Tom Ball
	DB Bill Hunt

RUSHING: Shanklin 182/732y, Riggins 61/246y, Jackson 60/202y
PASSING: Skahan 23-47/299y, 0TD, 48.9%;
Fenton 28-47/271y, 1TD, 59.6%
RECEIVING: Kampschr'der 18/278y, Buda 16/161y, Elias 15/124y
SCORING: Butler 21pts, Shanklin 18pts, Buda 15pts

1967 5-5

20 Stanford	21 WR Ben Olison / Tom Anderson
15 Indiana	18 T Harold Montgomery
15 Ohio	30 G Ken Wertzberger
10 Nebraska	0 C Dale Evans
26 Oklahoma State	15 G John Greene
28 Iowa State	14 T Keith Christensen
17 Kansas State	16 TE John Mosier
8 Colorado	12 QB Bobby Douglass
10 Oklahoma	14 WB John Jackson / Donnie Shanklin
17 Missouri	6 HB Junior Riggins
	FB J.C. Hixon / Mike Reeves
	DL Vern Vanoy
	DL Orville Turgeon
	DL Emery Hicks / Willie McDaniel
	DL Larry Dercher
	DL John Zook
	LB Mike Sweatman
	LB Mickey Doyle
	DB Eddie Hutchens
	DB Tom Ball
	DB Dave Morgan
	DB Bill Hunt / Drue Jennings

RUSHING: Douglass 175/415y, Riggins 99/279y, Reeves 46/243y
PASSING: Douglass 82-173/1326y, 7TD, 47.4%
RECEIVING: Mosier 37/495y, Anderson 14/171y,
Shanklin 10/169y
SCORING: Douglass 42pts, William Bell (K) 34pts, Riggins &
Mosier 24pts

1968 9-2

47 Illinois	7 E George McGowan
38 Indiana	20 T Keith Christensen
68 New Mexico	7 G Ken Wertzberger
23 Nebraska	13 C Dale Evans
49 Oklahoma State	14 G Dave Aikins
46 Iowa State	25 T Larry Brown / Grant Dahl
27 Colorado	14 TE John Mosier
23 Oklahoma	27 QB Bobby Douglass
38 Kansas State	29 HB John Jackson
21 Missouri	19 HB Donnie Shanklin / Junior Riggins
14 Penn State■	15 FB John Riggins
	DL John Zook
	DL Karl Salb
	DL Orville Turgeon
	DL Vern Vanoy
	DL Rudy Jacobcic
	LB Emery Hicks
	LB Mickey Doyle
	DB Dave Morgan
	DB Tommy Ball / Keith Lieppman
	DB Bill Hunt / Dale Holt
	DB Tom Anderson

RUSHING: John Riggins 139/866y, Shanklin 122/772y,
Douglass 148/495y
PASSING: Douglass 84-168/1316y, 12TD, 50%
RECEIVING: McGowan 32/592y, Mosier 25/281y,
Jackson 14/187y
SCORING: Douglass 72pts, William Bell (K) 66pts, Shanklin 60pts

1969 1-9

22 Texas Tech	38 E George McGowan
13 Syracuse	0 T Grant Dahl
7 New Mexico	16 G Dave Aikins
22 Kansas State	26 C Dale Evans
17 Nebraska	21 G Niles Hauser / John Weir
20 Iowa State	44 T Steve Lawson
25 Oklahoma State	28 TE John Mosier
14 Colorado	17 QB Phil Basler / Jim Ettinger
15 Oklahoma	31 WB Willie Amison
21 Missouri	69 HB Ron Jessie
	FB John Riggins
	DL Steve Carmichael
	DL Karl Salb
	DL Al Jacokcic
	DL Larry Brown / Gary Davenport
	DL Jim Bailey
	LB Emery Hicks
	LB Kenny Page
	DB Jim Hatcher
	DB Rich Hertel / John Mears
	DB George McGowan
	DB Dale Holt / Steve Roach

RUSHING: Riggins 170/662y, Jessie 131/603y, Amison 24/218y
PASSING: Basler 40-110/746y, 4TD, 36.4%
RECEIVING: Mosier 25/339y, Jessie 15/336y, McGowan 13/210y
SCORING: William Bell (K) 32pts, Amison & Basler 24pts

1970 5-6

48 Washington St.	31 WR Ron Jessie / Steve Natsues
0 Texas Tech	23 WR Marvin Foster / Lucious Turner
31 Syracuse	14 T Steve Lawson
49 New Mexico	23 G Bobby Childs
21 Kansas State	15 C Mike McCoy
20 Nebraska	41 G Gary Cooper
24 Iowa State	10 T Tom Gaughan
7 Oklahoma State	19 TE Larry Brown
29 Colorado	45 QB Dan Heck
24 Oklahoma	28 HB Steve Conley / Jerome Nelloms
17 Missouri	28 FB John Riggins
	DL Gery Palmer
	DL Pat Ryan
	DL Don Perkins
	DL Bob Tyus / Mike Sullivan
	LB Kenny Page / Tom Oakson
	LB Steve Roach
	LB Gary Davenport
	DB Mark Geraghty / Mike Burton
	DB Lee Hawkins / Dale Holt
	DB Gary Adams
	DB Jerry Evans / Dick Hertel

RUSHING: Riggins 209/1131y, Conley 117/535y, Nelloms 41/197y
PASSING: Heck 81-188/1169y, 10TD, 43.1%
RECEIVING: Jessie 18/308y, Foster 15/299y, Turner 14/243y
SCORING: Riggins 84pts, Bob Helmbacher (K) 50pts, Heck 34pts

1971 4-7

34 Washington St.	0 WR Marvin Foster
22 Baylor	0 WR Lucious Turner
7 Florida State	30 T Bruce Mitchell / John Bryant
20 Minnesota	38 G Bobby Childs
39 Kansas State	13 C Mike McCoy / Mike McDaniel
0 Nebraska	55 G Gary Cooper / Roger Bernhardt
24 Iowa State	40 T Tom Gaughan
10 Oklahoma State	17 TE John Schroll
14 Colorado	35 QB Dan Heck / Dave Jaynes
10 Oklahoma	56 HB Delvin Williams / Jerome Nelloms
7 Missouri	2 FB Steve Conley
	DL Eddie Sheats
	DL Phil Basler
	DL Tommy Oakson
	DL Gery Palmer
	DL Pat Ryan
	LB Kenny Page
	LB Steve Roach
	DB Lee Hawkins
	DB Mike Burton / Rocky Bron
	DB Gary Adams / Jerry Evans
	DB Mark Geraghty

RUSHING: Williams 102/509y, Conley 118/471y,
Nelloms 112/442y
PASSING: Jaynes 64-137/748y, 7TD, 46.7%
RECEIVING: Schroll 40/491y, Foster 15/255y, Turner 15/196y
SCORING: Conley 32pts, Schroll 32pts, Bob Helmbacher (K) 31pts

1972 4-7

17 Washington St.	18 WR Emmett Edwards / Ken Saathoff
52 Wyoming	14 WR Bruce Adams
22 Florida State	44 T John Bryant
34 Minnesota	28 G Jim Schumm / Gordon Stockemer
19 Kansas State	20 C Mike McDaniel
0 Nebraska	56 G Roger Bernhardt
8 Iowa State	34 T Don Perkins
13 Oklahoma State	10 TE John Schroll
8 Colorado	33 QB David Jaynes
7 Oklahoma	31 TB Jerome Nelloms / Delvin Williams
28 Missouri	17 FB Robert Miller / Vince O'Neil
	DL Don Goode / Dean Zook
	DL Gery Palmer
	DL Bill Skepnek / Mitch Sutton
	DL Pat Ryan
	LB Eddie Sheats
	LB Steve Towle
	LB Dean Baird / Tommy Oakson
	DB Mike Burton
	DB Rocky Bron
	DB Rick Mudge / Kurt Knoff
	DB Gary Adams

RUSHING: Nelloms 179/684y, Williams 67/352y, Miller 62/330y
PASSING: Jaynes 153-287/2253y, 15TD, 53.3%
RECEIVING: Adams 39/704y, Schroll 28/344y, Edwards 26/464y
SCORING: Adams 50pts, Miller 42pts, Bob Helmbacher (K) 40pts

1973 7-4-1

29 Washington St.	8 WR Emmett Edwards
28 Florida State	0 WR Bruce Adams
34 Minnesota	19 T John Bryant
27 Tennessee	28 G John Morgan
25 Kansas State	18 C Mike McDaniel
9 Nebraska	10 G Gordon Stockemer
22 Iowa State	20 T Dave Scott / Jerone Hodges
10 Oklahoma State	10 TE Ken Saathoff
17 Colorado	15 QB David Jaynes
20 Oklahoma	48 TB Delvin Williams
14 Missouri	13 FB Robert Miller
18 N. Carolina St.■	31 DL Don Goode
	DL Mitch Sutton
	DL Mike Lemon
	DL Federo Dillon
	DL Dean Zook
	LB Steve Towle / Mike Gardner
	LB Dean Baird
	DB Kurt Knoff
	DB Eddie Lewis
	DB Rocky Bron
	DB Jim David / Nolan Cromwell

RUSHING: Williams 198/762y, Miller 77/342y
PASSING: Jaynes 172-330/2131y, 13TD, 52.1%
RECEIVING: Edwards 49/802y, Williams 33/272y, Miller 27/238y
SCORING: Williams 60pts, Adams 44pts, Bob Swift 28pts

1974 4-7

14 Washington St.	7 WR Emmett Edwards
3 Tennessee	17 WR Bruce Adams
40 Florida State	9 T Dave Scott
28 Texas A&M	10 G Mike Englebrake
20 Kansas State	13 C John Morgan
0 Nebraska	56 G Gordon Stockemer
6 Iowa State	22 T Ace Boydston / Morris Pippen
13 Oklahoma State	24 TE Jim Michaels / Gregg Hosack
16 Colorado	17 QB Scott McMichael
14 Oklahoma	45 HB Laverne Smith / Bill Campfield
3 Missouri	27 FB Robert Miller
	DL Dean Zook
	DL Federo Dillon / Paul Van Saun
	DL Mike Lemon
	DL Mike Butler / Terry Beeson
	DL Les Barnes / Rick Kovach
	LB Steve Towle
	LB Odell Weidner / Don Pile
	DB Eddie Lewis
	DB Steve Taylor
	DB Kurt Knoff
	DB Nolan Cromwell

RUSHING: Smith 176/1181y, Miller 144/712y, Campfield 39/207y
PASSING: McMichael 74-156/1044y, 5TD, 47.4%
RECEIVING: Edwards 30/542y, Adams 17/349y, Smith 12/119y
SCORING: Smith 30pts, Miller 26pts, Mike Love (K) 22pts

1975 7-5

14 Washington St.	18 WR Waddell Smith
14 Kentucky	10 T Lindsey Mason / Blake Thompson
20 Oregon State	0 G Butch Mascarello
41 Wisconsin	7 C John Morgan
0 Nebraska	16 G Roger Hammond / Morris Pippen
21 Iowa State	10 T Dave Scott
19 Oklahoma State	35 TE Jim Michaels
28 Kansas State	0 QB Nolan Cromwell
23 Oklahoma	3 HB Bill Campfield / Marc Sharp (QB)
21 Colorado	24 HB Laverne Smith
42 Missouri	24 FB Norris Banks / Dennis Wright
19 Pittsburgh■	33 DL Tom Dinkel
	DL Mike Butler
	DL Jim Emerson / Dennis Balagna
	DL Franklin King
	DL Steve Jones / Harry Murphy
	LB Terry Beeson
	LB Rick Kovatch
	DB Eddie Lewis
	DB Steve Taylor / John O'Rear
	DB Kurt Knoff
	DB Chris Golub / Tom Fitch

RUSHING: Cromwell 218/1124y, Smith 126/864y, Banks 126/648y
PASSING: Cromwell 20-49/333y, 3TD, 40.8%
RECEIVING: Smith 9/197y, Michaels 7/72y, Sharp 5/56y
SCORING: Cromwell 54pts, Smith 48pts, Dennis Kerbel 32pts

1976 6-5

28 Oregon State	16 WR Waddell Smith
35 Washington St.	16 T Lindsey Mason
37 Kentucky	16 G Butch Mascarello
34 Wisconsin	24 C Mike Wellman
14 Oklahoma State	21 G Morris Pippin
10 Oklahoma	28 T Blake Thompson
24 Kansas State	14 TE Jim Michaels
3 Nebraska	31 QB Nolan Cromwell / Scott McMichael
17 Iowa State	31 HB Bill Campfield
17 Colorado	40 HB Laverne Smith
41 Missouri	14 FB Norris Banks
	DL Steve Jones
	DL Mike Butler
	DL Jim Emerson / Dennis Balagna
	DL Franklin King
	DL Jerry Calovich / Jim Young
	LB Terry Beeson
	LB Tom Dinkel (DL) / Tom Andalikiewicz
	DB Andy Reust / Caleb Rowe / Leroy Irvin
	DB Skip Sharp
	DB Tom Fitch
	DB Chris Golub

RUSHING: Smith 148/978y, Banks 137/559y, Cromwell 113/540y
PASSING: Cromwell 13-43/273y, 1TD, 30.2%
McMichael 16-45/144y, 1TD, 35.6%
RECEIVING: W Smith 10/221y, Campfield 6/76y, Michaels 6/66y
SCORING: Mike Hubach (K) 49pts, L Smith 48pts, Cromwell 42pts

1977 3-7-1

14 Texas A&M	28 WR David Verser / Rodney Olson
7 UCLA	17 T Mike Gay
14 Washington St.	12 G John Mascarello
9 Oklahoma	24 C Mike Wellman
7 Miami (Fla.)	14 G Greg Woods
17 Colorado	17 T Lindsay Mason / Dave Fletcher
0 Oklahoma State	21 TE Kirby Criswell
3 Iowa State	41 QB Brian Bethke / Jeff Hines
29 Kansas State	21 HB Max Ediger / Mike Higgins
7 Nebraska	52 HB Bill Campfield
24 Missouri	22 FB Norris Banks
	DL Tom Dinkel
	DL Franklin King
	DL John Algee / Charles Casey
	DL Mike Beal
	DL James German / Jim Zidd
	LB Monte Carbonell
	LB Scellars Young / Don Pile
	DB Wayne Ricks
	DB Caleb Rowe / Jimmy Little
	DB Tom Fitch
	DB LeRoy Irvin

RUSHING: Banks 162/655y, Ediger 73/443y, Campfield 58/398y
PASSING: Bethke 23-53/384y, TD, 43.4%
RECEIVING: Verser 11/220y, Ediger 7/120y, 3 tied w/ 4
SCORING: Mike Hubach (K) 25pts, Bethke 24pts, Higgins 18pts

1978 1-10

10 Texas A&M	37 WR David Verser
2 Washington	31 WR Kevin Murphy / Walker Little
28 UCLA	24 T Mike Gay
6 Miami	38 G Franklin King
7 Colorado	17 C Mike Wellman
16 Oklahoma	17 G Tom O'Dohrty
7 Oklahoma State	21 T Bobby Whitten
7 Iowa State	13 TE Kirby Criswell / Lloyd Sobek
21 Nebraska	63 QB Harry Sydney
0 Missouri	48 HB Mike Higgins
20 Kansas State	36 FB Dan Wagoner
	DL Jerry Calovich
	DL Charles Casey
	DL Joe McCraney / John Algee
	DL Greg Smith
	DL Jim Zidd
	LB Scellars Young
	LB Monte Carbonell
	DB Delvin Miller
	DB Dave Harris
	DB Frank Wattelet / Roger Foote
	DB LeRoy Irvin

RUSHING: Higgins 68/270y, Sydney 103/222y, Wagoner 41/213y
PASSING: Sydney 44-107/605y, 2TD, 41.1%
RECEIVING: Murphy 20/346y, Verser 15/217y, Little 10/125y
SCORING: Mike Hubach (K) 22pts, Sydney 20pts, Criswell & Higgins 12pts

1979 3-8

0 Pittsburgh	24 WR David Verser
7 Michigan	28 WR Jimmy Little / Kevin Murphy
37 No. Texas St.	18 T Dave Fletcher
27 Syracuse	45 G Jim Ragsdale
0 Nebraska	42 C Bob Fiss
24 Iowa State	7 G Bobby Whitten
17 Oklahoma State	30 T Kirk Tushaus
36 Kansas State	28 TE Lloyd Sobek
0 Oklahoma	38 QB Brian Bethke / Kevin Clinton
17 Colorado	31 HB Michael Higgins / Walter Mack
7 Missouri	55 FB Harry Sydney
	DL John McCray / Jeff Fox
	DL Stan Gardner
	DL Jim Jackson
	LB Chris Toburen
	LB Scellars Young
	LB Kyle McNorton / Monte Carbonell
	LB Kirby Criswell / Jim Zidd
	DB Joe Tumpich
	DB Delvin Miller
	DB Frank Wattelet
	DB LeRoy Irvin

RUSHING: Sydney 123/541y, Higgins 105/348y, Mack 72/257y
PASSING: Bethke 59-108/874y, 5TD, 54.6%
Clinton 55-143/570y, 0TD, 38.5%
RECEIVING: Verser 21/463y, Sydney 20/149y, 3 tied w/ 13
SCORING: Mike Hubach (K) 39pts, Verser 30pts, Higgins & Sydney 24pts

1980 4-5-2

7 Oregon	7 WR David Verser
3 Pittsburgh	18 WR Lester Mickens
9 Louisville	17 T Dave Wessling
23 Syracuse	8 G David Lawrence
0 Nebraska	54 C Bob Fiss
28 Iowa State (F-L)	17 G Fred Osborn
14 Okla. St (F-L)	14 T Bobby Whitten
20 Kansas State	18 TE Mike Kennaw / Jeff Schleicher
19 Oklahoma	21 QB Frank Seurer
42 Colorado	3 TB Kerwin Bell / Walter Mack
6 Missouri	31 FB Harry Sydney
	DL Al Bertsch / Gary Coleman
	DL Jeff Fox
	DL Gregg Smith
	DL Stan Gardner
	DL Hilton Dawson
	LB Chris Toburen
	LB Kyle McNorton
	DB Delvin Miller
	DB Robert McNeely
	DB Joe Tumpich
	DB Frank Wattelet

RUSHING: Bell 228/1114y, Mack 48/286y, Garfield Taylor (TB) 48/224y
PASSING: Seurer 64-146/797y, 5TD, 43.8%
RECEIVING: Verser 30/576y, Kennaw 15/153y, Schleicher 11/104y
SCORING: Bell 48pts, Bruce Kallmeyer (K) 39pts, Verser 30pts

1981 8-4

15 Tulsa	11 WR Russ Bastin
19 Oregon	10 WR Wayne Capers
21 Kentucky	16 T Dave Wessling
17 Arkansas State	16 G David Lawrence / Paul Fairchild
7 Oklahoma State	20 C Ed Bruce / John Prater
7 Oklahoma	45 G K.C. Brown
17 Kansas State	14 T Reggie Smith
15 Nebraska	31 TE Jeff Schleicher
24 Iowa State	11 QB Frank Seurer
27 Colorado	0 TB Garfield Taylor / Walter Mack
19 Missouri	11 FB E.J. Jones / Brad Butts
0 Mississippi St.■	10 DL Marky Alexander / Tim Freiss
	DL Guy Neighbors / Mark Wilbers
	DL Gregg Smith
	DL Broderick Thompson
	DL Bryan Horn
	LB Chris Toburen
	LB Kyle McNorton
	DB Dan Wagoner
	DB Tony McNeeley
	DB Robert Gentry / Roger Foote
	DB Gary Coleman / Jeff Colter

RUSHING: Taylor 167/728y, Mack 83/303y, Kerwin Bell (TB) 55/212y
PASSING: Seurer 89-176/1199y, 4TD, 50.6%
RECEIVING: Capers 36/629y, Bastin 16/221y, Taylor 14/106y
SCORING: Bruce Kallmeyer (K) 52pts, Taylor 38pts, Capers 24pts

1982 2-7-2

10 Wichita State	13 WR Bobby Johnson / Russ Bastin
30 TCU	19 WR Wayne Capers / Darren Green
13 Kentucky	13 T Renwick Atkins
15 Tulsa	20 G K.C. Brown
24 Oklahoma State	24 C Bennie Simecka
14 Oklahoma	38 G Craig Kirschbaum / Anthony Penny
7 Kansas State	36 T Reggie Smith
0 Nebraska	52 TE Sylvester Byrd / Ernie Wright
24 Iowa State	17 QB Frank Seurer
3 Colorado	28 TB Dino Bell / Robert Mimbs
10 Missouri	16 FB E.J. Jones
	DL Marky Alexander / Randall Amerine
	DL Broderick Thompson
	DL Walter Parrish
	DL Tim Freiss
	DL Carky Alexander / Willie Pless
	LB Mike Arbanas
	LB Eddie Simmons
	DB Rod Demerritte / Rod Madden
	DB Elvis Patterson
	DB Gary Coleman / Roger Foote
	DB Robert Gentry

RUSHING: Bell 110/370y, Jones 60/259y, Mimbs 66/201y
PASSING: Seurer 127-259/1625y, 7TD, 49%
RECEIVING: Capers 25/383y, Johnson 18/428y, Byrd 18/173y
SCORING: Bruce Kallmeyer (K) 44pts, Jones & Capers 18pts

1983 4-6-1

34 No. Illinois	37 WR Darren Green / Richard Estell
16 TCU	16 WR Bobby Johnson
57 Wichita State	6 T Renwick Atkins
26 Southern Cal	20 G Paul Fairchild
35 Iowa State	38 C Bennie Simecka
31 Kansas State	3 G K.C. Brown
10 Oklahoma State	27 T Reggie Smith
14 Oklahoma	45 TE Sylvester Byrd
23 Colorado	34 QB Frank Seurer
13 Nebraska	67 TB Kerwin Bell / Robert Mimbs
37 Missouri	27 FB E. J. Jones
	DL Elvis Patterson
	DL Carky Alexander
	DL Eldridge Avery
	DL Rod Timmons
	DL Joe Masaniou
	DL Len Gant
	LB Darnell Williams
	LB Willie Pless
	DB Jeffrey Colter
	DB Jeffrey Brown
	DB Derek Berry / Rodney Demerritte

RUSHING: Bell 115/498y, Mimbs 79/380y, Jones 98/417y
PASSING: Seurer 187-353/2789y, 14TD, 53%
RECEIVING: Johnson 58/1154y, Mimbs 27/315y, Jones 26/106y
SCORING: Bruce Kallmeyer 98pts, Johnson 42pts, Bell 30pts

1984 5-6

31 Wichita State	7 WR Richard Estell
16 Florida State	42 WR Skip Peete
6 Vanderbilt	41 T Jim Davis
17 North Carolina	23 G Doug Certain
33 Iowa State	14 C Bennie Simecka
7 Kansas State	24 G Paul Swenson / Gordon Schuler
10 Oklahoma State	47 T Bob Pieper
28 Oklahoma	11 TE Jeff Anderson
28 Colorado	27 QB Mike Norseth
7 Nebraska	41 TB Lynn Williams / Robert Mimbs
35 Missouri	21 FB Mark Henderson
	DL Phil Forte
	DL Bob Tucker
	DL Jon Stewart
	DL David Smith / Marvin Mattox
	LB Rick Bredesen
	LB Willie Pless
	LB Guy Gamble / Travis Hardy
	DB Alvin Walton
	DB Milt Garner
	DB Wayne Ziegler
	DB Arnold Fields

RUSHING: Williams 172/776y, Mimbs 100/494y, Norseth 94/100y
PASSING: Norseth 136-239/1682y, 9TD, 56.9%
RECEIVING: Peete 38/448y, Mimbs 28/291y, Estell 25/500y
SCORING: Dodge Schwartzburg (K) 66pts, Williams 48pts,
 3 tied w/ 18pts

1985 6-6

33 Hawaii	27 WR Richard Estell / Sandy McGee
42 Vanderbilt	16 WR Willie Vaughn / Johnny Holloway
37 Indiana State	10 T Jim Davis
20 Florida State	24 G Paul Swenson
44 E. Illinois	20 C Paul Oswald / Jay Allen
21 Iowa State	22 G Bryan Howard
38 Kansas State	7 T Bob Pieper
10 Oklahoma State	17 TE Sylvester Byrd
6 Oklahoma	48 QB Mike Norseth
3 Colorado	14 TB Lynn Williams / Mike Rogers
6 Nebraska	56 FB Arnold Fields
34 Missouri	20 DL Steve Nave
	DL Eldridge Avery
	DL Phil Forte
	LB Darnell Williams
	LB John Randolph
	LB Willie Pless
	LB Rick Bredeson
	DB Milt Garner
	DB Dan Crossman
	DB Travis Hardy
	DB Kevin Harder / Wayne Ziegler

RUSHING: Williams 86/373y, Fields 79/336y, Rogers 75/268y
PASSING: Norseth 227-408/2995y, 15TD, 55.6%
RECEIVING: Estell 70/1109y, Holloway 32/358y, McGee 31/476y
SCORING: Jeff Johnson (K) 83pts, Williams, Vaughn &
 Fields 30pts

1986 3-8

0 North Carolina	20 WR Ronnie Caldwell
16 Utah State	13 WR Willie Vaughn / Tony Harvey
20 Indiana State	6 T Jim Davis / Von Lacey
35 So. Illinois	23 G Steve Nave
10 Iowa State	13 C Paul Oswald
12 Kansas State	29 G Jay Allen
6 Oklahoma State	24 T Pete Popovich
3 Oklahoma	64 TE Mark Parks
0 Colorado	17 QB Mike Orth / Kelly Donohoe
0 Nebraska	70 TB Arnold Snell / Mike Rogers
0 Missouri	48 FB Mark Henderson
	DL Phil Forte / Teddy Newman
	DL Eldridge Avery
	DL Guy Gamble / David White
	DL Scott Carlson
	LB Stacy Henson
	LB Rick Bredeson
	LB Rick Clayton
	DB Mike Fisher
	DB Milt Garner
	DB Wayne Ziegler
	DB Jamey Steinhauser

RUSHING: Snell 163/672y, Rogers 40/132y, Henderson 33/114y
PASSING: Orth 144-290/1548y, 7TD, 49.7%
RECEIVING: Vaughn 41/341y, Caldwell 39/423y, Snell 34/250y
SCORING: Snell 30pts, Mac Smith (K) 18pts, 4 tied w/ 12pts

1987 1-9-1

0 Auburn	49 WR Ronnie Caldwell / Mark Parks (FB)
17 Kent State	31 WR Quintin Smith / Willie Vaughn
11 La. Tech	16 T Jim Davis
16 So. Illinois	15 G Bryan Howard
2 Nebraska	54 C Chip Budde
10 Colorado	35 G Jay Allen
28 Iowa State	42 T Bob Pieper
10 Oklahoma	71 TE John Baker
17 Kansas State	17 QB Kelly Donohue / Kevin Verdugo
17 Oklahoma State	49 TB Arnold Snell / Darryl Terrell
7 Missouri	19 FB Mike Rogers
	DL Eldridge Avery
	DL Mark Koncz / Von Lacey
	DL David White / David Gordon
	DL Teddy Newman
	LB Rick Clayton / Kyle Schenker
	LB Curtis Moore
	LB Rick Bredeson
	DB Milt Garner
	DB Rodney Harris / Bill Sutter
	DB Clint Normore
	DB Marvin Mattox

RUSHING: Snell 184/691y, Terrell 71/223y,
 Frank Hatchett (TB) 55/167y
PASSING: Donohoe 72-144/981y, 3TD, 50%
 Verdugo 52-112/569y, 1TD, 46.4%
RECEIVING: Baker 27/300y, Vaughn 25/672y, Smith 17/223y
SCORING: Louis Klemp (K) 35pts, Vaughn 24pts, 3 tied w/ 18pts

1988 1-10

14 Baylor	27 WR Quintin Smith
7 Auburn	56 WR Willie Vaughn
21 California	52 T Chris Perez
29 New Mexico St.	42 G Russ Bowen / Smith Holland
10 Nebraska	63 C Chip Budde
9 Colorado	21 G Dave Grattan
14 Iowa State	42 T Bill Hundelt
14 Oklahoma	63 TE John Baker
30 Kansas State	12 QB Kelly Donohue
24 Oklahoma State	63 TB.Tony Sands / Arnold Snell
17 Missouri	55 FB Roger Robben
	DL Mark Koncz
	DL John Fritch / Matt Nolen
	DL David Gordon / Dave Walton
	LB Dan Newbrough / Lance Flachsbarth
	LB Tony Barker / Mike Long
	LB Curtis Moore
	LB Paul Friday / Jason Tyrer
	DB Peda Samuel
	DB Rodney Harris
	DB Doug Terry / Jason Priest
	DB Deral Boykin

RUSHING: Sands 103/480y, Frank Hatchett (TB) 59/417y,
 Snell 85/399y
PASSING: Donohue 131-258/1844y, 9TD, 50.8%
RECEIVING: Vaughn 39/812y, Smith 30/426y, Hatchett 7/78y
SCORING: Brad Fleeman (K) 43pts, Vaughn 42pts, 3 tied w/ 18pts

1989 4-7

41 Montana State	17 WR Kenny Drayton / Jim New
28 Louisville	33 WR Quintin Smith
28 Kent State	21 T Chris Perez
3 Baylor	46 G John Fritch
6 Oklahoma	45 C Chip Budde
20 Iowa State	24 G Scott Imwalle / Marino Vidoli
17 Colorado	49 T Bill Hundelt
21 Kansas State	16 TE John Baker
24 Oklahoma State	37 QB Kelly Donohoe
14 Nebraska	51 TB Tony Sands / Frank Hatchett
46 Missouri	44 FB Maurice Hooks / Maurice Douglas
	DL David Gordon
	DL Gilbert Brown
	DL Gary Oatis / Mark Koncz
	LB Lance Flachsbarth
	LB Wes Swinford
	LB Roger Robben
	LB Dan Newbrough
	DB Hassan Bailey / Tim Hill
	DB Doug Terry
	DB Deral Boykin
	DB Jason Priest / Paul Friday

RUSHING: Sands 216/1109y, Hooks 43/206y, Hatchett 55/197y
PASSING: Donohue 141-256/2125y, 12TD, 55.1%
RECEIVING: Smith 50/898y, Drayton 25/444y, Baker 25/313y
SCORING: Sands 66pts, Smith & Brad Fleeman (K) 48pts

1990 3-7-1

10 Virginia	59 WR Rob Licursi / Jim New
38 Oregon State	12 WR Kenny Drayton
16 Louisville	28 T Chris Perez
17 Oklahoma	31 G Smith Holland / Dan Schmidt
34 Iowa State	34 C Chip Budde
0 Miami	34 G Scott Imwalle
10 Colorado	41 T Keith Loneker
27 Kansas State	24 TE Chad Fette
31 Oklahoma State	30 QB Chip Hilleary
9 Nebraska	41 TB Tony Sands / Chaka Johnson
21 Missouri	31 FB Maurice Douglas
	DL Gary Oatis / Brian Christian
	DL Dana Stubblefield
	DL Gilbert Brown
	DL Lance Flachsbarth
	LB Pat Rogan
	LB Curtis Moore
	LB Guy Howard
	DB Hassan Bailey
	DB Tim Hill
	DB Paul Friday
	DB Charley Bowen

RUSHING: Sands 186/757y, Hilleary 101/342y, Johnson 50/326y
PASSING: Hilleary 129-224/1730y, 7TD, 57.6%
RECEIVING: Drayton 34/506y, Licursi 28/452y, Fette 19/298y
SCORING: Dan Eichloff (K) 67pts, Sands 30pts, Douglas 24pts

1991 6-5

30 Toledo	7 WR Matt Gay / Jim New
23 Tulsa	17 WR Kenny Drayton
54 New Mexico St.	14 T Chris Perez
31 Virginia	19 G Hessley Hempstead
16 Kansas State	12 C Dan Schmidt
41 Iowa State	0 G Scot Imwalle
41 Oklahoma	3 T Keith Loneker
31 Oklahoma State	0 TE Dwayne Chandler
59 Nebraska	23 QB Chip Hilleary
30 Colorado	24 TB Tony Sands
53 Missouri	29 FB Roger Robben
	DL Kyle Moore / Lance Flachsbarth
	DL Gilbert Brown
	DL Dana Stubblefield
	DL Brian Christian
	LB G. Howard /Don Davis /Sylvester Wright
	LB Steve Harvey / Wes Swinford
	LB Hassan Bailey
	DB Robert Vaughn / Gerald McBurrows
	DB Tim Hill
	DB Doug Terry
	DB Paul Friday

RUSHING: Sands 273/1442y, Hilleary 93/400y, Robben 91/316y
PASSING: Hilleary 98-188/1267y, 6TD, 52.1%
RECEIVING: Drayton 34/439y, Chandler 18/345y, Gay 17/232y
SCORING: Dan Eichloff (K) 85pts, Hilleary 84pts, Sands 54pts

1992 8-4

49 Oregon State	20 WR Rob Licursi / Ashaundai Smith
62 Ball State	10 WR Matt Gay
40 Tulsa	7 T Khristopher Booth
23 California	27 G Hessley Hempstead
31 Kansas State	7 C Dan Schmidt
50 Iowa State	47 G John Jones
27 Oklahoma	10 T Keith Loneker
26 Oklahoma State	18 TE Dwayne Chandler / Rodney Harris
7 Nebraska	49 QB Chip Hilleary
18 Colorado	25 TB Maurice Douglas / George White
17 Missouri	22 FB/TE Monte Cozzens / Pete Vang
23 BYU■	20 DL Kyle Moore
	DL Chris Maumalanga / Gilbert Brown
	DL Dana Stubblefield
	DL Guy Howard / S. Wright / Ben Christian
	LB Don Davis / Ronnie Ward
	LB Larry Thiel / Steve Harvey
	LB Hassan Bailey
	DB Robert Vaughn
	DB Gerald McBurrows
	DB Kwamie Lassiter / Clint Bowen
	DB Charley Bowen

RUSHING: Douglas 198/899y, Hilleary 93/537y,
 Cozzens 115/527y
PASSING: Hilleary 106-215/1583y, 12TD, 49.3%
RECEIVING: Gay 30/425y, Chandler 17/398y, White 15/245y
SCORING: Dan Eichloff (K) 86pts, Douglas 76pts, Hilleary 38pts

1993 5-7

0 Florida State	42 WR Greg Ballard
46 W. Carolina	3 WR Ashaundai Smith / Robert Reed
14 Michigan State	31 T Rod Jones
16 Utah	41 G Hessley Hempstead
24 Colorado State	6 C Dan Schmidt / Joe Hornback
9 Kansas State	10 G John Jones
35 Iowa State	20 T Mark Allison / Chris Banks
21 Oklahoma	38 TE Dwayne Chandler
13 Oklahoma State	6 QB Asheiki Preston / Fredrick Thomas
20 Nebraska	21 TB June Henley / L.T. Levine
14 Colorado	38 RB Chris Powell / Costello Good
28 Missouri	0 DL Brian Christian / Jason Brown
	DL C. Maumalanga / Daryl Jones
	DL Mike Steele
	DL/LB Guy Howard / Steve Harvey
	LB Ronnie Ward
	LB Larry Thiel / Harold Harris
	LB Don Davis / Keith Rodgers
	DB Tony Blevins
	DB Gerald McBurrows
	DB Clint Bowen
	DB Robert Vaughn / Marlin Blakeney

RUSHING: Henley 233/1127y, Levine 123/542y, Preston 99/298y
PASSING: Preston 97-159/1233y, 3TD, 61%
Thomas 38-89/427y, 1TD, 42.7%
RECEIVING: Smith 27/256y, Reed 22/270y, Chandler 17/370y
SCORING: Henley 78pts, Dan Eichloff (K) 64pts, Preston 24pts

1994 6-5

35 Houston	13 WR Rodney Harris / Hosea Friday
17 Michigan State	10 WR Ashaundai Smith / George White
21 TCU	31 T Scott Whittaker / Rod Jones
72 UAB	0 G Hessley Hempstead
13 Kansas State	21 C Jared Smith
41 Iowa State	23 G John Jones
17 Oklahoma	20 T Mark Allison / Derek Brown
24 Oklahoma State	14 TE Jim Moore / Brent Willeford
17 Nebraska	45 QB Asheiki Preston
26 Colorado	51 TE L.T. Levine/June Henley/Mark Sanders
41 Missouri	31 FB Chris Powell
	DL Harold Harris / Derek Fairchild
	DL Sylvester Wright
	DL Darnell Britt / Brett McGraw
	DL Steve Harvey
	LB Don Davis
	LB Ronnie Ward / Jason Thoren
	LB Keith Rodgers
	DB Dorian Brew / Avery Randle
	DB Tony Blevins / Jason Harris
	DB Kwame Lassiter
	DB Gerald McBurrows

RUSHING: Levine 128/803y, Henley 130/599y, Sanders 60/322y
PASSING: Preston 88-156/1168y, 7TD, 56.4%
RECEIVING: Smith 22/426y, Moore 16/241y, White 16/201y
SCORING: Levine 66pts, Jeff McCord (K) 61pts, Sanders 30pts

1995 10-2

23 Cincinnati	18 WR Isaac Byrd
27 North Texas	10 WR Ashaundai Smith
38 TCU	20 T Rod Jones
20 Houston	13 G Chris Banks
40 Colorado	24 C Jim Stiebel / Jared Smith
34 Iowa State	7 G Cleve Roberts
38 Oklahoma	17 T Scott Whittaker
7 Kansas State	41 TE Jim Moore
42 Missouri	23 QB Mark Williams / Matt Johner
3 Nebraska	41 RB June Henley
22 Oklahoma State	17 RB L.T. Levine / Eric Galbreath
51 UCLA■	30 DL Dewey Houston / Dan Dercher
	DL Brett McGraw
	DL Kevin Kopp
	LB Keith Rodgers / Patrick Brown
	LB Jason Thoren
	LB Steve Bratten / Dick Holt
	LB Chris Jones / Freddie Hammonds
	DB Dorian Brew / Jason Harris
	DB Jaime Harris / Avery Randle
	DB Maurice Gaddie
	DB Charles Davis / Thad Warren

RUSHING: Levine 156/841y, Henley 158/766y, Williams 82/239y
PASSING: Williams 174-282y/1957y, 14TD, 61.7%
RECEIVING: Byrd 48/604y, Smith 41/550y, Henley 26/312y
SCORING: Jeff McCord (K) 60pts, Levine 54pts, Henley 48pts

1996 4-7

35 Ball State	10 WR Isaac Byrd
52 TCU	17 WR Andre Carter / John Gordon
42 Utah	45 T Scott Whittaker
52 Oklahoma	24 G Jim Stiebel (C) / Dameon Hunt
17 Texas Tech	30 C Jared Smith
7 Colorado	20 G Cleve Roberts
7 Nebraska	63 T Justin Glasgow
34 Iowa State	31 TE Jim Moore / Hosea Friday
12 Kansas State	38 QB Matt Johner / Ben Rutz
17 Texas	38 RB June Henley
25 Missouri	42 RB Eric Vann / Eric Galbreath
	DL Dewey Houston / Dan Dercher
	DL Brett McGraw
	DL Kevin Kopp
	LB Pat Brown
	LB Jason Thoren
	LB Ronnie Ward / Steve Bratten
	LB Chris Jones
	DB Jaime Harris
	DB Jason Harris
	DB Tony Blevins
	DB Maurice Gaddie / Michael Allen

RUSHING: Henley 302/1349y, Vann 51/176y
PASSING: Johner 96-185/1232y, 10TD, 51.9%
Rutz 59-103/823y, 7TD, 57.3%
RECEIVING: Byrd 53/840y, Henley 22/215y, Vann 20/284y
SCORING: Henley 108pts, Jeff McCord (K) 58pts, Byrd 48pts

1997 5-6

24 UAB	0 WR Eric Patterson / Akili Roberson
17 TCU	10 WR Tanner Hancock / Termaine Fulton
15 Missouri	7 WR Michael Chandler
7 Cincinnati	34 T Michael Lies
20 Oklahoma	17 G Dameon Hunt
7 Texas Tech	17 C Chris Enneking
6 Colorado	42 G Justin Glasgow
0 Nebraska	35 T Jerome Parks / Dan Dercher
34 Iowa State	24 TE Brian Gray
16 Kansas State	48 QB Zac Wegner / Matt Johner
31 Texas	45 RB Eric Vann / David Winbush
	DL Dion Johnson
	DL Brett McGraw
	DL Dewey Houston
	LB Patrick Brown
	LB Steve Bratten / J.J. Johnson
	LB Jason Thoren / Hanson Caston
	LB Ron Warner
	DB Jason Harris
	DB Jamie Harris / Michael Allen
	DB Tony Blevins
	DB Maurice Gaddie

RUSHING: Vann 196/796y, Winbush 61/338y,
Mitch Bowles (RB) 20/165y
PASSING: Wegner 66-144/970y, 4TD, 45.8%
Johner 32-74/419y, 1TD, 43.2%
RECEIVING: Chandler 21/311y, Vann 13/114y, Hancock 11/166y
SCORING: Joe Garcia (K) 51pts, Vann 36pts, Fulton 24pts

1998 4-7

28 Oklahoma State	38 WR Harrison Hill
23 Missouri	41 WR Termaine Fulton / Byron Gasaway
63 Illinois State	21 T Dan Dercher / Bob Smith
39 UAB	37 G Dameon Hunt / Marc Owen
21 Texas A&M	24 C Chris Enneking / Bob Schmidt
24 Baylor	31 G Justin Glasgow / Chuck Jarvis
0 Nebraska	41 T Michael Lies
33 Colorado	17 TE Jason Gulley / Brian Gray
6 Kansas State	54 QB Zac Wegner
23 North Texas	14 HB David Winbush / Mitch Bowles
20 Iowa State	23 FB Moran Norris
	DL Dion Johnson / Jeremy Hanak
	DL John Williams / Nate Dwyer
	DL Dion Rayford
	LB Hanson Caston
	LB Steve Bratten / Andrew LeClair
	LB J.J. Johnson / Marcus Rogers
	LB Pat Brown / Algie Atkinson
	DB Jamie Harris /Muhammad Abdul-Rahim
	DB Andrew Davison
	DB Chad Coellner / Greg Erb
	DB Michael Allen

RUSHING: Winbush 209/974y
PASSING: Wegner 91-186/1367y, 7TD, 48.9%
RECEIVING: Hill 28/391y
SCORING: Joe Garcia (K) 63pts

1999 5-7

13 Notre Dame	48 WR Harrison Hill
71 Cal-Northridge	14 WR Mike Chandler
17 Colorado	51 T John Oddonetto
13 San Diego State	41 G Dameon Hunt
27 SMU	9 C Chris Enneking
9 Kansas State	50 G Marc Owen / Chuck Jarvis
17 Texas A&M	34 T Justin Hartwig
21 Missouri	0 TE David Hurst / Jason Gulley
17 Nebraska	24 QB Dylen Smith / Zac Wegner
45 Baylor	10 HB David Winbush / Mitch Bowles
13 Oklahoma State	45 FB Moran Norris
31 Iowa State	28 DL Dion Johnson
	DL John Williams / Nate Dwyer
	DL Dion Rayford / Kareem Carter
	LB Algie Atkinson / Chaz Murphy
	LB Dariss Lomar / Marcus Rogers
	LB Andrew LeClair
	LB Tim Bowers
	DB Quincy Roe / Muhammad Abdul-Rahim
	DB Andrew Davison
	DB Carl Nesmith / Greg Erb
	DB Kareem High

RUSHING: Winbush 123/595y, Norris 107/537y, Bowles 89/444y
PASSING: Smith 135-263/1599y, 12TD, 51.3%
RECEIVING: Chandler 36/473y, Hill 29/506y, Winbush 18/135y
SCORING: Norris 54pts, Joe Garcia (K) 50pts, Winbush 42pts

2000 4-7

17 SMU	31 WR Harrison Hill / Algen Williams
23 UAB	20 WR Termaine Fulton / Roger Ross
42 Southern Illinois	0 T John Oddonetto
16 Oklahoma	34 G Bob Smith
13 Kansas State	52 C Nick Smith / Marc Owen
38 Missouri	17 G Chuck Jarvis
23 Colorado	15 T Justin Hartwig
39 Texas Tech	45 TE/WR David Hurst / Jason Gulley
17 Nebraska	56 QB Dylen Smith
16 Texas	51 HB David Winbush / Reggie Duncan
17 Iowa State	38 FB Moran Norris
	DL De'Nard Whitfield
	DL Nate Dwyer
	DL Ervin Holloman / Marquis Hayes
	LB Chaz Murphy
	LB Tim Bowers / Chris Doyle
	LB Marcus Rogers
	LB Algie Atkinson / Victor Bullock
	DB Andrew Davison
	DB Quincy Roe
	DB Carl Nesmith
	DB Kareem High / Bilal Cook

RUSHING: Winbush 163/701y
PASSING: Smith 140-306/1963y, 10TD, 45.8%
RECEIVING: Hill 47/591y, Ross 29/482y
SCORING: Joe Garcia (K) 59pts

2001 3-8

24 SW Missouri St.	10 WR Roger Ross / Byron Gasaway
17 UCLA	41 WR Termaine Fulton
16 Colorado	27 T Justin Sands
34 Texas Tech	31 G Bob Smith
10 Oklahoma	38 C Nick Smith
34 Missouri	38 G Kyle Grady
6 Kansas State	40 T Justin Hartwig
7 Nebraska	51 TE David Hurst / Adrian Jones
0 Texas	59 QB Mario Kinsey / Zach Dyer
7 Iowa State	49 HB Reggie Duncan / Marshell Chiles
27 Wyoming	14 FB/WR Austine Nwabuisi / Derick Mills
	DL Travis Watkins / David McMillan
	DL Nate Dwyer
	DL Marquis Hayes / Ervin Holloman
	DL Charlie Dennis
	LB Algie Atkinson
	LB Marcus Rogers / Banks Floodman
	LB Leo Eienne / Greg Cole
	DB Andrew Davison
	DB Carl Ivey
	DB Jamarei Bryant
	DB Jake Letourneau

RUSHING: Duncan 181/739y, Kinsey 130/225y, Chiles 34/133y
PASSING: Kinsey 88-202/1215y, 7TD, 43.6%
Dyer 43-89/460y, 3TD, 48.3%
RECEIVING: Ross 39/493y, Fulton 30/397y, Gasaway 18/200y
SCORING: Johnny Beck (K) 58pts, Kinsey & Duncan 20pts

2002 2-10

3 Iowa State	45 WR Byron Gasaway
20 UNLV	31 WR Brandon Rideau
44 SW Missouri St	24 WR Derick Mills / Mark Simmons
16 Bowling Green	39 T Justin Sands
43 Tulsa	33 G Tony Damiani
32 Baylor	35 C Greg Nicks
29 Colorado	53 G David Hurst (TE) / Justin Henry
22 Texas A&M	47 T Tony Coker / John Harvey
12 Missouri	36 TE/WR Adrian Jones / Marcellus Jones
0 Kansas State	64 QB Bill Whittemore / Jonas Weatherbie
7 Nebraska	45 RB Clark Green
20 Oklahoma State	55 DL Charlie Dennis
	DL Tim Allen / Brock Teddleton
	DL Travis Watkins
	DL David McMillan
	LB Nick Reid / Glenn Robinson
	LB Greg Cole
	LB Leo Etienne
	DB Remuise Johnson
	DB Donnie Amadi / Bobby Birhiray
	DB Johnny McCoy / Tony Stubbs
	DB Jake Letourneau / Zach Dyer (QB)

RUSHING: Green 119/519y, Whittemore 75/283y
PASSING: Whittemore 83-173/923y, 8TD, 48%
Dyer 20-42/211y, 1TD, 47.6%
RECEIVING: Gasaway 29/382y, Green 24/287y, Rideau 19/145y
SCORING: Gasaway & Whittemore 30pts, Johnny Beck (K) 19pts

2003 6-7

20 Northwestern	28 WR Charles Gordon (DB)/Mod'rck Johnson
46 UNLV	24 WR Mark Simmons
42 Wyoming	35 WR Brandon Rideau
41 Jacksonville St.	6 T Adrian Jones
35 Missouri	14 G Bob Whitaker
47 Colorado	50 C Joe Vaughn
28 Baylor	21 G Tony Coker / Travis Dambach
6 Kansas State	42 T Danny Lewis
33 Texas A&M	45 TE Lyonel Anderson / Denver Latimore
3 Nebraska	24 QB Bill Whittemore / Adam Barmann
21 Oklahoma State	44 RB Clark Green / John Randle (DB)
36 Iowa State	7 DL Cory Kipp / Monroe Weekley
26 N. Carolina St.■	56 DL Sid Bachman / Chuck Jones
	DL Reggie Curry / Tim Allen
	DL David McMillan
	LB Banks Floodman / Brandon Perkins
	LB Gabe Toomey
	LB Nick Reid
	DB Donnie Amadi / Kenneth Thompson
	DB Remuise Johnson / Shelton Simmons
	DB Jonathan Lamb
	DB Tony Stubbs

RUSHING: Green 204/968y, Whittemore 127/534y,
Randle 64/400y
PASSING: Whittemore 159-263/2385y, 18TD, 60.6%
RECEIVING: Gordon 57/769y, Rideau 51/677y, Green 44/464y
SCORING: Whittemore 60pts, Johnny Beck (K) 58pts, Green 48pts

2004 4-7

21 Tulsa	3 WR/FB Gary Heaggins / Austine Nwabuisi
63 Toledo	14 WR Brandon Rideau
17 Northwestern	20 WR Mark Simmons
30 Texas Tech	31 T Matt Thompson
8 Nebraska	14 G Bob Whitaker
31 Kansas State	28 C Joe Vaughn
10 Oklahoma	41 G David Ochoa
7 Iowa State	13 T Travis Dambach / Cesar Rodriguez
21 Colorado	30 TE Lyonel Anderson / Derek Fine
23 Texas	27 QB Adam Barmann / Brian Luke
31 Missouri	14 RB John Randle / Clark Green
	DL Jermial Ashley
	DL Travis Watkins / Greg Tyree
	DL Tim Allen / Brandon Perkins
	DL David McMillan
	LB Kevin Kane
	LB Gabe Toomey / Banks Floodman
	LB Nick Reid
	DB Charles Gordon
	DB Theo Baines / Ronnie Amadi
	DB Rodney Harris
	DB Tony Stubbs

RUSHING: Randle 147/540y, Green 87/309y
PASSING: Barmann 141-262/1427y, 12TD, 53.8%
Luke 40-65/467y, 3TD, 61.5%
RECEIVING: Rideau 51/597y, Simmons 48/553y, Randle 35/274y
SCORING: Randle 54pts, Rideau 42pts, Scott Webb (K) 35pts

2005 7-5

30 Florida Atlantic	19 WR/FB BrianMurph / Brandon McAnderson
36 Appalachian St.	8 WR Charles Gordon / Marcus Henry
34 Louisiana Tech	14 WR Mark Simmons
17 Texas Tech	30 T Cesar Rodriguez
3 Kansas State	12 G Bob Whitaker / Travis Dambach
3 Oklahoma	19 C David Ochoa
13 Colorado	44 G Ryan Cantrell / Jake Cox
13 Missouri	3 T Matt Thompson
40 Nebraska	15 TE Derek Fine
14 Texas	66 QB Jason Swanson / Brian Luke
24 Iowa State	21 RB Clark Green / Jon Cornish
42 Houston■	13 DL Jermial Ashley / Rodney Allen
	DL James McClinton
	DL Tim Allen / Brandon Perkins
	DL Charlton Keith
	LB Kevin Kane
	LB Banks Floodman
	LB Nick Reid
	DB Aqib Talib / Charles Gordon
	DB Theo Baines / Ronnie Amadi
	DB Rodney Fowler
	DB Jerome Kemp

RUSHING: Cornish 134/780y, Green 153/664y,
McAnderson 22/102y
PASSING: Swanson 105-190/1223y, 7TD, 55.3%
Luke 87-171/967y, 6TD, 50.9%
RECEIVING: Simmons 44/631y, Gordon 34/313y, Murph 33/368y
SCORING: Scott Webb (K) 69pts, Cornish 66pts, Simmons 26pts

2006 6-6

49 Northwestern St.	18 WR Brian Murph / Jonathan Lamb
21 La.-Monroe	19 WR Marcus Henry
31 Toledo	37 WR Dexton Fields
13 South Florida	7 T Cesar Rodriguez
32 Nebraska	39 G Bob Whitaker
18 Texas A&M	21 C David Ochoa
32 Oklahoma State	42 G Travis Dambach
35 Baylor	36 T Anthony Collins
20 Colorado	15 TE Derek Fine
41 Iowa State	10 QB Kerry Meier / Adam Barmann
39 Kansas State	20 RB Jon Cornish
17 Missouri	42 DL Russell Brorsen / Rodney Allen
	DL Wayne Wilder
	DL James McClinton
	DL Paul Como / John Larsen
	LB Joe Mortensen / Eric Washington
	LB Mike Rivera
	LB Arist Wright / James Holt
	DB Anthony Webb / Blake Bueltel
	DB Aqib Talib
	DB Darrell Stuckey / Justin Thornton
	DB Jerome Kemp

RUSHING: Cornish 250/1457y, Meier 99/344y,
Jake Sharp (RB) 21/129y
PASSING: Meier 104-184/1193y, 13TD, 56.5%
Barmann 82-150/911y, 3TD, 54.7%
RECEIVING: Fields 45/455y, Murph 43/467y, Fine 28/355y
SCORING: Scott Webb (K) 76pts, Cornish 54pts,
Fine & Meier 32pts

2007 12-1

52 C. Michigan	7 WR Marcus Henry
62 SE Louisiana	0 WR Dexton Fields
45 Toledo	13 WR Dezmon Briscoe / Tertavi Ingram
55 Fla. International	3 T Anthony Collins / Matt Darton
30 Kansas State	24 G Adrian Mayes
58 Baylor	10 C Ryan Cantrell
19 Colorado	14 G Chet Hartley
19 Texas A&M	11 T Cesar Rodriguez / Ian Wolfe
76 Nebraska	39 TE/WR Derek Fine / Kerry Meier
43 Oklahoma State	28 QB Todd Reesing
45 Iowa State	7 TB Brandon McAnderson / Jake Sharp
28 Missouri	36 DL Russell Brorsen / Jeff Wheeler
24 Virginia Tech■	21 DL Caleb Blakesley / Jake Laptad
	DL James McClinton / Todd Haselhorst
	DL John Larson
	LB James Holt
	LB Joe Mortensen
	LB Mike Rivera / Justin Springer
	DB Aqib Talib (WR)
	DB Chris Harris
	DB Darrel Stuckey
	DB Patrick Resby / Justin Thornton

RUSHING: McAnderson 190/1125y, Sharp 147/821y,
Reesing 92/197y
PASSING: Reesing 276-446/3486y, 33TD, 61.9%
RECEIVING: Fields 63/834y, Henry 54/1014y, Fine 46/394y
SCORING: Scott Webb (K) 120pts, McAnderson 96pts, Henry 60pts

2008 8-5

40 Fla. International	0 WR Johnathan Wilson
29 Louisiana Tech	0 WR Dezmon Briscoe / Raymond Brown
34 South Florida	37 WR Dexton Fields
38 Sam Houston St.	14 WR/TE Kerry Meier / Tim Biere
35 Iowa State	33 T Jeremiah Hatch
30 Colorado	14 G Adrian Mayes
31 Oklahoma	45 C Ryan Cantrell
21 Texas Tech	63 G Chet Hartley
52 Kansas State	21 T Jeff Spikes
35 Nebraska	45 QB Todd Reesing
7 Texas	35 RB Jake Sharp / Angus Quigley
40 Missouri	37 DL Russel Brorsen
42 Minnesota■	21 DL Cale Blakesley
	DL Richard Johnson / Jamal Greene
	DL Jake Laptad / Jeff Wheeler
	LB James Holt
	LB Joe Mortensen
	LB Mike Rivera / Arist Wright
	DB Kendric Harper / Phil Strozier
	DB Chris Harris / Ray Patterson (WR)
	DB Justin Thornton / Isiah Barfield
	DB Darrel Stuckey

RUSHING: Sharp 186/860y, Quigley 59/309y,
Jocques Crawford (RB) 62/232y
PASSING: Reesing 329-495/3888y, 32TD, 66.5%
RECEIVING: Meier 97/1045y, Briscoe 92/1407y, Wilson 43/573y
SCORING: Briscoe 90pts, Jacob Branstetter (K) & Sharp 78pts

2009 5-7

49 N. Colorado	3 WR Jonathan Wilson
34 UTEP	7 WR Kerry Meier
44 Duke	16 WR Dezmon Briscoe / Tertavian Ingram
41 Southern Miss	28 WR/TE Brad McDougald / Tim Biere
30 Colorado	34 G Brad Thorson (T)
13 Oklahoma	35 C Jeremiah Hatch
21 Texas Tech	42 G Sal Capra / Trevor Marrongelli
10 Kansas State	17 T Jeff Spikes (G)
17 Nebraska	31 QB Todd Reesing
20 Texas	51 RB Jake Sharp / Toben Opurum
39 Missouri	41 DL Maxwell Onyegbule / Jeff Wheeler
	DL Cale Blakesley
	DL Richard Johnson / John Williams
	DL Jake Laptad
	LB Huldon Tharp / Arist Wright
	LB Drew Dudley
	LB/DB Justin Springer / Justin Thornton
	DB Daymond Patterson / D.J. Beshears
	DB Chris Harris / Anthony Davis
	DB Lubbock Smith / Phillip Strozier
	DB Darrel Stuckey / Ryan Murphy

RUSHING: Opurum 133/554y, Sharp 102/429y,
Kale Pick (QB) 14/167y
PASSING: Reesing 313-496/3616y, 22TD, 63.1%
RECEIVING: Meier 102/985y, Briscoe 84/1337y, Wilson 35/449y
Sharp 34/266y, McDougald 33/318y
SCORING: Jacob Branstetter (K) 81pts, Briscoe 66pts,
Opurum 60pts

2010 3-9

3 No. Dakota St.	6 WR Daymond Patterson
28 Georgia Tech	25 WR Johnathan Wilson / Chris Omigie
16 So. Mississippi	31 WR/FB Brad McDougald (DB)/A.J. Steward
42 New Mexico St.	16 T Tann Hawkinson
7 Baylor	55 G Sal Capra
7 Kansas State	59 C Jeremiah Hatch
10 Texas A&M	45 G Duane Zlatnik / Trevor Marrongelli
16 Iowa State	28 T Brad Thorson
52 Colorado	45 TE Tim Biere
3 Nebraska	20 QB Jordan Webb / Quinn Mecham
14 Oklahoma State	48 RB D.J. Beshears / James Sims/ A. Quigley
7 Missouri	35 DL Toben Opurum / Kevin Young
	DL Richard Johnson
	DL Patrick Dorsey
	DL Jake Laptad
	LB Steven Johnson
	LB Justin Springer
	LB/DB Drew Dudley / Tyler Patmon
	DB Isiah Barfield / Clavin Rubles
	DB Chris Harris / Greg Brown
	DB Lubbock Smith / Prinz Kande
	DB Olaiton Oguntodu

RUSHING: Sims 168/742y, Quigley 71/262y, Beshears 55/213y
PASSING: Webb 121-214/1195y, 7TD, 56.5%
Mecham 61-102/554y, 4TD, 59.8%
RECEIVING: Patterson 60/487y, Wilson 38/387y,
McDougald 19/240y, Biere 19/228y, Sims 19/131y
SCORING: Jacob Branstetter (K) 49pts, Beshears & Biere 24pts

KANSAS STATE

Kansas State University (Founded 1863)
Manhattan, Kansas
Nickname: Wildcats
Colors: Purple and White
Stadium: Bill Snyder Family Stadium (1968) 52,200
Conference Affiliations: Big Seven (Charter member, 1948-56),
  Big Eight (1957-95), Big Twelve North (1996-present)

CAREER RUSHING YARDS	Attempts	Yards
Darren Sproles (2001-04)	815	4979
Daniel Thomas (2009-10)	545	2850
Eli Roberson (2000-03)	604	2818
Eric Hickson (1994-95, 97-98)	507	2537
Mike Lawrence (1994-97)	492	2265
J.J. Smith (1991-94)	491	2210
Isaac Jackson (1971-73)	492	2182
Josh Scobey (2000-01)	409	1981
Eric Gallon (1989-92)	447	1960
Cornelius Davis (1966-68)	506	1873

CAREER PASSING YARDS	Comp.-Att.	Yards
Josh Freeman (2006-08)	680-1151	8078
Lynn Dickey (1968-70)	501-994	6208
Chad May (1993-94)	385-687	5253
Carl Straw (1987-90)	385-833	5223
Eli Roberson (2000-03)	307-627	5099
Jonathan Beasley (1996-97, 99-2000)	259-544	4642
Michael Bishop (1997-98)	244-480	4401
Darrell Dickey (1979-82)	319-640	4098
Paul Watson (1988-91)	301-560	3963
Dennis Morrison (1970-72)	294-637	3428

CAREER RECEIVING YARDS	Catches	Yards
Kevin Lockett (1993-96)	217	3032
Jordy Nelson (2005-07)	206	2822
Michael Smith (1988-91)	179	2457
Aaron Lockett (1998-01)	137	2400
Quincy Morgan (1999-00)	106	2173
Dave Jones (1966-68)	127	1904
Mitch Running (1992-95)	133	1821
James Terry (2002-03)	92	1793
Brandon Banks (2008-09)	123	1754
Jermaine Moreira (2003-06)	114	1587

SEASON RUSHING YARDS	Attempts	Yards
Darren Sproles (2003)	306	1986
Daniel Thomas (2010)	298	1585
Darren Sproles (2002)	237	1465
Darren Sproles (2004)	244	1318
Daniel Thomas (2009)	247	1265

SEASON PASSING YARDS	Comp.-Att.	Yards
Josh Freeman (2007)	316-499	3353
Josh Freeman (2008)	224-382	2945
Michael Bishop (1998)	164-295	2844
Chad May (1993)	185-350	2682
Jonathan Beasley (2000)	156-313	2636

SEASON RECEIVING YARDS	Catches	Yards
Jordy Nelson (2007)	122	1606
James Terry (2003)	64	1232
Quincy Morgan (2000)	64	1166
Darnell McDonald (1998)	75	1092
Brandon Banks (2008)	67	1049

GAME RUSHING YARDS	Attempts	Yards
Darren Sproles (2004 vs. La.-Lafayette)	38	292
Darren Sproles (2003 vs. Missouri)	43	273
Mike Lawrence (1996 vs. Iowa State)	38	252

GAME PASSING YARDS	Comp.-Att.	Yards
Chad May (1993 vs. Nebraska)	30-51	489
Josh Freeman (2008 vs Oklahoma)	29-51	478
Michael Bishop (1998 vs. La.-Monroe)	23-40	441

GAME RECEIVING YARDS	Catches	Yards
Jordy Nelson (2007 vs. Iowa State)	14	214
Jordy Nelson (2007 vs. Missouri State)	15	209
Darnell McDonald (1997 vs. Syracuse)	7	206

GREATEST COACH:

He made his stamp on Kansas State football with a dedication to excellence not matched in school history. Bill Snyder will forever be associated with the program he built, with the stadium now named after him and his family.

Starting in 1989 from the bottom, Snyder built up Kansas State football piece-by-piece. Beating North Texas in the first year snapped the school's ungodly 30-game winless streak. Beating Oklahoma State in year two delivered the school's first Big Eight win in four years. Winning five games that year, 1990, earned Snyder the conference coach of the year award. It was the school's most wins in one season since 1982.

By 1991 the Wildcats were 7-4, winning seven games for the first time since 1954, grabbing the fourth spot in the conference with a 4-3 mark and winning the school's first road game in six years.

The building of the program was completed by 1993, when Snyder led KSU on a remarkable journey to the big-time of college football. They would win nine games that season, including the Copper Bowl, which was the first post-season win in school history, to begin a run during which they average 10 wins per season for the next eight years. With bowl victories, Top 10 finishes, All American honors and coaching awards, these were heady times. Even the end-of-the-season agony of 1998, when a spot in the BCS Championship Game was lost when the Wildcats fell in double overtime to Texas A&M in the Big 12 title game, was remarkable: Kansas State was one win away from a fight for the national championship! The Wildcats!

Plucked from Hayden Fry's coaching staff at Iowa, where he was offensive coordinator, Snyder had helped turn that program around and knew what he needed to do. As much as his weak non-conference scheduling helped secure some easy wins, the most important change to the program made by Snyder was in the attitude department. For a program that had become synonymous with losing, that was his most important gift.

KANSAS STATE'S 55 GREATEST SINCE 1953

OFFENSE

WIDE RECEIVER: Dave Jones, Kevin Lockett, Quincy Morgan, Jordy Nelson, Michael Smith
TIGHT END: Paul Coffman
TACKLE: Barrett Brooks, Jim Hmielewski, Damian Johnson, Todd Weiner, Ryan Young
GUARD: Andy Eby, Mo Latimore, Nick Leckey
CENTER: Randall Cummins, Quentin Neujahr
QUARTERBACK: Michael Bishop, Lynn Dickey, Josh Freeman, Chad May
RUNNING BACK: Isaac Jackson, J.J. Smith, Darren Sproles, Daniel Thomas
FULLBACK: Don Calhoun

DEFENSE

END: Manuel Barrera, Darren Howard, Bill Matan, James Walker
TACKLE: Tim Colston, Mario Fatafehi, Ron Nery, Reggie Singletary
LINEBACKER: Brooks Barta, Theopilis Bryant, Oscar Gibson, Danny Lankas, Mark Simoneau, Gary Spani
CORNERBACK: Chris Canty, Terence Newman, Thomas Randolph, Clarence Scott
SAFETY: Lamar Chapman, Jarrod Cooper, Barton Hundley, Jaime Mendez

SPECIAL TEAMS

RETURN SPECIALISTS: David Allen, Aaron Lockett
PLACE KICKER: Martin Gramatica
PUNTER: Tim Reyer

MULTIPLE POSITIONS

GUARD-TACKLE-TIGHT END: Bill Brittain
DEFENSIVE END-LINEBACKER: Ian Campbell

TWO-WAY PLAYERS

HALFBACK-DEFENSIVE BACK: Veryl Switzer
CENTER-GUARD-LINEBACKER: Ellis Rainsberger

PERFORMANCE FORMULA:
KANSAS STATE'S 10 BEST SEASONS

1997	1.6416	5 of 70
1999	1.6336	5 of 71
1998	1.6114	5 of 71
2002	1.5888	7 of 70
1995	1.5715	7 of 70
2000	1.5339	9 of 70
2003	1.4816	10 of 71
1996	1.4135	17 of 70
1994	1.4133	10 of 71
1993	1.3748	22 of 70

KANSAS STATE WILDCATS

Year	W-L-T	AP Poll	Conference Standing	Toughest Regular Season Opponents	Coach (Record at School)	Bowl Games		
1953	6-3-1		2t	Oklahoma 8-1-1, Missouri 6-4, Colorado 6-4	Bill Meek			
1954	7-3		5	Oklahoma 10-0, Colorado 7-2-1, Nebraska 6-4	Bill Meek (14-24-1)			
1955	4-6		3t	Oklahoma 10-0, Colorado 6-4, Wyoming 7-3	Bus Mertes			
1956	3-7		5t	Oklahoma 10-0, Michigan St. 7-2, Colorado 7-2-1, Wyoming 10-0	Bus Mertes			
1957	3-6-1		5t	Oklahoma 9-1, Michigan State 8-1, Colorado 6-3-1, Kansas 5-4-1	Bus Mertes			
1958	3-7		5	Oklahoma 9-1, Oklahoma State 7-3, Colorado 6-4, Wyoming 7-3	Bus Mertes			
1959	2-8		7	Oklahoma 7-3, Iowa State 7-3, Missouri 6-4, Oklahoma State 6-4	Bus Mertes (15-34-1)			
1960	1-9		8	Missouri 9-1, Minnesota 8-1, Kansas 7-2-1, Iowa State 7-3	Doug Weaver			
1961	2-8		8	Colorado 9-1, Missouri 7-2-1, Kansas 6-3-1	Doug Weaver			
1962	0-10		8	Missouri 7-1-2, Washington 7-1-2, Oklahoma 8-2, Nebraska 8-2	Doug Weaver			
1963	2-7		7	Nebraska 9-1, Oklahoma 8-2, Missouri 7-3	Doug Weaver			
1964	3-7		5t	Nebraska 9-1, Arizona State 8-2, New Mexico 9-2, Missouri 6-3-1	Doug Weaver			
1965	0-10		8	Nebraska 10-0, Missouri 7-2-1, Colorado 6-2-2, BYU 6-4	Doug Weaver			
1966	0-9-1		7t	Nebraska 9-1, Army 8-2, Colorado 7-3, Missouri 6-3-1, OU 6-4	Doug Weaver (8-60-1)			
1967	1-9		8	Oklahoma 9-1, Colorado 8-2, Missouri 7-3, Virginia Tech 7-3	Vince Gibson			
1968	4-6		6t	Penn State 10-0, Kansas 9-1, Oklahoma 7-3, Missouri 7-3	Vince Gibson			
1969	5-5		5t	Penn State 10-0, Missouri 9-1, Nebraska 8-2, Colorado 7-3	Vince Gibson			
1970	6-5		2t	Nebraska 10-0-1, Arizona State 10-0, Oklahoma 7-4	Vince Gibson			
1971	5-6		5t	Nebraska 12-0, Oklahoma 10-1, Colorado 9-3, ISU 8-3, FSU 8-3	Vince Gibson			
1972	3-8		8	Oklahoma 10-1, Nebraska 8-2-1, Colorado 8-3, Arizona State 9-2	Vince Gibson			
1973	5-6		6t	Oklahoma 10-0, Nebraska 8-2-1, Kansas 7-3-1, Missouri 7-4	Vince Gibson			
1974	4-7		7t	Oklahoma 11-0, Nebraska 8-3, Missouri 7-4, Miss. State 8-3	Vince Gibson (33-52)			
1975	3-8		8	Nebraska 10-1, Oklahoma 10-1, Colorado 9-2, Texas A&M 10-1	Ellis Rainsberger			
1976	1-10		8	Oklahoma 8-2-1, A&M 9-2, Colorado 8-3, Iowa St. 8-3, Ok. St 8-3	Ellis Rainsberger			
1977	2-9		8	Oklahoma 10-1, Nebraska 8-3, Iowa State 8-3, FSU 9-2, BYU 7-4	Ellis Rainsberger (5-28)			
1978	4-7		5t	Oklahoma 10-1, Nebraska 9-2, Missouri 7-4, ISU 8-3, Auburn 6-4-1	Jim Dickey			
1979	3-8		8	Nebraska 10-1, Oklahoma 10-1, Auburn 8-3, Oklahoma St. 7-4	Jim Dickey			
1980	3-8		7t	Oklahoma 9-2, Nebraska 9-2, Missouri 8-3, LSU 7-4	Jim Dickey			
1981	2-9		8	Nebraska 9-2, Wash. 9-2, Kansas 8-3, Missouri 7-4, Okla. State 7-4	Jim Dickey			
1982	6-5-1		4	Nebraska 11-1, Oklahoma 8-3, Arizona State 9-2	Jim Dickey	Independence	3 Wisconsin	14
1983	3-8		8	Nebraska 11-0, Missouri 7-4, Oklahoma St. 7-4, Kentucky 6-4-1	Jim Dickey			
1984	3-7-1		5t	Oklahoma 9-1-1, Nebraska 9-2, Okla. St. 9-2, So. Carolina 10-1	Jim Dickey (24-54-2), Lee Moon [1-8]			
1985	1-10		7t	Oklahoma 10-1, Nebraska 9-2, Oklahoma St. 8-3, Colorado 7-4	Stan Parrish			
1986	2-9		7	Oklahoma 10-1, Nebraska 9-2, Texas Tech 7-4	Stan Parrish			
1987	0-10-1		7t	Oklahoma 11-0, Nebraska 9-2, Oklahoma St. 9-2, Iowa 9-3	Stan Parrish (2-30-1)			
1988	0-11		8	Nebraska 11-1, Oklahoma 9-2, Oklahoma St. 9-2, Colorado 8-3	Bill Snyder			
1989	1-10		8	Colorado 11-0, Nebraska 10-1, Arizona State 6-4-1	Bill Snyder			
1990	5-6		6t	Colorado 10-1-1, Nebraska 9-2, Oklahoma 8-3	Bill Snyder			
1991	7-4		4	Washington 11-0, Nebraska 9-1-1, Colorado 8-2-1, Oklahoma 8-3	Bill Snyder			
1992	5-6		6t	Colorado 9-1-1, Nebraska 9-2, Kansas 7-4	Bill Snyder			
1993	9-2-1	20	3	Nebraska 11-0, Oklahoma 8-3, Colorado 7-3-1	Bill Snyder	Copper	52 Wyoming	17
1994	9-3	19	3	Nebraska 12-0, Colorado 10-1	Bill Snyder	Aloha	7 Boston College	12
1995	10-2	7	2t	Nebraska 11-0, Kansas 9-2, Colorado 9-2	Bill Snyder	Holiday	54 Colorado State	21
1996	9-3	17	N3	Nebraska 10-1, Colorado 9-2, Texas Tech 7-4, Rice 7-4	Bill Snyder	Cotton	15 BYU	19
1997	11-1	8	N2	Nebraska 11-0, Texas &M 9-2, Missouri 7-4	Bill Snyder	Fiesta	35 Syracuse	18
1998	11-2	10	N1	Nebraska 9-3, Texas 8-3, Missouri 7-4, Colorado 7-4	Bill Snyder	Alamo	34 Purdue	37
1999	11-1	6	N1t	Nebraska 10-1, Texas 9-3	Bill Snyder	Holiday	24 Washington	20
2000	11-3	9	N1t	Nebraska 9-2, Iowa State 8-3, Texas A&M 7-4, Texas Tech 7-5	Bill Snyder	Cotton	35 Tennessee	21
2001	6-6		N4t	Nebraska 11-1, Colorado 9-2, Texas A&M 8-4, Texas Tech 7-4	Bill Snyder	Insight.com	3 Syracuse	26
2002	11-2	7	N2	Texas 10-2, Southern Cal 10-2, Colorado 9-3, Oklahoma State 7-5	Bill Snyder	Holiday	34 Arizona State	27
2003	11-4	14	N1	Texas 10-2, Nebraska 9-3, Missouri 8-4	Bill Snyder	Fiesta	28 Ohio State	35
2004	4-7		N4t	Oklahoma 11-0, Colorado 7-4, Fresno State 8-3	Bill Snyder {see below}			
2005	5-6		N6	Texas Tech 9-2, Oklahoma 7-4, Colorado 7-4, Nebraska 7-4	Ron Prince			
2006	7-6		N2t	Louisville 11-1, Nebraska 9-3, Texas 9-3, Missouri 8-4	Ron Prince	Texas	10 Rutgers	37
2007	5-7		N4	Auburn 8-4, Texas 9-3, Kansas 11-1, Missouri 11-1	Ron Prince			
2008	5-7		N4t	Texas Tech 11-1, Oklahoma 12-1, Missouri 9-4	Ron Prince (17-20)			
2009	6-6		N2t	Texas Tech 8-4, Oklahoma 7-5, Nebraska 9-4	Bill Snyder			
2010	7-6		N3t	Nebraska 10-3, Oklahoma State 10-2, Missouri 10-2	Bill Snyder (149-80-1)	Pinstripe	34 Syracuse	36

TOTAL:	**269-370-7 .4218 (61 of 70)**	**Bowl Games since 1953:** **6-8 .4286 (54 of 70)**

GREATEST TEAM SINCE 1953: The 1998 squad came within three points of the BCS title game, falling to Texas A&M in the Big 12 title game. They were 11-0 at the time, and ranked no. 2 in the country.

1953 6-3-1
50 Drake 0 E Ed Pence / Wilbur Stocks
13 Colorado State 14 T Ron Marciniak / Ron Nery
27 Nebraska 0 G Tom O'Boyle / Bob Hilliard
20 Iowa State 12 C Ken Gowdy / Jim Furey
28 Colorado 14 G Dean Peck / Austin Gentry
21 Wichita 14 T Earl Meyer / Ron Clair
0 Oklahoma 34 E Ed Linta / Bob Smith
7 Kansas 0 QB Bob Dahnke / Bob Whitehead
6 Missouri 16 HB Gerald Cashman / Bernie Dudley
26 Arizona 26 HB Veryl Switzer / Corky Taylor
FB Bob Balderston / Doug Roether
RUSHING: Switzer 95/558y
PASSING: Dahnke 14-28/415y, 4TD, 50%
RECEIVING: Switzer 8/211y
SCORING: Switzer 49pts

1954 7-3
29 Colorado State 0 E L.D. Fitzgerald / Jim Rusher
21 Wyoming 13 T Ron Nery / Tito Cordelli
7 Missouri 35 G Bob Hilliard / Cletis Wilson
7 Nebraska 3 C Jim Furey / Chuck Zickefoose
20 Tulsa 13 G Ron Marciniak / George DeBitetto
0 Oklahoma 21 T Larry Hartshorn / Frank Rodman
28 Kansas 6 E Tom Ebert / Ed Linta
53 Drake 18 QB Bob Whitehead / Jim Logsdon
12 Iowa State 7 HB Corky Taylor / Bernie Dudley
14 Colorado 38 HB Bob Dahnke / Kenny Long /Tony
Addeo
FB Doug Roether / Bill Carrington
RUSHING: Taylor 72/529y, Roether 78/498y, Carrington 66/286y
PASSING: Logsdon 18-39/260y, 4TD, 46.2%
RECEIVING: Taylor 14/334y, Dahnke 8/95y, Addeo 6/97y
SCORING: Taylor 48pts, Rusher 25pts, Addeo & Whitehead 18pts

1955 4-6
7 Wyoming 12 E Jim Rushner / Don Zadnik
7 Iowa 28 T Ron Nery / Wally Carlson
0 Nebraska 16 G Ellis Rainsberger / Burt Schmidt
41 Marquette 0 C Jim Furey
13 Colorado 34 G Rudy Bletscher / George DeBitetto
9 Iowa State 7 T Frank Rodman / Jack Keelan
7 Oklahoma 40 E Chuck Zickefoose / George Laddish
46 Kansas 0 QB Bob Whitehead / Dick Corbin
21 Missouri 0 HB Ralph Pfeifer / Kenny Nesmith
0 Oklahoma A&M 28 HB Tony Addeo / Jerry Hayes
FB Doug Roether / Bill Carrington
RUSHING: Roether 74/272y, Pfeifer 54/252y, Addeo 50/226y
PASSING: Corbin 14-42/156y, TD, 33.3%
RECEIVING: Zadnik 9/110y, Hayes 5/83y, Wilson 4/21y
SCORING: Pfeifer 36pts, Rusher 18pts, Whitehead 18pts

1956 3-7
7 Oklahoma A&M 27 E Don Zadnik
0 Colorado 34 T Jack Keelan / Len LeGault
0 Oklahoma 66 G Don Martin / Jerry Sand
10 Nebraska 7 C Ellis Rainsberger
6 Missouri 20 G Rudy Bletscher / Wally Carlson
15 Wyoming 27 T Gene Meier
15 Kansas 20 E George Laddish / Jim Luzinski
41 Marquette 14 QB Dick Corbin / Keith Wilson
32 Iowa State 6 HB Kenny Nesmith / Ben Grosse
17 Michigan State 38 HB Gene Keady / Tony Addeo
FB Ralph Pfeifer
RUSHING: Wilson 103/341y, Keady 43/310y, Pfeifer 74/296y
PASSING: Corbin 16-49/378y, 5TD, 32.7%
RECEIVING: Keady 14/247y, Zadnik 10/179y, Nesmith 4/60y
SCORING: Keady 43pts, Nesmith 26pts, Grosse & Corbin 18pts

1957 3-6-1
7 Wyoming 12 E Don Zadnik
36 BYU 7 T Jack Keelan
7 Nebraska 14 G Gene Meier
7 Pacific 7 C Ellis Rainsberger
14 Colorado 42 G Donald Miles / Jaydee Stinson
14 Iowa State 10 T Wally Carlson
0 Oklahoma 13 E Jim Luzinski / George Laddish
7 Kansas 13 QB Dick Corbin / Les Krull
23 Missouri 21 HB Ralph Pfeifer / Ben Grosse
9 Michigan State 27 HB Gene Keady / Keith Wilson
FB Ray Glaze / Tony Tiro
RUSHING: Pfeifer 115/468y, Wilson 86/389y, Keady 38/332y
PASSING: Corbin 24-61/287y, TD, 39.3%
RECEIVING: Pfeifer 11/109y, Luzinski 9/117y, Zadnik 6/83y
SCORING: Pfeifer 24pts, Zadnik 15pts, 5 tied with 12pts

1958 3-7
17 Wyoming 14 E Joe Vader / Vern Osborne
3 Colorado 13 T John Stolte
13 Utah State 20 G Gene Meier / Don Martin
23 Nebraska 6 C Dick Boyd / Ralph Lambing
8 Missouri 32 G Dave Noblitt / Chester George
6 Oklahoma 40 T Ralph Peluso / Jim Speight
12 Kansas 21 E Cedric Price / Jim Luzinski
7 Oklahoma State 14 QB Les Krull / John Solmos
14 Iowa State 6 HB Ben Grosse/Dale Evans/Bill Gallagher
7 Michigan State 26 HB Max Falk / George Whitney
FB Terry Lee
RUSHING: Falk 74/295y, Lee 77/269y, Whitney 54/215y
PASSING: Krull 57-106/661y, 2TD, 53.8%
RECEIVING: Vader 21/219y, Price 17/230y, Luzinski 7/76y
SCORING: Grosse 41pts, Evans 18pts, Price 13pts

1959 2-8
0 Wichita 19 E Gary Lee Lafferty / Joe Vader
28 So. Dakota St. 12 T John Stolte / Don Darter
21 Oklahoma State 7 G Ron Carbone / Paul Kemp
17 Colorado 20 C Al Kouneski / Ralph Lambing
14 Kansas 33 G Larry Jones / Marlan Ray
0 Iowa State 26 T Ralph Peluso
0 Iowa 53 E Vern Osborne / Cedric Price
0 Oklahoma 36 QB John Solmos / Gary Kershner
0 Missouri 26 HB Dale Evans / Jack Richardson
29 Nebraska 14 HB Max Falk / George Whitney
FB J.B. Littlejohn / Gene Bessetti
RUSHING: Evans 70/245y, Falk 49/180y, Whitney 55/164y
PASSING: Solmos 49-114/585y, 3TD, 43%
RECEIVING: Evans 23/224y, Osborne 13/170y, Gallagher 10/82y
SCORING: Evans 24pts, Osborne 14pts, Richardson 14pts

1960 1-9
20 So Dakota State 6 E Darrell Elder
0 Kansas 41 T Dick Corrigan / Ray Slyter
7 Colorado 27 G Conrad Hardwick / John Winchester
7 Nebraska 17 C Al Kouneski
0 Missouri 45 G Marlan Ray / Ron Carbone
7 Oklahoma 49 T Tom Brettschneider / Dave Noblitt
7 Oklahoma State 28 QB Ron Blaylock / John Solmos
7 Iowa State 20 HB Jack Richardson / Larry O'Hara
16 Arizona 35 HB Dale Evans / Harold Haun
FB John Finfrock / Dave Laurie
RUSHING: Richardson 38/219y, Gallagher 10/117y, Solmos 44/102y
PASSING: Solmos 32-83/378y, 3TD, 38.6%
RECEIVING: Crenshaw 18/190y, Evans 17/205y, Elder 8/87y
SCORING: Blaylock 24pts, Crenshaw, Richardson & Solmos 12pts

1961 2-8
14 Indiana 8 E Darrell Elder
14 Air Force 12 T Marlan Ray / Neal Spence
0 Nebraska 24 G Conrad Hardwick / Tom Dowell
8 Kentucky 21 C Al Kouneski
0 Colorado 13 G Ken Nash
7 Iowa State 31 T Bill Hull / Dick Corrigan
6 Oklahoma 17 E Jack King / Dave Mehner
0 Kansas 34 QB Larry Corrigan / Tom Cooper
9 Missouri 27 HB Joel Searles / Spencer Puls
0 Oklahoma State 45 HB Bill Gallagher / Ralph McFillen
FB Benny Cochrun / David Noblitt
RUSHING: Searles 73/252y, Gallagh'r 68/230y, Cochrun 42/119y
PASSING: Corrigan 13-30/234y, 2TD, 43.3%
RECEIVING: Puls 7/123y, Mehner 6/46y, McFillen 5/49y
SCORING: McDonald 12pts, Barger 8pts, 6 tied with 6pts

1962 0-10
0 Indiana 21 E Darrel Elder / Carl Brown
0 Colorado 6 T Neal Spence / Dick Branson
0 Washington 41 G Conrad Hardwick / Joe Provenzano
0 Missouri 32 C Ron Lacy / Don Goodpasture
6 Nebraska 26 G Bob Mitts / Tom Dowell
0 Oklahoma 47 T Ken Nash / Bill Hull
0 Kansas 38 E Dennis Winfrey / Jack King
13 Arizona 14 QB Larry Corrigan / Doug Dusenbury
14 Iowa State 28 HB Larry Condit / Joel Searles
6 Oklahoma State 30 HB Ralph McFillen / Jerry condit
FB Willis Crenshaw / Benny Cochran
RUSHING: Crenshaw 88/331y, Searles 35/122y, Corrigan 82/115y
PASSING: Corrigan 28-84/441y, 2TD, 33.3%
RECEIVING: King 13/137y, James 6/81y, Winfrey 6/45y
SCORING: Crenshaw 12pts, 4 tied with 6pts

1963 2-7
24 BYU 7 E Ralph McFillen
0 San Jose State 16 T Dick Branson
7 Colorado 21 G Phil King
11 Missouri 21 C Dan Woodward
6 Nebraska 28 G Bob Mitts
9 Oklahoma 34 T Joe Provenzano
0 Kansas 34 E Bob Nichols / Spencer Puls
13 Texas Tech 51 QB Larry Corrigan / Jim Grechus (D)
21 Iowa State 10 HB Doug Dusenbury
HB Ron Barlow / Jerry Condit
FB Willis Crenshaw
RUSHING: Barlow 58/293y, Corrigan 109/215y, Crenshaw 43/197y
PASSING: Corrigan 58-127/634y, 3TD, 45.7%
RECEIVING: McFillen 29/328y, Puls 13/118y, Barlow 10/111y
SCORING: McFillen 20pts, Dusenbury 18pts, Corrigan 18pts

1964 3-7
7 Wisconsin 17 E Larry Condit
16 Colorado 14 T Dick Branson
0 Missouri 7 G Mike Penrod / Phil King
0 Nebraska 47 C Doug Nutter / Rich Wilkinson
0 Oklahoma 44 G Warren Klawiter / Bob Becker
0 Kansas 7 T Dave Langford / Dick Riggs
10 Arizona State 21 E Carl Brown
7 Iowa State 6 QB Ed Danieley
17 Oklahoma State 14 HB Doug Dusenbury
7 New Mexico 9 HB Jerry Condit
FB John Christensen / Ron Barlow
DL Bill Matan
DL Mike Beffa / Dave Langford
DL Willie Jones
DL Denby Blackwell
LB Bob Mitts
LB Max Martin
LB Dan Woodward / Jerry Cook
LB Charlie Cottle
DB Bob Sjogren
DB Jim Grechus
DB Larry Anderson
RUSHING: Condit 122/450y, Dusenbury 80/261y, Barlow 62/224y
PASSING: Danieley 36-79/358y, TD, 45.6%
RECEIVING: J. Condit 10/77y, L. Condit 9/170y, Brown 9/102y
SCORING: J. Condit 24pts, Cook 16pts, L. Condit & Danieley 12pts

1965 0-10
7 Indiana 19 E Rick Balducci / Bobby Nichols
3 BYU 21 T Dave Alexander / Phil King
0 Colorado 36 G Rich Wilkinson / Mike Goyne
6 Missouri 28 C Doug Nutter
0 Nebraska 41 G Warren Klawiter
0 Oklahoma 27 T Dave Langford
0 Kansas 34 E Bill Matan / Lodis Rhodes
14 Cincinnati 21 QB Vic Castillo / Mike White
6 Iowa State 38 HB Ed Danieley
7 Oklahoma State 31 HB Henry Howard
FB Charlie Cottle
DL Jerry Cook
DL Willie Jones / Art Strozier (OE)
DL Bill Salat / Carl Branson
DL Bill Greve
LB Mike Beffa
LB Dan Woodward
LB Max Martin
LB Marty Aubuchon / Steve Overton
DB Mitch Borota
DB Jim Grechus
DB Larry Anderson
RUSHING: Howard 84/279y, Cottle 81/253y, Danieley 35/101y
PASSING: Castillo 60-159/734y, 2TD, 37.7%
RECEIVING: Balducci 13/172y, Rhodes 13/138y, Strozier 11/142y
SCORING: Howard 12pts, Cook 11pts, 3 tied with 6

1966 0-9-1

6 Army	21 E Dave Jones
8 New Mexico	28 T Dave Alexander
0 Colorado	10 G Al Walczak / Dean Hokanson
0 Missouri	27 C Bob Stull
10 Nebraska	21 G Mike Goyne
14 Cincinnati	28 T Dave Langford
3 Kansas	3 E Bill Salat / Bill Greve
6 Oklahoma	37 QB Bill Nossek / Vic Castillo
13 Iowa State	30 WB Lodis Rhodes / Mike Duncan (D)
6 Oklahoma State	21 HB Cornelius Davis
	FB Ossie Cain
	DL Art Strozier
	DL Rich Wilkinson
	DL Ken Eckardt
	DL Dick Massieon
	DL Dick Wilkinson
	DL Bill Kennedy / Vernon Kraft
	LB Danny Lankas
	LB Steve Overton / Lon Austin
	DB Henry Howard
	DB Mitch Borota
	DB Wilbert Shaw

RUSHING: Davis 210/1028y, Cain 51/155y, Nossek 88/135y
PASSING: Castillo 44-113/617y, 2TD, 38.9%
RECEIVING: Jones 35/721y, Duncan 9/123y, Salat 9/92y
SCORING: Davis 36pts, Barnes 9pts, 3 tied with 6

1967 1-9

17 Colorado State	7 E Dave Jones
3 Virginia Tech	15 T Jim Moore
14 Nebraska	16 G John Watkins
0 Iowa State	17 G Al Walczak
7 Oklahoma	46 G Al Walczak
7 Arkansas	28 T Marty Allen
16 Kansas	17 E Art Strozier
6 Missouri	28 QB Bill Nossek
6 Colorado	40 WB Rick Balducci
14 Oklahoma State	49 HB Cornelius Davis
	FB Larry Brown
	DL Bill Kennedy / Jay Vader
	DL Bill Salat
	DL Ken Eckardt
	DL Mike Goyne
	DL Ron Bowen
	LB Lon Austin
	LB Danny Lankas
	DB Lodis Rhodes / Mike Bruhin
	DB Mike Duncan
	DB Greg Marn
	DB Mitch Borota

RUSHING: Davis 210/628y, Brown 50/282y
PASSING: Nossek 111-216/1220y, 3TD, 51.4%
RECEIVING: Jones 46/561y, Strozier 25/316y, Balducci 20/194y
SCORING: Davis 54pts, Bruhin 18pts, 3 tied with 6pts

1968 4-6

21 Colorado State	0 WR Mike Montgomery
9 Penn State	25 WR Dave Jones
34 Virginia Tech	19 T Lynn Larson
14 Iowa State	23 G Jim Carver
14 Colorado	37 C Ron Stevens / David Owens
20 Missouri	56 G Mike Kuhn
20 Oklahoma	35 T Dean Shaternick / Ira Gordon
12 Nebraska	0 QB Lynn Dickey / Bill Nossek
29 Kansas	38 WB Mack Herron
21 Oklahoma State	14 TB Larry Brown
	FB Cornelius Davis
	DL Manuel Barrera
	DL Tony Severino
	DL John Stucky
	DL Ken Eckardt / Arvyd Petrus
	DL John Acker
	LB Alan Steelman / Jim Dukelow
	LB Oscar Gibson
	DB Clarence Scott
	DB Ron Dickerson / Mike Bruhin
	DB Mike Kolich
	DB Greg Marn / Gary Godfrey

RUSHING: Brown 111/402y, Herron 71/309y, Davis 86/225y
PASSING: Dickey 125-258/1569y, 8TD, 48.4%
RECEIVING: Jones 46/622y, Herron 38/592y, Montgomery 20/227
SCORING: Herron 62pts, Davis 42pts, Max Arreguin (K) 28pts

1969 5-5

48 Baylor	15 E Sonny Yarnell / Charlie Collins
42 Arizona	27 T Lynn Larson
14 Penn State	17 G Jim Carver
26 Kansas	22 C Ron Stevens
34 Iowa State	7 G Dean Shaternick
59 Oklahoma	21 T Ira Gordon
38 Missouri	41 E Forrest Wells / Mike Creed
19 Oklahoma State	28 QB Lynn Dickey
7 Nebraska	10 WB Mack Herron
32 Colorado	45 HB Russell Harrison
	FB Mike Montgomery / Jerry Lawson
	DL Manuel Barrera
	DL Joe Colquitt
	DL John Stucky
	DL Ron Yankowski
	DL Mike Kuhn
	LB Alan Steelman / Oscar Gibson
	LB Jim Dukelow
	LB Randy Ross / Keith Best
	DB Clarence Scott
	DB Ron Dickerson
	DB Mike Kolich

RUSHING: Herron127/506y, Montgomery 81/399y, Harrison 88/293y
PASSING: Dickey 196-372/2476y, 14TD, 52.7%
RECEIVING: Herron 52/652y, Montgomery 28/217y, Wells 22/326y
SCORING: Herron 126pts, Max Arreguin (K) 53pts, Harrison 30pts

1970 6-5

37 Utah State	0 WR Jon Goerger / Sonny Yarnell
3 Kentucky	16 T Jim Carver
13 Arizona State	35 G David Payne
21 Colorado	20 C Steve Beyrle
15 Kansas	21 G Mo Latimore
0 Iowa State	0 T Dean Shaternick
19 Oklahoma	14 TE Mike Creed / Rick Fergerson
17 Missouri	13 QB Lynn Dickey
28 Oklahoma State	15 WB Henry Hawthorne
13 Nebraska	51 HB Bill Butler
7 Florida State	31 FB Mike Montgomery
	DL Jim Acker / Norm Dubois
	DL Charles Clarington / Leo Brouhard
	DL Ron Yankowski
	DL Mike Kuhn
	DL Joe Colquitt
	LB Oscar Gibson
	LB Keith Best
	LB Al Steelman / Gary Melcher
	DB Clarence Scott
	DB Ron Dickerson
	DB Mike Kolich

RUSHING: Butler 127/497y, Montgomery 133/436y, Hawthorne 90/399y
PASSING: Dickey 180-364/2163y, 7TD, 49.5%
RECEIVING: Montgomery 51/386y, Hawthorne 36/501y, Creed 28/481y
SCORING: Hawthorne 54pts, Max Arreguin (K) 31pts, Montgomery 26pts

1971 5-6

7 Utah State	10 WR Jon Goerger / Fred Merrill
19 Tulsa	10 T Del Acker
23 BYU	7 G Rick Heath / John Wells
21 Colorado	31 C Steve Beyrle
13 Kansas	39 G Mo Latimore
0 Iowa State	24 T Larry Anding
28 Oklahoma	75 TE Bill Brittain / Henry Childs
28 Missouri	12 QB Dennis Morrison
35 Oklahoma State	23 WB Mike Creed
17 Nebraska	44 HB Bill Butler / Isaac Jackson
28 Memphis State	21 FB Tim McLane / Bill Holman
	DL Norm Dubois / Bert Oettmeier
	DL Gary Glatz
	DL Clayton Ferguson / Don Alexander
	DL Leo Brouhard
	DL John O'Neill
	LB Joe Colquitt
	LB Keith Best
	LB Gary Melcher
	DB Kevin Vohoska / Ted Stealey
	DB Johnny Robertson
	DB Ron Coppenbarger

RUSHING: Butler 204/838y, Jackson 120/446y, Holman 56/229y
PASSING: Morrison 157-333/1780y, 8TD, 47.1%
RECEIVING: Childs 30/396y, Creed 24/329y, McLane 20/65y
SCORING: Butler 96pts, Goerger 32pts, Childs 22pts

1972 3-8

21 Tulsa	13 WR Jon Goerger
9 BYU	32 WR Bud Peterson
14 Arizona State	56 T Del Acker / Chuck Price
31 Tampa	7 G John Wells / Paul Steininger
17 Colorado	38 C Fred Rothwell
20 Kansas	19 G Larry Hopkins
22 Iowa State	25 T Bill Brittain
0 Oklahoma	52 TE Henry Childs
14 Missouri	31 QB Dennis Morrison
14 Oklahoma State	45 HB Isaac Jackson
7 Nebraska	59 FB Don Calhoun / Bill Holman
	DL Bert Oettmeier
	DL Gary Glatz / Clayton Ferguson
	DL Charles Clarington
	DL John O'Neill
	DL Roger Stucky
	LB Greg Jones
	LB Kevin Vohoska / Gordon Chambliss
	DB Ron Solt
	DB Terry Brown
	DB Gary Melcher / Donald Lareau
	DB Ron Coppenbarger

RUSHING: Calhoun 131/608y, Jackson 147/599y, Holman 58/177y
PASSING: Morrison 136-300/1596y, 9TD, 45.3%
RECEIVING: Goerger 57/612y, Childs 33/467y, Calhoun 15/85y
SCORING: Jackson 38pts, Calhoun 32pts, Childs 30pts

1973 5-6

10 Florida	21 WR Bud Peterson
21 Tulsa	0 WR Fred Merrill
17 Tampa	0 T Chuck Price
21 Memphis State	16 G Bill Brittain
18 Kansas	25 C Fred Rothwell
21 Iowa State	19 G John Wells
14 Oklahoma	56 T Bob Brandt / David Hernandez
7 Missouri	31 TE Henry Childs
9 Oklahoma State	28 QB Steve Grogan
21 Nebraska	50 HB Isaac Jackson
17 Colorado	14 FB Don Calhoun
	DL Willie Cullars
	DL Bert Oettmeier
	DL Hal Batdorf / Bill Crosby
	DL Lou Wegerer
	DL Charles Clarington
	LB Greg Jones / Dennis Gragg
	LB Theopilis Bryant
	DB Paul Smith
	DB Gordon Chambliss
	DB Terry Brown
	DB Kevin Vohoska

RUSHING: Jackson 225/1137y, Calhoun 120/539y, Grogan 188/372y
PASSING: Grogan 72-164/1050y, 4TD, 43.9%
RECEIVING: Childs 32/502y, Merrill 10/171y, Peterson 10/153y
SCORING: Jackson 60pts, Brimley 40pts, Grogan 32pts

1974 4-7

31 Tulsa	14 WR John Tuttle
17 Wichita State	0 WR Bud Peterson / Stan Ross
38 Pacific	7 T David Hernandez
16 Mississippi St.	21 G Floyd Dorsey / Bob Brandt
13 Kansas	20 C Tim Wasemiller
0 Kansas State	23 G Mark Zier
15 Missouri	63 T Gary Freeman / Pat Clerihan
5 Oklahoma State	52 TE Tom Winchell / Dave Chambliss
7 Nebraska	29 QB Steve Grogan / Arthur Bailey
33 Colorado	35 TB David Specht / L.T. Edwards
	19 FB Roscoe Scobey / Regan Steiner
	DL Lou Wegerer / Perry Viers
	DL Alton Carson
	DL Rickey Gray
	DL Kim Thomas
	DL Roy Shine / Charley Kilgore
	LB Theopilis Bryant
	LB Carl Pennington / Gary Spani
	DB Ron Solt / Paul Smith
	DB Rocky Osborn
	DB Gordon Chambliss / Jim Lembright
	DB Les Chaves / Dennis Frazee

RUSHING: Scobey 80/401y, Specht 68/344y, Steiner 65/219y
PASSING: Grogan 67-144/834y, 6TD, 46.5%
RECEIVING: Tuttle 24/346y, Ross 12/244y, Chambliss 12/135y
SCORING: David Cheves (K) 35pts, Bailey 30pts, Chambliss & Grogan 14pts

1975 3-8

17 Tulsa	16 WR Stan Ross / Manzy King / Kerwin Cox
32 Wichita State	0 T Chris Haag
17 Wake Forest	16 G Floyd Dorsey / Shelby Henderson
0 Texas A&M	10 C Tim Wasemiller
7 Iowa State	17 G Jim Rogers
3 Oklahoma	25 T Tom DeLaHunt / Mark Zier
3 Missouri	35 TE Paul Coffman
0 Kansas	28 QB Joe Hatcher
0 Nebraska	12 SB Greg Searcy / Mike Harris
3 Oklahoma State	56 HB Roscoe Scobey / Carlos Whitfield
7 Colorado	33 FB Verdell Jones
	DL Perry Viers
	DL Roy Shine
	DL Theopilis Bryant / Charley Kilgore
	DL Rickey Gray
	DL Vic Chandler
	LB Carl Pennington
	LB Gary Spani
	DB Rocky Osborn
	DB John Andrews
	DB Marvin Switzer
	DB Jim Lembright

RUSHING: Jones 78/373y, Scobey 87/320y, Cox 59/176y
PASSING: Hatcher 34-93/432y, 2TD, 36.6%
RECEIVING: Ross 13/192y, King 9/138y, Searcy 8/107y
SCORING: Bill Sinovic (K) 27pts, Harris 24pts, Scobey 12pts

1976 1-10

13 BYU	3 WR Eddy Whitley
14 Texas A&M	34 T Bob Thompson
0 Wake Forest	13 G Jim Cromleigh / Jim Rogers
10 Florida State	20 C John Hefferty
21 Missouri	28 G Mike Wakefield
0 Nebraska	51 T Phil Noel
14 Kansas	24 TE Paul Coffman
14 Iowa State	15 QB Wendell Henrikson
20 Oklahoma	49 SB Manzy King
21 Oklahoma State	45 HB Tony Brown / Roscoe Scobey
28 Colorado	35 FB Roosevelt Duncan / Ken Lovely
	DL Vic Chandler
	DL Roy Shine / Chester Jeffrey
	DL Theopilis Bryant
	DL Mike Osborn
	DL Perry Viers
	LB Carl Pennington
	LB Gary Spani
	DB Clyde Brinson
	DB Marvin Switzer
	DB Gary Bogue
	DB John Andrews

RUSHING: Brown 123/368y, Duncan 89/304y, Scobey 47/209y
PASSING: Henrikson 73-149/1066y, 4TD, 49%
RECEIVING: King 21/273y, Coffman 15/173y, Whitley 13/163y
SCORING: Brown 42pts, Bill Sinovic (K) 35pts,
 Lovely & Liebe 12pts

1977 1-10

0 BYU	39 WR Charlie Green
10 Florida State	18 T Bob Thompson
21 Wichita State	14 G Clint Davenport
21 Miss. St. (F-W)	24 C Malcolm Bussey / John Hafferty
9 Nebraska	26 G Floyd Dorsey
14 Oklahoma State	21 T Walt Wywadis / Phil Noel
13 Missouri	28 TE Paul Coffman
7 Oklahoma	42 QB Wendell Henrikson
21 Kansas	29 SB John Liebe / Manzy King
15 Iowa State	22 HB Mack Green / Ken Lovely
0 Colorado	23 FB Roosevelt Duncan
	DL Keith Nelms
	DL Chester Jeffrey
	DL Dave Kuklenski
	DL Rob Houchlin / Duane Dirk
	DL Mike Osborn / Tyrone Crews
	LB Gary Spani
	LB Randy Lorenzen
	DB Clyde Brinson / Robert Evans
	DB Nate Jones
	DB Brad Horchem / Bill Fisher
	DB Sam Owen / Brad Wagner

RUSHING: Green 192/707y, Duncan 66/272y, Lovely 65/221y
PASSING: Henrikson 72-163/882y, 3TD, 44.2%
RECEIVING: Green 33/634y, Coffman 25/427y, King 18/176y
SCORING: Coffman 20pts, Green, Lovely & Butler 18pts

1978 4-7

0 Arizona	31 WR Charlie Green
32 Auburn	45 WR Eugene Goodlow
14 Tulsa	24 T Jim Miller / Bobby Thompson
34 Air Force	21 G Ernie Navarro
18 Oklahoma State	7 C Chuck Bowling
14 Nebraska	48 G Malo Eteuini
14 Missouri	56 T Walt Wywadis
19 Oklahoma	56 TE Eddy Whitley
0 Iowa State	24 QB Dan Manucci
20 Colorado	10 HB Mack Green / L.J. Brown
36 Kansas	20 FB Roosevelt Duncan
	DL Chester Jeffrey
	DL Dave Kuklenski
	DL Rob Houchlin
	LB James Walker
	LB Bill Fisher
	LB Tom Faerber
	LB Tyrone Crews
	DB Ray Butler
	DB J.J. Miller
	DB Sam Owen
	DB Brad Horchem

RUSHING: Green 113/561y, Duncan 122/532y, Brown 62/337y
PASSING: Manucci 122-237/1808y, 9TD, 51.5%
RECEIVING: Green 39/616y, Goodlow 20/547y, Duncan 16/146y
SCORING: Duncan 48pts, Manucci 30pts, 3 tied with 24pts

1979 3-8

18 Auburn	26 WR John Liebe
22 Oregon State	16 WR Phil Pickard
19 Air Force	6 T Walt Wywadis
6 Tulsa	9 G Amos Donaldson
3 Iowa State	7 C Kerry Wilson
6 Oklahoma	38 G Chuck Bowling
19 Missouri	6 T Jim Miller
28 Kansas	36 TE Eddy Whitley
12 Nebraska	21 QB Darrel Ray Dickey / Sheldon Paris
15 Oklahoma State	42 HB L.J. Brown
6 Colorado	21 FB Roosevelt Duncan / Darryl Black
	DL James Walker
	DL Ben Landry / Steve Clark
	DL Monte Bennett
	DL D.L. Johnson / Wade Wentling
	LB Vic Koenning
	LB Tim Cole
	LB Tom Faerber
	LB Tyrone Crews
	DB Phil Switzer
	DB Sam Owen
	DB Brad Horchem / Mike Kopsky

RUSHING: Brown 148/668y, Duncan 87/326y, Dearring 70/282y
PASSING: Dickey 71-140/895y, 4TD, 50.7%
RECEIVING: Liebe 22/423y, Brown 20/145y, Whitley 18/228y
SCORING: Brown 30pts, Whitley 18pts, Liebe 16pts

1980 3-8

0 LSU	21 WR John Liebe
24 S. Dakota	3 WR Darryl Black
31 Arkansas State	7 T Doug Hoppock
0 Tulsa	3 G Kerry Benton
7 Iowa State	31 C Jim Kennedy
21 Oklahoma	35 G Amos Donaldson
3 Missouri	13 T Mike Ruzich
18 Kansas (F-W)	20 TE Mike Cox
8 Nebraska	55 QB Darrel Ray Dickey
0 Oklahoma State	10 HB L.J. Brown / Ernie Coleman
17 Colorado	14 FB Jeff Meyers
	DL James Walker
	DL Monte Bennett
	DL Mike Simeta
	DL Steve Clark
	LB Tim Cole
	LB Will Cokeley
	LB Vic Koenning
	DB Steve Schuster
	DB Gary Morrill / Greg Best
	DB Mike Kopsky
	DB Jim Bob Morris / Stan Weber

RUSHING: Brown 165/575y, Meyers 77/303y, Coleman 51/169y
PASSING: Dickey 80-168/1004y, 4TD, 47.6%
RECEIVING: Liebe 25/400y, Brown 19/140y, Black 16/243y
SCORING: Brown 42pts, Jim Jackson (K) 27pts, Coleman 24pts

1981 2-9

31 S. Dakota	10 WR Ernie Coleman / Ivan Pearl
3 Washington	20 WR Eric Mack / Rick Manning
17 Drake	18 T Randy Voelker / Jeff Koyl
21 Tulsa	35 G Jim Northcutt / Greg Pemberton
13 Missouri	58 C Jim Kennedy
3 Nebraska	49 G Tom Menas
14 Kansas	17 T Damian Johnson / Jeff Stevens
10 Iowa State	7 TE Mike Cox
21 Oklahoma	28 QB Darrel Ray Dickey
10 Oklahoma State	31 TB Mark Hundley
21 Colorado	24 FB Masi Toluao
	DL Stu McKinnon
	DL Reggie Singletary
	DL Mark Newton
	DL D.L. Johnson
	LB L.E. Madison
	LB Dan Ruzich
	LB Greg Strahm / Scott Wentzel
	DB Phil Switzer / Barton Hundley
	DB Greg Best
	DB Gary Morrill / Mike Kopsky
	DB Darren Gale / James Robinson

RUSHING: Toluao114/531y, Hundley 126/379y, Dickey 94/246y
PASSING: Dickey 75-158/974y, 7TD, 47.5%
RECEIVING: Coleman 13/229y, Pearl 12/177y, 3 tied w/ 11
SCORING: Hundley 36pts, Steve Willis (K) 36pts, Coleman &
 Pearl 18pts

1982 6-5-1

23 Kentucky	9 WR Mike Wallace
42 S. Dakota	3 WR Eric Mack
31 Wichita State	7 T Doug Hoppock
7 Arizona State	30 G Amos Donaldson
7 Missouri	7 C Jim Kennedy
13 Nebraska	42 G Tom Menas
36 Kansas	7 T Damian Johnson
9 Iowa State	3 TE Mike Cox / Eric Bailey
10 Oklahoma	24 QB Darrel Ray Dickey
16 Oklahoma State	24 TB Mark Hundley / Iosefatu Faraimo
33 Colorado	10 FB Masi Toluao / Charles Crawford
3 Wisconsin■	14 DL L.E. Madison
	DL Mike Simeta
	DL Jack Williamson
	DL Reggie Singletary
	DL Vic Koenning
	LB Dan Ruzich
	LB Will Cokeley
	DB Phil Switzer
	DB Greg Best
	DB Jim Bob Morris
	DB Gary Morrill

RUSHING: Faraimo 99/404y, Hundley 80/341y, Crawford 82/322y
PASSING: Dickey 93-174/1225y, 8TD, 53.4%
RECEIVING: Wallace 37/693y, Mack 13/209y, Bailey 9/96y
SCORING: Steve Willis (K) 60pts, Wallace 36pts, Hundley 24pts

1983 3-8

20 Long Beach St.	28 WR Mike Wallace
12 Kentucky	31 WR Eric Mack / Darrel Wild
20 TCU	3 T Damian Johnson
27 Wyoming	25 G Cal Switzer
10 Oklahoma	29 C Andrew Harding / Jim Northcutt
3 Kansas	31 G Bob Bessert
0 Missouri	38 T Jeff Koyl
25 Nebraska	51 TE Eric Bailey
21 Oklahoma State	20 QB Doug Bogue / Stan Weber
27 Iowa State	49 TB Greg Dageforde
21 Colorado	38 FB Charles Crawford
	DL L.E. Madison
	DL Reggie Singletary
	DL Kyle Clawson / Les Miller
	DL Greg Strahm
	DL Mark Newton
	LB Bob Daniels
	LB Bill Keeley
	DB Adrian Barber / Ivan Pearl
	DB Nelson Nickerson
	DB David Ast
	DB Jack Epps

RUSHING: Dageforde 153/677y, Weber 83/279y,
 Crawford 58/251y
PASSING: Bogue 61-119/851y, 5TD, 51.3%
RECEIVING: Wallace 32/466y, Bailey 20/269y, Wild 15/215y
SCORING: Steve Willis (K) 40pts, Dageforde 30pts, Weber 24pts

1984 3-7-1

14 Vanderbilt	26 WR Gerald Alphin
28 Tennessee Tech	12 WR Mike Wallace / Dick Warren
10 Texas Christian	42 T Damian Johnson
6 Oklahoma	24 G Cal Switzer
17 South Carolina	49 C Chuck Sander
24 Kansas	7 G Andrew Harding / Bob Bessert
21 Missouri	61 T Tim Stone
14 Nebraska	62 TE Eric Bailey
6 Oklahoma State	34 QB Stan Weber
7 Iowa State	7 HB Todd Moody / John Kendrick
38 Colorado	6 FB Dave Smith / Lemuel James
	DL Grady Newton
	DL Les Miller
	DL Renneth Reed
	DL Dwayne Castille
	DL Mark Newton
	LB Tim MacDonald
	LB Jeff Hurd / Bob Daniels
	DB Brad Lambert
	DB Barton Hundley
	DB Jack Epps
	DB David Ast

RUSHING: Weber 98/406y, Moody 51/288y, Kendrick 20/271
PASSING: Weber 58-114/602y, 3TD, 50.9%
RECEIVING: Bailey 15/171y, Alphin 14/256y, Wallace 12/170y
SCORING: Steve Willis (K) 51pts, Weber 24pts, Lambert 18pts

1985 1-10

10 Wichita State	16 WR Gerald Alphin / James Witherspoon
6 Northern Iowa	10 WR Dick Warren / Todd Elder
22 TCU	24 T Tim Stone / Dana Dimel
10 No. Texas St.	22 G Andy Harding
6 Oklahoma	41 C Chuck Sander
7 Kansas	38 G Bob Bessert
20 Missouri	17 T Rocky Dvorak
3 Nebraska	41 TE Kent Dean
3 Oklahoma State	35 QB Randy Williams / John Welch
14 Iowa State	21 HB John Kendrick / Todd Moody
0 Colorado	30 FB Ray Wilson
	DL Jeff Hurd
	DL Les Miller
	DL Renneth Reed
	DL Kevin Humphrey
	LB Tim MacDonald
	LB David Wallace
	LB Jack Epps
	DB Brad Lambert
	DB David Ast
	DB Scott Wentzel / Don Cliggett
	DB Barton Hundley

RUSHING: Kendrick 80/354y, Wilson 112/367y, Moody 94/343y
PASSING: Welch 55-116/659y, 4TD, 47.4%
 Williams 63-151/615y, 2TD, 41.7%
RECEIVING: Alphin 34/524y, Elder 16/154y, Moody 16/110y
SCORING: Mark Porter 27pts, Alphin 20pts, Williams &
 Elder 12pts

1986 2-9

35 Western Illinois	7 WR Clark Brown
7 Texas Tech	41 WR Dan Hughes / Todd Elder
0 No. Iowa	17 T Matt Garver
22 TCU	35 G Dana Dimel
10 Oklahoma	56 C Rob Goode
29 Kansas	12 G Bob Bessert
6 Missouri	17 T Rocky Dvorak
0 Nebraska	38 TE Kent Dean
3 Oklahoma State	23 QB Randy Williams
19 Iowa State	48 HB Tony Jordan / Todd Moody
3 Colorado	49 FB Ray Wilson
	DL Kevin Humphrey
	DL Jeff Hurd
	DL Jim Oehm
	LB Matt Wallerstedt
	LB Grady Newton
	LB Chris Smith
	LB David Baziel
	DB Steve Compton
	DB Robert Easterwood / Willie Halliburton
	DB Erick Harper / Marcus Miller
	DB Tyreese Herds / Brad Lambert

RUSHING: Jordan 202/738y, Moody 92/298y, Wilson 76/254
PASSING: Williams 88-197/1069y, 4TD, 44.7%
RECEIVING: Hughes 28/413y, Elder 16/250y, Jordan 15/196y
SCORING: Mark Porter (K) 44pts, Jordan 42pts, Hughes 12pts

1987 0-10-1

22 Austin Peay	26 WR Dan Hughes
14 Army	41 WR John Williams
13 Iowa	38 T Russ Strange
25 Tulsa	37 G Eric Zabelin
10 Missouri	34 C Chad Faulkner
10 Oklahoma	59 G Matt Garver
3 Nebraska	56 T Will McCain
7 Oklahoma State	56 TE Kent Dean
17 Kansas	17 QB Gary Swim
14 Iowa State	16 HB Tony Jordan / Maurice Henry
0 Colorado	41 FB Rick Lewis
	DL Jim Oehm
	DL Tim MacDonald / Doug Blackbourne
	DL Bobby Lawrence
	LB Matt Wallerstedt
	LB Grady Newton
	LB Lorne Whittle / David Wallace
	LB Dewayne Baziel
	DB Tyreese Herds
	DB Marcus Miller / Robert Easterwood
	DB Erick Harper
	DB Brad Lambert

RUSHING: Jordan 169/692y, Lewis 98/361y, Henry 46/166y
PASSING: Swim 115-235/1304y, 8TD, 48.9%
RECEIVING: Dean 38/481y, Jordan 23/136y, Williams 16/279y
SCORING: Mark Porter (K) 37pts, Dean 24pts, Williams 24pts

1988 0-11

9 Tulsa	35 WR Greg Washington
10 Iowa	45 WR Frank Hernandez / Mark Austin
16 Tulane	20 T Russ Strange
28 La. Tech	31 G Chad Faulkner
21 Missouri	52 C Paul Yniquez
24 Oklahoma	70 G Eric Zabelin
3 Nebraska	48 T Will McCain
27 Oklahoma State	45 TE Alan Friedrich
12 Kansas	30 QB Carl Straw
7 Iowa State	16 HB Tom Dillon / Sonny Ray Jones
14 Colorado	56 FB Lee Pickett
	DL James Enin-Okut / Elijah Alexander
	DL Jim Oehm / John Crawford
	DL Bobby Lawrence / Mark Young
	DL Doug Blackbourne / Alan Smith
	DL Danny Needham
	LB Maurice Henry
	LB Lorne Whittle / Erick Harper (DB)
	DB Tyreese Herds
	DB William Price / Dimitrie Scott
	DB Marcus Miller
	DB Emmett Bradford / Chris Thompson

RUSHING: Pickett 144/736y, Jones 46/216y, Dillon 37/214y
PASSING: Straw 191-358/1947y, 9TD, 53.4%
RECEIVING: Washington 69/928y, Friedrich 31/288y,
 Dillon 28/196y
SCORING: Washington 54pts, Mark Porter (K) 50pts,
 3 tied w/ 12pts

1989 1-10

0 Arizona State	31 WR Michael Smith
8 No. Iowa	10 WR Frank Hernandez
20 No. Illinois	37 T Will McCain
20 No. Texas State	17 G Chad Faulkner
7 Nebraska	58 C Paul Yniguez
13 Oklahoma State	17 G Eric Herrick / Shawn Fleming
3 Missouri	21 T Mike Orr / Toby Lawrence
16 Kansas	21 TE Alan Friedrich / Al Jones
11 Iowa State	36 QB Paul Watson / Carl Straw
19 Oklahoma	42 HB Pat Jackson / Richard Boyd
11 Colorado	59 FB Curtis Madden / Eric Gallon
	DL Ramon Davenport / Maurice Henry
	DL Anthony Williams
	DL Ekwensi Griffith / Robert Hubbell
	DL John Crawford
	DL Elijah Alexander
	LB Brooks Barta / Matt Hennesy
	LB Chris Patterson / James Enin-Okut
	DB Tyreese Herds
	DB Dimitrie Scott
	DB Marcus Miller
	DB Erick Harper / Danny Needham

RUSHING: Jackson 93/328y, Gallon 39/140y
PASSING: Straw 101-192/1095y, 3TD, 52.6%
 Watson 76-141/853y, 2TD, 53.9%
RECEIVING: Smith 70/816y, Hernandez 36/421y, Gallon 27/219y
SCORING: David Kruger (K) 27pts, Jackson 24pts,
 Hernandez 24pts

1990 5-6

27 W. Illinois	6 WR Michael Smith
52 New Mexico St.	7 WR Frank Hernandez
35 N. Illinois	42 T Mike Orr / Toby Lawrence
38 New Mexico	6 G Eric Wolford / Doug Warren
8 Nebraska	45 C Quentin Neujahr
23 Oklahoma State	17 G Doug Grush
10 Missouri	31 T David Gleue
24 Kansas	27 TE Russ Campbell
28 Iowa State	14 QB Carl Straw
7 Oklahoma	34 HB Pat Jackson
3 Colorado	64 FB Rod Schiller / Curtis Madden
	DL Elijah Alexander / Reggie Blackwell
	DL Tony Williams / Eric Clayton
	DL Jody Kilian / John Butler
	DL Steve Moten / Anthony Williams
	DL Ekwensi Griffith / Evan Simpson
	LB Brooks Barta / Chris Patterson
	LB James Enin-Okut
	DB William Price
	DB Rogerick Green
	DB Danny Needham
	DB C.J. Masters

RUSHING: Jackson 177/673y, Schiller 58/184y, Madden 22/90y
PASSING: Straw 153-277/2156y, 7TD, 55.2%
RECEIVING: Smith 46/796y, Hernandez 41/577y,
 Campbell 27/473y
SCORING: Jackson 54pts, Tate Wright (K) 53pts, Straw 36pts

1991 7-4

26 Indiana State	25 WR Frank Hernandez / Andre Coleman
41 Idaho State	7 WR Michael Smith
34 N. Illinois	17 T Mike Orr / David Gleue
3 Washington	56 G Toby Lawrence
16 Kansas	12 C Quentin Neujahr
31 Nebraska	38 G Eric Wolford
0 Colorado	10 T Doug Grush
7 Oklahoma	28 TE Russ Campbell
37 Iowa State	7 QB Paul Watson
32 Missouri	0 HB Eric Gallon / Kitt Rawlings
36 Oklahoma State	26 FB Curtis Madden
	DL Elijah Alexander
	DL Ekwensi Griffith / Tony Williams
	DL Kelly Greene
	DL Jody Kilian
	DL Reggie Blackwell
	LB Joe Boone / Chris Patterson
	LB Brooks Barta
	DB William Price
	DB Rogerick Green
	DB Jaime Mendez
	DB C. J. Masters / Greg Patterson

RUSHING: Gallon 224/1102y, Rawlings 41/172y, Smith 18/157y
PASSING: Watson 172-304/2312y, 10TD, 56.6%
RECEIVING: Smith 55/768y, Campbell 32/595y,
 Hernandez 23/231y
SCORING: Gallon 54pts, Tate Wright (K) 51pts, Smith 36pts

1992 5-6

27 Montana	12 WR Andre Coleman
35 Temple	14 WR Gerald Benton / Mitch Running
19 New Mexico St.	0 T Mike Orr / Barret Brooks
7 Kansas	31 G Toby Lawrence
16 Utah State	28 C Quentin Neujahr
7 Colorado	54 G Eric Wolford
14 Oklahoma	16 T Jim Hmielewski
22 Iowa State	13 TE Brian Rees
14 Missouri	27 QB Jason Smargiasso
10 Oklahoma State	0 RB Eric Gallon / J.J. Smith
24 Nebraska	38 FB Rod Schiller
	DL John Butler
	DL Steve Moten
	DL Jeff Simoneau / Darrell Harbert
	DL Ekwensi Griffith
	LB Brooks Barta
	LB Chris Patterson
	LB Brent Venables
	DB Kitt Rawlings
	DB Thomas Randolph
	DB Jaime Mendez
	DB C.J. Masters

RUSHING: Gallon 178/705y, Smith 50/232y
PASSING: Smargiasso 72-149/990y, 3TD, 48.3%
RECEIVING: Benton 38/603y, Coleman 25/336y, Rees 13/131y
SCORING: Smargiasso 48pts, Tate Wright (K) 28pts,
 Schiller 18 pts

1993 9-2-1

34 New Mexico St.	10 WR Kevin Lockett / Andre Coleman
38 W. Kentucky	13 WR Mitch Running
30 Minnesota	25 T Barret Brooks
36 UNLV	20 G Eric Wolford / Chris Oltmanns
10 Kansas	9 C Quentin Neujahr
28 Nebraska	45 G Bryan Campbell
16 Colorado	16 T Jim Hmielewski
21 Oklahoma	7 TE Brad Sieb
23 Iowa State	27 QB Chad May
31 Missouri	21 RB J.J. Smith
21 Oklahoma State	17 FB Rod Schiller
52 Wyoming■	17 DL Dirk Ochs
	DL Darrell Harbert
	DL Tim Colston
	DL John Butler
	LB Laird Veatch / Mike Ekeler
	LB Kirby Hocutt / DeShawn Fogle
	LB Percell Gaskins
	DB Thomas Randolph
	DB Kenny McEntyre
	DB Jaime Mendez / Steve Hanks
	DB Kitt Rawlings

RUSHING: Smith 190/758y, Schiller 505y
PASSING: May 185-350/2682y, 16TD, 52.9%
RECEIVING: Lockett 50/770y, Running 41/466y, Smith 20/247y
SCORING: Smith 72pts

1994 9-3

34 La-Lafayette	6 WR Kevin Lockett
27 Rice	18 WR Mitch Running
35 Minnesota	0 WR Tyson Schwieger / Ron Brown
21 Kansas	13 T Barret Brooks
6 Nebraska	17 G Chris Oltmanns / Kendyl Jocox
21 Colorado	35 C Jason Johnson
37 Oklahoma	20 G Ross Greenwood
38 Iowa State	20 T Jim Hmielewski
21 Missouri	18 TE Brian Lojka
23 Oklahoma State	6 QB Chad May
42 UNLV	3 RB J.J. Smith
7 Boston College■	12 DL Nyle Wiren
	DL Tim Colston
	DL Darrell Harbert
	DL Dirk Ochs
	LB Laird Veatch
	LB Kirby Hocutt
	LB Percell Gaskins
	DB Chris Canty
	DB Joe Gordon
	DB Mario Smith
	DB Chuck Marlowe

RUSHING: Smith 232/1073y
PASSING: May 200-337/2571y, 18TD, 59.3%
RECEIVING: Schwieger 44/564y, Lockett 39/583y,
  Running 31/441
SCORING: Smith 66pts, Schwieger 42pts,

1995 10-2

34 Temple	7 WR Kevin Lockett
23 Cincinnati	21 WR Mitch Running / Tyson Schwieger
67 Akron	0 T Chris Oltmanns
44 Northern Illinois	0 G Kendyl Jacox (C) / Brian O'Neil
30 Missouri	0 C Jason Johnson
23 Oklahoma State	17 G Jeremy Martin / Ross Greenwood
25 Nebraska	49 T Scott Heun
41 Kansas	7 TE Brian Lojka / Bobby Latiolais
49 Oklahoma	10 QB Matt Miller / Brian Kavanaugh
49 Iowa State	7 RB Eric Hickson / Mike Lawrence
17 Colorado	27 FB Dederick Kelly
54 Colorado State■	21 DL Nyle Wiren
	DL Tim Colston
	DL Ray Eagle / Andrew Timmons
	DL Dirk Ochs / Thad Swazer
	LB Travis Ochs
	LB DeShawn Fogle / LB David Damon
	LB Percell Gaskins
	DB Chris Canty
	DB Joe Gordon
	DB Mario Smith
	DB Chuck Marlowe

RUSHING: Hickson 158/816y, Lawrence 143/599y, Miller 129/309y
PASSING: Miller 154-240/2059y, 22TD, 64.2%
RECEIVING: Lockett 56/797y, Running 51/756y,
  Schwieger 39/438y
SCORING: Lockett 78pts, Martin Gramatica (K) 64pts,
  Miller & Hickson 48pts

1996 9-3

21 Texas Tech	14 WR Kevin Lockett
59 Indiana State	3 WR Jimmy Dean
35 Cincinnati	0 T Todd Weiner
34 Rice	7 G Ross Greenwood
3 Nebraska	39 C Jason Johnson
35 Missouri	10 G Kendyl Jacox / Jeremy Martin
23 Texas A&M	20 T Ryan Young
42 Oklahoma	35 TE Jarrett Grosdidier / Justin Swift
38 Kansas	12 QB Brian Kavanaugh
0 Colorado	12 TB Mike Lawrence / Marlon Charles
35 Iowa State	20 FB/WR Brian Goolsby / Andre Anderson
15 BYU■	19 DL Nyle Wiren
	DL Andrew Timmons
	DL Jerome Evans
	DL Thad Swazer
	LB Travis Ochs
	LB DeShawn Fogle
	LB Mark Simoneau
	DB Demetric Denmark / Lamar Chapman
	DB Chris Canty / Joe Gordon
	DB Mario Smith
	DB Clyde Johnson

RUSHING: Lawrence 209/982y
PASSING; Kavanagh 167-284/1893y, 20TD, 58.8%
RECEIVING: Lockett 72/882y
SCORING: Lawrence 60pts

1997 11-1

47 N. Illinois	7 WR Darnell McDonald
23 Ohio Univ.	20 WR Gavin Peries
58 Bowling Green	0 T Ryan Young
26 Nebraska	56 G Brien Hanley
41 Missouri	1 C Kendyl Jacox
36 Texas A&M	17 G Jeremy Martin
26 Oklahoma	7 T Todd Weiner
13 Texas Tech	2 TE Justin Swift
48 Kansas	16 QB Michael Bishop
37 Colorado	20 RB Eric Hickson / Mike Lawrence
28 Iowa State	3 FB Brian Goolsby
35 Syracuse■	18 DL Darren Howard
	DL Damion McIntosh
	DL Jerome Evans / Andrae Rowe
	DL Joe Bob Clements
	LB Travis Ochs
	LB Jeff Kelly
	LB Mark Simoneau
	DB Dyshod Carter
	DB Demetric Denmark / Gerald Neasman
	DB Lamar Chapman / Cephus Scott
	DB Jarrod Cooper

RUSHING: Hickson 169/750y, Lawrence 127/605y,
  Bishop 147/566y
PASSING: Bishop 80-185/1557y, 13TD, 43.2%
RECEIVING: McDonald 21/441y, Peries 19/404y, Swift 12/258y
SCORING: Gramatica 94pts, Hickson 60pts, Bishop 56pts

1998 11-2

66 Indiana State	0 WR Darnell McDonald
73 N. Illinois	7 WR Aaron Lockett / Gavin Peries
48 Texas	7 T Ryan Young
62 La-Monroe	7 G Brien Hanley
16 Colorado	9 C Randall Cummins
52 Oklahoma State	20 G Jeremy Martin
52 Iowa State	7 T Thomas Barnett / Milford Stephenson
54 Kansas	6 TE Justin Swift
49 Baylor	6 QB Michael Bishop
40 Nebraska	30 TB Eric Hickson
31 Missouri	25 FB Brian Goolsby
33 Texas A&M□	36 DL Joe Bob Clements / Monty Beisel
34 Purdue■	37 DL Andrae Rowe
	DL Damion McIntosh
	DL Darren Howard
	LB Travis Ochs
	LB Jeff Kelly / Ben Leber
	LB Mark Simoneau
	DB Dyshod Carter
	DB Jerametrius Butler / Gerald Neasman
	DB Lamar Chapman
	DB Jarrod Cooper

RUSHING: Hickson 169/902y
PASSING: Bishop 164-295/2844y, 23TD, 55.6%
RECEIVING: McDonald 75/1092y, Lockett 44/928y
SCORING: Martin Gramatica (K) 135pts

1999 11-1

40 Temple	0 WR Aaron Lockett
40 UTEP	7 WR Quincy Morgan
35 Iowa State	28 T Milford Stephenson
35 Texas	17 G Ian Moses
50 Kansas	9 C Randall Cummins
40 Utah State	0 G Andy Eby
44 Oklahoma State	21 T John Robertson
48 Baylor	7 TE Shad Meier
20 Colorado	14 QB Jonathan Beasley
15 Nebraska	41 TB Joe Hall / Frank Murphy / David Allen
66 Missouri	0 FB Johnno Lazetich
24 Washington■	20 DL Monty Beisel / Chris Johnson
	DL Mario Fatafehi
	DL Cliff Holloman
	DL Darren Howard
	LB Travis Litton
	LB Ben Leber
	LB Mark Simoneau
	DB Jerametrius Butler
	DB Dyshod Carter
	DB Lamar Chapman / John McGraw
	DB Jarrod Cooper

RUSHING: Hall 121/613y, Murphy 97/541y, Allen 74/364y
PASSING: Beasley 90-203/1805y, 14TD, 44.3%
RECEIVING: Morgan 42/1007y, Lockett 33/531y,
  George Williams (WR) 8/202y
SCORING: Jamie Rheem (K) 95pts, Allen & Morgan 57pts

2000 11-3

27 Iowa	7 WR Aaron Lockett / Martez Wesley
54 Louisiana Tech	10 WR Quincy Morgan
76 Ball State	0 T Milford Stephenson
55 North Texas	10 G Andy Eby / Nick Leckey
44 Colorado	21 C Randall Cummins
52 Kansas	13 G John Robertson
31 Oklahoma	41 T Thomas Barnett
28 Texas Tech	23 TE Shad Meier / Nick Warren
10 Texas A&M	26 QB Jonathan Beasley
56 Iowa State	10 TB Josh Scobey
29 Nebraska	28 FB Rock Cartwright
28 Missouri	24 DL Monty Beisel
24 Oklahoma□	27 DL Mario Fatafehi
35 Tennessee■	21 DL DeVane Robinson / Jerry Togiai
	DL Chris Johnson / Melvin Williams
	LB Terry Pierce / Warren Lott
	LB Ben Leber
	DB DeRon Tyler
	DB Jerametrius Butler/DeMarcus Faggins
	DB Dyshod Carter / Terence Newman
	DB Jon McGraw / Derrick Yates
	DB Jarrod Cooper / Milton Proctor

RUSHING: Scobey 169/718y, Beasley 149/499y,
  Chris Claybon (RB) 57/308y
PASSING: Beasley 156-313/2636y, 17TD, 49.8%
RECEIVING: Morgan 64/1166y, Lockett 36/584y, Wesley 20/365y
SCORING: Beasley 104pts, Jamie Rheem (K) 100pts, Scbey 96pts

2001 6-6

10 Southern Cal	6 WR Brandon Clark / Ricky Lloyd
64 New Mexico St.	0 WR Aaron Lockett
37 Oklahoma	38 T Matt Martin / Dralinn Burks
6 Colorado	16 G Nick Leckey
19 Texas Tech	38 C Steve Washington
24 Texas A&M	31 G Andy Eby (C) / John Robertson
40 Kansas	6 T Oshin Honarchian / Billy Miller
42 Iowa State	3 TE Nick Warren
21 Nebraska	31 QB Eli Roberson / Marc Dunn
40 Louisiana Tech	7 TB Josh Scobey
24 Missouri	3 FB Rock Cartwright
3 Syracuse■	26 DL Henry Bryant
	DL Justin Montgomery / Jerry Togiai
	DL Tank Reese
	DL Andrew Shull / Thomas Houchin
	LB Ben Leber
	LB Terry Pierce
	LB Josh Buhl
	DB DeMarcus Faggins / DeRon Tyler
	DB Terence Newman
	DB Jon McGraw
	DB Milton Proctor / Derrick Yates

RUSHING: Scobey 240/1263y, Roberson 142/643y,
  Cartwright 66/292y
PASSING: Roberson 54-136/855y, 4TD, 39.7%
RECEIVING: Lockett 24/357y, Lloyd 20/306y, Clark 19/346y
SCORING: Scobey 90pts, Roberson 56pts, Joe Rheem (K) 32pts

2002 11-2

48 W. Kentucky	3 WR Taco Wallace
68 La.-Monroe	0 WR James Terry / Davin Dennis
63 E. Illinois	13 T Thomas Barnett
27 Southern Cal	20 G Nick Leckey
31 Colorado	35 C Steve Washington
44 Oklahoma State	9 G Mike Johnson
14 Texas	17 T Billy Miller / Dralinn Burks
44 Baylor	10 TE Thomas Hill
64 Kansas	0 QB Ell Roberson / Marc Dunn
58 Iowa State	7 TB Darren Sproles
49 Nebraska	13 FB/TE Travis Wilson / Travon Magee
38 Missouri	0 DL Henry Bryant / Melvin Williams
34 Arizona State ■	27 DL Corey White / Justin Montgomery
	DL Tank Reese
	DL Andrew Shull / Thomas Houchin
	LB Bryan Hickman
	LB Terry Pierce
	LB Josh Buhl
	DB Randy Jordan / Jerry McCloud
	DB Terence Newman
	DB Bobby Walker / Jesse Tetuan
	DB Rashad Washington

RUSHING: Sproles 237/1465y, Roberson 202/1032y,
Daniel Davis (RB) 37/224y
PASSING: Roberson 91-175/1580y, 7TD, 52%,
Dunn 22-35/383y, 6TD, 62.9%
RECEIVING: Wallace 39/704y, Terry 28/561y, Hill 17/294y
SCORING: Sproles 104pts, Roberson 98pts, Joe Rheem (K) 80pts

2003 11-4

42 Cal	28 WR James Terry
41 Troy State	5 WR Antoine Polite / Davin Dennis
55 McNeese State	14 T Jon Doty
38 Massachusetts	7 G Ryan Lilja
20 Marshall	27 C Nick Leckey
20 Texas	24 G Mike Johnson
34 Oklahoma State	38 T Jeromey Clary
49 Colorado	20 TE Brian Casey / Thomas Hill
42 Kansas	6 QB Ell Roberson
38 Baylor	10 TB Darren Sproles
45 Iowa State	0 FB Travis Wilson
38 Nebraska	9 DL Andrew Shull / Scott Edmonds
24 Missouri	14 DL Justin Montgomery
35 Oklahoma □	7 DL Jermaine Berry
28 Ohio State ■	35 DL Tom Houchin / Kevin Huntley
	LB Bryan Hickman
	LB Ted Sims / Matt Butler
	LB Josh Buhl
	DB Randy Jordan
	DB Cedrick Williams / Louis Lavender
	DB Jesse Tetuan / James McGill
	DB Rashad Washington

RUSHING: Sproles 306/1986y, Roberson 227/975y
PASSING: Roberson 152-294/2545y, 24TD, 51.7%
RECEIVING: Terry 64/1232y, Polite 29/409y, Dennis 22/404y
SCORING: Sproles 114pts, Joe Rheem (K) 103pts,
Roberson 94pts

2004 4-7

27 W. Kentucky	13 WR Jermaine Moreira / Davin Dennis
21 Fresno State	45 WR Yamon Figurs / Tony Madison
40 La.-Lafayette	7 T Jon Doty
30 Texas A&M	42 G Malcolm Wooldridge
28 Kansas	31 C Mike Johnson
21 Oklahoma	31 G Mike Weiner
45 Nebraska	21 T Jeromey Clary
25 Texas Tech	35 TE Brian Casey
35 Missouri	24 QB Dylan Meier / Allen Webb
31 Colorado	38 TB Darren Sproles
23 Iowa State	37 FB Victor Mann
	DL Scott Edmonds
	DL Jermaine Berry
	DL Kevin Huntley / Derek Marso
	DL Tearrius George
	LB Brandon Archer
	LB Marvin Simmons
	LB Maurice Thurmond
	DB David Rose
	DB Cedrick Williams / Maurice Porter
	DB Bret Jones
	DB Jesse Tetuan

RUSHING: Sproles 244/1318y, Webb 127/418y, Meier 81/232y
PASSING: Meier 127-220/1436y, 9TD, 57.7%
RECEIVING: Moreira 39/406y, Sproles 32/223y, Figurs 31/483y
SCORING: Joe Rheem (K) 76pts, Sproles 68pts, Webb 48pts

2005 5-6

35 Fla. Internat'nal	21 WR Jordy Nelson
21 Marshall	19 WR Yamon Figurs
54 North Texas	7 T Jeromey Clary
21 Oklahoma	43 G John Hafferty
12 Kansas	3 C Jordan Bedore / Jacob Voegeli
20 Texas Tech	59 G Caleb Handy / Matt Boss
28 Texas A&M	30 T Greg Wafford
20 Colorado	23 TE/WR Rashaad Norwood/J. Moreira
17 Iowa State	45 QB Allan Evridge / Allen Webb
25 Nebraska	27 RB Thomas Clayton / Parrish Fisher
36 Missouri	28 FB/WR Victor Mann / Davin Dennis
	DL Blake Seiler Ian Campbell
	DL Quintin Echols
	DL Alphonso Moran / Derek Marso
	DL Tearrius George
	LB Brandon Archer
	LB Ted Sims / Zach Diles
	LB Maurice Mack
	DB Bryan Baldwin
	DB Byron Garvin / Justin McKinney
	DB Marcus Watts
	DB Maurice Porter / Kyle Williams

RUSHING: Clayton 137/637y, Fisher 48/289y, Evridge 102/203y
PASSING: Evridge 102-213/1365y, 6TD, 47.9%
Webb 62-105/850y, 9TD, 59%
RECEIVING: Nelson 45/669y, Moreira 35/485y, Dennis 20/281y
SCORING: Nelson 54pts, Jeff Snodgrass (K) 51pts, Clayton 30pts

2006 7-6

24 Illinois State	23 WR Jordy Nelson / Jermaine Moreira
45 Florida Atlantic	0 WR Yamon Figurs / Daniel Gonzalez
23 Marshall	7 T Greg Wafford (G) / Nick Stringer
6 Louisville	24 G Caleb Handy
3 Baylor	17 C Jordan Bedore / Brad Rooker
31 Oklahoma State	20 G Logan Robinson / Brock Unruh/
3 Nebraska	21 T Mike Frierson / Gerard Spexarth (G)
21 Missouri	41 TE Rashaad Norwood
31 Iowa State	10 TE Jeron Mastrud
34 Colorado	21 QB Josh Freeman / Dylan Meier
45 Texas	42 RB James Johnson / Leon Patton
20 Kansas	39 DL Ian Campbell
10 Rutgers ■	37 DL Steven Cline / Quintin Echols
	DL Blake Seiler / Alphonso Moran
	DL Rob Jackson
	LB Brandon Archer
	LB Zach Diles
	LB Reggie Walker / Marcus Perry
	DB Byron Garvin / Joshua Moore
	DB Justin McKinney / Bryan Baldwin
	DB Andrew Erker / Marcus Watts
	DB Kyle Williams

RUSHING: Patton 108/609y, Johnson 98/403y,
Thomas Clayton (RB) 67/322y
PASSING: Freeman 140-270/1780y, 6TD, 51.9%
Meier 72-141/775y, 3TD, 51.1%
RECEIVING: Nelson 39/547y, Norwood 36/358y, Figurs 28/418y
SCORING: Jeff Snodgrass (K) 83pts, Figurs & Patton 42pts

2007 5-7

13 Auburn	23 WR Jordy Nelson
34 San Jose State	14 WR Deon Murphy / Cedric Wilson
61 Missouri State	10 WR Daniel Gonzalez / Ernie Pierce
41 Texas	21 T Alesana Alesana
24 Kansas	30 G Logan Robinson / Brock Unruh
47 Colorado	20 C Trevor Viers / Jordan Bedore
39 Oklahoma St.	41 G Gerard Spexarth
51 Baylor	13 T Penisini Liu / Nick Stringer
20 Iowa State	31 TE Jeron Mastrud / Mike Pooschke
31 Nebraska	73 QB Josh Freeman
32 Missouri	49 RB James Johnson / Leon Patton
29 Fresno State	45 DL Moses Manu
	DL Steven Cline / Brandon Balkcom
	DL Rob Jackson
	LB Ian Campbell (DL) / Chris Patterson
	LB Reggie Walker / John Houlik
	LB Justin Roland
	LB Eric Childs
	DB Justin McKinney / Bryan Baldwin
	DB Byron Garvin / Ray Cheatham
	DB Chris Carney / Courtney Herndon
	DB Marcus Watts / Gary Chandler

RUSHING: Johnson 174/1106y, Patton 83/390y
PASSING: Freeman 316-499/3353y, 18TD, 63.3%
RECEIVING: Nelson 122/1606y, Murphy 57/605y, Johnson 34/220y
SCORING: Brooks Rossman (K) 110pts, Nelson 80pts,
Johnson 78pts

2008 5-7

45 North Texas	6 WR Brandon Banks / Aubrey Quarles
69 Montana State	10 WR Deon Murphy
29 Louisville	38 WR/TE Ernie Pierce / Brett Alstatt
45 La.-Lafayette	37 T Alesana Alesana / Edward Prince
28 Texas Tech	58 G Colten Freeze / Brock Unruh
44 Texas A&M	30 C Jordan Bedore / Zach Kendall
13 Colorado	14 G Gerard Spexarth / Eric Benoit
35 Oklahoma	58 T Nick Stringer / Penisini Liu (G)
21 Kansas	52 TE Jeron Mastrud
24 Missouri	41 QB Josh Freeman
28 Nebraska	56 RB Lamark Brown / Keithen Valentine
38 Iowa State	30 DL Eric Childs
	DL Brandon Balkcom / Daniel Calvin
	DL Brandon Harold
	DL Ian Campbell
	LB Reggie Walker / Ulla Pomele
	LB Alex Hrebec / Hansen Sekona
	LB Olu Hall / Antwon Moore
	DB Joshua Moore
	DB Ray Cheatham / Blair Irvin
	DB Tysn Hartman / Chris Carney
	DB Courtney Herndon / Gary Chandler

RUSHING: Brown 118/412y, Freeman 107/404y,
Logan Dold (RB) 82/333y
PASSING: Freeman 224-382/2945y, 20TD, 58.6%
RECEIVING: Banks 67/1049y, Mastrud 38/435y,
Murphy 37/555y
SCORING: Freeman 86pts, Brooks Rossman (K) 81pts,
Banks 66pts

2009 6-6

21 Massachusetts	17 WR Attrail Snipes
15 Louisiana	17 WR Brandon Banks / Collin Klein
9 UCLA	23 WR/FB Lamark Brown / Braden Wilson
49 Tennessee Tech	7 T Nick Stringer
24 Iowa State	23 G Zach Kendall
14 Texas Tech	66 C Wade Weibert (G) / Trevor Viers
62 Texas A&M	14 G Kenneth Mayfield / Colten Freeze
20 Colorado	6 T Clyde Aufner
30 Oklahoma	42 TE Jeron Mastrud
17 Kansas	10 QB Grant Gregory / Carson Coffman
12 Missouri	38 RB Daniel Thomas / Keithen Valentine
3 Nebraska	17 DL Jeffrey Fitzgerald / Eric Childs
	DL Raphael Guidry / Prizell Brown
	DL Daniel Calvin / Michael Abana
	DL Antonio Felder / Hansen Sekona
	LB John Houlik
	LB Ulla Pomele / Alex Hrebec
	LB/DB Kevin Rohleder / Troy Butler
	DB Joshua Moore / Darious Thomas
	DB Stephen Harrison / David Garrett
	DB Emmanuel Lamur
	DB Tysn Hartman

RUSHING: Thomas 247/1265y, Valentine 55/357y,
Gregory 106/308y
PASSING: Gregory 100-175/1096y, 4TD, 57.1%
Coffman 71-117/860y, 2TD, 60.7%
RECEIVING: Banks 56/705y, Snipes 28/424y, Thomas 25/257y
Mastrud 21/233y, Brown 18/215y
SCORING: Thomas 66pts, Josh Cherry (K) 63pts, Valentine 36pts

2010 7-6

31 UCLA	22 WR Chris Harper / Tramaine Thompson
48 Missouri State	24 WR A. Quarles/ Brod. Smith/Adrian Hilburn
27 Iowa State	20 T Manase Foketi / Ethan Douglas
17 Central Florida	13 G Zach Kendall
13 Nebraska	48 C Wade Weibert
59 Kansas	7 G Kenneth Mayfield
42 Baylor	47 T Clyde Aufner / Zach Hanson
14 Oklahoma State	24 TE Travis Tannahill / Andre McDonald
39 Texas	14 QB Carson Coffman / Collin Klein
28 Missouri	38 RB Daniel Thomas
36 Colorado	44 FB Braden Wilson
49 North Texas	41 DL Prizell Brown
34 Syracuse ■	36 DL Raphel Guidry / Brandon Harold
	DL Ray Kibble
	DL Antonio Felder
	LB Alex Hrebec
	LB Jarell Childs / Blake Slaughter
	LB/DB Tre Walker / David Garrett
	DB Stephen Harrison / Troy Butler
	DB Terrance Sweeney
	DB Ty Zimmerman / Emmanuel Lamur
	DB Tysn Hartman

RUSHING: Thomas 298/1585y, Klein 76/432y,
William Powell (RB) 23/250y
PASSING: Coffman 171-263/2060y, 14TD, 65%
RECEIVING: Quarles 51/760y, Hilburn 28/299y, Thomas 27/171y
SCORING: Thomas 116pts, Josh Cherry (K) 70pts, Coffman 54pts

KENTUCKY

University of Kentucky (Founded 1865)
Lexington, Kentucky
Nickname: Wildcats
Colors: Blue and White
Stadium: Commonwealth Stadium (1973) 67,606
Conference Affiliations: Southeastern (1933-present)

CAREER RUSHING YARDS	Attempts	Yards
Sonny Collins (1972-75)	777	3835
Moe Williams (1993-95)	618	3333
Rafael Little (2004-07)	580	2996
Mark Higgs (1984-87)	532	2892
George Adams (1981-84)	638	2648
Derrick Locke (2007-10)	518	2618
Artose Pinner (1999-2002)	438	2105
Marc Logan (1983-86)	389	1769
Derrick Ramsey (1975-77)	446	1764
Anthony White (1996-99)	364	1758

CAREER PASSING YARDS	Comp.-Att.	Yards
Jared Lorenzen (2000-03)	862-1514	10,354
André Woodson (2004-07)	791-1278	9360
Tim Couch (1996-98)	795-1184	8435
Mike Hartline (2007-10)	523-855	5680
Bill Ransdell (1983-86)	469-816	5564
Rick Norton (1963-65)	298-598	4514
Babe Parilli (1949-51)	331-592	4351
Randy Jenkins (1979-83)	363-699	4148
Pookie Jones (1991-93)	263-504	3459
Dusty Bonner (1997-99)	313-479	3380

CAREER RECEIVING YARDS	Catches	Yards
Craig Yeast (1995-98)	208	2899
Keenan Burton (2004-07)	189	2376
Derek Abney (2000-03)	197	2339
Dicky Lyons, Jr (2004, 06-08)	141	1752
Quentin McCord (1996, 98-2000)	112	1743
Randall Cobb (2008-10)	147	1636
Anthony White (1996-99)	194	1520
Felix Wilson (1977-79)	90	1508
Tom Hutchison (1960-62)	94	1483
Kevin Coleman (1995-98)	107	1428

SEASON RUSHING YARDS	Attempts	Yards
Moe Williams (1995)	294	1600
Artose Pinner (2002)	283	1414
Mark Higgs (1987)	193	1278
Sonny Collins (1973)	224	1213
Sonny Collins (1975)	248	1150

SEASON PASSING YARDS	Comp.-Att.	Yards
Tim Couch (1998)	400-553	4275
Tim Couch (1997)	363-547	3884
André Woodson (2007)	327-518	3709
Jared Lorenzen (2000)	321-559	3687
Andre' Woodson (2006)	264-419	3515

SEASON RECEIVING YARDS	Catches	Yards
Craig Yeast (1998)	85	1311
Steve Johnson (2007)	60	1041
Keenan Burton (2006)	77	1036
James Whalen (1999)	90	1019
Randall Cobb (2010)	84	1017

GAME RUSHING YARDS	Attempts	Yards
Moe Williams (1995 vs. South Carolina)	40	299
Moe Williams (1995 vs. Cincinnati)	40	272
Moe Williams (1995 vs. Mississippi State)	36	238

GAME PASSING YARDS	Comp.-Att.	Yards
Jared Lorenzen (2000 vs. Georgia)	39-58	528
Tim Couch (1998 vs. Arkansas)	47-67	499
Tim Couch (1998 vs. Louisville)	29-39	498

GAME RECEIVING YARDS	Catches	Yards
Craig Yeast (1998 vs. Vanderbilt)	16	269
Craig Yeast (1998 vs. Florida)	6	206
Rick Kestner (1964 vs. Mississippi)	9	185

GREATEST COACH:

Too often the time spent by Paul "Bear" Bryant in Lexington is considered merely a launching pad to further glory with other schools, with Alabama looming largest of all. But Bryant's success with the Kentucky program is unmatched by any other coach in the school's history. He won more games than anyone else, 60, while the 1950 team was named the best team of that year by computer expert Jeff Sagarin's ratings done decades after the season. That squad produced one of the greatest wins in Wildcats history with the stunning 13-7 victory over Oklahoma in the Sugar Bowl. The Cats went 3-1 in bowls under Bryant, which was the first post-season action in school history.

Although Bryant famously left Lexington over dissatisfaction with the football team's second-class status compared to Adolph Rupp's great basketball teams, he left quite a mark on the program. While it will be difficult for a Kentucky coach to match Bryant's .710 winning percentage or eight All Americans in eight seasons, the standard of excellence he demanded from his players is the same standard to be used by any coach. His legacy is an example to all that follow.

KENTUCKY'S 55 GREATEST SINCE 1953

OFFENSE

WIDE RECEIVER: Derek Abney, Tom Hutchinson, Howard Schnellenberger, Craig Yeast
TIGHT END: James Whalen
TACKLE: Sam Ball, Warren Bryant, Kris Comstock, Mike Pfeifer
GUARD: Ray Correll, Dermontti Dawson, Tom Dornbrook, Dan Fowler
CENTER: Rick Nuzum, Ken Roark
QUARTERBACK: Tim Couch, Rick Norton, André Woodson
RUNNING BACK: George Adams, Rodger Bird, Sonny Collins, Mark Higgs, Moe Williams
FULLBACK: Steve Campassi

DEFENSE

END: Dennis Johnson, Art Still, Jeff Van Note
TACKLE: Oliver Barnett, Richard Jaffe, Jim McCollom, Dewayne Robertson, Dave Roller
LINEBACKER: Joe Federspiel, Randy Holleran, Jim Kovach, Frank LeMaster, Wesley Woodyard
CORNERBACK: Kerry Baird, Darrell Cox, Trevard Lindley, Mike Siganos
SAFETY: Darryl Bishop, Melvin Johnson, Andy Molls, Dallas Owens

SPECIAL TEAMS

RETURN SPECIALIST: Calvin Bird
PLACE KICKER: Joe Worley
PUNTER: Glenn Pakulak

MULTIPLE POSITIONS

FULLBACK-WINGBACK-PUNTER: Larry Seiple
DEFENSIVE BACK-PUNTER: Paul Calhoun

TWO-WAY PLAYERS

TACKLE-DEFENSIVE TACKLE-KICKER-PUNTER: Lou Michaels
HALFBACK-END-LINEBACKER-DEFENSIVE BACK: Steve Meilinger
CENTER-LINEBACKER: Irv Goode
TACKLE-DEFENSIVE TACKLE: Herschel Turner
HALFBACK-FULLBACK-WIDE RECEIVER-DEFENSIVE BACK-KICK RETURNER: Dicky Lyons, Sr.

PERFORMANCE FORMULA:
KENTUCKY'S 10 BEST SEASONS

Year	Formula	Rank
1977	1.5904	7 of 70
1953	1.4264	11 of 69
1976	1.3302	19 of 70
1984	1.3010	19 of 70
1954	1.2744	25 of 69
1965	1.2473	17 of 70
1956	1.2390	27 of 69
1955	1.2245	27 of 69
2006	1.1864	34 of 72
1998	1.1708	31 of 71

948

KENTUCKY WILDCATS

Year	W-L-T	AP Poll	Conference Standing	Toughest Regular Season Opponents	Coach (Record at School)	Bowl Games		
1953	7-2-1	16	2t	Rice 8-2, Mississippi 7-2-1, Tennessee 6-4-1	Paul "Bear" Bryant (60-23-5)			
1954	7-3		3t	Mississippi 9-1, Maryland 7-2-1, Georgia Tech 7-3, Auburn 7-3	Blanton Collier			
1955	6-3-1		7t	Mississippi 9-1, Auburn 8-1-1, Vanderbilt 7-3	Blanton Collier			
1956	6-4		6t	Tennessee 10-0, Georgia Tech 9-1, Mississippi 7-3	Blanton Collier			
1957	3-7		12	Auburn 10-0, Mississippi 8-1-1, Tennessee 7-3, Florida 6-2-1	Blanton Collier			
1958	5-4-1		6t	LSU 10-0, Auburn 9-0-1, Mississippi 8-2	Blanton Collier			
1959	4-6		9	Mississippi 9-1, LSU 9-1, Georgia 9-1, Auburn 7-3	Blanton Collier			
1960	5-4-1		9	Mississippi 9-0-1, Auburn 8-2, Tennessee 6-2-2	Blanton Collier			
1961	5-5		7	LSU 9-1, Mississippi 9-1, Miami 7-3, Tennessee 6-4	Blanton Collier (41-36-3)			
1962	3-5-2		7t	Mississippi 9-0, LSU 8-1-1, Auburn 6-3-1, Miami 7-3	Charlie Bradshaw			
1963	3-6-1		11	Auburn 9-1, Mississippi 7-0-2, Va. Tech 8-2, LSU 7-3, Baylor 7-3	Charlie Bradshaw			
1964	5-5		2t	LSU 7-2-1, Florida State 8-1-1, Georgia 6-3-1, Auburn 6-4	Charlie Bradshaw			
1965	6-4		6t	Tennessee 7-1-2, Missouri 7-2-1, LSU 7-3, Georgia 6-4	Charlie Bradshaw			
1966	3-6-1		6	Georgia 9-1, Mississippi 8-2, Houston 8-2, Tennessee 7-3	Charlie Bradshaw			
1967	2-8		7	Tennessee 9-1, Indiana 9-1, Mississippi 7-3, LSU 7-3, Georgia 7-3	Charlie Bradshaw			
1968	3-7		7	Georgia 8-0-2, Tennessee 8-1-1, Missouri 7-3, LSU 7-3	Charlie Bradshaw (25-41-4)			
1969	2-8		9	LSU 9-1, Tennessee 9-1, Auburn 8-2, West Virginia 9-0-1	John Ray			
1970	2-9		8	Tennessee 10-1, 10-1, LSU 9-2, Auburn 8-2, Florida 7-4, UNC 8-3	John Ray			
1971	3-8		6t	Georgia 10-1, Auburn 9-1, Tennessee 9-2, Mississippi 9-2, LSU 8-3	John Ray			
1972	3-8		7t	Alabama 10-1, LSU 9-1-1, Tennessee 9-2, UNC 10-1, Georgia 7-4	John Ray (10-33)			
1973	5-6		5t	Alabama 11-0, LSU 9-2, Tennessee 8-3, Tulane 9-2	Fran Curci			
1974	6-5		3t	Auburn 9-2, Tennessee 8-2-1, Florida 7-3, Miami of Ohio 9-0-1	Fran Curci			
1975	2-8-1		5t	Penn State 9-2, Georgia 9-2, Florida 9-2, Maryland 8-2-1	Fran Curci			
1976	9-3	18	1t	Maryland 11-0, Georgia 10-1, Florida 8-3, Penn State 7-4	Fran Curci	Peach	21 North Carolina	0
1977	10-1	6	2	Penn State 10-1, LSU 8-3, UNC 8-2-1	Fran Curci			
1978	4-6-1		5t	Penn State 11-0, Georgia 9-1-1, Maryland 9-2, LSU 8-3	Fran Curci			
1979	5-6		4t	Tennessee 7-4, Indiana 7-4, LSU 6-5	Fran Curci			
1980	3-8		6	Georgia 11-0, Oklahoma 9-2, Alabama 9-2, Florida 7-4	Fran Curci			
1981	3-8		4t	Clemson 11-0, Georgia 10-1, Alabama 9-1-1	Fran Curci (47-51-2)			
1982	0-10-1		8t	Georgia 11-0, Clemson 9-1-1, LSU 8-2-1, Auburn 8-3, OU 8-3, Fla. 8-3	Jerry Claiborne			
1983	6-5-1		4	Auburn 10-1, Georgia 9-1-1, Florida 8-2-1, Tennessee 8-3	Jerry Claiborne	Hall of Fame	16 West Virginia	20
1984	9-3	19	4t	Florida 9-1-1, LSU 8-2-1, Tennessee 7-3-1, Georgia 7-4	Jerry Claiborne	Hall of Fame	20 Wisconsin	19
1985	5-6		7	LSU 9-1-1, Florida 9-1-1, Tennessee 8-1-2, Georgia 7-3-1	Jerry Claiborne			
1986	5-5-1		4t	LSU 9-2, Georgia 8-3, Virginia Tech 8-2-1, Mississippi 7-3-1	Jerry Claiborne			
1987	5-6		7t	LSU 9-1-1, Tennessee 9-2-1, Georgia 8-3	Jerry Claiborne			
1988	5-6		8t	Auburn 10-1, Alabama 8-3, LSU 8-3, Georgia 8-3	Jerry Claiborne			
1989	6-5		7t	Alabama 10-1, Tennessee 10-1, Auburn 9-2, Florida 7-4	Jerry Claiborne (41-46-3)			
1990	4-7		5	Mississippi 9-2, Florida 9-2, Tennessee 8-2-2	Bill Curry			
1991	3-8		10	Florida 10-1, Tennessee 9-2, Georgia 8-3, Mississippi State 7-4	Bill Curry			
1992	4-7		E5t	Georgia 9-2, Florida 8-3, Mississippi 8-3, Tennessee 8-3	Bill Curry			
1993	6-6		E3	Florida 9-2, Tennessee 9-1-1, Indiana 8-3	Bill Curry	Peach	13 Clemson	14
1994	1-10		E6	Florida 9-1-1, Auburn 9-1-1, Mississippi State 8-3, Tennessee 7-4	Bill Curry			
1995	4-7		E5	Florida 11-0, Tennessee 10-1, Auburn 8-3	Bill Curry			
1996	4-7		E4t	Florida 10-1, Alabama 9-2, LSU 9-2, Tennessee 9-2	Bill Curry (26-52)			
1997	5-6		E5	Tennessee 10-1, Florida 9-2, Georgia 9-2, LSU 8-3	Hal Mumme			
1998	7-5		E4	Tennessee 11-0, Florida 9-2, Arkansas 9-2, Georgia 8-3	Hal Mumme	Outback	14 Penn State	26
1999	6-6		E4	Florida 9-2, Tennessee 9-2, Mississippi State 9-2	Hal Mumme	Music City	13 Syracuse	20
2000	2-9		E6	Florida 9-2, Tennessee 8-3, LSU 7-4, Georgia 7-4	Hal Mumme (20-26)			
2001	2-9		E5	Tennessee 10-1, Florida 9-2, So. Car. 8-3, LSU 8-3, Georgia 8-3	Guy Morriss			
2002	7-5		E4t	Georgia 11-1, Arkansas 9-3, Florida 8-4, LSU 8-4, Tennessee 8-4	Guy Morriss (9-14)			
2003	4-8		E5t	Tennessee 10-2, Georgia 10-2, Florida 8-4, Arkansas 8-4	Rich Brooks			
2004	2-9		E5t	Auburn 11-0, Louisville 10-1, Tennessee 9-2, Georgia 9-2	Rich Brooks			
2005	3-8		E6	Florida 9-2, Georgia 9-2, Auburn 9-2, Louisville 9-2, South Carolina 7-4	Rich Brooks			
2006	8-5		E3t	Florida 11-1, Louisville 11-1, LSU 10-2, Tennessee 9-3, Georgia 8-4	Rich Brooks	Music City	28 Clemson	20
2007	8-5		E4t	LSU 10-2, Florida 9-3, Georgia 10-2, Tennessee 9-3	Rich Brooks	Music City	35 Florida State	28
2008	7-6		E6	Alabama 12-1, Florida 12-1, Georgia 9-3	Rich Brooks	Liberty	25 East Carolina	19
2009	7-6		E4t	Florida 12-1, Alabama 13-0, Tennessee 7-5	Rich Brooks (39-47)	Music City	13 Clemson	21
2010	6-7		E5	Auburn 13-0, South Carolina 9-4, Mississippi State 8-4	Joe "Joker" Phillips (6-7)	PapaJohn's.com	10 Pittsburgh	27

TOTAL: 271-355-13 .4343 (58 of 70)

Bowl Games since 1953: 5-6 .4545 (46 of 70)

GREATEST TEAM SINCE 1953: While the recruiting of some of the members of the 1977 team may not have been totally above-board, there is no denying how good they were on the field. Winning 10 of 11 games, including Penn State and its entire SEC schedule, the Wildcats finished no. 6 in the final AP Poll.

1953 7-2-1

6 Texas A&M	7 E Howard Schnellenberger
6 Mississippi	22 T Duke Curnutte
26 Florida	13 G Ray Correll
6 LSU	6 C Tommy Adkins
32 Mississippi St.	13 G Joe Koch
19 Villanova	0 T Harry Kirk
19 Rice	13 E Jim Proffitt
40 Vanderbilt	14 QB Bob Hardy
20 Memphis State	7 HB Steve Meilinger
27 Tennessee	21 HB Tom Fillion
	FB Ralph Paolone

RUSHING: Paolone 108/620y
PASSING: Hardy 24-47/418y, 5TD, 51%
RECEIVING: Meilinger 18/308y
SCORING: Hardy (QB-K) 37pts

1954 7-3

0 Maryland	20 E Howard Schnellenberger / Jerry Beatty
9 Mississippi	28 T Bill Wheeler / Duke Curnette
7 LSU	6 G Neil Lowry
21 Auburn	14 C Dave Kuhn
7 Florida	21 G Joe Koch / Ray Callahan
13 Georgia Tech	6 T Pete Kirk/Jack Butler/J.T. Frankenberger
28 Villanova	3 E Brad Mills / Dude Hennessey
19 Vanderbilt	7 QB Bob Hardy / Delmar Hughes
33 Memphis State	7 HB Dick Mitchell / Billy Mitchell
14 Tennessee	13 HB Dick Moloney / Don Netoskie
	FB Dick Rushing / Bobby Walker

RUSHING: Rushing 75/369y, Mitchell 81/361y, Moloney 39/215y
PASSING: Hardy 57-108/887y, 5TD, 52.7%
RECEIVING: Schnellenberger 19/254y, Mills 18/305y, Rushing 16/157y
SCORING: Hardy 29pts, Mitchell 24pts, Hughes (QB-K) 20pts

1955 6-3-1

7 LSU	19 E Howard Schnellenberger
21 Mississippi	14 T Bill Wheeler
28 Villanova	0 G Ray Callahan / Bob Collier
14 Auburn	14 C Dave Kuhn
14 Mississippi State	20 G O.E. Philpot / Archie Powers
10 Florida	7 T Lou Michaels / J.T. Frankenberger
20 Rice	16 E Brad Mills / Roger Pack
0 Vanderbilt	34 QB Bob Hardy / Delmar Hughes
41 Memphis State	7 HB Woody Herzog / Don Netoskie
23 Tennessee	0 HB Dick Moloney / Billy Mitchell
	FB Bob Dougherty / Bobby Walker

RUSHING: Dougherty 94/401y, Netoskie 54/276y, Walker 54/238y
PASSING: Hardy 58-106/777y, 8TD, 54.7%
RECEIVING: Schnellenberger 20/287y, Dougherty 9/87y
SCORING: Hardy 62pts, Schnellenberger 36pts, Hughes (QB-K) 16pts

1956 6-4

6 Georgia Tech	14 E Roger Pack / Doug Shively
7 Mississippi	37 T Lou Michaels
17 Florida	8 G Bob Collier
0 Auburn	13 C Dave Kuhn / Bill Livings
14 LSU	0 G Bob Bennett / Archie Powers
14 Georgia	7 T J.T. Frankenberger / Jack Butler
14 Maryland	0 E Al Zampino/John Cornelius/Jim Urbaniak
7 Vanderbilt	6 QB Delmar Hughes / Kenny Robertson
33 Xavier	0 HB Don Netoskie /W. Herzog/Ivan Curnutte
7 Tennessee	20 HB Bobby Cravens / Billy Mitchell
	FB Bob Dougherty / Cliff Tribble

RUSHING: Cravens 78/338y, Dougherty 73/277y, Netoskie 77/263y
PASSING: Hughes 14-42/206y, 3TD, 33.3%
RECEIVING: Shively 7/107y, Urbaniak 6/45y, Cornelius 3/65y
SCORING: Hughes (QB-K) 26pts, Mitchell 24pts, Curnutte 18pts

1957 3-7

0 Georgia Tech	13 E Jim Urbaniak / Doug Shively
0 Mississippi	15 T Lou Michaels
7 Florida	14 G Bob Collier / Bob Talamini
0 Auburn	6 C Dick Blocker /Bill Livings / Andy Schollett
0 LSU	21 G Cullen Wilson / Jim Miller / Demo Johns
14 Georgia	33 T Bobby Lindon / George Boone
53 Memphis State	7 E John Cornelius / Ronnie Cain
7 Vanderbilt	12 QB Lowell Hughes / Kenny Robertson
27 Xavier	0 HB Glenn Shaw / Woody Herzog
20 Tennessee	6 HB Bobby Cravens
	FB Cliff Tribble / Bobby Walker

RUSHING: Cravens 141/669y, Shaw 59/241y, Herzog 45/174y
PASSING: Hughes 40-83/447y, 2TD, 48.2%
RECEIVING: Urbaniak 13/194y, Cravens 13/143y, Cain 5/99y
SCORING: Cravens 24pts, Hughes 20pts, 2 tied w/ 18pts

1958 5-4-1

51 Hawaii	0 E Dickie Mueller / Ronnie Cain
13 Georgia Tech	0 T Bobby Lindon / Bob Hunt
6 Mississippi	27 G Bob Talamini / Bill Spicer
0 Auburn	8 C Dick Blocker/A.Schollett /Pascal Benson
7 LSU	32 G Jim Miller / Demo Johns
0 Georgia	28 T George Boone / Bull Wilson
33 Mississippi State	12 E Doug Shively / Tom Rodgers
0 Vanderbilt	0 QB Lowell Hughes / Jerry Eisaman
20 Xavier	6 HB Calvin Bird / Glenn Shaw
6 Tennessee	2 HB Bobby Cravens / Charlie Sturgeon
	FB Waymond Morris / Lloyd Hodge

RUSHING: Cravens 104/441y, Shaw 69/367y, Bird 51/168y
PASSING: Hughes 36-72/437y, 2TD, 50%
RECEIVING: Bird 21/373y, Cravens 11/93y, Cain 10/165y
SCORING: Bird 65pts, Eisaman 18pts, 3 tied w/ 12pts

1959 4-6

12 Georgia Tech	14 E Tom Rodgers / Howard Ledger
0 Mississippi	16 T George Boone / Bob Hunt
32 Detroit	7 G Bob Talamini / Jerry Dickerson
0 Auburn	33 C Lloyd Hodge / Irv Goode
0 LSU	9 G Don Sinor / Demo Johns/ Mel Chandler
7 Georgia	14 T Cullen Wilson / Bob Butler
22 Miami	3 E Dickie Mueller / Ronnie Cain
6 Vanderbilt	11 QB L.Hughes /J.Eisaman /Leeman Bennett
41 Xavier	0 HB Calvin Bird
20 Tennessee	0 HB Charlie Sturgeon
	FB Glenn Shaw / Jimmy Poynter

RUSHING: Sturgeon 101/417y, Shaw 95/345y, Bird 98/336y
PASSING: Hughes 30-67/375y, 1TD, 44.8%
Eisaman 29-71/310y, 4TD, 41.4%
RECEIVING: Bird 16/151y, Rodgers 10/154y, Cain 10/110y
SCORING: Bird (HB-K) 55pts, Sturgeon 18pts, 3 tied w/ 12 pts

1960 5-4-1

13 Georgia Tech	23 E Tom Hutchison / Dave Gash
6 Mississippi	21 T Junior Hawthorne / Bill Scott
7 Auburn	10 G Lloyd Hodge / Jim Yarbrough
55 Marshall	0 C Irv Goode / John Mutchler
3 LSU	0 G Jerry Dickerson / Mel Chandler
13 Georgia	17 T Bob Butler / Wayne Dixon
23 Florida State	0 E Dickie Mueller / Tommy Simpson
27 Vanderbilt	0 QB Jerry Eisaman/Jerry Woolum
49 Xavier	0 HB Calvin Bird / Bill Ransdell
10 Tennessee	10 HB Charlie Sturgeon / Gary Steward
	FB Jimmy Poynter / Gary Cochran

RUSHING: Sturgeon 58/291y, Poynter 54/208y, Ransdell 30/199y
PASSING: Woolum 63-125/767y, 3TD, 50.4%
RECEIVING: Hutchison 30/455y, Gash 19/293y, Bird 15/222y
SCORING: Hutchison, Bird & Ransdell 30pts

1961 5-5

7 Miami	14 E Tom Hutchison / Danny Riviero
6 Mississippi	20 T Junior Hawthorne
14 Auburn	12 G Jerry Dickerson
21 Kansas State	8 C Irv Goode / John Mutchler
14 LSU	24 G Mel Chandler / Jon Jurgens
15 Georgia	16 T Bob Butler / Herschel Turner
20 Florida State	0 E Dave Gash / Tommy Simpson
16 Vanderbilt	3 QB Jerry Woolum / John Rampulla
9 Xavier	0 HB Bill Ransdell
16 Tennessee	26 HB Gary Steward / Darrell Cox
	FB Howard Dunnebacke / Gary Cochran

RUSHING: Steward 79/285y, Ransdell 73/278y, Dunnebacke 67/276y
PASSING: Woolum 70-125/892y, 4TD, 56%
RECEIVING: Hutchison 32/543y, Gash 16/198y, Simpson 11/192y
SCORING: Hutchison 30pts, Clarkie Mayfield (K) 20pts, 3 w/18pts

1962 3-5-2

0 Florida State	0 E Tom Hutchison / Jim Komara
0 Mississippi	14 T Junior Hawthorne
6 Auburn	16 G Vince Semary / Jim Foley
27 Detroit	8 C Tommy Simpson / Clyde Richardson
0 LSU	7 G Jesse Grant / Jim Hill
7 Georgia	7 T Herschel Turner / Bob Brown
17 Miami	25 E Dave Gash / Bill Jenkins
7 Vanderbilt	0 QB Jerry Woolum / Bob Kosid
9 Xavier	14 HB Darrell Cox / Phil Pickett/ Clark Mayfield
12 Tennessee	10 HB Gary Steward / Ken Bocard
	FB Perky Bryant / Joe Parrott

RUSHING: Cox 81/363y, Bryant 108/326y, Steward 54/196y
PASSING: Woolum 83-157/1100y, 4TD, 52.8%
RECEIVING: Hutchinson 32/485y, Cox 18/310y, Bocard 10/127y
SCORING: Bryant 24pts, Cox & Bocard 12pts

1963 3-6-1

33 Virginia Tech	14 E Bill Jenkins
7 Mississippi	31 T Herschel Turner
13 Auburn	14 G Jim Foley
35 Detroit	18 C Clyde Richardson / Vince Semary (D)
7 LSU	28 G Jerry Murphy / Ed Smith / Bob Brown
14 Georgia	17 T Rich Tucci / Doug Davis
14 Miami	20 E Rick Kestner / Jim Komara
0 Vanderbilt	0 QB Rick Norton / Talbot Todd (D)
19 Baylor	7 HB Darrell Cox / Bobby Kosid
0 Tennessee	19 HB Roger Bird
	FB Ken Bocard / Perky Bryant

RUSHING: Bird 85/382y, Cox 58/293y, Bocard 60/219y
PASSING: Norton 79-182/1177y, 6TD, 41.2%
RECEIVING: Cox 20/333y, Kestner 15/230y, Bird 15/208y
SCORING: Bird, Cox & Bocard 24pts

1964 5-5

13 Detroit	6 E Rick Kestner
27 Mississippi	21 T Tony Manzonelli
20 Auburn	0 G Ed Stanko
6 Florida State	48 C Jim Miles / Calvin Winthrow
7 LSU	27 G Rich Machel
7 Georgia	21 T Sam Ball (DL)
21 West Virginia	26 E Bill Jenkins / John Andrighetti
22 Vanderbilt	21 QB Rick Norton
15 Baylor	17 HB Roger Bird / Frank Antonini
12 Tennessee	7 WB Larry Seiple / Tom Becherer
	FB Mike McGraw
	DL John Andrighetti / Dan Spanish
	DL Jerry Murphy / Howard Keyes
	DL Sam Ball (T) / Doug Davis
	DL Ed Stanko
	DL Tony Manzonelli / Rich Tucci
	DL Rick Kestner
	LB Jim Foley
	DB Mike McGraw
	DB Tom Becherer
	DB Joe David Smith / Talbott Todd
	DB Roger Bird

RUSHING: Bird 133/671y, Mike McGraw 104/370y, Antonini 51/146y
PASSING: Norton 106-202/1514y, 9TD, 52.4%
RECEIVING: Kestner 42/639y, Seiple 17/288y, Bird 14/191y
SCORING: Bird 60pts, Kestner 36pts, Tucci & Antonini 12 pts

1965 6-4

7 Missouri	0 E Rick Kestner / Dan Spanish
16 Mississippi	7 T Sam Ball
18 Auburn	23 G Jerry Murphy
26 Florida State	24 C Calvin Winthrow
21 LSU	31 G John Schornick
28 Georgia	10 T Doug Davis
28 West Virginia	8 E John Andrighetti
34 Vanderbilt	0 QB Rick Norton
21 Houston	38 WB Bob Windsor
3 Tennessee	19 HB Roger Bird
	FB Larry Seiple
	DL Jim Swart / Jim Gresham
	DL Tony Manzonelli
	DL Ed Stanko
	DL Rich Machel
	LB Ronnie Roberts / Jim Miles
	LB Mike McGraw
	LB Ken Curling
	LB Jim Komara
	DB Tom Becherer
	DB Terry Beadles
	DB Jerry Davis

RUSHING: Bird 179/646y, Seiple 103/446y
PASSING: Norton 113-214/1823y, 11TD, 52.8%
RECEIVING: Windsor 30/426y, Seiple 27/635y, Kestner 25/411y
SCORING: Bird 78pts, Seiple 56pts, Andrighetti (E-K) 19pts

1966 3-6-1

10 North Carolina	0 E Dan Spanish
0 Mississippi	17 T Dwight Little
17 Auburn	7 G Lou Wolf / Rich Machel
0 Virginia Tech	7 C Cal Winthrow
0 LSU	30 G Mike Cassity
15 Georgia	27 T Basil Mullins / Leonard Rush
14 West Virginia	14 E Derek Potter / Joe David Smith
14 Vanderbilt	10 QB Terry Beadles / Roger Walz
18 Houston	56 WB Larry Seiple
19 Tennessee	28 HB Bob Windsor
	FB Dicky Lyons / Donnie Britton
	DL Doug Van Meter
	DL Rich Machel / Jim Gresham
	DL Ken Curling
	DL George Katzenbach
	DL Jeff Van Note
	LB Mike McGraw
	LB Ronnie Roberts
	DB Bill Jansen
	DB Al Phaneuf
	DB Dicky Lyons / Tom Fee
	DB Jerry Davis

RUSHING: Windsor 101/356y, Seiple 81/256y, Lyons 56/177y
PASSING: Beadles 47-113/725y, 5TD, 41.6%,
RECEIVING: Seiple 28/499y, Spanish 22/346y, Windsor 11/132y
SCORING: Seiple 34pts, Lyons 24pts, Windsor 18pts

1967 2-8

10 Indiana	12 E Phil Thompson
13 Mississippi	26 T Dennis Drinnen / Kenny Wood (C-G)
7 Auburn	48 G Lou Wolf
14 Virginia Tech	24 C Bill Cartwright
7 LSU	30 G Dwight Little
7 Georgia	31 T Ronnie Roberts
22 West Virginia	7 TE Derek Potter
12 Vanderbilt	7 QB Dave Bair / Terry Beadles (DB)
12 Florida	28 WB Joe Jacobs / Dick Beard
7 Tennessee	17 HB Dicky Lyons / Roger Gann
	FB Keith Raynor / Donnie Britton
	DL Jeff Van Note
	DL Ken Curling (LB) / Mike Boulware
	DL George Katzenbach / Steve Koon
	DL Dick Palmer
	LB Bill Duke / Fred Conger
	LB Doug Van Meter
	LB Cary Shahid
	DB Don Holland / Tom Ferguson
	DB Al Phaneuf
	DB Phil Greer
	DB Chuck Blackburn / Bobby Abbott

RUSHING: Lyons 138/473y, Gann 66/245y, Beard 39/134y
PASSING: Bair 66-164/634y, 3TD, 40.3%
RECEIVING: Thompson 36/377y, Jacobs 30/316y, Potter 19/206y
SCORING: Lyons 73pts, Thompson 12pts, Dave Weld (K) 8pts

1968 3-7

12 Missouri	6 WR Vic King
14 Mississippi	30 T Bob Freibert / Dave Hardt
7 Auburn	26 G Lou Wolf
35 Oregon State	34 C Bill Cartwright / Pat Eckenrod
3 LSU	13 G Dennis Drinnen
14 Georgia	35 T George Katzenbach / Len Rush
35 West Virginia	16 TE Phil Thompson
0 Vanderbilt	6 QB Stan Forston / Dave Bair
14 Florida	16 WB Dick Beard
7 Tennessee	24 HB Dicky Lyons
	FB Roger Gann / Raynard Makin
	DL Jeff Van Note
	DL Mike Boulware / Steve Koon
	DL Dave Roller
	DL Doyle King
	DL Dick Palmer
	LB Cary Shahid
	LB Wilbur Hackett
	LB Bill Duke / Frank Rucks
	DB Paul Martin
	DB Phil Greer
	DB David Hunter

RUSHING: Lyons 134/392y, Beard 90/318y, Makin 63/245y
PASSING: Forston 48-129/643y, 1TD, 37.2%
    Bair 45-104/591y, 5TD, 44.4%
RECEIVING: Thompson 29/397y, King 29/375y, Lyons 11/201y
SCORING: Lyons 66pts, Bobby Jones (K) 21pts, Beard 18pts

1969 2-8

30 Indiana	58 WR Jim Grant
10 Mississippi	9 T Dave Hanson
3 Auburn	44 G Jerry Bentley
7 Virginia Tech	6 C Pat Eckenrod
10 LSU	37 G Fred Conger
0 Georgia	30 T Mike Boulware / Dave Hardt
6 West Virginia	7 TE Tom Crowe / Jim Mitchell
6 Vanderbilt	42 QB Bernie Scruggs / Steve Tingle
6 Florida	31 WB Steve Parrish
26 Tennessee	31 HB Roger Gann
	FB Bill Duke / Raynard Makin
	DL Dick Palmer
	DL Dave Roller
	DL Doyle King / Don Porterfield
	DL Roger Greer
	LB Bob Wixson
	LB Wilbur Hackett
	LB Joe Federspiel
	LB Rick Meunch
	DB Dave Van Meter
	DB Paul Martin / Joe Stephan
	DB David Hunter

RUSHING: Gann 180/646y, Duke 59/263y, Makin 36/116y
PASSING: Scruggs 80-183/969y, 3TD, 43%
RECEIVING: Grant 33/344y, Parrish 23/301y, Gann 22/329y
SCORING: Gann 30pts, Bob Jones (K) 20pts, Scruggs 12pts

1970 2-9

10 North Carolina	20 WR Jim Grant / Al Godwin
16 Kansas State	3 T Dave Hanson
17 Mississippi	20 G Jerry Bentley
15 Auburn	33 C Pat Eckenrod
6 Utah State	35 G Tom Clark
7 LSU	14 T Dave Pursell
3 Georgia	19 TE Tom Crowe / Jim Mitchell
27 N. Carolina St.	2 QB Bernie Scruggs
17 Vanderbilt	18 WB Jim Reed / Dave Hunter
13 Florida	24 TB Lee Clymer
0 Tennessee	45 FB Houston Hogg
	DL Dave Hardt
	DL Dave Roller
	DL Al Fish
	DL Don Porterfield
	LB Arvel Carroll / Rick Muench
	LB Wilbur Hackett
	LB Joe Federspiel
	LB Ken King
	DB Buzz Burnam
	DB Dave Van Meter
	DB Earl Swindle

RUSHING: Clymer 118/441y, Reed 86/231y, Scruggs 99/165y
PASSING: Scruggs 115-209/1181y, 7TD, 55%
RECEIVING: Grant 24/251y, Hunter 24/224y, Godwin 20/268y
SCORING: Bob Jones (K) 39pts, 4 tied w/ 12pts

1971 3-8

13 Clemson	10 WR Jim Grant
8 Indiana	26 T Rich Allen
20 Mississippi	34 G Jerry Bentley
6 Auburn	38 C Dan Neal
6 Ohio University	35 G Tom Crowe
13 LSU	17 T Harvey Sword
0 Georgia	44 TE Ray Barga / Jack Alvarez
33 Virginia Tech	27 QB Bernie Scruggs / Mike Fanuzzi
14 Vanderbilt	7 WB Doug Kotar / Mark Campbell
24 Florida	35 TB Lee Clymer
7 Tennessee	21 FB Arvel Carroll
	DL Jim Hovey
	DL Mike Doggendorf
	DL Jim McCollum / Bill Bushong
	DL Frank Kirschner
	LB Rick Muench
	LB Ken King / Tom Clark
	LB Joe Federspiel
	DB Buzz Burnham
	DB Jeff Woodcock
	DB Earl Swindle
	DB Darryl Bishop

RUSHING: Clymer 96/455y, Kotar 78/375y, Scruggs 114/374y
PASSING: Scruggs 44-102/554y, 3TD, 43.1%
RECEIVING: Grant 10/205y, Clymer 10/155y, Barga 7/119y
SCORING: Clymer & Tom Kirk (K) 24pts, Kotar 18pts

1972 3-8

25 Villanova	7 WR Jack Alvarez
0 Alabama	35 T Rich Allen
34 Indiana	35 G Tom Clark
17 Mississippi St.	13 C Dan Neal
20 North Carolina	31 G Harvey Sword
0 LSU	10 T Dave Margavage
7 Georgia	13 TE Ray Barga
7 Tulane	18 QB Dinky McKay
14 Vanderbilt	13 WB Gary Knutson
0 Florida	40 TB Sonny Collins
7 Tennessee	17 FB Doug Kotar
	DL Rick Fromm
	DL Ken Fuller / Ed Gusky
	DL Bubba McCollum
	DL Marty Marks
	DL Jim Hovey / Ken King (LB)
	LB Frank LeMaster
	LB Tom Ehlers / Tom Ranieri
	DB Earl Swindle
	DB Ben Thomas
	DB Darryl Bishop
	DB Buzz Burnham

RUSHING: Collins 128/502y, Knutson 117/450y, Kotar 105/361y
PASSING: McKay 80-185/879y, 1TD, 43.2%
RECEIVING: Alvarez 41/487y, Barga 28/307y
SCORING: Knutson 36pts, Kotar & Collins 20pts

1973 5-6

31 Virginia Tech	26 WR Jack Alvarez
14 Alabama	28 WR Ray Barga
3 Indiana	17 T Harvey Sword
42 Mississippi State	14 G Rich Allen
10 North Carolina	16 C Rick Nuzum
21 LSU	28 G Dave Margavage
12 Georgia	7 T Warren Bryant / Wally Pesuit
34 Tulane	7 TE Elmore Stephens
27 Vanderbilt	17 QB Mike Fanuzzi / Ernie Lewis
18 Florida	20 TB Sonny Collins
14 Tennessee	16 FB Doug Kotar
	DL Jim Hovey / Terry Haynes
	DL Fred Hamburg
	DL Bubba McCollum
	DL Pat Donley / Marty Marks
	DL Tom Ehlers
	LB Frank LeMaster
	LB Ned Lidval
	LB Mike Cassity
	DB Ben Thomas
	DB Jeff Woodcock
	DB Darryl Bishop

RUSHING: Collins 224/1213y, Kotar 110/431y, Fanuzzi 111/393y
PASSING: Fanuzzi 33-84/572y, 5TD, 39.3%
RECEIVING: Stephens 16/282y, Alvarez 11/182y, 2 tied w/ 7
SCORING: Collins 80pts, Ron Steele (K) 43pts, Stephens 26pts

1974 6-5

38 Virginia Tech	7 WR Randy Burke
3 West Virginia	16 WR Dallas Owens
28 Indiana	22 T Warren Bryant
10 Miami	14 G Dan Fowler / Ben Bransom
13 Auburn	31 C Rick Nuzum
20 LSU	13 G Ed Singleton
20 Georgia	24 T Wally Pesuit
30 Tulane	7 TE Elmore Stephens
38 Vanderbilt	12 QB Mike Fanuzzi
41 Florida	24 TB Sonny Collins
7 Tennessee	24 FB Steve Campassi
	DL Art Still / Rick Fromm
	DL Jerry Blanton
	DL Tom Ranieri
	DL Pat Donley
	DL Tom Ehlers
	LB Mike Emanuel / Jim Kovach
	LB Mike Cassity / Nid Lidvall
	DB Tony Gray
	DB Greg Woods
	DB Ray Carr / Mike Siganos
	DB Ben Thomas

RUSHING: Collins 177/970y, Fanuzzi 179/909y,
    Campassi 128/625y
PASSING: Fanuzzi 32-83/438y, 4TD 38.6%
RECEIVING: Burke 12/127y, Owens 10/147y, Stephens 9/135y
SCORING: Fanuzzi 66pts, John Pierce (K) 58pts, Collins 30pts

1975 2-8-1

27 Virginia Tech	8 WR Randy Burke
10 Kansas	14 WR Dallas Owens / Dave Trosper.
10 Maryland	10 T Warren Bryant
3 Penn State	10 G Dan Fowler?
9 Auburn	15 C Tom Dornbrook / Greg Nord
14 LSU	17 G Ed Singleton
13 Georgia	21 T Wally Pesuit
23 Tulane	10 TE Vin Hoover
3 Vanderbilt	13 QB Cliff Hite / Derrick Ramsey (TE)
7 Florida	48 TB Sonny Collins
13 Tennessee	17 FB Steve Campassi
	DL Art Still / Rick Fromm
	DL Jerry Blanton
	DL Tom Ranieri
	DL Bob Winkel / James Ramey
	DL Terry Haynes
	LB Jim Kovach
	LB Mike Emanuel
	DB Greg Woods
	DB Mike Siganos
	DB Ray Carr
	DB Ches Riddle / Tony Gray

RUSHING: Collins 248/1150y, Campassi 172/673y, Ramsey 100/375y
PASSING: Hite 35-101/430y, 2TD, 34.7%
RECEIVING: Hoover 18/198y, Burke 10/149y, Trosper 6/140y
SCORING: John Pierce (K) 42pts, Collins 30pts, Campassi 18pts

1976 9-3

38 Oregon State	13 WR Randy Burke
16 Kansas	37 T Warren Bryant
14 West Virginia	10 G Ed Smolder
22 Penn State	6 C Dave Hopewell
7 Miss. St. (F-W)	14 G Tom Dornbrook
21 LSU	7 T Steve Slates
7 Georgia	31 TE Charlie Dickerson
14 Maryland	24 QB Derrick Ramsey
14 Vanderbilt	0 WB Greg Woods
28 Florida	9 TB Chris Hill
7 Tennessee	0 FB Rod Stewart
21 North Carolina■	0 DL Art Still (TE)
	DL James Ramey / Richard Jaffe
	DL Jerry Blanton
	DL Bob Winkel / Tim Gooch
	DL David Stephens / Bud Diehl
	LB Jim Kovach
	LB Kelly Kirchbaum / Mike Martin
	DB Mike Siganos
	DB Ray Carr
	DB Dallas Owens / John Bow
	DB Rick Hayden

RUSHING: Ramsey 187/771y, Stewart 146/711y, Hill 124/606y
PASSING: Ramsey 51-103/659y, 7TD, 49.5%
RECEIVING: Burke 15/152y, Woods 10/142y, Hill 10/93y
SCORING: Ramsey 60pts, Stewart 32pts, John Pierce (K) 30pts

1977 10-1

10 North Carolina	7 WR Felix Wilson
6 Baylor	21 WR David Trosper
28 West Virginia	13 T Tom Kearns
24 Penn State	20 G Tom Dornbrook
23 Mississippi St.	7 C Dave Hopewell / Will Grant
33 LSU	13 G Dan Fowler
33 Georgia	0 T Larry Petkovsek
32 Virginia Tech	0 TE Greg Nord / Scott Petersen
28 Vanderbilt	6 QB Derrick Ramsey
14 Florida	7 TB Randy Brooks / Joe Dipre / Chris Hill
21 Tennessee	17 FB Freddie Williams
	DL Art Still
	DL Jerry Blanton
	DL Richard Jaffe
	DL James Ramey
	DL David Stephens / Bud Diehl
	LB Mike Martin
	LB Kelly Kirchbaum
	DB Larry Carter
	DB Rick Hayden / Ritchie Boyd
	DB Mike Siganos
	DB Dallas Owens

RUSHING: Ramsey 159/618y, Dipre 116/399y, Brooks 90/375y
PASSING: Ramsey 74-156/892y, 6TD, 48.4%
RECEIVING: Trosper 25/340y, Wilson 14/247y, Williams 10/87y
SCORING: Ramsey 80pts, Joe Bryant (K) 50pts, Dipre 20pts

1978 4-6-1

14 South Carolina	14 WR Felix Wilson
25 Baylor	21 WR Chris Hill
3 Maryland	20 T Larry Petkovsek
0 Penn State	30 G Dan Fowler
24 Mississippi	17 C Mark Keene
0 LSU	21 G Tom Kearns
16 Georgia	17 T Leon Shadowen
28 Virginia Tech	2 TE Greg Nord / Scott Petersen
53 Vanderbilt	2 QB Larry McCrimmon / Mike Deaton
16 Florida	18 TB Freddie Williams / Chris Hill
14 Tennessee	29 FB Randy Brooks/Henry Parks/R. Stewart
	DL Bud Diehl / David Stephens
	DL Bob Winkel
	DL Richard Jaffe
	DL James Ramey / Earl Wilson
	DL Craig Roberts
	LB Jim Kovach
	LB Kelly Kirchbaum / Lester Boyd
	DB Venus Meaux
	DB Rick Hayden
	DB Larry Carter
	DB Ritchie Boyd / Greg Motley

RUSHING: Williams 89/313y, Hill 62/281y, Parks 65/266y
PASSING: Deaton 54-105/623y, 51.4%
RECEIVING: Wilson 43/727y, Hill 17/311y, Williams 14/166y
SCORING: Tom Griggs (K) 33pts, Brooks 30pts, Wilson 24pts

1979 5-6

14 Miami	15 WR Felix Wilson
10 Indiana	18 WR Allan Watson
14 Maryland	7 T Steve Williams
6 West Virginia	10 G Tom Kearns
14 Mississippi	3 C Ken Roark
19 LSU	23 G Steve Hricenaki
6 Georgia	20 T Leon Shadowen
20 Bowling Green	14 TE Scott Petersen / Frank McDaniels
29 Vanderbilt	10 QB Terry Henry / Juan Portela
31 Florida	3 TB Chris Jones / Pete Venable
17 Tennessee	20 FB Shawn Donigan
	DL Jeff Dennis
	DL Tim Gooch
	DL Richard Jaffe / Effley Brooks
	DL Kevin Kearns / Luis Lopez
	DL Don Fielder
	LB Lester Boyd
	LB Chuck Smith
	DB Greg Motley / Chris Jacobs
	DB Greg Long
	DB Larry Carter
	DB Andy Molls

RUSHING: Donigan 187/847y, Jones 142/770y, Venable 92/460y
PASSING: Henry 30-76/408y, 5TD, 39.5%
RECEIVING: Wilson 33/534y, Jones 11/85y, Watson 7/92y
SCORING: Jones 46pts, Rick Strein (K) 28pts, Donigan 24pts

1980 3-8

17 Utah State	10 WR Allan Watson
7 Oklahoma	29 WR Greg Wimberly
30 Indiana	36 T Dave Bond
21 Bowling Green	20 G Robert Cobb / Brent Edwards
0 Alabama	45 C Ken Roark
10 LSU	17 G Richard Adams
0 Georgia	27 T Gerald Smyth
22 Tulane	24 TE Jim Campbell / Rob Mangas
31 Vanderbilt	10 QB Larry McCrimmon / Randy Jenkins
15 Florida	17 RB Charlie Jackson / Terry Henry
14 Tennessee	45 FB Randy Brooks
	DL Jeff Dennis
	DL Tim Gooch
	DL Effley Brooks / Kevin Kearns
	DL Earl Wilson
	DL Dave Lyons / Steve Willis
	LB Chuck Smith
	LB Scott Schroeder
	DB Venus Meaux
	DB Chris Jacobs
	DB Greg Motley / Andy Molls
	DB Greg Long

RUSHING: Brooks 137/578y, Henry 73/313y, Jackson 71/238y
PASSING: McCrimmon 69-137/1060y, 3TD, 50.4%
RECEIVING: Campbell 33/394y, Watson 30/536y, Wimberly 18/405y
SCORING: Tom Griggs (K) 43pts, Campbell & Brooks 24pts

1981 3-8

28 N. Texas State	6 WR Allan Watson
10 Alabama	19 WR Rick Massie
16 Kansas	21 T Gerald Smyth
3 Clemson	21 G Steve Williams / Dave Bond
14 South Carolina	28 C Steve Hricenak
10 LSU	24 G Doug Williams / Robert Cobb
0 Georgia	21 T Don Corbin
3 Virginia Tech	29 TE Jim Campbell / Rob Mangas
17 Vanderbilt	10 QB Randy Jenkins
12 Florida	33 TB Lawrence Lee / Pete Venable
21 Tennessee	10 FB Richard Abraham
	DL Don Fielder
	DL Jeff Smith
	DL Effley Brooks / John McVeigh
	DL Keith Martin / Chris Ference
	DL Dave Lyons / Don Roe
	LB John Grimsley
	LB Kevin McClelland
	DB Tom Petty / Benjie Johnson
	DB Kerry Baird
	DB Greg Long
	DB Andy Molls

RUSHING: Lee 78/275y, Abraham 69/193y, Venable 69/157y
PASSING: Jenkins 84-170/1079y, 6TD, 49.4%
RECEIVING: Massie 29/448y, Campbell 23/333y, Watson 11/132y
SCORING: Tom Griggs (K) 32pts, Henry Parks(TB)& Venable18pts

1982 0-10-1

9 Kansas State	23 WR Allan Watson / Rick Massie (TE)
8 Oklahoma	29 WR Joe Phillips
13 Kansas	13 T Gerald Smyth
6 Clemson	24 G Ron Bojalad / Don Portis
3 Auburn	18 C John Maddox
10 LSU	34 G Steve Williams
14 Georgia	27 T Don Corbin
3 Virginia Tech	29 TE Rob Mangas / Oliver White
10 Vanderbilt	23 QB Randy Jenkins / Doug Martin
13 Florida	39 TB George Adams
7 Tennessee	28 FB Shawn Donigan / Terry Henry
	DL Don Fielder / Brian Williams
	DL Effley Brooks
	DL Keith Martin
	DL John McVeigh
	DL Cam Jacobs / Frank Hare
	DL Dave Lyons / Don Roe
	LB John Grimsley
	LB Kevin McClelland / Scott Schroeder
	DB Kerry Baird
	DB Tom Petty / Gordon Jackson
	DB Andy Molls / David Meers

RUSHING: Adams 185/720y, Donigan 27/121y
PASSING: Jenkins 92-187/933y, 2TD, 49.2%
RECEIVING: Mangas 22/293y, Phillips 16/169y, Massie 14/162y
SCORING: Adams 32pts, Chris Caudell (K) 19pts, Mangas 12pts

1983 6-5-1

31 C. Michigan	14 WR Joe Phillips
31 Kansas State	12 WR Cisco Bryant
24 Indiana	13 T Don Corbin
26 Tulane	14 G Bob Shurtleff / Jim Richardson
21 Auburn	49 C Jerry Klein
21 LSU	13 G Ron Bojalad
21 Georgia	47 T Don Portis
13 Cincinnati	13 TE Oliver White
17 Vanderbilt	8 QB Randy Jenkins
7 Florida	24 TB George Adams / Lawrence Lee
0 Tennessee	10 FB Curt Cochran / Chris Derry
16 West Virginia■	20 DL Brian Williams
	DL Jeff Smith / Jon Dumbauld
	DL Frank Hare / David Thompson
	DL Cam Jacobs / Keith Martin
	DL Steve Mazza / Stacey Burrell
	LB Scott Schroeder
	LB John Grimsley
	LB Kevin McClelland
	DB Russell Hairston / Barry Alexander
	DB Paul Calhoun / Gordon Jackson
	DB Kerry Baird

RUSHING: Adams 166/763y, Lee 89/338y, Cochran 68/227y
PASSING: Jenkins 118-203/1272y, 10TD, 58.1%
RECEIVING: White 26/252y, Adams 24/154y, Phillips 22/255y
SCORING: Adams 50pts, Chris Caudell (K) 47pts, Bryant 24pts

1984 9-3

42 Kent State	0 WR Joe Phillips
48 Indiana	14 WR Eric Pitts / Cornell Burbage
30 Tulane	26 T Bob Shurtleff
27 Rutgers	14 G Joe Prince / Tom Richey
17 Mississippi St.	13 C Ken Pietrowiak
10 LSU	36 G Jim Reichwein
7 Georgia	37 T Vern Johnson
31 North Texas	7 TE Oliver White / Mark Wheeler
27 Vanderbilt	18 QB Bill Mansdell
17 Florida	25 TB George Adams/Marc Logan/Mark Higgs
17 Tennessee	12 FB Chris Derry
20 Wisconsin■	19 DL Brian Williams
	DL Jerry Reese / Jeff Smith
	DL Frank Hare / Tom Wilkins
	DL David Thompson
	DL Jon Dumbauld
	DL Steve Mazza
	LB Larry Smith / Jeff Kremer
	LB Cam Jacobs
	DB Gordon Jackson / Tony Mayes
	DB Maurice Douglass
	DB Paul Calhoun / Russell Hairston

RUSHING: Adams 253/1085y, Higgs 75/476y, Logan 84/400y
PASSING: Ransdell 148-266/1748y, 11TD, 55.6%
RECEIVING: Adams 33/330y, Phillips 28/305y, Derry 19/185y
SCORING: Adams 84pts, Joe Worley (K) 36pts, Phillips 32pts

1985 5-6

26 Bowling Green	30 WR Cornell Burbage
16 Tulane	11 WR Eric Pitts
27 Cincinnati	7 T Vernon Johnson / Bruce Bozick
26 Clemson	9 G Jim Reichwein
33 Mississippi St.	19 C Ken Pietrowiak
0 LSU	10 G Brad Myers / Dermontii Dawson
6 Georgia	26 T Tom Richey / Joe Prince
23 E. Tennessee St	13 TE Mark Wheeler / Matt Lucas
24 Vanderbilt	31 QB Bill Ransdell / Kevin Dooley
13 Florida	15 TB Marc Logan / Mark Higgs
0 Tennessee	42 FB Chris Derry
	DL Brian Williams
	DL Jerry Reese / John Shannon
	DL Tom Wilkins / Don Duckworth
	DL Stuart Stubbs / Mike Velotta
	DL Jon Dumbauld
	DL Steve Mazza
	LB Larry Smith
	LB Jeff Kremer / Chris Chenault
	DB Tony Mayes / David Johnson
	DB Maurice Douglass
	DB Russell Hairston

RUSHING: Logan 175/715y, Higgs 143/611y
PASSING: Ransdell 133-231/1744y, 5TD, 57.6%
 Dooley 51-108/537y, 5TD, 57.6%
RECEIVING: Logan 32/314y, Burbage 25/418y, Pitts 24/334y
SCORING: Joe Worley (K) 72pts, Higgs & Logan 30pts

1986 5-5-1

16 Rutgers	16 WR Cornell Burbage
37 Kent State	12 WR Eric Pitts
37 Cincinnati	20 T Greg Kunkel
32 S. Mississippi	0 G Dermontti Dawson
13 Mississippi	33 C Ken Lange
16 LSU	25 G Brad Myers / Butch Wilborn
9 Georgia	31 T Joe Prince
15 Virginia Tech	17 TE Mark Wheeler
34 Vanderbilt	22 QB Bill Ransdell
10 Florida	3 TB Ivy Joe Hunter / Mark Higgs
9 Tennessee	28 FB Marc Logan
	DL Carwell Gardner
	DL Jerry Reese / Oliver Barnett
	DL Tom Wilkins
	DL Vic Adams / Mike Velotta
	DL John Shannon / Doug Howser
	DL Jay Dortch / Guy Neal
	LB Larry Smith / Don Yarano
	LB Chris Chenault / Jeff Kremer
	DB David Johnson
	DB Tony Mayes / Ron Mack
	DB Ron Robinson

RUSHING: Hunter 103/621y, Logan 109/546y, Higgs 121/527y
PASSING: Ransdell 151-256/1610y, 3TD, 59%
RECEIVING: Burbage 24/331y, Pitts 23/238y, Higgs 20/182y
SCORING: Joe Worley (K) 70pts, Hunter & Logan 36pts

1987 5-6

41 Utah State	0 WR Tim Jones / Ray Gover
34 Indiana	15 WR Dee Smith
18 Rutgers	19 T Mike Pfeifer
28 Ohio University	0 G Butch Wilburn
35 Mississippi	6 C Brad Myers
9 LSU	34 G Dermontii Dawson
14 Georgia	17 T Greg Kunkel
14 Virginia Tech	7 TE Charlie Darrington
29 Vanderbilt	38 QB Kevin Dooley / Glenn Fohr
14 Florida	27 TB Mark Higgs / Ivy Joe Hunter
22 Tennessee	24 FB Andy Murray / Darren Bilberry
	DL Jay Dortch
	DL Jerry Reese
	DL John Shannon
	DL Vic Adams
	DL Oliver Barnett
	DL Tony Massey
	LB Jerry Kremer
	LB Chris Chenault
	DB David Johnson
	DB Ron Mack / Chris Tolbert
	DB Ron Robinson / Mark Sellers

RUSHING: Higgs 193/1278y, Hunter 100/503y, Murray 28/181y
PASSING: Fohr 74-163/973y, 6TD, 45.4%
RECEIVING: Darrington 26/365y, Smith 23/420y, Higgs 16/123y
SCORING: Joe Worley (K) 68pts, Higgs 60pts, Smith 56pts

1988 5-6

18 C. Michigan	7 WR Alfred Jones / John Bolden
10 Auburn	20 WR Ray Gover
15 Indiana	36 T Mike Nord
38 Kent State	14 G Dean Wilks / Brian Denham
27 Alabama	31 C Brian Cralle
12 LSU	15 G Joel Mazzella
16 Georgia	19 T Mike Pfeifer / Bo Smith
24 S. Illinois	10 TE Charlie Darrington
14 Vanderbilt	13 QB Glenn Fohr
19 Florida	24 TB Alfred Rawls / Ivy Joe Hunter
24 Tennessee	28 FB Andy Murray
	DL Oliver Barnett
	DL Vic Adams
	DL Jerry Bell / Mike Meiners
	DL Doug Hauser / Donnie Gardner
	LB Tony Massey
	LB Jay Dortch
	LB Chris Chenault
	LB Randy Holleran
	DB Chris Tolbert
	DB David Johnson
	DB Ron Robinson

RUSHING: Rawls 101/477y, Hunter 130/451y, Baker 89/373y
PASSING: Fohr 91-201/1260y, 5TD, 45.3%
RECEIVING: Hunter 17/160y, Jones 16/239y, Gover 16/215y
SCORING: Ken Willis (K) 57pts, Rawls 42pts, Hunter 36pts

1989 6-5

17 Indiana	14 WR John Bolden
13 North Carolina	6 WR Steve Philips / Phil Logan
3 Alabama	15 T Greg Lahr
12 Auburn	24 G Todd Perry / Bill Hulette
33 Rutgers	26 C David Crane
27 LSU	21 G Joel Mazzella
23 Georgia	34 T Mike Pfeifer
31 Cincinnati	0 TE Rodney Jackson / Mike Meece
15 Vanderbilt	11 QB Freddie Maggard
28 Florida	38 TB Alfred Rawls / Al Baker
10 Tennessee	31 FB Andy Murray
	DL Oliver Barnett
	DL Jerry Bell
	DL Joey Couch
	DL Donnie Gardner / Doug Houser
	LB Tony Massey / Tony Zigman
	LB Craig Benzinger
	LB Billy Swanson
	LB Jeff Brady
	DB Chris Tolbert
	DB Albert Burks
	DB Ron Robinson / Brad Armstead

RUSHING: Rawls 185/893y, Mike Thomas (TB) 48/213y,
 Baker 72/210y
PASSING: Maggard 130-231/1515y, 6TD, 56.3%
RECEIVING: Logan 28/337y, Rawls 15/182y, Murray 14/89y
SCORING: Ken Willis (K) 64pts, Rawls 62pts, Murray 24pts

1990 4-7

20 C. Michigan	17 WR Steve Phillips / Phil Logan
8 Rutgers	24 WR John Bolden / Kurt Johnson
24 Indiana	45 T Chuck Bradley
13 North Carolina	16 G Todd Perry
29 Mississippi	35 T Matt Branum / Travis Hahn
17 Mississippi St.	15 G Joel Mazzella
20 LSU	30 T Greg Lahr
26 Georgia	24 TE Rodney Jackson / Bobby Henderson
28 Vanderbilt	21 QB Freddie Maggard / Brad Smith
15 Florida	47 TB Al Baker
28 Tennessee	42 FB Terry Samuels / Craig Walker
	DL Dean Wells
	DL Jerry Bell / Jody Mathews/Brad Shuford
	DL Joey Couch
	DL Derrick Thomas
	LB Jeff Brady
	LB Randy Holleran
	LB Billy Swanson
	DB Sterling Ward
	DB Larry Jackson / Salim Shalid
	DB Gary Willis
	DB Brad Armstead

RUSHING: Baker 170/780y, Samuels 72/325y, Walker 59/195y
PASSING: Maggard 109-188/1051y, 6TD, 58%
 Smith 80-156/796y, 5TD, 51.3%
RECEIVING: Logan 37/565y, Baker 35/317y, Samuels 34/223y
SCORING: Baker 72pts, Doug Pelfrey (K) 54pts,
 Logan & Bolden 24pts

1991 3-8

23 Miami (Ohio)	20 WR Neal Clark
10 Indiana	13 WR Kurt Johnson
24 Kent State	6 T Chuck Bradley
14 Mississippi	35 G Todd Perry
6 Mississippi St.	31 C Matt Branum
26 LSU	29 G Jody Matthews / Mark Askin
27 Georgia	49 T Greg Lahr
20 Cincinnati	17 TE Neil Page
7 Vanderbilt	17 QB Pookie Jones / Brad Smith
26 Florida	35 TB Damon Hood / Carlos Collins
7 Tennessee	16 FB Terry Samuels / Craig Walker (TB)
	DL Dean Wells
	DL Joey Couch
	DL Jerry Bell / Damon Betz
	DL Derrick Thomas / Zane Beehn
	LB Duce Williams
	LB Marty Moore
	LB Reggie Smith
	DB Sterling Ward / Salim Shahid
	DB Don Robinson
	DB Adrian Sherwood / Gary Willis
	DB Brad Armstead / Melvin Johnson

RUSHING: Samuels 77/307y, Jones 97/271y, Walker 66/235y
PASSING: Jones 81-138/954y, 3TD, 58.7%
 Smith 53-94/561y, 3TD, 56.4%
RECEIVING: Clark 47/647y, Johnson 28/385y, Samuels 16/105y
SCORING: Doug Pelfrey (K) 50pts, Walker 36pts, Jones 24pts

1992 4-7

21 C. Michigan	14 WR Kurt Johnson / Tim Calvert
19 Florida	35 T Chuck Bradley
37 Indiana	25 G Todd Perry
13 South Carolina	9 C Matt Branum / David Parks
14 Mississippi	24 G Jody Matthews
27 LSU	25 T Mark Askin
7 Georgia	40 TE Neil Page / Corey Reeves
36 Mississippi St.	37 QB Pookie Jones
7 Vanderbilt	20 WB Matt Riazzi / Craig Walker
13 Cincinnati	17 TB Damon Hood (FB) / Donnie Redd
13 Tennessee	34 FB Terry Samuels
	DL Zane Beehn / Howard Carter
	DL Robert Stinson
	DL Damon Betz / Billy Lofton
	DL Dean Wells
	LB Duce Williams / David Snardon
	LB Marty Moore
	LB Reggie Smith / James Simpson
	DB Adrian Sherwood / Willie Cannon
	DB Don Robinson
	DB Brad Armstead
	DB Sterling Ward

RUSHING: Samuels 98/380y, Hood 84/321y, Jones 140/295y
PASSING: Jones 97-203/1434y, 5TD, 47.8%
RECEIVING: Johnson 20/318y, Samuels 19/127y, Calvert 16/330y
SCORING: Doug Pelfrey (K) 63pts, Hood 30pts, Samuels 24pts

1993 6-6

35 Kent State	0
20 Florida	24
8 Indiana	24
21 South Carolina	17
21 Mississippi	0
35 LSU	17
28 Georgia	33
26 Mississippi St.	17
7 Vanderbilt	12
6 East Carolina	3
0 Tennessee	48
13 Clemson ■	14

WR Mark Chatman / Troy Hobbs
T Chris Page / Aaron Purdie
G David Parks
C Wes Jackson
G Barry Rich
T Mark Askin
TE Terry Samuels
QB Pookie Jones
WB Alfonzo Browning / Matt Riazzi
TB Moe Williams / Randy Wyatt
FB Damon Hood
DL Zane Beehn
DL Billy Lofton / Robert Stinson
DL Jon Collins
DL Howard Carter
LB Duce Williams
LB Marty Moore
LB Darryl Conn / David Snardon
DB Willie Cannon
DB Don Robinson / Adrian Sherwood
DB Steven Hall / Melvin Johnson
DB Marcus Jenkins

RUSHING: Williams 164/928y, Hood 93/367y, Jones 130/288y
PASSING: Jones 85-163/1071y, 8TD, 52.2%
RECEIVING: Browning 20/335y, Chatmon 20/294y, Samuels 14/139y
SCORING: Jones 36pts, Juha Leonoff (K) 35pts, Williams 32pts

1994 1-10

20 Louisville	14
7 Florida	73
29 Indiana	59
9 South Carolina	23
14 Auburn	41
13 LSU	17
30 Georgia	34
7 Mississippi St.	47
6 Vanderbilt	24
14 NE Louisiana	21
0 Tennessee	52

WR Randy Wyatt / Isaac Curtis
WR Clyde Rudolph / Kio Sanford
T Aaron Purdie
G Barry Jones
C Dan Caruthers
G John Schlarman / Adam Kane
T Mark Askin
TE Chis Davis / Corey Reeves
QB Jeff Speedy / Antonio O'Ferral
TB Moe Williams
FB Damon Hood
DL Howard Carter / Robert Harris
DL Robert Stinson / Mike Schlegel
DL Roger Sullivan / Bill Verdonk
DL Kurt Supe / Chris Ward
LB David Snardon
LB Chad Hudson / Matt Neuss
LB Eric Wright / Donte Key
DB Steven Hall
DB Kiyo Wilson / Van Hiles / Carlos Collins
DB Melvin Johnson
DB Leman Boyd / George Harris

RUSHING: Williams 160/805, Hood 46/275y, Donnell Gordon (TB) 38/231y
PASSING: Speedy 54-119/580y, 1TD, 45.4%
O'Ferral 48-107/642y, 7TD, 44.9%
RECEIVING: Smith 27/375y, Curtis 13/176y, Sanford 12/145y
SCORING: Williams 30pts, Brian Sivinski (K) 27pts, Curtis 18pts

1995 4-7

10 Louisville	13
7 Florida	42
17 Indiana	10
35 South Carolina	30
21 Auburn	42
24 LSU	16
3 Georgia	12
32 Mississippi St.	42
10 Vanderbilt	14
33 Cincinnati	14
31 Tennessee	34

WR James Tucker / Craig Yeast
WR Antonio O'Ferral
T Barry Jones
G Andy Britt
C John Schlarman / Jason Watts
G Brandon Jackson
T Jonas Liening
TE Isaac Curtis / Darrin Clark
TE Marcus Cross
QB Billy Jack Haskins / Jeff Speedy
TB Moe Williams
DL Donte' Key / Kurt Supe
DL Mike Schlegel / Mark Jacobs
DL Marvin Major
DL Chris Ward / Jason Thomas
LB Lamont Smith
LB Mike Schnellenberger
LB David Snardon
DB Van Hiles / Littleton Ward
DB Steven Hall / Kiyo Wilson
DB Reggie Rusk
DB Leman Boyd / George Harris

RUSHING: Williams 294/1600y, Raymond McLaurin (TB) 60/260y, Haskins 107/160y
PASSING: Haskins 93-154/1176y, 4TD, 60.4%
RECEIVING: Yeast 24/337y, Tucker 19/230y, Williams 19/153y
SCORING: Williams 102pts, Brian Sivinski (K) 31pts, Haskins 24pts

1996 4-7

14 Louisville	38
3 Cincinnati	24
3 Indiana	0
0 Florida	65
7 Alabama	35
14 South Carolina	25
14 Louisiana State	41
24 Georgia	17
24 Mississippi St.	21
25 Vanderbilt	0
10 Tennessee	56

WR Craig Yeast / Quentin McCord
WR Jaysuma Simms / Norman Mason
WR Chad Spencer / Kevin Coleman
T Kris Comstock
G John Schlarman / DeAnthony Honaker
C Jason Watts
G Jeremy Streck / David De La Perralle
T Jonas Liening
TE Isaac Curtis III
QB Billy Jack Haskins / Tim Couch
TB Derick Logan / Raymond McLaurin
DL Kurt Supe
DL Jeff Tanner
DL Mark Jacobs / George Massey
DL Chris Ward
LB Dele Ali / Anwar Stewart
LB Mike Schellenberger
LB Lamont Smith / Jeff Snedegar
DB Van Hiles / Tony Woods
DB Littleton Ward
DB Kiyo Wilson / Chris Ford
DB Leman Boyd

RUSHING: Logan 190/700y, McLaurin 74/209y
PASSING: Haskins 93-175/967y, 5TD, 53.1%
Couch 32-84/276y, 1TD, 38.1%
RECEIVING: Yeast 26/378y, Curtis 22/188y, Mason 14/173y
SCORING: Brian Johnson (K) 31pts, Logan 30pts, Yeast & Mason 18pts

1997 5-6

38 Louisville	24
27 Mississippi St.	35
49 Indiana	7
28 Florida	55
40 Alabama	34
24 South Carolina	38
49 NE Louisiana	14
13 Georgia	23
28 LSU	63
21 Vanderbilt	10
31 Tennessee	59

WR Craig Yeast
WR Lance Mickelsen / Kio Sanford
T Jonas Liening
G Mike Webster
C Jason Watts
G John Schlarman
T Kris Comstock
TE Jimmy Haley / Darrin Clark
QB Tim Couch
WR/HB Kevin Coleman / A.J. Simon
FB Anthony White / Derek Homer
DL Lamont Smith
DL Marvin Major
DL Mark Jacobs
DL Anthony Watson / Bamidele Ali
LB Lee Wesley
LB Bob Holmberg
LB Jeff Snedegar / Ryan Murphy
DB Tony Woods / Evie Kelly
DB Littleton Ward
DB Willie Gary
DB Tremayne Martin

RUSHING: White 129/723y, Homer 88/502y
PASSING: Couch 363-547/3884y, 37TD, 66.4%
RECEIVING: Yeast 73/873y, White 59/453y, Coleman 52/621y
SCORING: Yeast 72pts, Coleman & White 48pts

1998 7-5

68 Louisville	34
52 E. Kentucky	7
31 Indiana	27
35 Florida	51
20 Arkansas	27
33 South Carolina	28
39 LSU	36
26 Georgia	28
37 Mississippi St.	35
55 Vanderbilt	17
21 Tennessee	59
14 Penn State ■	26

WR Craig Yeast
WR Kevin Coleman / Quentin McCord
WR Gary Davis / Lance Mickelsen
T Jonas Liening / Matt Brown
G Jeremy Streck
C Jason Watts
T Kris Comstock
TE Jimmy Haley / James Whalen
QB Tim Couch
RB Derek Homer / Anthony White
DL Gordon Crowe
DL Mark Jacobs / George Massey
DL Marvin Major
DL Dennis Johnson / Matt Layow
LB Jeff Snedegar
LB John Rader / Lee Wesley
LB Marlon McCree
DB Evie Kelly / Jeremy Bowie
DB Marvin Love
DB Jeff Zurcher / Willie Gary
DB David Johnson

RUSHING: Homer 137/716y, White 97/437y
PASSING: Couch 400-553/4275y, 36TD, 72.3%
RECEIVING: Yeast 85/1311y, White 78/582y, Coleman 42/588y
SCORING: Yeast 90pts, Seth Hanson (K) 81pts, Homer 42pts

1999 6-6

28 Louisville	56
45 Connecticut	14
44 Indiana	35
10 Florida	38
31 Arkansas	20
30 South Carolina	10
31 LSU	5
34 Georgia	49
22 Mississippi St.	23
19 Vanderbilt	17
21 Tennessee	56
13 Syracuse ■	20

WR Garry Davis / Kendrick Shanklin
WR Brad Pyatt / Dougie Allen
T Matt Brown
G Kip Sixberry
C Nolan DeVaughn
G Josh Parrish
T Omar Smith
TE James Whalen
QB Dusty Bonner
TB Derek Homer / A.J. Simon
FB Anthony White
DL Matt Layow / Anwar Stewart
DL Gordon Crowe / Jimmy Haley
DL George Massey
DL Dennis Johnson
LB Jeff Snedegar
LB Ryan Murphy
LB Marlon McCree
DB Eric Kelly
DB Kenneth Grant
DB Anthony Wajda
DB Willie Gary / Patrick Wiggins

RUSHING: White 121/562y, Homer 94/332y
PASSING: Bonner 303-465/3266y, 26TD, 65.2%
RECEIVING: Whalen 90/1019y, White 56/469y, Davis 26/312y
SCORING: Marc Samuel (K) 77pts, Whalen 62pts, White 48pts

2000 2-9

34 Louisville	40
27 South Florida	9
41 Indiana	34
31 Florida	59
17 Mississippi	35
17 South Carolina	20
0 LSU	34
30 Georgia	34
17 Mississippi St.	35
20 Vanderbilt	24
20 Tennessee	59

WR Quentin McCord
WR Dougie Allen/Neal Brown/Derek Abney
T Matt Brown
G Kip Sixberry
C Keith Chatelain
G Omar Smith (T) / Josh Parrish
T Antonio Hall
TE Derek Smith
QB Jared Lorenzen
HB/TE Derek Homer / Bobby Blizzard
FB/WR Chad Scott / Martez Johnson
DL Matt Layow
DL Jeremy Caudill
DL Dewayne Robertson
DL Otis Grigsby / Chris Demaree
LB Chris Gayton / Ronnie Riley
LB Ryan Murphy
LB Marlon McCree
DB Eric Kelly
DB Kenneth Grant / Derrick Tatum
DB Willie Gary / Anthony Wajda
DB/DL David Johnson / John Robinson

RUSHING: Scott 130/611y, Artose Pinner (FB) 39/188y, Lorenzen 76/140y
PASSING: Lorenzen 321-559/3687y, 19TD, 57.4%
RECEIVING: Smith 50/716y, McCord 45/799y, Abney 40/413y
SCORING: Seth Hanson (K) 68pts, McCord 36pts, Smith 34pts

2001 2-9

10 Louisville	36
28 Ball State	20
10 Florida	44
31 Mississippi	42
6 South Carolina	42
25 LSU	29
29 Georgia	43
14 Mississippi St.	17
56 Vanderbilt	30
35 Tennessee	38
15 Indiana	26

WR Derek Abney / Ernest Simms
WR Tommy Cook / Anthony Kelly
WR Dougie Allen / Aaron Boone
T Matt Brown / Matt Huff
G Keith Chatelain / Jason Rollins
C Nolan DeVaughn / Nick Seitze
G Josh Parrish
T Antonio Hall
TE Derek Smith / Chase Harp
QB Jared Lorenzen / Shane Boyd
TB Artose Pinner/M. Johnson/Chad Scott
DL Dennis Johnson
DL Dewayne Robertson / Ellery Moore
DL Jeremy Caudill / Derrick Johnson
DL Chris Demaree
LB Chris Gayton
LB Jamal White
LB Patrick Wiggins / Kamaal Ahmad
DB Derrick Tatum / Jeremy Bowie
DB Leonard Burress
DB Anthony Wajda
DB David Johnson

RUSHING: Pinner 100/441y, Johnson 54/242y, Scott 34/211y
PASSING: Lorenzen 167-292/2179y, 19TD, 57.2%
Boyd 85-154/852y, 4TD, 55.1%
RECEIVING: Abney 66/741y, Smith 30/396y, Allen 26/283y
SCORING: Abney 42pts, Boone 36pts

2002 7-5

22 Louisville	17 WR Tommy Cook / Chris Bernard
77 UTEP	17 WR Derek Abney
27 Indiana	17 T Matt Huff / Sylvester Miller
44 M. Tennessee	22 G Jason Rollins
34 Florida	41 C Nick Seitze
12 South Carolina	16 G Keith Chatelain
29 Arkansas	17 T Antonio Hall
24 Georgia	52 TE Chase Harp
45 Mississippi St.	24 QB Jared Lorenzen
30 LSU	33 TB Artose Pinner
41 Vanderbilt	21 FB/WR Kamphake / Aaron Boone
0 Tennessee	24 DL Otis Grigsby
	DL Dewayne Robertson / Ellery Moore
	DL Jeremy Caudill
	DL Vincent Burns
	LB Ronnie Riley
	LB Morris Lane / Dustin Williams
	DB Leonard Burress / Antoine Huffman
	DB Derrick Tatum / Earven Flowers
	DB Quentus Cumby / Claude Sagaille
	DB Mike Williams
	DB David Johnson

RUSHING: Pinner 283/1414y, Shane Boyd (QB) 12/124y
PASSING: Lorenzen 183-327/2267y, 24TD, 56%
RECEIVING: Boone 41/706y, Abney 40/569y, Pinner 37/264y
SCORING: Pinner 90pts, Abney & Boone 60pts

2003 4-8

24 Louisville	40 WR Derek Abney / Glenn Holt
37 Murray State	6 WR Tommy Cook / Chris Bernard
17 Alabama	27 T Matt Huff
34 Indiana	17 G Jason Rollins / Nate VanSickel
21 Florida	24 C Nick Seitze
21 South Carolina	27 G Sylvester Miller
35 Ohio Univ.	14 T Antonio Hall
42 Mississippi St.	17 TE Win Gaffron / J. Drobney / Bruce Fowler
63 Arkansas	71 QB Jared Lorenzen / Shane Boyd
17 Vanderbilt	28 TB Arliss Beach / Draak Davis
10 Georgia	30 FB/WR Alexis Bwenge / Keenan Burton
7 Tennessee	20 DL Jeremy Caudill
	DL Lamar Mills / Ellery Moore
	DL Vincent Burns
	LB Deion Holts / Raymond Fontaine
	LB Chad Anderson / Justin Haydock
	LB Dustin Williams
	LB Durrell White
	DB Bo Smith / Leonard Burress
	DB Earven Flowers
	DB Muhammad Abdullah/ Antoine Huffman
	DB Mike Williams / Claude Sagaille

RUSHING: Beach 103/386y, Bwenge 72/318y, Boyd 45/268y
PASSING: Lorenzen 191-336/2221y, 16TD, 56.8%
RECEIVING: Abney 51/616y, Bernard 33/532y, Cook 21/222y
SCORING: Taylor Begley (K) 55pts, Beach 48pts, 4 w/ 30pts

2004 2-9

0 Louisville	28 WR Glenn Holt / Jacob Tamme
51 Indiana	32 WR Scott Mitchell / Gerad Parker
3 Florida	20 T Michael Aitcheson
16 Ohio Univ.	28 G Jason Rollins / Trai Williams
17 Alabama	45 C Matt McCutchan
7 South Carolina	12 G Matt Huff
24 Auburn	42 T Hayden Lane / Eric Klope
7 Mississippi St.	22 TE Eric Scott / Jeremiah Drobney
17 Georgia	62 QB Shane Boyd
14 Vanderbilt	13 TB Rafael Little / Arliss Beach
31 Tennessee	37 FB Alexis Bwenge
	DL Ellery Moore
	DL Ricky Abren / Lamar Mills
	DL Trey Mielsch / Vincent Burns
	LB Joe Schuler / Cedric Koger
	LB Chad Anderson / Dustin Williams
	LB Jon Sumrall
	LB Durrell White / Ray Fontaine
	DB Antoine Huffman
	DB Earven Flowers / Karl Booker
	DB Muhammad Abdullah/Wes'y Woodyard
	DB Mike Williams / Marcus McClinton

RUSHING: Boyd 102/297y, Little 53/265y, Dixon 54/244y
PASSING: Boyd 138-263/1328y, 7TD, 52.5%
RECEIVING: Holt 49/415y, Mitchell 30/383y, Tamme 16/161y
SCORING: Taylor Begley (K) 47pts, Boyd 30pts,
Bwenge & Holt 18pts

2005 3-8

24 Louisville	31 WR Scott Mitchell / Tommy Cook
41 Idaho State	29 WR Glenn Holt / Keenan Burton
14 Indiana	38 T Fatu Turituri / Garry Williams
28 Florida	49 G Michael Aitcheson
16 South Carolina	44 C Matt McCutchan
7 Mississippi	13 G Trai Williams
13 Mississippi St.	7 T Hayden Lane / James Alexander
27 Auburn	49 TE Jacob Tamme / Jeremiah Drobney
48 Vanderbilt	43 QB André Woodson / Curtis Pulley
13 Georgia	45 TB Rafael Little
8 Tennessee	27 FB Alexis Bwenge / Arliss Beach
	DL B. Jay Parsons
	DL Jason Leger / Myron Pryor
	DL Troy Mielsch
	DL Durrell White / Nii Adjei Oninku
	LB Wesley Woodyard
	LB Braxton Kelley / Ben McGrath
	LB Joe Schuler / Raymond Fontaine
	DB Bo Smith / Shomari Moore
	DB Antoine Huffman / David Jones
	DB Muhammad Abdullah
	DB Roger Williams

RUSHING: Little 197/1045y, Beach 64/288y, Pulley 49/149y
PASSING: Woodson 146-253/1644y
RECEIVING: Little 46/449y, Tamme 29/251y, Burton 24/365y
SCORING: Taylor Begley (K) 63pts, Little 60pts, Beach 36pts

2006 8-5

28 Louisville	59 WR Keenan Burton
41 Texas State	7 WR Dicky Lyons, Jr.
31 Mississippi	1 WR Tommy Cook
7 Florida	26 G Christian Johnson / Fatu Turituri
45 C. Michigan	36 C Matt McCutchan
17 South Carolina	34 G Michael Aitcheson / Trai Williams
0 LSU	49 T Eric Scott / Hayden Lane
34 Mississippi St.	31 TE Jacob Tamme / T.C. Drake
24 Georgia	20 QB André Woodson
38 Vanderbilt	26 TB Rafael Little/Tony Dixon/Alfonso Smith
42 La.-Monroe	40 FB Terrell Bankhead / Maurice Grinter
12 Tennessee	17 DL Durrell White / Dominic Lewis
28 Clemson■	20 DL Lamar Mills / Ventrell Jenkins
	DL Myron Pryor
	DL Jeremy Jarmon / Nii Adjei Oninku
	LB Wesley Woodyard
	LB Braxton Kelley / Ben McGrath
	LB/DB Johnny Williams/Paul Warford
	DB Trevard Lindley / David Jones
	DB Karl Baker / Shomari Moore
	DB Marcus McClinton
	DB Roger Williams

RUSHING: Little 140/673y, Dixon 87/303y, Smith 60/250y
PASSING: Woodson 264-419/3515y, 31TD, 63%
RECEIVING: Burton 77/1036y, Lyons 50/822y, Tamme 32/386y
SCORING: Burton 78pts, Lones Seiber (K) 66pts, Lyons 54pts

2007 8-5

50 E. Kentucky	10 WR Keenan Burton
56 Kent State	20 WR Dicky Lyons / DeMoreo Ford
40 Louisville	34 T Garry Williams
42 Arkansas	29 G Zipp Duncan
45 Fla. Atlantic	17 C Eric Scott
23 South Carolina	38 G Jason Leger / Christian Johnson
43 Louisiana State	37 T Justin Jeffries
37 Florida	45 TE Jacob Tamme / T.C. Drake
14 Mississippi St.	31 QB André Woodson
27 Vanderbilt	20 TB Rafael Little/Tony Dixon/Derrick Locke
13 Georgia	24 FB/WR John Conner/Steve Johnson
50 Tennessee	52 DL Dominic Lewis / Jamil Paris
35 Florida State■	28 DL Corey Peters / Ricky Lumpkin
	DL Myron Pryor / Ventrell Jenkins
	DL Jeremy Jarmon / Travis Day
	LB Johnny Williams / Sam Maxwell
	LB Braxton Kelley / Micah Johnson
	LB Wesley Woodyard
	DB Paul Warford / Shomari Moore
	DB Trevard Lindley / E.J. Adams
	DB Marcus McClinton / Calvin Harrison
	DB Roger Williams / Ashton Cobb

RUSHING: Little 190/1013y, Locke 94/521y, Dixon 72/411y
PASSING: Woodson 327-518/3709y, 40TD, 63.1%
RECEIVING: Burton 66/741y, Johnson 60/1041y, Lyons 56/655y
SCORING: Lones Seiber (K) 99pts, Johnson 78pts, Burton 56pts

2008 7-6

27 Louisville	2 WR E.J. Adams / Kyrus Lanxter
38 Norfolk State	3 WR Dicky Lyons / Gene McCaskill
20 Mid. Tennessee	14 T Garry Williams / Billy Joe Murphy
41 W. Kentucky	3 G Zipp Duncan
14 Alabama	17 C Jorge Gonzalez
17 South Carolina	24 G Jess Beets / Jake Lanefski
21 Arkansas	20 T Justin Jeffries / Brad Durham
5 Florida	63 TE T.C. Drake / Maurice Grinter
14 Mississippi St.	13 QB Mike Hartline / Randall Cobb (WR)
38 Georgia	42 TB Tony Dixon / Alfonso Smith / D. Locke
24 Vanderbilt	31 FB John Conner
10 Tennessee	28 DL Jeremy Jarmon / Nii Adjei Oninku
25 East Carolina■	19 DL Corey Peters
	DL Myron Pryor / Ricky Lumpkin
	DL Ventrell Jenkins
	LB Braxton Kelley
	LB Micah Johnson / Sam Maxwell
	LB/DB Johnny Williams / Robbie McAtee
	DB Trevard Lindley
	DB David Jones / Shomari Moore
	DB Marcus McClinton / Calvin Harrison
	DB Ashton Cobb / Matt Lentz

RUSHING: Dixon 132/430y, Cobb 79/316y, Smith 74/313y
PASSING: Hartline 172-311/1666y, 9TD, 55.3%
Cobb 52-99/542y, 2TD, 52.5%
RECEIVING: Lyons 33/264y, Locke 23/195y, Lanxter 23/195y
SCORING: Lones Seiber (K) 67pts, Cobb 54pts, Dixon 42pts

2009 7-6

42 Miami (Ohio)	0 WR Chris Matthews / LaRod King
31 Louisville	27 WR Randall Cobb
7 Florida	41 T Zipp Duncan
20 Alabama	38 G Christian Johnson / Larry Warford
26 South Carolina	28 C Jorge Gonzalez
21 Auburn	14 G Stuart Hines
36 La.-Monroe	37 T Justin Jeffries / Brad Durham
24 Mississippi St.	31 TE Russ Bogue / T.C. Drake
37 E. Kentucky	12 QB Morgan Newton / Mike Hartline
24 Vanderbilt	13 TB Derrick Locke / Alfonso Smith
34 Georgia	27 FB/WR John Conner / Gene McCaskill
24 Tennessee	30 DL Taylor Wyndham / Collins Ukwu
13 Clemson■	21 DL Ricky Lumpkin
	DL Corey Peters
	DL DeQuin Evans / Chandler Burden
	LB Sam Maxwell
	LB Micah Johnson
	LB/DB Danny Trevathon / Paul Warford
	DB Trevard Lindley / Martavias Neloms
	DB Randay Burden / Taiedo Smith
	DB Winston Guy / Matt Lentz
	DB Calvin Harrison / Ashton Cobb

RUSHING: Locke 195/907y, Cobb 94/573y, Smith 60/245y
PASSING: Newton 75-135/706y, 6TD, 55.6%
Hartline 79-133/802y, 6TD, 59.4%
RECEIVING: Cobb 39/447y, Matthews 32/354y, Locke 31/284y
SCORING: Cobb 90pts, Lones Seiber (K) 73pts, Locke 54pts

2010 6-7

23 Louisville	16 WR Chris Matthews / Matt Roark
63 Wake Forest	28 WR Randall Cobb
47 Akron	10 WR/FB La'Rod King / Moncell Allen
14 Florida	48 T Chandler Burden
35 Mississippi	42 G Stuart Hines
34 Auburn	37 C Matt Smith
31 South Carolina	28 G Larry Warford
31 Georgia	44 T Brad Durham / B.J. Murphy (G)
17 Mississippi State	24 TE Jordan Aumiller / Tyler Robinson
49 Charleston So.	21 QB Mike Hartline / Morgan Newton
38 Vanderbilt	20 RB Derrick Locke / Donald Russell
14 Tennessee	24 DL Collins Ukwu
10 Pittsburgh■	27 DL Ricky Lumpkin / Shane McCord
	DL Mark Crawford / Luke McDermott
	DL DeQuin Evans / Taylor Wyndham
	LB Danny Trevathan / Qua Huzzie
	LB Ronnie Sweed / Ridge Wilson
	LB/DB Jacob Dufrene / Martarius Neloms
	DB Randall Burden
	DB Anthony Mosley
	DB Mychal Bailey
	DB Winston Guy

RUSHING: Locke 166/887y, Cobb 55/424y, Russell 64/293y
PASSING: Hartline 268-405/3178y, 23TD, 66.2%
Newton 25-43/265y, 0TD, 58.1%
RECEIVING: Cobb 84/1017y, Matthews 61/925y, King 36/478y
SCORING: Cobb 82pts, Craig McIntosh (K) 67pts, Locke 60pts

LOUISIANA STATE

Louisiana State University (Founded 1860)
Baton Rouge, Louisiana
Nickname: Tigers, Fighting Tigers
Colors: Purple and Gold
Stadium: Tiger Stadium (1924) 92,400
Conference Affiliations: Southeastern Conference
(Charter member, 1933-present)

CAREER RUSHING YARDS	Attempts	Yards
Kevin Faulk (1995-98)	856	4557
Dalton Hilliard (1982-85)	882	4050
Charles Alexander (1975-78)	855	4035
Harvey Williams (1986-90)	588	2904
Joseph Addai (2001-05)	490	2577
Terry Robiskie (1973-76)	578	2517
Charles Scott (2006-09)	424	2317
LaBrandon Toefield (2000-02)	511	2291
Rondell Mealey (1996-99)	453	2238
Garry James (1982-85)	491	2217

CAREER PASSING YARDS	Comp.-Atts.	Yards
Tommy Hodson (1986-89)	674-1163	9115
Jeff Wickersham (1982-85)	587-1005	6921
JaMarcus Russell (2004-06)	493-797	6625
Jamie Howard (1992-95)	459-934	6158
Herb Tyler (1995-98)	434-715	5876
Alan Risher (1980-82)	381-615	4585
Rohan Davey (1998-01)	286-478	4415
Josh Booty (1999-00)	307-623	3951
Jordan Jefferson (2008-10)	326-559	3838
Matt Mauck (2001-03)	310-529	3831

CAREER RECEIVING YARDS	Catches	Yards
Josh Reed (1999-01)	167	3001
Wendell Davis (1984-87)	183	2708
Eric Martin (1981-84)	152	2625
Michael Clayton (2001-03)	182	2582
Brandon LaFell (2006-09)	175	2517
Dwayne Bowe (2003-06)	154	2403
Tony Moss (1986-89)	132	2196
Craig Davis (2003-06)	141	2107
Early Doucet (2004-07)	160	2046
Andy Hamilton (1969-71)	100	1995

SEASON RUSHING YARDS	Attempts	Yards
Charles Alexander (1977)	311	1686
Kevin Faulk (1996)	248	1282
Kevin Faulk (1998)	229	1279
Dalton Hilliard (1984)	254	1268
Charles Scott (2008)	217	1174

SEASON PASSING YARDS	Comp.-Atts.	Yards
Rohan Davey (2001)	217-367	3347
JaMarcus Russell (2006)	232-342	3129
Matt Mauck (2003)	229-358	2825
Tommy Hodson (1989)	183-317	2655
Jeff Wickersham (1983)	193-337	2542

SEASON RECEIVING YARDS	Catches	Yards
Josh Reed (2001)	94	1740
Wendell Davis (1986)	80	1244
Josh Reed (2000)	65	1127
Michael Clayton (2003)	78	1079
Eric Martin (1983)	52	1064

GAME RUSHING YARDS	Attempts	Yards
Alley Broussard (2004 vs. Mississippi)	26	250
Kevin Faulk (1996 vs. Houston)	21	246
Charles Alexander (1977 vs. Oregon)	31	237

GAME PASSING YARDS	Comp.-Atts.	Yards
Rohan Davey (2001 vs. Alabama)	35-44	528
Tommy Hodson (1989 vs. Tennessee)	31-49	438
Jesse Daigle (1991 vs. Mississippi St.)	25-44	394

GAME RECEIVING YARDS	Catches	Yards
Josh Reed (2001 vs. Alabama)	19	293
Todd Kinchen (1991 vs. Mississippi St.)	9	248
Eric Martin (1983 vs. Alabama)	8	209

GREATEST COACH:

Say the name "Cholly Mac" to anyone in Louisiana over the age of 40 and one impression instantly comes to mind: the popular ball coach on the sidelines at Tiger Stadium, where he held court as head coach from 1962 to 1979. Add in his nine years as an assistant to first Gus Tinsley and then Paul Dietzel and Charles Youmans McClendon spent 27 mostly glorious years closely identified with LSU football.

As an assistant, McClendon helped LSU win the national championship in 1958. Deploying the three units, the "White Team," the "Go Team," and the "Chinese Bandits," that would soon become synonymous with Tigers football, the 1958 squad delivered a magical, title-winning season for LSU. After three more successful seasons, Dietzel left to become the head man at Army, and McClendon was elevated to the top job.

McClendon coached the Tigers to 137 wins and 13 bowl appearances during his 18 years as the LSU head coach. LSU finished in the final AP Poll 11 times during McClendon's tenure. He was awarded national coach of the year honors by the AFCA for the 1970 season, when his Tigers won the SEC.

McClendon was also associated with Paul "Bear" Bryant, his head coach at Kentucky and a rival for SEC glory at Alabama. Bryant had considerable success against McClendon and virtually all of his former players and assistants who moved up to become head coaches. With Alabama a huge power in the late 1970s, while LSU had slipped to also-ran status, "Cholly Mac" was replaced by a younger coach, Bo Rein. McClendon remained popular with the community and had the football practice facility named after him a few months after his death in 2001.

LOUISIANA STATE'S 55 GREATEST SINCE 1953

OFFENSE

WIDE RECEIVER: Michael Clayton, Wendell Davis, Andy Hamilton, Eric Martin, Josh Reed
TIGHT END: David LaFleur, Billy Truax
TACKLE: Ciron Black, Robert Dugas, Ralph Norwood, Andrew Whitworth
GUARD: Alan Faneca, Tyler LaFauci, Stephen Peterman
CENTER: Nacho Albergamo, Todd McClure, Ben Wilkerson
QUARTERBACK: Tommy Hodson, Bert Jones
RUNNING BACK: Charles Alexander, Kevin Faulk, Dalton Hilliard, Jerry Stovall
FULLBACK: Jimmy Taylor

DEFENSE

END: Roland Barbey, John Garlington, Gabe Northern, Marcus Spears
TACKLE: Steve Cassidy, Glenn Dorsey, Ronnie Estay, Chad Lavalais, Anthony McFarland, Fred Miller
LINEBACKER: Mike Anderson, Michael Brooks, Warren Capone, Bradie James, Albert Richardson, Roy Winston
CORNERBACK: James Britt, Patrick Peterson, Mike Williams
SAFETY: Tommy Casanova, Liffort Hobley, Greg Jackson, LaRon Landry

SPECIAL TEAMS

RETURN SPECIALISTS: Domanick Davis, Skyler Green
PLACE KICKER: David Browndyke
PUNTER: Chad Kessler

MULTIPLE POSITIONS

GUARD-TACKLE-DEFENSIVE TACKLE: Sid Fournet

TWO-WAY PLAYERS

CENTER-LINEBACKER: Max Fugler
HALFBACK-DEFENSIVE BACK: Billy Cannon, Johnny Robinson

PERFORMANCE FORMULA:
LOUISIANA STATE'S 10 BEST SEASONS

1958	1.7608	1 Of 70
2003	1.6784	3 of 71
1961	1.6631	2 of 71
2006	1.6507	3 of 72
2007	1.6496	1 of 70
1987	1.5816	5 of 69
1962	1.5653	4 of 70
2010	1.5497	9 of 71
1969	1.5474	8 of 70
2005	1.5336	8 of 70

LOUISIANA STATE TIGERS

Year	W-L-T	AP Poll	Conference Standing	Toughest Regular Season Opponents	Coach (Record at School)	Bowl Games		
1953	5-3-3		8	Texas 7-3, Alabama 6-2-3, Mississippi 7-2-1	Gaynell (Gus) Tinsley			
1954	5-6		9	Mississippi 9-1, Arkansas 8-2, Georgia Tech 7-3	Gaynell (Gus) Tinsley (35-34-6)			
1955	3-5-2		9	Maryland 10-0, Georgia Tech 8-1-1, Mississippi 9-1	Paul Dietzel			
1956	3-7		11	Georgia Tech 9-1, Texas A&M 9-0-1, Auburn 7-3	Paul Dietzel			
1957	5-5		6t	Mississippi 8-1-1, Rice 7-3, Tennessee 7-3	Paul Dietzel			
1958	11-0	1	1	Mississippi 8-2, Florida 6-3-1, Kentucky 5-4-1	Paul Dietzel	Sugar	7 Clemson	0
1959	9-2	3	2t	Mississippi 9-1, TCU 8-2, Florida 5-4-1	Paul Dietzel	Sugar	0 Mississippi	21
1960	5-4-1		8	Mississippi 9-0-1, Baylor 8-2, Florida 8-2	Paul Dietzel			
1961	10-1	4	2	Mississippi 9-1, Georgia Tech 7-3, Rice 7-3	Paul Dietzel (46-24-3)	Orange	25 Colorado	7
1962	9-1-1	7	3	Mississippi 9-0, Georgia Tech 7-2-1, Miami 7-3	Charles McClendon	Cotton	13 Texas	0
1963	7-4		5	Mississippi 7-0-2, Mississippi State 6-2-2, Rice 6-4	Charles McClendon	Bluebonnet	7 Baylor	14
1964	8-2-1	7	5	Alabama 10-0, Florida 7-3	Charles McClendon	Sugar	13 Syracuse	10
1965	8-3	8	6t	Alabama 8-1-1, Florida 7-3, Mississippi 6-4	Charles McClendon	Cotton	14 Arkansas	7
1966	5-4-1		6	Alabama 10-0, Miami 7-2-1, Florida 8-2	Charles McClendon			
1967	7-3-1		6	Tennessee 9-1, Alabama 8-1-1, Miami 7-3	Charles McClendon	Sugar	20 Wyoming	13
1968	8-3	19	3t	Alabama 8-2, Mississippi 6-3-1, Miami 5-5	Charles McClendon	Peach	31 Florida State	27
1969	9-1	10	2	Auburn 8-2, Mississippi 7-3, Alabama 6-4	Charles McClendon			
1970	9-3	7	1	Notre Dame 9-1, Auburn 8-2, Mississippi 7-3	Charles McClendon	Orange	12 Nebraska	17
1971	9-3	11	6	Alabama 11-0, Colorado 9-2, Notre Dame 8-2	Charles McClendon	Sun	33 Iowa State	15
1972	9-2-1	11	3	Alabama 10-1, Auburn 9-1, Mississippi 5-5	Charles McClendon	Bluebonnet	17 Tennessee	24
1973	9-3	13	2	Alabama 11-0, Mississippi 6-5, Tulane 9-2	Charles McClendon	Orange	9 Penn State	16
1974	5-5-1		9	Alabama 11-0, Texas A&M 8-3, Florida 7-3	Charles McClendon			
1975	4-7		9	Texas A&M 10-1, Alabama 10-1, Nebraska 10-1	Charles McClendon			
1976	6-4-1		7t	Nebraska 8-3-1, Alabama 8-3, Kentucky 7-4	Charles McClendon			
1977	8-4	15	3t	Alabama 10-1, Kentucky 10-1, Florida 6-4-1	Charles McClendon	Sun	14 Stanford	24
1978	8-4		4t	Alabama 10-1, Georgia 9-1-1	Charles McClendon	Liberty	15 Missouri	20
1979	7-5		3t	Alabama 11-0, Southern Cal 10-0-1, Florida State 11-0	Charles McClendon (135-61-7)	Tangerine	34 Wake Forest	10
1980	7-4		4t	Florida State 10-1, Alabama 9-2, Mississippi State 9-2	Jerry Stovall			
1981	3-7-1		8t	Alabama 9-1-1, Mississippi State 7-4, Florida 7-4	Jerry Stovall			
1982	8-3-1	11	2	Florida State 8-3, Alabama 7-4, Florida 7-4	Jerry Stovall	Orange	20 Nebraska	21
1983	4-7		9t	Florida 8-2-1, Alabama 7-4, Washington 7-4	Jerry Stovall (22-21-2)			
1984	8-3-1		1	Florida 9-1-1, Notre Dame 7-4, Southern Cal 8-3, Kentucky 8-3	Bill Arnsparger	Sugar	10 Nebraska	28
1985	9-2-1	20	2t	Florida 9-1-1, Alabama 8-2-1	Bill Arnsparger	Liberty	7 Baylor	21
1986	9-3	10	1	Texas A&M 9-2, Alabama 9-3, Georgia 8-3, Mississippi 7-3-1	Bill Arnsparger (26-8-2)	Sugar	15 Nebraska	30
1987	10-1-1	5	2	Texas A&M 9-2, Georgia 8-3, Alabama 7-4, Ohio State 6-4-1	Mike Archer	Gator	30 South Carolina	13
1988	8-4	19	1t	Miami 10-1, Auburn 10-1, Alabama 8-3, Florida 6-5	Mike Archer	Hall of Fame	10 Syracuse	23
1989	4-7		7t	Florida State 9-2, Alabama 10-1, Tennessee 10-1, Auburn 9-2	Mike Archer			
1990	5-6		7t	Florida State 9-2, Florida 9-2, Mississippi 9-2, Texas A&M 8-3	Mike Archer (27-18-1)			
1991	5-6		6t	Florida 10-1, Florida State 12-0, Alabama 10-1, Texas A&M 10-1	Curley Hallman			
1992	2-9		W6	Alabama 12-0, Texas A&M 12-0, Florida 8-4, Mississippi 8-3	Curley Hallman			
1993	5-6		W4t	Auburn 11-0, Tennessee 9-1-1, Texas A&M 10-1, Florida 9-2	Curley Hallman			
1994	4-7		W3	Florida 10-1-1, Alabama 11-1, Texas A&M 10-0-1	Curley Hallman (16-28)			
1995	7-4-1		W4	Florida 12-0, Auburn 8-3, Arkansas 8-4	Gerry DiNardo	Independence	45 Michigan State	26
1996	10-2	12	W1t	Florida 11-1, Alabama 9-2, Auburn 7-4	Gerry DiNardo	Peach	10 Clemson	7
1997	9-3	13	W1t	Florida 9-2, Auburn 9-2, Mississippi 7-4	Gerry DiNardo	Independence	27 Notre Dame	9
1998	4-7		W5	Florida 9-2, Georgia 8-3, Arkansas 9-2, Notre Dame 9-2	Gerry DiNardo			
1999	3-8		W6	Alabama 9-2, Florida 9-2, Mississippi State 9-2	Gerry DiNardo (32-24-1), Hal Hunter [1-0]			
2000	8-4	22	W1t	Florida 9-2, Auburn 9-2, Tennessee 8-3	Nick Saban	Peach	28 Georgia Tech	14
2001	10-3	7	W1t	Florida 9-2, Tennessee 10-1, Arkansas 7-4, Auburn 7-4	Nick Saban	Sugar	47 Illinois	34
2002	8-5		W1t	Alabama 10-3, Auburn 8-4, Virginia Tech 9-4, Arkansas 9-3	Nick Saban	Cotton	20 Texas	35
2003	13-1	2	W1t	Georgia 10-2, Mississippi 9-3, Florida 8-4	Nick Saban	Sugar	21 Oklahoma	14
2004	9-3	16	W2	Auburn 11-0, Georgia 9-2, Florida 7-4	Nick Saban (48-16)	Citrus	25 Iowa	30
2005	11-2	6	W1t	Alabama 9-2, Auburn 9-2, Florida 8-3	Les Miles	Peach	40 Miami	3
2006	11-2	3	W2t	Florida 11-1, Arkansas 10-2, Auburn 10-2, Tennessee 9-3	Les Miles	Sugar	41 Notre Dame	14
2007	12-2	1	W1	Virginia Tech 10-2, Florida 9-3, Auburn 8-4, Arkansas 8-4	Les Miles	BCS Title	38 Ohio State	24
2008	8-5		W3	Florida 12-1, Georgia 9-3, Alabama 12-1, Mississippi 8-4	Les Miles	Chick-fil-A	38 Georgia Tech	3
2009	9-4	17	W2	Florida 12-1, Alabama 13-0, Mississippi 8-4	Les Miles	Capital One	17 Penn State	19
2010	11-2	8	W2t	Mississippi State 8-4, Auburn 13-0, Alabama 9-3, Arkansas 10-2	Les Miles (62-17)	Cotton	41 Texas A&M	24

TOTAL: 425-226-19 .6485 (17 of 70)

Bowl Games since 1953: 21-15 .5833 (19 of 70)

GREATEST TEAM SINCE 1953: With all due respect to the very talented 2003 and 2007 national championship teams, they never really had a chance in this category. The 1958 edition of the Bengals captured the hearts of LSU fans with their inspirational play in producing the unlikeliest of championships. A young team coming off a 5-5 season in 1957, Louisiana State was expected to challenge for the SEC title in 1959. Showcasing its three units of players, the fresh and hungry Tigers instead sliced through Southern football in stunning fashion. After six wins they had earned a no. 1 spot in the AP Poll for the first time ever, which they held on to the top spot for the rest of an undefeated season and Sugar Bowl win.

1953 5-3-3
20 Texas	7	E Jim Mitchell / Richard DeSonier
7 Alabama	7	T William Harris / Sam Leake
42 Boston College	6	G Paul Miller
6 Kentucky	6	C Larry Jones / Gary Dildy
14 Georgia	6	G Andy Alford / Enos Parker
21 Florida	21	T Sid Fournet
16 Mississippi	27	E Al Guglielmo
14 Tennessee	32	QB Al Doggett / Win Turner
13 Mississippi St.	26	HB George Brancato
9 Arkansas	8	HB Vincent Gonzales
32 Tulane	13	FB Jerry Marchand / Tommy Davis

RUSHING: N/A
PASSING: N/A
RECEIVING: N/A
SCORING: N/A

1954 5-6
6 Texas	20	E Sammy Murphy / John Wood
0 Alabama	12	T Earl Leggett
Kentucky	6	E Enos Parker
20 Georgia Tech	30	C Harry Hodges / Durwood Graham
20 Texas Tech	13	G Gary Dildy / Paul Ziegler
20 Florida	7	T Sid Fournet
6 Mississippi	21	E Joe Tuminello
26 Chattanooga	19	QB Al Doggett / Win Turner
0 Mississippi St.	25	HB Matt Burns
7 Arkansas	6	HB Chuck Johns / Vince Gonzales
14 Tulane	13	FB O.K. Ferguson / Tommy Davis

RUSHING: Johns 88/408y, Gonzalez 95/356y, Prescott 48/216y
PASSING: Doggett 34-104/459y, 2TD, 32.7%
RECEIVING: Tuminello 13/181y, Gonzalez 9/150y, Wood 6/136y
SCORING: Gonzalez & Johns 24pts, Tuminello 18pts

1955 3-5-2
19 Kentucky	7	E Billy Smith / John Wood
0 Texas A&M	28	T Earl Leggett / Ed Fogg
20 Rice	20	G Don Scully / Ted Paris
0 Georgia Tech	7	C Harry Hodges / Durwood Graham
14 Florida	18	G Paul Ziegler
26 Mississippi	29	T Enos Parker
0 Maryland	13	E Joe Tuminello
34 Mississippi St.	7	QB Matt Burns / M.C. Reynolds
13 Arkansas	7	HB Chuck Johns
13 Tulane	13	HB Vince Gonzales / Joe May
		FB O.K. Ferguson / Lou Deutschmann

RUSHING: Ferguson 117/465y, Johns 97/455y, Gonzales 64/248y
PASSING: Reynolds 51-115/660y, 6TD, 44.3%
RECEIVING: Gonzales 17/216y, Johns 14/217y, Tuminello 9/129y
SCORING: Gonzales 32pts, Johns 24pts, Ferguson 18pts

1956 3-7
6 Texas A&M	9	E John Wood / Jim Mitchell
14 Rice	23	T Earl Leggett
7 Georgia Tech	39	G Don Scully / Larry Kahlden
0 Kentucky	14	C Ted Paris / Durwood Graham
6 Florida	21	G Paul Ziegler / Ed Cassidy
17 Mississippi	46	T Enos Parker / Al Aucoin
13 Oklahoma A&M	0	E Billy Hendrix / Billy Smith
13 Mississippi St.	32	QB M.C. Reynolds / Matt Burns
21 Arkansas	7	HB Joe May
7 Tulane	6	HB J.W. Brodnax / Jerry Johnston
		FB Jimmy Taylor

RUSHING: Taylor 117/552y, Brodnax 121/452y, May 40/130y
PASSING: Reynolds 30-70/385y, TD, 42.9%
RECEIVING: Brodnax 13/123y, Wood 4/97y, Johnston 4/83y
SCORING: Taylor (FB-K) 59pts, Brodnax 12pts, 5 tied w/ 6pts

1957 5-5
14 Rice	20	E Billy Hendrix / Scotty McClain
28 Alabama	0	T Lynn LeBlanc / Mel Branch
19 Texas Tech	14	G Larry Kahlden / Emile Fournet
20 Georgia Tech	13	C Max Fugler / Doug Skinner
21 Kentucky	0	G Ed Cassidy
14 Florida	22	T Al Aucoin / Jim Lavin
0 Vanderbilt	7	E Billy Smith
12 Mississippi	14	QB Win Turner / Warren Rabb
6 Mississippi St.	14	HB Billy Cannon
25 Tulane	6	HB J.W. Brodnax / Johnny Robinson
		FB Jimmy Taylor / Bob DeCrosta

RUSHING: Taylor 162/762y, Cannon 105/583y, Brodnax 75/259y
PASSING: Turner 16-41/231y, 2TD, 39%
RECEIVING: Cannon 11/199y, Brodnax 7/122y, Smith 7/94y
SCORING: Taylor (FB-K) 84pts, Cannon 36pts, Brodnax 18pts

1958 11-0
26 Rice	6	E Billy Hendrix / Scotty McClain
13 Alabama	3	T Lynn LeBlanc / Dave McCarty
20 Hardin-Simmons	6	G Larry Kahlden / Al Dampier
41 Miami	0	C Max Fugler / Bobby Greenwood
32 Kentucky	7	G Ed McCreedy / Mike Stupka
10 Florida	7	T Bo Strange / Jack Frayer
14 Mississippi	0	E Mickey Mangham / Don Norwood
50 Duke	18	QB Warren Rabb / Darryl Jenkins
7 Mississippi St.	6	HB Billy Cannon / Scooter Purvis
62 Tulane	0	HB Johnny Robinson / Donnie Daye
7 Clemson■	0	FB J.W. Brodnax / Tommy Davis

RUSHING: Cannon 115/686y, Robinson 86/480y, Purvis 60/253y
PASSING: Rabb 45-90/591y, 8TD, 50%
RECEIVING: Robinson 16/235y, Broadnax 10/63y, Cannon 9/162y
SCORING: Cannon 74pts, Robinson 42pts, Davis 32pts

1959 9-2
26 Rice	3	E Scotty McClain / Andy Bourgeois
10 TCU	0	T Mel Branch / Lynn LeBlanc
22 Baylor	0	G Emile Fournet / Roy Winston
27 Miami	3	C Max Fugler / John Langan
9 Kentucky	0	G Ed McCreedy / Tommy Lott
9 Florida	0	T Bo Strange / Duane Leopard
7 Mississippi	3	E Mickey Mangham / Gus Kinchen
13 Tennessee	14	QB Warren Rabb / Durel Matherne
27 Mississippi St.	0	HB Billy Cannon / Scooter Purvis
14 Tulane	6	HB Johnny Robinson / Wendell Harris
0 Mississippi■	21	FB Earl Gros / Donnie Daye

RUSHING: Cannon 139/598y, Robinson 84/316y, Gros 49/262y
PASSING: Rabb 33-65/422y, 4TD, 50.8%
RECEIVING: Robinson 16/181y, Cannon 11/161y, Daye 10/136y
SCORING: Cannon 44pts, Robinson 30pts, Harris (HB-K) 22pts

1960 5-4-1
9 Texas A&M	0	E Andy Bourgeois / Bob Flurry
3 Baylor	7	T Bob Richards / Don Estes
2 Georgia Tech	9	G Roy Winston
0 Kentucky	3	C Charles Strange
10 Florida	13	G Ed McCreedy/Eddie Habert/Monk Guillot
6 Mississippi	6	T Billy Booth / Rodney Guillot
35 South Carolina	6	E Mickey Mangham / Jack Gates
7 Mississippi St.	3	QB Lynn Amedee / Darryl Jenkins
16 Wake Forest	0	HB Jerry Stovall / Bo Campbell
17 Tulane	6	HB Wendell Harris / Ray Wilkins
		FB Donnie Daye / Charles Cranford

RUSHING: Stovall 65/298y, Harris 62/264y, Cranford 38/188y
PASSING: Amedee 31-67/438y, 4TD, 46.3%
RECEIVING: Stovall 12/114y, Harris 9/99y, Wilkins 9/74y
SCORING: Harris (HB-K) 34pts, Amedee, Campbell & Flurry 12pts

1961 10-1
3 Rice	16	E Gene Sykes / Danny Neumann
16 Texas A&M	7	T Don Estes / Ralph Pere
10 Georgia Tech	0	G Roy Winston / Robbie Hucklebridge
42 South Carolina	0	C Dennis Gaubatz / Gary Kinchen
24 Kentucky	14	G Monk Guillot / Eddie Habert
23 Florida	0	T Billy Booth / Rodney Guillot/Fred Miller
10 Mississippi	7	E Jack Gates / Billy Truax
30 North Carolina	0	QB L. Amedee/Jim Field/Dwight Robinson
14 Mississippi St.	6	HB Jerry Stovall/Bo Campbell/Tommy Neck
62 Tulane	0	HB Wend'll Harris/Ray Wilkins/Bud Soefker
25 Colorado■	7	FB Earl Gros / Steve Ward (D)

RUSHING: Gros 90/406y, Stovall 65/405y, Campbell 48/319y
PASSING: Amedee 40-94/485y, 2TD, 42.6%
RECEIVING: Harris 10/177y, Stovall 9/135y, Wilkins 9/72y
SCORING: Harris (HB-K) 94pts, Campbell & Gros 24pts

1962 9-1-1
21 Texas A&M	0	E Gene Sykes / Danny Neumann
6 Rice	6	T Don Estes / Ralph Pere
10 Georgia Tech	7	G Rodney Guillot / Remi Prudhomme
17 Miami	3	C Dennis Gaubatz / Gary Kinchen
7 Kentucky	0	G Robbie Huckelbridge / Eddie Habert
23 Florida	0	T Fred Miller
7 Mississippi	15	E Jack Gates / Billy Truax
5 TCU	0	QB Jimmy Field / Lynn Amedee
28 Mississippi St.	0	HB Jerry Stovall / Bo Campbell
38 Tulane	3	HB Danny LeBlanc / Ray Wilkins
13 Texas■	0	FB Steve Ward / Charles Cranford

RUSHING: Stovall 89/368y, Cranford 78/307y, Ward 59/278y
PASSING: Amedee 24-63/457y, 2TD, 38.1%
RECEIVING: Stovall 9/213y, Cranford 6/110y, Wilkins 5/55y
SCORING: Stovall 66pts, Amedee (QB-K) 33pts, Campbell 24pts

1963 7-4
14 Texas A&M	6	E Danny Neumann / Doug Moreau
12 Rice	21	T Ralph Pere / Ernest Maggiore
7 Georgia Tech	6	G Remi Prudhomme / Jerry Young
3 Miami	0	C Ruffin Rodrigue / Richard Granier
28 Kentucky	7	G Robbie Hucklebridge
14 Florida	0	T Milton Trosclair / Willis Langley
3 Mississippi	37	E Billy Truax / Mike Morgan
28 TCU	14	QB Pat Screen / Billy Ezell
6 Mississippi St.	7	HB Danny LeBlanc / Buddy Soefker
20 Tulane	0	FB Buddy Hamic / Don Schwab
7 Baylor■	14	

RUSHING: Schwab 108/553y, Labruzzo 78/395y, LeBlanc 103/388
PASSING: Screen 22-38/194y, 1TD, 57.9%
RECEIVING: Truax 10/112y, Labruzzo 8/71y, Schwab 6/83y
SCORING: Schwab 36pts, Moreau (E-K) 33pts, Labruzzo 30pts

1964 8-2-1
9 Texas A&M	6	WR Kenny Vairin / Bob O'Brien
3 Rice	0	WR Doug Moreau
20 North Carolina	3	T Dave McCormick / Charles Simmons
27 Kentucky	7	G Don Ellen
3 Tennessee	3	C Richard Granier
11 Mississippi	10	G Remi Prudhomme / John Aaron
9 Alabama	17	T George Rice / Tommy Powell
14 Mississippi St.	10	TE Walter Pillow / Billy Masters
13 Tulane	3	QB Pat Screen / Billy Ezell
6 Florida	20	TB Joe Labruzzo / Gawain DiBetta
13 Syracuse■	10	FB Donald Schwab
		DL Ernest Maggiore
		DL George Rice
		DL Mike Duhon / John Demarie
		DL Tommy Fussell / Remi Prudhomme
		DL Walter Pillow / Kenny Vairin
		LB Mike Vincent
		LB Ruffin Rodrigue
		DB Beau Colle
		DB White Graves
		DB Ken Cormier
		DB Billy Ezell / Charles Moore

RUSHING: Schwab 160/683y, Labruzzo 107/366y,
DiBetta 84/208y
PASSING: Screen 55-99/561y, TD, 55.6%
RECEIVING: Moreau 33/391y, Labruzzo 20/203y, DiBetta 9/88y
SCORING: Moreau (E-K) 73pts, 7 tied w/ 6pts

1965 8-3
10 Texas A&M	0	WR Doug Moreau
42 Rice	14	T Dave McCormick
7 Florida	14	G Eddie Banker
34 Miami	27	C Barry Wilson / Phil Johnson
31 Kentucky	21	G John Aaron
21 South Carolina	7	T Tommy Powell
0 Mississippi	23	TE Walter Pillow
7 Alabama	31	QB Nelson Stokley / Pat Screen
37 Mississippi St.	20	SB Billy Masters / Gawain Dibetta
62 Tulane	0	TB Joe Labruzzo / Jim Dousay
14 Arkansas■	7	FB Danny LeBlanc / Don Schwab
		DL Charles Moore / John Garlington
		DL George Rice
		DL Mike Duhon / John DeMarie
		DL Tommy Fussell
		DL Ernest Maggiore / Mike Robichaux
		LB Mike Vincent
		LB Bill Bass
		DB Jerry Joseph
		DB Beau Colle / Sammy Grezaffi
		DB Leonard Neumann
		DB Billy Ezell / Spike Pierce

RUSHING: Labruzzo 103/509y, Stokley 71/449y, Dousay 85/326y
PASSING: Stokley 32-50/468y, 3TD, 64%
RECEIVING: Moreau 29/468y, Labruzzo 15/167y, Masters 8/104y
SCORING: Moreau (E-K) 59pts, Labruzzo & Stokley 36pts

1966 5-4-1

28 South Carolina	12 WR Tommy Morel / George Haynes
15 Rice	17 T Terry Esthay
10 Miami	8 G Eddie Banker/Jerry Guillot/Pete Johnson
7 Texas A&M	7 C Barry Wilson
30 Kentucky	0 G Jimmy Hamic / Joe Reding
7 Florida	28 T Allen LeBlanc / Bill Bofinger
7 Mississippi	17 TE Bob O'Brien / Bob Hamlett
0 Alabama	21 QB Freddie Haynes / Nelson Stokley
17 Mississippi St.	7 SB Billy Masters
21 Tulane	7 TB Jim Dousay / Tommy Allen
	FB Gawain DiBetta
	DL Johnny Garlington
	DL Tommy Fussell
	DL Mike Duhon
	DL John Demarie
	DL Mike Robichaux / Wayne Sessions
	LB George Bevan
	LB Mike Pharis / Benny Griffin
	DB Jerry Joseph
	DB Gerry Kent / Barton Frye
	DB Sammy Grezaffi
	DB Leonard Neumann

RUSHING: Dousay 104/441y, Haynes 135/412y, Allen 93/355y
PASSING: Haynes 39-91/424y, 2TD, 42.9%
RECEIVING: Masters 24/241y, Morel 10/100y, Dousay 6/48y
SCORING: Allen 32pts, Steve Daniel (K) 24pts, DiBetta 18pts

1967 7-3-1

20 Rice	14 WR Tommy Morel
17 Texas A&M	6 T Terry Esthay / Larry McCaskill
37 Florida	6 G Tony Russell
15 Miami	17 C Barry Wilson
30 Kentucky	7 G Jerry Guillot / Joe Reding
14 Tennessee	17 T Bill Fortier / Allen LeBlanc
13 Mississippi	13 TE Bob Hamlett
6 Alabama	7 QB Nelson Stokley
55 Mississippi St.	0 SB Maurice LeBlanc / Jim West
41 Tulane	27 TB Tommy Allen / Jim Dousay
20 Wyoming■	13 FB Eddie Ray / Ken Newfield
	DL Johnny Garlington
	DL Jack Dyer / Donnie Bozeman
	DL Ronnie Manton / Ron Jeter
	DL Carlos Rabb / Fred Michaelson
	DL Jerry Kober / Tommy Youngblood
	LB Bill Thomason
	LB Benny Griffin
	DB Barton Frye
	DB Gerry Kent
	DB David Jones / Mike Ryan
	DB Sammy Grezaffi

RUSHING: Allen 106/534y, Dousay 101/456y, Stokley 106/299y
PASSING: Stokley 71-130/939y, 4TD, 54.6%
RECEIVING: Morel 28/404y, Ray 12/137y, LeBlanc 8/100y
SCORING: Roy Hurd (K) 41pts, Stokley & Allen 36pts

1968 8-3

13 Texas A&M	12 WR Tommy Morel
21 Rice	7 T Joe Reding / Red Ryder
48 Baylor	16 G Tony Russell
0 Miami	30 C Godfrey Zaunbrecher
13 Kentucky	3 G Jerry Guillot
10 TCU	7 T Bill Fortier / Larry McCaskill
24 Mississippi	27 TE Bob Hamlett
7 Alabama	16 QB Fred Haynes / Mike Hillman
20 Mississippi St.	16 SB Jim West / Maurice LeBlanc
34 Tulane	10 TB Tommy Allen /Frank Matte /Glenn Smith
31 Florida State■	27 FB Ken Newfield / Eddie Ray
	DL Mickey Christian / Buddy Millican
	DL John Sage / Donnie Bozeman
	DL Fred Michaelson
	DL Carlos Rabb / Billy Loftin
	DL Tommy Youngblood / Ricki Owens
	LB Mike Anderson
	LB Bill Thomason
	DB Barton Frye
	DB Gerry Kent
	DB James Earley / Don Addison
	DB James Lambert / Craig Burns

RUSHING: Newfield 85/441y, Allen 135/398y, Haynes 80/274y
PASSING: Hillman 64-118/787y, 5TD, 54.2%
RECEIVING: Morel 42/564y, West 17/185y, Hamlett 14/186y
SCORING: Mark Lumpkin (K) 40pts, Allen 30pts, Matte 18pts

1969 9-1

35 Texas A&M	6 WR Lonny Myles
42 Rice	0 T Red Ryder
63 Baylor	8 G Tony Russell
20 Miami	0 C Godfrey Zaunbrecher
37 Kentucky	10 G Mike Demarie
21 Auburn	20 T Mike Wright
23 Mississippi	26 TE Bill Stober
20 Alabama	15 QB Mike Hillman / Buddy Lee
61 Mississippi St.	6 SB Jim West / Andy Hamilton
27 Tulane	0 TB Jimmy Gilbert / Allen Shorey
	FB Eddie Ray
	DL Jerry Kober / Buddy Millican
	DL John Sage
	DL Fred Michaelson
	DL Arthur Davis / Donnie Bozeman
	LB Mike Anderson / Ricki Owens
	LB George Bevan
	LB Bill Thomason
	DB Tommy Casanova
	DB James Earley
	DB Craig Burns / Bill Norsworthy
	DB Don Addison

RUSHING: Ray 115/586y, Shorey 118/459y, Gilbert 85/325y
PASSING: Hillman 93-167/1180y, 8TD, 55.7%
RECEIVING: Myles 43/559y, West 25/283y, Stober 23/316y
SCORING: Mark Lumpkin (K) 62pts, Hamilton 42pts, Ray 32pts

1970 9-3

18 Texas A&M	20 WR Gerald Keigley / Jimmy LeDoux
24 Rice	0 WR Andy Hamilton
31 Baylor	10 T Charles Stuart / Glenn Alexander
34 Pacific	0 G Jimmy Elkins / Steve Martin
14 Kentucky	7 C Jack Jaubert
17 Auburn	9 G Mike Demarie
14 Alabama	9 T Mike Wright/Tom Besselman/Phil Murray
38 Mississippi St.	7 TE Ken Kavanaugh / Jay Michaelson
0 Notre Dame	3 QB Buddy Lee / Bert Jones
26 Tulane	14 TB Art Cantrelle / Chris Dantin
61 Mississippi	17 FB Jim Benglis / Del Walker
12 Nebraska■	17 DL Buddy Millican
	DL John Sage
	DL Ronnie Estay
	DL Arthur Davis / John Wood
	LB Mike Anderson
	LB Louis Cascio / Tommy Smith
	LB Richard Picou
	DB Tommy Casanova (TB)
	DB James Earley
	DB Bill Norsworthy / John Staggs
	DB Craig Burns

RUSHING: Cantrelle 247/892y, Dantin 102/350y, Casanova 48/194y
PASSING: Lee 73-138/1162y, 6TD, 52.9%
RECEIVING: Hamilton 39/870y, Kavanaugh 25/318y, Keigley 16/277y
SCORING: Mark Lumpkin (K) 53pts, Hamilton 48pts, Cantrelle 42pts

1971 9-3

21 Colorado	31 WR Gerald Keigley / Joe Fakier
37 Texas A&M	0 WR Andy Hamilton
38 Wisconsin	28 T Phil Murray / Steve Streete
38 Rice	3 G Jimmy Elkins / Loyd Daniel
48 Florida	7 C Jack Jaubert
17 Kentucky	13 G Mike Demarie
22 Mississippi	24 T Charles Stuart
7 Alabama	14 TE Ken Kavanaugh
28 Mississippi St.	3 QB Bert Jones / Paul Lyons
28 Notre Dame	8 TB Art Cantrelle / Chris Dantin
36 Tulane	7 FB Allen Shorey / Jim Benglis
33 Iowa State■	15 DL Skip Cormier / Jim Gainey
	DL Ronnie Estay
	DL Tyler Lafauci
	DL John Wood
	LB Lloyd Frye / Boyd Perry
	LB Louis Cascio / Warren Capone
	LB Richard Picou / Gary Champagne
	DB Tommy Casanova / Dale Cangelosi
	DB John Nagle / Norm Hodgins
	DB Joe Winkler
	DB Frank Racine / John Staggs

RUSHING: Cantrelle 133/649y, Dantin 105/445y, Lyons 101/394y
PASSING: Jones 66-119/945y, 9TD, 55.5%
Lyons 57-122/945y, 9TD, 46.7%
RECEIVING: Hamilton 45/854y, Kavanaugh 18/223y, Keigley 14/170y
SCORING: Jay Michaelson (K) 72pts, Hamilton 54pts, Lyons 38pts

1972 9-2-1

31 Pacific	13 WR Gerald Keigley
42 Texas A&M	17 WR Jimmy LeDoux
27 Wisconsin	7 T Phil Murray / Steve Streete
12 Rice	6 G Tyler Lafauci
10 Kentucky	7 C Logan Killen
17 Mississippi	0 G Loyd Daniel
21 Alabama	16 T Jimmy Elkins / Randy Russell
28 Mississippi St.	35 TE Brad Boyd / Chuck Williamson
3 Florida	14 QB Bert Jones
9 Tulane	3 TB Chris Dantin / Brad Davis
17 Tennessee■	3 FB Jim Benglis / Ken Addy
	24 DL Binks Miciotto / Skip Cormier
	DL Steve Cassidy / Tommy Butoud
	DL John Wood
	DL Jim Gainey
	LB Gary Champagne / Bo Harris
	LB Warren Capone
	LB Pepper Rutland
	DB Mike Williams
	DB Norm Hodgins / Dale Cangelosi
	DB John Staggs / Joe Winkler
	DB Frank Racine / Rand Dennis

RUSHING: Dantin 165/707y, Davis 114/560y, Rogers 63/274y
PASSING: Jones 103-199/1446y, 14TD, 51.8%
RECEIVING: Keigley 27/433y, Boyd 22/298y, LeDoux 22/295y
SCORING: Rusty Jackson (K) 46pts, Keigley 42pts, Boyd & LeDoux 30pts

1973 9-3

17 Colorado	6 WR Ben Jones / Al Coffee
28 Texas &M	23 WR Norm Hodgins / Richard Romain
24 Rice	9 T Doug Boutte
24 Florida	3 G Russel Heald / Clay Cain
20 Auburn	6 C Logan Killen
28 Kentucky	21 G Tyler Lafauci
33 South Carolina	29 T Richard Brooks
51 Mississippi	14 TE Brad Boyd
26 Mississippi St.	7 QB Mike Miley / Billy Broussard
7 Alabama	21 TB Brad Davis / Steve Rogers
0 Tulane	14 FB Brian Zeringue / Ken Addy
9 Penn State■	16 DL Binks Miciotto
	DL Steve Cassidy
	DL A.J. Duhe
	DL Ron Daily
	LB Gary Champagne
	LB Warren Capone
	LB Bo Harris
	DB Mike Williams
	DB Dale Cangelosi
	DB Mike Pike
	DB Frank Racine / Rand Dennis

RUSHING: Davis 173/904y, Rogers 86/386y, Lora Hinton (TB) 63/253y
PASSING: Miley 60-107/978y, 7TD, 56.1%
RECEIVING: Boyd 16/259y, Hodgins 12/234y, Jones 11/198y
SCORING: Rusty Jackson (K) 46pts, Davis 44pts, Miley 24pts

1974 5-5-1

42 Colorado	14 WR Ben Jones
14 Texas A&M	21 WR Bruce Hemphill / Richard Romain
10 Rice	10 T Doug Boutte
14 Florida	24 G Steve Ferrer / Clay Cain
20 Tennessee	10 C Phil Moses / Greg Bienvenu
13 Kentucky	20 G Roy Stuart / Pat Donahue
24 Mississippi	0 T Richard Brooks
0 Alabama	30 TE Brad Boyd
6 Mississippi St.	7 QB Billy Broussard
24 Tulane	22 HB Steve Rogers / Terry Robiskie
35 Utah	10 HB Brad Davis
	DL Ron Daily / Lew Sibley
	DL Steve Cassidy
	DL A.J. Duhe
	DL Kenny Bordelon
	LB Terry Hill / Thielen Smith
	LB Steve Lelekacs
	LB Bo Harris
	DB David Cook / Clinton Burrell
	DB Jimmy Knecht
	DB Rand Dennis/Mike Pike/Mike Leonard
	DB Mike Williams

RUSHING: Davis 169/701y, Rogers 131/600y, Robiskie 85/384y
PASSING: Broussard 41-103/700y, TD, 39.8%
RECEIVING: Boyd 18/275y, Romain 11/190y, Jones 8/191y
SCORING: Davis 54pts, Rusty Jackson (K) 37pts, Broussard 30pts

1975 5-6

7 Nebraska	10 WR Mike Quintela / Bruce Hemphill
8 Texas A&M	39 WR Carl Otis Trimble / Robert Dow
16 Rice	13 T Paul Lanoux
6 Florida	34 G Dennis Gardner / Craig Duhe
10 Tennessee	24 C Greg Bienvenu / Jimmy Oustalet
17 Kentucky	4 G Roy Stuart / Steve Ferrer
24 South Carolina	6 T Rock Raiford / Doug Boutte
13 Mississippi	17 TE Bo Dunphy / Mitch Dinkle
10 Alabama	23 QB Pat Lyons
6 Miss St. F-W	16 TB Terry Robiskie / Charles Alexander
42 Tulane	6 FB Harrison Francis / Thad Minaldi
	DL Lew Sibley
	DL Steve Cassidy
	DL A.J. Duhe / Dan Alexander
	DL Kenny Bordelon
	LB Terry Hill
	LB Jon Streete
	LB Thielen Smith / Blake Whitlach
	DB Clinton Burrell
	DB Dave Cook / Steve Jackson
	DB Ronnie Barber
	DB Mike Leonard

RUSHING: Robiskie 214/764y, Alexander 108/301y, Francis 64/252y
PASSING: Lyons 72-168/946y, 4TD, 42.9%
RECEIVING: Trimble 16/177y, Dow 14/245y, Robiskie 13/92y
SCORING: Robiskie 62pts, Trimble 18pts, Mike Conway (K) 16pts

1976 7-3-1

6 Nebraska	6 WR Bruce Hemphill / Mike Quintela
28 Oregon State	11 WR Carl Otis Trimble / Robert Dow
31 Rice	0 T Paul Lanoux
23 Florida	28 G Craig Duhe / Dennis Gardner
33 Vanderbilt	20 C Jay Whitley
7 Kentucky	21 G Roy Stuart
45 Mississippi	0 T Robert Dugas
17 Alabama	28 TE Mitch Dinkle / Cliff Lane
13 Miss. St. F-W	21 QB Pat Lyons / Steve Ensminger
17 Tulane	7 TB Terry Robiskie / Charles Alexander
35 Utah	7 FB Thad Minaldi / Kelly Simmons
	DL Lew Sibley
	DL Dan Alexander
	DL A.J. Duhe
	DL Butch Knight
	LB John Adams (DL) / Steve Ripple
	LB Jon Streete
	LB Blake Whitlatch
	DB Clinton Burrell / Ronnie Barber
	DB Steve Jackson
	DB Jackie Casanova / Gary Blacketter
	DB Mike Leonard

RUSHING: Robiskie 224/1117y, Alexander 155/876y, Simmons 71/352y
PASSING: Lyons 54-133/685y, 3TD, 40.6%
RECEIVING: Trimble 14/211y, Hemphill 11/167y, Robiskie 11/109y
SCORING: Robiskie 72pts, Mike Conway (K) 57pts, Alexander 42pts

1977 8-4

21 Indiana	24 WR Carlos Carson
77 Rice	0 WR Mike Quintela / Marcus Quinn
36 Florida	14 T Chris Rich
28 Vanderbilt	15 G Craig Duhe
13 Kentucky	33 C Jay Whitley
56 Oregon	17 G William Johnson / Spencer Smith
28 Mississippi	21 T Robert Dugas
3 Alabama	24 TE Cliff Lane
27 Mississippi St.	24 QB Steve Ensminger / David Woodley
20 Tulane	17 TB Charles Alexander
66 Wyoming	17 FB Kelly Simmons
14 Stanford■	24 DL Lew Sibley / Jay Blass
	DL George Atiyeh / Benjy Thibodeaux
	DL Gary Radecker / Kent Broha
	DL John Adams
	LB George Cupit / Thad Minaldi
	LB Steve Ripple
	LB Bobby Moreau / Lyman White
	DB Willie Teal
	DB Bob Conn / Chris Williams
	DB Jackie Casanova
	DB Jackie Lawton / Gary Blacketter

RUSHING: Alexander 311/1686y, Simmons 68/387y, Jerry Murphree 84/328y
PASSING: Ensminger 71-159/952y, 9TD, 44.7%
RECEIVING: Carson 23/552y, Quintela 18/215y, Alexander 12/80y
SCORING: Alexander 104pts, Carson 60pts, Mike Conway (K) 46pts

1978 8-4

24 Indiana	17 WR Carlos Carson
13 Wake Forest	11 WR Mike Quintela
37 Rice	7 T Chris Rich
34 Florida	21 G William Johnson / John Watson
17 Georgia	24 C Jay Whitley
21 Kentucky	0 G Lou de Launay
30 Mississippi	8 T Robert Dugas
10 Alabama	31 TE Cliff Lane
14 Mississippi St.	16 QB David Woodley / Steve Ensminger
40 Tulane	21 TB Charles Alexander
24 Wyoming	17 FB LeRoid Jones / Hokie Gajan (TB)
15 Missouri■	20 DL Lyman White
	DL Kent Broha / Ivan Phillips
	DL George Atiyeh
	DL Benjy Thiboeaux / Gary Radecker
	DL John Adams
	LB George Cupit
	LB Thad Minaldi / Tommy Frizzell
	DB James Britt
	DB Chris Williams
	DB Willie Teal
	DB Marcus Quinn

RUSHING: Alexander 281/1172y, Gajan 130/611y, Woodley 97/398y
PASSING: Woodley 79-154/995y, 3TD, 51.3%
RECEIVING: Quintela 30/352y, Alexander 28/263y, Carson 27/563y
SCORING: Alexander 96pts, Mike Conway (K) 68pts, Woodley 32pts

1979 7-5

44 Colorado	0 WR Carlos Carson
47 Rice	3 WR Jerry Murphree / Tracy Porter
12 Southern Cal	17 T Charles McDuff / Dave Koch
20 Florida	3 G Tom Tully
14 Georgia	21 C John Ed Bradley
23 Kentucky	19 G John Watson
19 Florida State	24 T Eddie Stanton
28 Mississippi	24 TE Greg LaFleur / Robert DeLee
0 Alabama	3 QB Steve Ensminger / David Woodley
21 Mississippi St.	3 RB Hokie Gajan/LeRoid Jones/Jesse Myles
13 Tulane	24 FB Danny Soileau / Jude Hernandez
34 Wake Forest■	10 DL Lyman White
	DL Benjy Thibodeaux
	DL George Atiyeh
	DL Ivan Phillips
	DL John Adams
	LB Tommy Frizzell
	LB Jerry Hill
	DB James Britt / Chris Williams
	DB Willie Teal
	DB Robert DeRutte
	DB Marcus Quinn

RUSHING: Gajan 134/568y, Jones 78/349y, Myles 56/211y
PASSING: Ensminger 80-175/1168y, 5TD, 45.9%
RECEIVING: Carson 39/608y, Porter 23/338y, Jerry Murphree (TB) 19/221y
SCORING: Don Barthel (K) & Woodley 42pts, Myles 36pts

1980 7-4

0 Florida State	16 WR Tracy Porter
21 Kansas State	0 WR Orlando McDaniel / Lionel Wallis
23 Colorado	20 T Robert DeLee
7 Rice	17 G Tom Tully
24 Florida	7 C John Watson (G) / Mike Gambrell
21 Auburn	17 G Greg Raymond
21 Kentucky	10 T Dave Koch
38 Mississippi	16 TE Greg LaFleur / Malcolm Scott
7 Alabama	28 QB Alan Risher
31 Mississippi St.	55 RB Jesse Myles / Mike Montz
24 Tulane	7 FB Hokie Gajan / Gene Lang
	DL Benjy Thibodeaux
	DL George Atiyeh / Leonard Marshall
	DL Ramsey Dunbar
	LB Lyman White
	LB Lawrence Williams
	LB Al Richardson
	LB Rydell Malancon / Tim Joiner
	DB James Britt
	DB Alvin Thomas
	DB Chris Williams
	DB Marcus Quinn

RUSHING: Myles 76/403y, Risher 155/362y, Gajan 90/316y
PASSING: Risher 82-143/971y, 9TD, 57.3%
RECEIVING: LaFleur 18/243y, Gajan 18/131y, Porter 14/318y
SCORING: David Johnston (K) 42pts, Risher 36pts, Porter & Montz 24pts

1981 3-7-1

7 Alabama	24 WR Orlando McDaniel
9 Notre Dame	27 WR Mark Johnson
27 Oregon state	24 T Bob Smith
28 Rice	14 G Tom Tully
10 Florida	24 C Mike Gambrell
7 Auburn	19 G David Koch
24 Kentucky	10 T Lance Smith / Clint Berry
14 Florida State	38 TE Malcolm Scott
27 Mississippi	27 QB Alan Risher
9 Mississippi St.	17 RB Jesse Myles / Eric Martin
7 Tulane	48 FB Mike Montz / Gene Lang / Lester Dunn
	DL Ramsey Dardar
	DL Greg Bowser / Bill Elko
	DL Leonard Marshall
	LB Lawrence Williams
	LB Gregg Dubroc / Tim Joiner
	LB Al Richardson
	LB Rydell Malancon
	DB Alvin Thomas / James Britt
	DB Eugene Daniel / Alex Clark
	DB Jeffery Dale
	DB Tommy Boudreaux

RUSHING: Myles 72/292y, Lang 55/227y, Martin 78/290y
PASSING: Risher 150-238/1780y, 5TD, 63.0%
RECEIVING: McDaniel 41/719y, Scott 34/433y, Myles 17/131y
SCORING: David Johnston (K) 47pts, 4 tied w/ 18pts

1982 8-3-1

45 Oregon State	7 WR Eric Martin
52 Rice	13 WR Herman Fontenot / Eric Ellington
24 Florida	13 T Clint Berry / John Harrell
24 Tennessee	24 G Mike Turner
34 Kentucky	10 C Mike Gambrell / Tommy Campbell
14 South Carolina	6 G Kevin Langford
45 Mississippi	8 T Lance Smith
20 Alabama	10 TE Malcolm Scott
24 Mississippi St.	27 QB Alan Risher
55 Florida State	21 TB Garry James
28 Tulane	31 FB Dalton Hilliard (TB) / M. Montz /J. Myles
20 Nebraska■	21 DL Bill Elko
	DL Ramsey Darbar / Greg Bowser
	DL Leonard Marshall
	LB Tim Joiner / Gregg Dubroc
	LB Rydell Malancon
	LB Al Richardson
	LB Lawrence Williams
	DB James Britt
	DB Eugene Daniel
	DB Jeffery Dale
	DB Liffort Hobley

RUSHING: Hilliard 193/901y, James 145/710y, Montz 48/280y
PASSING: Risher 149-234/1834y, 17TD, 63.7%
RECEIVING: Martin 45/817y, Hilliard 31/368y, Scott 28/264y
SCORING: Hilliard 96pts, Juan Betanzos (K) 77pts, James 54pts

1983 4-7

35 Florida state	40 WR Eric Martin
24 Rice	10 WR Herman Fontenot
40 Washington	14 T Clint Berry
17 Florida	31 G Jeff Fordham / Curt Gore
6 Tennessee	20 C Mike Gambrell / Tommy Campbell
13 Kentucky	21 G Kevin Langford
20 South Carolina	6 T Lance Smith
24 Mississippi	27 TE Mitch Andrews
26 Alabama	32 QB Jeff Wickersham
26 Mississippi St.	45 TB Dalton Hilliard / Garry James
20 Tulane	7 FB Gene Lang
	DL Eric Kittok
	DL Roland Barbay
	DL Clarence Osborne
	LB Gregg Dubroc / Michael Brooks
	LB Shawn Burks / Ricky Chatman
	LB Toby Caston
	LB Rydell Malancon / Freddie Lewis
	DB Alex Clark
	DB Eugene Daniel
	DB Jeffery Dale
	DB Liffort Hobley

RUSHING: Hill 177/747y, James 110/478y, Lang 61/252y
PASSING: Wickersham 193-337/2542y, 7TD, 57.3%
RECEIVING: Martin 52/1064y, Hill 31/248y, James 29/266y
SCORING: Juan Betanzos (K) 67pts, Wickersham 44pts, James & Hill 36pts

1984 8-3-1

21 Florida	21 WR Eric Martin
47 Wichita State	7 WR Herman Fontenot
27 Arizona	26 T John Harrell
23 Southern Cal	3 G Curt Gore
34 Vanderbilt	27 C Tommy Campbell
36 Kentucky	10 G Kevin Langford
22 Notre Dame	30 T Lance Smith
32 Mississippi	29 TE Mitch Andrews
16 Alabama	14 QB Jeff Wickersham
14 Mississippi St.	16 TB Garry James
33 Tulane	15 RB Dalton Hilliard
10 Nebraska■	28 DL Tommy Clapp / John Hazard
	DL Henry Thomas / George Henriquez
	DL Karl Wilson
	LB Gregg Dubroc
	LB Shawn Burks
	LB Ricky Chatman / Toby Caston
	LB Michael Brooks
	DB Kevin Guidry
	DB Norman Jefferson / James Pierson
	DB Jeffery Dale
	DB Liffort Hobley

RUSHING: Hilliard 254/1268y, James 131/462y,
 Jean Batiste (RB) 32/145y
PASSING: Wickersham 178-312/2165y, 12TD, 57.1%
RECEIVING: Martin 47/668y, Fontenot 25/349y, Andrews 24/225y
SCORING: Hilliard 84pts, Juan Betanzos (K) & James 54pts

1985 9-2-1

23 North Carolina	13 WR Wendell Davis
17 Colorado State	3 WR Rogie Magee
0 Florida	20 T Curt Gore
49 Vanderbilt	7 G Keith Melancon
10 Kentucky	0 C Nacho Albergamo
14 Mississippi	0 G Eric Andolsek / Jimmy Goodrum
14 Alabama	14 T John Hazard / Ralph Norwood
17 Mississippi St.	15 TE Mitch Andrews
10 Notre Dame	7 QB Jeff Wickersham
31 Tulane	19 TB Garry James
35 East Carolina	15 RB Dalton Hilliard
7 Baylor■	21 DL Roland Barbay
	DL Henry Thomas
	DL Karl Wilson / Tommy Clapp
	LB Ron Sancho
	LB Shawn Burks
	LB Toby Caston
	LB Michael Brooks
	DB Kevin Guidry / Willie Bryant
	DB Norman Jefferson / James Pierson
	DB Chris Carrier / Mike DeWitt
	DB Steve Rehage

RUSHING: Hilliard 258/1134y, James 105/567y
PASSING: Wickersham 209-346/2145y, 5TD, 60.4%
RECEIVING: James 50/414y, Magee 35/473y, Hilliard 34/313y
SCORING: Hilliard 84pts, Ron Lewis (K) 42pts, James 36pts

1986 9-3

35 Texas A&M	17 WR Wendell Davis
12 Miami (Ohio)	21 WR Rogie Magee
28 Florida	17 T Ralph Norwood
23 Georgia	14 G Keith Melancon
25 Kentucky	16 C Nacho Albergamo
30 North Carolina	3 G Eric Andolsek
19 Mississippi	21 T John Hazard
14 Alabama	10 TE Brian Kinchen
47 Mississippi St.	0 QB Tommy Hodson
21 Notre Dame	19 TB Sammy Martin / Harvey Williams
37 Tulane	17 RB Victor Jones / Garland Jean Baptiste
15 Nebraska■	30 DL Roland Barbay
	DL Henry Thomas
	DL Karl Wilson
	LB Ron Sancho / Oliver Lawrence
	LB Nicky Hazard / Darren Malbrough
	LB Toby Caston
	LB Eric Hill / Michael Brooks
	DB James Pierson
	DB Kevin Guidry / Steve Rehage
	DB Chris Carrier
	DB Greg Jackson / Norman Jefferson

RUSHING: Williams 178/700y, Martin 114/556y,
 Jean Batiste 50/260y
PASSING: Hodson 175-288/2261y, 19TD, 60.8%
RECEIVING: Davis 80/1244y, Martin 28/339y, Williams 27/272y
SCORING: Davis 66pts, David Browndyke (K) 61pts,
 Williams 36pts

1987 10-1-1

17 Texas A&M	3 WR Wendell Davis
56 Cal-St Fullerton	12 WR Rogie Magee
49 Rice	16 T Ralph Norwood / Kenny Davidson
13 Ohio Satte	13 G Ruffin Rodrigue
13 Florida	10 C Nacho Albergamo
26 Georgia	23 G Eric Andolsek
34 Kentucky	9 T Jim Hubicz / Robert Packnett
42 Mississippi	13 TE Brian Kinchen / Ronnie Haliburton
10 Alabama	22 QB Tommy Hodson
34 Mississippi St.	14 TB Harvey Williams / Sammy Martin
41 Tulane	36 FB Victor Jones
30 South Carolina■	13 DL Tommy Clapp
	DL Darrell Phillips
	DL Karl Dunbar
	LB Ron Sancho
	LB Darren Malbrough
	LB Nicky Hazard
	LB Oliver Lawrence / Eric Hill
	DB Willie Bryant / James Pierson
	DB Greg Jackson
	DB Chris Carrier
	DB Kevin Guidry

RUSHING: Williams 154/1001y, Martin 98/576y,
 Eddie Fuller (TB) 50/306y
PASSING: Hodson 162-265/2125y, 15TD, 61.1%
RECEIVING: Davis 72/993y, Martin 29/393y, Magee 20/327y
SCORING: David Browndyke (K) 83pts, Williams 72pts,
 Davis 42pts

1988 8-4

27 Texas A7M	0 WR Alvin Lee
34 Tennessee	9 WR Tony Moss
33 Ohio State	36 T Ralph Norwood / Jim Hubicz
6 Florida	19 G Ruffin Rodrigue / Steve Reading
7 Auburn	6 C Todd Coutee / Blake Miller
15 Kentucky	12 G Blake Miller / Jim Arnold
31 Mississippi	20 T Robert Packnett / Roger Hutchinson
19 Alabama	18 TE Ronnie Haliburton / Willie Williams
20 Mississippi St.	3 QB Tom Hodson / Mickey Guidry
3 Miami	44 TB Eddie Fuller / Slip Watkins
44 Tulane	14 FB Victor Jones / Jay Egloff
10 Syracuse■	23 DL Karl Dunbar
	DL Darrell Phillips
	DL Clint James / Marc Boutte
	LB Verge Ausberry / Mike Murla
	LB Ron Sancho / Mike Herbert
	LB Rudy Harmon / Eric Middleton
	LB Eric Hill
	DB Jimmy Young
	DB Jamie Bice / Corey Raymond
	DB Greg Jackson / Tony Houston
	DB Mike Mayes

RUSHING: Fuller 153/647y, Watkins 56/173y,
 Calvin Windom (TB) 45/154y
PASSING: Hodson 154-293/2074y, 13TD, 52.6%
RECEIVING: Moss 55/957y, Lee 40/537y, Fuller 32/375y
SCORING: David Browndyke (K) 77pts, Fuller 42pts, Moss 42pts

1989 4-7

16 Texas A&M	28 WR Alvin Lee / Todd Kinchen
21 Florida State	31 WR Tony Moss
57 Ohio Univ.	6 T Andy Martin / Jim Hubicz
13 Florida	16 G Ruffin Rodrigue
6 Auburn	10 C Blake Miller
21 Kentucky	27 G Jim Hubicz / Chris Truax
39 Tennessee	45 T Roger Hutchinson
35 Mississippi	30 TE Ronnie Haliburton
16 Alabama	32 QB Tom Hodson
44 Mississippi St.	20 TB Eddie Fuller / Harvey Williams
27 Tulane	7 FB Jay Egloff / Victor Jones
	DL Karl Dunbar
	DL Marc Boutte
	DL Clint James
	LB Oliver Lawrence
	LB Verge Ausberry
	LB Juan Cendoya
	LB Nigel Ventress
	DB Jimmy Young
	DB Corey Raymond
	DB Tony Houston
	DB Tommy Fabacher

RUSHING: Fuller 140/649y, Calvin Windom (TB) 57/209y,
 Williams 51/206y
PASSING: Hodson 183-317/2655y, 22TD, 57.7%
RECEIVING: Moss 59/934y, Fuller 38/477y, Kinchen 25/396y
SCORING: David Browndyke (K) 71pts, Fuller 60pts, Moss 56pts

1990 5-6

18 Georgia	13 WR Todd Kinchen
35 Miami (Oho)	7 WR Wesley Jacob / Marcus Carter
21 Vanderbilt	24 T Raymond Smoot (G) / Kevin Mawae
17 Texas A&M	8 G Darron Landry
8 Florida	34 C Blake Miller
30 Kentucky	20 G Chris Truax
3 Florida State	42 T Andy Martin
10 Mississippi	19 TE Harold Bishop
3 Alabama	24 QB Sol Graves / Chad Loup
22 Mississippi St.	34 TB Harvey Williams
16 Tulane	13 FB Sammy Seamster
	DL Leonard Harris / Scott Wharton
	DL Clayton Mouton
	DL Marc Boutte
	LB Mike Hewitt
	LB Anthony Williams
	LB David Walkup
	LB Roovelroe Swan
	DB Wayne Williams / Ray Adams
	DB Corey Raymond / Derril McCorvey
	DB Vincent Fuller
	DB Anthony Marshall

RUSHING: Williams 205/953y, Calvin Windom (TB) 56/228y,
 Seamster 36/161y
PASSING: Loup 75-141/975y, 3TD, 53.2%
RECEIVING: Kinchen 34/660y, Carter 24/299y, Williams 15/152y
SCORING: Pedro Suarez (K) 59pts, Williams 50pts, Carter 24pts

1991 5-6

10 Georgia	31 WR Todd Kinchen
7 Texas A&M	45 WR Wesley Jacob
16 Vanderbilt	14 T Ronnie Simnicht
0 Florida	16 G Kevin Mawae
70 Arkansas state	14 C Frank Godfrey
29 Kentucky	26 G Darron Landry
16 Florida State	27 T Bryan Madden / Andy Martin
25 Mississippi	22 TE Anthony Williams / Harold Bishop
17 Alabama	20 QB Chad Loup / Jesse Daigle
19 Mississippi St.	28 TB Vincent Fuller
39 Tulane	20 FB Leo Abel / Germaine Williams
	DL Clayton Mouton
	DL Scott Wharton
	DL Marc Boutte
	LB Mike Hewitt / Shawn King
	LB Ricardo Washington
	LB Reggie Walker
	LB Corey White
	DB Wayne Williams
	DB Corey Raymond
	DB Anthony Marshall / Robby Green
	DB Derriel McCorvey

RUSHING: Beckman 81/397y, Fuller 86/341y, Jacquet 39/220y
PASSING: Loup 102-174/1181y, 9TD, 58.6%
RECEIVING: Kinchen 53/855y, Fuller 24/227y, Jacob 22/334y
SCORING: Pedro Suarez (K) 59pts, Kinchen 42pts, Fuller 24pts

1992 2-9

22 Texas A&M	31 WR Scott Ray
24 Mississippi St.	3 WR Wesley Jacob
28 Auburn	30 T Kevin Mawae
14 Colorado State	17 G Darron Landry
0 Tennessee	20 C Frank Godfrey
21 Florida	28 G Ronnie Simnicht
25 Kentucky	27 T Bryan Madden
0 Mississippi	32 TE Harold Bishop
11 Alabama	31 QB Jamie Howard / Chad Loup
24 Tulane	12 TB Robert Davis
6 Arkansas	30 FB Odell Beckham / Robert Toomer
	DL Nate Miller
	DL Bo Davis
	DL Clayton Mouton / John Morgan
	LB James Gillyard
	LB Ricardo Washington/ Anthony Williams
	LB David Walkup
	LB Roovelroe Swan / Corey White
	DB Carlton Buckels
	DB Ray Adams
	DB Ivory Hilliard
	DB Derriel McCorvey

RUSHING: Davis 123/527y, Beckman 42/234y, Toomer 49/186y
PASSING: Howard 101-200/1349y, 5TD, 50.5%
RECEIVING: Ray 38/534y, Jacob 38/511y, Bishop 17/177y
SCORING: Toomer 32pts, Williams 24pts, Pedro Suarez (K) 23pts

1993 5-6

0 Texas A&M	24 WR Scott Ray / Brett Bech
18 Mississippi St.	16 WR Shedrick Wilson / Eddie Kennison
10 Auburn	34 T Ross Setters / Tom Turner
20 Tennessee	42 G Ben Bordelon / Mark King
38 Utah State	17 C Kevin Mawae
3 Florida	58 G Ronnie Simnicht
17 Kentucky	35 T Marcus Price
19 Mississippi	17 TE Harold Bishop / Chris Hill
17 Alabama	13 QB Jamie Howard / Chad Loup
24 Tulane	10 TB Jay Johnson
24 Arkansas	42 FB Robert Turner / Germaine Williams
	DL James Gillyard / Mike Hewitt
	DL Nate Miller / Robert Miller
	DL Ike Pullett / William Crowell
	DL Corey White / Gabe Northern
	LB Robert Deshotel
	LB Mike Calais
	LB Ricardo Washington
	DB Rodney Young
	DB Tory James
	DB Anthony Marshall
	DB Ivory Hilliard / Talvi Crawford

RUSHING: Johnson 106/558y, Toomer 82/295y, Williams 58/226y
PASSING: Howard 106-248/1319y, 7TD, 42.7%
RECEIVING: Bech 30/429y, Kennison 28/466y, Ray 25/366y
SCORING: Andre Lafleur (K) 59pts, Johnson 36pts, Toomer 24pts

1994 4-7

13 Texas A&M	18 WR Brett Bech
44 Mississippi St.	24 WR Eddie Kennison / Sheddrick Wilson
26 Auburn	30 T Marcus Price
17 South Carolina	18 G Mark King
18 Florida	42 C Mike Blanchard
17 Kentucky	13 G Adam Perry
21 Mississippi	34 T Sean Wells
17 Alabama	35 TE David LaFleur
19 Southern Miss	20 QB Jamie Howard / Melvin Hill
49 Tulane	25 TB Robert Toomer / Jermaine Sharp
30 Arkansas	12 FB/WR Andre Guerin / Chris Hill
	DL James Gillyard
	DL Nate Miller / Pete Ballis
	DL David Carmona / Chuck Wiley
	DL Gabe Northern
	LB Bobby Williams / Pat Rogers
	LB Mike Calais / Kimojha Brooks
	LB Allen Stansberry
	DB Rodney Young
	DB Tory James
	DB Ivory Hilliard
	DB Gary Pegues / Clarence Lenton

RUSHING: Sharp 135/750y, Toomer 150/491y,
Kevin Franklin (TB) 36/137y
PASSING: Howard 140-274/1997y, 13TD, 51.1%
Hill 35-59/429y, 4TD, 59.3%
RECEIVING: Bech 45/772y, Wilson 30/334y, Kennison 25/349y
SCORING: Andre LaFleur (K) 57pts, Kennison & Sharp 36pts

1995 7-4-1

17 Texas A&M	33 WR Eddie Kennison
34 Mississippi St.	16 WR Sheddrick Wilson / Chris Hill
12 Auburn	6 T Ben Bordelon
52 Rice	7 G Mark King
20 South Carolina	20 C Marcus Carmouche / Todd McClure
10 Florida	28 G Alan Faneca
16 Kentucky	24 T Sean Wells
49 North Texas	7 TE David LaFleur
3 Alabama	10 QB Jamie Howard / Herb Tyler
38 Mississippi	9 TB Kevin Faulk / Kendall Cleveland
28 Arkansas	0 FB Nicky Savoie
45 Michigan State■	26 DL Gabe Northern
	DL Anthony McFarland
	DL Chuck Wiley
	DL James Gillyard
	LB Pat Rogers
	LB Robert Deshotel
	LB Allen Stansberry
	DB Tory James
	DB Denard Walker / Troy Twillie
	DB Clarence Lenton
	DB Talvi Crawford / Greg Hill

RUSHING: Faulk 174/852y, Cleveland 137/562y
PASSING: Howard 112-212/1493y, 9TD, 52.8%
Tyler 45-69/589y, 5TD, 65.2%
RECEIVING: Wilson 60/845y, Kennison 45/739y, Hill 12/126y
SCORING: Andre LaFleur (K) 73pts, Cleveland 66pts, Faulk 42pts

1996 10-2

35 Houston	34 WR Larry Foster
19 Auburn	15 WR Tyrone Frazier
63 New Mexico St.	7 T Sean Wells
35 Vanderbilt	0 G Adam Perry
13 Florida	56 C Todd McClure
41 Kentucky	14 G Alan Faneca
28 Mississippi St.	20 T Ben Bordelon
0 Alabama	26 TE David LaFleur / Nicky Savoie
39 Mississippi	7 QB Herb Tyler
35 Tulane	17 TB Kevin Faulk / Rondell Mealey
17 Arkansas	7 FB Robert Tyler
10 Clemson■	7 DL Theo Williams
	DL Anthony McFarland
	DL Chuck Wiley
	DL Mike Sutton
	LB Pat Rogers
	LB Charles Smith
	LB Allen Stansberry
	DB Denard Walker
	DB Cedric Donaldson
	DB Mark Roman
	DB Greg Hill

RUSHING: Faulk 248/1282y, Mealey 603y
PASSING: Tyler 109-187/1688y, 7TD, 58.3%
RECEIVING: LaFleur 30/439y, Foster 26/446y, Frazier 17/336y
SCORING: Faulk 84pts, Mealey 60pts

1997 9-3

55 UTEP	3 WR Abram Booty / Tyrone Frazier
24 Mississippi St.	9 WR Larry Foster
28 Auburn	31 T Al Jackson
56 Akron	0 G Adam Perry
7 Vanderbilt	6 C Todd McClure
28 Florida	21 G Alan Faneca
21 Mississippi	36 T Trey Langley / Louis Williams
63 Kentucky	28 TE Furnell Hankton / Joe Domingeaux
27 Alabama	0 QB Herb Tyler
6 Notre Dame	24 TB Kevin Faulk / Cecil Collins / R. Mealey
31 Arkansas	21 FB Tommy Banks / Robert Tyler
27 Notre Dame■	9 DL Arnold Miller / Mike Sutton
	DL Chuck Wiley
	DL Anthony McFarland / Johnny Mitchell
	DL Kenny Mixon
	LB Charles Smith
	LB Joe Wesley
	DB Chris Cummings
	DB Cedric Donaldson / Troy Twillie
	DB Clarence LeBlanc
	DB Mark Roman
	DB Raion Hill / Chris Beard

RUSHING: Faulk 205/1144y, Mealey 112/664y, Collins 72/596y
PASSING: Tyler 127-209/1581y, 10TD, 60.8%
RECEIVING: Foster 43/579y, Booty 35/550y, Faulk 16/93y
SCORING: Faulk 90pts, Tyler 44pts, Mealey 42pts

1998 4-7

42 Arkansas State	6 WR Abram Booty
31 Auburn	19 WR Larry Foster
53 Idaho	20 T Louis Williams
27 Georgia	28 G Ryan Thomassie
10 Florida	22 C Todd McClure
36 Kentucky	39 G Trey Langley / Al Jackson
41 Mississippi St.	6 T Brandon Winey
31 Mississippi	37 TE Kyle Kipps
16 Alabama	22 QB Herb Tyler
36 Notre Dame	39 TB Kevin Faulk / Rondell Meaney
14 Arkansas	41 FB/WR Tommy Banks/Reggie Robinson
	DL Johnny Mitchell
	DL Anthony McFarland
	DL Jarvis Green / Kendrick Allen
	LB Arnold Miller / Theo Williams
	LB Joe Wesley
	LB Thomas Dunson / Charles Smith
	LB Aaron Adams / Jamal Hill
	DB Fred Booker / Chris Cummings
	DB Robert Davis / Damien Woods
	DB Mark Roman
	DB Clarence LeBlanc / Raion Hill

RUSHING: Faulk 229/1279y, Mealey 68/334y, Tyler 85/182y
PASSING: Tyler 153-250/2018y, 18TD, 61.2%
RECEIVING: Foster 56/722y, Booty 54/779y, Faulk 22/287y
SCORING: Faulk 102pts, Tyler 46pts, Mealey 36pts

1999 3-8

29 San Jose State	21 WR Jerel Myles
52 North Texas	0 WR Reggie Robinson / Abram Booty
7 Auburn	41 T Louis Williams
22 Georgia	23 G Al Jackson / Sam Forehand
10 Florida	31 C Jason Underwood
5 Kentucky	23 G Jason Baggett / Trey Langley
16 Mississippi St.	17 T Brandon Winey
23 Mississippi	42 TE Joe Domingeaux /Jamal Pack /K. Kipps
17 Alabama	23 QB Josh Booty
7 Houston	20 TB Rondell Mealey / Domanick Davis
35 Arkansas	10 FB Tommy Banks
	DL Johnny Mitchell
	DL Muskingum Barnes / Byron Dawson
	DL Kareem Mitchell
	LB Jarvis Green (DL) / Jeremy Lawrence
	LB Charles Smith / Bradie James
	LB Trev Faulk / Thomas Dunson
	LB Norman LeJeune / Lionel Thomas
	DB Robert Davis / Mark Roman
	DB Fred Booker
	DB Ryan Clark
	DB Clarence LeBlanc / Shane O'Toole

RUSHING: Mealey 170/637y, Davis 64/274y
PASSING: J. Booty 162-333/1830y, 7TD, 48.6%
RECEIVING: Myers 64/854y, A. Booty 26/374y, Robinson 25/362y
SCORING: Mealey 54pts, John Corbello (K) 48pts, 3 tied w/ 18pts

2000 8-4

58 W. Carolina	0 WR Josh Reed
28 Houston	13 WR Reggie Robinson / Jerel Myers
17 Auburn	34 T Rodney Reed / Brad Smalling
10 UAB	13 G Trey Langley / Dwayne Pierce
38 Tennessee	31 C Lou Williams
9 Florida	41 G Rob Sale
34 Kentucky	0 T Brandon Winey
45 Mississippi St.	38 TE Robert Royal / Joe Domingeaux
30 Alabama	28 QB Josh Booty / Rohan Davey
20 Mississippi	9 TB LaBrandon Toefield / Domanick Davis
3 Arkansas	14 FB Tommy Banks
28 Georgia Tech■	14 DL Kareem Mitchell / Kyle Kipps
	DL Howard Green / Chad Lavalais
	DL Muskingum Barnes / Byron Dawson
	DL Jarvis Green / Kenderick Allen
	LB Bradie James
	LB Trev Faulk
	LB Jeremy Lawrence
	DB Fred Booker / Damien James
	DB Demetrius Hookfin / Robert Davis
	DB Ryan Clark
	DB Lionel Thomas

RUSHING: Toefield 165/682y, Davis 123/445y
PASSING: Booty 145-290/2121y, 17TD, 50%
RECEIVING: Reed 65/1127y, Robinson 31/391y, Myers 29/347y
SCORING: John Corbello (K) 63pts, Reed 60pts, Royal &
Davis 30pts

2001 10-3

48 Tulane	17 WR Jerel Myers
31 Utah State	14 WR Josh Reed
18 Tennessee	26 T Rodney Reed
15 Florida	44 G Stephen Peterman
29 Kentucky	25 C Ben Wilkerson / Rob Sale (G)
42 Mississippi St.	0 G Dwayne Pierce
24 Mississippi	35 T Jason Baggett
35 Alabama	21 TE Robert Royal
30 M. Tennessee	14 TE/WR Joe Domingeaux / Michael Clayton
41 Arkansas	38 QB Rohan Davey
27 Auburn	14 TB LaBrandon Toefield / Domanick Davis
31 Tennessee□	20 DL Kyle Kipps / Kenderick Allen
47 Illinois■	34 DL Byron Dawson / Muskingum Barnes
	DL Chad Lavalais / Howard Green
	DL Jarvis Green
	LB Bradie James
	LB Trev Faulk
	LB Jeremy Lawrence
	DB Damien James / Erin Damond
	DB Demetrius Hookfin
	DB Ryan Clark
	DB Lionel Thomas / Norman LeJeune

RUSHING: Toefield 230/992y, Davis 75/406y,
Devery Henderson (TB) 47/273y
PASSING: Davey 217-367/3347y, 18TD, 59.1%
RECEIVING: Reed 94/1740y, Clayton 47/754y, Myers 39/461y
SCORING: Toefield 114pts, John Corbello (K) 83pts, Reed 46pts

2002 8-5

8 Virginia Tech	26 WR Jerel Myers
35 Citadel	10 WR Michael Clayton
33 Miami (Ohio)	7 T Andrew Whitworth
31 Mississippi St.	13 G Stephen Peterman
48 La-Lafayette	0 C Ben Wilkerson / John Young
36 Florida	7 G Rob Sale
38 South Carolina	14 T Rodney Reed
7 Auburn	31 TE Eric Edwards / Demetri Robinson
33 Kentucky	30 QB Matt Mauck / Marcus Randall
0 Alabama	31 TB Dominick Davis / LaBrandon Toefield
14 Mississippi.	13 FB/WR Solomon Lee / Reggie Robinson
20 Arkansas	21 DL Marcus Spears / Melvin Oliver
20 Texas■	35 DL Kenderick Allen / Byron Dawson
	DL Chad Lavalais
	DL Marquise Hill / Bryce Wyatt
	LB Lionel Turner / Cameron Vaughn
	LB Bradie James
	LB Jeremy Lawrence
	DB Randall Gay
	DB Demetrius Hookfin / Corey Webster
	DB Jack Hunt / Damien James
	DB Norman LeJeune

RUSHING: Davis 193/931y, Toefield 116/475y,
Joseph Addai (FB) 80/438y
PASSING: Randall 87-181/1173y, 7TD, 48.1%
Mauck 63-130/782y, 9TD, 48.5%
RECEIVING: Clayton 57/749y, Henderson 23/447y, Myers 17/181y
SCORING: John Corbello (K) 85pts, Henderson & Davis 48pts

2003 13-1

49 UL-Monroe	7 WR Devery Henderson
59 Arizona	13 WR Michael Clayton
35 W. Illinois	7 T Andrew Whitworth
17 Georgia	10 G Nate Livings / Rudy Niswanger
41 Mississippi State	6 C Ben Wilkerson
7 Florida	19 G Stephen Peterman / Terrell McGill
33 South Carolina	7 T Rodney Reed
31 Auburn	7 TE Eric Edwards
49 Louisiana Tech	10 QB Matt Mauck
27 Alabama	2 RB Justin Vincent / Joseph Addai
17 Mississippi	14 FB/WR David Jones (TE) / Skyler Green
55 Arkansas	24 DL Marcus Spears
34 Georgia□	13 DL Kyle Williams / Bryce Wyatt
21 Oklahoma■	14 DL Chad Lavalais
	DL Marquise Hill / Melvin Oliver
	LB Eric Alexander
	LB Lionel Turner
	LB Cameron Vaughn / Randall Gay
	DB Corey Webster
	DB Travis Daniels
	DB LaRon Landry / Ronnie Prude
	DB Jack Hunt / Jesse Daniels

RUSHING: Vincent 154/1001y, Addai 114/520y,
Alley Broussard (RB) 85/389y
PASSING: Mauck 229-358/2825y, 28TD, 64%
RECEIVING: Clayton 78/1079y, Henderson 53/861y,
Green 48/519y
SCORING: Henderson 66pts, Clayton & Vincent 60pts

2004 9-3

22 Oregon State	21 WR Craig Davis / Skyler Green
53 Arkansas State	3 WR Dwayne Bowe / Early Doucet
9 Auburn	10 WR David Jones
51 Mississippi St.	0 T Andrew Whitworth
16 Georgia	45 G Will Arnold / Terrell McGill
24 Florida	21 C Ben Wilkerson
24 Troy State	20 G Rudy Niswanger
24 Vanderbilt	7 T Nate Livings / Paris Hodges
26 Alabama	10 TE/FB Keith Zinger / Jacob Hester
27 Mississippi	24 QB Marcus Randall / JaMarcus Russell
43 Arkansas	14 RB Alley Broussard / Joseph Addai
25 Iowa■	30 DL Marcus Spears
	DL Claude Wroten / Glen Dorsey
	DL Kyle Williams
	DL Melvin Oliver / Kirston Pittman
	LB Lionel Turner
	LB Cameron Vaughn
	LB Kenneth Hollis / Ali Highsmith
	DB Corey Webster / Ronnie Prude
	DB Travis Daniels
	DB LaRon Landry
	DB Jesse Daniels

RUSHING: Broussard 142/867y, Addai 101/680y,
Justin Vincent (RB) 76/322y
PASSING: Randall 102-162/1269y, 9TD, 63%
Russell 73-144/1053y, 9TD, 50.7%
RECEIVING: Davis 43/659y, Bowe 39/597y, Addai 26/294y
SCORING: Broussard 60pts, Chris Jackson (K) 48pts, Addai 42pts

2005 11-2

35 Arizona State	31 WR Dwayne Bowe / Skyler Green
27 Tennessee	30 WR Craig Davis / Early Doucet
37 Mississippi St.	7 T Andrew Whitworth
34 Vanderbilt	6 G McGill / Arnold
21 Florida	17 C Rudy Niswanger
20 Auburn	17 G Nate Livings / Brett Helms
56 North Texas	3 T Brian Johnson
24 Appalachian St.	0 TE Keith Zinger / David Jones
16 Alabama	13 QB JaMarcus Russell / Matt Flynn
40 Mississippi	7 TB Joseph Addai / Justin Vincent
19 Arkansas	17 FB Kevin Steltz
14 Georgia□	34 DL Chase Pittman
40 Miami■	3 DL Kyle Williams
	DL Claude Wroten / Glenn Dorsey
	DL Melvin Oliver
	LB Ali Highsmith / E.J. Kuale
	LB Cameron Vaughn
	LB/DB Kenneth Hollis / Jonathan Zenon
	DB Chevis Jackson / Daniel Francis
	DB Ronnie Prude
	DB LaRon Landry
	DB Jesse Daniels / Craig Stelz

RUSHING: Addai 187/911y, Vincent 121/488y,
Shyrone Carey (TB) 59/234y
PASSING: Russell 188-311/2443y, 15TD, 60.5%
RECEIVING: Bowe 41/710y, Davis 35/559y, Green 32/268y
SCORING: Addai 60pts, Colt David (K) 57pts, Bowe 54pts

2006 11-2

45 UL-Lafayette	3 WR Dwayne Bowe
45 Arizona	3 WR Craig Davis / Early Doucet
3 Auburn	7 T Ciron Black
49 Tulane	7 G Herman Johnson / Will Arnold
48 Mississippi St.	17 C Brett Helms / Ryan Miller
10 Florida	23 G Brian Johnson
49 Kentucky	0 T Peter Dyakowski
38 Fresno State	6 TE Richard Dickson / Keith Zinger
28 Tennessee	24 QB JaMarcus Russell
28 Alabama	14 TB Justin Vincent / Keiland Williams
23 Mississippi	20 FB Jacob Hester
31 Arkansas	26 DL Tyson Jackson / Ryan Willis
41 Notre Dame■	14 DL Charles Alexander / Marlon Favorite
	DL Glenn Dorsey / Ricky Jean-Francios
	DL Chase Pittman
	LB/DB Darry Beckwith / Daniel Francis
	LB Luke Sanders / Jacob Cutrera
	LB Ali Highsmith
	DB Jonathan Zenon
	DB Chevis Jackson
	DB LaRon Landry
	DB Jesse Daniels / Craig Steltz

RUSHING: Hester 94/94/440y, Williams 76/436y,
Alley Broussard 74/281y
PASSING: Russell 232-342/3129y, 28TD, 67.8%
RECEIIVNG: Bowe 65/990y, Doucet 59/772y, Davis 56/836y
SCORING: Colt David (K) 74pts, Bowe 72pts, Doucet 60pts

2007 12-2

45 Mississippi St.	0 WR Brandon LaFell/ Demetrius Byrd
48 Virginia Tech	7 WR Early Doucet / Jared Mitchell
44 Middle Tenn.	0 WR/FB Chris Mitchell/Quinn Johnson
28 South Carolina	16 T Ciron Black
34 Tulane	9 G Herman Johnson
28 Florida	24 C Brett Helms
37 Kentucky	43 G Lyle Hitt / Ryan Miller
30 Auburn	24 T Carnell Stewart
41 Alabama	34 TE Keith Zinger / Richard Dickson
58 Louisiana Tech	10 QB Matt Flynn / Ryan Perrilloux
41 Mississippi	24 TB Jacob Hester / Keiland Williams
48 Arkansas	50 DL Tyson Jackson
21 Tennessee□	14 DL Glenn Dorsey / Al Woods
38 Ohio State■	24 DL Marlon Favorite / Drake Nevis
	DL Kirston Pittman
	LB/DB Luke Sanders / Danny McCray
	LB Darry Beckwith / Jacob Cutrera
	LB Ali Highsmith / Chad Jones
	DB Jonathan Zenon
	DB Chevis Jackson
	DB Curtis Taylor
	DB Craig Steltz

RUSHING: Hester 225/1103y, Williams 70/478y,
Trindon Holliday (TB) 53/364y
PASSING: Flynn 202-359/2407y, 21TD, 56.3%
Perrilloux 51-75/694y, 8TD, 68%
RECEIVING: Doucet 57/525y, LaFell 50/656y, Byrd 35/621y
SCORING: Colt David (K) 147pts, Hester 78pts, Williams,
Byrd & Charles Scott (TB) 42pts

2008 8-5

41 Appalachian St.	13 WR Brandon LaFell
41 North Texas	3 WR Demetrius Byrd / Terrance Toliver
26 Auburn	21 T Ciron Black
34 Mississippi St.	24 G Herman Johnson
21 Florida	51 C Brett Helms / Ryan Miller
24 South Carolina	17 G Lyle Hitt
38 Georgia	52 T Joseph Barksdale
35 Tulane	10 TE Richard Dickson
21 Alabama	27 QB Jarrett Lee / Andrew Hatch
40 Troy	31 TB Charles Scott / Keiland Williams
13 Mississippi	3 FB/WR Quinn Johnson / Chris Mitchell
30 Arkansas	31 DL Tyson Jackson
38 Georgia Tech■	3 DL Charles Alexander / R. Jean-Francois
	DL Marlon Favorite
	DL Kirston Pittman / Tremaine Johnson
	LB Darry Beckwith / Jacob Cutrera
	LB/DB Perry Riley / Chad Jones
	LB/DB Kelvin Sheppard / Danny McCray
	DB Chris Hawkins
	DB Jai Eugene / Patrick Peterson
	DB Curtis Taylor
	DB Harry Coleman

RUSHING: Scott 202/1109y, Williams 78/375y,
Richard Murphy (RB) 42/175y
PASSING: Lee 143-269/1873y, 14TD, 53.2%
Hatch 20-45/282y, 2TD, 55.6%
Jordan Jefferson (QB) 20-48/277y, 3TD, 41.7%
RECEIVING: LaFell 61/903y, Byrd 34/503y, Dickson 27/274y
SCORING: Scott 90pts, Colt David (K) 83pts, LaFell 48pts

2009 9-4

31 Washington	23 WR Terrance Tolliver / Reuben Randle
23 Vanderbilt	9 WR Brandon LaFell
31 La.-Lafayette	3 T Ciron Black
30 Mississippi State	26 G Josh Dworaczyk
20 Georgia	13 C T-Bob Hebert / P.J. Lonergan
3 Florida	13 G Lyle Hitt
31 Auburn	10 T Joe Barksdale
42 Tulane	0 TE Richard Dickson / Mitch Joseph
15 Alabama	24 QB Jordan Jefferson / Jarrett Lee
24 Louisiana Tech	16 TB Charles Scott/K. Williams/Stevan Ridley
23 Mississippi	23 FB/WR Thomas Parson / Chris Mitchell
33 Arkansas	30 DL Rahim Alem / Lavar Edwards
17 Penn State■	19 DL Al Woods
	DL Charles Alexander / Drake Nevis
	DL Lazarius Levingston/Chancey Aghayere
	LB Perry Riley
	LB Kelvin Sheppard / Jacob Cutrera
	LB Harry Coleman
	DB Patrick Peterson
	DB Chris Hawkins / Jai Eugene
	DB Chad Jones / Karnell Hatcher
	DB Brandon Taylor / Danny McCray

RUSHING: Scott 116/542y, Williams 70/368y,
Russell Shepard (QB) 45/277y
PASSING: Jefferson 112-296/2166y, 17TD, 61.5%
Lee 16-40/197y, 2TD, 40.0%
RECEIVING: LaFell 57/792y, Toliver 53/735y, Dickson 21/157y
SCORING: Josh Jasper (K) 85pts, LaFell 68pts, Scott 30pts

2010 11-2

30 North Carolina	24 WR Terrence Toliver
27 Vanderbilt	3 WR Rueben Randle / Deangelo Peterson
29 Mississippi State	7 T Joe Barksdale / Greg Shaw
20 West Virginia	14 G Josh Dworaczyk / Will Blackwell
16 Tennessee	14 C P.J. Lonergan
33 Florida	29 G T-Bob Hebert / Josh Williford
32 McNeese State	10 T Alex Hurst / Chris Faulk
7 Auburn	24 TE Chase Clement / Mitch Joseph
24 Alabama	21 QB Jordan Jefferson / Jarrett Lee
51 La.-Monroe	0 RB Stevan Ridley / Michael Ford
43 Mississippi	36 FB/WR James Stampley / Russell Shepard
23 Arkansas	31 DL Kendrick Adams / Chancey Aghayere
41 Texas A&M■	24 DL Lazarius Levingston / Michael Brockers
	DL Drake Nevis / Barkevious Mingo
	DL Lavar Edwards / Sam Montgomery
	LB Stefoin Francois
	LB Kelvin Sheppard
	LB Ryan Baker / Lamin Barrow
	DB Morris Claiborne / Jai Eugene
	DB Patrick Peterson / Ron Brooks
	DB Kornell Hatcher / Tyrann Mathieu
	DB Brandon Taylor/ Eric Reid/Craig Loston

RUSHING: Ridley 249/1147y, Jefferson 123/450y, Ford 45/244y
PASSING: Jefferson 118-209/1411y, 7TD, 56.5%
Lee 54-89/573y, 2TD, 60.7%
RECEIVING: Tolliver 41/579y, Randle 33/544y, Shepard 33/254y
SCORING: Josh Jasper (K) 120pts, Ridley 90pts, Jefferson 44pts

MARYLAND

University of Maryland (Founded 1856)
College Park, Maryland
Nickname: Terrapins or Terps
Colors: Red, Black, Yellow Gold, and White
Stadium: Byrd (1950) 51,500
Conference Affiliation: Atlantic Coast (Charter member 1953-present)

CAREER RUSHING YARDS	Attempts	Yards
LaMont Jordan (1997-2000)	807	4147
Charlie Wysocki (1978-81)	769	3317
Steve Atkins (1975-78)	625	2971
Lance Ball (2004-07)	549	2487
Bruce Perry (1999, 2001-03)	448	2424
Rick Badanjek (1982-85)	521	2417
Da'Rel Scott (2007-10)	430	2401
Louis Carter (1972-74)	561	2266
Alvin Blount (1983-86)	426	2158
Willie Joyner (1980-83)	437	2140

CAREER PASSING YARDS	Comp.-Att.	Yards
Scott Milanovich (1992-95)	650-982	7301
Chris Turner (2007-09)	547-918	6543
Boomer Esiason (1981-83)	461-850	6259
Scott McBrien (2002-03)	335-598	5169
Sam Hollenbach (2003-06)	417-679	5139
Neil O'Donnell (1987-89)	387-658	4989
Dan Henning (1985-87)	353-641	4560
Brian Cummings (1994-97)	344-594	4080
John Kaleo (1991-92)	305-537	3660
Stan Gelbaugh (1981-85)	251-454	3659

CAREER RECEIVING YARDS	Catches	Yards
Jermaine Lewis (1992-95)	193	2932
Torrey Smith (2008-10)	152	2218
Darrius Heyward-Bey (2006-08)	138	2089
Geroy Simon (1993-96)	185	2059
Aziz Abdur-Ra'oof (1984-87)	108	1895
Marcus Badgett (1989-92)	100	1748
Barry Johnson (1987-90)	106	1721
Greg Hill (1982-84)	97	1721
Ferrell Edmunds (1984-87)	101	1641
Guilian Gary (1998-2001)	113	1552

SEASON RUSHING YARDS	Attempts	Yards
LaMont Jordan (1999)	266	1632
Charlie Wysocki (1980)	334	1359
Steve Atkins (1978)	283	1261
Bruce Perry (2001)	219	1242
Chris Downs (2002)	208	1154

SEASON PASSING YARDS	Comp.-Att.	Yards
Scott Milanovich (1993)	279-431	3499
John Kaleo (1992)	286-482	3392
Dan Henning (1986)	196-353	2725
Scott McBrien (2003)	173-314	2672
Scott Zolak (1990)	225-418	2589

SEASON RECEIVING YARDS	Catches	Yards
Marcus Badgett (1992)	75	1240
Torrey Smith (2010)	67	1055
Jermaine Lewis (1993)	52	957
Jermaine Lewis (1995)	66	937
Geroy Simon (1994)	77	891

GAME RUSHING YARDS	Attempts	Yards
LaMont Jordan (1999 vs. Virginia)	37	306
Bruce Perry (2001 vs. Wake Forest)	30	276
Josh Allen (2003 vs. Virginia)	38	257

GAME PASSING YARDS	Comp.-Att.	Yards
Scott Milanovich (1993 vs. Va. Tech)	N/A-57	498
Scott Milanovich (1993 vs. W. Virginia)	35-54	451
John Kaleo (1992 vs. Clemson)	N/A-N/A	418

GAME RECEIVING YARDS	Catches	Yards
Marcus Badgett (1992 vs. Pittsburgh)	11	251
Jermaine Lewis (1993 vs. No. Carolina)	N/A	250
Torrey Smith (2010 vs. No. Carolina St.)	14	224

GREATEST COACH

Three coaches (Jim Tatum, Jerry Claiborne, and current head mentor Ralph Friedgen) have rescued Maryland from the wilderness and a fourth (Bobby Ross) won three straight Atlantic Coast Conference championships. The edge here goes to Tatum, based upon his having won a national title and owning the best winning percentage of .8191. Despite the one-year presence of legendary Paul "Bear" Bryant in 1945, it took the arrival of Big Jim and the installation of the Split-T offense in 1947 to send Maryland to the heights of Sugar and Gator Bowl victories, a regular season national championship in 1953, and another undefeated regular season in 1955.

Tatum had an entertaining faculty to irritate other coaches with his comments, much like a latter day Steve Spurrier. Tatum even agitated his good friend and mild-mannered Bud Wilkinson of Oklahoma after one of the two victories Wilkinson scored over Tatum in Orange Bowls in the 1950s. Tatum left abruptly to return to his alma mater, North Carolina, a few weeks after losing the Orange Bowl in January 1956.

Claiborne finished his 10-year stay in College Park with a 72-37-3 (.6563) record that included three straight ACC titles and a 20-game ACC win streak. Ross won 19 ACC games in row, while also winning three conferences titles in a row and posting a .6695 percentage.

MARYLAND'S 55 GREATEST SINCE 1953

OFFENSE

WIDE RECEIVER: Azizuddin Abdur-Ra'oof, Gary Collins, Jermaine Lewis, James Milling, Torrey Smith
TIGHT END: Vernon Davis, Ferrell Edmunds
TACKLE: Stan Jones, J.D. Maarleveld, Mike Sandusky, Roger Shoals
GUARD: Jack Davis, Len Lynch, Walter Rock
CENTER: Melvin Fowler, Kevin Glover
QUARTERBACK: Boomer Esiason, Scott Milanovich, Dick Shiner
RUNNING BACK: Steve Atkins, Bruce Perry, LaMont Jordan, Charlie Wysocki
FULLBACK: Rick Badanjek, Ralph Felton

DEFENSE

END: Russ Dennis, Shawne Merriman
TACKLE: Joe Campbell, Mark Duda, Randy White
GUARD: Bruce Mesner, Bruce Palmer, Paul Vellano
LINEBACKER: Rod Breedlove, Brad Carr, Chuck Faucette, E.J. Henderson, D'Qwell Jackson, Neal Olkewicz, Bob Pellegrini
CORNERBACK: Lloyd Burress, Keeta Covington, Domonique Foxworth, Lewis Sanders
SAFETY: Al Covington, Bob Smith, Madieu Williams

SPECIAL TEAMS

RETURN SPECIALISTS: Steve Suter
PLACEKICKER: Dale Castro, Steve Mike-Mayer
PUNTER: Brooks Barnard

MULTIPLE POSITIONS

FULLBACK-PLACEKICKER: Dick Bielski
HALFBACK-WIDE RECEIVER-DEFENSIVE BACK: Tom Brown

TWO-WAY PLAYERS

QUARTERBACK-SAFETY: Bernie Faloney
END-DEFENSIVE END-PUNTER: Bill Walker

PERFORMANCE FORMULA:
MARYLAND'S 10 BEST SEASONS

1953	1.7343	2 of 69
1955	1.6292	5 of 69
1976	1.5946	4 of 70
2001	1.4832	9 of 70
1954	1.4760	9 of 69
2003	1.4576	11 of 71
1985	1.4569	15 of 70
2002	1.4569	11 of 70
1974	1.4096	12 of 71
1975	1.3936	17 of 70

MARYLAND TERRAPINS

Year	W-L-T	AP Poll	Conference Standing	Toughest Regular Season Opponents	Coach (Record at School)	Bowl Games		
1953	10-1	1	1	Missouri 6-4, So. Carolina 7-3, Mississippi 7-2-1, Alabama 6-2-3	Jim Tatum	Orange	0 Oklahoma	7
1954	7-2-1	2	2	Kentucky 7-3, UCLA 9-0, Miami 8-1, South Carolina 6-4	Jim Tatum			
1955	10-1	3	1t	UCLA 9-1, Syracuse 5-3, Clemson 7-3	Jim Tatum (75-15-4)	Orange	6 Oklahoma	20
1956	2-7-1		4	Syracuse 7-1, Baylor 8-2, Miami 8-1-1, Tennessee 10-0	Tommy Mont			
1957	5-5		3t	Texas A&M 8-2, NC State 7-1-2, Duke 6-2-2, Tennessee 7-3	Tommy Mont			
1958	4-6		5	Clemson 8-2, North Carolina 6-4, Auburn 9-0-1, Navy 6-3	Tommy Mont (11-18-1)			
1959	5-5		3	Tennessee 9-1, Syracuse 10-0, Clemson 8-2	Tom Nugent			
1960	6-4		3	Texas 7-3, Duke 7-3, NC State 6-3-1, Penn State 6-3	Tom Nugent			
1961	7-3		3	Clemson 5-5, Syracuse 7-3, Penn State 7-3	Tom Nugent			
1962	6-4		3	Miami 7-3, Penn State 9-1, Duke 8-2, Clemson 6-4	Tom Nugent			
1963	3-7		5	NC State 8-2, North Carolina 8-2, Penn State 7-3, Navy 9-1	Tom Nugent			
1964	5-5		3t	Oklahoma 6-3-1, Penn State 6-4	Tom Nugent			
1965	4-6		5t	Syracuse 7-3, NC State 6-4, South Carolina 5-5	Tom Nugent (36-34)			
1966	4-6		3t	Syracuse 8-2, Clemson 6-4, Florida State 6-4	Lou Saban (4-6)			
1967	0-9		8	Oklahoma 9-1, Syracuse 8-2, NC State 8-2, Penn State 8-2	Bob Ward			
1968	2-8		7	Florida State 8-2, Syracuse 6-4, Penn State 10-0, Virginia 7-3	Bob Ward (2-17)			
1969	3-7		3t	West Virginia 9-1, South Carolina 7-3, Penn State 10-0	Roy Lester			
1970	2-9		6t	North Carolina 8-3, Penn State 7-3, West Virginia 8-3	Roy Lester			
1971	2-9		7	North Carolina 9-2, South Carolina 6-5, Penn State 10-1	Roy Lester (7-25)			
1972	5-5-1		3	NC State 7-3-1, North Carolina 10-1, Penn State 10-1	Jerry Claiborne			
1973	8-4	20	2	NC State 8-3, Penn State 11-0, Tulane 9-2	Jerry Claiborne	Peach	16 Georgia	17
1974	8-4	13	1	Alabama 11-0, Florida 8-3, NC State 9-2, Penn State 9-2	Jerry Claiborne	Liberty	3 Tennessee	7
1975	9-2-1	13	1	Tennessee 7-5, NC State 7-3-1, Penn State 9-2	Jerry Claiborne	Gator	13 Florida	0
1976	11-1	8	1	West Virginia 5-6, Duke 5-5-1, Kentucky 7-4, Cincinnati 8-3	Jerry Claiborne	Cotton	21 Houston	30
1977	8-4		3t	Clemson 8-2-1, Penn State 10-1, North Carolina 8-2-1	Jerry Claiborne	Hall of Fame	17 Minnesota	7
1978	9-3	20	2	NC State 8-3, Penn State 11-0, Clemson 10-1	Jerry Claiborne	Sun	0 Texas	42
1979	7-4		2t	Clemson 8-3, Penn St. 7-4, Wake Forest 8-3, No. Carolina 7-3-1	Jerry Claiborne			
1980	8-4		2	North Carolina 10-1, Pitt 10-1, Penn State 9-2, Clemson 6-5	Jerry Claiborne	Tangerine	20 Florida	35
1981	4-6-1		3	West Virginia 8-3, Florida 7-4, North Carolina 9-2, Clemson 11-0	Jerry Claiborne (72-37-3)			
1982	8-4	20	2	Penn State 10-1, West Va. 9-2, No. Carolina 7-4, Clemson 9-1-1	Bobby Ross	Aloha	20 Washington	21
1983	8-4		1	West Virginia 8-3, Pitt 8-2-1, Auburn 10-1, Clemson 9-1-1	Bobby Ross	Citrus	23 Tennessee	30
1984	9-3	12	1	West Virginia 7-4, Miami 8-4, Clemson 7-4, Virginia 7-2-2	Bobby Ross	Sun	28 Tennessee	27
1985	9-3	18	1	Penn State 11-0, West Virginia 7-3-1, Michigan 9-1-1, Miami 10-1	Bobby Ross	Cherry	35 Syracuse	18
1986	5-5-1		5	NC State 8-2-1, Boston College 7-4, Penn St. 11-0, Clemson 7-2-2	Bobby Ross (39-19-1)			
1987	4-7		5	Syracuse 11-0, Miami 11-0, Penn State 8-3, Clemson 9-2	Joe Krivak			
1988	5-6		4t	West Virginia 11-0, Syracuse 9-2, Duke 7-3-1, Clemson 9-2	Joe Krivak			
1989	3-7-1		6	West Virginia 8-2-1, Clemson 9-2, Michigan 10-1, Virginia 10-2	Joe Krivak			
1990	6-5-1		4	Clemson 9-2, Michigan 8-3, Georgia Tech 10-0-1, Penn State 9-2	Joe Krivak	Independence	34 Louisiana Tech	34
1991	2-9		6	Syracuse 9-2, Penn State 10-2, Clemson 9-1-1, NC State 9-2	Joe Krivak (20-34-1)			
1992	3-8		6	NC State 9-2-1, Penn State 7-4, No. Carolina 8-3, Florida St. 10-1	Mark Duffner			
1993	2-9		7t	No. Carolina 10-2, West Va. 11-0, Penn State 9-2, Florida St. 11-1	Mark Duffner			
1994	4-7		7	Duke 8-3, Fla. St. 9-1-1, No. Carolina 8-3, NC St. 8-3, Virginia 8-3	Mark Duffner			
1995	6-5		5t	Clemson 8-3, Louisville 7-4, Virginia 8-4, Florida State 9-2	Mark Duffner			
1996	5-6		6t	Virginia 7-4, West Va. 8-3, Clemson 7-4, Florida State 11-0	Mark Duffner (20-35)			
1997	2-9		8	Florida State 10-1, North Carolina 10-1, Clemson 7-4, Virginia 7-4	Ron Vanderlinden			
1998	3-8		7t	Virginia 9-2, West Virginia 8-3, Florida St. 11-1, Georgia Tech 9-2	Ron Vanderlinden			
1999	5-6		8t	Georgia Tech 8-3, Florida State 11-0, Virginia 7-4	Ron Vanderlinden			
2000	5-6		6t	Florida State 11-1, Clmson 9-2, NC State 7-4, Georgia Tech 9-2	Ron Vanderlinden (15-29)			
2001	10-2	11	1	No. Carolina 7-5, Georgia Tech 7-5, Florida St. 7-4, NC State 7-4	Ralph Friedgen	Orange	23 Florida	56
2002	11-3	13	2t	Notre Dame 10-2, Florida State 9-4, West Va. 9-3, NC State 10-3	Ralph Friedgen	Peach	30 Tennessee	3
2003	10-3	17	2	Florida State 10-2, West Virginia 8-4, Clemson 8-4	Ralph Friedgen	Gator	41 West Virginia	7
2004	5-6		8t	West Virginia 8-3, Florida St. 8-3, Virginia 8-3, Virginia Tech 10-2	Ralph Friedgen			
2005	5-6		Atl4t	Clemson 7-4, West Virginia 10-1, Florida St. 7-4, Boston College 8-3	Ralph Friedgen			
2006	9-4		Atl2t	West Virginia 10-2, Ga. Tech 8-4, Boston College 9-3, Wake Forest 10-2	Ralph Friedgen	Champs	24 Purdue	7
2007	6-7		Atl5t	West Virginia 10-2, Virginia 9-3, Clemson 9-3, Boston College 10-2	Ralph Friedgen	Emerald	14 Oregon State	21
2008	8-5		Atl3t	California 8-4, Virginia Tech 9-4, Florida State 8-4, Boston College 9-4	Ralph Friedgen	Humanitarian	42 Nevada	35
2009	2-10		Atl6	California 8-4, Rutgers 8-4, Clemson 8-5, Virginia Tech 9-3	Ralph Friedgen			
2010	9-4	23	Atl2t	West Virginia 9-3, Florida State 9-4, North Carolina State 8-4	Ralph Friedgen (75-50)	Military	51 East Carolina	20

TOTAL: 333-308-8 .5193 (43 of 70)

Bowl Games since 1953: 9-11-1 .4524 (47 of 70)

GREATEST TEAM SINCE 1953: Terrapins' 1953 (10-1) team blanked both SEC champion Alabama and runner-up Mississippi and was crowned undefeated national champions before losing 7-0 in Orange Bowl to Oklahoma. Maryland's unbeaten 1955 squad actually fared better in its 20-6 Orange Bowl loss to Oklahoma; Terps held a 6-0 lead at halftime and stayed within a touchdown under the end. Coach Jerry Claiborne's 1976 Terps team cruised through an undefeated regular season while permitting only 7.7 points-per-game. But, Maryland was stunned in the Cotton Bowl by Houston. In a close call, we go with Jim Tatum's 1953 Terrapins.

1953 10-1

20	Missouri	6 E Marty Crytzer / Paul Kramer
52	Wash'ton & Lee	0 T Bob Morgan / Ray Blackburn
20	Clemson	0 G Jack Bowersox / Bob Pellegrino
40	Georgia	13 C John Irvine
26	North Carolina	0 G George Palahunik
30	Miami	0 T Stan Jones / Tom Breunich
24	South Carolina	6 E Bill Walker / Russ Dennis
27	Geo. Wash'ton	6 QB Bernie Faloney
38	Mississippi	0 HB Chet "The Jet" Hanulak/Ronnie Waller
21	Alabama	0 HB Dick Nolan / Ed Vereb
0	Oklahoma	7 FB Ralph Felton / Dick Bielski

RUSHING: Hanulak 77/753y, Felton 100/556y, Nolan 50/259y
PASSING: Faloney 31-68/599y, 5TD, 45.6%
RECEIVING: Hanulak 10/152y, Waller 9/229y, Nolan 8/185y
SCORING: Faloney 54pts, Felton 53pts, Hanulak 36pts

1954 7-2-1

20	Kentucky	0 E Russ Dennis / Paul Kramer
7	UCLA	12 T Ralph Baierl / Ray Blackburn
13	Wake Forest	13 G Jack Bowersox
33	North Carolina	0 C Bob Pellegrini
7	Miami	9 G George Palahunik / Jack Davis
20	South Carolina	0 T Mike Sandusky / Tom Breunich
42	N. Carolina St.	14 E Bill Walker / Jim Parsons
16	Clemson	0 QB Charley Boxold / Frank Tamburello
48	Geo. Wash'ton	6 HB Ronnie Waller / Ed Vereb
74	Missouri	13 HB Joe Horning / Howard Dare
		FB Dick Bielski

RUSHING: Waller 66/592y, Bielski 79/405y, Horning 42/323y
PASSING: Boxold 23-59/525y, 6TD, 39.0%
RECEIVING: Walker 13/209y, Dare 7/104y, Dennis 6/186y
SCORING: Bielski (FB-K) 54pts, Waller 42pts, Dare 24pts

1955 10-1

13	Missouri	12 E Bill Walker / Jim Parsons
7	UCLA	0 T Al Wharton / Ed Heuring
20	Baylor	6 G Gene Dyson / Fred Tullai
28	Wake Forest	7 C Bob Pellegrini
25	North Carolina	7 G Jack Davis / Paul Tonetti
34	Syracuse	13 T Mike Sandusky / Joe Lazzarino
27	South Carolina	0 E Russ Dennis / Tim Flynn
13	LSU	0 QB Frank Tamburello / Lynn Beightol
25	Clemson	12 HB Ed Vereb
19	Geo. Wash'gton	0 HB Jack Healy / Howard Dare
6	Oklahoma	20 FB Fred Hamilton / Tom Selep

RUSHING: Vereb 113/643y, Dare 60/278y, Healy 56/276y
PASSING: Tamburello 28-58/497y, 4TDs, 48.3%
RECEIVING: Healy 10/182y, Dare 10/74y, Dennis 6/170y
SCORING: Vereb 96pts, Healy 24pts, Dare & Dennis 18pts

1956 2-7-1

12	Syracuse	26 E Gene Waters / Al Beardsley
6	Wake Forest	0 T Al Wharton / Ed Heuring
0	Baylor	14 G Paul Tonetti / George Kolarac
6	Miami	13 C Gene Alderton / Andy Main
6	North Carolina	34 G Jack Davis / Ron Athey
7	Tennessee	34 T Mike Sandusky / Don Healy
0	Kentucky	14 E Ed Cooke / Dick Porter
6	Clemson	6 QB John Fritsch / Lynn Beightol
0	South Carolina	13 HB Fred Hamilton / Ted Kershner
25	N. Carolina St.	14 HB Jack Healy / Ralph Hawkins
		FB Tom Selep / Tom Skarda

RUSHING: Selep 62/315y, Kershner 48/273y, Hamilton 75/269y
PASSING: Fritsch 23-52/219y, 0TDs, 44.2%
RECEIVING: Turner 7/74y, Hamilton 6/58y, Skarda 6/28y
SCORING: Fritsch (QB-K) 19pts, Dickie Lewis (QB) 12pts, 6 with 6pts

1957 5-5

13	Texas A&M	21 E Ed Cooke / Al Beardsley
13	N. Carolina St.	48 T Fred Cole / Kurt Schwarz
0	Duke	14 G Rod Breedlove
27	Wake Forest	0 C Gene Alderton / Andy Main
21	North Carolina	7 G Paul Tonetti
0	Tennessee	16 T Don Healy / Paul Stefl
10	South Carolina	6 E Ben Scotti / Bill Turner
7	Clemson	26 QB Bob Rusevlyan / Dickie Lewis
16	Miami	6 HB Ted Kershner / Howard Dare
12	Virginia	0 HB Fred Hamilton
		FB Jimmy Hatter / Phil Perlo

RUSHING: Kershner 41/227y, Rusevlyan 55/209y, Perlo 67/171y
PASSING: Rusevlyan 26-58/297y, 3TDs, 44.8%, Lewis 13-45/153y, 1TD, 28.9%
RECEIVING: Cooke 14/137y, Scotti 7/88y, Turner 6/61y
SCORING: Dare 24pts, John Fritsch (QB-K) 21pts, Rusevlyan (QB-K) 13pts

1958 4-6

0	Wake Forest	34 E Ron Shaffer / Vince Scott
21	N. Carolina St.	6 T Kurt Schwarz / Ed Nickla
0	Clemson	8 G Rod Breedlove
10	Texas A&M	14 C Vic Schwartz
0	North Carolina	27 G Tom Gunderman / Pete Boinis
7	Auburn	20 T Fred Cole
10	South Carolina	6 E Ben Scotti / Al Beardsley
14	Navy	40 QB Bob Rusevlyan
26	Miami	14 HB Ted Kershner / Gene Verardi
44	Virginia	6 HB Bob Layman / John Forbes
		FB Jim Joyce

RUSHING: Joyce 97/406y, Layman 59/278y, Forber 60/215y
PASSING: Rusevlyan 59-109/657y, 2TDs, 54.1%
RECEIVING: Scotti 18/282y, Shaffer 18/141y, Layman 12/151y
SCORING: Forbes 36pts, Rusevlyan 20pts, Layman 18pts

1959 5-5

27	West Virginia	7 E Gary Collins / Tony Scotti
0	Texas	26 T Kurt Schwarz
0	Syracuse	29 G Bill Lazaro / Pete Boinis
7	Wake Forest	10 C Vic Schwartz / Bob Hacker
14	North Carolina	7 G Tom Gunderman
6	South Carolina	22 T Joe Gardi
14	Navy	22 E Vince Scott / Ron Shaffer
28	Clemson	25 QB Dale Betty / Dick Novak
55	Virginia	12 HB Dwayne Fletcher
33	N. Carolina St.	28 HB-UB Rod Breedlove (G-LB) / Joe Mona
		FB Jim Joyce / Pat Drass

RUSHING: Joyce 137/567y, Fletcher 65/311y, Drass 77/264y
PASSING: Betty 39-76/552y, 9TDs, 51.3% Novak 32-72/486y, 4TDs, 44.4%
RECEIVING: Collins 14/350y, Scott 11/147y, Mona 9/53y
SCORING: Joyce 48pts, Scott 34pts, Collins 26pts

1960 6-4

31	West Virginia	8 E Gary Collins
0	Texas	34 T Gordon Bennett
7	Duke	20 G Dave Crossan
10	N. Carolina St.	13 C Bob Hacker
19	Clemson	17 G Bill Kirchiro
14	Wake Forest	13 T Tom Sankovich / Roger Shoals
15	South Carolina	0 E Walter Rock / Vince Scott
9	Penn State	28 QB Dale Betty / Dick Novak
22	North Carolina	19 HB Tom Brown / Dennis Condie
44	Virginia	12 HB-UB Everett Cloud / Joe Mona
		FB Pat Drass / John Forbes / Rex Collins

RUSHING: Drass 76/297y, R. Collins 48/201y, Condie 34/195y
PASSING: Betty 82-132/796y, 62.1%, 6TDs
RECEIVING: G.Collins 30/404, Mona 14/102y, Brown 11/120y
SCORING: G.Collins 26pts, Condie & Betty 24pts

1961 7-3

14	SMU	6 E Gary Collins / Tom Rae
24	Clemson	21 T Walter Rock / Dave Crossan
22	Syracuse	21 G Bill Kirchiro
8	North Carolina	14 C Bob Hacker
21	Air Force	0 G Tom Sankovich
10	South Carolina	20 T Roger Shoals
21	Penn State	17 E Dick Barlund / Henry Poniatowski
10	N. Carolina St.	7 QB Dick Novak / Dick Shiner
10	Wake Forest	7 HB Tom Brown /Ernie Arizzi /Dennis Condie
16	Virginia	28 HB-UB Jim Davidson
		FB Pat Drass

RUSHING: Arizzi 79/375y, Condie 68/236y, Novak 50/187y
PASSING: Shiner 58-111/921y, 7 TDs, 52.3%, Novak 55-99/487y, 5 TDs, 55.5%
RECEIVING: Collins 30/428y, Poniatowski 15/212y,
SCORING: John Hannigan (K) 56pts, Collins 24pts,

1962 6-4

7	SMU	0 WR Jerry Osler / Tom Rae
13	Wake Forest	2 WR Tom Brown / Mike Funk
14	N. Carolina St.	6 T Gordon Bennett / Dave Crossan
31	North Carolina	13 G Walter Rock
24	Miami	28 C Gene Feher
13	South Carolina	11 G Fred Joyce / Chester Detko
7	Penn State	23 T Roger Shoals / Norman Hatfield
7	Duke	10 TE-UB Bob Burton / Dave Nardo
14	Clemson	17 QB Dick Shiner / Ken Ambrusko (DB)
40	Virginia	18 TB Len Chiaverini
		FB Ernie Arizzi

RUSHING: Chiaverini 156/602y, Brown 35/189y, Arizzi 41/179y
PASSING: Shiner 121-203/1324y; 4TDs, 59.6%
RECEIVING: Brown 47/557y, Arizzi 26/247y, Funk 19/227y
SCORING: Brown 38pts, Shiner 36pts, Chiaverini 30pts

1963 3-7

14	N. Carolina St.	36 WR Howard Humphries / Andy Martin
13	South Carolina	21 WR Darryl Hill
12	Duke	30 T Olaf Drozdov
7	North Carolina	14 G Fred Joyce / Dick Melcher
21	Air Force	14 C Gene Feher
32	Wake Forest	0 G Joe Ferrante
15	Penn State	17 T Matt Arbutina / Larry Bagranoff
7	Navy	42 TE-UB Bob Burton
6	Clemson	21 QB Dick Shiner
21	Virginia	6 TB Jerry Fishman / Len Chiaverini

RUSHING: Fishman 116/480y, Chiaverini 93/312y,Arizzi 22/116y
PASSING: Shiner 108-222/1165y, 10TDs, 48.6%
RECEIVING: Hill 43/516y, Martin 19/238y, Humphries 12/116y
SCORING: Hill 55pts, Shiner 26pts, Fishman 24pts

1964 5-5

3	Oklahoma	13 WR Howard Humphries / Bill Pettit
24	South Carolina	6 WR Chip Myrtle
13	N. Carolina St.	14 T Joe Frattaroli
17	Duke	24 G Don Foran / Dave Markoe
10	North Carolina	9 C Charlie Martin
17	Wake Forest	21 G Jerry Fishman / Chick Krahling
9	Penn State	17 T Matt Arbutina
27	Navy	22 TE-UB Dick Absher / Doug Klingerman
34	Clemson	0 QB Phil Petry / Ken Ambusko (DB)
10	Virginia	0 TB Bo Hickey
		FB Walt Marciniak

RUSHING: Hickey 182/894y, Marciniak 114/440y, Petry 93/233y
PASSING: Petry 73-162/809y, 5TDs, 45.0%
RECEIVING: Absher 22/268y, Myrtle 13/190y, Pettit 11/122y
SCORING: Bernardo Bramson (K) 44pts, Hickey 30pts, Marciniak 24pts

1965 4-6

24	Ohio University	7 WRChip Myrtle/Billy Van Heus'n (HB-DB)
7	Syracuse	24 WR Bobby Collins / Andy Martin
10	Wake Forest	7 T Tom Cichowski
10	North Carolina	12 G Milan Vucin
7	N. Carolina St.	29 C Chick Krahling
27	South Carolina	14 G Dick Melcher
7	Navy	19 T Matt Arbutina
6	Clemson	0 TE Dick Absher / Doug Klingerman
27	Virginia	33 QB Phil Petry / Jim Corcoran
7	Penn State	19 HB Ernie Torain / Ken Ambrusko
		FB Walt Marciniak
		DL John Kenny
		DL Larry Bagranoff
		DL Jim Lavrusky / Ed Gunderman
		DL Bob York
		DL Mick Melcher
		LB Lorie McQueen
		LB George Stern / Alan Pastrana
		LB Ron Nalewak
		DB Fred Cooper / Lou Stickel
		DB Gary Miller
		DB Tony Santy / Bob Sullivan

RUSHING: Torain 93/370y, Marciniak 78/310y, Ambrusko 32/100y
PASSING: Petry 65-135/763y, 3TDs, 48.1%
RECEIVING: Absher 33/382y, Collins 25/462y, Klingerman 12/60y
SCORING: Bernardo Bramson (K) 36pts, Collins 24pts,

1966 4-6

7 Penn State	15 WR Billy Van Heusen (HB)
34 Wake Forest	7 WR Chip Myrtle / Bobby Collins (DB)
7 Syracuse	28 T Tom Cichowski
21 Duke	19 G Milan Vucin
28 West Virginia	9 C Joe Simoldoni / Larry Vince
14 South Carolina	2 G Chuck Tine / Ed Kane
21 N. Carolina St.	24 T Fred Gawlick / John Trachy
10 Clemson	14 TE Rick Carlson / Ron Pearson
17 Virginia	41 QB Alan Pastrana
21 Florida State	45 HB Ernie Torain /Wymard McQuown (FB)
	FB Billy Lovett / Ralph Donofrio
	DL Tom Plevin
	DL Ed Gunderman / Bob York
	DL John Miloszewski / Tom Myslinski
	DL Dick Absher (TE)
	LB Pat Baker / Mike Hoch
	LB Jim Lavrusky
	LB Art Brzostowski
	DB Fred Cooper
	DB Tony Santy / Carl Mortensen
	DB Lou Stickel
	DB John Hetrick

RUSHING: Lovett 98/451y, Torain 94/259y, Donofrio 48/119y
PASSING: Pastrana 102-195/1499y, 17TDs, 52.3%
RECEIVING: Van Heusen 25/536y, Donofrio 22/217y,
  Collins 18/276y
SCORING: Van Heusen 42pts, Torain 30pts,
  Bernardo Bramson (K) 30pts

1967 0-9

0 Oklahoma	35 WR Billy Van Heusen
3 Syracuse	7 WR Rick Carlson
9 N. Carolina St.	31 T Chuck Tine (G) / Fred Gawlick
0 North Carolina	14 G Ron Pearson
0 South Carolina	31 C Mike Stubljar / Ed Kane
3 Penn State	38 G Bruce Olecki
7 Clemson	28 T Tom Myslinski
17 Wake Forest	35 TE Bill Kirschensteiner / Tony Santy
7 Virginia	12 QB Chuck Drimal / Joe Tomcho
	TB Kenny Dutton
	FB Billy Lovett / Ralph Donofrio
	DL Lou Bracken / Ralph Sonntag
	DL John Dill
	DL Mike Grace
	DL Joe DiOrio / Tom Plevin
	DL Pat Baker / Hank Gareis
	LB Dan Kecman
	LB Jim Lavrusky
	LB Lou Stickel / Steve Ciambor
	DB Bob Colbert
	DB Mike Brant
	DB Bob Haley / Wally Stalnaker

RUSHING: Lovett 137/499y, Donofrio 81/331y, Dutton 81/246y
PASSING: Drimal 54-123/669y, 1TDs, 43.9%
RECEIVING: Carlson 24/309y, Van Heusen 15/256y,
  Dutton 15/155y
SCORING: Carlson 28pts, 3 with 6pts

1968 2-8

14 Florida State	24 E Ron Pearson / Lou Bracken
14 Syracuse	32 T Ralph Sonntag
28 Duke	30 G Ed Kane
33 North Carolina	24 C Mike Stubljar
21 South Carolina	19 G Bill Meister
11 N. Carolina St.	31 T Rich Slaninka
14 Wake Forest	38 E Rick Carlson
0 Clemson	16 QB Alan Pastrana
13 Penn State	57 TB Al Thomas / John King
23 Virginia	28 WB Sonny Demczuk
	FB Billy Lovett
	DL Bill Grant
	DL John Gebhardt
	DL Pete Mattia
	DL Tom Plevin / Mike Grace
	DL Hank Gareis
	LB Dean Landolt / John Dyer
	LB Dan Kecman
	LB Steve Ciambor
	DB Bob Haley
	DB Mike Brant / Kenny Dutton
	DB Wally Stalnaker

RUSHING: Lovett 217/963y Thomas 110/365y, King 88/301y
PASSING: Pastrana 81-172/1053y, 6TD, 47.1%
RECEIVING: Demczuk 23/215y, Carlson 21/359y,
  Pearson 14/189y
SCORING: Lovett 50pts, Carlson 35pts, King & Thomas 18pts

1969 3-7

7 West Virginia	31 WR Roland Merritt / Sonny Demczuk
7 N. Carolina St.	24 T Ralph Sonntag
19 Wake Forest	14 G Bill Meister
9 Syracuse	20 C Jim Stull
20 Duke	7 G Pat Burke
0 South Carolina	17 T Rich Slaninka / Bob MacBride
0 Clemson	40 TE Lou Bracken / Hank Barnes
21 Miami (Ohio)	34 QB Dennis O'Hara / Jeff Shugars
0 Penn State	48 TB Al Thomas
17 Virginia	14 WB Paul Fitzpatrick / Larry Marshall
	FB Tom Miller
	DL John Dill
	DL Charles Hoffman / Guy Roberts
	DL Pete Mattia
	DL James Hamley
	LB Hank Gareis
	LB John Dyer
	LB Dan Kecman / Bill Reilly
	LB Mike Brant
	DB Kenny Dutton / Len Massie
	DB Bob Colbert / Eric Moore
	DB Tony Greene

RUSHING: Miller 169/629y, Thomas 99/454y, O'Hara 80/254y
PASSING: Shugars 47-114/716y, 3TDs, 41.2%
RECEIVING: Merritt 19/499y, Demczuk 13/158y,
  Fitzpatrick 8/104y
SCORING: Fitzpatrick 20pts, Merritt, O'Hara, & Thomas 12pts

1970 2-9

3 Villanova	21 WR Floyd White
12 Duke	13 T Steve Fromang / Rich Slaninka
20 North Carolina	53 G Bill Meister / Pat Burke
11 Miami	18 C Ron Kecman / Len Santacroce
7 Syracuse	23 G Tim Brannan
21 South Carolina	15 T Bob MacBride
0 N. Carolina St.	6 TE Don Ratliff
11 Clemson	24 QB Jeff Shugars / Bob Tucker
0 Penn State	34 TB Art Seymore / Al Thomas
17 Virginia	14 WB Larry Marshall
10 West Virginia	20 FB Tom Miller / Scott Shank
	DL Guy Roberts
	DL Jim Watkins
	DL Pete Mattia
	DL Chris Cowdrey
	LB Ed McManus / Tim Brant
	LB Bill Reilly / John Dyer
	LB Ted Steiner
	LB Lee Branthover
	DB Eric Moore
	DB Len Massie
	DB Tony Greene

RUSHING: Seymore 221/945y, Thomas 95/384y, Shank 41/133y
PASSING: Shugars 75-175/836y, 3TDs, 42.9%
RECEIVING: Ratliff 26/242y, Seymore 16/309y, Shank 13/89y
SCORING: Tucker & Seymore 18pts, Thomas &
  Greg Fries (K) 12pts

1971 2-9

13 Villanova	28 WR Dan Bungori
35 N. Carolina St.	7 T Ray Bednar / Ken Scott
14 North Carolina	35 G Bill Meister
14 Wake Forest	18 C Ron Kecman
13 Syracuse	21 G Tim Brannan
6 South Carolina	35 T Ray Wethington
23 Florida	27 TE Dennis O'Hara
38 VMI	0 QB Al Neville / Jeff Shugars
27 Penn State	63 TB Monte Hinkle
14 Clemson	20 WB Bob Lane / Bill Emrich
27 Virginia	29 FB Art Seymore / Tom Miller
	DL Guy Roberts / Chris Cowdrey
	DL Jim Watkins
	DL Paul Vellano / Jim Boyles
	DL Don Ratliff / Jim Martell
	LB Tim Brant
	LB Ted Steiner
	LB Bill Reilly
	LB Lee Branthover / Darnell Tate
	DB Larry Marshall
	DB Len Massie
	DB Bob Tucker

RUSHING: Hinkle 117/457y, Seymore 103/309y, Miller 49/242y
PASSING: Neville 107-204/1275y, 10TD, 52.5%
RECEIVING: Bungori 32/490y, O'Hara 32/423y, Emrich 21/237y
SCORING: Kambiz Behbahani (K) 54pts, Bungori 48pts

1972 5-5-1

24 N. Carolina St.	24 WR Frank Russell / Dan Bungori
23 North Carolina	3 T Ray Wethington
28 VMI	16 G Ray Bednar
12 Syracuse	16 C Ron Kecman
23 Wake Forest	0 G Tim Brannan
37 Villanova	7 T Bart Purvis
14 Duke	20 TE Don Ratliff (DL)
0 Virginia	23 QB Bob Avellini / Al Neville
16 Penn State	46 TB Louis Carter / Art Seymore
31 Clemson	6 WB Jamie Franklin / Jerry Erhard
8 Miami	28 FB Mike Reitz / LeRoy Hughes
	DL Tim Brant
	DL Randy White
	DL Dave Visaggio / Guy Dietz
	DL Paul Vellano
	DL Ken Scott
	DL Chris Cowdrey
	LB Jim Santa / Steve Zannoni
	LB Kevin Benson / Kevin Ward
	DB Ken Schroy
	DB Bob Tucker
	DB Bob Smith

RUSHING: Carter 119/474y, Seymore 113/402y, Franklin 83/324y
PASSING: Avellini 98-170/1251y, 7TDs, 57.6%
RECEIVING: Ratliff 36/515y, Russell 30/472y, Bungori 24/339y
SCORING: Steve Mike-Mayer (K) 55pts, Carter & Ratliff 36pts

1973 8-4

13 West Virginia	20 WR Frank Russell / Walter White
23 North Carolina	3 T Frank Romano
31 Villanova	3 G John Vesce
38 Syracuse	0 C Robert Lange / Bob Lane
22 N. Carolina St.	24 G Bart Purvis
37 Wake Forest	0 T Stan Rogers
30 Duke	10 TE Don Weiss / Bob Raba
22 Penn State	42 QB Al Neville / Bob Avellini
33 Virginia	0 TB Louis Carter / Richard Jennings
28 Clemson	13 WB John Schultz / Kim Hoover
42 Tulane	9 FB Monte Hinkle / Joe Brancato
16 Georgia	17 DL Mickey Riggleman / Rod Sharpless
	DL Randy White
	DL Guy Dietz / Dave Visaggio
	DL Paul Vellano
	DL Ken Scott / Joe Campbell
	DL Kevin Ward / LeRoy Hughes
	LB Harry Walters / Jim Santa
	LB Kevin Benson
	DB Pat Ulam / Jim Brechbiel
	DB Ken Schroy
	DB Bob Smith

RUSHING: Carter 218/801y, Jennings 109/397y,
  Ben Kinard (QB) 88/366y
PASSING: Neville 51-92/554y, 4TDs, 55.4%
RECEIVING: Russell 39/468y, White 27/422y, Carter 12/99y
SCORING: Carter 84pts, Steve Mike-Mayer (K) 69pts,
  White 32pts

1974 8-4

16 Alabama	21 WR Frank Russell
10 Florida	17 T Frank Romano
24 North Carolina	12 G John Vesce
31 Syracuse	0 C Gene Ochap / Robert Lange
41 Clemson	0 G John Nash / Ed Fulton
47 Wake Forest	0 T Stan Rogers
20 N. Carolina St.	10 TE Bob Raba / Walter White
17 Penn State	24 QB Bob Avellini / Mark Manges
41 Villanova	0 TB Louis Carter
56 Duke	13 WB John Schultz
10 Virginia	0 FB Alan Bloomingdale
3 Tennessee	7 DL Rod Sharpless
	DL Randy White
	DL Dave Visaggio / Paul DiVito
	DL Guy Dietz
	DL Joe Campbell
	DL LeRoy Hughes
	LB Harry Walters
	LB Kevin Benson / Steve Zannoni
	DB Jim Brechbiel
	DB Ken Schroy
	DB Bob Smith

RUSHING: Carter 224/991y, Jennings 80/470y, Manges 43/233y
PASSING: Avellini 112-189/1648y, 7TD, 59.3%
RECEIVING: Russell 31/404y, White 27/440y, Carter 20/221y
SCORING: Steve Mike-Mayer (K) 79pts, Schultz 56pts,
  Carter 42pts

1975 9-2-1

41	Villanova	0
8	Tennessee	26
34	North Carolina	10
10	Kentucky	24
24	Syracuse	37
37	N. Carolina St.	22
27	Wake Forest	0
13	Penn State	15
21	Cincinnati	19
22	Clemson	20
62	Virginia	24
13	Florida	0

WR Kim Hoover
T Marion Koprowski
G Ed Fulton
C Gene Ochap
G John Nash
T Dave Conrad
TE Vince Kinney / Bob Raba
QB Larry Dick / Mark Manges
TB Jamie Franklin / Steve Atkins
WB John Schultz / Ricky Jennings
FB Tim Wilson / Dan DeCarlo
DL Bill Evans / Chip Garber
DL Ralph Fisher
DL Paul DiVito
DL Ted Klaube / Ernie Salley
DL Joe Campbell
DL LeRoy Hughes
LB Kevin Benson / Mike Miller
LB Brad Carr / George Shihda
DB Jim Brechbiel
DB Ken Roy
DB Pete Zachery / Joe Younge

RUSHING: Atkins 87/491y, Franklin 98/485y, Jennings 78/411y
PASSING: Dick 90-158/1190y, 8TDs, 57.0%
RECEIVING: Hoover 38/532y, Schultz 25/321y, Wilson 15/160y
SCORING: Mike Sochko (K) 67pts, Atkins 42pts, Schultz 38pts

1976 11-1

31	Richmond	7
24	West Virginia	3
42	Syracuse	28
20	Villanova	9
16	N. Carolina St.	6
17	Wake Forest	15
30	Duke	3
24	Kentucky	14
21	Cincinnati	0
20	Clemson	0
28	Virginia	0
21	Houston	30

WR Vince Kinney / Chuck White
T Tom Schick / Kervin Wyatt
G John Zernhelt / Ed Fulton
C Gene Ochap
G Mike Yeates
T Dave Conrad
TE Bob Raba / Eric Sievers
QB Mark Manges
TB Alvin Maddox / Steve Atkins
WB Dean Richards
FB Tim Wilson
DL Keith Calta / John Douglas
DL Ralph Fisher
DL Ted Klaube / Larry Seder
DL Ernie Salley / Bob Schwartz
DL Joe Campbell
DL Chip Garber
LB Mike Miller
LB Brad Carr
DB Ken Roy / Doug Harbert
DB Lloyd Burgess
DB Jonathan Claiborne

RUSHING: Maddox 141/678y, Atkins 108/621y, Wilson 138/610y
PASSING: Manges 81-139/1145y, 11TDs, 58.3%
RECEIVING: White 23/402y, Kinney 21/298y, Richards 15/190y
SCORING: Wilson 42pts, Mike Sochko (K) 36pts, 3 with 30pts

1977 8-4

21	Clemson	14
16	West Virginia	24
9	Penn State	27
20	N. Pacolina St.	24
24	Syracuse	10
35	Wake Forest	7
31	Duke	13
7	North Carolina	16
19	Villanova	13
27	Richmond	24
28	Virginia	0
17	Minnesota	7

WR Dean Richards / Vince Kinney
T Jim Ulam
G Glenn Chamberlain
C Don Rhodes
G Mike Yeates
T Larry Stewart
TE Eric Sievers
QB Mark Manges / Larry Dick
TB George Scott / Steve Atkins
WB Chuck White
FB Mickey Dudish
DL Joe Muffler
DL Ed Gall
DL Bruce Palmer
DL Ted Klaube
DL Charlie Jackson
DL Chip Garber
LB Neal Olkewicz
LB Brad Carr
DB Lloyd Burgess
DB Doug Harbert
DB Jonathan Claiborne

RUSHING: Scott 188/894y, Atkins 147/598y
PASSING: Dick 83-135/1351y, 5TDs, 61.5%, Manges 31-76/420y, 0TDs, 40.8%
RECEIVING: Kinney 32/505y, Richards 23/370y, White 21/325y
SCORING: Atkins 54pts, Scott 42pts, Ed Loncar (K) 32pts

1978 9-3

31	Tulane	7
24	Louisville	17
21	North Carolina	20
20	Kentucky	3
31	N. Carolina St.	7
24	Syracuse	9
39	Wake Forest	0
27	Duke	0
3	Penn State	27
17	Virginia	7
24	Clemson	28
0	Texas	42

WR Dean Richards / Gary Ellis
T Jim Ulam / Scott Franz
G Paul Glamp / Glenn Chamberlain
C Mike Simon
G Kervin Wyatt
T Kervin Stewart
TE Eric Sievers
QB Tim O'Hare / Mike Tice
TB Steve Atkins / Alvin Maddox
WB Jan Carinci
FB Mickey Dudish
DL Jimmy Shaffer
DL Ed Gall
DL Bruce Palmer
DL Marlin Van Horn
DL Charles Johnson
DL Joe Muffler / Pete Glamp
LB Neal Olkewicz
LB Brian Matera / Todd Benson
DB Lloyd Burgess
DB Steve Trimble
DB Ralph Lary / John Baldante

RUSHING: Atkins 283/1261y, Maddox 90/392y, Dudish 33/161y
PASSING: O'Hare 105-192/1388y, 4TDs, 54.7%
RECEIVING: Richards 35/575y, Sievers 21/258y, Carinci 21/229y
SCORING: Ed Loncar (K) 73pts, Atkins 66pts, Maddox 54pts

1979 7-4

24	Villanova	20
19	Clemson	0
35	Mississippi St.	14
7	Kentucky	14
7	Penn State	27
0	N. Carolina St.	7
17	Wake Forest	25
27	Duke	0
17	North Carolina	14
28	Louisville	7
17	Virginia	7

WR Gary Ellis / Mike Lewis
T Larry Stewart
G Paul Glamp
C Kyle Lorton
G Kervin Wyatt
T Scott Collins / Scott Fanz
TE John Tice
QB Mike Tice / Bob Milkovich
TB Charlie Wysocki / Wayne Wingfield
WB Jan Carinci
FB Rick Fasano / Tom Whittie
DL Jimmy Shaffer
DL Ed Gall / Mark Duda
DL Greg Vanderhout
DL Mike Corvino
DL Todd Benson
DL Pete Glamp
LB Darnell Dailey
LB Brian Matera / Todd Benson
DB Sam Medile
DB Steve Trimble
DB Ralph Lary / John Baldante

RUSHING: Wysocki 247/1140y, Wingfield 80/360y, Whittie 49/199y
PASSING: M.Tice 75-154/897y, 5TDs, 48.7%
RECEIVING: Carinci 30/375y, Lewis 12/166y, Ellis 11/176y
SCORING: Dale Castro (K) 70pts, Wysocki 48pts, Whittie 24pts

1980 8-4

7	Villanova	3
31	Vanderbilt	6
14	West Virginia	11
3	North Carolina	17
9	Pittsburgh	38
10	Penn State	24
11	Wake Forest	10
17	Duke	14
24	N. Carolina St.	0
34	Clemson	7
31	Virginia	0
20	Florida	35

WR Mike Lewis / Chris Havener
T Les Boring
G Bob Pacella
C Kyle Lorton / Bruce Byrom
G Brian Riendeau
T Scott Fanz
TE Eric Sievers / John Tice
QB Mike Tice
TB Charlie Wysocki / Wayne Wingfield
WB Jan Carinci
FB Rick Fasano / Jeff Rodenberger
DL Mark Wilson / Brad Senft
DL Ed Gall
DL Greg Vanderhout
DL Marlin Van Horn / Mike Corvino
DL Mark Duda / Todd Benson
DL Howard Eubanks / Joe Aulisi
LB Mike Muller / John Kreider
LB Joe Wilkins / Dave D'Addio
DB Lloyd Burgess
DB Steve Trimble / Ralph Lary
DB David Taylor / Bill McFadden

RUSHING: Wysocki 334/1359y, Wingfield 56/210y, Fasano 33/96y
PASSING: M. Tice 71-140/928y, 5TDs, 50.7%
RECEIVING: Havener 29/436y, Sievers 19/221y, Lewis 10/174y
SCORING: Wysocki 66pts, Dale Castro (K) 51pts, 2 with 18pts

1981 4-6-1

17	Vanderbilt	23
13	West Virginia	17
34	N. Carolina St.	9
17	Syracuse	13
10	Florida	15
45	Wake Forest	33
24	Duke	21
10	North Carolina	17
7	Tulane	14
7	Clemson	21
48	Virginia	7

WR Russell Davis
WR Mike Lewis
T Bob Gioia
G Ron Solt
C Todd Wright
G Vince Tomasetti / Len Lynch
T David Pacella
TE John Tice
QB Norman "Boomer" Esiason
TB Charlie Wysocki / Willie Joyner
FB John Nash
DL Mark Wilson / Brian Baker
DL Gurnest Brown
DL Greg Vanderhout
DL Mike Corvino
DL Mark Duda
DL Howard Eubanks / Joe Aulisi
LB Darnell Dailey
LB Mike Muller / Joe Wilkins
DB David Tayler
DB John Simmons / Lendell Jones
DB Bill McFadden / Wayne Wingfield

RUSHING: Wysocki 159/715y, Nash 115/459y, Joyner 57/181y
PASSING: Esiason 122-242/1635y, 9TDs, 50.4%
RECEIVING: Tice 31/353y, Davis 26/498y, Lewis 24/320y
SCORING: Jess Atkinson (K) 60pts, Wysocki 44pts, Lewis 32pts

1982 8-4

31	Penn State	39
18	West Virginia	19
23	N. Carolina St.	6
26	Syracuse	3
38	Indiana State	0
52	Wake Forest	31
49	Duke	22
31	North Carolina	24
18	Miami	17
22	Clemson	24
45	Virginia	14
20	Washington	21

WR Russell Davis
WR Mike Lewis / Greg Hill
T Harry Venezia
G Ron Solt
C Vince Tomasetti
G Len Lynch
T David Pacella
TE John Tice
QB Boomer Esiason
RB Willie Joyner / John Nash
RB Dave D'Addio / Rick Badanjek
DL J.D. Gross
DL Gurnest Brown
DL Mike Corvino
DL Frank Kalencik / Tyrone Furman
DL Mark Duda
DL Brian Baker / Howard Eubanks
LB Joe Wilkins
LB Mike Muller / Eric Wilson
DB Clarence Baldwin
DB Lendell Jones / Bobby Gunderman
DB Gil Hoffman

RUSHING: Joyner 177/1039y, Nash 83/434y, Badanjek 62/274y
PASSING: Esiason 176-314/2301y, 18TDs, 56.1%
RECEIVING: Tice 34/396y, Davis 27/445y, Hill 19/331y
SCORING: Jess Atkinson (K) 87pts, Badanjek 56pts, Joyner & Hill 42pts

1983 8-4

21	Vanderbilt	14
21	West Virginia	31
13	Pittsburgh	7
23	Virginia	3
34	Syracuse	13
36	Wake Forest	33
38	Duke	3
28	North Carolina	26
2	Auburn	35
27	Clemson	52
29	N. Carolina St.	6
23	Tennessee	30

WR Russell Davis
WR Greg Hill
T Greg Harraka
G Ron Solt
C Kevin Glover
G Shawn Benson
T Harry Venezia
TE Bill Rogers / Ron Fazio
QB Boomer Esiason
RB Willie Joyner
RB Rick Badanjek / Dave D'Addio
DL J.D. Gross
DL Pete Koch / Bruce Mesner
DL Tyrone Furman
DL Greg Thompson
DL Jim Joyce / Tom McHale
DL Brian Baker
LB Eric Wilson / Chuck Faucette
LB Bobby DePaul
DB Clarence Baldwin
DB Lendell Jones / Bobby Gunderman
DB Joe Kraus / Al Covington

RUSHING: Joyner 198/908y, Badanjek 131/635y, D'Addio 46/213y
PASSING: Esiason 163-294/2322y, 15TDs, 55.4%
RECEIVING: Davis 29/465y, Hill 27/570y, Badanjek 26/296y
SCORING: Jess Atkinson (K) 73pts, Badanjek 56pts, Hill 42pts

1984 9-3

7 Syracuse	23 WR Greg Hill / Eric Holder
14 Vanderbilt	23 WR Azizuddin "Ziz" Abdur-Ra'oof
20 Wake Forest	17 T Tony Edwards
38 Wake Forest	17 G Greg Harraka
24 Penn State	25 C Kevin Glover
44 N. Carolina St.	21 G Len Lynch
43 Duke	7 T Jeff Holinka / J.D. Maarleveld
34 North Carolina	23 TE Ferrell Edmunds / Chris Knight
42 Miami	40 QB Frank Reich / Stan Gelbaugh
41 Clemson	23 RB Alvin Blount / Tommy Neal
45 Virginia	34 RB Rick Badanjek
28 Tennessee 27	DL Scott Schankweiler
	DL Ted Chapman
	DL Bruce Mesner
	DL Greg Thompson / Tom Parker
	DL Duane Dunham / Scott Tye
	DL Steve Kelly
	LB Chuck Faucette / Kevin Walker
	LB Eric Wilson / Richie Petitbon
	DB Keeta Covington / Lewis Askew
	DB Bobby Gunderman / Donald Brown
	DB Al Covington

RUSHING: Badanjek 173/832y, Blount 128/759y, Neal 112/618y
PASSING: Reich 108-169/1446y, 9TDs, 63.9%,
Gelbaugh 78-133/1123y, 5TDs, 58.6%
RECEIVING: Hill 51/820y, Abdur-Ra'oof 25/438y, Blount 20/269y
SCORING: Badanjek 102pts, Jess Atkinson (K) 88pts,
Blount 48pts

1985 9-3

18 Penn State	20 WR Eric Holder / James Milling
31 Boston College	13 WR Ziz Abdur-Ra'oof
28 West Virginia	0 T J.D. Maarleveld
0 Michigan	20 G Jeff Holinka
31 N. Carolina St.	17 C Bill Hughes
26 Wake Forest	3 G Len Lynch / Dave Amend
40 Duke	10 T Tony Edwards / John Sorna
28 North Carolina	10 TE Ferrell Edmunds / Chris Knight
22 Miami	29 QB Stan Gelbaugh
34 Clemson	31 RB Alvin Blount / Stephon Scribner
33 Virginia	21 RB Rick Badanjek / Tommy Neal
35 Syracuse 18	DL Scott Tye
	DL Ted Chapman / Duane Dunham
	DL Bob Arnold / Robert Klein
	DL Bruce Mesner
	DL Sean Scott / Steve Kelly
	LB Richie Petitbon
	LB Scott Schankweiler / Kevin Walker
	LB Chuck Faucette
	DB Keeta Covington / Chad Sydnor
	DB Donald Brown / Lewis Askew
	DB Al Covington

RUSHING: Blount 171/828y, Badanjek 155/676y, Neal 62/362y
PASSING: Gelbaugh 166-311/2475y, 15TDs, 53.4%
RECEIVING: Abdur-Ra'oof 35/671y, Milling 26/415y,
Edmunds 21/314y
SCORING: Badanjek 72pts, Dan Plocki (K) 53pts, Blount 30pts

1986 5-5-1

10 Pittsburgh	7 WR Vernon Joines / James Milling
35 Vanderbilt	21 WR Ziz Abdur-Ra'oof
24 West Virginia	3 T Mark Agent
16 N. Carolina St.	28 G Joe Giuliano
25 Boston College	30 C Bill Hughes / John Rugg
21 Wake Forest	27 G Dave Amend
27 Duke	19 T John Sorna / Mark Hofland
30 North Carolina	32 TE Ferrell Edmunds / Blaine Rose
15 Penn State	17 QB Dan Henning
17 Clemson	17 RB Stephon Scribner
42 Virginia	10 RB Bren Lowery / Alvin Blount
	DL Terry Burke / O'Brien Alston
	DL Ted Chapman
	DL Bruce Mesner / Robert Klein
	DL Bob Arnold
	DL Warren Powers / Duane Dunham
	DL Sean Scott / Steve Kelly
	LB Chuck Faucette
	LB Kevin Walker / Richie Petitbon
	DB Keeta Covington
	DB Lewis Askew / Chad Sydnor
	DB J.B. Brown

RUSHING: Blount 119/505y, Neal 78/351y, Scribner 96/330y
PASSING: Henning 196-353/2725y, 15TDs, 55.5%
RECEIVING: Milling 33/650y, Edmunds 28/490y, Joines 28/395y
SCORING: Dan Plocki (K) 62pts, Neal 48pts, Milling 36pts

1987 4-7

11 Syracuse	25 WR Vernon Joines / James Milling
21 Virginia	19 WR Ziz Abdur-Ra'oof
25 West Virginia	7 T Mark Agent
14 N. Carolina St.	42 G Rich Nelson / John Rugg
16 Miami	46 C Bill Hughes
14 Wake Forest	0 G Dave Amend / Mike Kiselak
23 Duke	22 T Clarence Jones / Mark Hofland
14 North Carolina	27 TE Ferrell Edmunds / Blaine Rose
16 Penn State	21 QB Dan Henning / Neil O'Donnell
16 Clemson	45 RB Bren Lowery
24 Vanderbilt	34 RB Dennis Spinelli / Mike Anderson
	DL O'Brien Alston / Karl Edwards
	DL Robert Klein
	DL Bob Arnold
	DL Warren Powers / Duane Dunham
	DL Sean Scott
	LB Kevin Walker
	LB Richie Petitbon
	DB Mike Hollis
	DB Kevin Fowlkes / Irvin Smith
	DB J.B. Brown
	DB Chad Sydnor

RUSHING: Lowery 168/556y, Spinelli 73/249y, Anderson 41/162y
PASSING: Henning 157-287/1835y, 9TDs, 54.7%,
O'Donnell 71-111/913y, 4TDs, 64.0%
RECEIVING: Lowery 44/252y, Abdur-Ra'oof 39/617y,
Edmunds 35/603y
SCORING: Lowery 42pts, Dan Plocki (K) 34pts, Joines 32pts

1988 5-6

27 Louisville	16 WR Barry Johnson / Dean Green
24 West Virginia	55 WR Vernon Joines
30 N. Carolina St.	26 T Clarence Jones
9 Syracuse	30 G Rich Nelson
13 Georgia Tech	8 C Mark Agent
24 Wake Forest	27 G Mike Kiselak / John Rugg
34 Duke	24 T Mark Hofland / Ken Oberle
41 North Carolina	38 TE Blaine Rose / Dave Carr
10 Penn State	17 QB Neil O'Donnell
25 Clemson	49 RB Mike Beasley / Ricky Johnson
23 Virginia	24 RB Bren Lowery
	DL Karl Edwards / Mark Walsh
	DL Wayne Brunson
	DL Rick Fleece
	DL Warren Powers / Lubo Zizakovic
	DL Jack Bradford
	LB Scott Whittier / Matt D'Amico
	LB Scott Saylor
	DB Irvin Smith / Mike Hollis
	DB Kevin Fowlkes
	DB Chad Sydnor
	DB J.B. Brown

RUSHING: R.Johnson 136/635y, Beasley 115/528y,
Lowery 75/256y
PASSING: O'Donnell 160-267/1973y, 12TDs, 59.9%
RECEIVING: Joines 29/433y, Beasley 26/261y,
B.Johnson 24/348y
SCORING: Dan Plocki (K) 78pts, Beasley 48pts, R.Johnson 36pts

1989 3-7-1

6 N. Carolina St.	10 WR Dean Green / Richie Harris
10 West Virginia	14 WR Barry Johnson
23 W. Michigan	0 T Clarence Jones
7 Clemson	31 G Blaine Rose
21 Michigan	41 C Mark Agent / Mitch Suplee
24 Georgia Tech	28 G Mike Kiselak
27 Wake Forest	24 T Mark Hofland / Ken Oberle
25 Duke	46 TE Dave Carr
38 North Carolina	0 QB Neil O'Donnell
13 Penn State	13 RB Ricky Johnson / Dennis Spinelli
21 Virginia	48 RB Mike Anderson / Bren Lowery
	DL Jack Bradford / Greg Hines
	DL Larry Webster
	DL Rick Fleece
	DL Darren Drozdov / Lubo Zizakovic
	DL Mark Walsh
	LB Glenn Page
	LB Scott Saylor / Mike Jarmolowich
	DB Scott Rosen
	DB Mike Hollis
	DB Mike Thomas
	DB Ron Reagan

RUSHING: Lowery 100/482y, R.Johnson 112/469y,
Spinelli 43/224y
PASSING: O'Donnell 156-280/2103y, 10TDs, 55.7%
RECEIVING: B.Johnson 43/689y, Carr 25/358y,
R.Johnson 25/206y
SCORING: Dan DeArmas (K) 57pts, R. Johnson 48pts,
B.Johnson 36pts

1990 6-5-1

20 Virginia Tech	13 WR Gene Thomas
14 West Virginia	10 WR Barry Johnson
17 Clemson	18 T Clarence Jones
13 N. Carolina St.	12 G Kevin Arline
17 Michigan	45 C Mitch Suplee
3 Georgia Tech	31 G Ken Oberle / Ron Staffileno
41 Wake Forest	13 T O'Neil Glenn
23 Duke	20 TE Bret Boehly
10 North Carolina	34 QB Scott Zolak
10 Penn State	24 RB Troy Jackson / Mark Mason
35 Virginia	30 RB Frank Wycheck / Darren Colvin
34 Louisiana Tech 34	DL Greg Hines / Karl Edwards
	DL Larry Webster
	DL Rick Fleece / Ralph Orta
	DL Lubo Zizakovic
	DL Jack Bradford
	LB Glenn Page
	LB Scott Whittier
	DB Scott Rosen
	DB Mike Hollis
	DB Mike Thomas
	DB Ron Reagan

RUSHING: Jackson 176/662y, Mason 43/216y, Colvin 68/191y
PASSING: Zolak 225-418/2589y, 10TDs, 53.8%
RECEIVING: Wycheck 58/509y, B.Johnson 34/629y,
Boehly 32/350y
SCORING: Dan DeArmas (K) 65pts, Jackson & Thomas 30pts

1991 2-9

17 Virginia	6 WR Richie Harris / Marcus Badgett
7 Syracuse	31 WR Gene Thomas / Chad Wiestling
7 West Virginia	37 T Dave Hack
20 Pittsburgh	24 G Dave deBruin
10 Georgia Tech	34 C Mitch Suplee
23 Wake Forest	22 G Jade Dubis
13 Duke	17 T David Dunne
0 North Carolina	34 TE Brett Stevenson / Joe Cooper
7 Penn State	47 QB Jim Sandwisch
7 Clemson	40 RB Troy Jackson / Mark Mason
17 N. Carolina St.	20 RB Frank Wycheck / Doug Burnett
	DL Greg Hines
	DL Larry Webster
	DL Ralph Orta / Darren Drozdov
	DL Lubo Zizakovic
	DL Mark Sturdivant
	LB Dave Marrone
	LB Mike Jarmolowich
	DB Doug Thomas / Brendon Bertha
	DB Doug Lawrence / Mike Thomas
	DB Bill Inge
	DB Ron Reagan

RUSHING: Mason 82/452y, Jackson 123/414y, Burnett 42/195y
PASSING: Sandwisch 142-291/1499y, 6TDs, 48.8%
RECEIVING: Wycheck 45/438y, Thomas 21/209y, 2 with 16
SCORING: Dan DeArmas (K) 36pts, Jackson 30pts,
Mason 18pts

1992 3-8

15 Virginia	28 WR Marcus Badgett
10 N. Carolina St.	14 WR Frank Wycheck
33 West Virginia	34 WR Richie Harris / Wade Inge
13 Penn State	49 WR Dan Prunzik / Jermaine Lewis
47 Pittsburgh	34 T Steve Ingram
26 Georgia Tech	28 G Kevin Arline
23 Wake Forest	30 C Jamie Bragg
7 Duke	25 G Jade Dubis
24 North Carolina	31 T Dave Dunne / John Teter
21 Florida State	69 QB John Kaleo / Scott Milanovich
53 Clemson	23 RB Mark Mason / Doug Burnett
	DL Darren Drozdov / Rich Phoenix
	DL Jim Panagos / Madison Bradley
	DL Mark Sturdivant
	LB Darren Colvin / Jaime Flores
	LB Chad Wiestling / Mike Rodgers
	LB Mike Jarmolowich / Erick Wood
	LB Tim Brown
	DB Brandon Bertha
	DB Mike Lacy / Gene Green
	DB Scott Rosen / Raphael Wall
	DB Bill Inge / Ron Reagan

RUSHING: Mason 96/523y, Wycheck 77/369y, Burnett 94/323y
PASSING: Kaleo 286-482/3392y, 17TDs, 59.3%
RECEIVING: Badgett 75/1240y, Harris 56/518y, Prunzik 52/680y
SCORING: David DeArmas (K) 67pts, Badgett 54pts,
Burnett 36pts

1993 2-9

29 Virginia	43 WR Jason Kremus / Wade Inge
42 North Carolina	59 WR Jermaine Lewis / Walt Williams
37 West Virginia	42 WR Andrew Carter
28 Virginia Tech	55 WR Russ Weaver
7 Penn State	70 T Steve Ingram
0 Georgia Tech	38 G Jade Dubis / Erik Greenstein
26 Duke	18 C Jamie Bragg
0 Clemson	29 G Dave Hack
20 Florida State	49 T John Teter
21 N. Carolina St.	44 QB Scott Milanovich
33 Wake Forest	32 RB Mark Mason / Kameron Williams
	DL Sharrod Mack / Aaron Henne
	DL Madison Bradley / Johnnie Hicks
	DL Mark Sturdivant / Mike Gillespie
	LB Jaime Flores
	LB Ratcliff Thomas / Tim Brown
	LB Chad Wiestling / Erick Wood
	LB Mike Settles
	DB Gene Green / Orlando Strozier
	DB Andreal Johnson / Andre Martin
	DB Angel Guerra
	DB Raphael Wall / Lamont Gore

RUSHING: Mason 158/616y, Williams 28/111y
PASSING: Milanovich 279-431/3499y, 26TDs, 64.7%
RECEIVING: Weaver 69/606y, Lewis 52/957y, Carter 41/370y
SCORING: Lewis 42pts, Kremus 30pts, 4 with 18pts

1994 4-7

16 Duke	49 WR Geroy Simon
20 Florida State	52 WR Jermaine Lewis / Walt Williams
24 West Virginia	13 WR Russ Weaver
31 Wake Forest	7 WR Mancel Johnson / Richard Roberts
0 Clemson	13 T Steve Ingram / Darryl Gilliam
17 North Carolina	41 G Jade Dubis
42 Georgia Tech	27 C Jamie Bragg / Erik Greenstein
38 Tulane	10 G Dave Hack
45 N. Carolina St.	47 T Mark Motley / John Teter
21 Virginia	46 QB Scott Milanovich
16 Syracuse	21 RB Allen Williams / Brian Underwood
	DL Al Wallace
	DL Pat Ward
	DL Aaron Henne
	DL Eric Hicks
	LB Erick Wood
	LB Ratcliff Thomas / Tim Brown
	LB Mike Settles
	DB Wade Inge
	DB Andreal Johnson / Orlando Strozier
	DB Jermaine Stewart
	DB Raphael Wall / Lamont.Gore

RUSHING: Williams 129/649y, Underwood 41/180y
PASSING: Milanovich 229-333/2394y, 20TDs, 68.8%
RECEIVING: Simon 77/891y, Lewis 45/692y, Johnson 33/353y
SCORING:

1995 6-5

29 Tulane	10 WR Geroy Simon
32 North Carolina	18 WR Jermaine Lewis
31 West Virginia	17 WR Mancel Johnson / Bruce James
41 Duke	28 T Darryl Gilliam / Ryan Rezzelle
3 Georgia Tech	31 G Aaron Henne
9 Wake Forest	6 C Erik Greenstein
0 Clemson	17 G Pat Ward
0 Louisville	31 T Mark Motley / John Feugill
30 N. Carolina St.	13 TE Craig Fitzgerald / Eric Henry
18 Virginia	21 QB Scott Milanovich / Brian Cummings
17 Florida State	59 RB Buddy Rodgers / Brian Underwood
	DL Al Wallace / Eric Ogbogu
	DL Johnnie Hicks
	DL Tim Watson
	DL Eric Hicks / Anthony Jenkins
	LB Tim Brown / Eric Barton
	LB Ratcliff Thomas
	LB Mike Settles / Kendall Ogle
	DB A.J. Johnson / Paul Jackson
	DB Chad Scott
	DB Darrick Rather / Henry Baker
	DB Lamont Gore / Andre Hentz

RUSHING: Rodgers 158/718y, Underwood 73/290y
PASSING: Milanovich 125-188/1176y, 2TDs, 66.5%
  Cummings 98-166/1193y, 5TDs, 59.0%
RECEIVING: Lewis 66/937y, Simon 54/440y, Johnson 30/359y
SCORING: Rodgers & Joe O'Donnell (K) 46pts, Lewis 42pts

1996 5-6

30 N. Illinois	6 WR Geroy Simon / Troy Davidson
39 Ala.-Birm'ham	15 WR Walt Williams / Bruce James
3 Virginia	21 WR Mancel Johnson / Kendrick Walton
0 West Virginia	13 T Darryl Gilliam
8 N. Carolina St.	34 G Pat Ward
7 North Carolina	38 C Erik Greenstein
52 Wake Forest	0 G Mitch Watkins / Aaron Henne
22 Duke	19 T John Feugill / Ryan Rezelle
3 Clemson	35 TE Craig Fitzgerald / Tim Brown
13 Georgia Tech	10 QB Brian Cummings
10 Florida State	48 RB Brian Underwood / Buddy Rodgers
	DL Al Wallace
	DL Johnnie Hicks
	DL Tim Watson / Delbert Cowsette
	DL Eric Ogbogu / Eric Hicks
	LB Eric Barton
	LB Ratcliff Thomas
	LB Kendall Ogle / Erwyn Lyght
	DB A.J. Johnson / Bryn Boggs
	DB Chad Scott / Clifton Crosby
	DB Lamont Gore / Paul Jackson
	DB Andre Hentz / Henry Baker

RUSHING: Underwood 97/449y, Rodgers 100/447y,
  Harold Westley (RB) 116/421y
PASSING: Cummings 92-173/1127y, 7TDs, 53.2%
RECEIVING: Simon 35/534y, James 21/170y, Johnson 13/189y,
  Davidson 13/177y
SCORING: Joe O'Donnell (K) 48pts, Rodgers 36pts,
  Simon 26pts

1997 2-9

14 Ohio University	21 WR Doug Patterson / Bruce James
7 Florida State	50 WR Moises Cruz / Omar Cheeseboro
14 North Carolina	40 T Darryl Gilliam
24 Temple	21 G Brad Messina
16 Duke	10 C Ben Thomas
14 West Virginia	31 G Pat Ward / Eric Timothy
17 Wake Forest	35 T John Feugill
9 Clemson	20 TE Mike Hull
0 Virginia	45 QB Brian Cummings
28 N. Carolina St.	45 TB Lamont Jordan / Brian Underwood
18 Georgia Tech	37 FB Peter Timmins / Matt Kalapinski
	DL Eric Ogbogu / Eric Calendine
	DL Johnnie Hicks
	DL Delbert Cowsette / Kris Jenkins
	DL Eric Hicks
	LB Kendall Ogle / Jomo Huggins
	LB Eric Barton
	LB Erwyn Lyght
	DB Troy Davidson / Cliff Crosby
	DB Lynde Washington / Quinzy Fraser
	DB Lewis Sanders / Paul Jackson
	DB Henry Baker / Shawn Forte

RUSHING: Jordan 159/689y, Underwood 62/219y
PASSING: Cummings 154-255/1760y, 10TDs, 60.4%
RECEIVING: Cruz 29/337y, Rodgers 26/294y, Jordan 22/155y
SCORING: Rodgers & Brian Kopka (K) 30pts, Cheeseboro 24pts

1998 3-8

23 James Madison	15 WR Jermaine Arrington
19 Virginia	31 WR Moises Cruz / Omar Cheeseboro
20 West Virginia	42 T Brad Messina / Ryan Rezzelle
30 Temple	20 G Mike George
10 Florida State	24 C Melvin Fowler
0 Clemson	23 G Jamie Wu
10 Wake Forest	20 T John Feugill
14 Georgia Tech	19 TE John Waerig / Bruce James
13 North Carolina	24 QB Randall Jones / Ken Mastrole
42 Duke	25 TB LaMont Jordan / Harold Westley
21 N. Carolina St.	35 FB Matt Kalapinski
	DL Rasheed Simmons
	DL Delbert Cowsette
	DL Kris Jenkins / Chris Hayes
	DL Peter Timmins
	LB Aaron Thompson / Erwyn Lyght
	LB Eric Barton
	LB Kendall Ogle / Marlon Moore
	DB Cliff Crosby
	DB Renard Cox / Tony Okanlawon
	DB Paul Jackson
	DB Shawn Forte / Rod Littles

RUSHING: Jordan 170/902y, Kalapinski 75/370y,
  Westley 78/273y
PASSING: Mastrole 59-131/632y, TD, 45.0%,
  Jones 44-98/567y, 3 TDs, 44.9%
RECEIVING: Arrington 23/366y, Cruz 15/183y, Jordan 14/87y
SCORING: Brian Kopka (K) 58pts, Jordan 36pts, Kalapinski 24pts

1999 5-6

6 Temple	0 WR Guilian Gary / Omar Cheeseboro
51 W. Carolina	10 WR Jason Hatala / Jermaine Arrington
33 West Virginia	0 T Brad Messina
31 Georgia Tech	49 G Todd Wike
17 Wake Forest	14 C Melvin Fowler
30 Clemson	42 G Jamie Wu
45 North Carolina	7 T Matt Crawford
22 Duke	25 TE John Waerig / Jeff Dugan
17 N. Carolina St.	30 QB Calvin McCall
10 Florida State	49 TB LaMont Jordan / Bruce Perry
30 Virginia	34 FB Matt Kalapinski
	DL Peter Timmins
	DL Delbert Cowsette
	DL Kris Jenkins / Charles Hill
	DL Erwyn Lyght
	LB Marlon Moore
	LB Kevin Bishop / E.J. Henderson
	LB Aaron Thompson
	DB Lewis Sanders
	DB Renard Cox / Tony Okanlawon
	DB Shawn Forte
	DB Rod Littles / Tony Jackson

RUSHING: Jordan 266/1632y, McCall 79/256y, Perry 30/195y
PASSING: McCall 93-179/1264y, 5TDs, 52.0%
RECEIVING: Gary 24/257y, Jordan 19/208y, Arrington 17/302y
SCORING: Jordan 102pts

2000 5-6

17 Temple	10 WR Guilian Gary / Jason Hatala
17 West Virginia	30 WR Scooter Monroe / Moises Cruz
45 Middle Tenn.	27 T Tim Howard
7 Florida State	59 G Todd Wike
23 Virginia	31 C Melvin Fowler
14 Clemson	35 G Bob Krantz
37 Wake Forest	7 T Matt Crawford
20 Duke	9 TE Jeff Dugan
35 N. Carolina St.	28 QB Calvin McCall / Shaun Hill
10 North Carolina	13 TB LaMont Jordan / Mukala Sikyala
22 Georgia Tech	35 FB Matt Kalapinski
	DL Kris Jenkins
	DL Charles Hill / Landon Jones
	DL Durrand Roundtree / Scott Smith
	LB Aaron Thompson / Leroy Ambush
	LB Marlon Moye-Moore / Kevin Bishop
	LB E.J. Henderson / Leon Joe
	LB Mike Whaley
	DB Tony Okanlawon
	DB Curome Cox
	DB Shawn Forte / Randall Jones
	DB Tony Jackson / Rod Littles

RUSHING:Jordan 213/920y, Sikyala 40/190y, Hill 44/92y
PASSING: McCall 105-199/1533y, 5TDs, 52.8%
RECEIVING: Gary 40/568y, Dugan 25/319y, Jordan 21/287y
SCORING: Jordan 66pts, Brian Kopka (K) 50pts, Gary 42pts

2001 10-2

23 North Carolina	7 WR Guilian Gary / Scooter Monroe
50 E. Michigan	3 WR Jafar Williams
27 Wake Forest	20 T C.J. Brooks
32 West Virginia	20 G Todd Wike
41 Virginia	21 C Melvin Fowler
20 Georgia Tech	17 G Lamar Bryant
59 Duke	17 T Matt Crawford
31 Florida State	52 TE Jeff Dugan / Matt Murphy
47 Troy State	14 QB Shaun Hill
37 Clemson	20 TB Bruce Perry / Marc Riley
23 N. Carolina St.	19 FB James Lynch / Chad Killian
23 Florida56 DL Ryan Swift	
	DL C.J. Feldheim
	DL Durrand Roundtree
	LB Mike Whaley
	LB Aaron Thompson / Kevin Bishop
	LB E.J. Henderson / Monte Graves
	LB Leon Joe
	DB Tony Okanlawon/Dominique Foxw'rth
	DB Curome Cox
	DB Randall Jones
	DB Tony Jackson / Rod Littles

RUSHING: Perry 219/1242y Riley 85/338y, Hill 116/309y
PASSING: Hill 197-329/2380y, 13TDs, 59.9%
RECEIVING: Gary 49/727y, Perry 40/359y, Williams 39/425y
SCORING: Nick Novak (K) 89pts, Perry 72pts, Riley 60pts

2002 11-3

0 Notre Dame	22 WR Scooter Monroe / Derrick Fenner
44 Akron	14 WR Jafar Williams / Steve Suter
10 Florida State	37 T Eric Dumas / Stephon Heyer
45 E. Michigan	3 G C.J. Brooks
37 Wofford	8 C Todd Wike (G) / Kyle Schmitt
48 West Virginia	17 G Lamar Bryant
34 Georgia Tech	10 T Matt Crawford
45 Duke	12 TE Jeff Dugan
59 North Carolina	7 QB Scott McBrien
24 N. Carolina St.	21 TB Chris Downs / Bruce Perry
30 Clemson	12 FB James Lynch
13 Virginia	48 DL Jamahl Cochran / Shawne Merriman
32 Wake Forest	14 DL Randy Starks
30 Tennessee 3 DL C.J. Feldheim / William Shime
	DL Durrand Roundtree
	LB Leroy Ambush / William Kershaw
	LB E.J. Henderson / D'Qwell Jackson
	LB Leon Joe / Andrew Henley
	DB Curome Cox / Jamal Chance
	DB Domonique Foxworth
	DB Madieu Williams
	DB Dennard Wilson / Andrew Smith

RUSHING: Downs 208/1154y, Josh Allen (TB) 60/405y,
Perry 72/341y
PASSING: McBrien 162-284/2497y, 15TD, 57.0%
RECEIVING: Monroe 37/614y, Williams 28/562y,
Latrez Harrison (WR) 20/369y
SCORING: Nick Novak (K) 125pts, Downs 90pts, Allen 48pts

2003 10-3

13 N. Illinois	20 WR Steve Suter / Jo Jo Walker
10 Florida State	35 WR Latrez Harrison / Derrick Fenner, Jr.
61 Citadel	0 T Stephon Heyer
34 West Virginia	7 G C.J. Brooks
37 E. Michigan	13 C Kyle Schmitt
21 Clemson	7 G Lamar Bryant / Akil Patterson
33 Duke	20 T Eric Dumas
3 Georgia Tech	7 TE Jeff Dugan
59 North Carolina	21 QB Scott McBrien
27 Virginia	17 TB Josh Allen / Bruce Perry
26 N. Carolina St.	24 FB Bernard Fiddler
41 Wake Forest	28 DL Kevin Eli
41 West Virginia 7 DL C.J. Feldheim
	DL Randy Starks
	DL Shawne Merriman / Jamahl Cochran
	LB D'Qwell Jackson
	LB Leroy Ambush
	LB Leon Joe / William Kershaw
	DB Curome Cox
	DB Domonique Foxworth
	DB Madieu Williams / Andrew Smith
	DB Dennard Wilson

RUSHING: Allen 186/922y, Perry 147/713y,
Sam Maldonado (TB) 51/305y
PASSING: McBrien 173-314/2672y, 19TD, 55.1%
RECEIVING: Harrison 39/558y, Suter 29/471y, Walker 23/324y
SCORING: Nick Novak (K) 110pts, Allen 54pts,
McBrien & Perry 36pts

2004 5-6

23 N. Illinois	20 WR Derrick Fenner
45 Temple	22 WR Steve Suter / Jo Jo Walker
16 West Virginia	19 T Stephon Heyer
55 Duke	21 G C.J. Brooks / Donnie Woods
7 Georgia Tech	2 C Kyle Schmitt
3 N. Carolina St.	13 G Andrew Crummey / Russell Bonham
7 Clemson	10 T Lou Lombardo / Brandon Nixon
20 Florida State	17 TE Derek Miller/Vern Davis/Rob Abiamiri
0 Virginia	16 QB Joel Stratham / Sam Hollenbach
6 Virginia Tech	55 TB Josh Allen / Sammy Maldonado
13 Wake Forest	7 FB Maurice Smith
	DL Shawne Merriman
	DL Conrad Bolston / Rob Armstrong
	DL Henry Scott / Justin Duffie
	DL Kevin Eli
	LB David Holloway
	LB D'Qwell Jackson
	LB William Kershaw
	DB Gerrick McPhearson
	DB Domonique Foxworth
	DB Raymond Custis
	DB Chris Kelley

RUSHING: Maldonado 138/560y, Allen 144/533y,
Mario Merrills (TB) 33/124y
PASSING: Stratham 126-234/1590y, 8TD, 53.8%
RECEIVING: Fenner 35/430y, Davis 27/441y, Suter 23/270y
SCORING: Nick Novak (K) 69pts, Allen 36pts, Maldonado 30pts

2005 5-6

23 Navy	20 WR Derrick Fenner / Dan Melendez
24 Clemson	28 WR Jo Jo Walker / Drew Weatherly
19 West Virginia	31 T Jared Gaither / Derek Miller (TE)
22 Wake Forest	12 G Donnie Woods
45 Virginia	33 C Ryan McDonald
38 Temple	7 G Andrew Crummey / Russell Bonham
9 Virginia Tech	28 T Brandon Nixon
27 Florida State	35 TE Vernon Davis / Jason Goode
33 North Carolina	30 QB Sam Hollenbach
16 Boston College	31 TB Lance Ball / Mario Merrills
14 N. Carolina St.	20 FB Tim Cesa/Ricardo Dickerson/M.Deese
	DL Jeremy Navarre
	DL Conrad Bolston / Carlos Feliciano
	DL Jack Griffin / Dre Moore
	DL Trey Covington / Jermaine Lemons
	LB David Holloway
	LB D'Qwell Jackson
	LB William Kershaw / Wesley Jefferson
	DB Gerrick McPhearson / Isaiah Gardner
	DB Josh Wilson
	DB Christian Varner / J.J. Justice
	DB Milton Harris / Marcus Wimbush

RUSHING: Ball 189/903y, Merrills 82/313y,
Keon Lattimore 58/181y
PASSING: Hollenbach 192-315/2539y, 13TDs, 61.0%
RECEIVING: Davis 51/871y, Melendez 40/584y, Walker 35/480y,
Fenner 34/417y
SCORING: Daniel Ennis (K) 74pts, Ball & Davis 36pts

2006 9-4

27 Wm.& Mary	14 WR Derrius Heyward-Bey
24 Middle Tenn.	10 WR Danny Oquendo / Isaiah Williams
24 West Virginia	45 T Stephon Heyer
14 Florida Int'l	10 G Donnie Woods
23 Georgia Tech	27 C Edwin Williams
28 Virginia	26 G Andrew Crummey / Garrick Clig
26 N. Carolina St.	20 T Jared Gaither / Dane Randolph
27 Florida State	24 TE Dan Gronkowski / Joey Haynos
13 Clemson	12 QB Sam Hollenbach
14 Miami	13 TB Lance Ball / Josh Allen
16 Boston College	38 FB Keon Lattimore
24 Wake Forest	38 DL Jeremy Navarre
24 Purdue 7 DL Conrad Bolston / Carlos Feliciano
	DL Dre Moore
	DL Trey Covington / Barrod Heggs
	LB David Holloway / Dave Philistin
	LB Wesley Jefferson
	LB Erin Henderson / Moses Fokou
	DB Isaiah Gardner
	DB Josh Wilson
	DB Christian Varner / J.J. Justice
	DB Marcus Wimbush

RUSHING: Ball 174/815y, Lattimore 160/743y, Allen 33/98y
PASSING: Hollenbach 203-328/2371y, 15TD, 61.9%
RECEIVING: Heyward-Bey 45/694y, Haynos 37/369y,
Oquendo 34/396y, I. Williams 28/379y
SCORING: Dan Ennis (K) 92pts, Ball 48pts, Heyward-Bey 30pts

2007 6-7

31 Villanova	14 WR LaQuan Williams / Isaiah Williams
26 Florida Int'l	10 WR Darrius Heyward-Bey/Emani Lee-Odai
14 West Virginia	31 T Scott Burley / Bruce Campbell
24 Wake Forest	31 G Jaimie Thomas / Phil Costa
34 Rutgers	24 C Edwin Williams
28 Georgia Tech	26 G Andrew Crummey / Jack Griffin
17 Virginia	18 T Dane Randolph
17 Clemson	30 TE Dan Gronkowski / Joey Haynos
13 North Carolina	12 QB Chris Turner / Jordan Steffy
42 Boston College	35 TB Keon Lattimore / Lance Ball
16 Florida State	24 FB Cory Jackson / Jason Goode (H-B)
37 N. Carolina St.	0 DL Jeremy Navarre
14 Oregon State 21 DL Dre Moore
	DL Carlos Feliciano
	DL Trey Covington / Jermaine Lemons
	LB Moise Fokou / Adrian Moten
	LB Dave Philistin
	LB Erin Henderson / Rick Costa
	DB Isaiah Gardner / Anthony Wiseman
	DB Kevin Barnes / Noln Carroll
	DB J.J. Justice
	DB Christian Varner / Jeff Allen

RUSHING: Lattimore 213/805y, Ball 182/768y,
Da'Rel Scott (TB) 14/135y
PASSING: Turner 153-241/1958y, 7TD, 63.5%,
Steffy 70-104/686y, 2TD, 67.3%
RECEIVING: Heyward-Bey 51/786y, Haynos 30/318y,
I. Williams 25/395y
SCORING: Obi Egekeze (K) 87pts, Lattimore 78pts, Ball 72pts

2008 8-5

14 Delaware	7 WR Isaiah Williams / Torrey Smith
14 Middle Tenn.	24 WR Danny Oquendo / Cory Jackson (FB)
35 California	27 WR Darrius Heyward-Bey
51 E. Michigan	24 T Scott Burley
20 Clemson	17 G Jaimie Thomas
0 Virginia	31 C Edwin Williams
26 Wake Forest	0 G Phil Costa / Jack Griffin
27 N. Carolina St.	24 T Dane Randolph / Bruce Campbell
13 Virginia Tech	23 TE Dan Gronkowski
17 North Carolina	15 QB Chris Turner
3 Florida State	37 TB Da'Rel Scott / Davin Meggett
21 Boston College	28 DL Mack Frost / Dean Muhtadi
42 Nevada 35 DL Jeremy Navarre / Dion Armstrong
	DL Olugbemi Otulaja / Travis Ivey
	LB Trey Covington / Rick Costa
	LB Dave Philistin / Chase Bullock
	LB Alex Wujciak
	LB Moise Fokou / Derek Drummond
	DB Anthony Wiseman / Nolan Carroll
	DB Kevin Barnes / Jamari McCollough
	DB Terrell Skinner / Antwine Perez
	DB Jeff Allen

RUSHING: Scott 209/1133y, Meggett 89/457y,
Heyward-Bey 15/202y
PASSING: Turner 214-374/2516y, 13TD, 57.2%
RECEIVING: Heyward-Bey 42/609y, Oquendo 29/371y,
Gronkowski 29/287y, Smith 24/336y
SCORING: Obi Egekeze (K) 77pts, Scott 48pts,
Heyward-Bey 36pts

2009 2-10

13 California	52 WR Torrey Smith / Quintin McCree
38 James Madison	35 WR Adrian Cannon / Kerry Boykins
31 Middle Tenn.	32 WR Ronnie Tyler / Cory Jackson (FB)
13 Rutgers	34 T Bruce Campbell
24 Clemson	21 G Paul Pinegar (T) / Bennett Fulper
32 Wake Forest	42 C Phil Costa
9 Virginia	20 G Andrew Gonnella / Justin Lewis
13 Duke	17 T R.J. Dill
31 N. Carolina St.	18 TE Tommy Galt / Devonte Campbell
9 Virginia Tech	36 QB Chris Turner / Jamarr Robinson
26 Florida State	29 TB Da'Rel Scott / Davin Meggett
17 Boston College	19 DL Jared Harrell
	DL A.J. Francis
	DL Travis Ivey
	LB Deege Galt
	LB Adrian Moten
	LB Alex Wujciak
	LB Demetrius Hartsfield / Ben Pooler
	DB Anthony Wiseman
	DB Cameron Chism / Nolan Carroll
	DB Terrell Skinner / Antwine Perez
	DB Jamari McCollough / Kenny Tate

RUSHING: Scott 85/425y, Meggett 99/338y, Robinson 53/229y
PASSING: Turner 180-303/2069y, 10TD, 59.4%,
Robinson 46-85/482y, 2TD, 54.1%
RECEIVING: Smith 61/827y, Cannon 44/468y, Tyler 28/366y
Meggett 14/175y, T. Galt 14/146y
SCORING: Nick Ferrara (K) 80pts, Smith 48pts, Meggett 36pts

2010 9-4

17 Navy	14 WR Adrian Cannon / Quinton McCree
62 Morgan State	3 WR Torrey Smith / LaQuan Williams
17 West Virginia	31 T R.J. Dill
42 Florida Int'l	28 G Andrew Gonnella / Justin Gilbert
21 Duke	16 C Bennett Fulper
7 Clemson	31 G Justin Lewis / Pete White
24 Boston College	21 T Paul Pinegar (C) / Pete DeSouza
62 Wake Forest	14 TE Matt Furstenburg / Will Yeatman
20 Miami	26 QB Danny O'Brien / Jamarr Robinson
42 Virginia	23 TB Da'Rel Scott / Davin Meggett
16 Florida State	30 FB Taylor Watson / Haroon Brown
38 No. Carolina St.	31 DL Drew Gloster
51 East Carolina	20 DL A.J. Francis / Zachariah Kerr
	DL Joe Vellano
	DL Justin Anderson / Isaiah Ross
	LB Adrian Moten / Darin Drakeford
	LB Alex Wujciak / David Mackall
	LB Demetrius Hartsfield
	DB Trenton Hughes / Dexter McDougle
	DB Cameron Chism
	DB Kenny Tate / Eric Franklin
	DB Antwine Perez / Matt Robinson

RUSHING: Meggett 126/720y, Scott 122/708y,
D.J. Adams (TB) 67/239y
PASSING: O'Brien 192-337/2438y, 22TD, 57%
Robinson 26-49/349y, 4TD, 53.1%
RECEIVING: Smith 67/1055y, Cannon 36/324y, McCree 16/188y
SCORING: Travis Baltz (K) 95pts, Smith 72pts, Adams 66pts

MIAMI

University of Miami (Founded 1925)
Coral Gables, Florida
Nickname: Hurricanes
Colors: Orange, Green, and White
Stadium: Dolphin Stadium (1987) 76,500
Conference Affiliation: Independent (1953-90), Big East
(1991-2003), Atlantic Coast (2004-present)

CAREER RUSHING YARDS	Attempts	Yards
Ottis Anderson (1975-78)	691	3331
Edgerrin James (1996-98)	474	2960
James Jackson (1996-2000)	541	2953
Clinton Portis (1999-2001)	440	2523
Graig Cooper (2007-09)	430	2218
Danyell Ferguson (1992-96)	454	2214
Javarris James (2006-09)	505	2162
Willis McGahee (2001-02)	351	2067
Frank Gore (2001, 2003-04)	348	1975
Stephen McGuire (1989-92)	450	1953

CAREER PASSING YARDS	Comp.-Att.	Yards
Ken Dorsey (1999-02)	668-1153	9565
Gino Torretta (1989-92)	555-991	7690
Jacory Harris (2008-10)	508-870	6340
Vinny Testaverde (1982,84-86)	413-674	6058
Craig Erickson (1987-90)	420-752	6056
Ryan Clement (1994-97)	443-747	6004
Bernie Kosar (1983-84)	463-743	5971
Kyle Wright (2004-07)	478-807	5805
Steve Walsh (1986-88)	410-690	5369
Jim Kelly (1979-82)	376-676	5228

CAREER RECEIVING YARDS	Catches	Yards
Santana Moss (1997-2000)	143	2546
Reggie Wayne (1997-2000)	173	2510
Michael Irvin (1985-87)	143	2423
Lamar Thomas (1989-92)	144	2271
Leonard Hankerson (2007-10)	134	2160
Andre Johnson (2000-02)	92	1831
Eddie Brown (1983-84)	89	1754
Wesley Carroll (1989-90)	114	1722
Larry Brodsky (1979-81)	100	1696
Randal Hill (1987-90)	107	1643

SEASON RUSHING YARDS	Attempts	Yards
Willis McGahee (2002)	282	1753
Edgerrin James (1998)	242	1416
Ottis Anderson (1978)	224	1266
Clinton Portis (2001)	220	1200
Edgerrin James (1997)	184	1098

SEASON PASSING YARDS	Comp.-Att.	Yards
Bernie Kosar (1984)	262-416	3642
Ken Dorsey (2002)	222-393	3369
Craig Erickson (1990)	225-393	3363
Jacory Harris (2009)	242-406	3352
Vinny Testaverde (1985)	216-352	3238

SEASON RECEIVING YARDS	Catches	Yards
Leonard Hankerson (2010)	72	1156
Eddie Brown (1984)	59	1114
Andre Johnson (2002)	52	1092
Wesley Carroll (1990)	61	952
Santana Moss (1999)	54	899

GAME RUSHING YARDS	Attempts	Yards
Edgerrin James (1998 vs. UCLA)	39	299
Edgerrin James (1997 vs. Boston Coll.)	33	271
Smokey Roan (1980 vs. East Carolina)	33	249

GAME PASSING YARDS	Comp.-Att.	Yards
Gino Torretta (1991 vs. San Diego St.)	23-44	485
Gino Torretta (1989 vs. San Jose St.)	32-49	468
Craig Erickson (1990 vs. California)	32-47	467

GAME RECEIVING YARDS	Catches	Yards
Eddie Brown (1984 vs. Boston College)	10	220
Wesley Carroll (1990 vs. California)	11	208
Andre Johnson (2001 vs. Nebraska)	7	199

GREATEST COACH:

One could make an argument for four Miami coaches who have set a tremendous standard of winning. Jimmy Johnson won a national championship and finished second twice with a 34-2 record over a three-year span. Dennis Erickson took a national championship in his first year in Coral Gables, won a second title two years later, and finished third in the country two other times. Howard Schnellenberger got the Hurricanes flying by breaking through for the 1983 national championship at a time not long after the school considered dropping football. Larry Coker also won a national title in his first try and posted the greatest coaching record (35-3) in history over the first three years of a career.

Our pick is Butch Davis, who arrived in Coral Gables to keep afloat a program that had just received drastic NCAA-ordered cuts in scholarships. Although Davis' record of 51-20 pales in comparison to Johnson's 52-9 and Erickson's 63-9, he deserves tremendous credit for keeping the Hurricanes near the level of achievement to which they had become so accustomed. Davis' transition years of 1995-97 produced a record of 22-12, including the only losing season (5-6 in 1997) since 1979. Without his tremendous recruiting and coaching acumen, Miami could easily have slipped back into the dark days of the 1970s. And with such modern-day recruiting pressure as there is from in-state rivals Florida and Florida State, the Hurricanes could have sunk into oblivion.

Also in Davis' favor is that he brought polished classiness and a code of behavior to the school that hadn't been seen since the bad old days. Miami players actually acted like gentlemen under Davis, unlike the legendary flaunting of battle fatigues before the 1987 Fiesta Bowl and the landslide of unsportsmanlike penalties that the Hurricanes perpetrated in the 1991 Cotton Bowl.

MIAMI'S 55 GREATEST SINCE 1953

OFFENSE

WIDE RECEIVER: Eddie Brown, Michael Irvin, Andre Johnson, Santana Moss, Lamar Thomas
TIGHT END: Alfredo Roberts, Jeremy Shockey, Kellen Winslow, Jr.
TACKLE: Dan Connors, Juaquin Gonzalez, Bryant McKinnie, Leon Searcy
GUARD: Art Kehoe, Joe Kohut, Richard Mercier
CENTER: K.C. Jones, Jim Otto, Brett Romberg
QUARTERBACK: Ken Dorsey, Bernie Kosar, Vinny Testaverde
RUNNING BACK: Edgerrin James, Willis McGahee, Clinton Portis
FULLBACK: Don Bosseler, Alonzo Highsmith

DEFENSE

END: Ted Hendricks, Kenard Lang, Greg Mark, Daniel Stubbs
TACKLE: Jerome Brown, Cortez Kennedy, Russell Maryland, Warren Sapp
LINEBACKER: Michael Barrow, Maurice Crum, Ray Lewis, Dan Morgan, Winston Moss, Darrin Smith
CORNERBACK: Ronnie Lippett, Ryan McNeil, Burgess Owens, Antrel Rolle
SAFETY: Bennie Blades, Edward Reed, Sean Taylor, Darryl Williams

SPECIAL TEAMS

RETURN SPECIALISTS: Devin Hester, Kevin Williams
PLACE KICKER: Carlos Huerta
PUNTER: Freddie Capshaw

MULTIPLE POSITIONS

END-DEFENSIVE END-GUARD-LINEBACKER: Ed Weisacosky

TWO-WAY PLAYERS

HALFBACK-DEFENSIVE BACK: Whitey Rouviere
CENTER-LINEBACKER: Ernest Tobey

PERFORMANCE FORMULA:
MIAMI'S 10 BEST SEASONS

2001	1.9071	1 of 70
1988	1.8395	1 of 69
1987	1.8290	1 of 69
1991	1.8189	2 of 71
2000	1.7605	2 of 70
1989	1.7365	2 of 70
1986	1.7190	3 of 70
2002	1.7189	2 of 70
1990	1.6801	1 of 70
1983	1.6396	4 of 70

MIAMI HURRICANES

Year	W-L-T	AP Poll	Conference Standing	Toughest Regular Season Opponents	Coach (Record at School)	Bowl Games			
1953	4-5			Baylor 7-3, Maryland 10-0, Auburn 7-2-1	Andy Gustafson				
1954	8-1	11		Baylor 7-3, Maryland 7-2-1, Auburn 7-3, Florida 5-5	Andy Gustafson				
1955	6-3	14		Georgia Tech 8-1-1, Notre Dame 8-2, TCU 9-1, Pittsburgh 7-3	Andy Gustafson				
1956	8-1-1	6		TCU 7-3, Clemson 7-1-2, Florida 6-3-1, Pittsburgh 7-2-1	Andy Gustafson				
1957	5-4-1			Baylor 6-3, NC State 7-1-2, Florida 6-2-1	Andy Gustafson				
1958	2-8			Wisconsin 7-1-1, LSU 10-0, Boston College 7-3, Florida 6-3-1	Andy Gustafson				
1959	6-4			LSU 9-1, Auburn 7-3, South Carolina 6-4, Michigan State 5-4	Andy Gustafson				
1960	6-4			Auburn 8-2, Syracuse 7-2, Florida 8-2	Andy Gustafson				
1961	7-4			Penn State 7-3, Navy 7-3, Colorado 9-1, North Carolina 5-5	Andy Gustafson	Liberty	14	Syracuse	15
1962	7-4			LSU 8-1-1, Alabama 9-1, Northwestern 7-2, Florida 6-4	Andy Gustafson	Gotham	34	Nebraska	36
1963	3-7			LSU 7-3, North Carolina 8-2, Pittsburgh 9-1, Alabama 8-2	Andy Gustafson (93-65-3)				
1964	4-5-1			Florida St. 8-1-1, Georgia Tech 7-3, Boston College 6-3, Florida 7-3	Charlie Tate				
1965	5-4-1			Syracuse 7-3, LSU 7-3, Florida 7-3, Notre Dame 7-2-1	Charlie Tate				
1966	8-2-1	9		Colorado 7-3, Georgia 9-1, Southern Calif. 7-3, Florida 8-2	Charlie Tate	Liberty	14	Virginia Tech	7
1967	7-4	11+		Penn State 8-2, Auburn 6-4, Notre Dame 8-2	Charlie Tate	Bluebonnet	21	Colorado	31
1968	5-5			Southern Calif. 9-0-1, LSU 7-3, Penn State 10-0, Alabama 8-2	Charlie Tate				
1969	4-6			LSU 9-1, Houston 8-2, Florida 8-1-1	Charlie Tate				
1970	3-8			Georgia Tech 8-3, Florida 7-4, Houston 8-3	Charlie Tate [1-1] (34-27-3), Walt Kichefski [2-7]				
1971	4-7			Florida State 8-3, Notre Dame 8-2, Alabama 11-0, Houston 9-2	Fran Curci				
1972	5-6			Florida State 7-4, Texas 9-1, Notre Dame 8-2	Fran Curci (9-13)				
1973	5-6			Texas 8-2, Oklahoma 10-0-1, Alabama 11-0, Notre Dame 10-0	Pete Elliott				
1974	6-5			Auburn 9-2, Notre Dame 9-2, Alabama 11-0, Florida 8-3	Pete Elliott (11-11)				
1975	2-8			Oklahoma 10-1, Nebraska 10-1, Colorado 9-2, Florida 9-2	Carl Selmer				
1976	3-8			Pittsburgh 11-0, Notre Dame 8-3, Florida 8-3 Houston 9-2	Carl Selmer (5-16)				
1977	3-8			Ohio State 9-2, Penn State 10-1, Alabama 10-1, Notre Dame 10-1	Lou Saban				
1978	6-5			Florida State 8-3, Georgia Tech 7-4, Notre Dame 8-3	Lou Saban (9-13)				
1979	5-6			Florida State 11-0, Penn State 7-4, Alabama 11-0, Notre Dame 7-4	Howard Schnellenberger				
1980	9-3	18		Florida St. 10-1, Notre Dame 9-1-1, Miss. St. 9-2, Penn St. 9-2	Howard Schnellenberger	Peach	20	Virginia Tech	10
1981	9-2	8		Houston 7-3-1, Texas 9-1-1, Penn State 9-2, Florida State 6-5	Howard Schnellenberger				
1982	7-4			Florida 8-3, Florida State 8-3, Maryland 8-3	Howard Schnellenberger				
1983	11-1	1		Florida 8-2-1, Notre Dame 6-5, West Virginia 8-3	H. Schnell'nberger (41-16)	Orange	31	Nebraska	30
1984	8-5	18		Auburn 8-4, Florida 9-1-1, Maryland 8-3, Boston College 9-2	Jimmy Johnson	Fiesta	37	UCLA	39
1985	10-2	8		Florida 9-1-1, Oklahoma 10-1, Florida State 8-3, Maryland 8-3	Jimmy Johnson	Sugar	7	Tennessee	35
1986	11-1	2		Oklahoma 10-1, Florida State 6-4-1	Jimmy Johnson	Fiesta	10	Penn State	14
1987	12-0	1		Arkansas 9-3, Florida St. 10-1, Notre Dame 8-3, South Carolina 8-3	Jimmy Johnson	Orange	20	Oklahoma	14
1988	11-1	2		Florida St. 10-1, Michigan 8-2-1 Notre Dame 11-0, Arkansas 10-1	Jimmy Johnson (52-9)	Orange	23	Nebraska	3
1989	11-1	1		BYU 10-3, Iowa 8-4, Notre Dame 9-3, Florida State 10-2	Dennis Erickson	Sugar	33	Alabama	25
1990	10-2	3		BYU 10-2, Iowa 8-3, Florida State 9-2, Notre Dame 9-2	Dennis Erickson	Cotton	46	Texas	3
1991	12-0	1	1	Tulsa 9-2, Penn State 10-2, Florida State 10-2	Dennis Erickson	Orange	22	Nebraska	0
1992	11-1	3	1	Arizona 6-4-1, Florida State 10-1, Penn State 7-4, Syracuse 9-2	Dennis Erickson	Sugar	13	Alabama	34
1993	9-3	15	2	Virginia Tech 8-3, Colorado 7-3-1, Florida St. 11-1, West Va. 11-0	Dennis Erickson	Fiesta	0	Arizona	29
1994	10-2	6	1	Washington 7-4, Florida State 9-1-1, Virginia Tech 8-3	Dennis Erickson (63-9)	Orange	17	Nebraska	24
1995	8-3		1t	UCLA 7-4, Virginia Tech 9-2, Florida State 9-2, Syracuse 8-3	Butch Davis				
1996	9-3	14	1t	Florida State 11-0, East Carolina 8-3, Virginia Tech 10-1	Butch Davis	Carquest	31	Virginia	21
1997	5-6		5t	Arizona State 8-3, Florida State 10-1, Syracuse 9-3	Butch Davis				
1998	9-3	20	2t	Virginia Tech 8-3, Florida State 11-1, Syracuse 8-3, UCLA 10-1	Butch Davis	Micron PC	46	North Carolina State	23
1999	9-4	15	2	Penn State 9-3, Florida State 11-0, Virginia Tech 11-0	Butch Davis	Gator	28	Georgia Tech	13
2000	11-1	2	1	Washington 10-1, Florida State 11-1, Virginia Tech 10-1	Butch Davis (51-20)	Sugar	37	Florida	20
2001	12-0	1	1	Washington 8-3, Florida State 7-4, Syracuse 9-3	Larry Coker	Rose	37	Nebraska	14
2002	12-1	2	1	Florida 8-5, Florida State 9-5, Tennessee 8-5, Virginia Tech 10-4	Larry Coker	Fiesta	24	Ohio State	31
2003	11-2	5	1t	Florida 8-5, Florida State 10-3, Virginia Tech 8-5, Tennessee 10-3	Larry Coker	Orange	16	Florida State	14
2004	9-3	11	3t	Florida State 9-3, Louisville 11-1, Virginia Tech 10-3	Larry Coker	Peach	27	Florida	10
2005	9-3	17	Cstl2	Florida State 8-5, Clemson 8-4, Virginia Tech 11-2, Georgia Tech 7-5	Larry Coker	Peach	3	Louisiana State	40
2006	7-6		Cstl4	Louisville 11-1, Georgia Tech 9-4, Virginia Tech 10-2, Boston College 9-3	Larry Coker (60-15)	MPC Comp.	21	Nevada	20
2007	5-7		Cstl5	Oklahoma 10-2, Virginia 9-3, Virginia Tech 10-2, Boston College 10-2	Randy Shannon				
2008	7-6		Cstl3t	Florida 12-1, Florida State 8-4, Georgia Tech 9-3, Virginia Tech 9-4	Randy Shannon	Emerald	17	California	24
2009	9-4	19	Cstl3	Georgia Tech 11-2, Virginia Tech 9-3, Clemson 8-5	Randy Shannon	ChampsSports	14	Wisconsin	20
2010	7-6		Cstl2	Ohio State 11-1, Florida State 9-4, Maryland 8-4, Virginia Tech 11-2	Randy Shannon (28-23)	Sun	17	Notre Dame	33

TOTAL: 427-224-5 .6547 (15 of 70)   **Bowl Games since 1953:**   16-14 .5333 (29 of 70)

GREATEST TEAM SINCE 1953: There are, oh, so many Hurricane teams to choose from, but the 1987 (12-0) national champions, a 20-14 winner of the Orange Bowl over Oklahoma, get our nod as the greatest. Runners-up are plentiful, including (chronologically) 1954, 1956, 1983, 1986, 1988-92, 1994, and 2000-02. Larry Coker's fabulous coaching debut, an undefeated record in 2001, tops Miami's sterling group of teams in the Performance Formula.

1953 4-5

27	Florida State	0	E Bob Nolan / Tom Pepsin
13	Baylor	21	T Gene Bucilli
39	Clemson	7	G John Krotec / Joe Kohut
16	Nebraska	20	C Ernest Tobey
0	Maryland	30	G Norm French / Ted Lubas
0	Fordham	20	T Dan Tassotti / Ed Bucilli
20	Auburn	29	E Frank McDonald
26	Virginia Tech	0	QB Don James / J.B. Johnston
14	Florida	10	HB Bill Smith / Art Knust
			HB Whitey Rouviere / Ed "Porky" Oliver
			FB Gordon Malloy

RUSHING: Malloy 90/342y, Smith 60/290y, Rouviere 68/275y
PASSING: James 39-75/450y, 3TD, 52.0%
 Johnston 19-41/229y, TD, 46.3%
RECEIVING: McDonald 20/235y, Nolan 12/140y, Malloy 5/34y
SCORING: Rouviere & Smith 24pts, Oliver (HB-K) 23pts

1954 8-1

51	Furman	13	E Tom Pepsin / Bob Nolan
19	Baylor	13	T Allan Rodberg
26	Holy Cross	20	G John Krotec / Bob Cunio
27	Mississippi St.	13	C Ernest Tobey
9	Maryland	7	G Joe Kohut / Tom Pratt
75	Fordham	7	T Bob Della Valle
13	Auburn	14	E Frank McDonald / Don Johnson
23	Alabama	7	QB Mario Bonofiglio / Carl Garrigus
14	Florida	0	HB Gordon Malloy / Jack Losch
			HB Whitey Rouviere / Johnny Bookman
			FB Don Bosseler / Paul Hefti

RUSHING: Malloy 87/492y, Bosseler 110/424y,
 Garrigus 60/341y
PASSING: Garrigus 27-47/305y, 2TD, 57.4%,
 Bonofiglia 14-32/232y, 2TD, 43.8%
RECEIVING: McDonald 15/181y, Rouviere 7/81y,
 Bookman 4/111y, Losch 4/41y, Bosseler 4/12y
SCORING: Malloy 42pts, Bonofiglio (QB-K) 38pts,
 Garrigus 37pts

1955 6-3

6	Georgia Tech	14	E Bob Nolan / Phil Bennett
34	Florida State	0	T Allan Rodberg / George Vasu
0	Notre Dame	14	G John Krotec / Bob Cunio
19	TCU	21	C Mike Hudock / Vester Newcomb
21	Pittsburgh	7	G Joe Kohut / Tom Pratt
14	Boston College	7	T Bob Della Valle / Charley Hutchings
46	Bucknell	0	E Don Johnson / John Melwid
34	Alabama	12	QB Mario Bonofiglio / Sam Scarnecchia
7	Florida	6	HB Jack Losch/John Bookman/Ed Oliver
			HB Whit'y Rouviere / John Varone
			FB Don Bosseler / Paul Hefti

RUSHING: Bossler 104/435y, Losch 47/426y, Varone 46/324y
PASSING: Scarnecchia 31-49/485y, 2TD, 63.3%
RECEIVING: Rouviere 10/154y, Losch 7/206, Bookman 7/154y
SCORING: Losch (HB-K) 31pts, Bosseler, Hefti & Rouviere 18pts

1956 8-1-1

14	South Carolina	6	E Jack Johnson / Phil Bennett
27	Boston College	6	T Chuck DeVore / Charlie Diamond
13	Maryland	6	G Bob Cunio / Don Wallace
7	Georgia	7	C Mike Hudock / Vestor Newcomb
14	TCU	0	G Tom Pratt
20	Florida State	7	T Charley Hutchings / Gary Greaves
21	Clemson	0	E Don Johnson
18	West Virginia	0	QB Sam Scarnecchia / Bonnie Yarbrough
20	Florida	7	HB Joe Plevel / Johnny Bookman
7	Pittsburgh	14	HB John Varone / Ed Oliver
			FB Don Bosseler / Paul Hefti

RUSHING: Bosseler 161/723y, Oliver 53/194y, Varone 62/194y
PASSING: Scarnecchi 27-59/357y, TD, 45.8%
 Yarbrough 26-60/264y, 4TD, 43.3%
RECEIVING: Varone 10/107y, J. Johnson 8/98y, Bennett 7/90y
SCORING: Scarnecchia 42pts, Oliver (HB-K) 27pts,
 Bosseler 24pts

1957 5-4-1

0	Houston	7	E Bill Poole
13	Baylor	7	T Charlie Diamond / Frank Nodoline
13	North Carolina	20	G Don Wallace / Jim Crawford
0	N. Carolina St.	0	C Vester Newcomb / Bob Stewart
48	Kansas	6	G Bill Hayes / Bill Vasiloff
13	Villanova	7	T Gary Greaves
40	Florida State	13	E Phil Geatz
6	Maryland	16	QB Fran Curci
0	Florida	14	HB Joe Plevel / Bonnie Yarbrough (QB)
28	Pittsburgh	13	HB John Varone / Byron Blasko
			FB Bill Sandie / Harry Deiderich

RUSHING: Varone 79/460y, Curci 115/439y, Sandie 114/402y
PASSING: Curci 41-85/476y, 6TD, 48.2%
RECEIVING: Varone 11/108y, Plevel 7/78y, Geatz 7/41y
SCORING: Plevel 36pts, Varone 28pts, Curci (QB-K) 19pts

1958 2-8

0	Wisconsin	20	E Bill Poole / Doug Hildebrandt
14	Baylor	8	T Charlie Diamond
0	LSU	41	G Don Wallace / Dan Coughlin
2	Boston College	6	C Jim Otto
15	Vanderbilt	28	G Bill Hayes / Jack Novak
6	Florida State	17	T Gary Greaves / John O'Day
14	Maryland	26	E Phil Geatz / Jon Mirilovich
26	Houston	37	QB Fran Curci / Bonnie Yarbrough
9	Florida	12	HB Joe Plevel / Larry DiGiammarino
2	Oregon	0	HB George MacIntyre (QB) /Tom Fleming
			FB Frank Bouffard / Harry Deiderich

RUSHING: Bouffard 77/289y, Deiderich 39/180y,
 Fleming 47/173y
PASSING: Curci 46-76/493y, 2TD, 60.5%
 Yarbrough 32-80/509y, 2TD, 40.0%
RECEIVING: Plevel 17/141y, Hildebrandt 12/177y, Geatz 11/139y
SCORING: Bouffard, Bob Rosbaugh (HB) & DiGiammarino 18pts

1959 6-4

26	Tulane	7	E Bill Miller
7	Florida State	6	T John O'Day / Bill Watts
3	LSU	27	G Dan Coughlin / Larry Babb
23	Navy	8	C Jim Otto
6	Auburn	21	G Jack Novak / Tom Clark
3	Kentucky	22	T Charles Linning / Vic Savoca
14	North Carolina	7	E Frank Reinhart / Larry Wilson
23	South Carolina	6	QB Fran Curci
18	Michigan State	13	HB Jim Vollenweider
14	Florida	23	WB Bob Rosbaugh
			FB Frank Bouffard / Doug Davis

RUSHING: Bouffard 105/387y, Vollenweider 81/368y,
 Rosbaugh 67/295y
PASSING: Curci 100-195/1068y, 5TD, 51.3%
RECEIVING: Miller 33/395y, Rosbaugh 23/172y,
 Vollenweider 12/137y
SCORING: Bouffard 36pts, Rosbaugh 30pts, Al Dangel (K) 24pts

1960 6-4

29	North Carolina	12	E Bill Miller
6	Pittsburgh	17	T John O'Day / Vic Savoca
21	South Carolina	6	G Bill Diamond / Jerry Reynolds
7	Auburn	20	C Reuben Mills
10	Boston College	8	G Bob Eggert / Tom Clark
25	Florida State	7	T Charles Linning / Bill Watts
28	Notre Dame	21	E Larry Wilson / Frank Reinhart
14	Syracuse	21	QB Eddie Johns / Ray Timmons (DB)
0	Florida	18	HB Jim Vollenweider
23	Air Force	14	WB Ron Fritzsche / Nick Ryder (FB)
			FB Sam Fernandez

RUSHING: Johns 123/521y, Vollenweider 80/330y,
 Ryder 50/289y
PASSING: Johns 54-91/657y, 4TD, 59.3%
RECEIVING: Miller 26/413y, L. Wilson 14/155y
SCORING: Johns 42pts, Miller 32pts, Vollenweider 28pts

1961 7-4

7	Pittsburgh	10	E Bill Miller
14	Kentucky	7	T Stan Maluty / Dan Conners
25	Penn State	8	G Jerry Reynolds / Bill Diamond
9	Navy	17	C Charles Livingston
7	Colorado	9	G Bob Eggert / Jim O'Mahoney
10	North Carolina	0	T Bill Watts
32	Georgia	7	E Larry Wilson / Ben Rizzo
6	Tulane	0	QB George Mira
10	Northwestern	6	HB Nick Ryder (FB)
15	Florida	6	WB John Bahen / Nick Spinelli
14	Syracuse■	15	FB Jim Vollenweider / Sam Fernandez

RUSHING: Vollenweider 112/538y, Ryder 80/329y,
 Fernandez 47/198y
PASSING: Mira 81-172/1000y, 8TD, 47.1%
RECEIVING: Miller 44/648y, L. Wilson 21/310y, Spinelli 10/151y,
 Bahen 10/111y
SCORING: Vollenweider 24pts, Mira, Bahen & Spinelli 18pts

1962 7-4

23	Pittsburgh	14	E Bill Sparks / Ben Rizzo
21	TCU	20	T Dan Conners / Stan Maluty
7	Florida State	6	G Bob Strieter / Jerry Reynolds
3	LSU	17	C Bob Dentel
28	Maryland	24	G Jim O'Mahoney
21	Air Force	3	T Rowland Benson / Joe Smerdel
25	Kentucky	17	E Jim Simon / Bob Werl
3	Alabama	36	QB George Mira / Mark Panther (DB)
7	Northwestern	29	HB Nick Ryder / Ken Hunt
17	Florida	15	WB Nick Spinelli / Jack Sims
34	Nebraska■	36	FB John Bennett / John Sisk

RUSHING: Ryder 155/702y, Hunt 76/290y, Mira 73/166y
PASSING: Mira 146-306/1893y, 12TD, 47.7%
RECEIVING: Spinelli 33/506y, Sparks 26/339y, Sims 17/228y
SCORING: Ryder 44pts, Spinelli 36pts, Bob Wilson (K) 31pts

1963 3-7

0	Florida State	24	E Ed Weisacosky / Bob Werl
3	Purdue	0	T Dan Conners
10	Tulane	0	G Bob Strieter
0	LSU	3	C Bob Hart
14	Georgia	31	G Joe Smerdel / John Matlock
20	Kentucky	14	T Rowland Benson
16	North Carolina	16	E Bill Sparks / Fred Brown
21	Florida	27	QB George Mira
20	Pittsburgh	31	HB John Bennett/Russell Smith/R. Barth
12	Alabama	17	WB Nick Spinelli
			FB Pete Banaszak / John Sisk

RUSHING: Banaszak 97/461y, Bennett 62/197y, Barth 41/163y,
 Mira 59/163y
PASSING: Mira 172-334/2155y, 10TD, 51.5%
RECEIVING: Spinelli 41/501y, Sparks 27/435y,
 Weisacosky 20/299y
SCORING: Spinelli 28pts, Banaszak 18pts, 3 with 12pts

1964 4-5-1

0	Florida State	14	WR Don Cifra / Tom Coughlin
0	Georgia Tech	20	T Robert Brown / Ed Kraszewski
7	California	9	G Bernie Yaffa / Ed Weisacosky (LB)
20	Pittsburgh	20	C Norman Blanchard /John Matlock (DL)
14	Indiana	18	G Bruce Brinkos / Frank Beck
10	Detroit	7	T Harry Fersch / Eugene Trosch
21	Tulane	0	E Fred Brown / Frank Felicione
30	Boston College	0	QB Bob Biletnikoff / Andy Sixkiller (DB)
35	Vanderbilt	17	RB Russell Smith / Randy Barth
10	Florida	12	WB Jack Sims / Don Curtright (DB)
			FB Pete Banaszak / Fred Cassidy

RUSHING: Smith 84/370y, Biletnikoff 143/351y, Cassidy 36/203y
PASSING: Biletnikoff 85-159/920y, 5TD, 53.5%
RECEIVING: Coughlin 22/294y, Smith 18/140y, Sims 14/161y
SCORING: Biletnikoff 48pts, Cifra (WR-K) 25pts, Banaszak 24pts

1965 5-4-1

3	SMU	7	WR Tom Coughlin / James Cox
24	Syracuse	0	WR Jerry Daanen / Don Russo
16	Tulane	24	T Ed Kraszewski
27	LSU	34	G Bernie Yaffa / David Dice
44	Houston	12	C Norman Blanchard
14	Pittsburgh	28	G Tony Tocco / Frank Beck
20	Boston College	6	T Joe Mirto / Mike Haggerty
28	Vanderbilt	14	TE Steve Smith / Bob Stanley
16	Florida	13	QB Bill Miller / Bob Biletnikoff
0	Notre Dame	0	RB Russell Smith / Doug McGee
			FB Pete Banaszak / Fred Cassidy
			DL Bob Werl
			DL Gene Trosch
			DL John Tucek / Larry Bodie
			DL Leeroy Lewis
			DL Rex Wilson / Bill Schirmer
			LB Ken Corbin / Tom Hamilton
			LB Ed Weisacosky (DE)
			DB Richard Robinson / Don Curtright
			DB Ralph Hutchins / Tom Beier
			DB Jim Wahnee / Art Zachary
			DB Andy Sixkiller / Joe Mira

RUSHING: Banaszak 111/473y, Smith 66/289y, McGee 67/252y
PASSING: Miller 72-141/856y, 9TD, 51.1%
RECEIVING: Daanen 29/367y, Cox 17/285y, Coughlin 14/202y
SCORING: Curtright (DB-K) 41pts, Banaszak 30pts,
 Cassidy & Cox 24pts

1966 8-2-1

24 Colorado	3 WR James Cox / Steve Smith
20 Florida State	23 WR Jerry Daanen / Don Russo
8 LSU	10 T Joe Mirto
7 Georgia	6 G David Dice
14 Indiana	7 C Bill Chambless
10 Southern Cal	7 G Tony Tocco
10 Tulane	10 T Mike Haggerty
38 Pittsburgh	14 TE Larry LaPointe
44 Iowa	0 QB Bill Miller / David Olivo (HB)
21 Florida	16 RB John Acuff / Joe Mira
14 Virginia Tech■	7 FB Doug McGee / Fred Cassidy
	DL Ted Hendricks
	DL Gene Trosch
	DL John Tucek / Jerry Pierce
	DL Bob Taterek
	DL Phil Smith
	LB Ken Corbin
	LB John Barnett / Robert Czipulis
	DB Jimmy Dye
	DB Richard Robinson / Ralph Hutchins
	DB Hal Carew
	DB Tom Beier

RUSHING: McGee 100/377y, Acuff 73/277y, Olivo 106/259y
PASSING: Miller 84-155/1114y, 7TD, 54.2%
RECEIVING: Cox 41/627y, Daanen 17/192y, Smith 16/161y
SCORING: Ray Harris (K) 40pts, Daanen 24pts, Cox 24pts

1967 7-4

7 Northwestern	12 WR James Cox
8 Penn State	17 WR Jerry Daanen
34 Tulane	14 T Joe Mirto / Hank Urbanowicz (DT)
17 LSU	15 G Bill Chambless
58 Pittsburgh	0 C Don Brandy / Jim Schneider (T)
7 Auburn	0 G Charles Fullerton / Tom Hamilton
14 Virginia Tech	7 T Allan Folkins
49 Georgia Tech	7 TE Larry LaPointe
22 Notre Dame	24 QB David Olivo / Bill Miller
20 Florida	13 RB John Acuff / Vince Opalsky
21 Colorado■	31 RB Doug McGee / Joe Mira
	DL Ted Hendricks
	DL Bill Trout
	DL Jerry Pierce
	DL Bob Trocolor / Jim Kresl
	DL Tony Cline / Phil Smith
	LB Ken Corbin / Bob Czipulis
	LB John Barnett / Bob Taylor
	DB Jimmy Dye
	DB Richard Robinson / Tony Stawarz
	DB Hal Carew
	DB Bob Abbott

RUSHING: Acuff 112/572y, Opalsky 116/562y, Mira 54/204y
PASSING: Olivo 62-140/729y, 8TD, 44.3%,
Miller 22-63/358y, TD, 34.9%
RECEIVING: Cox 39/552y, Daanen 15/180y, LaPointe 7/72y
SCORING: Acuff & Opalsky 30pts, 3 with 24pts

1968 5-5

28 Northwestern	7 WR David Kalina / Van Golmont
10 Georgia Tech	7 WR Ray Bellamy
3 Southern Cal	28 T Jim Schneider / Robert Carlin
30 LSU	0 G James Chatlas
13 Virginia Tech	8 C Don Brandy / Allan Folkins (T)
6 Auburn	31 G Charles Fullerton
48 Pittsburgh	0 T George Hopgood
7 Penn State	22 TE Rick Strawbridge / Ray Heinly
6 Alabama	14 QB David Olivo
10 Florida	14 RB Vince Opalsky
	RB John Acuff / Bobby Best
	DL Ted Hendricks
	DL Bill Trout / Tom Colip
	DL Jerry Pierce / Mike Turner (OG)
	DL Robert Trocolor
	DL Tony Cline / Jim Kresl
	LB John Barnett / Bob Taylor
	LB Dick Sorensen / Bob Czipulis
	DB Bob Abbott Charles Parker
	DB Gregory Perez
	DB Tony Stawarz / Dean Stone
	DB Rod Taylor

RUSHING: Opalsky 152/446y, Best 84/301y, Acuff 49/140y
PASSING: Olivo 137-248/1727y, 9TD, 55.2%
RECEIVING: Kalina 43/628y, Bellamy 37/549y, Acuff 19/158y
SCORING: Jim Huff (K) 47pts, Opalsky 36pts, Kalina 24pts

1969 4-6

14 Florida State	16 WR David Kalina / Ray Bellamy
23 N. Carolina St.	13 WR Joe Schmidt
0 LSU	20 T James Chaltas / Gary McCormick
13 Memphis State	26 G George Hopgood / Mike Turner
14 Texas Christian	9 C James Schneider / Stan Bujalski
36 Houston	38 G Steve Henson / Wiley Matthews
30 Navy	10 T Larry Wilson / Ray Terzynski
6 Alabama	42 TE Kevin Griffin / Rick Strawbridge
49 Wake Forest	7 QB Kelly Cochrane
16 Florida	35 RB Vince Opalsky / Bobby Best
	RB Tom Sullivan / Steve Schaap
	DL Tony Cline / Jim Seely
	DL Bill Trout
	DL Bob Trocolor / Dick Trower
	DL Jim Kresl / Al Palewicz
	LB Paul Manard / Wayne Lawrence
	LB Dick Sorensen
	LB Jack Chauvet
	DB Charles Parker
	DB Gregory Perez / Jim Haviland
	DB Dean Stone
	DB Gary Mick

RUSHING: Opalsky 109/453y, Sullivan 79/319y, Best 56/233y
PASSING: Cochrane 121-243/1673y, 11TD, 49.8%
RECEIVING: Kalina 45/532y, Schmidt 36/651y, Griffin 14/217y,
Schaap 14/62y
SCORING: Jim Huff (K) 37pts, Opalsky & Sullivan 30pts

1970 3-8

36 William & Mary	14 WR Joe Schmidt / Bruce Bishop
21 Georgia Tech	31 WR Don Brennan / Dieter Matthes
18 Maryland	11 T Andrew Dorn
14 Tampa	31 G Jay Wilson
17 Pittsburgh	28 C Tom Turchetta / Stan Bujalski
3 Florida State	27 G Garry Vujanov / Steve Henson
16 Tulane	31 T Wiley Matthews / Maurice Kelly
8 Alabama	32 TE John Watson
16 Syracuse	56 QB Kelly Cochrane
14 Florida	13 RB Bobby Best / Chuck Foreman
3 Houston	36 RB Tom Sullivan
	DL Mike Barnes
	DL Dick Trower / Ken White
	DL Wayne Lawrence (LB)/ Ray Terzynski
	DL Mike Leary / Jack Chauvet
	LB Al Palewicz / Bo Dunn
	LB Jack Hendrickson / Bob Taylor
	LB Mike Riley / John Barlow
	DB Jim Haviland
	DB Burgess Owens / Buddy Scarborough
	DB Kurt Schottenheimer / Dean Stone
	DB Tony Stawarz

RUSHING: Sullivan 156/461y, Best 112/438y, Foreman 47/196y
PASSING: Cochrane 127-287/1348y, 7TD, 44.3%
RECEIVING: Schmidt 37/549y, Brennan 33/406y, Watson 16/176y
SCORING: Schmidt 26pts, Sullivan 24pts,
Mike Cummins (K) 19pts

1971 4-7

17 Florida State	20 WR Don Brennan / Bill Perkins
29 Wake Forest	10 WR Witt Beckman / Tracy Stubbs
41 Baylor	15 T Golden Ruel / Bill Murphy
0 Notre Dame	17 G Tom Turchetta
31 Navy	16 C Steve Gaunt
24 Army	13 G Wiley Matthews / Garry Vujanov
7 N. Carolina St.	13 T Stan Bujalski / Larry Wilson
3 Alabama	31 TE Kenny O'Connell / John Watson
6 Houston	27 QB John Hornibrook
16 Florida	45 RB Chuck Foreman
0 Syracuse	14 RB Tom Sullivan / Jack Brasington
	DL Mike Barnes / Herb Scott
	DL Dick Trower / Joe Geiger
	DL Tony Cristiani / Ken White
	DL Mike Leary
	LB Ron Proctor / Gary Altheide
	LB Harold Sears / Mike Riley
	LB Al Palewicz / Bo Dunn
	DB Burgess Owens
	DB Larry Lancaster / Bill Frohbose
	DB Jim Word / Bobby Taylor
	DB Daryl Reeh / Gary Mick

RUSHING: Foreman 191/951y, Sullivan 150/761y,
Brasington 29/110y
PASSING: Hornibrook 73-179/1006y, 2TD, 40.8%
RECEIVING: Beckman 21/288y, Sullivan 18/198y,
Perkins 15/249y
SCORING: Foreman 60pts, Mike Burke (K) 27pts,
Hornibrook 24pts

1972 5-6

14 Florida State	37 WR Walt Sweeting / Bill Perkins
10 Texas	23 WR Witt Beckman / Silvio Cardoso
3 Baylor	10 T Dennis Harrah
24 Tulane	21 G Golden Ruel / Bill Capraun
33 Houston	13 C Steve Gaunt / Wilmore Ritchie
28 Army	7 G Monk Laurenza / Jim Dittmar
51 UNLV	7 T Stan Bujalski / Fred Ross
0 Tampa	7 TE Phil Corrigan / Phil Iredale
17 Notre Dame	20 QB Ed Carney
28 Maryland	8 RB Chuck Foreman
6 Florida	17 RB Woody Thompson / Tom Smith
	DL Bo Dunn / Mike Daly
	DL Mike Barnes / Mike Leary
	DL Tony Cristiani / Ken White
	DL Rubin Carter / Jose Gonzalez
	DL Al Palewicz / Gary Altheide
	LB Mike Riley
	LB Harold Sears
	DB Greg Ingram / Mike Archer
	DB Bill Frohbose / Booker Cope
	DB Burgess Owens / Paul Horschel
	DB Gary Streicher / Eldridge Mitchell

RUSHING: Foreman 107/484y, Smith 91/457y,
Thompson 60/193y
PASSING: Carney 94-209/1399y, 6TD, 45.0%
RECEIVING: Foreman 37/557y, Beckman 18/322y,
Sweeting 12/190y
SCORING: Mike Burke (K) 44pts, Foreman 36pts, Carney 30pts

1973 5-6

20 Texas	15 WR Steve Marcantonio / Walt Sweeting
14 Florida State	10 T Dennis Hannah
20 Oklahoma	24 G Fred Ross
15 Boston College	10 C Wilmore Ritchie
7 Houston	30 G Jim Dittmar
34 Syracuse	23 T Bill Capraun
14 West Virginia	20 TE Phil Corrigan
19 Army	7 QB Ed Carney / Kary Baker / Coy Hall
13 Alabama	43 TB Woody Thompson / Johnny Williams
7 Florida	14 WB Jack Brasington / Silvio Cardoso
0 Notre Dame	44 FB Alan Reynaud / Dennis Breckner
	DL Mike Daly
	DL Jose Gonzalez / Gary Dunn
	DL Rubin Carter
	DL Tony Cristiani
	DL Gary Altheide
	LB Rick Liddell / Dominic Pisani
	LB Rich Griffiths / Clarence Corker
	DB Paul Horschel / Greg Ingram
	DB Gary Streicher / Bill Frohbose
	DB Eldridge Mitchell
	DB Booker Cope

RUSHING: Thompson 189/802y, Williams 65/429y,
Cardoso 52/153y
PASSING: Carney 41-94/658y, 3TD, 43.6%
Baker 31-83/412y, 0TD, 37.3%
RECEIVING: Marcantonio 35/568y, August 15/314y,
Sweeting 14/252y
SCORING: Thompson 48pts, Williams 24pts, Marcantonio &
Selmer 14pts

1974 6-5

20 Houston	3 WR Steve Marcantonio / Witt Beckman
28 Tampa	26 T Dennis Hannah
0 Auburn	3 G Bert Camut
35 Pacific	6 C George Demopoulos
21 West Virginia	20 G Joe Wysock / Steve Golding
7 Notre Dame	28 T Bill Capraun
14 Virginia Tech	7 TE Phil August / Mike Latimer
14 Florida State	21 QB Kary Baker / Ed Carney /Frank Glover
7 Alabama	28 TB Woody Thompson / Johnny Williams
14 Syracuse	7 WB Larry Cain
7 Florida	31 FB Alan Reynaud
	DL Steadman Scavella / Eddie Edwards
	DL Jose Gonzalez
	DL Rubin Carter
	DL Gary Dunn / Dennis Breckner
	DL Clarence Corker
	LB Rick Liddell
	LB Rich Griffiths / Gregg Wallick
	DB John Turner / Mike Archer
	DB Dave Sydnor
	DB Paul Horschel / Booker Cope
	DB Ernest Jones / Willie Jenkins

RUSHING: Thompson 78/343y, Williams 69/318y,
Tim Morgan (TB) 75/315y
PASSING: Baker 61-146/805y, 3TD, 41.8%
RECEIVING: Marcantonio 22/337y, Beckman 17/318y,
August 6/108y, Latimer 6/91y, Cain 6/65y
SCORING: Martin 30pts, Chris Dennis (K) 28pts, Williams 24pts

1975 2-8

23 Georgia Tech	38 WR Mike Adams / Phil August
17 Oklahoma	20 T Bob O'Gara / Frank Makaravich
16 Nebraska	31 G Bert Camut
10 Colorado	23 C George Demopoulos / Mike White
24 Houston	20 G Phil Iredale / Karl Monroe
7 Boston College	21 T Larry Brown / Dave Thompson
16 Navy	17 TE Charlie Claud / Dennis Jackson
24 Florida State	22 QB Kary Baker / Frank Glover
9 Notre Dame	32 TB Ottis Anderson / Tim Morgan
11 Florida	15 WB Larry Cain / Mike Latimer
	FB Larry Bates / Ray Ganong
	DL George Halas / John McGriff
	DL Eddie Edwards / Ronnie Walker
	DL Don Latimer
	DL Gary Dunn / Dennis Breckner
	DL Steadman Scavella / Larry Wilson
	LB Earl Monroe
	LB Gregg Wallick / Craig Cosden
	DB Ernest Jones / Bryan Ferguson
	DB John Turner / Eldridge Mitchell
	DB Joe Bettencourt / Mike Archer
	DB Willie Jenkins

RUSHING: Anderson 67/365y, Morgan 108/320y,
Don Martin (TB) 73/262y
PASSING: Baker 66-130/999y, 5TD, 50.8%
RECEIVING: August 25/419y, Anderson 11/128y, Cain 10/214y,
Claud 10/116y
SCORING: Chris Dennis (K) 53pts, Cain 30pts, Morgan 24pts

1976 3-8

47 Florida State	0 WR Phil August / Charlie Claud
3 Colorado	33 WR Larry Cain / Mike Adams
9 Nebraska	17 T Bob O'Gara
7 Duke	20 G Steve Golding / Karl Monroe
19 Pittsburgh	36 C Mike White
49 TCU	0 G Jim Standifer / Dusty Jackson
13 Boston College	6 T Larry Brown
7 Penn State	21 TE Dennis Jackson / Ricou deShaw
27 Notre Dame	40 QB E.J. Baker / Frank Glover
10 Florida	19 TB Ottis Anderson / Taylor Timmons
16 Houston	21 FB Woody Bennett / Ray Ganong
	DL George Halas / Larry Wilson
	DL Eddie Edwards / Ronnie Walker
	DL Don Latimer / Don Smith
	DL Dennis Breckner / Jim Browning
	DL Glenn Hill / Jim Maler
	LB Earl Monroe / Kevin Roberts
	LB Gregg Wallick / Craig Cosden
	DB John Turner
	DB Eldridge Mitchell / Rich Valerio
	DB Bryan Ferguson / Joe Bettencourt
	DB Willie Jenkins

RUSHING: Anderson 213/918y, Baker 100/208y,
Ganong 33/134y
PASSING: Baker 64-131/907y, 6TD, 48.9%
RECEIVING: Adams 24/345y, Cain 18/444y, August 15/314y
SCORING: Anderson 36pts, Chris Dennis (K) 36pts, 5 with 18pts

1977 3-8

0 Ohio State	10 WR Charlie Claud / Pat Walker
6 Georgia Tech	10 WR Gary Tokarski / Malcolm Simmons
23 Florida State	17 T Bob O'Gara
24 Pacific	3 G McKinley Griffin
14 Kansas	7 C Mike White / Tom Sedley
17 TCU	21 G Karl Monroe
7 Penn State	49 T Larry Brown / Charles Bloxsom
10 Tulane	13 TE Steve Alvers
0 Alabama	36 QB E.J. Baker / Kenny McMillian
14 Florida	31 TB Ottis Anderson / Taylor Timmons (FB)
10 Notre Dame	48 FB Woody Bennett / Chris Hobbs
	DL George Halas
	DL Tony Galente / Jim Browning
	DL Don Latimer / John McGriff
	DL Don Smith / Pat Millican
	DL Barry Gonzalez
	LB Earl Monroe / Herb Jackson
	LB Craig Cosden / Kevin Roberts
	DB Bryan Ferguson
	DB Gene Coleman / Rich Valerio
	DB Fred Azrak / Brian Eastburn
	DB John Turner

RUSHING: Anderson 187/782y, Timmons 129/466y,
Hobbs 57/219y
PASSING: McMillian 38-70/417y, 3TD, 54.3%
Baker 35-84/515y, 3TD, 41.7%
RECEIVING: Walker 21/234y, Anderson 20/243y, Alvers 14/249y
SCORING: Chris Dennis (K) 39pts, Anderson 24pts, Alvers 18pts

1978 6-5

7 Colorado	17 WR Jim Joiner
21 Florida State	31 WR E.J. Baker / Pat Walker
38 Kansas	6 T Charles Bloxsom / Frank Frazier
17 Auburn	15 G McKinley Griffin
19 Georgia Tech	24 C John Fenton / Tom Sedley
17 Utah State	16 G Karl Monroe
0 Notre Dame	20 T Jim Pokorney
16 Tulane	20 TE Steve Alvers / Mark Cooper
16 San Diego St.	14 QB Kenny McMillian / Mike Rodrique
21 Syracuse	9 TB Ottis Anderson (FB) / Gary Breckner
22 Florida	21 FB Ken Johnson
	DL Johnny Daniels
	DL Tony Galente / Lester Williams
	DL Don Smith / Don Krueger
	DL Barry Gonzalez
	LB Herb Jackson / Charles Cook
	LB Mozell Axson
	LB Scott Nicolas
	DB John Swain / Rich Valerio
	DB Gene Coleman
	DB Fred Azral / Fred Marion
	DB David Jefferson

RUSHING: Anderson 224/1266y, McMillian 125/405y,
Johnson 90/398y
PASSING: McMillian 53-108/611y, 3TD, 49.1%
RECEIVING: Joiner 15/235y, Baker 14/225y, Anderson 14/47y
SCORING: Anderson 68pts, Dan Miller (K) 46pts,
McMillian 24pts

1979 5-6

24 Louisville	12 WR Larry Brodsky / Malcolm Simmons
23 Florida State	40 WR Jim Joiner / Pat Walker
6 Louisiana Tech	0 T Steve Grady / Frank Frazier
13 Florida A&M	16 G Art Kehoe
20 San Diego St.	31 C John Fenton / Don Bailey
19 Boston College	8 G Jim Pokorney / Clem Barbarino
15 Syracuse	25 T John Canei
26 Penn State	10 TE Andy Baratta
0 Alabama	30 QB Mike Rodrigue / Jim Kelly
15 Notre Dame	40 RB Smokey Roan / Mark Rush
30 Florida	24 FB Chris Hobbs / Gary Breckner
	DL Barry Gonzalez / Johnny Daniels
	DL Lester Williams
	DL Jim Burt
	DL Bob Nelson / Tony Chickillo
	DL Tim Flanagan
	LB Jay Brophy / Scott Nicolas
	LB Mozell Axson / Charles Cook
	DB John Swain
	DB Gene Coleman
	DB David Jefferson
	DB Fred Marion

RUSHING: Hobbs 105/406y, Roan 97/307y, Breckner 47/179y
PASSING: Rodrigue 94-201/1197y, 2TD, 46.8%
Kelly 48-104/721y, 5TDs, 46.2%
RECEIVING: Brodsky 30/495y, Walker 24/625y, Joiner 24/293y
SCORING: Dan Miller (K) 57pts, Roan 24pts,
Walker & Joiner 18pts

1980 9-3

24 Louisville	10 WR Larry Brodsky / Mike Rodrigue
49 Florida A&M	0 WR Jim Joiner / Rocky Belk
14 Houston	7 T Dave Stewart
10 Florida State	9 G Art Kehoe / Clem Barbarino
14 Notre Dame	32 C John Fenton
31 Mississippi St.	34 G John Canei / Jim Pokorney
12 Penn State	27 T Frank Frazier
23 East Carolina	10 TE Mark Cooper / Andy Baratta
24 Vanderbilt	17 QB Jim Kelly
26 N. Texas St.	8 HB Smokey Roan / Mark Rush
31 Florida	7 FB Chris Hobbs / Gary Brackner
20 Virginia Tech■	10 DL Greg Zappala / Johnny Daniels
	DL Lester Williams
	DL Jim Burt
	DL Bob Nelson / Tony Chickillo
	DL Tim Flanagan
	LB Scott Nicolas / Jack Fernandez
	LB Mozell Axson
	DB John Swain / Rodney Bellinger
	DB Ronnie Lippett
	DB David Jefferson / Mark Smith
	DB Fred Marion

RUSHING: Roan 152/669y, Hobbs 111/437y, Rush 67/248y
PASSING: Kelly 109-206/1519y, 11TD, 52.9%
RECEIVING: Brodsky 33/570y, Rush 26/249y, Joiner 19/314y
SCORING: Dan Miller (K) 64pts, Rush 36pts, Roan 30pts

1981 9-2

21 Florida	20 WR Larry Brodsky
12 Houston	7 WR Mike Rodrigue
7 Texas	14 T Dave Stewart
48 Vanderbilt	16 G Mike Moore
10 Mississippi St.	14 C Don Bailey
31 East Carolina	6 G Clem Barbarino
17 Penn State	14 T John Canei / Frank Frazier
27 Florida State	19 TE Glenn Dennison / Mark Cooper
21 Virginia Tech	14 QB Jim Kelly
14 N. Carolina St.	6 HB Smokey Roan / Keith Griffin
37 Notre Dame	15 FB Chris Hobbs / Speedy Neal
	DL Isaiah West
	DL Lester Williams
	DL Bob Nelson
	DL Tony Chickillo
	DL Tim Flanagan / Danny Brown
	LB Scott Nicolas / Greg Brown
	LB Jay Brophy
	DB Dave Ditthardt
	DB Ronnie Lippett
	DB David Jefferson / Jamie Boone
	DB Fred Marion / Ken Calhoun

RUSHING: Roan 111/364y, Hobbs 75/295y, Neal 58/209y
PASSING: Kelly 168-285/2403y, 14TD, 58.9%
RECEIVING: Brodsky 37/631y, Rodrigue 29/478y,
Dennison 29/270y
SCORING: Dan Miller (K) 77pts, Rodrigue 26pts, Rush 26pts

1982 7-4

14 Florida	17 WR Rocky Belk
31 Houston	12 WR Stanley Shakespeare
14 Virginia Tech	8 T Mark Cooper
25 Michigan State	22 G Mike Moore
28 Louisville	6 C Don Bailey
14 Notre Dame	16 G Alvin Ward
31 Mississippi St.	14 T John Canei
7 Florida State	24 TE Glenn Dennison / Mark Cooper
17 Maryland	18 QB Mark Richt / Jim Kelly
41 N. Carolina St.	3 HB Keith Griffin / Mark Rush
19 Cincinnati	13 FB Speedy Neal / Albert Bentley
	DL Isaiah West / Julio Cortes
	DL Fred Robinson / Willie Broughton
	DL Tony Fitzgerald
	DL Tony Chickillo / Eric Larkin
	DL Joe Kohlbrand / Danny Brown
	LB Greg Brown / Ken Sisk
	LB Jay Brophy
	DB Rodney Bellinger / Dave Ditthardt
	DB Ronnie Lippett
	DB Eddie Williams
	DB Ken Calhoun / Jamie Boone

RUSHING: Griffin 131/473y, Neal 123/446y, Rush 72/265y
PASSING: Richt 71-149/838y, 4TD, 47.7%,
Kelly 51-81/585y, 3TD, 63.0%
RECEIVING: Belk 35/646y, Neal 31/274y, Rush 30/384y
SCORING: Jeff Davis (K) 61pts, Neal 48pts, Rush 36pts

1983 11-1

3 Florida	28 WR Eddie Brown
29 Houston	7 WR Stanley Shakespeare
35 Purdue	0 T Paul Bertucelli
20 Notre Dame	0 G Juan Comendeiro / Mike Moore
56 Duke	17 C Ian Sinclair
42 Louisville	14 G Alvin Ward
31 Mississippi St.	7 T Dave Heffernan
37 Cincinnati	7 TE Glenn Dennison
20 West Virginia	3 QB Bernie Kosar
12 East Carolina	7 HB Albert Bentley / Keith Griffin
17 Florida State	16 FB Speedy Neal
31 Nebraska■	30 DL Danny Brown / Joe Kohlbrand
	DL Fred Robinson / Dallas Cameron
	DL Tony Fitzpatrick
	DL Kevin Fagan
	DL Julio Cortes
	LB Jay Brophy / Jack Fernandez
	LB Ken Sisk / Bruce Fleming
	DB Rodney Bellinger / Dave Ditthardt
	DB Reggie Sutton / Keith Walker
	DB Eddie Williams
	DB Ken Calhoun

RUSHING: Bentley 144/722y, Griffin 101/447y, Neal 66/295y
PASSING: Kosar 201-327/2329y, 15TD, 61.5%
RECEIVING: Dennison 54/594y, Shakespeare 34/452y,
Bentley 32/294y
SCORING: Jeff Davis (K) 64pts, Neal, Brown & Bentley 36pts

1984 8-5
20 Auburn	18 WR Eddie Brown / Brian Blades
32 Florida	20 WR Stanley Shakespeare
14 Michigan	22 T Paul Bertucelli
28 Purdue	17 G Juan Comendeiro / Mike Moore
3 Florida State	38 C Ian Sinclair
38 Rice	3 G Alvin Ward
31 Notre Dame	13 T Dave Heffernan
49 Cincinnati	25 TE Willie Smith / Alfredo Roberts
27 Pittsburgh	7 QB Bernie Kosar
38 Louisville	23 HB Darryl Oliver / Melvin Bratton
40 Maryland	42 FB Alonzo Highsmith
45 Boston College	47 DL Julio Cortes
37 UCLA■	39 DL Dallas Cameron
	DL Willie Lee Broughton
	DL Kevin Fagan / Paul O'Connor
	DL Joe Kohlbrand
	LB Winston Moss
	LB John McVeigh / Bruce Fleming
	DB Darrell Fullington / Lucious Delegal
	DB Greg Jones / Reggie Sutton
	DB Willie Martinez
	DB Ken Calhoun

RUSHING: Highsmith 146/906y, Oliver 93/407y, Bratton 49/279y
PASSING: Kosar 262-416/3642y, 25TD, 63.0%
RECEIVING: Smith 66/852y, Brown 59/1114y, Shakespeare 38/621y
SCORING: Greg Cox (K) 82pts, Highsmith 66pts, Brown 54pts

1985 10-2
23 Florida	35 WR Brian Blades / Brett Perriman
48 Rice	20 WR Michael Irvin
45 Boston College	10 T Paul Bertucelli / Matt Patchan
27 East Carolina	15 G Dave Alekna
38 Cincinnati	0 C Greg Rakoczy
27 Oklahoma	14 G Paul O'Connor
45 Louisville	7 T Ed Davis / John O'Neill
35 Florida State	27 TE Willie Smith / Charles Henry
29 Maryland	22 QB Vinny Testaverde
24 Colorado State	3 RB Warren Williams / Darryl Oliver
58 Notre Dame	7 FB Alonzo Highsmith / Melvin Bratton
7 Tennessee■	35 DL Kevin Fagan / Daniel Stubbs
	DL Derwin Jones
	DL Jerome Brown
	DL John McVeigh / Victor Morris
	LB Randy Shannon
	LB Bruce Fleming / Winston Moss
	LB Rod Carter
	DB Donald Ellis
	DB Tolbert Bain
	DB Darrell Fullington / Bennie Blades
	DB Selwyn Brown

RUSHING: Williams 89/522y, Highsmith 117/451y, Bratton 67/285y
PASSING: Testaverde 216-352/3238y, 21TD, 61.4%
RECEIVING: W. Smith 48/669y, Irvin 46/840y, Br.Blades 30/657y
SCORING: Greg Cox (K) 82pts, Irvin 54pts, Bratton 48pts

1986 11-1
34 South Carolina	14 WR Brett Perriman / Brian Blades
23 Florida	15 WR Michael Irvin
61 Texas Tech	11 T Maurice Maddox / Matt Patchan
28 Oklahoma	16 G Dave Alekna
34 N. Illinois	0 C Greg Rakoczy / Rod Holder
58 West Virginia	14 G Paul O'Connor
45 Cincinnati	13 T Scott Provin / John O'Neill
41 Florida State	23 TE Alfredo Roberts / Charles Henry
37 Pittsburgh	10 QB Vinny Testaverde
23 Tulsa	10 RB Melvin Bratton / Warren Williams
36 East Carolina	10 FB Alonzo Highsmith / Cleveland Gary
10 Penn State■	14 DL Daniel Stubbs
	DL Derwin Jones / Dan Sileo
	DL Jerome Brown
	DL Bill Hawkins
	LB Winston Moss / Randy Shannon
	LB George Mira Jr.
	LB Rod Carter
	DB Donald Ellis / Bubba McDowell
	DB Tolbert Bain
	DB Bennie Blades / Darrell Fullington
	DB Selwyn Brown / Kevin McCutcheon

RUSHING: Highsmith 105/442y, Williams 80/399y, Bratton 84/380y
PASSING: Testaverde 175-276/2557y, 26TD, 63.4%
RECEIVING: Irvin 53/868y, Perriman 34/647y, Highsmith 30/416y
SCORING: Irvin 66pts, Highsmith 48pts, Bratton 48pts

1987 12-0
31 Florida	4 WR Brian Blades / Brett Perriman
51 Arkansas	7 WR Michael Irvin / Randal Hill
26 Florida State	25 T Matt Patchan / Darren Bruce
46 Maryland	16 G Scott Provin
48 Cincinnati	10 C Rod Holder / Bobby Garcia
41 East Carolina	3 G Mike Sullivan
54 Miami (Ohio)	3 T John O'Neill
27 Virginia Tech	13 TE Alfredo Roberts / Charles Henry
24 Toledo	14 QB Steve Walsh
24 Notre Dame	0 RB Warren Williams / Leonard Conley
20 South Carolina	16 FB Melvin Bratton / Cleveland Gary
20 Oklahoma■	14 DL Daniel Stubbs
	DL Derwin Jones
	DL Dan Sileo / Greg Mark
	DL Bill Hawkins
	LB Randy Shannon / Bernard Clark
	LB George Mira Jr.
	LB Rod Carter / Maurice Crum
	DB Bubba McDowell / Donald Ellis
	DB Tolbert Bain
	DB Bennie Blades
	DB Darrell Fullington / Selwyn Brown

RUSHING: Williams 135/673y, Bratton 119/473y, Conley 66/423y
PASSING: Walsh 176-298/2249y, 19TD, 59.1%
RECEIVING: Irvin 44/715y, Williams 30/309y, Br. Blades 29/394y
SCORING: Greg Cox (K) 94pts, Bratton 66pts, Gary 42pts

1988 11-1
31 Florida State	0 WR Randal Hill
31 Michigan	30 WR Andre Brown / Dale Dawkins
23 Wisconsin	3 T Mike Sullivan / Darren Bruce
55 Missouri	0 G Rod Holder
30 Notre Dame	31 C Bobby Garcia
57 Cincinnati	3 G Darren Handy
31 East Carolina	7 T John O'Neill
34 Tulsa	3 TE Rob Chudzinski
44 LSU	3 QB Steve Walsh / Craig Erickson
18 Arkansas	16 RB Leonard Conley / Shannon Crowell
41 BYU	17 RB Cleveland Gary
23 Nebraska■	3 DL Greg Mark
	DL Russell Maryland
	DL Jimmie Jones
	DL Bill Hawkins / Willis Peguese
	LB Randy Shannon / Richard Newbill
	LB Bernard Clark
	LB Rod Carter / Maurice Crum
	DB Donald Ellis / Bobby Harden
	DB Bubba McDowell / Kenny Berry
	DB Charles Pharms
	DB Bobby Harden

RUSHING: Gary 117/480y, Conley 122/476y, Crowell 62/240y
PASSING: Walsh 233-390/3115y, 29TD, 59.7%
RECEIVING: Gary 57/655y, A. Brown 47/746y, Dawkins 31/488y
SCORING: Carlos Huerta (K) 107pts, Gary 66pts, A. Brown 48pts

1989 11-1
51 Wisconsin	3 WR Randal Hill / Lamar Thomas
31 California	3 WR Wesley Carroll / Dale Dawkins
38 Missouri	7 T Mike Sullivan
26 Michigan State	20 G Rod Holder
56 Cincinnati	0 C Bobby Garcia
48 San Jose State	16 G Darren Handy
10 Florida State	24 T Leon Searcy
40 East Carolina	10 TE Rob Chudzinski
24 Pittsburgh	3 QB Craig Erickson / Gino Torretta
42 San Diego St.	6 RB Leonard Conley
27 Notre Dame	10 FB Stephen McGuire / Alex Johnson
33 Alabama■	25 DL Greg Mark / Shane Curry
	DL Russell Maryland
	DL Cortez Kennedy
	DL Willis Peguese
	LB Richard Newbill / Darrin Smith
	LB Bernard Clark / Michael Barrow
	LB Maurice Crum
	DB Kenny Berry / Bobby Harden
	DB Ryan McNeil / Roland Smith
	DB Charles Pharms
	DB Hurlie Brown

RUSHING: Conley 134/529y, McGuire 106/519y, Johnson 62/347y
PASSING: Erickson 147-273/2007y, 16TDs, 53.8%
Torretta 101-177/1325y, 8TD, 57.1%
RECEIVING: Dawkins 54/833y, Carroll 53/770y, Hill 42/652y
SCORING: Carlos Huerta (K) 101pts, McGuire 60pts, Dawkins 42pts

1990 10-2
21 BYU	28 WR Randall Hill
52 California	24 WR Lamar Thomas
48 Iowa	21 WR Wesley Carroll / Horace Copeland
31 Florida State	22 T Leon Searcy
34 Kansas	0 G Rudy Barber
20 Notre Dame	29 C Kelvin Harris
45 Texas Tech	10 G Claude Jones
45 Pittsburgh	0 T Mike Sullivan / Mario Cristobal
42 Boston College	12 TE Rob Chudzinski / Coleman Bell
33 Syracuse	7 QB Craig Erickson
30 San Diego St.	28 RB Stephen McGuire / Darryl Spencer
46 Texas■	3 DL Anthony Hamlet / Shane Curry
	DL Russell Maryland / Eric Miller
	DL Mark Caesar
	DL Kevin Patrick / Rusty Medearis
	LB Darrin Smith
	LB Michael Barrow
	LB Maurice Crum / Jessie Armstead
	DB Roland Smith
	DB Ryan McNeil
	DB Darryl Williams
	DB Charles Pharms

RUSHING: McGuire 150/621y, Leonard Conley (RB) 78/464y, Alex Johnson (RB) 60/281y
PASSING: Erickson 225-393/3363y, 22TD, 57.3%
RECEIVING: Carroll 61/952y, Hill 44/653y, Thomas 43/742y
SCORING: Carlos Huerta (K) 101pts, McGuire 66pts, Conley 42pts

1991 12-0
31 Arkansas	3 WR Horace Copeland / Chris T. Jones
40 Houston	10 WR Lamar Thomas / Kevin Williams (TB)
34 Tulsa	10 T Leon Searcy
40 Oklahoma State	3 G Rudy Barber
26 Penn State	20 C Kelvin Harris / Tirrell Greene
55 Long Beach St.	0 G Claude Jones / Kipp Vickers
36 Arizona	9 T Mario Cristobal
27 West Virginia	3 TE Joe Moore / Coleman Bell
17 Florida State	16 QB Gino Torretta
19 Boston College	14 TB Darryl Spencer / Larry Jones
39 San Diego St.	12 FB Stephen McGuire / Martin Patton
22 Nebraska■	0 DL Kevin Patrick
	DL Anthony Hamlet / Patrick Riley
	DL Mark Caesar / Eric Miller
	DL Rusty Medearis
	LB Darrin Smith
	LB Michael Barrow
	LB Jessie Armstead
	DB Herbert James / Dexter Seigler
	DB Ryan McNeil / Terris Harris
	DB Darryl Williams
	DB Charles Pharms / Hurlie Brown

RUSHING: McGuire 123/608y, Jones 65/326y, Patton 75/242y
PASSING: Torretta 205-371/3095y, 20TD, 55.3%
RECEIVING: Thomas 39/623y, Copeland 31/592y, Spencer 28/380y
SCORING: Carlos Huerta (K) 88pts, McGuire 54pts, Patton 42pts

1992 11-1
24 Iowa	7 WR Horace Copeland
38 Florida A&M	0 WR Lamar Thomas / Kevin Williams
8 Arizona	7 T Carlos Etheredge
19 Florida State	16 G Diego London / Rudy Barber
17 Penn State	14 C Tirrell Greene
45 Texas Christian	10 G Kipp Vickers
43 Virginia Tech	23 T Mario Cristobal / Zev Lumelski
35 West Virinia	23 TE Coleman Bell
48 Temple	0 QB Gino Torretta
16 Syracuse	10 TB Darryl Spencer / Danyell Ferguson
63 San Diego St.	17 FB Donnell Bennett / Larry Jones
13 Alabama■	34 DL Darren Krein
	DL Patrick Riley
	DL Mark Caesar / Warren Sapp
	DL Kevin Patrick / Rusty Medearis
	LB Darrin Smith
	LB Michael Barrow
	LB Jessie Armstead
	DB Ryan McNeil
	DB Dexter Seigler / Paul White
	DB Terris Harris
	DB Casey Greer / Hurlie Brown

RUSHING: Bennett 97/421y, Jones 85/328y, Ferguson 63/305y
PASSING: Torretta 228-402/3060y, 19TD, 56.7%
RECEIVING: Copeland 47/769y, Thomas 47/701y, Bell 43/634y
SCORING: Dane Prewitt (K) 78pts, Thomas 60pts, Bennett & Jones 36pts

1993 9-3

23 Boston College	7 WR Chris T. Jones / A.C. Tellison
21 Virginia Tech	2 WR Jonathan Harris / Jammi German
35 Colorado	29 T Ricky Perry
30 Ga. Southern	7 G Rudy Barber
10 Florida State	28 C. K.C. Jones
49 Syracuse	0 G Tirrell Greene
42 Temple	7 T Zev Lumelski
35 Pittsburgh	7 TE Syii Tucker / Dietrich Clausell
31 Rutgers	17 QB Frank Costa / Ryan Collins
14 West Virginia	17 TB Donnell Bennett / James Stewart
41 Memphis	17 FB Larry Jones
0 Arizona ■	29 DL Darren Krein / Kenny Holmes
	DL Kenny Lopez / Patrick Riley
	DL Warren Sapp
	DL Kevin Patrick
	LB Corwin Francis / Robert Bass
	LB Ray Lewis
	LB Rohan Marley
	DB Dexter Seigler
	DB Paul White / Carlos Jones
	DB C.J. Richardson
	DB Terris Harris

RUSHING: Stewart 105/604y, Bennett 143/563y,
L. Jones 57/400y
PASSING: Collins 112-188/1555y, 14TD, 59.6%
Costa 107-199/1324y, 5TD, 53.8%
RECEIVING: C.T. Jones 45/700y, Harris 38/496y,
Tellison 26/547y
SCORING: Dane Prewitt (K) 68pts, Bennett 48pts, Stewart 36pts

1994 10-2

56 Ga. Southern	0 WR Chris T. Jones / A.C. Tellison
47 Arizona State	10 WR Jammi German / Jonathan Harris
20 Washington	38 T Zev Lumelski
24 Rutgers	3 G Alan Symonette (C)
34 Florida State	20 C K.C. Jones
38 West Virginia	6 G Tirrell Greene
24 Virginia Tech	3 T Ricky Perry / J Ina
27 Syracuse	6 TE Syii Tucker / Gerard Daphnis
17 Pittsburgh	12 QB Frank Costa / Ryan Collins
38 Temple	14 TB Al Shipman / Danyell Ferguson
23 Boston College	7 FB James Stewart / Larry Jones
17 Nebraska ■	24 DL Kenard Lang
	DL Patrick Riley
	DL Warren Sapp
	DL Kenny Holmes
	LB Corwin Francis / Twan Russell
	LB Ray Lewis
	LB James Burgess / Rohan Marley
	DB Carlos Jones
	DB Chad Wilson
	DB C.J. Richardson
	DB Malcolm X. Pearson / Earl Little

RUSHING: Stewart 147/724y, Shipman 45/454y,
L. Jones 88/409y, Ferguson 74/405y,
PASSING: Costa 168-313/2443y, 15 TD, 53.7%
RECEIVING: C.T. Jones 39/664y, German 33/391y,
Harris 25/327y
SCORING: Dane Prewitt (K) 74pts, Stewart 72pts,
C.T. Jones 36pts

1995 8-3

8 UCLA	31 WR Yatil Green / Tony Gaiter
49 Florida A&M	3 WR Jammi German / Magic Benton
7 Virginia Tech	13 T Kerlin Blaise
17 Florida State	41 G Alan Symonette / Richard Mercier
56 Rutgers	21 C K.C. Jones
17 Pittsburgh	16 G Mike Wehner
36 Temple	12 T J Ina
35 Baylor	14 TE Syii Tucker / Gerard Daphnis
17 Boston College	14 QB Ryan Clement
17 West Virginia	12 TB Dan'l Ferguson/D. McMillan/Tr't Jones
35 Syracuse	24 FB Derrick Harris / Carlo Joseph
	DL Kenard Lang
	DL Denny Fortney / Michael Lawson
	DL Marvin Davis / Jason McCullough
	DL Kenny Holmes
	LB Twan Russell
	LB Ray Lewis
	LB James Burgess / Antonio Coley
	DB Carlos Jones / Nick Ward
	DB Earl Little
	DB Tremain Mack / Jack Hallmon
	DB Chris Gibson / Eugene Ridgely

RUSHING: Ferguson 212/1069y, McMillan 81/322y,
Jones 28/125y
PASSING: Clement 119-201/1638y, 7TD, 59.2%
RECEIVING: German 41/730y, Green 25/476y,
Ferguson 22/248y
SCORING: Ferguson 78pts

1996 9-3

30 Memphis	7 WR Yatil Green / Magic Benton
52 Citadel	6 WR Tony Gaiter / Jermaine Chambers
33 Rutgers	0 T Kerlin Blaise
45 Pittsburgh	9 G Richard Mercier
16 Florida State	34 C K.C. Jones
6 East Carolina	31 G Mike Wehner
10 West Virginia	7 T J Ina / Freeman Brown
57 Temple	26 TE Chris C. Jones / Gerard Daphnis
7 Virginia Tech	21 QB Ryan Clement
43 Boston College	26 TB Dyral McMill'n/T. Jones/Edg'r'n James
38 Syracuse	31 FB Carlo Joseph / Nick Williams
31 Virginia ■	21 DL Kenard Lang / Derrick Ham
	DL Michael Lawson / Chad Pegues
	DL Denny Fortney
	DL Kenny Holmes / Matt Sweeney
	LB Antonio Coley / Michael Smith
	LB James Burgess / Cliff Jackson
	LB Twan Russell
	DB Carlos Jones / Duane Starks
	DB Earl Little / Nate Brooks
	DB Tremain Mack
	DB Marcus Wimberly / Eugene Ridgley

RUSHING: McMillan 111/565y
PASSING: Clement 148-246/1983y, 18TD, 60.2%
RECEIVING: Green 44/746y
SCORING: Andy Crosland (K) 77pts

1997 5-6

45 Baylor	14 WR Daryl Jones / Santana Moss
12 Arizona State	23 WR Reggie Wayne / Omar Rolle
17 Pittsburgh	21 T Kerlin Blaise
17 West Virginia	28 G Carlos Callejas
0 Florida State	47 C Mike Wehner / Ty Wise
45 Boston College	44 G Damond Neely
47 Temple	15 T Robert Sampson / Robert Hall
42 Arkansas State	10 TE Bubba Franks / Mondriel Fulcher
25 Virginia Tech	27 QB Ryan Clement / Scott Covington
51 Rutgers	23 TB Edgerrin James / James Jackson
13 Syracuse	33 FB Carlo Joseph / Nick Williams
	DL Derrick Ham / Quincy Hipps
	DL Damione Lewis
	DL Chad Pegues
	DL Denny Fortney / Matt Sweeney
	LB Dan Morgan
	LB Rod Mack / Nate Webster
	LB Michael Smith / Jevon Rhodes
	DB Duane Starks / Leonard Myers
	DB Nate Brooks
	DB Eugene Ridgely / Delvin Brown
	DB Dennis Scott / Jeff Popovich

RUSHING: James 184/1098y, Jackson 81/595y,
Dyral McMillan (TB) 31/144y
PASSING: Clement 157-267/2089y, 10TD, 58.8%
RECEIVING: Wayne 48/640y, Franks 19/294y, James 19/250y
SCORING: James 84pts, Andy Crosland (K) 61pts,
Jackson 36pts

1998 9-3

66 E. Tenn. St.	17 WR Reggie Wayne / Andre King
38 Cincinnati	12 WR Santana Moss
20 Virginia Tech	27 T Robert Hall / Robert Sampson
53 Rutgers	17 G Richard Mercier
14 Florida State	26 C Ty Wise
34 West Virginia	31 G Brett Romberg
35 Boston College	17 T Joaquin Gonzalez
42 Temple	7 TE Bubba Franks
38 Pittsburgh	10 QB Scott Covington
13 Syracuse	66 TB Edgerrin James / Najeh Davenport
49 UCLA	45 FB Mondriel Fulcher
46 N. Carolina St. ■	23 DL Derrick Ham
	DL Damione Lewis
	DL Matt Sweeney / Michael Lawson
	DL Quincy Hipps / Michael Boireau
	LB Dan Morgan
	LB Nate Webster / Rod Mack
	LB Michael Smith
	DB Leonard Myers
	DB Markese Fitzgerald / Michael Rumph
	DB Al Blades / Delvin Brown
	DB Edward Reed / Jeff Popovich

RUSHING: James 242/1416y, James Jackson (TB) 82/545y
Davenport 55/387y
PASSING: Covington 159-270/2301y, 19TD, 58.9%
RECEIVING: Wayne 42/629y, Moss 30/631y, King 28/397y
SCORING: James 114pts, Andy Crosland (K) 72pts, Moss 48pts

1999 9-4

23 Ohio State	12 WR Reggie Wayne / Andre King
57 Florida A&M	3 WR Santana Moss / Daryl Jones
23 Penn State	27 T Greg Laffere / Robert Hall
23 East Carolina	17 G Richard Mercier
21 Florida State	31 C Ty Wise
31 Boston College	28 G Martin Bibla
28 West Virginia	20 T Joaquin Gonzalez
33 Pittsburgh	3 TE Bubba Franks
10 Virginia Tech	43 QB Kenny Kelly / Ken Dorsey
55 Rutgers	0 TB James Jackson / Clinton Portis
45 Temple	13 FB Mondriel Fulcher / Will McPartland
55 Temple	0 DL William Joseph
28 Georgia Tech ■	13 DL Matt Sweeney / Adrian Wilson
	DL Damione Lewis / Matt Walters
	DL Michael Boireau
	LB Chris Campbell
	LB Nate Webster / Rod Mack
	LB Dan Morgan
	DB Leonard Myers / Phillip Buchanon
	DB Michael Rumph
	DB Edward Reed / James Lewis
	DB Al Blades / Jeff Popovich

RUSHING: Portis 143/838y, Jackson 169/782y,
Jarrett Payton (TB) 53/262y
PASSING: Kelly 141-259/1913y, 15 TD, 54.4%,
Dorsey 74-120/807y, 10 TD, 61.7%
RECEIVING: Moss 54/899y, Franks 45/565y, Wayne 40/
SCORING: Andy Crosland (K) 82pts, Jackson 62pts, Portis 60pts

2000 11-1

61 McNeese State	14 WR Reggie Wayne / Daryl Jones
29 Washington	34 WR Santana Moss
47 West Virginia	10 T Bryant McKinnie
64 Rutgers	6 G Greg Laffere / Sherko Haji-Rasouli
27 Florida State	24 C Brett Romberg
45 Temple	31 G Martin Bibla / Vernon Carey
42 Louisiana Tech	31 T Joaquin Gonzalez
35 Pittsburgh	7 QB Ken Dorsey
26 Syracuse	0 TB James Jackson / Clinton Portis
52 Boston College	6 FB Najeh Davenport
37 Florida ■	20 DL Jamaal Green
	DL William Joseph
	DL Damione Lewis / Matt Walters
	DL Cornelius Green
	LB Chris Campbell / Ken Dangerfield
	LB Dan Morgan
	LB Howard Clark / Jonathan Vilma
	DB Phillip Buchanon / Leonard Myers
	DB Michael Rumph / Markese Fitzgerald
	DB Edward Reed
	DB Al Blades / James Lewis

RUSHING: Jackson 201/1006y, Portis 77/485y, Davenport 65/308y
PASSING: Dorsey 188-322/2737y, 25TD, 58.4%
RECEIVING: Moss 45/748y, Wayne 43/755y, Shockey 21/296y
SCORING: Todd Sievers (K) 85pts, Jackson 78pts, Moss 66pts

2001 12-0

33 Penn State	7 WR Daryl Jones / Kevin Beard
61 Rutgers	0 WR Andre Johnson / Ethenic Sands
43 Pittsburgh	21 T Bryant McKinnie
38 Troy State	7 G Sherko Haji-Rasouli / Ed Wilkins
49 Florida State	27 C Brett Romberg
45 West Virginia	3 G Martin Bibla
38 Temple	0 T Joaquin Gonzalez
18 Boston College	7 TE Jeremy Shockey
59 Syracuse	0 QB Ken Dorsey
65 Washington	7 TB Clinton Portis / Frank Gore
26 Virginia Tech	24 FB Najeh Davenport/Willis McGahee (TB)
37 Nebraska ■	14 DL Jerome McDougle
	DL William Joseph
	DL Matt Walters / Vince Wilfork
	DL Andrew Williams / John Square
	LB Chris Campbell
	LB Jonathan Vilma / Howard Clark
	LB D.J. Williams / Jamaal Green
	DB Phillip Buchanon / Markese Fitzgerald
	DB Michael Rumph
	DB Edward Reed
	DB James Lewis / Maurice Sikes

RUSHING: Portis 220/1200y, Gore 62/562y, McGahee 67/314y
PASSING: Dorsey 184-318/2652y, 23TD, 57.9%
RECEIVING: Shockey 40/519y, Johnson 37/682y, Sands 26/385y
SCORING: Todd Sievers (K) 119pts, Portis 66pts, Johnson 60pts

2002 12-1

63 Florida A&M	17 WR Kevin Beard / Roscoe Parrish
41 Florida	16 WR Andre Johnson /Jason Geathers (TB)
44 Temple	21 T Carlos Joseph
38 Boston College	6 G Sherko Haji-Rasouli
48 Connecticut	14 C Brett Romberg
28 Florida State	27 G Chris Myers
40 West Virginia	23 T Vernon Carey
42 Rutgers	17 TE Kellen Winslow, Jr / Eric Winston
26 Tennessee	3 QB Ken Dorsey
28 Pittsburgh	21 TB Willis McGahee / Jarrett Payton
49 Syracuse	7 FB Quadtrine Hill
56 Virginia Tech	45 DL Jerome McDougle
24 Ohio State ■	31 DL William Joseph
	DL Matt Walters / Vince Wilfork
	DL Jamaal Green / John Square
	LB Roger McIntosh / Howard Clark
	LB Jonathan Vilma
	LB D.J. Williams
	DB Kelly Jennings / Alfonso Marshall
	DB Antrel Rolle / Glenn Sharpe
	DB Sean Taylor
	DB Maurice Sykes / Greg Threat

RUSHING: McGahee 282/1753y, Geathers 68/398y,
 Payton 50/223y
PASSING: Dorsey 222-393/3369y, 28 TD, 56.5%
RECEIVING: Winslow 57/726y, Johnson 52/1092y,
 McGahee 27/355y
SCORING: McGahee 168pts, Todd Sievers (K) 105pts,
 Johnson 54pts

2003 11-2

48 Louisiana Tech	9 WR Ryan Moore / Roscoe Parrish
38 Florida	33 WR Kevin Beard / Jason Geathers (TB)
38 East Carolina	3 T Eric Winston
33 Boston College	14 G Vernon Carey
22 West Virginia	20 C Joel Rodriguez
22 Florida State	14 G Chris Myers (C) / Joe McGrath
52 Temple	14 T Carlos Joseph / Rashad Butler
7 Virginia Tech	31 TE Kellen Winslow, Jr. / Kevin Everett
6 Tennessee	10 QB Brock Berlin / Derrick Crudup
17 Syracuse	10 TB Jarrett Payton / Frank Gore
34 Rutgers	9 FB Quadtrine Hill
28 Pittsburgh	14 DL Baraka Atkins / Bryan Pata
16 Florida State ■	14 DL Orien Harris / Kareem Brown
	DL Vince Wilfork / John Square
	DL Thomas Carroll
	LB Darrell McClover / Roger McIntosh
	LB Jonathan Vilma
	LB D.J. Williams / Leon Williams
	DB Alfonso Marshall / Kelly Jennings
	DB Antrel Rolle
	DB Sean Taylor / Brandon Meriweather
	DB Maurice Sikes

RUSHING: Payton 182/985y, Moss 107/511y, Gore 89/468y
PASSING: Berlin 211-352/2419y, 12TD, 59.9%
RECEIVING: Winslow 60/605y, Moore 44/637y, Parrish 24/322y
SCORING: Jon Peattie (K) 103pts, Payton 48pts, Moss 30pts

2004 9-3

16 Florida State	10 WR Roscoe Parrish / Ryan Moore
48 Louisiana Tech	0 WR Darnell Jenkins / Sinorice Moss
38 Houston	13 T Rashad Butler / Eric Winston
27 Georgia Tech	3 G Tony Tella
41 Louisville	38 C Joel Rodriguez
45 N. Carolina St.	31 G Tyler McMeans / Derrick Morse
28 North Carolina	31 T Chris Myers
17 Clemson	24 TE Kevin Everett / Greg Olsen
31 Virginia	21 QB Brock Berlin
52 Wake Forest	7 TB Frank Gore / Tyrone Moss
10 Virginia Tech	16 FB Quadtrine Hill / Talib Humphrey
27 Florida ■	10 DL Baraka Atkins
	DL Orien Harris / Kareem Brown
	DL Santonio Thomas / Thomas Carroll
	DL Javon Nanton / Bryan Pata
	LB Roger McIntosh / Jon Beason
	LB Leon Williams
	LB Tavares Gooden / Romeo Davis
	DB Kelly Jennings / Devin Hester (WR)
	DB Antrel Rolle
	DB Anthony Reddick/Brand'n Meriweath'r
	DB Greg Threat / Marcus Maxey

RUSHING: Gore 197/945y, Moss 102/445y, Hill 20/111y
PASSING: Berlin 195-348/2680y, 22TD, 56.0%
RECEIVING: Parrish 43/693y, Everett 23/310y, Jenkins 21/230y,
 Moss 20/351y
SCORING: Jon Peattie (K) 90pts, Parrish 60pts, Gore 48pts

2005 9-3

7 Florida State	10 WR Sinorice Moss / Lance Leggett
36 Clemson	30 WR Ryan Moore / Darnell Jenkins
23 Colorado	3 T Eric Winston
27 South Florida	7 G Tyler McMeans
52 Duke	7 C Anthony Wollschlager
34 Temple	3 G Tony Tella / Andrew Bain
34 North Carolina	16 T Rashad Butler
27 Virginia Tech	7 TE Greg Olsen / Chris Zellner
47 Wake Forest	17 QB Kyle Wright
10 Georgia Tech	14 TB Tyrone Moss / Charlie Jones
25 Virginia	17 FB Quadtrine Hill
3 LSU ■	40 DL Bryan Pata / Javon Nanton
	DL Baraka Atkins / Kareem Brown
	DL Orien Harris
	DL Thomas Carroll / Calais Campbell
	LB Rocky McIntosh / Leon Williams
	LB Romeo Davis / Glenn Cook
	LB Jon Beason
	DB Kelly Jennings / Devin Hester (WR)
	DB Marcus Maxey
	DB Kenny Phillips / Greg Threat
	DB Brandon Meriweather / Lovon Ponder

RUSHING: T. Moss 137/701y, Jones 123/507y,
 Derron Thomas 47/150y, Hill 19/138y
PASSING: Wright 180-307/2403y, 18TDs, 58.6%
RECEIVING: S. Moss 37/614y, Olsen 31/451y, Hill 29/252y,
 Moore 28/464y
SCORING: Jon Peattie (K) 79pts, T. Moss 72pts, S. Moss 36pts

2006 7-6

10 Florida State	13 WR Lance Leggett / Ryan Moore
51 Florida A&M	10 WR Sam Shields / Darnell Jenkins
7 Louisville	31 T Reggie Youngblood
14 Houston	13 G Andrew Bain
27 North Carolina	7 C Anthony Wollschlager
35 Florida Int'l	0 G Derrick Morse / Alex Pou
20 Duke	15 T Jason Fox / Chris Rutledge
23 Georgia Tech	30 TE Greg Olsen / Dedrick Epps
10 Virginia Tech	17 TE Chris Zellner / DajLeon Farr
13 Maryland	14 QB Kyle Wright / Kirby Freeman
7 Virginia	17 RB Javarris James / Charlie Jones
17 Boston College	14 DL Baraka Atkins / Eric Moncur
21 Nevada ■	20 DL Bryan Pata / Kareem Brown
	DL Teraz McCray
	DL Calais Campbell
	LB Tavares Gooden
	LB Glenn Cook / Darryl Sharpton
	LB Jon Beason / Romeo Davis
	DB Glenn Sharpe / Chavez Grant
	DB Randy Phillips / Bruce Johnson
	DB Lovon Ponder
	DB Brandon Meriweather / Kenny Phillips

RUSHING: James 175/802y, Tyrone Moss (RB) 66/285y,
 Jones 61/206y
PASSING: Wright 152-250/1655y, 8 TDs, 60.8%,
 Freeman 59-108/872y, 7 TDs, 54.6%
RECEIVING: Olsen 40/489y, Leggett 38/584y, Shields 37/501y

2007 5-7

31 Marshall	3 WR Darnell Jenkins / Sam Shields
13 Oklahoma	51 WR Lance Leggett / Kayne Farquharson
23 Florida Int'l	9 T Jason Fox
34 Texas A&M	17 G Andrew Bain / Orlando Franklin
24 Duke	14 C John Rochford
27 North Carolina	33 G Derrick Morse
14 Georgia Tech	17 T Reggie Youngblood / Chris Rutledge
37 Florida State	29 TE Chris Zellner / Richard Gordon
16 N. Carolina St.	19 QB Kyle Wright / Kirby Freeman
0 Virginia	48 RB Javarris James / Charlie jones
14 Virginia Tech	44 FB Jerrell Mabry / Graig Cooper
14 Boston College	28 DL Eric Moncur / Vegas Franklin
	DL Joe Joseph / Antonio Dixon
	DL Teraz McCray / Dwayne Hendricks
	DL Calais Campbell
	LB Colin McCarthy
	LB Tavares Gooden
	LB Spencer Adkins / Darryl Sharpton
	DB Bruce Johnson / DeMarcus Van Dyke
	DB Carlos Armour / Randy Phillips
	DB Kenny Phillips
	DB Willie Cooper

RUSHING: Cooper 125/682y, James 159/582y,
 Derron Thomas (RB) 40/200y
PASSING: Wright 141-241/1747y, 12TD, 58.5%
RECEIVING: Jenkins 31/619y, Shields 27/346y, Leggett 15/238y
SCORING: Francesco Zampogna (K) 50pts, Cooper 30pts,
 James 24pts

2008 7-6

52 Charleston So.	7 WR Laron Byrd / Travis Benjamin
3 Florida	26 WR Sam Shields / Kayne Farquharson
41 Texas A&M	23 WR Aldarius Johnson / Thearon Collier
24 North Carolina	28 T Jason Fox / Reggie Youngblood
39 Florida State	41 G Orlando Franklin
20 C. Florida	14 C Xavier Shannon
49 Duke	31 G A.J. Trump / Joel Figueroa
16 Wake Forest	10 T Chris Rutledge
24 Virginia	17 TE Dedrick Epps / Chris Zellner
16 Virginia Tech	14 QB Robert Marve / Jacory Harris
23 Georgia Tech	41 RB Graig Cooper / Javarris James
28 N. Carolina St.	38 DL Steven Wesley / Allen Bailey
17 California ■	24 DL Joe Joseph / Antonio Dixon
	DL Dwayne Hendricks / Marcus Forson
	DL Marcus Robinson / Adewale Ojomo
	LB Darryl Sharpton / Romeo Davis
	LB Glenn Cook
	LB Sean Spence / Colin McCarthy
	DB Brandon Harris / Chavez Grant
	DB Bruce Johnson
	DB Anthony Reddick
	DB JoJo Nicolas / Ryan Hill

RUSHING: Cooper 171/841y, James 68/286y, Marve 59/116y
PASSING: Marve 116-213/1293y, 9TD, 54.5%
 Harris 118-194/1195y, 12TD, 60.8%
RECEIVING: Johnson 31/332y, Cooper 29/113y, Collier 26/324y,
SCORING: Matt Bosher (K) 94pts, Cooper 36pts,
 Benjamin, Byrd & James 24pts

2009 9-4

38 Florida State	34 WR Laron Byrd / Aldarius Johnson
33 Georgia Tech	17 WR Leonard Hankerson / Travis Benjamin
7 Virginia Tech	31 T Jason Fox
21 Oklahoma	20 G Orlando Franklin
48 Florida A&M	16 C A.J. Trump
27 C. Florida	7 G Joel Figueroa
37 Clemson	40 T Matt Pipho
28 Wake Forest	27 TE Dedrick Epps / Tervaris Johnson
52 Virginia	14 QB Jacory Harris
24 North Carolina	33 RB Graig Cooper / Javarris James
34 Duke	16 FB Mike James
31 South Florida	10 DL Steven Wesley / Marcus Robinson
14 Wisconsin ■	20 DL Joe Joseph
	DL Josh Holmes / Micanor Regis
	DL Allen Bailey / Andrew smith
	LB Colin McCarthy / Jordan Futch
	LB Daryll Sharpton
	LB Sean Spence / Ramon Buchanon
	DB Brandon Harris / Chavez Grant
	DB Sam Shields / Demarcus Van Dyke
	DB Randy Phillips / Vaughn Telemaque
	DB Jared Campbell / Ray-Ray Armstrong

RUSHING: Cooper 134/695y, Damien Berry (RB) 93/616y
 J. James 103/492y
PASSING: Harris 242-406/3352y, 24TDs, 59.6%
RECEIVING: Hankerson 45/801y, Byrd 33/460y, Benjamin 29/501y
SCORING: Matt Bosher (K) 92pts, Damien Berry (RB) 48pts,
 Hankerson & James 36pts

2010 7-6

45 Florida A&M	0 WR Travis Benjamin / Kendal Thompkins
24 Ohio State	36 WR Leonard Hankerson / Aldarius Johnson
31 Pittsburgh	3 WR/FB LaRon Byrd / Pat Hill
30 Clemson	21 T Orlando Franklin / Joel Figueroa
17 Florida State	45 G Harland Gunn
28 Duke	13 C Tyler Horn
33 North Carolina	10 G Brandon Washington / Brandon Linder
19 Virginia	24 T Sentrel Henderson / Jermaine Johnson
26 Maryland	20 TE Richard Gordon / Chase Ford
35 Georgia Tech	10 QB Jacory Harris / Stephen Morris
17 Virginia Tech	31 HB Damien Berry/Mike James/Lamar Miller
20 South Florida	23 DL Allen Bailey
17 Notre Dame ■	33 DL Micanor Regis / Josh Holmes
	DL Marcus Forston
	DL Olivier Vernon / Adewale Ojomo
	LB Ramon Buchanan
	LB Colin McCarthy / Kelvin Cain
	LB Sean Spence
	DB Ryan Hill / DeMarcus Van Dyke
	DB Brandon Harris / Brandon McGee
	DB Vaughn Telemaque
	DB JoJo Nicolas / Ray Ray Armstrong

RUSHING: Berry 190/899y, Miller 108/646y, James 70/398y
PASSING: Harris 148-270/1793y, 14TD, 54.8%
 Morris 82-153/1240y, 7TD, 53.6%
RECEIVING: Hankerson 72/1156y, Benjamin 43/743y,
 Byrd 41/441y
SCORING: Hankerson 78pts, Matt Bosher (K) 76pts, Miller 44pts

MICHIGAN

University of Michigan (Founded 1817)
Ann Arbor, Michigan
Nickname: Wolverines
Colors: Maize and Blue
Stadium: Michigan Stadium (1927) 106,201
Conference Affiliation: Big Ten (Charter member 1895-present)

CAREER RUSHING YARDS	Attempt	Yards
Mike Hart (2004-07)	1015	5040
Anthony Thomas (1997-2000)	924	4472
Jamie Morris (1984-87)	809	4393
Tyrone Wheatley (1991-94)	688	4178
Butch Woolfolk (1978-81)	718	3861
Chris Perry (2000-03)	811	3696
Rob Lytle (1973-76)	557	3317
Billy Taylor (1969-71)	587	3072
Gordon Bell (1973-75)	535	2900
Tim Biakabutuka (1993-95)	472	2810

CAREER PASSING YARDS	Comp.-Att.	Yards
Chad Henne (2004-07)	828-1387	9715
John Navarre (2000-03)	765-1366	9254
Elvis Grbac (1989-92)	522- 835	6460
Todd Collins (1991-94)	457- 711	5858
Jim Harbaugh (1983-86)	387- 620	5449
Tom Brady (1996-99)	443- 711	5351
Steve Smith (1980-83)	324- 648	4860
Brian Griese (1993-97)	355- 606	4383
Rick Leach (1975-78)	250- 537	4284

CAREER RECEIVING YARDS	Catches	Yards
Braylon Edwards (2001-04)	252	3541
Anthony Carter (1979-82)	161	3076
Amani Toomer (1992-95)	143	2657
David Terrell (1998-2000)	152	2317
Mario Manningham (2005-07)	137	2310
Tai Streets (1995-98)	144	2284
Marquise Walker (1998-2001)	176	2269
Jason Avant (2002-05)	169	2247
Greg McMurtry (1986-89)	111	2163
Desmond Howard (1989-91)	134	2146

SEASON RUSHING YARDS	Attempts	Yards
Tim Biakabutuka (1995)	303	1818
Anthony Thomas (2000)	319	1733
Jamie Morris (1987)	282	1703
Denard Robinson (2010)	256	1702
Chris Perry (2003)	338	1674

SEASON PASSING YARDS	Comp.-Att.	Yards
John Navarre (2003)	270-456	3331
John Navarre (2002)	248-448	2905
Chad Henne (2004)	240-399	2743
Jim Harbaugh (1986)	180-277	2729
Tom Brady (1998)	214-350	2636

SEASON RECEIVING YARDS	Catches	Yards
Braylon Edwards (2004)	97	1330
Mario Manningham (2007)	72	1174
Marquise Walker (2001)	86	1143
Braylon Edwards (2003)	85	1138
David Terrell (2000)	67	1130

GAME RUSHING YARDS	Attempts	Yards
Ron Johnson (1968 vs. Wisconsin)	31	347
Tim Biakabutuka (1995 vs. Ohio State)	37	313
Jon Vaughn (1990 vs. UCLA)	32	288

GAME PASSING YARDS	Comp.-Att.	Yards
John Navarre (2003 vs. Iowa)	26-49	389
Tom Brady (1998 vs. Ohio State)	31-56	375
Chad Henne (2007 vs. Florida)	25-39	373

GAME RECEIVING YARDS	Catches	Yards
Roy Roundtree (2010 vs. Illinois)	9	246
Jack Clancy (1966 vs. Oregon State)	10	197
Tai Streets (1998 vs. Minnesota)	6	192

GREATEST COACH:

There can be only one Michigan coach, and that is the incomparable Glenn "Bo" Schembechler. Even with a great roster of coaches that includes Fielding Yost, Fritz Crisler, Bennie Oosterbaan, and Lloyd Carr, Schembechler is the all-time winner with a 194-47-5 (.7988) record. Schembechler won 13 of Michigan's 42 Big Ten championships.

Schembechler authored an immediate hit in his first season when his Wolverines upset Ohio State 24-12 to snap a 22-game win streak by the Buckeyes. That win secured Schembechler his first Rose Bowl trip.

But the night before the 1970 Rose Bowl, Schembechler suffered a mild heart attack. It was almost as if that illness ruined the coach's future bowl record. Schembechler suffered through a mysterious 5-12 post season mark and lost five Rose Bowls before his 1980 team, led by Anthony Carter, Ed Muransky, and Mel Owens, finally beat Washington in Pasadena.

Still, Schembechler presented such a strong voice of achievement that he became the face of the University of Michigan.

MICHIGAN'S 55 BEST SINCE 1953

OFFENSE

WIDE RECEIVER: Anthony Carter, Jack Clancy, Braylon Edwards, Marquise Walker
TIGHT END: Jim Mandich, Jerame Tuman
TACKLE: Dan Dierdorf, John "Jumbo" Elliott, Jake Long, Ed Muransky, Greg Skrepenak
GUARD: Kurt Becker, Mark Donahue, Steve Hutchinson, Reggie McKenzie
CENTER: David Baas, Steve Everitt
QUARTERBACK: Elvis Grbac, Jim Harbaugh, Chad Henne
RUNNING BACK: Mike Hart, Jamie Morris, Anthony Thomas, Tyrone Wheatley
FULLBACK: Rob Lytle

DEFENSE

END: Glen Steele, LaMarr Woodley
TACKLE: Curtis Greer, Mike Hammerstein, Chris Hutchinson, Bill Yearby
NOSE GUARD: William Carr, Mark Messner, Rob Renes
LINEBACKER: Erick Anderson, Jarrett Irons, Ron Simpkins, Sam Sword, Mike Taylor
CORNER BACK: Dave Brown, Brad Cochran, Garland Rivers
SAFETY: Tom Curtis, Tom Darden, Randy Logan, Ernest Shazor, Tripp Welborne

SPECIAL TEAMS

RETURN SPECIALISTS: Steve Breaston, Desmond Howard
PLACEKICKER: Remy Hamilton
PUNTER: Monte Robbins

MULTIPLE POSITIONS

QUARTERBACK-FULLBACK-LINEBACKER: Lou Baldacci
QUARTERBACK-HALFBACK-KICKER-PUNTER: Bob Timberlake

TWO-WAY PLAYERS

END-DEFENSIVE END-PUNTER-KICKER: Ron Kramer
CORNERBACK-WIDE RECEIVER-KICK RETURNER: Charles Woodson

PERFORMANCE FORMULA:
MICHIGAN'S 10 BEST SEASONS

1997	1.7413	3 of 70
1985	1.7015	2 of 70
1973	1.6563	6 of 70
1964	1.6353	3 of 70
1976	1.6286	3 of 70
1974	1.6244	3 of 71
1991	1.6157	5 of 71
2006	1.6109	5 of 72
1972	1.5955	7 of 70
1978	1.5916	5 of 70

MICHIGAN WOLVERINES

Year	W-L-T	AP Poll	Conference Standing	Toughest Regular Season Opponents	Coach (Record at School)	Bowl Games		
1953	6-3	20	5t	Iowa 5-3-1, Illinois 7-1-1, Michigan State 8-1, Ohio State 6-3	Bennie Oosterbaan			
1954	6-3	15	2t	Army 7-2, Minnesota 7-2, Ohio State 9-0	Bennie Oosterbaan			
1955	7-2	12	3	Michigan State 8-1, Army 6-3, Illinois 5-3-1, Ohio State 7-2	Bennie Oosterbaan			
1956	7-2	7	2	Michigan State 7-2, Minnesota 6-1-2, Iowa 8-1, Ohio State 6-3	Bennie Oosterbaan			
1957	5-3-1		6	Michigan State 8-1, Iowa 7-1-1, Ohio State 8-1	Bennie Oosterbaan			
1958	2-6-1		8	Navy 6-3, Iowa 7-1-1, Ohio State 6-1-2	Bennie Oosterbaan (63-33-4)			
1959	4-5		7	Missouri 6-4, Northwestern 6-3, Wisconsin 7-2, Illinois 5-3-1	Chalmers "Bump" Elliott			
1960	5-4		5t	Oregon 7-2-1, Duke 7-3, Minnesota 8-1, Ohio State 7-2	Bump Elliott			
1961	6-3		6	Michigan State 7-2, Minnesota 7-2, Duke 7-3, Ohio State 8-0-1	Bump Elliott			
1962	2-7		10	Nebraska 8-2, Minnesota 6-2-1, Wisconsin 8-1, Ohio State 6-3	Bump Elliott			
1963	3-4-2		5	Navy 9-1, Michigan State 6-2-1, Illinois 7-1-1, Ohio State 5-3-1	Bump Elliott			
1964	9-1	4	1	Purdue 6-3, Illinois 6-3, Ohio State 7-2	Bump Elliott	Rose	34 Oregon State	7
1965	4-6		7t	Georgia 6-4, Michigan State 10-0, Purdue 7-2-1, Ohio State 7-2	Bump Elliott			
1966	6-4		3t	Oregon State 7-3, Michigan State 9-0-1, Purdue 8-2	Bump Elliott			
1967	4-6		5t	Indiana 9-1, Minnesota 8-2, Ohio State 6-3	Bump Elliott			
1968	8-2	12	2	California 7-3-1, Indiana 6-4, Minnesota 6-4, Ohio State 9-0	Bump Elliott (51-42-2)			
1969	8-3	9	1t	Missouri 9-1, Purdue 8-2, Ohio State 8-1	Glenn "Bo" Schembechler	Rose	3 Southern California	10
1970	9-1	9	2t	Washington 6-4, Ohio State 9-0	Bo Schembechler	Rose	12 Stanford	13
1971	11-1	6	1	Northwestern 7-4, Michigan State 6-5, Ohio State 6-4	Bo Schembechler			
1972	10-1	6	1t	UCLA 8-3, Purdue 6-5, Ohio State 9-1	Bo Schembechler			
1973	10-0-1	6	1t	Stanford 7-4, Minnesota 7-4, Ohio State 9-0-1	Bo Schembechler			
1974	10-1	3	1t	Michigan State 7-3-1, Wisconsin 7-4, Ohio State 10-1	Bo Schembechler	Orange	6 Oklahoma	14
1975	8-2-2	8	2	Stanford 6-4-, Michigan State 7-4, Ohio State 11-0	Bo Schembechler	Rose	6 Southern California	14
1976	10-2	3	1t	Stanford 6-5, Minnesota 6-5, Ohio State 8-2-1	Bo Schembechler	Rose	20 Washington	27
1977	10-2	9	1t	Texas A&M 8-3, Mich. State 7-3-1, Minnesota 7-4, Ohio State 9-2	Bo Schembechler	Rose	10 Southern California	17
1978	10-2	5	1t	Notre Dame 8-3, Mich. State 8-3, Purdue 8-2-1, Ohio State 7-3-1	Bo Schembechler	Gator	15 North Carolina	17
1979	8-4	18	3	Notre Dame 7-4, Indiana 7-4, Purdue 9-2, Ohio State 11-0	Bo Schembechler	Rose	23 Washington	6
1980	10-2	4	1	Notre Dame 9-1-1, South Carolina 8-3, Purdue 8-3, Ohio State 9-2	Bo Schembechler	Bluebonnet	33 UCLA	14
1981	9-3	12	3t	Navy 7-3-1, Iowa 8-3, Ohio State 8-3	Bo Schembechler	Rose	14 UCLA	24
1982	8-4		1	UCLA 9-1-1, Iowa 7-4, Illinois 7-4, Ohio State 8-3	Bo Schembechler	Sugar	7 Auburn	9
1983	9-3	8	2	Washington 8-3, Iowa 9-2, Illinois 10-1, Ohio State 8-3	Bo Schembechler	Holiday	17 BYU	24
1984	6-6		6t	Miami 8-4, Washington 10-1, Wisconsin 7-3-1, Ohio State 9-2	Bo Schembechler	Fiesta	27 Nebraska	23
1985	10-1-1	2	2	Maryland 8-3, Iowa 10-1, Ohio State 8-3	Bo Schembechler	Rose	15 Arizona State	22
1986	11-2	8	1t	Florida State 6-4-1, Iowa 8-3, Ohio State 9-3	Bo Schembechler	Hall of Fame	28 Alabama	24
1987	8-4	19	4	Notre Dame 8-3, Michigan State 8-2-1, Iowa 9-3, Indiana 8-3	Bo Schembechler	Rose	22 Southern California	14
1988	9-2-1	4	1	Notre Dame 11-0, Miami 10-1, Iowa 6-3-3, Indiana 7-3-1	Bo Schembechler (194-47-5)	Rose	10 Southern California	17
1989	10-2	8	1	Notre Dame 11-1, Michigan State 7-4, Illinois 9-2, Ohio State 8-3	Bo Schembechler	Rose	23 Washington	
1990	9-3	7	1t	No. Dame 9-2, Mich. St. 7-3-1, Iowa 8-3, Illinois 8-3, Ohio St. 7-3-1	Gary Moeller	Gator	35 Mississippi	3
1991	10-2	6	1	Notre Dame 9-3, Florida State 10-2, Iowa 10-1, Ohio State 8-3	Gary Moeller	Rose	14 Washington	34
1992	9-0-3	5	1	Notre Dame 9-1-1, Illinois 6-4-1, Ohio State 8-2-1	Gary Moeller	Rose	38 Washington	31
1993	8-4	21	4t	Notre Dame 10-1, Penn St. 9-2, Wisconsin 9-1-1, Ohio State 9-1-1	Gary Moeller	Hall of Fame	42 North Carolina State	7
1994	8-4	12	3	Colorado 10-1, Penn State 11-0, Ohio State 9-3	Gary Moeller (44-13-3)	Holiday	24 Colorado State	14
1995	9-4	19	3t	Virginia 8-4, Northwestern 10-1, Penn State 9-3, Ohio State 11-1	Lloyd Carr	Alamo	20 Texas A&M	22
1996	8-4	20	5t	Colorado 9-2, Northwestern 9-2, Penn State 10-2, Ohio State 10-1	Lloyd Carr	Outback	14 Alabama	17
1997	12-0	1	1	Penn State 9-2, Wisconsin 8-4, Ohio State 10-2	Lloyd Carr	Rose	21 Washington State	16
1998	10-3	12	1t	Notre Dame 9-2, Penn State 8-3, Wisconsin 10-1, Ohio State 10-1	Lloyd Carr	Citrus	45 Arkansas	31
1999	10-2	5	2t	Wisconsin 9-2, Michigan State 9-2, Penn State 9-3	Lloyd Carr	Orange	35 Alabama	34
2000	9-3	11	1t	Wisconsin 8-4, Purdue 8-3, Northwestern 8-3, Ohio State 8-3	Lloyd Carr	Citrus	31 Auburn	28
2001	8-4	20	2	Washington 8-3, Illinois 10-1, Ohio State 7-4	Lloyd Carr	Citrus	17 Tennessee	45
2002	10-3	9	3	Notre Dame 10-2, Penn State 9-3, Ohio State 13-0	Lloyd Carr	Outback	38 Florida	30
2003	10-3	6	1	Iowa 9-3, Minnesota 9-3, Purdue 9-3, Ohio State 10-2	Lloyd Carr	Rose	14 Southern California	28
2004	9-3	14	1t	Iowa 10-1, Purdue 7-4, Ohio State 7-4	Lloyd Carr	Rose	37 Texas	38
2005	7-5		3t	Notre Dame 9-3, Wisconsin 9-3, Penn State 10-1, Ohio State 9-2	Lloyd Carr	Alamo	28 Nebraska	32
2006	11-2	8	2t	Notre Dame 10-2, Wisconsin 11-1, Penn State 8-4, Ohio State 12-0	Lloyd Carr	Rose	18 Southern California	32
2007	9-4	18	2t	Oregon 8-4, Illinois 9-3, Wisconsin 9-3, Ohio State 11-1	Lloyd Carr (122-40)	Capital One	41 Florida	35
2008	3-9		9t	Utah 12-0, Penn State 11-1, Ohio State 10-2	Rich Rodriguez			
2009	5-7		10t	Iowa 10-2, Penn State 10-2, Wisconsin 9-3, Ohio State 10-2	Rich Rodriguez			
2010	7-6		7t	Michigan State 11-1, Wisconsin 11-1, Ohio State 11-1	Rich Rodriguez (15-22)	Gator	14 Mississippi State	52

TOTAL: 459-184-12 .7099 (7 of 70)

Bowl Games since 1953: 16-20 .4444 (49 of 70)

GREATEST TEAM SINCE 1953: One could make a great argument against coach Lloyd Carr's 1997 national champions, but as close as Bo Schembechler got his Wolverines to perfection (such as his 1971, 1972, 1973, 1974, 1980, and 1985 teams), the 1997 Wolverines edition won them all. So the 1997 squad, perhaps less star-studded than other Michigan teams but still led by Brian Griese, Steve Hutchinson, Jerame Tuman, Glen Steele, and Heisman winner Charles Woodson, earns its spot at the top in Ann Arbor.

1953 6-3

50	Washington	0	E Bob Topp
26	Tulane	7	T Art Walker / Dick Strozewski
14	Iowa	13	G Don Dugger
20	Northwestern	12	C John Morrow / Dick O'Shaughnessy
0	Minnesota	22	G Richard Beison
24	Pennsylvania	14	T Jim Balog / Ron Geyer
3	Illinois	19	E Gene Knutson / John Vaselenak
6	Michigan State	14	QB Lou Baldacci / Duncan McDonald
20	Ohio State	0	HB Ted Kress / Tony Cline
			HB Tony Branoff / Ed Hickey
			FB Dick Balzhiser / Bob Hurley

RUSHING: Branoff 101/501y, Kress 101/339y, Hurley 47/282y
PASSING: McDonald 20-46/293y, 4TD, 43.5%
  Baldacci 21-51/285y, TD, 41.2%
  Kress 19-43/238y, TD, 44.2%
RECEIVING: Topp 23/331y, Knutson 11/201y, Branoff 11/151y
SCORING: Branoff (HB-K) 39pts, Kress 36pts,
  Baldacci (QB-K) 25pts

1954 6-3

14	Washington	0	E Ron Kramer
7	Army	26	T Art Walker
14	Iowa	13	G Ted Cachey / Dick Hill
7	Northwestern	0	C John Peckham / Jim Bates
34	Minnesota	0	G Ed Meads / Jim Fox
9	Indiana	13	T Bill Kolesar / Lionel Sigman
14	Illinois	7	E Tom Maentz / Dave Williams
33	Michigan State	7	QB Lou Baldacci (FB) / Jim Maddock
7	Ohio State	21	HB Dan Cline / Ted Hendricks
			HB Tony Branoff / Ed Hickey
			FB Fred Baer / Dave Hill

RUSHING: Baer 107/439y, Cline 97/340y, Hickey 45/169y,
  Baldacci 46/152y
PASSING: Maddock 16-35/293y, TD, 45.7%,
  Cline 15-43/281y, 3TD, 34.9%
  Duncan McDonald (QB) 15-36/237y, TD, 41.7%
RECEIVING: Kramer 23/303y, Baldacci 8/211y, Cline 6/61y
SCORING: Kramer (E-K) 32pts, Baldacci (QB-K) 31pts,
  Baer & Cline 18pts

1955 7-2

42	Missouri	7	E Ron Kramer
14	Michigan State	7	T Jim Orwig / Bill Kolesar
26	Army	2	G Dick Hill / Jim Fox
14	Northwestern	2	C Jim Bates / John Peckham
14	Minnesota	13	G Ed Meads
33	Iowa	21	T Lionel Sigman / John Morrow
6	Illinois	25	E Tom Maentz / John Vaselenak
30	Indiana	0	QB Jim Maddock / Jim Van Pelt
0	Ohio State	17	HB Terry Barr / Jim Pace
			HB Tony Branoff / Ed Hickey
			FB Lou Baldacci (QB) / Dave Hill

RUSHING: Branoff 86/387y, Barr 63/245y, Baldacci 69/218y
PASSING: Maddock 20-52/343y, 38.5%
RECEIVING: Kramer 12/224y, Maentz 11/253y, Barr 4/74y
SCORING: Kramer (E-K) 36pts, Barr 30 pts, Baldacci 24pts

1956 7-2

42	UCLA	13	E Ron Kramer
0	Michigan State	9	T Jim Orwig
48	Army	14	G Dick Hill
34	Northwestern	20	C Mike Rotunno
7	Minnesota	20	G Clem Corona / Marv Nyren
17	Iowa	14	T Lionel Sigman / Jim Davies
17	Illinois	7	E Tom Maentz / Charlie Brooks
49	Indiana	26	QB Jim Van Pelt / Jim Maddock
19	Ohio State	0	HB Jim Pace / Bob Ptacek
			HB Terry Barr / Mike Shatusky
			FB John Herrnstein / Jim Byers

RUSHING: Pace 103/498y, Herrnstein 123/475y, Barr 60/366y
PASSING: Maddock 20-42/213y, 47.6%,
  Ptacek 15-23/245y, 65.2%, Van Pelt 15-33/221y, 45.5%
RECEIVING: Kramer 18/353y, Pace 7/155y, Ptacek 7/53y
SCORING: Barr & Herrnstein 42pts, Kramer (E-K) 35pts

1957 5-3-1

16	Southern Cal	6	E Gary Prahst
26	Georgia	0	T Jim Orwig / Dick Heynen
6	Michigan State	35	G Larry Faul
34	Northwestern	14	C Gene Snider / Jerry Goebel
24	Minnesota	7	G Marv Nyren
21	Iowa	21	T Jim Davies / Willie Smith
19	Illinois	20	E Walter Johnson / Bob Boshoven
27	Indiana	13	QB Jim Van Pelt / Stan Noskin
14	Ohio State	31	HB Jim Pace / Bob Ptacek
			HB Mike Shatusky / Brad Myers
			FB John Herrnstein

RUSHING: Pace 123/664y, Myers 69/252y, Ptacek 60/161y
PASSING: Van Pelt 42-80/629y, 52.5%
RECEIVING: Prahst 15/233y, Pace 11/122y, Myers 9/159y
SCORING: Pace 60pts, Van Pelt 26pts, Myers 24pts

1958 2-6-1

20	Southern Cal	19	E Gary Prahst
12	Michigan State	12	T George Genyk / Willie Smith
14	Navy	20	G Alex Callahan
24	Northwestern	55	C Jim Dickey
20	Minnesota	19	G Jerry Marciniak
14	Iowa	37	T Don Deskins
8	Illinois	21	E Walter Johnson
8	Indiana	8	QB Bob Ptacek / Stan Noskin
14	Ohio State	20	HB Brad Myers / Darrell Harper
			HB Fred Julian
			FB John Herrnstein / Tony Rio

RUSHING: Harper 55/309y, Myers 81/201y, Julian 45/180y
PASSING: Ptacek 65-115/763y, 56.5%
RECEIVING: Prahst 22/313y, Myers 17/169y, Harper 13/137y
SCORING: Ptacek 26pts, W. Johnson 26pts, Harper 22pts

1959 4-5

15	Missouri	20	E John Halstead / Scott Maentz
8	Michigan State	34	T Tom Jobson
18	Oregon State	7	G George Genyk
7	Northwestern	20	C Gerry Smith / Todd Grant
14	Minnesota	6	G Alex Callahan / Mike Fillichio
10	Wisconsin	19	T Jon Schopf / Jared Bushong
20	Illinois	15	E Bob Johnson / George Mans
7	Indiana	26	QB Stan Noskin
23	Ohio State	14	HB Darrell Harper / Bennie McRae
			HB Fred Julian / Brad Myers
			FB Tony Rio / Ken Tureaud

RUSHING: Julian 72/289y, McRae 76/242y, Harper 67/224y
PASSING: Noskin 61-115/747y, 53.0%
RECEIVING: Johnson 20/264y, Rio 8/90y, Halstead 6/77y
SCORING: Harper 31pts, Halstead 21pts, Rio 18pts

1960 5-4

21	Oregon	0	E Scott Maentz / John Halstead
17	Michigan State	24	T Tom Jobson
31	Duke	6	G Lee Hall / Paul Poulos
14	Northwestern	7	C Gerry Smith / John Walker
0	Minnesota	10	G Dick Syring / Joe O'Donnell
13	Wisconsin	16	T Jon Schopf / Guy Curtis
8	Illinois	7	E Bob Johnson / George Mans
29	Indiana	7	QB Dave Glinka
0	Ohio State	7	HB Bennie McRae / Reid Bushong
			HB Dennis Fitzgerald / Dave Raimey
			FB Ken Tureaud / Bill Tunnicliff

RUSHING: McRae 80/352y, Raimey 62/292y, Fitzgerald 66/263y
PASSING: Glinka 54-124/755y, 43.5%
RECEIVING: Johnson 15/230y, Mans 9/136y, Maentz 7/128y
SCORING: Raimey 36pts, Fitzgerald 22pts, Tunnicliff 18pts

1961 6-3

29	UCLA	6	E Scott Maentz / Bob Brown
38	Army	8	T John Houtman / Tom Keating
0	Michigan State	28	G John Minko / Frank Maloney
16	Purdue	14	C John Walker
20	Minnesota	23	G Ben Hall
28	Duke	14	T Jon Schopf / Guy Curtis
38	Illinois	6	E George Mans
23	Iowa	14	QB Dave Glinka
20	Ohio State	50	HB Bennie McRae
			HB Dave Raimey / Ed Hood
			FB Bill Tunnicliff / Ken Tureaud

RUSHING: McRae 75/453y, Raimey 99/496y, Tunnicliff 96/396y
PASSING: Glinka 46-96/588y, 47.9%
RECEIVING: Mans 15/149y, McRae 10/210y, Brown 6/127y
SCORING: Raimey 48pts, McRae 36pts, Bickle 32pts

1962 2-7

13	Nebraska	25	E Bob Brown / Ben Farabee
17	Army	7	T John Houtman / Tom Keating
0	Michigan State	28	G John Minko / John Marcum
0	Purdue	37	C Jim Green / Lou Pavloff
0	Minnesota	17	G Dave Kurz
12	Wisconsin	34	T Joe O'Donnell
14	Illinois	12	E Jim Conley / Bill Laskey
14	Iowa	28	QB Bob Chandler / Bob Timberlake (HB)
0	Ohio State	28	HB Jack Strobel / Harvey Chapman
			HB Dave Raimey / Tom Pritchard
			FB Wayne Sparkman / Bill Dodd

RUSHING: Raimey 124/385y, Sparkman 35/133y
PASSING: Chandler 29-63/401y, 46.0%,
  Timberlake 16-34/179y, 47.1%
RECEIVING: Chapman 11/223y, Timberlake 11/164y,
  Raimey 11/45y
SCORING: Raimey 30pts, Timberlake (QB-HB-K) 14pts

1963 3-4-2

27	SMU	16	E Jim Conley/Craig Kirby/J'hn Henders'n
13	Navy	26	T Tom Keating / Charles Ruzicka
7	Michigan State	7	G Joe O'Donnell
12	Purdue	23	C Tom Cecchini / Brian Patchen
0	Minnesota	6	G Rich Hahn / Dick Ries
27	Northwestern	0	T Bill Yearby
14	Illinois	8	E Bill Laskey / Jeff Hoyne
21	Iowa	21	QB Bob Timberlake / Frosty Evashevski
10	Ohio State	14	HB Jack Clancy / John Rowser
			HB Dick Wells / Dick Rindfuss
			FB Mel Anthony

RUSHING: Anthony 103/394y, Timberlake 98/231y,
  Rindfuss 58/211y
PASSING: Timberlake 47-98/593y, 48.0%
RECEIVING: Henderson 27/330y, Kirby 13/166y,
  Rindfuss 10/100y
SCORING: Henderson 32pts, Anthony 30pts,
  Timberlake (QB-K) 27pts

1964 9-1

24	Air Force	7	E Jim Conley/Steve Smith/B. Farabee (DE)
21	Navy	0	T Charles Kines / Don Bailey
17	Michigan State	10	G Dave Butler / Dennis Flanagan (LB)
20	Purdue	21	C Brian Patchen
19	Minnesota	12	G John Marcum
35	Northwestern	0	T Tom Mack
21	Illinois	6	E John Henderson / Craig Kirby
34	Iowa	20	QB Bob Timberlake / Wally Gabler
10	Ohio State	0	HB Jim Detwiler / Rick Syger (DB)
34	Oregon State ■	7	HB Carl Ward / Rick Volk (DB)
			FB Mel Anthony / Dave Fisher
			DL Bill Laskey / Clayton Wilhite
			DL Bill Yearby
			DL Bob Mielke / Bill Keating
			DL Arnie Simkus
			DL Ben Farabee (E) / Stan Kemp
			LB Tom Cecchini / Barry Dehlin
			LB Frank Nunley / Dennis Flanagan (G)
			DB Dick Rindfuss
			DB Mike Bass / Dick Wells
			DB Rick Syger (HB)/Frosty Evash'vski (QB)
			DB Rick Volk (HB)

RUSHING: Anthony 132/579y, Timberlake 144/574y,
  Ward 91/427y
PASSING: Timberlake 63-127/807y, 49.6%
RECEIVING: Henderson 27/393y, Detwiler 10/184y,
  Smith 8/131y
SCORING: Timberlake 80pts, Anthony 36pts,
  Detwiler & Ward18pts

1965 4-6

31	North Carolina	24	E Steve Smith / Craig Kirby
10	California	7	T Charles Kines / Bill Keating (DT)
7	Georgia	15	G Ken Wright / Dennis Flanagan (LB)
7	Michigan State	24	C Joe Dayton / Paul D'Eramo
15	Purdue	17	G Don Bailey / Henry Hanna
13	Minnesota	14	T Tom Mack
50	Wisconsin	14	E Jack Clancy
23	Illinois	3	QB Wally Gabler / Dick Vidmer
22	Northwestern	34	HB Rick Syger (DB) / Jim Detwiler
7	Ohio State	9	HB Carl Ward / Ernie Sharpe
			FB Dave Fisher / Dennis Morgan
			DL Jeff Hoyne / Tom Pullen / Stan Kemp
			DL Bill Yearby / Bill Keating (OT)
			DL Bob Mielke
			DL Paul Johnson / Charles Ruzicka
			DL Rocky Rosema / Clayton Wilhite
			LB Tom Cecchini
			LB Frank Nunley / Dennis Flanagan (G)
			DB Dick Wells / Rick Syger (HB)
			DB John Rowser
			DB Mike Bass
			DB Rick Volk

RUSHING: Ward 112/639y, Fisher 139/575y, Gabler 85/265y
PASSING: Gabler 58-125/825y, 4TD, 46.4%
RECEIVING: Clancy 52/762y, Smith 22/314y, Sharpe 4/62y
SCORING: Gabler 42pts, Sygar 39pts, Fisher 24pts

SCORES, LINEUPS, AND STATISTICS

1966 6-4
41 Oregon State	0 WR Jack Clancy
17 California	7 T Ray Phillips / Bill Hardy
7 North Carolina	21 G Henry Hanna
7 Michigan State	20 C Joe Dayton
21 Purdue	22 G Don Bailey
49 Minnesota	0 T Jim Hribal
28 Wisconsin	17 TE Warren Sipp / Clayton Wilhite
21 Illinois	28 QB Dick Vidmer
28 Northwestern	20 HB Jim Detwiler / Ron Johnson
17 Ohio State	3 HB Carl Ward / Ernie Sharpe
	FB Dave Fisher
	DL Rocky Rosema / Jon Kramer
	DL Bob Mielke / Dick Williamson
	DL Dave Porter
	DL Paul Johnson
	DL Tom Stincic
	LB Barry Dehlin / Dennis Morgan
	LB Frank Nunley
	DB John Rowser
	DB Mike Bass
	DB Rick Sygar
	DB Rick Volk

RUSHING: Fisher 131/673y, Ward 128/499y, Detwiler 86/413y
PASSING: Vidmer 117-226/1611y, 10TD, 51.8%
RECEIVING: Clancy 76/1079y, Ward 10/146y, Detwiler 9/165y
SCORING: Detwiler 60pts, Sygar 50pts, Ward 42pts

1967 4-6
10 Duke	7 WR Jim Berline
9 California	10 T Bob Penksa
21 Navy	26 G Ray Phillips
0 Michigan State	34 C Joe Dayton
20 Indiana	27 G Bob Baumgartner / Stan Broadnax
15 Minnesota	20 T Pete Mair
7 Northwestern	3 TE Jim Mandich
21 Illinois	14 QB Dennis Brown / Dick Vidmer
27 Wisconsin	14 HB John Gabler / Ernie Sharpe
14 Ohio State	24 HB Ron Johnson
	FB Garvie Craw / Warren Sipp
	DL Jon Kramer
	DL Dave Porter
	DL Dennis Monthei / Jerry Miklos
	DL Dick Williamson / Jim Wilhite
	DL Phil Seymour
	LB Dennis Morgan / Bob Wedge
	LB Rocky Rosema / Tom Stincic (DL)
	DB Brian Healy
	DB George Hoey / Barry Pierson
	DB Tom Curtis
	DB Jerry Hartman

RUSHING: Johnson 220/1005y, Brown 137/358y, Sipp 24/104y
PASSING: Brown 82-156/913y, 52.6%, Vidmer 38-88/376y, 43.2%
RECEIVING: Berline 54/624y, Mandich 26/256y, Gabler 20/173y
SCORING: Johnson 48pts, Brown 24pts, Berline 18pts

1968 8-2
7 California	21 WR Bill Harris / Jerry Imsland
31 Duke	10 T Bob Penksa / Jack Harpring
32 Navy	9 G Dick Caldarazzo / Bob Baumgartner
28 Michigan State	14 C Dave Denzin
27 Indiana	22 G Stan Broadnax
33 Minnesota	20 T Dan Dierdorf
35 Northwestern	0 TE Jim Mandich
36 Illinois	0 QB Dennis Brown
34 Wisconsin	9 HB Ron Johnson / John Gabler
14 Ohio State	50 WB Paul Staroba
	FB Garvie Craw / Warren Sipp
	DL Tom Stincic
	DL Tom Goss
	DL Henry Hill / Jerry Miklos
	DL Dan Parks / Jim Wilhite
	DL Phil Seymour
	LB Ed Moore / Tim Killian
	LB Cecil Pryor / Marty Huff
	DB Brian Healy
	DB George Hoey / Barry Pierson
	DB Tom Curtis
	DB Jerry Hartman / Bob Wedge

RUSHING: Johnson 255/1391y, Craw 81/307y, Brown 115/215y
PASSING: Brown 109-209/1562y, 12TD, 52.2%
RECEIVING: Mandich 43/576y, Imsland 19/269y, Harris 16/369y
SCORING: Johnson 116pts, Killian (K) 37pts, Mandich 18pts

1969 8-3
42 Vanderbilt	14 WR Bill Harris / Paul Staroba
45 Washington	7 T Jack Harpring
17 Missouri	40 G Bob Baumgartner
31 Purdue	20 C Guy Murdock / Tim Killian
12 Michigan State	23 G Dick Caldarazzo / Frank Titas
35 Minnesota	9 T Dan Dierdorf
35 Wisconsin	7 TE Jim Mandich / Mike Hankwitz
57 Illinois	0 QB Don Moorhead
51 Iowa	6 TB Glenn Doughty / Billy Taylor
24 Ohio State	12 WB John Gabler
3 Southern Cal ■	10 FB Garvie Craw
	DL Cecil Pryor / Butch Carpenter
	DL Fred Grambau / Dan Parks
	DL Henry Hill / Al Francis
	DL Pete Newell
	DL Mike Keller
	LB Ed Moore / Mike Taylor
	LB Marty Huff
	DB Brian Healy
	DB Barry Pierson
	DB Tom Curtis
	DB Tom Darden / Frank Gusich

RUSHING: Taylor 141/864y, Doughty 150/625y, Moorhead 170/625y
PASSING: Moorhead 103-210/1261y, 5TD, 49.0%
RECEIVING: Mandich 50/662y, Harris 15/302y, Hankwitz 13/155y
SCORING: Craw 78pts, Moorhead 54pts, Taylor 48pts

1970 9-1
20 Arizona	9 WR Paul Staroba / Bill Harris
17 Washington	3 T Jack Harpring
14 Texas A&M	10 G Reggie McKenzie
29 Purdue	0 C Guy Murdock / Bill Hart
34 Michigan State	20 G Tom Coyle / Werner Hall
39 Minnesota	13 T Dan Dierdorf
29 Wisconsin	15 TE Paul Seymour
42 Illinois	0 QB Don Moorhead
55 Iowa	0 TB Billy Taylor / Lance Sheffler
9 Ohio State	20 WB Glenn Doughty / Bill Berutti (WR)
	FB Fritz Seyferth
	DL Phil Seymour / Butch Carpenter
	DL Fred Grambau / Dick McCoy
	DL Henry Hill
	DL Pete Newell / Tom Beckman
	DL Mike Keller
	LB Mike Taylor / Ed Moore
	LB Marty Huff / Tom Kee
	DB Frank Gusich
	DB Bruce Elliott / Bo Rather
	DB Jim Betts
	DB Tom Darden

RUSHING: Taylor 197/911y, Moorhead 97/368y, Seyferth 86/333y, Henry 70/314y
PASSING: Moorhead 87-190/1167y, 8TD, 45.8%
RECEIVING: Staroba 35/519y, Doughty 22/298y, Seymour 13/194y
SCORING: Taylor 68pts, Seyferth 48pts, Dana Coin (K) & Scheffler 30pts

1971 11-1
21 Northwestern	6 WR Bo Rather / Mike Oldham
56 Virginia	0 T Jim Coode
38 UCLA	0 G Reggie McKenzie
46 Navy	0 C Guy Murdock
24 Michigan State	13 G Tom Coyle / Jerry Schumacher
35 Illinois	6 T Jim Brandstatter
35 Minnesota	7 TE Paul Seymour / Paul Seal
61 Indiana	7 QB Tom Slade / Kevin Casey
63 Iowa	7 TB Billy Taylor / Alan "Cowboy" Walker
20 Purdue	17 WB Glenn Doughty / Larry Gustafson
10 Ohio State	7 FB Ed Shuttlesworth / Fritz Seyferth
12 Stanford ■	13 DL Butch Carpenter / Clint Spearman
	DL Fred Grambau / Dave Gallagher
	DL Greg Ellis / Walt Sexton
	DL Tom Beckman
	DL Mike Keller
	LB Tom Kee / Dana Coin
	LB Mike Taylor
	DB Bruce Elliott / Tom Drake
	DB Randy Logan
	DB Tom Darden
	DB Frank Gusich / Geoff Steger

RUSHING: Taylor 249/1297y
PASSING: Slade 27-63/364y, 2TD, 42.9%
RECEIVING: Doughty 16/203y
SCORING: Dana Coin (K) 79pts

1972 10-1
7 Northwestern	0 WR Bo Rather / Clint Haslerig
26 UCLA	9 T Jim Coode
41 Tulane	7 G Mike Hoban
35 Navy	7 C Dennis Franks / Bill Hart
10 Michigan State	0 G Tom Coyle / Jerry Schumacher
31 Illinois	7 T Paul Seymour / Tom Poplawski
42 Minnesota	0 TE Paul Seal
21 Indiana	6 QB Dennis Franklin / Tom Slade
31 Iowa	0 TB Chuck Heater
9 Purdue	6 WB Gil Chapman / Larry Gustafson
11 Ohio State	14 FB Ed Shuttlesworth
	DL Clint Spearman
	DL Fred Grambau / Tony Smith
	DL Greg Ellis / Walt Sexton
	DL Dave Gallagher / Doug Troszak
	DL Walt Williamson / Don Coleman
	LB Tom Kee / Craig Mutch
	LB Steve Strinko / Carl Russ
	DB Tom Drake
	DB Dave Brown / Linwood Harden
	DB Randy Logan / Roy Burks
	DB Greg Koss / Barry Dotzauer

RUSHING: Shuttlesworth 157/723y, Franklin 143/511y
PASSING: Franklin 59-123/818y, 6TD, 48.0%
RECEIVING: Seal 18/243y
SCORING: Shuttlesworth 66pts

1973 10-0-1
31 Iowa	7 WR Jim Smith / Jeff Steger
47 Stanford	10 T Jim Coode / Curtis Tucker
14 Navy	0 G Mike Hoban / Kirk Lewis
24 Oregon	0 C Dennis Franks
31 Michigan State	0 G Tom Jensen / Dave Metz
35 Wisconsin	6 T Steve King / Pat Tumpane
34 Minnesota	7 TE Paul Seal / George Przygodski
49 Indiana	13 QB Dennis Franklin / Tom Slade
21 Illinois	6 TB Gordon Bell
34 Purdue	9 WB Clint Haslerig / Gil Chapman
10 Ohio State	10 FB Ed Shuttlesworth / Chuck Heater
	DL Dan Jilek / Don Coleman (LB)
	DL Doug Troszak / Jeff Perlinger
	DL Tim Davis / Bill Hoban / Don Warner
	DL Dave Gallagher
	DL Walt Williamson / Don Eaton
	LB Steve Strinko / Mike Day
	LB Carl Russ / Jovan Vercel
	DB Tom Drake
	DB Dave Brown
	DB Dave Elliott / Roy Burks
	DB Don Dufek/Greg Koss/Barry Dotzauer

RUSHING: Shuttlesworth 193/745y, Franklin 101/425y
PASSING: Franklin 36-67/534y, 4TD, 53.7%
RECEIVING: Seal 14/254y
SCORING: Mike Lantry (K) 66pts

1974 10-1
24 Iowa	7 WR Jim Smith / Max Richardson
31 Colorado	0 T Bill Dufek
52 Navy	0 G Kirk Lewis / Les Miles
27 Stanford	16 C Dennis Franks
21 Michigan State	7 G Tom Jensen / Dave Metz
24 Wisconsin	20 T Steve King / Pat Tumpane
49 Minnesota	0 TE Greg DenBoer / George Przygodksi
21 Indiana	7 QB Dennis Franklin
14 Illinois	6 TB Gordon Bell / Rob Lytle
51 Purdue	0 WB Gil Chapman / Jeff Steger
10 Ohio State	12 FB Chuck Heater / Scott Corbin
	DL Dan Jilek
	DL Jeff Perlinger / Greg Morton
	DL Tim Davis / Rick Koschalk
	DL John Hennessy / Larry Banks
	DL Mike Holmes
	LB Steve Strinko / John Anderson
	LB Carl Russ / Calvin O'Neal
	DB Tom Drake / Derek Howard
	DB Dave Brown / Kurt Kampe
	DB Dave Elliott / Dwight Hicks
	DB Don Dufek / Jerry Zuver

RUSHING: Bell 174/1048y
PASSING: Franklin 58-104/933y, 8TD, 55.8%
RECEIVING: Chapman 23/378y, Smith 21/392y
SCORING: Bell 66pts

1975 8-2-2
23 Wisconsin	6 WR Curt Stevenson / Max Richardson
19 Stanford	19 T Bill Dufek / Bob Lang
14 Baylor	14 G Kirk Lewis / Les Miles
31 Missouri	7 C John Czirr / Walt Downing
16 Michigan State	6 G Mark Donahue / Jerry Szara
69 Northwestern	0 T Steve King / Mike Kenn
55 Indiana	7 TE George Przygodski / Gene Johnson
28 Minnesota	21 QB Rick Leach
28 Purdue	0 TB Gordon Bell / Harlan Huckleby
21 Illinois	15 WB Jim Smith
14 Ohio State	21 FB Rob Lytle (TB) / Russell Davis
6 Oklahoma■	14 DL Dan Jilek / Mike Holmes
	DL Jeff Perlinger / Bill Hoban
	DL Tim Davis / Rick Koschalk
	DL Greg Morton / John Hennessy
	DL John Anderson / Greg Strinko
	LB Tom Seabron / Rex Mackall
	LB Calvin O'Neal / Jerry Vogele
	DB Derek Howard / Jim Bolden
	DB Jim Pickens / Kurt Kampe
	DB Dwight Hicks / Dave Whiteford
	DB Don Dufek / Jerry Zuver

RUSHING: Bell 273/1388y
PASSING: Leach 32-100/680y, 3TD, 32.0%
RECEIVING: Smith 24/553y
SCORING: Bell 84pts

1976 10-2
40 Wisconsin	27 WR Curt Stevenson / Max Richardson
51 Stanford	0 T Bill Dufek / Mike Kenn
70 Navy	14 G Kirk Lewis / Greg Bartnick
31 Wake Forest	0 C Walt Downing
42 Michigan State	10 G Mark Donahue
38 Northwestern	7 T Jon Geisler / Bob Lang
35 Indiana	0 TE Gene Johnson
45 Minnesota	0 QB Rick Leach
14 Purdue	16 TB Harlan Huckleby
38 Illinois	0 WB Jim Smith
22 Ohio State	0 FB Rob Lytle / Russell Davis
6 Southern Cal■	14 DL John Anderson / Curtis Greer
	DL John Hennessy / William Jackson
	DL Steve Anderson / Steve Graves
	DL Greg Morton
	DL Calvin O'Neal
	LB Jerry Meter / Jerry Vogele
	LB Ron Simpkins / Tom Seabrun
	DB Derek Howard / Jim Bolden
	DB Jim Pickens
	DB Dwight Hicks
	DB Mike Jolly / Jerry Zuver

RUSHING: Lytle 221/1469y, Leach 114/638y
PASSING: Leach 50-105/973y, 13TD, 47.6%
RECEIVING: Smith 26/714y
SCORING: Lytle 96pts

1977 10-2
37 Illinois	9 WR Curt Stevenson / Max Richardson
21 Duke	9 T Mike Kenn
14 Navy	7 G John Powers / Greg Bartnick
41 Texas A&M	3 C Walt Downing
24 Michigan State	14 G Mark Donahue / Jerry Szara
56 Wisconsin	0 T Jon Geisler / Mike Leoni
0 Minnesota	16 TE Gene Johnson / Doug Marsh
23 Iowa	6 QB Rick Leach
63 Northwestern	20 TB Harlan Huckleby / Stanley Edwards
40 Purdue	7 WB Ralph Clayton
14 Ohio State	6 FB Russell Davis / Kevin King
20 Washington■	27 DL Dale Keitz / Chris Godfrey
	DL Mike Trgovac / Steve Graves
	DL Curtis Greer / Gary Weber
	LB John Anderson / Tom Seabron
	LB Jerry Meter / Dave Harding
	LB Ron Simpkins
	LB Mel Owens / Bob Hollway
	DB Mike Harden
	DB Jim Pickens / Derek Howard
	DB Dwight Hicks / Gene Bell
	DB Mike Jolly / Woody Brown

RUSHING: Davis 225/1092y, Huckleby N/A/743y, Leach 115/375y
PASSING: Leach 90-174/1348y, 15TD, 51.7%
RECEIVING: Clayton 24/477y
SCORING: Davis 54pts

1978 10-2
31 Illinois	0 WR Rodney Feaster / Alan Mitchell
28 Notre Dame	14 T Bill Dufek / Mike Leoni
52 Duke	0 G John Arbeznik
21 Arizona	17 C George Lilja / Steve Nauta
15 Michigan State	24 G John Powers / Kurt Becker
42 Wisconsin	0 T Jon Geisler / Bubba Paris
42 Minnesota	10 TE Doug Marsh / Gene Johnson
34 Iowa	0 QB Rick Leach
59 Northwestern	14 TB Harlan Huckleby / Roosevelt Smith
24 Purdue	6 WB Ralph Clayton
14 Ohio State	3 FB Russell Davis / Lawrence Reid
10 Southern Cal■	17 DL Dale Keitz / Chris Godfrey
	DL Mike Trgovac / Jim Humphries
	DL Curtis Greer / Gary Weber
	LB Tom Seabron / Bob Needham
	LB Andy Cannavino / Tim Malinak
	LB Ron Simpkins / Jerry Meter
	LB Bob Hollway / Tom Seabron
	DB Mark Braman / Tony Jackson
	DB Mike Jolly
	DB Mike Harden / Gerald Diggs
	DB Gene Bell / Stu Harris

RUSHING: Huckleby 154/741y, Leach 145/611y
PASSING: Leach 78-158/1283y, 17TD, 49.4%
RECEIVING: Clayton 25/546y
SCORING: Leach 72pts

1979 8-4
49 Northwestern	7 WR Anthony Carter / Alan Mitchell
10 Notre Dame	12 T Ed Muransky / Tom Garrity
28 Kansas	9 G John Arbeznik
14 California	10 C George Lilja
21 Michigan State	7 G Kurt Becker
31 Minnesota	21 T Bubba Paris
27 Illinois	7 TE Doug Marsh / Norm Betts
27 Indiana	21 QB John Wangler / Rich Hewlett
54 Wisconsin	0 TB Stanley Edwards / Butch Woolfolk
21 Purdue	24 WB Ralph Clayton / Rodney Feaster
15 Ohio State	18 FB Lawrence Reid / Jerry Ingram
15 North Carolina■	17 DL Dale Keitz / Cedric Coles
	DL Mike Trgovac
	DL Curtis Greer / Chris Godfrey
	LB Ben Needham / Tom Keller
	LB Andy Cannavino
	LB Ron Simpkins / Paul Girgash
	LB Mel Owens / Robert Thompson
	DB Mark Braman / Marion Body
	DB Mike Jolly
	DB Mike Harden / Keith Bostic
	DB Jeff Reeves / Stu Harris

RUSHING: Woolfolk 191/990y
PASSING: Wangler 78-130/1431y, 8TD, 60.0%
RECEIVING: Marsh 33/612y
SCORING: Woolfolk 78pts

1980 10-2
17 Northwestern	10 WR Anthony Carter
27 Notre Dame	29 WR Alan Mitchell / Fred Brockington
14 South Carolina	17 T Ed Muransky / Rich Stenger
38 California	13 G Kurt Becker / John Powers
27 Michigan State	23 C George Lilja / Tom Dixon
37 Minnesota	14 G Jerry Diorio / Stefan Humphries
45 Illinois	14 T Bubba Paris
35 Indiana	0 TE Norm Betts / Craig Dunaway
24 Wisconsin	0 QB John Wangler /Rich Hewlett /S. Smith
26 Purdue	0 TB Butch Woolfolk / Stanley Edwards
9 Ohio State	3 FB Jerald Ingram / Kerry Smith
23 Washington■	6 DL Cedric Coles
	DL Mike Trgovic / Jeff Shaw
	DL Winfred Carraway / Kelly Keough
	LB Carlton Rose / Robert Thompson
	LB Andy Cannavino / Jim Herrmann
	LB Paul Girgash / Mike Boren
	LB Mel Owens
	DB Marion Body
	DB Evan Cooper / Jeff Reeves
	DB Tony Jackson / Jerry Burgei
	DB Keith Bostic / Gerald Diggs

RUSHING: Woolfolk 196/1042y
PASSING: Wangler 117-212/1522y, 16TD, 55.2%
RECEIVING: Carter 51/818y
SCORING: Carter 84pts

1981 9-3
14 Wisconsin	21 WR Anthony Carter
25 Notre Dame	7 WR Vince Bean
21 Navy	16 T Ed Muransky / Rich Strenger
38 Indiana	17 G Kurt Becker / Doug James
38 Michigan State	20 C Tom Dixon
7 Iowa	9 G Stefan Humphries
38 Northwestern	0 T Bubba Paris / Clay Miller
34 Minnesota	13 TE Norm Betts / Craig Dunaway
70 Illinois	21 QB Steve Smith
28 Purdue	10 TB Butch Woolfolk / Lawrence Ricks
9 Ohio State	14 FB Stanley Edwards / Jerald Ingram
33 UCLA■	14 DL Mike Hammerstein / Tony Osbun
	DL Mike Trgovic / Al Sincich
	DL Wilfred Carraway
	LB Carlton Rose
	LB Paul Girgash / Mike Boren
	LB Jim Herrmann / Ben Needham
	LB Robert Thompson
	DB Marion Body
	DB Evan Cooper / Jeff Reeves
	DB Tony Jackson / Jerry Burgei
	DB Keith Bostic

RUSHING: Woolfolk 253/1459y
PASSING: Smith 97-210/1661y, 15TD, 46.2%
RECEIVING: Carter 50/952y
SCORING: Smith 74pts

1982 8-4
20 Wisconsin	9 WR Vince Bean / Giovanni Johnson
17 Notre Dame	23 WR Anthony Carter
27 UCLA	31 T Rich Strenger
24 Indiana	10 G Stefan Humphries
31 Michigan State	17 C Tom Dixon
29 Iowa	7 G Jerry DiOrio
49 Northwestern	14 T Doug James
52 Minnesota	14 TE Craig Dunaway
16 Illinois	10 QB Steve Smith
52 Purdue	24 TB Lawrence Ricks / Rick Rogers
14 Ohio State	24 FB Dan Rice / Eddie Garrett
14 UCLA■	24 DL Kevin Brooks / Dave Meredith
	DL Al Sincich
	DL Wilfred Carraway
	LB Carlton Rose
	LB Paul Girgash
	LB Mike Boren
	LB Robert Thompson
	DB Jerry Bergei / Marion Body
	DB Tony Gant / John Lott
	DB Evan Cooper
	DB Keith Bostic

RUSHING: Ricks 266/1388y
PASSING: Smith118-227/1735y, 14TD, 52.0%
RECEIVING: Carter 43/1982y
SCORING: Ali Haji-Sheikh (K) 77pts

1983 9-3
20 Washington St.	17 WR Vince Bean / Triando Markray
24 Washington	25 T Clay Miller
38 Wisconsin	21 G Jerry DiOrio / Art Balourdos
43 Indiana	18 C Tom Dixon
42 Michigan State	0 G Stefan Humphries
35 Northwestern	0 T Doug James
16 Iowa	13 TE Sim Nelson
6 Illinois	16 TE Sim Nelson / Milt Carthens
42 Purdue	10 QB Steve Smith
58 Minnesota	10 TB Rick Rogers / Kerry Smith
24 Ohio State	21 FB Eddie Garr'tt/Greg Arms'r'ng/Dan Rice
7 Auburn■	9 DL Vince DeFelice / Mike Hammerstein
	DL Al Sincich
	DL Kevin Brooks / David Meredith
	LB Carlton Rose
	LB Mike Reinhold / Tim Anderson
	LB Mike Mallory
	LB Rodney Lyles
	DB Brad Cochran
	DB John Lott
	DB Evan Cooper
	DB Tony Gant

RUSHING: Rogers 209/1002y
PASSING: S. Smith106-205/1420y, 13TD, 51.7%
RECEIVING: Nelson 41/494y
SCORING: Bob Bergeron (K) 76pts

1984 6-6

22 Miami	14 WR Steve Johnson / Triando Markray
11 Washington	20 WR Vince Bean / Paul Jokisch
20 Wisconsin	14 T Clay Miller
14 Indiana	6 G Bob Tabachino
7 Michigan State	19 C Art Balourdos
31 Northwestern	0 G Doug James
0 Iowa	26 T Mark Hammerstein
26 Illinois	18 TE Sim Nelson
29 Purdue	31 QB Jim Harbaugh / Chris Zurbrugg
31 Minnesota	7 TB Jamie Morris / Gerald White
6 Ohio State	21 FB Bob Perryman / Eddie Garrett
17 BYU■	24 DL Mike Hammerstein / Vince DeFelice
	DL Al Sincich / Joe Gray
	DL Kevin Brooks
	LB Jim Scarcelli
	LB Tim Anderson / Andy Moeller
	LB Mike Mallory
	LB Rodney Lyles
	DB Brad Cochran
	DB Garland Rivers
	DB Doug Mallory / Ivan Hicks
	DB Tony Gant

RUSHING: Morris 118/574y
PASSING: Harbaugh 60-111/718y, 3TD, 54.1%
RECEIVING: Nelson 40/459y
SCORING: Bob Bergeron (K) 60pts

1985 10-1-1

20 Notre Dame	12 WR Paul Jokisch
34 South Carolina	3 WR John Kolesar
20 Maryland	0 T John "Jumbo" Elliott
33 Wisconsin	6 G Bob Tabachino / Michael Dames
31 Michigan State	0 C John Vitale
10 Iowa	12 G Mike Husar
42 Indiana	15 T Clay Miller
3 Illinois	3 TE Eric Kattus / Jeff Brown
47 Purdue	0 QB Jim Harbaugh
48 Minnesota	7 TB Jamie Morris
27 Ohio State	17 FB Bob Perryman / Gerald White
27 Nebraska■	23 DL Billy Harris
	DL Mark Messner
	DL Mike Hammerstein
	LB Tim Schulte / Carlitos Bostic
	LB Andy Moeller
	LB Mike Mallory / Andree McIntyre
	LB Dieter Heren / Todd Schulte
	DB Brad Cochran
	DB Garland Rivers / Rick Hassel
	DB Ivan Hicks / Doug Mallory
	DB Tony Gant

RUSHING: Morris 197/1030y
PASSING: Harbaugh 145-227/1976y, 18TD, 63.9%
RECEIVING: Kattus 38/582y, Jokisch 35/681y
SCORING: Mike Gillette (K) 78pts

1986 11-2

24 Notre Dame	23 WR Paul Jokisch / Ken Higgins
31 Oregon State	12 WR Greg McMurtry / John Kolesar
20 Florida State	18 T Mike Husar / Jerry Quaerna
34 Wisconsin	17 G Michael Dames / Dave Chester
27 Michigan State	6 C John Vitale
20 Iowa	17 G Mark Hammerstein
38 Indiana	14 T John "Jumbo" Elliott
69 Illinois	13 TE Jeff Brown / Derrick Walker
31 Purdue	7 QB Jim Harbaugh
17 Minnesota	20 TB Jamie Morris / Thomas Wilcher
26 Ohio State	24 FB Bob Perryman / Gerald White
27 Hawaii	10 DL Dave Folkertsma
15 Arizona State■	22 DL Billy Harris
	DL Mark Messner
	LB Tim Schulte / John Willingham
	LB Andy Moeller / Todd Schulte
	LB Andree McIntyre / J.J. Grant
	LB Dieter Heren
	DB Erik Campbell
	DB Garland Rivers
	DB Tony Gant
	DB Ivan Hicks / Doug Mallory

RUSHING: Morris 212/1086y, Perryman 117/543y,
   Wilcher 91/397y
PASSING: Harbaugh 180-277/2729y, 10TD, 65.0%
RECEIVING: White 38/408y, Higgins 33/621y, Morris 33/287y
SCORING: Mike Gillette (K) 59pts, White 50pts,
   Harbaugh & Perryman 48pts

1987 8-4

7 Notre Dame	26 WR Greg McMurtry / Chris Calloway
44 Washington St.	18 WR John Kolesar
49 Long Beach St.	0 T Mike Husar / Dean Dingman
49 Wisconsin	0 G Michael Dames
11 Michigan State	17 C John Vitale
37 Iowa	10 G David Chester
10 Indiana	14 T John "Jumbo" Elliott
29 Northwestern	6 TE Derrick Walker / Jeff Brown
30 Minnesota	20 QB Demetrius Brown
17 Illinois	14 TB Jamie Morris
20 Ohio State	23 FB Jarrod Bunch / Phil Webb
28 Alabama■	24 DL Billy Harris
	DL Mark Messner
	DL John Herrmann
	LB Steven Thibert
	LB J.J. Grant
	LB Andree McIntyre
	LB Bobby Abrams / Tim Williams
	DB Tripp Welborne
	DB David Arnold
	DB Erik Campbell
	DB Doug Mallory

RUSHING: Morris 282/1703y
PASSING: Brown 80-168/1251y, 11TD, 47.6%
RECEIVING: McMurtry 21/474y
SCORING: Morris 90pts

1988 9-2-1

17 Notre Dame	19 WR Greg McMurtry
30 Miami	31 WR John Kolesar / Chris Calloway
19 Wake Forest	9 T Greg Skrepenak
62 Wisconsin	14 G Dean Dingman / Michael Dames
17 Michigan State	3 C John Vitale
17 Iowa	17 G Mike Husar / David Chester
31 Indiana	6 T Tom Dohring
52 Northwestern	7 TE Jeff Brown / Derrick Walker
22 Minnesota	7 QB Michael Taylor
38 Illinois	9 TB Tony Boles / Tim Williams
34 Ohio State	31 FB Leroy Hoard
22 Southern Cal■	14 DL Brent White / John Herrmann
	DL T.J. Osman
	DL Mark Messner
	LB Alex Marshall
	LB J.J. Grant
	LB Erick Anderson
	LB Bobby Abrams
	DB David Key
	DB David Arnold / Todd Plate
	DB Tripp Welborne
	DB Vada Murray

RUSHING: Boles 262/1408y, Hoard 130/752y, Williams 41/236y
PASSING: Taylor 76-112/957y, 5TD, 62.3%
   D. Brown 48-84/775y, 6TD, 57.1%
RECEIVING: McMurtry 27/470y, Kolesar 18/356y,
   Calloway 18/272y
SCORING: Mike Gillette (K) 97pts, Hoard 66pts, Boles 54pts

1989 10-2

19 Notre Dame	24 WR Greg McMurtry
24 UCLA	23 WR Chris Calloway
41 Maryland	21 T Greg Skrepenak
24 Wisconsin	0 G Matt Elliott / Joe Cocozzo
10 Michigan State	7 C Steve Everitt
26 Iowa	21 G Dean Dingman
38 Indiana	10 T Tom Dohring
42 Purdue	27 TE Derrick Walker
24 Illinois	10 QB Michael Taylor / Elvis Grbac
49 Minnesota	15 TB Tony Boles / Allen Jefferson
28 Ohio State	18 FB Leroy Hoard / Jarrod Bunch
10 Southern Cal■	17 DL Brent White / Mike Evans
	DL Michael Teeter
	DL Chris Hutchinson
	LB Alex Marshall / Brian Townsend
	LB J. J. Grant / John Milligan
	LB Erick Anderson
	LB Bobby Abrams
	DB David Key
	DB Lance Dottin / Todd Plate
	DB Tripp Welborne
	DB Vada Murray / Otis Williams

RUSHING: Boles 131/839y, Hoard 162/832y, Jefferson 65/380y
PASSING: Taylor 74-121/1081y, 11TD, 61.2%
   Grbac 73-116/824y, 8TD, 62.9%
RECEIVING: McMurtry 41/711y, Calloway 31/425y,
   Boles 16/224y
SCORING: John Carlson (K) 76pts, Boles 66pts, McMurtry 42pts

1990 9-3

24 Notre Dame	28 WR Desmond Howard
38 UCLA	15 WR Derrick Alexander / Yale Van Dyne
45 Maryland	17 T Greg Skrepenak
41 Wisconsin	3 G Matt Elliott (C) / Joe Cocozzo
27 Michigan State	28 C Steve Everitt
23 Iowa	24 G Dean Dingman
45 Indiana	19 T Tom Dohring
38 Purdue	13 TE Dave Diebolt / Tony McGee
22 Illinois	17 QB Elvis Grbac
35 Minnesota	18 TB Jon Vaughn / Ricky Powers
16 Ohio State	13 FB Jarrod Bunch
35 Mississippi■	3 DL Mike Evans
	DL T.J. Osman
	DL Chris Hutchinson / Steve Rekowski
	LB Martin Davis / Brian Townsend
	LB John Milligan / Chris Bohn
	LB Erick Anderson / Dave Dobreff
	LB Neil Simpson / Alex Marshall
	DB David Key
	DB Lance Dottin / Todd Plate
	DB Tripp Welborne
	DB Vada Murray / Corwin Brown

RUSHING: Vaughn 216/1364y, Powers 144/748y,
   Bunch 103/515y
PASSING: Grbac 155-266/1911y, 21 TDs, 58.3%
RECEIVING: Howard 63/1025y, Alexander 31/450y,
   Vaughn 20/123y
SCORING: John Carlson (K) 95pts, Howard 72pts, Vaughn 54pts

1991 10-2

35 Boston College	13 WR Desmond Howard
24 Notre Dame	14 WR Yale Van Dyne
31 Florida State	51 T Greg Skrepenak
43 Iowa	24 G Matt Elliott / Doug Skene
45 Michigan State	28 C Steve Everitt
24 Indiana	16 G Joe Cocozzo
52 Minnesota	6 T Rob Doherty
42 Purdue	0 TE Dave Diebolt / Tony McGee
59 Northwestern	14 QB Elvis Grbac
20 Illinois	0 TB Ricky Powers / Jesse Johnson
31 Ohio State	3 FB Burnie Legette / Greg McThomas
14 Washington■	34 DL Mike Evans
	DL Buster Stanley / Ninef Aghakhan
	DL Chris Hutchinson / Tony Henderson
	LB Brian Townsend / Martin Davis
	LB Steve Morrison / Marcus Walker
	LB Erick Anderson
	LB Neil Simpson / Matt Dyson
	DB Dwayne Ware
	DB Lance Dottin / Alfie Burch
	DB Otis Williams / David Ritter
	DB Corwin Brown

RUSHING: Powers 240/1197y, Johnson 107/634y,
   Wheatley 86/548y
PASSING: Grbac 165-254/2085y, 25TD, 65.0%
RECEIVING: Howard 62/985y, Van Dyne 39/500y,
   Johnson 16/180y
SCORING: Howard 138pts, John Carlson (K) 82pts,
   Powers & Wheatley 54pts

1992 9-0-3

17 Notre Dame	17 WR Derrick Alexander / Amani Toomer
35 Oklahoma State	3 WR Walter Smith / Felman Malveaux
61 Houston	7 T Trezelle Jenkins
52 Iowa	28 G Doug Skene (T) / Shawn Miller
35 Michigan State	10 C Steve Everitt
31 Indiana	3 G Joe Cocozzo
63 Minnesota	13 T Rob Doherty
24 Purdue	17 TE Tony McGee
40 Northwestern	7 QB Elvis Grbac / Todd Collins
22 Illinois	22 TB Tyrone Wheatley / Jesse Johnson
13 Ohio State	13 FB Burnie Legette
38 Washington■	31 DL Buster Stanley
	DL Tony Henderson
	DL Chris Hutchinson / Ninef Aghakhan
	LB Martin Davis
	LB Steve Morrison / Greg McThomas
	LB Marcus Walker / David Dobreff
	LB Matt Dyson
	DB Dwayne Ware / Coleman Wallace
	DB Ty Law / Alfie Burch
	DB Shonte Peoples / Pat Maloney
	DB Corwin Brown

RUSHING: Wheatley 185/1357y, Johnson 155/792y,
   Ricky Powers (TB) 53/254y
PASSING: Grbac 129-199/1640y, 17TD, 64.8%
RECEIVING: Alexander 50/740y, McGee 32/350y,
   Smith 22/301y
SCORING: Wheatley 102pts

1993 8-4

41 Washington St.	14 WR Derrick Alexander / Mercury Hayes
23 Notre Dame	27 WR Walter Smith / Amani Toomer
42 Houston	21 T Jon Runyan (G) / Thomas Guynes
24 Iowa	7 G Shawn Miller
7 Michigan State	17 C Marc Milia / Rod Payne
21 Penn State	13 G Joe Marino
21 Illinois	24 T Trezelle Jenkins / Mike Sullivan
10 Wisconsin	13 TE Marc Burkholder
25 Purdue	10 QB Todd Collins
58 Minnesota	7 TB Tyr'ne Wheatley / Ricky Powers
28 Ohio State	0 FB Che Foster
42 N. Carolina St.■	7 DL Buster Stanley / Damon Denson
	DL Jason Horn / Tony Henderson
	DL Ninef Aghakhan / Steve Rekowski
	LB Gannon Dudlar / Trevor Pryce
	LB Jarrett Irons / Bobby Powers
	LB Steve Morrison / Mike Vanderbeek
	LB Matt Dyson / Shawn Collins
	DB Ty Law
	DB Alfie Bunch
	DB Shonte Peoples / Deollo Anderson
	DB Chuck Winters

RUSHING: Wheatley 207/1129y, Ed Davis (TB) 93/441y, Powers 75/288y
PASSING: Collins 189-296/2509y, 17TD, 63.9%
RECEIVING: Alexander 35/621y, Smith 31/325y, Hayes 30/496y
SCORING: Wheatley 84pts, Peter Elezovic (K) 64pts, Alexander 36pts

1994 8-4

34 Boston College	26 WR Amani Toomer
26 Notre Dame	24 WR Mercury Hayes / Walter Smith
26 Colorado	27 T Jon Runyan
29 Iowa	14 G Thomas Guynes / Zach Adami
40 Michigan State	20 C Rod Payne
24 Penn State	31 G Joe Marino
19 Illinois	14 T Trezelle Jenkins / Mike Sullivan
19 Wisconsin	31 TE Jay Riemersma
45 Purdue	23 QB Todd Collins
38 Minnesota	22 TB Tyrone Wheatley / Tim Biakabutuka
6 Ohio State	22 FB Che Foster
24 Colorado State■	14 DL Glen Steele
	DL Trent Zenkewicz
	DL Tony Henderson
	DL Jason Horn
	LB Matt Dyson / Trevor Pryce
	LB Jarrett Irons
	LB Rob Swett / David Bowens
	DB Ty Law / Charles Woodson
	DB Woodrow Hankins / Deon Johnson
	DB Clarence Thompson
	DB Chuck Winters

RUSHING: Wheatley 194/1064y, Biakabutuka 117/713y
PASSING: Collins 172-264/2356y, 11TD, 65.2%
RECEIVING: Toomer 49/1033y, Hayes 33/548y, Riemersma 33/336y
SCORING: Remy Hamilton (K) 101pts

1995 9-4

18 Virginia	17 WR Amani Toomer / Tyrone Butterfield
38 Illinois	14 WR Mercury Hayes / Seth Smith
24 Memphis	7 T Jon Runyan / Jon Jansen
23 Boston College	13 G Zach Adami
38 Miami (Ohio)	19 C Rod Payne
13 Northwestern	19 G Joe Marinaro / Damon Denson
34 Indiana	17 T Thomas Guynes
52 Minnesota	17 TE Jay Riemersma / Mark Campbell
25 Michigan State	28 QB Brian Griese / Scott Dreisbach
5 Purdue	0 TB Tim Biakabutuka / Ed Davis
17 Penn State	27 FB Chris Floyd / Chris Howard
31 Ohio State	23 DL Glen Steele
20 Texas A&M■	22 DL Trent Zenkewicz / Steve Evans
	DL William Carr / Ben Huff
	DL Jason Horn
	LB David Bowens / Brent Blackwell
	LB Jarrett Irons / Clint Copenhaver
	LB Rob Swett / Sam Sword
	DB Clarence Thompson
	DB Charles Woodson / Woodrow Hankins
	DB Steve King
	DB Chuck Winters

RUSHING: Biakabutuka 279/1724y, Davis 69/217y, Chris Williams (TB) 53/191y
PASSING: Griese 118-215/1395y, 11TD, 54.9%
Dreisbach 56-106/850y, 3TD, 52.8%
RECEIVING: Hayes 46/888y, Riemersma 40/360y, Toomer 39/623y
SCORING: Remy Hamilton (K) 91pts

1996 8-4

20 Illinois	8 WR Tai Streets / Charles Woodson (DB)
20 Colorado	13 WR Russell Shaw / Marcus Knight
20 Boston College	14 T Jon Runyan
38 UCLA	9 G Zach Adami
16 Northwestern	17 C Rod Payne
27 Indiana	20 G Damon Denson
44 Minnesota	10 T Thomas Guynes
45 Michigan State	29 TE Jerame Tuman / Mark Campbell
3 Purdue	29 QB Scott Dreisbach / Brian Griese
17 Penn State	29 TB Chris Howard / Clarence Williams
13 Ohio State	9 FB Chris Floyd
14 Alabama■	17 DL Glen Steele / Juaquin Feazell
	DL Ben Huff / Chris Ziemann
	DL William Carr
	DL David Bowens / James Hall
	LB Clint Copenhaver
	LB Jarrett Irons / Sam Sword
	LB Sam Sword / Rob Swett
	DB Woodrow Hankins / Andre Weathers
	DB Charles Woodson (WR)
	DB Marcus Ray
	DB Daydrion Taylor / Tommy Hendricks

RUSHING: Williams 202/837y, Howard 160/725y, Woodson 6/152y
PASSING: Dreisbach 149-269/2025y, 12TD, 55.4%
Griese 35-61/513y, 3TD, 57.4%
RECEIVING: Streets 44/730y, Tuman 33/524y, Shaw 33/384y
SCORING: Remy Hamilton (K) 83pts

1997 12-0

27 Colorado	3 WR Tai Streets
38 Baylor	3 WR Russell Shaw/Charles Woodson (DB)
21 Notre Dame	14 T Jeff Backus
37 Indiana	0 G Steve Hutchinson
23 Northwestern	6 C Zach Adami
28 Iowa	24 G Chris Ziemann / David Brandt
23 Michigan State	7 T Jon Jansen
24 Minnesota	29 TE Jerame Tuman / Mark Campbell
34 Penn State	8 QB Brian Griese
26 Wisconsin	16 TB Chris Howard / Anthony Thomas
20 Ohio State	14 FB Chris Floyd
21 Washington St.■	16 DL Glen Steele / Juaquin Feazell
	DL Rob Renes / Eric Wilson
	DL Josh Williams
	DL James Hall
	LB Clint Copenhaver / Chris Singletary
	LB Sam Sword / Rob Swett
	LB Dhani Jones / Eric Mayes / Ian Gold
	DB Andre Weathers / James Whitley
	DB Charles Woodson (WR)
	DB Marcus Ray
	DB Tommy Hendricks / William Peterson

RUSHING: Howard 180/868y, Thomas 130/529y, Clarence Williams (TB) 57/264y
PASSING: Griese 175-277/2042y, 14TD, 63.2%
RECEIVING: Howard 35/263y, Tuman 27/404y, Streets 24/349y
SCORING: Kraig Baker (K) 74pts, Howard 48pts, Thomas 30pts

1998 10-3

20 Notre Dame	36 WR Marcus Knight
28 Syracuse	38 WR Tai Streets / David Terrell
59 E. Michigan	20 T Jeff Backus
29 Michigan State	17 G Steve Hutchinson
12 Iowa	9 C David Brandt
12 Northwestern	6 G Chris Ziemann / Steve Frazier
21 Indiana	10 T Jon Jansen
15 Minnesota	10 TE Jerame Tuman / Mark Campbell
27 Penn State	0 QB Tom Brady
27 Wisconsin	10 TB Anthony Thomas / Clarence Williams
16 Ohio State	31 FB Aaron Shea / Ray Jackson
48 Hawaii	17 DL Juaquin Feazell
45 Arkansas■	31 DL Rob Renes
	DL Josh Williams / Jake Frysinger
	LB James Hall
	LB Dhani Jones
	LB Sam Sword
	LB Clint Copenhaver / Ian Gold
	DB James Whitley
	DB Andre Weathers
	DB DeWayne Patmon
	DB Marcus Ray / Tommy Hendricks

RUSHING: Thomas 146/761y, Williams 126/568y, Justin Fargas (TB) 77/277y
PASSING: Brady 200-323/2427y, 14TD, 61.9%
RECEIVING: Streets 60/906y, Knight 41/597y, Tuman 27/247y
SCORING: Hayden Epstein (K) 93pts, Thomas 72pts, Streets 66pts

1999 9-3

26 Notre Dame	22 WR David Terrell / DiAllo Johnson
37 Rice	3 WR Marcus Knight / Marquise Walker
18 Syracuse	13 T Jeff Backus
21 Wisconsin	16 G Steve Hutchinson
38 Purdue	12 C David Brandt / Steve Frazier (G)
31 Michigan State	34 G Jonathan Goodwin / Chris Ziemann
29 Illinois	35 T Maurice Williams / Ben Mast (G)
34 Indiana	31 TE Shawn Thompson / Bill Seymour
37 Northwestern	3 QB Tom Brady / Drew Henson
31 Penn State	27 TB Anthony Thomas
24 Ohio State	17 FB Aaron Shea / B.J. Askew
35 Alabama■	34 DL Josh Williams
	DL Rob Renes
	DL Eric Wilson / Larry Foote
	LB Grady Brooks / Victor Hobson
	LB Ian Gold
	LB Dhani Jones
	LB James Hall
	DB James Whitley
	DB Todd Howard
	DB DeWayne Patmon / Cato June
	DB Tommy Hendricks

RUSHING: Thomas 283/1257y, Terrell 5/89y, Askew 23/70y
PASSING: Brady 180-295/2217y, 16TD, 61.0%
RECEIVING: Terrell 61/888y, Knight 36/766y, Walker 31/331y, Shea 31/239y
SCORING: Thomas 96pts

2000 9-3

42 Bowling Green	7 WR David Terrell
38 Rice	7 WR Marquise Walker
20 UCLA	23 T Jeff Backus
35 Illinois	31 G Steve Hutchinson
13 Wisconsin	10 C David Brandt
31 Purdue	32 G Jonathan Goodwin / Ben Mast (C)
58 Indiana	0 T Maurice Williams
14 Michigan State	0 TE Bill Seymour
51 Northwestern	54 QB Drew Henson / John Navarre
33 Penn State	11 TB Anthony Thomas / Chris Perry
38 Ohio State	26 FB B.J. Askew
31 Auburn■	28 DL Eric Wilson
	DL Grant Bowman
	DL Shawn Lazarus
	DL Dan Rumishek
	LB Eric Brackins / Carl Diggs
	LB Larry Foote
	LB Victor Hobson
	DB James Whitley / Jeremy LeSueur
	DB Todd Howard / Brandon Williams
	DB DeWayne Patmon
	DB Julius Curry / Charles Drake

RUSHING: Thomas 319/1773y, Perry 77/417y, Walter Cross (TB) 27/151y
PASSING: Henson 146-237/2146y, 18TD, 61.6%
RECEIVING: Terrell 71/1130y, Walker 49/699y
SCORING: Thomas 108pts, Hayden Epstein (K) 50pts

2001 8-4

31 Miami (Ohio)	13 WR Marquise Walker / Calvin Bell
18 Washington	23 WR Ronald Bellamy / Tyrece Butler
38 W. Michigan	21 T Demetrius Solomon
45 Illinois	20 G Jonathan Goodwin / David Baas
20 Penn State	0 C Kurt Anderson / Ben Mast
24 Purdue	10 G Dave Petruziello
32 Iowa	26 T Tony Pape
24 Michigan State	26 TE Bill Seymour / Bennie Joppru
31 Minnesota	10 QB John Navarre
20 Wisconsin	17 TB Chris Perry / David Underwood
20 Ohio State	26 FB B.J. Askew
17 Tennessee■	45 DL Dan Rumishek
	DL Norman Heuer / John Wood
	DL Shawn Lazarus / Grant Bowman
	DL Shantee Orr / Larry Stevens
	LB Victor Hobson
	LB Larry Foote
	LB Eric Brackins / Carl Diggs
	DB Marlin Jackson
	DB Todd Howard / Brandon Williams
	DB Cato June
	DB Charles Drake

RUSHING: Askew 199/902y, Perry 129/495y, Bell 15/169y
PASSING: Navarre 207-385/2435y, 19TD, 53.8%
RECEIVING: Walker 86/1143y, Seymour 27/279y, Askew 26/236y
SCORING: Hayden Epstein (K) 77pts, Askew 72pts, Walker 66pts

2002 10-3

31 Washington	29 WR Calvin Bell / Tyrece Butler
35 W. Michigan	12 WR Ronald Bellamy / Braylon Edwards
23 Notre Dame	25 T Courtney Morgan / Adam Stenavich
10 Utah	7 G David Baas
45 Illinois	28 C Dave Pearson
27 Penn State	24 G Ben Mast / Matt Lentz
23 Purdue	21 T Tony Pape
9 Iowa	34 TE Bennie Joppru
49 Michigan State	3 QB John Navarre
41 Minnesota	24 TB Chris Perry / David Underwood
21 Wisconsin	14 FB B.J. Askew / Kirk Moundros
9 Ohio State	14 DL Dan Rumishek / Shantee Orr
38 Florida■	30 DL Grant Bowman
	DL Norman Heuer / Shawn Lazarus
	DL Larry Stevens
	LB Victor Hobson / Pierre Woods
	LB Carl Diggs / Scott McClintock
	LB Zach Kaufman
	DB Marlin Jackson / Marcue Curry
	DB Jeremy LeSueur / Brandon Williams
	DB Cato June
	DB Charles Drake / Ernest Shazor

RUSHING: Perry 264/1110y, Askew 110/568y,
Underwood 36/105y
PASSING: Navarre 248-448/2905y, 21TD, 55.4%
RECEIVING: Edwards 67/1032y, Joppru 53/579y,
Bellamy 46/530y
SCORING: Perry 84pts, Edwards 60pts, Askew 42pts

2003 10-3

45 C. Michigan	7 WR Steve Breaston / Jason Avant
50 Houston	3 WR Braylon Edwards / Calvin Bell
38 Notre Dame	0 T Adam Stenavich / Courtney Morgan
27 Oregon	31 G David Baas
31 Indiana	17 C Dave Pearson
27 Iowa	30 G Matt Lentz
38 Minnesota	35 T Tony Pape
56 Illinois	14 TE Tim Massaquoi / Tyler Ecker
31 Purdue	3 QB John Navarre
27 Michigan State	20 TB Chris Perry / David Underwood
41 Northwestern	10 FB Kevin Dudley
35 Ohio State	21 DL Alain Kashama
14 Southern Cal ■	28 DL Grant Bowman
	DL Norman Heuer
	DL Larry Stevens / LaMarr Woodley
	LB Pierre Woods / Zach Kaufman
	LB Carl Diggs / Scott McClintock
	LB Lawrence Reid
	DB Jeremy LaSueur / Leon Hall
	DB Markus Curry
	DB Marlin Jackson / Jon Shaw
	DB Ernest Shazor

RUSHING: Perry 338/1674y, Underwood 52/270y,
Jerome Jackson (TB) 29/187y
PASSING: Navarre 270-456/3331y, 24TD, 59.2%
RECEIVING: Edwards 85/1138y, Avant 47/772y, Perry 44/367y
SCORING: Perry 108pts,

2004 9-3

43 Miami (Ohio)	10 WR Jason Avant / Steve Breaston
20 Notre Dame	28 WR Braylon Edwards
24 San Diego State	21 T Adam Stenavich
30 Iowa	17 G Rueben Riley / Leo Henige
35 Indiana	14 C David Baas (G) / Mark Bihl
27 Minnesota	24 G Matt Lentz
30 Illinois	19 T Jake Long / Mike Kolodziej
16 Purdue	14 TE Tim Massaquoi / Tyler Ecker
45 Michigan State	37 QB Chad Henne
42 Northwestern	20 TB Mike Hart / David Underwood
21 Ohio State	37 FB Kevin Dudley
37 Texas■	38 DL Larry Harrison / Rondell Biggs
	DL Gabriel Watson
	DL Pat Massey
	LB LaMarr Woodley (DL) / Pierre Woods
	LB Lawrence Reid
	LB Scott McClintock / Dave Harris
	LB Roy Manning / Prescott Burgess
	DB Marlin Jackson / Grant Mason
	DB Markus Curry / Leon Hall
	DB Ryan Mundy
	DB Ernest Shazor

RUSHING: Hart 282/1455y, Max Martin (TB) 32/132y,
Underwood 29/129y
PASSING: Henne 240-399/2743y, 25TD, 60.2%
RECEIVING: Edwards 97/1330y, Avant 38/447y,
Breaston 34/291y
SCORING: Garrett Rivas (K) 94pts, Edwards 90pts, Hart 60pts

2005 7-5

33 N. Illinois	17 WR Jason Avant / Mario Manningham
10 Notre Dame	17 WR Steve Breaston / Carl Tabb
55 E. Michigan	0 T Adam Stenavich
20 Wisconsin	23 G Leo Henige
34 Michigan State	31 C Adam Kraus (G)
20 Minnesota	23 G Matt Lentz
27 Penn State	25 T Rueben Riley (G) / Jake Long
23 Iowa	20 TE Tyler Ecker / Tim Massaquoi
33 Northwestern	17 QB Chad Henne
41 Indiana	14 TB Mike Hart / Kevin Grady
21 Ohio State	25 FB Will Paul
28 Nebraska■	32 DL Pat Massey
	DL Gabe Watson
	DL Alan Branch
	DL LaMarr Woodley
	LB Prescott Burgess
	LB David Harris
	LB Pierre Woods / Chris Graham
	DB Leon Hall
	DB Grant Mason / Brandon Harrison
	DB Willis Barringer
	DB Jamar Adams

RUSHING: Hart 150/662y, Grady 121/483y,
Jerome Jackson (TB) 54/228y, Max Martin (TB) 53/226y
PASSING: Henne 223-382/2526y, 23TD, 58.4%
RECEIVING: Avant 82/1007y, Manningham 27/433y,
Breaston 26/291y
SCORING: Garrett Rivas (K) 90pts, Avant 48pts,
Manningham 36pts

2006 11-2

27 Vanderbilt	7 WR Mario Manningham / Adrian Arrington
41 C. Michigan	17 WR Steve Breaston
47 Notre Dame	21 T Jake Long
27 Wisconsin	13 G Adam Kraus
28 Minnesota	14 C Mark Bihl
31 Michigan State	13 G Alex Mitchell
17 Penn State	10 T Rueben Riley
20 Iowa	6 TE Tyler Ecker / Mike Massey
17 Northwestern	3 QB Chad Henne
34 Ball State	26 TB Mike Hart / Jerome Jackson
34 Indiana	3 FB Obi Oluigbo
39 Ohio State	42 DL Rondell Biggs / Tim Jamison
18 Southern Cal■	32 DL Terrance Taylor / Will Johnson
	DL Alan Branch
	DL LaMarr Woodley
	LB Shawn Crable
	LB David Harris
	LB Prescott Burgess / Chris Graham
	DB Leon Hall / Brandon Harrison
	DB Morgan Trent / Charles Stewart
	DB Willis Barringer / Ryan Mundy
	DB Jamar Adams / Brandent Englemon

RUSHING: Hart 318/1562y, Brandon Minor (TB) 42/238y,
Jackson 28/213y
PASSING: Henne 203-328/2508y, 22TD, 61.9%
RECEIVING: Breaston 58/670y, Arrington 40/544y,
Manningham 38/703y
SCORING: Garrett Rivas (K) 93pts, Hart 86pts,
Manningham 54pts

2007 9-4

32 Appalachian St.	34 WR Mario Manningham
7 Oregon	39 WR Adrian Arrington / Greg Mathews
38 Notre Dame	0 T Jake Long
14 Penn State	9 G Adam Kraus / Tim McAvoy
28 Northwestern	16 C Justin Boren
33 E. Michigan	22 G Jeremy Ciulla / Alex Mitchell
48 Purdue	21 T Stephen Schilling / Mark Ortmann
27 Illinois	17 TE Carson Butler / Mike Massey
34 Minnesota	10 QB Chad Henne / Ryan Mallett
28 Michigan State	24 TB Mike Hart / Carlos Brown
21 Wisconsin	37 FB Mark Moundros
3 Ohio State	14 DL Tim Jamison
41 Florida■	35 DL Terrance Taylor
	DL Will Johnson
	DL Brandon Graham
	LB Shawn Crable
	LB Obi Ezeh / John Thompson
	LB Chris Graham / Brandon Logan
	DB Morgan Trent / Brandon Harrison
	DB Donovan Warren
	DB Brandent Englemon / Stevie Brown
	DB Jamar Adams / Charles Stewart

RUSHING: Hart 265/1361y, Brandon Minor (TB) 90/385y,
Brown 75/382y
PASSING: Henne 162-278/1938y, 17TD, 58.3%,
Mallett 61-141/892y, 7TD, 43.3%
RECEIVING: Manningham 72/1174y, Arrington 67/882y,
Mathews 39/366y
SCORING: Hart 84pts, Manningham 72pts, K.C. Lopata (K) 61pts

2008 3-9

25 Utah	27 WR Greg Mathews / James Rogers
16 Miami (Ohio)	6 WR Darryl Stonum / Zion Babb
17 Notre Dame	35 WR Martavious Odoms / Toney Clemons
27 Wisconsin	25 T Mark Ortmann (G) / Perry Dorrestein
20 Illinois	45 G Tim McAvoy / John Ferrara
10 Toledo	13 C David Molk
17 Penn State	46 G David Moosman
21 Michigan State	35 T Stephen Schilling
42 Purdue	48 TE Carson Butler / Kevin Koger
29 Minnesota	6 QB Steven Threet / Nick Sheridan
14 Northwestern	21 TB Sam McGuffie / Brandon Minor
7 Ohio State	42 DL Brandon Graham / Ryan Van Bergen
	DL Terrance Taylor
	DL Will Johnson / Mike Martin
	DL Tim Jamison
	LB John Thompson / Austin Panter
	LB Obi Ezeh
	LB Jonas Mouton / Marell Evans
	DB Morgan Trent
	DB Donovan Warren / Boubacar Cissoko
	DB Stevie Brown
	DB Brandon Harrison / Charles Stewart

RUSHING: Minor 103/533y, McGuffie 118/486y, Shaw 42/215y
PASSING: Threet 102-200/1105y, 9TD, 51.0%,
Sheridan 63-137/613y, 2TD, 46.0%
RECEIVING: Odoms 49/443y, Mathews 35/409y,
McGuffie 19/175y
SCORING: Minor 66pts, K.C. Lopata (K) 57pts, McGuffie 24pts

2009 5-7

31 W. Michigan	7 WR Greg Mathews
38 Notre Dame	34 WR Junior Hemingway / Darryl Stonum
45 E. Michigan	17 WR Martavious Odoms / Ray Roundtree
36 Indiana	33 T Mark Ortmann
20 Michigan State	26 G Stephen Schilling / John Ferrara
28 Iowa	30 C David Moosman (G) / David Molk
63 Delaware State	6 G Mark Huyge (T) / Patrick Orameh
10 Penn State	35 T Perry Dorrestein
13 Illinois	38 TE Kevin Koger
36 Purdue	38 QB Tate Forcier / Denard Robinson
24 Wisconsin	45 TB Carlos Brown / Brandon Minor
10 Ohio State	21 DL Brandon Graham / Will Heininger
	DL Mike Martin
	DL Ryan Van Bergen
	LB Craig Roh / Brandon Herron
	LB Stevie Brown / Brandon Smith
	LB Obi Ezeh
	LB Jonas Mouton / Kevin Leach
	DB Troy Woolfolk / J.T. Floyd
	DB Donovan Warren / Boubacar Cissoko
	DB Mike Williams
	DB Jordan Kovacs

RUSHING: Minor 96/502y, Brown 81/480y, Robinson 69/351y
Vincent Smith (TB) 48/276y, Forcier 118/240y
PASSING: Forcier 165-281/2050y, 13TD, 58.7%
RECEIVING: Roundtree 32/434y, Mathews 29/352y,
Odoms 22/257y, Hemingway 16/268y, Koger 16/220y
SCORING: Jason Olesnavage (K) 75pts, Minor 48pts,
Brown & Robinson 30pts

2010 7-6

30 Connecticut	10 WR Darryl Stonum / Martavious Odoms
28 Notre Dame	24 WR Roy Roundtree / Kelvin Grady
42 Massachusetts	37 WR/FB Junior Hemingway/ John McColgan
65 Bowling Green	21 T Taylor Lewan
42 Indiana	35 G Stephen Schilling / Kevin Leach
17 Michigan State	34 C David Molk
28 Iowa	38 G Patrick Omameh
31 Penn State	41 T Perry Dorrestein / Mark Huyge
67 Illinois	65 TE Kevin Koger / Martell Webb
27 Purdue	16 QB Denard Robinson
28 Wisconsin	48 TB Vincent Smith / Michael Shaw
7 Ohio State	37 DL Ryan Van Bergen
14 Mississippi St.■	52 DL Mike Martin / Adam Patterson
	DL Greg Banks / J.B. Fitzgerald (LB)
	LB Craig Roh (DE) / Kenny Demens
	LB Kenny Demens / Obi Ezeh
	LB Jonas Mouton / Mark Moundros
	LB Carvin Johnson / Thomas Gordon
	DB J.T. Floyd / Courtney Avery
	DB James Rogers
	DB Cameron Gordon (LB) / Ray Vinopal
	DB Jordan Kovacs

RUSHING: Robinson 256/1702y, Smith 136/601y, Shaw 75/402y
PASSING: Robinson 182-291/2570y, 18TD, 62.5%
Forcier 54-84/597y, 4TD, 64.3%
RECEIVING: Roundtree 72/935y, Stonum 49/633y,
Hemingway 32/593y
SCORING: Robinson 84pts, Shaw 54pts,
Seth Broekhuizen (K) 51pts

MICHIGAN STATE

Michigan State University (Founded 1855)
East Lansing, Michigan
Nickname: Spartans
Colors: Green and White
Stadium: Spartan Stadium (1957) 75,005
Conference Affiliations: Big Ten (1950-present)

CAREER RUSHING YARDS	Attempts	Yards
Lorenzo White (1984-87)	1082	4887
Javon Ringer (2005-08)	843	4398
Tico Duckett (1989-92)	836	4212
Blake Ezor (1986-89)	800	3749
Sedrick Irvin (1996-98)	755	3504
T.J. Duckett (1999-2001)	621	3379
Duane Goulbourne (1992-94, 1996)	627	2848
Steve Smith (1977-80)	524	2676
Eric Allen (1969-71)	521	2654
Jehuu Caucrick (2004-07)	532	2395

CAREER PASSING YARDS	Comp.-Att.	Yards
Jeff Smoker (2000-03)	685-1150	8932
Drew Stanton (2003-06)	543-846	6524
Brian Hoyer (2005-08)	500-896	6159
Kirk Cousins (2008-10)	456-709	5815
Dave Yarema (1982-86)	464-767	5809
Ed Smith (1976-78)	418-789	5706
Bill Burke (1996-99)	416-766	5463
Jim Miller (1990-93)	467-746	5037
Todd Schultz (1994-97)	360-593	4273
Tony Banks (1994-95)	301-496	4129

CAREER RECEIVING YARDS	Catches	Yards
Andre Rison (1985-88)	146	2992
Charles Rogers (2001-02)	135	2821
Kirk Gibson (1975-78)	112	2347
Courtney Hawkins (1988-91)	138	2210
Plaxico Burress (1998-99)	131	2155
Mark Dell (2007-10)	133	2136
Gari Scott (1996-99)	134	2095
Eugene Byrd (1975-76, 1978-79)	114	2082
Mark Ingram (1983-86)	95	1944
Derrick Mason (1993-96)	120	1914

SEASON RUSHING YARDS	Attempts	Yards
Lorenzo White (1985)	419	2066
Javon Ringer (2008)	390	1637
Lorenzo White (1987)	357	1572
Blake Ezor (1988)	322	1496
Eric Allen (1971)	259	1494

SEASON PASSING YARDS	Comp.-Att.	Yards
Jeff Smoker (2003)	302-488	3395
Drew Stanton (2005)	236-354	3077
Kirk Cousins (2010)	226-338	2825
Brian Hoyer (2007)	223-376	2725
Kirk Cousins (2009)	198-328	2680

SEASON RECEIVING YARDS	Catches	Yards
Charles Rogers (2001)	67	1470
Charles Rogers (2002)	68	1351
Devin Thomas (2007)	79	1260
Plaxico Burress (1999)	66	1142
Courtney Hawkins (1989)	60	1080

GAME RUSHING YARDS	Attempts	Yards
Eric Allen (1971 vs. Purdue)	29	350
Lorenzo White (1987 vs. Indiana)	56	292
Lorenzo White (1985 vs. Indiana)	25	286

GAME PASSING YARDS	Comp.-Att.	Yards
Bill Burke (1999 vs. Michigan)	21-36	400
Jeff Smoker (2001 vs. Fresno State)	22-32	376
Ed Smith (1978 vs. Indiana)	20-30	369

GAME RECEIVING YARDS	Catches	Yards
Charles Rogers (2001 vs. Fresno State)	10	270
Plaxico Burress (1999 vs. Michigan)	10	255
Andre Rison (1988 vs. Georgia)	9	252

GREATEST COACH:

Hugh "Duffy" Daugherty was so witty and engaging with the sports writers of his day that if he coached 25 years later he might today be John Madden with computer games with his name on the cover.

Things started poorly for Daugherty as he stepped into the big shoes of Biggie Munn who had put Michigan State on the football map. He went 3-6 in his rookie year as head coach the year after Munn earned a Rose Bowl win and a no. 3 final ranking. But in his second year, Daugherty returned the Spartans to the Rose Bowl to again defeat UCLA with what some people believe was the greatest of all Spartan teams.

In 19 seasons, Daugherty won 109 games, the most in Michigan State coaching history and played a big role in the 1966 season in which his Spartans and Notre Dame played one of the most famous games of all time.

MICHIGAN STATE'S 55 GREATEST SINCE 1953

OFFENSE

WIDE RECEIVER: Plaxico Burgess, Kirk Gibson, Andre Rison, Charles Rogers, Devin Thomas
TIGHT END: Mark Brammer, Billy Joe DuPree
TACKLE: Flozell Adams, Brian DeMarco, Bob Kula, Tony Mandarich
GUARD: Ed Budde, Joe DeLamielleure, Ron Saul
CENTER: Dave Behrman
QUARTERBACK: Earl Morrall, Drew Stanton
RUNNING BACK: Eric Allen, Tico Duckett, Sedrick Irvin, Clinton Jones, Javon Ringer, Lorenzo White
FULLBACK: Bob Apisa

DEFENSE

END: Charles "Bubba" Smith, Robaire Smith, Sam Williams
TACKLE: Charles Bailey, Larry Bethea, Ron Curl
MIDDLE GUARD: Harold Lucas
LINEBACKER: Carl Banks, Dan Bass, Dan Currie, Ron Goovert, Percy Snow, George Webster
CORNER BACK: Herb Adderley, Jim Burroughs, Amp Campbell, Renaldo Hill
SAFETY: Harlan Barnett, Allen Brenner, Bill Simpson, Brad Van Pelt

SPECIAL TEAMS

RETURN SPECIALISTS: DeAndra Cobb, Herb Haygood
PLACE KICKER: Morten Anderson, Paul Edinger
PUNTER: Greg Montgomery, Ray Stachowicz

TWO-WAY PLAYERS

END-DEFENSIVE END: Don Dohoney
TACKLE-DEFENSIVE TACKLE: Norm Masters
WINGBACK-DEFENSIVE BACK: Walt Kowalczyk
FULLBACK-DEFENSIVE BACK: George Saimes

PERFORMANCE FORMULA:
MICHIGAN STATE'S 10 BEST SEASONS

1955	1.7010	2 of 69
1966	1.6794	3 of 70
1965	1.6773	1 of 70
1953	1.5782	5 of 69
1957	1.5634	6 of 69
1999	1.5389	7 of 71
1987	1.4855	9 of 69
1961	1.4555	8 of 71
1978	1.4523	11 of 70
2010	1.4368	15 of 71

MICHIGAN STATE SPARTANS

Year	W-L-T	AP Poll	Conference Standing	Toughest Regular Season Opponents	Coach (Record at School)	Bowl Games			
1953	9-1	3	1	Iowa 5-3-1, Ohio State 6-3, Michigan 6-3	Clar'ce "Biggie" Munn (54-9-2)	Rose	28	UCLA	20
1954	3-6			Wisconsin 7-2, Minnesota 7-2, Ohio State 9-0	Hugh "Duffy" Daugherty				
1955	9-1	2	2	Michigan 7-2, Notre Dame 8-2, Illinois 5-3-1	Duffy Daugherty	Rose	17	UCLA	14
1956	7-2	9	4t	Michigan 7-2, Minnesota 6-1-2	Duffy Daugherty				
1957	8-1	3	2	Michigan 5-3-1, Wisconsin 6-3, Notre Dame 7-3	Duffy Daugherty				
1958	3-5-1		10	Purdue 6-1-2, Wisconsin 7-1-1, Ohio State 6-1-2	Duffy Daugherty				
1959	5-4		2	Iowa 5-4, Purdue 5-2-2, Northwestern 6-3, Miami 6-4	Duffy Daugherty				
1960	6-2-1	15	4	Pittsburgh 4-3-3, Iowa 8-1, Ohio State 7-2	Duffy Daugherty				
1961	7-2	8	3	Wisconsin 6-3, Michigan 6-3, Minnesota 7-2	Duffy Daugherty				
1962	5-4		5t	Minnesota 6-2-1, Northwestern 7-2	Duffy Daugherty				
1963	6-2-1	10	2t	North Carolina 8-2, South California 7-3, Illinois 7-1-1	Duffy Daugherty				
1964	4-5		6	Southern California 7-3, Michigan 8-1, Notre Dame 9-1	Duffy Daugherty				
1965	10-1	2	1	UCLA 7-2-1, Ohio State 7-2-1, Purdue 7-2-1, Notre Dame 7-2-1	Duffy Daugherty	Rose	12	UCLA	14
1966	9-0-1	2	1	Michigan 6-4, Purdue 8-2, Notre Dame 9-0-1	Duffy Daugherty				
1967	3-7		5t	So. Calif. 9-1, Min'sota 8-2, No. Dame 8-2, Indiana 9-1, Purdue 8-2	Duffy Daugherty				
1968	5-5		7	Michigan 8-2, Notre Dame 7-2-1, Ohio State 9-0, Purdue 8-2	Duffy Daugherty				
1969	4-6		9	Notre Dame 8-1-1, Ohio State 8-1, Michigan 8-2, Purdue 8-2	Duffy Daugherty				
1970	4-6		5t	Notre Dame 9-1, Ohio State 9-0, Michigan 9-1	Duffy Daugherty				
1971	6-5		3t	Notre Dame 8-2, Michigan 11-0, Northwestern 7-4	Duffy Daugherty (109-69-5)				
1972	5-5-1		4	So. California 11-0, Notre Dame 8-2, Michigan 10-1, Ohio State 9-1	Dennis Stoltz				
1973	5-6		4t	UCLA 9-2, Notre Dame 10-0, Michigan 10-0-1, Ohio State 9-0-1	Dennis Stoltz				
1974	7-3-1	12	3	Notre Dame 9-2, Michigan 10-1, Ohio State 10-1	Dennis Stoltz (19-13-1)				
1975	7-4		3t	Ohio State 11-0, Notre Dame 8-3, Michigan 8-2-1	Darryl Rogers				
1976	4-6-1		7t	Ohio State 8-2-1, Notre Dame 8-3, Michigan 10-1	Darryl Rogers				
1977	7-3-1		3	Notre Dame 10-1, Michigan 10-1, Minnesota 7-4	Darryl Rogers				
1978	8-3	12	1t	Purdue 8-2-1, So. Calif. 11-1, Notre Dame 8-3, Michigan 10-1	Darryl Rogers (24-28-2)				
1979	5-6		7t	Notre Dame 7-4, Michigan 8-3, Purdue 9-2, Ohio State 11-0					
1980	3-8		9	Notre Dame 9-1-1, Michigan 9-2, Purdue 8-3, Ohio State 9-2	Frank "Muddy" Waters				
1981	5-6		6t	Ohio State 8-3, Michigan 8-3, Iowa 8-3	Muddy Waters				
1982	2-9		8t	Illinois 7-4, Ohio State 8-3, Miami 7-4, Michigan 8-3	Muddy Waters (10-23)				
1983	4-6-1		7	Illinois 10-1, Michigan 9-2, Ohio State 8-3, Iowa 9-2	George Perles	Cherry	6	Army	10
1984	6-6		6t	Notre Dame 7-4, Purdue 7-4, Ohio State 9-2, Wisconsin 7-3-1	George Perles	All-American	14	Georgia Tech	17
1985	7-5		4t	Arizona State 8-3, Iowa 10-1, Michigan 9-1-1	George Perles				
1986	6-5		5t	Arizona State 9-1-1, Iowa 8-3, Michigan 11-0	George Perles				
1987	9-2-1	8	1	So. Calif. 8-3, Notre Dame 8-3, Fla. St. 10-1, Iowa 9-3, Indiana 8-3	George Perles	Rose	20	Southern California	17
1988	6-5-1		2	Notre Dame 11-0, Florida State 10-1, Michigan 8-2-1	George Perles	Gator	27	Georgia	34
1989	8-4	16t	3t	Notre Dame 11-1, Miami 10-1, Michigan 10-1, Illinois 9-2	George Perles	Aloha	33	Hawaii	13
1990	8-3-1	16	1t	Notre Dame 9-2, Iowa 8-3, Michigan 8-3, Illinois 8-3	George Perles	John Hancock	17	Southern California	16
1991	3-8		6t	Notre Dame 9-3, Michigan 10-1, Ohio State 8-3	George Perles				
1992	5-6		3	Notre Dame 9-1-1, Boston Coll. 8-2-1, Michigan 8-0-3, Ohio St. 8-2-1	George Perles	Liberty	7	Louisville	18
1993	6-6		7	Notre Dame 10-1, Ohio State 9-1-1, Penn St. 9-2, Wisconsin 9-1-1	George Perles (68-56-4)				
1994	5-6		5t	Michigan 7-4, Ohio State 9-3, Penn State 11-0	Nick Saban	Independence	26	LSU	45
1995	6-5-1		5	Nebraska 11-0, Michigan 9-3, Penn State 8-3	Nick Saban	Sun	38	Stanford	0
1996	6-6		5t	Nebraska 10-1, Iowa 8-3, Michigan 8-3, Penn State 10-2	Nick Saban	Aloha	23	Washington	51
1997	7-5		6t	Michigan 11-0, Ohio State 10-2, Penn State 9-2	Nick Saban				
1998	6-6		6	Notre Dame 9-2, Michigan 9-3, Ohio State 10-1, Penn State 8-3	Nick Saban				
1999	10-2	7	2t	Oregon 8-3, Michigan 9-2, Wisconsin 9-2, Penn State 9-3	Nick Saban (34-24), Bobby Williams [1-0]	Citrus	37	Florida	34
2000	5-6		9t	Notre Dame 9-2, Wisconsin 8-4, Michigan 8-3, Ohio State 8-3	Bobby Williams	Silicon Valley	44	Fresno State	35
2001	7-5		8t	Iowa 6-5, Michigan 8-3, Purdue 6-5	Bobby Williams				
2002	4-8		8t	Notre Dame 10-2, Iowa 11-1, Michigan 9-3, Penn State 9-3	Bobby Williams (15-17), Morris Watts [2-2]				
2003	8-5		4t	Iowa 9-3, Minnesota 9-3, Michigan 10-2	John L. Smith	Alamo	3	Nebraska	17
2004	5-7		5t	Iowa 10-1, Michigan 9-2, Wisconsin 9-2	John L. Smith				
2005	5-6		10	Notre Dame 9-2, Ohio State 9-2, Penn State 10-2	John L. Smith				
2006	4-8		10t	Notre Dame 10-2, Michigan 11-1, Ohio State 12-0	John L. Smith (22-26)	Champs Sports	21	Boston College	24
2007	7-6		7t	Wisconsin 9-3, Ohio State 11-1, Michigan 8-4	Mark Dantonio	Capital One	12	Georgia	24
2008	9-4	24	3	California 8-4, Northwestern 9-3, Ohio State 10-2, Penn State 11-1	Mark Dantonio	Alamo	31	Texas Tech	41
2009	6-7		6t	C. Michigan 11-2, Wisconsin 9-3, Iowa 10-2, Penn State 10-2	Mark Dantonio (33-19)	Capital One	7	Alabama	49
2010	11-2	14	1t	Notre Dame 7-5, Wisconsin 11-1, Penn State 7-5	Mark Dantonio				

TOTAL: 355-274-13 .5631 (31 of 70)

Bowl Games since 1953: 8-12 .4000 (57 of 70)

GREATEST TEAM SINCE 1953: The Michigan State Spartans of 1966 edge the 1955 team only slightly on the basis of one of the greatest defensive units of all time. The 1966 Spartans included Charles Bailey, Ron Goovert, Phil Hoag, Jess Phillips, Charles "Bubba" Smith, Charles "Mad Dog" Thornhill, and the greatest Monster-back ever in football history in George Webster. The 1955 Spartans had a slightly superior offense with Walt "The Sprinting Blacksmith" Kowalczyk, John "Thunder" Lewis, Norm Masters, Earl Morrall, and Clarence Peaks.

1953 9-1

21 Iowa	7 E Bill Quinlan / Ellis Duckett
21 Minnesota	0 T Jim Jebb
26 TCU	19 G Ferris Hallmark / Embry Robinson
47 Indiana	18 C Jim Neal
0 Purdue	6 G Hank Bullough / Bill Ross
34 Oregon State	6 T Larry Fowler / Randy Schrecengost
28 Ohio State	13 E Don Dohoney
14 Michigan	6 QB Tom Yewcic / Earl Morrall
21 Marquette	15 HB Leroy Bolden / Jim Ellis
28 UCLA■	20 WB Billy Wells
	FB Evan Slonac

RUSHING: Bolden 127/691y, Slonac 75/396y, Wells 69/262y
PASSING: Yewcic 34-80/489y, 7TD, 42.5%,
Morrall 17-31/279y, 2TD, 54.8%
RECEIVING: Duckett 10/169, Slonac 7/105y, 3 with 6
SCORING: Bolden 48pts, Wells, Ellis & Slonac 36pts

1954 3-6

10 Iowa	14 E John Lewis / Bill Quinlan
0 Wisconsin	6 T Randy Schrecengost /Embry Robinson
21 Indiana	14 G Hank Bullough / Ferris Hallmark
19 Notre Dame	20 C Joe Badaczewski / Fred Rody
13 Purdue	27 G Norm Masters
13 Minnesota	19 T Roland Dotsch / Buck Nystrom
54 Washington St.	6 E Jim Hinesly / Ellis Duckett
7 Michigan	33 QB Earl Morrall / Johnny Matsock
40 Marquette	10 HB Leroy Bolden / Clarence Peaks
	WB Bert Zagers
	FB Gerry Planutis / Gary Lowe

RUSHING: Peaks 45/321y, Bolden 63/292y, Matsock 70/268y
PASSING: Morrall 39-99/795y, 6TD, 39.4%
RECEIVING: Hinesly 15/231y, Lewis 10/338y,
Don Kauth (E) 8/102y
SCORING: Bolden 30pts, Lewis & Peaks 24pts

1955 9-1

20 Indiana	13 E John Lewis / Bob Jewett
7 Michigan	14 T Norm Masters
38 Stanford	14 G Dan Currie / Embry Robinson
21 Notre Dame	7 C Joe Badaczewski / John Matsko
21 Illinois	7 G Carl Nystrom / Dale Hollern
27 Wisconsin	0 T Pat Burke / Tom Saidock
27 Purdue	0 E Dave Kaiser / Jim Hinesly
42 Minnesota	14 QB Earl Morrall
33 Marquette	0 HB Clarence Peaks / Jerry Musatti
17 UCLA■	14 WB Walt Kowalczyk / Vic Zucco
	FB Gerry Planutis / Gary Lowe

RUSHING: Kowalczyk 82/584y, Planutis 78/385y, Peaks 82/376y
PASSING: Morrall 42-68/941y, 5TD, 61.8%
RECEIVING: Kaiser 12/343y, Jewett 9/164y, Peaks 7/120y
SCORING: Planutis (FB-K) 52pts, Kowalczyk 36pts, Peaks 30pts

1956 7-2

21 Stanford	7 E Tony Kolodziej / Sam Williams
9 Michigan	0 T Tom Saidock
53 Indiana	6 G Dan Currie
47 Notre Dame	14 C John Matsko / Don Berger
13 Illinois	20 G Ellison Kelly / Archie Matsos
33 Wisconsin	0 T Pat Burke / Fran O'Brien
12 Purdue	9 E Dave Kaiser/Jim Hinesly/Harold Dukes
13 Minnesota	14 QB Pat Wilson / Jim Ninowski
38 Kansas State	17 HB Clarence Peaks / Dennis Mendyk
	WB Walt Kowalczyk
	FB Don Gilbert / Vic Zucco

RUSHING: Mendyk 85/495y, Gilbert 48/260y, Peaks 52/235y
PASSING: Wilson 20-39/414y, 1TD, 51.3%,
Ninowski 13-31/237y, 4TD, 41.9%
RECEIVING: Hinesly 9/131y, Kolodziej 7/221y, Duke 5/105y
SCORING: Mendyk 42pts, Gilbert 30pts,
Wilson & Peaks (HB-K) 24pts

1957 8-1

54 Indiana	0 E Sam Williams / Bob Jewett
19 California	0 T Fran O'Brien
35 Michigan	6 G John Middleton
13 Purdue	20 C Dan Currie / Don Berger
19 Illinois	14 G Ellison Kelly
21 Wisconsin	7 T Pat Burke / Palmer Pyle
34 Notre Dame	6 E Dave Kaiser
42 Minnesota	13 QB Jim Ninowski / Mike Panitch
27 Kansas State	9 HB Blanche Martin / Dean Look
	WB Walt Kowlaczyk / Art Johnson
	FB Don Gilbert

RUSHING: Kowalczyk 101/545y, Martin 100/528y, Johnson 56/71y
PASSING: Ninowski 45-79/718y, 6 TDs, 57.0%
RECEIVING: Kaiser 19/267y, Williams 11/236y, Johnson 8/71y
SCORING: Kowalczyk 54pts, Martin & Johnson 42pts

1958 3-5-1

32 California	12 E Sam Williams
12 Michigan	12 T Fran O'Brien
22 Pittsburgh	8 G John Middleton
6 Purdue	14 C Archie Matsos
0 Illinois	16 G Ellison Kelly
7 Wisconsin	9 T Cliff LaRose / Palmer Pyle
0 Indiana	6 E Dick Barker
12 Minnesota	39 QB Mike Panitch / Greg Montgomery
26 Kansas State	7 HB Jim Wulff / Dean Look / Al Luplow
	WB Art Johnson / Herb Adderley
	FB Don Arend

RUSHING: Look 90/328y, Johnson 84/326y, Lulow 64/236y
PASSING: Panitch 16-37/250y, 3 TDs, 43.2%,
Montgomery 11-35/217y, TD, 314%
RECEIVING: Williams 15/242y, Adderley 6/100y, Barker 6/92y
SCORING: Look (QB-K) 24pts, Barker 18pts, 3 with 12pts

1959 5-4

7 Texas A&M	9 E Fred Arbanas
34 Michigan	8 T Ed McLucas / Pete Kakela
8 Iowa	37 G Fred Boylan
19 Notre Dame	0 C Dave Manders
14 Indiana	6 G Don Wright / Mickey Walker
24 Ohio State	30 T Palmer Pyle
15 Purdue	0 E Art Brandstatter / Jim Corgiat
15 Northwestern	10 QB Dean Look
13 Miami	18 HB Herb Adderley
	WB Gary Ballman / Bob Bercich
	FB Blanche Martin

RUSHING: Adderley 93/419y
PASSING: Look 49-100/785y, 9 TDs, 49.0%
RECEIVING: Adderley 13/265y
SCORING: Ballman 30pts

1960 6-2-1

7 Pittsburgh	7 E Fred Arbanas / Lonnie Sanders
24 Michigan	17 T Pete Kakela
15 Iowa	27 G Fred Boylan / Ed Budde
21 Notre Dame	0 C Dave Manders
35 Indiana	0 G Dave Behrman / George Azar
0 Ohio State	21 T Jim Kanicki / Jim Bobbitt
17 Purdue	13 E Art Brandstatter / Ernie Clark
21 Northwestern	18 QB Tom Wilson
43 Detroit	15 HB Herb Adderley
	WB Gary Ballman / Wayne Fontes
	FB Ron Hatcher / Carl Charon

RUSHING: Hatcher 59/361y, Ballman 51/295y, Adderley 68/261y
PASSING: Wilson 46-109/761y, 8TD, 42.2%
RECEIVING: Adderley 9/154y, Hatcher 6/82y, Brandstatter 5/95y
SCORING: Brandstatter (E-K) 37pts, Ballman 36pts,
Charon 24pts

1961 7-2

20 Wisconsin	0 E Lonnie Sanders
31 Stanford	3 T Pete Kakela / Jim Kanicki
28 Michigan	0 G Ed Budde / George Azar
17 Notre Dame	7 C Dave Manders
35 Indiana	0 G Charles Brown / Tony Kumiega
0 Minnesota	13 T Dave Behrman / Dave Herman
6 Purdue	7 E Art Brandstatter / Ernie Clark
21 Northwestern	13 QB Pete Smith
34 Illinois	7 HB Sherman Lewis / Wayne Fontes (E)
	HB Dewey Lincoln / Gary Ballman
	FB George Saimes / Ron Hatcher

RUSHING: Saimes 82/451y, Lewis 64/399y, Lincoln 72/374y
PASSING: Smith 42-94/630y, 5TD, 44.7%
RECEIVING: Sanders 15/247y, Brandstatter 10/134y,
Ballman 7/69y
SCORING: Saimes 48pts, Lewis 38pts, Brandstatter (E-K) 19pts

1962 5-4

13 Stanford	16 E Ernie Clark
38 North Carolina	6 T Ed Budde / Jim Kanicki
28 Michigan	0 G George Azar
31 Notre Dame	7 C Dave Behrman
26 Indiana	8 G Steve Mellinger / Mike Currie
7 Minnesota	28 T Jim Bobbitt / Dave Herman
9 Purdue	17 E Matt Snorton / Ed Lothamer
31 Northwestern	7 QB Pete Smith
6 Illinois	7 HB Sherman Lewis / Ron Rubick
	HB Dewey Lincoln / Lonnie Sanders
	FB George Saimes

RUSHING: Saimes 122/642y, Lewsi 98/590y, Rubick 68/429y
PASSING: Smith 18-52/241y, 3TD, 34.6%
RECEIVING: Sanders 7/109y, Snorton 6/89y, Lewis 6/79y
SCORING: Lewis 58pts, Saimes 54pts, Rubick 24pts

1963 6-2-1

31 North Carolina	0 E Dan Underwood / Tom Krzemienski
10 Southern Cal	13 T Jerry Rush / Jim Kanicki
7 Michigan	7 G George Azar
20 Indiana	3 C Dave Behrman
15 Northwestern	7 G Steve Mellinger / Mike Currie
30 Wisconsin	13 T Jim Bobbitt / Dave Herman
23 Purdue	0 E Matt Snorton / Ed Lothamer
12 Notre Dame	7 QB Steve Juday / Ed Proebstle
0 Illinois	16 HB Sherman Lewis
	HB Ron Rubick
	FB Roger Lopes / Dewey Lincoln

RUSHING: Lopes 138/601y, Lewis 90/577y, Lincoln 65/188y
PASSING: Juday 30-68/509y, 5TD, 44.1%
RECEIVING: Lewis 11/303y, Krzemienski 9/117y,
Lothamer 5/72y
SCORING: Lewis 48pts, Lopes 42pts, Lou Bobich (K) 17pts

1964 4-5

15 North Carolina	21 WR Gene Washington / Dave McCormick
17 Southern Cal	7 T Jerry Rush / Jerry West (G)
10 Michigan	17 G Gary Rugg / Steve Millinger
20 Indiana	27 C Don Ross
24 Northwestern	6 G John Karpinski / John Walsh
22 Wisconsin	6 T Dick Flynn / Rahn Bentley
21 Purdue	7 TE Tom Krzemienski
7 Notre Dame	34 QB Steve Juday
0 Illinois	16 HB Dick Gordon / John Tinnick
	HB Clinton Jones / Harry Ammons
	FB Eddie Cotton / Larry Mackey
	DL Doug Roberts / George Webster
	DL Don Bierowicz
	DL Harold Lucas
	DL Buddy Owens
	DL Bob Viney / Charles "Bubba" Smith
	LB Ron Goovert / Phil Hoag
	LB Charles Thornhill
	DB Herman Johnson / Larry Lukasik
	DB Don Japinga / Jerry Jones
	DB Lou Bobich
	DB Charley Migyanka

RUSHING: Gordon 123/741y, Jones 72/350y, Cotton 48/183y
PASSING: Juday 79-148/894y, 9 TDs, 53.4%
RECEIVING: Washington 35/542y, Krzemienski 15/175y,
Gordon 13/81y
SCORING: Jones & Washington 30pts, Krzemienski 18pts

1965 10-1

13 UCLA	3 WR Gene Washington
23 Penn State	0 T Joe Przybycki
22 Illinois	12 G Norm Jenkins
24 Michigan	7 C Boris Dimitroff
32 Ohio State	7 G John Karpinski
14 Purdue	10 T Jerry West / Dave Techlin
49 Northwestern	7 TE Jim Proebstle
35 Iowa	0 QB Steve Juday
27 Indiana	13 HB Dwight Lee
12 Notre Dame	3 HB Clinton Jones
12 UCLA■	14 FB Eddie Cotton / Bob Apisa
	DL Bubba Smith
	DL Buddy Owens
	DL Harold Lucas
	DL Don Bierowicz
	DL Bob Viney
	LB Ron Goovert
	LB Charles Thornhill
	LB George Webster
	DB Jim Summers / Larry Lukasik
	DB Don Japinga / Sterling Armstrong
	DB Jess Phillips

RUSHING: Jones 165/787y, Apisa 122/666y, Lee 109/411y
PASSING: Juday 89-168/1173y, 7TD, 53.0%
RECEIVING: Washington 40/638y, Jones 26/308y
SCORING: Jones 74pts, Apisa 56pts, Dick Kenney (K) 53pts

1966 9-0-1

28 N. Carolina St.	10 WR Gene Washington
42 Penn State	8 T Joe Przybycki
26 Illinois	10 G Tony Conti
20 Michigan	7 C Lawrence Smith / Ron Ranieri
11 Ohio State	8 G Dave Techlin / Mitch Pruiett
41 Purdue	20 T Jerry West
22 Northwestern	0 TE Allen Brenner
56 Iowa	7 QB Jimmy Raye
37 Indiana	19 HB Dwight Lee / Dick Berlinski
10 Notre Dame	10 HB Clinton Jones / Frank "Muddy" Waters
	FB Bob Apisa / Regis Cavender
	DL Bubba Smith / George Chatlos
	DL Charles Bailey
	DL Pat Gallinagh
	DL Nick Jordan
	DL Phil Hoag
	LB Ron Goovert
	LB Charles Thornhill / Bob Brawley (DL)
	LB George Webster
	DB Sterling Armstrong / Jim Summers
	DB Drake Garrett / Jerry Jones
	DB Jess Phillips

RUSHING: Jones 159/784y, Apisa 86/445y, Raye 122/436y
PASSING: Raye 62-123/1110y, 10TD, 50.4%
RECEIVING: Washington 27/677y, Brenner 22/357y, Lee 7/53y
SCORING: Apisa 54pts, Dick Kenney (K) 45pts,
Cavender & Washington 42pts

1967 3-7

7 Houston	37 WR Frank Foreman
17 Southern Cal	21 T Joe Pryzbycki / Larry Smith
35 Wisconsin	7 G Mitchell Pruiett / Don Baird
34 Michigan	0 C Ron Ranieri / Ted Bohn
0 Minnesota	21 G Tony Conti
12 Notre Dame	24 T Ron Saul / Eddy McLoud (C)
7 Ohio State	21 TE Allen Brenner / Maurice Haynes
13 Indiana	14 QB Jimmy Raye
7 Purdue	21 HB Dwight Lee / Muddy Waters
41 Northwestern	27 HB LaMarr Thomas / Dick Berlinski
	FB Bob Apisa / Regis Cavender
	DL George Chatlos
	DL Charles Bailey
	DL Ken Little / Frank Traylor
	DL Nick Jordan / Don Law
	DL Rich Saul
	LB Robert Lange / Kermit Smith
	LB Robert Super
	DB Sterling Armstrong
	DB Drake Garrett / Bill Ware
	DB Muddy Waters (HB) / Wade Payne
	DB Paul Lawson / Steve Garvey

RUSHING: Lee 116/497y, Thomas 74/311y, Raye 92/247y,
Cavender 34/175y
PASSING: Raye 42-107/580y, 4TD, 39.3%
RECEIVING: Brenner 26/462y, Waters 18/220y,
Foreman/10/135y
SCORING: Lee 42pts, Brenner 28pts

1968 5-5

14 Syracuse	10 WR Frank Foreman / Gordon Bowdell
28 Baylor	10 WR Muddy Waters / Charles Wedemeyer
39 Wisconsin	0 T Dave Van Elst / Gary Nowak
14 Michigan	28 G Don Baird / Mike Tobin
13 Minnesota	14 C Eddy McLoud
21 Notre Dame	17 G Ron Saul / Dave Thomas
20 Ohio State	25 T Craig Wycinsky
22 Indiana	24 TE Bruce Kulesza
0 Purdue	9 QB Bill Triplett / Bill Feraco
31 Northwestern	14 HB Tommy Love / Don Highsmith
	FB Dick Berlinski / Regis Cavender
	DL Wilt Martin / Calvin Fox
	DL Charles Bailey
	DL William Dawson / Jack Zindel
	DL Ron Curl / Michael Young
	DL Rich Saul
	LB Don Law / Gary Palmentier
	LB Mike Hogan / Jay Breslin (DB)
	DB Ken Heft / Clifton Hardy
	DB Harold Phillips
	DB Kermit Smith
	DB Allen Brenner (WR)

RUSHING: Love 177/729y
PASSING: Triplett 47-90/714y, 4TD, 52.2%
RECEIVING: Foreman 29/456y
SCORING: Feraco 42pts

1969 4-6

27 Washington	11 WR Frank Foreman
23 SMU	15 WR Gordon Bowdell / Steve Kough
28 Notre Dame	42 T Dave Van Elst
21 Ohio State	54 G Don Baird / Mike Tobin
23 Michigan	12 C Tom Beard / Morgan Justice
18 Iowa	19 G Ron Saul
0 Indiana	16 T Craig Wycinsky / Vic Mittelberg
13 Purdue	41 TE Bruce Kulesza
-10 Minnesota	14 QB Bill Triplett
39 Northwestern	7 HB Don Highsmith / Eric Allen
	FB Kermit Smith / Earl Anderson
	DL Wilt Martin
	DL Ron Curl / Gary Nowak
	DL Bill Dawson
	DL Wilt Martin / Ron Joseph
	DL Rich Saul / Dave Thomas
	LB Don Law / Errol Roy / Gary Van Elst
	LB Gary Parmentier / Ken Little
	DB Clifton Hardy
	DB Harold Phillips
	DB Brad McLee
	DB Jay Breslin / Ralph Wiebala

RUSHING: Highsmith 209/937y
PASSING: Triplett 37-117/715y, 6TD, 31.6%
RECEIVING: Foreman 22/537y
SCORING: Highsmith 44pts

1970 4-6

16 Washington	42 WR Gordon Bowdell
28 Washington St.	14 WR Randy Davis
0 Notre Dame	29 T Robert McClowry (C) / Jim Nicholson
0 Ohio State	29 G Joe DeLamielleure / Chris King
20 Michigan	34 C Tom Beard
37 Iowa	0 G Mike Tobin
32 Indiana	7 T Vic Mittelberg / Brian McConnell
24 Purdue	14 TE Billy Joe DuPree
13 Minnesota	23 QB Mike Rasmussen / George Mihaiu
20 Northwestern	23 TB Eric Allen / Bill Triplett (QB-WR)
	FB Henry Matthews / Mark Charette
	DL Doug Halliday / Ralph Wielba
	DL Bill Dawson
	DL Ernie Hamilton / Gary Parmentier
	DL Wilt Martin / Duane McLaughlin
	DL Dave Thomas / Jay Breslin
	LB Mike Hogan / Tom Barnum
	LB Gail Clark / Calvin Fox
	DB Doug Barr / Mark Sokoll
	DB Harold Phillips
	DB Brad Van Pelt / Tom Kutchinski
	DB Brad McLee / Clifton Hardy

RUSHING: Allen 186/811y
PASSING: Rasmussen 91-199/1344y, 9TD, 45.7%
RECEIVING: Bowdell 34/495y
SCORING: Allen 60pts

1971 6-5

10 Illinois	0 WR Steve Kough
0 Georgia Tech	10 WR Doug Barr
31 Oregon State	14 T Jim Nicholson / Scott Miltenberger
2 Notre Dame	14 G Joe DeLamielleure
13 Michigan	24 C Errol Roy (G) / Bob Mills
28 Wisconsin	31 G Dennis Macholz / Mark Loper
34 Iowa	3 T Brian McConnell / Bob McClowry
43 Purdue	10 TE Billy Joe DuPree / Tom Brown
17 Ohio State	10 QB Mike Rasmussen / George Mihaiu
40 Minnesota	28 HB Eric Allen / Jesse Williams
7 Northwestern	28 FB Henry Matthews
	DL Doug Halliday / Ernie Hamilton
	DL Wilt Martin / Gary Van Elst
	DL Bill Dawson / Chris King
	DL Ron Curl / Duane McLaughlin
	DL Tom Kronner
	LB Ron Kumiega / Mark Charette
	LB Dan Kulikowski / Ray Nester
	DB Bill Simpson / Paul Hayner
	DB Frank Timmons / Mike Holt
	DB Brad Van Pelt
	DB Mark Niesen / Ralph Wiebala (LB)

RUSHING: Allen 259/1494y,
PASSING: Rasmussen 32-88/642y, 3TD, 36.4%
RECEIVING: DuPree 25/414y
SCORING: Allen 110pts

1972 5-5-1

24 Illinois	0 WR Mike Jones / Mark Grua
16 Georgia Tech	21 T Joe DeLamielleure
6 Southern Cal	51 G Jim Nicholson
0 Notre Dame	16 C Bob McClowry / Bob Mills
0 Michigan	10 G Dennis Macholz
31 Wisconsin	0 T Marvin Roberts / Craig Omerod
6 Iowa	6 TE Billy Joe DuPree / Mike Danielewicz
22 Purdue	12 QB Mark Niesen / George Mihaiu
10 Ohio State	12 HB David Brown
10 Minnesota	14 HB Mike Holt / Damond Mays
24 Northwestern	14 FB Arnold Morgado / Jim Bond
	DL Brian McConnell
	DL John Shinsky / Jim Taubert
	DL Chris King
	DL Gary Van Elst
	DL Ernie Hamilton / Tom Kronner
	LB Gail Clark / Mark Charette
	LB Ray Nester / Ken Alderson
	DB Bill Simpson / Cheadrick Harriatte
	DB Frank Timmons / Bruce Harms
	DB Brad Van Pelt
	DB Paul Hayner

RUSHING: Brown 123/575y
PASSING: Mihaiu 25-55/367y, 0TD, 45.4%
RECEIVING: DuPree 23/406y
SCORING: Niesen 24pts

1973 5-6

10 Northwestern	14 WR Michael Hurd / Mike Danielewisz
14 Syracuse	8 WR Damond Mays / Dane Fortney
21 UCLA	34 T Ray Spencer / John Ruzich
10 Notre Dame	14 G Greg Croxton
0 Michigan	31 C Bob Mills / Charles Ane, Jr.
3 Illinois	6 G Charles Wilson
10 Purdue	7 T Phil Smolinski / Rich Pawlak
21 Wisconsin	0 TE Mike Cobb
0 Ohio State	35 QB Charles Baggett
10 Indiana	9 TB David Brown / Mike Holt
15 Iowa	6 FB Clarence Bullock / Levi Jackson
	DL Tom Kronner / Otto Smith
	DL Jim Taubert
	DL Ron Kumienga / Kim Rowekamp
	DL John Shinsky / Greg Schaum
	DL Mike Duda
	LB Terry McClowry
	LB Ray Nester / Pat McClowry
	DB Mark Niesen
	DB Bruce Harms
	DB Bill Simpson / Tom Hannon
	DB Paul Hayner

RUSHING: Bullock 113/496y
PASSING: Baggett 38-94/516y, 0TD, 46.4%
RECEIVING: Hurd 11/163y
SCORING: Dirk Kryt (K) 38pts

1974 7-3-1

41 Northwestern	7 WR Michael Hurd
19 Syracuse	0 WR Mike Jones / Dane Fortney
14 UCLA	56 T Tony Bruggenthies / William Brown
14 Notre Dame	19 G Greg Croxton
7 Michigan	21 C Charles Ane, Jr.
21 Illinois	21 G Charles Wilson
31 Purdue	7 T Ray Spencer / Greg Bewton
28 Wisconsin	21 TE Mike Cobb
16 Ohio State	13 QB Charles Baggett
19 Indiana	10 TB Rich Baes
60 Iowa	21 FB Levi Jackson / Clarence Bullock
	DL Otto Smith
	DL Jim Taubert
	DL Kim Rowekamp
	DL Greg Schaum
	DL Mike Duda
	LB Terry McClowry
	LB Pat McClowry
	DB John Breslin / Joe Hunt
	DB Mike Imhoff / Ken Jones
	DB Tom Hannon
	DB Tom Graves

RUSHING: Jackson 153/942y, Baes 181/754y, Baggett 137/748y
PASSING: Baggett 48-105/965y, 10TD, 45.7%
RECEIVING: Hurd 18/373y, Jones 12/299y, Fortney 5/119y
SCORING: Baggett 66pts, Baes 56pts, Hans Nielsen (K) 40pts

1975 7-4

0 Ohio State	21 WR Dane Fortney
14 Miami (Ohio)	13 WR Kirk Gibson
37 N. Carolina St.	15 T Tony Bruggenthies
10 Notre Dame	3 G Greg Croxton
6 Michigan	16 C Al Pitts
38 Indiana	15 G Ray Spencer
19 Illinois	21 T Greg Brewton / Tom Cole
10 Purdue	20 TE Mike Cobb
14 Indiana	6 QB Charles Baggett
47 Northwestern	14 TB Rich Baes
27 Iowa	23 FB Levi Jackson / Tyrone Wilson
	DL Rich Washington / Otto Smith
	DL Larry Bethea
	DL Kim Rowekamp (LB) / Tom Standal
	DL Greg Schaum
	DL Craig Fedore / Mike Dean
	LB Paul Ruszinski / Willie Smith
	LB Pat McClowry / Greg Young
	DB John Breslin / Mike Imhoff
	DB Joe Hunt
	DB Tom Hannon
	DB Tom Graves

RUSHING: Jackson 230/1063y, Baggett 171/645y, Baes 135/531y
PASSING: Baggett 42-88/854y, 4TD, 47.7%
RECEIVING: Byrd 10/266y, Cobb 10/151y, Gibson 9/262y
SCORING: Hans Nielsen (K) 52pts, Baggett 42pts, Jackson 30pts

1976 4-6-1

21 Ohio State	49 WR Eugene Byrd / Dan DeRose
21 Wyoming	10 WR Kirk Gibson
31 N. Carolina St.	31 T Jim Hinesly
6 Notre Dame	24 G Tony Marek / Mike Densmore
10 Michigan	42 C Al Pitts
10 Minnesota	14 G Tom Cole
31 Illinois	23 T Tony Bruggenthies / John Malinosky
45 Purdue	13 TE Mike Cobb / Mark Brammer
23 Indiana	0 QB Ed Smith
21 Northwestern	42 TB Rich Baes
17 Iowa	30 FB Levi Jackson / Jim Earley
	DL Angelo Fields / Melvin Land
	DL Craig Lonce / Doug Lantz
	DL Larry Bethea
	LB Otto Smith
	LB Paul Rudzinski / Larry Savage
	LB Dan Bass
	LB Craig Fedore
	DB Ken Jones / Jerome Stanton
	DB Mike Imhoff / Mark Anderson
	DB Tom Hannon
	DB Dave Duda / John Breslin

RUSHING: Baes 187/931y
PASSING: Smith 132-257/1749y, 13TD, 51.3%
RECEIVING: Gibson 39/748y
SCORING: Hans Nielsen (K) 60pts

1977 7-3-1

19 Purdue	14 WR Edgar Wilson
21 Washington St.	23 WR Kirk Gibson / Barry Harris
34 Wyoming	16 T Jim Hinesly
6 Notre Dame	16 G Mike Densmore
14 Michigan	24 C Al Pitts
13 Indiana	13 G Rod Strata / Jim Sciarini
9 Wisconsin	7 T John Malinosky
49 Illinois	20 TE Mark Brammer
29 Minnesota	10 QB Ed Smith
44 Northwestern	3 TB Leroy McGee / Bruce Reeves
22 Iowa	16 FB Jim Earley
	DL Melvin Land
	DL Bernard Hay / Kim Rowekamp
	DL Larry Bethea
	LB Mike Dean
	LB Paul Rudzinski
	LB Dan Bass
	LB Craig Fedore
	DB Mike Imhoff / Alan Davis
	DB Jerome Stanton / Jim Burroughs
	DB Mark Anderson
	DB Tom Graves

RUSHING: McGee 162/720y, Earley 109/668y, Reeves 53/266y
PASSING: Smith 117-240/1731y, 10TD, 48.8%
RECEIVING: Brammer 27/385y, Wilson/23/418y, Gibson 22/531y
SCORING: Hans Nielsen (K) 78pts, McGee & Gibson 36pts

1978 8-3

14 Purdue	21 WR Eugene Byrd
49 Syracuse	21 WR Kirk Gibson
9 Southern Cal	30 T Jim Hinesly
25 Notre Dame	29 G Mike Densmore
24 Michigan	15 C Matt Foster
49 Indiana	14 G Rod Strata
55 Wisconsin	2 T Craig Lonce
59 Illinois	19 TE Mark Brammer
33 Minnesota	9 QB Ed Smith / Bert Vaughn
52 Northwestern	3 TB Steve Smith / Larry McGee
42 Iowa	7 FB Lonnie Middleton
	DL Angelo Fields
	DL Bernard Hay
	DL Melvin Land
	LB Larry Savage
	LB Mike Decker / Steve Otis
	LB Dan Bass
	LB John McCormick /Johnny Lee Haynes
	DB Jerome Stanton / Jim Burroughs
	DB Mike Marshall
	DB Mark Anderson
	DB Tom Graves

RUSHING: S. Smith 115/772y, McGee 78/465y, Derek Hughes 42/408y
PASSING: E. Smith 169-292/2226y, 20TD, 57.9%
RECEIVING: Byrd 43/718y, Gibson 42/806y, Brammer 33/360y
SCORING: Morten Andersen (K) 73pts, Gibson 54pts, S. Smith 48pts

1979 5-6

33 Illinois	16 WR Samson Howard / Jim Williams
41 Oregon	17 WR Eugene Byrd
24 Miami (Ohio)	21 T Angelo Fields
3 Notre Dame	27 G Mike Densmore / Marv Mantos
7 Michigan	21 C Matt Foster
29 Wisconsin	38 G Rod Strata / Jeff Wiska
7 Purdue	14 T Ted Grabenhorst
0 Ohio State	42 TE Mark Brammer / Al Kimichik
42 Northwestern	7 QB Bert Vaughn / Bryan Clark
31 Minnesota	17 TB Steve Smith / Derek Hughes
23 Iowa	33 FB Lonnie Middleton
	DL Jack Kirkling / Tanya Webb
	DL Bernard Hay
	DL Pat Mitten / Ike Griffin
	LB Larry Savage
	LB Dan Bass
	LB Steve Otis / Mike Decker
	LB John McCormick
	DB Van Williams / Carl Williams
	DB Jim Burroughs / Chris Van Pelt
	DB Mark Anderson
	DB Alan Davis / Rick Milhizer

RUSHING: Smith 204/972y, Hughes 118/626y, Bruce Reeves (TB) 43/213y
PASSING: Clark 64-131/800y, 4TD, 48.9%, Vaughn 57-128/729y, 4 TDs, 44.5%
RECEIVING: Byrd 30/559y, Brammer 23/288y, Williams 16/180y
SCORING: Hughes 66pts, Morten Andersen (K) 58pts, Byrd 26pts

1980 3-8

17 Illinois	20 WR Ted Jones / Jim Williams
7 Oregon	35 WR Otis Grant / Tony Gilbert
33 W. Michigan	7 T Jeff Wiska
21 Notre Dame	26 G Marv Mantos / Joe Jacquemain
23 Michigan	27 C Tom Piette
7 Wisconsin	17 G Rod Strata
25 Purdue	36 T Dave Whittle / Mike Densmore (G)
16 Ohio State	48 TE Al Kimichik
42 Northwestern	10 QB John Leister / Bert Vaughn
30 Minnesota	12 TB Steve Smith
0 Iowa	41 FB Andy Schramm / Tony Ellis
	DL Joe Stevens / Ron Mitchem
	DL Johnny Lee Haynes
	DL Bernard Hay / Calvin Perkins
	DL Smiley Creswell
	LB George Cooper
	LB James Neely / Terry Bailey
	LB John McCormick
	DB Chris Van Pelt / Mike Marshall
	DB Nate Hannah / Van Williams
	DB Thomas Morris / Tim Cunningham
	DB Carl Williams / Rick Milhizer

RUSHING: Smith 154/667y
PASSING: Leister 103-247/1569y, 10TD, 41.7%
RECEIVING: Jones 40/568y
SCORING: Morten Andersen (K) 57pts

1981 5-6

17 Illinois	27 WR Daryl Turner / Ted Jones
13 Ohio State	27 WR Otis Grant
10 Bowling Green	7 T Jeff Wiska / Jack Kirkling
7 Notre Dame	20 G Joe Jacquemain
20 Michigan	38 C Tom Piette / Ken Stockwell
33 Wisconsin	14 G Marv Mantos
26 Purdue	27 T Walter Schramm
26 Indiana	3 TE Al Kimichik / Terry Tanker
61 Northwestern	14 QB Bryan Clark / John Leister
43 Minnesota	36 TB Lance Hawkins / Aaron Roberts
7 Iowa	36 FB Darrin McClelland / Tony Ellis
	DL Smiley Creswell
	DL Howard McAdoo / Calvin Perkins
	DL Johnny Lee Haynes
	DL Joe Stevens / Isaac Griffin
	LB George Cooper
	LB Steve Maidlow / Terry Bailey
	LB Carl Banks
	DB Jim Burroughs / Chris Van Pelt
	DB Carter Kamana / Nate Hannah
	DB Thomas Morris
	DB Tim Cunningham / Carl Williams

RUSHING: Roberts 94/461y, Hawkins 87/321y, James Hodo (TB) 48/188y
PASSING: Clark 109-204/1521y, 14TD, 53.6%, Leister 90-186/1097y, 5TD, 48.4%
RECEIVING: Jones 44/624y, Kimichik 39/383y, Turner 31/635y
SCORING: Morten Andersen (K) 73pts, Jones & Grant 30pts

1982 2-9

16 Illinois	23 WR Daryl Turner / Ted Jones
10 Ohio State	31 WR Otis Grant
22 Miami	25 T Jack Kirkling
3 Notre Dame	11 G Randy Lark
17 Michigan	31 C Ken Stockwell / Tom Piette
23 Wisconsin	24 G Marv Mantos
21 Purdue	24 T Walter Schramm
22 Indiana	14 TE Thomas Robinson / Terry Tanker
24 Northwestern	28 QB John Leister / Dave Yarema
26 Minnesota	7 TB Tony Ellis / Aaron Roberts
18 Iowa	24 FB Darrin McClelland / Marcus Toney
	DL Joe Stevens
	DL Smiley Creswell
	DL Calvin Perkins/Joe Curran/J.Woj'h'ski
	DL Howard McAdoo / Tom Allan
	DL Carl Banks
	LB Jim Neely / Greg Lauble
	LB Jim Morrissey / Steve Maidlow
	DB Chris Van Pelt / Lonnie Young
	DB Carter Kamana / Nate Hannah
	DB Darryl Dixon / James Smith
	DB Tim Cunningham / Carl Williams

RUSHING: Ellis 179/671y, Roberts 68/256y, McClelland 55/221y
PASSING: Leister 119-251/1321y, 4TD, 47.4%, Yarema 46-80/528y, 4TD, 57.5%
RECEIVING: Grant 36/547y, Jones 34/486y, McClelland 26/144y
SCORING: Ralf Mojsiejenko (K) 58pts, Ellis 42pts, Roberts 30pts

1983 4-6-1

23 Colorado	17 WR Daryl Turner / Joel Waller
28 Notre Dame	23 WR John Hurt/Larry Jackson/Mark Ingr'm
10 Illinois	20 T Scott Auer
29 Purdue	29 G Randy Lark / John Wojciechowski
0 Michigan	42 C Mark Napolitan / Ken Stockwell
12 Indiana	24 G Pat Shurmur / Tyrone Rhodes
11 Ohio State	21 T Jim Bob Lamb / Mitch Wachman (G)
34 Minnesota	10 TE Butch Rolle / Terry Tanker
9 Northwestern	3 QB Clark Brown / Dave Yarema
6 Iowa	12 TB Bobby Morse / Aaron Roberts
0 Wisconsin	32 FB Carl Butler / Keith Gates
	DL Tom Allan / Leroy Shepherd
	DL Jim Rinella / Joe Curran
	DL David Wolff
	DL Kelly Quinn
	LB Derek Bunch / Thomas Tyree
	LB Jim Morrissey
	LB Carl Banks / Warren Lester
	DB Nate Hannah / Lonnie Young
	DB Terry Lewis
	DB Phil Parker / Paul Bobbitt
	DB Tim Cunningham / Darryl Dixon

RUSHING: Butler 126/549y, Gates 134/542y, Roberts 49/145y
PASSING: Brown 82-141/837y, 4TD, 58.2%, Yarema 33-52/383y, 3TD, 63.5%
RECEIVING: Turner 28/549y, Morse 21/151y, Rolle 16/169y
SCORING: Ralf Mojsiejenko 46pts, Turner 30pts, Gates 24pts

MICHIGAN STATE

1984 6-6
24 Colorado
20 Notre Dame
7 Illinois
10 Purdue
19 Michigan
13 Indiana
20 Ohio State
20 Minnesota
27 Northwestern
17 Iowa
10 Wisconsin
6 Army■

21 WR Larry Jackson / Dempsey Norman
24 WR Mark Ingram / Bob Wasczenski
40 T Doug Rogers
13 G Alan Akana / Jeff Stump
7 C Mark Napolitan
6 G John Wojciechowski
23 T Steve Bogdalek
13 TE Butch Rolle / Veno Belk
10 QB Dave Yarema
16 TB Carl Butler / Lorenzo White
20 FB Keith Gates / Bobby Morse
10 DL Kelly Quinn
DL Jim Rinella / Joe Curran
DL David Wolff / Doug Rogers
DL Tom Allan/John Jones/Greg Thornton
LB Anthony Bell / Derek Bunch
LB Jim Morrissey
LB Thomas Tyree / Tim Moore
DB Lonnie Young
DB Terry Lewis
DB Phil Parker
DB Paul Bobbitt

RUSHING: White 142/616y, Butler 149/581y, Gates 79/362y
PASSING: Yarema 119-222/1477y, 11TD, 53.6%
RECEIVING: Ingram 22/499y, Belk 20/220y, Gates 20/152y
SCORING: Ralf Mojsiejenko (K) 45pts, Butler 36pts, Ingram 26pts

1985 7-5
12 Arizona State
10 Notre Dame
7 W. Michigan
31 Iowa
0 Michigan
17 Illinois
31 Purdue
31 Minnesota
35 Indiana
32 Northwestern
41 Wisconsin
14 Georgia Tech■

3 WR Andre Rison
27 WR Mark Ingram
3 T Tony Mandarich
35 G Doug Rogers / Jeff Stump
31 C Pat Shurmur / Mitch Wachman
31 G John Wojciechowski
24 T Steve Bogdalek
26 TE Butch Rolle / Veno Belk
16 QB Dave Yarema / Bobby McAllister
0 TB Lorenzo White / Craig Johnson
7 FB Bobby Morse / Keith Gates
17 DL Kelly Quinn / Mark Beaudoin
DL Mark Nichols
DL Joe Curran / Dave Wolff
DL John Jones / Warren Lester
LB Anthony Bell / Rob Stradley
LB Shane Bullough
LB Tim Moore / Kurt Larson
DB Todd Krumm
DB Ron Rowe / Keith Fisher
DB Phil Parker
DB Dean Altobelli / Paul Bobbitt

RUSHING: White 419/2066y, Johnson 32/225y, Morse 40/144y
PASSING: Yarema 66-116/840y, 10TD, 56.9%, McAllister 40-88/577y, 2TD, 45.5%
RECEIVING: Ingram 34/745y, Morse 25/182y, Rison 19/280y
SCORING: White 102pts, Chris Caudell (K) 47pts, Ingram 30pts

1986 6-5
17 Arizona State
20 Notre Dame
45 W. Michigan
21 Iowa
6 Michigan
29 Illinois
37 Purdue
52 Minnesota
14 Indiana
21 Northwestern
23 Wisconsin

20 WR Andre Rison / Willie Bouyer
15 WR Mark Ingram
10 T Tony Mandarich
24 G Vince Tata / Doug Rogers
27 C Pat Shurmur
21 G Mark Hill / Mel Richendollar (T)
3 T David Houle
23 TE Mike Sargent / Rich Gicewicz
17 QB Dave Yarema
24 TB Lorenzo White / Craig Johnson
13 FB Bobby Morse
DL Joe Bergin / Jim Szymanski
DL Mark Nichols
DL Dave Wolff / Travis Davis
DL John Budde
LB Tim Moore
LB Shane Bullough
LB Rob Stradley / Kurt Larson
DB John Miller
DB Todd Krumm / Ron Rowe
DB Maurice Chamberlain / Paul Bobbitt
DB Dean Altobelli

RUSHING: White 164/633y, Morse 87/398y, Johnson 78/345y
PASSING: Yarema 200-297/2581y, 16 TDs, 67.3%
RECEIVING: Rison 54/966y, Morse 39/282y, Ingram 35/672y
SCORING: Chris Caudell (K) 61pts

1987 9-2-1
27 Southern Cal
8 Notre Dame
3 Florida State
19 Iowa
17 Michigan
38 Northwestern
14 Illinois
13 Ohio State
45 Purdue
27 Indiana
30 Wisconsin
20 Southern Cal■

13 WR Andre Rison
31 WR Willie Bouyer
31 T Tony Mandarich
14 G Bob Kula
11 C Pat Shurmur
0 G Vince Tata
14 T David Houle / Kevin Robbins
7 TE Mike Sargent / Rich Gicewicz
3 QB Bobby McAllister
3 TB Lorenzo White / Blake Ezor
9 FB James Moore / Joe Pugh
17 DL Joe Bergin / Jim Szymanski
DL Mark Nichols
DL Travis Davis / Chris Soehnlen
DL John Budde
LB Tim Moore / Carlos Jenkins
LB Percy Snow
LB Kurt Larson / Dixon Edwards
DB Derrick Reed
DB Harlon Barnett / Lenier Payton
DB Todd Krumm
DB John Miller

RUSHING: White 357/1572y, Ezor 133/617y, McAllister 136/298y
PASSING: McAllister 71-139/1171y, 6TD, 51.1%
RECEIVING: Rison 34/785y, White 12/115y, Sargent 10/83y
SCORING: White 96pts, John Langeloh (K) 79pts, Rison 30pts

1988 6-5-1
13 Rutgers
3 Notre Dame
7 Florida State
10 Iowa
3 Michigan
36 Northwestern
28 Illinois
20 Ohio State
48 Purdue
38 Indiana
36 Wisconsin
27 Georgia■

17 WR Andre Rison / Brian Smolinski
20 WR Willie Bouyer / Bernard Wilson
30 T Tony Mandarich
10 G Bob Kula (T) / Eric Moten
17 C David Martin
3 G Vince Tata
21 T Kevin Robbins
10 TE Rich Gicewicz / Duane Young
3 QB Bobby McAllister
12 TB Blake Ezor / Hyland Hickson
0 FB Steve Montgomery / James Moore
34 DL Matt Vanderbeek / Chris Willertz
DL Jason Ridgeway / Cliff Confer
DL Travis Davis
DL John Budde / Chris Soehnlen
LB Carlos Jenkins
LB Percy Snow
LB Kurt Larson / Dixon Edwards
DB Derrick Reed / Alan Haller
DB Ventson Donelson
DB Lenier Payton / Harlon Barnett
DB John Miller / Mike Iaquaniello

RUSHING: Ezor 322/1496y, Hickson 74/385y, McAllister 105/351y
PASSING: McAllister 80-154/1406y, 9TD, 51.9%
RECEIVING: Rison 39/961y, Montgomery 10/76y, Young 8/122y
SCORING: John Langeloh (K) 83pts, Ezor 66pts, Rison 48pts

1989 8-4
49 Miami (Ohio)
13 Notre Dame
20 Miami
17 Iowa
7 Michigan
10 Illinois
28 Purdue
51 Indiana
21 Minnesota
76 Northwestern
31 Wisconsin
33 Hawaii■

0 WR James Bradley / Brian Smolinski
21 WR Courtney Hawkins
26 T Bob Kula
14 G Eric Moten
10 C Jeff Pearson
14 G Matt Keller / Roosevelt Wagner
21 T Jim Johnson
20 TE Duane Young / Kurt Prins
7 QB Dan Enos
14 TB Blake Ezor / Tico Duckett
3 FB Steve Montgomery / Rob Roy
13 DL Matt Vanderbeek / Jim Szymanski
DL Tim Ridinger / Bobby Wilson
DL Travis Davis
DL Chris Willertz / Bill Johnson
LB Carlos Jenkins / Tony Briningstool
LB Percy Snow / Brian Jones
LB Dixon Edwards Chuck Bullough
DB Alan Haller / Todd Murray
DB Ventson Donelson
DB Mike Iaquaniello
DB Harlon Barnett / Freddie Wilson

RUSHING: Ezor 267/1299y, Duckett 103/593y, Hyland Hickson (TB) 76/325y
PASSING: Enos 153-240/2066y, 9TD, 63.8%
RECEIVING: Hawkins 60/1080y, Bradley 22/437y, Young 15/130y
SCORING: Ezor 114pts, John Langeloh (K) 72pts, Enos & Hawkins 36pts

1990 8-3-1
23 Syracuse
19 Notre Dame
34 Rutgers
7 Iowa
28 Michigan
13 Illinois
55 Purdue
45 Indiana
28 Minnesota
29 Northwestern
14 Wisconsin
17 Southern Cal■

23 WR James Bradley / Brian Smolinski
20 WR Courtney Hawkins
10 T Toby Heaton / Roosevelt Wagner
12 G Eric Moten
27 C Jeff Pearson
15 G Matt Keller
33 T Jim Johnson
20 TE Duane Young / Kurt Prins
16 QB Dan Enos
22 TB Tico Duckett / Hyland Hickson
9 FB Rob Roy
16 DL Cliff Confer / Mike Edwards
DL Bobby Wilson
DL Bill Reese
DL Bill Johnson
LB Carlos Jenkins / Rob Fredrickson
LB Chuck Bullough / Brian Jones
LB Dixon Edwards
DB Eddie Brown / Todd Murray
DB Alan Haller / Myron Bell
DB Mike Iaquaniello
DB Freddie Wilson / Steve Wasylk

RUSHING: Duckett 257/1394y, Hickson 234/1196y, Enos 91/133y
PASSING: Enos 137-220/1677y, 4TD, 62.3%
RECEIVING: Bradley 32/517y, Hawkins 31/474y, Hickson 14/151y
SCORING: Hickson 90pts, John Langeloh (K) 74pts, Duckett 66pts

1991 3-8
3 C. Michigan
10 Notre Dame
7 Rutgers
0 Indiana
28 Michigan
20 Minnesota
17 Ohio State
13 Northwestern
20 Wisconsin
17 Purdue
27 Illinois

20 WR Mark MacFarland / Mill Coleman
49 WR Courtney Hawkins / Tim Bryan
14 T Shane Hannah
31 G Toby Heaton
45 C Chris Piwowarczyk
12 G Roosevelt Wagner / Brett Lorius
27 T Jim Johnson
16 TE Mitch Lyons / Kurt Prins
9 QB Jim Miller / Bret Johnson
27 TB Tico Duckett / Sebastian Small
24 FB Tony Rollin / Brice Abrams
DL John MacNeill
DL Ed O'Bradovich / Aaron Jackson
DL Bill Reese / Willie Hill
DL Bill Johnson / Eric White
LB Matt Christensen / Rob Fredrickson
LB Chuck Bullough
LB Ernest Steward
DB Brian Winters / Todd Murray
DB Alan Haller / Stan Callender
DB Corey Keyes / Brian Vooletich
DB Myron Bell / Steve Wasylk

RUSHING: Duckett 272/1204y, Small 65/215y
PASSING: Miller 130-218/1368y, 6TD, 59.6%
RECEIVING: Hawkins 47/656y, Duckett 17/136y, 3 with 16
SCORING: Jim DelVerne (K) 52pts, Hawkins & Duckett 30pts

1992 5-6
20 C. Michigan
31 Notre Dame
0 Boston College
42 Indiana
10 Michigan
20 Minnesota
17 Ohio State
27 Northwestern
26 Wisconsin
35 Purdue
10 Illinois

24 WR Mark MacFarland / Demetrice Martin
52 WR Mill Coleman (QB) / Napoleon Outlaw
14 T Shane Hannah
31 G Toby Heaton
35 C Mark Birchmeier / Jeff Graham
15 G Bob Denton / Brett Lorius
27 T Brian DeMarco / Colin Cronin
26 TE Mitch Lyons / Bob Organ
10 QB Jim Miller / Bret Johnson
13 TB Tico Duckett / Craig Thomas
14 FB Brice Abrams / Tony Rollin
DL Juan Hammonds
DL Robert McBride / Dale Person
DL Bill Reese / Aaron Jackson
DL Mike Edwards / Rich Glover
LB Matt Christensen
LB Ty Hallock
LB Rob Fredrickson
DB Stan Callender
DB Myron Bell
DB Damian Manson / Brian Winters
DB Steve Wasylk

RUSHING: Duckett 204/1021y, Thomas 155/887y, Coleman 23/62y
PASSING: Miller 122-191/1400y, 2TD, 63.9%
RECEIVING: Coleman 37/586y, Lyons 36/400y, McFarland 16/230y
SCORING: Thomas 90pts, Bill Stoyanovich (K) 50pts, Duckett 42pts

1993 6-6

31 Kansas	14 WR Napoleon Outlaw / Nigea Carter
14 Notre Dame	36 WR Mill Coleman
48 C. Michigan	34 T Shane Hannah
17 Michigan	7 G Colin Cronin
21 Ohio State	28 C Mark Birchmeier
24 Iowa	10 G Brett Lorius
0 Indiana	10 T Brian DeMarco
31 Northwestern	29 TE Bob Organ / Jay Greene
27 Purdue	24 QB Jim Miller
37 Penn State	38 TB Craig Thomas / Duane Goulbourne
20 Wisconsin	41 FB Brice Abrams / Scott Greene
7 Louisville■	18 DL Juan Hammonds
	DL Aaron Jackson / Dale Person
	DL Yakini Allen / Zeb Jones
	DL Rich Glover / Robert McBride
	LB Matt Christensen
	LB Reggie Garnett / Greg Anderson
	LB Rob Frederickson / Ricardo Jackson
	DB Stan Callender
	DB Myron Bell / Demetrice Martin
	DB Steve Wasylk / Aldi Henry
	DB Damian Manson

RUSHING: Goulbourne 196/973y, Thomas 193/889y
PASSING: Miller 215-336/2269y, 9TD, 64.0%
RECEIVING: Coleman 48/671y, Organ 33/306y,
S. Greene 31/306y
SCORING: Bill Stoyanovich (K) 65pts, Thomas 54pts,
Goulbourne 48pts

1994 5-6

10 Kansas	17 WR Nigea Carter / Muhsin Muhammad
20 Notre Dame	21 WR Mill Coleman / Derrick Mason
45 Miami (Ohio)	10 T Shane Hannah / Flozell Adams
29 Wisconsin	10 G Colin Cronin
20 Michigan	40 C Mark Birchmeier
7 Ohio State	23 G Bob Denton / Don Walker
14 Iowa	19 T Brian DeMarco
27 Indiana	21 TE Bob Organ / Josh Keur
35 Northwestern	17 QB Tony Banks
42 Purdue	30 TB Duane Goulbourne / Marc Renaud
31 Penn State	59 FB Scott Greene
	DL Juan Hammonds / Robert McBride
	DL Aaron Jackson
	DL Yakini Allen / Dale Person
	LB Matt Christensen
	LB Yakini Allen
	LB Reggie Garnett
	LB Ike Reese
	DB Stan Callender
	DB Demetrice Martin
	DB Robert Shurelds / Luke Bencie
	DB Damian Manson / Brian Echols

RUSHING: Goulbourne 214/930y, Renaud 96/529,
Greene 68/375y
PASSING: Banks 145-238/2040y, 11TD, 60.9%
RECEIVING: Greene 42/452y, Coleman 25/400y, Carter 16/430y
SCORING: Chris Gardner (K) 72pts,

1995 6-5-1

10 Nebraska	50 WR Derrick Mason / Nigea Carter
30 Louisville	7 WR Muhsin Muhammad
35 Purdue	35 T Flozell Adams
25 Boston College	21 G Brian Mosallam
7 Iowa	21 C Matt Beard
27 Illinois	21 G Tony Popovski / Scott Shaw
34 Minnesota	31 T Bob Denton / Dave Mudge
14 Wisconsin	45 TE Josh Keur / Marcus Chapman
28 Michigan	25 QB Tony Banks
31 Indiana	13 TB Marc Renaud / Tyrone Crenshaw
20 Penn State	24 FB Scott Greene / Travis Reece
26 LSU■	45 DL Jabbar Threats / Tim Laws (LB)
	DL Robert McBride / Desmond Thomas
	DL Chris Smith / Guy Reid
	DL Yakini Allen / Dimitrius Underwood
	LB Carl Reaves / Dwayne Hawkins
	LB Reggie Garnett
	LB Ike Reese
	DB Ray Hill / Amp Campbell
	DB Demetrice Martin / Brian Echols
	DB Sorie Kanu
	DB Marvin Wright

RUSHING: Renaud 200/978y, Greene 117/542y,
Crenshaw 21/131y
PASSING: Banks 134-214/1741y, 8TD, 62.6%
RECEIVING: Mason 47/713y, Muhammad 41/696y,
Greene 33/291y
SCORING: Greene 96pts, Chris Gardner (K) 67pts

1996 6-6

52 Purdue	14 WR Nigea Carter
14 Nebraska	55 WR Derrick Mason
20 Louisville	30 T Flozell Adams
47 E. Michigan	0 G Brian Mosallam
30 Iowa	37 C Matt Beard
42 Illinois	14 G Scott Shaw
27 Minnesota	9 T Dave Mudge
30 Wisconsin	13 TE Josh Keur / Kyle Rance
29 Michigan	45 QB Todd Schultz / Bill Burke
38 Indiana	15 TB Duane Goulbourne / Sedrick Irvin
29 Penn State	32 FB Garrett Gould
0 Stanford■	38 DL Courtney Ledyard / Pete Govens
	DL Robert Newkirk
	DL Chris Smith / Desmond Thomas
	DL Dimitrius Underwood
	LB Mike Austin/ Tyrone Garland
	LB Reggie Garnett / Dwayne Hawkins
	LB Ike Reese
	DB Ray Hill / Aric Morris
	DB Amp Campbell
	DB Sorie Kanu / Shawn Wright
	DB Lemar Marshall / Dan Hackenbracht

RUSHING: Irvin 237/1067y, Goulbourne 213/942y,
Tyrone Crenshaw (TB) 32/152y
PASSING: Schultz 130-209/1693y, 7TD, 62.2%
RECEIVING: Mason 53/865y, Irvin 40/337y, Carter 33/546y
SCORING: Irvin 108pts

1997 7-5

42 W. Michigan	10 WR Gari Scott
51 Memphis	21 WR Octavis Long / Lavaile Richardson
23 Notre Dame	7 T Flozell Adams
31 Minnesota	10 G Shaun Mason
38 Indiana	6 C Jason Strayhorn
17 Northwestern	19 G Scott Shaw / Mike Schutz
7 Michigan	23 T Dave Mudge / Casey Jensen
13 Ohio State	37 TE Josh Keur / Kyle Rance / Brad Rainco
21 Purdue	22 QB Todd Schultz / Bill Burke
27 Illinois	17 TB Sedrick Irvin / Billy Greene
49 Penn State	14 FB Garrett Gould / Leroy McFadden
23 Washington■	51 DL Robaire Smith
	DL Robert Newkirk / Pete Govens
	DL Desmond Thomas / Artie Steinmetz
	DL Dimitrius Underwood / Jace Saylor
	LB Courtney Ledyard / Dwayne Hawkins
	LB Mike Austin / T.J. Turner
	LB Ike Reese / Wes Kammer
	DB Ray Hill / Richard Newsome
	DB Amp Campbell
	DB Sorie Kanu
	DB Aric Morris / Lemar Marshall

RUSHING: Irvin 231/1211y, Mark Renaud (TB) 133/740y,
McFadden 72/322y
PASSING: Schultz 163-275/1783y, 16TD, 59.3%
RECEIVING: Irvin 39/339y, Scott 36/566y, Keur 34/355y
SCORING: Irvin 78pts

1998 6-6

16 Colorado State	23 WR Plaxico Burress / Lavaile Richardson
14 Oregon	48 WR Gari Scott / Herb Haygood
45 Notre Dame	23 T Dave Sucura
17 Michigan	29 G Paul Harker
38 C. Michigan	7 C Jason Strayhorn / Mike Neal
38 Indiana	31 G Casey Jensen
18 Minnesota	19 T Greg Robinson-Randall / Matt Bonito
29 Northwestern	5 TE Chris Baker
28 Ohio State	24 QB Bill Burke
24 Purdue	25 TB Sedrick Irvin / Lloyd Clemons
41 Illinois	9 FB Garett Gould / Leroy McFadden
28 Penn State	51 DL Jace Saylor
	DL Robert Newkirk
	DL Pete Govens / Desmond Thomas
	DL Robaire Smith / Julian Peterson
	LB Courtney Ledyard / Sean Banks
	LB T.J. Turner
	LB Josh Thornhill / Shawn Wright
	DB Renaldo Hill
	DB Lemar Marshall / Amp Campbel
	DB Sorie Kanu
	DB Aric Morris / Richard Newsome

RUSHING: Irvin 272/1230y, Clemons 73/364y,
Shawn Foster (TB) 22/126y
PASSING: Burke 195-358/2595y, 19TD, 54.5%
RECEIVING: Burress 65/1013y, Scott 58/843y, Irvin 28/210y
SCORING: Paul Edinger (K) 94pts, Irvin 60pts, Burress 48pts

1999 10-2

27 Oregon	20 WR Plaxico Burress / Lavaile Richardson
51 E. Michigan	7 WR Gari Scott / Herb Haygood
23 Notre Dame	13 T Siitupe Peko
27 Illinois	10 G Dave Sucura
49 Iowa	3 C Casey Jensen / Mike Neal
34 Michigan	31 G Shaun Mason
28 Purdue	52 T Greg Robinson-Randall / Matt Bonito
10 Wisconsin	40 TE Chris Baker / Ivory McCoy
23 Ohio State	7 QB Bill Burke
34 Northwestern	0 TB Lloyd Clemons / T.J. Duckett
35 Penn State	28 FB Dawan Moss
37 Florida ■	34 DL Nick Myers / Hubert Thompson
	DL Josh Shaw / Jace Saylor
	DL Desmond Thomas
	DL Robaire Smith
	LB Julian Peterson / Pierre Wilson
	LB T.J. Turner / Mike Austin
	LB Josh Thornhill / Shawn Wright
	DB Amp Campbell / Cedric Henry
	DB Renaldo Hill
	DB Richard Newsome
	DB Aric Morris

RUSHING: Clemons 191/959y, Duckett 118/606y,
Shawn Foster (TB) 39/197y
PASSING: Burke 173-312/2214y, 20TD, 55.4%
RECEIVING: Burress 66/1142y, Baker 38/391y, Scott 30/483y
SCORING: Paul Edinger (K) 103pts, Burress 72pts, Duckett 62pts

2000 5-6

34 Marshall	24 WR Laveile Richardson
13 Missouri	10 WR Herb Haygood / Shawn Foster
27 Notre Dame	21 T Siitupe Peko (C) / Ulish Booker
17 Northwestern	37 G Dave Sucura
16 Iowa	21 C Brian Ottney
10 Wisconsin	17 G Shaun Mason
0 Michigan	14 T Matt Bonito
14 Illinois	10 TE Chris Baker / Ivory McCoy
13 Ohio State	27 QB Jeff Smoker / Ryan Van Dyke
30 Purdue	10 TB T.J. Duckett / Little John Flowers
23 Penn State	42 FB Dawan Moss
	DL Nick Myers (LB) / Jabari Hendricks
	DL Jace Saylor
	DL Josh Shaw / Kyle Rasmussen
	DL Greg Taplin / Dimitry Bernard
	LB T.J. Turner / Richard Brown (DB)
	LB Josh Thornhill
	LB Drew Young / Matt Dawes
	DB Cedric Henry / DeMario Suggs
	DB Renaldo Hill
	DB Richard Newsome / Lorenzo Guess
	DB Thomas Wright / Duron Bryan

RUSHING: Duckett 240/1353y, Flowers 54/281y,
Tyrell Dorch (TB) 36/210y
PASSING: Smoker 103-197/1365y, 6TD, 52.3%,
Van Dyke 70-122/796y, 4TD, 57.4%
RECEIVING: Richardson 40/459y, Haygood 35/539y,
Baker 33/461y
SCORING: David Schaefer (K) 51pts, Duckett 42pts, Moss 18pts

2001 7-5

35 C. Michigan	21 WR Charles Rogers
17 Notre Dame	10 WR Herb Haygood / B.J. Lovett
26 Northwestern	27 T Ulish Booker
31 Iowa	28 G Joe Tate / Joe Patrick
19 Minnesota	28 C Brian Ottney
42 Wisconsin	28 G William Whitticker
26 Michigan	24 T Steve Stewart / Sean Poole
28 Indiana	37 TE Chris Baker
14 Purdue	24 QB Jeff Smoker / Ryan Van Dyke
37 Penn State	42 TB T.J. Duckett / Little John Flowers
55 Missouri	7 FB Dawan Moss
44 Fresno State■	35 DL Josh Shaw / Greg Taplin
	DL Kyle Rasmussen
	DL Kevin Vickerson
	DL Nick Myers / Clifford Dukes
	LB Mike Labinjo / Ivory McCoy
	LB Josh Thornhill
	LB Ronald Stanley / Mark Goebel
	DB Cedric Henry
	DB Broderick Nelson / DeMario Suggs
	DB Lorenzo Guess / Robert Flagg
	DB Thomas Wright

RUSHING: Duckett 263/1420y, Flowers 69/296y, Moss 25/93y
PASSING: Smoker 166-262/2579y, 21TD, 63.4%,
Van Dyke 37-67/569y, 4TD, 55.2%
RECEIVING: Rogers 67/1470y, Hagood 57/808y, Baker 40/548y
SCORING: Rogers 96pts, Duckett 78pts, Dave Raynor (K) 60pts

2002 4-8

56 E. Michigan	7 WR Charles Rogers
27 Rice	10 WR B.J. Lovett
22 California	46 WR Ziehl Kavanaght / Robert Strickland
17 Notre Dame	21 T Ulish Booker
39 Northwestern	24 G Joe Tate
16 Iowa	44 C Brian Ottney
7 Minnesota	28 G Paul Harker / William Whittiker
24 Wisconsin	42 T Steve Stewart
3 Michigan	49 TE Eric Knott / Jason Randall
56 Indiana	21 QB Damon Dowdell / Jeff Smoker
42 Purdue	45 RB David Richard / Jaren Hayes
7 Penn State	61 DL Greg Taplin
	DL Kyle Rasmussen
	DL Kevin Vickerson
	DL Clifford Dukes / Lonnie Simmons
	LB Monquiz Wedlow
	LB Ronald Stanley / Mark Goebel
	LB Mike Labinjo
	DB Cedric Henry / DeMario Suggs
	DB Broderick Nelson / Roderick Maples
	DB Jason Harmon / Robert Flagg
	DB Thomas Wright

RUSHING: Richard 133/654y, Dawan Moss (RB) 125/592y, Hayes 61/340y
PASSING: Smoker 114-203/1593y, 13TD, 56.2%, Dowdell 92-165/1097y, 10TD, 55.8%
RECEIVING: Rogers 68/1351y, Knott 35/349y, Lovett 33/383y
SCORING: Rogers 78pts, Dave Raynor (K) 64pts, Richard 30pts

2003 8-5

26 W. Michigan	21 WR Matt Trannon / Ziehl Kavanaght
44 Rutgers	28 WR Aaron Alexander / Kyle Brown
19 Louisiana Tech	20 WR Agim Shabaj
22 Notre Dame	16 T Stefon Wheeler / Sean Poole
20 Iowa	10 G Joe Tate
31 Indiana	3 C Chris Morris
49 Illinois	14 G Paul Harker / William Whittiker
44 Minnesota	38 T Steve Stewart
20 Michigan	27 TE Eric Knott / Jason Randall
23 Ohio State	33 QB Jeff Smoker
21 Wisconsin	56 RB Jaren Hayes / Tyrell Dortch
41 Penn State	10 DL Greg Taplin
3 Nebraska■	17 DL Matthias Askew / Keith Vickerson
	DL Kyle Rasmussen / Greg Yeaster
	DL Clifford Dukes
	LB Seth Mitchell / Monquiz Wedlow
	LB Ronald Stanley / Mark Goebel
	LB Mike Labinjo
	DB Darren Barnett / Ashton Watson
	DB Roderick Maples
	DB Jason Harmon / Greg Cooper
	DB Eric Smith / Derron Ware

RUSHING: Hayes 145/609y, Dortch 65/279y
PASSING: Smoker 302-488/3395y, 21TD, 61.9%
RECEIVING: Shabaj 57/692y, Hayes 48/414y, Alexander 44/522y
SCORING: Dave Raynor (K) 105pts, Hayes 48pts, Shabaj 30pts

2004 5-7

14 Rutgers	19 WR Matt Trannon / Aaron Alexander
24 C. Michigan	7 WR Agim Shabaj / Jerramy Scott
24 Notre Dame	31 WR Kyle Brown
30 Indiana	20 T Stefon Wheeler
16 Iowa	38 G Kyle Cook
38 Illinois	25 C Chris Morris
37 Michigan	17 G William Whitticker
19 Ohio State	45 T Sean Poole
49 Wisconsin	32 TE Eric Knott / Jason Randall
13 Penn State	14 QB Drew Stanton / Damon Dowdell
38 Hawaii	37 RB DeAndra Cobb / Jason Teague
	41 DL Clifton Ryan
	DL Brandon McKinney
	DL Keillith Vickerson / Demato Peko
	DL Clifford Dukes
	LB David Herron / Kaleb Thornh
	LB Ronald Stanley
	LB Tyrell Dortch
	DB Jaren Hayes / Ashton Watson
	DB Roderick Maples
	DB Jason Harmon / Greg Cooper
	DB Eric Smith / Cole Corey

RUSHING: Cobb 96/728y, Teague 150/688y, Stanton 96/687y
PASSING: Stanton 141-220/1601y, 8TD, 64.1%, Dowdell 66-114/657y, 4TD, 57.9%
RECEIVING: Scott 39/444y, Trannon 36/405y, Shabaj 29/308y
SCORING: Dave Raynor (K) 105pts, Teague 62pts, Stanton 36pts

2005 5-6

49 Kent State	14 WR Matt Trannon / Kerry Reed
42 Hawaii	14 WR Kyle Brown / Terry Love
44 Notre Dame	41 WR Jerramy Scott
61 Illinois	14 T Stefon Wheeler / Tom Kaczmarek
31 Michigan	34 G Kyle Cook
24 Ohio State	35 C Chris Morris
14 Northwestern	49 G Gordon Niebylski / Roland Martin
46 Indiana	15 T Mike Gyetvai
1 Purdue	28 TE Kellen Davis / Ryan Woods
18 Minnesota	41 QB Drew Stanton
22 Penn State	31 RB Jevon Ringer / Jason Teague
	DL Clifton Ryan
	DL Brandon McKinney / David Stanton
	DL Domata Peko
	DL Michael Bazemore
	LB SirDarean Adams
	LB Kaleb Thornton
	LB David Herron
	DB Ashton Watson / Jaren Hayes
	DB Demond Williams
	DB Greg Cooper / Otis Wiley
	DB Eric Smith

RUSHING: Ringer 122/817y, Jehuu Caulcrick (RB) 89/478y, Teague 78/420y, Stanton 121/338y
PASSING: Stanton 236-354/3077y, 22TDs, 66.7%
RECEIVING: Scott 49/722y, Trannon 40/573y, Brown 36/546y
SCORING: Jehuu Caulcrick (RB) 42pts, John Goss (K) 40pts, Scott 36pts

2006 4-8

27 Idaho	17 WR Matt Trannon
52 E. Michigan	20 WR Kerry Reed / Terry Love
38 Pittsburgh	23 WR Jerramy Scott / T.J. Willams
37 Notre Dame	40 T Pete Clifford / Mike Gyetvai
20 Illinois	23 G Kyle Cook / Daniel Zynn
13 Michigan	31 C John Masters
7 Ohio State	38 G Roland Martin
41 Northwestrn	38 T Jesse Miller
21 Indiana	46 TE Kellen Davis / Dwayne Holmes
15 Purdue	17 QB Drew Stanton / Brian Hoyer
18 Minnesota	31 RB Jehuu Caulcrick / Javon Ringer
13 Penn State	17 DL Ervin Baldwin
	DL Clifton Ryan
	DL Ogemdi Nwagbuo / David Stanton
	DL Justin Kershaw / Jonal Saint-Dic
	LB SirDarean Adams
	LB Kaleb Thornton
	LB David Herron / Steve Juarez
	DB Demond Williams
	DB Greg Cooper / Kendell Davis-Clark
	DB Otis Wiley
	DB Nehemiah Warrick / Travis Key

RUSHING: Ringer 86/497y, Stanton 110/445y, Caulcrick 108/426y
PASSING: Stanton 164-269/1807y, 12TD, 61.0%, Hoyer 82-144/863y, 4TD, 56.9%
RECEIVING: Reed 64/775y, Trannon 44/518y, Scott 26/339y
SCORING: Brett Swenson (K) 78pts, Caulcrick 42pts, Reed & Stanton 30pts

2007 9-4

55 Ala.-Birm'ham	18 WR Mark Dell / Deon Curry
28 Bowling Green	17 WR Devin Thomas
17 Pittsburgh	13 T Pete Clifford
31 Notre Dame	14 G Kenny Shane
34 Wisconsin	37 C Joel Nitchman / John Masters
41 Northwestern	48 G Roland Martin / Mike Gyetvai
52 Indiana	27 T Jesse Miller
1 Ohio State	24 TE Kellen Davis
27 Iowa	34 QB Brian Hoyer
24 Michigan	28 RB Javon Ringer / Jehuu Caulcrick
48 Purdue	31 FB Jeff McPherson / Devin Pritchett
35 Penn State	31 DL Jonal Saint-Dic / Brandon Long
21 Boston College■	24 DL Ogemdi Nwagbuo / Oren Wilson
	DL Justin Kershaw
	DL Ervin Baldwin
	LB Greg Jones / SirDarean Adams
	LB Kaleb Thornhill
	LB Eric Gordon
	DB Kendell Davis-Clark / Chris L. Rucker
	DB Ross Weaver / Ashton Henderson
	DB Otis Wiley / Travis Key
	DB Nehemiah Key

RUSHING: Ringer 245/1447y, Caulcrick 222/872y, Thomas 27/177y
PASSING: Hoyer 223-376/2725y, 20TD, 59.3%
RECEIVING: Thomas 79/1260y, Ringer 35/295y, Davis 32/513y
SCORING: Caulcrick 126pts, Brett Swenson (K) 98pts, Thomas 48pts

2008 9-4

31 California	38 WR Mark Dell
42 E. Michigan	10 WR Blair White / Jeff McPherson (FB)
17 Florida Atlantic	0 WR B.J. Cunningham / Deon Curry
23 Notre Dame	7 T Rocco Cironi
42 Indiana	29 G Joel Foreman / Mike Bacon
16 Iowa	13 C Joel Nitchman
37 Northwestern	20 G Roland Martin
7 Ohio State	45 T Jesse Miller
35 Michigan	21 TE Charlie Gantt / Garrett Celek
25 Wisconsin	24 QB Brian Hoyer
21 Purdue	7 TB Javon Ringer
18 Penn State	49 DL Brandon Long
12 Georgia■	24 DL Oren Wilson
	DL Justin Kershaw
	DL Trevor Anderson / Dwayne Holmes
	LB Greg Jones / Brandon Denson
	LB Adam Decker
	LB Eric Gordon / Ryan Allison
	DB Chris Rucker / Jeremy Ware
	DB Ross Weaver / Johnny Adams
	DB Dan Fortener / Kendell Davis-Clark
	DB Otis Wiley / Marcus Hyde

RUSHING: Ringer 390/1637y, Andre Anderson (TB) 26/97y
PASSING: Hoyer 180-353/2404y, 9TD, 51.0%
RECEIVING: White 43/659y, Cunningham 41/528y, Dell 36/679y
SCORING: Ringer 132pts, Brett Swenson (K) 100pts, Gantt 24pts

2009 6-7

44 Montana State	3 WR Blair White / Mark Dell
27 C. Michigan	29 WR B.J. Cunningham / Keshawn Martin
30 Notre Dame	33 T Rocco Cironi
26 Wisconsin	38 G Joel Foreman
24 Michigan	20 C Joel Nitchman (G) / John Stipek
24 Northwestern	14 G Brendon Moss (T) / Jared McGaha
13 Iowa	14 T D.J. Young (G)
34 Minnesota	15 TE Brian Linthicum
49 W. Michigan	42 TE Charlie Gantt
40 Purdue	14 QB Kirk Cousins / Keith Nichol (WR)
14 Penn State	35 TB Larry Caper / Caulton Ray
31 Texas Tech■	42 DL Trevor Anderson
	41 DL Oren Wilson
	DL Jerel Worthy / Kevin Pickelman
	DL Colin Neely / Tyler Hoover
	LB Eric Gordon / Chris Norman
	LB Greg Jones / Adam Decker
	LB Brandon Denson / Jon Misch
	DB Jeremy Ware / Ross Weaver
	DB Chris Rucker / Kendell Davis-Clark
	DB Dan Fortener / Tenton Robinson
	DB Marcus Hyde / Roderick Jenrette

RUSHING: Caper 120/468y, Edwin Baker (TB) 85/427y, Martin 18/219y, Glenn Winston (TB) 60/204y
PASSING: Cousins 198-328/2680y, 19TD, 60.4%, Nichol 49-91/764y, 7TD, 53.8%
RECEIVING: White 70/990y, Cunningham 48/641y, Dell 26/449y, Gantt 22/348y, Linthicum 20/266y
SCORING: Brett Swenson (K) 101pts, White 54pts, Martin 42pts

2010 11-2

38 W. Michigan	14 WR Mark Dell / Bennie Fowler
30 Fla. Atlantic	17 WR Keith Nichol / Keshawn Martin
34 Notre Dame	31 WR/FB B.J. Cunningham / Nick Bendzuck
45 No. Colorado	17 T D.J. Young
34 Wisconsin	24 G Joel Foreman
34 Michigan	17 C John Stipek
26 Illinois	6 G Chris McDonald / Jared McGaha (T)
35 Northwestern	27 T J'Michael Deane
6 Iowa	37 TE Charlie Gantt / Brian Linthicum (G)
31 Minnesota	8 QB Kirk Cousins
35 Purdue	31 TB Edwin Baker / Le'Veon Bell
28 Penn State	22 DL Tyler Hoover / Denzel Drone
7 Alabama■	49 DL Jerel Worthy
	DL Kevin Pickelman / Blake Treadwell
	DL Colin Neely / Johnathan Strayhorn
	LB Eric Gordon / Max Bullough
	LB Greg Jones / Steve Gardiner
	LB Chris Norman / Jon Misch
	DB Chris Rucker / Darqueze Dennard
	DB Johnny Adams
	DB Trenton Robinson / Isaiah Lewis
	DB Marcus Hyde

RUSHING: Baker 207/1201y, Bell 107/605y
PASSING: Cousins 226-338/2825y, 20TD, 66.9%
RECEIVING: Dell 51/788y, Cunningham 50/611y, Martin 32/394y
SCORING: Dan Conroy (K) 87pts, Baker 78pts, Cunningham 54pts

MINNESOTA

University of Minnesota (Founded 1851)
Minneapolis, Minnesota
Nickname: Golden Gophers
Colors: Maroon and Gold
Stadium: Hubert H. Humphrey Metrodome (1982) 64,111
Conference Affiliation: Big Ten (Charter Member, 1896-present)

CAREER RUSHING YARDS	Attempts	Yards
Darrell Thompson (1986-89)	936	4654
Laurence Maroney (2003-05)	660	3933
Thomas Hamner (1996-99)	882	3810
Marion Barber III (2001-04)	575	3276
Chris Darkins (1992-95)	643	3235
Marion Barber (1977-80)	660	3094
Tellis Redmon (1999-01)	486	2481
Amir Pinnix (2004-07)	462	2439
Garry White (1977-80)	444	2353
Francis "Pug" Lund (1932-34)	416	2264

CAREER PASSING YARDS	Comp.-Att.	Yards
Adam Weber (2007-10)	909-1594	10,917
Bryan Cupito (2003-06)	513-918	7446
Cory Sauter (1994-97)	539-945	6834
Asad Abdul-Khaliq (2000-03)	481-847	6660
Marquel Fleetwood (1989-92)	465-876	5279
Rickey Foggie (1984-87)	311-628	5162
Mike Hohensee (1981-82)	392-722	4792
Tim Schade (1993-94)	322-627	3986
Tony Dungy (1973-76)	274-586	3515
Billy Cockerham (1996-99)	252-485	3483

CAREER RECEIVING YARDS	Catches	Yards
Eric Decker (2006-09)	227	3119
Ron Johnson (1998-01)	198	2989
Tutu Atwell (1994-97)	171	2640
Ernie Wheelwright (2004-07)	159	2434
Ryan Thelwell (1994-96)	136	2232
Jared Ellerson (2002-05)	111	2054
Luke Leverson (1996-99)	132	1843
Omar Douglas (1990-93)	130	1681
Dwayne McMullen (1981-84)	95	1627
Aaron Osterman (1990-94)	111	1598

SEASON RUSHING YARDS	Attempts	Yards
Laurence Maroney (2005)	281	1464
Chris Darkins (1994)	277	1443
Thomas Hamner (1999)	308	1426
Darrell Thompson (1986)	242	1376
Tellis Redmon (2000)	293	1368

SEASON PASSING YARDS	Comp.-Att.	Yards
Adam Weber (2007)	258-449	2895
Bryan Cupito (2006)	214-359	2819
Adam Weber (2008)	255-410	2761
Adam Weber (2010)	205-368	2679
Cory Sauter (1995)	204-338	2600

SEASON RECEIVING YARDS	Catches	Yards
Ron Johnson (2000)	61	1125
Eric Decker (2008)	84	1074
Ryan Thelwell (1996)	54	1051
Chester Cooper (1981)	58	1012
Tutu Atwell (1997)	58	924

GAME RUSHING YARDS	Attempts	Yards
Chris Darkins (1995 vs. Purdue)	38	294
Clarence Schutte (1924 vs. Illinois)	N/A	282
Kent Kitzmann (1977 vs. Illinois)	57	266

GAME PASSING YARDS	Comp.-Att.	Yards
Tim Schade (1993 vs. Penn State)	34-66	478
Mike Hohensee (1981 vs. Ohio State)	37-67	444
Adam Weber (2009 vs. Michigan State)	19-31	416

GAME RECEIVING YARDS	Catches	Yards
Ryan Thelwell (1996 vs. Ball State)	8	228
Omar Douglas (1993 vs. Penn State)	11	193
Eric Decker (2008 vs. Indiana)	13	190

GREATEST COACH:

In 1960 the University of Minnesota was the only game in town for sports-starved fans of the Gopher State. The Lakers had moved to Los Angeles earlier that year and the baseball Twins and NFL Vikings would begin play in 1961, so for the fall of 1960 all eyes were on the local college football squad. Having finished last in the Big 10 in 1959, the team may not have been able to provide a proper showing for the fan, although they were sure to play hard as always. Instead, the Gophers dazzled from the get-go, drubbing favored Nebraska 26-14 before running off four straight Big 10 wins, three by shutouts including a 10-0 blanking of rival Michigan. Suddenly the fact that coach Murray Warmath's Gophers were the only game in town did not matter—who needed the pros! The match-up would be against powerful Iowa, ranked no. 1 in the country. Suddenly the game had more meaning than the Floyd of Rosedale Trophy. With guard Tom Brown cementing the Big Ten MVP and Outland trophies, the Gophers clocked the Hawkeyes on the road 27-10.

The Gophers lost the following week to a struggling Purdue unit, and eventually to Washington in the Rose Bowl, but 1960 is still a magical worst-to-first run for the Gophers who nonetheless captured a national championship, the school's first since 1941.

Coach Warmath, who played for General Neyland at Tennessee, became a state hero. His 1961 team won the last Rose Bowl the school has appeared in, beating UCLA, and he had a couple of other runs to the top half of the Big 10. He rebuilt the Gophers by pulling in talent from outside the state, like quarterback Sandy Stephens from Pennsylvania, to compliment the big, but not too fast, local players. In 18 years, Warmath went 86-78-7.

MINNESOTA'S 55 GREATEST SINCE 1953

OFFENSE

WIDE RECEIVER: Tutu Atwell, Eric Decker, Ron Johnson, Ryan Thelwell
TIGHT END: Doug Kingsriter, Matt Spaeth, Ben Utecht
TACKLE: Keith Ballard, Ken Dallafior, Matt Herkenhoff, Rian Melander
GUARD: Dick Enderle, Mark Setterstrom, Troy Wolkow
CENTER: Greg Eslinger, Ben Hamilton, Greg Larson
QUARTERBACK: Rickey Foggie, Adam Weber
RUNNING BACK: Marion Barber III, Paul Giel, Laurence Maroney, Tellis Redmon, Darrell Thompson
FULLBACK: John King

DEFENSE

END: Steve Neils, Karon Riley, Bob Stein, Lamanzer Williams
TACKLE: Tom Brown, Carl Eller, Karl Mecklenberg, Steve Midboe, Mike Sunvold
LINEBACKER: Jim Fahnhorst, Bruce Holmes, Wayne King, Bill Light, Pete Najarian
CORNERBACK: Ukee Dozier, Kerry Glenn, Willie Middlebrooks
SAFETY: Tyrone Carter, Kraig Lofquist, Sean Lumpkin, Tom Sakal, Jeff Wright

SPECIAL TEAMS

RETURN SPECIALIST: Rick Upchurch
PLACE KICKER: Chip Lohmiller, Dan Nystrom
PUNTER: Preston Gruening

MULTIPLE POSITIONS

CENTER-GUARD-TACKLE: Randy Rasmussen
HALFBACK-FULLBACK: Bob McNamara

TWO-WAY PLAYERS

END-DEFENSIVE END: Aaron Brown
TACKLE-DEFENSIVE TACKLE: Bobby Bell

PERFORMANCE FORMULA:
MINNESOTA'S 10 BEST SEASONS

1961	1.4842	6 of 71
1960	1.4787	6 of 70
1956	1.4472	11 of 69
2003	1.4100	14 of 71
1962	1.3789	17 of 70
1999	1.3131	18 of 71
1954	1.3055	21 of 69
1967	1.3027	20 of 71
2005	1.2516	24 of 70
2002	1.1589	34 of 70

MINNESOTA GOLDEN GOPHERS

Year	W-L-T	AP Poll	Conference Standing	Toughest Regular Season Opponents	Coach (Record at School)	Bowl Games		
1953	4-4-1		5	Michigan State 8-1, Illinois 7-1-1, Iowa 5-3-1	Wes Fesler (10-13-4)			
1954	7-2		4	Wisconsin 7-2, Michigan 6-3 Iowa 5-4	Murray Warmath			
1955	3-6		8	Michigan State 9-1, Michigan 7-2, Southern Cal 6-4	Murray Warmath			
1956	6-1-2	12	3	Iowa 8-1, Michigan 7-2, Michigan State 7-2	Murray Warmath			
1957	4-5		8	Michigan State 8-1, Iowa 7-1-1, Wisconsin 6-3	Murray Warmath			
1958	1-8		9	Iowa 7-1-1, Wisconsin 7-1-1, Illinois 4-5	Murray Warmath			
1959	2-7		10	Wisconsin 7-2, Illinois 5-3-1, Iowa 5-4	Murray Warmath			
1960	8-2	1	1t	Iowa 8-1, Purdue 4-4-1, Illinois 5-4	Murray Warmath	Rose	7 Washington	17
1961	8-2	6	2	Michigan State 7-2, Missouri 7-2-1, Wisconsin 6-3	Murray Warmath	Rose	21 UCLA	3
1962	6-2-1	10	2	Wisconsin 8-1, Missouri 7-1-2, Northwestern 7-2	Murray Warmath			
1963	3-6		9	Illinois 7-1-1, Nebraska 9-1, Army 7-3	Murray Warmath			
1964	5-4		4t	Michigan 8-1, Nebraska 9-1, Illinois 6-3	Murray Warmath			
1965	5-4-1		3t	Missouri 7-2-1, Purdue 7-2-1, Southern Cal 7-2-1	Murray Warmath			
1966	4-5-1		5	Purdue 8-2, Michigan 6-4, Missouri 6-3-1	Murray Warmath			
1967	8-2		1t	Purdue 8-2, Indiana 9-1, Nebraska 6-4	Murray Warmath			
1968	6-4		3t	Southern Cal 9-0-1, Michigan 8-2, Purdue 8-2	Murray Warmath			
1969	4-5-1		4	Ohio State 8-1, Michigan 8-2, Purdue 8-2	Murray Warmath			
1970	3-6-1		7	Ohio State 9-0, Nebraska 10-0-1, Michigan 9-1	Murray Warmath			
1971	4-7		6t	Nebraska 11-0, Michigan 11-0, Northwestern 7-4	Murray Warmath (87-78-7)			
1972	5-6		5	Ohio State 9-1, Michigan 10-1, Nebraska 8-2-1	Cal Stoll			
1973	7-4		3	Ohio State 9-0-1, Michigan 10-0-1, Nebraska 8-2-1	Cal Stoll			
1974	4-7		7t	Ohio State 10-1, Michigan 10-1, Nebraska 8-3	Cal Stoll			
1975	6-5		7t	Ohio State 10-1, Michigan 8-1-2, Michigan State 7-4	Cal Stoll			
1976	6-5		3t	Michigan 10-1, Ohio State 8-2-1, Indiana 5-6	Cal Stoll			
1977	7-5		5	Michigan 10-1, Ohio State 9-2, Washington 9-2	Cal Stoll	Hall of Fame	7 Maryland	17
1978	6-5		5	Michigan 10-1, Michigan State 8-3, UCLA 8-3	Cal Stoll (39-39)			
1979	4-6-1		6	Ohio State 11-0, Southern Cal 10-0-1, Purdue 9-2	Joe Salem			
1980	5-6		5	Michigan 9-2, Ohio State 9-2, Southern Cal 8-2-1	Joe Salem			
1981	6-5		6t	Iowa 8-3, Michigan 8-3, Ohio State 8-3	Joe Salem			
1982	3-8		10	Ohio State 8-3, Michigan 8-3, Iowa 7-4	Joe Salem			
1983	1-10		10	Nebraska 12-0, Illinois 10-1, Michigan 9-2	Joe Salem (19-35-1)			
1984	4-7		8	Nebraska 9-2, Ohio State 9-2, Purdue 7-4	Lou Holtz			
1985	7-5		6	Iowa 10-1, Oklahoma 10-1, Michigan 9-1-1	Lou Holtz (10-12) / John Gutekunst [1-0]	Independence	20 Clemson	13
1986	6-6		3t	Oklahoma 10-1, Michigan 11-1, Ohio State 9-3	John Gutekunst	Liberty	14 Tennessee	21
1987	6-5		6t	Iowa 9-3, Michigan 7-4, Indiana 8-3	John Gutekunst			
1988	2-7-2		9	Michigan 8-2-1, Washington State 8-3, Indiana 7-3-1	John Gutekunst			
1989	6-5		5	Michigan 10-1, Nebraska 10-1, Michigan State 7-4	John Gutekunst			
1990	6-5		6	Nebraska 9-2, Michigan 8-3, Iowa 8-3	John Gutekunst			
1991	2-9		10	Michigan 10-1, Iowa 10-1, Colorado 8-2-1	John Gutekunst (29-36-2)			
1992	2-9		10	Michigan 8-0-3, Colorado 9-1-1, Ohio State 8-2-1	Jim Wacker			
1993	4-7		8t	Penn State 9-2, Wisconsin 9-1-1, Michigan 7-4	Jim Wacker			
1994	3-8		11	Penn State 11-0, Kansas State 9-2, Michigan 8-3	Jim Wacker			
1995	3-8		10	Northwestern 10-1, Ohio State 11-1, Michigan 9-3	Jim Wacker			
1996	4-7		9t	Ohio State 10-1, Michigan 8-3, Northwestern 9-2	Jim Wacker (16-39)			
1997	3-9		9t	Michigan 11-0, Ohio State 10-2, Penn State 9-2	Glen Mason			
1998	5-6		7t	Ohio State 10-1, Wisconsin 10-1, Michigan 9-3	Glen Mason			
1999	8-4	18	4t	Wisconsin 9-2, Penn State 9-3, Purdue 7-4	Glen Mason	Sun	20 Oregon	24
2000	6-6		4t	Purdue 8-3, Northwestern 8-3, Ohio State 8-3	Glen Mason			
2001	4-7		10t	Illinois 10-1, Michigan 8-3, Toledo 9-2	Glen Mason			
2002	8-5		7	Ohio State 13-0, Iowa 11-1, Michigan 9-3	Glen Mason	Music City	29 Arkansas	14
2003	10-3	20	4t	Michigan 10-2, Iowa 9-3, Michigan State 8-4	Glen Mason	Sun	31 Oregon	30
2004	7-5		8	Iowa 9-2, Michigan 9-2, Wisconsin 9-2	Glen Mason	Music City	20 Alabama	16
2005	7-5		7	Penn State 10-1, Ohio State 9-2, Iowa 7-4	Glen Mason	Music City	31 Virginia	34
2006	6-6		6t	Ohio State 12-0, Michigan 11-1, Wisconsin 11-1	Glen Mason (64-56)	Insight	41 Texas Tech	44
2007	1-11		11	Ohio State 11-1, Michigan 8-4, Illinois 9-3, Wisconsin 9-3	Tim Brewster			
2008	7-6		6t	Ohio State 10-2, Northwestern 9-3, Iowa 8-4	Tim Brewster	Insight	21 Kansas	42
2009	6-7		8	Wisconsin 9-3, Penn State 10-2, Ohio State 10-2, Iowa 10-2	Tim Brewster	Insight	13 Iowa State	14
2010	3-9		9t	Wisconsin 11-1, Ohio State 11-1, Michigan State 11-1	Tim Brewster (15-30) / Jeff Horton [2-3]			

TOTAL: 287-332-11 .4643 (51 of 70)

Bowl Games since 1953: 5-8 .3846 (60 of 70)

GREATEST TEAM SINCE 1953: The 1960 edition of the Golden Gophers (8-2), surprise winner of the national championship, was the school's best team in the modern era. Winning with defense, Minnesota featured a powerful line, led by Bobby Bell, Tom Brown, Bob Deegan, and Greg Larson, that shut out three opponents.

1953 4-4-1

7 Southern Cal	17 E Jim Soltau
0 Michigan State	21 T Gordon Holz / Ron Hansen
30 Northwestern	13 G Robert Hagemeister / Rocky Elton
7 Illinois	27 C Gerald Helgeson
22 Michigan	0 G Mike Falls / Jerome Rau
35 Pittsburgh	14 T Stavros Canakes
28 Indiana	20 E Robert Rutford / Phil McElroy
0 Iowa	27 QB Gino Cappelletti
21 Wisconsin	21 HB Paul Giel
	HB Bob McNamamra / Mike Sullivan
	FB Melvin Holme / John Baumgartner

RUSHING: Giel 198/749y, McNamara 59/286y, Holme 64/267y
PASSING: Giel 50-93/590y, 53.8%, 4TD
RECEIVING: McNamara 15/204y, Soltan 12/156y, Cappelletti 12/139y
SCORING: Giel 54pts, Cappelletti 36pts, Home & Quist 12pts

1954 7-2

19 Nebraska	7 E Jim Soltau / Tom Juhl
46 Pittsburgh	7 T Gordon Holz / Chuck Kubes
26 Northwestern	7 G Robert Hagemeister
19 Illinois	6 C Dean Maas
0 Michigan	34 G Mike Falls / Rocky Elton
19 Michigan State	13 T Bob Hobert / Clint Andrus
44 Oregon State	6 E Phil McElroy
22 Iowa	20 QB Gino Cappelletti / Dale Quist
0 Wisconsin	27 HB Darrell Cochran / Pinky McNamara
	HB Bob McNamara
	FB John Baumgartner / Ken Yackel

RUSHING: B. McNamara 112/708y, Baumgartner 53/376y,
PASSING: Cappelletti 28-65/434y, 43.8%, 4 TD
RECEIVING: P. McNamara 12/117y, B. McNamara 10/193y,
SCORING: B. McNamara 66pts, Cappelletti (QB-K) 31pts, Cochran 18pts

1955 3-6

0 Washington	30 E Tom Juhl / Ken Fischman
6 Purdue	7 T Erle Ukkelberg / Robert Hagemeister
18 Northwestern	7 G Bob Rasmussen
13 Illinois	21 C Dean Maas
13 Michigan	14 G Mike Falls
25 Southern Cal	19 T Bob Hobert / Frank Youso
0 Iowa	26 E Franz Koenecke
14 Michigan State	42 QB Don Swanson / Dick Larson
21 Wisconsin	6 HB Pinky McNamara / Bob Schultz
	HB Dick Borstad / Darrell Cochran
	FB Ken Yackel / Rhody Tuszka

RUSHING: Borstad 96/440y, Schultz 48/302y, McNamara 42/185y
PASSING: Larson 12-27/253y, 2TD, 44.4%
RECEIVING: Juhl 11/172y, McNamara 5/102y, Koeneke 4/99y
SCORING: Schultz 24pts, Borstad & Swanson 18pts

1956 6-1-2

34 Washington	14 E Tom Juhl / Bob Schmidt
21 Purdue	14 T Frank Youso / Ed Buckingham
0 Northwestern	0 G Bob Rasmussen / Dave Burkholder
16 Illinois	13 C Dean Maas
20 Michigan	7 G Paul Barrington / Kelvin Kleber
9 Pittsburgh	6 T Bob Hobert / Dave Herbold
0 Iowa	7 E Perry Gehring / Jon Jelacic
14 Michigan State	13 QB Bobby Cox / Dick Larson
13 Wisconsin	13 HB Ken Bombardier / Pinky McNamara
	HB Bob Schultz / Dave Lindblom
	FB Dick Borstad / Bob Blakely

RUSHING: Cox 130/553y, Schultz 62/290y, Bombardier 48/213y
PASSING: Cox 18-53/240y, 3TD, 34%
RECEIVING: Lindblom 12/156y, Schultz 7/86y, McNamara 5/46y
SCORING: Cox 36pts, Borstad (FB-K) 29pts, 3 tied w/ 12pts

1957 4-5

46 Washington	7 E Perry Gehring / Bob Schmidt
21 Purdue	17 T Norman Sixta / Mike Wright
41 Northwestern	6 G Dave Burkholder / Ev Gerths
13 Illinois	34 C Bill Jukich / Bernard Svendsen
7 Michigan	24 G Bob Rasmussen / Dave Herbold
34 Indiana	0 T Jerry Wallin / Frank Youso
20 Iowa	44 E Jon Jelacic / Ken Schultz
13 Michigan State	42 QB Bobby Cox / Dick Larson
6 Wisconsin	14 HB Bob Soltis / Dave Lindblom
	HB Bob Schultz/Bill Chorske/K. Bombardier
	FB Rhody Tuszka/Dick Borstad/B. Blakely

RUSHING: Blakely 65/324y, Cox 84/315y, Borstad 45/234y
PASSING: Cox 19-53/268y, 4TD, 35.8%
RECEIVING: Schultz 7/94y, Chorske 6/113y, Bombardier 5/74y
SCORING: Blakely (FB-K) 45pts, Borstad (FB-K) 22pts

1958 1-8

21 Washington	24 E Perry Gehring / Tom Moe
7 Pittsburgh	13 T Mike Wright / Norman Sixta
3 Northwestern	7 G Ev Gerths
8 Illinois	20 C Bernard Svendsen / Greg Larson
19 Michigan	20 G Tom Brown / Jerome Shetler
0 Indiana	6 T Jerry Wallin
6 Iowa	28 E Ken Schultz / Bruce Hammond
39 Michigan State	12 QB Jimmy Reese / Larry Johnson
12 Wisconsin	27 HB Bob Soltis / Gary Melchert
	HB Bill Kauth / Arlie Bomstad
	FB Roger Hagberg / Jim Rogers

RUSHING: Kauth 92/361y, Hagberg 73/261y, Soltis 52/252y
PASSING: Johnson 17-51/406y, 3TD, 33.3%
RECEIVING: Soltis 11/172y, Moe 10/238y, Kauth 9/144y
SCORING: Kauth 30pts, Hagberg & Johnson 18pts

1959 2-7

12 Nebraska	32 E Tom Moe /Dick Larson /Dick Johnson
24 Indiana	14 T Mike Wright / Jerry Friend
0 Northwestern	6 G Jerry Shelter / John Mulvena
6 Illinois	14 C Greg Larson
6 Michigan	14 G Tom Brown
20 Vanderbilt	6 T Arnold Osmundson / Frank Brixius
0 Iowa	33 E Tom Hall / Bob Deegan
23 Purdue	29 QB Sandy Stephens / Larry Johnson
7 Wisconsin	11 HB Arlie Bomstad / Judge Dickson
	HB Bill Kauth / Tom King
	FB Tom Robbins / Roger Hagberg

RUSHING: Robbins 93/339y, Hagberg 50/239y, Bomstad 55/225y
PASSING: Johnson 39-92/497y, 2TD, 42.4%
RECEIVING: Hall 22/322y, Kauth 8/70y, Moe 7/86y
SCORING: Stephens 20pts, Robbins & Hagberg 12pts

1960 8-1

26 Nebraska	14 E Dick Larson / Tom Hall
42 Indiana	0 T Bobby Bell / Bob Frisbee
7 Northwestern	0 G John Mulvena / Dean Odegard
21 Illinois	10 C Greg Larson / Jerry Annis
10 Michigan	0 G Tom Brown
48 Kansas State	7 T Frank Brixius / Dick Miller
27 Iowa	10 E Bob Deegan
14 Purdue	23 QB Sandy Stephens / Larry Johnson
26 Wisconsin	7 HB Dave Mulholland / Judge Dickson
7 Washington■	17 HB Bill Munsey / Tom King / Bill Kauth
	FB Roger Hagberg / Jim Rogers

RUSHING: Hagberg 90/399y, Munsey 51/225y, Rogers 57/218y
PASSING: Stephens 20-52/305y, 2TD, 38%
RECEIVING: Hall 10/135y, Deegan 6/148y, King 5/35y
SCORING: Stephens 54pts, Rogers (FB-K) 49pts, Hagberg 18pts

1961 8-2

0 Missouri	6 E Tom Hall
14 Oregon	7 T Carl Eller / Jim Wheeler
10 Northwestern	3 G Julian Hook / John Mulvena
33 Illinois	0 C Bob Frisbee / Dick Enga
23 Michigan	20 G Robin Tellor / Jack Perkovich
13 Michigan State	0 T Bobby Bell
16 Iowa	9 E Bob Deegan / John Campbell
10 Purdue	7 QB Sandy Stephens
21 Wisconsin	23 HB Dave Mulholland / Tom King
21 UCLA■	3 HB Bill Munsey / Jim Cairns
	FB Judge Dickson / Jerry Jones

RUSHING: Stephens 110/487y, Dickson 82/275y, Munsey 56/211y
PASSING: Stephens 47-142/794y, 9TD, 33.1%
RECEIVING: Hall 9/197y, Cairns 8/156y, Jones 6/65y
SCORING: Stephens 38pts, Campbell 20pts, Hall 18pts

1962 6-2-1

0 Missouri	0 E Bob Prawdzik / Myron Rognlie
21 Navy	0 T Carl Eller
22 Northwestern	34 G Julian Hook
17 Illinois	0 C Paul Benson
17 Michigan	0 G Jack Perkovich / Larry Hartse
28 Michigan State	7 T Bobby Bell / Milt Sunde
10 Iowa	0 E John Campbell / Ray Zitzlaff
7 Purdue	6 QB Duane Blaska / Jerry Pelletier
9 Wisconsin	14 HB Bill Munsey / Bill Crockett
	HB Jim Cairns / Paul Ramseth (DB)
	FB Jerry Jones / Dick Enga

RUSHING: Jones 98/450y, Cairns 51/224y, Munsey 68/203y
PASSING: Blaska 71-154/862y, 8TD, 46.1%
RECEIVING: Cairns 14/221y, Rognlie 11/154y, Munsey 8/85y
SCORING: Cairns 27pts, Jones 24pts, Collin Versich (K) 19pts

1963 3-6

7 Nebraska	14 E Bob Bruggers / Myron Rognlie
24 Army	8 T Milt Sunde
8 Northwestern	15 G Willie Costanza / Bill Dallman
6 Illinois	16 C Frank Marchlewski / Joe Pung (D)
6 Michigan	0 G Larry Hartse
6 Indiana	24 T Carl Eller
13 Iowa	27 E Aaron Brown / John Rajala
11 Purdue	13 QB Bob Sadek / Paul Ramseth (D)
14 Wisconsin	0 HB Dick Harren/Al Harris/Kraig Lofquist (D)
	HB Jerry Pelletier / Stan Skjei
	FB Mike Reid / Jay Sharp

RUSHING: Reid 102/392y, Pelletier 56/250y, Sharp 43/147y
PASSING: Sadek 58-128/647y, 2TD, 45.3%
RECEIVING: Pelletier 9/105y, Bruggers 6/98y, Harren 6/80y
SCORING: Reid (FB-K) 31pts, Sadek 24pts, Pelletier 12pts

1964 5-4

21 Nebraska	26 E Kent Kramer / Kenny Last
26 Cal	20 T Gale Gillingham / Jim Fulgham
21 Northwestern	18 G Paul Faust / Charles Killian
0 Illinois	14 C Frank Marchlewski
12 Michigan	19 G Randy Staten
21 Indiana	0 T Don Rosen
14 Iowa	13 E Aaron Brown
14 Purdue	7 QB John Hankinson
7 Wisconsin	14 HB Ray Whitlow / Mike Orman
	HB Fred Farthing (FB) / Bill Crockett
	FB Mike Reid
	DL Aaron Brown
	DL Fred Nord / Don Rosen
	DL Brian Callahan
	DL Bill Costanza
	DL Jim Fulgham / Jon Staebler
	DL Bob Bruggers
	LB Joe Pung
	LB Mike Reid / Jerome Newsom
	DB Bill Bevan / Andrew Haines
	DB Kraig Lofquist
	DB Stan Skjei

RUSHING: Farthing 113/433y, Hankinson 78/178y, Reid 62/176y
PASSING: Hankinson 86-178/1084y, 8TD, 48.3%
RECEIVING: Brown 27/267y, Last 21/308y, Kramer 17/342y
SCORING: Reid (FB-K) 39pts, Kramer 24pts, Hankinson & Farthing 18pts

1965 5-4-1

20 Southern Cal	20 WR Kenny Last
13 Washington St.	14 WR Kent Kramer / Chet Anderson
6 Missouri	17 T Don Rosen
42 Indiana	18 G Paul Faust
14 Iowa	3 C Charles Killian
14 Michigan	13 G Randolph Staten
10 Ohio State	11 T Gale Gillingham
27 Northwestern	22 TE Aaron Brown
0 Purdue	35 QB John Hankinson
42 Wisconsin	7 TB David Colburn / Richard Peterson
	FB Joe Holmberg
	DL John Rajala
	DL McKinley Boston
	DL Brian Callahan
	DL James Fulgham
	DL Bob Bruggers
	LB Tim Wheeler
	LB Gary Reierson
	DB Jerome Newsom
	DB Stewart Maples
	DB Tom Sakal
	DB Mike Condo

RUSHING: Holmberg 106/352y, Colburn 58/268y, Peterson 62/222y
PASSING: Hankinson 111-214/1477y, 8TD, 51.9%
RECEIVING: Last 31/463y, Brown 24/333y, Kramer 19/232y
SCORING: Hankinson 42pts, Holmberg, Deryl Ramey (K) & Peterson 24pts

1966 4-5-1

0 Missouri	24 WR Charlie Sanders / Chip Litten
35 Stanford	21 WR Chet Anderson
14 Kansas	16 T Ezell Jones
7 Indiana	7 G Dick Enderle / Tom Fink
17 Iowa	0 C Chuck Killian
0 Michigan	49 G Andy Brown / Bill Christison
17 Ohio State	7 T Ron Klick
28 Northwestern	13 TE Kenny Last
0 Purdue	16 QB Curtis Wilson / Larry Carlson
6 Wisconsin	7 TB Hubie Bryant / John Wintermute
	FB Dennis Cornell / Ray Whitlow
	DL Bob Stein
	DL McKinley Boston
	DL Ed Duren / Bob Bedney
	DL Jerry Hermann / Ron Kamzelski
	DL John Williams
	LB Tim Wheeler
	LB Gary Reierson
	LB Jerry Newsom
	DB Dick Seitz / Gene Hatfield
	DB Tom Sakal
	DB Mike Condo

RUSHING: Wilson 138/546y, Wintermute 87/284y, Bryant 34/209y
PASSING: Carlson 56-108/599y, 5TD, 51.8%
RECEIVING: Last 30/356y, Anderson 17/174y, Litten 8/112y
SCORING: Last 30pts, Wilson 24pts, Jerry Beven (K) 13pts

1967 8-2

13 Utah	12 WR Chip Litten
0 Nebraska	7 WR Mike Curtis / Hubie Bryant
23 SMU	3 T John Williams
10 Illinois	7 G Dick Enderle
21 Michigan State	0 C Steve Lundeen
20 Michigan	15 G Andy Brown / Tom Fink
10 Iowa	0 T Ezell Jones
12 Purdue	41 TE Charlie Sanders
33 Indiana	7 QB Curtis Wilson
21 Wisconsin	14 TB George Kemp / John Wintermute
	FB Jim Carter
	DL Bob Stein
	DL Ron Kamzelski
	DL Ed Duren
	DL McKinley Boston
	DL Del Jessen
	LB Wayne King
	LB Noel Jenke
	LB Dave Nixon
	DB Dennis Hale
	DB Tom Sakal
	DB Mike Condo

RUSHING: Carter 142/519y, Kemp 100/349y, Wilson 87/272y
PASSING: Wilson 33-76/543y, 6TD, 43.4%
RECEIVING: Sanders 21/276y, Litten 16/296y, Bryant 10/166y
SCORING: Wilson 48pts, Litten 24pts, Stein (DE-K) 20pts

1968 6-4

20 Southern Cal	29 WR Chip Litten
14 Nebraska	17 WR Mike Curtis / Walt Bowser
24 Wake Forest	19 T Alvin Hawes
17 Illinois	10 G Dick Enderle
14 Michigan State	13 C Steve Lundeen / Bob Eastlund
20 Michigan	33 G Tom Fink
28 Iowa	35 T Ezell Jones
27 Purdue	13 TE Ray Parson
20 Indiana	6 QB Phil Hagen / Ray Stephens
23 Wisconsin	15 TB Barry Mayer / George Kemp
	FB Jim Carter
	DL Del Jessen
	DL Jim Pahula
	DL Steve Thompson / Bill Laakso
	DL Ron Kamzelski
	DL Bob Stein
	LB Wayne King
	LB Rich Crawford / John Darkenwald
	LB Noel Jenke
	DB Doug Roalstad
	DB Dennis Hale
	DB Jeff Wright

RUSHING: Mayer 130/662y, Carter 96/423y, Kemp 75/288y
PASSING: Hagen 75-157/771y, 4TD, 47.8%
RECEIVING: Parson 30/333y, Litten 27/481y, Kemp 13/124y
SCORING: Carter 64pts, Maurice Forte (FB), Jeff Nygren (K) & Mayer 18pts

1969 4-5-1

26 Arizona State	48 WR Kevin Hamm
35 Ohio U.	35 T John Thompson
14 Nebraska	42 G Bill Christison
7 Indiana	17 C Ted Burke / Bob Eastlund
7 Ohio State	34 G Vern Winfield
9 Michigan	35 T Alvin Hawes
35 Iowa	7 TE Ray Parson
28 Northwestern	21 QB Phil Hagen
14 Michigan State	10 HB Barry Mayer
35 Wisconsin	10 HB George Kemp / Terry Addison
	FB Jim Carter / Ernie Cook
	DL Leon Trawick
	DL Mike Goldberg / Jim O'Brien
	DL Bill Light
	DL Tony Pahula
	DL Jack Babcock
	LB Bob Bailey
	LB Rich Crawford
	LB Ron Anderson
	DB Gary Hohman
	DB Walt Bowser
	DB Jeff Wright

RUSHING: Mayer 162/745y, Carter 121/575y, Cook 60/304y
PASSING: Hagen 109-208/1266y, 6TD, 52.4%
RECEIVING: Parson 27/391y, Mayer 17/137y, Hamm 15/165y
SCORING: Carter 54pts, Jeff Nygren (K) & Cook 30pts

1970 3-6-1

12 Missouri	34 WR Kevin Hamm
49 Ohio U.	7 WR George Honza
10 Nebraska	35 T Alvin Hawes
23 Indiana	0 G Paul Tollefson
8 Ohio State	28 C Bob Eastlund
13 Michigan	39 G Vern Winfield
14 Iowa	14 T John Thompson
14 Northwestern	28 TE Doug Kingsriter
23 Michigan State	13 QB Craig Curry
14 Wisconsin	39 TB Barry Mayer
	FB Ernie Cook
	DL Tom Chandler
	DL Mike Goldberg
	DL Steve Thompson
	DL Tom Lavaty / Jim O'Brien
	LB Rich Crawford
	LB Bill Light
	LB Ron King
	DB Ron Anderson
	DB Walt Bowser
	DB Jeff Wright
	DB Mike White

RUSHING: Cook 107/495y, Mayer 89/422y, Curry 94/295y
PASSING: Curry 103-228/1315y, 6TD, 45.3%
RECEIVING: Kingsriter 26/362y, Cook 18/82y, Hamm 17/269y
SCORING: Cook 44pts, Lou Clare (K) 38pts, Curry 30pts

1971 4-7

28 Indiana	0 WR Kevin Hamm
7 Nebraska	35 WR Mel Anderson / George Honza
20 Washington St.	31 T Jack Babcock
38 Kansas	20 G Lee Rankin / Paul Tollefson
13 Purdue	27 C Dale Hegland
19 Iowa	14 G Vern Winfield
7 Michigan	35 T Bart Buetow
12 Ohio State	14 TE Doug Kingsriter
20 Northwestern	41 QB Craig Curry
25 Michigan State	40 TB John Marquesen / Jim Henry
23 Wisconsin	21 FB Ernie Cook
	DL Tom Chandler
	DL John Krol
	DL Clayton Schewer
	DL Steve Neils
	LB Jeff Gunderson / Scott Irwin
	LB Bill Light
	LB Ron King
	DB Mike Perfetti
	DB Farrell Sheridan
	DB Paul Wright / Steve Politano
	DB Tim Alderson

RUSHING: Cook 177.881y, Curry 119/380y, Marquesen 64/224y
PASSING: Curry 118-266/1691y, 9TD, 44.3%
RECEIVING: Kingsriter 28/379y, Hamm 27/404y, Cook 19/143y
SCORING: Curry 48pts, Cook & Mel Anderson (K) 36pts

1972 5-6

23 Indiana	27 WR Keith Fahnhorst
6 Colorado	38 WR George Honza
0 Nebraska	49 T Matt Herkenhoff
48 Kansas	34 G Darrel Bunge
3 Purdue	28 C Bob Veldman
43 Iowa	14 G Dale Hegland
0 Michigan	42 T Dennis Maloney
19 Ohio State	27 TE Doug Kingsriter
35 Northwestern	29 QB Bob Morgan
14 Michigan State	10 TB Doug Beaudoin
14 Wisconsin	6 FB John King
	DL Steve Neils
	DL Keith Simons
	DL Clayton Schewer
	DL Bob Bailey
	LB Tom MacLeod
	LB Paul Glanton
	LB Ollie Bakken
	DB Greg Engebos
	DB Mike White
	DB Tim Alderson
	DB Todd Randall / Steve Politano

RUSHING: King 237/1164y, Morgan 188/595y, Beaudoin 105/513y
PASSING: Morgan 32-89/475y, 2TD, 36%
RECEIVING: Kingsriter 16/178y, Fahnhorst 13/224y, Honza 8/153y
SCORING: King 76pts, Beaudoin, Morgan & Steve Goldberg (K) 24pts

1973 7-4

7 Ohio State	56 WR Keith Fahnhorst
41 N. Dakota	14 WR Vince Fuller
19 Kansas	34 T Matt Herkenhoff
7 Nebraska	48 G Darrel Bunge
24 Indiana	3 C Jeff Selleck
31 Iowa	23 G Dale Hegland
7 Michigan	34 T Greg Shoff
52 Northwestern	43 TE Dale Henricksen
34 Purdue	7 QB John Lawing
19 Illinois	16 TB Rick Upchurch / Larry Powell
19 Wisconsin	17 FB John King
	DL Steve Neils
	DL Keith Simons
	DL Jeff Gunderson
	DL Dan Christensen
	LB Mike Steidl
	LB Ollie Bakken
	LB Paul Glanton
	DB Greg Engebos
	DB Orville Gilmore
	DB Doug Beaudoin
	DB Todd Randall

RUSHING: Upchurch 141/841y, King 131/533y, Powell 95/481y
PASSING: Lawing 23-48/276y, 3TD, 47.9%
RECEIVING: Fahnhorst 10/102y, Henricksen 7/100y
SCORING: Upchurch 56pts, Steve Goldberg (K) 36pts, Lawing 30pts

1974 4-7

19 Ohio State	34 WR Vince Fuller
42 N. Dakota	30 WR Dale Henrickson
9 TCU	7 T Art Meadowcroft
0 Nebraska	54 G Brien Harvey
3 Indiana	34 C Jeff Selleck
23 Iowa	17 G Dale Hegland
0 Michigan	49 T Greg Shoff
13 Northwestern	21 TE Scott Puchtel / Bill Sims
24 Purdue	20 QB Tony Dungy
14 Illinois	17 TB Rick Upchurch / Sam Brady
14 Wisconsin	49 FB J. Dexter Pride / John Jones
	DL Jeff Smith
	DL Keith Simons
	DL George Washington
	DL Mike Ramerth
	DL Mike Byrne
	LB Greg Gerths
	LB Ollie Bakken
	DB Greg Engebos
	DB Bob Weber / Orvile Gilmore
	DB Doug Beaudoin / Tommie Ash
	DB George Adzick / Kirby Kuklenski

RUSHING: Upchurch 153/942y, Pride 115/472y, Dungy 141/417y
PASSING: Dungy 39-94/612y, 5TD, 41.5%
RECEIVING: Upchurch 14/209y, Puchtel 13/149y, Fuller 10/174y
SCORING: Upchurch 54pts, Steve Goldberg (K) 31pts, Pride 24pts

1975 6-5

14 Indiana	20 WR Ron Kullas
38 W. Michigan	0 WR Mike Jones
10 Oregon	7 T Art Meadowcroft
21 Ohio U.	0 G Roger Plath
23 Illinois	42 C Dave Nolander
15 Michigan State	38 G Brien Harvey
31 Iowa	7 T Jeff Morrow
21 Michigan	28 TE Scott Puchtel / Bill Sims
33 Northwestern	9 QB Tony Dungy
6 Ohio State	38 TB Bubby Holmes / John Mathews
24 Wisconsin	3 FB J. Dexter Pride / Jim Perkins
	DL Jeff Smith
	DL Keith Simons
	DL George Washington
	DL Steve Midboe
	DL Mark Merrill
	LB Steve Craine / Michael Hunt
	LB Steve Stuart
	DB Tom Luckemeyer
	DB Bob Weber
	DB George Adzick
	DB Doug Beaudoin

RUSHING: Holmes 132/573y, Pride 137/565y, Mathews 73/272y
PASSING: Dungy 123-225/1515y, 15TD, 54.7%
RECEIVING: Kullas 42/545y, Jones 29/473y, Sims 14/217y
SCORING: Brian Kocourek (K) 46pts, Perkins 36pts, Dungy 30pts

1976 6-5

32 Indiana	13 WR Ron Kullas / Jeff Anhorn
28 Washington St.	14 WR Mike Jones
21 W. Michigan	10 T Jeff Morrow
7 Washington	38 G Brien Harvey
29 Illinois	14 C Mark Slater
14 Michigan State	10 G Greg Shoff
12 Iowa	22 T Terry Matula
0 Michigan	45 TE Glenn Bourquin
38 Northwestern	10 QB Tony Dungy
3 Ohio State	9 TB Kent Kitzmann /S. Breault /J. Mathews
17 Wisconsin	26 FB Jim Perkins / Bubby Holmes
	DL Mark Merrill
	DL Steve Midboe
	DL George Washington
	DL Doug Friberg / Steve Cunningham
	DL Ron Wrobel
	LB Michael Hunt
	LB Steve Stewart
	DB Tom Luckemeyer / Orville Gilmore
	DB Bobby Weber
	DB George Adzick
	DB Brian Snyder

RUSHING: Kitzmann 168/696y, Dungy 109/348y, Breault 85/327y
PASSING: Dungy 104-234/1291y, 4TD, 44.4%
RECEIVING: Kullas 33/372y, Anhorn 14/216y, Mathews 13/97y
SCORING: Perkins 78pts, Paul Rogind (K) 39pts, Dungy 30pts

1977 7-5

10 W. Michigan	0 WR Jeff Anhorn / Elmer Bailey
7 Ohio State	38 T Dennis Fitzpatrick / Marty Stein
27 UCLA	13 G Bryson Hollimon
19 Washington	17 C Mark Slater
6 Iowa	18 G Gary Acromite / Desi Williamson
10 Northwestern	7 T Jeff Morrow
16 Michigan	0 TE Glenn Bourquin
22 Indiana	34 QB Wendell Avery / Mark Carlson
10 Michigan State	29 WB Steve Breault
21 Illinois	0 TB Marion Barber
13 Wisconsin	7 FB Kent Kitzmann / Jeff Thompson
7 Maryland■	17 DL Mark Merrill
	DL Steve Midboe
	DL Doug Friberg
	DL Jim Ronan
	DL Stan Sytsma
	LB Michael Hunt
	LB Steve Stewart
	DB Bobby Weber
	DB Tom Luckemeyer / Ken Foxworth
	DB Keith Edwards / Brian Snyder
	DB Keith Brown

RUSHING: Kitzmann 151/647y, Barber 128/582y, Thompson 79/279y
PASSING: Avery 33-76/461y, 3TD, 43.4%
RECEIVING: Anhorn 16/217y, Bailey 15/250y, Breault 6/61y
SCORING: Paul Rogind (K) 68pts, Kitzmann 24pts, Thompson 18pts

1978 6-5

38 Toledo	12 WR Elmer Bailey
10 Ohio State	27 T Marty Stein
3 UCLA	17 G Ken Wypyszynski
14 Oregon State	17 C Steve Tobin
22 Iowa	20 G Darell Schwen
38 Northwestern	14 T Greg Murtha
10 Michigan	42 TE Glenn Bourquin
32 Indiana	31 QB Mark Carlson / Wendell Avery
9 Michigan State	33 WB Jeff Thompson / Ray Dilulo
24 Illinois	6 TB Marion Barber
49 Wisconsin	48 FB Kent Kitzmann / Garry White
	DL Tom Murphy / Steve Cunningham
	DL Alan Blanshaw
	DL Doug Friberg
	DL Jim Ronan
	DL Stan Sytsma
	LB Jack Johnson
	LB Ed Burns
	DB Ken Foxworth
	DB Keith Brown
	DB Keith Edwards
	DB Brian Snyder

RUSHING: Barber 247/1210y, Kitzmann 100/339y, Roy Artis (TB) 60/280y
PASSING: Carlson 64-113/736y, 3TD, 56.6%
RECEIVING: Bailey 27/464y, Barber 22/171y, Bourquin 19/279y
SCORING: Barber 62pts, Paul Rogind (K) 52pts, Bailey 26pts

1979 4-6-1

24 Ohio U.	10 WR Elmer Bailey
17 Ohio State	21 WR Jeff Anhorn / Roy Artis
14 Southern Cal	48 T Ken Dallafior
38 Northwestern	8 G Darell Schwen
31 Purdue	14 C Steve Tobin
21 Michigan	31 G Tom Fitzpatrick
24 Iowa	7 T Greg Murtha
17 Illinois	17 TE Glenn Bourquin
24 Indiana	42 QB Mark Carlson
17 Michigan State	31 TB Marion Barber / Glenn Lewis
37 Wisconsin	42 FB Garry White
	DL Tom Murphy
	DL Alan Blanshaw
	DL Dave Gardner
	DL Kevin Kellin / Marty Stein
	DL Steve Cunninham
	LB Jack Johnson
	LB Todd Peterson / Glenn Howard
	DB Dana Noel
	DB Glenn Cardelli
	DB Mike Robb / Mike Peppe
	DB Keith Edwards

RUSHING: White 135/861y, Barber 127/540y, Lewis 60/300y
PASSING: Carlson 177-300/2188y, 11TD, 59%
RECEIVING: Bailey 37/552y, Anhorn 28/392y, Bourquin 28/270y
SCORING: Barber 72pts, Paul Rogind (K) 58pts, White 48pts

1980 5-6

38 Ohio U.	14 WR Kelvin Jenkins
0 Ohio State	47 WR Chester Cooper
7 Southern Cal	24 T Ken Dallafior
49 Northwestern	21 G Todd Hallstrom / Eric Peterson
7 Purdue	21 C Ed Olson
14 Michigan	37 G Bill Humphries
24 Iowa	6 T Kent Penovich
21 Illinois	18 TE Mike Curtis
31 Indiana	7 QB Tim Salem
12 Michigan State	30 TB Marion Barber
7 Wisconsin	25 FB Garry White / Duane Gregory
	DL Fred Orgas
	DL Steve Bisch / Rene Capo
	DL Kevin Kellin
	DL Jeff Schuh
	LB Jim Fahnhorst
	LB Glenn Howard
	LB Glen Cieslewicz / Virgil Thomas
	DB Dana Noel
	DB Ken Foxworth
	DB Rick Withus
	DB Mike Robb

RUSHING: White 177/959y, Barber 154/769y, Gregory 59/275y
PASSING: Salem 81-170/887y, 2TD, 47.6%
RECEIVING: White 15/177y, Cooper 14/210y, Jenkins 13/158y
SCORING: Barber 66pts, White 54pts, Jim Gallery (K) 42pts

1981 6-5

19 Ohio U.	13 WR Chester Cooper
16 Purdue	13 WR Ron Weckbacker
42 Oregon State	12 T Ken Dallafior
29 Illinois	38 G Bill Humphries
35 Northwestern	23 C Ed Olson
16 Indiana	17 G Randy Rasmussen
12 Iowa	10 T Wally Kersten
13 Michigan	34 TE Jay Carroll / Mike Curtis
35 Ohio State	31 QB Mike Hohensee
36 Michigan State	43 TB Walter Ross / Tony Hunter
21 Wisconsin	26 FB Frank Jacobs/Bob Stroup/Manny Henry
	DL Anthony Davis / Jimmie James
	DL Karl Mecklenburg / Brent Harms
	DL Kevin Kellin
	DL Fred Orgas
	LB Jim Fahnhorst
	LB Glenn Howard
	LB Glen Cieslewicz
	DB Andre' Harris
	DB Glenn Cardelli
	DB Mike Robb / Mike Peppe
	DB Rick Withus

RUSHING: Jacobs 147/636y, Henry 71/372y, Hunter 41/217y
PASSING: Hohensee 182-362/2412y, 20TD, 50.3%
RECEIVING: Cooper 58/1012y, Weckbacker 29/364y, Jacobs 23/129y
SCORING: Jim Gallery (K) 65pts, Jacobs 54pts, Carroll & Cooper 36pts

1982 3-8

57 Ohio U.	3 WR Lonnie Farlow
36 Purdue	10 WR Dwayne McMullen
41 Washington St.	11 T Mark VonderHaar / Steve Bisch
24 Illinois	42 G Bill Humphries
21 Northwestern	31 C Ed Olson
21 Indiana	40 G Randy Rasmussen
16 Iowa	21 T Todd Hallstrom / Keith Gehrke
14 Michigan	52 TE Mike Curtis / Jay Carroll
10 Ohio State	35 QB Mike Hohensee
7 Michigan State	26 TB Tony Hunter / Valdez Baylor
0 Wisconsin	24 FB Bob Stroup / Alan Reid
	DL Fred Orgas / Anthony Davis
	DL Kevin Kellin / Ivan Zubar
	DL Karl Mecklenburg
	DL Jimmy James / John Wood
	LB Eric Johnson / Glen Cieslewicz
	LB Peter Najarian
	LB Joe Christopherson
	DB Kerry Glenn
	DB Phil Sutton
	DB Rick Witthus / Glenn Cardelli
	DB Craig White

RUSHING: Hunter 69/395y, Reid 57/290y, Baylor 61/233y
PASSING: Hohensee 210-360/2380y, 13TD, 58.3%
RECEIVING: McMullen 41/640y, Curtis 34/383y, Reid 33/280y
SCORING: Jim Gallery (K) 61pts, Hunter & McMullen 30pts

1983 1-10

21 Rice	17 WR Fred Hartwig / Lungen Howard
13 Nebraska	84 WR Dwayne McMullen
20 Purdue	32 T Jim Hobbins
18 Ohio State	64 G Bob Anderson / Ray Hitchcock
31 Indiana	38 C Randy Rasmussen
17 Wisconsin	56 G Jeff Moritko
8 Northwestern	19 T Jon Lilleberg
10 Michigan State	34 TE Jay Carroll / Kevin Starks
23 Illinois	50 QB Brett Sadek / Greg Murphy
10 Michigan	58 TB Valdez Baylor / Tony Hunter
10 Iowa	61 FB David Puk / Kevin Wilson
	DL Scott Tessier
	DL Ivan Zubar / Craig Graffunder
	DL Craig Paulson
	DL Anthony Burke / Bruce Holmes
	LB Jerry Keeble / Mark Dusabeck
	LB Peter Najarian
	LB Joe Christopherson
	DB Kerry Glenn
	DB Phil Sutton / Duane Dutrieuille
	DB Andy Hare / Andre' Harris
	DB Craig White

RUSHING: Puk 73/287y, Baylor 55/229y, Wilson 61/197y
PASSING: Murphy 115-242/1410y, 6TD, 47.5%
RECEIVING: Carroll 37/459y, McMullen 28/393y, Hartwig 28/333y
SCORING: Jim Gallery (K) 51pts, McMullen 30pts, Baylor 24pts

1984 4-7

31 Rice	24 WR Dwayne McMullen
7 Nebraska	38 WR Mel Anderson / Andy Hare
10 Purdue	34 T Dan Rechtin
22 Ohio State	35 G Jon Lilleberg / Ray Hitchcock
33 Indiana	24 C John Kelly
17 Wisconsin	14 G Jeff Moritko
28 Northwestern	31 T Mark VanderHaar
13 Michigan State	20 TE Kevin Starks
3 Illinois	48 QB Rickey Foggie
7 Michigan	31 TB Tony Hunter / Valdez Baylor
23 Iowa	17 FB David Puk / Kevin Wilson
	DL Mark Dusbabek
	DL Pat Hart / Craig Graffunder
	DL Steve Thompson
	DL Gary Hadd / Craig Paulson
	DL Bruce Holmes
	LB Joe Christopherson / Glen Cieslewicz
	LB Peter Najarian / Larry Joyner
	DB Kerry Glenn
	DB Andre' Harris / Lungen Howard
	DB Scott Tessier / Duane Dutrieuille
	DB Donovan Small

RUSHING: Foggie 145/647y, Puk 67/334y, Hunter 71/308y
PASSING: Foggie 57-121/1036y, 10TD, 47.1%
RECEIVING: McMullen 26/594y, Anderson 17/247y, Starks 14/136y
SCORING: Chip Lohmiller (K) 53pts, McMullen 30pts, 4 tied w/ 18pts

1985 7-5

28 Wichita State	14 WR Mel Anderson / Eugene Gailord
62 Montana	17 WR Gary Couch / Andy Hare
7 Oklahoma	13 T Jim Hobbins
45 Purdue	15 G Troy Wolkow
21 Northwestern	10 C Ray Hitchcock
22 Indiana	7 G Jon Lilleberg
19 Ohio State	23 T Dan Rechtin
26 Michigan State	31 TE Kevin Starks / Craig Otto
27 Wisconsin	18 QB Rickey Foggie
7 Michigan	48 TB Valdez Baylor
9 Iowa	31 FB David Puk
20 Clemson■	13 DL Anthony Burke
	DL Doug Mueller / Gary Hadd
	DL Steve Thompson
	LB Mark Dusbabek
	LB Bruce Holmes
	LB Peter Najarian
	LB Larry Joyner
	DB Duane Dutrieuille
	DB Matt Martinez
	DB Donovan Small
	DB David Williams

RUSHING: Baylor 99/582y, Foggie127/451y, Puk 87/405y
PASSING: Foggie 65-141/1370y, 7TD, 46.1%
RECEIVING: Anderson 22/520y, Starks 16/275y, Couch 14/494y
SCORING: Chip Lohmiller (K) 67pts, Foggie 54pts, Baylor 38pts

1986 6-6

31 Bowling Green	7 WR Mel Anderson
0 Oklahoma	63 WR Gary Couch / Jason Bruce
20 Pacific	24 T Jim Hobbins
36 Purdue	9 G Paul Anderson
44 Northwestern	23 C Ray Hitchcock
19 Indiana	17 G Troy Wolkow
0 Ohio State	33 'T Norries Wilson
23 Michigan State	52 TE Craig Otto
27 Wisconsin	20 QB Rickey Foggie
20 Michigan	17 TB Darrell Thompson
27 Iowa	30 FB Kevin Wilson / Roselle Richardson
14 Tennessee■	21 DL Anthony Burke
	DL Gary Hadd / Doug Mueller
	DL Steve Thompson
	LB Mark Dusbabek / Jon Melander
	LB Bruce Holmes
	LB Don Pollard / Jon Leverenz
	LB Larry Joyner
	DB Duane Dutrieuille
	DB Matt Martinez / Chuck McCree
	DB Donovan Small
	DB Steve Franklin / David Williams

RUSHING: Thompson 217/1240y, Foggie 117/349y, Richardson 51/273y
PASSING: Foggie 87-191/1265y, 8TD, 45.5%
RECEIVING: Anderson 24/353y, Thompson 21/198y, Couch 11/218y
SCORING: Thompson 66pts, Chip Lohmiller (K) 59pts, Foggie 50pts

1987 6-5

24 N. Iowa	7 WR Chris Gaiters
32 California	23 WR Jason Bruce / Gary Couch
30 C. Michigan	10 T Dan Liimatta
21 Purdue	19 G Paul Anderson
45 Northwestern	33 C Brian Williams
17 Indiana	18 G Troy Wolkow
9 Ohio State	42 T Dan Rechtin
17 Illinois	27 TE Craig Otto
20 Michigan	30 QB Rickey Foggie
22 Wisconsin	19 TB Darrell Thompson
20 Iowa	34 FB Roselle Richardson
	DL Trint Trip
	DL Doug Mueller
	DL Gary Hadd
	LB Ron Goetz
	LB Jon Leverenz
	LB Terry Hrycak / Mac Stephens
	LB Brian Bonner
	DB Frank Jackson
	DB Charles McCree
	DB Doug Evans
	DB David Williams

RUSHING: Thompson 224/1229y, Foggie 121/591y, Marcus Evans (TB) 60/303y
PASSING: Foggie 83-175/1232y, 8TD, 47.4%
RECEIVING: Otto 22/309y, Couch 17/241y, Gaiters 13/231y
SCORING: Thompson 78pts, Chip Lohmiller (K) 75pts, Foggie 36pts

1988 2-7-2

9 Washington St.	41 WR Chris Gaiters
35 Miami (Ohio)	3 WR Jason Bruce
31 N. Illinois	20 T Mark Drabczak / Jon Melander
10 Purdue	14 G Chris Thome / Mark Drabczak
28 Northwestern	28 C Brian Williams
13 Indiana	33 G J.J. Lennon
6 Ohio State	13 T Dan Liimatta / John Selvestra
27 Illinois	27 TE Craig Otto / Shane Strain
7 Michigan	22 QB Scott Schaffner
7 Wisconsin	14 TB Darrell Thompson
22 Iowa	31 FB Octavius Gould
	DL Mike Sunvold
	DL Trint Tripp / Gary Isakson
	DL Ross Ukkelberg
	DL Skeeter Akre / Anthony Bryant
	LB Ron Goetz
	LB Joel Staats / Eddie Miles
	LB Mac Stephens
	DB Andre Thaddies / James King
	DB Chuck McCree
	DB Sean Lumpkin / Les O'Hara
	DB Joel Brown

RUSHING: Thompson 210/910y, Gould 77/326y
PASSING: Schaffner 106-191/1234y, 7TD, 55.5%
RECEIVING: Gaiters 42/564y, Bruce 32/447y, Gould 16/151y
SCORING: Thompson 54pts, Brent Berglund (K) 51pts, Gaiters 30pts

1989 6-5

30 Iowa State	20 WR Pat Tingelhoff / Steve Rhem
0 Nebraska	48 WR Chris Gaiters
34 Indiana State	14 T Dan Liimatta
35 Purdue	15 G J.J. Lennon
20 Northwestern	18 C Chris Thome
18 Indiana	28 G Mark Drabczak / Craig Hendrickson
37 Ohio State	41 T Jon Melander
24 Wisconsin	22 TE Shane Strain / Trey Whitson
7 Michigan State	21 QB Scott Schaffner / Marquel Fleetwood
15 Michigan	49 TB Darrell Thompson
43 Iowa	7 FB Pat Cummings
	DL Skeeter Akre / Anthony Bryant
	DL Bob Coughlin
	DL Mike Sunvold
	DL Eddie Miles
	LB Joel Staats / Mac Stephens
	LB Jon Leverenz
	LB Ron Goetz
	DB Derek Fisher / Andre Thaddies
	DB Fred Foggie
	DB Sean Lumpkin
	DB Les O'Hara / Frank Jackson

RUSHING: Thompson 260/1139y, Marcus Evans (TB) 64/220y, Shaffner 76/125y
PASSING: Schaffner 101-190/1373y, 7TD, 53.2%
RECEIVING: Gaiters 31/366y, Tingelhoff 26/369y, Strain 17/202y
SCORING: Brent Berglund (K) 66pts, Thompson 62pts, Fleetwood 20pts

1990 6-5

29 Utah	35 WR Kevin Grant / Paul Hopewell
20 Iowa State	16 WR Pat Tingelhoff
0 Nebraska	56 T Keith Ballard
19 Purdue	7 G Craig Hendrickson
35 Northwestern	25 C Chris Thome
12 Indiana	0 G Ted Harrison
23 Ohio State	52 T Mark Drabczak
21 Wisconsin	3 TE Patt Evans
16 Michigan State	28 QB Marquel Fleetwood / Scott Schaffner
18 Michigan	35 TB Mark Smith
31 Iowa	24 FB James King / Chuck Rios
	DL Ben Williams
	DL Gary Isakson
	DL Mike Sunvold
	DL Skeeter Akre
	LB Joel Staats
	LB William Collins / Andre Davis
	LB Russ Heath
	DB Derek Fisher
	DB Drinon Mays
	DB Sean Lumpkin
	DB Frank Jackson

RUSHING: Smith 196/700y, Fleetwood 92/268y, Rios 66/231y
PASSING: Fleetwood 95-171/1199y, 6TD, 55.6% Schaffner 49-86/597y, 6TD, 55.9%
RECEIVING: Grant 28/413y, Evans 22/244y, Smith 18/149y
SCORING: Brent Berglund (K) 58pts, Smith 36pts, Fleetwood 30pts

1991 2-9

26 San Jose State	20 WR Paul Hopewell / John Lewis
0 Colorado	58 WR Keswic Joiner
13 Pittsburgh	14 T Keith Ballard
3 Illinois	24 G Scott Hendrickson / Rob Rogers
6 Purdue	3 C Frank Brixius
12 Michigan State	20 G Ted Harrison
6 Michigan	52 T Patrick O'Brien / Neil Fredenburg
8 Indiana	34 TE Patt Evans
6 Ohio State	35 QB Marquel Fleetwood
16 Wisconsin	19 TB Antonio Carter / Mark Smith
8 Iowa	23 FB James King / Chuck Rios
	DL Ben Williams
	DL Gary Isakson / Ed Hawthorne
	DL Dennis Cappella
	DL Anthony Bryant
	LB Joel Staats / William Collins
	LB Andre Davis
	LB Russ Heath
	DB Derek Fisher
	DB Drinon Mays
	DB Sean Lumpkin
	DB Andre Thaddies / Ken Sebree

RUSHING: Carter 165/660y, Rios 66/233y, Smith 46/191y
PASSING: Fleetwood 155-264/1642y, 5TD, 58.7%
RECEIVING: Evans 35/454y, Rios 27/175y, Joiner 26/361y
SCORING: Hopewell 22pts, Mike Chalberg (K) 17pts, Fleetwood & Joiner 12pts

1992 2-9

30 San Jose State	39 WR John Lewis
20 Colorado	21 WR Omar Douglas
33 Pittsburgh	41 WR Aaron Osterman / Lewis Garrison
18 Illinois	17 T Keith Ballard
20 Purdue	24 G Rob Rogers
15 Michigan State	20 C Neil Fredenburg
13 Michigan	63 G Prince Pearson
17 Indiana	24 T Chris Fowlkes
0 Ohio State	17 TE Michael Dean / Steve Cambrice
6 Wisconsin	34 QB Marquel Fleetwood
28 Iowa	13 TB Antonio Carter / Chris Darkins
	DL Dennis Cappella
	DL Doyle Cockrell
	DL Ed Hawthorne
	DL Andy Kratochvil
	LB Andy Veit
	LB Andre Davis
	LB Russ Heath
	DB Drinon Mays
	DB Ken Sebree / Derek Fisher
	DB Jeff Rosga / Dan Li Santi
	DB Rod Narcisse / Justin Conzemius

RUSHING: Carter 133/572y, Darkins 78/357y, Fleetwood 116/319y
PASSING: Fleetwood 192-385/2168y, 7TD, 49.9%
RECEIVING: Douglas 61/669y, Osterman 41/592y, Lewis 34/392y
SCORING: Aaron Piepkorn (K) 66pts, Fleetwood 30pts, Douglas 20pts

1993 4-7

20 Penn State	38 WR Lewis Garrison / Tony Levine
27 Indiana State	10 WR Omar Douglas
25 Kansas State	30 WR Aaron Osterman / Rishon Early
17 San Diego State	48 T Rob Rogers
19 Indiana	23 G Chris Fowlkes
59 Purdue	56 C Neil Fredenburg
28 Northwestern	26 G Rick Thome
28 Wisconsin	21 T David Vertin
20 Illinois	23 TE Eric Dalen
7 Michigan	58 QB Tim Schade / Scott Eckers
3 Iowa	21 TB Chris Darkins / A. Carter / Chuck Rios
	DL Dennis Cappella / Jerome Davis
	DL Doyle Cockrell
	DL Ed Hawthorne
	DL Andy Kratochvil
	LB Andy Veit
	LB Russ Heath
	LB Craig Sauer / Lance Wolklow
	DB Juan Hunter / Drinon Mays
	DB Roderick Narcisse
	DB Jeff Rosga / Moses Taylor
	DB Justin Conzemius

RUSHING: Darkins 124/610y
PASSING: Tim Schade 135-286/1648y, 8TD, 47.2%
RECEIVING: Douglas 60/880y, Rios 48/488y, Osterman 32/402y
SCORING: Douglas 66pts, Mike Chalberg (K) 50pts

1994 3-8

3 Penn State	56 WR Aaron Osterman / Ryan Thelwell
33 Pacific	7 WR Chuck Rios
40 San Diego State	17 WR Johnny Woodson
0 Kansas State	35 T Mike Giovinetti / Gann Brooks
20 Indiana	27 G Pat O'Brien
37 Purdue	49 C Todd Jesewitz
31 Northwestern	37 G Rich Thome
17 Wisconsin	14 T David Vertin
17 Illinois	21 TE Mark Tangen / Matt Reem
22 Michigan	38 QB Tim Schade
42 Iowa	49 RB Chris Darkins
	DL Trevor Walker
	DL Ed Hawthorne
	DL Doyle Cockrell / Kevin Holmes
	DL Jerome Davis / Ogun Akbar
	LB Justin Conzemius
	LB Ben Langford / Dan LiSanti
	LB Craig Sauer / Peter Hiestand
	DB Juan Hunter / Terrance Blayne
	DB Rodney Heath
	DB Rishon Early / Moses Taylor
	DB Crawford Jordan

RUSHING: Darkins 277/1443y, Javon Jackson (RB) 41/208y
PASSING: Schade 187-341/2338y, 14TD, 54.8%
RECEIVING: Rios 52/436y, Osterman 38/604y, Woodson 28/326y
SCORING: Darkins 78pts, M Chalberg (K) 76pts, Osterman 30pts

1995 3-8

31 Ball State	7 WR Ryan Thelwell
17 Syracuse	27 WR Johnny Woodson / Greg Nelson
55 Arkansas State	7 WR Tony Levine / Tutu Atwell
39 Purdue	38 T Mike Giovinetti
17 Northwestern	27 G Chris Bergstrom
31 Michigan State	34 C Todd Jesewitz
17 Michigan	52 G Toby Anderson
21 Ohio State	49 T Gann Brooks
27 Wisconsin	34 TE Matt Reem/Paul Kratochvil/MarkTangen
14 Illinois	48 QB Cory Sauter
3 Iowa	45 RB Chris Darkins / Rafael Cooper
	DL Ogun Akbar / Lamanzer Williams
	DL Antoine Richard / Troy Duerr
	DL Kevin Holmes / Ralph Green
	DL Jerome Davis / Peter Hiestand
	LB Justin Conzemius
	LB Ben Langford / Parc Williams
	LB Craig Sauer
	DB Rodney Heath
	DB Terrance Blayne / Craig Scruggs
	DB Crawford Jordan
	DB Rishon Early / Don Williams

RUSHING: Darkins 164/825y, Cooper 112/471y, Javon Jackson (RB) 43/201y
PASSING: Sauter 204-338/2600y, 18TD, 60.4%
RECEIVING: Thelwell 58/775y, Atwell 41/735y, Levine 38/396y
SCORING: Mike Chalberg (K) 65pts, Thelwell 38pts, Darkins & Atwell 36pts

1996 4-7

30 Northeastern La.	3 WR Ryan Thelwell
26 Ball State	23 WR Greg Nelson
35 Syracuse	33 WR Tutu Atwell
27 Purdue	30 T Luke Herkenhoff / Luke Glime
24 Northwestern	26 G Chris Bergstrom
9 Michigan State	27 C Gregg James / Jeff Baldauf
10 Michigan	44 G Tim Socha
28 Wisconsin	45 T Gann Brooks
23 Illinois	45 TE Paul Kratochvil
24 Iowa	21 QB Cory Sauter
	43 RB Thomas Hamner / Byron Evans
	DL Raymond Baylor / Antoine Richard
	DL Ogun Akbai / Mark Cross
	DL Jerome Davis
	LB Danny Dalton / Lamanzer Williams
	LB Parc Williams
	LB Rufus Smith / Don Williams
	LB Ben Langford
	DB Rodney Heath
	DB Craig Scruggs / Mari Moore
	DB Rishon Early / Crawford Jordan
	DB Tyrone Carter

RUSHING: Hamner 195/883y, Evans 69/314y
PASSING: Sauter 200-352/2578y, 14TD, 56.8%
RECEIVING: Atwell 62/822y, Thelwell 54/1051y, Nelson 31/287y
SCORING: Adam Bailey (K) 58pts, Atwell 40pts, Thelwell 30pts

1997 3-9

3 Hawaii	17 WR Greg Nelson / Luke Leverson
53 Iowa State	29 WR Tutu Atwell
20 Memphis	17 T Jon Albrecht / Luke Herkenhoff
43 Houston	45 G Luke Glime
10 Michigan State	31 C Ben Hamilton
43 Purdue	59 G Pat Hau
15 Penn State	16 T Tim Socha
21 Wisconsin	22 TE Alex Hass
3 Michigan	24 QB Cory Sauter
3 Ohio State	31 RB Thomas Hamner / Byron Evans
24 Indiana	12 FB/TE Justin Hall / Troy Duerr
0 Iowa	31 DL Raymond Baylor / Mark Cross
	DL Antoine Richard
	DL Dyron Russ / Josh Rawlings
	DL Lamanzer Williams
	LB Sean Hoffman
	LB Parc Williams
	LB Rufus Smith / Ben Mezera
	DB Jimmy Wyrick
	DB Craig Scruggs
	DB Crawford Jordan / Keith Dimmy
	DB Tyrone Carter

RUSHING: Hamner 170/663y, Evans 69/364y, Antoine Henderson (RB) 51/205y
PASSING: Sauter 126-234/1576y, 8TD, 53.9%
RECEIVING: Atwell 58/924y, Leverson 28/400y, Nelson 13/182y
SCORING: Adam Bailey (K) 68pts, Atwell 42pts, Hamner 32pts

1998 5-6

17 Arkansas State	14 WR Luke Leverson
14 Houston	7 WR Ron Johnson
41 Memphis	14 WR/TE Antoine Henderson / Zach Vevea
21 Purdue	56 T Adam Haayer
17 Penn State	27 G Pat Hau (T) / Jon Albrecht
15 Ohio State	45 C Ben Hamilton
19 Michigan State	18 G Ryan Roth
10 Michigan	15 T Erik Larson / Troy Duerr
7 Wisconsin	26 TE Alex Hass
19 Indiana	20 QB Billy Cockerham / Andy Persby
49 Iowa	7 RB Thomas Hamner
	DL Jon Michals / Rufus Smith
	DL Antoine Richard
	DL John Schlecht / Dyron Russ
	DL Curtese Poole
	LB Parc Williams
	LB Sean Hoffman
	LB Ben Mezera
	DB Willie Middlebrooks / Travis Graham
	DB Craig Scruggs
	DB Keith Dimmy / Delvin Jones
	DB Tyrone Carter

RUSHING: Hamner 209/838y, Byron Evans (RB) 51/327y, Cockerham 127/311y
PASSING: Cockerham 92-180/1150y, 11TD, 51.1%
RECEIVING: Leverson 60/854y, Johnson 38/395y, Henderson 16/178y
SCORING: Leverson 60pts, Adam Bailey (K) 53pts, Hamner & Johnson 24pts

1999 8-4

33 Ohio	7 WR Luke Leverson
35 La.-Monroe	0 WR Ron Johnson
55 Illinois State	0 WR Arland Bruce
33 Northwestern	14 T Adam Haayer
17 Wisconsin	20 G Derek Burns
37 Illinois	7 C Ben Hamilton
17 Ohio State	20 G Ryan Roth
28 Purdue	33 T Josh Rawlings
24 Penn State	23 TE Alex Hass / Zach Venca
44 Indiana	20 QB Billy Cockerham
25 Iowa	21 TB Thomas Hamner
20 Oregon■	24 DL Dyron Russ
	DL Jon Michals / Matt Anderle
	DL John Schlecht
	DL Karon Riley
	LB Astein Osei / Jimmy Henry
	LB Sean Hoffman
	LB Ben Mezera
	DB Trevis Graham / Jimmy Wyrick
	DB Willie Midlebrooks
	DB Delvin Jones / Jack Brewer
	DB Tyrone Carter

RUSHING: Hamner 308/1426y, Cockerham 168/831y, Byron Evans 69/314y
PASSING: Cockerham 147-276/2091y, 15TD, 53.3%
RECEIVING: Johnson 43/574y, Leverson 41.547y, Hamner 21/305y
SCORING: Dan Nystrom (K) 92pts, Hamner 78pts, Cockerham 60pts

2000 6-6

47 La.-Monroe	10 WR Ron Johnson
17 Ohio Univ.	23 WR Jack Brewer (S) / Jermaine Mays
34 Baylor	9 WR Elvin Jones / Tony Patterson
24 Purdue	38 T Aam Haayer
44 Illinois	10 G Derek Burns
25 Penn State	16 C Ben Hamilton
29 Ohio State	17 G Ryan Roth
43 Indiana	51 T Jake Kuppe
35 Northwestern	41 TE Ben Utecht / Scooter Baugus
20 Wisconsin	41 QB Travis Cole / Asad Abdul-Khaliq
27 Iowa	24 RB Tellis Redmon / Thomas Tapeh
30 N. Carolina St.■	38 DL Karon Riley
	DL John Schlecht
	DL Matt Anderle / Maurice White
	DL Greg White
	LB Curtese Poole / Justin Hall
	LB Sean Hoffman / Jimmy Henry
	LB Ben Mezera
	DB Willie Middlebrooks / Trevis Graham
	DB Mike Lehan
	DB Delvin Jones
	DB Clorenzo Griffin

RUSHING: Redmon 293/1368y, Tapeh 81/344y, Abdul-Khaliq 42/200y
PASSING: Cole 147-252/1982y, 11TD, 58.3%, Abdul-Khaliq 51-95/676y, 7TD, 53.7%
RECEIVING: Johnson 61/1125y, Redmon 32/327y, Brewer 22/286y
SCORING: Dan Nystrom (K) 109pts, Johnson & Redmon 66pts

2001 4-7

7 Toledo	38 WR Ron Johnson
44 La.-Lafayette	14 WR Antoine Burns / Tony Patterson
28 Purdue	35 T Jake Kuppe
14 Illinois	25 G Akeem Akinwale
17 Northwestern	23 C Derek Burns
28 Michigan State	19 G Jeremiah Carter
66 Murray State	10 T Matt Anderle
28 Ohio State	31 TE Ben Utecht / Scooter Baugus
10 Michigan	31 QB Asad Abdul-Khaliq / Travis Cole
24 Iowa	42 RB Tellis Redmon / Marion Barber III
42 Wisconsin	31 FB/WR Thomas Tapeh / Antoine Henderson
	DL Astein Osei / Zach Vevea
	DL Dan Kwapinski
	DL Darrell Reid
	DL Greg White
	LB Bradley Vance
	LB Phil Archer
	LB/DB Jimmy Henry / Justin Isom
	DB Michael Lehan
	DB Ukee Dozier / Justin Fraley (LB)
	DB Jack Brewer
	DB Eli Ward / Dominique Sims

RUSHING: Redmon 185/1091y, Barber 118/742y, Abdul-Khaliq 69/266y
PASSING: Abdul-Khaliq 107-187/1393y, 12TD, 57.2%, Cole 58-115/765y, 5TD, 50.4%
RECEIVING: Johnson 56/895y, Burns 30/470y, Henderson 23/235y
SCORING: Dan Nystrom (K) 64pts, Johnson 54pts, Barber 42pts

2002 8-5

42 SW Texas State	0 WR Aaron Hosack / Jared Ellerson
35 La-Lafayette	11 WR Antoine Burns / Danny Upchurch
31 Toledo	21 T Jeremiah Carter
41 Buffalo	17 G Mark Setterstrom
15 Purdue	28 C Greg Eslinger
31 Illinois	10 G Joe Quinn
45 Northwestern	42 T Jake Kuppe / Rian Melander
28 Michigan State	7 TE Ben Utecht
3 Ohio State	34 TE/WR Scooter Baugus / Tony Patterson
24 Michigan	41 QB Asad Abdul-Khaliq / Kamrath
21 Iowa	45 RB Terry Jackson / Thomas Tapeh
31 Wisconsin	49 DL Paul Nixon / Charlton Keith
29 Arkansas■	14 DL Dan Kwapinski / Anthony Montgomery
	DL Darrell Reid
	DL Mark Losli
	LB Terrance Campbell / Justin Fraley
	LB Ben West
	LB B. Vance / Phil Archer / Kyle McKenzie
	DB Michael Lehan / Ken Williams
	DB Ukee Dozier / Mike Wojciechowski
	DB Eli Ward
	DB Justin Isom

RUSHING: Jackson 239/1317y, Tapeh 181/906y, Abdul-Khaliq 86/322y
PASSING: Abdul-Khaliq 165-315/2190y, 19TD, 52.4%
RECEIVING: Burns 44/526y, Utecht 37/480y, Hosack 29/649y
SCORING: Dan Nystrom (K) 102pts, Tapeh 60pts, Jackson 42pts

2003 10-3

49 Tulsa	10 WR Aaron Hosack
48 Troy State	7 WR/RB Jared Ellerson / Laurence Maroney
42 Ohio	20 T Rian Melander
48 La-Lafayette	14 G Mark Setterstrom
20 Penn State	14 C Greg Eslinger
42 Northwestern	17 G Joseph Quinn
35 Michigan	38 T Joe Ainslie / Mike Nicholson
38 Michigan State	44 TE Ben Utecht
36 Illinois	10 TE/FB/WR Matt Spaeth/T.Tapeh/T.Pattersn
55 Indiana	7 QB Asad Abdul-Khaliq
37 Wisconsin	34 TB Marion Barber / Terry Jackson
22 Iowa	40 DL Mark Losli / Mario Reese
31 Oregon■	30 DL Anthony Montgomery / Dan Kwapinski
	DL Darrell Reid
	DL Paul Nixon / Eric Clark
	LB Terrance Campbell
	LB Ben West
	LB Lyle McKenzie / Brian Smith
	DB Ukee Dozier
	DB Trumaine Banks / John Pawielski
	DB Eli Ward
	DB Justin Isom / Justin Fraley

RUSHING: Barber 207/1196y, Maroney 162/1121y, Tapeh 119/570y
PASSING: Abdul-Khaliq 158-250/2401y, 17TD, 63.2%
RECEIVING: Hosack 51/814y, Ellerson 44/909y, Patterson 21/257y
SCORING: Barber 102pts, Rhys Lloyd (K) 101pts, Maroney & Tapeh 66pts

2004 7-5

63 Toledo	21 WR Jared Ellerson
37 Illinois State	21 WR Ernest Wheelwright / Jakari Wallace
34 Colorado State	16 T Rian Melander
43 Northwestern	17 G Mark Setterstrom
16 Penn State	7 C Greg Eslinger
24 Michigan	27 G Brandon Harston
17 Michigan State	51 T Joe Ainslie
45 Illinois	0 TE/FB Jarod Posthumus / Justin Valentine
21 Indiana	30 TE Matt Spaeth
14 Wisconsin	38 QB Bryan Cupito
27 Iowa	29 TB Marion Barber / Laurence Maroney
20 Alabama■	16 DL Eric Clark / Mario Reese
	DL Mark Losli
	DL Anthony Montgomery
	DL Darrell Reid
	LB Terrance Campbell
	LB Kyle McKenzie
	LB Dominique Sims
	DB Trumaine Banks / Jamal Harris
	DB Ukee Dozier
	DB John Pawielski / Brandon Owens
	DB Justin Fraley / Quentin White

RUSHING: Maroney 217/1348y, Barber 231/1269y
PASSING: Cupito 123-261/2097y, 14TD, 47.1%
RECEIVING: Ellerson 37/521y, Wheelwright 30/654y, Spaeth 24/298y
SCORING: Rhys Lloyd (K) 79pts, Maroney 72pts, Barber 66pts

2005 7-5

41 Tulsa	10 WR E. Wheelwright / Jakari Wallace
56 Colorado State	24 WR Logan Payne / Jared Ellerson
46 Florida Atlantic	7 T Steve Shidell
42 Purdue	35 G Mark Setterstrom
14 Penn State	44 C Greg Eslinger
23 Michigan	20 G Mike Nicholson
34 Wisconsin	38 T Tony Brinkhaus
31 Ohio State	45 TE Matt Spaeth
42 Indiana	21 TE/FB Jarod Posthumus/J. Valentine
41 Michigan State	18 QB Bryan Cupito
28 Iowa	52 RB Laurence Maroney / Gary Russell
31 Virginia■	34 DL Steve Davis / Willie VanDeSteeg
	DL Anthony Montgomery
	DL Mark Losli / Todd Meisel
	DL Keith Lipka
	LB John Shevlin
	LB Kyle McKenzie
	LB Mike Sherels / Mario Reese
	DB Trumaine Banks
	DB Jamal Harris
	DB John Pawielski
	DB Dominic Jones / Brandon Owens

RUSHING: Maroney 281/1464y, Russell 186/1130y, Amir Pinnix (RB) 78/467y
PASSING: Cupito 176-297/2530y, 19TD, 59.3%
RECEIVING: Wheelwright 37/568y, Payne 37/529y, Spaeth 26/333y
SCORING: Russell 114pts, Jason Giannini (K) 75pts, Maroney 66pts

2006 6-7

44 Kent State	0 WR Ernie Wheelwright / Eric Decker
17 California	42 WR Logan Payne / Mike Chambers
62 Temple	0 T Steve Shidell
21 Purdue	27 G Tyson Swaggert
14 Michigan	28 C Tony Brinkhaus / Matt DeGeest
27 Penn State	28 G Nedward Tavale
12 Wisconsin	48 T Joe Ainslie
10 N. Dakota State	9 TE Matt Spaeth
0 Ohio State	44 TE/FB Jack Simmons/Justin Valentine
63 Indiana	26 QB Bryan Cupito
31 Michigan State	18 RB Amir Pinnix / Alex Daniels
34 Iowa	24 DL Willie VanDeSteeg
41 Texas Tech■	44 DL Todd Meisel / John Jakel
	DL Neel Allen
	DL Steve Davis
	LB Mario Reese / John Shevlin
	LB Mike Sherels
	LB Deon Hightower
	DB Trumaine Banks / Duran Cooley
	DB Jamal Harris / Desi Steib
	DB Dominique Barber
	DB Dominic Jones

RUSHING: Pinnix 252/1272y, Daniels 67/309y, Jay Thomas (RB) 37/225y
PASSING: Cupito 214-359/2819y, 22TD, 59.6%
RECEIVING: Payne 59/804y, Spaeth 47/564y, Wheelwright 26/437y
SCORING: Pinnix 60pts, Jason Giannini (K) 59pts, Payne 54pts

2007 1-11

31 Bowling Green	32 WR Eric Decker
41 Miami (Ohio)	35 WR Tray Herndon / Ralph Spry
39 Florida Atlantic	42 WR Ernie Wheelwright
31 Purdue	45 T Steve Shidell
7 Ohio State	30 G Ned Tavale / Ryan Ruckdashel
20 Indiana	40 C Tony Brinkhaus
48 Northwestern	49 G D.J. Burris / Jeff Tow-Arnett
21 N. Dakota State	27 T Matt DeGeest / Dominic Alford
10 Michigan	34 TE Jack Simmons / Nick Tow-Arnett
17 Illinois	44 QB Adam Weber
16 Iowa	21 RB Duane Bennett / Amir Pinnix
34 Wisconsin	41 DL Willie VanDeSteeg/Derrick Onwuachi
	DL Eric Small / Garrett Brown
	DL Todd Meisel / Neel Allen
	DL Lee Campbell
	LB Steve Davis
	LB Deon Hightower / Mike Sherels
	LB John Shevlin / Kevin Mannion
	DB Jamal Harris / Kyle Theret
	DB Ryan Collado / Desi Steib
	DB Duran Cooley / Curtis Thomas
	DB Dom Barber

RUSHING: Weber 146/617y, Pinnix 106/563y, Bennett 107/442y
PASSING: Weber 258-449/2895y, 24TD, 57.5%
RECEIVING: Decker 67/909y, Wheelwright 66/775y, Spry 23/226y
SCORING: Wheelwright 56pts, Decker 54pts, Joel Monroe (K) 49pts

2008 7-6

31 N. Illinois	27 WR Eric Decker / Brandon Green
42 Bowling Green	17 WR Ben Kuznia
35 Montana State	23 WR Ralph Spry / Brodrick Smith
37 Fla. Atlantic	3 T Jason Meinke / Dominic Alford
21 Ohio State	34 G D.J. Burris / Ryan Orton
16 Indiana	7 C Jeff Tow-Arnett / Trey Davis
27 Illinois	20 G Nedward Tavale / Chris Bunders
17 Purdue	6 T Ryan Wynn
17 Northwestern	24 TE Jack Simmons / Nick Tow-Arnett
6 Michigan	29 QB Adam Weber
32 Wisconsin	35 RB DeLeon Eskridge / Shady Salamon
0 Iowa	55 DL Willie VanDeSteeg
21 Kansas■	42 DL Eric Small
	DL Garrett Brown
	DL/LB Derrick Onwuachi / Steve Davis
	LB Lee Campbell
	LB Deon Hightower
	LB Simoni Lawrence / Kevin Mannion
	DB Traye Simmons
	DB Marcus Sherels / Ryan Collado
	DB Tramaine Brock / Mike Rallis
	DB Kyle Theret

RUSHING: Eskridge 184/678y, Weber 127/233y, Salamon 49/181y
PASSING: Weber 255-410/2761y, 15TD, 62.2%
RECEIVING: Decker 84/1074y, Simmons 36/331y, Kuznia 31/310y
SCORING: Joel Monroe (K) 70pts, Decker 50pts, Eskridge 42pts

2009 6-7

23 Syracuse	20 WR Eric Decker / Da'Jon McKnight
20 Air Force	13 WR Troy Stoudermire
21 California	35 T Dom Alford / Matt Stommes
35 Northwestern	24 G Chris Bunders / Jewhan Edwards
28 Wisconsin	31 C D.J. Burris / Jeff Tow-Arnett
35 Purdue	20 G Matt Carufel / Ryan Orton
0 Penn State	20 T Jeff Willis
7 Ohio State	38 TE Nick Tow-Arnett
42 Michigan State	34 QB Adam Weber / MarQueis Gray (WR)
32 Illinois	35 RB Duane Bennett / DeLeon Eskridge
16 S. Dakota St.	13 FB/WR Jon Hoese / Brandon Green
0 Iowa	12 DL Barrett Moen
13 Iowa State■	14 DL Garrett Brown / Brandon Kirksey
	DL Eric Small
	DL Cedric McKinley / Anthony Jacobs
	LB Simoni Lawrence
	LB Lee Campbell
	LB Nate Triplett / Keanon Cooper
	DB Traye Simmons / Michael Carter
	DB Marcus Sherels / Ryan Collado
	DB Kyle Theret
	DB Kim Royston

RUSHING: Bennett 98/376y, Kevin Whaley (RB) 88/367y, Eskridge 74/294y, Gray 47/265y
PASSING: Weber 191-367/2582y, 13TD, 52.0%
RECEIVING: Decker 50/758y, N. Tow-Arnett 37/505y, Stoudermire 26/306y, Green 21/293y, McKnight 17/311y
SCORING: Eric Ellestad (K) 70pts, Bennett 48pts, Decker 30pts

2010 3-9

24 Mid. Tennessee	17 WR Da'Jon McKnight
38 South Dakota	41 WR MarQueis Gray / Bryant Allen
21 Southern Cal	32 T Ed Olson / Dominic Alford
23 N. Illinois	34 G Chris Bunders
28 Northwestern	29 C D.J. Burris
23 Wisconsin	41 G Matt Carufel / Ryan Orton
17 Purdue	28 T Jeff Wills / Ryan Winn
1 Penn State	33 TE Eric Lair
10 Ohio State	52 QB Adam Weber
8 Michigan State	31 RB Duane Bennett / DeLeon Eskridge
38 Illinois	34 FB/TE Jon Hoese / Curtis Hughes
27 Iowa	24 DL D.L. Wilhite / Matt Garin
	DL Jewhan Edwards
	DL Brandon Kirksey / Austin Hahn
	DL Anthony Jacobs
	LB Mike Rallis / Ryan Grant
	LB Gary Tinsley / Aaron Hill
	LB Keanon Cooper / Spencer Reeves
	DB Troy Stoudermire / Christyn Lewis
	DB Brock Vereen/M. Carter/John Johnson
	DB Ryan Collado / Kyle Henderson
	DB Kyle Theret / James Manuel

RUSHING: Eskridge 193/698y, Bennett 123/529y, Weber 52/156y
PASSING: Weber 205-368/2679y, 20TD, 55.7%
RECEIVING: McKnight 48/750y, Gray 42/587y, Lair 39/526y
SCORING: Eric Ellestad (K) 64pts, McKnight 60pts, Eskridge 44pts

MISSISSIPPI

University of Mississippi (often known as Ole Miss) (Founded 1844)
Oxford, Mississippi
Nickname: Rebels
Colors: Cardinal Red and Navy Blue
Stadium: Vaught-Hemingway Stadium at Hollingsworth Field
 (1915) 60,856
Conference Affiliation: Southeastern (Charter member, 1933-present)

CAREER RUSHING YARDS	Attempts	Yards
Deuce McAllister (1997-2000)	616	3060
Joe Gunn (1998-2001)	630	2749
Kayo Dottley (1947-50)	478	2654
Dou Innocent (1991-92, 1994-95)	494	2322
BenJarvis Green-Ellis (2006-07)	464	2137
Leon Perry (1976-79)	471	2135
Brandon Bolden (2008-10)	290	2132
Dexter McCluster (2006-09)	304	1955
Charlie Flowers (1957-59)	307	1730
John Avery (1996-97)	347	1650

CAREER PASSING YARDS	Comp.-Att.	Yards
Eli Manning (2000-03)	829-1363	10,119
Romaro Miller (1997-2000)	497-902	6311
Kent Austin (1981-85)	566-981	6184
John Fourcade (1978-81)	445-819	5412
Jevan Snead (2008-09)	375-678	5394
Mark Young (1985-88)	410-809	4971
Archie Manning (1968-70)	402-761	4753
Russ Shows (1989-92)	279-560	3778
Josh Nelson (1994-95)	311-558	3703
Stewart Patridge (1994-97)	310-510	3564

CAREER RECEIVING YARDS	Catches	Yards
Shay Hodge (2008-09)	173	2646
Chris Collins (2000-03)	198	2621
Willie Green (1986-89)	126	2274
Grant Heard (1996-2000)	142	2029
J.R. Ambrose (1984-87)	118	2012
Mike Wallace (2006-08)	101	1910
Cory Peterson (1996-99)	135	1842
Bill Flowers (2001-04)	149	1795
Mike Espy (2002-05)	136	1779
Michael Harmon (1979-82)	119	1760

SEASON RUSHING YARDS	Attempts	Yards
Kayo Dottley (1949)	208	1312
Dexter McCluster (2009)	181	1169
BenJarvis Green-Ellis (2007)	230	1137
Deuce McAllister (1998)	212	1082
Kayo Dottley (1950)	191	1007

SEASON PASSING YARDS	Comp.-Att.	Yards
Eli Manning (2003)	275-441	3600
Eli Manning (2002)	279-481	3401
Eli Manning (2001)	259-408	2948
Jevon Snead (2008)	194-327	2762
Stewart Patridge (1997)	228-352	2667

SEASON RECEIVING YARDS	Catches	Yards
Shay Hodge (2009)	70	1135
Chris Collins (2003)	77	949
Willie Green (1989)	41	816
Chris Collins (2002)	55	812
LeMay Thomas (1995)	56	801

GAME RUSHING YARDS	Attempts	Yards
Dexter McCluster (2009 vs. Tennessee)	25	282
Dou Innocent (1995 vs. Miss. State)	39	242
Randy Baldwin (1990 vs. Tulane)	17	241

GAME PASSING YARDS	Comp.-Att.	Yards
Archie Manning (1969 vs. Alabama)	33-52	436
Eli Manning (2002 vs. Arkansas)	42-56	414
John Darnell (1989 vs. Arkansas State)	23-35	412

GAME RECEIVING YARDS	Catches	Yards
Eddie Small (1993 vs. Vanderbilt)	6	210
Pat Coleman (1989 vs. Arkansas State)	6	200
Floyd Franks (1969 vs. Alabama)	13	191

GREATEST COACH:

Gentleman Johnny Vaught, a Texan who came to the deep south in 1947, provided the University of Mississippi with its greatest stretch of football in the late 1940s into the first half of the 1960s. From Vaught's first season in beautiful Oxford when he took the Rebels to the Southeastern Conference title through 1963 when he won his sixth conference crown, Ole Miss enjoyed a 137-32-8 overall mark. Mississippi has never won another conference championship other than the half-dozen Vaught wrought.

Mississippi enjoyed a five-year stretch from 1959 to 1963 when it consistently was the best team in the land. The Rebels ran off a 46-4-3 record, a staggering .8962 winning percentage. Two of the losses were by less than a touchdown and came in bowl games to two other great coaches: Darrell Royal of Texas in the 1962 Cotton Bowl and Bear Bryant of Alabama in the 1964 Sugar Bowl.

So, why didn't Ole Miss win any national championships amid two undefeated and four one-loss seasons? The perception was that the Rebels played a weak schedule, although they were good enough to finish second in the AP Poll in both 1959 and '60. And, their opponents' winning percentage from 1953-63 was .5463, better than the SEC's average for opponents over that time.

With the exception of LSU and Tennessee, however, Ole Miss rarely played against the SEC's best. In the 17 years, from 1947 to 1963, Mississippi played only nine games (6-3) against Alabama, Auburn, Florida, Georgia, and Georgia Tech. The Rebs went 3-1 against Auburn in 1949-53 before the Tigers peaked, lost to Georgia Tech in the 1953 Sugar Bowl, beat Georgia in 1955, beat Florida in 1948 and in the Gator Bowl following the 1958 season, and lost to Alabama in the 1964 Sugar Bowl. They didn't face neighboring Alabama at any time in the regular season between 1933 and 1965, but its annual SEC slate was loaded with relative conference lightweights Kentucky, Mississippi State, Tulane, and Vanderbilt.

Still, there is no coach in Ole Miss history who can touch Johnny Vaught.

MISSISSIPPI'S 55 GREATEST SINCE 1953

OFFENSE

WIDE RECEIVER: Chris Collins, Floyd Franks, Grant Heard, Willie Green
TIGHT END: Rufus French, Kris Mangum, Wesley Walls
TACKLE: Gene Hickerson, Terrence Metcalf, Crawford Mims
GUARD: Buddy Alliston, Bookie Bolin, Stan Hindman, Everett Lindsay, Marvin Terrell
CENTER: Chuck Hinton
QUARTERBACK: Jake Gibbs, Archie Manning, Eli Manning
RUNNING BACK: John Avery, Randy Baldwin, Deuce McAllister, Dou Innocent
FULLBACK: Billy Ray Adams, Charlie Flowers

DEFENSE

END: Derrick Burgess, Freddie Joe Nunn, Kelvin Prichett, Ralph "Catfish" Smith
TACKLE: Rex Reed Boggan, Jim Dunaway, Jim Urbanek, Ben Williams
LINEBACKER: Kenny Dill, Larry Grantham, Abdul Jackson, Jackie Simpson, Eddie Strong, Patrick Willis
CORNERBACK: Aldunis Brice, Tommy James, Ken Lucas
SAFETY: Glenn Cannon, Billy Clay, Matt Grier, Chris Mitchell

SPECIAL TEAMS

RETURN SPECIALISTS: Doug Cunningham
PLACE KICKER: Jonathan Nichols
PUNTER: Jim Miller, Bill Smith

MULTIPLE POSITIONS

FULLBACK-LINEBACKER-PLACE KICKER: Paige Cothren
QUARTERBACK-SAFETY-PUNT RETURNER: Ray Brown
WIDE RECEIVER-RUNNING BACK: Dexter McCluster

TWO-WAY PLAYERS

HALFBACK-DEFENSIVE BACK: Jimmy Patton
END-DEFENSIVE END: Bob Drewry

PERFORMANCE FORMULA:
MISSISSIPPI'S 10 BEST SEASONS

1959	1.7660	2 of 70
1960	1.7541	1 of 70
1962	1.7390	1 of 70
1955	1.6561	3 of 69
1961	1.6418	4 of 71
1969	1.5030	14 of 70
1957	1.5997	3 of 69
1954	1.5028	8 of 69
1966	1.4698	9 of 70
1958	1.4662	9 of 70

MISSISSIPPI REBELS

Year	W-L-T	AP Poll	Conference Standing	Toughest Regular Season Opponents	Coach (Record at School)	Bowl Games		
1953	7-2-1		2t	Kentucky 7-2-1, Auburn 7-2-1, Maryland 10-0	Johnny Vaught			
1954	9-2	6	1	Kentucky 7-3, Arkansas 8-2, Mississippi State 6-4	Johnny Vaught	Sugar	0 Navy	21
1955	10-1	10	1	Kentucky 6-3-1, Vanderbilt 7-3	Johnny Vaught	Cotton	14 Texas Christian	13
1956	7-3		4	Houston 7-2-1, Arkansas 6-4, Tennessee 10-0	Johnny Vaught			
1957	9-1-1	7	2	Vanderbilt 5-3-2, Arkansas 6-4, Tennessee 7-3, Miss. State 6-2-1	Johnny Vaught	Sugar	39 Texas	7
1958	9-2	11	3	Kentucky 5-4-1, LSU 10-0	Johnny Vaught	Gator	7 Florida	3
1959	10-1	2	2t	Vanderbilt 5-3-2, Arkansas 8-2, LSU 9-1, Tennessee 5-4-1	Johnny Vaught	Sugar	21 Louisiana State	0
1960	10-0-1	2	1	Memphis State 8-2, Arkansas 8-2, LSU 5-4-1, Tennessee 6-2-2	Johnny Vaught	Sugar	14 Rice	6
1961	9-2	5	3	Arkansas 8-2, LSU 9-1, Tennessee 6-4	Johnny Vaught	Cotton	7 Texas	12
1962	10-0	3	1	Memphis State 8-1, Houston 6-4, LSU 8-1-1	Johnny Vaught	Sugar	17 Arkansas	13
1963	7-1-2	7	1	Memphis State 9-0-1, LSU 7-3, Mississippi State 6-2-2	Johnny Vaught	Sugar	7 Alabama	12
1964	5-5-1		7	Florida 7-3, LSU 7-2-1	Johnny Vaught	Bluebonnet	7 Tulsa	14
1965	7-4		5	Alabama 8-1-1, Florida 7-3, LSU 7-3, Tennessee 7-1-2	Johnny Vaught	Liberty	13 Auburn	7
1966	8-3	11+	4	Alabama 10-0, Georgia 9-1, Houston 8-2, Tennessee 7-3	Johnny Vaught	Bluebonnet	0 Texas	19
1967	6-4-1		4	Alabama 8-1-1, Georgia 7-3, LSU 6—3-1, Tennessee 9-1	Johnny Vaught	Sun	7 Texas-El Paso	14
1968	7-3-1		6t	Alabama 8-2, Georgia 8-0-2, LSU 7-3, Tennessee 8-1-1	Johnny Vaught	Liberty	34 Virginia Tech	17
1969	8-3	8	5	Alabama 6-4, Houston 8-2, LSU 9-1, Tennessee 9-1	Johnny Vaught	Sugar	27 Arkansas	22
1970	7-4		4	Alabama 6-5, Houston 8-3, LSU 9-2	Johnny Vaught {see below}			
1971	10-2	17	4t	Alabama 11-0, Georgia 10-1, LSU 8-3	Billy Kinard	Peach	41 Georgia Tech	18
1972	5-5		7t	Auburn 9-1, Alabama 10-1, LSU 9-1-1	Billy Kinard			
1973	6-5		3	Florida 7-4, Alabama 11-0, LSU 9-2	Billy Kinard (16-9), Johnny Vaught [5-3], (190-65-12)			
1974	3-8		10	Missouri 7-4, Alabama 11-0, Tennessee 6-3-2, Miss. State 8-3	Ken Cooper			
1975	6-5		2t	Texas A&M 10-1, Alabama 10-1, Georgia 9-2	Ken Cooper			
1976	6-5		6	Alabama 8-3, Georgia 10-1, Mississippi State 9-2	Ken Cooper			
1977	6-5		6	Alabama 10-1, Notre Dame 10-1, South Carolina 8-1-1, LSU 8-3	Ken Cooper (21-23)			
1978	5-6		7t	Missouri 7-4, Georgia 9-1-1, LSU 8-3	Steve Sloan			
1979	4-7		5t	Georgia 6-5, South Carolina 8-3, Tulane 9-2, Tennessee 7-4	Steve Sloan			
1980	3-8		7	Florida 7-4, Miami 8-3, Alabama 9-2, LSU 7-4	Steve Sloan			
1981	4-6-1		8t	Florida 7-4, Miami 9-2, Alabama 9-1-1, So. Mississippi 9-1-1	Steve Sloan			
1982	4-7		9t	Arkansas 8-2-1, Georgia 11-0, Vanderbilt 8-3, LSU 8-2-1	Steve Sloan (20-34-1)			
1983	7-5		5t	Alabama 7-4, Georgia 9-1-1, Tennessee 8-3	Billy Brewer	Independence	3 Air Force	9
1984	4-6-1		9t	Arkansas 7-3-1, Auburn 8-4, LSU 8-2-1, Tennessee 7-3-1	Billy Brewer			
1985	4-6-1		6	Arkansas 9-2, Auburn 8-3, LSU 9-1-1, Tennessee 8-2-1	Billy Brewer			
1986	8-3-1		2t	Arkanas 9-2, Georgia 8-3, LSU 9-2	Billy Brewer	Independence	20 Texas Tech	17
1987	3-8		7t	Arkansas 9-3, Georgia 8-3, LSU 9-1-1, Tennessee 9-2-1	Billy Brewer			
1988	5-6		6t	Arkansas 10-1, Georgia 8-3, Alabama 8-3, LSU 8-3	Billy Brewer	Liberty	42 Air Force	29
1989	8-4		4t	Arkansas 10-1, Alabama 10-1, Tennessee 10-1	Billy Brewer			
1990	9-3	21	3t	Auburn 7-3-1, Tennessee 8-2-2	Billy Brewer	Gator	3 Michigan	35
1991	5-6		9	Georgia 8-3, Tennessee 9-2, Mississippi State 7-4	Billy Brewer			
1992	9-3	20	W2	Georgia 9-2, Alabama 12-0, Mississippi State 7-4	Billy Brewer	Liberty	13 Air Force	0
1993	5-6		W4t	Auburn 11-0, Alabama 8-2-1	Billy Brewer			
1994	4-7		W4t	Auburn 9-1-1, Florida 9-1-1, Alabama 11-0, Miss. State 8-3	Billy Brewer (71-63-3)			
1995	6-5		W5	Auburn 8-3, Florida 11-0, Alabama 8-3	Tommy Tuberville			
1996	5-6		W5t	Tennessee 9-2, Alabama 9-3, LSU 9-2	Tommy Tuberville			
1997	8-4	22	W4t	Auburn 9-2, Tennessee 10-1, LSU 8-3, Georgia 9-2	Tommy Tuberville	Motor City	34 Marshall	31
1998	7-5		W4	Alabama 7-4, Arkansas 9-2, Georgia 8-3, Miss. State 8-3	Tommy Tuberville (25-20), David Cutcliffe [1-0]	Independence	35 Texas Tech	18
1999	8-4	22	W3t	Alabama 9-2, Arkansas 7-4, Georgia 7-4, Miss. State 9-2	David Cutcliffe	Independence	27 Oklahoma	25
2000	7-5		W3t	Auburn 9-2, LSU 7-4, Georgia 7-4, Mississippi State 7-4	David Cutcliffe	Music City	38 West Virginia	49
2001	7-4		W3t	Auburn 7-4, LSU 8-3, Arkansas 7-4, Georgia 8-3	David Cutcliffe			
2002	7-6		W5	Florida 8-4, Alabama 10-3, Arkansas 9-3, Georgia 11-1, LSU 8-4	David Cutcliffe	Independence	27 Nebraska	23
2003	10-3		W1t	Florida 8-4, Arkansas 8-4, LSU 11-1	David Cutcliffe	Cotton	31 Oklahoma State	28
2004	4-7		W3t	Memphis 8-3, Tennessee 9-2, Auburn 11-0, LSU 9-2	David Cutcliffe (43-30)			
2005	3-8		W5t	Alabama 9-2, Auburn 9-2, LSU 10-2	Ed Orgeron			
2006	4-8		W4t	Wake Forest 10-2, Arkansas 10-2, Auburn 10-2, LSU 10-2	Ed Orgeron			
2007	3-9		W6t	Missouri 11-1, Florida 9-3, Georgia 10-2, LSU 10-2	Ed Orgeron (10-25)			
2008	9-4	14	W2	Florida 12-1, Alabama 12-1	Houston Nutt	Cotton	47 Texas Tech	34
2009	9-4	20	W3	Alabama 13-0, Auburn 7-5, Tennessee 7-5, LSU 9-3	Houston Nutt	Cotton	21 Oklahoma State	7
2010	4-8		W6	Alabama 9-3, Arkansas 10-2, Auburn 13-0, LSU 10-2	Houston Nutt (22-16)			

TOTAL: 379-263-12 .5887 (24 of 70)   **Bowl Games since 1953:**   20-9 .6897 (2 of 70)

GREATEST TEAM SINCE 1953: Mississippi's 1959 squad lost a heart-breaker to undefeated LSU at Tiger Stadium and rebounded to easily take measure of the Bayou Bengals by 21-0 in a Sugar Bowl rematch. Ole Miss finished 10-1 and was voted national champions by minor services Dunkel and Berryman. Years later, Jeff Sagarin of *USA TODAY* retroactively declared the Rebels as champs. Johnny Vaught's Rebs, led by Jake Gibbs, Charlie Flowers, Marvin Terrell, and Larry Grantham, serve as Ole Miss' greatest team of the modern era.

1953 7-2-1

39	Chattanooga	6	E Bob Adams / Bob Drewry
22	Kentucky	6	T Dick Weiss
0	Auburn	13	G Ray James / Buddy Alliston
28	Vanderbilt	6	C Ed Beatty
45	Tulane	14	G Crawford Mims / Archie Shepherd
28	Arkansas	0	T Henry Linton
27	LSU	16	E George Harris / Dave Dickerson
40	N. Texas St.	7	QB Lea Paslay / Eagle Day
0	Maryland	38	HB Harold Lofton/Jimmy Patton/Earl Blair
7	Mississippi St.	7	HB Billy Kinard / Allen "Red" Muirhead
			FB Bobby "Slick" McCool

RUSHING: McCool 127/564y
PASSING: Paslay 32-66/713y, 48.5%
RECEIVING: Blair 10/213y
SCORING: Blair & McCool 42pts

1954 9-2

35	N. Texas St.	12	E George Harris / Bobby Fisher
28	Kentucky	9	T Dick Weiss / Billy Yelverton
52	Villanova	0	G Ray James / Buddy Alliston
22	Vanderbilt	7	C Bobby McKinney / Gene Dubuisson
34	Tulane	7	G Archie Shepherd
0	Arkansas	6	T Rex Reed Boggan
21	LSU	6	E Bob Drewry / Dave Dickerson
51	Memphis State	0	QB Eagle Day / Houston Patton
26	Houston	0	HB Jimmy Patton / Earl Blair
14	Mississippi St.	0	HB Red Muirhead / Billy Kinard
0	Navy■	21	FB Bobby McCool / Paige Cothren

RUSHING: Muirhead 63/443y, McCool 88/418y,
  J. Patton 48/343y, Cothren 64/310y
PASSING: Day 40-85/879y, 4TD, 47.0%,
  H. Patton 29-62/511y, 3TD, 46.8%
RECEIVING: Blair 18/472y, Muirhead 13/138y, J. Patton 9/139y
SCORING: Muirhead 60pts, J. Patton (HB-K) 37pts,
  Cothren (FB-K) 31pts

1955 10-1

26	Georgia	13	E Bobby Fisher / Leon "Buddy" Harbin
14	Kentucky	21	T Dick Weiss / Billy Yelverton
33	N. Texas St.	0	G Buddy Alliston
13	Vanderbilt	0	C Gene Dubuisson / Jerry Stone
27	Tulane	13	G Charles Duck / Jackie Simpson
17	Arkansas	7	T Dick Goehe / Gene Hickerson
29	LSU	26	E Bob Drewry / Dave Dickerson
39	Memphis State	6	QB Eagle Day / John Blalack
27	Houston	11	HB Eddie Crawford / Earl Blair
26	Mississippi St.	0	HB Billy Kinard / Billy Lott
14	TCU■	13	FB Paige Cothren / Bill Hurst

RUSHING: Cothren 93/520y, Blair 54/286y, Kinard 66/281y
PASSING: Day 47-95/724y, 8TD, 49.5%
RECEIVING: Kinard 23/371y, Crawford 7/108y, Williams 6/116y
SCORING: Cothren (FB-K) 74pts, Kinard, Blalack & Blair 24pts

1956 7-3

45	N. Texas St.	0	E Buddy Harbin / Billy Templeton
37	Kentucky	7	T Billy Yelverton
14	Houston	0	G Jackie Simpson
16	Vanderbilt	0	C Jerry Stone / Milt Crain
3	Tulane	10	G Charles Duck / Earl McKay
0	Arkansas	14	T Gene Hickerson
46	LSU	17	E Don Williams / Warren Jenkins
26	Memphis State	0	QB Ray Brown / John Blalack
7	Tennessee	27	HB Eddie Crawford / Leroy Reed
13	Mississippi St.	7	HB Billy Lott / Lea Paslay
			FB Paige Cothren / Jerry Baker

RUSHING: Cothren 115/560y, Crawford 67/357y, Lott 36/241y
PASSING: Brown 40-84/653y, 4TD, 47.6%,
  Blalack 33-67/474y, 3TD, 49.2%
RECEIVING: Reed 14/278y, Crawford 14/217y, Williams 7/118y
SCORING: Brown 52pts, Cothren (FB-K) 46pts, Crawford 36pts

1957 9-1-1

44	Trinity	0	E Billy Templeton / Larry Grantham
15	Kentucky	0	T Wayne West / Robert Owens
34	Hardin-Simmons	7	G Jackie Simpson / Harold Cooper
28	Vanderbilt	0	C Milt Crain
50	Tulane	0	G Willie Henderson / Bull Churchwell
6	Arkansas	12	T Gene Hickerson / Aubrey Sanders
20	Houston	7	E Don Williams / Warren Jenkins
14	LSU	12	QB Ray Brown / Bobby Franklin
14	Tennessee	7	HB Cowboy Woodruff / Kent Lovelace
7	Mississippi St.	7	HB Billy Lott / Leroy Reed
39	Texas■	7	FB Bill Hurst / Charlie Flowers

RUSHING: Brown 99/530y, Hurst 112/527y, Flowers 59/438y
PASSING: Brown 24-53/308y, 6TD, 45.3%,
  Franklin 10-25/134y, 2TD, 40.0%
RECEIVING: Lott 5/71y, Reed, Williams, Hall & Lovelace with 4
SCORING: Brown (QB-K) 42pts, Woodruff 30pts,
  Lovelace & Lott 24pts

1958 9-2

17	Memphis State	0	E Larry Grantham / Billy Templeton
27	Kentucky	6	T Rudolph Smith / Bull Churchwell
21	Trinity	0	G Harold Cooper / Richard Price
19	Tulane	8	C Milt Crain / Ken Kirk
24	Hardin-Simmons	0	G Marvin Terrell
14	Arkansas	12	T Aubrey Sanders / Bob Khayat
0	LSU	14	E Warren Jenkins
56	Houston	7	QB Bobby Franklin / Billy Brewer
16	Tennessee	18	HB Cowboy Woodruff
21	Mississippi St.	0	HB Kent Lovelace / Tommy Taylor
7	Florida■	3	FB Charlie Flowers / James Anderson

RUSHING: Flowers 107/559y,Lovelace 71/324y,Franklin 71/250y
PASSING: Franklin 56-121/710y, 10TD, 46.3%
RECEIVING: Lovelace 14/178y,Grantham 12/182y,Jenkins 9/97y
SCORING: Franklin (QB-K) 39pts, Khayat (T-K) 34pts

1959 10-1

16	Houston	0	E Larry Grantham / Ralph "Catfish" Smith
16	Kentucky	0	T Charles Kempinska / Joe Robertson
43	Memphis State	0	G Richard Price / Warner Alford
33	Vanderbilt	0	C Ken Kirk / Fred Lentjes
53	Tulane	7	G Marvin Terrell / Bob Khayat
28	Arkansas	0	T Robert Owens / Bob Benton
3	LSU	7	E Johnny Brewer / Jerry Daniels
58	Chattanooga	0	QB B'by Franklin/Jake Gibbs/Billy Brewer
37	Tennessee	7	HB George Blair / Cowboy Woodruff
42	Mississippi St.	0	HB Bobby Crespino / Dewey Partridge
21	LSU■	0	FB Charlie Flowers / James Anderson

RUSHING: Flowers 141/733y, Anderson 66/317y, Blair 49/249y
PASSING: Gibbs 46-94/755y, 6TD, 48.9%
RECEIVING: Partridge 13/142y, Daniels 11/164y,
  Grantham 10/162y
SCORING: Flowers 66pts, Gibbs 42pts, Khayat (G-K) 40pts

1960 10-0-1

42	Houston	0	E Catfish Smith / Jerry Daniels
21	Kentucky	6	T Jerry Brown / Joe Robertson
31	Memphis State	20	G Richard Price / Warner Alford
26	Vanderbilt	0	C Fred Lentjes / Allen Green
26	Tulane	13	G Bookie Bolin
10	Arkansas	7	T Jim Dunaway / Bob Benton
6	LSU	6	E Johnny Brewer
45	Chattanooga	0	QB Jake Gibbs / Doug Elmore
24	Tennessee	3	HB George Blair / Art Doty
35	Mississippi St.	9	HB Bobby Crespino / Louis Guy
14	Rice■	6	FB James Anderson / Billy Ray Adams

RUSHING: Anderson 104/505y, Adams 67/348y, Doty 58/299y
PASSING: Gibbs 66-109/970y, 12TD, 60.6%
RECEIVING: Crespino 30/408y, Doty 13/138y, Anderson 10/165y
SCORING: Anderson 42pts, Green (C-K) 31pts

1961 9-2

16	Arkansas	0	E Catfish Smith / Reed Davis
20	Kentucky	6	T Jerry Brown / Whaley Hall
33	Florida State	0	G Billy Ray Jones
47	Houston	7	C Fred Lentjes / Richard Ross
41	Tulane	0	G Bookie Bolin
47	Vanderbilt	0	T Jim Dunaway
7	LSU	10	E Woody Dabbs / Wesley Sullivan
54	Chattanooga	0	QB Doug Elmore / Glynn Griffing
24	Tennessee	10	TB Art Doty / Chuck Morris
37	Mississippi St.	7	WB Louis Guy / A.J. Holloway
7	Texas■	12	FB Billy Ray Adams / Buck Randall

RUSHING: Adams 91/575y, Elmore 77/345y, Randall 48/200y
PASSING: Elmore 50-84/741y, 6TD, 59.4%,
  Griffing 46-91/785y, 10TD, 50.5%
RECEIVING: Smith 14/254y, Holloway 14/148y, Adams 11/198y
SCORING: Adams 60pts, Sullivan (E-K) 51pts

1962 10-0

21	Memphis State	7	E Allen Brown
14	Kentucky	0	T Whaley Hall / James Roberts
40	Houston	7	G Fred Kimbrell
21	Tulane	0	C Richard Ross / Kenny Dill
35	Vanderbilt	0	G Don Dickson
15	LSU	7	T Jim Dunaway
52	Chattanooga	7	E Woody Dabbs / Wesley Sullivan
19	Tennessee	6	QB Glynn Griffing
13	Mississippi St.	6	TB Chuck Morris
17	Arkansas■	13	WB Louis Guy
			FB Perry Lee Dunn / Buck Randall

RUSHING: Griffing 74/278y, Morris 52/272y, Dunn 61/262y
PASSING: Griffing 72-122/882y, 11TD, 59.0%
RECEIVING: Guy 24/295y, Morris 17/149y, Brown 11/134y
SCORING: Guy 48pts, Sullivan 20pts
  Dabbs, Dunn & Randall 18pts

1963 7-1-2

0	Memphis State	0	E Allen Brown / Billy Carl Irwin
31	Kentucky	7	T Whaley Hall / Bo Aldridge
20	Houston	6	G Bobby Robinson / Rodney Mattina
21	Tulane	0	C Kenny Dill
27	Vanderbilt	7	G Stan Hindman
37	LSU	3	T Cecil Ford / James Harvey
41	Tampa	0	E Reed Davis / Joe Pettey
20	Tennessee	0	QB Perry Lee Dunn / Jim Weatherly
10	Mississippi St.	10	TB Mike Dennis / Billy Sumrall
7	Alabama	12	WB Bill Clay / Larry Smith
			FB Fred Roberts / Frank Kinard

RUSHING: Roberts 70/273y, Dennis 68/227y, Weatherly 61/202y
PASSING: Weatherly 52-96/676y, 7TD, 54.2%,
  Dunn 51-89/820y, 9TD, 57.3%
RECEIVING: Brown 16/221y, Dennis 13/217y, Smith 13/200y
SCORING: Billy Carl Irwin (K) 38pts, Dennis 36pts,
  Weatherly & Roberts 24pts

1964 5-5-1

30	Memphis State	0	E Allen Brown / Roy Heidel
21	Kentucky	27	T Tommy Lucas / Bo Aldridge
31	Houston	9	G Bobby Robinson / John Turner (LB)
14	Florida	30	C Chuck Hinton / Ray Beddingfield (LB)
14	Tulane	9	G Stan Hindman / Don Windham (LB)
7	Vanderbilt	7	T James Harvey / Joe Dean
10	LSU	11	E Rocky Fleming / Joe Pettey
36	Tampa	0	QB Jim Weatherly / Charles Myers (DB)
30	Tennessee	0	TB Mike Dennis / Brent Caston (DB)
17	Mississippi St.	20	WB Dave Wells / Billy Clay (DB)
7	Tulsa■	14	FB Frank Kinard / Tommy Luke (DB)

RAUSHING: Dennis 134/571y, Weatherly 79/262y,
  Kinard 68/253y
PASSING: Weatherly 91-170/1034y, 5TD, 53.5%
RECEIVING: Dennis 29/276y, Brown 24/229y, Wells 15/194y
SCORING: Billy Carl Irwin (K) 42pts, Dennis 36pts,
  Weatherly 30pts

1965 7-4

34	Memphis State	14	WR Rocky Fleming
7	Kentucky	16	T James Harvey / Bobby Hendrix
16	Alabama	17	G Kenny Smith
0	Florida	17	C Chuck Hinton
24	Tulane	7	G Stan Hindman
24	Vanderbilt	7	T Tommy Lucas
23	LSU	0	TE Steve Terracin / Mac Haik
3	Houston	17	QB Jimmy Heidel / Jody Graves
14	Tennessee	13	TB Mike Dennis
21	Mississippi St.	0	WB Doug Cunningham / Dave Wells
13	Auburn■		FB Bobby Wade / Don Street
			DL John Maddox / Jerry Richardson
			DL Dan Sartin
			DL Jimmy Keyes / Ronnie Fowler
			DL Jim Urbanek
			DL Kelley Roberts / Marvin McQueen
			LB Lee Garner / Mike Nelson
			LB Mac McClure
			DB Tommy James / Tommy Luke
			DB Billy Clay / Bruce Dillingham
			DB Brent Caston / Gerald Warfield
			DB Jimmy Haddock

RUSHING: Dennis 152/525y, Wade 97/459y, Heidel 119/202y
PASSING: Heidel 52-95/586y, 3TD, 54.7%
RECEIVING: Dennis 23/246y, Cunningham 16/109y,
  Fleming 8/153y
SCORING: Dennis 48pts, Keyes (DL-K) 43pts, Heidel 24pts

1966 8-3

13 Memphis State	0 WR Mac Haik
17 Kentucky	0 T Bobby Hendrix (G) / Bob Vaughan
7 Alabama	17 G Reed Webb / Mike Swetland
3 Georgia	9 C Chuck Hinton
14 Southern Miss	7 G Mike Magee
27 Houston	6 T Alan Bush
17 LSU	0 TE Hank Shows / Steve Terracin
14 Tennessee	7 QB Bruce Newell / Jody Graves
34 Vanderbilt	0 TB Doug Cunningham / Steve Hindman
24 Mississippi St.	0 WB Rocky Fleming / Bill Matthews
0 Texas■	19 FB Bobby Wade / Don Street
	DL Jerry Richardson
	DL Dan Sartin / James Shows
	DL Jimmy Keyes
	DL Jim Urbanek
	DL Marvin McQueen
	LB Mac McClure / Frank Trapp
	LB Lee Garner / Sammy Graves
	DB Tommy Luke / Tommy James
	DB Bruce Dillingham / Robert Bailey
	DB Brent Caston
	DB Gerald Warfield

RUSHING: Cunningham 139/653y, Wade 153/599y, Street 40/166y
PASSING: Newell 54-101/702y, 6TD, 53.5%, Graves 23-67/293y, TD, 34.3%
RECEIVING: Haik 20/267y, Cunningham 20/132y, Fleming 15/153y
SCORING: Keyes (DL-K) 50pts, Cunningham 42pts, Matthews 18pts

1967 6-4-1

17 Memphis State	27 WR Mac Haik / Jim Sullivan
26 Kentucky	13 T Alan Bush
7 Alabama	21 G Mike Magee
29 Georgia	20 C Jim Parkes
23 Southern Miss	14 G Mike Swetland / Bobby Hendrix
14 Houston	13 T Bob Vaughan / Jim Farmer
13 LSU	13 TE Hank Shows / Chip Stewart
7 Tennessee	20 QB Bruce Newell
28 Vanderbilt	7 TB Steve Hindman / Bo Bowen
10 Mississippi St.	3 WB Carol Carpenter / Bill Matthews
7 Texas■	14 FB Bobby Wade / Don Street
	DL Jerry Richardson
	DL Buz Morrow
	DL Dan Sartin
	DL Claude Herard
	DL Jim Urbanek
	DL Mac McClure / Bobo Uzzle
	LB Frank Trapp
	LB Jimmy Keyes / Sammy Graves
	DB Tommy James / Robert Bailey
	DB Bruce Dillingham
	DB Glenn Cannon / Jimmy Haddock

RUSHING: Hindman 215/829y, Wade 72/325y, Bowen 56/181y
PASSING: Newell 53-121/663y, 6TD, 43.8%
RECEIVING: Haik 33/475y, Hindman 12/88y, Matthews 8/80y, Carpenter 8/64y
SCORING: Keyes (LB-K) 41pts, Haik 36pts, Hindman 30pts

1968 7-3-1

21 Memphis State	7 WR Floyd Franks / Riley Myers
30 Kentucky	14 T Buddy Mitchell / Owen Holder
10 Alabama	8 G Billy Coker
7 Georgia	21 C Jim Parkes
21 Southern Miss	13 G Skip Jernigan
7 Houston	29 T Worthy McClure / Murray Williams
27 LSU	24 TE Hank Shows
38 Chattanooga	16 QB Archie Manning / Terry Collier
0 Tennessee	31 TB Steve Hindman
17 Mississippi St.	17 WB Vernon Studdard / Wyck Neely
34 Virginia Tech ■	17 FB Bo Bowen
	DL Hap Farber / John Gilliland
	DL Buz Morrow
	DL Putt Crull / Jeff Horn
	DL Claude Herard
	DL Dennis Coleman / George Lotterhos
	LB Joe Blount
	LB Frank Trapp / Fred Brister
	DB Ray Heidel / Bill Jones
	DB Bobby Garrigues
	DB Glenn Cannon
	DB Robert Bailey

RUSHING: Hindman 129/475y, Bowen 132/469y, Manning 110/208y
PASSING: Manning 127-263/1510y, 8TD, 48.3%, Collier 26-56/271y, 1TD, 46.4%
RECEIVING: Franks 27/319y, Shows 27/276y, Hindman 21/197y
SCORING: Hindman 42pts, Perry Lee King (K) 37pts, Manning 30pts

1969 8-3

28 Memphis State	3 WR Floyd Franks / Buddy Jones
9 Kentucky	10 WR Vernon Studdard / Riley Myers
32 Alabama	33 T Buddy Mitchell
25 Georgia	17 G Billy Coker
69 Southern Miss	7 C Wimpy Winther
11 Houston	25 G Skip Jernigan
26 LSU	23 T Worthy McClure
21 Chattanooga	0 TE Jim Poole
38 Tennessee	0 QB Archie Manning
48 Mississippi State	22 TB Leon Felts / Randy Reed
27 Arkansas■	22 FB Bo Bowen
	DL Hap Farber / John Gilliland
	DL Buz Morrow
	DL Larry Thomas
	DL Claude Herard / John Aldridge
	DL Dennis Coleman
	LB Fred Brister / Paul Dongieux
	LB Joe Blount / Crowell Armstrong
	DB Bob Knight / Bill Jones
	DB Wyck Neely / Ray Heidel
	DB Glenn Cannon / Danny Hooker
	DB Bill Van Devender

RUSHING: Manning 124/502y, Bowen 95/447y, Felts 87/288y
PASSING: Manning 154-265/1762y, 9TD, 58.1%
RECEIVING: Franks 54/720y, Poole 43/456y, Myers 26/262y
SCORING: Manning 86pts, Bowen 30pts, Perry Lee King (K) 25pts

1970 7-4

47 Memphis State	13 WR Floyd Franks
20 Kentucky	17 WR Vernon Studdard / Buddy Jones
48 Alabama	23 T Buddy Mitchell / Robert Burke
31 Georgia	21 G Billy Coker / Dave Bridgers
14 Southern Miss	30 C Wimpy Winther
26 Vanderbilt	16 G Skip Jernigan
24 Houston	13 T Worthy McClure
44 Chattanooga	7 TE Jim Poole
14 Mississippi St.	19 QB Archie Manning / Shug Chumbler
17 LSU	61 TB Randy Reed (FB) / Bob Knight
28 Auburn■	35 FB Luther Webb / Gerald Havard
	DL Preston Carpenter / John Gilliland
	DL Elmer Allen / Larry Torgerson
	DL John Aldridge
	DL Dennis Coleman
	LB Crowell Armstrong
	LB Paul Dongieux / Jeff Horn
	LB Fred Brister
	DB Ray Heidel / Frank McKellar
	DB Wyck Neely / Freddie Farmer
	DB Danny Hooker
	DB Bill Van Devender / Tommy Magee

RUSHING: Reed 157/668y, Knight 105/476y, Manning 80/113y
PASSING: Manning 121-233/1481y, 14TD, 51.9%, Chumbler 34-86/419y, 5TD, 39.5%
RECEIVING: Franks 46/668y, Poole 32/333y, Reed 31/325y
SCORING: Knight & Poole (TE-K) 48pts, Reed & Franks 42pts

1971 10-2

29 Long Beach St.	13 WR Riley Myers
49 Memphis State	21 WR Bill Barry / Leon Felts
34 Kentucky	20 T John Wohlgemuth / Robert Burke
6 Alabama	40 G Art Bressler
7 Georgia	38 C Chuck Wood
20 Southern Miss	6 G Dave Parham
28 Vanderbilt	7 T John Gregory
24 LSU	22 TE Jim Poole / Butch Veazey
28 Tampa	27 QB Norris Weese / Kenny Lyons
49 Chattanooga	10 TB Greg Ainsworth / Randy Reade
48 Mississippi St.	0 FB Gene Allen / Jim Porter
41 Georgia Tech■	18 DL Jim Stuart / Preston Carpenter
	DL Elmer Allen
	DL Steve Burkhalter
	DL Reggie Dill / Tom Monsour
	LB Crowell Armstrong
	LB Paul Dongieux
	LB Bob Bailess / James Horne
	DB Dwayne Franks / Stan Moley
	DB Danny Harris
	DB Mickey Fratesi / Jimmy Causey
	DB Henry Walsh

RUSHING: Ainsworth 134/629y, Weese 125/488y, Reed 76/299y
PASSING: Weese 56-102/650y, 5TD, 54.9%, Lyons 46-71/594y, 9TD, 64.8%
RECEIVING: Myers 27/390y, Barry 24/281y, Poole 19/224y
SCORING: Ainsworth 66pts, Cloyce Hinton (K) 54pts, Myers & Weese 30pts

1972 5-5

34 Memphis State	29 WR Bill Jordan / Bill Malouf (QB)
21 South Carolina	0 WR Bill Barry
13 Southern Miss	9 T Don Leathers
13 Auburn	19 G Art Bressler
13 Georgia	14 C Pete Boone
0 Florida	16 G Danny Mikul
31 Vanderbilt	7 T John Gregory
16 LSU	17 TE Butch Veazey
0 Tennessee	17 QB Norris Weese
51 Mississippi St.	14 TB Greg Ainsworth / Jim Porter
	FB Gene Allen
	DL Mackey McKinzie
	DL Bill May
	DL Jim Stuart / Ben Williams
	DL Reggie Dill
	LB Mel Richardson / Terry Kilpatrick
	LB Bob Bailess
	LB Stump Russell
	DB Stan Moley
	DB Henry Walsh
	DB Harry Harrison
	DB Mickey Fratesi

RUSHING: Ainsworth 161/634y, Weese 154/542y, Allen 62/288y
PASSING: Weese 77-163/917y, 11TD, 47.2%
RECEIVING: Veazey 29/374y, Barry 17/184y, Allen 17/169y
SCORING: Veazey 48pts, Weese, Allen & Ainsworth 30pts

1973 6-5

24 Villanova	6 WR Danny Stallings / Bill Small
0 Missouri	17 WR Rick Kimbrough
13 Memphis State	17 T Dick Lawrence
41 Southern Miss	0 G Art Bressler
7 Auburn	14 C Chuck Wood
0 Georgia	20 G Bill Marshall / Sam Correo
13 Florida	10 T Dave Parham / James Hickman
24 Vanderbilt	14 TE Butch Veasey
14 LSU	51 QB Norris Weese / Kenny Lyons
28 Tennessee	18 TB Larry Kramer / James Reed
38 Mississippi St.	10 FB Paul Hofer / Gene Allen
	DL Greg Markow
	DL Pete Robertson / Bill May
	DL Ben Williams
	DL Gary Turner
	LB Bob Bailess / Stump Russell
	LB Jim Stuart
	LB Terry Kilpatrick / Bill Steele
	DB Pete Markow
	DB Gary Hall
	DB Harry Harrison
	DB Mickey Fratesi

RUSHING: Hofer 123/642y, Kramer 139/577y, Reed 103/470y
PASSING: Weese 32-55/401y, 2TD, 58.2%, Lyons 26-76/297y, TD, 34.2%
RECEIVING: Kimbrough 29/459y, Veazey 16/180y, Stallings 12/144y
SCORING: Stephen Lavinghouze (K) 52pts, Kimbrough & Weese 30pts

1974 3-8

10 Missouri	0 WR Bill Small
7 Memphis State	15 WR Rick Kimbrough
20 Southern Miss	14 T Dick Lawrence
21 Alabama	35 G James Hickman
0 Georgia	49 C John MacNeill
7 South Carolina	10 G Sam Correro
14 Vanderbilt	24 T James Mason
0 LSU	24 TE Jim Winstead / Curtis Weathers
17 Tennessee	29 QB Kenny Lyons / Tim Ellis
13 Mississippi St.	31 TB James Reed / Larry Kramer
26 Tulane	10 FB Paul Hofer
	DL Greg Markow / Bill Farriss
	DL Mackey McKinzie
	DL Ben Williams / Mike Pittman
	DL Gary Turner
	LB George Stuart
	LB Kem Coleman
	LB Stump Russell
	DB George Nasif / Dan Murff
	DB Johnny Hatch
	DB Gary Hall
	DB Pete Markow / Les Sutherland

RUSHING: Reed 110/461y, Hofer 66/305y, Kramer 80/287y
PASSING: Lyons 51-132/583y, TD, 38.6%, Ellis 28-53/427y, 5TD, 52.8%
RECEIVING: Kimbrough 23/271y, Weathers 16/227y, Reed 13/229y
SCORING: Stephen Lavinghouze (K) 31pts, Lyons 30pts, Reed 24pts

1975 6-5

10 Baylor	20 WR Bill Small
0 Texas A&M	7 WR Rick Kimbrough
3 Tulane	14 T Dick Lawrence
24 Southern Miss	8 G Robert Henry
6 Alabama	32 C John MacNeill
28 Georgia	13 G Chuck Kota
29 South Carolina	35 T James Hickman
17 Vanderbilt	7 TE Robert Fabris
17 LSU	13 QB Tim Ellis / Stan Bounds
23 Tennessee	6 TB Michael Sweet / James Reed
13 Mississippi St.	7 FB Paul Hofer / James Storey
	DL Bill Farris
	DL Lawrence Johnson
	DL Ben Williams
	DL Mike Pittman / Pete Robertson
	DL Gary Turner
	LB Kem Coleman / Eddie Cole
	LB George Stuart / Larry Dantzler
	DB George Nasif
	DB Charlie Moss
	DB Rickye Hicks / Brad Pittman
	DB Gary Jones

RUSHING: Sweet 146/653, Hofer 90/413y, Storey 75/389y
PASSING: Ellis 49-92/621y, 4TD, 53.3%
  Bounds 31-65/277y, 1TD, 47.7%
RECEIVING: Kimbrough 31/407y, Sweet 16/152y, Small 14/220y
SCORING: Stephen Lavinghouze (K) 48pts, Sweet 42pts,
  Reed 24pts

1976 6-5

16 Memphis State	21 WR Robert Fabris
10 Alabama	7 WR Mark Clark / Danny Fischer
34 Tulane	7 T Fernando Harvey
28 Southern Miss	0 G Roy Grant
0 Auburn	10 C Reggie Pace
21 Georgia	17 G Randy White
7 South Carolina	10 T Terrance Walker
20 Vanderbilt	3 TE Curtis Weathers
0 LSU	45 QB Tim Ellis
6 Tennessee	32 TB Leon Perry / Reg Woullard
11 Mississippi St.	28 FB James Storey / Michael Sweet (TB)
	DL Bob Grefseng
	DL Bryan Niebuhr / James Jordan
	DL Pete Robertson / Charlie Cage
	DL Mike Pittman
	DL George Plasketes
	LB Kem Coleman
	LB George Stuart / Eddie Cole
	DB George Nasif
	DB Charlie Moss
	DB Rickye Hicks
	DB Brad Pittman

RUSHING: Sweet 118/513y, Storey 98/338y, Perry 53/305y
PASSING: Ellis 59-132/740y, 4TD, 46.4%
RECEIVING: Fabris 20/220y, Clark 12/120y, Weathers 10/213y
SCORING: Hoppy Langley (K) 40pts, Sweet 20pts,
  Woullard & Perry 18pts

1977 6-5

7 Memphis State	3 WR Robert Fabris / Roy Coleman
13 Alabama	34 WR Les Kimbrough
20 Notre Dame	13 T Jimmy Hawkins
19 Southern Miss	27 G Mickey Thames
15 Auburn	21 C Chuck Commiskey
13 Georgia	14 G Randy White
17 South Carolina	10 T Terrance Walker
26 Vanderbilt	14 TE Curtis Weathers
21 LSU	28 QB Tim Ellis / Bobby Garner
43 Tennessee	14 TB Leon Perry / Freddie Williams
14 Mississippi St.	18 FB James Storey / Roger Gordon
	DL Bob Grefseng
	DL Charlie Cage
	DL Bryan Niebuhr
	DL Lawrence Johnson / Quentin McDonald
	DL George Plasketes
	LB Eddie Cole / Brian Moreland
	LB Kem Coleman / Eddy Householder
	DB Jon Fabris / Willie Burns
	DB Al Dotson / Joel Stewart
	DB Gary Jones
	DB William Day

RUSHING: Storey 143/564y, Perry 110/479y, Williams 80/433y
PASSING: Ellis 35-78/551y, 4TD, 44.9%,
  Garner 33-56/462y, 3TD, 58.9%
RECEIVING: Weathers 23/395y, Fabris 11/160y, Williams 9/56y
SCORING: Storey 60pts, Hoppy Langley (K) 46pts, 3 with 24pts

1978 5-6

14 Memphis State	7 WR Curtis Weathers / Norm Seawright
14 Missouri	45 WR Ken Toler / Les Kimbrough
16 Southern Miss	13 T Dennis Watkins
3 Georgia	42 G Mickey Thames / Gregg Jefcoat
17 Kentucky	24 C Mike "Coot" Russell
17 South Carolina	18 G David Traxler
35 Vanderbilt	10 T Murray Whitaker
8 LSU	30 TE Billy Wise / Billy Denny
13 Tulane	3 QB B'by Garn'r/J.Fourcade/Roy Coleman
17 Tennessee	41 TB Freddie Williams
27 Mississippi St.	7 FB Leon Perry / Jarratt Price
	DL Bob Grefseng
	DL Charlie Cage / John Johnson
	DL James Jordan / Bryan Niebuhr
	DL Lawrence Johnson
	DL John Peel
	LB Brian Moreland / Eddie Cole
	LB Eddy Householder
	DB Brad White
	DB John Fabris
	DB Phil Freightman
	DB Jerry Spore

RUSHING: Perry 148/673y, Williams 137/627y, Fourcade 90/227y
PASSING: Garner 51-79/512y, 1TD, 64.6%,
  Fourcade 36-86/461y, 2TD, 41.9%,
  Coleman 33-69/448y, 1TD, 47.8%
RECEIVING: Williams 30/232y, Weathers 22/361y, Toler 17/208y
SCORING: Hoppy Langley (K) 51pts, Williams 26pts,
  Fourcade & Coleman 18pts

1979 4-7

38 Memphis State	34 WR Ken Toler / Michael Harmon
7 Missouri	33 WR Freddie Williams / Norm Seawright
8 Southern Miss	38 T David Traxler
21 Georgia	24 G Gregg Jefcoat
3 Kentucky	14 C Coot Russell / Chuck Commiskey
14 South Carolina	21 G Terrence Walker
63 Vanderbilt	28 T Mark Moore
24 LSU	28 TE Billy Wise / Billy Denny
15 Tulane	49 QB John Fourcade
44 Tennessee	20 TB Leon Perry
14 Mississippi St.	9 FB Kinney Hooper
	DL James Otis / Jimmy Hawkins
	DL John Johnson / Tony Dalton
	DL James Jordan
	DL Quentin McDonald
	DL John Peel / Rich Vacca
	LB Nakita Williams / Brian Moreland
	LB Eddy Householder
	DB Mike Fountain
	DB Brad White / Dan Caccamo
	DB Phil Freightman
	DB Joel Stewart

RUSHING: Perry 160/678y, Fourcade 128/493y,
  Hooper 110/459y
PASSING: Fourcade 115-196/1521y, 7TD, 58.7%
RECEIVING: Toler 23/441y, Wise 18/181y, Williams 17/285y
SCORING: Perry 62pts, Hoppy Langley (K) 41pts, Fourcade 36pts

1980 3-8

20 Texas A&M	23 WR Ken Toler / Michael Harmon
61 Memphis State	7 WR Breck Tyler / Gino English
35 Alabama	59 T Pat Phenix
24 Tulane	26 G Chris Cottam
22 Southern Miss	28 C Coot Russell
21 Georgia	28 G Chuck Commiskey
3 Florida	15 T Mark Moore
27 Vanderbilt	14 TE Billy Wise
16 LSU	38 QB John Fourcade
20 Tennessee	9 TB Buford McGee / Malvin Gipson
14 Mississippi St.	19 FB Kinney Hooper
	DL James Otis
	DL Tony Dalton
	DL Andy Shaw / Matthew Lovelady
	DL Ken Dotson / Bryan Kennedy
	DL Keith Fourcade / Bentley Burgess
	LB Nakita Williams / Lee Cole
	LB Danny Robertson / Phil Wylie
	DB Mike Fountain / Joel Stewart
	DB Melvin Brown
	DB Johnny Burrow / Brad White
	DB Wally Knox / Bobo Thomas

RUSHING: Hooper 155/619y, Fourcade 125/402y, Gipson 65/348y
PASSING: Fourcade 157-286/1897y, 13TD, 54.9%
RECEIVING: Tyler 33/535y, Toler 27/553y, Harmon 20/246y
SCORING: Toler 54pts, Todd Gatlin (K) 43pts, Fourcade 36pts

1981 4-6-1

19 Tulane	18 WR Michael Harmon / James Harbour
20 South Carolina	13 WR Breck Tyler / Gino English
7 Memphis State	3 T Mike Stearns
13 Arkansas	27 G Steve Searfoss / Tony Dalton
7 Alabama	38 C Steve Herring
7 Georgia	37 G John Allen
3 Florida	49 T Pat Phenix
23 Vanderbilt	27 TE Greg Walker
27 LSU	27 QB John Fourcade / Kelly Powell
20 Tennessee	28 TB Malvin Gipson / Buford McGee
21 Mississippi St.	17 FB Andre "Hammerhead" Thomas
	DL Bryan Kennedy / Carl Lewis
	DL Quentin McDonald / Matthew Lovelady
	DL Andre Townsend
	DL James Otis / Bob Blakemore
	LB Lee Cole / Johnny Armstrong
	LB Nakita Williams / Keith Fourcade
	LB Thomas Hubbard / Kinney Hooper
	DB Melvin Brown
	DB Lee Davis / Skip Lane
	DB Roger Clark / Barry Wilburn
	DB Johnny Burrow / Wally Knox

RUSHING: Thomas 128/548y, Gipson 94/330y, McGee 65/205y
PASSING: J. Fourcade 137-251/1533y, 3TD, 54.6%
RECEIVING: Harmon 46/750y, Gipson 21/130y, McGee 19/138y
SCORING: Todd Gatlin (K) 43pts, J. Fourcade 42pts,
  Thomas 36pts

1982 4-7

27 Memphis State	10 WR James Harbour / Timmy Moffett
28 Southern Miss	19 WR Michael Harmon / Gino English
14 Alabama	42 T Alan Partin / Mark Friedrichsen
12 Arkansas	14 G Tony Dalton / Stephen Searfoss
10 Georgia	33 C Steve Herring
27 TCU	9 G John Allen / Bobby Clark
10 Vanderbilt	19 T Pat Phenix
8 LSU	45 TE Michael Smith / Greg Walker
45 Tulane	14 QB Kent Austin
17 Tennessee	30 TB Buford McGee / Kinney Hooper
10 Mississippi St.	27 FB Hamm'rhe'd Thomas/Arthur Humphrey
	DL Bryan Kennedy
	DL Arnold Seymour / Ken Dotson
	DL Andre Townsend
	DL Freddie Joe Nunn / Matthew Lovelady
	LB Keith Fourcade / James Otis / Lee Cole
	LB Nakita Williams / Danny Robertson
	LB Thomas Hubbard / Jerry Stewart
	DB Joe Hall / Lee Davis
	DB Melvin Brown
	DB Barry Wilburn / Johnny Burrow
	DB Johnny Armstrong / Carl Lewis

RUSHING: Thomas 173/686y, Humphrey 99/414y,
  Hooper 66/227y
PASSING: Austin 186-307/2026y, 12TD, 60.6%
RECEIVING: McGee 42/365y, Harmon 41/583y,
  Harbour 35/512y
SCORING: Todd Gatlin (K) 48pts, Thomas 38pts, Harmon 30pts

1983 7-5

17 Memphis State	37 WR Timmy Moffett
23 Tulane	27 WR Jamie Holder / Andree Rodgers
0 Alabama	40 T Eric Sheehan / Mark Friedrichsen
13 Arkansas	10 G Bobby Clark
7 Southern Miss	27 C Wayne Pierce
11 Georgia	36 G John Allen
20 TCU	7 T Greg Walker / Eric Denmark
21 Vanderbilt	14 TE Michael Smith
27 LSU	24 QB Kent Austin / Kelly Powell
13 Tennessee	10 TB Buford McGee / Nathan Wonsley
24 Mississippi St.	23 FB Arthur Humphrey / Frank Porter
3 Air Force ■	9 DL Carl Lewis / Matthew Lovelady
	DL Bob Blakemore
	DL Terry Williamson
	DL Andre Townsend / Benton Reed
	DL Freddie Joe Nunn / Dwight Bingham
	LB Lee Cole/Joe Brewer/ Dwayne Nesmith
	LB Thomas Hubbard / Jerry Stewart
	DB Eric Truitt
	DB Lee Davis
	DB Roger Clark / Johnny Armstrong
	DB Joe Hall / Barry Wilburn

RUSHING: McGee 141/580y, Humphrey 138/536y,
  Wonsley 62/212y
PASSING: Austin 107-211/1077y, 3TD, 50.7%,
  Powell 60-104/568y, 5TD, 57.7%
RECEIVING: McGee 39/272y, Moffett 35/541y, Holder 25/282y
SCORING: McGee 42pts, Neil Teevan (K) 36pts,
  Moffett & Smith 24pts

1984 4-6-1

22 Memphis State	6 WR Timmy Moffett / Andree Rodgers
14 Arkansas	14 WR James Harbour / Jamie Holder
14 Louisiana Tech	8 T Eric Sheehan
19 Tulane	14 G Bobby Clark
13 Auburn	17 C Wayne Pierce
12 Georgia	18 G Tony Rayburn
10 Southern Miss	13 T Greg Walker / Eric Denmark
20 Vanderbilt	37 TE Mario Perry / Michael Smith
29 LSU	32 QB Kent Austin
17 Tennessee	41 TB Nathan Wonsley
24 Mississippi St.	3 FB Arthur Humphrey / Thunder Smith
	DL Jay Webb
	DL Bob Blakemore
	DL Terry Williamson / Michael Portis
	DL Benton Reed / Mike Fitzsimmons
	DL Freddie Joe Nunn
	LB Dan Boyce / Reed Killion
	LB Fuzzy Huddleston / Jeff Herrod
	DB Howard Moss / Eric Truitt
	DB Lee Davis
	DB Johnny Armstrong / Everett Flakes
	DB Barry Wilburn

RUSHING: Wonsley 116/479y, Humphrey 121/439y,
  Smith 47/162y
PASSING: Austin 177-302/1889y, 8TD, 58.6%
RECEIVING: Wonsley 36/248y, Moffett 33/486y,
  Harbour 24/362y
SCORING: Jon Howard (K) 52pts, Wonsley 50pts,
  Humphrey & Moffett 24pts

1985 4-6-1

17 Memphis State	17 WR J.R. Ambrose / Andree Rodgers
19 Arkansas	24 WR Jamie Holder / Daren Johnson
18 Arkansas State	16 T Ross Genovese / Jay Schimmel
27 Tulane	10 G Bobby Clark
0 Auburn	41 C Jud Alexander (G) / Nubbin Ross
21 Georgia	49 G Tony Rayburn
35 Vanderbilt	7 T Eric Sheehan / Todd Irvin
0 LSU	14 TE Mario Perry
14 Notre Dame	37 QB Kent Austin / Mark Young
14 Tennessee	34 TB Nathan Wonsley / Shawn Sykes
45 Mississippi St.	27 FB Joe Mickles
	DL Jay Webb / Wesley Walls
	DL Mike Fitzsimmons
	DL Michael Portis
	DL Benton Reed / Lester Brinkley
	DL Lopaz Jones
	LB Jeff Herrod / Dan Boyce
	LB Fuzzy Huddleston / Bubba Dickey
	DB Steven Moore / Eric Truitt
	DB Jonathan Shelley
	DB Jeff Noblin
	DB Everett Flakes / Howard Moss

RUSHING: Wonsley 116/462y, Mickens 44/192y, Sykes 50/189y
PASSING: Austin 89-147/1116y, 8TD, 60.5%
  Young 27-58/358y, 4TD, 46.5%
RECEIVING: Ambrose 38/708y, Sykes 21/192y, Holder 18/240y
SCORING: Bryan Owen (K) 44pts, Ambrose 36pts,
  Wonsley 30pts

1986 8-3-1

28 Memphis State	6 WR Ricky Myers / Willie Green
0 Arkansas	21 WR J.R. Ambrose / Bryan Owen/Bill Smith
10 Arkansas State	10 T Jay Schimmel / James King
35 Tulane	10 G Derek King / Danny Hoskins
10 Georgia	14 C Rob Goff / Steve Sutton
33 Kentucky	13 G Rich Adamcik / Jeff Rhodes
21 SW Louisiana	20 T Todd Irvin
28 Vanderbilt	12 TE Mario Perry / Greg Lee
21 LSU	19 QB Mark Young / Chris Osgood
10 Tennessee	22 TB Willie Goodloe / Lightning Sykes
24 Mississippi St.	3 FB Joe Mickles / Tony Dentley
	DL Wesley Walls / Ben Morris
	DL Mike Fitzsimmons
	DL Darryl Smith / Lance Hathcock
	DL Rodney Lowe
	DL Arthur Scott / Lopaz Jones
	LB Jeff Herrod / Fuzzy Huddleston
	LB Robert Smith / Bubba Dickey
	DB Don Price / Jonathan Shelley
	DB Steven Moore
	DB Jeff Noblin
	DB Howard Moss

RUSHING: Goodloe 119/526y, Mickles 89/359y, Sykes 49/191y
PASSING: Young 87-178/1154y, 8TD, 48.9%,
  Osgood 43-78/530y, 2TD, 55.1%
RECEIVING: Ambrose 32/578y, Myers 30/468y, Sykes 20/173y
SCORING: Bryan Owen (K) 52pts, Myers 30pts, 3 tied w/24pts

1987 3-8

10 Memphis State	16 WR Willie Green / Reid Hines
10 Arkansas	31 WR J.R. Ambrose / Bobby Martin
47 Arkansas State	10 T Jay Schimmel / James King
24 Tulane	31 G Derek King / Danny Hoskins
14 Georgia	31 C Dawson Pruett
6 Kentucky	35 G Rich Adamcik
24 SW Louisiana	14 T Todd Irvin
42 Vanderbilt	14 TE Shawn Sowder / Greg Lee
13 LSU	42 QB Mark Young / John Darnell
13 Tennessee	55 TB Lightning Sykes / Chuck Cleveland
20 Mississippi St.	30 FB Ed Thigpen / Joe Mickles
	DL Wesley Walls / Lopaz Jones
	DL Darryl Smith
	DL Dan Wigley / Lester Brinkley
	DL Arthur Scott
	LB Jeff Herrod / Tony "Gator" Bennett
	LB Robert Smith / Bubba Dickey
	LB Shawn Cobb
	DB Don Price / Chris Mitchell
	DB Stevon Moore
	DB Todd Sandroni / Derrick Lindsay
	DB Howard Moss / Rodney Lowe

RUSHING: Sykes 88/379y, Cleveland 73/32y, Thigpen 57/296y
PASSING: Young 140-261/1490y, 9TD, 53.6%,
  Darnell 54-95/675y, 2 TD, 56.8%
RECEIVING: Ambrose 42/515y, Green 34/588y, Sykes 23/242y
SCORING: Bryan Owen (K) 59pts, Willie Goodloe (TB) 36pts,
  Darnell & Sowder 24pts

1988 5-6

24 Memphis State	6 WR Willie Green / Jeffrey Holder
15 Florida	27 WR Reid Hines / Pat Coleman
13 Arkansas	21 T Bubba Dickey
2 Georgia	36 G Jeff Rhodes
22 Alabama	12 C Dawson Pruett / Vince Bonham
25 Arkansas State	22 G Derek King / Tim Brown
36 Vanderbilt	28 T James King / Adrian Strother
20 LSU	31 TE Wesley Walls / Shawn Sowder
9 Tulane	14 QB Mark Young
12 Tennessee	20 TB Lightning Sykes / Jim Earl Thomas
33 Mississippi St.	6 FB Joe Mickles
	DL Doug Jacobs / Dan Wigley
	DL Kelvin Pritchett / Darryl Smith
	DL Rodney Lowe / Lester Brinkley
	LB Lopaz Jones
	LB Shawn Cobb / Reggie Parrott
	LB Keith Thompson / Pete Harris
	LB Tony Bennett / Arthur Scott
	DB Don Price / Chris Mitchell
	DB Stevon Moore
	DB Todd Sandroni / Chauncey Godwin
	DB Roger Hancock

RUSHING: Mickles 115/528y, Sykes 63/337y, Thomas 40/157y
PASSING: Young 156-312/1969y, 10TD, 50.0%
RECEIVING: Green 38/648y, Walls 36/426y, Mickles 21/189y
SCORING: Bryan Owen (K) 51pts, Coleman 42pts, Mickles 38pts

1989 8-4

20 Memphis State	13 WR Willie Green / Jeffrey Holder
24 Florida	19 WR Pat Coleman / Reid Hines
34 Arkansas State	31 T Adrian Strother / Mike Easton
17 Arkansas	24 G Jeff Rhodes
21 Alabama	62 C Dawson Pruett
17 Georgia	13 G Tim Brown / Everett Lindsay
32 Tulane	28 T Lee Lott
24 Vanderbilt	16 TE Rich Gebbia / Daniel Westmoreland
30 LSU	35 QB John Darnell
21 Tennessee	33 RB Ed Thigpen / Tyrone Ashley (WR)
21 Mississippi St.	11 RB Randy Baldwin
42 Air Force ■	29 DL Doug Jacobs
	DL Kelvin Prichett / Jim Lentz
	DL Darryl Smith / Dan Wigley
	LB Keith Thompson / Phillip Kent
	LB Shawn Cobb
	LB Pete Harris
	LB Tony Bennett
	DB Don Price / Danny Boyd
	DB Chauncey Godwin
	DB Jeff Carter / Chuckie Mullins
	DB Chris Mitchell

RUSHING: Baldwin 107/642y, Thigpen 80/327y, Ashley 33/182y
PASSING: Darnell 167-301/2326y, 11TD, 55.5%
RECEIVING: Green 41/816y, Coleman 32/595y,
  Baldwin 22/170y
SCORING: Baldwin 60pts, Brian Lee (K) & Thigpen 32pts,

1990 9-3

23 Memphis State	21 WR Jeffrey Holder / Tyrone Montgomery
10 Auburn	24 WR Vincent Brownlee / Darrick Owens
21 Arkansas	17 T Adrian Strother
31 Tulane	21 G Everett Lindsay / Monty Perry
35 Kentucky	29 C Dawson Pruett
28 Georgia	12 G Cliff Dew / David Herring
42 Arkansas State	13 T Lee Lott / Clint Conlee
14 Vanderbilt	13 TE Tyji Armstrong / Louis Gordon
19 LSU	10 QB Russ Shows / Tom Luke
13 Tennessee	22 RB Ed Thigpen
21 Mississippi St.	9 RB Randy Baldwin
	DL Doug Jacobs / Brian Cagle
	DL Jim Lentz / Victor Lester
	DL Kelvin Pritchett / Jack Muirhead
	LB Phillip Kent / Kevin Ingram
	LB Shawn Cobb
	LB Pete Harris / Gary Abide
	LB Roger Hancock
	DB Danny Boyd / Dwayne Amos
	DB Chauncey Godwin / Tyrone Ashley
	DB Jeff Carter
	DB Chris Mitchell

RUSHING: Baldwin 163/970y, Luke 106/519y, Thigpen 96/422y
PASSING: Shows 57-126/953y, 45.2%, 6TD,
  Luke 51-107/853y, 4TD, 47.7%
RECEIVING: Owens 18/305y, Holder 17/260y,
  Montgomery 15/386y
SCORING: Baldwin 78pts, Brian Lee (K) 41pts,
  Brownlee & Luke 24pts

1991 5-6

22 Tulane	3 WR Darrick Owens / Eddie Small
10 Memphis State	0 WR Vincent Brownlee / Germaine Kohn
13 Auburn	23 T Wesley Melton
38 Ohio University	14 G Everett Lindsay
24 Arkansas	17 C Cliff Dew
35 Kentucky	14 G David Herring / James Holcombe
17 Georgia	37 T Clint Conlee
27 Vanderbilt	30 TE Tyji Armstrong / Thomas McLeish
22 LSU	25 QB Russ Shows / Tom Luke
25 Tennessee	36 TB Tyrone Ashley / Dou Innocent
9 Mississippi St.	24 FB Marvin Courtney
	DL Artis Ford / Phillip Kent
	DL Jim Lentz / Sean O'Malley
	DL Chad Brown / Jack Muirhead
	LB Kevin Ingram / Phillip Kent
	LB Gary Abide
	LB Pete Harris / Lynn Ross
	LB Derrick King
	DB Danny Boyd / Lance Whiteside
	DB Chauncey Godwin / Gerald Vaughn
	DB Jeff Carter
	DB Johnny Dixon

RUSHING: Ashley 82/503y, Courtney 99/454y, Innocent 67/327y
PASSING: Shows 99-198/1369y, 4TD, 50.0%,
  Luke 33-62/655y, 7TD, 53.2%
RECEIVING: Owens 23/329y, Courtney 22/258y, Small 19/311y,
  Ashley 19/248y
SCORING: Courtney 68pts, Brian Lee (K) 64pts, Brownlee 30pts

1992 9-3

45 Auburn	21 WR Eddie Small
35 Tulane	9 WR Germaine Kohn / Joe Woods
9 Vanderbilt	31 T Sebastian "Snake" Williams
11 Georgia	37 G Everett Lindsay (T)
24 Kentucky	14 C James Holcombe (G) / Darrell Moncus
17 Arkansas	3 G Wesley Melton (T) / Joel Jordan
10 Alabama	31 T Clint Conlee / Burkes Brown
32 LSU	0 TE Thomas McLeish / Chris Turner
17 Memphis State	12 QB Russ Shows
13 Louisiana Tech	6 TB Cory Philpot / Dou Innocent
17 Mississippi St.	10 FB Marvin Courtney
13 Air Force ■	0 DL Abdul Jackson (LB)
	DL Sean O'Malley / Brian Mays
	DL Artis Ford
	DL Chad Brown
	DL Cassius Ware (LB)
	LB Dewayne Dotson (DL) / Lynn Ross
	LB Michael Lowery
	DB Danny Boyd
	DB Dwayne Amos / Lance Whiteside
	DB Tony Collier
	DB Johnny Dixon

RUSHING: Philpot 190/994y, Courtney 89/339y,
  Innocent 53/217y
PASSING: Shows 118-224/1400y, 9TD, 52.7%
RECEIVING: Small 39/558y, Kohn 29/377y, Courtney 15/143y,
  Philpot 15/84y
SCORING: Brian Lee (K) 70pts, Courtney 32pts, Shows 30pts

1993 5-6

12 Auburn	16 WR Eddie Small (TE) / LeMay Thomas
40 Tenn.-Chatt'ga	7 WR Roell Preston / Ta'Boris Fisher
49 Vanderbilt	7 T Wesley Melton / Jeff Miller
31 Georgia	14 G Chris May
0 Kentucky	21 C Darrell Moncus / Skip Joyce
19 Arkansas	0 G Skip Jordan
14 Alabama	19 T Clint Conlee / Ahmed Shahid
17 LSU	19 TE Frank Wilson / Chris Turner
3 Memphis State	19 QB Lawrence Adams
44 Northern Illinois	0 TB Marvin Courtney / Mark Smith
13 Mississippi St.	20 FB Jeremy Veasley / Renard Brown
	DL Tim Bowens / David Harris
	DL Huck Ferguson / Sean O'Malley
	DL Norman Hand / Brian Mays
	LB Dewayne Dotson
	LB Gary Abide
	LB Abdul Jackson
	LB Cassius Ware
	DB Aldunis Brice
	DB Tony Collier / Derek Jones
	DB Michael Lowery
	DB Johnny Dixon / Antonious Bonner

RUSHING: Courtney 71/343y, Veasley 78/342y, Smith 56/300y
PASSING: Adams 110-195/1415y, 13TD, 56.4%
RECEIVING: Preston 35/455y, Small 33/624y, Smith 14/101y
SCORING: Walter Grant (K) 59pts, Small 36pts, 3 with 18pts

1994 4-7

17 Auburn	22 WR Ta'Boris Fisher
59 Southern Illinois	3 WR LeMay Thomas / John Knight
20 Vanderbilt	14 WR Roell Preston
14 Georgia	17 T Jeff Miller / Boyd Kitchen
14 Florida	38 G Chris May / Jonathan Casey
7 Arkansas	31 C Darrell Moncus
10 Alabama	21 G Shannon Provencher / David Evans
34 LSU	21 T James Holcombe / Skip Joyce
16 Memphis	17 TE Kris Mangum / Chris Turner
38 Tulane	0 QB Josh Nelson
17 Mississippi St.	21 RB Dou Innocent / Mark Smith
	DL Sid Carmichael
	DL Stacy Wilson / Ed Fortson
	DL Huck Ferguson
	DL Norman Hand
	DL David McGowan
	LB Nate Wayne / Kyle Wicker
	LB Abdul Jackson
	DB Alundis Brice / Fred Thomas
	DB Derek Jones
	DB Antonious Bonner / David Knott
	DB Michael Lowery

RUSHING: Innocent 182/910y, Smith 113/436y,
 Moine Nicholson (RB) 27/143y
PASSING: Nelson 168-308/2028y, 15TD, 54.5%
RECEIVING: Fisher 41/483y, Preston 38/688y, Thomas 24/290y,
 Innocent 24/206y
SCORING: Tim Montz (K) 66pts, Preston 48pts,
 Innocent & Smith 30pts

1995 6-5

13 Auburn	46 WR Ta'Boris Fisher / Andre Hollis
56 Indiana State	10 WR LeMay Thomas / Stuart Brown
18 Georgia	10 WR Moine Nicholson / Damon Bilbrew
10 Florida	28 T Omar Edwards
20 Tulane	17 G Chris May / Shannon Provencher
6 Arkansas	13 C Darrell Moncus
9 Alabama	23 G Jonathan Casey
21 Vanderbilt	10 T Skip Joyce / Orlando Trainer
34 Memphis	3 TE Kris Mangum / Frank Wilson
9 LSU	38 QB Josh Nelson / Paul Head
13 Mississippi St.	10 RB Dou Innocent / Mark Smith
	DL Renard Brown / Morris Scott
	DL Ed Fortson / David Evans
	DL Greg Childs / Devon Coburn
	DL Trey Wicker / David McGowan
	LB Michael Lowery / Nate Wayne
	LB Kyle Wicker
	LB Paul Winfield / Broc Kreitz
	DB Gary Thigpen / David Knott
	DB Derek Jones
	DB Keith Campbell / Lawrence Adams
	DB Walker Jones / Kyron Motton

RUSHING: Innocent 192/868y, Smith 101/358y,
 Artie Moore (RB) 40/217y
PASSING: Nelson 143-250/1675y, 9TD, 57.2%,
 Head 70-113/748y, 5TD, 61.9%
RECEIVING: Thomas 56/801y, Fisher 45/493y,
 Mangum 36/391y
SCORING: Tim Montz (K) 56pts, Innocent & Nicholson 30pts

1996 5-6

38 Idaho State	14 WR Andre Rone / Lawrence Adams (DB)
31 VMI	7 WR Orlando Trainer / Grant Heard
28 Auburn	45 WR Damon Bilbrew / Cory Peterson
20 Vanderbilt	9 T Devon Coburn / Kendrick Hickman
3 Tennessee	41 G Omar Edwards / Todd Wade
0 Alabama	37 C Matt Luke
38 Arkansas State	21 G Shannon Provencher
7 Arkansas	13 T Boyd Kitchen
1 LSU	39 TE Kris Mangum / Rufus French
31 Georgia	27 QB Paul Head / Stewart Partridge
0 Mississippi St.	17 RB John Avery / Artie Moore
	DL Kyle Wicker / Morris Scott
	DL David Evans / Michael Boone
	DL Quentin Wilson / Comone Fisher
	DL Andre Harrison / Johnny Jones
	LB Walker Jones / Eli Anding
	LB Nate Wayne / Armegis Spearman
	LB Broc Kreitz / Al Rice
	DB Gary Thigpen
	DB Derek Jones / Malikia Griffin
	DB Timothy Strickland / Jason Clingan
	DB Ronnie Heard

RUSHING: Avery 181/788y, Moore 107/341y,
 Tony Cannion (RB) 49/191y
PASSING: Head 104-172/1014y, 5TD, 60.5%,
 Partridge 79-154/876y, 3TD, 51.3%
RECEIVING: Fisher 40/417y, Mangum 29/264y, Heard 21/291y
SCORING: Tim Montz (K) 47pts, Avery & Moore 42pts

1997 8-4

24 C. Florida	23 WR Grant Heard / Andre Rone
23 SMU	15 WR Cory Peterson / Robert Reed
9 Auburn	19 T Devon Coburn
15 Vanderbilt	3 G Terrence Metcalf / Keydrick Vincent
17 Tennessee	31 C Matt Luke / Charlie Perkins
36 LSU	21 G Boyd Kitchen
20 Alabama	29 T Todd Wade / Tuten Reyes
19 Arkansas	9 TE Rufus French
41 Tulane	24 QB Stewart Partridge / Romaro Miller
14 Georgia	21 TB John Avery / Deuce McAllister
15 Mississippi St.	14 FB Eli Anding
34 Marshall■	31 DL Johnny Jones / Morris Scott
	DL Michael Boone / Mitch Baker
	DL Derrick Burgess / Comone Fisher
	DL Andre Harrison / Robert Gates
	LB Walker Jones
	LB Nate Wayne / Armegis Spearman
	LB Broc Kreitz / Al Rice
	DB Gary Thigpen
	DB Malikia Griffin
	DB Timothy Strickland
	DB Ronnie Heard / Jason Clingan

RUSHING: Avery 166/862y, McAllister 94/402y,
 Tony Cannion (TB) 49/210y
PASSING: Partridge 228-352/2667y, 12TD, 64.8%
RECEIVING: French 43/345y, Peterson 40/527y, Rone 36/513y
SCORING: Avery 48pts, Steve Lindsay (K) 47pts,
 Alishma Alexander (TB) & McAllister 24pts

1998 7-5

30 Memphis	10 WR Grant Heard
0 Auburn	17 WR Cory Peterson / Sheldon Morris
30 Vanderbilt	6 T Todd Wade / John McGarvey
48 SMU	41 G Shane Grice / John Keith
30 South Carolina	28 C Matt Luke / Charlie Perkins
17 Alabama	20 G Keydrick Vincent / Terrence Metcalf
30 Arkansas State	17 T Tuten Reyes
37 LSU	31 TE Rufus French / Adam Bettis
0 Arkansas	34 QB Romaro Miller
17 Georgia	24 TB Deuce McAllister / Joe Gunn
6 Mississippi St.	28 FB Charles Stackhouse
35 Texas Tech■	18 DL Morris Scott / Derrick Burgess
	DL Kendrick Clancy / Mitch Baker
	DL Michael Boone / Comone Fisher
	DL Shane Elam / Tyler Williams
	LB Ronnie Heard
	LB Armegis Spearman / Chad Cook
	LB Eddie Strong / Al Rice
	DB Gary Thigpen / Ken Lucas (WR)
	DB Timothy Strickland
	DB Anthony Magee
	DB Kenny Woods / Syniker Taylor

RUSHING: McAllister 239/1161y, Gunn 188/560y,
 Tony Cannion (TB) 56/202y
PASSING: Miller 198-349/2489y, 14TD, 56.7%
RECEIVING: Peterson 44/655y, Heard 40/559y, French 39/432y
SCORING: McAllister 60pts, Peterson & Gunn 38pts

1999 8-4

3 Memphis	0 WR Maurice Flournoy / Grant Heard
38 Arkansas State	14 WR Cory Peterson / Jamie Armstrong
34 Vanderbilt	37 T Todd Wade
24 Auburn	17 G Shane Grice / Terrence Metcalf
36 South Carolina	10 C Ben Claxton
20 Tulane	13 G Keydrick Vincent
24 Alabama	30 T Tuten Reyes
42 LSU	23 TE Adam Bettis / Doug Ziegler
38 Arkansas	16 QB Romaro Miller
17 Georgia	20 TB Joe Gunn / Deuce McAllister
20 Mississippi St.	23 FB Toward Sanford / Charles Stackhouse
27 Oklahoma■	25 DL Derrick Burgess / Justin Blake
	DL Kendrick Clancy / Anthony Sims
	DL Comone Fisher / Michael Boone
	DL Shane Elam / Antoinne Scott
	LB Armegis Spearman / Kevin Thomas
	LB Eddie Strong / Chad Cook
	LB Shawn Johnson / Al Rice
	DB Ken Lucas (WR) / Justin Coleman
	DB Timothy Strickland
	DB Syniker Taylor
	DB L.J. Taylor / Anthony Magee

RUSHING: Gunn 187/978y, McAllister 168/930y, Sanford 24/127y
PASSING: Miller 165-298/2201y, 16TD, 55.4%
RECEIVING: Peterson 51/661y, Flournoy 24/269y,
 McAllister 23/256y
SCORING: McAllister 90pts, Les Binkley (K) 87pts, Gunn 42pts

2000 7-5

49 Tulane	20 WR Grant Heard / Omar Rayford
27 Auburn	35 WR L.J. Taylor / Jamie Armstrong
12 Vanderbilt	7 T Terrence Metcalf
35 Kentucky	17 G Shane Grice
35 Arkansas State	10 C Ben Claxton
7 Alabama	45 G Keydrick Vincent / Matt Koon
43 UNLV	40 T Belton Johnson
38 Arkansas	24 TE Doug Zeigler
9 LSU	20 QB Romaro Miller / Eli Manning
14 Georgia	32 TB Deuce McAllister / Joe Gunn
45 Mississippi St.	30 FB Charles Stackhouse
38 West Virginia■	49 DL Derrick Burgess
	DL Anthony Sims
	DL Kenny Jackson
	DL Shane Elam
	LB Lanier Goethie / Kevin Thomas
	LB Chad Cook / Ryan Hamilton
	LB Shawn Johnson
	DB Ken Lucas
	DB Justin Colemen
	DB Syniker Taylor
	DB Anthony Magee / Kenny Woods

RUSHING: McAllister 159/767y, Gunn 125/382y,
 Stackhouse 37/182y
PASSING: Miller 161-295/2012y, 14TD, 54.6%,
 Manning 16-33/170y, 2TD, 48.5%
RECEIVING: Heard 44/655y, Taylor 23/339y, Rayford 19/229y
SCORING: McAllister 102pts, Les Binkley (K) 64pts

2001 7-4

49 Murray State	14 WR Chris Collins / Bill Flowers
21 Auburn	27 WR Jason Armstead / Jamie Armstrong
42 Kentucky	31 T Terrence Metcalf
35 Arkansas State	17 G German Bello / Doug Buckles
27 Alabama	24 C Ben Claxton
45 Middle Tenn.	17 G Marcus Johnson
35 LSU	24 T Belton Johnson
56 Arkansas	58 TE Doug Zeigler / Mitch Skrmetta
15 Georgia	35 QB Eli Manning
28 Mississippi St.	36 TB Joe Gunn / Robert Williams
38 Vanderbilt	28 FB Charles Stackhouse / Toward Sanford
	DL Charlie Anderson / Ryan Hamilton
	DL Anthony Sims
	DL Kenny Jackson / Jesse Mitchell
	DL Cory Robinson / Josh Cooper
	LB Eddie Strong
	LB Lanier Goethie / Kevin Thomas
	LB L.P. Spence / Rob Robertson
	DB Justin Coleman / Desmon Johnson
	DB Syniker Taylor
	DB Von Hutchins / Eric Oliver
	DB Matt Grier / Marcus Woodson

RUSHING: Gunn 200/870y, Stackhouse 75/330y, Williams 42/200y
PASSING: Manning 259-408/2948y, 31TD, 63.5%
RECEIVING: Collins 54/692y, Armstrong 40/470y,
 Armstead 32/413y
SCORING: Gunn 60pts, Jonathan Nichols (K) 56pts,
 Sanford 48pts

2002 7-6

31 La.-Monroe	3 WR Bill Flowers/Kerry Johnson/Mike Espy
38 Memphis	16 WR Taye Biddle/Chris Collins/J.Armstead
28 Texas Tech	42 T Tre Stallings
45 Vanderbilt	38 G Doug Buckles
17 Florida	14 C Ben Claxton / Justin Sawyer
52 Arkansas State	17 G Marcus Johnson
7 Alabama	42 T Belton Johnson / Clifford Woodruff
28 Arkansas	48 TE Eric Rice / Doug Zeigler / Bo Hartsfield
24 Auburn	21 QB Eli Manning
17 Georgia	31 TB Ronald McClendon / Tremaine Turner
13 LSU	14 FB Rick Razzano / Toward Sanford
24 Mississippi St.	12 DL Josh Cooper / Germaine Landrum
27 Nebraska■	23 DL Yahrek Johnson / McKinley Boykin
	DL Jesse Mitchell
	DL Charlie Anderson / Mike Gibson
	LB Eddie Strong / Ryan Hamilton
	LB Justin Wade / Lanier Goethie
	DB Von Hutchins / Wes Scott
	DB Travis Johnson / Chris Knight
	DB Travis Blanchard / Desmon Jonson
	DB Eric Oliver
	DB Matt Grier / Kelvin Robinson

RUSHING: McClendon 96/378y, Robert Williams (TB) 61/307y
Turner 79/300y
PASSING: Manning 279-481/3401y, 21TD, 58.0%
RECEIVING: Collins 55/812y, Flowers 53/588y, Espy 30/465y
SCORING: Jonathan Nichols (K) 85pts, Collins 60pts,
Vaughn Pearson (TB) 38pts

2003 10-3

24 Vanderbilt	21 WR Chris Collins / Bill Flowers
34 Memphis	44 WR Mike Espy / Kerry Johnson
59 La.-Monroe	14 T Tre Stallings
45 Texas Tech	49 G Doug Buckles
20 Florida	17 C Justin Sawyer / Chris Spencer
55 Arkansas State	0 G Marcus Johnson
43 Alabama	28 T Clifford Woodruff
19 Arkansas	7 TE Erid Rice / Jimmy Brooks
43 South Carolina	40 QB Eli Manning
24 Auburn	20 RB Tremaine Turner / Vashon Pearson
14 LSU	17 FB Lorenzo Townsend / Rick Razzano
31 Mississippi St.	0 DL Josh Cooper / Jayme Mitchell
31 Oklahoma St.■	28 DL Jesse Mitchell / McKinley Boykin
	DL Daniel Booth / Michael Bozeman
	DL Charlie Anderson
	LB Justin Wade / Ken Bournes
	LB L.P. Spence / Brian Lester
	DB Travis Johnson / Bryan Brown
	DB Von Hutchins
	DB Travis Blanchard / Wes Scott
	DB Eric Oliver
	DB Kelvin Robinson

RUSHING: Turner 173/809y, Pearson 94/398y,
Ronald McClendon (RB) 55/331y
PASSING: Manning 275-441/3600y, 29TD, 62.4%
RECEIVING: Collins 77/949y, Flowers 39/543y, Espy 30/542y
SCORING: Jonathan Nichols (K) 124pts, Collins 42pts,
Turner 36pts

2004 4-7

13 Memphis	20 WR Bill Flowers / Mario Hill
7 Alabama	28 WR Taye Biddle / Mike Espy
26 Vanderbilt	23 T Bobby Harris
32 Wyoming	37 G Doug Buckles
28 Arkansas St.	21 C Chris Spencer
3 South Carolina	28 G Marcus Johnson (T) / Tony Bonds
17 Tennessee	21 T Tre Stallings
14 Auburn	35 TE Eric Rice/Lawrence Lilly/Jim'y Brooks
3 Arkansas	35 QB Ethan Flatt / Michael Spurlock
24 LSU	27 RB Vashon Pearson / Alan Abrams
20 Mississippi St.	3 FB Rick Razzano / Lorenzo Townsend
	DL Jayme Mitchell / Brandon Jenkins
	DL McKinley Boykin / Andrew Wicker
	DL Michael Bozeman
	DL Cory Robinson / Corvelli Haynes
	LB Rob Robertson / Gary Pack
	LB Brian Lester / Patrick Willis
	DB Travis Johnson / Nate Banks
	DB Trumaine McBride
	DB Charles Clark
	DB Eric Oliver
	DB Kelvin Robinson / Iroko Ayodele

RUSHING: Pearson 158/807y, Lane 60/309y, Abrams 56/275y
PASSING: Flatt 123-220/1530y, 6TD, 55.9%
RECEIVING: Hill 36/426y, Flowers 29/349y, Johnson 27/338y
SCORING: Jonathan Nichols (K) 79pts, Jacobs 30pts,
Lane 20pts

2005 3-8

10 Memphis	6 WR Taye Biddle / Robert Lane (QB)
23 Vanderbilt	31 WR Larry Kendrick (RB)
14 Wyoming	24 WR Mario Hill / Mike Espy
10 Tennessee	27 T Bobby Harris
27 Citadel	7 G Andrew Wicker / David Traxler
10 Alabama	13 C Darryl Harris / Tony Bonds
13 Kentucky	7 G Michael Oher / Thomas Eckers
3 Auburn	27 T Tre Stallings
17 Arkansas	28 TE Jimmy Brooks / Robert Hough
7 LSU	40 QB Michael Spurlock (RB) / Ethan Flatt
14 Mississippi St.	35 RB Mico McSwain / Antonio Turner (FB)
	DL Jayme Mitchell
	DL Michael Bozeman
	DL McKinley Boykin / Jeremy Garrett
	DL Corvelli Haynes / Chris Bowers
	LB Garry Pack
	LB Patrick Willis
	LB Kelvin Robinson
	DB Travis Johnson / Nate Banks
	DB Trumaine McBride
	DB Charles Clark
	DB Jamarca Sanford / Bryan Brown

RUSHING: McSwain 124/612y, Turner 30/79y, Kendrick 43/77y
PASSING: Spurlock 142-267/1703y, 7TDs, 53.2%
RECEIVING: Espy 52/543y, Biddle 35/487y, Hill 34/524y
SCORING: Espy 24pts, Matt Hinkle (K) 21pts, McSwain 18pts

2006 4-8

28 Memphis	25 WR Mike Wallace / Shay Hodge
7 Missouri	34 WR Mico McSwain (RB) / Marshay Green
14 Kentucky	31 T Michael Oher
3 Wake Forest	27 G Andrew Wicker
9 Georgia	14 C Corey Actis
17 Vanderbilt	10 G John Jerry
23 Alabama	26 T Maurice Miller / Darryl Harris
3 Arkansas	38 TE Lawrence Lilly / Robert Hough
17 Auburn	23 QB Brent Schaeffer
27 Northwestern St.	7 RB BenJarvis Green-Ellis / Bruce Hall
20 LSU	23 FB Jason Cook
20 Mississippi St.	17 DL Greg Hardy
	DL Brandon Jenkins / Jeremy Garrett
	DL Marcus Tillman / Peria Jerry
	DL Chris Bowers / Viciente DeLoach
	LB Rory Johnson / Garry Pack
	LB Patrick Willis
	LB Quentin Taylor
	DB Trumaine McBride / Dustin Mouzon
	DB Nate Banks
	DB Charles Clark
	DB Jamarca Sanford / Bryan Brown

RUSHING: Green-Ellis 234/1000y, Hall 32/182y,
McSwain 27/140y
PASSING: Schaeffer 115-244/1442y, 9TDs, 47.1%
RECEIVING: Wallace 24/410y, Green 19/174y, Hodge 16/193y
SCORING: Joshua Shene (K) 62pts, Green-Ellis 42pts,
Green 18pts

2007 3-9

23 Memphis	21 WR Mike Wallace / Michael Hicks
25 Missouri	38 WR Marshay Green / Dexter McCluster
17 Vanderbilt	31 T Michael Oher
24 Florida	30 G Reid Neely
17 Georgia	45 C Corey Actis / Thomas Eckers (G)
24 Louisiana Tech	0 G John Jerry
24 Alabama	27 T Maurice Miller / Darryl Harris
8 Arkansas	44 TE Robert Lane / Shay Hodge (WR)
3 Auburn	17 QB Seth Adams / Brent Schaeffer
38 Northwestern St.	31 RB BenJarvus Green-Ellis / Bruce Hall
24 LSU	41 FB Jason Cook
14 Mississippi St.	17 DL Marcus Tillman / Antonio Turner
	DL Brandon Jenkins / Jeremy Garrett
	DL Peria Jerry
	DL Greg Hardy / Vicinente DeLoach
	LB Ashlee Palmer
	LB Tony Fein / Brandon Thomas
	LB Jamie Phillips / Jonathan Cornell
	DB Dustin Mouzon / Terrell Jackson
	DB Nate Banks / Cassius Vaughn
	DB Johnny Brown / Kendrick Lewis
	DB Jamarca Sanford / Allen Walker

RUSHING: Green-Ellis 230/1137y, Hall 53/234y,
Schaeffer 33/155y
PASSING: Adams 163-297/1979y, 12TD, 54.9%
RECEIVING: Hodge 43/593y, Wallace 38/716y, Green 31/260y,
McCluster 27/326y
SCORING: Joshua Shene (K) 57pts, Wallace 44pts,
Green-Ellis & Hodge 36pts

2008 9-4

41 Memphis	24 WR Shay Hodge / Lionel Breaux
28 Wake Forest	30 WR Mike Wallace /Dexter McCluster (RB)
34 Samford	10 T Michael Oher
17 Vanderbilt	23 G Reid Neely / Darryl Harris
31 Florida	30 C Daverin Geralds
20 South Carolina	31 G Maurice Miller
20 Alabama	24 T John Jerry
23 Arkansas	21 TE Gerald Harris / David Traxler
7 Auburn	7 QB Jevon Snead
59 La.-Monroe	0 RB Codera Eason / Brandon Bolden
31 LSU	13 FB Jason Cook / Andy Hartman
45 Mississippi St.	0 DL Marcus Tillman / Emmanuel Stephens
47 Texas Tech■	34 DL Ted Lurent / Lawon Scott
	DL Peria Jerry
	DL Kentrell Lockett / Chris Bowers
	LB Allen Walker / Lamar Brumfield
	LB Jonathan Cornell / Tony Fein
	LB Ashlee Palmer / Patrick Trahan
	DB Marshay Green
	DB Cassius Vaughn / Dustin Mouzon
	DB Kendrick Lewis / Johnny Brown
	DB Jamarca Sanford

RUSHING: McCluster 109/655y, Eason 140/647y,
Bolden 98/542y
PASSING: Snead 184-327/2762y, 26TD, 56.3%
RECEIVING: Hodge 44/725y , McCluster 44/625y ,
Wallace 39/784y
SCORING: Joshua Shene (K) 103pts, Hodge & Wallace 48pts

2009 9-4

45 Memphis	14 WR Shay Hodge / Lionel Breaux
53 SE Louisiana	6 WR Markeith Summers / Pat Patterson
10 South Carolina	16 T Bradley Sowell
23 Vanderbilt	7 G Reid Neely (T) / Alex Washington
3 Alabama	22 C Daverin Geralds
48 Ala.-Birmingham	13 G Brandon Green / Rishaw Johnson
30 Arkansas	17 T John Jerry (G) / Bobbie Massie
20 Auburn	33 TE Gerald Harris / Ferbia Allen
38 N. Arizona	14 QB Jevon Snead
42 Tennessee	17 RB Dexter McCluster (WR)/Brand'n Bolden
25 LSU	23 FB Andy Hartmann / Derrick Davis
27 Mississippi St.	41 DL Marcus Tillman
21 Oklahoma State■	7 DL Jerrell Powe / Ted Laurent
	DL Lawon Scott
	DL Kentrell Lockett
	LB Allen Walker / Lamar Brumfield
	LB Jonathan Cornell
	LB Patrick Trahan
	DB Marshay Green / Marcus Temple
	DB Cassius Vaughn / Jeremy McGee
	DB Kendrick Lewis
	DB Johnny Brown

RUSHING: McCluster 181/1169y, Bolden 129/614y
Rodney Scott (RB) 35/138y, Cordera Eason (RB) 36/133y
PASSING: Snead 191-351/2632y, 20TD, 54.4%
RECEIVING: Hodge 70/1135y, McCluster 44/520y, Bolden 20/209y
SCORING: Joshua Shene (K) 88pts, McCluster 66pts, Hodge 48pts

2010 4-8

48 Jacksonville St.	49 WR Markeith Summers / Korvic Neat
27 Tulane	13 WR Ja-Mes Logan / Melvin Harris
14 Vanderbilt	28 WR Lionel Breaux / Jesse Grandy
55 Fresno State	38 T Bradley Sowell
42 Kentucky	35 G Alex Washington / Patrick Junen
10 Alabama	23 C A.J. Hawkins / Evan Swindall
24 Arkansas	38 G Jared Duke / Logan Clair
31 Auburn	51 T Bobby Massie
43 La.-Lafayette	21 TE Ferbia Allen / E.J. Epperson (FB)
14 Tennessee	52 QB Jeremiah Masoli / Nathan Stanley
36 LSU	43 RB Brandon Bolden / Jeff Scott
23 Mississippi State	31 DL Wayne Dorsey / Jason Jones
	DL Jerrell Powe / LeMark Armour
	DL Ted Laurent / Lawon Scott
	DL Gerald Rivers / Kentrell Lockett
	LB Joel Kight / D.T. Shackelford (DL)
	LB Jonathan Cornell / Mike Marry
	LB Allen Walker
	DB Marcus Temple / Charles Sawyer
	DB Jeremy McGee / Tony Grimes
	DB Damien Jackson / Fon Ingram
	DB Johnny Brown

RUSHING: Bolden 163/976y, Masoli 121/544y, Scott 66/429y
PASSING: Masoli 167-296/2039y, 14TD, 56.4%
Stanley 17-32/261y, 3TD, 53.1%
RECEIVING: Bolden 32/344y, Harris 30/408y, Logan 29/387y
Summers 28/575y
SCORING: Bolden 102pts, Bryson Rose (K) 91pts,
Masoli & Summers 36pts

MISSISSIPPI STATE

Mississippi State University (Founded 1878)
Mississippi State, Mississippi, near Starkville, Mississippi
Nickname: Bulldogs, Maroons
Colors: Maroon and White
Stadium: Davis Wade Stadium at Scott Field (1914) 55,082
Conference Affiliation: Southeastern (Charter member, 1933-present)

CAREER RUSHING YARDS	Attempts	Yards
Anthony Dixon (2006-09)	910	3994
Jerious Norwood (2002-05)	573	3212
Walter Packer (1973-76)	483	2820
Michael Davis (1991-94)	578	2721
Michael Haddix (1979-82)	425	2558
James Johnson (1997-98)	453	2452
Dennis Johnson (1974-77)	428	2284
John Bond (1980-83)	572	2280
Direnzo Miller (1998-01)	403	2209
Kenny Roberts (1989-92)	376	2070

CAREER PASSING YARDS	Comp.-Att.	Yards
Wayne Madkin (1998-01)	462-887	6336
Kevin Fant (2000-03)	461-866	5631
Derrick Taite (1993-96)	362-734	5232
Don Smith (1983-86)	342-738	5229
John Bond (1980-83)	307-665	4621
Tony Shell (1988-90)	349-715	4292
Tommy Pharr (1967-69)	339-648	3720
Omarr Conner (2003-06)	269-507	3080
Tyson Lee (2008-09)	283-481	2963
Rockey Felker (1972-74)	207-424	2961

CAREER RECEIVING YARDS	Catches	Yards
Mardye McDole (1977-80)	116	2214
David Smith (1968-70)	162	2168
Eric Moulds (1993-95)	118	2022
Justin Jenkins (2000-03)	139	1974
Sammy Milner (1968-70)	146	1806
Danny Knight (1980-83)	81	1773
Terrell Grindle (1999-02)	119	1724
Bill Buckley (1971-73)	102	1632
Fred Hadley (1984, 86-88)	86	1520
Willie Harris (1989-92)	74	1391

SEASON RUSHING YARDS	Attempts	Yards
Anthony Dixon (2009)	257	1391
James Johnson (1998)	236	1383
Wayne Jones (1973)	212	1193
Jerious Norwood (2005)	191	1136
Keffer McGee (1995)	235	1072

SEASON PASSING YARDS	Comp.-Att.	Yards
Dave Marler (1978)	163-287	2422
Don Smith (1985)	143-312	2332
Derrick Taite (1995)	165-309	2241
Kevin Fant (2003)	186-351	2151
Todd Jordan (1993)	131-294	1935

SEASON RECEIVING YARDS	Catches	Yards
Mardye McDole (1978)	48	1035
David Smith (1970)	74	987
Danny Knight (1982)	37	924
Sammy Milner (1968)	64	909
Justin Jenkins (2003)	62	880

GAME RUSHING YARDS	Attempts	Yards
Jerious Norwood (2005 vs. Houston)	24	257
Anthony Dixon (2009 vs. Kentucky)	33	252
James Johnson (1998 vs. Alabama)	36	237

GAME PASSING YARDS	Comp.-Att.	Yards
Derrick Taite (1994 vs. Tulane)	21-30	466
Dave Marler (1978 vs. Alabama)	28-46	429
Wesley Carroll (2007 vs. Arkansas)	29-51	421

GAME RECEIVING YARDS	Catches	Yards
David Smith (1970 vs. Texas Tech)	12	215
Sammy Milner (1968 vs. Texas Tech)	9	208
Danny Knight (1982 vs. Florida)	9	208
Jamayel Smith (2007 vs. Arkansas)	10	208

GREATEST COACH:

For taking the Bulldogs to six bowl games, an appearance in the SEC championship game, and a 10-win season in his 10 years, Jackie Sherrill gets the nod as Mississippi State's greatest coach of the last 56 years.

With 10 different head men in 54 seasons, it is easy to see why Mississippi State is a tough place to coach. It is the second-favorite school in a small state with less-than-average high school player depth and considerably less than average finances at the disposal of the alumni and community.

Perhaps most indicative of Mississippi State's plight is the case of Hall of Fame coach Darrell Royal, who took his first head coaching position in Starkville in 1954. After leading the Maroons to two winning seasons, Royal left for the University of Washington where a player revolt had just disposed of the coach and conference sanctions were on the way. Royal, fortunately, got out of Seattle after a year and found his home for greatness at the University of Texas.

Because not every school was interested in a controversial mastermind, Mississippi State attracted Jackie Sherrill in 1991, and, except for a severe downturn in his last three years, Sherrill delivered the first winning stretch since the win-and-forfeit-filled years of Bob Tyler in the 1970s. Sherrill went a somewhat-miraculous 66-49-2 in his first 10 years.

MISSISSIPPI STATE'S 55 GREATEST SINCE 1953

OFFENSE

WIDE RECEIVER: Mardye McDole, Sammy Milner, Eric Moulds
TIGHT END: Johnny Baker, David Smith
TACKLE: Jesse James, John James, Floyd "Pork Chop" Womack
GUARD: Ricky Byrd, Wayne Harris, Scott Suber, Pat Watson
CENTER: Harold Easterwood, Tom Goode
QUARTERBACK: John Bond, Wayne Madkin, Jackie Parker
RUNNING BACK: Arthur Davis, Anthony Dixon, Michael Haddix, James Johnson, Jerious Norwood
FULLBACK: Hoyle Granger, Dennis Johnson

DEFENSE

END: Willie Evans, Billy Jackson, Tyrone Keys, Jimmy Webb
TACKLE: Glen Collins, Tommy Neville, Nate Williams
NOSE GUARD: Harvey Hull
LINEBACKER: Daniel Boyd, Johnie Cooks, Ray Costict, Quinton Culberson, Dwayne Curry, Mario Haggan, James Williams
CORNERBACK: Frank Dowsing, Walt Harris, Ken Phares, Fred Smoot
SAFETY: Stan Black, Ashley Cooper, Rob Fesmire, Pig Prather

SPECIAL TEAMS

RETURN SPECIALISTS: Tony James, Walter Packer
PLACE KICKER: Scott Westerfield
PUNTER: Jeff Walker

MULTIPLE POSITIONS

CENTER-LINEBACKER: D.D. Lewis
GUARD-PLACE KICKER: Justin Canale

TWO-WAY PLAYERS

QUARTERBACK-SAFETY: Billy Stacy
END-DEFENSIVE END: Ron Bennett

PERFORMANCE FORMULA:
MISSISSIPPI STATE'S 10 BEST SEASONS

1963	1.4180	13 of 70
1999	1.4079	12 of 71
1976	1.3895	18 of 70
1957	1.3710	14 of 69
1974	1.3683	15 of 71
1953	1.3276	17 of 69
2010	1.3144	22 of 71
1980	1.3097	21 of 70
2000	1.2905	20 of 70
1994	1.2509	28 of 71

MISSISSIPPI STATE BULLDOGS

Year	W-L-T	AP Poll	Conference Standing	Toughest Regular Season Opponents	Coach (Record at School)	Bowl Games		
1953	5-2-3		5	Auburn 7-2-1, Kentucky 7-2-1, Texas Tech 10-1, Mississippi 7-2-1	Murray Warmath (10-6-3)			
1954	6-4		6t	Miami 8-1, Mississippi 9-1	Darrell Royal			
1955	6-4		6	Tennessee 6-3-1, Kentucky 6-3-1, Auburn 8-1-1, Mississippi 8-1-1	Darrell Royal (12-8)			
1956	4-6		8t	Florida 6-3-1, Houston 7-2-1, Auburn 7-3, Mississippi 7-3	Wade Walker			
1957	6-2-1	14	3t	Tennessee 7-3, Florida 6-2-1, Auburn 10-0, Mississippi 8-1-1	Wade Walker			
1958	3-6		12	Florida 6-3-1, Auburn 9-01, LSU 10-0, Mississippi 8-2	Wade Walker			
1959	2-7		12	Georgia 9-1, Alabama 7-1-2, LSU 9-1, Mississippi 9-1	Wade Walker			
1960	2-6-1		11	Tennessee 6-2-2, Alabama 8-1-1, Auburn 8-2, Mississippi 9-0-1	Wade Walker			
1961	5-5		10t	Memphis State 8-2, Alabama 10-0, LSU 9-1, Mississippi 9-1	Wade Walker (22-32-2)			
1962	3-6		9	Alabama 9-1, Auburn 6-3-1, LSU 8-1-1, Mississippi 9-0	Paul Davis			
1963	7-2-2	11+	4	Memphis State 9-0-1, Alabama 8-2, Auburn 9-1, Mississippi 7-0-2	Paul Davis	Liberty	16 North Carolina State	12
1964	4-6		8	Florida 7-3, Alabama 10-0, LSU 7-2-1, Mississippi 5-4-1	Paul Davis			
1965	4-6		9t	Florida 7-3, Alabama 8-1-1, LSU 7-3, Mississippi 6-4	Paul Davis			
1966	2-8		9t	Georgia 9-1, Florida 8-2, Alabama 10-0, Mississippi 8-2	Paul Davis (20-28-2)			
1967	1-9		9t	Georgia 7-3, Houston 7-3, Florida State 7-2-1, Alabama 8-1-1	Charley Shira			
1968	0-8-2		9	Alabama 8-2, Florida State 8-2, LSU 7-3	Charley Shira			
1969	3-7		10	Florida 8-1-1, Houston 8-2, Auburn 8-2, LSU 9-1, Mississippi 7-3	Charley Shira			
1970	6-5		7t	Houston 8-3, Texas Tech 8-3, Auburn 8-2, LSU 9-2	Charley Shira			
1971	2-9		10	Georgia 10-1, Tenn'see 9-2, Alabama 11-0, Auburn 9-1, Mississippi 9-2	Charley Shira			
1972	4-7		9	Auburn 9-1, Alabama 10-1, LSU 9-1-1	Charley Shira (16-45-2)			
1973	4-5-2		8t	Florida 7-4, Alabama 11-0, LSU 9-2	Bob Tyler			
1974	9-3		4t	Florida 8-3, Alabama 11-0, Auburn 9-2	Bob Tyler	Sun	26 North Carolina	24
1975	6-4-1		9t	Georgia 9-2, Florida 9-2, Alabama 10-1	Bob Tyler			
1976	9-2	20	3t	Florida 8-3, Kentucky 7-4, Alabama 8-3	Bob Tyler			
1977	5-6		9t	Washington 8-3, Kentucky 10-1, Alabama 10-1, LSU 8-3	Bob Tyler			
1978	6-5		7t	Florida State 8-3, Alabama 10-1, LSU 8-3	Bob Tyler (39-25-3)			
1979	3-8		8	Florida State 11-0, Alabama 11-0, Auburn 8-3	Emory Bellard			
1980	9-3	19	2t	Florida 7-4, Southern Miss. 8-3, Miami 8-3, Alabama 9-2, LSU 7-4	Emory Bellard	Sun	17 Nebraska	31
1981	8-4	17	3	Miami 9-2, Alabama 9-1-1, Southern Miss. 9-1-1	Emory Bellard	Hall of Fame	10 Kansas	0
1982	5-6		8	Florida 8-3, Georgia 11-0, Auburn 8-3, Alabama 7-4, LSU 8-2-1	Emory Bellard			
1983	3-8		8	Florida 8-2-1, Georgia 9-1-1, Miami 10-1, Auburn 10-1	Emory Bellard			
1984	4-7		9t	Florida 9-1-1, Kentucky 8-3, Auburn 8-4, LSU 8-2-1	Emory Bellard			
1985	5-6		9	Florida 9-1-1, Auburn 8-3, Alabama 8-2-1, LSU 9-1-1	Emory Bellard (37-42)			
1986	6-5		7t	Auburn 9-2, Alabama 9-3, LSU 9-2, Mississippi 7-3-1	Rockey Felker			
1987	4-7		7t	Tennessee 9-2-1, Auburn 9-1-1, Alabama 7-4, LSU 9-1-1	Rockey Felker			
1988	1-10		10	Georgia 8-3, Auburn 10-1, Alabama 8-3, LSU 8-3	Rockey Felker			
1989	5-6		9	Florida 7-4, Auburn 9-2, Alabama 10-1, Mississippi 7-4	Rockey Felker			
1990	5-6		8t	Tennessee 8-2-2, Florida 9-2, Mississippi 9-2	Rockey Felker (21-34)			
1991	7-5		4t	Tennessee 9-2, Florida 10-1, Alabama 10-1	Jackie Sherrill	Liberty	15 Air Force	38
1992	7-5		W3	Florida 8-4, Alabama 12-0, Mississippi 8-3	Jackie Sherrill	Peach	17 North Carolina	21
1993	3-6-2		W5	Florida 9-2, Auburn 11-0, Alabama 8-2-1	Jackie Sherrill			
1994	8-4	24	W2	Tennessee 7-4, Auburn 9-1-1, Alabama 11-0	Jackie Sherrill	Peach	24 North Carolina State	28
1995	3-8		W6	Tennessee 10-1, Auburn 8-3, Alabama 8-3	Jackie Sherrill			
1996	5-6		W4	Auburn 7-4, LSU 9-2, Alabama 9-3	Jackie Sherrill			
1997	7-4		W4t	LSU 8-3, Georgia 9-2, Auburn 9-2, Mississippi 7-4	Jackie Sherrill			
1998	8-5		W1	Kentucky 7-4, Alabama 7-4, Arkansas 9-2	Jackie Sherrill	Cotton	11 Texas	38
1999	10-2	13	W2	Alabama 9-2, Arkansas 7-4, Mississippi 7-4	Jackie Sherrill	Peach	17 Clemson	7
2000	8-4	24	W3t	Florida 9-2, Auburn 9-2, LSU 7-4, Mississippi 7-4	Jackie Sherrill	Independence	43 Texas A&M	41
2001	3-8		W6	BYU 12-1, South Carolina 8-3, Florida 9-2, LSU 8-3	Jackie Sherrill			
2002	3-9		W6	Auburn 8-4, LSU 8-4, Alabama 10-3, Tennessee 8-4, Arkansas 9-3	Jackie Sherrill			
2003	2-10		W6	Oregon 8-4, LSU 11-1, Tennessee 10-2, Mississippi 9-3	Jackie Sherrill (74-76-2)			
2004	3-8		W6	Auburn 11-0, LSU 9-2, Florida 7-4	Sylvester Croom			
2005	3-8		W5t	Auburn 9-2, Georgia 10-2, Florida 8-3, Alabama 9-2	Sylvester Croom			
2006	3-9		W6	Auburn 10-2, LSU 10-2, West Virginia 10-2, Arkansas 10-2	Sylvester Croom			
2007	8-5		W3t	LSU 10-2, Auburn 8-4, Tennessee 9-3, West Virginia 10-2	Sylvester Croom	Liberty	10 Central Florida	3
2008	4-8		W4t	Georgia Tech 9-3, LSU 7-5, Alabama 12-1, Mississippi 8-4	Sylvester Croom (21-38)			
2009	5-7		W4t	LSU 9-3, Georgia Tech 11-2, Houston 10-3, Florida 12-1, Alabama 13-0	Dan Mullen			
2010	9-4	15	W5	Alabama 9-3, Arkansas 10-2, Auburn 13-0, LSU 10-2	Dan Mullen (13-11)	Gator	52 Michigan	52

TOTAL: 281-341-14 .4528 (53 of 70)   **Bowl Games since 1953:** 7-5 .5833 (Tied 20 of 70)

GREATEST TEAM SINCE 1953: Jackie Sherrill's 1999 Bulldogs won 10 games, and, using the nation's top-rated defense (222.5 yards per game), shut down Clemson in the Peach Bowl, a virtual home game for the Tigers. The Bulldogs' defensive secondary surely was the best five-man group for any time that constantly used a "nickel package." The defensive backs included corner backs Fred Smoot and Robert Bean, safeties Ashley Cooper, Tim Nelson, and Pig Prather, and reserves Eugene Liger, Eugene Clinton, and Josh Morgan. Only 17 points separated Mississippi State from losses to Alabama and Arkansas and a possible undefeated season. Coach Paul Davis' 1963 champions of the Liberty Bowl also rank near the top of Mississippi State's list. That edition of the Maroons posted a 7-2-2 record against the nation's toughest schedule.

1953 5-2-3

34	Memphis State	6	E John McKee
26	Tennessee	0	T Tom Morris
21	N. Texas State	6	G Murphy Robertson / Scott Suber
21	Auburn	21	C Harold Easterwood
13	Kentucky	32	G Bill Zimmerman / Max Williams
7	Alabama	7	T Jim Barron
20	Texas Tech	27	E John Katusa / Levaine Hollingshead
21	Tulane	0	QB Jackie Parker
26	LSU	13	HB Don Morris / Zerk Wilson
7	Mississippi	7	HB Arthur Davis / Lou Venier
			FB George Suda / Charles Evans

RUSHING: Evans 109/549y, Suda 98/465y, Parker 75/208y
PASSING: Parker 41-69/603y, 7TD, 59.4%
RECEIVING: Davis 11/150y, Wilson 8/170y, Venier 6/77y, Hollingshead 6/56y
SCORING: Parker 65pts, Wilson & Davis 24pts

1954 6-4

27	Memphis State	7	E Ron Bennett / Jim Ross
7	Tennessee	19	T Bill Glasgow / Ted Vallas
46	Arkansas State	13	G Scott Suber (T) / Bill Dooley
14	Tulane	0	C Harold Easterwood
13	Miami	27	G Max Williams / Bill Zimmerman
12	Alabama	7	T Jim Barron
0	Florida	7	E Levaine Hollingshead / Jimmy Vincent
48	N. Texas St.	26	QB Bobby Collins / Bill Stanton
25	LSU	0	HB Joe Silveri / Jim Harness
0	Mississippi	14	HB Arthur Davis / Lou Venier
			FB Charles Evans

RUSHING: Davis 132/670y, Evans 69/384y, Silveri 37/313y
PASSING: Collins 20-45/337y, 3TD, 44.4%
RECEIVING: Hollingshead 11/180y, Davis 7/103y, Ross 3/81y, Harness 3/65y, Silveri 3/37y
SCORING: Davis 60pts, Silveri (HB-K) 25pts, Harness (HB-K) 20pts

1955 6-4

14	Florida	20	E Ron Bennett
13	Tennessee	7	T Don Conkel / Gil Hastings
33	Memphis State	0	G Scott Suber
14	Tulane	0	C Speights Duncan / Jimmy Dodd
20	Kentucky	14	G Max Williams / Bill Dooley
26	Alabama	7	T Jim Barron
20	N. Texas State	7	E Jim Ross / Levaine Hollingshead
26	Auburn	27	QB Bill Stanton / Jim Bain
7	LSU	34	HB Jim Harness / William Earl Morgan
0	Mississippi	26	HB Arthur Davis / Jim Tait
			FB Frank Sabbatini / Molly Halbert

RUSHING: Davis 61/282y, Harness 62/280y, Morgan 47/262y
PASSING: Stanton 13-29/323y, 4TD, 44.8%
RECEIVING: Bennett 7/162y, Morgan 3/117y, Davis 3/48y, Hollingshead 3/40y
SCORING: Morgan (HB-K) 43pts, Harness (HB-K) 19pts, Davis & Tait 18pts

1956 4-6

0	Florida	26	E Ron Bennett
7	Houston	18	T Don Conkel / Ernie Galloway
19	Georgia	7	G Billy Fulton / Billy King
18	Trinity	6	C Jimmy Dodd
19	Arkansas State	9	G Wylie Drayton / Wayne Mangum
12	Alabama	13	T Gil Hastings / Sam Latham
14	Tulane	20	E Levaine Hollingshead
20	Auburn	27	QB Billy Stacy / Tom Miller
32	LSU	13	HB Molly Halbert / Bubber Trammell
7	Mississippi	13	HB Jim Tait
			FB Frank Sabbatini

RUSHING: Stacy 138/613y, Sabbatini 88/421y, Halbert 58/336y
PASSING: Stacy 32-71/464y, 3TD, 45.1%
RECEIVING: Bennett 15/227y, Hollingshead 7/103y, Halbert 5/76y
SCORING: Stacy 36pts, Sabbatini (FB-K) 33pts, Halbert 18pts

1957 6-2-1

10	Memphis State	6	E John Benge
9	Tennessee	14	T Bobby Tribble
47	Arkansas State	13	G Jack Benson
29	Florida	20	C Jimmy Dodd
25	Alabama	13	G Wylie Drayton / J.E. Logan
27	Tulane	6	T Sam Latham
7	Auburn	15	E Charles Weatherly / Ned Brooks
14	LSU	6	QB Billy Stacy / Tom Miller
7	Mississippi	7	HB Bubber Trammell / Wm. Earl Morgan
			HB Gil Peterson / Robert Collins
			FB Molly Halbert / Jack Batte

RUSHING: Halbert 76/386y, Stacy 110/350y, Peterson 51/254y
PASSING: Stacy 13-41/248y, 31.7%
RECEIVING: Peterson 7/95y, Weatherly 4/87y, 3 with 3
SCORING: Halbert 42pts, Collins 30pts, Peterson (HB-K) 25pts

1958 3-6

14	Florida	7	E P.L. Blake / Ned Brooks
8	Tennessee	13	T Bobby Tribble
28	Memphis State	8	G Jack Benson
38	Arkansas State	0	C Jim Poteete / Tom Goode
7	Alabama	9	G J.E. Logan / Wayne Mangum
12	Kentucky	33	T Ken Irby / Walter Suggs
14	Auburn	33	E Lavalle White / Robert Neaves
6	LSU	7	QB Billy Stacy / Tom Miller
0	Mississippi	21	HB Bubber Trammell / Willie Daniel
			HB Gil Peterson / Robert Collins
			FB Jack Batte / Bill Schoenrock

RUSHING: Batte 62/292y, Stacy 107/269y, Trammell 49/255y
PASSING: Stacy 32-70/388y, 2TD, 45.7%
RECEIVING: Blake 6/85y, White 5/68y, Collins 5/56y, Peterson 5/46y
SCORING: Stacy 20pts, Peterson (HB-K) 20pts, Batte 18pts

1959 2-7

13	Florida	14	E Lavalle White / David Kelley
6	Tennessee	22	T Floyd Powers / Ray Osborne
49	Arkansas State	14	G Buck Kennedy / Robert Shaw
0	Georgia	15	C Tom Goode
28	Memphis State	23	G Curtis Lloyd / Bennie Stacy
0	Alabama	10	T Walter Suggs
0	Auburn	31	E Ed Smith / Ned Brooks
0	LSU	27	QB Billy Hill / John Correro
0	Mississippi	42	HB Willie Daniel / Bobby Bethune
			HB Pat Shute / Lee Welch
			FB G.T. Thomas / Walter Flowers

RUSHING: Hill 63/257y, Daniel 48/214y, Bethune 39/181y
PASSING: Hill 25-62/248y, TD, 40.3%, Correro 21-35/251y, 2TD, 60.0%
RECEIVING: Welch 14/127y, Shute 8/97y, Smith 8/91y
SCORING: Hill 18pts, Bethune 12pts, Jerry Wade (K) 8pts

1960 2-6-1

10	Houston	14	E David Kelley / Randy Hutto
0	Tennessee	0	T Floyd Powers / Ray Osborne
29	Arkansas State	9	G Robert Shaw
17	Georgia	20	C Tom Goode
21	Memphis State	0	G Curtis Lloyd / Benny Stacy
0	Alabama	7	T Walter Suggs
12	Auburn	27	E Johnny Baker
3	LSU	7	QB Billy Hill / Charlie Furlow
9	Mississippi	35	HB Pat Shute / Bobby Bethune
			HB Lee Welch
			FB Mackie Weaver / Billy Tohill

RUSHING: Weaver 88/354y, Hill 76/344y, Bethune 49/224y
PASSING: Furlow 63-114/599y, 2TD, 55.3%
RECEIVING: Welch 12/98y, Shute 11/64y, Baker 9/100y, Bethune 9/93y
SCORING: Hill 20pts, Sammy Dantone (K) 19pts, Weaver 18pts

1961 5-5

6	Texas Tech	0	E David Kelley
10	Houston	7	T Howard Benton
3	Tennessee	7	G Robert Shaw
38	Arkansas State	0	C Brownie Walker
7	Georgia	10	G Benny Stacy
23	Memphis State	16	T Bobby Garvin
0	Alabama	24	E Johnny Baker
11	Auburn	10	QB John Correro/Charlie Furlow/Billy Hill
6	LSU	14	HB Jimmy Jenkins / Hal Green
7	Mississippi	37	HB Lee Welch / Billy Cook
			FB Mackie Weaver / Sammy Dantone

RUSHING: Hill 85/337y, Weaver 97/312y, Cook 42/198y
PASSING: Furlow 36-65/389y, 0TD, 55.4%, Hill 27-53/299y, TD, 50.9%, Correro 18-38/234y, 2TD, 47.4%
RECEIVING: Baker 22/323y, Welch 12/116y, Cook 10/102y, Jenkins 10/46y
SCORING: Sammy Dantone (K) 27pts, Welch 14pts, Cook 12pts

1962 3-6

9	Florida	19	E Gene Gibbs / Randy Hutto
7	Tennessee	6	T Howard Benton
35	Tulane	6	G Pat Watson / Hilton Ball
9	Houston	3	C Brownie Walker / Jon Windham
7	Memphis State	28	G Tommy Ranager
0	Alabama	20	T Tommy Neville
3	Auburn	9	E Johnny Baker
0	LSU	28	QB Charlie Furlow / Sonny Fisher
6	Mississippi	13	HB Ode Burrell / Jimmy Jenkins
			HB John Sparks / Billy Cook
			FB Mackie Weaver / Sammy Dantone

RUSHING: Burrell 71/310y, Weaver 49/157y, Cook 33/113y
PASSING: Furlow 62-111/744y, 3TD, 55.9%
RECEIVING: Burrell 24/204y, Hutto 14/189y, Baker 9/135y, Cook 9/114y
SCORING: Burrell 30pts, Sammy Dantone (K) 20pts, Hutto 12pts

1963 7-2-2

43	Howard College	0	E Bill McGuire
9	Florida	9	T Bob Dugan
7	Tennessee	0	G Pat Watson
31	Tulane	10	C Jon Windham
20	Houston	0	G Ronnie Kirkland / Justin Canale
10	Memphis State	17	T Tommy Neville
19	Alabama	20	E Tommy Inman
13	Auburn	10	QB Sonny Fisher
7	LSU	6	HB Ode Burrell/Mickey Edw'rds/Dan Bl'nd
10	Mississippi	10	HB Price Hodges/John Sparks/Billy Cook
16	N. Carolina St.■	12	FB Hoyle Granger

RUSHING: Granger 113/481y, Burrell 81/330y, Hodges 50/221y
PASSING: Fisher 36-74/353y, 2TD, 48.6%
RECEIVING: Inman 12/179y, Burrell 11/86y, McGuire 4/58y
SCORING: Burrell 42pts, Canale (G-K) 37pts, 4 with 12

1964 4-6

7	Texas Tech	21	E Tommy Inman
13	Florida	16	T Grady Bolton / Bubba Hampton
13	Tennessee	14	G Richard Weaver / Hilton Ball
17	Tulane	6	C Bootsie Larsen / Pat Watson
48	Southern Miss	7	G Justin Canale / Tom Folliard (DL)
18	Houston	13	T Frankie Bell / Tommy Neville
6	Alabama	23	E Harland Reed / Bill McGuire
3	Auburn	12	QB Don Edwards / Ashby Cook
10	LSU	14	HB Marcus Rhoden / Dan Bland
20	Mississippi	17	HB Price Hodges / Larry Swearengen
			FB Hoyle Granger / James Carroll

RUSHING: Granger 129/604y, Rhoden 58/384y, Hodges 79/282y
PASSING: Cook 35-61/426y, 2TD, 57.4%, Edwards 27-61/298y, TD, 44.3%
RECEIVING: Inman 21/338y, Hodges 14/84y, Rhoden 11/94y
SCORING: Rhoden 42pts, Canale (G-K) 34pts, Bland 24pts

1965 4-6

36	Houston	0	WR Don Saget / Dave Nugent
18	Florida	13	T Mike Duckworth
48	Tampa	7	G Bubba Hampton
27	Southern Miss	9	C Bootsie Larsen
13	Memphis State	33	G Richard Weaver / Bill Stevens
15	Tulane	17	T Sherman Douglas / George Barron
7	Alabama	10	TE Harland Reed
18	Auburn	25	QB Ashby Cook / Bill Buckner
20	LSU	37	HB Marcus Rhoden / Billy Moore
0	Mississippi	21	HB Dan Bland
			FB Hoyle Granger / Barry Cotney
			DL Jimbo Lane / C.R. Reed
			DL Duane Moore / Jerry Rosetti
			DL Grady Bolton
			DL Fred Corley
			DL Ed Hudgins / Glenn Higgins
			DL Bobby Carollo
			LB Jim Lightsey / Greg Baggett
			LB D.D. Lewis / Lewis Newton
			DB Marvin Cornelius
			DB Tommy Corbett / Jim Courtney
			DB James Carroll / Bill Kiser

RUSHING: Granger 108/449y, Rhoden 67/242y, Bland 54/212y
PASSING: Cook 78-162//1032y, 8TD, 48.1%
RECEIVING: Saget 24/373y, Rhoden 19/158y, Reed 18/187y
SCORING: Rhoden 42pts

1966 2-8

17 Georgia	20 E Harlan Reed / Harry Ivy
7 Flordia	28 T Hilton Pittman / Ed Hudgins
20 Richmond	0 G Jerry Jackson / Bill Canale
10 Southern Miss	9 C D.D. Lewis (LB) / Bill Nelson
0 Houston	28 G Jerry Rosetti / Bill Dear
0 Florida State	10 T Bubba Hampton
14 Alabama	27 E Richard Eaton / Dave Nugent
0 Auburn	13 QB Don Saget / Ronnie Coleman
7 LSU	17 TB Tommy Garrison / Prentis Calhoun
0 Mississippi	24 WB Marcus Rhoden / Joe Culpepper
	FB Bob Haller / Mike Wade
	DL Ray Reed
	DL Fred Corley / John Castleberry
	DL Ray Dedeaux
	DL Stu Scheer / Bill Thomas
	LB Leslie Newton / Rich Santagata
	LB D.D. Lewis (C)
	LB Calvin Harrison / Ted Carmical
	LB Jerry Beach / Bill Rucker
	DB Johnny Woitt / Jerry Woods
	DB Tommy Corbett / Bill Stevens
	DB Bill Kiser / Jimmy Courtney

RUSHING: Rhoden 75/295y, Saget 91/150y, Haller 40/109y
PASSING: Saget 69-166/753y, 2TD, 41.6%
RECEIVING: Rhoden 31/365y, Reed 16/232y, Nugent 13/137y
SCORING: Saget 18pts, James Neill (K) 15pts,
  Rhoden & Calhoun 12pts

1967 1-9

0 Georgia	30 E Sonny Shamburger / Tom Abernathy
7 Florida	24 T Hilton Pittman / Ed Hudgins
7 Texas Tech	3 G Jerry Jackson / Barry Bordelon
14 Southern Miss	21 C Bill Nelson
6 Houston	43 G Ted Carmical
12 Florida State	24 T Ronnie Gray / Bobby Knight
0 Alabama	13 E Stu Scheer (DL) / Don Saget
0 Auburn	36 QB Tommy Pharr
0 LSU	55 TB Tommy Garrison / Lennis Stevens
3 Mississippi	10 WB Marcus Rhoden / Joe Culpepper
	FB Tommy Corbett / Bobby Gossett
	DL Glenn Rhodes
	DL Glenn Higgins
	DL Duaine "Sappo" Moore / Hugh Adams
	DL Justin Alfred
	DL Gene Wood
	LB D.D. Lewis (C)
	LB Calvin Harrison / Joe Jennings
	DB Johnny Woitt (WB)
	DB Conn Canale / Louis D'Avignon
	DB Bill Kiser
	DB Jim Courtney

RUSHING: Pharr 136/326y, Garrison 90/255y, Stevens 47/123y
PASSING: Pharr 26-71/279y, 4TD, 36.6%,
  Saget 21-48/231y, 0TD, 43.8%
RECEIVING: Woitt 8/82y, Hardwich 6/65y, 3 with 5
SCORING: Woitt 18pts, 4 with 6pts

1968 0-8-2

13 Louisiana Tech	20 WR Sammy Milner/S'nny Shamb'rg'r (TE)
0 Auburn	26 T Rusty Dunaway / Freddy Russell
14 Florida	31 G Jerry Jackson
14 Southern Miss	47 C Bill Nelson
28 Texas Tech	28 G Ted Carmical
17 Tampa	24 T Hilton Pittman
13 Alabama	20 TE David Smith / Ronnie Moore
14 Florida State	27 QB Tommy Pharr
16 LSU	20 TB Andy Rhodes
17 Mississippi	17 WB Buddy Newsom / Lynn Zeningue
	FB Don Dudley / Bobby Gossett
	DL Bill Thomas / Richard Carver
	DL Stu Scheer / Justin Alfred
	DL Jack Thomas / Durwood Stephens
	DL Hugh Adams / Jan Gwin
	DL Gene Wood
	LB Joe Jennings
	LB Calvin Harrison
	DB Conn Canale
	DB Al Morrell / Dwight Sisk
	DB Buddy Hardwich / Don Shanks
	DB Dickie Carpenter

RUSHING: Pharr 141/239y, Gossett 58/170y, Dudley 38/156y
PASSING: Pharr 173-319/1838y, 9TD, 54.2%
RECEIVING: Milner 64/909y, Smith 38/425y, Gossett 22/174y
SCORING: Milner 30pts, H.F. Culver (K) 20pts, 4 with 18pts

1969 3-7

17 Richmond	14 WR Sammy Milner
35 Florida	47 T Joe Edwards
0 Houston	74 G Roye Carnell / Tate Marsh
34 Southern Miss	20 C Ronnie Gray
30 Texas Tech	26 G Joe Hart / Butch Yarbrough
17 Florida State	20 T Freddy Russell
19 Alabama	23 TE David Smith
13 Auburn	52 QB Tommy Pharr
6 LSU	61 TB Steve Whaley
22 Mississippi	48 WB Terry Smithart / Jim Patridge
	FB Don Dudley / Bobby Gossett
	DL Jim McAlpin / Gene Wood
	DL Jack Thomas
	DL Jerry Conrad
	DL Mike Eaton
	LB Dickie Carpenter / Joe Jennings
	LB Mike Wade / Chuck Dees
	LB Steve Brown / Jim Nelson
	DB Buddy Newsom
	DB Bill Lancaster
	DB Bill Crick
	DB Joel Holliman / Jay Hughes

RUSHING: Whaley 89/275y, Dudley 71/250y, Patridge 36/78y
PASSING: Pharr 140-258/1603y, 11TD, 54.3%
RECEIVING: Milner 64/745y, Smith 50/756y, 3 with 14
SCORING: Whaley 42pts, Milner 38pts, Smith 30pts

1970 6-5

14 Oklahoma State	13 WR Sammy Milner / Bob Anger
13 Florida	34 WR David Smith / Steve Natale
20 Vanderbilt	6 T Joe Edwards / Greg Fountain
7 Georgia	6 G Butch Yarbrough
14 Houston	31 C Tate Marsh / Alex Romanoff
20 Texas Tech	16 G Joe Hart
51 Southern Miss	15 T Preston Payne
6 Alabama	35 TE Bob Young
0 Auburn	56 QB Joe Reed
7 LSU	38 TB Lewis Grubbs
19 Mississippi	14 FB Don Dudley / Steve Stoots
	DL Jim McAlpin / Bob Kimbrough
	DL Jerry Conrad
	DL Mike Eaton
	DL Jack Hall / Robbie Armstrong
	LB Joel Holliman
	LB Chuck Dees
	LB Chick King / Jim Nelson
	DB Ken Phares
	DB Frank Dowsing
	DB Emile Petro / Anthony Walker
	DB Steve Whaley / Billy Southward

RUSHING: Grubbs 155/644y, Reed 155/316y, Dudley 39/194y
PASSING: Reed 138-294/1616y, 8TD, 46.9%
RECEIVING: Smith 74/987y, Milner 18/153y, Young 11/127y
SCORING: Grubbs 48pts, Reed 42pts, Smith 38pts

1971 2-9

7 Oklahoma State	26 WR Tommy Strahan / Bill Buckley
13 Florida	10 T Danny West (G)
19 Vanderbilt	49 G Joe Edwards (T)
7 Georgia	35 C Gen Wardlow
9 Florida State	27 G Butch Yarbrough
24 Lamar	7 T Larry Greenlee / Preston Payne
7 Tennessee	10 TE Eric Hoogatt
10 Alabama	41 QB Hal Chealander / Billy Baker
21 Auburn	30 TB Lewis Grubbs
3 LSU	28 WB Jay Hughes / Dick McElroy (FB)
0 Mississippi	48 FB Wayne Jones / Steve Whaley
	DL Jim McAlpin
	DL Jerry Conrad
	DL Robert Bell / Mike Eaton
	DL Jack Hall / Robbie Armstrong
	LB Joel Holliman
	LB Chuck Dees
	LB Jim Nelson / Chick King
	LB Billy Southward
	DB Ken Phares
	DB Frank Dowsing
	DB Emile Petro

RUSHING: Grubbs 134/419y, Jones 79/285y, Baker 67/184y
PASSING: Chealander 66-155/937y, 2TD, 42.6%
RECEIVING: Hoggatt 28/365y, Strahan 21/346y, Hughes 16/215y
SCORING: Glenn Ellis (K) 30pts, Jones 24pts, Grubbs 18pts

1972 4-7

3 Auburn	14 WR Tommy Strahan
42 NE Louisiana	7 T Jerry Johnston
10 Vanderbilt	6 G Danny West / Jim Touchet
13 Florida	28 C Gene Wardlaw
13 Kentucky	17 G Greg Fountain
13 Florida State	25 T Larry Thompson / Roger Cook
26 Southern Miss	7 TE Bob Bozeman / Glenn Ellis
27 Houston	13 QB Melvin Barkum / Rockey Felker
14 Alabama	58 TB Lewis Grubbs
14 LSU	28 WB Bill Buckley
14 Mississippi	51 FB Wayne Jones / Dick McElroy
	DL Allen Brantley / Larry McCullough
	DL Jimmy Webb
	DL Robert Hall
	DL Jack Hall
	LB John David Calhoun
	LB Johnny Bruce
	LB Bill Wilkerson / Tommy Gatlin
	DB Ken Phares
	DB Frank Dowsing
	DB Emile Petro / Billy Baker
	DB Billy Southward / Don Magee

RUSHING: Barkum 132/522y, Grubbs 116/517y, Jones 105/387y
PASSING: Felker 74-161/992y, 6TD, 46.0%,
  Barkum 38-96/591y, 2TD, 39.6%
RECEIVING: Buckley 47/776y, Strahan 21/308y, Braswell 13/226y
SCORING: Barkum, Buckley & Grubbs 36pts

1973 4-5-2

21 NE Louisiana	21 WR Tommy Strahan
52 Vanderbilt	21 T Roger Cook / Sam Nichols
33 Florida	12 G Keith Temple
14 Kentucky	42 C Richard Keys
37 Florida State	12 G Greg Fountain
18 Louisville	7 T Danny West / Larry Thompson
10 Southern Miss	10 TE Danny Malone / Bob Bozeman
0 Alabama	35 QB Rockey Felker / Mike Monaghan
17 Auburn	31 TB Stan Murray / Melvin Barkum
7 LSU	26 WB Bill Buckley
10 Mississippi	38 FB Wayne Jones
	DL Jimmy Webb / Wally Cox
	DL Chuck Brislin
	DL Bobby Walden / Jackie Chapman
	DL Larry McCullough / Sidney Key
	LB Tommy Gatlin
	LB Calvin Hymel / Johnny Bruce
	LB Harvey Hull
	DB Steve Freeman
	DB Larry Buie / Willie Lee
	DB Bobby Wallace
	DB Leon Alexander

RUSHING: Jones 212/1193y, Felker 51/272y, Murray 69/270y
PASSING: Felker 60-106/782y, 9 TD, 56.6%,
  Monaghan 45-105/557y, 2TD, 42.9%
RECEIVING: Buckley 41/661y, Strahan 26/394y, Malone 13/121y
SCORING: Sam Nickles (K) 47pts, Buckley 44pts, Jones 36pts

1974 9-3

49 William & Mary	7 WR Melvin Barkum
38 Georgia	14 WR Sandy Braswell / Stan Black
13 Florida	29 T Jim Touchet
21 Kansas State	16 G Keith Temple
37 Lamar	21 C Richard Keys
29 Memphis State	28 G Sam Nichols
56 Louisville	7 T Jim Eidson
0 Alabama	35 TE Howard Lewis / Bob Bozeman
20 Auburn	24 QB Rockey Felker
7 LSU	6 TB Walter Packer /
31 Mississippi	13 FB Dennis Johnson (TB) / James Smith
26 North Carolina■	24 DL Wally Cox
	DL Jimmy Webb
	DL Harvey Hull
	DL Larry Gillard / Sidney Key
	DL Ronnie Everett
	LB Ray Costict / Andy Miller
	LB Calvin Hymel
	DB Steve Freeman / Larry Buie
	DB Willie Lee / Richard Blackmore
	DB Bobby Wallace
	DB Mike Lawrence

RUSHING: Packer 157/994y, Johnson 90/522y, Felker 149/446y
PASSING: Felker 73-155/1147y, 8TD, 47.1%
RECEIVING: Lewis 21/330y, Barkum 19/296y, Black 14/266y
SCORING: Felker 46pts, Sam Nickles (K) 45pts, Johnson 42pts

1975 6-4-1

17 Memphis State	7 WR Duncan McKenzie / Steve White
6 Georgia	28 WR Gavin Rees
10 Florida	27 T Duane McNeil / Joe Soileau
7 So. Miss.(F-L)	3 G Chuck Brislin
28 Rice (F-L)	14 C Richard Keys
15 No. Texas State	12 G Sam Nichols
28 Louisville (F-L)	14 T Jim Eidson
10 Alabama	21 TE Howard Lewis
21 Auburn (F-L)	21 QB Bruce Threadgill
16 LSU (F-L)	6 TB Walter Packer / Terry Vitrano
7 Mississippi	13 FB Dennis Johnson / Clarence Harmon
	DL Wally Cox / Raymond Peyton
	DL Larry Gillard
	DL Harvey Hull / Perry Tanksley
	DL Sidney Key
	DL Will Coltharp
	LB Ray Costict / Jerald Porter
	LB Calvin Hymel / Andy Miller
	DB Henry Davison
	DB Larry Buie / Willie Lee
	DB Stan Black
	DB Bobby Wallace / Gerald Jackson

RUSHING: Packer 180/1012y, Johnson 72/372y, Harmon 74/427y
PASSING: Threadgill 43-123/575y, 2TD, 35.0%
RECEIVING: Rees 18/292y, White 10/145y, Johnson 7/73y
SCORING: Kinney Jordan (K) 53pts, Packer 44pts, Johnson 18pts

1976 9-2

7 N. Tex. St. (F-L)	0 WR Gavin Rees / Robert Chatman
30 Louisville (F-L)	21 T Mark Trogdon
30 Florida	34 G Fred Rainer
38 Cal-Pom'a (F-L)	0 C Richard Keys
14 Kentucky (F-L)	7 G Perry Tanksley
42 Memphis St.(F-L)	33 T Sam Nichols
14 So. Miss. (F-L)	6 TE Duncan McKenzie / Bobby Molden
17 Alabama	34 QB Bruce Threadgill
28 Auburn (F-L)	19 HB Walter Packer
21 LSU (F-L)	13 HB Clarence Harmon / Len Copeland
28 Mississippi (F-L)	11 FB Dennis Johnson
	DL Raymond Peyton / Wally Cox
	DL Larry Gillard
	DL Harvey Hull / Perry Tanksley
	DL John Carter
	DL Will Coltharp
	LB Ray Costict
	LB Jerald Porter / Mike Lawrence
	DB Henry Davison
	DB Kenny Johnson / Richard Blackmore
	DB Stan Black
	DB Gerals Jackson

RUSHING: Johnson 152/859y, Packer 96/633y, Threadgill 160/554y
PASSING: Threadgill 45-89/807y, 7TD, 50.6%
RECEIVING: Chatman 15/277y, Rees 14/321y, Johnson 7/94y, McKenzie 7/67y
SCORING: Kinney Jordan (K) 61pts, Johnson 42pts, Packer 36pts

1977 5-6

17 N. Tex. St. (F-L)	15 WR Mardye McDole / Steve White
27 Wash'gton (F-L)	18 T Mark Trogden
22 Florida	24 G Mike Edwards / Alan Massey
24 Kansas St. (F-L)	21 C Chris Quillian
7 Kentucky	23 G Perry Tanksley
13 Memphis State	21 T Joe Soileau
7 Southern Miss	14 TE Duncan McKenzie
7 Alabama	37 QB Bruce Threadgill
27 Auburn (F-L)	13 HB James Jones / James Otis Doss
24 LSU	27 HB Len Copeland
18 Mississippi (F-L)	14 FB Dennis Johnson
	DL Raymond Peyton
	DL Larry Gillard / Lonnie Greene
	DL Mark Hitt
	DL Mark White / Tyrone Keys
	DL Bobby Molden
	LB Mike Lawrence
	LB Jerald Porter
	DB Henry Davison
	DB Bill Lee / Larry Dixon
	DB Kenny Johnson
	DB Gerald Jackson

RUSHING: Johnson 114/529y, Jones 67/400y, Copeland 68/329y
PASSING: Threadgill 91-219/1317y, 7TD, 41.6%
RECEIVING: McDole 29/510y, Robert Chatman (WR) 22/266y, Johnson 14/176y
SCORING: Dave Marler (K) 57pts, Copeland 30pts, Johnson & Jones 24pts

1978 6-5

28 W. Texas State	0 WR Mardye McDole
17 N. Texas State	5 WR Robert Chatman
44 Memphis State	14 T Roman Grace
0 Florida	34 G Matt Edwards
17 Southern Miss	22 C Chris Quillian
55 Florida State	27 G Alan Massey
34 Tennessee	21 T Alan Hartlein
14 Alabama	35 TE Bill Maxey
0 Auburn	6 QB Dave Marler
16 LSU	14 TB James Jones
7 Mississippi	27 FB Fred Collins / James Otis Doss
	DL Raymond Peyton
	DL Tyrone Keys / Chuck Maier
	DL Mitchell Street
	DL Keith Jackson
	DL Don Edwards / Bobby Molden
	LB Johnie Cooks
	LB Rusty Martin
	DB Henry Monroe
	DB Richard Blackmore / Willie Jackson
	DB Kenny Johnson
	DB Gerald Jackson

RUSHING: Jones 130/687y, Collins 83/402y, Doss 29/136y
PASSING: Marler 163-287/2422y, 11TD, 56.8%
RECEIVING: McDole 48/1035y, Jones 24/237y, Ellis 20/301y, Chatman 20/290y
SCORING: Jones 84pts, McDole 42pts, Marler 33pts

1979 3-8

13 Memphis State	14 WR Mardye McDole / David Ellis
14 Maryland	35 T Roman Grace
24 Florida	10 G Matt Edwards
28 Tennessee	9 C Kent Hull / Bill Bell
6 Florida State	17 G Alan Massey / Wayne Harris
48 Marshall	0 T Alan Hartlein
7 Southern Miss	21 TE Arthur Wiley / Jerry Price
7 Alabama	24 QB Tony Black / Dwayne Brown
3 Auburn	14 HB Michael Haddix
3 LSU	21 HB Stanley Howell / Len Copeland
9 Mississippi	14 FB Fred Collins / Donald Ray King
	DL Tyrone Keys
	DL Keith Jackson / Chuck Maier
	DL Lonnie Greene
	DL Glen Collins / Earnie Barnes
	LB Don Edwards
	LB Curtis Hill / Johnie Cooks
	LB Rusty Martin
	DB Willie Jackson / Larry Friday
	DB Don Burrell
	DB Kenny Johnson
	DB Rob Fesmire

RUSHING: Collins 128/591y, Howell 58/425y, Haddix 60/399y
PASSING: Black 23-62/363y, 2TD, 37.1%, Brown 21-62/274y, 2TD, 33.9%
RECEIVING: McDole 20/380y, Ellis 7/125y, Jones 4/29y
SCORING: Collins 26pts, Haddix & Danny Brown (K) 24pts

1980 9-3

34 Memphis State	7 WR David Ellis / Glen Young
31 Louisiana Tech	11 T Roman Grace
24 Vanderbilt	14 G Matt Edwards
15 Florida	21 C Kent Hull
28 Illinois	21 G Wayne Harris
17 Southern Miss	42 T Alan Massey
34 Miami	31 TE Jerry Price
24 Auburn	21 QB John Bond
6 Alabama	3 HB Michael Haddix / George Wonsley
55 LSU	31 WB Mardye McDole
19 Mississippi	14 FB Donald Ray King / Fred Collins
17 Nebraska■	31 DL Tyrone Keys
	DL Earnie Barnes / Ricky George
	DL Glen Collins
	DL Billy Jackson / Mike McEnany
	LB Don Edwards
	LB Curtis Stowers / Johnie Cooks
	LB Rusty Marrtin
	DB Willie Jackson
	DB Steve Johnson / Lawrence Evans
	DB Larry Friday
	DB Rob Fesmire

RUSHING: Haddix 133/724y, Bond 131/720y, King 147/642y
PASSING: Bond 59-133/849y, 5TD, 44.4%
RECEIVING: McDole 19/289y, Haddix 13/122y, Yoiung 11/218y, Ellis 11/187y
SCORING: McDole 42pts, Haddix & King 36pts

1981 8-4

20 Memphis State	3 WR Glen Young
29 Vanderbilt	9 T Roman Grace
28 Florida	7 G Bill Bell
3 Missouri	14 C Kent Hull
37 Colorado State	27 G Wayne Harris
14 Miami	10 T Bobby Miketinas
21 Auburn	17 TE Jerry Price
10 Alabama	13 QB John Bond
6 Southern Miss	7 HB Michael Haddix / Danny Knight
17 LSU	9 WB Danny Knight
17 Mississippi	21 FB Donald Ray King / Al Ricky Edwards
10 Kansas■	0 DL Billy Jackson
	DL Earnie Barnes / Ricky George
	DL Glen Collins
	DL Mike McEnany
	LB Curtis Stowers
	LB Johnie Cooks
	LB John Miller
	DB Steve Johnson / Cookie Jackson
	DB Lawrence Evans / Kenneth Johnson
	DB Greg Williams
	DB Rob Fesmire

RUSHING: Haddix 110/622y, King 152/581y, Bond 133/339y
PASSING: Bond 65-144/875y, 4TD, 45.1%
RECEIVING: Young 19/263y, Price 18/271y, Haddix 10/90y
SCORING: Dana Moore 30pts, King 24pts, Haddix & Lamar Windham (HB) 20pts

1982 5-6

30 Tulane	21 WR Danny Knight / Glen Young
31 Arkansas State	10 T Tony Sartor
41 Memphis State	17 G Bill Bell
17 Florida	27 C Kent Hull
22 Georgia	29 G Wayne Harris
14 Southern Miss	20 T Bobby Miketinas
14 Miami	31 TE Jerry Price
17 Auburn	35 QB John Bond
12 Alabama	20 HB Michael Haddix
27 LSU	24 HB George Wonsley / Lamar Windham
27 Mississippi	10 FB Henry Koontz / Al Rickey Edwards
	DL Billy Jackson
	DL Earnie Barnes
	DL Ricky George
	DL Mike McEnany
	LB Clay Peacher
	LB Ermon Green
	LB John Miller / Calvin Zanders
	DB Steve Johnson
	DB Kenneth Johnson
	DB Gary Lambert
	DB Tom Nichols

RUSHING: Haddix 122/813y, Bond 144/609y, Koontz 91/397y
PASSING: Bond 91-183/1591y, 7TD, 49.7%
RECEIVING: Knight 37/924y, Young 15/249y, Aldredge 14/223y
SCORING: Haddix 54pts, Knight 42pts, Dana Moore (K) 39pts

1983 3-8

14 Tulane	9 WR Danny Knight
38 Navy	10 T Alvin Robinson / Frank Harbin
12 Florida	35 G Rusty Brown / Kevin Walker
7 Georgia	20 C Mike McDonald
6 Southern Miss	31 G Don Scamardo
7 Miami	31 T Ken Leikam / Danny Sanders (G)
13 Auburn	28 TE Corwyn Aldredge
18 Alabama	35 QB John Bond
13 Memphis State	30 HB George Wonsley
45 LSU	26 HB Lamar Windham
23 Mississippi	24 FB Al Ricky Edwards / Henry Koontz
	DL Eddie Hornback
	DL Elvis Butler
	DL Pat Swoopes / Darrell Moore
	DL Carsno Mitchell
	LB Clay Peacher
	LB Billy Jackson / Ermon Green CHECK
	LB Calvin Zanders
	DB Cookie Jackson / Kirby Jackson
	DB Kenneth Johnson
	DB Gary Lambert / R.J. McKenna
	DB Tom Nichols

RUSHING: Bond 164/612y, Koontz 84/366y, Edwards 92/355y
PASSING: Bond 92-205/1306y, 2TD, 44.9%
RECEIVING: Knight 34/671y, Aldredge 16/219y, Windham 15/126y
SCORING: Bond 78pts, Artie Cosby (K) 47pts, Koontz 18pts

1984 4-7

30 Tulane	3 WR Art Mordecai
14 Colorado State	9 T Joe Estay
30 Missouri	47 G Stan Sims
12 Florida	27 C Garry Frank
27 Southern Miss	18 G Danny Sanders
13 Kentucky	17 T Alvin Robinson / Frank Harbin
12 Memphis State	23 TE Corwyn Aldredge
21 Auburn	24 QB Don Smith
20 Alabama	24 TB Jim Cumberbatch
16 LSU	14 WB Louis Clark
3 Mississippi	24 FB Mikel Williams
	DL Mike Guttuso
	DL Elvis Butler
	DL Pat Swoopes
	DL William French
	LB Ermon Green / Cedric Corse
	LB Aaron Pearson
	LB Leon Cannon
	DB Kirby Jackson
	DB Bennie Thomas / Bruce Plummer
	DB R.J. McKenna
	DB Tom Nichols

RUSHING: Smith 128/545y, Cumberbatch 83/478y,
Williams 107/446y
PASSING: Smith 75-176/1236y, 6TD, 42.6%
RECEIVING: Williams 23/177y, Mordecai 19/387y, Clark 16/338y
SCORING: Artie Cosby (K) 56pts, Smith 54pts, Williams 30pts

1985 5-6

22 Arkansas State	14 WR James Bloodworth
30 Syracuse	3 T Garry Frank
23 Southern Miss	20 G Stan Sims / Scott Wilbanks
22 Florida	36 C Paul Young
31 Memphis State	28 G Rusty Brown
19 Kentucky	33 T John Fitzgerald / Alvin Robinson
31 Tulane	27 TE Louis Clark
9 Auburn	21 QB Don Smith
28 Alabama	44 HB Calvin Robinson / Kenny Rogers
15 LSU	17 HB Jeff Patton
27 Mississippi	45 TB Hank Phillips / Rodney Peters
	DL Mike Guttuso / Michael Simmons
	DL Darrell Moore
	DL Pat Swoopes
	DL Eric Mell
	LB Cedric Corse
	LB Aaron Pearson
	LB Leon Cannon
	DB Kirby Jackson
	DB Bruce Plummer
	DB R.J. McKenna
	DB Brian Hutson

RUSHING: Smith 190/308y, Phillips 97/447y, Peters 55/236y
PASSING: Smith 143-312/2332y, 15TD, 45.8%
RECEIVING: Patton 34/416y, Rogers 25/362y,
Bloodworth 23/479y
SCORING: Artie Cosby (K) 51pts, Smith 42pts, Bloodworth 30pts

1986 6-5

24 Syracuse	17 WR Louis Clark
27 Tennessee	23 WR Fred Hadley
24 Southern Miss	28 T Alvin Robinson
16 Florida	10 G Durward Minor / Carl Middleton
34 Memphis State	17 C Tommy Goode
24 Arkansas State	9 G Stan Sims
34 Tulane	27 T Harold Rials / Jerome McLaurin
6 Auburn	35 TE Heath Jackson / Gary Gleason
3 Alabama	38 QB Don Smith
0 LSU	47 TB Rodney Peters / Marcus Bush
3 Mississippi	24 FB Michael Taylor
	DL Anthony Butts
	DL Garry Frank / Jason Little
	DL Michael Simmons
	LB Jesse Anderson
	LB Darren Martin
	LB Cedric Corse / Dwayne King
	LB Jerry Leggett
	DB Bruce Plummer
	DB Kirby Jackson
	DB Asa Bennett / Milton Smith
	DB Brian Hutson

RUSHING: Smith 159/740y, Peters 84/367y, Bush 54/268y
PASSING: Smith 120-244/1609y, 10TD, 49.2%
RECEIVING: Hadley 28/529y, Clark 24/378y, Lowe 14/249y
SCORING: Artie Cosby (K) 57pts, Smith 36pts, 4 with 18pts

1987 4-7

31 SW Louisiana	3 WR Darrell Kennybrew
10 Tennessee	38 WR Fred Hadley / John Moore
14 Louisiana Tech	13 T Kevin Englehardt / Tony Robetrson
3 Florida	38 G Durward Minor
9 Memphis State	6 C Tommy Goode
14 Southern Miss	18 G Stan Sims
7 Auburn	38 T Mike Hendershot / Gary Frank
18 Alabama	21 TE Jesse Anderson / Sam Wright
19 Tulane	30 QB Mike Davis / Eric Underwood
14 LSU	34 TB Hank Phillips / David Fair
30 Mississippi	20 FB Rodney Peters
	DL Michael Simmons / Bill Knight
	DL Anthony Butts
	DL Bobby Barlow / Ryan Ford
	LB Darren Martin
	LB Keith Neal / Jeremiah Sangster
	LB Lenard Hooker / James Williams
	LB Cedric Corse
	DB Milton Smith / Eddie Myles
	DB Bernard McCullough
	DB Bo Russell / Asa Bennett
	DB Michael Taylor

RUSHING: Phillips 184/848y, Albert Williams (QB) 79/287y,
Fair 30/251y
PASSING: Davis 60-129/779y, 2TD, 46.5%,
Underwood 48-83/582y, 3TD, 57.8%
RECEIVING: Hadley 28/499y, Kenneybrew 21/305y,
Anderson 20/324y
SCORING: Joel Logan (K) 53pts, Phillips 48pts, Wade 20pts

1988 1-10

21 Louisiana Tech	14 WR Jerry Bouldin
20 Vanderbilt	24 WR Fred Hadley
35 Georgia	42 T Mike Hendershot
0 Florida	17 G Derrick Dean
10 Memphis State	31 C Tony Robertson
21 Southern Miss	38 G Durwood Minor
0 Auburn	33 T Kenny Stewart
34 Alabama	53 TE Sam Wright
3 LSU	20 QB Tony Shell / Eric Underwood
22 Tulane	27 TB Jesse Anderson / Hank Phillips
6 Mississippi	33 FB Jerrod Young
	DL Desmond Bates / Ryan Ford
	DL Bill Knight
	DL Bobby Barlow
	DL Robert Young
	LB Darren Martin
	LB James Williams
	LB Reggie Stewart
	DB Milton Smith / Jerry Myers
	DB Bernard McCullough / Eddie Myles
	DB Albert Williams / Asa Bennett
	DB Bo Russell

RUSHING: Anderson 102/468y, Phillips 72/317y, Young 56/237y
PASSING: Shell 153-335/1884y, 13TD, 45.7%
RECEIVING: Hadley 29/477y, Wright 29/334y,
Anderson 28/333y, Bouldin 28//429y
SCORING: Joel Logan (K) 50pts, Hadley & Bouldin 30pts

1989 5-6

42 Vanderbilt	7 WR John Parker / Jerry Bouldin
26 Southern Miss	23 WR John Moore / Chris Firle
6 Georgia	23 T John James
0 Florida	21 G Ricky Byrd
28 NE Louisiana	14 C Byron Jordan
35 Memphis State	10 G Tony Robertson
0 Auburn	14 T Derrick Dean
10 Alabama	23 TE Jesse Anderson / Sam Wright
27 Tulane	7 QB Tony Shell / Todd Jordan
20 LSU	44 RB William Prince / Kenny Roberts
11 Mississippi	21 FB Treddis Anderson / Todd Morris
	DL Bill Knight / Robert Young
	DL Demetrius Hill / Rodney Stowers
	DL Bobby Barlow
	LB Derrell Robertson
	LB James Williams / Dewayne King
	LB Reggie Stewart
	LB Marc Woodard
	DB Milton Smith
	DB Eddie Myles
	DB Rocky Nabors
	DB Bo Russell

RUSHING: Roberts 108/511y
PASSING: Shell 45-87/499y, 2TD, 51.7%
RECEIVING: Anderson 21/230y
SCORING: Joel Logan (K) 47pts

1990 5-6

7 Tennessee	40 WR Jerry Bouldin
27 Cal-Fullerton	13 WR Chris Firle
13 Southern Miss	10 T John James
21 Florida	34 G Ricky Byrd
15 Kentucky	17 C Byron Jordan
38 Tulane	17 G Shea Bell
16 Auburn	17 T Kenny Stewart
0 Alabama	0 TE Trenell Edwards / Treddis Anderson
27 Memphis State	23 QB Tony Shell / Wm. "Sleepy" Robinson
34 LSU	22 RB Ken Rob'rts/Tay Gall'way/Tony Jam's
9 Mississippi	21 FB Jerrod Young / David Fair
	DL Ryon Ford / Desmond Bates
	DL Demetrius Hill / Rodney Stowers
	DL Robert Young / Kevin Henry
	LB Keith Joseph
	LB Daniel Boyd
	LB Reggie Stewart / Keo Coleman
	LB Marc Woodard
	DB Lee Lipscomb
	DB Eddie Myles / Tony Harris
	DB Lance Aldridge / Kelvin Knight
	DB Albert Williams

RUSHING: Roberts 93/523y
PASSING: Shell 151-293/1909y, 10TD, 51.5%
RECEIVING: Bouldin 32/447y
SCORING: Jeff Logan (K) 49pts

1991 7-5

47 Cal-Fullerton	3 WR Tony James / Charlie Davidson
13 Texas	6 WR Willie Harris / Chris Firle
48 Tulane	0 T John James
24 Tennessee	26 G Bill Sartin
7 Florida	29 C Lee Ford
31 Kentucky	6 G Shea Bell
23 Memphis State	28 T Michael Montgomery
24 Auburn	17 TE Trenell Edwards
7 Alabama	13 QB Sleepy Robinson / Greg Plump
28 LSU	19 RB Kenny Roberts / Michael Davis
24 Mississippi	9 FB William Prince
15 Air Force■	38 DL Kevin Henry
	DL Nate Williams / Arleye Gibson
	DL Jerome Brown / Rodney Stowers
	LB Keith Joseph
	LB Daniel Boyd
	LB Keo Coleman / Juan Long
	LB Marc Woodard
	DB Tony Harris
	DB Edward Williams
	DB Kelvin Knight / Lance Aldridge
	DB Frankie Luster

RUSHING: Robinson 154/543y, Roberts 69/439y, Davis 70/435y
PASSING: Robinson 77-141/1167y, 8TD, 54.6%
RECEIVING: Harris 24/529y, James 16258y, Roberts 15/159y
SCORING: Chris Gardner (K) 60pts, Davis & Robinson 30pts

1992 7-4

28 Texas	10 WR Orlando Truitt / Chris Jones
3 LSU	24 WR Willie Harris / Bernard Euell
20 Memphis State	16 T John James / Melvin Hayes
30 Florida	6 G Bill Sartin
14 Auburn	7 C Lee Ford / Brian Anderson
6 South Carolina	21 G Shea Bell
56 Arkansas State	6 T Jesse James
37 Kentucky	36 TE Kendell Watkins
10 Arkansas	3 QB Greg Plump
21 Alabama	30 RB Kenny Roberts
10 Mississippi	17 FB Michael Davis
17 North Carolina■	21 DL Kevin Henry / Herman Carroll
	DL Arleye Gibson
	DL Jerome Brown / Tim Foster
	LB Keith Joseph
	LB Danial Keith
	LB Juan Long / Wesley Leasy
	LB Johnny Curtis / Lateef Travis
	DB Walt Harris
	DB Edward Williams / Charlie Davidson
	DB Kelvin Knight
	DB Frankie Luster

RUSHING: Roberts 106/597y
PASSING: Plump 54-129/863y, 4TD, 41.9%
RECEIVING: Harris 35/574y
SCORING: Chris Gardner (K) 58pts

1993 3-6-2

35 Memphis State	45 WR Chris Jones / Eric Moulds
16 LSU	18 WR Bernard Euell / Kenny Causey
36 Tulane	10 T Henry McCann
24 Florida	38 G Melvin Hayes
17 Auburn	31 C Brian Anderson
23 South Carolina	0 G Jason Wisner
15 Arkansas State	15 T Jesse James
17 Kentucky	26 TE Kendell Watkins
13 Arkansas	13 QB Todd Jordan / Derrick Taite
25 Alabama	36 RB Michael Davis / Kevin Bouie
20 Mississippi	13 FB Fred McCrary
	DL Herman Carroll / Colby McCullough
	DL Arleye Gibson
	DL Jimmie Myles / Koche Anderson
	LB Mike James
	LB Dwayne Curry / Reggie Wilson
	LB Wesley Leasy
	LB Lateef Travis
	DB Walt Harris
	DB Charlie Davidson
	DB Andre Bennett
	DB Johnnie Harris / Scott Gumina

RUSHING: Davis 205/883y
PASSING: Jordan 131-294/1935y, 11TD, 44.6%
RECEIVING: Jones 24/541y
SCORING: Tom Burke (K) 69pts, Davis 44pts

1994 8-4

17 Memphis	6 WR Chris Jones / Bernard Euell
24 LSU	44 WR Eric Moulds / Nakia Greer
24 Tennessee	21 T Melvin Hayes / Henry McCann
49 Arkansas State	3 G Purvis Hunt / Brad Ainsworth
18 Auburn	42 C Brian Anderson
41 South Carolina	36 G Jason Wisner
66 Tulane	22 T Jesse James / Robert Hicks
47 Kentucky	7 TE Kendell Watkins
17 Arkansas	7 QB Derrick Taite
25 Alabama	29 RB Michael Davis / Keffer McGee
21 Mississippi	17 FB Fred McCrary / Kevin Bouie
24 N. Carolina St.■	28 DL Brent Smith / Larry Williams
	DL Jimmie Myles / Al Cotton
	DL James Grier / Corey Sears
	LB Mike James / Michael Lindsey
	LB Dwayne Curry / Conley Earls
	LB Wesley Leasy
	LB Scott Gumina / Paul Lacoste
	DB Walt Harris
	DB Charlie Davidson / Clay Mack
	DB Andre Bennett
	DB Johnnie Harris

RUSHING: Davis 196/929y, Bouie 157/896y, McGee 15/94y
PASSING: Taite 110-220/1806y, 14TD, 50.0%
RECEIVING: Moulds 39/845y, Jones 15/258y, McCrary 15/134y
SCORING: Tom Rogers (K) 70pts, Davis 60pts

1995 3-8

28 Memphis	18 WR Chris Jones / Michael Brown
16 LSU	34 WR Eric Moulds / Cameron Floyd
30 Baylor	21 T Brent Smith
14 Tennessee	52 G Henry McCann
32 NE Louisiana	34 C Brian Anderson / Dan Hoover
20 Auburn	48 G Brian Ainsworth
39 South Carolina	65 T Brian Wright / Robert Hicks
42 Kentucky	32 TE John Jennings / Reginald Kelly
21 Arkansas	26 QB Derrick Taite
9 Alabama	14 RB Keffer McGee / Robert Isaac
10 Mississippi	13 FB Nakia Greer
	DL Larry Williams / Dereck Rush
	DL Corey Sears / Eric Dotson
	DL Terry Day / Raymond Gee
	DL James Grier / Michael Lindsey
	LB Dwayne Curry
	LB Paul Lacoste
	LB Gregory Favors
	DB Walt Harris
	DB Izell McGill / Chauncey McGee
	DB Bernard Euell / Anthony Derricks
	DB Jimmy Lipscomb / Eric Daniel

RUSHING: McGee 235/1072y, Greer 47/199y, Isaac 20/109y
PASSING: Taite 165-309/2241y, 16TD, 53.4%
RECEIVING: Moulds 62/779y, McGee 27/295y, Jones 23/400y
SCORING: McGee 92pts

1996 5-6

31 Memphis	10 WR Lamont Woodberry / Jeremy Jones
23 Louisiana Tech	38 WR Lahitia Grant / Matthew Butler
14 South Carolina	10 T Brent Smith / Alan Smith
19 Georgia	38 G Henry McCann / Stoney Price
15 Auburn	49 C Dan Hoover / Eric Allen
20 LSU	28 G Brad Ainsworth / Burt Ashley
59 NE Louisiana	0 T Robert Hicks / Sam Baker
21 Kentucky	24 TE John Jennings / Reginald Kelly
17 Alabama	16 QB Derrick Taite / Matt Wyatt
13 Arkansas	16 RB Robert Isaac / Keffer McGee
17 Mississippi	0 FB Nakia Greer
	DL Greg Favors / Larry Campbell
	DL Eric Dotson
	DL James Grier / Kevin Sluder
	DL Terry Day / Cornell Menafee
	LB Dwayne Curry
	LB Paul Lacoste
	LB Earnest Garner / Dereck Rush
	DB Adesola Badon
	DB Izell McGill
	DB Kendall Roberson / Tim Nelson
	DB Eric Brown

RUSHING: Isaac 117/527y, McGee 73/481y,
  Tony Buckhalter (RB) 75/295y, Greer 51/249y
PASSING: Taite 75-171/1009y, 6TD, 43.9%,
  Wyatt 64-130/830y, 7TD, 49.2%
RECEIVING: Woodberry 27/305y, Grant 22/333y, Isaac 12/172y
SCORING: Brian Hazelwood (K) 49pts, Grant 30pts

1997 7-4

13 Memphis	10 WR Lamont Woodberry / Troy Belcher
35 Kentucky	27 WR Kevin Prentiss / Matthew Butler
9 LSU	24 T Anthony Kapp / Floyd Womack
37 South Carolina	17 G Stoney Price / Craig Moore
0 Georgia	47 C Eric Allen / Michael Fair
24 NE Louisiana	10 G Randy Thomas
35 C. Florida	28 T Robert Hicks / Tron Thomas
20 Auburn	0 TE John Jennings / Reginald Kelly
32 Alabama	20 QB Matt Wyatt / Rob Morgan
7 Arkansas	17 RB James Johnson / Robert Isaac
14 Mississippi	15 FB Nakia Greer / Dennis McKinley
	DL Greg Favors / Larry Campbell
	DL Eric Dotson / Kenwoynne Smith
	DL Conley Earls / John Hilliard
	DL James Grier / Cornell Menafee
	LB Jamaal Dinkins / Edward Yeates
	LB Barron Simpson / Bert Keys
	LB Dereck Rush
	DB Kendall Roberson / Adesola Badon
	DB Izell McGill / Kenzaki Jones
	DB Anthony Derricks / Eric Daniel
	DB Eric Brown / Tim Nelson

RUSHING: Johnson 217/1069y, Isaac 116/562y, Greer 26/108y
PASSING: Wyatt 92-201/1369y, 6TD, 45.8%
RECEIVING: Woodberry 24/342y, Prentiss 20/385y,
  Butler 19/335y
SCORING: Johnson 72pts, Brian Hazelwood (K) 70pts

1998 8-5

42 Vanderbilt	0 WR Kevin Cooper
14 Memphis	6 WR Kevin Prentiss / Matthew Butler
23 Oklahoma State	42 T Floyd "Pork Chop" Womack
38 South Carolina	0 G Stoney Price
38 Auburn	21 C Eric Allen
53 E. Tenn. St.	6 G Randy Thomas
6 LSU	41 T Anthony Kapp / Wes Shivers
35 Kentucky	37 TE John Jennings / Terrence McCaskey
26 Alabama	14 QB Wayne Madkin / Matt Wyatt
22 Arkansas	21 RB James Johnson / Dicenzo Miller
28 Mississippi	6 FB Dennis McKinley
14 Tennessee ▢	24 DL Edward Smith / Alvin McKinley
11 Texas■	38 DL Larry Campbell
	DL John Hilliard / Kenwoynne Smith
	DL Kevin Sluder
	DL Cornell Menafee
	LB Bert Keys / Jamaal Dinkins
	LB Barrin Simpson
	DB Kendall Roberson / Adesola Badon
	DB Robert Bean
	DB Kenzaki Jones / Eric Daniel
	DB Tim Nelson / Ashley Cooper

RUSHING: Johnson 236/1383y, Miller 55/290y,
  Chris Rainey (TB) 40/167y
PASSING: Madkin 96-199/1532y, 11TD, 48.2%
RECEIVING: Prentiss 38/681y, Cooper 25/298y, Kelly 12/140y
SCORING: Brian Hazelwood (K) 77pts, Johnson 72pts

1999 10-2

40 Middle Tenn. St.	7 WR Kelvin Love / Larry Huntington
13 Memphis	10 WR Matthew Butler
29 Oklahoma State	11 T Pork Chop Womack
17 South Carolina	0 G Michael Fair
42 Vanderbilt	14 C Paul Mooney
18 Auburn	16 G Kenric Fairchild
17 LSU	16 T Wes Shivers
23 Kentucky	22 TE C.J. Sirmones / Donald Lee
7 Alabama	19 QB Wayne Madkin
9 Arkansas	14 RB Dicenzo Miller / Dontae Walker
23 Mississippi	20 FB Justin Griffith
17 Clemson■	7 DL Conner Stephens
	DL John Hilliard / Dorsett Davis
	DL Alvin McKinley
	DL Kevin Sluder / Ellis Wyms
	DL Cornell Menafee
	LB Barrin Simpson / Barris Grant
	DB Fred Smoot
	DB Robert Bean / Eugene Liger
	DB Ashley Cooper
	DB Tim Nelson / Eugene Clinton
	DB Pig Prather / Josh Morgan

RUSHING: Walker 76/384y, Miller 76/238y,
  Chris Rainey (RB) 68/218y
PASSING: Madkin 135-257/1884y, 10TD, 52.5%
RECEIVING: Love 43/834y, Griffith 37/380y, Butler 28/327y
SCORING: Scott Westerfield (K) 76pts

2000 8-4

17 Memphis	3 WR Terrell Grindle
44 BYU	28 WR Larry Huntington / Harold Lindsey
19 South Carolina	23 T Pork Chop Womack/Derrick Thompson
47 Florida	35 G Courtney Lee
17 Auburn	10 C Michael Fair
38 LSU	45 G Tommy Watson
61 Middle Tenn.	35 T Kenric Fairchild
35 Kentucky	17 TE Donald Lee
29 Alabama	7 QB Wayne Madkin
10 Arkansas	17 RB Dicenzo Miller / Dontae Walker
30 Mississippi	45 FB Kenny Williamson / Justin Griffith
43 Texas A&M■	41 DL Rob Knight
	DL Ellis Wyms
	DL Toby Golliday / Wilie Blade
	DL Dorsett Davis
	LB Conner Stephens
	LB Mario Haggan
	DB Fred Smoot
	DB Kendall Roberson / Shawn Byrdsong
	DB Josh Morgan
	DB Eugene Clinton
	DB Pig Prather

RUSHING: Miller 160/1005y, Walker 148/795y, Madkin 69/179y
PASSING: Madkin 138-246/1908y, 8TD, 56.1%
RECEIVING: Grindle 31/436y, Miller 24/344y,
  Huntington 19/361y, Griffith 19/240y
SCORING: Scott Westerfield (K) 73pts, Miller 72pts, Walker 54pts

2001 3-8

30 Memphis	10 WR Terrell Grindle / Ray Ray Bivines
14 South Carolina	16 WR Justin Jenkins
0 Florida	52 T Derrick Thompson / David Stewart
14 Auburn	16 G Donald Tucker
9 Troy State	21 C Blake Jones
0 LSU	42 G Tommy Watson
17 Kentucky	14 T Kenric Fairchild
17 Alabama	24 TE Donald Lee
21 Arkansas	24 QB Wayne Madkin / Kevin Fant
36 Mississippi	28 TB Dicenzo Miler / Dontae Walker
38 BYU	41 FB Justin Griffith
	DL Dwayne Robertson / Kamau Jackson
	DL Kahlil Nash
	DL Tommy Kelly / Ronald Fields
	DL Dorsett Davis
	DL Conner Stephens / Jason Clark
	LB Mario Haggan / T.J. Mawhinney
	DB Shawn Byrdsong / Walter Burdett
	DB Demetric Wright / Eugene Liger
	DB Korey Banks
	DB Josh Morgan
	DB Pig Prather

RUSHING: Miller 132/676y, Walker 136/548y,
  Fred Reid (TB) 25/108y
PASSING: Madkin 93-185/1012y, 5TD, 50.3%,
  Fant 93-185/1012y, 5TD, 50.3%
RECEIVING: Jenkins 42/661y, Grindle 40/463y, Miller 19/337y
SCORING: Jenkins 50pts, John Michael Marlin (K) 44pts,
  Miller 42pts

2002 3-9

13 Oregon	36 WR Terrell Grindle / Ray Ray Bivines
51 Jacksonville St.	13 WR Justin Jenkins
14 Auburn	42 T Carl Hutchins
13 LSU	31 G Brad Weathers / Will Rogers
10 South Carolina	34 C Blake Jones / Kyle Watson
11 Troy State	8 G Donald Tucker / Chris McNeil
29 Memphis	17 T David Stewart
24 Kentucky	45 TE Donald Lee
14 Alabama	28 QB Kevin Fant / Kyle York
17 Tennessee	35 TB Jerious Norwood / Fred Reid
19 Arkansas	26 FB Justin Griffith
12 Mississippi	24 DL Tommy Kelly / Jason Clark
	DL Ronald Fields
	DL Kahil Nash
	DL Kamau Jackson / Willie Evans
	LB Mario Haggan / Marvin Byrdsong
	LB T.J. Mawhinney
	DB Korey Banks / Milas Randle
	DB Walter Burdett
	DB Kevin Dockery
	DB Josh Morgan / Michael Gholar
	DB Darren Williams / Gabe Wallace

RUSHING: Griffith 91/471y, Norwood 66/394y, Reid 97/338y
PASSING: Fant 163-311/1918y, 10TD, 52.4%
RECEIVING: Bivines 40/511y, Grindle 34/608y, Jenkins 28/273y
SCORING: Brent Smith (K) 64pts,
  Reid & Dontae Walker (TB) 30pts

2003 2-10

34 Oregon	42 WR Justin Jenkins / McKinley Scott
28 Tulane	31 WR Ray Ray Bivines / Omarr Conner
35 Houston	42 T Richard Burch
6 LSU	41 G Will Rogers
30 Vanderbilt	21 C Blake Jones / Chris McNeil
35 Memphis	27 G Otis Riddley/Donovan Davis/J Wadley
13 Auburn	45 T David Stewart
17 Kentucky	42 TE Aaron Lumpkin
0 Alabama	38 QB Kevin Fant
21 Tennessee	59 TB Jerious Norwood / Nick Turner
6 Arkansas	52 FB Darnell Jones
0 Mississippi	31 DL Tommy Kelly
	DL Deljuan Robinson / Lennie Day
	DL Ronald Fields / Kahil Nash
	DL Willie Evans / Kamau Jackson
	LB Jason Clark / Clarence McDougal
	LB T.J. Mawhinney / Kenny Kern
	LB Marvin Byrdsong / Chris Swain
	DB Odell Bradley / Quinton Culberson
	DB Kevin Dockery / Bernard Vinson
	DB Darren Williams / Gabe Wallace
	DB Jeramie Johnson / Slovakia Griffith

RUSHING: Turner 123/696y, Norwood 121/642y,
  Fred Reid 32/157y
PASSING: Fant 186-351/2151y, 14TD, 53.0%
RECEIVING: Jenkins 62/880y, Scott 29/391y, Bivines 26/324y
SCORING: Jenkins 56pts, Brent Smith (K) 43pts, Turner 42pts

2004 3-8

28 Tulane	7 WR Tee Milons / McKinley Scott
14 Auburn	43 WR Will Prosser
7 Maine	9 T Richard Burch
0 LSU	51 G Brian Anderson / Johnny Wadley
13 Vanderbilt	31 C Chris McNeil
13 Ala.-Birm'ham	27 G Will Rogers
38 Florida	31 T David Stewart
22 Kentucky	7 TE Eric Butler / Blake Pettit
14 Alabama	30 QB Omarr Conner
21 Arkansas	24 HB Jerious Norwood / Fred Reid
3 Mississippi	20 FB Bryson Davis / Darnell Jones
	DL Michael Heard / Deljuan Robinson
	DL Ronald Fields
	DL Andrew Powell / Corey Clark
	DL Willie Evans
	LB Clarence McDougal / Gabe O'Neal
	LB Kenny Kern / Titus Brown
	LB Quinton Culberson / Marvin Byrdsong
	DB Kevin Dockery / Jamaal Johnson
	DB David Heard / Mario Bobo
	DB Slovakia Griffith
	DB Darren Williams / Jeramie Johnson

RUSHING: Norwood 195/1050y, Reid 82/393y, Conner 67/115y
PASSING: Conner 107-206/1224y, 6TD, 51.9%
RECEIVING: Prosser 24/328y, Milons 24/285y, Butler 15/166y
SCORING: Norwood 42pts, Keith Andrews (K) 39pts,
  Butler 24pts

2005 3-8

38 Murray State	6 WR Tee Milons
0 Auburn	28 WR Will Prosser
21 Tulane	14 T Brian Anderson
10 Georgia	23 G Anthony Strauder / Anthony Dunning
7 LSU	37 C Chris McNeil
9 Florida	35 G Royce Blackledge / Johnny Wadley/
16 Houston	28 T Avery House
7 Kentucky	13 TE Eric Butler
0 Alabama	17 QB Omarr Conner (WR) / Mike Henig
10 Arkansas	44 HB Jerious Norwood / Brandon Thornton
35 Mississippi	14 FB Bryson Davis
	DL Michael Heard / Titus Brown
	DL Andrew Powell
	DL Deljuan Robinson / Corey Clark
	DL Willie Evans
	LB Anthony Littlejohn / Gabe O'Neal
	LB Quinton Culberson
	LB Clarence McDougal / Jamar Chaney
	DB Kevin Dockery
	DB David Heard / Jamaal Johnson
	DB Jeramie Johnson
	DB Demario Bobo / Keith Fitzhugh

RUSHING: Norwood 191/1136y, Thornton 47/225y,
  Demarcus Johnson (HB) 24/117y
PASSING: Conner 86-167/903y, 8TDs, 51.5%,
  Henig 60-135/621y, 2TDs, 44.4%
RECEIVING: Prosser 28/286y, Norwood 19/96y, Milons 18/214y
SCORING: Norwood 48pts, Keith Andrews (K) 26pts, Butler 18pts

2006 3-9

0 South Carolina	15 WR Tony Burks / Lance Long
0 Auburn	34 WR Will Prosser/Aubrey Bell/Jam'l Smith
29 Tulane	32 T J.D. Hamilton / Michael Brown
16 Ala.-Birm'ham	10 G Anthony Strauder / Michael Gates
17 LSU	48 C Royce Blackledge
14 West Virginia	42 G Brian Anderson
35 Jacksonville St.	3 T Craig Jenkins
24 Georgia	27TE Eric Butler/Jason Husband/D. Sherrod
31 Kentucky	34 QB Mike Henig / Omarr Conner (WR)
24 Alabama	16 HB Anthony Dixon / Brandon Thornton
14 Arkansas	28 FB Bryson Davis / Casey Rogers
17 Mississippi	20 DL Michael Heard
	DL Andrew Powell
	DL Deljuan Robinson / Antonio Johnson
	DL Titus Brown
	LB Gabe O'Neal / Anthony Littlejohn
	LB Quinton Culberson
	LB Jamar Chaney
	DB Derek Pegues
	DB David Heard
	DB Jeramie Johnson
	DB Keith Fitzhugh / De'Mon Glanton

RUSHING: Dixon 169/668y, Thornton 60/230y,
  Arnil Stallworth (HB) 42/137y
PASSING: Henig 74-169/1201y, 7D, 43.8%,
  Conner 76-135/943y, 3TD, 56.3%
RECEIVING: Burks 35/850y, Long 25/177y, Smith 20/335y
SCORING: Dixon 60pts, Adam Carlson (K) 45pts, Burks 30pts

2007 8-5

0 LSU	45 WR Tony Burks / Co-Eric Riley
38 Tulane	17 WR Jamayel Smith / Aubrey Bell
19 Auburn	14 T Michael Brown
31 Gardner-Webb	15 G Anthony Strauder
21 South Carolina	38 C Royce Blackledge
30 Ala.-Birm'ham	13 G Craig Jenkins / Michael Gates
21 Tennessee	33 T J.D. Hamilton
13 West Virginia	38 TE Dezmond Sherrod / Eric Butler
31 Kentucky	14 QB Wesley Carroll / Michael Henig
17 Alabama	12 RB Anthony Dixon / Christian Ducre
31 Arkansas	45 FB Eric Hoskins / Brandon Hart
17 Mississippi	14 DL Titus Brown
10 Central Florida■	3 DL Jessie Bowman
	DL Kyle Love / Cortez McCraney
	DL Avery Hannibal
	LB Gabe O'Neal / Tim Bailey
	LB Jamar Chaney / Jamon Hughes
	LB Dominic Douglas / Anthony Littlejohn
	DB Anthony Johnson / Demario Bobo
	DB Marcus Washington / Jasper O'Quinn
	DB Derek Pegues
	DB De'Mon Glanton / Keith Fitzhugh

RUSHING: Dixon 287/1066y, Ducre 112/487y,
  Justin Williams (RB) 21/96y
PASSING: Carroll 134-255/1392y, 9TD, 52.5%,
  Henig 36-78/447y, TD, 46.2%
RECEIVING: Smith 33/510y, Burks 33/444y,
  Jason Husband (TE) 16/193y, Ducre 16/83y
SCORING: Dixon 96pts, Adam Carlson (K) 63pts,
  Burks, Ducre, & Smith 18pts

2008 4-8

14 Louisiana Tech	22 WR Aubrey Bell / Co-Eric Riley
34 S.E. Louisiana	10 WR Brandon McRae / Jamayel Smith
2 Auburn	3 T Derek Sherrod / Mark Melichar
7 Georgia Tech	38 G Anthony Strauder
24 LSU	34 C J.C. Brignone (G) / D.J. Looney
17 Vanderbilt	14 G Michael Gates / Craig Jenkins
3 Tennessee	34 T Quentin Saulsberry
31 Middle Tenn.	22 TE Nelson Hurst / Marcus Green
13 Kentucky	14 QB Tyson Lee / Wesley Carroll
7 Alabama	32 HB Anthony Dixon / Christian Ducre
31 Arkansas	28 FB Eric Hoskins / Brandon Hart
0 Mississippi	45 DL Tim Bailey
	DL Jessie Bowman
	DL Cortez McCraney / Kyle Love
	DL Sean Ferguson / Charles Burns
	LB K.J. Wright
	LB Dominic Douglas / Jamar Chaney
	LB Karlin Brown / Anthony Johnson
	DB Jasper O'Quinn
	DB Marcus Washington / Charles Mitchell
	DB Derek Pegues / Zach Smith
	DB Keith Fitzhugh / De'Mon Glanton

RUSHING: Dixon 197/869y, Ducre 56/222y,
  Robert Elliott (HB) 18/61y
PASSING: Lee 153-260/1519y, 7TD, 58.8%,
  Carroll 55-115/560y, 3TD, 47.8%
RECEIVING: McRae 51/518y, Bell 31/271y, Smith 23/302y,
  Amil Stallworth (FB) 23/273y
SCORING: Dixon 54pts, Adam Carlson (K) 43pts,
  Ducre & McRae 18pts

2009 5-7

45 Jackson State	7 WR Brandon McRae / Chad Bumphis
24 Auburn	49 WR O'Neal Wilder / Leon Berry
15 Vanderbilt	3 T Derek Sherrod / Mark Melichar
26 LSU	30 G Quentin Saulsberry
31 Georgia Tech	42 C J.C. Brignone
24 Houston	31 G Craig Jenkins
27 Middle Tenn.	6 T Addison Lawrence
19 Florida	29 TE Marcus Green / Kendrick Cook
31 Kentucky	24 QB Tyson Lee / Chris Relf
3 Alabama	31 HB Anthony Dixon
21 Arkansas	42 FB Christian Ducre
41 Mississippi	27 DL Pernell McPhee / Nick Bell
	DL Charles Burns / Josh Boyd
	DL Kyle Love / Fletcher Cox
	DL Sean Ferguson / Brandon Cooper
	LB K.J. Wright
	LB Jamar Chaney
	LB Chris White / Jamie Jones
	DB Maurice Langston / Damein Anderson
	DB Marcus Washington / Corey Broomfield
	DB Zach Smith / Johnthan Banks
	DB Charles Mitchell / Wade Bonner

RUSHING: Dixon 257/1391y, Relf 76/500y, Ducre 45/263y,
  Robert Elliott (HB) 44/221y
PASSING: Lee 130-221/1444y, 4TD, 58.8%,
  Relf 22-41/283y, 5TD, 53.7%
RECEIVING: Bumphis 32/375y, Green 27/306y, Wilder 14/236y
  Berry 14/170y
SCORING: Dixon 72pts, Derek DePasquale (K) 52pts
  Bumphis & Sean Brauchle (K) 31pts

2010 9-4

49 Memphis	7 WR Chris Smith / Leon Berry
14 Auburn	17 WR Arceto Clark
7 LSU	29 WR Chad Bumphis / Brandon Heavens
24 Georgia	12 T Derek Sherrod
49 Alcorn State	16 G Gabe Jackson / Tobias Smith
47 Houston	24 C J.C. Brignone
10 Florida	7 G Quentin Saulsberry (C)/Mark Melichar
29 UAB	24 T Addison Lawrence
24 Kentucky	17 QB Chris Relf / Tyler Russell
10 Alabama	30 RB Vick Ballard / Robert Elliott
31 Arkansas	38 FB/TE Pat Hanrah'n(DL)/Brand'n Hend'rs'n
31 Mississippi	23 DL Pernell McPhee
52 Michigan■	14 DL Josh Boyd
	DL Fletcher Cox / Devin Jones
	DL S. Ferguson/ James Carmon / Nick Bell
	LB Emmanuel Gatling / Cameron Lawrence
	LB Chris White
	LB K.J. Wright / Mike Hunt
	DB Johnthan Banks / Maurice Langston
	DB Corey Broomfield
	DB Nickoe Whitley / Wade Bonner
	DB Charles Mitchell / Zack Smith

RUSHING: Ballard 186/968y, Relf 194/713y,
  LaDarius Perkins (RB) 101/566y
PASSING: Relf 129-220/1789y, 13TD, 58.6%,
  Russell 39-67/635y, 5TD, 58.2%
RECEIVING: Bumphis 44/634y, Clark 25/362y, Smith 24/264y
SCORING: Ballard 120pts, Derek DePasquale (K) 58pts,
  Perkins 36pts

MISSOURI

University of Missouri (Founded 1839)
Columbia, Missouri
Nickname: Tigers
Colors: Old Gold and Black
Stadium: Faurot Field at Memorial Stadium (1926) 68,349
Conference Affiliations: Big Seven (Charter Member 1948-57),
  Big Eight (1958-95), Big Twelve North (1996-present)

CAREER RUSHING YARDS	Attempts	Yards
Brad Smith (2002-05)	799	4289
Zack Abron (2000-03)	692	3198
Brock Olivo (1994-97)	686	3026
Devin West (1995-98)	567	2954
Darrell Wallace (1984-87)	574	2607
Tony Temple (2004-07)	466	2552
Corby Jones (1995-98)	559	2533
James Wilder (1978-80)	487	2357
Joe Moore (1968-70)	453	2244
Derrick Washington (2007-09)	403	2085

CAREER PASSING YARDS	Comp.-Att.	Yards
Chase Daniel (2005-08)	1094-1609	12,515
Brad Smith (2002-05)	835-1484	8799
Jeff Handy (1991-94)	618-1058	6959
Blaine Gabbert (2008-10)	568-933	6822
Phil Bradley (1977-80)	437-798	5352
Marlon Adler (1982-85)	347-642	5231
Kent Kiefer (1989-90)	348-589	4497
Corby Jones (1995-98)	257-516	3697
Phil Johnson (1990-92)	291-520	3600
Steve Pisarkiewicz (1974-76)	236-509	3413

CAREER RECEIVING YARDS	Catches	Yards
Danario Alexander (2006-09)	191	2778
Justin Gage (1999-02)	200	2704
Chase Coffman (2005-08)	247	2659
Jeremy Maclin (2007-08)	182	2315
Martin Rucker (2004-07)	203	2175
Victor Bailey (1990-92)	128	2144
Will Franklin (2004-07)	143	2125
Linzy Collins (1989-90)	102	1760
Kenny Holly (1990-93)	151	1708
Tommy Saunders (2005-08)	150	1600

SEASON RUSHING YARDS	Attempts	Yards
Devin West (1998)	283	1578
Brad Smith (2003)	212	1406
Joe Moore (1969)	260	1312
Brad Smith (2005)	229	1301
Zack Abron (2003)	219	1155

SEASON PASSING YARDS	Comp.-Att.	Yards
Chase Daniel (2008)	385-528	4335
Chase Daniel (2007)	384-563	4306
Blaine Gabbert (2009)	262-445	3593
Chase Daniel (2006)	287-452	3527
Blaine Gabbert (2010)	301-475	3186

SEASON RECEIVING YARDS	Catches	Yards
Danario Alexander (2009)	113	1781
Jeremy Maclin (2008)	102	1260
Victor Bailey (1992)	75	1210
Justin Gage (2002)	82	1075
Jeremy Maclin (2007)	80	1055

GAME RUSHING YARDS	Attempts	Yards
Devin West (1998 vs. Kansas)	33	319
Brad Smith (2003 vs. Texas Tech)	19	291
Tony Temple (2007 vs. Arkansas)	24	281

GAME PASSING YARDS	Comp.-Att.	Yards
Jeff Handy (1992 vs. Oklahoma State)	43-73	480
Blaine Gabbert (2009 vs. Baylor)	30-51	468
Kent Kiefer (1989 vs. Kansas)	29-44	444

GAME RECEIVING YARDS	Catches	Yards
Justin Gage (2001 vs. Baylor)	13	236
Justin Gage (2002 vs. Bowling Green)	16	236
Danario Alexander (2009 vs. Kansas)	15	233

GREATEST COACH:

Columbia, Missouri, is perhaps the one place in the college football world where Dan Devine is truly appreciated for his talents as a head coach and athletic director. And perhaps he never should have left Columbia, where he carved out a fantastic 92-38-7 record from 1958-70. For it was with the Tigers that Devine fashioned a Hall of Fame career, reaching the final Top 10 in four of his 13 years with the Tigers. Not until 2007 did Missouri again crack the final Top 10 since he departed after the 1970 season.

Missouri was not Devine's first head coaching job. After a four-year stint as an assistant at Michigan State, Devine traveled west to take over the Arizona State program. His three-year record with the Sun Devils was a lofty 27-3-1, which earned him the attention of the folks at Missouri. With Frank Broyles leaving for Arkansas after only one year with Missouri, Devine received the offer to coach the once-strong Tigers who had fallen a bit in recent times.

Devine needed two years to finish the rebuilding effort begun by Broyles. By 1960 everything was in place. Winning with a punishing defense—the Tigers were 8-0 before an opponent reached double figures in points scored, and victim no. 9 Oklahoma fell 41-19—and an opportune offense, Missouri reached a no. 1 ranking. Alas, pesky Kansas knocked them from those heights in a bitter loss later forfeited to Missouri. But 1960 was still memorable.

The Tigers remained a very good team under Devine, if not a national title contender. There were more memorable games and quite a few memorable players. But his home state Green Bay Packers called and the pull of home and the professional ranks was too great to ignore. Then, after a mixed run with the Packers, Devine was lured back into the collegiate ranks, but by Notre Dame, a school whose attraction for a young Irish American born a few days before Knute Rockne's Fighting Irish beat Stanford in the January 1925 Rose Bowl must have been profound. As with the Packers, Devine's time spent in South Bend featured some good moments and some bad. He won the national championship in 1977, a feat he would have been hard-pressed to achieve with the Tigers.

He retired after the 1980 season with an overall collegiate record of 172-57-9. After returning to Arizona State in an administrative capacity, he came back to help Missouri once more as AD from 1992-94.

MISSOURI'S 55 GREATEST SINCE 1953

OFFENSE

WIDE RECEIVER: Victor Bailey, Justin Gage, Mel Gray, Jeremy Maclin, Joe Stewart
TIGHT END: Chase Coffman, Kellen Winslow
TACKLE: Ed Blaine, John Clay, Conrad Goode, Francis Peay, Morris Towns
GUARD: Scott Anderson, Mark Bedosky, Mike Carroll, Mark Jones
CENTER: Brad Edelman, Rob Riti, Adam Spieker
QUARTERBACK: Phil Bradley, Chase Daniel, Brad Smith
RUNNING BACK: Tony Galbreath, Joe Moore, Brock Olivo, Devin West
FULLBACK: James Wilder

DEFENSE

END: Bobby Bell, Conrad Hitchler, Brian Smith, Justin Smith
TACKLE: Jeff Gaylord, Mark Kuhlmann, Bruce Van Dyke, Jay Wallace, Lorenzo Williams
LINEBACKER: John Douglass, Chris Garlich, Darren MacDonald, Travis McDonald, Sean Weatherspoon
CORNERBACK: Adrian Jones, John Moseley, Roger Wehrli, Bill Whitaker
SAFETY: DeMontie Cross, Erik McMillan, Dennis Poppe, Eric Wright

SPECIAL TEAMS

RETURN SPECIALIST: Mike Fink
PLACE KICKER: Jeff Jacke
PUNTER: Kyle Pooler

TWO-WAY PLAYERS

END-DEFENSIVE END: Danny LaRose
HALFBACK-DEFENSIVE BACK: Johnny Roland
TACKLE-DEFENSIVE END: Russ Washington

PERFORMANCE FORMULA:
MISSOURI'S 10 BEST SEASONS

1960	1.6032	3 of 70
2007	1.5821	4 of 70
1969	1.5516	7 of 70
2010	1.4809	12 of 71
1982	1.4516	10 of 70
1965	1.4228	9 of 70
1968	1.3899	13 of 70
2008	1.3781	13 of 71
1998	1.3462	24 of 71
1978	1.3303	19 of 70

MISSOURI TIGERS

Year	W-L-T	AP Poll	Conference Standing	Toughest Regular Season Opponents	Coach (Record at School)	Bowl Games		
1953	6-4		2t	Maryland 10-0, Oklahoma 8-1-1, Kansas State 6-3-1	Don Faurot			
1954	4-5-1		3t	Oklahoma 10-0, Colorado 7-2-1, Nebraska 6-4	Don Faurot			
1955	1-9		7	Oklahoma 10-0, Maryland 10-0, Michigan 7-2	Don Faurot			
1956	4-5-1		3	Oklahoma 10-0, Colorado 7-2-1, Oregon State 7-2-1	Don Faurot (101-79-10)			
1957	5-4-1		3t	Oklahoma 9-1, Texas A&M 8-2, Colorado 6-3-1	Frank Broyles (5-4-1)			
1958	5-4-1		2	Oklahoma 9-1, Colorado 6-4, SMU 6-4	Dan Devine			
1959	6-5	18	2	Oklahoma 7-3, Penn State 8-2, Iowa State 7-3	Dan Devine	Orange	0 Georgia	14
1960	10-1	5	1	Kansas 7-2-1, Iowa State 7-3, Penn State 6-3, Colorado 6-4	Dan Devine	Orange	21 Navy	14
1961	7-2-1	11	2t	Colorado 9-1, Minnesota 7-2, Kansas 6-3-1	Dan Devine			
1962	8-1-2		2	Nebraska 8-2, Oklahoma 8-2, Minnesota 6-2-1, Kansas 6-3-1	Dan Devine	Bluebonnet	14 Georgia Tech	10
1963	7-3		3	Nebraska 9-1, Oklahoma 8-2, Northwestern 5-4	Dan Devine			
1964	6-3-1		4	Nebraska 9-1, Utah 8-2, Oklahoma 6-3-1	Dan Devine			
1965	8-2-1	6	2	Nebraska 10-0, UCLA 7-2-1, Colorado 6-2-2	Dan Devine	Sugar	20 Florida	18
1966	6-3-1		3t	Nebraska 9-1, UCLA 9-1, Colorado 7-3	Dan Devine			
1967	7-3		4	Oklahoma 9-1, Colorado 8-2, Nebraska 6-4	Dan Devine			
1968	8-3	9	3	Kansas 9-1, Oklahoma 7-3, Army 7-3	Dan Devine	Gator	35 Alabama	10
1969	9-2	6	1t	Nebraska 8-2, Michigan 8-2, Colorado 7-3	Dan Devine	Orange	3 Penn State	10
1970	5-6		4t	Nebraska 10-0-1, Notre Dame 9-1, Air Force 9-2, Oklahoma 7-4	Dan Devine (92-38-7)			
1971	1-10		8	Nebraska 12-0, Oklahoma 10-1, Colorado 9-2, Stanford 8-3	Al Onofrio			
1972	6-6		5	Oklahoma 10-1, Nebraska 8-2-1, Notre Dame 8-2, Colorado 8-3	Al Onofrio	Fiesta	35 Arizona State	49
1973	8-4	17	4	Oklahoma 10-0, Nebraska 8-2-1, Kansas 7-3-1	Al Onofrio	Sun	34 Auburn	17
1974	7-4		2t	Oklahoma 11-0, Nebraska 8-3, Baylor 8-3	Al Onofrio			
1975	6-5		5t	Oklahoma 10-1, Alabama 10-1, Michigan 8-1-2, Nebraska 10-1	Al Onofrio			
1976	6-5		6	Southern Cal 10-1, Oklahoma 8-2-1, Ohio St. 8-2-1, Colorado 8-3	Al Onofrio			
1977	4-7		5	Oklahoma 10-1, Nebraska 8-3, Arizona State 9-2, Iowa State 8-3	Al Onofrio (38-41)			
1978	8-4	15	3t	Alabama 10-1, Oklahoma 10-1, Nebraska 9-2, Notre Dame 8-3	Warren Powers	Liberty	20 Louisiana State	15
1979	7-5		4	Oklahoma 11-1, Nebraska 10-1, Texas 9-2	Warren Powers	Hall of Fame	24 South Carolina	14
1980	8-4		3	Oklahoma 9-2, Nebraska 9-2, Penn State 9-2	Warren Powers	Liberty	25 Purdue	28
1981	8-4	19	5	Nebraska 9-2, Oklahoma 6-4-1, Mississippi State 7-4	Warren Powers	Tangerine	19 Southern Mississippi	17
1982	5-4-2		5	Nebraska 11-1, Oklahoma 8-3, Texas 9-2	Warren Powers			
1983	7-5		2t	Nebraska 11-0, Illinois 10-1, Oklahoma State 7-4	Warren Powers	Holiday	17 BYU	21
1984	3-7-1		5t	Oklahoma 9-1-1, Nebraska 9-2, Oklahoma St. 9-2, Wisconsin 7-3-1	Warren Powers (46-33-3)			
1985	1-10		7t	Oklahoma 10-1, Nebraska 9-2, Oklahoma State 8-3, Texas 8-3	Woody Widenhofer			
1986	3-8		6	Oklahoma 10-1, Nebraska 9-2, Colorado 6-5	Woody Widenhofer			
1987	5-6		5	Oklahoma 11-0, Syracuse 11-0, Nebraska 10-1, Oklahoma St. 9-2	Woody Widenhofer			
1988	3-7-1		6	Miami 10-1, Nebraska 11-1, Oklahoma 9-2, Oklahoma St. 9-2	Woody Widenhofer (12-31-1)			
1989	2-9		7	Colorado 11-0, Miami 10-1, Nebraska 10-1	Bob Stull			
1990	4-7		6t	Colorado 10-1-1, Nebraska 9-2, Oklahoma 8-3	Bob Stull			
1991	3-7-1		7	Nebraska 9-1-1, Colorado 8-2-1, Oklahoma 8-3, Baylor 8-3	Bob Stull			
1992	3-8		6t	Texas A&M 12-0, Colorado 9-1-1, Nebraska 9-2	Bob Stull			
1993	3-7-1		6t	Nebraska 11-0, Texas A&M 10-1, Kansas State 8-2-1, OU 8-3	Bob Stull (15-38-2)			
1994	3-8-1		6	Nebraska 12-0, Colorado 10-1, Kansas State 9-2	Larry Smith			
1995	3-8		7t	Nebraska 11-0, Colorado 9-2, Kansas State 9-2, Texas Tech 8-3	Larry Smith			
1996	5-6		N4	Nebraska 11-0, Colorado 9-2, Kansas State 9-2, Texas 7-4	Larry Smith			
1997	7-5	23	N3	Nebraska 11-0, Kansas State 10-1, Ohio State 10-2	Larry Smith	Holiday	24 Colorado State	35
1998	8-4	21	N2t	Ohio State 10-1, Texas A&M 10-2, Kansas St. 11-0, Nebraska 9-3	Larry Smith	Insight	34 West Virginia	31
1999	4-7		N5t	Nebraska 10-1, Kansas State 10-1, Texas 9-3, Texas A&M 8-3	Larry Smith			
2000	3-8		N5t	Kansas State 10-2, Nebraska 9-2, Texas 9-2, Iowa State 9-2	Larry Smith (33-46-1)			
2001	4-7		N4t	Texas 10-1, Colorado 9-2, Nebraska 11-1, Iowa State 7-4	Gary Pinkel			
2002	5-7		N5	Oklahoma 10-2, Kansas State 10-2, Colorado 9-3	Gary Pinkel			
2003	8-5		N3	Oklahoma 12-0, Kansas State 10-3, Nebraska 9-3	Gary Pinkel	Independence	14 Arkansas	27
2004	5-6		N3t	Oklahoma 11-0, Texas 10-1, Colorado 7-4, Oklahoma State 7-4	Gary Pinkel			
2005	7-5		N2t	Texas 11-0, Colorado 7-4, Nebraska 7-4	Gary Pinkel	Independence	38 South Carolina	31
2006	8-5		N2t	Nebraska 9-3, Oklahoma 10-2, Texas A&M 9-3	Gary Pinkel	Sun	38 Oregon State	39
2007	12-2	4	N1t	Illinois 9-3, Oklahoma 10-2, Texas Tech 8-4, Kansas 11-1	Gary Pinkel	Cotton	38 Arkansas	7
2008	10-4	19	N1t	Nebraska 8-4, Oklahoma State 9-3, Texas 11-1, Oklahoma 12-1	Gary Pinkel	Alamo	30 Northwestern	23
2009	8-5		N2t	Nevada 8-4, Nebraska 9-4, Oklahoma State 9-3, Texas 13-0	Gary Pinkel	Texas	13 Navy	35
2010	10-3	18	N1t	San Diego State 9-4, Texas A&M 9-4, Oklahoma 11-2, Nebraska 10-3	Gary Pinkel (77-49)	Insight	24 Iowa	27

TOTAL: 333-303-17 .5230 (41 of 70) **Bowl Games since 1953:** 12-10 .5455 (26 of 70)

GREATEST TEAM SINCE 1953: Although the 2007 Tigers set a school record for victories with 12, the 1960 Missouri Tigers remain to this day the only squad to earn a no. 1 ranking in school history. Of course, that mark was reached during the regular season and was not maintained by season's end thanks to a loss to Kansas. After averaging five wins per season for the four previous years, the Tigers were expected to be improved but no one expected a national title contender. Still, the Tigers rolled through the first nine games of their schedule, posting 3 shutouts along the way, to earn that no. 1 spot. After the costly loss to the Jayhawks, the Tigers regrouped to beat Navy in the Orange Bowl to finish the season ranked no. 5.

1953 6-4

6	Maryland	20	E John Wilson / Jim Jennings
14	Purdue	7	T Clyde Boyd / Charles Phillips
27	Colorado	16	G Terry Roberts / Tony Karakas
7	SMU	20	C Loyd Ray Brown / Norden Stefanides
6	Iowa State	13	G Ted Follin / Jake Shiveley
23	Nebraska	7	T Al Portney / Charley Bull
14	Indiana	7	E Pete Corpeny / John David Hurley
7	Oklahoma	14	QB Vic Eaton / Tony Scardino
16	Kansas State	6	HB Bob Schoonmaker / James Milne
10	Kansas	6	HB Edwin Merrifield / Jack Fox
			FB Bob Bauman / Ray Detring

RUSHING: Bauman 90/405y
PASSING: Eaton 24-53/364y, 4TD, 45.3%
RECEIVING: Corpeny 12/179y
SCORING: Schoonmaker 36pts

1954 4-5-1

0	Purdue	31	E Jim Jennings / Pete Corpeny
35	Kansas State	7	T Gene Campbell / Charley Bull
6	SMU	25	G Carl Osterloh / Terry Roberts
20	Indiana	14	C Norden Stefanides / Tony Karakas
32	Iowa State	14	G Jake Shiveley
19	Nebraska	25	T Al Portney / Chuck Mehrer
19	Colorado	19	E Hal Burnine / John David Hurley
13	Oklahoma	34	QB Vic Eaton / Tony Scardino
41	Kansas	18	HB Jimmy Hunter / Ray Detring
13	Maryland	74	HB Jack Fox / Bob Schoonmaker
			FB Bob Bauman

RUSHING: Bauman 60/293y, Hunter 45/239y, Fox 48/233y
PASSING: Eaton 36-74/609y, 6TD, 48.6%
RECEIVING: Burnine 22/405y, Jenning 11/171y, Musgrave 8/113y
SCORING: Fox 47pts, Hunter 30pts, Bauman & Jennings 18pts

1955 1-9

12	Maryland	13	E Hal Burnine / Terry Roberts
7	Michigan	42	T Chuck Mehrer / Frank Czapla
14	Utah	20	G Bob Lee / Bobby Gooch
6	SMU	13	C Terry Roberts / Carl Osterloh
14	Iowa State	20	G Jim Martin / Tony Karakas
12	Nebraska	18	T Al Portney / Merv Johnson
20	Colorado	12	E Bill Craig / Larry Plumb
0	Oklahoma	10	QB Jimmy Hunter / Dave Doane
0	Kansas State	21	HB Jerry Curtright / Dick Stuber / Bill Rice
7	Kansas	13	HB John Powell / Sonny Stringer
			FB Carl Wynn / Gene Roll

RUSHING: Roll 99/432y, Wynn 50/199y, Curtright 33/163y
PASSING: Doane 52-113/774y, 4TD, 46%
RECEIVING: Burnine 44/594y, Wynn 13/144y, Stringer 6/95y
SCORING: Hunter & Wynn 18pts, Burnine & Doane 12pts

1956 4-5-1

13	Oregon State	19	E George Boucher / Bill McKinney
7	Purdue	16	T Merv Johnson
25	SMU	33	G Pete Jensen / Don Chadwick
42	No. Dakota St.	0	C Carl Osterloh / Skip Schulz
20	Kansas State	6	G Jim Martin / Paul Browning
34	Iowa State	0	T Frank Czapla / Chuck Mehrer
14	Nebraska	15	E Larry Plumb / Bill Craig
14	Colorado	14	QB Jimmy Hunter / Dave Doane
14	Oklahoma	67	HB Hank Kuhlmann / Sonny Stringer
15	Kansas	13	HB Charley James / Fred Henger
			FB George Cramer / Gene Roll

RUSHING: Kuhlmann 87/440y, Cramer 89/393y, Hunter 91/301y
PASSING: Hunter 42-91/567y, 2TD, 46.2%
RECEIVING: James 30/362y, Henger 8/68y, Plumb 7/107y
SCORING: Kuhlmann 37pts, James 30pts, Cramer 24pts

1957 5-4-1

7	Vanderbilt	7	E George Boucher / Dale Pidcock
35	Arizona	13	T Merv Johnson
0	Texas A&M	28	G Charley Rash / Pete Jensen
7	SMU	6	C Tom Swaney
35	Iowa State	13	G Don Chadwick
14	Nebraska	13	T Mike Magac / Bob Lee
9	Colorado	6	E Bill McKinney / L. Plumb / Bennie Alburtis
14	Oklahoma	39	QB Phil Snowden / Ken Clemenson
21	Kansas State	23	HB Bob Haas / Jerry Cutright
7	Kansas	9	HB Charley James / George Cramer
			FB Hank Kuhlmann

RUSHING: Kuhlmann 136/554y, Snowden 64/207y, Curtright 25/171y
PASSING: Snowden 24-57/299y, 3TD, 42.1%
RECEIVING: James 12/132y, McKinney 5/68y, Alburtis 4/35y
SCORING: Kuhlmann 48pts, Snowden 36pts, Rash 20pts

1958 5-4-1

8	Vanderbilt	12	E Russ Sloan / George Boucher
14	Idaho	10	T Owen Worstell
0	Texas A&M	12	G Charlie Rash
19	SMU	32	C Tom Swaney / Bill Feind
32	Kansas State	8	G Don Chadwick
14	Iowa State	8	T Mike Magac
31	Nebraska	0	E Danny LaRose / Dale Pidcock
33	Colorado	9	QB Phil Snowden / Bob Haas
0	Oklahoma	39	HB Mel West / Hank Kuhlmann
13	Kansas	13	HB Norris Stevenson
			FB Ed Mehrer / Jim Miles

RUSHING: West 131/642y, Kuhlmann 89/369y, Stevenson 77/307y
PASSING: Snowden 46-86/550y, 3TD, 54.5%
RECEIVING: Sloan 16/211y, LaRose 14/215y, Boucher 6/57y
SCORING: Snowden 37pts, West 24pts, Sloan 18pts

1959 6-5

8	Penn State	19	E Russ Sloan / Gordon Smith
20	Michigan	15	T Bill Wegener / Ed Blaine
14	Iowa State	0	G Paul Henley / Paul Gravis
2	SMU	23	C Tom Swaney / Bill McCartney
0	Oklahoma	23	G Rockne Calhoun
9	Nebraska	0	T Mike Magac
20	Colorado	21	E Danny LaRose / Dale Pidcock
13	Air Force	0	QB Phil Snowden / Bob Haas
26	Kansas State	0	HB Mel West / Fred Brossart (D)
13	Kansas	9	HB Donnie Smith / Norris Stevenson
9	Georgia ■	14	FB Ed Mehrer / Jim Miles

RUSHING: West 122/556y, Smith 74/377y, Stevenson 60/267y
PASSING: Snowden 33-83/415y, 4TD, 39.8%
RECEIVING: Sloan 13/128y, LaRose 9/142y, Smith 8/121y
SCORING: Smith 24pts, Sloan 18pts, West 18pts

1960 10-1

20	SMU	0	E Gordon Smith / Russ Sloan
28	Oklahoma State	7	T Ed Blaine
21	Penn State	8	G Paul Henley / T Smith
34	Air Force	8	C Mike Langan / Bill McCartney
45	Kansas State	0	G Paul Garvis / Tom Hertz
35	Iowa State	8	T Rockne Calhoun / Max Moyer
28	Nebraska	0	E Danny Larose / Conrad Hitchler
16	Colorado	6	QB Ron Taylor
41	Oklahoma	19	HB Mel West / Norm Beal
7	Kansas (F-W)	23	HB Donnie Smith / Norris Stevenson
21	Navy ■	14	FB Andy Russell / Ed Mehrer

RUSHING: West 138/650y, Stevenson 85/610y, Smith 86/357y
PASSING: Taylor 23-44/302y, 4TD, 52.3%
RECEIVING: LaRose 10/151y, Smith 6/63y, Hitchler 4/50y
SCORING: Smith 78pts, Tobin 39pts, Stevenson 36pts

1961 7-2-1

28	Washington St.	6	E Don Wainwright / John Sevcik
6	Minnesota	0	T Bill Wegener / Jerry Wallach
14	California	14	G Paul Henley
10	Oklahoma State	0	C Bill McCartney / Jim Vermillion
13	Iowa State	0	G Paul Garvis / Tom Hertz
10	Nebraska	0	T Ed Blaine / Bill Siekierski
6	Colorado	7	E Conrad Hitchler / George Seals
0	Oklahoma	7	QB Ron Taylor / Daryl Krugman
27	Kansas State	9	HB Norm Beal / Turner
10	Kansas	7	HB Bill Tobin / Carl Crawford
			FB Andy Russell

RUSHING: Russell 100/412y, Beal 57/287y, Tobin 87/236y
PASSING: Taylor 31-62/428y, 0TD, 50.0%
RECEIVING: Hitchler 8/124y, Russell 7/100y, Tobin 7/66y
SCORING: Tobin (HB-K) 38pts, Taylor 24pts, Russell 18pts

1962 8-1-2

21	California	10	E John Sefcik / Don Wainwright
0	Minnesota	0	T Dave Gill
17	Arizona	7	G Tom Hertz
32	Kansas State	0	C Jim Vermillion / Gene Oliver (E)
23	Oklahoma State	6	G Roger Phillips
21	Iowa State	6	T Jerry Wallach
16	Nebraska	7	E Conrad Hitchler / George Seals
57	Colorado	0	QB Jim Johnson
0	Oklahoma	13	HB Bill Tobin
3	Kansas	3	HB Johnny Roland
14	Georgia Tech ■	10	FB Paul Underhill / Andy Russell

RUSHING: Roland 159/830y, Underhill 110/462y, Tobin 76/347y
PASSING: Johnson 12-33/198y, 1TD, 36.4%
RECEIVING: Roland 6/59y, Tobin 3/75y, 4 tied w/ 2
SCORING: Roland 78pts, Tobin 28pts, Bill Leistritz (HB-K) 20pts

1963 7-3

12	Northwestern	23	E John Sevcik
7	Arkansas	6	T Bobby Brown
24	Idaho	0	G Ron Lurie
21	Kansas State	11	C Gene Oliver
28	Oklahoma	6	G Ralph Kubinski
7	Iowa State	0	T Dave Gill
12	Nebraska	13	E Harry Abell / George Seals
28	Colorado	7	QB Gary Lane
3	Oklahoma	13	HB Ted Saussele
9	Kansas	7	HB Monroe Phelps / Ken Boston
			FB Gus Otto/Carl Reese / P. Underhill

RUSHING: Reese 67/300y, Lane 111/300y, Phelps 60/265y
PASSING: Lane 51-113/710y, 3TD, 45.1%
RECEIVING: Saussele 8/115y, Sevcik 8/107y, Phelps 7/73y
SCORING: Lane 36pts, Leistritz 23pts, Phelps & Boston 18pts

1964 6-3-1

14	California	21	E Tom Lynn / Robert Ritter
23	Utah	6	T Francis Peay / Don Snyder
7	Oklahoma State	10	G Bobby Brown
7	Kansas State	0	C Joe Buerkle
17	Air Force	7	G Tom Wyrostek / Dave Holsinger
10	Iowa State	0	T Jerry Crumpler / Butch Allison
0	Nebraska	9	E Jim Waller / Bud Abell
16	Colorado	7	QB Gary Lane
14	Oklahoma	14	HB Johnny Roland / Ray Thorpe
34	Kansas	14	HB Earl Denny / Charlie Brown
			FB Carl Reese / Gus Otto
			DL Bud Abell
			DL Bruce Van Dyke
			DL Bill Powell
			DL Don Nelson
			DL Butch Allison
			DL Tom Lynn / Dan Schuppan
			LB Gus Otto
			LB Rich Bernsen
			DB Johnny Roland / Gary Grossnickle
			DB Ken Boston
			DB Vince Tobin

RUSHING: Lane 100/432y, Brown 99/349y, Reese 83/299y
PASSING: Lane 50-119/770y, 7TD, 42%
RECEIVING: Waller 13/121y, Denny 10/222y, Brown 7/136y
SCORING: Lane 26pts, Brown 26pts, Bates 18pts

1965 8-2-1

0	Kentucky	7	E Monroe Phelps / Ray West
13	Oklahoma State	0	T Francis Peay
17	Minnesota	6	G Mike Eader / Jim Willsey
28	Kansas State	14	C Al Chettle / Dick Kistner
14	UCLA	14	G Bruce Van Dyke / Gary Frieders
23	Iowa State	7	T Butch Allison
14	Nebraska	16	E Jim Waller
20	Colorado	7	QB Gary Lane / Johnny Roland
30	Oklahoma	0	HB Charlie Brown
44	Kansas	20	HB Earl Denny
20	Florida ■	18	FB Carl Reese
			DL Russ Washington / Dan Schuppan
			DL Bruce Van Dyke
			DL Bill Powell
			DL Don Nelson
			DL Ron Snyder
			DL Tom Lynn
			LB Rich Bernsen
			LB Bob Ziegler
			DB Ken Boston
			DB Johnny Roland
			DB Gary Grossnickle

RUSHING: Brown 174/937y, Reese 139/520y, Lane 84/450y
PASSING: Lane 45-106/544y, 4TD, 42.5%
RECEIVING: Phelps 17/207y, Brown 11/99y, Waller 11/96y
SCORING: Lane 54pts, Roland 36pts, Bill Bates (K) 34pts

1966 6-3-1

24	Minnesota	0 E Marty Berg
21	Illinois	14 T Jim Anderson / Roger Short
15	UCLA	24 G Jim Willsey / Bob Parker
27	Kansas State	0 C Rich Kistner
7	Oklahoma State	0 G Al Pepper
10	Iowa State	10 T Mike Wempe
0	Nebraska	35 E Chuck Weber / Jim Juras
0	Colorado	26 QB Gary Kombrink / Steve Sharp
10	Oklahoma	7 HB Charlie Brown
7	Kansas	0 HB Earl Denny

FB Barry Lischner / Bob Powell
DL Elmer Benhardt
DL Bill Powell
DL Carl Garber
DL Don Nelson
DL Lee Mungai
DL Dan Schuppan
LB John Douglas
LB John Spengel / Rich Bernsen
DB Jim Whitaker
DB Roger Wehrli
DB Gary Grossnickle

RUSHING: Brown 139/544y, Ewing 43/225y, Kombrink 122/212y
PASSING: Kombrink 32-77/433y, 1TD, 41.6%
RECEIVING: Weber 14/157y, Brown 12/54y, Denny 11/276y
SCORING: Bill Bates (K) 27pts, Weber 18pts, Denny 14pts

1967 7-3

21	SMU	0 E Marty Berg
13	Northwestern	6 T Mike Wempe
17	Arizona	3 G Jim Willsey
9	Colorado	23 C Conway Rees
23	Iowa State	7 G Al Pepper / Mike Carroll
0	Oklahoma	7 T Russ Washington / Jim Anderson
7	Oklahoma State	0 E Chuck Weber
28	Kansas State	6 QB Gary Kombrink
10	Nebraska	7 HB Ron McBride
6	Kansas	17 HB Larry Moore / Jon Staggers

FB Barry Lischner
DL Elmer Benhardt
DL Curtis Jones / Robert Boyd
DL Carl Garber
DL Lee Mungai
DL Jay Wallace
DL Bill Schmitt / Russ Washington
LB John Douglas
LB Roger J Boyd
DB Roger Wehrli
DB Butch Davis
DB John Meyer

RUSHING: Lischner 174/647y, Kombrink 169/520y,
 McBride 50/199y
PASSING: Kombrink 34-97/452y, 1TD, 35%
RECEIVING: Weber 15/212y, Brown 8/105y, Berg 7/71y
SCORING: Jay Wallace (K) 27pts, Lischner 24pts, Kombrink 18pts

1968 8-3

6	Kentucky	12 WR Chuck Weber / Mel Gray
44	Illinois	0 T Jim Anderson
7	Army	3 G Joe Clark / Sam Adams
27	Colorado	14 C Conway Rees / Gene Hertz
16	Nebraska	14 G Tom Crnko
56	Kansas State	20 T Mike Carroll
42	Oklahoma State	7 TE Tom Shyrock
42	Iowa State	7 QB Terry McMillan / Garnett Phelps
14	Oklahoma	28 HB Greg Cook
19	Kansas	21 HB Jon Staggers
35	Alabama■	10 FB Ron McBride / James Harrison

DL Elmer Benhardt
DL Mark Kuhlman
DL Carl Garber
DL Roger Boyd
DL Jay Wallace
DL Bill Schmitt
LB Jerry Boyd / Nip Weisenfels
LB Steve Lundholm
DB Roger Wehrli
DB Butch Davis
DB George Fountain / Dennis Poppe

RUSHING: Cook 161/693y, Staggers 94/385y, McBride 83/367y
PASSING: McMillan 56-113/745y, 4TD, 50%
RECEIVING: Staggers 19/171y, Gray 14/337y, Cook 14/103y
SCORING: Harrison 48pts, Cook 30pts, 5 tied with 24pts

1969 9-2

19	Air Force	17 WR Mel Gray
37	Illinois	6 T Larron Jackson
40	Michigan	17 G Dan Kelley
17	Nebraska	7 C Bob Wilson / Ron Sloan
31	Oklahoma State	21 G Tom Crnko / Mickey Kephart
24	Colorado	31 T Mike Carroll
41	Kansas State	38 TE Tom Shyrock
44	Oklahoma	10 QB Terry McMillan
40	Iowa State	13 HB Jon Staggers
69	Kansas	21 HB Joe Moore
3	Penn State■	10 FB Ron McBride

DL Joe Hauptman / John Brown
DL Mark Kuhlman
DL John Cowan / Steve Mizer
DL Mike Bennett / Dan Borgard
DL Adam Vital
DL Sam Adams
LB Steve Lundholm
LB Nip Weisenfels
DB George Fountain
DB Butch Davis
DB Dennis Poppe

RUSHING: Moore 260/1312y, McBride 83/316y, Staggers 76/273y
PASSING: McMillan 105-233/1963y, 18TD, 45.1%
RECEIVING: Gray 26/705y, Henley 19/320y, Shyrock 15/176y
SCORING: Henry Brown (K) 71pts, Gray 60pts, Staggers &
 McMillan 42pts

1970 5-6

38	Baylor	0 WR John Henley
34	Minnesota	12 WR Mel Gray
14	Air Force	37 T Larron Jackson
40	Oklahoma State	20 G Ray Bell
7	Nebraska	21 C Bob Wilson
7	Notre Dame	24 G Mickey Kephart
30	Colorado	16 T Eric Lowder
13	Kansas State	17 TE Tyrone Walls
13	Oklahoma	28 QB Mike Farmer / Chuck Roper
19	Iowa State	31 HB Joe Moore / Bill Mauser
28	Kansas	17 FB James Harrison

DL Mike Bennett
DL John Cowan
DL Jay Wallace
DL John Brown
DL Adam Vital
DL Steve Mizer
LB Mike McKee / Nip Weisenfels
LB Samuel Britts
DB Lorenzo Brinkley / George Fountain
DB Henry Stuckey
DB Pete Buha / Paul Fink

RUSHING: Harrison 127/702y, Moore 127/610y, Mauser 126/505y
PASSING: Roper 105-235/1097y, 1TD, and 49%
RECEIVING: Henley 39/481y, Walls 28/311y, Gray 27/449y
SCORING: Jack Bastable (K) 60pts, Moore 36pts, Farmer 32pts

1971 1-10

0	Stanford	19 WR John Henley
6	Air Force	7 T Jim Schnietz
24	SMU	12 G Ray Bell
4	Army	22 C Scott Sodergren
0	Nebraska	36 G Mark Clark / Ohris Kirley
16	Oklahoma State	37 T Mickey Kephart / Kelley Curbow
7	Colorado	27 TE John Kelsey / Chuck McMurry
12	Kansas State	28 SB Mike Fink / Chuck Link
3	Oklahoma	20 QB Chuck Roper / Ed Johndrow
17	Iowa State	45 HB Jack Bastable
2	Kansas	7 FB Don Johnson

DL John Brown / Dan McDonough
DL John Cowan
DL Steve Mizer
DL Dan Borgard
LB Bob Orsi
LB Bob Luther
LB Mike McKee
LB Samuel Britts
DB Lorenzo Brinkley
DB Henry Stuckey
DB Pete Buha

RUSHING: Johnson 98/360y, Bastable 119/304y, Mauser 57/206y
PASSING: Roper 62-131/613y, 3TD, 54.9%
 Johndrow 49-112/475y, 1TD, 43.8%
RECEIVING: Henley 25/247y, Link 23/177y, Fink 21/191y
SCORING: Greg Hill (K) 23 pts, Fink & Henley 12pts

1972 6-6

24	Oregon	22 WR Jim Sharp
0	Baylor	27 WR Jack Bastable / Chuck Link (HB)
34	California	27 T Kelley Curbow
16	Oklahoma State	17 G Chris Kirley
0	Nebraska	62 C Scott Sodergren
30	Notre Dame	26 G Scott Anderson
20	Colorado	17 T Jim Schnietz
31	Kansas State	14 TE John Kelsey / Don Muse
6	Oklahoma	17 QB John Cherry
6	Iowa State	5 HB Tommy Reamon
17	Kansas	28 FB Ray Bybee / Don Johnson
35	Arizona State■	49 DL J.L. Doak

DL Larry Frost / Dennis Vanarsdall
DL Lynn Evans
DL Dan McDonough
DL Dave Johnston / Steve Schreiber
LB Scott Pickens / Bob Keeney
LB Tom Kellett
DB Ken Gregory / Steve Yount
DB John Moseley
DB Mike Fink
DB Bob Pankey / Brad Brown

RUSHING: Reamon 115/454y, Bybee 88/449y, Johnson 120/406y
PASSING: Cherry 52-131/861y, 5TD, 39.7%
RECEIVING: Bastable 20/362y, Reamon 11/110y, Sharp 9/208y
SCORING: Greg Hill (K) 61pts, Johnson 24pts, 3 tied with 18pts

1973 8-4

17	Mississippi	0 WR Jim Sharp / Mark Miller
31	Virginia	7 T Jim Schneitz
27	North Carolina	14 G Don Buck
17	SMU	7 C Scott Anderson
13	Nebraska	12 G Steve Sadich
13	Oklahoma State	9 T Kelley Curbow
13	Colorado	17 TE Don Muse / John Kelsey (T)
31	Kansas State	7 SB Bill Ziegler
3	Oklahoma	31 QB John Cherry / Ray Smith
7	Iowa State	17 TB Tommy Reamon / Leroy Moss
13	Kansas	14 FB Ray Bybee
34	Auburn■	17 DL Steve Schreiber / Bob Keeney

DL Dennis Vanarsdall
DL Herris Butler / Frank Caldwell
DL Mark Johnson
DL Bob McRoberts
LB Scott Pickens
LB Lynn Evans
DB John Moseley
DB Kenny Downing
DB Tony Gillick
DB Steve Yount

RUSHING: Reamon 149/610y, Bybee 127/563y, Moss 114/373y
PASSING: Cherry 59-120/743y, 5TD, 49.2%
RECEIVING: Miller 17/256y, Sharp 15/244y, Kelsey 7/71y
SCORING: Greg Hill (K) 63pts, Reamon 24pts, Cherry &
 Sharp 18pts

1974 7-4

0	Mississippi	10 WR Mark Miller
28	Baylor	21 T Morris Towns
9	Arizona State	0 G Steve Sadich
20	Wisconsin	59 C Mike Owens
21	Nebraska	10 G Don Buck
7	Oklahoma State	31 T D.W. Johnston
30	Colorado	24 TE Don Muse
52	Kansas State	15 SB Bill Ziegler
0	Oklahoma	37 QB Steve Pisarkiewicz / Ray Smith
10	Iowa State	7 HB Tony Galbreath / Joe Stewart
27	Kansas	3 FB Ray Bybee

DL Bob McRoberts
DL Mark Johnson
DL Tom Cooper / Steve Meyer
DL Dave Johnston
DL Bob Keeney
LB Lynn Evans
LB Scott Pickens
DB Rob Fitzgerald
DB Kenny Downing
DB Steve Yount
DB Tony Gillick

RUSHING: Galbreath 197/870y, Bybee 79/433y, Stewart 54/243y
PASSING: Pisarkiewicz 70-156/828y, 6TD, 44.9%
RECEIVING: Miller 38/522y, Galbreath 16/130y, Muse 11/158y
SCORING: Galbreath 48pts, Miller 36pts, Tim Gibbons (K) 32pts

1975 6-5

20 Alabama	7 WR Henry Marshall
30 Illinois	20 T James Taylor
27 Wisconsin	21 G Joel Yearian
7 Michigan	31 C Larry McDevitt / Mike Owens
41 Oklahoma State	14 G Tom Kowalczyk
20 Colorado	31 T Morris Towns
35 Kansas State	3 TE Charlie Douglass
7 Nebraska	30 SB Joe Stewart / Randy Grossart
44 Iowa State	14 QB Steve Pisarkiewicz
27 Oklahoma	28 HB Tony Galbreath / Curtis Brown
24 Kansas	42 FB John Blakeman / Rich Dansdill
	DL Dale Smith / Tom Garavaglia
	DL Randy Frisch / Blaine Henningsen
	DL Steve Meyer
	DL Tom Cooper / Keith Morrissey
	DL Bob McRoberts
	LB Tom Hodge
	LB Mark Kirkpatrick / Bill Culp
	DB Kenny Downing
	DB Bruce Carter
	DB Rob Fitzgerald / Larry Davis
	DB Chuck Banta / Jim Leavitt

RUSHING: Galbreath 183/777y, Brown 113/636y, Blakeman 85/385y
PASSING: Pisarkiewicz 113-232/1792y, 11TD, 48.7%
RECEIVING: Marshall 44/945y, Grossart 27/366y, Galbreath 18/195y
SCORING: Tim Gibbons (K) 72pts, Galbreath 60pts, Marshall 54pts

1976 6-5

46 Southern Cal	25 WR Leo Lewis
6 Illinois	31 T James Taylor
22 Ohio State	21 G Joel Yearian
24 North Carolina	3 C Larry McDevitt
28 Kansas State	21 G Tom Kowalczyk
17 Iowa State	21 T Morris Towns
34 Nebraska	24 TE Kellen Winslow
19 Oklahoma State	20 SB Joe Stewart
16 Colorado	7 QB Pete Woods / Steve Pisarkiewicz
20 Oklahoma	27 TB Curtis Brown / Dean Leibson
14 Kansas	41 FB Rich Dansdill
	DL Dale Smith
	DL Curtis Kirkland / Don Cole
	DL Rickie Sutherland / Randy Frisch
	DL Keith Morrissey
	DL Steve Hamilton
	LB Tom Hodge
	LB Chris Garlich
	DB Bob Fitzgerald
	DB Bruce Carter
	DB Mike Newman / Jim Leavitt
	DB Chuck Banta

RUSHING: Brown 169/844y, Dansdill 125/669y, Leibson 69/351y
PASSING: Woods 59-131/996y, 9TD, 45.0%
Pisarkiewicz 53-121/793y, 6TD, 43.8%
RECEIVING: Stewart 45/834y, Lewis 30/394y, Winslow 16/240y
SCORING: Tim Gibbons (K) 62pts, Lewis 48pts, Stewart 44pts

1977 4-7

10 Southern Cal	27 WR Leo Lewis
7 Illinois	11 WR Joe Stewart
21 California	28 T James Taylor / Wayne Washington
15 Arizona State	0 G Mark Clark
0 Iowa State	7 C Pete Allard
17 Oklahoma	21 G Mark Jones
28 Kansas State	13 T Howard Richards / Bruce Whitmer
24 Colorado	14 TE Kellen Winslow
10 Nebraska	21 QB Pete Woods / Phil Bradley
41 Oklahoma State	14 TB Earl Gant / Dave Newman
22 Kansas	24 FB Annise Davis / Rich Dansdill
	DL David Legg / Eugene Twellman
	DL Ron Suda / James Mathews
	DL Rickie Sutherland
	DL Keith Morrissey
	DL Steve Hamilton / Bill Anderson
	LB William Bess
	LB Chris Garlich / Oliver Burbage
	DB Russ Calabrese
	DB Terry Newman
	DB Jim Leavitt
	DB Steve Mally

RUSHING: Gant 144/769y, Davis 105/437y, Bradley 139/372y
PASSING: Woods 65-127/785y, 4TD, 51.2%
RECEIVING: Stewart 27/384y, Winslow 25/358y, Lewis 24/273y
SCORING: Jeff Brockhaus (K) 49pts, Davis 30pts, Bradley 24pts

1978 8-4

3 Notre Dame	0 WR Lamont Downer
20 Alabama	38 WR Leo Lewis
45 Mississippi	14 T Dave Guender
23 Oklahoma	45 G Mark Jones
45 Illinois	3 C Pete Allard
26 Iowa State	13 G Stan Lechner
56 Kansas State	14 T Howard Richards
27 Colorado	28 TE Kellen Winslow
20 Oklahoma State	35 QB Phil Bradley
48 Kansas	0 HB Earl Gant / Gerry Ellis
35 Nebraska	31 FB James Wilder
	DL Wendell Ray
	DL Ken Bungarda
	DL Bennie Smith / Norm Goodman
	DL Steve Hamilton
	DL Kurt Petersen / Tony Green
	LB William Bess / Eric Berg
	LB Chris Garlich
	DB Johnnie Poe
	DB Russ Calabrese / Bill Whitaker
	DB Eric Wright
	DB Larry Lauderdale

RUSHING: Wilder 160/873y, Gant 138/789y, Ellis 66/336y
PASSING: Bradley 136-226/1780y, 12TD, 60.2%
RECEIVING: Winslow 29/479y, Lewis 28/376y, Downer 22/331y
SCORING: Wilder 72pts, Jeff Brockhaus (K) 56pts, Gant 48pts

1979 7-5

45 San Diego State	15 WR Lee Wagner / Ken Blair
14 Illinois	6 WR David Newman
33 Mississippi	7 T Dave Guender
0 Texas	21 G Mark Jones
13 Oklahoma State	14 C Brad Edelman
13 Colorado	7 G Stan Lechner
3 Kansas State	19 T Howard Richards
20 Nebraska	23 TE Andy Gibler
18 Iowa State	9 QB Phil Bradley
22 Oklahoma	24 HB Gerry Ellis
55 Kansas	7 FB James Wilder
24 So. Carolina■	14 DL Tony Green
	DL Kurt Petersen
	DL Norm Goodman
	DL Bennie Smith
	DL Wendell Ray
	LB Lester Dickey
	LB Eric Berg
	DB Johnnie Poe
	DB Bill Whitaker / Chip Powell
	DB Kevin Potter
	DB Eric Wright

RUSHING: Wilder 155/645y, Ellis 121/584y Bradley 131/316y
PASSING: Bradley 127-236/1448y, 5TD, 53.8%
RECEIVING: Gibler 23/316y, Ellis 23/285y, Newman 21/216y
SCORING: Ellis 54pts, Ron Verrilli (K) 33pts, Jeff Brockhaus (K) 27pts

1980 8-4

47 New Mexico	16 WR Ken Blair
52 Illinois	7 WR Ron Fellows
31 San Diego State	7 T Wayne Washington
21 Penn State	29 G Kevin Sadler
30 Oklahoma State	7 C Brad Edelman
45 Colorado	7 G Stan Lechner
13 Kansas State	3 T Howard Richards
16 Nebraska	38 TE Andy Gibler
14 Iowa State	10 QB Phil Bradley
7 Oklahoma	17 HB Andy Hill
31 Kansas	6 FB James Wilder
25 Purdue ■	28 DL Wendell Ray
	DL Bennie Smith
	DL Jerome Sally
	DL Randy Jostes / Rodney Skillman
	DL Ray Stephens / Tony Green
	LB Lester Dickey
	LB Van Darkow
	DB Johnnie Poe
	DB Bill Whitaker
	DB Eric Wright
	DB Kevin Potter

RUSHING: Wilder 172/839y, Hill 113/425y, Meyer 47/315y
PASSING: Bradley 132-242/1632y, 12TD, 54.5%
RECEIVING: Fellows 33/586y, Gibler 26/298y, Hill 22/273y
SCORING: Ron Verrilli (K) 67pts, Wilder 54pts, Hill 42pts

1981 8-4

24 Army	10 WR James Caver
42 Rice	10 WR Curtland Thomas
34 Louisville	3 T Andy Ekern
14 Mississippi St.	3 G John Millearty
58 Kansas State	13 C Brad Edelman / Tony Bruns
13 Iowa State	34 G Bernie Laster
0 Nebraska	6 T Conrad Goode
12 Oklahoma State	16 TE Andy Gibler
30 Colorado	14 QB Mike Hyde
19 Oklahoma	14 RB Bobby Meyer / George Shorthose
11 Kansas	19 RB Bill White
19 Southern Miss■	17 DL Ken Judd
	DL Rodney Skillman / Randy Jostes
	DL Jerome Sally
	DL Jeff Gaylod
	DL Taft Sales
	LB Van Darkow
	LB David McNeel / Jay Wilson
	DB Demetrious Johnson
	DB Raymond Hairston / Jeff Smith
	DB Steve Crapo
	DB Kevin Potter

RUSHING: Meyer 180/791y, White 106/458y, Shorthose 46/165y
PASSING: Hyde 123-249/1471y, 8TD, 49.4%
RECEIVING: Caver 33/509y, Gibler 27/223, Meyer 24/235y
SCORING: Bob Lucchesi (K) 51pts, Meyer 48pts, Hyde 30pts

1982 5-4-2

28 Colorado State	14 WR James Caver
23 Army	10 WR Curtland Thomas / Craig White
0 Texas	21 T Andy Ekern
28 East Carolina	9 G Jim Dempsey
7 Kansas State	7 C Phil Greenfield
17 Iowa State	17 G Bernie Laster
19 Nebraska	23 T Conrad Goode
20 Oklahoma State	30 TE Andy Gibler
35 Colorado	14 QB Marlon Adler / Brad Perry
14 Oklahoma	41 TB Santio Barbosa
16 Kansas	10 FB Tracey Mack
	DL Bobby Bell
	DL Randy Jostes
	DL Jim Lockette
	DL Rodney Skillman
	DL Taft Sales (LB) / Ken Judd
	LB Jay Wilson
	LB Ken Harlan
	DB Jeff Smith
	DB Demetrious Johnson / Terry Matichak
	DB Raymond Hairston
	DB Kevin Potter

RUSHING: Mack 120/484y, Barbosa 102/365y, Snowden 65/263y
PASSING: Adler 79-140/1242y, 7TD, 56.4%
Perry 70-124/839y, 6TD, 56.5%
RECEIVING: Caver 41/634y, Gibler 25/453y, Thomas 17/378y
SCORING: Caver 24pts, Thomas 24pts, Gibler 20pts

1983 7-5

28 Illinois	18 WR Andy Hill
20 Wisconsin	21 WR George Shorthose / Craig White
17 Utah State	10 T Conrad Goode
6 East Carolina	13 G Tom Hornof
59 Colorado	20 C Phil Greenfield
13 Nebraska	34 G Bernard Laster
38 Kansas State	0 T Scott Shockley
41 Iowa State	18 TE Greg Krahl
10 Oklahoma	0 QB Marlon Adler
16 Oklahoma State	10 TB Eric Drain
27 Kansas	37 FB Santio Barbosa / Jon Redd
17 BYU■	21 DL Bobby Bell
	DL Mike Scott
	DL Steve Leshe
	DL Bob Curry
	DL Taft Sales / Lenson Staples
	LB Tracey Mack
	LB Jay Wilson
	DB Jeff Hooper
	DB Terry Matichak
	DB Tom Hawkins
	DB Jerome Caver

RUSHING: Drain 167/684y, Barbosa 91/367y, Riley 87/324y
PASSING: Adler 102-175/1603y 11TD, x%
RECEIVING: Shorthose 32/483y, White 23/393y, Hill 15/315y
SCORING: Adler 72pts, Burditt 64pts, Drain 24pts

1984 3-7-1

24 Illinois	30 WR Andy Hill
34 Wisconsin	35 WR George Shorthose
47 Mississippi St.	30 T Leon Clay
14 Notre Dame	16 G Phil Pettey
52 Colorado	7 C Phil Greenfield / Craig Suntrup
23 Nebraska	33 G Nick Llewellyn / Mike Penny
61 Kansas State	21 T Dave Kniptash
14 Iowa State	14 TE Tony Davis
7 Oklahoma	49 QB Marlon Adler / Warren Seitz
13 Oklahoma State	31 HB Eric Drain
21 Kansas	35 FB Jon Redd
	DL Erik McMillan / Dick Chapura
	DL Pat Burns / Robert Curry
	DL Steve Leshe
	DL Michael Scott
	DL Gary Justis / Lenson Staples
	LB Bo Sherrill
	LB Tracey Mack
	DB Terry Matichak
	DB Tony Facinelli / Ron Floyd
	DB Jeff Hooper / Cameron Riley
	DB Jerome Caver

RUSHING: Redd 119/668y, Drain 138/596y, Seitz 92/382y
PASSING: Adler 77-144/1128y, 7TD, 53.5%
RECEIVING: Shorthose 33/601y, Hill 25/445y, Davis 25/326y
SCORING: Drain 60pts, Brad Burditt (K) 53pts, Adler & Seitz 36pts

1985 1-10

23 Northwestern	27 WR Herbert Johnson
17 Texas	21 WR Victor Moore / Craig Lammers
17 Indiana	36 T Dave Kniptash
32 California	39 G Jeff Rigman
7 Colorado	38 C Dal Lockwood / Mike Penny
20 Nebraska	28 G Phil Pettey
17 Kansas State	20 T John Clay
28 Iowa State	27 TE Pat Thetford / Joe Close
6 Oklahoma	51 QB Marlon Adler / Warren Seitz
19 Oklahoma State	21 HB Darrell Wallace
20 Kansas	34 FB Mike Scott / Eric Drain / Jon Redd
	DL Dick Chapura
	DL Darryl Darling / Steve Leshe
	DL Rick Klohmann
	LB Terry Walker / Mike Vestweber
	LB Buck Stinson / Bo Sherrill
	LB Eric Troy / Bond Howery
	LB Steve Vandegrift
	DB Tony Facinilli
	DB Ron Floyd / Cordell McKinney
	DB Cameron Riley / Stan Long
	DB Erik McMillan

RUSHING: Wallace 226/1120y, Boyd 35/170y, Adler 80/122y
PASSING: Adler 89-183/1258y, 7TD, 48.6%
RECEIVING: Johnson 49/806y, Thetford 21/254y, Lammers 15/214y
SCORING: Tom Whelihan (K) 64pts, Wallace 30pts, Johnson 26pts

1986 3-8

24 Utah State	10 WR Herbert Johnson / Victor Moore
25 Texas	27 WR Robert Delpino
24 Indiana	41 T John Clay
9 Syracuse	41 G Phil Pettey
12 Colorado	17 C Dal Lockwood
17 Nebraska	48 G Jeff Rigman
17 Kansas State	6 T Ted Romney
14 Iowa State	37 TE Joe Close / Brent Peterson
0 Oklahoma	77 QB Ronnie Cameron / Jeff Henningsen
48 Kansas	0 HB Darrell Wallace
6 Oklahoma State	10 FB Ed Esson
	DL Dick Chapura
	DL Darryl Darling
	DL Jeff Cross
	LB Gary Justis
	LB Terry Walker
	LB Darren MacDonald / Mike Vestweber
	LB Steve Vandegrift
	DB Adrian Jones
	DB Pat Ray
	DB Erik McMillan
	DB Cameron Riley / Stan Long

RUSHING: Wallace 211/872y, Cameron 120/365y, Vernon Boyd (HB) 38/233y
PASSING: Cameron 49-111/654y, 6TD, 44.1% Henningsen 40-82/506y, 4 TD, 48.8%
RECEIVING: Johnson 17/167y, Delpino 16/299y, Moore 14/290y
SCORING: Tom Whelihan (K) 62pts, Wallace 30pts, Cameron 30pts

1987 5-6

23 Baylor	18 WR Craig Lammers
28 Northwestern	3 T Carl Bax
17 Indiana	20 G Jeff Rigman
13 Syracuse	24 C Curtis Wilson
34 Kansas State	10 G Chris Lowe / Pete Scott
42 Iowa State	17 T Phil Schreiber / Andy Lock
20 Oklahoma State	24 TE Tim Bruton / Mike Boliaux
7 Nebraska	42 QB John Stollenwerck / Ronnie Cameron
10 Colorado	27 HB Darrell Wallace
13 Oklahoma	17 HB Robert Delpino
19 Kansas	7 FB Tommie Stowers
	DL Steve Vandegrift
	DL Darryl Darling
	DL Jeff Cross / Kevin White
	DL Ben Corl / Lee Johnson
	LB Darren MacDonald
	LB Reggie Ballard / Ron Walters
	LB Jerold Fletcher / Kirk Ekern
	DB Adrian Jones
	DB Pat Ray
	DB Charles Murphy
	DB Erik McMillan

RUSHING: Delpino 115/750y, Stowers 151/707y, Wallace 126/552y
PASSING: Stollenwerck 60-137/831y, 3TD, 43.8%
RECEIVING: Lammers 16/253y, Bruton 13/174y, Hagens 11/147y
SCORING: Tom Whelihan (K) 64pts, Delpino 54pts, Wallace 30pts

1988 3-7-1

35 Utah State	21 WR Craig Lammers / Ronnie Cameron
7 Houston	31 T Carl Bax / Rick Trumball
28 Indiana	28 G Pete Scott
0 Miami	55 C Curtis Wilson
52 Kansas State	21 G David Washington / Jay Greenwood
3 Iowa State	21 T Andy Lock
21 Oklahoma State	49 TE Tim Bruton / Larry Linthacum
18 Nebraska	26 QB Corey Welch / Brad Fitzmaurice
8 Colorado	45 HB Michael Jones / Jim White
7 Oklahoma	16 HB Smiley Elmore
55 Kansas	17 FB Tommie Stowers
	DL Steve Vandegrift / Ben Corl
	DL Darryl Darling
	DL Kevin White / Mario Johnson
	DL Lee Johnson
	LB A.J. Miller
	LB Darren MacDonald
	LB Ron Walters / Brian Reeves
	DB Adrian Jones
	DB Pat Ray
	DB Charles Murphy / Sharron Washington
	DB Otis Smith / Harry Colon/ Darrell Bryant

RUSHING: Stowers 143/667y, Jones 85/463y, Elmore 80/410y
PASSING: Welch 23-53/524y, 1TD, 43.4% Fitzmaurice 35-79/425y, 3TD, 44.3%
RECEIVING: Bruton 26/447y, Lammers 16/226y, Cameron 13/173y
SCORING: Jeff Jacke (K) 50pts, Elmore 48pts, Jones 42pts

1989 2-9

14 TCU	10 WR Linzy Collins
7 Indiana	24 WR Damon Mays
7 Miami	38 T Don Wright / Rick Trumball
3 Arizona State	19 G Pete Scott
3 Colorado	49 C Brad Funk
7 Nebraska	50 G Jay Greenwood
21 Kansas State	9 T Andy Lock / Ken Christensen
30 Oklahoma State	31 TE Tim Bruton / Larry Linthacum
14 Oklahoma	52 QB Kent Kiefer
21 Iowa State	35 HB Michael Jones / Jim White
44 Kansas	46 FB Tommie Stowers
	DL Kevin White
	DL Mario Johnson / Chris Russell
	DL Lee Johnson
	LB Stacy Elliott / A.J. Miller
	LB Darren MacDonald
	LB Andy Titone / Tom Reiner
	LB Mike Ringgenberg
	DB Adrian Jones / Brad Scrivner
	DB Otis Smith / Cordell McKinney
	DB Leon Fisher / Sharron Washington
	DB Ted LePage

RUSHING: Stowers 142/547y, Jones 87/343y, White 36/125y
PASSING: Kiefer 183-314/2314y, 12TD, 58.3%
RECEIVING: Collins 46/803y, Stowers 28/268y, Bruton 27/305y
SCORING: Stowers 36pts, Jones & Dan Baker (K) 30pts

1990 4-7

19 TCU	20 WR Linzy Collins
45 Utah State	10 WR Damon Mays
7 Indiana	58 T Rick Trumball
30 Arizona State	9 G Mike Bedosky
31 Colorado	33 C Brad Funk / Doug Hembrough
21 Nebraska	69 G Don Wright
31 Kansas State	10 T Russ McCullough
28 Oklahoma State	48 TE Tim Bruton
10 Oklahoma	55 QB Kent Kiefer
25 Iowa State	27 HB Sean Moore / Ronnell Kayhill
31 Kansas	21 FB Mike Jones
	DL Rick Lyle
	DL Mario Johnson
	DL George Hunt
	DL Rob Harper
	LB Mike Ringgenberg
	LB Tom Reiner
	LB Jerold Fletcher
	DB Sharron Washington
	DB Maurice Benson
	DB Niu Sale / Jermaine Wilkins
	DB Harry Colon

RUSHING: Jones 100/485y, Kayhill 94/391y, Moore 74/237y
PASSING: Kiefer 165-275/2183y, 11TD, 60%
RECEIVING: Collins 56/957y, Jones 41/405y, Bruton 31/360y
SCORING: Jones 60pts, Jeff Jacke (K) 53pts, Kayhill 48pts

1991 3-7-1

23 Illinois	19 WR Byron Chamberlain / Kenny Holly
21 Baylor	47 WR Victor Bailey / Kenneth Dunn
22 Indiana	27 T Doug Hembrough (C)
31 Memphis State	21 G Mike Bedosky
7 Colorado	55 C Brad Funk / Tim Alvarado (T)
6 Nebraska	7 G Don Wright
22 Iowa State	63 T Russ McCullough
16 Oklahoma	23 TE A.J. Ofodile
0 Kansas State	56 QB Phil Johnson
29 Kansas	32 TB Ronnell Kayhill / Joe Freeman
	53 FB/WR Mike Washington / Skip Leach
	DL Rick Lyle / Jon Watkins
	DL Mario Johnson
	DL George Hunt
	DL Stacy Elliott / Tim Burke
	LB Kent Gardner / Jermaine Wilkins
	LB Darryl Major / Will Bass
	LB Tom Reiner / Travis McDonald
	DB Maurice Benson / Javan Lenhardt
	DB Jason Oliver
	DB Sharron Washington
	DB Brad Scrivner

RUSHING: Washington 101/420y, Freeman 54/267y, Kayhill 69/186y
PASSING: Johnson 167-311/2029y, 14TD, 53.7%
RECEIVING: Chamberlain 39/464y, Kayhill 32/299y, Holly 31/399y
SCORING: Jeff Jacke (K) 50pts, Kayhill 42pts, Chamberlain & Bailey 24pts

1992 3-8

17 Illinois	24 WR Victor Bailey
13 Texas A&M	26 WR Kenny Holly
10 Indiana	20 T Coby Crowl
44 Marshall	21 G Bob Petrus
0 Colorado	6 C Doug Hembrough
26 Oklahoma State	28 G Mike Bedosky
24 Nebraska	34 T Gene Snisky
14 Iowa State	28 TE Kent Gardner / A.J. Ofodile
17 Oklahoma	51 QB Phil Johnson / Jeff Handy
27 Kansas State	14 TB Joe Freeman / Ryan Lyons
22 Kansas	17 FB Ronnell Kayhill / Mike Schlef
	DL Stacy Elliott
	DL Steve Martin / Quentin Hayden
	DL George Hunt / Jon Watkins
	DL Rick Lyle
	LB Mike Ringgenberg / Darryl Major
	LB Travis McDonald
	LB/DB Andre White / Jermaine Wilkins
	DB Kevin McIntosh
	DB Jason Oliver
	DB Jerome Madison / Montana Waggoner
	DB Maurice Benson

RUSHING: Freeman 98/360y, Kayhill 94/328y, Lyons 43/151y
PASSING: Handy 196-329/2463y, 13TD, 59.6%
RECEIVING: Bailey 75/1210y, Holly 60/663y, Kayhill 41/395y
SCORING: Jeff Jacke 70pts, Bailey 36pts, Freeman & Kayhill 30pts

1993 3-7-1

31 Illinois	3 WR Jeff Holly
0 Texas A&M	73 WR Brian Sallee
3 West Virginia	35 T Tim Alvarado
10 SMU	10 G Matt Pearce
18 Colorado	30 C Matt Burgess
42 Oklahoma State	9 G Mike Bedosky
7 Nebraska	49 T Trey O'Neil
37 Iowa State	34 TE A.J. Ofodile
23 Oklahoma	42 QB Jeff Handy
21 Kansas State	31 TB Joe Freeman
0 Kansas	28 FB Mike Washington / Antwan Johnson
	DL Damon Simon / Marc Pedrotti
	DL Steve Martin / Earl Brooks
	DL Matt Murray / George Hunt
	DL Rick Lyle
	LB Darryl Major
	LB Travis McDonald
	LB Detrick Wells
	DB Kevin McIntosh
	DB Jason Oliver / Javan Lenhardt
	DB Andre White / Bo Adams
	DB Jerome Madison / Montana Waggoner

RUSHING: Freeman 136/675y, Washington 82/407y
PASSING: Handy 174-291/1901y, 12TD, 59.8%
RECEIVING: Holly 58/623y, Sallee 34/406y
SCORING: Kyle Pooler (K) 38pts

1994 3-8-1

17 Tulsa	20 WR Brian Sallee
0 Illinois	42 WR Rahsetnu Jenkins / Frank Jones
16 Houston	0 T Trey O'Neil
10 West Virginia	34 G Mike Morris / Matt Dowil
23 Colorado	38 C Russ Appel
24 Oklahoma State	15 G Rafe Parsons / Chris Barrows
7 Nebraska	42 T Chris Buck / Tim Keith
34 Iowa State	20 TE Bill Lingerfelt / Lamont Frazier
13 Oklahoma	30 QB Jeff Handy
18 Kansas State	21 TB Joe Freeman / Brock Olivo
14 Kansas	31 FB Mike Washington / Ron Janes
32 Hawaii	32 DL Marc Pedrotti
	DL Steve Martin
	DL Jon Sanft / Matt Murray
	DL Damon Simon / Jon Safley
	LB Chris Singletary / Kay Blake
	LB Darryl Major (DL) / Darryl Chatman
	LB Travis McDonald
	DB Kevin McIntosh
	DB Clayton Baker / Derrick Miller
	DB DeMontie Cross / Jerome Madison
	DB Andre White / Bo Adams

RUSHING: Olivo 142/614y, Freeman 129/509y, Washington 46/151y
PASSING: Handy 200-349/2030y, 12TD, 57.3%
RECEIVING: Sallee 58/616y, Jenkins 40/482y, Frazier 34/301y
SCORING: Kyle Pooler (K) 48pts, Olivo 36pts, Jones 20pts

1995 3-8

17 North Texas	20 WR Eddie Brooks / Jay Murchison
10 Bowling Green	17 WR Lou Shepherd / Martez Young
14 Texas Tech	41 T Travis Biebel
31 NE Louisiana	22 G Mike Morris
0 Kansas State	30 C Russ Appel / Chris Barrows (G)
0 Nebraska	57 G Cliff Smith
26 Oklahoma State	30 T Chris Buck
9 Oklahoma	13 TE Bill Lingerfelt / Jake Steuve
23 Kansas	42 QB Corby Jones / Brandon Corso
0 Colorado	21 TB Brock Olivo
45 Iowa State	31 FB Ernest Blackwell / Antwan Johnson
	DL Brian Cracraft / Justin Wyatt
	DL Jon Sanft / Tim Mittelstadt
	DL Steve Martin
	DL Pat Ivey
	LB Kay Blake
	LB Darryl Chatman
	LB Joe Love
	DB Shad Criss
	DB Clayton Baker / Derrick Miller
	DB DeMontie Cross
	DB Bo Adams

RUSHING: Olivo 232/985y, Jones 78/368y, Blackwell 33/220y
PASSING: Corso 59-136/623y, 3TD, 43.4%
RECEIVING: Olivo 17/101y, Lingerfelt 13/202y, Brooks 13/116y
SCORING: Mark Norris (K) 41pts, Olivo 38pts, Jones 24pts

1996 5-6

10 Texas	40 WR Eddie Brooks / Ricky Ross
16 Memphis	19 WR Rahsetnu Jenkins
38 Clemson	24 T Travis Biebel / Craig Heimburger
31 Iowa State	45 G Mike Morris
27 SMU	26 C Russ Appel (G) / Steve Haag
10 Kansas State	35 G Rob Riti / Cliff Smith
35 Oklahoma State	28 T Todd Neimeyer
13 Colorado	41 TE Bill Lingerfelt / Jake Steuve
7 Nebraska	51 QB Corby Jones / Kent Skornia
49 Baylor	42 TB Brock Olivo / Devin West
42 Kansas	25 FB Ron Janes
	DL Eric Douglas / Jeff Marriott
	DL Donnell Jones / David Rowe
	DL Brian Cracraft
	DL Justin Wyatt
	LB Kevin Ford / Sam Josue
	LB Darryl Chatman / Al Sterling
	LB Joe Love / Barry Odom
	DB Shad Criss / Randy Potter
	DB Clayton Baker
	DB DeMontie Cross / Harold Piersey
	DB Caldrinoff Easter

RUSHING: Olivo 157/749y, Jones 130/742y, West 116/649y
PASSING: Skornia 61-118/701y, 5TD, 51.7%
Jones 54-105/624y, 5TD, 51.4%
RECEIVING: Jenkins 29/419y, Olivo 22/165y, Brooks 17/236y
SCORING: Mark Norris (K) 58pts, Jones 54pts, Olivo 42pts

1997 7-5

44 E. Michigan	24 WR Jay Murchison
7 Kansas	15 WR Kent Layman / Torey Coleman
42 Tulsa	21 T Travis Biebel
10 Ohio State	31 G Mike Morris
45 Iowa State	21 C Rob Riti
11 Kansas State	41 G Cliff Smith / Craig Heimburger
37 Texas	29 T Todd Neimeyer
51 Oklahoma State	50 TE Eddie Brooks / Jake Steuve
41 Colorado	31 QB Corby Jones
38 Nebraska	45 TB Brock Olivo
42 Baylor	24 FB Ron Janes / Ernest Blackwell
	DL Brian Cracraft / Steve Erickson
	DL Justin Wyatt
	DL Donnell Jones
	DL Marquis Gibson
	LB Sam Josue / Al Sterling
	LB Kevin Ford
	LB Barry Odom
	DB Shad Criss
	DB Carlos Posey / Wade Perkins
	DB Harold Piersey
	DB Caldrinoff Easter

RUSHING: Jones 188/887y, Olivo 155/678y, Blackwell 72/551y
PASSING: Jones 102-191/1658y, 12TD, 53.4%
RECEIVING: Brooks 24/311y, Layman 21/534y, Coleman 14/233y
SCORING: Jones 84pts, Scott Knickman 76pts, Olivo 72pts

1998 8-4

37 Bowling Green	0 WR Kareem Wise / John Dausman
41 Kansas	23 WR Kent Layman
14 Ohio State	35 T Chris Meredith / Aaron Crittendon
35 Northwestern St.	14 G Cliff Smith / Jeff Hellerstedt
35 Iowa State	19 C Rob Riti
20 Oklahoma	6 G Craig Heimburger
13 Nebraska	20 T Todd Neimeyer
28 Texas Tech	26 TE Jake Steuve / Dwayne Blakley
38 Colorado	14 QB Corby Jones
14 Texas A&M	17 TB Devin West
25 Kansas State	31 FB Rob West / Sean Benton
34 West Virginia ■	31 DL Justin Smith
	DL Justin Wyatt
	DL Jeff Marriott / Pat Mingucci
	DL Steve Erickson
	LB Marquis Gibson
	LB Al Sterling / Damonte Robinson
	LB Barry Odom
	DB Carlos Posey
	DB Wade Perkins / Julian Jones
	DB Harold Piersey
	DB Caldrinoff Easter

RUSHING: West 283/1578y, Jones 168/536y, West 32/165y
PASSING: Jones 87-178/1281y, 9TD, 48.9%
RECEIVING: Layman 26/495y, Dausman 18/364y, Wise 9/143y
SCORING: West 108pts, Jones 66pts, Tim Geiger (K) 23pts

1999 4-7

28 UAB	28 WR Kent Layman / Travis Garvin
48 W. Michigan	34 WR Kareem Wise
10 Nebraska	40 T Aaron Crittendon
27 Memphis	17 G Mike Hayes
39 Colorado	46 C Rob Riti
21 Iowa State	24 G Joe Glauberman
0 Kansas	21 T Justin Bland
34 Texas Tech	7 TE Dwayne Blakley / Brandon Ford
0 Oklahoma	37 QB Jim Dougherty / Kirk Farmer
14 Texas A&M	51 TB DeVaughn Black / Zain Gilmore
0 Kansas State	66 FB Joseph Chirumbolo
	DL Pat Mingucci / Cedric Harden
	DL Jeff Marriott
	DL Steve Erickson
	DL Justin Smith
	LB Danny McCamy / Pat Duffy
	LB Jamonte Robinson / Sean Doyle
	LB Barry Odom
	DB Andre Roberson / Terrence Curry
	DB Carlos Posey / Larry Hollinquest
	DB Julian Jones
	DB Clarence Jones

RUSHING: Gilmore 188/764y, Black 169/740y
PASSING: Dougherty 109-219/1304y, 4TD, 49.8%
RECEIVING: Garvin 36/608y, Wise 29/316y, Spencer 28/265y
SCORING: Brad Hammerich (K) 52pts, Blakley & Gilmore 36pts

2000 3-8

50 Western Illinois	20 WR Justin Gage
9 Clemson	62 WR Eric Spencer
10 Michigan State	13 WR John Dausman/Tay Jackson/T. Curry
24 Nebraska	42 T Aaron Crittendon / Joe Glauberman (G)
24 Oklahoma State	10 G Adrian Cole / Rob Droege
17 Kansas	38 C A.J. Ricker
12 Texas	46 G Mike Hayes
20 Iowa State	39 T Justin Bland
18 Colorado	28 TE Dwayne Blakley
47 Baylor	22 QB Darius Outlaw / Kirk Farmer
24 Kansas State	28 TB Zain Gilmore / Zack Abron
	DL Danny McCamy / Michael Gavins
	DL Pat Mingucci
	DL Cedric Harden
	DL Justin Smith
	LB Pat Duffy / David Monroe
	LB Jamonte Robinson / Daryl Whittington
	LB Sean Doyle / Duke Revard
	DB Antoine Duncan / Larry Hollinquest
	DB Julian Jones
	DB Clarence Jones
	DB Gary Anthony / Marcus Caldwell

RUSHING: Gilmore 139/632y, Abron 140/502y, Outlaw 110/259y
PASSING: Outlaw105-225/1391y, 9TD, 46.7%
Farmer 50-102/669y, 3TD, 49%
RECEIVING: Gage 44/709y, Spencer 35/493y, Blakley 18/211y
SCORING: Gilmore 42pts, Brad Hammerich (K) 36pts, Abron & Outlaw 30pts

2001 4-7

13 Bowling Green	20 WR Justin Gage
40 SW Texas	6 WR Thomson Omboga / Marcus James
3 Nebraska	36 T Aaron Crittendon
41 Oklahoma State	38 G Adrian Cole / Rob Droege
14 Iowa State	20 C A.J. Ricker
38 Kansas	34 G Mike Hayes
16 Texas	35 T Justin Bland
24 Colorado	38 TE Dwayne Blakley
41 Baylor	24 QB Kirk Farmer / Darius Outlaw
3 Kansas State	24 TB Zack Abron / Zain Gilmore
7 Michigan State	55 RB/WR Joe Chirumbolo / Tay Jackson
	DL Antwaun Bynum / Nick Tarpoff
	DL Keith Wright
	DL Cedric Harden / Chris Ryan
	DL Dan Davis
	LB Sean Doyle
	LB Jamonte Robinson / James Kinney
	DB Antoine Duncan
	DB R.J. Jones / Michael Harden
	DB Clarence Jones
	DB Tauras Ferguson
	DB Gary Anthony / Kevin Johnson

RUSHING: Abron 157/783y, Farmer 59/379y, Gilmore 90/347y
PASSING: Farmer 135-285/1567y, 13TD, 47.4%
RECEIVING: Gage 74/920y, Blakley 34/362y, Omboga 15/158y
SCORING: Brad Hammerich (K) 56pts, Gage 32pts, Abron 30pts

2002 5-7

33 Illinois
41 Ball State
28 Bowling Green
44 Troy State
24 Oklahoma
13 Nebraska
38 Texas Tech
36 Kansas
35 Iowa State
35 Colorado
33 Texas A&M
0 Kansas State

20 WR Justin Gage
6 WR Darius Outlaw / Thomson Omboga
51 WR Marcus James / Sean Coffey
7 T Rob Droege
31 G Tony Palmer
24 C A.J. Ricker
52 G Cliff Young / Joe Gianino
12 T Scott Paffrath
42 TE Ben Fredrickson / J.D. McCoy
42 QB Brad Smith
27 TB Zack Abron / T.J. Leon
38 DL Antwaun Bynum / Nick Tarpoff
DL Russ Bell / C.J. Mosley
DL Keith Wright
DL Atiyyah Ellison / Terrell Mills
LB Sean Doyle
LB James Kinney
DB Antoine Duncan / R.J. Jones
DB Michael Harden / A.J. Kincade
DB Marcus King / Brandon Barnes
DB Jason Simpson / Gary Anthony
DB Tauras Ferguson

RUSHING: Smith 193/1029y, Abron 176/758y, Leon 62/285y
PASSING: Smith 196-366/2333y, 15TD, 53.6%
RECEIVING: Gage 82/1075y, Outlaw 46/552y, Omboga 21/253y
SCORING: Abron 102pts, Mike Matheny (K) 67pts, Gage 54pts

2003 8-5

22 Illinois
35 Ball State
37 E. Illinois
41 M. Tennessee
14 Kansas
41 Nebraska
13 Oklahoma
62 Texas Tech
16 Colorado
45 Texas A&M
14 Kansas State
45 Iowa State
14 Arkansas■

15 WR Sean Coffey
7 WR Thomson Omboga
0 WR Darius Outlaw
40 T Rob Droege
35 G Tony Palmer / Joe Gianino
24 C A. J. Ricker
34 G Cliff Young
31 T Steven Sanchez / Scott Paffrath
21 TE J. D. McCoy / Victor Sesay
22 QB Brad Smith
24 TB Zack Abron
7 DL Brian Smith / Xzavie Jackson
27 DL C. J. Mosley
DL Atiyyah Ellison / Russ Bell
DL Zach Ville
LB Brandon Barnes / Henry Sweat
LB James Kinney
DB Calvin Washington / Terrence Curry
DB Michael Harden / A.J. Kincade
DB Nino Williams
DB Jason Simpson / David Overstreet
DB Dedrick Harrington / Quincy Wade

RUSHING: Smith 212/1406y, Abron 219/1155y,
Damien Nash (TB) 89/462y
PASSING: Smith 211-350/1977y, 11TD, 60.3%
RECEIVING: Omboga 52/466y, Outlaw 41/417y, Coffey 27/341y
SCORING: Smith 118pts, Abron 84pts, Mike Matheny (K) 74pts

2004 5-6

52 Arkansas State
14 Troy State
48 Ball State
17 Colorado
30 Baylor
20 Texas
17 Oklahoma State
3 Nebraska
24 Kansas State
14 Kansas
17 Iowa State

20 WR Brad Ekwerekwu
24 WR Sean Coffey
0 WR/TE Thomson Omboga / Victor Sesay
9 T Tony Clinker / Tyler Luellen
10 G Tony Palmer
28 C Adam Spieker
20 G Joe Gianino
24 T Scott Paffrath
35 TE Martin Rucker
31 QB Brad Smith
14 TB Damien Nash / Marcus Woods
DL Xzavie Jackson
DL Atiyah Ellison
DL C.J. Mosley
DL Zach Ville
LB Henry Sweat / Marcus Bacon
LB James Kinney
LB David Richard / Dedrick Harrington
DB Marcus King / A.J. Kincade
DB Shirdonya Mitchell
DB Jason Simpson / David Overstreet
DB Nino Williams

RUSHING: Nash 164/792y, Smith 165/553y, Woods 101/428y
PASSING: Smith 191-369/2185y, 17TD, 51.8%
RECEIVING: Coffey 39/648y, Omboga 39/392y, Sesay 31/314y
SCORING: Coffey60pts, Joe Tantarelli (K) 57pts, Nash 50pts

2005 7-5

44 Arkansas State
35 New Mexico
52 Troy
20 Texas
38 Oklahoma State
27 Iowa State
41 Nebraska
3 Kansas
12 Colorado
31 Baylor
28 Kansas State
38 South Carolina■

17 WR Sean Coffey / Tommy Saunders
45 WR Brad Ekwerekwu
21 WR Will Franklin
51 T Tyler Luellen
31 G Tony Palmer
24 C Adam Spieker
24 G Mike Cook
13 T Joel Clinger
41 TE Martin Rucker / Chase Coffman
16 QB Brad Smith
36 RB Marcus Woods / Tony Temple
31 DL Brian Smith
DL Lorenzo Williams
DL Jamar Smith
DL Stryker Sulak / Xzavie Jackson
LB Derrick Ming / Brock Christopher
LB Dedrick Harrington
LB Marcus Bacon
DB Marcus King / William Moore
DB A. J. Kincade
DB Jason Simpson/Domono Johnson
DB David Overstreet

RUSHING: Smith 229/1301y, Temple 81/437y, Woods 93/435y
PASSING: Smith 237-399/2304y, 13TD, 59.4%
RECEIVING: Rucker 47/567y, Coffman 47/503y, Coffey 40/448y
SCORING: Smith 100pts, Adam Crossett (K)
81pts, Ekwerekwu & Woods 30pts

2006 8-5

47 Murray State
34 Mississippi
27 New Mexico
31 Ohio
28 Colorado
38 Texas Tech
19 Texas A&M
41 Kansas State
10 Oklahoma
20 Nebraska
16 Iowa State
42 Kansas
38 Oregon State■

7 WR Tommy Saunders
7 WR Will Franklin / Jared Perry
17 WR/TE Brad Ekwerekwu/C. Coffman
6 T Tyler Luellen
13 G Ryan Madison / Monte Wyrick
21 C Adam Spieker
25 G Mike Cook
21 T Joel Clinger
26 TE Martin Rucker
34 QB Chase Daniel
21 RB Tony Temple
17 DL Brian Smith / Stryker Sulak
39 DL Lorenzo Williams / Jamar Smith
DL Ziggy Hood / DeMarcus Scott
DL Xzavie Jackson
LB Brock Christopher
LB Dedrick Harrington
LB Marcus Bacon
DB Darnell Terrell
DB David Overstreet/Cornelius Brown
DB Brandon Massey / William Moore

RUSHING: Temple 193/1063y, Daniel 147/379y,
Jimmy Jackson (RB) 32/123y
PASSING: Daniel 287-452/3527y, 28TD, 63.5%
RECEIVING: Coffman 58/638y, Rucker 53/511y, Franklin 48/829y
SCORING: Jeff Wolfert (K) 99pts, Coffman 54pts, Temple 42pts

2007 12-2

40 Illinois
38 Mississippi
52 W. Michigan
38 Illinois State
41 Nebraska
31 Oklahoma
41 Texas Tech
42 Iowa State
55 Colorado
40 Texas A&M
49 Kansas State
36 Kansas
17 Oklahoma□
38 Arkansas■

34 WR William Franklin
25 WR Jeremy Maclin / Danario Alexander
24 WR Tommy Saunders
17 T Tyler Luellen
6 G Ryan Madison / Monte Myrick
41 C Adam Spieker
10 G Kurtis Gregory
28 T Colin Brown
10 TE Martin Rucker / Chase Coffman
26 QB Chase Daniel
32 RB Tony Temple / Jimmy Jackson
29 DL Tommy Chavis
38 DL Ziggy Hood
7 DL Loren Williams
DL Stryker Sulak
LB Brock Christopher / Luke Lambert
LB Sean Weatherspoon
LB/DB Van Alexander / Del Howard
DB Carl Gettis
DB Darnell Terrell / Hardy Ricks
DB William Moore / Castin Bridges
DB Justin Garrett / Cornelius Brown

RUSHING: Temple 186/1039y, Maclin 51/375y, Jackson 67/331y
PASSING: Daniel 384-563/4306y, 33TD, 68.2%
RECEIVING: Rucker 84/834y, Maclin 80/1055y, Coffman 52/531y
SCORING: Jeff Wolfert (K) 130pts, Maclin 96pts, Temple 78pts

2008 10-4

52 Illinois
52 SE Missouri
69 Nevada
42 Buffalo
52 Nebraska
23 Oklahoma State
31 Texas
53 Colorado
31 Baylor
41 Kansas State
52 Iowa State
37 Kansas
21 Oklahoma□
30 Northwestern■

42 WR Jared Perry
3 WR Jeremy Maclin
17 WR Tommy Saunders
21 T Elvis Fisher
17 G Ryan Madison
28 C Tim Barnes
56 G Kurtis Gregory
0 T Colin Brown
28 TE Chase Coffman / Andrew Jones
24 QB Chase Daniel
20 RB Derrick Washington
40 DL Tommy Chavis / Jacquies Smith
62 DL Ziggy Hood
23 DL Jaron Baston
DL Stryker Sulak
LB Sean Witherspoon
LB Brock Christopher
LB/DB Luke Lambert / Kenji Jackson
DB Castin Bridges / Tru Vaughns
DB Carl Gettis
DB William Moore
DB Justin Garrett

RUSHING: Washington 177/1036y, Maclin 40/293y,
Daniel 69/281y
PASSING: Daniel 385-528/4335y, 39TD, 72.9%
RECEIVING: Maclin 102/1260y, Coffman 90/987y,
Saunders 72/873y
SCORING: Jeff Wolfert (K) 133pts, Washington 114pts
Maclin 102pts

2009 8-5

37 Illinois
27 Bowling Green
52 Furman
31 Nevada
12 Nebraska
17 Oklahoma State
7 Texas
36 Colorado
32 Baylor
38 Kansas State
34 Iowa State
41 Kansas
13 Navy■

9 WR Jared Perry / Brandon Gerau
20 WR Danario Alexander
12 WR Wes Kemp
21 T Elvis Fisher
27 G Austin Wuebbels
33 C Tim Barnes
41 G Kurtis Gregory
17 T Dan Hoch
40 TE/WR Andrew Jones / Jerrel Jackson
12 QB Blaine Gabbert
24 TB Derrick Washington / De'Vion Moore
39 DL Brian Coulter / Jacquies Smith
35 DL Dominique Hamilton / Terrell Resonno
DL Jaron Baston
DL Aldon Smith
LB Sean Weatherspoon
LB Will Ebner / Luke Lambert
LB Andrew Gachkar / Zaviar Gooden
DB Carl Gettis
DB Kevin Rutland / Kip Edwards
DB Jarrell Harrison / Kenji Jackson
DB Jasper Simmons

RUSHING: Washington 190/865y, Moore 63/258y,
Kendial Lawrence (TB) 52/219y
PASSING: Gabbert 262-445/3593y, 24TD, 58.9%
RECEIVING: Alexander 113/1781y, Perry 46/696y,
J. Jackson 37/458y, Kemp 23/418y
SCORING: Grant Ressel (K) 117pts, Alexander 84pts,
Washington 60pts

2010 10-3

23 Illinois
50 McNeese State
27 San Diego State
51 Miami (OH)
26 Colorado
30 Texas A&M
36 Oklahoma
17 Nebraska
17 Texas Tech
38 Kansas State
14 Iowa State
35 Kansas
24 Iowa■

13 WR Jerrel Jackson / Rolandis Woodland
6 WR Wes Kemp
24 WR T.J. Moe
13 T Elvis Fisher
0 G Jayson Palmgren / Travis Ruth (C)
9 C Tim Barnes
27 G Austin Wuebbels
31 T Dan Hoch / Jack Meiner (TE)
24 TE Michael Egnew
28 QB Blaine Gabbert
0 TB De'Vion Moore / Henry Josey
7 DL Jacquies Smith / Michael Sam
27 DL Terrel Resonno
DL Dominique Hamilton / Jimmy Burge
DL Aldon Smith / Brad Madison
LB Zaviar Gooden
LB Will Ebner / Andrew Wilson
LB Andrew Gachkar
DB Carl Gettis / Kip Edwards
DB Kevin Rutland / E.J. Gaines
DB Jarrell Harrison / Jasper Simmons
DB Kenji Jackson

RUSHING: Moore 99/517y, Josey 76/437y
Kendial Lawrence (TB) 73/422y
PASSING: Gabbert 301-475/3186y, 16TD, 63.4%
RECEIVING: Moe 92/1045y, Egnew 90/762y, Jackson 50/656y,
Kemp 39/420y
SCORING: Grant Ressel (K) 96pts, Moore 48pts, Moe 42pts

NEBRASKA

University of Nebraska (Founded 1869)
Lincoln, Nebraska
Nickname: Cornhuskers
Colors: Scarlet & Cream
Stadium: Memorial (1923) 81,067
Affiliation: Big Six (1928-47), Big Seven (1948-59), Big Eight (1960-95), Big Twelve North (1996-2010), Big Ten (2011-present)

CAREER RUSHING YARDS	Attempts	Yards
Mike Rozier (1981-83)	668	4780
Ahman Green (1995-97)	574	3880
Eric Crouch (1998-2001)	648	3434
Roy Helu, Jr. (2007-10)	578	3404
Calvin Jones (1991-93)	461	3153
Ken Clark (1987-89)	494	3037
I.M. Hipp (1977-79)	495	2814
Lawrence Phillips (1993-95)	449	2777
Dahrran Diedrick (1999-2002)	502	2745
Cory Ross (2002-05)	597	2743

CAREER PASSING YARDS	Comp.-Att.	Yards
Zac Taylor (2005-06)	470-821	5850
Joe Ganz (2006-08)	381-585	5125
Dave Humm (1972-74)	353-637	5035
Jerry Tagge (1969-71)	348-581	4704
Eric Crouch (1998-2001)	312-606	4481
Tommie Frazier (1992-95)	232-469	3521
Turner Gill (1980-83)	231-428	3317
Vince Ferragamo (1975-76)	224-389	3224
Jammal Lord (2000-03)	193-404	2848
Steve Taylor (1985-88)	184-404	2815

CAREER RECEIVING YARDS	Catches	Yards
Johnny Rodgers (1970-72)	143	2479
Nate Swift (2005-08)	166	2476
Terrence Nunn (2004-07)	136	1762
Todd Peterson (2005-08)	108	1602
Niles Paul (2007-10)	103	1532
Matt Davison (1997-2000)	93	1456
Maurice Purify (2006-07)	91	1444
Marlon Lucky (2005-08)	135	1379
Matt Herian (2002-06)	65	1243
Irving Fryar (1981-83)	67	1196

SEASON RUSHING YARDS	Attempts	Yards
Mike Rozier (1983)	275	2148
Ahman Green (1997)	278	1877
Lawrence Phillips (1994)	286	1722
Mike Rozier (1982)	242	1689
Ken Clark (1988)	232	1497

SEASON PASSING YARDS	Comp.-Atts.	Yards
Joe Ganz (2008)	285-420	3568
Zac Taylor (2006)	233-391	3197
Zac Taylor (2005)	237-430	2653
Sam Keller (2007)	205-325	2422
Zac Lee (2009)	177-302	2143

SEASON RECEIVING YARDS	Catches	Yards
Johnny Rodgers (1972)	55	942
Nate Swift (2008)	63	941
Johnny Rodgers (1971)	53	872
Maurice Purify (2007)	57	814
Niles Paul (2009)	40	796

GAME RUSHING YARDS	Attempts	Yards
Roy Helu, Jr. (2010 vs. Missouri)	28	307
Calvin Jones (1991 vs. Kansas)	27	294
Mike Rozier (1983 vs. Kansas)	31	285

GAME PASSING YARDS	Comp.-Atts.	Yards
Joe Ganz (2007 vs. Kansas State)	30-40	510
Joe Ganz (2007 vs. Colorado)	31-58	484
Sam Keller (2007 vs. Ball State)	29-37	438

GAME RECEIVING YARDS	Catches	Yards
Matt Davison (1998 vs. Texas A&M)	10	167
Chuck Malito (1976 vs. Hawaii)	4	166
Guy Ingles (1969 vs. Oklahoma State)	5	163

GREATEST COACH:

There is no denying that Bob Devaney brought Nebraska out of the football wilderness in the 1960s and won the school's first national title in 1970 and went back-to-back by repeating in 1971.

But, Devaney's hand-picked successor, Dr. Tom Osborne, won two-and-a-half times more games than his mentor and established himself as one of the all-time great coaches during 25 years in the head coach's chair.

Osborne also went back-to-back on his long-awaited national championships, winning it in 1994 and '95. Only a couple of poor officiating calls cost Osborne's Huskers a win in the Orange Bowl after the 1993 season, or he would have been the only coach to ever have won three straight titles. Osborne retired to enter politics after the 1997 season, but returned as athletic director during a desperate year in 2007.

Osborne enjoyed a 255-49-3 record, and at the time of his retirement, he was sixth all-time in Division 1-A victories. Nebraska earned a spectacular 60-3 record in Osborne's last five years.

NEBRASKA'S 55 GREATEST SINCE 1953

OFFENSE

WIDE RECEIVER: Matt Davison, Irving Fryar, Maurice Purify, Johnny Rodgers
TIGHT END: Junior Miller
TACKLE: Kelvin Clark, Chris Dishman, Bob Newton, Zach Wiegert
GUARD: Bob Brown, Will Shields, Dean Steinkuhler, Brenden Stai, Aaron Taylor
CENTER: Rik Bonness, Dave Rimington
QUARTERBACK: Eric Crouch, Tommie Frazier, Joe Ganz, Turner Gill
RUNNING BACK: Ahman Green, Calvin Jones, Jeff Kinney, Jarvis Redwine, Mike Rozier
FULLBACK: Tom Rathman, Cory Schlesinger

DEFENSE

END: Adam Carriker, Willie Harper, Jimmy Williams, Grant Wistrom
TACKLE: John Dutton, Larry Jacobson, Neil Smith, Ndamukong Suh
NOSE GUARD: Rich Glover, Wayne Mehlan, Danny Noonan
LINEBACKER: Trev Alberts, Mike Knox, Marc Munford, Broderick Thomas
CORNER BACK: Ralph Brown, Keyuo Craver, Wonder Monds
SAFETY: Josh Bullocks, Mike Brown, Bret Clark, Mike Minter

SPECIAL TEAMS

RETURN SPECIALISTS: DeJuan Groce, Josh Davis
PLACE KICKER: Kris Brown
PUNTER: Kyle Larson

MULTIPLE POSITIONS

HALFBACK-QUARTERBACK-DEFENSIVE BACK: Pat Fischer

TWO-WAY PLAYER

HALFBACK-CORNERBACK: Kent McCloughan

PERFORMANCE FORMULA:
NEBRASKA'S 10 BEST SEASONS

1995	1.9434	1 of 70
1971	1.9154	1 of 70
1997	1.8146	1 of 70
1994	1.7935	2 of 71
1983	1.7712	1 of 70
1982	1.7474	2 of 70
1999	1.7193	2 of 71
1996	1.6975	5 of 70
1970	1.6889	3 of 70
1980	1.6798	4 of 70

NEBRASKA CORNHUSKERS

Year	W-L-T	AP Poll	Conference Standing	Toughest Regular Season Opponents	Coach (Record at School)	Bowl Games		
1953	3-6-1		4t	Illinois 7-1-1, Kansas State 6-3-1, Oklahoma 8-1-1	Bill Glassford			
1954	6-5		2	Minnesota 7-2, Colorado 7-2-1, Oklahoma 10-0	Bill Glassford	Orange	7 Duke	34
1955	5-5		2	Ohio State 7-2, Texas A&M 7-2-1, Pittsburgh 7-3, Oklahoma 10-0	Bill Glassford (31-35-3)			
1956	4-6		4	Ohio State 6-3, Colorado 7-2-1, Baylor 8-2, Oklahoma 10-0	Pete Elliott (4-6)			
1957	1-9		7	Washington State 6-4, Army 7-2, Oklahoma 9-1	Bill Jennings			
1958	3-7		6	Penn State 6-3-1, Purdue 6-1-2, Syracuse 8-1, Oklahoma 9-1	Bill Jennings			
1959	4-6		6	Texas 9-1, Oklahoma 7-3, Iowa State 7-3	Bill Jennings			
1960	4-6		6t	Texas 7-3, Minnesota 8-1, Iowa State 7-3, Army 6-3-1, Missouri 9-1	Bill Jennings			
1961	3-6-1		5t	Syracuse 7-3, Missouri 7-2-1, Kansas 6-3-1, Colorado 9-1	Bill Jennings (15-34-1)			
1962	9-2		3	Missouri 7-1-2, Kansas 6-3-1, Oklahoma 8-2	Bob Devaney	Gotham	36 Miami	34
1963	10-1	5	1	Air Force 7-3, Missouri 7-3, Oklahoma 8-2	Bob Devaney	Orange	13 Auburn	7
1964	9-2	6	1	Missouri 6-3-1, Kansas 6-4, Oklahoma 6-3-1	Bob Devaney	Cotton	7 Arkansas	10
1965	10-1	5	1	TCU 6-4, Colorado 6-2-2, Missouri 7-2-1	Bob Devaney	Orange	28 Alabama	39
1966	9-2	6	1	Colorado 7-3, Missouri 6-3-1, Oklahoma 6-4	Bob Devaney	Sugar	7 Alabama	34
1967	6-4		5t	Minnesota 8-2, Colorado 8-2, Oklahoma 9-1	Bob Devaney			
1968	6-4		4t	Kansas 9-1, Missouri 7-3, Oklahoma 7-3	Bob Devaney			
1969	9-2	11	1t	Southern California 9-0-1, Missouri 9-1, Colorado 7-3	Bob Devaney	Sun	45 Georgia	6
1970	11-0-1	1	1	Southern California 6-4-1, Colorado 6-4, Oklahoma 7-4	Bob Devaney	Orange	17 LSU	12
1971	13-0	1	1	Colorado 9-2, Iowa State 8-3, Oklahoma 10-1	Bob Devaney	Orange	38 Alabama	6
1972	9-2-1	4	1	UCLA 8-3, Colorado 8-3, Oklahoma 10-1	Bob Devaney (101-20-2)	Orange	40 Notre Dame	6
1973	9-2-1	7	2t	UCLA 9-2, NC State 8-3, Kansas 7-3-1, Oklahoma 10-0-1	Tom Osborne	Cotton	19 Texas	3
1974	9-3	9	2t	Wisconsin 7-4, Missouri 7-, Oklahoma 11-0	Tom Osborne	Sugar	13 Florida	10
1975	10-2	9	1t	Kansas 7-4, Oklahoma State 7-4, Colorado 9-2, Oklahoma 10-1	Tom Osborne	Fiesta	14 Arizona State	17
1976	9-3-1	9	4t	Colorado 8-3, Oklahoma State 8-3, Iowa State 8-3, Oklahoma 8-2-1	Tom Osborne	Bluebonnet	27 Texas Tech	24
1977	9-3	12	2t	Alabama 10-1, Iowa State 8-3, Colorado 7-3-1, Oklahoma 10-1	Tom Osborne	Liberty	21 North Carolina	17
1978	9-3	8	1t	Alabama 10-1, Oklahoma 10-1, Missouri 7-4	Tom Osborne	Orange	24 Oklahoma	31
1979	10-2	9	2	Penn State 7-4, Oklahoma State 7-4, Oklahoma 10-1	Tom Osborne	Cotton	14 Houston	17
1980	10-2	7	2	Penn State 9-2, Florida State 10-1, Oklahoma 9-2	Tom Osborne	Sun	31 Mississippi State	17
1981	9-3	11	1	Iowa 8-3, Penn State 9-2, Kansas 8-3	Tom Osborne	Orange	15 Clemson	22
1982	12-1	3	1	Iowa 7-4, Penn State 10-1, Auburn 8-3, Oklahoma 8-3	Tom Osborne	Orange	21 LSU	20
1983	12-1	2	1	Penn State 7-4-1, Oklahoma State 7-4, Missouri 7-4, Oklahoma 8-4	Tom Osborne	Orange	30 Miami	31
1984	10-2	4	1t	UCLA 8-3, Oklahoma State 9-2, Oklahoma 9-1-1	Tom Osborne	Sugar	28 LSU	10
1985	9-3	11	2	Florida State 8-3, Oklahoma State 8-3, Oklahoma 10-1	Tom Osborne	Fiesta	23 Michigan	27
1986	10-2	5	3	Florida State 6-4-1, Oklahoma 10-1	Tom Osborne	Sugar	30 LSU	15
1987	10-2	6	2	UCLA 9-2, South Carolina 8-3, Oklahoma State 9-2, Oklahoma 11-0	Tom Osborne	Fiesta	28 Florida State	31
1988	11-2	10	1	UCLA 9-2, Oklahoma State 9-2, Colorado 8-3, Oklahoma 9-2	Tom Osborne	Orange	3 Miami	23
1989	10-2	11	2	Minnesota 6-5, Colorado 11-0, Oklahoma 7-4	Tom Osborne	Fiesta	17 Florida State	41
1990	9-3	24	2t	Baylor 6-4-1, Colorado 10-1-1, Oklahoma 8-3	Tom Osborne	Citrus	21 Georgia Tech	45
1991	9-2-1	15	1t	Washington 11-0, Colorado 8-2-1, Oklahoma 8-3	Tom Osborne	Orange	0 Miami	22
1992	9-3	14	1	Washington 9-2, Arizona State 6-5, Colorado 9-1-1	Tom Osborne	Orange	14 Florida State	27
1993	11-1	3	1	UCLA 8-3, Kansas State 8-2-1, Colorado 7-3-1, Oklahoma 8-3	Tom Osborne	Orange	16 Florida State	18
1994	13-0	1	1	West Virginia 7-5, Kansas State 9-2, Colorado 10-1	Tom Osborne	Orange	24 Miami	17
1995	12-0	1	1	Michigan St. 6-4-1, Kansas State 9-2, Colorado 9-2, Kansas 9-2	Tom Osborne	Fiesta	62 Florida	24
1996	11-2	6	N1	Arizona State 11-0, Kansas State 9-2, Colorado 9-2	Tom Osborne	Orange	41 Virginia Tech	21
1997	13-0	2	N1	Washington 7-4, Kansas State 10-1, Missouri 7-4	Tom Osborne (255-49-3)	Orange	42 Tennessee	17
1998	9-4	19	N2	Texas A&M 10-2, Texas 8-3, Kansas State 11-0	Frank Solich	Holiday	20 Arizona	23
1999	12-1	3	N1	Texas 9-3, Texas A&M 8-3, Kansas State 10-1	Frank Solich	Fiesta	31 Tennessee	21
2000	10-2	8	N2	Notre Dame 9-2, Oklahoma 11-0, Kansas State 10-2	Frank Solich	Alamo	66 Northwestern	17
2001	11-2	8	N1t	Rice 8-4, Oklahoma 10-2, Colorado 9-2	Frank Solich	Rose	14 Miami	37
2002	7-7		N4	Penn State 9-3, Texas 10-2, Kansas St. 10-2, Colorado 9-3	Frank Solich	Independence	23 Mississippi	27
2003	10-3	19	N2	Oklahoma State 9-3, Missouri 8-4, Texas 10-2, Kansas State 10-3	Frank Solich (58-19) / Bo Pelini [1-0]	Alamo	17 Michigan State	3
2004	5-6		N3t	Pittsburgh 8-3, Oklahoma 11-0	Bill Callahan			
2005	8-4		N2t	Iowa State 7-4, Texas Tech 9-2, Oklahoma 7-4, Colorado 7-4	Bill Callahan	Alamo	32 Michigan	28
2006	9-5		N1	Southern California 10-2, Texas 9-3, Texas A&M 9-3	Bill Callahan	Cotton	14 Auburn	17
2007	5-7		N5t	Southern California 10-2, Missouri 11-1, Texas 9-3, Kansas 11-1	Bill Callahan (27-22)			
2008	9-4		N1t	Virginia Tech 9-4, Missouri 9-4, Texas Tech 11-1, Oklahoma 12-1	Bo Pelini	Gator	26 Clemson	21
2009	10-4	14	N1	Virginia Tech 9-3, Texas Tech 8-4, Oklahoma 7-5, Texas 13-0	Bo Pelini	Holiday	33 Arizona	0
2010	10-4	20	N1t	Oklahoma State 10-2, Missouri 10-2, Texas A&M 9-3, Oklahoma 11-2	Bo Pelini (30-12)	Holiday	7 Washington	19

TOTAL:　504-178-7 .7366 (3 of 70)　　　**Bowl Games since 1953:**　24-22 .5217 (32 of 70)

GREATEST TEAM SINCE 1953: Although there are four national championship teams to choose from, the Nebraska Cornhuskers team that gets the nod is the 1995 edition that crushed Florida in the Fiesta Bowl title game by 62-24. Although the offensive line had a very slight drop-off from the 1994 national champions, with the departures of Brenden Stai and Zach Wiegert, nicely replaced by Chris Dishman and Aaron Taylor, the Huskers more than made up with a healthy Tommie Frazier at quarterback and outstanding new starters on defense in Jason Peter, Grant Wistrom, and Mike Minter.

1953 3-6-1
12 Oregon	20 E Andy Loehr
21 Illinois	21 T Bill Connor
0 Kansas State	27 G Charles Bryant
6 Pittsburgh	14 C Tom Oliver
20 Miami	16 G Donn Glantz / Robert Wagner
7 Missouri	23 T Jerry Minnick / Bill Halloran
9 Kansas	0 E John Schobacker
27 Iowa State	19 QB John Bordogna / Dan Brown
10 Colorado	14 HB Dennis Korinek / Jon McWilliams
7 Oklahoma	30 HB Bob Smith / Rex Fischer
	FB Ray Novak

RUSHING: Smith 136/704y
PASSING: N/A
RECEIVING: Loehr 16/188y
SCORING: N/A

1954 6-5
7 Minnesota	19 E Andy Loehr / Jon McWilliams
39 Iowa State	14 T Bill Halloran / Jerry Peterson
3 Kansas State	7 G Charles Bryant
27 Oregon State	7 C Bob Oberlin / LaVerne Torczon
20 Colorado	6 G Robert Wagner / Bob Berguin (C)
25 Missouri	19 T Don Glantz / Jack Fleming
41 Kansas	20 E Bill Giles / Jack Braley
7 Pittsburgh	21 QB Dan Brown / Don Erway / Rex Fischer
7 Oklahoma	55 HB Ron Clark / Don Comstock
50 Hawaii	0 HB Willie Greenlaw / Dennis Korinek
7 Duke■	34 FB Bob Smith

RUSHING: N/A
PASSING: N/A
RECEIVING: N/A
SCORING: N/A

1955 5-5
0 Hawaii	6 E LeRoy Butherus/Jack Braley /Don Hewitt
20 Ohio State	28 T LaVerne Torczon / Don Rhoda
16 Kansas State	0 G Jerry Peterson
0 Texas A&M	27 C Jack Post / Bob Berguin
7 Pittsburgh	21 G Don Kampe / Tom Taylor
18 Missouri	12 T Jack Fleming / Jerry Wheeler
19 Kansas	14 E Jon McWilliams / Larry Westervelt
10 Iowa State	7 QB Don Erway
37 Colorado	20 HB Rex Fischer / Frank Nappi
0 Oklahoma	41 HB Willie Greenlaw / Hank Johnson
	FB Jerry Brown/John Edwards/George Cifra

RUSHING: Fischer 133/599y, Greenlaw 113/584y, Cifra 42/121y
PASSING: Erway 21-58/312y, 4TD, 36.2%
RECEIVING: McWilliams 14/239y, Greenlaw 9/165y, Butherus 7/147y
SCORING: Erway (QB-K) 55pts, Greenlaw 30pts, Fischer 24pts

1956 4-6
34 South Dakota	6 E Martin Hilding / Clarence Cook
7 Ohio State	34 T Don Kampe / Don Rhoda
9 Iowa State	7 G LaVerne Torczon / Art Klein
7 Kansas State	10 C Bob Berguin / Max Kitzelman
14 Indiana	19 G Jim Murphy / Jerry Petersen
0 Colorado	16 T Jerry Wheeler / Jack Fleming
15 Missouri	14 E Mike Lee
26 Kansas	20 QB George Harshman/Roy Stinnett
7 Baylor	26 HB Frank Nappi / Bill Hawkins
6 Oklahoma	54 HB Larry Naviaux / Willie Greenlaw
	FB Jerry Brown / Dick McCashland

RUSHING: Brown 129/690y, Naviaux 73/403y, Hawkins 42/254y
PASSING: Stinnett 12-22/171y, 1TD, 54.5%
RECEIVING: Nappi 13/139y, Hilding 7/84y, Cook 5/88y
SCORING: Brown 30pts, Hawkins & Greenlaw (HB-K) 18pts

1957 1-9
12 Washington St.	34 E Bill Hawkins / Marlin Hilding
0 Army	42 T Don Rhoda
14 Kansas State	7 G Jerry Peterson / Stu Howerter
0 Pittsburgh	34 C Dick McCashland
9 Syracuse	26 G Don Kampe / LeRoy Zentic
13 Missouri	14 T Don Olson / Jerry Wheeler
12 Kansas	14 E Mike Lee / Clarence Cook
0 Iowa State	13 QB Harry Tolly / Roy Stinnett
0 Colorado	27 HB Doug Thomas /C. Zaruba/Benny Dillard
7 Oklahoma	32 HB Larry Naviaux / Gene Sandage
	FB Jerry Brown / George Cifra

RUSHING: Brown 97/398y, Thomas 72/244y, Naviaux 72/217y
PASSING: Stinnett 8-22/140y, 0TD, 35.6%
RECEIVING: Thomas 6/79y, Cook 4/80y, Lee 4/48y
SCORING: Stinnett 18pts, Thomas 12pts, Cifra 8pts

1958 3-7
14 Penn State	7 E Mike Eger / Bill Bohanan
0 Purdue	28 T Duane Mongerson
7 Iowa State	6 G Dennis Emanuel / John Ponseigo
6 Kansas State	23 C Don Fricke
0 Syracuse	38 G Leroy Zentic / Dick Kosier
16 Colorado	27 T Joe Gacusana / Allen Wellman
0 Missouri	31 E Roland McDole / Guy Sapp
7 Kansas	29 QB George Harshman / Harry Tolly
14 Pittsburgh	6 HB Pat Fischer / Max Martz
7 Oklahoma	40 HB Larry Naviaux / Roy Stinnett
	FB Dick McCashland / Carroll Zaruba

RUSHING: Naviaux 74/261y,McCashland 86/257y,Zaruba 47/164y
PASSING: Harshman 13-32/201y, 2TD, 40.6%
RECEIVING: Fischer 7/39y, White 6/137y, Bohanan 6/49y
SCORING: Harshman (QB-K) 15pts, Naviaux 14pts, Fischer 12pts

1959 4-6
0 Texas	20 E Roger Brede/ John Bond/Rich McDaniel
32 Minnesota	12 T George Haney / Duane Mongerson
7 Oregon State	6 G Don Olson
3 Kansas	10 C Jim Moore / Mick Tingelhoff
7 Indiana	23 G LeRoy Zentic / Dick Kosier
0 Missouri	9 T Ron McDole / Allen Wellman
25 Oklahoma	21 E Don Purcell / Max Martz
6 Iowa State	18 QB Harry Tolly / Ron Meade / Tom Kramer
14 Colorado	12 HB Pat Fischer
14 Kansas State	29 HB Carroll Zaruba / Clay White
	FB Don Fricke / Noel Martin

RUSHING: Zaruba 82/463y, Fischer 87/300y, White 50/203y
PASSING: Tolly 19-53/200y, 4TD, 35.8%
RECEIVING: White 7/54y, Brede 6/66y, 3 tied w/ 4
SCORING: Zaruba 80pts, White & Meade 18pts

1960 4-6
14 Texas	13 E Bill Comstock
14 Minnesota	26 T George Haney
7 Iowa State	10 G Darrell Cooper / Tyrone Robertson
17 Kansas State	17 C Don Fricke / Mick Tingelhoff
14 Army	9 G Gary Toogood / Dick Kosier
6 Colorado	19 T Ron McDole
0 Missouri	28 E Don Purcell
0 Kansas	31 QB Pat Fischer
6 Oklahoma State	7 HB Pat Clare / Bennie Dillard
17 Oklahoma	14 HB Warren Powers / Clay White
	FB Bill Thornton / Noel Martin

RUSHING: Thornton 96/422y, Fischer 97/381y, Clare 37/169y
PASSING: Fischer 9-35/161y, 1TD, 25.7%
RECEIVING: White 6/72y, Purcell 3/39y, Thornton 3/21y
SCORING: Fischer 32pts, Thornton 26pts, Dillard 18pts

1961 3-6-1
33 North Dakota	0 E Don Purcell / Larry Tomlinson
14 Arizona	14 T Robert Jones
24 Kansas State	0 G Dwain Carlson / John Kirby
6 Syracuse	28 C Mick Tingelhoff / Ron Michka
6 Oklahoma State	14 G Tyrone Robertson / Gary Toogood
0 Missouri	10 T Bob Brown / Lloyd Voss
6 Kansas	28 E Jim Huge / Dick McDaniel
16 Iowa State	13 QB Dennis Claridge / Ron Meade
0 Colorado	7 HB Warren Powers / Willie Ross
14 Oklahoma	21 HB Rudy Johnson / Dennis Stuewe
	FB Bill Thornton (HB) / Bill Comstock

RUSHING: Thornton 127/618y, Ross 45/198y, Johnson 41/193y
PASSING: Claridge 38-104/464y, 3TD, 36.5%
RECEIVING: McDaniel 14/158y, Purcell 12/173y, Stuewe 9/88y
SCORING: Thornton 30pts, Ross 24pts, Meade (QB-K) 23pts

1962 9-2
53 South Dakota	0 E Larry Donovan /Dick Callahan/Mike Eger
25 Michigan	13 T Tyrone Robertson
36 Iowa State	22 G Dwain Carlson
19 N. Carolina St.	14 C Ron Michka
26 Kansas State	6 G Bob Brown
31 Colorado	6 T Lloyd Voss
7 Missouri	16 E Bill Comstock / Jim Huge
40 Kansas	16 QB Dennis Claridge
14 Oklahoma State	0 HB Willie Ross
6 Oklahoma	34 HB Kent McCloughan
36 Miami■	34 FB Warren Powers / Bill Thornton

RUSHING: Ross 89/431y, Claridge 104/370y, Powers 49/279y
PASSING: Claridge 56-128/829y, 4TD, 43.8%
RECEIVING: Huge 11/208y, Callahan 10/189y, Eger 9/109y
SCORING: Claridge 64pts, Thornton 22pts, Ross 20pts

1963 10-1
58 So. Dakota St.	7 E Larry Tomlinson
14 Minnesota	7 T Larry Kramer / Bob Jones
21 Iowa State	7 G John Kirby / John Dervin
13 Air Force	17 C Ron Michka / Lyle Sittler
28 Kansas State	6 T Bob Brown
41 Colorado	6 T Lloyd Voss / Monte Kiffin
13 Missouri	12 E Dick Callahan / Tony Jeter
23 Kansas	9 QB Dennis Claridge / Fred Duda
20 Oklahoma State	16 HB Will Ross/Maynard Smidt/Dave Thiesen
29 Oklahoma	20 HB Bobby Hohn / Kent McCloughan
13 Auburn■	6 FB Rudy Johnson (QB) / Bruce Smith

RUSHING: Johnson 91/573y, Ross 92/496y, McCloughan 51/261y
PASSING: Claridge 31-66/440y, 3TD, 46.8%
RECEIVING: Jeter 9/151y, Tomlinson 9/129y, Callahan 8/157y
SCORING: Johnson 50pts, Claridge 36pts, Duda 32pts

1964 9-2
56 So. Dakota St.	0 E Freeman White
26 Minnesota	21 T Larry Kramer
14 Iowa State	7 G John Dervin
28 South Carolina	6 C Lyle Sittler
47 Kansas State	0 G Ron Griesse
21 Colorado	3 T Dennis Carlson
9 Missouri	0 E Tony Jeter
14 Kansas	7 QB Bobby Churchich / Fred Duda
27 Oklahoma State	14 HB Kent McCloughan
7 Oklahoma	17 HB Bobby Hohn / Harry Wilson
7 Arkansas■	10 FB Frankie Solich / Bruce Smith
	DL Mike Grace / Bill Haug
	DL John Strohmyer
	DL Walt Barnes
	DL Dick Czap
	DL Langston Coleman
	LB Bernie McGinn
	LB Mike Kennedy
	DB Joe McNulty
	DB Bill Johnson
	DB Ted Vactor
	DB Larry Wachholtz

RUSHING: Solich 87/444y, McCloughan 96/367y, Hohn 74/344y
PASSING: Churchich 54-102/893y, 7TD, 52.9%
RECEIVING: Jeter 18/219y, White 17/338y, McCloughan 11/213y
SCORING: McCloughan 72pts, Solich 30pts, Churchich 24pts

1965 10-1
34 TCU	14 E Tony Jeter
27 Air Force	17 T Dennis Carlson
44 Iowa State	0 G LaVerne Allers
37 Wisconsin	0 C Kelly Petersen
41 Kansas State	0 G Jim Osberg / Wayne Meylan
38 Colorado	13 T Jim Brown
16 Missouri	14 E Freeman White / Dennis Richnafsky
42 Kansas	6 QB Fred Duda / Bob Churchich
21 Oklahoma State	17 HB Ron Kirkland / Charlie Winters
21 Oklahoma	9 HB Harry Wilson
28 Alabama■	39 FB Frank Solich / Pete Tatman
	DL Jerry Patton / Len Janik
	DL Dick Czap
	DL Wayne Meylan / Jerry Murphy
	DL Walt Barnes
	DL Langston Coleman / Ivan Zimmer
	LB Mike Kennedy
	LB Lynn Senkbeil
	DB Bill Johnson
	DB Kaye Carstens
	DB Marv Mueller / Ted Vactor
	DB Larry Wachholtz

RUSHING: Wilson 120/672y, Solich 107/580y, Kirkland 79/522y
PASSING: Duda 46-110/632y, 6TD, 41.8%
RECEIVING: White 28/458y, Richnafsky 13/133y, Jeter 11/158y
SCORING: Wachholtz (S-K) 45pts, Winters 42pts, White 38pts

1966 9-2

14 TCU	10 E Tom Penney / Dennis Richnafsky
28 Utah State	7 T Gary Brichacek
12 Iowa State	6 G Jim Osberg
31 Wisconsin	3 C Kelly Petersen
21 Kansas State	10 G LaVerne Allers
21 Colorado	19 T Bob Pickens
35 Missouri	0 E Dennis Morrison / Miles Kimmel
24 Kansas	13 QB Bob Churchich
21 Oklahoma State	6 HB Ben Gregory (LB) / Ron Kirkland
9 Oklahoma	10 HB Harry Wilson
7 Alabama■	34 FB Pete Tatman / Dick Davis
	DL Jerry Patton
	DL Jim McCord
	DL Wayne Meylan
	DL Carel Smith
	DL Langston Coleman
	LB Rick Coleman / Barry Alvarez
	LB Lynn Senkbeil
	DB Dennis Thorell
	DB Kaye Carstens
	DB Larry Wachholtz
	DB Marv Mueller

RUSHING: Wilson 138/635y, Tatman 107/418y, Gregory 93/418y
PASSING: Churchich 96-174/1136y, 4TD, 55.2%
RECEIVING: Penney 24/286y, Morrison 22/271y, Wilson 16/216y
SCORING: Gregory & Wachholtz (DB-K) 42pts, Wilson & Churchich 24pts

1967 6-4

17 Washington	7 WR Dennis Richafsky / Tom Penney
7 Minnesota	0 T Bob Taucher
16 Kansas State	14 G Mel Brichacek
0 Kansas	10 C Roger Kudrna
16 Colorado	21 G Carl Ashman / Joe Armstrong
29 TCU	0 T Glenn Patterson
12 Iowa State	0 TE Dennis Morrison
9 Oklahoma State	0 QB Frank Patrick
7 Missouri	10 HB Ben Gregory
14 Oklahoma	21 HB Joe Orduna
	FB Dick Davis
	DL Frank Avolio / Ivan Zimmer
	DL Jim McCord
	DL Wayne Meylan
	DL Jerry Patton
	DL Mike Wynn
	LB Barry Alvarez
	LB Ken Geddes / Adrian Fiala / Dan Kobza
	DB Al Larson / Bob Best
	DB Jim Hawkins
	DB Dana Stephenson
	DB Marv Mueller

RUSHING: Davis 162/717y, Orduna 116/457y, Gregory 130/412y
PASSING: Patrick 116-233/1449y, 7TD, 49.6%
RECEIVING: Richnafsky 36/422y, Morrison 19/282y, Penney 17/216y
SCORING: Bill Bomberger (K) 29pts, 4 tied w/ 18pts

1968 6-4

13 Wyoming	10 WR Tom Penney / Guy Ingles
31 Utah	0 T Ed Hansen
17 Minnesota	14 G Joe Armstrong / Carl Ashman
13 Kansas	23 C Joe Buda
14 Missouri	16 G Mel Brickacek / Wally Winter
21 Oklahoma State	20 T Glenn Patterson
24 Iowa State	13 TE Jim McFarland
0 Kansas State	12 QB Ernie Sigler
22 Colorado	6 HB Joe Orduna
0 Oklahoma	47 HB Mick Ziegler / Larry Frost
	FB Dick Davis
	DL Mike Wynn
	DL Bob Liggett
	DL Bill Hornbacher / Dan Kobza
	DL Tom Linstroth / Dave Walline
	DL Sherwin Jarmon
	LB Ken Geddes
	LB Jerry Murtaugh
	DB Al Larson
	DB Randy Reeves / Jim Hawkins
	DB Dana Stephenson
	DB Bob Best

RUSHING: Orduna 186/677y, Davis 158/606y, Dan Schneiss (FB) 28/115y
PASSING: Sigler 73-144/907y, 6TD, 50.7%
RECEIVING: Penney 25/424y, McFarland 23/244y, Frost 14/152y
SCORING: Orduna 60pts, Paul Rogers (K) 35pts, McFarland 24pts

1969 9-2

21 Southern Cal	31 WR Guy Ingles
14 Texas A&M	0 T Wally Winter / Bob Newton
42 Minnesota	14 G Carl Ashman
7 Missouri	17 C Glenn Patterson
21 Kansas	17 G Gale Williams
13 Oklahoma State	3 T Paul Topliff
20 Colorado	7 TE Jim McFarland
17 Iowa State	3 QB Jerry Tagge / Van Brownson
10 Kansas State	7 IB Larry Frost
44 Oklahoma	6 WB Jeff Kinney
45 Georgia■	6 FB Mike Green / Dan Schneiss
	DL Mike Wynn
	DL Dave Walline
	DL Ken Geddes
	DL Bob Liggett
	DL Sherwin Jarmon
	LB Jerry Murtaugh
	LB Adrian Fiala
	DB Randy Reeves
	DB Jim Anderson
	DB Al Larson
	DB Dana Stephenson

RUSHING: Kinney 177/546y, Schneiss 63/334y, Green 50/196y
PASSING: Tagge 101-177/1302y, 3TD, 57.1%
RECEIVING: Kinney 41/433y, McFarland 30/381y, Ingles 26/408y
SCORING: Kinney 68pts, Paul Rogers (K) 45pts, Brownson 24pts

1970 11-0-1

36 Wake Forest	12 WR Guy Ingles
21 Southern Cal	21 T Wally Winter
28 Army	0 G Dick Rupert
35 Minnesota	10 C Doug Dumler
21 Missouri	7 G Donnie McGhee / Carl Johnson
41 Kansas	20 T Bob Newton
65 Oklahoma State	31 TE Jerry List
29 Colorado	13 QB Jerry Tagge / Van Brownson
54 Iowa State	29 IB Jeff Kinney / Joe Orduna
51 Kansas State	13 WB Johnny Rodgers
28 Oklahoma	21 FB Dan Schneiss
17 LSU■	12 DL John Adkins
	DL Larry Jacobson
	DL Eddie Periard
	DL Dave Walline
	DL Willie Harper
	LB Jerry Murtaugh
	LB Bob Terrio
	DB Joe Blahak
	DB Jim Anderson
	DB Bill Kosch
	DB Dave Morock

RUSHING: Orduna 187/834y, Kinney 146/661y, Schneiss 69/330y
PASSING: Tagge 104-165/1383y, 12TD, 63%
RECEIVING: Rodgers 35/665y, Ingles 34/603y, List 19/215y
SCORING: Orduna 86pts, Paul Rogers (K) 69pts, Rodgers 66pts

1971 13-0

34 Oregon	7 WR Woody Cox
35 Minnesota	7 T Daryl White
34 Texas A&M	7 G Dick Rupert
42 Utah State	6 C Doug Dumler
36 Missouri	0 G Keith Wortman
55 Kansas	0 T Carl Johnson / Al Austin
41 Oklahoma State	13 TE Jerry List
31 Colorado	7 QB Jerry Tagge
37 Iowa State	0 IB Jeff Kinney / Gary Dixon
44 Kansas State	17 WB Johnny Rodgers
35 Oklahoma	31 FB Bill Olds / Maury Damkroger
38 Alabama■	6 DL Willie Harper
	DL Bill Janssen / John Dutton
	DL Rich Glover
	DL Larry Jacobsen
	DL John Adkins
	LB Jim Branch / Pat Morrell
	LB Bob Terrio
	DB Bill Kosch
	DB Joe Blahak
	DB Dave Mason
	DB Jim Anderson

RUSHING: Kinney 222/1037y, Dixon 139/501y, Olds 73/500y
PASSING: Tagge 143-239/2019y, 17TD, 59.8%
RECEIVING: Rodgers 53/872y, Cox 24/356y, Kinney 23/252y
SCORING: Rodgers 102pts, Kinney 96pts, Rich Sanger (K) 75pts

1972 9-2-1

17 UCLA	20 WR Bob Revelle / Frosty Anderson
37 Texas A&M	7 T Daryl White
77 Army	7 G Bob Wolfe / Dan Anderson
49 Minnesota	0 C Doug Dumler
62 Missouri	0 G Mike Beran
56 Kansas	0 T Marvin Crenshaw
34 Oklahoma State	0 TE Jerry List
33 Colorado	10 QB Dave Humm
23 Iowa State	23 IB Gary Dixon / Jeff Moran
59 Kansas State	7 WB Johnny Rodgers
14 Oklahoma	17 FB Bill Olds / Maury Damkroger
40 Notre Dame■	6 DL Steve Manstedt
	DL John Dutton
	DL Rich Glover
	DL Bill Janssen / Monte Johnson
	DL Willie Harper
	LB Jim Branch / Bob Nelson
	LB John Pitts / Tom Ruud
	DB Dave Mason
	DB Randy Borg
	DB Joe Blahak
	DB George Kyros / Bob Thornton

RUSHING: Dixon 130/506y, Olds 62/341y, Jeff Moran 54/303y
PASSING: Humm 140-266/2074y, 17TD, 52.6%
RECEIVING: Rodgers 55/942y, Revelle 38/486y, List 21/339y
SCORING: Rodgers 102pts, Rich Sanger (K) 76pts, Dixon & Dave Goeller (IB) 48pts

1973 9-2-1

40 UCLA	13 WR Frosty Anderson / Dave Shamblin
31 N. Carolina St.	14 T Daryl White
20 Wisconsin	16 G Tom Alward
48 Minnesota	7 C Rik Bonness
12 Missouri	13 G Dan Anderson
10 Kansas	9 T Marvin Crenshaw / Al Austin
17 Oklahoma State	17 TE Brent Longwell
28 Colorado	16 QB Dave Humm
31 Iowa State	7 IB Tony Davis
50 Kansas State	21 WB Ritch Bahe
0 Oklahoma	27 FB Maury Damkroger
19 Texas■	3 DL Steve Manstedt
	DL Ron Pruitt
	DL John Bell / Willie Thornton
	DL John Dutton
	DL Bob Martin
	LB Tom Ruud / John Starkebaum
	LB Bob Nelson
	DB Randy Borg
	DB Zaven Yaralian
	DB Mark Heydorff / Wonder Monds
	DB Bob Thornton

RUSHING: Davis 254/1008y, John O'Leary 72/326y, Bahe 49/293y
PASSING: Humm 109-196/1526y, 12TD, 55.6%
RECEIVING: Bahe 30/406y, Anderson 26/504y, Longwell 19/235y
SCORING: Davis 78pts, Rich Sanger (K) 52pts, Anderson 48pts

1974 9-3

61 Oregon	7 WR Ritch Bahe / Chuck Malito
20 Wisconsin	21 T Mark Doak
49 Northwestern	7 G Tom Alward
54 Minnesota	0 C Rik Bonness / Rich Duda
10 Missouri	21 G Stan Hegener
56 Kansas	0 T Marvin Crenshaw
7 Oklahoma State	3 TE Larry Mushinskie / Brad Jenkins
31 Colorado	15 QB Dave Humm
23 Iowa State	13 IB Monte Anthony / John O'Leary
35 Kansas State	7 WB Don Westbrook
14 Oklahoma	28 FB Tony Davis
13 Florida■	10 DL Tom Pate
	DL Ron Pruitt
	DL John Lee
	DL Mike Fultz
	DL Bob Martin
	LB Tom Ruud
	LB Bob Nelson / John Starkebaum
	DB Ardell Johnson
	DB Jim Burrow / Dave Butterfield
	DB Wonder Monds
	DB George Kyros / Mark Heydorff

RUSHING: Anthony 109/587y, Davis 106/526y, O'Leary 100/499y
PASSING: Humm 104-175/1435y, 12TD, 59.4%
RECEIVING: Westbrook 33/508y, Davis 19/185y, Bahe 15/214y
SCORING: Westbrook 60pts, Mike Coyle (K) 55pts, Anthony & O'Leary 36pts

1975 10-2

10	LSU	7	WR Bobby Thomas / Chuck Malito
45	Indiana	0	T Bob Lingenfelter
56	TCU	14	G Dan Schmidt
31	Miami	16	C Rik Bonness
16	Kansas	0	G Greg Jorgensen
28	Oklahoma State	20	T Steve Hoins
63	Colorado	21	TE Larry Mushinskie
30	Missouri	7	QB Vince Ferragamo / Terry Luck
12	Kansas State	0	IB Monte Anthony / John O'Leary
52	Iowa State	0	WB Curtis Craig / Tom Heiser
10	Oklahoma	35	FB Tony Davis
14	Arizona State ■	17	DL Ray Phillips
			DL Jerry Wied
			DL John Lee
			DL Mike Fultz
			DL Bob Martin
			LB Clete Pillen
			LB Jim Wightman
			DB Dave Butterfield
			DB Wonder Monds
			DB Jimmy Burrow
			DB Chuck Jones

RUSHING: Anthony 161/723y, Davis 141/619y, O'Leary 121/599y
PASSING: Ferragamo 79-134/1153y, 12TD, 59%
RECEIVING: Thomas 24/501y, Davis 16/175y, Malito 15/230y
SCORING: Mike Coyle (K) 68pts, O'Leary 48pts, Anthony & Thomas 42pts

1976 9-3-1

6	LSU	6	WR Chuck Malito / Bobby Thomas
45	Indiana	13	T Bob Lingenfelter
64	TCU	10	G Greg Jorgensen
17	Miami	9	C Tom Davis
24	Colorado	12	G Dan Schmidt
51	Kansas State	0	T Steve Hoins
24	Missouri	34	TE Ken Spaeth
31	Kansas	3	QB Vince Ferragamo
14	Oklahoma State	10	IB Rick Berns / Monte Anthony
28	Iowa State	37	WB Dave Shamblin / Curtis Craig
17	Oklahoma	20	FB Dodie Donnell
68	Hawaii	3	DL Tony Samuel
27	Texas Tech ■	24	DL Ron Pruitt
			DL Jeff Pullen
			DL Mike Fultz
			DL Ray Phillips
			LB Jim Wightman
			LB Clete Pillen
			DB Ted Harvey
			DB Dave Butterfield
			DB Kent Smith
			DB Larry Valasek

RUSHING: Berns 155/854y, Anthony 148/594y, Donnell 104/486y
PASSING: Ferragamo 145-254/2071y, 20TD, 57%
RECEIVING: Malito 30/615y, Thomas 30/561y, Spaeth 18/251y
SCORING: Al Eveland (K) 73pts, Berns 54pts, Thomas 48pts

1977 9-3

10	Washington St.	19	WR Tim Smith
31	Alabama	24	T Kelvin Clark
31	Baylor	10	G Greg Jorgensen
31	Indiana	13	C Tom Davis
26	Kansas State	9	G Steve Lindquist / Brett Moritz
21	Iowa State	24	T Stan Waldemore
33	Colorado	15	TE Ken Spaeth
31	Oklahoma State	14	QB Tom Sorley / Randy Garcia
21	Missouri	10	IB I.M. Hipp / Rick Berns
52	Kansas	7	WB Curtis Craig
7	Oklahoma	38	FB Dodie Donnell
21	North Carolina ■	14	DL Tony Samuel
			DL Rod Horn / Barney Cotton
			DL Kerry Weinmaster
			DL Randy Poeschl / Dan Pensick
			DL George Andrews
			LB Tom Vering / Jeff Carpenter
			LB Lee Kunz
			DB Ted Harvey
			DB Rene Anderson
			DB Jim Pillen
			DB Larry Valasek

RUSHING: Hipp 197/1301y, Berns 121/662y, Craig 44/337y
PASSING: Garcia 38-94/568y, 3TD, 40.4%
Sorley 42-83/558y, 2TD, 50.6%
RECEIVING: Smith 23/371y, Spaeth 23/300y, Berns 9/79y
SCORING: Billy Todd (K) 64pts, Hipp 62pts, Berns 60pts

1978 9-3

3	Alabama	20	WR Tim Smith / Frank Lockett
36	California	26	T Kelvin Clark
56	Hawaii	10	G Barney Cotton
69	Indiana	17	C Kelly Saalfeld
23	Iowa State	0	G Steve Lindquist
48	Kansas State	14	T Tom Ohrt / Steve Glenn
52	Colorado	14	TE Junior Miller / Jeff Finn
22	Oklahoma State	14	QB Tom Sorley
63	Kansas	21	IB Rick Berns / I.M. Hipp
17	Oklahoma	14	WB Kenny Brown
31	Missouri	35	FB Andra Franklin
24	Oklahoma ■	31	DL Lawrence Cole / Derrie Nelson
			DL Rod Horn / David Clark
			DL Kerry Weinmaster / Oudious Lee
			DL Bill Barnett / Dan Pensick
			DL George Andrews
			LB Bruce Dunning
			LB Lee Kunz
			DB Tim Fischer
			DB Andy Means
			DB Jim Pillen
			DB Russell Gary / Jeff Hansen

RUSHING: Hipp 173/936y, Berns 164/933y, Franklin 83/419y
PASSING: Sorley 102-174/1571y, 12TD, 58.6%
RECEIVING: Miller 30/560y, Brown 23/367y, Smith 19/241y
SCORING: Billy Todd (K) 72pts, Berns 66pts, Hipp 42pts

1979 10-2

35	Utah State	14	WR Tim Smith
24	Iowa	21	T Dan Steiner
42	Penn State	17	G John Havekost
57	New Mexico St.	0	C Kelly Saalfeld
42	Kansas	0	G Randy Schleusener
36	Oklahoma State	0	T Mark Goodspeed
38	Colorado	10	TE Junior Miller
23	Missouri	20	QB Jeff Quinn / Tim Hager
21	Kansas State	12	IB Jarvis Redwine / I.M. Hipp.
34	Iowa State	3	WB Kenny Brown
14	Oklahoma	17	FB Andra Franklin
14	Houston ■	17	DL Lawrence Cole
			DL Rod Horn / Dan Pensick
			DL Kerry Weinmaster / Oudious Lee
			DL Bill Barnett
			DL Derrie Nelson
			LB Brent Williams
			LB Kim Baker / Tom Vering
			DB Ric Lindquist
			DB Mark LeRoy
			DB Russell Gary
			DB Andy Means

RUSHING: Redwine 148/1042y, Hipp 125/577y, Franklin 98/543y
PASSING: Quinn 47-91/624y, 4TD, 51.6%
Hager 46-90/680y, 6TD, 51.1%
RECEIVING: Smith 30/477y, Miller 21/409y, Brown 10/134y
SCORING: Dean Sukup (K) 74pts, Redwine 54pts, Miller 42pts

1980 10-2

55	Utah	9	WR Todd Brown / John Noonan
57	Iowa	0	T Dan Hurley
21	Penn State	7	G Joe Adams
14	Florida State	18	C Dave Rimington
54	Kansas	0	G Randy Schleusener
48	Oklahoma State	7	T Randy Theiss
45	Colorado	7	TE Jeff Finn / Steve Davies
38	Missouri	16	QB Jeff Quinn
55	Kansas State	8	IB Jarvis Redwine / Roger Craig
35	Iowa State	0	WB Anthony Steels / Tim McCrady
17	Oklahoma	21	FB Andra Franklin
31	Mississippi St. ■	17	DL Jimmy Williams
			DL David Clark
			DL Curt Hineline
			DL Henry Waechter
			DL Derrie Nelson
			LB Brent Williams
			LB Kim Baker / Steve Damkroger
			DB Andy Means / Rodney Lewis
			DB Ric Lindquist
			DB Sammy Sims
			DB Russell Gary

RUSHING: Redwine 156/1119y, Craig 180/769y,
Craig Johnson (IB) 72/679y
PASSING: Quinn 96-157/1337y, 14TD, 61.1%
RECEIVING: Brown 28/416y, Finn 20/217y, McCrady 12/195y
SCORING: Craig 90pts, Kevin Seibel (K) 63pts, Redwine 54pts

1981 9-3

7	Iowa	10	WR Todd Brown
34	Florida State	14	T Randy Theiss
24	Penn State	30	G Mike Mandelko
17	Auburn	3	C Dave Rimington
59	Colorado	0	G Tom Carlstrom
49	Kansas State	3	T Dan Hurley
6	Missouri	0	TE John Williams
31	Kansas	15	QB Turner Gill / Mark Mauer
54	Oklahoma State	7	IB Roger Craig / Mike Rozier
31	Iowa State	7	WB Anthony Steels
37	Oklahoma	14	FB Phil Bates
15	Clemson ■	22	DL Jimmy Williams
			DL Toby Williams
			DL Jeff Merrell
			DL Henry Waechter
			DL Tony Felici
			LB Steve Damkroger
			LB Brent Evans
			DB Rodney Lewis
			DB Ric Lindquist
			DB Sammy Sims
			DB Jeff Krejci

RUSHING: Craig 173/1060y, Rozier 151/943y, Bates 94/555y
PASSING: Gill 47-91/619y, 9TD, 51.6%
RECEIVING: Williams 22/282y, Steels 15/187y, Brown 14/277y
SCORING: Kevin Seibel (K) 52pts, Bates 48pts,
Craig & Rozier 36pts

1982 12-1

42	Iowa	7	WR Todd Brown
68	New Mexico St.	0	T Randy Theiss
24	Penn State	27	G Dean Steinkuhler
41	Auburn	7	C Dave Rimington
40	Colorado	14	G Mike Mandelko
42	Kansas State	13	T Jeff Kwapick
23	Missouri	19	TE Jamie Williams
52	Kansas	0	QB Turner Gill
48	Oklahoma State	10	IB Mike Rozier / Roger Craig
48	Iowa State	10	WB Irving Fryar
28	Oklahoma	24	FB Doug Wilkening
37	Hawaii	16	DL Bill Weber / Dave Ridder
21	LSU ■	20	DL Toby Williams
			DL Jeff Merrell
			DL Rob Stuckey
			DL Tony Felici / Scott Strasburger
			LB Steve Damkroger / Brent Evans
			LB Steve McWhirter / Mike Knox
			DB Neil Harris / Dave Burke
			DB Bret Clark
			DB Allen Lyday
			DB Kris van Norman

RUSHING: Rozier 242/1689y, Craig 119/586y,
Jeff Smith (IB) 56/569y
PASSING: Gill 90-166/1182y, 11TD, 54.2%
RECEIVING: Fryar 24/346y, Brown 23/399y, Williams 21/222y
SCORING: Rozier 102pts, Kevin Seibel (K) 82pts,
Smith & Wilkening 48pts

1983 12-1

44	Penn State	6	WR Ricky Simmons / Scott Kimball
56	Wyoming	20	T Scott Raridon
84	Minnesota	13	G Dean Steinkuhler
42	UCLA	10	C Mark Traynowicz
63	Syracuse	7	G Harry Grimminger
14	Oklahoma State	10	T Mark Behning
34	Missouri	13	TE Monte Engebritson / Todd Frain
69	Colorado	19	QB Turner Gill
51	Kansas State	25	IB Mike Rozier
72	Iowa State	29	WB Irving Fryar
67	Kansas	13	FB Mark Schellen
28	Oklahoma	21	DL Bill Weber / Dave Ridder
30	Miami ■	31	DL Mike Keeler / Doug Herrmann
			DL Mike Tranmer / Ken Graeber
			DL Rob Stuckey / Jim Skow
			DL Scott Strasburger
			LB Mark Daum
			LB Mike Knox
			DB Neil Harris
			DB Dave Burke
			DB Bret Clark
			DB Mike McCashland

RUSHING: Rozier 275/2148y, Gill 109/531y, Schellen 77/450y
PASSING: Gill 94-170/1516y, 14TD, 55.3%
RECEIVING: Fryar 40/780y, Simmons 13/137y, Kimball 12/207y
SCORING: Rozier 174pts, Gill 66pts, Fryar 64pts

1984 10-2

42 Wyoming	7 WR Scott Kimball
38 Minnesota	7 T Tom Morrow
42 UCLA	3 G Greg Orton
9 Syracuse	17 C Mark Traynowicz
17 Oklahoma State	3 G Harry Grimminger
33 Missouri	23 T Mark Behning
24 Colorado	7 TE Todd Frain / Brian Hiemer
62 Kansas State	14 QB Travis Turner / Craig Sundberg
44 Iowa State	0 IB Jeff Smith / Doug DuBose
41 Kansas	7 WB Shane Swanson
7 Oklahoma	17 FB Tom Rathman
28 LSU ■	10 DL Scott Strasburger
	DL Rob Stuckey
	DL Ken Graeber
	DL Chris Spachman
	DL Bill Weber
	LB Mark Daum
	LB Marc Munford
	DB Dave Burke
	DB Neil Harris
	DB Bret Clark
	DB Mike McCashland

RUSHING: DuBose 156/1040y, Smith 177/935y, Rathman 75/381y
PASSING: Sundberg 53-84/740y, 4TD, 63.1%
Turner 37-75/541y, 4TD, 49.3%
RECEIVING: Swanson 16/203y, Frain 15/218y, Hiemer 12/174y
SCORING: Turner 60pts, DuBose 48pts, Smith 44pts

1985 9-3

13 Florida State	17 WR Robb Schnitzler / Rod Smith
52 Illinois	25 T Tim Roth
63 Oregon	0 G Brian Blankenship
38 New Mexico	7 C Bill Lewis
34 Oklahoma State	24 G John McCormick
28 Missouri	20 T Tom Welter
17 Colorado	7 TE Todd Frain
41 Kansas State	3 QB McCathorn Clayton / Travis Turner
49 Iowa State	0 IB Doug DuBose / Paul Miles
56 Kansas	6 WB Roger Lindstrom / Von Sheppard
7 Oklahoma	27 FB Tom Rathman
23 Michigan ■	27 DL Gregg Reeves
	DL Chris Spachman
	DL Danny Noonan
	DL Jim Skow
	DL Brad Smith / Scott Tucker
	LB Marc Munford / Mike Knox
	LB Kevin Parsons
	DB Brian Davis
	DB Bryan Siebler / Chris Carr
	DB Brian Washington
	DB Dennis Watkins

RUSHING: DuBose 203/1161y, Rathman 118/689y, Miles 102/689y
PASSING: Clayton 28-78/602y, 3TD, 35.9%
RECEIVING: Schnitzler 16/382y, Sheppard 9/281y, Smith 8/121y
SCORING: Dale Klein (K) 77pts, DuBose & Rathman 48pts

1986 10-2

34 Florida State	17 WR Rod Smith / Robb Schnitzler
59 Illinois	14 T Rob Maggard
48 Oregon	14 G Stan Parker
27 South Carolina	24 C Mark Cooper
30 Oklahoma State	10 G John McCormick
48 Missouri	17 T Tom Welter
10 Colorado	20 TE Todd Millikan / Tom Banderas
38 Kansas State	0 QB Steve Taylor
35 Iowa State	14 IB Keith Jones / Tyreese Knox
70 Kansas	0 WB Dana Brinson / Von Sheppard
17 Oklahoma	20 FB Ken Kaelin / Micah Heibel
30 LSU ■	15 DL Broderick Thomas
	DL Chris Spachman / Neil Smith
	DL Danny Noonan
	DL Lee Jones
	DL Tony Holloway
	LB Marc Munford
	LB Kevin Parsons
	DB Brian Davis
	DB Charles Fryar
	DB Brian Washington / Jeff Tomjack
	DB Bryan Siebler

RUSHING: Jones 161/830y, Taylor 130/537y, Knox 70/419y
PASSING: Taylor 52-124/808y, 7TD, 41.9%
RECEIVING: Brinson 14/208y, Smith 12/190y, Millikan 11/230y
SCORING: Jones 84pts, Dale Klein (K) 81pts, Taylor 54pts

1987 10-2

56 Utah State	12 WR Rod Smith
42 UCLA	33 T Bob Sledge
35 Arizona State	28 G Andy Keeler
30 South Carolina	21 C Jake Young
54 Kansas	2 G John McCormick
35 Oklahoma State	0 T Kevin Lightner
56 Kansas State	3 TE Tom Banderas / Todd Millikan
42 Missouri	7 QB Steve Taylor
42 Iowa State	3 IB Keith Jones
7 Oklahoma	17 WB Dana Brinson
24 Colorado	7 FB Micah Heibel
28 Florida State ■	31 DL Broderick Thomas
	DL Neil Smith
	DL Lawrence Pete / Mike Murray
	DL Tim Rother
	DL Jeff Jamrog
	LB LeRoy Etienne
	LB Steve Forch
	DB Lorenzo Hicks
	DB Charles Fryar
	DB Mark Blazek / Tim Jackson
	DB Brian Washington

RUSHING: Jones 170/1232y, Taylor 130/659y,
Tyreese Knox (IB) 62/428y
PASSING: Taylor 57-123/902y, 13TD, 46.3%
RECEIVING: Smith 21/329y, Millikan 13/287y, Brinson 13/189y
SCORING: Jones 80pts, Chris Drennan (K) 71pts, Taylor 48pts

1988 11-2

23 Texas A&M	14 WR Morgan Gregory
63 Utah State	13 T Bob Sledge / Tom Punt
28 UCLA	41 G Andy Keeler
47 Arizona State	16 C Jake Young / Jeff Anderson
48 UNLV	6 G John Nelson
63 Kansas	10 T Doug Glaser
63 Oklahoma State	42 TE Todd Millikan / Monte Kratzenstein
48 Kansas State	3 QB Steve Taylor
26 Missouri	18 IB Ken Clark
51 Iowa State	6 WB Richard Bell / Dana Brinson
7 Colorado	0 FB Bryan Carpenter
7 Oklahoma	3 DL Willie Griffin
3 Miami ■	23 DL Lawrence Pete / Mike Murray
	DL Paul Brunghardt / Kent Wells
	LB Broderick Thomas
	LB Chris Callendo / Pat Tyrance
	LB LeRoy Etienne
	LB Jeff Mills
	DB Charles Fryar
	DB Lorenzo Hicks
	DB Reggie Cooper
	DB Tim Jackson / Mark Blazek

RUSHING: Clark 232/1497y, Taylor 157/826y, Carpenter 72/498y
PASSING: Taylor 72-151/1067y, 11TD, 47.7%
RECEIVING: Gregory 20/239y, Millikan 16/308y, Brinson 11/148y
SCORING: Taylor 80pts, Clark 74pts, Gregg Barrios (K) &
Millikan 42pts

1989 10-2

48 N. Illinois	17 WR Morgan Gregory / Jon Bostick
42 Utah	30 T Tom Punt / Terry Eyman
48 Minnesota	0 G Jim Wanek
35 Oregon State	7 C Jake Young
58 Kansas State	7 G Bill Borbora
50 Missouri	7 T Doug Glaser / Erik Wiegert
48 Oklahoma State	23 TE Monte Kratzenstein / Bill Washington
49 Iowa State	17 QB Gerry Gdowski
21 Colorado	27 IB Ken Clark / Leodis Flowers
51 Kansas	14 WB Richard Bell / Nate Turner
42 Oklahoma	25 FB Bryan Carpenter
17 Florida State ■	41 DL Kent Wells / Kenny Walker
	DL Mike Murray
	DL Ray Valladad / Joe Sims
	LB Mike Croel
	LB Pat Tyrance
	LB Mike Petko / Randall Jobman
	LB Jeff Mills / Travis Hill
	DB Bruce Pickens
	DB Tahaun Lewis / Tyrone Legette
	DB Reggie Cooper
	DB Marvin Sanders / Tyrone Byrd

RUSHING: Clark 198/1196y, Gdowski 117/925y, Flowers 66/493y
PASSING: Gdowski 71-136/1326y, 19TD, 52.2%
RECEIVING: Gregory 19/282y, Bell 18/357y, Bostick 12/289y
SCORING: Gdowski 78pts, Gregg Barrios (K) 75pts, Clark 72pts

1990 9-3

13 Baylor	0 WR Jon Bostick
60 N. Illinois	14 T Tom Punt
56 Minnesota	0 G Jim Wanek
31 Oregon State	7 C David Edeal
45 Kansas State	8 G Will Shields / Erik Wiegert
69 Missouri	21 T Brian Boerboom
31 Oklahoma State	3 TE Johnny Mitchell / William Washington
45 Iowa State	13 QB Mickey Joseph / Mike Grant
12 Colorado	27 IB Leodis Flowers / Scott Baldwin
41 Kansas	9 WB Nate Turner / Tyrone Hughes
10 Oklahoma	45 FB Omar Soto / Lance Lewis
21 Georgia Tech ■	45 DL Joe Sims
	DL Pat Engelbert
	DL Kenny Walker
	LB Travis Hill
	LB Mike Petko
	LB Pat Tyrance
	LB Mike Croel
	DB Bruce Pickens
	DB Tahaun Lewis / Tyrone Leggette
	DB Tyrone Byrd
	DB Reggie Cooper

RUSHING: Flowers 149/940y, Baldwin 92/579y, Joseph 91/554y
PASSING: Joseph 34-78/624y, 11TD, 43.6%
Grant 32-69/484y, 4TD, 46.4%
RECEIVING: Bostick 19/375y, Mitchell 11/282y, Hughes 10/113y
SCORING: Gregg Barrios (K) 87pts, Joseph 62pts, Flowers 54pts

1991 9-2-1

59 Utah State	28 WR Jon Bostick
71 Colorado State	14 T Lance Lundberg
21 Washington	36 G Erik Wiegert (T) / Dave Jensen
18 Arizona State	9 C Bill Ziegelbein / Jim Scott
49 Oklahoma State	8 G Will Shields
38 Kansas State	31 T Brian Boerboom
63 Missouri	6 TE Johnny Mitchell / William Washington
19 Colorado	19 QB Keithen McCant
59 Kansas	23 IB Derek Brown / Calvin Jones
38 Iowa State	13 WB Nate Turner
19 Oklahoma	15 FB/WR Lance Lewis / Tyrone Hughes
0 Miami ■	22 DL Kevin Ramaekers / Jaime Liewer
	DL Pat Engelhart
	DL John Parrella
	LB Travis Hill
	LB Mike Petko
	LB Mike Anderson
	LB David White / Trev Alberts
	DB Curtis Cotton / Kenny Wilhite
	DB Tyrone Legette
	DB Tyrone Byrd
	DB Steve Carmer

RUSHING: Brown 230/1313y, Jones 108/900y, McCant 117/654y
PASSING: McCant 97-168/1454y, 13TD, 57.7%
RECEIVING: Mitchell 31/534y, Bostick 24/419y, Hughes 12/208y
SCORING: Jones & Brown 84pts, Byron Bennett (K) 78pts

1992 9-3

49 Utah	22 WR Tyrone Hughes / Corey Dixon
48 Middle Tenn. St.	7 T Lance Lundberg
14 Washington	29 G Ken Mehlin
45 Arizona State	24 C Jim Scott
55 Oklahoma St.	0 G Will Shields
34 Missouri	24 T Zach Wiegert
52 Colorado	7 TE Will Washington / Gerald Armstrong
49 Kansas	7 QB Tommie Frazier / Mike Grant
10 Iowa State	19 IB Derek Brown / Calvin Jones
33 Oklahoma	9 WB Vincent Hawkins / Abdul Muhammad
38 Kansas State	24 FB Lance Lewis
14 Florida State ■	27 DL John Parrella
	DL David Noonan / Terry Conneally
	DL Bruce Moore
	LB Travis Hill
	LB Mike Anderson / Darren Williams
	LB Ed Stewart
	LB Trev Alberts / David White
	DB Kenny Wilhite
	DB John Reece
	DB Tyrone Byrd / Troy Dumas
	DB Steve Carmer / Tobey Wright

RUSHING: Jones 168/1210y, Brown 169/1011y, Lewis 62/482y
PASSING: Frazier 44-100/727y, 10TD, 44%
Grant 46-92/479y, 5TD, 50%
RECEIVING: Jones 14/162y, Trumane Bell (WR) 14/124y,
Dixon 13/279y
SCORING: Jones 90pts, Byron Bennett (K) 71pts, Frazier &
Armstrong 42pts

1993 11-1

76 North Texas	14 WR Corey Dixon / Reggie Baul
50 Texas Tech	27 T Lance Lundberg
14 UCLA	13 G Rob Zatechka
48 Colorado State	13 C Ken Mehlin (G) / Aaron Graham
27 Oklahoma State	13 G Brenden Stai
45 Kansas State	28 T Zach Wiegert
49 Missouri	7 TE Gerald Armstrong / Trumane Bell
21 Colorado	17 QB Tommie Frazier
21 Kansas	20 IB Calvin Jones / Lawrence Phillips
49 Iowa State	17 WB Abdul Muhammad / Matt Shaw (TE)
21 Oklahoma	7 FB Cory Schlesinger
16 Florida State ■	18 DL Kevin Ramaekers
	DL Terry Connealy
	LB Donta Jones / Bruce Moore
	LB Ernie Beler / Lorenzo Brinkley
	LB Mike Anderson / Daren Williams
	LB Ed Stewart
	LB Trev Alberts
	DB Barron Miles
	DB Tyrone Williams / Troy Dumas
	DB John Reece
	DB Toby Wright

RUSHING: Jones 185/1043y, Frazier 126/704y, Phillips 92/508y
PASSING: Frazier 77-162/1159y, 12TD, 47.5%
RECEIVING: Muhammad 25/383y, Dixon 17/320y, Bell 12/187y
SCORING: Jones 78pts, Byron Bennett (K) 71pts, Frazier 54pts

1994 13-0

31 West Virginia	0 WR Reggie Baul / Brendan Holbein
42 Texas Tech	16 T Rob Zatechka
49 UCLA	21 G Joel Wilks / Aaron Taylor
70 Pacific	21 C Aaron Graham
42 Wyoming	32 G Brenden Stai
32 Oklahoma State	3 T Zach Wiegert
17 Kansas State	6 TE Matt Shaw / Mark Gilman
42 Missouri	7 QB Brook Berringer / Tommie Frazier
24 Colorado	7 IB Lawrence Phillips
45 Kansas	14 WB Abdul Muhammad / Clester Johnson
28 Iowa State	12 FB Cory Schlesinger / Jeff Makovicka
13 Oklahoma	3 DL Christian Peter
24 Miami ■	17 DL Terry Connealy
	LB Dwayne Harris
	LB Troy Dumas
	LB Phil Ellis / Doug Colman
	LB Ed Stewart
	LB Donta Jones / Grant Wistrom
	DB Barron Miles
	DB Tyrone Williams
	DB Tony Veland
	DB Kareem Moss

RUSHING: Phillips 286/1722y, Frazier 33/248y
PASSING: Berringer 94-151/1295y, 10TD, 62.3%
RECEIVING: Muhammad 23/360y, Phillips 22/172y, Baul 17/300y
SCORING: Phillips 96pts,

1995 12-0

64 Oklahoma State	21 WR Reggie Baul / Brendan Holbein
50 Michigan State	10 T Chris Dishman
77 Arizona State	28 G Aaron Taylor
49 Pacific	7 C Aaron Graham
35 Washington St.	21 G Steve Ott
57 Missouri	0 T Eric Anderson / Adam Treu
49 Kansas State	25 TE Mark Gilman / Tim Carpenter
44 Colorado	21 QB Tommie Frazier
73 Iowa State	14 IB A. Green/L. Phillips/ Damon Benning
41 Kansas	3 WB Clester Johnson / Jon Vedral
37 Oklahoma	0 FB Jeff Mackovicka
62 Florida ■	24 DL Jared Tomich / Chad Kelsay
	DL Christian Peter
	DL Jason Peter
	DL Grant Wistrom
	LB Jay Foreman / Jamel Williams
	LB Doug Colman / Phil Ellis/Jon Hesse
	LB Terrell Farley / Ryan Terwilliger
	DB Michael Booker / Eric Stokes
	DB Tyrone Williams
	DB Tony Veland
	DB Mike Minter

RUSHING: Green 141/1086y, Frazier 97/604y, Phillips 71/547y
PASSING: Frazier 92-163/1362y, 17TD, 56.4%
RECEIVING: Johnson 22/367y, Baul 17/304y, Gilman 16/256y
SCORING: Kris Brown (K) 97pts, Green 96pts, Frazier 86pts

1996 11-2

55 Michigan State	14 WR Brendan Holbein
0 Arizona State	19 T Adam Treu
65 Colorado State	9 G Chris Dishman
39 Kansas State	3 C Aaron Taylor
49 Baylor	0 G Jon Zatechka
24 Texas Tech	10 T Eric Anderson
63 Kansas	7 TE Tim Carpenter / Vershan Jackson
73 Oklahoma	21 QB Scott Frost
51 Missouri	7 IB Ahman Green / D. Evans/D. Benning
49 Iowa State	14 WB Jon Vedral
17 Colorado	12 FB Brian Schuster / Joel Makovicka
27 Texas ☐	37 DL Jared Tomich / Chad Kelsay
41 Virginia Tech ■	21 DL Jeff Ogard / Jason Wiltz
	DL Jason Peter
	DL Grant Wistrom / Mike Rucker
	LB Jamel Williams
	LB Jon Hesse / Jay Foreman
	LB Terrell Farley / Ryan Terwilliger
	DB Michael Booker
	DB Ralph Brown
	DB Eric Stokes / Eric Warfield
	DB Mike Minter / Octavious McFarlin

RUSHING: Green 155/917y, Evans 148/776y, Benning 85/465y
PASSING: Frost 104-200/1440y, 13TD, 52%
RECEIVING: Holbein 23/335y, Vedral 20/300y, Jackson 13/220y
SCORING: Kris Brown (K) 86pts, Evans 84pts, Frost 54pts

1997 13-0

59 Akron	14 WR Jeff Lake / Kenny Cheatham
38 Central Florida	24 T Fred Pollack
27 Washington	14 G Aaron Taylor
56 Kansas State	26 C Josh Heskew
49 Baylor	21 G Jon Zatechka
29 Texas Tech	0 T Eric Anderson
35 Kansas	0 TE Tim Carpenter / Vershan Jackson
69 Oklahoma	7 QB Scott Frost
45 Missouri	38 IB Ahman Green
77 Iowa State	14 WB Lance Brown / Shevin Wiggins
27 Colorado	24 FB Joel Makovicka
54 Texas A&M ☐	15 DL Chad Kelsay / Mike Rucker
42 Tennessee ■	17 DL Jason Wiltz / Steve Warren
	DL Jason Peter
	DL Grant Wistrom
	LB Brian Shaw / Tony Ortiz
	LB Jay Foreman / Carlos Polk
	LB Octavious McFarlin / Eric Johnson
	DB Erwin Swiney / Jerome Peterson
	DB Ralph Brown
	DB Eric Warfield
	DB Mike Brown

RUSHING: Green 278/1877y, Frost 176/1095y, Makovicka 105/685y
PASSING: Frost 88-159/1237y, 5TD, 55.4%
RECEIVING: Cheatham 14/191y, Green 14/105y, Brown 12/226y
SCORING: Green 132pts, Kris Brown (K) 115pts, Frost 114pts

1998 9-4

56 Louisiana Tech	26 WR Kenny Cheatham / Matt Davison
38 Ala.-Birm'ham	7 T Adam Julich
24 California	3 G James Sherman / Dominic Raiola
55 Washington	7 C Josh Heskew
24 Oklahoma State	17 G Ben Gessford / Russ Hochstein
21 Texas A&M	28 T Jason Schwab
41 Kansas	0 TE Sheldon Jackson / T.J. DeBates
20 Missouri	13 QB Bobby Newcombe / Eric Crouch
16 Texas	20 IB C. Buckhalter / DeAngelo Evans
42 Iowa State	7 WB Shevin Wiggins / Lance Brown
30 Kansas State	40 FB Joel Makovicka
16 Colorado	14 DL Chad Kelsay
20 Arizona ■	23 DL Jason Wiltz
	DL Loran Kaiser warren
	DL Mike Rucker / Kyle Vanden Bosch
	LB Tony Ortiz / Brian Shaw
	LB Jay Foreman
	LB Eric Johnson
	DB Erwin Swiney / Keyuo Craver
	DB Ralph Brown
	DB Mike Brown
	DB Clint Finley / Joe Walker

RUSHING: Buckhalter 142/799y, Crouch 96/459y, Mackovicka 97/458y
PASSING: Crouch 49-101/601y, 4TD, 48.5%
  Newcombe 50-79/712y, 1TD, 63.3%
RECEIVING: Davison 32/394y, Wiggins 22/326y, Jackson 19/343y
SCORING: Kris Brown (K) 89pts, Newcombe & Buckhalter 48pts

1999 12-1

42 Iowa	7 WR Matt Davison / Wilson Thomas
45 California	0 T Adam Julch
20 So. Mississippi	13 G James Sherman
40 Missouri	10 C Dominic Raiola
38 Oklahoma State	14 G Russ Hochstein
49 Iowa State	14 T Dave Volk
20 Texas	24 TE T.J. DeBates / Tracey Wistrom
24 Kansas	17 QB Eric Crouch
37 Texas A&M	0 IB Dan Alexander / Correll Buckhalter
41 Kansas State	15 WB Sean Applegate / Bob Newcombe (QB)
33 Colorado	30 FB Willie Miller
22 Texas ☐	6 DL Aaron Wills
31 Tennessee ■	21 DL Steve Warren / Jason Lohr
	DL Loran Kaiser
	DL Kyle Vanden Bosch / Chris Kelsay
	LB Tony Ortiz / Brian Shaw
	LB Carlos Polk
	LB Eric Johnson / Julius Jackson
	DB Keyuo Craver
	DB Ralph Brown / DeJuan Groce
	DB Clint Finley / Dion Booker
	DB Mike Brown

RUSHING: Crouch 180/889y, Alexander 134/865y, Buckhalter 111/662y
PASSING: Crouch 83-160/1269y, 7TD, 51.9%
RECEIVING: Davison 29/441y, Newcombe 19/238y, Wistrom 16/429y
SCORING: Crouch 102pts, Josh Brown (K) 88pts, Alexander 50pts

2000 10-2

49 San Jose State	13 WR Matt Davison
27 Notre Dame	24 T Dave Volk
42 Iowa	13 G Toniu Fonoti
42 Missouri	24 C Dominic Raiola
49 Iowa State	27 G Russ Hochstein
56 Texas Tech	3 T Jason Schwab
59 Baylor	0 TE Tracey Wistrom / John Gibson
14 Oklahoma	31 QB Eric Crouch
56 Kansas	17 IB Dan Alexander (FB) / Correll Buckhalter
28 Kansas State	29 WB Bobby Newcombe
34 Colorado	32 FB Willie Miller
66 Northwestern ■	17 DL Chris Kelsay / Demoine Adams
	DL Jason Lohr
	DL Loran Kaiser / Jeremy Slechta
	DL Kyle Vanden Bosch
	LB Scott Shanle
	LB Carlos Polk
	LB Randy Stella / Mark Vedral
	DB Keyuo Craver
	DB Erwin Swiney / DeJuan Groce
	DB Dion Booker / Troy Watchorn
	DB Joe Walker / Clint Finley

RUSHING: Alexander 182/1154y, Crouch 169/971y, Buckhalter 106/750y
PASSING: Crouch 75-156/1101y, 11TD, 48.1%
RECEIVING: Davison 21/389y, Wistrom 19/314y, Newcombe 19/249y
SCORING: Crouch 120pts, Josh Brown (K) 75pts, Buckhalter & Alexander 48pts

2001 11-2

21 TCU	7 WR Wilson Thomas
42 Troy State	14 T Dave Volk
27 Notre Dame	10 G Toniu Fonoti
48 Rice	3 C John Garrison
36 Missouri	3 G Jon Rutherford
48 Iowa State	14 T Dan Vili Waldrop
48 Baylor	7 TE Tracey Wistrom / Aaron Golliday
41 Texas Tech	31 QB Eric Crouch
20 Oklahoma	10 IB Dahrran Diedrick / Thunder Collins
51 Kansas	7 WB John Gibson
31 Kansas State	21 FB Judd Davies / Steve Kriewald
36 Colorado	62 DL Chris Kelsay / Justin Smith
14 Miami ■	37 DL Jon Clanton
	DL Jeremy Slechta / Casey Nelson
	DL Demoine Adams
	LB Scott Shanle
	LB Jamie Burrow / Barrett Ruud
	LB Mark Vedral
	DB Keyuo Craver / Lornell McPherson
	DB DeJuan Groce
	DB Dion Booker / Pat Ricketts
	DB Willie Amos /Philip Bland/ Erwin Swiney

RUSHING: Diedrick 233/1299y, Crouch 203/1115y, Collins 94/678y
PASSING: Crouch 105-189/1510y, 7TD, 55.6%
RECEIVING: Thomas 37/616y, Wistrom 21/323y, Collins 19/189y
SCORING: Crouch 116pts, Diedrick 92pts, Josh Brown (K) 64pts

2002 7-7

48 Arizona State
31 Troy State
44 Utah State
7 Penn State
14 Iowa State
38 McNeese State
24 Missouri
21 Oklahoma State
38 Texas A&M
24 Texas
45 Kansas
13 Kansas State
13 Colorado
23 Mississippi ■

10 WR Wilson Thomas / Ross Pilkington
16 T Richie Incognito
13 G Mike Erickson
40 C John Garrison
36 G Wes Cody
14 T Dan Vili Waldrop / Nick Povendo
13 TE Aaron Golliday/Jon Bowling/Matt Herian
24 QB Jammal Lord
31 IB Dahrran Diedrick / David Horne
27 WB Troy Hassebroek / John Klem
7 FB Judd Davies
49 DL Chris Kelsay / Justin Smith
28 DL Ryon Bingham / Le Kevin Smith
27 DL Patrick Kabongo / Jon Clanton
DL Trevor Johnson / Demoine Adams
LB Scott Shanle
LB Barrett Ruud
LB Demorrio Williams / T.J. Hollowell
DB Fabian Washington / Pat Ricketts
DB DeJuan Groce
DB Philip Bland / Lannie Hopkins
DB Josh Bullocks / Lornell McPherson

RUSHING: Lord 251/1412y, Diedrick 179/931y, Horne 127/651y
PASSING: Lord 95-204/1362y, 12TD, 46.6%
RECEIVING: Thomas 30/353y, Pilkington 14/301y, Josh Davis (IB) 10/58y
SCORING: Josh Brown (K) 88pts, Lord 48pts, Horne 42pts

2003 10-3

17 Oklahoma State
31 Utah State
18 Penn State
38 Southern Miss
30 Troy State
24 Missouri
48 Texas A&M
28 Iowa State
7 Texas
24 Kansas
9 Kansas State
31 Colorado
17 Michigan State ■

7 WR Ross Pilkington
7 T Richie Incognito
10 G Mike Erickson
14 C Josh Sewell
0 G Jake Andersen / Brandon Koch
41 T Dan Vili Waldrop
12 TE Matt Herian
0 QB Jammal Lord
31 IB Cory Ross / Cory Ross
3 WB Mark LeFlore / Isaiah Fluellen
38 FB Judd Davies
22 DL Benard Thomas
3 DL Ryon Bingham / Patrick Kabongo
DL Le Kevin Smith / Titus Adams
DL Trevor Johnson
LB T.J. Hollowell
LB Barrett Ruud
LB Demorrio Wiliams
DB Fabian Washington
DB Pat Ricketts / Lornell McPherson
DB Josh Bullocks / Jerrell Pippens
DB Daniel Bullocks

RUSHING: Lord 215/948y, Davis 138/600y, Ross 130/575y
PASSING: Lord 85-176/1305y, 6TD, 48.3%
RECEIVING: Herian 22/484y, Pilkington 22/338y, LeFlore 19/197y
SCORING: David Dyches (K) 74pts, Lord 60pts, Davies 30pts

2004 5-6

56 W. Illinois
17 Southern Miss
24 Pittsburgh
14 Kansas
10 Texas Tech
59 Baylor
21 Kansas State
24 Missouri
27 Iowa State
3 Oklahoma
20 Colorado

17 WR Ross Pilkington / Grant Mulkey
21 WR Terrence Nunn / Mark LeFlore
17 T Mike Erickson
8 G Brandon Koch
70 C Kurt Mann
27 G Jake Andersen
45 T Seppo Evwaraye
3 TE Matt Herian / Dusty Keiser
34 QB Joe Dailey
30 IB Cory Ross / Brandon Jackson
26 FB Steve Kriewald / Tierre Green
DL Benard Thomas
DL Le Kevin Smith
DL Titus Adams
DL Adam Carriker / Jay Moore
LB Stewart Bradley
LB Barrett Ruud
LB Chad Sievers / Ira Cooper
DB Fab Washington / Kellen Huston
DB Lornell McPherson / Cortney Grixby
DB Josh Bullocks
DB Daniel Bullocks

RUSHING: Ross 207/1102y, Jackson 85/390y, Green 44/284y
PASSING: Dailey 153-311/2025y, 17TD, 49.2%
RECEIVING: Pilkington 27/337y, Herian 24/308y, Ross 21/262y
SCORING: Ross 48pts, Sandro DeAngelis (K) 45pts, Jackson 36pts

2005 8-4

25 Maine
31 Wake Forest
7 Pittsburgh
27 Iowa State
31 Texas Tech
23 Baylor
24 Missouri
24 Oklahoma
15 Kansas
27 Kansas State
30 Colorado
32 Michigan ■

7 WR Terrence Nunn
3 WR Nate Swift / Frantz Hardy
6 WR Isaiah Fluellen / Grant Mulkey
20 T Corn'lius Fuamatu-Thomas/L. Murtha
34 G Greg Austin / Jared Helming
14 C Kurt Mann
41 G Brandon Koch
31 T Seppo Evwaraye / Matt Slauson
40 TE J.B. Phillips / Josh Mueller
25 QB Zac Taylor
3 RB Cory Ross /Marlon Lucky/Cody Glenn
28 DL Jay Moore / Wali Muhammad
DL Titus Adams
DL LeKevin Smith
DL Adam Carriker / Barry Turner
LB Adam Ickes / Stewart Bradley
LB Corey McKeon
LB Bo Ruud / Lance Brandenburgh
DB Cortney Grixby
DB Tierre Green / Zackary Bowman
DB Blake Tiedtke
DB Daniel Bullocks

RUSHING: Ross 225/882y, Glenn 45/131y, Lucky 43/129y
PASSING: Taylor 237-430/2653y, 19TDs, 55.1%
RECEIVING: Swift 45/641y, Nunn 43/495y, Ross 43/392y
SCORING: Jordan Congdon (K) 88pts, Ross 48pts, Nunn & Swift 42pts

2006 9-5

49 Louisiana Tech
56 Nicholls State
10 Southern Cal
56 Troy
39 Kansas
28 Iowa State
21 Kansas State
20 Texas
29 Oklahoma State
34 Missouri
28 Texas A&M
37 Colorado
7 Oklahoma □
14 Auburn ■

10 WR Terrence Nunn / Nate Swift
7 WR Maurice Purify / Todd Peterson
28 T Chris Patrick / Lydon Murtha
0 G Greg Austin / Andy Christensen
32 C Brett Byford / Kurt Mann
14 G Mike Huff
3 T Matt Slauson / Carl Nicks
22 TE Matt Herian/J.B. Phillips/Josh Mueller
41 QB Zac Taylor
20 RB Brandon Jackson / Marlon Lucky
27 FB Dane Todd
14 DL Jay Moore
21 DL Ola Dagunduro
17 DL Barry Cryer / Ndamukong Suh
DL Adam Carriker / Barry Turner
LB Stewart Bradley /Lance Brandenburgh
LB Corey McKeon
LB Bo Ruud / Steve Octavien
DB Cortney Grixby
DB Andre Jones
DB Andrew Shanle
DB Tierre Green

RUSHING: Jackson 188/989y, Lucky 141/728y, Cody Glenn (RB) 71/370y, Kenny Wilson (RB) 75/335y
PASSING: Taylor 233-391/3197y, 26TD, 59.6%
RECEIVING: Nunn 42/597y, Purify 34/630y, Jackson 33/313y, Lucky 32/383y, Swift 22/374y
SCORING: Jordan Congdon (K) 70pts, Jackson 60pts, Cody Glenn (RB) 48pts

2007 5-7

52 Nevada
20 Wake Forest
31 Southern Cal
41 Ball State
35 Iowa State
6 Missouri
14 Oklahoma State
14 Texas A&M
25 Texas
39 Kansas
73 Kansas State
51 Colorado

10 WR Nate Swift / Todd Peterson
17 WR Terrence Nunn / Frantz Hardy
49 WR Maurice Purify
40 T Carl Nicks
17 G Jacob Hickman
41 C Brett Byford
45 G Mike Huff (T) / Jaivorio Burkes
36 T Lydon Murtha / Matt Slauson (G)
28 TE J.B. Phillips / Sean Hill
76 QB Sam Keller / Joe Ganz
31 IB Marlon Lucky / Andy Sand (FB)
65 DL Barry Turner
DL Ndamukong Suh / Dan Titchener
DL Ty Steinkuhler / Kevin Dixon
DL Zach Potter
LB Bo Ruud
LB Corey McKeon / Phillip Dillard
LB Steve Octavien / Lance Brandenburgh
DB Anthony Murillo / Zackary Bowman
DB Cortney Grixby / Anthony Blue
DB Tierre Green
DB Larry Asante / Ben Eisenhart

RUSHING: Lucky 206/1090y, Quentin Castille (IB) 76/343y, Roy Helu (IB) 45/209y
PASSING: Keller 205-325/2422y, 14TD, 63.1%
Ganz 89-152/1435y, 16TD, 58.6%
RECEIVING: Lucky 75/705y, Purify 57/814y, Swift 36/520y, Nunn 35/452y
SCORING: Lucky 74pts, Alex Henery (K) 69pts, Purify 54pts

2008 9-4

47 W. Michigan
35 San Jose State
38 New Mexico St.
30 Virginia Tech
17 Missouri
31 Texas Tech
35 Iowa State
32 Baylor
28 Oklahoma
45 Kansas
56 Kansas State
40 Colorado
26 Clemson ■

24 WR Nate Swift / Menelik Holt
12 WR Todd Peterson / Niles Paul
7 T Mike Smith / Jaivorio Burkes
35 G Keith Williams / Mike Huff
52 C Jacob Hickman
37 G Matt Slauson
7 T Lydon Murtha / Marcel Jones
20 TE Mike McNeill / Hunter Teafatiller
62 QB Joe Ganz
35 IB Marlon Lucky / Roy Helu, Jr.
28 FB Thomas Lawson / Dreu Young (TE)
31 DL Zach Potter
21 DL Ndamukong Suh
DL Ty Steinkuhler
DL Pierre Allen
LB Tyler Wortman
LB Phillip Dillard
LB Cody Glenn / Blake Lawrence
DB Anthony West / Lance Thorell
DB Armando Murillo / Eric Hagg
DB Matt O'Hanlon / Rickey Thenarse
DB Larry Asante / Prince Amukamara

RUSHING: Helu 125/803y, Lucky 125/517y, Quentin Castille (IB) 106/467y
PASSING: Ganz 285-420/3568y, 25TD, 67.9%
RECEIVING: Swift 63/941y, Peterson 62/786y, McNeill 32/442y
SCORING: Alex Henery (K) 110pts, Swift 66pts, Lucky 48pts

2009 10-4

40 Florida Atlantic
38 Arkansas State
15 Virginia Tech
55 La.-Lafayette
27 Missouri
10 Texas Tech
7 Iowa State
20 Baylor
10 Oklahoma
31 Kansas
17 Kansas State
28 Colorado
12 Texas □
33 Arizona ■

3 WR Menelik Holt / Khiry Cooper
9 WR Niles Paul / Curenski Gilleylen
16 T Mike Smith
0 G Keith Williams / Derek Meyer
12 C Jacob Hickman
31 G Ricky Henry
9 T Marcel Jones / P.J. Jones
10 TE Mike McNeill / Dreu Young
3 QB Zac Lee / Cody Green
18 IB Roy Helu, Jr. / Rex Burkhead
3 FB Tyler Legate
20 DL Barry Turner / Cameron Meredith
13 DL Ndamukong Suh
0 DL Jared Crick
DL Pierre Allen
LB Sean Fisher
LB Will Compton
LB Phillip Dillard / Blake Lawrence
DB Alfonzo Dennard / Anthony West
DB Prince Amukamara / Dejon Gomes
DB Matt O'Hanlon
DB Larry Asante / Eric Hagg

RUSHING: Helu 220/1147y, Burkhead 81/346y, Lee 103/171y
PASSING: Lee 177-302/2143y, 14TD, 58.6%
RECEIVING: Paul 40/796y, McNeill 28/259y, Helu 19/149y, Gilleylen 17/302y
SCORING: Alex Henery (K) 110pts, Helu 60pts, Paul 38pts

2010 10-4

49 W. Kentucky
38 Idaho
56 Washington
17 So. Dakota St.
48 Kansas State
13 Texas
51 Oklahoma State
31 Missouri
31 Iowa State
20 Kansas
6 Texas A&M
45 Colorado
20 Oklahoma □
7 Washington ■

10 WR Brandon Kinnie / Tim Marlowe
17 WR Niles Paul / Mike McNeill (TE)
21 T Jeremiah Sirles
3 G Keith Williams
13 C Mike Caputo / Justin Jackson
20 G Ricky Henry
41 T D.J. Jones
17 TE Ben Cotton
30 TE/FB Kyler Reed / Tyler Legate
3 QB Tyler Martinez / Cody Green
9 IB Roy Helu, Jr. / Rex Burkhead
17 DL Cameron Meredith
23 DL Baker Steinkuhler / Terrence Moore
19 DL Jared Crick
DL Pierre Allen
LB Lavonte Davis / Eric Martin
LB/DB Will Compton / Courtney Osborne
DB Prince Amukamara
DB Alfonzo Dennard
DB Eric Hagg
DB Dejon Gomes / P.J. Smith
DB Austin Cassidy / Rickey Thenarse

RUSHING: Helu 188/1245y, Martinez 162/966y, Burkhead 172/951y
PASSING: Martinez 116-196/1631y, 10TD, 59.2%
Green 33-60/340y, 3TD, 55%
RECEIVING: Kinnie 44/494y, Paul 39/516y, Reed 22/396y, McNeill 21/346y
SCORING: Alex Henery (K) 108pts, Martinez 72pts, Helu 66pts

NORTH CAROLINA

University of North Carolina (Founded 1789)
Chapel Hill, North Carolina
Nickname: Tar Heels
Colors: Carolina Blue and White
Stadium: Kenan Memorial Stadium (1927) 60,000
Conference Affiliation: Atlantic Coast (Charter member, 1953-present)

CAREER RUSHING YARDS

	Attempts	Yards
Amos Lawrence (1977-80)	881	4391
Mike Voight (1973-76)	826	3971
Leon Johnson (1993-96)	797	3693
Kelvin Bryant (1979-82)	599	3267
Don McCauley (1968-70)	603	3172
Ethan Horton (1981-84)	604	3074
Natrone Means (1990-92)	605	3074
Charlie Justice (1946-49)	526	2634
Tyrone Anthony (1980-83)	464	2516
Ronnie McGill (2003-06)	529	2393

CAREER PASSING YARDS

	Comp.-Att.	Yards
T.J. Yates (2007-10)	795-1277	9377
Darian Durant (2001-04)	701-1159	8755
Ronald Curry (1998-01)	345-695	4987
Jason Stanicek (1991-94)	372-622	4683
Mike Thomas (1991-95)	302-573	4368
Matt Kupec (1976-79)	305-552	3840
Chris Keldorf (1996-97)	305-519	3795
Mark Maye (1984, 86-87)	263-468	3459
Kevin Anthony (1983-85)	296-528	3412
Scott Stankavage (1980-83)	272-497	3363

CAREER RECEIVING YARDS

	Catches	Yards
Hakeem Nicks (2006-08)	181	2840
Corey Holliday (1989-93)	155	2447
Octavus Barnes (1994-97)	129	2398
Sam Aiken (1999-02)	146	2205
Na Brown (1995-98)	165	2086
L.C. Stevens (1995-98)	120	2002
Jarwarski Pollock (2002-05)	177	1958
Kory Bailey (1998-01)	139	1939
Art Weiner (1946-49)	106	1733
Jesse Holley (2003-06)	126	1760

SEASON RUSHING YARDS

	Attempts	Yards
Don McCauley (1970)	324	1720
Mike Voight (1976)	315	1407
Mike Voight (1975)	259	1250
Derrick Fenner (1986)	200	1250
Ethan Horton (1984)	238	1247

SEASON PASSING YARDS

	Comp.-Att.	Yards
T.J. Yates (2010)	282-422	3418
T.J. Yates (2007)	218-365	2655
Darian Durant (2003)	234-389	2551
Mike Thomas (1975)	185-332	2436
Chris Keldorf (1996)	201-338	2347

SEASON RECEIVING YARDS

	Catches	Yards
Hakeem Nicks (2008)	68	1222
Sam Aiken (2002)	68	990
Octavus Barnes (1995)	53	970
Hakeem Nicks (2007)	74	958
Dwight Jones (2010)	62	946

GAME RUSHING YARDS

	Attempts	Yards
Derrick Fenner (1986 vs. Virginia)	39	328
Kennard Martin (1988 vs. Duke)	39	291
Amos Lawrence (1977 vs. Virginia)	36	286

GAME PASSING YARDS

	Comp.-Att.	Yards
T.J. Yates (2010 vs. Florida State)	24-35	439
Darian Durant (2002 vs. Arizona State)	25-40	417
Chris Keldorf (1997 vs. TCU)	25-41	415

GAME RECEIVING YARDS

	Catches	Yards
Randy Marriott (1987 vs. Georgia Tech)	9	247
Dwight Jones (2010 vs. Florida State)	8	233
Jheranie Boyd (2010 vs. LSU)	6	221

GREATEST COACH:

The choice for best North Carolina coach since 1953 was a difficult one, with the main contestants possessing very similar records. But Mack Brown gets the nod due to a more difficult schedule. He did just about everything right as head coach in Chapel Hill, building the Tar Heels into a Top 10 program. But ACC king Florida State was his Achilles Heel, as the Seminoles beat Brown's Tar Heels every year they played (1992-97) before the coach departed for Texas.

With that handicap, Brown was still able to steer North Carolina to three second place finishes in the conference and final national rankings of no. 10 in 1996 and no. 6 in 1997. Coming to Chapel Hill from Tulane with the reputation as an offensive wunderkind, Brown built both sides of the ball into feared units. Every year he seemed to lose All American defenders, yet every year there was someone new who did the job just as well.

Brown did the same good-job-but-there-was-someone-better work with Texas until 2005, when there was no school better at the game of football than his Longhorns.

NORTH CAROLINA'S 55 GREATEST SINCE 1953

OFFENSE

WIDE RECEIVER: Sam Aiken, Corey Holliday, Hakkem Nicks
TIGHT END: Freddie Jones, Charles Waddell
TACKLE: Brian Blados, Brian Chacos, Kevin Donnalley, Jerry Sain
GUARD: Ed Chalupka, David Drechsler, Ken Huff, Ron Rusnak, Ron Wooten
CENTER: Mark Cantrell, Rick Donnalley
QUARTERBACK: Darian Durant, T.J. Yates
RUNNING BACK: Kelvin Bryant, Ethan Horton, Leon Johnson, Amos Lawrence, Don McCauley, Mike Voight
FULLBACK: Ken Willard

DEFENSE

END: Greg Ellis, Marcus Jones, Julius Peppers, Ryan Sims
TACKLE: Carlton Bailey, William Fuller, Dee Hardison, Donnell Thompson
LINEBACKER: Buddy Curry, Kivuusama Mays, Darrrell Nicholson, Brian Simmons, Lawrence Taylor, Mike Wilcher
CORNERBACK: Lou Angelo, Ricky Barden, Dre' Bly, Greg Poole
SAFETY: Dexter Reid, Steve Streater, Bracey Walker

SPECIAL TEAMS

RETURN SPECIALISTS: Bosley Allen, Brandon Tate
PLACE KICKER: Josh McGee
PUNTER: Brian Schmitz

MULTIPLE POSITIONS

LINEBACKER-SAFETY: Jimmy DeRatt
CENTER-TACKLE: Harris Barton

TWO-WAY PLAYERS

GUARD-LINEBACKER: Bill Koman
QUARTERBACK-DEFENSIVE BACK: Jack Cummings
END-DEFENSIVE END: Al Goldstein

PERFORMANCE FORMULA:
NORTH CAROLINA'S 10 BEST SEASONS

1980	1.6006	6 of 70
1972	1.5778	8 of 70
1997	1.5769	8 of 70
1996	1.5638	7 of 70
1981	1.5180	9 of 70
1982	1.4080	16 of 70
1979	1.4028	13 of 70
1993	1.3983	18 of 70
1977	1.3748	15 of 70
1963	1.3637	15 of 70

NORTH CAROLINA TAR HEELS

Year	W-L-T	AP Poll	Conference Standing	Toughest Regular Season Opponents	Coach (Record at School)	Bowl Games			
1953	4-6		3t	Maryland 10-0, Notre Dame 9-0-1, Duke 7-2-1, Tennessee 6-4-1	George Barclay				
1954	4-5-1		3	Notre Dame 9-1, Maryland 7-2-1, Duke 7-2-1, Georgia 6-3-1	George Barclay				
1955	4-6		3t	Oklahoma 10-0, Maryland 10-0, Notre Dame 8-2, Duke 7-2-1	George Barclay (11-18-1)				
1956	2-7-1		3	Oklahoma 10-0, Tennessee 10-0, South Carolina 7-3	Jim Tatum				
1957	6-4		4	Navy 8-1-1, No. Carolina St. 7-1-2, Clemson 7-3, Duke 6-2-2	Jim Tatum				
1958	6-4		4	Clemson 8-2, Notre Dame 6-4, South Carolina 6-4	Jim Tatum (16-13-1)				
1959	5-5		2	Clemson 8-2, Wake Forest 6-4, South Carolina 6-4, Miami 6-4	Jim Hickey				
1960	3-7		6	Tennessee 6-2-2, No. Carolina St. 6-3-1, Duke 7-3, Maryland 6-4	Jim Hickey				
1961	5-5		2	LSU 9-1, Duke 7-3, Maryland 7-3, Miami 7-3	Jim Hickey				
1962	3-7		4t	Duke 8-2, Ohio State 6-3, Clemson 6-4, Maryland 6-4	Jim Hickey				
1963	9-2		1	North Carolina State 8-2, Michigan State 6-2-1, Clemson 5-4-1	Jim Hickey	Gator	35	Air Force	0
1964	5-5		3t	LSU 7-2-1, Georgia 6-3-1	Jim Hickey				
1965	4-6		5t	Ohio State 7-2, Notre Dame 7-2-1, Duke 6-4, No. Carolina St. 6-4	Jim Hickey (36-45)				
1966	2-8		8	Notre Dame 9-0-1, Georgia 9-1, Clemson 6-4, Michigan 6-4	Bill Dooley				
1967	2-8		7	North Carolina State 8-2, Clemson 6-4	Bill Dooley				
1968	3-7		8	Virginia 7-2, Air Force 7-3, North Carolina State 6-4, Florida 6-3-1	Bill Dooley				
1969	5-5		3t	Florida 8-1-1, South Carolina 7-3, Air Force 6-4	Bill Dooley				
1970	8-4		2t	Duke 6-5, Wake Forest 6-5, Tulane 7-4	Bill Dooley	Peach	26	Arizona State	48
1971	9-3		1	Notre Dame 8-2, Duke 6-5, Wake Forest 6-5	Bill Dooley	Gator	3	Georgia	7
1972	11-1	12	1	Ohio State 9-1, North Carolina State 7-3-1, East Carolina 9-2	Bill Dooley	Sun	32	Texas Tech	28
1973	4-7		6	North Carolina State 8-3, Maryland 8-3, Missouri 7-4	Bill Dooley				
1974	7-5		2t	North Carolina State 9-2, Maryland 8-3, Clemson 7-4, Pitt 7-4	Bill Dooley	Sun	24	Mississippi State	26
1975	3-7-1		6	Ohio St. 10-1, Maryland 8-2-1, No. Dame 8-3, No. Carolina St 7-3-1	Bill Dooley				
1976	9-3		2	Florida 8-3, Kentucky 8-3, Missouri 6-5	Bill Dooley	Peach	0	Kentucky	21
1977	8-3-1	17	1	Kentucky 10-1, Clemson 8-2-1, North Carolina St. 7-4, Maryland 7-4	Bill Dooley (69-53-2)	Liberty	17	Nebraska	21
1978	5-6		4	Clemson 10-1, Maryland 9-2, North Carolina State 8-3, Pitt 8-3	Dick Crum				
1979	8-3-1	15	5	Pitt 10-1, Clemson 8-3, Wake Forest 8-3, Maryland 7-4, NC St. 7-4	Dick Crum	Gator	17	Michigan	15
1980	11-1	10	1	Maryland 8-3, North Carolina State 6-5	Dick Crum	Bluebonnet	16	Texas	7
1981	10-2	9	2	Clemson 11-0, Duke 6-5	Dick Crum	Gator	31	Arkansas	27
1982	8-4	18	3t	Clemson 9-1-1, Pitt 9-2, Maryland 8-3, North Carolina State 6-5	Dick Crum	Sun	26	Texas	10
1983	8-4		2	Clemson 9-1-1, Maryland 8-3, Florida State 7-4	Dick Crum	Peach	3	Florida State	28
1984	5-5-1		3	Boston College 9-2, Maryland 8-3, Virginia 7-2-2, Clemson 7-4	Dick Crum				
1985	5-6		5	LSU 9-1-1, Florida State 8-3, Maryland 8-3, Georgia Tech 8-2-1	Dick Crum				
1986	7-4-1		2	LSU 9-2, North Carolina State 8-2-1, Clemson 7-2-2, FSU 6-4-1	Dick Crum	Aloha	21	Arizona	30
1987	5-6		6	OU 11-0, Auburn 9-1-1, Clemson 9-2, UVA 7-4, Wake Forest 7-4	Dick Crum (72-43-1)				
1988	1-10		7	Auburn 10-1, Clem. 9-2, OU 9-2, No. Carolina St. 7-3-1, Duke 7-3-1	Mack Brown				
1989	1-10		8	Virginia 10-2, Clemson 9-2, Duke 8-3, North Carolina St. 7-4	Mack Brown				
1990	6-4-1		5	Georgia Tech 10-0-1, Clemson 9-2, Virginia 8-3	Mack Brown				
1991	7-4		5	No. Carolina St. 9-2, Clemson 8-2-1, UVA 8-2-1, Georgia Tech 7-5	Mack Brown				
1992	9-3	19	3	Florida State 10-1, North Carolina State 9-2-1, Virginia 7-4	Mack Brown	Peach	21	Mississippi State	17
1993	10-3	21	2	Florida State 10-1, Clemson 8-3, North Carolina St. 7-4, Virginia 7-4	Mack Brown	Gator	10	Alabama	24
1994	8-4		3t	Florida State 9-1-1, North Carolina State 8-3, Duke 8-3, Virginia 8-3	Mack Brown	Sun	31	Texas	35
1995	7-5	27	5	Florida State 9-2, Clemson 8-3, Virginia 8-4, Georgia Tech 6-5	Mack Brown	Carquest	20	Arkansas	10
1996	10-2	10	2	Florida State 11-0, Clemson 7-4, Virginia 7-4, Houston 7-4	Mack Brown	Gator	20	West Virginia	13
1997	11-1	6	2	Florida State 10-1, Clemson 7-4, Virginia 7-4, Georgia Tech 6-5	Mack Brown (69-46-1)	Gator	42	Virginia Tech	3
					Carl Torbush [1-0]	Las Vegas	20	San Diego State	13
1998	7-5		4t	FSU 11-1, Virginia 9-2, Georgia Tech 9-2, North Carolina St. 7-5	Carl Torbush				
1999	3-8		9	Florida State 11-0, Georgia Tech 8-3, Virginia 7-4, Houston 7-4	Carl Torbush				
2000	6-5		6	FSU 11-1, Clemson 9-2, Georgia Tech 9-2, North Carolina St. 7-4	Carl Torbush (17-18)				
2001	8-5		3	Oklahoma 11-1, Maryland 10-1, Texas 10-2, Florida State 7-4	John Bunting	Peach	16	Auburn	10
2002	3-9		8	North Carolina State 10-3, Maryland 10-3, Texas 10-2, FSU 9-4	John Bunting				
2003	2-10		9	Florida State 10-2, Maryland 9-3, Clemson 8-4, Wisconsin 7-5	John Bunting				
2004	6-6		3t	Virginia Tech 10-2, Florida State 8-3, Miami 8-3, Virginia 8-3	John Bunting	Continental	24	Boston College	37
2005	5-6		Cst4	Va Tech 10-2, Miami 9-2, Louisville 9-2, Wisconsin 9-3, BC 8-3	John Bunting				
2006	3-9		Cst5	Virginia Tech 10-2, Wake Forest 10-2, ND 10-2, Rutgers 10-2	John Bunting (27-45)				
2007	4-8		Cst4	Virginia 9-3, South Florida 9-3, Virginia Tech 10-2	Butch Davis				
2008	8-5		Cst3t	Virginia Tech 9-4, Boston College 9-4, Georgia Tech 9-3	Butch Davis	Meineke Care	30	West Virginia	31
2009	8-5		Cst4	Georgia Tech 11-2, Virginia Tech 9-3, Miami 9-3, Boston College 8-4	Butch Davis	Meineke Care	17	Pittsburgh	19
2010	8-5		Cst 3t	LSU 10-2, Virginia Tech 11-2, North Carolina State 8-4	Butch Davis (28-23)	Music City	30	Tennessee	27

TOTAL: 343-304-8 .5298 (37 of 70)

Bowl Games since 1953: 13-12 .5200 (33 of 70)

GREATEST TEAM SINCE 1953: The 1980 team won 11 games and the ACC crown behind a great offensive line that opened holes for two 1,000-yard backs and a hard-hitting defense. Five of coach Dick Crum's Tar Heels received All American notice that season.

1953 4-6

29 N. Carolina St.	7 E Ken Yarborough (T) / Tom Adler
39 Wash'gt'n & Lee	0 T Frank Fredere / Jim McCreedy
18 Wake Forest	13 G Jimmy Neville
0 Maryland	26 C Bill Koman / Howard Seawell
14 Georgia	27 G Ed Patterson / Miles Gregory
6 Tennessee	20 T Thad Eure
0 South Carolina	18 E Norm Lane / Will Frye
14 Notre Dame	34 QB Marshall Newman
33 Virginia	7 HB Ken Keller / Larry Parker
20 Duke	35 HB Connie Gravitte
	FB Billy Williams / Dick Lackey

RUSHING: Keller 83/432y
PASSING: Newman 26-81/297y, 3TD, 32.1%
RECEIVING: Adler 13/145y
SCORING: Keller (HB-K) 37pts

1954 4-5-1

20 N. Carolina St.	6 E Will Frye
7 Tulane	7 T Jack Maultsby
7 Georgia	21 G Jimmy Neville
0 Maryland	33 C Bill Koman
14 Wake Forest	7 G Ed Patterson / John Jones
20 Tennessee	26 T Roland Perdue
21 South Carolina	19 E Norman Lane
13 Notre Dame	42 QB Len Bullock / Marshall Newman
26 Virginia	14 HB Ken Keller / Larry Parker
12 Duke	47 HB Connie Gravitte / Ed Sutton
	FB Don Klochak / Bill Kirkman

RUSHING: Klochak 55/361y
PASSING: Bullock 31-55/283y, 3TD, 56.4%
RECEIVING: Frye 12/100y
SCORING: Keller (HB-K) 33pts

1955 3-7

6 Oklahoma	13 E Will Frye
25 N. Carolina St.	18 T Jack Maultsby / John Bilich
7 Georgia	28 G Bill Koman
7 Maryland	25 C George Stavnitski / Jimmy Jones
0 Wake Forest	25 G Jackie Lineberger / John Jones
7 Tennessee	48 T Roland Perdue / Dick Smith
32 South Carolina	14 E Buddy Payne / Norman Lane
7 Notre Dame	27 QB Dave Reed / Buddy Sasser (HB)
26 Virginia	14 HB Ken Keller / Larry McMullen
0 Duke	6 HB Ed Sutton / Joel Temple
	FB Don Lear / Howie Williams

RUSHING: Keller 105/353y, Sutton 52/349y, Lear 35/186y
PASSING: Reed 25-73/418y, 1TD, 34.2%
RECEIVING: Frye 13/181y, Temple 6/102y, Sutton 6/101y
SCORING: Keller 21pts, Sutton, Reed & Sasser 18pts

1956 2-7-1

6 N. Carolina St.	26 E Buddy Payne / Larry Muschamp
0 Oklahoma	36 T Phil Blazer / Leo Russavage
0 South Carolina	14 G Jimmy Jones
12 Georgia	26 C Ronnie Koes / Fred Swearingen
34 Maryland (F-L)	6 G Don Kemper
6 Wake Forest	6 T Stuart Pell / Don Redding
0 Tennessee	20 E Charlie Robinson / Dick Ellington
21 Virginia (F-L)	7 QB Dave Reed / Curt Hathaway
14 Notre Dame	21 HB Larry McMullen / Emil DeCantis
6 Duke	21 HB Ed Sutton / Daley Goff / Jim Varnum
	FB Wallace Vale / John Haywood

RUSHING: Sutton 120/748y, DeCantis 43/214y, Vale 50/176y
PASSING: Reed 22-54/313y, 4TD, 40.7%
RECEIVING: Sutton 14/159y, Payne 6/116y, DeCantis 5/84y
SCORING: Sutton 42pts, DeCantis 18pts, Blazer (T-K) 8pts

1957 6-4

0 N. Carolina St.	7 E Buddy Payne
26 Clemson	0 T Leo Russavage / Stuart Pell
13 Navy	9 G Fred Swearingen
20 Miami	13 C Ronnie Koes
7 Maryland	21 G Jack Lineberger / Ed Furjanic
14 Wake Forest	7 T Phil Blazer / Don Redding
0 Tennessee	35 E Mac Turlington / Don Kemper
28 South Carolina	6 QB Jack Cummings / Curt Hathaway
21 Duke	13 HB Emil DeCantis / Jim Shuler
13 Virginia	20 HB Daley Goff
	FB Ed Lipski / Bob Shupin / Don Coker

RUSHING: Goff 69/272y, Lipski 50/305y, Coker 44/135y
PASSING: Cummings 39-76/640y, 4TD, 51.3%
RECEIVING: Payne 12/204y, Goff 10/124y, DeCantis 9/137y
SCORING: Payne 18pts, Dave Reed (QB) & Shuler 12pts

1958 6-4

14 N. Carolina St.	21 E Al Goldstein / Mac Turlington
21 Clemson	26 T Phil Blazer
8 Southern Cal	7 G Fred Swearingen / Bob Shupin (FB)
6 South Carolina	0 C Ronnie Koes / Rip Hawkins
27 Maryland	0 G Fred Mueller
26 Wake Forest	7 T Don Redding / Don Stallings
21 Tennessee	7 E Don Kemper / John Schroeder
42 Virginia	0 QB Jack Cummings
24 Notre Dame	34 HB Wade Smith / Emil DeCantis
6 Duke	7 HB Danny Droze / Sonny Folckomer
	FB Don Klochak / Don Coker

RUSHING: Smith 102/449y, DeCantis 78/371y, Klochak 60/321y
PASSING: Cummings 68-134/1139y, 11TD, 50.7%
RECEIVING: Goldstein 24/490y, Smith 11/194y, Kemper 10/131y
SCORING: Klochak 34pts, Smith 30pts, 4 tied w/ 18pts

1959 5-5

18 Clemson	20 E John Schroederr / Mike Greenday
8 Notre Dame	28 T Don Stallings / John Stunda
20 N. Carolina St.	12 G Frank Riggs / Fred Mueller
19 South Carolina	6 C Rip Hawkins / Jim Davis
7 Maryland	14 G Jim LeCompte / Bob Shupin
21 Wake Forest	19 T John Hegarty / Moose Butler
7 Tennessee	29 E Al Goldstein
7 Miami	14 QB Jack Cummings / Ray Farris
41 Virginia	0 HB Wade Smith / Milam Wall
50 Duke	0 HB Gib Carson / Sonny Folckomer
	FB Don Kolchak / Bob Elliott / Joe Davies

RUSHING: Smith 87/414y, Klochak 76/278y, Davies 45/202y
PASSING: Cummings 63-144/889y, 4TD, 43.8%
RECEIVING: Goldstein 20/328y, Smith 12/181y, Schroeder 12/158y
SCORING: Klochak 30pts, Wall 24pts, 4 tied w/ 18pts

1960 3-7

0 N. Carolina St.	3 E John Schroeder / John Runco
12 Miami	29 T John Stunda / Tony Hennessey
12 Notre Dame	9 G Fred Mueller / Frank Riggs
12 Wake Forest	13 C Rip Hawkins
6 South Carolina	22 G Jim LeCompte / Jack Tillery
14 Tennessee	27 T John Hegarty / Ben Gallagher
0 Clemson	24 E Conrad Sloop / Mike Greenday
19 Maryland	22 QB Ray Farris
7 Duke	6 HB Gib Carson / Skip Clement
35 Virginia	8 HB S. Folckomer / Milam Wall / Lenny Beck
	FB Bob Elliott / Joe Davies

RUSHING: Elliott 88/356y, Carson 78/307y, Farris 126/257y
PASSING: Farris 63-143/865y, 3TD, 44.1%
RECEIVING: Schroeder 15/202y, Clement 12/153y, Runco 11/182y
SCORING: Farris 36pts, Elliott (FB-K) 33pts, Clement 12pts

1961 5-5

27 N. Carolina St.	22 E Conrad Sloop / John Runco
0 Clemson	27 T Vic Esposito / Jim Alderman
14 Maryland	8 G Benton McMillan / Sam Loflin
17 South Carolina	0 C Joe Craver
0 Miami	10 G Jim LeCompte / Duff Greene
22 Tennessee	21 T John Hegarty / Jim Shumate
0 LSU	30 E Bob Lacey / George Knox
3 Duke	6 QB Ray Farris / Junior Edge (DB)
14 Wake Forest	17 HB Gib Carson / Lenny Beck
24 Virginia	0 HB Jim Addison / Ward Marslender
	FB Bob Elliott / Joe Davies

RUSHING: Carson 116/406y, Elliott 98/361y, Addison 86/265y
PASSING: Farris 72-159/875y, 2TD, 45.3%
RECEIVING: Addison 16/110y, Carson 15/147y, Lacey 10/161y
SCORING: Elliott (FB-K) 39pts, Carson 26pts, Farris 24pts

1962 3-7

6 N. Carolina St.	7 E Bob Lacey / John Hammett
7 Ohio State	41 T Vic Esposito / John Hill
6 Michigan State	38 G Buddy Cozart / Duff Greene
13 Maryland	31 C Joe Craver
19 South Carolina	14 G Jack Tillery / Richy Zarro
23 Wake Forest	14 T Tony Hennessey
6 Clemson	17 E Steve Yates / Chris Hanburger (D)
11 Virginia	7 QB Junior Edge
7 Notre Dame	21 HB Ron Tuthill / Roger Smith
14 Duke	16 HB Ward Marslender / Ron Jackson
	FB Ken Willard / Eddie Kesler

RUSHING: Willard 119/466y, Kesler 51/157y, Tuthill 38/94y
PASSING: Edge 103-185/1234y, 7TD, 55.7%
RECEIVING: Lacey 44/668y, Tuthill 14/98y, Marslender 13/136y
SCORING: Lacey 35pts, Willard 30pts, Jackson 12pts

1963 9-2

11 Virginia	7 E Bob Lacey / John Hammett
0 Michigan State	31 T Gene Sigmon / John Hill
21 Wake Forest	0 G Jerry Cabe
14 Maryland	7 C Chris Hanburger / Glenn Ogburn
31 N. Carolina St.	10 G Richy Zarro / Clint Eudy / Jay Malobicky
7 South Carolina	0 T Vic Esposito / Cole Kortner
28 Georgia	7 E John Atherton / Joe Robinson
7 Clemson	11 QB Junior Edge / Gary Black
27 Miami	16 HB Ken Willard / Ron Tuthill
16 Duke	14 WB Ronnie Jackson / Dave Braine
35 Air Force ■	0 FB Eddie Kesler / Frank Bowman

RUSHING: Willard 185/742y, Kesler 76/314y, Edge 81/279y
PASSING: Edge 94-179/1205y, 5TD, 52.5%
RECEIVING: Lacey 51/568y, Robinson 19/259y, Hammett 19/246y
SCORING: Willard 44pts, Edge 36pts, Braine (HB-K) 21pts

1964 5-5

13 N. Carolina St.	14 E Bill Darnall / Jim Harrington
21 Michigan State	15 T John Hill
23 Wake Forest	0 G Charlie Davis
3 LSU	20 C Ed Stringer / Glenn Ogburn
9 Maryland	10 G Jay Malobicky
24 South Carolina	6 T John Harmon
8 Georgia	24 E John Atherton / Billy Axselle
29 Clemson	0 QB Gary Black / Danny Talbott
27 Virginia	31 HB Ken Willard
21 Duke	15 WB Ronnie Jackson
	FB Eddie Kesler
	DL Frank Gallagher
	DL Charlie Davis / Clint Eudy
	DL Joe Frantangelo
	DL Hank Sadler
	DL Bo Wood
	LB Chris Hanburger
	LB Richy Zarro
	DB Eddie Kesler
	DB Ron Tuthill
	DB Dave Braine / Tommy Ward
	DB Gary Black / Alan McArthur

RUSHING: Willard 228/835y, Kesler 95/465y, Black 80/261y
PASSING: Black 82-174/1038y, 7TD, 47.1%
RECEIVING: Jackson 34/512y, Willard 24/29y, Atherton 13/130y
SCORING: Willard 54pts, Jackson 30pts, Braine (DB-K) 21pts

1965 4-6

24 Michigan	31 E Bob Hume / Charlie Carr
14 Ohio State	3 T John Harmon / Chuck Alexander
17 Virginia	21 G Charlie Davis
10 N. Carolina St.	7 C Ed Stringer
12 Maryland	10 G Jay Malobicky
10 Wake Forest	12 T Tom Ingle
35 Georgia	47 TE John Atherton
17 Clemson	13 QB Danny Talbott
0 Notre Dame	17 WB Bud Phillips
7 Duke	34 HB Max Chapman / Dave Riggs
	FB Tom Lampman
	DL Bo Wood
	DL Hank Sadler
	DL Joe Frantangelo
	DL Hank Barden
	DL Jim Masino
	LB Jay Malobicky
	LB Bill Spain
	DB Jack Davenport
	DB Bill Edwards
	DB Bill Darnall
	DB Alan McArthur / Gene Link

RUSHING: Lampman 108/444y, Chapman 103/415y, Talbott 96/397y
PASSING: Talbott 103-217/1084y, 3TD, 47.5%
RECEIVING: Hume 30/263y, Atherton 29/433y, Carr 14/124y
SCORING: Talbott (QB-K) 70pts, Chapman & Riggs 18pts

1966 2-8

0 Kentucky	10 WR Charlie Carr
10 N. Carolina St.	7 T Tom Ingle
21 Michigan	7 G Mike Richey (T) / Ev Cowan
0 Notre Dame	32 C Chip Bradley
0 Wake Forest	3 G Chuck Alexander / Pat Shea
3 Georgia	28 T Terry Rowe
3 Clemson	27 T Bob Hume
14 Air Force	20 QB Danny Talbott / Jeff Beaver / Tim Karrs
25 Duke	41 HB Dave Riggs / Bud Phillips
14 Virginia	21 HB Dick Wesolowski / Tom Lampman
	FB Mark Mazza
	DL Bo Wood
	DL Tom Renedo
	DL Jim Masino
	DL Hank Sadler
	DL Lyn Duncan
	LB Bill Spain / Dave Ringwalt
	LB Brent Milgram / Mike Horvat
	DB Bill Darnall
	DB Landy Blank
	DB Jack Davenport
	DB Gene Link / Gayle Bomar

RUSHING: Riggs 110/399y, Wesolowski 87/299y, Talbott 74/188y
PASSING: Talbott 69-122/691y, 2TD, 56.6%
RECEIVING: Carr 52/490y, Hume 32/331y, Phillips 22/262y
SCORING: Bill Dodson (K) 20pts, Talbott (QB-K) 16pts, 4 tied w/12

1967 2-8

7 N. Carolina St.	13 WR Charlie Carr
10 South Carolina	16 T Steve Burdulis / Tom Ingle
11 Tulane	36 G Ev Cowan
7 Vanderbilt	21 C Chip Bradley
8 Air Force	10 G Ed Chalupka / Lou Pukal
14 Maryland	0 T Mike Richey
10 Wake Forest	20 TE Tom Cantrell / Peter Davis
0 Clemson	17 QB Gayle Bomar / Jeff Beaver
17 Virginia	40 TB Dave Riggs / Saul Zemaitis
20 Duke	9 WB Doug David / Dick Wesolowski
	FB Tommy Dempsey
	DL Lyn Duncan
	DL Jim Masino
	DL Mike Smith
	DL Battle Wall / Mike Hollifield
	DL Neil Rogers
	DL Tim Karrs
	LB Mark Mazza / Mike Horvat
	LB Bob Hanna
	DB Jack Davenport
	DB Ron Lowry / Landy Blank
	DB Ken Price

RUSHING: Bomar 193/529y, Dempsey 130/501y, Zemaitis 52/208y
PASSING: Bomar 79-158/873y, 4TD, 50%
RECEIVING: Davis 30/338y, Carr 28/273y, David 10/115y
SCORING: Dempsey 24pts, Don Hartig, Jr. (K) 22pts, Bomar 16pts

1968 3-7

6 N. Carolina St.	38 WR Bill Kelly / Peter Davis
27 South Carolina	32 T Ev Cowan
8 Vanderbilt	7 G Jim Papai
24 Maryland	33 C Chip Bradley
22 Florida	7 G Ed Chalupka
31 Wake Forest	48 T Mike Richey
15 Air Force	28 TE Tony Blanchard
6 Virginia	41 QB Gayle Bomar
14 Clemson	24 TB Saul Zemaitis / Don McCauley
25 Duke	14 WB Dick Wesolowski (FB) / Bucky Perry
	FB Ken Borries
	DL Tim Karrs
	DL Mike Smith
	DL Mike Hollifield
	DL Battle Wall
	DL Ron Grzybowski
	DL Ron Lowry
	LB Bob Hanna
	LB Mark Mazza
	DB John Harris
	DB Rusty Ross / David Jackson
	DB Ken Price

RUSHING: Bomar 165/495y, Zemaitis 119/460y, McCauley 74/345y
PASSING: Bomar 87-189/1229y, 8TD, 46%
RECEIVING: McCauley 23/313y, Blanchard 22/337y, Davis 22/300y
SCORING: Don Hartig, Jr (K) 38pts, Bomar 32pts, Blanchard 30pts

1969 5-5

3 N. Carolina St.	10 WR Ricky Lanier (QB) / Steve Alvis
6 South Carolina	14 T Paul Hoolahan / Mike Bobbitt
38 Vanderbilt	22 G Jim Hambacher
10 Air Force	20 C Keith Hicks / Bob Hanna
2 Florida	52 G Ed Chalupka
23 Wake Forest	3 T Sam Bounds
12 Virginia	0 TE Tony Blanchard
61 VMI	11 QB Johnny Swofford / Paul Miller
32 Clemson	15 TB Don McCauley
13 Duke	17 WB Lewis Jolley / Bucky Perry
	FB Saul Zemaitis
	DL Bill Brafford / Jan Smith
	DL Bud Grissom / Eric Hyman
	DL Tom Cantrell
	DL Bill Richardson
	DL Flip Ray
	DL Judge Mattocks
	LB John Bunting / Sam Cook
	LB Jim Webster / Ricky Packard
	DB David Jackson
	DB Rusty Culbreth / Richard Garrett
	DB Ken Price

RUSHING: McCauley 204/1092y, Lanier 86/370y, Zemaitis 86/311y
PASSING: Swofford 33-74/487y, 4TD, 44.6%
RECEIVING: Blanchard 23/320y, McCauley 14/238y, Jolley 9/143y
SCORING: McCauley 66pts, Don Hartig, Jr. (K) 45pts, Jolley 14pts

1970 8-4

20 Kentucky	10 WR Ricky Lanier / Ken Taylor
19 N. Carolina St.	0 T Mike Bobbitt / Jerry Sain
53 Maryland	20 G Ron Grzybowski
10 Vanderbilt	7 C Keith Hicks
21 South Carolina	35 G Jim Hambacher
17 Tulane	24 T Paul Hoolahan
13 Wake Forest	14 TE Tony Blanchard / Johnny Cowell
30 Virginia	15 QB Paul Miller
62 VMI	13 TB Don McCauley / Ike Oglesby
42 Clemson	7 WB Lewis Jolley
59 Duke	34 FB Geof Hamlin
26 Arizona State■	48 DL Bill Brafford
	DL Flip Ray
	DL Bill Richardson
	DL Bud Grissom
	DL Jan Smith / Gene Brown
	LB John Bunting / Sam Cook
	LB Rocky Packard
	LB Jim Webster
	DB Lou Angelo
	DB Greg Ward
	DB Richard Stilley / Richard Garrett

RUSHING: McCauley 324/1720y, Oglesby 126/562y, Hamlin 55/195y
PASSING: Miller 45-80/728y, 8TD, 56.3%
RECEIVING: Jolley 20/358y, Blanchard 16/239y, McCauley 15/235y
SCORING: McCauley 126pts, Ken Craven (K) 62pts, Oglesby & Jolley 36pts

1971 9-3

28 Richmond	0 WR Earle Bethea
27 Illinois	0 T Robert Pratt
35 Maryland	14 G Robert Walters / Billy Newton
27 N. Carolina St.	7 C Bob Thornton
29 Tulane	37 G Ron Rusnak
0 Notre Dame	16 T Jerry Sain
7 Wake Forest	3 TE Johnny Cowell / Ken Taylor
36 William & Mary	35 QB Paul Miller
26 Clemson	13 TB Ike Oglesby
32 Virginia	20 WB Lewis Jolley / Billy Sigler
38 Duke	0 FB Geof Hamlin
3 Georgia■	7 DL Bill Brafford
	DL Bud Grissom
	DL John Anderson / Terry Taylor
	DL Eric Hyman / Bob Vandenbrock
	DL Gene Brown
	LB John Bunting
	LB Ricky Packard
	LB Jim Webster / Mike Mansfield
	DB Lou Angelo
	DB Rusty Culbreth
	DB Richard Stilley / Phil Lamm

RUSHING: Jolley 117/712y, Hamlin 134/594y, Oglesby 118/504y
PASSING: Miller 75-146/1041y, 9TD, 51.4%
RECEIVING: Jolley 23/367y, Cowell 21/223y, Sigler 9/119y
SCORING: Jolley 68pts, Ken Craven (K) 63pts, Miller 38pts

1972 11-1

28 Richmond	18 WR Earle Bethea / Pat Norton
31 Maryland	26 T Robert Pratt
34 N. Carolina St.	33 G Ken Huff
14 Ohio State	29 C Bob Thornton
31 Kentucky	20 G Ron Rusnak
21 Wake Forest	0 T Jerry Sain
26 Clemson	10 TE Ken Taylor
23 Virginia	3 QB Nick Vidnovic
14 Duke	0 TB Ike Oglesby/Sammy Johnson/Billy Hite
42 East Carolina	19 WB Jimmy Jerome / Ted Leverenz
28 Florida	24 FB Tim Kirkpatrick / Dickie Oliver
32 Texas Tech■	28 DL Bill Chapman / Ted Elkins
	DL Peter Talty / Ronnie Robinson
	DL Eric Hyman
	DL Gene Brown
	LB Tom Embrey / Gary Cowan
	LB Terry Taylor
	LB Mike Mansfield
	LB Jimmy DeRatt
	DB Lou Angelo
	DB Phil Lamm
	DB Greg Ward

RUSHING: Oglesby 148/707y, Johnson 103/484y, Hite 118/451y
PASSING: Vinovic 69-143/1096y, 10TD, 48.3%
RECEIVING: Jerome 22/326y, Taylor 19/286y, Bethea 12/278y
SCORING: Ellis Alexander (K) 56pts, Vidnovic 36pts, Johnson 30pts

1973 4-7

34 William & Mary	27 WR Earle Bethea / Pat Norton
3 Maryland	23 T Billy Newton / John Frerotte
14 Missouri	27 G Ken Huff
26 N. Carolina St.	28 C Gary Ulicny
16 Kentucky	10 G Robert Walters
0 Tulane	16 T Robert Pratt
28 East Carolina	27 TE Charles Waddell
40 Virginia	44 QB Nick Vidnovic / Billy Paschall
29 Clemson	37 TB Sammy Johnson / Jim Betterson
42 Wake Forest	0 WB Jimmy Jerome / Ted Leverenz
10 Duke	27 FB Dickie Oliver
	DL Ted Elkins
	DL Ronnie Robinson / Steve Early
	DL Terry Taylor
	DL Peter Talty / Rod Broadway
	DL Tom Embrey
	LB Gary Cowan / Terry Cantrell
	LB Jimmy DeRatt
	LB Mark DiCarlo
	DB Phil Lamm
	DB Russ Conley / Kip Arnall
	DB Earl Chesson

RUSHING: Johnson 183/1006y, Betterson 83/414y, Mike Voight (TB) 49/281y
PASSING: Paschall 65-116/837y, 7TD, 56%
RECEIVING: Jerome 24/309y, Waddell 21/242y, Leverenz 20/252y
SCORING: Ellis Alexander (K) 48pts, Johnson 44pts, Leverenz 24pts

1974 7-5

42 Ohio Univ.	7 WR Pat Norton
31 Wake Forest	0 T Mark Griffin / Tommy Burkett
12 Maryland	24 G David Barrett / Craig Funk
45 Pittsburgh	29 C Mark Cantrell
28 Georgia Tech	29 G Ken Huff
33 N. Carolina St.	14 T John Frerotte
23 South Carolina	31 TE Charles Waddell / Andy Chacos
24 Virginia	10 QB Chris Kupec
32 Clemson	54 TB Jim Betterson / Mike Voight
56 Army	42 WB Jimmy Jerome
14 Duke	13 FB Dickie Oliver
24 Mississippi St.■	26 DL Bill Perdue / Chuck Austin
	DL Rod Broadway / Brian Hughes
	DL Ronnie Robinson
	DL Scott Reynolds / Dee Hardison
	DL Ted Elkins
	LB Billy Murphy / Gary Cowan
	LB Tom Embrey
	DB Russ Conley
	DB Ronny Johnson
	DB Bobby Trott
	DB Jimmy DeRatt

RUSHING: Betterson 209/1082y, Voight 203/1033y, Oliver 52/256y
PASSING: Kupec 104-150/1474y, 12TD, 69.3%
RECEIVING: Jerome 47/837y, Norton 23/310y, Waddell 17/206y
SCORING: Voight 66pts, Betterson & Kupec 54pts

1975 3-7-1

33 William & Mary	7 WR Ray Stanford
7 Maryland	34 T Mark Griffin
7 Ohio State	32 G Mark Salzano / Scott Davison
31 Virginia	28 C Mark Cantrell
14 Notre Dame	21 G Craig Funk
20 N. Carolina St.	21 T Tommy Burkett
17 East Carolina	38 TE Brooks Williams / Mike Corbin
9 Wake Forest	21 QB Billy Paschall
35 Clemson	38 TB Mike Voight / Jim Betterson
17 Tulane	15 WB Charlie Williams / Mel Collins
17 Duke	17 FB Brian Smith / Bob Loomis
	DL Chuck Austin / Ken Sheets
	DL Dee Hardison
	DL Roger Shonosky
	DL Rod Broadway
	DL Bill Perdue
	LB Bobby Gay / Mike Duffy
	LB Bobby Trott
	DB Russ Conley
	DB John Daw / Bobby Cale
	DB Jeff Caldwell
	DB Ronny Johnson

RUSHING: Voight 259/1250y, Betterson 95/407y, Smith 46/207y
PASSING: Paschall 93-180/1195y, 10TD, 51.7%
RECEIVING: Williams 24/290y, Collins 20/321y, Stanford 17/175y
SCORING: Voight 66pts, Tom Biddle (K) 41pts, Collins 24pts

1976 9-3

14 Miami (Ohio)	10 WR Walker Lee
24 Florida	21 T Mark Griffin
12 Northwestern	0 G John Rushing
34 Army	32 C Mark Cantrell
3 Missouri	24 G Craig Funk
13 N. Carolina St.	21 T Bobby Hukill / Tommy Burkett
12 East Carolina	10 TE Brooks Williams
34 Wake Forest	14 QB Matt Kupec / Bernie Menapace
27 Clemson	23 TB Mike Voight
31 Virginia	6 WB Mel Collins / Billy Mabry
39 Duke	38 FB Billy Johnson / Bob Loomis
0 Kentucky■	21 DL Ken Sheets
	DL Dee Hardison
	DL Roger Shonosky / Dave Simmons
	DL T.K. McDaniels
	DL Bill Perdue
	LB Ronnie Dowdy / Mike Finn
	LB Buddy Curry
	DB Russ Conley
	DB Bobby Cale
	DB Ronny Johnson
	DB Alan Caldwell

RUSHING: Voight 15/1407y, Johnson 80/411y, Loomis 56/223y
PASSING: Kupec 52-99/751y, 2TD, 52.5%
RECEIVING: Collins 14/185y, Mabry 12/116y, Lee 11/158y
SCORING: Voight 110pts, Tom Biddle (K) 62pts, Menapace 20pts

1977 8-3-1

7 Kentucky	10 WR Walker Lee
31 Richmond	0 T Steve Junkman
41 Northwestern	7 G John Rushing / Lowell Eakin
7 Texas Tech	10 C Scott Davison
24 Wake Forest	3 G Mike Salzano
27 N. Carolina St.	14 T Bobby Hukill
17 South Carolina	0 TE Brooks Williams / Mike Finn
16 Maryland	7 QB Matt Kupec
13 Clemson	13 TB Amos Lawrence / Doug Paschal
35 Virginia	14 WB Mel Collins
16 Duke	3 FB Billy Johnson / Bob Loomis
17 Nebraska■	21 DL Ken Sheets
	DL Dee Hardison
	DL Dave Simmons / Bunn Rhames
	DL Rod Broadway
	DL T.K. McDaniels
	LB Bobby Gay / Ronnie Dowdy
	LB Buddy Curry
	DB Ricky Barden
	DB Bobby Cale
	DB Bernie Menapace
	DB Alan Caldwell

RUSHING: Lawrence 193/1211y, Johnson 83/357y, Paschal 81/324y
PASSING: Kupec 59-105/715y, 7TD, 56.2%
RECEIVING: Williams 19/218y, Lee 16/220y, Collins 12/158y
SCORING: Tom Biddle (K) 66pts, Lawrence 38pts, Johnson 24pts

1978 5-6

14 East Carolina	10 WR Jim Rouse / Delbert Powell
20 Maryland	21 WR Jeff Grey / Wayne Tucker
16 Pittsburgh	20 T Steve Junkman
3 Miami of Ohio	7 G Ron Wooten
34 Wake Forest	29 C Rick Donnalley / Mark Sugg
7 N. Carolina St.	34 G Mike Salzano
24 South Carolina	22 T Bobby Hukill
18 Richmond	27 TE Bob Loomis
9 Clemson	13 QB Matt Kupec / Chuck Sharpe
38 Virginia	20 TB Amos Lawrence
16 Duke	15 FB Doug Paschal
	DL Donnell Thompson / Harry Stanback
	DL Dave Simmons
	DL Bunn Rhames / John Brugos
	LB Ken Sheets
	LB T.K. McDaniels
	LB Buddy Curry
	LB Darrell Nicholson
	DB Ricky Barden
	DB Bobby Cale
	DB Bernie Menapace
	DB Francis Winters

RUSHING: Lawrence 234/1043y, Paschal 105/499y, Terence Burrell (TB) 60/197y
PASSING: Kupec 71-121/787y, 6TD, 58.7%
Sharp 57-121/691y, 5TD, 47.1%
RECEIVING: Loomis 31/432y, Grey 20/291y, Rouse 20/279y
SCORING: Jeff Hayes (K) 43pts, Loomis 42pts, Paschal & Sharp 24pts

1979 8-3-1

28 South Carolina	0 WR Wayne Tucker / Phil Farris
17 Pittsburgh	7 WR Jeff Grey
41 Army	3 T Steve Junkmann
35 Cincinnati	14 G Ron Wooten
19 Wake Forest	24 C Rick Donnalley
35 N. Carolina St.	21 G Mark Suggs / David Drechsler
24 East Carolina	24 T Carl Hackley / Mike Marr
14 Maryland	17 TE Mike Chatham
10 Clemson	19 QB Matt Kupec
13 Virginia	7 TB Amos Lawence
37 Duke	16 FB Doug Paschal / Billy Johnson
17 Michigan■	15 DL Donnell Thompson
	DL Bob Duncan / Paul Davis
	DL John Brugos / Harry Stanback
	LB Calvin Daniels
	LB Darrell Nicholson
	LB Buddy Curry
	LB Lawrence Taylor
	DB Alana Burrus
	DB David Singleton
	DB Steve Streater
	DB Ricky Barden

RUSHING: Lawrence 225/1019y, Paschal 177/835y, Johnson 78/365y
PASSING: Kupec 123-227/1587y, 18TD, 54.2%
RECEIVING: Chatham 29/448y, Paschal 24/168y, Grey 17/230y
SCORING: Lawrence 60pts, Jeff Hayes (K) 53pts, Chatham 48pts

1980 11-1

35 Furman	13 WR Jon Richardson
9 Texas Tech	3 WR Victor Harris / Wayne Tucker
17 Maryland	3 T David Drechsler
33 Georgia Tech	0 G Ron Wooten
27 Wake Forest	9 C Rick Donnalley
28 N. Carolina St.	8 G Ron Spruill
31 East Carolina	3 T Mike Marr
7 Oklahoma	41 TE Shelton Robinson / Mike Chatham
24 Clemson	19 QB Rod Elkins
26 Virginia	3 TB Amos Lawrence / Kelvin Bryant
44 Duke	21 FB Billy Johnson / Walt Sturdivant
16 Texas■	7 DL Donnell Thompson
	DL Paul Davis
	DL Harry Stanback
	LB Calvin Daniels
	LB Darrell Nicholson
	LB Lee Shaffer
	LB Lawrence Taylor
	DB Greg Poole / David Singleton
	DB Tyress Bratton
	DB Steve Streater
	DB Billy Jackson

RUSHING: Lawrence 229/1118y, Bryant 177/1039y, Johnson 103/433y
PASSING: Elkins 81-160/1002y, 11TD, 50.6%
RECEIVING: Chatham 20/239y, Harrison 16/210y, Richardson 15/206y
SCORING: Lawrence 90pts, Bryant 72pts, Jeff Hayes (K) 55pts

1981 10-2

56 East Carolina	0 WR Jon Richardson
49 Miami of Ohio	7 WR Mark Smith
56 Boston College	14 T Brian Blados
28 Georgia Tech	7 G David Drechsler
48 Wake Forest	10 C Steve McGrew / Brian Johnston
21 N. Carolina St.	10 G Ron Spruill
13 South Carolina	31 T Mike Marr
17 Maryland	10 TE Shelton Robinson
8 Clemson	10 QB Rod Elkins / Scott Stankavage
17 Virginia	14 TB Kelvin Bryant / Tyrone Anthony
31 Duke	10 FB Alan Burrus
31 Arkansas■	27 DL William Fuller
	DL Steve Fortson
	DL Jack Parry
	LB Mike Wilcher
	LB Lee Shaffer / Chris Ward
	LB Darrell Nicholson
	LB Calvin Daniels
	DB Greg Poole
	DB Walter Black
	DB Sammy Johnson / Darryl Lucas
	DB Billy Jackson / Willie Harris

RUSHING: Bryant 152/1015y, Anthony 146/699y, Burrus 98/463y
PASSING: Elkins 69-136/994y, 9TD, 50.7%
RECEIVING: Richardson 28/373y, Smith 19/368y, Anthony 14/165y
SCORING: Bryant 108pts, Jeff Hayes (K) 54pts, Anthony 48pts

1982 8-4

6 Pittsburgh	7 WR Earl Winfield
34 Vanderbilt	10 WR Victor Harrison / Mark Smith
62 Army	8 T Brian Blados
41 Georgia Tech	0 G David Drechsler
24 Wake Forest	7 C Steve McGrew / Brian Johnston
41 N. Carolina St.	9 G Ron Spruill / Greg Naron
24 Maryland	31 T Joe Conwell
13 Clemson	16 TE Doug Sickels / Arnold Franklin
27 Virginia	14 QB Scott Stankavage / Rod Elkins
17 Duke	23 TB Kelvin Bryant /T. Anthony / EthanHorton
33 Bowling Green	14 FB James Jones / Eddie Colson
26 Texas■	10 DL William Fuller
	DL Steve Fortson
	DL Jack Parry
	LB Mike Wilcher
	LB Chris Ward
	LB Bill Sheppard / Micah Moon
	LB Aaron Jackson
	DB Greg Poole / Larry James
	DB Walter Black
	DB Steve Hendrickson / Sam Johnson
	DB Willie Harris

RUSHING: Bryant 228/1064y, Anthony 118/697y, Horton 126/576y
PASSING: Stankavage 78-158/1124y, 11TD, 49.4%
RECEIVING: Harrison 30/489y, Smith 27/479y, Bryant 24/249y
SCORING: Brooks Barwick (K) 97pts, Horton 54pts, Bryant 42pts

1983 8-4

24 South Carolina	8 WR Earl Winfield / Larry Griffin
24 Memphis State	10 WR Mark Smith
48 Miami of Ohio	17 T Brian Blados
51 William & Mary	20 G Greg Naron
38 Georgia Tech	21 C Harris Barton
30 Wake Forest	10 G Willy Austin
42 N. Carolina St.	14 T Joe Conwell
26 Maryland	28 TE Arnold Franklin / Dave Truitt
3 Clemson	16 QB Scott Stankavage
14 Virginia	17 TB Tyrone Anthony / Ethan Horton
34 Duke	27 FB Eddie Colson
3 Florida State■	28 DL William Fuller
	DL Ronnie Snipes
	DL Brian Johnston
	LB Butch Griffin
	LB Micah Moon
	LB Bill Sheppard
	LB Aaron Jackson / Jeff Blaylock
	DB Larry James
	DB Walter Black / Steve Moss
	DB Steve Hendrickson
	DB Willie Harris

RUSHING: Horton 200/1107y, Anthony 184/1063y, Colson 79/425y
PASSING: Stankavage 147-249/1721y, 16TD, 59%
RECEIVING: Smith 40/580y, Franklin 25/271y, Truitt 18/204y
SCORING: Brooks Barwick (K) 73pts, Horton & Smith 48pts

1984 5-5-1

30 Navy	33 WR Eric Streater / Eric Lewis
20 Boston College	52 WR Earl Winfield
23 Kansas	17 T Harris Barton (C) / Pat Sheehan
12 Clemson	20 G Greg Naron
3 Wake Forest	14 C Mark Sigmon
28 N. Carolina St.	21 G C.A. Brooks
30 Memphis State	27 T Bobby Pope
23 Maryland	34 TE Arnold Franklin
24 Georgia Tech	17 QB Kevin Anthony
24 Virginia	24 TB Ethan Horton / William Humes
17 Duke	15 FB Eddie Colson
	DL Donnie Wallace /Tim Goad/B. Johnston
	DL Dennis Barron / Carlton Bailey
	DL Reuben Davis / Jeff Ray
	LB Troy Simmons
	LB Micah Moon
	LB Carl Carr
	LB Noel McEachern / Ron Burton
	DB Larry James
	DB Walter Bailey / Derrick Donald
	DB Tim Morrison
	DB Barry James / Steve Hendrickson

RUSHING: Horton 238/1047y, Colson 72/355y, Humes 60/302y
PASSING: Anthony 146-265/1786y, 8TD, 55.1%
RECEIVING: Winfield 34/527y, Franklin 27/315y, Horton 25/254y
SCORING: Kenny Miller (K) 66pts, Horton 54pts, Streater & Anthony 24pts

1985 5-6

21 Navy	19 WR Earl Winfield
13 LSU	23 WR Eric Streater
51 VMI	7 T Harris Barton
0 Georgia Tech	31 G Pat Sheehan
34 Wake Forest	14 C Ralph Phifer / Jeff Garnica
21 N. Carolina St.	14 G C.A. Brooks
0 Florida State	20 T Daryl Parham / Creighton Incorminias
10 Maryland	28 TE Arnold Franklin
21 Clemson	20 QB Kevin Anthony / Jonathan Hall
22 Virginia	24 TB William Humes / Derrick Fenner
21 Duke	23 FB Brad Lopp
	DL Carlton Bailey / Chris Jacobs
	DL Donnie Wallace / Reuben Davis
	DL Tim Goad / Mike Johnson
	DL Ron Burton / Noel McEachern
	LB Brett Rudolph
	LB Carl Carr
	DB Howard Feggins / Walter Bailey
	DB Larry Griffin / Derrick Donald
	DB Daryl Johnston
	DB Antonio Goss
	DB Norris Davis

RUSHING: Humes 115/515y, Lopp 101/407y, Fenner 92/393y
PASSING: Anthony 142-249/1546y, 11TD, 57%
RECEIVING: Winfield 47/696y, Streater 24/424y, Humes 21/175y
SCORING: Winfield 54pts, Lee Gliarmis (K) 37pts, Humes 30pts

1986 7-4-1

45 Citadel	14 WR Eric Streater
20 Kansas	0 WR Eric Lewis / Randy Marriott
10 Florida State	10 T Harris Barton
21 Georgia Tech	20 G Ralph Phifer / Steve Steinbacher
40 Wake Forest	30 C Jeff Garnica
34 N. Carolina St.	35 G Pat Crowley
3 LSU	30 T Creighton Incorminias / Darrell Hamilton
32 Maryland	30 TE David Truitt
10 Clemson	38 QB Mark Maye / Jonathan Hall
27 Virginia	7 TB Derrick Fenner / Eric Starr
42 Duke	35 FB Brad Lopp / James Thompson
21 Arizona■	30 DL Ron Burton / Noel McEachern
	DL Reuben Davis
	DL Tim Goad / Carlton Bailey
	DL Kubi Kalombo
	LB Mitch Wike / Leonard Dempsey
	LB Brett Rudolph
	DB Walter Bailey
	DB Derrick Donald
	DB Danny Burmeister / Dan Vooletich
	DB Skeet Baldwin / Jim Jauch
	DB Norris Davis / Howard Feggins

RUSHING: Fenner 200/1250y, Starr 73/478y, Thompson 72/341y
PASSING: Maye 110-176/1401y, 10TD, 62.5%
RECEIVING: Streater 37/601y, Smith 17/266y, Keller 16/113y
SCORING: Lee Gliarmis (K) 63pts, Fenner 36pts, Lewis & Starr 30pts

1987 5-6

34 Illinois	14 WR Eric Lewis
0 Oklahoma	28 WR Quinton Smith / Randy Marriott
30 Georgia Tech	23 T Darrell Hamilton
45 Navy	14 G Steve Steinbacher / Ralph Phifer
10 Auburn	20 C Jeff Garnica
14 Wake Forest	22 G Pat Crowley
17 N. Carolina St.	14 T Creighton Incorminias
27 Maryland	14 TE Daryl Parham / John Keller
10 Clemson	13 QB Mark Maye
17 Virginia	20 TB Eric Starr / Torin Dorn
10 Duke	25 FB James Thompson
	DL Tim Goad
	DL Carlton Bailey
	DL Cecil Gray / Reuben Davis
	LB Antonio Goss
	LB John Reed / Noel McEachern
	LB Brett Rudolph
	LB Mitch Wike
	DB Derrick Donald / Skeet Baldwin
	DB Howard Feggins / Victor Bullock
	DB Dan Vooletich
	DB Norris Davis

RUSHING: Starr 142/550y, Dorn 88/479y, Thompson 86/375y
PASSING: Maye 143-270/1965y, 9TD, 53%
RECEIVING: Marriott 36/634y, Lewis 27/496y, Smith 21/289y
SCORING: Kenny Miller (K) 62pts, Lewis 32pts, 3 tied w/ 30pts

1988 1-10

10 South Carolina	31 WR Eric Blount / Kurt Green
0 Oklahoma	28 WR Randy Marriott
34 Louisville	38 T Darrell Hamilton / Dennis Clemons
21 Auburn	47 G Steve Steinbacher / Carl Watts
24 Wake Forest	42 C Jeff Garnica
3 N. Carolina St.	48 G Pat Crowley
20 Georgia Tech	17 T Creighton Incorminias / Tim Brooks
38 Maryland	41 TE Damon Hueston / John Keller
14 Clemson	37 QB Jonathan Hall / Todd Burnett
24 Virginia	27 TB Torin Dorn / Kennard Martin
29 Duke	35 FB James Thompson
	DL Cecil Gray
	DL Dennis Tripp / Chris Jacobs
	DL Roy Barker
	LB Antonio Goss
	LB John Reed / Eric Gash
	LB Bernard Timmons /Karekin Cunningham
	LB Dwight Hollier
	DB Larry Whiteside / Doxie Jordan
	DB Skeet Baldwin / Clarence Carter
	DB Victor Bullock / Terrence Fedd
	DB Dan Vooletich / Stuffy Hewitt

RUSHING: Martin 193/1146y, Dorn 102/451y, Thompson 59/205y
PASSING: Hall 51-129/675y, 4TD, 39.5%
Burnett 52-97/497y, 3TD, 53.6%
RECEIVING: Marriott 34/498y, Thompson 21/97y, Blount 17/211y
SCORING: Martin 66pts, Clint Gwaltney (K) 32pts, Marriott 30pts

1989 1-10

49 VMI	7 WR Julius Reese / Joey Jauch
6 Kentucky	13 WR Randall Felton / Bucky Brooks
6 N. Carolina St.	40 T Kevin Donnalley
7 Navy	12 G Alec Millen
16 Wake Forest	17 C Carl Watts
17 Virginia	50 G Pat Crowley / Andy Dinkin
14 Georgia Tech	17 T Andrew Oberg
0 Maryland	38 TE Craig Brown / Ethan Albright
3 Clemson	35 QB Jonathan Hall / Chuckie Burnette
20 South Carolina	27 TB Aaron Staples / Eric Blount
0 Duke	41 FB Michael Benefield
	DL Cecil Gray / Alex Simakas
	DL Roy Barker / J.R. Boldin
	DL Dennis Tripp / Rickie Shaw
	LB Willie Joe Walker
	LB Eric Gash
	LB Dwight Hollier
	LB Tommy Thigpen / Bernard Timmons
	DB Torin Dorn
	DB Clarence Carter / Cliff Baskerville
	DB Reggie Clark / Cookie Massey
	DB Rondell Jones / Doxie Jordan

RUSHING: Staples 114/463y, Blount 86/409y, Randy Jordan (TB) 67/261y
PASSING: Burnette 44-133/520y, 2TD, 33.1%
Hall 50-113/581y, 2TD, 44.2%
RECEIVING: Felton 37/495y, Blount 19/102y, Jauch 13/263y
SCORING: Benefield & Clint Gwaltney (K) 30pts, Staples 24pts

1990 6-4-1

34 Miami of Ohio	0 WR Julius Reese / Corey Holliday
5 South Carolina	27 WR Joey Jauch
48 Connecticut	21 T Kevin Donnalley
16 Kentucky	13 G Brian Bollinger
9 N. Carolina St.	12 C Randall Parsons / Bryan Lindsey
31 Wake Forest	24 G Andy Dinkin
13 Georgia Tech	13 T Andrew Oberg / Rickie Shaw
34 Maryland	10 TE Deems May
3 Clemson	20 QB Todd Burnett
10 Virginia	24 TB Natrone Means / Eric Blount
24 Duke	22 FB Mike Faulkerson
	DL Roy Barker / Austin Robbins
	DL Alex Simakas / J.R. Boldin
	DL Dennis Tripp / Curt Brown
	LB Eric Gash
	LB Dwight Hollier
	LB Tommy Thigpen / Bernard Timmons
	LB Jonathan Perry
	DB Doxie Jordan / Thomas Smith
	DB Cliff Baskerville / Sean Crocker
	DB Rondell Jones / Bracey Walker
	DB Cookie Massey

RUSHING: Means 168/849y, Blount 92/381y, Faulkerson 61/180y
PASSING: Burnett 112-219/1339y, 4TD, 51.1%
RECEIVING: Holliday 28/488y, Means 24/229y, Reese 23/291y
SCORING: Clint Gwaltney (K) 85pts, Means 68pts, 4 tied w/ 12pts

1991 7-4

51 Cincinnati	16 WR Corey Holliday
20 Army	12 WR Joey Jauch / Randall Felton
7 N. Carolina St.	24 T Rickie Shaw
59 William & Mary	36 G Andy Dinkin / Scott Falise
24 Wake Forest	10 C Randall Parsons
9 Virginia	14 G Brian Bollinger
14 Georgia Tech	35 T Andrew Oberg
24 Maryland	0 TE Deems May
6 Clemson	21 QB Chuckie Burnette / Jason Stanicek
21 South Carolina	17 TB Natrone Means / Randy Jordan
47 Duke	14 FB William Henderson / Mike Faulkerson
	DL Roy Barker / Curt Brown
	DL J.R. Boldin / Curtis Parker
	DL Austin Robbins
	LB Eric Gash
	LB Tommy Thigpen / Ray Jacobs
	LB Rick Steinbacher / Dwight Hollier
	LB Jonathan Perry / Bernardo Harris
	DB Sean Crocker / Cliff Baskerville
	DB Thomas Smith
	DB Rondell Jones
	DB Cookie Massey / Bracey Walker

RUSHING: Means 201/1030y, Jordan 124/618y, Henderson 45/252y
PASSING: Burnette 81-130/939y, 4TD, 62.3%
RECEIVING: Holliday 40/504y, Means 23/178y, Jauch 15/169y
SCORING: Means 66pts, Clint Gwaltney (K) 64pts, Jordan 54pts

1992 9-3

35 Wake Forest	17 WR Corey Holliday
28 Furman	0 WR Bucky Brooks / Randall Felton
22 Army	9 T Curtis Parker
20 N. Carolina St.	27 G Shawn Hocker / Russell Babb
28 Navy	14 C Randall Parsons
13 Florida State	36 G Scott Falise
27 Virginia	7 T Ethan Albright
26 Georgia Tech	14 TE Greg DeLong
31 Maryland	24 QB Jason Stanicek / Mike Thomas
7 Clemson	40 TB Natrone Means / Randy Jordan
31 Duke	28 FB Mike Faulkerson
21 Mississippi St.■	17 DL Curt Brown / Michael Payne
	DL J. R. Boldin / Troy Barnett
	DL Austin Robbins / Greg Black
	LB Bernardo Harris
	LB Tommy Thigpen / Kerry Mock
	LB Rick Steinbacher / Mike Morton
	LB Jonathan Perry / Ray Jacobs
	DB Cliff Baskerville
	DB Sean Crocker / Thomas Smith
	DB Rondell Jones
	DB Bracey Walker

RUSHING: Means 236/1195y, Faulkerson 69/286y, Jordan 59/255y
PASSING: Stanicek 83-144/1082y, 4TD, 57.6%
Thomas 54-114/831y, 3TD, 47.4%
RECEIVING: Holliday 37/588y, Felton 22/279y, Brooks 21/400y
SCORING: Means 80pts, Tripp Pignetti (K) 70pts, Brooks 20pts

1993 10-3

31 Southern Cal	9 WR Corey Holliday
44 Ohio Univ.	3 WR Bucky Brooks / Marcus Wall
59 Maryland	42 T Curtis Parker
7 Florida State	33 G Shawn Hocker
35 N. Carolina St.	14 C Pat Conneely
45 UTEP	39 G Scott Falise / Russell Babb
45 Wake Forest	35 T Ethan Albright
41 Georgia Tech	3 TE Freddie Jones / Greg DeLong
10 Virginia	17 QB Jason Stanicek
24 Clemson	0 TB Curtis Johnson / Leon Johnson
42 Tulane	10 FB Malcolm Marshall / William Henderson
38 Duke	24 DL Michael Payne / Marcus Jones
10 Alabama■	24 DL Troy Barnett
	DL Austin Robbins
	LB Bernardo Harris
	LB Kerry Mock / Eddie Mason
	LB Rick Steinbacher / Mike Morton
	LB Ray Jacobs
	DB Jimmy Hitchcock / Lawrence Winslow
	DB Sean Crocker
	DB Bracey Walker
	DB Sean Boyd

RUSHING: C. Johnson 173/1034y, L. Johnson 179/1012y, Stanicek 109/406y
PASSING: Stanicek 139-217/1878y, 12TD, 64.1%
RECEIVING: Holliday 50/867y, L. Johnson 29/233y, Brooks 25/514y
SCORING: L. Johnson 100pts, Tripp Pignetti (K) 86pts, C. Johnson 72pts

1994 8-4

27 TCU	17 WR Octavus Barnes
49 Tulane	0 WR Marcus Wall / Darrin Ashford
18 Florida State	31 T Byron Thomas
28 SMU	24 G Jerness Gethers / Pat Conneely
31 Georgia Tech	24 C Don Meredith / Jeff Saturday
41 Maryland	17 G Mike Hobgood / Russell Babb
10 Virginia	34 T Roge Purgason
31 N. Carolina St.	17 TE Greg DeLong
17 Clemson	28 QB Jason Stanicek / Mike Thomas
50 Wake Forest	0 TB Leon Johnson / Curtis Johnson
41 Duke	40 FB Malcolm Marshall / William Henderson
31 Texas■	35 DL Oscar Sturgis / Greg Ellis
	DL Greg Black
	DL Riddick Parker
	DL Marcus Jones
	LB Kerry Mock
	LB Mike Morton
	LB Eddie Mason / James Hamilton
	DB Jimmy Hitchcock / Terry Billups
	DB Fuzzy Lee / Omar Brown
	DB Eric Thomas
	DB Sean Boyd

RUSHING: L. Johnson 151/805y, C. Johnson 146/721y, Stanicek 88/281y
PASSING: Stanicek 96-166/1222y, 7TD, 57.8%
  Thomas 39-83/715y, 8TD, 47%
RECEIVING: Barnes 32/609y, Wall 29/569y, L. Johnson 29/266y
SCORING: Tripp Pignetti (K) 73pts, Wall 66pts, L. Johnson 60pts

1995 7-5

9 Syracuse	20 WR Octavus Barnes
18 Maryland	32 WR Marcus Wall / L.C. Stevens/ D. Ashford
17 Louisville	10 T Byron Thomas / Ryan Hoffman
62 Ohio Univ.	0 G Mike Baxter / Mike Hobgood
22 Virginia	17 C Jeff Saturday
25 Georgia Tech	27 G Brian Honeycutt / Jerness Gethers
31 Wake Forest	7 T Russell Babb / Scott Overbeck
10 Clemson	17 TE Freddie Jones / Marc Montoro
12 Florida State	28 QB Mike Thomas
28 Duke	24 TB Leon Johnson / Jonathan Linton (FB)
30 N. Carolina St.	28 FB Chris Watson
20 Arkansas■	10 DL Greg Ellis
	DL Marcus Jones / Vonnie Holliday
	DL Rick Terry
	DL Russell Davis / Mike Pringley
	LB James Hamilton / Kevin Addis
	LB Kivuusama Mays
	LB Brian Simmons
	DB Fuzzy Lee
	DB Terry Billups / Reggie Love
	DB Sean Boyd
	DB Omar Brown / Eric Thomas

RUSHING: Johnson 225/963y, Linton 90/350y, Mike Geter (TB) 30/134y
PASSING: Thomas 185-332/2436y, 10TD, 55.7%
RECEIVING: Johnson 54/408y, Barnes 53/970y, Wall 28/424y
SCORING: Johnson 74pts, Scott Caparelli (K) 51pts, Barnes 32pts

1996 10-2

45 Clemson	0 WR L.C. Stevens
27 Syracuse	10 WR Na Brown / Octavus Barnes
16 Georgia Tech	0 T Byron Thomas / Ryan Hoffman
0 Florida State	13 G Jerness Gethers / Joe Ellison
45 Wake Forest	6 C Jeff Saturday
38 Maryland	7 G Mike Hobgood / Brian Honeycutt
42 Houston	14 T Mike Baxter
52 N. Carolina St.	20 TE Freddie Jones
28 Louisville	10 QB Chris Keldorf
17 Virginia	20 TB Leon Johnson / Jonathan Linton
27 Duke	10 FB Chris Watson
20 West Virginia■	13 DL Greg Ellis
	DL Vonnie Holliday
	DL Rick Terry
	DL Mike Pringley / Russell Davis
	LB James Hamilton
	LB Kivuusama Mays
	LB Brian Simmons / Keith Newman
	DB Dre Bly
	DB Robert Williams
	DB Omar Brown
	DB Greg Williams / Jomo Legins

RUSHING: Johnson 242/913y, Linton 55/200y, Maurice McGregor (TB) 42/132y
PASSING: Keldorf 201-338/2347y, 23TD, 59.5%
RECEIVING: Brown 52/534y, Stevens 44/771y, Johnson 39/381y
SCORING: Johnson 72pts, Josh McGee (K) 63pts, Stevens 42pts

1997 11-1

23 Indiana	6 WR L.C. Stevens / Jason Peace
28 Stanford	17 WR Na Brown / Octavus Barnes
40 Maryland	14 T Ryan Hoffman / John Surigao
48 Virginia	20 G Mike Gimbol
31 TCU	10 C Jeff Saturday
30 Wake Forest	12 G Mike Hobgood / Joe Ellison
20 N. Carolina St.	7 T Mike Baxter
16 Georgia Tech	13 TE Alge Crumpler
3 Florida State	20 QB Chris Keldorf / Oscar Davenport
17 Clemson	10 TB Jonathan Linton / Mike Geter
50 Duke	14 FB Dean Dyer / Ronnie Robinson
42 Virginia Tech■	3 DL Greg Ellis
	DL Vonnie Holliday
	DL Russell Davis / Nate Hobgood-Chittick
	LB Mike Pringley / Ebenezer Ekuban
	LB Keith Newman / Brandon Spoon
	LB Kivuusama Mays
	LB Brian Simmons
	DB Dre Bly
	DB Robert Williams
	DB Omar Brown
	DB Greg Williams / Jomo Legins

RUSHING: Linton 248/1004y, Geter 55/245y
PASSING: Keldorf 104-181/1448y, 12TD, 57.5%
  Davenport 115-183/1380y, 7TD, 62.8%
RECEIVING: Brown 55/610y, Stevens 45/727y, Peace 32/418y
SCORING: Josh McGee (K) 70pts, Linton 66pts, Barnes 30pts

1998 7-5

10 Miami (Ohio)	13 WR Na Brown
34 Stanford	37 WR L.C. Stevens / Kory Bailey
21 Georgia Tech	43 T John Surigao
21 Clemson	14 G James Wagstaff / Mike Gimbol
29 Pittsburgh	10 C Ryan Carfley / Cam Holland
38 Wake Forest	31 G Bryan Jones
13 Florida State	39 T Kareem Ellis / Joe Ellison
24 Maryland	13 TE Allen Mogridge
13 Virginia	30 QB Oscar Davenport / Ronald Curry
28 Duke	6 TB Rufus Brown / Ronnie Robinson
37 N. Carolina St.	34 FB Dean Dyer
20 San Diego St.■	13 DL Ebenezer Ekuban
	DL Marcus Dow / Ryan Sims
	DL Sherrod Peace / Russell Davis
	DL Mike Pringley
	LB Sedrick Hodge / Merceda Perry
	LB Brandon Spoon
	LB Keith Newman
	DB Steve Fisher
	DB Dre Bly
	DB Antwon Black / Billy-Dee Greenwood
	DB Jomo Legins / Quinton Savage

RUSHING: Brown 133/534y, Curry 80/419y, Dyer 84/258y
PASSING: Davenport 100-182/1208, 8TD, 54.9%
  Curry 66-147/975y, 6TD, 44.9%
RECEIVING: Brown 55/897y, Bailey 38/363y, Stevens 25/414y
SCORING: Josh McGee (K) 72pts, Brown & Dyer 42pts

1999 3-8

17 Virginia	20 WR Jason Peace
42 Indiana	30 WR Kory Bailey / Greg Harris
10 Florida State	42 T Kareem Ellis
20 Clemson	31 G Mike Gimbol
24 Georgia Tech	31 C Ryan Carfley / Cam Holland
12 Houston	20 G Bryan Jones
7 Maryland	45 T Allen Mogridge
3 Furman	28 TE Alge Crumpler / Dauntae Finger
3 Wake Forest	19 QB Ronald Curry / Luke Huard
10 N. Carolina St.	6 TB Rufus Brown / A. Sanders / David Davis
38 Duke	0 FB Dean Dyer
	DL Julius Peppers
	DL Ryan Sims
	DL Sherrod Peace/Anthony Perkins
	DL Ross McAllister / Joey Evans
	LB Quincy Monk / Shawn Woodard
	LB Merceda Perry / Tim Burgess
	LB Sedrick Hodge
	DB Anthony Anderson / Jason Horton
	DB Errol Hood
	DB Billy-Dee Greenwood
	DB Quinton Savage / David Bomar

RUSHING: Davis 69/303y, Saunders 75/297y, Brown 74/275y
PASSING: Curry 54-110/682y, 3TD, 49.1%
RECEIVING: Bailey 25/418y, Peace 23/373y, Crumpler 20/191y
SCORING: Josh McGee (K) 66pts, Dyer 18pts, 5 tied w/ 12pts

2000 6-5

30 Tulsa	9 WR Bosley Allen / Sam Aiken
35 Wake Forest	14 WR Kory Bailey / Jamal Jones
14 Florida State	63 T Louis Marchetti / Greg Woofler
20 Maryland	15 G Cam Holland
28 Georgia Tech	42 C Adam Metts
20 N. Carolina St.	38 G Isaac Morford
24 Clemson	38 T James Wagstaff
6 Virginia	17 TE Alge Crumpler
20 Pittsburgh	17 QB Ronald Curry
13 Maryland	10 TB Brandon Russell / Willie Parker
59 Duke	21 FB Anthony Saunders
	DL Julius Peppers
	DL Ryan Sims
	DL Anthony Perkins / Will Chapman
	DL Ross McAllister / Joey Evans
	LB Sedrick Hodge
	LB Brandon Spoon
	LB Quincy Monk
	DB Michael Waddell / Kevin Knight
	DB Errol Hood
	DB David Bomar / Dexter Reid
	DB DeFonte Coleman / B.-D. Greenwood

RUSHING: Russell 145/508y, Parker 84/355y, Curry 119/351y
PASSING: Curry 163-304/2325y, 11TD, 53.6%
RECEIVING: Allen 40/634y, Bailey 32/550y, Aiken 29/410y
SCORING: Jeff Reed (K) 78pts, Allen & Curry 36pts

2001 8-5

27 Oklahoma	41 WR Bosley Allen / Sam Aiken
9 Maryland	23 WR Kory Bailey / Chesley Borders
14 Texas	44 T Greg Woofter / Skip Seagraves
41 Florida State	9 G Jupiter Wilson / Isaac Morford
17 N. Carolina St.	9 C Adam Metts
24 East Carolina	21 G Jeb Terry
30 Virginia	24 T Willie McNeil / Jason Brown
23 Clemson	3 TE Zach Hilton / Doug Brown
21 Georgia Tech	28 QB Ronald Curry / Darian Durant
31 Wake Forest	32 TB Andre' Williams / Willie Parker
52 Duke	17 FB Madison Hedgecock / Richard Moore
19 SMU	10 DL Joey Evans
16 Auburn■	10 DL Will Chapman / Anthony Perkins
	DL Ryan Sims
	DL Julius Peppers / Isaac Mooring
	LB Quincy Monk
	LB Merceda Perry
	LB David Thornton
	DB Michael Waddell
	DB Errol Hood / Kevin Knight
	DB Dexter Reid
	DB Billy-Dee Greenwood

RUSHING: Williams 170/520y, Parker 83/400y, Curry 89/253y
PASSING: Durant 142-223/1843y, 17TD, 63.7%
  Curry 62-134/1005y, 8TD, 46.3%
RECEIVING: Aiken 46/789y, Bailey 44/608y, Allen 39/562y
SCORING: Jeff Reed (K) 72pts, Aiken 48pts, Bailey 36pts

2002 3-9

21 Miami (Ohio)	27 WR Sam Aiken
30 Syracuse	22 WR Chesley Borders / Jawarski Pollock
21 Texas	52 T Willie McNeil
13 Georgia Tech	21 G Jupiter Wilson / Steven Bell
38 Arizona State	35 C Jason Brown
17 N. Carolina St.	34 G Jeb Terry / Kyle Ralph
27 Virginia	37 T Skip Seagrave
0 Wake Forest	31 TE Zach Hilton / Bobby Blizzard
7 Maryland	59 QB Darian Durant / C.J. Stephens
12 Clemson	42 TB Jacque Lewis/Will Parker/Mahlon Carey
14 Florida State	40 FB James Faison / Madison Hedgecock
23 Duke	21 DL Jocques Dumas / Isaac Mooring
	DL Chase Page
	DL Kendall High / Donti Coats
	DL Tommy Davis / Will Chapman
	LB Malcolm Stewart / Isaiah Robinson
	LB Doug Justice
	LB Clarence Gaddy / Devllen Bullard
	DB Michael Waddell / Derrick Johnson
	DB Kevin Knight
	DB Dexter Reid
	DB DeFonte Coleman / Chris Curry

RUSHING: Lewis 130/574y, Parker 70/236y, Carey 56/216y
PASSING: Durant 147-248/2122y, 16TD, 59.3%
  Stephens 80-156/921y, 4TD, 51.3%
RECEIVING: Aiken 68/990y, Borders 32/499y, Pollock 31/464y
SCORING: Dan Orner (K) 53pts, Blizzard & Borders 30pts

2003 2-10

0 Florida State	37 WR Derrele Mitchell / Brandon Russell
47 Syracuse	49 WR Jarwarski Pollock / Mike Mason
27 Wisconsin	38 T Willie McNeil
34 N. Carolina St.	47 G Jupiter Wilson
13 Virginia	38 C Jason Brown
28 East Carolina	17 G Jeb Terry
31 Arizona State	33 T Skip Seagraves / Brian Chacos
28 Clemson	36 TE Bob Blizzard /Jon Hamlett /John Dunn
21 Maryland	59 QB Darian Durant
42 Wake Forest	34 TB Ronnie McGill / Chad Scott
24 Georgia Tech	41 TB Jacque Lewis / Willie Parker
22 Duke	30 DL Madison Hedgecock / Alden Blizzard
	DL Jonas Seawright / Isaiah Thomas
	DL Chase Page / Jocques Dumas
	DL Tommy Davis / Shelton Bynum
	LB Melik Brown / Jeff Longhany
	LB Devllen Bullard / Doug Justice
	LB Larry Edwards
	DB Lionell Green / Michael Waddell
	DB Derrick Johnson / Chris Hawkins
	DB Dexter Reid
	DB Mahlon Carey / Michael Harris

RUSHING: McGill 128/654y, Durant 91/396y, Lewis 61/374y
PASSING: Durant 234-389/2551y, 18TD, 60.2%
RECEIVING: Pollock 71/745y, Lewis 34/391y, Mason 22/313y
SCORING: Dan Orner (K) 71pts, McGill 42pts, Durant &
  Lewis 36pts

2004 6-6

49 William & Mary	38 WR Derrele Mitchell / Mike Mason
24 Virginia	56 WR Jawarski Pollock / Jesse Holley
34 Georgia Tech	13 T Brian Chacos
0 Louisville	34 G Charlston Gray / Steven Bell
16 Florida State	38 C Jason Brown
30 N. Carolina St.	24 G Kyle Ralph
16 Utah	46 T Willie McNeil
31 Miami	28 TE Scott Brumett / J. Dumas / Jon Hamlett
24 Virginia Tech	27 QB Darian Durant
31 Wake Forest	24 TB Chad Scott / Jacque Lewis
40 Duke	17 FB Madison Hedgecock
24 Boston College ■	37 DL Kyndraus Guy / Brian Rackley
	DL Jonas Seawright
	DL Shelton Bynum / Khalif Mitchell
	DL Tommy Davis / Melik Brown
	LB Tommy Richardson / Mahlon Carey
	LB Fred Sparkman / Doug Justice
	LB Jeff Longhany / Larry Edwards
	DB Jacoby Watkins
	DB Cedrick Holt / Lionell Green
	DB Kareen Taylor / Linwood Williams
	DB Gerald Sensabaugh

RUSHING: Scott 143/796y, Lewis 74/557y,
  Ronnie McGill (TB) 79/419y
PASSING: Durant 178-299/2238y, 17TD, 59.5%
RECEIVING: Pollock 45/408y, Holley 30/456y, Mitchell 21/354y
SCORING: Connor Barth (K) 77pts, Scott 54pts, McGill 36pts

2005 5-6

21 Georgia Tech	27 WR Jesse Holley / Jarwarski Pollock
5 Wisconsin	14 WR Mike Mason / Wallace Wright
31 N. Carolina St.	24 T Brian Chacos
31 Utah	17 G Charlston Gray
14 Louisville	69 C Steven Bell
7 Virginia	5 G Kyle Ralph
16 Miami	34 T Skip Seagraves
16 Boston College	14 TE Jon Hamlett
30 Maryland	33 QB Matt Baker
24 Duke	21 TB R. McGill / Barrington Edwards
3 Virginia Tech	30 FB/TE Rikki Cook / Justin Phillips
	DL Brian Rackley / Kentwan Balmer
	DL Chase Page
	DL Shelton Bynum / Kyndraus Guy
	DL Tommy Davis
	LB Larry Edwards / Victor Worsley
	LB Durell Mapp / Doug Justice
	LB Tommy Richardson
	DB Jacoby Watkins / Quinton Person
	DB Cedrick Holt / Bryan Bethea
	DB Kareen Taylor
	DB Trimane Goddard / Mahlon Carey

RUSHING: McGill 130/530y, Edwards 114/397y,
  Cooter Arnold (TB) 48/187y
PASSING: Baker 180-346/2345y, 9TD, 52%
RECEIVING: Holley 47/670y, Pollock 30/341y, Mason 22/372y
SCORING: Connor Barth (K) 56pts, McGill 30pts, 5 w/ 12pts

2006 3-9

16 Rutgers	21 WR Jesse Holley
10 Virginia Tech	35 WR Hakeem Nicks / Brooks Foster
45 Furman	42 T Brian Chacos
7 Clemson	52 G Charlston Gray
7 Miami	27 C Scott Lenahan
20 South Florida	37 G Calvin Darity
0 Virginia	23 T Ben Lemming(C)/Garrett Reynolds
17 Wake Forest	24 TE Jon Hamlett
26 Notre Dame	45 QB Joe Dailey / Cam Sexton
0 Georgia Tech	7 TB Ronnie McGill / B. Edwards
23 N. Carolina St.	9 FB Nick Starcevic
45 Duke	44 DL Brian Rackley
	DL Kentwan Balmer / Kyndraus Guy
	DL Shelton Bynum / Cam Thomas
	DL Hilee Taylor / Melik Brown
	LB Larry Edwards / Chase Rice
	LB Victor Worsley / Mark Paschal
	LB Durell Mapp
	DB Jacoby Watkins / Bryan Bethea
	DB Quinton Person/ Jermaine Strong
	DB Kareen Taylor / Cooter Arnold
	DB D. J. Walker

RUSHING: McGill 192/790y, Edwards 91/330y,
PASSING: Dailey 112-195/1316y, 7TD, 57.4%
  Sexton 57-136/840y, 4TD, 41.9%
RECEIVING: Nicks 39/660y, Foster 38/486y, Holley 37/406y
SCORING: Connor Barth (K) 54pts, McGill 48pts, Nicks 24pts

2007 4-8

37 James Madison	14 WR Brandon Tate
31 East Carolina	34 WR Hakeem Nicks / Brooks Foster
20 Virginia	22 T Kyle Jolly
10 South Florida	37 G Aaron Stahl
10 Virginia Tech	17 C Scott Lenahan / Lowell Dyer
33 Miami	27 G Calvin Darity
15 South Carolina	21 T Garrett Reynolds
10 Wake Forest	37 TE Richard Quinn
16 Maryland	13 QB T.J. Yates
27 No. Carolina St.	31 TB Johnny White / Anthony Elzy
25 Georgia Tech	27 HB/FB Zack Pianalto / Bobby Rome
20 Duke	14 DL Hilee Taylor
	DL Aleric Mullins / Marvin Austin
	DL Kentwan Balmer / Tavares Brown
	DL E.J. Wilson / Darrius Massenburg
	LB Durell Mapp / Wesley Flagg
	LB Mark Paschal / Quan Sturdivant
	LB/DB Bruce Carter/Kendric Williams
	DB Charles Brown
	DB Kendric Burney / Richie Rich
	DB Deunta Williams
	DB Trimane Goddard

RUSHING: White 95/399y, Elzy 92/321y,
  Greg White (TB) 59/300y
PASSING: Yates 218-365/2655y, 14TD, 59.7%
RECEIVING: Nicks 74/958y, Foster 29/417y, Tate 25/479y
SCORING: Connor Barth (K) 78pts, Tate 42pts, Elzy 32pts

2008 8-5

35 McNeese State	27 WR Hakeem Nicks / Cooter Arnold
44 Rutgers	12 WR Brooks Foster / Brandon Tate
17 Virginia Tech	20 T Kyle Jolly
28 Miami	24 G Alan Pelc / Bryan Bishop
38 Connecticut	12 C Lowell Dyer / Aaron Stahl (G)
29 Notre Dame	24 G Calvin Darity
13 Virginia	16 T Garrett Reynolds
45 Boston College	24 TE Richard Quinn / Zack Piavalto
28 Georgia Tech	7 QB T.J. Yates / Cam Sexton
15 Maryland	17 TB Shaun Draughn / Ryan Houston
10 N. Carolina St.	41 FB/WR Bobby Rome / Greg Little (TB)
28 Duke	20 DL E.J. Wilson
30 West Virginia ■	31 DL Marvin Austin / Tydreke Powell
	DL Cam Thomas
	DL Robert Quinn
	LB Quan Sturdivant
	LB Mark Paschal / Chase Rice
	LB Bruce Carter
	DB Jordan Hemby
	DB Kendric Burney
	DB Deunta Williams
	DB Trimane Goddard / Da'Norris Searcy

RUSHING: Draughn 198/866y, Little 78/339y, Houston 77/299y
PASSING: Sexton 94-168/1261y, 9TD, 56%
  Yates 81-135/1168y, 11TD, 60%
RECEIVING: Nicks 68/1222y, Foster 30/334y, Tate 16/376y
  Draughn 16/81y
SCORING: Nicks 78pts, Casey Barth (K) 63pts, Houston 48pts

2009 8-5

40 Citadel	6 WR Greg Little
12 Connecticut	10 WR Erik Highsmith / Jheranie Boyd
31 East Carolina	17 T Kyle Jolly
6 Georgia Tech	24 G Jonathan Cooper / Greg Elleby
3 Virginia	16 C Cam Holland / Lowell Dyer
42 Georgia Southern	12 G Alan Pelc
27 Florida State	30 T Mike Ingersoll
20 Virginia Tech	17 TE Zack Pianalto
19 Duke	6 QB T.J. Yates
33 Miami	24 TB Shaun Draughn / Ryan Houston
31 Boston College	13 FB/TE Devon Ramsey / Ed Barham
27 N. Carolina St.	28 DL E.J. Wilson / Quinton Coples
17 Pittsburgh ■	19 DL Cam Thomas / Michael McAdoo
	DL Marvin Austin / Tydreke Powell
	DL Robert Quinn
	LB Quan Sturdivant
	LB Zach Brown / Kevin Reddick
	LB Bruce Carter / Kennedy Tinsley
	DB Charles Brown / Melvin Williams
	DB Kendric Burney
	DB Deunta Williams
	DB Da'Norris Searcy

RUSHING: Houston 191/713y, Draughn 124/567y, Little 29/166y
PASSING: Yates 214-355/2136y, 14TD, 60.3%
RECEIVING: Little 62/724y, Highsmith 37/425y, Pianalto 33/334y
  Draughn 21/125y
SCORING: Casey Barth (K) 97pts, Houston 54pts, Little 36pts

2010 8-5

24 LSU	30 WR Dwight Jones / Jheranie Boyd
24 Georgia Tech	30 WR Erik Highsmith / Joshua Adams
17 Rutgers	13 T James Hurst / Carl Gaskins
42 East Carolina	17 G Jonathan Cooper / Travis Bond
21 Clemson	16 C Cam Holland
44 Virginia	10 G Alan Pelc
10 Miami	33 T Mike Ingersoll
21 William & Mary	17 TE Zack Pianalto / Ed Barham
37 Florida State	35 QB T.J. Yates
10 Virginia Tech	26 HB Curtis Byrd / Ryan Taylor
25 N. Carolina St.	29 TB Johnny White/Anthony Elzy/S. Draughn
24 Duke	19 DL Tim Jackson / Jared McAdoo
30 Tennessee ■	27 DL Quinton Coples / Jordan Nix
	DL Tydreke Powell
	DL Donte Paige-Moss / Kareem Martin
	LB Quan Sturdivant / Zach Brown
	LB Kevin Reddick
	LB Bruce Carter / Herman Davidson
	DB K. Burney/ Tre Boston/ Mywan Jackson
	DB Jabari Price / LeCount Fantroy
	DB Deunta Williams / Matt Merletti
	DB Da'Norris Searcy / Gene Robinson

RUSHING: White 130/720y, Draughn 129/637y, Elzy 72/296y
PASSING: Yates 282-422/3418y, 19TD, 66.8%
RECEIVING: Jones 62/946y, Taylor 36/330y, Pianalto 30/311y
  Highsmith 25/348y
SCORING: Casey Barth (K) 95pts, White 42pts, Draughn 36pts

NORTH CAROLINA STATE

North Carolina State University (Founded 1889)
Raleigh, North Carolina
Nickname: Wolfpack
Colors: Red and White
Stadium: Carter-Finley (1966) 60,000
Conference Affiliation: Atlantic Coast (1953-present)

CAREER RUSHING YARDS	Attempts	Yards
Ted Brown (1975-78)	860	4602
Joe McIntosh (1981-84)	729	3642
Tremayne Stephens (1994-97)	680	3553
Ray Robinson (1998-2001)	649	2781
Anthony Barbour (1988-89, 91-92)	474	2575
Stan Fritts (1972-74)	534	2542
Andre Brown (2005-08)	523	2539
Willie Burden (1971-73)	491	2529
T.A. McLendon (2002-04)	542	2479
Billy Ray Vickers (1976-79)	489	2189

CAREER PASSING YARDS	Comp.-Att.	Yards
Philip Rivers (2000-03)	1087-1710	13,484
Jamie Barnette (1996-99)	637-1243	9461
Russell Wilson (2008-10)	682-1180	8545
Terry Harvey (1991, 93-95)	442-785	5925
Shane Montgomery (1987-89)	421-746	5298
Erik Kramer (1985-86)	334-616	4602
Dave Buckey (1972-75)	303-524	4286
Daniel Evans (2005-08)	370-681	4004
Tim Esposito (1983-84)	333-585	3847
Terry Jordan (1989-92)	303-504	3695

CAREER RECEIVING YARDS	Catches	Yards
Torry Holt (1995-98)	191	3379
Jerricho Cotchery (2000-03)	200	3119
Owen Spencer (2007-10)	126	2441
Eddie Goines (1991-94)	147	2351
Nasrallah "Naz" Worthen (1984-88)	131	2247
Mike Quick (1978-81)	116	1934
T.J. Williams (2002-05)	98	1916
Koren Robinson (1999-2000)	110	1914
Chris Coleman (1996-99)	122	1909
Bryan Peterson (1999-2002)	139	1894

SEASON RUSHING YARDS	Attempts	Yards
Ted Brown (1978)	302	1350
Ted Brown (1977)	218	1251
Anthony Barbour (1992)	199	1204
Joe McIntosh (1981)	222	1190
Stan Fritts (1974)	245	1169

SEASON PASSING YARDS	Comp.-Att.	Yards
Philip Rivers (2003)	348-483	4491
Russell Wilson (2010)	308-527	3563
Philip Rivers (2002)	262-418	3353
Jamie Barnette (1998)	193-377	3169
Philip Rivers (2000)	237-441	3054

SEASON RECEIVING YARDS	Catches	Yards
Terry Holt (1998)	88	1604
Jerricho Cotchery (2003)	86	1369
Jerricho Cotchery (2002)	67	1192
Torry Holt (1997)	62	1099
Koren Robinson (2000)	62	1061

GAME RUSHING YARDS	Attempts	Yards
Ted Brown (1977 vs. Penn State)	37	251
Andre Brown (2005 vs. So. Miss.)	32	248
Ted Brown (1975 vs. Clemson)	24	227

GAME PASSING YARDS	Comp.-Att.	Yards
Shane Montgomery (1989 vs. Duke)	37-73	535
Philip Rivers (2003 vs. Kansas)	37-45	475
Jamie Barnette (1998 vs. Baylor)	24-55	469

GAME RECEIVING YARDS	Catches	Yards
Terry Holt (1998 vs. Baylor)	11	255
Terry Holt (1998 vs. Clemson)	11	225
Jerricho Cotchery (2003 vs. N. Carolina)	9	217

GREATEST COACH:

While Lou Holtz left quite an impression in his four years in Raleigh with a 33-12-3 record and a best-ever 11th ranking following the 1974 season, it was Dick Sheridan, a highly underrated coach, who followed a couple of losing regimes and took the Wolfpack to six bowl games in seven years from 1986-92.

Sheridan affected a stronger defense and more balanced attack behind quarterback Erik Kramer and receivers Naz Worthen and Heywood Jeffires to jump from three wins to eight in his first year of 1986.

After two straight second place finishes in the ACC, Sheridan resigned due to poor health after the 1992 season when NC State was ranked 17th in the final AP Poll.

NORTH CAROLINA STATE'S 55 GREATEST SINCE 1953

OFFENSE

WIDE RECEIVER: Jerricho Cotchery, Eddie Goines, Torry Holt, Mike Quick, Koren Robinson, Nasrallah "Naz" Worthen
TIGHT END: Pat Hovance, T.J. Williams
TACKLE: Darrell Dess, Collice Moore, Glenn Sasser
GUARD: Bill Rearick, John Stec, Bill Yoest
CENTER: Carey Metts, Jim Ritcher
QUARTERBACK: Roman Gabriel, Shane Montgomery, Philip Rivers
RUNNING BACK: Ted Brown, Willie Burden, Dick Christy, Joe McIntosh, Tremayne Stephens
FULLBACK: Stan Fritts

DEFENSE

END: Ray Agnew, Manny Lawson, Pete Soklasky, Mario Williams
TACKLE: Dennis Byrd, Ron Carpenter, Bubba Green, Bert Wilder
LINEBACKER: Darrien Covington, Lavar Fisher, Tyler Lawrence, Stephen Tulloch, Vaughan Johnson
CORNERBACK: Lloyd Harrison, Danny LeGrande, Sebastian Savage, Ralph Stringer
SAFETY: Jesse Campbell, Mike Devine, Tony Golmont, Mike Reid, Woodrow Wilson

SPECIAL TEAMS

RETURN SPECIALISTS: Darrell Blackman, Fred Combs
PLACE KICKER: Marc Primanti
PUNTER: Austin Herbert

MULTIPLE POSITIONS

QUARTERBACK-FULLBACK-PUNTER: Johnny Evans

TWO-WAY PLAYERS

END-DEFENSIVE END: John Collar
HALFBACK-CORNERBACK: Claude Gibson

PERFORMANCE FORMULA:
NORTH CAROLINA STATE'S 10 BEST SEASONS

1973	1.4593	14 of 70
1972	1.4265	14 of 70
1967	1.4165	12 of 71
1974	1.4116	11 of 71
2002	1.4019	16 of 70
1957	1.3880	13 of 69
1978	1.3457	18 of 70
2010	1.3287	20 of 71
1994	1.3185	20 of 71
1992	1.3151	17 of 70

NORTH CAROLINA STATE WOLFPACK

Year	W-L-T	AP Poll	Conference Standing	Toughest Regular Season Opponents	Coach (Record at School)	Bowl Games			
1953	1-9		7	Duke 7-2-1, Army 7-1-1, West Virginia 8-1	Horace Hendrickson (4-16)				
1954	2-8		8	Virginia Tech 8-0-1, Duke 7-2-1, Maryland 7-2-1, West Va. 8-1	Earle Edwards				
1955	4-5-1		7	Duke 7-2-1, Virginia Tech 6-3-1, West Virginia 8-2	Earle Edwards				
1956	3-7		6	Va. Tech 7-2-1, Clemson 7-1-2, South Carolina 7-3, Penn St. 6-2-1	Earle Edwards				
1957	7-1-2	15	1	North Carolina 6-4, Clemson 7-3, Duke 6-2-2	Earle Edwards				
1958	2-7-1		7	North Carolina 6-4, Mississippi Southern 9-0, Clemson 8-2	Earle Edwards				
1959	1-9		7t	Clemson 8-2, Wake Forest 6-4, Wyoming 9-1, South Carolina 6-4	Earle Edwards				
1960	6-3-1		2	Duke 7-3, UCLA 7-2-1, Arizona State 7-3	Earle Edwards				
1961	4-6		5t	Wyoming 6-1-2, Alabama 10-0, Duke 7-3, Maryland 7-3	Earle Edwards				
1962	3-6-1		4t	Nebraska 8-2, Southern Miss. 9-1, Duke 8-2	Earle Edwards				
1963	8-3		1t	North Carolina 8-2, Virginia Tech 8-2	Earle Edwards	Liberty	12	Mississippi State	16
1964	5-5		1	Alabama 10-0, Virginia Tech 6-4, Florida State 8-1-1	Earle Edwards				
1965	6-4		1t	Clemson 5-5, South Carolina 5-5, Florida 7-3, Duke 6-4	Earle Edwards				
1966	5-5		2	Michigan State 9-0-1, Florida 8-2, Clemson 6-4	Earle Edwards				
1967	9-2	11+	2	Florida State 7-2-1, Houston 7-3, Penn State 8-2	Earle Edwards	Liberty	14	Georgia	7
1968	6-4		1	Oklahoma 7-3, SMU 7-3, Virginia 7-3, Florida State 8-2	Earle Edwards				
1969	3-6-1		2	South Carolina 7-3, Houston 8-2, Penn State 10-0	Earle Edwards				
1970	3-7-1		5	North Carolina 8-3, Florida 7-4, Tulane 7-4	Earle Edwards (77-88-8)				
1971	3-8		6	North Carolina 9-2, Penn State 10-1	Al Michaels (3-8)				
1972	8-3-1	17	2	North Carolina 10-1, Georgia 7-4, Penn State 10-1	Lou Holtz	Peach	49	West Virginia	13
1973	9-3	16	1	Nebraska 8-2-1, Maryland 8-3, Penn State 11-0	Lou Holtz	Liberty	31	Kansas	18
1974	9-2-1	11	2t	Clemson 7-4, Maryland 8-3, Penn State 9-2	Lou Holtz	Bluebonnet	31	Houston	31
1975	7-4-1		3t	Florida 9-2, Maryland 8-2-1, Penn State 9-2	Lou Holtz (33-12-3)	Peach	10	West Virginia	13
1976	3-7-1		4t	Maryland 11-0, North Carolina 9-2, Penn State 7-4	Bo Rein				
1977	8-4		3	North Carolina 8-2-1, Clemson 8-2-1, Penn State 10-1	Bo Rein	Peach	24	Iowa State	14
1978	9-3	18	3	Maryland 9-2, Clemson 10-1, Penn State 11-0	Bo Rein	Citrus	30	Pittsburgh	17
1979	7-4	15	1	Wake Forest 8-3, Auburn 8-3, Clemson 8-3, South Carolina 8-3	Bo Rein (27-18-1)				
1980	6-5		3	So. Carolina 8-3, No. Carolina 10-1, Maryland 8-3, Penn St. 9-2	Monte Kiffin				
1981	4-7		5	North Carolina 9-2, Clemson 11-0, Penn State 9-2, Miami 9-2	Monte Kiffin				
1982	6-5		4t	Maryland 8-3, North Carolina 7-4, Clemson 9-1-1, Penn St. 11-0	Monte Kiffin (16-17)				
1983	3-8		6t	North Carolina 8-3, Clemson 9-1-1, Maryland 8-3	Tom Reed				
1984	3-8		6t	Maryland 8-3, Clemson 7-4, South Carolina 10-1, Virginia 7-2-2	Tom Reed				
1985	3-8		6t	Georgia Tech 8-2-1, Maryland 8-3, Clemson 6-5, Virginia 6-5	Tom Reed (9-24)				
1986	8-3-1		2t	North Carolina 7-3-1, Clemson 7-2-2	Dick Sheridan	Peach	24	Virginia Tech	25
1987	4-7		3t	Pittsburgh 8-3, Clemson 9-2, South Carolina 8-3	Dick Sheridan				
1988	8-3-1		3	Clemson 9-2, South Carolina 8-3, Virginia 7-4, Duke 7-3-1	Dick Sheridan	Peach	28	Iowa	23
1989	7-5		4t	Clemson 9-2, Virginia 10-2, Duke 8-3	Dick Sheridan	Copper	10	Arizona	17
1990	7-5		6	Georgia Tech 10-0-1, Virginia 8-3, Clemson 9-2	Dick Sheridan	All America	31	Southern Mississippi	27
1991	9-3	24	2	North Carolina 7-4, Clemson 9-1-1, Virginia 8-2-1	Dick Sheridan	Peach	34	East Carolina	37
1992	9-3-1	17	2	Florida St. 10-1, North Carolina 8-3, Virginia 7-4, Wake Forest 7-4	Dick Sheridan (52-29-3)	Gator	10	Florida	27
1993	7-5		5	North Carolina 10-2, Clemson 8-3, Florida State 11-1	Mike O'Cain	Hall of Fame	7	Michigan	42
1994	9-3	17	2	North Carolina 8-3, Duke 8-3, Florida State 9-1-1, Virginia 8-3	Mike O'Cain	Peach	28	Mississippi State	24
1995	3-8		7	Virginia 8-4, Florida State 9-2, Clemson 8-3, Alabama 8-3	Mike O'Cain				
1996	3-8		6t	Florida State 11-0, Alabama 9-3, North Carolina 9-2	Mike O'Cain				
1997	6-5		6	Syracuse 9-3, North Carolina 10-1, Florida State 10-1	Mike O'Cain				
1998	7-5		4	Florida State 11-1, Syracuse 8-3, Georgia Tech 9-2, Virginia 9-2	Mike O'Cain				
1999	6-6		5t	Texas 9-3, Florida State 11-0, Georgia Tech 8-3	Mike O'Cain (41-40)	Micron PC	38	Minnesota	30
2000	8-4		5	Georgia Tech 9-2, Clemson 9-2, Florida State 11-1	Chuck Amato	Tangerine	34	Pittsburgh	19
2001	7-5		5	No. Carolina 7-5, Ga. Tech 7-5, Florida State 7-4, Maryland 10-1	Chuck Amato	Gator	28	Notre Dame	6
2002	11-3	12	4	Maryland 10-3, Virginia 8-5, Florida State 9-4	Chuck Amato	Tangerine	56	Kansas	26
2003	8-5		4t	Ohio State 10-2, Clemson 8-4, Florida State 10-2, Maryland 9-3	Chuck Amato				
2004	5-6		8t	Virginia Tech 10-2, Miami 8-3, Florida State 8-3	Chuck Amato				
2005	7-5		Atl4t	Virginia Tech 10-2, Florida State 8-4, Boston College 8-3	Chuck Amato	Meineke	14	South Florida	0
2006	3-9		Atl6	Boston College 9-3, Wake Forest 10-2, Georgia Tech 9-3	Chuck Amato (49-37)				
2007	5-7		Atl5t	Boston College 10-2, Clemson 9-3, Virginia 9-3, Wake Forest 8-4	Tom O'Brien				
2008	6-7		Atl3t	Boston College 9-4, Florida State 8-4, North Carolina 8-4	Tom O'Brien	Papajohns.com	23	Rutgers	29
2009	5-7		Atl5	Pittsburgh 9-3, Boston College 8-4, Clemson 8-5, Virginia Tech 9-3	Tom O'Brien				
2010	9-4	25	Atl2t	C. Florida 10-3, Virginia Tech 11-2, Florida State 9-4, Maryland 8-4	Tom O'Brien (25-25)	Champs Sports	23	West Virginia	7

TOTAL: 333-307-15 .5198 (42 of 70)   **Bowl Games since 1953:**   14-8-1 .6304 (6 of 70)

GREATEST TEAM SINCE 1953: Although coach Chuck Amato's 2002 Wolfpack edition fell into a three-game nosedive, it rallied to beat Florida State with an all-out blitzing defense. That regular season finale victory at Carter-Finley Stadium meant North Carolina State had won 10 games in a season for the first time ever. The Wolfpack went on to trounce Notre Dame in the Gator Bowl. Although the 2002 Wolfpack sits fifth of school's list of Performance Formula Bests, it is only marginally behind coach Lou Holtz's top-rated 1973 Liberty Bowl champions.

1953 1-9

7 North Carolina	29 E Harry Lodge
7 Geo. Wash'ton	20 T Ken Urgovitch / Ben Kapp
27 Davidson	7 G Ed Mazgaj / John Bagonis
7 Wake Forest	20 C Dick Tonn
0 Duke	31 G Al D'Angelo
6 William & Mary	7 T C.M. Price / Bob Dunnigan
6 Pittsburgh	40 E Henry Brown
0 West Virginia	61 QB Eddie West
13 Florida State	23 HB Billy Teer / Paul Smith
7 Army	27 HB Chris Frauenhofer / Colbert Micklem
	FB Don Langston / Monte Seehorn

RUSHING: Langston 74/326y, Teer 51/182y, Micklem 35/153y
PASSING: West 39-113/595y, 0TD, 34.5%
RECEIVING: Brown 11/166y, Lodge 8/80y, Micklem 5/78y
SCORING: Langston 24pts, West 19pts, Seehorn 12pts

1954 2-8

21 Virginia Tech	30 E Harry Lodge / Ronnie Gall
6 North Carolina	20 T Bob Dunnigan / Henry Spivey
0 Wake Forest	26 G Mike Nardone / Darrell Dess
26 William & Mary	0 C Dick Tonn
7 Florida State	13 G Al D'Angelo / John Szuchan
7 Duke	21 T C.M. Price / John Bagonis
6 Furman	7 E Henry Brown / John Lowe
14 Maryland	42 QB Eddie West / Billy Franklin
14 Richmond	6 HB George Marinkov / Billy Teer
3 West Virginia	28 HB Monte Seehorn / John Zubaty
	FB Don Langston / Harrison McKeever

RUSHING: Marinkov 101/419y, Zubaty 98/324y,
Langston 62/259y
PASSING: West 43-90/482y, 3TD, 47.8%
RECEIVING: Marinkov 14/108y, Lodge 13/179y, Lowe 9/84y,
Brown 6/78y
SCORING: Marinkov & Zubaty 18pts, Langston & West 12pts

1955 4-5-1

0 Florida State	7 E John Collar / Ronnie Gall
7 Duke	33 T John Szuchan / Dick DeAngelis
18 North Carolina	25 G Al D'Angelo
13 Wake Forest	13 C Dick Tonn / Jim Oddo
34 Villanova	13 G Mike Nardone
33 Furman	7 T Henry Spivey / Darrell Dess
40 Boston Univ.	13 E Henry Brown / John Lowe
26 Virginia Tech	34 QB Eddie West
28 William & Mary	21 HB Dick Hunter / John Zubaty
7 West Virginia	27 HB Dick Christy / George Marinkov
	FB Tony Guerrieri

RUSHING: Christy 85/602y, Marinkov 61/364y, Hunter 64/339y
PASSING: West 42-87/660y, 7 TD, 48.3%
RECEIVING: Collar 14/231y, Christy 12/197y, Hunter 7/171y
SCORING: Hunter 48pts, Collar 30pts, West 30pts

1956 3-7

26 North Carolina	6 E John Collar / Ronnie Gall
6 Virginia Tech	35 T John Szuchan / Dick DeAngelis
7 Clemson	13 G Francis Tokar / Joe Rodri
0 Florida State	14 C Jim Oddo
20 Dayton	0 G Bill Rearick
0 Duke	42 T Darrell Dess / Henry Spivey
0 Wake Forest	13 E Bob Pepe / John Lowe
14 South Carolina	7 QB Bill Franklin / Frank Cackovic
7 Penn State	14 HB Dick Hunter
14 Maryland	25 HB Dick Christy / George Marinkov
	FB Tony Guerrieri / Wally Prince

RUSHING: Christy 119/589y, Hunter 86/369y, Marinkov 52/159y
PASSING: Franklin 18-45/275y, 4 TD, 40.0%,
Cackovic 15-49/217y, TD, 30.6%,
Tom Katich (QB) 13-21/144y, 2 TD, 61.9%
RECEIVING: Pepe 12/171y, Collar 11/157y, Gall 8/124y
SCORING: Christy 19pts, Collar 18pts, Pepe 12pts

1957 7-1-2

7 North Carolina	0 E John Collar
48 Maryland	13 T Dick DeAngelis
13 Clemson	7 G Francis Tokar / Joe Rodri
7 Florida State	0 C Jim Oddo / Bill Hill
0 Miami	0 G Bill Rearick / Ed Hordubay
14 Duke	14 T Darrell Dess
19 Wake Forest	0 E Bob Pepe
6 William & Mary	7 QB Tom Katich / Frank Cackovic
12 Virginia Tech	0 HB Dick Hunter / Ken Trowbridge
29 South Carolina	26 HB Dick Christy / Ron Podwika
	FB Tony Guerrieri / Don Hafer

RUSHING: Christy 144/626y, Hunter 104/475y, Hafer 53/230y
PASSING: Katich 11-29/182y, 2 TD, 37.9%,
Ernie Driscoll (QB) 10-25/162y, 3 TD, 40.0%
RECEIVING: Christy 10/211y, Hunter 5/75y, Podwicka 4/31y
SCORING: Christy (HB-K) 83pts, Hunter 34pts, 6 with 6pts

1958 2-7-1

21 North Carolina	14 E Jim Crain / Finley Read
6 Maryland	21 T Larry Dixon / Alex Gilleskie
26 Virginia	14 G Bill Rearick
7 Wake Forest	13 C Bill Hill / Ron Savage
6 William & Mary	13 G Joe Rodri / Frank Marocco
13 Duke	14 T Kelly Minyard
14 Virginia Tech	14 E Bob Pepe / George Vollmar
14 Miss. Southern	26 QB Frank Cackovic / Gerry Mancini
6 Clemson	13 HB Ken Trowbridge / Bernie Latusick
7 South Carolina	12 HB Ron Podwika / Randy Harrell
	FB Arnold Nelson / Don Hafer

RUSHING: Trowbridge 113/495y, Nelson 84/325y,
Podwika 68/221y
PASSING: Cackovic 42-108/487y, 3 TD, 38.9%
RECEIVING: Pepe 15/203y, Harrell 6/46y, Trowbridge 6/24y
SCORING: Nelson 24pts, Pepe 18pts, Harrell 18pts

1959 1-9

15 Virginia Tech	13 E Dick Drexler
12 North Carolina	20 T Dick Reynolds / Collice Moore
0 Clemson	23 G Alex Gillespie
14 Wake Forest	17 C Paul Balonick
15 Duke	17 G Frank Marocco
0 Wyoming	26 T Kelly Minyard / John Lawrence
14 Miss. Southern	19 E George Vollmar / Jim Tapp
12 UCLA	21 QB Roman Gabriel
7 South Carolina	12 HB Claude Gibson / Bernie Latusick
28 Maryland	33 HB Ron Podwika
	FB Arnold Nelson / Ken Nye

RUSHING: Podwika 96/379y, Nye 36/160y, Latusick 43/153y
PASSING: Gabriel 81-134/832y, 3 TD, 60.4%
RECEIVING: Podwika 23/181y, Gibson 19/224y, Tapp 13/148y
SCORING: Podwicka 30pts, Gabriel 24pts, Tapp & Latusick 14pts

1960 6-3-1

29 Virginia Tech	14 E John Morris / George Vollmar
3 North Carolina	0 T Collice Moore
26 Virginia	7 G Joe Bushofsky
13 Maryland	10 C Bill Hill
3 Duke	17 G Alex Gillespie
0 UCLA	7 T Dick Reynolds
20 Miss. Southern	13 E Jim Tapp / Dennis Kroll
14 Wake Forest	12 QB Roman Gabriel
22 Arizona State	25 HB John Stanton / Al Taylor
8 South Carolina	8 HB Claude Gibson
	FB Roger Moore / Jim D'Antonio

RUSHING: Taylor 93/303y, Stanton 62/270y, Gabriel 98/174y
PASSING: Gabriel 105-186/1182y, 8 TD, 56.5%
RECEIVING: Morris 18/218y, Vollmar 16/270y, Taylor 16/111y
SCORING: Gabriel 42pts, Taylor 18pts, D'Antonio 16pts

1961 4-6

14 Wyoming	15 E John Morris
22 North Carolina	27 T Bert Wilder / Jake Shaffer
21 Virginia	14 G Joe Bushofsky / Harry Puckett
7 Alabama	26 C Walt Kudryan
7 Wake Forest	0 G Bill Sullivan / Graham Singleton
6 Duke	17 T Nick Maravich
7 Miss. Southern	6 E Dennis Kroll / John Gill
7 Maryland	10 QB Roman Gabriel
33 South Carolina	14 HB Al Taylor / Joe Scarpati
0 Clemson	20 HB Mike Clark / Carson Bosher
	FB Jim D'Antonio / Roger Moore

RUSHING: D'Antonio 47/232y, Gabriel 97/196y,
Scarpati 43/164y
PASSING: Gabriel 99-186/937y, 8 TD, 53.2%
RECEIVING: Morris 24/325y, Taylor 17/96y, Scarpati 14/150y
SCORING: Gabriel 26pts, D'Anyonio, Scarpati & Bosher 18pts

1962 3-6-1

7 North Carolina	6 E Bob Faircloth
0 Clemson	7 T Bert Wilder
6 Maryland	14 G Harry Puckett
14 Nebraska	19 C Oscar Overcash / Walt Kudryan
0 Southern Miss.	30 G Skip Matthews
14 Duke	21 T Chuck Wachtel
10 Georgia	10 E Don Montgomery
6 South Carolina	17 QB Jim Rossi / Bill Kriger
24 Virginia	12 HB Tony Koszarsky / Mike Clark
27 Wake Forest	3 HB Joe Scarpati
	FB Roger Moore / Pete Falzarano

RUSHING: Koszarsky 64/244y, Rossi 123/216y,
Scarpati 62/210y
PASSING: Rossi 66-130/792y, 4TD, 50.8%
RECEIVING: Scarpati 18/214y, Montgomery 9/108y,
Faircloth 8/95y, Koszarsky 8/64y
SCORING: Scarpati 30pts, Koszarsky 12pts, Rossi 12pts

1963 8-3

36 Maryland	14 E Don Montgomery
14 Southern Miss.	0 T Rosie Amato
7 Clemson	3 G Bennett Williams
18 South Carolina	6 C Oscar Overcash
10 North Carolina	31 G Bill Sullivan / Jack Schafer
21 Duke	7 T Bert Wilder / Chuck Wachtel
15 Virginia	9 E Ray Barlow
13 Virginia Tech	7 QB Jim Rossi
0 Florida State	14 HB Tony Koszarsky / Mike Clark
42 Wake Forest	0 HB Joe Scarpati / James Guin
12 Mississippi St. ■	16 FB Pete Falzarano

RUSHING: Rossi 139/423y, Clark 54/325y, Falzarano 75/316y
PASSING: Rossi 70-141/783y, 8 TD, 49.6%
RECEIVING: Scarpati 24/273y, Guin 12 136y, Clark 8/53y
SCORING: Koszarsky 30pts, Scarpati 24pts,
Gus Andrews (K) 22pts

1964 5-5

14 North Carolina	13 E Bill Hall
9 Clemson	0 T Glenn Sasser / Rosie Amato
14 Maryland	13 G Bennett Williams
0 Alabama	21 C Charles Bradburn / Lou DeAngelis
3 Duke	35 G Silas Snow
24 Virginia	15 T Steve Parker
17 South Carolina	14 E Tony Golmont / Ray Barlow
19 Virginia Tech	28 QB Ron Skosnik / Charlie Noggle
6 Florida State	28 HB Shelby Mansfield / Dan DeArment
13 Wake Forest	27 HB Gary Rowe / Larry Brown
	FB Pete Falzarano

RUSHING: Falzarano 78/324y, Mansfield 77/312y,
Skosnik 91/267y
PASSING: Skosnik 45-93/566y, 7TD, 48.4%
RECEIVING: Rowe 16/210y, Mansfield 11/128y,
DeArment 10/102y
SCORING: Rowe 24pts, Wendell Coleman (HB) 18pts,
Noggle 18pts

1965 6-4

7 Clemson	21 E Bill Gentry
13 Wake Forest	11 T Dave Ellis
7 South Carolina	13 G John Stec
7 North Carolina	10 C Charles Bradburn
6 Florida	28 G Flake Campbell
29 Maryland	7 T Steve Warren
13 Virginia	0 E Harry Martell
21 Duke	0 QB Charlie Noggle
3 Florida State	0 HB Shelby Mansfield / Page Ashby
28 Iowa	20 WB Gary Rowe / Wendell Coleman
	FB Dan Golden / Bill Wyland
	DL Pete Sokalsky
	DL Dennis Byrd
	DL Bob Smith
	DL Trent Holland
	DL Gary Whitman
	LB Gus Andrews / Chuck Amato
	LB Dave Everett
	DB Larry Brown
	DB Art McMahon
	DB Bill James
	DB Tony Golmont

RUSHING: Mansfield 175/618y, Noggle 149/344y,
Wyland 46/162y
PASSING: Noggle 55-109/533y, 0TD, 50.5%
RECEIVING: Rowe 20/270y, Mansfield 16/145y,
Coleman 12/129y
SCORING: Mansfield 36pts, Harold Deters (K) 32pts,
Noggle 18pts

1966 5-5

10 Michigan State	28 E Harry Martell
7 North Carolina	10 T Bill Gentry (TE) / Lloyd Spangler
15 Wake Forest	12 G John Stec
21 South Carolina	31 C Carey Metts
10 Florida	17 G Terry Jenkins
33 Duke	7 T Steve Warren / Richard Chapman
42 Virginia	21 TE Don Donaldson
24 Maryland	21 QB Jim Donnan / Charlie Noggle
6 Southern Miss.	7 HB Don DeArment
23 Clemson	14 WB Gary Rowe
	FB Bill Wyland / Bobby Hall
	DL Mark Capuano / Pete Sokalsky
	DL Dennis Byrd
	DL Terry Brookshire
	DL Trent Holland
	DL Gary Whitman
	LB Chuck Amato / Ron Jackson
	LB Dave Everett
	DB Fred Combs
	DB Art McMahon
	DB Bill James
	DB Greg Williams

RUSHING: DeArment 175/727y
PASSING: Donnan 74-158/859y, 2TD, 46.8%
RECEIVING: Rowe 47/571y
SCORING: DeArment 54pts, Harold Deters (K) 49pts

1967 9-2

13 North Carolina	7 E Harry Martell
24 Buffalo	6 T Lloyd Spangler
20 Florida State	10 G Norman Cates
16 Houston	6 C Carey Metts
31 Maryland	6 G Flake Campbell
24 Wake Forest	7 T Steve Warren
28 Duke	7 TE Don Donaldson
30 Virginia	8 QB Jim Donnan
8 Penn State	13 HB Tony Barchuck / Charlie Bowers
6 Clemson	14 WB Bobby Hall
14 Georgia■	7 FB Settle Dockery
	DL Pete Sokalsky
	DL Dennis Byrd
	DL Terry Brookshire
	DL Trent Holland
	DL Mark Capuano
	LB Chuck Amato
	LB Mike Hilka
	DB Bill Morrow
	DB Fred Combs
	DB Greg Williams
	DB Art McMahon

RUSHING: Barchuck 175/600y
PASSING: Donnan 79-156/980y, 9TD, 50.6%
RECEIVING: Martell 27/390y
SCORING: Gerald Warren (K) 70pts

1968 6-4

10 Wake Forest	6 E George Botsko / Charles Tope
38 North Carolina	8 T Dick Chapman
14 Oklahoma	28 G Robby Evans / Don Bumgarner
14 So. Methodist	35 C Carey Metts
36 South Carolina	12 G Don Jordan
19 Virginia	0 T Marvin Tharp
31 Maryland	11 E Wayne Lewis
19 Clemson	24 QB Jack Klebe / Darrell Moody
17 Duke	15 HB Charlie Bowers / Jim Hardin
7 Florida State	48 WB Bobby Hall / Jimmy Lisk
	FB Settle Dockery / Dave Rodgers
	DL Mark Capuano
	DL Art Hudson / Henry Billger
	DL Andy Solonoski / Pete Sowirka
	DL Ron Carpenter
	DL Bob Follweiler / Steve Rummage
	LB Mike Hilka
	LB Steve Diacont / Pete Bailey
	DB Dick Idol
	DB Paul Reid / Jim Smith
	DB Jack Whitley
	DB Gary Yount

RUSHING: Bowers 197/706y, Hall 92/506y, Klebe 144/498y
PASSING: Klebe 57-120/746y, 5 TD, 47.5%
RECEIVING: Hall 17/231y, Lisk 15/225y, Lewis 9/147y
SCORING: Gerald Warren (K) 49pts, Bowers 42pts, 2 with 24pts

1969 3-6-1

21 Wake Forest	22 E Wayne Lewis / Pete Sowirka
10 North Carolina	3 T Ed Nicholas
24 Maryland	7 G Robby Evans
13 Miami	23 C Dan Sarik
16 South Carolina	21 G Don Jordan
31 Virginia	0 T Marvin Tharp
25 Duke	25 E Robert McLean
13 Houston	34 QB Darrell Moody
22 Florida State	33 HB Charlie Bowers / Jim Hardin
8 Penn State	33 WB Leon Mason / Walter Altman
	FB Dave Rodgers
	DL Steve Rummage
	DL Dan Medlin
	DL George Smith
	DL Ron Carpenter
	DL Bob Follweiler
	LB Mike Hilka
	LB Steve Diacont
	DB Jim Smith
	DB Van Walker / Dave Adamczyk
	DB Jack Whitley
	DB Gary Yount

RUSHING: Bowers 180/693y, Mason 110/658y, Moody 126/252y
PASSING: Moody 44-101/434y, TD, 43.6%
RECEIVING: Lewis 15/148y, Mason 13/204y, McLean 8/92y
SCORING: Moody 42pts, Mike Charron (K) 37pts, Mason 32pts

1970 3-7-1

6 Richmond	7 E George Botsko
0 North Carolina	19 T Ed Nicholas
7 South Carolina	7 G Bill Yoest
6 Florida	14 C Bill Culbertson
23 East Carolina	6 G John Saunderson
6 Duke	22 T Bill Phillips
6 Maryland	0 E Pete Sowirka
2 Kentucky	27 QB Dennis Britt / Pat Korsnick
21 Virginia	16 HB Paul Sharp / Jim Hardin
13 Wake Forest	16 WB Pat Kenney / Don Bradley
0 Tulane	31 FB Dave Rodgers
	DL Steve Rummage
	DL Dan Medlin
	DL George Smith
	DL Roger McSwain
	DL Clyde Chesney / Bill Clark
	LB Stauber Wilson
	LB Bryan Wall
	DB Jim Smith
	DB Bill Miller
	DB Van Walker
	DB Jack Whitley / Tommy Siegfried
	DB Bob Divens

RUSHING: Kenney 66/310y, Rodgers 83/265y, Hardin 65/211y
PASSING: Korsnick 46-91/427y, 0 TD, 50.5%,
Britt 27-86/304y, 5 TD, 31.4%
RECEIVING: Kenney 19/249y, Bradley 12/73y, Botsko 10/145y
SCORING: Mike Charron (K) 28pts, Kenney 18pts, Altman 12pts

1971 3-8

21 Kent State	23 WR Steve Lester
7 Maryland	35 T Heber Whitley
6 South Carolina	24 G Howard Bradburn / Craig John
7 North Carolina	27 C Bill Culbertson
21 Wake Forest	14 G John Saunderson
13 Duke	41 T John Elliott / Rick Druschel
15 East Carolina	31 TE Gary Saul / Mark Cassidy
10 Virginia	14 QB Bruce Shaw/Dennis Britt/Pat Korsnick
13 Miami	7 HB Willie Burden
3 Penn State	35 WB Mike Stultz / Pat Kenney
31 Clemson	23 FB Gary Moser / Charley Young
	DL Bill Clark
	DL Dan Medlin
	DL George Smith
	DL Roger McSwain
	DL Brian Krueger / Clyde Chesney
	LB Stauber Wilson
	LB Bryan Wall
	DB Bobby Pilz
	DB Bill Miller
	DB Van Walker
	DB Bob Divens / Tommy Siegfried

RUSHING: Burden 228/910y, Young 85/385y, Stultz 60/228y
PASSING: Shaw 53-127/681y, 4 TD, 41.7%,
Korsnik 24-55/281y, 2 TD, 43.6%,
Britt 11-28/220y, TD, 39.3%
RECEIVING: Stultz 24/481y, Burden 22/222y, Lester 20/211y
SCORING: Burden 50pts, Stultz 36pts, Sam Harrell (K) 20pts

1972 8-3-1

24 Maryland	24 WR Steve Lester / Don Buckey
43 Syracuse	20 WR Pat Kenney
33 North Carolina	34 T Allen Sitterle
22 Georgia	28 G Bob Blanchard
17 Duke	0 C Justus Everett
42 Wake Forest	13 G Bill Yoest
38 East Carolina	16 T Rick Druschel
42 South Carolina	24 TE Harvey Willis
35 Virginia	14 QB Bruce Shaw / Dave Buckey
22 Penn State	37 RB Willie Burden / Charley Young
42 Clemson	17 FB Stan Fritts / Roland Hooks
49 West Virginia ■	13 DL Brian Krueger
	DL Sam Senneca / George Bell
	DL Mike Daley
	DL John Goeller
	DL Jim Nelson
	LB Ed Hoffman
	LB Bryan Wall / Stauber Wilson
	DB Bobby Pilz / Mike Stultz
	DB Bill Miller
	DB Tommy Siegfried
	DB Bob Divens

RUSHING: Fritts 145/689y, Young 118/611y, Burden 114/605y
PASSING: Shaw 91-175/1708y, 9 TD, 52.0%
RECEIVING: Kenney 38/832y, Don Buckey 18/293y,
Burden 18/267y
SCORING: Fritts 106pts, Ron Sewell (K) 49pts, Burden 44pts

1973 9-3

57 East Carolina	8 WR John Gargano / George Gantt
43 Virginia	23 WR Don Buckey
14 Nebraska	31 T Allen Sitterle
12 Georgia	31 G Bob Blanchard
28 North Carolina	26 C Justus Everett
24 Maryland	22 G Bill Yoest
29 Clemson	6 T Rick Druschel
56 South Carolina	35 TE Harvey Willis / Pat Hovance
29 Penn State	35 QB Dave Buckey / Bruce Shaw
21 Duke	3 RB Willie Burden / Charley Young
52 Wake Forest	13 FB Stan Fritts / Roland Hooks (RB)
31 Kansas■	18 DL Brain Krueger
	DL Sam Senneca / Frank Haywood
	DL Doug Carter / Dan Meier
	DL Craig Xander / Mark Wilks
	DL John Goeller
	LB Mike Daley / Kirby Shimp
	LB Ken Sheesley
	DB Bobby Pilz
	DB Mike Stultz
	DB Mike Devine
	DB Bob Divens / Eddie Poole

RUSHING: Burden 150/1014y, Fritts 144/684y, Young 114/661y
PASSING: Dave Buckey 53-101/762y, 7 TD, 52.5%,
Shaw 40-94/610y, 3 TD, 42.6%
RECEIVING: Don Buckey 24/439y, Burden 15/157y, 3 with 11
SCORING: Fritts 78pts, Ron Sewell (K) 53pts, Burden 48pts

1974 9-2-1

33 Wake Forest	15 WR Don Buckey
35 Duke	21 WR John Gargano / Elijah Marshall
31 Clemson	10 T Mike Fagan
28 Syracuse	22 G Bob Blanchard
24 East Carolina	20 C Justus Everett
22 Virginia	21 G Tom Serfass
14 North Carolina	33 T Rich Lehr
10 Maryland	20 TE Pat Hovance / Ricky Knowles
42 South Carolina	27 QB Dave Buckey / Johnny Evans (FB)
12 Penn State	7 TB Roland Hooks / Tommy London
35 Arizona State	14 FB Stan Fritts
31 Houston■	31 DL Clarence Cotton
	DL Sam Senneca
	DL Tom Higgins
	DL Frank Haywood / John Goeller
	DL Ron Banther
	LB Mike Daley
	LB Jack Hall
	DB Eddie Poole / Joe Robinson
	DB Ralph Stringer
	DB Mike Devine
	DB Bob Devins

RUSHING: Fritts 245/1169y, Hooks 136/850y, Evans 45/227y
PASSING: Dave Buckey 105-162/1481y, 8 TD, 64.8%
RECEIVING: Don Buckey 26/452y, Hooks 20/246y,
Hovance 19/259y
SCORING: Hooks 82pts, Fritts 72pts, John Huff (K) 32pts

1975 7-4-1

26 East Carolina	3 WR Don Buckey
22 Wake Forest	30 WR Pat Hovance (TE) / Elijah Marshall
8 Florida	7 T Bill Druschel / Larry Shavis
15 Michigan State	37 G Ed Callaway / Glenn Genis
27 Indiana	0 C Lou Alcamo
22 Maryland	37 G Tom Serfass
21 North Carolina	20 T Mike Fagan
45 Clemson	7 TE B.J. Lyttle / Ricky Knowles
28 South Carolina	21 QB Dave Buckey / Johnny Evans (FB)
15 Penn State	14 RB Ted Brown / Richard Carter
21 Duke	21 FB Scott Wade/Ricky Adams/Tim Johnson
10 West Virginia■	13 DL Jeff Easter
	DL Jim Henderson / Doug Carter
	DL Tom Higgins
	DL Dan Meier
	DL Clarence Cotton / Ron Banther
	LB Jim Stowe / Bill Cherry
	LB Jack Hall / Greg Walker
	DB Mike Miller / Darryl Jackson
	DB Ralph Stringer
	DB Richard Wheeler
	DB Eddie Poole

RUSHING: Brown 142/913y, Adams 79/376y, Evans 98/331y
PASSING: Dave Buckey 113-201/1511y, 6 TD, 56.2%
RECEIVING: Don Buckey 34/551y, Marshall 21/363y, Brown 16/160y
SCORING: Brown 84pts, Evans 31pts, Johnson 30pts

1976 3-7-1

12 Furman	18 WR Elijah Marshall
18 Wake Forest	20 WR David Moody / Mike Crabtree
14 East Carolina	23 T Bill Druschel
31 Michigan State	31 G Larry Shavis
24 Indiana	21 C Ed Callaway (G) / Tom Lindner
6 Maryland	16 G Reggie Jackson
21 North Carolina	13 T Mike Fagan
38 Clemson	21 TE Ricky Knowles
7 South Carolina	27 QB Johnny Evans / Kevin Scanlon
20 Penn State	41 TB Ted Brown
14 Duke	28 FB Ricky Adams / Timmy Johnson
	DL Jon Hall
	DL Frank Hitt / Bubba Green
	DL A.W. Jenkins
	DL Tom Prongay / Tim Gillespie
	DL Ron Banther
	LB Bill Cherry / Kyle Wescoe
	LB Jack Hall / Bill Cowher
	DB Alan Baltrus / Tommy London
	DB Richard Carter / Larry Eberheart
	DB Tom Ebner / Mike Miller
	DB Richard Wheeler / Mike Nall

RUSHING: Brown 198/517y, Evans 163/517y, Johnson 52/288y
PASSING: Evans 77-163/942y, 3 TD, 47.2%
RECEIVING: Brown 25/239y, Marshall 13/234y, Knowles 13/190y
SCORING: Brown 78pts, Evans 44pts, Jay Sherril (K) 41pts

1977 8-4

23 East Carolina	28 WR Elijah Marshall
14 Virginia	0 WR Randy Hall / Terry Crite
38 Syracuse	0 T Chris Dieterich
41 Wake Forest	14 G Tim Gillespie
24 Maryland	20 C Jim Ritcher
17 Auburn	15 G Rodger Parker / Ed Callaway
14 North Carolina	27 T Frank Hitt
3 Clemson	7 TE Jim Stowe / Lin Dawson
7 South Carolina	3 QB Johnny Evans
17 Penn State	21 TB Ted Brown
37 Duke	32 FB Billy Ray Vickers / Timmy Johnson
24 Iowa State■	14 DL Joe Hannah / Jon Hall
	DL Tom Prongay / Brian O'Doherty
	DL A.W. Jenkins
	DL Simon Gupton
	DL Doug Cullen / Marion Gale
	LB Kyle Wescoe / James Butler
	LB Bill Cowher
	DB Tommy London / Donnie LeGrande
	DB Richard Carter
	DB Ralph Stringer
	DB Woodrow Wilson

RUSHING: Brown 218/1251y, Vickers 148/726y, Ricky Adams (FB) 51/279y
PASSING: Evans 93-203/1357y, 8 TD, 45.8%
RECEIVING: Brown 24/164y, Marshall 20/418y, Hall 13/311y
SCORING: Brown 84pts, Jay Sherrill (K) 55pts, 4 with 12pts

1978 9-3

29 East Carolina	13 WR Buster Ray / Mike Jukes
27 Syracuse	19 WR Randy Hall / Mike Quick
29 West Virginia	15 T Chris Dieterich
34 Wake Forest	10 G Chuck Stone
7 Maryland	31 C Jim Ritcher
34 North Carolina	9 T Tim Gillespie
10 Clemson	33 T Frank Hitt / Chris Carr / Chris Koehne
22 South Carolina	13 TE Lin Dawson
10 Penn State	19 QB Scott Smith
24 Duke	10 TB Ted Brown
24 Virginia	21 FB Billy Ray Vickers
30 Pittsburgh■	17 DL James Butler / Mike Owens
	DL Brian O'Doherty
	DL John Stanaton
	DL Simon Gupton / Bubba Green
	DL Jon Hall / Joe Hannah
	LB Kyle Wescoe / Marion Gale
	LB Bill Cowher
	DB Ronnie Lee / Eddie Jackson
	DB Donnie LeGrande
	DB Mike Nall
	DB Woodrow Wilson

RUSHING: Brown 302/1350y, Vickers 144/600y, Smith 130/304y
PASSING: Smith 50-101/741y, 0 TD, 49.5%
RECEIVING: Brown 17/197y, Quick 11/270y, Dawson 9/164y, Vickers 9/60y
SCORING: Nathan Ritter (K) 76pts, Brown 66pts, Vickers 50pts

1979 7-4

34 East Carolina	20 WR Lee Jukes / Eddie Jackson
31 Virginia	27 WR Mike Quick
38 West Virginia	14 T Chris Carr / Todd Eckerson
17 Wake Forest	14 G Chuck Stone
31 Auburn	44 C Jim Ritcher
7 Maryland	0 G Chris Dieterich
21 North Carolina	35 T Chris Koehne
16 Clemson	13 TE Lin Dawson
28 South Carolina	30 QB Scott Smith
7 Penn State	9 RB Dwight Sullivan
28 Duke	7 RB Billy Ray Vickers
	DL Brian O'Doherty / Bubba Green
	DL John Stanton
	DL Simon Gupton / Dennis Owens
	LB David Horning
	LB Dann Lute
	LB Robert Abraham
	LB Joe Hannah
	DB Ronnie Lee / Eric Williams
	DB Donnie LeGrande
	DB Mike Nall
	DB Woodrow Wilson

RUSHING: Sullivan 150/665y, Vickers 152/636y, Smith 189/451y
PASSING: Smith 75-138/1093y, 5 TD, 54.3%
RECEIVING: Quick 30/524y, Dawson 15/201y, Sullivan 10/51y, Jukes 7/195y
SCORING: Smith 78pts, Nathan Ritter (K) 54pts, Sullivan 36pts

1980 6-5

42 William & Mary	0 WR Mike Quick
27 Virginia	13 WR Randy Phelps / Curtis Rein
7 Wake Forest	27 T Todd Eckerson
10 South Carolina	30 G Doug Howard
17 Appalachian St.	14 C Jeff Nyce / Frank Sisto
8 North Carolina	28 G Chuck Long / Earnest Butler
24 Clemson	20 T Chris Koehne
0 Maryland	24 TE Lin Dawson / Todd Baker
13 Penn State	21 QB Tol Avery / Ron Laraway
38 Duke	21 TB Wayne McLean
36 East Carolina	14 FB Eddie Jackson / Andre Marks
	DL David Horning / David Shelton
	DL Bubba Green
	DL Al Della Porta / Greg Mathews
	DL Dennis Owens / Todd Blackwell
	DL Ricky Etheridge
	LB Robert Abraham / Sam Grooms
	LB Neal Musser / Sam Key
	DB Dee Dee Hoggard
	DB Perry Williams
	DB Hillery Honeycutt
	DB Louie Meadows

RUSHING: McLean 147/706y, Jackson 103/488y, Avery 142/456y
PASSING: Avery 98-184/1114y, 6 TD, 53.3%
RECEIVING: Quick 43/632y, Jackson 11/133y, Dawson 11/116y
SCORING: Nathan Ritter (K) 50pts, Avery 48pts, Jackson 30pts

1981 4-7

27 Richmond	21 WR Mike Quick
28 Wake Forest	23 WR Ken Jenkins / Dee Whitley
31 East Carolina	10 T Todd Eckerson
9 Maryland	34 G Earnest Butler / Steve Saulnier
30 Virginia	24 C Jeff Nyce
10 North Carolina	21 G Chuck Long
7 Clemson	17 T Chris Koehne
12 South Carolina	20 TE Bobby Longmire / Rufus Friday
15 Penn State	22 QB Tol Avery / Ron Laraway
7 Duke	17 TB Joe McIntosh / Larmount Lawson
5 Miami	14 FB Dwight Sullivan / John Peterson
	DL Dann Lute
	DL David Shelton / Doug Howard
	DL Al Della Porta / Greg Mathews
	DL Dennis Owens
	DL Ricky Etheridge
	LB Robert Abraham
	LB Sam Key / Vaughan Johnson
	DB Donnie LeGrande / Dee Dee Hoggard
	DB Perry Williams
	DB Eric Williams / Nat Brown
	DB Louie Meadows / Mike Wright

RUSHING: McIntosh 222/1190y, Lawson 104/406y, Sullivan 56/334y
PASSING: Avery 70-129/825y, 3 TD, 50.0%
RECEIVING: Quick 32/508y, Longmire 12/116y, McIntosh 11/97y
SCORING: Todd Auten (K) 48pts, McIntosh 30pts, Avery & Quick 18pts

1982 6-5

26 Furman	0 WR Ricky Wall
33 East Carolina	26 WR Ken Jenkins / Stanley Davis
30 Wake Forest	0 T Doug Howard / Chuck Long
6 Maryland	23 G Earnest Butler
16 Virginia	13 C Dean Shavlik / Jeff Nyce
9 North Carolina	41 G A.V. Richards / Steve Saulnier
29 Clemson	38 T Joe Millinichik
33 South Carolina	3 TE Tim Foster / Bobby Longmire
0 Penn State	54 QB Tol Avery
21 Duke	16 TB Joe McIntosh / Mike Miller
3 Miami	41 FB Andre Marks / Rickey Isom
	DL Frank Bush / Raymond Phillips
	DL David Shelton
	DL Mitch Rushing / Anthony Hicks
	DL Todd Blackwell / Greg Steele
	DL Darryl Harris / Markus Hager
	LB Andy Hendel / Mark Franklin
	LB Vaughan Johnson
	DB Dee Dee Hoggard / Ken Loney
	DB Perry Williams / Nat Brown
	DB Eric Williams
	DB Don Wilson

RUSHING: McIntosh 183/780y, Miller 89/450y, Larmount Lawson (TB) 53/237y
PASSING: Avery 126-224/1396y, 8 TD, 56.2%
RECEIVING: Wall 23/412y, Foster 19/240y, Marks 19/27y
SCORING: Mike Cofer (K) 42pts, McIntosh 36pts, Miller 30pts

1983 3-8

16 East Carolina	22 WR Paul Brothers / Stanley Davis
45 Citadel	0 WR Ricky Wall / Chris Cook
14 Virginia	26 T A.V. Richards / Larry Brunette (G)
38 Wake Forest	15 G Greg Steele
10 Georgia Tech	20 C Dean Shavlik
14 North Carolina	42 G Steve Saulnier
17 Clemson	27 T Joe Millinichik
17 South Carolina	31 TE Jeff Brown / Tim Foster
33 Appalachian St.	7 QB Tim Esposito
26 Duke	27 TB Joe McIntosh / Mike Miller
6 Maryland	29 FB Vince Evans / Rickey Isom
	DL Barry Amatucci
	DL Todd Blackwell / Mitch Rushing
	DL Raymond Phillips
	LB Frank Bush
	LB Andy Hendel
	LB Vaughan Johnson
	LB Darryl Harris / Mark Franklin
	DB Nat Brown / Ken Loney
	DB Nelson Jones
	DB John McRorie / Don Wilson
	DB Dwayne Greene

RUSHING: McIntosh 217/1081y, Joe Greene (TB) 44/268y, Miller 54/216y
PASSING: Esposito 190-323/2096y, 8 TD, 58.8%
RECEIVING: Brown 41/354y, Wall 25/371y, McIntosh 21/215y
SCORING: Mike Cofer (K) 54pts, McIntosh 30pts, Greene 24pts

1984 3-8

43	Ohio University	6 WR Haywood Jeffires
30	Furman	34 WR Phil Brothers / Ricky Wall
15	Wake Forest	24 T A.V. Richards
31	East Carolina	22 G Johnny Smith
27	Georgia Tech	22 C Ron Kosor
21	Maryland	44 G Larry Burnette
21	North Carolina	28 T Joe Millinichik
34	Clemson	35 TE Jeff Brown / Ralph Britt
28	South Carolina	35 QB Tim Esposito
0	Virginia	45 TB Joe McIntosh / Vince Evans
13	Duke	16 FB Rickey Isom / Mike Miller
		DL Raymond Phillips / Brian Bullock
		DL Sandy Kea / Kent Winstead
		DL Reggie Singletary / Mark Shaw
		LB Frank Bush
		LB Pat Teague / Dan Holder
		LB Mark Franklin
		LB Don Herron / Benny Pegram
		DB Nelson Jones / Ricky Morris
		DB Jeff Byrd
		DB John McRorie / Jeff Gethers
		DB Dwayne Greene / Michael Bowser

RUSHING: Evans 198/883y, McIntosh 107/591y,
Joe Greene (TB) 84/456y
PASSING: Esposito 143-262/1751y, 10 TD, 54.6%
RECEIVING: Brown 33/243y, Isom 23/215y, Jeffires 22/405y
SCORING: Mike Cofer (K) 78pts, Evans 48pts,
McIntosh & Jeffires 24pts

1985 3-8

14	East Carolina	33 WR Haywood Jeffires / Naz Worthen
18	Georgia Tech	28 WR Phil Brothers / Danny Peebles
20	Wake Forest	17 T Joey Page / Bill Leach
20	Furman	42 G Chuck Massaro / Lenny Schultz
17	Maryland	31 C Jeff Hojnacki / Ron Kosor (G)
10	Pittsburgh	24 G Jeff Strum / Johnny Smith
14	North Carolina	21 T Joe Millinichik
10	Clemson	39 TE Ralph Britt / Johnny Davis
21	South Carolina	17 QB Erik Kramer
23	Virginia	22 TB Vince Evans / Mike Miller
19	Duke	31 FB Fred Stone / Rickey Isom
		DL Raymond Phillips
		DL Kent Winstead / Sandy Kea
		DL Grady Harris / Dillard Andrews
		DL Reggie Singletary
		LB Don Herron
		LB Kelvin Crooms
		LB Pat Teague / Albert Miller
		LB Mark Franklin
		DB Derrick Taylor / Nelson Jones
		DB Jeff Gethers
		DB Michael Bowser

RUSHING: Evans 172/712y, Miller 39/126y,
Frank Harris (TB) 41/122y
PASSING: Kramer 189-339/2510y, 16 TD, 55.8%
RECEIVING: Jeffires 36/542y, Brothers 34/563y,
Worthen 26/505y
SCORING: Brothers & Jeffires 36pts, Kelly Hollodick (K) 34pts

1986 8-3-1

38	East Carolina	10 WR Haywood Jeffires / Danny Peebles
14	Pittsburgh	14 WR Naz Worthen / Mack Jones
42	Wake Forest	38 T Bill Leach
28	Maryland	16 G John Inman / Lenny Schultz
21	Georgia Tech	59 C Chuck Massaro
35	North Carolina	34 G Johnny Smith / Jeff Strum
27	Clemson	3 T Joey Page
23	SouthCarolina	22 TE Ralph Britt / Todd Fisher
16	Virginia	20 QB Erik Kramer / Cam Young
29	Duke	15 TB Bobby Crumpler / Frank Harris
31	W. Carolina	18 FB Steve Salley / Mal Crite
24	Virginia Tech■	25 DL Ray Agnew / John Adleta
		DL Sandy Kea
		DL Grady Harris / Brian Bullock
		LB Scott Wilson / Scott Auer
		LB Kelvin Crooms
		LB Pat Teague / Fred Stone
		LB Greg Harris / Mark Smith
		DB Nelson Jones
		DB Derrick Taylor / Izel Jenkins
		DB Michael Brooks
		DB Jeff Hairston / Chris Johnson

RUSHING: Crumpler 152/581y, Harris 71/329y, Salley 64/282y,
Crite 63/254y
PASSING: Kramer 145-277/2092y, 14 TD, 52.3%
RECEIVING: Worthen 41/686y, Jeffires 40/591y, Britt 24/279y
SCORING: Mike Cofer (K) 72pts, Crumpler 56pts, Worthen 32pts

1987 4-7

14	East Carolina	32 WR Danny Peebles / Eugene Peters
0	Pittsburgh	34 WR Mack Jones / Mike Kavulic
3	Wake Forest	21 T Lance Hammond / Brock Miller
42	Maryland	14 G Lenny Schultz
17	Georgia Tech	0 C Chuck Massaro
14	North Carolina	17 G Jeff Strum
30	Clemson	28 T Joey Page
0	South Carolina	48 TE Bobby Harrell / Todd Fisher
14	E. Tenn. State	29 QB Shane Montgomery / Preston Poag
47	Duke	45 TB Bobby Crumpler / Chris Williams
31	Virginia	34 FB Mal Crite / Todd Varn
		DL Ray Agnew
		DL Kent Winstead
		DL John Adleta
		LB Mark Smith
		LB Clayton Henry / Ray Frost
		LB Grant Slavin / Fred Stone
		LB Scott Wilson / Scott Auer
		DB Joe Johnson / Al Byrd
		DB Izel Jenkins
		DB Michael Brooks
		DB Chris Johnson / Fernandus Vinson

RUSHING: Crumpler 143/571y, Crite 98/463y, Varn 51/182y
PASSING: Montgomery 81-153/1144y, 7 TD, 52.9%
Poag 71-148/741y, 6 TD, 48.0%
RECEIVING: Jones 23/403y, Peebles 22/313y, Varn 20/290y
SCORING: Bryan Carter (K) 47pts, Crumpler 42pts, Varn 30pts

1988 8-3-1

45	W. Carolina	6 WR Naz Worthen / Chris Corders
14	Wake Forest	6 WR Danny Peebles
26	Maryland	30 T Brock Miller
14	Georgia Tech	6 G Lance Hammond
49	E. Tenn. State	0 C Chuck Massaro
48	North Carolina	3 G John Huggins
10	Clemson	3 T Scott Adell
7	South Carolina	23 TE Bobby Harrell
14	Virginia	19 QB Shane Montgomery / Preston Poag
43	Duke	43 TB Tyrone Jackson / Chris Williams
14	Pittsburgh	3 FB Mal Crite / Todd Varn
28	Iowa■	23 DL Ray Agnew
		DL John Adleta / Elijah Austin
		DL Derick Debnam / Kenny Fondren
		LB Bobby Houston
		LB Billy Ray Haynes / Ray Frost
		LB Fred Stone / Corey Edmond
		LB Scott Auer
		DB Al Byrd
		DB Joe Johnson
		DB Fernandus "Snake" Vinson
		DB Jesse Campbell / Eddie Cashion

RUSHING: Jackson 119/464y, Crite 82/285y, Williams 80/258y
PASSING: Montgomery 123-198/1522y, 8 TD, 62.1%
RECEIVING: Worthen 55/868y, Peebles 23/436y, Varn 18/213y
SCORING: Damon Hartman (K) 51pts, Worthen 42pts

1989 7-5

10	Maryland	6 WR Chris Corders
38	Georgia Tech	28 WR Mike Kavulic / Al Byrd
27	Wake Forest	17 T Lance Hammond
40	North Carolina	6 G Rich Pokrant
42	Kent State	22 C Kent Jordan / Charlie Cobb
35	Mid. Tenn. St.	4 G Clyde Hawley
10	Clemson	30 T Scott Adell
20	South Carolina	10 TE Lance Hammond / Todd Harrison
9	Virginia	20 QB Shane Montgomery
26	Duke	35 TB Anthony Barbour / Chris Williams
23	Virginia Tech	25 FB Todd Varn / Greg Manior
10	Arizona■	17 DL Ray Agnew
		DL Elijah Austin / Ricky Logo
		DL Derick Debnam / Mike Jones
		LB Bobby Houston / Andreas O'Neal
		LB Billy Ray Haynes
		LB Lee Knight / Corey Edmond
		LB Mark Thomas
		DB Barry Anderson / Sebastian Savage
		DB Joe Johnson
		DB Snake Vinson
		DB Jesse Campbell / Eddie Cashion

RUSHING: Barbour 108/412y, Jackson 96/390y, Varn 89/337y
PASSING: Montgomery 217-395/2632y, 16 TD, 54.9%
RECEIVING: Kavulic 46/745y, Corder 42/528y, Varn 41/333y
SCORING: Damon Hartman (K) 84pts, Corders 36pts,
Varn 20pts

1990 7-5

67	W. Carolina	0 WR Charles Davenport (QB) / Al Byrd
13	Georgia Tech	21 WR Bobby Jurgens / Reggie Lawrence
20	Wake Forest	15 T Mike Gee / Marc Hubble
12	Maryland	13 G Rich Pokrant
12	North Carolina	5 G Charlie Cobb
56	Appalachian St.	0 G Clyde Hawley
0	Virginia	31 T Scott Woods
17	Clemson	24 TE Todd Harrison / Alex Nicholson
38	South Carolina	29 QB Terry Jordan
16	Virginia Tech	20 TB Gary Downs / Aubrey Shaw
16	Duke	0 FB Greg Manior / Ledell George
31	Southern Miss■	27 DL Mike Jones
		DL Ricky Logo
		DL Elijah Austin
		LB Tyler Lawrence / Clayton Henry
		LB Billy Ray Haynes
		LB David Merritt / Ray Frost
		LB Corey Edmond / Mark Thomas
		DB Sebastian Savage / Wade Burton
		DB Joe Johnson
		DB Snake Vinson / Dexter Royal
		DB Jesse Campbell

RUSHING: Manior 97/406y, Downs 94/397y, Shaw 93/395y
PASSING: Jordan 101-179/1221y, 6 TD, 56.4%,
Davenport 44-82/565y, 3 TD, 53.7%
RECEIVING: Shaw 34/288y, George 20/139y, Byrd 15/172y
SCORING: Damon Hartman (K) 44pts, Shaw 42pts,
Downs 36pts

1991 9-3

7	Virginia Tech	0 WR Ray Griffits
47	Kent State	0 WR Charles Davenport / Robert Hinton
30	Wake Forest	3 T Scott Adell
24	North Carolina	7 G Clyde Hawley
28	Georgia Tech	21 C Todd Ward
15	Marshall	14 G Mike Gee
19	Clemson	29 T Scott Woods
38	South Carolina	21 TE Todd Harrison / Neal Auer
10	Virginia	42 QB Terry Jordan / Geoff Bender
32	Duke	31 TB Anthony Barbour / Aubrey Shaw
20	Maryland	17 FB Greg Manior / Chris Cotton
34	East Carolina■	37 DL John Akins
		DL Ricky Logo
		DL Mark Thomas / Carl Reeves
		LB Tyler Lawrence
		LB Billy Ray Haynes / Gregg Giannamore
		LB David Merritt
		LB Clayton Henry / Kevin Battle
		DB Sebastian Savage / Wade Burton
		DB Dewayne Washington / William Strong
		DB Mike Reid
		DB Ricky Turner

RUSHING: Barbour 124/769y, Manior 79/272y, Shaw 59/257y
PASSING: Bender 76-167/949y, 7 TD, 45.5%,
Jordan 38-68/511y, 4 TD, 55.9%,
Terry Harvey (QB) 40-72/523y, 0 TD, 55.6%
RECEIVING: Davenport 33/558y, George 25/225y,
Harrison 15/205y
SCORING: Damon Hartman (K) 62pts, Downs 30pts,
Davenport 26pts

1992 9-3-1

24	Iowa	14 WR Ray Griffis / Robert Hinton
35	Appalachian St.	10 WR Reggie Lawrence / Eddie Goines
14	Maryland	10 T Eric Tayor / Scott Woods
13	Florida State	34 G Shawn Johnson
27	North Carolina	20 C Todd Ward
13	Georgia Tech	16 G Mike Gee
48	Texas Tech	13 T George Hegamin
13	Georgia Tech	13 TE Neal Auer
20	Clemson	6 QB Terry Jordan / Geoff Bender
31	Virginia	7 TB Anthony Barbour / Gary Downs
45	Duke	27 FB Greg Manior / Ledel George
42	Wake Forest	14 DL John Akins
10	Florida■	27 DL Ricky Logo
		DL Carl Reeves
		LB Tyler Lawrence
		LB Damien Covington
		LB David Merritt / Gregg Giannamore
		LB Keith Battle
		DB Sebastian Savage
		DB Dewayne Washington / William Strong
		DB Mike Reid
		DB Ricky Turner

RUSHING: Barbour 199/1204y, Manior 123/634y,
Downs 45/198y
PASSING: Jordan 164-256/1963y, 9 TD, 64.1%
RECEIVING: Goines 46/580y, Auer 27/275y, Hinton 23/323y
SCORING: Steve Videtich (K) 80pts, Barbour 54pts,
Manior 36pts

1993 7-5

20 Purdue	7 WR Robert Hinton
34 Wake Forest	16 WR Eddie Goines
14 North Carolina	35 T Eric Taylor / Hearth Woods
14 Clemson	20 G Steve Keim
36 Texas Tech	34 C Todd Ward
24 Marshall	17 G Chris Hennie-Roed
28 Georgia Tech	23 T Scott Woods / George Hegamin
34 Virginia	29 TE Ryan Schultz
20 Duke	21 QB Terry Harvey / Geoff Bender
44 Maryland	21 TB Gary Downs / Brian Fitzgerald
3 Florida State	62 FB Ledel George
7 Michigan■	42 DL Loren Pinkney / John Akins
	DL Eric Counts / Nick Kukulinski
	DL Carl Reeves / Mike Harrison
	LB Tyler Lawrence / Jon Rissler
	LB Damien Covington
	LB Gregg Giannamore / Carlos Pruitt
	LB Eddie Gallon / Mike Moore
	DB William Strong
	DB Dewayne Washington
	DB Ricky Bell / Kenny Harris
	DB James Walker / Allen Johnson

RUSHING: Downs 173/835y, George 62/346y,
Fitzgerald 45/199y
PASSING: Harvey 131-235/1837y, 14TD, 55.7%
Bender 63-113/817y, 6TD, 55.8%
RECEIVING: Goines 48/929y, Hinton 29/442y, George 29/253y
SCORING: Goines 64pts, Steve Videtich (K) 62pts, Downs 60pts

1994 9-3

20 Bowling Green	15 WR Mike Guffie / Jimmy Grissett
29 Clemson	12 WR Eddie Goines
38 W. Carolina	13 T Heath Woods / Scott Woods
21 Georgia Tech	13 G Steve Keim
14 Louisville	35 C Kenneth Redmond
34 Wake Forest	3 G Jonathan Redmond
17 North Carolina	31 T Chris Hennie-Roed
47 Maryland	45 TE Dallas Dickerson / Mark Thomas
24 Duke	23 QB Terry Harvey / Geoff Bender
3 Florida State	34 TB Tremayne Stephens / Brian Fitzgerald
30 Virginia	27 FB Rod Brown
28 Mississippi St.■	24 DL Jon Rissler
	DL Carl Reeves
	DL Mike Harrison / George Williams
	DL Eric Counts
	LB Morocco Brown / Steven McKnight
	LB Damien Covington / Ron Melnik
	LB Eddie Gallon
	DB Ricky Bell
	DB William Strong
	DB Kenny Harris
	DB James Walker

RUSHING: Stephens 125/791y, Brown 105/563y,
Fitzgerald 97/408y
PASSING: Harvey 116-199/1466y, 8 TD, 58.3%
Bender 52-94/637y, 3 TD, 55.3%
RECEIVING: Goines 39/624y, Fitzgerald 23/191y,
Grissett 20/183y
SCORING: Steve Videtich (K) 77pts, Brown 30pts

1995 3-8

33 Marshall	16 WR Mike Guffie
24 Virginia	29 WR Jimmy Grissett / Greg Addis
17 Florida State	77 T Tom Dobalis
0 Baylor	14 G Steve Keim
22 Clemson	43 C Kenneth Redmond
11 Alabama	27 G Jonathan Redmond / Lonnie Gilbert
41 Duke	38 T Terrence Boykin
13 Maryland	30 TE Mark Thomas
19 Georgia Tech	27 QB Terry Harvey / Jose Laureano
52 Wake Forest	23 TB Tremayne Stephens
28 North Carolina	30 FB Rod Brown
	DL Brad Collins / Darwin Walker
	DL George Williams / Mark Lawrence
	DL Jon Rissler / Clayton Simon
	LB Bobbie Cotton / Kit Carpenter
	LB Morocco Brown
	LB Ron Melnik
	LB Duan Everett
	DB Ricky Bell / Rodney Redd
	DB Hassan Shamsid-Deen
	DB James Walker / Damon Wyche
	DB Kenny Harris

RUSHING: Stephens 186/849y, Brown 117/526y, King 22/124y
PASSING: Harvey 155-279/2099y, 16 TD, 55.6%
RECEIVING: Guffie 49/810y, Grissett 37/570y, Addis 34/433y
SCORING: Marc Primanti (K) 60pts

1996 3-8

16 Georgia Tech	28 WR Jimmy Grissett / Alvis Whitted
17 Florida State	51 WR Torry Holt / Chris Coleman
21 Purdue	42 T Ian Rafferty
34 Maryland	8 G Alex Santos
19 Alabama	24 C Seamus Murphy / Justin Burroughs
14 Virginia	62 G Lonnie Gilbert
20 North Carolina	52 T Tom Dombalis
44 Duke	22 TE Mark Thomas / Jason McGeorge
17 Clemson	40 QB Jamie Barnette / Jose Laureano
37 Wake Forest	22 TB Tremayne Stephens /Rahshon Spikes
29 East Carolina	50 FB Rod Brown / Carlos King
	DL Clayton Simon / Bobbie Cotten
	DL George Williams
	DL Lateef Patterson / Mark Lawrence
	DL Brad Collins / Devon Smith
	LB Kit Carpenter / Kevin Turks
	LB Morocco Brown / Tim Ramseur
	LB Duan Everett
	DB Hassan Shamsid-Deen
	DB Rodney Redd / Marcelle Hough
	DB Damon Wyche / Eric Riddick
	DB Kenny Harris

RUSHING: Stephens 165/771y, King 50/227y, Brown 55/226y
PASSING: Barnette 102-226/1594y, 9 TD, 45.1%,
Loreano 55-110/750y, 3 TD, 50.0%
RECEIVING: Grissett 50/751y, Holt 24/415y, Thomas 18/248y
SCORING: Marc Primanti (K) 84pts, Grissett 32pts,
Stephens 30pts

1997 6-5

32 Syracuse	31 WR Chris Coleman / Alvis Whitted
45 Duke	14 WR Torry Holt
17 Clemson	19 T Ian Rafferty
41 N. Illinois	14 G Alex Santos
18 Wake Forest	19 C Seamus Murphy / Justin Burroughs
17 Georgia Tech	27 G Lonnie Gilbert
7 North Carolina	20 T Todd Boyle
35 Florida State	48 TE Mark Thomas
45 Maryland	28 QB Jamie Barnette
31 Virginia	24 TB Treamyne Stephens /Rahshon Spikes
37 East Carolina	24 FB Carlos King / Jeff Butler
	DL Bobbie Cotten / Kyle Blalock
	DL George Williams
	DL Tom Loughlin / Andre Wray
	DL Brad Collins / Clint Johnson
	LB Morocco Brown / Kit Carpenter
	LB Sheldon Kee
	LB Duan Everett / Derek Roberts
	DB Hassan Shamsid-Deen
	DB Tony Scott / Lloyd Harrison
	DB Jason Perry
	DB Eric Riddick / Damon Wyche

RUSHING: Stephens 204/1142y, King 70/380y, Spikes 67/297y
PASSING: Barnette 171-302/2378y, 19 TD, 56.6%
RECEIVING: Holt 62/1099y, Thomas 29/271y, King 20/207y
SCORING: Holt 96pts, Chris Hensler (K) 69pts, Stephens 60pts,

1998 7-5

34 Ohio	31 WR Chris Coleman / Ryan Hamrick
24 Florida State	7 WR Torry Holt
30 Baylor	33 T Ian Rafferty
38 Syracuse	17 G Ryan Knudtson
24 Georgia tech	47 C Justin Burroughs / J.J. Jones
27 Duke	24 G Alex Rice / Alex Santos
13 Virginia	23 T Todd Boyle
46 Clemson	39 TE Michael Foushee / Devon Smith
38 Wake Forest	27 QB Jamie Barnette
35 Maryland	21 TB Rahshon Spikes / Ray Robinson
34 North Carolina	37 FB Jeff Butler
23 Miami■	46 DL Bobbie Cotten
	DL Jeff Fisher / Rashad Streets
	DL Darius Bryant /Nate Goodson/Jeff Kuh
	DL Greg Derrick / Clint Johnson
	LB Levar Fisher
	LB Edrick Smith / Sheldon Kee
	LB Clayton White / Corey Lyons
	DB Lloyd Harrison
	DB Tony Scott / Anthony Cason
	DB Jason Perry
	DB Rodney Redd

RUSHING: Robinson 154/822y, Spikes 99/381y, Butler 34/125y
PASSING: Barnette 193-377/3169y, 18 TD, 51.2%
RECEIVING: Holt 88/1604y, Coleman 52/876y, Hamrick 16/323y
SCORING: Holt 80pts, Robinson 60p;ts

1999 6-6

23 Texas	20 WR Koren Robinson / Chris Coleman
10 South Carolina	0 WR Ryan Hamrick / Bryan Peterson
38 William & Mary	9 T Jarvis Borum
11 Florida State	42 G John Fletcher / Ryan Knudtson (C)
7 Wake Forest	31 C Derek Green / Keegan Weir
35 Clemson	31 G Alex Santos
26 Virginia	47 T Todd Boyle
31 Duke	24 TE Andy Vanderveer/Tramayne Simmons
21 Georgia Tech	48 QB Jamie Barnette
30 Maryland	17 TB Ray Robinson / Rahshon Spikes
6 North Carolina	10 FB Derek Roberts
6 East Carolina	23 DL Brian Jamison / George Anderson
	DL Jeff Fisher
	DL Nate Goodson
	DL Clint Johnson / Corey Smith
	LB Clayton White / William Pannell (DL)
	LB Dantonio Burnette / Edrick Smith
	LB Levar Fisher / Corey Lyons
	DB Lloyd Harrison
	DB Tony Scott
	DB Brian Williams / Terrence Holt
	DB Adrian Wilson

RUSHING: Spikes 140/636y, R. Robinson 112/438y,
K. J. Stone (TB) 21/81y
PASSING: Barnette 171-338/2320y, 13 TD, 50.6%
RECEIVING: K. Robinson 48/853y, Coleman 41/487y,
Peterson 21/274y
SCORING: Kent Passingham (K) 52pts, Spikes 36pts,
Barnete 30pts

2000 8-4

38 Arkansas State	31 WR Koren Robinson
41 Indiana	38 WR Bryan Peterson / Eric Leak
41 SMU	0 T Jarvis Borum
30 Georgia Tech	23 G William Brown
27 Clemson	34 C Derek Green / Keegan Weir
38 North Carolina	20 G Alex Rice
14 Florida State	58 T Reggie Poole
28 Maryland	35 TE Willie Wright / Andy Vanderveer
35 Duke	31 QB Philip Rivers
17 Virginia	24 TB Ray Robinson
32 Wake Forest	14 FB Cotra Jackson / Derek Roberts
38 Minnesota■	30 DL Corey Smith
	DL Darius Bryant
	DL Nate Goodson
	DL Drew Wimsatt
	LB Clayton White / Brian Jamison
	LB Dantonio Burnette
	LB Levar Fisher / William Pannell
	DB James Walker
	DB Brian Williams / Anthony Cason
	DB Terrence Holt
	DB Adrian Wilson

RUSHING: R. Robinson 193/788y, Jackson 35/177y,
K. Robinson 15/104y
PASSING: Rivers 237-441/3054y, 25 TD, 53.7%
RECEIVING: K. Robinson 62/1061y, R. Robinson 41/366y,
Leak 32/396y
SCORING: K. Robinson 84pts, Kent Passingham (K) 75pts

2001 7-5

35 Indiana	14 WR Jericho Cotchery
26 SMU	17 WR Bryan Peterson / Troy Graham
9 North Carolina	17 T Chris Colmer
17 Wake Forest	14 G William Brown
37 Clemson	45 C Derek Green / Keegan Weir
17 Georgia Tech	27 G Joe Lardino / Tim Turner
24 Virginia	0 T Scott Kooistra
55 Duke	31 TE Sean Berton
34 Florida State	28 QB Philip Rivers
19 Maryland	23 TB Ray Robinson
27 Ohio	7 FB Cotra Jackson
19 Pittsburgh■	34 DL Corey Smith / Drew Wimsatt
	DL Terrance Martin / Ricky Fowler
	DL Jerrick Hall / Darius Bryant
	DL George Anderson / Sean Price
	LB Freddie Aughtry-Lindsay
	LB Dantonio Burnette
	LB Levar Fisher / Sean Locklear
	DB Brian Williams
	DB J.J. Washington / Marcus Hudson
	DB Terrence Holt
	DB Julius Patterson

RUSHING: Robinson 190/733y, Jackson 40/174y
PASSING: Rivers 240-368/2586y, 16 TD, 65.2%
RECEIVING: Robinson 52/376y Peterson 48/657y,
Cotchery 41/483y
SCORING: Robinson 68pts, Adam Kiker (K) 63pts

2002 11-3

34 New Mexico	14 WR Jericho Cotchery
34 E. Tenn. State	0 WR Bryan Peterson / Dovonte Edwards
65 Navy	19 WR Sterling Hicks / Joe Gray (TE)
32 Wake Forest	13 T Chris Colmer
51 Texas Tech	48 G Shane Riggs
56 Massachusetts	24 C Jed Paulsen / Brandon Sanders
34 North Carolina	17 G Sean Locklear
24 Duke	22 T Scott Kooistra
38 Clemson	6 TE Sean Berton / John Ritcher
17 Georgia Tech	24 QB Philip Rivers
21 Maryland	24 TB T.A. McLendon / Josh Brown
9 Virginia	14 DL George Anderson
17 Florida State	7 DL Terrance Martin
28 Notre Dame■	6 DL Jerrick Hall
	DL Sean Price / Drew Wimsatt
	LB Freddie Aughtry-Lindsay
	LB Dantonio Burnette / Oliver Hoyte
	LB Pat Thomas / Manny Lawson
	DB Lamont Reid / Greg Golden (TB)
	DB Marcus Hudson
	DB Terrence Holt / Victor Stephens
	DB Andre Maddox

RUSHING: McLendon 245/1101y, Brown 123/483y, Golden 60/265y
PASSING: Rivers 262-418/3353y, 20 TD, 62.7%
RECEIVING: Cotchery 67/1192y, Peterson 42/559y, McLendon 42/354y
SCORING: McLendon 108pts, Rivers 60pts, Austin Herbert (K) 53pts

2003 8-5

59 W. Carolina	20 WR Jerricho Cotchery
24 Wake Forest	38 WR Lamart Barrett / Tramain Hall
38 Ohio State	44 WR Brian Clark / Richard Washington
49 Texas Tech	21 T John McKeon
47 North Carolina	34 G Ricky Fowler
21 Georgia Tech	29 C Jed Paulsen
31 Connecticut	24 G Antoine Colvin
17 Clemson	15 T Sean Locklear / Derek Morris
28 Duke	21 TE T.J. Williams
51 Virginia	37 QB Philip Rivers
44 Florida State	50 TB T.A. McLendon / Cotra Jackson
24 Maryland	26 DL Mario Williams / Maurice Charles
56 Kansas■	26 DL John McCargo
	DL Dwayne Herndon / Alan Halloway
	DL Renaldo Moses / James Martin
	LB Freddie Aughtry-Linds'y/Man'y Laws'n
	LB Oliver Hoyte
	LB Pat Thomas / Stephen Tulloch
	DB Greg Golden / A.J. Davis
	DB Lamont Reid / Dovonte Edwards
	DB Troy Graham / Victor Stephens
	DB Andre Maddox

RUSHING: Mclendon 130/608y, Josh Brown (TB) 50/186y, Hall 36/142y
PASSING: Rivers 348-483/4491y, 34TD, 72.0%
RECEIVING: Cotchery 86/1369y, Hall 69/799y, Washington 44/500y, McLendon 40/368y
SCORING: Adam Kiker (K) 92pts, McLendon 66pts, Cotchery 62pts

2004 5-6

42 Richmond	0 WR Lamart Barrett / Brian Clark
14 Ohio State	22 WR Tramain Hall
17 Virginia Tech	16 WR Richard Washington / John Dunlap
27 Wake Forest	21 T Chris Colmer
24 North Carolina	30 G Leroy Harris / James Newby
13 Maryland	3 C Luke Iatahn / Jed Paulsen
31 Miami	45 G John McKeon / Ricky Fowler
20 Clemson	26 T Derek Morris / Jon Holt
14 Georgia Tech	24 TE T.J. Williams
10 Florida State	17 QB Jay Davis
52 East Carolina	14 TB T.A. McLendon / Reggie Davis
	DL Mario Williams / Raymond Brooks
	DL John McCargo / DeMario Pressley
	DL DeMarcus "Tank" Tyler
	DL Manny Lawson
	LB Pat Thomas /Freddie Aughtry-Lindsay
	LB Oliver Hoyte / Pat Lowery
	LB Stephen Tulloch
	DB Lamont Reid / A.J. Davis
	DB Dovonte Edwards
	DB Troy Graham / Marcus Hudson
	DB Andre Maddox

RUSHING: McLendon 167/770y, R. Davis 46/227y, Darrell Blackman (TB) 52/206y
PASSING: J. Davis 175-313/2104y, 12TD, 55.9%
RECEIVING: Williams 31/382y, Washington 29/348y, Hall 28/324y, Barrett 24/326y
SCORING: John Deraney (K) 68pts, McLendon 42pts, Hall & R. Davis 24pts

2005 7-5

16 Virginia Tech	20 WR Lamart Barrett / Sterling Hicks
54 E. Kentucky	10 WR Tramain Hall
24 North Carolina	31 WR Brian Clark
17 Georgia Tech	14 T James Newby
10 Clemson	31 G John McKeon
19 Wake Forest	27 C Leroy Harris
21 Southern Miss	17 G Dwayne Herndon
20 Florida State	15 T Derek Morris
10 Boston College	30 TE T.J. Williams / Anthony Hill
24 Middle Tenn.	3 QB Jay Davis / Marcus Stone
20 Maryland	14 TB Darrell Blackman / Andre Brown
14 South Florida■	0 DL Mario Williams
	DL DeMario Pressley / John McCargo
	DL Tank Tyler
	DL Manny Lawson / Renaldo Moses
	LB LeRue Rumph
	LB Oliver Hoyte / Patrick Lowery
	LB Stephen Tulloch
	DB A.J. Davis
	DB Marcus Hudson / Jimmie Sutton III
	DB Miguel Scott
	DB Garland Heath / DaJuan Morgan

RUSHING: Brown 129/667y, Toney Baker (TB) 124/546y, Blackman 46/203y
PASSING: Davis 108-180/1267y, 6TD, 60.0%, Stone 75-154/1015y, 8TD, 48.7%
RECEIVING: Williams 36/407y, Hall 28/343y, Clark 25/537y
SCORING: John Deraney (K) 73pts, Baker, Brown, & Clark 36pts

2006 3-9

23 Appalachian St.	10 WR John Dunlap / Donald Bowens
17 Akron	20 WR Darrell Blackman / Lamart Barrett
17 Southern Miss	37 T James Newby
17 Boston College	15 G Kalani Heppe
24 Florida State	20 C Leroy Harris (G) / Tank Tyler (DT)
23 Wake Forest	25 G Curtis Crouch
20 Maryland	26 T Jon Holt / Meares Green
7 Virginia	14 TE Anthony Hill
23 Georgia Tech	21 QB Daniel Evans / Marcus Stone
14 Clemson	20 TB Andre Brown / Jamelle Eugene
9 North Carolina	23 FB Toney Baker / John Bedics
16 East Carolina	21 DL Willie Young / Raymond Brooks
	DL Tank Tyler (C) / Ted Larsen
	DL DeMario Pressley
	DL Martel Brown
	LB LeRue Rumph / James Martin
	LB Patrick Lowery
	LB Ernest Jones / Reggie Davis
	DB A.J. Davis / Levin Neal
	DB Jimmie Sutton III
	DB Miguel Scott / DaJuan Morgan
	DB Garland Heath

RUHING: Baker 157/688y, Brown 124/658y, Eugene 17/60y
PASSING: Evans 163-307/1843y, 6TD, 53.1%, Stone 33-69/345y, 4TD, 47.8%
RECEIVING: Hill 45/478y, Dunlap 30/392y, Blackman 27/358y, Barrett 27/241y, Baker 21/177y
SCORING: John Deraney (K) 58pts, Baker 36pts, Blackman, Brown, & Dunlap 24pts

2007 5-7

23 Central Florida	25 WR John Dunlap / Darrell Davis
17 Boston College	37 WR Darrell Blackman / Donald Bowens
38 Wofford	17 T Julian Williams / Jake Vermiglio
20 Clemson	42 G Kalani Heppe
10 Louisville	29 C Luke Lathan
10 Florida State	27 G Curtis Crouch / Yomi Ojo
34 East Carolina	20 T Meares Green (G) / Jeraill McCuller
29 Virginia	24 TE Marcus Stone / Matt Kushner
19 Miami	16 QB Daniel Evans / Harrison Beck
31 North Carolina	27 RB Jamelle Eugene / Andre Brown
18 Wake Forest	38 FB Pat Bedics / Toney Baker
0 Maryland	37 DL Martel Brown / Littleton Wright
	DL DeMario Pressley / John Bedics
	DL Alan-Michael Cash / Markus Kuhn
	DL Willie Young / Antoine Holmes
	LB LeRue Rumph
	LB James Martin / John Ware
	LB Ernest Jones / Nathaniel Irving
	DB DeAndre Morgan / J.C. Neal
	DB Jeremy Gray / Jimmie Sutton III
	DB Miguel Scott / Javon Walker
	DB DaJuan Morgan / Robbie Leonard

RUSHING: Eugene 172/667y, Brown 95/447y, Curtis Underwood (RB) 19/84y
PASSING: Evans 194-339/2030y, 12TD, 57.2%, Beck 85-160/903y, 2TD, 53.1%
RECEIVING: Dunlap 45/375y, Eugene 42/263y, Bowens 41/598y, Blackman 41/593y
SCORING: Steven Hauschka (K) 73pts, Eugene 36pts, Brown 30pts

2008 6-7

0 South Carolina	34 WR Owen Spencer / T.J. Graham
34 William & Mary	24 WR Jarvis Williams / Darrell Davis
9 Clemson	27 T Jake Vermiglio / Julian Williams
30 East Carolina	24 G John Bedics
10 South Florida	41 C Ted Larsen
31 Boston College	38 G Meares Green
17 Florida State	26 T Jeraill McCuller
24 Maryland	27 TE Anthony Hill / George Bryan
27 Duke	17 QB Russell Wilson / Harrison Beck
21 Wake Forest	27 RB Andre Brown / Jamelle Eugene
41 North Carolina	10 FB Taylor Gentry / Harrison Ritcher
38 Miami	28 DL Shea McKeen / Markus Kuhn
23 Rutgers■	29 DL Antoine Holmes / Keith Willis
	DL Alan-Michael Cash / LeRoy Burgess
	DL Willie Young / Jeff Rieskamp
	LB Robbie Leonard
	LB Ray Michel
	LB Nate Irving / Dwayne Maddox
	DB DeAndre Morgan / Koyal George
	DB Jeremy Gray
	DB J.C. Neal / Scott Bradsher
	DB Justin Byers / Clem Johnson

RUSHING: Brown 175/767y, Eugene 95/442y, Wilson 116/388y
PASSING: Wilson 150-275/1955y, 17TD, 54.5%, Beck 34-80/592y, 2TD, 42.5%
RECEIVING: Spencer 31/691y, Brown 29/309y, Jar. Williams 26/432y, Eugene 26/224y
SCORING: Josh Czajkowski (K) 81pts, Brown 54pts, Spencer 30pts

2009 5-7

3 South Carolina	7 WR Jarvis Williams / Darrell Davis
65 Murray State	7 WR Owen Spencer / T.J. Graham
45 Gardner-Webb	14 T Jake Vermiglio
38 Pittsburgh	31 G Julian Williams
24 Wake Forest	30 C Ted Larsen
28 Duke	49 G R.J. Mattes / Andy Barbee
20 Boston College	52 T Jeraill McCuller
42 Florida State	45 TE George Bryan / Matt Kushner
38 Maryland	31 QB Russell Wilson
23 Clemson	43 RB Toney Baker / Jamelle Eugene
10 Virginia Tech	38 FB Taylor Gentry / Harrison Ritcher
28 North Carolina	27 DL Shea McKeen / Michael Lemon
	DL LeRoy Burgess
	DL Alan-Michael Cash
	DL Willie Young
	LB Audie Cole / Bobby Floyd (DB)
	LB Ray Michel / Sterling Lucas
	LB Dwayne Maddox / Terrell Manning
	DB C.J. Wilson / Koyal George
	DB DeAndre Morgan / Jarvis Byrd
	DB Brandon Bishop / Justin Byers
	DB Clem Johnson / Earl Wolff

RUSHING: Baker 160/773y, Eugene 99/309y, Wilson 103/260y
PASSING: Wilson 224-378/3027y, 31TD, 59.3%
RECEIVING: Jar. Williams 45/547y, Bryan 40/422y, Spencer 30/765y, Baker 28/355y
SCORING: Josh Czajkowski (K) 74pts, Jar. Williams 66pts, Baker 54pts

2010 9-4

48 W. Carolina	7 WR Jarvis Williams / Jay Smith
28 Central Florida	21 WR Owen Spencer / T.J. Graham
30 Cincinnati	19 T Jake Vermiglio / Rob Crisp
45 Georgia Tech	28 G Andrew Wallace
30 Virginia Tech	41 C Camden Wentz
44 Boston College	17 G Zach Allen / Gary Gregory
27 East Carolina	33 T R.J. Mattes / Mikel Ovargaard
28 Florida State	24 TE George Bryan
13 Clemson	14 QB Russell Wilson
38 Wake Forest	1 HB Dean Haynes / Mustafa Greene
29 North Carolina	25 FB/WR Taylor Gentry / Darrell Davis
31 Maryland	38 DL Jeff Rieskamp / Michael Lemon
23 West Virginia■	7 DL Nafanu Mageo
	DL J.R. Sweezy / Brian Slay
	DL David Akinniyi / Audi Augustin
	LB Audie Cole
	LB Nate Irving
	LB Terrell Manning
	DB C.J. Wilson
	DB David Amerson / Justin Byers
	DB Brandan Bishop / Dontae Johnson
	DB Earl Wolff

RUSHING: Greene 134/597y, Wilson 143/435y, Haynes 83/320y
PASSING: Wilson 308-527/3563y, 28TD, 58.4%
RECEIVING: Spencer 60/912y, Williams 52/713y, Bryan 35/369y
SCORING: Josh Czajkowski (K) 102pts, Wilson 54pts, Greene & Williams 36pts

NORTHWESTERN

Northwestern University (Founded 1851)
Evanston, Illinois
Nickname: Wildcats
Colors: Purple and White
Stadium: Ryan Field (1926) 47,130
Conference Affiliation: Big 10 (charter member, 1896-present)

CAREER RUSHING YARDS	Attempts	Yards
Damien Anderson (1998-01)	953	4485
Tyrell Sutton (2005-08)	731	3886
Darnell Autry (1994-96)	787	3793
Bob Christian (1987-90)	612	2643
Jason Wright (2000-03)	489	2625
Noah Herron (2001-04)	462	2524
Greg Boykin (1972-76)	601	2465
Mike Adamle (1968-70)	483	2015
Stanley Davenport (1984-87)	522	1946
Byron Sanders (1987-88)	451	1840

CAREER PASSING YARDS	Comp.-Att.	Yards
Brett Basanez (2002-05)	913-1584	10,580
Len Williams (1990-93)	644-1076	7487
C.J. Bachér (2005-08)	664-1105	7319
Zak Kustok (1999-01)	507-920	5822
Mike Greenfield (1984-87)	497-933	5803
Sandy Schwab (1982-85)	533-975	5679
Steve Schnur (1993-96)	443-785	5612
Mike Kafka (2006-09)	408-637	4265
Maurie Daigneau (1969-71)	298-659	4237
Mike Kerrigan (1979-81)	379-797	4094

CAREER RECEIVING YARDS	Catches	Yards
D'Wayne Bates (1995-98)	210	3370
Richard Buchanan (1987-90)	197	2474
Ross Lane (2005-08)	163	2068
Eric Peterman (2005-08)	160	2011
Shaun Herbert (2003-06)	168	1926
Lee Gissendaner (1990-93)	156	1878
Kunle Patrick (2000-03)	171	1873
Mark Philmore (2002-05)	163	1768
Scott Yelvington (1973-76)	122	1762
Brian Musso (1994-97)	132	1709

SEASON RUSHING YARDS	Attempts	Yards
Damien Anderson (2000)	311	2063
Darnell Autry (1995)	387	1785
Tyrell Sutton (2005)	250	1474
Darnell Autry (1996)	280	1452
Jason Wright (2003)	267	1388

SEASON PASSING YARDS	Comp.-Att.	Yards
C.J. Bachér (2007)	318-521	3656
Brett Basanez (2005)	314-497	3622
Mike Kafka (2009)	319-492	3430
Brett Basanez (2004)	247-460	2838
Sandy Schwab (1982)	234-416	2735

SEASON RECEIVING YARDS	Catches	Yards
D'Wayne Bates (1998)	83	1245
D'Wayne Bates (1996)	75	1196
Richard Buchanan (1989)	94	1115
Jeremy Ebert (2010)	62	953
Andrew Brewer (2009)	57	925

GAME RUSHING YARDS	Attempts	Yards
Mike Adamle (1969 vs. Wisconsin)	40	316
Byron Sanders (1987 vs. Minnesota)	46	295
Damien Anderson (2000 vs. Indiana)	36	292

GAME PASSING YARDS	Comp.-Att.	Yards
Mike Kafka (2009 vs. Auburn)	47-78	532
C.J. Bachér (2007 vs. Michigan St.)	38-48	520
Brett Basanez (2004 vs. TCU)	39-62	513

GAME RECEIVING YARDS	Catches	Yards
Jim Lash (1972 vs. Purdue)	9	226
Todd Sheets (1980 vs. Purdue)	11	226
Jon Harvey (1982 vs. Michigan)	17	208

GREATEST COACH:

The task was considered impossible. In the 20 seasons since Northwestern went 7-4 under Alex Agase in 1971, the program went 38-179-3. The program was not only down, it had been counted out by the time they lost 34 straight games from 1979 to 1982.

But there was soon to be a new era for Wildcats football. Gary Barnett, an assistant coach for eight very successful seasons at Colorado, became the new head coach in Evanston. The Buffaloes had been rebuilt from Big Eight doormat to national champion, so Barnett knew that nothing was impossible. He also knew that in the past six seasons, five Big 10 member teams had won or shared conference titles. With discipline, good coaching, and better recruiting, he could turn the impossible into reality.

And he did. It took four seasons, but the talent level needed to be brought up to the rest of the conference. That it had was made evident by the opening game of what would prove to be a magical season: 1995. Huge underdog Northwestern stunned Notre Dame 17-15, and suddenly the name Gary Barnett was better known. Michigan, Penn State, Wisconsin, Iowa all fell as Northwestern swept its conference schedule. They were off to the Rose Bowl for the first time since 1949, which was the only bowl season to date for the Cats.

Barnett lost that game to Southern California to finish the season 10-2, but as a follow up, Northwestern went 9-3 the next season to prove that they were not one-hit wonders. Two mediocre seasons followed and the Barnett was off to Colorado.

Although he won more games than he lost with Colorado, his time in Boulder will be remembered more for the unraveling of his career. Under Barnett there were a host recruiting improprieties, and he trivialized rape allegations by former kicker Katie Hnida. Immediately after the end of the 2005 season, Barnett's contract was bought out.

NORTHWESTERN'S 55 GREATEST SINCE 1953

OFFENSE

WIDE RECEIVER: D'Wayne Bates, Richard Buchanan, Jim Lash, Barry Pearson
TIGHT END: Cas Banaszek, Steve Craig
TACKLE: Justin Chabot, Andy Cvercko, Gene Gossage, Chris Hinton
GUARD: Jack Cvercko, Matt O'Dwyer, Ryan Padgett, Mike Sikich
CENTER: James Andreotti, Rob Johnson, Jack Rudnay
QUARTERBACK: Brett Basanez, Tommy Myers, Steve Schnur
RUNNING BACK: Damien Anderson, Darnell Autry, Ron Burton, Tyrell Sutton
FULLBACK: Mike Stock

DEFENSE

END: Casey Dailey, Wil Hembly, Dwayne Missouri, Corey Wootten
TACKLE: Jim Anderson, Luis Castillo, Keith Cruise
LINEBACKER: Kevin Bentley, Pat Fitzgerald, Barry Gardner, Napoleon Harris, Adam Kadela,
 Chuck Kern, Tim McGarigle, Ed Sutter
CORNERBACK: Harold Blackmon, Jack Dustin, Chris Martin, Brett Whitley
SAFETY: Jeff Backes, Pat Geegan, Eric Hutchinson, Pete Shaw

SPECIAL TEAMS

RETURN SPECIALISTS: Lee Gissendaner, Brian Musso
PLACE KICKER: Brian Gowins
PUNTER: John Kidd

MULTIPLE POSITIONS

LINEBACKER-DEFENSIVE BACK: Phil Clark
HALFBACK-FULLBACK: Mike Adamle

TWO-WAY PLAYERS

GUARD-LINEBACKER: Al Viola
CENTER-LINEBACKER: Larry Onesti

PERFORMANCE FORMULA:
NORTHWESTERN'S 10 BEST SEASONS

1995	1.5607	8 of 70
1962	1.4444	12 of 70
1996	1.2944	23 of 70
1959	1.2711	17 of 70
2000	1.2588	26 of 70
1963	1.1911	29 of 70
2008	1.1897	35 of 71
2005	1.1885	29 of 70
1958	1.1790	24 of 70
1970	1.1586	28 of 70

NORTHWESTERN WILDCATS

Year	W-L-T	AP Poll	Conference Standing	Toughest Regular Season Opponents	Coach (Record at School)	Bowl Games		
1953	3-6		10	Illinois 7-1-1, Ohio State 6-3, Michigan 6-3, Wisconsin 6-2-1	Bob Voigts			
1954	2-7		8t	Ohio State 9-0, Wisconsin 7-2, Minnesota 7-2, Southern Cal 8-3	Bob Voigts (33-39-1)			
1955	0-8-1		10	Michigan 7-2, Ohio State 7-2, Miami (Ohio) 9-0, Illinois 5-3-1	Lou Saban (0-8-1)			
1956	4-4-1		6	Minnesota 6-1-2, Michigan 7-2, Ohio State 6-3, Tulane 6-4	Ara Parseghian			
1957	0-9		10	Ohio State 8-1, Iowa 7-1-1, Oregon State 8-2, Wisconsin 6-3	Ara Parseghian			
1958	5-4		7	Iowa 7-1-1, Wisconsin 7-1-1, Ohio State 6-1-2, Purdue 6-1-2	Ara Parseghian			
1959	6-3		5	Wisconsin 7-2, Oklahoma 7-3, Illinois 5-3-1	Ara Parseghian			
1960	5-4		5t	Iowa 8-1, Minnesota 8-1, Michigan State 6-2-1	Ara Parseghian			
1961	4-5		7t	Ohio State 8-0-1, Minnesota 7-2, Michigan State 7-2, Wisconsin 6-3	Ara Parseghian			
1962	7-2		3t	Wisconsin 8-1, Minnesota 6-2-1, Ohio State 6-3, Miami 7-3	Ara Parseghian			
1963	5-4		5t	Illinois 7-1-1, Michigan State 6-2-1, Missouri 7-3, Ohio State 5-3-1	Ara Parseghian (36-35-1)			
1964	3-6		7t	Michigan 8-1, Ohio State 7-2, Oregon State 8-2, Illinois 6-3	Alex Agase			
1965	4-6		6	Michigan State 10-0, Notre Dame 7-2-1, Florida 7-3	Alex Agase			
1966	3-6-1		7	Notre Dame 9-0-1, Michigan St. 9-0-1, Florida 8-2, Oregon St. 7-3	Alex Agase			
1967	3-7		8	Purdue 8-2, Missouri 7-3, Miami 7-3, Ohio State 6-3	Alex Agase			
1968	1-9		8t	Ohio State 9-0, Southern Cal 9-0-1, Purdue 8-2, Michigan 8-2	Alex Agase			
1969	3-7		5t	Southern Cal 9-0-1, Ohio State 8-1, Notre Dame 8-1-1, UCLA 8-1-1	Alex Agase			
1970	6-4		2t	Ohio State 9-0, Notre Dame 9-1, UCLA 6-5	Alex Agase			
1971	7-4		2	Michigan 11-0, Notre Dame 8-2, Ohio State 6-4	Alex Agase			
1972	2-9		10	Michigan 10-1, Ohio State 9-1, Notre Dame 8-2	Alex Agase (32-58-1)			
1973	4-7		4t	Notre Dame 10-0, Ohio State 9-0-1, Minnesota 7-4, Pitt 6-4-1	John Pont			
1974	3-8		7t	Ohio State 10-1, Nebraska 8-3, Notre Dame 9-2, MSU 7-3-1	John Pont			
1975	3-8		9	Michigan 8-1-2, Notre Dame 8-3, Arizona 9-2	John Pont			
1976	1-10		10	Michigan 10-1, Notre Dame 8-3, North Carolina 9-2	John Pont			
1977	1-10		10	Michigan 10-1, Ohio State 9-2, Arizona State 9-2, UNC 8-2-1	John Pont (12-43)			
1978	0-10-1		10	Michigan 10-1, Michigan State 8-3, Purdue 7-2-1, Ohio State 7-3-1	Rick Venturi			
1979	1-10		10	Ohio State 11-0, Purdue 9-2, Michigan 8-3, Indiana 7-4	Rick Venturi			
1980	0-11		10	Washington 9-2, Michigan 9-2, Ohio State 9-2, Purdue 8-3	Rick Venturi (1-31-1)			
1981	0-11		10	Iowa 8-3, Michigan 8-3, Arkansas 8-3, Ohio State 8-3	Dennis Green			
1982	3-8		8t	Michigan 8-3, Ohio State 8-3, Iowa 7-4, Illinois 7-4	Dennis Green			
1983	2-9		8t	Illinois 10-1, Michigan 9-2, Iowa 9-2, Washington 8-3, Ohio St. 8-3	Dennis Green			
1984	2-9		9	Washington 10-1, Ohio State 9-2, Wisconsin 7-3-1, Purdue 7-4	Dennis Green			
1985	3-8		9t	Iowa 10-1, Ohio State 8-3, Michigan State 7-4, Illinois 6-4-1	Dennis Green (10-45)			
1986	4-7		8t	Ohio State 9-3, Iowa 8-3	Francis Peay			
1987	2-8-1		9	Michigan State 8-2-1, Iowa 9-3, Indiana 8-3, Michigan 7-4	Francis Peay			
1988	2-8-1		7t	Michigan 8-2-1, Army 9-2, Indiana 7-3-1	Francis Peay			
1989	0-11		10	Michigan 10-1, Illinois 9-2, MSU 7-4, Air Force 8-3-1, Duke 8-3	Francis Peay			
1990	2-9		8t	Iowa 8-3, Illinois 8-3, Ohio State 73-1, Michigan State 7-3-1	Francis Peay			
1991	3-8		8t	Michigan 10-1, Iowa 10-1, Ohio State 8-3	Francis Peay (13-51-2)			
1992	3-8		6t	Notre Dame 9-1-1, Michigan 8-0-3, Ohio State 8-2-1, BC 8-2-1	Gary Barnett			
1993	2-9		10t	Notre Dame 10-1, Ohio State 9-1-1, Wisconsin 9-1-1, Penn St. 9-2	Gary Barnett			
1994	3-7-1		10	Penn State 11-0, Ohio State 9-3, Wisconsin 6-4-1, ND 6-4-1	Gary Barnett			
1995	10-2	8	1	Notre Dame 9-2, Michigan 9-3, Penn State 9-3, Iowa 7-4	Gary Barnett	Rose	32 Southern Cal	41
1996	9-3	15	1t	Penn State 10-2, Iowa 8-3, Michigan 8-3	Gary Barnett	Citrus	28 Tennessee	48
1997	5-7		8	Michigan 11-0, Ohio State 10-2, Penn State 9-2, Purdue 8-3	Gary Barnett			
1998	3-9		11	Wisconsin 10-1, Ohio State 10-1, Michigan 9-3, Penn State 8-3	Gary Barnett (35-45-1)			
1999	3-8		10	Michigan 9-2, Michigan State 9-2, Wisconsin 9-2, Minnesota 8-3	Randy Walker			
2000	8-4		1t	TCU 10-1, Michigan 8-3, Wisconsin 8-4, Purdue 8-3	Randy Walker	Alamo	17 Nebraska	66
2001	4-7		10t	Illinois 10-1, Ohio State 7-4, Iowa 6-5	Randy Walker			
2002	3-9		10t	Ohio State 13-0, Iowa 11-1, Penn State 9-3, TCU 9-2	Randy Walker			
2003	6-7		7t	Ohio State 10-2, Michigan 10-2, Purdue 9-3, Minnesota 9-3	Randy Walker	Motor City	24 Bowling Green	28
2004	6-6		4	Michigan 9-2, Wisconsin 9-2, Arizona State 8-3, Ohio State 7-4	Randy Walker			
2005	7-5		3t	Penn State 10-1, Ohio State 9-2, Wisconsin 9-3, Iowa 7-4	Randy Walker (37-46)	Sun	38 UCLA	50
2006	4-8		8t	Ohio State 12-0, Wisconsin 11-1, Michigan 11-1	Pat Fitzgerald			
2007	6-6		7t	Ohio State 11-1, Michigan 8-4, Purdue 7-5, Ilinois 9-3	Pat Fitzgerald			
2008	9-4		4t	Iowa 8-4, Michigan State 9-3, Ohio State 10-2	Pat Fitzgerald	Alamo	23 Missouri	30
2009	8-5		4t	Penn State 10-2, Iowa 10-2, Wisconsin 9-3	Pat Fitzgerald	Outback	35 Auburn	38
2010	7-6		7t	Michigan State 11-1, Penn State 7-5, Wisconsin 11-1	Pat Fitzgerald (34-29)	Dallas Classic	38 Texas Tech	45

TOTAL: 215-403-7 .3496 (69 of 70)   **Bowl Games since 1953:**   0-8 .0000 (70 of 70)

GREATEST TEAM SINCE 1953: Winning 10 games and earning a rare Rose Bowl bid makes the 1995 squad the choice here, although the talented but thin 1962 Wildcats, coached by Ara Parseghian, did hold the nation's no. 1 spot for two weeks before a late-season collapse.

1953 3-6

35	Iowa State	0
33	Army	20
13	Minnesota	30
12	Michigan	20
27	Pittsburgh	21
13	Ohio State	27
13	Wisconsin	34
6	Indiana	14
14	Illinois	39

E Joe Collier / Ziggie Niepokoj
T John Roche / Merl Searcy
G Ron Riba / LeRoy Anderson
C John Damore / Don Haffner
G Fred Nosal / Frank Hren
T John Young / Sanford Sacks
E Ed Demyan / John Biever
QB Dick Thomas / John Rearden
HB Nick Chandler / Lloyd Israels
HB Dick Ranicke / Jim Troglio
FB Bob Lauter / Gerald Weber

RUSHING: Troglio 50/312y
PASSING: Thomas 74-145/933y, 6TD, 51%
RECEIVING: Collier 22/354y
SCORING: Lauter 30pts

1954 2-7

27	Iowa State	14
7	Southern Cal	12
7	Minnesota	26
0	Michigan	7
7	Pittsburgh	14
7	Ohio State	14
13	Wisconsin	34
13	Indiana	14
20	Illinois	7

E Ziggie Niepokoj / Fred Nosal
T John Young / Sanford Sacks
G Bob Higley / Frank Hren
C John Damore / Ted Ringer
G Ron Riba / John Lohbauer
T Billy Williams / John Roche
E Jack Stillwell / Fred Duhart
QB John Rearden / Dale Pienta
HB Jim Troglio / Bob King
HB Dick Ranicke / George Gondek
FB Bob Lauter

RUSHING: Lauter 102/371y, Ranicke 88/270y, Troglio 56/254y
PASSING: Pienta 25-62/394y, 2TD, 40.3%
RECEIVING: Niepokoj 15/157y, Stillwell 9/197y, Nosal 8/125y
SCORING: Six players tied w/ 12pts

1955 0-8-1

14	Miami (Ohio)	25
0	Tulane	21
7	Minnesota	18
2	Michigan	14
14	Indiana	20
0	Ohio State	49
14	Wisconsin	41
8	Purdue	46
7	Illinois	7

E Jack Stillwell / Fred Nosal
T Sanford Sacks / Al Weyhrich
G John Lohbauer / Tom Williams
C Ted Ringer
G Al Viola / John Eldridge
T John Smith
E Kurt Krueger / Cliff Peart / Stan Dwyer
QB Dale Pienta / Jack Ellis
HB Jim Troglio / Ollie Lindborg
HB Jerry Weber / Frank Jeske
FB E. Quinn/Wayne Glassman/John Foster

RUSHING: Troglio 66/287y, Weber 57/260y, Quinn 38/137y
PASSING: Ellis 22-49/165y, 1TD, 44.9%
RECEIVING: Stillwell 11/242y, Krueger 7/90y, Quinn 6/17y
SCORING: Jerry Eber (K) 18pts, 6 tied w/ 6pts

1956 4-4-1

14	Iowa State	13
13	Tulane	20
0	Minnesota	0
20	Michigan	34
13	Indiana	19
2	Ohio State	6
17	Wisconsin	7
14	Purdue	0
14	Illinois	13

E Ben Napolski
T Andy Cvercko / Al Weyhrich
G John Lohbauer / Tom Williams
C Ted Ringer
G Al Viola
T John Smith
E Cliff Peart
QB Dale Pienta / Jack Ellis
HB Bobby McKeiver / George Gondek
HB Willmer Fowler
FB Eddie Quinn / Chuck Jerasa

RUSHING: McKeiver 115/592y, Quinn 94/358y, Fowler 63/304y
PASSING: Ellis 19-44/248y, 2TD, 43.2%
RECEIVING: McKeiver 11/251y, Napolski 8/83y, Peart 6/99y
SCORING: McKiever 38pts, Fowler 18pts, Peart & Quinn 12pts

1957 0-9

6	Stanford	26
13	Oregon State	22
6	Minnesota	41
14	Michigan	34
0	Iowa	6
6	Ohio State	47
12	Wisconsin	41
0	Purdue	27
0	Illinois	27

E Ben Napolski / Doug Asad / Dick Moser
T Andy Cvercko
G John Lake / Jack Siatta
C Jim Andreotti
G Al Viola / Pete Arena
T Al Weyhrich / Gene Gossage
E Cliff Peart / Fred Williamson
QB Chip Holcomb / John Talley
HB Bobby McKeiver / Ron Burton
HB Willmer Fowler / Sam Johnson
FB Eddie Quinn

RUSHING: Burton 74/389y, Fowler 74/294y, McKeiver 65/240y
PASSING: Holcomb 41-91/395y, 2TD, 45.1%
RECEIVING: McKeiver 16/120y, Williamson 15/168y, Moser 9/61y
SCORING: Burton 18pts, Quinn 13pts, McKiever 8pts

1958 5-4

29	Washington St.	28
28	Stanford	0
7	Minnesota	3
55	Michigan	24
20	Iowa	26
21	Ohio State	0
13	Wisconsin	17
6	Purdue	23
20	Illinois	27

E Elbert Kimbrough / Irv Cross
T Andy Cvercko
G Joe Abbatiello
C Jim Andreotti
G Russ Asala / Pete Arena
T Gene Gossage
E Doug Asad / Fred Williamson
QB Dick Thornton
HB Ron Burton / Ray Purdin
HB Willmer Fowler / Sam Johnson
FB Mike Stock/Mark Johnston/Fred Hecker

RUSHING: Burton 141/613y, Thornton 110/250y, Fowler 63/246y
PASSING: Thornton 53-122/828y, 7TD, 43.4%
RECEIVING: Burton 19/392y, Kimbrough 14/148y, Williamson 9/199y
SCORING: Burton 76pts, Thornton 42pts, Purdin 24pts

1959 6-3

45	Oklahoma	13
14	Iowa	10
6	Minnesota	0
20	Michigan	7
30	Notre Dame	24
30	Indiana	13
19	Wisconsin	24
10	Michigan State	10
0	Illinois	28

E Irv Cross / Doug Asad
T Dewitt Hoopes
G Joe Abbatiello / Russ Asala
C Jim Andreotti
G Pete Arena
T Gene Gossage
E Elbert Kimbrough / Paul Yanke
QB John Talley / Larry Wood (D)
HB Ron Burton
HB Ray Purdin / Mark Johnston
FB Mike Stock

RUSHING: Stock 109/400y, Burton 65/357y, Purdin 58/307y
PASSING: Talley 44-100/783y, 4TD, 44%
RECEIVING: Kimbrough 16/235y, Burton 14/138y, Purdin 12/278y
SCORING: Burton 36pts, Stock 34pts, Purdin 32pts

1960 5-4

19	Oklahoma	3
0	Iowa	42
0	Minnesota	7
7	Michigan	14
7	Notre Dame	6
21	Indiana	3
21	Wisconsin	0
18	Michigan State	21
14	Illinois	7

E Irv Cross / Paul Yanke
T Bud Melvin / George Thomas
G Wayne Chamberlain / James Lutz
C Larry Onesti (D)/Dick Nichols/Ike Smith
G Russ Asala / Chuck Urbanic
T Fate Echols / Jack Cvercko
E Elbert Kimbrough
QB Dick Thornton / Larry Wood (D)
HB Al Kimbrough / Frank Johnson
HB Ray Purdin / Larry Benz
FB Mike Stock

RUSHING: Stock 133/536y, Thornton 115/225y
PASSING: Thornton 54-128/901y, 6TD, 42.2%
RECEIVING: E. Kimbrough 26/378y, A. Kimbrough 8/136y
SCORING: Stock 39pts, A. Kimbrough & E. Kimbrough 18pts

1961 4-5

45	Boston College	0
28	Illinois	7
3	Minnesota	10
0	Ohio State	10
12	Notre Dame	10
14	Indiana	8
10	Wisconsin	29
13	Michigan State	21
6	Miami	10

E Chuck Logan / Dick Machalski
T Bud Melvin / Ike Smith
G Larry Zeno / Chuck Urbanic
G Jay Robertson / Larry Onesti (LB)
G Kent Pike / Burt Petkus
T Fate Echols
E Pat Riley / Ray Dillon / Dave Cox
QB Tom O'Grady / Bob Eickhoff
HB Willie Stinson / Albert Kimbrough
HB L. Benz / Chuck Brainerd / Bob Snider
FB Bill Swingle / Paul Flatley

RUSHING: Swingle 79/483y, O'Grady 65/251y, Eickhoff 48/201y
PASSING: O'Grady 28-59/320y, 1TD, 47.5%
RECEIVING: Logan 13/130y, Stinson 10/158y, Cox 9/100y
SCORING: Swingle 30pts, Flatley 18pts, Dave Damm (K?) 17pts

1962 7-2

37	South Carolina	20
45	Illinois	0
34	Minnesota	22
18	Ohio State	14
35	Notre Dame	6
26	Indiana	21
6	Wisconsin	37
7	Michigan State	31
29	Miami	7

WR Paul Flatley
E Chuck Logan
T George Thomas / Mike Schwager
G Larry Zeno / Burt Petkus
C Jay Robertson / Jerry Goshgarian (D)
G Jack Cvercko / Kent Pike
T Joe Szczecko
E Gary Crum/George Burman/Jim Benda
QB Tommy Myers / Rollie Wahl (DB)
HB W. Stinson /Dick McCauley /Larry Benz
FB Bill Swingle / Steve Murphy

RUSHING: Stinson 88/418y, Swingle 66/291y, McCauley 57/273y
PASSING: Myers 116-195/1537y, 13TD, 59.5%
RECEIVING: Flatley 45/626y, Crum 16/166y, Logan 11/136y
SCORING: Murphy 56pts, Flatley 36pts, Swingle 34pts

1963 5-4

23	Missouri	12
34	Indiana	21
9	Illinois	10
15	Minnesota	8
37	Miami (Ohio)	6
7	Michigan State	15
6	Michigan	27
14	Wisconsin	17
17	Ohio State	8

E Chuck Logan / Pat Riley (DE)
T Joe Szczecko / Tim Ziemke
G Tim Powell / Fred Tuerk
C Joe Cerne / Dick Uhlir (LB)
G Don Robinson / Rich Lawton
T Mike Schwager / Kent Pike
E George Burman / Gary Crum
QB Tommy Myers / Rollie Wahl (DB)
HB Dick McCauley / James Dau (DB)
FB Bill Swingle / Steve Murphy

RUSHING: Stinson 115/368y, McCauley 66/302y, Murphy 59/253y
PASSING: Myers 93-179/1398y, 6TD, 52%
RECEIVING: Crum 22/417y, Logan 22/352y, Burman 12/209y
SCORING: Murphy 36pts, Pete Stamison (K) 33pts, Stinson 24pts

1964 3-6

7	Oregon State	3
14	Indiana	13
6	Illinois	17
18	Minnesota	21
27	Miami (Ohio)	28
6	Michigan State	24
0	Michigan	35
17	Wisconsin	13
0	Ohio State	10

E Dick Smith
T Jim Burns
G Rich Olson
G Joe Cerne
G Don Robinson
T Mike Schwager
G Cas Banaszek
QB Tommy Myers
HB Dick McCauley
HB Ron Rector / Woody Campbell
FB Steve Murphy / Bob McKelvey
DL Pat Riley
DL Mike Beinor
DL Larry Zeno
DL Jeff Brooke
DL Joe Szczecko
DL Dave Cyranoski
LB Jim Haugsness
LB Wade Clark
DB Phil Clark
DB Mike Buckner
DB Jim Dau

RUSHING: Murphy 109/377y, Rector 76/332y, McKelvey 23/139y
PASSING: Myers 72-160/901y, 2TD, 45%
RECEIVING: Banaszek 27/317y, Smith 11/193y, Rector 11/145y
SCORING: Murphy 36pts, Rector 18pts, Smith 12pts

1965 4-6

14	Florida	24
20	Indiana	0
7	Notre Dame	38
15	Oregon State	7
7	Wisconsin	21
9	Iowa	0
7	Michigan State	49
22	Minnesota	27
34	Michigan	22
6	Illinois	20

E Dick Smith / Mike Donaldson
T Jerry Oberdorf
G Jeff Brooke
C Jim Haugsness / Mike Shea
G Bruce Gunstra / Tom Nunamaker
T Jim Burns / John Brlas
E Cas Banaszek
QB Denny Boothe / Dave Milam
HB Woody Campbell / Larry Gates
HB Ron Rector
FB Bob McKelvey
DL John McCambridge
DL Ken Ramsey
DL Mike Beinor
DL Jim Burns
DL Bob Tubbs
LB Phil Clark
LB Bob OtterBacher
LB Denny Yanta
DB Mike Buckner
DB Bob Hampton
DB Tom Garretson

RUSHING: McKelvey 175/587y, Campbell 86/373y, Rector 82/345y
PASSING: Boothe 42-102/487y, 2TD, 41.2%
RECEIVING: Banaszek 30/333y, Donaldson 17/203y, Smith 9/122y
SCORING: McKelvey 48pts, Rector 38pts, Dean Dickie (K) 17pts

1966 3-6-1

7	Florida	43 E Roger Murphy
14	Indiana	26 T John Brlas
7	Notre Dame	35 G Ron Silver
14	Oregon State	6 C Jack Rudnay / John Eggemeyer
3	Wisconsin	3 G Bruce Gunstra
24	Iowa	15 T Tom Ziolkowski
0	Michigan State	22 E Cas Banaszek
13	Minnesota	28 QB Bill Melzer / Dennis Boothe
20	Michigan	28 HB Woody Campbell
35	Illinois	7 HB Chico Kurzawski / Larry Gates
		FB Bob McKelvey / Mike Bradburn
		DL John McCambridge
		DL Ken Ramsey / Sandy Smith
		DL Justin Ramp / Bruce Gunstra
		DL Walt Geister / Mark Proskine
		DL Bob Tubbs
		LB John Cornell
		LB Dennis Coyne
		LB Al Koranda / Bob OtterBacher
		DB Tom Garretson / Dennis White
		DB Phil Clark
		DB Bob Hampton

RUSHING: McKelvey 128/459y, Campbell 114/364y, Kurzawski 49/215y
PASSING: Melzer 94-176/1171y, 7TD, 53.4%
RECEIVING: Murphy 51/777y, Banaszek 31/272y, Kurzawski 14/193y
SCORING: Dick Emmerich (K) Murphy 24pts, Kurzawski 18pts

1967 3-7

12	Miami	7 E Don Anderson / Bruce Hubbard
6	Missouri	13 T Don Denny
16	Purdue	25 G Angelo Loukas
6	Rice	50 C Jack Rudnay
2	Ohio State	6 G Bruce Gunstra
17	Wisconsin	13 T Tom Ziolkowski
3	Michigan	7 E Jeff Buckner
39	Iowa	24 QB Bill Melzer
21	Illinois	27 HB Chico Kurzawski
27	Michigan State	41 HB Bob Olson
		FB John Anstey / Dick Emmerich
		DL Mark Proskine
		DL Frank Mullins / Harvey Blue
		DL John Brandt
		DL Ed Paquette / Roland Collins
		LB John Cornell
		LB Mike Hudson
		LB Ron Mied
		LB Don Ross / Ray Forsthoffer
		DB Dennis White
		DB Denny Coyne
		DB Tom Garretson

RUSHING: Olson 143/507y, Kurzawski 165/477y, Anstey 66/228y
PASSING: Melzer 101-215/1146y, TD, 47%
RECEIVING: Anderson 33/376y, Kurzawski 29/326y, Buckner 18/189y
SCORING: Kurzawski 42pts, Emmerich (FB-K) 35pts, Melzer 30pts

1968 1-9

7	Miami	28 WR Bruce Hubbard
7	Southern Cal	24 T Don Denny
6	Purdue	43 G Mike Sikich / John Hoerster
7	Notre Dame	27 C Jack Rudnay / Joe Zigulich
21	Ohio State	45 G Angelo Loukas
13	Wisconsin	10 T Tom Ziokowski
0	Michigan	35 TE Pat Harrington / Jon Hittman
34	Iowa	68 QB Dave Shelbourne
0	Illinois	14 HB Chico Kurzawski / Craig Smeeton
14	Michigan State	31 HB Ken Luxton / Mike Adamle
		FB Bob Olson / Dick Emmerich
		DL John Cornell / Ed Paquette
		DL Bill Galler
		DL John Rodman / Frank Mullins
		DL Mark Proskine / Roland Collins
		LB Don Ross
		LB Joel Hall
		LB Ray Forsthoffer / Jeff Rockenbach
		LB Mike Hudson
		DB Denny White
		DB Rich Dean / Brad Somers
		DB Rich Field / Harold Daniels

RUSHING: Olson 90/342y, Kurzawski 90/299y, Emmerich 59/224y
PASSING: Shelbourne 105-251/1358y, 7TD, 41.8%
RECEIVING: Hubbard 33/551y, Harrington 17/163y, Hittman 15/214y
SCORING: Emmerich 35pts, Kurzawski & Smeeton 18pts

1969 3-7

10	Notre Dame	35 WR Bruce Hubbard / Jerry Brown
6	Southern Cal	48 WR Ken Luxton / Barry Pearson
0	UCLA	36 T Paul Gary
10	Illinois	6 G Mike Sikich
27	Wisconsin	7 C Joe Zigulich
20	Purdue	45 G John Hoerster / Terry Ekl
6	Ohio State	35 T John Bradley / Jerry Combs
21	Minnesota	28 TE Jon Hittman
30	Indiana	27 QB Maurie Daigneau / Dave Shelbourne
7	Michigan State	39 HB Mike Adamle / Craig Smeeton
		FB Mike Hudson
		DL Wil Hemby
		DL George Keporos / Jeff Rockenbach
		DL Bill Galler
		DL John Rodman
		LB Jack Derning
		LB Don Ross / John Vorhees
		LB Joel Hall
		DB Rick Telander
		DB Gary Holland
		DB Eric Hutchinson
		DB Mike Coughlin / Jack Dustin

RUSHING: Adamle 140/666y, Hudson 127/554y, Smeeton 28/103y
PASSING: Daigneau 85-191/1276y, 7TD, 47.3%
RECEIVING: Hubbard 25/384y, Luxton 21/284y, Adamle 17/260y
SCORING: Adamle & Hudson 30pts, Bill Planisek (K) 29pts

1970 6-4

14	Notre Dame	35 WR Jim Lash / Tony Koenings
7	UCLA	12 WR Barry Pearson
20	SMU	21 T John Rodman
48	Illinois	0 G Mike Sikich
24	Wisconsin	14 C Joe Zigulich
38	Purdue	14 G John Hoerster
10	Ohio State	24 T Jon Hittman
28	Minnesota	14 TE Tom McCreight
21	Indiana	7 QB Maurie Daigneau
23	Michigan State	20 HB Al Robinson
		FB Mike Adamle
		DL Wil Hemby
		DL Jim Anderson
		DL Pat Kershaw / Frank Bliss
		DL Jerry Combs
		LB John Vorhees
		LB Jack Derning / Pat McNamara
		LB Joel Hall
		DB Jack Dustin
		DB Rick Telander
		DB Mike Coughlin
		DB Eric Hutchinson

RUSHING: Adamle 304/1255y, Robinson 174/556y
PASSING: Daigneau 88-204/1228y, 10TD, 43.1%
RECEIVING: Pearson 33/552y, Lash 16/289y, Robinson 15/165y
SCORING: Adamle 60pts, Bill Planisek (K) 45pts, Robinson 30pts

1971 7-4

6	Michigan	21 WR Jim Lash
7	Notre Dame	50 WR Barry Pearson
12	Syracuse	6 T Dave Glantz
24	Wisconsin	11 G Donnie Haynes / Tom Dickinson
28	Iowa	3 C Dave Dybas
20	Purdue	21 G Tom McCreight
24	Indiana	10 T Paul Gary
7	Illinois	24 TE Steve Craig
41	Minnesota	20 QB Maurie Daigneau
14	Ohio State	10 HB Al Robinson
28	Michigan State	7 FB Randy Anderson / Harold Smith
		DL Wil Hemby
		DL Pat Kershaw
		DL Jim Anderson
		DL George Keporos
		LB Mike Varty
		LB John Vorhees
		LB Jack Derning
		DB Jack Dustin
		DB Jerry Brown
		DB Eric Hutchinson
		DB Mike Coughlin

RUSHING: Robinson 277/881y, Anderson 135/480y
PASSING: Daigneau 125-264/1733y, 6TD, 47.3%
RECEIVING: Pearson 48/674y, Lash 34/523y, Anderson 15/84y
SCORING: Anderson 60pts, Bill Planisek (K) 34pts, Robinson 30pts

1972 2-9

0	Michigan	7 WR Jim Lash
0	Notre Dame	37 WR Steve Harris / Pat McNamara
27	Pittsburgh	22 T Dave Glantz
14	Wisconsin	21 G Donnie Haynes
12	Iowa	23 C Ray Felton (G) / Dave Dybas
0	Purdue	37 G Paul Hiemenz / Larry Lilja
23	Indiana	14 T Larry Mishler
13	Illinois	43 TE Steve Craig
29	Minnesota	35 QB Mitch Anderson
14	Ohio State	27 HB Greg Boykin / Stan Key
14	Michigan State	24 FB Harold Smith / Jim Trimble
		DL Frank Bliss
		DL Jim Anderson
		DL George Petrak / Joe Verzino
		DL Rob Mason / Jamie Summerfelt
		LB Doug Belko / Al Draper
		LB Steve Anenen
		LB Art Riley
		DB Greg Strunk
		DB Bob Beutel
		DB Greg Swanson
		DB Pete Wessel / Pete Shaw

RUSHING: Boykin 159/625y, Trimble 93/339y, Key 71/290y
PASSING: Anderson 95-187/1333y, 7TD, 50.8%
RECEIVING: Lash 36/667y, Craig 29/362y, Boykin 11/100y
SCORING: Boykin 38pts, Craig 28pts, Dave Skarin (K) 26pts

1973 4-7

14	Michigan State	10 WR Bill Stevens / Steve Harris
0	Notre Dame	44 WR Wayne Fredrickson
14	Pittsburgh	21 T James Foskett
12	Ohio U.	14 G Donnie Haynes
31	Iowa	15 C Larry Lilja
10	Purdue	21 G Ray Felton
0	Ohio State	60 T Paul Hiemenz
43	Minnesota	52 TE Steve Craig
21	Indiana	20 QB Mitch Anderson
34	Wisconsin	36 TB Stan Key / Rich Boothe
9	Illinois	6 FB Greg Boykin / Jim Trimble
		DL Doug Belko
		DL John Holliday
		DL Paul Maly
		DL Jamie Summerfelt / Darryl Brandford
		DL Rob Mason
		LB Mike Varty
		LB Steve Anenen
		DB Neil Little / Charles Hickerson
		DB Pete Wessel
		DB Greg Swanson
		DB Pete Shaw

RUSHING: Key 197/894y, Boothe 101/416y, Boykin 98/350y
PASSING: Anderson 91-197/1224y, 12TD, 46.2%
RECEIVING: Craig 30/479y, Stevens 15/246y, Harris 15/240y
SCORING: Craig & Key 36pts, Jim Blazevich (K) 30pts

1974 3-8

7	Michigan State	41 WR Bill Stevens / Pat McNamara
3	Notre Dame	49 WR Wayne Fredrickson / Mike Darraugh
7	Nebraska	49 T James Foskett / Richard Dembowski
14	Oregon	10 G Mark Ruff / DeWayne Shambley
10	Iowa	35 C Larry Lilja
26	Purdue	31 G Ron Kuceyeski
7	Ohio State	55 T Paul Hiemenz
21	Minnesota	13 TE Scott Yelvington
24	Indiana	22 QB Mitch Anderson
7	Wisconsin	52 TB Jim Pooler
14	Illinois	28 FB Jim Trimble / Rich Boothe
		DL Doug Belko
		DL John Holliday
		DL Randy Kuceyeski / Frank Malec
		DL Marty Szostak
		DL Rob Mason
		LB Carl Patrnchak
		LB Joe Patrnchak
		DB Steve Scardina
		DB Rob Dean / Doug Baske
		DB Mark Harlow / Neil Little
		DB James Hutchings / Malcolm Hunter

RUSHING: Pooler 216/949y, Trimble 118/525y, Boothe 100/375y
PASSING: Anderson 101-225/1282y, 7TD, 44.9%
RECEIVING: Yelvington 37/417y, Fredrickson 14/219y, Boothe 11/109y
SCORING: Pooler 54pts, Jim Blazevich (K) 26pts, 4 tied w/ 12pts

1975 3-8

31 Purdue	25 WR Scott Yelvington
10 N. Illinois	3 T Rich Dembowski / Joe Corona
7 Notre Dame	31 G Carl Peterson
6 Arizona	41 C Paul Jasinskis
30 Indiana	0 G Ron Kuceyeski
0 Michigan	69 T Tony Ardizzone
14 Wisconsin	17 TE Dan Cleary
21 Iowa	24 QB Randy Dean
9 Minnesota	33 HB Jim Pooler / Mark Bailey
14 Michigan State	47 HB Greg Boykin
7 Illinois	28 FB Rich Boothe

DL Kevin Sprouse
DL John Holliday / Darryl Brandford
DL Paul Maly / Randy Kuceyeski
DL Marty Szostak / Mike Weitzman
DL Terry Brantley / Garry Ogden
LB Al Benz / Lodi Vercelli
LB Blaine Ogilvie / Greg Stanley
DB Mark Harlow / Guy Knafelc
DB Neil Little / Mike Taylor
DB Pete Shaw
DB Rob Dean / Jack Gavin

RUSHING: Boykin 239/1105y, Boothe 114/425y, Pooler 89/305y
PASSING: Dean 101-200/1315y, 3TD, 50.3%
RECEIVING: Yelvington 50/686y, Pooler 16/213y, Bailey 11/118y
SCORING: Boykin 54pts, Nick Mirkopulos (K) 35pts,
  Yelvington 24pts

1976 1-10

19 Purdue	31 WR Scott Yelvington
0 North Carolina	12 WR Mark Bailey / Rob Dean
0 Notre Dame	48 T Jim Foskett / Don Herzog
15 Arizona	27 G Rudi Tanck
0 Indiana	7 C Carl Peterson / DeWayne Shambley
7 Michigan	38 G Dan Henderson
25 Wisconsin	28 T Tony Ardizzone
10 Iowa	13 TE Wally Kasprzycki
10 Minnesota	38 QB Randy Dean
42 Michigan State	21 TB Greg Boykin / Pat Geegan
6 Illinois	48 FB Matt Reitzug / Jim Whims

DL Garry Ogden
DL Mike Weitzman
DL Paul Maly
DL Marty Szostak
DL Kevin Sprouse
LB Al Benz / Scott Duncan
LB Greg Stanley
DB Guy Knafelc / Steve Bobowski
DB Neil Little
DB Malcolm Hunter
DB Pete Shaw

RUSHING: Geegan 154/537y, Whims 126/405y, Boykin 105/385y
PASSING: Dean 87-177/1384y, 8TD, 49.2%
RECEIVING: Yelvington 34/649y, Bailey 32/496y, Dean 11/215y
SCORING: Bailey & Yelvington 24pts, Geegan & Poulos 20pts

1977 1-10

0 Iowa	24 WR Mark Bailey
3 Arizona State	35 WR Mike Taylor / Todd Sheets
7 North Carolina	41 T Don Herzog
7 Wisconsin	19 G Frank Malec
3 Indiana	28 C Mike Fiedler / Greg Soderberg
7 Minnesota	13 G Rudi Tanck / Dan Henderson
15 Ohio State	35 T Tony Ardizzone
16 Purdue	28 TE Dan Cleary
20 Michigan	63 QB Stuart Stranski / Dana Hemphill
3 Michigan State	44 TB Dave Mishler / Sam Rushing
21 Illinois	7 FB Matt Reitzug / Harold Gilmore

DL Curt Grelle / Dean Payne / Kevin Berg
DL Marty Szostak
DL Lodi Vercelli
DL Mike Weitzman
DL Mike Kendzicky
LB Paul Maly / Blaine Ogilvie
LB Scott Duncan / Greg Stanley
DB Steve Bobowski
DB Guy Knafelc / Stephen Scardina
DB Malcolm Hunter
DB Pat Geegan

RUSHING: Mishler 115/520y, Reitzug 103/445y, Rushing 72/236y
PASSING: Stranski 37-95/541y, 4TD, 38.9%
RECEIVING: Bailey 22/347y, Taylor 11/138y, Sheets 8/199y
SCORING: Poulos 21pts, Mishler & Reitzug 18pts

1978 0-10-1

0 Illinois	0 WR Mike McGee
3 Iowa	20 T John Schober
7 Wisconsin	28 G Bill Draznik / Kevin Kenyon
7 Colorado	55 C Mike Fiedler
14 Arizona State	56 G Jim Ford
10 Indiana	38 T Michael Kranz
14 Minnesota	38 TE Wally Kasprzycki / Sam Poulos
20 Ohio State	63 QB Kevin Strasser
0 Purdue	31 TB Tim Hill / Lou Tiberi
14 Michigan	59 WB Tom North / Steve Bogan
3 Michigan State	52 FB Mike Cammon / Dave Mishler

DL Mike Kendzicky / Bruce Robinett
DL Brian Stasiewicz / Robert Taylor
DL Joe Corona / James Dunlea
DL Charles Rogers / Bill Gildner
LB Dean Payne / Tim Lawrence
LB Chuck Kern
LB Kevin Berg
DB Dave Hoffman
DB Guy Knafelc / Steve Bobowski
DB Tom McGlade
DB Pat Geegan / Ben Butler

RUSHING: Cammon 73/322y, Hill 65/195y, Mishler 55/168y
PASSING: Strasser 151-307/1526y, 6TD, 49.2%
RECEIVING: Hill 24/122y, Bogan 22/353y, McGee 22/298y
SCORING: Bogan 36pts, Strasser 18pts, Nick Mirkopulos (K)15pts

1979 1-10

7 Michigan	49 WR Todd Sheets
27 Wyoming	22 T John Schober / Bill Greer
21 Syracuse	54 G Bill Draznik / Robert Taylor
8 Minnesota	38 C Mike Fiedler
7 Ohio State	16 G Kevin Kenyon
6 Iowa	58 T Jim Ford
0 Indiana	30 TE Wally Kasprzycki / Sam Poulos
16 Purdue	20 QB Mike Kerrigan / Chris Capstran
7 Michigan State	42 TB Jeff Cohn / Tim Hill / Mike Cammon
3 Wisconsin	28 WB Steve Bogan / Dave Bahoric
13 Illinois	29 FB Dave Callaway / Dave Mishler

DL Bruce Robinett
DL Curt Grelle / Brian Stasiewicz
DL Norm Wells
LB Chris Hinton / Kevin Berg
LB Scott Duncan / Jim Miller
LB Chuck Kern
LB Dean Payne
DB Roosevelt Groves / Mark Adams
DB Lou Tiberi
DB Ben Butler / John Burns
DB Jay Anderson / Tom McGlade

RUSHING: Cohn 117/426y, Cammon 49/236y, Hill 59/174y
PASSING: Kerrigan 82-195/961y, 4TD, 42.1%
  Capstran 52-101/491y, 51.5%
RECEIVING: Sheets 43/614y, Poulos 31/245y, Bogan 17/253y
SCORING: Bogan & Mishler 24pts, Poulos 23pts

1980 0-11

9 Illinois	35 WR Todd Sheets
10 Michigan	17 T Bob Pratt
7 Washington	45 G Kelby Brown / Pat Erdman
21 Syracuse	42 C Bill Gerber
21 Minnesota	49 G Robert Taylor (T) / Bill Draznik
0 Ohio State	63 T Jim Ford
3 Iowa	25 TE John Finn / Chris Hinton
20 Indiana	35 QB Mike Kerrigan
31 Purdue	52 TB Jeff Cohn / Ricky Edwards
10 Michigan State	42 WB Dave Bahoric / Todd Jenkins
19 Wisconsin	89 FB Dave Mishler

DL Richard Moore
DL Brian Stasiewicz / Tom Maul
DL Bill Gildner (LB) / Terry Harrell (LB)
LB Chris Hinton / Kenny Gregory
LB Chuck Kern / Don Bambauer
LB Steve Pals/Jer Woods/Lenson Staples
LB Chris Capstran / Jim Karstens
DB Roosevelt Groves
DB Lou Tiberi / Percy Holden
DB Mike Guendling / David Hoffman
DB Bobby Anderson

RUSHING: Cohn 137/503y, Mishler 82/286y, Edwards 32/102y
PASSING: Kerrigan 173-337/1816y, 12TD, 51.3%
RECEIVING: Sheets 33/570y, Mishler 27/135y, Cohn 24/162y
SCORING: Jay Anderson (K) 37pts, Sheets 24pts, 4 tied w/ 18pts

1981 0-11

20 Indiana	21 WR Dave Bahoric / Steve Kaiser
7 Arkansas	38 WR Steve Bogan / Todd Jenkins
0 Utah	42 T Robert Taylor
0 Iowa	64 G Kelby Brown / Phil Leonard
23 Minnesota	35 C Jack Kreider
0 Purdue	35 G Jim Crowder / Steve McGill
0 Michigan	38 T Bob Pratt
0 Wisconsin	52 TE Chris Hinton / Paul Mosby
14 Michigan State	61 QB Kevin Villars / Mike Kerrigan
6 Ohio State	70 HB Kenny Watkins / Marc Hujik
12 Illinois	49 FB Dave Callaway / Jim Browne

DL Keith Cruise / Jerald Wolff
DL Chris Capstran / Leon Rallings
DL Richard Moore / Bill Gildner
LB Alex Moyer
LB Jim Bobbitt / Chris Natzke
LB Rich Raffin / Darin Morgan
LB Mike Guendling
DB Greg Washington / Jankeith Gatewood
DB Lou Tiberi
DB Fred Sobeck / Dean Koester
DB Bobby Anderson / David Shaw

RUSHING: Browne 52/162y, Villars 70/98y, Hujik 25/93y
PASSING: Kerrigan 124-265/1317y, 7TD, 46.8%,
  Villars 77-148/773y, 3TD, 52%
RECEIVING: Browne 24/140y, Callaway 20/143y, Hinton 19/265y
SCORING: Bogan 24pts, Bahoric & Hujik 12pts

1982 3-8

13 Illinois	49 WR Todd Jenkins
0 Indiana	30 WR Tony Coates / Kevin Villars
13 Miami (Ohio)	27 T Chris Hinton
31 N. Illinois	6 G Bob Pratt / David Dallstream
7 Iowa	45 C Phil Leonard (G) / Gregg Damminga
31 Minnesota	21 G Chris Banaszak
21 Purdue	34 T Jack Vandenberghe
14 Michigan	49 TE Jon Harvey / Steve Kaiser
20 Wisconsin	54 QB Sandy Schwab
28 Michigan State	24 TB Ricky Edwards / Tracey Parsons
28 Ohio State	40 FB Casey Cummings / Danny Hurwitz

DL Tom Flaherty / Daryl Newell
DL Keith Cruise
DL Kim Hawley / Jerald Wolff / Bill Prince
LB Alex Moyer
LB Jim Bobbitt / Jim Murauskis
LB Darin Morgan / Rich Raffin
LB Mike Guendling / Jim Karstens
DB Jankeith Gatewoood / Kenny Watkins
DB Roosevelt Groves
DB Scott Sanderson / Joe Morton
DB Bill Kornegay / Dean Koester

RUSHING: Edwards 157/668y, Parsons 28/97y
PASSING: Schwab 234-416/2735y, 14TD, 56.3%
RECEIVING: Harvey 52/807y, Jenkins 49/701y, Edwards 41/342y
SCORING: Edwards 54pts, Schwab 30pts, Harvey 24pts

1983 2-9

0 Washington	34 WR Todd Jenkins / Eric Anderson
0 Syracuse	35 WR Tony Coates
10 Indiana	8 T Matt Burbach/ D. Dudzinski/ Mike Meskill
0 Wisconsin	49 G Chris Banaszak / Bill Balmer
21 Iowa	61 C John Yale / Phil Leonard
0 Michigan	35 G Gregg Damminga / David Dallstream
19 Minnesota	8 T Jack Vandenberghe
17 Purdue	48 TE Jon Harvey
3 Michigan State	9 QB Sandy Schwab / Steve Burton
7 Ohio State	55 HB Rickey Edwards
24 Illinois	56 FB Casey Cummings / Mark Ignatowicz

DL Keith Cruise
DL Daryl Newell / Ted Karras
DL Jerald Wolff / Bill Prince
LB Alex Moyer
LB Jim Bobbitt
LB Darin Morgan
LB Mike Guendling
DB Charles Plant / David Dixon
DB Undra Lofton
DB Orville Nevels / Joe Morton
DB Kenny Watkins / Scott Sanderson

RUSHING: Edwards 183/561y, Claudell Robertson (FB) 24/73y
PASSING: Schwab 188-334/1838y, 6TD, 56.3%
RECEIVING: Edwards 83/570y, Harvey 39/549y, Coates 24/354y
SCORING: John Duvic (K) 27pts, Harvey 24pts, Edwards 18pts

1984 2-9

16 Illinois	24 WR Marc Bumgarner / Brett Whitley
0 Washington	26 WR Tony Coates
12 Syracuse	13 T Dave Dudzinski
40 Indiana	37 G Mario Zappia
16 Wisconsin	31 C Phil Leonard
3 Iowa	31 G Steve Hofmann
0 Michigan	31 T Jack Vandenberghe
31 Minnesota	28 TE Ralph Jackson
7 Purdue	49 QB Sandy Schwab / Mike Greenfield
10 Michigan State	27 HB Tracy Parsons / Stanley Davenport
3 Ohio State	52 FB Casey Cummings
	DL Keith Cruise
	DL Ted Karras / Bob Dirkes
	DL Daryl Newell
	LB Alex Moyer
	LB Jim Torkelson / Jim Bobbitt
	LB Darin Morgan
	LB Ellery Bennett
	DB Kevin Brown
	DB Jankeith Gatewood
	DB Scott Sanderson
	DB Charles Plant

RUSHING: Cummings 79/386y, Davenport 84/244y, Parsons 83/242y
PASSING: Schwab 93-198/845y, 2TD, 47%, Greenfield 80-149/733y, 3TD, 53.7%
RECEIVING: Cummings 28/131y, Coates 25/311y, Jackson 20/246y
SCORING: John Duvic (K) 48pts, Parsons 24pts, Davenport & Duncan 12pts

1985 3-8

17 Duke	40 WR Marc Bumgarner
27 Missouri	23 WR Curtis Duncan / Rudy Germany
38 N. Illinois	16 T Daryl Newell
7 Indiana	26 G Mario Zappia
10 Minnesota	21 C John Yale / Clint Gregg
17 Wisconsin	14 G Steve Hofmann
10 Iowa	49 T Matt Burbach / Tom Nicklas / Mike Baum
7 Purdue	31 TE Bob Driscoll / Rich Borresen
17 Ohio State	35 QB Mike Greenfield
0 Michigan State	32 HB Stanley Davenport / Brian Nuffer
20 Illinois	45 FB Casey Cummings
	DL Jerald Wolff
	DL Bob Dirkes
	DL Ted Karras
	DL Tom Flaherty
	LB Rich Myers / Bob Bucaro / David Dixon
	LB Jim Torkelson / Alan Brown
	LB Mike Witteck
	DB Todd Krehbiel
	DB Dirk Adams / Hughes
	DB Brett Whitley
	DB Charles Plant / Kyle Palmer

RUSHING: Davenport 149/598y, Cummings 50/186y
PASSING: Greenfield 199-335/2152y, 5TD, 59.4%
RECEIVING: Nuffer 40/328y, Davenport 32/235y, Duncan 31/498y
SCORING: John Duvic (K) 48pts, Davenport 30pts, Greenfield 24pts

1986 4-7

6 Duke	17 WR George Jones / Randy McClellan
25 Army	18 WR Curtis Duncan
37 Princeton	0 T Jeff Stainton
7 Indiana	24 G Steve Hofmann
23 Minnesota	44 C John Yale
27 Wisconsin	35 G Tom Nicklas
20 Iowa	27 T Michael Baum
16 Purdue	17 TE Rich Borresen (WR) / Bob Driscoll
9 Ohio State	30 QB Mike Greenfield
24 Michigan State	21 HB Brian Nuffer / Stanley Davenport
23 Illinois	18 FB Claudell Robertson / Ron Burton
	DL Dave Helding
	DL Ted Karras
	DL Bob Dirkes
	DL Kelvin Scott
	LB Bob Bucaro/ Charles Plant/ John Ruden
	LB Alan Brown
	LB Tom Kaukialo
	DB Brett Whitley / Kyle Palmer
	DB Jeff Robinson
	DB Todd Krehbiel
	DB Rich Myers

RUSHING: Davenport 181/703y, Greenfield 109/418y, Nuffer 93/381y
PASSING: Greenfield 126-250/1653y, 7TD, 50.4%
RECEIVING: Duncan 29/437y, Borresen 25/331y, Jones 17/259y
SCORING: John Duvic (K) 77pts, Davenport 36pts, Nuffer 24pts

1987 2-8-1

16 Duke	31 WR George Jones
3 Missouri	28 WR Randy McClellan
16 N. Illinois	16 T Kevin Smith
18 Indiana	35 G Steve Hofmann
33 Minnesota	45 C Jeff Freeman
0 Michigan State	38 G Jeff Stainton
27 Wisconsin	24 T Michael Baum
6 Michigan	29 TE Bob Driscoll
24 Iowa	52 QB Mike Greenfield
15 Purdue	20 HB Byron Sanders / Stanley Davenport
28 Illinois	10 FB Curtis Spears
	DL Andre Walker / Paul Schuler
	DL Doug Pennington
	DL Darryl Ashmore/D. Helding/Bob Jamsek
	DL Kevin Peterson (LB) / Mike Vickery
	LB Bob Bucaro
	LB Alan Brown
	LB Tom Kaukialo
	DB Brett Whitley
	DB Terry Thomas / Jeff Robinson
	DB Kyle Palmer
	DB Rich Myers

RUSHING: Sanders 187/778y, Greenfield 142/425y, Davenport 108/401y
PASSING: Greenfield 92-199/1265y, 6TD, 46.2%
RECEIVING: Jones 40/668y, McClellan 26/373y, Driscoll 15/181y
SCORING: Ira Adler (K) 48pts, Greenfield 36pts, McClellan & Sanders 24pts

1988 2-8-1

21 Duke	31 WR Randy McClellan / Marcus Lang
27 Air Force	62 WR Pat New / Richard Buchanan
7 Army	23 T Bret Dirks / Michael Baum
17 Indiana	48 G Dirk Disper / Mihailo Panovich
28 Minnesota	28 C Kurt Minko
3 Michigan State	36 G Brian Tichy / D.R. Callentine
35 Wisconsin	14 T Derrill Vest / Stan Holsen
7 Michigan	52 TE Bob Griswold / Randy Rowe
10 Iowa	35 QB Greg Bradshaw
28 Purdue	7 HB Byron Sanders / Bob Christian
9 Illinois	14 FB Steve Rosholt
	DL John Broeker
	DL Darryl Ashmore
	DL Michael Baum / Andre Walker
	DL Kurt Lundergreen / Doug Martin
	LB Kevin Peterson
	LB Thomas Homco / Ed Sutter
	LB Dan Freveletti / Matt Witt
	DB David Eaton / Terry Thomas
	DB Jeff Robinson
	DB Dwight James / Steve Siewert
	DB Kyle Palmer / John Ivlow

RUSHING: Sanders 264/1062y, Christian 98/413y, Bradshaw 67/137y.
PASSING: Bradshaw 129-257/1550y, 9TD, 50.2%
RECEIVING: Sanders 41/514y, Christian 22/294y, McClellan 18/227y
SCORING: Christian 44pts, Ira Adler (K) 39pts, Buchanan 36pts

1989 0-11

31 Duke	41 WR Randy McClellan
31 Air Force	48 WR Richard Buchanan
27 Rutgers	38 T Stan Holsen / Todd McClish
11 Indiana	43 G Tobin Buckner
18 Minnesota	20 C David Woollard (G) / Kurt Minko
31 Wisconsin	35 G Brian Tichy
22 Iowa	35 T Derrill Vest
27 Ohio State	52 TE Bob Griswold
15 Purdue	46 QB Tim O'Brien
14 Michigan State	76 HB Bob Christian
14 Illinois	63 FB Steve Rosholt
	DL John Broeker
	DL Darryl Ashmore / Mike Lowe
	DL Dan Freveletti
	DL Ed Feaster / Frank Boudreaux
	LB Ed Sutter
	LB Matt Witt / David Sanderson
	LB Thomas Homco
	DB Terry Thomas / Sheridan Wilks
	DB Greg Gill / John Ivlow
	DB Dwight James
	DB David Eaton

RUSHING: Christian 277/1291y, Rosholt 44/126y
PASSING: O'Brien 207-334/2218y, 14TD, 62%
RECEIVING: Buchanan 94/1115y, McClellan 36/341y, Christian 26/199y
SCORING: Christian 74pts, Buchanan 56pts, Ira Adler (K) 43pts

1990 2-9

24 Duke	27 WR Richard Buchanan
14 Rice	31 WR Chip Morris / Mark Benson
24 N. Illinois	7 T Stan Holsen
0 Indiana	42 G Tobin Buckner
25 Minnesota	35 C Brian Tichy (G) / Brendan Bentley
44 Wisconsin	34 G Pat Norton / Jeff Pietrowski
14 Iowa	56 T David Woollard / Eric Wenzel
7 Ohio State	48 TE David Cross
13 Purdue	33 QB Len Williams
22 Michigan State	29 RB Bob Christian
23 Illinois	28 RB Curt Zipfel / Eric Dixon
	DL Frank Boudreaux / Jim Zajicek
	DL Dan Freveletti
	DL John Broeker
	LB Jason Cunningham / Ed Feaster
	LB Thomas Homco / Adam Schell
	LB Ed Sutter
	LB David Sanderson
	DB Terry Thomas
	DB Dwight James / Willie Lindsey
	DB Pat New
	DB Greg Gill / David Eaton

RUSHING: Christian 237/939y, Dixon 58/217y, Williams 111/140y
PASSING: Williams 150-262/1700y, 12TD, 57.3%
RECEIVING: Buchanan 60/834y, Christian 39/328y, Morris 14/196y
SCORING: Ira Adler (K) 58pts, Christian 56pts, Buchanan 42pts

1991 3-8

7 Rice	36 WR Lee Gissendaner
18 Rutgers	22 WR Mark Benson
41 Wake Forest	14 T Stan Holsen
14 Purdue	17 G Brian Tichy
6 Indiana	44 C David Woollard
3 Ohio State	34 G Pat Norton / Matt O'Dwyer
17 Illinois	11 T Darryl Ashmore
16 Michigan State	13 TE David Cross
14 Michigan	59 QB Len Williams
10 Iowa	24 RB Curt Zipfel / Dennis Lundy
14 Wisconsin	32 RB Eric Dixon
	DL John Hellebusch
	DL Dan Freveletti
	DL Frank Boudreaux
	LB Jason Cunningham
	LB Ed Sutter
	LB Steve Ostrowski / Mike Golarz
	LB Thomas Homco
	DB Willie Lindsey
	DB Anthony Purkett
	DB Marlon Collins
	DB Dwight James

RUSHING: Lundy 142/615y, Dixon 64/245y, Williams 155/207y
PASSING: Williams 131-212/1630y, 10TD, 61.8%
RECEIVING: Benson 45/831y, Zipfel 22/138y, Gissendaner 19/234y
SCORING: Benson 42pts, Brian Leahy (K) 32pts, Williams 24pts

1992 3-8

7 Notre Dame	42 WR Patrick Wright
0 Boston College	49 WR Lee Gissendaner
24 Stanford	35 WR Chris Gamble
28 Purdue	14 T Matt O'Dwyer
3 Indiana	28 G Pat Norton / Tobin Buckner
7 Ohio State	31 C Rob Johnson
27 Illinois	26 G Brad Draga / Ryan Padgett
26 Michigan State	27 T Jeff Jimmar / Todd Baczek
7 Michigan	40 TE David Cross / Luther Morris
14 Iowa	56 QB Len Williams
27 Wisconsin	25 RB Dennis Lundy / Chuck Robinson
	DL Frank Boudreaux
	DL Nick Walker
	DL John Hellebusch
	LB Jason Cunningham
	LB Steve Ostrowski
	LB Tom Christian / Hugh Williams
	LB Steve Shine
	DB Willie Lindsey / Korey Singleton
	DB Anthony Purkett
	DB William Bennett / Jason Green
	DB Greg Gill

RUSHING: Lundy 164/688y, Williams 148/119y, Robinson 29/117y
PASSING: Williams 181-286/2110y, 11TD, 63.3%
RECEIVING: Gissendaner 68/846y, Lundy 30/260y, Gamble 21/267y
SCORING: Gissendaner 54pts, Brian Leahy (K) 36pts, Lundy 24pts

1993 2-9

12 Notre Dame	27 WR Chris Gamble / Patrick Wright
22 Boston College	21 WR Lee Gissendaner
26 Wake Forest	14 WR Michael Senters / Dave Beazley
3 Ohio State	51 T Matt O'Dwyer
14 Wisconsin	53 G Justin Chabot / Brian Kardos
26 Minnesota	28 C Rob Johnson
0 Indiana	24 G Ryan Padgett
13 Illinois	20 T Todd Baczek
29 Michigan State	31 TE Luther Morris / Shane Graham
19 Iowa	23 QB Len Williams
21 Penn State	43 RB Dennis Lundy / Chuck Robinson
	DL Joe Reiff / Matt Rice
	DL Bill Koziel / Nick Walker
	DL John Hellebusch
	LB Mike Warren / Geoff Shein
	LB Steve Ostrowski
	LB Hugh Williams
	LB Steve Shine
	DB Rodney Ray / Anthony Purkett
	DB Chris Martin
	DB William Bennett
	DB Korey Singleton

RUSHING: Lundy 170/617y, Robbie Glanton (RB) 36/159y, Robinson 49/105y
PASSING: Williams 182-316/2047y, 11TD, 57.6%
RECEIVING: Gissendaner 58/669y, Senters 27/364y, Gamble 25/304y
SCORING: Sam Valenzisi (K) 49pts, Lundy 44pts, Gissendaner 30pts

1994 3-7-1

15 Notre Dame	42 WR Michael Senters
41 Stanford	41 WR Chris Gamble
14 Air Force	10 T Justin Chabot
15 Ohio State	17 G Ryan Padgett
14 Wisconsin	46 C Rob Johnson
37 Minnesota	31 G Matt O'Dwyer
20 Indiana	7 T Todd Baczek
7 Illinois	28 TE Shane Graham
17 Michigan State	35 TE Luther Morris / Joe Burns
13 Iowa	49 QB Tim Hughes / Steve Schnur
17 Penn State	45 RB Dennis Lundy / Darnell Autry
	DL Larry Curry / Joe Reiff
	DL Bill Koziel
	DL Matt Rice
	LB Mike Warren
	LB Hugh Williams / Pat Fitzgerald
	LB Danny Sutter
	LB Geoff Shein
	DB Rodney Ray / B.J. Winfield
	DB Chris Martin / Hudhaifa Ismaeli
	DB William Bennett
	DB Korey Singleton

RUSHING: Lundy 260/1189y, Autry 120/556y
PASSING: Hughes 61-132/774y, 4TD, 46.2%
Schnur 61-117/899y, 5TD, 52.1%
RECEIVING: Senters 28/385y, Morris 18/246y, Gamble 17/324y
SCORING: Sam Valenzisi (K) 60pts, Lundy 48pts, Gamble 24pts

1995 10-2

17 Notre Dame	15 WR D'Wayne Bates
28 Miami (Ohio)	30 WR Dave Beazley / Brian Musso
30 Air Force	6 T Paul Janus / Chad Pugh
31 Indiana	7 G Ryan Padgett
19 Michigan	13 C Rob Johnson
27 Minnesota	17 G Justin Chabot
35 Wisconsin	0 T Brian Kardos
17 Illinois	14 TE Darren Drexler / Shane Graham
21 Penn State	10 QB Steve Schnur
31 Iowa	20 RB Darnell Autry
23 Purdue	8 FB Matt Hartl
32 Southern Cal■	41 DL Mike Warren / Keith Lozowski
	DL Rodney Rice
	DL Larry Curry / Ray Robey / Joe Reiff
	DL Casey Dailey
	LB Danny Sutter
	LB Pat Fitzgerald / Don Holmes
	LB Geoff Shein / Tim Scharf
	DB Rodney Ray
	DB Chris Martin / Hudhaifa Ismaeli
	DB William Bennett
	DB Eric Collier

RUSHING: Autry 387/1785y, Adrian Autry (RB) 32/118y
PASSING: Schnur 141-257/1792y, 9TD, 54.9%
RECEIVING: Bates 49/889y, Autry 27/168y, Hartl 21/221y
SCORING: Autry 108pts, Sam Valenzisi (K) 60pts, Bates 32pts

1996 9-3

27 Wake Forest	28 WR D'Wayne Bates
38 Duke	13 WR Toussaint Waterman / Brian Musso
28 Ohio Univ.	7 T Paul Janus
35 Indiana	17 G Kevin Peterson / Bryan LaBelle
17 Michigan	16 C Nathan Strikwerda
26 Minnesota	24 G Justin Chabot
34 Wisconsin	30 T Brian Kardos
27 Illinois	24 TE Darren Drexler
9 Penn State	34 QB Steve Schnur
40 Iowa	13 RB Darnell Autry / Adrian Autry
27 Purdue	24 FB Mike McGrew
28 Tennessee■	48 DL Keith Lozowski
	DL Matt Rice
	DL Joe Reiff / Bobby Russ
	DL Casey Dailey
	LB Barry Gardner
	LB Pat Fitzgerald
	LB Tim Scharf
	DB Hudhaifa Ismaeli / Gerald Conoway
	DB Josh Barnes
	DB Mike Nelson
	DB Eric Collier

RUSHING: D. Autry 280/1452y, A. Autry 112/421y
PASSING: Schnur 221-368/2632y, 17TD, 60.1%
RECEIVING: Bates 75/1196y, Musso 51/515y
SCORING: Autry 108pts, Brian Gowins (K) 82pts, Bates 72pts

1997 5-7

24 Oklahoma	0 WR Brian Musso
20 Wake Forest	27 WR Toussaint Waterman / Jon Burden
24 Duke	20 T Bryan LaBelle
34 Rice	40 G Brian Hemmerle
9 Purdue	21 C Nate Strikwerda / Ty Garner
25 Wisconsin	26 G Chris Leeder
6 Michigan	23 T Paul Janus
19 Michigan State	17 TE Jay Tant / Joel Stuart
6 Ohio State	49 QB Tim Hughes
27 Penn State	30 RB Adrian Autry
34 Illinois	21 FB Matt Hartl / Levelle Brown
15 Iowa	14 DL Keith Lozowski
	DL KeJuan DuBose
	DL Bobby Russ
	DL Casey Dailey / Thor Schmidt
	LB Barry Gardner
	LB Kevin Buck / Conrad Emmerich
	LB Preston Letts / Anwawn Jones
	DB Fred Wilkerson / Gerald Conoway
	DB Mike Nelson / Josh Barnes
	DB Mike Nelson
	DB Eric Collier

RUSHING: Autry 244/1049y, Faraji Leary (RB) 62/257y, Brian Marshall (RB) 42/150y
PASSING: Hughes 142-270/1862y, 11TD, 52.6%
RECEIVING: Musso 58/865y, Stuart 23/279y, Burden 22/303y
SCORING: Brian Gowins (K) 79pts, Musso 50pts, Autry 44pts

1998 3-9

41 UNLV	7 WR D'Wayne Bates
10 Duke	44 WR John Burden
23 Rice	14 T Ryan Friedrich / Mike Souza
7 Wisconsin	38 G Lance Clelland / Mark Perry
10 Illinois	13 C Adam Fay /Ty Garner
24 Iowa	26 G Jack Harnedy /Brian Hemmerle
6 Michigan	12 T Bryan LaBelle / Blake Henry
10 Ohio State	36 TE Jay Tant
5 Michigan State	29 QB Gavin Hoffman
21 Purdue	56 RB Damien Anderson / Brian Marshall
10 Penn State	41 FB Levelle Brown / Sean Bennett
47 Hawaii	21 DL Thor Schmidt / Salem Simon
	DL Darryl Hodge
	DL Jeff Dyra /Javiar Collins
	DL Dwayne Missouri
	LB Barry Gardner
	LB Conrad Emmerich / Preston Letts
	LB Kevin Buck / Napoleon Harris
	DB Fred Wilkerson
	DB Harold Blackmon
	DB Mike Nelson
	DB Mycal Jones / Kyle Sanders

RUSHING: Anderson 164/537y, Marshall 98/296y, Bennett 32/160y
PASSING: Hoffman 176-323 /2199y, 13TD, 54.5%
RECEIVING: Bates 83/1245y, Tant 30/327y, Bennett17/228y
SCORING: Brian Gowins (K) 72pts, Bates 54pts, Anderson 24pts

1999 3-8

3 Miami (Ohio)	28 WR Aaron Burrell / Jon Schweighardt
17 TCU	7 WR S. Simmons/T. Johnson/D. Thompson
15 Duke	12 T Leon Brockmeier
23 Purdue	31 G Wayne Lucier
14 Minnesota	33 C Austin King
17 Indiana	34 G Mark Perry (C) / Brian Hemmerle
23 Iowa	21 T Mike Souza
19 Wisconsin	35 TE Jay Tant
3 Michigan	37 QB Zak Kustok / Nick Kreinbrink
0 Michigan State	34 RB Damien Anderson
7 Illinois	29 FB Ian Miller / John Cerasani (TE)
	DL Dwayne Missouri
	DL Javier Collins / Jeff Dyra
	DL Darryl Hodge / Jeff Baer
	DL Salem Simon
	LB Kevin Bentley
	LB Conrad Emmerich / Billy Silva
	LB Napoleon Harris
	DB Shegun Cummings-John
	DB Harold Blackmon
	DB Rashad Morton
	DB Mycal Jones / Kyle Sanders

RUSHING: Anderson 306/1128y, Kustok 92/209y, Louis Ayeni (RB) 44/160y
PASSING: Kustok 70-153/741y, 3TD, 45.8%
Kreinbrink 60-158/774y, 4TD, 38%
RECEIVING: Johnson 23/354y, Thompson 22/162y, Tant 17/203y
SCORING: Tim Long (K) 47pts, Johnson 24pts, Anderson 18pts

2000 8-4

35 N. Illinois	17 WR Teddy Johnson / Roger Jordan
38 Duke	5 WR Sam Simmons / Kunle Patrick
14 TCU	41 WR/FB Jon Schweighardt /Vincent Cartaya
47 Wisconsin	44 T Leon Brockmeier
37 Michigan State	17 G Lance Clelland
52 Indiana	33 C Austin King
28 Purdue	41 G Jeff Roehl
41 Minnesota	35 T Mike Souza
54 Michigan	51 TE David Farman
17 Iowa	27 QB Zak Kustok
61 Illinois	23 RB Damien Anderson
17 Nebraska■	66 DL Dwayne Missouri
	DL Pete Chapman / Salem Simon
	DL Javiar Collins
	DL Conrad Emmerich
	LB Napoleon Harris
	LB Billy Silva
	LB Kevin Bentley / Pat Durr
	DB Harold Blackmon
	DB Raheem Covington
	DB Rashad Morton / Sean Wieber
	DB Rashidi Wheeler

RUSHING: Anderson 293/1914y, Kustok 152/450y, Kevin Lawrence (RB) 69/348y
PASSING: Kustok 191-328/2251y, 18TD, 58.2%
RECEIVING: Simmons 35/474y, Schweighardt 34/339y, Patrick 32/363y
SCORING: Anderson 132pts, Tim Long (K) 84pts, Kustok 54pts

2001 4-7

37 UNLV	28 WR Sam Simmons
44 Duke	7 WR Jon Schweighardt
27 Michigan State	26 WR Kunle Patrick
20 Ohio State	38 T Leon Brockmeier
23 Minnesota	17 G Lance Clelland
35 Penn State	38 C Austin King
27 Purdue	32 G Jeff Roehl
21 Indiana	56 T Mike Souza
16 Iowa	59 TE David Farman
42 Bowling Green	43 QB Zak Kustok
28 Illinois	34 RB Damien Anderson / Kevin Lawrence
	DL Salem Simon / Onaje Grimes
	DL Matt Anderson / Thomas Derricks
	DL Colby Clark / Luis Castillo
	DL Napoleon Harris
	LB Pat Durr
	LB Billy Silva
	LB Kevin Bentley
	DB Raheem Covington
	DB Marvin Ward / Chasda Martin
	DB Mark Roush / Sean Wieber
	DB Marvin Brown / Dominique Price

RUSHING: Anderson 172/757y, Kustok 175/580y, Lawrence 57/291y
PASSING: Kustok 231-404/2692y, 20TD, 57.2%
RECEIVING: Patrick 56/672y, Simmons 50/807y, Schweighardt 43/469y
SCORING: Kustok 66pts, David Wasielewski (K) 60pts, Anderson & Simmons 48pts

2002 3-9

3 Air Force	52 WR Kunle Patrick / Jeff Backes (RB)
24 TCU	48 WR Jon Schweighardt / Ashton Aikens
26 Duke	21 WR Roger Jordan / Mark Philmore
49 Navy	40 T Trai Essex
24 Michigan State	39 G Matt Ulrich
16 Ohio State	27 C Austin King
42 Minnesota	45 G Jeff Roehl (T) / Carl Matejka
0 Penn State	49 T Derek Martinez / Zach Streif
13 Purdue	42 TE/RB Joe Wohlscheid / Noah Herron
41 Indiana	37 QB Brett Basanez / Tony Stauss
10 Iowa	62 RB Jason Wright
24 Illinois	31 DL Loren Howard / Onaje Grimes
	DL Colby Clark / Ray Bogenrief
	DL Luis Castillo / Matt Anderson
	DL David Thompson / Barry Cofield
	LB Braden Jones / Eric VanderHorst
	LB John Pickens / Vincent Cartaya
	LB Doug Szymul / Tim McGarigle
	DB Raheem Covington
	DB Herschel Henderson / Marvin Ward
	DB Jarvis Adams / Dominique Price
	DB Mark Roush / Torri Stuckey

RUSHING: Wright 219/1234y, Herron 66/365y, Backes 23/124y
PASSING: Basanez 190-325/2204y, 7TD, 58.5%
RECEIVING: Schweighardt 58/719y, Patrick 49/558y,
  Philmore 31/245y
SCORING: Wright 78pts, David Wasieleski (K) 56pts, Herron 42pts

2003 6-7

28 Kansas	20 WR Kunle Patrick / Shaun Herbert
21 Air Force	22 WR Roger Jordan / Mark Philmore
14 Miami (Ohio)	44 WR Ashton Aikens / Brandon Horn
28 Duke	10 T Trai Essex
0 Ohio State	20 G Ike Ndukwe
17 Minnesota	42 C Trevor Rees
37 Indiana	31 G Matt Ulrich (C) / Bill Newton
16 Wisconsin	7 T Zach Strief
14 Purdue	34 TE Ray Bogenrief / Joe Wohlscheid
17 Penn State	7 QB Brett Basanez
10 Michigan	41 RB Jason Wright / Noah Herren
37 Illinois	20 DL Loren Howard
24 Bowling Green■	28 DL Luis Castillo / Ryan Keenan
	DL Colby Clark
	DL Barry Cofield / David Thompson
	LB Tim McGarigle
	LB Pat Durr
	LB John Pickens
	DB Jeff Backes / Marquice Cole
	DB Dominique Price / Bryan Heinz
	DB Torri Stuckey
	DB Marvin Ward / Louis Ayeni

RUSHING: Wright 267/1388y, Herron 119/739y,
  Terrell Jordan (RB) 46/253y
PASSING: Basanez 162-302/1916y, 4TD, 53.6%
RECEIVING: Jordan 31/442y, Patrick 32/32/274y,
  Philmore 23/228y
SCORING: Wright 126pts, Herron 36pts, Brian Huffman (K) 28pts

2004 6-6

45 TCU	48 WR Mark Philmore / Shaun Herbert
21 Arizona State	30 WR Ashton Aikens
20 Kansas	17 WR Josh Fields / Kim Thompson
17 Minnesota	43 WR/TE Brandon Horn / Taylor Jones
33 Ohio State	27 T Trai Essex
31 Indiana	24 G Ike Ndukwe
12 Wisconsin	24 C Trevor Rees
13 Purdue	10 G Matt Ulrich
14 Penn State	7 T Zach Strief
20 Michigan	42 QB Brett Basanez
28 Illinois	21 RB Noah Herron / Terrell Jordan
41 Hawaii	49 DL Barry Cofield
	DL Colby Clark
	DL Luis Castillo
	DL David Thompson / Loren Howard
	LB Tim McGarigle / Adam Kadela
	LB John Pickens / Demetrius Eaton
	LB Nick Roach
	DB Marvin Ward
	DB Jeff Backes / Herschel Henderson
	DB Dominique Price
	DB Bryan Heinz

RUSHING: Herron 274/1381y, Jordan 65/315y, Basanez 83/258y
PASSING: Basanez 247-460/2838y, 12TD, 53.7%
RECEIVING: Philmore 54/633y, Fields 48/560y, Herron 36/351y
SCORING: Herren 90pts, Brian Huffman (K) 44pts, Basanez 30pts

2005 7-5

38 Ohio University	14 WR Mark Philmore / Rasheed Ward
38 N. Illinois	37 WR Jonathan Fields
21 Arizona State	52 WR Shaun Herbert / Ross Lane
29 Penn State	34 WR/TE Kim Thompson / Erryn Cobb
51 Wisconsin	48 T Dylan Thiry / Vince Clarke
34 Purdue	29 G Joe Tripodi
49 Michigan State	14 C Austin Matthews / Joel Belding
17 Michigan	33 G Ryan Keenan
28 Iowa	27 T Zach Streif
7 Ohio State	48 QB Brett Basanez
38 Illinois	21 RB Tyrell Sutton
38 UCLA■	50 DL Kevin Mims / David Ngene
	DL John Gill / Trevor Schultz
	DL Barry Cofield
	DL Mark Koehn / Corey Wootton
	LB Adam Kadela
	LB Tim McGarigle
	LB Nick Roach / Eddie Simpson
	DB Marquice Cole
	DB Deante Battle / Cory Dious
	DB Hersch'l Henderson/R. McPherson
	DB Frederic Tarver / Brendan Smith

RUSHING: Sutton 250/1474y, Basanez 113/423y,
  Gerard Hamlett (RB) 32/174y
PASSING: Basanez 314-497/3622y, 21TD, 63.2%
RECEIVING: Herbert 79/862y, Fields 60/555y, Philmore 55/662y
SCORING: Sutton 106pts, Joel Howells (K) 78pts,
  Basanez & Philmore 42pts

2006 4-8

21 Miami (Ohio)	3 WR Kim Thompson / Eric Peterman
17 New Hampshire	34 WR Ross Lane / Rasheed Ward
14 E. Michigan	6 WR Shaun Herbert / Sam Cheatham
21 Nevada	31 T Dylan Thiry / Desmond Taylor
7 Penn State	33 G Joe Tripodi
9 Wisconsin	41 C Trevor Rees
10 Purdue	31 G Joel Belding / Adam Crum
38 Michigan State	41 T Ryan Keenan / Austin Matthews
3 Michigan	17 TE Erryn Cobb
21 Iowa	7 QB C. J. Bachér / Mike Kafka
10 Ohio State	54 RB Tyrell Sutton / Terrell Jordan
27 Illinois	16 DL Corey Wootton
	DL John Gill / Mark Koehn
	DL Kevin Mims / David Ngene
	DL/LB Adam Hahn / Mike Dinard
	LB Nick Roach / Eddie Simpson
	LB Adam Kadela
	LB Demetrius Eaton
	DB Marquice Cole/Sherrick McManis
	DB Deante Battle
	DB Reggie McPherson
	DB Brendan Smith

RUSHING: Sutton 189/1000y, Kafka 48/263y,
  Terrell Jordan 66/219y
PASSING: Bachér 95-161/1172y, 6TD, 59%
  Kafka 55-96/494y, 1TD, 57.3%
  Andrew Brewer 37-74/344y, 0TD, 50%
RECEIVING: Herbert 47/494y, Sutton 40/261y, Lane 30/401y
SCORING: Joel Howells (K) 48pts, Sutton 42pts, Jordan 30pts

2007 6-6

27 Northeastern	0 WR Eric Peterman
36 Nevada	31 WR Tonjua Jones/Kim Thompson
14 Duke	20 WR Ross Lane / Jeff Yarbrough
7 Ohio State	58 WR/SB Rasheed Ward/Brendan Mitchell
16 Michigan	28 T Dylan Thiry
48 Michigan State	41 G Adam Crum (C)/Desmond Taylor
49 Minnesota	48 C Trevor Rees
26 E. Michigan	14 G Joel Belding
17 Purdue	35 T Kurt Mattes
17 Iowa	28 QB C.J. Bachér
31 Indiana	28 RB Tyrell Sutton / Omar Conteh
22 Illinois	41 DL Kevin Mims / David Ngene
	DL Adam Hahn
	DL John Gill
	DL Corey Wootton
	LB Mike Dinard / Eddie Simpson
	LB Adam Kadela / Malcolm Arrington
	LB Prince Kwateng / Quentin Davie
	DB Deante Battle
	DB Sherrick McManis
	DB Reggie McPherson
	DB Brad Phillips / Brendan Smith

RUSHING: Sutton 108/522y, Conteh 96/447y,
  Brandon Roberson (RB) 76/348y
PASSING: Bachér 318-521/3656y, 19TD, 61%
RECEIVING: Peterman 66/744y, Lane 49/649y, Thompson 46/678y
SCORING: Amado Villarreal (K) 72pts, Lane 44pts, Conteh 42pts

2008 9-4

30 Syracuse	10 WR Rasheed Ward
24 Duke	20 WR Ross Lane / Andrew Brewer
33 S. Illinois	7 WR Eric Peterman
16 Ohio	8 WR Josh Rooks / Jeremy Ebert
22 Iowa	17 T Al Netter
20 Michigan State	37 G Keegan Kennedy
48 Purdue	26 C Ben Burkett
19 Indiana	21 G Doug Bartels
24 Minnesota	17 Desmond Taylor (G) / Kurt Mattes
10 Ohio State	45 QB C.J. Bachér / Mike Kafka
21 Michigan	14 TB T.Sutton/Stephen Simmons/O.Conteh
27 Illinois	10 DL Corey Wootton
23 Missouri■	30 DL Corbin Bryant / Adam Hahn
	DL John Gill
	DL Kevin Mims / Vince Browne
	LB Prince Kwateng
	LB Nate Williams / Malcolm Arrington
	LB Quentin Davie
	DB Sherrick McManis
	DB Jordan Mabin
	DB Brendan Smith
	DB Brad Phillips (LB) / Brian Peters

RUSHING: Sutton 184/890y, Kafka 68/321y, Conteh 73/235y
PASSING: Bachér 245-408/2432y, 17TD, 60%
  Kafka 32-46/330y, 2TD, 69.6%
RECEIVING: Lane 60/640y, Peterman 59/737y, Ward 51/526y
SCORING: Amado Villarreal (K) 90pts, Sutton 48pts,
  Peterman 36pts

2009 8-5

47 Towson State	14 WR Zeke Markshausen / Jeremy Ebert
27 E. Michigan	24 WR Sidney Stewart / Demetrius Fields
34 Syracuse	37 WR Andrew Brewer
24 Minnesota	35 T Al Netter
27 Purdue	21 G Keegan Grant / Desmond Taylor
16 Miami (Ohio)	6 C Ben Burkett
14 Michigan State	24 G Doug Bartels
29 Indiana	28 T Kurt Mattes / Neal Deiters
13 Penn State	34 QB Mike Kafka
17 Iowa	10 SB Drake Dunsmore / Josh Rooks
21 Illinois	16 TB Scott Concannon / Arby Fields
33 Wisconsin	31 DL Corey Wooten / Kevin Watt
35 Auburn■	38 DL Corbin Bryant
	DL Marshall Thomas / Adam Hahn
	DL Vince Browne
	LB David Arnold / Ben Johnson
	LB Nate Williams
	LB Quentin Davie
	DB Sherrick McManis / Demetrius Dugar
	DB Jordan Mabin
	DB Brendan Smith / Brian Peters
	DB Brad Phillips / Jared Carpenter

RUSHING: Fields 82/302y, Kafka 150/295y,
  Concannon 68/241y, Stephen Simmons (TB) 59/233y
PASSING: Kafka 319-492/3430y, 16TD, 64.8%
RECEIVING: Markshausen 91/858y, Brewer 57/925y,
  Dunsmore 47/523y, Stewart 42/470y
SCORING: Stefan Demos (K) 88pts, Kafka & Brewer 54pts

2010 7-6

23 Vanderbilt	21 WR Demetrius Fields / Charles Brown
37 Illinois State	3 WR Jeremy Ebert
30 Rice	13 WR Sidney Stewart
30 C. Michigan	25 T Al Netter
29 Minnesota	28 G Brian Mulroe
17 Purdue	20 C Ben Burkett
27 Michigan State	35 G Keegan Grant / Doug Bartels
20 Indiana	17 T Patrick Ward
21 Penn State	35 QB Dan Persa / Evan Watkins
21 Iowa	17 SB Drake Dunsmore / Arby Fields
27 Illinois	48 RB Mike Trumpy / Jacob Schmidt
23 Wisconsin	70 DL Kevin Watt / Quentin Williams
38 Texas Tech■	45 DL Corbin Bryant
	DL Jack DiNardo / Brian Arnfelt
	DL Vince Browne
	LB Quentin Davie / David Nwabuisi
	LB Nate Williams / Ben Johnson
	LB Bryce McNaul / Damien Proby
	DB Jordan Mabin
	DB Justan Vaughn
	DB Brian Peters / Hunter Bates
	DB David Arnold / Jared Carpenter

RUSHING: Trumpy 116/530y, Persa 164/519y
  Adonis Smith (RB) 41/196y
PASSING: Persa 222-302/2581y, 15TD, 73.5%
  Watkins 36-70/378y, 2TD, 51.4%
RECEIVING: Ebert 62/953y, Stewart 40/454y, Dunsmore 40/381y
SCORING: Stefan Demos (K) 82pts, Persa 54pts, Ebert 48pts

NOTRE DAME

University of Notre Dame (Founded 1842)
Notre Dame, Indiana (near South Bend)
Nickname: Fighting Irish
Colors: Gold and Blue
Stadium: Notre Dame Stadium (1930) 80,795
Conference Affiliation: Independent

CAREER RUSHING YARDS	Attempts	Yards
Autry Denson (1995-98)	854	4318
Allen Pinkett (1982-85)	889	4131
Vagas Ferguson (1976-79)	673	3472
Darius Walker (2004-06)	693	3249
Julius Jones (1999-2001, 03)	634	3018
Jerome Heavens (1975-78)	590	2682
Phil Carter (1979-82)	557	2409
George Gipp (1917-20)	369	2341
Randy Kinder (1993-96)	404	2295
Tony Brooks (1987-91)	423	2274

CAREER PASSING YARDS	Comp.-Att.	Yards
Brady Quinn (2003-06)	929-1602	11762
Jimmy Clausen (2007-09)	695-1110	8148
Ron Powlus (1994-97)	558-969	7602
Steve Beuerlein (1983-86)	473-850	6527
Rick Mirer (1989-92)	377-698	5997
Jarious Jackson (1996-99)	306-536	4820
Joe Theismann (1968-70)	290-509	4411
Terry Hanratty (1966-68)	304-550	4152
Joe Montana (1975-78)	268-515	4121
Blair Kiel (1980-83)	297-609	3650

CAREER RECEIVING YARDS	Catches	Yards
Golden Tate (2007-09)	157	2707
Jeff Samardzija (2003-06)	179	2593
Michael Floyd (2008-10)	171	2539
Derrick Mayes (1992-95)	129	2512
Tim Brown (1984-87)	137	2493
Tom Gatewood (1969-71)	157	2283
Rhema McKnight (2002-06)	170	2277
Maurice Stovall (2002-05)	130	2195
Jim Seymour (1966-68)	138	2113
Tony Hunter (1979-82)	120	1897

SEASON RUSHING YARDS	Attempts	Yards
Vagas Ferguson (1979)	301	1437
Allen Pinkett (1983)	252	1394
Reggie Brooks (1992)	167	1343
Julius Jones (2003)	229	1268
Autry Denson (1997)	264	1268

SEASON PASSING YARDS	Comp.-Att.	Yards
Brady Quinn (2005)	292-450	3919
Jimmy Clausen (2009)	289-425	3722
Brady Quinn (2006)	289-467	3426
Jimmy Clausen (2008)	268-440	3172
Jarious Jackson (1999)	184-316	2753

SEASON RECEIVING YARDS	Catches	Yards
Golden Tate (2009)	93	1496
Jeff Samardzija (2005)	77	1249
Maurice Stovall (2005)	69	1149
Tom Gatewood (1970)	77	1123
Jack Snow (1964)	60	1114

GAME RUSHING YARDS	Attempts	Yards
Julius Jones (2003 vs. Pittsburgh)	24	262
Vagas Ferguson (1978 vs. Georgia Tech)	30	255
Phil Carter (1980 vs. Michigan State)	40	254

GAME PASSING YARDS	Comp.-Att.	Yards
Joe Theismann (1970 vs. Southern Cal)	33-58	526
Brady Quinn (2005 vs. Michigan State)	33-60	487
Brady Quinn (2005 vs. BYU)	32-41	467

GAME RECEIVING YARDS	Catches	Yards
Jim Seymour (1966 vs. Purdue)	13	276
Golden Tate (2009 vs. Washington)	9	244
Jack Snow (1964 vs. Wisconsin)	9	217

GREATEST COACH:

For immediately bringing the Notre Dame program back to its past level of glory, and maintaining that level despite intense pressure and stringent school requirements, Ara Parseghian is the greatest head coach to work in South Bend since 1953. Wooed from a Northwestern program at which he regularly beat the Irish, Parseghian took over a team that had just finished a poor 2-7 in 1963 and immediately re-installed a winning environment at the football-crazy school. Unbelievably, Notre Dame rebounded to great heights at once, winning the first nine games of 1964. It was then that he suffered one of his biggest disappointments, as Southern Cal rallied from 17-0 deficit to pull out a late 20-17 upset that prevented the Irish from winning their first consensus national championship since 1949.

After dipping to a 7-2-1 record in 1965, Notre Dame won Parseghian his first national title with one of the finest teams in school history. Scoring 362 points while allowing only 38, Notre Dame held onto the number one ranking at season's end despite a famous 10-10 tie with Michigan State. Unfortunately with sports history defining personalities with quick "bites," Parseghian is most remembered for not being aggressive with his play-calling at the end of that game than for winning the championship. That the title should have vindicated him is often ignored.

But did he set the bar too high for himself? Winning 25 games over that opening three-year span, with one national title and one near title, should have set Parseghian for life, and he was certainly granted a level of respect by most for the remainder of his time at Notre Dame. But losing two games in each of the next three seasons, with three straight losses to in-state rival Purdue, and not being able to beat Southern California from 1967 to 1972 (0-4-2), began to take its toll on the coach's support and health. Despite annual Top 10 finishes for the remainder of the 1960s and a return to bowl play with a split of Cotton Bowls with Texas following the 1969 and 1970 seasons, Parseghian began to hear that he could not win the big ones. After dipping to an 8-3 mark in 1972, Notre Dame bounced back with a perfect critic-answering 11-0 season that included a memorable 24-23 win over no. 1 Alabama in the Sugar Bowl. Parseghian was back on top, but still not getting enough sleep. He coached one more season, capped with one more win over Bear Bryant and then moved on to announcing. He was 51.

NOTRE DAME'S 55 GREATEST SINCE 1953

OFFENSE

WIDE RECEIVER: Tim Brown, Tom Gatewood, Jeff Samardzija, Jim Seymour, Golden Tate
TIGHT END: Dave Casper, Ken MacAfee
TACKLE: Tim Foley, Art Hunter, George Kunz
GUARD: Dick Arrington, Larry DiNardo, Tom Regner, Aaron Taylor
CENTER: Dave Huffman, John Scully
QUARTERBACK: Joe Montana, Brady Quinn, Tony Rice, Joe Theismann
RUNNING BACK: Autry Denson, Vagas Ferguson, Allen Pinkett
FULLBACK: Jerome Bettis, Larry Conjar

DEFENSE

END: Ross Browner, Alan Page, Walt Patulski, Anthony Weaver
TACKLE: Kevin Hardy, Greg Marx, Mike McCoy, Steve Niehaus, Bryant Young, Chris Zorich
LINEBACKER: Jim Carroll, Bob Crable, Bob Golic, Jim Lynch, Bob Olson, Michael Stonebreaker
CORNERBACK: Luther Bradley, Clarence Ellis, Todd Lyght, Bobby Taylor
SAFETY: Jeff Burris, Dave Duerson, Tom Schoen, Mike Townsend

SPECIAL TEAMS

RETURN SPECIALISTS: Raghib "Rocket" Ismail
PLACE KICKER: John Carney
PUNTER: Craig Hentrich

MULTIPLE POSITIONS

QUARTERBACK-FULLBACK-DEFENSIVE BACK-PUNTER-KICKER: Paul Hornung

TWO-WAY PLAYERS

QUARTERBACK-DEFENSIVE BACK: Ralph Guglielmi
GUARD-LINEBACKER: Al Ecuyer

PERFORMANCE FORMULA:
NOTRE DAME'S 10 BEST SEASONS

1966	1.8314	1 of 70
1973	1.7913	2 of 70
1988	1.7860	2 of 69
1977	1.7519	1 of 70
1989	1.7466	1 of 70
1953	1.7360	1 of 69
1970	1.6812	4 of 70
1992	1.6548	3 of 70
1993	1.6481	4 of 70
1964	1.6100	5 of 70

NOTRE DAME FIGHTING IRISH

Year	W-L-T	AP Poll	Conference Standing	Toughest Regular Season Opponents	Coach (Record at School)	Bowl Games		
1953	9-0-1	2		Oklahoma 8-1-1, Georgia Tech 8-2-1, Iowa 5-3-1	Frank Leahy (87-11-9)			
1954	9-1	4		Navy 7-2, Southern California 8-3, Purdue 5-4	Terry Brennan			
1955	8-2	9		Michigan State 8-1, Southern California 6-4, Miami 6-3	Terry Brennan			
1956	2-8			Oklahoma10-0, Iowa 8-1, Michigan State 7-2	Terry Brennan			
1957	7-3	10		Oklahoma 10-0, Michigan State 8-1, Navy 8-1-1	Terry Brennan			
1958	6-4	17		Iowa 7-1-1, Army 8-0-1, Purdue 6-1-2	Terry Brennan (32-18)			
1959	5-5	17		Southern California 8-2, Pittsburgh 6-4, Northwestern 6-3	Joe Kuharich			
1960	2-8			Iowa 8-1, Navy 9-1, Michigan State 6-2-1	Joe Kuharich			
1961	5-5			Michigan State 7-2, Syracuse 7-3, Duke 7-3	Joe Kuharich			
1962	5-5			Southern California10-0, Wisconsin 8-1, Oklahoma 8-2	Joe Kuharich (17-23)			
1963	2-7			Navy 9-1, Pittsburgh 9-1, Michigan State 6-2-1	Hugh Devore (2-7)			
1964	9-1	3		Southern California 7-3, Purdue 6-3, Michigan State 4-5	Ara Parseghian			
1965	7-2-1	9		Michigan State 10-0, Southern California 7-2-1, Purdue 7-2-1	Ara Parseghian			
1966	9-0-1	1		Michigan State 9-0-1, Purdue 8-2, Southern California 7-3	Ara Parseghian			
1967	8-2	5		Southern California 9-1, Purdue 8-2, Miami 7-3	Ara Parseghian			
1968	7-2-1	5		Southern California 9-0-1, Purdue 8-2, Oklahoma 7-3	Ara Parseghian			
1969	8-2-1	5		Southern California9-0-1, Purdue 8-2, Air Force 6-4	Ara Parseghian	Cotton	17 Texas	21
1970	10-1	2		Southern California 6-4-1, Louisiana State 9-2, Georgia Tech 8-3	Ara Parseghian	Cotton	24 Texas	11
1971	8-2	13		Southern California 6-4-1, Louisiana State 8-3, Northwestern 7-4	Ara Parseghian			
1972	8-3	14		Southern California 11-0, Missouri 6-5, Air Force 6-4	Ara Parseghian	Orange	6 Nebraska	40
1973	11-0	1		Southern California 9-1-1, Pittsburgh 6-4-1, Air Force 6-4	Ara Parseghian	Sugar	24 Alabama	23
1974	10-2	6		Southern California 9-1-1, Michigan State 7-3-1, Pittsburgh 7-4	Ara Parseghian (95-17-4)	Orange	13 Alabama	11
1975	8-3			Pittsburgh 7-4, Southern California 7-4, Michigan State 7-4	Dan Devine			
1976	9-3	12		Pittsburgh 11-0, Southern California 10-1, Alabama 8-3	Dan Devine	Gator	20 Penn State	9
1977	11-1	1		Pittsburgh 8-2-1, Southern California 7-4, Clemson 8-2-1	Dan Devine	Cotton	38 Texas	10
1978	9-3	7		Southern California 11-1, Michigan 10-1, Michigan State 8-3	Dan Devine	Cotton	35 Houston	34
1979	7-4			Southern California 10-0-1, Purdue 9-2, Michigan 8-3	Dan Devine			
1980	9-2-1	9		Michigan 9-2, Alabama 9-2, Southern California 8-2-1	Dan Devine (53-16-1)	Sugar	10 Georgia	17
1981	5-6			Penn State 9-2, Miami 9-2, Michigan 8-3	Gerry Faust			
1982	6-4-1			Penn State 9-2, Pittsburgh 9-2, Southern California 8-3	Gerry Faust			
1983	7-5			Miami 10-1, Air Force 9-2, Pittsburgh 8-2-1	Gerry Faust	Liberty	19 Boston College	18
1984	7-5			Southern California 8-3, Louisiana State 8-2-1, Miami 8-4	Gerry Faust	Aloha	20 SMU	27
1985	5-6			Penn State 11-0, Michigan 9-1-1, Miami 10-1	Gerry Faust (30-26-1)			
1986	5-6			Penn State 11-0, Michigan 11-1, Alabama 9-3	Lou Holtz			
1987	8-4	17		Miami 11-0, Michigan State 8-2-1, Southern California 8-3	Lou Holtz	Cotton	10 Texas A&M	35
1988	12-0	1		Miami 10-1, Southern California 10-1, Michigan 8-2-1	Lou Holtz	Fiesta	34 West Virginia	21
1989	12-1	2		Miami 10-1, Southern California 8-2-1, Michigan 10-1	Lou Holtz	Orange	21 Colorado	6
1990	9-3	6		Miami 10-1, Penn State 9-2, Michigan 8-3	Lou Holtz	Orange	9 Colorado	10
1991	10-3	13		Penn State 10-2, Michigan 10-1, Tennessee 9-2	Lou Holtz	Sugar	39 Florida	28
1992	10-1-1	4		Michigan 8-0-3, Stanford 9-3, Penn State 7-4	Lou Holtz	Cotton	28 Texas A&M	3
1993	11-1	2		Florida State 11-1, Boston College 7-3, Michigan 7-4	Lou Holtz	Cotton	24 Texas A&M	21
1994	6-5-1			Florida State 9-1-1, Michigan 7-4, Boston College 6-4-1	Lou Holtz	Fiesta	24 Colorado	41
1995	9-3	11		Ohio State 11-1, Southern California 8-2-1, Northwestern 10-1	Lou Holtz	Orange	26 Florida State	31
1996	8-3	19		Ohio State 10-1, Washington 9-2, Texas 8-4	Lou Holtz (100-30-2)			
1997	7-6			Michigan 11-0, Louisiana State 8-3, Purdue 8-3	Bob Davie	Independence	9 LSU	27
1998	9-3	22		Michigan 9-3, Purdue 8-4, Southern California 8-4	Bob Davie	Gator	28 Georgia Tech	35
1999	5-7			Tennessee 9-2, Michigan 9-2, Michigan State 9-2	Bob Davie			
2000	9-3	15		Nebraska 9-2, Purdue 8-3, Texas A&M 7-4	Bob Davie	Fiesta	9 Oregon State	41
2001	5-6			Tennessee 10-2, Nebraska 11-1, Stanford 9-2	Bob Davie (35-25)			
2002	10-3	17		Southern California 10-2, Michigan 9-3, Maryland 10-3	Ty Willingham	Gator	6 North Carolina State	28
2003	5-7			Southern California 11-1, Michigan 10-2, Florida State 10-2	Ty Willingham			
2004	6-6			Southern California 12-0, Tennessee 9-2, Michigan 9-2	Ty Willingham (21-16)	Insight	21 Oregon State	38
2005	9-3	9		Southern California 12-1, Michigan 7-5, Michigan State 5-6	Charlie Weis	Fiesta	20 Ohio State	34
2006	10-3	17		Southern California 10-2, Michigan 11-1, Penn State 8-4	Charlie Weis	Sugar	14 Louisiana State	41
2007	3-9			Penn State 8-4, Michigan 8-4, Boston College 10-2, So. California 10-2	Charlie Weis			
2008	7-6			Michigan State 9-3, Pittsburgh 9-3, Southern California 11-1	Charlie Weis	Hawaii	49 Hawaii	21
2009	6-6			Southern California 8-4, Navy 9-4, Pittsburgh 9-3, Stanford 8-4	Charlie Weis (35-27)			
2010	8-5			Michigan State 11-1, Stanford 11-1, Utah 10-2	Brian Kelly (8-5)	Sun	33 Miami	17

| TOTAL: | | 437-210-9 .6730 (12 of 70) | | | Bowl Games since 1953: | 14-15 .4828 (40 of 70) | | |

GREATEST TEAM SINCE 1953: The 1966 (9-0-1) national champions, who shut out six of ten opponents, get the nod here. Although too much attention is focused on coach Ara Parseghian's conservative play-calling at the end of the tie with Michigan State, that game and the entire impressive performance by both sides of the ball get too overlooked. A match-up with undefeated Alabama in a bowl game could have been memorable.

1953 9-0-1
28	Oklahoma	21 E Dan Shannon / Paul Matz
37	Purdue	7 T Frank Varrichione / Sam Palumbo
23	Pittsburgh	14 G Ray Lemek / Pat Bisceglia
27	Georgia Tech	14 C Jim Schrader / Dick Szymanski
38	Navy	7 G Minnie Mavraides / Jack Lee
28	Pennsylvania	20 T Art Hunter
34	North Carolina	14 E Don Penza / Walter Cabral
14	Iowa	14 QB Ralph Guglielmi
48	Southern Cal	14 HB Joe Heap / Dick Fitzgerald
40	SMU	14 HB Johnny Lattner
		FB Neil Worden

RUSHING: Worden 145/859y, Lattner 134/651y, Heap 62/314y
PASSING: Guglielmi 52-113/792y, 8TD, 46%
RECEIVING: Heap 22/335y, Lattner 14/204y
SCORING: Worden 66pts, Lattner 30pts

1954 9-1
21	Texas	0 E Dan Shannon / Don George
14	Purdue	27 T Sam Palumbo / George Nicula
33	Pittsburgh	0 G Ray Lemek / Pat Bisceglia
20	Michigan State	19 C Dick Szymanski / Jim Mense
6	Navy	0 G Jack Lee
42	Penn	7 T Frank Varrichione / Wayne Edmonds
42	North Carolina	13 E Paul Matz
34	Iowa	18 QB Ralph Guglielmi
23	Southern Cal	17 HB Joe Heap
26	SMU	14 HB Jim Morse / Paul Reynolds
		FB Don Schaefer / Paul Hornung

RUSHING: Schaefer 141/766y, Heap 110/594y, Morse 68/345y
PASSING: Guglielmi 68-127/1162y, 53.5%
RECEIVING: Heap 18/369y, Matz 16/224y, Morse 15/236y
SCORING: Heap 48pts, Schaefer (FB-K) 40pts, Morse 31pts

1955 8-2
17	SMU	0 E Dick Prendergast
19	Indiana	0 T Wayne Edmonds / George Nicula
14	Miami	0 G Pat Bisceglia
7	Michigan State	21 C Jim Mense
22	Purdue	7 G John McMullan / Bob Gaydos
21	Navy	7 T Ray Lemek / Ed Sullivan
46	Penn	14 E Gene Kapish / Bob Scannell
27	North Carolina	7 QB Paul Hornung
17	Iowa	14 HB Dean Studer / Aubrey Lewis
20	Southern Cal	42 HB Jim Morse
		FB Don Schaefer

RUSHING: Schaefer 145/638y, Hornung 92/472y, Studer 88/439y
PASSING: Hornung 46-103/743y, 9TD, 44.7%
RECEIVING: Morse 17/424y, Kapish 11/142y, Prendergast 8/105y
SCORING: Hornung 47pts, Morse 36pts, Schaefer 34pts

1956 2-8
13	SMU	19 E Dick Royer / Dick Prendergast
20	Indiana	6 T Frank Geremia / Angelo Mosca
14	Purdue	28 G Gene Hedrick / Dick Shulsen
14	Michigan State	47 C Ed Sullivan
0	Oklahoma	40 G Al Ecuyer / Bob Gaydos
7	Navy	33 T Bronko Nagurski
13	Pittsburgh	26 E Gary Myers / Bob Wetoska
21	North Carolina	14 QB Paul Hornung
8	Iowa	48 HB Aubrey Lewis / Frank Reynolds
20	Southern Cal	28 HB Jim Morse / Bob Ward
		FB Chuck Lima / Jim Just

RUSHING: Hornung 94/420y, Lewis 59/292y, Ward 38/170y
PASSING: Hornung 59-111/917y, 3TD, 53.2%
RECEIVNG: Morse 20/442y, Lewis 11/170y, Lima 7/105y
SCORING: Hornung 56pts, Ward 18pts, Lewis & Reynolds 12pts

1957 7-3
12	Purdue	0 E Dick Royer / Dick Prendergast
26	Indiana	0 T Chuck Puntillo / Frank Geremia
23	Army	21 G Jim Schaaf
13	Pittsburgh	7 C Bob Scholtz
6	Navy	20 G Al Ecuyer
6	Michigan State	34 T Bronko Nagurski / Don Lawrence
7	Oklahoma	0 E Monty Stickles/Gary Myers/Bob Wetoska
13	Iowa	21 QB Bob Williams
40	Southern Cal	12 HB Frank Reynolds
54	SMU	21 HB Dick Lynch / Jim Just
		FB Nick Pietrosante / Ron Toth

RUSHING: Pietrosante 90/449y, Lynch 77/287y, Toth 49/214y
PASSING: Williams 53-106/565y, 3TD, 50%
RECEIVING: Lynch 13/128y, Stickles 11/183y, Wetoska 8/141y
SCORING: Stickles 32pts, Lynch 30pts, Williams 24pts

1958 6-4
18	Indiana	0 E Monty Stickles / Dick Royer
14	SMU	6 T Frank Geremia / Bronko Nagurski
2	Army	14 G Jim Schaaf / Dick Shulsen
9	Duke	7 C Bob Scholtz / Myron Pottios
22	Purdue	29 G Al Ecuyer / Ken Adamson
40	Navy	20 T Chuck Puntillo / Don Lawrence
26	Pittsburgh	29 E Bob Wetoska / Gary Myers
34	North Carolina	24 QB Bob Williams / George Izo
21	Iowa	31 HB Red Mack
20	Southern Cal	13 HB Jim Crotty / Bob Scarpitto
		FB Nick Pietrosante

RUSHING: Pietrosante 117/549y, Mack 71/429y, Crotty 67/315y
PASSING: Izo 68-118/1067y, 9TD, 57.6%
RECEIVNG: Stickles 20/328y, Crotty 13/137y, Wetoska 12/210y
SCORING: Stickles 60pts, Mack 36pts, Pietrosante 26pts

1959 5-5
28	North Carolina	8 E Monty Stickles
7	Pudue	28 T Ollie Flor / Joe Carollo
28	California	6 G Nick Buoniconti / Al Sabal
0	Michigan State	19 C Bob Scholtz
24	Northwestern	30 G Ken Adamson
25	Navy	22 T Bob Bill / George Williams
10	Georgia Tech	14 E Pat Heenan / Les Traver
13	Pittsburgh	28 QB Don White / George Izo
20	Iowa	19 HB George Sefcik / Angelo Dabiero
16	Southern Cal	6 HB Bob Scarpitto / Red Mack
		FB Gerry Gray / Jim Crotty

RUSHING: Gray 50/256y, Sefcik 43/206y, Scarpitto 59/199y
PASSING: Izo 44-95/661y, 6TD, 46.3%
RECEIVING: Scarpitto 15/297y, Heenan 12/198y, Stickles 11/235y
SCORING: Scarpitto 48pts, Stickles (E-K) 37pts, 3 tied w/ 18pts

1960 2-8
21	California	7 E Les Traver
19	Purdue	51 T George Williams / Bob Bill
7	North Carolina	12 G Myron Pottios / Nick Buoniconti
0	Michigan State	21 C Ed Hoerster / John Linehan
6	Northwestern	7 G Norb Roy
7	Navy	14 T Joe Carollo / Ed Burke
13	Pittsburgh	20 E Denny Murphy / Max Burnell
21	Miami	28 QB Daryle Lamonica / George Haffner
0	Iowa	28 HB George Sefcik / Frank Minik
17	Southern Cal	0 HB Angelo Dabiero / Bob Scarpitto
		FB Mike Lind / Joe Perkowski

RUSHING: Dabiero 80/325y, Sefcik 50/248y, Scarpitto 51/228y
PASSING: Haffner 30-108/548y, 3TD, 27.8%
RECEIVING: Traver 14/225y, Scarpitto 8/164y, Burke 6/84y
SCORING: Scarpitto 30pts, Dabiero & Lamonica 18pts

1961 5-5
19	Oklahoma	6 E Les Traver / Jim Kelly
22	Purdue	20 T Bob Bill / Roger Wilke
30	Southern Cal	0 G Nick Buoniconti / Bob Lehmann
7	Michigan State	17 C Tom Hecomovich / Ed Hoerster
10	Northwestern	12 G Norb Roy
10	Navy	13 T Joe Carollo
26	Pittsburgh	20 E Denny Murphy / Tom Goberville
17	Syracuse	15 QB Daryle Lamonica / Frank Budka
21	Iowa	42 HB George Sefcik
13	Duke	37 HB Angelo Dabiero
		FB Mike Lind / Gerry Gray

RUSHING: Dabiero 92/637y, Lind 87/450y, Sefcik 72/335y
PASSING: Budka 40-95/636y, 3TD, 42.1%
RECEIVING: Traver 17/349y, Dabiero 10/201y, Kelly 9/138y
SCORING: Joe Perkowski (K) 31pts, Dabiero & Lind 24pts

1962 5-5
13	Oklahoma	7 E Tom Goberville / Clay Stephens
6	Purdue	24 T Nick Etten / Gene Penman
8	Wisconsin	17 G Jim Carroll / Ken Maglicic
7	Michigan State	31 C Ed Hoerster
6	Northwestern	35 G Bob Lehmann / Wayne Allen
20	Navy	12 T George Bednar / Ed Burke
43	Pittsburgh	22 E Jim Kelly
21	North Carolina	7 QB Daryle Lamonica / Frank Budka
35	Iowa	12 HB Ron Bliey / Tom MacDonald (D)
0	Southern Cal	25 HB Don Hogan / Denny Phillips
		FB Gerry Gray / Joe Farrell

RUSHING: Hogan 90/454y, Farrell 70/278y, Bliey 57/167y
PASSING: Lamonica 64-128/821y, 6TD, 50%
RECEIVING: Kelly 41/523y, Hogan 12/146y, Stephens 5/93y
SCORING: Farrell, Kelly and Lamonica 24pts

1963 2-7
9	Wisconsin	14 E Jim Kelly / Dave Pivec
6	Purdue	7 T Dick Arrington
17	Southern Cal	14 G Bob Lehmann
27	UCLA	12 C Norm Nicola / Tom Kostelnik
14	Stanford	24 G Jim Carroll / John Atamian
14	Navy	35 T John Meyer / George Bednar
7	Pittsburgh	27 E Tom Goberville
7	Michigan State	12 QB Frank Budka / Tom Longo (D)
	Iowa-cancelled	HB Joe Farrell / B. Wolski/ Tom MacDonald
7	Syracuse	14 HB Jack Snow / Ron Bliey / Bill Pfeiffer (D)
		FB Joe Kantor

RUSHING: Kantor 88/330y, Wolski 70/320y, Bliey 30/115y
PASSING: Budka 21-40/239y, 4TD, 52.5%
RECEIVING: Kelly 18/264y, Snow 6/82y, Pivec 6/76y
SCORING: Budka 24pts, Ken Ivan (K) 15pts, 4 tied w/ 12pts

1964 9-1
31	Wisconsin	7 E Jack Snow
34	Purdue	15 T Bob Meeker
34	Air Force	7 G John Atamian
24	UCLA	0 C Norm Nicola
28	Stanford	6 G Dick Arrington
40	Navy	0 T John Meyer / Jim Snowden
17	Pittsburgh	15 E Phil Sheridan
34	Michigan State	7 QB John Huarte
28	Iowa	0 HB Bill Wolski
17	Southern Cal	20 HB Nick Eddy
		FB Joe Farrell / Joe Kantor
		DL Don Gmitter
		DL Kevin Hardy
		DL Tom Regner
		DL Alan Page
		LB Jim Lynch / Arunas Vasys
		LB Tom Kostelnik
		LB Jim Carroll
		LB Ken Maglicic
		DB Tom Longo
		DB Tony Carey
		DB Nick Rassas

RUSHING: Wolski 136/657y, Eddy 98/490y, Farrell 93/387y
PASSING: Huarte 114-205/2062y, 16TD, 55.6%
RECEIVING: Snow 60/1114y, Sheridan 20/320y, Eddy 16/352y
SCORING: Wolski 66pts, Snow 56pts, Eddy 44pts

1965 7-2-1
48	California	6 E Tom Talaga / Don Gmitter
21	Purdue	25 T Bob Meeker
38	Northwestern	7 G Tom Regner
17	Army	0 C George Goeddeke
28	Southern Cal	7 G Dick Arrington
29	Navy	3 T Tom Sullivan / Rudy Konieczny
69	Pittsburgh	13 E Phil Sheridan
17	North Carolina	0 QB Bill Zloch
3	Michigan State	12 HB Bill Wolski
0	Miami	0 HB Nick Eddy
		FB Larry Conjar
		DL Harry Long / Tom Rhoads
		DL Pete Duranko
		DL Dick Arrington
		DL Alan Page
		LB Jim Lynch
		LB John Horney
		LB Mike McGill
		LB Dave Martin
		DB Tom Longo
		DB Tony Carey
		DB Nick Rassas

RUSHING: Eddy 115/582y, Conjar 137/535y, Wolski 103/452y
PASSING: Zloch 36-88/558y, 3TD, 40.9%
RECEIVING: Eddy 13/233y, Sheridan 10/140y, Gmitter 6/155y
SCORING: Wolski 52pts, Ken Ivan (K) 48pts, Conjar 42pts

1966 9-0-1

26 Purdue	14 E Jim Seymour
35 Northwestern	7 T Paul Seiler
35 Army	0 G Tom Regner
32 North Carolina	0 C George Goeddeke
38 Oklahoma	0 G Dick Swatland
31 Navy	7 T Bob Kuechenberg / Rudy Konieczny
40 Pittsburgh	0 E Don Gmitter
64 Duke	0 QB Terry Hanratty / Coley O'Brien
10 Michigan State	10 HB Nick Eddy
51 Southern Cal	0 HB Rocky Bleier
	FB Larry Conjar
	DL Tom Rhoads
	DL Pete Duranko
	DL Kevin Hardy
	DL Alan Page
	LB John Horney / Mike McGill
	LB Jim Lynch
	LB John Pergine
	LB Dave Martin
	DB Tom O'Leary
	DB Jim Smithberger
	DB Tom Schoen

RUSHING: Eddy 78/553y, Conjar 112/521y, Bleier 63/282y
PASSING: Hanratty 78-147/1247y, 8TD, 53.1%
RECEIVING: Seymour 48/862y, Bleier 17/209y, Eddy 15/123y
SCORING: Eddy 60pts, Seymour 48pts, Joe Azzaro (K) 47pts

1967 8-2

41 California	8 WR Jim Seymour
21 Purdue	28 T Jim Reilly
56 Iowa	6 G Tom McKinley
7 Southern Cal	24 C Steve Quinn
47 Illinois	7 G Dick Swatland
24 Michigan State	12 T George Kunz
43 Navy	14 TE Jim Winegardner
38 Pittsburgh	0 QB Terry Hanratty
36 Georgia Tech	3 HB Rocky Bleier
24 Miami	22 HB Bob Gladieux / Dan Harshman
	FB Jeff Zimmerman
	DL Bob Kuechenberg
	DL Kevin Hardy / Mike McCoy
	DL Eric Norri
	DL Chick Lauck
	LB John Pergine
	LB Mike McGill
	LB Bob Olson
	LB Dave Martin
	DB Jim Smithberger
	DB Tom O'Leary
	DB Tom Schoen

RUSHING: Zimmerman 133/591y, Gladieux 84/384y, Bleier 77/357y
PASSING: Hanratty 110-206/1439y, 9TD, 53.4%
RECEIVING: Seymour 37/515y, Gladieux 23/297y, Bleier 16/171y
SCORING: Joe Azzaro (K) 61pts, Zimmerman 54pts, 3 tied w/ 42pts

1968 7-2-1

45 Oklahoma	21 WR Jim Seymour
22 Purdue	37 T Jim Reilly
51 Iowa	28 G Larry DiNardo
27 Northwestern	7 C Tim Monty / Mike Oriard
58 Illinois	8 G Tom McKinley
17 Michigan State	21 T George Kunz
45 Navy	14 TE Jim Winegardner
56 Pittsburgh	7 QB Terry Hanratty / Joe Theismann
34 Georgia Tech	6 HB Coley O'Brien
21 Southern Cal	21 HB Bob Gladieux
	FB Ron Dushney
	DL Bob Kuechenberg
	DL Mike McCoy
	DL Eric Norri
	DL Chick Lauck
	LB Tim Kelly
	LB Bob Olson
	LB Joe Freebery
	LB Larry Schumacher
	DB John Gasser
	DB Chuck Zloch
	DB Don Reid

RUSHING: Gladieux 152/713y, Dushney 108/540y, O'Brien 64/314y
PASSING: Hanratty 116-197/1466y, 10TD, 58.9%, Theismann 27-49/451y, 1 TD, 55.1%
RECEIVING: Seymour 53/736y, Gladieux 37/442y, O'Brien 16/272y
SCORING: Gladieux 84 pts, Scott Hempel (K) 60pts, O'Brien 42pts

1969 8-2-1

35 Northwestern	10 WR Tom Gatewood
14 Purdue	28 T Jim Reilly
42 Michigan State	28 G Larry DiNardo
45 Army	0 C Mike Oriard
14 Southern Cal	14 G Gary Kos
37 Tulane	0 T Terry Brennan
47 Navy	0 TE Dewey Poskon / Tom Lawson
49 Pittsburgh	7 QB Joe Theismann
38 Georgia Tech	20 HB Ed Ziegler / Andy Huff
13 Air Force	6 HB Denny Allan
17 Texas■	21 FB Bill Barz
	DL Walt Patulski
	DL Mike McCoy
	DL Mike Kadish
	DL Fred Swendsen
	LB Tim Kelly
	LB Larry Schumacher
	LB Bob Olson
	LB John Raterman
	DB John Gasser
	DB Ralph Stepaniak
	DB Clarence Ellis

RUSHING: Allan 148/612y, Ziegler 94/483y, Theismann 116/378y
PASSING: Theismann 108-192/1531y, 13TD, 56.3%
RECEIVING: Gatewood 47/743y, Barz 24/262y, Poskon 13/176y
SCORING: Scott Hempel (K) 56pts, Allan 54pts, Gatewood 48pts

1970 10-1

35 Northwestern	14 WR Tom Gatewood
48 Purdue	0 T Mike Martin
29 Michigan State	0 G Larry DiNardo
51 Army	10 C Dan Novakov
24 Missouri	7 G Gary Kos
56 Navy	7 T John Dampeer
46 Pittsburgh	14 TE Mike Creaney
10 Georgia Tech	7 QB Joe Theismann
3 LSU	0 HB Ed Gulyas
28 Southern Cal	38 HB Denny Allan
24 Texas■	11 FB Bill Barz
	DL Walt Patulski
	DL Mike Kadish / Mike Zikas
	DL Greg Marx
	DL Bob Neidert
	LB Tim Kelly
	LB Eric Patton
	LB Jim Wright
	LB Rick Thomann
	DB Clarence Ellis
	DB Ralph Stepaniak
	DB Mike Crotty

RUSHING: Gulyas 118/534y, Allan 111/401y, Theismann 123/384y
PASSING: Theismann 155-268/2429y, 16TD, 57.8%
RECEIVING: Gatewood 77/1123y, Creaney 17/399y, Barz 13/127y
SCORING: Scott Hempel (K) 48pts, Allan 48pts, Gatewood 44pts

1971 8-2

50 Northwestern	7 WR Tom Gatewood
8 Purdue	7 T Jim Humbert / Dave Casper
14 Michigan State	2 G Frank Pomarico
17 Miami	0 C Dan Novakov
16 North Carolina	0 G John Kondrk
14 Southern Cal	28 T John Dampeer
21 Navy	0 TE Mike Creaney
56 Pittsburgh	7 QB Bill Etter / Cliff Brown
21 Tulane	7 HB Ed Gulyas
8 LSU	28 HB Bob Minnix / Larry Parker
	FB Andy Huff / John Cieszkowski
	DL Walt Patulski
	DL Mike Kadish
	DL Greg Marx
	DL Fred Swendsen
	LB Jim Musuraca
	LB Eric Patton
	LB Jim O'Malley / Ken Schlezes (DB)
	LB Rick Thomann
	DB Clarence Ellis
	DB Ralph Stepaniak
	DB Mike Crotty

RUSHING: Minnix 78/337y, Cieszkowski 69/316y, Parker 80/299y
PASSING: Brown 56-111/669y, 4TD, 50.5%,
RECEIVING: Gatewood 33/417y, Creaney 11/151y, Parker 10/109y
SCORING: Bob Thomas (K) 36pts, Minnix 34pts, Gulyas 30pts

1972 8-3

37 Northwestern	0 WR Willie Townsend
35 Purdue	14 T Dave Casper
16 Michigan State	0 G Frank Pomarico
42 Pittsburgh	16 C Dave Drew
26 Missouri	30 G Gerry DiNardo
21 TCU	0 T John Dampeer
42 Navy	23 TE Mike Creaney
21 Air Force	7 QB Tom Clements
20 Miami	17 HB Darryll Dewan / Gary Diminick
23 Southern Cal	45 HB Eric Penick
6 Nebraska■	40 FB Andy Huff
	DL Tom Freistroffer / Tim Sullivan
	DL Steve Niehaus / Kevin Nosbusch
	DL Greg Marx
	DL George Hayduk
	LB Tim Sullivan / Tim Rudnick (DB)
	LB Jim O'Malley
	LB Drew Mahalic
	LB Jim Musuraca
	DB Mike Townsend
	DB Reggie Barnett
	DB Ken Schlezes

RUSHING: Penick 124/727y, Huff 155/567y, Diminick 71/377y
PASSING: Clements 83-162/1163y, 8TD, 51.2%
RECEIVING: Townsend 25/369y, Creaney 17/321y, Diminick 14/143y
SCORING: Huff 60pts, Bob Thomas (K) 55pts, Penick 30pts

1973 11-0

44 Northwestern	0 WR Pete Demmerle
20 Purdue	7 T Steve Neece
14 Michigan State	10 G Frank Pomarico
28 Rice	0 C Mark Brenneman
62 Army	3 G Gerry DiNardo
23 Southern Cal	14 T Steve Sylvester
44 Navy	7 TE Dave Casper
31 Pittsburgh	10 QB Tom Clements
48 Air Force	15 HB Art Best
44 Miami	0 HB Eric Penick
24 Alabama■	23 FB Wayne Bullock
	DL Ross Browner
	DL Steve Niehaus / Kevin Nosbusch
	DL Mike Fanning
	DL Jim Stock
	LB Greg Collins
	LB Gary Potemba
	LB Drew Mahalic / Sherm Smith
	DB Reggie Barnett
	DB Tim Rudnick
	DB Mike Townsend
	DB Luther Bradley

RUSHING: Bullock 162/752y, Best 118/700y, Penick 102/586y
PASSING: Clements 60-113/882y, 8TD, 53.1%
RECEIVING: Demmerle 26/404y, Casper 19/317y, Bullock 8/83y
SCORING: Bob Thomas (K) 70pts, Bullock 66pts, Penick 42pts

1974 10-2

31 Georgia Tech	7 WR Pete Demmerle
49 Northwestern	3 T Steve Neece / Ed Bauer
20 Purdue	31 G Al Wujciak
19 Michigan State	14 C Mark Brenneman
10 Rice	3 G Gerry DiNardo
48 Army	0 T Steve Sylvester
38 Miami	7 TE Robin Weber / Ken MacAfee
14 Navy	6 QB Tom Clements
14 Pittsburgh	10 HB Art Best / Mark McLane
38 Air Force	0 HB Al Samuel / Ron Goodman
24 Southern Cal	55 FB Wayne Bullock
13 Alabama■	11 DL Steve Niehaus
	DL Kevin Nosbusch
	DL Mike Fanning
	DL Jim Stock
	LB Greg Collins
	LB Tom Eastman / Marv Russell
	LB Drew Mahalic
	DB Reggie Barnett
	DB Randy Payne
	DB John Dubenetzky
	DB Randy Harrison

RUSHING: Bullock 203/855y, Samuel 95/525y, Clements 95/369y
PASSING: Clements 122-215/1549y, 8TD, 56.7%
RECEIVING: Demmerle 43/667y, Goodman 14/149y, MacAfee 14/146y
SCORING: Bullock 72pts, Dave Reeve (K) 59pts, Demmerle 36pts

1975 8-3

17 Boston College	3 WR Ted Burgmeier / Dan Kelleher
17 Purdue	0 T Ed Bauer
31 Northwestern	7 G Al Wujciak
3 Michigan State	10 C Steve Quehl
21 North Carolina	14 G Ernie Hughes
31 Air Force	30 T Pat Pohlen
17 Southern Cal	24 TE Ken MacAfee
31 Navy	10 QB Rick Slager / Joe Montana
24 Georgia Tech	3 HB Al Hunter
20 Pittsburgh	34 HB Mark McLane
32 Miami	9 FB Jerome Heavens / Jim Browner
	DL Ross Browner
	DL Steve Niehaus
	DL Jeff Weston
	DL Willie Fry
	LB Jim Stock
	LB Bob Golic / Tom Eastman
	LB Doug Becker / Pete Johnson
	DB Tom Lopienski
	DB Luther Bradley
	DB Mike Banks
	DB Randy Harrison

RUSHING: Heavens 129/756y, Hunter 117/558y, Browner 104/394y
PASSING: Slager 66-139/686y, 2TD, 47.5%, Montana 28-66/507y, 4TD, 42.4%
RECEIVING: MacAfee 26/333y, McLane 21/277y, Kelleher 12/171y
SCORING: Dave Reeve (K) 57pts, Hunter 48pts, Heavens & McAfee 30pts

1976 9-3

10 Pittsburgh	31 WR Dan Kelleher
23 Purdue	0 T Harry Woebkenberg
48 Northwestern	0 G Mike Carney / Ted Horansky
24 Michigan State	6 C Dave Huffman
41 Oregon	0 G Ernie Hughes
13 South Carolina	6 T Steve McDaniel
27 Navy	21 TE Ken MacAfee
14 Georgia Tech	23 QB Rick Slager
21 Alabama	18 HB Al Hunter
40 Miami	27 HB Mark McLane / Tom Domin
13 Southern Cal	17 FB Vagas Ferguson / Willard Browner
20 Penn State■	9 DL Ross Browner
	DL Ken Dike
	DL Mike Calhoun
	DL Willie Fry
	LB Steve Heimkreiter
	LB Bob Golic
	LB Doug Becker
	DB Luther Bradley
	DB Ted Burgmeier
	DB Jim Browner
	DB Joe Restic

RUSHING: Hunter 233/1058y, Ferguson 81/350y, Terry Eurick (HB) 46/230y
PASSING: Slager 86-172/1281y, 11TD, 41.2%
RECEIVING: MacAfee 34/483y, Kelleher 24/522y, Hunter 15/189y
SCORING: Hunter 78pts, Dave Reeve (K) 56pts, Kelleher 26pts

1977 11-1

19 Pittsburgh	9 WR Kris Haines
13 Mississippi	20 T Tim Foley
31 Purdue	24 G Ted Horansky
16 Michigan State	6 C Dave Huffman
24 Army	0 G Ernie Hughes
49 Southern Cal	19 T Steve McDaniel
43 Navy	10 TE Ken MacAfee
69 Georgia Tech	14 QB Joe Montana / Rusty Lisch
21 Clemson	17 HB Vagas Ferguson / Terry Eurick
49 Air Force	0 WB Dave Waymer / Tom Domin
48 Miami	10 FB Jerome Heavens
38 Texas■	10 DL Ross Browner
	DL Ken Dike
	DL Mike Calhoun / Jeff Weston
	DL Willie Fry / Scott Zettek
	LB Steve Heimkreiter
	LB Bob Golic
	LB Doug Becker
	DB Luther Bradley
	DB Ted Burgmeier
	DB Jim Browner
	DB Joe Restic

RUSHING: Heavens 229/994y, Ferguson 80/493y, Dave Mitchell (FB) 82/303y
PASSING: Montana 99-189/1604y, 11TD, 52%, Lisch 51-94/568y, 6TD, 54%
RECEIVING: MacAfee 54/797y, Haines 28/587y, Heavens 12/133y
SCORING: Dave Reeve (K) 75pts, Eurick 42pts, Ferguson 42pts

1978 9-3

0 Missouri	3 WR Kris Haines
14 Michigan	28 WR Pete Holohan / Jim Stone (HB)
10 Purdue	6 T Rob Martinovich
29 Michigan State	25 G Jim Hautman
26 Pittsburgh	17 C Dave Huffman
38 Air Force	15 G Tim Huffman
20 Miami	0 T Tim Foley
27 Navy	7 TE Dennis Grindinger
31 Tennessee	14 QB Joe Montana
38 Georgia Tech	21 HB Vagas Ferguson
25 Southern Cal	27 FB Jerome Heavens
35 Houston■	34 DL Jay Case
	DL Jeff Weston
	DL Mike Calhoun
	DL John Hankerd
	LB Steve Heimkreiter
	LB Bob Golic
	LB Bobby Leopold / Mike Whittington
	DB Dave Waymer
	DB Tom Gibbons
	DB Jim Browner
	DB Joe Restic

RUSHING: Ferguson 211/1192y, Heavens 178/728y, Stone 28/109y
PASSING: Montana 141-260/2010y, 10TD, 54.2%
RECEIVING: Haines 32/699y, Holohan 20/301y, Ferguson 20/171y
SCORING: Ferguson 48pts, Chuck Male (K) 41pts, Montana 36pts

1979 7-4

12 Michigan	10 WR Tony Hunter
22 Purdue	28 WR Pete Holohan
27 Michigan State	3 T Rob Martinovich
21 Georgia Tech	13 G John Leon / Ted Horansky
38 Air Force	13 C John Scully
23 Southern Cal	42 G Tim Huffman
18 South Carolina	17 T Tim Foley
14 Navy	0 TE Dean Masztak
18 Tennessee	40 QB Rusty Lisch
10 Clemson	16 HB Vagas Ferguson
40 Miami	15 FB John Sweeney / Ty Barber
	DL John Hankerd
	DL Scott Zettek
	DL Kevin Griffith / Pat Kramer
	DL Joe Gramke
	LB Mike Whittington / Mark Zavagnin
	LB Bob Crable
	LB Bobby Leopold
	DB Dave Waymer
	DB John Krimm / Dave Duerson
	DB Steve Cichy
	DB Tom Gibbons

RUSHING: Ferguson 301/1437y, Barber 40/172y, Jim Stone (HB) 37/156y
PASSING: Lisch 108-208/1781y, 4TD, 51.9%
RECEIVING: Masztak 28/428y, Hunter 27/690y, Holohan 22/386y
SCORING: Ferguson 102pts, Chuck Male (K) 63pts, 5 tied with 12pts

1980 9-2-1

31 Purdue	10 WR Tony Hunter
29 Michigan	27 WR Pete Holohan
26 Michigan State	21 T Mike Shiner
32 Miami	14 G Bob Burger / Robb Gagnon
30 Army	3 C John Scully
20 Arizona	3 G Tom Thayer / Tim Huffman
33 Navy	0 T Phil Pozderac
3 Georgia Tech	3 TE Dean Masztak / Nick Vehr
7 Alabama	0 QB Blair Kiel / Mike Courey
24 Air Force	10 HB Phil Carter / Jim Stone
3 Southern Cal	20 FB John Sweeney
10 Georgia■	37 DL John Hankerd
	DL Joe Gramke / Don Kidd
	DL Pat Kramer / Tim Marshall
	DL Scott Zettek
	LB Mark Zavagnin
	LB Bob Crable
	LB Joe Rudzinski
	DB Stacey Toran
	DB John Krimm
	DB Dave Duerson / Steve Cichy
	DB Tom Gibbons

RUSHING: Stone 192/908y, Carter 186/822y, Sweeney 50/202y
PASSING: Kiel 48-124/531y, 0TD, 38.7%
RECEIVING: Hunter 23/303y, Holohan 21/296y, Masztak 8/97y
SCORING: Harry Oliver (K) 73pts, Stone 42pts, Carter 36pts

1981 5-6

27 LSU	9 WR Joe Howard / Mike Boushka
7 Michigan	25 T Tom Thayer
14 Purdue	15 G Randy Ellis / Mike Kelley
20 Michigan State	7 C Mark Fischer
13 Florida State	19 G Mike Shiner / Larry Kissner
7 Southern Cal	14 T Phil Pozderac
38 Navy	0 TE Dean Masztak
35 Georgia Tech	3 QB Blair Kiel / Tim Koegel
35 Air Force	7 TB Phil Carter / Greg Bell (WB)
21 Penn State	24 WB Tony Hunter (TE) / John Moseley
15 Miami	37 FB John Sweeney
	DL Jon Autry / Tony Belden
	DL Tim Marshall
	DL Bob Clasby / Joe Gramke
	DL Kevin Griffith
	LB Mark Zavagnin
	LB Bob Crable
	LB Joe Rudzinski / Rick Naylor
	DB Stacey Toran
	DB John Krimm
	DB Dave Duerson
	DB Rod Bone

RUSHING: Carter 165/727y, Bell 92/512y, Sweeney 36/168y
PASSING: Kiel 67-151/936y, 7TD, 44.4%
RECEIVING: Hunter 28/387y, Howard 17/463y, Carter 14/57y
SCORING: Harry Oliver (K) 46pts, Carter 36pts, Bell 30pts

1982 6-4-1

23 Michigan	17 WR Joe Howard
28 Purdue	14 WR Mike Haywood
11 Michigan State	3 T Mike Kelley
16 Miami	14 G Tom Thayer (C) / Neil Maune
13 Arizona	16 C Mark Fischer
13 Oregon	13 G Randy Ellis
27 Navy	10 T Larry Williams
31 Pittsburgh	16 TE Tony Hunter
14 Penn State	24 QB Blair Kiel
17 Air Force	30 TB Phil Carter / Allen Pinkett
13 Southern Cal	17 FB Larry Moriarty
	DL Kevin Griffith
	DL Mike Gann
	DL Jon Autry
	DL Bob Clasby
	LB Mike Larkin
	LB Mark Zavagnin
	LB Rick Naylor
	DB Chris Brown
	DB Stacey Toran
	DB Joe Johnson
	DB Dave Duerson

RUSHING: Carter 179/715y, Pinkett 107/532y, Moriarty 88/520y
PASSING: Kiel 118-219/1273y, 3TD, 53.9%
RECEIVING: Hunter 42/507y, Howard 28/524y, Moriarty 18/170y
SCORING: Mike Johnston (K) 76pts, Moriarty 42pts, Pinkett 36pts

1983 7-5

52 Purdue	6 WR Joe Howard
23 Michigan State	28 WR Milt Jackson
0 Miami	20 T Larry Williams / Mike Shiner
27 Colorado	3 G Tim Scannell / Tom Doerger
30 South Carolina	6 C Mike Kelley
42 Army	0 G Neil Maune
27 Southern Cal	6 T Mike Perrino / Greg Golic
28 Navy	12 TE Mark Bavaro
16 Pittsburgh	21 QB Steve Beuerlein / Blair Kiel
30 Penn State	34 TB Allen Pinkett
22 Air Force	23 FB Chris Smith / Mark Brooks
19 Boston College■	18 DL Mike Golic
	DL Mike Gann
	DL Jon Autry / Mike Griffin
	DL Greg Dingens / Eric Dorsey
	LB Mike Kovaleski / Robert Banks
	LB Tony Furjanic
	LB Rick Naylor
	DB Pat Ballage
	DB Stacey Toran / Tony Wilson
	DB Chris Brown
	DB Joe Johnson

RUSHING: Pinkett 252/1394y, Smith 77/421y
PASSING: Beuerlein 75-145/1061y, 4TD, 51.7%
RECEIVING: Pinkett 28/288y, Howard 27/464y, Jackson 23/438y
SCORING: Pinkett 110pts, Mike Johnston (K) 69pts, Greg Bell (TB) 30pts

1984 7-5

21 Purdue	23 WR Joe Howard / Tim Brown
24 Michigan State	20 WR Milt Jackson
55 Colorado	14 T Tom Doerger / Ron Plantz
16 Missouri	14 G Tim Scannell
13 Miami	31 C Mike Kelley
7 Air Force	21 G Larry Williams / John Askin
32 South Carolina	36 T Mike Perrino
30 LSU	22 TE Mark Bavaro / Ricky Gray
18 Navy	17 QB Steve Beuerlein
44 Penn State	7 TB Allen Pinkett
19 Southern Cal	7 FB Chris Smith / Mark Brooks
20 SMU■	27 DL Mike Gann
	DL Mike Griffin
	DL Wally Kleine
	LB Mike Golic / Rick DiBernardo
	LB Robert Banks
	LB Mike Kovaleski / Ron Weissenhofer
	LB John McCabe /T. Furjanic /Mike Larkin
	DB Troy Wilson / Mike Haywood
	DB Pat Ballage
	DB Joe Johnson
	DB Steve Lawrence / Hiawatha Francisco

RUSHING: Pinkett 275/1105y, Smith 61/260y, Brooks 34/131y
PASSING: Beuerlein 140-232/1920y, 7TD, 60.3%
RECEIVING: Bavaro 32/395y, Jackson 28/363y, Brown 28/340y
SCORING: Pinkett 108pts, John Carney (K) 76pts, Jackson 24pts

1985 5-6

12 Michigan	20 WR Reggie Ward
27 Michigan State	10 WR Tim Brown
17 Purdue	35 T Tom Doerger / Jay Underwood
15 Air Force	21 G Tim Scannell
24 Army	10 C Ron Plantz
37 Southern Cal	3 G Shawn Heffern
41 Navy	17 T Mike Perrino
37 Mississippi	14 TE Tom Rehder / Joel Williams
6 Penn State	36 QB Steve Beuerlein
7 LSU	10 TB Allen Pinkett
7 Miami	58 FB Frank Stams
	DL Greg Dingens / Mike Larkin
	DL Eric Dorsey / Mike Kiernan
	DL Wally Kleine / Jeff Kunz
	LB Cedric Figaro
	LB Mike Kovaleski
	LB Tony Furjanic
	LB Robert Banks
	DB Mike Haywood / Marv Spence
	DB Troy Wilson
	DB Pat Ballage
	DB Steve Lawrence

RUSHING: Pinkett 255/1100y, Hiawatha Francisco (TB) 60/252y,
  Stams 44/164y
PASSING: Beuerlein 107-214/1335y, 3TD, 50%
RECEIVING: Brown 25/397y, Ward 24/355y, Pinkett 17/135y
SCORING: Pinkett 66pts, John Carney (K) 60pts, Brown 30pts

1986 5-6

23 Michigan	24 WR Milt Jackson
15 Michigan State	20 WR Tim Brown
41 Purdue	9 T Tom Rehder / John Askin
10 Alabama	28 G Tom Freeman
9 Pittsburgh	10 C Chuck Lanza
31 Air Force	3 G Shawn Heffrem
33 Navy	14 T Byron Spruell
61 SMU	29 TE Joel Williams
19 Penn State	24 QB Steve Beuerlein
19 LSU	21 TB Mark Green / Anthony Johnson
38 Southern Cal	37 FB Pernell Taylor
	DL Robert Banks
	DL Mike Griffin
	DL Wally Kleine
	LB Dave Butler / Flash Gordon
	LB Cedric Figaro
	LB Mike Kovaleski
	LB Ron Weissenhofer
	DB Troy Wilson
	DB Marv Spence
	DB Brandy Wells / George Streeter
	DB Steve Lawrence

RUSHING: Green 96/406y, Johnson 80/349y, Taylor 69/284y
PASSING: Beuerlein 151-259/2211y, 3TD, 58.3%
RECEIVING: Brown 45/910y, Jackson 31/592y, Green 25/242y
SCORING: John Carney (K) 87pts, Brown 54pts, Johnson &
  Taylor 30pts

1987 8-4

26 Michigan	7 WR Pat Terrell / Reggie Ward
31 Michigan State	8 WR Tim Brown
44 Purdue	20 T Tom Rehder
22 Pittsburgh	30 G Tom Freeman
35 Air Force	14 C Chuck Lanza
26 Southern Cal	15 G Jeff Pearson / Tim Grunhard
56 Navy	13 T Byron Spruell
32 Boston College	25 TE Andy Heck
37 Alabama	6 QB Tony Rice / Terry Andrysiak
20 Penn State	21 TB Mark Green / Ricky Watters
0 Miami	24 FB Anthony Johnson
10 Texas A&M■	35 DL Tom Gorman
	DL Mike Griffin
	DL Jeff Kunz / Bryan Flannery
	LB Flash Gordon
	LB Cedric Figaro
	LB Wes Pritchett
	LB Ned Bolcar
	DB Marv Spence
	DB Stan Smagala
	DB George Streeter
	DB Brandy Wells / Corny Southall

RUSHING: Green 146/861y, Watters 69/373y, Johnson 78/366y
PASSING: Rice 35-82/663y, 1TD, 42.7%
  Andrysiak 30-58/480y, 2TD, 51.7%
RECEIVING: Brown 39/846y, Green 13/98y, Watters 6/70y
SCORING: Ted Gradel (K) 75pts, Johnson 66pts, Brown 44pts

1988 12-0

19 Michigan	17 WR Raghib Ismail / Steve Alaniz
20 Michigan State	3 WR Pat Eilers / Ricky Watters
52 Purdue	7 T Andy Heck
42 Stanford	14 G Tim Ryan
30 Pittsburgh	20 C Mike Heldt
31 Miami	30 G Tim Grunhard / Winston Sandri
41 Air Force	13 T Dean Brown
22 Navy	7 TE Derek Brown / Frank Jacobs
54 Rice	11 QB Tony Rice
21 Penn State	3 TB Mark Green / Tony Brooks
27 Southern Cal	10 FB Anthony Johnson / Braxston Banks
	DL George Williams
	DL Chris Zorich
	DL Jeff Alm
	LB Frank Stams
	LB Mike Stonebreaker
	LB Wes Pritchett
	LB Andre Jones / Arnold Ale / F. Gordon
	DB Todd Lyght
	DB Stan Smagala
	DB George Streeter
	DB Pat Terrell / Corny Southall

RUSHING: Rice 121/700y, Brooks 117/667y, Green 135/646y
PASSING: Rice 70-138/1176y, 8TD, 50.7%
RECEIVING: Watters 15/286y, Green 14/155y, Ismail 12/331y
SCORING: Reggie Ho (K) 59pts, Rice 56pts, Green 42pts

1989 12-1

36 Virginia	13 WR Pat Eilers
24 Michigan`	19 WR Raghib Ismail
21 Michigan State	13 T Mike Brennan
40 Purdue	9 G Tim Ryan
27 Stanford	17 C Mike Heldt
41 Air Force	27 G Tim Grunhard
28 Southern Cal	24 T Dean Brown
45 Pittsburgh	7 TE Derek Brown
41 Navy	0 QB Tony Rice
59 SMU	6 TB Ricky Watters
34 Penn State	23 FB Anthony Johnson
10 Miami	27 DL Bob Dahl
21 Colorado■	6 DL Chris Zorich
	DL Jeff Alm
	LB Scott Kowalkowski
	LB Donn Grimm
	LB Ned Bolcar
	LB Andre Jones / Devon McDonald
	DB Todd Lyght
	DB Stan Smagala / Rod Smith
	DB D'Juan Francisco
	DB Pat Terrell

RUSHING: Rice 174/884y, Watters 118/791y, Johnson 131/515y
PASSING: Rice 68-137/1122y, 2TD, 49.6%
RECEIVING: Ismail 27/535y, Brown 13/204y, Watters 13/196y
SCORING: Johnson 78pts, Craig Hentrich (K) 68pts, Watters 66pts

1990 9-3

28 Michigan	24 WR Tony Smith
20 Michigan State	19 WR Raghib Ismail
37 Purdue	11 T Gene McGuire
31 Stanford	36 G Tim Ryan
57 Air Force	27 C Mike Heldt
29 Miami	20 G Mirko Jurkovic
31 Pittsburgh	22 T Justin Hall / Winston Sandri
52 Navy	31 TE Derek Brown
34 Tennessee	29 QB Rick Mirer
21 Penn State	24 TB Ricky Watters / Tony Brooks
10 Southern Cal	6 FB Rodney Culver
9 Colorado■	10 DL George Williams
	DL Chris Zorich / Eric Jones
	DL Bob Dahl
	LB Scott Kowalkowski
	LB Andre Jones / Devon McDonald
	LB Michael Stonebreaker
	LB Demetrius DuBose / Donn Grimm
	DB Todd Lyght / Greg Lane
	DB Rod Smith / Reggie Brooks
	DB Greg Davis
	DB Will Clark/Tom Carter/George Poorman

RUSHING: Culver 150/710y, Watters 108/579y, Ismail 67/537y
PASSING: Mirer 110-200/1824y, 8TD, 55%
RECEIVING: Ismail 32/699y, Smith 15/229y, Brown 15/220y
SCORING: Craig Hentrich (K) 89pts, Watters 48pts, Culver 42pts

1991 10-3

49 Indiana	27 WR Tony Smith
14 Michigan	24 WR Lake Dawson / Ray Griggs
49 Michigan State	10 T Lindsay Knapp
45 Purdue	20 G Aaron Taylor / Tim Ruddy
42 Stanford	26 C Gene McGuire
42 Pittsburgh	7 G Mirko Jurkovic
28 Air Force	15 T Justin Hall / Todd Norman
24 Southern Cal	20 TE Derek Brown
38 Navy	0 QB Rick Mirer
34 Tennessee	35 TB Rodney Culver / Tony Brooks
13 Penn State	35 FB Jerome Bettis
48 Hawaii	42 DL Devon McDonald
39 Florida■	28 DL Junior Bryant / Troy Ridgley
	DL Bryant Young
	DL Eric Jones / Germaine Holden
	LB John Covington / Anthony Peterson
	LB Demetrius DuBose
	LB Pete Bercich / Jim Flanigan
	DB Jeff Burris
	DB Tom Carter
	DB Rod Smith / Greg Davis
	DB Willie Clark

RUSHING: Bettis 168/972y, Brooks 147/894y, Culver 101/550y
PASSING: Mirer 132-234/2117y, 18TD, 56.4%
RECEIVING: Smith 42/789y, Dawson 24/433y, Brown 22/325y
SCORING: Bettis 120pts, Craig Hentrich (K) 63pts, Mirer 54pts

1992 10-1-1

42 Northwestern	7 WR Lake Dawson
17 Michigan	17 WR Ray Griggs / Adrian Jarrell
52 Michigan State	31 T Lindsey Knapp
48 Purdue	0 G Aaron Taylor
16 Stanford	33 C Tim Ruddy
52 Pittsburgh	21 G Todd Norman / Mark Zataveski
42 BYU	16 T Justin Hall
38 Navy	7 TE Irv Smith
54 Boston College	7 QB Rick Mirer
17 Penn State	16 TB Reggie Brooks
31 Southern Cal	23 FB Jerome Bettis / Dean Lytle
28 Texas A&M■	3 DL Devon McDonald
	DL Bryant Young
	DL Jim Flanigan
	DL Brian Hamilton / Germaine Holden
	DL Karmeeleyah McGill
	LB Demetrius DeBose / Pete Bercich
	LB Anthony Peterson
	DB Tom Carter
	DB Greg Lane
	DB Jeff Burris
	DB Bobby Taylor / John Covington (DL)

RUSHING: Brooks 167/1343y, Bettis 154/825y,
  Lee Becton (TB) 68/373y
PASSING: Mirer 120-234/1876y, 15TD, 51.3%
RECEIVING: Dawson 25/462y, Smith 20/262y, Griggs 17/312y
SCORING: Brooks 86pts, Craig Hentrich (K) 74pts, Bettis 72pts

1993 11-1

27 Northwestern	12 WR Clint Johnson / Derrick Mayes
27 Michigan	23 WR Lake Dawson / Mike Miller
36 Michigan State	14 T Aaron Taylor
17 Purdue	0 G Mark Zataveski
48 BYU	20 C Tim Ruddy / Lance Johnson
44 Pittsburgh	0 G Ryan Leahy / Jeremy Akers
45 BYU	20 T Todd Norman
31 Southern Cal	13 TE Pete Chryplewicz / Oscar McBride
58 Navy	27 QB Kevin McDougal
31 Florida State	24 TB Lee Becton
39 Boston College	41 FB Roy Zellars / Marc Edwards
24 Texas A&M ■	21 DL Brian Hamilton
	DL Bryant Young
	DL Jim Flanigan
	DL Oliver Gibson / Thomas Knight
	DL/LB Renaldo Wynn / Bert Berry
	LB Justin Goheen
	LB Pete Bercich
	DB Greg Lane
	DB Bobby Taylor
	DB Jeff Burris
	DB John Covington

RUSHING: Becton 164/1044y, Kinder 89/537y, Zellars 99/494y
PASSING: McDougal 98-159/1541y, 7TD, 61.6%
RECEIVING: Dawson 25/395y, Mayes 24/512y, Miller 19/412y
SCORING: Kevin Pendergast (K) 87pts, Edwards & Zellars 48pts

1994 6-5-1

42 Northwestern	15 WR Derrick Mayes
24 Michigan	26 WR Mike Miller / Charles Stafford
21 Michigan State	20 T Mike McGlinn / Chris Clevenger
39 Purdue	21 G Dusty Zeigler (C) / Jeremy Akers
34 Stanford	15 C Mark Zataveski
11 Boston College	30 G Ryan Leahy / Steve Masetic
14 BYU	21 T Mike Doughty
58 Navy	21 TE Oscar McBride
16 Florida State	23 QB Ron Powlus
42 Air Force	30 TB Lee Becton / Randy Kinder
17 Southern Cal	17 FB Ray Zellars / Marc Edwards
24 Colorado ■	41 DL Brian Hamilton
	DL Oliver Gibson
	DL Paul Grasmanis / Germaine Holden
	LB Bert Berry / Jeremy Nau
	LB Jeremy Sample
	LB Justin Goheen
	LB Renaldo Wynn
	DB Bobby Taylor
	DB Shawn Wooden
	DB Brian Magee
	DB Travis Davis

RUSHING: Kinder 119/702y, Becton 100/550y, Zellars 79/466y
PASSING: Powlus 119-222/1729y, 19TD, 53.6%
RECEIVING: Mayes 47/847y, Stafford 18/254y, Miller 17/276y
SCORING: Mayes 68pts, Stefan Schroffner (K) 48pts, Zellars 30pts

1995 9-3

15 Northwestern	17 WR Derrick Mayes
35 Purdue	28 WR Charles Stafford / Emmett Mosley
41 Vanderbilt	0 T Chris Clevenger
55 Texas	27 G Dusty Ziegler
26 Ohio State	45 C Rick Kaczenski
29 Washington	21 G Ryan Leahy
28 Army	27 T Mike Doughty / Mike Rosenthal
38 Southern Cal	10 TE Pete Chryplewicz
20 Boston College	10 QB Ron Powlus
35 Navy	17 TB Randy Kinder / Autry Denson
44 Air Force	14 FB Marc Edwards
26 Florida State ■	31 DL Renaldo Wynn
	DL Paul Grasmanis
	DL Cory Bennent
	LB Bert Berry
	LB Kinnon Tatum
	LB Lyron Cobbins
	LB Kory Minor
	DB Allen Rossum / Ivory Covington
	DB Shawn Wooden
	DB LaRon Moore
	DB Brian Magee

RUSHING: Kinder 143/809y, Edwards 140/717y, Denson 137/695y
PASSING: Powlus 124-217/1853y, 12TD, 57.1%
RECEIVING: Mayes 48/881y, Edwards 25/361y, Mosley 17/268y
SCORING: Edwards 76pts, Kinder 60pts, Denson 48pts

1996 8-3

14 Vanderbilt	7 WR Malcolm Johnson
35 Purdue	0 WR Emmett Mosley
27 Texas	24 T Chris Clevenger
16 Ohio State	29 G Jeremy Akers / Jerry Wisne
54 Washington	20 C Rick Kaczenski
17 Air Force	20 G Mike Rosenthal / Tim Ridder
54 Navy	27 T Mike Doughty
48 Boston College	13 TE Pete Chryplewicz
60 Pittsburgh	6 QB Ron Powlus
62 Rutgers	0 TB Autry Denson / Robert Farmer
20 Southern Cal	27 FB Marc Edwards / Jaime Spencer
	DL Renaldo Wynn
	DL Alton Maidon
	DL Melvin Dansby / Corey Bennett
	LB Kory Minor
	LB Lyron Cobbins
	LB Kinnon Tatum
	LB Bert Berry
	DB Ivory Covington
	DB Allen Rossum
	DB Jarvis Edison / Deke Cooper
	DB Benny Guilbeaux / A'Jani Sanders

RUSHING: Denson 202/1179y, Farmer 78/660y, Edwards 83/381y
PASSING: Powlus 133-232/1942y, 12TD, 57.3%
RECEIVING: Chryplewicz 27/331y, Johnson 25/449y, Mosley 24/369y
SCORING: Denson 66pts, Edwards 62pts, Jim Sanson (K) 57pts

1997 7-6

17 Georgia Tech	13 WR Malcolm Johnson
17 Purdue	28 WR Bobby Brown / Raki Nelson
7 Michigan State	23 T Mike Doughty
14 Michigan	21 G Mike Rosenthal
15 Stanford	33 C Rick Kaczenski
45 Pittsburgh	21 G Jerry Wisne
17 Southern Cal	20 T Luke Petitgout / Chris Clevenger
52 Boston College	20 TE Jabari Holloway / Tim Ridder
21 Navy	17 QB Ron Powlus
24 LSU	6 TB Autry Denson
21 West Virginia	14 FB Ken Barry / Joey Goodspeed
23 Hawaii	22 DL Melvin Dansby
9 LSU ■	27 DL Corey Bennett / Lance Legree
	DL Brad Williams / Kurt Belisk
	LB Kory Minor
	LB Jimmy Friday
	LB Bobbie Howard / Grant Irons
	LB Lammont Bryant
	DB Allen Rossum / Ty Goode
	DB Ivory Covington
	DB Deveron Harper / Jarvis Edison
	DB Benny Guilbeaux / A'Jani Sanders

RUSHING: Denson 264/1268y, Clement Stokes (TB) 75/344y, Barry 35/186y
PASSING: Powlus 182-298/2078y, 9TD, 61.1%
RECEIVING: Brown 45/543y, Johnson 42/596y, Denson 30/175y
SCORING: Denson 78pts, Brown 36pts, Jim Sanson (K) 30pts

1998 9-3

36 Michigan	20 WR Malcolm Johnson
23 Michigan State	45 WR Bobby Brown / David Givens
31 Purdue	30 T Luke Petitgout
33 Stanford	15 G Jerry Wisne / Mike Gandy
28 Arizona State	9 C John Merandi
20 Army	17 G Tim Ridder
27 Baylor	3 T Mike Rosenthal
31 Boston College	26 TE Jabari Holloway / Dan O'Leary
30 Navy	0 QB Jarious Jackson
39 LSU	36 TB Autry Denson
0 Southern Cal	10 FB Jamie Spencer
28 Georgia Tech ■	35 DL Anthony Weaver
	DL Lance Legree / Antwon Jones
	DL Brad Williams
	LB Kory Minor
	LB Jimmy Friday / Anthony Denman
	LB Bobbie Howard
	LB Lamont Bryant / Grant Irons
	DB Brock Williams / Ty Goode
	DB Deveron Harper
	DB A'Jani Sanders / Deke Cooper
	DB Tony Driver / Benny Guilbeaux

RUSHING: Denson 251/1176y, Jackson 113/441y, Spencer 54/256y
PASSING: Jackson 104-188/1740y, 13TD, 55.3%
RECEIVING: Johnson 43/692y, Holloway 15/262y, Brown 13/286y
SCORING: Denson 90pts, Jim Sanson (K) 64pts, Johnson 38pts

1999 5-7

48 Kansas	13 WR Bobby Brown / David Givens
22 Michigan	26 WR Joey Getherall / Raki Nelson
23 Purdue	28 T Jordan Black / Kurt Vollers
13 Michigan State	23 G Jim Jones
34 Oklahoma	30 C John Merandi
48 Arizona State	17 G Mike Gandy
25 Southern Cal	24 T John Teasdale
28 Navy	24 TE Jabari Holloway
14 Tennessee	38 QB Jarious Jackson
21 Pittsburgh	37 TB Tony Fisher / Julius Jones
29 Boston College	31 FB Joey Goodspeed / Tom Lopienski
37 Stanford	40 DL Grant Irons
	DL Anthony Weaver / Lance Legree
	DL Brad Williams
	DL Lamont Bryant
	LB Joe Ferrer / Rocky Boiman
	LB Ronnie Nicks / Tyreo Harrison
	LB Anthony Denman
	DB Clifford Jefferson
	DB Devaron Harper
	DB Deke Cooper
	DB A'Jani Sanders

RUSHING: Fisher 156/783y, Jackson 140/464y, Jones 75/375y
PASSING: Jackson 184-316/2753y, 17TD, 58.2%
RECEIVING: Brown 36/608y, Getherall 35/436y, Nelson 23/395y
SCORING: Fisher 44pts, Jackson 42pts, Jim Sanson (K) 41pts

2000 9-3

24 Texas A&M	10 WR Javin Hunter / Joey Getherall
24 Nebraska	27 WR David Givens
23 Purdue	21 T Jordan Black
21 Michigan State	27 G Jim Jones
20 Stanford	14 C Jeff Faine
45 Navy	14 G Mike Gandy
42 West Virginia	28 T Kurt Vollers
34 Air Force	31 TE Jabari Holloway / Dan O'Leary
28 Boston College	16 QB Matt LoVecchio / Arnaz Battle
45 Rutgers	17 TB Tony Fisher /J. Jones/Terrance Howard
38 Southern Cal	21 FB Tom Lopienski / Jason Murray
9 Oregon State ■	41 DL Anthony Weaver
	DL B. J. Scott / Andy Wisne
	DL Lance Legree
	DL Ryan Roberts / Grant Irons
	LB Rocky Boiman
	LB Tyreo Harrison
	LB Anthony Denman
	DB Brock Williams / Jason Beckstrom
	DB Shane Walton / Clifford Jefferson
	DB Tony Driver
	DB Ron Israel / Glenn Earl

RUSHING: Jones 162/657y, Fisher 132/607y, Howard 75/424y
PASSING: LoVecchio 73-125/980y, 11TD, 58.4%
RECEIVING: Givens 25/310y, Getherall 17/323y, Hunter 13/256y
SCORING: Nicholas Setta (K) 74pts, Fisher 54pts, Jones 48pts

2001 5-6

10 Nebraska	27 WR Javin Hunter
10 Michigan State	17 WR David Givens / Arnaz Battle
3 Texas A&M	24 T Jordan Black (G) / Brennan Curtin
24 Pittsburgh	7 G Sean Mahan
34 West Virginia	24 C Jeff Faine
27 Southern Cal	16 G Sean Milligan
17 Boston College	21 T Kurt Vollers
18 Tennessee	28 TE John Owens
34 Navy	16 QB Carlyle Holiday / Matt LoVecchio
13 Stanford	17 TB Julius Jones / Tony Fisher
24 Purdue	18 FB Tom Lopienski
	DL Anthony Weaver
	DL Darrell Campbell / Kyle Budinscak
	DL Cedric Hilliard / Andy Wisne
	DL Ryan Roberts / Grant Irons
	LB Rocky Boiman
	LB Tyreo Harrison
	LB Courtney Watson
	DB Vontez Duff / Clifford Jefferson
	DB Shane Walton / Jason Beckstrom
	DB Donald Dykes / Glenn Earl
	DB Ron Israel / Gerome Sapp

RUSHING: Jones 168/718y, Holiday 156/666y, Fisher 78/384y
PASSING: Holiday 73-144/784y, 3TD, 50.7%
RECEIVING: Hunter 37/387y, Givens 33/317y, Jones 9/57y
SCORING: Nicholas Setta (K) 68pts, Jones 42pts, Fisher 26pts

2002 10-3

22 Maryland	0 WR Omar Jenkins / Maurice Stovall
24 Purdue	17 WR Arnaz Battle
25 Michigan	23 T Jordan Black / Jim Molinaro
21 Michigan State	17 G Sean Mahan
31 Stanford	7 C Jeff Faine
14 Pittsburgh	6 G Sean Milligan
21 Air Force	14 T Brennan Curtin
34 Florida State	24 TE Gary Godsey
7 Boston College	14 QB Carlyle Holiday
30 Navy	23 TB Ryan Grant
42 Rutgers	0 FB Tom Lopienski / Rashon Powers-Neal
13 Southern Cal	44 DL Kyle Budinscak / Justin Tuck
6 N. Carolina St.■	28 DL Darrell Campbell
	DL Cedric Hilliard / Greg Pauly
	DL Ryan Roberts
	LB Derek Curry
	LB Mike Goolsby
	LB Courtney Watson / Brandon Hoyte
	DB Vontez Duff
	DB Shane Walton / Preston Jackson
	DB Glenn Earl
	DB Gerome Sapp / Garron Bible

RUSHING: Grant 261/1085y, Powers-Neal 77/333y, Holiday 92/200y
PASSING: Holiday 129-257/1788y, 10TD, 50.2%
RECEIVING: Battle 58/786 y, Jenkins 37/633y, Stovall 18/312 y
SCORING: Nicholas Setta (K) 74pts, Grant 54pts, Battle 32 pts

2003 5-7

29 Washington St.	26 WR Omar Jenkins
0 Michigan	38 WR Rhema McKnight
16 Michigan State	22 T Jim Molinaro
10 Purdue	23 G Mark LeVoir
20 Pittsburgh	14 C Bob Morton
14 Southern Cal	45 G Dan Stevenson / Jamie Ryan
25 Boston College	27 T Ryan Harris
0 Florida State	37 TE Billy Palmer/Jared Clark/Tony Fasano
27 Navy	24 QB Brady Quinn / Carlyle Holiday (WR)
33 BYU	14 TB Julius Jones / Ryan Grant
57 Stanford	7 FB Rashon Powers-Neal / Josh Schmidt
12 Syracuse	38 DL Kyle Budinscik / Victor Abiamiri
	DL Darrell Campbell
	DL Cedric Hilliard / Greg Pauly
	DL Justin Tuck
	LB Derek Curry
	LB Brandon Hoyte
	LB Courtney Watson
	DB Vontez Duff / Jason Beckstrom
	DB Preston Jackson / Dwight Ellick
	DB Quentin Burrell / Glenn Earl
	DB Garron Bible

RUSHING: Jones 229/1268y, Grant 143/510y
PASSING: Quinn 157-332/1831y, 9TD, 47.3%
RECEIVING: McKnight 47/600y, Jenkins 36/344y, Stovall 22/421y
SCORING: Jones 60pts, D.J. Fitzpatrick (K) 53pts, Nicholas Setta (K) 32pts

2004 6-6

17 BYU	20 WR Maurice Stovall / Jeff Samardzija
28 Michigan	20 WR Rhema McKnight / Matt Shelton
31 Michigan State	24 T Ryan Harris
38 Washington	3 G Bob Morton / Dan Santucci
16 Purdue	41 C John Sullivan
23 Stanford	15 G Dan Stevenson
27 Navy	9 T Mark LeVoir
23 Boston College	24 TE Anthony Fasano / Billy Palmer
13 Tennessee	13 TE/FB Marcus Freeman / R. Powers-Neal
38 Pittsburgh	41 QB Brady Quinn
10 Southern Cal	41 RB Ryan Grant / Darius Walker
21 Oregon State■	38 DL Justin Tuck / Victor Abiamiri
	DL Greg Pauly
	DL Derek Landri
	DL Kyle Budinscak
	LB Mike Goolsby
	LB Derek Curry
	LB/DB Brandon Hoyte / Mike Richardson
	DB Dwight Ellick / Carlos Campbell
	DB Preston Jackson / Freddie Parrish
	DB Quentin Burrell
	DB Tom Zbikowski

RUSHING: Walker 185/786y, Grant 127/515y, Marcus Wilson (RB) 35/138y
PASSING: Quinn 191-353/2586y, 17TD, 54.1%
RECEIVING: McKnight 42/610y, Fasano 27/367y, Stovall 21/313y
SCORING: David Fitzpatrick (K) 67pts, Walker 42pts, Shelton 36pts

2005 9-3

42 Pittsburgh	21 WR Maurice Stovall
17 Michigan	10 WR Jeff Samardzija
41 Michigan State	44 T Ryan Harris
36 Washington	17 G Dan Santucci
49 Purdue	28 C John Sullivan / Bob Morton
31 Southern Cal	34 G Dan Stevenson
49 BYU	23 T Mark LeVoir
41 Tennessee	21 TE Anthony Fasano
42 Navy	21 TE/WR John Carlson / Matt Shelton
34 Syracuse	10 QB Brady Quinn
38 Stanford	31 RB Darius Walker
20 Ohio State■	34 DL Victor Abiamiri / Justin Brown
	DL Trevor Laws
	DL Derek Landri
	DL Ronald Talley / Chris Frome
	LB Brandon Hoyte
	LB Corey Mays
	LB Maurice Crum
	DB Ambrose Wooden / Leo Ferrine
	DB Mike Richardson
	DB Chinedum Ndukwe
	DB Tom Zbikowski

RUSHING: Walker 253/1196y, Travis Thomas (RB) 63/248y
PASSING: Quinn 292-450/3919y, 32TD, 64.9%
RECEIVING: Samardzija 77/1249y, Stovall 69/1149y, Fasano 47/576y
SCORING: Samardzija 90pts, D. J. Fitzpatrick (K) 85pts, Walker 68pts

2006 10-3

14 Georgia Tech	10 WR Rhema McKnight/Chase Anastasio
41 Penn State	17 WR Jeff Samardzija
21 Michigan	47 WR/FB David Grimes/Ashley McConnell
40 Michigan State	37 T Ryan Harris
35 Purdue	21 G Dan Santucci
31 Stanford	10 C John Sullivan
20 UCLA	17 G Bob Morton / Brian Mattes
38 Navy	14 T Sam Young
45 North Carolina	26 TE John Carlson / Marcus Freeman
39 Air Force	17 QB Brady Quinn
41 Army	9 RB Darius Walker
24 Southern Cal	44 DL Victor Abiamiri
14 Louisiana St.■	41 DL Trevor Laws
	DL Derek Landri
	DL Chris Frome / Ronald Talley
	LB Joe Brockington / Mitchell Thomas
	LB Maurice Crum
	LB/DB Travis Thomas / Darrin Walls
	DB Terrell Lambert / Ambrose Wooden
	DB Mike Richardson
	DB Chinedum Ndukwe
	DB Tom Zbikowski / Ray Herring

RUSHING: Walker 255/1267y, James Aldridge (RB) 37/142y
PASSING: Quinn 289-467/3426y, 37TD, 61.9%
RECEIVING: Samardzija 78/1017y, McKnight 67/907y, Walker 56/391y
SCORING: McKnight 90pts, Samardzija 78pts, Carl Gioia (K) 73pts

2007 3-9

3 Georgia Tech	33 WR Duval Kamara / Robby Parris
10 Penn State	31 WR David Grimes / George West
0 Michigan	38 T Sam Young
14 Michigan State	91 G Mike Turkovich
19 Purdue	33 C John Sullivan / Dan Wenger (G)
20 UCLA	6 G Eric Olsen / Matt Carufel
14 Boston College	27 T Paul Duncan
0 Southern Cal	38 TE John Carlson / Will Yeatman
44 Navy	46 QB Jimmy Clausen / Evan Sharpley
24 Air Force	41 RB James Aldridge / Armando Allen
28 Duke	7 FB Asaph Schwapp / Junior Jabbie
21 Stanford	14 DL Trevor Laws
	DL Pat Kuntz / Ian Williams
	DL Justin Brown / Dwight Stephenson
	LB John Ryan / Kerry Neal
	LB Maurice Crum
	LB Joe Brockington
	LB Brian Smith / Anthony Vernaglia
	DB Darrin Walls / Ambrose Wooden
	DB Terrell Laimbert
	DB David Bruton / Kyle McCarthy
	DB Tom Zbikowski

RUSHING: Aldridge 121/463y, Allen 86/348y, Robert Hughes (RB) 53/294y
PASSING: Clausen 138-245/1254y, 7TD, 56.3%, Sharpley 77-140/736y, 5TD, 55%
RECEIVING: Carlson 40/372y, Kamara 32/357y, Parris 29/361y
SCORING: Brandon Walker (K) 40pts, Travis Thomas (RB) 30pts, Hughes & Kamara 24pts

2008 7-6

21 San Diego State	13 WR Golden Tate
35 Michigan	17 WR Michael Floyd / David Grimes
7 Michigan State	23 WR/TE Duval Kamara / Wil Yeatman
38 Purdue	21 T Michael Turkovich
28 Stanford	21 G Eric Olsen
24 North Carolina	29 C Dan Wenger
33 Washington	7 G Chris Stewart / Trevor Robinson
33 Pittsburgh	36 T Sam Young
0 Boston College	17 TE Kyle Rudolph
27 Navy	21 QB Jimmy Clausen
23 Syracuse	24 RB Armando Allen / Robert Hughes
3 Southern Cal	38 DL Justin Brown / Ethan Johnson
49 Hawaii■	21 DL Pat Kuntz
	DL Ian Williams / John Ryan
	LB Kerry Neal / Darius Fleming
	LB Brian Smith / Toryan Smith
	LB Maurice Crum, Jr. / Steve Quinn
	LB/DB Harrison Smith / Sergio Brown
	DB Terrail Lambert / Robert Blanton
	DB Raeshon McNeil
	DB David Bruton
	DB Kyle McCarthy

RUSHING: Allen 134/585y, Hughes 112/382y, James Aldridge (RB) 91/357y
PASSING: Clausen 268-440/3172y, 25TD, 60.9%
RECEIVING: Tate 58/1080y, Floyd 48/719y, Allen 50/355y
SCORING: Brandon Walker (K) 81pts, Tate 66pts, Floyd 42pts

2009 6-6

35 Nevada	0 WR Michael Floyd / Robby Parris
34 Michigan	38 WR Golden Tate
33 Michigan State	30 WR Duval Kamara / John Goodman
24 Purdue	21 T Paul Duncan
37 Washington	30 G Chris Stewart
27 Southern Cal	34 C Eric Olsen
20 Boston College	16 G Trevor Robinson / Dan Wenger
40 Washington St.	14 T Sam Young
21 Navy	23 TE Kyle Rudolph / Mike Ragone
22 Pittsburgh	27 QB Jimmy Clausen
30 Connecticut	33 RB Armando Allen / Robert Hughes
38 Stanford	45 DL Kapron Lewis-Moore
	DL Ethan Johnson
	DL Ian Williams
	DL John Ryan / Kerry Neal (LB)
	LB Manti Te'o / Darius Fleming (DL)
	LB Brian Smith / Toryan Smith
	LB Harrison Smith (DB) / Scott Smith
	DB Robert Blanton / Gary Gray
	DB Darrin Walls
	DB Sergio Brown
	DB Kyle McCarthy

RUSHING: Allen 142/697y, Hughes 88/416y, Tate 25/186y
PASSING: Clausen 289-425/3722y, 28TD, 68.0%
RECEIVING: Tate 93/1496y, Floyd 44/795y, Rudolph 33/364y, Allen 28/216y, Parris 25/227y
SCORING: Tate 108pts, Nick Tausch (K) 69pts, Floyd 54pts

2010 8-5

23 Purdue	12 WR Theo Riddick / John Goodman
24 Michigan	28 WR Michael Floyd / Robby Toma
31 Michigan State	34 WR T.J. Jones / Duval Kumara
14 Stanford	37 T Zack Martin
31 Boston College	13 G Chris Stewart
23 Pittsburgh	7 C Braxston Cave
44 W. Michigan	20 G Trevor Robinson
17 Navy	35 T Taylor Dever / Matt Romine
27 Tulsa	28 TE Tyler Eifert / Kyle Rudolph
28 Utah	3 QB Dayne Crist / Tommy Rees
27 Army	3 RB Armando Allen / Cierre Wood
20 Southern Cal	16 DL Ethan Johnson / Hafis Williams
33 Miami■	17 DL Ian Williams / Sean Cwynar
	DL Kapron Lewis-Moore
	LB Darius Fleming / Prince Shembo
	LB Carlo Calabrese / Brian Smith
	LB Manti Te'o
	LB Kerry Neal / Steve Filer
	DB Darrin Walls / Robert Blanton
	DB Gary Gray
	DB Harrison Smith
	DB Zeke Motta / Jamoris Slaughter

RUSHING: Wood 119/603y, Allen 107/514y, Robert Hughes (RB) 68/300y
PASSING: Crist 174-294/2033y, 15TD, 59.2%, Rees 100-164/1106y, 12TD, 61%
RECEIVING: Floyd 79/1025y, Riddick 40/414y, Rudolph 28/328y
SCORING: David Ruffer (K) 91pts, Floyd 72pts, Wood 30pts

OHIO STATE

The Ohio State University (Founded 1870)
Columbus, Ohio
Nickname: Buckeyes
Colors: Scarlet and Gray
Stadium: Ohio (1922) 102,329
Conference Affiliation: Big Ten (1913-present)

CAREER RUSHING YARDS	Attempts	Yards
Archie Griffin (1972-75)	924	5589
Eddie George (1992-95)	683	3768
Tim Spencer (1979-82)	644	3553
Chris Wells (2006-08)	585	3382
Keith Byars (1982-85)	619	3200
Pepe Pearson (1994-97)	659	3121
Carlos Snow (1987-89, 91)	610	2974
Michael Wiley (1996-99)	509	2951
Antonio Pittman (2004-06)	557	2945
Raymont Harris (1990-93)	574	2649

CAREER PASSING YARDS	Comp.-Att.	Yards
Art Schlichter (1978-81)	497-951	7547
Bobby Hoying (1992-95)	498-858	7232
Joe Germaine (1996-98)	439-741	6370
Greg Frey (1987-92)	443-835	6316
Terrelle Pryor (2008-10)	477-783	6177
Steve Bellisari (1998-2001)	286-759	5878
Troy Smith (2003-06)	420-670	5720
Mike Tomczak (1981-84)	376-675	5569
Jim Karsatos (1983-86)	359-629	5089
Craig Krenzel (2000-03)	329-579	4493

CAREER RECEIVING YARDS	Catches	Yards
Michael Jenkins (2000-03)	165	2898
David Boston (1996-98)	191	2855
Gary Williams (1979-82)	154	2792
Cris Carter (1984-86)	168	2725
Santonio Holmes (2003-05)	140	2295
Doug Donley (1977-80)	106	2252
Dee Miller (1995-98)	132	2090
Ted Ginn (2004-06)	135	1943
Joey Galloway (1991-94)	108	1894
Brian Robiskie (2005-08)	127	1866

SEASON RUSHING YARDS	Attempts	Yards
Eddie George (1995)	328	1927
Keith Byars (1984)	336	1764
Archie Griffin (1974)	256	1695
Chris Wells (2007)	274	1609
Archie Griffin (1973)	247	1577

SEASON PASSING YARDS	Comp.-Att.	Yards
Joe Germaine (1998)	230-384	3330
Bobby Hoying (1995)	211-341	3269
Terrelle Pryor (2010)	210-323	2772
Art Schlichter (1981)	183-350	2551
Troy Smith (2006)	203-311	2542

SEASON RECEIVING YARDS	Catches	Yards
David Boston (1998)	85	1435
Terry Glenn (1995)	64	1411
Cris Carter (1986)	69	1127
Michael Jenkins (2002)	61	1076
Dee Miller (1997)	58	981

GAME RUSHING YARDS	Attempts	Yards
Eddie George (1995 vs. Illinois)	36	314
Keith Byars (1984 vs. Illinois)	39	274
Archie Griffin (1973 vs. Iowa)	30	246

GAME PASSING YARDS	Comp.-Att.	Yards
Art Schlichter (1981 vs. Florida State)	31-52	458
Joe Germaine (1997 vs. Penn State)	29-43	378
Greg Frey (1989 vs. Minnesota)	20-31	362

GAME RECEIVING YARDS	Catches	Yards
Terry Glenn (1995 vs. Pittsburgh)	9	253
Santonio Holmes (2004 vs. Marshall)	10	224
Gary Williams (1981 vs. Florida State)	13	220

GREATEST COACH:

Ohio State has had some great coaches, but there truly is only one. That would be Woodrow Wayne "Woody" Hayes, the Buckeye mentor with the most wins under his belt at 205. At the time of Hayes' departure from Ohio State at the end of 1978, his win total (including 33 he earned at Denison and Miami of Ohio) stood as fourth highest behind Amos Alonzo Stagg (314), Pop Warner (313), and Bear Bryant (284).

Hayes won or shared 12 Big Ten titles in his 28 seasons at the helm of the Scarlet-and-Gray. He also earned at least a share of the national championships voted by media or coaches in 1954, 1957, and 1968.

OHIO STATE'S 55 GREATEST SINCE 1953

OFFENSE

WIDE RECEIVER: David Boston, Cris Carter, Joey Galloway, Terry Glenn, Michael Jenkins
TIGHT END: Doug France, John Frank
TACKLE: John Hicks, Orlando Pace, Kurt Schumacher, Jim Tyrer
GUARD: Ken Fritz, Jim Lachey, Jim Parker
CENTER: LeCharles Bentley
QUARTERBACK: Bobby Hoying, Rex Kern, Art Schlichter, Troy Smith
RUNNING BACK: Keith Byars, Eddie George, Archie Griffin
FULLBACK: Bob Ferguson, Pete Johnson, Jim Otis, Bob White

DEFENSE

END: Bob Brudzinski, Jim Houston, Will Smith, Mike Vrabel
TACKLE: Pete Cusick, Quinn Pitcock, Dan Wilkinson
NOSE GUARD: Jim Stillwagon
LINEBACKER: Tom Cousineau, Randy Gradishar, A.J. Hawk, Thomas "Pepper" Johnson, James Laurinaitis, Marcus Marek, Chris Spielman, Steve Tovar
CORNER BACK: Tim Anderson, Neal Colzie, Ted Provost, Shawn Springs, Antoine Winfield
SAFETY: Mike Doss, Tim Fox, Jack Tatum

SPECIAL TEAMS

RETURN SPECIALST: Ted Ginn
PLACE KICKER: Mike Nugent
PUNTER: Tom Tupa

MULTIPLE POSITIONS

HALFBACK-END: Paul Warfield

TWO-WAY PLAYER

HALFBACK-CORNERBACK: Howard "Hopalong" Cassady

PERFORMANCE FORMULA:
OHIO STATE'S 10 BEST SEASONS

2002	1.7588	1 of 70
1996	1.7332	3 of 70
1954	1.7278	2 of 69
1998	1.7269	2 of 71
1968	1.7198	1 of 70
1975	1.7158	1 of 70
2006	1.7135	1 of 72
2010	1.6989	3 of 71
1973	1.6964	5 of 70
2005	1.6423	5 of 70

OHIO STATE BUCKEYES

Year	W-L-T	AP Poll	Conference Standing	Toughest Regular Season Opponents	Coach (Record at School)	Bowl Games		
1953	6-3		4	Illinois 7-1-1, Wisconsin 6-2-1, Michigan State 8-1, Michigan 6-3	Woodrow W. "Woody" Hayes			
1954	10-0	1	1	Iowa 5-4, Wisconsin 7-2, Purdue 5-3-1, Michigan 6-3	Woody Hayes	Rose	20 Southern California	7
1955	7-2	5	1	Stanford 6-3-1, Duke 7-2-1, Michigan 7-2	Woody Hayes			
1956	6-3	15	4t	Penn State 6-2-1, Iowa 8-1, Michigan 7-2	Woody Hayes			
1957	9-1	2	1	TCU 5-4-1, Wisconsin 6-3, Iowa 7-1-1, Michigan 5-3-1	Woody Hayes			
1958	6-1-2	8	3	Indiana 5-3-1, Wisconsin 7-1-1, Purdue 6-1-2, Iowa 7-1-1	Woody Hayes			
1959	3-5-1		8t	Southern California 8-2, Illinois 5-3-1, Purdue 5-2-2, Wisconsin 7-2	Woody Hayes			
1960	7-2	8	3	Michigan State 6-2-1, Iowa 8-1, Michigan 5-4	Woody Hayes			
1961	8-0-1	2	1	TCU 3-5-2, UCLA 7-3, Wisconsin 6-3, Michigan 6-3	Woody Hayes			
1962	6-3		3t	Northwestern 7-2, Wisconsin 8-1, Oregon 6-3-1	Woody Hayes			
1963	5-3-1		2t	Illinois 7-1-1, Southern Calif. 7-3, Penn State 7-3, Northwestern 5-4	Woody Hayes			
1964	7-2	9	2	Illinois 6-3, Southern Calif. 7-3, Michigan 8-1	Woody Hayes			
1965	7-2	11+	2	Illinois 6-4, Michigan State 10-0, Minnesota 5-4-1	Woody Hayes			
1966	4-5		6	Washington 6-4, Michigan State 9-0-1, Michigan 6-4	Woody Hayes			
1967	6-3		4	Purdue 8-2, Illinois 4-6, Michigan 4-6	Woody Hayes			
1968	10-0	1	1	SMU 7-3, Purdue 8-2, Michigan 8-2	Woody Hayes	Rose	27 Southern California	16
1969	8-1	4	1t	Minnesota 4-5-1, Purdue 8-2, Michigan 8-2	Woody Hayes			
1970	9-1	5	1	Duke 6-5, Northwestern 6-4, Michigan 9-1	Woody Hayes	Rose	17 Stanford	27
1971	6-4		3t	Colorado 9-2, Michigan State 6-5, Northwestern 7-4, Michigan 11-0	Woody Hayes			
1972	9-2	9	1t	North Carolina 10-1, Michigan State 5-5-1, Michigan 10-1	Woody Hayes	Rose	17 Southern California	42
1973	10-0-1	2	1t	Minnesota 7-4, Michigan 10-0-1	Woody Hayes	Rose	42 Southern California	21
1974	10-2	4	1t	SMU 6-4-1, Wisconsin 7-4, Michigan State 7-3-1, Michigan 10-1	Woody Hayes	Rose	17 Southern California	18
1975	11-1	4	1	Michigan State 7-4, Penn State 9-2, UCLA 8-2-1, Michigan 8-2-1	Woody Hayes	Rose	10 UCLA	23
1976	9-2-1	6	1t	Penn State 7-4, UCLA 9-1-1, Michigan 10-1	Woody Hayes	Orange	27 Colorado	10
1977	9-3	11	1t	Minnesota 7-4, Oklahoma 10-1, Michigan 10-1	Woody Hayes	Sugar	6 Alabama	35
1978	7-4-1		4	Penn State 11-0, Purdue 8-2-1, Michigan 10-1	Woody Hayes (205-61-10)	Gator	15 Clemson	17
1979	11-1	4	1	Syracuse 6-5, Indiana 7-4, Michigan 8-3	Earle Bruce	Rose	16 Southern California	17
1980	9-3	15	2t	Arizona State 7-4, UCLA 9-2, Michigan 9-2	Earle Bruce	Fiesta	19 Penn State	31
1981	9-3	15	1t	Wisconsin 7-4, Illinois 7-4, Michigan 8-3	Earle Bruce	Liberty	31 Navy	28
1982	9-3	12	2	Florida State 8-3, Illinois 7-4, Michigan 8-3	Earle Bruce	Holiday	47 BYU	17
1983	9-3	9	4	Oklahoma 8-4, Iowa 9-2, Illinois 10-1, Michigan 9-2	Earle Bruce	Fiesta	28 Pittsburgh	23
1984	9-3	13	1	Iowa 7-4-1, Purdue 7-4, Illinois 7-4, Wisconsin 7-3-1	Earle Bruce	Rose	17 Southern California	20
1985	9-3	14	4t	Colorado 7-4, Iowa 10-1, Michigan 9-1-1	Earle Bruce	Citrus	10 BYU	7
1986	10-3	7	1t	Alabama 9-3, Washington 8-2-1, Iowa 8-3, Michigan 11-1	Earle Bruce	Cotton	28 Texas A&M	12
1987	6-4-1		5	LSU 9-1-1, Indiana 8-3, Michigan St. 8-2-1, Iowa 9-3, Michigan 7-4	Earle Bruce (81-26-1)			
1988	4-6-1		7	Syracuse 9-2, LSU 8-3, Indiana 7-3-1, Iowa 6-3-3, Michigan 8-2-1	John Cooper			
1989	8-4	24	3t	Southern California 8-2-1, Illinois 9-2, Michigan 10-1	John Cooper	Hall of Fame	14 Auburn	31
1990	7-4-1		5	Southern California 8-3-1, Illinois 8-3, Iowa 8-3, Michigan 8-3	John Cooper	Liberty	11 Air Force	23
1991	8-4		3t	Illinois 6-5, Iowa 10-1, Indiana 6-4-1, Michigan 10-1	John Cooper	Hall of Fame	17 Syracuse	24
1992	8-3-1	18	2	Syracuse 9-2, Illinois 6-4-1, Michigan 8-0-3	John Cooper	Citrus	14 Georgia	21
1993	10-1-1	11	1t	Penn State 9-2, Wisconsin 9-1-1, Indiana 8-3, Michigan 7-4	John Cooper	Holiday	28 BYU	21
1994	9-4	14	2	Washington 7-4, Penn State 11-0, Michigan 7-4	John Cooper	Citrus	17 Alabama	24
1995	11-2	6	2	Washington 7-3-1, Notre Dame 9-2, Penn State 8-3, Michigan 9-3	John Cooper	Citrus	14 Tennessee	20
1996	11-1	2	1	Notre Dame 9-3, Penn State 10-2, Iowa 8-3, Michigan 8-3	John Cooper	Rose	20 Arizona State	17
1997	10-3	12	2t	Iowa 7-4, Penn State 9-2, Michigan State 7-4, Michigan 11-0	John Cooper	Sugar	14 Florida State	31
1998	11-1	2	1t	West Virginia 8-3, Penn State 8-3, Michigan 9-3	John Cooper	Sugar	24 Texas A&M	14
1999	6-6		8t	Wisconsin 9-2, Penn State 9-3, Michigan State 9-2, Michigan 9-2	John Cooper			
2000	8-4		4	Wisconsin 8-4, Purdue 8-3, Michigan 8-3	John Cooper (111-43-4)	Outback	7 South Carolina	24
2001	7-5		3	UCLA 7-4, Illinois 10-1, Michigan 8-3	Jim Tressel	Outback	28 South Carolina	31
2002	14-0	1	1	Texas Tech 8-5, Washington St. 10-2, Penn St. 9-3, Michigan 9-3	Jim Tressel	Fiesta	31 Miami	24
2003	11-2	4	2t	Iowa 9-3, Michigan Sate 8-4, Purdue 9-3, Michigan 10-2	Jim Tressel	Fiesta	35 Kansas State	28
2004	8-4	20	2t	Wisconsin 9-2, Iowa 10-1, Michigan 9-2	Jim Tressel	Alamo	33 Oklahoma State	7
2005	10-2	4	1t	Texas 12-0, Iowa 7-4, Penn St. 10-1, No'western 7-4, Michigan 7-4	Jim Tressel	Fiesta	34 Notre Dame	20
2006	12-1	2	1	Texas 9-3, Penn State 8-4, Michigan 11-1	Jim Tressel	BCS Title	14 Florida	41
2007	11-2	5	1	Penn State 8-4, Wisconsin 9-3, Illinois 9-3, Michigan 8-4	Jim Tressel	BCS Title	24 Louisiana State	38
2008	10-3	9	1t	Southern California 11-1, Michigan State 9-3, Penn State 11-1	Jim Tressel	Fiesta	21 Texas	24
2009	11-2	5	1	Southern California 8-4, Wisconsin 9-3, Penn State 10-2, Iowa 10-2	Jim Tressel	Rose	26 Oregon	17
2010	12-1	5	1t	Wisconsin 11-1, Penn State 7-5, Iowa 7-5	Jim Tressel (106-22)	Sugar	31 Arkansas	26

| TOTAL: | | 493-146-13 .7661 (1 of 70) | | | Bowl Games since 1953: | | 18-21 .4615 (45 of 70) | |

GREATEST TEAM SINCE 1953: Considering Ohio State has won national championships in 1954, 1957, 1968, and 2002, it may come as a surprise that Woody Hayes' 1973 10-0-1 team gets the nod as the Buckeyes' best. The 1973 squad, led by Brian Baschnagel, Cornelius Greene, Archie Griffin, John Hicks, and Greg Schumacher on offense and Neal Colzie, Pete Cusick, Tim Fox, and Randy Gradishar on defense, surged through its first eight opponents by a 361-26 point differential. Next came a stunning 10-10 deadlock with Michigan in Ann Arbor which seemed to ruin everything. But, in a surprise conference vote, the Buckeyes were sent to the Rose Bowl where they scored their largest Pasadena victory by 42-21 over Southern California.

1953 6-3

36	Indiana	12
33	California	19
20	Illinois	41
12	Pennsylvania	6
20	Wisconsin	19
27	Northwestern	13
13	Michigan State	28
21	Purdue	6
0	Michigan	20

12 E Dean Dugger / Tom Hague
19 T George Jacoby / Jim Schumacher
41 G Mike Takacs / Robert Roberts
6 C Ken Vargo / Bob Thornton
19 G Jim Reichenbach
13 T Don Swartz / Francis Machinsky
28 E Bob Joslin / Dick Brubaker
6 QB John Borton / Dave Leggett (FB)
20 HB Howard "Hopalong" Cassady
HB Jerry Harkrader / Carroll Howell
FB Bobby Watkins (HB) / George Rosso

RUSHING: Watkins 153/875y, Cassady 86/514y,
Leggett 69/104y
PASSING: Borton 45-86/522y, 4TD, 52.2%
Leggett 35-81/468y, 2TD, 43.2%
RECEIVING: Hague 19/275y, Cassady 16/273y, Dugger 11/139y
SCORING: Watkins 66pts, Cassady 48pts, Hague (E-K) 28pts,
Thurlow "Tad" Weed (K) 16pts

1954 10-0

28	Indiana	0
21	California	13
40	Illinois	7
20	Iowa	14
31	Wisconsin	14
14	Northwestern	7
26	Pittsburgh	0
28	Purdue	6
21	Michigan	7
20	Southern Cal■	7

0 E Dean Dugger / Bill Michael
13 T Dick Hilinski
7 G Jim Parker
14 C Ken Vargo / Bob Thornton
14 G Jim Reichenbach / Dave Weaver
7 T Frank Machinsky / Jerry Krisher
0 E Dick Brubaker / Fred Kriss
6 QB Dave Leggett
7 HB Hopalong Cassady / Jerry Harkrader
7 HB Bobby Watkins / Jim Roseboro
FB Hubert Bobo / Jack Gibbs

RUSHING: Cassady 123/701y, Watkins 119/660y, Bobo 69/401y,
Leggett 116/302y
PASSING: Leggett 52-106/643y, 8TD, 49.1%
RECEIVING: Cassady 13/148y, Brubaker 12/120y, Dugger 9/144y,
Watkins 8/93y
SCORING: Watkins (HB-K) 64pts, Cassady 48pts,
Thurlow "Tad" Weed (K) 27pts, Leggett 24pts

1955 7-2

28	Nebraska	20
0	Stanford	6
27	Illinois	12
14	Duke	20
26	Wisconsin	16
49	Northwestern	0
20	Indiana	13
20	Iowa	10
17	Michigan	0

20 E Bill Michael / Tom Spears
6 T Francis Machinsky
12 G Jim Parker
20 C Ken Vargo
16 G Aurealius Thomas
0 T Richard Guy / Don Stoeckel
13 E Leo Brown / Fred Kriss
10 QB Frank Ellwood / Bill Booth
0 HB Hopalong Cassady
HB James Roseboro / Jerry Harkrader
FB Don Vicic / Galen Cisco

RUSHING: Cassady 161/958y, Roseboro 62/379y, Vicic 63/269y
PASSSING: Ellwood 9-23/60y, 2TD, 39.1%
RECEIVING: Michael 4/50y, Roseboro 3/40y, 3 with 2
SCORING: Cassady 90pts, Ellwood 30pts, Kriss 29pts

1956 6-3

34	Nebraska	7
32	Stanford	10
26	Illinois	6
6	Penn State	7
21	Wisconsin	0
6	Northwestern	2
35	Indiana	14
0	Iowa	6
0	Michigan	19

7 E Bill Michael / Fred Kriss
10 T John Martin / Dick Schafrath
6 G Jim Parker / Tom Baldacci
7 C Tom Dillman
0 G Aurealius Thomas
2 T Richard Guy
14 E Leo Brown
6 QB Frank Ellwood
19 HB Don Clark / Don Sutherin
HB James Roseboro
FB Galen Cisco / Don Vicic

RUSHING: Clark 139/797y, Roseboro 152/712y, Cisco 64/438y
PASSING: Ellwood 7-20/86y, 4TD, 35.0%,
Clark 3-7/88y, TD, 42.9%
RECEIVING: Brown 8/151y, Roseboro 4/82y, Cisco 2/18y
SCORING: Clark & Roseboro 42pts, Ellwood 39pts

1957 9-1

14	TCU	18
35	Washington	7
21	Illinois	7
56	Indiana	0
16	Wisconsin	13
47	Northwestern	6
20	Purdue	7
17	Iowa	13
31	Michigan	14
10	Oregon■	7

18 E Jim Houston / Russ Bowermaster
7 T Dick Schafrath
7 G Bill Jobko / Tom Baldacci
0 C Dan Fronk
13 G Aurealius Thomas
6 T Jim Marshall / Al Crawford
7 E Leo Brown / Tom Morgan
13 QB Frank Kremblas
14 HB Don Clark / Don Sutherin
7 HB Dick LeBeau / Joe Cannavino
FB Bob White / Galen Cisco

RUSHING: Clark 132/737y, White 114/645y, LeBeau 85/360y
PASSING: Kremblas 20-47/337y, 3TD, 42.5%
RECEIVING: LeBeau 7/91y, Brown 7/83y, Clark 5/63y
SCORING: Kremblas (QB-K) 55pts, Clark 54pts, LeBeau 48pts

1958 6-1-2

23	SMU	20
12	Washington	7
19	Illinois	13
49	Indiana	8
7	Wisconsin	7
0	Northwestern	21
14	Purdue	14
38	Iowa	28
20	Michigan	14

20 E Jim Houston / Sam Tidmore
7 T Jim Tyrer / Al Crawford
13 G Dan James / Oscar Hauer
8 C Dan Fronk
7 G Ernie Wright
21 T Jim Marshall / Birtho Arnold
14 E Dick Schafrath / Russ Bowermaster
28 QB Frank Kremblas / Jerry Fields
14 HB Don Clark / Jim Herbstreit
HB Dick LeBeau / Tom Matte
FB Bob White

RUSHING: White 218/859y, Clark 114/582y, Kremblas 56/219y
PASSING: Kremblas 16-42/281y, 0TD, 38.1%
RECEIVING: Clark 8/110y, LeBeau 8/110y, Houston 4/127y
SCORING: White 72pts, Clark 36pts, David Kilgore (K) 18pts

1959 3-5-1

14	Duke	13
0	Southern Cal	17
0	Illinois	9
15	Purdue	0
3	Wisconsin	12
30	Michigan State	24
0	Indiana	0
7	Iowa	16
14	Michigan	23

13 E Tom Perdue / Charles Bryant
17 T Rich Michael
9 G Mike Ingram / Don Young
0 C Dick Anders / Jene Watkins
12 G Ernie Wright / Gabe Hartman
24 T Jim Tyrer
0 E Jim Houston
16 QB Tom Matte (HB) / Jerry Fields
23 HB Bob Ferguson / Bill Wentz
HB Ronnie Houck / Jim Herbstreit
FB Bob White / Roger Detrick

RUSHING: Ferguson 61/371y, White 96/312y, Detrick 55/231y
PASSING: Matte 28-51/439y, 4TD, 54.9%,
Fields 20-53/260y, TD, 37.7%
RECEIVING: Houston 11/214y, Bryant 11/153y, Perdue 7/74y
SCORING: David Kilgore (K) 19pts, Houston 18pts

1960 7-2

24	SMU	0
20	Southern Cal	0
34	Illinois	7
21	Purdue	24
34	Wisconsin	7
21	Michigan State	10
36	Indiana	7
12	Iowa	35
7	Michigan	0

0 E Charles Bryant / Tom Perdue
0 T Alan Fiers / Bob Vogel
7 G Donald Young / Oscar Hauer
24 C Bill Armstrong / Gary Moeller (LB)
7 G Gabe Hartman / Mike Ingram (LB)
10 T Jim Tyrer / Daryl Sanders
7 E Bob Middleton / Sam Tidmore
35 QB Tom Matte / Bill Mrukowski
0 HB Bill Wentz / Ed Ulmer / Jim Herbstreit
HB Bob Klein / Bill Hess / Ron Houck
FB Bob Ferguson / Roger Detrick

RUSHING: Ferguson 160/853y, Matte 161/682y, Detrick 55/235y
PASSING: Matte 50-95/737y, 8TD, 52.6%
RECEIVING: Bryant 17/336y, Klein 10/110y, Middleton 7/104y
SCORING: Ferguson 78pts, Klein 32pts, Ben Jones (K) 25pts

1961 8-0-1

7	TCU	7
13	UCLA	3
44	Illinois	0
10	Northwestern	0
30	Wisconsin	21
29	Iowa	13
16	Indiana	7
22	Oregon	12
50	Michigan	20

7 E Charles Bryant / Tom Perdue
3 T Bob Vogel / George Tolford
7 G Tom Jenkins / Mike Ingram (LB)
0 C Bill Armstrong / Gary Moeller (LB)
21 G Rod Foster/Larry Stephens/Wes Mirick
7 T Daryl Sanders / Jack Roberts
7 E Bob Middleton / Ormonde Ricketts
12 QB J. Mummey /J. Sparma /B. Mrukowski
20 HB Paul Warfield / Ron Houck / Bill Hess
HB Matt Snell / Bob Klein / Ed Ulmer
FB Bob Ferguson / Dave Tingley

RUSHING: Ferguson 202/938y, Warfield 77/420y,
Mummey 69/392y
PASSING: Mrukowski 23-35/231y, TD, 65.7%
Sparma 16-38/341y, 6TD, 42.1%,
Mummey 6-14/106y, TD, 42.9%
RECEIVING: Bryant 15/270y, Warfield 9/120y, Middleton 6/52y
SCORING: Ferguson 68pts, Warfield 36pts, D.V'R'ph'st (K) 35pts

1962 6-3

41	North Carolina	7
7	UCLA	9
51	Illinois	15
14	Northwestern	18
14	Wisconsin	7
14	Iowa	28
10	Indiana	7
26	Oregon	7
28	Michigan	0

7 E Ormonde Ricketts / Bill Spahr
9 T Bob Vogel / Ed Orazen
15 G Tom Jenkins / Al Parker
18 C Bill Armstrong / Gary Moeller (LB)
7 G Rod Foster /Wayne Betz /Ray Krstolic
28 T Daryl Sanders / Dan Porretta
7 E Bob Middleton / Matt Snell
7 QB B. Mrukowski/J. Mummey/J. Sparma
0 HB Paul Warfield/Bob Scott/Arn'd Chonko
HB Bob Klein / Bill Hess / Don Harkins
FB D've Francis/B. Butts/D. Katterhenrich

RUSHING: Francis 119/624y, Mummey 66/370y,
Warfield 57/367y
PASSING: Sparma 30-71/288y, 2TD, 42.2%
Mrukowski 7-18/42y, 0TD, 38.9%
RECEIVING: Ricketts 9/79y, Warfield 8/139y, Snell 8/66y
SCORING: Francis 42pts, Dick VanRaaphorst (K) 25pts

1963 5-3-1

17	Texas A&M	0
21	Indiana	0
20	Illinois	20
3	Southern Cal	32
13	Wisconsin	10
7	Iowa	3
7	Penn State	10
8	Northwestern	17
14	Michigan	10

0 E Greg Lashutka / Bill Spahr
0 T Jim Davidson/Ed Oraz'n/B'rnie Stanley
20 G Tom Jenkins / Tom Bugel
32 C Tom Federle / Dwight Kelley (LB)
10 G Dan Porretta / Bill Ridder
3 T Doug Van Horn / Charles Mamula
10 E Ormonde Ricketts / Tom Kienfuss
17 QB Don Unverferth / Arnold Chonko (DB)
10 HB Paul Warfield (E) / Tom Barrington
HB Tyrone Barnett / Don Harkins
FB Matt Snell / Will Sander /Steve Dreffer

RUSHING: Snell 134/491y, Barrington 61/264y, Warfield 62/260y
PASSING: Unverferth 48-117/586y, 4TD, 41.0%
RECEIVING: Warfield 22/266y, Spahr 7/97y, Ricketts 7/72y
SCORING: Dick VanRaaphorst (K) 34pts, Snell 30pts,
Warfield 24pts

1964 7-2

27	SMU	8
17	Indiana	9
26	Illinois	0
17	Southern Cal	0
28	Wisconsin	3
21	Iowa	19
0	Penn State	27
10	Northwestern	0
0	Michigan	10

8 E Bob Stock / Bill Spahr
9 T Jim Davidson / Ed Orazen
0 G Ted Andrick / Ray Pryor / Tom Bugel
0 C Tom Federle / Dwight Kelley (LB)
3 G Dan Porretta / Bill Ridder
19 T D'g Van Horn/Gary Miller/G'r'd Kasunic
27 E John Palmer / Greg Lashutka
0 QB Don Unverferth / Arnold Chonko (DB)
10 HB Tom Barrington / John Fill / Jim Nein
HB Bo Rein / Don Harkins
FB Will Sander/Steve Dreffer/D'g Drenik

RUSHING: Sander 147/626y, Rein 73/281y, Barrington 66/206y
PASSING: Unverferth 73-160/871y, 4TD, 45.6%
RECEIVING: Rein 22/320y, Stock 18/215y, Lashutka 12/136y
SCORING: Sander 42pts, Robert Funk (K) 38pts, Rein 18pts

1965 7-2

3	North Carolina	14
23	Washington	21
28	Illinois	14
7	Michigan State	32
20	Wisconsin	10
11	Minnesota	10
17	Indiana	10
38	Iowa	0
9	Michigan	7

14 E Billy Anders
21 T Mike Current
14 G Ted Andrick
32 C Ray Pryor
10 G Doug Van Horn (T-DT) / Bill Eachus
10 T Dick Anderson
10 E Greg Lashutka
0 QB Don Unverferth
7 HB Tom Barrington (FB)
HB Bo Rein / Nelson Adderley
FB Will Sander
DL Jim Baas
DL Gary Miller
DL Bill Ridder
DL Larry Snyder
DL Dick Himes
LB Tom Bugel
LB John McCoy
LB Dwight Kelley
DB John Fill
DB Stan Hamlin
DB Bob Walden / Tom Portsmouth

RUSHING: Barrington 139/554y, Sander 134/530y, Rein 38/201y
PASSING: Unverferth 99-191/1061y, 4TD, 51.8%
RECEIVING: Rein 29/328y, Anders 25/244y, Lashutka 22/226y
SCORING: Sander 48pts, Robert Funk 40pts, Barrington 36pts

1966 4-5

14 TCU	7 E Billy Anders
22 Washington	38 T Mike Current
9 Illinois	10 G John Kelley
8 Michigan State	11 C Ray Pryor
24 Wisconsin	13 G John Palmer / Bill Eachus
7 Minnesota	17 T Dave Foley
7 Indiana	0 E Rufus Mayes
14 Iowa	10 QB Bill Long
3 Michigan	17 HB Rudy Hubbard / Arnold Fontes
	HB Bo Rein
	FB Paul Hudson
	DL Jim Baas
	DL Dick Himes
	DL Vic Stottlemyer
	DL Gary Miller
	DL Nick Roman
	LB Mark Stier / Kim Anderson
	LB Dirk Worden
	LB John McCoy / John Muhlbach
	DB John Fill
	DB Jim Nein
	DB Tom Portsmouth

RUSHING: Rein 103/456y, Hudson 120/427y Hubbard 18/78y
PASSING: Long 106-192/1180y, 6TD, 55.2%
RECEIVING: Anders 55/671y, Rein 26/281y, Hubbard 11/105y
SCORING: Hudson 36pts, Gary Cairnes (K) 26pts, Anders 14pts

1967 6-3

7 Arizona	14 E Billy Anders
30 Oregon	0 T Dick Himes
6 Purdue	41 G John Kelley
6 Northwestern	2 C John Muhlbach / Jim Roman
13 Illinois	17 G Alan Jack
21 Michigan State	7 T Dave Foley
17 Wisconsin	15 E Rufus Mayes
21 Iowa	10 QB Bill Long / Gerald Ehrsam
24 Michigan	14 HB Dave Brungard / Lonnie Gillian
	HB Rudy Hubbard
	FB Jim Otis / Paul Huff
	DL Dave Whitfield
	DL Paul Schmidlin
	DL Dwight Fertig / Vic Stottlemyer
	DL Bill Urbanik / Brad Nielsen
	DL Nick Roman
	LB Mark Stier / Mike Radtke
	LB Dirk Worden
	LB Jim Nein
	DB Ted Provost
	DB Sam Elliott
	DB Tom Portsmouth / Mike Polaski

RUSHING: Otis 141/530y, Brungard 110/515y, Huff 83/273y
PASSING: Long 44-102/563y, 2TD, 43.1%
RECEIVING: Anders 28/403y, Hubbard 13/98y, Otis 7/48y
SCORING: Long 30pts, Gary Cairnes (K) 25pts,
Huff & Anders 24pts

1968 10-0

35 SMU	14 E Jan White
21 Oregon	6 T Dave Foley
13 Purdue	0 G Tom Backhaus / Brian Donovan
45 Northwestern	21 C John Muhlbach
31 Illinois	24 G Alan Jack / Phil Strickland
25 Michigan State	20 T Rufus Mayes / Charles Hutchison
43 Wisconsin	8 E Bruce Jankowski / Richard Kuhn
33 Iowa	27 QB Rex Kern
50 Michigan	14 HB John Brockington (FB) / Leo Hayden
27 Southern Cal■	16 HB Larry Zelina / Dave Brungard
	FB Jim Otis
	DL Dave Whitfield
	DL Paul Schmidlin / Bill Urbanik
	DL Jim Stillwagon
	DL Brad Nielsen
	DL Mark Debevc / Mike Radtke
	LB Doug Adams
	LB Mark Stier
	DB Ted Provost
	DB Tim Anderson / Mike Polaski
	DB Mike Sensibaugh
	DB Jack Tatum

RUSHING: Otis 219/985y, Kern 131/534y, Zelina 39/338y
PASSING: Kern 75-131/972y, 7TD, 57.2%
RECEIVING: Jankowski 31/328y, White 21/283y, Zelina 18/327y
SCORING: Otis 102pts, Kern 48pts, Jim Roman (K) 36pts

1969 8-1

62 TCU	0 E Jan White / Dick Kuhn
41 Washington	14 T Dave Cheney
54 Michigan State	21 G Brian Donovan / Tom Backhaus
34 Minnesota	7 C Tom DeLeone
41 Illinois	0 G Alan Jack / Ted Kurz
35 Northwestern	6 T Charles Hutchison
62 Wisconsin	7 E Bruce Jankowski
42 Purdue	14 QB Rex Kern
12 Michigan	24 HB Leo Hayden
	HB Larry Zelina / Lonnie Gillian
	FB Jim Otis / John Brockington
	DL Dave Whitfield
	DL Paul Schmidlin
	DL Jim Stillwagon
	DL Bill Urbanik
	DL Mark Debevc
	LB Doug Adams
	LB Phil Strickland / Stan White
	DB Ted Provost
	DB Tim Anderson
	DB Mike Sensibaugh
	DB Jack Tatum

RUSHING: Otis 225/1027y, Kern 109/583y, Hayden 63/344y
PASSING: Kern 68-135/1002y, 9TD, 50.4%
RECEIVING: Jankowski 23/404y, White 23/308y, Zelina 15/271y
SCORING: Otis 96pts, Kern 54pts, White 42pts

1970 9-1

56 Texas A&M	13 E Jan White
34 Duke	10 T Dave Cheney
29 Michigan State	0 G Dick Kuhn / Brian Donovan
28 Minnesota	8 C Tom DeLeone
48 Illinois	29 G Phil Strickland / Charles Bonica
24 Northwestern	10 T John Hicks
24 Wisconsin	7 E Bruce Jankowski
10 Purdue	7 QB Rex Kern / Ron Maciejowski
20 Michigan	9 HB Leo Hayden
17 Stanford■	27 HB Tom Campana / Larry Zelina
	FB John Brockington
	DL Mark Debevc
	DL George Hasenohrl
	DL Jim Stillwagon
	DL Shad Williams / Ralph Holloway
	DL Ken Luttner
	LB Doug Adams
	LB Stan White
	LB Jack Tatum
	DB Harry Howard
	DB Tim Anderson
	DB Mike Sensibaugh

RUSHING: Brockington 261/1142y, Hayden 132/767y,
Kern 112/597y
PASSING: Kern 45-98/470y, 3 TD, 45.9%,
Maciejowski 22-50/397y, TD, 44.0%
RECEIVING: White 17/171y, Zelina 13/212y, Jankowski 12/235y,
Brockington 12/64y
SCORING: Brockington 102pts, Fred Schram (K) 54pts,
Kern 42pts

1971 6-4

52 Iowa	21 WR Jimmie Harris / Fred Pagac
14 Colorado	20 T Dan Scott / Merv Teague
35 California	3 G Jim Kregel
24 Illinois	10 C Tom DeLeone
27 Indiana	7 G Chuck Bonica
31 Wisconsin	6 T Rick Simon
14 Minnesota	12 TE Rick Middleton
10 Michigan State	17 QB Don Lamka / Greg Hare
10 Northwestern	14 HB Rick Galbos
7 Michigan	10 HB Morris Bradshaw / Dick Wakefield
	FB John Bledsoe / Randy Keith
	DL Tom Marendt
	DL George Haenohrl
	DL Dan Cutillo / Shad Williams
	DL Ken Luttner
	LB Vic Koegel
	LB Randy Gradishar
	LB Stan White
	DB Harry Howard
	DB Tom Campana
	DB Jeff Davis
	DB Rick Seifert

RUSHING: Galbos 141/540y, Bradshaw 65/340y, Lamka 107/308y
PASSING: Lamka 54-107/718y, 2TD, 50.5%
RECEIVING: Wakefield 31/432y, Middleton 11/152y, 2 with 9
SCORING: Lamka & Fred Schram (K) 48pts, Bradshaw 30pts

1972 9-2

21 Iowa	0 WR Mike Bartaszek / Morris Bradshaw
29 North Carolina	14 T Merv Teague / Doug France
35 California	18 G Jim Kregal
26 Illinois	7 C Steve Myers / Steve Luke
44 Indiana	7 G Chuck Bonica / Larry Wiggins
28 Wisconsin	20 T John Hicks
27 Minnesota	19 TE Fred Pagac / Ted Powell
12 Michigan State	19 QB Greg Hare
27 Northwestern	14 HB Archie Griffin
14 Michigan	11 HB Richard Galbos / Brian Baschnagel
17 Southern Cal■	42 FB Harold "Champ" Henson /Randy Keith
	DL Van DeCree / Maike Scannell
	DL George Hasenohrl
	DL Pete Cusick / Shad Williams
	DL Jim Cope / Tom Marendt
	LB Arnie Jones / Vic Koegel
	LB Randy Gradishar / Ken Kuhn
	LB Rick Middleton
	DB Lou Mathis / Doug Plank
	DB Neal Colzie
	DB Jeff Davis / John Hughes
	DB Richard Seifert / Rich Parsons

RUSHING: Griffin 159/867y, Henson 193/795y, Hare 87/365y
PASSING: Hare 55-111/815y, 3TD, 49.5%
RECEIVING: Galbos 11/235y, Baschnagel 10/145y, Pagac 8/68y
SCORING: Henson 120pts, Blair Conway (K) 41pts,
Hare & Keith 24pts

1973 10-0-1

56 Minnesota	7 WR Mike Bartoszek / Dave Hazel
37 TCU	3 T Kurt Schumacher
27 Washington St.	3 G Jim Kregel
24 Wisconsin	0 C Steve Myers
37 Indiana	7 G Dick Mack
60 Northwestern	0 T John Hicks
30 Illinois	0 TE Fred Pagac
35 Michigan State	0 QB Cornelius Greene / Greg Hare
55 Iowa	13 TB Archie Griffin / Elmer Lippert
10 Michigan	10 WB Brian Baschnagel / Tim Holycross
42 Southern Cal■	21 FB Bruce Elia / Pete Johnson
	DL Van DeCree
	DL Arnie Jones
	DL Pete Cusick
	DL Jim Cope
	LB Vic Koegel / Ken Kuhn
	LB Randy Gradishar
	LB Rick Middleton
	DB Neal Colzie
	DB Steve Luke / Jeff Davis
	DB Tim Fox
	DB Rich Parsons / Bruce Ruhl

RUSHING: Griffin 247/1577y, Greene 126/720y, Elia 106/429y
PASSING: Greene 20-46/343y, 2TD, 43.4%,
Hare 11-30/224y, 3TD, 36.6%
RECEIVING: Pagac 9/159y, Griffin 5/32y, Hazel 4/121y,
Holycross 4/76y
SCORING: Elia 84pts, Greene 74pts, Blair Conway (K) 60pts

1974 10-2

34 Minnesota	19 WR Dave Hazel
51 Oregon State	10 T Kurt Schumacher / Lou Pietrini
28 SMU	9 G Ted Smith
42 Washington St.	7 C Steve Myers
52 Minnesota	7 G Dick Mack
49 Indiana	9 T Scott Dannelley
55 Northwestern	7 TE Doug France / Mike Bartoszek
49 Illinois	7 QB Cornelius Greene
13 Michigan State	16 TB Archie Griffin
35 Iowa	10 WB Brian Baschnagel / Lenny Willis
12 Michigan	10 FB Pete Johnson / Champ Henson
17 Southern Cal■	18 DL Van DeCree / Bob Brudzinski
	DL Nick Buonamici
	DL Pete Cusick
	DL Jim Cope
	LB Ken Kuhn / Brian Bowers
	LB Arnie Jones
	LB Bruce Elia
	DB Neal Colzie
	DB Steve Luke
	DB Tim Fox / Bruce Ruhl
	DB Rich Parsons / Doug Plank

RUSHING: Griffin 256/1695y, Greene 155/842y, Henson 88/433y
PASSING: Greene 58-97/939y, 9TD, 59.7%
RECEIVIVNG: Baschnagel 19/244y, Bartoszek 15/240y,
Hazel 11/272y
SCORING: Tom Klaban (K) 79pts, Griffin & Henson 72pts

1975 11-1

21 Michigan State	0 WR Lenny Willis
17 Penn State	9 T Chris Ward
32 North Carolina	7 G Ted Smith
41 UCLA	20 C Rick Applegate / Ron Ayers
49 Iowa	0 G Bill Lukens
56 Wisconsin	0 T Scott Dannelley
35 Purdue	6 TE Larry Kain / Jimmy Moore
24 Indiana	14 QB Cornelius Greene
40 Illinois	3 TB Archie Griffin / Jeff Logan
38 Minnesota	6 WB Brian Baschnagel
21 Michigan	14 FB Pete Johnson
10 UCLA■	23 DL Pat Curto
	DL Eddie Beamon
	DL Aaron Brown
	DL Nick Buonamici
	DL Bob Brudzinski / Kelton Danzler
	LB Ken Kuhn / Tom Cousineau
	LB Ed Thompson
	DB Craig Cassady / Max Midlam
	DB Bruce Ruhl / Leonard Mills
	DB Tim Fox
	DB Ray Griffin

RUSHING: Griffin 262/1450y, Johnson 227/1059y, Greene 136/518y
PASSING: Greene 68-121/1066y, 6TD, 56.1%
RECEIVING: Baschnagel 24/362y, Willis 17/350y, Griffin 14/170y
SCORING: Johnson 156pts, Tom Klaban (K) 64pts, Greene 48pts

1976 9-2-1

49 Michigan State	21 WR Herman Jones / Bob Hyatt
12 Penn State	7 T Chris Ward
21 Missouri	22 G Jim Savoca
10 UCLA	10 C Mark Lang
34 Iowa	14 G Bill Lukens
30 Wisconsin	20 T Lou Pietrini / Doug Mackie
24 Purdue	3 TE Greg Storer / Joe Robinson
47 Indiana	7 QB Rod Gerald / Jim Pacenta
42 Illinois	10 TB Jeff Logan / Ron Springs
9 Minnesota	3 WB Jim Harrell
0 Michigan	22 FB Pete Johnson / Paul Campbell
27 Colorado■	10 DL Bob Brudzinski
	DL Nick Buonamici / Mark Sullivan
	DL Aaron Brown
	DL Eddie Beamon / Byron Cato
	DL Kelton Danzler
	LB Tom Cousineau
	LB Ed Thompson
	DB Mike Guess
	DB Tom Roche / Bruce Ruhl
	DB Joe Allegro / Duncan Griffin
	DB Ray Griffin

RUSHING: Logan 218/1248y, Johnson 186/724y, Gerald 116/465y
PASSING: Pacenta 28-54/404y, TD, 51.8%, Gerald 14-40/245y, 0TD, 35.0%
RECEIVING: Harrell 14/288y, Storer 11/161y, Logan 5/44y
SCORING: Johnson 114pts, Tom Skladany (K) 59pts, Logan & Gerald 42pts

1977 9-3

10 Miami	0 WR Jim Harrell / Herman Jones
38 Minnesota	7 TE Jimmy Moore / Greg Storer
28 Oklahoma	29 T Chris Ward
35 SMU	7 G Mark Lang / Ernie Andria
46 Purdue	0 C Tim Vogler / Doug Porter
27 Iowa	6 G Ken Fritz
35 Northwestern	15 T Joe Robinson
42 Wisconsin	0 TE Bill Jaco
35 Illinois	0 QB Rod Gerald
35 Indiana	7 TB Jeff Logan (FB) / Ron Springs
6 Michigan	14 FB Paul Campbell / Joel Payton
6 Alabama■	35 DL Paul Ross
	DL Byron Cato
	DL Aaron Brown
	DL Gary Dunn / Eddie Beamon
	DL Kelton Dansler
	LB Tom Cousineau
	LB Dave Adkins
	DB Mike Guess
	DB Leonard Mills
	DB Joe Allegro
	DB Ray Griffin

RUSHING: Springs 200/1166y, Logan 107/606y, Campbell 103/457y
PASSING: Gerald 67-114/1016y, 4TD, 58.8%
RECEIVING: Springs 16/90y, Harrell 14/348y, Jaco 10/109y
SCORING: Payton 80pts, Vlade Janakievski (K) 65pts, Gerald & Springs 42pts

1978 7-4-1

0 Penn State	19 WR Rod Gerald
27 Minnesota	10 WR Doug Donley
34 Baylor	28 T Keith Ferguson
35 SMU	35 G Ken Fritz
16 Purdue	27 C Tim Vogler / Tom Waugh
31 Iowa	7 G Jim Savoca / Ernie Andria
63 Northwestern	20 T Joe Robinson / Tim Brown
49 Wisconsin	14 TE Jimmy Moore / Ron Barwig
45 Illinois	7 QB Art Schlichter
21 Indiana	18 TB Ron Springs / Calvin Murray
3 Michigan	14 FB Paul Campbell / Ric Volley
15 Clemson■	17 DL Gary Dunn / Luther Henson
	DL Mark Sullivan
	DL Byron Cato
	LB Paul Ross
	LB Tom Cousineau
	LB Alvin Washington
	LB Kelton Dansler
	DB Mike Guess
	DB Ray Ellis
	DB Vince Skillings
	DB Todd Bell

RUSHING: Campbell 142/591y, Schlichter 157/590y, Springs 124/585y
PASSING: Schlichter 87-175/1250y, 4TD, 49.7%
RECEIVING: Donley 24/510y, Gerald 16/314y, Springs 13/78y
SCORING: Schlichter 78pts, Campbell 54pts, Vlade Janakievski (K) 43pts

1979 11-1

31 Syracuse	8 WR Gary Williams / Chuck Hunter
21 Minnesota	17 WR Doug Donley
45 Washington St.	29 T Tim Burke
17 UCLA	13 G Ernie Andria / Scott Burris
16 Northwestern	7 C Tom Waugh
47 Indiana	6 G Ken Fritz
59 Wisconsin	0 T Joe Lukens
42 Michigan State	0 TE Bill Jaco / Brad Dwelle
44 Illinois	7 QB Art Schlichter
34 Iowa	7 TB Calvin Murray / Tim Spencer
18 Michigan	15 FB Ric Volley / Paul Campbell
16 Southern Cal■	17 DL Luther Henson / Gary Dunn
	DL Tim Sawicki / Mark Sullivan
	DL Jerome Foster
	LB Keith Ferguson
	LB Marcus Marek
	LB Al Washington
	LB Jim Laughlin
	DB Mike Guess
	DB Ray Ellis
	DB Vince Skillings
	DB Todd Bell

RUSHING: Murray 173/872y, Volley 112/565y, Schlichter 133/430y
PASSING: Schlichter 105-200/1816y, 14 TD, 52.5%
RECEIVING: Donley 37/800y, Williams 25/479y, Murray 19/239y
SCORING: Vlade Janakievski 97pts, Schlichter 54pts, Murray 42pts

1980 9-3

31 Syracuse	21 WR Gary Williams
47 Minnesota	0 WR Doug Donley / Cedric Anderson
38 Arizona State	21 T Joe Smith
0 UCLA	17 G Scott Burris
63 Northwestern	0 C Jim DeLeone
27 Indiana	17 G Joe Lukens
21 Wisconsin	0 T Luther Henson
48 Michigan State	16 TE Brad Dwelle / John Frank
49 Illinois	42 QB Art Schlichter
41 Iowa	7 TB Calvin Murray / Jimmy Gayle
3 Michigan	9 FB Tim Spencer / Vaughn Broadnax
19 Penn State■	31 DL Chris Riehm
	DL Mark Sullivan
	DL Jerome Foster
	LB Keith Ferguson
	LB Marcus Marek
	LB Glen Cobb / John Epitropoulos
	LB Al Washington
	DB Vince Skillings
	DB Ray Ellis
	DB Rod Gorley / Bob Murphy
	DB Todd Bell

RUSHING: Murray 195/1267y, Spencer 108/577y, Gayle 61/326y
PASSING: Schlichter 122-226/1930y, 15 TD, 54.0%
RECEIVING: Donley 43/887y, Williams 39/682y, Murray 21/204y
SCORING: Vlade Janakievski (K) 90pts, Murray & Spencer 48pts

1981 9-3

34 Duke	13 WR Gary Williams / Thad Jemison
27 Michigan State	13 WR Cedric Anderson
24 Stanford	19 T William Roberts
27 Florida State	36 G Scott Zalenski / Dave Medich
21 Wisconsin	24 C Jim DeLeone
34 Illinois	27 G Joe Lukens
29 Indiana	10 T Joe Smith
45 Purdue	33 TE John Frank / Brad Dwelle
31 Minnesota	35 QB Art Schlichter
70 Northwestern	6 TB Tim Spencer / Jimmy Gayle
14 Michigan	9 FB Vaughn Broadnax / Craig Dunn
31 Navy■	28 DL Chris Riehm
	DL Nick Miller
	DL Jerome Foster
	LB Mike D'Andrea
	LB Marcus Marek
	LB Glen Cobb
	LB Anthony Griggs / Ben Lee
	DB Kelvin Bell
	DB Shaun Gayle
	DB Garcia Lane
	DB Doug Hill

RUSHING: Spencer 226/1217y, Gayle 153/732y, Broadnax 50/184y
PASSING: Schlichter 183-350/2551y 17 TD, 52.3%
RECEIVING: Williams 50/941y, Frank 45/449y, Anderson 31/564y
SCORING: Bob Atha (K) 88pts, Spencer 74pts, Gayle 54pts

1982 9-3

21 Baylor	14 WR Gary Williams / Thad Jemison
31 Michigan State	10 WR Cedric Anderson
20 Stanford	23 T William Roberts
17 Florida State	34 G Scott Zalenski
0 Wisconsin	6 C Craig Pack
26 Illinois	21 G Joe Lukens
49 Indiana	25 T Jim Carson / Joe Smith
38 Purdue	6 TE John Frank / Brad Dwelle
35 Minnesota	10 QB Mike Tomczak
40 Northwestern	28 TB Tim Spencer / Jimmy Gayle
24 Michigan	14 FB Vaughn Broadnax
47 BYU■	17 DL Chris Riehm
	DL Spencer Nelms / Kirk Loudermilk
	DL Jerome Foster
	LB Rowland Tatum
	LB Marcus Marek
	LB Glen Cobb
	LB Curt Curtis
	DB Garcia Lane
	DB Shaun Gayle / Doyle Lewis
	DB Kelvin Bell
	DB Doug Hill / Lamar Kuechler

RUSHING: Spencer 273/1538y, Gayle 142/647y, Broadnax 103/514y
PASSING: Tomczak 96-187/1602y, 8 TD, 51.3%
RECEIVING: Williams 40/690y, Frank 26/326y, Anderson 20/552y
SCORING: Spencer 90pts, Rich Spangler (K) 68pts, Broadnax 54pts

1983 9-3

31 Oregon	6 WR Thad Jemison / Doug Smith
24 Oklahoma	14 WR Cedric Anderson / Jay Holland
14 Iowa	20 T William Roberts / Jim Carson
69 Minnesota	18 G Kirk Lowdermilk
33 Purdue	22 C Joe Dooley
13 Illinois	63 G Scott Zalenski / Jim Lachey
21 Michigan State	11 T Mark Krerowicz
45 Wisconsin	27 TE John Frank
56 Indiana	17 QB Mike Tomczak
55 Northwestern	7 TB Keith Byars / Roman Bates
21 Michigan	24 FB Vaughn Boardnax / Barry Walker
28 Pittsburgh■	23 DL Dave Crecelius
	DL Spencer Nelms
	DL Dave Morrill / Darryl Lee
	LB Orlando Lowry
	LB Clark Backus
	LB Rowland Tatum
	LB Curt Curtis / Byron Lee
	DB Garcia Lane
	DB Shaun Gayle
	DB KelvinBell
	DB Doug Hill / Steve Hill

RUSHING: Byars 222/1199y, Broadnax 84/346y, Bates 53/293y
PASSING: Tomczak 131-237/1942y, 13 TD, 55.3%
RECEIVING: Frank 45/641y, Jemison 35/558y, Anderson 26/524y
SCORING: Byars 132pts, Rich Spangler (K) 62pts, Broadnax 30pts

1984 9-3

22 Oregon State	14 WR Cris Carter / Doug Smith
44 Washington St.	0 WR Mike Lanese / Dino Dawson
45 Iowa	26 T Rory Graves
35 Minnesota	22 G Jim Lachey
23 Purdue	28 C Kirk Lowdermilk / Bob Maggs
45 Illinois	38 G Scott Zalenski
23 Michigan State	20 T Mark Krerowicz
14 Wisconsin	16 TE Ed Taggart / Judd Groza
50 Indiana	7 QB Mike Tomczak
52 Northwestern	3 TB Keith Byars / John Wooldridge
21 Michigan	6 FB Roman Bates / Barry Walker
17 Southern Cal■	20 DL Dave Crecelius
	DL Tony Giuliani
	DL Dave Morrill / Darryl Lee
	LB Dennis Hueston / Eric Kumerow
	LB Larry Kolic
	LB Pepper Johnson
	LB Byron Lee
	DB Greg Rogan / Steve Hill
	DB William White
	DB Terry White
	DB Sonny Gordon

RUSHING: Byars 336/1764y, Wooldridge 108/633y,
  Walker 30/154y
PASSING: Tomczak 145-244/1952y, 10 TD, 59.4%
RECEIVING: Byars 42/479y, Carter 41/648y, Lanese 41/618y
SCORING: Byars 144pts, Rich Spangler 87pts, Carter 48pts

1985 9-3

10 Pittsburgh	7 WR Cris Carter
36 Colorado	13 WR Mike Lanese
48 Washington St.	32 T Rory Graves
28 Illinois	31 G Jeff Uhlenhake
48 Indiana	7 C Bob Maggs
41 Purdue	27 G Jim Gilmore
23 Minnesota	19 T Larry Kotterman
22 Iowa	13 TE Ed Taggart / John Hutchison
35 Northwestern	17 QB Jim Karsatos
7 Wisconsin	12 TB John Wooldridge/V.Workman/K.Byars
17 Michigan	27 FB George Cooper
10 BYU■	7 DL Fred Ridder / Ray Holliman
	DL Darryl Lee / Henry Brown
	LB Eric Kumerow
	LB Chris Spielman
	LB Larry Kolic
	LB Pepper Johnson / Scott Leach
	LB Byron Lee
	DB William White
	DB Greg Rogan / Steve Hill
	DB Terry White
	DB Sonny Gordon / Sean Bell

RUSHING: Wooldridge 174/820y, Cooper 129/581y,
  Workman 68/321y, Byars 55/213y
PASSING: Karsatos 177-289/2311y, 19 TD, 61.2%
RECEIVING: Carter 58/950y, Lanese 31/552y, Taggart 31/327y
SCORING: Rich Spangler (K) 77pts, Wooldrdige 54pts,
  Carter 48pts

1986 10-3

10 Alabama	16 WR Cris Carter
7 Washington	40 WR Nate Harris / Everett Ross
13 Colorado	10 T Joe Staysniak / Tim Moxley
64 Utah	6 G Jeff Uhlenhake
14 Illinois	0 C Bob Maggs
24 Indiana	22 G Greg Zackeroff
39 Purdue	11 T Larry Kotterman
33 Minnesota	0 TE Ed Taggart / John Hutchison
31 Iowa	10 QB Jim Karsatos / Tom Tupa
30 Northwestern	9 TB Vince Workman / Jaymes Bryant
30 Wisconsin	17 FB George Cooper
24 Michigan	26 DL Mike Showalter / Henry Brown
28 Texas A&M■	12 DL Fred Ridder / Mike Sullivan
	LB Eric Kumerow
	LB Chris Spielman
	LB Mike Lee / John Sullivan
	LB Darryl Lee
	LB Scott Leach / Derek Isaman
	DB William White / Ray Jackson
	DB Greg Rogan
	DB David Brown
	DB Sonny Gordon

RUSHING: Workman 210/1030, Bryant 141/656y,
  Cooper 113/467y
PASSING: Karsatos 145-272/2122y, 13 TD, 53.3%
RECEIVING: Carter 69/1127y, Harris 30/496y, Workman 19/157y
SCORING: Matt Frantz (K) 71pts, Carter 66pts, Workman 54pts

1987 6-4-1

24 West Virginia	3 WR Anthony Cupe / Gary Clift
24 Oregon	14 WR Everett Ross
13 Louisiana State	13 T Joe Staysniak
10 Illinois	6 G Karl Coles
10 Indiana	31 C Jeff Uhlenhake
20 Purdue	17 G Greg Zackeroff
42 Minnesota	9 T Tim Moxley
7 Michigan State	13 TE Alex Higdon / Jeff Ellis
24 Wisconsin	26 QB Tom Tupa
27 Iowa	19 TB Vince Workman (WR) / Carlos Snow
23 Michigan	20 FB George Cooper
	DL Ray Holliman
	DL Mike Sullivan
	DL Kenneth Coleman / Mike Showalter
	LB Eric Kumerow
	LB Chris Spielman
	LB John Sullivan / Fred Ridder
	LB Mike McCray
	DB William White
	DB Zack Dumas / Greg Rogan
	DB David Brown
	DB Ray Jackson

RUSHING: Workman 118/470y, Snow 99/381y, Cooper 86/347y
PASSING: Tupa 134-242/1786y, 12TD, 55.4%
RECEIVING: Ross 29/585y, Workman 26/354y, Higdon 2/252y
SCORING: Matt Frantz (K) 56pts, Snow 36pts, Ross 30pts

1988 4-6-1

26 Syracuse	9 WR Jeff Graham / Marc Hicks
5 Pittsburgh	42 WR Bobby Olive / Bernard Edwards
36 LSU	33 T Joe Staysniak / Mike Kuri
12 Illinois	31 G Jeff Davidson
7 Indiana	41 C Jeff Uhlenhake
26 Purdue	31 G Greg Zackeroff
13 Minnesota	6 T Tim Moxley
10 Michigan State	20 TE Jeff Ellis
34 Wisconsin	12 QB Greg Frey
24 Iowa	24 TB Carlos Snow / Jaymes Bryant
31 Michigan	34 FB Bill Matlock / Scotty Graham
	DL Ken Coleman / Mike Showalter
	DL Mike Sullivan / Pat Thomas
	DL Derek MacCready
	LB Srecko Zizakovic / John Kacherski
	LB Orlondo Craig / Andrew Gurd
	LB John Sullivan
	LB Michael McCray / Patrick Rogan
	DB Zack Dumas
	DB Vinnie Clark / Dwight Smith
	DB David Brown / Mark Pelini
	DB Jim Peel

RUSHING: Snow 152/775y, Matlock 69/317y, Bryant 52/245y
PASSING: Frey 152-293/2028y, 8TD, 51.9%
RECEIVING: Ellis 40/492y, Graham 27/438y, Olive 25/370y
SCORING: Pat O'Morrow (K) 77pts, Snow 42pts, 7 with 12pts

1989 8-4

37 Oklahoma State	13 WR Jeff Graham / Greg Beatty
3 Southern Cal	42 WR Bobby Olive / Brian Stablein
34 Boston College	29 T Joe Staysniak
14 Illinois	34 G Jeff Davidson
35 Indiana	31 C Dan Beatty
21 Purdue	3 G Karl Coles
41 Minnesota	37 T Tim Moxley
52 Northwestern	27 TE Jim Palmer
28 Iowa	0 QB Greg Frey
42 Wisconsin	22 TB Carlos Snow / Dante Lee
18 Michigan	28 FB Scotty Graham
14 Auburn■	31 DL Rich Frimel / Mike Showalter
	DL Pat Thomas
	DL Alonzo Spellman
	LB Srecko Zizakovic
	LB Judah Herman
	LB Steve Tovar
	LB Derek Isaman
	DB Zack Dumas
	DB Vinnie Clark
	DB David Brown / Foster Paulk
	DB Mark Pelini / Bryan Cook

RUSHING: Snow 190/990y, Graham 183/977y, Lee 83/503y
PASSING: Frey 144-246/2132y, 13 TD, 58.5%
RECEIVING: Graham 32/608y, Palmer 28/308y, Olive 23/379y
SCORING: Snow 80pts, Graham 66pts, Pat O'Morrow (K) 63pts

1990 7-4-1

17 Texas Tech	10 WR Bobby Olive / Brian Stablein
31 Boston College	10 WR Jeff Graham / Bernard Edwards
26 Southern Cal	35 T Alan Kline
20 Illinois	31 G John Peterson / Len Hartman
27 Indiana	27 C Dan Beatty
42 Purdue	2 G Roy Nichols / Rod Smith
52 Minnesota	23 T Mick Shoaf
48 Northwestern	7 TE Gary Lickovitch / Jeff Ellis
27 Iowa	26 QB Greg Frey
35 Wisconsin	10 TB Robert Smith / Butler By'not'e
13 Michigan	16 FB Scottie Graham / Raymont Harris
11 Air Force■	23 DL Alonzo Spellman / Derrick Foster
	DL Greg Smith
	DL Rich Frimel / Dave Monnot
	LB Jay Koch / Mark Williams
	LB Steve Tovar
	LB Tom Lease / Judah Herman
	LB Jason Simmons
	DB Foster Paulk / Tim Walton
	DB Vinnie Clark / Bryan Cook
	DB Mark Pelini
	DB Jim Peel / Roger Harper

RUSHING: Smith 164/1064y, Harris 115/508y,
  S.Graham 70/246y
PASSING: Frey 129-249/1952y, 16 TD, 51.8%
RECEIVING: J.Graham 39/760y, Olive 37/589y,
  Edwards 12/179y
SCORING: Tim Williams (K) 76pts, J.Graham 56pts, Harris 54pts

1991 8-4

38 Arizona	14 WR Brian Stablein / Joey Galloway
23 Louisville	15 WR Bernard Edwards
33 Washington St.	19 T Alan Kline
31 Wisconsin	16 G Len Hartman
7 Illinois	10 C Paul Long / Jack Thrush
34 Northwestern	3 G Dave Monnot / Rod Smith
27 Michigan State	17 T Jason Winrow
9 Iowa	16 TE Cedric Saunders
35 Minnesota	6 QB Kent Graham / Kirk Herbstreit
20 Indiana	16 TB Carlos Snow / Butler By'not'e
3 Michigan	31 FB Scottie Graham
17 Syracuse■	24 DL Alonzo Spellman
	DL Greg Smith
	DL Rich Frimel
	LB Mark Williams
	LB Steve Tovar
	LB Judah Herman
	LB John Kacherski / Jason Simmons
	DB Foster Paulk
	DB Bryan Cook / Tim Walton
	DB Roger Harper
	DB Chico Nelson

RUSHING: Snow 169/828y, By'not'e 152/648y,
  S. Graham 66/374y
PASSING: K. Graham 79-153/1018y, 4TD, 51.6%
RECEIVING: Edwards 27/381y, Stablein 26/381y,
  Galloway 14/255y
SCORING: Tim Williams (K) 63pts, Snow 54pts,
  By'not'e & S. Graham 30pts

1992 8-3-1

20 Louisville	19 WR Brian Stablein
17 Bowling Green	6 WR Chris Sanders / Joey Galloway
35 Syracuse	12 T Alan Kline
16 Wisconsin	20 G Len Hartman
16 Illinois	18 C Paul Long / Jack Thrush
31 Northwestern	3 G Dave Monnot / Rod Smith (C)
27 Michigan State	17 T Jason Winrow / Korey Stringer
38 Iowa	15 TE Cedric Saunders
17 Minnesota	0 QB Kirk Herbstreit
27 Indiana	10 TB Rob't Smith / But'r By'not'e / E.George
13 Michigan	13 FB Jeff Cothran / Raymont Harris
14 Georgia■	21 DL Derrick Foster / Randall Brown
	DL Dan Wilkinson / Pete Beckman
	DL Greg Smith / Matt Bonhaus
	DL Jason Simmons
	LB Mark Williams
	LB Steve Tovar / Lorenzo Styles
	LB Craig Powell / Alex Rodriguez
	DB Tim Walton / Tito Paul
	DB Bryan Cook / Marlon Kerner
	DB Roger Harper / Walter Taylor
	DB Chico Nelson

RUSHING: Smith 147/819y, Harris 106/463y, Cothran 98/410y
PASSING: Herbstreit 155-264/1904y, 4 TD, 58.7%
RECEIVING: Stablein 53/643y, Saunders 28/342y,
  Sanders 22/360y
SCORING: Tim Williams (K) 79pts, Smith 60pts,
  George & Harris 30pts

1993 10-1-1

34 Rice	7 WR Joey Galloway
21 Washington	12 WR Chris Sanders / Terry Glenn
63 Pittsburgh	28 T Alan Kline
51 Northwestern	3 G Jason Winrow / Juan Porter
20 Illinois	12 C Jack Thrush / Brian Smith
28 Michigan State	21 G Dave Monnot
45 Purdue	24 T Korey Stringer
24 Penn State	6 TE Cedric Saunders / D.J. Jones
14 Wisconsin	14 QB Bobby Hoying
23 Indiana	17 TB Butler By'not'e / Raymont Harris
0 Michigan	28 FB Jeff Cothran
28 BYU■	21 DL Randall Brown / Mike Vrabel
	DL Dan Wilkinson
	DL Luke Fickell
	DL Jason Simmons / Randall Brown
	LB Mark Williams
	LB Lorenzo Styles
	LB Craig Powell
	DB Tim Walton / Tito Paul
	DB Marlon Kerner
	DB Walter Taylor / Tim Patillo
	DB Chico Nelson / Anthony Gwinn

RUSHING: Harris 273/1344y, Eddie George (TB) 42/223y
PASSING: Hoying 109-202/1570y, 8TD, 54.0%
RECEIVING: Galloway 47/946y
SCORING: Galloway 78pts, Harris 72pts, Tim Williams (K) 69pts

1994 9-4

34 Fresno State	10 WR Joey Galloway / Buster Tillman
16 Washington	25 WR Chris Sanders / Terry Glenn
27 Pittsburgh	3 T Orlando Pace
52 Houston	0 G LeShun Daniels
17 Northwestern	15 C Juan Porter
10 Illinois	24 G Jamie Sumner
23 Michigan State	7 T Korey Stringer / Eric Gohlstin
48 Purdue	14 TE D.J. Jones / Ricky Dudley
14 Penn State	63 QB Bobby Hoying / Stanley Jackson
24 Wisconsin	3 TB Eddie George / Pepe Pearson
32 Indiana	17 FB Nicky Sualua
22 Michigan	6 DL Mike Vrabel
17 Alabama■	24 DL Luke Fickell
	DL Matt Bonhaus / Randall Brown
	DL Matt Finkes
	LB Craig Powell
	LB Lorenzo Styles
	LB Greg Bellisari / Kevin Johnson
	DB Shawn Springs
	DB Marlon Kerner
	DB Tim Patillo
	DB Tito Paul / Anthony Gwinn

RUSHING: George 276/1442y, Pearson 85/338y,
  Jackson 45/202y
PASSING: Hoying 170-301/2335y, 19TD, 56.5%
RECEIVING: Galloway 44/669y, Sanders 35/533y,
  Tillman 33/455y
SCORING:

1995 11-2

38 Boston College	6 WR Buster Tillman / Dee Miller
30 Washington	20 WR Terry Glenn / Dimitrious Stanley
54 Pittsburgh	14 T Orlando Pace
45 Notre Dame	26 G Le Shun Daniels
28 Penn State	25 C Juan Porter
27 Wisconsin	16 G Jamie Sumner
28 Purdue	0 T Eric Gohlstin
56 Iowa	35 TE Rickey Dudley
49 Minnesota	21 QB Bobby Hoying / Stanley Jackson
41 Illinois	3 TB Eddie George / Pepe Pearson
42 Indiana	3 FB Nicky Sualua / D.J. Jones
23 Michigan	31 DL Mike Vrabel / Jeff Wilson
14 Tennessee■	20 DL Luke Fickell
	DL Matt Bonhaus / Winfield Garnett
	DL Matt Finkes / John Day
	LB Ryan Miller
	LB Greg Bellisari
	LB Kevin Johnson
	DB Shawn Springs
	DB Ty Howard / Antoine Winfield
	DB Anthony Gwinn / Damon Moore
	DB Rob Kelly / Che Bryant

RUSHING: George 328/1927y, Pearson 83/385y,
  Jermon Jackson 38/19y
PASSING: Hoying 211-341/3269y, 29TD, 61.9%
RECEIVING: Glenn 64/1411y, Georga 47/417y, Dudley 37/575y
SCORING: George 150pts, Glenn 102pts

1996 11-1

70 Rice	7 WR David Boston / Dimitrious Stanley
72 Pittsburgh	0 WR Dee Miller / Michael Wiley
29 Notre Dame	16 T Orlando Pace
38 Penn State	7 G Le Shun Daniels / Drew Elford
17 Wisconsin	14 C Juan Porter
42 Purdue	14 G Rob Murphy / Ben Gilbert
38 Iowa	26 T Eric Gohlstin
45 Minnesota	0 TE D.J. Jones / John Lumpkin
48 Illinois	0 QB Joe Germaine / Stanley Jackson
27 Indiana	17 TB Pepe Pearson / Jermon Jackson
9 Michigan	13 FB Matt Calhoun / Matt Keller
20 Arizona State■	17 DL Mike Vrabel
	DL Luke Fickell / Jim Bell
	DL Winfield Garnett
	DL Matt Finkes / John Day
	LB Greg Bellisari / Jerry Rudzinski
	LB Andy Katzenmoyer
	LB Ryan Miller
	DB Shawn Springs / Ahmed Plummer
	DB Ty Howard / Antoine Winfield
	DB Rob Kelly
	DB Damon Moore / Che Bryant

RUSHING: Pearson 286/1373y, Joe Montgomery (TB) 68/460y,
  J. Jackson 51/319y
PASSING: S. Jackson 81-151/1239y, 11TD, 53.6%,
  Germaine 71-130/1062y, 13TD, 54.6%
RECEIVING: Stanley 38/705y, Boston 29/430y, Pearson 18/214y
SCORING: Pearson 102pts

1997 10-3

24 Wyoming	10 WR David Boston
44 Bowling Green	13 WR Dee Miller / Reggie Germany
28 Arizona	20 T Tyson Walter
31 Missouri	10 G Rob Murphy
23 Iowa	7 C Eric Gohlstin (T) / Kurt Murphy
27 Penn State	31 G Ben Gilbert
31 Indiana	0 T Brooks Burris
49 Northwestern	6 TE John Lumpkin
37 Michigan State	13 QB Joe Germaine / Stanley Jackson
31 Minnesota	3 TB Pepe Pearson / Michael Wiley
41 Illinois	6 FB Matt Keller
14 Michigan	20 DL Rodney Bailey / Jeff Wilson
14 Florida State■	31 DL Jim Bell / Joe Brown
	DL Winfield Garnett
	DL Matt LaVrar
	LB Kevin Johnson / Na'il Diggs
	LB Andy Katzenmoyer
	LB Jerry Rudzinski / Courtland Bullard
	DB Ahmed Plummer
	DB Antoine Winfield / David Mitchell
	DB Gary Berry / Percy King
	DB Damon Moore / Che Bryant

RUSHING: Pearson 170/809y, Wiley 102/579y, Keller 53/237y
PASSING: Germaine 119-184/1674y, 15TD, 64.7%,
  Jackson 75-125/1021y, 8TD, 60.0%
RECEIVING: Boston 70/930y, Miller 52/902y, Keller 17/142y
SCORING: Dave Stultz (K) 86pts, Boston 84pts, Pearson 60pts

1998 11-1

34 West Virginia	17 WR David Boston
49 Toledo	0 WR Dee Miller
35 Missouri	14 T Tyson Walter
28 Penn State	9 G Rob Murphy
41 Illinois	0 C Kurt Murphy / LeCharles Bentley
45 Minnesota	15 G Ben Gilbert / Tam Hopkins
36 Northwestern	10 T Brooks Burris
38 Indiana	7 TE John Lumpkin / Steve Wisniewski
24 Michigan State	28 QB Joe Germaine
45 Iowa	14 TB Michael Wiley / Joe Montgomery
31 Michigan	16 FB Matt Keller / Jamar Martin
24 Texas A&M■	14 DL Rodney Bailey
	DL Joe Brown
	DL Ryan Pickett
	DL Brent Johnson
	LB Na'il Diggs
	LB Andy Katzenmoyer / Chris Kirk
	LB Jerry Rudzinski / Courtland Bullard
	DB Ahmed Plummer / Nate Clements
	DB Antoine Winfield
	DB Gary Berry
	DB Damon Moore / Percy King

RUSHING: Wiley 182/1147y, Montgomery 109/670y,
  Jonathan Wells (TB) 34/167y, Keller 32/128y
PASSING: Germaine 209-346/3108y, 24TD, 60.4%
RECEIVING: Boston 74/1330y, Miller 58/887y, Wiley 22/160y
SCORING: Boston 78pts, Wiley 66pts

1999 6-6

12 Miami	23 WR Reggie Germany
42 UCLA	20 WR Ken-Yon Rambo
40 Ohio	16 T Tyson Walter
34 Cincinnati	20 G Mike Gurr / Rob Murphy
17 Wisconsin	42 G Kurt Murphy
25 Purdue	22 G LeCharles Bentley (C) / Ben Gilbert
10 Penn State	23 T Henry Fleming
20 Minnesota	17 TE Darnell Sanders
41 Iowa	11 QB Steve Bellisari / Austin Moherman
7 Michigan State	23 TB Michael Wiley / Jonathan Wells
20 Illinois	46 FB Matt Keller
17 Michigan	24 DL Rodney Bailey
	DL Ryan Pickett
	DL Mike Collins / Joe Brown
	DL Brent Johnson / James Cotton
	LB Na'il Diggs
	LB Jason Ott
	LB Jerry Rudzinski
	DB Ahmed Plummer
	DB Nate Clements / Derek Ross
	DB Donnie Nickey / Gary Berry
	DB Mike Doss / Percy King

RUSHING: Wiley 183/952y, Bellisari 116/332y, Wells 51/292y
PASSING: Bellisari 101-224/1616y, 12TD, 45.1%
RECEIVING: Germany 43/656y, Rambo 41/833y, Wiley 14/153y
SCORING: Wiley 68pts

2000 8-4

43 Fresno State	10 WR Reggie Germany / Vaness Profit
27 Arizona	17 WR Ken-Yon Rambo / Chad Cocchio
27 Miami (Ohio)	16 T Adrien Clarke / Ivan Douglas
45 Penn State	6 G Mike Gurr / Alex Stepanovich
23 Wisconsin	7 C LeCharles Bentley
17 Minnesota	29 G Tam Hopkins / Shane Olivea
38 Iowa	10 T Henry Fleming
27 Purdue	31 TE Darnell Sanders
27 Michigan State	13 QB Steve Bellisari
24 Illinois	21 TB Derek Combs / Jonathan Wells
26 Michigan	38 FB Jamar Martin
7 So. Carolina■	24 DL Rodney Bailey
	DL Ryan Pickett
	DL Mike Collins / Tim Anderson
	DL Brent Johnson
	LB Courtland Bullard
	LB Matt Wilhelm / Fred Pagac, Jr.
	LB Joe Cooper
	DB Nate Clements
	DB David Mitchell / Derek Ross
	DB Donnie Nickey
	DB Mike Doss

RUSHING: Combs 175/888y, Wells 136/598y, Bellisari 107/179y
PASSING: Bellisari 163-310/2319y, 13TD, 52.6%
RECEIVING: Rambo 53/794y, Sanders 23/270y,
  Germany 22/366y
SCORING: Dan Stultz (K) 91pts

2001 7-5

28 Akron	14 WR Michael Jenkins
6 UCLA	13 WR Chris Vance
27 Indiana	14 T Adrien Clarke
38 Northwestern	20 G Alex Stepanovich
17 Wisconsin	20 C LeCharles Bentley
27 San Diego St.	12 G Bryce Bishop
27 Penn State	29 T Tyson Walter / Shane Olivea
31 Minnesota	28 TE Darnell Sanders / Ben Hartsock
35 Purdue	9 QB Steve Bellisari
22 Illinois	34 TB Jonathan Wells / Lydell Ross
26 Michigan	20 FB Jamar Martin
28 So. Carolina■	31 DL Darrion Scott / Kenny Peterson
	DL Tim Anderson
	DL Mike Collins
	DL Will Smith
	LB Courtland Bullard / Robert Reynolds
	LB Matt Wilhelm / Fred Pagac, Jr.
	LB Cie Grant
	DB Derek Ross
	DB Richard McNutt
	DB Donnie Nickey / Will Allen
	DB Mike Doss

RUSHING: Wells 251/1294y
PASSING: Bellisari 119-220/1919y, 10TD, 54.1%
RECEIVING: Jenkins 49/988y
SCORING: Wells 96pts

2002 14-0

45 Texas Tech	21 WR Michael Jenkins
51 Kent State	17 WR Chris Gamble (DB) / Chris Vance
25 Washington St.	7 T Ivan Douglas / Rob Sims
23 Cincinnati	19 G Adrien Clarke / Michael Stafford
45 Indiana	17 C Alex Stepanovich
27 Northwestern	16 G Bryce Bishop
50 San Jose State	7 T Shane Olivea
19 Wisconsin	14 TE Ben Hartsock / Ryan Hamby
13 Penn State	7 QB Craig Krenzel
34 Minnesota	3 TB Maurice Clarett / Lydell Ross
10 Purdue	6 FB Brandon Joe / Brandon Schnittker
23 Illinois	16 DL Darrion Scott / Simon Fraser
14 Michigan	9 DL Kenny Peterson / David Thompson
31 Miami ■	24 DL Tim Anderson
	DL Will Smith
	LB Robert Reynolds
	LB Matt Wilhelm
	LB Cie Grant / A.J. Hawk
	DB Dustin Fox / E.J. Underwood
	DB Richard McNutt / Chris Gamble (WR)
	DB Donnie Nickey
	DB Mike Doss

RUSHING: Clarett 222/1237y, Ross 166/619y, Maurice Hall (TB) 78/370y
PASSING: Krenzel 148-249/2110y, 12 TD, 59.4%
RECEIVING: Jenkins 61/1076y, Gamble 31/499y, Hartsock 17/137y
SCORING: Mike Nugent (K) 120pts, Clarett 108pts, Ross & Jenkins 36pts

2003 11-2

28 Washington	9 WR Michael Jenkins / Drew Carter
16 San Diego St.	13 WR Santonio Holmes / Bam Childress
44 N. Carolina St.	38 T Rob Sims
24 Bowling Green	17 G Adrien Clarke
20 Northwestern	0 C Alex Stepanovich (G) / Nick Mangold
10 Wisconsin	17 G Bryce Bishop
19 Iowa	10 T Shane Olivea / Mike Kne
35 Indiana	6 TE Ben Hartsock / Ryan Hamby
21 Penn State	20 QB Craig Krenzel / Scott McMullen
33 Michigan State	23 TB Lydell Ross / Maurice Hall
16 Purdue	13 FB Branden Joe / Brandon Schnittker
21 Michigan	35 DL Simon Fraser / Quinn Pitcock
35 Kansas State ■	28 DL Darrion Scott
	DL Tim Anderson
	DL Will Smith
	LB Robert Reynolds / Bobby Carpenter
	LB Fred Pagac, Jr. / Mike D'Andrea
	LB A.J. Hawk
	DB Dustin Fox
	DB Chris Gamble (WR) / Ashton Youboty
	DB Nate Salley / Brandon Mitchell
	DB Will Allen

RUSHING: Ross 193/826y, Hall 97/316y, Krenzel 109/255y
PASSING: Krenzel 153-278/2040y, 15 TD, 55.0%
RECEIVING: Jenkins 55/834y, Hartsock 33/290y, Holmes 32/549y
SCORING: Mike Nugent (K) 86pts, Ross 60pts, Jenkins 48pts

2004 8-4

27 Cincinnati	6 WR Roy Hall / Bam Childress
24 Marshall	21 WR Santonio Holmes / Ted Ginn, Jr.
22 N. Carolina St.	14 T Rob Sims / Steve Rehring
27 Northwestern	33 G Doug Datish / T.J. Downing
13 Wisconsin	24 C Nick Mangold
7 Iowa	33 G Mike Kne
30 Indiana	7 T Kirk Barton / Tim Shafer
21 Penn State	10 TE Ryan Hamby / Rory Nicol
32 Michigan State	19 QB Justin Zwick / Troy Smith
17 Purdue	24 TB Lydell Ross / Antonio Pittman / M. Hall
37 Michigan	21 FB Branden Joe / Brandon Schnittker
33 Oklahoma St. ■	7 DL Simon Fraser
	DL Marcus Green / David Patterson
	DL Quinn Pitcock
	DL Jay Richardson / Mike Kudla
	LB Bobby Carpenter
	LB Anthony Schlegel / Mike D'Andrea
	LB A.J. Hawk
	DB Ashton Youboty / Dustin Fox
	DB E.J. Underwood
	DB Nate Salley / Brandon Mitchell
	DB Donte Whitner / Tyler Everett

RUSHING: Ross 117/475y, Pittman 72/403y, Smith 82/401y
PASSING: Zwick 98-187/1209y, 6TD, 52.4%, Smith 68-122/896y, 8TD, 55.7%
RECEIVING: Holmes 55/769y, Ginn 25/359y, Hall 17/230y, Childress 17/205y
SCORING: Mike Nugent (K) 102pts, Ginn & Holmes 48pts

2005 10-2

34 Miami (Ohio)	14 WR Santonio Holmes
22 Texas	25 WR Anthony Gonzalez
27 San Diego State	6 WR Ted Ginn
31 Iowa	6 T Doug Datish
10 Penn State	17 G Rob Sims
35 Michigan State	24 C Nick Mangold
41 Indiana	10 G T.J. Downing
45 Minnesota	31 T Kirk Barton / Alex Boone
40 Illinois	2 TE Ryan Hamby
48 Northwestern	7 QB Troy Smith
25 Michigan	21 TB Antonio Pittman / Maurice Wells
34 Notre Dame ■	20 DL David Patterson / Jay Richardson
	DL Marcus Green / Joel Penton
	DL Quinn Pitcock
	DL Mike Kudla
	LB Bobby Carpenter
	LB Anthony Schlegal / John Kerr
	LB A.J. Hawk
	DB Ashton Youboty
	DB Tyler Everett / Malcolm Jenkins
	DB Nate Salley
	DB Donte Whitner / Brandon Mitchell

RUSHING: Pittman 243/1331y, Smith 136/611y, Wells 61/199y
PASSING: Smith 149-237/2282y, 16TD, 62.9%
RECEIVING: Holmes 53/977y, Ginn 51/803y, Gonzalez 28/373y
SCORING: Josh Huston (K) 110pts, Holmes & Smith 66pts, Ginn & Pittman 42pts

2006 12-1

35 N. Illinois	12 WR Roy Hall / Brian Robiskie
24 Texas	7 WR Anthony Gonzalez / Brian Hartline
37 Cincinnati	7 WR Ted Ginn
28 Penn State	6 T Alex Boone
38 Iowa	17 G Steve Rehring / Tim Schaefer (T)
35 Bowling Green	7 C Doug Datish
38 Michigan State	10 G T.J. Downing
44 Indiana	3 T Kirk Barton
44 Minnesota	0 TE Rory Nicol
17 Illinois	10 QB Troy Smith
54 Northwestern	10 TB Antonio Pittman / Chris Wells
42 Michigan	39 DL Jay Richardson
14 Florida ■	41 DL David Patterson / Joel Penton
	DL Quinn Pitcock
	DL Vernon Gholston
	LB Marcus Freeman
	LB James Laurinaitis / Larry Grant
	LB John Kerr / Ross Homan
	DB Malcolm Jenkins
	DB Antonio Smith / Donald Washington
	DB Jamario O'Neal
	DB Brandon Mitchell

RUSHING: Pittman 242/1233y, Wells 104/576y, Smith 72/204y
PASSING: Smith 203-311/2542y, 30TD, 65.3%
RECEIVING: Ginn 59/781y, Gonzalez 51/734y, Robiskie 29/383y
SCORING: Pittman 84pts, Aaron Pettrey (K) 79pts, Ginn 66pts, Gonzalez 48pts

2007 11-2

38 Youngstown St.	6 WR Brian Robiskie / Raymond Small
20 Akron	2 WR Brian Hartline
33 Washington	14 T Alex Boone
58 Northwestern	7 G Steve Rehring
30 Minnesota	7 C Jim Cordle
23 Purdue	7 G Ben Person
48 Kent State	3 T Kirk Barton
24 Michigan State	17 TE Rory Nicol / Jake Ballard
37 Penn State	17 QB Todd Boeckman
38 Wisconsin	17 TB Chris "Beanie" Wells / Maurice Wells
21 Illinois	28 FB Dionte Johnson
14 Michigan	3 DL Cameron Heyward / Robert Rose
28 LSU ■	38 DL Nader Abdallah / Todd Denlinger
	DL Doug Worthington
	DL Vernon Gholston
	LB Larry Grant / Austin Spitler
	LB James Laurinaitis
	LB Marcus Freeman / Brian Rolle
	DB Donald Washington
	DB Malcolm Jenkins / Chimdi Chekwa
	DB Anderson Russell
	DB Kurt Coleman

RUSHING: C. Wells 274/1609y, M. Wells 103/367y, Brandon Saine (TB) 60/267y
PASSING: Boeckman 191-299/2379y, 25TD, 63.9%
RECEIVING: Robiskie 55/935y, Hartline 52/694y, Small 20/267y
SCORING: Ryan Pretorius (K) 102pts, C. Wells 90pts, Robiskie 66pts

2008 10-3

43 Youngstown St.	0 WR Brian Robiskie / Ray Small
26 Ohio U.	14 WR Brian Hartline / Dane Sanzenbacher
3 Southern Cal	35 T Alex Boone
28 Troy	10 G Jim Cordle (C) / Steve Rehring
34 Minnesota	21 C Mike Brewster
20 Wisconsin	17 G Ben Person
16 Purdue	3 T Bryant Browning
45 Michigan State	7 TE Rory Nicol / Jake Ballard
6 Penn State	13 TE Brandon Smith
45 Northwestern	10 QB Tyrelle Pryor / Todd Boeckman
30 Illinois	20 TB Beanie Wells / Dan Herron
42 Michigan	7 DL Lawrence Wilson / Cameron Heyward
21 Texas ■	24 DL Doug Worthington / Dexter Larimore
	DL Nader Abdallah / Todd Denlinger
	DL Thaddeus Gibson
	LB Marcus Freeman / Tyler Moeller
	LB James Laurinaitis
	LB Ross Homan / Jermale Hines (DB)
	DB Chimdi Chekwa / Donald Washington
	DB Malcolm Jenkins
	DB Anderson Russell
	DB Kurt Coleman

RUSHING: B. Wells 207/1197y, Pryor 139/631y, Herron 89/439y
PASSING: Pryor 100-165/1311y, 12TD, 60.6%, Boeckman 57-93/620y, 5TD, 61.3%
RECEIVING: Robiskie 42/535y, Hartline 21/479y, Sanzenbacher 21/272y
SCORING: Ryan Pretorius (K) 83pts, Robiskie & B. Wells 48pts

2009 11-2

31 Navy	27 WR DeVier Posey / Taurian Washington
15 Southern Cal	18 WR Dane Sanzenbacher / Ray Small
38 Toledo	0 T Jim Cordle / Andrew Miller
30 Illinois	0 G Justin Boren
33 Indiana	14 C Mike Brewster
31 Wisconsin	13 G Bryant Browning
18 Purdue	26 T J.B. Shugarts / Mike Adams
38 Minnesota	7 TE Jake Ballard / Jake Stoneburner
45 New Mexico St.	2 QB Tyrelle Pryor
24 Penn State	7 TB Dan Herron / Brandon Saine
27 Iowa	24 FB Zach Boren
21 Michigan	10 DL Cameron Heyward / Nathan Williams
26 Oregon ■	17 DL Doug Worthington
	DL Dexter Larimore / Todd Denlinger
	DL Thaddeus Gibson / Lawrence Wilson
	LB Austin Spitler
	LB Brian Rolle
	LB Ross Homan
	DB Chimdi Chekwa
	DB Devon Torrence / Andre Amos
	DB Jamale Hines (LB) / Anderson Russell
	DB Kurt Coleman

RUSHING: Pryor 162/779y, Saine 145/739y, Herron 153/600y
PASSING: Pryor 167-295/2094y, 18TD, 56.6%
RECEIVING: Posey 60/828y, Sanzenbacher 36/570y, Saine 17/224y, Small 15/175y, Ballard 14/150y
SCORING: Aaron Pettrey (K) 72pts, Herron & Posey 48pts, Pryor 44pts

2010 12-1

45 Marshall	7 WR Dane Sanzenbacher
36 Miami	24 WR DeVier Posey
43 Ohio	7 T Mike Adams
73 E. Michigan	20 G Justin Boren
24 Illinois	13 C Mike Brewster
38 Indiana	10 G Bryant Browning
18 Wisconsin	31 T J.B. Shugarts
49 Purdue	0 TE Jake Stoneburner / Reid Fragel
52 Minnesota	10 QB Terrelle Pryor
38 Penn State	14 TB Dan Herron / Brandon Saine
20 Iowa	17 FB Zach Boren
37 Michigan	7 DL Nathan Williams / Solomon Thomas
31 Arkansas ■	26 DL Dexter Larimore
	DL John Simon
	DL Cameron Heyward
	LB Ross Homan / Jon Newsome
	LB Brian Rolle / Storm Klein
	LB/DB Andrew Sweat / Tyler Moeller
	DB Chimdi Chekwa
	DB Devon Torrence
	DB Jermale Hines / Aaron Gant
	DB Orhian Johnson / C.J. Barnett

RUSHING: Herron 216/1155y, Pryor 135/754y, Saine 70/337y
PASSING: Pryor 210-323/2772y, 27TD, 65%
RECEIVING: Sanzenbacher 55/948y, Posey 53/848y, Saine 23/195y
SCORING: Devin Barclay (K) 122pts, Herron 96pts, Sanzenbacher 72pts

OKLAHOMA

University of Oklahoma (Founded 1890)
Norman, Oklahoma
Nickname: Sooners
Colors: Crimson and Cream
Stadium: Memorial Stadium at Owen Field (1925) 82,112
Conference Affiliations: Big Seven (Charter Member, 1948-57), Big
Eight (1958-95), Big Twelve South (1996-present)

CAREER RUSHING YARDS	Attempts	Yards
Billy Sims (1975-79)	593	4118
Joe Washington (1972-75)	675	4071
Adrian Peterson (2004-06)	408	4045
Steve Owens (1967-69)	958	4041
Quentin Griffin (1999-02)	744	3938
DeMarco Murray (2007-10)	759	3685
De'Mond Parker (1996-98)	579	3403
Stanley Wilson (1979-82)	567	3198
Greg Pruitt (1970-72)	422	3122
Chris Brown (2006-09)	627	2923

CAREER PASSING YARDS	Comp.-Att.	Yards
Sam Bradford (2007-09)	594-893	8403
Jason White (1999-04)	627-990	7922
Landry Jones (2009-10)	666-1066	7916
Josh Heupel (1999-00)	654-1025	7456
Cale Gundy (1990-93)	460-808	6686
Nate Hybl (2000-02)	464-791	5091
Bobby Warmack (1966-68)	259-475	3744
Paul Thompson (2002-06)	246-409	3095
Jack Mildren (1969-71)	170-358	3092
Eric Moore (1995-98)	168-393	2675

CAREER RECEIVING YARDS	Catches	Yards
Ryan Broyles (2008-10)	266	3429
Mark Clayton (2001-04)	221	3241
Juaquin Iglesias (2005-08)	202	2861
Malcolm Kelly (2005-07)	144	2285
Antwone Savage (1999-02)	157	2009
Eddie Hinton (1966-68)	123	1894
Corey Warren (1990-93)	106	1785
Manuel Johnson (2005-08)	119	1710
Curtis Fagan (1999-02)	135	1689
Jermaine Gresham (2006-08)	111	1629

SEASON RUSHING YARDS	Attempts	Yards
Adrian Peterson (2004)	339	1925
Billy Sims (1978)	256	1896
Quentin Griffin (2002)	287	1884
Greg Pruitt (1971)	196	1760
Billy Sims (1979)	248	1670

SEASON PASSING YARDS	Comp.-Att.	Yards
Sam Bradford (2008)	328-483	4720
Landry Jones (2010)	405-617	4718
Josh Heupel (1999)	349-553	3850
Jason White (2003)	278-451	3846
Josh Heupel (2000)	305-472	3606

SEASON RECEIVING YARDS	Catches	Yards
Ryan Broyles (2010)	131	1622
Mark Clayton (2003)	83	1425
Juaquin Iglesias (2008)	74	1150
Ryan Broyles (2009)	89	1120
Eddie Hinton (1968)	64	1034

GAME RUSHING YARDS	Attempts	Yards
Greg Pruitt (1971 vs. Kansas State)	19	294
De'Mond Parker (1997 vs. Texas)	31	291
Billy Sims (1979 vs. Missouri)	36	282

GAME PASSING YARDS	Comp.-Att.	Yards
Sam Bradford (2008 vs. Kansas)	36-53	468
Landry Jones (2010 vs. Oklahoma State)	37-62	468
Landry Jones (2010 vs. Colorado)	32-46	453

GAME RECEIVING YARDS	Catches	Yards
Ryan Broyles (2010 vs. Colorado)	9	208
Manuel Johnson (2008 vs. TCU)	5	206
Juaquin Iglesias (2008 vs. Kansas)	12	191

GREATEST COACH:

In today's game, recruiting is national. Players from one end of the coast to the other are recruited by programs without too much emphasis placed on geography.

In the 1950s, that was not the case, at least not with the Oklahoma Sooners of Bud Wilkinson. Filling his roster annually with the best Oklahoma had to offer, plus some star Texans (almost always from up North), Wilkinson won with what he had on hand. Why go to California or Pennsylvania when Muskogee, Oklahoma, produced the Burris brothers, Max Boydston, and Bo Bollinger?

Coaxed back into coaching by Oklahoma head coach Jim Tatum, Wilkinson succeeded his friend one year later, in 1947, when Tatum departed for Maryland. Wilkinson "only" won seven games that first year; he would win eight or more games for the next 11 seasons. In eight of those seasons he won 10 or more games, with perfect records in four seasons. His Sooners won national titles in 1950, 1955, and 1956 and conference titles 12 straight years. He not only coached Oklahoma through a 47-game win streak, which remains the national record, but a 31-game win streak early in his career. He retired with a 145-29-4 record.

OKLAHOMA'S 55 GREATEST SINCE 1953

OFFENSE

WIDE RECEIVER: Ryan Broyles, Mark Clayton, Eddie Hinton
TIGHT END: Max Boydston, Keith Jackson
TACKLE: Jammal Brown, Bob Kalsu, Louis Oubre, Mike Vaughan
GUARD: Terry Crouch, Bill Krisher, Luke Phillips, Greg Roberts
CENTER: Tom Brahaney, Bob Harrison
QUARTERBACK: Sam Bradford, Josh Heupel, Jamelle Holieway
RUNNING BACK: Tommy McDonald, Steve Owens, Adrian Peterson, Greg Pruitt, Billy Sims, Joe Washington
FULLBACK: Jim Grisham

DEFENSE

END: Jimbo Elrod, Cedric Jones, Kevin Murphy, Darrell Reed
TACKLE: Rick Bryan, Tony Casillas, Reggie Kinlaw, Derland Moore, Lee Roy Selmon, Lucious Selmon
LINEBACKER: Brian Bosworth, Rocky Calmus, George Cumby, Daryl Hunt, Carl MacAdams, Rod Shoate
CORNERBACK: Derrick Strait, Clendon Thomas
SAFETY: Rickey Dixon, Jimmy Harris, Zac Henderson, Roy Williams

SPECIAL TEAMS

RETURN SPECIALIST: Antonio Perkins, Antwone Savage
PLACE KICKER: Uwe von Schamann
PUNTER: Jeff Ferguson

MULTIPLE POSITIONS

FULLBACK-CENTER-LINEBACKER: Jerry Tubbs

TWO-WAY PLAYERS

CENTER-LINEBACKER: Kurt Burris
CENTER-LINEBACKER: Jerry Tubbs
TACKLE-DEFENSIVE TACKLE: Ralph Neely
TIGHT END-DEFENSIVE END-PUNTER: Steve Zabel

PERFORMANCE FORMULA:
OKLAHOMA'S 10 BEST SEASONS

1974	1.8484	1 of 71
2000	1.8104	1 of 70
1973	1.8007	1 of 70
1986	1.7913	1 of 70
1971	1.7667	3 of 70
1972	1.7577	2 of 70
1955	1.7521	1 of 69
1985	1.7395	1 of 70
1954	1.7374	1 of 69
1956	1.7260	1 of 69

OKLAHOMA SOONERS

Year	W-L-T	AP Poll	Conference Standing	Toughest Regular Season Opponents	Coach (Record at School)	Bowl Games			
1953	9-1-1	4	1	Notre Dame 9-0-1, Texas 7-3, Oklahoma A&M 7-3	Bud Wilkinson	Orange	7	Maryland	0
1954	10-0	3	1	Colorado 7-2-1, Kansas State 7-3, Nebraska 6-4	Bud Wilkinson				
1955	11-0	1	1	Pittsburg 7-3, Colorado 6-4, Texas 5-5	Bud Wilkinson	Orange	20	Maryland	6
1956	10-0	1	1	Colorado 7-2-1, Nebraska 4-6	Bud Wilkinson				
1957	10-1	4	1	Notre Dame 7-3, Texas 6-3-1, Oklahoma St. 6-3-1, Colorado 6-3-1	Bud Wilkinson	Orange	48	Duke	21
1958	10-1	5	1	Texas 7-3, Oklahoma State 7-3, Colorado 6-4	Bud Wilkinson	Orange	21	Syracuse	6
1959	7-3	15	1	Texas 9-1, Iowa State 7-3, Northwestern 6-3, Missouri 6-4	Bud Wilkinson				
1960	3-6-1		5	Missouri 9-1, Kansas 7-2-1, Texas 7-3, Iowa State 7-3	Bud Wilkinson				
1961	5-5		4	Texas 9-1, Colorado 9-1, Missouri 7-2-1, Kansas 6-3-1	Bud Wilkinson				
1962	8-3	8	1	Texas 9-0-1, Nebraska 8-2, Kansas 6-3-1	Bud Wilkinson	Orange	0	Alabama	17
1963	8-2	9	2	Texas 10-0, Nebraska 9-1, Southern California 7-3	Bud Wilkinson (145-29-4)	Gator	19	Florida State	36
1964	6-4-1		2	Nebraska 9-1, Texas 9-1, Southern California 7-3	Gomer Jones				
1965	3-7		5	Nebraska 10-0, Missouri 7-2-1, Colorado 6-2-2, Texas 6-4	Gomer Jones (9-11-1)				
1966	6-4		5	Notre Dame 9-0-1, Nebraska 9-1, Missouri 6-3-1	Jim Mackenzie (6-4)				
1967	10-1	3	1	Colorado 8-2, Missouri 7-3, Texas 6-4, Nebraska 6-4	Chuck Fairbanks	Orange	26	Tennessee	24
1968	7-4	11	1t	Kansas 9-1, Texas 8-1-1, Notre Dame 7-2-1, Missouri 7-3	Chuck Fairbanks	Bluebonnet	27	SMU	28
1969	6-4		4	Texas 10-0, Missouri 9-1, Nebraska 8-2, Colorado 7-3	Chuck Fairbanks				
1970	7-4-1	20	2t	Texas 10-0, Nebraska 10-0-1, Colorado 6-4	Chuck Fairbanks	Bluebonnet	24	Alabama	24
1971	11-1	2	2	Nebraska 12-0, Colorado 9-2, Texas 8-2, Iowa State 8-3	Chuck Fairbanks	Sugar	40	Auburn	22
1972	11-1	2	5	Texas 9-1, Nebraska 8-2-1, Colorado 8-3	Chuck Fairbanks (52-15-1)	Sugar	14	Penn State	0
1973	10-0-1	3	1	Southern Cal 9-1-1, Texas 8-2, Nebraska 8-2-1, Kansas 7-3-1	Barry Switzer				
1974	11-0	1	1	Nebraska 8-3, Texas 8-3, Missouri 7-4	Barry Switzer				
1975	11-1	1	1t	Nebraska 10-1, Texas 9-2, Colorado 9-2, Kansas 7-4	Barry Switzer	Orange	14	Michigan	6
1976	9-2-1	5	1t	Nebraska 8-3-1, Colorado 8-3, Iowa St. 8-3, Oklahoma State 8-3	Barry Switzer	Fiesta	41	Wyoming	7
1977	10-2	7	1	Texas 11-0, Ohio State 9-2, Nebraska 8-3, Colorado 7-3-1	Barry Switzer	Orange	6	Arkansas	31
1978	11-1	3	1t	Nebraska 9-2, Texas 8-3, Iowa State 8-3, Missouri 7-4	Barry Switzer	Orange	31	Nebraska	24
1979	11-1	3	1	Nebraska 10-1, Texas 9-2, Oklahoma State 7-4	Barry Switzer	Orange	24	Florida State	7
1980	10-2	3	1	Nebraska 9-2, North Carolina 10-1, Texas 7-4, Missouri 7-4	Barry Switzer	Orange	18	Florida State	17
1981	7-4-1	20	2	Texas 9-1-1, Southern Cal 9-2, Nebraska 9-2, Missouri 7-4	Barry Switzer	Sun	40	Houston	14
1982	8-4	16	2	Nebraska 11-1, Texas 9-2, West Virginia 9-2, Southern Cal 8-3	Barry Switzer	Fiesta	21	Arizona State	32
1983	8-4		2	Nebraska 12-0, Texas 11-0, Ohio State 8-3, Oklahoma State 7-4	Barry Switzer				
1984	9-2-1	6	1t	Nebraska 9-2, Oklahoma State 9-2, Texas 7-3-1	Barry Switzer	Orange	17	Washington	28
1985	11-1	1	1	Miami 10-1, Nebraska 9-2, Texas 8-3, Oklahoma State 8-3	Barry Switzer	Orange	25	Penn State	10
1986	11-1	3	1	Miami 11-0, Nebraska 9-2, UCLA 7-3-1	Barry Switzer	Orange	42	Arkansas	8
1987	11-1	3	1	Nebraska 10-1, Oklahoma State 9-2, Colorado 7-4	Barry Switzer	Orange	14	Miami	20
1988	9-3	14	2	Nebraska 11-1, Southern Cal 10-1, Oklahoma State 9-2	Barry Switzer (157-29-4)	Citrus	6	Clemson	13
1989	7-4		3	Colorado 11-0, Nebraska 10-1, Arizona 7-4	Gary Gibbs				
1990	8-3	17	2t	Texas 10-1, Colorado 10-1-1, Nebraska 9-2	Gary Gibbs				
1991	9-3	16	3	Nebraska 9-1-1, Colorado 8-2-1	Gary Gibbs	Gator	48	Virginia	14
1992	5-4-2		4	Colorado 9-1-1, Nebraska 9-2, Kansas 7-4	Gary Gibbs				
1993	9-3	17	4	Nebraska 11-0, Texas A&M 10-1, Kansas St. 8-2-1, Colorado 7-3-1	Gary Gibbs	Hancock	41	Texas Tech	10
1994	6-6		4	Nebraska 12-0, Texas A&M 10-0-1, Colorado 10-1, Kansas St. 9-2	Garry Gibbs (44-23-2)	Copper	6	BYU	31
1995	5-5-1		6	Nebraska 11-0, Texas 10-1-1, Kansas State 9-2, Kansas 9-2	H. Schnellenberger (5-5-1)				
1996	3-8		S5t	Nebraska 10-1, Kansas State 9-2, Texas 7-4, Texas Tech 7-4	John Blake				
1997	4-8		S5t	Nebraska 11-0, Kansas St. 10-1, Texas A&M 9-2, Syracuse 9-3	John Blake				
1998	5-6		S4t	Texas A&M 10-2, Texas 8-3, Missouri 7-4	John Blake (12-22)				
1999	7-5		S2t	Texas 9-3, Texas A&M 8-3	Bob Stoops	Independence	25	Mississippi	27
2000	13-0	1	S1	Kansas State 10-2, Texas 9-2, Nebraska 9-2	Bob Stoops	Orange	13	Florida State	2
2001	11-2	6	S2	Texas 10-1, Nebraska 11-1, Texas A&M 7-4	Bob Stoops	Cotton	10	Arkansas	3
2002	12-2	5	S1	Texas 10-2, Alabama 9-3, Colorado 9-3	Bob Stoops	Rose	34	Washington State	14
2003	12-2	3	S1	Texas 10-2, Oklahoma State 9-3, Texas Tech 7-4	Bob Stoops	Sugar	14	LSU	21
2004	12-1	3	S1	Texas 10-1, Oklahoma State 7-4, Texas Tech 7-4, Texas A&M 7-4	Bob Stoops	Orange	19	Southern California	55
2005	8-4	22	S2t	Texas 11-0, TCU 10-1, UCLA 9-2, Texas Tech 9-2, Nebraska 7-4	Bob Stoops	Holiday	17	Oregon	14
2006	11-3	11	S1	Texas 9-3, Texas A&M 9-3, Missouri 8-4, Oregon 7-5	Bob Stoops	Fiesta	42	Boise State	43
2007	11-3	8	S1	Texas 9-3, Missouri 11-1, Texas Tech 8-4	Bob Stoops	Fiesta	28	West Virginia	48
2008	12-2	5	S1t	TCU 10-2, Texas 11-1, Texas Tech 11-1, Oklahoma State 9-3	Bob Stoops	BCS Title	14	Florida	24
2009	8-5		S3t	BYU 10-2, Miami 9-3, Texas 13-0, Nebraska 9-4	Bob Stoops	Sun	31	Stanford	27
2010	12-2	6	S1t	Missouri 10-2, Texas A&M 9-3, Oklahoma State 10-2, Nebraska 9-3	Bob Stoops (129-31)	Fiesta	49	Connecticut	20

TOTAL: 505-162-11 .7529 (2 of 70)   **Bowl Games since 1953:**   23-15-1 .6026 (15 of 70)

GREATEST TEAM SINCE 1953: With six national championship teams since 1953, Oklahoma proves a challenge when selecting one of its teams as the school's best. Still, one had to be chosen, and the 1974 team is the winner. With the Selmon brothers, Rod Shoate, Joe Washington, et al, the Sooners were loaded, but really any of a number of teams could have won this prize.

1953 9-1-1

21	Notre Dame	28 E Carl Allison / Joe Mobra
7	Pittsburgh	7 T Don Brown / Dick Bowman
19	Texas	14 G Melvin Brown / Bo Bolinger
45	Kansas	0 C Kurt Burris (G) / Gene Mears
27	Colorado	20 G J.D. Roberts / Cecil Morris
34	Kansas State	0 T Roger Nelson / Doc Hearon
14	Missouri	7 E Max Boydston (FB) / Kay Keller
47	Iowa State	7 QB Gene Calame / Buddy Leake
30	Nebraska	7 HB Jack Ging / Bob Herndon
42	Oklahoma A&M	7 HB Larry Grigg
7	Maryland■	7 FB Bob Burris / Jerry Donaghey

RUSHING: Grigg 130/792y, Burris 78/516y, Calame 132/367y
PASSING: Leake 9-21/138y, 2TD, 42.9%
 Calame 5-23/61y, 0TD, 21.7%
RECEIVING: Allison 5/94y, Boydston 4/88y, Ging 4/52y
SCORING: Grigg 78pts, Green 32pts, Herndon & Ging 24pts

1954 10-0

27	California	13 E Carl Allison / Tommy Pearson
21	TCU	16 T Cal Woodworth / Don Brown
14	Texas	7 G Bo Bolinger
65	Kansas	0 C Kurt Burris / Gene Mears
21	Kansas State	0 G Cecil Morris / John Sain
13	Colorado	6 T Edmon Gray / Emery Link
40	Iowa State	0 E Max Boydston / John Bell
34	Missouri	13 QB Gene Calame / Jimmy Harris
55	Nebraska	7 HB Buddy Leake / Tommy McDonald
14	Oklahoma A&M	0 HB Bob Herndon / Tom Carroll
		FB Jerry Tubbs / Bob Burris

RUSHING: Herndon 98/588y, Harris 73/427y, Tubbs 63/387y
PASSING: Leake 12-26/249y, 3TD, 46.2%
RECEIVING: Boydston 11/276y, Allison 7/109y, Herndon 7/108y
SCORING: Leake 79pts, Herndon 54pts, Calame 30pts

1955 11-0

13	North Carolina	6 E Don Stiller / Joe Mobra
26	Pittsburgh	14 T Cal Woodworth / Bob Loughridge
20	Texas	0 G Bo Bolinger / Wayne Greenlee
44	Kansas	6 C Jerry Tubbs / Bobby Darnell
56	Colorado	21 G Cecil Morris / Bill Krisher
40	Kansas State	7 T Edmon Gray / Buddy Cockrell
20	Missouri	0 E John Bell / Bob Timberlake
52	Iowa State	0 QB Jimmy Harris / Jay O'Neal
41	Nebraska	0 HB Tommy McDonald / Clendon Thomas
53	Oklahoma A&M	0 HB Bob Burris / Carl Dodd
20	Maryland■	6 FB Billy Pricer/Dennit Morris/Bill Brown

RUSHING: McDonald 103-702y, Thomas 71/487y, Burris 106/445y
PASSING: McDonald 17-24/265y, 0TD, 70.8%
RECEIVING: Burris 8/104y, Bell 7/109y, Mobra 6/126y
SCORING: McDonald 96pts, Burris 66pts, Thomas 54pts

1956 10-0

36	North Carolina	0 E Don Stiller / Ross Coyle
66	Kansas State	0 T Edmon Gray / Hugh Ballard
45	Texas	0 G Joe Oujesky / Ken Northcutt
34	Kansas	12 C Jerry Tubbs / Bob Harrison
40	Notre Dame	0 G Bill Krishner / Doyle Jennings
27	Colorado	19 T Tom Emerson / Buddy Cockrell
44	Iowa State	0 E John Bell / Bob Timberlake
67	Missouri	14 QB Jimmy Harris / Jay O'Neal
54	Nebraska	6 HB Tommy McDonald / Jackie Sandefer
53	Oklahoma A&M	0 HB Clendon Thomas / Carl Dodd
		FB Billy Pricer / Dennit Morris

RUSHING: McDonald 119/853y, Thomas 104/817y, Harris 76/362y
PASSING: Harris 23-37/482y, 8TD, 62.2%
RECEIVING: McDonald 12/282y, Thomas 12/241y, Stiller 5/118y
SCORING: Thomas 108pts, McDonald 102pts, Dodd 39pts

1957 10-1

26	Pittsburgh	0 E Don Stiller / Ross Coyle
40	Iowa State	14 T Byron Searcy / Jerry Thompson
21	Texas	7 G Ken Northcutt / Joe Oujesky
47	Kansas	0 C Bob Harrison / Jim Davis
14	Colorado	13 G Bill Krishner / Dick Corbitt
13	Kansas State	0 T Doyle Jennings / Benton Ladd
39	Missouri	14 E Joe Rector / Dick Carpenter
0	Notre Dame	7 QB Carl Dodd / David Baker
32	Nebraska	7 HB Clendon Thomas / Prentice Gautt
53	Oklahoma State	6 HB Jackie Sandefer / Bobby Boyd
48	Duke■	21 FB Dennit Morris / Dave Rolle

RUSHING: Thomas 130/816y, Morris 81/376y, Sandefer 77/354y
PASSING: Baker 12-18/261y, 3TD, 66.7%
RECEIVING: Carpenter 8/90, Stiller 5/86y, Coyle 4/114y
SCORING: Thomas 54pts, Dodd 45pts, Baker 37pts

1958 10-1

47	West Virginia	14 E Ross Coyle / Ed "Wahoo" McDaniel
6	Oregon	0 T Steve Jennings / Jere Durham
14	Texas	15 G Jerry Thompson / Jerry Payne
43	Kansas	0 C Bob Harrison
40	Kansas State	6 G Dick Corbitt / Jim Davis
23	Colorado	7 T Gilmer Lewis / Jim Lawrence
20	Iowa State	0 E Joe Rector / Jerry Tillery
39	Missouri	0 QB David Baker/Bobby Boyd/Bob Cornell
40	Nebraska	7 HB Prentice Gautt (FB) / Jimmy Carpenter
7	Oklahoma State	0 HB Jackie Sandefer / Dick Carpenter
21	Syracuse■	6 FB Brewster Hobby / Dave Rolle

RUSHING: Gautt 105/627y, Hobby 82/387y, Baker 119/339y
PASSING: Boyd 24-50/353y, 5TD, 48%
RECEIVING: D.Carpenter 11/103y, Sandefer 10/102y, Tillery 7/129y
SCORING: Boyd 36pts, Baker 34pts, J. Carpenter 32pts

1959 7-3

13	Northwestern	45 E Ed "Wahoo" McDaniel / Phil Lohman
42	Colorado	12 T Gilmer Lewis / Billy White
12	Texas	19 G Jerry Thompson (T) / Jerry Payne
23	Missouri	0 C Jim Davis (G) / Jim Byerly
7	Kansas	6 G Billy Jack Moore / Karl Milstead
21	Nebraska	25 T Tom Cox / Jere Durham
36	Kansas State	0 E Ronny Payne / Jerry Tillery
28	Army	20 QB Bobby Boyd / Bob Cornell
35	Iowa State	12 HB Mike McClellan / Jackie Holt
17	Oklahoma State	7 HB Brewster Hobby / Dick Carpenter
		FB Prentice Gautt / Ronnie Hartline

RUSHING: Gautt 130/674y, Boyd 144/508y, Hartline 85/487y
PASSING: Boyd 19-54/256y, 0TD, 35.2%
RECEIVING: Hobby 10/143y, Carpenter 7/121y, Holt 6/97y
SCORING: Boyd 62pts, Hartline 26pts, Davis 25pts

1960 3-6-1

3	Northwestern	19 E Ronny Payne / Phil Lohmann
15	Pittsburgh	14 T Billy White / H.O. Estes
0	Texas	24 G Duane Cook / Leon Cross
13	Kansas	13 C Jim Byerly / Wayne Lee
49	Kansas State	7 G Karl Milstead / John Tatum
0	Colorado	7 T Tom Cox / Marshall York
6	Iowa State	10 E Jerry Tillery / Paul Benien
19	Missouri	41 QB Jimmy Carpenter / Bennett Watts
14	Nebraska	17 HB Mike McClellan / Melvin Sandersfield
17	Oklahoma State	6 HB Don Dickey / Bill Meacham / Paul Lea
		FB Ronnie Hartline / Gary Wylie

RUSHING: Hartline 138/682y, McClellan 55/295y,
 Meacham 58/204y
PASSING: Carpenter 25-40/357y, 3TD, 62.5%
RECEIVING: Meacham 8/86y, McClellan 7/87y, Payne 6/140y
SCORING: McClellan 30pts, Carpenter & Sandersfield 20pts

1961 5-5

6	Notre Dame	19 E Ronny Payne / James McCoy
15	Iowa State	21 T Billy White
7	Texas	28 G Karl Milstead / Jimmy Gilstrap
0	Kansas	10 C Wayne Lee / Johnny Tatum
14	Colorado	22 G Leon Cross / George Jarman
17	Kansas State	6 T Tom Cox / Dennis Ward
7	Missouri	0 E Dale Perini / Paul Benien
14	Army	8 QB BobPage/Bill Van Burkleo/Monte Deere
21	Nebraska	14 HB Mike McClellan / Paul Lea
21	Oklahoma State	13 HB Jimmy Carpenter / Gary Wylie
		FB Phil Lohmann / Dick Beattie

RUSHING: McClellan 82/508y, Lohmann 98/436y, Carp.105/342y
PASSING: Page 13-45/233y, 2TD, 28.9%
RECEIVING: Carpenter 12/143y, McClellan 10/125y, Payne 6/84y
SCORING: Page 38pts, Carpenter 24pts, McClellan 18pts

1962 8-3

7	Syracuse	3 E John Flynn / Glen Condren
7	Notre Dame	13 T Dennis Ward
6	Texas	9 G Newt Burton / Jimmy Gilstrap
13	Kansas	7 C Wayne Lee
47	Kansas State	0 G Leon Cross / Larry Vermillion
62	Colorado	0 T James Cook
41	Iowa State	0 E Rick McCurdy / John Porterfield
13	Missouri	0 QB Monte Deere
34	Nebraska	6 HB Joe Don Looney / Paul Lea
37	Oklahoma State	6 HB Virgil Boll/Gary Wylie/Jackie Dempsey
0	Alabama■	17 FB Jim Grisham

RUSHING: Looney 137/852y, Grisham 147/711y,
 Dempsey 41/192y
PASSING: Deere 38-65/789y, 9TD, 58.5%
RECEIVING: Flynn 10/247y, Boll 10/237y, Looney 7/119y
SCORING: Looney 62pts, Grisham 48pts, Dempsey 24pts

1963 8-2

31	Clemson	14 E John Porterfield/John Flynn/Ron Harmon
17	Southern Cal	12 T Ralph Neely
7	Texas	28 G Carl Schreiner
21	Kansas	18 C John Garrett
34	Kansas State	9 G Newt Burton
35	Colorado	0 T George Stokes / Glenn Condren
24	Iowa State	14 E Rick McCurdy
-13	Missouri	3 QB Bobby Page
20	Nebraska	29 HB Jackie Cowan / Joe Don Looney
34	Oklahoma State	10 HB Virgil Boll / Lance Rentzel
		FB Jim Grisham

RUSHING: Grisham 153/861y, Rentzel 59/387y
PASSING: Page 13-45/198y, 2TD, 28.9%
RECEIVING: McCurdy 9/112y, Flynn 8/115y, Harmon 5/79y
SCORING: Grisham 48pts, George Jarman (K) 38pts,
 3 tied w/ 18pts

1964 6-4-1

13	Maryland	3 E Ben Hart
14	Southern Cal	40 T Ralph Neely
7	Texas	28 G Carl Schreiner
14	Kansas	15 C Bill Carlyle
44	Kansas State	0 G Newt Burton
14	Colorado	11 T Butch Metcalf
30	Iowa State	0 E Gordon Brown
14	Missouri	14 QB Bobby Page / John Hammond
17	Nebraska	7 HB Larry Brown
21	Oklahoma State	16 HB Lance Rentzel
19	Florida State■	36 FB Jim Grisham
		DL Al Bumgardner
		DL Bill Hill / Jerry Goldsby
		DL Glenn Condren
		DL Rick McCurdy
		DL Vern Burkett
		DL James Riley
		LB David Voiles
		LB Carl McAdams
		DB Charles Mayhue / Rod Crosswhite
		DB W.S. Thomas / Eugene Ross
		DB Larry Shields

RUSHING: Grisham 146/725y, Rentzel 89/491y, Brown 58/267y
PASSING: Hammond 16-38/284y, 1TD, 42.1%
 Page 15-35/280y, 3TD, 42.9%
RECEIVING: Rentzel 18/268y, Hart 8/255y, G. Brown 7/139y
SCORING: Rentzel 36pts, Metcalf (T-K) 28pts, Page & Hart 24pts

1965 3-7

9	Pittsburgh	13 E Bob Kalsu
0	Navy	10 T Ed Hall
0	Texas	19 G Wes Butts / Mark Kosmos
21	Kansas	7 C Bill Carlyle
27	Kansas State	0 G Bob Vardeman / Rick Goodwin
0	Colorado	13 T Jim Riley / Mike Oliver
24	Iowa State	20 E Gordon Brown
0	Missouri	30 QB Gene Cagle / John Hammond
9	Nebraska	21 WB Tommy Pannell
16	Oklahoma State	17 HB Ben Hart / Ron Shotts
		FB Larry Brown
		DL Phil Wetherbee / Jim Riley
		DL Larry Crutchmer / Joe Poslick
		DL Vern Burkett / Granville Liggins
		DL Mike Base
		DL John Koller
		LB Alan Henderson / Bob Flanagan
		LB Carl McAdams
		DB Rod Crosswhite / Al Knight
		DB Bob Stephenson
		DB Eugene Ross
		DB Mike Ringer / Ray Haynes

RUSHING: L. Brown 102/344y, Cagle 82/340y, Shotts 90/317y
PASSING: Cagle 34-80/382y, 0TD, 42.5%
RECEIVING: G. Brown 35/413y, Hart 12/115y, Pannell 7/96
SCORING: Cagle 24pts, Shotts 20pts, L. Brown 18pts

1966 6-4

17 Oregon	0 WR Ben Hart
33 Iowa State	11 T Ed Hall
18 Texas	9 G Ron Winfrey
35 Kansas	0 C Robert Edward Craig / Don Kindley
0 Notre Dame	38 G Mark Kosmos / Vern Burkett
21 Colorado	24 T Bob Kalsu
37 Kansas State	6 E Randy Meacham
7 Missouri	10 QB Bobby Warmack
10 Nebraska	9 WB Eddie Hinton
14 Oklahoma State	15 HB Ron Shotts / James Ray Jackson
	FB Gary Harper
	DL Bobbie Robinson
	DL Jim Riley
	DL John Titsworth
	DL John Koller / Ray Haynes
	DL Granville Liggins / Larry Crutchmer (LB)
	LB Harry Hettmannsperger
	LB Ricky Burgess / Rick Goodwin
	DB Rodney Crosswhite
	DB Bob Stephenson
	DB Eugene Ross
	DB Steve Barrett

RUSHING: Shotts 149/535y, Jackson 106/489y, Warmack 103/335y
PASSING: Warmack 57-103/843y, 4TD, 55.3%
RECEIVING: Hart 33/565y, Hinton 26/341y, Shotts 8/67y
SCORING: Mike Vachon (K) 44pts, Hinton 42pts, Shotts 30pts

1967 10-1

21 Washington St.	0 WR Joe Killingsworth
35 Maryland	0 T Byron Bigby
7 Texas	9 G Eddie Lancaster
46 Kansas State	7 C Robert Edward Craig
7 Missouri	0 G Ken Mendenhall
23 Colorado	0 T Bob Kalsu
52 Iowa State	14 TE Steve Zabel
14 Kansas	10 QB Bob Warmack
21 Nebraska	14 WB Eddie Hinton
38 Oklahoma State	14 TB Ron Shotts / Steve Owens
26 Tennessee	24 FB Mike Harper / Richard Baldridge
	DL John Koller
	DL Dick Paaso
	DL Granville Liggins
	DL John Titsworth
	DL Jim Files
	LB Rick Goodwin
	LB Don Pfrimmer
	DB Bruce Stensrud
	DB Bob Stephenson / Joe Pearce
	DB Gary Harper / F. Wayne Nelson
	DB Steve Barrett

RUSHING: Owens 190/808y, Shotts 176/726y, Hinton 40/250y
PASSING: Warmack 80-151/1136y, 8TD, 53%
RECEIVING: Hinton 28/427y, Zabel 22/333y, Killingsworth 18/250y
SCORING: Owens 72pts, Shotts 42pts, Hinton 36pts

1968 7-4

21 Notre Dame	45 WR Joe Killingsworth / Johnny Barr
28 N. Carolina St.	14 T Byron Bigby
20 Texas	26 G Bill Elfstrom
42 Iowa State	7 C Ken Mendenhall
27 Colorado	41 G Eddie Lancaster
35 Kansas State	20 T Jack Porter
27 Kansas	23 TE Steve Zabel / Bo Denton
28 Missouri	14 QB Bob Warmack
47 Nebraska	0 WB Eddie Hinton
41 Oklahoma State	7 TB Steve Owens
27 SMU■	28 FB Mike Harper
	DL Larry MacDuff / Steve Zabel
	DL Dick Paaso
	DL Johnny Watson / Joe Kusiak
	DL John Titsworth
	DL Jim Files
	LB Steve Casteel
	LB Don Pfrimmer
	DB Bruce Stensrud
	DB Rickey Hetherington / Joe Pearce
	DB Gary Harper
	DB Steve Barrett

RUSHING: Owens 357/1536y, Harper 57/279y, Warmack 103/266y
PASSING: Warmack 106-186/1548y, 10TD, 57%
RECEIVING: Hinton 60/967y, Zabel 19/237y, Owens 10/94y
SCORING: Owens 126pts, Hinton & Bruce Derr (K) 36pts

1969 6-4

48 Wisconsin	21 WR John Shelley / Everett Marshall
37 Pittsburgh	8 T Ken Mendenhall
17 Texas	27 G Bill Elfstrom
42 Colorado	30 C Glenn Dewberry
21 Kansas State	59 G Stephen Tarlton
37 Iowa State	14 T Darryl Emmert (G) / Nelson Todd
10 Missouri	44 TE Steve Zabel
31 Kansas	15 QB Jack Mildren
14 Nebraska	44 WR Roy Bell / Geoffrey Nordgren
28 Oklahoma State	27 TB Steve Owens
	FB Mike Harper
	DL Vince La Rosa / Albert Qualls
	DL Kevin Grady
	DL Lionell Day
	DL Johnny Watson
	DL Bruce DeLoney
	LB Steve Aycock
	LB Steve Casteel
	DB Rick Heatherton / Glenn King
	DB Joe Pearce
	DB Jim Files
	DB Monty Johnson

RUSHING: Owens 358/1523y, Bell 81/467y, Mildren 127/345y
PASSING: Mildren 79-172/1319y, 9TD, 45.9%
RECEIVING: Zabel 22/203y, Bell 15/215y, Nordgren 13/188y
SCORING: Owens 138pts, Mildren 46pts, Bruce Derr (K) 45pts

1970 7-4-1

28 SMU	11 WR Willie Franklin / Jon Harrison
21 Wisconsin	7 T Ronnie Stacy / Darryl Emmert
14 Oregon State	23 G Ken Jones
9 Texas	41 C Tom Brahaney / Glenn Dewberry
23 Colorado	15 G Dean Unruh / Stephen Tarleton
14 Kansas State	19 T Johnny Watson
29 Iowa State	28 TE Al Chandler
28 Missouri	13 QB Jack Mildren
28 Kansas	24 WB Joe Wylie
21 Nebraska	28 TB Greg Pruitt / Roy Bell
66 Oklahoma State	6 FB Leon Crosswhite
24 Alabama■	24 DL Ray Hamilton / Vince La Rosa
	DL Lionell Day / Albert Qualls
	DL Kevin Grady
	DL Rick Mason / Johnny Watson
	LB Gary Baccus / Ford Phillips
	LB Steve Aycock
	LB Steve Casteel / Mark Driscoll
	DB Glenn King / Larry Roach
	DB Geoff Nordgren / Steve O'Shaughnessy
	DB John Shelley
	DB Monty Johnson

RUSHING: Wylie 159/984y, Crosswhite 124/568y, Bell 82/329y
PASSING: Mildren 54-110/818y, 7TD, 49%
RECEIVING: Pruitt 19/240y, Harrison 11/272y, Chandler 9/172y
SCORING: Wylie 78pts, Pruitt 44pts, Bruce Derr (K) 43pts

1971 11-1

30 SMU	0 WR Jon Harrison
55 Pittsburgh	29 T Dean Unruh
33 Southern Cal	20 G Darryl Emmert
48 Texas	27 C Tom Brahaney
45 Colorado	17 G Ken Jones
75 Kansas State	28 T Robert Jensen
43 Iowa State	12 TE Al Chandler
20 Missouri	3 QB Jack Mildren
56 Kansas	10 WB Joe Wylie / Roy Bell
31 Nebraska	35 HB Greg Pruitt
58 Oklahoma State	14 FB Leon Crosswhite
40 Auburn■	22 DL Ray Hamilton
	DL Lucious Selmon
	DL Derland Moore
	DL Mike Struck
	LB Albert Qualls
	LB Steve Aycock
	LB Mark Driscoll
	DB Glenn King / Ken Pope
	DB Steve O'Shaughnessy
	DB Geoff Nordgren / Larry Roach
	DB John Shelly

RUSHING: Pruitt 178/1665y, Mildren 193/1140y, Crosswhite 136/666y
PASSING: Mildren 31-64/878y, 10TD, 48.4%
RECEIVING: Harrison 17/494y, Chandler 8/223y, Pruitt 4/108y
SCORING: Mildren 106pts, Pruitt 102pts, John Carroll (WR-K) 80pts

1972 11-1

49 Utah State	0 WR Tinker Owens / John Carroll
68 Oregon	3 T Dean Unruh
53 Clemson	3 G John Roush
27 Texas	0 C Tom Brahaney
14 Colorado	20 G Ken Jones
52 Kansas State	0 T Eddie Foster
20 Iowa State	6 TE Al Chandler
17 Missouri	6 QB Dave Robertson
31 Kansas	3 HB Joe Washington / Joe Wylie
17 Nebraska	14 HB Greg Pruitt
38 Oklahoma State	15 FB Leon Crosswhite
14 Penn State■	0 DL Gary Baccus / Dewey Selmon
	DL Derland Moore
	DL Lucious Selman
	DL Ray Hamilton
	DL Vic Kearney
	LB Jon Milstead
	LB Rod Shoate
	DB Ken Pope
	DB Larry Roach
	DB Randy Hughes
	DB Danny Ruster

RUSHING: Pruitt 152/938y, Washington 115/630y, Crosswhite 139/614y
PASSING: Robertson 56-110/1054y, 9TD, 50.9%
RECEIVING: Carroll 17/343y, Owens 17/298y, Chandler 14/301y
SCORING: Pruitt 84pts, Rick Fulcher (K) 65pts, Washington 44pts

1973 10-0-1

42 Baylor	14 WR Tinker Owens / Billy Brooks
7 Southern Cal	7 T Eddie Foster
24 Miami	20 G John Roush
52 Texas	13 C Kyle Davis
34 Colorado	7 G Terry Webb
56 Kansas State	14 T Jerry Arnold
34 Iowa State	17 TE Wayne Hoffman
31 Missouri	3 QB Steve Davis
48 Kansas	20 HB Tim Welch
27 Nebraska	0 HB Joe Washington
45 Oklahoma State	18 FB Waymon Clark
	DL Gary Baccus
	DL Dewey Selmon
	DL Lucious Selmon
	DL Lee Roy Selmon / Jimbo Elrod
	DL Mike Struck
	LB Dave Smith
	LB Rod Shoate
	DB Clyde Powers / Tony Peters
	DB Ken Pope
	DB Durwood Keeton
	DB Randy Hughes

RUSHING: Washington 176/1173y, Clark 209/1014y, Davis 179/887y
PASSING: Davis 38-92/934y, 9TD, 41.3%
RECEIVING: Owens 16/472y, Brooks 12/310y, Hoffman 5/121y
SCORING: Davis 108pts, Rick Fulcher (K) 67pts, Washington 60pts

1974 11-0

28 Baylor	11 WR Tinker Owens / Billy Brooks
72 Utah State	3 T Jerry Arnold
63 Wake Forest	0 G John Roush
16 Texas	13 C Kyle Davis
49 Colorado	14 G Terry Webb
63 Kansas State	0 T Mike Vaughn
28 Iowa State	10 TE Wayne Hoffman
37 Missouri	0 QB Steve Davis
45 Kansas	14 WR Grant Burget
28 Nebraska	14 HB Joe Washington
44 Oklahoma State	13 FB Jim Littrell
	DL Ron Waters
	DL Anthony Bryant
	DL Dewey Selmon
	DL Lee Roy Selmon
	DL Jimbo Elrod
	LB Gary Gibbs
	LB Rod Shoate
	DB Sidney Brown
	DB Tony Peters / Eric Van Camp
	DB Randy Hughes
	DB Zac Henderson

RUSHING: Washington 194/1321y, Littrell 124/837y, Davis 165/659y
PASSING: Davis 26-63/601y, 11TD, 41.3%
RECEIVING: Owens 18/413y, Brooks 7/176y, Hoffman 6/98y
SCORING: Washington 84pts, Tony DiRienzo (K) 57pts, Davis 54pts

1975 11-1

62 Oregon	7 WR Tinker Owens / Billy Brooks
46 Pittsburgh	10 T Kurt Baldischwiler / Jaime Melendez
20 Miami	17 G Chez Evans
21 Colorado	20 C Dennis Buchanan
24 Texas	17 G Terry Webb / Greg Roberts
25 Kansas State	3 T Mike Vaughan
39 Iowa State	7 TE Victor Hicks / Craig Lund
27 Oklahoma State	7 QB Steve Davis
3 Kansas	23 HB Elvis Peacock
28 Missouri	27 HB Joe Washington
35 Nebraska	10 FB Horace Ivory /Jim Littrell / Jim Culbreath
14 Michigan■	6 DL Mike Phillips
	DL Lee Roy Selmon
	DL Dewey Selmon
	DL Anthony Bryant
	DL Jimbo Elrod
	LB Bill Dalke / Daryl Hunt
	LB Jaime Thomas
	DB Sidney Brown / Terry Peters
	DB Jerry Anderson
	DB Zac Henderson
	DB Scott Hill / Mike Birks

RUSHING: Washington 171/871y, Ivory 102/649y, Davis 171/512y
PASSING: Davis 19-56/438y, 1TD, 33.9%
RECEIVING: Owens 9/241y, Brooks 5/114y, Washington 4/56y
SCORING: Washington 74pts, Tony DiRienzo (K)72pts, Peacock 38pts

1976 9-2-1

24 Vanderbilt	3 WR Steve Rhodes / Lee Hover
28 California	17 T Leo Martin / Karl Baldischwiler
24 Florida State	9 G Greg Roberts
24 Iowa State	10 C Jody Farthing
6 Texas	6 G Jaime Melendez
28 Kansas	10 T Mike Vaughan
24 Oklahoma State	31 TE Victor Hicks / Reggie Mathis
31 Colorado	42 QB Thomas Lott / Dean Blevins
49 Kansas State	20 HB Elvis Peacock
27 Missouri	20 HB Horace Ivory
20 Nebraska	17 FB Kenny King / Jim Culbreath
41 Wyoming■	7 DL Victor Brown / Anthony Bryant
	DL Phil Tabor
	DL Reggie Kinlaw / David Hudgens
	DL Richard Murray
	DL Mike Phillips / Greg Sellmyer
	LB Bill Dalke / Obie Moore
	LB Daryl Hunt
	DB Sidney Brown / Bud Hebert
	DB Jerry Anderson / Terry Peters
	DB Jerry Reese
	DB Zac Henderson / Scott Hill

RUSHING: King 141/791y, Ivory 111/741y, Lott 143/630y
PASSING: Blevins 18-44/370y, 2TD, 40.9%
RECEIVING: Rhodes 6/160y, Hover 4/145y, Hicks 3/45y
SCORING: Uwe von Schamann (K) 61pts, Lott 42pts, King 24pts

1977 10-2

25 Vanderbilt	23 WR Steve Rhodes / Bobby Kimball
62 Utah	24 T Karl Baldischwiler
29 Ohio State	28 G Jaime Melendez
24 Kansas	9 C Paul Tabor / Jody Farthing
6 Texas	13 G Greg Roberts
21 Missouri	17 T Sam Clapham
35 Iowa State	16 TE Victor Hicks / Reggie Mathis
42 Kansas State	7 QB Thomas Lott / Dean Blevins
61 Oklahoma State	28 HB Elvis Peacock
52 Colorado	14 HB Billy Sims / David Overstreet
38 Nebraska	7 FB Kenny King
6 Arkansas■	31 DL Bruce Taton / Barry Burget
	DL Dave Hudgens / Phil Tabor
	DL Reggie Kinlaw
	DL Richard Murray
	DL Reggie Mathis
	LB George Cumby
	LB Daryl Hunt
	DB Terry Peters / Bud Hebert
	DB Mike Babb / Darrol Ray
	DB Zac Henderson
	DB Sherwood Taylor

RUSHING: Lott 139/760y, Peacock 121/695y, King 114/640y
PASSING: Blevins 16-29/347y, 4TD, 55.2%, Lott 16-36/314y, 4 TD, 44.4%
RECEIVING: Kimball 13/199y, Rhodes 12/226y, Hicks 5/120y
SCORING: Uwe von Schamann (K) 89pts, Lott 74pts, Peacock 60pts

1978 11-1

35 Stanford	29 WR Bobby Kimball / Steve Rhodes
52 West Virginia	10 T Louis Oubre
66 Rice	7 G Paul Tabor
45 Missouri	23 C Jody Farthing
31 Texas	10 G Greg Roberts
17 Kansas	16 T Sam Claphan
34 Iowa State	6 TE Forrest Valora
56 Kansas State	19 QB Thomas Lott
28 Colorado	7 HB Billy Sims
14 Nebraska	18 HB David Overstreet / Fred Nixon
62 Oklahoma State	7 FB Kenny King
31 Nebraska■	24 DL Reggie Mathis / Barry Burget
	DL John Goodman
	DL Reggie Kinlaw
	DL Phil Tabor
	DL Bruce Taton
	LB George Cumby
	LB Daryl Hunt
	DB Basil Banks
	DB Jay Jimerson
	DB Darrol Ray
	DB Mike Babb / Sherwood Taylor

RUSHING: Sims 231/1762y, King 99/779y, Lott 111/577y
PASSING: Lott 21-55/440y, 6TD, 38.2%
RECEIVING: Kimball 12/198y, Rhodes 9/211y, Nixon 5/109y
SCORING: Sims 120pts, Uwe von Schamann (K) 80pts, Lott 54pts

1979 11-1

21 Iowa	6 WR Steve Rhodes / Bobby Grayson
49 Tulsa	13 T Louis Oubre
63 Rice	21 G Terry Crouch
49 Colorado	24 C Paul Tabor
7 Texas	16 G Don Key
38 Kansas State	6 T Ed Culver / Lyndle Byford
38 Iowa State	9 TE Forrest Valora
38 Oklahoma State	7 QB J.C. Watts
38 Kansas	0 HB David Overstreet / Fred Nixon
24 Missouri	22 HB Billy Sims
17 Nebraska	14 FB Stanley Wilson / Weldon Ledbetter
24 Florida State■	7 DL Barry Burget
	DL Keith Gary
	DL Johnny Lewis
	DL Richard Turner
	DL John Goodman / Bruce Taton
	LB George Cumby
	LB Barry Dittman
	DB Bud Hebert / Mike Babb
	DB Basil Banks / Jay Jimerson
	DB Darrol Ray
	DB Sherwood Taylor

RUSHING: Sims 248/1670y, Wilson 119/696y
PASSING: Watts 41-85/821y, 4TD, 48.2%
RECEIVING: Rhodes 15/346y, Nixon 15/293y
SCORING: Sims 138pts,

1980 10-2

29 Kentucky	7 WR Steve Rhodes / Bobby Grayson
14 Stanford	31 T Louis Oubre
82 Colorado	42 G Terry Crouch
13 Texas	20 C Bill Bechtold
35 Kansas State	21 G Don Key
42 Iowa State	7 T Ed Culver / Lyndle Byford
41 North Carolina	7 TE Forest Valora
21 Kansas	19 QB J.C. Watts
17 Missouri	17 HB Buster Rhymes / Chet Winters
21 Nebraska	17 HB David Overstreet
63 Oklahoma State	7 FB Stanley Wilson
18 Florida State■	17 DL Orlando Flanagan / Mike Weddington
	DL Scott Dawson / Keith Gary
	DL Johnny Lewis / John Blake
	DL Richard Turner
	DL Steve Whaley
	LB Mike Coast
	LB Mike Reilly / Sherdeill Breathett
	DB Darrell Songy / Basil Banks
	DB Byron Paul / Gary Lowell
	DB Steve Haworth
	DB Jay Jimerson / Ken Sitton

RUSHING: Overstreet 96/678y, Watts 163/663y, Wilson 120/659y
PASSING: Watts 35-78/905y, 2TD, 44.9%
RECEIVING: Grayson 14/389y, Rhodes 10/251y, Valora 5/152y
SCORING: Watts 108pts, Rhymes 60pts, Mike Keeling (K) 54pts

1981 7-4-1

37 Wyoming	20 WR Bobby Grayson / Paul Clewis
24 Southern Cal	28 T Ed Culver / Elbert Graham
7 Iowa State	7 G Terry Crouch
14 Texas	34 C Bill Bechtold
45 Kansas	7 G Don Key / Steve Williams
42 Oregon State	3 T Lyndle Byford
49 Colorado	0 TE Jeff Williams
28 Kansas State	21 QB Darrell Shepard / Kelly Phelps
14 Missouri	19 WB Buster Rhymes
14 Nebraska	37 HB Chet Winters/ Alvin Ross / Steve Sewell
27 Oklahoma State	3 FB Stanley Wilson
40 Houston■	14 DL John Truitt
	DL Bob Slater
	DL Johnnie Lewis
	DL Rick Bryan
	DL Steve Whaley
	LB Thomas Benson
	LB Jackie Shipp
	DB Barrion Walker
	DB Elbert Watts
	DB Dwight Drane
	DB Gary Lowell / Keith Stanberry

RUSHING: Wilson 156/1008y, Shepard 122/774y, Rhymes 68/442y
PASSING: Shepard 26-56/371y, 3TD, 50%
RECEIVING: Grayson 12/249y, Clewis 7/88y, 2 tied w/ 5
SCORING: Shepard 80pts, Mike Keeling (K) 45pts, Rhymes 32pts

1982 8-4

27 West Virginia	41 WR Paul Clewis / David Carter
29 Kentucky	8 T Rocky Hubble / Eric Pope
0 Southern Cal	12 G Paul Parker
13 Iowa State	3 C Chuck Thomas / Paul Ferrer
28 Texas	22 G Steve Williams
38 Kansas	14 T Brent Burks / Sidney Dodd
27 Oklahoma State	9 TE Johnny Fontenette
45 Colorado	10 QB Kelly Phelps
24 Kansas State	10 HB Fred Sims / Chet Winters
41 Missouri	14 HB Marcus DuPree
24 Nebraska	28 FB Stanley Wilson / Weldon Ledbetter
21 Arizona State■	32 DL Kevin Murphy
	DL Rick Bryan
	DL John Blake
	DL Bob Slater / Danny Wilson
	DL Daryl Goodlow / John Truitt
	LB Jackie Shipp
	LB Thomas Benson
	DB Dwight Drane / Steve Haworth
	DB Scott Case
	DB Keith Stanberry
	DB Darrell Songy

RUSHING: DuPree 129/905y, Wilson 172/835y, Sims 116/625y
PASSING: Phelps 33-91/492y, 1TD, 36.3%
RECEIVING: Carter 11/218y, Clewis 9/137y, Wilson 6/65y
SCORING: DuPree 78pts, Mike Keeling (K) 46pts, Phelps 42pts

1983 8-4

27 Stanford	14 WR Buster Rhymes
14 Ohio State	24 T Brent Burks / Sidney Dodd
28 Tulsa	18 G Paul Parker
29 Kansas State	10 C Chuck Thomas
16 Texas	28 G Jeff Pickett / Eric Pope
21 Oklahoma State	20 T David Dillingham
49 Iowa State	11 TE Johnny Fontenette
45 Kansas	14 QB Danny Bradley
0 Missouri	10 HB Steve Sewell / Derrick Shepard
41 Colorado	28 HB Earl Johnson / Marcus Dupree
21 Nebraska	28 FB Spencer Tillman
21 Hawaii	17 DL Daryl Goodlow
	DL Rick Bryan
	DL Tony Casillas
	DL Bob Slater
	DL Kevin Murphy
	LB Thomas Benson
	LB Jackie Shipp
	DB Jim Rockford
	DB Dwight Drane
	DB Keith Stanberry
	DB Scott Case

RUSHING: Tillman 188/1047y, Johnson 148/945y, Bradley 128/426y
PASSING: Bradley 61-143/1125y, 7TD, 42.7%
RECEIVING: Rhymes 32/747y, Shepard 19/314y, Sewell 9/116y
SCORING: Tillman 60pts, Johnson & Tim Lashar (K) 50pts

1984 9-2-1

19 Stanford	7 WR Derrick Shepard / Buster Rhymes
42 Pittsburgh	10 T Brent Burks
34 Baylor	15 G Eric Pope
24 Kansas State	6 C Chuck Thomas
15 Texas	15 G Jeff Pickett
12 Iowa State	10 T David Dillingham
11 Kansas	28 TE Keith Jackson
49 Missouri	7 QB Danny Bradley
42 Colorado	17 HB Steve Sewell
17 Nebraska	17 HB Spencer Tillman / Patrick Collins
24 Oklahoma State	14 FB Lydell Carr
17 Washington■	28 DL Darrell Reed
	DL Jeff Tupper / Richard Reed
	DL Tony Casillas
	DL Tommy Flemons / Steve Bryan
	DL Troy Johnson
	LB Paul Migliazzo / Dante Jones
	LB Brian Bosworth
	DB Andre Johnson / Rickey Dixon
	DB Jim Rockford / Brian Hall
	DB Keith Stanberry / Tony Rayburn
	DB Sonny Brown

RUSHING: Carr 138/625y, Sewell 98/577y, Tillman 119/449y
PASSING: Bradley 67-130/971y, 8TD, 51.5%
RECEIVING: Shepard 24/305y, Sewell 16/315y, Jackson 15/223y
SCORING: Tim Lashar (K) 63pts, Bradley 48pts, Sewell, 42pts

1985 11-1

13 Minnesota	7 WR Derrick Shepard
41 Kansas State	6 T Mark Hutson
14 Texas	7 G Eric Pope
14 Miami	27 C Travis Simpson
59 Iowa State	14 G Paul Ferrer
48 Kansas	6 T Anthony Phillips
51 Missouri	6 TE Keith Jackson
31 Colorado	0 QB Jamelle Holieway / Troy Aikman
27 Nebraska	7 HB Anthony Stafford/ L. Perry/ Damon Stell
13 Oklahoma State	0 HB Patrick Collins / Don Maloney
35 SMU	13 FB Lydell Carr
25 Penn State■	10 DL Darrell Reed
	DL Jeff Tupper
	DL Tony Casillas
	DL Steve Bryan
	DL Kevin Murphy
	LB Paul Migliazzo / Dante Jones
	LB Brian Bosworth
	DB Derrick White
	DB Derrick Crudup / Ledell Glenn
	DB Tony Rayburn / Ricky Dixon
	DB Sonny Brown / David Vickers

RUSHING: Carr 188/883y, Holieway 161/861y
PASSING: Holieway 24-58/517y, 5TD, 41.4%
RECEIVING: Jackson 20/486y
SCORING: Tim Lashar (K) 88pts

1986 11-1

38 UCLA	3 WR Derrick Shepard / Carl Cabbiness
63 Minnesota	0 T Greg Johnson
16 Miami	28 G Mark Hutson
56 Kansas State	10 C Travis Simpson
47 Texas	12 G Anthony Phillips
19 Oklahoma State	0 T Jon Phillips
38 Iowa State	0 TE Keith Jackson
64 Kansas	3 QB Jamelle Holieway
77 Missouri	0 WB Patrick Collins
28 Colorado	0 HB Spencer Tillman / Earl Johnson
20 Nebraska	17 FB Lydell Carr / Leon Perry
42 Arkansas■	8 DL Troy Johnson
	DL Steve Bryan
	DL Dante Williams
	DL Richard Reed
	DL Darrell Reed / Mike Mantle
	LB Dante Jones / Paul Migliazzo
	LB Brian Bosworth
	DB Sonny Brown
	DB Derrick White / Lonnie Finch
	DB Rickey Dixon
	DB David Vickers

RUSHING: Holieway 139/811y, Carr 101/548y, Johnson 72/537y
PASSING: Holieway 30-63/541y, 4TD, 47.6%
RECEIVING: Jackson 14/403y, Shepard 13/198y, Cabbiness 6/110y
SCORING: Tim Lashar (K) 96pts, Collins, Holieway & Jackson 48pts

1987 11-1

69 North Texas	14 WR Carl Cabbiness / Artie Guess
28 North Carolina	0 T Jon Phillips
65 Tulsa	9 G Mark Hutson
56 Iowa State	3 C Bob Latham
44 Texas	9 G Anthony Phillips
59 Kansas State	10 T Greg Johnson
24 Colorado	6 TE Keith Jackson
71 Kansas	10 QB Jamelle Holieway / Charles Thompson
29 Oklahoma State	10 HB Anthony Stafford
17 Missouri	13 HB Patrick Collins
17 Nebraska	7 FB Lydell Carr / Rotnei Anderson
14 Miami■	20 DL Darrell Reed
	DL Darren Kilpatrick / Scott Evans
	DL Dante Williams
	DL Curtice Williams
	DL Troy Johnson
	LB Richard Dillon / Keith Kaspar
	LB Dante Jones
	DB Lonnie Finch
	DB Derrick White
	DB David Vickers
	DB Rickey Dixon

RUSHING: Holieway 142/860y, Thompson 105/731y, Carr 105/676y
PASSING: Holieway 21-62/548y, 7TD, 33.8%
RECEIVING: Jackson 13/358y, Cabbiness 10/235y, 2 tied w/ 3
SCORING: R.D. Lashar (K) 89pts, Holieway & Thompson 60pts

1988 9-3

28 North Carolina	0 WR Eric Bross / Artie Guess
28 Arizona	10 T Terron Manning
7 Southern Cal	23 G Larry Medice / Mike Sawatzky
35 Iowa State	7 C Mike Wise
28 Texas	10 G Anthony Phillips
70 Kansas State	24 T Mark Van Keirsbilck
17 Colorado	14 TE Adrian Cooper
63 Kansas	14 QB Charles Thompson / Jamelle Holieway
31 Oklahoma State	28 HB Mike Gaddis
16 Missouri	7 HB Anthony Stafford
3 Nebraska	7 FB Leon Perry
6 Clemson■	13 DL Wayne Dickson
	DL Scott Evans
	DL Tony Woods
	DL Curtice Williams / Tom Backes
	DL James Goode
	LB Keith Kaspar
	LB Frank Blevins
	DB Kem McMichel
	DB Kevin Thompson
	DB Jerry Parks
	DB Scott Garl

RUSHING: Thompson 145/829y, Perry 110/546y, Gaddis 80/516y
PASSING: Holieway 27-41/548y, 5TD, 65.9%
RECEIVING: Bross 14/279y, Perry 7/125y, Guess 5/88y
SCORING: Thompson 56pts, R.D. Lashar (K) 52pts, Perry 42pts

1989 7-4

73 New Mexico	3 WR Eric Bross / Artie Guess
33 Baylor	7 T Terron Manning
3 Arizona	6 G Mike Sawatzky
45 Kansas	6 C Mike Wise
37 Oklahoma State	15 G Larry Medice
24 Texas	28 T Mark Van Keirsbilck
43 Iowa State	40 TE Adrian Cooper
3 Colorado	20 QB Steve Collins
52 Missouri	14 HB Ted Long / Dewell Brewer
42 Kansas State	19 HB Mike Gaddis / Dewell Lewis
25 Nebraska	42 FB Leon Perry
	DL James Goode / Tracy Gordon
	DL Tom Backes / Stacey Dillard
	DL Dante Williams
	DL Scott Evans
	DL Wayne Dickson
	LB Frank Blevins
	LB Chris Wilson
	DB Jason Belser / Greg DeQuasie
	DB Charles Franks
	DB Terry Ray
	DB Kevin Thompson

RUSHING: Gaddis 110/829y, Brewer 118/584y, Perry 132/582y
PASSING: Collins 18-49/442y, 3TD, 36.7%
RECEIVING: Guess 9/357y, Bross 6/121y, Cooper 5/46y
SCORING: R.D. Lashar (K) 84pts, Gaddis 60pts, Perry 54pts

1990 8-3

34 UCLA	14 WR Corey Warren / Artie Guess
52 Pittsburgh	10 T Jeff Miller
52 Tulsa	10 G Mike Sawatzky
31 Kansas	17 C Randy Wallace
31 Oklahoma State	17 G Larry Medice
13 Texas	14 T Brandon Houston
31 Iowa State	33 TE Adrian Cooper
23 Colorado	32 QB Cale Gundy
55 Missouri	10 HB Ted Long / Otis Taylor
34 Kansas State	7 HB Dewell Brewer
45 Nebraska	10 FB Kenyon Rasheed / Mike McKinley
	DL Reggie Barnes
	DL Tom Backes / Corey Mayfield
	DL Stacey Dillard
	DL Scott Evans
	DL James Goode
	LB Chris Wilson
	LB Joe Bowden
	DB Charles Franks
	DB Darnell Walker
	DB Jason Belser / Greg DeQuasie
	DB Terry Ray

RUSHING: Brewer 154/872y, Rasheed 124/661y, McKinley 88/534y
PASSING: Gundy 54-109/904y, 4TD, 49.5%
RECEIVING: Cooper 13/301y, Taylor 13/217y, Guess 11/129y
SCORING: R.D. Lashar (K) 95pts, Rasheed 60pts, Brewer 48pts

1991 9-3

40 North Texas	2 WR Ted Long
55 Utah State	21 WR Corey Warren
27 Virginia Tech	17 T Brian Brauninger
29 Iowa State	8 G Paul Moriarty
7 Texas	10 C Randy Wallace
17 Colorado	34 G Jeff Resler
41 Kansas	3 T Brandon Houston
28 Kansas State	7 TE Joey Mickey
56 Missouri	16 QB Cale Gundy
21 Oklahoma State	6 TB Mike Gaddis / Dewell Brewer
14 Nebraska	19 FB Mike McKinley / Kenyon Rasheed
48 Virginia■	14 DL Trey Tippens
	DL Stacey Dillard
	DL Corey Mayfield / Ricky Wren
	DL Proctor Land
	DL Reggie Barnes
	LB Joe Bowden
	LB Chris Wilson / Mike Coats
	DB Darnell Walker
	DB Charles Franks / Drew Christmon
	DB Terry Ray
	DB Jason Belser

RUSHING: Gaddis 221/1240y, Rasheed 77/355y, McKinley 88/346y
PASSING: Gundy 91-172/1228y, 8TD, 42.9%
RECEIVING: Warren 26/366y, Long 24/302y, Mickey 13/127y
SCORING: Gaddis 84pts, Scott Blanton (K) 43pts, McKinley & Rasheed 24pts

1992 5-4-2

34 Texas Tech	9 WR Albert Hall / P.J. Mills
61 Arkansas State	0 WR Corey Warren
10 Southern Cal	20 T Paul Moriarty
14 Iowa State	3 G Broderick Roberson
24 Texas	34 C J.R. Conrad
24 Colorado	24 G Jeff Resler
10 Kansas	27 T Jason Comer
16 Kansas State	14 TE Joey Mickey
55 Missouri	17 QB Cale Gundy
15 Oklahoma State	15 TB Earnest Williams / Dewell Brewer
9 Nebraska	33 FB Kenyon Rasheed
	DL Joe Correia
	DL David Campbell / Ricky Wren
	DL Russell Allen / Cedric Jones
	LB Aubrey Beavers
	LB Mike Coats
	LB Tremayne Green / Mario Freeman
	LB Reggie Barnes / Trey Tippens
	DB William Shankle / Darrius Johnson
	DB Darnell Walker
	DB Maylon Wesley
	DB John Anderson / Drew Christmon

RUSHING: Brewer 120/521y, Williams 101/514y, Rasheed 106/426y
PASSING: Gundy 131-227/1914y, 9TD, 57.7%
RECEIVING: Warren 35/659y, Hall 21/234y, Mills 18/296y
SCORING: Scott Blanton (K) 75pts, Williams 30pts, Brewer & Hall 24pts

OKLAHOMA

1993 9-3

35 TCU	3 WR Albert Hall
44 Texas A&M	14 WR Corey Warren
41 Tulsa	20 T Ben Cavil / J.R. Conrad
24 Iowa State	7 G Joe Carollo / Broderick Roberson
38 Texas	17 C Chuck Langston
10 Colorado	27 G Milton Overton
38 Kansas	21 T Harry Stamps
7 Kansas State	23 TE Rickey Brady
42 Missouri	23 QB Cale Gundy
31 Oklahoma State	0 TB James Allen
7 Nebraska	21 FB Terry Collier / Dwayne Chandler
41 Texas Tech ■	10 DL David Campbell / Russell Allen
	DL Joe Correia / Ricky Wren
	DL Cedric Jones
	LB Aubrey Beavers
	LB Mike Coats / Tremayne Green
	LB Mario Freeman
	LB Brent DeQuasie
	DB Darrius Johnson
	DB Shankle
	DB John Anderson
	DB Larry Bush

RUSHING: Allen 153/739y, Collier 88/463y, Moore 70/325y
PASSING: Gundy 144-243/2096y, 14TD, 59.3%
RECEIVING: Brady 35/536y, Warren 26/387y, Hall 21/366y
SCORING: Scott Blanton (K) 71pts, Chandler 60pts, Gundy 36pts

1994 6-6

30 Syracuse	29 WR Albert Hall / Mike McDaniel
14 Texas A&M	36 WR P.J. Mills
17 Texas Tech	11 T Harry Stamps
34 Iowa State	6 G Ben Cavil
10 Texas	17 C Chuck Langston
7 Colorado	45 G Milton Overton (TE) / Bruce McClure
20 Kansas	17 T J.R. Conrad
20 Kansas State	37 TE Stephen Alexander / Jason Harmon
30 Missouri	13 QB Garrick McGee
33 Oklahoma State	14 TB James Allen / Jeff Frazier
3 Nebraska	13 FB Jerald Moore / Dwayne Chandler
6 BYU ■	31 DL David Campbell / Barron Tanner
	DL Fred Lewis / Martin Chase
	DL Cedric Jones
	LB Collin Rosenberg / Broderick Simpson
	LB Mario Freeman
	LB Tyrell Peters
	LB Brent DeQuasie / Stirling Luckey
	DB Larry Bush
	DB Darrius Johnson
	DB Anthony Fogle
	DB Rod Henderson / John Anderson

RUSHING: Moore 129/659y, Allen 136/543y, Frazier 69/370y
PASSING: McGee 149-284/1909y, 8TD, 52.4%
RECEIVING: Hall 36/515y, Mills 29/432y, Allen 18/155y
SCORING: Moore 66pts, Scott Blanton (K) 44pts, McDaniel 22pts

1995 5-5-1

38 San Diego State	22 WR JaJuan Penny
24 SMU	10 WR P.J. Mills
51 North Texas	10 T Harry Stamps
17 Colorado	38 G Milton Overton
39 Iowa State	26 C Chuck Langston
24 Texas	24 G Joe Carollo
17 Kansas	38 T J.R. Conrad / Bruce McClure
13 Missouri	9 TE Stephen Alexander
10 Kansas State	49 QB Eric Moore
0 Oklahoma State	12 TB James Allen
0 Nebraska	37 FB Jerald Moore
	DL Stirling Luckey / Rod Manuel / T. Smith
	DL Baron Tanner
	DL Martin Chase / Arthur Atkins
	DL Cedric Jones
	LB Broderick Simpson
	LB Tyrell Peters
	LB Brent DeQuasie
	DB Darrius Johnson
	DB Larry Bush
	DB Anthony Fogle / Rod Henderson
	DB Maylon Wesley

RUSHING: J. Moore 165/1001y, Allen 87/338y, E. Moore 91/231y
PASSING: E. Moore 90-200/1375y, 7TD, 45.0%
RECEIVING: Alexander 43/580y, Mills 25/507y, Moore 19/216y
SCORING: Jeremy Alexander (K) 65pts, J. Moore 62pts, Mills 26pts

1996 3-8

7 TCU	20 WR Michael McDaniel / Chris Blocker
31 San Diego State	51 WR Gerald Williams / Jarrail Jackson
24 Tulsa	31 T Barry Giles / Sammy Williams
24 Kansas	52 G Derrick Nelson
30 Baylor	27 C Bruce McClure
28 Baylor	24 G Chris Campbell
35 Kansas State	42 T Jay Smith
21 Nebraska	73 TE Stephen Alexander / Jason Freeman
27 Oklahoma State	17 QB Justin Fuente / Eric Moore
16 Texas A&M	33 TB De'Mond Parker / James Allen
12 Texas Tech	22 FB Dwayne Chandler / Michael Rose
	DL Rod Manuel
	DL Kelly Gregg
	DL Barton Tanner
	DL Martin Chase
	LB Travian Smith (DL) / Chris Justice
	LB Tyrell Peters
	LB Broderick Simpson / Dale Allen
	DB Cedric Stephens / Mike Woods
	DB Anthony Fogle
	DB Gana Joseph
	DB Terry White / Dan Beisiegel

RUSHING: Parker 180/1184y, Allen 163/768y, Moore 46/181y
PASSING: Fuente 91-196/1271y, 8TD, 46.4%
RECEIVING: McDaniel 28/553y, Alexander 22/438y, Allen 18/152y
SCORING: Parker 60pts, Jeremy Alexander (K) 57pts, McDaniel 36pts

1997 4-8

0 Northwestern	24 WR Jarrail Jackson / Gerald Williams
36 Syracuse	34 WR Mo Little / Chris Blocker
36 California	40 T Scott Kempenich
35 Louisville	14 G Tim Macias / Barry Giles
17 Kansas	20 C Bruce McClure
24 Texas	27 G Adam Carpenter/Greg Moyer/J.
Bronson	
24 Baylor	23 T Sammy Williams
7 Kansas State	26 TE Stephen Alexander
7 Nebraska	69 QB Justin Fuente / Eric Moore / B. Daniels
7 Oklahoma State	30 TB De'Mond Parker
7 Texas A&M	51 FB Jermaine Fazande / Michael Rose
32 Texas Tech	21 DL Corey Callens
	DL Kelly Gregg
	DL Martin Chase
	DL Cornelius Burton / Rocky Bright
	LB Travian Smith
	LB C.L. Ivy / Sedric Jones
	LB Dale Allen / Terrance Malone
	DB Corey Ivy / Pee Wee Woods
	DB Mike Woods
	DB Gana Joseph
	DB Terry White

RUSHING: Parker 194/1143y, Fazande 105/491y, Moore 66/265y
PASSING: Fuente 69-129/1018y, 2TD, 53.5%
RECEIVING: Alexander 29/450y, Little 27/390y, Parker 11/140y
SCORING: Jeremy Alexander (K) 41pts, Parker 36pts, Moore & Fazande 30pts

1998 5-6

37 North Texas	9 WR Jarrail Jackson / Ahmed Kabba
10 TCU	9 WR/HB Chris Blocker / Jay Fazande (FB)
12 California	13 T Scott Kempenich / Stocker McDougle
25 Colorado	27 G Bubba Burcham / Jason Bronson
3 Texas	34 C Matt O'Neal
6 Missouri	20 G Adam Carpenter / Jay Smith
26 Oklahoma State	41 T Tim Macias
17 Iowa State	14 TE Jason Freeman
0 Texas A&M	29 QB Jake Sills/ Brandon Daniels /Eric Moore
28 Baylor	16 HB De'Mond Parker
20 Texas Tech	17 FB Seth Littrell / Jermaine Fazande
	DL Cornelius Burton
	DL Kelly Gregg
	DL Ryan Fisher / Jeremy Wilson-Guest
	DL Rocky Bright
	LB Ontei Jones
	LB Brandon Moore
	LB Rocky Calmus / Dale Allen
	DB Mike Woods
	DB Corey Ivy
	DB Terry White / Rodney Rideau
	DB Gana Joseph

RUSHING: Parker 204/1077y, Littrell 55/205y, Fazande 42/161y
PASSING: Sills 39-83/502y, 5TD, 47.0%
RECEIVING: Blocker 14/206y, Parker 14/176y, Jackson 12/218y
SCORING: Matt Reeves (K) 42pts, Parker 36pts, Kabba & Fazande 18pts

1999 7-5

49 Indiana State	0 WR Jarrial Jackson / Curtis Fagan
41 Baylor	10 WR Brandon Daniels / Antwone Savage
42 Louisville	21 T Al Baysinger / Frank Romero
30 Notre Dame	34 G Jay Smith
28 Texas	38 C Matt O'Neal
51 Texas A&M	6 G Bubba Burcham
24 Colorado	38 T Stocker McDougle
37 Missouri	0 TE Trent Smith / Chris Hammons
31 Iowa State	10 QB Josh Heupel
28 Texas Tech	38 HB Mike Thornton / Quentin Griffin
44 Oklahoma State	44 FB Seth Littrell / Reggie Skinner
25 Mississippi ■	27 DL Corey Callens
	DL Ryan Fisher
	DL Bary Holleyman / Ramon Richardson
	DL Cornelius Burton / Corey Heinecke
	LB Roger Steffen / Brandon Moore
	LB Torrance Marshall
	LB Rocky Calmus
	DB Mike Woods
	DB Pee Wee Woods / Michael Thompson
	DB Rodney Rideau
	DB William Bartee / Roy Williams

RUSHING: Thornton 78/383y, Griffin 44/285y, Skinner 50/283y
PASSING: Heupel 310-500/3460y, 30TD, 62.0%
RECEIVING: Daniels 50/572y, Jackson 44/583y, Savage 31/426y
SCORING: Tim Duncan (K) 88pts, Littrell 48pts, Jackson 42pts

2000 13-0

55 UTEP	14 WR Antwone Savage / Curtis Fagan
45 Arkansas State	7 WR Andre Woolfolk
42 Rice	14 T Frank Romero
34 Kansas	16 G Howard Duncan / Al Baysinger
63 Texas	14 C Bubba Burcham
41 Kansas State	31 G Mike Skinner
31 Nebraska	14 T Scott Kempenich
56 Baylor	7 TE Trent Smith
35 Texas A&M	31 QB Josh Heupel
27 Texas Tech	13 TB Quentin Griffin / Renaldo Works
12 Oklahoma State	7 FB/WR Seth Littrell / Josh Norman
27 Kansas State□	24 DL Corey Heinecke
13 Florida State■	2 DL Ryan Fisher
	DL Kory Klein / Ramon Richardson
	DL Corey Callens
	LB Roger Steffen / Ontei Jones
	LB Torrance Marshall
	LB Rocky Calmus
	DB Michael Thompson
	DB Derrick Strait
	DB J.T. Thatcher / Brandon Everage
	DB Roy Williams

RUSHING: Griffin 189/783y, Works 83/377y, Savage 12/160y
PASSING: Heupel 280-433/3392y, 20TD, 64.7%
RECEIVING: Savage 48/598y, Griffin 45/406y, Fagan 40/567y
SCORING: Tim Duncan (K) 98pts, Griffin 96pts, Fagan 48pts

2001 11-2

41 North Carolina	27 WR Mark Clayton / Antwone Savage
44 Air Force	3 WR Curtis Fagan
37 North Texas	10 WR/HB Josh Norman / Chris Toney
38 Kansas State	37 T Frank Romero
14 Texas	3 G Howard Duncan
38 Kansas	10 C Vince Carter
33 Baylor	17 G Mike Skinner
10 Nebraska	20 T Wes Sims/ Jerod Fields / Jammal Brown
58 Tulsa	0 TE Trent Smith
31 Texas A&M	10 QB Nate Hybl / Jason White
30 Texas Tech	13 RB Quentin Griffin / Renaldo Works
13 Oklahoma State	16 DL Corey Heinecke / Dan Cody
10 Arkansas■	3 DL Kory Klein
	DL Tommie Harris / Dusty Dvoracek
	DL Jimmy Wilkerson / Jonathan Jackson
	LB Brandon Moore
	LB Teddy Lehman
	LB Rocky Calmus
	DB Andre Woolfolk (WR) / Antonio Perkins
	DB Derrick Strait
	DB Brandon Everage
	DB Roy Williams

RUSHING: Griffin 201/860y, Works 48/297y, White 52/164y
PASSING: Hybl 245-411/2391y, 14TD, 59.6%
White 73-113/681y, 5TD, 64.6%
RECEIVING: Smith 65/585y, Griffin 64/472y, Norman 52/479y
SCORING: Tim Duncan (K) 114pts, Griffin 66pts, Savage, Smith & Works 36pts

2002 12-2

37 Tulsa	0 WR Curtis Fagan / Mark Clayton
37 Alabama	27 WR Will Peoples
68 UTEP	0 WR/RB Antwone Savage / Renaldo Works
31 South Florida	14 T Wes Sims
31 Missouri	24 G Brad Davis / Kelvin Chiasson
35 Texas	24 C Vince Carter / Chris Bush
49 Iowa State	3 G Mike Skinner / Davin Joseph
27 Colorado	11 T Jammal Brown
26 Texas A&M	30 TE Trent Smith
49 Baylor	9 QB Nate Hybl
60 Texas Tech	15 RB Quentin Griffin / Kejuan Jones
28 Oklahoma State	38 DL Jimmy Wilkerson
29 Colorado□	7 DL Tommie Harris / Lynn McGruder
34 Washington St.■	14 DL Kory Klein / Dusty Dvoracek
	DL Jonathan Jackson
	LB Teddy Lehman
	LB Lance Mitchell
	LB/DB Pasha Jackson / Matt McCoy
	DB Andre Woolfolk / Antonio Perkins
	DB Derrick Strait
	DB Brandon Everage
	DB Eric Bassey / Brandon Shelby

RUSHING: Griffin 287/1884y, Jones 165/613y, Works 34/152y
PASSING: Hybl 209-363/2538y, 24TD, 57.6%
RECEIVING: Smith 46/396y, Peoples 39/571y, Savage 35/438y
SCORING: Griffin 108pts, Trey DiCarlo (K) 106pts, Jones 84pts

2003 12-2

37 North Texas	3 WR Jejuan Rankins / Will Peoples
20 Alabama	13 WR Mark Clayton
52 Fresno State	28 WR/FB Brandon Jones / J.D. Runnels
59 UCLA	24 T Wes Sims
53 Iowa State	7 G Kelvin Chaisson
65 Texas	13 C Vince Carter / Chris Bush
34 Missouri	13 G Davin Joseph
34 Colorado	20 T Jammal Brown
52 Oklahoma State	9 TE Lance Donley / Bubba Moses
77 Texas A&M	0 QB Jason White
41 Baylor	3 RB Kejuan Jones / Renaldo Works
56 Texas Tech	25 DL Jonathan Jackson
7 Kansas State□	35 DL Dusty Dvoracek / Lynn McGruder
14 LSU■	21 DL Tommie Harris / Kory Klein
	DL Dan Cody / Larry Birdine
	LB G. Allen/ Wayne Chambers/ L. Mitchell
	LB Teddy Lehman
	DB/LB Brodney Pool / Pasha Jackson
	DB Derrick Strait
	DB Antonio Perkins
	DB Brandon Everage
	DB Donte Nicholson

RUSHING: Jones 225/925y, Works 146/716y,
  Donta Hickson (RB) 78/306y
PASSING: White 278-451/3846y, 40TD, 61.6%
RECEIVING: Clayton 83/1425y, Jones 46/709y, Rankins 33/406y
SCORING: Trey DiCarlo (K) 131pts, Clayton 90pts, K. Jones 84pts

2004 12-1

40 Bowling Green	24 WR Brandon Jones / Mark Bradley
63 Houston	13 WR Travis Wilson / Will Peoples
31 Oregon	7 WR Mark Clayton
28 Texas Tech	13 T Wes Sims
12 Texas	0 G Kelvin Chaisson / Chris Bush (C)
31 Kansas State	21 C Vince Carter (G)
41 Kansas	10 G Davin Joseph
38 Oklahoma State	35 T Jammal Brown
42 Texas A&M	35 TE/FB James Moses / J.D. Runnels
30 Nebraska	3 QB Jason White
35 Baylor	0 RB Adrian Peterson / Kejuan Jones
42 Colorado□	3 DL Dan Cody
19 Southern Cal■	55 DL Carl Pendleton / Remi Ayodele
	DL Lynn McGruder / Dusty Dvoracek
	DL Jonathan Jackson / Larry Birdine
	LB Clint Ingram
	LB Lance Mitchell
	LB Rufus Alexander / Gayron Allen
	DB Antonio Perkins (RB) / Brandon Shelby
	DB Donte Nicholson
	DB Brodney Pool
	DB Eric Bassey / Chijioke Onyenegecha

RUSHING: Peterson 339/1925y, Jones 129/513y
PASSING: White 255-390/3205y, 35TD, 65.4%
RECEIVING: Clayton 66/876y, Wilson 50/660y, Jones 27/345y
SCORING: Peterson 90pts, Trey DiCarlo (K) 69pts, Wilson 66pts

2005 8-4

10 TCU	17 WR Juaquin Iglesias/Jejuan Rankins
31 Tulsa	15 WR Travis Wilson/ Paul Thompson(QB)
31 UCLA	41 WR Malcolm Kelly/Manuel Johnson
43 Kansas State	21 T Davin Joseph
12 Texas	45 G Kelvin Chaisson
19 Kansas	3 C Chris Bush / Jon Cooper
37 Baylor	30 G Chris Chester / J. D. Quinn
31 Nebraska	24 T Chris Messner / Branndon Braxton
36 Texas A&M	30 TE/FB Joe Jon Finley / J.D. Runnels
21 Texas Tech	23 QB Rhett Bomar
42 Oklahoma State	14 RB Adrian Peterson / KeJuan Jones
17 Oregon■	14 DL Calvin Thibodeaux
	DL Remi Ayodele / Cory Bennett
	DL Dusty Dvoracek
	DL C. J. Ah You / Larry Birdine
	LB Rufus Alexander / Lewis Baker
	LB Zach Latimer
	LB Clint Ingram
	DB D. J. Wolfe / Nic Harris
	DB Eric Bassey / Jason Carter
	DB Reggie Smith / C. Onyenegecha
	DB Darien Williams

RUSHING: Peterson 220/1104y, Jones 86/280y,
  Jacob Gutierrez (RB) 48/254y
PASSING: Bomar 167-308/2018y, 10TD, 54.2%
RECEIVING: Kelly 33/471y, Wilson 25/310y, Runnels 20/205y
SCORING: Peterson 84pts, Garrett Hartley (K) 79pts,
  Jones & Bomar 24pts

2006 11-3

24 UAB	17 WR Juaquin Iglesias / Fred Strong
37 Washington	20 WR Malcolm Kelly
33 Oregon	34 WR/FB M. Johnson / Brody Eldridge
59 Middle Tenn.	0 T Chris Messner
10 Texas	28 G George Robinson
34 Iowa State	9 C Jon Cooper / Chase Beeler
24 Colorado	3 G Brandon Walker
26 Missouri	10 T Branndon Braxton / Trent Williams
17 Texas A&M	16 TE Joe Jon Finley
34 Texas Tech	24 QB Paul Thompson
36 Baylor	10 RB Adrian Peterson / Allen Patrick
27 Oklahoma State	21 DL C. J. Ah You / Calvin Thibodeaux
21 Nebraska□	7 DL Steven Coleman/Carl Pendleton
42 Boise State■	43 DL Cory Bennett/ DeMarcus Granger
	DL Larry Birdine
	LB Rufus Alexander / Lewis Baker
	LB Zach Latimer / Demarrio Pleasant
	LB/DB Curtis Lofton / Nic Harris
	DB Marcus Walker / D. J. Wolfe
	DB Lendy Holmes
	DB Darien Williams / Keenan Clayton
	DB Reggie Smith / Jason Carter

RUSHING: Peterson 188/1012y, Patrick 169/761y,
  Chris Brown (RB) 70/343y
PASSING: Thompson 204-336/2667y, 22TD, 60.7%
RECEIVING: Kelly 62/993y, Iglesias 41/514y, Johnson 36/378y
SCORING: Garrett Hartley (K) 106pts, Peterson 78pts, Kelly 60pts

2007 11-3

79 North Texas	10 WR Malcolm Kelly
51 Miami	13 WR Juaquin Iglesias/Quentin Chaney
54 Utah State	3 T Phil Loadholt
62 Tulsa	21 G George Robinson
24 Colorado	27 C Jon Cooper
28 Texas	21 G Brandon Walker / Brian Simmons
41 Missouri	31 T Trent Williams / Branndon Braxton
17 Iowa State	7 TE Joe Jon Finley / Jermaine Gresham
42 Texas A&M	14 TE/WR Brody Eldridge/Manuel Johnson
52 Baylor	21 QB Sam Bradford
27 Texas Tech	34 RB Allen Patrick / DeMarco Murray
49 Oklahoma St.	17 DL Auston English/Alan Davis/Jeremy Beal
38 Missouri□	17 DL Gerald McCoy / Cory Bennett
28 West Virginia■	48 DL DeMarc Granger / Adrian Taylor
	DL Alonzo Dotson / Darie Williams
	LB Curtis Lofton
	LB Lewis Baker
	LB/DB Ryan Reynolds / Lendy Holmes
	DB Marcus Walker
	DB Reggie Smith
	DB Nic Harris
	DB D.J. Wolfe

RUSHING: Patrick 173/1009y, Murray 127/764y,
  Chris Brown (RB) 158/611y
PASSING: Bradford 237-341/3121y, 36TD, 69.5%
RECEIVING: Iglesias 68/907y, Kelly 49/821y, Gresham 37/518y
SCORING: Garret Hartley (K) 110pts, Murray 90pts, Gresham 66pts

2008 12-2

57 Chattanooga	2 WR Juaquin Iglesias
52 Cincinnati	26 WR Manuel Johnson / Quentin Chaney
55 Washington	14 WR/TE Ryan Broyles / Brody Eldridge
35 TCU	45 T Phil Loadholt
49 Baylor	17 G George Robinson
35 Texas	45 C Jon Cooper
45 Kansas	31 G Brandon Walker
58 Kansas State	35 T Trent Williams
62 Nebraska	28 TE Jermaine Gresham
66 Texas A&M	28 QB Sam Bradford
65 Texas Tech	21 TB DeMarco Murray / Chris Brown
61 Oklahoma State	41 DL Auston English / Frank Alexander
62 Missouri□	21 DL Gerald McCoy
14 Florida■	24 DL Adrian Taylor
	DL Jeremy Beal
	LB Keenan Clayton
	LB Ryan Reynolds / Austin Box
	LB Travis Lewis
	DB Dominque Franks
	DB Brian Jackson
	DB Lendy Holmes
	DB Nic Harris / Quinton Carter

RUSHING: Brown 217/1220y, Murray 179/1002y,
  Mossis Madu (RB) 115/475y
PASSING: Bradford 328-483/4720y, 50TD, 67.9%
RECEIVING: Iglesias 74/1150y, Gresham 66/950y,
  Broyles 46/687y
SCORING: Brown 126pts, Jimmy Stevens (K) 118pts,
  Murray 108pts

2009 8-5

13 BYU	14 WR Cameron Kenney / Brandon Caleb
64 Idaho State	0 WR Ryan Broyles / Adron Tennell
45 Tulsa	0 WR/FB DeJuan Miller / Matt Clapp
20 Miami	21 T Trent Williams / Eric Mensik (TE)
33 Baylor	7 G Brian Simmons(T) / Cory Brandon(T)
13 Texas	16 C Ben Habern / Brody Eldridge(G-TE)
35 Kansas	13 G Stephen Good (C) / Tavar Jeffries
42 Kansas State	30 T Jarvis Jones (G) / Tyler Evans
3 Nebraska	10 TE James Hanna (T)/Trent Ratterree (WR)
65 Texas A&M	10 QB Landry Jones / Sam Bradford
13 Texas Tech	41 RB Chris Brown / DeMarco Murray
27 Oklahoma State	0 DL Jeremy Beal
31 Stanford■	27 DL Adrian Taylor
	DL Gerald McCoy
	DL Auston English / Frank Alexander
	LB Keenan Clayton / Ronnell Lewis
	LB Ryan Reynolds / Austin Box
	LB Travis Lewis
	DB Dominque Franks
	DB Brian Jackson
	DB Quinton Carter
	DB Sam Proctor / Jonathan Nelson

RUSHING: Brown 182/749y, Murray 171/705y,
  Jermie Calhoun (RB) 45/220y
PASSING: Jones 261-449/3198y, 26TD, 58.1%
  Bradford 39-69/562y, 2TD, 56.5%
RECEIVING: Broyles 89/1120y, Murray 41/522y, Miller 36/434
  Caleb 26/408y, Tennell 24/297y
SCORING: Broyles 102pts, Murray 72pts, Jimmy Stevens (K) 60pts

2010 12-2

31 Utah State	24 WR Kenny Stills / Cameron Kenney
47 Florida State	17 WR Ryan Broyles / Dejuan Miller
27 Air Force	24 WR/TE Trey Franks / Trent Ratterree
31 Cincinnati	29 T Don Stephenson / Jarvis Jones
28 Texas	20 G Gabe Ikard / Stephen Good
52 Iowa State	0 C Ben Habern
27 Missouri	36 G Tyler Evans / Brian Lepak
43 Colorado	10 T Eric Mensik
19 Texas A&M	33 TE James Hanna
45 Texas Tech	7 QB Landry Jones
53 Baylor	24 RB DeMarco Murray / Roy Finch
47 Oklahoma State	41 DL Jeremy Beal / Casey Walker
23 Nebraska□	20 DL Stacy McGee/Pryce Macon/David King
48 Connecticut■	20 DL Adrian Taylor / Jamarkus McFarland
	DL Frank Alexander / Ronnell Lewis
	LB Tom Wort / Austin Box
	LB Travis Lewis
	LB/DB Joseph Ibiloye / Tony Jefferson
	DB Jamell Fleming / Aaron Colvin
	DB Demontre Hurst / Javon Harris
	DB Quinton Carter
	DB Jonathan Nelson

RUSHING: Murray 282/1214y, Finch 85/398y,
  Mossis Madu (RB) 59/254y
PASSING: Jones 405-617/4718y, 38TD, 65.6%
RECEIVING: Broyles 131/1622y, Murray 71/594y, Stills 61/786y
SCORING: Murray 120pts, Jimmy Stevens (K) 110pts, Broyles 84pts

OKLAHOMA STATE

Oklahoma State University (Founded 1890)
Stillwater, Oklahoma
Nickname: Cowboys
Colors: Orange and Black
Stadium: Boone Pickens Stadium (1920) 60,000
Conference Affiliations: Missouri Valley (1925-56), Independent (1957-59), Big Eight (1960-95), Big Twelve South (1996-present)

CAREER RUSHING YARDS	Attempts	Yards
Thurman Thomas (1984-87)	898	4595
Terry Miller (1974-77)	848	4581
David Thompson (1993-96)	848	4314
Kendall Hunter (2007-10)	708	4181
Barry Sanders (1986-88)	523	3556
Ernest Anderson (1979-83)	713	3529
Tatum Bell (2000-03)	657	3409
Gerald Hudson (1988-90)	513	2921
Keith Toston (2006-09)	473	2725
Shawn Jones (1980-84)	636	2698

CAREER PASSING YARDS	Comp.-Att.	Yards
Zac Robinson (2006-09)	610-999	8317
Mike Gundy (1986-89)	604-1035	7997
Josh Fields (2000-03)	445-815	6090
Tone Jones (1993-96)	402-819	4812
Brandon Weeden (2008-10)	358-538	4533
Tony Lindsay (1997-00)	281-529	4002
Aso Pogi (2000-02)	335-583	3673
Rusty Hilger (1981-84)	280-515	3640
Bobby Reid (2005-07)	226-424	3143
Tony Pounds (1970-71)	189-402	2663

CAREER RECEIVING YARDS	Catches	Yards
Rashaun Woods (2000-03)	293	4414
Hart Lee Dykes (1985-88)	203	3171
D'Juan Woods (2003-06)	154	2604
Adarius Bowman (2004-07)	145	2516
Dez Bryant (2007-09)	147	2425
Justin Blackmon (2009-10)	131	2042
Hermann Eben (1968-70)	114	1973
Curtis Mayfield (1987-90)	93	1507
Dick Graham (1969-71)	97	1458
Brandon Pettigrew (2005-08)	112	1450

SEASON RUSHING YARDS	Attempts	Yards
Barry Sanders (1988)	344	2628
Ernest Anderson (1982)	353	1877
Terry Miller (1977)	314	1680
Gerald Hudson (1990)	279	1642
Thurman Thomas (1987)	251	1613

SEASON PASSING YARDS	Comp.-Att.	Yards
Brandon Weeden (2010)	342-511	4277
Josh Fields (2002)	226-408	3145
Zac Robinson (2008)	204-314	3064
Zac Robinson (2007)	201-333	2824
Josh Fields (2003)	184-338	2494

SEASON RECEIVING YARDS	Catches	Yards
Justin Blackmon (2010)	111	1782
Rashaun Woods (2002)	107	1695
Dez Bryant (2008)	87	1480
Rashaun Woods (2003)	77	1367
Hart Lee Dykes (1988)	74	1278

GAME RUSHING YARDS	Attempts	Yards
Barry Sanders (1988 vs. Texas Tech)	44	332
David Thompson (1996 vs. Baylor)	38	321
Barry Sanders (1988 vs. Kansas State)	42	320

GAME PASSING YARDS	Comp.-Att.	Yards
Brandon Weeden (2010 vs. Baylor)	34-42	435
Zac Robinson (2007 vs. Texas)	30-42	430
Mike Gundy (1989 vs. Kansas)	27-35	429

GAME RECEIVING YARDS	Catches	Yards
Adarius Bowman (2006 vs. Kansas)	13	300
Dez Bryant (2008 vs. Houston)	9	236
Rashaun Woods (2003 vs. SMU)	13	232

GREATEST COACH:

The race for this spot was hotly contested but Les Miles captures the prize largely due to his record versus rival Oklahoma. After lettering at Michigan (1974-5) under Bo Schembechler, Miles went into coaching at his alma mater in 1980. Two years later he followed Michigan assistant Bill McCartney to Colorado where he helped in the rebuilding effort. In 1987 he returned to Ann Arbor to assist in eight hugely successful years for the Wolverines, who went bowling each year including four Rose Bowls.

Miles's next stop was Stillwater, Oklahoma, where he became offensive coordinator under head coach Bob Simmons.

Of course every aspiring college head coach these days needs some NFL experience and Miles moved on to the Dallas Cowboys, with whom he coached tight ends. Oklahoma State had three straight losing seasons without Miles, which cost Simmons his job, and the school reached out to their former assistant. Miles was now a head coach.

Year one was a struggle with seven losses, including a five-game losing streak. But the fortunes of the Cowboys and Miles changed with a stunning final game road upset of no. 4 ranked Oklahoma, the defending national champions. With the stars of that win, quarterback Josh Fields and wide receiver Rashaun Woods, returning along with a host of other starters, there was renewed hope in Stillwater. Oklahoma State delivered with eight wins in 2002 and another victory over Oklahoma. The Cowboys parlayed a talented core of players into a nine-win season in 2003—the most for a Cowboys team since 1988—and a berth in the Cotton Bowl.

The Cowboys lost a great deal of talent after 2003, but Miles may have done his best coaching in leading them to seven wins and another bowl berth. Unfortunately the attention he had generated attracted the interest of Louisiana State, which hired him away for the 2005 season.

OKLAHOMA STATE'S 55 GREATEST SINCE 1953

OFFENSE

WIDE RECEIVER: Adarius Bowman, Dez Bryant, Hart Lee Dykes, Hermann Eben, Rashaun Woods
TIGHT END: Alonzo Mayes, Brandon Pettigrew
TACKLE: Paul Blair, Corey Hilliard, Russell Okung, John Ward, Byron Woodard
GUARD: Bon Boatwright, David Koenig, Kevin Igo, Chris Stanley
CENTER: Gary Chlouber, Jon Kolb
QUARTERBACK: Josh Fields, Mike Gundy, Zac Robinson
RUNNING BACK: Ernest Anderson, Terry Miller, Barry Sanders, Thurman Thomas
FULLBACK: Walt Garrison

DEFENSE

END: Rick Antle, Daria Butler, Jason Gildon, Dexter Manley
TACKLE: Phillip Dokes, Gary Lewis, John Little, Leslie O'Neal, James White, Kevin Williams
LINEBACKER: Keith Burns, John Corker, Matt Monger, Ricky Young, Cleveland Vann
CORNERBACK: Tony Banfield, Benny Goodwin, Darrent Williams
SAFETY: Alvin Brown, Harry Cheatwood, John Gates, Mark Moore

SPECIAL TEAMS

RETURN SPECIALIST: Terance Richardson
PLACE KICKER: Larry Roach
PUNTER: Cliff Parsley

MULTIPLE POSITIONS

CENTER-GUARD-TACKLE: Derrel Gofourth

TWO-WAY PLAYERS

HALFBACK-DEFENSIVE BACK: Bill Bredde
END-DEFENSIVE END-PUNTER: Jim Wood
WIDE RECEIVER-CORNERBACK-RETURNER: R.W. McQuarters

PERFORMANCE FORMULA:
OKLAHOMA STATE'S 10 BEST SEASONS

2010	1.5988	8 of 71
1988	1.5252	11 of 69
1984	1.5086	5 of 70
1987	1.4306	11 of 69
1976	1.4288	14 of 70
1958	1.4206	13 of 70
2008	1.3368	20 of 71
1975	1.3352	20 of 70
1983	1.3035	23 of 70
1953	1.2942	21 of 69

OKLAHOMA STATE COWBOYS

Year	W-L-T	AP Poll	Conference Standing	Toughest Regular Season Opponents	Coach (Record at School)	Bowl Games		
1953	7-3		1t	Oklahoma 8-1-1, Texas Tech 10-1, Detroit 6-4	J.B. Whitworth			
1954	5-4-1		3	Oklahoma 10-0, Wichita 9-1, Texas Tech 7-2-1	J.B. Whitworth (22-27-2)			
1955	2-8		4	Oklahoma 10-0, Texas Tech 7-2-1, Colorado A&M 8-2	Cliff Speegle			
1956	3-5-2		2t	Oklahoma 10-0, Arkansas 6-4, Houston 7-2-1, Tulsa 7-2-1	Cliff Speegle			
1957	6-3-1			Oklahoma 9-1, Arkansas 6-4, Kansas 5-4-1	Cliff Speegle			
1958	8-3	19		Oklahoma 9-1, Air Force 9-0-1, Tulsa 7-3	Cliff Speegle	Blue Grass	15 Florida State	6
1959	6-4			Oklahoma 7-3, Arkansas 8-2, Kansas 5-5	Cliff Speegle			
1960	3-7		6	Missouri 9-1, Arkansas 8-2, Kansas 7-2-1, Iowa State 7-3	Cliff Speegle			
1961	4-6		6	Colorado 9-1, Missouri 7-2-1, Kansas 6-3-1, Wichita 8-2	Cliff Speegle			
1962	4-6		6	Arkansas 9-1, Missouri 7-1-2, Oklahoma 8-2, Nebraska 8-2	Cliff Speegle (36-42-3)			
1963	1-8		8	Texas 10-0, Nebraska 9-1, Oklahoma 8-2, Missouri 7-3	Phil Cutchin			
1964	4-6		5	Arkansas 10-0, Nebraska 9-1, Oklahoma 6-3-1, Missouri 6-3-1	Phil Cutchin			
1965	3-7		6	Arkansas 10-0, Nebraska 10-0, Missouri 7-2-1, Texas Tech 8-2	Phil Cutchin			
1966	4-5-1		3	Nebraska 9-1, Arkansas 8-2, Houston 8-2, Colorado 7-3	Phil Cutchin			
1967	4-5-1		5	Oklahoma 9-1, Colorado 8-2, Missouri 7-3, Texas 6-4	Phil Cutchin			
1968	3-7		6	Arkansas 9-1, Kansas 9-1, Texas 8-1, Missouri 7-3	Phil Cutchin (19-38-2)			
1969	5-5		5t	Arkansas 9-1, Missouri 9-1, Nebraska 8-2, Houston 8-2	Floyd Gass			
1970	4-7		6	Nebraska 10-01, Arkansas 9-2, Oklahoma 7-4, Houston 8-3	Floyd Gass			
1971	4-6-1		5	Nebraska 12-0, Oklahoma 10-1, Arkansas 8-2-1, Colorado 9-2	Floyd Gass (13-18-1)			
1972	6-5		3t	Oklahoma 10-1, Nebraska 8-2-1, Colorado 8-3	Dave Smith (6-5)			
1973	5-4-2		4	Oklahoma 10-0-1, Nebraska 8-2-1, Texas Tech 9-1, Missouri 7-4	Jim Stanley	Fiesta	16 BYU	6
1974	7-5		4	Oklahoma 11-0, Baylor 8-3, Nebraska 8-3	Jim Stanley			
1975	7-4		5	Oklahoma 10-1, Nebraska 10-1, Arkansas 9-2, Kansas 7-4	Jim Stanley	Tangerine	49 BYU	21
1976	9-3	14	1	Oklahoma 8-2-1, Nebraska 8-2-1, Colorado 8-3	Jim Stanley			
1977	4-7		7	Oklahoma 10-1, Arkansas 10-1, Iowa State 8-3, Nebraska 8-3	Jim Stanley (35-31-2)			
1978	3-8		5	Oklahoma 10-1, Nebraska 9-2, Arkansas 9-2, Florida State 8-3	Jimmy Johnson			
1979	7-4		3	Oklahoma 10-1, Nebraska 10-1, Arkansas 10-1, So. Carolina 8-3	Jimmy Johnson			
1980	3-7-1		5	Oklahoma 9-2, Washington 9-2, Nebraska 9-2, Missouri 8-3	Jimmy Johnson			
1981	7-5		3	Nebraska 9-2, Oklahoma 6-4-1, Kansas 8-3	Jimmy Johnson	Independence	16 Texas A&M	33
1982	4-5-2		3	Nebraska 11-1, Oklahoma 8-3, Tulsa 10-1	Jimmy Johnson (29-25-3)			
1983	8-4		4	Nebraska 12-0, Missouri 7-4, Oklahoma 7-4	Pat Jones	Bluebonnet	24 Baylor	14
1984	10-2	7	3	Oklahoma 9-1-1, Nebraska 9-2	Pat Jones	Gator	21 South Carolina	14
1985	8-4		3	Oklahoma 10-1, Nebraska 9-2, Colorado 7-4, Washington 6-5	Pat Jones	Gator	23 Florida State	34
1986	6-5		4	Oklahoma 10-1, Nebraska 9-2, Colorado 6-5	Pat Jones			
1987	10-2	11	3	Oklahoma 11-0, Nebraska 10-1	Pat Jones	Sun	35 West Virginia	33
1988	10-2	11	3	Nebraska 11-1, Oklahoma 9-2, Colorado 8-3, Texas A&M 7-4	Pat Jones	Holiday	62 Wyoming	14
1989	4-7		5	Colorado 11-0, Nebraska 10-1, Texas Tech 8-3, Ohio State 8-3	Pat Jones			
1990	4-7		6t	Colorado 10-1-1, Nebraska 9-2, Florida 9-2, Oklahoma 8-3	Pat Jones			
1991	0-10-1		8	Miami 11-0, Nebraska 8-2-1, Oklahoma 8-3, Colorado 8-2-1	Pat Jones			
1992	4-6-1		5	Colorado 9-1-1, Nebraska 9-2, Michigan 8-0-3, Kansas 7-4	Pat Jones			
1993	3-8		8	Nebraska 11-0, Kansas State 8-2-1, Oklahoma 8-3, Colorado 7-3-1	Pat Jones			
1994	3-7-1		7t	Nebraska 12-0, Colorado 10-1, Kansas State 9-2, Baylor 7-4	Pat Jones (62-60-3)			
1995	4-8		5t	Nebraska 11-0, Colorado 9-2, Tennessee 10-1, Kansas State 9-2	Bob Simmons			
1996	5-6		S5	Colorado 9-2, Texas 7-4, Texas Tech 7-4	Bob Simmons			
1997	8-4	25	S2t	Texas A&M 9-2, Missouri 7-4, Texas Tech 6-5	Bob Simmons	Alamo	20 Purdue	33
1998	5-6		S4	Kansas State 11-0, Texas A&M 10-2, Nebraska 9-3, Texas 8-3	Bob Simmons			
1999	5-6		S5	Nebraska 10-1, Kansas State 10-1, Miss. State 9-2, Texas 9-3	Bob Simmons			
2000	3-8		S5	Oklahoma 11-0, Texas 9-2, Texas A&M 7-4	Bob Simmons (30-38)			
2001	4-7		S5	Oklahoma 10-2, Texas 10-1, Colorado 9-2, Texas A&M 7-4	Les Miles			
2002	8-5		S4	Oklahoma 10-2, Texas 10-2, Kansas State 10-2, UCLA 7-5	Les Miles	Houston	33 Southern Mississippi	23
2003	9-4		S3	Oklahoma 12-0, Kansas State 10-3, Texas 10-2, Nebraska 9-3	Les Miles	Cotton	28 Mississippi	31
2004	7-5		S5	Oklahoma 110-0, Texas 10-1, Texas A&M 7-4, Texas Tech 7-4	Les Miles (28-21)	Alamo	7 Ohio State	33
2005	4-7		S6	Texas 11-0, Texas Tech 9-2, Oklahoma 7-4, Colorado 7-4	Mike Gundy			
2006	6-6		S5t	Oklahoma 11-2, Texas 9-3, Nebraska 9-3, Texas A&M 9-3	Mike Gundy)			
2007	7-6		S3t	Georgia 10-2, Texas 9-3, Kansas 11-1, Oklahoma 10-2	Mike Gundy	Insight	49 Indiana	33
2008	9-4	16	S4	Missouri 9-4, Texas 11-1, TexasTech 11-1, Oklahoma 21-1	Mike Gundy	Holiday	31 Oregon	42
2009	9-4		S2	Houston 10-3, Texas 13-0, Texas Tech 8-4, Oklahoma 7-5	Mike Gundy	Cotton	7 Mississippi	21
2010	11-2	13	S1t	Tulsa 9-3, Texas A&M 9-3, Nebraska 10-3, Oklahoma 11-2	Mike Gundy (46-29)	Alamo	36 Arizona	10

TOTAL: 316-314-15 .5016 (46 of 70)   **Bowl Games since 1953:**   11-7 .6111 (13 of 70)

GREATEST TEAM SINCE 1953: Although the 2010 squad had a similarly excellent season--riding offensive firepower to a top 20 ranking and the top rung in our performance formula--the 1988 Oklahoma State squad, whose high-powered offense was headed by the incomparable Barry Sanders, may not have beaten Oklahoma and Nebraska, but they put up enough of a fight while sweeping the rest of the slate to top our ballot. Despite the 2,163 yards thrown by quarterback Mike Gundy, coach of the 2010 team, and the 74 receptions for 1,278 yards by wideout Hart Lee Dykes, the show was firmly Sanders's and he shone despite the full attention of every defender in rushing for 2,628 yards and scoring 234 points.

1953 7-3

20	Hardin-Simmons	0	E John Weigle /Ken McCullough
7	Arkansas	6	T Leland Kendall / Jack Hutchison
13	Texas Tech	27	G Bud Godsoe / Don Holcomb
14	Wichita	7	C Pat Fitter / Jim Lutes
14	Houston	7	G Buddy Ryan / John Payne (C)
14	Detroit	18	T Dale Meinert
28	Tulsa	14	E Bob LaRue
20	Wyoming	14	QB Bobby Andrew / Bobby Green
41	Kansas	14	HB Bill Bredde
7	Oklahoma	42	HB Dorsey Gibson
			FB Earl Lunsford

RUSHING: Lunsford 147/748y, Bredde 114/645y, Gibson 58/361y
PASSING: Green 16-35/219y, 1 TD, 45.7%
    Andrew 15-37/139y, 0 TD, 40.5%
RECEIVING: LaRue 12/122y, Weigle 7/69y, Bredde 5/88y
SCORING: Bredde, Lunsford & Gibson 36pts

1954 5-4-1

14	Wyoming	6	E Ken McCullough / Lee Snider
14	Texas A&M	6	T Leland Kendall / Hal Rinker
13	Texas Tech	13	G Don Holcomb
13	Wichita	22	C Jim Lutes / John Payne
7	Houston	14	G Dale Meinert (T) / Buddy Ryan
7	Hardin-Simmons	13	T Jack Hutchison / Hal Mahany
12	Tulsa	0	E Bob LaRue
34	Detroit	19	QB Fred Duvall / Fred Meyers
47	Kansas	12	HB Joel Favara / Harvey Romans
0	Oklahoma	14	HB Bill Whitt / Keith Kashmer
			FB Earl Lunsford

RUSHING: Lunsford 140/761y, Favara 58/288y, Whitt 47/246y
PASSING: Duvall 8-28/195y, 2TD, 28.6%
RECEIVING: LaRue 9/106y, Spencer 8/119y, 3 tied w/4
SCORING: Lunsford 54pts, Favara 18pts,
    Don Holcomb (K) & Kashwer 12pts

1955 2-8

0	Arkansas	21	E Choppy Spencer / Bill Williams
6	Texas Tech	24	T Dwaine Underwood / John McQuiston
7	Wichita	14	G Buddy Ryan / Bob Van Landingham
13	Houston	21	C Vern Womack / Bob Greenhaw
0	Detroit	7	G Jerry Budzik / Wayne Coble
14	Tulsa	0	T Jack Hutchison / Hal Mahaney
13	Colorado State	20	E Bob Curtis / Jon Evans
7	Kansas	12	QB Tom Pontius
28	Kansas State	0	HB Harvey Romans / John Jacob
0	Oklahoma	53	HB Forrest Campbell / Keith Kashmer
			FB Earl Lunsford / Joel Favara

RUSHING: Lunsford 140/596y
PASSING: Pontius 39-95/764y
RECEIVING: Spencer 18/319y
SCORING: Lunsford 30pts

1956 3-5-2

27	Kansas State	7	E McL Odell / Roland Butler
7	Arkansas	19	T Joe Holt / Ted Smith
32	Wichita	6	G Wayne Coble / Vandiver Childs
14	Tulsa	14	C John Calvin / Fred Latham
0	Houston	13	G Barry West / Howard Keys
13	Kansas	21	T Jim Howard / Dwaine Underwood
13	Texas Tech	13	E Jim Wood / Jack Motley / Jon Evans
0	LSU	13	QB Johnny Allen / Bill Borum
25	Detroit	7	HB Duane Wood / Jim Wiggins
0	Oklahoma	53	HB Keith Kashmer / Joel Favara
			FB Everett Wood / Larry Rundle

RUSHING: Wiggins 90/473y, D. Wood 87 393y, Rundle 62/278y
PASSING: Allen 23-55/380y, 1TD, 41.8%
RECEIVING: J. Wood 9/190y, Motley 8/95y, D. Wood 5/109y
SCORING: Wood 44pts, Favara 24pts, Wiggins & Borum 18pts

1957 6-3-1

0	Arkansas	12	E Jim Wood / Jon Evans
25	No. Texas St.	19	T Jim Howard / Joe Holt
26	Wichita	0	G Vandiver Childs
28	Tulsa	13	C John Calvin / Don Garner
6	Houston	6	G H.J. Green / Ros McAdams
13	Texas Tech	0	T McLindley Odell / Sonny Keys
39	Wyoming	6	E Jack Motley / Don Hitt
7	Kansas	13	QB Dick Soergel / Dave Cross
32	Hardin-Simmons	7	HB Duane Wood
6	Oklahoma	53	HB Jim Wiggins / Vernon Sewell
			FB Larry Rundle / Everett Wood

RUSHING: Wiggins 108/418y, Rundle 85/405y, D. Wood 61/271y
PASSING: Soergel 34-85/587y, 6TD, 40%
RECEIVING: J. Wood 16/316y, Wiggins 11/134y, Hitt 9/121y
SCORING: Wiggins 62pts, D. Wood & Rundle 19pts

1958 8-3

31	Denver	14	E C.J. Harkey
21	No. Texas St.	14	T Sonny Keys
43	Wichita	12	G Vandiver Childs
16	Tulsa	24	C Fred Latham
7	Houston	0	G John Calvin
19	Cincinnati	14	T Jim Howard
29	Air Force	33	E Jim Wood
14	Kansas State	7	QB Dick Soergel
6	Kansas	3	HB Duane Wood
0	Oklahoma	7	HB Jim Wiggins / Tony Banfield
15	Florida State ■	6	FB Forrest Campbell / Larry Rundle

RUSHING: D. Wood 100/573y, Wiggins 95/342y, Campbell 84/324y
PASSING: Soergel 42-91/616y, 5TD, 46.2%
RECEIVING: J. Wood 21/282y, D. Wood 11/191y, Wiggins 10/168y
SCORING: D. Wood 56pts, Wiggins 36pts, J. Wood 20pts

1959 6-4

9	Cincinnati	22	E Bill Dodson / George Walstad
7	Arkansas	13	T Frank Parker / Gary Cutsinger
27	Kansas State	21	G Richard DuPree
26	Tulsa	0	C Don Hitt / Charles Willingham
19	Houston	12	G James Frazier
34	Wichita	14	T Harold Beaty / John Ed Gardner
18	Marquette	12	E Blanchard Reel / C.J. Harkey
20	Denver	12	QB Dick Soergel
14	Kansas	28	HB Tony Banfield
7	Oklahoma	17	HB David Cross / Chester Pittman
			FB Jim Dillard / Vernon Sewell

RUSHING: Dillard 111/582y, Banfield 120/455y, Sewell 103/453y
PASSING: Soergel 93-155/1100y, 8TD, 60%
RECEIVING: Dodson 21/286y, Cross 17/168y, Banfield 13/156y,
SCORING: Banfield 66pts, Cross 25pts, Dillard 24pts

1960 3-7

0	Arkansas	9	E Bill Dodson / Blanchard Reel
7	Missouri	28	T Gary Cutsinger / Gerald Benn
28	Tulsa	7	G David Wilks / Lynn Pitts
7	Houston	12	C James Frazier
7	Kansas	14	G Charles Willingham (C) / Rod Replogle
6	Iowa State	13	T Harold Beaty / Frank Parker
28	Kansas State	7	E George Walstad / Ben Kraybill
7	Nebraska	6	QB John Maisel / Jim Elliott
6	Colorado	13	HB Tommy Jackson / Dick Buck (FB)
6	Oklahoma	17	HB Chester Pittman / Lonie Buchner
			FB Jim Dillard / Bob Adcock

RUSHING: Dillard 153/631y, Pittman 55/312y, Jackson 67/268y
PASSING: Elliott 10-30/90y, 0TD, 33.3%
RECEIVING: Dodson 7/41y, Jackson 6/110y, Buchner 5/62y
SCORING: Dillard 30pts, 4 tied w/ 12pts

1961 4-6

7	Iowa State	14	E George Walstad / Rod Replogle
0	Colorado	24	T Frank Parker
26	Tulsa	0	G Gary Cutsinger
0	Missouri	10	C Bill York / Jerry Runyan / Roy Peck
14	Nebraska	6	G Leland Slack / Charles Upton
8	Kansas	42	T Jim Dale Sellers / John Ed Gardner
13	Wichita	25	E Ben Kraybill/Don Brewington/Tom Ward
28	Houston	24	QB Bill Leming / Jim Elliott / Mike Miller
45	Kansas State	0	HB Jim Dillard
13	Oklahoma	21	HB Don Derrick / Tommy Jackson
			FB Bill McFarland

RUSHING: Dillard 128/627y, McFarland 82/331y, Derrick 53/213y
PASSING: Miller 37-86/371y, 0TD, 43%
RECEIVING: Brewington 14/215y, Dillard 14/71y, Ward 11/106y
SCORING: McFarland 42pts, Dillard 24pts, Davis 20pts

1962 4-6

7	Arkansas	34	E Don Brewington / Rodney Replogle
17	Tulsa	7	T Jerry Hammond / Jim Dale Sellers
36	Colorado	16	G Darrell Powell / Charles Upton
6	Missouri	23	C Jerry Runyan / Gary Bob Howard
17	Kansas	36	G Bennie Cravatt / Leland Slack
7	Iowa State	34	T John Ed Gardner / Rodney Cutsinger
12	Army	7	E Tom Ward/Don Karns/Marcus Hendricks
0	Nebraska	14	QB Mike Miller
30	Kansas State	6	HB Don Derrick / Bill Parent / Mutual Bryant
6	Oklahoma	37	HB Wardell Hollis/T.Jackson/David Hannah
			FB B. McFarland/Bob Adcock/Geo.Thomas

RUSHING: Derrick 110/539y, Hollis 69/331y, McFarland 38/177y
PASSING: Miller 81-180/1056y, 9TD, 45%
RECEIVING: Karns 21/328y, Brewington 19/243y, Hollis 12/95y
SCORING: Derrick 24pts, Hannah 24pts, Thomas 18pts

1963 1-8

0	Arkansas	21	E Bill McFarland / Lynn Chadwick
7	Texas	34	T Charles Harper / Leon Ward
0	Colorado	25	G Leland Slack
6	Missouri	28	C Hugh McCrabb
7	Kansas	41	G Gary Bob Howard
28	Iowa State	33	T Rusty Martin
33	Tulsa	24	E Jack Jacobson
16	Nebraska	20	QB Mike Miller
10	Oklahoma	34	HB Franklin Jeff Williams / Larry Elliott
			HB Bill Parent / Wardell Hollis
			FB George Thomas / Walt Garrison

RUSHING: Thomas 88/399y, Garrison 59/387y, Williams 48/216y
PASSING: Miller 64-127/674y, 1TD, 50.4%
RECEIVING: Jacobson 22/282y, Williams 10/64y, Chadwick 8/80y
SCORING: Miller 30pts, Thomas 24pts, Mickey Durkee (K) 17pts

1964 4-6

10	Arkansas	14	E Lynn Chadwick / Jack Jacobsen
29	Iowa State	14	T J.B. Christian
10	Missouri	7	G Peter Francis
14	Colorado	10	C Jim Click / Leon Ward
13	Kansas	14	G Rodney Cutsinger
1	Tulsa	61	T Harold Akin
31	Wichita	7	E Tony Sellari
14	Nebraska	27	QB Glenn Baxter
14	Kansas State	17	HB Franklin Jeff Williams / Larry Elliott
16	Oklahoma	21	HB David Dickerson
			FB Walt Garrison
			DL Jack Jacobson
			DL Dennis Randall
			DL Hugh McCrabb
			DL Charley Harper
			DL Rusty Martin
			DL George Thomas
			LB Leon Ward / Jim Click
			LB Ron Alexander
			DB Franklin Jeff Williams
			DB Wardell Hollis / Larry Elliott
			DB Jerry Gill / Happy Settle

RUSHING: Garrison 176/730y, Baxter 89/239y, Elliott 64/161y
PASSING: Baxter 55-136/845y, 4TD, 40.4%
RECEIVING: Sellari 17/238y, Williams 11/126y, Chadwick 10/208y
SCORING: Mickey Durkee (K) 37pts, Garrison 36pts, Baxter 30pts

1965 3-7

14	Arkansas	28	E Tony Sellari
0	Missouri	13	T Harold Akin
17	Tulsa	14	G J.B. Christian
11	Colorado	34	C Jim Click
14	Texas Tech	17	G Pete Francis / John Matlock
0	Kansas	9	T Tim Havern
10	Iowa State	14	E Lynn Chadwick
17	Nebraska	21	QB Glenn Baxter / Buddy Burris
31	Kansas State	7	HB Dan Lawson / Larry Elliott
17	Oklahoma	16	HB Dave Dickerson
			FB Walt Garrison
			DL Bill Young
			DL Hugh McCrabb
			DL David Davis / Jimmy Goodwin
			DL Charley Harper
			DL Dennis Randall
			DL Doug Cathey
			LB Jay Lavender
			LB Verne Miller
			DB Willard Nahrgang / Happy Settle
			DB Jerry Gill
			DB Harry Cheatwood

RUSHING: Garrison 217/924y, Burris 83/205y, Lawson 57/191y
PASSING: Baxter 43-112/574y, 2TD, 38.4%
RECEIVING: Sellari 21/226y, Chadwick 18/209y, 2 tied w/ 7
SCORING: Mickey Durkee (K) 37pts, Garrison 30pts, Baxter 18pts

1966 4-5-1

10	Arkansas	14 E Jerry Philpott / Ken Wallace
9	Houston	35 T J.B. Christian
11	Colorado	10 G Charlie Gasch / Ken McSwane
0	Missouri	7 C Jon Kolb
10	Kansas	7 G Jim Carreker / Art Fleak
14	Iowa State	14 T John Matlock / Tim Havern
7	Texas Tech	10 E Tony Sellari
6	Nebraska	21 QB Ronnie Johnson
21	Kansas State	6 WB Happy Settle / Buddy Burris
15	Oklahoma	14 HB Tom Boone

FB Jack Reynolds / Larry Gosney
DL Bill Young
DL Terry Bacigallipo
DL David Davis
DL Dennis Randall
DL Doug Cathey
LB Leon Ward
LB Rick McCoin / Ron Freeman (DL)
DB Terry Brown
DB Dan Lawson / Willard Nahrgang
DB Jerry Gill
DB Harry Cheatwood

RUSHING: Reynolds 153/585y, Boone 110/390y, Gosney 52/188y
PASSING: Johnson 60-127/659y, 2TD, 47.2%
RECEIVING: Philpott 28/312y, Settle 16/222y, Sellari 10/98y
SCORING: Reynolds & Johnson 24pts, Craig Kessler (K)19pts

1967 4-5-1

0	Air Force	0 E Jerry Philpott
7	Arkansas	6 T John Ward / Bruce Pieratt
0	Texas	19 G Jim Carreker
15	Kansas	26 C Jon Kolb
10	Colorado	7 G Ken McSwane
0	Missouri	7 T Jim Moeller / Art Fleak
0	Nebraska	9 E Jack Crissup / Steve Gray
28	Iowa State	14 QB Ronnie Johnson / Bruce Scott
49	Kansas State	14 WB Terry Brown
14	Oklahoma	38 HB Larry Gosney / Tommy Boone

FB Jack Reynolds
DL Joe Esch / Verne Miller
DL Bill Young
DL Dave Baughman / Jimmy Goodwin
DL John Little
DL Doug Cathey
LB Rick McCoin
LB Gary Darnell
DB Larry Kirkland / Willard Nahrgang
DB Benny Goodwin
DB Charles Trimble / Dick Bechtol
DB Harry Cheatwood

RUSHING: Reynolds 134/643y, Gosney 95/386y, Johnson 93/215y
PASSING: Johnson 42-91/494y, 3TD, 46.2%
 Scott 28-60/377y, 0TD, 46.7%
RECEIVING: Brown 34/425y, Philpott 20/216y, Crissup 5/74y
SCORING: Gosney 36pts, Johnson 24pts, Craig Kessler (K) 19pts

1968 3-7

15	Arkansas	32 WR Hermann Eben
3	Texas	31 T John Ward
21	Houston	17 G Tommy Noles/Jim Kelley/Brian Martin
14	Kansas	49 C Jon Kolb
20	Nebraska	21 G Fred Moore / Art Fleak
7	Missouri	42 T David Gaile
34	Colorado	17 TE Tom Dearinger
26	Iowa State	17 QB Ronnie Johnson
14	Kansas State	21 WB Terry Brown
7	Oklahoma	41 TB Bub Deerinwater / Wayne Hallmark

FB Jack Reynolds / Duane Porter
DL Joe Esch
DL Dave Baughman
DL John Little
DL Jerry Sherk
DL Jerry Philpott / Joe Coyle
LB Gary Darnell
LB Larry Gosney
DB Benny Goodwin
DB Larry Kirkland
DB John Gates
DB Charles Trimble / David Davis

RUSHING: Porter 75/307y, Hallmark 70/258y, Reynolds 73/248y
PASSING: Johnson 121-247/1438y, 5TD, 49%
RECEIVING: Brown 54/688y, Dearinger 34/369y, Eben 25/303y
SCORING: Johnson 50pts, Hallmark 20pts,
 Bob Cutburth (QB-K) 16pts

1969 5-5

0	Arkansas	39 WR Hermann Eben
24	Houston	18 WR Dick Graham
17	Texas Tech	10 T John Ward
21	Missouri	31 G Carl Armstrong
3	Nebraska	13 C Tommy Noles
28	Kansas	25 G Fred Moore
28	Kansas State	19 T David Gaile / Dan Blackard
14	Colorado	17 TE Tom Dearinger
35	Iowa State	0 QB Bob Cutburth
27	Oklahoma	28 HB Wayne Hallmark / Bobby Cole

FB Bub Deerinwater
DL Joe Coyle
DL Gill Barnes
DL John Little
DL Jerry Sherk
LB Steve Farris
LB Joe Crews / Woody Roof
LB Gary Darnell
DB Larry Kirkland / David Davis
DB Tom Carraway
DB John Gates
DB Benny Goodwin

RUSHING: Deerinwater 135/587y, Cole 45/190y, Hallmark 58/181y
PASSING: Cutburth 111-275/1593y, 16TD, 40.4%
RECEIVING: Eben 41/733y, Dearinger 24/263y, Graham 17/209y
SCORING: Eben 42pts, Cutburth 36pts, Uwe Pruss (K) 35pts

1970 4-7

13	Mississippi St.	14 WR Hermann Eben
7	Arkansas	23 WR Dick Graham
26	Houston	17 T Danny Blackard
20	Missouri	40 G Dan Heiker
34	TCU	20 C Tommy Noles
31	Nebraska	65 G Fred Moore
19	Kansas	7 T Bob Bridges
15	Kansas State	28 TE Tom Dearinger
6	Colorado	30 QB Tony Pounds
36	Iowa State	27 HB Bobby Cole
6	Oklahoma	66 FB Jimmy Williams

DL Don Geier
DL Gill Barnes
DL John Carter / Tim Potts
DL Joe Coyle / John Allen
LB George Farris / Doug Tarrant
LB Joe Crews
LB Barty Chappell
DB Eugene Jefferson / Glenn Bonner
DB Tom Carraway / David Davis
DB Lee Stover
DB John Gates

RUSHING: Cole 167/685y, Williams 132/498y, Graham 50/223y
PASSING: Pounds 133-269/1871y, 15TD, 49.4%
RECEIVING: Eben 48/937y, Graham 39/618y, Dearinger 14/161y
SCORING: Graham 48pts, Eben 44pts, Cole 30pts

1971 4-6-1

26	Mississippi St.	7 WR Reuben Gant / Steve Pettes
10	Arkansas	31 WR Dick Graham
24	Virginia Tech	16 T Mike Treece
14	TCU	14 G Bon Boatwright / Bard Peevy
37	Missouri	16 C Bert Jacobson
13	Nebraska	41 G Dick O'Connell / Pat Yates
17	Kansas	10 T Mike Clendennen
23	Kansas State	35 TE Charlie Beall / Eddie Garrett
6	Colorado	40 QB Tony Pounds / Brent Blackman
0	Iowa State	54 HB Bobby Cole
14	Oklahoma	58 FB Cleveland Vann / Tommy Lee Woods

DL Don Geier
DL Jimmy Williams
DL Barry Price
DL Jay Cruse
LB Joe Crews / David Ennis / Robert Bacon
LB Bubba Bain
LB Mark Hatley
DB Tom Carraway
DB Eugene Jefferson
DB Glenn Bonner
DB Travis Wilkey

RUSHING: Cole 176/631y, Vann 65/240y, Blackman 77/219y
PASSING: Pounds 56-133/792y, 5TD, 42.1%
RECEIVING: Graham 41/631y, Cole 14/98y, Gant 8/181y
SCORING: Blackman & Graham 30pts, Uwe Pruss (K) 26pts

1972 6-5

21	UT-Arlington	3 WR Steve Pettes
23	Arkansas	24 WR Alton Gerard (HB) / Tom Stremme
31	Colorado	6 T Tom Wolf
17	Missouri	16 G Pat Yates
32	Virginia Tech	34 C Bert Jacobson
20	Baylor	7 G Bon Boatwright
0	Nebraska	34 T Mike Clendennen
10	Kansas	13 TE Reuben Gant / Eddie Garrett
45	Kansas state	14 QB Brent Blackman
45	Iowa State	14 HB Fountain Smith
15	Oklahoma	38 FB George Palmer

DL Glenn Robinson
DL Barry Price
DL Jimmy Williams
DL Gilbert Barnes
DL Doug Tarrant
LB David Ennis
LB Cleveland Vann
LB Bubba Bain / Jessie Hudson
DB Darryll Stewart / Mike Terry
DB Alvin Brown
DB Lee Stover

RUSHING: Palmer 193/937y, Blackman 166/842y, Smith 90/610y
PASSING: Blackman 30-102/572y, 6TD, 29.4%
RECEIVING: Pettes 9/194y, Gant 8/151y, Stremme 5/120y
SCORING: Garrett (TE-K) 55pts, Gerard 42pts, Blackman 32pts

1973 5-4-2

56	UT-Arlington	7 WR Steve Pettes / Ricky Taylor
28	Arkansas	6 T Tom Wolf
70	So. Illinois	7 G Calvin Payne / Mike Kennedy
7	Texas Tech	20 C Gary Chlouber
9	Missouri	13 G Bon Boatwright
17	Nebraska	17 T Mike Clendennen
10	Kansas	10 TE Reuben Gant
28	Kansas State	9 WB Leonard Thompson
38	Colorado	24 QB Brent Blackman
12	Iowa State	28 HB Alfred Nelms / Fountain Smith
18	Oklahoma	45 FB George Palmer

DL James White / Tony Buck
DL Carl Devorce / Phil Dokes
DL Barry Price
DL Calvin Miller
DL Glenn Robinson
LB Jesse Hudson / Brent Robinson
LB Cleveland Vann
DB Mike Terry / Reggie Pierson
DB Darryl Stewart
DB Lee Stover
DB Alvin Brown

RUSHING: Blackman 175/809y, Palmer 160/657y,
 Thompson 90/518y
PASSING: Blackman 40-110/602y, 3TD, 36.4%
RECEIVING: Gant 19/447y, Pettes 9/125y, Taylor 7/132y
SCORING: Abby Daigle (K) 53pts, Thompson 38pts,
 Blackman & Palmer 36pts

1974 7-5

59	Wichita State	0 WR Gerald Bain / Sam Lisle
26	Arkansas	7 T Tom Wolf
14	Baylor	31 G Gene Ritz / Jim Ledford
13	Texas Tech	14 C Gary Chlouber
31	Missouri	9 G S.L. Stephens
3	Nebraska	7 T Derrel Gofourth
24	Kansas	13 TE John Boyer / Bruce Blankenship
29	Kansas State	5 WB Skip Taylor / Leonard Thompson
20	Colorado	37 QB Charlie Weatherbie
14	Iowa State	12 HB Terry Miller / Kenny Walker
13	Oklahoma	44 FB George Palmer / Robert Turner
16	BYU ■	6 DL Jesse Hudson / Mike Allen

DL Phil Dokes
DL Carl Devorce
DL James White / Calvin Miller
DL Tony Buck
LB Brent Robinson
LB Marcellous Mitchell
DB Reggie Pierson
DB Bob Shephard
DB Darnell Myers
DB Mike Terry

RUSHING: Palmer 99/516y, Miller 87/334y, Thompson 77/323y
PASSING: Weatherbie 42-113/622y, 2TD, 37.2%
RECEIVING: Bain 16/336y, Lisle 7/128y, Boyer 7/69y
SCORING: Abby Daigle (K) 58pts, Weatherbie 32pts, Walker 30pts

1975 7-4

34 Wichita State	0 WR Gerald Bain
20 Arkansas	13 T Larry Harris
61 No. Texas St.	7 G Derrel Gofourth
17 Texas Tech	16 C Gary Chlouber
14 Missouri	41 G Jim Ledford
20 Nebraska	28 T Mark Perrelli
35 Kansas	19 TE Bruce Blankenship
7 Oklahoma	27 WB Sam Lisle / Ricky Taylor
7 Colorado	17 QB Scott Burk / Charlie Weatherbie
56 Kansas State	3 HB Terry Miller
14 Iowa State	7 FB Robert Turner
	DL Daria Butler
	DL Phil Dokes
	DL Richard Allen
	DL James White
	DL Bobby Douglas / Lorenzo Turner
	LB John Weimer / Don Edwards
	LB Brent Robinson
	DB Willie Lester / Gary Irions
	DB Clifton Sullivan
	DB Darnell Meyers
	DB Jerry Cramer / Joe Avanzini

RUSHING: Miller 179/1026y, Turner 185/992y, Burk 95/277y
PASSING: Burk 20-58/300y, 2TD, 34.5%
Weatherbie 23-46/563y, 5TD, 50%
RECEIVING: Lisle 16/384y, Bain 15/307y, Taylor 15/269y
SCORING: Miller 66pts, Turner 54pts, Bain 24pts

1976 9-3

33 Tulsa	21 WR Sam Lisle
10 Arkansas	16 WR Ricky Taylor / Gerald Bain
16 No. Texas St.	10 T Mark Perrelli
21 Kansas	14 G Jim Ledford / Craig Simmons
10 Colorado	20 C Derrel Gofourth (T) / Mike Ritz
31 Oklahoma	24 G Ron Baker
20 Missouri	19 T Robert Ringwall
10 Nebraska	14 TE Bruce Blankenship / Steve Stephens
45 Kansas State	21 QB Charlie Weatherbie / Harold Bailey
42 Iowa State	21 HB Terry Miller
42 UTEP	13 FB Robert Turner / Skip Taylor
49 BYU■	21 DL Daria Butler
	DL Chris Dawson
	DL Richard Allen
	DL Phil Dokes
	DL Lorenzo Turner
	LB John Weimer
	LB John Corker
	DB Milton Kirven
	DB Willie Lester / Clifton Sullivan
	DB Peter Coppola
	DB Gary Irions

RUSHING: Miller 291/1714y, Turner 131/561y,
Weatherbie 133/418y
PASSING: Weatherbie 42-109/779y, 4TD, 38.5%
RECEIVING: Lisle 23/387y, Taylor 9/149y, Bain 7/152y
SCORING: Miller 138pts, Abby Daigle (K) 65pts, Turner 48pts

1977 4-7

34 Tulsa	17 WR Gerald Bain
6 Arkansas	28 WR L.P. Williams
54 UTEP	0 T Jim Clark / Dudley Stephenson
17 Florida State	25 G Craig Simmons
13 Colorado	29 C Dave Monroe
21 Kansas State	14 G Reggie Hall / Reggie Richardson
21 Kansas	0 T Milton Hardaway
14 Nebraska	31 TE Steve Stephens / Don Echols
28 Oklahoma	61 QB Randy Stephenson / Harold Bailey
14 Missouri	41 HB Terry Miller
13 Iowa State	21 FB SkipTaylor / Vince Orange
	DL Daria Butler
	DL Chris Dawson
	DL Joe Avanzini
	DL Michael Robinson / Curtis Boone
	DL Mike Edwards / Dexter Manley
	LB John Corker
	LB Larry Jackson / George Suda
	DB Gregg Johnson
	DB Willie Lester
	DB Peter Coppola
	DB Gary Irions

RUSHING: Miller 319/1680y, Bailey 91/456y, Taylor 63/310y
PASSING: Stephenson 22-61/386y, 2TD, 36.1%
RECEIVING: Bain 16/349y, Williams 11/233y, Orange 8/52y
SCORING: Miller 84pts, Colin Ankerson (K) 37pts, 3 tied w/18pts

1978 3-8

10 Wichita State	20 WR L.P. Williams
20 Florida State	38 WR Mel Campbell/Jim Cowins /Ron Ingram
7 Arkansas	19 T Jody Tillman
7 No. Texas St.	12 G Craig Simmons
7 Kansas State	18 C Dave Monroe
24 Colorado	20 G Reggie Richardson
21 Kansas	7 T Marty Shepherd
14 Nebraska	22 TE Steve Stephens
35 Missouri	20 QB Scott Burk
15 Iowa State	28 HB Ed Smith / Terry Suellentrop
7 Oklahoma	62 FB Worley Taylor
	DL Curtis Boone
	DL Billy Wells
	DL Jerry Winchester
	DL Roger Taylor
	LB Mike Edwards
	LB John Corker
	LB Rick Antle
	DB Gregg Johnson
	DB John Odom / Gary Irions
	DB Peter Coppola
	DB Darnell Scott

RUSHING: Taylor 176/807y, Suellentrop 70/321y, Smith 50/181y
PASSING: Burk 50-134/722y, 2TD, 37.3%
RECEIVING: Williams 14/166y, Campbell 8/153y, Stephens 8/83y
SCORING: Burk & Suellentrop 32pts, Colin Ankerson (K) 29pts

1979 7-4

25 No. Texas St.	7 WR James Cowins
16 Wichita State	6 WR Ron Ingram
7 Arkansas	27 T Paul Speight
16 So. Carolina	23 G Drew Hetzler
14 Missouri	13 C Kevin Bennett
0 Nebraska	36 G Reggie Richardson
30 Kansas	17 T Roger Taylor / Jody Tillman
7 Oklahoma	38 TE Don Echols
21 Colorado	20 QB Harold Bailey / John Doerner
42 Kansas State	15 HB Ed Smith / Terry Suellentrop
13 Iowa State	10 FB Worley Taylor
	DL Rick Antle
	DL Curtis Boone
	DL Steve Heinzler
	DL Dean Prater
	DL Dexter Manley
	LB John Corker
	LB Ricky Young
	DB Greg Hill
	DB Jerry Lewis
	DB Pete DiClementi
	DB Gregg Johnson

RUSHING: Taylor 216/994y, Smith 53/220y, Suellentrop 42/212y
PASSING: Bailey 94-210/1301y, 5TD, 44.8%
RECEIVING: Echols 20/293y, Taylor 20/193y, Ingram 19/323y
SCORING: Colin Ankerson (K) 55pts, Ingram & Taylor 24pts

1980 3-7-1

19 W. Texas St.	20 WR Mel Campbell
20 Arkansas	33 WR Ron Ingram
18 Washington	24 T Roy Hackett
7 Missouri	30 G Drew Hetzler
7 Nebraska	48 C Kevin Bennett
14 Kansas (F-W)	14 G Mark Granger
15 San Diego State	6 T Roger Taylor
42 Colorado	7 TE James Cowins / John Chesley
10 Kansas State	0 QB Houston Nutt /Jim Traber/John Doerner
21 Iowa State	23 TB Ed Smith
14 Oklahoma	63 FB Earnest Anderson / Worley Taylor
	DL Butch Crites / Louis Blackwell
	DL Curtis Boone
	DL Dean Prater
	DL Gary Lewis / Steve Heinzler
	DL Dexter Manley
	LB Mike Green
	LB Ricky Young
	DB Greg Hill
	DB Rod Fisher
	DB Chris Rockins / Pete DiClementi
	DB Gregg Johnson

RUSHING: Smith 158/613y, Anderson 103/438y, Taylor 97/326y
PASSING: Traber 46-99/619y, 3TD, 46.5%
Nutt 43-83/574y, 3TD, 51.8%
RECEIVING: Campbell 39/536y, Ingram 16/246y, Cowins 15/191y
SCORING: Colin Ankerson (K) 39pts, Smith 36pts, Campbell 32pts

1981 7-5

23 Tulsa	21 WR Mark Cromer
16 San Diego State	23 WR Terry Young / Ron Ingram
9 No. Texas St.	0 T John Cegielski
20 Kansas	7 G Paul Speight / Kevin Igo
10 Colorado	11 C Doug Freeman
19 Louisville	11 G Mark Granger
16 Missouri	12 T Russell Graham
7 Nebraska	54 TE John Chesley
31 Kansas State	10 QB John Doerner / Rusty Hilger
27 Iowa State	7 TB Shawn Jones / James Evans
3 Oklahoma	27 FB Ernest Anderson
16 Texas A&M■	33 DL Rodney Harding
	DL Louis Blackwell
	DL Gary Lewis
	DL Gary Chachere
	DL Allen Benson / Brent Guy
	LB Mike Green
	LB Ricky Young
	DB Greg Hill
	DB Raymond Polk / Rod Fisher
	DB Pete DiClementi
	DB Chris Rockins

RUSHING: Jones 209/788y, Anderson 129/678y, Evans 70/253y
PASSING: Doerner 79-145/877y, 4TD, 54.5%
RECEIVING: Chesley 26/350y, Young 22/284y, Cromer 19/347y
SCORING: Larry Roach (K) 71pts, Chesley 26pts, Jones 24pts

1982 4-5-2

27 No. Texas St.	6 WR Mark Cromer
15 Tulsa	25 WR Terry Young
22 Louisville	28 T John Cegielski
24 Kansas	24 G Kevin Igo
25 Colorado	25 C Doug Freeman
9 Oklahoma	27 G Paul Speight
30 Missouri	20 T Russ Graham
10 Nebraska	48 TE John Chesley / Barry Hanna
24 Kansas State	16 QB Ike Jackson / Rusty Hilger
49 Iowa State	13 TB Ernest Anderson
6 San Diego State	35 FB Kelly Cook
	DL Brent Guy
	DL Gary Chachere
	DL Gary Lewis
	DL Keith Brown / Tim Reeves
	DL Rodney Harding
	LB Mike Green
	LB James Spencer
	DB Greg Hill
	DB Rod Brown / Rod Fisher
	DB Chris Rockins
	DB Raymond Polk

RUSHING: Anderson 353/1877y, Harry Roberts (TB) 77/378y,
Cook 40/218y
PASSING: Jackson 100-198/1254y, 7TD, 50.5%
RECEIVING: Young 35/507y, Cromer 28/409y, Anderson 21/103y
SCORING: Larry Roach (K) 65pts, Anderson 58pts, Cromer 24pts

1983 8-4

20 No. Texas St.	13 WR Malcolm Lewis / Bobby Riley
27 Cincinnati	17 WR Jamie Harris
34 Texas A&M	15 T John Cegielski
9 Tulsa	0 G Kevin Igo
10 Nebraska	14 C David Tucker
20 Oklahoma	21 G Ralph Partida
27 Kansas	10 T Paul Blair
40 Colorado	14 TE John Chesley / Barry Hanna
20 Kansas State	21 QB Rusty Hilger
10 Missouri	16 TB Shawn Jones / Earnest Anderson
30 Iowa State	7 FB Kelly Cook / Arthur Price
24 Baylor■	14 DL James Ham / Warren Thompson
	DL Rodney Harding
	DL John Washington
	DL Leslie O'Neal
	DL Harry Roberts (DB) / David Webb
	LB Matt Monger
	LB James Spencer
	DB Chris Rockins
	DB Rod Fisher
	DB Adam Hinds
	DB Rod Brown / Mark Moore

RUSHING: Jones 225/956y, Anderson 148/631y,
Kenny Zachary (TB) 82/337y
PASSING: Hilger 94-171/1247y, 11TD, 55.0%
RECEIVING: Harris 45/618y, Chesley 32/354y, Lewis 26/419y
SCORING: Larry Roach (K) 81pts, Harris & Jones 42pts

1984 10-2

45 Arizona State	3 WR Malcolm Lewis / Terry Werner
31 Bowling Green	14 WR Jamie Harris / Bobby Riley
19 San Diego State	16 T Chuck Shanklin
31 Tulsa	7 G Derek Burton
3 Nebraska	17 C David Tucker
47 Kansas	10 G Ralph Partida
20 Colorado	14 T Paul Blair
34 Kansas State	6 TE Barry Hanna
31 Missouri	13 QB Rusty Hilger
16 Iowa State	10 TB Thurman Thomas / Shawn Jones
14 Oklahoma	24 FB Kelly Cook
21 South Carolina■	14 DL James Ham / Warren Thompson
	DL Rodney Harding
	DL John Washington
	DL Leslie O'Neal
	DL Harry Roberts / David Webb
	LB Matt Monger
	LB Ricky Adams
	DB Mike Hudson
	DB Mark Moore
	DB Adam Hinds
	DB Rod Brown

RUSHING: Thomas 205/843y, Jones 133/676y,
  Charles Crawford (TB) 110/477y
PASSING: Hilger 165-281/2048y, 8TD, 58.7%
RECEIVING: Hanna 35/385y, Harris 28/431y, Lewis 26/414y
SCORING: Larry Roach (K) 78pts, Thomas 42pts, Harris 32pts

1985 8-4

31 Washington	17 WR Terry Werner
10 No. Texas St.	9 WR Bobby Riley
45 Miami (Ohio)	10 T Chuck Shanklin
25 Tulsa	13 G Derek Burton
24 Nebraska	34 C David Tucker
17 Kansas	10 G Doug Meacham
14 Colorado	11 T Paul Blair
35 Kansas State	3 TE J.R. Dillard
21 Missouri	19 QB Ronnie Williams
10 Iowa State	15 TB Thurman Thomas
9 Oklahoma	13 FB Will Timmons
23 Florida State■	34 DL Warren Thompson
	DL John Washington
	DL Dana Hawkins
	DL Leslie O'Neal
	DL Ricky Shaw
	LB Ricky Adams
	LB James Ham
	DB DeMise Williams
	DB Melvin Gilliam / Windell Yancy
	DB Mark Moore
	DB Mike Hudson

RUSHING: Thomas 327/1650y, Mitch Nash (TB) 48/167y,
  Timmons 43/159y
PASSING: Williams 141-291/1757y, 8TD, 48.5%
RECEIVING: Riley 36/659y, Werner 27/321y, Thomas 25/142y
SCORING: Thomas 102pts, Joey O'Donnell (K) 42pts,
  Williams 14pts

1986 6-5

21 SW Louisiana	20 WR Hart Lee Dykes
23 Tulsa	27 WR Kevin Simien
12 Houston	28 T Byron Woodard
23 Illinois State	7 G Doug Meacham
10 Nebraska	30 C Tony Wilkins
0 Oklahoma	19 G Chris Stanley
24 Kansas	6 T Mike Wolfe / Mike Zentic
14 Colorado	31 TE J.R. Dillard
23 Kansas State	3 QB Mike Gundy / Ronnie Williams
21 Iowa State	14 TB Thurman Thomas / Barry Sanders
10 Missouri	6 FB Garrett Limbrick
	DL Ricky Shaw
	DL Leonard Jackson
	DL Marcus Jones
	DL David Bailey
	LB Jerry Deckard
	LB Sim Drain / Robert Nunn
	LB Chris Pegram
	DB Melvin Gilliam
	DB DeMise Williams
	DB Mark Moore
	DB Mike Hudson

RUSHING: Thomas 173/741y, Sanders 74/325y,
  Mitch Nash (TB) 82/291y
PASSING: Gundy 117-225/1525y, 8TD, 52%
RECEIVING: Dykes 60/814y, Dillard 18/190y, Thomas 18/150y
SCORING: Dykes 42pts, Thomas 30pts, Joey O'Donnell (K) 20pts

1987 10-2

39 Tulsa	28 WR Jarrod Green / Ronnie Williams
35 Houston	0 WR Hart Lee Dykes
35 Wyoming	29 T Jason Kidder / Mike Wolfe
36 SW Louisiana	0 G Chris Stanley
42 Colorado	17 C John Boisvert
0 Nebraska	35 G Doug Meacham
24 Missouri	20 T Byron Woodard
56 Kansas State	7 TE Brien Keith / J.R. Dillard
10 Oklahoma	29 QB Mike Gundy
49 Kansas	17 TB Thurman Thomas / Barry Sanders
48 Iowa State	27 FB Garrett Limbrick
35 West Virginia■	33 DL Ricky Shaw
	DL David Bailey
	DL Brandon Colbert / Kim Johnson
	DL Marcus Jones
	DL Ron Williams
	LB Sim Drain / Chris Pegram
	LB Robert Nunn / Vernon Victor
	DB Melvin Gilliam
	DB Wade Weller
	DB Jerry Deckard
	DB Rod Smith

RUSHING: Thomas 251/1613y, Sanders 105/603y
PASSING: Gundy 170-287/2106y, 13TD, 59.2%
RECEIVING: Dykes 61/978y, Williams 26/304y, Green 24/259y
SCORING: Thomas 104pts, Sanders 84pts,
  Cary Blanchard (K) 67pts

1988 10-2

52 Miami (Ohio)	20 WR Hart Lee Dykes
52 Texas A&M	15 WR Jarrod Green
56 Tulsa	35 T Mike Wolfe
41 Colorado	21 G Chris Stanley
42 Nebraska	63 C John Boisvert
49 Missouri	21 G Jason Kidder
45 Kansas State	27 T Byron Woodard
28 Oklahoma	31 TE Vance Vice
63 Kansas	24 QB Mike Gundy
49 Iowa State	28 TB Barry Sanders
45 Texas Tech	42 FB Garrett Limbrick
62 Wyoming■	14 DL David Bailey
	DL Brandon Colbert
	DL Ruben Oliver
	DL Stacey Satterwhite / Shawn Mackey
	DL Devin Jones / Rod Gaines
	LB Torrance Cummings
	LB Sim Drain
	DB Melvin Gilliam
	DB Mike Clark / Jason Juhl
	DB Lamar McGriggs
	DB Rod Smith

RUSHING: Sanders 344/2628y, Gerald Hudson (TB) 47/369y,
  Limbrick 45/223y
PASSING: Gundy 153-236/2163y, 19 TD, 64.8%
RECEIVING: Dykes 74/1278y, Green 20/309y, Sanders 19/106y
SCORING: Sanders 234pts, Cary Blanchard (K) 100pts,
  Dykes 90pts

1989 4-7

10 Tulsa	20 WR Curtis Mayfield
13 Ohio State	37 WR Jarrod Green / Brent Parker
15 Texas Tech	31 T Josh Arrott
27 Wyoming	7 G Brent Davis
15 Oklahoma	37 C Pete Surette
17 Kansas State	13 G Scott Webb
23 Nebraska	48 T Keith Roller
31 Missouri	30 TE Vance Vice / Mark Walker
37 Kansas	34 QB Mike Gundy
17 Colorado	41 TB Gerald Hudson / Vernon Brown
21 Iowa State	31 FB Cecil Wilson
	DL Brandon Colbert
	DL Ruben Oliver
	DL Stacey Satterwhite
	DL Shawn Mackey
	LB George Bright
	LB Mike Woolridge
	LB Sim Drain
	DB Mike Clark
	DB Joe King / Cornell Cannon
	DB Jay Fleischman
	DB Rod Smith

RUSHING: Hudson 187/910y, Brown 140/511y, Wilson 56/193y
PASSING: Gundy 164-287/2203y, 14TD, 57.1%
RECEIVING: Mayfield 49/879y, Green 30/441y, Parker 18/198y
SCORING: Cary Blanchard (K) 82pts, Mayfield & Green 24pts

1990 4-7

10 Tulsa	3 WR Curtis Mayfield
7 Florida	50 WR Robert Kirksey
33 No. Iowa	23 T Josh Arrott / Matt Jose
21 TCU	40 G Brian Bobo
17 Oklahoma	31 C Pete Surette
17 Kansas State	23 G Scott Hall
3 Nebraska	31 T Scott Webb
48 Missouri	28 TE Scott Copeland
30 Kansas	31 QB Kenny Ford / Earl Wheeler
22 Colorado	41 TB Gerald Hudson
25 Iowa State	17 FB Cecil Wilson
	DL Jason Gildon
	DL Eric Garmond / Ruben Oliver
	DL Stacey Satterwhite
	DL George Bright
	LB Mike Woolridge
	LB Chris Calhoun / Clarence Nobles
	LB Richie Ansley
	DB Mike Clark
	DB Joe King / Terry Henley
	DB Jay Fleischman
	DB Charles Verner / Scott Harmon

RUSHING: Hudson 279/1642y, Ford 67/332y, Wilson 74/309y
PASSING: Wheeler 53-112/727y, 2TD, 47.3%,
  Ford 40-98/450y, 4TD, 40.8%
RECEIVING: Kirksey 29/486y, Mayfield 28/455y,
  Ronnie Fisher (TB) 11/68y
SCORING: Cary Blanchard (K) 63pts, Hudson 60pts,
  Vernon Brown (TB) 24pts

1991 0-10-1

7 Tulsa	13 WR Robert Kirksey
3 Arizona State	30 WR Bert Milliner
21 TCU	24 T Matt Jose
3 Miami	40 G Brian Bobo
15 Nebraska	49 C Pete Surette
7 Missouri	41 G Josh Arrott / Anthony Greenlee
6 Iowa State	6 T Mike Butler
0 Kansas	31 TE Scott Copeland
12 Colorado	16 QB Kenny Ford / Brent Scott
6 Oklahoma	21 TB Rafael Denson / Russell Berrien
26 Kansas State	36 FB Roger Franks / L.G. Thompson
	DL Andre Thompson / Eric Garmond
	DL Brandon Colbert
	DL Stacey Satterwhite
	DL Jason Gildon
	LB Mike Woolridge
	LB Clarence Nobles / Arthur Davis
	LB Chaucer Funchess / Chris Calhoun
	DB Mike Clark
	DB Carlos Erving / Terry Henley
	DB Cornell Cannon / Jay Fleischman
	DB Scott Harmon

RUSHING: Denson 150/568y, Berrien 113/349y, Ford 87/147y
PASSING: Ford 111-238/1377y, 7TD, 46.6%
RECEIVING: Milliner 47/631y, Kirksey 42/604y,
  Mark Cheatwood (WR) 18/230y
SCORING: Kirksey & Rick Myers (K) 30pts, Milliner 18pts

1992 4-6-1

35 Indiana State	3 WR Shannon Culver
3 Michigan	35 WR Mark Cheatwood / Bert Milliner
24 Tulsa	19 T Matt Jose
11 TCU	13 G Anthony Greenlee
0 Nebraska	55 C Scott Hall
28 Missouri	26 G Scott Waterbury
27 Iowa State	21 T Mike Butler
18 Kansas	26 TE/WR Steve Keith / Rafael Denson (TB)
0 Colorado	28 QB Gary Porter / Andy Loveland
15 Oklahoma	15 TB John White / Mark Williams
0 Kansas State	10 FB Roger Franks / Marc Spatz
	DL Mike Woolridge
	DL David Brooks / Jason Bufford
	DL Elmer Williams
	DL Jason Gildon
	LB Keith Burns
	LB Richie Ansley
	LB Carlos Erving
	DB Terry Henley
	DB Todd Fisher
	DB Cornell Cannon
	DB Scott Harmon

RUSHING: Denson 99/435y, White 101/368y, Williams 112/315y
PASSING: Porter 96-188/1280y, 7TD, 51.1%
RECEIVING: Culver 41/629y, Denson 22/303y, Milliner 10/160y
SCORING: Lawson Vaughn (K) 41pts, Denson 32pts, Culver 26pts

1993 3-8

45 SW Missouri St.	7 WR Shannon Culver / Kris Lofton
16 Tulsa	10 WR Rafael Denson
10 Arizona State	12 T Matt Jose / Derek Leinen
27 TCU	22 G Anthony Greenlee / Bryan Guillory
13 Nebraska	27 C Bryan Hope / Scott Hall
9 Missouri	42 G Alan Orts / Scott Waterbury
7 Iowa State	20 T Mike Butler
6 Kansas	13 TE/WR Derek Jones / Fred Thomas
14 Colorado	31 QB Tone Jones / Gary Porter
0 Oklahoma	31 TB Daryl Johnson / David Thompson
17 Kansas State	21 FB Marc Spatz / Joe Jefferson
	DL Jevon Langford
	DL Lorenzo Green
	DL Tyler Williams
	DL Jason Gildon
	LB Keith Burns
	LB Richie Ansley
	LB Linc Harden / Eric Hobbs
	DB Delvin Myles / Jitu Criddle
	DB Cleavon Williams
	DB Scott Harmon
	DB Charles Verner

RUSHING: Thompson 111/466y, Johnson 97/401,
 Jefferson 89/331y
PASSING: Jones 54-111/608y, 1TD, 48.6%
 Porter 37-69/478y, 2TD, 53.6%
RECEIVING: Denson 27/356y, Culver 23/346y, Thomas 14/182y
SCORING: Lawson Vaughn (K) 52pts, Denson 24pts,
 Louis Adams (FB) & Jefferson 18pts

1994 3-7-1

31 No. Illinois	14 WR Kris Lofton / Mark Cheatwood
10 Baylor	14 WR Rafael Denson
17 Tulsa	10 T Derek Leinen
36 North Texas	34 G Scott Waterbury
3 Nebraska	32 C Bryan Hope
15 Missouri	24 G Alan Orts
31 Iowa State	31 T Calvin Menepee / Josh Henson
14 Kansas	24 TE Derek Jones
3 Colorado	17 QB Tone Jones
14 Oklahoma	33 TB David Thompson / Andre Richardson
6 Kansas State	23 FB Joe Jefferson
	DL Jevon Langford
	DL Lorenzo Green
	DL Tyler Williams / Jay Grosfield
	DL Demetrius Crowder / Norman Williams
	LB Linc Harden
	LB Eric Hobbs
	LB James Elliott / Alamu Bailey
	DB Johnny Jones
	DB Jeroid Johnson / Cleavon Williams
	DB Louis Adams
	DB Trent Fisher / Jitu Criddle

RUSHING: Thompson 186/819y, Richardson 121/774
 Jefferson 58/216y
PASSING: Jones 114-256/1468y, 8TD, 44.5%
RECEIVING: Denson 40/713y, Cheatwood 14/174y,
 Richardson 12/97y
SCORING: Lawson Vaughn (K) 46pts, Thompson 30pts,
 Denson 24pts

1995 4-8

21 Nebraska	64 WR Kent Luck / Willie Grissom
23 Tulsa	24 WR Terrance Richardson
35 SW Missouri St.	7 T Derek Leinen
25 Wyoming	45 G Bryan Guillory / Scott Waterbury
0 Tennessee	31 C Bryan Hope
17 Kansas State	23 G Josh Henson
30 Missouri	26 T Calvin Menepee / Jeremy Offutt
14 Iowa State	38 TE Alonzo Mayes / Roger Pfeiffer
32 Colorado	45 QB Tone Jones
12 Oklahoma	0 TB David Thompson
17 Kansas	22 FB Geoff Grenier / Brian Aikins
24 Hawaii	20 DL Lorenzo Green
	DL Norman Williams
	DL Jay Grosfield
	DL/ LB Jamal Williams / Josh Green
	LB Louis Adams
	LB Alamu Bailey
	LB Jevan Langford / Billy Stone
	DB Johnny Jones / Jeroid Johnson
	DB R.W. McQuarters
	DB Trent Fisher
	DB Kevin Williams / Courtney Garner

RUSHING: Thompson 256/1509y, Richardson 115/705y
 Jones 95/125y
PASSING: Jones 104-218/1185y, 7TD, 47.7%
RECEIVING: Mayes 32/421y, Richardson 17/145y,
 Grissom 16/159y
SCORING: Jones 62pts, Lawson Vaughn (K) 58pts,
 Thompson 54pts

1996 5-6

23 SW Missouri St.	20 WR Willie Grissom / Kent Luck
3 Texas Tech	31 WR Terrance Richardson
30 Tulsa	9 T Derek Leinen
31 Utah State	17 G Adam Davis / Blaine Cook
14 Texas	71 C Josh Henson (G) / Reynell Lavigne
13 Colorado	35 G Jeremy Offutt / Jorge Arceo
28 Iowa State	27 T Calvin Menephee
28 Missouri	35 TE Alonzo Mayes
19 Texas A&M	38 QB Tone Jones
17 Oklahoma	27 TB David Thompson
37 Baylor	17 FB/TE Brian Aikins / Roger Pfieffer
	DL Jay Grosfield
	DL Denshio Cook / Courtney Mallory
	DL Kevin Kemp / Brandon Ashley
	LB Andrel Waddle / Tarrell Knawls
	LB Raymond Cato
	LB Kenyatta Wright / Josh Green
	LB Louis Adams
	DB Jitu Criddle
	DB J.B. Flowers / Alvin Porter
	DB R.W. McQuarters / Courtney Garner
	DB Trent Fisher

RUSHING: Thompson 293/1524y, Richardson 89/447y,
 Jones 71/170y
PASSING: Jones 130-234/1551y, 8TD, 55.6%
RECEIVING: Mayes 30/512y, Richardson 29/376y,
 Thompson 20/225y, Grissom 20/225y
SCORING: Thompson 78pts, Tim Sydnes (K) 63pts,
 Richardson 36pts

1997 8-4

21 Iowa State	14 WR R.W. McQuarters / Sean Love
31 SW Louisiana	7 WR Willie Grissom / Daunte Hill
35 Fresno State	0 T David Camacho
38 NE Louisiana	7 G Josh Henson
42 Texas	16 C Jeremy Offutt
33 Colorado	29 G Adam Davis
50 Missouri	51 T Calvin Menepee
25 Texas A&M	28 TE Alonzo Mayes / Josh Lind
30 Oklahoma	7 QB Tony Lindsay / Chris Chaloupka
3 Texas Tech	27 TB Nathan Simmons / Jamaal Fobbs
24 Baylor	14 FB/TE Brian Aikins / Garrett Steggs
20 Purdue■	33 DL Alton Weaver / Taber LeBlanc
	DL Jamal Williams
	DL Cortney Mallory
	LB Andrel Waddle
	LB Tarrell Knauls
	LB Kenyatta Wright
	LB Jack Golden
	DB R. W. McQuarters
	DB Kevin Williams
	DB Ricky Thompson / Maurice Simpson
	DB Trent Alexander

RUSHING: Fobbs 161/846y, Simmons 166/711y,
 Lindsay 151/564y
PASSING: Lindsay 76-123/1172y, 9TD, 61.8%
RECEIVING: Mayes 29/424y, Grissom 14/166y, Steggs 13/172y
SCORING: Tim Sydnes (K) 68pts, Lindsay 56pts, Mayes 42pts

1998 5-6

38 Kansas	28 WR Willie Grissom
20 Tulsa	35 WR Sean Love / Terrance Richardson
42 Mississippi St.	23 T David Camacho / Reynell Lavigne
17 Nebraska	24 G Adam Davis
17 Texas Tech	24 C Jeremy Offutt
20 Kansas State	52 G Jorge Arceo
41 Oklahoma	26 T Josh Lind
6 Texas A&M	17 TE Marcellus Rivers / Garrett Steggs
34 Texas	37 QB Tony Lindsay
44 SW Louisiana	20 TB Nathan Simmons
24 Baylor	10 FB Jeremy Halferty / Brian Aikins
	DL Taber LeBlanc
	DL Alton Weaver / Zac Akin
	DL Cortney Mallory
	DL Andrel Waddle
	LB Tarrell Knauls / Dwayne Levels
	LB Kenyatta Wright / Clint Metcalf
	LB Raymond Cato / Troy West
	DB Adams Edwards / Marcus Jones
	DB Evan Howell
	DB Ricky Thompson
	DB Trent Alexander

RUSHING: Simmons 204/937y, Lindsay 151/592y, Fobbs 89/409y
PASSING: Lindsay 97-196/1442y, 7TD, 49.5%
RECEIVING: Richardson 25/337y, Rivers 22/335y,
 Grissom 21/278y
SCORING: Tim Sydnes (K) 76pts, Lindsay 64pts,
 Simmons & Aikins 30pts

1999 5-6

24 La. Lafayette	7 WR Terrance Richardson
46 Tulsa	9 WR Ethan Howell
11 Mississippi St.	29 T Josh Lind
14 Nebraska	38 G Adam Davis / Blaine Cook
41 Texas Tech	21 C Reynell Lavigne
21 Kansas State	44 G Adam Davis
3 Texas A&M	21 T Kyle Eaton / Bryan Phillips
21 Texas	34 TE Brian Blackwood / Khary Jackson
45 Kansas	13 QB Tony Lindsay / B.J. Tiger
34 Baylor	14 TB Nathan Simmons / Jamaal Fobbs
7 Oklahoma	44 FB/TE Jeremy Halferty / Marcellus Rivers
	DL Juqua Thomas / Zac Warner
	DL Cortney Mallory
	DL Zac Akin
	DL Kevin Williams
	LB Jack Golden
	LB Kenyatta Wright / Dwayne Levels
	LB Tarrell Knauls
	DB Evan Howell / Jacoby Shepherd
	DB Alvin Porter
	DB Adam Edwards
	DB/LB J.B. Flowers / Raymond Cato

RUSHING: Fobbs 110/544y, Simmons 114/285y, Tiger 73/259y
PASSING: Lindsay 61-116/767y, 5TD, 52.6%
RECEIVING: Howell 32/496y, Rivers 27/336y, Richardson 21/232y
SCORING: Tim Sydnes (K) 58pts, Rivers & Simmons 24pts

2000 3-8

36 Tulsa	26 WR Rashaun Woods / Willie Young
23 SW Texas St.	0 WR/TE Gabe Lindsay / Marcellus Rivers
6 So. Mississippi	28 T Kyle Eaton
7 Texas	42 G Jeff Machado
10 Missouri	24 C Jon Vandrell
26 Iowa State	33 G Bryan Phillips
21 Colorado	37 T Josh Lind / Jason Russell
16 Texas A&M	21 TE Brian Blackwood / Khary Jackson
0 Texas Tech	58 QB Aso Pogi / Tony Lindsay
50 Baylor	22 TB Reggie White
7 Oklahoma	12 FB/WR Tim Burrough / Jamaal Fobbs
	DL Juqua Thomas
	DL Zac Akin
	DL Kevin Williams
	DL Zac Warner / Sean Barry
	LB Chris Carter
	LB Dwayne Levels
	LB Terrence Robinson
	DB Michael Cooper
	DB Chris Massey
	DB Robbie Gillem / Marcus Jones
	DB Elbert Craig

RUSHING: White 210/1049y, Tatum Bell (TB) 49/251y,
 Pogi 85/159y
PASSING: Pogi 139-247/1550y, 6TD, 56.3%
RECEIVING: Fobbs 31/334y, Woods 29/329y, Lindsay 28/359y
SCORING: Seth Condley (K) 55pts, Pogi 36pts, White 24pts

2001 4-7

9 Southern Miss	17 WR Rashaun Woods
30 La. Tech	23 WR John Lewis
7 Texas A&M	21 T Kyle Eaton
24 Northwestern St.	0 G Jeff Machado
38 Missouri	41 C Jon Vandrell
17 Texas	45 G Bryan Phillips
14 Iowa State	28 T Jason Russell / Sam Mayes
19 Colorado	22 TE Mark Milosevich
30 Texas Tech	49 QB Aso Pogi
38 Baylor	22 TB Tatum Bell
16 Oklahoma	13 FB/WR Mike Denard / T. D. Bryant
	DL Greg Richmond
	DL LaWaylon Brown
	DL Kevin Williams / Clay Coe
	DL Khreem Smith
	LB Terrence Robinson
	LB Dwayne Levels
	DB Michael Cooper / Darrent Williams
	DB R. Holmes/ KobinaAmoo/ PaulJones
	DB Elbert Craig / Kirk Milligan
	DB Marcus Jones
	DB Roger Bombach / Chris Massey

RUSHING: Bell 197/776y, Richard Schwarz (TB) 36/113y,
PASSING: Pogi 179-296/1854y, 11TD, 60.5%
RECEIVING: Woods 80/1023y, Bryant 38/368y, Lewis 24/455y
SCORING: Luke Phillips (K) 72pts, Woods 60pts, Bell 36pts

2002 8-5

36 Louisiana Tech	39 WR Rashaun Woods
45 Northern Iowa	10 WR John Lewis / Willie Young / T.D. Bryant
24 UCLA	38 T Kyle Eaton
52 SMU	16 G Chris Akin / Corey Curtis
15 Texas	17 C Ben Buie / Bryon Machado
9 Kansas State	44 G Sam Mayes
24 Nebraska	21 T Jason Russell
28 Texas A&M	23 TE Billy Bajema / Charlie Johnson
24 Texas Tech	49 QB Josh Fields
55 Kansas	20 TB Tatum Bell / Seymore Shaw
63 Baylor	28 FB Burrough / Mike Denard
38 Oklahoma	28 DL Greg Richmond / Kyle Beck
33 Southern Miss■	23 DL Kevin Williams
	DL LaWaylon Brown
	DL Antonio Smith / Khreem Smith
	LB Paul Duren
	LB Terrence Robinson / Lawrence Pinson
	DB Darrent Williams
	DB Vernon Grant / Riklan Holmes-Miller
	DB Chris Massey
	DB Elbert Craig
	DB Kirk Milligan / Fath' Carter

RUSHING: Bell 175/1096y, Shaw 89/498y,
 Vernand Morency (TB) 58/269y
PASSING: Fields 226-408/3145y, 31TD, 55.4%
RECEIVING: Woods 107/1695y, Lewis 34/577y, Bryant 31/351y
SCORING: Woods 102pts, Luke Phillips (K) 88pts, Bell 78pts

2003 9-4

7 Nebraska	17 WR Rashaun Woods
48 Wyoming	24 WR D'Juan Woods
42 SW Missouri St.	3 T Matt Hardison / Doug Koenig
52 SMU	6 G Chris Akin (C) / Caleb Noble
56 La.-Lafayette	3 C Ben Buie
38 Kansas State	34 G Sam Mayes
51 Texas Tech	49 T Corey Hilliard / Kellen Davis
38 Texas A&M	10 TE Billy Bajema / Charlie Johnson
9 Oklahoma	52 QB Josh Fields
16 Texas	55 TB Tatum Bell / Vernand Morency
44 Kansas	21 FB/WR Shawn Willis / Gabe Lindsay
38 Baylor	21 DL Greg Richmond
28 Mississippi■	31 DL Brad Girtman / Efe Mowarin
	DL Clay Coe
	DL Antonio Smith / Khreem Smith
	LB Paul Duren / Pagitte McGee
	LB Victor DeGrate / Lawrence Pinson
	DB Robert Jones
	DB Darrent Williams / Dan McLemore
	DB Elbert Craig / Jamaar Ransom
	DB Jon Holland
	DB Vernon Grant / Fath' Carter

RUSHING: Bell 213/1286y, Morency 135/918y,
 Seymore Shaw (TB) 58/363y
PASSING: Fields 184-338/2494y, 21TD, 54.4%
RECEIVING: R. Woods 77/1367y, D. Woods 31/479y,
 Lindsay 24/191y
SCORING: Luke Phillips (K) 103pts, Bell 96pts, R. Woods 90pts

2004 7-5

31 UCLA	20 WR D'Juan Woods
38 Tulsa	21 T Corey Hilliard
59 SMU	7 G David Koenig/Doug Bird/Corey Curtis
36 Iowa State	7 C Chris Akin
42 Colorado	14 G Sam Mayes
20 Texas A&M	36 T Kellen Davis
20 Missouri	17 TE Billy Bajema
35 Oklahoma	38 TE Charlie Johnson
35 Texas	56 QB Donovan Woods
49 Baylor	21 TB Vernand Morency / Seymore Shaw
15 Texas Tech	31 FB/WR Shawn Willis / Prentiss Elliott
7 Ohio State■	33 DL Marque Fountain
	DL Efe Mowarin / Nathan Peterson
	DL Clay Coe
	DL Darnell Smith
	LB Paul Duren / Pagitte McGee
	LB Lawrence Pinson / Victor DeGrate
	DB Darren Williams / Dan McLemore
	DB Robert Jones
	DB Jan Holland
	DB Jamie Thompson / Jamar Ransom
	DB Vernon Grant

RUSHING: Morency 250/1454y, Shaw 79/371y,
 Dn. Woods 111/364y
PASSING: Woods 82-153/1491y, 13TD, 53.6%
RECEIVING: D'J Woods 29/650y, Bajema 18/264y, Elliott 17/295y
SCORING: Jason Ricks (K) 79pts, Morency 78pts,
 Dn. Woods 60pts

2005 4-7

15 Montana State	10 WR D'Juan Woods / Tom Devereaux
23 Florida Atlantic	3 WR Ricky Price / Errick McCown
20 Arkansas State	10 WR/TE Luke Frazier / Paschal Smith
0 Colorado	34 T Charlie Johnson / Adam Gourley
31 Missouri	38 G David Koenig
23 Texas A&M	62 C David Washington
0 Iowa State	37 G Kellen Davis
28 Texas	47 T Corey Hilliard
24 Texas Tech	17 TE Brandon Pettigrew
34 Baylor	44 QB Bobby Reid / Al Pena
23 Oklahoma	42 RB Mike Hamilton / Julius Crosslin
	DL Jerry Don Bray / Darnell Smith
	DL Ryan McBean
	DL Xavier L.-Kennedy / Larry Brown
	DL Victor DeGrate
	LB Pat Duren
	LB L. Pinson / Rodrick Johnson
	LB Jamar Ransom
	DB Calvin Mickens / Martel Van Zant
	DB Daniel McLemore
	DB Don. Woods(QB)/Stephen James
	DB Jamie Thompson/ Chase Holland

RUSHING: Hamilton 193/961y, Crosslin 71/231y,
 Reid 61/139y
PASSING: Pena 89-179/1102y, 8TD, 49.7%
 Reid 52-108/602y, 2TD, 48.1%
RECEIVING: Woods 56/879y, Hamilton 20/161y, Price 16/238y
SCORING: Crosslin 74pts, Bruce Redden (K) 56pts, Woods 50pts

2006 7-6

52 Missouri State	10 WR D'Juan Woods
35 Arkansas State	7 WR Adarius Bowman
48 Florida Atlantic	8 T Russell Okung / Brady Bond
25 Houston	34 G David Koenig
27 Kansas State	31 C David Washington
42 Kansas	32 G Kurt Seifried
33 Texas A&M	34 T Corey Hilliard
41 Nebraska	29 TE Justin Waller
10 Texas	36 TE Brandon Pettigrew
66 Baylor	24 QB Bobby Reid
24 Texas Tech	30 RB Dantrell Savage / Mike Hamilton
21 Oklahoma	27 DL Marque Fountain / Darnell Smith
34 Alabama■	31 DL Ryan McBean
	DL Larry Brown
	DL Victor DeGrate / Nathan Peterson
	LB Jeremy Nethon
	LB Rodrick Johnson
	LB Patrick Lavine / Chris Collins
	DB Martel Van Zant
	DB Jacob Lacey / Perrish Cox
	DB Andre Sexton
	DB Donovan Woods / Quinton Moore

RUSHING: Savage 126/820y, Keith Totson (RB) 106/631y,
 Hamilton 97/546y
PASSING: Reid 148-267/2266y, 24TD, 55.4%
RECEIVING: Bowman 60/1181y, Woods 38/596y,
 Pettigrew 24/310y
SCORING: Jason Ricks (K) 77pts, Bowman 72pts,
 Savage & Totson 48pts

2007 7-6

14 Georgia	35 WR Adarius Bowman / Seth Newton
42 Florida Atlantic	6 WR Jeremy Broadway / Dez Bryant
23 Troy	41 T Russell Okung
49 Texas Tech	45 G David Koenig
39 San Houston St.	3 C Andrew Lewis (G)/David Washington
23 Texas A&M	24 G Steve Denning
45 Nebraska	14 T Brady Bond
41 Kansas State	39 TE Brandon Pettigrew
35 Texas	38 TE/FB Justin Waller / Zach Carter
28 Kansas	43 QB Zac Robinson / Bobby Reid
45 Baylor	14 RB Dantrell Savage / Kendall Hunter
17 Oklahoma	49 DL Marque Fountain / Derek Burton
49 Indiana■	33 DL Jeremy Chatham
	DL Maurice Cummings / Tonga Tea
	DL Nathan Peterson
	LB Donovan Woods / Rodrick Johnson
	LB Patrick Lavine / Chris Collins
	LB/DB Jeremy Nethon / Quinton Moore
	DB Perrish Cox / Martel Van Zant
	DB Jacob Lacey / Terrance Anderson
	DB Ricky Price
	DB Andre Sexton

RUSHING: Savage 223/1272y, Robinson 140/847y,
 Hunter 107/696y
PASSING: Robinson 201-333/2824y, 23TD, 60.4%
 Reid 26-49/275y, 1TD, 53.1%
RECEIVING: Bowman 67/1006y, Bryant 43/622y, Pettigrew 35/540y
SCORING: Savage 66pts, Jason Ricks (K) 62pts, Robinson 54pts

2008 9-4

39 Washington St.	13 WR Dez Bryant
56 Houston	37 WR DeMarcus Conner / Damian Davis
57 Missouri State	13 T Russell Okung
55 Troy	24 G Andrew Lewis
56 Texas A&M	28 C David Washington
28 Missouri	23 G Steve Denning
34 Baylor	6 T Brady Bond
24 Texas	28 TE Brandon Pettigrew / Wilson Youman
59 Iowa State	17 QB Zac Robinson
20 Texas Tech	56 RB Kendell Hunter / Keith Toston
30 Colorado	17 FB/WR Bryant Ward / Bo Bowling
41 Oklahoma	61 DL Ugo Chinasa
31 Oregon■	42 DL Tonga Tea / Swanson Miller
	DL/DB Jeray Chatham / T.J. Bell
	DL Derek Burton / Jeremiah Price
	LB Andre Sexton
	LB Orie Lemon / Donald Booker
	LB Patrick Lavine
	DB Perrish Cox / Terrance Anderson
	DB Jacob Lacey
	DB Quinton Moore
	DB Ricky Price

RUSHING: Hunter 241/1555y, Toston 102/686y,
 Robinson 146/562y
PASSING: Robinson 204-314/3064y, 25TD, 65%
RECEIVING: Bryant 87/1480y, Pettigrew 42/472y,
 Hunter 22/198y
SCORING: Bryant 128pts, Dan Dailey (K) 110pts, Hunter 102pts

2009 9-4

24 Georgia	10 WR Hubert Anyiam / Dez Bryant
35 Houston	45 WR DeMarcus Conner / Justin Blackmon
41 Rice	24 WR/FB Josh Cooper / Beau Johnson
56 Grambling	6 T Russell Okung
36 Texas A&M	31 G Noah Franklin
33 Missouri	17 C Andrew Lewis
34 Baylor	7 G Lane Taylor / Anthony Morgan
14 Texas	41 T Brady Bond / Andrew Mitchell
34 Iowa State	8 TE Wilson Youman / Cooper Bassett
24 Texas Tech	17 QB Zac Robinson
31 Colorado	28 TB Keith Toston / Kendall Hunter
0 Oklahoma	27 DL Jeremiah Price / Jamie Blatnick
7 Mississippi■	21 DL Swanson Miller
	DL Derek Burton
	DL Ugo Chinasa
	LB Andre Sexton
	LB Donald Booker
	LB Patrick Lavine
	DB Perrish Cox / Andrew McGee
	DB Terrance Anderson
	DB Markelle Martin / Johnny Thomas
	DB Lucien Antoine / Victor Johnson

RUSHING: Toston 227/1218y, Hunter 89/382y, Robinson 111/305y,
 Johnson 77/304y
PASSING: Robinson 180-301/2084y, 15TD, 59.8%
RECEIVING: Anyiam 42/515y, Toston 25/261y, Blackmon 20/260y,
 Cooper 20/234y, Bryant 17/323y
SCORING: Dan Bailey (K) 85pts, Toston 74pts,
 Bryant & Johnson 30pts

2010 11-2

65 W. Kentucky	17 WR Justin Blackmon / Josh Cooper
41 Troy	38 WR Tracy Moo'e/H. Anyiam/Isaiah And'rs'n
65 Tulsa	28 WR Colton Chelf / Bo Bowling
38 Texas A&M	35 T Nick Martinez
54 Louisiana	28 G Jonathan Rush
34 Texas Tech	17 C Grant Garner
41 Nebraska	51 G Lane Taylor
24 Kansas State	14 T Levy Adcock
55 Baylor	28 QB Brandon Weeden
33 Texas	16 HB Kendall Hunter / Jeremy Smith
48 Texas	14 FB/RB Bryant Ward / Joseph Randle
41 Oklahoma	47 DL Ugo Chinasa / Darius Hart
36 Arizona■	10 DL Chris Donaldson
	DL Shane Jarka / Nigel Nicholas
	DL Jamie Blatnick / Richetti Jones
	LB Shawn Lewis / James Thomas
	LB Orie Lemon
	LB Justin Gent
	DB Andrew McGee / Devin Hedgepeth
	DB Brodrick Brown
	DB Johnny Thomas / Victor Johnson
	DB Markelle Martin

RUSHING: Hunter 271/1548y, Randle 82/452y, Smith 56/262y
PASSING: Weeden 342-511/4277y, 34TD, 66.9%
RECEIVING: Blackmon 111/1782y, Cooper 68/736y,
 Bowling 42/437y, Randle 37/427y
SCORING: Dan Bailey (K) 149pts, Blackmon 132pts, Hunter 96pts

OREGON

University of Oregon (1876)
Eugene, Oregon
Nickname: Ducks
Colors: Green and Yellow
Stadium: Autzen Stadium (1967) 54,000
Conference Affiliations: Pacific Coast (Charter Member, 1916-58), Independent (1959-63), Pacific 8/10 (1964-present)

CAREER RUSHING YARDS	Carries	Yards
Derek Loville (1986-89)	811	3296
LaMichael James (2009-10)	524	3277
Jonathan Stewart (2005-07)	516	2891
Terrence Whitehead (2002-05)	611	2832
Sean Burwell (1990-93)	668	2758
Ricky Whittle (1992-95)	590	2545
Jeremiah Johnson (2005-08)	349	2336
Bobby Moore (1969-71)	474	2306
Maurice Morris (2000-01)	466	2237
Don Reynolds (1972-74)	443	2210

CAREER PASSING YARDS	Comp-Att	Yards
Bill Musgrave (1987-90)	634-1104	8343
Danny O'Neil (1991-94)	636-1132	8301
Kellen Clemens (2002-05)	613-1005	7555
Joey Harrington (1998-2001)	512-928	6911
Chris Miller (1983-86)	560-1015	6681
Dan Fouts (1970-72)	482-956	5995
Akili Smith (1997-98)	323-571	5148
Dennis Dixon (2004-07)	444-695	5129
Tony Graziani (1993-96)	362-670	4498
Jack Henderson (1975-77)	411-842	4360

CAREER RECEIVING YARDS	Catches	Yards
Samie Parker (2000-03)	178	2761
Tony Hartley (1996-99)	160	2744
Keenan Howry (1999-02)	173	2698
Demetrius Williams (2002-05)	162	2660
Jaison Williams (2005-08)	174	2546
Cristin McLemore (1992-95)	162	2498
Jeff Maehl (2007-10)	178	2311
Terry Obee (1986-89)*	122	2233
Lew Barnes (1983-85)	117	2048
Bob Newland (1968-70)	125	1941

SEASON RUSHING YARDS	Carries	Yards
LaMichael James (2010)	294	1731
Jonathan Stewart (2007)	280	1722
LaMichael James (2009)	230	1546
Saladin McCullough (1997)	267	1343
Reuben Droughns (1999)	277	1234

SEASON PASSING YARDS	Comp-Att	Yards
Akili Smith (1998)	215-371	3763
Danny O'Neil (1993)	223-360	3224
Bill Musgrave (1989)	231-401	3081
Joey Harrington (2000)	214-405	2967
Darron Thomas (2010)	222-361	2881

SEASON RECEIVING YARDS	Catches	Yards
Bob Newland (1970)	67	1123
Samie Parker (2003)	77	1088
Jeff Maehl (2010)	77	1076
Pat Johnson (1997)	55	1072
Demetrius Williams (2005)	59	1059

GAME RUSHING YARDS	Carries	Yards
Onterrio Smith (2001 vs. Washington St.)	26	285
LaMichael James (2010 vs. Stanford)	31	257
Jonathan Stewart (2007 vs. So. Florida)	23	253

GAME PASSING YARDS	Comp-Att	Yards
Bill Musgrave (1989 vs. BYU)	26-44	489
Ryan Perry-Smith (1996 vs. Arizona State)	29-56	468
Danny O'Neil (1994 vs. Penn State)	41-61	465

GAME RECEIVING YARDS	Catches	Yards
Tony Hartley (1998 vs. Washington)	9	242
Derrick Deadwiler (1993 vs. Cal)	11	234
Cristin McLemore (1993 vs. Stanford)	11	230

GREATEST COACH:

In taking the Oregon football program to never-before heights of success, Mike Bellotti quickly become an institution in Eugene. In becoming the winningest coach in Oregon history, with 116, Bellotti became so successful that the expectations for the program have become higher than once thought possible. His hand-picked successor, and former offensive coordinator, Chip Kelly is now expected to lead the Ducks to challenge for the Pac-10 title, a January bowl bid, and a spot in the nation's Top 10. This for a school that went 24 years (1965-88) without reaching seven wins in any season.

Bellotti arrived in 1989 as the offensive coordinator. Things quickly changed for that side of the ball and the Ducks became much more explosive. In his very first year, the Ducks broke the school record for points scored. In his final year as coordinator, 1994, Oregon went to the Rose Bowl for the first time since 1957 and, in a losing effort, outgained Penn State, considered to have one of the best offenses in college football history.

As the head man, the yards gained and games won continued to pile up. This despite the annual struggle to recruit against power programs like Southern California. But Bellotti and his staffs were always able to get the most out of Oregon players, even without too many future All-Pros dotting his roster. Just a look at the top yardage producers during his tenure will bear out that Bellotti was a genius at getting excellent results from smart and solid, if not overly talented, players.

OREGON'S 55 GREATEST SINCE 1953

OFFENSE

WIDE RECEIVER: Lew Barnes, Bob Newland, Terry Obee, Samie Parker
TIGHT END: Russ Francis, Justin Peelle
TACKLE: Steve Barnett, Tom Drougas, Jack Patera, Adam Snyder
GUARD: John McKean, Mark Richards, Gary Zimmerman
CENTER: Bob Peterson, Dave Tobey
QUARTERBACK: Dan Fouts, Joey Harrington, Bill Musgrave
RUNNING BACK: Reuben Droughns, LaMichael James, Derek Loville, Maurice Morris, Jim Shanley, Jonathan Stewart
FULLBACK: Josh Line

DEFENSE

END: Matt Brock, Matt LaBounty, Saul Patu, Mike Walter
TACKLE: George Dames, Vince Goldsmith, Haloti Ngata, Rollin Putzier
LINEBACKER: Bruce Beekley, Joe Farwell, Tom Graham, Darrell Mehl, Kevin Mitchell
CORNERBACK: Rashad Bauman, Mario Clark, Alex Molden, Chris Oldham, Jim Smith
SAFETY: Patrick Chung, Chad Cota, Steve Donnelly, Anthony Newman

SPECIAL TEAMS

RETURN SPECIALISTS: Keenan Howry, Pat Johnson
PLACE KICKER: Jared Siegel
PUNTER: Mike Preacher

MULTIPLE POSITIONS

HALFBACK-WIDE RECEIVER: Bobby Moore

TWO-WAY PLAYERS

QUARTERBACK-DEFENSIVE BACK: George Shaw
GUARD-DEFENSIVE END: Dave Wilcox
HALFBACK-DEFENSIVE BACK: Mel Renfro

PERFORMANCE FORMULA:
OREGON'S 10 BEST SEASONS

2010	1.6412	5 of 71
2001	1.6207	5 of 70
2009	1.5086	10 of 72
2000	1.4919	10 of 70
2005	1.4604	11 of 70
2007	1.4343	12 of 70
2008	1.4244	11 of 71
1959	1.3740	14 of 70
1999	1.3466	15 of 71
1994	1.3354	18 of 71

OREGON DUCKS

Year	W-L-T	AP Poll	Conference Standing	Toughest Regular Season Opponents	Coach (Record at School)	Bowl Games		
1953	4-5-1		8	UCLA 8-1, Stanford 6-3-1, Southern California 6-3-1	Len Casanova			
1954	6-4		3	UCLA 8-0, Southern California 8-3, San Jose 7-3	Len Casanova			
1955	6-4		4	Oregon State 6-3, Colorado 6-4, USC 6-4, Utah 6-3, Stanford 6-3-1	Len Casanova			
1956	4-4-2		4t	USC 8-2, Oregon State 7-2-1, Pittsburgh 7-2-1, Colorado 7-2-1, UCLA 7-3	Len Casanova			
1957	7-4		1t	UCLA 8-2, Oregon State 8-2, Stanford 6-4, Washington St. 6-4	Len Casanova	Rose	7 Ohio State	10
1958	4-6		5	Oklahoma 9-1, Washington St. 7-3, California 7-3, Oregon State 6-4	Len Casanova			
1959	8-2			Washington 9-1, Washington St. 6-4	Len Casanova			
1960	7-3-1			Washington 9-1, Oregon State 6-3-1, Utah 7-3	Len Casanova	Liberty	12 Penn State	41
1961	4-6			Ohio State 8-0-1, Minnesota 7-2, Arizona 8-1-1	Len Casanova			
1962	6-3-1			Texas 9-0-1, Washington 7-1-2, Oregon State 8-2	Len Casanova	Sun	21 SMU	14
1963	8-3			Penn State 7-3, Washington 6-4	Len Casanova			
1964	7-2-1			Oregon State 8-2, Penn State 6-4, Washington 6-4	Len Casanova			
1965	4-5-1		6t	Washington St. 7-3, Stanford 6-3-1, BYU 6-4	Len Casanova			
1966	3-7		8	Oregon State 7-3, Oklahoma 6-4, Washington 6-4	Len Casanova (82-73-8)			
1967	2-8		7t	Southern California 9-1, Colorado 8-2, Oregon State 7-2-1, Ohio State 6-3	Jerry Frei			
1968	4-6		5t	Ohio State 9-0, Southern Cal 9-0-1, California 7-3-1, Oregon State 7-3	Jerry Frei			
1969	5-5-1		5	UCLA 8-1-1, Utah 8-2, Stanford 7-2-1, Oregon State 6-4	Jerry Frei			
1970	6-4-1		2t	Air Force 9-2, Stanford 8-3, Washington 6-4, Southern California 6-4-1	Jerry Frei			
1971	5-6		5	Nebraska 12-0, Texas 8-2, Stanford 8-3, Washington 8-3	Jerry Frei (22-29-2)			
1972	4-7		6t	Southern California 11-0, Oklahoma 10-1, UCLA 8-3, Washington 8-3	Dick Enright			
1973	2-9		5t	Michigan 10-0-1, Southern California 9-1-1, Arizona State 10-1, UCLA 9-2	Dick Enright (6-16)			
1974	2-9		8	Southern California 9-1-1, Nebraska 8-3, UCLA 6-3-2, California 7-3-1	Don Read			
1975	3-8		6	Oklahoma 10-1, UCLA 8-2-1, California 8-3, Southern California 7-4	Don Read			
1976	4-7		7t	Southern California 10-1, Notre Dame 8-3, UCLA 9-1-1	Don Read (9-24)			
1977	2-9		7	Washington 7-4, Southern California 7-4, Stanford 8-3, LSU 8-3, UCLA 7-4	Rich Brooks			
1978	2-9		8	Southern California 10-1, Stanford 8-3, UCLA 8-3, BYU 9-3	Rich Brooks			
1979	6-5		3t	Purdue 9-2, Washington 9-2, Arizona 6-3-1	Rich Brooks			
1980	6-3-2		5	Southern California 8-2-1, UCLA 8-2, Washington 9-2	Rich Brooks			
1981	2-9		9	Washington 9-2, Arizona St. 9-2, Washington St. 8-2-1, UCLA 7-3-1	Rich Brooks			
1982	2-8-1		9	UCLA 9-1-1, Washington 9-2, Southern California 8-3, Arizona State 9-2	Rich Brooks			
1983	4-6-1		6t	Ohio State 8-3, Washington 8-3, UCLA 6-4-1	Rich Brooks			
1984	6-5		7t	Washington 10-1, Southern California 8-3, UCLA 8-3	Rich Brooks			
1985	5-6		6	Nebraska 9-2, Arizona 8-3, Washington 6-5	Rich Brooks			
1986	5-6		7	Arizona State 9-1-1, Nebraska 9-2, Arizona 8-3, Washington 8-3	Rich Brooks			
1987	6-5		4t	UCLA 9-2, Southern California 8-3, Arizona State 6-4-1, Washington 6-4-1	Rich Brooks			
1988	6-6		6t	Southern California 10-1, UCLA 9-2, Washington St. 8-3	Rich Brooks			
1989	8-4		2t	BYU 10-2, Arizona 7-4, Washington 7-4	Rich Brooks	Independence	27 Tulsa	24
1990	8-4		3	Washington 9-2, BYU 10-2, Colorado 6-4-1, Arizona 7-4	Rich Brooks	Freedom	31 Colorado State	32
1991	3-8		9t	Washington 11-0, California 9-2, UCLA 8-3, Stanford 8-3	Rich Brooks			
1992	6-6		6t	Washington 9-2, Stanford 9-3, Hawaii 10-2, Washington St. 8-3	Rich Brooks	Independence	35 Wake Forest	39
1993	5-6		8t	Arizona 9-2, California 8-4, Southern California 7-5	Rich Brooks			
1994	9-4	11	1	USC 7-3-1, Arizona 8-3, Washington St. 7-4, Utah 9-2	Rich Brooks (91-109-4)	Rose	20 Penn State	38
1995	9-3	18	3	Stanford 7-3-1, Washington 7-3-1, UCLA 7-4	Mike Bellotti	Cotton	6 Colorado	38
1996	6-5		5t	Arizona State 11-0, Washington 9-2, Stanford 6-5	Mike Bellotti			
1997	7-5		7t	Washington St. 10-1, UCLA 9-2, Arizona State 8-3, Washington 7-4	Mike Bellotti	Las Vegas	41 Air Force	13
1998	8-4		3t	UCLA 10-1, Arizona 11-1, Southern California 8-4	Mike Bellotti	Aloha	43 Colorado	51
1999	9-3	19	2t	Michigan State 9-2, Washington 7-4, Oregon State 7-4	Mike Bellotti	Sun	24 Minnesota	20
2000	10-2	7	1t	Oregon State 10-1, Washington 10-1, Wisconsin 8-4	Mike Bellotti	Holiday	35 Texas	30
2001	11-1	2	1	Washington St. 9-2, Washington 8-3, Stanford 9-2	Mike Bellotti	Fiesta	38 Colorado	16
2002	7-6		8	USC 10-2, Washington St. 10-2, Arizona State 8-5, Oregon St. 8-4	Mike Bellotti	Seattle	17 Wake Forest	38
2003	8-5		3t	Michigan 10-2, Washington St. 9-3, Utah 10-2	Mike Bellotti	Sun	30 Minnesota	31
2004	5-6		5t	Oklahoma 11-0, California 10-1, Arizona State 8-3	Mike Bellotti			
2005	10-2	12t	2	USC 12-0, California 7-4, Fresno State 8-4	Mike Bellotti	Holiday	14 Oklahoma	17
2006	7-6		5t	USC 12-0, Oklahoma 10-2, California 9-3, Oregon State 9-4	Mike Bellotti	Las Vegas	8 Brigham Young	38
2007	9-4	23	4t	Michigan 8-4, So. California 10-2, Arizona State 10-2, Oregon State 8-4	Mike Bellotti	Sun	56 South Florida	21
2008	10-3	10	2t	Boise State 12-0, Southern California 11-1, Oregon State 8-4	Mike Bellotti (116-55)	Holiday	42 Oklahoma State	31
2009	10-3	11	1	Boise State 13-0, Stanford 8-4, Arizona 8-4, Oregon State 8-4	Chip Kelly	Rose	17 Ohio State	26
2010	12-1	3	1	Stanford 11-1, Southern California 8-5	Chip Kelly (22-4)	BCS Title	19 Auburn	22

TOTAL: 344-295-13 .5376 (34 of 70)

Bowl Games since 1953: 8-13 .3810 (61 of 70)

GREATEST TEAM SINCE 1953: What if? The 2001 Ducks finished second in the nation after routing Colorado in the Fiesta Bowl, 38-16, but would have preferred a shot at undefeated Miami in the Rose Bowl for the BCS title. Still, an 11-1 record—marking the first time that Oregon ever won 11 games in a season--and the highest-ever ranking made for a special year. As for the 2010 Oregon Ducks, they enjoyed a special season too. But with the Pac 10 down all season, their won-loss ledger was largely devoid of meaningful victories.

1953 4-5-1

20 Nebraska	12 E John Reed / Charles Greenley
0 Stanford	7 T Hal Reeve / Lon Stiner
0 UCLA	12 G Ken Sweitzer / Don Hedgepeth
0 Washington St.	7 C Ron Pheister
6 Washington	14 G Jack Patera
26 San Jose State	13 T Keith Tucker / Harry Johnson
13 Southern Cal	7 E Emery Barnes / Dick Mobley
26 Idaho	6 QB George Shaw / Barney Holland
0 California	0 HB Dick James / Ted Anderson
0 Oregon State	7 HB Farrell Albright / Walter Gaffney
	FB Cecil Hodges / Dean Van Leuven

RUSHING: Jarnes 106/479y, Albright 67/248y, Shaw 62/215y
PASSING: Shaw 49-119/652y, 3TD, 44.2%
RECEIVING: Reed 15/152y, Shaw 13/197y, Hodges 10/58y
SCORING: James 36pts, Shaw 23pts, Gaffney 12pts

1954 6-4

41 Idaho	0 E Hal Reeve / Phil McHugh
13 Stanford	18 T Keith Tucker / Dave Lowe
6 Utah	7 G Reanous Cochran / Jerry Nelson
33 California	27 C Ron Pheister
14 Southern Cal	24 G Jack Patera
26 San Jose State	7 T Lon Stiner / Harry Johnson
26 Washington	7 E Dick Mobley / Leroy Campbell
0 UCLA	41 QB George Shaw
26 Washington St.	14 HB Dick James / Tom Crabtree
33 Oregon State	14 HB Walt Gaffney / Lloyd Powell
	FB Jasper McGee / Dean Van Leuven

RUSHING: McGee 88/380y, James 93/359y, Shaw 80/178y
PASSING: Shaw 91-196/1358y, 10TD, 46.4%
RECEIVING: James 24/394y, McHugh 19/233y, Reeve 17/257y
SCORING: James 66pts, Shaw 35pts, McGee 30pts

1955 6-4

14 Utah	13 E George Slender / J.C. Wheeler
15 Southern Cal	42 T Lon Stiner
7 Washington	19 G Reanous Cochran / Harry Mondale
6 Colorado	13 C Nick Markulis / Art Weber
21 California	0 G Spike Hillstrom / Jack Hilficker
46 Arizona	27 T John Raventos / Harry Johnson
25 Idaho	0 E Phil McHugh / Bill Tarrow
35 Washington St.	0 QB Tom Crabtree / Jack Crabtree
7 Stanford	44 HB Dick James / Jack Brown
28 Oregon State	0 HB Jim Shanley / Hank Loumena
	FB Jack Morris / Larry Rose

RUSHING: Shanley 100/711y, James 115/596y, Morris 110/501y
PASSING: T. Crabtree 24-63/335y, 2TD, 38.1%
RECEIVING: Shanley 8/139y, McHugh 7/96y, Loumena 6/98y
SCORING: Morris (FB-K) 68pts, Shanley 54pts, Slender 18pts

1956 4-4-2

35 Colorado	0 E J.C. Wheeler / Bruce Brenn
21 Idaho	14 T Chuck Austin / Jerry Kershner
0 UCLA	6 G Harry Mondale / Reanous Cochran
7 Washington	20 C Norm Chapman / Nick Markulis
7 Stanford	21 G Spike Hillstrom
7 Pittsburgh	14 T John Raventos / Jim Linden
28 California	6 E Phil McHugh / Ron Stover
7 Washington St.	7 QB Tom Crabtree / Jack Crabtree
7 Southern Cal	0 HB Leroy Phelps / Jack Brown
14 Oregon State	14 HB Jim Shanley / Hank Loumena
	FB Jack Morris / Fred Miklancis

RUSHING: Morris 137/519y, Shanley 102/453y, Phelps 51/232y
PASSING: T. Crabtree 28-65/366y, 2TD, 43.1%
RECEIVING: McHugh 11/139y, Shanley 9/173y, Brenn 4/50y
SCORING: Shanley 30pts, Morris (FB-K) 19pts, 2 tied w/ 18pts

1957 7-4

9 Idaho	6 E J.C. Wheeler / Alden Kimbrough
3 Pittsburgh	6 T Jerry Kershner / Darrel Aschbacher
21 UCLA	0 G Harry Mondale / Joe Schaffeld
26 San Jose State	0 C Bob Peterson
14 Washington St.	13 G Bob Grottkau / Will Reeve
24 California	6 T Jim Linden
27 Stanford	26 E Ron Stover
6 Washington	13 QB Jack Crabtree
16 Southern Cal	7 HB Charley Tourville / Willie West
7 Oregon State	10 HB Jim Shanley
7 Ohio State ■	10 FB Jack Morris / Chuck Osborne

RUSHING: Shanley 168/664y, Morris 104/611y, Tourville 71/321y
PASSING: Crabtree 55-99/624y, 4TD, 55.5%
RECEIVING: Stover 24/247y, Shanley 14/221y, Morris 9/58y
SCORING: Shanley 54pts, Morris (FB-K) 43pts, Crabtree 26pts

1958 4-6

27 Idaho	0 E Alden Kimbrough / Greg Altenhofen
0 Oklahoma	6 T Darrell Aschbacher
25 Southern Cal	0 G Will Reeve / Bob Heard
0 Washington St.	6 C Bob Peterson / Dave Fish
6 California	23 G Bob Grottkau / Joe Schaffeld
0 Washington	9 T Jim Linden / Jim Keele
12 Stanford	0 E Ron Stover / Pete Welch
3 UCLA	7 QB Dave Grosz / Paul Grover
20 Oregon State	0 HB Willie West / Dave Grayson
0 Miami	2 HB Charlie Tourville / Herm McKinney
	FB Marlan Holland / Dave Powell

RUSHING: West 101/470y, Holland 94/342y, Powell 76/318y
PASSING: Grosz 42-91/468y, 2TD, 46.2%
RECEIVING: West 18/140y, McKinney 11/115y, Altenhofen 9/129y
SCORING: Grosz & Powell 12pts, West & Clarke 8pts

1959 8-2

28 Stanford	27 E Alden Kimbrough / Fred Siler
21 Utah	6 T John Wilcox / Riley Mattson
14 Washington St.	6 G John Willener
35 San Jose State	12 C Bob Peterson / Joe Clesceri
21 Air Force	3 G Dave Urell / Mike Rose
12 Washington	13 T Tom Keele
45 Idaho	7 E Greg Altenhofen
20 California	18 QB Dave Grosz
7 Washington St.	6 HB Willie West
7 Oregon State	15 HB Dave Grayson / Cleveland Jones
	FB Dave Powell / Harry Needham

RUSHING: Powell 126/495y, West 108/428y, Grosz 88/318y
PASSING: Grosz 67-139/865y, 8TD, 48.2%
RECEIVING: C Jones 17/205y, West 17/187y, Kimbrough 17/182y
SCORING: West 48pts, Powell & Needham 30pts

1960 7-3-1

33 Idaho	6 E Paul Bauge / Jerry Tarr
0 Michigan	21 T Ron Snidow / Riley Mattson
20 Utah	17 G Mike Rose / Al Weigel
33 San Jose State	0 C Joe Clesceri / Bill Swain
21 Washington St.	12 G Dave Urell / Mickey Ording
20 California	0 T Steve Barnett / Ron Anderson
6 Washington	7 E Len Burnett/G. Willener/Kent Petersen
27 Stanford	6 QB Dave Grosz
20 West Virginia	6 HB Dave Grayson
14 Oregon State	14 HB Cleveland Jones / Mickey Bruce
12 Penn State	41 FB Bruce Snyder / Jim Josephson

RUSHING: Grayson 117/631y, Jones 80/511y, Snyder 72/237y
PASSING: Grosz 57-141/910y, 7TD, 40.4%
RECEIVING: Jones 25/402y, Burnett 10/207y, Grayson 6/85y
SCORING: Jones (HB-K) 46pts, Grosz 30pts, Josephson 24pts

1961 4-6

51 Idaho	0 E Kent Peterson / Paul Burleson
6 Utah	14 T Ron Snidow / Ron Anderson
7 Minnesota	14 G Al Weigel / Ed Thomas
6 Arizona	15 C Rich Dixon / Bill Swain
21 San Jose State	6 G Mickey Ording / Bill Del Baiggio
7 Washington	6 T Steve Barnett
19 Stanford	7 E Greg Willener / Dick Imwalle
21 Washington St.	22 QB Doug Post / Ron Veres
12 Ohio State	22 HB Mel Renfro / Ben Brown
2 Oregon State	6 HB Mike Gaechter / Lu Bain
	FB Jim Josephson / Duane Cargill

RUSHING: Renfro 61/335y, Josephson 81/287y, Cargill 43/236y
PASSING: Post 48-113/662y, 3TD, 42.5%
RECEIVING: Petersen 18/209y, Burleson 11/222y, Gaechter 11/167y
SCORING: Renfro & Bain 24pts, Burleson & Josephson 18pts

1962 6-3-1

13 Texas	25 E Paul Burleson / Dick Imwalle
35 Utah	8 T Ron Snidow / Milt Kanehe
14 San Jose State	0 G Ed Thomas
31 Rice	12 C Rich Dixon
35 Air Force	20 G Mickey Ording
21 Washington	21 T Steve Barnett / Ray Johnson
28 Stanford	14 E Greg Willener / Dave Wilcox (D)
28 Washington St.	10 QB Bob Berry / Doug Post
7 Ohio State	26 HB Mel Renfro / Lu Bain
17 Oregon State	20 HB Larry Hill / Monte Fitchett
	FB Jim Josephson /Bruce Snyder/D. Cargill

RUSHING: Renfro 126/753y, Hill 84/534y, Josephson 52/256y
PASSING: Berry 62-115/995y, 6TD, 53.9%
RECEIVING: Willener 19/263y, Renfro 16/298y, Imwalle 11/221y
SCORING: Renfro 78pts, Berry 36pts, Buck Corey (K) 35pts

1963 8-3

7 Penn State	17 E Rich Schwab / Ray Palm
36 Stanford	7 T Pat Matson / Milt Kanehe
35 West Virginia	0 G Ron Jones / Mark Richards (D)
41 Idaho	21 C Dave Toby / Oliver McKinney (D)
28 Arizona	12 G Dave Wilcox
19 Washington	26 T Lowell Dean / Ray Johnson
21 San Jose State	13 E Dick Imwalle / Buck Corey
21 Washington St.	13 QB Bob Berry
28 Indiana	22 HB Mel Renfro / Dennis Keller
31 Oregon State	14 HB Larry Hill / H.D. Murphy
21 SMU ■	14 FB Lu Bain / Tim Casey (D)

RUSHING: Renfro 82/452y, Keller 65/294y, Hill 50/269y
PASSING: Berry 101-171/1675y, 16TD, 59.1%
RECEIVING: Imwalle 23/401y, Schwab 22/455y, Renfro 18/260y
SCORING: Renfro 39pts, Bain & Schwab 30pts

1964 7-2-1

20 BYU	13 WR Corky Sullivan / Charles Miller
22 Pittsburgh	13 WR/LH Steve Bunker / Bill O'Toole
22 Penn State	14 T Pat Matson
14 Idaho	8 G Dale Wilson
21 Arizona	0 C Dave Tobey
7 Washington	0 G Mark Richards
8 Stanford	10 T Lowell Dean
21 Washington St.	21 TE Ray Palm
29 Indiana	21 QB Bob Berry
6 Oregon State	7 HB Dennis Keller
	FB Dick Winn
	DL Robb Haskins / Jerry Parsons
	DL Jim Kollman
	DL Jack Clark
	DL Gary Davis
	DL Ancer Haggerty
	DL Oliver McKinney
	LB Tim Casey
	DB Ron Martin
	DB Les Palm
	DB Tim Temple
	DB Dave Fluke

RUSHING: Winn 103/345y, Keller 108/317y
PASSING: Berry 108-208/1478y, 15TD, 51.9%
RECEIVING: Palm 42/570y, Sullivan 32/541y, Bunker 29/385y
SCORING: Keller 36pts, Bunker 32pts, Palm 30pts

1965 4-5-1

17 Pittsburgh	15 WR Ray Palm
31 Utah	14 WR Dennis Keller
27 BYU	14 T Pat Matson
14 Stanford	3 G Dale Wilson
18 Air Force	18 C Bill Smith
20 Washington	24 G Mark Richards
17 Idaho	14 T Jim Kollman / Dan Archer
7 Washington St.	27 TE Steve Bunker
0 California	24 QB Tom Trovato / Mike Brundage
14 Oregon State	19 HB Bill O'Toole / Scott Cress
	FB Dick Winn
	DL Robb Haskins
	DL Jerry Inman
	DL Ancer Haggerty
	DL Gary Davis / Jack Clark
	DL Ray Eaglin
	LB Dave Tobey
	LB Tim Casey
	DB Tim Temple / Ken Klein
	DB Les Palm
	DB Jim Smith
	DB Cam Molter

RUSHING: Winn 96/423y, O'Toole 44/145y, Cress 59/144y
PASSING: Brundage 85-180/1127y, 9TD, 47.2%
RECEIVING: Bunker 51/838y, Palm 39/585y, Cress 19/242y
SCORING: Bunker 56pts, Marc Scholl (K) 31pts, Cress 30pts

1966 3-7

0 Oklahoma	17 WR Steve Bunker / Lachlan Heron
14 Utah	17 WR Scott Cress (HB) / Jim Evenson
7 San Jose State	21 T Roger Stahlhut / Tom Wooton
7 Stanford	3 G Ross Carter / Jim Nicolaisen
17 Air Force	6 C Bill Smith
13 Washington	14 G Warner Wong
28 Idaho	7 T Dan Archer
13 Washington St.	14 TE Lefty Hendrickson / Steve Reina
10 Arizona State	14 QB Mike Barnes / Mike Brundage
15 Oregon State	20 HB Steve Jones (FB) / Claxton Welch
	FB Arlan Elms / Kent Grote
	DL Cam Molter
	DL Jack Rust / Bob Lawrence
	DL George Dames
	DL Jeff MacRae / Jim Kollmann
	DL Pat Helfrich
	LB Harry Cartales
	LB Gunther Cunningham
	LB Omri Hildreth
	DB Jim Smith
	DB Ken Klein / Les Palm
	DB Tim Temple

RUSHING: S Jones 158/542y, Welch 50/196y, Barnes 77/143y
PASSING: Barnes 49-128/710y, 4TD, 38.3%
RECEIVING: Cress 28/402y, Bunker 23/272y, Hendrickson 12/165y
SCORING: Cress 18pts, Reina 14pts, Jones & Brundage 12pts

1967 2-8

13 California	21 WR Denny Schuler / Steve Kantola
13 Colorado	17 WR Roger Smith / John Roche
0 Utah	21 T Joe Phillips
0 Ohio State	30 G John Luger / Keith Hedges
0 Washington	26 C Tom Wooton
31 Idaho	6 G Nick Shur / Jim Nicolaisen
6 Southern Cal	28 T Warner Wong / Bruce Schneider
17 Washington St.	13 TE Lynn Hendrickson / Scott Cress
14 Stanford	17 QB Eric Olson / Tom Blanchard
10 Oregon State	14 TB Claxton Welch
	FB Jim Evenson
	DL Cam Molter
	DL Jack Rust
	DL George Dames
	DL Jeff MacRae
	DL Dennis Gassner / Bill Thomas
	LB Kent Grote
	LB Keith Sherman
	DB Jim Smith
	DB Jack Gleason / Jim Franklin
	DB Steve Hilbert
	DB Omri Hildreth

RUSHING: Welch 130/474y, Evenson 123/407y
PASSING: Olson 51-123/840y, 7TD, 41.5%
RECEIVING: Smith 26/402y, Hendrickson 14/174y, Cress 12/167y
SCORING: Welch & Marc Scholl (K) 18pts, 3 tied w/ 12pts

1968 4-6

7 Colorado	28 WR Greg Lindsey / Bob Newland
12 Stanford	28 WR Roger Smith / Denny Schuler
6 Ohio State	21 T Warner Wong
3 Washington	0 G Nick Shur
23 Idaho	8 C Tom Wooton
14 Utah	6 G John Luger
13 Southern Cal	20 T Joe Phillips
27 Washington St.	13 TE Dave Roberson
8 California	36 QB Eric Olson / John Harrington
19 Oregon State	41 TB Claxton Welch / Stan Hearn
	FB Greg Marshall / Rocky Pamplin
	DL Dennis Gassner
	DL Jack Rust
	DL George Dames
	DL Jim Nicolaisen / Jim Wathey
	DL Mike Kish
	LB Keith Sherman
	LB Kent Grote
	DB Jack Gleason
	DB Jim Franklin
	DB Steve Hilbert / Bill Brauner
	DB Omri Hildreth / Cam Sinclair

RUSHING: Welch 141/505y, Marshall 84/231y, Hearn 61/209y
PASSING: Olson 48-90/796y, 6TD, 53.3%
RECEIVING: Schuler 30/351y, Lindsey 20/463y, Newland 13/178y
SCORING: Lindsey 24pts, Hearn & Schuler 18pts

1969 5-5-1

28 Utah	17 WR Bob Newland
0 Stanford	28 WR Bobby Moore
25 Washington St.	24 T Ralph Pettingell / Tom Drougas
34 San Jose State	36 G Mark Andrews / John McKean
13 Air Force	60 C Brad Halverson / Jim Figoni
22 Washington	7 G Jack Stambaugh
58 Idaho	14 T Joe Phillips / Kim Laiolo
17 Army	17 TE Andy Maurer
10 UCLA	13 QB Tom Blanchard / John Harrington
7 Oregon State	10 TB Pat Verutti / Rocky Pamplin
57 Hawaii	16 FB Greg Marshall / Alan Pitcaithley
	DL Dennis Gassner
	DL Jim Wathey
	DL Dave Walker
	DL Steve Buettner
	DL Mike Kish
	LB Tom Graham
	LB Dane Smith / Steve Rennie
	DB Lionel Coleman
	DB Bill Drake
	DB Jim Franklin
	DB Jack Gleason

RUSHING: Verutti 151/682y, Pamplin 84/390y, Stan Hearn (TB) 44/185y
PASSING: Blanchard 106-184/1488y, 12TD, 57.6%
RECEIVING: Moore 54/786y, Newland 45/640y, Maurer 22/354y
SCORING: Moore 92pts, Ken Woody (K) 37pts, Pamplin 36pts

1970 6-4-1

31 California	24 WR Bob Newland
16 Illinois	20 WR Leland Glass
10 Stanford	33 T Tom Drougas
28 Washington St.	13 G John McKean / Mark Andrews
41 UCLA	40 C Jim Figoni
49 Idaho	13 G Jack Stambaugh
10 Southern Cal	7 T Tim Stokes
23 Washington	25 TE Greg Marshall / Greg Specht (WR)
46 Air Force	35 QB Dan Fouts
22 Army	22 TB Bobby Moore
9 Oregon State	24 FB Jim Anderson / Thurman Anderson
	DL Ray Reeves
	DL Dave Walker
	DL Mike Johnson / Mike Williams
	DL Steve Buettner
	LB Steve Rennie
	LB Mike McConnell
	LB Tom Graham
	DB Lionel Coleman
	DB Bill Drake
	DB Fred Manuel
	DB Bill Brauner / Bob Green

RUSHING: Moore 203/924y, J. Anderson 69/390y, T. Anderson 60/176y
PASSING: Fouts 188-361/2390y, 16TD, 52.1%
RECEIVING: Newland 67/1123y, Glass 45/659y, Moore 45/455y
SCORING: Moore 74pts, Newland 44pts, Ken Woody (K) 43pts

1971 5-6

7 Nebraska	34 WR Greg Specht
36 Utah	29 WR Leland Glass
17 Stanford	38 T Tom Drougas
7 Texas	35 G LeFrancis Arnold
28 Southern Cal	23 C Jim Figoni
23 Washington	21 G John McKean
34 San Jose State	14 T Tim Stokes
21 Washington St.	31 TE Chuck Bradley
23 Air Force	14 QB Dan Fouts
10 California	17 HB Bobby Moore
29 Oregon State	30 FB Greg Herd / Jim Anderson
	DL Keith Davis
	DL Art Webb / Mike Bollinger
	DL Tim Guy / Rich Osterkamp
	DL Steve Buettner
	LB Mike McConnell
	LB Bruce Johnson / Tom Graham
	LB Steve Rennie
	DB Fred Manuel
	DB Bill Drake
	DB Bobby Green / Dave Pieper
	DB Bill Steber / Greg Brosterhous

RUSHING: Moore 249/1211y, Anderson 101/400y, Herd 70/308y
PASSING: Fouts 123-247/1564y, 9TD, 49.8%
RECEIVING: Glass 46/584y, Specht 36/454y, Moore 32/324y
SCORING: Moore 60pts, Herd 42pts, Larry Battle (K) 40pts

1972 4-7

22 Missouri	24 WR Greg Specht / Greg Lindsey
34 Arizona	7 T Tim Stokes
3 Oklahoma	68 T LeFrancis Arnold
20 UCLA	65 G Chuck Bradley / Carl Nickerson
17 Washington	23 G Mike Bolliger
14 Washington St.	31 T Ron Hunt
15 Stanford	13 TE George Martin / Russ Francis
0 Southern Cal	18 QB Dan Fouts
12 California	31 TB Don Reynolds
27 San Jose State	2 SB/WR Maurice Anderson / Bob Palm
30 Oregon State	3 FB Henderson Martin
	DL Tim Guy
	DL Mike Pulver / Reggie Lewis
	DL Art Webb
	DL Greg Brosterhous / Keith Davis
	LB Mike Jodoin
	LB Mike Popovich / Bill Meyer
	LB Bobby Green / Steve Herr
	DB Fred Manuel
	DB Jack Conners
	DB Steve Donnelly
	DB Dave Pieper

RUSHING: Reynolds 52/421y, Anderson 96/259y, Martin 61/206y
PASSING: Fouts 171-348/2041y, 12TD, 49.1%
RECEIVING: Specht 52/710y, Palm 24/418y, Anderson 23/211y
SCORING: Anderson, Reynolds & Specht 26pts

1973 2-9

20 Arizona State	26 WR Greg Lindsey / Pat McNally
17 Air Force	24 WR Bob Palm / Maurice Anderson
17 Utah	35 T Tim Guy
0 Michigan	24 G LeFrancis Arnold
41 California	10 C Mike Popovich
10 Southern Cal	31 G Mike Bollinger
58 Washington	0 T Ron Hunt
14 Washington St.	21 TE Russ Francis
7 UCLA	27 QB Herb Singleton / Norval Turner
7 Stanford	24 TB Don Reynolds / Rick Kane
14 Oregon State	17 FB Eugene Brown / Greg Herd
	DL George Martin
	DL Reggie Lewis
	DL Art Webb / Dave Morgan
	DL Don Johnson
	LB Mike Jodoin
	LB Bill Meyer
	LB Bobby Green
	DB Mario Clark
	DB Jack Conners
	DB Steve Donnelly
	DB Tim Slapnicka / Chuck Wills

RUSHING: Reynolds 226/1002y, Kane 90/430y, Herd 37/180y
PASSING: Singleton 109-234/1333y, 10TD, 46.6%
RECEIVING: Francis 31/495y, Palm 27/407y, Lindsey 22/255y
SCORING: Palm (WR-K) 47pts, Reynolds 42pts, Kane 30pts

1974 2-9

7 Nebraska	61 WR Wayne Johnson / Greg Bauer
27 Air Force	23 WR Bob Palm
23 Utah	16 T Chris Haake
10 Northwestern	14 G Ross Duman / Laird Riffle
10 California	40 C Carl Nickerson
7 Southern Cal	16 G Ken Bondelie / Chuck Thomas
0 Washington	66 T Ron Hunt
16 Washington St.	21 TE Kevin Culligan
0 UCLA	21 QB Norval Turner
9 Stanford	17 TB Don Reynolds
16 Oregon State	35 FB Rick Kane / George Bennett
	DL George Martin
	DL Greg Gibson
	DL Dave Morgan
	DL Dave Freeman / Don Johnson
	LB Darrell Mehl
	LB Tom Yaru
	LB Bobby Green
	DB Mario Clark
	DB Frank Ehret / Jo Jo White
	DB Steve Donnelly
	DB Tim Slapnicka / Chuck Wills

RUSHING: Reynolds 165/787y, Kane 120/499y, Bennett 43/157y
PASSING: Turner 99-202/1261y, 5TD, 49%
RECEIVING: Palm 31/466y, Reynolds 19/140y, Bauer 15/248y
SCORING: Stan Woodfill (K) 38pts, Turner 24pts, Palm 18pts

1975 3-8

7 Oklahoma	62 WR Greg Bauer
2 San Jose State	5 WR Wayne Johnson
7 Minnesota	10 T Ron Hunt
17 Washington	27 G Tim Overall / Chuck Thomas
7 California	34 C Fred Quillan
3 Southern Cal	17 G Les Duman / Laird Riffle
18 Utah	7 T John Rosette
26 Washington St.	14 TE Kevin Culligan
17 UCLA	50 QB Jack Henderson
30 Stanford	33 RB Eugene Brown / Tommy Garrett
14 Oregon State	7 RB George Bennett

DL Mel Cook / John Reed
DL Greg Gibson
DL Rod Rickert
DL Dave Morgan / Rob Plath
DL Don Johnson
LB Tom Yaru / Kim Netting
LB Darrell Mehl
DB Mario Clark
DB Reggie Grant
DB Chuck Wills
DB Bruce Jensen / Brian Rekofke

RUSHING: Bennett 175/805y, Garrett 34/134y, Brown 40/123y
PASSING: Henderson 151-321/1492y, 6TD, 47%
RECEIVING: Bauer 52/616y, Johnson 29/250y, Bennett 18/84y
SCORING: Stan Woodfill (K) 48pts, Bennett 42pts, Bauer 24pts

1976 4-7

17 Colorado State	3 WR Greg Bauer
0 Southern Cal	53 WR Tom Cafferty / Bill Vincent
21 Utah	13 T Raul Martinez
27 Utah State	9 G Larry Ermini
10 California	27 C Fred Quillan
0 Notre Dame	41 G Bill Hoffman / Les Duman
7 Washington	14 T John Rosette
22 Washington St.	43 TE Jeff Butts
0 UCLA	46 QB Jack Henderson
17 Stanford	28 TB Jim Johnson / Dennis Bullock
23 Oregon State	14 FB George Bennett

DL Mel Cook
DL Rob Plath
DL Rod Rickert
DL Rudy Bryan
DL John Reed / Larry Williams
LB Bruce Beekley / Kim Nutting
LB Darrell Mehl
DB Reggie Grant
DB Darrell Mellum / Steve Brouchet
DB Brian Refofke
DB Craig Feola / Darrell Mellum

RUSHING: Johnson 89/356y, Bennett 105/324y, Bullock 42/179y
PASSING: Henderson 157-298/1582y, 6TD, 52.7%
RECEIVING: Bauer 53/632y, Cafferty 21/358y, Vincent 19/283y
SCORING: Roy Geiger (K) 42pts, Henderson 20pts, Bennett 18pts

1977 2-9

16 Georgia	27 WR Tom Cafferty
29 TCU	24 WR Ken Page
10 Wisconsin	22 T Matt Hamstreet
10 Stanford	20 G Steve Greatwood / Jon Gragg
0 Washington	54 C Fred Quillan / Steve Nado
15 Southern Cal	33 G Bill Hoffman
17 LSU	56 T Pete Laughlin / Pat McDougall
20 Washington St.	56 TE Bill Vincent / Dan Clark
3 UCLA	21 QB Jack Henderson
16 Cal	48 TB Ed Ratliff / Dennis Bullock
28 Oregon State	16 FB Kim Nutting / Vince Williams

DL Mel Cook
DL Rob Plath
DL Vince Goldsmith
DL Scott Setterlund / Rudy Bryan
DL Willie Blasher
LB Tim Beyer / Bryan Hinkle
LB Bruce Beekley
DB Mike Chriss / David Haynes
DB Reggie Grant / Rick Hudnell
DB Bruce Jensen
DB Kenny Bryant

RUSHING: Nutting 101/357y, Williams 71/316y, Wood 38/190y
PASSING: Henderson 108-223/1286y, 5TD, 48.4%
RECEIVING: Page 40/591y, Cafferty 30/393y, Bullock 22/196y
SCORING: Roy Geiger (K) 52pts, Nutting 24pts, Page 18pts

1978 2-9

7 Colorado	24 WR Paul Bachtold
10 Southern Cal	37 WR Curt Jackson
10 TCU	14 T Bill Hoffman
19 Wisconsin	22 G Kevin Anderson / Jamey Mathews
18 California	21 C Steve Kleffner / Mike Delegato
16 BYU	17 G Steve Greatwood
14 Washington	20 T Pete Laughlin / Pat McDougall
31 Washington St.	7 TE Tim Beyer
21 UCLA	23 QB Mike Kennedy / Tim Durando
3 Arizona	24 TB Ed Radcliff / Dwight Robertson
24 Oregon State	3 FB Vince Williams / Jeff Wood

DL Neil Elshire
DL Vince Goldsmith
DL Scott Setterlund / Mike Kesler
DL Terry Dion
LB Mike Berkich / Bryan Hinkle
LB Bruce Beekley
LB Willie Blasher
DB Rick Hudnell
DB Jerome Covington / Rock Richmond
DB Mike Nolan
DB Kenny Bryant / Jim Johnson

RUSHING: Williams 183/842y, Wood 94/347y, Robertson 58/300y
PASSING: Kennedy 58-136/683y, 4TD, 42.6%
  Durando 54-134/620y, 1TD, 40.3%
RECEIVING: Jackson 21/237y, Bachtold 18/310y, Williams 15/181y
SCORING: Pat English (K) 37pts, Robertson 30pts, Bachtold 18pts

1979 6-5

33 Colorado	19 WR Rick Ward
17 Michigan State	41 WR Curt Jackson / Don Coleman
17 Washington	21 T Kevin McGill
7 Purdue	13 G Kevin Anderson
19 California	14 C Mike Delegato
13 Arizona	24 G Steve Greatwood
17 Air Force (F-L)	9 T Pat McDougall
37 Washington St.	26 TE Tim Tyler / Greg Hogensen
16 Stanford	7 QB Reggie Ogburn
0 UCLA	35 TB Dwight Robertson / Reggie Young
24 Oregon State	3 FB Vince Williams / Jeff Wood

DL Neil Elshire
DL Vince Goldsmith
DL Scott Setterlund / Mike Kesler
DL Terry Dion
LB Bryan Hinkle / Andy Vobora
LB Chris Cosgrove
LB Mike Berkich
DB Rock Richmond
DB Steve Brown
DB Mike Nolan
DB Joe Figures

RUSHING: Ogburn 156/644y, Robertson 100/454y, Young 64/402y
PASSING: Ogburn 71-139/905y, 6TD, 51.1%
RECEIVING: Ward 16/217y, Robertson 15/94y, Jackson 14/206y
SCORING: Robertson 54pts, Doug Jollymour (K) 33pts,
  Pat English (K) 23pts

1980 6-3-2

25 Stanford	35 WR Greg Moser
7 Kansas	7 WR Curt Jackson / Mark James
35 Michigan State	7 T Jeff Kubitz
34 Washington	10 G Jamey Mathews
6 California	31 C Mike Delegato
7 Southern Cal	7 G Stu Yatsko / Scott Shepard
32 UNLV	9 T Kevin McGill
20 Washington St.	10 TE Greg Hogenson / Tim Tyler
20 UCLA	14 QB Reggie Ogburn / Kevin Lusk
40 Oregon State	21 TB Reggie Brown / Dwight Robertson
37 Arizona State	42 FB Charlie Bisharat / Terrance Jones

DL Rich Schwartz
DL Vince Goldsmith / Bill Lowder
DL Scott Setterland
DL Mike Walter / Gordon Bledsoe
LB Bryan Hinkle
LB Ed Hagerty
LB Andy Vobura
DB Ross Gibbs / Dennis Clay
DB Steve Brown
DB Mike Nolan
DB Joe Figures / Gary Beck

RUSHING: Brown 171/775y, Ogburn 130/527y, Bisharat 59/313y
PASSING: Ogburn 99-183/1257y, 8TD, 54.1%
RECEIVING: Moser 32/611y, Jackson 24/361y, Brown 22/165y
SCORING: Ogburn 42pts, Robertson 36pts,
  Doug Jollymour (K) 32pts

1981 2-9

16 Fresno State	23 WR Greg Moser
10 Kansas	19 WR Osborn Thomas / Jon Brosterhous
34 Pacific	0 T Tim Ellis
3 Washington	17 G Paul Sanborn / Stu Yatsko
0 Arizona State	24 C Mike Delegato / Gary Zimmerman (DL)
14 Arizona	18 G Craig Kaylor
10 Air Force	20 T Jeff Pew / Brian Castle
11 UCLA	18 TE Tim Tyler / Greg Hogensen
7 Washington St.	39 QB Kevin Lusk / Mike Owens
3 Stanford	42 TB Reggie Brown / Harry Billups
47 Oregon State	17 FB Vince Williams / Ladaria Johnson

DL Gordon Bledsoe / Steve Baack
DL Steve Johnson / Michael Gray
DL Bill Lowder
DL Mike Walter
LB Andy Vobora / Cliff Gibson
LB Chris Cosgrove / Mike Berkich
LB Dwight Ford / Ed Hagerty
DB Steve Brown
DB Ross Gibbs / Dennis Clay
DB Gary Beck
DB Joe Figures

RUSHING: Brown 177/690y, Williams 65/241y, Johnson 32/155y
PASSING: Lusk 86-174/864y, 4TD, 49.4%
RECEIVING: Moser 39/605y, Brown 34/180y, Thomas 25/319y
SCORING: Doug Jollymour (K) 47pts, Brown & Billups 18pts

1982 2-8-1

3 Arizona State	24 WR G. Moser/Rourke Lowe/Eugene Young
13 San Jose State	18 WR Osborn Thomas
4 Fresno State	10 T Tim Ellis
21 Washington	37 G Scott Shepard / Paul Sanborn
7 Southern Cal	38 C Ryan Zinke
7 California	10 G Gary Zimmerman / Craig Kaylor
13 Notre Dame	13 T Jeff Pew / Brian Castle
12 UCLA	40 TE Doug Herman
3 Washington St.	10 QB Mike Jorgensen / Kevin Lusk
13 Arizona	42 TB Ladaria Johnson / Dwight Robertson
7 Oregon State	6 FB Terrance Jones

DL Steve Baack
DL Bill Lowder / Michael Gray
DL Steve Johnson / Dan Ralph
DL Mike Walter
LB Chris Gibson / Jerry Mickels
LB Chris Cosgrove
LB Dwight Ford
DB Steve Brown / Wendell Cason
DB Dennis Clay
DB Jeff Williams
DB Doug Judge / Devall Webster

RUSHING: Jones 165/715y, Johnson 75/332y, Robertson 37/142y
PASSING: Jorgensen 33-74/393y, 2TD, 44.6%
RECEIVING: Thomas 30/369y, Moser 10/156y, Lowe 10/149y
SCORING: Todd Lee (K) 23pts, Thomas 18pts, Jones 12pts

1983 4-6-1

15 Pacific	21 WR Kwante Hampton / Osborn Thomas
6 Ohio State	31 WR Lew Barnes
15 Houston	14 T Scott Shepard
34 San Jose State	44 G Brad Smith / Ken Warner / Lino Vaccher
24 California	17 C Ryan Zinke
19 Arizona	10 G Gary Zimmerman
3 Washington	32 T Greg Schwab / Ed Stringer
7 Washington St.	24 TE Doug Herman / Rich Gaiser
13 UCLA	24 QB Mike Jorgensen / Mike Owens
16 Stanford	7 TB Kevin McCall
0 Oregon State	0 FB Ladaria Johnson / Kevin Wilhite

DL Steve Baack
DL Dan Ralph
DL Dave Maley / Terry Youngblood
DL John Byrne / Dale Dorning
LB Jerry Mikels / Dan Devaney
LB Lerry Wilson / Bob Hudetz
LB E.J. Duffy
DB Wendell Cason
DB Don Brown / Danny McCalister
DB Jeff Williams / Dan Wilken
DB Doug Judge / Ron Johnson

RUSHING: Johnson 85/394y, McCall 90/331y, Wilhite 63/225y
PASSING: Jorgensen 72-174/938y, 5TD, 41.4%
RECEIVING: Barnes 30/625y, McCall 26/171y, Hampton 17/297y
SCORING: Paul Schwabe (K) 43pts, Barnes 36pts, McCall 24pts

1984 6-5

28 Long Beach St.	17 WR Scott Holman
27 Colorado	20 WR Lew Barnes
21 California	14 T Greg Schwab
30 Pacific	14 G Brad Smith / Ray Wheatley
14 Arizona	28 C Ken Warner
9 Southern Cal	19 G Craig Kaylor
10 Washington	17 T Steve Jenson
41 Washington St.	50 TE Doug Herman
20 UCLA	18 QB Chris Miller
10 Arizona State	44 TB Kevin McCall / Tony Cherry
31 Oregon State	6 FB Alex Mack
	DL Dale Dorning
	DL Dave Maley / Rollin Putzier
	DL David Culp / Rob Marshall
	DL John Byrne
	LB Dan Devaney / Don Pellum
	LB Bob Hudetz
	LB Todd Welch
	DB Wendell Cason
	DB Ed Hulbert
	DB Dan Wilken / Jeff Williams
	DB Doug Judge

RUSHING: Cherry 87/569y, McCall 143/561y, Mack 69/244y
PASSING: Miller 145-289/1712y, 10TD, 50.2%
RECEIVING: McCall 39/317y, Barnes 37/634y, Herman 30/376y
SCORING: Matt MacLeod (K) 63pts, Barnes 42pts, McCall 34pts

1985 5-6

42 Washington St.	39 WR Scott Holman
17 Colorado	21 WR Lew Barnes
45 Stanford	28 T Greg Schwab
0 Nebraska	63 G Lino Vaccher
13 Washington	19 C Garrett Holmes / Ken Warner
24 California	27 G Brad Smith
49 San Diego St.	37 T Drew Smetana / Jeff Stefanick
35 San Jose State	13 TE Bobby DeBisschop / Eric Elliott
8 Arizona	20 QB Chris Miller
34 Oregon State	13 TB Tony Cherry
6 Southern Cal	20 FB Alex Mack / Kevin Wilhite
	DL Matt Brock
	DL Rollin Putzier
	DL Dave Maley / Rob Marshall
	DL John Byrne
	LB Dan Devaney / Darrin Golka
	LB Jerry Mikels
	LB E.J. Duffy
	DB Ron Johnson / Don Brown
	DB Ed Hulbert
	DB Anthony Newman
	DB Doug Judge

RUSHING: Cherry 211/1006y, Willhite 50/195y, Mack 33/117y
PASSING: Miller 182-329/2237y, 18TD, 55.3%
RECEIVING: Barnes 50/789y, Cherry 39/245y, Holman 29/477y
SCORING: Cherry 60pts, Matt MacLeod (K) 58pts, Barnes 42pts

1986 5-6

21 San Jose State	14 WR Jan Cespedes/Sam Archer/Terry Obee
32 Colorado	30 WR Rod Green / J.J. Birden
17 Arizona	41 T Tony Borba
14 Nebraska	48 G Chris Husko
21 Southern Cal	35 C Garrett Holmes / Gary Gilbert
17 Arizona State	37 G Brad Smith
7 Stanford	41 T Jeff Stefanick
3 Washington	38 TE Bobby DeBisschop
27 California	9 QB Chris Miller
27 Washington St.	17 TB Latin Berry/Derek Loville/James Harper
49 Oregon State	28 FB Kevin Willhite / Alan Jackson
	DL Matt Brock / Joe Mansfield
	DL Rollin Putzier
	DL Dave Maley / David Cusano
	DL Rob Marshall / Joe Taylor
	LB Mike Blakey / Scott Kozak / John Wolf
	LB Mark Kearns / Tom Talbot/ Darrin Golka
	LB Dan Devaney
	DB Clifford Hicks / LaRoy Montgomery
	DB Don Brown / Brett Young
	DB Ed Hulbert
	DB Anthony Newman / Tim Cooper

RUSHING: Loville 140/544y, Berry 63/291y, Willhite 42/189y
PASSING: Miller 216-356/2503y, 12TD, 60.7%
RECEIVING: DeBisschop 40/500y, Loville 35/236y, Green 29/512y
SCORING: Loville 60pts, Matt MacLeod (K) 59pts, Berry 24pts

1987 6-5

10 Colorado	7 WR Terry Obee / J.J. Birden
14 Ohio State	24 WR Rod Green / Tony Hargain
25 San Diego St.	20 T Eric Hunter / Gary Robertson
29 Washington	22 G Andy Sunia / Todd Kunzman
34 Southern Cal	27 C Gary Gilbert
10 UCLA	41 G Chris Husko
10 Stanford	13 T Jeff Stefanick
6 California	20 TE Tim Parker / Joe Meerten
17 Arizona State	37 QB Bill Musgrave
31 Washington St.	17 TB Derek Loville / Russell Lawson
44 Oregon State	0 FB Latin Berry / Randy Willhite
	DL Matt Brock
	DL Rollin Putzier
	DL Devin FitzPatrick / Joe Taylor
	LB Scott Kozak / Bjarne Jensen
	LB Mark Kearns
	LB Tom Talbot
	LB Mike Blakey
	DB Ron Gould
	DB Brett Young / Chris Oldham
	DB Thom Kaumeyer / Derek Horton
	DB Anthony Newman

RUSHING: Loville 165/591y, Berry 82/313y, Lawson 43/131y
PASSING: Musgrave 139-234/1836y, 13TD, 59.4%
RECEIVING: Obee 33/640y, Parker 22/263y, Birden 19/399y
SCORING: Kirk Dennis (K) 66pts, Loville 48pts, Obee 24pts

1988 6-6

49 Long Beach St.	0 WR Sam Archer
43 Washington St.	28 WR Terry Obee
7 Stanford	3 T Curt Dykes
34 San Diego St.	13 G Chris Husko
14 Southern Cal	42 C Scot Boatright / Gary Gilbert
52 Idaho State	7 G Andy Sunia / Rick Hunt
17 Washington	14 T Todd Kunzman / Todd Kaanapu
20 Arizona State	21 TE Joe Meerten / Kolya Tefft
6 UCLA	16 QB Doug Musgrave / Pete Nelson
27 Arizona	41 TB Derek Loville
10 Oregon State	21 FB Latin Berry / Randy Willhite
17 Hawaii	41 DL Matt Brock
	DL David Cusano
	DL Joe Taylor / Devinn FitzPatrick
	LB Scott Kozak
	LB Scott Whitney
	LB Mark Kearns / Leroy Ale
	LB Peter Brantley
	DB Brett Young
	DB Chris Oldham / Daryl Reed
	DB Thom Kaumeyer / Mark Winn
	DB Derek Horton / Rory Dairy

RUSHING: Loville 265/1202y, Berry 103/424y, Willhite 27/106y
PASSING: Nelson 66-140/897y, 4TD, 47.1%
Musgrave 62-121/815y, 8TD, 51.2%
RECEIVING: Obee 33/596y, Archer 31/490y, Loville 19/182y
SCORING: Loville & Kirk Dennis (K) 80pts, Obee 44pts

1989 8-4

35 California	19 WR Tony Hargain / Joe Reitzug
44 Iowa	6 WR Terry Obee
17 Stanford	18 T Curt Dykes / Todd Kaanapu
16 Arizona	10 G Chris Husko
38 Washington St.	51 C Colin Hall / Scott Boatright
14 Washington	20 G Brian Hanable / Andy Sunia
27 Arizona State	7 T Todd Kunzman (G) / David Collinsworth
52 Long Beach St.	10 TE Joe Meerten / Jeff Thomason
41 BYU	45 QB Bill Musgrave
38 UCLA	20 TB Derek Loville
30 Oregon state	21 FB Latin Berry / Dondre Bausley
27 Tulsa■	24 DL Matt LaBounty
	DL David Cusano / Marcus Woods
	DL Andre Williams
	LB Bjarne Jensen / Andy Conner
	LB Mark Kearns
	LB Joe Farwell
	LB Peter Brantley
	DB Chris Oldham / Steve Kemp
	DB Daryl Reed
	DB Derek Horton / Eric Castle
	DB Rory Dairy

RUSHING: Loville 244/959y, Berry 100/542y, Bausley 52/235y
PASSING: Musgrave 231-401/3081y, 22TD, 57.6%
RECEIVING: Obee 46/741y, Hargain 40/686y, Reitzug 34/511y
SCORING: Gregg McCallum (K) 109pts, Loville 84pts, Obee 34pts

1990 8-4

42 San Diego St.	21 WR Joe Reitzug
55 Idaho	23 WR Michael McClellan / Anthony Jones
17 Arizona	22 T Todd Kaanapu
32 BYU	16 G Andy Sunia / Jon Tattersall
52 Utah State	7 C Scot Boatright / Collin Hall
17 Washington	38 G Bud Bowie / Greg Phillips
27 Arizona State	7 T David Collinsworth / Todd Gydesen
31 Stanford	0 TE Jeff Thomason / Vince Ferry
28 UCLA	24 QB Bill Musgrave
3 California	28 TB Sean Burwell
6 Oregon State	3 FB Ngalu Kelemani / Juan Shedrick
31 Colorado St.■	32 DL Matt LaBounty
	DL Marcus Woods
	DL Jeff Cummins / Romeo Bandison
	LB Andy Conner
	LB James Bautista
	LB Joe Farwell
	LB Peter Brantley
	DB Daryl Singleton / Muhammad Oliver
	DB Daryle Smith
	DB Eric Castle / Steve Kemp
	DB Rory Dairy

RUSHING: Burwell 223/969y, Kelemani 108/425y, Shedrick 45/188y
PASSING: Musgrave 202-348/2611y, 17TD, 57.5%
RECEIVING: Reitzug 40/639y, McClellan 36/525y, Burwell 35/340y
SCORING: Gregg McCallum (K) 81pts, Burwell 68pts, Kelemani 38pts

1991 3-8

40 Washington St.	14 WR Ronnie Harris
28 Texas Tech	13 WR Anthony Jones
21 Utah	24 T Todd Gydesen
14 Southern Cal	30 G Jon Tattersall
29 New Mexico St.	6 C Greg Phillips
7 California	45 G Bud Bowie / Heath Howington
7 Washington	29 T David Collingsworth
13 Stanford	33 TE Jeff Thomason
21 Arizona State	24 QB Danny O'Neil / Brett Salisbury
7 UCLA	16 TB Sean Burwell / Donovan Moore
3 Oregon State	14 FB Juan Shedrick
	DL Matt LaBounty
	DL Marcus Woods
	DL Romeo Bandison
	LB Andy Conner
	LB James Bautista
	LB Joe Farwell
	LB Ernest Jones / Terrell Edwards
	DB Muhammad Oliver
	DB Daryle Smith / Herman O'Berry
	DB Eric Castle
	DB Chad Cota / Paul Rodriguez

RUSHING: Burwell 139/510y, Moore 94/375y, Shedrick 50/219y
PASSING: O'Neill 55-115/73y, 7TD, 47.8%
RECEIVING: Jones 34/435y, Harris 25/311y, Thomason 21/298y
SCORING: Gregg McCallum (K) 36pts, Jones 32pts, Harris 18pts

1992 6-6

21 Hawaii	24 WR Derrick Deadwiler / Ronnie Harris
7 Stanford	21 WR Anthony Jones
16 Texas Tech	13 T David Collinsworth
59 UNLV	6 G Jon Tattersall
30 Arizona State	20 C Tom Curran
10 Southern Cal	32 G Mike DiFonzo / Heath Howington
3 Washington	24 T Steve Hardin / Justin Starck
34 Washington St.	17 TE Vince Ferry / Willy Tate
37 California	17 QB Danny O'Neill
6 UCLA	9 TB Sean Burwell / Ricky Whittle
7 Oregon State	0 FB Juan Shedrick
35 Wake Forest■	39 DL Jeff Cummins
	DL Romeo Bandison
	DL Gary Williams
	LB Terrell Edwards
	LB David Massey / Jeremy Asher
	LB Joe Farwell
	LB Ernest Jones
	DB Alex Molden
	DB Herman O'Berry
	DB Eric Castle
	DB Chad Cota / Paul Rodriguez

RUSHING: Burwell 193/822y, Whittle 133/634y, Shedrick 49/186y
PASSING: O'Neill 176-316/2152y, 11TD, 55.7%
RECEIVING: Burwell 35/293y, Harris 32/496y, Deadwiler 29/414y
SCORING: Tommy Thompson (K) 85pts, Burwell 56pts, Harris 32pts

1993 5-6

23	Colorado State	9 WR	Derrick Deadwiler / Dameron Ricketts
35	Montana	30 WR	Cristin McLemore / Kory Murphy
13	Illinois	7 T	Steve Hardin / Paul Wiggins
41	California	42 G	Eric Barnes
13	Southern Cal	24 C	Tom Curran / Heath Howington (G)
45	Arizona State	36 G	Mike DiFonzo
6	Washington	21 T	Justin Starck
46	Washington St.	23 TE	Willy Tate / Josh Wilcox
10	Arizona	31 QB	Danny O'Neil
34	Stanford	38 TB	Sean Burwell / Ricky Whittle
12	Oregon State	15 FB	Juan Shedrick / Pulou Malepea
		DL	Gary Williams
		DL	Silila Malepeai
		DL	Romeo Bandison / Troy Bailey
		LB	John Taumoepeau / Eugene Jackson
		LB	Dave Massey / Rich Ruhl
		LB	Jeremy Asher
		LB	Ernest Jones
		DB	Alex Molden
		DB	Isaac Walker / LaMont Woods
		DB	Dante Lewis / Jeff Sherman
		DB	Chad Cota

RUSHING: Burnell 113/457y, Whittle 67/284y, Shedrick 48/183y
PASSING: O'Neil 223-360/3224y, 22TD, 61.9%
RECEIVING: Deadwiler 52/811y, McLemore 50/791y,
  Tate 32/512y
SCORING: Tommy Thompson (K) 72pts, McLemore 60pts,
  Deadwiler 30pts

1994 9-4

58	Portland State	16 WR	Dameron Ricketts / Kory Murphy
16	Hawaii	36 WR	Cristin McLemore / Pat Johnson
16	Utah	34 T	Willy Rife (G) / Paul Wiggins
40	Iowa	18 G	Eric Reid
22	Southern Cal	7 C	Mark Gregg / Dave Cuttrell
7	Washington St.	21 G	Tasi Malepeai / Bob Baldwin
23	California	7 T	Steve Hardin
31	Washington	20 TE	Josh Wilcox
10	Arizona	9 QB	Danny O'Neil / Tony Graziani
34	Arizona State	10 TB	Dino Philyaw / Ricky Whittle
55	Stanford	21 FB	Dwayne Jones / Pulou Maleapeai
17	Oregon State	13 DL	Troy Bailey
20	Penn State■	38 DL	Silila Maleapeai
		DL	Mark Schmidt / Mark Slymen
		LB	Reggie Jordan / Derrick Barnes
		LB	Jeremy Asher
		LB	Rich Ruhl
		LB	Paul Jensen
		DB	Alex Molden / Isaac Walker
		DB	Herman O'Berry / Kenny Wheaton
		DB	Jeff Sherman
		DB	Chad Cota

RUSHING: Philyaw 181/716y, Whittle 130/606y,
  Marcel Stewart (TB) 38/141y
PASSING: O'Neil 182-341/2212y, 22TD, 53.4%
RECEIVING: McLemore 42/564y, Ricketts 42/534y,
  Johnson 30/472y
SCORING: Matt Belden (K) 76pts, Philyaw 66pts, McLemore &
  Whittle 54pts

1995 9-3

27	Utah	20 WR	Dameron Ricketts / Jibiri Hodge
34	Illinois	31 WR	Cristin McLemore / Pat Johnson
38	UCLA	31 T	Paul Wiggins
21	Stanford	28 G	Eric Reid
45	Pacific	7 C	Mark Gregg
52	California	30 G	Tasi Malepeai / Bob Baldwin
26	Washington St.	7 T	David Weber / Willy Rife
24	Arizona State	35 TE	Josh Wilcox
24	Washington	22 QB	Tony Graziani
17	Arizona	13 TB	Ricky Whittle / Kevin Parker
12	Oregon State	10 FB	A.J. Jelks / Eric Winn
6	Colorado■	38 DL	Troy Bailey / Desmond Byrd
		DL	Bryant Jackson
		DL	Mark Schmidt
		LB	Paul Jensen
		LB	Jeremy Asher
		LB	Rich Ruhl
		LB	Derrick Barnes / Reggie Jordan
		DB	Alex Molden
		DB	Kenny Wheaton / LaMont Woods
		DB	Isaac Walker
		DB	Brian Collins / Dante Lewis

RUSHING: Whittle 260/1021y, Graziani 81/236y, Parker 46/221y
PASSING: Graziani 231-426/2604y, 13TD, 54.2%
RECEIVING: McLemore 64/1036y, Whittle 55/437y,
  Wilcox 36/456y
SCORING: Whittle 78pts, Josh Smith (K) 77pts, Wilcox 30pts

1996 6-5

30	Fresno State	27 WR	Jibiri Hodge / Dameron Ricketts
44	Nevada	30 WR	Damon Griffin / Pat Johnson
35	Colorado State	28 T	Paul Wiggins
44	Washington St.	55 G	Bob Baldwin / Willy Rife
27	Arizona State	48 C	Mark Gregg
22	UCLA	41 G	Tasi Malepeai
24	Stanford	27 T	David Weber
14	Washington	33 TE	Josh Wilcox
49	Arizona	31 QB	Tony Graziani / Ryan Perry-Smith
40	California	23 TB	Saladin McCullough / Derien Latimer
49	Oregon State	13 FB	Eric Winn / A.J. Jelks
		DL	Desmond Byrd
		DL	Bryant Jackson
		DL	Mark Schmidt / Caleb Smith
		DL	Reggie Jordan
		LB	Chris Vandiver / Peter Sirmon
		LB	Ryan Klaasen / Garth White
		LB	Derrick Barnes / Derek Allen
		DB	Kenny Wheaton
		DB	LaMont Woods / Ronnie Gipson
		DB	Brandon McLemore / Jaiya Figueras
		DB	Chris Young / Michael Fletcher

RUSHING: McCullough 122/685y, Latimer 61/268y,
  Jerry Brown (TB) 42/215y
PASSING: Perry-Smith 125-241/1874y, 12TD, 51.9%
  Graziani 92-171/1353y, 8TD, 53.8%
RECEIVING: Griffin 43/711y, Wilcox 28/425y, Hodge 26/421y
SCORING: McCullough 90pts, Josh Smith (K) 78pts, Griffin 42pts

1997 7-5

16	Arizona	9 WR	Pat Johnson / Tony Hartley
24	Nevada	20 WR	Donald Haynes / Ray Brust
43	Fresno State	40 T	Marco Aguirre
49	Stanford	58 G	Stefan deVries
13	Washington St.	24 C	Deke Moen / Seaton Daly
31	UCLA	39 G	Michael Klews (T) / Lee Gundy
31	Utah	13 T	David Weber
22	Southern Cal	24 TE	Blake Spence
31	Washington	28 QB	Akili Smith / Jason Maas
31	Arizona State	52 TB	Saladin McCullough
48	Oregon State	30 FB	Eric Winn
41	Air Force■	13 DL	Caleb Smith / Terry Miller
		DL	Desmond Byrd
		DL	Leie Sualua
		DL	Saul Patu
		LB	Peter Sirmon
		LB	Garth White
		LB	Dietrich Moore / Ryan Klaasen
		DB	Eric Edwards / Tamoni Joiner
		DB	Jaiya Figueras
		DB	Rashad Bauman
		DB	Michael Fletcher / Brandon McLemore

RUSHING: McCullough 267/1343y, Smith 89/378y,
PASSING: Smith 108-200/1385y, 13TD, 54%
  Maas 104-187/1631y, 18TD, 55.6%
RECEIVING: Johnson 55/1072y, Spence 38/632y, Hartley 31/461y
SCORING: McCullough 72pts, Johnson 54pts,
  Joshua Smith (K) 51pts

1998 8-4

48	Michigan State	14 WR	Damon Griffin
33	UTEP	26 WR	Tony Hartley / Donald Haynes
58	San Jose State	3 T	Marco Aguirre / Mike Klews (G)
63	Stanford	28 G	Stefan deVries
51	Washington St.	29 C	Deke Moen
38	UCLA	41 G	Lee Gundy
17	Southern Cal	13 T	Scott Fergus / Josh Beckett
3	Arizona	38 TE	Jed Weaver
27	Washington	22 QB	Akili Smith
51	Arizona State	19 TB	Reuben Droughns/ Derien Latimer
41	Oregon State	44 FB	Chris Young / Chad Chance
43	Colorado■	51 DL	Terry Miller
		DL	Caleb Smith / Masi Heamish
		DL	Leie Sualua
		DL	Saul Patu
		LB	Aaron Cheuvront
		LB	Chris Vandiver / Peter Sirmon
		LB	Dietrich Moore
		DB	Eric Edwards
		DB	Rashad Bauman / Tamoni Joiner
		DB	Brandon McLemore / Justin Wilcox
		DB	Michael Fletcher / Gary Barker

RUSHING: Droughns 112/824y, Latimer 90/306y,
  Herman Ho-Ching (TB) 89/296y
PASSING: Smith 215-371/3763y, 32TDs, 58%
RECEIVING: Griffin 58/1038y, Hartley 48/1015y, Weaver 39/623y
SCORING: Nathan Villegas (K) 117pts, Droughns 66pts,
  Hartley 60pts

1999 9-3

20	Michigan State	27 WR	Keenan Howry / Marshaun Tucker
47	UTEP	28 WR	Tony Hartley
72	Nevada	10 T	Scott Fergus / Al Cotton
33	Southern Cal	33 G	Deke Moen (C) / Jim Adams
20	Washington	34 C	Ryan Schmid
29	UCLA	34 G	Lee Gundy
44	Arizona	41 T	Josh Beckett
20	Arizona State	17 TE	Enyi Nwamuo / Justin Peelle
52	Washington St.	10 QB	A.J. Feeley / Joey Harrington
24	California	19 TB	Reuben Droughns
25	Oregon State	14 FB	Todd Brooks / Derien Latimer
24	Minnesota■	20 DL	Terry Miller
		DL	Caleb Smith / Jason Nikolao
		DL	Faiva Talaeai
		DL	Saul Patu
		LB	Matt Smith
		LB	Peter Sirmon
		LB	Dietrich Moore / Garrett Sabol
		DB	Brian Johnson / Tamoni Joiner
		DB	Justin Wilcox
		DB	Brandon McLemore
		DB	Michael Fletcher

RUSHING: Droughns 277/1234y, Herman Ho-Ching (TB) 54/198y,
  Latimer 38/177y
PASSING: Feeley 136-259/1951y, 14TD, 52.5%
  Harrington 84-158/1180y, 10TD, 53.2%
RECEIVING: Hartley 56/881y, Tucker 32/481y, Howry 29/452y
SCORING: Nathan Villegas (K) 63pts, Droughns 62pts,
  Josh Frankel (K) 51pts

2000 10-2

36	Nevada	7 WR	Keenan Howry
23	Wisconsin	27 WR	Marshaun Tucker / Jason Willis
42	Idaho	13 T	Jim Adams
29	UCLA	10 G	Ryan Schmid (C) / Josh Jones
23	Washington	16 C	Jeff Austin
28	Southern Cal	17 G	Joey Forster / Corey Chambers
14	Arizona	10 T	Lee Gundy
56	Arizona State	55 TE	Justin Peelle
27	Washington St.	24 QB	Joey Harrington
25	California	17 TB	Maurice Morris
13	Oregon State	23 FB	Josh Line
35	Texas■	30 DL	Jason Nikalao
		DL	Zack Freiter / Seth McEwen
		DL	Jed Boice
		DL	Saul Patu
		LB	Matt Smith
		LB	Michael Callier / Kevin Mitchell
		LB	Garrett Sabol / Wesly Mallard
		DB	Rashad Bauman
		DB	Steve Smith
		DB	Ryan Mitchell / Gary Barker
		DB	Rasuli Webster / Keith Lewis

RUSHING: Morris 286/1188y, Allan Amundson (TB) 67/283y,
  Harrington 66/124y
PASSING: Harrington 214-405/2967y, 22TD, 52.8%
RECEIVING: Howry 52/780y, Tucker 51/882y, Peelle 24/388y
SCORING: Josh Frankel (K) 76pts, Morris 60pts, Harrington 48pts

2001 11-1

31	Wisconsin	28 WR	Jason Willis / Samie Parker
24	Utah	10 WR	Keenan Howry
24	Southern Cal	22 T	Jim Adams
38	Utah State	21 G	Ryan Schmid
63	Arizona	28 C	Dan Weaver
48	California	7 G	Joey Forster
42	Stanford	49 T	Corey Chambers
24	Washington St.	17 TE	Justin Peelle / George Wrightster
42	Arizona State	24 QB	Joey Harrington
21	UCLA	20 TB	Maurice Morris / Onterrio Smith
17	Oregon State	14 FB	Josh Line
38	Colorado■	16 DL	Seth McEwan
		DL	Zack Freiter
		DL	Chris Tetterton
		DL	Darrell Wright
		LB	David Moretti
		LB	Kevin Mitchell
		LB	Wesly Mallard
		DB	Rashad Bauman
		DB	Steve Smith
		DB	Keith Lewis
		DB	Rasuli Webster

RUSHING: Smith 175/1058y, Morris 180/1049y
PASSING: Harrington 214-364/2764y, 27TD, 58.8%
RECEIVING: Howry 52/682y, Willis 43/448y, Parker 41/748y
SCORING: Howry 72pts, Jared Siegel (K) 71pts, Morris &
  Smith 60pts

2002 7-6

36 Mississippi St.	13 WR Samie Parker
28 Fresno State	24 WR Keenan Howry / Jason Willis
58 Idaho	21 T Adam Snyder / Robin Knebel
41 Portland State	0 G Nick Steitz / Corey Chambers
31 Arizona	14 C Dan Weaver
31 UCLA	30 G Joey Forster
42 Arizona State	45 T Michael Delagrange / Phil Finzer
33 Southern Cal	44 TE George Wrighster
41 Stanford	14 QB Jason Fife
21 Washington St.	32 TB Onterrio Smith / Terrence Whitehead
14 Washington	42 FB Matt Floberg
24 Oregon State	45 DL Seth McEwen / Ed Wangler
17 Wake Forest■	38 DL Haloti Ngata / Kai Smalley
	DL Igor Olshansky
	DL Darrell Wright / Rod Wright
	LB David Moretti
	LB Kevin Mitchell / Jerry Matson
	LB Garret Graham / David Martin
	DB Steven Moore
	DB Aaron Gipson / Marques Binns
	DB Keith Lewis
	DB Rasuli Webster / Marley Tucker

RUSHING: Smith 244/1141y, Whitehead 63/272y,
Allan Amundson (TB) 42/228y
PASSING: Fife 190-367/2752y, 24TD, 51.8%
RECEIVING: Parker 49/724y, Wrighster 41/568y, Howry 40/784y
SCORING: Jared Siegel (K) 109pts, Smith 72pts, Parker 48pts

2003 8-5

42 Mississippi St.	34 WR Samie Parker / Kellen Taylor
31 Nevada	23 WR Demetrius Williams
48 Arizona	10 T Mike DeLaGrange (G)
31 Michigan	27 G Nick Steitz
16 Washington St.	55 C Dan Weaver
13 Utah	17 G Adam Snyder (T) / Ian Reynoso
14 Arizona State	59 T Robin Knebel
35 Stanford	0 TE Tim Day
10 Washington	42 QB Kellen Clemens
21 California	17 TB Terrence Whitehead / Chris Vincent
31 UCLA	13 FB Matt Floberg / Dante Rosario
34 Oregon State	20 DL Igor Olshansky
30 Minnesota■	31 DL Robby Valenzuela / Quinn Dorsey
	DL Junior Siavii
	DL Devan Long
	LB Kevin Mitchell
	LB Jerry Matson
	LB David Martin
	DB Steven Moore / Rodney Woods
	DB Justin Phinisee / Aaron Gipson
	DB Keith Lewis
	DB Marley Tucker

RUSHING: Whitehead 192/737y, Fife 42/225y,
Washington 33/174y
PASSING: Clemens 182-304/2400y, 18TD, 59.9%
Fife 64-120/879y, 6TD, 53.3%
RECEIVING: Parker 77/1088y, Williams 51/935y,
Whitehead 28/253y
SCORING: Jared Siegel (K) 84pts, Williams 48pts, Parker &
Whitehead 42pts

2004 5-6

24 Indiana	30 WR Demetrius Williams / Keith Allen
7 Oklahoma	31 WR Marcus Maxwell
48 Idaho	10 T Adam Snyder
13 Arizona State	28 G Nick Steitz
41 Washington St.	38 C Enoka Lucas
28 Arizona	14 G Ian Reynoso
16 Stanford	13 T Robin Knebel
31 Washington	6 TE Tim Day
27 California	28 QB Kellen Clemens
26 UCLA	34 TB Terrence Whitehead
21 Oregon State	50 FB Dante Rosario
	DL Chris Solomona
	DL Rob Valenzuela
	DL Haloti Ngata / Matt Toeaina
	DL Devan Long
	LB Ramone Reed
	LB Jerry Matson
	LB Anthony Trucks
	DB Aaron Gipson / Marques Binns
	DB Justin Phinisee
	DB J.D. Nelson
	DB Marley Tucker / Jackie Bates

RUSHING: Whitehead 200/1144y, Clemens 118/190y,
Ken Washington (TB) 48/161y
PASSING: Clemens 223-372/2548y, 22TD, 59.9%
RECEIVING: Williams 47/593y, White 44/405y, Day 35/457y
SCORING: Jared Siegel (K) 58pts, White & Day 48pts

2005 10-2

38 Houston	24 WR Demetrius Williams
47 Montana	14 WR James Finley / Garren Strong
37 Fresno State	34 WR Cameron Colvin /Jaison Williams
13 Southern Cal	45 T Max Ungar
44 Stanford	20 G Josh Tschirgi
31 Arizona State	17 C Enoka Lucas
45 Washington	21 G Palauni Ma Sun / Ian Reynoso
28 Arizona	21 T Geoff Schwartz
27 California	20 TE Tim Day
34 Washington St.	31 QB Kellen Clemens / Dennis Dixon
56 Oregon State	14 TB T. Whitehead / Jonathan Stewart
14 Oklahoma■	17 DL Devan Long
	DL Haloti Ngata
	DL Matt Toeaina / Cole Linehan
	DL Darius Sanders / Victor Filipe
	LB Brent Haberly
	LB Blair Phillips / A. J. Tuitele
	DB Aaron Gipson / Jackie Bates
	DB Justin Phinisee
	DB J. D. Nelson
	DB Anthony Trucks
	DB Patrick Chung

RUSHING: Whitehead 156/679y, Clemens 69/228y, Stewart
53/188y
PASSING: Clemens 185-289/2406y, 19TD, 64%
Dixon 69-104/777y, 6TD, 66.3%
RECEIVING: D. Williams 59/1059y, Finley 57/571y,
Whitehead 52/490y
SCORING: Paul Martinez (K) 83pts, D. Williams 66pts,
Stewart 54pts

2006 7-6

48 Stanford	10 WR Jaison Williams/ Cameron Colvin
31 Fresno State	24 WR Brian Paysinger / Garren Strong
34 Oklahoma	33 WR Jordan Kent / James Finley
48 Arizona State	13 T Max Ungar
24 California	45 G Josh Tschirgi / Jon Teague
30 UCLA	20 C Enoka Lucas / Mark Lewis
23 Washington St.	34 G Palauni Ma Sun
55 Portland State	12 T Geoff Schwartz / Jacob Hucko
34 Washington	14 TE Dante Rosario
10 Southern Cal	35 QB Dennis Dixon / Brady Leaf
10 Arizona	37 TB J. Stewart / Jeremiah Johnson
28 Oregon State	30 DL Darius Sanders
8 BYU■	38 DL Matt Toeaina
	DL David Faaeteete / Jeremy Gibbs
	DL Nick Reed / Cole Linehan
	LB A. J. Tuitele / Brent Haberly
	LB Blair Phillips
	DB Jairus Byrd
	DB Walter Thurmond
	DB J. D. Nelson
	DB Kwame Agyeman / Jon Pope
	DB Patrick Chung

RUSHING: Stewart 183/981y, Johnson 103/644y, Dixon 94/442y
PASSING: Dixon 197-322/2143y, 12TD, 61.2%
Leaf 86-155/917y, 6TD, 55.5%
RECEIVING: Williams 68/984y, Kent 44/491y, Rosario 42/426y
SCORING: Paul Martinez (K) 83pts, Stewart 66pts,
Johnson 62pts

2007 9-4

48 Houston	27 WR Jaison Williams / Derrick Jones
39 Michigan	7 WR Brian Paysinger / Aaron Pflugrad
52 Fresno State	21 WR Garren Strong / Cameron Colvin
55 Stanford	31 T Fenuki Tupou / Jacob Hucko
24 California	31 G Josh Tschirgi / Pat So'oalo
53 Washington St.	7 C Max Unger
55 Washington	34 G Mark Lewis
24 Southern Cal	17 T Geoff Schwartz
35 Arizona State	23 TE Ed Dickson
24 Arizona	34 QB Dennis Dixon / Brady Leaf
0 UCLA	16 TB Jonathan Stewart / Andre Crenshaw
31 Oregon State	38 DL Will Tukuafu
56 South Florida■	21 DL David Faaeteete
	DL Jeremy Gibbs / Cole Linehan
	DL Nick Reed
	LB Kwame Agyeman / A.J. Tuitele
	LB John Bacon / Kevin Garrett
	LB Jerome Boyd
	DB Jairus Byrd / Willie Glasper
	DB Walter Thurmond
	DB Matthew Harper
	DB Patrick Chung

RUSHING: Stewart 280/1722y, Dixon 105/583y, Crenshaw 82/415y
PASSING: Dixon 172-254/2136y, 20TD, 67.7%
Leaf 34-72/276y, 0TD, 47.2%
RECEIVING: Williams 55/844y, Dickson 43/453y, Strong 27/249y
SCORING: Matt Evensen (K) 102pts, Stewart 78pts, Dixon 54pts

2008 10-3

44 Washington	10 WR Jaison Williams
66 Utah State	24 WR Jeff Maehl
32 Purdue	26 WR Terence Scott
32 Boise State	37 T Fenuki Tupuo
63 Washington St.	14 G Jordan Holmes / Jeff Kendall (C)
10 Southern Cal	44 C Max Unger (T)
31 UCLA	24 G Mark Lewis / Riley Showalter
54 Arizona State	20 T C.E. Kaiser / Bo Thran (G)
16 California	26 TE Ed Dickson
35 Stanford	28 QB Jeremiah Masoli / Justin Roper
55 Arizona	45 TB Jeremiah Johnson / LeGarrette Blount
65 Oregon State	38 DL Will Tukuafu
42 Oklahoma St.■	31 DL Ra'Shon Harris
	DL Cole Linehan
	DL Nick Reed
	LB Spencer Paysinger
	LB Casey Matthews / John Bacon
	LB Jerome Boyd
	DB Jairus Byrd
	DB Walter Thurmond/ Talmadge Jackson
	DB T.J. Ward
	DB Patrick Chung

RUSHING: Johnson 168/1201y, Blount 137/1002y,
Masoli 127/718y
PASSING: Masoli 136-239/1744y, 13TD, 56.9%
Roper 48-91/610y, 3TD, 52.7%
RECEIVING: Scott 50/751y, Maehl 39/421y, Williams 36/473y
SCORING: Blount 104pts, Johnson 78pts,
Matt Evensen (K) 68pts

2009 10-3

8 Boise State	19 WR D.J. Davis / Jamere Holland
38 Purdue	36 WR Jeff Maehl
31 Utah	24 WR/TE Lavasier Tuinei / David Paulson
42 California	3 T Bo Thran (G) / Darion Weems
52 Washington St.	6 G Carson York
24 UCLA	10 C Jordan Holmes
43 Washington	19 G Mark Asper
47 Southern Cal	20 T C.E. Kaiser / Nick Cody
42 Stanford	51 TE Ed Dickson
44 Arizona State	21 QB Jeremiah Masoli / Nate Costa
44 Arizona	41 RB LaMichael James / Andrew Crenshaw
37 Oregon State	33 DL Will Tukuafu
17 Ohio State■	26 DL Brandon Bair
	DL Blake Ferras
	DL Kenny Rowe
	LB Eddie Pleasant / Michael Clay
	LB Casey Matthews
	LB Spencer Paysinger
	DB Walter Thurmond / Anthony Gildon
	DB Talmadge Jackson / Cliff Harris
	DB T.J. Ward / Marvin Johnson
	DB Javes Lewis / John Boyett

RUSHING: James 230/1546y, Masoli 121/668y,
Kenjon Barner (RB) 61/366y
PASSING: Masoli 177-305/2147y, 15TD, 58.0%
RECEIVING: Maehl 53/696y, Dickson 42/551y, Tuinei 24/217y
Davis 23/233y
SCORING: Morgan Flint (K) 104pts, James 84pts, Masoli 76pts

2010 12-1

72 New Mexico	0 WR D.J. Davis
48 Tennessee	12 WR Jeff Maehl
69 Portland State	0 WR Lavasier Tuinei / Josh Huff
42 Arizona State	31 T Bo Thran (G) / Darrion Weems
52 Stanford	31 G Carson York
43 Washington St.	23 C Jordan Holmes
60 UCLA	13 G C.E. Kaiser
53 Southern Cal	32 T Mark Asper
53 Washington	16 TE David Paulson
15 Washington	13 QB Darron Thomas
48 Arizona	29 RB LaMichael James / Kenjon Barner
37 Oregon State	20 DL Terrell Turner / Dion Jordan
19 Auburn■	22 DL Zac Clark / Wade Keliikipi
	DL Brandon Bair
	DL Kenny Rowe
	LB Spencer Paysinger / Michael Clay
	LB Casey Mattews / Boseko Lokombo
	LB Josh Kaddu / Bryson Littlejohn
	DB Cliff Harris / Anthony Gildon
	DB Talmadge Jackson
	DB John Boyett / Javes Lewis
	DB Eddie Pleasant / Marvin Johnson

RUSHING: James 294/1731y, Barner 91/551y, Thomas 93/486y
PASSING: Thomas 222-361/2881y, 30TD, 61.5%
RECEIVING: Maehl 77/1076y, Davis 42/470y, Tuinei 36/396y
SCORING: James 114pts, Rob Beard (K) 97pts, Maehl 74pts

OREGON STATE

Oregon State University (1868)
Corvallis, Oregon
Nickname: Beavers
Colors: Orange and Black
Stadium: Reser Stadium (1953) 45,674
Conference Affiliations: Pacific Coast (Charter member, 1916-1958),
    Independent (1959-63), Pacific 8/10 (1964-present)

CAREER RUSHING YARDS	Carries	Yards
Ken Simonton (1998-01)	1041	5044
Jacquizz Rodgers (2008-10)	788	3877
Yvenson Bernard (2004-07)	876	3862
Steven Jackson (2001-03)	743	3625
Dave Schilling (1969-71)	641	2552
Pete Pifer (1964-66)	474	2233
Bill Enyart (1966-68)	492	2155
J.J. Young (1991-94)	361	2084
Sam Baker (1950-52)	487	1947
Ken Carpenter (1946-49)	441	1910

CAREER PASSING YARDS	Comp-Att	Yards
Derek Anderson (2001-04)	768-1515	11249
Jonathan Smith (1998-01)	638-1261	9680
Erik Wilhelm (1985-88)	870-1480	9393
Sean Canfield (2006-09)	552-861	5970
Matt Moore (2005-06)	440-733	5733
Terry Baker (1960-62)	233-454	3476
Lyle Moevao (2007-09)	291-509	3410
Ed Singler (1979-82)	281-513	3399
Alvin White (1973-74)	250-557	3099
Steve Endicott (1969-71)	227-456	2940

CAREER RECEIVING YARDS	Catches	Yards
Mike Hass (2002-05)	220	3924
James Newsom (2000-03)	213	3572
Sammie Stroughter (2005-08)	164	2623
Reggie Bynum (1982-85)	149	2231
James Rodgers (2007-10)	177	2064
Robb Thomas (1985-88)	138	2043
Roddy Tompkins (1996-99)	118	1845
Steve Coury (1976-79)	135	1837
Phil Ross (1985, 87-89)	153	1827
Vern Burke (1962-63)	117	1799

SEASON RUSHING YARDS	Carries	Yards
Steven Jackson (2002)	319	1690
Ken Simonton (2000)	284	1559
Steven Jackson (2003)	350	1545
Ken Simonton (1999)	294	1486
Jacquizz Rodgers (2009)	273	1440

SEASON PASSING YARDS	Comp-Att	Yards
Derek Anderson (2003)	261-510	4058
Derek Anderson (2004)	279-515	3615
Derek Anderson (2002)	211-449	3313
Sean Canfield (2009)	303-446	3271
Jonathan Smith (1999)	207-425	3053

SEASON RECEIVING YARDS	Catches	Yards
Mike Hass (2005)	90	1532
Mike Hass (2004)	86	1379
James Newsom (2003)	81	1306
Sammie Stroughter (2006)	74	1293
James Newsom (2002)	74	1284

GAME RUSHING YARDS	Carries	Yards
Bill Enyart (1968 vs. Utah)	50	299
Steven Jackson (2002 vs. California)	35	239
Ken Simonton (2000 vs. Southern Cal)	37	234

GAME PASSING YARDS	Comp-Att	Yards
Derek Anderson (2003 vs. So. Cal)	34-60	485
Jonathan Smith (1998 vs. Washington)	17-32	469
Erik Wilhelm (1987 vs. Akron)	27-44	461

GAME RECEIVING YARDS	Catches	Yards
Mike Hass (2004 vs. Boise State)	12	293
Robb Thomas (1987 vs. Akron)	9	230
Mike Hass (2003 vs. Stanford)	8	225

GREATEST COACH:

Tommy Prothro's background was in baseball and the military. His father, Doc Prothro, was a major league player and manager, and his uncle, Clifton Cates, was commandant of the United States Marine Corps. But despite good baseball skills and 39 months served as a lieutenant in the Navy during World War II, football is where Prothro made his mark.

Despite growing up in Memphis, playing for Wallace Wade at Duke and working as an assistant at Western Kentucky and Vanderbilt, it was the Pacific Coast where Prothro fulfilled his ambition. Red Sanders, the head man at Vandy, took Prothro west with him when he received the UCLA job in 1949. Prothro oversaw the team's use of the Single Wing, which helped bring the Bruins the UPI championship for an undefeated 1954 season.

That success enabled Prothro to get the head job in Corvallis. He was an immediate hit, winning six games in 1955 to finish second in the Pacific Coast Conference, and then 7 games in year two to not only capture the conference crown but gain the school's second Rose Bowl berth.

Prothro coached the Beavers for eight more seasons, earning a second Rose Bowl bid after the 1964 season. That game, a 34-7 loss to Michigan, would be his last as coach of Oregon State. He returned to UCLA, where he won 41 games in six years. After 104 wins as a college coach, Prothro spent the rest of his career in the pros, coaching the Los Angeles Rams and San Diego Chargers and then finishing in the Cleveland Browns front office.

OREGON STATE'S 55 GREATEST SINCE 1953

OFFENSE

WIDE RECEIVER: Vern Burke, Reggie Bynum, Mike Hass, James Newsom, Robb Thomas
TIGHT END: Phil Ross
TACKLE: Ted Bates, Jeff Hart, Rich Koeper, John Witte
GUARD: Fletcher Keister, Aaron Koch, Dave Marlette, Roy Schuening
CENTER: John Didion, Chris Gibson, Greg Krpalek
QUARTERBACK: Derek Anderson, Terry Baker, Jonathan Smith
RUNNING BACK: Yvenson Bernard, Joe Francis, Steven Jackson, Jacquizz Rodgers, Ken Simonton
FULLBACK: Pete Pifer, Dave Schilling

DEFENSE

END: Inoke Breckterfield, DeLawrence Grant, Jim Sherbert
TACKLE: Dwan Edwards, Craig Hanneman, Jess Lewis, Eric Manning, Jon Sandstrom, Tom Schillinger, Esera Tuaolo
LINEBACKER: Nick Barnett, Steve Brown, Bob Horn, Jack O'Billovich, Skip Vanderbundt
CORNERBACK: Dan Espalin, Charlie Olds, Dennis Weathersby
SAFETY: Armon Hatcher, Jim Lilly, Mitch Meeuwsen, Lavance Northington, Reggie Tongue

SPECIAL TEAMS

RETURN SPECIALISTS: Ray Taroli, Mark Waletich
PLACE KICKER: Alexis Serna
PUNTER: Gary Houser

TWO-WAY PLAYERS

FULLBACK-LINEBACKER: Bill Enyart

PERFORMANCE FORMULA:
OREGON STATE'S 10 BEST SEASONS

2000	1.5833	7 of 70
1962	1.5111	6 of 70
1967	1.3769	15 of 71
1956	1.3754	17 of 69
2008	1.3517	16 of 71
1957	1.3291	17 of 69
2006	1.3205	23 of 72
1968	1.3170	20 of 70
1964	1.2759	16 of 70
2007	1.2603	25 of 70

OREGON STATE BEAVERS

Year	W-L-T	AP Poll	Conference Standing	Toughest Regular Season Opponents	Coach (Record at School)	Bowl Games		
1953	3-6		6	UCLA 8-1, Michigan State 8-1, Southern California 6-3-1, Stanford 6-3-1	Kip Taylor			
1954	1-8		8t	UCLA 8-0, Minnesota 7-2, Southern Cal 8-3, Oregon 6-4, Nebraska 6-4	Kip Taylor (20-36)			
1955	6-3		2	UCLA 9-1, Stanford 6-3-1, Oregon 6-4	Tommy Prothro			
1956	7-3-1	10	1	Southern California 8-2, UCLA 7-3, Washington 5-5	Tommy Prothro	Rose	19 Iowa	35
1957	8-2		1t	UCLA 8-2, Washington State 6-4, Stanford 6-4	Tommy Prothro			
1958	6-4		4	California 7-3, Washington State 7-3, Wyoming 7-3	Tommy Prothro			
1959	3-7			Washington 8-1, Oregon 8-2, Southern California 8-2, Washington St. 6-4	Tommy Prothro			
1960	6-3-1			Washington 9-1, Iowa 8-1, Oregon 7-2-1, Houston 6-4	Tommy Prothro			
1961	5-5			Syracuse 7-3, Wisconsin 6-3, Arizona State 7-3, Washington 5-4-1	Tommy Prothro			
1962	9-2	11*		Washington 7-1-2, Oregon 6-3-1, West Virginia 8-2	Tommy Prothro	Liberty	6 Villanova	0
1963	5-5			Syracuse 8-2, Southern Cal 7-3, Baylor 7-3, Oregon 7-3, Washington 6-4	Tommy Prothro			
1964	8-3	8	1	Oregon 7-2-1, Syracuse 7-3, Washington 6-4	Tommy Prothro (63-37-2)	Rose	7 Michigan	34
1965	5-5		7	Southern California 7-2-1, Syracuse 7-3, Washington State 7-3	Dee Andros			
1966	7-3		2t	Southern California 7-3, Washington 6-4, Michigan 6-4	Dee Andros			
1967	7-2-1	7	2t	Southern California 9-1, Purdue 8-2, UCLA 7-2-1, Arizona State 8-2	Dee Andros			
1968	7-3	15t	2	Southern California 9-0-1, Arizona State 8-2, Stanford 6-3-1	Dee Andros			
1969	6-4		4	Southern California 9-0-1, UCLA 8-1-1, Stanford 7-2-1, Arizona State 8-2	Dee Andros			
1970	6-5		6t	Stanford 8-3, Houston 7-4, Oklahoma 7-4, Oregon 6-4-1	Dee Andros			
1971	5-6		2	Georgia 10-1, Arizona State 10-1, Washington 8-3, Stanford 8-3	Dee Andros			
1972	2-9		8	Southern California 11-0, UCLA 8-3, Washington 8-3, Arizona State 9-2	Dee Andros			
1973	2-9		5t	UCLA 9-2, Southern California 9-1-1, Arizona State 10-1, Stanford 7-4	Dee Andros			
1974	3-8		5t	Southern Cal 9-1-1, Ohio State 10-1, California 7-3-1, UCLA 6-3-2	Dee Andros			
1975	1-10		7	UCLA 8-2-1, California 8-3, Southern Cal 7-4, Stanford 6-4-1, Kansas 7-4	Dee Andros (51-64-1)			
1976	2-10		7t	Southern California 10-1, UCLA 9-1-1, Kentucky 8-3, LSU 6-4-1	Craig Fertig			
1977	2-9		8	Washington 9-2, Stanford 8-3, ASU 9-2, BYU 9-2, So. Cal 7-4, UCLA 7-4	Craig Fertig			
1978	3-7-1		9	So Cal 11-1, UCLA 8-3, ASU 8-3, BYU 9-3, Stanford 7-4, Washington 7-4	Craig Fertig			
1979	1-10		10	Southern California 10-0-1, Washington 9-2, Oregon 6-5	Craig Fertig (8-36-1)			
1980	0-11		10	Washington 9-2, UCLA 9-2, Oregon 6-3-2, Arizona State 8-4, Texas 7-4	Joe Avezzano			
1981	1-10		10	Southern California 9-1, Washington 9-2, Washington State 8-2-1	Joe Avezzano			
1982	1-9-1		10	Washington 9-2, ASU 9-2, LSU 8-2-1, Southern Cal 8-3, California 7-4	Joe Avezzano			
1983	2-8-1		9	Washington 8-3, Arizona 7-3-1, Washington St. 7-4, Arizona State 6-4-1	Joe Avezzano			
1984	2-9		9	Washington 10-1, Ohio State 9-2, UCLA 8-3, Arizona 7-4	Joe Avezzano (6-47-2)			
1985	3-8		9	UCLA 8-2-1, Arizona 8-3	Dave Kragthorpe			
1986	3-8		10	Michigan 11-1, Washington 8-2-1, Stanford 8-3, Arizona 8-3	Dave Kragthorpe			
1987	2-9		10	UCLA 9-2, Southern California 8-3, Georgia 8-3, Washington 6-4-1	Dave Kragthorpe			
1988	4-6-1		8	Southern California 10-1, UCLA 9-2, Washington St. 8-3, Arizona 7-4	Dave Kragthorpe			
1989	4-7-1		6	Nebraska 10-1, Southern California 8-2-1, Oregon 7-4, Washington 7-4	Dave Kragthorpe			
1990	1-10		10	Nebraska 9-2, Southern California 8-3-1, Oregon 8-3, Arizona 7-4	Dave Kragthorpe (17-48-2)			
1991	1-10		9t	Washington 11-0, California 9-2, UCLA 8-3, Stanford 8-3	Jerry Pettibone			
1992	1-9-1		10	Washington 9-2, Stanford 9-3, Washington St. 8-3, Arizona 6-4-1	Jerry Pettibone			
1993	4-7		7t	Arizona 9-2, UCLA 8-3, California 8-4, Southern Cal 7-5, Washington 7-4	Jerry Pettibone			
1994	4-7		7t	Oregon 9-3, Arizona 8-3, Southern California 7-3-1, Washington St. 7-4	Jerry Pettibone			
1995	1-10		10	Oregon 9-2, Southern California 8-2-1, Stanford 7-3-1, Washington 7-3-1	Jerry Pettibone			
1996	2-9		10	Arizona State 11-0, Washington 9-2	Jerry Pettibone (13-52-1)			
1997	3-8		10	UCLA 9-2, Arizona State 8-3, Washington 7-4	Mike Riley			
1998	5-6		8t	Arizona 11-1, UCLA 10-1, Oregon 8-3, Southern California 8-4	Mike Riley			
1999	7-5		5	Oregon 8-3, Stanford 7-4, Washington 7-4	Dennis Erickson	O'ahu	17 Hawaii	23
2000	11-1	4	1t	Washington 10-1, Oregon 9-2	Dennis Erickson	Fiesta	41 Notre Dame	9
2001	5-6		7	Oregon 10-1, Washington St. 9-2, Fresno 11-2, Washington 8-3	Dennis Erickson			
2002	8-5		4t	Southern California 10-2, Arizona State 8-5, Oregon 7-5, UCLA 7-5	Dennis Erickson (31-17)	Insight	13 Pittsburgh	38
2003	8-5		5t	Southern California 11-1, Washington St. 9-3, Oregon 8-4	Mike Riley	Las Vegas	55 New Mexico	14
2004	7-5		3t	Southern California 11-0, California 10-1, Arizona State 8-3	Mike Riley	Insight	38 Notre Dame	21
2005	5-6		7	Oregon 10-1, UCLA 9-2, Louisville 9-2, California 7-4, Boise State 9-3	Mike Riley			
2006	10-4	21	3	Southern California 10-2, Boise State 12-0, California 9-3, Oregon 7-5	Mike Riley	Sun	39 Missouri	38
2007	9-4	25	3	Cincinnati 9-3, Arizona State 10-2, Southern California 10-2, Oregon 8-4	Mike Riley	Emerald	21 Maryland	14
2008	9-4	18	2t	Penn State 11-1, Southern California 11-1, Utah 12-0, Oregon 9-3	Mike Riley	Sun	3 Pittsburgh	0
2009	8-5		2t	Cincinnati 12-0, Arizona 8-4, Southern California 8-4, Oregon 10-2	Mike Riley	Las Vegas	20 Brigham Young	44
2010	5-7		5t	TCU 12-0, Boise State 11-1, Stanford 11-1, Oregon 12-0	Mike Riley (69-54)			

TOTAL: 262-369-9 .4164 (63 of 70)   **Bowl Games since 1953:**   7-5 .5833 (tied 20 of 70)

GREATEST TEAM SINCE 1953: Coach Dennis Erickson's 2000 squad takes top honors, unleashing an explosive offense that averaged 33.3 points per game. Quarterback Jonathan Smith, tailback Ken Simonton, and wideouts Chad Johnson and T.J. Houshmandzadeh paced an attack that led to a Pac-10 co-championship and 41-9 rout of Notre Dame in the Fiesta Bowl.

1953 3-6
0	UCLA	41 E Richard Van Lom / Andy Skief
0	California	26 T Ron Ashbacher / Bob Riggert
0	Washington	28 G Charles Ferguson / Joel Calavan
0	Stanford	21 C Joe Fulwyler / Laird Brattain
0	Southern Cal	37 G Bill Johnson / Art Keith
19	Idaho	0 T James Luster / Howard Buettgenbach
6	Michigan State	34 E Wes Ediger
7	Washington St.	0 QB Jim Withrow/Dick Mason/Ron Siegrist
7	Oregon	0 HB Chuck Brackett / Jack Peterson
		HB Ralph Carr / Ken Brown / Jim Rock
		FB Tom Little / Jack Pinion

RUSHING: N/A
PASSING: N/A
RECEIVING: N/A
SCORING: N/A

1954 1-8
13	Idaho	0 E Richard Van Lom / Laird Brattain
7	Washington	17 T John Hall / Howard Buettgenbach
6	Washington St.	34 G Jim Roberts / Bob Riggert
7	Nebraska	27 C Bob Frommelt
0	UCLA	61 G Bill Johnson / John Sniffen
0	Southern Cal	34 T Ron Aschbacker
6	Minnesota	44 E Wes Ediger / Leon Hittner
7	California	46 BB Bob Clark / Jim Withrow
14	Oregon	33 HB Arlo Wenstrand / Dick Mason
		HB Jack Peterson/Tom Berry/Ray Westfall
		FB Chuck Marsh / Ernie Zwarlen

RUSHING: Mason 67/283y, Wenstrand 53/196y, Berry 50/142y
PASSING: Withrow 37-94/432y, 2TD, 39.4%
RECEIVING: Hittner 22/222y, Ediger 11/93y, Brattain 8/103y
SCORING: Mason 18pts, 5 tied w/ 12pts

1955 6-3
33	BYU	0 E Norm Thiel / Dwayne Fournier
10	Stanford	0 T John Witte
0	UCLA	38 G Bob Riggert / John Sniffen
7	Pacific	13 C Larry Stevens/Bob Hadraba/Dick Corrick
14	Washington St.	6 G Vern Ellison / Ron Daniels
13	Washington	7 T Howard Buettgenbach / Dave Jesmer
16	Idaho	14 E Bob DeGrant
33	California	14 BB Ron Siegrist
0	Oregon	28 TB Joe Francis / Ray Westfall
		WB Sam Wesley / Dick Mason
		FB Tom Berry / Arlo Wenstrand

RUSHING: Berry 71/378y, Francis 65/296y, Wenstrand 43/237y
PASSING: Westfall 7-20/139y, 2TD, 35%
RECEIVING: Wesley 11/235y, DeGrant 4/117y, Mason 4/67y
SCORING: Wesley 33pts, Berry 30pts, Mason & Wenstrand 18pts

1956 7-3-1
19	Missouri	13 E Norm Thiel / Dwayne Fournier
13	Southern Cal	21 T John Witte / Clark Cubbage
13	Iowa	14 G John Sniffen / Bob McKittrick
21	California	13 C Buzz Randall / Dick Corrick
21	Washington St.	6 G Jim Brackins / Vern Ellison
21	UCLA	7 T Dave Jesmer / Ted Bates
28	Washington	20 E Bob DeGrant / Frank Negri
20	Stanford	9 BB Gerry Laird / Ted Searle
14	Idaho	10 TB Joe Francis / Paul Lowe
19	Iowa■	35 WB Earnel Durden / Sterling Hammick
		FB Tom Berry / Nub Beamer

RUSHING: Durden 71/508y, Berry 139/487y, Lowe 113/407y
PASSING: Francis 27-48/377y, 4TD, 56.3%
RECEIVING: DeGrant 10/105y, Negri 8/113y, Durden 6/205y
SCORING: Berry 43pts, Durden & Lowe 36pts

1957 8-2
20	Southern Cal	0 E Dwayne Fournier
34	Kansas	6 T Dave Jesmer / Ed Kaohelaulii
22	Northwestern	13 G Bob McKittrick
20	Idaho	0 C Buzz Randall
7	UCLA	26 G Jim Brackins / Ron Daniels
6	Washington	19 T Ted Bates
39	Washington St.	25 E Bob DeGrant / Jerry Doman
21	California	19 BB Ted Searle / Gary Lukehart
24	Stanford	14 TB Joe Francis / Larry Sanchez
10	Oregon	7 HB Earnel Durden / Sterling Hammoack
		FB Nub Beamer / Jim Stinnette

RUSHING: Beamer 172/760y, Francis 119/626y, Durden 71/398y
PASSING: Francis 32-54/456y, 3TD, 59.3%
RECEIVING: DeGrant 19/239y, Fournier 10/177y, Thompson 5/99y
SCORING: Francis 54pts, Beamer 48pts, Durden 36pts

1958 6-4
0	Southern Cal	21 E Jerry Doman / Aaron Thomas
12	Kansas	0 T Ed Kaohelaulii / Howard Hogan
14	UCLA	0 G Jim Brackins
0	Wyoming	28 C Bruce Hake / Doug Bashor
20	Idaho	6 G Sonny Sanchez / Dennis Brundage
14	Washington	12 T Ted Bates
14	California	8 E Don Thiel / Roger Johnson
0	Washington St.	7 BB Gary Lukehart / Derald Swift
24	Stanford	16 TB Dainard Paulson / Paul Lowe
0	Oregon	20 WB John Horrollo /E. Durden/Grimm Mason
		FB Nub Beamer / Jim Stinnette

RUSHING: Beamer 108/434y, Paulson 93/54y, Stinnette 45/208y
PASSING: Paulson 10-27/146y, 2TD, 37%
RECEIVING: Thomas 9/172y, Doman 6/82y, Thiel 5/63y
SCORING: Beamer 28pts, Mason & Lowe 12pts

1959 3-7
6	Southern Cal	27 E Aaron Thomas / Jerry Doman
14	Texas Tech	15 T Ed Kaohelaulii / Neil Plumley
6	Nebraska	7 G George Enderle / Denny Pieters
7	Michigan	18 C Doug Bashor/Bruce Hake/John Hadraba
66	Idaho	18 G Sonny Sanchez / John Cadwell
24	California	20 T H. Hogan / Mike Kline / Earl Woodward
0	Washington St.	14 E Don Thiel / George Thompson
6	Washington	13 BB Marne Palmateer
22	Stanford	39 TB Don Kasso/D. Paulson/Larry Sanchez
15	Oregon	7 WB Art Gilmore / Ron Miller
		FB Jim Stinnette / Chuck Marshall

RUSHING: Kasso 94/345y, Stinnette 119/304y, Miller 38/195y
PASSING: Sanchez 19-45/305y, 3TD, 42.2%
RECEIVING: Thomas 11/150y, Doman 10/156y, Miller 8/144y
SCORING: Kasso (TB-K) 40pts, Stinnette 30pts, Gilmore 20pts

1960 6-3-1
14	Southern Cal	0 E Aaron Thomas / Skip Russell
12	Iowa	22 T Mike Kline / Frank Greminger
29	Houston	20 G Denny Pieters / George Gnoss
20	Indiana	6 C Dick DeBischop / Doug Bashor
28	Idaho	8 G Ross Cariaga
29	Washington	30 T Neil Plumley / Earl Woodward
6	California	14 E Amos Marsh / Leon Criner
20	Washington St.	10 BB Tim Anderson / Marne Palmateer
25	Stanford	21 TB Don Kasso / Terry Baker
14	Oregon	14 WB Grimm Mason/Art Gilmore/G. Hilliard
		FB Chuck Marshall / Bill Monk

RUSHING: Baker 111/610y, Kasso 110/511y, Marshall 79/341y
PASSING: Baker 60-117/863y, 3TD, 51.3%
RECEIVING: Hilliard 13/196y, Marsh 10/183y, Gilmore 9/169y
SCORING: Kasso 46pts, Marshall 42pts, Baker 34pts

1961 5-5
8	Syracuse	19 E Roger Johnson / Don Kasso (HB)
0	Stanford	34 T Mike Kline
44	Idaho	6 G Mike Dolby / George Gnoss
20	Wisconsin	23 C John Farrell / Marne Palmeteer
23	Arizona State	24 G Ross Cariaga
14	Washington St.	6 T Neil Plumley
3	Washington	0 E Fred Jones
35	BYU	0 QB Terry Baker
6	Oregon	2 HB Leroy Whittle / Bill Monk / John Thomas
12	Houston	23 HB Hank Rivera / Gene Hilliard
		FB Tom Gates / Bruce Williams

RUSHING: Whittle 81/364y, Gates 86/357y, Baker 73/355y
PASSING: Baker 61-134/875y, 5TD, 45.5%
RECEIVING: Kasso 20/258y, Johnson 11/179y, Whittle 9/110y
SCORING: Whittle 26pts, Williams 24pts, Thomas 22pts

1962 9-2
39	Iowa State	35 E Vern Burke
8	Iowa	28 T Jim Funston / Joe Bonilla
27	Stanford	0 G George Gnoss / Warren Cole
13	Washington	14 C Dick DeBisschop / Doug Suckling
40	Pacific	6 G Ross Cariaga / Don Doman
51	West Virginia	22 T Jerry Neil (E) / Rich Koeper
32	Idaho	0 E Fred Jones / Len Frketich
18	Washington St.	12 QB Terry Baker
24	Colorado State	14 HB Leroy Whittle / Dan Espalin
20	Oregon	17 HB Dan Sieg / Art O'Grady
6	Villanova■	0 FB Bruce Williams / Booker Washington

RUSHING: Baker 115/538y, Whittle 81/396y, Washington 65/328y
PASSING: Baker 112-203/1738y, 15TD, 55.2%
RECEIVING: Burke 69/1007y, Frketich 10/139y, Whittle 9/139y
SCORING: Burke 64pts, Baker 58pts, Williams 44pts

1963 5-5
29	Utah	14 E Vern Burke / Thurman Bell (D)
41	Colorado	6 T Ken Brusven / Joe Bonilla
22	Baylor	15 G Dave Gould / Ron Doman
7	Washington	34 C Hoyt Keeney / Jack O'Billovich (D)
30	Washington St.	6 G Tom Holley / Al Funston
8	Syracuse	31 T Rich Koeper / Bill Stellmacher
10	Stanford	7 E Len Frketich / Doug McDougal
15	Indiana	20 QB Gordon Queen
22	Southern Cal	28 HB Tim Osmer / Olvin Moreland
14	Oregon	31 HB Leroy Whittle / Dan Espalin
		FB Charlie Shaw / Booker Washington

RUSHING: Shaw 75/459y, Whittle 69/392y, Washington 59/269y
PASSING: Queen 84-183/1281y, 16TD, 45.9%
RECEIVING: Burke 48/792y, McDougal 14/223y, Frketich 11/160y
SCORING: Burke 56pts, Frketich, Bruce Williams (FB) & Espalin 18pts

1964 8-3
3	Northwestern	7 E Bob Grim / Scott Miller
14	Colorado	7 T Bill Stellmacher / Ken Brusven
13	Baylor	6 G Warren Cole / Norm Winton
9	Washington	7 C Hoyt Keeney / Rockne Freitas
10	Idaho	7 G Al Funston / Jerry Neil
31	Syracuse	13 T Rich Koeper / Jim Wilkin
24	Washington St.	7 E Len Frketich / Doug McDougal
24	Indiana	14 QB Paul Brothers / Gordon Queen
7	Stanford	16 HB Olvin Moreland / Marv Crowston
7	Oregon	6 HB Cliff Watkins / Charlie Shaw
7	Michigan■	34 FB Booker Washington
		DL Greg Hartman / Thurman Bell
		DL Dennis Rozario / Ron Aarts
		DL Dave Gould
		DL Doug John
		DL George Carr
		DL Al East
		LB Dick Ruhl
		LB Jack O'Billovich
		DB Dan Sieg / Tom Osmer
		DB Jim Smith
		DB Dan Espalin

RUSHING: Brothers 151/451y, Watkins 85/340y, Washington 70/302y
PASSING: Brothers 75-144/1036y, 7TD, 52.1
RECEIVING: Moreland 35/428y, Grim 11/142y, Frketich 7/154y
SCORING: Steve Clark (K) 40pts, Brothers 30pt, Watkins 12pts

1965 5-5
12	Illinois	10 E Lew Scott / Craig Cording
7	Iowa	27 T Bill Stellmacher
12	Southern Cal	26 G Joel Heacock
7	Northwestern	15 C Al Frei
16	Idaho	14 G Joe Reid
10	Utah	6 T Jeff Hardrath / Jim Wilkin
8	Washington St.	10 E Mike Sullivan
13	Syracuse	12 QB Paul Brothers
21	Washington	28 WB Fred Schweer / Cliff Watkins
19	Oregon	14 HB Bob Grim / Chuck Crabtree
		FB Pete Pifer
		DL Greg Hartman
		DL Dennis Rozario
		DL Dave Gould
		DL Doug John
		DL Mark Gartung / George Carr
		DL Al East
		LB Jack O'Billovich
		LB Russ Kuhns
		DB Thurman Bell
		DB Jim Smith / Lew Scott
		DB Tim Osmer

RUSHING: Pifer 234/1095y, Grim 87/398y, Brothers 118371y
PASSING: Brothers 45-121/416y, 4TD, 37.2%
RECEIVING: Schweer 15/127y, Grim 10/86y, Scott 6/77y
SCORING: Pifer 36pts, Brothers 24pts, Mike Haggard (K) 15pts

1966 7-3

0 Michigan	41 E Roger Cantlon / Harry Gunner
17 Iowa	3 T Jim Wilkin
0 Southern Cal	21 G Dave Marlette
6 Northwestern	14 C Rockne Freitas
14 Idaho	7 G Joe Reid
18 Arizona State	17 T Wayne Valley / Jeff Hardrath
41 Washington St.	13 E Gary Houser / Mike Sullivan
31 Arizona	12 QB Paul Brothers
24 Washington	13 WB Bob Grim
20 Oregon	15 HB Jerry Belcher / Don Summers
	FB Pete Pifer
	DL Greg Hartman
	DL Dennis Rozario
	DL Skip Diaz
	DL Mark Gartung / Jon Sandstrom
	DL Jess Lewis
	DL Tom Coccione
	LB Bill Enyart
	LB Russ Kuhns / Jim Godfrey
	DB Charles Olds
	DB Don Welch
	DB Scott Eaton

RUSHING: Pifer 230/1088y, Grim 71/470y, Brothers 95/271y
PASSING: Brothers 55-122/610y, 3TDs, 45.1%
RECEIVING: Grim 25/289y, Cantlon 8/76y, Houser 6/90y
SCORING: Pifer 72pts, Mike Haggard (K) 31pts, Brothers 24pts

1967 7-2-1

13 Stanford	7 E Roger Cantlon
27 Arizona State	21 T Nick Rogers / Lee Jamison
38 Iowa	18 G Dave Marlette
6 Washington	13 C John Didion
13 BYU	31 G Clyde Smith
22 Purdue	14 T Van Smith / Roger Stalick
35 Washington St.	7 E Gary Houser
16 UCLA	16 QB Steve Preece
3 Southern Cal	0 WB Billy Main
14 Oregon	10 HB Jerry Belcher / Don Summers
	FB Bill Enyart
	DL Mike Leep / Harry Gunner
	DL Jess Lewis
	DL Jon Sandstrom
	DL Bill Nelson / Bob Jeremiah
	DL Ron Boley
	DL Mike Foote / Rich LaSalle
	LB Skip Vanderbundt
	LB Fred Milton / Mike Groff
	DB Don Whitney / Don Welch
	DB Charles Olds / Rick Harrington
	DB Mark Waletich

RUSHING: Enyart 201/851y, Main 112/564y, Preece 138/376y
PASSING: Preece 47-129/737y, 3TDs, 36.4%
RECEIVING: Cantlon 14/214y, Main 11/202y, Houser 10/103y
SCORING: Enyart 48pts, Mike Haggard (K) 43pts, Preece &
Main 36pts

1968 7-3

20 Iowa	21 E Roger Cantlon
24 Utah	21 T Kent Scott
35 Washington	21 G Rocky Rasley
34 Kentucky	35 C John Didion
28 Arizona State	9 G Clyde Smith
16 Washington St.	8 T Roger Stalick
29 Stanford	7 E Nick Rogers / Bill Plumeau
45 UCLA	21 QB Steve Preece
13 Southern Cal	17 WB Billy Main
41 Oregon	19 HB Don Summers
	FB Bill Enyart
	DL Mike Foote (LB) / Rich LaSalle
	DL Tom Greerty / Craig Hanneman
	DL Jon Sandstrom
	DL Bill Nelson / Dale Branch
	DL Ron Boley
	DL Jerry Belcher
	LB Mike Groff / Louis Armstrong
	LB Wally Johnson
	DB Charles Olds
	DB Don Whitney / Mel Easley
	DB Larry Rich

RUSHING: Enyart 293/1304y, Main 125/634y, Summers 83/283y
PASSING: Preece 55-126/881y, 5TD, 43.7%
RECEIVING: Cantlon 23/409y, Main 14/230y, Rogers 6/109y
SCORING: Enyart 102pts, Main 84pts, Larry Rich (K) 21pts

1969 6-4

0 UCLA	37 E Jeff Kolberg / Jim Scheele
42 Iowa	14 T Dave Nirenberg / Jim Davidson
30 Arizona State	7 G Steve Morton / Rob Jurgenson
7 Southern Cal	31 C Mike White
10 Washington	6 G Dan Zellick
3 Utah	7 T Chris Haag
0 Stanford	33 TE Bill Plumeau
35 California	3 QB Steve Endicott
38 Washington St.	3 WB Billy Main / Larry Watson
10 Oregon	7 HB Bryce Huddleston
	FB Dave Schilling
	DL Jim Sherbert
	DL Jess Lewis
	DL Dale Branch
	DL Bill Nelson
	DL Craig Hanneman
	DL Rich LaSalle / Rex Behnke
	LB Wally Johnson / Jim Blackford
	LB Jack Faulkender
	DB Mel Easley
	DB Don Whitney
	DB Larry Rich

RUSHING: Schilling 173/635y, Main 110/423y,
Huddleston 76/372y
PASSING: Endicott 93-190/1251y, 10TD, 48.9%
RECEIVING: Main 21/282y, Kolberg 18/305y, Plumeau 15/259y
SCORING: Main 42pts, Mike Nehl (K) 37pts, Schilling 30pts

1970 6-5

9 UCLA	14 WR Jeff Kolberg
21 Iowa	14 T Dave Nirenberg
23 Oklahoma	14 G Rob Jurgenson
13 Southern Cal	45 C Jack Turnbull
31 Utah	21 G Dan Zellick
16 Houston	19 T Chris Viet
20 Washington	29 TE Clark Hoss
10 Stanford	48 QB Jim Kilmartin / Steve Endicott
16 California	10 WB Sal Cirrincione / Bill Carlquist
28 Washington St.	16 HB Ralph Show
24 Oregon	9 FB Dave Schilling
	DL Jim Sherbert
	DL Scott Freeburn / Duane Defrees
	DL Bob Jossis
	DL Mark Dippel
	DL Craig Hanneman
	DL Steve Bielenberg
	LB Butch Wicks
	LB Steve Brown / Jack Faulkender
	DB Dennis Draper
	DB Dave Graham
	DB Jim Lilly

RUSHING: Schilling 254/1084y, Carlquist 78/339y,
Cirrincione 65/295y
PASSING: Kilmartin 39-90/463y, 5TD, 43.3%
RECEIVING: Kolberg 39/534y, Hoss 19/285y,
Cirrincione 10/81y
SCORING: Carlquist 38pts, Lynn Boston (K) 33pts,
Kolberg & Schilling 30pts

1971 5-6

25 Georgia	56 WR Jeff Kolberg
33 Iowa	19 T Jim Davidson
14 Michigan State	31 G Dave Nirenberg
34 UCLA	17 C Jack Turnbull
27 California	30 G Terry Nimz
24 Arizona State	18 T Chris Veit / John Todd
14 Washington	38 TE Clark Hoss
24 Stanford	31 QB Steve Endicott
22 Arizona	34 WB Bill Carlquist / Jerry McBurney
21 Washington St.	14 HB Mike Maestri
30 Oregon	29 FB Dave Schilling / Roger Smith
	DL Steve Bielenberg
	DL Scott Woods
	DL Tex Gschwandtner / Billy Winchester
	DL Fred Hauck
	DL Duane Defrees
	DL Jim Sherbert
	LB Butch Wicks
	LB Steve Brown
	DB Dave Graham / Bruce Fry
	DB Dennis Draper / Bill Bartley
	DB Jim Lilly

RUSHING: Schilling 214/833y, Smith 124/483y, Carlquist 85/331y
PASSING: Endicott 105-203/1334y, 9TD, 51.7%
RECEIVING: Kolberg 35/525y, Hoss 24/284y, Schilling 18/127y
SCORING: Schilling 60pts, Lynn Boston (K) 48pts, Smith 36pts

1972 2-9

8 San Diego State	17 WR Ron Stewart / Greg Mobley
6 Southern Cal	51 T Kurt Jurgenson
11 Iowa	19 G Rob Jurgenson
29 BYU	3 C Greg Krpalek
7 Arizona State	38 G Terry Nimz
7 UCLA	37 T Fred Jaross / Jeff Hart
7 Washington St.	37 TE Rod Petersen
11 Stanford	17 QB Scott Spiegelberg / Tom Hickey
16 Washington	23 WB Wilson Morris
26 California	23 HB Mike Maestri / Bob McKenzie
3 Oregon	30 FB Mike Davenport
	DL Duane Defrees
	DL Lee Nielsen / Mike Shannon
	DL Billy Winchester
	DL Jim Mott
	LB Butch Wicks
	LB Steve Brown
	LB Craig Fair / Chris Lunde
	DB Bill Bartley
	DB Wayne Leitner
	DB Jim Lilly
	DB Dan Sanders

RUSHING: Davenport 120/538y, Morris 54/233y, Maestri 44/183y
PASSING: Spiegelberg 22-56/278y, 2TD, 39.3%
RECEIVING: Petersen 17/232y, Maestri 9/93y, Stewart 8/75y
SCORING: Ken McGrew (K) 23pts, 4 tied w/ 12pts

1973 2-9

9 Auburn	18 WR Ron Stewart
16 SMU	35 WR Lee Overton
14 BYU	37 T Jeff Hart
7 Southern Cal	21 G Mike Kobielsky
31 Washington	7 C Greg Krpalek
14 California	24 G Doug Doyle
14 Arizona State	44 T Jeff Worth
23 Stanford	24 TE Rod Petersen
7 Washington St.	13 QB Alvin White
14 UCLA	56 HB Ray Taroli / Bill Cecil
17 Oregon	14 FB Dick Maurer
	DL Dennis Boyd
	DL Jerry Hackenbruck
	DL Lee Nielsen
	DL Jim Mott / Fred Anderson
	LB Tim Warner
	LB Bob Horn / Bob Harris
	LB Craig Fair
	DB Kirk Byers
	DB Ron Bradford
	DB Dan Sanders
	DB Dennis Downey

RUSHING: Maurer 95/393y, Taroli 99/380y, Cecil 52/217y
PASSING: White 130-301/1437y, 5TD, 43.2%
RECEIVING: Maurer 33/326y, Overton 21/351y, Stewart 18/185y
SCORING: Rick Kulaas (K) 40pts, Maurer 30pts, 3 tied w/ 24pts

1974 3-8

15 Syracuse	23 WR Grant Boustead
35 Georgia	48 WR Lee Overton
10 Ohio State	51 T Jeff Hart
30 SMU	37 G Mike Kobeilsky
23 Washington	9 C Greg Krpalek
14 California	17 G Jim Walker
10 Southern Cal	31 T Ken Maurer / Jeff Worth
13 Stanford	17 TE David Brown
17 Washington St.	3 QB Alvin White
14 UCLA	33 HB Elvin Momon / Charles Smith
35 Oregon	16 FB Dick Maurer
	DL Dennis Boyd
	DL Jerry Hackenbruck
	DL Casey Keller
	DL Fred Anderson
	LB Gene Dales / Clarence Smithey
	LB Bob Horn
	LB Rob Nairne
	DB Kirk Byers
	DB Dick Sheehy / Mike McLaughlin
	DB Dan Sanders
	DB Dennis Downey

RUSHING: Momon 120/479y, Maurer 89/343y, Smith 81/324y
PASSING: White 120-256/1662y, 5TD, 46.9%
RECEIVING: Brown 26/383y, Overton 19/356y, Boustead 16/298y
SCORING: Rick Kulaas (K) 42pts, Maurer 36pts, Smith &
White 24pts

1975 1-10

0 San Diego State	25 WR Larry Clark / Grant Boustead
7 Southern Cal	24 WR Lee Overton
0 Kansas	20 T Ken Maurer / Dan Wood
12 Grambling	19 G Wally Remmers / Craig Spiegelberg
8 Colorado State	17 C Greg Marshall / Tony Banaszak
24 California	51 G Mike Kobielsky
7 Washington	35 T Kurt Jurgensen
22 Stanford	28 TE Phil Wroblicky
7 Washington St.	0 QB Kyle Grossart / Steve Gervais
9 UCLA	31 TB Rich Dodge / Johnny Taylor
7 Oregon	14 FB Ron Cuie/ Larry Dozier/ Jerome Shelton
	DL Ernie Richarson / Randy Rosa
	DL Dennis Boyd
	DL Rob Nairne / Fred Anderson
	DL Jerry Wilkinson / Gene Dales
	DL Ken Burke / Tom Chamberlain
	LB Bob Horn
	LB Bill Ford / Cory Osenga
	DB J.R. Jones
	DB Oscar Williams
	DB Jay Locey
	DB Dick Sheehy / Wayne King

RUSHING: Dodge 126/558y, Cuie 131/338y, Taylor 65/247y
PASSING: Grossart 89-185/969y, 4TD, 48.1%
RECEIVING: Wroblicky 27/370y, Overton 20/219y, Clark 14/161y
SCORING: Cuie & Keith Nelson (K) 14pts, 3 tied w/ 12pts

1976 2-10

16 Kansas	28 WR Dwayne Hall / Matt Hammack
13 Kentucky	38 WR Lee Overton
11 LSU	28 T Vern Ward
3 Syracuse	21 G Larry Winkler
12 Washington	24 C Jim Walker
10 California	9 G Jeff Worth / Wally Remmers
0 Southern Cal	56 T Craig Spiegelberg /Kevin Donaghue (DL)
3 Stanford	24 TE Tom Chamberlain / Dave Patapoff
24 Washington St.	29 QB Dave White / Scott Richardson
14 UCLA	45 TB James Fields / Jarvis Redwine
14 Oregon	23 FB Steve Bozan / Charlie Smith
59 Hawaii	0 DL Clarence Smithey / Jerry Wilkinson
	DL Greg Marshall
	DL Joel Malone / Troy Gusick
	DL Dennis Boyd / Russ Harris
	LB Bill Ford / Kent Howe
	LB Kent Peyton
	LB Rob Nairne / Cory Osenga
	DB Lenny Holmes / Johnnie Jones
	DB Kerry Justin
	DB Jay Locey
	DB Tom Stevens

RUSHING: Fields 163/649y, Smith 45/309y, Bozan 59/241y
PASSING: White 47-100/552y, 2TDs, 47%
RECEIVING: Overton 30/382y, Hammack 21/261y, Hall 20/295y
SCORING: Kieron Walford (K) 39pts, Fields 36pts, Overton 26pts

1977 2-9

24 Syracuse	12 WR Dwayne Hall / Karl Halberg
10 Southern Cal	17 WR Steve Coury
31 Arizona State	33 T Vern Ward
10 Tennessee	41 G Larry Winkler
24 BYU	19 C Jim Walker / Dennis Vanderwall
17 California	41 G Kevin Donaghue
6 Washington	14 T Gordy Neumann
7 Stanford	26 TE Terry Beck / Chris Smith
10 Washington St.	24 QB John Norman
18 UCLA	48 TB James Fields / Willie Johnson
16 Oregon	28 FB Byron Kellar / Rich Johnson
	DL Tom Schillinger / Rich Harris
	DL Greg Marshall
	DL Troy Guscik / Joel Malone
	DL Clarence Smithey
	LB Kent Peyton
	LB Kent Howe
	LB Gene Dales / Reggie Williams
	DB Kerry Justin
	DB Lenny Holmes
	DB Rob Emmons
	DB Tom Stevens

RUSHING: Fields 191/740y, Johnson 69/201y, Kellar 47/189y
PASSING: Norman 90-200/929y, 6TD, 45%
RECEIVING: Coury 36/458y, Halberg 22/274y, Kellar 14/87y
SCORING: Kieron Walford (K) 51pts, Fields 32pts, Kahoonei 24pts

1978 3-7-1

7 BYU	10 WR Steve Coury / Dwayne Hall
7 Arizona	21 WR Karl Halberg
13 Tennessee	13 T Doug Johnston / Eric Pettigrew
0 Washington	34 G Brian Stack
17 Minnesota	14 C Roger Levasa / Gregg McDonald
7 Southern Cal	38 G Kevin Donaghue
6 Stanford	24 T Craig Spiegelberg / Rich Humphreys
32 Washington St.	31 TE Chris Smith / Iris Hawkins
15 UCLA	13 QB Steve Smith
22 Arizona State	44 TB Willie Johnson / Tim Sim
3 Oregon	24 FB Mike Smith / James Fields
	DL Jerry Wilkinson
	DL Tom Schillinger
	DL Craig Roussell
	DL Nick Westerberg
	LB Kent Howe
	LB Kent Peyton / Harv Childress
	LB Reggie Williams
	DB Noble Franklin
	DB Tim Smith
	DB Lenny Holmes
	DB Dan Wells / Tom Stevens

RUSHING: Johnson 100/324y, Smith 80/312y, Sim 63/179y
PASSING: Smith 96-196/1182y, 7TD, 49%
RECEIVING: Coury 31/502y, Hall 25/408y, Sim 20/181y
SCORING: Kieron Walford (K) 32pts, Smith 24pts, Coury & Hall 18pts

1979 1-10

16 New Mexico	35 WR Justin Willis / Dan Fidel
5 Southern Cal	42 WR Steve Coury
16 Kansas State	22 T Rick Loberg / Joe Carnahan
0 Arizona State	45 G Brian Stack
0 Washington	41 C Roger Levaska
0 California	45 G Matt Reinhard
14 San Jose State	24 T Rich Humphreys
33 Stanford	31 TE Chris Smith
42 Washington St.	45 QB Scott Richardson
18 Arizona	42 TB Darryl Minor
3 Oregon	24 FB Tony Robinson / Mike Smith
	DL Nick Westerberg
	DL Tom Schillinger
	DL Craig Roussell / Darren Couts
	DL Paul Franklin
	LB Rudy Guice
	LB Harv Childress
	LB Terry Batchelder / David Howard
	DB Tim Smith
	DB Noble Franklin / Dee Ward
	DB Leroy Edwards
	DB Dan Wells

RUSHING: Robinson 143/525y, Minor 93/357y, Smith 74/295y
PASSING: Richardson 145-291/1645y, 6TD, 49.8%
RECEIVING: Coury 66/842y, Robinson 23/150y, Minor 20/175y
SCORING: Coury 36pts, Kieron Walford (K) 31pts, Robinson 26pts

1980 0-11

10 Wyoming	30 WR Dan Fidel / Lane McLaughlin
14 Arizona State	42 WR Victor Simmons
0 Texas	35 T Eric Pettigrew
6 Washington	41 G Kevin Donaghue
6 California	27 C Roger Levasa
21 Long Beach St.	31 G Matt Reinhard
13 Stanford	54 T Rich Humphreys
7 Washington St.	28 TE Ron Vogel
21 Oregon	40 QB Ed Singler / Scott Richardson
7 Arizona	24 TB Randy Holmes / Jaimy Patton
3 UCLA	34 FB Tony Robinson
	DL Eric Bosworth / Rudy Guice
	DL Tyrone Howard
	DL Darren Couts / Angelo Dilullo
	DL Nick Westerberg
	DL Craig Sowash / Bob Johnson
	LB Lew Wilson / Carl Keever
	LB James Gracio / Derek Warren
	DB Kellen Young
	DB Forrest Pellum / Dee Ward
	DB Mark Hettum
	DB Terry Harris / Marty Brooks

RUSHING: Robinson 213/882y, Holmes 106/379y, Patton 34/171y
PASSING: Singler 106-180/1166y, 3TD, 58.9%
RECEIVING: Robinson 38/291y, Simmons 37/500y, Vogel 28/320y
SCORING: Robinson 54pts, Chris Mangold (K) 24pts, Simmons & Holmes 12pts

1981 1-10

31 Fresno State	28 WR Tim Sim
24 LSU	27 WR Victor Simmons
12 Minnesota	42 T Eric Pettigrew
22 Southern Cal	56 G Jim Wilson
0 Washington St.	23 C Roger Levasa / Bob Kornmann
17 Washington	56 G Pete Grossnicklaus / Rick Meggers
3 Oklahoma	42 T Joe Carnahan
3 California	45 TE Chris Smith / Ron Vogel
9 Stanford	63 QB Ed Singler
7 Arizona	40 TB Darryl Minor
17 Oregon	47 FB Randy Holmes
	DL Rudy Guice / Eric Bosworth
	DL Tyrone Howard
	DL Angelo Dilullo / Ron Heller
	DL Darren Couts / Dwayne Jackola
	DL Craig Sowash
	LB James Gracio / Derek Warren
	LB Jerome Boyd
	DB Reggie Dupee / Kenny Taylor
	DB Steve Holsberry
	DB Terry Harris
	DB Tony Fuller / Tom Critser

RUSHING: Holmes 148/637y, Minor 101/456y
PASSING: Singler 118-220/1500y, 5TD, 53.6%
RECEIVING: Simmons 43/703y, Smith 30/319y, Vogel 13/140y
SCORING: Chris Mangold (K) 41pts, Holmes 20pts, Simmons 18pts

1982 1-9-1

12 Arizona	38 WR Tim Sim
7 LSU	45 WR Claude Dixon / Reggie Bynum
13 San Jose State	17 T Dwayne Jackola
5 Stanford	45 G Herb Wilson
14 Washington St.	14 C Mark Bonner
17 Washington	34 G Rick Meggers / Joe Parry
0 Southern Cal	38 T Joe Carnahan
14 California	28 TE Ron Vogel
16 Arizona State	30 QB Ed Singler / Jeff Seay
30 Montana	10 TB James Terrell / Lucius High
6 Oregon	7 FB Bryce Oglesby
	DL Tyrone Howard
	DL Joe Phillips / Angelo Dilullo
	DL Maurice Porter
	LB Bob Johnson / Eric Bosworth
	LB James Murphy / Derrick Warren
	LB Jerome Boyd
	LB Craig Sowash / John Saleaumua
	DB Forrest Pellum
	DB Kenny Taylor
	DB Terry Harris / Reggie Dupee
	DB Steve Holsberry / Tony Fuller

RUSHING: Oglesby 126/676y, Terrell 64/333y, High 57/182y
PASSING: Seay 69-147/889y, 46.9%
Singler 53-103/698y, 1TD, 51.5%
RECEIVING: Vogel 27/280y, Oglesby 25/255y, Dixon 15/345y
SCORING: Chris Mangold (K) 44pts, Singler 14pts, 3 tied w/ 12pts

1983 2-8-1

6 Arizona	50 WR Robert Adams / Claude Dixon
51 Portland State	14 WR Reggie Bynum / Larry Clemons
10 Southern Cal	33 T Dwayne Jackola
14 Colorado	38 G Herb Wilson (T) / Mike Terry
21 UNLV	35 C Jack Lester
7 Washington	34 G Rick Meggers / Darrick Brilz
19 California	45 T Tom Emmons
31 Stanford	18 TE Mike Laverty / Tracy Abernathy
9 Washington St.	27 QB Ladd McKittrick / Jeff Seay
3 Arizona State	38 TB Randy Holmes / Donald Beavers
0 Oregon	0 FB Bryce Oglesby
	DL Angelo Dilulo
	DL John Gonzalez
	DL Charles Naone / Paul Hayes
	LB Willie Stubblefield
	LB James Murphy
	LB Ron Heller
	LB Bob Johnson
	DB Kenny Taylor
	DB Jonathon Harrington / DeMonty Price
	DB Reggie Dupee / Bernie Wilson
	DB Tony Fuller

RUSHING: Oglseby 171/878y, Holmes 73/219y, Beavers 46/175y
PASSING: McKittrick 74-191/1106y, 4TD, 38.7%
RECEIVING: Bynum 24/580y, Oglesby 20/156y, Adams 15/284y
SCORING: Bynum 42pts, Marty Breen (K) 37pts, Oglesby 30pts

1984 2-9

14 Ohio State	22 WR Claude Dixon
8 Arizona	27 WR Reggie Bynum
41 Wyoming	14 T Dwayne Jackola / Garth Rouse
22 Idaho	41 G Doug Wright / Darrick Brilz
7 Washington	19 C Jack Lester
9 California	6 G Frank Jones / Dave Giacomelli
10 Arizona State	45 T Tom Emmons
21 Stanford	28 TE Duane Stan / Brad Miller
3 Washington St.	20 QB Ricky Greene / Steve Steenwyk
17 UCLA	26 TB Donald Beavers
6 Oregon	31 FB Tony Green / Darvin Malone
	DL John Gonzalez
	DL Angelo Dilullo
	DL Bob Cline / Gino Mingo
	DL Charles Naone
	LB Ron Heller
	LB Mike Sodaro / Paul Saunders
	LB Osia Lewis
	DB Kenny Taylor / Terry Brown
	DB Lavance Northington
	DB Reggie Dupee
	DB Bernie Wilson

RUSHING: Beavers 99/392y, Green 66/315y, Malone 95/312y
PASSING: Greene 69-140/927y, 1TD, 49.3%
  Steenwyk 62-133/772y, 3TD, 46.6%
RECEIVING: Bynum 51/711y, Dixon 37/465y, Stan 14/233y
SCORING: Beavers & Jim Nielsen (K) 24pts,
  Marty Breen (K) 22pts

1985 3-8

43 Idaho	28 WR Robert Adams
23 California	20 WR Reggie Bynum / Dave Montagne
24 Fresno State	33 T Tom Emmons / Garth Rouse
6 Grambling	23 G Darrick Brilz
0 Southern Cal	63 C Jack Lester
0 Washington St.	34 G Dave Giacomelli / Curt Olsen
21 Washington	20 T Doug Wright
6 Arizona	27 TE Ron Heller (DL) / Phil Ross
24 Stanford	39 QB Rich Gonzales / Erik Wilhelm
0 UCLA	41 TB Carl Lane / Jerry Jordan
13 Oregon	34 FB Darvin Malone
	DL Gino Mingo
	DL Phil Afieri / Paul Saunders
	DL Bob Cline
	DL Rich Haggerty / Andre Todd
	LB Osia Lewis
	LB Jeff Schneider
	LB Harold Johnson / Jim Cureton
	DB Lavance Northington
	DB Don Odegard
	DB Jaime Norman / Scott Monson
	DB Michael Lopez

RUSHING: Malone 134/554y, Lane 39/163y,
  Erick Montgomery (TB) 24/94y,
PASSING: Gonzales 94-181/986y, 3TD, 51.9%
  Wilhelm 86-145/890y, 9TD, 59.3%
RECEIVING: Bynum 61/703y, Malone 30/206y, Montagne 29/358y
SCORING: Bynum 42pts, Jim Nielsen (K) 40pts, Lane 14pts

1986 3-8

0 Fresno State	27 WR Dave Montagne
12 Michigan	31 WR Eric Ory
7 Stanford	17 T Darrick Brilz
14 Washington St.	24 G Jeff Talamantes
14 California	12 C Dave Orndorff
12 Arizona	23 G Paul Hopkins
34 Boise State	3 T Dave Giacomelli
0 UCLA	49 TE Damon Medlock
12 Washington	28 QB Erik Wilhelm
10 BYU	7 TB Carl Lane / Erick Montgomery
28 Oregon	49 FB Dowell Williams / Pat Chaffey
	DL Gino Mingo
	DL Paul Carberry
	DL Rich Haggerty
	DL Paul Alfieri
	LB Terry Page / Mike Matthews
	LB Jeff Schneider
	LB Harold Johnson / Jim Cureton
	DB Kevin Scott
	DB Teddy Johnson
	DB Don Odegard
	DB Bronco Mendenhall

RUSHING: Chaffey 47/232y, Lane 51/201y, Montgomery 27/131y
PASSING: Wilhelm 283-470/2871y, 8TD, 60.2%
RECEIVING: Montagne 78/862y, Williams 45/323y,
  Medlock 37/313y
SCORING: Marty Breen (K) 41pts, Chaffey 18pts, 4 tied w/ 12pts

1987 2-9

7 Georgia	41 WR Roland Hawkins / Bryant Hill
36 San Jose State	34 WR Robb Thomas
16 Texas	61 T Ken Kiff / Mike Bailey
14 Southern Cal	48 G Kenny Felix / Hector Meza
42 Akron	26 C Dave Orndorff
17 Arizona	31 G Paul Hopkins / Jeff Mori
21 Arizona State	30 T Owen Hooven
12 Washington	28 TE Phil Ross
17 UCLA	52 QB Erik Wilhelm
7 Stanford	38 TB Brian Taylor / Erick Montgomery
0 Oregon	44 FB Dowell Williams / Brian Swanson
	DL Tom Vettrus
	DL Phil Alfieri
	DL Rich Haggerty
	DL Brent Mann / Esera Tuaolo
	LB Bronco Mendenhall / Ray Giacomelli
	LB Jeff Schneider / Mike Mathews
	LB Scott Sanders / Jim Cureton
	DB Teddy Johnson / David Brannon
	DB Kevin Scott / Don Odegard
	DB Andre Harris
	DB Lavance Northington

RUSHING: Taylor 97/411y, Swanson 23/72y, Williams 20/64y
PASSING: Wilhelm 226-423/2736y, 17TD, 53.4%
RECEIVING: Thomas 58/891y, Ross 56/625y, Taylor 49/364y
SCORING: Thomas 60pts, Troy Bussanich (K) 51pts, Taylor 24pts

1988 4-6-1

13 Arizona	24 WR Bryant Hill
41 San Jose State	27 WR Robb Thomas
17 California	16 T Ken Kiff
21 Colorado	28 G Hector Meza
21 Fresno State	10 C Rob Jack
21 UCLA	38 G Pete Steffen (T) / Kenny Felix
20 Stanford	20 T Mike Bailey
20 Southern Cal	41 TE Phil Ross
24 Arizona State	30 QB Erik Wilhelm
27 Washington St.	36 TB Brian Taylor
21 Oregon	10 FB Pat Chaffey / Brian Swanson
	DL Esera Tuaolo
	DL Tom Vettrus
	DL Pellom McDaniels
	LB Ray Giacomelli
	LB Bruce Sanders
	LB Mike Mathews
	LB Jim Cureton / Scott Sanders
	DB Calvin Nicholson
	DB Billy Hughely / David Brannon
	DB Andre Harris
	DB Larry Vladic / Teddy Johnson

RUSHING: Chaffey 113/475y, Taylor 88/403y, Swanson 64/250y
PASSING: Wilhelm 275-442/2896y, 18TD, 62.2%
RECEIVING: Thomas 58/763y, Chaffey 45/540y, Ross 30/347y
SCORING: Troy Bussanich (K) 64pts, Chaffey 42pts,
  Thomas 36pts

1989 4-7-1

20 Stanford	16 WR Maurice Wilson / Lloyd Bailey
3 Washington St.	41 WR Reggie Hubbard / Jason Kent
37 Boise State	30 T Brad D'Ancona / Derek Nelons
7 Nebraska	35 G Matt Irvin / Dan Blus
18 Fresno State	35 C Rob Jack / Johnny Feinga
17 Arizona State	17 G Pete Steffen
18 UCLA	17 T Mike Bailey
25 California	14 TE Phil Ross
6 Southern Cal	48 QB Nick Schichtle / Matt Booher
14 Washington	51 TB Reggie Pitchford / Jerrell Waddell
21 Oregon	30 FB Pat Chaffey
21 Hawaii	23 DL Mike Maggiore
	DL Esera Tuaolo
	DL Pellom McDaniels
	LB Bruce Sanders / Todd McKinley
	LB Martin Billings / Doug Lewis
	LB Todd Sahlfeld / Paul Hill
	LB Scott Sanders
	DB Brian Beck / Torey Overstreet
	DB Brent Huff
	DB Billy Hughely / Scott Thompson
	DB Larry Vladic

RUSHING: Chaffey 205/714y, Booher 93/125y, Pitchford 41/118y
PASSING: Schichtle 93-187/1378y, 7TD, 49.7%
  Booher 122-201/1242y, 4TD, 60.7%
RECEIVING: Chaffey 46/457y, Ross 36/415y, Kent 31/436y
SCORING: Chaffey 80pts, Troy Bussanich (K) 55pts, Wilson 18pts

1990 1-10

15 Montana	22 WR Maurice Wilson
12 Kansas	38 WR Kevin Strasser / Craig Palos
20 UNLV	45 T Brad D'Ancona
3 Stanford	37 G Christian Miller
7 Nebraska	31 C Tom Nordquist
35 Arizona	21 G Fletcher Keister / Matt Miner
24 Washington St.	55 T Adam Albaugh
17 UCLA	26 TE George Breland / Jason Blum
9 Arizona State	34 QB Matt Booher / Fred Schweer
5 Southern Cal	56 TB Reggie Pitchford / Dwayne Owens
3 Oregon	6 FB James Jones
	DL Chad de Sully / Corey Brannon
	DL Esera Tuaolo / Thomas Bookman
	DL Martin Billings
	LB Mark Price / Rickey Fizer
	LB Todd Sahlfeld / Tony O'Billovich
	LB Eric Davis / Tim Slone
	LB Doug Lewis / Todd McKinney
	DB Brian Beck
	DB Zechariah Davis
	DB Brent Huff / Earl Zackery
	DB Dennis Edwards / Scott Thompson

RUSHING: Owens 87/364y, Jones 104/364y, Pitchford 78/313y
PASSING: Booher 100-183/892y, 3TD, 54.7%
RECEIVING: Wilson 41/425y, Pitchford 29/150y, Breland 17/173y
SCORING: Jones 38pts, Pitchford 36pts, Jamie Burke (K) 30pts

1991 1-10

10 Utah	22 WR Maurice Wilson / Kenyan Branscomb
9 UNLV	23 T Jason Downs
20 Fresno State	24 G Christian Miller / Fletcher Keister
7 Washington St.	55 C Tom Nordquist
7 Arizona State	24 G Adam Albaugh / Jim Buchanan
7 UCLA	44 T John Garrett
10 Stanford	40 TE Jason Blum
21 Arizona	45 QB Ed Browning / Mark Olford / Ian Shields
14 California	27 HB J.J. Young
6 Washington	58 HB Chad Paulson / Jason Barry
14 Oregon	3 FB Chris Morton / James Jones
	DL Chad de Sully
	DL Corey Brannon / Tom Holmes
	DL Sailusi Pouliivaati
	DL Rickey Fizer
	LB Rico Petrini
	LB Todd Sahlfeld
	LB Mark Price
	DB William Ephraim
	DB Zechariah Davis
	DB Dennis Edwards
	DB Michael Hale / Brent Huff

RUSHING: Paulson 79/490y, Morton 89/353y, Barry 38/245y
PASSING: Browning 13-43/171y, 0TD, 30.2%
RECEIVING: Wilson 10/155y, Branscomb 5/76y,
  Kevin Strasser (WR) 5/47y
SCORING: Jamie Burke (K) 32pts, Shields 24pts, Olford 18pts

1992 1-9-1

20 Kansas	49 WR Maurice Wilson / Kenyan Branscomb
46 Fresno State	36 T Adam Albaugh / Jim Buchanan
14 Arizona	14 G Fletcher Keister
9 Utah	42 C Johnny Feinga
0 California	42 G Jason Downs
10 Washington St.	35 T John Garrett
13 Arizona State	40 TE Ray Penniman
21 Stanford	27 QB Mark Olford
14 UCLA	26 HB Jason Barry / Dwayne Owens
16 Washington	45 HB Chad Paulson
0 Oregon	7 FB J.D. Stewart / John Young
	DL Chad de Sully
	DL Alai Kalaniuvalu / Eric Hale
	DL Sailusi Pouliivaati
	DL Rickey Fizer
	LB Kane Rogers / Corey Huot
	LB Tony O'Billovich
	DB William Ephraim / Reggie Tongue
	DB Herschel Currie
	DB Zechariah Davis
	DB Michael Hale

RUSHING: Olford 167/525y, Owens 63/415y, Paulson 78/381y
PASSING: Olford 22-64/331y, 0TD, 34.4%
RECEIVING: Branscomb 11/174y, Wilson 7/113y
SCORING: Owens 36pts, Paulson 30pts, Jamie Burke (K) 28pts

1993 4-7

27 Wyoming	16 WR Mark Olford / Chris Cross
30 Fresno State	48 T Adam Albaugh / Tim Camp
6 Washington St.	51 G Starling Latu
0 Arizona	33 C Johnny Feinga
30 Arizona State	14 G Alai Kalaniuvalu / Jason Downs
42 Pacific	7 T John Garrett
9 Southern Cal	34 TE Ray Penniman / Brad Barcroft
17 UCLA	20 QB Rahim Muhammad / Ian Shields
27 Stanford	31 HB J.J. Young
21 Washington	28 HB Chad Paulson / Cameron Reynolds
15 Oregon	12 FB John Young /J.D. Stewart /S. Thomas
	DL Chad de Sully
	DL Tom Holmes / Packy Ena
	DL Mark Schultz
	LB Dennis Edwards
	LB Rico Petrini / Cory Huot
	LB Kane Rogers
	LB Tony O'Billovich
	DB William Ephraim
	DB Basheer Elahee / Herschel Currie
	DB Reggie Tongue
	DB Michael Hale

RUSHING: Young 136/955y, Muhammad 87/400y,
   Paulson 64/383y
PASSING: Muhammad 7-29/124y, 2TD, 24.1%
RECEIVING: Cross 8/92y, Olford 7/69y,
   Sylvester Green (WR) 5/42y
SCORING: Young 54pts, Reynolds & Paulson 30pts

1994 4-7

16 Arizona State	22 WR Joe Douglass / Sylvester Green
44 Wyoming	31 T Tim Camp
14 Fresno State	24 G Starling Latu / Brad Thompson
10 Arizona	30 C Johnny Feinga
19 Southern Cal	27 G Darin Borter
23 UCLA	14 T John Garrett
29 Stanford	35 TE Brad Barcroft / Justin Moore
10 Washington	24 QB Don Shanklin
24 Pacific	12 HB J.J. Young
21 Washington St.	3 HB Cameron Reynolds
13 Oregon	17 FB J.D. Stewart / Sedrick Thomas
	DL David Kiepke
	DL Tom Holmes
	DL Tony Huot
	LB Cory Huot
	LB Rico Petrini
	LB Kane Rogers
	LB Packy Ena / Eric Hale
	DB William Ephraim
	DB Marc Williams / Basheer Elahee
	DB Reggie Tongue
	DB Michael Hale

RUSHING: Young 148/891y, Shanklin 132/630y, Stewart 119/499y
PASSING: Shanklin 29-73/560y, 1TD, 39.7%
RECEIVING: Reynolds 10/231y, Douglass 9/137y
SCORING: Young 60pts, Randy Lund (K) 39pts, Shaw 36pts

1995 1-10

14 Idaho	7 WR Chris Cross / Terrance Blackwell
10 Pacific	23 T Tim Camp
27 North Texas	30 G Darin Borter (C) / Jarrod Owens
11 Arizona State	20 C Jamie Critchlow
16 Washington	26 G Brad Thompson
14 Washington St.	40 T Phil Lafler
12 California	13 TE Larry Ramirez / Justin Moore
3 Stanford	24 QB Don Shanklin / Tim Alexander
9 Arizona	14 HB Mark Olford
10 Southern Cal	28 HB Cameron Reynolds
10 Oregon	12 FB J.D. Stewart / Sedrick Thomas
	DL Brian Rogers / Bryan Ludwick
	DL Tony Huot
	DL Tom Holmes
	DL David Kiepke / Inoke Breckterfield
	LB Ahmani Johnson
	LB Kane Rogers
	LB Marc Williams
	DB Andrae Holland
	DB Armon Hatcher
	DB Reggie Tongue
	DB Larry Bumpus

RUSHING: Alexander 109/439y, Stewart 68/421y, Olford 83/336y
PASSING: Alexander 25-76/400y, 0TD, 32.9%
RECEIVING: Reynolds 13/219y, Blackwell 13/175y, Cross 11/163y
SCORING: Randy Lund (K) & Olford 38pts, Reynolds 30pts

1996 2-9

14 Montana	35 WR Roddy Tompkins / Sylvester Green
17 Southern Cal	46 T Grant Forman
10 Baylor	42 G Freddie Perez / Charles Hatcher
42 California	48 C Jamie Critchlow
3 Washington St.	24 G Brad Thompson
26 Stanford	12 T Jarrod Owens
7 Arizona	33 TE Joe Kuykendall
14 Arizona State	29 QB Tim Alexander / David Moran
3 Washington	42 HB Shayzar Hawkins / DeShawn Williams
67 N. Illinois	28 HB Akili King
13 Oregon	49 FB Darron Kirkman
	DL Inoke Breckterfield
	DL Tony Huot
	DL Tom Huthoefer
	LB Bryan Ludwick
	LB Nathan McAtee / Anthony Murray
	LB Brian Rogers
	LB Bryan Jones / Marc Williams
	DB Robert Ruffin
	DB Andrae Holland
	DB Buster Elahee / Larry Bumpus
	DB Armon Hatcher

RUSHING: King 182/740y, Alexander 80/566y, Kirkman 104/566y
PASSING: Alexander 34-94/328y, 2TD, 36.2%
RECEIVING: Williams 18/173y, Tompkins 15/296y, Reynolds 8/148y
SCORING: King 42pts

1997 3-8

33 North Texas	7 WR Roddy Tompkins
24 Stanford	27 WR Robert Prescott / Greg Ainsworth
10 Arizona State	13 T Matt Gartung
26 San Jose State	12 G Larry Ramirez / Keith DiDomenico
24 Utah State	16 C Aaron Koch
10 UCLA	34 G Freddie Perez
17 Washington	45 T Trey Hyde
14 California	33 TE Joe Kuykendall / Martin Maurer
7 Arizona	27 QB Tim Alexander
0 Southern Cal	23 TB Ricky Walker / DeShawn Williams
30 Oregon	48 FB John Lazetich
	DL Jason Mageo / Alex Sawatzke
	DL Shawn Ball / Bob McKane
	DL James Greule / Aaron Wells
	DL Imoke Breckterfield
	LB Brian Rogers
	LB Nathan McAtee / Jonathan Jackson
	LB Bryan Jones
	DB Andrae Holland
	DB Buster Elahee / Larry Bumpus
	DB Terrence Carroll
	DB Armon Hatcher

RUSHING: Alexander 127/288y, Walker 80/274y,
   Jason Dandridge (TB) 54/190y
PASSING: Alexander 157-327/1745y, 6TD, 48%
RECEIVING: Ainsworth 49/600y, Tompkins 46/538y,
   Prescott 24/424y
SCORING: Jose Cortez (K) 51pts, Tompkins, Walker &
   Jason Dandridge (TB) 18pts

1998 5-6

48 Nevada	6 WR Roddy Tompkins / James Battle
27 Baylor	17 WR Tim Alexander
20 Southern Cal	40 WR Greg Ainsworth
3 Arizona State	24 T Jason White
20 Utah State	16 G Larry Ramirez / Jared Cornell
30 Stanford	23 C Keith DiDomenico
7 Arizona	28 G Aaron Koch
34 Washington	35 T Matt Gartung
19 California	20 TE Joe Kuykendall
34 UCLA	41 QB Terrance Bryant / Jonathan Smith
44 Oregon	41 TB Ken Simonton / Jason Dandridge
	DL Inoke Breckterfield
	DL Aaron Wells
	DL Shawn Ball / James Greule
	DL Jamil Brathwaite
	LB Brian Rogers / Micah Moore
	LB Jonathan Jackson
	LB Bryan Jones
	DB Andrae Holland
	DB Keith Heyward-Johnson / Ricky Walker
	DB Terrence Carroll
	DB Armon Hatcher

RUSHING: Simonton 224/1028y, Dandridge 55/277y
PASSING: Bryant 136-272/1362y, 4TD, 50%
RECEIVING: Ainsworth 58/749y, Alexander 52/620y,
   Battle 31/563y
SCORING: Jose Cortez (K) 80pts, Simonton 78pts,
   Dandridge 24pts

1999 7-5

28 Nevada	13 WR Imani Percoats/ T.J. Houshmandzadeh
46 Fresno State	23 WR Robert Prescott
48 Ga. Southern	41 WR Roddy Tompkins
29 Southern Cal	37 T Jason White
21 Washington	47 G Robert Sykes
17 Stanford	21 C Keith DiDomenico
55 UCLA	7 G Aaron Koch
27 Washington St.	13 T Mitch White
17 California	7 TE Martin Maurer / Bennie Johnson
28 Arizona	20 QB Jonathan Smith
14 Oregon	25 TB Ken Simonton
17 Hawaii■	23 DL DeLawrence Grant
	DL Aaron Wells
	DL Shawn Ball
	DL Toalei Talataina / LaDairis Jackson
	LB Darnell Robinson
	LB Jonathan Jackson
	LB James Allen / Tevita Moala
	DB Keith Heyward-Johnson
	DB Dennis Weathersby
	DB Calvin Carlyle
	DB Terrance Carroll

RUSHING: Simonton 294/1486y, Antonio Battle (TB) 50/211y
PASSING: Smith 207-425/3053y, 15TD, 48.7%
RECEIVING: Percoats 51/816y, Prescott 49/614y,
   Tompkins 28/580y
SCORING: Simonton 118pts, Ryan Cesca (K) 58pts,
   Tompkins 30pts

2000 11-1

21 E. Washington	19 WR Chad Johnson
28 New Mexico	20 WR T.J. Houshmandzadeh
35 San Diego St.	3 WR Robert Prescott / Seth Trimmer
31 Southern Cal	21 T Vincent Sandoval
30 Washington	33 G Robert Sykes
38 Stanford	6 C Chris Gibson
44 UCLA	38 G Jared Cornell
38 Washington St.	9 T Mitch White
38 California	32 TE Martin Maurer
33 Arizona	9 QB Jonathan Smith
23 Oregon	13 TB Ken Simonton / Patrick McCall
41 Notre Dame■	9 DL DeLawrence Grant
	DL Eric Manning
	DL Ryan Atkinson / Dwan Edwards
	DL LaDairis Jackson
	LB Darnell Robinson
	LB Richard Seigler
	LB James Allen / Nick Barnett
	DB Keith Hayward-Johnson
	DB Dennis Weathersby
	DB Calvin Carlyle
	DB Terrence Carroll / Jake Cookus

RUSHING: Simonton 284/1559y, McCall 129/658y,
   Antonio Battle (TB) 47/178y,
PASSING: Smith 170-338/2773y, 20TD, 50.3%
RECEIVING: Houshmandzadeh 48/730y, Johnson 37/806y,
   Maurer 36/465y
SCORING: Simonton 116pts, Ryan Cesca (K) 94pts,
   Johnson 48pts

2001 5-6

24 Fresno State	44 WR Cole Clasen / Shawn Kintner
27 New Mexico St.	22 WR James Newson
7 UCLA	38 WR Seth Trimmer / George Gillett
27 Washington St.	34 T Lee Davis
38 Arizona	3 G Mike Kuykendall
24 Arizona State	41 C Chris Gibson
19 California	10 G Kanan Sanchez
13 Southern Cal	16 T Vincent Sandoval
49 Washington	24 TE Tim Euhus
45 N. Arizona	10 QB Jonathan Smith
14 Oregon	17 TB Ken Simonton / Steven Jackson
	DL Noah Happe
	DL Eric Manning
	DL Dwan Edwards
	DL Kyle Rosselle / Dan Rothwell
	LB Nick Barnett
	LB Richard Seigler
	LB James Allen
	DB Dennis Weathersby
	DB Terrell Roberts
	DB Mitch Meeuwsen
	DB Jake Cookus

RUSHING: Simonton 239/971y, Jackson 74/390y,
   Patrick McCall (TB) 54/203y
PASSING: Smith 180-317/2427y, 14TD, 56.8%
RECEIVING: Newson 57/968y, Euhus 27/316y, Clasen 23/250y
SCORING: Ryan Cesca (K) 59pts, Simonton 54pts, Jackson 42pts

2002 8-5

49 E. Kentucky	10 WR Shawn Kintner / Jayson Boyd
35 Temple	3 WR Kenny Farley / Cole Clasen
47 UNLV	17 WR James Newsom
59 Fresno State	19 T Mike Kuykendall (G) / Brian Kilkenny
0 Southern Cal	22 G David Lose
35 UCLA	43 C Matt Brock
9 Arizona State	13 G Kanan Sanchez
24 California	13 T Doug Nienhuis
38 Arizona	3 TE Tim Euhus / Dan Haines
29 Washington	41 QB Derek Anderson
31 Stanford	21 TB Steven Jackson
45 Oregon	24 DL Noah Happe
13 Pittsburgh■	38 DL Eric Manning
	DL Dwan Edwards / James Lee
	DL Bill Swancutt
	LB Nick Barnett
	LB Richard Seigler
	LB Erik Tuma / Jonathan Pollard
	DB Terrell Roberts
	DB Dennis Weathersby
	DB Lawrence Turner
	DB Calvin Carlyle / Mitch Meeuwsen

RUSHING: Jackson 319/1690y, Dwight Wright (TB) 84/383y
PASSING: Anderson 211-449/3313y, 47%, 25 TD
RECEIVING: Newsom 74/1284y, Farley 29/526y, Clasen 23/273y
SCORING: Jackson 102pts, Kirk Yliniemi (K) 90pts, Newsom 72pts

2003 8-5

13 Arizona	24 WR James Newson
41 San Jose State	27 WR Kenny Farley
17 California	16 WR Mike Hass / George Gillett
21 Colorado	28 T Brian Kilkenny (G) / Brandon Lockheart
21 Fresno State	10 G David Lose
21 UCLA	38 C Matt Brock
20 Stanford	20 G Kanan Sanchez
20 Southern Cal	41 T Doug Nienhuis
24 Arizona State	30 TE Tim Euhus
27 Washington St.	36 QB Derek Anderson
21 Oregon	10 TB Steven Jackson
28 Southern Cal	52 DL Jayson Jean-Baptiste / Dan Rothwell
55 New Mexico■	14 DL Ben Siegert
	DL Dwan Edwards
	DL Bill Swancutt
	LB Trent Bray / Seth Lacey
	LB Richard Seigler
	LB Jonathan Pollard / Chaz Scott
	DB Aric Williams
	DB Brandon Browner
	DB Mitch Meeuwsen
	DB Lawrence Turner

RUSHING: Jackson 350/1545y, Dwight Wright (TB) 89/350y
PASSING: Anderson 261-510/4058y, 24TD, 51.2%
RECEIVING: Newson 81/1306y, Euhus 49/645y, Hass 44/1013y
SCORING: Jackson 132pts, Kirk Yliniemi (K) 103pts, Hass & Euhus 42pts

2004 7-5

21 LSU	22 WR Mike Hass
34 Boise State	53 WR Marcel Love
17 New Mexico	7 WR Anthony Wheat-Brown / George Gillett
14 Arizona State	27 T Adam Koets
7 California	49 G Josh Linehan
29 Washington	14 C Matt Brock
38 Washington St.	19 G Roy Schueing
28 Arizona	14 T Doug Nienhuis
20 Southern Cal	28 TE Joe Newton
24 Stanford	19 QB Derek Anderson
50 Oregon	21 TB Dwight Wright / Ryan Cole
38 Notre Dame■	21 DL Joe Lemma
	DL Ben Siegert
	DL Sir Henry Anderson / Alvin Smith
	DL Bill Swancutt
	LB Keith Ellison
	LB Trent Bray
	LB Jonathan Pollard / Chaz Scott
	DB Aric Williams
	DB Brandon Browner
	DB Mitch Meeuwsen
	DB Sabby Piscitelli

RUSHING: Wright 209/784y, Cole 80/210y
PASSING: Anderson 279-515/3615y, 29TD, 54.2%
RECEIVING: Hass 86/1379y, Newton 56/687y, Love 40/523y
SCORING: Alexis Serna (K) 90pts, Wright 48pts, Newton & Hass 42pts

2005 5-6

41 Portland State	14 WR Mike Hass
30 Boise State	27 WR Anthony Wheat-Brown
27 Louisville	63 WR Josh Hawkins
24 Arizona State	42 T Adam Koets
44 Washington St.	33 G Jeremy Perry
23 California	20 C Kyle DeVan
28 UCLA	51 G Roy Schueing
27 Arizona	29 T Josh Linehan / Andy Levitre
18 Washington	10 TE Dan Haines / Jason Vandiver
17 Stanford	20 QB Matt Moore / Ryan Gunderson
14 Oregon	56 TB Yvenson Bernard
	DL Joe Lemma / Joe Rudulph
	DL Alvin Smith / Ben Siegert
	DL Sir Henry Anderson
	DL Jeff Van Orsow
	LB Keith Ellison
	LB Trent Bray
	LB Andy Darkins / Derrick Doggett
	DB Keenan Lewis
	DB Brandon Hughes/ Gerard Lawson
	DB Al Afalava / Lamar Herron
	DB Sabby Piscitelli

RUSHING: Bernard 299/1321y, Nate Wright (TB) 10/45y
PASSING: Moore 211-355/2711y, 11TD, 59.4%
Gunderson 54-102/542y, 2TD, 52.9%
RECEIVING: Hass 90/1532y, Wheat-Brown 40/400y, Hawkins 38/393y
SCORING: Alexis Serna (K) 101pts, Bernard 84pts, Hass 36pts

2006 10-4

56 E. Washington	17 WR Sammie Stroughter
14 Boise State	42 WR A. Wheat-Brown/Ruben Jackson
38 Idaho	0 WR Brandon Powers
13 California	41 T Adam Koets
6 Washington St.	13 G Jeremy Perry / Adam Speer
27 Washington	17 C Kyle DeVan
17 Arizona	10 G Roy Schueing
33 Southern Cal	31 T Andy Levitre / Josh Linehan
44 Arizona State	10 TE Joe Newton / Jason Vandiver
7 UCLA	25 QB Matt Moore
30 Stanford	7 TB Yvenson Bernard
30 Oregon	28 DL Joe Lemma / Dorian Smith
35 Hawaii	32 DL Ben Siegert
39 Missouri■	38 DL Curtis Coker/ William Aka'ola Vea
	DL Jeff Van Orsow
	LB Derrick Doggett
	LB Alan Darlin
	LB Joey LaRocque
	DB Keenan Lewis / Coye Francies
	DB Brandon Hughes
	DB Al Afalava / Bryan Payton
	DB Sabby Piscitelli

RUSHING: Bernard 296/1307y, Clinton Polk (TB) 63/248y
PASSING: Moore 229-378/3022y, 18TD, 60.6%
RECEIVING: Stroughter 74/1293y, Bernard 43/276y, Powers 39/433y
SCORING: Alexis Serna (K) 111pts, Bernard 80pts, Stroughter 48pts

2007 9-4

24 Utah	7 WR Darrell Catchings/Sammie Stroughter
3 Cincinnati	34 WR Anthony Brown / James Rodgers
61 Idaho State	10 WR/TE Brandon Powers / Gabe Miller
32 Arizona State	44 T Tavita Thompson / Ryan Pohl
14 UCLA	40 G Adam Speer / Jeremy Perry
31 Arizona	16 C Kyle DeVan
31 California	28 G Roy Schueing (T) / Gregg Peat
23 Stanford	6 T Andy Levitre
3 Southern Cal	24 TE Howard Croom
29 Washington	23 QB Sean Canfield / Lyle Moevao
52 Washington St.	17 TB Yvenson Bernard / Matt Sieverson
38 Oregon	31 DL Dorian Smith / Victor Butler
21 Maryland■	14 DL Gerard Lee / William 'Akau'ola Vea
	DL Curtis Coker
	DL Jeff Van Orsow
	LB Derrick Doggett
	LB Alan Darlin
	LB Joey LaRocque
	DB Keenan Lewis / Tim Clark
	DB Brandon Hughes / Gerard Lawson
	DB Al Afalava / Bryan Payton
	DB Daniel Drayton / Greg Laybourn

RUSHING: Bernard 275/1214y, Rodgers 50/586y, Sieverson 85/344y
PASSING: Canfield 165-286/1661y, 9TD, 57.7%
Moevao 77-147/876y, 2TD, 52.4%
RECEIVING: Brown 39/550y, Bernard 36/179y, Catchings 33/386y
SCORING: Alexis Serna (K) 92pts, Bernard 84pts, Rodgers 24pts

2008 9-4

28 Stanford	36 WR Sammie Stroughter
14 Penn State	45 WR James Rodgers / Darrell Catchings
45 Hawaii	7 WR/TE Shane Morales / Brady Camp
27 Southern Cal	21 T Andy Levitre
28 Utah	31 G Adam Speer
66 Washington St.	13 C Alex Linnenkohl
34 Washington	13 G Gregg Peat
27 Arizona State	25 T Tavita Thompson / Mike Remmers
34 UCLA	6 TE Howard Croom
34 California	21 QB Lyle Moevao / Sean Canfield
19 Arizona	17 TB Jacquizz Rodgers / Ryan McCants
38 Oregon	65 DL Victor Butler
3 Pittsburgh■	0 DL Pernell Booth
	DL Stephen Paea / Mitchel Hunt
	DL Slade Norris
	LB Keaton Kristick
	LB Bryant Cornell
	LB Keith Pankey
	DB Keenan Lewis
	DB Brandon hughes / Tim Clark
	DB Al Afalava / Suaesi Tuimaunei
	DB Greg Laybourn

RUSHING: Jac. Rodgers 259/1253y, Jam. Rodgers 46/408y, McCants 85/337y
PASSING: Moevao 214-361/2534y, 19TD, 59.3%
Canfield 56/84/703y, 6TD, 66.7%
RECEIVING: Stroughter 70/1040y, Morales 54/743y, Jam. Rodgers 51/607y
SCORING: Justin Kahut (K) 94pts, Jac. Rodgers 72pts, Jam. Rodgers 60pts

2009 8-5

34 Portland State	7 WR Damola Adeniji / Markus Wheaton
23 UNLV	21 WR James Rodgers
18 Cincinnati	28 WR/FB Jordan Bishop / Will Darkins
32 Arizona	37 T Michael Philipp
28 Arizona State	17 G Grant Johnson
38 Stanford	28 C Alex Linnenkohl
36 Southern Cal	42 G Gregg Peat
26 UCLA	19 T Mike Remmers
31 California	14 TE Brady Camp / Howard Croom
48 Washington	21 QB Sean Canfield
42 Washington St.	10 RB Jacquizz Rodgers
33 Oregon	37 DL Ben Terry / Gabe Miller
20 BYU■	44 DL Brennan Olander / Latu Moala
	DL Stephen Paea
	DL Kevin Frahm / Matt LaGrone
	LB Keaton Kristick
	LB David Pa'aluhi
	LB Dwight Roberson / Keith Pankey
	DB James Dockery
	DB Tim Clark / Brandon Hardin
	DB Lance Mitchell
	DB Cameron Collins / Suaesi Tuimaunei

RUSHING: Jac. Rodgers 273/1440y, Jam. Rodgers 58/303y, Jovan Stevenson (RB) 26/137y
PASSING: Canfield 303-446/3271y, 21TD, 67.9%
RECEIVING: Jam. Rodgers 91/1034y, Jac. Rodgers 78/522y, Adeniji 57/807y, Joe Haluhuni (SB) 35/486y
SCORING: Jac. Rodgers 132pts, Justin Kahut (K) 111pts, Jam. Rodgers 62pts

2010 5-7

21 TCU	30 WR Markus wheaton / James Rodgers
35 Louisville	28 WR Aaron Nichols / Jordan Bishop
24 Boise State	37 WR/FB Joe Halahuni / Will Darkins
31 Arizona State	28 T Michael Philipp / Wilder McAndrews
29 Arizona	27 G Grant Johnson
34 Washington	35 C Alex Linnenkohl
35 California	7 G Burke Ellis
14 UCLA	17 T Mike Remmers
14 Washington St.	31 TE Brady Camp / John Reese
36 Southern Cal	7 QB Ryan Katz
0 Stanford	38 TB Jacquizz Rodgers
20 Oregon	37 DL Gabe Miller
	DL Stephen Paea
	DL Brennan Olander / Kevin Frahm
	DL Dominic Glover / Taylor Henry
	LB Keith Pankey
	LB Rueben Robinson / Tony Wilson
	LB Dwight Roberson
	DB James Dockery / Jordan Poyer
	DB Brandon Hardin / Cameron Collins
	DB Lance Mitchell
	DB Suaesi Tuimaunei / Anthony Watkins

RUSHING: Jac. Rodgers 256/1184y, Wheaton 27/220y
PASSING: Katz 213-355/2401y, 18TD, 60%
RECEIVING: Wheaton 55/675y, Jac. Rodgers 44/287y, Nichols 31/336y, Halahuni 30/390y
SCORING: Jac. Rodgers 96pts, Justin Kahut (K) 51pts, Halahuni 36pts

PENN STATE

Pennsylvania State University (Founded 1855)
University Park, Pennsylvania (near State College, Pennsylvania)
Nickname: Nittany Lions
Colors: Blue and White
Stadium: Beaver (1960) 107,282
Affiliations: Independent (1887-1992), Big Ten (1993-present)

CAREER RUSHING YARDS	Attempts	Yards
Evan Royster (2007-10)	686	3932
Curt Warner (1979-82)	649	3398
Tony Hunt (2003-06)	654	3320
Blair Thomas (1985-87, 89)	606	3301
Curtis Enis (1995-97)	565	3256
D.J. Dozier (1983-86)	624	3227
Larry Johnson (1999-2002)	460	2953
Lydell Mitchell (1969-71)	501	2934
Ki-Jana Carter (1992-94)	395	2829
Matt Suhey (1976-79)	633	2818

CAREER PASSING YARDS	Comp.-Att.	Yards
Zack Mills (2001-04)	606-1082	7212
Tony Sacca (1988-91)	401-824	5869
Daryll Clark (2006-09)	444-738	5742
Chuck Fusina (1975-78)	371-665	5382
Kerry Collins (1991-94)	370-657	5304
Anthony Morelli (2004-07)	460-821	5279
Todd Blackledge (1980-82)	341-658	4812
Wally Richardson (1992, 94-96)	378-692	4419
Kevin Thompson (1996-99)	263-495	3710
John Hufnagel (1970-72)	225-408	3545

CAREER RECEIVING YARDS	Catches	Yards
Bobby Engram (1991, 93-95)	167	3026
Deon Butler (2005-08)	179	2771
Jordan Norwood (2005-08)	158	2015
Bryant Johnson (1999-2002)	110	2008
Kenny Jackson (1980-83)	109	2006
O.J. McDuffie (1988-92)	125	1988
Joe Jurevicius (1994-97)	94	1894
Jack Curry (1965-67)	117	1837
Terry Smith (1988-91)	108	1825
Derrick Williams (2005-08)	161	1743

SEASON RUSHING YARDS	Attempts	Yards
Larry Johnson (2002)	271	2087
Lydell Mitchell (1971)	254	1567
Ki-Jana Carter (1994)	198	1539
John Cappelletti (1973)	286	1522
Blair Thomas (1987)	268	1414

SEASON PASSING YARDS	Comp.-Att.	Yards
Daryll Clark (2009)	232-381	3003
Kerry Collins (1994)	176-264	2679
Anthony Morelli (2007)	234-402	2651
Daryll Clark (2008)	192-321	2592
Tony Sacca (1991)	169-292	2488

SEASON RECEIVING YARDS	Catches	Yards
Bobby Engram (1995)	63	1084
Bobby Engram (1994)	52	1029
O.J. McDuffie (1992)	63	977
Freddie Scott (1994)	47	973
Bryant Johnson (2002)	48	917

GAME RUSHING YARDS	Attempts	Yards
Larry Johnson (2002 vs. Indiana)	28	327
Larry Johnson (2002 vs. Illinois)	31	279
Larry Johnson (2002 vs. Michigan St.)	19	279

GAME PASSING YARDS	Comp.-Att.	Yards
Zack Mills (2002 vs. Iowa)	23-44	399
Michael Robinson (2003 vs. Wisconsin)	22-53	379
Mike McQueary (1997 vs. Pittsburgh)	21-36	366

GAME RECEIVING YARDS	Catches	Yards
Dean Butler (2006 vs. Northwestern)	11	216
O.J. McDuffie (1992 vs. Boston College)	11	212
Bobby Engram (1995 vs. Purdue)	9	203

GREATEST COACH:

There is little argument that one person personifies everything about Penn State football: head coach Joe Paterno. The Brooklyn, N.Y., native played effectively as an Ivy League quarterback-defensive back in the late 1940s at Brown University. After graduation, he followed his former Brown head coach, Rip Engle, to Penn State in 1950 to become an offensive assistant coach. When Engle retired in 1966, Paterno was named to head the Nittany Lions football program at age 39, a somewhat late start for a head coach who would win more games than nearly every other coach. Paterno stayed remarkably loyal to Penn State and in 2007 surpassed the immortal Amos Alonzo Stagg (University of Chicago, 1892-1932) with 42 years of head coaching at a single institution. Paterno won the most games at one major school in the history of college football.

Paterno guided Penn State to the 1982 and 1986 national championships. Four of Paterno's other Penn State teams—1968, 1969, 1973, and 1994—were undefeated but failed to be voted national champions. Since Paterno became coach in 1966, there were more than 800 head coaching changes at other FBS schools.

Paterno was the only coach to win all four of the original and traditional New Year's Day bowl games—Rose, Sugar, Cotton and Orange Bowls—and he owned a 6-0 record in the Fiesta Bowl. In 2006, he was selected by the National Football Foundation for the College Football Hall of Fame. Paterno was the 1986 Sports Illustrated "Sportsman-of-the-Year."

In a remarkable gesture uncommon in the coaching and athletic profession, Paterno and his wife Sue donated several $ million to the Penn State Library Fund.

PENN STATE'S 55 GREATEST SINCE 1953

OFFENSE

WIDE RECEIVER: Deon Butler, Bobby Engram, Kenny Jackson, Bryant Johnson
TIGHT END: Kyle Brady, Ted Kwalick
TACKLE: Levi Brown, Keith Dorney, Irv Pankey, Kareem McKenzie
GUARD: Sean Farrell, Jeff Hartings, Tom Rafferty, Steve Wisniewski
CENTER: Roger Duffy, Keith Radecic
QUARTERBACK: Todd Blackledge, Kerry Collins, Chuck Fusina
RUNNING BACK: Ki-Jana Carter, Curtis Enis, Lydell Mitchell, Blair Thomas, Curt Warner
FULLBACK: Franco Harris

DEFENSE

END: Courtney Brown, Tamba Hali, Michael Haynes, Dave Robinson
TACKLE: Bruce Clark, Tim Johnson, Jimmy Kennedy, Mike Reid
LINEBACKER: LaVar Arrington, Navorro Bowman, Greg Buttle, Shane Conlin, Dan Connor, Jack Ham, Lance Mehl, Paul Posluszny
CORNERBACK: Duffy Cobbs, Shelly Hammonds, George Landis, Brian Miller
SAFETY: Pete Harris, Kim Herring, Shawn Mayer, Michael Zordich

SPECIAL TEAMS

RETURN SPECIALIST: O.J. McDuffie
PLACE KICKER: Matt Bahr
PUNTER: John Bruno

MULTIPLE POSITIONS

QUARTERBACK-RUNNING BACK-WIDE RECEIVER: Michael Robinson
TAILBACK-FULLBACK: Matt Suhey
LINEBACKER-PUNT RETURNER: Dennis Onkontz

PERFORMANCE FORMULA:
PENN STATE'S 10 BEST SEASONS

1994	1.8165	1 of 71
1969	1.7879	1 of 70
1986	1.7652	2 of 70
1973	1.7632	3 of 70
1982	1.7587	1 of 70
1977	1.7375	2 of 70
1968	1.7198	1 of 70
1971	1.6875	4 of 70
1978	1.6816	3 of 70
1981	1.6749	3 of 70

PENN STATE NITTANY LIONS

Year	W-L-T	AP Poll	Conference Standing	Toughest Regular Season Opponents	Coach (Record at School)	Bowl Games		
1953	6-3			Wisconsin 6-2-1, Syracuse 5-3-1, West Virginia 8-1	Charles "Rip" Engle			
1954	7-2	20		West Virginia 8-1, TCU 4-6	Rip Engle			
1955	5-4			Army 6-3, Navy 6-2-1, Syracuse 5-3, Pittsburgh 7-3	Rip Engle			
1956	6-2-1			Army 5-3-1, Ohio State 6-3, Syracuse 7-1, Pittsburgh 7-2-1	Rip Engle			
1957	6-3			Army 7-2, Vanderbilt 5-3-2, Syracuse 5-3-1, West Virginia 7-2-1	Rip Engle			
1958	6-3-1			Army 8-0-1, Syracuse 8-1, Pittsburgh 5-4-1	Rip Engle			
1959	9-2	11		Missouri 6-4, Syracuse 10-0, Pittsburgh 6-4	Rip Engle	Liberty	7 Alabama	0
1960	7-3	16		Missouri 9-1, Army 6-3-1, Syracuse 7-2, Pittsburgh 4-3-3	Rip Engle	Liberty	41 Oregon	12
1961	8-3	18		Navy 7-3, Miami 7-3, Syracuse 7-3, Maryland 7-3	Rip Engle	Gator	30 Georgia Tech	15
1962	9-2	9		Navy 5-5, Syracuse 5-5, West Virginia 8-2, Pittsburgh 5-5	Rip Engle	Gator	7 Florida	17
1963	7-3	10		Oregon 7-3, Army 7-3, Syracuse 8-2, Pittsburgh 9-1	Rip Engle			
1964	6-4			Oregon 7-2-1, Syracuse 7-3, West Virginia 7-3, Ohio State 7-2	Rip Engle			
1965	5-5			Michigan State 10-0, UCLA 7-2-1, Syracuse 7-3	Rip Engle (104-48-4)			
1966	5-5			Michigan State 9-0-1, UCLA 9-1, Syracuse 8-2, Georgia Tech 9-1	Joe Paterno			
1967	8-2-1	10		Miami 7-3, UCLA 8-2, NC State 8-2	Joe Paterno	Gator	17 Florida State	17
1968	11-0	2		West Virginia 7-3, Army 7-3, Syracuse 6-4	Joe Paterno	Orange	15 Kansas	14
1969	11-0	2		Colorado 7-3, Kansas State 5-5, West Virginia 9-1	Joe Paterno	Orange	10 Missouri	3
1970	7-3	18		Colorado 6-4, Boston College 8-2, Syracuse 6-4, West Virginia 8-3	Joe Paterno			
1971	11-1	5		West Virginia 7-4, Tennessee 9-2	Joe Paterno	Cotton	30 Texas	6
1972	10-2	10		Tennessee 9-2, West Virginia 8-3, NC State 7-3-1	Joe Paterno	Sugar	0 Oklahoma	14
1973	12-0	5		Stanford 7-4, Air Force 6-4, Maryland 8-3, NC State 8-3	Joe Paterno	Orange	16 Louisiana State	9
1974	10-2	7		Stanford 5-4-2, Maryland 8-3, NC State 9-2, Pittsburgh 7-4	Joe Paterno	Cotton	41 Baylor	20
1975	9-3	10		Ohio State 11-0, West Virginia 8-3, Maryland 8-2-1, Pittsburgh 7-4	Joe Paterno	Sugar	6 Alabama	13
1976	7-5			Ohio State 8-2-1, Kentucky 7-4, Pittsburgh 11-0	Joe Paterno	Gator	9 Notre Dame	20
1977	11-1	5		Maryland 7-4, Kentucky 10-1, Pittsburgh 8-2-1	Joe Paterno	Fiesta	42 Arizona State	30
1978	11-1	4		Ohio State 7-3-1, Maryland 9-2, NC State 8-3, Pittsburgh 8-3	Joe Paterno	Sugar	7 Alabama	14
1979	8-4	20		Nebraska 10-1, NC State 7-4, Temple 9-2, Pittsburgh 10-1	Joe Paterno	Liberty	9 Tulane	6
1980	10-2	8		Nebraska 9-2, Missouri 8-3, Maryland 8-3, Miami 8-3, Pitt 10-1	Joe Paterno	Fiesta	31 Ohio State	19
1981	10-2	3		Nebraska 9-2, Miami 9-2, Alabama 9-1-1, Pittsburgh 10-1	Joe Paterno	Fiesta	26 Southern California	10
1982	11-1	1		Maryland 8-3, Nebraska 11-1, Alabama 7-4, West Va. 9-2, Pitt 9-2	Joe Paterno	Sugar	27 Georgia	23
1983	8-4-1			Nebraska 12-0, Iowa 9-2, Boston College 9-2, Pittsburgh 8-2-1	Joe Paterno	Aloha	13 Washington	10
1984	6-5			Iowa 7-4-1, Texas 7-3-1, Maryland 8-3, Boston College 9-2	Joe Paterno			
1985	11-1	3		Maryland 8-3, Ala 8-2-1, Syracuse 7-4, West Virginia 7-3-1	Joe Paterno	Orange	10 Oklahoma	25
1986	12-0	1		Boston College 8-3, Alabama 9-3	Joe Paterno	Fiesta	14 Miami	10
1987	8-4			Syracuse 11-0, Pittsburgh 8-3, Notre Dame 8-3	Joe Paterno	Citrus	10 Clemson	35
1988	5-6			Syracuse 9-2, Alabama 8-3, West Virginia 11-0, Notre Dame 11-0	Joe Paterno			
1989	8-3-1	15		Virginia 10-2, Alabama 10-1, West Virginia 8-2-1, Notre Dame 11-1	Joe Paterno	Holiday	50 Brigham Young	39
1990	9-3	11		Texas 10-1, Southern Calif. 8-3-1, Alabama 7-4, Notre Dame 9-2	Joe Paterno	Blockbuster	17 Florida State	24
1991	11-2	3		Brigham Young 8-2-1, Miami 11-0, Notre Dame 9-3,	Joe Paterno	Fiesta	42 Tennessee	17
1992	7-5	24		Miami 11-0, Boston College 8-2-1, Notre Dame 9-1-1,	Joe Paterno	Blockbuster	3 Stanford	24
1993	10-2	8	3	Michigan 7-4, Ohio State 9-1-1, Indiana 8-3,	Joe Paterno	Citrus	31 Tennessee	13
1994	12-0	2	1	Southern California 7-3-1, Michigan 7-4, Ohio State 9-3,	Joe Paterno	Rose	38 Oregon	20
1995	9-3	13	3t	Ohio State 11-1, Northwestern 10-1, Michigan 9-3	Joe Paterno	Outback	43 Auburn	14
1996	11-2	7	3t	Ohio State 10-1, Iowa 8-3, Indiana 8-3, Northwestern 9-2	Joe Paterno	Fiesta	38 Texas	15
1997	9-3	16	2t	Ohio State 10-2, Michigan 11-0, Purdue 8-3	Joe Paterno	Citrus	6 Florida	21
1998	9-3	17	5	Ohio State 10-1, Michigan 9-3, Wisconsin 10-1	Joe Paterno	Outback	26 Kentucky	14
1999	10-3	13	4t	Minnesota 8-3, Michigan 9-2, Michigan State 9-2	Joe Paterno	Alamo	24 Texas A&M	0
2000	5-7		5t	Toledo 10-1, Ohio State 8-3, Purdue 8-3, Michigan 8-3	Joe Paterno			
2001	5-6		4t	Miami 11-0, Ohio State 7-4, Illinois 10-1, Michigan 8-3	Joe Paterno			
2002	9-4	16	4	Iowa 11-1, Michigan 9-3, Ohio State 13-0	Joe Paterno	Capital One	9 Auburn	13
2003	3-9		9t	Nebraska 10-3, Minnesota 10-3, Iowa 10-3, Ohio State 11-2	Joe Paterno			
2004	4-7		9	Boston College 9-3, Wisconsin 9-3, Iowa 10-2, Ohio State 8-4	Joe Paterno			
2005	11-1	3	1t	Ohio State 10-2, Michigan 7-5, Wisconsin 10-3	Joe Paterno	Orange	26 Florida State	23
2006	9-4	24	4t	Notre Dame 10-2, Ohio State 12-0, Michigan 11-1, Wisconsin 11-1	Joe Paterno	Outback	20 Tennessee	10
2007	9-4		5t	Michigan 8-4, Illinois 9-3, Wisconsin 9-3, Ohio State 11-1	Joe Paterno	Alamo	24 Texas A&M	17
2008	11-2	8	1t	Oregon State 8-4, Ohio State 10-2, Iowa 8-4, Michigan State 9-3	Joe Paterno	Rose	24 Southern California	38
2009	11-2	9	2t	Temple 9-3, Iowa 10-2, Ohio State 10-2	Joe Paterno	Capital One	19 Louisiana State	17
2010	7-6		4t	Alabama 9-3, Ohio State 11-1, Michigan State 11-1	Joe Paterno (401-135-3)	Outback	24 Florida	37

TOTAL: 487-174-5 .7350 (4 of 70)   **Bowl Games since 1953:** 27-13-1 .6707 (3 of 70)

GREATEST TEAM SINCE 1953: Penn State's 1986 (12-0) national champions, upset winner of the Fiesta Bowl over no. 1 Miami, probably was coach Joe Paterno's most balanced club. The 1982 champions were great on defense and the undefeated 1994 team had one of the greatest offenses ever. The 2005 Nittany Lions came within one second of a win at Michigan and an undefeated season. The College Football Performance Formula favors Paterno's 1994 club. You decide.

1953 6-3

0	Wisconsin	20 E Don Malinak / Jack Sherry
7	Pennsylvania	13 T Roosevelt Grier / Dan DeFalco
35	Boston Univ.	13 G Sam Green
20	Syracuse	14 C Don Balthaser / Frank Reich
27	TCU	21 G Keith Horn
19	West Virginia	20 T Otto Kneidinger
28	Fordham	21 E Jim Garrity / Jesse Arnelle
54	Rutgers	26 QB Tony Rados
17	Pittsburgh	0 HB Buddy Rowell / Lenny Moore
		HB Ron Younker
		FB Bill Straub

RUSHING: Moore 108/601y
PASSING: Rados 81-171/1025y, 8TD, 47.4%
RECEIVING: Garrity 30/349y
SCORING: Garrity (E-K) 44pts

1954 7-2

14	Illinois	12 E Jesse Arnelle / Jack Sherry
13	Syracuse	0 T Roosevelt Grier
34	Virginia	7 G Sam Green / Sam Valentine
14	West Virginia	19 C Don Balthaser / Frank Reich
7	TCU	20 G Earl Shumaker
35	Pennsylvania	13 T Otto Kneidinger
39	Holy Cross	7 E Jim Garrity
37	Rutgers	14 QB Bobby Hoffman
13	Pittsburgh	0 HB Lenny Moore
		HB Ron Younker
		FB Bill Straub

RUSHING: Moore 136/1082y
PASSING: Bailey 33-80/393y, 4TD, 41.3%
RECEIVING: Sherry 11/160y
SCORING: Moore 78pts

1955 5-4

35	Boston Univ.	0 E Paul North / Ned Finkbeiner
6	Army	35 T Otto Kneidinger / Walt Mazur
26	Virginia	7 G Sam Valentine / Dick DeLuca
14	Navy	34 C Frank Reich / Ed Kleinst
7	West Virginia	21 G Earl Shumaker / John Arnst
20	Penn	0 T Jack Calderone
21	Syracuse	20 E Les Walters / Jack Farls
34	Rutgers	13 QB Bobby Hoffman / Milt Plum
0	Pittsburgh	20 HB Lenny Moore
		HB Billy Kane / Bobby Allen
		FB Bill Straub / Frank Della Penna

RUSHING: Moore 138/697y
PASSING: Hoffman 25-53/355y, TD, 47.2%
RECEIVING: Kane 9/184y
SCORING: Moore & Plum (QB-K) 30pts

1956 6-2-1

34	Pennsylvania	0 E Les Walters / Paul North
7	Army	14 T Walt Mazur
43	Holy Cross	0 G Sam Valentine / Joe Sabal
7	Ohio State	6 C Dan Radakovich / Steve Garban
16	West Virginia	6 G Dick DeLuca / John Arnst
9	Syracuse	13 T Jack Calderone / Clint Law
40	Boston Univ.	7 E Jack Farls / Doug Mechling
14	N. Carolina St.	7 QB Milt Plum / Al Jacks
7	Pittsburgh	7 HB Dave Kasparian / Bruce Gilmore
		HB Billy Kane
		FB Emil Caprara / Maurice Schleicher

RUSHING: Kane 105/544y
PASSING: Plum 40-75/675y, 6TD, 53.3%
RECEIVING: Kane 16/232y
SCORING: Kane 42pts

1957 6-3

19	Pennsylvania	14 E Les Walters / Paul North
13	Army	27 T Bill Wehmer
21	William & Mary	13 G Joe Sabal / Bud Kohlhaas
20	Vanderbilt	32 C Charlie Ruslavage / Steve Garban
20	Syracuse	12 G Richie McMillen
27	West Virginia	6 T Joe Bohart / Andy Stynchula
20	Marquette	7 E Jack Farls / Ron Markiewicz
14	Holy Cross	10 QB Al Jacks / Richie Lucas
13	Pittsburgh	14 HB Dave Kasparian / Bruce Gilmore
		HB Andy Moconyi / Fran Paolone
		FB Maurice Schleicher / Emil Caprara

RUSHING: Kasperian 122/469y
PASSING: Jacks 53-103/673y, 5TD, 51.5%
RECEIVING: Walters 24/440y
SCORING: Kasparian 48pts

1958 6-3-1

7	Nebraska	14 E Maurice Schleicher
43	Pennsylvania	0 T Tom Mulraney / Bill Wehmer
0	Army	26 G Charlie Ruslavage / Sam Stellatella
40	Marquette	8 C Steve Garban
34	Boston Univ.	0 G Bill Popp
6	Syracuse	14 T Andy Stynchula / Joe Bohart
36	Furman	0 E Norm Neff / John Bozick
14	West Virginia	14 QB Richie Lucas / Al Jacks
32	Holy Cross	0 HB Dave Kasparian / Bruce Gilmore
25	Pittsburgh	21 HB Jim Kerr / Don Jonas
		FB Pat Botula / Andy Moconyi

RUSHING: Kasparian 98/381y, Botula 82/342y, Gilmore 52/288y
PASSING: Lucas 36-80/483y, 3TD, 45%,
  Jacks 27-69/285, TD, 39.1%
RECEIVING: Schleicher 9/127y, Kapsarian 9/107y, Neff 9/106y
SCORING: Kasparian 46pts, Lucas 40pts, Kerr (HB-K) 30pts

1959 9-2

19	Missouri	8 E Henry Oppermann / John Bozick
21	VMI	0 T Andy Stynchula / Charles Janerette
58	Colgate	20 G Bud Kohlhaas / Sam Stellatella
17	Army	11 C Jay Huffman
21	Boston Univ.	12 G Bill Popp / Frank Korbini
20	Illinois	9 T Tom Mulraney / Stew Barber
28	West Virginia	10 E Norm Neff / Bob Mitinger
18	Syracuse	20 QB Richie Lucas / Galen Hall
46	Holy Cross	0 HB Dick Hoak/Roger Kochman/Dick Pae
7	Pittsburgh	22 HB Jim Kerr / Ed Caye
7	Alabama■	0 FB Pat Botula / Sam Sobczak

RUSHING: Lucas 99/325y
PASSING: Lucas 58-117/913y, 5TD, 49.6%
RECEIVING: Hoak 14/167y
SCORING: Lucas & Kerr (HB-K) 36pts

1960 7-3

20	Boston Univ.	0 E Henry Oppermann / Dave Robinson
8	Missouri	21 T Stew Barber / Charlie Sieminski
27	Army	16 G Dick Wilson / Joe Blasentine
15	Syracuse	21 C Jay Huffman / Bill Saul
8	Illinois	10 G Bill Popp
34	West Virginia	13 T Jim Smith / Gerry Farkas
28	Maryland	9 E Jim Schwab / Bob Mitinger /Dave Truitt
33	Holy Cross	8 QB Galen Hall / Dick Hoak
14	Pittsburgh	3 HB Don Jonas / Ed Caye / Al Gurski
41	Oregon■	12 HB Jim Kerr / Dick Pae
		FB Sam Sobczak/Dave Hayes/B'dy Torris

RUSHING: Kerr 93/389y, Sobczak 70/287y, Hoak 66/284y
PASSING: Hall 39-89/448y, 5TD, 43.8%,
  Hoak 25-46/396y, 5TD, 54.3%
RECEIVING: Kerr 13/163y, Oppermann 13/131y, Truitt 6/100y,
  Jonas 6/87y
SCORING: Kerr (HB-K) 52pts, Gursky, Opperman & Torris 18pts

1961 8-3

20	Navy	10 E Jim Schwab / Dave Robinson
8	Miami	25 T Charlie Sieminski / Terry Monaghan
32	Boston Univ.	0 G Joe Blasentine
6	Army	10 C Jay Huffman / Bill Saul
14	Syracuse	0 G Harrison Rosdahl / Dick Wilson
33	California	16 T Jim Smith / Gerry Farkas
17	Maryland	21 E Bob Mitinger / Dick Anderson
20	West Virginia	6 QB Galen Hall / Pete Liske / Don Caum
31	Holy Cross	14 HB Roger Kochman / Al Gursky
47	Pittsburgh	26 HB Don Jonas / Junior Powell
30	Georgia Tech■	15 FB Buddy Torris / Dave Hayes

RUSHING: Kochman 129/666y, Torris 105/490y, Hayes 66/253y
PASSING: Hall 50-97/951y, 8TD, 51.5%
RECEIVING: Schwab 16/257y, Powell 15/332y,
  Kochman 10/226y
SCORING: Kochman 56pts, Jonas 47pts, Torris 24pts

1962 9-2

41	Navy	7 E Dick Anderson / Bud Yost
20	Air Force	6 T Charlie Sieminski
18	Rice	7 G Joe Blasentine / Bernie Sabol
6	Army	9 C Joe Galardi / Jim Williams
20	Syracuse	19 G Harrison Rosdahl / Glenn Ressler
23	California	21 T Terry Monaghan / Gerry Farkas
23	Maryland	7 E Dave Robinson / Bill Bowes
34	West Virginia	6 QB Pete Liske / Ron Coates
48	Holy Cross	20 HB Roger Kochman / Frank Hershey
16	Pittsburgh	0 HB Junior Powell / Al Gursky
7	Florida■	17 FB Dave Hayes / Buddy Torris

RUSHING: Kochman 120/652y, Hayes 74/291y, Torris 64/264y
PASSING: Liske 91-162/1037y, 12TD, 56.2%
RECEIVING: Powell 32/303y, Robinson 17/178y, Gursky 16/152y
SCORING: Kochman 48pts, Hayes 42pts, Powell 38pts

1963 7-3

17	Oregon	7 E Bill Bowes / Don Caum
17	UCLA	14 T Sandy Buchan
28	Rice	7 G Glenn Ressler / Ed Stewart
7	Army	10 C Ralph Baker
0	Syracuse	9 G Bernie Sabol
20	West Virginia	9 T John Simko / John Deibert
17	Maryland	15 E Dick Anderson / Jerry Sandusky
10	Ohio State	7 QB Pete Liske / Ron Coates
28	Holy Cross	14 HB Junior Powell/Chris Weber/Joe Vargo
21	Pittsburgh	22 HB Gary Klingensmith / Frank Hershey
		FB Ed Stuckrath / Tom Urbanik

RUSHING: Klingensmith 102/450y, Stuckrath 62/306y,
  Urbanik 66/236y
PASSING: Liske 87-161/1117y, 10TD, 54.0%
RECEIVING: Anderson 21/229y, Caum 18/371y, Powell 18/231y
SCORING: Coates (QB-K) 33pts, Klingensmith 24pts,
  Caum 24pts

1964 6-4

8	Navy	21 E Bill Huber / Jerry Sandusky
14	UCLA	21 T Joe Bellas / John Deibert
14	Oregon	22 G Chuck Ehlinger / Ellery Seitz
6	Army	2 C Glenn Ressler / Bob Andronici
14	Syracuse	21 G Ed Stewart / Steve Schreckengaust
37	West Virginia	8 T John Simko
17	Maryland	9 E Bill Bowes / Bud Yost
27	Ohio State	0 QB Gary Wydman / Dick Gingrich (DB)
24	Houston	7 HB Gary Klingensmith / Mike Irwin
28	Pittsburgh	0 HB Don Kunit / Joe Vargo (DB)
		FB Tom Urbanik / Ed Stuckrath

RUSHING: Urbanik 134/625y
PASSING: Wydman 70-149/832y, TD, 47.0%
RECEIVING: Huber 25/347y
SCORING: Urbanik 48pts

1965 5-5

0	Michigan State	23 E Bill Huber
22	UCLA	24 T Joe Bellas
17	Boston College	0 G Chuck Ehlinger
21	Syracuse	28 C Bob Andronici / Bill Lenkaitis (T)
44	West Virginia	6 G Steve Schreckengaust
17	California	21 T Gary Eberle / Ed Lenda
21	Kent State	6 E Jack Curry
14	Navy	6 QB Jack White / Tom Sherman
27	Pittsburgh	30 HB Don Kunit / Roger Grimes
19	Maryland	7 HB Mike Irwin (DB)
		FB Dave McNaughton / Dirk Nye
		DL Rich Buzin
		DL Dave Rowe / Mike McBath
		DL Bryan Hondru / Tom McGrath
		DL Jerry Sandusky
		LB John Runnells
		LB Jim Kollar
		LB Bob Kane / Jim Litterelle
		DB Bob Riggle
		DB John Sladki
		DB Dick Gingrich
		DB Bob Capretto

RUSHING: McNaughton 193/884y, Kunit 94/425y, Irwin 56/398y
PASSING: White 98-205/1275y, 6TD, 47.8%
RECEIVING: Curry 42/572y, Irwin 17/217y, Huber 15/192y
SCORING: Irwin 42pts, McNaughton 42pts,
  Sherman (QB-K) 36pts

1966 5-5

15 Maryland	7 WR Jack Curry
8 Michigan State	42 T John Kulka
0 Army	11 G Jim Kollar
30 Boston College	21 C Bill Lenkaitis
11 UCLA	49 G Bryan Hondru
38 West Virginia	6 T Rich Buzin / John Sain
33 California	15 TE Ted Kwalick
10 Syracuse	12 QB Tom Sherman (DB) / Jack White
0 Georgia Tech	21 TB Bobby Campbell
48 Pittsburgh	24 WB Mike Irwin / Roger Grimes
	FB Dan Lucyk / Bill Rettig
	DL Bill Morgan
	DL Mike McBath
	DL Mike Reid
	DL Dave Rowe / Tom McGrath
	DL Frank Pringle / Bob Vukmer
	LB John Runnells
	LB Jim McCormick
	LB Jim Litterelle
	DB John Sladki
	DB Tim Montgomery
	DB Bob Capretto

RUSHING: Campbell 79/482y, Lucyk 91/480y, Irwin 48/205y
PASSING: Sherman 58-135/943y, 6TD, 42.9%
RECEIVING: Curry 34/584y, Kwalick 22/377y, Irwin 13/182y
SCORING: Sherman (QB-K) 57pts, Campbell 42pts,
Kwalick 26pts

1967 8-2-1

22 Navy	23 WR Jack Curry
17 Miami	8 T John Kulka
15 UCLA	17 G Bob Yowell / Don Coccoli
50 Boston College	28 C Bill Lenkaitis
21 West Virginia	14 G Dave Bradley
29 Syracuse	20 T Rich Buzin
38 Maryland	3 TE Ted Kwalick
13 N. Carolina St.	8 QB Tom Sherman
35 Ohio University	14 HB Charlie Pittman / Bobby Campbell
42 Pittsburgh	6 HB Paul Johnson
17 Florida State■	17 FB Don Abbey / Dan Lucyk
	DL Frank Spaziani / Frank Pringle
	DL Jim Letterelle
	DL Mike McBath
	DL Dave Rakiecki / Tom McGrath
	DL Steve Smear
	LB Dennis Onkontz
	LB Jim Kates / Jim McCormick
	LB Pete Johnson
	DB Neal Smith
	DB Tim Montgomery
	DB Bob Capretto

RUSHING: Pittman 119/580y, Abbey 93/386y, Campbell 36/247y
PASSING: Sherman 104-205/1616y, 13TD, 50.7%
RECEIVING: Curry 41/681y, Kwalick 33/563y, Abbey 10/148y
SCORING: Abbey 88pts, Pittman 42pts, Kwalick 28pts

1968 11-0

31 Navy	6 WR Leon Angevine / Charlie Wilson
25 Kansas State	9 T John Kulka
31 West Virginia	20 G Charlie Zapiec
21 UCLA	6 C Warren Koegel
29 Boston College	0 G Tom Jackson
28 Army	24 T Dave Bradley / Dave Mercinko
22 Miami	7 TE Ted Kwalick
57 Maryland	13 QB Chuck Burkhart
65 Pittsburgh	9 HB Bobby Campbell
30 Syracuse	12 HB Charlie Pittman
15 Kansas■	14 FB Tom Cherry
	DL Frank Spaziani
	DL Mike Reid / John Ebersole
	DL Steve Smear
	DL Lincoln Lippincott
	LB Dennis Onkontz
	LB Jim Kates
	LB Gary Hull / Dave Rakiecki
	LB Jack Ham / Pete Johnson
	DB Paul Johnson
	DB Mike Smith / George Landis
	DB Neal Smith

RUSHING: Pittman 186/950y, Campbell 127/751y,
Cherry 77/256y
PASSING: Burkhart 87-177/1170y, 6TD, 49.2%
RECEIVING: Kwalick 31/403y, Angevine 17/226y,
Pittman 14/196y
SCORING: Pittman 84pts, Campbell 44pts,
Bob Garthwaite (K) 43pts

1969 11-0

45 Navy	22 WR Greg Edmonds
27 Colorado	3 T Vic Surma
17 Kansas State	14 G Bob Holuba
20 West Virginia	0 C Warren Koegel
15 Syracuse	14 G Charlie Zapiec
42 Ohio University	3 T Tom Jackson
38 Boston College	16 TE Pete Johnson
48 Maryland	0 QB Chuck Burkhart / Mike Cooper
27 Pittsburgh	7 HB Charlie Pittman / Gary Deuel
33 N. Carolina St.	8 HB Lydell Mitchell
10 Missouri■	3 FB Franco Harris
	DL Gary Hull / Dave Rakiecki
	DL Mike Reid
	DL Steve Smear
	DL John Ebersole
	LB Jack Ham
	LB Mike Smith
	LB Jim Kates / Dave Radakovich
	LB Dennis Onkontz
	DB Paul Johnson
	DB George Landis
	DB Neal Smith

RUSHING: Pittman 134/751y, Harris 115/643y, Mitchell 113/616y
PASSING: Burkhart 59-114/805y, TD, 51.8%
RECEIVING: Edmonds 20/246y, Mitchell 13/206y, Harris 12/189y
SCORING: Pittman 66pts, Harris 64pts, Mike Reitz (K) 54pts

1970 7-3

55 Navy	7 WR Greg Edmonds / John Skarzynski
13 Colorado	41 T Vic Surma
16 Wisconsin	29 G Bob Holuba
28 Boston College	3 C Warren Koegel
7 Syracuse	24 G Bob Knechtel
38 Army	14 T Dave Joyner
42 West Virginia	8 TE Jim McCord / John Hull
34 Maryland	0 QB J.Hufnagel/Mike Cooper/Bob Parsons
32 Ohio University	22 HB Lydell Mitchell
35 Pittsburgh	15 HB Joel Ramich / Gary Deuel
	FB Franco Harris
	DL Bruce Bannon
	DL Frank Ahrenhold / Doug Allen
	DL Jim Heller
	DL Steve Prue / Marshall Wagner
	LB Jack Ham
	LB Gary Hull
	LB John Skorupan
	LB Gary Gray
	DB George Landis
	DB Mike Smith
	DB Gregg Ducatte

RUSHING: Mitchell 134/751y, Harris 142/675y, Ramich 90/353y
PASSING: Cooper 32-64/429y, 4TD, 50.0%,
Parsons 30-61/353y, 3TD, 49.2%,
Hufnagel 24-56/321y, TD, 42.9%
RECEIVING: Edmonds 38/506y, Skarzynski 12/165y,
Mitchell 9/110y
SCORING: Harris 48pts, Edmonds 36pts, Mitchell 36pts

1971 11-1

56 Navy	3 WR Scott Skarzynski
44 Iowa	14 T Craig Lyle
16 Air Force	14 G Carl Schaukowitch
42 Army	0 C Don Gersh / Mike Botts
31 Syracuse	0 G Bob Knechtel
66 Texas Christian	14 T Dave Joyner
35 West Virginia	7 TE Bob Parsons / Gary Debes
63 Maryland	27 QB John Hufnagel
35 N. Carolina St.	3 HB Lydell Mitchell
55 Pittsburgh	18 WB Glen Cole
11 Tennessee	31 FB Franco Harris / Tom Donchez
30 Texas■	6 DL Bruce Bannon / Gary Hager
	DL Frank Ahrenhold / Jack Aumiller
	DL Jim Heller / John Booth
	DL Jim Laslavic
	LB Charlie Zapiec / Ed O'Neil
	LB Tom Hull
	LB Gary Gray / Jim Trent
	LB John Skorupan / Paul Pasqualoni
	DB Chuck Mesko / John Cappelletti
	DB Buddy Ellis
	DB Gregg Ducatte

RUSHING: Mitchell 254/1567y, Harris 123/684y,
Hufnagel 79/346y
PASSING: Hufnagel 86-136/1185y, 10TD, 63.2%
RECEIVING: Parsons 30/489y, Mitchell 16/154y,
Skarzynski 12/204y
SCORING: Mitchell 174pts, Alberto Vitiello (K) 74pts,
Harris 42pts

1972 10-2

21 Tennessee	28 WR Scott Skarzynski / Jimmy Scott
21 Navy	10 WR Gary Hayman
14 Iowa	10 T Paul Gabel
35 Illinois	17 G Carl Schaukowitch
45 Army	0 C Jack Baiorunos
17 Syracuse	0 G Mark Markovich / Phil LaPorta
28 West Virginia	19 T Charlie Getty
46 Maryland	16 TE Don Natale / Bob Rickenbach
37 N. Carolina St.	22 QB John Hufnagel
45 Boston College	26 TB John Cappelletti / Walt Addie
49 Pittsburgh	27 FB Bob Nagle
0 Oklahoma■	14 DL Bruce Bannon
	DL Randy Crowder
	DL Jim Heller / Mike Hartenstine
	DL Dave Graf / Gary Hager
	LB John Skorupan
	LB Ed O'Neil / Chris Devlin
	LB Jim Laslavic
	LB Larry Ludwig / Tom Hull
	DB Buddy Ellis
	DB Jack Koniszewski / Steve Davis
	DB Gregg Ducatte

RUSHING: Cappelletti 233/1117y, Addie 64/314y, Nagle 57/238y
PASSING: Hufnagel 115-216/2039y, 15TD, 53.5%
RECEIVING: Natale 30/460y, Cappelletti 16/138y,
Hayman 14/205y
SCORING: Cappelletti 78pts, Alberto Vitiello (K) 63pts,
Hufnagel 38pts

1973 12-0

20 Stanford	6 WR Gary Hayman
39 Navy	0 WR Chuck Herd / Jimmy Scott
27 Iowa	8 T Phil LaPorta
19 Air Force	9 G John Nessel / Paul Gabel
54 Army	3 C Jack Baiorunos
49 Syracuse	6 G Mark Markovich
62 West Virginia	14 T Charlie Getty
42 Maryland	22 TE Dan Natale / Gary Debes
35 N. Carolina St.	29 QB Tom Shuman
49 Ohio University	10 TB John Cappelletti / Walt Addie
35 Pittsburgh	13 FB Bob Nagle / Tom Donchez
16 LSU■	9 DL Greg Murphy
	DL Mike Hartenstine
	DL Randy Crowder
	DL Dave Graf
	LB Chris Devlin
	LB Tom Hull
	LB Doug Allen
	LB Ed O'Neil
	DB Buddy Ellis
	DB Jim Bradley
	DB Scott Mitchell

RUSHING: Cappelletti 286/1522y, Nagle 77/343y, Addie 43/311y
PASSING: Shuman 83-161/1375y, 13TD, 51.6%
RECEIVING: Hayman 30/525y, Natale 21/359y, Herd 10/197y
SCORING: Cappelletti 102pts, Chris Bahr (K) 70pts, Nagle 42pts

1974 10-2

24 Stanford	20 WR Jim Eaise / Jerry Jeram
6 Navy	7 T Brad Benson
27 Iowa	0 G Tom Rafferty
21 Army	14 C Jack Baiorunos
55 Wake Forest	0 G George Reihner / Mark Thomas
30 Syracuse	14 T Jeff Bleamer
21 West Virginia	12 TE Dan Natale
24 Maryland	17 QB Tom Shuman
7 N. Carolina St.	12 TB Woody Petchel / Walt Addie
35 Ohio University	16 WB Jimmy Cefalo
31 Pittsburgh	10 FB Tom Donchez / Duane Taylor
41 Baylor■	20 DL Greg Murphy
	DL Mike Hartenstine
	DL John Quinn
	DL Dennis Zmudzin
	LB Chris Devlin
	LB Greg Buttle
	LB Rich Kriston / Kurt Allerman
	LB Buddy Tesner
	DB Tom Odell
	DB Mike Johnson
	DB Jim Bradley / Jim Hite

RUSHING: Donchez 195/880y, Taylor 81/412y, Cefalo 53/328y
PASSING: Shuman 97-183/1355y, 12TD, 53.0%
RECEIVING: Jeram 17/259y, Donchez 17/176y, Natale 16/219y
SCORING: Donchez 48pts, Taylor 36pts, Reihner 36pts

1975 9-3

26 Temple	25 WR Dick Barvinchak / Tom Donovan
34 Stanford	14 WR Jimmy Cefalo
9 Ohio State	17 T Brad Benson
30 Iowa	10 G Tom Rafferty / Greg Kubas
10 Kentucky	3 C Ron Argenta / Rich Knechtel
39 West Virginia	0 G George Reihner / Mark Thomas
19 Syracuse	7 T Dave Shukri
31 Army	0 TE Dave Stutts / Mickey Shuler
15 Maryland	13 QB John Andress
14 N. Carolina St.	15 TB Woody Petchel / Rich Mauti
7 Pittsburgh	6 FB Duane Taylor / Larry Suhey
6 Alabama■	13 DL Ron Crosby / Bill Banks
	DL Ron Coder / Greg Christian
	DL John Quinn / Mark Ewing
	DL Dennis Zmudzin
	LB Kurt Allerman
	LB Greg Buttle
	LB Jim Rosecrans / Randy Sidler
	LB Ron Hostetler / Tom DePaso
	DB Tom Odell / Bernard Robinson
	DB Mike Johnson / John Bush
	DB Gary Petercuskie

RUSHING: Petchel 148/621y, Taylor 123/556y, Geise 54/252y
PASSING: Andress 71-149/991y, 2TD, 47.7%
RECEIVING: Barvinchak 17/327y, Shuler 12/135y, Donovan 12/130y
SCORING: Chris Bahr (K) 73pts, Petchel 30pts, Mauti & Taylor 24pts

1976 7-5

15 Stanford	12 WR Tom Donovan / Scott Fitzkee
7 Ohio State	12 WR Jimmy Cefalo
6 Iowa	7 T Brad Benson
6 Kentucky	22 G Greg Kubas
38 Army	16 C Keith Dorney
27 Syracuse	3 G George Reihner (DL) / Tony Williott
33 West Virginia	0 T Paul Renaud
31 Temple	30 TE Mickey Shuler
41 N. Carolina St.	20 QB Chuck Fusina / John Andress
21 Miami	7 TB Steve Geise / Mike Guman
7 Pittsburgh	24 FB Matt Suhey / Bob Torrey
9 Notre Dame■	20 DL Bill Banks
	DL Matt Millen / Bruce Clark
	DL Randy Sidler / Tony Petruccio
	DL Joe Lally
	LB Ron Hostetler
	LB Rick Donaldson
	LB Tom DePaso
	LB Paul Suhey / Doug Hostetler
	DB Neil Hutton
	DB Bill Crummy
	DB Gary Petercuskie

RUSHING: Geise 116/560y, Suhey 125/487y, Guman 95/470y
PASSING: Fusina 88-167/1260y, 11TD, 52.7%
RECEIVING: Shuler 21/281y, Cefalo 14/295y, Donovan 13/258y
SCORING: Guman 48pts, Cappozzoli 43pts, Suhey 32pts

1977 11-1

45 Rutgers	7 WR Scott Fitzkee / Bob Bassett
31 Houston	14 WR Jimmy Cefalo
27 Maryland	9 T Keith Dorney
20 Kentucky	24 G Marty Sierocinski
16 Utah State	7 C Chuck Correal
31 Syracuse	24 G Eric Cunningham
49 West Virginia	28 T Irv Pankey
49 Miami	7 TE Mickey Shuler
21 N. Carolina St.	17 QB Chuck Fusina
44 Temple	7 TB Steve Geise / Mike Guman
15 Pittsburgh	13 FB Matt Suhey / Bob Torrey
42 Arizona State■	30 DL Bill Banks
	DL Bruce Clark
	DL Randy Sidler / Tony Petruccio
	DL Matt Millen
	DL Joe Lally / Fred Ragucci
	LB Ron Hostetler / Tom DePaso
	LB Rick Donaldson
	LB Paul Suhey / Lance Mehl
	DB Neil Hutton / Karl McCoy
	DB Grover Edwards
	DB Gary Petercuskie

RUSHING: Suhey 139/638y, Geise 143/550y, Torrey 78/456y
PASSING: Fusina 142-246/2221y, 15TD, 57.7%
RECEIVING: Shuler 33/600y, Cefalo 28/507y, Fitzkee 18/372y
SCORING: Matt Bahr (K) 81pts, Suhey 48pts, Cefalo 48pts

1978 11-1

10 Temple	7 WR Scott Fitzkee / Scott Hettinger
26 Rutgers	10 WR Tom Donovan / Bob Bassett
19 Ohio State	0 T Keith Dorney
26 SMU	21 G Jim Romano
58 TCU	0 C Chuck Correal
30 Kentucky	0 G Eric Cunningham
45 Syracuse	15 T Paul Renaud / Jim Brown
49 West Virginia	21 TE Irv Pankey
27 Maryland	3 QB Chuck Fusina
19 N. Carolina St.	10 TB Matt Suhey / Mike Guman (DB)
17 Pittsburgh	10 FB Booker Moore / Bob Torrey
7 Alabama■	14 DL Larry Kubin
	DL Bruce Clark
	DL Matt Millen / Greg Jones
	DL Joe Lally
	LB Lance Mehl / Doug Hostetler
	LB Steve Griffiths
	LB Rick Donaldson
	LB Paul Suhey / Micky Urquhart
	DB Karl McCoy
	DB Grover Edwards / Tom Wise
	DB Pete Harris

RUSHING: Suhey 184/720y, Moore 143/602y, Guman 91/351y
PASSING: Fusina 137-242/1859y, 11TD, 56.6%
RECEIVING: Fitzkee 37/630y, Guman 18/181y, Bassett 15/285y
SCORING: Matt Bahr (K) 97pts

1979 8-4

45 Rutgers	10 WR Scott Hettinger / Tom Wise
14 Texas A&M	27 WR Tom Donovan
17 Nebraska	42 T Bill Dugan
27 Maryland	7 G Mike Munchak
24 Army	3 C Bob Jagers / Jim Romano
35 Syracuse	7 G Sean Farrell
31 West Virginia	6 T Irv Pankey
10 Miami	26 TE Brad Scovill
9 N. Carolina St.	7 QB Dayle Tate / Frank Rocco
22 Temple	7 TB Matt Suhey / Curt Warner
14 Pittsburgh	29 FB Booker Moore
9 Tulane■	6 DL Larry Kubin
	DL Bruce Clark / Pete Kugler
	DL Greg Jones
	DL Matt Millen / Leo Wisniewski
	DL Gene Gladys
	LB Lance Mehl
	LB Steve Griffiths / Rick Donaldson
	DB Karl McCoy / Grover Edwards
	DB Giuseppe Harris
	DB Matt Bradley
	DB Micky Urquhart

RUSHING: Suhey 185/973y, Moore 131/555y, Warner 84/391y
PASSING: Tate 92-176/1179y, 8TD, 52.3%
RECEIVING: Scovill 26/331y, Donovan 21/254y, Suhey 13/99y
SCORING: Herb Menhardt (K) 70pts, Moore 54pts, Suhey 42pts

1980 10-2

54 Colgate	10 WR Tom Wise/Kevin Baugh/Gr'gg Garrity
25 Texas A&M	9 WR Micky Urquhart / Kenny Jackson
7 Nebraska	21 T Bill Dugan / Bill Contz
29 Missouri	21 G John Wojtowicz
24 Maryland	10 C Bob Jagers / Jim Romano
20 West Virginia	15 G Sean Farrell
27 Miami	12 T Dave Laube
21 N. Carolina St.	13 TE Brad Scovill/V'to Kab/Mike McCloskey
50 Temple	7 QB Todd Blackledge / Jeff Hostetler
9 Pittsburgh	14 TB Curt Warner / Joel Coles
31 Ohio State■	19 FB Booker Moore / Mike Meade
	DL Gene Gladys / Larry Kubin
	DL Leo Wisniewski
	DL Greg Jones
	DL Pete Kugler / Frank Case
	DL Rich D'Amico / Walker Lee Ashley
	LB Chet Parlavecchio
	LB Steve Griffiths / Ed Pryts
	DB Grover Edwards / Guiseppe Harris
	DB Paul Lankford
	DB Matt Bradley
	DB Pete Harris / Dan Biondi

RUSHING: Warner 196/922y, Moore 120/707y, Coles 75/406y
PASSING: Blackledge 76-159/1037y, 7TD, 47.8%, Hostetler 18-42/247y, TD, 42.9%
RECEIVING: Jackson 21/386y, Scovil 18/277y, Baugh 13/188y, Warner 13/92y
SCORING: Herb Menhardt (K) 71pts, Warner 48pts, Jackson 30pts

1981 10-2

52 Cincinnati	0 WR Kenny Jackson
30 Nebraska	24 WR Kevin Baugh / Gregg Garrity
30 Temple	0 T Bill Contz / Jim Brown
38 Boston College	7 G Mike Munchak
41 Syracuse	16 C Jim Romano
30 West Virginia	7 G Sean Farrell
14 Miami	17 T Dave Laube
22 N. Carolina St.	15 TE Mike McCloskey / Vito Kab
16 Alabama	31 QB Todd Blackledge
24 Notre Dame	21 TB Curt Warner
48 Pittsburgh	14 FB Jon Williams / Mike Meade
26 Southern Cal■	10 DL Rich D'Amico / Ken Kelley
	DL Leo Wisniewski
	DL Dave Opfar / Pete Speros (OG)
	DL Greg Gattuso
	DL Walker Lee Ashley
	LB Chet Parlavecchio
	LB Ed Pryts / Scott Radecic
	DB Guiseppe Harris
	DB Paul Lankford
	DB Matt Bradley / Harry Hamilton
	DB Dan Biondi

RUSHING: Warner 171/1044y, Williams 142/667y, Meade 100/475y
PASSING: Blackledge 104-207/1557y, 12TD, 50.2%
RECEIVING: Garrity 23/415y, McCloskey 20/308y, Jackson 19/440y
SCORING: Brian Franco (K) 81pts, Warner 48pts, Williams 42pts

1982 11-1

31 Temple	14 WR Gregg Garrity / Kevin Baugh
39 Maryland	31 WR Kenny Jackson
49 Rutgers	14 T Bill Contz / Stan Short
27 Nebraska	24 G Dick Maginnis
21 Alabama	42 C Mark Battaglia
28 Syracuse	7 G Pete Speros / Dave Laube
24 West Virginia	0 T Ron Heller
52 Boston College	17 TE Mike McCloskey / Kirk Bowman
54 N. Carolina St.	0 QB Todd Blackledge
24 Notre Dame	14 TB Curt Warner / Skeeter Nichols
19 Pittsburgh	10 FB Jon Williams / Joel Coles
27 Georgia■	23 DL Walker Lee Ashley
	DL Dave Opfar / Joe Hines
	DL Greg Gattuso
	DL Ken Kelley / Steve Sefter
	LB Al Harris / Carmen Masciantonio
	LB Scott Radecic
	LB Dave Paffenroth / Rogers Alexander
	DB Chris Sydnor / Mike Zordich
	DB Roger Jackson
	DB Mark Robinson / Dan Biondi
	DB Harry Hamilton / Brian McCann

RUSHING: Warner 198/1041y, Williams 110/609y, Nichols 40/228y
PASSING: Blackledge 161-292/2218y, 22TD, 55.1%
RECEIVING: Jackson 41/697y, Garrity 32/509y, Warner 24/335y
SCORING: Warner 78pts, Nick Gancitano (K) 56pts, Jackson 48pts

1983 8-4-1

6 Nebraska	44 WR Kenny Jackson
3 Cincinnati	14 WR Kevin Baugh
34 Iowa	42 T Stan Short
23 Temple	18 G Jeff Woofter
36 Rutgers	25 C Nick Haden
34 Alabama	28 G Todd Moules (DL) / Dick Maginnis
17 Syracuse	6 T Ron Heller
41 West Virginia	23 TE Dean DiMidio / Kirk Bowman
17 Boston College	27 QB Doug Strang / Dan Lonergan
38 Brown	21 TB D. J. Dozier / Tony Mumford
34 Notre Dame	30 FB Jon Williams
24 Pittsburgh	24 DL Bob White
13 Washington■	10 DL Joe Hines / Mike Russo
	DL Greg Gattuso
	LB Chris Collins
	LB Scott Radecic
	LB Carmen Masciantonio
	LB Shane Conlin / Rogers Alexander
	DB Michael Zordich
	DB Lance Hamilton / Mark Fruehan
	DB Harry Hamilton
	DB Chris Sydnor / Mark Robinson

RUSHING: Dozier 174/1002y, Williams 115/590y, Mumford 74/331y
PASSING: Strang 134-259/1944y, 19TD, 51.7%
RECEIVING: Baugh 36/547y, Jackson 28/483y, DiMidio 19/355y, Dozier 19/189y
SCORING: Nick Gancitano (K) 85pts, Dozier 48pts, Jackson 48pts

1984 6-5

15 Rutgers	12 WR Herb Bellamy
20 Iowa	17 WR Rocky Washington / Eric Hamilton
56 William & Mary	18 T Stan Short
3 Texas	28 G Jeff Woofter
25 Maryland	24 C Nick Haden / Keith Radecic
0 Alabama	6 G Mitch Frerotte
21 Syracuse	3 T Chris Conlin
14 West Virginia	17 TE Dean DiMidio / Brian Siverling
37 Boston College	30 QB Doug Strang / John Shaffer
7 Notre Dame	44 TB Tony Mumford / D.J. Dozier
11 Pittsburgh	31 FB Steve Smith / Tim Manoa
	DL Bob White
	DL Mike Russo
	DL Todd Moules / Mike Garrett
	DL Dan Morgan
	LB Shane Conlin / Rogers Alexander
	LB Carmen Masciantonio / Chris Collins
	LB Don Graham / Trey Bauer
	DB Chris Sydnor / Duffy Cobbs
	DB Lance Hamilton
	DB Michael Zordich / Drew Bycoskie
	DB Ray Isom

RUSHING: Dozier 125/691y,
PASSING: Strang 134-259/1944y, 5TD, 51.7%
RECEIVING: Bellamy 16/306y
SCORING: Nick Gancitano (K) 49pts

1985 11-1

20 Maryland	18 WR Ray Roundtree / Darrell Giles
27 Temple	25 WR Eric Hamilton / Michael Timpson
17 East Carolina	10 T Mark Sickler / Stan Clayton
17 Rutgers	10 G Mitch Frerotte
19 Alabama	17 C Rob Smith / Keith Radecic (G)
24 Syracuse	20 G Todd Moules
27 West Virginia	0 T Chris Conlin / Dan Morgan
16 Boston College	12 TE Dean DiMidio / Brian Siverling
31 Cincinnati	10 QB John Shaffer
36 Notre Dame	6 TB D.J. Dozier
31 Pittsburgh	0 FB Steve Smith / Tim Manoa
10 Oklahoma■	25 DL Bob White
	DL Mike Russo
	DL Tim Johnson
	DL Don Graham
	LB Shane Conlin
	LB Trey Bauer / Bob Ontko
	LB Rogers Alexander / Pete Giftopoulos
	DB Duffy Cobbs
	DB Lance Hamilton / Eddie Johnson
	DB Michael Zordich
	DB Ray Isom

RUSHING: Dozier 154/723y
PASSING: Shaffer 103-228/1366y, 8TD, 45.2%
RECEIVING: Roundtree 15/285y
SCORING: Massimo Manca (K) 91pts,

1986 12-0

45 Temple	15 WR Ray Roundtree / Darrell Giles
26 Boston College	14 WR Eric Hamilton / Michael Timpson
42 East Carolina	17 T Mark Sickler / Stan Clayton
31 Rutgers	6 G Steve Wisniewski / Rich Kuzy
23 Cincinnati	17 C Keith Radecic
42 Syracuse	3 G Dan Morgan
23 Alabama	3 T Chris Conlin
19 West Virginia	0 TE Brian Siverling / Bob Mrosko
17 Maryland	15 QB John Shaffer
24 Notre Dame	19 TB D.J. Dozier / Blair Thomas
34 Pittsburgh	14 FB Steve Smith / Tim Manoa
14 Miami■	10 DL Bob White
	DL Mike Russo / Matt Johnson
	DL Tim Johnson / Pete Curkendall
	LB Don Graham
	LB Trey Bauer
	LB Pete Giftopoulos / Mike Beckish
	LB Shane Conlin
	DB Duffy Cobbs
	DB Eddie Johnson
	DB Marques Henderson / Sherrod Rainge
	DB Ray Isom

RUSHING: Dozier 171/811y, Manoa 98/546y, Thomas 60/504y
PASSING: Shaffer 114-204/1510y, 9TD, 55.9%
RECEIVING: Dozier 26/287y, Siverling 21/279y, Hamilton 19/387y
SCORING: Massimo Manca (K) 79pts, Dozier 72pts, Thomas 30pts

1987 8-4

45 Bowling Green	19 WR Ray Roundtree / Mike Alexander
13 Alabama	24 WR Michael Timpson
41 Cincinnati	0 T Stan Clayton
27 Boston College	17 G Steve Wisniewski
27 Temple	13 C Roger Duffy / Mike Wolf
35 Rutgers	21 G Rich Kuzy
21 Syracuse	48 T Mark Sickler / Tim Freeman
25 West Virginia	21 TE Paul Pomfret / Bob Mrosko
21 Maryland	16 QB Matt Knizner
0 Pittsburgh	10 TB Blair Thomas / Gary Brown
21 Notre Dame	20 FB John Greene / Sean Redman
10 Clemson■	35 DL Pete Curkendall
	DL Aaotaoa Polamalu
	DL Rich Schonewolf
	LB Keith Karpinski / Quintus McDonald
	LB Trey Bauer
	LB Pete Giftopoulos / Andre Powell
	LB Scott Gob / Kurt Bernier
	DB Gary Wilkerson
	DB Eddie Johnson / Willie Thomas
	DB Brian Chizmar
	DB Andre Collins / Sherrod Rainge

RUSHING: Thomas 268/1414y, Greene 90/473y, Brown 42/273y
PASSING: Knizner 113-223/1478y, 7TD, 50.7%
RECEIVING: Thomas 23/300y, Alexander 20/286y, Timpson 19/296y
SCORING: Thomas 80pts, Eric Etze (K) 48pts, Greene 48pts

1988 5-6

42 Virginia	14 WR David Daniels / Terry Smith
23 Boston College	20 WR Michael Timpson
16 Rutgers	21 T Tim Freeman
45 Temple	9 G Steve Wisniewski
35 Cincinnati	9 C Roger Duffy
10 Syracuse	24 G Ed Monaghan
3 Alabama	8 T Jeff Brubaker
30 West Virginia	51 TE Dave Jakob
17 Maryland	10 QB Tony Sacca / Tom Bill
7 Pittsburgh	14 TB Gary Brown / Leroy Thompson
3 Notre Dame	21 FB John Greene / Sam Gash
	DL Rich Schonewolf
	DL Dave Szott / Eric Renkey
	DL Bob Mrosko / Frank Giannetti
	LB Keith Karpinski
	LB Scott Gob / Mark D'Onofrio
	LB Andre Collins
	LB Quintus McDonald
	DB Willie Thomas
	DB Sherrod Rainge / Matt Baggett
	DB Brian Chizmar / Neil Hamilton
	DB Eddie Johnson / Darren Perry

RUSHING: Brown 136/689y, Thompson 108/401y, Greene 77/342y
PASSING: Sacca 54-146/821y, 4TD, 37.0%
RECEIVING: Timpson 22/342y, Jakob 20/274y, Daniels 16/322y
SCORING: Brown 44pts, Gash 42pts, Ray Tarasi (K) 40pts

1989 8-3-1

6 Virginia	14 WR David Daniels
42 Temple	3 WR Terry Smith
7 Boston College	3 T Matt McCartin / Paul Siever
16 Texas	12 G Dave Szott
17 Rutgers	0 C Roger Duffy
34 Syracuse	12 G Ed Monaghan / Sean Love
16 Alabama	17 T Tim Freeman
19 West Virginia	9 TE Dave Jakob / Al Golden
13 Maryland	13 QB Tony Sacca / Tom Bill
23 Notre Dame	34 TB Blair Thomas / Gerry Collins
16 Pittsburgh	13 FB John Gerak / Leroy Thompson
50 BYU■	39 DL Frank Giannetti / Todd Burger
	DL Jim Deter
	DL Rich Schonewolf
	LB Mark D'Onofrio
	LB Brian Chizmar
	LB Andre Collins / Keith Goganious
	LB Geoff Japchen / Reggie Givens
	DB Hernon Henderson
	DB Willie Thomas / Leonard Humphries
	DB Darren Perry
	DB Matt Baggott / Sherrod Rainge

RUSHING: Thomas 264/1341y, Collins 62/293y, Thompson 54/184y
PASSING: Sacca 56-137/694y, 6TD, 40.9%, Bill 43-88/605y, 3 TD, 48.9%
RECEIVING: Daniels 22/362y, Thomas 18/118y, Jakob 17/194y
SCORING: Ray Tarasi (K) 77pts, Thomas 30pts, Daniels 24pts

1990 9-3

13 Texas	17 WR David Daniels / Troy Drayton
14 Southern Cal	19 WR Terry Smith / Tisen Thomas
28 Rutgers	0 T Pat Duffy
48 Temple	10 G Greg Huntington
27 Syracuse	21 C Rob Luedeke
40 Boston College	21 G Dave Brzenchek / Paul Siever
9 Alabama	0 T Matt McCartin
31 West Virginia	19 TE Al Golden / Rick Sayles
24 Maryland	10 QB Tony Sacca
24 Notre Dame	21 TB Leroy Thompson / Gary Brown
22 Pittsburgh	17 FB Sam Gash / Brian O'Neal
17 Florida State■	24 DL Frank Giannetti / Todd Burger
	DL Jim Deter
	DL Lou Benfatti
	LB Reggie Givens / Ivory Gethers
	LB Mark D'Onofrio / Brett Wright
	LB Keith Goganious
	LB Rich McKenzie
	DB Leonard Humphries
	DB Greg Fusetti / Mark Graham
	DB Darren Perry
	DB Willie Thomas

RUSHING: Thompson 152/573y, Brown 82/359y, Gash 95/315y
PASSING: Sacca 122-249/1866y, 10TD, 49.0%
RECEIVING: Daniels 31/538y, Smith 29/530y, Thompson 20/245y
SCORING: Craig Fayak (K) 74pts, Thompson 48pts, Gash 30pts

1991 11-2

34 Georgia Tech	22 WR Terry Smith / Chip LaBarca
81 Cincinnati	0 WR O.J. McDuffie
10 Southern Cal	21 T Paul Siever (G) / Todd Rucci
33 BYU	7 G Mac Gallagher / Mike Malinoski
28 Boston College	21 C Greg Huntington
24 Temple	7 G John Gerak
20 Miami	26 T Todd Burger / Derick Pickett
37 Rutgers	17 TE Al Golden / Kyle Brady
51 West Virginia	6 QB Tony Sacca
47 Maryland	7 TB Richie Anderson / Shelly Hammonds
35 Notre Dame	13 FB Sam Gash / Brian O'Neal
32 Pittsburgh	20 DL Eric Ravotti / Tyoka Jackson
42 Tennessee■	17 DL Jim Deter
	DL Lou Benfatti
	LB Reggie Givens / Ivory Gethers
	LB Mark D'Onofrio / Brett Wright
	LB Keith Goganious
	LB Rich McKenzie
	DB Leonard Humphries / Mark Graham
	DB Derek Bochna
	DB Darren Perry
	DB Lee Rubin / Tony Pittman

RUSHING: Anderson 152/779y, Gash 87/391y, Hammonds 63/363y
PASSING: Sacca 169-292/2488y, 21TD, 57.9%
RECEIVING: Smith 55/846y, McDuffie 46/790y, Anderson 21/255y
SCORING: Craig Fayak (K) 93pts

1992 7-5

24 Cincinnati	20 WR Tisen Thomas / Chip LaBarca
49 Temple	8 WR O.J. McDuffie
52 E. Michigan	7 T Todd Rucci / Derick Pickett
49 Maryland	13 G Mike Malinoski
38 Rutgers	24 C E.J. Sandusky / Bucky Greeley
14 Miami	17 G John Gerak
32 Boston College	35 T Greg Huntington
40 West Virginia	26 TE Troy Drayton / Kyle Brady
17 Brigham Young	30 QB John Sacca / Kerry Collins
16 Notre Dame	17 TB Richie Anderson / Ki-Jana Carter
57 Pittsburgh	13 FB Brian O'Neal
3 Stanford■	24 DL Tyoka Jackson / Todd Atkins
	DL Vin Stewart / Todd Burger
	DL Lou Benfatti
	LB Reggie Givens
	LB Brett Wright / Brian Gelzheiser
	LB Phil Yeboah-Kodie / Willie Smith
	LB Rich McKenzie / Eric Clair
	DB Mark Graham / Marlon Forbes
	DB Shelly Hammonds / Tony Pittman
	DB Derek Bochna
	DB Lee Rubin / Chris Cisar

RUSHING: Anderson 195/900y, O'Neal 81/458y, Carter 42/264y
PASSING: Sacca 81-155/1118y, 9TD, 52.3%, Collins 64-137/925y, 4TD, 46.7%
RECEIVING: McDuffie 63/977y, Drayton 36/488y, Anderson 16/98y
SCORING: Anderson 116pts

1993 10-2

38 Minnesota	20 WR Bobby Engram
21 Southern Cal	20 WR Chip LaBarca / Phil Collins
31 Iowa	0 T Marco Rivera
31 Rutgers	7 G Jeff Hartings / Keith Conlin
70 Maryland	7 C Bucky Greeley / Barry Tielsch
13 Michigan	21 G Mike Malinoski
6 Ohio State	24 T Derick Pickett / Andre Johnson
38 Indiana	31 TE Kyle Brady
28 Illinois	14 QB Kerry Collins / John Sacca
43 Northwestern	21 TB Ki-J'a Carter/Mike Archie/Steph'n Pitts
38 Michigan State	37 FB Brian O'Neal / Jon Witman
31 Tennessee■	13 DL Tyoka Jackson
	DL Eric Clair
	DL Lou Benfatti / Todd Atkins
	LB Eric Ravotti
	LB Brian Gelzheiser
	LB Brian Monaghan / Phil Yeboah-Kodie
	LB Rob Holmberg / Willie Smith
	DB Shelly Hammonds
	DB Marlon Forbes / Tony Pittman
	DB Derek Bochna / Cliff Dingle
	DB Lee Rubin

RUSHING: Carter 155/1026y
PASSING: Collins 127-250/1605y, 13TD, 50.8%
RECEIVING: Engram 48/873y,
SCORING: Craig Fayak (K) 79pts

1994 12-0

56 Minnesota	3 WR Bobby Engram
38 Southern Cal	14 WR Freddie Scott / Chris Campbell
61 Iowa	21 T Andre Johnson
55 Rutgers	27 G Jeff Hartings
48 Temple	21 C Bucky Greeley
31 Michigan	24 G Marco Rivera
63 Ohio State	14 T Keith Conlin
35 Indiana	29 TE Kyle Brady / Keith Olsommer
35 Illinois	31 QB Kerry Collins
45 Northwestern	17 TB Ki-Jana Carter / Mike Archie
59 Michigan State	31 FB Jon Witman / Brian Milne
38 Oregon■	20 DL Todd Atkins / Brad Scioli
	DL Chris Mazyck / Brandon Noble
	DL Vin Stewart / Eric Clair
	DL Jeff Perry / Chris Snyder
	LB Willie Smith / Terry Killens
	LB Brian Gelzheiser
	LB Phil Yeboah-Kodie
	DB Mark Tate / Jason Collins
	DB Brian Miller / Tony Pittman
	DB Clint Holes
	DB Cliff Dingle / Brian King / Kim Herring

RUSHING: Carter 198/1539y, Archie 52/303y, Milne 56/267y
PASSING: Collins 176-264/2679y, 21TD, 66.7%
RECEIVING: Engram 52/1029y, Scott 47/973y, Brady 27/365y
SCORING: Carter 138pts

1995 9-3

24 Texas Tech	23 WR Bobby Engram
66 Temple	14 WR Freddie Scott
59 Rutgers	34 T Andre Johnson / Jason Henderson
9 Wisconsin	17 G Jeff Hartings
25 Ohio State	28 C Barry Tielsch
26 Purdue	23 G Marco Rivera / Phil Ostrowski
41 Iowa	27 T Keith Conlin
45 Indiana	21 TE Keith Olsommer
10 Northwestern	21 QB Wally Richardson
27 Michigan	17 TB Mike Archie / Curtis Enis /Step'n Pitts
24 Michigan State	20 FB Jon Witman / Brian Milne
43 Auburn■	14 DL Todd Atkins / Chris Snyder
	DL Brad Scioli
	DL Brandon Noble
	DL Terry Killens (LB) / Anthony Cleary
	LB Aaron Collins
	LB Gerald Filardi / Clint Searce
	LB Jim Nelson
	DB Mark Tate
	DB Brian Miller
	DB Clint Holes / Chuck Penzenik
	DB Kim Herring / Jason Collins

RUSHING: Enis 113/683y, Archie 97/512y, Pitts 68/468y
PASSING: Richardson 193-335/2198y, 18TD, 57.6%
RECEIVING: Engram 63/1084y, Scott 34/347y,
  Olsommer 23/197y
SCORING: Brett Conway (K) 85pts,

1996 11-2

24 Southern Cal	7 WR Joe Jurevicius
24 Louisville	7 WR Chris Campbell / Joe Nastasi
49 No. Illinois	0 T Jason Henderson / Ryan Fagan
41 Temple	0 G Phil Ostrowski
23 Wisconsin	20 C Barry Tielsch
7 Ohio State	38 G Pete Marczyk / Brad Jones
31 Purdue	14 T John Blick / Bill Anderson
20 Iowa	21 TE Keith Olsommer / Bob Stephenson
48 Indiana	26 QB Wally Richardson
34 Northwestern	9 TB Curtis Enis / Chris Eberly
29 Michigan	17 FB Aaron Harris/Jason Sload/A't'y Cleary
32 Michigan State	29 DL Chris Snyder / Courtney Brown
38 Texas■	15 DL Brandon Noble
	DL Matt Fornadel / Mike Buzin
	DL Brandon Short
	LB Aaron Collins
	LB Gerald Filardi
	LB Jim Nelson
	DB Mark Tate
	DB Brian Miller / Shano Prater
	DB Shawn Lee / Derek Fox
	DB Kim Herring

RUSHING: Enis 224/1210y, Harris 105/587y, Eberly 55/281y
PASSING: Richardson 145-279/1732y 7TD, 52.0%
RECEIVING: Jurevicius 41/869y, Enis 32/291y, Nastasi 21/234y
SCORING: Brett Conway (K) 93pts,

1997 9-3

34 Pittsburgh	17 WR Joe Jurivicius / Titcus Pettigrew
52 Temple	10 WR Chafie Fields / Joe Nastasi
57 Louisville	21 T Floyd Wedderburn
41 Illinois	6 G Eric Cole / Gabe Tincher
31 Ohio State	27 C Kevin Conlin
16 Minnesota	15 G Phil Ostrowski / Ryan Fagan
30 Northwestern	27 T John Blick
8 Michigan	34 TE Cuncho Brown / Brad Scioli
42 Purdue	17 QB Mike McQueary
35 Wisconsin	10 TB Curtis Enis / Cordell Mitchell
14 Michigan State	49 FB Aaron Harris / Anthony Cleary
6 Florida■	21 DL Courtney Brown
	DL Imani Bell / David Fleischhauer
	DL Matt Fornadel
	DL Chris Snyder
	LB Aaron Collins / LaVar Arrington
	LB Brandon Short
	LB Jim Nelson / Aaron Gatten
	DB Anthony King
	DB Shino Prater / David Macklin
	DB Shawn Lee / James Boyd
	DB Jason Collins

RUSHING: Enis 228/1363y, Harris 42/261y, Mitchell 38/236y
PASSING: McQueary 146-255/2211y, 17TD, 57.3%
RECEIVING: Jurevicius 39/817y, Enis 25/215y, Fields 23/374y
SCORING: Enis 122pts

1998 9-3

34 Southern Miss	6 WR Chafie Fields / Titcus Pettigrew
48 Bowling Green	3 WR Corey Jones / Joe Nastasi
20 Pittsburgh	13 T Floyd Wedderburn
9 Ohio State	28 G Kareem McKenzie / Gabe Tincher
27 Minnesota	17 C Eric Cole
31 Purdue	13 G Ryan Fagan / Greg Ransom
27 Illinois	0 T John Blick / Jordan Caruso
0 Michigan	27 TE Cuncho Brown / Tony Stewart
41 Northwestern	10 QB Kevin Thompson
3 Wisconsin	24 TB Cordell Mitchell / Eric McCoo
51 Michigan State	28 FB Mike Cerimele / Aaron Harris
26 Kentucky■	14 DL Courtney Brown
	DL David Fleischhauer / Imani Bell
	DL Bob Jones
	DL Brad Scioli
	LB LaVar Arrington / Aaron Gatten
	LB Brandon Short
	LB Mac Morrison / Ron Graham
	DB Anthony King / Bhawoh Jue
	DB David Macklin
	DB Shawn Lee / James Boyd
	DB Derek Fox

RUSHING: McCoo 127/822y, Mitchell 99/511y, Cerimele 52/261y
PASSING: Thompson 121-226/1691y, 6TD, 53.5%
RECEIVING: Jones 27/368y, Fields 25/369y, Brown 21/245y
SCORING: Travis Forney (K) 89pts, Cerimele 48pts, Harris 30pts

1999 10-3

41 Arizona	7 WR Chafie Fields
70 Akron	24 WR Eddie Drummond / Sam Crenshaw
20 Pittsburgh	17 T Kareem McKenzie
27 Miami	23 G Jordan Caruso
45 Indiana	24 C Francis Spano / Rich Stankewicz
31 Iowa	7 G Eric Cole
23 Ohio State	10 T John Blick
31 Purdue	25 TE Tony Stewart / John Gilmore
27 Illinois	7 QB Kevin Thompson / Rashard Casey
23 Minnesota	24 TB Eric McCoo / Cordell Mitchell
27 Michigan	31 FB Mike Cerimele / Aaron Harris
28 Michigan State	35 DL Courtney Brown
24 Texas A&M■	0 DL David Fleischhauer
	DL Jimmy Kennedy / Imani Bell
	DL Justin Kurpeikis / Bob Jones
	LB LaVar Arrington
	LB Brandon Short / Maurice Daniels
	LB Mac Morrison / Ron Graham
	DB Anthony King / Bhawoh Jue
	DB David Macklin
	DB Askari Adams / James Boyd
	DB Derek Fox

RUSHING: McCoo 148/739y, Casey 76/290y, Harris 50/206y
PASSING: Thompson 133-242/1916y, 13TD, 55.0%
RECEIVING: Fields 39/692y, Drummond 35/652y,
  Gilmore 22/259y, McCoo 22/249y
SCORING: Travis Forney (K) 107pts

2000 5-7

5 Southern Cal	29 WR Eddie Drummond / Tony Johnson
6 Toledo	24 WR Kenny Watson
67 Louisiana Tech	7 T Kareem McKenzie
0 Pittsburgh	12 G Jordan Caruso
6 Ohio State	45 C Matt Schmitt / Francis Spano
22 Purdue	20 G Joe Iorio / Joe Hartings
16 Minnesota	25 T Imani Bell
39 Illinois	25 TE Tony Stewart / John Gilmore
27 Indiana	24 QB Rashard Casey
23 Iowa	26 TB Eric McCoo / Larry Johnson
11 Michigan	33 FB Mike Cerimele
42 Michigan State	23 DL Michael Haynes / Bob Jones
	DL Jimmy Kennedy
	DL Anthony Adams / T.J. Gholston
	DL Justin Kurpeikis
	LB Shamar Finney / Aaron Gatten
	LB Ron Graham / Yaacov Yisreal
	LB Eric Sturdifen
	DB Bruce Branch
	DB Bhawoh Jue
	DB Titcus Pettigrew
	DB James Boyd / Shawn Mayer

RUSHING: McCoo 140/692y, L. Johnson 75/358y,
  Casey 112/315y
PASSING: Casey 163-309/2001y, 14TD, 52.8%
RECEIVING: Stewart 38/451y, Drummond 29/365y,
  McCoo 26/288y
SCORING: Ryan Primanti (K) 64pts, McCoo 54pts, Casey 30pts

2001 5-6

7 Miami	33 WR Bryant Johnson / Eddie Drummond
6 Wisconsin	18 WR Tony Johnson
18 Iowa	24 T Gus Felder
0 Michigan	20 G Greg Ransom
38 Northwestern	35 C Joe Iorio
29 Ohio State	27 G Tyler Lenda
38 Southern Miss	20 T Chris McKelvy
28 Illinois	33 TE John Gilmore / R.J. Luke
28 Indiana	14 QB Zack Mills / Matt Senneca
42 Michigan State	37 TB Larry Johnson / Eric McCoo
14 Virginia	20 FB Mick Blosser / Sean McHugh
	DL Bob Jones
	DL Jimmy Kennedy
	DL Anthony Adams
	DL Michael Haynes
	LB Deryck Toles / LaMar Stewart
	LB Shamar Finney
	LB Ron Graham
	DB Bryan Scott
	DB Bruce Branch / Rich Gardner
	DB Shawn Mayer
	DB Yaacov Yisrael

RUSHING: L. Johnson 71/337y, McCoo 82/265y,
  Omar Easy (TB) 45/196y
PASSING: Mills 127-230/1669y, 9TD, 55.2%,
  Senneca 54-126/755y, 3 TDs, 42.9%
RECEIVING: B. Johnson 51/866y, T. Johnson 27/504y,
  Gilmore 25/284y
SCORING: McCoo 54pts, Robbie Gould (K) 47pts,
  L. Johnson 42pts

2002 9-4

27 C. Florida	24 WR Bryant Johnson
40 Nebraska	7 WR Tony Johnson
49 Louisiana Tech	17 T Gus Felder
35 Iowa	42 G Chris McKelvy / E.Z. Smith
34 Wisconsin	31 C Joe Iorio
24 Michigan	27 G Tyler Lenda
49 Northwestern	0 T Matt Schmidt
7 Ohio State	13 TE Casey Williams / Mike Lukac
18 Illinois	7 QB Zack Mills / Michael Robinson
35 Virginia	14 TB Larry Johnson
58 Indiana	25 FB Paul Jefferson / Sean McHugh
61 Michigan State	7 DL John Bronson
9 Auburn ■	13 DL Jimmy Kennedy
	DL Anthony Adams
	DL Michael Haynes
	LB LaMar Stewart / Deryck Toles
	LB Gino Capone / Andy Ryland
	LB Derek Wake
	DB Bryan Scott
	DB Rich Gardner / Anwar Phillips
	DB Shawn Mayer
	DB Chris Harrell

RUSHING: L. Johnson 271/2087y, Robinson 50/263y,
Mills 87/210y
PASSING: Mills 188-333/2417y, 17TD, 56.5%
RECEIVING: B. Johnson 48/917y, L. Johnson 41/349y,
T. Johnson 34/549y
SCORING: L. Johnson 140pts, Robbie Gould (K) 93pts,
Robinson 36pts

2003 3-9

23 Temple	10 WR Tony Johnson / Ernie Terrell
14 Boston College	27 WR Gerald Smith / Kinta Palmer
10 Nebraska	18 T Levi Brown
32 Kent State	10 G Scott Davis / Charles Rush
14 Minnesota	20 C Dave Costlow
23 Wisconsin	30 G Tyler Reed / Nick Marmo
14 Purdue	28 T Chris McKelvy / Damone Jones
14 Iowa	26 TE Mike Lukac / Matt Kranchick
20 Ohio State	21 QB Zack Mills / Michael Robinson (TB)
7 Northwestern	17 TB Austin Scott
52 Indiana	7 FB Sean McHugh
10 Michigan State	41 DL Matt Rice / John Bronson
	DL Tamba Hali
	DL Ed Johnson / Jay Alford
	DL Lavon Chisley / Sam Ruhe
	LB Deryck Toles
	LB Gino Capone
	LB Derek Wake
	DB Alan Zemaitis / Anwar Phillips
	DB Rich Gardner
	DB Chris Harrell / Andrew Guman
	DB Yaacov Yisrael / Calvin Lowry

RUSHING: Scott 100/436y, Robinson 107/396y,
McHugh 54/256y
PASSING: Mills 136-251/1404y, 6TD, 54.2%,
Robinson 62-138/892y, 5TD, 44.9%
RECEIVING: Johnson 32/445y, Maurice Humphrey (WR) 30/410y,
McHugh 27/185y
SCORING: Robbie Gould (K) 49pts, Scott 36pts,
Johnson & McHugh 24pts

2004 4-7

48 Akron	10 WR Gerald Smith / Mark Rubin
7 Boston College	21 WR Michael Robinson (QB-TB)
37 C. Florida	13 T Levi Brown
3 Wisconsin	16 G Charles Rush
7 Minnesota	16 C E.Z. Smith
13 Purdue	20 G Tyler Reed
4 Iowa	6 T John Wilson / Andrew Richardson
10 Ohio State	21 TE Isaac Smolko / John Bronson
7 Northwestern	14 QB Zack Mills / Chris Gantner
22 Indiana	18 TB Tony Hunt / Austin Scott
37 Michigan State	13 FB Paul Jefferson
	DL Derek Wake
	DL Scott Paxson / Ed Johnson
	DL Jay Alford / Tamba Hali
	DL Matt Rice / Amani Purcell
	LB Paul Posluszny
	LB Dan Connor
	LB Tim Shaw
	DB Alan Zemaitis
	DB Anwar Phillips
	DB Andrew Guman
	DB Calvin Lowry / Paul Cronin

RUSHING: Hunt 169/818y, Scott 55/321y, Robinson 49/172y
PASSING: Mills 155-268/1722y, 9TD, 57.8%
RECEIVING: Hunt 39/334y, Robinson 33/485y, Smolko 21/192y
SCORING: Robbie Gould (K) 43pts, Hunt 42pts, Mills 32pts

2005 11-1

23 South Florida	13 WR Derrick Williams / Ethan Kilmer
42 Cincinnati	24 WR Deon Butler / Jordan Norwood
40 C. Michigan	3 T Levi Brown
34 Northwestern	29 G Charles Rush
44 Minnesota	14 C Lance Antolick / E.Z. Smith
17 Ohio State	10 G Tyler Reed / Robert Price
25 Michigan	27 T Andrew Richardson
63 Illinois	10 TE Isaac Smolko
33 Purdue	15 QB Michael Robinson
35 Wisconsin	14 TB Tony Hunt / Austin Scott
31 Michigan State	22 FB BranDon Snow
26 Florida State ■	23 DL Tamba Hali
	DL Scott Paxson
	DL Jay Alford
	DL Matthew Rice / Jim Shaw
	LB Dan Connor / Tyrell Sales
	LB Tim Shaw
	LB Paul Posluszny
	DB Alan Zemaitis
	DB Anwar Philips / Justin King (WR)
	DB Chris Harrell / Paul Cronin
	DB Calvin Lowry

RUSHING: Hunt 174/1047y, Robinson 163/806y, Scott 66/273y
PASSING: Robinson 162-311/2350y, 17TD, 52.1%
RECEIVING: Butler 37/691y, Norwood 32/422y,
Williams 22/289y
SCORING: Kevin Kelly (K) 99pts, Robinson 66pts, Butler 54pts

2006 9-4

34 Akron	16 WR Derrick Williams/A.Wallace/Chris Bell
17 Notre Dame	41 WR Deon Butler / Jordan Norwood
37 Youngstown St.	3 T Levi Brown
6 Ohio State	28 G Robert Price / Gerald Cadogan
33 Northwestern	7 C A.Q. Shipley
28 Minnesota	27 G Rich Ohrnberger
10 Michigan	17 T John Shaw / Chris Auletta
26 Illinois	12 TE Andrew Quarless / Kevin Darling
12 Purdue	0 QB Anthony Morelli
3 Wisconsin	13 TB Tony Hunt / Rodney Kinlaw
47 Temple	0 FB Matt Hahn / BranDon Snow
17 Michigan State	13 DL Jim Shaw
20 Tennessee ■	10 DL Ed Johnson
	DL Jay Alford
	DL Josh Gaines / Jim Shaw
	LB Dan Connor
	LB Sean Lee / Tim Shaw
	LB Paul Posluszny / Tyrell Sales
	DB Justin King
	DB Tony Davis / Knowledge Timmons
	DB Donnie Johnson / Nolan McCready
	DB Anthony Scirrotto

RUSHING: Hunt 277/1386y, Kinlaw 39/199y, Wallace 8/153y
PASSING: Morelli 208-386/2424y, 11TD, 53.9%
RECEIVING: Butler 48/637y, Norwood 45/472y Williams 40/440y
SCORING: Kevin Kelly (K) 96pts, Hunt 84pts,
Williams & Daryll Clark (QB) 18pts

2007 9-4

59 Florida Int'l	0 WR Derrick Williams / Jordan Norwood
31 Notre Dame	10 WR Deon Butler /Terrell Golden /Chris Bell
45 Buffalo	24 T Gerald Cadogan
9 Michigan	14 G Rich Ornsberger
20 Illinois	27 C A.Q. Shipley
27 Iowa	7 G Mike Lucian / John Shaw
38 Wisconsin	7 T Dennis Lanbolt
36 Indiana	31 TE Andrew Quarless / Mickey Shuler
17 Ohio State	37 QB Anthony Morelli
26 Purdue	19 TB Reggie Kinlaw / Austin Scott
31 Temple	0 FB Matt Hahn / Dan Lawlor
31 Michigan State	35 DL Josh Gaines
24 Texas A&M ■	17 DL Jared Odrick / Abe Koroma
	DL Chris Baker / Phillip Taylor
	DL Maurice Evans
	LB Sean Lee
	LB Dan Connor
	LB Tyrell Sales
	DB Lydell Sargeant / A.J. Wallace
	DB Justin King
	DB Tony Davis / Lee Rubin
	DB Anthony Scirrotto

RUSHING: Kinlaw 243/1329y, Evan Royster (TB) 82/513y,
Scott 69/302y
PASSING: Morelli 234-402/2651y, 19TD, 58.2%
RECEIVING: Williams 55/529y, Butler 47/633y, Norwood 40/484y
SCORING: Kevin Kelly (K) 110pts, Kinlaw 60pts, Scott 36pts

2008 11-2

66 Cstl. Carolina	10 WR Deon Butler / Jordan Norwood
45 Oregon State	14 WR Derrick Williams / Graham Zug
55 Syracuse	13 T Gerald Cadogan
45 Temple	3 G Rich Ornberger
38 Illinois	24 C A.Q. Shipley
20 Purdue	6 G Stefen Wisniewski
48 Wisconsin	7 T Dennis Landolt
46 Michigan	17 TE Mickey Shuler, Jr. / Andrew Quarless
13 Ohio State	6 QB Daryll Clark
23 Iowa	24 TB Evan Royster / Stephfon Green
34 Indiana	7 FB Dan Lawlor
49 Michigan State	18 DL Aaron Maybin / Maurice Evans
24 Southern Cal ■	38 DL Jared Odrick
	DL Ollie Ogbu / Abe Korona
	DL Josh Gaines
	LB Tyrell Sales
	LB Josh Hull
	LB Navorro Bowman / Bani Gbadyu
	DB Tony Davis
	DB Lydell Sargeant / A.J. Wallace
	DB Anthony Scirrotto / Drew Astorino
	DB Mark Rubin

RUSHING: Royster 191/1236y, Green 105/578y, Clark 79/282y
PASSING: Clark 192-321/2592y, 19TD, 59.8%
RECEIVING: Butler 47/810y, Williams 44/485y,
Norwood 41/637y
SCORING: Kevin Kelly (K) 120pts, Royster 72pts,
Clark & Williams 60pts

2009 11-2

31 Akron	7 WR Derek Moye / Chaz Powell
28 Syracuse	7 WR Graham Zug / Patrick Mauti
31 Temple	6 T Dennis Landolt
10 Iowa	21 G Johnnie Troutman / Matt Stankiewitch
35 Illinois	17 C Stefen Wisniewski
52 E. Illinois	3 G Lou Eliades
20 Minnesota	0 T Alo Poti / DeOn'tae Pannell (G)
35 Michigan	10 TE Andrew Quarless / Mickey Shuler, Jr.
34 Northwestern	13 QB Daryll Clark
7 Ohio State	24 TB Evan Royster / Stephfon Green
31 Indiana	20 FB Joe Suhey
42 Michigan State	14 DL Jerome Hayes / Eric Latimore
19 LSU ■	17 DL Jared Odrick
	DL Ollie Ogbu / Devon Still
	DL Jack Crawford
	LB Sean Lee / Bani Gbadyu
	LB Josh Hull
	LB Navorro Bowman / Nathan Stupar
	DB A.J. Wallace / Knowledge Timmons
	DB D'Anton Lynn / Stephon Morris
	DB Nick Sukay / Cedric Jeffries
	DB Drew Astorino

RUSHING: Royster 205/1169y, Green 71/319y, Clark 82/211y
PASSING: Clark 232-681/3003y, 24TD, 60.9%
RECEIVING: Moye 48/785y, Zug 46/600y, Quarless 41/536y
Powell 28/366y
SCORING: Collin Wagner (K) 91pts, Royster 48pts,
Clark & Zug 42pts

2010 7-6

44 Youngstown St.	14 WR Derek Moye
3 Alabama	24 WR Brett Brackett / Graham Zug
24 Kent State	0 WR Justin Brown / Devon Smith
22 Temple	13 T Quinn Barham
3 Iowa	24 G Johnnie Troutman / DeOn'tae Pannell
13 Illinois	33 C Doug Klopacz
33 Minnesota	21 G Stefen Wisniewski / Mike Farrell
41 Michigan	31 T Chima Okoli / Lou Eliades
35 Northwestern	21 QB Rob Borden / Matt McGloin
14 Ohio State	38 RB Evan Royster / Silas Redd
41 Indiana	24 FB/TE Joe Suhey / Garry Gilliam
22 Michigan State	28 DL Pete Massaro / Eric Latimore
24 Florida ■	37 DL Ollie Ogbu / James Terry
	DL Devon Still / Sean Stanley
	DL Jack Crawford / Jordan Hill
	LB Michael Manti / Nate Stupar
	LB Chris Colasanti / Gerald Hodges
	LB Bani Gbadyu / Khairi Fortt
	DB D'Anton Lynn
	DB Stephon Morris / Chazz Powell
	DB Nick Sukay / Malcolm Willis
	DB Drew Astorino / Andrew Dailey

RUSHING: Royster 208/1014y, Redd 77/437y
PASSING: McGloin 118-215/1548y, 14TD, 54.9%
Bolden 112-193/1360y, 5TD, 58%
RECEIVING: Moye 53/885y, Brackett 39/525y, Brown 33/452y
SCORING: Collin Wagner (K) 94pts, Moye 48pts, Royster 42pts

PITTSBURGH

University of Pittsburgh (Founded 1787)
Pittsburgh, Pennsylvania
Nickname: Panthers
Colors: Royal Blue and Old Gold
Stadium: Heinz Field (2001) 65,050
Affiliations: Independent (1890-1990), Big East (1991-present)

CAREER RUSHING YARDS	Attempts.	Yards
Tony Dorsett (1973-76)	1133	6526
Curvin Richards (1988-90)	584	3192
Craig Heyward (1984, 86-87)	681	3086
Dion Lewis (2009-10)	544	2860
LeSean McCoy (2007-08)	584	2816
Billy West (1993-97)	455	2803
Elliott Walker (1974-77)	481	2748
Curtis Martin (1991-94)	518	2643
Kevan Barlow (1997-2000)	508	2438
Bryan Thomas (1978, 80-82)	447	2141

CAREER PASSING YARDS	Comp.-Att.	Yards.
Alex Van Pelt (1989-92)	865-1503	11,267
Dan Marino (1979-82)	693-1204	8597
Tyler Palko (2002, 2004-06)	645-1075	8343
Rod Rutherford (2000-03)	458-842	6724
John Congemi (1983-86)	550-994	6467
Bill Stull (2005-09)	418-681	5252
John Ryan (1992-95)	338-626	4334
David Priestley (1999-2001)	380-475	4262
Rick Trocano (1977-1980)	N/A	4219
John Turman (1999-2000)	240-461	3783

CAREER RECEIVING YARDS	Catches	Yards
Antonio Bryant (1999-2001)	173	3061
Dietrich Jells (1991-95)	160	3003
Latef Grim (1998-2000)	178	2680
Larry Fitzgerald (2002-03)	161	2677
Greg Lee (2003-05)	127	2470
Jonathan Baldwin (2008-10)	128	2337
Dwight Collins (80-83)	133	2264
Gordon Jones (75-78)	133	2230
Henry Tuten (1987-89)	92	1758
Oderick Turner (2006-09)	122	1681

SEASON RUSHING YARDS	Attempts	Yards
Tony Dorsett (1976)	370	2150
Dion Lewis (2009)	325	1799
Craig Heyward (1987)	387	1791
Tony Dorsett (1973)	288	1686
Tony Dorsett (1975)	255	1686

SEASON PASSING YARDS	Comp.-Att.	Yards
Rod Rutherford (2003)	247-413	3679
Alex Van Pelt (1992)	245-407	3163
Tyler Palko (2004)	230-409	3067
Alex Van Pelt (1989)	192-347	2881
Dan Marino (1981)	226-380	2876

SEASON RECEIVING YARDS	Catches	Yards
Larry Fitzgerald (2003)	92	1672
Antonio Bryant (2000)	73	1457
Greg Lee (2004)	68	1297
Jonathan Baldwin (2009)	57	1111
Latef Grim (1999)	75	1106

GAME RUSHING YARDS	Attempts	Yards
Tony Dorsett (1975 vs. Notre Dame)	23	303
Ray Graham (2010 vs. FIU)	29	277
Kevan Barlow (2000 vs. West Virginia)	33	272

GAME PASSING YARDS	Comp.-Att.	Yards
Pete Gonzalez (1997 vs. Rutgers)	N/A	470
John Congemi (1986 vs. Navy)	N/A	446
John Ryan (1994 vs. West Virginia)	N/A	433

GAME RECEIVING YARDS	Caught	Yards
Dietrich Jells (1994 vs. West Virginia)	5	225
Antonio Bryant (2000 vs. Boston College)	8	222
Antonio Bryant (1999 vs. Virginia Tech)	13	215

GREATEST COACH:

Johnny Majors may have brought Pittsburgh back to the big time and won a national championship in 1976, but it was Jackie Sherrill, for all his negatives, that really put the Panthers consistently in the mix for national honors.

Sherrill had the Panthers in the AP Poll's top 10 four times in his five years at the helm in Pittsburgh's Oakland section. When it comes to won-loss records, Sherrill was 50-9-1 (.8417) at Pitt, while Majors finished 45-45-1 due to his second tour of duty (1993-96) during which things worked out much for the worse.

PITTSBURGH'S 55 GREATEST SINCE 1953

OFFENSE

WIDE RECEIVER: Antonio Bryant, Larry Fitzgerald, Latef Grim, Gordon Jones, Greg Lee
TIGHT END: Jim Corbett, Joe Walton
TACKLE: Jimbo Covert, Randy Dixon, Bill Fralic, Mark May
GUARD: Tom Brzoza, Jeff Christy, Mark Stepnoski
CENTER: Russ Grimm, Jim Sweeney
QUARTERBACK: Matt Cavanaugh, John Congemi, Dan Marino
RUNNING BACK: Tony Dorsett, Craig Heyward, Curtis Martin, Curvin Richards
FULLBACK: Rick Leeson, Randy McMillan

DEFENSE

END: Chris Doleman, Hugh Green, Rickey Jackson, Michael Woods
TACKLE: Sean Gilbert, Randy Holloway, Bill Maas, Bill Neill, Mark Spindler
NOSE GUARD: Al Romano, Tony Siragusa
LINEBACKER: H.B. Blades, Gerald Hayes, Jerry Olsavsky, Sal Sunseri, Tom Tumulty
CORNERBACK: Steve Israel, Tim Lewis, Darrelle Rivas, Carlton Williamson
SAFETY: Tom Flynn, Bob Jury

SPECIAL TEAMS

RETURN SPECIALISTS: Dietrich Jells, Hank Poteat
PLACE KICKER: Fred Cox
PUNTER: Brian Greenfield

MULTIPLE POSITIONS

HALFBACK-QUARTERBACK-DEFENSIVE BACK: Paul Martha
SAFETY-FULLBACK: Dan Crossman

TWO-WAY PLAYERS

END-DEFENSIVE END: Mike Ditka
TACKLE-DEFENSIVE TACKLE: Bob Pollock

PERFORMANCE FORMULA:
PITTSBURGH'S 10 BEST SEASONS

1980	1.7291	1 of 70
1976	1.7271	1 of 70
1981	1.7121	2 of 70
1979	1.6379	5 of 70
1977	1.6333	6 of 70
1963	1.5782	2 of 70
1982	1.4987	6 of 70
2009	1.4523	13 of 72
1975	1.4035	15 of 70
1983	1.3691	16 of 70

PITTSBURGH PANTHERS

Year	W-L-T	AP Poll	Conference Standing	Toughest Regular Season Opponents	Coach (Record at School)	Bowl Games			
1953	3-5-1			West Virginia 8-1, Oklahoma 8-1-1, Notre Dame 9-0-1	Lowell "Red" Dawson				
1954	4-5			Southern California 8-3, Minnesota 7-2, Notre Dame 9-1, Navy 7-2, West Virginia 8-1, Ohio State 9-0, Penn State 7-2	Red Dawson (9-11-1), Tom Hamilton [4-2], (7-9)				
1955	7-4	11		Oklahoma 10-0, Navy 6-2-1, Duke 7-2-1, Miami 6-3, West Va. 8-2	John Michelosen	Sugar	0	Georgia Tech	7
1956	7-3-1	13		Syracuse 7-1, Minnesota 6-1-2, Penn State 6-2-1, Miami 8-1-1	John Michelosen	Gator	14	Georgia Tech	21
1957	4-6			Oklahoma 9-1, Army 7-2, Notre Dame 7-3, West Virginia 7-2-1	John Michelosen				
1958	5-4-1			Army 8-0-1, Syracuse 8-1, Notre Dame 6-4, Penn State 6-3-1	John Michelosen				
1959	6-4	20		Southern California 8-2, TCU 8-2, Syracuse 10-0, Penn State 8-2	John Michelosen				
1960	4-3-3			UCLA 7-2-1, Michigan State 6-2-1, Syracuse 7-2, Army 6-3-1	John Michelosen				
1961	3-7			Miami 7-3, UCLA 7-3, Navy 7-3, Syracuse 7-3, Penn State 7-3	John Michelosen				
1962	5-5			Miami 7-3, West Virginia 8-2, Army 6-4, Penn State 9-1	John Michelosen				
1963	9-1	4		Navy 9-1, Syracuse 8-2, Army 7-3, Penn State 7-3	John Michelosen				
1964	3-5-2			Oregon 7-2-1, West Virginia 7-3, Syracuse 7-3, Notre Dame 9-1	John Michelosen				
1965	3-7			Syracuse 7-3, Notre Dame 7-2-1, Southern California 7-2-1	John Michelosen (56-49-7)				
1966	1-9			UCLA 9-1, Army 8-2, Syracuse 8-2, Notre Dame 9-0-1, Miami 7-2-1	Dave Hart				
1967	1-9			UCLA 7-2-1, Syracuse 8-2, No. Dame 8-2, Army 8-2, Penn St. 8-2	Dave Hart				
1968	1-9			W. Va. 7-3, Air Force 7-3, No. Dame 7-2-1, Army 7-3, Penn St.10-0	Dave Hart (3-27)				
1969	4-6			UCLA 8-1-1, West Va. 9-1, Notre Dame 8-1-1, Penn State 10-0	Carl Depasqua				
1970	5-5			West Va. 8-3, Notre Dame 9-1, Boston College 8-2, Penn St. 7-3	Carl DePasqua				
1971	3-8			Oklahoma 10-1, Boston College 9-2, No. Dame 8-2, Penn St. 10-1	Carl DePasqua				
1972	1-10			Fla. St. 7-4, UCLA 8-3, No. Dame 8-2, West Va. 8-3, Penn St. 10-1	Carl DePasqua (13-29)				
1973	6-5-1			Georgia 6-4-1, Boston College 7-4, No. Dame 10-0, Penn St. 11-0	Johnny Majors	Fiesta	7	Arizona State	28
1974	7-4			Boston College 8-3, Temple 8-2, Notre Dame 9-2, Penn State 9-2	Johnny Majors				
1975	8-4	15		Georgia 9-2, Oklahoma 10-1, Notre Dame 8-3, Penn State 9-2	Johnny Majors	Sun	33	Kansas	19
1976	12-0	1		Notre Dame 8-3, Penn State 7-4	Johnny Majors {see below}	Sugar	27	Georgia	3
1977	9-2-1	8		Notre Dame 10-1, Florida 6-4-1, Army 7-4, Penn State 10-1	Jackie Sherrill	Gator	34	Clemson	3
1978	8-4			Notre Dame 8-3, Florida State 8-3, Navy 8-3, Penn State 11-0	Jackie Sherrill	Citrus	17	North Carolina State	30
1979	11-1	7		Temple 9-2, Washington 8-3, Navy 7-4, Penn State 7-4	Jackie Sherrill	Fiesta	16	Arizona	10
1980	11-1	2		Boston College 7-4, Maryland 8-3, Fla. State 10-1, Penn State 9-2	Jackie Sherrill	Gator	37	South Carolina	9
1981	11-1	4		Illinois 7-4, West Virginia 8-3, Penn State 9-2	Jackie Sherrill (50-9-1)	Sugar	24	Georgia	20
1982	9-3	10		North Carolina 7-4, Florida St. 8-3, West Va. 9-2, Penn State 10-1	Serafino "Foge" Fazio	Cotton	3	Southern Methodist	7
1983	8-3-1	18		Tennessee 8-3, Maryland 8-3, West Virginia 8-3, Penn State 7-4-1	Foge Fazio	Fiesta	23	Ohio State	28
1984	3-7-1			BYU 12-0, Oklahoma 9-1-1, South Carolina 10-1, Miami 8-4	Foge Fazio				
1985	5-5-1			Ohio State 8-3, West Virginia 7-3-1, Syracuse 7-4, Penn State 11-0	Foge Fazio (25-18-3)				
1986	5-5-1			NC State 8-2-1, Miami 11-0, Penn State 11-0	Mike Gottfried				
1987	8-4			BYU 9-3, Notre Dame 8-3, Syracuse 11-0, Penn State 8-3	Mike Gottfried	Bluebonnet	27	Texas	32
1988	6-5			West Va. 11-0, Notre Dame 11-0, NC State 7-3-1, Syracuse 9-2	Mike Gottfried				
1989	8-3-1	19		West Va. 8-2-1, Notre Dame 11-1, Miami 10-1, Penn State 7-3-1	Mike Gottfried (26-17-2), Paul Hackett [1-0]	Sun	31	Texas A&M	28
1990	3-7-1			Okla. 8-3, Louisv'le 9-1-1, No. Dame 9-2, Miami 9-2, Penn St. 9-2	Paul Hackett				
1991	6-5			Notre Dame 9-3, Syracuse 9-2, E. Carolina 10-1, Penn State 10-2	Paul Hackett				
1992	3-9			Notre Dame 9-1-1, Syracuse 9-2, Penn State 7-4, Hawaii 10-2	Paul Hackett (13-20-1), Sal Sunseri [0-1]				
1993	3-8		6	Ohio State 9-1-1, Notre Dame 10-1, West Va. 11-0, Miami 9-2	Johnny Majors				
1994	3-8		7	Texas 7-4, Ohio State 9-3, Virginia Tech 8-3, Miami 10-1	Johnny Majors				
1995	2-9		8	Texas 10-1-1, Ohio St. 11-1, Va. Tech 9-2, Miami 8-3, Syr'cuse 8-3	Johnny Majors				
1996	4-7		5	W. Va. 8-3, Ohio St. 10-1, Miami 8-3, Syracuse 8-3, No. Dame 8-3	Johnny Majors (45-45-1)				
1997	6-6		3t	Penn State 9-2, Syracuse 9-3, Virginia Tech 7-4, West Virginia 7-4	Walt Harris	Liberty	7	Southern Mississippi	41
1998	2-9		8	Penn St. 8-3, Va. Tech 8-3, Syracuse 8-3, West Va. 8-3, Miami 8-3	Walt Harris				
1999	5-6		6t	Penn State 9-3, Boston College 8-3, Virginia Tech 11-0, Miami 8-4	Walt Harris				
2000	7-5		3t	Virginia Tech 10-1, Miami 10-1	Walt Harris	Insight.com	29	Iowa State	37
2001	7-5		3t	Miami 11-0, Syracuse 9-3, Virginia Tech 8-3	Walt Harris	Tangerine	34	North Carolina State	19
2002	9-4	19	3	Notre Dame 10-2, Virginia Tech 9-4, Miami 10-1, West Va. 9-3	Walt Harris	Insight.com	38	Oregon State	13
2003	8-5		3	Virginia Tech 8-4, West Virginia 8-4, Miami 10-2	Walt Harris	Continental Tire	16	Virginia	23
2004	8-4	25	1t	Boston College 8-3, Notre Dame 6-5, West Virginia 8-3	Walt Harris (52-44)	Fiesta	7	Utah	35
2005	5-6		3t	Notre Dame 9-2, Nebraska 7-4, Louisville 9-2, West Virginia10-1	Dave Wannstedt				
2006	6-6		5	Rutgers 10-2, So. Florida 8-4, West Virginia 10-2, Louisville 11-1	Dave Wannstedt				
2007	5-7		5t	Connecticut 9-3, Virginia 9-3, Cincinnati 9-3, So. Florida 9-3, W. Va. 10-2	Dave Wannstedt				
2008	9-4		2t	Iowa 8-4, Cincinnati 11-2, West Virginia 8-4	Dave Wannstedt	Sun	0	Oregon State	3
2009	10-3	15	2t	Navy 9-4, West Virginia 9-3, Cincinnati 12-0	Dave Wannstedt	Meineke Care	19	North Carolina	17
2010	8-5		1t	Utah 10-2, Connecticut 8-4, West Virginia 9-3	Dave Wannstedt (43-31), Phil Bennett [1-0]	Papajohn's	27	Kentucky	10

TOTAL: 333-300-16 .5254 (40 of 70) **Bowl Games since 1953:** 11-12 .4783 (41 of 70)

GREATEST TEAM SINCE 1953: Although the storied 1976 team won the national championship, the 1980 Pittsburgh Panthers were a remarkable team with four future College Football Hall of Famers in the lineup: Tackles Jimbo Covert and Mark May, defensive end Hugh Green, and quarterback Dan Marino. Pitt outscored their opponents (which had a .5991 winning percentage) by 20.83 points per game, and finished no. 2 in the country after destroying South Carolina in the Gator Bowl.

1953 3-5-1

7 West Virginia	17 E Joe Zombek / Bob McQuaide
7 Oklahoma	7 T Bill Cessar / Rich Gatz
14 Nebraska	6 G Harold Hunter / Ed Stowe
14 Notre Dame	23 C Ed Johnson
21 Northwestern	27 G John Cenci / Paul Blanda
14 Minnesota	35 T Eldred Kraemer
26 Virginia	0 E Dick Deitrick
40 N. Carolina St.	6 QB Henry Ford / Pete Neft
0 Penn State	17 HB Ray DiPasquale / John Jacobs
	HB Richie McCabe / Ray Ferguson
	FB Bobby Epps / Bobby Grier

RUSHING: Epps 100/424y, Grier 20/241y, McCabe 57/199y
PASSING: Ford 33-80/305y, 3TD, 41.3%
RECEIVING: Deitrick 13/139y, Zombek 11/95y, Ferguson 5/81y,
SCORING: Epps 24pts, Ford 18pts, Blanda (G-K) 13pts

1954 4-5

7 Southern Cal	27 E Joe Walton / Bob McQuaide
7 Minnesota	46 T Bob Pollock / Lou Pallatella
0 Notre Dame	33 G Ed Stowe / Harold Hunter
21 Navy	19 C John Cenci
14 Northwestern	7 G Al Bolkovac
13 West Virginia	10 T Eldred Kramer
0 Ohio State	26 E John Paluck / Dick Sherer
21 Nebraska	7 QB Pete Neft / Rudy Mattioli
0 Penn State	13 HB Henry Ford (QB)
	HB Ambrose "Bags" Bagamery
	HB Tom Jenkins / Bobby Grier

RUSHING: Ford 95/322y, Salvaterra 73/296y, Jenkins 63/203y
PASSING: Salvaterra 19-57/286y, 3TD, 33.3%
RECEIVING: McQuaide 8/78y, Ford 5/103y, Walton 4/15y
SCORING: Bagamery (HB-K) 23pts, Salvaterra 18pts, Ford 12pts

1955 7-4

27 California	7 E Joe Walton / Fred Glatz
22 Syracuse	12 T Bob Pollock / Jim McCusker
14 Oklahoma	26 G Harold Hunter
0 Navy	21 C John Cenci / Ed Bose
21 Nebraska	7 G Al Bolkovac / Bill Schmitt
26 Duke	7 T Herman Canil / Ron Kissel
7 Miami	21 E John Paluck / Bob Rosborough
18 Virginia	7 QB Corny Salvaterra / Pete Neft
26 West Virginia	7 HB Corky Cost / Dick Bowen
20 Penn State	0 HB Lou Cimarolli / Ray DiPasquale
0 Georgia Tech■	7 FB Tom Jenkins / Bobby Grier

RUSHING: Cimarolli 57/339y, Bowen 64/303y, Salvaterra 73/279y
PASSING: Salvaterra 25-54/329y, 4TD, 46.3%
RECEIVING: Walton 16/241y, Paluck 8/65y, Cost 5/77y
SCORING: Walton 48pts, Cimarolli, Grier & Jenkins 18pts

1956 7-3-1

14 West Virginia	13 E Joe Walton / Dick Scherer
14 Syracuse	7 T Bob Pollock / Jim McCusker
0 California	14 G Vince Scorsone
27 Duke	14 C Charley Brueckman
14 Oregon	7 G Dan Wisniewski / Dick Carr
6 Minnesota	9 T Herman Canil / Ron Kissel
26 Notre Dame	13 E Bob Rosborough / Fred Glatz
20 Army	7 QB Corny Salvaterra / Darrell Lewis
7 Penn State	7 HB Dick Bowen / Dick Haley / Corky Cost
7 Miami	7 HB Jim Theordore / Ray DiPasquale
14 Georgia Tech■	21 FB Tom Jenkins / Ralph Jelic

RUSHING: Salvaterra 123/504y, Theodore 91/405y, Jelic 69/398y
PASSING: Salvaterra 33-88/500y, 7TD, 37.5%
RECEIVING: Walton 21/360y, Cost 5/82y, Rosborough 4/44y
SCORING: Walton 36pts, Salvaterra 31pts, Bagamery 17pts

1957 4-6

0 Oklahoma	26 E Dick Scherer
6 Oregon	3 T Ron Kissel / Ken Montanari
20 Southern Cal	14 G John Guzik
34 Nebraska	0 C Charley Brueckman / Don Crafton
13 Army	29 G Dan Wisniewski / Dick Carr
7 Notre Dame	13 T Jim McCusker / Bill Lindner
21 Syracuse	24 E Jim Zanos / Art Gob
6 West Virginia	7 QB Bill Kaliden / Ivan Toncic
14 Penn State	13 HB Dick Haley / John Flara
13 Miami	28 HB Jim Theodore / Joe Scisly
	FB Fred Riddle / Dick Bowen (HB)

RUSHING: Riddle 76/407y,
PASSING: Kaliden 40-93/519y, 2TD, 43.0%
RECEIVING: Scherer 20/403y,
SCORING: Scherer 30pts, Gob 18pts, 3 with 12pts

1958 5-4-1

27 UCLA	6 E Mike Ditka / Jim Zanos
17 Holy Cross	0 T Ken Montanari
13 Minnesota	7 G John Guzik
8 Michigan State	22 C Don Crafton / Serafino "Foge" Fazio
15 West Virginia	8 G Ed Michaels
14 Army	14 T Bill Lindner
13 Syracuse	16 E Art Gob / Joe Pullekines
29 Notre Dame	26 QB Bill Kaliden / Ivan Toncic
6 Nebraska	14 HB Dick Haley / Chuck Reinhold
21 Penn State	25 HB Joe Scisly/Andy Sepsi/Curt Plowman
	FB Fred Riddle / Jim Cunningham

RUSHING: Haley 93/311y, Riddle 105/310y, Scisly 72/266y
PASSING: Toncic 49-69/641y, 4TD, 71.0%
  Kaliden 39-81/549y, 3TD, 48.1%
RECEIVING: Ditka 18/252y, Haley 14/232y, Riddle 12/117y
SCORING: Haley 42pts

1959 6-4

21 Marquette	15 E Mike Ditka
0 Southern Cal	23 T Ken Montanari / Ernie Westwood
25 UCLA	21 G Regis Coustillac / Paul Hodge
12 Duke	0 C Foge Fazio / Andy Kuzneski
14 West Virginia	23 G Larry Vignali / Bob Guzik
3 Texas Christian	13 T Bill Lindner / Dick Mills
0 Syracuse	35 E Ron Delfine / Steve Jastrzembski
22 Boston College	14 QB Ivan Toncic
28 Notre Dame	13 HB Bob Clemens / Chuck Reinhold
22 Penn State	7 HB Fred Cox /Joe Scisly /Curt Plowman
	FB Jim Cunningham / Fred Riddle

RUSHING: Cox 47/392y, Cunningham 80/326y, Scisly 45/224y
PASSING: Toncic 56-133/667y, 8TD, 42.1%
RECEIVING: Ditka 16/249y, Jastrzembski 8/141y, Cox 8/112y
SCORING: Cox (HB-K) 41pts

1960 4-3-3

7 UCLA	8 E Mike Ditka
7 Michigan State	7 T Dick Mills / Bob Budavich
14 Oklahoma	15 G Regis Coustillac / Paul Hodge
17 Miami	6 C Andy Kuzneski
42 West Virginia	0 G Larry Vignali / Bob Guzik
7 Texas Christian	7 T Gary Kaltenbach
10 Syracuse	0 E Steve Jastrzembski / Ron Delfine
20 Notre Dame	13 QB Jim Traficant / Dave Kraus
7 Army	7 HB Bob Clemens / Chuck Reinhold
3 Penn State	14 HB Fred Cox / John Yaccino
	FB Jim Cunningham

RUSHING: Clemens 74/349y, Cox 82/333y,
  Cunningham 89/303y
PASSING: Traficant 29-57/407y, 4TD, 50.9%
  Kraus 17-39/149y, TD, 43.6%
RECEIVING: Ditka 11/229y, Cox 11/177y, Jastrzembski 7/125y
SCORING: Cox 42pts

1961 3-7

10 Miami	7 E Steve Jastrzembski
13 Baylor	16 T Gary Kaltenbach / Bob Ostrosky
17 Washington	22 G Regis Coustillac / Tom Brown
6 West Virginia	20 C Andy Kuzneski
6 UCLA	20 G Larry Vignali
28 Navy	14 T Bob Guzik / Ed Adamchik
9 Syracuse	28 E Heywood Haser / John Kuprok
20 Notre Dame	26 QB Jim Traficant
10 Southern Cal	9 HB Ed Clark / Bob Clemens
26 Penn State	47 HB Fred Cox / Paul Martha (QB)
	FB Rick Leeson / Lou Slaby

RUSHING: Leeson 103/452y, Clark 57/213y, Martha 44/212y
PASSING: Traficant 32-67/437y, 2TD, 47.8%
RECEIVING: Kuprok 18/247y, Cox 12/148y, Jastrzembski 7/99y
SCORING: Leeson 24pts

1962 5-5

14 Miami	23 E Al Grigaliunas / Joe Kuzneski
24 Baylor	14 T Gary Kaltenban
26 California	24 G Tom Brown / John Draksler
8 West Virginia	15 C Charles Alborn / Paul Cercel
8 UCLA	6 G Ralph Conrad / Ray Popp
9 Navy	32 T Ed Adamchik / Ernie Borghetti
24 Syracuse	6 E Bob Long
22 Notre Dame	43 QB Jim Traficant
7 Army	6 HB Ed Clark / John Ozimek
0 Penn State	16 HB Paul Martha (QB) / Dennis Chillinsky
	FB Rick Leeson / John Telesky

RUSHING: Leeson 104/481y, Clark 75/407y, Martha 78/351y
PASSING: Traficant 39-88/611y, 3TD, 44.3%
RECEIVING: Martha 12/246y, Grigalunas 9/128y, 3 with 5
SCORING: Martha 44pts, Leeson 32pts, Clark & Traficant 12pts

1963 9-1

20 UCLA	0 E Al Grigaliunas / Bill Howley
13 Washington	6 T Ernie Borghetti
35 California	15 G Jeff Ware / Jim Irwin
13 West Virginia	10 C Marty Schottenheimer / Charles Alborn
12 Navy	24 G Ray Popp
35 Syracuse	27 T Ed Adamchik / Ron Linaberg
27 Notre Dame	7 E Joe Kuzneski / John Jenkins
28 Army	0 QB Freddie Mazurek / Kenny Lucas
31 Miami	20 HB Bill Bodle / Eric Crabtree
22 Penn State	21 HB Paul Martha / Bob Roeder
	FB Rick Leeson / John Telesky

RUSHING: Mazurek 132/646y, Leeson 98/501y, Martha 89/485y
PASSING: Mazurek 74-127/949y, 5TD, 58.3%
RECEIVING: Kuzneski 21/258y, Howley 18/235y, Bodle 17/183y
SCORING: Mazurek 46pts

1964 3-5-2

12 UCLA	17 E Mike Rosborough / Bill Howley
13 Oregon	22 T Dennis Bernick
34 William & Mary	7 G Ray Popp / Bernard LaQuinta
14 West Virginia	0 C Paul Cercel/Marty Schottenheimer(LB)
20 Miami	20 G Bob Sorochak / Joe Novogratz
14 Navy	14 T Ron Linaburg
6 Syracuse	21 E Mitchell Zalnasky / Tom Black
15 Notre Dame	17 QB Freddie Mazurek / Kenny Lucas
24 Army	8 HB Jim Dodaro / Bill Bodle
0 Penn State	28 HB Eric Crabtree / Dale Stewart
	FB Barry McKnight

RUSHING: McKnight 129/551y, Mazurek 123/481y,
  Crabtree 75/344y
PASSING: Mazurek 53-93/686y, 3TD, 57.0%
RECEIVING: Rosborough 16/151y, Crabtree 14/255y,
  Zalnasky 14/156y
SCORING: McKnight 50pts

1965 3-7

15 Oregon	17 E Mickey Rosborough
13 Oklahoma	9 T Tom Raymond / Bob Guzinsky
48 West Virginia	63 G Gabe Tamburino
13 Duke	21 C Fred Hoaglin
0 Navy	12 G Tom Qualey
28 Miami	14 T James Jones (DL)
13 Syracuse	51 E Mitch Zalnasky / Bob Longo
13 Notre Dame	69 QB Kenny Lucas
0 Southern Cal	28 HB Bob Dyer / Dewey Chester
30 Penn State	27 HB Eric Crabtree / Gerry Rife
	FB Barry McKnight / Mike Raklewicz
	DL Ed Assid
	DL Bob Guzinsky / Bob Trethaway
	DL Dave Drake
	DL Al Keiser
	DL Phil Dahar / Greg Keller
	LB Joe Novogratz
	LB Jim Flanigan
	LB Tom Mitrakos / Bill Boucek
	DB Tippy Pohl
	DB Mickey Depp / Bob Bazylak
	DB Dale Stewart / Joe Curtin

RUSHING: McKnight 124/406y, Crabtree 84/372y, Dyer 75/307y
PASSING: Lucas 144-268/1921y, 10TD, 53.7%
RECEIVING: Crabtree 45/724y, Rosborough 32/364y,
  Zalnasky 32/340y
SCORING: Crabtree 44pts

1966 1-9

14 UCLA	57 WR Bob Longo
7 Duke	14 T Ed Whittaker / Bob Trethaway
15 California	30 G Dick Miale
17 West Virginia	14 C Bob Taylor
7 Navy	24 G Dave Randour
0 Army	28 T Dave Raudman / John Schmidt
0 Syracuse	33 TE Mickey Rosborough (WB)/Frank Hartz
0 Notre Dame	40 QB Ed James
14 Miami	38 TB Joe Jones / Dewey Chester
24 Penn State	48 WB Skip Orszulak / Gerry Rife
	FB Mike Raklewicz
	DL Art Alois / Richard Genter
	DL Dave Drake
	DL Brian Bubnis
	DL Greg Keller / Tom Mitrakos (C)
	LB Ed Gallin
	LB Jim Flanigan
	LB Lou Parrott / Tom DeMelfi
	DB Paul Killian / Tippy Pohl
	DB Joe Curtin
	DB Mickey Depp
	DB Bob Dyer / Bob Bazylak

RUSHING: Raklewicz 110/324y, Jones 97/273y,Chester 38/112y
PASSING: James 91-193/1162y, 7TD, 47.2%
RECEIVING: Longo 46/732y, Rosborough 30/311y, Orszulak 16/167y
SCORING: Longo 30pts, Jones 18pts, Howard Heit (K) 11pts

1967 1-9

8 UCLA	40 WR Bob Longo
6 Illinois	34 T Tom Mitrakos
0 West Virginia	15 G Art Alois (T) / Warren Allen
13 Wisconsin	11 C Chuck Hutchko
0 Miami	58 G Ray Radakovich / Ed Sadowski
21 Navy	22 T Dave Mancuso
7 Syracuse	14 TE George "Doc" Medich / Frank Hartz
0 Notre Dame	38 QB Bob Bazylak / Jeff Barr
12 Army	21 HB Gary Cramer
6 Penn State	42 WB Skip Orszulak / Joe McCain
	FB Mike Raklewicz / Jeff Brown
	DL Terry Hoover / Paul Naponick
	DL Dave Drake
	DL Ed Whittaker
	DL Bob Ellis
	LB Lou Parrott
	LB Eugene Yajko
	LB Ed Gallin / Greg Keller
	DB Joe Curtin / George Pribish
	DB Paul Killian / Mike Elliott
	DB Mickey Depp
	DB Dave Dibbley

RUSHING: Cramer 78/312y, Brown 33/149y, McCain 23/116y
PASSING: Bazylak 55-124/679y, 2TD, 44.3%
RECEIVING: Longo 40/548y, McCain 26/370y, Medich 23/269y
SCORING: McCain 17pts, Longo 12pts, Barr 12pts

1968 1-9

7 UCLA	63 WR Bill Piconis
15 West Virginia	38 T Bill Beinecke
14 William & Mary	3 G Dave Mancuso
17 Syracuse	50 C Dave Magyar / Chuck Hutchko
16 Navy	17 G Art Alois
14 Air Force	27 T Ed Whittaker
0 Miami	48 TE Doc Medich
7 Notre Dame	56 QB Dave Havern
0 Army	26 HB Denny Ferris
9 Penn State	65 WB Skip Orszulak / Joe McCain
	FB Tony Esposito
	DL Bob Ellis
	DL John Stevens
	DL Bruce Harkiewicz
	DL Paul Naponick
	LB Geoff Brown
	LB Ed Gallin / Ralph Cindrich
	LB Lloyd Weston
	DB Charles Hall
	DB Dave Dibbley
	DB Jeff Barr
	DB George Pribish

RUSHING: Ferris 120/472y, Esposito 51/150y, Garnett 50/134y
PASSING: Havern 140-287/1810y, 7TD, 48.7%
RECEIVING: Orszulak 50/725y, McCain 33/421y, Medich 29/330y
SCORING: Orszulak 24pts, Ferris 14pts, 3 with 12pts

1969 4-6

8 UCLA	42 WR Steve Moyer
8 Oklahoma	37 WR Bill Peconis / Skip Orszulak
14 Duke	12 T Bill Beinecke
46 Navy	19 G Ed Sadowski
22 Tulane	26 C Dave Magyer
18 West Virginia	49 G John Simpson
21 Syracuse	20 T Rodney Fedorchak
7 Notre Dame	49 TE Doc Medich
15 Army	6 QB Jim Friedl
7 Penn State	27 HB Denny Ferris / Dave Garnett
	FB Tony Esposito / Mike Raklewicz
	DL Bob Ellis
	DL Lloyd Weston
	DL John Stevens / Bruce Harkiewicz
	DL Jack Dykes
	LB Geoff Brown / Dave McGrath
	LB Ralph Cindrich
	LB Joe Carroll / Bob Dyer
	DB Charles Hall
	DB Bryant Salter / Mike Bannon
	DB Dave Dibbley / Joe Curtin
	DB George Pribish

RUSHING: Esposito 201/743y, Ferris 127/469y, Garnett 35/149y
PASSING: Friedl 128-263/1277y, 11TD, 48.9%
RECEIVING: Moyer 48/437y, Medich 39/424y, Pilconis 19/205y
SCORING: Ferris 42pts, Esposito 36pts, Medich 32pts

1970 5-5

15 UCLA	24 WR Steve Moyer
15 Baylor	10 WR Bill Peconis
27 Kent State	6 T Bill Beinecke
10 Navy	8 G Dan Lynn
36 West Virginia	35 C Bob Kuziel
28 Miami	17 G John Simpson
13 Syracuse	43 T Bruce Harkiewicz
14 Notre Dame	46 TE Joel Klimek
6 Boston College	21 QB John Hogan / Dave Havern
15 Penn State	35 HB Denny Ferris
	FB Tony Esposito / Phil Sgrignoli
	DL John Stevens
	DL Howard Broadhead
	DL Lloyd Weston
	DL Hank Alford / Jack Dykes
	LB George Feher
	LB Dave McGrath
	LB Joe Carroll
	DB Charles Hall
	DB Reggie Frye
	DB J.D. Lewis
	DB Bryant Salter

RUSHING: Esposito 160/623y, Ferris 158/595y, Sgrignoli 47/204y
PASSING: Hogan 72-140/801y, 3TD, 51.4%, Havern 60-106/638y, 3TD, 56.6%
RECEIVING: Ferris 35/506y, Moyer 32/312y, Klimek 28/329y
SCORING: Ferris 54pts, Esposito 42pts, Spicko 19pts

1971 3-8

29 UCLA	25 WR Steve Moyer / Doug Gindin
29 Oklahoma	55 T Ernie Webster / Dave Blandino
9 West Virginia	20 G Dan Lynn / Joe Kovacic
36 Navy	35 C Bob Kuziel
8 Tulane	33 G John Simpson
22 Boston College	40 T Dave Wannstedt / John Robb
31 Syracuse	21 TE Joel Klimek / Leslie Block
7 Notre Dame	56 QB Dave Halvern / John Hogan
14 Army	17 HB Stan Ostrowski / Bill Englert
18 Penn State	55 HB John Chatman / John Moss
13 Florida State	31 FB Lou Julian / Paul Felinczak
	DL James Buckman
	DL Howard Broadhead
	DL Jack Dykes / Art Venzin
	DL Glenn Hyde
	DL Andy Mollura / Eric Knisley
	LB Ralph Cindrich / George Feher
	LB Joe Carroll / Gary Patterson
	DB Ed Marstellar / Lance Wall
	DB Reggie Frye / Dan Rullo
	DB Lou Cecconi / Lloyd Rodgers
	DB Bill Adams / Joe Herndon

RUSHING: Julian 101/368y, Felinczek 85/313y, Chatman 61/309y
PASSING: Havern 108-207/1197y, 11TD, 52.1%
RECEIVING: Klimek 39/452y, Moyer 37/522y, Ginkin 19/278y
SCORING: Moyer 32pts, Block 30pts, Knisley 26pts

1972 1-10

7 Florida State	19 WR Todd Toerper / Lance Wall
28 UCLA	38 T Dave Wannstedt / Paul Yuna
13 Air Force	41 G Reynold Stoner
22 Northwestern	27 C Mike Carey / Anthony Kuzneski
6 Tulane	38 G Ernie Webster / Joe Kovacic
16 Notre Dame	42 T Dave Blandino
35 Boston College	20 TE Les Block / Rod Huth
6 Syracuse	10 QB John Hogan
20 West Virginia	38 HB Stan Ostrowski / John Chatman
13 Navy	28 HB Bill Englert / Lou Cecconi
27 Penn State	49 FB Dave Janasek / Paul Felinczak
	DL Jim Buckman / Gary Roos
	DL Glenn Hyde
	DL Art Venzin / Spencer Potter
	DL Dave Jancisin
	DL Eric Knisley / John Moss
	LB Ken Paieski/Lou Julian/Gary Patters'n
	LB Carlos Hamlin / George Feher
	DB Reggie Frye
	DB Ed Marstellar / Glenn Hodge
	DB Dan Rullo
	DB Mike Bulino / Joe Herndon

RUSHING: Ostrowski 140/514y, Englert 81/354y, Cecconi 48/184y
PASSING: Hogan 91-191/1250y, 14TD, 47.6%
RECEIVING: Toerper 34/501y, Englert 20/213y, Wall 18/298y, Ostrowski 18/255y
SCORING: Ostrowski 26pts, Toerper 20pts, Wall 18pts

1973 6-5-1

7 Georgia	7 WR Bruce Murphy
14 Baylor	20 WR Todd Toerper
21 Northwestern	14 T Dave Wannstedt
6 Tulane	24 G Reynold Stoner
35 West Virginia	7 C Mike Carey
28 Boston College	14 G Ray Olsen
22 Navy	17 T Dave Blandino
28 Syracuse	14 TE Stan Ostrowski / Leslie Block
10 Notre Dame	31 QB Bill Daniels
34 Army	0 TB Tony Dorsett
13 Penn State	35 FB Dave Janasek
7 Arizona State ■	28 DL Jim Buckmon
	DL Don Parrish
	DL Gary Burley
	DL Glenn Hyde / Dave Jancisin
	DL Tom Perko
	LB Rod Kirby
	LB Mike Bulino
	LB Kelcy Daviston
	DB Dennis Moorhead
	DB David Spates
	DB Glenn Hodge

RUSHING: Dorsett 288/1586y, Daniels 149/440y, Janasek 61/292y
PASSING: Daniels 84-176/1170y, 3TD, 47.7%
RECEIVING: Murphy 20/325y, Toerper 16/228y, Ostrowski 13/159y
SCORING: Dorsett 72pts, Daniels 62pts, Carson Long (K) 48pts

1974 7-4

9 Florida State	6 WR Karl Farmer / Todd Toerper
27 Georgia Tech	17 T Joe Stone
7 Southern Cal	16 G Reynold Stoner
29 North Carolina	45 C Mike Carey
31 West Virginia	14 G Tom Brzoza
35 Boston College	11 T Theo Lawrence
13 Navy	11 TE Jim Corbett
21 Syracuse	13 QB Bill Daniels
35 Temple	24 TB Tony Dorsett / Elliott Walker
10 Notre Dame	14 WB Bruce Murphy
10 Penn State	31 FB Bob Hutton / Dave Janasek
	DL Cecil Johnson
	DL Al Romano
	DL Gary Burley
	DL Don Parrish / Randy Holloway
	DL Tom Perko
	LB Arnie Weatherington
	LB Kelcy Daviston
	LB Mike Bulino / Larry Felton
	DB David Spates
	DB Glenn Hodge
	DB Dennis Moorhead

RUSHING: Dorsett 220/1004y, Walker 63/431y, Murphy 51/295y
PASSING: Daniels 71-121/919y, 9TD, 587.%
RECEIVING: Murphy 25/400y, Farmer 18/285y, Corbett 16/202y
SCORING: Dorsett 66pts, Carson Long (K) 45pts, Walker 38pts

1975 8-4

19 Georgia	9 WR Gordon Jones / Willie Taylor
10 Oklahoma	46 WR Rodney Clark / Karl Farmer
47 William & Mary	0 T John Hanhauser
14 Duke	0 G Matt Carroll
55 Temple	6 C John Pelusi / Mike Shaffer
52 Army	20 G Tom Brzoza
0 Navy	17 T Joe Stone
38 Syracuse	0 TE Jim Corbett
14 West Virginia	17 QB Robert Haygood / Matt Cavanaugh
34 Notre Dame	20 TB Tony Dorsett
6 Penn State	7 FB Elliott Walker / Bob Hutton
33 Kansas■	19 DL Ed Wilamowski
	DL Don Parrish
	DL Al Romano
	DL Randy Holloway
	DL Randy Cozens / Cecil Johnson
	LB Tom Perko / Al Chesley
	LB Arnie Weatherington / Jim Cramer
	DB Dennis Moorhead
	DB James Wilson / Leroy Felder
	DB Bob Jury
	DB Jeff Delaney

RUSHING: Dorsett 255/1686y, Walker 161/903y,
  Haygood 123/336y
PASSING: Haygood 42-78/687y, 4TD, 53.9%
  Cavanaugh 30-65/488y, 7TD, 46.2%
RECEIVING: Corbett 24/322y, Jones 22/385y, Dorsett 11/191y
SCORING: Dorsett 96pts, Carson Long (K) 76pts, Walker 54pts

1976 12-0

31 Notre Dame	10 WR Gordon Jones
42 Georgia Tech	14 WR Willie Taylor / Randy Reutershan
21 Temple	7 T John Hanhauser
44 Duke	31 G Matt Carroll
27 Louisville	6 C John Pelusi
36 Miami	19 G Tom Brzoza / George Link
45 Navy	0 T Joe Stone / George Messich
23 Syracuse	13 TE Jim Corbett
37 Army	7 QB Matt Cavanaugh / Robert Haygood
24 West Virginia	16 TB Tony Dorsett
24 Penn State	7 FB Elliott Walker
27 Georgia■	3 DL Cecil Johnson / Desmond Robinson
	DL Don Parrish
	DL Al Romano / Dave Logan
	DL Randy Holloway
	DL Arnie Weatherington / Ed Wilamowski
	LB Jim Cramer / Desmond Robinson
	LB Al Chesley / Gary Tyra
	DB Mike Balzer / Steve Gaustad
	DB Leroy Felder / Larry Felton
	DB Bob Jury / James Wilson
	DB Jeff Delaney / Dave DiCiccio

RUSHING: Dorsett 370/2150y, Walker 85/389y,
  Cavanaugh 98/366y
PASSING: Cavanaugh 65-110/1046y, 9TD, 59.1%
RECEIVING: Corbett 34/538y, Jones 21/386y, Taylor 18/320y
SCORING: Dorsett 140pts, Carson Long (K) 99pts,
  Jones & Cavanaugh 30pts

1977 9-2-1

9 Notre Dame	19 WR Gordon Jones
28 William & Mary	6 WR Willie Taylor / Randy Reutershan
76 Temple	0 T Art Bortnick
45 Boston College	7 G Matt Carroll
17 Florida	17 C Tom Brzoza / Walt Brown
34 Navy	17 G Walter Link
28 Syracuse	21 T Kurt Brechbill
48 Tulane	0 TE Steve Gaustad
44 West Virginia	3 QB Matt Cavanaugh / Rick Trocano
52 Army	26 TB Elliott Walker / Larry Sims
13 Penn State	15 FB Freddy Jacobs
34 Clemson■	3 DL Dave Diciccio / Mike Lenosky
	DL Dave Logan / Bill Neill
	DL Jerry Boyarsky
	DL Randy Holloway
	DL Hugh Green
	LB Jeff Pelusi
	LB Al Chesley / Steve Fedell
	DB James Wilson / Jo Jo Heath
	DB Leroy Felder
	DB Bob Jury / Mike Balzer
	DB Jeff Delaney

RUSHING: Walker 172/1025y, Jacobs 121/672y,
  Trocano 63/265y
PASSING: Cavanaugh 110-187/1844y, 15 TDs, 58.8%
RECEIVING: Jones 45/793y, Gausted 31/514y,
  Reutershan 17/311y
SCORING: Walker 90pts, Jones 66pts, Mark Schubert (K) 65pts

1978 8-4

24 Tulane	6 WR Gordon Jones
20 Temple	12 WR Willie Collier / Ralph Still
20 North Carolina	16 T Bob Gruber / Kurt Brechbill
32 Boston College	15 G Dan Fidler / Emil Boures
17 Notre Dame	26 C Walt Brown
7 Florida State	3 G Matt Carroll
11 Navy	21 T Mark May
18 Syracuse	17 TE Steve Gaustad
52 West Virginia	7 QB Rick Trocano
35 Army	17 RB Freddy Jacobs / Larry Sims
10 Penn State	17 RB Ray "Rooster" Jones
17 N. Carolina St.■	30 DL Greg Meisner
	DL Dave Logan / Jerry Boyarsky
	DL Bill Neill
	LB Hugh Green
	LB Al Chesley
	LB Jeff Pelusi / Desmond Robinson
	LB Dave DiCiccio / Rickey Jackson
	DB Lynn Thomas
	DB Mike Balzer / Carlton Williamson
	DB Jo Jo Heath
	DB Jeff Delaney

RUSHING: Jacobs 152/634y, R. Jones 150/617y, Sims 72/323y
PASSING: Trocano 138-283/1648y, 5TD, 48.8%
RECEIVING: Jones 45/666y
SCORING: Jacobs 54pts

1979 11-1

24 Kansas	0 WR Ralph Still / Willie Collier
7 North Carolina	17 WR Larry Sims
10 Temple	9 T Bob Gruber / Ed Gallagher
28 Boston College	7 G Emil Boures / Dan Fidler
35 Cincinnati	0 C Russ Grimm
26 Washington	14 G Jim Morsillo / Bert Bertagna
24 Navy	7 T Mark May
28 Syracuse	21 TE Benji Pryor / Mike Dombrowski
24 West Virginia	17 QB Rick Trocano / Dan Marino
40 Army	0 HB Freddy Jacobs / Rooster Jones
29 Penn State	14 FB Randy McMillan / Russell Carter
16 Arizona■	10 DL Rickey Jackson / Steve Fedell
	DL Greg Meisner / Jimbo Covert
	DL Jerry Boyarsky / Dave Bucklew
	DL Bill Neill
	DL Hugh Green
	LB Jeff Pelusi / Sal Sunseri
	LB Mark Reichard / Yogi Jones
	DB Carlton Williamson / Butch Baierl
	DB Lynn Thomas / Pappy Thomas
	DB Jo Jo Heath / Terry White
	DB Mike Christ / Barry Compton

RUSHING: McMillan 184/802y, Jones 105/407y, Jacobs 90/316y
PASSING: Marino 130-222/1680y, 10TD, 58.6%
RECEIVING: Pryor 45/588y, Still 43/580y, Jacobs 22/176y
SCORING: Mark Schubert (K) 71pts, McMillan 60pts, Still 42pts

1980 11-1

14 Boston College	6 WR Willie Collier / Julius Dawkins
18 Kansas	3 WR Dwight Collins / Larry Sims
36 Temple	2 T Jimbo Covert
38 Maryland	9 G Rob Fada
22 Florida State	36 C Russ Grimm
42 West Virginia	14 G Emil Boures
30 Tennessee	6 T Mark May
43 Syracuse	6 TE Benji Pryor / Mike Dombrowski
41 Louisville	23 QB Dan Marino / Rick Trocano
45 Army	7 HB Joe McCall / Artrell Hawkins
14 Penn State	9 FB Randy McMillan / Wayne DiBartola
37 South Carolina ■	9 DL Greg Meisner / Dave Bucklew
	DL Jerry Boyarsky / Jay Pelusi
	DL Bill Neill
	LB Hugh Green
	LB Sal Sunseri / Mark Reichard
	LB Steve Fedell
	LB Rickey Jackson / Michael Woods
	DB Terry White / Tim Lewis
	DB Lynn Thomas / Pappy Thomas
	DB Carlton Williamson
	DB Tom Flynn

RUSHING: McMillan 134/633y, McCall 105/453y,
  DiBartola 40/160y
PASSING: Marino 109-211/1513y, 14TD, 51.7%,
  Trocano 78-144/1246y, 10TD, 54.2%
RECEIVING: Pryor 43/538y, Collins 37/777y, Collier 32/537y
SCORING: Dave Trout (K) 71pts, Collins 60pts, McMillan 54pts

1981 11-1

26 Illinois	6 WR Julius Dawkins / Bill Wallace
38 Cincinnati	7 WR Dwight Collins / Barry Compton
42 South Carolina	28 T Jimbo Covert
17 West Virginia	0 G Rob Fada
42 Florida State	14 C Emil Boures / Anthony Magnelli
23 Syracuse	10 G Ron Sams / Paul Dunn
29 Boston College	24 T Bill Fralic / Greg Christy
47 Rutgers	3 TE John Brown / Clint Wilson
48 Army	0 QB Dan Marino
35 Temple	0 HB Bryan Thomas / Joe McCall
14 Penn State	48 FB Wayne DiBartolo / Marlon McIntyre
24 Georgia■	20 DL Chris Doleman / Al Wenglikowski
	DL Dave Pezzuoli
	DL J.C. Pelusi
	DL Bill Maas
	DL Michael Woods
	LB Sal Sunseri / Ray Lao
	LB Rich Kraynak / Caeser Aldisert
	DB Pappy Thomas / Troy Hill
	DB Tim Lewis / Melvin Dean
	DB Tom Flynn

RUSHING: Thomas 217/1132y, DiBartola 158/716y,
  McCall 50/179y
PASSING: Marino 226-380/2876y, 37TD, 59.5%
RECEIVING: Dawkins 46/767y, Thomas 46/451y, Brown 43/530y
SCORING: Dawkins 96pts, Ray Everett (K) 61pts, Brown 48pts

1982 9-3

7 North Carolina	6 WR Julius Dawkins
37 Florida State	17 WR Dwight Collins
20 Illinois	3 T Jimbo Covert
16 West Virginia	13 G Rob Fada
38 Temple	17 C Jim Sweeney
14 Syracuse	0 G Ron Sams
63 Louisville	14 T Bill Fralic
16 Notre Dame	31 TE John Brown / Clint Wilson
24 Army	6 QB Dan Marino
52 Rutgers	6 TB Bryan Thomas / Joe McCall
10 Penn State	19 FB Marlon McIntyre / Marc Bailey
3 SMU■	7 DL Bill Maas
	DL Dave Puzzuoli
	DL J. C. Pelusi / Tim Quense
	LB Michael Woods / Michael Brooks
	LB Yogi Jones
	LB Rich Kraynak / Caesar Aldisert
	LB Al Wenglikowski / Chris Doleman
	DB Tim Lewis
	DB Troy Hill / Melvin Dean
	DB Peep Short
	DB Tom Flynn

RUSHING: Thomas 219/955y
PASSING: Marino 221-378/2432y, 17TD, 58.5%
RECEIVING: Thomas 54/404y
SCORING: Eric Schubert (K) 69pts

1983 8-3-1

13 Tennessee	3 WR Dwight Collins
35 Temple	0 WR Bill Wallace
7 Maryland	13 T Tony Brown
21 West Virginia	24 G Mike Dorundo
17 Florida State	16 C Jim Sweeney
55 Louisville	10 G Bob Brown
21 Navy	14 T Bill Fralic
13 Syracuse	10 TE Clint Wilson
21 Notre Dame	16 QB John Congemi
38 Army	7 RB Joe McCall
24 Penn State	24 RB Marc Bailey / Marlon McIntyre
23 Ohio State■	28 DL Bill Maas
	DL Bob Schilken
	DL Tim Quense
	LB Al Wenglikowski
	LB Caesar Aldisert
	LB Troy Benson / Steve Apke
	LB Chris Doleman
	DB Troy Hill
	DB Melvin Dean
	DB Ray Weatherspoon
	DB Tom Flynn

RUSHING: McCall 197/961y, Bailey 86/451y, McIntyre 82/414y
PASSING: Congemi 170-286/1940y, 16TD, 59.4%
RECEIVING: Wallace 45/727y, Collins 33/433y, McCall 26/253y
SCORING: Wallace 48pts, Eric Schubert (K) 47pts, McCall 42pts

1984 3-7-1

14 BYU	20 WR Bill Wallace
10 Oklahoma	42 WR Jeff Casper / Chuck Scales (HB)
12 Temple	13 T Bill Fralic
10 West Virginia	28 G Greg Christy
17 East Carolina	10 C Barry Pettyjohn
21 South Carolina	45 G Bob Brown / Mike Dorundo
7 Miami	27 T Randy Dixon / Tony Brown
28 Navy	28 TE Dexter Edmonds / Tom Johnson
7 Syracuse	13 QB John Congemi
21 Tulane	10 HB Ch'les Gladman/C. "Ironh'd" Heyward
31 Penn State	11 FB Marc Bailey / Marlon McIntyre
	DL Bill Sapio / Mark Rich
	DL Lorenzo Freeman / Jon Carter
	DL Walter Johnson
	DL Bob Buczkowski
	DL Bob Schilken / Tom Crawford
	LB Chris Doleman / Caesar Aldisert
	LB Troy Benson
	DB Keith Tinsley / John Lewis
	DB Melvin Dean
	DB Reggie Smith
	DB Bill Callahan

RUSHING: Heyward 123/529y, Gladman 134/525y, McIntyre 50/250y
PASSING: Congemi 93-174/1102y, 9TD, 53.4%
RECEIVING: Wallace 43/610y, Scales 22/431y, McIntyre 12/54y
SCORING: Wallace 48pts, Mark Brasco (K) 32pts, Heywood 26pts

1985 5-5-1

31 Purdue	30 WR Reggie Williams / Michael Stewart
7 Ohio State	10 WR Matt Stennett / Chuck Scales
22 Boston College	29 T Randy Dixon
10 West Virginia	10 G Mike Dorundo
42 South Carolina	7 C Barry Pettyjohn
24 N. Carolina St.	10 G Bob Sign
38 Rutgers	10 T Tony Brown
7 Navy	21 TE Clint Wilson / David Shuck
0 Syracuse	12 QB John Congemi
21 Temple	17 TB Charles Gladman / Brian Davis
0 Penn State	31 RB Tom Brown / Darnell Stone
	DL Bill Sapio / Jon Carter
	DL Bob Buczkowski
	DL Dennis Atiyeh / Bob Schilken
	DL Walter Johnson / Lorenzo Freeman
	DL Tony Woods / Burt Grossman
	LB Steve Apke / Jerry Wall /Brian Shields
	LB Matt Lavigna / Jerry Olsavsky
	DB Teryl Austin / Quintin Jones
	DB John Lewis / Billy Owens
	DB Bill Callahan
	DB Troy Washington

RUSHING: Gladman 194/1085y, Brown 85/386y, Davis 60/298y Stone 60/228y
PASSING: Congemi 122-241/1377y, 6TD, 50.6%
RECEIVING: Scales 34/446y, Wilson 16/177y, Stewart 13/209y, R. Williams 9/125y, Stennett 7/100y
SCORING: Gladman 36pts, Mark Brasco (K) 34pts, Scales & Congemi 24pts

1986 5-5-1

7 Maryland	10 WR Reggie Williams / Billy Osborn
14 N. Carolina St.	14 WR Chuck Scales / Michael Stewart
41 Purdue	26 T Tom Ricketts
48 West Virginia	16 G Bob Sign / Dean Caliguire
13 Temple	19 C Chip Backauskas / Ed Miller
10 Notre Dame	9 G Mark Stepnoski
56 Navy	14 T Randy Dixon
20 Syracuse	24 TE Vernon Kirk
10 Miami	37 QB John Congemi
20 Rutgers	6 TB Charles Gladman / Ironhead Heyward
14 Penn State	34 FB Tom Brown / Mark LaVigna
	DL Tony Woods / Jon Carter
	DL Walter Johnson
	DL Tony Siragusa
	DL Burt Grossman / Carnel Smith
	LB Steve Apke / Jerry Wall
	LB Jerry Olsavsky
	LB Ezekial Gadson
	DB Quintin Jones
	DB Gary Richard
	DB Billy Owens / Troy Washington
	DB Teryl Austin

RUSHING: Heyward 171/756y
PASSING: Congemi 165-293/2048y, 11TD, 56.3%
RECEIVING: Osborn 33/414y
SCORING: Jeff Van Horne (K) 62pts

1987 8-4

27 BYU	17 WR Reggie Williams / Henry Tuten
34 N. Carolina St.	0 WR Billy Osborn/Micha'l Stew'rt/H. Heard
21 Temple	24 T Tom Ricketts
6 West Virginia	3 G Dean Caliguire / Bill Cherpak
10 Boston College	13 C Ed Miller / Chip Backauskas
30 Notre Dame	22 G Mark Stepnoski
10 Navy	6 T Roman Matusz
10 Syracuse	24 TE Eric Seaman / David Shuck
17 Rutgers	0 QB Sal Genilla / Darnell Dickerson
10 Penn State	0 TB Craig "Ironhead" Heyward
28 Kent State	5 FB Prentiss Wright / Louis Riddick
27 Texas■	32 DL Jon Carter
	DL Marc Spindler
	DL Tony Siragusa
	DL Burt Grossman / Carnel Smith
	LB Jerry Wall
	LB Jerry Olsavsky / Jeff Christy
	LB Ezekial Gadson
	DB Quintin Jones / Teryl Austin
	DB Gary Richard
	DB Troy Washington
	DB Billy Owens / Dan Crossman

RUSHING: Heyward 387/1791y, Adam Walker (TB) 38/214y, Riddick 40/175y
PASSING: Genilla 80-145/1051y, 7TD, 55.2%, Dickerson 35-93/375y, TD, 37.6%
RECEIVING: Williams 31/535y, Osborn 26/341y, Heyward 22/207y
SCORING: Heyward 78pts, Jeff VanHorne 53pts, Heard & Osborn 24pts

1988 6-5

59 Northern Iowa	10 WR Henry Tuten / Bill Osborn
42 Ohio State	10 WR Reggie Williams
10 West Virginia	31 T Scott Miller
31 Boston College	34 G Chris Goetz / Bill Cherpak
20 Notre Dame	30 C Dean Caliguire
42 Temple	7 G Mark Stepnoski
52 Navy	6 T Roman Matusz
20 Rutgers	10 TE Tom Huebner / Dave Tanczos
14 Penn State	7 QB Darnell Dickerson
3 N. Carolina St.	14 TB Curvin Richards / Adam Walker
7 Syracuse	24 FB Dan Crossman / Ron Redmon
	DL Burt Grossman
	DL Nelson Walker / Tom Sims
	DL Marc Spindler / Mike Chalenski
	DL Carnel Smith
	LB Curtis Bray
	LB Jerry Olsavsky
	LB Ricardo McDonald
	DB Alonzo Hampton
	DB Cornell Holloway
	DB Louis Riddick
	DB Troy Washington / Doug Hetzler

RUSHING: Richards 207/1228y
PASSING: Dickerson 104-213/1599y, 7TD, 48.8%
RECEIVING: Tuten 37/571y
SCORING: Scott Kaplan (K) 53pts

1989 8-3-1

38 Pacific	3 WR Henry Tuten
29 Boston College	10 WR Reggie Williams / Olando Truitt
30 Syracuse	23 T Scott Miller
31 West Virginia	31 G Bill Cherpak / Jeff Christy
27 Temple	3 C Chris Sestilli
31 Navy	14 G Chris Goetz
7 Notre Dame	45 T Roman Matusz
3 Miami	24 TE Lionel Sykes / Eric Seaman
47 East Carolina	42 QB Alex Van Pelt
13 Penn State	16 TB Curvin Richards / Glenn Deveaux
26 Rutgers	29 FB Ronald Redmon
31 Texas A&M■	28 DL Keith Hamilton
	DL Tom Sims / Richard Allen
	DL Mark Spindler / Jon Baker
	DL Carnel Smith / Mark Gunn
	LB Curtis Bray / Prentiss Wright
	LB Craig Gob
	LB Ricardo McDonald
	DB Alonzo Hampton / Dave Coleman
	DB Barry Threats / Robert Bradley
	DB Louis Riddick
	DB Dan Crossman / Doug Hetzler

RUSHING: Richards 232/1282y
PASSING: Van Pelt 192-347/2881y, 17TD, 55.3%
RECEIVING: Tuten 41/975y
SCORING: Ed Frazier (K) 77pts

1990 3-7-1

35 Ohio University	3 WR Darnell Dickerson (QB)
29 Boston College	6 WR Olanda Truitt
10 Oklahoma	52 T Scott Miller
20 Syracuse	20 G Jeff Christy
24 West Virginia	38 C Chris Sestilli
45 Rutgers	21 G Gary Gorajewski
20 Louisville	27 T Mike LiVorio
22 Notre Dame	31 TE Eric Seaman / Dave Moore
0 Miami	45 QB Alex Van Pelt
18 Temple	28 TB Glenn Deveaux / Curvin Richards
17 Penn State	22 FB Ronald Redmon / Ricky Turner
	DL Keith Hamilton
	DL Sean Gilbert
	DL Mark Gunn
	LB Curtis Bray / Heath Snell
	LB Craig Gob
	LB Prentiss Wright / Nelson Walker
	LB Ricardo McDonald
	DB Marcus Washington / Dave Coleman
	DB Tinker Harris / Steve Israel
	DB Louis Riddick
	DB Doug Hetzler

RUSHING: Richards 145/682y
PASSING: Van Pelt 201-351/2427y, 14TD, 57.3%
RECEIVING: Truitt 49/895y
SCORING: Scott Kaplan (K) 50pts

1991 6-5

34 West Virginia	3 WR Chris Bouyer / Junior Green
35 Southern Miss	14 WR Dietrich Jells
26 Temple	7 T Scott Miller / Mike LiVorio
14 Minnesota	13 G Jeff Christy / Lawson Mollica
24 Maryland	20 C Chris Sestilli
7 Notre Dame	42 G Gary Gorojewski / Shawn Abinet
27 Syracuse	31 T Reuben Brown
23 East Carolina	24 TE Eric Seaman / Dave Moore
12 Boston College	38 QB Alex Van Pelt
22 Rutgers	17 TB Curtis Martin / Jermaine Williams
20 Penn State	32 FB Glenn Deveaux
	DL Keith Hamilton
	DL Tom Barndt
	DL Sean Gilbert / Mike Kelly
	LB Nelson Walker
	LB Tom Tumulty
	LB Charles Williams
	LB Ricardo McDonald
	DB Dave Coleman
	DB Steve Israel / Tinker Harris
	DB Lex Perkins / Chris Hupko
	DB Doug Whaley

RUSHING: Williams 137/682y
PASSING: Van Pelt 227-398/2796y, 15TD, 57.0%
RECEIVING: Moore 51/505y
SCORING: Scott Kaplan (K) 55pts

1992 3-9

51 Kent	10 WR Dietrich Jells / Junior Green
6 West Virginia	44 WR Billy Davis / Chad Askew
16 Rutgers	21 T Reuben Brown
41 Minnesota	33 G Lawson Mollica / Dave Kristofic
34 Maryland	47 C Chris Sestilli
21 Notre Dame	52 G Gary Gorojewski
27 Temple	20 T Mike LiVorio / Matt Bloom
31 East Carolina	37 TE Rob Coons / Raymond Belvin
10 Syracuse	41 QB Alex Van Pelt
10 Louisville	31 TB Curtis Martin / Tim Colicchio
13 Penn State	57 FB Carl Hagins / Lyron Brooks
23 Hawaii	36 DL Mike Halapin
	DL Tom Barndt
	DL Matt Hosilyk
	LB Gerald Simpson / Dell Seagraves
	LB Jason Chavis
	LB Shawn Abinet
	LB Charles Williams
	DB Derrick Parker
	DB Vernon Lewis / Jay Jones
	DB Lex Perkins / Anthony Dorsett
	DB Doug Whaley / David Sumner

RUSHING: Colicchio 139/743y
PASSING: Van Pelt 245-407/3163y, 20TD, 60.2%
RECEIVING: Jells 55/1091y
SCORING: Sean Conley (K) 75pts

1993 3-8

14 Southern Miss	10 WR Junior Green / Dietrich Jells
21 Virginia Tech	63 WR Billy Davis / Curtis Anderson
28 Ohio State	63 T Reuben Brown
7 Louisville	29 G Dave Kristofic
0 Notre Dame	44 C Lawson Mollica
21 Syracuse	24 G Lamont Liggett
21 West Virginia	42 T Matt Bloom / Brian Curran
21 Rutgers	10 TE Raymond Belvin / Lyron Brooks
7 Miami	35 QB John Ryan / Ken Ferguson
0 Boston College	33 TB Curtis Martin / Billy West
28 Temple	18 FB Chad Dukes / Maurice Washington
	DL Zatiti Moody
	DL Mike Halapin / Matt Hosilyk
	DL Tom Barndt
	DL Mike Mohring
	LB Gerald Simpson
	LB Tom Tumulty / Hayes Clark
	LB Jon McCray / Tony Reardon
	DB Denorse Mosley/Anth'ny Dorsett(WR)
	DB Maurice Williams / Jay Jones
	DB Doug Whaley
	DB David Sumner / Jim Williams

RUSHING: Martin 210/1075y, West 58/244y, Dukes 25/143y
PASSING: Ryan 115-203/1284y, 6 TDs, 56.7%
RECEIVING: Martin 33/249y, Green 25/335y, Davis 24/346y
SCORING: Martin 52pts, West 42pts, Steve Kalmanides 32pts

1994 3-8

28 Texas	30 WR Dietrich Jells / Mark Butler
30 Ohio University	16 WR Billy Davis / Curtis Anderson
3 Ohio State	27 T Rueben Brown
9 Boston College	21 G Reggie Thomas / Tim Glass
29 Louisville	33 C Lawson Molica
7 Syracuse	31 G Jeff Craig
41 West Virginia	47 T Matt Bloom / Tony Orlandini
7 Virginia Tech	45 TE Dell Seagraves
45 Temple	19 QB John Ryan
12 Miami	17 TB Billy West / Curtis Martin
35 Rutgers	21 FB Vince Williams / Maurice Washington
	DL Zatiti Moody
	DL Mike Halapin
	DL Tyler Young / Tim Robbins
	DL Tom Barndt / Mike Mohring
	LB Hayes Clark / Jon McCray
	LB Tom Tumulty / Jason Chavis
	LB Gerald Simpson
	DB Denorse Mosley
	DB Anthony Dorsett
	DB David Sumner / John Jenkins
	DB Jim Williams

RUSHING: West 252/1358y
PASSING: Ryan 87-144/1294y, 14TD, 60.4%
RECEIVING: Davis 51/731y
SCORING: David Merrick (K) 62pts

1995 2-9

17 Washington St.	13 WR Dietrich Jells / Sadiq Durham
66 E. Michigan	30 WR Curtis Anderson / Mark Butler
27 Texas	38 T Matt Hosilyk
14 Ohio State	54 G Jon Marzoch
16 Virginia Tech	26 C Reggie Thomas
0 Boston College	17 G Jeff Craig
27 Temple	29 T Tony Orlandini / Mike Schultz
16 Miami	17 TE Dell Seagraves
24 Rutgers	42 QB John Ryan / Pete Gonzalez
10 Syracuse	42 TB Demetrius Harris / Chris Patton
0 West Virginia	21 FB Craig Schneider
	DL Zatiti Moody
	DL Mike Halapin / Frank Moore
	DL Tyler Young / Mike Mohring
	DL Jared Miller / Marlin Young
	LB Tom Tumulty / Jim Williams
	LB Jon McCray / Phil Clarke
	LB David Sumner / Rodney Humphrey
	DB Rasshad Whitmill
	DB Anthony Dorsett
	DB John Jenkins
	DB Chuck Brown

RUSHING: Harris 137/610y, Patton 67/264y, Schneider 53/155y
PASSING: Ryan 115-232/1439y, 9TD, 49.6%,
Gonzalez 30-76/478y, 3TD, 39.5%
RECEIVING: Jells 48/789y, Durham 38/
SCORING: Chris Ferencik (K) 59pts

1996 4-7

0 West Virginia	34 WR Jake Hoffart
52 Kent	14 WR Mark Butler / Vital Joseph
35 Houston	42 T Jeff Craig
0 Ohio State	72 G Jon Marzoch
0 Miami	45 C Reggie Thomas
53 Temple	52 G Brian Minehart
7 Syracuse	55 T Tony Orlandini
17 Virginia Tech	34 TE John Jones / Kirk McMullen
20 Boston College	13 QB Mark Lytle / Pete Gonzalez
6 Notre Dame	60 TB Billy West / Dwayne Schulters
24 Rutgers	9 FB Chris Schneider
	DL Trey McCray / Jason Soboleski
	DL Kenny Pegram / Chris Dilba
	DL Demond Gibson / Frank Moore
	DL Jared Miller
	LB Phil Clarke / Djems Don
	LB Rod Humphrey / Julian Graham
	LB Ernest Coakley
	DB Chuck Brown / Rasshad Whitmill
	DB Curtis Anderson / Hank Poteat
	DB John Jenkins
	DB Curtis McGhee (LB) / Seth Hornack

RUSHING: West 145/687y
PASSING: Lytle 105-214/1249y, 8TD, 49.1%
RECEIVING: Hoffart 39/667y
SCORING: Schulters 60pts, Chris Fedencik (K) 38pts,

1997 6-6

45 SW Louisiana	13 WR Jake Hoffart
17 Penn State	34 WR Terry Murphy / Jackie Womack
35 Houston	24 T Tony Orlandini
21 Miami	17 G Jon Marzoch / Ben Kopp
13 Temple	17 C Andrew Grischow
21 Notre Dame	45 G Reggie Thomas
55 Rutgers	48 T Ethan Weidle / Jason Dugger
21 Boston College	22 TE Juan Williams
27 Syracuse	32 QB Pete Gonzalez / Matt Lytle
30 Virginia Tech	23 RB Dwayne Schulters / Kevan Barlow
41 West Virginia	38 FB Tony Thompson / Chris Schneider
7 Southern Miss■	41 DL Marlin Young
	DL Jeff McCurley / Demond Gibson
	DL Frank Moore / Kenny Pegram
	DL Julian Graham
	LB Phil Clarke / Ken Kshubara
	LB Rod Humphrey / Brian Jacobs
	LB Eric Kasperowicz / Karim Thompson
	DB Chuck Brown / Hank Poteat
	DB Tray Crayton
	DB John Jenkins / D.J. Dinkins
	DB Curtis McGhee

RUSHING: Schulters 169/861y
PASSING: Gonzalez 211-374/2829y, 31TD, 56.4%
RECEIVING: Hoffart 69/852y, Murphy 46/873y
SCORING: Murphy 78pts

1998 2-9

48 Villanova	41 WR Terry Murphy / R.J. English
13 Penn State	20 WR Latef Grim / Kenney Ketchen
7 Virginia Tech	27 T Ryan Hansen
35 Akron	0 G Jeff McCurley
10 North Carolina	29 C Andrew Grischow
21 Rutgers	25 G Ethan Weidle
28 Syracuse	45 T Mark Browne
33 Temple	34 TE Ben Kopp / Kirk McMullen
15 Boston College	23 QB Matt Lytle
10 Miami	38 RB Kevan Barlow / Brandon Williams
14 West Virginia	52 FB Chris Schneider / Chris Feola
	DL Marlin Young
	DL Ken Pegram / Mike White
	DL Demond Gibson / Mike Bosnic
	DL Juliann Graham / Brandon Dewey
	LB Nick Cole / Amir Purifoy
	LB Phil Clarke / Ryan Gonsales
	LB Karim Thompson
	DB Hank Poteat / Chiffon Allen
	DB Tray Crayton / Chuck Brown
	DB D.J. Dinkins
	DB Seth Hornack / Mark Ponko

RUSHING: Barlow 121/533y
PASSING: Lytle 159-306/2092y, 16TD, 52.0%
RECEIVING: Grim 60/906y, Murphy 40/563y
SCORING: Grim 60pts

1999 5-6

30 Bowling Green	10 WR Antonio Bryant / Kenney Ketchen
17 Penn State	20 WR Latef Grim / Julius Dixon
30 Kent State	23 T Ryan Hansen
55 Temple	24 G Khiawatha Downey
17 Syracuse	24 C Jeff McCurley / Chad Reed
16 Boston College	20 G Bryan Anderson
38 Rutgers	15 T Ethan Weidle
17 Virginia Tech	30 TE Ben Kopp / Kirk McMullen
3 Miami	33 QB John Turman / David Priestley
37 Notre Dame	27 RB Kevan Barlow / Nick Goings
21 West Virginia	52 FB Mark Moothart / Chris Feola
	DL Julian Graham / Ryan Smith
	DL Mike White / Brandon Dewey
	DL Demond Gibson
	DL Bryan Knight / Nigel Neal
	LB Gerald Hayes / Amir Purifoy
	LB Ryan Gonsales
	LB Karim Thompson / Brian Beinecke
	DB Hank Poteat
	DB Chiffon Allen / Demetrious Rich
	DB Ramon Walker / D.J. Dinkins
	DB Mark Ponko / Seth Hornack

RUSHING: Barlow 141/630y, Goings 110/469y, Feola 24/114y
PASSING: Priestley 92-158/1305y, 6TD, 58.2%,
Turman 92-192/1301y, 10TD, 47.9%
RECEIVING: Grim 75/1106y, Bryant 51/844y, McMullen 14/184y,
Goings 14/135y
SCORING: Nick Lotz (K) 69pts, Goings 48pts, Barlow 42pts

2000 7-5

30 Kent State	7 WR Antonio Bryant / R.J. English
34 Bowling Green	16 WR Latef Grim / Lamar Slade
12 Penn State	0 T Matt Browne / Matt Morgan
29 Rutgers	17 G Jon Schall
17 Syracuse	24 C Chad Reed / Jeff McCurley (G)
42 Boston College	26 G Bryan Anderson (C)
34 Virginia Tech	37 T Khiawatha Downey
17 North Carolina	20 TE Mike Bosnic / Kris Wilson
7 Miami	35 QB John Turman / David Priestley
7 Temple	0 RB Kevan Barlow / Nick Goings
38 West Virginia	28 FB Lousaka Polite
29 Iowa State■	37 DL Ryan Smith
	DL Mike White / Penny Semaia
	DL Joe Conlin / Darrell McMurray
	DL Bryan Knight / Nigel Neal
	LB Gerald Hayes / Brandon Williams
	LB Amir Purifoy / Ryan Gonsales
	LB Brian Beinecke / Lewis Moore
	DB Shawntae Spencer
	DB Shawn Robinson/Wm."Tutu"Ferguson
	DB Ramon Walker
	DB Mark Ponko

RUSHING: Barlow 219/1167y, Goings 75/296y, Polite 36/109y
PASSING: Turman 148-269/2482y, 20TD, 55.0%,
Priestley 57-103/829y, 5TD, 55.3%
RECEIVING: Bryant 73/1457y, Grim 39/595y, Polite 16/118y
SCORING: Bryant 78pts, Nick Lotz (K) 59pts, Barlow 54pts

2001 7-5

31 E. Tenn. St.	0 WR Antonio Bryant
26 S. Florida	35 WR R.J. English / Lamar Slade
21 Miami	43 T Rob Petitti
7 Notre Dame	24 G Dan LaCarte / Jon Schall
10 Syracuse	42 C Chad Reed
7 Boston College	45 G Bryan Anderson / Penny Semaia
33 Temple	7 T Matt Morgan
38 Virginia Tech	7 TE Kris Wilson
42 Rutgers	0 QB David Priestley / Rod Rutherford
23 West Virginia	17 RB Raymond Kirkley / Marcus Furman
24 Ala.-Birm'ham	6 FB Lousaka Polite
34 N. Carolina St.■	19 DL Brian Guzek
	DL Trye Young
	DL Joe Conlin / Darell McMurray
	DL Bryan Knight / Claude Harriott
	LB Lewis Moore
	LB Gerald Hayes / Ryan Gonsales
	LB Brian Beinecke / Brandon Williams
	DB Shawntae Spencer / Tutu Ferguson
	DB Torrie Cox / Shawn Robinson
	DB Ramon Walker / Corey Humphries
	DB Mark Ponko

RUSHING: Kirkley 166/672y, Rutherford 81/255y,
Furman 42/242y
PASSING: Priestley 165-280/2128y, 18TD, 58.9%
RECEIVING: Bryant 49/760y
SCORING: Nick Lotz (K) 74pts, Bryant 54pts

2002 9-4

27 Ohio University	14 WR Lamar Slade / Roosevelt Bynes
12 Texas A&M	14 WR Larry Fitzgerald / Yogi Roth
26 Ala.-Birm'ham	20 T Rob Petitti
23 Rutgers	3 G Dan LaCarte / Penny Semaia
37 Toledo	19 C Chad Reed
48 Syracuse	24 G Bryan Anderson
6 Notre Dame	14 T Matt Morgan
28 Boston College	16 TE Kris Wilson / Erik Gill
19 Virginia Tech	21 QB Rod Rutherford
29 Temple	22 RB Brandon Miree / Raymond Kirkley
21 Miami	28 FB Lousaka Polite
17 West Virginia	24 DL Brian Guzek / Kevin Harris
38 Oregon State ■	13 DL Dan Stephens
	DL Vince Crochunis
	DL Claude Harriott
	LB Lewis Moore / Charles Spencer
	LB Gerald Hayes
	LB Brian Beinecke / Malcolm Postell
	DB Shawn Robinson / Shantae Spencer
	DB Torrie Cox / Tutu Ferguson
	DB Tez Morris / Corey Humphries
	DB Tyrone Gilliiard / Gary Urschler

RUSHING: Miree 214/943y, Rutherford 182/398y, Polite 52/211y
PASSING: Rutherford 192-367/2783y, 22TD, 52.3%
RECEIVING: Fitzgerald 69/1005y, Slade 48/649y,
Bynes 18/404y, Wilson 18/389y
SCORING: Fitzgerald 72pts, David Abdul (K) 67pts,
Rutherford 36pts

2003 8-5

43 Kent State	3 WR Greg Lee / Prencell Brockenbrough
42 Ball State	21 WR Larry Fitzgerald
31 Toledo	35 T Rob Petiti
37 Texas A&M	26 G Dan LaCarte
14 Notre Dame	20 C Jon Schall / Justin Belarski
42 Rutgers	32 G John Simonitis
34 Syracuse	14 T Matt Morgan
24 Boston College	13 TE Kris Wilson
31 Virginia Tech	28 QB Rod Rutherford
31 West Virginia	52 RB Jawan Walker / Brandon Miree
30 Temple	16 FB Lousaka Polite
14 Miami	28 DL Claude Harriott / Azzie Beagnyam
16 Virginia ■	23 DL Vince Crochunis
	DL Dan Stephens
	DL Thomas Smith
	LB Brian Bennett / H.B. Blades
	LB Lewis Moore
	LB Malcolm Postell / J.J. Horne
	DB Shantae Spencer
	DB Tutu Ferguson / Bernard "Josh" Lay
	DB Tez Morris
	DB Tyrone Gilliard

RUSHING: Miree 115/573y, Walker 107/407y, Polite 70/258
PASSING: Rutherford 247-413/3679y, 37TD, 59.8%
RECEIVING: Fitzgerald 92/1672y, Wilson 44/643y,
Brockenbrough 35/616y
SCORING: Fitzgerald 132pts, David Abdul (K) 76pts,
Wilson 54pts

2004 8-4

24 Ohio University	3 WR Greg Lee
17 Nebraska	24 WR Joe DelSardo / Marcus Furman
41 Furman	38 T Rob Petitti
17 Connecticut	29 G Charles Spencer
27 Temple	22 C Justin Belarski
20 Boston College	17 G John Simonitis / Matt Maiers
41 Rutgers	17 T Mike McGlynn / Dale Williams
31 Syracuse	38 TE Erik Gill
41 Notre Dame	38 QB Tyler Palko
16 West Virginia	13 RB Raymond Kirkley / Tim Murphy (FB)
43 S. Florida	14 FB Kellen Campbell / Justin Acierno
7 Utah ■	35 DL Charles Sallet / Azzie Beagnyam
	DL Vince Crochunis
	DL Dan Stephens
	DL Thomas Smith / Keith Hill
	LB H.B. Blades / Brian Bennett
	LB Clint Session
	LB Malcolm Postell / J.J. Horne
	DB Darrelle Rives
	DB Josh Lay / Mike Phillips
	DB Tez Morris / Jemeel Brady
	DB Tyrone Gilliard

RUSHING: Kirkley 154/560y, Murphy 88/334y, Palko 129/139y
PASSING: Palko 230-409/3067y, 24TD, 56.2%
RECEIVING: Lee 68/1297y, DelSardo 49/573y, Gill 25/433y,
Furman 25/236y
SCORING: Josh Cummings (K) 89pts, Lee 60pts, Kirkley 36pts

2005 5-6

21 Notre Dame	42 WR Derek Kinder / Joe DelSardo
10 Ohio University	16 WR Greg Lee
6 Nebraska	7 T Charles Spencer
41 Youngstown St.	0 G C.J. Davis / Dale Williams
29 Rutgers	37 C Joe Villani
38 Cincinnati	20 G John Simonitis
31 South Florida	17 T Mike McGlynn
34 Syracuse	17 TE Erik Gill / Darrell Strong
20 Louisville	42 QB Tyler Palko
24 Connecticut	0 TB L. Stephens-Howling / Raym'd Kirkley
13 West Virginia	45 FB Tim Murphy / Kellen Campbell
	DL Chris McKillop
	DL Phil Tillman
	DL Thomas Smith / Rashaad Duncan
	DL Charles Sallet
	LB Derron Thomas / Scott McKillop
	LB H.B. Blades / Clint Session
	LB J.J. Horne / Brian Bennett
	DB Josh Lay
	DB Darrelle Revis
	DB Tez Morris
	DB Sam Bryant / Mike Phillips

RUSHING: Stephens-Howling 96/434y,
Rashad Jennings (TB) 86/411y, Kirkley 82/352y
PASSING: Palko 193-341/2392y, 17TD, 56.6%
RECEIVING: Lee 49/962y, Kinder 37/374y, Gill 21/244y
SCORING: Josh Cummings (K) 61pts, Lee 44pts, Palko 36pts

2006 6-6

38 Virginia	13 WR Derek Kinder / Marcel Pestano
33 Cincinnati	15 WR Oderick Turner
23 Michigan State	38 T Jeff Otah
51 Citadel	6 G C.J. Davis
45 Toledo	3 C Joe Villani
21 Syracuse	11 G Joe Thomas / John Simonitis
52 C. Florida	7 T Mike McGlynn
10 Rutgers	20 TE Steve Buches/Darrell Strong/N.Byham
12 South Florida	22 QB Tyler Palko
45 Connecticut	46 TB LaRod Stephens-Howling
27 West Virginia	45 FB Conredge Collins
24 Louisville	48 DL Joe Clermond
	DL Rashaad Duncan / Corey Davis
	DL Gus Mustakas
	DL Chris McKillop / Doug Fulmer
	LB Clint Session / Scott McKillop
	LB H.B. Blades
	LB Brian Bennett / Tommie Campbell
	DB Kennard Cox
	DB Darrelle Revis
	DB Mike Phillips / Eric Thatcher
	DB Sam Bryant

RUSHING: Stephens-Howling 178/893y, Shane Brooks (TB)
50/218y, Collins 29/115y, Kevin Collier 33/115y
PASSING: Palko 220-322/2871y, 25TD, 68.3%
RECEIVING: Kinder 57/847y, Turner 44/660y, Pestrano 28/424y,
Buches 26/302y
SCORING: Conor Lee (K) 83pts, Stephens-Howling 60pts,
Turner 48pts

2007 5-7

27 E. Michigan	3 WR Oderick Turrner / Maurice Williams
34 Grambling	10 WR T.J. Porter / Marcel Pestano
13 Michigan State	17 T Jeff Otah
14 Connecticut	34 G C.J. Davis
14 Virginia	44 C Chris Vangas
45 Navy	48 G Joe Thomas / John Bachman
24 Cincinnati	17 T Mike McGlynn (G) / Jason Pinkston
17 Louisville	24 TE Nate Byham/Darrell Strong/John Pelusi
20 Syracuse	17 QB Pat Bostick / Kevan Smith
16 Rutgers	20 TB LeSean McCoy / L. Stephens-Howling
37 South Florida	48 FB Conredge Collins
13 West Virginia	9 DL Joe Clermond
	DL Rashaad Duncan / John Malecki
	DL Ernest Williams / Tommie Duhart
	DL Chris McKillop / Greg Romeus
	LB Adam Gunn
	LB Scott McKillop
	LB Shane Murray / Jemeel Brady
	DB Kennard Cox / Jovani Chappel
	DB Aaron Berry / Ricky Gary
	DB Eric Thatcher
	DB Mike Phillips

RUSHING: McCoy 276/1328y, Stephens-Howling 78/320y,
Collins 33/110y
PASSING: Bostick 155-252/1500y, 8TD, 61.5%
RECEIVING: Porter 37/329y, Turner 36/496y, McCoy 33/244y,
Strong 29/328y
SCORING: McCoy 90pts, Conor Lee (K) 82pts, Turner 34pts

2008 9-4

17 Bowling Green	27 WR Oderick Turner / Jonathan Baldwin
27 Buffalo	16 WR Derek Kinder / T.J. Porter
21 Iowa	20 T Jason Pinkston
34 Syracuse	24 G C.J. Davis (C) / Dominic Williams
26 South Florida	21 C Robb Houser
42 Navy	21 G John Malecki
34 Rutgers	54 T Joe Thomas
36 Notre Dame	33 TE Nate Byham / John Pelusi
41 Louisville	7 QB Bill Stull
21 Cincinnati	28 TB LeSean McCoy / L. Stephens-Howling
19 West Virginia	15 FB Conredge Collins
34 Connecticut	10 DL Jabaal Sheard
0 Oregon State ■	3 DL Rashaad Duncan
	DL Mick Williams / Gus Mustakas
	DL Greg Romeus
	LB Greg Williams / Adam Gunn
	LB Scott McKillop
	LB Austin Ransom
	DB Jovani Chappel / Ricky Gary
	DB Aaron Berry
	DB Eric Thatcher
	DB Dom DeCicco / Elijah Fields

RUSHING: McCoy 308/1488y, Stephens-Howling 77/312y,
Collins 21/85y
PASSING: Stull 188-330/2356y, 9TD, 57.0%
RECEIVING: Kinder 36/422y, McCoy 32/305y, Porter 25/357y,
Cedric McGee (WR) 23/201y, Turner 21/298y
SCORING: McCoy 126pts, Conor Lee (K) 98pts,
Stephens-Howling 30pts

2009 10-3

38 Youngstown St.	3 WR Jonathan Baldwin / Mike Shanahan
54 Buffalo	27 WR Oderick Turner / Cedric McGee
27 Navy	14 T Jason Pinkston
31 N. Carolina St.	38 G Joe Thomas
35 Louisville	10 C Robb Houser
24 Connecticut	21 G John Malecki
24 Rutgers	17 T Lucas Nix
41 South Florida	14 TE Nate Byham / Dorin Dickerson
37 Syracuse	10 QB Bill Stull
27 Notre Dame	22 TB Dion Lewis
16 West Virginia	19 FB Henry Hynoski
44 Cincinnati	45 DL Jabaal Sheard / Brandon Lindsey
19 North Carolina ■	17 DL Gus Mustakas / Myles Caragein
	DL Mick Williams
	DL Greg Romeus
	LB Greg Williams
	LB Adam Gunn / Dan Mason
	LB Max Gruder
	DB Jovani Chappel
	DB Aaron Berry / Ricky Gary
	DB Jarred Holley / Elijah Fields
	DB Dom DiCicco / Andrew Taglianetti

RUSHING: Lewis 325/1799y, Ray Graham (TB) 61/349y,
Hynoski 24/107y
PASSING: Stull 209-321/2633y, 21TD, 65.1%
RECEIVING: Baldwin 57/1091y, Dickerson 49/529y, Lewis 25/189y
Turner 21/227y
SCORING: Dan Hutchins (K) 115pts, Lewis 108pts, Dickerson 60pts

2010 8-5

24 Utah	27 WR Mike Shanahan / Devin Street
38 New Hampshire	16 WR Jonathan Baldwin
3 Miami	31 T Jason Pinkston
44 Florida Intl.	17 G Chris Jacobson
17 Notre Dame	23 C Alex Karabin
45 Syracuse	14 G Lucas Nix (T) / Greg Gaskins
41 Rutgers	21 T Jordan Gibbs
20 Louisville	3 TE Mike Cruz
28 Connecticut	30 QB Tino Sunseri
17 South Florida	10 TB Dion Lewis / Ray Graham
10 West Virginia	35 FB/WR Henry Hynoski / Brock DeCicco
28 Cincinnati	10 DL Jabaal Sheard
27 Kentucky ■	10 DL Chas Alecxih
	DL Miles Caragein
	DL Brandon Lindsey / Greg Romeus
	LB Greg Williams
	LB Max Gruder
	LB Tristan Roberts / Dan Mason
	DB Antwaan Reed
	DB Ricky Gary
	DB Jarred Holley
	DB Dom DeCicco (LB) / Jason Hendricks

RUSHING: Lewis 219/1061y, Graham 148/922y
PASSING: Sunseri 223-346/2572y, 16TD, 64.5%
RECEIVING: Baldwin 53/822y, Shaw 43/589y, Lewis 27/216y
SCORING: Dan Hutchins (K) 94pts, Lewis 78pts, Graham 60pts

PURDUE

Purdue University (Founded 1869)
West Lafayette, Indiana
Nickname: Boilermakers
Colors: Old Gold and Black
Stadium: Ross-Ade (1924) 62,500
Conference Affiliation: Big Ten (Charter member, 1895-present)

CAREER RUSHING YARDS	Attempts	Yards
Mike Alstott (1992-95)	644	3635
Kory Sheets (2005-08)	664	3341
Otis Armstrong (1970-72)	670	3315
Scott Dierking (1973-76)	578	2863
Montrell Lowe (1999-2002)	612	2648
Edwin Watson (1994-97)	530	2520
Harry Szulborski (1946-49)	478	2478
Corey Rogers (1991-95)	489	2436
Jerod Void (2002-05)	569	2429
Leroy Keyes (1966-68)	356	2094

CAREER PASSING YARDS	Comp.-Att.	Yards
Drew Brees (1997-2000)	1026-1678	11,792
Curtis Painter (2005-08)	987-1648	11,163
Mark Herrmann (1977-80)	772-1309	9946
Kyle Orton (2001-04)	786-1336	9337
Scott Campbell (1980-83)	609-1060	7636
Jim Everett (1981-85)	572- 965	7411
Eric Hunter (1989-92)	422- 818	5598
Mike Phipps (1967-69)	375- 733	5423
Rick Trefzger (1993-96)	383- 663	5063
Bob Griese (1964-66)	358- 627	4541

CAREER RECEIVING YARDS	Catches	Yards
John Standeford (2000-03)	266	3788
Taylor Stubblefield (2001-04)	325	3629
Dorien Bryant (2004-07)	292	3548
Brian Alford (1994-97)	164	3029
Vinny Sutherland (1997-2000)	176	2370
Greg Orton (2005-08)	203	2356
Dave Young (1977-80)	180	2316
Steve Griffin (1982-85)	146	2234
Bart Burrell (1977-80)	140	2126
Tim Stratton (1998-2001)	204	2088

SEASON RUSHING YARDS	Attempts	Yards
Mike Alstott (1995)	243	1436
Otis Armstrong (1972)	243	1361
Mike Alstott (1994)	202	1188
Kory Sheets (2008)	234	1131
Joey Harris (2002)	250	1115

SEASON PASSING YARDS	Comp.-Att.	Yards
Curtis Painter (2006)	315-530	3985
Drew Brees (1998)	361-569	3983
Drew Brees (1999)	337-554	3909
Curtis Painter (2007)	356-569	3846
Drew Brees (2000)	309-512	3668

SEASON RECEIVING YARDS	Catches	Yards
John Standeford (2002)	75	1307
Chris Daniels (1999)	121	1236
Brian Alford (1997)	59	1228
John Standeford (2003)	86	1150
Keith Smith (2009)	91	1100

GAME RUSHING YARDS	Attempts	Yards
Otis Armstrong (1972 vs. Indiana)	32	276
Mike Alstott (1995 vs. Indiana)	25	264
Ralph Bolden (2009 vs. Toledo)	21	234

GAME PASSING YARDS	Comp.-Att.	Yards
Curtis Painter (2007 vs. Cen. Michigan)	35-54	546
Drew Brees (1998 vs. Minnesota)	31-36	522
Kyle Orton (2004 vs. Indiana)	33-54	522

GAME RECEIVING YARDS	Catches	Yards
Chris Daniels (1999 vs. Michigan State)	21	301
Selwyn Lymon (2006 v. Notre Dame)	8	238
Brian Alford (1997 vs. Minnesota)	4	215

GREATEST COACH:

When Joe Tiller headed into retirement after the 2008 season, he left a bit of a quandary behind over the issue of Purdue's greatest coach since 1953. Tiller won the most games (87) while bringing a renaissance to Purdue with a dynamic passing attack that produced a ripple effect throughout the Big Ten Conference. In his first season in 1997, Tiller's Boilermakers turned their record from 3-8 into 9-3 and won the school's first bowl game since 1980. In his 12 seasons, Tiller also developed three outstanding quarterbacks in Drew Brees, Kyle Orton, and Curtis Painter.

Another coach, however, gets the nod as the Boilermakers' best, owing to his .6705 winning percentage, compared to Tiller's .5839. Jack Mollenkopf is in the College Hall of Fame, but one would never know it from the lack of mention his name receives today. All Mollenkopf did was to take one of the lesser lights of the Big Ten and lead the Boilermakers to their first-ever Rose Bowl, a 14-13 win over Southern California in January 1967.

Before Mollenkopf was through in West Lafayette by the end of the 1960s he had built 84 wins against 39 losses and nine ties. His teams consistently finished in the upper half of the Big Ten.

Also fans shouldn't forget Hall of Famer Jim Young, who didn't stay long at Purdue but brought bowl victories in three straight seasons during his five-year stay.

PURDUE'S 55 GREATEST SINCE 1953

OFFENSE 26

WIDE RECEIVER: Bruce Alford, Jim Beirne, Dorien Bryant, Larry Burton, Bob Hadrick, John Standeford, Taylor Stubblefield
TIGHT END: Tim Stratton, Dave Young
TACKLE: Joe Krupa, Matt Light, Gene Selawski, Karl Singer
GUARD: Tom Luken, Ron Maltony, Stan Sczurek
CENTER: Larry Kaminski
QUARTERBACK: Drew Brees, Len Dawson, Bob Griese, Mark Herrmann, Mike Phipps
RUNNING BACK: Otis Armstrong, Rodney Carter, Scott Dierking
FULLBACK: Mike Alstott, Perry Williams

DEFENSE 22

END: Rosevelt Colvin, Shaun Phillips, Blane Smith, Keena Turner, Harold Wells
TACKLE: Don Brumm, Dave Butz, Ken Novak, Jerry Shay
NOSE GUARD: Chuck Kyle, Jeff Zgonina
LINEBACKER: Niko Koutouvides, James Looney, Brock Spack, Fred Strickland
CORNERBACK: Tim Foley, Steve Jackson, Charles King, Rod Woodson
SAFETY: Marc Foster, John Charles, Stuart Schweigart

SPECIAL TEAMS 6

RETURN SPECIALIST: Stan Brown
PLACE KICKER; Travis Dorsch
PUNTER: Shawn McCarthy

MULTIPLE POSITIONS

HALFBACK-WINGBACK-CORNERBACK: Leroy Keyes

TWO-WAY PLAYERS

GUARD-LINEBACKER: Tom Bettis
END-DEFENSIVE END: Lamar Lundy

PERFORMANCE FORMULA: PURDUE'S 10 BEST SEASONS

1967	1.5414	4 of 71
1966	1.5229	7 of 70
1968	1.4684	8 of 70
1958	1.4622	10 of 70
1969	1.4395	20 of 70
1998	1.4076	17 of 71
1979	1.3801	15 of 70
1965	1.3720	10 of 70
1978	1.3684	16 of 70
1997	1.3573	17 of 70

PURDUE BOILERMAKERS

Year	W-L-T	AP Poll	Conference Standing	Toughest Regular Season Opponents	Coach (Record at School)	Bowl Games		
1953	2-7		8	Notre Dame 9-0-1, Duke 7-2-1, Wisconsin 6-2-1	Stu Holcomb			
1954	5-3-1		6	Notre Dame 9-1, Duke 7-2-1 Wisconsin 7-2, Ohio State 9-0	Stu Holcomb			
1955	5-3-1		4	Notre Dame 8-2, Illinois 5-3-1, Michigan State 8-1	Stu Holcomb (35-42-4)			
1956	3-4-2		7t	Minnesota 6-1-2, Iowa 8-1, Michigan State 7-2	Jack Mollenkopf			
1957	5-4		4t	Notre Dame 7-3, Wisconsin 6-3, Michigan State 8-1, Ohio State 8-1	Jack Mollenkopf			
1958	6-1-2	13	4	Wisconsin 7-1-1, Notre Dame 6-4, Ohio State 6-1-2, Indiana 5-3-1	Jack Mollenkopf			
1959	5-2-2		2t	Wisconsin 7-2, Iowa 5-4, Illinois 5-3-1, Michigan State 5-4	Jack Mollenkopf			
1960	4-4-1		5t	UCLA 7-2-1, Ohio State 7-2, Iowa 8-1, Minnesota 8-1	Jack Mollenkopf			
1961	6-3	12	4	Washington 5-4-1, Iowa 5-4, Michigan State 7-2, Minnesota 7-2	Jack Mollenkopf			
1962	4-4-1		5	Washington 7-1-2, Miami (Ohio) 8-1-1, Minnesota 6-2-1	Jack Mollenkopf			
1963	5-4		4	Wisconsin 5-4, Illinois 7-1-1, Michigan State 6-2-1	Jack Mollenkopf			
1964	6-3		3	Notre Dame 9-1, Michigan 8-1, Illinois 6-3	Jack Mollenkopf			
1965	7-2-1	11+	3t	Notre Dame 7-2-1, Michigan State 10-0, Illinois 6-4	Jack Mollenkopf			
1966	9-2	7	2	Notre Dame 9-0-1, SMU 8-2, Michigan State 9-0-1	Jack Mollenkopf	Rose	14 Southern California	13
1967	8-2	9	1t	Notre Dame 8-2, Ohio State 6-3, Minnesota 8-2, Indiana 9-1	Jack Mollenkopf			
1968	8-2	10	3	Notre Dame 7-2-1, Ohio State 9-0, Minnesota 6-4, Indiana 6-4	Jack Mollenkopf			
1969	8-2	18	3	Notre Dame 8-1-1, Stanford 7-2-1, Michigan 8-2, Ohio State 8-1	Jack Mollenkopf (84-39-9)			
1970	4-6		8	Notre Dame 9-1, Stanford 8-3, Michigan 9-1, Ohio State 9-0	Bob DeMoss			
1971	3-7		6t	Washington 8-3, Notre Dame 8-2, Northwestern 7-4, Michigan 11-0	Bob DeMoss			
1972	6-5		3	Washington 8-3, Notre Dame 8-2, Michigan 10-1	Bob DeMoss (13-18)			
1973	5-6		4t	Miami (Ohio) 10-0, Notre Dame 10-0, Michigan 10-0-1	Alex Agase			
1974	4-6-1		6	Miami (Ohio) 9-0-1, Notre Dame 9-2, Michigan St. 7-3-1, Michigan 10-1	Alex Agase			
1975	4-7		3t	Notre Dame 8-3, Miami (Ohio) 10-1, Ohio State 11-0, Michigan 8-2-1	Alex Agase			
1976	5-6		3t	Notre Dame 8-3, Southern Calif. 10-1, Ohio State 8-2-1, Michigan 10-1	Alex Agase (18-25-1)			
1977	5-6		6t	Michigan State 7-3-1, Notre Dame 10-1, Ohio State 9-2, Michigan 10-1	Jim Young			
1978	9-2-1	13	3	Michigan State 8-3, Notre Dame 8-3, Ohio State 7-3-1, Michigan 10-1	Jim Young	Peach	41 Georgia Tech	21
1979	10-2	10	2	Notre Dame 7-4, Michigan 8-3, Indiana 7-4	Jim Young	Bluebonnet	27 Tennessee	22
1980	9-3	17	2t	Notre Dame 9-1-1, UCLA 9-2, Michigam 9-2	Jim Young	Liberty	28 Missouri	25
1981	5-6		8t	Ohio State 8-3, Iowa 8-3, Michigan 8-3	Jim Young (38-19-1)			
1982	3-8		7	Illinois 7-4, Ohio State 8-3, Iowa 7-4, Michigan 8-3	Leon Burnett			
1983	3-7-1		6	Miami 10-1, Ohio State 8-3, Iowa 9-2, Michigan 9-2	Leon Burnett			
1984	7-5		2t	Miami 10-1, Ohio State 9-2, Michigan 8-2-1	Leon Burnett	Peach	24 Virginia	27
1985	5-6		7	Ohio State 8-3, Michigan 9-1-1, Iowa 10-1	Leon Burnett			
1986	3-8		8t	Ohio State 9-3, Michigan 11-1, Iowa 8-3	Leon Burnett (21-34-1)			
1987	3-7-1		6	Notre Dame 8-3, Iowa 9-3, Michigan 8-2-1, Indiana 8-3	Fred Akers			
1988	4-7		6	Notre Dame 11-0, Iowa 6-3-3, Indiana 7-3-1	Fred Akers			
1989	3-8		8	Notre Dame 11-1, Illinois 9-2, Ohio State 8-3, Michigan 10-1	Fred Akers			
1990	2-9		8t	Washington 9-2, Notre Dame 9-2, Illinois 8-3, Michigan 8-, Iowa 8-3	Fred Akers (12-31-1)			
1991	4-7		6t	California 9-2, Notre Dame 9-3, Iowa 10-1, Michigan 10-1	Jim Colletto			
1992	4-7		6t	Notre Dame 9-1-1, Michigan 8-0-3	Jim Colletto			
1993	1-10		10t	Notre Dame 10-1, Wisconsin 9-1-1, Ohio State 9-1-1, Michigan 7-4	Jim Colletto			
1994	4-5-2		9	Notre Dame 6-4-1, Wisconsin 6-4-1, Ohio State 9-3, Michigan 7-4	Jim Colletto			
1995	4-6-1		9	Notre Dame 9-2, Ohio State 11-1, Michigan 9-3, Northwestern 10-1	Jim Colletto (20-43-3)			
1996	3-8		8	Penn State 10-2, Ohio State 10-1, Northwestern 9-2	Joe Tiller			
1997	9-3	15	2t	Wisconsin 8-4, Penn State 9-2	Joe Tiller	Alamo	33 Oklahoma State	20
1998	9-4	24	4	Southern Calif. 8-4, Notre Dame 9-2, Wisconsin 10-1, Penn State 8-3	Joe Tiller	Alamo	37 Kansas State	34
1999	7-5	25	6t	Miami 8-4, Minnesota 8-3, Michigan 9-2, Michigan 9-2	Joe Tiller	Outback	25 Georgia	28
2000	8-4	13	1t	Notre Dame 9-2, Michigan 8-3, Northwestern 8-3, Ohio State 8-3	Joe Tiller	Rose	24 Washington	34
2001	6-6		4t	Michigan 8-3, Illinois 10-1, Ohio State 7-4	Joe Tiller	Sun	27 Washington State	33
2002	7-6		5t	Notre Dame 10-2, Iowa 11-1, Michigan 9-3, Ohio State 13-0	Joe Tiller	Sun	34 Washington	24
2003	9-4	18	2t	Wisconsin 7-5, Michigan 10-2, Ohio State 10-2	Joe Tiller	Capital One	27 Georgia	34
2004	7-5		5t	Wisconsin 9-2, Michigan 9-2, Iowa 10-1	Joe Tiller	Sun	23 Arizona State	27
2005	5-6		8	Notre Dame 9-2, Wisconsin 9-3, Penn State 10-1	Joe Tiller			
2006	8-6		4t	Notre Dame 10-2, Wisconsin 11-1, Penn State 8-4, Hawaii 10-3	Joe Tiller	Champs	7 Maryland	24
2007	8-5		7t	Ohio State 11-1, Michigan 8-4, Penn State 8-4	Joe Tiller	Motor City	51 Central Michigan	48
2008	4-8		9t	Oregon 9-3, Penn State 11-1, Ohio State 10-2, Northwestern 9-3	Joe Tiller (87-62)			
2009	5-7		7	Oregon 10-2, Northwestern 8-4, Ohio State 10-2, Wisconsin 9-3	Danny Hope			
2010	4-8		9t	Notre Dame 7-5, Ohio State 11-1, Wisconsin 11-1, Michigan State 11-1	Danny Hope (9-15)			

TOTAL: 315-298-18 .5135 (44 of 70)

Bowl Games since 1953: 8-7 .5333 (30 of 70)

GREATEST TEAM SINCE 1953: Purdue offers two excellent teams from which to choose its best. They are the Boilermaker squads from 1966 and 1979, quarterbacked by a pair of greats: Bob Griese and Mark Herrmann. The nod here goes to the 1966 team which supported Griese with two All-America players in receiver Jim Beirne and safety John Charles. There also were four linemen, guard Charles Erlenbaugh and tackle Jack Calcaterra on offense and defensive linemen Lance Olssen and George Olion, who contributed heavily along with sophomore superstar-in-the-making, cornerback Leroy Keyes.

1953 2-7

7	Missouri	14	E Jim Wojciehowski / Bob Springer
7	Notre Dame	37	T Raymond Pacer / Frank Paparazzo
14	Duke	20	G Walt Houston / Dick Skibinski
19	Wisconsin	28	C Walt Cudzik / Glenn Knecht
6	Michigan State	0	G Tom Bettis
0	Illinois	21	T Joe Krupa
0	Iowa	26	E Len Zyzda / John Kerr / Tom Redinger
6	Ohio State	21	QB Froncie Gutman / Roy Evans
30	Indiana	0	HB Ed Neves / Ed Zembal
			HB Karl Herkommer / Rex Brock
			FB Max Schmaling / Jim Reichert

RUSHING: Neves 55/245y, Schmaling 36/201y, Brock 34/146y
PASSING: Evans 30-76/514y, 3TD, 39.5%
RECEIVING: Brock 9/187y, Kerr 7/130y, Redinger 5/63y
SCORING: Gutman 18pts, Dan Pobojewski (FB) 12pts, Reichert (FB-K) 7pts

1954 5-3-1

31	Missouri	0	E Lamar Lundy / Bob Springer
27	Notre Dame	14	T Frank Paparazzo / Dick Murley
13	Duke	13	G Walter Houston / Dick Skibinski
6	Wisconsin	20	C John Allen
27	Michigan State	13	G Tom Bettis / Bob Clasey
28	Illinois	14	T Joe Krupa
14	Iowa	25	E John Kerr/Bob Khoenle/Len Zyzda
6	Ohio State	28	QB Len Dawson / Froncie Gutman
13	Indiana	7	HB Rex Brock / Jim Whitmer
			HB Ed Zembal / Jim Peters
			FB Bill Murakowski / Phil Ehrman

RUSHING: Murakowski 93/404y
PASSING: Dawson 87-167/1464y, 52.1%
RECEIVING: Kerr 20/337y
SCORING: N/A

1955 5-3-1

14	Pacific	7	E Lamar Lundy
7	Minnesota	6	T Ken Panfil / Dick Murley
0	Wisconsin	9	G Dick Skibinski / Ed Voytek
20	Iowa	20	C Neil Habig / John Simerson
7	Notre Dame	22	G Bob Clasey
13	Illinois	0	T Joe Krupa
0	Michigan State	27	E Bob Khoenle / Len Zyzda
46	Northwestern	8	QB Len Dawson
6	Indiana	4	HB Tommy Fletcher / Jim Whitmer
			HB Erich Barnes / Ed Neves / Jim Peters
			FB Bill Murakowski / Mel Dillard

RUSHING: Murakowski 125/493y, Whitmer 58/273y, Peters 44/175y
PASSING: Dawson 87-155/1005y, 7 TD, 56.1%
RECEIVING: Khoenle 18/162y, Lundy 16/221y, Whitmer 16/146y
SCORING: Murakowski & Neves 18pts, Whitmer & Peters 12pts

1956 3-4-2

16	Missouri	7	E Lamar Lundy
14	Minnesota	21	T Nick Mumley / Ron Sabal
28	Notre Dame	14	G Jim Shea / Ed Voytek
6	Wisconsin	6	C Neil Habig / Dale Snelling
20	Iowa	21	G Bob Clasey / John Jardine
7	Illinois	7	T Wayne Farmer
9	Michigan State	12	E Bob Khoenle / Tom Frankhauser
0	Northwestern	14	QB Len Dawson
39	Indiana	20	HB Tom Fletcher / Kenny Mikes
			HB Erich Barnes / John Brideweser
			FB Mel Dillard

RUSHING: Dillard 193/873y, Fletcher 89/398y, Barnes 52/217y
PASSING: Dawson 69-130/856y, 7 TD, 53.1%
RECEIVING: Lundy 15/248y, Barnes 12/137y, Dillard 10/99y
SCORING: Dillard 48pts, Fletcher (HB-K) 25pts, Lundy 24pts

1957 5-4

0	Notre Dame	12	E Erich Barnes/Len Jardine/Rich Brooks
17	Minnesota	21	T Ed Dwyer / Nick Mumley
14	Wisconsin	23	G Ron Sabal
20	Michigan State	13	C Neil Habig
37	Miami (Ohio)	6	G John Jardine / Bill Spillane (T)
21	Illinois	6	T Wayne Farmer / Gene Selawski
7	Ohio State	20	E Tom Frankhauser / John Crowl
27	Northwestern	0	QB Bob Spoo / Ross Fichtner
35	Indiana	13	HB Kenny Mikes / Tommy Fletcher
			HB Erich Barnes / Leonard Wilson
			FB Mel Dillard / Bob Jarus

RUSHING: Jarus 72/278y, Dillard 79/265y, Mikes 50/257y
PASSING: Fichtner 23-58/355y, 4 TD, 39.7%
RECEIVING: Frankhauser 12/228y, Brooks 5/124y, 5 with 3
SCORING: Fletcher 34pts, Mikes 30pts, Dillard 19pts

1958 6-1-2

28	Nebraska	0	E Rich Brooks / Len Jardine
24	Rice	0	T Jerry Beabout / Nick Mumley
6	Wisconsin	31	G Fred Brandel / Shug Turner
14	Michigan State	6	C Terry Sheehan / Sam Joyner
29	Notre Dame	22	G Ron Maltony / Jake Ciccone
31	Illinois	8	T Gene Selawski / Dale Rems
14	Ohio State	14	E Tom Frankhauser / John Crowl
23	Northwestern	6	QB Bernie Allen/ Bob Spoo/Ross Fichtner
15	Indiana	15	HB Tom Barnett / Joe Kulbacki
			HB Leonard Wilson / Clyde Washington
			FB Bob Jarus / Jack Laraway

RUSHING: Jarus 115/396y, Wilson 71/331y, Kulbacki 49/246y
PASSING: Fichtner 25-67/414y, 4 TD, 37.3%
RECEIVING: Frankhauser 13/300y, Brooks 7/104y, 3 with 3
SCORING: Jarus 60pts, Wilson & Laraway 24pts

1959 5-2-2

0	UCLA	0	E Rich Brooks / Jack Elwell
28	Notre Dame	7	T Jerry Beabout / Moose Mincevich
21	Wisconsin	0	G Fred Brandel / Jake Ciccone
0	Ohio State	15	C Sam Joyner / Phil Kardasz
14	Iowa	7	G Stan Sczurek / Ron Maltony
7	Illinois	7	T Bob Becker / Dale Rems
0	Michigan State	15	E Len Jardine / Wedge Winters
29	Minnesota	23	QB Bernie Allen / Ross Fichtner
10	Indiana	7	HB Joe Kulbacki / Jim Tiller
			HB Leonard Wilson / Clyde Washington
			FB Bob Jarus/Jack Laraway /Willie Jones

RUSHING: Laraway 65/281y, Wilson 56/216y, Kulbacki 52/204y
PASSING: Allen 33-86/416y, 4 TD, 38.4%
RECEIVING: Wilson 8/75y, Brooks 7/113y, Jardine 5/121y, Washington 5/39y
SCORING: Jarus & Washington 18pts, Allen 15pts

1960 4-4-1

27	UCLA	27	E Jack Elwell / Jim Kubinski
51	Notre Dame	19	T Jerry Beabout / Bill Currie
13	Wisconsin	24	G Stan Sczurek / Moose Mincevich
24	Ohio State	21	C Phil Kardasz/Don Paltani/J'n Behanna
14	Iowa	21	G Ron Maltony / Tom Krysinski
12	Illinois	14	T Don Brumm / Pat Russ
13	Michigan State	17	E Forest Farmer
23	Minnesota	14	QB Bernie Allen / Maury Gutman
35	Indiana	6	HB Jim Tiller / Tom Bloom
			HB Dave Miller / Bob Wiater
			FB Willie Jones / Tom Yakubowski

RUSHING: Jones 124/575y, Yakubowski 86/310y, Tiller 64/253y
PASSING: Allen 61-103/765y, 5 TD, 59.2%
RECEIVING: Tiller 21/237y, Elwell 12/230y, Farmer 7/126y
SCORING: Allen 54pts, Tiller 42pts, Jones 36pts

1961 6-3

13	Washington	6	E Jack Elwell / Harold Wells
20	Notre Dame	22	T Don Brumm / Larry Bowie
19	Miami (Ohio)	6	G Stan Sczurek / Wally Florence
14	Michigan	16	C John Behanna / Don Paltani
9	Iowa	0	G Tom Krysinski
23	Illinois	9	T Pat Russ
7	Michigan State	6	E Forest Farmer
7	Minnesota	10	QB Ron DiGravio / Ron Meyer
34	Indiana	12	HB Tom Bloom / Tom Boris
			HB Dave Miller / Bob Wiater
			FB Gene Donaldson / Roy Walker

RUSHING: Walker 123/491y, Bloom 38/236y, Donaldson 51/178y
PASSING: DiGravio 52-100/861y, 6 TD, 52.0%
RECEIVING: Elwell 16/343y, Bloom 14/128y, Boris 8/178y
SCORING: Skip Ohl (K) 32pts, Walker 24pts, DiGravio & Elwell 18pts

1962 4-4-1

7	Washington	7	E Don Brooks / Dave Ellison
24	Notre Dame	6	T Don Brumm / Nate Jackson
7	Miami (Ohio)	10	G Wally Florence / George Pappas
37	Michigan	0	C Don Paltani / Henry Dudgeon
26	Iowa	3	G Bob Lake / Babe DiFilippo
10	Illinois	14	T Ron Richnafsky / Jim Garcia
17	Michigan State	9	E John Greiner / Forest Farmer
6	Minnesota	7	QB Ron DiGravio / Ron Meyer
7	Indiana	12	HB Dave Miller / Tom Fugate
			HB Tom Bloom / Charlie King
			FB Roy Walker / Gene Donaldson

RUSHING: Walker 97/427y, Donaldson 46/249y, King 62/247y
PASSING: DiGravio 34-92/629y, 7 TD, 37.0%
RECEIVING: Bloom 13/217y, King 10/142y, Greiner 10/117y
SCORING: Skip Ohl (K) 32pts, DiGravio & Bloom 18pts

1963 5-4

0	Miami	3	E Bob Hadrick / Don Brooks
7	Notre Dame	6	T Jerry Shay / Harold Wells
20	Wisconsin	38	G Wally Florence / Jim Hales
23	Michigan	12	C Henry Dudgeon / Larry Kaminski
14	Iowa	0	G Bob Lake / Sal Ciampi
21	Illinois	41	T Bob Hopp / Jim Garcia
0	Michigan State	23	E Dave Ellison
13	Minnesota	11	QB Ron DiGravio / Ken Eby
21	Indiana	15	HB Randy Minniear / Jim Morel
			HB Gordon Teter / John Kuzniewski
			FB Terry Marccoline / Gene Donaldson

RUSHING: Kuzniewski 62/242y, Donaldson 68/212y, Minniear 27/103y
PASSING: DiGravio 88-161/1108y, 8 TD, 54.7%
RECEIVING: Hadrick 29/388y, Morel 17/233y, Teter 11/113y
SCORING: DiGravio 20pts, 6 with 12pts

1964 6-3

17	Ohio University	0	E Bob Hadrick
15	Notre Dame	34	T Bob Hopp / Lou DeFilippo
28	Wisconsin	7	G George Pappas
21	Michigan	20	C Ed Flanagan
19	Iowa	14	G Sal Ciampi
26	Illinois	14	T Karl Singer
7	Michigan State	21	E Rich Ruble
7	Minnesota	14	QB Bob Griese
28	Indiana	22	HB Jim Morel / Randy Minniear (FB)
			HB Gordon Teter
			FB Bill Harmon
			DL Harold Wells
			DL Jerry Shay
			DL Jack Calcaterra
			DL Jim Garcia
			DL Jim Long
			LB Pat Conley
			LB Bill Howard
			DB Ken Eby / John Charles
			DB George Catavolos
			DB Charles King
			DB John Kuzniewski

RUSHING: Teter 152/614y, Minniear 126/438y, Griese 82/147y
PASSING: Griese 76-156/934y, 5 TD, 48.7%
RECEIVING: Hadrick 37/441y, Morel 18/240y, Teter 10/101y
SCORING: Minniear 54pts, Griese 46pts, Teter 24pts

1965 7-2-1

38	Miami (Ohio)	0	WR Bob Hadrick
25	Notre Dame	21	T Babe DiFilippo / Bob Hopp
14	SMU	14	G Charles Erlenbaugh / Jim Hales
17	Iowa	14	C Larry Kaminski
17	Michigan	15	G Sal Ciampi / Chuck Kuzneski
10	Michigan State	14	T Karl Singer / Jim Bonk
0	Illinois	21	TE Jim Beirne
45	Wisconsin	7	QB Bob Griese
35	Minnesota	0	HB Jim Finley
26	Indiana	21	HB Gordon Teter
			FB Randy Minniear / John Kuzniewski
			DL Jim Long
			DL Jerry Shay
			DL Jack Calcaterra / Bob Sebeck
			DL Mike Barnes
			DL George Olion
			LB Pat Labus / Bob Yunaska
			LB Pat Conley / Francis Burke
			DB George Catavolos
			DB John Charles
			DB Charles King
			DB Lou Sims

RUSHING: Teter 123/490y, Minniear 98/349y, Kuzniewski 73/263y
PASSING: Griese 142-238/1719y, 11 TD, 60.0%
RECEIVING: Hadrick 47/562y, Finley 33/424y, Beirne 29/384y
SCORING: Griese 62pts, Kuzniewski 48pts, Bierne & Teter 24pts

1966 9-2

42 Ohio University	3 WR Jim Beirne
14 Notre Dame	26 T Mike Barnes / Jim Bonk
35 SMU	23 G Charles Erlenbaugh
35 Iowa	0 C Pat Labus
22 Michigan	21 G Chuck Kuzneski / Bob Sebeck
20 Michigan State	41 T Jack Calcaterra
25 Illinois	21 TE Marion Griffin
23 Wisconsin	0 QB Bob Griese
16 Minnesota	0 HB Lou Sims / Bob Baltzell
51 Indiana	6 FB Perry Williams
14 Southern Cal■	13 DL George Olion
	DL Fred Rafa / Clanton King (LB)
	DL Chuck Kyle
	DL Lance Olssen
	DL Robert Holmes
	LB Bob Yunaska / Francis Burke
	LB Pat Conley
	DB Leroy Keyes
	DB Bob Corby / Dennis Cirbes
	DB George Catavolos
	DB John Charles

RUSHING: Williams 179/689y, Baltzell 67/245y, Griese 71/215y
PASSING: Griese 130-215/1749y, 12 TD, 60.5%
RECEIVING: Beirne 64/768y, Finley 26/438y, Griffin 17/198y
SCORING: Griese 81pts, Williams 54pts, Bierne 50pts

1967 8-2

24 Texas A&M	20 WR Jim Beirne / Bob Dillingham
28 Notre Dame	21 T Jim Bonk
25 Northwestern	16 G Clanton King (LB) / Dave Piper
41 Ohio State	6 C Walter Whitehead / Mike Frame
14 Oregon State	22 G Bob Sebeck / Gary Roberts
41 Iowa	22 T Dave Stydahar (DL)
42 Illinois	9 TE Marion Griffin
41 Minnesota	12 QB Mike Phipps
21 Michigan State	7 HB Bob Baltzell
14 Indiana	19 HB Leroy Keyes (DB)
	FB Perry Williams
	DL George Olion
	DL Fred Rafa (OT) / Bill Yanchar
	DL Chuck Kyle
	DL Lance Olssen
	DL Robert Holmes
	LB Dick Marvel
	LB Francis Burke / Bob Yunaska
	DB Dennis Cirbes
	DB Tim Foley
	DB Don Webster / Larry Emch
	DB Bob Corby

RUSHING: Keyes 149/986y, Williams 177/746y, Phipps 86/220y
PASSING: Phipps 118-243/1800y, 11 TD, 48.6%
RECEIVING: Beirne 45/643y, Keyes 45/758y, Griffin 17/196y
SCORING: Keyes 114pts, Williams 66pts, Baltzell 53pts

1968 8-2

44 Virginia	6 WR Bob Dillingham
37 Notre Dame	22 T Clanton King
43 Northwestern	6 G Gary Roberts / Clinton Turner
0 Ohio State	13 C Mike Frame / Walter Whitehead
28 Wake Forest	27 G Dave Stydahar
44 Iowa	14 T Paul DeNuccio / Donnie Green
35 Illinois	17 TE Marion Griffin / Mike Engelbrecht
13 Minnesota	27 QB Mike Phipps
9 Michigan State	0 HB Jim Kirkpatrick / Randy Cooper (DB)
38 Indiana	35 HB Leroy Keyes / Stan Brown
	FB Perry Williams
	DL Bill McKoy
	DL Bill Yanchar
	DL Chuck Kyle
	DL Alex Davis / Ron Maree
	DL Dennis Wirgowski / Willie Nelson
	LB Bob Yunaska
	LB Veno Paraskevas / Dick Marvel
	DB Tim Foley / John Reilly
	DB Don Webster / Richard Mahurt
	DB Larry Emch
	DB Steve deGrandmaison

RUSHING: Keyes 189/1003y, Williams 138/553y,
   Kirkpatrick 69/370y
PASSING: Phipps 88-169/1096y 3 TD, 52.1%
RECEIVING: Dillingham 35/456y, Keyes 33/428y,
   Kirkpatrick 10/99y
SCORING: Keyes 90pts, Williams 54pts, Jeff Jones (K) 39pts

1969 8-2

42 TCU	35 WR Greg Fenner
28 Notre Dame	14 WR Stan Brown
36 Stanford	35 T Paul DeNuccio
20 Michigan	31 G Tim Huxhold
35 Iowa	31 C Walter Whitehead
45 Northwestern	20 G Tom Luken
49 Illinois	22 T Donnie Green
41 Michigan State	13 TE Ashley Bell / Mike Cota
14 Ohio State	42 QB Mike Phipps
44 Indiana	21 HB Randy Cooper / Scott Clayton
	FB John Bullock
	DL Bill McKoy
	DL Bill Yanchar
	DL Tom Bayless / Dave Beigh
	DL Ron Maree
	DL Dennis Wirgowski
	LB Veno Paraskevas
	LB Jim Teal
	DB Tim Foley
	DB Sammy Carter / Richard Mahurt
	DB Mike Renie
	DB Steve deGrandmaison

RUSHING: Cooper 171/697y, Bullock 74/349y, Phipps 97/218y
PASSING: Phipps 169-321/2527y, 23 TD, 52.6%
RECEIVING: Bell 49/669y, Brown 32/725y, Cooper 29/377y
SCORING: Brown 108pts, Bell 66pts, Jeff Jones (K) 56pts

1970 4-6

15 TCU	0 WR Darryl Stingley
0 Notre Dame	48 WR Stan Brown
26 Stanford	14 T Paul DeNuccio / Alan Dick
0 Michigan	29 G Tim Huxhold / Clinton Turner
24 Iowa	3 C Kenneth Watkins
14 Northwestern	48 G Tom Luken
21 Illinois	23 T Donnie Green
14 Michigan State	24 TE Ashley Bell / Mike Cota
7 Ohio State	10 QB Gary Danielson / Chuck Piebes
40 Indiana	0 HB Otis Armstrong / Jack Spellman
	FB Ron North / Scott Clayton
	DL John Handy / Rick Tekavec
	DL Ron Maree / Bronco Keser
	DL Doug Molls / Gregg Bingham
	DL Alex Davis / Steve Nurrenbern
	DL Gary Hrivnak
	LB Jim Teal
	DB Arnold Carter / Mike Renie
	DB Mike McDaniel / Charlie Potts
	DB Steve deGrandmaison
	DB Randy Cooper

RUSHING: Armstrong 213/1009y, North 88/339y,
   Clayton 45/201y
PASSING: Piebes 44-90/430y, 0 TD, 48.9%,
   Danielson 39-98/546y, 2 TD, 39.8%
RECEIVING: Stingley 23/286y, Brown 17/221y, Bell 13/161y,
   Armstrong 13/148y
SCORING: Brown 54pts, Clayton 24pts, Armstrong 18pts

1971 3-7

35 Washington	38 WR Rick Sayers
7 Notre Dame	8 WR Darryl Stingley (HB)
45 Iowa	13 T Tim Huxhold
27 Minnesota	13 G Kenneth Watkins / Rich Ostriker
21 Northwestern	20 C Bob Hoidahl
7 Illinois	21 G Mike Williams
10 Michigan State	43 T Tom Luken (G) / Donn Smith
10 Wisconsin	14 TE Ashley Bell / Mike Cota
17 Michigan	20 QB Gary Danielson / Steve Burke
31 Indiana	38 HB Otis Armstrong
	FB Ron North / Scott Clayton
	DL Steve Baumgartner / Joe Tenkman
	DL Dave Butz
	DL Gregg Bingham / Doug Molls
	DL Bronco Keser
	DL Gary Hrivnak
	LB Rick Schavietello / Mark Gefert
	LB Jim Teal
	DB Carl Capria / Mike Renie
	DB Sammy Carter
	DB Chuck Piebes
	DB Charlie Potts

RUSHING: Armstrong 214/945y, Stingley 60/248y, North 57/157y
PASSING: Danielson 89-154/1467y, 10 TD, 57.8%
RECEIVING: Sayers 39/573y, Stingley 36/734y, Bell 18/239y
SCORING: Armstrong 60pts, Stingley 44pts,
   Mike Renie (K) 39pts

1972 6-5

14 Bowling Green	17 WR Rick Sayers / Dan Roman
21 Washington	22 WR Stan Brown / Bob Herrick
14 Notre Dame	35 T Donn Smith
24 Iowa	0 G Ralph Perretta / Steve Schaefer
28 Minnesota	3 C Frank DiLieto
37 Northwestern	0 G Rich Ostriker
20 Illinois	14 T Don Myers / Mike Albright
12 Michigan State	22 TE Gary Hrivnak / Barry Santini
27 Wisconsin	6 QB Gary Danielson / Bo Bobrowski
6 Michigan	9 HB Otis Armstrong
42 Indiana	7 FB Jack Spellman / Skip Peterson
	DL Joe Tenkman / Mike Barr
	DL Dave Butz
	DL Gregg Bingham
	DL Bronco Keser
	DL Steve Baumgartner
	LB Mark Gefert
	LB Joe Monago / Ron North
	DB Arnold Carter
	DB Bill Knox / Fred Cooper
	DB Carl Capria / Chuck Piebes
	DB Tim Racke

RUSHING: Armstrong 243/1361y, Spellman 84/323y,
   Danielson 108/274y
PASSING: Danielson 50-138/735y, 2 TD, 36.2%
RECEIVING: Sayers 16/196y, Stingley 10/236y, Roman 9/114y
SCORING: Armstrong 66pts, Bobrowski 41pts,
   Howard Conner (K) 34pts

1973 5-6

14 Wisconsin	13 WR Larry Burton / Dan Roman
19 Miami (Ohio)	24 WR Bob Herrick / Errol Patterson
7 Notre Dame	20 T Steve Schaefer
27 Duke	7 G Jeff Romack
13 Illinois	15 C Frank DiLieto
21 Northwestern	10 G Ralph Perretta
7 Michigan State	10 T Ken Long
48 Iowa	23 TE Barry Santini / Jon Walling
7 Minnesota	34 QB Bo Bobrowski
9 Michigan	34 TB Mike Northington / Skip Peterson (FB)
28 Indiana	23 FB Pete Gross / Mike Pruitt
	DL Joe Tenkman / Rick Oliver
	DL Ken Novak / Steve Nurrenbern
	DL Mark Gorgal / Chuk Keever
	DL Stan Parker / Jon Zwitt
	DL Bob Hoftiezer
	LB Rick Schavietello / Cedric Evans
	LB Mark Gefert / Randy Clark
	DB Bill Knox / Alex DiMarzio
	DB Fred Cooper
	DB Tim Racke
	DB Carl Capria / Jim Wood

RUSHING: Gross 133/560y, Bobrowski 139/549y,
   Northington 126/502y
PASSING: Bobrowski 57-135/849y, 4 TD, 42.2%
RECEIVING: Burton 15/271y, Herrick 14/207y, Roman 12/156y
SCORING: Bobrowski 48pts, Northington 42pts,
   Howard Conner (K) 25pts

1974 4-6-1

14 Wisconsin	28 WR Larry Burton
7 Miami (Ohio)	7 WR Reggie Arnold / Paul Beery
31 Notre Dame	20 T Jeff Stapleton
14 Duke	16 G Tom Gibson
23 Illinois	27 C Jim Polak
31 Northwestern	26 G Ralph Perretta
7 Michigan State	31 T Connie Zelencik / Ken Long
38 Iowa	14 TE Barry Santini
20 Minnesota	24 QB Mark Vitali / Mike Terrizzi
0 Michigan	51 TB Mike Northington / Scott Dierking
38 Indiana	17 FB Pete Gross / Mike Pruitt
	DL Rick Oliver
	DL Ken Novak
	DL Mark Gorgal / Roger Ruwe
	DL Stan Parker
	DL Ron Hardy
	LB Joe Sullivan
	LB Bob Manella
	DB Alex DiMarzio / Pat Harris
	DB Fred Cooper
	DB Jim Wood / Dwight Lewis
	DB Tom Andres / Antjony Thompson

RUSHING: Dierking 164/779y, Pruitt 102/613y, Gross 105/390y
PASSING: Vitali 68-145/1006y, 8 TD, 46.9%
RECEIVING: Burton 38/702y, Arnold 11/187y, Beery 11/152y
SCORING: Vitali 44pts, Steve Schmidt (K) 34pts, Dierking 30pts

1975 4-7

25 Northwestern	31 WR Reggie Arnold / Jesse Townsend
0 Notre Dame	17 WR Paul Beery
6 Southern Cal	17 T Jeff Stapleton
3 Miami (Ohio)	14 G Tom Gibson
14 Wisconsin	17 C Jim Polak
26 Illinois	24 G Connie Zelencik
6 Ohio State	35 T Ken Long
20 Michigan State	10 TE Nigel Wirgowski
0 Michigan	28 QB Mark Vitali
19 Iowa	18 TB Scott Dierking
9 Indiana	7 FB Mike Pruitt
	DL Blane Smith
	DL Ken Novak
	DL Roger Ruwe / Mark Gorgal
	DL Jon Zwitt
	DL Kim Cripe
	LB Joe Sullivan / Mike Burgamy
	LB Bob Mannella
	DB Jerome King
	DB Mike Northington
	DB Pat Harris
	DB Mark Travline

RUSHING: Dierking 180/914y, Pruitt 217/899y, Vitali 52/132y
PASSING: Vitali 46-127/728y, 3 TD, 36.2%
RECEIVING: Beery 27/454y, Townsend 17/276y, Arnold 11/167y
SCORING: Dierking 42pts, Steve Schmidt (K) 38pts,
Pruitt & Beery 18pts

1976 5-6

31 Northwestern	19 WR Raymond Smith / Jesse Townsend
0 Notre Dame	23 WR Reggie Arnold
13 Southern Cal	31 T John LeFeber
42 Miami (Ohio)	20 G Tom Gibson
18 Wisconsin	16 C Jay Venzin / Ricj Wetendorf
17 Illinois	21 G Connie Zelencik
3 Ohio State	24 T Dave Lafary
13 Michigan State	45 TE Nigel Wirgowski
16 Michigan	14 QB Mark Vitali
21 Iowa	0 TB Scott Dierking
14 Indiana	20 FB John Skibinski
	DL Blane Smith
	DL Cleveland Crosby
	DL Ken Loushin
	DL Chris Barr
	DL Kim Cripe
	LB Fred Arrington / Kevin Motts
	LB Bob Mannella
	DB Jerome King
	DB Mike Northington / Pat Harris
	DB Rock Supan
	DB Paul Beery

RUSHING: Dierking 201/1000y, Skibinski 173/871y,
Vitali 100/317y
PASSING: Vitali 73-172/1184y, 0 TD, 42.4%
RECEIVING: Arnold 16/287y, Skibinski 13/118y, Smith 11/233y
SCORING: Dierking 68pts, Vitali 48pts, Skibinski 24pts

1977 5-6

14 Michigan State	19 WR Raymond Smith
44 Ohio University	7 WR Reggie Arnold
24 Notre Dame	31 T Mike Barberich
26 Wake Forest	17 G John Finucan / Dale Schwan
0 Ohio State	46 C Pete Quinn / Steve Schlundt
22 Illinois	29 G Steve McKenzie
34 Iowa	21 T John LeFeber
28 Northwestern	16 TE Dave Young / Tim Eubank
22 Wisconsin	0 QB Mark Herrmann
7 Michigan	40 TB Mike Brown / Bob Williams
10 Indiana	21 FB John Skibinski
	DL Lee Larkins
	DL Marcus Jackson / Calvin Clark
	DL Roger Ruwe
	DL Jeff Senica
	DL Keena Turner
	LB Fred Arrington
	LB Kevin Motts
	DB Jerome King
	DB Pat Harris
	DB Rock Supan
	DB Willie Harris / Paul Beery

RUSHING: Skibinski 147/665y, Williams 99/362y, Brown 77/318y
PASSING: Herrmann 175-319/2153y, 18 TD, 54.9%
RECEIVING: Arnold 44/840y, Smith 38/565y, Skibinski 32/221y
SCORING: Scott Sovereen (K) 59pts, Arnold 48pts,
Skibinski 32pts

1978 9-2-1

21 Michigan State	14 WR Bart Burrell / Raymond Smith
24 Ohio University	0 WR Mike Harris
6 Notre Dame	10 T Henry Fiel
14 Wake Forest	7 G Dale Schwan
27 Ohio State	16 C Pete Quinn
13 Illinois	0 G John LeFeber
34 Iowa	7 T Steve McKenzie
31 Northwestern	0 TE Dave Young / Tim Eubank
24 Wisconsin	24 QB Mark Herrmann
6 Michigan	24 TB Russell Pope / Wally Jones
20 Indiana	7 FB John Macon / Mike Augustyniak
41 Georgia Tech■	21 DL Ruben Floyd
	DL Calvin Clark
	DL Ken Loushin
	DL Marcus Jackson
	DL Keena Turner
	LB Kevin Motts
	LB Mark Johanson / Mike Marks
	DB Wayne Smith
	DB Rick Moss
	DB Willie Harris
	DB Rock Supan

RUSHING: Macon 225/913y, Pope 164/673y,
Augustyniak 52/308y
PASSING: Herrmann 152-274/1904y, 14 TD, 55.5%
RECEIVING: Pope 35/292y, Harris 34/495y, Burrell 31/467y
SCORING: Scott Sovereen (K) 73pts, Pope 36pts, Burrell 26pts

1979 10-2

41 Wisconsin	20 WR Bart Burrell / Raymond Smith
21 UCLA	31 WR Mike Harris
28 Notre Dame	22 T Henry Fiel
13 Oregon	7 G Dale Schwan
14 Minnesota	31 C Pete Quinn
28 Illinois	14 G Don Hall
14 Michigan State	7 T Steve McKenzie
20 Northwestern	16 TE Dave Young
20 Iowa	14 QB Mark Herrmann
24 Michigan	21 TB Wally Jones / Ben McCall
37 Indiana	21 FB Mike Augustyniak / John Macon
27 Tennessee■	22 DL Tom Kingsbury
	DL Calvin Clark
	DL Ken Loushin
	DL Marcus Jackson
	DL Keena Turner
	LB Kevin Motts
	LB James Looney / Mike Marks
	DB Wayne Smith
	DB Bill Kay
	DB Robert Williams / Marcus McKinnie
	DB Tim Seneff

RUSHING: Jones 183/754y, Macon 113/488y, McCall 80/451y
PASSING: Herrmann 203-348/2377y, 16 TD, 58.3%
RECEIVING: Young 55/584y, Burrell 40/607y, Smith 31/421y
SCORING: Young 60pts, Jones 48pts, John Seibel (K) 40pts

1980 9-3

10 Notre Dame	31 WR Bart Burrell
12 Wisconsin	6 WR Steve Bryant
14 UCLA	23 T Henry Fiel / Claybon Fields
28 Miami (Ohio)	3 G Tim Hull
21 Minnesota	7 C Pete Quinn
45 Illinois	20 G Ray Gunner
36 Michigan State	25 T Tom Jelesky
52 Northwestern	31 TE Dave Young
58 Iowa	13 QB Mark Herrmann
0 Michigan	26 TB Jimmy Smith / Wally Jones
24 Indiana	23 FB John Macon / Ben McCall (TB)
28 Missouri■	25 DL Paul Hanna / Chris Scott
	DL Tom Munro
	DL Calvin Clark
	LB Tom Kingsbury
	LB James Looney
	LB Mike Marks
	LB David Frye
	DB Robert Williams
	DB Bill Kay
	DB Marcus McKinnie / Bob Lashley
	DB Tim Seneff

RUSHING: Smith 139/657y, McCall 113/507y, Macon 116/450y
PASSING: Herrmann 242-368/3212y, 23 TD, 65.8%
RECEIVING: Young 70/959y, Burrell 40/607y, Bryant 50/892y
SCORING: Rick Anderson (K) 86pts, Young & Smith 54pts

1981 5-6

27 Stanford	19 WR Joe Linville
13 Minnesota	16 WR Steve Bryant
15 Notre Dame	14 T Jim Fritzsche
14 Wisconsin	20 G Ray Gunner
44 Illinois	20 C Paul Royer
35 Northwestern	0 G Claybon Fields
27 Michigan State	26 T Tom Jelesky
33 Ohio State	45 TE Cliff Benson
7 Iowa	33 QB Scott Campbell
10 Michigan	28 TB Jeff Feulner /Jimmy Smith/Eric Jordan
17 Indiana	20 FB Bruce King
	DL Matt Hernandez
	DL Casey Moore
	DL Chris Scott
	LB Andy Gladstone
	LB Brock Spack
	LB Mark Brown
	LB David Frye
	DB Robert Williams
	DB Derrick Taylor
	DB Marcus McKinnie / Bob Lashley
	DB Tim Seneff

RUSHING: Smith 152/540y, Fuelner 55/287y, Jordan 62/287y
PASSING: Campbell 185-321/2686y, 18 TD, 57.6%
RECEIVING: Bryant 60/971y, Linville 33/475y, Benson 33/458y
SCORING: Bryant 68pts, Tim Clark (K) 41pts, Smith 36pts

1982 3-8

14 Stanford	35 WR Steve Griffin / Joe Linville
10 Minnesota	36 WR Everett Pickens / Dave Retherford
14 Notre Dame	28 T Claybon Fields
31 Wisconsin	35 G Mike Brown / John Fitzpatrick
34 Illinois	38 C Paul Royer
34 Northwestern	21 G Chris Prince
24 Michigan State	21 T Paul Alekna / Tom Jelesky
6 Ohio State	38 TE Cliff Benson
16 Iowa	7 QB Scott Campbell
21 Michigan	52 TB Melvin Gray
7 Indiana	13 FB Rodney Carter / Timothy Richardson
	DL Matt Hernandez
	DL Brad Hornor
	DL Chris Scott / Derek Wimberly
	LB Andy Gladstone
	LB Brock Spack
	LB Mark Brown
	LB David Frye / Jason Houston
	DB Don Anderson
	DB Eric Jordan
	DB Ray Wallace
	DB Bob Lashley / Kennedy Wilson

RUSHING: Gray 195/916y, Carter 87/343y, Richardson 19/94y
PASSING: Campbell 218-399/2626y, 14 TD, 54.6%
RECEIVING: Benson 50/762y, Gray 38/299y, Carter 34/301y
SCORING: Tim Clark (K) 47pts, Gray 36pts, Benson 30pts

1983 3-7-1

6 Notre Dame	52 WR Jeff Price / Steve Griffin
0 Miami	35 WR Dave Retherford
32 Minnesota	20 T Doug Isbell
29 Michigan State	29 G John Fitzpatrick / Jerry Boat (C)
22 Ohio State	33 C Butch Adler
14 Iowa	31 G Mark Drenth
21 Illinois	35 T Paul Alekna
48 Northwestern	17 TE Cliff Benson / Marty Scott
10 Michigan	42 QB Scott Campbell / Jim Everett
38 Wisconsin	42 TB Melvin Gray / Lloyd Hawthorne
31 Indiana	24 FB Bruce King / Eric Jordan
	DL Andy Gladstone
	DL Chris Scott / Bob Ziltz
	DL Brad Hornor / Kevin Holley
	DL Derek Wimberly / Melvin Menke
	DL Derrick Hoskins
	LB Brock Spack
	LB Jason Houston / Kevin Sumlin
	DB Don Anderson
	DB Ray Wallace
	DB Rod Woodson
	DB Kennedy Wilson

RUSHING: Gray 190/849y, Jordan 81/521y, Hawthorne 95/490y
PASSING: Campbell 183-305/2031y, 12 TD, 60.0%
RECEIVING: Price 40/633y, Benson 34/326y, Griffin 24/270y
SCORING: Gray 60pts, Tim Clark (K) 43pts,
Benson & Hawthorne 30pts

SCORES, LINEUPS, AND STATISTICS

1984 7-5
23 Notre Dame
17 Miami
34 Minnesota
13 Michigan State
28 Ohio State
3 Iowa
20 Illinois
49 Northwestern
31 Michigan
13 Wisconsin
31 Indiana
24 Virginia ■

21 WR Steve Griffin
28 WR Rick Brunner / Jeff Price
10 T Paul Alekna
10 G Drew Banks / Dave Jaumotte
23 C Jerry Boat / Rick Skibinski
40 G Mark Drenth
34 T Doug Isbell
7 TE Marty Scott / Jack Beery
29 QB Jim Everett / Doug Downing
30 TB Ray Wallace / Rodney Carter
24 FB Bruce King
27 DL Tony Visco / Fred Strickland
DL Melvin Menke
DL Brad Hornor / Bob Ziltz
DL Kevin Holley / Derek Wimberly
DL Don Baldwin
LB Jason Houston / Merkle Williams
LB Keith Sumlin / Bill Mulchrone
DB Don Anderson / Jeff Lee
DB Cris Dishman / Tommy Lee Myers
DB Rod Woodson
DB Kennedy Wilson

RUSHING: Wallace 145/587y, Carter 135/449y, King 91/416y
PASSING: Everett 249-431/3256y, 18 TD, 57.8%
RECEIVING: Griffin 64/1060y, Scott 46/556y, King 33/355y, Carter 33/275y
SCORING: Mike Rendina (K) 74pts, Wallace 36pts, Griffin 30pts

1985 5-6
30 Pittsburgh
37 Ball State
35 Notre Dame
15 Minnesota
30 Illinois
27 Ohio State
24 Michigan State
31 Northwestern
0 Michigan
24 Iowa
34 Indiana

31 WR Steve Griffin / Jon Hayes
18 WR Rick Brunner / Mark Jackson
17 T Mark Drenth / Kieth Brown
45 G Vince Panfil / Bruce Crites
24 C Rick Skibinski
41 G Bret Brunnel / Todd Tyrie
28 T Mike Connors
7 TE Marty Scott / Jack Beery
47 QB Jim Everett
27 TB Rodney Carter / James Medlock
21 FB Ray Wallace
DL Don Baldwin
DL Brad Hornor / Anthony Rose
DL Kevin Holley / Derek Wimberly
DL Bob Ziltz
LB Tony Visco / Merkle Williams
LB Keith Sumlin / Matt Morgan
LB Fred Strickland
DB Mike Weaver
DB Cris Dishman
DB Rod Woodson / Marc Foster
DB Kennedy Wilson / Damon Taylor

RUSHING: Wallace 100/522y, Medlock 68/259y, Carter 71/216y
PASSING: Everett 285-450/3651y, 23 TD, 63.3%
RECEIVING: Carter 98/1099y, Jackson 43/732y, Wallace 43/514y
SCORING: Jonathan Briggs (K) 63pts, Wallace 54pts, Carter & Medlock 42pts

1986 3-8
20 Ball State
26 Pittsburgh
9 Notre Dame
9 Minnesota
27 Illinois
11 Ohio State
3 Michigan State
17 Northwestern
7 Michigan
14 Iowa
17 Indiana

3 WR Rick Brunner / Lance Scheib
41 WR Jon Hayes / Calvin Williams
41 T Keith Brown
36 G Bruce Crites
34 C Todd Tyrie
39 G DeWayne Penn / Jim Richmond
37 T Mike Connors
16 TE Jack Beery
31 QB Jeff George / Doug Downing
42 TB Jerry Chancy / James Medlock
15 FB Tony Grant
DL Bill Hitchcock
DL Chris Keevers
DL Kevin Holley
DL Bill Gildea
LB Fred Strickland
LB Keith Sumlin
DB Rod Woodson (WR)
DB Mike Weaver
DB Marc Foster / Scott Kalinoski
DB Ronnie Beeks

RUSHING: Medlock 137/488y, Chancy 43/151y, Woodson 15/93y
PASSING: George 122-227/1217y, 4 TD, 53.7%
RECEIVING: Chancy 46/257y, Brunner 35/496y, Grant 24/188y
SCORING: Jonathan Briggs (K) 48pts, Scheib 30pts, Chancy 18pts

1987 3-7-1
10 Washington
22 Louisville
20 Notre Dame
19 Minnesota
9 Illinois
17 Ohio State
14 Iowa
49 Wisconsin
3 Michigan State
20 Northwestern
14 Indiana

28 WR Anthony Hardy / Lance Scheib
22 WR Calvin Williams
44 T Mike Connors
21 G Anthony Rose
3 C Bruce Crites
20 G Keith Brown
38 T Jim Richmond
14 TE Brad Schumacher
45 QB Doug Downing / Shawn McCarthy
15 TB Darren Myles / Jerry Chancy
35 FB James Medlock / Scott Nelson
DL Tony Visco
DL Chris Keevers
DL Bill Hitchcock / Ken Kushner
DL Scott Conover / Donzel Leggett
LB Jerrol Williams
LB Fred Strickland
LB Art DuBose
DB Cris Dishman
DB Steve Jackson
DB Marc Foster / Scott Kalinoski
DB Derrick Kelson

RUSHING: Medlock 175/634y, Myles 109/363y, Nelson 11/40y
PASSING: McCarthy 98-177/1088y, 5 TD, 55.4%
Downing 102-200/1065y, 6 TD, 51.0%
RECEIVING: Hardy 58/723y, Williams 42/585y, Chancy 39/276y
SCORING: Jonathan Briggs (K) 59pts, Myles 48pts, Williams 36pts

1988 4-7
6 Washington
33 Ohio University
7 Notre Dame
14 Minnesota
0 Illinois
31 Ohio State
7 Iowa
9 Wisconsin
3 Michigan State
7 Northwestern
7 Indiana

20 WR Todd Moore / Curtis McManus
10 WR Calvin Williams
52 T Bruce Brineman
10 G Derick Schmidt
20 C Bruce Crites / Bob Dressel (DL)
26 G Jason Cegielski
31 T Teko Johnson
6 TE Dwayne O'Connor
48 QB Brian Fox
28 TB Jarrett Scales / Ray Graham
52 FB Ernie Schramayr / Jerome Sparkman
DL Scott Conover / Dennis Dotson
DL Bill Hitchcock
DL Ken Kushner / Bryan Madden
DL Donzel Leggett
LB Jerrol Williams
LB Darrin Trieb
LB Tyrone Starks / Jim Schwantz
DB Steve Jackson
DB Derrick Kelson
DB Marc Foster / Reggie Broussard
DB Ronnie Beeks / Terry Johnson

RUSHING: Scales 112/362y,
PASSING: Fox 121-235/1250y, 7 TD, 51.5%
RECEIVING: Williams 37/479y, O'Connor 24/276y,
SCORING: Larry Sullivan (K) 34pts,

1989 3-8
27 Miami (Ohio)
9 Washington
7 Notre Dame
15 Minnesota
2 Illinois
3 Ohio State
21 Michigan State
27 Michigan
46 Northwestern
0 Iowa
15 Indiana

10 WR Robert Oglesby / Rod Dennis
38 WR Calvin Williams / Abe Hoskins
40 T Bruce Brineman / Jim Wormsley
35 G Derick Schmidt / Larry Taylor
14 C Bob Dressel
21 G Jason Cegielski
28 T Bill Hitchcock / Scott Conover
42 TE Dwayne O'Connor
15 QB Eric Hunter / Steve Letnich
24 TB Jerome Sparkman
14 FB Tony Vinson / Earl Coleman
DL Frank Kmet / Donzel Leggett
DL Jeff Zgonina
DL Ken Kushner / Kris Burns
DL Dennis Dotson / Peyton Minter
LB Eric Beatty
LB Darrin Trieb
LB Jim Schwantz
DB Steve Jackson
DB Derrick Kelson
DB Nat Martin / Jarrett Scales
DB Terry Johnson

RUSHING: Sparkman 118/451y, Vinson 39/92y, Coleman 22/52y
PASSING: Hunter 91-178/1368y, 11 TD, 51.1%
RECEIVING: Williams 51/630y, Vinson 30/327y, Sparkman 28/239y
SCORING: Williams 42pts, Larry Sullivan (K) 40pts, Dennis 36pts

1990 2-9
14 Washington
41 Indiana State
11 Notre Dame
7 Minnesota
0 Illinois
2 Ohio State
33 Michigan State
13 Michigan
33 Northwestern
9 Iowa
14 Indiana

20 WR Rodney Dennis
13 WR Curtis McManus
37 WR Ernest Calloway
19 WR Jeff Hill / Jimmy Young
34 T Denny Chronopoulos
42 G Larry Taylor
55 C Bob Dressel
38 G Jason Cegielski
13 T Scott Conover
38 QB Eric Hunter
28 RB Tony Vinson / John Oglesby
DL Frank Kmet
DL Jeff Zgonina
DL Kris Burns
DL Peyton Minter
LB Tom McNeil
LB Eric Beatty
LB Jim Schwantz
DB Steve Jackson
DB Jarrett Scales
DB Nat Martin
DB Terry Johnson

RUSHING: Vinson 49/198y, Oglesby 48/131y, Galen Morrow (RB) 41/120y
PASSING: Hunter 200-366/2355y, 12 TD, 54.6%
RECEIVING: Calloway 47/541y, McManus 45/581y, Hill 31/277y
SCORING: Hunter 44pts, McManus 24pts, Steve Wambold (K) 22pts

1991 4-7
49 E. Michigan
18 California
20 Notre Dame
17 Northwestern
3 Minnesota
21 Iowa
0 Michigan
14 Illinois
27 Michigan State
22 Indiana

3 WR Ernest Calloway
42 WR Tedman Brown / Rodney Dennis
45 T Derick Schmidt
14 G Denny Chronopoulos / David Bratton
6 C Bob Dressel / Nick Mamula
9 G Elvin Caldwell
31 T Kevin Janiak
42 TE Scott Green / Tony Simmons
41 QB Eric Hunter / Matt Pike
17 TB Jeff Hill / Corey Rogers
24 FB Arlee Conners / Earl Coleman
DL Frank Kmet / James Cole
DL Jeff Zgonina
DL Robert Hardin / Eric Gray
LB Trent Decatur
LB Peyton Minter / Kevin Strickland
LB Eric Beatty
LB Jim Schwantz / Don Delvy
DB Tank Adams
DB Jimmy Young
DB Pat Johnson
DB Rick Smith / Ikee Dozier

RUSHING: Hill 116/678y, Rogers 108/502y, Conners 69/325y
PASSING: Hunter 77-162/1018y, 7 TD, 47.5%, Pike 29-61/436y, 3 TD, 47.5%
RECEIVING: Calloway 24/475y, Dennis 19/312y, Brown 12/199y
SCORING: Joe O'Leary (K) 43pts, Coleman & Rogers 36pts

1992 4-7
41 California
29 Toledo
0 Notre Dame
14 Northwestern
24 Minnesota
16 Wisconsin
27 Iowa
17 Michigan
17 Illinois
13 Michigan State
13 Indiana

14 WR Jermaine Ross
33 WR Ernest Calloway
48 T Elvin Caldwell / Ryan Grigson
28 G David Bratton
20 C Nick Mamula / Bill Clince
19 G Chris Sedoris
16 T Kevin Janiak / Alfie Hill
24 TE Scott Green / Tony Simmons
20 QB Matt Pike / Eric Hunter / Scott Hoffman
35 TB Jeff Hill / Arlee Conners
10 FB Mike Alstott
DL Eric Gray / Jarrod Walker
DL Jeff Zgonina
DL James Cole / Ben Metzger
LB Romond Batten
LB Eric Beatty
LB Bart Conley / Aaron Hall
LB Don Delvy
DB Tank Adams / Courtland Byrd
DB Jimmy Young
DB Pat Johnson
DB Ikee Dozier / Chad Buckland

RUSHING: Conners 154/676y
PASSING: Hunter 54-112/857y, 3TD, 48.2%,
RECEIVING: Ross 26/579y, Calloway 24/363y
SCORING: Joe O'Leary (K) 67pts, Conners 24pts

1993 1-10

7 N. Carolina St.	20 WR Jermaine Ross / Kirk Olivadotti
28 W. Michigan	13 WR Jeff Hill / Terry Samuel
0 Notre Dame	17 T Alfie Hill
10 Illinois	28 G Elvin Caldwell / Damon Lewis
56 Minnesota	59 C Bill Clince / Emmett Zitelli
28 Wisconsin	42 G Chris Sedoris
24 Ohio State	45 T Ryan Grigson / Mike Cardona
17 Iowa	26 TE Scott Green / Tony Simmons
10 Michigan	25 QB Rick Trefzger / Matt Pike
24 Michigan State	27 TB Corey Rogers / Arlee Conners
17 Indiana	24 FB Mike Alstott
	DL Jayme Washel / Jarrod Walker
	DL Darnell Howard / Eric Gray
	DL James Cole / Ben Metzger
	LB Romond Batten
	LB Aaron Hall / Bob O'Connor
	LB Bart Conley
	LB Joe Hagins / Chris Coeppen
	DB John Jackson / Kevin Nolan
	DB Jimmy Young
	DB Pat Johnson / Brian Lohman
	DB Ikee Dozier / Brian Thurman

RUSHING: Alstott 153/816y, Rogers 153/746y, Conners 26/119y
PASSING: Trefzger 90-154/1247y, 7 TD, 58.4%
Pike 71-139/997y, 4 TD, 51.1%
RECEIVING: Hill 35/559y, Ross 31/493y, Alstott 30/407y
SCORING: Alstott 84pts, Brad Bobich (K) 45pts,
Rogers & Hill 24pts

1994 4-5-2

51 Toledo	17 WR Burt Thornton
49 Ball State	21 WR Craig Allen
21 Notre Dame	39 T Ryan Grigson / Alfie Hill
22 Illinois	16 G Damon Lewis
49 Minnesota	37 C Emmett Zitelli
27 Wisconsin	27 G Chris Sedoris
14 Ohio State	48 T Mike Cardona
21 Iowa	21 TE Charlie Stephens
23 Michigan	45 QB Rick Trefzger / Billy Dicken
30 Michigan State	42 TB Corey Rogers / Edwin Watson
29 Indiana	33 FB Mike Alstott
	DL Matt Kingsbury
	DL Jayme Washel
	DL Jon Krick / Ben Metzger
	DL Mike Burchfield / Darnell Howard
	LB Bart Conley
	LB Aaron Hall
	LB Chike Okeafor
	DB John Jackson
	DB Derrick Brown
	DB Joe Hagins / Lee Brush
	DB Reggie Johnson

RUSHING: Alstott 202/1188y, Rogers 146/764y, Watson 59/272y
PASSING: Trefzger 74-131/1137y, 3 TD, 56.5%,
Dicken 44-82/593y, 3 TD, 53.7%
RECEIVING: Thornton 45/726y, Alstott 23/298y, Allen 16/294y
SCORING: Alstott 86pts

1995 4-6-1

26 West Virginia	24 WR Brian Alford / Isaac Jones
28 Notre Dame	35 WR Craig Allen / Kirk Olivadotti
35 Michigan State	35 T Alfie Hill
35 Ball State	13 G Emmett Zitelli / Damon Lewis
38 Minnesota	39 C Chris Sedoris / Brian Nicley
23 Penn State	26 G Mark Fischer / Dan Maly
0 Ohio State	28 T John Hoogendoorn
38 Wisconsin	27 TE Charlie Stephens / Jon Blackman
0 Michigan	5 QB Rick Trefzger / Billy Dicken
8 Northwestern	23 TB Edwin Watson / Kendall Matthews
51 Indiana	14 FB Mike Alstott
	DL Craig Williams / Chukie Nwokorie
	DL Jayme Washel
	DL Leo Perez
	DL Jon Krick
	LB Aaron Hall / Willie Fells
	LB Bob O'Connor / Noble Jones
	LB Chike Oleafor / Joe Hagins
	DB Jamel Coleman
	DB Derrick Winston / Tommy Triplett
	DB Derrick Brown
	DB Willie Burroughs / Lee Brush

RUSHING: Alstott 243/1436y, Watson 102/553y, Rogers 82/424y
PASSING: Trefzger 123-208/1521y, 6 TD, 59.1%
RECEIVING: Alford 34/686y, Allen 21/347y, Olivadotti 20/203y
SCORING: Alstott 68pts.

1996 3-8

14 Michigan State	52 WR Brian Alford / Robert Tolbert
0 Notre Dame	35 WR Willie Tillman / Isaac Jones
6 West Virginia	20 T Nick Sweeney / Jim Niedrach
42 N. Carolina St.	21 G Emmett Zitelli
30 Minnesota	27 C Brian Nicley
14 Penn State	31 G Wayne Finchum / Chad Manning
14 Ohio State	42 T Mark Fischer
25 Wisconsin	33 TE Brandon Jewell
9 Michigan	3 QB Rick Trefzger / John Reeves (DB)
24 Northwestern	27 TB Kendall Matthews / Lee Johnson
16 Indiana	33 FB Edwin Watson
	DL Craig Williams / Chukie Nwokorie
	DL Jon Krick / Greg Smith
	DL Leo Perez / David Nugent
	DL Rosevelt Colvin
	LB Joe Hagins / Mike Rose
	LB Chris Koeppen / Noble Jones
	LB Chike Okeafor
	DB Jamal Coleman
	DB Derrick Winston / Mike Hawthorne
	DB Derrick Brown
	DB Willie Burroughs / Lee Brush

RUSHING: Watson 194/768y, Matthews 123/471y,
Reeves 52/157y
PASSING: Trefzger 96-170/1158y, 8 TD, 56.5%,
Reeves 51-102/772y, 6 TD, 50.0%
RECEIVING: Alford 63/1057y, Tillman 40/557y, Watson 25/220y
SCORING: Alford 72pts

1997 9-3

22 Toledo	36 WR Brian Alford / Vinny Sutherland
28 Notre Dame	17 WR Gabe Cox / Chris Daniels
28 Ball State	14 WR Isaac Jones / Chris Clopton
21 Northwestern	9 T Mark Fischer / Brandon Gorin
59 Minnesota	43 G Brian Nicley
45 Wisconsin	20 C Jim Niedrach
48 Illinois	3 G Chukky Okobi
17 Iowa	35 T Dan Maly / Pete VanderWeele
22 Michigan State	21 TE Jon Blackman / Matt Light
17 Penn State	42 QB Billy Dicken / Drew Brees
56 Indiana	7 RB Edwin Watson / Eric Haddad
33 Oklahoma St.■	20 DL Chukie Nwokorie / Rocco Fogio
	DL Greg Smith / Brent Botts
	DL Leo Perez / Ian Allen
	DL Rosevelt Colvin / Warren Moore
	LB Willie Burroughs / Lee Johnson
	LB Willie Fells / Noble Jones
	LB Mike Rose
	DB Lamar Conard / Henry Bell
	DB Mike Hawthorne
	DB Adrian Beasley
	DB Lee Brush / Billy Gustin

RUSHING: Watson 162/886y, Matthews 79/560y, Dicken 89/308y
PASSING: Dicken 206-373/2811y, 19 TD, 55.2%,
Brees 19-42/232y, 0 TD, 45.2%
RECEIVING: Alford 59/1167y, Jones 38/416y,
Sutherland 33/345y
SCORING: Watson 80pts, Shane Ryane (K) 72pts, Alford 62pts

1998 9-4

17 Southern Cal	27 WR Chris Daniels / Vinny Sutherland
21 Rice	19 WR Isaac Jones / Gabe Cox
35 C. Florida	7 WR Randall Lane
30 Notre Dame	31 T Matt Light
56 Minnesota	21 G David Cohen
24 Wisconsin	31 C Jim Niedrach
13 Penn State	31 G Chukky Okobi
42 Illinois	9 T Brandon Gorin
36 Iowa	14 TE Tim Stratton
56 Northwestern	21 QB Drew Brees
25 Michigan State	24 RB J. Crabtree / Dondre Johnson
52 Indiana	7 DL Chike Okeafor / Chukie Nwokorie
37 Kansas State■	34 DL Matt Mitrione
	DL David Nugent
	DL Rosevelt Colvin / Brian Dinkins
	LB Jason Loerzel
	LB Willie Fells
	LB Willie Burroughs / Mike Rose
	DB Chris Clopton
	DB Da'Shann Austin / Henry Bell
	DB Billy Gustin / Lamar Conard
	DB Adrian Beasley

RUSHING: Crabtree 152/648y, Johnson 96/433y,
Eric Haddad (RB) 44/211y
PASSING: Brees 361-569/3983y, 39 TD, 63.4%
RECEIVING: Jones 83/899y, Lane 67/940y, Cox 55/647y
SCORING: Travis Dorsch (K) 96pts, Cox 48pts, Lane 46pts

1999 7-5

47 C. Florida	13 WR Vinny Sutherland
28 Notre Dame	23 WR Chris Daniels / Chris James
58 C. Michigan	16 WR Randall Lane / Seth Morales
31 Northwestern	23 T Matt Light
12 Michigan	38 G Gene Mruczkowski
22 Ohio State	25 C Jim Niedrach
52 Michigan State	28 G Chukky Okobi
25 Penn State	31 T Brandon Gorin
33 Minnesota	28 TE Tim Stratton
21 Wisconsin	28 QB Drew Brees
30 Indiana	24 RB Montrell Lowe / J. Crabtree
25 Georgia■	28 DL Brian Dinkins
	DL Matt Mitrione
	DL David Nugent
	DL Akin Ayodele
	LB Jason Loerzel
	LB Willie Fells / Joe Odom
	LB Mike Rose
	DB Chris Clopton / James Dunnigan
	DB Mike Hawthorne / Da'Shann Austin
	DB Lamar Conard / Ralph Turner
	DB Adrian Beasley / Ben Smith

RUSHING: Lowe 158/754y, Crabtree 43/251y, Brees 70/181y
PASSING: Brees 301-494/3531y, 21 TD, 60.9%
RECEIVING: Daniels 109/1133y, Stratton 48/585y, Lane 47/630y
SCORING: Travis Dorsch (K) 92pts, Sutherland 56pts,
Daniels 42pts

2000 8-4

48 C. Michigan	0 WR Vinny Sutherland / A.T. Simpson
45 Kent State	10 WR John Standeford
21 Notre Dame	23 WR Seth Morales / Donald Winston
38 Minnesota	24 T Matt Light
20 Penn State	22 G Gene Mruczkowski
32 Michigan	31 C Chukky Okobi
41 Northwestern	28 G Ian Allen / Rob Turner
30 Wisconsin	24 T Brandon Gorin
31 Ohio State	27 TE Tim Stratton
10 Michigan State	30 QB Drew Brees
41 Indiana	13 RB Montrell Lowe / Sedrick Brown
24 Washington■	34 DL Shaun Phillips
	DL Craig Terrill / Brent Botts
	DL Matt Mitrione
	DL Akin Ayodele
	LB Gilbert Gardner
	LB Joe Odom
	LB Landon Johnson
	DB Ashante Woodyard
	DB Chris Clopton
	DB Stuart Schweigert / Brady Doe
	DB Ralph Turner

RUSHING: Lowe 226/998y, Brees 95/521y, Brown 44/260y
PASSING: Brees 309-512/3668y, 26 TD, 60.4%
RECEIVING: Sutherland 72/1014y, Standeford 67/744y,
Stratton 58/605y
SCORING: Sutherland 84pts, Travis Dorsch (K) 81pts

2001 6-6

19 Cincinnati	14 WR John Standeford / A.T. Simpson
33 Akron	14 WR Taylor Stubbefield / Chris James
35 Minnesota	28 WR Seth Morales / Gary Heaggans
23 Iowa	14 T Pete Lougheed
10 Michigan	24 G Seab Rufolo
32 Northwestern	27 C Gene Mruczkowski
13 Illinois	38 G Kelly Kitchel / Max Miller
9 Ohio State	35 T Kelly Butler / Tyler Moore
24 Michigan State	14 TE Tim Stratton
7 Indiana	13 QB Kyle Orton / Brandon Hance
18 Notre Dame	24 RB Montrell Lowe / Joey Harris
27 Washington St.■	33 DL Shaun Phillips
	DL Matt Mitrione / Craig Tirrell
	DL Brandon Johnson
	DL Akin Ayondele
	LB Landon Johnson / Jason Loerzel
	LB Joe Odom
	LB Niko Koutouvides / Gilbert Gardner
	DB Ashante Woodyard / Jacques Reeves
	DB Antwaun Rogers
	DB Stuart Schweigert / Ben Smith
	DB Ralph Turner / Deaunte Ferrell

RUSHING: Lowe 183/640y, Harris 58/255y, Hance 112/242y
PASSING: Hance 136-258/1529y, 8 TD, 52.7%
Orton 107-216/1105y, 4 TD, 49.5%
RECEIVING: Stubblefield 73/910y, Stratton 59/509y,
Standeford 47/587y
SCORING: Travis Dorsch (K) 86pts, Hance 30pts,
Standeford, Lowe & Morales 24pts

SCORES, LINEUPS, AND STATISTICS

2002 7-6

51 Illinois State	10 WR John Standeford / Seth Morales
17 Notre Dame	24 WR Taylor Stubblefield
28 W. Michigan	24 WR Ray Williams / Anthony Chambers
21 Wake Forest	24 T Pete Lougheed
28 Minnesota	15 G Nick Hardwick
28 Iowa	31 C Gene Mruczkowski / Matt Turner
31 Illinois	38 G Rob Turner / Max Miler
21 Michigan	23 T Kelly Butler
42 Northwestern	13 TE Charles Davis
6 Ohio State	10 QB Kyle Orton / Brandon Kirsch
45 Michigan State	42 RB Joey Harris / Brandon Jones
34 Indiana	10 DL Shaun Phillips
34 Washington■	24 DL Craig Terrill / Brandon Villarreal
	DL Brent Grover / Brandon Johnson
	DL Kevin Nesfield / Vedran Dzolovio
	LB Landon Johnson
	LB Niko Koutouvides / Jon Goldsberry
	LB Joe Odom / Gilbert Gardner
	DB Jacques Reeves / Sean Petty
	DB Antwaun Rogers
	DB Stuart Schweigert / Deaunte Ferrell
	DB Ralph Turner

RUSHING: Harris 250/1115y, Jones 127/668y, Kirsch 72/423y
PASSING: Orton 192-317/2257y, 13 TD, 60.6%,
Kirsch 79-134/1067y, 8 TD, 59.0%
RECEIVING: Stubblefield 77/789y, Standeford 75/1307y,
Chambers 28/228y
SCORING: Berin Lacevic (K) & Standeford 78pts,
Jerod Void (RB) 60pts

2003 9-4

27 Bowling Green	28 WR John Standeford / Kyle Ingraham
16 Wake Forest	10 WR Taylor Stubblefield
59 Arizona	7 WR Ray Williams / Anthony Chaambers
23 Notre Dame	10 T Mike Otto
43 Illinois	10 G Matt Turner
28 Penn State	14 C Nick Hardwick
26 Wisconsin	23 G Tyler Moore
3 Michigan	31 T Kelly Butler
34 Northwestern	14 TE Charles Davis
27 Iowa	14 QB Kyle Orton
13 Ohio State	16 RB Jerod Void / Brandon Jones
24 Indiana	16 DL Shaun Phillips
27 Georgia■	34 DL Craig Terrill / Brandon Villarreal
	DL Brent Grover
	DL Kevin Nesfield / Ray Edwards
	LB Gilbert Gardner / Bobby Iwuchukwu
	LB Niko Koutouvides
	LB Landon Johnson
	DB Jacques Reeves
	DB Antwaun Rogers
	DB Stuart Schweigert / Kyle Smith
	DB Bernard Pollard / Deaunte Ferrell

RUSHING: Void 235/952y, Jerome Brooks (RB) 79/349y,
Jones 77/286y
PASSING: Orton 251-414/2885y, 15TD, 60.6%
RECEIVING: Stubblefield 86/835y, Standeford 77/1150y,
Chambers 25/222y
SCORING: Ben Jones (K) 111pts, Void 78pts,
Standeford, Williams & Jones 24pts

2004 7-5

51 Syracuse	0 WR Kyle Ingraham / Brian Hare
59 Ball State	7 WR Taylor Stubblefield / Dorien Bryant
38 Illinois	30 WR Ray Williams / Jon Goldsberry (FB)
41 Notre Dame	16 T Mike Otto
20 Penn State	13 G Uche Nwaneri
17 Wisconsin	20 C Rob Turner
14 Michigan	16 G Tyler Moore
10 Northwestern	13 T David Owen
21 Iowa	23 TE Charles Davis / Jeff Bennett
24 Ohio State	17 QB Kyle Orton / Brandon Kirsch
63 Indiana	24 RB Jerod Void / Brandon Jones
23 Arizona State■	27 DL Anthony Spencer / Rob Ninkovich
	DL Brandon Villarreal
	DL Brent Grover
	DL Ray Edwards
	LB Bobby Iwuchukwu / Cliff Avril
	LB George Hall
	LB Stanford Kegler
	DB Antwaun Rogers / Paul Long
	DB Brian Hickman
	DB Kyle Smith / Torri Williams
	DB Bernard Pollard

RUSHING: Void 159/625y, Jones 113/477y, Orton 80/112y
PASSING: Orton 236-389/3090y, 31TD, 60.7%,
Kirsch 58-94/711y, 7TD, 61.7%
RECEIVING: Stubblefield 89/1095y, Ingraham 51/624y,
Bryant 38/584y, Davis 34/416y
SCORING: Stubblefield 96pts, Ben Jones (K) 79pts,
Ingraham 42pts

2005 5-6

49 Akron	24 WR Kevin Noel / Ray Williams (DB)
31 Arizona	24 WR Dorien Bryant / Andre Chattams
35 Minnesota	42 WR Kyle Ingraham / Brian Hare
28 Notre Dame	49 T Mike Otto
17 Iowa	34 G Robbie Powell
29 Northwestern	34 C Matt Turner
20 Wisconsin	31 G Jordan Grimes
15 Penn State	33 T Sean Sester
28 Michigan State	21 TE Charles Davis
37 Illinois	3 QB Brandon Kirsch / Curtis Painter
41 Indiana	14 RB Jerod Void / Kory Sheets
	DL Anthony Spencer / Eugene Bright
	DL Brandon Villarreal
	DL Brent Glover / Alex Magee
	DL Rob Ninkovich / Ray Edwards
	LB Bobby Iwuchukwu / Cliff Avril
	LB George Hall
	LB Kyle Williams/Dan Bick/St'nf'rd Keglar
	DB Ray Williams (WR) / Paul Long
	DB Zach Logan / Brian Hickman
	DB Kyle Smith / Brandon Whittington
	DB Bernard Pollard

RUSHING: Void 130/696y, Sheets 104/571y, Painter 52/251y
PASSING: Kirsch 152-257/1727y, 7TDs, 59.1%,
Painter 89-170/932y, 3TDs, 52.4%
RECEIVING: Bryant 80/960y, Ingraham 41/500y, Davis 26/311y
SCORING: Ben Jones (K) 64pts, Sheets & Void 60pts

2006 8-6

60 Indiana State	35 WR Selwyn Lymon
38 Miami (Ohio)	31 WR Dorien Bryant
38 Ball State	28 WR Greg Orton / Jake Standeford
27 Minnesota	21 T Mike Otto
21 Notre Dame	35 G Uche Nwaneri
17 Iowa	47 C Robbie Powell
31 Northwestern	10 G Jordan Grimes
3 Wisconsin	24 T Sean Sester
0 Penn State	12 TE Dustin Keller / Desmond Tardy
17 Michigan State	15 QB Curtis Painter
42 Illnois	31 RB Kory Sheets / Jaycen Taylor
28 Indiana	19 DL Cliff Avril (LB) / Mike McDonald
35 Hawaii	42 DL Jermaine Guynn / Ryan Baker
7 Maryland■	24 DL Alex Magee
	DL Anthony Spencer
	LB Dan Bick / Al Royal
	LB George Hall
	LB Stanford Keglar
	DB Royce Adams / Aaron Lane
	DB Terrell Vinson/Zach Logan/D. Pender
	DB Brandon Erwin / Keith Smith
	DB Justin Scott

RUSHING: Sheets 158/780y, Taylor 113/677y, Bryant 19/150y
PASSING: Painter 315-530/3985y, 22TD, 59.4%
RECEIVING: Bryant 87/1068y, Orton 58/790y, Keller 56/771y,
Lymon 33/580y
SCORING: Sheets 78pts, Chris Summers (K) 70pts,
Bryant 48pts

2007 8-5

52 Toledo	24 WR Greg Orton
52 E. Michigan	6 WR Dorien Bryant
45 C. Michigan	22 WR Selwyn Lymon / Jake Standeford
45 Minnesota	31 T Sean Sester
33 Notre Dame	19 G Zach Reckman
7 Ohio State	23 C Robbie Powell
21 Michigan	48 G Jordan Grimes / Justin Pierce
31 Iowa	6 T Zach Jones / Elliott Hood
35 Northwestern	17 TE Dustin Keller
19 Penn State	26 QB Curtis Painter
31 Michigan State	48 RB Kory Sheets / Jaycen Taylor
24 Indiana	27 DL Cliff Avril
51 C. Michigan■	48 DL Ryan Baker
	DL Alex Magee
	DL Keyon Brown / Eugene Bright
	LB Anthony Heygood
	LB Josh Ferguson / Dan Bick
	LB Stanford Keglar
	DB Terrell Vinson
	DB David Pender / Royce Adams
	DB Brandon King
	DB Justin Scott

RUSHING: Sheets 168/859y, Taylor 107/560y,
Dan Dierking (RB) 42/181y
PASSING: Painter 356-569/3846y, 29TD, 62.2%
RECEIVING: Bryant 87/936y, Keller 68/881y, Orton 67/752y,
Lymon 40/450y
SCORING: Chris Summers (K) 95pts, Sheets 78pts, Bryant 48pts

2008 4-8

42 N. Colorado	10 WR Greg Orton
26 Oregon	32 WR Desmond Tardy / Keith Smith
32 C. Michigan	25 WR Brandon Whittington / Jeff Lindsay
21 Notre Dame	38 T Zach Reckman / Garret Miller
6 Penn State	20 G Eric Hedstrom / Jared Zwilling
3 Ohio State	16 C Cory Benton
26 Northwestern	48 G Ken Plue / Justin Pierce
6 Minnesota	17 T Zach Jones / Sean Sester (G)
48 Michigan	42 TE Jerry Wasikowski / Colton McKey
7 Michigan State	21 QB Curtis Painter / Justin Siller
17 Iowa	22 RB Kory Sheets
62 Indiana	10 DL Alex Magee
	DL Mike Neal
	DL Ryan Baker / Jermaine Guynn
	DL Ryan Kerrigan / Keyon Brown
	LB Anthony Heygood
	LB Chris Carlino
	LB Joe Holland / Nickcaro Golding
	DB David Pender / Royce Adams
	DB Brandon King / Mike Conway
	DB Torri Williams / Josh McKinley
	DB Frank Duong / Dwight Mclean (LB)

RUSHING: Sheets 234/1131y, Siller 60/167y,
Heygood (LB-RB) 1/61y
PASSING: Painter 227-379/2400y, 13TD, 59.9%,
Siller 59-106/496y, 3TD, 55.7%
RECEIVING: Orton 69/720y, Tardy 67/876y, Smith 49/486y,
Sheets 37/253y
SCORING: Sheets 102pts, Carson Wiggs (K) 43pts, Orton 32pts

2009 5-7

52 Toledo	31 WR Aaron Valentin / Cortez Smith
36 Oregon	38 WR Keith Smith / Dan Dierking (FB)
21 N. Illinois	28 WR Keith Carlos / Royce Adams
21 Notre Dame	24 T Dennis Kelly
21 Northwestern	27 G Zach Reckman / Rick Schmeig
20 Minnesota	35 C Jared Zwilling
26 Ohio State	18 G Ken Plue
24 Illinois	14 T Zach Jones
0 Wisconsin	37 TE Kyle Adams / Jeff Lindsay
38 Michigan	36 QB Joey Elliott
37 Michigan State	40 RB Ralph Bolden / Jaycen Taylor
38 Indiana	21 DL Gerald Gooden / Robert Maci
	DL Mike Neal / Nick Mondek
	DL Kawann Short
	DL Ryan Kerrigan / Keyon Brown
	LB Jason Werner
	LB Chris Carlino
	LB Joe Holland
	DB David Pender
	DB Brandon King
	DB Torri Williams / Josh McKinley
	DB Dwight Mclean / Albert Evans

RUSHING: Bolden 200/935y, Taylor 70/387y, Elliott 87/268y
PASSING: Painter 267-433/3026y, 22TD, 61.7%
RECEIVING: K. Smith 91/1100y, Valentin 54/621y,
K. Adams 29/249y, Carlos 21/242y, Bolden 20/261y
SCORING: Carson Wiggs (K) 82pts, Bolden 66pts, Valentin 48pts

2010 4-8

12 Notre Dame	23 WR Cortez Smith / Gary Bush / Keith Smith
31 W. Illinois	21 WR Antavian Edison / O.J. Ros
24 Ball State	13 WR/TE Justin Siller / Jeff Lindsay
20 Toledo	31 T Dennis Kelly
20 Northwestern	17 G Justin Pierce
28 Minnesota	17 C Peters Drey
0 Ohio State	49 G Ken Plue / Rick Schmeig
10 Illinois	44 T Nick Mondek
13 Wisconsin	34 TE Kyle Adams / Gabe Holmes
16 Michigan	27 QB Rob Henry / Robert Marve
31 Michigan State	35 RB Dan Dierking / Keith Carlos
31 Indiana	34 DL Gerald Gooden
	DL Bruce Gaston / Brandon Taylor
	DL Kawann Short
	DL Ryan Kerrigan
	LB Jason Werner / Will Lucas
	LB Dwayne Beckford
	LB/DB Joe Holland / Normando Harris
	DB Ricardo Allen / Charlton Williams
	DB Josh Johnson / Mike Eargle
	DB Albert Evans / Max Charlot
	DB Logan Link

RUSHING: Henry 104/547y, Dierking 118/530y, Carlos 56/314y
PASSING: Henry 86-162/996y, 8TD, 53.1%
Marve 67-99/512y, 3TD, 67.7%
Sean Robinson (QB) 44-91/301y, 2TD, 48.4%
RECEIVING: Adams 36/244y, Smith 33/434y, Edison 32/316y
SCORING: Carson Wiggs (K) 72pts, Dierking 30pts, 3 tied w/24pts

RUTGERS

Rutgers University, State University of New Jersey (Founded 1776)
New Brunswick, New Jersey
Nickname: Scarlet Knights
Color: Scarlet
Stadium: Rutgers (1994) 41,500
Conference Affiliations: Independent (1952-57; 1962-90), Middle
Atlantic (1958-61), Big East (Charter member, 1991-present)

CAREER RUSHING YARDS

	Attempts	Yards
Ray Rice (2005-07)	910	4926
Terrell Willis (1993-95)	588	3114
J.J. Jennings (1971-73)	650	2935
Bruce Presley (1992-95)	552	2792
Brian Leonard (2003-06)	678	2775
Glen Kehler (1975-78)	537	2567
Jacki Crooks (1996-99)	570	2434
Bryant Mitchell (1966-68)	495	2286
Albert Smith (1982-85)	542	2269
Henry Benkert (1921-24)	N/A	2124

CAREER PASSING YARDS

	Comp.-Att.	Yards
Mike Teel (2005-08)	661-1142	9398
Ryan Hart (2002-05)	735-1217	8482
Scott Erney (1986-89)	614-1128	7188
Mike McMahon (1997-99)	482-974	6608
Ray Lucas (1992-95)	514-908	5896
Eric Hochberg (1982-85)	337-639	3825
Bert Kosup (1974-77)	214-448	3613
Tom Tarver (1989-91)	285-518	3607
Ed McMichael (1978-90)	292-474	3584
Leo Gasiencia (1970-72)	230-448	2801

CAREER RECEIVING YARDS

	Catches	Yards
Kenny Britt (2006-08)	178	3043
Tres Moses (2001-05)	192	2522
Tim Brown (2006-09)	114	2272
Andrew Baker (1981-84)	127	2268
Marco Battaglia (1992-95)	171	2221
Jim Guarantano (1989-92)	158	2065
Clark Harris (2003-06)	143	2015
Tiquan Underwood (2005-08)	132	1931
Chris Brantley (1990-93)	144	1914
Brian Leonard (2003-06)	207	1868

SEASON RUSHING YARDS

	Attempts	Yards
Ray Rice (2007)	380	2012
Ray Rice (2006)	335	1794
J.J. Jennings (1973)	303	1353
J.J. Jennings (1972)	287	1262
Terrell Willis (1993)	195	1261

SEASON PASSING YARDS

	Comp.-Att.	Yards
Mike Teel (2008)	243-396	3418
Ryan Hart (2004)	295-453	3154
Mike Teel (2007)	203-349	3147
Ryan Hart (2003)	234-398	2714
Scott Erney (1989)	208-374	2536

SEASON RECEIVING YARDS

	Catches	Yards
Kenny Britt (2008)	87	1371
Kenny Britt (2007)	62	1232
Tim Brown (2009)	55	1150
Tiquan Underwood (2007)	65	1100
Tres Moses (2004)	81	1056

GAME RUSHING YARDS

	Attempts	Yards
Ray Rice (2007 vs. Ball State)	35	280
Ray Rice (2007 vs. Army)	34	243
Terrell Willis (1994 vs. Temple)	35	232

GAME PASSING YARDS

	Comp.-Att.	Yards
Mike Teel (2008 vs. Louisville)	21-26	447
Scott Erney (1988 vs. Vanderbilt)	35-55	436
Mike McMahon (1997 vs. Army)	26-42	386

GAME RECEIVING YARDS

	Catches	Yards
Tiquan Underwood (2007 vs. Buffalo)	10	248
Jack Emmer (1966 vs. Holy Cross)	13	237
Andrew Baker (1983 vs. Penn State)	5	210

GREATEST COACH:

As a player his nickname was "Flinging Frank," in honor of his quarterbacking skills that led Rutgers to 27 wins during the late 1940s. As a coach Frank Burns was commonly referred to as the "Major," more so for the character with the same name on *M.A.S.H.* than for any authoritarian tendencies. Burns is honored in this space for two reasons. For one, he won more games than any Rutgers coach; Burns sported a 78-43-1 mark for the years 1973-83. Burns will always be remembered for the 1976 season, when he guided the Scarlet Knights to a lofty 11-0 record.

The second reason for Burns's inclusion here is that he kept Rutgers respectable while their schedule was revamped in an effort to go big-time. The 1976 schedule included only three schools that would be now considered Division 1A, Tulane, Louisville and Navy, and they all had losing records that season. The next year Penn State returned to opponent list—the two teams had squared off in the 1950s—and by 1978 Rutgers was in their first bowl game, played in its home state of New Jersey and titled the Garden State Bowl. In 1979 they played, and beat, Tennessee, and in 1980 the Scarlet Knights narrowly lost to Alabama. By 1983, Burns's final season, they had begun playing Penn State, Boston College, Syracuse, Army and West Virginia on an annual basis, while removing many of the smaller programs, including Princeton, a team they first played in 1869 in what is acknowledged as the first collegiate football game. While the win totals naturally decreased, the team under Burns was rarely an easy victim for these more-established teams.

RUTGERS' 55 GREATEST SINCE 1953

OFFENSE

WIDE RECEIVER: Andrew Baker, Kenny Britt, Jim Guarantano, Tres Moses
TIGHT END: Marco Battaglia
TACKLE: Anthony Davis, Kevin Kurdyla, Steve Tardy, Jeremy Zuttah
GUARD: Lee Getz, John Glass, Tony Hoeflinger, Andy Tighe
CENTER: Travis Broadbent, Frank Naylor, Darnell Stapleton
QUARTERBACK: Scott Erney, Mike Teel
RUNNING BACK: Billy Austin, J.J. Jennings, Ray Rice, Terrell Willis
FULLBACK: Glen Kehler, Brian Leonard

DEFENSE

END: Ryan Neill, Raheem Orr, Nate Toran
TACKLE: John Alexander, Eric Foster, Dan Gray, Dino Mangiero, Bill Pickel, Ed Steward, Harry Swayne
LINEBACKER: Jim Dumont, Jim Hughes, Sam Picketts, Lee Schneider, Tyronne Stowe, Elnardo Webster, Shawn Williams
CORNERBACK: Ed Jones, Nate Jones, Devin McCourty, Ken Smith
SAFETY: Deron Cherry, Courtney Greene, Malik Jackson

SPECIAL TEAMS

RETURN SPECIALISTS: Willie Foster, Marshall Roberts
PLACE KICKER: Jeremy Ito
PUNTER: Mike Barr

MULTIPLE POSITIONS

QUARTERBACK-RUNNING BACK: Bruce Van Ness

TWO-WAY PLAYERS

END-DEFENSIVE END: Bob Simms
CENTER-LINEBACKER: Alex Kroll

PERFORMANCE FORMULA:
RUTGERS' 10 BEST SEASONS

2006	1.5298	11 of 72
1976	1.4729	11 of 70
1958	1.3347	15 of 70
1984	1.2763	22 of 70
1979	1.2460	22 of 70
2009	1.2421	29 of 72
2007	1.2300	29 of 70
2008	1.2287	31 of 71
1961	1.0966	32 of 71
1960	1.0692	43 of 70

RUTGERS SCARLET KNIGHTS

Year	W-L-T	AP Poll	Conference Standing	Toughest Regular Season Opponents	Coach (Record at School)	Bowl Games		
1953	2-6			Penn State 6-3, Princeton 5-4, Virginia Tech 5-5	Harvey Harman			
1954	3-6			Princeton 7-2, Lehigh 8-1	Harvey Harman			
1955	3-5			Princeton 7-2, Penn State 5-4, Delaware 8-1, Lehigh 7-2	Harvey Harman (74-44-2)			
1956	3-7			Princeton 7-2, Boston College 5-3, Lehigh 7-2	John Stiegman			
1957	5-4			Penn State 7-2, Princeton 5-3-1, Colgate 5-2-2	John Stiegman			
1958	8-1	20	1	Princeton 6-3, Delaware 5-3	John Stiegman			
1959	6-3		5	Delaware 8-1, Connecticut 6-3	John Stiegman (22-15)			
1960	8-1		1	Princeton 7-2, Bucknell 7-2	John Bateman			
1961	9-0	15	1	Columbia 6-3, Princeton 5-4	John Bateman			
1962	5-5			Princeton 5-4, Villanova 7-2, Delaware 7-2	John Bateman			
1963	3-6			Princeton 7-2, Delaware 8-0, Harvard 5-2-2	John Bateman			
1964	6-3			Princeton 9-0, Colgate 7-2	John Bateman			
1965	3-6			Princeton 8-1, Colgate 6-3-1	John Bateman			
1966	5-4			Army 8-2, Princeton 7-2, Colgate 8-1-1	John Bateman			
1967	4-5			Army 8-2, Princeton 6-3	John Bateman			
1968	8-2			Army 7-3, Delaware 7-3, Lafayette 7-3	John Bateman			
1969	6-3			Delaware 8-2, Connecticut 5-4	John Bateman			
1970	5-5			Delaware 8-2, Harvard 7-2	John Bateman			
1971	4-7			Army 6-4, Cornell 8-1, Delaware 9-1	John Bateman (73-51)			
1972	7-4			Army 6-4, Cornell 6-3	Frank Burns			
1973	6-5			Air Force 6-4, Tampa 8-3, Delaware 8-3	Frank Burns			
1974	7-3-1			Harvard 7-2, Hawaii 6-5, Lehigh 7-3	Frank Burns			
1975	9-2			Syracuse 6-5, Lehigh 9-2, Hawaii 6-5	Frank Burns			
1976	11-0	17		Colgate 8-2, Louisville 4-7	Frank Burns			
1977	8-3			Penn State 10-1, Colgate 10-1, Lehigh 9-2	Frank Burns	Garden State	18 Arizona State	34
1978	9-3			Penn State 11-0, Temple 7-3-1, Massachusetts 8-3	Frank Burns			
1979	8-3			Penn State 7-4, Tennessee 7-4, Temple 9-2	Frank Burns			
1980	7-4			Alabama 9-2, West Virginia 6-6	Frank Burns			
1981	5-6			Pittsburgh 10-1, Alabama 9-1, West Virginia 8-3	Frank Burns			
1982	4-7			Penn State 10-1, Pittsburgh 9-2, West Virginia 9-2, Auburn 8-3	Frank Burns			
1983	3-8			Boston College 9-2, Tennessee 8-3, West Virginia 8-3, PSU 7-4-1	Frank Burns (77-44-1)			
1984	7-3			Boston College 9-2, Army 7-3-1, Kentucky 8-3, Penn State 6-5	Dick Anderson			
1985	2-8-1			Penn State 11-0, Florida 9-1-1, Tennessee 8-1-2, West Va. 7-3-1	Dick Anderson			
1986	5-5-1			Penn State 11-0, Boston College 8-3	Dick Anderson			
1987	6-5			Syracuse 11-0, Pittsburgh 8-3, Penn State 8-3	Dick Anderson			
1988	5-6			West Virginia 11-0, Syracuse 9-2, Army 9-2, Michigan State 6-4-1	Dick Anderson			
1989	2-7-2			West Virginia 8-2-1, Penn State 7-3-1, Pittsburgh 7-3-1	Dick Anderson (27-34-4)			
1990	3-8			Penn State 9-2, Michigan State 7-3-1, Syracuse 6-4-2	Doug Graber			
1991	6-5			Penn State 10-2, Syracuse 9-2	Doug Graber			
1992	7-4		3	Syracuse 9-2, Boston College 8-2-1, Penn State 7-4	Doug Graber			
1993	4-7		7	West Virginia 11-0, Miami 9-2, Penn St. 9-2, BC 8-3, Virginia Tech 8-3	Doug Graber			
1994	5-5-1		6	Penn State 11-0, Miami 10-1, Virginia Tech 8-3, Syracuse 7-4	Doug Graber			
1995	4-7		6	Virginia Tech 9-2, Penn State 8-3, Miami 8-3, Syracuse 8-3	Doug Graber (29-36-1)			
1996	2-9		7	Va Tech 10-1, Army 10-1, Miami 8-3, ND 8-3, N'vy 8-3, Syracuse 8-3	Terry Shea			
1997	0-11		8	Syracuse 8-4, Virginia Tech 7-4, West Virginia 7-4, Navy 7-4	Terry Shea			
1998	5-6		6t	Miami 8-3, Syracuse 8-3, Virginia Tech 8-3, West Virginia 8-3	Terry Shea			
1999	1-10		8	Virginia Tech 11-0, Texas 9-3, Boston College 8-3, Miami 8-4	Terry Shea			
2000	3-8		8	Miami 10-1, Virginia Tech 10-1, Notre Dame 9-2, Pittsburgh 7-4	Terry Shea (11-44)			
2001	2-9		8	Miami 11-0, Syracuse 9-3, Virginia Tech 8-3, Boston College 7-4	Greg Schiano			
2002	1-11		8	Miami 12-0, Notre Dame 10-2, Va Tech 8-3, Pitt 8-3, BC 8-3, West Va. 9-3	Greg Schiano			
2003	5-7		6t	Miami 10-2, Virginia Tech 8-4, Pitt 8-4, West Virginia 8-4, Navy 8-3	Greg Schiano			
2004	4-7		6t	Navy 9-2, Boston College 8-3, Pitt 8-3, West Virginia 8-3	Greg Schiano	Insight	40 Arizona State	45
2005	7-5		3t	West Virginia 10-1, Louisville 9-2, Navy 7-4	Greg Schiano	Texas	37 Kansas State	10
2006	11-2	12	2t	Louisville 11-1, West Virginia 10-2, South Florida 8-4, Navy 9-3	Greg Schiano	International	52 Ball State	30
2007	8-5		5t	Cincinnati 9-3, South Florida 9-3, West Virginia 10-2	Greg Schiano	Papajohns.com	29 North Carolina State	23
2008	8-5		2t	North Carolina 8-4, West Virginia 8-4, Cincinnati 11-2	Greg Schiano	St. Petersburg	45 Central Florida	24
2009	9-4		4t	Cincinnati 12-0, Pittsburgh 9-3, West Virginia 9-3	Greg Schiano			
2010	4-8		8	North Carolina 7-5, Connecticut 8-4, Pitt 8-4, West Virginia 9-3	Greg Schiano (59-63)			

TOTAL: 306-304-6 .5046 (45 of 70)   **Bowl Games since 1953:**   4-2 .6667 (4 of 70)

GREATEST TEAM SINCE 1953: Although they were not able to cap a great season with a January bowl game, the 2006 Rutgers team takes top honors over the undefeated Scarlet Knights of 1976 due to their tougher schedule. Rutgers was one of the best Cinderella stories of 2006, finishing no. 12 in the country.

1953 2-6

20	Virginia Tech	13 E Tom Nathaniel / August Johnson
7	Princeton	9 T Marv Blumenstock / Jim Marco
20	Brown	27 G Jim O'Brien / Bob Howard
13	Fordham	40 C Joe Daddario
12	Colgate	33 G Ken Bossow / Dick Hemmer
14	Lafayette	13 T Les Miller / Bill Doliber
26	Penn State	54 E Jim Davis / Bruce Johnson
13	Columbia	27 QB John Fennell / Don Dreier
		HB Frank Triggs / Ron Mastrola
		HB Steve Johnson / Bob Kelley
		FB Angelo Ianucci / Don Duncan

RUSHING: N/A
PASSING: N/A
RECEIVING: N/A
SCORING: N/A

1954 3-6

8	Princeton	10 E Don Felber / Ed Farrell
7	Fordham	13 T Marv Blumenstock / Tom Mullowney
14	Colgate	26 G Jim O'Brien / Bob Howard
7	William & Mary	14 C Brian O'Hearn
3	Lehigh	33 G Dick Hemmer / Ken Bossow
25	Temple	0 T Ed Evans / Tony DeSantis
7	Lafayette	0 E Paul Stitik / Al Mitlehner
14	Penn State	37 QB John Fennell / Bill Gatyas
45	Columbia	12 HB S. Johnson/ Bob Kelley/ Greg Holmes
		HB Ron Mastrola / Bob Redman
		FB Angelo Iannucci / John Laverty

RUSHING: Laverty 41/191y, Kelley 34/177y, Holmes 27/86y
PASSING: Gatyas 2-13/8y 0TD, 15.4%
RECEIVING: Stitik 11/87y, Felber 8/167y, Farrell 5/66y
SCORING: Laverty & Kelley 12pts

1955 3-5

7	Princeton	41 E Don Felber / Ed Burkowski
21	Muhlenburg	0 T Jim Marco / Wally Lindquist
14	Brown	12 G Bob Howard / George Wilson
14	Lehigh	21 C Tony DeSantis / Dave Pooley
7	Delaware	33 G Richard Murar / Mike Fisher
7	Lafayette	16 T Art Robinson / Ed Evans
13	Penn State	34 E Al Mitlehner / Ed Farrell
12	Columbia	6 QB Bill Gatyas / Toshimasa Hosoda
		HB Leroy Lusardi / Greg Holmes
		HB Bob Kelley
		FB John Laverty / Bob Bear

RUSHING: Lusardi 74/319y, Laverty 59/307y, Bear 38/103y
PASSING: Bill Whitacre (QB) 18-41/234y, TD, 43.9%,
Gatyas 15-35/175y, 2TD, 42.9%
RECEIVING: Laverty 5/40y, Lusardi 4/40y
SCORING: Gatyas 25pts, Laverty 24pts, 3 with 6pts

1956 3-7

33	Ohio Wesleyan	13 E Don Felber / John Canal
6	Princeton	28 T Dick Pfeiffer
7	Connecticut	27 G Larry Muschiatti / Richard Murar
6	Colgate	48 C Dave Pooley (E) / Bob Naso
0	Boston College	32 G Ed Burkowski/Ron Sabo/Joe Polidoro
13	Lehigh	27 T Art Robinson / Mike Fisher
20	Lafayette	19 E Dutch Wermuth / Henry D'Andrea
0	Delaware	22 BB Bill Whitacre / Sam Crosby
20	William & Mary	6 TB Billy Austin / Bill Gatyas
12	Columbia	18 WB Jay Hunton/John Laverty/ Bob Max
		FB Bill Hopwood / Lloyd Seaman

RUSHING: Austin 123/380y, Hopwood 42/139y, Hunton 33/131y
PASSING: Austin 17-41/230y, 2TD, 41.5%
RECEIVING: Hunton 15/408y, Whitacre 7/94y, Wermuth 5/84y
SCORING: Hunton 36pts, Austin 24pts, Max 18pts

1957 5-4

0	Princeton	7 E Bob Simms / John Canal
14	Connecticut	7 T Dick Pfeiffer / Bob Clark
48	Colgate	6 G Larry Muschiatti
7	Lehigh	13 C Dick Oberlander / Don Mozzochi
26	Richmond	13 G Ron Sabo
19	Delaware	23 T Bill Pulley
34	Lafayette	19 E Dutch Wermuth / Dave Pooley
7	William & Mary	38 BB Sam Crosby / Dick Garretson
26	Columbia	7 TB Billy Austin / Bruce Webster
		WB Bob Max
		FB Lloyd Seaman / Bill Hopwood

RUSHING: Austin 193/946y, Seaman 52/249y, Max 23/160y
PASSING: Austin 38-80/479y, 3TD, 47.5%,
RECEIVING: Simms 12/180y, Canal 11/174y, Wermuth 11/129y
SCORING: Austin 74pts, Seaman 29pts, Max 12pts

1958 8-1

28	Princeton	0 E Dutch Wermuth
21	Colgate	7 T Jud Pahls
23	Richmond	12 G Larry Muschiatti
57	Bucknell	12 C Don Mozzochi / Armand Glassman
44	Lehigh	13 G Bob Clark / Jim Horner
37	Delaware	20 T Bill Pulley / Bob Blanchfield
12	Quantico	13 E Bob Simms / George Darlington
61	Columbia	0 BB Sam Crosby
		TB Billy Austin / Bruce Webster
		WB Arny Byrd / Dick Pencek
		FB Jim Rogers / Bill Tully / Lloyd Seaman

RUSHING: Austin 145/747y, Byrd 42/193y, Seaman 41/182y
PASSING: Webster 40-74/513y, 5TD, 54.1%,
Austin 22-44/284y, 8TD, 50.0%
RECEIVING: Simms 33/468y, Wermuth 10/112y, Crosby 9/80y
SCORING: Austin 106pts, Simms 64pts, Byrd 16pts

1959 6-3

8	Princeton	6 E Bob Simms / Paul Benke
20	Connecticut	8 T Jud Pahls / Pat Dilemms
15	Colgate	12 G Bill Pulley / Bill Libby
8	Bucknell	15 C Lester Senft / Larry Makaravich
23	Lehigh	0 G Jim Horner / Bob Harrison
14	Delaware	34 T Bob Blanchfield
16	Lafayette	14 E Bob Clark / Del Coston
12	Villanova	6 BB Dick Lawrence / Frank Lugossy
16	Columbia	26 TB Sam Mudie / Bill Wolff / Bill Speranza
		WB Arny Byrd / Pierce Frauenheim
		FB Bill Tully / Jim Rogers / Steve Simms

RUSHING: Rogers 54/161y, Wolff 51/153y, Speranza 47/143y
PASSING: Mudie 20-50/339y, TD, 40.0%,
RECEIVING: B. Simms 19/345y, Pencek 12/404y, Byrd 4/125y
SCORING: B. Simms 20pts, Paul Mullert (WB-K) 15pts, 4 with 12

1960 8-1

13	Princeton	8 E George Darlington / Dick Lawrence
19	Connecticut	6 T Jud Pahls / Tony Simonelli
49	Colgate	12 G Lester Senft / Bob Harrison
23	Bucknell	19 C Alex Kroll / Larry Makaravich
8	Lehigh	0 G Jim Horner / Larry Brown
12	Villanova	14 T Bob Blanchfield / John Pregnolato
36	Lafayette	8 E Paul Benke / Marv Engle
22	Delaware	0 QB Sam Mudie / Bill Speranza
43	Columbia	2 HB Dick Webb / Bill Thompson
		HB Arny Byrd / Pierce Frauenheim
		FB Steve Simms / Bill Tully

RUSHING: Simms 102/613y, Thompson 46/272y,
Frauenheim 35/202y
PASSING: Mudie 34-77/452y, 4TD, 44.2%
RECEIVING: Byrd 18/269y, Engle 8/145y, Simms 8/106y
SCORING: Simms, Byrd & Thompson 36pts

1961 9-0

16	Princeton	13 E Bill Craft / Bob Flower
35	Connecticut	12 T Tony Simonelli / Gus Giebelhaus
21	Bucknell	6 G Bob Harrison / Tom Kocaj
32	Lehigh	15 C Alex Kroll
20	Pennsylvania	6 G Tony Hoeflinger
37	Lafayette	6 T George Elias / Tom Tappen
27	Delaware	19 E Lee Curley / Marv Engle
26	Colgate	6 QB Sam Mudie / Bill Speranza
32	Columbia	19 HB Bill Thompson / Doug Reeser
		HB Pierce Frauenheim / Bob Yaksick
		FB Steve Simms

RUSHING: Simms 103/614y, Mudie 80/403y, Thompson 67/372y
PASSING: Speranza 15-46/318y, 3TD, 32.6%
RECEIVING: Curley 12/274y, Frauenheim 6/108y, Flower 5/77y
SCORING: Mudie 70pts, Frauenheim32pts,
Simms & Speranza 30pts

1962 5-5

7	Princeton	15 E Bob Flower/ Jerry Melcon/Jim Hackett
9	Connecticut	15 T Tony Simonelli / Gus Giebelhaus
27	Colgate	15 G John Hurt / Jeff Grote
29	Lehigh	12 C Jon Paulson / Bob Norton
12	Pennsylvania	7 G Tony Hoeflinger
40	Lafayette	0 T George Elias / Tom Tappen
6	Delaware	23 E Bill Craft / Lee Sherman
12	Villanova	34 QB Bob Yaksick / Dick Novak
22	Columbia	6 HB Bill Thompson / Bill Herring (DB)
0	Virginia	41 HB Keith Krayer/P. Strelick/Bill Green (DB)
		FB Ritchie Poad/Drew Carollo/D. Viggiano

RUSHING: Thompson 99/405y, Carollo 79/284y,
Yaksick 100/239y
PASSING: Yaksick 36-87/502y, 5TD, 41.4%
RECEIVING: Craft 23/426y, Flower 8/103y, Strelick 8/73y
SCORING: Yaksick 36pts, Craft 30pts, Thompson 20pts

1963 3-6

0	Princeton	24 E Jim Hackett / Werner Frentop
0	Harvard	28 T Gus Giebelhaus
8	Colgate	28 G Frank Kuch
30	Lehigh	6 C Jon Paulson / Pete Savidge
6	Pennsylvania	9 G Tony Hoeflinger / Bruce Lawrence
21	Boston Univ.	6 T Bill Sparks / Rich VonBischoffshausen
49	Lafayette	0 E Fran Pease / Bob Stohrer
3	Delaware	14 QB Dave Stout
28	Columbia	35 HB John Canavan / Jim D'Antonio
		HB Paul Strelick / Chet Ward
		FB Don Viggiano / Bob Brendel (E)

RUSHING: Viggiano 86/404y, Ward 65/344y, Strelick 60/218y
PASSING: Stout 58-120/634y, 634y, TD, 48.3%
RECEIVING: Strelick 27/242y, D'Antonio 6/64y, Brendel 5/92y
SCORING: Brendel 24pts, Stout 20pts, Ward & Viggiano 18pts

1964 6-3

7	Princeton	10 E Fran Pease
9	Connecticut	3 T Rich VonBischoffshausen
20	Lehigh	7 G Gene Renna
10	Pennsylvania	7 C Pete Savidge / Bob Norton
38	Columbia	35 G Bruce Lawrence
9	Boston Univ.	0 T Ron Kenny
31	Lafayette	6 E Bob Stohrer / John Emmer
18	Delaware	27 QB Roger Kalinger
7	Colgate	20 HB Chet Ward / Ralf Stegmann
		HB Charley Mudie
		FB Bob Brendel
		DL Garth Weber
		DL Bill Sparks
		DL Tom Connelly
		DL Jerry Sertick
		DL Werner Frentrop
		LB Bob Brush
		LB Bob Schroeder
		LB Don Viggiano
		DB John Canavan
		DB Dave Stout (QB)
		DB George Lamb / Bill Green

RUSHING: Brendel 125/464y, Stegman 61/318y, Ward 88/285y
PASSING: Kalinger 84-158/916y, 4TD, 53.2 %
RECEIVING: Emmer 22/306y, Stohrer 21/235y, Mudie 20/187y
SCORING: Ward 30pts, Kalinger 26pts, Brendel 24pts

1965 3-6

6	Princeton	32 E Bob Brendel
17	Connecticut	8 T Jim Hackett
6	Lehigh	0 G Marty Frankiewicz / Jack Liddy
6	Army	23 C Pete Savidge
7	Columbia	12 G Gene Renna
0	Boston Univ.	30 T Ron Kenny
18	Lafayette	23 E Bob Stohrer
14	Holy Cross	0 QB Fred Eckert / Jack Callaghan
10	Colgate	24 HB Ralf Stegmann / Chet Ward
		HB Charley Mudie / Jim Baker
		FB Rich Capria / Jack Hohnstine
		DL Garth Weber
		DL Jerry Sertick
		DL Tom Connelly
		DL Sampson Brown
		DL Scott Lewendon
		LB Bob Schroeder
		LB Bob Brush / Don Riesett (FB)
		LB Lou Tepper
		DB Chet Ward
		DB George Lamb / Jack Prigger
		DB Jack Emmer (OE)

RUSHING: Capri 58/242y, Stegman 62/222y, Mudie 72/196y
PASSING: Eckert 38-92/412y, TD, 41.3%
Callaghan 38-73/456y, 2TD, 52.1%
RECEIVING: Stohrer 19/201y, Mudie 18/243y, Brendel 15/158y
SCORING: Hohnstine, Riesett & Stohrer 12pts

1966 5-4

12 Princeton	16 E Jim Higgins
17 Yale	14 T Dave Zimmerman
42 Lehigh	14 G Walt Stasiak / Alan Greenberg
9 Army	14 C Tom Vitolo / Bob Schroeder
37 Columbia	34 G Jim Julian
16 Boston Univ.	7 T Ron Kenny (DL) / Rich Koprowski
32 Lafayette	28 E Jack Emmer
12 Holy Cross	24 QB Fred Eckert / Pete Savino
7 Colgate	26 HB Bryant Mitchell
	HB Jim Baker / Ralf Stegmann
	FB Don Riesett / Mel Brown
	DL Scott Lewendon
	DL Bob Schroeder
	DL Joe Urbanick / John Liddy
	DL Sampson Brown
	DL Garth Weber
	LB Chuck Bowers
	LB Lou Tepper / Bill Cintolo
	LB Bob Higgins / Rich Bing
	DB Denny McGorry
	DB Sid Rhines
	DB Jack Prigger

RUSHING: Mitchell 133/540y, Riesett 96/305y, Brown 36/156y
PASSING: Eckert 44-94/756y, 6TD, 46.8%
RECEIVING: Emmer 41/701y, Stegmann 13/216y, Baker 9/180y
SCORING: Mitchell 42pts, Jim Dulin (K) 36pts, Baker 32pts

1967 4-5

21 Princeton	22 E Jim Higgins
14 Lehigh	7 T Dave Zimmerman
29 Delaware	21 G Alan Greenberg
3 Army	14 C Tom Vitolo
13 Columbia	24 G Jim Julian
27 Lafayette	3 T Rich Koprowski
7 Massachusetts	30 E Bob Stonebraker / Paul Hohne
10 Holy Cross	21 QB Bruce Van Ness (HB) / Pete Savino (E)
31 Colgate	28 HB Bryant Mitchell
	HB Jim Baker
	FB Don Riesett / Mel Brown
	DL Scott Lewendon
	DL Lee Schneider
	DL Len Novelli / John Niemyer
	DL Dennis Dutch
	DL Rick Bonsall
	LB Rich Bing
	LB Chuck Bowers / Bill Regan
	LB Bob Higgins
	DB Sid Rhines / Jim Renshaw
	DB Jack Prigger
	DB John Pollock

RUSHING: Mitchell 124/542y, Van Ness 101/389y, Riesett 59/258y
PASSING: Van Ness 44-104/504y, 5TD, 2.3%
RECEIVING: Baker 20/242y, Stonebreaker 12/232y, Brown 9/132y
SCORING: Mitchell 36pts, Jim Dulin (K) 27pts, Baker 26pts

1968 8-2

37 Lafayette	7 WR Al Fenstemacher
20 Princeton	14 E Jim Benedict
16 Cornell	17 T Mike Kizis
29 Lehigh	26 G Alan Greenberg
0 Army	24 C John Orrizzi
28 Columbia	17 G Dave Zimmerman
23 Delaware	14 T Rich Koprowski
27 Connecticut	15 E Bob Stonebraker
41 Holy Cross	14 QB Rich Policastro / Bruce Van Ness
55 Colgate	34 TB Bryant Mitchell
	FB Mel Brown
	DL Rick Bonsall
	DL Jim DiGiacinto
	DL Len Novelli
	DL Mike Pellowski / Andy Naporano
	LB Rich Bing
	LB Drew Forgash
	LB Lee Schneider
	LB Larry Clymer
	DB Pete Savino
	DB Jim Renshaw
	DB John Pollock

RUSHING: Mitchell 238/1204y, Brown 74/31y, Van Ness 81/280y
PASSING: Policastro 68-122/994y, 15TD, 55.7%
Van Ness 42-107/656y, 5TD, 39.3%
RECEIVING: Stone 31/448y, Fenstemacher 22/432y, Benedict 19/315y
SCORING: Mitchell 54pts, Jim Julian (K) 46pts, Stonebreaker 36pts

1969 6-3

44 Lafayette	22 WR Al Fenstemacher
29 Princeton	0 E Jim Benedict
21 Cornell	7 T Murray Bakst
7 Lehigh	17 G Bob Coppola
20 Navy	6 C John Orrizzi
21 Columbia	14 G Mike Kizis
0 Delaware	44 T John Bauer
22 Connecticut	28 E Bob Stonebraker / Randy Bokesch
48 Colgate	12 QB Rich Policastro
	TB Bruce Van Ness / Larry Robertson
	FB Steve Ferrughelli
	DL Andy Naporano
	DL Paul Milea / Gary Martin
	DL Len Novelli
	DL Mike Pellowski
	LB Drew Forgash
	LB Lee Schneider
	LB Sam Picketts
	LB Larry Clymer
	DB Jim Renshaw
	DB John Miller
	DB Sam Chapman

RUSHING: Ferrughelli 131/564y, Robertson 95/405y,
Van Ness 105/375y
PASSING: Policastro 149-258/1690y, 14TD, 57.8%
RECEIVING: Benedict 48/650y, Van Ness 24/244y,
Fenstemacher 22/291y
SCORING: Van Ness 48pts, Robertson 36pts, Benedict 18pts

1970 5-5

41 Lafayette	16 WR Al Fenstermacher
14 Princeton	41 WR Bob Carney / Bruce Miller
9 Harvard	39 T Mike Kizis
9 Lehigh	7 G Murray Bakst / Bob Coppola
21 Delaware	51 C Gary Tinney
14 Columbia	30 G Dave Rinehimer
21 Bucknell	7 T John Bauer
6 Boston Univ.	3 TE Larry Christoff / Jim Fallon
37 Holy Cross	7 QB Mike Yancheff / Leo Gasienica
30 Colgate	12 TB Larry Robertson
	FB Steve Ferrughelli / Bill Donaldson
	DL Andy Naporano
	DL Alan Bain
	DL Kevin O'Connor / Greg Sivess
	DL Mike Pellowski / Bob Zieniuk
	LB Larry Clymer / Brill Beierle
	LB Sam Picketts
	LB Andy Malekoff
	LB Gary Martin / Jim Liguori
	DB Joe Epps
	DB John Miller
	DB Sam Chapman

RUSHING: Robertson 101/397y, Ferrughelli 100/368y,
Miller 47/165y
PASSING: Yancheff 93-185/974y, 8TD, 50.3%
RECEIVING: Fenstemacher 27/254y, Christoff 16/164y,
Ferrughelli 15/137y
SCORING: John Pesce (K) 33pts, Robertson, Ferrughelli &
Christoff 24pts

1971 4-7

7 Lafayette	13 WR Bob Carney
33 Princeton	18 WR Bruce Miller / Andy Byers
17 Cornell	31 T Doug Davis
14 Lehigh	35 G Andy Tighe
7 Delaware	48 C Vic Lapkowicz
16 Columbia	17 G Dave Rinehimer
13 Bucknell	14 T Scott Spencer / Sam Turner
17 Army	30 TE Larry Christoff
14 Holy Cross	13 QB Leo Gasienica / Gary Smolyn
28 Colgate	16 TB Larry Robertson / J.J. Jennings
27 Morgan State	8 FB Bill Donaldson
	DL Bob Wilusz
	DL Steve Allen
	DL Marty Benante / Jack Salemi
	DL Bob Dillard
	LB Roy Malinak
	LB Sam Picketts / Frank Zukas
	LB Andy Malekoff
	LB Gary Martin
	DB Bob Oldt
	DB Ed Jones (TB) / Joe Epps
	DB Bob Shutte

RUSHING: Robertson 133/405y, Donaldson 84/337y,
Jennings 60/320y
PASSING: Gasienica 98-197/1148y, 9TD, 49.7%
RECEIVING: Carney 30/351y, Christoff 25/246y,
Robertson 23/314y
SCORING: Robertson 42pts, John Pesce (K) 31pts,
Miller & Jennings 24pts

1972 7-4

14 Holy Cross	24 WR Bob Carney / Tom Sweeney
41 Lehigh	13 WR Bruce Miller
6 Princeton	7 T Bob Morton
22 Cornell	36 G Andy Tighe
21 Lafayette	7 C Vic Lapkowicz / Bruce Montigney
28 Army	35 G Dave Rinehimer
6 Columbia	3 T Scott Spencer
21 Connecticut	13 TE Larry Christoff
51 Boston Univ.	7 QB Leo Gasienica
37 Morgan State	14 TB J.J. Jennings
43 Colgate	13 FB Charley D. Ponziano
	DL Bob Dillard
	DL Steve Allen
	DL Jack Salemi/Marty Benante/Alan Bain
	DL Roy Malinak / Dwight Lipscomb
	LB Andy Malekoff / Paul Krasnavage
	LB John Witkowski
	LB Frank Zukas
	DB Tony Pawlik / Bob Oldt
	DB Len Boone
	DB Andy Mazer
	DB Gary Smolyn

RUSHING: Jennings 287/1262y, Ron Shycko (TB) 106/432y,
Ponziano 52/128y
PASSING: Gasienica 107-198/1409y, 8TD, 54%
RECEIVING: Christoff 27/278y, Sweeney 23/369y,
Carney 19/279y
SCORING: John Pesce (K) 56pts, Jennings 54pts,
Gasienica 42pts

1973 6-5

31 Lehigh	13 WR Tom Sweeney
39 Princeton	14 WR Bill Bolash
22 Massachusetts	25 T Bob Morton
35 Lafayette	6 G Andy Tighe
24 Delaware	7 C Bruce Montigney / Andy Zdobylak
28 Columbia	2 G Dale Sipos / Art Thompson
19 Connecticut	27 T Scott Spencer
13 Air Force	31 TE Ken Hall
27 Holy Cross	7 QB John Piccirillo / Gary Smolyn
0 Colgate	42 TB J.J. Jennings
6 Tampa	34 FB Ron Shycko
	DL Bob Dillard
	DL Jack Salemi
	DL Steve Allen
	DL Dwight Lipscomb / Nate Toran
	LB Paul Krasnavage
	LB John Witkowski
	LB Tom Holmes
	DB Ed Jones
	DB Len Boone / Andy Farkas
	DB Tony Pawlik
	DB Andy Mazer

RUSHING: Jennings 303/1353y, Shycko 95/485y, Bolash 31/313y
PASSING: Piccirillo 26-63/415y, 2TD, 41.3%
Smolyn 28-51/337y, 3TD, 54.9%
RECEIVING: Sweeney 28/479y, Bolash 15/173y, Hall 11/156y
SCORING: Jennings 128pts, Tighe (G-K) 35pts, Sweeney 18pts

1974 7-3-1

16 Bucknell	14 WR Joe Yacaginsky / Dustin Bryan
6 Princeton	6 T Tony Ray
24 Harvard	21 G Linwood Taylor
37 Lehigh	16 C Andy Zdobylak
15 William & Mary	28 G Art Thompson
20 Air Force	3 T Bill Fenn / Nick Sauter
7 Connecticut	9 TE Pete Clark / Mark Debes
35 Lafayette	0 QB Bert Kosup
6 Boston Univ.	0 HB Bill Bolash
62 Colgate	21 HB Mike Fisher / Keith Davis
16 Hawaii	28 FB Curt Edwards
	DL Nate Toran
	DL John Alexander
	DL Tom Mannon / Steve Hoffman
	DL Paul Krasnavage
	DL Dwight Lipscomb / Edgar Robinson
	LB Paul Lewis / Elvin Washington
	LB Tom Holmes
	DB Ed Jones
	DB Andy Farkas
	DB Tony Pawlik
	DB Jim Teatom

RUSHING: Edwards 189/889y, Fisher 102/622y, Bolash 79/288y
PASSING: Kosup 63-150/1070y, 9TD, 42.0%
RECEIVING: Bryan 18/266y, Yacaginsky 14/250y,
Mark Twitty (WR) 9/314y
SCORING: Kosup 36pts, Edwards 30pts, Bill Bradley (K) 26pts

1975 9-2

47 Bucknell	3 WR Mark Twitty / Dusty Bryan
7 Princeton	10 T Jim O'Halloran
7 Hawaii	3 G Jim Clements / Dan Pfabe
20 Lehigh	34 C John Fedorchak / Ray Kinch
24 William & Mary	0 G Tony Ray
41 Columbia	0 T Bill Fenn / Nick Sauter
35 Connecticut	8 TE Jon Walling / Mark Debes
48 Lafayette	6 QB Jeff Rebholz / Matt Allison
41 Boston Univ.	3 HB Mark Lassiter / Keith Davis
56 Colgate	14 HB Mike Fisher
21 Syracuse	10 FB Curt Edwards
	DL Nate Toran
	DL John Alexander
	DL Rich Wagner
	DL Dan Gray
	LB Dwight Lipscomb
	LB Elvin Washington / Tim Blanchard
	LB Tom Holmes
	DB Henry Jenkins
	DB Dave Figueroa / Reggie Moultrie
	DB Bob Davis
	DB Jim Teatom / Sammie Davis

RUSHING: Edwards 236/1157y, Fisher 127/545y, Lassiter 93/532y
PASSING: Rebholz 33-69/715y, 8TD, 47.8%
 Allison 44-81/510y, 6TD, 54.3%
RECEIVING: Twitty 24/544y, Walling 11/141y,
 Jeff Greczyn (FB) 8/46y
SCORING: Edwards 66pts, Fisher 54pts, Twitty 42pts

1976 11-0

13 Navy	3 WR Mark Twitty
19 Bucknell	7 T Jim O'Halloran / John Gallo
17 Princeton	0 G Dan Pfabe
21 Cornell	14 C John Fedorchak
38 Connecticut	0 G John Bucci / Ray Kinch
28 Lehigh	21 T Nick Sauter
47 Columbia	0 TE Jon Walling / Mark Debes
24 Massachusetts	7 QB Bert Kosup
34 Louisville	0 HB Mark Lassiter
29 Tulane	20 HB Mike Fisher
17 Colgate	9 FB Glen Kehler / Jeff Greczyn
	DL Nate Toran
	DL John Alexander / Dino Mangiero
	DL Rich Wagner
	DL Dan Gray
	LB Len Davis
	LB Tim Blanchard / Elvin Washington
	LB Jim Hughes
	DB Don Harris
	DB Henry Jenkins / Reggie Moultrie
	DB Bob Davis
	DB Jim Teatom

RUSHING: Kehler 151/764y, Lassiter 168/750y, Fisher 138/459y
PASSING: Kosup 69-141/1098y, 6TD, 48.9%
RECEIVING: Twitty 29/514y, Walling 18/236y, Fisher 9/119y
SCORING: Kennan Startzell (K) 65pts, Lassiter 60pts, Fisher 50pts

1977 8-3

7 Penn State	45 WR Walt Hynoski / Tim Odell
0 Colgate	23 T Kevin Kurdyla / Guy Sarna
36 Bucknell	14 G Dan Pfabe / Pete Honeyford
10 Princeton	6 C John Fedorchak
30 Cornell	14 G John Bucci
48 Connecticut	18 T John Gallo
20 Lehigh	0 TE George Carter
22 William & Mary	21 QB Bert Kosup
14 Temple	24 HB Mark Lassiter / Lester Johnson
47 Tulane	8 HB Mike Fisher
63 Boston Univ.	8 FB Glen Kehler
	DL Phil Parkins / Rick Baldwin
	DL Dino Mangiero
	DL Dan Gray
	DL Pete Zimmerman / Ed Steward
	LB Len Davis / Dan McMahon
	LB Elvin Washington
	LB Tim Blanchard
	DB Ken Smith / Bob Hynoski
	DB Reggie Moultrie
	DB Bob Davis
	DB Sammie Davis / Len McBroom

RUSHING: Kehler 164/866y, Lassiter 102/602y, Fisher 86/409y
PASSING: Kosup 82-157/1445y, 10TD, 52.2%
RECEIVING: Carter 17/391y, Odell 16/273y, Hynoski 13/270y
SCORING: Fisher 60pts, Kennan Startzell (K) 54pts,
 Johnson 48pts

1978 9-3

10 Penn State	26 WR Walt Hynoski / Tim Odell
27 Bucknell	13 T Kevin Kurdyla
24 Princeton	0 G Pete Honeyford
28 Yale	27 C John Bucci
10 Connecticut	0 G Mike Kubas
24 Villanova	9 T John Gallo
69 Columbia	0 TE George Carter
21 Massachusetts	11 QB Bob Hering / Ed McMichael
13 Temple	10 HB Ted Blackwell / Lester Johnson
31 Holy Cross	21 HB David Dorn
0 Colgate	14 FB Glen Kehler
18 Arizona State■	34 DL Phil Parkins
	DL Dino Mangiero
	DL Ed Steward
	DL Mike Rutemeyer / Pete Zimmerman
	LB Dan McMahon
	LB Tim Blanchard
	LB Jim Hughes
	DB Ken Smith
	DB Bob Hynoski
	DB Deron Cherry
	DB Mark Freeman

RUSHING: Kehler 212/883y, Blackwell 120/532y,
 Johnson 82/342y
PASSING: Hering 88-193/1193y, 5TD, 45.6%
RECEIVING: Dorn 27/535y, Hynoski 20/284y, Odell 13/245y,
 Carter 13/185y
SCORING: Kennan Startzell (K) 76pts, Dorn 54pts,
 Blackwell 34pts

1979 8-3

28 Holy Cross	0 WR Tim Odell
10 Penn State	45 WR David Dorn (TB)
16 Bucknell	14 T Kevin Kurdyla
38 Princeton	14 G Pete Honeyford
20 Temple	41 C Frank Naylor
26 Connecticut	14 G Mike Kubas / Tony Cella
24 William & Mary	0 T Rich Spitzer / Frank Cerone
13 Tennessee	7 TE George Carter / Steve Pfirman
20 Army	0 QB Ed McMichael
17 Villanova	32 HB Ted Blackwell / Albert Ray
31 Louisville	7 FB Bryant Moore
	DL Bill Pickel / Kevin Conlon
	DL Dino Mangiero / Ralph Ivy
	DL Nasario Dunn
	DL Mike Rustemeyer
	LB Mike Knight / Jeff Blanchard
	LB Jim Dumont / Nick Marotta
	LB Ed Steward (DL)
	DB Ken Smith
	DB Jerry Smith / Mark Piniero
	DB Mark Freeman
	DB Deron Cherry

RUSHING: Ray 107/567y, Blackwell 100/527y, Dorn 90/356y
PASSING: McMichael 124-211/1529y, 7TD, 58.8%
RECEIVING: Odell 34/466y, Dorn 27/468y, Carter 15/176y
SCORING: Dorn 74pts, Kennan Startzell (K) 65pts, Ray 30pts

1980 7-4

21 Temple	3 WR Tim Odell
24 Cincinnati	7 WR David Dorn / Dave Palumbo
44 Princeton	13 T Kevin Kurdyla
44 Cornell	3 G Pete George
13 Alabama	17 C Frank Naylor
18 William & Mary	21 G Mike Kubas / Tony Cella
9 Syracuse	17 T Rich Spitzer
37 Army	21 TE Steve Pfirman
19 Virginia	17 QB Ed McMichael
15 West Virginia	24 TB Albert Ray
35 Colgate	13 FB Ted Blackwell / Bryant Moore
	DL Andy Carino
	DL Bill Pickel
	DL Mike Rustemeyer / Bill Beschner
	DL Ken Bercier
	DL Ed Steward
	LB Mike Knight / Jeff Blanchard
	LB Keith Woetzel
	DB William Hill
	DB Ken Smith / Dan Errico
	DB Mark Piniero / Bob Ciampaglio
	DB Deron Cherry

RUSHING: Ray 187/778y, Blackwell 162/748y, Moore 58/240y
PASSING: McMichael 146-229/1761y, 10TD, 63.8%
RECEIVING: Odell 49/718y, Blackwell 36/276y, Ray 20/112y
SCORING: Alex Falcinelli (K) 69pts, Blackwell 44pts, Odell 32pts

1981 5-6

29 Syracuse	27 WR Eric Johnson
13 Colgate	5 WR Andrew Baker
3 Virginia	0 T Tony Cella
0 Cincinnati	10 G Pete George
31 Cornell	17 C Frank Naylor
17 Army	0 G Jeff Kurdyla / Jim Zurich
12 Temple	24 T Rich Spitzer
7 Alabama	31 TE Steve Pfirman / Brian Crockett
3 Pittsburgh	47 QB Ralph Leek / Keith Hudak
3 West Virginia	20 TB Albert Ray/Dwayne Hooper/Joe Burke
21 Boston College	27 FB Bryant Moore
	DL Andy Carino
	DL Bill Pickel / Bill Beschner
	DL Ray Moore
	DL Mike Rustemeyer / Charles Bounty
	DL Ken Bercier / Jim Dumont
	LB Keith Woetzel
	LB Bob Dumont / Jack Hotz
	DB Carl Howard
	DB Dan Errico
	DB Mark Piniero
	DB Bob Ciampaglio

RUSHING: Ray 180/679y, Hooper 84/300y, Moore 51/229y
PASSING: Leek 80-167/926y, 5TD, 47.9%
RECEIVING: Ray 31/228y, Pfirman 24/246y Baker 18/356y
SCORING: Alex Falcinelli (K) 47pts, Baker & Burke 18pts

1982 5-6

8 Syracuse	31 WR Eric Johnson / Boris Pendergrass
14 Penn State	49 WR Andrew Baker
10 Temple	7 T Tony Cella
27 William & Mary	17 G Clement Udovich / Lamont Green
24 Army	3 C Joe DiGilio
13 Boston College	14 G John Owens
34 Colgate	17 T Rich Spitzer / Mike Brenner
20 Richmond	14 TE Alan Andrews
7 Auburn	30 QB Jacque LaPrarie / Eric Hochberg
17 West Virginia	44 TB Albert Smith/Vernon Williams/Joe
Burke	
6 Pittsburgh	52 FB Bryant Moore
	DL Lionel Washington / Barry Buchowski
	DL Bill Beschner / Tony Sagnella
	DL Jeff Kurdyla / George Pickel
	DL Bill Pickel / Randy Hannis
	DL Bob Dumont
	LB Jim Dumont
	LB Keith Woetzel / Mercer Hedgeman
	DB Carl Howard
	DB Harold Young
	DB Bill Houston
	DB Bob Ciampaglio

RUSHING: Smith 130/466y, Moore 104/449y, Burke 72/254y
PASSING: LaPrarie 100-186/1164y, 7TD, 53.8%
RECEIVING: Johnson 35/444y, Baker 30/472y,
 Andrews 18/242y
SCORING: Alex Falcinelli (K) 52pts, Smith 24pts,
 Baker & Andrews 18pts

1983 3-8

22 Connecticut	5 WR Boris Pendergrass
22 Boston College	42 WR Andrew Baker
13 Syracuse	17 T Jim Keating / Mike Brenner
25 Penn State	36 G Clement Udovich
12 Army	20 C Joe DiGilio
29 Colgate	25 G Joe Pennucci
35 William & Mary	28 T John Owens
0 Tennessee	7 TE Alan Andrews / Scott Drake
7 Cincinnati	18 QB Jacque LaPrarie / Eric Hochberg
7 West Virginia	35 TB Albert Smith / Len Bellezza
23 Temple	24 FB Vernon Williams
	DL Bob Dumont
	DL Bob Beschner / Barry Buchowski
	DL Jeff Kurdyla / Randy Hannis
	DL Tony Sagnella / Harry Swayne
	LB Tyronne Stowe / Mercer Hedgeman
	LB Jim Dumont / Matt Bachman
	LB Lionel Washington
	DB Harold Young
	DB Carl Howard / Joe Corbin
	DB Bill Houston / John Cummins
	DB Dan Errico

RUSHING: Smith 122/572y, Williams 92/404y, Bellezza 55/299y
PASSING: LaPrarie 104-203/1275y, 7TD, 51.2%,
 Hochberg 61-100/814y, 4 TDs, 61.0%
RECEIVING: Andrews 48/472y, Baker 37/857y,
 Pendergrass 22/292y
SCORING: Tom Angstadt (K) 49pts, Smith 36pts, Andrews 24pts

1984 7-3

12 Penn State	15 WR Boris Pendergrass
10 Temple	9 WR Andrew Baker
19 Syracuse	0 T Mike Brenner
43 Cincinnati	15 G Clement Udovich
14 Kentucky	27 C Joe DiGilio
14 Army	7 G Lee Getz
38 Louisville	21 T Jim Keating / Tony Rigole
23 Boston College	35 TE Alan Andrews / Scott Drake
23 West Virginia	19 QB Eric Hochberg
17 Colgate	7 TB Albert Smith

FB Vernon Williams / Curt Stephens
DL Tom Duffy
DL Barry Buchowski
DL George Pickel
DL Tony Sagnella / Harry Swayne
LB Lionel Washington
LB Roy Oake
LB Tyronne Stowe
DB Harold Young
DB Steve Twamley
DB John Cummins
DB Jacque LaPrarie / Roger Pollard

RUSHING: Smith 178/869y, Williams 90/398y, Stephens 57/269y
PASSING: Hochberg 162-305/1905y, 9TD, 53.1%
RECEIVING: Baker 42/583y, Andrews 40/511y, Pendergrass 25/420y
SCORING: Tom Angstadt (K) 77pts, Smith 54pts, Baker 18pts

1985 2-8-1

28 Florida	28 WR Greg Raffaelli / Eric Young
16 Army	20 WR Roy Hoover / Brian Cobb
10 Penn State	17 T Mike Brenner / Tony Rigole
10 Boston College	20 G Clement Udovich
13 Temple	14 C Glenn Fine / Mike Dillon
10 Pittsburgh	38 G Lee Getz
20 Richmond	17 T Jim Keating
0 Tennessee	40 TE Scott Drake / Bruce Campbell
0 West Virginia	27 QB Joe Gagliardi / Eric Hochberg
28 Colgate	14 TB Albert Smith / Henry Henderson
14 Syracuse	31 FB Matt Prescott (TB) / Curtis Stephens

DL Alec Hoke
DL George Pickel
DL Harry Swayne / George Bankos
DL Tony Sagnella
LB Jim Pickel
LB Matt Bachman / Roy Oake
LB Tyronne Stowe
DB Jean Austin
DB Steve Twamley
DB Luis Moro
DB Will Dunster / Derek Baker

RUSHING: Smith 112/362y, Prescott 45/266y, Reynold Walbrook (TB) 71/275y
PASSING: Gagliardi 128-220/1273y, 6TD, 58.2%, Hochberg 79-169/752y, 4TD, 46.7%
RECEIVING: Smith 36/244y, Drake 28/239y, Campbell 20/213y
SCORING: Smith 42pts, Tom Angstadt (K) 28pts, Walbrook 18pts

1986 5-5-1

11 Boston College	9 WR Eric Young
16 Kentucky	16 WR Brian Cobb
48 Cincinnati	28 T John Kutz / Steve Tardy
16 Syracuse	10 G Doug Strickland
6 Penn State	13 C Mike Dillon
3 Florida	13 G Lee Getz
35 Army	7 T Marshall Haegley / Bill Hiros
41 Louisville	0 TE Bruce Campbell
17 West Virginia	24 QB Scott Erney / Joe Gagliardi
6 Pittsburgh	20 TB Matt Prescott / Dan Lipsett
22 Temple	29 FB Curtis Stephens

DL Tom Duffy
DL Harry Swayne
DL Doug Kokoskie
DL George Bankos / Scott Miller
LB Alec Hoke
LB Matt Bachman
LB Tyronne Stowe
DB Sean Washington
DB Steve Twamley / Jean Austin
DB Derek Baker
DB Luis Moro / Darrin Czellecz

RUSHING: Prescott 155/606y, Stephens 113/419y, Lipsett 49/186y
PASSING: Erney 96-190/1160y, 6TD, 50.5%, Gagliardi 90-139/9924y, 7TD, 64.8%
RECEIVING: Campbell 30/323y, Young 28/331y, Stephens 27/205y
SCORING: Doug Giesler (K) 56pts, Prescott 42pts, Cobb 32pts

1987 6-5

10 Cincinnati	7 WR Eric Young
3 Syracuse	20 WR Tyrone McQueen
19 Kentucky	18 T Bill Milano / Bill Hiros
7 Duke	0 G Doug Strickland
21 Penn St.	35 C Nick Urda / Jeff Erickson
38 Boston College	24 G John Kutz / Bill Dubiel
27 Army	14 T Steve Tardy
13 Vanderbilt	27 TE Bruce Campbell
0 Pittsburgh	17 QB Scott Erney
13 West Virginia	27 TB Henry Henderson / Mike Botti
17 Temple	14 FB Curtis Stephens

DL Chris Evans
DL Scott Miller
DL Carter Giles / Joe Savoy
DL Chuck Paugh
LB Alec Hoke
LB Paul Garea / Pat Udovich
LB Bob Speidel
DB Jean Austin
DB Sean Washington
DB Derek Baker
DB Darrin Czellecz

RUSHING: Henderson 158/846y, Botti 72/397y, Stephens 78/359y
PASSING: Erney 122-225/1369y, 7TD, 54.2%
RECEIVING: Young 25/364y, Campbell 25/200y, McQueen 22/314y
SCORING: Carmen Sclafani (K) 54pts, Stephens 30pts, Young & Henderson 24pts

1988 5-6

17 Michigan State	13 WR Eric Young / Tyrone McQueen
30 Vanderbilt	31 WR Brett Mersola
21 Penn State	16 T Bill Hiros / Bill Milano
38 Cincinnati	9 G John Kutz / Bill Dubiel
20 Syracuse	34 C Jeff Erickson
17 Boston College	6 G Nick Urda
24 Army	34 T Steve Tardy
30 Temple	35 TE James Jenkins / Scott Blanche
10 Pittsburgh	20 QB Scott Erney
24 West Virginia	35 TB James Cann / Henry Henderson
41 Colgate	22 FB Mike Botti

DL Larry Muno / Mike Conlan
DL Scott Paugh / Scott Miller
DL George Bankos / Steve Tomkins
DL Carter Giles
LB Tim Lester
LB Pat Udovich
LB Doug Kokoskie
DB Darrin Czellecz
DB John Blanton / Rusty Mayes
DB Derek Baker
DB Jeff Newman / Glenn Miller

RUSHING: Botti 161/715y, Cann 104/401y, Henderson 40/167y
PASSING: Erney 188-339/2123y, 13TD, 55.5%
RECEIVING: Young 48/592y, McQueen 31/341y, Mersola 25/388y
SCORING: Carmen Sclafani (K) 79pts, Botti 42pts, Cann 30pts

1989 2-7-2

17 Cincinnati	17 WR Tyrone McQueen
31 Ball State	31 WR Gary Melton / Randy Jackson
9 Boston College	7 T Bill Milano
38 Northwestern	27 G Nick Urda
0 Penn State	17 C Jeff Erickson / Travis Broadbent
26 Kentucky	33 G Steve Tardy / Tim Christ
28 Syracuse	49 T Bill Hiros
14 Army	35 TE Scott Blanche
20 West Virginia	21 QB Scott Erney
33 Temple	36 TB James Cann
29 Pittsburgh	46 FB Mike Botti

DL Scott Miller / Pete Kofitsas
DL Marty Mayes
DL Joe Savoy / Chuck Paugh
DL Tim Lester / James Jenkins
LB Pat Udovich
LB Bob Speidel / Mike Bouchard
LB Elinardo Webster / Shawn Williams
DB Rusty Mayes / Marshall Roberts
DB Ron Allen / Glenn Miller
DB Vaughn McKoy / John Blanton
DB Darrin Czellecz

RUSHING: Cann 117/429y, Botti 93/319y, Erney 69/139y
PASSING: Erney 208-374/2536y, 15TD, 55.6%
RECEIVING: Cann 42/507y, McQueen 39/449y, Melton 33/410y
SCORING: Cann 66pts, Doug Giesler (K) 55pts, Botti 34pts

1990 3-8

24 Kentucky	8 WR Jim Guarantano
28 Colgate	17 WR Gary Melton / Chris Brantley
0 Penn State	28 T Allen Mitchell
10 Michigan State	34 G Maurice Owens / Doug Kavulich
14 Boston College	19 C Travis Broadbent
21 Pittsburgh	45 G Tim Christ
0 Syracuse	42 T Don Forbes / Dave Clark
20 Akron	17 TE James Jenkins / John Murphy
31 Army	35 QB Tom Tarver / Derek McCord
3 West Virginia	28 TB Bill Bailey / Antoine Moore
22 Temple	29 FB Tekay Dorsey

DL Scott Miller
DL Marty Mayes
DL Kory Kozak / Mike Spitzer
LB Shawn Williams / Mike Conlan
LB Jamil Jackson / Luis Bido
LB Todd Lane
LB Elnardo Webster
DB Ron Allen
DB Rusty Mayes
DB Willie Wilkes / Jay Bellamy
DB Malik Jackson / Shaun Smith

RUSHING: Dorsey 131/505y, Bailey 125/499y, Moore 45/261y
PASSING: Tarver 107-188/1348y, 8TD, 56.9%
RECEIVING: Jenkins 31/325y, Guarantano 26/386y, Brantley 18/366y
SCORING: John Benestad (K) 37pts, Bailey & Jenkins 18pts

1991 6-5

20 Boston College	13 WR Gary Melton / Chris Brantley
22 Duke	42 WR Jim Guarantano
22 Northwestern	18 T Ken Dammann
14 Michigan State	7 G Joe Ciaffoni
14 Army	12 C Travis Broadbent
40 Maine	19 G Tim Christ
17 Penn State	37 T Allen Mitchell
7 Syracuse	21 TE Chris Stoll
3 West Virginia	28 QB Tom Tarver
17 Pittsburgh	22 TB Antoine Moore / Bill Bailey
41 Temple	0 FB Tekay Dorsey

DL Andrew Beckett
DL Mike Spitzer
DL Kory Kozak
LB Shawn Williams
LB Jamil Jackson
LB Todd Lane / Luis Bido
LB Elnardo Webster / Robert Sneathen
DB Ron Allen / Tim Geckeler
DB Marshall Roberts / Keith Price
DB Jay Bellamy / Doug Atkins
DB Malik Jackson / Shaun Smith

RUSHING: Moore 145/627y, Mitter 107/495y, Bailey 60/219y
PASSING: Tarver 164-307/1969y, 10TD, 53.4%
RECEIVING: Guarantano 62/740y, Brantley 30/400y, Melton 27/433y
SCORING: Bailey & Moore 36pts, John Benestad (K) 31pts

1992 7-4

20 Boston College	37 WR Chris Brantley / Lance Evina
41 Colgate	0 WR Jim Guarantano / Mario Henry
21 Pittsburgh	16 T Ken Dammann
40 Navy	0 G Joe Ciaffoni
24 Penn State	38 C Travis Broadbent
28 Syracuse	50 G Doug Kavulich
45 Army	10 T Scott Vaughn
50 Virginia Tech	49 TE Chris Stoll / Marco Battaglia
24 Cincinnati	26 QB Bryan Fortay / Ray Lucas
13 West Virginia	9 RB Bruce Presley / Tekay Dorsey
35 Temple	10 RB Craig Mitter

DL Andrew Beckett
DL Mike Spitzer
DL Keif Bryant / Roger Jeffries
LB Shawn Williams
LB Jamil Jackson
LB Todd Lane / George Stewart
LB Bob Sneathen
DB Jay Bellamy / Tim Geckeler
DB Marshall Roberts / Keith Price
DB Doug Adkins
DB Malik Jackson

RUSHING: Presley 148/817y
PASSING: Fortay 1608y, 16TD, Lucas 61-105/836y, 4TD, 58.1%
RECEIVING: Guarantano 56/755y, Brantley 40/559y, Battaglia 17/219y
SCORING: John Benestad (K) 71pts, Presley 54pts, Brantley & Guarantano 36pts

1993 4-7

68 Colgate	6 WR Chris Brantley
39 Duke	38 WR Mario Henry
7 Penn State	31 T Ken Dammann
62 Temple	0 G Scott Patkochis
21 Boston College	31 C John Bleich
45 Army	38 G Kareem Williams (C) / Mike Spitzer
42 Virginia Tech	49 T Scott Vaughn
10 Pittsburgh	21 TE Marco Battaglia
22 West Virginia	58 QB Ray Lucas / Bryan Fortay
17 Miami	31 TB Bruce Presley / Terrell Willis
18 Syracuse	31 FB/WR Bill Bailey / Ed Walker

DL Rashod Swinger / Jim Guarnera
DL Andrew Beckett
DL Keif Bryant
DL Bob Sneathen / Anthony Cauthen
LB Jamil Jackson / Brian Sheridan
LB George Stewart / Mike Brestle
LB Shane Spells / Rusty Swartz
DB Marshall Roberts / Tim Geckeler
DB Michael Fullman / Keith Price
DB Jay Bellamy / Shaun Smith
DB Malik Jackson / Mark Washington

RUSHING: Willis 195/1261y, Presley 126/741y, Lucas 67/220y
PASSING: Lucas 109-188/1011y, 7TD, 58%
  Fortay 59-107/766y, 9TD, 55.1%
RECEIVING: Brantley 56/589y, Battaglia 27/329y, Henry 23/294y
SCORING: Willis 80pts, John Benestad (K) 50pts, Brantley 44pts

1994 5-5-1

28 Kent State	6 WR Reggie Funderburk
17 West Virginia	12 WR Steve Harper / Jonathan Gibbs
36 Syracuse	37 T Ken Dammann
27 Penn State	55 G Kareem Williams
3 Miami	24 C John Bleich
16 Army	14 G Chris Kennedy
14 Cincinnati	9 T Robert Barr
7 Boston College	7 TE Marco Battaglia
38 Temple	21 QB Ray Lucas
34 Virginia Tech	41 TB Bruce Presley / Terrell Willis
21 Pittsburgh	35 FB/WR Wes Bridges / Chris Hutton

DL James Guarnera
DL Rashod Swinger
DL Keif Bryant
DL Robert Sneathen
LB Rusty Swartz / Brian Sheridan
LB Rahsaan Giddings
LB Alcides Catanho
DB Curtis Tribbitt
DB Derek Ward / Keith Price
DB Thomas Kelly
DB Mark Washington

RUSHING: Willis 216/1080y, Presley 126/546y, Lucas 67/157y
PASSING: Lucas 156-268/1869y, 16TD, 58.2%
RECEIVING: Battaglia 58/779y, Funderburk 55/751y, Harper 60pts
SCORING: Funderburk 48pts, Eddie Duborg (K) 43pts, Willis 30pts

1995 4-7

14 Duke	24 WR Reggie Funderburk / Chris Hutton
27 Navy	17 WR Steve Harper / Bill Powell
34 Penn State	59 T Jack McKiernan / Michael Theokas
17 Syracuse	27 G Matt Brown
21 Miami	56 C Pat Gorman
17 Virginia Tech	45 G Chris Kennedy
42 Pittsburgh	24 T Robert Barr
26 West Virginia	59 TE Marco Battaglia
45 Tulane	40 QB Ray Lucas
23 Temple	20 RB Terrell Willis
38 Boston College	41 RB Bruce Presley / Chad Bosch

DL Rudy Smith
DL Rashod Swinger
DL Joey Jones / Shawn Devlin
DL Charles Woolridge
LB Rashon Giddings
LB Brian Sheridan
LB Rusty Swartz
DB Cameron Chadwick / Kevin Williams
DB Derek Ward
DB Thomas Kelly / Norris Crawford
DB Mark Washington / Aaron Brady

RUSHING: Willis 177/773y, Presley 147/678y, Bosch 71/356y
PASSING: Lucas 188-347/2180y, 16TD, 54.2%
RECEIVING: Battaglia 69/894y, Funderburk 54/546y, Harper 35/417y
SCORING: Battaglia 62pts, Nick Mike-Mayer (K) 54pts, Harper 42pts

1996 2-9

38 Villanova	28 WR Andy Holland
6 Navy	10 WR Steven Harper
0 Miami	33 T Kerry Ware / Pete Donnelly
14 Virginia Tech	30 G Ben French
0 Syracuse	42 C Jack McKiernan
21 Army	42 G Matt Fleming / Bryan Raftery
13 Boston College	37 T T.J. Spizzo
28 Temple	17 TE Rob Seeger / Jason Curry / Ron Keller
14 West Virginia	55 QB Mike Stephans / Ralph Sacca
0 Notre Dame	62 HB Chad Bosch / Jacki Crooks
9 Pittsburgh	24 FB Gary Fauntleroy

DL Chris Cebula / Mike DeLucia
DL Rashod Swinger / Bryan Yeager
DL Shawn Devlin
DL Charles Woolridge / Rusty Swartz
LB Roger Wingate / Gil Ross
LB Aaron Brady / Art Dreher
LB Taman Bryant
LB Norris Crawford / Dax Strohmeyer
DB Peter Clarke / Cameron Chadwick
DB Derek Ward
DB Thomas Kelly

RUSHING: Bosch 111/523y, Crooks 76/268y, Fauntleroy 50/183y
PASSING: Stephans 73-172/918y, 4TD, 42.4%, Sacca 36-80/356y, 3TD, 45.0%
RECEIVING: Harper 25/321y, Holland 20/288y, Bosch 15/163y
SCORING: Nick Mike-Mayer (K) 26pts, Bosch 24pts, Seeger 18pts

1997 0-11

19 Virginia Tech	59 WR Andy Holland / Walter King
14 Texas	48 WR Steven Harper / Bill Powell
7 Navy	36 T Shaun O'Hara / Kerry Ware
21 Boston College	35 G Ben French
0 West Virginia	48 C Jack McKiernan
3 Syracuse	50 G Pete Donnelly / Clint Hunt
35 Army	37 T Ryan Comeau
48 Pittsburgh	55 TE Chris Hutton / Billy Woodard
7 Temple	49 QB Mike McMahon / Brendan Edmonds
14 Wake Forest	28 HB Jacki Crooks
23 Miami	51 FB Joe Diggs / Gary Fauntleroy

DL Chris Cebula
DL Bryan Yeager / Mike Belh
DL Charles Woolridge
DL Wayne Hampton / Billy Tulloch
LB Aaron Brady
LB Brian Sheridan / Joe Hynes
LB Norris Crawford (DB) / Roger Wingate
DB Reggie Stephens
DB Kevin Williams
DB Gil Ross / Thomas Kelly
DB Tarell Freeney

RUSHING: Crooks 174/758y, Robinson 52/273y, Fauntleroy 52/99y
PASSING: McMahon 104-212/1259y, 6TD, 49.1%
RECEIVING: Holland 28/276y, Crooks 24/135y, Powell 22/335y
SCORING: Crooks 26pts, Fauntleroy & King 24pts

1998 5-6

7 Richmond	6 WR Andy Holland
14 Boston College	41 WR Bill Powell
14 Syracuse	70 T Shaun O'Hara (C) / Ben French (G)
27 Army	15 G Pete Donnelly
17 Miami	53 C Mike DeLucia
25 Pittsburgh	21 G Iosefa Puaauli / Rich Mazza
24 Tulane	52 T Ryan Comeau
21 Temple	10 TE Billy Woodard
36 Navy	33 QB Mike McMahon
14 West Virginia	28 HB Jacki Crooks / Dennis Thomas
7 Virginia Tech	47 FB/WR Gary Fauntleroy / Chris Hutton

DL Marcus Perry
DL Ansel George-Shields / Thomas Petko
DL Mike Belh
DL Wayne Hampton
LB Dax Strohmeyer (DL) / Gil Ross
LB Aaron Brady
LB Jabari Moore / Wes Robertson
DB Garrett Shea
DB Reggie Stephens
DB Alan Davis / Ben Martin
DB Tarell Freeney / Dante Siciliano

RUSHING: Crooks 159/821y, Thomas 108/418y, Fauntleroy 50/161y
PASSING: McMahon 143-276/2203y, 12TD, 51.8%
RECEIVING: Powell 37/730y, Hutton 34/531y, Holland 21/298y
SCORING: Steven Barone (K) 44pts, Powell, Fauntleroy & Crooks 24pts

1999 1-10

7 California	21 WR Walter King / Aaron Martin
21 Texas	38 WR Errol Johnson / Sean Carty
7 Boston College	27 T Shaun O'Hara
10 Wake Forest	17 G Rich Mazza
20 Virginia Tech	58 C Mike DeLucia
16 West Virginia	62 G Iosefa Puaauli
15 Pittsburgh	38 T Ben French
28 Temple	56 TE L.J. Smith / Shin Black
7 Navy	34 QB Mike McMahon / Chad Schwenk
24 Syracuse	21 HB Jacki Crooks / Jason Ohene
0 Miami	55 FB Dennis Thomas

DL Wayne Hampton / Julian Ross
DL Thomas Petko
DL Mike Belh / Ansel George-Shields
DL Jack Bloom / Greg Pyszczymuka
LB Mike Pridgeon / Wes Robertson
LB Jabari Moore / Nate Leonard
LB Dax Strohmeyer / Brian Bender
DB Tony Berry
DB Robert Crenshaw
DB Nate Colon / Shahib White
DB David Griffin / Brian Bender

RUSHING: Crooks 161/587y, Thomas 37/180y, Ohene 27/100y
PASSING: McMahon 66-146/989y, 5TD, 45.2%, Schwenk 72-125/845y, 3 TD, 57.6%
RECEIVING: Johnson 35/507y, King 29/453y, Smith 26/418y
SCORING: Steve Barone (K) 30pts, Crooks 20pts, Smith 18pts

2000 3-8

34 Villanova	21 WR Walter, King / Aaron Martin
59 Buffalo	0 WR Errol Johnson
0 Virginia Tech	49 T Howard Blackwood
17 Pittsburgh	29 G Rich Mazza
6 Miami	64 C Jeremy Womack
14 Temple	48 G Mike Esposito / Travis Mills
28 Navy	21 T Julian Ross
13 Boston College	42 TE L.J. Smith
24 West Virginia	31 QB Mike McMahon / Chad Schwenk
17 Notre Dame	45 HB/WR Jason Ohene / Josh Hobbs
21 Syracuse	49 FB Dennis Thomas / Seth Stanton

DL Marcus Perry / Bill Tulloch
DL Tom Petko / Will Burnett
DL Greg Pyszczymuka / Jason Malakoski
LB Wes Robertson / Peter Mendez
LB M. Davis/Bill Hambrecht/Nate Leonard
LB Tarell Freeney / Gary Brackett
LB Torrance Heggie / Dennis McCormack
DB Brandon Haw
DB Deway Thompson / Tony Berry
DB Shahib White / Shawn Seabrooks
DB Nate Colon / Ben Martin

RUSHING: Thomas 137/587y, Ohene 58/304y, McMahon 68/243y
PASSING: McMahon 169-340/2157y, 18TD, 49.7%
RECEIVING: Johnson 46/555y, Smith 34/374y, King 26/398y
SCORING: Steve Barone (K) 47pts, Johnson 30pts, Thomas 24pts

2001 2-9

31 Buffalo	15 WR Aaron Martin
0 Miami	61 WR Delrico Fletcher / Tres Moses
0 Virginia Tech	50 T Trohn Carswell / Howard Blackwood
19 Connecticut	20 G Marty Pyszczymuka
17 Syracuse	24 C Bryan Boehrer
5 Temple	30 G Mike Esposito (C) / Travis Mills
23 Navy	17 T Brian Duffy
7 West Virginia	80 TE L.J. Smith / Rob Ring
0 Pittsburgh	42 QB Ryan Cubit
7 Boston College	38 HB Dennis Thomas / Ravon Anderson
10 California	20 FB Seth Stanton / Ray Pilch

DL Alfred Peterson / Torrance Heggie
DL Billy Tulloch / Ron Jenerette
DL Greg Pyszczymuka / Davon Clark
DL Ryan Neill / Raheem Orr
LB Brad Cunningham / Brian Hohmann
LB Gary Brackett
LB Mitchell Davis / Brian Bender
DB Tony Berry
DB Nate Jones / DeWayne Thompson
DB Shawn Seabrooks
DB Nate Colon / Tarell Freeney

RUSHING: Thomas 97/372y, Anderson 69/344y, Marcus Jones (TB) 101/327y
PASSING: Cubit 120-268/1433y, 9TD, 44.8%
RECEIVING: Smith 30/282y, Martin 25/523y, Fletcher 19/200y
SCORING: Ryan Sands (K) 26pts, Smith & Martin 18pts

2002 1-11

19 Villanova	37 WR Aaron Martin / Jerry Andre
11 Buffalo	34 WR Shawn Tucker / Chris Baker
44 Army	0 T Trohn Carswell / Mike Williamson
3 Pittsburgh	23 G Sameeh McDonald / Mike Esposito
14 Tennessee	35 C Marty Pyscczymuka
0 West Virginia	40 G Brian Duffy / Rich McManis
14 Virginia Tech	35 T Howard Blackwood
14 Syracuse	45 TE L.J. Smith / Chris Loomis
17 Miami	42 QB Ryan Hart / Ryan Cubit / Ted Trump
17 Temple	20 HB Clarence Pittman / Markis Facyson
0 Notre Dame	42 FB Ray Pilch
14 Boston College	44 DL Raheem Orr / Val Barnaby
	DL Will Burnett / Davon Clark
	DL Gary Gibson
	DL Ryan Neill / Alfred Peterson
	LB Brian Hohmann
	LB Gary Brackett
	LB Brian Bender
	DB Brandon Haw / Eddie Grimes
	DB Nate Jones / DeWayne Thompson
	DB Shawn Seabrooks
	DB Jarvis Johnson / Jason Grant

RUSHING: Facyson 124/398y, Pittman 126/316y, Nugent 29/125y
PASSING: Trump 71-155/740y, 4TD, 45.8%
  Cubit 64-141/657y, 5TD, 45.4%
  Hart 51-111/479y, 2TD, 45.9%
RECEIVING: Smith 32/384y, Martin 30/284y, Hobbs 27/324y
SCORING: Ryan Sands (K) 33pts, Smith 20pts, Martin 18pts

2003 5-7

24 Buffalo	10 WR Shawn Tucker / Marcus Daniels
28 Michigan State	44 WR Tres Moses / Jerry Andre
36 Army	21 T Mike Williamson
48 Navy	27 G Brian Duffy / Rich McManis
22 Virginia Tech	48 C Marty Pyszczymuka
19 West Virginia	34 G John Glass
32 Pittsburgh	42 T Ron Green / Sameeh McDonald
30 Temple	14 TE Ray Pilch / Clark Harris
31 Connecticut	38 QB Ryan Hart
25 Boston College	35 RB Justise Hairston / Markis Facyson
10 Miami	34 FB Brian Leonard
24 Syracuse	7 DL Raheem Orr
	DL Gary Gibson
	DL Luis Rivas / David Harley
	DL Alfred Peterson / Piana Lukabu
	LB Brian Bender / Brian Hohmann
	LB Will Gilkison / DeVraun Thompson
	LB William Beckford / Brad Cunningham
	DB Nate Jones
	DB Brandon Haw / Eddie Grimes
	DB Jason Grant / Jason Nugent
	DB Jarvis Johnson / Bryan Durango

RUSHING: Leonard 213/880y, Hairston 137/550y,
  Facyson 42/207y
PASSING: Hart 234-398/2714y, 15TD, 58.8%
RECECIVING: Leonard 53/488y, Moses 52/536y, Tucker 50/726y
SCORING: Leonard 86pts, Ryan Sands (K) 60pts, Hairston 48pts

2004 4-7

19 Michigan State	14 WR Tres Moses
24 New Hampshire	35 WR Chris Baker / Marcus Daniels
29 Kent State	21 T Ron Green / Jeremy Zuttah
31 Syracuse	41 G Brian Duffy
37 Vanderbilt	34 C Ray Pilch
16 Temple	6 G John Glass
17 Pittsburgh	41 T Saheem McDonald / Pedro Sosa
30 West Virginia	35 TE Clark Harris / Sam Johnson
10 Boston College	21 QB Ryan Hart
21 Navy	54 RB Justise Hairston / Clarence Pittman
35 Connecticut	41 FB Brian Leonard
	DL Val Barnaby / Piana Lukabu
	DL Gary Gibson
	DL David Harley
	DL Ryan Neill / Alfred Peterson
	LB Terry Bynes / William Gilkison
	LB DeVraun Thompson
	LB William Beckford
	DB Joe Porter
	DB Derrick Roberson
	DB Ron Girault / Jason Nugent
	DB Jarvis Johnson

RUSHING: Leonard 199/732y, Hairston 53/146y
PASSING: Hart 295-453/3154y, 17TD, 65.1%
RECEIVING: Moses 81/1056y, Leonard 61/518y, Harris 53/725y
SCORING: Jeremy Ito (K) 73pts, Leonard 54pts, Moses 32pts

2005 7-5

30 Illinois	33 WR Tres Moses
38 Villanova	6 WR Shawn Tucker
17 Buffalo	3 T Pedro Sosa
37 Pittsburgh	29 G Jeremy Zuttah / Mike Fladell
14 West Virginia	27 C Darnell Stapleton
31 Syracuse	9 G John Glass / Mike Gilmartin
26 Connecticut	24 T Sameeh McDaniel
31 Navy	21 TE Clark Harris / Sam Johnson
31 South Florida	45 QB Ryan Hart / Mike Teel
5 Louisville	56 TB Ray Rice
44 Cincinnati	9 FB Brian Leonard
40 Arizona State	45 DL Val Barnaby / Jamal Westerman
	DL Ramel Meekins
	DL Luis Rivas
	DL Ryan Neill
	LB Chenry Lewis / Terry Byrnes
	LB Devraun Thompson
	LB Quintero Frierson / Will Gilkison
	DB Derrick Roberson / Joe Porter
	DB Corey Barnes / Manny Collins
	DB Ron Girault
	DB Courtney Greene

RUSHING: Rice 195/1120y, Leonard 173/740y
PASSING: Hart 155-255/2135y, 18TD, 60.8%
  Teel 51-101/683y, 2TD, 50.5%
RECEIVING: Leonard 55/568y, Moses 45/758y, Harris 38/584y
SCORING: Leonard 102pts, Jeremy Ito (K) 100pts,
  Moses & Rice 30pts

2006 11-2

21 North Carolina	16 WR Tiquan Underwood/ Willie Foster
33 Illinois	0 WR Dennis Campbell / Kenny Britt
24 Ohio University	7 T Pedro Sosa
56 Howard	7 G Mike Fladell
22 South Florida	20 C Darnell Stapleton
34 Navy	0 G Cam Stephenson
20 Pittsburgh	10 T Jeremy Zuttah
24 Connecticut	13 TE Clark Harris / Sam Johnson
28 Louisville	25 QB Mike Teel
11 Cincinnati	30 TB Ray Rice
38 Syracuse	7 FB Brian Leonard
39 West Virginia	41 DL William Beckford
37 Kansas State ■	10 DL Ramel Meekins
	DL Eric Foster
	DL Jamal Westerman
	LB Brandon Renkart
	LB Devraun Thompson
	LB Quintero Frierson
	DB Manny Collins / Derrick Roberson
	DB Jason McCourty
	DB Ron Girault / Devin McCourty
	DB Courtney Greene

RUSHING: Rice 335/1794y, Leonard 93/423y,
  Kordell Young (TB) 29/138y
PASSING: Teel 164-296/2135y, 12TD, 55.4%
RECEIVING: Leonard 38/294y, Harris 34/493y, Britt 29/440y
SCORING: Rice 120pts, Jeremy Ito (K) 107pts, Leonard 30pts

2007 8-5

38 Buffalo	3 WR Kenny Britt / Tim Brown
41 Navy	24 WR Tiquan Underwood
59 Norfolk State	0 T Pedro Sosa
24 Maryland	34 G Mike Fladell
23 Cincinnati	28 C Ryan Blaszczyk
38 Syracuse	14 G Anthony Davis / Kevin Haslem (T)
30 South Florida	27 T Jeremy Zuttah
3 West Virginia	13 TE Chris Rudanovic / Kevin Brock
19 Connecticut	38 QB Mike Teel / Jabu Lovelace
41 Army	6 TB Ray Rice
20 Pittsburgh	16 FB Andres Morales / Jack Corcoran
38 Louisville	41 DL Jamal Westerman
52 Ball State ■	30 DL Eric Foster
	DL Pete Tverdov / Vantrise Studivant
	DL George Johnson / Gary Watts
	LB Kevin Malast / Joe Lefeged (DB)
	LB Damaso Munoz
	LB Brandon Renkart
	DB Jason McCourty
	DB Devin McCourty
	DB Courtney Greene
	DB Ron Girault / Glen Lee

RUSHING: Rice 380/2012y, Lovelace 82/332y
  Mason Robinson (TB) 36/202y
PASSING: Teel 203-349/3147y, 20TD, 58.2%
RECEIVING: Underwood 65/1100y, Britt 62/1232y, Rice 25/239y
SCORING: Rice 150pts, Jeremy Ito (K) 120pts, Britt 48pts

2008 8-5

7 Fresno State	24 WR Kenny Britt
12 North Carolina	44 WR Tiquan Underwood / Tim Brown
21 Navy	23 T Anthony Davis
38 Morgan State	0 G Caleb Ruch / Howard Barbieri
17 West Virginia	24 C Ryan Blasczcyk
12 Connecticut	13 G Art Forst / Mike Gilmartin (T)
54 Pittsburgh	10 T Kevin Haslem (G)
35 Syracuse	34 TE Kevin Brock / Shamar Graves
49 South Florida	17 QB Mike Teel
30 Army	16 RB Kordell Young / Jourdan Brooks
63 Louisville	3 FB/WR Jack Corcoran / Dennis Campbell
29 N. Carolina St. ■	14 DL George Johnson
	23 DL Pete Tverdov / Blair Bines
	DL Alex Silvestro
	DL Jamal Westerman / Jonathan Freeny
	LB Ryan D'Imperio
	LB Kevin Malast
	LB Manny Abreu / Damaso Munoz
	DB Jason McCourty
	DB Devin McCourty / Zaire Kitchen
	DB Courtney Greene
	DB Joe Lefeged

RUSHING: Young 142/554y, Brooks 100/516y
  Joe Martinek (RB) 76/404y
PASSING: Teel 243-396/3418y, 25TD, 61.4%
RECEIVING: Britt 87/1371y, Underwood 40/494y,
  Brown 27/565y
SCORING: San San Te (K) 81pts, Britt 48pts, Brown 42pts

2009 9-4

15 Cincinnati	47 WR Tim Brown
45 Howard	7 WR Mohamed Sanu / Tim Wright
23 Fla. International	15 T Anthony Davis / Desmond Stapleton
34 Maryland	13 G Art Forst
42 Texas Southern	0 C Ryan Blaszczyk
17 Pittsburgh	24 G Howard Barbieri / Desmond Wynn
27 Army	10 T Kevin Haslem
28 Connecticut	24 TE Shamar Graves / D.C. Jefferson
31 South Florida	0 QB Tom Savage / Dom Natale
13 Syracuse	31 RB Joe Martinek / Jourdan Brooks
34 Louisville	14 FB Jack Corcoran
21 West Virginia	24 DL George Johnson / Jonathan Freeny
45 Central Florida ■	24 DL Charlie Noonan / Eric LeGrand
	DL Scott Vallone
	DL Alex Silvestrio
	LB Antonio Lowery / Steve Beauharnais
	LB Ryan D'Imperio
	LB Damaso Munoz
	DB David Rowe / Brandon Bing
	DB Devin McCourty
	DB Zaire Kitchen / Billy Anderson
	DB Joe Lefeged / Khaseem Greene

RUSHING: Martinek 206/967y, Sanu 62/346y, Brooks 60/282y
PASSING: Savage 149-285/2211y, 14TD, 52.3%
RECEIVING: Brown 55/1150y, Sanu 51/639y, Graves 14/159y
SCORING: San San Te (K) 93pts, Brown & Martinek 54pts,
  Sanu 52pts

2010 4-8

31 Norfolk State	0 WR Mark Harrison / Keith Stroud
19 Florida Intl.	14 WR Mohamed Sanu (QB)
13 North Carolina	17 WR/TE Jeremy Deering(RB)/Evan Lampert
14 Tulane	17 T Desmond Stapleton
27 Connecticut	24 G Desmond Wynn
23 Army	20 C Howard Barbieri
21 Pittsburgh	41 G Caleb Ruch / Antwan Lowery (FB)
27 South Florida	28 T Art Forst (TE) / Devon Watkins
10 Syracuse	13 TE D.C. Jefferson
38 Cincinnati	69 QB Chas Dodd / Tom Savage
13 Louisville	40 RB Joe Martinek / Jordan Thomas
14 West Virginia	35 DL Alex Silvestro
	DL Charlie Noonan
	DL Scott Vallone
	DL Jonathan Freeny
	LB Manny Abreu / Ka'Lial Glaud
	LB Steve Beauharnais
	LB Antonio Lowery
	DB David Rowe / Duron Harmon
	DB Brandon Bing / Marcus Cooper
	DB Khaseem Greene
	DB Joe Lefeged

RUSHING: Thomas 95/417y, Deering 77/352y, Sanu 59/309y
PASSING: Dodd 123-223/1637y, 11TD, 55.2%
  Savage 43-83/521y, 2TD, 51.8%
  Sanu 6-9/160y, 3TD, 66.7%
RECEIVING: Harrison 44/829y, Sanu 44/418y, Stroud 17/157y
SCORING: San San Te (K) 68pts, Harrison 54pts, Sanu 38pts

SOUTH CAROLINA

University of South Carolina (Founded 1801)
Columbia, South Carolina
Nickname: Gamecocks
Colors: Garnet and Black
Stadium: Williams-Brice (1934) 80,250
Conference Affiliations: Southern (1933-52), Atlantic Coast (1953-70), Independent (1971-91), Southeastern (1992-present)

CAREER RUSHING YARDS	Attempts	Yards
George Rogers (1977-80)	954	5205
Brandon Bennett (1991-94)	681	3055
Harold Green (1986-1989)	702	3005
Steve Wadiak (1948-51)	543	2878
Thomas Dendy (1982-85)	494	2767
Johnnie Wright (1977-81)	552	2589
Jay Lynn Hodgin (1972-74)	515	2478
Kevin Long (1973-76)	447	2372
Clarence Williams (1974-76)	440	2311
Cory Boyd (2003-07)	464	2267

CAREER PASSING YARDS	Comp.-Att.	Yards
Todd Ellis (1986-89)	747-1350	9953
Steve Taneyhill (1992-95)	753-1245	8782
Stephen Garcia (2008-10)	528-903	6753
Blake Mitchell (2004-07)	482-794	5992
Anthony Wright (1995-98)	432-796	5681
Phil Petty (1998-2001)	454-861	5652
Tommy Suggs (1968-70)	355-672	4916
Bobby Fuller (1990-91)	373-634	4896
Dondrial Pinkins (2000-04)	265-504	3459
Jeff Grantz (1972-75)	231-455	3440

CAREER RECEIVING YARDS	Catches	Yards
Kenny McKinley (2005-08)	207	2781
Sterling Sharpe (1983, 1985-87)	169	2497
Zola Davis (1995-98)	164	2354
Alshon Jeffery (2009-10)	134	2280
Sidney Rice (2005-06)	142	2233
Robert Brooks (1988-91)	156	2211
Jermale Kelly (1997-2000)	153	2181
Philip Logan (1974-77)	105	2063
Fred Zeigler (1967-69)	146	1876
Troy Williamson (2002-04)	91	1754

SEASON RUSHING YARDS	Attempts	Yards
George Rogers (1980)	324	1894
George Rogers (1979)	311	1681
Marcus Lattimore (2010)	249	1197
Kevin Long (1975)	190	1133
Duce Staley (1996)	218	1116

SEASON PASSING YARDS	Comp.-Att.	Yards
Todd Ellis (1987)	241-432	3206
Steve Taneyhill (1995)	261-389	3094
Stephen Garcia (2010)	224-349	3059
Todd Ellis (1986)	205-340	3020
Stephen Garcia (2009)	239-432	2862

SEASON RECEIVING YARDS	Catches	Yards
Alshon Jeffery (2010)	88	1517
Sidney Rice (2005)	70	1143
Sterling Sharpe (1986)	74	1106
Sidney Rice (2006)	72	1090
Kenny McKinley (2007)	77	968

GAME RUSHING YARDS	Attempts	Yards
Brandon Bennett (1991 vs. E. Tenn. St.)	31	278
Jeff Grantz (1973 vs. Ohio University)	N/A	260
Steve Wadiak (1950 vs. Clemson)	N/A	256

GAME PASSING YARDS	Comp.-Att.	Yards
Steve Taneyhil (1995 vs. Miss. State)	38-44	473
Steve Taneyhill (1994 vs. E. Carolina)	39-58	451
Todd Ellis (1987 vs. East Carolina)	N/A	425

GAME RECEIVING YARDS	Catches	Yards
Troy Williamson (2004 vs. South Florida)	6	210
Zola Davis (1998 vs. Vanderbilt)	14	206
Fred Zeigler (1968 vs. Virginia)	12	199

GREATEST COACH

He was an Ohio guy who played for the slumping program of the University of Cincinnati. He was a sure-handed but slow-footed, do-it-all kind of running back for the New York Giants for 14 seasons. And 10 years after leaving the NFL, Joe Morrison became a successful coach at a school where a lot of people thought no one could succeed.

South Carolina has a tremendously loyal fan base which has packed their stadium for many years of up and down football. (As an old joke used to go: "What do Billy Graham and Sparky Woods have in common? Answer: They are the only two people who can get 72,000 people at Williams-Brice Stadium to stand up and shout 'Oh! Jesus!'")

Despite the emotional support of Gamecock fans, two coaches with national championships on their resumes—Paul Dietzel and Lou Holtz—left Columbia with losing records. Even current coach Steve Spurrier, another former national champion coach, has experienced mixed results at South Carolina.

The sad part of the Joe Morrison story is that he died of a heart attack after the 1988 season at the relatively young age of 51. He was just beginning to pull the Gamecocks out of the doldrums with three bowl trips in six years and seasons of 10-2, 8-4, and 8-4, but he never was able to see just how far South Carolina could soar.

SOUTH CAROLINA'S 55 GREATEST SINCE 1953

OFFENSE

WIDE RECEIVER: Robert Brooks, Zola Davis, Sidney Rice, Sterling Sharpe, Troy Williamson, Fred Zeigler
TIGHT END: Clyde Bennett
TACKLE: Sam DeLuca, Melvin Paige, Chuck Slaughter, Travelle Wharton
GUARD: Steve Courson, Frank Mincevich, Del Wilkes
CENTER: Leon Cunningham
QUARTERBACK: Todd Ellis, Steve Taneyhill, Anthony Wright
RUNNING BACK: Brandon Bennett, Thomas Dendy, George Rogers, Derek Watson
FULLBACK: Andrew Pinnock, Stanley Pritchett, Warren Muir

DEFENSE

END: Kalimba Edwards, Andrew Provence
TACKLE: John LeHeup, Don Somma
NOSE GUARD: Roy Hart, Langston Moore
LINEBACKER: John Abraham, Tommy Addison, J.D. Fuller, Corey Miller, Garry Mott, James Seawright
CORNERBACK: Sheldon Brown, Bobby Bryant, Deandre Eiland, Dick Harris, Dunta Robinson, Rick Sanford
SAFETY: Brad Edwards, Rashad Faison, Bryant Gilliard, Ko Simpson

SPECIAL TEAMS

RETURN SPECIALISTS: King Dixon, Horace Smith
PLACE KICKER: Collin Mackie
PUNTER: Max Runager

MULTIPLE POSITIONS:

TAILBACK-WIDE RECEIVER- KICK RETURNER: Ryan Brewer

TWO-WAY PLAYER:

HALFBACK-DEFENSIVE BACK: Alex Hawkins

PERFORMANCE FORMULA:
SOUTH CAROLINA'S 10 BEST SEASONS

1987	1.3928	16 of 69
1984	1.3797	11 of 70
1953	1.3602	16 of 69
2001	1.3368	18 of 70
1979	1.3249	16 of 70
2010	1.3196	21 of 71
1980	1.3097	22 of 70
2006	1.2847	27 of 72
2000	1.2751	25 of 70
1973	1.1853	23 of 70

SOUTH CAROLINA GAMECOCKS

Year	W-L-T	AP Poll	Conference Standing	Toughest Regular Season Opponents	Coach (Record at School)	Bowl Games		
1953	7-3		3t	Duke 7-2-1, Maryland 10-0, West Virginia 8-1	Rex Enright			
1954	6-4		4	Army 7-2, West Virginia 8-1, Maryland 7-2-1, Duke 7-2-1	Rex Enright			
1955	3-6		7	Navy 6-2-1, Clemson 7-3, Maryland 10-0, Duke 7-2-1	Rex Enright (64-69-7)			
1956	7-3		3	Miami 8-1-1, Clemson 7-1-2	Warren Giese			
1957	5-5		7	Duke 6-2-2, Texas 6-3-1, Clemson 7-3, NC State 7-1-2	Warren Giese			
1958	7-3		2	Army 8-0-1, North Carolina 6-4, Clemson 8-2,	Warren Giese			
1959	6-4		4t	Georgia 9-1, Clemson 8-2, Miami 6-4	Warren Giese			
1960	3-6-1		5	Duke 7-3, Georgia 6-4, Miami 6-4, NC State 6-3-1	Warren Giese (28-21-1)			
1961	4-6		5t	Duke 7-3, LSU 9-1, Maryland 7-3	Marvin Bass			
1962	4-5-1		4t	Northwestern 7-2, Duke 8-2, Maryland 6-4, Clemson 6-4	Marvin Bass			
1963	1-8-1		6	NC State 8-2, North Carolina 8-2, Memphis State 9-0-1	Marvin Bass			
1964	3-5-2		6	Georgia 6-3-1, Nebraska 9-1, Florida 7-3	Marvin Bass			
1965	5-5		1t	Tennessee 7-1-2, LSU7-3, Alabama 8-1-1	Marvin Bass (17-29-4)			
1966	1-9		7	Georgia 9-1, Tennessee 7-3, Alabama 10-0	Paul Dietzel			
1967	5-5		3	Georgia 7-3, Florida State 7-2-1, Alabama 8-1-1	Paul Dietzel			
1968	4-6		4	Georgia 8-0-2, Florida State 8-2, Virginia 7-3, Virginia Tech 7-3	Paul Dietzel			
1969	7-4		1	Georgia 5-4-1, Florida State 6-3-1, Tennessee 9-1	Paul Dietzel	Peach	3 West Virginia	14
1970	4-6-1		4	Georgia Tech 8-3, North Carolina 8-3, Tennessee 10-1	Paul Dietzel			
1971	6-5		-	Florida State 8-3, Georgia 10-1, Tennessee 9-2	Paul Dietzel			
1972	4-7		-	Georgia Tech 6-4-1, NC State 7-3-1, Florida State 7-4	Paul Dietzel			
1973	7-4		-	Houston 10-1, LSU 9-2, NC State 8-3	Paul Dietzel			
1974	4-7		-	Houston 8-3, North Carolina 7-4, NC State 9-2, Clemson 7-4	Paul Dietzel (42-53-1)			
1975	7-5		-	Georgia Tech 7-4, Georgia 9-2, NC State 7-3-1	Jim Carlen	Tangerine	7 Miami (Ohio)	20
1976	6-5		-	Georgia 10-1, Baylor 7-3-1, Notre Dame 8-3	Jim Carlen			
1977	5-7		-	Miami (Ohio) 10-1, North Carolina 8-2-1, Clemson 8-2-1	Jim Carlen			
1978	5-5-1		-	Georgia 9-1-1, Georgia Tech 7-4, NC State 8-3	Jim Carlen			
1979	8-4		-	North Carolina 7-3-1, Florida St. 11-0, Wake Forest 8-3, Clemson 8-3	Jim Carlen	Fame	14 Missouri	24
1980	8-4		-	Southern Calif. 8-2-1, Michigan 9-2, Georgia 11-0	Jim Carlen	Gator	9 Pittsburgh	37
1981	6-6		-	Georgia 10-1, Pittsburgh 10-1, North Carolina 9-2, Clemson 11-0	Jim Carlen (45-36-1)			
1982	4-7		-	Georgia 11-0, LSU 8-2-1, Florida State 8-3, Clemson 9-1-1	Richard Bell (4-7)			
1983	5-6		-	North Carolina 8-3, Georgia 9-1-1, Clemson 9-1-1	Joe Morrison			
1984	10-2	11	-	Georgia 7-4, Notre Dame 7-4, Florida State 7-3-1, Clemson 7-4	Joe Morrison	Gator	14 Oklahoma State	21
1985	5-6		-	Michigan 9-1-1, Georgia 7-3-1, Florida State 8-3	Joe Morrison			
1986	3-6-2		-	Miami 11-0, Georgia 8-3, Nebraska 9-2, Va. Tech 8-2-1, NC St. 8-2-1	Joe Morrison			
1987	8-4	15	-	Georgia 8-3, Nebraska 10-1, Clemson 9-2, Miami 11-0	Joe Morrison	Gator	13 LSU	30
1988	8-4		-	Georgia 8-3, NC State 7-3-1, Florida State 10-1, Clemson 9-2	Joe Morrison (39-28-2)	Liberty	10 Indiana	34
1989	6-4-1		-	Duke 8-3, West Virginia 8-2-1, Florida State 9-2, Clemson 9-2	Sparky Woods			
1990	6-5		-	Georgia Tech 10-0-1, Florida State 9-2, Clemson 9-2	Sparky Woods			
1991	3-6-2		-	East Carolina 10-1, NC State 9-2, Florida State 10-2, Clemson 9-1-1	Sparky Woods			
1992	5-6		E4	Georgia 9-2, Alabama 12-0, Tennessee 8-3, Florida 8-4	Sparky Woods			
1993	4-7		E4t	Tennessee 9-1-1, Florida 9-2, Clemson 8-3	Sparky Woods (24-28-3)			
1994	7-5		E4	Mississippi State 8-3, Tennessee 7-4, Florida 9-1-1	Brad Scott	Carquest	24 West Virginia	21
1995	4-6-1		E4	Arkansas 7-4, Tennessee 10-1, Florida 11-0, Clemson 8-3	Brad Scott			
1996	6-5		E3	Auburn 7-4, Tennessee 9-2, Florida 10-1, Clemson 7-4	Brad Scott			
1997	5-6		E4	Georgia 9-2, Tennessee 10-1, Flordia 9-2, Clemson 7-4	Brad Scott			
1998	1-10		E6	Marshall 10-1, Arkansas 9-2, Tennessee 11-0, Florida 9-2	Brad Scott (23-32-1)			
1999	0-11		E6	Mississippi State 9-2, Tennessee 9-2, Florida 9-2	Lou Holtz			
2000	8-4	19	E2t	Georgia 7-4, Miss. St. 7-4, Tennessee 8-3, Florida 9-2, Clemson 9-2	Lou Holtz	Outback	24 Ohio State	7
2001	9-3	13	E3t	Georgia 8-3, Tennessee 10-1, Florida 9-2, Clemson 6-5	Lou Holtz	Outback	31 Ohio State	28
2002	5-7		E4	Georgia 11-1, LSU 8-4, Tennessee 8-4, Arkansas 9-3, Florida 8-4	Lou Holtz			
2003	5-7		E4	Georgia 10-2, Tennessee 10-2, LSU 11-1, Mississippi 9-3	Lou Holtz (33-37)			
2004	6-5		E3t	Georgia 9-2, Tennessee 9-2, Florida 7-4	Steve Spurrier			
2005	7-5		E2t	Georgia 10-2, Alabama 9-2, Auburn 9-2, Florida 8-3	Steve Spurrier	Independence	31 Missouri	38
2006	8-5		E5	Auburn 10-2, Tennessee 9-3, Arkansas 10-2, Florida 11-1	Steve Spurrier	Liberty	44 Houston	36
2007	6-6		E4t	Georgia 10-2, LSU 10-2, Tennessee 9-3, Florida 9-3	Steve Spurrier			
2008	7-6		E3t	Georgia 9-3, Mississippi 8-4, Florida 12-1	Steve Spurrier	Outback	10 Iowa	31
2009	7-6		E4t	Mississippi 8-4, Alabama 13-0, Florida 12-1	Steve Spurrier	Papajohn's.com	7 Connecticut	20
2010	9-5	22	E1	Auburn 13-0, Alabama 9-3, Arkansas 10-2	Steve Spurrier (44-33)	Chick-fil-A	17 Florida State	26

TOTAL: 315-317-13 .4984 (47 of 70)

Bowl Games since 1953: 4-11 .2667 (69 of 70)

GREATEST TEAM SINCE 1953: Joe Morrison's 1984 Gamecocks team that went 10-2 was a terrific selection. But, because only two years earlier, South Carolina had gone 0-11, Lou Holtz's 2001 squad that upset Ohio State for a second straight year in the Outback Bowl is judged to be the school's best in 54 seasons. The Gamecocks of 2001 won nine and lost three against a tough SEC schedule (plus Boise State, Bowling Green, and Clemson) that won .5789 percent of its games.

1953 7-3

7	Duke	20	E Joe Silas / Spec Granger
25	Citadel	0	T Harry Lovell / Charlie Camp
19	Virginia	0	G Bob King
27	Furman	13	C Leon Cunningham / Hugh Bell
14	Clemson	7	G Frank Mincevich / Bill Covington
6	Maryland	24	T Hugh Merck
18	North Carolina	0	E Clyde Bennett
20	West Virginia	14	QB Johnny Gramling / Hal Lewis
49	Wofford	0	HB Gene Wilson / Mike Caskey
13	Wake Forest	19	HB Carl Brazell / Blackie Kincaid
			FB Bill Wohrman / Crosby Lewis

RUSHING: Wilson 77/502y, Caskey 55/340y
PASSING: Gramling 68-132/1045y, 8TD, 51.5%
RECEIVING: Bennett 23/413y
SCORING: Wilson 36pts

1954 6-4

34	Army	20	E Buddy Frick / Joe Silas
6	West Virginia	26	T Harry Lovell
27	Furman	7	G Bill Covington / Bill Floyd
13	Clemson	8	C Leon Cunningham / Hugh Bell
0	Maryland	20	G Frank Mincevich
19	North Carolina	21	T Sam DeLuca / Crosby Lewis
27	Virginia	0	E Spec Granger / Larry Gosnell
7	Duke	26	QB Mackie Prickett / Hal Lewis
20	Wake Forest	19	HB Mike Caskey / Bill Tarrer
19	Citadel	6	HB Carl Brazell / Tommy Woodlee
			FB Bill Wohrman / Jim Jarrett

RUSHING: Caskey 83/556y
PASSING: Prickett 68-116/682y, 1TD, 58.6%
RECEIVING: Brazell 29/241y
SCORING: Prickett (QB-K) 43pts

1955 3-6

26	Wofford	7	E Buddy Frick / Billy Rivers
19	Wake Forest	34	T Hugh Merck
0	Navy	26	G Dick Covington / Nelson Weston
19	Furman	0	C Hugh Bell / Harry Crowley
14	Clemson	28	G Tommy Addison / Bill Floyd
0	Maryland	27	T Sam DeLuca / Crosby Lewis
14	North Carolina	32	E Julius Derrick / Larry Gosnell
7	Duke	41	QB Mackie Prickett / Hal Lewis
21	Virginia	14	HB Mike Caskey / Bobby Drawdy
			HB Carl Brazell
			FB Bobby Barrett / Jim Jarrett

RUSHING: Brazell 46/305y, Caskey 65/274y
PASSING: Prickett 35-73/513y, 47.9%
RECEIVING: Brazell 11/162y, Frick 7/195y
SCORING: Brazell 30pts

1956 7-3

26	Wofford	13	E Buddy Frick / Billy Rivers
7	Duke	0	T John Kompara / Tony Byers
6	Miami	14	G Jimmy Merck / Nelson Weston
14	North Carolina	0	C Lawton Rogers / Dwight Keith
27	Virginia	13	G Tommy Addison / Rick Ericsson
0	Clemson	7	T Sam DeLuca
13	Furman	6	E Julius Derrick / Weems Baskin
7	N. Carolina St.	14	QB Mackie Prickett
13	Maryland	0	HB King Dixon / Frank Destino
13	Wake Forest	0	HB Alex Hawkins
			FB Bobby Barrett / Don Johnson

RUSHING: Dixon 136/655y, Hawkins 130/566y,
Johnson 76/415y
PASSING: Prickett 15-44/193y, 34.1%
RECEIVING: Hawkins 10/91y, Dixon 7/126y, Derrick 7/108y
SCORING: Hawkins (HB-K) 41pts, Dixon (HB-K) 24pts, Prickett 18pts

1957 5-5

14	Duke	26	E Julius Derrick / Jimmy Duncan
26	Wofford	0	T Don Rogers / Ed Pitts
27	Texas	21	G Nelson Weston / Corky Gaines
58	Furman	13	C Charlie Johnson / Lawton Rogers
0	Clemson	13	G Tommy Addison / Jimmy Merck
6	Maryland	10	T John Kompara
6	North Carolina	28	E Eddie Beall / Buddy Mayfield
13	Virginia	0	QB Bobby Bunch / Steve Satterfield
26	N. Carolina St.	29	HB King Dixon / Frank Destino
26	Wake Forest	7	HB Alex Hawkins / Heyward King
			FB Don Johnson / John Saunders

RUSHING: Hawkins 109/450y, Johnson 100/405y, Dixon 73/272y
PASSING: Hawkins 9-12/153y, 2TD, 75.0%
RECEIVING: Derrick 6/126y, King 4/41y, Hawkins 4/37y
SCORING: Hawkins (HB-K) 35pts, Dixon (HB-K) 30pts

1958 7-3

8	Duke	0	E Jimmy Duncan / Jerry Frye
8	Army	45	T Don Rogers / Bill Jerry
24	Georgia	14	G Corky Gaines
0	North Carolina	6	C Lawton Rogers / Dwight Keith
26	Clemson	6	G Jimmy Merck / Jake Bodkin
6	Maryland	10	T Ed Pitts / John Kompara
32	Furman	7	E Bucky Walker / Weems Baskin
28	Virginia	14	QB Bobby Bunch
12	N. Carolina St.	7	HB King Dixon / Joe Gomes
24	Wake Forest	7	HB Alex Hawkins
			FB John Saunders / Bob Farmer

RUSHING: Saunders 128/653y, Hawkins 100/474y, Dixon 79/323y
PASSING: Bunch 13-23/177y, 56.5%, Hawkins 8-13/120y, 61.5%
RECEIVING: Dixon 10/189y, Hawkins 10/141y, Walker 4/25y
SCORING: Hawkins (HB-K) 42pts, Saunders 36pts, 2 with 32pts

1959 6-4

12	Duke	7	E Jerry Frye / Jimmy Duncan
30	Furman	0	T Bill Jerry / Kirk Phares
30	Georgia	14	G Jack Ashton / Don Miles
6	North Carolina	19	C John Gordon
0	Clemson	27	G Jake Bodkin
22	Maryland	6	T Ed Pitts / Sam Fewell
32	Virginia	20	E Jack Pitt / Bob Drost
6	Miami	26	QB Steve Satterfield / Buddy Bennett
12	N. Carolina St.	7	HB Joe Gomes / Steve Kopian
20	Wake Forest	43	HB Ken Norton / Jimmy Hunter
			FB John Saunders / Phil Lavoie

RUSHING: Lavoie 122/522y, Norton 79/396y, Gomes 49/263y
PASSING: Satterfield 17-44/180y, 2TD, 38.6%
RECEIVING: Hunter 9/60y, Gomes 6/69y, Pitt 5/72y
SCORING: Lavoie 60pts, Satterfield 38pts, Norton 22pts

1960 3-6-1

0	Duke	31	E Jerry Frye
6	Georgia	38	T Wayne Shiflet / Frank Staley
6	Miami	21	G Don Miles
22	North Carolina	6	C Jim Nemeth / John Gordon
0	Maryland	15	G Jake Bodkin / Howard Sohm
6	LSU	35	T Sam Fewell / Harold Jones
2	Clemson	12	E Jack Pitt / Bob Drost
8	N. Carolina St.	8	QB Jim Costen / Dave Sowell
41	Wake Forest	20	HB Reggie Logan / Billy Gambrell
26	Virginia	0	HB Ken Kilrea / Jimmy Hunter
			FB Bob Farmer

RUSHING: Buddy Bennett (QB) 80/401y, Sowell 58/355y,
Day 50/178y
PASSING: Sowell 17-38/190y, TD, 44.7%,
Costen 16-47/130y, 0TD, 34.0%
RECEIVING: Gambrell 12/106y, Melvin Harris (HB) 10/100y,
Logan 6/54y
SCORING: Bennett 18pts, Costen & Pitt 14pts,

1961 4-6

6	Duke	7	E John Caskey / Larry Rucker
10	Wake Forest	7	T Joel Goodrich
14	Georgia	17	G Dave Adam
0	LSU	42	C Richard Lomas / Everette Crats
0	N.Carolina	17	G John Jones
20	Maryland	10	T Jim Moss / Tommy Gibson
20	Virginia	28	E Ken Lester / Bob Drost
21	Clemson	14	QB Jim Costen / Dave Sowell
14	N. Carolina St.	38	HB Billy Gambrell / Jack Morris
23	Vanderbilt	7	HB Henry Crosby
			FB Carl Huggins / Dick Day

RUSHING: Day 100/400y, Gambrell 75/327y, Costen 72/157y
PASSING: Costen 61-146/764y, 3TD, 41.8%
RECEIVING: Gambrell 24/243y, Caskey 15/267y, Crosby 11/169y
SCORING: Gambrell 32pts, Dave Findley (K) & Costen 24pts

1962 4-5-1

20	Northwestern	37	E John Caskey / Larry Rucker
8	Duke	21	T Dwaine Godfrey / Joel Goodrich
7	Georgia	7	G John Jones
27	Wake Forest	6	C Richard Lomas / Everette Crafts
14	North Carolina	19	G Tommy Gibson / Dave Pope
11	Maryland	13	T Jim Moss / Joe Prehodka
40	Virginia	6	E Ken Lester / Roy Chatman
17	N. Carolina St.	6	QB Dan Reeves
26	Detroit	13	HB Billy Grambrell/Marty Rosen/Larry Gill
17	Clemson	20	HB Sammy Anderson / Charley Williams
			FB Dick Day / Ed Holler / Pete Divenere

RUSHING: Gambrell 105/582y, Reeves 148/471y,
Divenere 71/265y, Day 57/254y
PASSING: Reeves 66-131/930y, 7TD, 50.4%
RECEIVING: Gambrell 21/226y, Anderson 14/239y
SCORING: Gambrell & Reeves 50pts, Caskey & Anderson 18pts

1963 1-8-1

14	Duke	22	E Billy Nies / Larry Rucker
21	Maryland	13	T Len Sears / Bobby Collins
7	Georgia	27	G Mike Kirkpatrick / Forbes Patterson
6	N. Carolina St.	18	C Johnny King
10	Virginia	10	G Ed Hertwig / Dan Legat
0	N. Carolina	7	T Tom Gibson / Jerry Soles
0	Tulane	20	E Roy Chatman / Doug Senter
0	Memphis State	9	QB Dan Reeves
19	Wake Forest	20	HB Marty Rosen
20	Clemson	24	HB Larry Gill / Ronnie Lamb
			FB Pete Divenere / Carl Huggins

RUSHING: Rosen 86/382y, Huggins 62/283y, Divenere 35/128y
PASSING: Reeves 62-146/657y, 5TD, 42.5%
RECEIVING: Gill 14/188y, Wilburn 11/153y, Rosen 10/89y
SCORING: Rosen 24pts, Wilburn 18pts,
Huggins & Jack McCathern (K) 12pts

1964 3-5-2

9	Duke	9	WR J.R. Wilburn
6	Maryland	24	T Len Sears / Dennis Darling
7	Georgia	7	G Dan Legat / Wilbur Hodge
6	Nebraska	28	C Jon Linder / Bobby Gunnels (LB)
0	Florida	37	G Ed Hertwig / Paul Phillips (DL)
6	North Carolina	24	T Bobby Collins / Steve Cox
14	N. Carolina St.	17	TE Doug Senter / John Breeden
17	Citadel	14	QB Dan Reeves / Jim Rogers (DB)
23	Wake Forest	13	TB Marty Rosen / Jule Smith
7	Clemson	3	WB Larry Gill / Ronnie Lamb

RUSHING: Branson 85/276y, Rosen 65/273y, Reeves 103/232y
PASSING: Reeves 83-164/974y, 4TD, 50.6%
RECEIVING: Wilburn 21/236y, Gill 18/207y, Smith 13/188y
SCORING: Rosen 30pts, Reeves 18pts,
Jack McCathern (K) 17pts

1965 5-5

13	Citadel	3	WR J.R. Wilburn
15	Duke	20	T Bobby Collins / Dennis Darling
13	N. Carolina St.	7	G Dave Berry / John Dyer
3	Tennessee	24	C Johnny Gobble / Jon Linder
38	Wake Forest	7	G Billy Nelson
7	LSU	21	T Randy Harbour
14	Maryland	27	TE Wayne Tucker / Mike Ragin
17	Virginia	7	QB Mike Fair / Jim Rogers
14	Alabama	35	TB Ben Garnto / Jule Smith
17	Clemson	16	WB Ronnie Lamb
			FB Phil Branson / Jimmy Killen
			DL Doug Senter / Leroy Bailey
			DL Steve Cox
			DL Bill Dickens
			DL Len Sears / Jerry Soles
			DL Butch Williams / Bob McCullough
			LB Dan Legat / Bob Cole
			LB Bobby Gunnels
			DB Benny Galloway
			DB Bobby Bryant (WB) / Paul Harmon
			DB Dave Truby
			DB Butch Reeves / Stan Juk

RUSHING: Garnto 90/437y, Branson 108/415y,
Bennie Galloway (TB) 34/137y
PASSING: Fair 89-175/1049y, 2TD, 50.9%
RECEIVING: Wilburn 38/562y, Garnto 16/156y, Lamb 9/92y
SCORING: Jimmy Poole (K) 32pts, Smith 18pts, 5 with 12pts

1966 1-9

12 LSU	28 WR Johnny Gregory / Mac Perry
7 Memphis State	16 T Hyrum Pierce / Bob Wehmeyer
0 Georgia	7 G Dave Berry
31 N.Carolina St.	21 C Jimmy Gobble / Tom Wingard
6 Wake Forest	10 G Donnie Rose
17 Tennessee	29 T Paul Phillips / Billy Nelson
2 Maryland	14 TE Randy Harbour / Ken Thornton
10 Florida State	32 QB Mike Fair / Ted Wingard
0 Alabama	24 TB Benny Galloway / Jimmy Killen
10 Clemson	35 WB Ben Garnto
	FB Jim Mulvihill / Curtis Williams
	DL Gene Schwarting
	DL Jerry Soles / Paul Phillips
	DL Charles Thompson / Ron Hunch
	DL Don Somma / Joe Komoroski
	DL Lynn Hodge / Leroy Bailey
	LB Bob Cole / David Grant
	LB Bill Dickens
	DB Toy McCord / Wally Medlin
	DB Bobby Bryant
	DB Wally Orrel / Tim Bice
	DB Stan Juk / Gary Musgrove

RUSHING: Galloway 130/580y, Garnto 99/440y, Fair 88/190y
PASSING: Fair 31-82/467y, 2TD, 37.8%,
 Wingard 19-48/268y, TD, 39.6%
RECEIVING: Garnto 19/242y, Gregory 17/299y,
 Galloway 16/211y
SCORING: Jimmy Poole (K) 19pts, Garnto 18pts, 3 with 12pts

1967 5-5

34 Iowa State	3 WR Fred Zeigler / Andy Chavous
16 North Carolina	10 T Bob Mauro / Bob Wehmeyer
21 Duke	17 G Bob Morris / Johnny Glass
0 Georgia	21 C Jimmy Gobble
0 Florida State	17 G Tom Wingard
24 Virginia	23 T Hyrum Pierce / John Dyer
31 Maryland	0 TE Johnny Gregory / John King
21 Wake Forest	35 QB Mike Fair
0 Alabama	17 HB Ben Garnto / Rudy Holloman
12 Clemson	23 HB Roy Don Reeves / Fletcher Spigner
	FB Warren Muir
	DL Gene Schwarting / Billy Tharp
	DL Joe Komoroski
	DL Dave Grant / John Tominach
	DL Don Somma
	DL Dave Lucas
	LB Bob Cole / Ron Buch
	LB Tim Bice / Don Buckner
	DB Toy McCord / Butch Reeves
	DB Pat Watson / Bob White
	DB Wally Orrel / Wally Medlin
	DB Jim Mulvihill / Candler Boyd

RUSHING: Muir 188/805y, Garnto 88/274y, Fair 133/258y
PASSING: Fair 79-165/970y, TD, 47.9%
RECEIVING: Zeigler 35/370y, Gregory 13/226y, Reeves 9/125y,
 Holloman 9/119y
SCORING: Fair 42pts, Muir 36pts, Jimmy Poole (K) 25pts

1968 4-6

7 Duke	14 WR Fred Zeigler
32 North Carolina	27 WR Johnny Gregory
20 Georgia	21 T Dave DeCamilla
12 N. Carolina St.	36 G Don Buckner
19 Maryland	21 C Bob Mauro
28 Florida State	35 G Chris Bank
49 Virginia	28 T Tony Fusaro
34 Wake Forest	17 TE Gene Schwarting
6 Virginia Tech	17 QB Tommy Suggs / Randy Yoakum
7 Clemson	3 HB Rudy Holloman / Benny Galloway
	FB Warren Muir
	DL Lynn Hodge
	DL John Coleman / Jimmy Poston
	DL Dave Grant (LB)
	DL Rusty Ganas
	DL Dave Lucas
	LB Tim Bice (DL) / Benny Padgett
	LB Al Usher
	DB Tyler Hellams
	DB Pat Watson
	DB Roy Don Reeves
	DB Wally Orrel

RUSHING: Holloman 111/530y, Muir 112/460y,
 Galloway 76/251y
PASSING: Suggs 110-207/1544y, 13TD, 53.1%
RECEIVING: Zeigler 59/848y, Gregory 20/268y,
 Holloman 20/238y
SCORING: Zeigler & Muir 36pts, Billy DuPre (K) 29pts

1969 7-4

27 Duke	20 WR Fred Zeigler
14 North Carolina	6 WR Ken Walkup / Tom Trevillian
16 Georgia	41 T Dave DeCamilla
21 N. Carolina St.	16 G Tony Fusaro
17 Virginia Tech	16 C Ken Ross
17 Maryland	0 G Chris Bank
9 Florida State	34 T Rick Hipkins
14 Tennessee	29 TE Doug Hamrick / Billy Freeman
24 Wake Forest	9 QB Tommy Suggs / Randy Yoakum
27 Clemson	13 TB Rudy Holloman / Billy Ray Rice
3 West Virginia ■	14 FB Warren Muir
	DL Lynn Hodge
	DL Jimmy Poston
	DL Mack Lee Tharpe / Pat Kohout
	DL Rusty Ganas
	DL Dave Lucas
	LB Don Buckner / Benny Padgett
	LB Gregg Crabb / Al Usher
	DB Dick Harris
	DB Pat Watson / Don Bailey
	DB Jimmy Nash / Tyler Hellams
	DB Bo Davies / Candler Boyd

RUSHING: Muir 223/969y, Holloman 116/402y, Rice 31/130y
PASSING: Suggs 109-196/1342y, 7TD, 55.6%
RECEIVING: Zeigler 52/658y, Holloman 26/350y,
 Hamrick 19/240y
SCORING: Billy DuPre (K) 51pts, Muir 48pts, Holloman 42pts

1970 4-6-1

20 Georgia Tech	23 WR Tom Trevillian / Jackie Brown
43 Wake Forest	7 WR Jim Mitchell / Mike Haggard
7 N. Carolina St.	7 T Dave DeCamilla
24 Virginia Tech	7 G Richie Moye
35 North Carolina	21 C Danny Dyches
15 Maryland	21 G Chris Bank / Dennis Ford
13 Florida State	21 T Rick Hipkins / Bill Boyte
34 Georgia	52 TE Doug Hamrick / Billy Freeman
18 Tennessee	20 QB Tommy Suggs
38 Duke	42 TB Billy Ray Rice / Chuck Mimms
38 Clemson	32 FB Tommy Simmons / Bob Miranda
	DL Don Brant
	DL Jimmy Poston
	DL Pat Kohout / Mack Lee Tharpe
	DL John LeHeup / Rusty Ganas
	DL Joe Wingard
	LB Al Usher / Benny Padgett
	LB Greg Crabb
	DB Dick Harris
	DB Jimmy Nash
	DB Bo Davies
	DB Candler Boyd / Tyler Hellams

RUSHING: Simmons 165/572y, Rice 83/401y, Miranda 36/154y
PASSING: Suggs 136-269/2030y, 14TD, 50.6%
RECEIVING: Mitchell 41/842y, Hamrick 38/418y,
 Haggard 21/357y
SCORING: Billy DuPre (K) 58pts, Simmons 48pts, Mitchell 44pts

1971 6-5

24 Georgia Tech	7 WR Jackie Brown
12 Duke	28 WR Jim Mitchell
24 N. Carolina St.	6 T Darrell Austin
7 Memphis State	3 G Richie Moye
34 Virginia	14 C Steve Wade
35 Maryland	6 G Dennis Ford
18 Florida State	49 T Dave Cash
0 Georgia	24 TE Billy Freeman
6 Tennessee	35 QB Glenn Morris
24 Wake Forest	7 TB Carlton Haywood
7 Clemson	17 FB Tommy Simmons
	DL Bob Rose
	DL Joe Regalis
	DL Pat Kohout
	DL John LeHeup
	DL Monty Matthews
	LB Rick Brown
	LB Gregg Crabb
	DB Dick Harris
	DB Jimmy Nash
	DB Bo Davies
	DB Tyler Hellams

RUSHING: Simmons 126/430y
PASSING: Morris 104-229/1313y, 45.4%
RECEIVING: Mitchell 47/618y
SCORING: Simmons 42 pts

1972 4-7

16 Virginia	24 WR Jackie Brown
6 Georgia.Tech	34 WR Mike Haggard / Eddie Muldrow
0 Mississippi	21 T Roger Toy
34 Memphis State	7 G Rick Anthony
41 Appalachian St.	7 C Jimmy Privette
8 Miami (Ohio)	21 G Jerry Witherspoon
24 N. Carolina St.	42 T Buck Thompson
35 Wake Forest	3 TE Marty Woolbright
20 Virginia Tech	45 QB Bobby Grossman / Bill Troup
24 Florida State	21 TB Jay Lynn Hodgin
6 Clemson	7 FB Tom Armein
	DL Bob Roe
	DL Darrell Austin
	DL Dana Carpenter
	DL John LeHeup
	DL Tony Pepper / Gary McLaren
	LB Rick Brown
	LB Phil Wallace
	DB Tom Zipperly
	DB Thad Rowe
	DB C.A. Wilson
	DB Neville Files

RUSHING: Hodgin 188/675y, Parson 56/172y, Cregar 37/155y,
 Randy Spinks (TB) 17/129y, Grossman 46/127y
PASSING: Grossman 61-117/884y, 11TD, 52.1%,
 Troup 56-129/758y, 4TD, 43.4%
RECEIVING: Haggard 46/639y, Brown 32/436y,
 Woolbright 15/175y, Muldrow 14/272y
SCORING: Haggard & Hodgin 48pts, Tommy Bell (K) 35pts

1973 7-4

41 Georgia Tech	28 WR Mike Haggard / Mike Farrell
19 Houston	27 WR Eddie Muldrow
11 Miami (Ohio)	13 T Buck Thompson
27 Virginia Tech	24 G Rick Anthony
28 Wake Forest	12 C Darrell Austin
30 Ohio University	22 G Jerry Witherspoon
29 LSU	33 T Dave Cash
35 N. Carolina St.	56 TE Marty Woolbright
35 Appalachian St.	14 QB Jeff Grantz
42 Florida State	12 HB Jay Lynn Hodgin
32 Clemson	20 HB Randy Spinks
	DL Monty Matthews
	DL Dana Carpenter
	DL Andy Levantis
	DL Gary McLaren
	LB Grahl Phillips
	LB Bill Cregar
	LB Garry Mott
	DB Henry Laws
	DB Tom Zipperly
	DB C.A. Wilson
	DB Thad Rowe

RUSHING: Hodgin 172/862y
PASSING: Grantz 62-121/864y, 51.2%
RECEIVING: Haggard 46/639y
SCORING: Bobby Marino (K) 65pts

1974 4-7

20 Georgia Tech	35 WR Mike Farrell
14 Duke	20 WR Eddie Muldrow
14 Georgia	52 T Buck Thompson
14 Houston	24 G Brad Kline
17 Virginia Tech	31 C Mike McCabe
10 Mississippi	23 G Jerry Witherspoon
31 North Carolina	23 T Bubba Shugart
27 N. Carolina St.	42 TE Steve Blackman
21 Appalachian St.	18 QB Jeff Grantz
34 Wake Forest	21 HB Jay Lynn Hodgin
21 Clemson	39 HB Clarence Williams / Randy Chastain
	DL Tony Pepper
	DL Stan James
	DL Kerry DePasquale
	DL Russ Manzari
	LB Grahl Phillips
	LB Gary McLaren
	LB Bill Cregar
	DB Henry Laws
	DB Tom Zipperly / Keith Colson
	DB Bill Currier
	DB Zeb Shue

RUSHING: Hodgin 154/941y, Long 81/490y, Bass 107/460y
PASSING: Grantz 39-95/642y, 3TD, 41.1%,
 Bass 18-39/245y, 0TD, 46.2%
RECEIVING: Farrell 18/258y, Thomas 16/278y, Muldrow 15/346y
SCORING: Hodgin 40pts, Williams 30pts,
 Grantz & Bobby Marino (K) 24pts

1975 7-5

23 Georgia Tech
24 Duke
20 Georgia
24 Baylor
41 Virginia
35 Mississippi
6 LSU
21 N. Carolina St.
34 Appalachian St.
37 Wake Forest
56 Clemson
7 Miami (Ohio) ■

17 WR Philip Logan
16 WR Scott Thomas / Stevie Stephens
28 T E.Z. Smith
13 G Brad Kline
14 C Mike McCabe
29 G Steve Courson
24 T Jerome Provence
28 TE Brian Nemeth
39 QB Jeff Grantz
26 TE Clarence Williams / Randy Chastain
20 FB Kevin Long
20 DL Scott Blackman / John Dantonio
DL Joe McGregor
DL Bubba Shugart / David Prezioso
DL Kerry DePasquale
DL Russ Manzari / John Dantonio
LB Garry Mott
LB Ricky Payne / John Green
DB Henry Laws / Lance Garrett
DB Jacyn Adamski
DB Bill Currier
DB Andy Nelson

RUSHING: Long 190/1133y, Williams 190/1073y, Grantz 141/473y
PASSING: Grantz 120-216/1815y, 16TD, 55.6%
RECEIVING: Logan 39/716y, Stephens 24/308y, Thomas 15/204y
SCORING: Grantz 72pts, Bobby Marino (K) 64pts, Williams 60pts

1976 6-5

21 Appalachian St.
27 Georgia Tech
24 Duke
12 Georgia
17 Baylor
35 Virginia
10 Mississippi
6 Notre Dame
27 N. Carolina St.
7 Wake Forest
9 Clemson

10 WR Philip Logan / Stevie Stephens
17 WR Zion McKinney / Gene Wilson
6 T Jerome Provence
20 G Tami Tarbush
18 C Danny Clancy
7 G Steve Courson / Tony Penny
7 T Mike Fralic
13 TE Don Stewart / Ben Cornett
7 QB Ron Bass
10 HB Clarence Williams
28 FB Kevin Long / Steve Dorsey
DL Scott Blackman
DL Joe McGregor
DL Bubba Shugart / Roscoe Watson
DL Charles Barber / Kerry DePasquale
DL Russ Manzari / John Dantonio
LB David Prezioso
LB John Green / Tim Singleton
DB Lance Garrett
DB Rick Sanford / Mike Tisdale
DB Bill Currier
DB Jacyn Adamski

RUSHING: Williams 174/873y, Long 174/746y, McKinney 33/237y, Dorsey 61/233y
PASSING: Bass 110-199/1320y, 9TD, 55.3%
RECEIVING: Logan 41/678y, Williams 23/180y, Stephens 14/165y
SCORING: Britt Parrish (K) 53pts, Long 50pts, Logan 36pts

1977 5-7

32 Appalachia● St.
17 Georgia Tech
42 Miami (Ohio)
13 Georgia
19 East Carolina
21 Duke
10 Mississippi
0 North Carolina
3 N. Carolina St.
24 Wake Forest
27 Clemson
7 Hawaii

17 WR Philip Logan / John Bailey
0 WR Zion McKinney / Gene Wilson
19 T Jerome Provence
15 G Tami Tarbush / Fred David
16 C Danny Clancy
25 G Tony Penny
7 T Mike Fralic
17 TE Don Stewart / Willie Scott
7 QB Ron Bass
14 TB Spencer Clark / George Rogers
31 FB Steve Dorsey / Johnnie Wright
24 DL Scott Blackman
DL Joe McGregor / Chuck Allen
DL Bill Janus / Roscoe Watson
DL Steve Burnish / Fred Sinclair
DL John Dantonio / Roger Woolbright
LB David Prezioso / Bob Orkis
LB Tim Singleton
DB Mike Tisdale
DB Rick Sanford
DB Lance Garrett / Robert Perlotte
DB Curtis Boyd / Nat Veal

RUSHING: Clark 135/777y, Rogers 143/623y, Dorsey 94/418y
PASSING: Bass 82-176/1140y, 4TD, 46.6%
RECEIVING: Logan 21/415y, McKinney 15/178y, Rogers 14/185y
SCORING: Britt Parrish (K) 53pts, Clark 48pts, Dorsey 36pts

1978 5-5-1

45 Furman
14 Kentucky
12 Duke
27 Georgia
3 Georga Tech
24 Ohio University
18 Mississippi
22 North Carolina
13 N. Carolina St.
37 Wake Forest
23 Clemson

10 WR John Bailey
14 WR Zion McKinney
16 T Chuck Slaughter / Bill Lane
10 G Fred David
6 C Danny Clancy
7 G Steve Gettel / Tony Penny
17 T George Schechterly
24 TE Ben Cornett / Willie Scott
22 QB Garry Harper
14 TB Johnnie Wright / Spencer Clark
41 FB George Rogers / Steve Dorsey
DL Brett Boyd / Roger Woolbright
DL Steve Bernish
DL Bill Janus / W.T. Williams
DL Fred Sinclair / Chuck Allen
DL John Dantonio
LB Tim Singleton
LB Scott Wade
DB Andy Hastings / Mark Bridges
DB Rick Sanford
DB Robert Perlotte
DB Lou Biondi / Nat Veal

RUSHING: Rogers 176/1006y, Wright 176/903y, Dorsey 53/220y
PASSING: Harper 62-135/776y, 7TD, 45.9%
RECEIVING: McKinney 19/281y, Scott 13/127y, Wright 9/54y
SCORING: Wright 42pts, Rogers 38pts, Eddie Leopold (K) 35pts

1979 8-4

0 North Carolina
24 W. Michigan
35 Duke
27 Georgia
23 Oklahoma State
21 Mississippi
17 Notre Dame
30 N. Carolina St.
7 Florida State
35 Wake Forest
13 Clemson
14 Missouri ■

28 WR Horace Smith
7 WR Zion McKinney
0 T Chuck Slaughter
20 G Fred David
16 C Quay Farr
14 G Steve Gettel
18 T George Schechterly
28 TE Ben Cornett / Willie Scott
27 QB Garry Harper
14 TB George Rogers
9 FB Steve Dorsey / Johnnie Wright
24 DL Brett Bond
DL Steve Bernish
DL Fred Sinclair
DL Chuck Allen
DL Arthur Broussard
LB Tim Singleton
LB Scott Wade
DB Andy Hastings
DB Mark Bridges
DB Robert Perlotte
DB Lou Biondi

RUSHING: Rogers 311/1681y
PASSING: Harper 73-143/929y, 51.0%
RECEIVING: McKinney 23/387y
SCORING: Rogers 54pts

1980 8-4

37 Pacific
73 Wichita State
13 Southern Cal
17 Michigan
30 N.Carolina St.
20 Duke
49 Cincinnati
10 Georgia
45 Citadel
39 Wake Forest
6 Clemson
9 Pittsburgh ■

0 WR Tim Gillespie / John Bailey
0 WR Horace Smith
23 T George Schechterly / Rubin Proctor
14 G Joe Doyle
10 C Mark Austin
7 G Steve Gettel
7 T Chuck Slaughter
13 TE Willie Scott / Ben Cornett
24 QB Garry Harper
28 TB George Rogers
27 FB Johnnie Wright / Carl West
37 DL Phil Ellis
DL Andrew Provence
DL Emanuel Weaver
DL Chuck Allen / Donnie McDaniel
DL Hal Henderson
LB Walt Kater / J.D. Fuller
LB Ed Baxley / Mike Durrah
DB Harry Skipper / Chuck Finney
DB Mark Bridges / Troy Thomas
DB Robert Perlotte / Gary Burger
DB Pat Bowen

RUSHING: Rogers 324/1894y, Wright 90/481y, West 33/341y
PASSING: Harper 90-177/1266y, 5TD, 50.8%
RECEIVING: Scott 34/469y, Smith 26/455y, Gillespie 17/249y
SCORING: Rogers 84pts, Eddie Leopard (K) 78pts, Harper 36pts

1981 6-6

23 Wake Forest
13 Mississippi
17 Duke
0 Georgia
28 Pittsburgh
28 Kentucky
21 Virginia
31 North Carolina
20 N. Carolina St.
21 Pacific
13 Clemson
10 Hawaii

6 WR Ira Hillary / Jerry Aubin
20 WR Horace Smith
3 T Tim Dyches (G) / Ricky Elliott
24 G Cas Danielowski / Joe Doyle
42 C Mark Austin
14 G Del Wilkes
3 T Chuck Slaughter / Fred Chalmers
13 TE Chris Corley / DeWayne Chivers
12 QB Gordon Beckham / Terry Bishop
23 TB Johnnie Wright / Kent Hagood
29 FB Dominique Blasingame / Todd Berry
33 DL Phil Ellis
DL Andrew Provence
DL Emanuel Weaver / Rickey Hagood
DL Mike Vargo / Frank Wright
DL Karey Johnson / Hal Henderson
LB J.D. Fuller / James Sumpter
LB James Seawright / Mike Durrah
DB Harry Skipper / Chuck Finney
DB Troy Thomas
DB Robert Perlotte / Tony Rambo
DB Pat Bowen

RUSHING: Wright 212/834y, Hagood 83/336y, Blasingame 60/238y
PASSING: Beckham 92-180/1221y, 9TD, 50.8%
RECEIVING: Smith 27/451y, Blasingame 17/135y, Hillary 14/248y
SCORING: Mark Fleetwood (K) 57pts, Berry 36pts, Wright 30pts

1982 4-7

41 Pacific
30 Richmond
17 Duke
18 Georgia
37 Cincinnati
23 Furman
6 LSU
3 N. Carolina. St.
26 Florida State
17 Navy
6 Clemson

6 WR Chris Wade
10 WR Ira Hillary
30 T Rusty Russell
34 G Cas Danielowski
10 C Kenny Gil
28 G Tim Dyches
14 T Jim Walsh
33 TE Chris Corley
56 QB Gordon Beckham / Bill Bradshaw
14 TB Thomas Dendy / Quinton Lewis
24 FB Dominique Blasingame / Todd Berry
DL Andrew Provence
DL Rickey Hagood
DL Frank Wright / Paul Martin
LB Phil Ellis
LB J.D. Fuller / James Seawright
LB Paul Vogel / Mike Durrah
LB Skip Minton / Karey Johnson
DB Harry Skipper
DB Earl Johnson / Troy Thomas
DB Chuck Finney
DB Pat Bowen / Glenn LeGrande

RUSHING: Dendy 140/848y, Berry 134/577y, Blasingame 56/226y, Lewis 52/206y
PASSING: Beckham 63-146/725y, 7TD, 43.2%, Bradshaw 58-119/536y, 2TD, 48.7%
RECEIVING: Corley 24/163y, Hiillary 19/332y, Wade 14/286y, Berry 14/121y
SCORING: Mark Fleetwood (K) 70pts, Dendy 24pts, 3 with 18pts

1983 5-6

8 North Carolina
24 Miami (Ohio)
31 Duke
13 Georgia
38 Southern Cal
6 Notre Dame
6 LSU
31 N. Carolina St.
30 Florida State
31 Navy
13 Clemson

24 WR Eric Poole / Chris Wade
3 WR Ira Hillary / Bill Bradshaw
14 T Jeff Teague
31 G Jim Walsh
14 C Tom Garner
30 G Cas Danielowski
20 T Rusty Russell
17 TE Dominique Blasingame
45 QB Allen Mitchell
7 RB Thomas Dendy / Quinton Lewis
22 RB Kent Hagood / Todd Berry
DL James Sumpter
DL Paul Martin
DL Rickey Hagoood
DL Willie McIntee
LB J.D. Fuller
LB Mike Durragh
LB Kenneth Robinson
DB Chris Major
DB Earl Johnson
DB Bryant Gilliard
DB Gary Ryan

RUSHING: Dendy 133/725y, Hagood 105/653y, Lewis 50/243y
PASSING: Mitchell 80-172/1142y, 5TD, 46.5%
RECEIVING: Hillary 30/422y, Blasingame 19/309y, Dendy 18/172y, Poole 15/240y
SCORING: Mark Fleetwood (K) 59pts

1984 10-2

31 Citadel	24 WR Eric Poole / Bill Bradshaw
21 Duke	0 WR Ira Hillary
17 Georgia	10 T Carl Womble
49 Kansas State	17 G Jim Walsh
45 Pittsburgh	21 C Tom Garner
36 Notre Dame	32 G Del Wilkes
42 East Carolina	20 T Bill Barnhill
35 N. Carolina St.	28 TE Chris Corley
38 Florida State	26 QB Allen Mitchell / Mike Hold
21 Navy	38 RB Thomas Dendy / Raynard Brown
22 Clemson	21 RB Quinton Lewis / Kent Hagood
14 Oklahoma St.■	21 DL James Sumpter
	DL James Wright
	DL Glenn Woodley
	DL Willie McIntee
	LB James Seawright
	LB Paul Vogel
	LB Carl Hill
	DB Chris Major
	DB Otis Morris
	DB Bryant Gilliard
	DB Joe Brooks

RUSHING: Dendy 103/634y, Lewis 97/572y, Hagood 82/551y
PASSING: Hold 64-137/1385y, 8TD, 46.7%, Mitchell 53-99/780y, 7TD, 53.5%
RECEIVING: Hillary 27/564y, Corley 19/389y, Bradshaw 15/305y
SCORING: Scott Hagler (K) 69pts, Dendy 48pts, Hold 32pts

1985 5-6

56 Citadel	17 WR Ryan Bethea / Eric Poole
20 Appalachian St.	13 WR Sterling Sharpe / Hardin Brown
3 Michigan	34 T Charles Gowan
21 Georgia	35 G Ray Carpenter
7 Pittsburgh	42 C Leonard Burton
28 Duke	7 G David Poinsett
52 E.Carolina	10 T Buddy Quarles / Dru Mims
7 N. Carolina St.	21 TE Danny Smith
14 Florida State	56 QB Mike Hold / Allen Mitchell
34 Navy	31 RB Thomas Dendy / Anthony Smith
17 Clemson	24 RB Kent Hagood / Raynard Brown
	DL Willie McIntee / Ricky Daniels
	DL Tom Chalkin / David Hodge
	DL Fitzgerald Davis
	DL Tony Guyton / Derrick Little
	LB Kenneth Robinson
	LB Glenn Peacock / Willie Hill
	LB Carl Hill / Shed Diggs
	DB Chris Major
	DB Robert Robinson
	DB Greg Philpot / Ken Sally
	DB Joe Brooks

RUSHING: Dendy 118/560y, Hagood 95/474y, A. Smith 55/386y
PASSING: Hold 107-208/1596y, 7TD, 51.4%
RECEIVING: Sharpe 32/471y, D. Smith 22/379y, Poole 18/397y
SCORING: Scott Hagler (K) 59pts, Dendy, Hold & Hagood 36pts

1986 3-6-2

14 Miami	34 WR Danny Smith / Kevin White
20 Virginia	30 WR Ryan Bethea
45 W. Carolina	24 T Curtis Hill / Kenny Haynes
26 Georgia	31 G Charles Gowan / Paul Shivers
24 Nebraska	27 C Woody Myers
27 Virginia Tech	27 G Deron Farina / David Poinsett
38 East Carolina	3 T Mark Fryer
22 N. Carolina St.	23 QB Todd Ellis
28 Florida State	45 WB Raynard Brown / Vic McConnell
48 Wake Forest	21 WB Sterling Sharpe
21 Clemson	21 RB Anthony Smith / Harold Green
	DL Kevin Hendrix / Kurt Wilson
	DL Fitzgerals Davis / Tommy Chaikin
	DL Roy Hart / Brendon McCormack
	DL Derrick Frazier / Willie McIntee
	LB Kenneth Robinson / Curtis Kilgore
	LB Derrick Little / Matt McKernan
	LB Shed Diggs / Zip Zanders
	DB Chris Major / Ron Rabune
	DB Robert Robinson
	DB Greg Philpot / Ken Sally
	DB Brad Edwards / Ron Rabune

RUSHING: A. Smith 96/469y, Green 108/388y, Sharpe 23/104y
PASSING: Ellis 205-340/3020y, 20TD, 60.3%
RECEIVING: Sharpe 74/1106y, Brown 28/289y, Bethea 27/572y
SCORING: Sharpe 72pts, Scott Hagler (K) 67pts, Green 42pts

1987 8-4

24 Appalachian St.	3 WR Danny Smith
31 W. Carolina	6 WR Ryan Bethea
6 Georgia	13 T John Morrell
21 Nebraska	30 G Charles Gowan
40 Va. Tech	10 C Woody Myers / Randy Harwell
58 Virginia	10 G Calvin Stephehs / Paul Shivers
34 East Carolina	12 T Mark Fryer
48 N. Carolina St.	7 QB Todd Ellis
30 Wake Forest	0 WB Sterling Sharpe / Carl Platt
20 Clemson	7 WB Kevin White / Hardin Brown
16 Miami	20 RB Harold Green / Keith Bing
13 LSU■	30 DL Scott Winsdor / Patrick Hinton
	DL Kurt Wilson / Tommy Chaikin
	DL Roy Hart / Tim High
	DL Brendon McCormack / Derrick Frazier
	DL Shed Diggs / Kevin Hendrix
	LB Matt McKernan
	LB Derrick Little
	DB Robert Robinson / Stephane Williams
	DB Norman Floyd
	DB Brad Edwards / Ron Rabune
	DB Greg Philpot / Ken Sally

RUSHING: Green 229/1022y, Bing 54/305y, Greg Welch (RB) 21/132y
PASSING: Ellis 241-432/3206y, 10TD, 55.8%
RECEIVING: Sharpe 62/915y, Bethea 45/689y, White 42/353y
SCORING: Collin Mackie (K) 113pts, Green 96pts, Sharpe 54pts

1988 8-4

31 North Carolina	10 WR Robert Brooks
38 W. Carolina	0 WR Eddie Miller
17 E. Carolina	0 T Ike Harris / Kenny Haynes
23 Georgia	10 G Paul Shivers / Charles Gowan
35 Appalachian St.	9 G Randy Harwell
26 Virginia Tech	24 G Calvin Stephens / Dany Branch
0 Georgia Tech	34 T Mark Fryer
23 N. Carolina St.	7 QB Todd Ellis
0 Florida State	59 WB Carl Platt
19 Navy	7 RB Harold Green
10 Clemson	29 FB Keith Bing / Mike Dingle
10 Indiana■	34 DL Scott Windsor (LB) / Kevin Hendrix
	DL Marty Dye / Theartis Woodard
	DL Tim High / Kurt Wilson
	DL Derrick Frazier / Patrick Blackwell
	DL David Taylor
	LB Patrick Hinton / Mike Tolbert
	LB Matt McKernan / Corey Miller
	LB Derrick Little
	DB Robert Robinson
	DB Stephane Williams / Dale Campbell
	DB Ron Rabune/Pat Turner/Mike Conway

RUSHING: Green 164/606y, Dingle 92/386y, Bing 56/196y
PASSING: Ellis 198-391/2353y, 9TD, 50.6%
RECEIVING: Green 36/315y, Brooks 34/508y, Platt 34/460y
SCORING: Collin Mackie (K) 82pts, Dingle & Brooks 30pts

1989 6-4-1

27 Duke	21 WR Robert Brooks
17 Virginia Tech	17 WR Eddie Miller / Carl Platt
21 West Virginia	45 T Ike Harris
21 Georgia Tech	10 G Kenny Haynes / Antoine Rivens
24 Georgia	20 C Curt High / Hal Hamrick
47 East Carolina	14 G Dany Branch
24 W. Carolina	3 T Calvin Stephens
10 N. Carolina St.	20 TE David Hodge
10 Florida State	35 QB Todd Ellis
27 North Carolina	20 TB Harold Green / Mike Dingle
0 Clemson	45 FB George Rush / Ken Watson
	DL Corey Miller / Troy Duke
	DL Tim High
	DL Curtis Godwin / Patrick Blackwell
	DL Marty Dye / Trent Simpson
	LB Scott Windsor / Mike Conway
	LB Robert Gibson / Joe Reaves
	LB Patrick Hinton
	LB David Taylor
	DB Erik Anderson
	DB Keith McDonald / Antonio Walker
	DB Leon Harris / Stephane Williams

RUSHING: Green 201/989y, Dingle 110/502y, Albert Haynes (TB) 65/293y
PASSING: Ellis 103-187/1374y, 10TD, 55.1%
RECEIVING: Brooks 34/471y, Miller 17/342y, Platt 17/308y, Rush 17/129y
SCORING: Collin Mackie (K) 59pts, Dingle & Green 36pts

1990 6-5

21 Duke	10 WR Robert Brooks
27 North Carolina	5 WR Eddie Miller
35 Virginia Tech	24 T Ike Harris / Rich Sweet
6 Georgia Tech	27 G Antoine Rivens
37 East Carolina	7 C Hal Hamrick
35 Citadel	38 G Jay Killen
29 N. Carolina St.	38 T Calvin Stephens / Scott Cooley
10 Florida State	41 TE Charles Steward / Mathew Campbell
38 Southern Illinois	13 QB Bobby Fuller
15 Clemson	24 TB Mike Dingle
29 West Virginia	10 FB Ken Watson
	DL Corey Miller
	DL Kurt Wilson
	DL Marty Dye / Cedric Bembery
	DL Gerald Dixon
	LB Joe Reaves / Eric Brown
	LB Patrick Hinton
	LB Ernest Dixon
	DB Antonio Walker
	DB Cedric Surratt
	DB Keith McDonald / Bru Pender
	DB Leon Harris

RUSHING: Dingle 187/746y
PASSING: Fuller 171-294/2372y, 13TD, 58.2%
RECEIVING: Brooks 33/548y
SCORING: Collin Mackie (K) 76pts

1991 3-6-2

24 Duke	24 WR Robert Brooks
16 West Virginia	21 WR Eddie Miller / Asim Penny
28 Virginia Tech	21 T Ernest Dye
20 East Carolina	31 G Antoine Rivens
55 E. Tenn. State	7 C Jay Killen
12 Louisiana Tech	12 G Kenny Farrell / Vincent Dinkins
23 Georgia Tech	14 T Rich Sweet / Kevin Rosenkrans
21 N. Carolina St.	38 TE Mike Whitman / Mathew Campbell
10 Florida State	38 QB Bobby Fuller
17 North Carolina	21 TB Brandon Bennett / Albert Haynes
24 Clemson	41 FB Leroy Jeter / Rob DeBoer
	DL Bobby Brown / David Turnipseed
	DL Cedric Bembery
	DL Marty Dye / Troy Duke
	LB Gerald Dixon / Joe Reaves
	LB Ernest Dixon
	LB Eric Brown
	LB Robert Gibson / Keith Franklin
	DB Toby Cates / Frank Adams
	DB Jerry Inman
	DB Bru Pender / Norman Greene
	DB Tony Watkins

RUSHING: Bennett 154/702y, DeBoer 73/285y, Haynes 33/139y
PASSING: Fuller 202-340/2524y, 15TD, 59.4%
RECEIVING: Brooks 33/548y, Miller 31/592y, Pitchko 31/470y
SCORING: Bennett 54pts, Brooks & Miller 30pts

1992 5-6

6 Georgia	28 WR Toby Cates / Asim Penny
7 Arkansas	45 T Ernest Dye
18 East Carolina	20 G Antoine Rivens
9 Kentucky	13 C Vincent Dinkins
7 Alabama	48 G Kenny Farrell
21 Mississippi St.	6 T Corey Louchiey / James Dexter
21 Vanderbilt	17 TE Boomer Foster
24 Tennessee	23 TE Mike Whitman / Mathew Campbell
14 LSU	13 QB Steve Taneyhill
9 Florida	14 TB Brandon Bennett / Mike Reddick
24 Clemson	13 FB Rob DeBoer
	DL David Turnipseed
	DL Cedric Bembery
	DL Jahmal Pettiford / Mike Washington
	DL Eric Sullivan
	LB Eric Brown
	LB Ernest Dixon
	LB Hank Campbell / Lawrence Mitchell
	DB Frank Adams / Reggie Richardson
	DB Jerry Inman / Ron Nealy
	DB Norman Greene
	DB Tony Watkins / Shawn Sterling

RUSHING: Bennett 152/646y
PASSING: Taneyhill 86-162/1272y, 7TD, 53.1%
RECEIVING: Bennett 22/194y
SCORING: Marty Simpson (K) 50pts

1993 4-7

23	Georgia	21
17	Arkansas	18
34	Louisiana Tech	3
17	Kentucky	21
6	Alabama	17
27	East Carolina	3
0	Mississippi St.	23
22	Vanderbilt	0
3	Tennessee	55
26	Florida	37
13	Clemson	16

WR Toby Cates / Terrell Harris
WR Chris Alford / Corey Bridges
T Luther Dixon
G John Harrison
C Vincent Dinkins
G James Dexter / Anton Gunn
T Corey Louchiey
TE Mathew Campbell / James Cummings
QB Steve Taneyhill
TB Brandon Bennett / Mike Reddick
FB Rob DeBoer / Stanley Pritchett
DL Stacy Evans / David Turnipseed
DL Eric Sullivan
DL Jahmal Pettiford
LB Mike Landry / Hank Camobell
LB James Flowers
LB Eric Brown / Chris Rumph
LB Ernest Dixon / Aubrey Brooks
DB Frank Adams / Terry Cousin
DB Jerry Inman / Ron Nealy
DB Norman Greene
DB Tony Watkins

RUSHING: Bennett 194/853y
PASSING: Taneyhill 149-291/1930y, 6TD, 51.2%
RECEIVING: Cates 27/541y
SCORING: Reed Morton (K) 57pts

1994 7-5

21	Georgia	24
14	Arkansas	0
31	Louisiana Tech	6
23	Kentucky	9
18	LSU	17
42	East Carolina	56
36	Mississippi St.	41
19	Vanderbilt	16
22	Tennessee	31
17	Florida	48
33	Clemson	7
24	West Virginia■	21

WR Toby Cates / Marcus Robinson
WR Darrel Nicklow / Corey Bridges
T Randy Wheeler
G Delvin Herring
C Vincent Dinkins / Paul Beckwith
G Luther Dixon
T James Dexter
TE Boomer Foster
QB Steve Taneyhill
TB Brandon Bennett / Mike Reddick
FB Stanley Pritchett
DL Chris Rumpf
DL Eric Sullivan
DL David Turnipseed
DL Stacy Evans
LB Hank Campbell
LB Ronnie Smith
LB Aubrey Brooks
DB Ron Nealy / Lee Wiggins
DB Corey Bell / Terry Cousin
DB Ben Washington
DB Tony Watts

RUSHING: Bennett 181/782y, Pritchett 130/601y
PASSING: Taneyhill 231-367/2259y, 20TD, 62.9%
RECEIVING: Bennett 43/324y, Cates 42/588y
SCORING: Pritchett 62pts, Reed Morton (K) 58pts

1995 4-6-1

23	Georgia	42
21	Arkansas	51
68	Louisiana Tech	21
30	Kentucky	35
20	LSU	20
77	Kent	14
65	Mississippi St.	39
52	Vanderbilt	14
21	Tennessee	56
7	Florida	63
17	Clemson	38

WR Zola Davis / Kerry Hood
WR Monty Means / Darrel Nicklow
T Randy Wheeler
G Jamar Nesbit
C Luther Dixon / Paul Beckwith
G Travis Whitfield
T James Dexter
TE Jason Lawson
QB Steve Taneyhill
TB Duce Staley / Mike Reddick
FB Stanley Pritchett
DL Maynard Caldwell
DL Henry Taylor
DL Eric Sullivan
DL Selvesta Miller
LB Hank Campbell / Benji Young
LB Ronnie Smith / Shane Burnham
LB Aubrey Brooks
DB Ron Nealy
DB Joe Troupe / Terry Cousin
DB Arturo Freeman
DB Ben Washington

RUSHING: Staley 127/736y, Pritchett 86/333y, Reddick 30/146y
PASSING: Taneyhill 261-389/3094y, 29TD, 67.1%
RECEIVING: Pritchett 62/664y, Davis 58/911y, Means 46/657y
SCORING: Pritchett 76pts

1996 6-5

33	C. Florida	14
23	Georgia	14
7	East Carolina	23
10	Mississippi St.	14
24	Auburn	28
25	Kentucky	14
23	Arkansas	17
27	Vanderbilt	0
14	Tennesee	31
25	Florida	52
34	Clemson	31

WR Zola Davis / Marcus Robinson
WR Corey Bridges / Ben Fleming
T Jamar Nesbit / Reggie Baker
G Ed Hrubiec
C Paul Beckwith
G Travis Whitfield
T Randy Wheeler / Andray Spearman
TE Jason Lawson / Trevon Matthews
QB Anthony Wright
TB Duce Staley / Troy Hambrick
FB Steve Mixon
DL Maynard Caldwell / Matt Marsters
DL Henry Taylor
DL Michael Maddox
DL Selvesta Miller / John Abraham
LB Benji Young / Corey Atkins
LB Shane Burnham
LB Darren Hambrick
DB Lee Wiggins
DB Terry Cousin / Keris Sullivan
DB Arturo Freeman / Ray Green
DB Ben Washington

RUSHING: Staley 218/1116y, Hambrick 43/281y, Scott Moritz (TB) 50/172y
PASSING: Wright 131-244/1850y, 8TD, 53.7%
RECEIVING: Bridges 28/399y, Staley 28/253y, Davis 24/303y, Robinson 21/505y
SCORING: Staley 54pts

1997 5-6

33	C. Florida	31
15	Georgia	31
26	East Carolina	0
17	Mississippi St.	37
6	Auburn	23
38	Kentucky	24
39	Arkansas	13
35	Vanderbilt	3
7	Tennessee	22
21	Florida	48
21	Clemson	47

WR Zola Davis / Jermale Kelly
WR Kerry Hood / Ben Flemng
T Jamar Nesbit
G Ed Hrubiec
C Paul Beckwith / Scott Browne
G Travis Whitfield
T Andray Spearman
TE Trevon Matthews / Trey Pennington
QB Anthony Wright
RB Troy Hambrick / Boo Williams
FB Steve Mixon / Jacob Bush
DL Selvesta Miller / Matt Martsers
DL Henry Taylor
DL Cecil Caldwell
DL John Abraham / Anthony Overstreet
LB Corey Atkins / Andre Offing
LB Shane Burnham / Marco Henderson
LB Daron Brooker / Ryan Koop
DB Lee Wiggins / Keris Sullivan
DB Kevin Brooks / Homer Torrance
DB Arturo Freeman
DB Ben Washington / Maurice Henderson

RUSHING: Hambrick 115/604y, Williams 117/348y, Scott Moritz (TB) 55/189y
PASSING: Wright 139-252/1685y, 18TD, 55.2%
RECEIVING: Kelly 43/618y, Davis 34/407y, Hood 26/320y
SCORING: Kelly 60pts, Hood 36pts

1998 1-10

38	Ball State	20
3	Georgia	17
21	Marshall	24
0	Mississippi St.	38
28	Mississippi	30
28	Kentucky	33
28	Arkansas	41
14	Vanderbilt	17
14	Tennessee	49
14	Florida	33
19	Clemson	28

WR Zola Davis / Kerry Hood
WR Jermale Kelly / Ben Fleming
T Jamar Nesbit / Kevin Johnson
G Jason Cox / Kevin Rivers
C Scott Browne
G Philip Jones
T Melvin Paige
TE Trevon Matthews
QB Anthony Wright
TB Troy Hambrick / Boo Williams
FB Steve Mixon / Antione Nesmith
DL John Stamper
DL Errol Rochester
DL Cecil Caldwell
DL Kalimba Edwards
LB Corey Atkins
LB Kenneth Harney / Andre Offing
LB John Abraham / Marco Henderson
DB Homer Torrance
DB Kevin Brooks
DB Maurice Henderson / O'Rondai Cox
DB Ray Green / Willie Offord

RUSHING: Hambrick 144/701y, Williams 51/239y, Nesmith 53/188y, Mixon 42/153y
PASSING: Wright 145-273/1899y, 10TD, 53.1%, Penn 55-112/642y, 7TD, 49.1%
RECEIVING: Davis 48/733y, Kelly 44/555y, Fleming 24/336y, Williams 24/335y
SCORING: Courtney Leavitt (K) 37pts, Davis 30pts, Hambrick & Kelly 24pts

1999 0-11

0	N. Carolina St.	10
9	Georgia	24
3	East Carolina	21
0	Mississippi St.	17
10	Mississippi	36
10	Kentucky	30
14	Arkansas	48
10	Vanderbilt	11
7	Tennessee	30
3	Florida	20
21	Clemson	31

WR Kerry Hood
WR Jermale Kelly
T Trey Pennington
G Cedric Williams
C Scott Browne
G Phillip Jones
T Melvin Paige
TE Trevon Matthews
QB Phil Petty / Mikal Goodman
TB Derek Watson
FB Andrew Pinnock / Antione Nesmith
DL John Stamper
DL Cleveland Pinkney
DL Cecil Caldwell
DL Kalimba Edwards
LB Corey Atkins
LB Andre Offing / Kenneth Harney
LB John Abraham
DB Sheldon Brown
DB Kevin House
DB Arturo Freeman / Ray Green
DB Rashad Faison / Willie Offord

RUSHING: Watson 111/394y, Pinnock 73/261y, Brewer 35/163y
PASSING: Petty 65-146/803y, TD, 44.5%, Goodman 32-65/572y, 3TD, 49.2%
RECEIVING: Kelly 24/366y, Hood 16/287y, Nesmith 15/200y
SCORING: Steve Florio (K) 32pts, Pinnock 18pts, 5 with 6

2000 8-4

31	New Mexico St.	0
21	Georgia	10
41	E. Michigan	6
23	Mississippi St.	19
17	Alabama	27
20	Kentucky	17
27	Arkansas	7
30	Vanderbilt	14
14	Tennessee	17
21	Florida	41
14	Clemson	16
24	Ohio State■	7

WR Jermale Kelly / Ryan Brewer (TB)
WR Brian Scott / James Adkisson
T Watts Wharton / Travelle Wharton
G Cedric Williams
C Scott Browne
G C.J. Frye / Kevin Rivers
T Melvin Paige
TE Thomas Hill
QB Phil Petty
TB Derek Watson
FB Andrew Pinnock / Travis Lewis
DL Dennis Quinn / John Stamper
DL Cleveland Pinkney
DL Cecil Caldwell
DL Kalimba Edwards
LB Shannon Wadley
LB Andre Offing / Kenny Harney
DB Andre Goodman / Kevin House
DB Sheldon Brown
DB Deandre Eiland / Antione Nesmith
DB Willie Offord / Jonathan Martin
DB Rashad Faison

RUSHING: Watson 187/1066y, Pinnock 110/406y, Brewer 33/175y
PASSING: Petty 170-315/2285y, 8TD, 54.0%
RECEIVING: Kelly 42/640y, Brewer 36/418y, Scott 35/560y
SCORING: Watson 72pts

2001 9-3

32	Boise State	13
14	Georgia	9
16	Mississippi St.	14
37	Alabama	36
42	Kentucky	6
7	Arkansas	10
46	Vanderbilt	14
10	Tennessee	17
38	Wofford	14
17	Florida	54
20	Clemson	15
31	Ohio State■	28

WR Ryan Brewer (TB) / Corey Alexander
WR Brian Scott /Carlos Spikes / M. Ages
T Travelle Wharton
G Cedric Williams
C Larrell Johnson / C.J. Frye
G Shane Hall / Phillip Jones
T Melvin Paige / Watts Sanderson
TE Rod Trafford / Hart Turner
QB Phil Petty / Corey Jenkins
TB Derek Watson
FB Andrew Pinnock / Travis Lewis
DL John Stamper
DL Langston Moore / Willie Sams
DL Dennis Quinn / George Gause
LB Kalimba Edwards / Rod Thomas
LB Jermaine Lemon /
LB Kenny Harney / Shannon Wadley
DB Andre Goodman
DB Sheldon Brown / Brian Elam
DB Antione Nesmith / Deandre Eiland
DB Willie Offord / Jonathan Martin
DB Rashad Faison / Dunta Robinson

RUSHING: Pinnock 115/622y, Watson 139/618y, Jenkins 59/303y
PASSING: Petty 164-288/1926y, 12TD, 56.9%
RECEIVING: Scott 47/730y, Brewer 37/352y, Watosn 27/218y
SCORING: Pinnock 72pts, Daniel Weaver (K) 72pts, Watson 44pts

2002 5-7

34 New Mexico St.	24 WR Ryan Brewer (TB) / James Adkisson
21 Virginia	34 WR Michael Ages / Troy Williamson
7 Georgia	13 T Travelle Wharton
42 Temple	21 G Lenny Williams
20 Vanderbilt	14 C C.J. Frye / Na'shan Goddard
34 Mississippi St.	10 G Shane Hall
16 Kentucky	12 T Watts Sanderson
14 LSU	38 TE Hart Turner
10 Tennessee	18 QB Corey Jenkins / Dondrial Pinkins
0 Arkansas	23 TB Daccus Turman / Kenny Irons
7 Florida	28 FB Andrew Pinnock
20 Clemson	27 DL Dennis Quinn / Jason Capers
	DL Langston Moore
	DL Moe Thompson
	LB George Gause (DL) / Jermaine Lemon
	LB Lance Laury
	LB Jeremiah Garrison
	DB Dunta Robinson
	DB Taqiy Muhammad / Ted Crawford
	DB Rashad Faison / Jamacia Jackson
	DB Deandre Eiland
	DB Jonathan Martin

RUSHING: Jenkins 160/655y, Pinnock 124/563y, Irons 47/201y
PASSING: Jenkins 100-180/1334y, 7TD, 55.6%
RECEIVING: Brewer 28/299y, Ages 22/331y, Williamson 17/491y
SCORING: Daniel Weaver (K) 54pts, Pinnock 32pts, 3 with 24pts

2003 5-7

14 La-Lafayette	7 WR Matthew Thomas / Taqiy Muhammad
31 Virginia	7 WR Troy Williamson
7 Georgia	31 T Jabari Levey / Jeff Barnes
42 Ala.-Birm'ham	10 G Travelle Wharton
20 Tennessee	23 C John Strickland / Chris White
27 Kentucky	21 G Jonathan Alston
7 LSU	33 T Na'Shan Goddard / Stephen Sene
35 Vanderbilt	24 TE Hart Turner / Brian Brownlee
40 Mississippi	43 QB Condrial Pinkins
6 Arkansas	28 TB Demetris Summers
22 Florida	24 FB Daccus Turman
17 Clemson	63 DL Moe Thompson / Jason Capers
	DL Freddy Saint-Preux
	DL Darrell Shropshire
	DL George Gause
	LB Lance Laury / Orus Lambert
	LB Marcus Lawrence
	LB Jeremiah Garrison / Rodriques Wilson
	DB Dunta Robinson / Tremaine Tyler
	DB Deandre Eiland / Ted Crawford
	DB Jamacia Jackson
	DB Jermaine Harris / Corey Peoples

RUSHING: Turman 132/646y, Summers 124/638y,
  Pinkins 95/254y
PASSING: Pinkins 162-322/2127y, 10TD, 50.3%
RECEIVING: Williamson 31/428y, Thomas 24/442y,
  Newton 22/277y
SCORING: Daniel Weaver (K) 49pts, Turman 42pts,
  Pinkins 32pts

2004 6-5

31 Vanderbilt	6 WR Matthew Thomas / Noah Whiteside
16 Georgia	20 WR Troy Williamson
34 South Florida	3 T Jabari Levey
17 Troy	7 G Chris White (C) / Woodly Telfort
20 Alabama	3 C John Strickland
28 Mississippi	31 G Jonathan Alston
12 Kentucky	7 T Na'Shan Goddard
29 Tennessee	43 TE Brian Brownlee
35 Arkansas	32 QB Dondrial Pinkins / Syvelle Newton
14 Florida	48 TB Demetris Summers / Daccus Turman
7 Clemson	29 FB Cory Boyd / Gonzie Gray
	DL Moe Thompson
	DL Darrell Shrophire / Marque Hall
	DL Preston Thorne / Jason Capers
	DL George Gause
	LB Ricardo Hurley
	LB Marcus Lawrence / Orus Lambert
	LB Rodriques Wilson
	DB Tremaine Tyler / Taqiy Muhammad
	DB Fred Bennett
	DB Ko Simpson
	DB Jamacia Jackson / Jermaine Harris

RUSHING: Summers 88/487y, Boyd 62/309y, Newton 104/262y
PASSING: Newton 70-131/1093y, 6TD, 53.4%,
  Pinkins 68-108/880y, 4TD, 63.0%
RECEIVING: Williamson 43/835y, Boyd 35/347y,
  Whiteside 20/290y
SCORING: Josh Brown (K) 57pts, Williamson 42pts,
  Newton 30pts

2005 7-5

24 C. Florida	15 WR Kris Clark / Carlos Thomas (DB)
15 Georgia	17 WR Sidney Rice
14 Alabama	37 WR Kenny McKinley / Noah Whiteside
45 Troy	20 T Jabari Levey
7 Auburn	48 G Freddy St.-Preux/Thomas Colem'n (T)
44 Kentucky	16 C Chris White
35 Vanderbilt	28 G James Thompson / Kyle Bishop
16 Tennessee	15 T Na'Shan Goddard
14 Arkansas	10 TE Carson Askins/Andy Boyd/Jn. Hannah
30 Florida	22 QB Blake Mitchell / Syvelle Newton (WR)
9 Clemson	13 TB Mike Davis / Daccus Turman
31 Missouri■	38 DL Jordin Lindsey / Josh Johnson
	DL Chris Tucker / Stanley Doughty
	DL De'Adrian Coley
	DL Orus Lambert / Charles Silas
	LB Lance Laury / Marvin Sapp
	LB Ricardo Hurley
	LB Dustin Lindsey /Mike West/Cody Wells
	DB Johnathan Joseph
	DB Fred Bennett / Carlos Thomas (WR)
	DB Ko Simpson
	DB Tremaine Tyler / Brandon Isaac

RUSHING: Davis 146/666y, Turman 59/245y, Newton 21/150y
PASSING: Mitchell 186-315/2370y, 17TD, 59.0%
RECEIVING: Rice 70/1143y, Newton 27/297y,
  McKinley 25/291y, Clark 20/245y
SCORING: Rice 78pts, Josh Brown (K) 62pts, Davis 30pts

2006 8-5

15 Mississippi St.	0 WR Sidney Rice / Freddie Brown
0 Georgia	18 WR Kenny McKinley / Noah Whiteside
27 Wofford	20 T Hutch Eckerson / Gurminder Thind
45 Florida Atlantic	6 G Thomas Coleman / William Brown
17 Auburn	24 C Chris White
24 Kentucky	17 G Seth Edwards / Garrett Anderson
31 Vanderbilt	13 T Jamon Meredith / Justin Sorensen
24 Tennessee	31 TE Andy Boyd / Robert Pavlovic
20 Arkansas	26 QB Blake Mitchell/Syv'le Newt'n (WR-DB)
16 Florida	17 TB Cory Boyd / Mike Davis
52 Middle Tenn.	7 FB Lanard Stafford
31 Clemson	28 DL Casper Brinkley
44 Houston■	36 DL Joel Reeves / Stanley Doughty
	DL Nathan Pepper / Marque Hall
	DL Ryan Brown / Jordin Lindsey
	LB Rodney Oaulk / Marvin Sapp
	LB Jasper Brinkley / Dakota Walker
	LB Cody Wells / Yvan Banag
	DB Carlos Thomas / Captain Munnerlyn
	DB Fred Bennett
	DB Stoney Woodson
	DB Chris Hampton / Emanuel Cook

RUSHING: C. Boyd 164/823y, Davis 100/474y, Newton 86/330y
PASSING: Mitchell 135-202/1789y, 10TD, 66.8%,
  Newton 95-162/1316y, 12TD, 58.6%
RECEIVING: Rice 72/1090, McKinley 51/880y, C. Boyd 35/406y
SCORING: Ryan Succop (K) 85pts, C. Boyd & Rice 60pt

2007 6-6

28 La.-Lafayette	14 WR Dion Lecorn /Moe Brown /Jared Cook
16 Georgia	12 WR Kenny McKinley / Freddie Brown
38 S. Carolina State	3 T Jamon Meredith
16 LSU	28 G Seaver Brown/Jam's Th'mps'n/G. Thind
38 Mississippi St.	21 C William Brown
38 Kentucky	23 G Lemuel Jeanpierre / Garrett Anderson
21 North Carolina	15 T Justin Sorensen
6 Vanderbilt	17 TE Andy Boyd
24 Tennessee	27 QB Blake Mitchell / Chris Smelley
36 Arkansas	48 TB Cory Boyd / Mike Davis
31 Florida	51 FB Lanard Stafford
21 Clemson	23 DL Casper Brinkley
	DL Ladi Ajiboye / Nathan Pepper
	DL Marque Hall / Kenrick Ellis
	DL Eric Norwood / Jonathan Williams
	LB Rodney Paulk
	LB Marvin Sapp / Jasper Brinkley
	LB Cliff Matthews / Cody Wells
	DB Carlos Thomas
	DB Captain Munnerlyn / Stoney Woodson
	DB Darian Stewart / Brandon Isaac
	DB Emanuel Cook / Chris Hampton

RUSHING: C. Boyd 180/903y, Davis 114/518y,
  Chris Culliver (WR) 5/31y
PASSING: Mitchell 152-255/1747y, 10TD, 59.6%,
  Smelley 92-162/1176y, 9TD, 56.8%
RECEIVING: McKinley 77/968y, C. Boyd 36/405y, Cook 30/421y,
  Lecorn 27/315y, Davis 23/224y
SCORING: Ryan Succop (K) 76pts, C. Boyd 60pts, McKinley 54pts

2008 7-6

34 N. Carolina St.	0 WR Mark Barnesw / Moe Brown
17 Vanderbilt	24 WR Kenny McKinley
7 Georgia	14 T Jarriel King / Hutch Eckerson
23 Wofford	13 G Jamon Meredith / Heath Batchelor
26 Ala.-Birm'ham	13 C Garrett Anderson
31 Mississippi	24 G Terrence Campbell/Lemuel Jeanpierre
24 Kentucky	17 T Justin Sorensen
27 Tennessee	24 TE Jared Cook / Weslye Saunders
34 Arkansas	6 QB Chris Smelley / Stephen Garcia
6 Florida	21 TB Mike Davis / Eric Baker
14 Clemson	56 FB Patrick DiMarco
7 Iowa■	31 DL Jordin Lindsey / Clifton Geathers
	31 DL Nathan Pepper / Travian Robertson
	DL Ladi Ajiboye
	DL Cliff Matthews
	LB Darian Stewart (DB)
	LB Jasper Brinkley / Dustin Lindsey
	LB Eric Norwood / Marvin Sapp
	DB Stoney Woodson / Carlos Thomas
	DB Captain Munnerlyn
	DB Chris Culliver / Akeem Auguste
	DB Emanuel Cook

RUSHING: Davis 163/573y, Garcia 70/198y, Baker 46/182y
PASSING: Smelley 169-302/1922y, 14TD, 56.0%,
  Garcia 65-122/832y, 6TD, 53.3%
RECEIVING: McKinley 54/642y, J. Cook 37/573y,
  Brown 30/391y, Barnes 27/346y
SCORING: Ryan Succop (K) 90pts, Davis & McKinley 24pts

2009 7-6

7 N. Carolina St.	3 WR Moe Brown/Steph'n Flint/Jason Barnes
37 Georgia	41 WR Alshon Jeffery / Tori Gurley
38 Florida Atlantic	16 T Jarriel King / Kyle Nunn
16 Mississippi	10 G Garrett Anderson / Terrence Campbell
38 S. Carolina St.	14 C Lemuel Jeanpierre
28 Kentucky	26 QB T.J. Johnson / Garrett Chisolm
6 Alabama	20 T Hutch Eckerson / Quintin Richardson
14 Vanderbilt	7 TE Weslye Saunders / Justice Cunningham
13 Tennessee	31 QB Stephen Garcia
16 Arkansas	33 TB Kenny Miles / Brian Maddox
14 Florida	24 FB Patrick DiMarco
34 Tennessee	17 DL Clifton Geathers / Devin Taylor
7 Connecticut■	20 DL Nathan Pepper / Travian Robertson
	DL Ladi Ajiboye
	DL Cliff Matthews
	LB Antonio Allen
	LB Shaq Wilson / Josh Dickerson
	LB Eric Norwood / Tony Straughter
	DB Stephon Gilmore
	DB Akeem Auguste
	DB Chris Culliver
	DB Darian Stewart

RUSHING: Miles 117/626y, Maddox 102/307y,
  Jarvis Giles (TB) 52/277y
PASSING: Garcia 239-432/2862y, 17TD, 55.3%
RECEIVING: Jeffery 46/763y, Brown 33/491y, Saunders 32/353y
  Gurley 31/440y
SCORING: Spencer Lanning (K) 79pts, Maddox 48pts, Jeffery 36pts

2010 9-5

41 Southern Miss.	13 WR Alshon Jeffery
17 Georgia	6 WR Tori Gurley
38 Furman	19 WR D.L. Moore / Ace Sanders
27 Auburn	35 T Jarriel King / Kyle Nunn
35 Alabama	21 G Garrett Chisolm / Terrence Campbell
28 Kentucky	31 C T.J. Johnson
21 Vanderbilt	7 G Rokevious Watkins
38 Tennessee	24 T Hutch Eckerson
20 Arkansas	41 QB Stephen Garcia
36 Florida	14 TB Marcus Lattimore / Brian Maddox
69 Troy	24 FB/TEPatrick DiMarco/Justice Cunningham
29 Clemson	7 DL Devin Taylor
17 Auburn□	56 DL Travian Robertson
17 Florida State■	26 DL Ladi Ajiboye / Melvin Ingram
	DL Cliff Matthews
	LB Josh Dickerson / Rodney Paulk
	LB Tony Slaughter / Quin Smith
	LB/DB Antonio Allen / Damario Jeffery
	DB Stephon Gilmore / Marty Markett
	DB Chris Culliver / C.C. Whitlock
	DB D.J. Swearinger / Akeem Auguste
	DB DeVonte Holloman

RUSHING: Lattimore 249/1197y, Maddox 74/391y, Garcia 105/222y
PASSING: Garcia 224-349/3059y, 20TD, 64.2%
RECEIVING: Jeffery 88/1517y, Gurley 44/465y, Lattimore 29/412y
SCORING: Lattimore 114pts, Spencer Lanning (K) 102pts,
  Jeffery 54pts

SOUTHERN CALIFORNIA

University of Southern California (Founded 1880)
Los Angeles, California
Nickname: Trojans
Colors: Cardinal and Gold
Stadium: Los Angeles Coliseum (1923) 93,607
Conference Affiliations: Pacific Coast (1922-1958),
  AAWU (1959-1967), Pacific 8/10 (1968-present)

CAREER RUSHING YARDS	Attempts	Yards
Charles White (1976-79)	1147	6245
Marcus Allen (1978-81)	932	4810
Anthony Davis (1972-74)	784	3724
Ricky Bell (1973-76)	710	3689
O.J. Simpson (1967-68)	674	3423
Mike Garrett (1963-65)	612	3221
Reggie Bush (2003-05)	433	3169
LenDale White (2003-05)	541	3159
Fred Crutcher (1981, 83-85)	670	2815
Sultan McCullough (1999-2002)	611	2800

CAREER PASSING YARDS	Comp.-Att.	Yards
Carson Palmer (1998-2002)	927-1569	11,818
Matt Leinart (2002-05)	807-1245	10,693
Rob Johnson (1991-94)	676-1046	8472
Rodney Peete (1985-88)	630-1081	8225
John David Booty (2005-07)	518-832	6125
Matt Barkley (2009-10)	447-729	5526
Brad Otton (1994-96)	410-718	5359
Todd Marinovich (1989-90)	415-674	5001
Sean Salisbury (1982-83, 85)	346-602	4481
Paul McDonald (1977-79)	299-501	4138

CAREER RECEIVING YARDS	Catches	Yards
Johnnie Morton (1990-93)	201	3201
Dwayne Jarrett (2004-06)	216	3138
Kareem Kelly (1999-2002)	204	3104
Steve Smith (2003-06)	190	3019
Keary Colbert (2000-03)	207	2964
Keyshawn Johnson (1994-95)	168	2796
R. Jay Soward (1996-99)	161	2672
Mike Williams (2002-03)	176	2579
John Jackson (1986-89)	163	2379
Randy Simmrin (1975-77)	100	2015

SEASON RUSHING YARDS	Attempts	Yards
Marcus Allen (1981)	433	2427
Charles White (1979)	332	2050
Ricky Bell (1975)	385	1957
O.J. Simpson (1968)	383	1880
Charles White (1978)	374	1859

SEASON PASSING YARDS	Comp.-Att.	Yards
Carson Palmer (2002)	309-489	3942
Matt Leinart (2005)	283-431	3815
Rob Johnson (1993)	308-449	3630
Matt Leinart (2003)	255-402	3556
John David Booty (2006)	269-436	3347

SEASON RECEIVING YARDS	Catches	Yards
Johnnie Morton (1993)	88	1520
Keyshawn Johnson (1995)	102	1434
Keyshawn Johnson (1994)	66	1362
Mike Williams (2003)	95	1314
Dwayne Jarrett (2006)	91	1274

GAME RUSHING YARDS	Attempts	Yards
Ricky Bell (1976 vs. Washington State)	51	347
Marcus Allen (1981 vs. Washington St.)	44	289
Marcus Allen (1981 vs. Indiana)	40	274

GAME PASSING YARDS	Comp.-Att.	Yards
Carson Palmer (2002 vs. Oregon)	31-42	448
Carson Palmer (2002 vs. Notre Dame)	32-46	425
Mike Van Raaphorst (1999 vs. Stanford)	25-51	415

GAME RECEIVING YARDS	Catches	Yards
R. Jay Soward (1996 vs. UCLA)	6	260
Johnnie Morton (1993 vs. Wash. St.)	8	229
Mike Williams (2002 vs. Oregon)	13	226

GREATEST COACH:

Had Pete Carroll, winner of back-to-back national championships in 2003-04, stayed at USC and not moved on to the Seattle Seahawks in 2010, he very well may have secured the crown of greatest Trojan coach. Carroll enjoyed a Rockne-like .8348 winning percentage in nine years at the Los Angeles campus.

But the Cardinal and Gold coaching throne room remains open for John McKay, the author of three national championships and nine conference crowns in 16 years at Southern California. McKay's overall record at USC stood at 127-40-8 for a .7486 percentage.

McKay was well known for his recruiting ability and his sense of humor. What made his hiring in 1960 so unusual was that no one in the ample Los Angeles press corps hardly had heard of him. The reason was that McKay's contacts with USC were through scouting he had done while on the staff of his alma mater, Oregon.

McKay didn't invent the I-Formation, but he popularized the dynamic offense. Although the Trojans rushed and passed with equal ability out of the Power-I, McKay was best known for his brilliant tailbacks, including Mike Garrett, O.J. Simpson, Anthony Davis, and Ricky Bell, running behind great offensive lines.

SOUTHERN CALIFORNIA'S 55 GREATEST SINCE 1953

OFFENSE

WIDE RECEIVER: Kerry Colbert, Dwayne Jarrett, Keyshawn Johnson, Johnnie Morton
TIGHT END: Fred Davis, Charle Young
TACKLE: Sam Baker, Tony Boselli, Ron Mix, Marv Montgomery, Keith Van Horne, John Vella, Ron Yary
GUARD: Brad Budde, Roy Foster, Pat Howell, Bruce Matthews
CENTER: Tony Slaton
QUARTERBACK: Matt Leinart, Carson Palmer
RUNNING BACK: Marcus Allen, Reggie Bush, Mike Garrett, O.J. Simpson, Charles White
FULLBACK: Sam Cunningham, Mosi Tatupu

DEFENSE

END: Jimmy Gunn, Kenechi Udeze, Charles Weaver
TACKLE: Al Cowlings, Sedrick Ellis, John Grant, Gary Jeter, Mike Patterson
NOSE GUARD: George Achica
LINEBACKER: Damon Bame, Chris Claiborne, Junior Seau, Lofa Tatupu, Richard Wood, Adrian Young
CORNERBACK: Tyrone Hudson, Brian Kelly, Nate Shaw
SAFETY: Ronnie Lott, Tim McDonald, Troy Polamalu, Dennis Thurman

SPECIAL TEAMS

RETURN SPECIALISTS: Anthony Davis, Curtis Conway, Lynn Swann
PLACE KICKER: Quin Rodriguez
PUNTER: Tom Malone

TWO-WAY PLAYER

HALFBACK-DEFENSIVE BACK: Jon Arnett

PERFORMANCE FORMULA:
SOUTHERN CALIFORNIA'S 10 BEST SEASONS

1972	1.8483	1 of 70
2004	1.8345	1 of 72
2005	1.7879	2 of 70
1978	1.7412	1 of 70
2008	1.7263	3 of 71
2003	1.7025	1 of 71
2002	1.6967	3 of 70
1962	1.6898	2 of 70
1979	1.6568	4 of 70
1967	1.6464	1 of 71

SOUTHERN CALIFORNIA TROJANS

Year	W-L-T	AP Poll	Conference Standing	Toughest Regular Season Opponents	Coach (Record at School)	Bowl Games		
1953	6-3-1		3	Stanford 6-3-1, UCLA 8-1, Notre Dame 9-0-1	Jess Hill			
1954	8-4	17	2	Pittsburgh 4-5, Oregon 6-4, UCLA 9-0, Notre Dame 9-1	Jess Hill	Rose	7 Ohio State	20
1955	6-4	13	6	Washington 5-4-1, Stanford 6-3-1, UCLA 9-1, Notre Dame 8-2	Jess Hill			
1956	8-2	18	2t	Oregon State 7-2-1, Washington 5-5, UCLA 7-3	Jess Hill (45-17-1)			
1957	1-9		7t	Oregon State 8-2, Oregon 7-3, UCLA 8-2, Notre Dame 7-3	Don Clark			
1958	4-5-1		3	California 7-3, Washington State 7-3, Notre Dame 6-4	Don Clark			
1959	8-2	14	1t	Pittsburgh 6-4, Washington 9-1, UCLA 5-4-1, Notre Dame 5-5	Don Clark (13-16-1)			
1960	4-6		2	Ohio State 7-2, Washington 9-1, Baylor 8-2, UCLA 7-2-1	John McKay			
1961	4-5-1		2t	Georgia Tech 7-3, Iowa 5-4, UCLA 7-3	John McKay			
1962	11-0	1	1	Duke 8-2, Washington 7-1-2, Notre Dame 5-5	John McKay	Rose	42 Wisconsin	37
1963	7-3	11+	2	Oklahoma 8-2, Michigan St. 6-2-1, Ohio St. 5-3-1, Washington 6-4	John McKay			
1964	7-3	10	1t	Oklahoma 6-3-1, Ohio State 7-2, Notre Dame 9-1	John McKay			
1965	7-2-1	10	2	Minnesota 5-4-1, Notre Dame 7-2-1, UCLA 7-2-1	John McKay			
1966	7-4	11+	1	Oregon State 7-3, Miami 7-2-1, UCLA 9-1, Notre Dame 9-0-1	John McKay	Rose	13 Purdue	14
1967	10-1	1	1	Texas 6-4, Notre Dame 8-2, Oregon State 7-2-1, UCLA 7-2-1	John McKay	Rose	14 Indiana	3
1968	9-1-1	4	1	Stanford 6-3-1, California 7-3-1, Oregon St. 7-3, Notre Dame 7-2-1	John McKay	Rose	16 Ohio State	27
1969	10-0-1	3	1	Nebraska 8-2, Stanford 7-2-1, Notre Dame 8-1-1, UCLA 8-1-1	John McKay	Rose	10 Michigan	3
1970	6-4-1	15	6	Nebraska 10-0-1, Stanford 8-3, Washington 6-4, Notre Dame 9-1	John McKay			
1971	6-4-1	20	2	Alabama 11-0, Oklahoma 10-1, Stanford 8-3, Notre Dame 8-2	John McKay			
1972	12-0	1	1	Washington 8-3, UCLA 8-3, Notre Dame 8-2	John McKay	Rose	42 Ohio State	17
1973	9-2-1	8	1	Oklahoma 10-0-1, Notre Dame 10-0, UCLA 9-2	John McKay	Rose	21 Ohio State	42
1974	10-1-1	2	1	Pittsburgh 7-4, California 7-3-1, UCLA 6-3-2, Notre Dame 9-2	John McKay	Rose	18 Ohio State	17
1975	8-4	17	5	Notre Dame 8-3, California 8-3, UCLA 8-2-1	John McKay (127-40-8)	Liberty	20 Texas A&M	0
1976	11-1	2	1	Missouri 6-5, Stanford 6-5, UCLA 9-1-1, Notre Dame 8-3	John Robinson	Rose	14 Michigan	6
1977	8-4	13	2t	Alabama 10-1, Notre Dame 10-1, Stanford 8-3, Washington 8-3	John Robinson	Bluebonnet	47 Texas A&M	28
1978	12-1	2	1	Alabama 10-1, Michigan State 8-3, UCLA 8-3, Notre Dame 8-3	John Robinson	Rose	17 Michigan	10
1979	11-0-1	2	1	Notre Dame 7-4, Arizona 6-4-1, Washington 8-3	John Robinson	Rose	17 Ohio State	16
1980	8-2-1	11	3	South Carolina 8-3, Washington 9-3, UCLA 9-3, Notre Dame 9-1-1	John Robinson			
1981	9-3	14	2	Tennessee 7-4, Washington St. 8-2-1, Wash'gton 9-2, UCLA 7-3-1	John Robinson	Fiesta	10 Penn State	26
1982	8-3	15	3t	Florida 8-3, Oklahoma 8-3, Arizona State 9-2, UCLA 9-1-1	John Robinson {see below}			
1983	4-6-1		3	Florida 8-2-1, Washington State 7-4, Washington 8-3	Ted Tollner			
1984	9-3	10	1	LSU 8-3, Washington 10-1, UCLA 8-3, Notre Dame 7-4	Ted Tollner	Rose	20 Ohio State	17
1985	6-6		4t	Baylor 8-3, Arizona State 8-3, UCLA 8-2-1	Ted Tollner	Aloha	3 Alabama	24
1986	7-5		4t	Washington 8-2-1, Arizona State 9-1-1, Stanford 8-3, UCLA 7-3-1	Ted Tollner (26-20-1)	Citrus	7 Auburn	16
1987	8-4	18	1t	Michigan State 8-2-1, Notre Dame 8-3, UCLA 9-2	Larry Smith	Rose	17 Michigan State	20
1988	10-2	7	1	Oklahoma 9-2, UCLA 9-2, Notre Dame 11-0	Larry Smith	Rose	14 Michigan	22
1989	9-2-1	8	1	Illinois 9-2, Ohio State 8-3, Notre Dame 11-1	Larry Smith	Rose	17 Michigan	10
1990	8-4-1	20	2	Penn State 9-2, Washington 9-2, Ohio State 7-3-1, Notre Dame 9-2	Larry Smith	John Hancock	16 Michigan State	17
1991	3-8		8	Penn State 10-2, Notre Dame 9-3, Washington 11-0, UCLA 8-3	Larry Smith			
1992	6-5-1		3t	Washington 9-2, Wash. St. 8-3, Stanford 9-3, Notre Dame 9-1-1	Larry Smith (44-25-3)	Freedom	7 Fresno State	24
1993	8-5		1t	North Carolina 10-2, Penn State 9-2, Arizona 9-2, Notre Dame 10-1	John Robinson	Freedom	28 Utah	21
1994	8-3-1	13	2t	Penn State 11-0, Oregon 9-3, Arizona 8-3	John Robinson	Cotton	55 Texas Tech	14
1995	9-2-1	12	1t	Notre Dame 9-2, Washington 7-3-1, Stanford 7-3-1, UCLA 7-4	John Robinson	Rose	41 Northwestern	32
1996	6-6		5t	Penn St. 10-2, Arizona St. 11-0, Washington 9-2, Notre Dame 8-3	John Robinson			
1997	6-5		5t	Florida State 10-1, Washington St. 10-1, Arizona St. 8-3, UCLA 9-2	John Robinson (112-40-4)	Sun	19 Texas Christian	28
1998	8-5		3t	Florida State 11-1, UCLA 10-1, Notre Dame 9-2	Paul Hackett			
1999	6-6		6t	Hawaii 8-4, Oregon 8-3, Stanford 8-3	Paul Hackett (11-13)			
2000	5-7		8t	Oregon State 10-1, Oregon 9-2, Notre Dame 9-2	Pete Carroll			
2001	6-6		5	Oregon 10-1, Stanford 9-2, Washington 8-3	Pete Carroll	Las Vegas	6 Utah	10
2002	11-2	4	1	Auburn 8-4, Colorado 9-3, Washington State 10-2, Arizona St. 8-5	Pete Carroll	Orange	38 Iowa	17
2003	12-1	1	1	Auburn 7-5, Hawaii 8-5, Washington State 9-3	Pete Carroll	Rose	28 Michigan	14
2004	12-0	1	1	Virginia Tech 10-2, California 10-1, Arizona State 8-3	Pete Carroll	Orange	55 Oklahoma	19
2005	12-1	2	1	Oregon 10-1, Notre Dame 9-2, California 7-4, UCLA 9-2	Pete Carroll	Rose	38 Texas	41
2006	11-2	4	1t	Arkansas 10-2, Nebraska 9-3, California 9-3, Notre Dame 10-2	Pete Carroll	Rose	32 Michigan	18
2007	11-2	3	1t	Oregon 8-4, Oregon State 8-4, Arizona State 10-2	Pete Carroll	Rose	49 Illinois	17
2008	12-1	3	1	Ohio State 10-2, Oregon State 8-4, Oregon 9-3, California 8-4	Pete Carroll	Rose	38 Penn State	24
2009	9-4	22	5t	Ohio State 10-2, Oregon 10-2, Stanford 8-4, Arizona 8-4	Pete Carroll (96-19)	Emerald	24 Boston College	13
2010	8-5		3t	Hawaii 10-3, Stanford 11-1, Oregon 12-0	Lane Kiffin (8-5)			

| **TOTAL:** | | | | 465-191-18 .7033 (8 of 70) | **Bowl Games since 1953:** | 22-14 .6111 (12 of 70) | | |

GREATEST TEAM SINCE 1953: There are so many Trojan fish in football's "greatest" sea, but the choice is the 2004 juggernaut that featured an offense with quarterback Matt Leinart, running backs Reggie Bush and Len Dale White, and receivers Dwayne Jarrett and Steve Smith. USC beat two 10-win teams in Virginia Tech and California and crushed Oklahoma in the BCS championship Orange Bowl by 55-19. Kudos also to John McKay's 1969 and '72 titlists and especially John Robinson's 1979 squad, which featured Marcus Allen, Chip Banks, Brad Budde, Roy Foster, Ronnie Lott, Paul McDonald, Don Mosebar, Dennis Smith, and Keith Van Horne.

1953 6-3-1
29	Washington St.	13	E Ron Miller / Al Baldock
17	Minnesota	7	T Mario DaRe
27	Indiana	14	G Ed Pucci / George Galli
13	Washington	13	C Dick Petty / Vern Sampson
37	Oregon State	0	G George Timberlake / Orlando Ferrante
32	California	20	T Ed Fouch / Frank Thompson
7	Oregon	13	E Tom Nickoloff / Leon Clarke
23	Stanford	20	QB George Bozanic
0	UCLA	13	TB Aramis Dandoy / Desmond Koch
14	Notre Dame	48	WB Lindon Crow / Bob Buckley
			FB Harold Han / Leon Sellers

RUSHING: Dandoy 113/578y, Crow 49/235y, Han 48/196y
PASSING: Dandoy 24-55/242y, TD, 43.6%
RECEIVING: Nickoloff 16/214y, Miller 13/181y, Bozanic 8/66y
SCORING: Dandoy 42pts, Han 24pts, Sam Tsagalakis (G-K) & Koch (TB-K) 21pts

1954 8-4
39	Washington St.	0	E Leon Clarke / Chuck Leimbach
27	Pittsburgh	7	T Mario DaRe / George Bellotti
12	Northwestern	7	G George Galli / John Miller
7	TCU	20	C Marv Goux
24	Oregon	14	G Orlando Ferrante / Dick Enright
29	California	27	T Ed Fouch
34	Oregon State	0	E Chuck Greenwood / Chuck Griffith
21	Stanford	7	QB Jim Contratto / Frank Hall
41	Washington	0	TB Aramis Dandoy / Jon Arnett
0	UCLA	34	WB Lindon Crow
17	Notre Dame	23	FB Gordon Duvall / Jim Decker
7	Ohio State■	20	

RUSHING: Arnett 87/478y, Dandoy 74/356y, Crow 86/353y, Duvall 46/245y
PASSING: Contratto 32-77/702y, 9TD, 41.6%, Arnett 17-30/164y, 0TD, 56.7%, Hall 15-32/187y, TD, 46.9%
RECEIVING: Clarke 12/227y, Crow 7/274y, Leimbach 7/84y, Contratto 7/65y
SCORING: Arnett (TB-K) 55pts, Crow 36pts, Dandoy 30pts

1955 6-4
50	Washington St.	12	E Leon Clarke / Chuck Griffith
42	Oregon	15	T Dick Enright / George Belotti
19	Texas	5	G George Galli / Ron Miller
0	Washington	7	C Marv Goux/Vern Sampson/Karl Rubke
33	Wisconsin	21	G Orlando Ferrante
33	California	6	T Fabian Abram / Ron Fletcher
19	Minnesota	25	E Chuck Leimbach / Bing Bordier
20	Stanford	28	QB Jim Contratto / Frank Hall
7	UCLA	17	TB Jon Arnett / Ernie Zampese
42	Notre Dame	20	WB Don Hickman / Ron Brown
			FB C.R. Roberts / Gordon Duvall

RUSHING: Arnett 141/672y, Roberts 72/469y, Duvall 70/372y
PASSING: Contratto 22-55/406y, 5TD, 40.0%
RECEIVING: Clarke 15/215y, Leimbach 14/150y, Griffith 9/145y
SCORING: Arnett 108pts, Roberts & Duvall 36pts

1956 8-2
44	Texas	20	E Don McFarland / Hillard Hill
21	Oregon State	13	T Dick Enright / George Belotti
13	Wisconsin	6	G Ben Lardizabal / Walt Gurasich
35	Washington	7	C Karl Rubke / Walt Gorrell
19	Stanford	27	G Laird Willott / Frank Fiorentino
28	Washington St.	12	T Ron Fletcher / Fabian Abram
20	California	7	E Chuck Leimbach / Bob Voiles
0	Oregon	7	QB Frank Hall / Ells Kissinger
10	UCLA	7	TB Jon Arnett / Ernie Zampese
28	Notre Dame	20	WB Don Hickman / Tony Ortega
			FB C.R. Roberts / Jim Decker

RUSHING: Roberts 120/775y, Arnett 99/625y, Zampese 106/500y
PASSING: Hall 10-23/196y, 2TD, 43.5%
RECEIVING: Ortega 7/223y, Hill 7/88y, Voiles 5/109y
SCORING: Arnett (TB-K) 43pts, Roberts 36pts, Zampese (TB-K) 25pts

1957 1-9
0	Oregon State	20	E Lindsy Hubby / Don Voyne
6	Michigan	16	T Monte Clark / Gary Finneran
14	Pittsburgh	20	G Ben Lardizabal / Walt Gurasich
0	California	12	C Ken Antle
12	Washington St.	13	G Frank Fiorentino
19	Washington	12	T Mike Henry / Rod Humenuik
7	Stanford	35	E Ron Mix / Larry Boies
7	Oregon	16	QB Willie Wood / Tom Maudlin
9	UCLA	20	HB Rex Johnston / Don Buford
12	Notre Dame	40	HB Tony Ortega / Clark Holden
			FB Jim Conroy (QB) / Ed Isherwood

RUSHING: Johnston 74/304y, Buford 59/192y, Ortega 59/156y
PASSING: Maudlin 48-100/552y, 0TD, 48.0%
RECEIVING: Boies 14/144y, Voyne 10/130y, Ortega 8/102y
SCORING: Johnston 25pts, Voyne & Maudlin 12pts

1958 4-5-1
21	Oregon State	0	E Hillard Hill / Luther Hayes
19	Michigan	20	T Dan Ficca / Gary Finneran
7	North Carolina	8	G Frank Fiorentino
0	Oregon	25	C Ken Antle / Bob Edwards
12	California	14	G Mike McKeever
14	Washington St.	6	T Monte Clark / Ron Mix
29	Stanford	6	E Marlin McKeever / George Van Vliet
21	Washington	6	QB Willie Wood / Tom Maudlin
15	UCLA	15	HB Angelo Coia / Don Buford / Bob Arnett
13	Notre Dame	20	HB Rex Johnston / Jerry Traynham
			FB Clark Holden / Jerry Persinger

RUSHING: Buford 64/306y, Johnston 48/248y, Coia 48/237y
PASSING: Maudlin 41-95/535y, 4TD, 43.2%
RECEIVING: Hill 11/319y, Marlin McKeever 6/105y, Buford 5/44y
SCORING: Hill 36pts, Maudlin 20pts, Johnston 16pts

1959 8-2
27	Oregon State	6	E Luther Hayes / George Van Vliet
23	Pittsburgh	0	T Gary Finneran / Dan Ficca
17	Ohio State	0	G Al Bansavage
22	Washington	15	C Dave Morgan
30	Stanford	28	G Mike McKeever
14	California	7	T Ron Mix
36	West Virginia	0	E Marlin McKeever
17	Baylor	8	QB Al Prukop / Willie Wood / Ben Charles
3	UCLA	10	HB Jerry Traynham / Angelo Coia
6	Notre Dame	16	HB Bob Levingston / Lynn Gaskill
			FB Clark Holden / Hal Tobin

RUSHING: Traynham 123/583y, Holden 93/393y,Gaskill 40/290y
PASSING: Charles 20-46/348y, 4TD, 43.5%, Wood 17-58/283y, 3TD, 29.3%, Prukop 11-30/131y, 0TD, 36.7%
RECEIVING: Hayes 9/179y, Marlin McKeever 9/107y, Coia 8/76y
SCORING: Holden 30pts, Coia 22pts, Jim Conroy (FB) 20pts

1960 4-6
0	Oregon State	14	E Dave Washington / George Van Vliet
6	TCU	7	T Mike Bundra
0	Ohio State	20	G Britt Williams
10	Georgia	3	C Dave Morgan
27	California	10	G Mike McKeever / Roger Mietz
21	Stanford	10	T Dan Ficca / John Wilkins
0	Washington	34	E Marlin McKeever
14	Baylor	35	QB Al Prukop / Bill Nelsen
17	UCLA	6	HB Jerry Traynham / Alan Shields
0	Notre Dame	17	HB Bob Levingston / Lynn Gaskill
			FB Hal Tobin / Ben Wilson / Jim Bates

RUSHING: Tobin 61/318y, Shields 56/233y, Nelsen 90/186y
PASSING: Nelsen 29-72/446y, 3TD, 40.3%
RECEIVING: Marlin McKeever 15/218y, Ken Del Conte (HB) 8/91y
SCORING: Tobin 18pts, Don Zachik (HB-K) 17pts, Gaskill 12pts

1961 4-5-1
7	Georgia Tech	27	E Hal Bedsole / Phil Hoover
21	SMU	16	T Frank Buncom / Roger Clark
34	Iowa	35	G Britt Williams / John Ratliff
0	Notre Dame	30	C Skip Johnson / Dave Morgan
28	California	14	G Pete Lubisich
14	Illinois	10	T Mike Bundra / Marv Marinovich
0	Washington	0	E Warren Stephenson / Ben Rosin
30	Stanford	15	QB Bill Nelsen / Pete Beathard
9	Pittsburgh	10	HB Ken Del Conte / Willie Brown
7	UCLA	10	HB Jim Maples / Lynn Gaskill
			FB Ben Wilson /Hal Tobin/Rich McMahon

RUSHING: Wilson 139/619y, Brown 58/333y, Beathard 54/290y
PASSING: Beathard 40-83/482y, 3TD, 48.2%, Nelsen 39-86/683y, 4TD, 45.3%
RECEIVING: Bedsole 27/525y, Brown 11/132y, Maples 8/115y
SCORING: Bedsole 38pts, Beathard 30pts, Nelsen & Wilson 24pts

1962 11-0
14	Duke	7	E Hal Bedsole / Fred Hill
33	SMU	3	T Marv Marinovich / Bob Svihus
7	Iowa	0	G John Ratliff / Damon Bame (LB)
32	California	6	C Larry Sagouspe / Armando Sanchez
28	Illinois	16	G Pete Lubisich / Bill Fisk
14	Washington	0	T Gary Kirner / Randy Jones
39	Stanford	14	E Gary Potter / John Brownwood
13	Navy	6	QB Pete Beathard / Bill Nelsen
14	UCLA	3	HB Ken Del Conte / Gary Hill
25	Notre Dame	0	HB Willie Brown / Loran Hunt
42	Wisconsin■	37	FB Ben Wilson / Ernie Pye / Ernie Jones

RUSHING: Brown 88/574y, Wilson 85/311y, Beathard 100/290y
PASSING: Beathard 54-107/948y, 10TD, 50.5%, Nelsen 36-80/682y, 8TD, 45.0%
RECEIVING: Bedsole 33/827y, Brown 20/291y, Del Conte 8/67y
SCORING: Bedsole 68pts, Brown & Beathard 30pts

1963 7-3
14	Colorado	0	E Hal Bedsole
12	Oklahoma	17	T Mike Giers / Bob Svihus
13	Michigan State	10	G Bill Fisk
14	Notre Dame	17	C Armando Sanchez / Larry Sagouspe
36	Ohio State	3	G Mac Byrd / Damon Bame (LB)
7	Washington	22	E John Thomas / Fred Hill
25	Stanford	11	QB Pete Beathard / Craig Fertig
28	Oregon State	22	HB Mike Garrett
26	UCLA	6	HB Willie Brown
			FB Ernie Pye / Tom Lupo / Ron Heller

RUSHING: Garrett 128/833y, Brown 80/387y, Heller 65/247y
PASSING: Beathard 66-140/944y, 5TD, 47.1%, Fertig 41-77/545y, 5TD, 53.2%
RECEIVING: Brown 34/448y, Bedsole 22/365y, Garrett 10/78y
SCORING: Brown 44pts, Beathard 30pts, Garrett 26pts

1964 7-3
21	Colorado	0	E Dave Moton / John Brownwood
40	Oklahoma	14	T Bob Svihus / Mike Giers
7	Michigan State	17	G Bill Fisk / Doug Patrick
31	Texas A&M	7	C Paul Johnson
0	Ohio State	17	G Frank Lopez / Mac Byrd
26	California	21	T Jeff Smith / Chuck Arrobio
13	Washington	14	E Fred Hill / Ty Salness
15	Stanford	10	QB Craig Fertig / Gary Hill (DB)
34	UCLA	13	HB Mike Garrett / Nate Shaw (DB)
20	Notre Dame	17	HB Rod Sherman / Ed Blecksmith
			FB Ernie Pye/ Ron Heller/ Tom Lupo (DB)

RUSHING: Garrett 217/948y, Heller 95/441y, Sherman 35/234y
PASSING: Fertig 109-209/1671y, 11TD, 52.2%
RECEIVING: Hill 33/436y, Sherman 24/446y, Garrett 17/227y
SCORING: Garrett 62pts, Sherman 38pts, Richard Brownell (K) 21pts

1965 7-2-1
20	Minnesota	20	E Dave Moton
26	Wisconsin	6	T Chuck Arrobio / Mike Scarpace
26	Oregon State	12	G Frank Lopez
34	Washington	0	C Paul Johnson
14	Stanford	0	G Jim Homan
7	Notre Dame	28	T Ron Yary
35	California	0	E John Thomas
28	Pittsburgh	0	QB Troy Winslow
16	UCLA	20	TB Mike Garrett / Don McCall
56	Wyoming	6	WB Rod Sherman
			FB Mike Hull / Gary Fite
			DL Ray May
			DL Jim Vellone
			DL Larry Petrill / Jerry Conroy
			DL Doug Patrick / Gary Magner
			DL Jim Walker / Tim Rossovich
			LB Eddie King / Adrian Young
			LB Jeff Smith / Marv Bain
			DB Phil Lee
			DB Nate Shaw
			DB Mike Hunter
			DB Ed Blecksmith / Mickey Upton (HB)

RUSHING: Garrett 267/1440y, Winslow 81/319y, Sherman 49/277y
PASSING: Winslow 78-127/1019y, 11TD, 61.4%
RECEIVING: Moton 29/493y, Sherman 24/296y,Thomas 16/198y
SCORING: Garrett 96pts, Sherman 52pts, Moton 30pts

1966 7-4

10 Texas	6 E Ron Drake
38 Wisconsin	3 T Mike Scarpace
21 Oregon State	0 G Steve Barry
17 Washington	14 C Jim Ferguson / John Baccitich
21 Stanford	7 G Jim Homan
30 Clemson	0 T Ron Yary
7 Miami	10 E Bob Klein / Bob Miller
35 California	9 QB Troy Winslow / Toby Page
7 UCLA	14 TB Don McCall / Steve Grady
0 Notre Dame	51 WB Rod Sherman / Jim Lawrence
13 Purdue■	14 FB Mike Hull / Dan Scott
	DL Ray May
	DL Denis Moore
	DL Larry Petrill
	DL Gary Magner / Jerry Hayhoe
	DL Tim Rossovich
	LB Adrian Young
	LB Eddie Young / Jim Snow
	DB Mike Battle
	DB Nate Shaw
	DB Phil Lee
	DB Pat Cashman / Bill Jaroncyk

RUSHING: McCall 127/560y, Hull 75/502y, Sherman 79/303y
PASSING: Winslow 82-138/1023y, 6TD, 59.4%
RECEIVING: Drake 52/607y, Sherman 42/445y, 12/179y
SCORING: Sherman 38pts, McCall 30pts, Drake 24pts

1967 10-1

49 Washington St.	0 WR Earl McCullough / Ron Drake
17 Texas	13 T Ron Yary
21 Michigan State	17 G Mike Scarpace
30 Stanford	0 C Dick Allmon
24 Notre Dame	7 G Steve Lehmer / Fred Khasigian
23 Washington	6 T Mike Taylor
28 Oregon	6 TE Bob Klein / Bob Miller
31 California	12 QB Steve Sogge / Toby Page
0 Oregon State	3 TB O.J. Simpson / Steve Grady
21 UCLA	20 WB Jim Lawrence / Rikki Aldridge
14 Indiana■	3 FB Dan Scott / Mike Hull
	DL Tim Rossovich
	DL Gary Magner
	DL Ralph "Chip" Oliver
	DL Willard Scott / Tony Terry
	DL Jimmy Gunn
	LB Adrian Young / Gerry Shaw
	LB Jim Snow / Ty Salness
	DB Mike Battle
	DB Nate Shaw / Sandy Durko
	DB Bill Jaroncyk
	DB Pat Cashman

RUSHING: Simpson 291/1543y, Scott 84/349y, Grady 69/279y
PASSING: Sogge 75-151/1032y, 7TD, 49.7%
RECEIVING: McCullough 30/540y, Lawrence 20/319y, Simpson 10/109y, Miller 10/80y
SCORING: Simpson 78pts, Aldridge 46pts, McCullough 30pts

1968 9-1-1

29 Minnesota	20 WR Bob Chandler / Sam Dickerson
24 Northwestern	7 T Sid Smith
28 Miami	3 G Fred Khasigian
27 Stanford	24 C Dick Allmon
14 Washington	7 G Steve Lehmer
20 Oregon	13 T Jack O'Malley
35 California	17 TE Bob Klein / Bob Miller
17 Oregon State	13 QB Steve Sogge
28 UCLA	16 TB O.J. Simpson / Wilson Bowie
21 Notre Dame	21 WB Jim Lawrence
16 Ohio State■	27 FB Dan Scott / Humphrey Covington
	DL Jim Grissum / Bill Hayhoe
	DL Al Cowlings
	DL Willard Scott / Bill Redding
	DL Tony Terry
	DL Jimmy Gunn
	LB Jim Snow / Mike Haluchak
	LB John Blanche / Bob Jensen
	DB Sandy Durko / John Young
	DB Mike Battle
	DB Ron Ayala
	DB Gerry Shaw

RUSHING: Simpson 383/1880y, Scott 73/270y, Covington 12/58y
PASSING: Sogge 122-207/1454y, 9TD, 58.9%
RECEIVING: Lawrence 26/386y, Simpson 26/211y, Klein 23/237y
SCORING: Simpson 138pts, Ayala (K) 47pts, Dickerson 18pts

1969 10-0-1

31 Nebraska	21 WR Sam Dickerson / Terry DeKraai
48 Northwestern	6 WR Bob Chandler / Gary Orcutt
31 Oregon State	7 T Sid Smith
26 Stanford	24 G Fred Khasigian
14 Notre Dame	14 C Bill Redding
29 Georgia Tech	18 G Steve Lehmer / Wayne Yary
14 California	9 T John Vella / Marv Montgomery
28 Washington St.	7 TE Gerry Mullins
16 Washington	7 QB Jimmy Jones / Jim Fassell
14 UCLA	12 TB Clarence Davis / Mike Berry
10 Michigan■	3 FB Charlie Evans / Humphrey Covington
	DL Jimmy Gunn
	DL Al Cowlings
	DL Willard Scott / Tony Terry
	DL Tody Smith / Gary McArthur
	DL Charlie Weaver
	LB Bob Jensen
	LB Greg Slough / Mike Haluchak
	DB Sandy Durko
	DB Tyrone Hudson
	DB John Young / Ron Ayala
	DB Gerry Shaw

RUSHING: Davis 297/1351y, Evans 76/328y, Berry 83/328y
PASSING: Jones 88-210/1230y, 13TD, 41.9%
RECEIVING: Dickerson 24/473y, DeKraai 19/215y, Chandler 17/279y
SCORING: Davis 54pts, Ayala (K) 45pts, Dickerson 36pts

1970 6-4-1

42 Alabama	21 WR Sam Dickerson
21 Nebraska	21 WR Bob Chandler / Mike Morgan
48 Iowa	0 T Pete Adams / Marv Montgomery
45 Oregon State	13 G Allan Graf / Mike Ryan
14 Stanford	24 C Dave Brown
28 Washington	25 G Wayne Yary
7 Oregon	10 T John Vella
10 California	13 TE Gerry Mullins / Charles Young
70 Washington St.	33 QB Jimmy Jones / Mike Rae
20 UCLA	45 TB Clarence Davis / Mike Berry
38 Notre Dame	28 FB Sam "Bam" Cunn'ngh'm/Ch'rlie Evans
	DL Charlie Weaver / Ken Carter
	DL John Grant
	DL Tody Smith / John Skiles
	DL Willie Hall / Jim Grissum
	LB Mike Haluchak / Ron Preston
	LB Greg Slough
	LB John Papadakis
	DB Walt Failor
	DB Bruce Dyer
	DB Tyrone Hudson
	DB Ron Ayala / Curt Timmons

RUSHING: Davis 214/972y, Cunningham 76/488y
PASSING: Jones 121-234/1877y, 10TD, 51.7%
RECEIVING: Chandler 41/590y, Dickerson 24/527y, Young 16/322y, Cunningham 16/167y
SCORING: Davis 66pts, Ayala (K) 55pts, Cunningham 44pts

1971 6-4-1

10 Alabama	17 WR Edesel Garrison / Mike Morgan
24 Rice	0 WR Lynn Swann
28 Illinois	0 T Pete Adams / Bob Shaputis
20 Oklahoma	33 G Mike Ryan / Allen Gallaher
23 Oregon	28 C Dave Brown
18 Stanford	33 G Allan Graf
28 Notre Dame	14 T John Vella / Steve Riley
28 California	0 TE Charles Young
30 Washington St.	20 QB Jimmy Jones / Mike Rae
13 Washington	12 TB Lou Harris / Charles Hinton
7 UCLA	7 FB Bam Cunningham / Ray Washmera
	DL Mike McGirr
	DL John Grant
	DL John Skiles / George Follett
	DL Scott Weber
	LB Charles Anthony / Bob Eriksen
	LB Willie Hall
	LB John Papadakis
	DB Skip Thomas
	DB Bruce Dyer
	DB Artimus Parker
	DB Steve Fate

RUSHING: Harris 167/801y, Cunningham 159/742y, Jones 87/267y
PASSING: Jones 89-161/995y, 7TD, 55.3%, Rae 38-79/599y, 7TD, 48.1%
RECEIVING: Swann 27/305y, Garrison 25/475y, Young 23/298y
SCORING: Rae (QB-K) 37pts, Young 36pts, 3 with 30pts

1972 12-0

31 Arkansas	10 WR Edesel Garrison / John McKay
51 Oregon State	6 WR Lynn Swann / Dave Boulware
55 Illinois	20 T Pete Adams
51 Michigan State	6 G Allan Graf / Booker Brown
30 Stanford	21 C Dave Brown
42 California	14 G Mike Ryan
34 Washington	7 T Steve Riley / Allan Gallaher
30 Oregon	0 TE Charles Young
44 Washington St.	3 QB Mike Rae / Pat Haden
24 UCLA	7 TB Anthony Davis / Rod McNeill
45 Notre Dame	23 FB Bam Cunningham / Manfred Moore
42 Ohio State■	17 DL Dale Mitchell
	DL John Grant
	DL Monte Doris / George Follett
	DL Jeff Winans / Glenn Byrd
	DL James Sims / Ed Powell
	LB Richard Wood
	LB Charles Anthony / Ray Rodriguez
	DB Charles Hinton / Marvin Cobb
	DB Eddie Johnson / Charles Phillips
	DB Artimus Parker
	DB Steve Fate

RUSHING: Davis 207/1191y, McNeill 131/567y, Cunningham 102/349y
PASSING: Rae 114-199/1754y, 5TD, 57.3%, Haden 34-72/468y, 7TD, 47.2%
RECEIVING: Young 29/470y, Swann 27/543y, McKay 26/342y
SCORING: Davis 114pts, Rae (QB-K) 103pts, Cunningham 78pts

1973 9-2-1

17 Arkansas	0 WR John McKay
23 Georgia Tech	6 WR Lynn Swann / Dave Boulware
7 Oklahoma	7 T Bill Bain
21 Oregon State	7 G Mike Cordell
46 Washington St.	35 C Bob McCaffrey
31 Oregon	10 G Booker Brown
14 Notre Dame	23 T Steve Riley
50 California	14 TE Jim Obradovich
27 Stanford	26 QB Pat Haden
42 Washington	19 TB Anthony Davis / Allen Carter
23 UCLA	13 FB Manfred Moore / Rod McNeill
21 Ohio State■	42 DL James Sims
	DL Gary Jeter
	DL Monte Doris
	DL Art Riley
	DL Ed Powell / Ray Rodriguez (LB)
	LB Richard Wood / Dale Mitchell
	LB Charles Anthony / Kevin Bruce
	DB Danny Reece
	DB Marvin Cobb
	DB Artimus Parker
	DB Charles Phillips

RUSHING: Davis 276/1112y, McNeill 142/763y, Carter 43/294y
PASSING: Haden 137-247/1832y, 13TD, 55.5%
RECEIVING: Swann 42/714y, McKay 28/434y, Obradovich 17/284y
SCORING: Davis 90pts, Chris Limahelu (K) 73pts, Swann 42pts

1974 10-1-1

7 Arkansas	22 WR John McKay
16 Pittsburgh	7 WR Shelton Diggs
41 Iowa	3 T Marvin Powell
54 Washington St.	7 G Joe Davis
16 Oregon	7 C Bob McCaffrey
31 Oregon State	10 G Bill Bain
15 California	15 T Steve Knutson
34 Stanford	10 TE Jim Obradovich
42 Washington	11 QB Pat Haden
34 UCLA	9 TB Anthony Davis / Allen Carter
55 Notre Dame	24 FB Ricky Bell / Dave Farmer
18 Ohio State■	17 DL Gary Jeter
	DL Otha Bradley
	DL Art Riley
	LB Ed Powell / David Lewis
	LB Richard Wood / Clay Matthews
	LB Mario Celotto / Dale Mitchell
	LB Kevin Bruce
	DB Danny Reece
	DB Ron Bush
	DB Marvin Cobb
	DB Charles Phillips / Doug Hogan

RUSHING: Davis 301/1421y, Carter 111/580y, Bell 45/299y
PASSING: Haden 70-149/988y, 13TD, 47.0%
RECEIVING: McKay 34/550y, Davis 15/96y, Obradovich 9/121y
SCORING: Davis 110pts, Chris Limahelu (K) 69pts, McKay 48pts

1975 8-4

35 Duke	7 WR Randy Simmrin
24 Oregon State	7 WR Shelton Diggs
19 Purdue	6 T Marvin Powell
27 Iowa	16 G Joe Davis
28 Washington St.	10 C Mike Cordell
17 Oregon	3 G Donnie Hickman
24 Notre Dame	17 T Melvin Jackson
14 California	28 TE Mike Howell
10 Stanford	13 QB Vince Evans / Rob Hertel
7 Washington	8 TB Ricky Bell
22 UCLA	25 FB Mosi Tatupu
20 Texas A&M■	0 DL Walt Underwood
	DL Harold Steele / Tim Rhames
	DL Gary Jeter
	LB David Lewis
	LB Clay Matthews / Dale Logie
	LB Rod Martin / Mario Celotto
	LB Eric Williams
	DB Danny Reece / Ricky Odom
	DB Ron Bush
	DB Dennis Thurman
	DB Clint Strozier / Doug Hogan

RUSHING: Bell 385/1957y, Tatupu 82/425y, Evans 104/246y
PASSING: Evans 35-112/695y, 3TD, 31.3%
RECEIVING: Simmrin 26/478y, Bell 4/100y, Diggs 4/75y, Howell 4/58y
SCORING: Bell 88pts, Glen Walker (K) 49pts, Evans 32pts

1976 11-1

25 Missouri	46 WR Randy Simmrin
53 Oregon	0 WR Shelton Diggs
31 Purdue	13 T Marvin Powell
55 Iowa	0 G Brad Budde / Pat Howell
23 Washington St.	14 C Gary Bethel
56 Oregon State	0 G Donnie Hickman
20 California	6 T Otis Page
48 Stanford	24 TE William Gay / Jim Obradovich
20 Washington	3 QB Vince Evans
24 UCLA	14 TB Ricky Bell / Charles White
17 Notre Dame	13 FB Mosi Tatupu / Dave Farmer
14 Michigan■	6 DL Walt Underwood / Vinny Van Dyke
	DL Harold Steele / Rich Dimler
	DL Gary Jeter / Ed Gutierrez
	LB David Lewis
	LB Clay Matthews
	LB Rod Martin / Mario Celotto
	LB Eric Williams / Garry Cobb
	DB Ricky Odom / Carter Hartwig
	DB Ron Bush
	DB Dennis Thurman
	DB Clint Strozier

RUSHING: Bell 280/1433y, White 156/858y, Tatupu 56/391y
PASSING: Evans 75-177/1440y, 10TD, 53.7%
RECEIVING: Diggs 37/655y, Simmrin 32/653y, Bell 14/85y
SCORING: Bell 86pts, Glen Walker (K) 71pts, White 66pts

1977 8-4

27 Missouri	10 WR Calvin Sweeney / Howard Studdard
17 Oregon State	10 WR Randy Simmrin / Kevin Williams
51 TCU	0 T Anthony Munoz
41 Washington St.	7 G Brad Budde
20 Alabama	21 C Gary Bethel
33 Oregon	15 G Pat Howell
19 Notre Dame	49 T John Schumacher
14 California	17 TE William Gay
49 Stanford	0 QB Rob Hertel
10 Washington	28 TB Charles White / Dwight Ford
29 UCLA	27 FB Mosi Tatupu / Lynn Cain
47 Texas A&M■	28 DL Walt Underwood
	DL Rich Dimler
	DL Myron Lapka / Ty Sperling
	DL Ed Gutierrez
	LB Dennis Johnson
	LB Clay Matthews / Mario Celotto
	LB Garry Cobb / Larry McGrew
	DB Larry Braziel / Carter Hartwig
	DB Ricky Odom
	DB Dennis Thurman
	DB Willie Crawford / Ronnie Lott

RUSHING: White 185/1478y, Ford 98/763y, Tatupu 78/416y
PASSING: Hertel 132-245/2145y, 19TD, 53.9%
RECEIVING: Simmrin 41/840y, Sweeney 33/564y, Gay 13/128y
SCORING: Frank Jordan (K) 68pts, White 54pts, Cain 42pts

1978 12-1

17 Texas Tech	9 WR Calvin Sweeney / Dan Garcia
37 Oregon	10 WR Kevin Williams / Vic Rakhshani
24 Alabama	14 T Keith Van Horne
30 Michigan State	9 G Brad Budde
7 Arizona State	20 C Ray Peters
38 Oregon State	7 G Pat Howell
42 California	17 T Otis Page / Anthony Munoz
13 Stanford	7 TE James Hunter
28 Washington	10 QB Paul McDonald
17 UCLA	10 TB Charles White / Dwight Ford
27 Notre Dame	25 FB Lynn Cain / Marcus Allen
21 Hawaii	5 DL Myron Lapka
17 Michigan■	10 DL Rich Dimler
	DL Ty Sperling / Dennis Edwards
	DL Garry Cobb / Chip Banks
	LB Riki Gray / Charlie Moses
	LB Dennis Johnson
	LB Larry McGrew / Eric Scoggins
	DB Carter Hartwig / Herb Ward
	DB Tim Lavender / Larry Braziel
	DB Dennis Smith
	DB Ronnie Lott / Willie Crawford

RUSHING: White 374/1859y, Cain 187/977y, Ford 62/265y
PASSING: McDonald 115-203/1690y, 19TD, 56.7%
RECEIVING: Sweeney 32/644y, White 22/193y, Williams 17/317y
SCORING: White 86pts, Frank Jordan (K) 68pts, Williams 60pts

1979 11-0-1

21 Texas Tech	7 WR Kevin Williams / Dan Garcia
42 Oregon State	5 WR Vic Rakhshani / Ray Butler
48 Minnesota	14 T Keith Van Horne
LSU	12 G Brad Budde
50 Washington St.	21 C Chris Foote
21 Stanford	21 G Roy Foster
42 Notre Dame	23 T Don Mosebar / Bruce Mathews (G)
24 California	14 TE Hoby Brenner / James Hunter
34 Arizona	7 QB Paul McDonald
24 Washington	17 TB Charles White / Michael Hayes
49 UCLA	14 FB Marcus Allen
17 Ohio State■	16 DL Myron Lapka / Byron Darby
	DL Ty Sperling / George Achica
	DL Dennis Edwards
	LB Chip Banks / Mike McDonald
	LB Dennis Johnson
	LB Riki Gray / Steve Busick
	LB Larry McGrew / Eric Scoggins
	DB Herb Ward
	DB Jeff Fisher / Joey Browner
	DB Dennis Smith
	DB Ronnie Lott / Kenney Moore

RUSHING: White 332/2050y, Allen 114/649y, Hayes 64/348y
PASSING: McDonald 164-264/2223y, 18TD, 62.1%
RECEIVING: Garcia 29/492y, Williams 25/491y, Butler 23/337y
SCORING: White 114pts, Eric Hipp (K) 67pts, Allen & Williams 48pts

1980 8-2-1

20 Tennessee	17 WR Kevin Williams / Malcolm Moore
23 South Carolina	13 WR Vic Rakhshani / Jeff Simmons
24 Minnesota	7 T Keith Van Horne
23 Arizona State	21 G Bruce Matthews
27 Arizona	10 C Allen Pugh
7 Oregon	7 G Roy Foster
60 California	7 T Don Mosebar
34 Stanford	9 TE Hoby Brenner / James Hunter
10 Washington	20 QB Gordon Adams
17 UCLA	20 TB Marcus Allen / Anthony Gibson
20 Notre Dame	3 FB Paul DiLulo / Michael Harper
	DL Byron Darby / August Curley
	DL George Achica / Charles Ussery
	DL Dennis Edwards / Keith Browner
	LB Chip Banks
	LB Riki Gray
	LB Steve Busick
	LB Eric Scoggins
	DB Joey Browner
	DB Jeff Fisher / Don Jones
	DB Dennis Smith
	DB Ronnie Lott

RUSHING: Allen 354/1563y, Harper 55/274y, Gibson 46/226y
PASSING: Adams 104-179/1237y, 7TD, 58.1%
RECEIVING: Allen 30/231y, Brenner 26/315y, Simmons 21/309y
SCORING: Allen 84pts, Eric Hipp (K) 65pts, Harper, Simmons & Williams 24pts

1981 9-3

43 Tennessee	7 WR John Kamana / Malcolm Moore
21 Indiana	0 WR Jeff Simmons / Timmy White
28 Oklahoma	24 T Don Mosebar
56 Oregon State	22 G Bruce Matthews
10 Arizona	13 C Tony Slaton
25 Stanford	17 G Roy Foster
14 Notre Dame	7 T Kelly Thomas
41 Washington St.	17 TE Fred Cornwell
21 California	3 QB John Mazur
3 Washington	13 TB Marcus Allen / Fred Crutcher
22 UCLA	21 FB Todd Spencer / Bob McClananahan
10 Penn State■	26 DL Keith Browner
	DL George Achica / John Harvey
	DL Charles Ussery / Byron Darby
	DL Dennis Edwards
	LB August Curley
	LB Chip Banks / Jeff Brown / Neil Hope
	LB Jack Del Rio / Tim Sullivan
	DB Joe Turner
	DB Troy West
	DB Marv Williams
	DB Joey Browner

RUSHING: Allen 433/2427y, Spencer 62/377y, Crutcher 36/268y
PASSING: Mazur 93-194/1128y, 7TD, 47.9%
RECEIVING: Allen 34/256y, Simmons 28/543y, Moore 15/230y
SCORING: Allen 138pts, Steve Jordan (K) 65pts, 4 with 12pts

1982 8-3

9 Florida	17 WR Jeff Simmons
28 Indiana	7 WR Timmy White
12 Oklahoma	0 T Don Mosebar
38 Oregon	7 G Bruce Matthews
41 Stanford	21 C Tony Slaton
38 Oregon State	0 G Joe Murray
10 Arizona State	17 T Kelly Thomas
42 California	0 TE Fred Cornwell / Pat McCool
48 Arizona	41 QB Sean Salisbury / Scott Tinsley
19 UCLA	20 TB Todd Spencer / Anthony Gibson
17 Notre Dame	13 FB Kennedy Pola / John Kamana
	DL Brian Luft / Duane Bickett
	DL George Achica / Matt Koart
	DL Byron Darby / August Curley
	LB Keith Browner
	LB Neil Hope / Tim Sullivan
	LB Riki Gray /
	LB Jack Del Rio / Jeff Brown
	DB Darrel Hopper
	DB Troy West / Matt Johnson
	DB Tony Brewer
	DB Joey Browner

RUSHING: Spencer 141/596y, Gibson 140/581y
PASSING: Salisbury 82-142/1062y, 6TD, 57.7%, Tinsley 74-127/879y, 4TD, 58.3%
RECEIVING: Simmons 56/973y, White 24/404y, Spencer 15/163y
SCORING: Steve Jordan (K) 68pts, Spencer 54pts, Gibson & Simmons 30pts

1983 4-6-1

19 Florida	19 WR Hank Norman
33 Oregon State	10 WR Timmie Ware / Joe Cormier
20 Kansas	26 T James Fitzpatrick
14 South Carolina	38 G Jeff Bregel
38 Washington St.	17 C Tony Slaton
14 Arizona State	34 G Tom Hallock
6 Notre Dame	27 T Ken Ruettgers / Mike Lamb
19 California	9 TE Fred Cornwell
30 Stanford	7 QB Sean Salisbury
0 Washington	24 TB Michael Harper / Fred Crutcher
17 UCLA	27 FB Kennedy Pola / John Kamana
	DL Brian Luft
	DL Tony Colorito / Dave Purling
	DL Matt Koart
	LB Keith Browner
	LB Duane Bickett
	LB Jeff Brown / Neil Hope
	LB Jack Del Rio
	DB Tommy Haynes / Darrel Hopper
	DB Duaine Jackson / Matt Johnson
	DB Tony Brewer
	DB Jerome Tyler

RUSHING: Harper 151/685y, Crutcher 121/528y, Spencer 93/364y
PASSING: Salisbury 142-248/1882y, 10TD, 57.3%
RECEIVING: Norman 31/407y, Cormier 28/416y, Ware 23/481y
SCORING: Steve Jordan (K) 56pts, Harper 36pts, Ware 30pts

1984 9-3

42 Utah State	7 WR Hank Norman
6 Arizona State	3 WR Timmie Ware / Joe Cormier
3 LSU	23 T James Fitzpatrick
29 Washington St.	27 G Jeff Bregel
19 Oregon	9 C Tom Cox / Andy Baroncelli
17 Arizona	14 G Tom Hallock
31 California	7 T Ken Ruettgers
20 Stanford	11 TE Mark Boyer
16 Washington	7 QB Tim Green
10 UCLA	29 TB Fred Crutcher / Ryan Knight
7 Notre Dame	19 FB Kennedy Pola
20 Ohio State ■	17 DL Brian Luft
	DL Tony Colorito
	DL Brent Moore / Dave Purling
	LB Keith Biggers
	LB Duane Bickett
	LB Neil Hope
	LB Jack Del Rio
	DB Tommy Haynes / Matt Johnson
	DB Duaine Jackson / Darrel Hopper
	DB Tim McDonald
	DB Jerome Tyler

RUSHING: Crutcher 307/1155y, Knight 121/489y, Lee 42/268y
PASSING: Green 116-224/1448y, 5TD, 51.8%
RECEIVING: Norman 39/643y, Cormier 33/364y, Ware 28/425y
SCORING: Steve Jordan (K) 73pts, Crutcher 60pts, Knight 30pts

1985 6-6

20 Illinois	10 WR Hank Norman
13 Baylor	20 WR Randy Tanner / Al Washington
0 Arizona State	24 T James Fitzpatrick
63 Oregon State	0 G Jeff Bregel
30 Stanford	6 C Tom Fox
3 Notre Dame	37 G Dave Cadigan
31 Washington St.	13 T Gaylord Kuamoo
6 California	14 TE Joe Cormier
17 Washington	20 QB Sean Salisbury / Rodney Peete
17 UCLA	13 TB Ry'n Kn'ght/F.Crutch'r/Aar'n Emanuel
20 Oregon	6 FB Kennedy Pola
3 Alabama ■	24 DL Tony Colorito / Gary Willison
	DL Brent Moore
	DL Matt Koart
	LB Garrett Breeland
	LB Keith Davis
	LB Sam Anno
	LB Marcus Cotton
	DB Louis Brock
	DB Matt Johnson
	DB Tim McDonald
	DB Jerome Tyler

RUSHING: Knight 195/732y, Crutcher 145/621y, Emanuel 97/472y
PASSING: Salisbury 98-172/1180y, 6TDs, 57.0%
RECEIVING: Cormier 44/409y, Norman 39/635y, Tanner 12/216y
SCORING: Don Shafer (K) 71pts, Crutcher 36pts, Knight 24pts

1986 7-5

31 Illinois	16 WR Ken Henry
17 Baylor	14 WR Randy Tanner
20 Washington	10 T Dave Cadigan
35 Oregon	21 G Jeff Bregel
14 Washington St.	34 C John Katnik
20 Arizona State	29 G Brent Parkinson
10 Stanford	0 T Bruce Parks
20 Arizona	13 TE Erik McKee
28 California	3 QB Rodney Peete
25 UCLA	45 TB Ryan Knight / Aaron Emanuel
37 Notre Dame	38 FB Todd Steele / Leroy Holt
7 Auburn ■	16 DL Deryl Henderson
	DL Dan Owens
	DL Tim Ryan
	LB Ron Brown
	LB Keith Davis
	LB Rex Moore
	LB Marcus Cotton
	DB Louis Brock
	DB Greg Coauette
	DB Tim McDonald
	DB Junior Thurman

RUSHING: Knight 148/536y, Emanuel 128/495y, Steele 51/216y
PASSING: Peete 160-305/2138y, 10TD, 52.5%
RECEIVING: Henry 43/807y, Tanner 29/408y, McKee 17/154y
SCORING: Don Shafer (K) 65pts, Henry & Knight 42pts

1987 8-4

13 Michigan State	27 WR Erik Affholter
23 Boston College	17 WR Randy Tanner / John Jackson
31 California	14 T Dave Cadigan
48 Oregon State	14 G Brent Parkinson
27 Oregon	34 C John Katnik
37 Washington	23 G Mark Tucker
15 Notre Dame	26 T John Guerrero
42 Washington St.	7 TE Paul Green
39 Stanford	24 QB Rodney Peete
12 Arizona	10 TB Steven Webster
17 UCLA	13 FB Leroy Holt
17 Michigan St. ■	20 DL Dan Owens
	DL Don Gibson
	DL Tim Ryan
	DL Bill Stokes
	LB Delmar Chesley / Scott Ross
	LB Keith Davis
	LB Marcus Cotton
	DB Chris Hale / Dwayne Garner
	DB Greg Coauette
	DB Mark Carrier
	DB Cleveland Colter

RUSHING: Webster 239/1109y, Holt 128/496y, Lockwood 42/233y
PASSING: Peete 197-332/2709y, 21TD, 59.3%
RECEIVING: Affholter 44/649y, Jackson 37/5578y, Green 31/317y
SCORING: Quin Rodriguez (K) 74pts, Tanner 44pts, Jackson 42pts

1988 10-2

34 Boston College	7 WR Erik Affholter
24 Stanford	20 WR John Jackson / Gary Wellman
23 Oklahoma	7 T Brent Parkinson
38 Arizona	15 G Mark Tucker
42 Oregon	14 C Brad Leggett
28 Washington	27 G Dan Barnes
41 Oregon State	20 T John Guerrero
35 California	3 TE Scott Galbraith
50 Arizona State	0 QB Rodney Peete
10 Notre Dame	27 TB Aaron Emanuel / Scott Lockwood
31 UCLA	22 FB Leroy Holt
14 Michigan ■	22 DL Dan Owens
	DL Don Gibson
	DL Tim Ryan
	DL Michael Williams
	LB Scott Ross / Junior Seau
	LB Delmar Chesley
	LB Craig Hartsuyker / Brian Tuliau
	DB Chris Hale
	DB Ernest Spears
	DB Mark Carrier
	DB Cleveland Colter

RUSHING: Emanuel 108/545y, Holt 122/540y, Lockwood 117/527y
PASSING: Peete 223-359/2812y, 18TDs, 62.1%
RECEIVING: Affholter 68/952y, Jackson 48/609y, Wellman 21/377y
SCORING: Quin Rodriguez (K) 76pts, Emanuel 54pts, Affholter 52pts

1989 9-2-1

13 Illinois	14 WR Gary Wellman
66 Utah State	10 WR John Jackson
42 Ohio State	3 T Bill Schultz
18 Washington St.	17 G Mark Tucker
24 Washington	16 C Brad Leggett
31 California	15 G Brent Parkinson
24 Notre Dame	28 T Pat Harlow
19 Stanford	0 TE Scott Galbraith
48 Oregon State	6 QB Todd Marinovich
24 Arizona	3 TB Ricky Ervins / Aaron Emanuel
10 UCLA	10 FB Leroy Holt
17 Michigan ■	10 DL Dan Owens
	DL Gene Fruge
	DL Tim Ryan
	LB Junior Seau
	LB Delmar Chesley
	LB Scott Ross
	LB Michael Williams
	DB Dwayne Garner
	DB Ernest Spears
	DB Mark Carrier
	DB Cleveland Colter

RUSHING: Ervins 269/1395y, Holt 123/619y, Emanuel 57/272y
PASSING: Marinovich 219-352/2578y, 16TDs, 62.2%
RECEIVING: Jackson 62/964y, Ervins 39/221y, Holt 28/269y
SCORING: Quin Rodriguez (K) 73pts

1990 8-4-1

34 Syracuse	16 WR Larry Wallace / Johnnie Morton
19 Penn State	14 WR Gary Wellman
0 Washington	31 T Michael Moody
35 Ohio State	26 G Derrick Deese
30 Washington St.	17 C Craig Gibson / David Apolskis
37 Stanford	22 G Mark Tucker
26 Arizona	35 T Pat Harlow
13 Arizona State	6 TE Frank Griffin
31 California	31 QB Todd Marinovich
56 Oregon State	7 TB Mazio Royster / Ricky Ervins
45 UCLA	42 FB Scott Lockwood
6 Notre Dame	10 DL Don Gibson
16 Michigan St. ■	17 DL Gene Fruge
	DL Terry McDaniels
	LB Kurt Barber
	LB Scott Ross
	LB Brian Tuliau
	LB Craig Hartsuyker
	DB Calvin Holmes
	DB Mike Salmon / Jason Oliver
	DB Marcus Hopkins
	DB Stephon Pace

RUSHING: Royster 235/1168y, Lockwood 118/534y, Ervins 90/393y
PASSING: Marinovich 196-322/2423y, 15TDs, 60.9%
RECEIVING: Wellman 66/1015y, Royster 25/199y, Lockwood 22/186y
SCORING: Quin Rodriguez 94pts, Royster 48pts, Ervins & Wellman 30pts

1991 3-8

10 Memphis State	24 WR Johnnie Morton / Travis Hannah
21 Penn State	10 WR Larry Wallace / Curtis Conway (QB)
25 Arizona State	32 T Michael Moody
30 Oregon	14 G Derrick Deese / Titus Tuiasosososopo
34 Washington St.	27 C Craig Gibson
21 Stanford	24 G Kris Pollack (T) / Joel Crisman
20 Notre Dame	24 T Tony Boselli
30 California	52 TE Yonnie Jackson / Bradford Banta
3 Washington	14 QB Reggie Perry / Rob Johnson
14 Arizona	31 TB Deon Strother / Mazio Royster
21 UCLA	24 FB Scott Lockwood / Raoul Spears
	DL Terry McDaniels / Jason Uhl
	DL Mike Hinz / Thomas Holland
	DL David Webb / Matt Willig
	LB Lamont Hollinquest (DB) / Kurt Barber
	LB Matt Gee
	LB Gideon Murrell / Brian Williams
	LB Willie McGinest
	DB Calvin Holmes
	DB Jason Oliver / Jerald Henry
	DB Mike Salmon
	DB Stephon Pace / Bruce Luizzi

RUSHING: Strother 129/614y, Royster 111/542y, Estrus Crayton (TB) 69/405y
PASSING: Perry 131-255/1574y, 3 TDs, 51.4%
RECEIVING: Morton 49/662y, Jackson 27/302y, Conway 21/240y
SCORING: Cole Ford (K), Strother & Royster 42pts

1992 6-5-1

31 San Diego State	31 WR Johnnie Morton
20 Oklahoma	10 WR Curtis Conway
10 Washington	17 T Tony Boselli
32 Oregon	10 G Joel Crisman / Clay Hattabaugh
27 California	24 C Craig Gibson
31 Washington St.	21 G Kris Pollock / Robert Loya
23 Arizona State	13 T Len Gorecki / Norberto Garrido
9 Stanford	23 TE Bradford Banta
14 Arizona	7 QB Rob Johnson
37 UCLA	38 TB Estrus Crayton / Deon Strother
23 Notre Dame	31 FB Wes Bender / Michael Jones
7 Fresno State ■	24 DL David Webb / Terry McDaniels
	DL Mike Hinz
	DL Shannon Jones / Thomas Holland
	DL Willie McGinest
	LB Jeff Kopp
	LB Brian Williams
	DB Jerald Henry
	DB Jason Oliver / John Herpin
	DB Mike Salmon
	DB Stephon Pace / Reggie Perry
	DB Jason Sehorn / Scott Fields

RUSHING: Crayton 183/700y
PASSING: Johnson 163-285/2118y, 12TD, 57.2%
RECEIVING: Conway 49/764y, Morton 49/756y
SCORING: Cole Ford (K) 58pts

1993 8-5

9 N. Carolina St.	31 WR Johnnie Morton
49 Houston	7 WR Ken Grace / Edwin Hervey
20 Penn State	21 T Tony Boselli
34 Washington St.	3 G Kris Pollack
7 Arizona	38 C Craig Gibson
24 Oregon	13 G Joel Crisman
34 Oregon State	9 T Norberto Garrido
13 Notre Dame	31 TE Bradford Banta / Johnny McWilliams
42 California	14 QB Rob Johnson / Kyle Wachholtz
45 Stanford	20 TB Deon Strother / Shawn Walters
22 Washington	17 FB Rory Brown
21 UCLA	27 DL Matt Keneley
28 Utah■	21 DL Terry McDaniels
	DL Thomas Holland
	DL Willie McGinest
	LB Brian Williams / Doug Cunningham
	LB Jeff Kopp
	LB Joe Barry
	DB Jason Sehorn
	DB John Herpin / Jerald Henry
	DB Jason Oliver / Micah Phillips
	DB Mike Salmon / Sammy Knight

RUSHING: Walters 156/711y
PASSING: Johnson 308-449/3630y, 29TD, 68.6%
RECEIVING: Morton 88/1520y
SCORING: Morton 86pts

1994 8-3-1

24 Washington	17 WR Ken Grace / Edward Hervey
14 Penn State	38 WR Keyshawn Johnson
37 Baylor	27 T Tony Boselli
7 Oregon	22 G Chris Brymer / Clay Hattabaugh
27 Oregon State	19 C Jeremy Hogue
27 Stanford	20 G Kris Pollack / Phalen Pounds
61 California	0 T Norberto Garrido / Kyle Ramsey
23 Washington St.	10 TE Johnny McWilliams / John Allred
45 Arizona	28 QB Rob Johnson / Brad Otton
19 UCLA	31 TB Shawn Walters / Leonard Green
17 Notre Dame	17 FB Terry Barnum / Rodney Sermons
55 Texas Tech■	14 DL Matt Keneley
	DL Darrell Russell
	DL Willie Lowery / Elic Mahone
	LB Brian Williams / Israel Ifeanyi
	LB Jeff Kopp / Brian Haas
	LB Errick Herrin / Donn Cunnigan
	LB Errol Small / Junior Rickman
	DB Brian Kelly / Jerald Henry
	DB John Herpin / Quincy Harrison
	DB Mario Bradley / Micah Phillips
	DB Sammy Knight

RUSHING: Walters 193/976y, Green 68/343y, Sermons 78/249y
PASSING: R. Johnson 186-276/2499y, 15TDs, 67.4%, Otton 55-92/787y, 6TDs, 59.8%
RECEIVING: K. Johnson 66/1362y, Barnum 34/302y, Grace 27/319y
SCORING: Cole Ford (K) 82pts

1995 9-2-1

45 San Jose State	7 WR Larry Parker / Billy Miller
45 Houston	10 WR Keyshawn Johnson / Chris Miller
31 Arizona	10 T John Michels / Ken Bowen
31 Arizona State	0 G Kyle Ramsey / David Pratchard
26 California	16 C Jeremy Hogue / Jonathan Himebauch
26 Washington St.	14 G Phalen Pounds
10 Notre Dame	38 T Norberto Garrido
21 Washington	21 TE Johnny McWilliams / John Allred
31 Stanford	30 QB Kyle Wachholtz / Brad Otton
28 Oregon State	10 TB Delon Washington / Rodney Sermons
20 UCLA	24 FB Terry Barnum / Shawn Walters
41 Northwestern■	32 DL Marcus Bonds / Willie Lowery
	DL Matt Keneley / Stuart Gage
	DL Darrell Russell / Rome Douglas
	DL Israel Ifeanyi / George Perry
	LB Scott Fields
	LB Errick Herrin
	LB Brian Haas / Mark Cusano
	DB Brian Kelly / Ken Haslip
	DB Daylon McCullough / Quincy Harrison
	DB Micah Phillips / Rashard Cook
	DB Sammy Knight / Grant Pearsall

RUSHING: Washington 220/1058y, Sermons 60/244y
PASSING: Otton 130-220/1532y, 12TD, 61.3%, Wachholtz 105-171/1231y, 11TD, 61.4%
RECEIVING: Johnson 90/1218y, Barnum 29/268y, Parker 24/26
SCORING: Johnson 42pts

1996 6-6

7 Penn State	24 WR Billy Miller / Mike Bastianelli
55 Illinois	3 WR Chris Miller / Larry Parker
46 Oregon State	17 T Ken Bowen / Faasea Mailo
26 Houston	9 G Chris Brymer / David Pratchard
15 California	22 C Jonathan Himebauch
14 Arizona	7 G Travis Claridge
35 Arizona State	48 T Rome Douglas
29 Washington St.	24 TE John Allred / Junior Rickman
10 Washington	21 QB Brad Otton / John Fox
20 Stanford	24 TB Delon Washington / LaVale Woods
41 UCLA	48 FB Rodney Sermons
27 Notre Dame	20 DL George Perry / Lawrence Larry
	DL Matt Keneley / Cedric Jefferson
	DL Darrell Russell / Marc Matock
	DL Willie Lowery / Aaron Williams
	LB Mark Cusano
	LB Chris Claiborne / Taso Papadakis
	LB Sammy Knight (DB) / Ryan Tyiska
	DB Brian Kelly / Ken Haslip
	DB Daylon McCutcheon / Chad Morton
	DB Darnell Lacy
	DB Grant Pearsall / David Gibson

RUSHING: Woods 119/601y, Washington 112/370y, Sermons 54/256y
PASSING: Otton 196-370/2649y, 20TD, 53.0%
RECEIVING: C. Miller 43/793y, Sermons 39/315y, Allred 27/283y, Bastianelli, 24/391y
SCORING: Adam Abrams (K) 72pts

1997 6-5

7 Florida State	14 WR Billy Miller / Mike Bastianelli
21 Washington St.	28 WR R. Jay Soward
27 California	17 T Phalen Pounds
35 UNLV	21 G Chris Brymer / David Pratchard
7 Arizona State	35 C Jonathan Himebauch
20 Notre Dame	17 G Travis Claridge
24 Oregon	22 T Ken Bowen / Rome Douglas
0 Washington	27 TE Antoine Harris
45 Stanford	21 QB John Fox / Mike Van Raaphorst
23 Oregon State	0 TB Delon W'sh'ngt'n/Malaefou MacK'nzie
24 UCLA	31 FB Rodney Sermons / Ted Iacenda
	DL George Perry
	DL Marc Matock / Ennis Davis
	DL Cedric Jefferson / Aaron Williams
	DL Sultan Abdul-Malik
	LB David Gibson (DB) / Ryan Tyiska
	LB Chris Claiborne
	LB Mark Cusano
	DB Brian Kelly
	DB Daylon McCutcheon
	DB Chad Morton / Darnell Lacy
	DB Rashard Cook /Antuan Simmons (LB)

RUSHING: Washington 125/444y, MacKenzie 96/332y
PASSING: Fox 153-280/1940y, 12TD, 54.6%
RECEIVING: Miller 56/649y, Soward 48/831y, Bastianelli 33/376y
SCORING: Soward 66pts, Adam Abrams (K) 55pts, 3 with 18pts

1998 8-5

27 Purdue	17 WR Billy Miller / Larry Parker
35 San Diego State	9 WR R. Jay Soward
40 Oregon State	20 T Ken Bowen / Brent McCaffrey
10 Florida State	30 G Jason Grain
35 Arizona State	24 C Matt McShane
31 California	32 G Travis Claridge
42 Washington St.	14 T Rome Douglas / Matt Welch
13 Oregon	17 TE Antoine Harris
33 Washington	10 QB John Fox / Carson Palmer
34 Stanford	9 TB Chad Morton / Petros Papadakis
17 UCLA	34 FB Ted Iacenda / Marvin Powell
10 Notre Dame	0 DL Lawrence Larry
19 TCU■	28 DL Aaron Williams
	DL Ennis Davis / Todd Keneley
	DL Sultan Abdul-Malik
	LB Zeke Moreno
	LB Chris Claiborne
	LB David Gibson (DB) / Marc Cusano
	DB Antuan Simmons
	DB Daylon McCutcheon
	DB Rashard Cook / Darnell Lacy
	DB Grant Pearsall

RUSHING: Morton 188/967y, Papadakis 90/360y, Frank Strong (TB) 37/193y
PASSING: Palmer 113-207/1475y, 6TD, 54.6%
RECEIVING: Miller 46/556y, Soward 38/615y, Parker 25/476y
SCORING: Papadakis 42pts, Morton & Soward 36pts

1999 6-6

62 Hawaii	7 WR Windrell Hayes / Kareem Kelly
24 San Diego State	21 WR R. Jay Soward
30 Oregon	33 T Brent McCaffrey
37 Oregon State	29 G Trevor Roberts / Faaesea Mailo
24 Arizona	31 C Eric Denmon
24 Notre Dame	25 G Zach Wilson
31 Stanford	35 T Travis Claridge
7 California	17 TE Antoine Harris
16 Arizona State	26 QB Carson Palmer / Mike Van Raaphorst
31 Washington St.	28 TB Chad Morton / Sultan McCullough
17 UCLA	7 FB Charlie Landrigan
45 Louisiana Tech	19 DL Lawrence Ford / S. Adbul-Shaheed
	DL Ryan Nielsen
	DL Ennis Davis
	DL Matt Childers / Todd Keneley
	LB Sultan Abdul-Malik / Kori Dickerson
	LB Zeke Moreno
	LB Marcus Steele
	DB Antuan Simmons
	DB Kris Richard / Jason Oliver
	DB Ifeanyi Ohalete
	DB Frank Strong / Troy Polamalu

RUSHING: Morton 244/1057y, McCullough 90/413y
PASSING: Van Raaphorst 139-258/1758y, 8TD, 53.9%
RECEIVING: Kelly 54/902y, Hayes 52/696y, Soward 48/581y
SCORING: Morton 90pts, David Newbury (K) 69pts, Hayes, Kelly, & Soward 24pts

2000 5-7

29 Penn State	5 WR Kareem Kelly / Steve Stevenson
17 Colorado	14 WR Matt Nickels / Keary Colbert
34 San Jose State	24 T Brent McCaffrey / Jacob Rogers
21 Oregon State	31 G Trevor Roberts / Eric Torres
15 Arizona	31 C Lenny Vandermade
17 Oregon	28 G Zach Wilson
30 Stanford	32 T Faaesea Mailo
16 California	28 TE Antonie Harris / Scott Huber
44 Arizona State	38 QB Carson Palmer
27 Washington St.	33 TB Sultan McCullough/Malaefou M'K'nzie
38 UCLA	35 FB Charlie Landrigan / Petros Papadakis
21 Notre Dame	38 DL Shamsud-Din Adul-Shaheed
	DL Ennis Davis
	DL Bernard Riley / Ryan Nielsen
	DL Sultan Abdul-Malik / Lonnie Ford
	LB Chris Prosser
	LB Aaron Graham / Mike Pollard
	LB Zeke Moreno / Darryl Knight
	DB Kris Richard
	DB Chris Cash
	DB Frank Strong / DeShaun Hill
	DB Troy Polamalu

RUSHING: McCullough 227/1163y, MacKenzie 41/284y
PASSING: Palmer 228-415/2914y, 16TD, 54.9%
RECEIVING: Kelly 55/796y, Colbert 33/480y, Nickles 32/408y
SCORING: Papadakis 48pts, McCullough 36pts

2001 6-6

21 San Jose State	10 WR Kareem Kelly
6 Kansas State	10 WR Keary Colbert / Marcel Allmond
22 Oregon	24 T Jacob Rogers
16 Stanford	21 G Lenny Vandermade
24 Washington	27 C Norm Katnik
48 Arizona State	17 G Zach Wilson
16 Notre Dame	27 T Eric Torres
41 Arizona	34 TE Kori Dickerson / Doyal Butler
16 Oregon State	13 QB Carson Palmer
55 California	14 TB Sultan McCullough
27 UCLA	0 FB Charlie Landrigan / Sunny Byrd
6 Utah■	10 DL Kenechi Udeze / Omar Nazel
	DL Bernard Riley
	DL Shaun Cody / Ryan Nielsen
	DL Lonnie Ford / Bobby DeMars
	LB Chris Prosser
	LB Mike Pollard / Aaron Graham
	LB Matt Grootegoed / Henry Wallace
	DB Kris Richard / Antuan Simmons
	DB Chris Cash / Darrell Rideaux
	DB Frank Strong / DeShaun Hill
	DB Troy Polamalu

RUSHING: McCullough 115/467y, Byrd 113/329y, Palmer 82/282y
PASSING: Palmer 206-351/2567y, 13TDs, 58.7%
RECEIVING: Kelly 46/768y, Colbert 32/404y, Landrigan 29/351y
SCORING: David Davis (K) 76pts,

2002 11-2

24 Auburn	17 WR Kareem Kelly / Mike Williams
40 Colorado	3 WR Keary Colbert
20 Kansas State	27 T Jacob Rogers
22 Oregon State	0 G Lenny Vandermade / Eric Torres (T)
27 Washington St.	30 C Norm Katnik / Derek Graf (G)
30 California	28 G Zach Wilson
41 Washington	21 T Winston Justice
44 Oregon	33 TE Alex Holmes / Gregg Guenther
49 Stanford	17 QB Carson Palmer
34 Arizona State	13 TB Sultan McCullough / Justin Fargas
52 UCLA	21 FB Malaefou MacKenzie / Chad Pierson
44 Notre Dame	13 DL Omar Nazel
38 Iowa■	17 DL Mike Patterson / Bernard Riley
	DL Shaun Cody
	DL Kenechi Udeze
	LB Matt Grootegoed
	LB Mike Pollard
	LB Melvin Simmons
	DB Darrell Rideaux / William Buchanon
	DB Marcell Allmond / Ronald Nunn
	DB DeShaun Hill
	DB Troy Polamalu / Jason Leach

RUSHING: McCullough 179/814y, Fargas 161/715y, Hershel Dennis (TB) 49/198y
PASSING: Palmer 309-489/3942y, 33TD, 63.2%
RECEIVING: Williams 81/1265y, Colbert 71/1029y, Kelly 46/605y
SCORING: Ryan Killeen (K) 95pts, Williams 84pts, MacKenzie 54pts

2003 12-1

23 Auburn	0 WR Mike Williams
35 Brigham Young	18 WR Keary Colbert / Steve Smith
61 Hawaii	32 T Jacob Rogers
31 California	34 G Lenny Vandermade
37 Arizona State	17 C Norm Katnik
44 Stanford	21 G Fred Matua / John Drake
45 Notre Dame	14 T Winston Justice
43 Washington	23 TE Gregg Guenther / Dominique Byrd
43 Washington St.	16 QB Matt Leinart
45 Arizona	0 TB Hershel Dennis / LenDale White
47 UCLA	22 FB Brandon Hancock / Lee Webb
52 Oregon State	28 DL Kenechi Udeze
28 Michigan■	14 DL Mike Patterson
	DL Shaun Cody
	DL Omar Nazel / Frostee Rucker
	LB Matt Grootegoed / Dallas Sartz
	LB Lofa Tatupu
	LB Melvin Simmons / Collin Ashton
	DB Will Poole / Keith Arbot
	DB Marcell Allmond
	DB Jason Leach
	DB Darnell Bing

RUSHING: White 141/754y, Dennis 137/661y, Reggie Bush (TB) 90/521y
PASSING: Leinart 255-402/3556y, 38TD, 63.4%
RECEIVING: Williams 95/1314y, Colbert 69/1013y, Smith 17/319y, Guenther 17/167y, Reggie Bush (TB) 15/314y
SCORING: Ryan Killeen (K) 122pts, Williams 96pts, White 84pts

2004 13-0

24 Virginia Tech	13 WR Dwayne Jarrett / Jason Mitchell
49 Colorado State	0 WR Steve Smith / Chris McFoy
42 Brigham Young	10 T Sam Baker
31 Stanford	28 G John Drake / Jeff Byers
23 California	17 C Ryan Kalil
45 Arizona State	7 G Fred Matua
38 Washington	0 T Taitusi Lutui
42 Washington St.	12 TE Alex Holmes / Dominique Byrd
28 Oregon State	20 QB Matt Leinart
49 Arizona	9 TB Reggie Bush / LenDale White
41 Notre Dame	10 FB Lee Webb / David Kirtman
29 UCLA	24 DL Frostee Rucker
55 Oklahoma■	19 DL Mike Patterson
	DL Shaun Cody / Manuel Wright
	DL Lawrence Jackson
	LB Dallas Sartz
	LB Lofa Tatupu
	LB Matt Grootegoed / Keith Rivers
	DB Justin Wyatt / Ronald Nunn
	DB Eric Wright / Keith Arbot
	DB Jason Leach
	DB Darnell Bing / Scott Ware

RUSHING: White 203/1103y, Bush 143/908y, Desmond Reed (TB) 31/182y
PASSING: Leinart 269-412/3322y, 33TD, 65.3%
RECEIVING: Jarrett 55/849y, Bush 43/509y, Smith 42/660y, Byrd 37/384y
SCORING: Ryan Killeen (K) 112pts, White 102pts, Bush 90pts

2005 12-1

63 Hawaii	17 WR Dwayne Jarrett
70 Arkansas	17 WR Steve Smith
45 Oregon	13 T Sam Baker
38 Arizona State	28 G Taitusi Lutui
42 Arizona	21 C Ryan Kalil
34 Notre Dame	31 G Fred Matua
51 Washington	24 T Winston Justice
55 Washington St.	13 TE Dominique Byrd
51 Stanford	21 QB Matt Leinart
35 California	10 TB Reggie Bush / LenDale White
50 Fresno State	42 FB David Kirtman
66 UCLA	19 DL Frostee Rucker
38 Texas■	41 DL Sedrick Ellis / Travis Tofi
	DL LaJuan Ramsey
	DL Lawrence Jackson
	LB Thomas Williams / Brian Cushing
	LB Oscar Lua / Rey Maualuga
	LB Collin Ashton / Keith Rivers
	DB Justin Wyatt
	DB John Walker / Josh Pinkard
	DB Scott Ware / Ryan Ting
	DB Darnell Bing / Brandon Ting

RUSHING: Bush 200/1740y, White 197/1302y, Desmond Reed 19/137y
PASSING: Leinart 283-431/3815y, 28TD, 65.7%
RECEIVING: Jarrett 91/1274y, Smith 60/957y, Bush 37/478y
SCORING: White 156pts, Mario Danelo (K) 116pts, Bush 114pts

2006 11-2

50 Arkansas	14 WR Dwayne Jarrett / Patrick Turner
28 Nebraska	10 WR Steve Smith / Chris McFoy
20 Arizona	3 T Sam Baker
28 Washington St.	22 G Drew Radovich
26 Washington	20 C Ryan Kalil
28 Arizona State	21 G Chilo Rachal
31 Oregon State	33 T Kyle Williams
42 Stanford	0 TE Fred Davis
35 Oregon	10 QB John David Booty
23 California	9 TB Chauncey Washington / C.J. Gable
44 Notre Dame	24 FB Stanley Havili / Ryan Powdrell
9 UCLA	13 DL Brian Cushing (LB)
32 Michigan■	18 DL Sedrick Ellis
	DL Chris Barrett / Fili Moala
	DL Lawrence Jackson
	LB Dallas Sartz / Thomas Williams
	LB Rey Maualuga / Oscar Lua
	LB Keith Rivers / Kaluka Maiava
	DB Terrell Thomas / Kevin Thomas
	DB Cary Harris
	DB Taylor Mays
	DB Kevin Ellison

RUSHING: Washington 157/744y, Emmanuel Moody (TB) 79/459y, Gable 111/434y
PASSING: Booty 269-436/3347y, 29TD, 61.7%
RECEIVING: Smith 71/1083y, Jarrett 70/1015y, Davis 38/352y
SCORING: Mario Danelo (K) 89pts, Jarrett 72pts, Washington 56pts

2007 11-2

38 Idaho	10 WR Patrick Turner / David Ausberry
49 Nebraska	31 WR Vidal Hazelton / Ronald Johnson
47 Washington St.	14 T Sam Baker / Butch Lewis
27 Washington	24 G Jeff Byers / Alatini Malu
23 Stanford	24 C Matt Spanos / Kristofer O'Dowd
20 Arizona	13 G Chilo Rachal / Zack Heberer
38 Notre Dame	0 T Drew Radovich / Charles Brown
17 Oregon	24 TE Fred Davis
24 Oregon State	3 QB John David Booty / Mark Sanchez
24 California	17 TB Chauncey Washington / Joe McKnight
44 Arizona State	24 FB Stanley Havili
24 UCLA	7 DL Lawrence Jackson
49 Illinois■	17 DL Sedrick Ellis
	DL Fili Moala
	DL Kyle Moore / Everson Griffen
	LB Brian Cushing / Thomas Williams
	LB Rey Maualuga / Luther Brown
	LB Keith Rivers / Kaluka Maiava
	DB Cary Harris / Shareece Wright
	DB Terrell Thomas
	DB Taylor Mays
	DB Kevin Ellison

RUSHING: Washington 195/969y, Stafon Johnson (TB) 98/673y, McKnight 94/540y
PASSING: Booty 215-340/2361y, 23TD, 63.2%, Sanchez 69-114/695y, 7TD, 60.5%
RECEIVING: Davis 62/881y, Hazelton 50/540y, Turner 48/569y
SCORING: David Buehler (K) 100pts, Washington 72pts, Davis 48pts

2008 12-1

52 Virginia	7 WR Patrick Turner / Vidal Hazelton
35 Ohio State	3 WR Damian Williams / Ronald Johnson
21 Oregon State	27 T Charles Brown
44 Oregon	10 G Jeff Byers
28 Arizona State	0 C Kristofer O'Dowd
69 Washington St.	0 G Alex Parsons / Zack Heberer
17 Arizona	10 T Butch Lewis / Nick Howell
56 Washington	0 TE Anthony McCoy / Blake Ayles
17 California	3 QB Mark Sanchez
45 Stanford	23 TB C.J. Gable / Stafon Johnson
38 Notre Dame	3 FB Stanley Havili
28 UCLA	7 DL Clay Matthews (LB) / Everson Griffen
38 Penn State■	24 DL Christian Tupou / Averell Spicer
	DL Fili Moala
	DL Kyle Moore
	LB Brian Cushing / Michael Morgan
	LB Rey Maualuga
	LB Kaluka Maiava / Malcolm Smith
	DB Josh Pinkard / Kevin Thomas
	DB Cary Harris / Shareece Wright
	DB Taylor Mays
	DB Kevin Ellison / Will Harris

RUSHING: S. Johnson 138/705y, Joe McKnight (TB) 89/659y, Gable 107/617y
PASSING: Sanchez 241-366/3207y, 34TD, 65.8%
RECEIVING: Williams , Turner , R. Johnson , Havili
SCORING: David Buehler (K) 92pts, Gable & Turner 60pts, S. Johnson & Williams 54pts

2009 9-4

56 San Jose State	3 WR Ronald Johnson / David Ausberry
18 Ohio State	15 WR Damian Williams / Brice Butler
13 Washington	16 T Charles Brown
27 Washington St.	6 G Jeff Byers (C)
30 California	3 C Kristofer O'Dowd
34 Notre Dame	27 G Alex Parsons / Butch Lewis
42 Oregon State	36 T Tyron Smith
20 Oregon	47 TE Anthony McCoy/ Rhett Ellison/ B. Ayles
14 Arizona State	9 QB Matt Barkley / Aaron Corp
21 Stanford	55 TB Joe McKnight / Allen Bradford
28 UCLA	7 FB Stanley Havili
17 Arizona	21 DL Wes Horton / Nick Perry
24 Boston College■	13 DL Christian Tupou
	DL Jurell Casey / Armond Armstead
	DL Everson Griffen / Malik Jackson
	LB Devon Kennard (DL) / Shane Horton
	LB Chris Gallipo
	LB Malcolm Smith / Michael Morgan
	DB Kevin Thomas / T.J. Bryant
	DB Josh Pinkard / Shareece Wright
	DB Taylor Mays
	DB Will Harris

RUSHING: McKnight 164/1014y, Bradford 115/668y, Stafon Johnson (TB) 32/157y
PASSING: Barkley 211-352/2735y, 15TD, 59.9%
RECEIVING: Williams 70/1010y, Johnson 34/378y, McCoy 22/457y Havili 22/298y, McKnight 22/146y
SCORING: Jordan Congdon (K) 77pts, McKnight 50pts, Bradford & Williams 48pts

2010 8-5

49 Hawaii	36 WR Robert Woods / Brandon Carswell
17 Virginia	14 WR Ronald Johnson / Brice Butler
32 Minnesota	21 T Matt Kalil
50 Washington St.	16 G Butch Lewis / Michael Reardon
31 Washington	32 C Kristofer O'Dowd
35 Stanford	37 G Khaled Holmes
48 California	14 T Tyson Smith
32 Oregon	53 TE Rhett Ellison / Jordan Cameron
34 Arizona State	33 QB Matt Barkley / Mitch Mustain
24 Arizona	21 TB Marc Tyler / Allen Bradford
7 Oregon State	36 FB/WR Stanley Havili / David Ausberry
16 Notre Dame	20 DL Armond Armstead
28 UCLA	14 DL DaJohn Harris
	DL Jurell Casey
	DL Nick Perry / Wes Horton
	LB Michael Morgan / Shane Horton
	LB Devon Kennard / Malcolm Smith
	LB/DB Chris Gallipo / Torin Harris
	DB Shareece Wright / Brian Baucham
	DB Nickell Robey
	DB T.J. McDonald / Tony Burnett
	DB Jawanza Starling / Marshall Jones

RUSHING: Tyler 171/913y, Bradford 110/794y, C.J. Gable (TB) 53/253y
PASSING: Barkley 236-377/2791y, 26TD, 62.6% Mustain 41-73/348y, 1TD, 56.2%
RECEIVING: Woods 65/792y, Johnson 64/692y, Havili 32/396y
SCORING: Joe Houston (K) 73pts, Tyler 60pts, Johnson 58pts

STANFORD

Stanford University (Founded 1891)
Palo Alto, California
Nicknames: Cardinal (since 1972), Indians (prior to 1972)
Colors: Cardinal Red and White
Stadium: Stanford (1921) 50,000
Conference Affiliations: Pacific Coast (1918-58), AAWU (1959-68),
   Pac-8/10 (1969-present)

CAREER RUSHING YARDS	Attempts	Yards
Darrin Nelson (1977-78, 80-81)	703	4033
Toby Gerhart (2006-09)	671	3522
Brad Muster (1984-87)	686	2940
Anthony Bookman (1994-97)	514	2523
Mike Mitchell (1993-97)	535	2446
Glyn Milburn (1990-92)	460	2178
Brian Allen (1998-2001)	482	2117
Kerry Carter (1999-2002)	538	2039
Anthony Kimble (2005-08)	415	1940
Tommy Vardell (1988-91)	418	1789

CAREER PASSING YARDS	Comp.-Att.	Yards
Steve Stenstrom (1991-1994)	833-1320	10,531
John Elway (1979-82)	774-1246	9349
John Paye (1983-86)	715-1198	7669
Jim Plunkett (1968-70)	530-962	7544
Todd Husak (1996-1999)	465-872	6564
Guy Benjamin (1974-77)	488-808	5946
Andrew Luck (2009-10)	425-660	5913
Trent Edwards (2003-06)	487-865	5429
Jason Palumbis (1988, 1990-91)	442-708	4954
Chris Lewis (2000-03)	350-713	4346

CAREER RECEIVING YARDS	Catches	Yards
Troy Walters (1996-99)	244	3986
DeRonnie Pitts (1997-2000)	222	2942
Justin Armour (1991-94)	154	2482
Mark Bradford (2003-07)	169	2431
Ken Margerum (1977-80)	141	2430
Darrin Nelson (1977-78, 80-81)	214	2368
Ed McCaffrey (1986-87, 89-90)	146	2333
Brian Manning (1993-96)	140	2280
Emile Harry (1981-84)	123	2270
Jeff James (1984-87)	154	2265

SEASON RUSHING YARDS	Attempts	Yards
Toby Gerhart (2009)	343	1871
Stepfan Taylor (2010)	223	1137
Toby Gerhart (2008)	210	1136
Tommy Vardell (1991)	226	1084
Darrin Nelson (1977)	183	1069

SEASON PASSING YARDS	Comp.-Att.	Yards
Steve Stenstrom (1993)	300-455	3627
Andrew Luck (2010)	263-372	3338
John Elway (1982)	262-405	3242
Todd Husak (1998)	233-447	3092
Steve Dils (1978)	247-391	2943

SEASON RECEIVING YARDS	Catches	Yards
Troy Walters (1999)	74	1456
Troy Walters (1997)	86	1206
Gene Washington (1968)	71	1117
Justin Armour (1994)	67	1092
DeRonnie Pitts (1998)	74	1012

GAME RUSHING YARDS	Attempts	Yards
Toby Gerhart (2009 vs. Oregon)	38	223
Jon Volpe (1988 vs. Washington)	29	220
Darrin Nelson (1977 vs. San Jose St.)	20	211

GAME PASSING YARDS	Comp.-Att.	Yards
Todd Husak (1998 vs. Oregon State)	N/A	450
Steve Dils (1978 vs. Washington State)	32-51	430
Andrew Luck (2009 vs. Arizona)	21-35	423

GAME RECEIVING YARDS	Catches	Yards
Troy Walters (1999 vs. UCLA)	9	278
Darrin Nelson (1981 vs. Arizona State)	9	237
Justin Armour (1994 vs. UCLA)	11	220

GREATEST COACH

Bill Walsh, who contributed two tours of duty at Stanford, is rightfully considered a football genius but not especially for his work with the Cardinal for whom he was 34-24-1.

John Ralston won the most games of any of Stanford's 12 coaches during the last 54 years, but more importantly he guided the Cardinal to back-to-back Rose Bowl upset wins in the early 1970s. So, Ralston gets credit as Stanford's greatest since 1953.

STANFORD'S 55 GREATEST SINCE 1953

OFFENSE

WIDE RECEIVER: Tony Hill, Ken Margerum, James Lofton, Troy Walters, Gene Washington
TIGHT END: Chris Burford, Sam Morley
TACKLE: Kwame Harris, Gordon King, Malcolm Snider, Bob Whitfield
GUARD: Jack Chapple, Marv Harris, Eric Heitman, Alex Karakazoff
CENTER: John Macaulay, Mike McLaughlin
QUARTERBACK: Guy Benjamin, John Brodie, John Elway, Jim Plunkett, Steve Stenstrom
RUNNING BACK: Toby Gerhart, Glyn Milburn, Darrin Nelson
FULLBACK: Brad Muster, Tommy Vardell

DEFENSE

END: Pat Donovan, Duncan McColl, Garin Veris, Kaile Wong
TACKLE: Willie Howard, Pete Lazetich, Gary Pettigrew, Dave Tipton
LINEBACKER: Ron George, Don Parish, Gordon Riegel, Jeff Siemon, Dave Wyman
CORNERBACK: Kevin Baird, Darrien Gordon, Kevin Scott
SAFETY: John Lynch, Oshiomogho Atogwe, Dick Ragsdale, Tank Williams, Vaughn Williams

SPECIAL TEAMS

RETURN SPECIALIST: Brian Allen, Luke Powell
PLACE KICKER: Rod Garcia
PUNTER: Ken Nabor

MULTIPLE POSITIONS

TACKLE-DEFENSIVE TACKLE: Blaine Nye
RUNNING BACK-LINEBACKER: Coy Wire

TWO-WAY PLAYER

TACKLE-DEFENSIVE TACKLE: Paul Wiggin

PERFORMANCE FORMULA:
STANFORD'S 10 BEST SEASONS

2010	1.6586	4 of 71
1992	1.4761	10 of 70
1969	1.4703	17 of 70
1970	1.4346	11 of 70
2001	1.3895	15 of 70
1971	1.3886	14 of 70
1955	1.3797	15 of 69
1978	1.3762	14 of 70
1986	1.3266	20 of 70
1953	1.3222	19 of 69

STANFORD CARDINAL

Year	W-L-T	AP Poll	Conference Standing	Toughest Regular Season Opponents	Coach (Record at School)	Bowl Games			
1953	6-3-1	19	2	Illinois 7-1-1, UCLA 8-1, Southern California 6-3-1, California 4-4-2	Chuck Taylor				
1954	4-6		6	Oregon 6-4, Navy 7-2, UCLA 9-0, Southern California 8-3	Chuck Taylor				
1955	6-3-1	16	3	Oregon State 6-3, Ohio State 7-2, Michigan State 8-1, UCLA 9-1	Chuck Taylor				
1956	4-6		6	Michigan State 7-2, So. Calif. 8-2, UCLA 7-3, Oregon State 7-2-1	Chuck Taylor				
1957	6-4		5	UCLA 8-2, Oregon 7-3, Southern Calif. 8-2, Oregon State 8-2	Chuck Taylor (40-29-2)				
1958	2-8		7	Washington State 7-3, Air Force 9-0-1, California 7-3	Jack Curtice				
1959	3-7		5	Oregon 8-2, Wisconsin 7-2, Washington 9-1, Southern Cal. 8-2	Jack Curtice				
1960	0-10		5	Washington 9-1, UCLA 7-2-1, Oregon 7-2-1, Oregon State 6-3-1	Jack Curtice				
1961	4-6		4t	Michigan State 7-2, Washington 5-4-1, UCLA 7-3,	Jack Curtice				
1962	5-5		3	Oregon State 8-2, Washington 7-1-2, Southern California 10-0	Jack Curtice (14-36)				
1963	3-7		6	Oregon 7-3, Washington 6-4, Southern California 7-3	John Ralston				
1964	5-5		5	Notre Dame 9-1, Oregon 7-2-1, Southern Calif. 7-3, Oregon St. 8-2	John Ralston				
1965	6-3-1		5t	Southern California 7-2-1, UCLA 7-2-1	John Ralston				
1966	5-5		8	Southern California 7-3, Washington 6-4, UCLA 9-1	John Ralston				
1967	5-5		5t	Oregon State 7-2-1, Southern Calif. 9-1, UCLA 7-2-1, Army 8-2	John Ralston				
1968	6-3-1		3	Air Force 7-3, Southern Calif. 9-0-1, Oregon State 7-3, California 7-3-1	John Ralston				
1969	7-2-1	19	2t	Purdue 8-2, Southern Calif. 9-0-1, UCLA 8-1-1	John Ralston				
1970	9-3	8	1	Arkansas 9-2, Oregon 6-4-1, Southern Calif. 6-4-1, Air Force 9-2	John Ralston	Rose	27	Ohio State	17
1971	9-3	10	1	Army 6-4, Washinton 8-3, Southern California 6-4-1	John Ralston (55-36-3)	Rose	13	Michigan	12
1972	6-5		6t	West Virginia 8-3, Southern Calif. 11-0, Washington 8-3, UCLA 8-3	Jack Christiansen				
1973	7-4		3	Penn State 11-0, Michigan 10-0-1, UCLA 9-2, Southern Calif. 9-1-1	Jack Christiansen				
1974	5-4-2		2	Penn State 9-2, Michigan 10-1, Southern California 9-2-1	Jack Christiansen				
1975	6-4-1		3t	Penn State 9-2, Notre Dame 8-3, California 8-3, UCLA 8—2-1	Jack Christiansen				
1976	6-5		3	Michigan 10-1, UCLA 9-1-1, Southern California 10-1	Jack Christiansen (30-22-3)				
1977	9-3	15	2t	Colorado 7-3-1, Washington 8-3	Bill Walsh	Sun	24	Louisiana State	14
1978	8-4	17	4t	Oklahoma 10-1, UCLA 8-3, Southern California 11-1	Bill Walsh (see below)	Bluebonnet	25	Georgia	22
1979	5-5-1		6	Tulane 9-2, Southern Calif. 10-0-1, Arizona 6-4-1	Rod Dowhower (5-5-1)				
1980	6-5		6t	Oklahoma 9-2, UCLA 9-2, Washington 9-2, Southern Calif. 8-2-1	Paul Wiggin				
1981	4-7		6t	Ohio State 8-3, Southern Calif. 9-2, Arizona State 9-2, Washington 9-2	Paul Wiggin				
1982	5-6		7	Arizona State 9-2, Washington 9-2, UCLA 9-1-1	Paul Wiggin				
1983	1-10		10	Oklahoma 8-4, Illinois 10-1, Washington 8-3, Arizona 7-3-1	Paul Wiggin (16-28)				
1984	5-6		7t	Oklahoma 9-1-1, Washington 10-1, Southern California 8-3	Jack Elway				
1985	4-7		7t	Texas 8-3, UCLA 8-2-1, Arizona 8-3, Arizona State 8-3	Jack Elway				
1986	8-4		4t	San Jose State 9-2, Washington 8-2-1, UCLA 7-3-1, Arizona 8-3	Jack Elway	Gator	21	Clemson	27
1987	5-6		5t	San Jose State 10-1, UCLA 9-2, Southern California 8-3	Jack Elway				
1988	3-6-2		9	Southern Calif. 10-1 Notre Dame 11-0, UCLA 9-2	Jack Elway (25-29-2)				
1989	3-8		7t	Arizona 7-4, Oregon 7-4, Notre Dame 11-1, Southern Calif. 8-2-1	Dennis Green				
1990	5-6		6t	Colorado 10-1-1, Notre Dame 9-2, Washington 9-2	Dennis Green				
1991	8-4	22	2t	Washington 11-0, Colorado 8-2-1, Notre Dame 9-3, California 9-2	Dennis Green (16-18)	Aloha	17	Georgia Tech	18
1992	10-3	9	1t	Texas A&M 12-0, Notre Dame 9-1-1, Washington 9-2	Bill Walsh	Blockbuster	24	Penn State	3
1993	4-7		8t	Colorado 7-3-1, UCLA 8-3, Notre Dame 10-1, Arizona 9-2	Bill Walsh				
1994	3-7-1		7t	Arizona 8-3, Southern California 7-3-1, Oregon 9-3	Bill Walsh (34-24-1)				
1995	7-4-1		4	Oregon 9-2, Washington7-3-1, Southern California 8-2-1	Tyrone Willingham	Liberty	13	East Carolina	19
1996	7-5		3	Utah 8-3, Washington9-2, Arizona State 11-0	Tyrone Willingham	Sun	38	Michigan State	0
1997	5-6		7t	North Carolina 10-1, UCLA 9-2, Washington State 10-1	Tyrone Willingham				
1998	3-8		8t	Arizona 11-1, Notre Dame 9-2, UCLA 10-1	Tyrone Willingham				
1999	8-4		1	Texas 9-3, Oregon State 7-4, Washington 7-4	Tyrone Willingham	Rose		9 Wisconsin	17
2000	5-6		4	Texas 9-2, Notre Dame 9-2, Oregon State 10-1, Washington 10-1	Tyrone Willingham				
2001	9-3	16	2t	Washington State 9-2, Oregon 10-1, Washington 8-3	Tyrone Willingham (44-36-1)	Seattle	14	Georgia Tech	24
2002	2-9		9t	Notre Dame 10-2, Washington State 10-2, Southern California 10-2	Buddy Teevens				
2003	4-7		8t	Southern California 11-1, Washington State 9-3, Oregon 8-4	Buddy Teevens				
2004	4-7		8t	Southern California 12-0, Arizona State 8-3, California 10-1	Buddy Teevens (10-23)				
2005	5-6		4t	Oregon 10-1, UCLA 9-2, Southern California 12-0, Notre Dame 9-2	Walt Harris				
2006	1-11		10	Navy 9-3, Notre Dame 10-2, Southern California 10-2, California 9-3	Walt Harris (6-17)				
2007	4-8		7t	Oregon 8-4, So. California 10-2, Arizona State 10-2, Oregon State 8-4	Jim Harbaugh				
2008	5-7		6t	TCU 11-1, Oregon 9-3, Southern California 11-1, California 8-4	Jim Harbaugh				
2009	8-5		2t	Arizona 8-4, Oregon 10-2, Southern California 8-4, California 8-4	Jim Harbaugh	Sun	27	Oklahoma	31
2010	12-1	4	2	Notre Dame 7-5, Oregon 12-0, Southern California 8-5	Jim Harbaugh (29-21)	Orange	40	Virginia Tech	12

TOTAL: 310-317-13 .4945 (48 of 70)   **Bowl Games since 1953:**   7-6 .5385 (28 of 70)

GREATEST TEAM SINCE 1953: The Performance Formula does not lie. While the 1970 and '71 Cardinal teams won back-to-back Rose Bowls, the 2010 team owns by far the best formula at Stanford since 1953. Coach Jim Harbaugh's last Stanford squad posted the school's best winning percentage since 1940. The 2010 Cardinal offered a hard-hitting defense and a tremendous offense, sparked by Andrew Luck, one of the nation's great passers, and an effective ground attack led by unheralded youngster Stepfan Taylor, who did yeoman's work replacing Toby Gerhart, the nation's rushing yards leader in 2009.

1953 6-3-1

20 Pacific	25 E Sam Morley
7 Oregon	0 T Matt Armitage
21 Illinois	33 G Phil Watson
21 Oregon State	0 C Ted Tanner / Jerry Goldberg
13 Washington	20 G Norm Manoogian / Len Doster
48 Washington St.	7 T Barry Smith / Win Wedge
20 Southern Cal	19 E John Steinberg / John Stewart
54 San Jose State	23 QB Bobby Garrett
21 California	0 HB Ron Cook
	21 HB Ernie Dorn / Bill Rogers
	FB Jarvis Watson / Bill Tarr

RUSHING: Cook 80/424y, Dorn 75/292y, Watson 69/281y
PASSING: Garrett 118-205/1637y, 17TD, 57.6%
RECEIVING: Morley 45/594y, Steinberg 32/425y, Cook 19/326y
SCORING: Cook 54pts, Garrett 38pts, Morley 36pts

1954 4-6

13 Pacific	12 E John Stewart / Bob Gergen
18 Oregon	13 T Win Wedge / Chris Marshall
12 Illinois	2 G Donn Carswell
0 Navy	25 C Jerry Goldberg / Bob Long / Joe Long
0 UCLA	72 G Roy Krickeberg / Tony Mosich
13 Washington	7 T Matt Armitage / Paul Wiggin
26 Washington St.	30 E Paul Camera / Jerry Beattie
7 Southern Cal	21 QB Jerry Gustafson / John Brodie
14 San Jose State	19 HB Harry Hugasian / Jeri McMillin
20 California	28 HB Ernie Dorn / Gordy Young
	FB Bill Tarr / Jerry Angove

RUSHING: N/A
PASSING: N/A
RECEIVING: N/A
SCORING: N/A

1955 6-3-1

33 Pacific	14 E John Stewart
0 Oregon State	10 T Chris Marshall
6 Ohio State	0 G Donn Carswell
14 Michigan State	38 C Joe Long
13 UCLA	21 G Tony Mosich
7 Washington	7 T Paul Wiggin
34 San Jose State	18 E Jerry Beatie / Gary Van Galder
28 Southern Cal	20 QB John Brodie / Jerry Gustafson
44 Oregon	7 HB Paul Camera / Jeri McMillin
19 California	0 HB Ernie Dorn / Gordy Young
	FB Bill Tarr

RUSHING: Tarr 172/687y, Young 47/249y, McMillin 65/215y
PASSING: Brodie 76-133/1024y, 5TD, 57.1%
RECEIVING: Stewart 23/296y, Camera 22/330y,
  Van Galder 20/232y
SCORING: Tarr 48pts, Camera 30pts, Brodie 24pts

1956 4-6

40 Washington St.	26 E Carl Isaacs / Ben Robinson
7 Michigan State	21 T Troy Barbee
20 Ohio State	32 G Donn Carswell / Armand DeWeese
40 San Jose State	20 C Russ Steele / Bob Long
21 Oregon	7 G Noel Robinson / Bob Peterson
27 Southern Cal	19 T Paul Wiggin
13 UCLA	14 E Gary Van Galder / Joel Freis
19 Oregon State	20 QB John Brodie
13 Washington	34 HB Paul Camera / Jeri McMillin
18 California	20 HB Gordy Young / Al Harrington
	FB Lou Valli / Jerry Angove / Doug Dick

RUSHING: Valli 120/628y, Young 98/394y, Dick 31/137y
PASSING: Brodie 139-240/1633y, 12TDs, 57.9%
RECEIVING: Camera 28/350y, Isaacs 25/348y, Valli 21/176y
SCORING: Valli 60pts, Isaacs (E-K) 31pts, Mike Raftery (K) 25pts

1957 6-4

47 San Jose State	7 E Ben Robinson / Joel Freis
26 Northwestern	6 T Troy Barbee / John Kidd
7 Rice	34 G Don Manoukian
18 Washington St.	21 C Russ Steele
21 Washington	14 G Noel Robinson / Bob Peterson
20 UCLA	6 T Armond DeWeese
26 Oregon	27 E Gary Van Galder
35 Southern Cal	7 QB Jack Douglas / Bob Nicolet
14 Oregon State	24 HB Jeri McMillin / Jack Taylor
14 California	12 HB Al Harrington / Roy Stephen
	FB Chuck Shea / Lou Valli / Rick McMillen

RUSHING: Shea 163/840y, Harrington 90/419y, McMillen 64/263y
PASSING: Douglas 78-146/957y, 9TD, 53.5%
RECEIVING: Van Galder 18/182y, Freis 14/218y, Taylor 11/123y
SCORING: Shea 48pts, Harrington (HB-K) 36pts, McMillen 24pts

1958 2-8

6 Washington St	40 E Irv Nikolai / Joel Freis
7 Rice	30 T Troy Barbee
0 Northwestern	28 G Don Dawson
22 Washington	12 C Roch Conklin / Doug Pursell
0 Air Force	16 G Russ Steele / Bob Peterson
21 UCLA	19 T Eric Provita / Dean Hinshaw
6 Southern Cal	29 E Chris Burford
0 Oregon	12 QB Bob Nicolet / Dick Norman
16 Oregon State	24 HB Skip Face / Rick McMillen
15 California	16 HB John Bond / Jim Byrer
	FB Gil Dowd / Doug Dick

RUSHING: Dick 60/252y, McMillen 40/233y, Dowd 54/176y
PASSING: Nicolet 77-146/724y, 2TD, 52.7%
  Norman 76-133/717y, 3TD, 57.1%
RECEIVING: Burford 45/493y, Nikolai 32/343y, Bond 17/177y
SCORING: Face (HB-K) 29pts, McMillen & Burford 14pts

1959 3-7

27 Oregon	28 E Ben Robinson / Irv Nikolai
14 Wisconsin	16 T Phil Burkland
21 Pacific	6 G Ron Fernandez / Tom Walsh
0 Washington	10 C Doug Pursell
28 Southern Cal	30 G Larry Lacey
19 Washington St.	36 T Gary Pike / Dean Hinshaw
54 San Jose State	38 E Chris Burford
13 UCLA	55 QB Dick Norman / Rod Sears
39 Oregon State	22 HB Dick Bowers / John Bond
17 California	20 HB Mac Wylie / Gil Dowd
	FB Skip Face / Rick McMillen

RUSHING: Face 96/362y, Wylie 56/247y, McMillen 59/200y
PASSING: Norman 152-263/1963y, 11TD, 57.8%
RECEIVING: Burford 61/757y, Robinson 34/595y,
  Bowers 17/229y, Bond 17/194y
SCORING: Face (FB-K) 100pts, Burford 36pts

1960 0-10

14 Washington St.	15 E Steve Pursell
7 Wisconsin	24 T Carlton Simons
9 Air Force	32 G Ron Fernandes / Tom Walsh
10 Washington	29 C Doug Pursell / Chris Cottle
20 San Jose State	34 G Errol Scott
8 UCLA	26 T Dean Hinshaw / Randy Vahan
6 Southern Cal	21 E Dale Ostrander
6 Oregon	27 QB Dick Norman
21 Oregon State	21 HB Mac Wylie
10 California	21 HB Gil Dowd / Hal Steuber
	FB Skip Face

RUSHING: Dowd 116/477y, Face 96/430y, Steuber 43/200y
PASSING: Norman 95-201/1057y, 4TD, 47.3%
RECEIVING: Face 29/270y, Wylie 25/377y, Ostrander 19/270y
SCORING: Face (FB-K) 47pts, Dowd 30pts, Steuber 14pts

1961 4-6

9 Tulane	7 E Steve Pursell
34 Oregon State	0 T Frank Atkinson / Al Hildebrand
3 Michigan State	31 G Tom Walsh / Marvin Harris
17 San Jose State	6 C Chris Cottle
0 Washington	13 G Errol Scott / Frank Dubofsky
0 UCLA	20 T Carlton Simons / Randy Vahan
7 Oregon	19 E George Honore / Chris Jessen
15 Southern Cal	30 QB Rod Sears
0 Washington St.	30 HB Gary Craig / Stan Lindskog
20 California	7 HB Dan Spence / Hal Steuber
	FB Ken Babajian / Ed Cummings

RUSHING: Babajian 55/189y, Craig 50/185y, Lindskog 42/178y
PASSING: Sears 37-82/358y, TD, 45.1%
RECEIVING: Honore 22/225y, Pursell 13/132y, Spence 8/41y
SCORING: Babajian 24pts, Lindskog 17pts,
  Craig & Tony DeLellis (K) 12pts

1962 5-5

6 Tulane	3 E Bob Howard / Chris Jessen
16 Michigan State	13 T Al Hildebrand / Charlie Buehler
0 Oregon State	27 G Marvin Harris
6 Washington St.	21 C Carlton Simons
0 Washington	14 G Frank Dubofsky
17 UCLA	7 T Frank Atkinson / Bob Nichols
14 Oregon	28 E Frank Patitucci
14 Southern Cal	39 QB Steve Thurlow / Clark Weaver
21 San Jose State	9 HB Jack Lodato
30 California	13 HB Gary Sargent / Stan Lindskog
	FB Ken Babajian / Ed Cummings

RUSHING: Lodato 84/357y, Babajian 66/229y, Weaver 84/219y
PASSING: Thurlow 55-115/768y, TD, 47.8%
  Weaver 38-80/416y, 3TD, 47.5%
RECEIVING: Patitucci 22/259y, Howard 20/272y, Jessen 17/234y
SCORING: Weaver 18pts, Lindskog 16pts

1963 3-7

29 San Jose State	13 E Bob Howard / Chuck McCormick
7 Oregon	36 T Al Hilebrand / Chuck Hartwig
9 UCLA	10 G Jack Chapple
13 Rice	23 C Marvin Harris
11 Washington	19 G John Wilbur / Joe Neal
24 Notre Dame	14 T Bob Nichols / Dick Leeuwenburg
7 Oregon State	10 E Frank Patitucci
11 Southern Cal	25 QB Dick Berg / Don Cook / Clark Weaver
15 Washington St.	32 HB Steve Thurlow / Ray Handley
28 California	17 HB Dick Ragsdale / Jack Lodato
	FB Ken Babajian / Glenn Myers

RUSHING: Thurlow 92/495y, Ragsdale 57/317y, Handley 43/178y
PASSING: Berg 29-62/301y, TD, 46.8%, Cook 14-25/179y, TD, 56.0%
RECEIVING: Howard 11/174y, Ragsdale 11/129y, Patitucci 9/141y
SCORING: Ragsdale 38pts, Braden Beck (K) 36pts, Thurlow 32pts

1964 5-5

23 Washington St.	29 E John Mason / Braden Beck
10 San Jose State	8 T Dick Leeuwenburg
20 UCLA	27 G Joe Neal / Ed Ptacek
34 Rice	7 C Carl Schrader
0 Washington	6 G Larry Volmert / Bruce Kehrli
6 Notre Dame	28 T John Wilbur / Fergus Flanagan
10 Oregon	8 E Mike Connelly
10 Southern Cal	15 QB Terry DeSylvia / Dave Lewis
16 Oregon State	7 HB Ray Handley
21 California	3 HB Jack Lodato (DB) / Bob Blunt
	FB John Read / Pete Middlekauff
	DL Guy Rounsaville
	DL Mike Hibler
	DL Tom Ross
	DL Bob Nichols
	DL Gary Pettigrew
	DL Bob Howard
	LB Bob Rath / Glenn Myers
	LB Jack Chapple
	DB Craig Ritchey
	DB Dick Ragsdale
	DB John Guillory

RUSHING: Handley 197/936y, Read 89/301y, Blunt 27/114y
PASSING: DeSylvia 39-48/451y, 1TD, 54.9%
  Dick Berg (QB) 26-48/278y, 0TD, 52.9%
RECEIVING: Mason 22/250y, Connelly 17/266y, Handley 15/86y
SCORING: Beck 42pts, Handley 24pts

1965 6-3-1

26 San Jose State	6 E Mike Connelly
7 Navy	7 T Blaine Nye
17 Air Force	16 G Bruce Kehrli / Rich Derby
17 Oregon	14 C Tim Sheehan
0 Southern Cal	14 G Delos Brown
31 Army	14 T John Wilbur
8 Washington	41 E Bob Conrad / John Mason
16 Tulane	0 QB Dave Lewis / Terry DeSylvia
13 UCLA	30 HB Ray Handley
9 California	7 HB Phil Humphreys / Bob Blunt
	FB John Read
	DL Tom Hazelrigg
	DL Al Wilburn
	DL Bill Ogle
	DL Mike Hibler
	DL Tom Ross / Allen Mohrman
	DL Roger Clay
	LB Mike Pavko
	LB Bob Rath / Marty Brill
	DB Craig Ritchey
	DB John Guillory / Donn Renwick
	DB Dale Rubin

RUSHING: Handley 163/654y, Read 125/553y, Lewis 124/183y
PASSING: Lewis 94-183/1257y, 5TD, 51.4%
RECEIVING: Connelly 29/366y, Conrad 24/242y,
  Humphreys 13/164y
SCORING: Handley 44pts, DeSylvia 34pts

1966 5-5

25 San Jose State	21 WR Bob Conrad
21 Minnesota	35 WR Tim Abena / Bob Blunt
33 Tulane	14 T George Buehler / Bob Shore
3 Oregon	7 G Rich Derby / Larry Volmert
7 Southern Cal	21 C Tim Sheehan
6 Illinois	3 G Don Swartz / Phil Messer
20 Washington	22 T Bob Heffernan / Mal Snider
21 Air Force	6 TE John Mason / Tom Weingartner
0 UCLA	10 QB Gene Washington
13 California	7 RB Dave Lewis (QB) / Bill Shoemaker
	FB Jack Root
	DL Al Wilburn
	DL Bill Ogle / Bob Bittner
	DL Blaine Nye / Mike Miller
	DL Mike Hibler
	DL Allen Mohrman
	DL Tom Hazelrigg
	LB John Read / Marty Brill
	LB Andy Carrigan / Mike Pavko
	DB John Guillory
	DB Donn Renwick
	DB David Nelson / Mark Marquess

RUSHING: Root 136/571y, Washington 101/362y, Lewis 72/228y
PASSING: Washington 35-102/479y, 4TD, 34.3%
Lewis 28-52/395y, TD, 53.8%
RECEIVING: Conrad 45/555y, Blunt 21/376y, Mason 7/65y
SCORING: Root 36pts, Shoemaker (RB-K) 31pts, Washington 20pts

1967 5-5

7 Oregon State	13 WR Gene Washington
21 Kansas	20 WR Jim Cross / Andy Vanderschoot
28 San Jose State	14 T George Buehler (TE)
0 Southern Cal	30 G Bob Shore (T)
31 Washington St.	10 C Tom Giallonardo / Don Swartz
16 UCLA	21 G George Crooks / Phil Messer
20 Army	24 T Mal Snider
14 Washington	7 TE Phil Schneider
17 Oregon	14 QB Chuck Williams / Mark Marquess
3 California	26 HB Nate Kirtman / Howie Williams
	FB Jack Root / Greg Broughton
	DL Stu Kellner
	DL Blaine Nye
	DL John de la Forest / Bob Bittner
	DL Bill Nicholson
	DL Don Parish / Tom Hazelrigg
	LB Andy Carrigan / Tom Weingartner
	LB Marty Brill
	LB Pat Preston / John Haygood
	DB Dick Oliver / Bob Rinker
	DB Donn Renwick
	DB Tom Massey

RUSHING: Kirtman 130/573y, H. Williams 85/347y, Root 95/271y
PASSING: C. Williams 76-153/923y, 7TD, 49.7%
RECEIVING: Washington 48/575y, Cross 31/303y, Bill Shoemaker (HB) 8/110y
SCORING: Bill Shoemaker (HB-K) 47pts, Root 36pts, Cross 18pts

1968 6-3-1

68 San Jose State	20 WR Gene Washington / Jack Lasater
28 Oregon	12 WR Jim Cross / Mark Marquess
24 Air Force	13 T Bob Shore / Pete Seymour
24 Southern Cal	27 G George Crooks / Mike Willard
21 Washington St.	21 C Tom Giallonardo / John Sande
17 UCLA	20 G Phil Messer
7 Oregon State	29 T Mal Snider
35 Washington	20 TE Bob Moore
24 Pacific	0 QB Jim Plunkett
20 California	0 HB Howie Williams / Bubba Brown
	FB Greg Broughton
	DL Tom Weingartner
	DL Bill Nicholson
	DL George Buehler
	DL Doug McKenzie / Bob Bittner
	DL Stu Kellner
	LB Don Parish
	LB Pat Preston / Andy Carrigan
	LB Bill Shoemaker / Dennis Moore
	DB Dick Oliver
	DB Dick Keller
	DB Tom Massey / Jim Kauffman

RUSHING: Williams 105/499y, Brown 88/492y, Broughton 102/352y
PASSING: Plunkett 142-268/2156y, 14TD, 52.9%
RECEIVING: Washington 71/1117y, Moore 28/389y, Lasater 14/347y
SCORING: Washington 54pts, Plunkett 36pts, Shoemaker 30pts

1969 7-2-1

63 San Jose State	21 WR Jack Lasater / Jim Cross
28 Oregon	0 WR Randy Vataha
35 Purdue	36 T Pete Seymour
24 Southern Cal	26 G George Crooks / Dan Lightfoot
49 Washington St.	0 C John Sande
20 UCLA	20 G Bob Reinhard
33 Oregon State	0 T Dave Sharp
21 Washington	7 TE Bob Moore
47 Air Force	34 QB Jim Plunkett / Don Bunce
29 California	28 RB Bubba Brown / Jackie Brown
	FB Howie Williams / Hillary Shockley
	DL Jack Schultz / Wade Killefer
	DL Dave Tipton
	DL Pete Lazetich
	DL Jody Graves / Tim McClure
	DL Bill Alexander
	LB Dennis Moore / Jeff Siemon
	LB Pat Preston
	LB Don Parish / Ron Kadziel (TE)
	DB Rich Keller / Miles Moore
	DB Dick Oliver / Mike Ewing
	DB Jim Kauffman

RUSHING: B. Brown 127/588y, Williams 114/494y, J. Brown 51/209y
PASSING: Plunkett 197-336/2673y, 20TD, 58.6%
RECEIVING: Moore 38/476y, Vataha 35/691y, Lasater 34/515y
SCORING: Steve Horowitz (K) 71pts, Williams 60pts, B. Brown & Vataha 30pts

1970 9-3

34 Arkansas	28 WR Jack Lasater / Eric Cross
34 San Jose State	3 WR Randy Vataha / Demea Washington
33 Oregon	10 T Bill Meyers / Larry Jones
14 Purdue	26 G Terrell Smith / Doug Adams
24 Southern Cal	14 C John Sande / Dennis Sheehan
63 Washington St.	16 G Dan Lightfoot
9 UCLA	7 T Steve Jubb
48 Oregon State	10 TE Bob Moore / Bill Scott
29 Washington	22 QB Jim Plunkett
14 Air Force	31 RB Jackie Brown / Reggie Sanderson
14 California	22 FB Hillary Shockley / Jim Kehl
27 Ohio State■	17 DL Dave Tipton
	DL Pete Lazetich / Tim McClure
	DL Bill Alexander / Larry Butler
	DL Greg Sampson / Jody Graves
	LB Ron Kadziel / Dennis Moore
	LB Jeff Siemon / Phil Satre
	LB Mike Simone
	DB Charles McCloud
	DB Benny Barnes / Mike Ewing
	DB Jack Schultz / Pat Moore
	DB Jim Kauffman / Steve Murray

RUSHING: Shockley 171/622y, J.Brown 125/568y, Plunkett 78/183y
PASSING: Plunkett 191-358/2715y, 18TD, 53.3%
RECEIVING: Vataha 48/844y, Moore 34/562y, J. Brown 31/375y
SCORING: Steve Horowitz (K) 60pts, J. Brown 50pts, Shockley 48pts

1971 9-3

19 Missouri	0 WR Miles Moore / Eric Cross
38 Army	3 WR John Winesberry
38 Oregon	17 T Bill Meyers
3 Duke	9 G Younger Klipper
17 Washington	6 C Dennis Sheehan
33 Southern Cal	18 G Lee Fair / Doug Adams
23 Washington St.	24 T Tim Schaklich
31 Oregon State	24 TE Bill Scott
20 UCLA	9 QB Don Bunce
12 San Jose State	13 HB Jackie Brown / Reggie Sanderson
14 California	0 FB Hillary Shockley / Jim Kehl
13 Michigan■	12 DL Roger Cowan
	DL Pete Lazetich
	DL Larry Butler
	DL Greg Sampson / Pierre Perreault
	LB Jim Merlo / Pat Moore
	LB Jeff Siemon
	LB Mike Simone
	DB Charles McCloud
	DB Benny Barnes
	DB Tim Robnett
	DB Randy Poltl / John Ferguson

RUSHING: Brown 124/479y, Sanderson 75/326y, Bunce 122/248y
PASSING: Bunce 162-297/2265y, 13TD, 54.5%
RECEIVING: Moore 38/816y, Winesberry 37/543y, Scott 31/393y
SCORING: Rod Garcia (K) 66pts, Brown & Moore 36pts

1972 6-5

44 San Jose State	0 WR Miles Moore
10 Duke	6 WR Eric Cross / Reggie Ishman
42 West Virginia	35 T Keith Rowen
21 Southern Cal	30 G Younger Klipper
24 Washington	0 C Bill Reid
13 Oregon	15 G Chuck Cordes / Lee Fair
17 Oregon State	11 T Mike Askea
23 UCLA	28 TE Bill Scott
13 Washington St.	27 QB Mike Boryla
21 California	24 HB John Winesberry
39 Hawaii	7 FB Reggie Sanderson / Scott Laidlaw
	DL Roger Cowan / Jim Ferguson
	DL Peter Hansel
	DL Barry Reynolds
	DL Pierre Perreault / Roger Stillwell
	LB Jim Merlo
	LB Dennis Peterson
	DB Charles McCloud
	DB John Ferguson / John "Doc" Blanchard
	DB Randy Poltl
	DB Dennis Bragonier / Gary Murray

RUSHING: Winesberry 125/536y, Sanderson 137/426y, Laidlaw 84/268y
PASSING: Boryla 183-350/2284y, 14TD, 52.3%
RECEIVING: Cross 53/730y, Moore 27/418y, Scott 27/372y
SCORING: Rod Garcia (K) 55pts, Cross 54pts, Winesberry 42pts

1973 7-4

6 Penn State	20 WR Bill Singler / Eric Test
10 Michigan	47 WR Reggie Ishman / Tony Hill
23 San Jose State	12 T Keith Rowen
24 Illinois	0 G Gary Anderson
13 UCLA	59 C Bill Reid
23 Washington	14 G Bruce Blackstone
45 Washington St.	14 T Todd Anderson
24 Oregon State	23 TE Glen Stone / Ted Pappas
26 Southern Cal	27 QB Mike Boryla
24 Oregon	7 HB John Winesberry
26 California	17 FB Scott Laidlaw
	DL Roger Stillwell
	DL Peter Hansel
	DL Joe Martin / Drew Palin
	DL Pat Donovan
	LB Gordon Riegel / John Snider
	LB Folrest Martin
	LB Gerald Church
	DB Doc Blanchard
	DB John Ferguson
	DB Randy Poltl
	DB Jim Kaffen

RUSHING: Laidlaw 145/639y,
PASSING: Boryla 140-256/1629y, 17TD, 54.7%
RECEIVING: Singler 31/501y, Ishman 27/398y, Laidlaw 19/155y
SCORING: Rod Garcia (K) 76pts, Test 36pts, Laidlaw & Singler 30pts

1974 5-4-2

20 Penn State	24 WR Bill Singler / Eric Test
7 Illinois	41 WR Tony Hill / Brad Williams
21 San Jose State	21 T Keith Rowen
16 Michigan	27 G Tom Tipton
13 UCLA	13 C Todd Anderson
34 Washington	17 G Alex Karakozoff
20 Washington St.	18 T Gary Anderson
17 Oregon State	13 TE Ted Pappas
10 Southern Cal	34 QB Mike Cordova / Guy Benjamin
17 Oregon	0 HB Ron Inge / Dave Tenn
22 California	20 FB Scott Laidlaw
	DL Roger Stillwell
	DL Drew Palin
	DL Pat Donovan
	LB Gordon Riegel
	LB John Snider
	LB Folrest Martin / Rich Merlo
	LB Gerald Church
	DB Paul Skrabo
	DB Rich Waters / Gerald Wilson
	DB Doc Blanchard
	DB Jeff Siemens / Larry McGovern

RUSHING: Laidlaw 156/636y, Inge 92/355y, Tenn 33/134y
PASSING: Cordova 128-295/1569y, 10TD, 43.4%
RECEIVING: Hill 34/542y, Test 34/419y, Williams 24/305y
SCORING: Mike Langford (K) 65pts, Laidlaw 30pts, Singler 24pts

1975 6-4-1

14 Penn State	34 WR Bill Singler / Bill Kellar
19 Michigan	19 WR Tony Hill
34 San Jose State	36 T Gordon King
67 Army	14 G Alex Karakozoff
21 UCLA	31 C Todd Anderson
24 Washington	21 G Al TenBruggencate / Bill Hubbard
54 Washington St.	14 T Gary Anderson
28 Oregon State	22 TE Ted Pappas / Mark Hoaglin
13 Southern Cal	10 QB Mike Cordova
33 Oregon	30 HB Ron Inge / John Finley
15 California	48 FB Don Stevenson
	DL Duncan McColl
	DL John Harris
	DL Geoff Kieburtz / Bruce Barker
	LB Phil Francis
	LB Ray Cardinalli
	LB Rich Merlo
	LB Gerald Church / Jeff Barton
	DB Larry Reynolds / Ray Anderson
	DB Savann Thompson
	DB Rich Waters / Ralph Phillips
	DB Gerald Wilson

RUSHING: Stevenson 138/650y, Inge 90/439y, Finley 70/343y
PASSING: Cordova 106-231/1311y, 11TD, 45.9%
RECEIVING: Hill 55/916y, Pappas 29/332y, Inge 27/231y
SCORING: Mike Langford (K) 60pts, Hill 42pts, Inge 36pts

1976 6-5

12 Penn State	15 WR Bill Kellar
0 Michigan	51 WR Tony Hill / James Lofton
28 San Jose State	23 T Gordon King
20 Army	21 G Al TenBruggencate
20 UCLA	38 C Mark Hill / Dan McCann
34 Washington	28 G Bill Hubbard
22 Washington St.	16 T Gary Anderson
24 Oregon State	3 TE Mark Hoaglin / David Strong
24 Southern Cal	48 QB Guy Benjamin
28 Oregon	17 HB Ron Inge
27 California	24 FB Don Stevenson / Phil Francis
	DL Duncan McColl
	DL John Harris
	DL Geoff Kieburtz / Jack Moller
	LB Bruce Barker / Charles Evans
	LB Ray Cardinalli
	LB Gordy Ceresino
	LB Jeff Barton
	DB Larry Reynolds
	DB Savann Thompson
	DB Ralph Phillips
	DB Rich Waters

RUSHING: Stevenson 121/452y, Francis 67/299y, Inge 66/267y
PASSING: Benjamin 170-295/1982y, 12TD, 57.6%
RECEIVING: Hill 44/696y, Kellar 34/447y, Stevenson 23/187y
SCORING: Mike Michel (K) 61pts, Hill 48pts, Lofton 24pts

1977 9-3

21 Colorado	27 WR Bill Kellar
21 Tulane	17 WR James Lofton
37 Illinois	24 T Gordon King
20 Oregon	10 G Brent Saylor / Jim Stephens
32 UCLA	28 C Dan McCann
21 Washington	45 G Mark Hill
31 Washington St.	29 T Gene Engle
26 Oregon State	7 TE Mitch Pleis
0 Southern Cal	49 QB Guy Benjamin
31 San Jose State	26 HB Darrin Nelson / John Finley
21 California	3 FB Phil Francis
24 LSU■	14 DL Chuck Evans
	DL Dan Floyd
	DL Geoff Kieburtz
	DL Bruce Barker / Dean Wilson
	LB Terry Rennaker / Milt McColl
	LB Gordy Ceresino / Tom Hall
	LB Ray Cardinalli
	DB John Pigott / Larry Reynolds
	DB Rick Parker / Savann Thompson
	DB Robby Chapman / Keith Burcham
	DB Ralph Phillips

RUSHING: Nelson 183/1069y, Finley 114/456y, Francis 88/373y
PASSING: Benjamin 208-330/2521y, 19TD, 63.0%
RECEIVING: Lofton 53/931y, Nelson 50/524y, Kellar 46/653y
SCORING: Lofton 74pts, Ken Naber (K) 60pts, Nelson 36pts

1978 8-4

29 Oklahoma	35 WR Ken Margerum / Andre Tyler
38 San Jose State	9 WR James Lofton / Gordon Banks
35 Illinois	10 T Brian Holloway
17 Tulane	14 G Paul Hibler / Brent Saylor
26 UCLA	27 C John Macauley
31 Washington	34 G Jim Stephens
43 Washington St.	27 T Gene Engle
24 Oregon State	6 TE Mitch Pleis / Pat Bowe
7 Southern Cal	13 QB Steve Dills
21 Arizona State	14 HB Darrin Nelson
30 California	10 FB Phil Francis / Jim Brown
25 Georgia■	22 DL Chuck Evans
	DL Doug Rogers / Dan Floyd
	DL Dean Wilson
	LB Milt McColl / Terry Rennaker
	LB Gordy Ceresino
	LB Steve Budinger / Bo Boxold
	LB Kevin Bates / Tom Hall
	DB John Pigott
	DB Rick Parker / Savann Thompson
	DB Robby Chapman / Keith Burcham
	DB Steve Foley / Kent Stalwick

RUSHING: Nelson 167/1061y, Francis 106/455y, Brown 69/248y
PASSING: Dils 247-391/2943y, 22TD, 63.2%
RECEIVING: Margerum 53/942y, Nelson 50/446y, Francis 49/378y
SCORING: Ken Naber (K) 65pts, Nelson 60pts, Margerum 54pts

1979 5-5-1

10 Tulane	33 WR Andre Tyler
45 San Jose State	29 WR Ken Margerum
13 Army	17 T Brian Holloway
33 Boston College	14 G Mike Neill / Paul Hibler
27 UCLA	24 C John Macauley
21 Southern Cal	21 G John Delmare
30 Arizona	10 T Andre Hines
31 Oregon State	33 TE Pat Bowe
28 Arizona State	21 QB Turk Schonert / John Elway
7 Oregon	16 RB Vincent White
14 California	21 RB Mike Dotterer / Greg Hooper
	DL Chuck Evans
	DL Doug Rogers / Craig Awbrey
	DL Doug Wilson / Steve Ballinger
	LB Milt McColl / Terry Rennaker
	LB Craig Zellmer / Gary Wimmer
	LB Dave Morze / Vince Williams
	LB Kevin Bates / Jay Summers
	DB Steve Gervais
	DB Rick Parker / Rod Gilmore
	DB Steve Foley / Kevin MacMillan
	DB Joe St. Geme

RUSHING: White 104/475y, Dotterer 97/366y, Hooper 52/238y
PASSING: Schonert 148-221/1927y, 19TD, 67.0%,
Elway 50-96/544y, 6TD, 52.1%
RECEIVING: Tyler 45/652y, Margerum 41/733y, Dotterer 35/316y
SCORING: Margerum 60pts, Ken Naber (K) 55pts, Dotterer 48pts

1980 6-5

35 Oregon	25 WR Andre Tyler / Eric Mullins
19 Tulane	14 WR Ken Margerum / Mike Tolliver
13 Boston College	30 T Brian Holloway
31 Oklahoma	14 G Mike Neill
35 San Jose State	21 C John Macauley
21 UCLA	35 G Chris Rose / John Delmare
24 Washington	27 T Jim Dykstra / Bo Mattson
48 Washington St.	34 TE Chris Dressel / Jim Clymer
54 Oregon State	13 QB John Elway
9 Southern Cal	34 RB Darrin Nelson / Vincent White
23 California	28 FB Jim Brown / Rob Moore
	DL Doug Rogers
	DL Craig Awbrey
	DL Duker Dapper / Kevin Lamar
	LB Milt McColl
	LB Craig Zellmer
	LB Dave Morze / Gary Wimmer
	LB Jay Summers
	DB Rick Gervais / Rod Gilmore
	DB Kevin Baird
	DB Kevin MacMillan
	DB Vaughn Williams

RUSHING: Nelson 161/889y, White 57/303y, Brown 45/163y
PASSING: Elway 248-379/2889y, 27TD, 65.4%
RECEIVING: Tyler 53/737y, Nelson 47/552y, Margerum 44/691y
SCORING: Margerum 66pts, Ken Naber (K) 56pts, Nelson 50pts

1981 4-7

19 Purdue	27 WR Emile Harry / Don Lonsinger
6 San Jose State	28 WR Mike Tolliver / Eric Mullins
19 Ohio State	24 T Jim Dykstra
13 Arizona	17 G Mike Neill / Chris Rose
26 UCLA	23 C John Macaulay
17 Southern Cal	25 G Dennis Engel / Mike Teeuws
36 Arizona State	62 T Matt Moran
31 Washington	42 TE Chris Dressel
63 Oregon State	9 QB John Elway
42 Oregon	3 RB Darrin Nelson / Vincent White
42 California	21 FB Rob Moore / Mike Dotterer
	DL Doug Rogers
	DL Pat Mitchel / Terry Jackson
	DL John Bergren
	LB Jay Summers
	LB Don Stubblefield / Craig Zellmer
	LB Dave Morze / Gary Wimmer
	LB Tom Hall / Kevin Bates
	DB Kevin Baird
	DB Eric Price / Charles Hutchins
	DB Steve Lemon / Kevin MacMillan
	DB Vaughn Williams / Darrell Grissum

RUSHING: Nelson 192/1014y, White 72/417y, Moore 46/218y
PASSING: Elway 214-366/2674y, 20TD, 58.4%
RECEIVING: Nelson 67/846y, White 41/431y, Tolliver 33/639y
SCORING: Nelson 96pts, Mark Harmon (K) 66pts, Tolliver 42pts

1982 5-6

35 Purdue	14 WR Emile Harry
31 San Jose State	35 WR Mike Tolliver / Eric Mullins
23 Ohio State	20 T Jeff Deaton
45 Oregon State	5 G Matt Moran
17 Arizona State	21 C Mike Teeuws
21 Southern Cal	41 G Dennis Engel / Brent Martin
31 Washington St.	26 T Chris Rose
43 Washington	31 TE Chris Dressel
27 Arizona	41 QB John Elway
35 UCLA	38 RB Mike Dotterer / Vincent White
20 California	25 FB Greg Hooper / Kuaulana Park
	DL John Bergren
	DL Terry Jackson
	DL Pat Mitchel / Mike Wyman
	LB Garin Veris
	LB Matt Soderlund / Dave Wyman
	LB Gary Wimmer / Don Stubblefield
	LB Kevin Bates
	DB Kevin Baird
	DB Eric Price / Rod Gilmore
	DB Vaughn Williams
	DB Charles Hutchins

RUSHING: Dotterer 113/535y, White 88/494y, Hooper 34/200y
PASSING: Elway 262-405/3242y, 24TD, 64.6%
RECEIVING: White 68/677y, Harry 44/763y, Dressel 44/580y
SCORING: White 92pts, Mark Harmon (K) 78pts, Dotterer 60pts

1983 1-10

14 Oklahoma	27 WR Emile Harry
7 Illinois	17 WR Mike Tolliver / Eric Mullins
10 San Jose State	23 T Jeff Deaton
11 Arizona State	29 G Matt Moran
21 UCLA	39 C Brent Martin
15 Washington	32 G Tom Prukop
31 Arizona	22 T John Barns
18 Oregon State	31 TE Greg Baty / Dan Westerfield
7 Southern Cal	30 QB John Paye
7 Oregon	16 RB Thomas Henley
18 California	27 FB Shawn Avant / Marshall Dillard
	DL John Bergren
	DL Pat Mitchel / Terry Jackson
	DL Mike Wyman
	LB Garin Veris
	LB Matt Soderlund
	LB Dave Wyman / Mike Noble
	LB Tom Briehl / Joe Cain
	DB Kevin Baird
	DB Eric Price
	DB Vaughn Williams
	DB Charles Hutchings / Darrell Grissum

RUSHING: Henley 66/228y, Avant 42/165y, Dillard 38/155y
PASSING: Paye 150-297/1971y, 10TD, 49.1%
RECIVING: Tolliver 58/656y, Harry 44/829y, Clymer 23/277y
SCORING: Mark Harmon (K) 43pts, Harry 36pts, Henley 20pts

1984 5-6

7 Oklahoma	19 WR Emile Harry
34 Illinois	19 WR Jeff James / Carl Morris
28 San Jose State	27 T Jeff Deaton
10 Arizona State	28 G Matt Moran
23 UCLA	21 C Brent Martin
15 Washington	37 G Tom Prukop
42 Washington St.	49 T John Barns
28 Oregon State	21 TE Greg Baty / Eric Snelson
11 Southern Cal	20 QB John Paye / Fred Buckley
14 Arizona	28 RB Thomas Henley / Kevin Scott
27 California	10 FB Brad Muster
	DL Garin Veris
	DL Terry Jackson
	DL Pat Mitchel / Mike Wyman
	LB Joe Krupok
	LB Matt Soderlund
	LB Dave Wyman / Mike Noble
	LB Tom Briehl
	DB Toi Cook
	DB Eric Price / Walt Harris
	DB Darrell Grissum
	DB Joe Cain

RUSHING: Muster 184/823y, Scott 70/375y, Henley 63/276y
PASSING: Buckley 81-166/940y, 5TD, 48.8%,
  Paye 77-147/848y, 4TD, 52.4%
RECEIVING: Muster 31/228y, Harry 25/482y, Henley 22/250y
SCORING: Mark Harmon (K) 65pts, Henley 30pts, Harry 26pts

1985 4-7

41 San Jose State	7 WR Carl Morris / Henry Green
28 Oregon	45 WR Jeff James
34 Texas	38 T Jeff Marchin / Robbie Coffin
22 San Diego State	41 G Andy Sinclair
9 UCLA	34 C Kurt Josephson
6 Southern Cal	30 G Tom Nye / Guy Bunyard
28 Arizona	17 T John Barns
0 Washington	34 TE Greg Baty / Eric Snelson
39 Oregon State	24 QB John Paye
14 Arizona State	21 RB Thomas Henley (WR) / Kevin Scott
24 California	22 FB Brad Muster (RB) / Brian Morris
	DL Joe Lortie / Sean Scheller
	DL Eric Volta
	DL Tony Leiker
	LB Tom Prukop / Chris Weber
	LB Matt Soderlund
	LB Jack Gilmete
	LB Kurt Colehower / Bill Fiander
	DB Toi Cook
	DB Walt Harris / Kevin Richardson
	DB Brad Humphreys / Mark Hashimoto
	DB Bruce Richardson

RUSHING: Muster 140/521y, B. Morris 55/180y, Scott 38/148y
PASSING: Paye 271-405/2589y, 10TD, 66.9%
RECEIVING: Muster 78/654y, Baty 61/690y, James 42/658y
SCORING: Muster 62pts, David Sweeney (K) 61pts

1986 8-4

31 Texas	20 WR Thomas Henley / Carl Morris
28 San Jose State	10 WR Jeff James
17 Oregon State	7 T Kurt Josephson / Robbie Coffin
17 San Diego State	10 G Tom Nye / John Mahoney
14 Washington	24 C Andy Sinclair
41 Oregon	7 G Andy Papathanassiou
0 Southern Cal	10 T John Zentner / Jeff Marchin
42 Washington St.	12 TE Eric Snelson
28 UCLA	23 QB John Paye
11 California	17 RB Kevin Scott / Brian Morris
29 Arizona	24 FB Brad Muster
21 Clemson■	27 DL Joe Lortie
	DL Eric Volta
	DL Tony Leiker
	LB Barry McKeever
	LB Dave Wyman / Mike Noble
	LB Kevin Richardson / Darron Bennett
	LB Kurt Colehower
	DB Toi Cook
	DB Walt Harris
	DB Brad Humphreys
	DB Bruce Richardson

RUSHING: Muster 243/1053y, Scott 43/168y, B. Morris 33/162y
PASSING: Paye 217-349/2261y, 14TD, 62.2%
RECEIVING: Muster 61/565y, James 52/779y, Henley 28/431y
SCORING: Muster 78pts, James 48pts, David Sweeney (K) 44pts

1987 5-6

21 Washington	31 WR Ed McCaffrey
17 Colorado	31 WR Jeff James
17 San Jose State	24 T Jon Summers
0 UCLA	49 G Chuck Gillingham / John Mahoney
44 Washington St.	7 C Andy Sinclair / Dan Nash
44 San Diego State	40 G Andy Papathanassiou
13 Oregon	10 T John Zentner
13 Arizona	23 TE James Price · Eric Snelson
24 Southern Cal	39 DB Brian Johnson
38 Oregon State	7 RB Brad Muster
31 California	7 FB Jon Volpe
	DL Lester Archambeau
	DL Ray Huckestein / Eric Volta
	DL Sean Scheller / Joe Lortie
	LB Rob Hinkley / Barry McKeever
	LB Jono Tunney / Kevin Mescher
	LB Kevin Richardson
	LB Kurt Colehower / Bruce Lang
	DB Alan Grant
	DB Kevin Scott / Brad Cook
	DB Brad Humphreys
	DB Bruce Richardson

RUSHING: Muster 119/543y, Volpe 111/379y,
PASSING: Johnson 112-203/1510y, 11TD, 55.2%
RECEIVING: James 42/516y, McCaffrey 30/533y, Muster 24/222y
SCORING: Muster 48pts, John Hopkins (K) 38pts, Volpe 36pts

1988 3-6-2

20 Southern Cal	24 WR Ed McCaffrey
31 San Diego State	10 WR Walter Batson
3 Oregon	7 T Jon Summers / Mike Kohlmoos
14 Notre Dame	42 G Andy Papathanassiou
44 San Jose State	12 C Andy Sinclair / Dan Nash
24 Arizona State	3 G Chuck Gillingham / John Mahoney
20 Oregon State	20 T Darran Baird
25 Washington	28 QB Jason Palumbis / Brian Johnson
21 Washington St.	24 SB Chris Walsh
17 UCLA	27 SB Charlie Young / Scott Eschelman
19 California	19 FB Jon Volpe / Tommy Vardell
	DL Lester Archambeau
	DL Ray Huckestein / Buck Roggeman
	DL Scott Palmbush
	LB Rob Hinckley
	LB Jono Tunney
	LB Kevin Richardson
	LB Bruce Lang
	DB Alan Grant
	DB Kevin Scott
	DB Tony Trousset
	DB Rob Englehardt

RUSHING: Volpe 228/1027y, Eschelman 37/169y, Vardell 12/27y
PASSING: Palumbis 128-228/1569y, 8TD, 56.1%,
  Johnson 72-135/767y, 3TD, 53.3%
RECEIVING: Young 43/560y, Walsh 41/480y, Green 27/351y
SCORING: John Hopkins (K) 82pts, Volpe 36pts

1989 3-8

3 Arizona	19 WR Ed McCaffrey / Turner Baur
16 Oregon State	20 WR Jon Pinckney / Walter Batson
18 Oregon	7 T Bob Whitfield
33 San Jose State	40 G Chris Dalman
17 Notre Dame	27 C Chuck Gilligham (G) / Rick Pallow
13 Washington St.	31 G Andy Papathanassiou
24 Utah	27 T Darran Baird / John Carpenter
0 Southern Cal	19 TE James Price / Cory Booker
17 UCLA	14 QB Steve Smith / Brian Johnson
22 Arizona State	30 RB J.J. Lasley / Gary Taylor / Galen
Foster	
24 California	14 FB Scott Eschelman / Tommy Vardell
	DL Lester Archambeau
	DL Aaron Rembisz / Estevan Avila
	DL Scott Palmbush / Matt Borkowski
	LB Bob Hinckley / Chris Hawkins
	LB Jono Tunney
	LB Dave Garnett
	LB Bruce Lang / Charles Lough
	DB Alan Grant
	DB Kevin Scott / Albert Richardson
	DB Tony Trousset
	DB Jimmy Klein

RUSHING: Eschelman 77/334y, Vardell 60/237y, Lasley 40/185y
PASSING: Smith 150-270/1502y, 7TD, 55.6%,
  Johnson 95-153/1057y, 4TD, 62.1%
RECEIVING: McCaffrey 53/871y, Price 45/391y,
  Eschelman 36/203y
SCORING: John Hopkins (K) 82pts, Pinckney 32pts,
  McCaffrey 24pts

1990 5-6

17 Colorado	21 WR Ed McCaffrey / Chris Walsh
31 UCLA	32 WR Jon Pinckney / Vaughn Bryant
37 Oregon State	3 T Bob Whitfield
23 San Jose State	29 G Brian Cassidy
36 Notre Dame	31 C Chris Dalman
22 Southern Cal	37 G Chuck Gillingham
16 Washington	52 T Steve Hoyem / Darran Baird
0 Oregon	31 TE Paul Nickel / Turner Baur
31 Washington St.	13 QB Jason Palumbis
23 Arizona	10 RB Glyn Milburn
27 California	25 FB Tommy Vardell / Jon Volpe
	DL Matt Borkowski / Tyler Batson
	DL Aaron Rembisz / Frank Busalacchi
	DL Estevan Avila
	LB Ron George
	LB Jono Tunney
	LB Tom Williams / Dan Byers
	LB Dave Garnett
	DB Darrien Gordon / Albert Richardson
	DB Kevin Scott
	DB Seyon Albert
	DB Jimmy Klein / John Lynch

RUSHING: Milburn 152/729y, Vardell 120/441y, Volpe 42/148y
PASSING: Palumbis 234-341/2579y, 11TD, 68.6%
RECEIVING: Milburn 64/632y, McCaffrey 61/917y, Walsh 29/386y
SCORING: Vardell 84pts, John Hopkins (K) 65pts,
  McCaffrey 56pts

1991 8-4

7 Washington	42 WR Chris Walsh / David Shaw
23 Arizona	28 WR Jon Pinckney / Justin Armour
28 Colorado	21 T Bob Whitfield
26 Notre Dame	42 G Brian Cassidy
56 Cornell	6 C Glen Cavanaugh
24 Southern Cal	21 G Chris Dalman
40 Oregon State	10 T Steve Hoyem / Derron Klafter
33 Oregon	13 TE Turner Baur / Ryan Wetnight
27 UCLA	10 QB Steve Stenstrom / Jason Palumbis
49 Washington St.	14 RB Glyn Milburn
38 California	21 FB Tommy Vardell
17 Georgia Tech■	18 DL Tyrone Parker
	DL Jason Fisk / Aaron Rembisz
	DL Estevan Avila / Tyler Batson
	LB Ron George
	LB Coy Gibbs
	LB Tom Williams / Jimmy Klein
	LB Dave Garnett / Tommy Knecht
	DB Darrien Gordon
	DB Vaughn Bryant / Ron Reddell
	DB Seyon Albert / Albert Richardson
	DB John Lynch

RUSHING: Vardell 226/1084, Milburn 131/598y, Lasley 32/120y
PASSING: Stenstrom 119-197/1683y, 15TD, 60.4%,
  Palumbis 80-139/806y, 0TD, 57.6%
RECEIVING: Walsh 66/934y, Milburn 40/454y, Pinckney 27/448y
SCORING: Vardell 120pts, Aaron Mills (K) 58pts,
  Milburn & Walsh 36pts

1992 10-3

7 Texas A&M	10 WR Mike Cook / David Shaw
21 Oregon	7 WR Justin Armour / Tyler Batson
35 Northwestern	24 T Jeff Bailey / Seth Dittman
37 San Jose State	13 G Brian Cassidy / T.J. Gaynor
33 Notre Dame	16 C Glen Cavanaugh
19 UCLA	7 G Chris Dalman / Jeff Buckey
6 Arizona	21 T Steve Hoyem
27 Oregon State	21 TE Ryan Wetnight / Tony Cline
7 Washington	41 QB Steve Stenstrom
23 Southern Cal	9 RB Glyn Milburn / Ellery Roberts
40 Washington St.	3 FB J.J. Lasley / Ethan Allen
41 California	21 DL Tyrone Parker
24 Penn State■	3 DL Jason Fisk
	DL Estevan Avila / David Carder
	LB Ron George
	LB Coy Gibbs / Toby Norwood
	LB Tom Williams
	LB Dave Garnett Jason White
	DB Darrien Gordon
	DB Vaughn Bryant / Kwame Ellis
	DB Seyon Albert
	DB John Lynch

RUSHING: Milburn 177/851y, Roberts 132/627y, Lasley 58/245y
PASSING: Stenstrom 197-335/2399y, 14TD, 58.8%
RECEIVING: Cook 51/649y, Lasley 38/380y, Milburn 37/405y
SCORING: Eric Abrams (K) 79pts, Milburn 78pts, Armour 42pts

1993 4-7

14 Washington	31 WR Justin Armour
31 San Jose State	28 WR David Shaw / Brian Manning
41 Colorado	37 T Seth Dittman
25 UCLA	28 G Mike Jerich
20 Notre Dame	48 C T.J. Gaynor / Glen Cavanaugh
24 Arizona	27 G Jeff Buckey
30 Arizona State	38 T Steve Hoyem
31 Oregon State	27 TE Tony Cline / Jeff Hansen
20 Southern Cal	45 QB Steve Stenstrom
38 Oregon	34 RB Ellery Roberts
17 California	46 FB Ethan Allen
	DL Tyrone Parker
	DL Jason Fisk / John Hebert
	DL David Carder / Pete Swanson
	LB Jason White
	LB Coy Gibbs
	LB Toby Norwood
	LB Nick Wattts / Brian Batson
	DB Eliel Swinton / Kwame Ellis
	DB Vaughn Bryant / Jami Webb
	DB Kevin Garnett
	DB David Walker

RUSHING: Roberts 111/419y, Allen 46/260y, Mitchell 47/124y
PASSING: Stenstrom 300-455/3627y, 27TD, 65.9%
RECEIVING: Allen 52/313y, Armour 51/764y, Cline 42/465y
SCORING: Eric Abrams (K) 67pts, Armour 36pts, Roberts 30pts

1994 3-7-1

41 Northwestern	41 WR Justin Armour / David Shaw
51 San Jose State	20 WR Brian Manning / Mark Harris
10 Arizona	34 T Seth Dittman
15 Notre Dame	34 G Mike Jerich
35 Arizona State	36 C T.J. Gaynor
20 Southern Cal	27 G Brad Badger
35 Oregon State	29 T Jeff Buckey
30 UCLA	31 TE Tony Cline
46 Washington	28 QB Steve Stenstrom / Scott Frost (DB)
21 Oregon	55 RB Anthony Bookman / Mike Mitchell
23 California	24 FB Ethan Allen / Adam Salina
	DL Kailee Wong / Bryan Werner
	DL Jason Fisk / John Hebert
	DL Pete Swanson / David Carder
	LB Jason White / Chris Draft
	LB Mark Hall
	LB Coy Gibbs
	LB Jon Haskins / Brian Batson
	DB Leroy Pruitt
	DB Jami Webb / Eliel Swinton
	DB Charles Young
	DB Kadar Hamilton / David Walker

RUSHING: Bookman 129/577y, Mitchell 43/323y, Allen 70/282y
PASSING: Stenstrom 217-333/2822y, 16TD, 65.2%
RECEIVING: Armour 67/1092y, Manning 46/899y, Allen 40/391y
SCORING: Eric Abrams (K) 55pts, Bookman & Armour 42pts

1995 7-4-1

47 San Jose State	33 WR Mark Harris / Damon Dunn
27 Utah	20 WR Brian Manning / Marlon Evans
24 Wisconsin	24 T Nathan Parks
28 Oregon	21 G Brad Badger / Matt Motherway
30 Arizona State	28 C T.J. Gaynor
28 Washington	38 G Ryan Waters / Andrew Kroeker
28 UCLA	42 T Jeff Buckey
24 Oregon State	3 TE Greg Clark / Derek Hubbard
30 Southern Cal	31 QB Mark Butterfield
36 Washington St.	24 RB Anthony Bookman / Mike Mitchell
29 California	24 FB Adam Salina / Greg Comella
13 East Carolina■	19 DL Jason White / Kailee Wong
	DL John Hebert
	DL Pete Swanson
	DL David Carder
	LB Brian Batson / Nicodemus Watts
	LB Chris Draft
	LB Mike Hall / Jon Haskins
	DB Leroy Pruitt
	DB Kwame Ellis / Corey Hill
	DB Josh Madsen / Charles Young
	DB Eliel Swinton

RUSHING: Bookman 181/872y, Mitchell 129/593y, Comella 63/245y
PASSING: Butterfield 194-333/2533y, 19TD, 58.3%
RECEIVING: Harris 57/984y, Manning 40/616y, Clark 23/260y
SCORING: Eric Abrams (K) 81pts

1996 7-5

10 Utah	17 WR Damon Dunn/Jeff Allen/Andre Kirwan
25 San Jose State	2 WR Brian Manning / Troy Walters
0 Wisconsin	14 T Nathan Parks
6 Washington	27 G Brad Badger
27 Oregon	24 C Mike McLaughlin
12 Oregon State	26 G Andrew Kroeker
9 Arizona State	41 T Jeff Cronshagen
21 UCLA	20 TE Greg Clark / Derek Hubbard
24 Southern Cal	20 QB Chad Hutchinson / Todd Husak
33 Washington St.	17 TB Mike Mitchell / Anthony Bookman
42 California	21 FB Adam Salina /Greg Comella/Jon Ritchie
38 Michigan St.■	0 DL Kailee Wong
	DL Carl Hansen
	DL Pete Swanson
	DL Bryan Werner
	LB Brian Batson
	LB Chris Draft
	LB Jon Haskins
	DB Leroy Pruitt
	DB Corey Hill
	DB Josh Madsen
	DB Eliel Swinton / Kadar Hamilton

RUSHING: Mitchell 164/809y, Bookman 82/274y, Comella 38/115y
PASSING: Hutchinson 190-312/2134y, 10TD, 60.9%
RECEIVING: Manning 37/383y, Dunn 35/452y, Walters 32/444y
SCORING: Kevin Miller (K) 57pts

1997 5-6

28 San Jose State	12 WR Damon Dunn / DeRonnie Pitts
17 North Carolina	28 WR Troy Walters
27 Oregon State	24 T Jeff Cronshagen
58 Oregon	49 G Joe Fairchild / Matt Motherway
33 Notre Dame	15 C Mike McLaughlin
22 Arizona	28 G Eli Burriss / Andrew Kroeker
14 Arizona State	31 T Geoff Wilson
7 UCLA	27 TE Tommy Hanson / Russell Stewart
21 Southern Cal	45 QB Chad Hutchinson
28 Washington St.	38 TB Anthony Bookman / Mike Mitchell
21 California	20 FB Greg Comella / Jon Ritchie
	DL Kailee Wong
	DL Carl Hanson / Andrew Currie
	DL Willie Howard
	DL Bryan Werner
	LB Jon Haskins / Sharcus Steen
	LB Chris Draft
	LB Donnie Spragan / Marc Stockbauer
	DB Chris Johnson / Frank Primus
	DB Corey Hill
	DB Alistair White
	DB Kadar Hamilton / Than Merrill

RUSHING: Bookman 122/800y, Mitchell 152/597y, Ritchie 17/95y
PASSING: Hutchinson 189-315/2101y, 10TD, 60.0%
RECEIVING: Walters 86/1206y, Dunn 54/578y, Mitchell 17/118y
SCORING: Walters 60pts, Bookman 44pts, Kevin Miller (K) 43pts

1998 3-8

23 San Jose State	35 WR DeRonnie Pitts / Dave Davis
14 Arizona	31 WR Troy Walters / Jeff Allen
37 North Carolina	34 T Jeff Cronshagen
28 Oregon	63 G Joe Fairchild
15 Notre Dame	33 C Mike McLaughlin
23 Oregon State	30 G Andrew Kroeker / Jon Abendschein
38 Arizona State	44 T Geoff Wilson / Brian Donoghue
24 UCLA	28 TE Russell Stewart
9 Southern Cal	34 QB Todd Husak / Joe Borchand
38 Washington St.	28 RB Coy Wire / J.C. Lacey / Brian Allen
10 California	3 FB Maxwell Stevenson / Emory Brock
	DL Sam Benner
	DL Andrew Currie / Travis Pfeifer
	DL Willie Howard
	DL Riall Johnson
	LB Donnie Spragan
	LB Sharcus Steen / Matt Friedrichs
	LB Marc Stockbauer
	DB Chris Johnson
	DB Brian Taylor / Ruben Carter
	DB Tim Smith / Tank Williams
	DB Aaron Focht / Simba Hodari

RUSHING: Wire 85/298y, Lacey 73/279y, B. Allen 76/154y
PASSING: Husak 233-447/3092y, 17TD, 52.1%
RECEIVING: Pitts 74/1012y, Walters 52/880y, Davis 48/707y
SCORING: Kevin Miller (K) 59pts, Pitts 42pts, Davis 38pts

1999 8-4

17 Texas	69 WR DeRonnie Pitts / Dave Davis
54 Washington St.	17 WR Troy Walters / Tafiti Uso
50 Arizona	22 T Jeff Cronshagen
42 UCLA	32 G Zach Quaccia / Joe FAirchild
39 San Jose State	44 C Mike McLaughlin
21 Oregon State	17 G Eric Heitmann
35 Southern Cal	31 T Greg Schindler
30 Washington	35 TE Russell Stewart / Matt Wright
50 Arizona State	30 QB Todd Husak / Joe Borchard
31 California	13 RB Brian Allen / Kerry Carter / Coy Wire
40 Notre Dame	37 FB Casey Moore / Emory Brock
9 Wisconsin■	17 DL Sam Benner
	DL Andrew Currie
	DL Willie Howard
	DL Austin Lee
	LB Riall Johnson
	LB Sharcus Steen
	LB Marc Stockbauer
	DB Chris Johnson
	DB Frank Primus / Ruben Carter
	DB Tank Williams
	DB Tim Smith / Aaron Focht

RUSHING: Allen 115/604y, Carter 87/330y, Wire 88/317y
PASSING: Husak 176-308/2688y, 18TD, 57.1%
RECEIVING: Walters 74/1456y, Pitts 58/853y, Davis 30/522y
SCORING: Mike Biselli (K) 91pts, Walters 60pts, Pitts 48pts

2000 5-6

24 Washington St.	10 WR DeRonnie Pitts / Jamien McCullum
27 San Jose State	40 WR Ryan Wells / Luke Powell
27 Texas	24 T Kirk Chambers
3 Arizona	27 G Zach Quaccia (C) / Paul Weinacht
14 Notre Dame	20 C Mike Holman
6 Oregon State	38 G Eric Heitmnn
32 Southern Cal	30 T Kwame Harris
28 Washington	31 TE Russell Stewart / Brett Pierce
35 UCLA	37 QB Randy Fasani / Chris Lewis
29 Arizona State	7 RB Kerry Carter / Brian Allen
36 California	30 FB Casey Moore
	DL Marcus Hoover / Sam Benner
	DL Matt Leonard / Trey Freeman
	DL Willie Howard / Travis Pfeifer
	DL Austin Lee
	LB Riall Johnson
	LB Matt Friedrichs / Anthony Gabriel
	LB Coy Wire
	DB Ruben Carter / Brian Taylor
	DB Ryan Fernandez
	DB Tank Williams
	DB Aaron Focht / Simba Hodari

RUSHING: Carter 179/729y, Allen 117/460y, Moore 50/224y
PASSING: Fasani 93-180/1400y, 11TD, 51.7%
　　　　Lewis 92-204/1179y, 8TD, 45.1%
RECEIVING: Pitts 77/882y, Wells 19/201y, Powell 18/502y
SCORING: Pitts 50pts, Mike Biselli (K) 47pts, Carter 42pts

2001 9-3

38 Boston College	22 WR Ryan Wells / Teyo Johnson
51 Arizona State	28 WR Luke Powell
21 Southern Cal	16 T Kirk Chambers
39 Washington St.	45 G Eric Heitmann / Paul Weinacht
49 Oregon	42 C Zach Quaccia
38 UCLA	28 G Greg Schindler
28 Washington	42 T Kwame Harris
51 Arizona	37 TE Brett Pierce
35 California	28 QB Randy Fasani / Chris Lewis
17 Notre Dame	13 RB Brian Allen / Kenneth Tolon
41 San Jose State	14 FB Casey Moore / Kerry Carter
14 Georgia Tech■	24 DL Marcus Hoover / Louis Hobson
	DL Craig Albrecht
	DL Travis Pfeifer
	DL Austin Lee / Drew Caylor
	LB Anthony Gabriel
	LB Matt Friedrichs
	LB Coy Wire
	DB Ruben Carter
	DB Ryan Fernandez / Garry Cobb
	DB Tank Williams
	DB Colin Branch / Simba Hodari

RUSHING: Allen 174/899y, Carter 123/456y, Tolon 54/346y
PASSING: Fasani 86-167/1479y, 13TD, 51.5%
　　　　Lewis 90-163/1277y 12TD, 55.2%
RECEIVING: Powell 40/790y, Johnson 38/565y, Wells 31/519y
SCORING: Mike Biselli (K) 78pts, Carter 60pts, Allen 56pts

2002 2-9

27 Boston College	34 WR Teyo Johnson / Ryan Wells
63 San Jose State	26 WR Luke Powell
24 Arizona State	65 T Kirk Chambers
7 Notre Dame	31 G Paul Weinacht
11 Washington St.	36 C Tom Kolich
16 Arizona	6 G Greg Schindler
18 UCLA	28 T Kwame Harris
14 Oregon	41 TE Alex Smith / Brett Pierce
17 Southern Cal	49 QB Chris Lewis / Kyle Matter
21 Oregon State	31 RB Kerry Carter / Kenneth Tolon
7 California	30 FB Casey Moore
	DL Amon Gordon / Will Svitek
	DL Trey Freeman / Junior Oshinowo
	DL Matt Leonard
	DL Louis Hobson / Julian Jenkins
	LB Jon Alston / Michael Craven
	LB David Bergeron / Jake Covault
	LB Jared Newberry / Brian Gaffney
	DB Stanley Wilson / T.J. Rushing
	DB Leigh Torrence
	DB Oshiomogho Atogwe
	DB Colin Branch

RUSHING: Carter 149/524y, Moore 54/348y, Tolon 66/346y
PASSING: Matter 116-214/1219y, 8TD, 5.2%, Lewis 68-139/712y, 5TD, 48.9%
RECEIVING: Johnson 41/467y, Smith 30/380y, Powell 25/268y
SCORING: Johnson 52pts, Michael Sgroi (K) 50pts, Tolon 24pts

2003 4-7

31 San Jose State	10 WR Luke Powell / Greg Camarillo
18 BYU	14 WR Gerren Crochet / Mark Bradford
17 Washington	28 T Kirk Chambers
21 Southern Cal	44 G Ismail Simpson
14 Washington St.	24 C Drew Caylor / Brian Head
0 Oregon	35 G Jeff Edwards / Josiah Vinson
21 UCLA	14 T Mike Sullivan / Jon Cochran
38 Arizona State	27 TE Brett Pierce / Matt Traverso
3 Oregon State	43 TE Alex Smith / Patrick Danahy
16 California	28 QB Chris Lewis / Trent Edwards
7 Notre Dame	57 RB Kenneth Tolon / J.R. Lemon
	DL Will Svitek
	DL Amon Gordon
	DL Babatunde Oshinowo
	DL Louis Hobson / Julian Jenkins
	LB Jared Newberry / Brian Gaffney
	LB David Bergeron / Jon Alston
	LB Michael Craven / Kevin Schimmelmann
	DB T.J. Rushing / Stanley Wilson
	DB Leigh Torrence
	DB Oshiomogho Atogwe
	DB Trevor Hooper

RUSHING: Tolon 150/522y, Lemon 118/467y, David Marrero (RB) 37/115y
PASSING: Lewis 100-207/1178y, 8TD, 48.3%, Edwards 77-170/750y, 4TD, 45.3%
RECEIVING: Powell 45/520y, Bradford 37/587y, Smith 24/185y
SCORING: Michael Sgroi (K) 42pts, Powell & Lemon 24pts

2004 4-7

43 San Jose State	3 WR Mark Bradford / Greg Camarillo
37 BYU	10 WR Evan Moore / Justin McCullum
28 Southern Cal	31 T Jon Cochran
27 Washington	13 G Ismail Simpson
15 Notre Dame	23 C Brian Head / Mikal Brewer (G)
23 Washington St.	17 G Josiah Vinson
13 Oregon	16 T Jeff Edwards
0 UCLA	21 TE Alex Smith / Patrick Danahy
31 Arizona State	34 QB Trent Edwards / T.C. Ostrander
19 Oregon State	24 RB J.R. Lemon / Kenneth Tolon
6 California	41 FB Kris Bonifas
	DL Scott Scharff / Will Svitek
	DL Babatunde Oshinowo
	DL Julian Jenkins
	LB Jon Alston / Timi Wusu
	LB David Bergeron / Nick Silva
	LB Kevin Schimmelmann / Michael Okwo
	LB Jared Newberry
	DB Stanley Wilson / T.J. Rushing
	DB Leigh Torrence
	DB Oshiomogho Atogwe
	DB Brandon Harrison

RUSHING: Lemon 93/440y, Tolon 116/422y, Jones 38/87y
PASSING: Edwards 149-274/1732y, 9TD, 54.4%, Ostrander 56-126/914y, 4TD, 44.4%
RECEIVING: Smith 52/706y, Moore 39/616y, Bradford 34/482y
SCORING: Michael Sgroi (K) 70pts, Lemon & Moore 36pts

2005 5-6

41 Navy	38 WR Mark Bradford / Justin McCullum
17 Cal-Davis	20 WR Gerren Crochet
20 Oregon	44 T Allen Smith / Jeff Edwards
24 Washington St.	21 G Josiah Vinson
20 Arizona	16 C Tim Mattran / BrianHead
45 Arizona State	35 G Alex Fletcher (C) / Ismail Simpson
27 UCLA	30 T Jon Cochran
21 Southern Cal	51 TE Matt Traverso / Patrick Danahy
20 Oregon State	17 QB Trent Edwards / T.C. Ostrander
3 California	27 RB Anthony Kimble / Jason Evans
31 Notre Dame	38 FB Nick Frank
	DL Udeme Udofia
	DL Babatunde Oshinowo
	DL Gustav Rydstedt
	DL Julian Jenkins
	LB Jon Alston / Michael Craven
	LB Kevin Schimmelmann / Michael Okwo
	LB Mike Silva / Tim Wasu
	DB Nick Sanchez
	DB T.J. Rushing / Calvin Armstrong
	DB David Lofton / Trevor Hooper
	DB Brandon Harrison

RUSHING: Evans 72/248y, Kimble 66/244y, J.R. Lemon (RB) 76/222y
PASSING: Edwards 168-268/1934y, 17TD, 62.7%
RECEIVING: Bradford 37/609y, McCullum 36/539y, Crochet 29/387y
SCORING: Michael Srgoi (K) 77pts, Bradford 36pts, McCullum 30pts

2006 1-11

10 Oregon	48 WR Richard Sherman / Austin Yancey
34 San Jose State	35 WR Kelton Lynn / Evan Moore
9 Navy	37 T Allen Smith
10 Washington St.	36 G Josiah Vinson / Ismail Simpson
0 UCLA	31 C Alex Fletcher / Mikal Brewer
10 Notre Dame	31 G Jon Cochran
7 Arizona	20 T Jeff Edwards / Chris Marinelli
3 Arizona State	38 TE Jim Dray / Matt Traverso
0 Southern Cal	42 QB Trent Edwards / T.C. Ostrander
20 Washington	3 RB Anthony Kimble / Toby Gerhart
7 Oregon State	30 FB Emeka Nnoli
17 California	26 DL Chris Horn
	DL Ekom Udefia
	DL Pannel Egboh
	LB Udeme Udofia
	LB Pat Maynor / Brian Bulcke
	LB Michael Okwo / Fred Campbell
	LB Clinton Snyder / Will Powers
	DB Nick Sanchez / Wopamo Osaisai
	DB Brandon Harrison / Tim Sims
	DB David Lofton
	DB Trevor Hooper / Bo McNally

RUSHING: Kimble 114/470y, Gerhart 106/375y, Nnoli 19/49y
PASSING: Edwards 94-156/1027y, 6TD, 60.3%, Ostrander 72-158/918y, 3TD, 45.6%
RECEIVING: Sherman 34/581y, Lynn 19/254y, Dray 19/178y, Kimble 19/156y
SCORING: Aaron Zagory (K) 37pts, Moore & Sherman 18pts

2007 4-8

17 UCLA	45 WR Mark Bradiord / Richard Sherman
37 San Jose State	0 WR Evan Moore
31 Oregon	55 T Ben Muth / Allen Smith
3 Arizona State	41 G Mikal Brewer
24 Southern Cal	23 C Tim Mattran
36 TCU	38 G Alex Fletcher
21 Arizona	20 T Chris Marinelli
6 Oregon State	23 TE Jim Dray / Austin Gunder
9 Washington	27 QB T.C. Ostrander / Tavita Pritchard
17 Washington St.	33 RB Anthony Kimble / Jeremy Stewart
14 Notre Dame	21 FB Owen Marecic / Josh Catron
20 California	13 DL Pannel Egboh
	DL Chris Horn
	DL Levirt Griffin / Ekom Udofia
	DL Erik Lorig / Udeme Udofia
	LB Clinton Snyder
	LB Pat Maynor
	LB Chike Amajoyi / Nick Macaluso
	DB Nick Sanchez / Tim Sims
	DB Wopamo Osaisai / Kris Evans
	DB Austin Yancy
	DB Bo McNally / Taylor Skaufel

RUSHING: Kimble 115/509y, Stewart 105/343y, Tyrone McGraw (RB) 64/294y
PASSING: Ostrander 130-229/1422y, 7TD, 56.8%, Pritchard 97-194/1114y, 5TD, 50.0%
RECEIVING: Bradford 51/642y, Sherman 39/651y, Moore 39/481y
SCORING: Derek Belch (K) 71pts, Kimble 48pts, Sherman 24pts

2008 5-7

36 Oregon State	28 WR Ryan Whalen / Richard Sherman
17 Arizona State	41 WR Doug Baldwin / Delano Howell
14 TCU	31 T Ben Muth
23 San Jose State	10 G Chase Beeler / Bert McBride
35 Washington	28 C Alex Fletcher
21 Notre Dame	28 G Andrew Phillips
24 Arizona	23 T Chris Martinelli (G) / Matt Kopa
20 UCLA	23 TE Austin Gunder / Jim Dray (WR)
58 Washington St.	7 QB Tavita Pritchard / Alex Loukas
28 Oregon	35 TB Toby Gerhart / Anthony Kimble
23 Southern Cal	45 FB Owen Marecic
16 California	37 DL Pannel Egboh / Tom McAndrew
	DL Ekom Udofia / Brian Bulcke
	DL Sione Fua / Matt Masifilo
	DL Erik Lorig
	LB Clinton Snyder / Will Powers
	LB Nick Macaluso / Chike Amajoyi
	LB Pat Maynor
	DB Wopamo Osaisai
	DB Kris Evans / Michael Thomas
	DB Sean Wiser / Taylor Skaufel
	DB Bo McNally

RUSHING: Gerhart 210/1136y, Kimble 120/717y, Loukas 36/186y
PASSING: Pritchard 147-254/1633y, 10TD, 57.9%
RECEIVING: Whalen 41/508y, Baldwin 23/332y, Gunder 17/145y
SCORING: Gerhart 90pts, Aaron Zagory (K) 77pts, Kimble 42pts

2009 8-5

39 Washington St.	13 WR Ryan Whalen / Griff Whalen
17 Wake Forest	24 WR Chris Owusu / Warren Rueland (TE)
42 San Jose	17 T Jonathan Martin / Al Smith
34 Washington	14 G Andrew Phillips
24 UCLA	16 C Chase Beeler
28 Oregon State	38 G David DeCastro
38 Arizona	43 T Chris Martinelli (G) / Matt Kopa
33 Arizona State	14 TE Jim Dray / Cobi Fleener
51 Oregon	42 QB Andrew Luck / Tavita Pritchard
55 Southern Cal	21 TB Toby Gerhart
28 California	34 FB Owen Marecic
45 Notre Dame	38 DL Thomas Keiser / Tom McAndrew
27 Oklahoma■	31 DL Ekom Udofia
	DL Sione Fua / Matt Masifilo
	DL Chase Thomas / Erik Lorig
	LB Will Powers
	LB Clinton Snyder / Nick Macaluso
	LB Shayne Skov / Chike Amajoyi
	DB Richard Sherman / Kris Evans
	DB Corey Gatewood / Johnson Bademosi
	DB Bo McNally / Austin Yancy
	DB Delano Howell / Taylor Skaufel

RUSHING: Gerhart 343/1871y, Luck 61/354y, Stepfan Taylor (RB) 56/303y
PASSING: Luck 162-288/2575y, 13TD, 56.2%
RECEIVING: Whalen 57/926y, Owusu 37/682y, Fleener 21/266y
SCORING: Gerhart 172pts, Nate Whitaker (K) 101pts, Owusu 48pts

2010 12-1

52 Sacramento State	0 WR Doug Baldwin / Griff Whalen
35 UCLA	0 WR Ryan Whalen / Chris Owusu
68 Wake Forest	24 T Jonathan Martin
37 Notre Dame	14 G Andrew Phillips
31 Oregon	52 C Chase Beeler
37 Southern Cal	35 G David DeCastro
38 Washington St.	28 T Derek Hall
41 Washington	0 TE Coby Fleener / Konrad Reuland
42 Arizona	17 QB Andrew Luck
17 Arizona State	13 RB Stepfan Taylor / Anthony Wilkerson
48 California	14 FB Owen Marecic / James McGillicuddy
38 Oregon State	0 DL Matthew Masifilo
40 Virginia Tech■	12 DL Sione Fua
	DL/DB Brian Bulcke / Taylor Skaufel
	LB Chase Thomas (DL)
	LB Owen Marecic / Max Bergen
	LB Shayne Skov / Chike Amajoyi
	LB Thomas Keiser (DL)
	DB Richard Sherman
	DB Johnson Bademosi / Barry Browning
	DB Michael Thomas / Austin Yancy
	DB Delano Howell

RUSHING: Taylor 223/1137y, Luck 55/453y, Wilkerson 89/408y
PASSING: Luck 263-372/3338y, 32TD, 70.7%
RECEIVING: Baldwin 58/857y, R. Whalen 41/439y, Fleener 28/434y, Taylor 28/266y
SCORING: Nate Whitaker (K) 112pts, Taylor 96pts, Baldwin 56pts

SYRACUSE

Syracuse University (founded 1870)
Syracuse, New York
Nickname: Orangemen, Orange
Colors: Orange and Blue
Stadium: Carrier Dome (1980) 49,250
Conference Affiliations: Independent (1889-1990), Big East
  (Charter member, 1991-present)

CAREER RUSHING YARDS	Attempts	Yards
Joe Morris (1978-81)	813	4299
Walter Reyes (2001-04)	625	3424
Delone Carter (2006, 08-10)	646	3104
Larry Csonka (1965-67)	594	2934
James Mungro (1998-01)	529	2869
Floyd Little (1964-66)	504	2704
David Walker (1989-92)	503	2643
Dee Brown (1997-00)	493	2626
Bill Hurley (1975-79)	685	2551
Damien Rhodes (2002-05)	545	2461

CAREER PASSING YARDS	Comp.-Att.	Yards
Marvin Graves (1990-93)	563-943	8466
Donovan McNabb (1995-98)	548-938	8389
Don McPherson (1983-87)	367-687	5812
Perry Patterson (2003-06)	456-862	5220
R.J. Anderson (2000-03)	358-679	4698
Troy Nunes (1999-02)	362-618	4578
Bill Hurley (1975-79)	228-465	3398
Ryan Nassib (2008-10)	238-426	2756
Todd Norley (1982-85)	250-482	2661
Bernie Custis (1948-50)	196-424	2617

CAREER RECEIVING YARDS	Catches	Yards
Marvin Harrison (1992-95)	135	2728
Shelby Hill (1990-93)	139	2296
Rob Moore (1987-89)	106	2122
Scott Schwedes (1983-86)	139	2111
Mike Williams (2006-07, 2009)	133	2044
Rob Carpenter (1989-90)	93	1656
Quinton Spotwood (1996-99)	105	1653
Art Monk (1976-79)	102	1644
Kevin Johnson (1995-98)	98	1584
Mike Siano (1982-85)	93	1574

SEASON RUSHING YARDS	Attempts	Yards
Joe Morris (1979)	238	1372
Walter Reyes (2003)	253	1347
Delone Carter (2010)	231	1233
Joe Morris (1981)	261	1194
James Mungro (2001)	248	1170

SEASON PASSING YARDS	Comp.-Att.	Yards
Marvin Graves (1993)	171-280	2547
Donovan McNabb (1997)	145-265	2488
Don McPherson (1987)	129-229	2341
Ryan Nassib (2010)	202-358	2334
Marvin Graves (1992)	146-242	2296

SEASON RECEIVING YARDS	Catches	Yards
Marvin Harrison (1995)	56	1131
Rob Moore (1989)	53	1064
Tommy Kane (1987)	44	968
Shelby Hill (1993)	56	937
Rob Carpenter (1990)	52	895

GAME RUSHING YARDS	Attempts	Yards
Joe Morris (1979 vs. Kansas)	23	252
Walter Reyes (2003 vs. Central Florida)	31	241
Dee Brown (2000 vs. Rutgers)	24	239

GAME PASSING YARDS	Comp.-Att.	Yards
Marvin Graves (1992 vs. Rutgers)	18-28	425
Andrew Robinson (2007 vs. Louisville)	17-26	423
Andrew Robinson (2007 vs. Cincinnati)	29-47	419

GAME RECEIVING YARDS	Catches	Yards
Scott Schwedes (1985 vs. Boston College)	8	249
David Tyree (2002 vs. Virginia Tech)	9	229
Marvin Harrison (1995 vs. West Virginia)	9	213

GREATEST COACH:

When Ben Schwartzwalder began coaching Syracuse football in 1949, the program was in the midst of a four-game losing streak to middling Ivy League Columbia. By his fourth year, the Orangemen were playing Alabama in the Orange Bowl. True, they were routed in that game, but Syracuse football was back on the national stage. In 1956, buoyed by the talents of halfback Jimmy Brown, the Orangemen were in the Top Ten and facing TCU in the Cotton Bowl.

With enthusiasm and a fierce determination, Schwartzwalder, who was a 152-pound center under Greasy Neale at West Virginia and a hero in World War II, had crafted an Eastern power out of the Orangemen. Beginning in 1958, they would have to be considered on the national stage as well. For the next 10 years the Orangemen would win seven or more games (when that meant something) nine times, including the dream 11-0 season in 1959 that produced a national title. Proving that they were more than just a regional power, that squad beat Kansas, Maryland, and UCLA in Los Angeles. They capped that dream season with a 23-14 beating of Texas in the Cotton Bowl.

Schwartzwalder was certainly ahead of the curve with his racial integration of football teams, and when the rest of the nation caught up, his win totals dropped off. Still there is no denying a record of 153-91-3, six bowl appearances, four Lambert Trophies for Eastern excellence, and one national championship.

SYRACUSE'S 55 GREATEST SINCE 1953

OFFENSE

WIDE RECEIVER: Rob Carpenter, Marvin Harrison, Rob Moore, Scott Schwedes
TIGHT END: Chris Gedney, John Mackey
TACKLE: Gary Bugenhagen, Craig Wolfley, Bob Yates
GUARD: Roger Davis, Matt Tarullo, Stan Walters
CENTER: Al Bemiller, John Flannery, Pat Killorin
QUARTERBACK: Marvin Graves, Donovan McNabb, Don McPherson
RUNNING BACK: Jimmy Brown, Ernie Davis, Floyd Little, Joe Morris
FULLBACK: Larry Csonka, Jim Nance

DEFENSE

END: Rob Burnett, Paul Frase, Dwight Freeney
TACKLE: Joe Ehrmann, Tim Green, Ted Gregory, Arthur Jones, Art Thoms
LINEBACKER: Keith Bulluck, Jim Collins, Kevin Mitchell, Ray Preston, Tony Romano, Terry Wooden
CORNERBACK: Kevin Abrams, Tony Kyasky, Jim Ridlon
SAFETY: Donovan Darius, Cliff Ensley, Tom Myers, Markus Paul, Rob Thomson

SPECIAL TEAMS

RETURN SPECIALISTS: Kevin Johnson, Jim Turner
PLACE KICKER: Gary Anderson, David Jacobs
PUNTER: Pat O'Neill

MULTIPLE POSITIONS

TAILBACK-WIDE RECEIVER: Art Monk

TWO-WAY PLAYERS

END-DEFENSIVE END: Fred Mautino, Walt Sweeney
HALFBACK-QUARTERBACK-DEFENSIVE BACK: Ger Schwedes

PERFORMANCE FORMULA:
SYRACUSE'S 10 BEST SEASONS

1959	1.8698	1 of 70
1992	1.5138	7 of 70
1991	1.4941	14 of 71
1958	1.4904	7 of 70
1996	1.4758	12 of 70
1960	1.4594	9 of 70
2001	1.4520	14 of 70
1963	1.4417	11 of 70
1988	1.4395	13 of 69
1995	1.3962	16 of 70

SYRACUSE ORANGE

Year	W-L-T	AP Poll	Conference Standing	Toughest Regular Season Opponents	Coach (Record at School)	Bowl Games		
1953	5-3-1			Illinois 7-1-1, Penn State 6-3	Ben Schwartzwalder			
1954	4-4			Penn State 7-2, Boston University 7-2, Colgate 5-2-2	Ben Schwartzwalder			
1955	5-3			Maryland 10-0, West Virginia 8-2, Pittsburgh 7-3, Army 6-3	Ben Schwartzwalder			
1956	7-2	8		Pittsburgh 7-2-1, Penn State 6-2-1, Army 5-3-1, West Virginia 6-4	Ben Schwartzwalder	Cotton	27 TCU	28
1957	5-3-1			West Virginia 7-2-1, Penn State 6-3, Holy Cross 5-3-1	Ben Schwartzwalder			
1958	8-2	9		Boston College 7-3, Penn State 6-3, Pitt 5-4-1, Cornell 6-3	Ben Schwartzwalder	Orange	6 Oklahoma	21
1959	11-0	1		Penn State 8-2, Pittsburgh 6-4, UCLA 5-4-1, Navy 5-4-1	Ben Schwartzwalder	Cotton	23 Texas	14
1960	7-2	19		Kansas 7-2-1, Penn State 6-3, Army 6-3-1	Ben Schwartzwalder			
1961	8-3	14		Penn State 7-3, Maryland 7-3, Holy Cross 7-3	Ben Schwartzwalder	Liberty	15 Miami	14
1962	5-5			Penn State 9-1, Oklahoma 8-2, Boston College 8-2, West Virginia 8-2	Ben Schwartzwalder			
1963	8-2			Pittsburgh 9-1, Penn State 7-3, Boston College 6-3, Kansas 5-5	Ben Schwartzwalder			
1964	7-4			Oregon State 8-2, West Virginia 7-3, Penn State 6-4, Boston College 6-3	Ben Schwartzwalder	Sugar	10 LSU	13
1965	7-3			UCLA 7-2-1, West Virginia 6-4, Boston College 6-4	Ben Schwartzwalder			
1966	8-3			UCLA 9-1, Florida State 6-4	Ben Schwartzwalder	Gator	12 Tennessee	18
1967	8-2			UCLA 7-2-1, Penn State 8-2, Navy 5-4-1	Ben Schwartzwalder			
1968	6-4			Penn State 10-0, West Virginia 7-3, California 7-3-1	Ben Schwartzwalder			
1969	5-5			Penn State 10-0, West Virginia 9-1, Boston College 5-4	Ben Schwartzwalder			
1970	6-4			Penn State 7-3, West Virginia 8-3, Houston 8-3	Ben Schwartzwalder			
1971	5-5-1			Penn State 10-1, Boston College 9-2, West Virginia 7-4, Northwestern 7-4	Ben Schwartzwalder			
1972	5-6			Penn State 10-1, West Virginia 8-3, North Carolina State 7-3-1	Ben Schwartzwalder			
1973	2-9			Penn State 11-0, Maryland 8-3, Pittsburgh 6-4-1, Boston College 7-4	Ben Schwartzwalder (153-91-3)			
1974	2-9			North Carolina State 9-1-1, Maryland 8-3, Penn State 7-4, Pittsburgh 7-4	Frank Maloney			
1975	6-5			Penn State 9-2, Rutgers 9-2, Maryland 8-2-1, West Virginia 8-3	Frank Maloney			
1976	3-8			Pittsburgh 11-0, Maryland 11-0, Boston College 8-3, Penn State 7-4	Frank Maloney			
1977	6-5			Penn State 10-1, Pittsburgh 8-2-1, Washington 7-4, Maryland 7-4	Frank Maloney			
1978	3-8			Penn St. 11-0, Maryland 9-2, Pitt 8-3, FSU 8-3, Navy 8-3, MSU 8-3	Frank Maloney			
1979	7-5			Ohio State 11-0, Pitt 10-1, Penn State 7-4, Navy 7-4, Temple 9-2	Frank Maloney	Independence	31 McNeese State	7
1980	5-6			Pittsburgh 10-1, Penn State 9-2, Ohio State 9-2, Navy 8-3	Frank Maloney (32-46)			
1981	4-6-1			Pittsburgh 10-1, Penn State 9-2, West Virginia 8-3, Navy 7-3-1	Dick MacPherson			
1982	2-9			Penn State 10-1, Pittsburgh 9-2, West Va. 9-2, BC 8-2-1, Maryland 8-3	Dick MacPherson			
1983	6-5			Nebraska 12-0, Pittsburgh 8-2-1, West Virginia 8-3, Maryland 8-3, BC 9-2	Dick MacPherson			
1984	6-5			Florida 9-1-1, Nebraska 9-2, BC 9-2, Maryland 8-3, Rutgers 7-3	Dick MacPherson			
1985	7-5			Penn State 11-0, West Virginia 7-3-1	Dick MacPherson	Cherry	18 Maryland	35
1986	5-6			Penn State 11-0, Virginia Tech 8-2-1, Boston College 8-3	Dick MacPherson			
1987	11-0-1	4		Penn State 8-3, Pittsburgh 8-3	Dick MacPherson	Sugar	16 Auburn	16
1988	10-2	13		West Virginia 11-0, Pittsburgh 6-5	Dick MacPherson	Hall of Fame	23 LSU	10
1989	8-4			Florida State 9-2, West Virginia 8-2-1, Penn State 7-3-1, Pittsburgh 7-3-1	Dick MacPherson	Peach	19 Georgia	18
1990	7-4-2			Miami 9-2, Penn State 9-2, Southern California 8-3-1	Dick MacPherson (66-46-4)	Aloha	28 Arizona	0
1991	10-2	11		Florida 10-1, Florida State 10-2, Rutgers 6-5	Paul Pasqualoni	Hall of Fame	24 Ohio State	17
1992	10-2	6	2	Miami 11-0, Ohio State 8-2-1, Boston College 8-2-1, Rutgers 7-4	Paul Pasqualoni	Fiesta	26 Colorado	22
1993	6-4-1		5	West Virginia 11-0, Miami 9-2, Virginia Tech 8-3, Boston College 8-3	Paul Pasqualoni			
1994	7-4		3t	Miami 10-1, Virginia Tech 8-3, Boston College 6-4-1	Paul Pasqualoni			
1995	9-3	19	3	Virginia Tech 9-2, Miami 8-3	Paul Pasqualoni	Gator	41 Clemson	0
1996	9-3	22	1t	Virginia Tech 10-1, Miami 8-3, Army 10-1, North Carolina 9-2	Paul Pasqualoni	Liberty	30 Houston	17
1997	9-4	21	1	Wisconsin 8-4, West Virginia 7-4, Virginia Tech 7-4	Paul Pasqualoni	Fiesta	18 Kansas State	35
1998	8-4	25	1	Tennessee 11-0, Michigan 9-3, West Virginia 8-3, Miami 8-3, Va. Tech 8-3	Paul Pasqualoni	Orange	10 Florida	31
1999	7-5		4t	Virginia Tech 11-0, Michigan 9-2, Boston College 8-3, Miami 8-4	Paul Pasqualoni	Music City	20 Kentucky	13
2000	6-5		3t	Miami 10-1, Virginia Tech 10-1, Pittsburgh 7-4	Paul Pasqualoni			
2001	10-3	14	2	Miami 11-0, Tennessee 9-2, Virginia Tech 8-3, BC 7-4, Auburn 7-4	Paul Pasqualoni	Insight.com	26 Kansas State	3
2002	4-8		6t	Miami 12-0, West Virginia 9-3, Va. Tech 8-3, BC 8-3, Pittsburgh 8-3	Paul Pasqualoni			
2003	6-6		6t	Miami 10-2, Virginia Tech 8-4, Pittsburgh 8-4, West Virginia 8-4	Paul Pasqualoni			
2004	6-6		1t	West Virginia 8-3, Boston College 8-3, Pittsburgh 8-3, Auburn 8-4	Paul Pasqualoni (107-59)	Champs Sports	14 Georgia Tech	51
2005	1-10		8	West Virginia 10-1, Notre Dame 9-2, Louisville 9-2 Florida State 7-4	Greg Robinson			
2006	4-8		7t	West Virginia 10-2, Louisville 11-1, Rutgers 10-2, Wake Forest 11-2	Greg Robinson			
2007	2-10		8	Illinois 9-3, West Virginia 10-2, South Florida 9-3, Connecticut 9-3	Greg Robinson			
2008	3-9		7t	Northwestern 9-3, Penn State 11-1, Pittsburgh 9-3, Cincinnati 11-2	Greg Robinson (10-37)			
2009	4-8		7t	Penn State 10-2, West Virginia 9-3, Cincinnati 12-0, Pittsburgh 9-3	Doug Marrone			
2010	8-5		4	Pittsburgh 8-4, West Virginia 9-3, Connecticut 8-4	Doug Marrone (12-13)	Pinstripe	36 Kansas State	34

TOTAL: 359-275-8 .5654 (29 of 70)   **Bowl Games since 1953:** 13-8-1 .6136 (11 of 70)

GREATEST TEAM SINCE 1953: For an out-of-the-way, far-north area and football program fighting for identity, the 1959 national champion Syracuse Orangemen hold a special place in their combined histories. For Syracuse natives that year, the cold weather seemed a bit more tolerable, the financial strain facing upstate New York cities like Syracuse was a bit less stressful. For the Orange had conquered the nation. With Ger Schwedes, Ernie Davis, et al, operating behind the "Sizable Seven" offensive line, they averaged 451 yards per game, while the incredible defense allowed 193 yards *total* for the entire 11-0 season.

1953 5-3-1

42	Temple	0	E Pete Schwert / Herb Steigler
14	Boston Univ.	14	T Les McClelland / Paul Slick
20	Fordham	13	G Sam Johnson / Cal Smith
14	Penn State	20	C Ted Kukowski
13	Illinois	20	G Bob Fleck / Mike Skop
21	Holy Cross	0	T James George / Paul Kernaklian
26	Cornell	0	E Neil Brenneman / Tom Richardson
34	Colgate	18	QB Pat Stark / Bruce Yancey (HB)
13	Villanova	14	HB Bob Leberman
			HB Lyle Carlson/Art Troilo/Ray Perkins
			FB Don Laaksonen / Al Vergara

RUSHING: Leberman 110/513y
PASSING: Stark 73-141/1045y, 8TD, 51.8%
RECEIVING: Perkins 18/212y
SCORING: Leberman 38pts

1954 4-4

28	Villanova	6	E Pete Schwert / Don Althouse
0	Penn State	13	T Paul Kernaklian
19	Boston Univ.	41	G Cal Smith / Rudy Farmer
6	Illinois	34	C Paul Slick
25	Holy Cross	20	G Mike Skop / Ed Bailey
6	Cornell	14	T Joe Cappadonna / Jerry Cashman
31	Colgate	12	E Tom Richardson / Jim Ridlon
20	Fordham	7	QB Mickey Rich / Eddie Albright
			HB Sam Alexander / Jimmy Brown
			HB Ray Perkins / Art Troilo
			FB Don Laaksonen / Bill Wetzel

RUSHING: Perkins 98/499y, Brown 75/439y, Troilo 30/199y
PASSING: Rich 17-52/234y, 1TD, 32.7%
RECEIVING: Richardson 6/107y, Schwert 5/77y, Perkins 3/30y
SCORING: Perkins 47pts, Brown 26pts

1955 5-3

12	Pittsburgh	22	E Don Althouse
27	Boston Univ.	12	T Jim Brill
13	Army	0	G Rudy Farmer / Cal Smith
13	Maryland	34	C Joe Krivak / Bill Brown
49	Holy Cross	9	G Chuck Strid / Pete Schwert
20	Penn State	21	T Jerry Cashman
26	Colgate	19	E Tom Richardson / Dick Lasse
20	West Virginia	13	QB Eddie Albright
			HB Jimmy Brown / Ed Ackley
			HB Jim Ridlon / Bill Micho
			FB Don Laaksonen / Bill Brown

RUSHING: Brown 128/666y, Micho 26/147y, Ackley 26/141y
PASSING: Albright 19-34/324y, 7TD, 55.9%
RECEIVING: Althouse 10/173y, Ridlon 6/176y, Brown 5/44y
SCORING: Brown 55pts, Ridlon 42pts, Albright 24pts

1956 7-2

26	Maryland	12	E Nick Baccile / Don Althouse
7	Pittsburgh	14	T Chuck Strid / Gerry Hershey
27	West Virginia	20	G Rudy Farmer / Mike Bill
7	Army	0	C Bill Brown / Joe Krivak
21	Boston Univ.	7	G Ed Bailey
13	Penn State	9	T Jerry Cashman
41	Holy Cross	20	E Dick Lasse / Dick Aloise
61	Colgate	7	QB Chuck Zimmerman / Ferd Kuczala
27	TCU■	28	HB Jimmy Brown
			HB Jim Ridlon / Ernie Jackson
			FB Alan Cann / Ed Coffin

RUSHING: Brown 158/986y, Cann 46/306y, Ridlon 71/267y
PASSING: Zimmerman 18-42/272y, 2TD, 42.9%
RECEIVING: Ridlon 8/153y, Lasse 5/124y, Brown 5/56y
SCORING: Brown 106pts, Ridlon 19pts, 4 tied w/ 12pts

1957 5-3-1

7	Iowa State	7	E Glenn Preising / Dick Aloise
27	Boston Univ.	7	T Chuck Strid
34	Cornell	0	G Al Benecick / Lou Mautino
26	Nebraska	9	C Mike Bill
12	Penn State	20	G Gerry Hershey / George Stock
24	Pittsburgh	21	T Ron Luciano / Roger Davis
19	Holy Cross	20	E Dick Laase
34	Colgate	6	QB Chuck Zimmerman / Fred Kuczala
0	West Virginia	7	HB Tom Stephens / Dave Baker
			HB Dan Fogerty / Ernie Jackson
			FB Ed Coffin / Ger Schwedes

RUSHING: Coffin 106/448y, Stephens 70/306y, Schwedes 45/196y,
PASSING: Zimmerman 53-96/770y, 5TD, 55.2%
RECEIVING: Lasse 16/202y, Stephens 13/190y, Coffin 10/175y
SCORING: Stephens 42pts, Coffin 30pts, Zimmerman 19pts

1958 8-2

24	Boston College	14	E Dave Baker / Tom Gilburg
13	Holy Cross	14	T Bob Yates / Al Gerlick
55	Cornell	0	G Roger Davis / Maury Youmans
38	Nebraska	0	C Dave Applehof / Al Bemiller
14	Penn State	6	G Al Benecick / Bruce Tarbox
16	Pittsburgh	13	T Ron Luciano / Gerry Hershey
42	Boston Univ.	0	E Fred Mautino / Gerry Skonieczki
47	Colgate	0	QB Chuck Zimmerman / Dan Fogarty
15	West Virginia	12	HB Tom Stephens / Mark Weber
6	Oklahoma■	21	HB Ger Schwedes / Whitey Reimer
			FB Ed Keiffer / Art Baker

RUSHING: Schwedes 83/360y, Stephens 78/351y, Baker 63/295y
PASSING: Zimmerman 46-76/645y, 7 TD, 60.5%
RECEIVING: Schwedes 13/117y, Stephens 11/173y, Baker 10/231y
SCORING: Zimmerman 54pts, Stephens 44pts, Reimer 26pts

1959 11-0

35	Kansas	21	E Gerry Skonieczki
29	Maryland	0	T Bob Yates / Al Gerlick
32	Navy	6	G Roger Davis
42	Holy Cross	6	C Al Bemiller / Dave Applehof
44	West Virginia	0	G Bruce Tarbox
35	Pittsburgh	0	T John Brown / Maury Youmans
20	Penn State	18	E Fred Mautino / Tom Gilburg
71	Colgate	0	QB Dave Sarette / Dick Easterly
46	Boston Univ.	0	HB Ernie Davis
36	UCLA	8	HB Ger Schwedes (QB) / Mark Weber
23	Texas■	14	FB Art Baker

RUSHING: Davis 98/686y, Schwedes 90/567y, Baker 100/507y
PASSING: Sarette 49-83/763y, 10TD, 59%
RECEIVING: Mautino 17/215y, Schwedes 15/231y, Skonieczky 13/256y
SCORING: Schwedes 100pts, Davis 64pts, Weber 36pts

1960 7-2

35	Boston Univ.	7	E Walt Sweeney / Ken Ericson
14	Kansas	7	T Tom Gilburg / Leon Cholakis
15	Holy Cross	6	G Dave Fiedler
21	Penn State	15	C Al Bemiller / Bob Stem
45	West Virginia	0	G Bruce Tarbox / Otis Godfrey
0	Pittsburgh	10	T Dave Meggyesy / John Brown
6	Army	9	E Fred Mautino / Dave Baker
46	Colgate	6	QB Dave Sarette / Dick Easterly
21	Miami	14	HB Ernie Davis / Mark Weber
			HB Don King / John Mackey / Pete Brokaw
			FB Art Baker

RUSHING: Davis 112/877y, Baker 80/390y, Brokaw 52/333y
PASSING: Sarette 30-65/327y, 4TD, 46.2%
RECEIVING: Mautino 14/171y, Davis 11/141y, Ericson 6/82y
SCORING: Davis 62pts, Brokaw 30pts, Ericson (E-K) 29pts

1961 8-3

19	Oregon State	8	E Walt Sweeney / John Snider
29	West Virginia	14	T Dick Feidler / Stan Sokol
21	Maryland	22	G George Francovitch / Ray Seager
28	Nebraska	6	C Bob Stem / Henry Huettner
0	Penn State	14	G Tom Spillett / Jim Mazurek / Len Slaby
34	Holy Cross	6	T Dave Meggyesy / John Brown
28	Pittsburgh	9	E John Mackey
51	Colgate	3	QB Dave Sarette
15	Notre Dame	17	HB Ernie Davis / Don King
28	Boston College	13	HB Dick Easterly / Pete Brokaw
15	Miami■	14	FB Gerry Fallon/Bill Meyers/BillSchoonover

RUSHING: Davis 150/823y, Fallon 66/299y, Meyers 23/163y
PASSING: Sarette 55-106/813y, 9TD, 51.9%
RECEIVING: Davis 16/157y, Mackey 15/321y, Easterly 12/207y
SCORING: Davis 94pts, Ken Ericson (E-K) 33pts, Mackey 26pts

1962 5-5

3	Oklahoma	7	E Walt Sweeney / Dick Bowman
2	Army	9	T Leon Cholakis / Gerry Everling
12	Boston College	0	G Ray Seager / Jim Mazurek
19	Penn State	20	C Gene Stancin / Len Slaby
30	Holy Cross	20	G Dave Meggysey
6	Pittsburgh	24	T John Paglio
34	Navy	6	E John Mackey / Jim Cripps
35	Geo. Washington	0	QB Walley Mahle / Walt Sofsian
6	West Virginia	17	HB Don King / Bill Schoonover
12	UCLA	7	HB Mike Koski / Rich King / Nat Duckett
			FB Jim Nance / Ed Conti (LB)

RUSHING: Nance 84/417y, King 58/325y, Mahle 87/303y
PASSING: Mahle 33-71/455y, 3TD, 46.5%
RECEIVING: Mackey 8/131y, King 7/79y, Bowman 7/77y
SCORING: Mahle 40pts, King 36ots, Mackey 24pts

1963 8-2

32	Boston College	21	E Dick Bowman / Brad Clarke
0	Kansas	10	T Tom Wilhelm / Gerald Everling
48	Holy Cross	0	G John Salerno / John Paglio
29	UCLA	7	C Len Slaby / Ed Conti (LB)
9	Penn State	0	G Jim Mazurek / Paul Houle
31	Oregon State	8	T Tony Scibelli / H. Huettner / Bob Meehan
27	Pittsburgh	35	E Jim Cripps / George Fair
15	West Virginia	13	QB Wally Mahle / Ted Holman
50	Richmond	0	HB Bill Hunter / Rich King
14	Notre Dame	7	HB Mike Koski / Nate Duckett
			FB Jim Nance / Bill Schoonover

RUSHING: Mahle 78/457y, Hunter 56/270y, Koski 44/239y
PASSING: King 37-80/675y, 5TD, 46.3%
RECEIVING: Bowman 10/190y, Clarke 9/112y, Cripps 9/107y
SCORING: Koski 38pts, John Paglio (T-K) 27pts, Duckett 25pts

1964 7-4

14	Boston College	21	E Jim Cripps / Brad Clarke
38	Kansas	6	T Harris Wienke / Tom Wilhelm
34	Holy Cross	8	G Howie McCard
39	UCLA	0	C Pat Killorin
21	Penn State	14	G Tony Scibelli
13	Oregon State	31	T Gary Bugenhagen
21	Pittsburgh	6	E Harris Elliott
27	Army	15	QB Wally Mahle
20	Virginia Tech	15	HB Floyd Little
27	West Virginia	28	HB Ray Oyer
10	LSU■	13	FB Jim Nance
			DL George Fair
			DL Dave Archer
			DL Gerald Everling / John Krok
			DL Paul Houle
			DL Herb Strecker
			LB Jim Cheyunski
			LB Terry Roe
			LB Murray Johnson
			DB Ted Holman / Bill Hunter
			DB Charley Brown
			DB Rich King / Harold Rooney

RUSHING: Nance 190/951y, Little 149/828y, Mahle 93/390y
PASSING: Mahle 31-80/324y, 2TD, 38.8%
RECEIVING: Little 16/248y, Clarke 10/87y, Cripps 7/69y
SCORING: Nance 78pts, Little 72pts, Mahle 36pts

1965 7-3

14	Navy	6	E Ed Schreck / John McGuire
0	Miami	24	T Ray Paglio
24	Maryland	7	G Howie McCard
14	UCLA	24	C Pat Killorin
28	Penn State	21	G Harris Wienke
32	Holy Cross	6	T Tony Scibelli
51	Pittsburgh	13	E Dick Towne / Harris Elliott
12	Oregon State	13	QB Rick Cassata
41	West Virginia	19	HB Floyd Little
21	Boston College	13	HB Mike Koski
			FB Larry Csonka / Ron Oyer
			DL Steve Chomyszak / Herb Stecker
			DL Dennis Fitzgibbons
			DL John Krok
			DL Gary Bugenhagen / Joe Dziekonski
			DL Harris Elliot
			LB Roger Smith / Paul Nettelbladt
			LB Jim Cheyunski / Larry Csonka
			LB Terry Roe
			DB Charley Brown
			DB Ted Holman / Ed Mantie
			DB George Fair

RUSHING: Little 193/1065y, Csonka 136/795y, Koski 35/187y
PASSING: Cassata 47-104/525y, 2TD, 45.2%
RECEIVING: Little 21/248y, Towne 7/70y, Elliott 7/54y
SCORING: Little 114pts, Csonka 24pts, Dziekonski (K-DT) 20pts

1966 8-3

12	Baylor	35	E Ed Schreck
12	UCLA	31	T Harris Wienke
28	Maryland	7	G Jim LeMessurier
28	Navy	14	C Tom Rosia
30	Boston College	0	G Bill Benecick
28	Holy Cross	6	T Gary Bugenhagen
33	Pittsburgh	7	E Dick Towne
12	Penn State	10	QB Rick Cassata / Jim Del Gaizo
37	Florida State	21	WB Tom Coughlin / Ed Allen
34	West Virginia	7	HB Floyd Little
12	Tennessee ■	18	FB Larry Csonka
			DL Herb Stecker
			DL Dennis Fitzgibbons
			DL John Krok
			DL Art Thoms
			DL Dave Casmay / Bill Wosilius
			LB Steve Zegalia
			LB Paul Nettelbladt
			LB Jerry Ruccio / Terry Roe
			DB Tony Kyasky / Ed Mantie
			DB Tom George / Cliff Ensley
			DB Bill Zanieski

RUSHING: Csonka 197/1012y, Little 162/811y, Allen 35/182y
PASSING: Cassata 41-85/472y, 4TD, 48.2%
  Del Gaizo 34-83/418y, 5TD, 40.9%
RECEIVING: Schreck 14/175y, Towne 14/139y, Little 13/86y
SCORING: Little 92pts, Csonka 44pts, Alex Gousseff (K) 30pts

1967 8-2

7	Baylor	0	E Dennis Kleinback
23	West Virginia	6	T Ed Nowicki (E) / Dennis Fitzgibbons
7	Maryland	3	G Jim Pritzlaff / Dave McCard
14	Navy	27	C Jim Murphy
20	California	14	G Ed Schreck
20	Penn State	29	T Jim LeMessurier
14	Pittsburgh	7	E Jack Jones
41	Holy Cross	7	QB Rick Cassata
32	Boston College	20	WB Tom Coughlin
32	UCLA	14	HB Bill During / Ed Mantie
			FB Larry Csonka
			DL Steve Zegalia / Lou Gubitosa
			DL Bill Coghill
			DL Dennis Fitzgibbons / Gerald Beach
			DL Art Thoms / Bill Smith
			DL Dave Casmay
			LB Bob Bancroft
			LB Jim Cheyunski
			LB Bill Zanieski
			DB Tony Kyasky
			DB Tom Hermanowski / Ed Mantie
			DB Cliff Ensley

RUSHING: Csonka 261/1127y, Cassata 126/474y,
  Coughlin 42/256y
PASSING: Cassata 92-176/992y, 8TD, 52.3%
RECEIVING: Coughlin 26/257y, Jones 22/215y, Csonka 11/125y
SCORING: Csonka 62pts, Mantie (HB-K) 37pts, Cassata 36pts

1968 6-4

10	Michigan State	14	E Tony Gabriel
32	Maryland	14	T Andrew Fusco
20	UCLA	7	G Dave McCard
50	Pittsburgh	17	C Gerry Vogt
0	California	43	G Jim Pritzlaff
47	Holy Cross	0	T John Cherundolo
31	William & Mary	0	E John Massis
44	Navy	6	QB Paul Paolisso
6	West Virginia	23	WB John Bulicz
12	Penn State	30	HB John Godbolt / Ron Trask
			FB Al Newton
			DL Lou Gubitosa
			DL Ray White
			DL Gerry Beach
			DL Art Thoms
			DL Steve Zegalia
			LB Bob Schoonmaker / Bill Smith
			LB Jerry Ruccio / John Protz
			LB Bob Bancroft
			DB Tony Kyasky
			DB Gary Bletsch / Tom Hermanowski
			DB Cliff Ensley

RUSHING: Newton 126/618y, Godbolt 68/321y, Bulicz 46/244y
PASSING: Paolisso 87-164/939y, 6TD, 53%
RECEIVING: Massis 29/400y, Gabriel 28/365y, Bulicz 17/167y
SCORING: George Jakowenko (K) 46pts, Godbolt 36pts,
  5 tied w/ 18pts

1969 5-5

14	Iowa State	13	WR Tony Gabriel
0	Kansas	13	T Andrew Fusco
43	Wisconsin	7	G Dave McCard
20	Maryland	9	C Gerry Vogt
14	Penn State	15	G Jim Pritzlaff
20	Pittsburgh	21	T John Cherundolo
23	Arizona	0	TE Bill Maddox
15	Navy	0	QB Randy Zur
10	West Virginia	13	WB Greg Allen / Mike Chlebeck
10	Boston College	35	HB Ron Trask / John Godbolt
			FB Al Newton
			DL Clarence McGill
			DL Joe Ehrmann
			DL Ted Lachowicz
			DL Ray White
			DL Dick Kokosky
			LB Don Dorr
			LB John Protz
			LB Bob Bancroft / Bob Rust
			DB Duane Walker
			DB Tommy Myers
			DB Gary Bletsch

RUSHING: Newton 154/689y, Allen 81/362y, Zur 112/195y
PASSING: Zur 73-148/816y, 1TD, 49.3%
RECEIVING: Gabriel 30/419y, Allen 15/212y, 3 tied w/ 10
SCORING: George Jakowenko (K) 45pts, Newton & Zur 24pts

1970 6-4

15	Houston	42	WR Tony Gabriel
14	Kansas	31	T Ray Jarosz
0	Illinois	27	G Stan Walters
23	Maryland	7	C Doug Auld
24	Penn State	7	G Chuck Chulada
23	Navy	8	T Dan Yochum
43	Pittsburgh	13	TE Rick Steiner
31	Army	29	QB Randy Zur / Paul Paolisso
19	West Virginia	28	WB Ray White
56	Miami	16	TB Roger Praetorius
			FB Marty Januszkiewicz
			DL Lou Gubitosa
			DL Joe Ehrmann
			DL Ted Lachowicz
			DL Bill Coghill / Ray White
			DL Rich Kokosky
			LB Len Masci
			LB Dave King / Howard Goodman
			LB Chuck Boniti
			DB Robin Griffin
			DB Gary Bletsch
			DB Tommy Myers

RUSHING: Januszkiewicz 199/769y, Praetorius 114/474y,
  White 30/244y
PASSING: Paolisso 33-71/370y, 5TD, 46.5%
RECEIVING: Gabriel 28/402y, Steiner 8/67y, White 6/45y
SCORING: Januszkiewicz 48pts, Gabriel 44pts,
  George Jakowenko (K) 38pts

1971 5-5-1

20	Wisconsin	20	WR Gary Sweat
6	Northwestern	12	T Ray Jarosz
7	Indiana	0	G Ross Sposato
21	Maryland	13	C Doug Auld
0	Penn State	31	G Dave Lapham / Charles Chulada
63	Holy Cross	21	T Stan Walters / Dan Yochum
21	Pittsburgh	31	TE Rick Steiner
3	Boston College	10	QB Bob Woodruff / Franklin Ruggiero
14	Navy	17	WB Brian Hambleton / Ron Page
28	West Virginia	24	TB Roger Praetorius
14	Miami	0	FB Marty Januszkiewicz
			DL Charles Boniti
			DL Len Campolieto
			DL Ted Lachowicz
			DL Bill Coghill
			DL Steve Joslin
			LB Dave King
			LB Howard Goodman
			LB Ken Bohannon
			DB Robin Griffin
			DB Ken Sawyer
			DB Tommy Myers

RUSHING: Praetorius 169/705y, Januszkiewicz 148/623y
  Rosella 17/130y
PASSING: Woodruff 74-132/910y, 2TD, 56.1%
RECEIVING: Steiner 24/310y, Sweat 23/345y, Hambleton 20/226y
SCORING: Praetorius 66pts, Page 24pts, Erie Baugher (K) 22pts

1972 5-6

17	Temple	10	WR Brian Hambleton / Chris Hoornbeck
20	N. Carolina St.	43	T Larry Boynton
7	Wisconsin	31	G Charles Chulada
16	Maryland	12	C Mike McNeely / Ray Mills
2	Indiana	10	G Ross Sposato
30	Navy	14	T Dave Lapham
0	Penn State	17	TE Rick Steiner
10	Pittsburgh	6	QB Bob Woodruff / Bob Sutton
0	Boston College	37	WB Greg Allen / Mike Bright / Ron Page
27	Army	6	TB Roger Praetorius / Bob Barlette
12	West Virginia	43	FB Marty Januszkiewicz / Steve Webster
			DL Chuck Smyrl / Greg Steen
			DL Joe Ehrmann
			DL Ed Zamaitis / Jeff Hopkins
			DL Skip Dalrymple
			DL Ray Preston
			LB Dave King
			LB Charles Boniti
			LB Walter Delikat / Len Masci
			DB Ken Sawyer / Jim Longley
			DB George Yencho
			DB Gary Sweat

RUSHING: Januszkiewicz 126/618y, Praetorius 144/593y
  Barlette 68/275y
PASSING: Woodruff 63-136/649y, TD, 46.3%
RECEIVING: Hambleton 15/156y, Steiner 15/150y,
  Petchel 13/131y
SCORING: Januszkiewicz 30pts, Bernie Ruoff (K) 29pts,
  Praetorius 24pts

1973 2-9

14	Bowling Green	41	WR Joe Brennan
8	Michigan State	14	T Larry Boynton
7	Washington	21	G Tom Morgan
0	Maryland	38	C Mike McNeely
14	Navy	23	G Dave Lapham
6	Penn State	49	T Steve Scully / John Spillett
23	Miami	34	TE Bob Petchel
14	Pittsburgh	28	QB Bob Mitch
5	Holy Cross	3	WB Brian Hambleton (WR) / Tim Williams
24	Boston College	13	TB B. Barlette/ Jim Donoghue/ Phil Raleigh
14	West Virginia	24	FB Ron Page / Steve Webster
			DL Jim Jerome / Tony Sidoni
			DL Dave Laputka
			DL Ed Zamaitis / Ken Stach
			DL Skip Dalrymple / Steve Joslin
			DL Greg Steen
			LB Chuck Smyrl / Walt Delikat
			LB Rick Schmitt / Lindy Hess
			LB Steve Dolce / Bill Zanovitch
			DB Gary Sweat
			DB Jim Longley / John Rafferty
			DB Ken Sawyer / Kevin Morrissey

RUSHING: Mitch 139/448y, Barlette 92/367y, Raleigh 49/207y
PASSING: Mitch 58-139/722y, 2TD, 41.7%
RECEIVING: Petchel 22/183y, Brennan 19/290y,
  Hambleton 14/177y
SCORING: Hambleton & Mitch 24pts, Bernie Ruoff (K) 19pts

1974 2-9

23	Oregon State	15	WR Lonnie Allgood / Joe Brennan
14	Kent State	20	WR Don Magee
0	Michigan State	19	T Jose St. Victor
22	N. Carolina St.	28	G Kevin Moss / Kosta Kobakof
0	Maryland	31	C Mike McNeeley
17	Navy	9	G Tom Morgan / Don Wells
14	Penn State	30	T Jeremy Scharoun / Steve Scully
13	Pittsburgh	21	TE Bob Petchel
11	West Virginia	39	QB Jim Donoghue
0	Boston College	45	TB Ken Kinsey
7	Miami	14	FB Mike Bright / Steve Webster
			DL Jim Jerome
			DL Ed Zamaitis / Ken Clarke
			DL Steve Dolce
			DL Nick Marsella
			DL Greg Steen / Dave Tate
			LB Ray Preston
			LB Joe Echert
			DB Jim Kiles / Larry King
			DB Keith Moody / Bob Mitch
			DB John Rafferty / Nate Wright
			DB Tim Moresco

RUSHING: Kinsey 152/610y, Bright 80/299y, Donoghue 139/196y
PASSING: Donoghue 68-136/938y, 4TD, 50%
RECEIVING: Allgood 22/477y, Petchel 21/206y, Magee 11/124
SCORING: Bernie Ruoff (K) 25pts, Kinsey 20pts, Magee 16pts

1975 6-5

24 Villanova	17 WR Lonnie Allgood
10 Iowa	7 WR Don Magee
31 Tulane	13 T Jose St. Victor
7 Maryland	24 G Glenn Williams / Rick Rosen
6 Navy	10 C Bill Varvari
7 Penn State	19 G Don Wells
22 Boston College	14 T Larry Archis
0 Pittsburgh	38 TE Mike Jones / George Yost
37 Virginia	0 QB Jim Donoghue / Bob Mitch
20 West Virginia	19 TB Bob Avery / Bill Hurley / Jim Grubbs
10 Rutgers	21 FB Earl Vaughn / Tom Voyda
	DL Jim Jerome
	DL Bernie Winters / Gerry Martin
	DL Ken Clarke
	DL Bill Zanovitch
	DL Dave Tate
	LB Ray Preston
	LB Linwood Hess
	DB Nate Wright
	DB Keith Moody
	DB Larry King
	DB Tim Moresco

RUSHING: Vaughn 118/470y, Avery 100/460y, Donoghue 121/280y
PASSING: Donoghue 52-118/832y, 5TD, 44.1%
RECEIVING: Allgood 27/477y, Magee 19/276y, Jones 16/208y
SCORING: Dave Jacobs (K) 58pts, Vaughn & Grubbs 24pts

1976 3-8

7 Bowling Green	22 WR Mike Jones / Brian Ishman
3 Iowa	41 WR Don Magee / Art Monk
28 Maryland	42 T Neil Barton / Craig Wolfley
21 Oregon State	3 G Glenn Williams / Larry Archis
3 Tulane	0 C Paul Colvin
3 Penn State	27 G Don Wells
24 Temple	16 T Jose St. Victor
13 Pittsburgh	23 TE Rich Rosen
10 Navy	27 QB Bill Hurley
14 Boston College	28 TB Bob Avery
28 West Virginia	34 FB Earl Vaughn
	DL Gerry Martin
	DL Bernie Winters
	DL Willie McCullough
	DL Ken Clarke
	DL Jay Brennan / Tim Trapasso
	LB Jim Collins / Steve Spinney
	LB Bill Zanovitch
	DB DeShawn Hawkins
	DB Nate Wright / Warren Harvey
	DB Tim Moresco
	DB Larry King

RUSHING: Hurley 185/716y, Avery 128/562y, Vaughn 106/530y
PASSING: Hurley 38-95/638y, 5TD, 40%
RECEIVING: Jones 16/240y, Magee 13/271y, Rosen 6/68y
SCORING: Dave Jacobs (K) 40pts, Avery 30pts, Sessler 24pts

1977 6-5

12 Oregon State	24 WR Mike Jones
0 N. Carolina St.	38 WR Bruce Semall
22 Washington	20 T Neil Barton
30 Illinois	20 G Don Wells
10 Maryland	24 C Paul Colvin
24 Penn State	31 G Larry Archis (T) / Glenn Williams
21 Pittsburgh	28 T Craig Wolfley
6 Virginia	3 TE Rich Rosen
45 Navy	34 QB Bill Hurley
20 Boston College	3 TB Art Monk
28 West Virginia	9 FB Bob Avery
	DL Bob Tate / Kevin Yard
	DL Ken Clarke
	DL Willie McCullough
	DL Bernie Winters
	DL Jerry Martin
	LB John Kinley
	LB Chris Shaffer
	DB Larry King
	DB Terry O'Leary
	DB John Patterson (RB) / Joe Caruso
	DB Warren Harvey

RUSHING: Hurley 200/625y, Monk 110/566y, Avery 131/561y
PASSING: Hurley 108-201/1455y, 8TD, 53.7%
RECEIVING: Monk 41/590y, Jones 25/301y, Semall 22/332y
SCORING: Dave Jacobs (K) 70pts, Avery 54pts, Monk 36pts

1978 3-8

0 Florida State	28 WR Mike Jones / Greg Williams
19 N. Carolina St.	27 WR Paul Zambuto / Brian Ishman
21 Michigan State	49 T Bruce Babcock / John McCollom
14 Illinois	28 G Glenn Williams
31 West Virginia	15 C Andy Gissinger / Joe Hodges
9 Maryland	24 G Larry Archis
15 Penn State	45 T Craig Wolfley
17 Pittsburgh	18 TE Bruce Semall/Tim Trapasso/Tony Sidor
20 Navy	17 QB Tim Wilson / Ron Farneski
37 Boston College	23 TB Art Monk
9 Miami	21 FB Joe Morris / Dennis Hartman
	DL Mike Gyetvay
	DL Ron Richardson / Fred Lang
	DL Mike Rotunda / Willie McCullough
	DL John Cameron
	LB Mike Zunic / Robert Tate
	LB Jim Collins
	LB Tom Seibert / Ken Kollar
	DB John Patterson
	DB Warren Harvey
	DB Terry O'Leary
	DB Bob Arkeilpane

RUSHING: Morris 170/1001y, Monk 136/573y, Wilson 128/289y
PASSING: Wilson 22-68/345y, TD, 32.4%
Farneski 21-51/241y, 2TD, 41.2%
RECEIVING: Monk 19/293y, Semall 6/63y, Williams 6/62y
SCORING: Dave Jacobs (K) 66pts, Monk 30pts, Mandeville 24pts

1979 7-5

8 Ohio State	31 WR Brian Ishman
24 West Virginia	14 WR Art Monk
54 Northwestern	21 T Drew Gissinger
52 Washington St.	25 G Tony Hazzan
45 Kansas	27 C Joe Hodges
17 Temple	49 G Craig Wolfley
7 Penn State	35 T John McCollom
25 Miami	15 TE Tony Sidor
21 Pittsburgh	28 QB Bill Hurley
30 Navy	14 TB Joe Morris
10 Boston College	27 FB Ken Mandeville
31 McNeese State ■	7 DL John Kinley
	DL Mike Connors
	DL Chris Shaffer
	DL John Cameron
	LB Mike Zunic
	LB Jim Collins
	LB Ken Kollar / Tom Seibert
	DB Cedric Hinton
	DB Russell Spitz
	DB Ike Bogasian
	DB Bob Arkeilpane

RUSHING: Morris 238/1372y, Hurley 203/813y, Mandeville 105/397y
PASSING: Hurley 79-158/1276y, 6TD, 50%
RECEIVING: Monk 40/716y, Ishman 17/278y, Sidor 15/235y
SCORING: Hurley 74pts, Gary Anderson (K) 73pts, Morris 42pts

1980 5-6

21 Ohio State	31 WR Tony Sidor / Marcus Hackett
36 Miami (Ohio)	24 WR Paul Zambuto
42 Northwestern	21 T Drew Gissinger
8 Kansas	23 G Tony Hazzan
31 Temple	7 C Gerry Feehery
7 Penn State	24 G John Lally
17 Rutgers	9 T John McCollom
6 Pittsburgh	43 TE Chris Jilleba
3 Navy	6 QB Dave Warner
16 Boston College	27 TB Joe Morris / Glenn Moore
20 West Virginia	7 FB Ken Mandeville
	DL Mike Charles
	DL Chris Hand / Ralph Joline
	DL Herb Butzke
	DL Jim Kimmel / Ken Kollar
	LB Mike Zunic
	LB Jim Collins
	LB Craig Bingham
	DB Cedric Hinton
	DB Russ Spitz
	DB Gerald Kilpatrick / Ike Bogasian
	DB Bob Arkeilpane / Derek Frederickson

RUSHING: Morris 144/732y, Warner 153/532y, Mandeville 118/516y
PASSING: Warner 81-167/1008y, 3TD, 48.5%
RECEIVING: Sidor 23/288y, Jilleba 17/237y, Mandeville 13/128y
SCORING: Gary Anderson (K) 49pts, Warner 42pts, Morris 36pts

1981 4-6-1

27 Rutgers	29 WR Willie Sydnor
19 Temple	31 WR Paul Zambuto
14 Illinois	17 T Jim McAndrews
21 Indiana	7 G Tony Hazzan
16 Maryland	17 C Gerry Feehery
10 Penn State	41 G John Lally
47 Colgate	23 T John McCollom
23 Navy	24 TE Marty Chalk
27 Boston College	35 QB Dave Warner
27 West Virginia	17 TB Joe Morris
	24 FB Brent Ziegler
	DL Mike Charles
	DL Herb Butzke
	DL Blaise Winter
	LB Guy Ruff
	LB Chris Hand / Craig Bingham
	LB Tony Romano
	LB Mike Gyetvay / Mike Zunic
	DB Ron Hobby
	DB Ed Koban
	DB Gerald Kilpatrick
	DB Derek Fredrickson

RUSHING: Morris 261/ 1194y, Ziegler 151/418y, Jack Gilligan (TB) 47/151y
PASSING: Warner 120-233/1445y, 7TD, 53.8%
RECEIVING: Sydnor 29/418y, Zambuto 22/337y, Chalk 21/261y
SCORING: Gary Anderson (K) 76pts, Morris 68pts, Warner 42pts

1982 2-9

31 Rutgers	8 WR Marcus Hackett
18 Temple	23 WR Nick Bruckner
10 Illinois	47 T Mark Ehde
10 Indiana	17 G Joe Nett
3 Maryland	26 C Gerry Feehery
7 Penn State	28 G Matt Walker
0 Pittsburgh	14 T Ted Cirillo
49 Colgate	15 TE Bob Brotzki / Tom Stephens
18 Navy	20 QB Todd Norley / Steve Peach
13 Boston College	20 TB Jaime Covington / Glenn Moore
0 West Virginia	26 FB Brent Ziegler
	DL Mike Charles
	DL Tim Green / Bill Pendock
	DL Blaise Winter / Jamie Kimmel
	LB Chris Hand
	LB Rudy Reed / Bernie King
	LB Tony Romano
	LB Rich Roche
	DB Ed Koban / John Roos
	DB Ron Hobby
	DB Derek Frederickson
	DB Vic Bellamy

RUSHING: Covington 171/774y, Ziegler 89/393y, Moore 49/218y
PASSING: Norley 70-134/833y, TD, 52.2%
RECEIVING: Bruckner 24/374y, Ziegler 22/202y, Covington 20/183y
SCORING: Russ Carpentieri (K) 43pts, Covington 36pts, Ziegler 26pts

1983 6-5

6 Temple	17 WR Mike Siano
22 Kent State	10 WR Mike Morris / Scott Schwedes
35 Northwestern	0 T Bob Brotzki
17 Rutgers	13 G Tom Stephens
7 Nebraska	63 C Jack Simko
13 Maryland	34 G Matt Walker
6 Penn State	17 T Doug Marrone
10 Pittsburgh	13 TE Marty Chalk
14 Navy	7 QB Todd Norley
21 Boston College	10 TB Jaime Covington
27 West Virginia	16 FB Bruce Ziegler / Harold Gayden
	DL Blaise Winter
	DL Bill Pendock
	DL Tim Green
	LB Jaime Kimmel
	LB Rick Roche
	LB Bernard King / Rudy Reed
	LB Tony Romano
	DB Ed Koban
	DB John Roos
	DB Ron Hobby
	DB Vic Bellamy

RUSHING: Covington 143/606y, Gayden 108/514y, Ziegler 76/308y
PASSING: Norley 87-177/999y, 5TD, 49.2%
RECEIVING: Schwedes 21/261y, Siano 20/341y, Ziegler 19/122y
SCORING: Don McAulay (K) 64pts, Gayden 30pts, Covington 24pts

1984 6-5

23 Maryland	7 WR Mike Siano
13 Northwestern	12 WR Scott Schwedes
0 Rutgers	19 T Bob Brotzki
17 Nebraska	9 G Stephens
0 Florida	16 C Jack Simko
10 West Virginia	20 G Steve Villanti
3 Penn State	21 T Doug Marrone
27 Army	16 TE Jim Tait / Marty Chalk
13 Pittsburgh	7 QB Todd Norley / Mike Kmetz
29 Navy	0 HB Jaime Covington
16 Boston College	24 FB Harold Gayden
	DL Tim Green
	DL Ted Gregory
	DL Jeff Knauff
	LB Jerry Kimmel
	LB Bernie King
	LB Rudy Reed
	LB Gerry Allen
	DB David Lee
	DB John Roos
	DB Ron Hobby
	DB Vic Bellamy

RUSHING: Covington 201/745y, Gayden 121/478y, Kmetz 41/160y
PASSING: Norley 93-171/829y, 5TD, 54.4%
RECEIVING: Schwedes 37/506y, Siano 27/381y, Covington 25/147y
SCORING: Don McAulay (K) 59pts, Gayden 24pts, Covington & Schwedes 18pts

1985 7-5

3 Mississippi St.	30 WR Scott Schwedes
34 Kent State	0 WR Mike Siano
14 Virginia Tech	24 T Bob Brotzki
48 Louisville	0 G Hans Wiederkehr
20 Penn State	24 C Jim Leible
29 Temple	14 G Craig Stoeppel / Tom Watson (T)
12 Pittsburgh	0 T Doug Marrone
24 Navy	20 TE Jim Tait
41 Boston College	21 QB Don McPherson / Mike Kmetz
31 Rutgers	14 TB Robert Drummond / Byron Abraham
10 West Virginia	13 FB Roland Grimes
18 Maryland■	35 DL Jerry Kimmel / Wes Dove
	DL Ted Gregory
	DL Tim Green
	LB Doug Pina / Keith Friberg
	LB Tim Pidgeon
	LB Rudy Reed
	LB Jerome Hall
	DB Dave Lee
	DB Jeff Mangram
	DB Markus Paul / Pete Ewald
	DB Cooper Gardiner

RUSHING: McPherson 157/489y, Drummond 86/407y, Abraham 62/325y
PASSING: McPherson 85-159/1469y, 12TD, 53.5%
RECEIVING: Siano 46/852y, Schwedes 34/692y, Tait 18/215y
SCORING: Don McAulay (K) 80pts, Schwedes & Siano 48pts

1986 5-6

17 Mississippi St.	24 WR Scott Schwedes
28 Army	33 WR Tommy Kane
17 Virginia Tech	26 T Craig Stoeppel
10 Rutgers	16 G John Garrett
41 Missouri	9 C Jim Leible
3 Penn State	42 G Tom Watson
27 Temple	24 T Shawn Garrity
24 Pittsburgh	20 TE Pat Kelly
31 Navy	22 QB Don McPherson
9 Boston College	27 TB Robert Drummond
34 West Virginia	23 FB Daryl Johnston / Harold Gayden
	DL Wes Dove
	DL John Dominic
	DL Paul Frase
	LB Roger Remo
	LB Terry Wooden
	LB Tim Pidgeon
	LB Derek Ward
	DB Pete Ewald
	DB Chris Ingram
	DB Jeff Mangram
	DB Markus Paul / Jim Sheedy

RUSHING: McPherson 191/523y, Johnston 102/469y, Gayden 79/258y
PASSING: McPherson 142-269/1827y, 12TD, 52.8%
RECEIVING: Schwedes 47/652y, Kelly 20/239y, Kane 19/337y
SCORING: Tim Vesling (K) 67pts, Schwedes 42pts, McPherson 36pts

1987 11-0-1

25 Maryland	11 WR Tommy Kane
20 Rutgers	3 WR Deval Glover
24 Miami (Ohio)	10 T Craig Stoeppel
35 Virginia Tech	21 G John Garrett
24 Missouri	13 C John Garrett
48 Penn State	21 G Blake Bednarz
52 Colgate	6 T Turnell Sims
24 Pittsburgh	10 TE Pat Kelly
45 Boston College	17 QB Don McPherson
34 Navy	10 HB Robert Drummond / Michael Owens
32 West Virginia	31 FB Daryl Johnston
16 Auburn■	16 DL Paul Frase
	DL Ted Gregory / Alain Greer
	DL Rob Burnett
	LB Terry Wooden / John Dominic
	LB Derek Ward / Don Bucey
	LB David Bavaro
	LB Keith Friberg
	DB Chris Ingram
	DB David Holmes
	DB Markus Paul
	DB Jeff Mangram

RUSHING: Drummond 124/746y, Johnston 116/564y, Owens 88/531y
PASSING: McPherson 129-229/2341y, 22TD, 56.3%
RECEIVING: Kane 44/968y, Kelly 24/392y, Glover 20/369y
SCORING: Tim Vesling (K) 88pts, Kane 84pts, Owens 38pts

1988 10-2

31 Temple	21 WR Rob Moore
9 Ohio State	26 WR Deval Glover
35 Virginia Tech	0 T Mike Bernard
20 Maryland	9 G Gary McCummings
34 Rutgers	20 C John Flannery
24 Penn State	10 G Blake Bednarz
38 East Carolina	14 T Turnell Sims
49 Navy	21 TE Pat Davis
45 Boston College	20 QB Todd Philcox
9 West Virginia	31 TB Robert Drummond / Michael Owens
24 Pittsburgh	7 FB Daryl Johnston
23 LSU■	10 DL George Rooks / Mark Swinson
	DL Fred DeRiggi
	DL Rob Burnett
	LB Keith Friberg
	LB Terry Wooden
	LB Dan Bucey
	LB David Bavaro
	DB Chris Ingram
	DB David Holmes
	DB Jeff Mangram
	DB Markus Paul

RUSHING: Drummond 124/747y, Johnston 128/645y, Owens 94/460y
PASSING: Philcox 141-234/2076y, 16TD, 60.2%
RECEIVING: Moore 44/797y, Glover 41/580y, Davis 27/424y
SCORING: Kevin Greene (K) 82pts, Moore 68pts, Drummond 42pts

1989 8-4

43 Temple	3 WR Rob Moore
10 Army	7 WR Rob Carpenter
23 Pittsburgh	30 T Mike Bernard
10 Florida State	41 G Gary McCummings
12 Penn State	34 C John Flannery
49 Rutgers	28 G Blake Bednarz
18 East Carolina	16 T Turnell Sims
23 Boston College	11 TE Andrew Dees
38 Navy	17 QB Bill Schaar / Mark McDonald
17 West Virginia	24 HB Michael Owens
24 Louisville	13 FB Duane Kinnon
19 Georgia■	18 DL George Rooks
	DL Fred DeRiggi
	DL Rob Burnett
	LB Alban Brown / Brian LeBaron
	LB Dan Bucey
	LB David Bavaro
	LB Terry Wooden
	DB Greg Walker / Ousmane Bary
	DB Sean Whiteman
	DB Rob Thomson
	DB Tim Sandquist

RUSHING: Owens 211/1018y, Kinnon 92/352y, Chris Chavers (HB) 16/112y
PASSING: Schaar 107-169/1625y, 9TD, 63.3% McDonald 63-88/748y, 3TD, 71.6%
RECEIVING: Moore 53/1064y, Carpenter 41/761y, Kinnon 39/429y
SCORING: John Biskup (K) 67pts, Moore 56pts, Owens 48pts

1990 7-4-2

16 Southern Cal	34 WR Shelby Hill / Chris Gedney
19 Temple	9 WR Rob Carpenter
23 Michigan State	23 T Mike Bernard
20 Pittsburgh	20 G Gary McCummings
49 Vanderbilt	14 C John Flannery
21 Penn State	27 G Terrence Wisdom / Dan Erickson
42 Rutgers	0 T Turnell Sims
26 Army	14 TE Andrew Dees
35 Boston College	6 QB Marvin Graves
24 Tulane	26 TB David Walker / Terry Richardson
31 West Virginia	7 FB Duane Kinnon
7 Miami	33 DL George Rooks
28 Arizona■	0 DL Kevin Mitchell
	DL Frank Conover
	LB Brian LeBaron
	LB Garland Hawkins
	LB Glen Young
	LB Dan Conley
	DB Greg Walker
	DB Dwayne Joseph / Ousmane Bary
	DB Tim Sandquist
	DB Rob Thomson

RUSHING: Walker 150/730y, Richardson 60/320y, Kinnon 65/290y
PASSING: Graves 115-200/1711y, 9TD, 57.5%
RECEIVING: Carpenter 52/895y, Hill 33/558y, Gedney 24/332y
SCORING: John Biskup (K) 63pts, Walker 42pts, Graves 40pts

1991 10-2

37 Vanderbilt	10 WR Shelby Hill
31 Maryland	17 WR Qadry Ismail
38 Florida	21 T John Capachione
24 Tulane	0 G Jerry Sharp / John Nilsen
14 Florida State	46 C John Reagan
20 East Carolina	23 G Terrence Wisdom
31 Pittsburgh	27 T Andrew Dees
21 Rutgers	7 TE Chris Gedney
27 Temple	6 QB Marvin Graves
38 Boston College	16 TB David Walker / Terry Richardson
16 West Virginia	10 FB Al Wooten
24 Ohio State■	17 DL George Rooks
	DL Kevin Mitchell
	DL Jim Wentworth / Ernie Brown
	LB Jo Jo Wooden / Chip Todd
	LB Garland Hawkins
	LB Glen Young
	LB John Lusardi
	DB Greg Walker
	DB Dwayne Joseph
	DB Tim Sandquist
	DB Tony Montemorra

RUSHING: Walker 169/969y, Richardson 82/341y, Ismail 12/216y
PASSING: Graves 131-221/1912y, 10TD, 59.3%
RECEIVING: Ismail 37/693y, Gedney 25/322y, Hill 21/321y
SCORING: John Biskup (K) 85pts, Walker 48pts, Ismail 42pts

1992 10-2

42 East Carolina	21 WR Shelby Hill
31 Texas	21 WR Qadry Ismail
12 Ohio State	35 T Chuck Bull
15 Louisville	9 G Jerry Sharp
50 Rutgers	28 C John Reagan
20 West Virginia	17 G Terrence Wisdom
38 Temple	7 T Kyle Adams / Melvin Tuten
41 Pittsburgh	10 TE Chris Gedney
28 Virginia Tech	9 QB Marvin Graves
27 Boston College	10 TB David Walker / Terry Richardson
10 Miami	16 FB Al Wooten
26 Colorado■	22 DL Ernie Brown
	DL Kevin Mitchell
	DL James Spencer
	LB Garland Hawkins
	LB Glen Young
	LB Dan Conley
	LB Jo Jo Wooden (DL) / Chip Todd
	DB Ousmane Bary / Doug Womack
	DB Dwayne Joseph
	DB Tony Jones
	DB Bob Grosvenor

RUSHING: Walker 168/855y, Richardson 61/336y, Wooten 75/312y
PASSING: Graves 146-242/2296y, 14TD, 60.3%
RECEIVING: Ismail 36/625y, Gedney 34/587y, Hill 29/480y
SCORING: John Biskup (K) 81pts, Wooten 42pts, Graves 34pts

1993 6-4-1

35	Ball State	12 WR Marvin Harrison
41	East Carolina	22 WR Shelby Hill
21	Texas	21 T Melvin Tuten
24	Cincinnati	21 G Cy Ellsworth
29	Boston College	23 C John Reagan
24	Pittsburgh	21 G Dave Wohlabaugh
0	Miami	49 T Kyle Adams
0	West Virginia	43 TE Eric Chenoweth
52	Temple	3 QB Marvin Graves
24	Virginia Tech	45 TB Terry Richardson / Kirby Dar Dar
31	Rutgers	18 FB Al Wooten

DL Ernie Brown
DL Kevin Mitchell (LB) / Ed Hobson
DL Wilky Bazile
LB Scott Freeney
LB Chip Todd
LB Nate Hemsley / Greg Shaw
LB Dana Cottrell
DB Dwayne Joseph
DB Bryce Bevill
DB Darrell Parker / Tony Jones
DB Bob Grosvenor

RUSHING: Richardson 104/526y, Dar Dar 347y
PASSING: Graves 171-280/2547y, 15TD, 61.1%
RECEIVING: Hill 56/937y, Harrison 41/813y
SCORING: Pat O'Neill (K) 61pts, Harrison 42pts

1994 7-4

29	Oklahoma	30 WR Marvin Harrison
34	Cincinnati	19 WR Sir Mawn Wilson
27	Rutgers	36 T Melvin Tuten
21	East Carolina	18 G Cy Ellsworth
28	Virginia Tech	20 C Dave Wohlabaugh
31	Pittsburgh	7 G Shelton Prescott
49	Temple	42 T Jim Ledger
6	Miami	27 TE Eric Chenoweth
0	Boston College	31 QB Kevin Mason
21	Maryland	16 TB Kirby Dar Dar / Malcolm Thomas
0	West Virginia	13 FB Terry Morris / Roy Willis

DL Wilky Bazile
DL Ed Hobson
DL Dave Rebar
LB Scott Freeney
LB Dan Conley / Dana Cottrell
LB Antwaune Ponds
LB Chris Marques
DB Bryce Bevill / Rod Gadson
DB Kevin Abrams
DB Tony Jones
DB Darrell Parker

RUSHING: Dar Dar 188/853y, Thomas 113/642y, Mason 144/369y
PASSING: Mason 105-187/1627y, 10TD, 56.1%
RECEIVING: Harrison 37/761y, Wilson 16/251y, Chenoweth 11/150y
SCORING: Dar Dar 72pts, Mason 48pts, Harrison 36pts.

1995 9-3

20	North Carolina	9 WR Marvin Harrison
24	East Carolina	27 WR Sir Mawn Wilson / Deon Maddux
27	Minnesota	17 T Jim Ledger
27	Rutgers	17 G Cy Ellsworth / John Michaelidis
31	Temple	14 C Harvey Pennypacker
52	E. Michigan	24 G Shelton Prescott
22	West Virginia	0 T Brent Warren / Brad Patkochis
7	Virginia Tech	31 TE Roland Williams / Kaseem Sinceno
42	Pittsburgh	10 QB Donovan McNabb
58	Boston College	29 TB Malcolm Thomas / Kyle McIntosh
24	Miami	35 FB Terry Morris / Rob Konrad
41	Clemson■	0 DL Scott Freeney / Antonio Anderson

DL Jeff Danish / Jason Walters
DL Chris Marques / Dave Rebar (LB)
LB Dulayne Morgan / George Meyers
LB Antwaune Ponds / Mike Brown
LB Nate Hemsley
LB Dana Cottrell
DB Rod Gadson / Phil Nash
DB Kevin Abrams / Anthony Walker
DB Donovin Darius
DB Darrell Parker

RUSHING: Thomas 124/603y, McNabb 63/433y, McIntosh 59/338y
PASSING: McNabb 128-207/1991y, 16TD, 61.8%
RECEIVING: Harrison 56/1131y, Thomas 19/183y, Wilson 16/211y
SCORING: Olindo Mare (K) 74pts, Harrison 60pts, Thomas 54pts

1996 9-3

10	North Carolina	27 WR Kaseem Sinceno (TE) / Jim Turner
33	Minnesota	35 WR Greg Maddox / Quinton Spotwood
52	Virginia Tech	21 T Brad Patkochis
42	Rutgers	0 G Scott Kiernan / John Michaelidis
55	Pittsburgh	7 C Harvey Pennypacker / Cory Bowen
45	Boston College	17 G Shelton Prescott
30	West Virginia	7 T Brent Warren
31	Tulane	7 TE Roland Williams
42	Army	17 QB Donovan McNabb
36	Temple	15 TB Malcolm Thomas
31	Miami	38 FB Rob Konrad
30	Houston■	17 DL Dana Cottrell / Michael Brown

DL George Meyers
DL Antonio Anderson
DL Scott Freeney / Jeff Danish
LB Jason Walters / Stanakeane Gibbs
LB Nathaniel Helmsley
LB Antwaune Ponds
DB Kevin Abrams / Phil Nash
DB Donovon Darius
DB Walkers / Keith Bulluck
DB Rod Gadson

RUSHING: Thomas 166/891y, McNabb 97/458y, Konrad 93/361y
PASSING: McNabb 118-215/1776y, 19TD, 54.9%
RECEIVING: Maddox 23/344y, Turner 20/383y, Spotwood 17/326y
SCORING: Nathan Trout (K) 85pts, Thomas 60pts, Williams 30pts

1997 9-4

34	Wisconsin	0 WR Quinton Spotwood / Kevin Johnson
31	N Carolina St.	32 WR Jim Turner
34	Oklahoma	36 T Brad Patkochis / Jeff Pilon
3	Virginia Tech	31 G Scott Kiernan
30	Tulane	19 C Cory Bowen
56	East Carolina	0 G Brent Warren
50	Rutgers	3 T Mark Baniewicz
60	Temple	7 TE Roland Willams / Kaseem Sinceno
40	West Virginia	10 QB Donovan McNabb
20	Boston College	13 TB Kyle McIntosh / Dee Brown
32	Pittsburgh	27 FB Rob Konrad / Nick Sudano
33	Miami	13 DL Jason Walters
18	Kansas State■	35 DL Jeff Danish

DL Brian Coleman / Derrick Corley
DL Dulayne Morgan
LB Morlon Greenwood
LB Antwaune Ponds
LB Keith Bulluck / Stan Gibbs
DB Phil Nash
DB Rod Gadson
DB Donovan Darius
DB Tebucky Jones / Jason Poles

RUSHING: McIntosh 181/898y, Brown 118/555y, McNabb 110/404y
PASSING: McNabb 145-265/2488y, 20TD, 54.7%
RECEIVING: Spotwood 41/797y, Johnson 32/612y, Turner 23/488y
SCORING: Nathan Trout (K) 79pts, Spotwood 72pts, Brown 48pts

1998 8-4

33	Tennessee	34 WR Kevin Johnson
38	Michigan	28 WR Quinton Spotwood / Darryl Daniel
70	Rutgers	14 T Mark Baniewicz
17	N. Carolina St.	38 G Scott Kiernan
63	Cincinnati	21 C Cory Bowen / Patrick Alexander
42	Boston College	25 G William O'Donnell / Joseph Burton
45	Pittsburgh	28 T Jeff Pilon
28	West Virginia	35 TE Stephen Brominski
28	Virginia Tech	26 QB Donovan McNabb
38	Temple	7 TB Kyle McIntosh
66	Miami	13 FB Rob Konrad
10	Florida■	31 DL Marc Pilon / Donald Dinkins

DL Brian Coleman
DL Rickie Simpkins
DL Maynard Pettijohn
LB Morlon Greenwood / Vernon Banks
LB Keith Bulluck
LB Stanakeane Gibbs
DB Will Allen / Kyle McIntosh
DB Phillip Nash
DB Quentin Harris
DB Jason Poles / Charles Burton

RUSHING: McIntosh 137/742y, McNabb 135/438y, Konrad 93/417y
PASSING: McNabb 157-251/2134y, 22TD, 62.5%
RECEIVING: Johnson 60/894y, Daniel 22/263y, Konrad 20/196y
SCORING: Nathan Trout (K) 94pts, Johnson 84pts, Konrad 54pts

1999 7-5

35	Toledo	12 WR Quinton Spotwood / Malik Campbell
47	C. Michigan	7 WR Patrick Woodcock / Jeffrey Lowe
13	Michigan	18 T Mark Baniewicz
30	West Virginia	7 G William O'Donnell
47	Tulane	17 C Corey Bowen
24	Pittsburgh	17 G Joseph Burton / Sean O'Connor
0	Virginia Tech	62 T Jeff Pilon
23	Boston College	24 TE Stephen Brominski / Mike Bennett
27	Temple	10 QB Troy Nunes / Madei Williams
21	Rutgers	24 TB Dee Brown
13	Miami	45 FB James Mumgro / Kyle Johnson
20	Kentucky■	13 DL Maynard Pettijohn

DL Rickie Simpkins
DL Eric Downing / Derrick Corley
DL Donald Dinkins / Dwight Freeney
LB Morlon Greenwood
LB Keith Bulluck
LB Clifton Smith / Vernon Banks
DB Will Allen
DB Willie Ford / David Bird
DB Quentin Harris
DB Ian McIntosh

RUSHING: Brown 145/741y, Mumgro 116/537y, Johnson 32/157y
PASSING: Nunes 95-161/1141y, 11TD, 59%
Williams 55-110/742y, 2TD, 50%
RECEIVING: Spotwood 32/380y, Woodcock 24/402y, Brominski 20/287y
SCORING: Nathan Trout (K) 76pts, Mungro 36pts, 3 tied w/ 24pts

2000 6-5

63	Buffalo	7 WR Malik Campbell / Maurice Jackson
10	Cincinnati	12 WR Pat Woodcock / David Tyree
17	East Carolina	34 T P.J. Alexander
42	Brigham Young	14 G Sean O'Connor
24	Pittsburgh	17 C Nick Romeo
13	Boston College	20 G Vaughn Smith / Emerson Kilgore
14	Virginia Tech	22 T Joe Burton / Giovanni DeLoatch
31	West Virginia	27 TE Graham Manley / Jeremie Frazier
31	Temple	12 QB Troy Nunes / R.J. Anderson
0	Miami	26 TB Dee Brown / James Mungro
49	Rutgers	21 FB George Scott / Chris Davis

DL Duke Pettijohn
DL Rick Simpkins
DL Eric Downing / Louis Gachelin
DL Dwight Freeney / Mark Holtzman
LB Morlon Greenwood
LB Clifton Smith
LB J.R. Johnson / Jameel Dumas
DB Will Allen
DB Willie Ford / Will Hunter
DB Quentin Harris
DB Keeon Walker

RUSHING: Brown 172/1031y, Mungro 115/797y
PASSING: Nunes 94-154/1366y, 8TD, 61%
Anderson 42-91/512y, 2TD, 46.2%
RECEIVING: Woodcock 29/453y, Campbell 26/319y, Jackson 20/337y
SCORING: Brown 68pts, Mike Shafer (K) 56pts, Mungro 42pts

2001 10-3

7	Georgia Tech	13 WR Maurice Jackson / Johnnie Morant
9	Tennessee	33 WR Malik Campbell / David Tyree
21	Central Florida	10 T P.J. Alexander
31	Auburn	14 G Joe Burton
44	East Carolina	30 C Nick Romeo
24	Rutgers	17 G Sean O'Connor
42	Pittsburgh	10 T Giovanni DeLoatch / Kevin Sampson
45	Temple	3 TE Graham Manley / Joe Donnelly
22	Virginia Tech	14 QB R.J. Anderson / Troy Nunes
24	West Virginia	13 TB James Mungro
0	Miami	59 FB Kyle Johnson
39	Boston College	28 DL Josh Thomas
26	Kansas State■	3 DL Christian Ferrara

DL Mark Holtzman / Louis Gachelin
DL Dwight Freeney
LB Jameel Dumas
LB Clifton Smith
LB Charles Burton / Rich Scanlon
DB Latroy Oliver / Will Hunter
DB Willie Ford
DB Quentin Harris
DB Keeon Walker

RUSHING: Mungro 267/1282y, Anderson 125/228y, Johnson 53/210y
PASSING: Anderson 77-158/1236y, 6TD, 48.7%
Nunes 58-105/734y, 5TD, 55.2%
RECEIVING: Morant 20/502y, Jackson 19/254y, Tyree 18/233y
SCORING: Mungro 108pts, Collin Barber (K) 37pts, Anderson 30pts

2002 4-8

21 Brigham Young	42 WR Jamel Riddle / Johnnie Morant
22 North Carolina	30 WR David Tyree / Jared Jones
63 Rhode Island	17 T Adam Terry / Quinn Ojinnaka
34 Auburn	37 G Erik Kaloyanides
24 Pittsburgh	48 C Nick Romeo
16 Temple	17 G Matt Tarullo
7 West Virginia	34 T Kevin Sampson
45 Rutgers	14 TE Lenny Cusumano / Joe Donnelly
38 Central Florida	35 QB R.J. Anderson / Troy Nunes
50 Virginia Tech	42 TB Walter Reyes / Damien Rhodes
20 Boston College	41 FB Chris Davis / Barry Baker
7 Miami	49 DL Josh Thomas / Julian Pollard
	DL Louis Gachelin
	DL Christian Ferrara / Brian Hooper
	DL James Wyche / Ryan LaCasse
	LB Jameel Dumas
	LB Clifton Smith
	LB Rich Scanlon
	DB Latroy Oliver
	DB Will Hunter / Steve Gregory
	DB O'Neil Scott / Maurice McClain
	DB Keeon Walker / Anthony Smith

RUSHING: Reyes 182/1135y, Rhodes 138/568y, Baker 21/116y
PASSING: Nunes 115-198/1337y, 8TD, 58.1%
 Anderson 58-134/899y, 4TD, 43.3%
RECEIVING: Riddle 41/626y, Tyree 36/559y, Morant 24/327y
SCORING: Reyes 104pts, Collin Barber (K) 66pts, Rhodes 56pts

2003 6-6

49 North Carolina	47 WR Johnnie Morant
20 Louisville	20 WR Jared Jones / Rashard Williams
38 Central Florida	14 T Adam Terry
34 Toledo	7 G Steve Franklin
7 Virginia Tech	51 C Nick Romeo
39 Boston College	14 G Matt Tarullo
14 Pittsburgh	34 T Kevin Sampson
41 Temple	17 TE Lenny Cusumano / Joe Donnelly
10 Miami	17 QB R.J. Anderson
23 West Virginia	34 TB Walter Reyes
7 Rutgers	24 FB Thump Belton
38 Notre Dame	12 DL Josh Thomas / Julian Pollard
	DL Louis Gachelin
	DL Christian Ferrara
	DL James Wyche
	LB Kelvin Smith
	LB Rich Scanlon
	LB Kellen Pruitt
	DB Steve Gregory / Thomas Whitfield
	DB Troy Swittenburg / Terrell Lemon
	DB Anthony Smith
	DB Diamond Ferri

RUSHING: Reyes 253/1347y, Anderson 99/262y, Belton 35/168y
PASSING: Anderson 186-310/2164y, 10TD, 60%
RECEIVING: Morant 46/799y, Reyes 38/375y, Jones 37/355y
SCORING: Reyes 128pts, Collin Barber (K) 69pts, Anderson &
 Morant 30pts

2004 6-6

0 Purdue	51 WR Jared Jones / Landel Bembo
37 Buffalo	17 WR Steve Gregory / Andre Fontenette
19 Cincinnati	7 T Adam Terry
10 Virginia	31 G Jason Greene
41 Rutgers	31 C Matt Tarullo
13 Florida State	17 G Steve Franklin
6 West Virginia	27 T Quinn Ojinnaka
42 Connecticut	30 TE Joe Kowalewski
38 Pittsburgh	31 QB Perry Patterson / Joe Fields
24 Temple	34 TB Walter Reyes / Damien Rhodes
43 Boston College	17 FB Greg Hanoian / Breyone Evans
14 Georgia Tech■	51 DL James Wyche / Ryan LaCasse
	DL Tony Jenkins / Chris Thorner
	DL Kader Drame
	DL Julian Pollard
	LB Kelvin Smith
	LB Jerry Mackey / Troy Swittenburg
	LB Kellen Pruitt / Luke Cain
	DB DeAndre LaCaille / O'Neill Scott
	DB Tanard Jackson
	DB Anthony Smith
	DB Diamond Ferri (TB)

RUSHING: Rhodes 153/870y, Reyes 148/803y, Ferri 29/173y
PASSING: Patterson 168-289/1851y, 7TD, 58.1%
 Fields 13-29/192y, TD, 44.8%
RECEIVING: Jones 43/621y, Gregory 38/420y, Rhodes 18/246y
SCORING: Rhodes & Collin Barber (K) 66pts, Reyes 42pts

2005 1-10

7 West Virginia	15 WR Rice Moss
31 Buffalo	0 WR Tim Lane
24 Virginia	27 T Carroll Madison (G) / Kurt Falke
14 Florida State	38 G Jason Greene / Mike Sklarosky
7 Connecticut	26 C Justin Outten
9 Rutgers	31 G Steve Franklin
7 Pittsburgh	34 T Quinn Ojinnaka
16 Cincinnati	22 TE Joe Kowalewski / Alex Shor
0 South Florida	27 QB Perry Patterson / Joe Fields
10 Notre Dame	34 TB Damien Rhodes
17 Louisville	41 FB/TE Steve McDonald/B. Darlington
	DL James Wyche
	DL Chris Thorner
	DL Kader Drame / Tony Jenkins
	DL Ryan LaCasse / Jarneel McClain
	LB Kellen Pruitt
	LB Kelvin Smith
	LB Tommy Harris / Jerry Mackey
	DB Tanard Jackson
	DB Steve Gregory
	DB Anthony Smith
	DB Dewayne Davis

RUSHING: Rhodes 219/900y, Kareem Jones (TB) 42/108y
PASSING: Patterson 130-273/1504y, 6TD, 47.6%
 Fields 9-28/155y, 0TD, 32.1%
RECEIVING: Lane 27/341y, Moss 26/359y, Rhodes 23/270y
SCORING: Rhodes 42pts, John Barker (K) 24pts,
 Ricky Krautman (K) 20pts

2006 4-8

10 Wake Forest	20 WR Rice Moss / Mike Williams
13 Iowa	20 WR Tim Lane / Taj Smith
31 Illinois	21 T Corey Chavers / Marvin McCall
34 Miami (Ohio)	14 G C. Madison (T) / Mike Sklarosky
40 Wyoming	34 C Justin Outten
11 Pittsburgh	21 G Ryan Durand
17 West Virginia	41 T Eugene Newsome
13 Louisville	28 TE Tom Ferron / J. Nesheiwat
3 Cincinnati	17 QB Perry Patterson
10 South Florida	27 TB Curtis Brinkley / Delone Carter
20 Connecticut	14 FB/TE S. McDonald/Brandon Darlington
7 Rutgers	38 DL Lee Williams / Brandon Gilbeaux
	DL Tony Jenkins / Arthur Jones
	DL C. Thorner / Cornelius Campbell
	DL Jameel McClain
	LB Luke Cain / Nick Chestnut
	LB Kelvin Smith
	LB Jerry Mackey
	DB Tanard Jackson
	DB Terrell Lemon
	DB Joe Fields / A. J. Brown
	DB Dewayne Davis

RUSHING: Carter 156/713y, Brinkley 139/571y
PASSING: Patterson 158-300/1865y, 12TD, 52.7%
RECEIVING: Ferron 30/351y, Williams 24/461y, Moss 23/272y
SCORING: Patrick Shadle (K) 69pts, Williams 26pts
 Carter & Smith 24pts

2007 2-10

12 Washington	42 WR Taj Smith / Rice Moss
0 Iowa	35 WR Mike Williams
20 Illinois	41 T Corey Chavers
38 Louisville	35 G Carroll Madison
14 Miami (Ohio)	17 C Jim McKenzie / Marvin McCall (G)
14 West Virginia	55 G Ryan Durand
14 Rutgers	38 T Larry Norton
20 Buffalo	12 TE Jewad Nesheiwat
17 Pittsburgh	20 QB Andrew Robinson/Cameron Dantley
10 South Florida	41 TB Curtis Brinkley / Doug Hogue
7 Connecticut	30 FB/TE Tony Fiammetta / Mike Owen
31 Cincinnati	52 DL Brandon Gilbeaux
	DL Arthur Jones / Bud Tribbey
	DL Tony Jenkins / Nick Santiago
	DL Jameel McClain / Lee Williams
	LB Vincenzo Giruzzi / Mike Stenclik
	LB Jake Flaherty / Patrick Cantey
	LB Ben Maljovec / Mike Mele
	DB Nick Chestnut / Nico Scott
	DB Dowayne Davis
	DB Joe Fields / Max Suter
	DB Mike Holmes / A.J. Brown

RUSHING: Brinkley 111/371y, Hogue 77/251y
PASSING: Robinson 154-292/2192y, 13TD, 52.7%
 Dantley 48-90/558y, 5TD, 53.3%
RECEIVING: Williams 60/837y, Smith 44/822y, Nesheiwat 17/270y
SCORING: Williams 60pts, Patrick Shadle (K) 53pts, Smith 30pts

2008 3-9

10 Northwestern	30 WR Lavar Lobdell / Grant Mayes
28 Akron	42 WR Donte Davis / Marcus Sales
13 Penn State	55 T Tucker Baumbach
30 Northeastern	21 G Ryan Bartholomew / Nick Lepak
24 Pittsburgh	34 C Jim McKenzie
6 West Virginia	17 G Ryan Durand
13 South Florida	45 T Corey Chavers
28 Louisville	21 TE Mike Owen
17 Rutgers	35 QB Cam Dantley
14 Connecticut	39 TB Curtis Brinkley
24 Notre Dame	23 FB Tony Fiammetta / Doug Hogue
10 Cincinnati	30 DL Jared Kimmel / Anthony Perkins
	DL Arthur Jones
	DL Nick Santiago
	DL Vince Giruzzi
	LB Derrell Smith
	LB Jake Flaherty
	LB Mike Mele
	DB Mike Holmes / Paul Chiara
	DB Kevyn Scott / Nico Scott
	DB Max Suter / Bruce Williams (WR)
	DB A.J. Brown / Randy McKinnon

RUSHING: Brinkley 237/1164y, Hogue 35/232y,
 Antwan Bailey (RB) 33/221y
PASSING: Dantley 121-251/1298y, 11 TD, 48.2%
RECEIVING: Davis 29/312y, Owen 19/175y, Fiammetta 16/127y
SCORING: Patrick Shadle (K) 67 pts, Brinkley 42 pts, Hogue 18 pts

2009 4-8

20 Minnesota	23 WR Marcus Sales / Donte Davis
7 Penn State	28 WR Alec Lemon / Lavar Lobdell
37 Northwestern	34 WR Mike Williams / Cody Catalina
41 Maine	24 T Nick Speller / Josh White
20 South Florida	34 G Ryan Bartholomew (C)
13 West Virginia	34 C Jim McKenzie
28 Akron	14 G Tucker Baumbach / Adam Rosner
7 Cincinnati	28 T Jonathan Meldrum / Andrew Tiller (G)
10 Pittsburgh	37 TE Mike Owen / Nick Provo / Carl Cutler
9 Louisville	10 QB Greg Paulus
31 Rutgers	13 RB Delone Carter / Antwon Bailey
31 Connecticut	56 DL Mikhail Marinovich
	DL Arthur Jones / Bud Tribbey
	DL Andrew Lewis
	DL Chandler Jones / Jared Kimmel
	LB Doug Hogue
	LB Derrell Smith / Mike Stenclik
	LB E.J. Carter / Ryan Gillum
	DB Kevyn Scott / Phillip Thomas
	DB Da'Mon Merkerson / Nico Scott
	DB Mike Holmes
	DB Max Suter / Shamarko Thomas

RUSHING: Carter 236/1021, Bailey 67/312y
PASSING: Paulus 193-285/2024y, 13TD, 67.7%
RECEIVING: Williams 49/746y, Lemon 29/295y, Sales 28/324y
 Bailey 27/200y, Davis 24/257y
SCORING: Carter 72pts, Ryan Lichtenstein (K) 66pts,
 Williams 36pts

2010 8-5

29 Akron	3 WR Van Chew / Marcus Sales
20 Washington	41 WR Alec Lemon
38 Maine	14 T Justin Pugh
42 Colgate	7 G Zack Chibane
13 South Florida	9 C Ryan Bartholomew
14 Pittsburgh	45 G Andrew Tiller
19 West Virginia	14 T Michael Hay / Andrew Phillips
31 Cincinnati	17 TE Jose Cruz
20 Louisville	28 QB Ryan Nassib
13 Rutgers	10 RB Delone Carter / Antwan Bailey
6 Connecticut	23 FB/TE Adam Harris / Nick Provo
7 Boston College	16 DL Mikhail Marinovich / Brandon Sharpe
36 Kansas State■	34 DL Andrew Lewis / Anthony Perkins
	DL Bud Tribbey
	DL Chandler Jones / Torrey Ball
	LB Marquis Spruill
	LB Derrell Smith
	LB Doug Hogue
	DB Da'Mon Merkerson / Kevyn Scott
	DB Mike Holmes / Jeremi Wilkes
	DB Phillip Thomas / Orlando Fisher
	DB Shamarko Thomas / Max Suter

RUSHING: Carter 231/1233y, Bailey 114/554y
PASSING: Nassib 202-358/2334y, 19TD, 56.4%
RECEIVING: Chew 41/611y, Bailey 35/306y, Provo 33/365y
 Lemon 32/397y
SCORING: Ross Krautman (K) 84pts, Carter 54pts,
 Bailey & Chew 30pts

TENNESSEE

University of Tennessee (Founded 1794)
Knoxville, Tennessee
Nickname: Volunteers, Vols
Colors: Bright Orange and White
Stadium: Neyland Stadium at Shields-Watkins Field (1921) 102,037
Affiliations: Southeastern Conference (1933-present)

CAREER RUSHING YARDS	Att.	Yards
Travis Henry (1997-2000)	556	3078
Arian Foster (2005-08)	650	2964
James Stewart (1991-94)	531	2890
Johnnie Jones (1981-84)	517	2852
Jamal Lewis (1997-99)	487	2677
Cedric Houston (2001-04)	501	2634
Jay Graham (1993-96)	540	2609
Montario Hardesty (2005-09)	560	2391
Curt Watson (1969-71)	529	2364
Reggie Cobb (1987-89)	445	2360

CAREER PASSING YARDS	Comp.-Att.	Yards
Peyton Manning (1994-97)	863-1381	11,201
Casey Clausen (2000-03)	775-1270	9707
Erik Ainge (2004-07)	733-1210	8700
Andy Kelly (1988-91)	514-846	6397
Jeff Francis (1985-88)	476-768	5867
Tee Martin (1996-99)	326-588	4592
Jonathan Crompton (2006-09)	348-629	4187
Heath Shuler (1991-93)	316-513	4088
Alan Cockrell (1981-83)	317-568	3823
Jimmy Streater (1976-79)	241-467	3433

CAREER RECEIVING YARDS	Catches	Yards
Joey Kent (1993-96)	183	2814
Marcus Nash (1994-97)	177	2447
Peerless Price (1995-98)	147	2298
Robert Meacham (2004-06)	125	2140
Cedric Wilson (1997-2000)	159	2137
Tim McGee (1982-85)	123	2042
Denarius Moore (2007-10)	112	2004
Larry Seivers (1974-76)	117	1924
Carl Pickens (1989-91)	109	1875
Anthony Hancock (1978-81)	106	1826

SEASON RUSHING YARDS	Attempts	Yards
Travis Stephens (2001)	291	1464
Jay Graham (1995)	272	1438
Jamal Lewis (1997)	232	1364
Montario Hardesty (2009)	282	1345
Travis Henry (2000)	253	1314

SEASON PASSING YARDS	Comp.-Att.	Yards
Peyton Manning (1997)	287-477	3819
Erik Ainge (2007)	325-519	3522
Peyton Manning (1996)	243-380	3287
Erik Ainge (2006)	233-348	2989
Casey Clausen (2001)	227-354	2969

SEASON RECEIVING YARDS	Catches	Yards
Robert Meachan (2006)	71	1298
Marcus Nash (1997)	76	1170
Joey Kent (1996)	68	1080
Joey Kent (1995)	69	1055
Kelley Washington (2001)	64	1010

GAME RUSHING YARDS	Attempts	Yards
Chuck Webb (1989 vs. Mississippi)	35	294
Chuck Webb (1990 vs. Arkansas)	26	250
Tony Thompson (1990 vs. Miss. State)	22	248

GAME PASSING YARDS	Comp.-Att.	Yards
Peyton Manning (1997 vs. Kentucky)	N/A	523
Peyton Manning (1996 vs. Florida)	37-65	492
Peyton Manning (1997 vs. Northwestern)	27-39	408

GAME RECEIVING YARDS	Catches	Yards
Kelley Washington (2001 vs. LSU)	11	256
Denarius Moore (2010 vs. South Carolina)	6	228
Johnny Mills (1966 vs. Kentucky)	9	225

GREATEST COACH

He arrived as head coach as a fill-in for ailing Johnny Majors, but before the 1992 season was over the rug had been pulled from under Majors and the coaching throne in Knoxville had been dusted off for Phillip Fulmer.

Since then, Fulmer won at least shares of six SEC divisional titles, two SEC championships, and the 1998 national championship title. During a spectacular four-year run that featured All American quarterback Peyton Manning, Tennessee earned a 45-5 record during the 1995-98 seasons. He stayed at or near the top of the winning percentage list for active coaches. Through 2008, Fullmer has enjoyed a 151-52-1 record for a .7426 winning percentage.

Yet Fulmer never seemed to be fully appreciated by Volunteer fans. He was dismissed during the latter stages of a disappointing, offense-failed 2008 season, Fulmer's 17th in Knoxville.

TENNESSEE'S 55 GREATEST SINCE 1953

OFFENSE

WIDE RECEIVER: Richmond Flowers, Joey Kent, Robert Meachem, Carl Pickens, Larry Seivers
TIGHT END: Buddy Cruze, Austin Denney
TACKLE: Antone Davis, Michael Munoz, Arron Sears
GUARD: Cosey Coleman, Harry Galbreath, Bill Johnson, Chip Kell, Bill Mayo, Charles Rosenfelder
CENTER: Bob Johnson
QUARTERBACK: Casey Clausen, Andy Kelly, Peyton Manning
RUNNING BACK: Reggie Cobb, Travis Henry, Jamal Lewis, Travis Stephens
FULLBACK: Curt Watson

DEFENSE

END: Shaun Ellis, Leonard Little, Will Overstreet
TACKLE: John Henderson, Darris McCord, Reggie White
NOSE GUARD: Steve DeLong
LINEBACKER: Frank Emanuel, Steve Kiner, Paul Naumoff, Jack Reynolds, Raynoch Thompson, Jackie Walker, Al Wilson
CORNERBACK: Albert Dorsey, Roland James, Jim Weatherford
SAFETY: Eric Berry, Eddie Brown, Dale Carter, Deon Grant, Bobby Majors

SPECIAL TEAMS

RETURN SPECIALIST: Willie Gault
PLACE KICKER: John Becksvoort
PUNTER: Jimmy Colquitt, Ron Widby

MULTIPLE POSITIONS

TAILBACK-DEFENSIVE BACK-PUNTER: Johnny Majors
QUARTERBACK-TAILBACK-WINGBACK: Charles Fulton

TWO-WAY PLAYERS

TACKLE-DEFENSIVE TACKLE: John Gordy
FULLBACK-LINEBACKER: Tommy Bronson

PERFORMANCE FORMULA:
TENNESSEE'S 10 BEST SEASONS

1998	1.7711	1 of 71
1956	1.6891	3 of 69
1995	1.6789	3 of 70
1970	1.6769	5 of 70
1997	1.6389	6 of 70
1989	1.6368	5 of 70
2001	1.6016	6 of 70
1985	1.5978	5 of 70
1993	1.5806	7 of 70
1972	1.5763	9 of 70

TENNESSEE VOLUNTERS

Year	W-L-T	AP Poll	Conference Standing	Toughest Regular Season Opponents	Coach (Record at School)	Bowl Games		
1953	6-4-1		7	Duke 7-2-1, Alabama 6-2-3, Kentucky 7-2-1	Harvey Robinson			
1954	4-6		11t	Duke 7-2-1, Georgia Tech 7-3, Kentucky 7-3	Harvey Robinson (10-10-1)			
1955	6-3-1		4	Duke 7-2-1, Georgia Tech 8-1-1, Kentucky 6-3-1, Vanderbilt 7-3	Bowden Wyatt			
1956	10-1	2	1	Auburn 7-3, Georgia Tech 9-1, Mississippi 7-3	Bowden Wyatt	Sugar	7 Baylor	13
1957	8-3	13	5	Auburn 10-0, Mississippi State 6-2-1, Mississippi 8-1-1	Bowden Wyatt	Gator	3 Texas A&M	0
1958	4-6		5	Auburn 9-0-1, Florida State 7-3, Mississippi 8-2	Bowden Wyatt			
1959	5-3-1		8	Auburn 7-3, Alabama 7-1-2, LSU 9-1, Mississippi 9-1	Bowden Wyatt			
1960	6-2-2		5t	Auburn 8-2, Alabama 8-1, Mississippi 9-0-1	Bowden Wyatt			
1961	6-4		4t	Alabama 10-0, Georgia tech 7-3, Mississippi 9-1	Bowden Wyatt			
1962	4-6		10	Auburn 6-3-1, Georgia Tech 7-2-1, Alabama 9-1, Mississippi 9-0	Bowden Wyatt (49-29-4)			
1963	5-5		8	Auburn 9-1, Alabama 8-2, Mississippi 7-0-2	Jim McDonald (5-5)			
1964	4-5-1		10	Auburn 6-4, Alabama 10-0, LSU 7-2-1, Georgia Tech 7-3	Doug Dickey			
1965	8-1-2	7	3t	Alabama 8-1-1, Georgia Tech 6-3-1, UCLA 7-2-1	Doug Dickey	Bluebonnet	27 Tulsa	6
1966	8-3	11+	5	Georgia Tech 9-1, Alabama 10-0, Army 8-2, Mississippi 8-2	Doug Dickey	Gator	18 Syracuse	12
1967	9-2	2	1	UCLA 7-2-1, Alabama 8-1-1, LSU 6-3-1, Mississippi 6-3-1	Doug Dickey	Orange	24 Oklahoma	26
1968	8-2-1	13	2	Georgia 8-0-2, Alabama 8-2, Mississippi 6-3-1	Doug Dickey	Cotton	13 Texas	36
1969	9-2	15	1	Auburn 8-2, Alabama 6-4, Southern Calif. 9-0-1, Mississippi 7-3	Doug Dickey (46-15-4)			
1970	11-1	4	2t	Auburn 8-2, Georgia Tech 8-3, Florida 7-4	Bill Battle	Sugar	34 Air Force	13
1971	10-2	9	4t	Auburn 9-1, Alabama 11-0, Penn State 10-1	Bill Battle	Liberty	14 Arkansas	13
1972	10-2	8	4	Penn State 10-1, Auburn 9-1, Alabama 10-1, Georgia 7-4	Bill Battle	Bluebonnet	24 LSU	17
1973	8-4	19	4	Kansas 7-3-1, Alabama 11-0, Georgia 6-4-1	Bill Battle	Gator	19 Texas Tech	28
1974	7-3-2	20	7	UCLA 6-3-2, Auburn 9-2, Alabama 11-0, Vanderbilt 7-3-1	Bill Battle	Liberty	7 Maryland	3
1975	7-5		5	Maryland 8-2-1, UCLA 8-2-1, Alabama 10-1, Vanderbilt 7-4	Bill Battle			
1976	6-5		7t	Alabama 8-3, Florida 8-3, Kentucky 7-4	Bill Battle (59-22-2)			
1977	4-7		9	California 7-4, Alabama 10-1, Florida 6-4-1, Kentucky 10-1	Johnny Majors			
1978	5-5-1		4t	UCLA 8-3, Alabama 10-1, Notre Dame 8-3	Johnny Majors			
1979	7-5		5t	Auburn 8-3, Alabama 11-0, Rutgers 8-3, Notre Dame 7-4	Johnny Majors	Bluebonnet	22 Purdue	27
1980	5-6		6	Georgia 1-0, Southern Calif. 8-2-1, Alabama 9-2, Pittsburgh 10-1	Johnny Majors			
1981	8-4		4t	Georgia 10-1, Southern Calif. 9-2, Alabama 9-1-1	Johnny Majors	Garden State	28 Wisconsin	21
1982	6-5-1		5	Auburn 8-3, LSU 8-2-1, Alabama 7-4, Vanderbilt 8-3	Johnny Majors	Peach	22 Iowa	28
1983	9-3		3t	Pittsburgh 8-2-1, Auburn 10-1, Alabama 7-4	Johnny Majors	Citrus	30 Maryland	23
1984	7-4-1		5t	Army 7-3-1, Auburn 8-4, Florida 9-1-1, Kentucky 8-3	Johnny Majors	Sun	27 Maryland	28
1985	9-1-2	4	1	UCLA 8-2-1, Auburn 8-3, Florida 9-1-1, Alabama 8-2-1, Ga. Tech 8-2-1	Johnny Majors	Sugar	35 Miami	7
1986	7-5		6	Auburn 9-2, Alabama 9-3, Mississippi 7—3-1	Johnny Majors	Liberty	21 Minnesota	14
1987	10-2-1	14	3	Iowa 9-3, Auburn 9-1-1, Alabama 7-4	Johnny Majors	Peach	27 Indiana	22
1988	5-6		6t	Georgia 8-3, LSU 8-3, Auburn 10-1, Wash. State 8-3, Alabama 8-3	Johnny Majors			
1989	11-1	5	1t	Duke 8-3, Auburn 9-2, Alabama 10-1, Mississippi 7-4	Johnny Majors	Cotton	31 Arkansas	27
1990	9-2-2	8	1	Colorado 10-1-1, Florida 9-2, Notre Dame 9-2, Mississippi 9-2	Johnny Majors	Sugar	23 Virginia	22
1991	9-3	14	3	UCLA 8-3, Florida 10-1, Alabama 10-1, Nótre Dame 9-3	Johnny Majors	Fiesta	17 Penn State	42
1992	9-3	12	E3	Georgia 9-2, Florida 8-4, Alabama 12-0	Johnny Majors [5-3], (116-62-8), Phillip Fulmer [4-0]	Hall Fame	38 Boston College	23
1993	9-2-1	12	E2	Florida 9-2, Alabama 8-2-1, Louisville 8-3	Phillip Fulmer	Citrus	13 Penn State	31
1994	8-4	22	E2	Florida 9-1-1, Mississippi State 8-3, Alabama 11-0	Phillip Fulmer	Gator	45 Virginia Tech	23
1995	11-1	3	E2	Florida 11-0, Arkansas 7-4, Alabama 8-3	Phillip Fulmer	Citrus	20 Ohio State	14
1996	10-2	9	E2	Florida 11-1, Alabama 9-3	Phillip Fulmer	Citrus	48 Northwestern	28
1997	11-2	7	E1	UCLA 9-2, Florida 9-2, Georgia 9-2	Phillip Fulmer	Orange	17 Nebraska	42
1998	13-0	1	E1	Syracuse 8-3, Florida 9-2, Georgia 8-3	Phillip Fulmer	Fiesta	23 Florida State	16
1999	9-3	9	E2	Florida 9-2, Georgia 7-4, Alabama 9-2, Arkansas 7-4	Phillip Fulmer	Fiesta	21 Nebraska	31
2000	8-4	25	E2t	Florida 9-2, LSU 7-4, Georgia 7-4, South Carolina 7-4	Phillip Fulmer	Cotton	21 Kansas State	35
2001	11-2	4	E1	Syracuse 9-3, Florida 9-2, LSU 8-3, Georgia 8-3, So. Carolina 8-3	Phillip Fulmer	Citrus	45 Michigan	17
2002	8-5		E3	Arkansas 9-3, Georgia 11-1, Alabama 10-3, Miami 10-1	Phillip Fulmer	Peach	3 Maryland	30
2003	10-3	15	E1t	Florida 8-4, Georgia 10-2, Miami 10-2	Phillip Fulmer	Peach	14 Clemson	27
2004	10-3	13	E1	Auburn 11-0, Georgia 9-2	Phillip Fulmer	Cotton	38 Texas A&M	7
2005	5-6		E4t	Florida 8-3, Georgia 10-2, Alabama 9-2, No. Dame 9-2	Phillip Fulmer			
2006	9-4	25	E2	California 9-3, Florida 11-1, LSU 10-2, Arkansas 10-2	Phillip Fulmer	Outback	10 Penn State	20
2007	10-4	12	E1t	California 6-6, Florida 9-3, Georgia 10-2	Phillip Fulmer	Outback	21 Wisconsin	17
2008	5-7		E5	Florida 11-1, Georgia 9-3, Alabama 12-0	Phillip Fulmer (151-52-1)			
2009	7-6		E2t	Florida 12-1, Auburn 7-5, Alabama 13-0, Mississippi 8-4	Lane Kiffin (7-6)	Chick-fil-A	14 Virginia Tech	37
2010	6-7		E3t	Oregon 12-0, LSU 10-2, Alabama 9-3, South Carolina 9-4	Derek Dooley (6-7)	Music City	27 North Carolina	30

| **TOTAL:** | | | 449-208-20 .6780 (11 of 70) | | **Bowl Games since 1953:** | 22-18 .5500 (25 of 70) | | |

GREATEST TEAM SINCE 1953: With apologies to the 1998 national championship team, the 1956 Tennessee edition gets the nod here. Undefeated, the Volunteers of 1956 escaped the classic 6-0 match-up with undefeated Georgia Tech, but somehow spit the bit against a good but far from great Baylor team in the Sugar Bowl. Led by Bill Anderson, Tommy Bronson, Buddy Cruze, Bobby Gordon, John Gordy, Johnny Majors, and Roger Urbano, the Vols were perhaps the last of the great teams that ran the precise, powerful Single Wing offense.

1953 6-4-1

0 Mississippi St.	26 E Mack Franklin / Dan Sekanovich
7 Duke	21 T Bob Fisher / Tom Hensley
40 Chattanooga	7 G Frank McCroskey / Bill Hubbard
0 Alabama	0 C Bob Cloninger / Lamar Leachman
59 Louisville	6 G John Powell
20 No. Carolina	6 T Darris McCord
32 LSU	14 E Roger Rotroff / Bill Spoone
9 Florida	7 BB Hal Hubbard / Bill Barbish
21 Kentucky	27 TB Jimmy Wade / Dave Griffith
33 Vanderbilt	6 WB Jerry Hyde / Hugh Garner
19 Houston	33 FB Ted Schwanger / Tom Tracy

RUSHING: Wade 158/675y, Schwanger 83/477y, Tracy 71/336y
PASSING: Wade 25-63/451y, 5TD, 39.7%
RECEIVING: Hyde 8/173y, Rotroff 8/157y, Sekanovich 7/134y
SCORING: Wade 72pts, Tracy (FB-K) 35pts,
Tom Priest (FB-K) 21pts

1954 4-6

19 Mississippi St.	7 E Edd Cantrell / Buddy Cruze
6 Duke	7 T Charlie Rader / Bob Williams
20 Chattanooga	14 G Charlie Coffey / Bruce Burnham
0 Alabama	27 C Lamar Leachman / Bubba Howe
14 Dayton	7 G Charley Scholes
26 North Carolina	20 T Darris McCord / John Gordy
7 Georgia Tech	28 E Terry Sweeney / Roger Urbano
0 Florida	14 BB Jimmy Beutel
13 Kentucky	14 TB Jimmy Wade / Johnny Majors
0 Vanderbilt	26 WB Hugh Garner / Bobby Brengle
	FB Tom Tracy / Pat Oleksiak (TB)

RUSHING: Tracy 116/794y, Majors 95/416y, Oleksiak 81/300y
PASSING: Majors 8-24/107y, 0TD, 33.3%,
Oleksiak 7-31/79y, 3TD, 22.6%
RECEIVING: Garner 5/57y, Sweeney 4/54y, Tracy 3/9y
SCORING: Tracy (FB-K) 31pts, Major 18pts, Brengle & Wade 12pts

1955 6-3-1

7 Mississippi St.	13 E Buddy Cruze / Edd Cantrell
0 Duke	21 T Charlie Rader / Jim Smelcher
13 Chattanooga	0 G Bruce Burnham
20 Alabama	0 C Bubba Howe / Lamar Leachman
53 Dayton	7 G Charlie Coffey / Bill Johnson
48 North Carolina	7 T John Gordy
7 Georgia Tech	7 E Roger Urbano
20 Florida	0 BB Jimmy Beutel
0 Kentucky	23 TB Johnny Majors / Bobby Gordon
20 Vanderbilt	14 WB Bob Hibbard / Bill Anderson
	FB Tommy Bronson / Tom Priest

RUSHING: Majors 183/657y, Bronson 100/429y, Gordon 47/254y
PASSING: Majors 36-65/476y, 5TD, 55.4%
RECEIVING: Cruze 12/232y, Urbano 10/121y, Beutel 7/66y
SCORING: Majors 36pts, Bronson 24pts, Cruze 24pts

1956 10-1

35 Auburn	7 E Buddy Cruze / Edd Cantrell
33 Duke	20 T Charlie Rader
42 Chattanooga	20 G Bruce Burnham
24 Alabama	0 C Bubba Howe
34 Maryland	7 G Charlie Coffey / Bill Johnson
20 North Carolina	0 T John Gordy
6 Georgia Tech	0 E Roger Urbano
27 Mississippi	7 BB Jimmy Beutel / Stockton Adkins
20 Kentucky	7 TB Johnny Majors / Bobby Gordon
27 Vanderbilt	7 WB Bill Anderson / Bob Hibbard
7 Baylor■	13 FB Tommy Bronson / Carl Smith

RUSHING: Bronson 105/562y, Majors 108/549y, Smith 67/341y
PASSING: Majors 36-59/552y, 5TD, 61.0%
RECEIVING: Cruze 20/357y, Anderson 10/216y, Urbano 10/103y
SCORING: Bronson 48pts, Carter 42pts, Majors 42pts

1957 8-3

0 Auburn	7 E Landon Darty
14 Mississippi St.	9 T Jim Smelcher / Bo Shafer
28 Chattanooga	13 G Lon Herzbrun / Bobby Urbano
14 Alabama	0 C Dave Stottlemyer
16 Maryland	0 G Bill Johnson
35 North Carolina	0 T Frank Kolinsky / Joe Schaffer
21 Georgia Tech	6 E Tommy Potts / Murray Armstrong
7 Mississippi	14 BB Stockton Adkins
6 Kentucky	20 TB Bobby Gordon / Al Carter
20 Vanderbilt	6 WB Bill Anderson
3 Texas A&M■	0 FB Tommy Bronson / Carl Smith

RUSHING: Gordon 167/526y, Bronson 103/395y, Smith 65/304y
PASSING: Gordon 20-40/260y, 2TD, 50.0%
RECEIVING: Potts 10/123y, Anderson 6/102y
SCORING: Gordon 54pts, Smith 24pts, Bronson 18pts

1958 4-6

0 Auburn	13 E Mike LaSorsa / Murray Armstrong
13 Mississippi St.	8 T Bo Shafer / Labron Shields
7 Georgia Tech	21 G Bobby Urbano
14 Alabama	7 C Ray Brann
0 Florida State	10 G Coy Franklin / Wayne Grubb
7 North Carolina	21 T Joe Schaffer
6 Chattanooga	14 E Tommy Potts / Cotton Letner
18 Mississippi	16 BB Jim Cartwright
2 Kentucky	6 TB Billy Majors / Gene Etter
10 Vanderbilt	6 WB Don Stephens / Bobby Sandlin
	FB Carl Smith / Neyle Sollee

RUSHING: Majors 148/294y, Smith 94/255y, Etter 66/189y
PASSING: Majors 17-25/215y, 2TD, 68.0%,
Etter 14-31/166y, 1TD, 45.2%
RECEIVING: Armstrong 14/195y, Stephens 10/91y, LaSorsa 5/54y
SCORING: Majors, Smith, & Armstrong 12pts

1959 5-4-1

3 Auburn	0 E Mike LaSorsa
22 Mississippi St.	6 T Lebron Shields
7 Georgia Tech	14 G Joe Lukowski
7 Alabama	7 C Ray Moss
23 Chattanooga	0 G Wayne Grubb
29 North Carolina	7 T Joe Schaffer
14 LSU	13 E Cotton Letner / Marvin Phillips
0 Mississippi	37 BB Jim Cartwright
0 Kentucky	20 TB Billy Majors/Glenn Glass/Gene Etter
0 Vanderbilt	14 WB Ken Waddell / Don Leake
	FB Bunny Orr / Neyle Sollee

RUSHING: Glass 75/261y, Majors 105/232y, Orr 55/198y
PASSING: Etter 22-36/298y, 3TD, 61.1%,
Majors 14-27/122y, 51.9%
RECEIVING: Letner 8/92y, Leake 7/129y, LaSorsa 7/78y
SCORING: Etter (TB-K) 27pts, Glass 24pts,
Cartwright & Phillips 12pts

1960 6-2-2

10 Auburn	3 E Mike LaSorsa
0 Mississippi St.	0 T Cliff Marquart / Ken Frost
62 Tampa	7 G Paul Inglett
20 Alabama	7 C Mike Lucci / L.T. Helton
35 Chattanooga	0 G Wayne Grubb / Don Patterson
27 North Carolina	14 T Don Cissell / Tom Williams
7 Georgia Tech	14 E Cotton Letner
3 Mississippi	24 BB Jim Cartwright / Wayne Coleman
10 Kentucky	10 TB Billy Majors/Glenn Glass/Geo. Canale
35 Vanderbilt	0 WB Ken Waddell / Charles Wyrick
	FB Bunny Orr / J.W. Carter

RUSHING: Glass 90/478y, Orr 61/267y, Canale 47/225y
PASSING: Glass 11-26/167y, 2TD, 42.3%,
Etter 10-17/78y, 0TD, 58.8%
RECEIVING: Waddell 8/60y, Leake 7/92y, LaSorsa 4/30y
SCORING: Glass 48pts, Letner (E-K) 33pts, Wyrick 24pts

1961 6-4

21 Auburn	24 E Mike Stratton
17 Mississippi St.	3 T Cliff Marquart / Kenny Brown
52 Tulsa	6 G Joe Foxall / Paul Inglett
3 Alabama	34 C Mike Lucci / L.T. Helton
20 Chattanooga	7 G Larry Richards / Bob Dalton
21 North Carolina	22 T Paul Tilson / Tom Williams
10 Georgia Tech	6 E Buddy Fisher / Pat Augustine
10 Mississippi	24 BB Wayne Coleman
26 Kentucky	16 TB Glenn Glass / Mallon Faircloth
41 Vanderbilt	7 WB Charles Wyrick / Hubert McClain
	FB Bunny Orr / J.W. Carter

RUSHING: Faircloth 123/475y, Orr 67/332y, Glass 59/261y
PASSING: Faircloth 31-52/460y, 8TD, 59.6%
RECEIVING: McClain 11/149y, Stratton 9/142y, Wyrick 7/87y
SCORING: Faircloth 36pts, Gary Cannon (K) 33pts,

1962 4-6

21 Auburn	22 E Whit Canale / John Hudson
6 Mississippi St.	7 T Kenny Brown / Paul Tilson
0 Georgia Tech	17 G Ned Sullivan / Joe Foxall
7 Alabama	27 C L.T. Helton
48 Chattanooga	14 G Bob Dalton / Larry Richards
23 Wake Forest	0 T Tom Williams
28 Tulane	16 E Pat Augustine / Al Tanara
6 Mississippi	19 BB Wayne Coleman
10 Kentucky	12 TB Mallon Faircloth / George Canale
30 Vanderbilt	0 WB John Paty / Wayne Waff
	FB Jimmy Sullivan / Pat Canini

RUSHING: G. Canale 79/455y, Faircloth 140/376y
PASSING: Bobby Morton (TB) 20-40/305y, 3TD, 50.0%,
Faircloth 15-49/261y, 2TD, 30.6%
RECEIVING: Hudson 15/259y, Waff 8/121y, Tanara 6/77y
SCORING: George Shuford (K) 25pts, G. Canale 24pts

1963 5-5

34 Richmond	6 E Bob Frazier / Al Tanara
19 Auburn	23 T Bob Zvolerin / Jim Lowe
0 Mississippi St.	7 G Ned Sullivan / Bob Dalton
7 Georgia Tech	23 C Frank Emanuel /Norbert Ackerman, Jr.
0 Alabama	35 G Steve DeLong
49 Chattanooga	7 T Dick Evey / Tom Johnson
26 Tulane	0 E Buddy Fisher / Glenn Gray
0 Mississippi	20 QB Mallon Faircloth / Hal Wantland
19 Kentucky	0 BB Ken Honea
14 Vanderbilt	0 WB Bob Petrella / Billy Tomlinson
	FB Stan Mitchell / Pat Canini

RUSHING: Faircloth 137/652y,Mitchell 103/477y, Canini 53/274y
PASSING: Faircloth 137/509y, 3TD, 41.3%
RECEIVING: Fisher 12/242y, Petrella 12/130y, Gray 8/120y
SCORING: Wantland, Faircloth, & Mitchell 24pts

1964 4-5-1

10 Chattanooga	6 E Johnny Mills / Whit Canale
0 Auburn	3 T Gerald Woods
14 Mississippi St.	13 G Terry Bird / Bill Danychuk
16 Boston College	14 C Reggie Jellicorse / Frank Emanuel (LB)
8 Alabama	19 G Steve DeLong
3 LSU	3 T Bill Cameron / Carl Ellis (DL)
22 Georgia Tech	14 E Paul Naumoff / Al Tanara
0 Mississippi	30 QB Art Galiffa / David Leake
7 Kentucky	12 HB Hal Wantland / Harold Stancell (DB)
0 Vanderbilt	7 WB Jackie Cotton / Bobby Petrella (DB)
	FB Stan Mitchell (WB) / Jack Patterson

RUSHING: Mitchell 94/325y, Wantland 102/222y,
Patterson 65/203y
PASSING: Galiffa 29-59/338y, TD, 49.2%,
RECEIVING: Wantland 21/284y, Mitchell 9/89y, Mills 5/67y
SCORING: Wantland 32pts, Fred Martin (K) 18pts

1965 8-1-2

21 Army	0 E Austin Denney
13 Auburn	13 T John Boyton / Terry Bird
24 South Carolina	3 G Gerald Woods
7 Alabama	7 C Reggie Jellicorse
17 Houston	8 G Bobby Gratz
21 Georgia Tech	7 T Jim Lowe
13 Mississippi	14 E Johnny Mills
19 Kentucky	3 QB Charles Fulton / Dewey Warren
21 Vanderbilt	3 TB Walter Chadwick / Billy Tomlinson
37 UCLA	34 WB Hal Wantland
27 Tulsa■	6 FB Stan Mitchell
	DL Paul Naumoff / Mack Gentry
	DL Bobby Morel / Bobby Franklin
	DL Bill Cameron
	DL Bobby Frazier / Glenn Gray
	LB Frank Emanuel
	LB Tom Fisher
	LB Doug Archibald
	DB Harold Stancell
	DB Jerry Smith
	DB Bob Petrella

RUSHING: Chadwick 101/470y, Mitchell 106/464y,
Fulton 118/298y
PASSING: Warren 44-79/588y, 3TD, 55.7%,
Fulton 29-59/425y, 4TD, 49.2%
RECEIVING: Mills 23/328y, Wantland 21/305y, Denney 14/206y
SCORING: David Leake (K) 39pts, Chadwick & Mitchell 30pts

1966 8-3

28 Auburn	0 E Austin Denney
23 Rice	3 T John Boynton
3 Georgia Tech	6 G Charles Rosenfelder / Joe Graham
10 Alabama	11 C Bob Johnson
29 So. Carolina	17 G Robbie Franklin / Elliott Gammage
38 Army	7 T Terry Bird
28 Chattanooga	10 E Johnny Mills
7 Mississippi	14 QB Dewey Warren
28 Kentucky	19 TB Charles Fulton (WB)/Walter Chadwick
28 Vanderbilt	0 WB Richmond Flowers / Bill Baker
18 Syracuse■	12 FB Richard Pickens / Bob Mauriello
	DL Neal McMeans / Jim McDonald
	DL Mack Gentry
	DL Bobby Morel
	DL Derrick Weatherford / Dick Williams
	DL Nick Showalter
	LB Paul Naumoff / Rick Marino
	LB Doug Archibald
	LB Jimmy Glover / Jim Bates
	DB Harold Stancell
	DB Jerry Smith / Albert Dorsey
	DB Bill Young / Skip Edwards

RUSHING: Fulton 109/463y, Pickens 62/321y, Mauriello 42/192y
PASSING: Warren 136-229/1716y, 18TD, 59.0%
RECEIVING: Mills 48/725y, Flowers 35/407y, Denney 21/264y
SCORING: Denney 42pts, Gary Wright (K) 40pts,
    Flowers & Warren 30pts

1967 9-2

16 UCLA	20 WR Terry Dalton / Gary Kreis
27 Auburn	13 T Elliott Gammage
24 Georgia Tech	13 G Joe Graham / Jerry Holloway
24 Alabama	13 C Bob Johnson
17 LSU	14 G Charles Rosenfelder
38 Tampa	0 T John Boynton
35 Tulane	14 TE Ken DeLong
20 Mississippi	7 QB Dewey Warren / Bubba Wyche
17 Kentucky	7 TB Walter Chadwick /Charles Fulton (QB)
41 Vanderbilt	14 WB Richmond Flowers / Bill Baker
24 Oklahoma■	26 FB Richard Pickens
	DL Neal McMeans / Steve Carroll
	DL Dick Williams
	DL Jimmy Hahn / Rick Marino
	DL Derrick Weatherford
	DL Jim McDonald
	LB Jack Reynolds / Nick Showalter
	LB Steve Kiner
	LB Jimmy Glover
	DB Jim Weatherford
	DB Albert Dorsey
	DB David Murphy / Mike Jones

RUSHING:Chadwick 144/645y,Pickens 111/587y,Fulton 69/328y
PASSING: Warren 78-132/1053y, 6TD, 59.1%
RECEIVING: Flowers 41/585y, DeLong 20/216y, Dalton 15/173y
SCORING: Chadwick 66pts, Karl Kremser (K) 60pts,
    Flowers 24pts

1968 8-2-1

17 Georgia	17 WR Gary Kreis / Mike Price
24 Memphis State	17 T Clifton Stewart
52 Rice	0 G Don Denbo / David Browne
24 Georgia Tech	7 C Chip Kell
10 Alabama	9 G Charles Rosenfelder
42 UCLA	18 T Jerry Holloway
14 Auburn	28 TE Ken DeLong / Terry Dalton
31 Mississippi	0 QB Bubba Wyche / Bobby Scott
24 Kentucky	7 TB Richmond Flowers / Lanny Pearce
10 Vanderbilt	7 WB Bill Baker / Lester McClain
13 Texas■	36 FB Richard Pickens
	DL Neal McMeans / Ronnie Drummonds
	DL Dick Williams / Steve Carroll
	DL James Woody
	DL Frank Yanossy
	DL Jim McDonald / Vic Dingus
	LB Jack Reynolds
	LB Steve Kiner
	LB Nick Showalter / Wayne Smith
	DB Jim Weatherford / Tom Callaway
	DB Tim Priest / Mike Jones
	DB Bill Young

RUSHING: Pickens 133/736y, Flowers 111/375y,
    Pearce 35/170y
PASSING: Wyche 134-237/1539y, 14TD, 56.1%
RECEIVING: DeLong 34/393y, McClain 29/329y, Kreis 25/334y,
    Flowers 25/180y
SCORING: Karl Kremser (K) 46pts, Flowers 42pts,
    McClain 36pts

1969 9-2

31 Tenn-Chatt'ga	0 WR Gary Kreis
45 Auburn	19 T Steve Robinson
55 Memphis St.	16 G Don Denbo
26 Georgia Tech	8 C Mike Bevans
41 Alabama	14 G Chip Kell
17 Georgia	3 T Joe Balthrop
29 So. Carolina	14 TE Ken DeLong / Gary Theiler
0 Mississippi	38 QB Bobby Scott
31 Kentucky	26 TB Don McLeary / Bobby Patterson
40 Vanderbilt	27 WB Lester McClain / Bobby Majors
13 Florida■	14 FB Curt Watson
	DL James Woody / Ronnie Drummonds
	DL Steve Carroll
	DL Frank Yanossy
	DL Vic Dingus / Tom Bennett
	LB Steve Kiner
	LB Jack Reynolds / Ray Nettles
	LB Jackie Walker
	LB Benny Dalton
	DB Tim Priest / Don Carpenter
	DB Mike Jones / Tom Callaway
	DB Bill Young / Wayne Spain

RUSHING: Watson 146/807y, McCleary 121/493y,
    Patterson 47/171y
PASSING: Scott 92-191/1352y, 14TD, 48.2%
RECEIVING: Kreis 38/609y, DeLong 22/235y, McClain 17/333y
SCORING: George Hunt (K) 65pts, Scott & Watson 36pts

1970 11-1

28 Southern Miss	3 WR Joe Thompson
23 Auburn	36 T Steve Robinson
48 Army	3 G Don Denbo / Phillip Fulmer
17 Georgia Tech	6 C Mike Bevans
24 Alabama	0 G Chip Kell
38 Florida	7 T Joe Balthrop
41 Wake Forest	7 TE Gary Theiler
20 South Carolina	18 QB Bobby Scott
45 Vanderbilt	0 TB Don McLeary
24 Vanderbilt	6 WB Lester McClain / Stan Trott
28 UCLA	17 FB Curt Watson / Steve Wold
34 Air Force■	13 DL Manley Mixon / Tom Bennett
	DL Bill Emendorfer
	DL Frank Howell / John Wagster
	DL Ronnie Drummonds
	LB Jackie Walker
	LB Ray Nettles
	LB Jamie Rotella / James Woody
	DB Conrad Graham
	DB David Allen / Phil Pierce
	DB Tim Priest
	DB Bobby Majors

RUSHING: Watson 190/791y, Wold 84/435y, McLeary 103/353y
PASSING: Scott 118-252/1697, 14TD, 46.9%
RECEIVING: Thompson 37/502y, McClain 24/341y,
    Theiler 22/237y
SCORING: George Hunt (K) 72pts, Watson 48pts, McLeary 36pts

1971 10-2

48 Cal-S. Barbara	6 WR Joe Thompson / Sonny Leach
9 Auburn	10 T Gaylon Hill
20 Florida	13 G Phillip Fulmer
10 Georgia Tech	6 C Tom Johnson
15 Alabama	32 G Bill Emendorfer
10 Mississippi St.	7 T Joe Balthrop
38 Tulsa	3 TE Gary Theiler
35 South Carolina	6 QB Jim Maxwell / Chip Howard
21 Kentucky	7 TB Curt Watson
19 Vanderbilt	7 WB Stan Trott / George Silvey
31 Penn State	11 FB Bill Rudder / Steve Chancey
14 Arkansas■	13 DL Ken Lambert / Tom Bennett
	DL John Wagster
	DL Frank Howell
	DL Carl Johnson
	LB Jackie Walker
	LB Ray Nettles
	LB Jamie Rotella
	DB Conrad Graham
	DB David Allen
	DB Eddie Brown / Tim Townes
	DB Bobby Majors

RUSHING: Watson 193/766y, Rudder 78/414y,
    Chancey 89/388y
PASSING: Maxwell 46-102/544y, TD, 45.0%
RECEIVING: Thompson 15/247y, Theiler 12/191y,
    Chancey 10/55y
SCORING: George Hunt (K) 66pts, Watson 54pts,
    Chancey 18pts

1972 10-2

34 Georgia Tech	3 WR Emmon Love / Jimmy Young
28 Penn State	21 T Gene Killion
45 Wake Forest	6 G Gaylon Hill
6 Auburn	10 C Steve Urubek / Tom Johnson
38 Memphis State	7 G Bill Emendorfer
10 Alabama	17 T David Shaffer
34 Hawaii	2 TE Sonny Leach
14 Georgia	0 QB Condredge Holloway
17 Mississippi	0 TB Haskel Stanback / Paul Careathers
17 Kentucky	7 WB Chip Howard
30 Vanderbilt	10 FB Steve Chancey / Bill Rudder
24 LSU■	17 DL Ken Lambert
	DL Robert Pulliam
	DL John Wagster
	DL Carl Johnson
	LB Jamie Rotella
	LB Art Reynolds
	LB Eddie Wilson
	DB Conrad Graham
	DB David Allen
	DB Tim Townes
	DB Eddie Brown

RUSHING: Stanback 183/890y, Rudder 88/420y,
    Holloway 123/266y
PASSING: Holloway 73-120/807y, 3TD, 60.8%
RECEIVING: Love 20/280y, Young 19/270y, Leach 13/182y
SCORING: Stanback 78pts, Ricky Townsend (K) 67pts,
    3 with 18pts

1973 8-4

21 Duke	17 WR Emmon Love / Stanley Morgan
37 Army	18 T Gene Killian / Steve Cone
21 Auburn	0 G Mike Caldwell / Mickey Marvin
28 Kansas	27 C Steve Urubek
20 Georgia Tech	14 G Mike Rotella / Phil Clabo
21 Alabama	42 T David Shaffer
39 TCU	7 TE Mitchell Gravitt / Tommy West
31 Georgia	35 QB Condredge Holloway
18 Mississippi	28 TB Haskel Stanback
16 Kentucky	14 WB Chip Howard / Tim Fitchpatrick
20 Vanderbilt	17 FB Bill Rudder
19 Texas Tech■	28 DL Sammy Hair / Ronnie McCartney
	DL Robert Pulliam
	DL David Poley / Joe Gallagher
	DL David Campbell
	LB Eddie Wilson / Bill Bandemier
	LB Art Reynolds
	LB Steve Poole / Hank Walter
	DB Nick Carmichael
	DB Jon Murdic / Russ Rabenstein
	DB Jim Watts
	DB Eddie Brown

RUSHING: Stanback 165/682y, Holloway 128/433y,
    Rudder 75/426y
PASSING: Holloway 89-154/1149y, 10TD, 57.8%
RECEIVING: Morgan 22/511y, Love 20/256y, Yarbrough 16/185y
SCORING: Ricky Townsend (K) 60pts, Stanback 42pts,
    Holloway 28pts

1974 7-3-2

17 UCLA	17 WR Larry Seivers / John Yarbrough
17 Kansas	3 T Larry Satterfield / Dave Brady
0 Auburn	21 G Steve Cone
17 Tulsa	10 C Paul Johnson
10 LSU	20 G Mickey Marvin
6 Alabama	28 T Phil Clabo / Roger Higginbotham
29 Clemson	28 TE Tommy West
34 Memphis State	6 QB Condredge Holloway
29 Mississippi	17 TB Stanley Morgan (WB) / Mike Gayles
24 Kentucky	7 WB Tim Fitchpatrick
21 Vanderbilt	21 FB Paul Careathers / Dale Fair
7 Maryland■	3 DL Ron McCartney
	DL Robert Pulliam
	DL David Page
	DL Kevin Davis / David Poley
	LB Hank Walter
	LB Steve Poole
	LB Andy Spiva
	DB Jim Watts
	DB Jon Murdic
	DB Ernie Ward
	DB Mike Mauck

RUSHING: Morgan 1128/723y, Gayles 120/472y,
    Careathers 72/296y
PASSING: Holloway 76-133/1146y, 5TD, 57.1%
RECEIVING: Seivers 25/347y, Yarbrough 19/247y,
    West 14/248y
SCORING: Morgan 84pts, Ricky Townsend (K) 44pts,
    Gayles 24pts

1975 7-5

26 Maryland	8 WR Larry Seivers / John Yarbrough
28 UCLA	34 T Brent Watson
21 Auburn	17 G Joe Gallagher
24 LSU	10 C Paul Johnson
7 Alabama	30 G Mickey Marvin
14 N. Texas St.	21 T Dave Brady
28 Colorado State	7 TE Tommy West
40 Utah	7 QB Randy Wallace / Gary Roach
6 Mississippi	23 TB Stanley Morgan / Mike Gayles
17 Kentucky	13 WB Tim Fitchpatrick
14 Vanderbilt	17 FB Terry Moore
28 Hawaii	6 DL Ron McCartney
	DL Jim Woofter
	DL David Page
	DL Kevin Davis
	LB Russ Williams
	LB Steve Poole
	LB Andy Spiva
	DB Russ Rabenstein / Thomas Rowsey
	DB David Parsons / Bill Cole
	DB Ernie Ward
	DB Mike Mauck

RUSHING: Morgan 133/809y, Gayles 137/559y, Moore 48/211y
PASSING: Wallace 72-145/1318y, 8TD, 49.7%
RECEIVING: Seivers 41/840y, Yarbrough 21/344y, West 16/233y
SCORING: Morgan 60pts, Gayles 46pts, Jim Gaylor (K) 39pts

1976 6-5

18 Duke	21 WR Larry Seivers
31 TCU	0 T Brent Watson
28 Auburn	38 G Joe Gallagher
21 Clemson	19 C Robert Shaw / Steve Porter
42 Georgia Tech	7 G Mickey Marvin
13 Alabama	20 T Dave Brady / Scott Farrar
18 Florida	20 TE John Murphy / John Duvall
21 Memphis State	14 QB Randy Wallace
32 Mississippi	6 TB Frank Foxx / Kelsey Finch
0 Kentucky	7 WB Stanley Morgan (TB) / Billy Arbo
13 Vanderbilt	10 FB Mike Gayles / Bobby Emmons
	DL Charles Anderson
	DL Jim Woofter
	DL Danny Jenkins
	DL Kevin Davis / Dennis Wolfe
	LB Andy Spiva
	LB Greg Jones
	LB Craig Puki
	DB David Parsons / Jeff Moore
	DB Thomas Rowsey
	DB Russ Williams
	DB Roland James / Mike Mauck

RUSHING: Morgan 90/388y, Foxx 73/371y, Gayles 60/331y
PASSING: Wallace 68-130/1046y, 4TD, 52.4%
RECEIVING: Seivers 51/737y, Morgan 14/317y, Arbo 5/74
SCORING: Morgan 68pts, Jim Gaylor (K) 43pts, 3 with 24pts

1977 4-7

17 California	27 WR Jeff Moore
24 Boston College	18 T Ralph Bullard
12 Auburn	14 G Scott Farrar
41 Oregon State	10 C Robert Shaw
8 Georgia Tech	24 G Jay Williams / Bill Marren
10 Alabama	24 T Brent Watson
17 Florida	27 TE Reggie Harper / Kyle Aguillard
27 Memphis State	14 QB Jimmy Streater / Pat Ryan
14 Mississippi	43 TB Kelsey Finch
17 Kentucky	21 WB Billy Arbo
42 Vanderbilt	7 FB Nate Sumpter / Jesse Briggs
	DL Jesse Turnbow / Glenn Tucker
	DL Jim Noonan / Johnny Chavis
	DL Danny Jenkins
	DL David Barron
	LB Lyonel Stewart / Chris Bolton
	LB Greg Jones
	LB Greg Davis / Kim Logan
	DB Roland James
	DB Thomas Rowsey / Johnny Watts
	DB Russ Williams / Chip Linebarier
	DB Val Barksdale / Clark Duncan

RUSHING: Finch 154/770y, Streater 136/397y, Sumpter 55/319y
PASSING: Streater 59-105/742y, 4TD, 56.2%
RECEIVING: Harper 30/331y, Arbo 20/314y, Moore 18/275y
SCORING: Finch 56pts, Jim Gaylor (K) 51pts, Streater 50pts

1978 5-5-1

0 UCLA	13 WR Jeff Moore
13 Oregon State	13 T Phil Sutton
10 Auburn	29 G Charlton Webb
31 Army	13 C Robert Shaw
17 Alabama	30 G Bill Marren
21 Mississippi St.	34 T Jay Williams
34 Duke	0 TE Reggie Harper
14 Notre Dame	31 QB Jimmy Streater
41 Mississippi	17 TB Kelsey Finch
29 Kentucky	14 WB Billy Arbo
41 Vanderbilt	15 FB Frank Foxx / Hubert Simpson
	DL Steve Davis
	DL Lee North / Lee Otis Burton
	DL Jim Noonan
	DL Brad White / Johnny Chavis
	DL Dennis Wolfe
	LB Chris Bolton / Danny Spradlin
	LB Craig Puki
	DB Roland James
	DB Junior Reid / Wilbert Jones
	DB Greg Gaines
	DB Clark Duncan / Chip Linebarier

RUSHING: Streater 146/593y, Simpson 105/524y, Finch 105/408y
PASSING: Streater 101-198/1418y, 4TD, 51.0%
RECEIVING: Harper 31/356y, Moore 27/502y, Arbo 18/276y
SCORING: Alan Duncan (K) 65pts, Streater 60pts, Foxx & Finch 24pts

1979 7-5

28 Boston College	16 WR Anthony Hancock
51 Utah	18 T Phil Sutton
35 Auburn	17 G Mike Jester
9 Mississippi St.	28 C Lee North
31 Georgia Tech	0 G Bill Marren / Jay Williams
17 Alabama	27 T Tim Irwin
7 Rutgers	13 TE Reggie Harper
40 Notre Dame	18 QB Jimmy Streater / Jeff Olszewski
20 Misssissippi	44 TB James Berry / Glenn Ford
20 Kentucky	17 WB Phil Ingram
31 Vanderbilt	10 FB Hubert Simpson / Terry Daniels
22 Purdue■	27 DL Steve Davis / Mike L. Cofer
	DL Kenny Jones / Lee Otis Burton
	DL Jim Noonan
	DL Brad White
	DL Brian Ingram
	LB Danny Spradlin
	LB Craig Puki / Chris Bolton
	DB Roland James / Wilbert Jones
	DB Danny Martin
	DB Greg Gaines / Val Barksdale
	DB Bill Bates

RUSHING: Simpson 157/792y, Berry 118/516y, Streater 82/377y
PASSING: Streater 6\80-161/1256y, 9TD, 49.7%
RECEIVING: Hancock 34/687y, Harper 24/323y, Ingram 15/225y
SCORING: Alan Duncan (K) 63pts, Simpson 42pts, Streater 42pts

1980 5-6

15 Georgia	16 WR Mike Miller / Willie Gault
17 Southern Cal	20 T Rory Cunningham
35 Washington State	23 G Bill Marren
42 Auburn	0 C Lee North
23 Georgia Tech	10 G Dwight Wilson / Jay Williams (T)
0 Alabama	27 T Tim Irwin / Jani Trupovnieks
6 Pittsburgh	30 TE Reggie Harper / Mike "Go" Cofer
13 Virginia	16 QB Steve Alatorre / Jeff Olszewski
9 Mississippi	20 TB Terry Daniels / Glenn Ford
45 Kentucky	14 WB Anthony Hancock
51 Vanderbilt	13 FB James Berry
	DL Mike "Stop" Cofer / Lamont Jeffers
	DL Chris Wampler / Reggie White
	DL Jim Noonan / Leonard Jackson
	DL Brad White
	DL Mike Casteel
	LB Danny Spradlin
	LB Chris Bolton
	DB Wilbert Jones / Lee Jenkins
	DB Danny Martin
	DB Greg Gaines (LB) / Val Barksdale
	DB Bill Bates

RUSHING: Berry 131/543y, Daniels 100/363y, Ford 61/223y
PASSING: Alatorre 58-119/747y, 5TD, 48.7%, Olszewski 43-75/594y, 4TD, 57.3%
RECEIVING: Hancock 33/580y, Gault 14/240y, Harper 13/131y
SCORING: Alan Duncan (K) 52pts, Berry 50pts, Gault 24pts

1981 8-4

0 Georgia	44 WR Mike Miller
7 Southern Cal	43 T Jani Trupovnieks
42 Colorado State	0 G David James / Steve Knight
10 Auburn	7 C Lee North
19 Alabama	38 G Bill Mayo
28 Memphis State	9 T John Matthews / Curt Singer
24 Wichita State	21 TE "Go" Cofer
28 Mississippi	20 QB Steve Alatorre / Jeff Olszewski
10 Kentucky	21 TB James Berry
38 Vanderbilt	34 WB Willie Gault / Anthony Hancock
28 Wisconsin■	21 FB Alvin Toles / Doug Furnas
	DL Mike Terry
	DL Chris Wampler
	DL Leonard Jackson
	DL Reggie White
	DL Brian Ingram / Ricky Holt
	LB Lemont H. Jeffers / Reggie McKenzie
	LB "Stop" Cofer / Mark Burns
	DB Lee Jenkins
	DB Carlton Peoples
	DB Daryl Harper
	DB Bill Bates

RUSHING: Berry 129/500y, Furnas 81/409y, Toles 47/220y
PASSING: Alatorre 81-154/1171y, 8TD, 52.6%
RECEIVING: Hancock 32/437y, Gault 22/479y, Berry 15/86y
SCORING: Fuad Reveiz (K) 46pts, Hancock 36pts, Berry 36pts

1982 6-5-1

24 Duke	25 WR Willie Gault
23 Iowa State	23 T Curt Singer
14 Auburn	24 G Mike Furnas / David James
10 Washington St.	3 C Glenn Streno
24 LSU	24 G Bill Mayo
35 Alabama	28 T John Matthews
21 Georgia Tech	31 TE Kenny Jones
29 Memphis State	3 QB Alan Cockrell
30 Mississippi	17 TB Chuck Coleman / Johnnie Jones
28 Kentucky	7 WB Darryal Wilson / Mike Miller
21 Vanderbilt	28 FB Doug Furnas / Alvin Toles
22 Iowa■	28 DL Mike Terry
	DL Mike Casteel / Chris Wampler
	DL Steve Kluge
	DL Reggie White
	DL Mike "Stop" Cofer
	LB Reggie McKenzie / Duan Henry
	LB Joe Cofer / Carl Zander
	DB Lee Jenkins / Tommy Sims
	DB Carlton Peoples
	DB Joe Cozart / Doug Parrish
	DB Bill Bates

RUSHING: Coleman 113/600y, J. Jones 93/421y, D. Furnas 55/221y
PASSING: Cockrell 174-294/2021, 12TD, 59.2%
RECEIVING: Gault 50/668y, Miller 24/368y, Wilson 23/308y
SCORING: Fuad Reveiz (K) 101pts, Gault 30pts, Coleman 30pts

1983 9-3

3 Pittsburgh	13 WR Clyde Duncan / Tim McGee
31 New Mexico	6 T Curt Singer
14 Auburn	37 G Mike Furnas
45 Citadel	6 C Glenn Streno
20 Louisiana State	6 G Bill Mayo
41 Alabama	34 T Steve Knight
37 Georgia Tech	3 TE John Matthews/Jeff Smith/John Cook
7 Rutgers	0 QB Alan Cockrell
10 Mississippi	13 TB Johnnie Jones / Sam Henderson
10 Kentucky	0 WB Lenny Taylor
34 Vanderbilt	24 FB Randall Morris
30 Maryland■	23 DL Reggie White
	DL Johnny Williams
	DL Mark Studaway
	LB Reggie McKenzie / Ricky Holt
	LB Carl Zander
	LB Alvin Toles
	LB Dale Jones / David Scandrett
	DB Tommy Sims
	DB Terry Brown
	DB Joe Cofer
	DB Charles Davis

RUSHING: Jones 191/1116y, Henderson 97/432y, Morris 80/412y
PASSING: Cockrell 128-243/1683y, 13TD, 52.7%
RECEIVING: Duncan 33/640y, Taylor 26/372y, Morris 21/137y
SCORING: Fuad Reveiz (K) 78pts, Duncan 36pts, Jones 30pts

1984 7-4-1

34 Wash. State	27 WR Eric Swanson
27 Utah	21 T David Douglas
24 Army	24 G Bill Mayo
10 Auburn	29 C Raleigh McKenzie
30 Florida	43 G Todd Upton
28 Alabama	27 T Bruce Wilkerson
24 Georgia Tech	21 TE Jeff Smith / John Cook
41 Memphis State	9 QB Tony Robinson
41 Mississippi	17 TB Johnnie Jones / Charles Wilson
12 Kentucky	17 WB Tim McGee
29 Vanderbilt	13 FB William Howard / B.B. Cooper
27 Maryland ■	28 DL Jim Dunkin
	DL Robbie Scott
	DL Tony Simmons
	LB Alvin Toles
	LB Dale Jones
	LB Carl Zander
	LB Reggie McKenzie
	DB Tommy Sims
	DB Terry Brown / Victor Peppers
	DB Charles Davis
	DB Joe Cofer (LB) / Charles Benton

RUSHING: Jones 229/1290y, Howard 89/452y, Wilson 36/195y
PASSING: Robinson 156-253/ 1963y, 14TD, 61.7%
RECEIVING: McGee 54/809y, Smith 26/416y, Howard 24/231y
SCORING: Fuad Reveiz (K) 89pts, Jones 66pts, McGee 36pts

1985 9-1-2

26 UCLA	26 WR Eric Swanson / Joey Clinkscales
38 Auburn	20 T David Douglas / Daryle Smith
31 Wake Forest	29 G John Bruhin / Tony Williams
10 Florida	17 C Todd Kirk
16 Alabama	14 G Harry Galbreath
6 Georgia Tech	6 T Bruce Wilkerson
40 Rutgers	0 TE Jeff Smith
17 Memphis State	7 QB Daryl Dickey / Tony Robinson
34 Mississippi	14 TB Keith Davis / Jeff Powell
42 Kentucky	0 WB Tim McGee
30 Vanderbilt	0 FB William Howard / Sam Henderson
35 Miami ■	7 DL Mark Hovanic
	DL Robby Scott
	DL Fred Bennett / Richard Brown
	LB Bryan Kimbro / Tyrone Robinson
	LB Dale Jones
	LB Kelly Ziegler
	LB Darrin Miller
	DB Tommy Sims / Terry McDaniel
	DB Terry Brown / Victor Peppers
	DB Charles Davis
	DB Chris White

RUSHING: Davis 141/684y, Powell 55/235y,
  Pete Panuska (TB) 39/182y
PASSING: Robinson 91-143/1246, 8TD, 63.6%,
  Dickey 85-131/1161y, 10TD, 63.6%
RECEIVING: McGee 50/947y, Davis 25/168y, Swanson 24/300y
SCORING: Carlos Reveiz (K) 102pts, McGee 42pts,
  Clinkscales & Swanson 24pts

1986 7-5

35 New Mexico	21 WR Joey Clinkscales / Anthony Miller
23 Mississippi St.	27 T Daryle Smith
8 Auburn	34 G Harry Galbreath
26 Texas-El Paso	16 C Todd Kirk / Ray Robinson
21 Army	25 G John Bruhin
28 Alabama	56 T Bruce Wilkerson
13 Georgia Tech	14 TE Tim Hendrix / John Rollins
33 Memphis State	3 QB Jeff Francis
22 Mississippi	10 TB Keith Davis
28 Kentucky	9 WB Terence Cleveland
35 Vanderbilt	20 FB William Howard / Charles Wilson
21 Minnesota ■	14 DL Robby Scott / Marion Hobby
	DL Brian Hunt / Mike Whitehead
	DL Mark Hovanic
	LB Bryan Kimbro
	LB Dale Jones
	LB Kelly Ziegler / Keith DeLong
	LB Darrin Miller / Milton Gordon
	DB Terry McDaniel
	DB Victor Peppers
	DB Andre Creamer
	DB Charles Davis

RUSHING: Howard 177/787y, Wilson 61/301y, Davis 57/293y
PASSING: Francis 150-233/1946y, 9TD, 64.4%
RECEIVING: Clinkscales 37/511y, A. Miller 36/667y,
  Cleveland 22/364y
SCORING: Howard 86pts, Carlos Reveiz (K) 55pts,
  A. Miller 30pts

1987 10-2-1

23 Iowa	22 WR Thomas Woods
49 Colorado State	3 T Kevin Simons
38 Mississippi St.	10 G Harry Galbreath
20 Auburn	20 C Todd Kirk
38 California	12 G John Bruhin
22 Alabama	41 T Phil Stuart
29 Georgia Tech	15 TE Nate Middlebrooks
18 Boston College	20 QB Jeff Francis
41 Louisville	10 TB Reggie Cobb / Keith Davis
55 Mississippi	13 WB Terence Cleveland
24 Kentucky	22 FB William Howard / Charles Wilson
38 Vanderbilt	36 DL Marion Hobby
27 Indiana ■	22 DL Brian Hunt / Charles McRae
	DL Mark Hovanic / David Johnson
	LB Mike Kelley
	LB Keith DeLong
	LB Kelly Ziegler / Charles Kimbrough
	LB Darrin Miller
	DB Terry McDaniel
	DB Victor Peppers
	DB Cedric Kline / Andre Creamer
	DB Kelly Days / Tony Nelson

RUSHING: Cobb 237/1197y, K. Davis 64/440y, Howard 79/313y
PASSING: Francis 121-201/1512y, 8TD, 60.2%
RECEIVING: Woods 26/335y, Cleveland 23/417y,
  Howard 17/153y
SCORING: Cobb 120pts, Phil Reich (K) 88pts, Howard 36pts

1988 5-6

17 Georgia	28 WR Thomas Woods
26 Duke	31 WR Terence Cleveland / Alvin Harper
9 LSU	34 T Kevin Simons
6 Auburn	38 G Antone Davis / Doug Baird
24 Washington St.	52 C Ray Robinson / John Fisher
20 Alabama	28 G Eric Still
38 Memphis State	25 T Phil Stewart
10 Boston College	7 TE Nate Middlebrooks
20 Mississippi	12 QB Jeff Francis
28 Kentucky	24 TB Reggie Cobb / Keith Davis
14 Vanderbilt	7 FB John Rollins / Greg Amsler
	DL Mark Moore / David Johnson
	DL Shazzon Bradley / Martin Williams
	DL Marion Hobby
	LB Bryan Kimbro / Kacy Rodgers
	LB Keith DeLong
	LB Earnest Fields / Mike Kelley
	LB Tracy Hayworth
	DB Preston Warren
	DB Jeremy Lincoln
	DB Cedric Kline
	DB Kelly Days / Tony Nelson

RUSHING: Cobb 118/547y, K. Davis 60/287y, Amsler 63/213y
PASSING: Francis 191-314/2237y, 13TD, 60.8%
RECEIVING: Woods 58/689y, Harper 37/487y, Cobb 17/126y
SCORING: Chip McCallum (K) 36pts, Woods 36pts,
  Harper 30pts

1989 11-1

17 Colorado State	14 WR Thomas Woods / Anthony Morgan
24 UCLA	6 WR Alvin Harper / Terence Cleveland
28 Duke	6 T Antone Davis
21 Auburn	14 G Tom Myslinski
17 Georgia	14 C John Fisher
30 Alabama	47 G Eric Still
45 LSU	39 T Charles McRae
52 Akron	9 TE Mark Adams / Von Reeves
33 Mississippi	21 QB Andy Kelly / Sterling Henton
31 Kentucky	10 TB Chuck Webb / Reggie Cobb
17 Vanderbilt	10 FB Roland Poles / Greg Amsler
31 Arkansas ■	27 DL Marion Hobby
	DL Mark Moore
	DL Martin Williams / Carey Bailey
	DL Tracy Hayworth
	LB Darryl Hardy
	LB Shazzon Bradley
	LB Earnest Fields / Kacy Rodgers
	DB Keith Denson
	DB Preston Warren / J. J. McCleskey
	DB Jason Julian / Carl Pickens
	DB Kelly Days / Mark Fletcher

RUSHING: Webb 209/1236y, Cobb 90/616y,
  Tony Thompson (TB) 71/300y
PASSING: Kelly 92-156/1299y, 7TD, 59.0%
RECEIVING: Woods 34/511y, Amsler 23/244y, Harper 13/246y,
  Morgan 13/226y
SCORING: Greg Burke (K) 75pts, Webb 72pts, Amsler 42pts

1990 9-2-2

31 Colorado	31 WR Carl Pickens
55 Pacific	7 WR Alvin Harper / Craig Faulkner
40 Mississippi St.	7 T Antone Davis
56 Texas-El Paso	0 G Tom Myslinski
26 Auburn	26 C John Fisher
45 Florida	3 G Doug Baird
6 Alabama	9 T Charles McRae
41 Temple	20 TE Mark Adams / Von reeves
29 Notre Dame	34 QB Andy Kelly
22 Mississippi	13 TB Tony Thompson / Tavio Henson
42 Kentucky	28 FB Roland Poles / Greg Amsler
49 Vanderbilt	20 DL Kacy Rodgers / Chris Mims
23 Virginia ■	22 DL Carey Bailey / Shazzon Bradley
	DL Mark Moore
	DL Chuck Smith
	LB Darryl Hardy
	LB Shon Walker
	LB Earnest Fields
	DB Jeremy Lincoln
	DB Floyd Miley
	DB Dale Carter
	DB Mark Fletcher

RUSHING: Thompson 219/1261y, Henson 39/234y,
  Amsler 52/196y
PASSING: Kelly 179-304/2241y, 14TD, 58.9%
RECEIVING: Pickens 53/917y, Harper 37/567y, Amsler 20/185y
SCORING: Greg Burke (K) 107pts, Thompson 96pts,
  Harper 48pts

1991 9-3

28 Louisville	11 WR Carl Pickens
30 UCLA	16 WR Craig Faulkner / J. J. McCleskey
26 Mississippi St.	24 T Bernard Dafney / Rodney Gordon
30 Auburn	21 G Tom Myslinski
18 Florida	35 C John Fisher / Brian Spivey
19 Alabama	24 G Mike Stowell
52 Memphis State	24 T Patrick Lenoir
35 Notre Dame	34 TE Mark Adams / Von Reeves
36 Mississippi	25 QB Andy Kelly
16 Kentucky	7 TB James Stewart / Aaron Hayden
45 Vanderbilt	0 FB Mario Brunson / Kenneth Campbell
17 Penn State ■	42 DL Chris Mims / Kacy Rodgers
	DL Shazzon Bradley
	DL J.J. Surlas
	DL Chuck Smith
	LB Darryl Hardy
	LB Shon Walker / Reggie Ingram
	LB Earnest Fields
	DB Jeremy Lincoln
	DB Floyd Miley
	DB Dale Carter / Mark Fletcher
	DB David Bennett / Roderick Lewis

RUSHING: Stewart 190/939y, Hayden 145/704y,
  Mose Phillips (TB) 36/ 234y
PASSING: Kelly 228-361/2759y, 15TD, 63.2%
RECEIVING: Pickens 49/877y, Faulkner 35/509y,
  McCleskey 35/391y
SCORING: John Becksvoort (K) 73pts, Hayden & Stewart 48pts

1992 9-3

38 S.W. Louisiana	3 WR Cory Fleming / Kendrick Jones
34 Georgia	31 WR Craig Faulkner
31 Florida	14 T Mike Stowell
40 Cincinnati	0 G Bubba Miller
20 Louisiana State	0 C Brian Spivey / Jason Layman
24 Arkansas	25 G Jeff Smith
10 Alabama	17 T Rodney Gordon / Leslie Ratliffe
23 South Carolina	24 TE David Horn / Robert Todd
26 Memphis State	21 QB Heath Shuler
34 Kentucky	13 TB Charlie Garner / James Stewart
29 Vanderbilt	25 FB Mario Brunson / Mose Phillips
38 Boston College ■	23 DL James Wilson / Shane Bonham
	DL Jeff Tullis
	DL J. J. Surlas / Paul Yatkowski
	DL Todd Kelly
	LB George Kidd / Jesse Sanders
	LB Reggie Ingram / Willie Richards
	LB Ben Talley
	DB Tavio Henson / Steve Session
	DB Tracy Smith / DeRon Jenkins
	DB Jason Parker / Victor Brown
	DB J. J. McCleskey (WR) / David Bennett

RUSHING: Garner 154/928y, Stewart 85/386y,
  Aaron Hayden (TB) 63/321y
PASSING: Shuler 130-224/1712y, 10TD, 58.0%
RECEIVING: Fleming 40/490y, Faulkner 31/462y, Jones 17/172y
SCORING: John Becksvoort (K) 83pts, Shuler 66pts,
  Stewart 48pts

1993 9-2-1

50 Louisiana Tech	0 WR Cory Fleming
38 Georgia	6 WR Craig Faulkner / Billy Williams
34 Florida	41 T Jason Layman
42 Louisiana State	20 G Kevin Mays
52 Duke	19 C Bubba Miller
28 Arkansas	14 G Jeff Smith
17 Alabama	17 T Leslie Ratliffe
55 South Carolina	3 TE David Horn
45 Louisville	10 QB Heath Shuler
48 Kentucky	0 TB Charlie Garner / James Stewart
62 Vanderbilt	14 FB Mario Brunson / Mose Phillips
13 Penn State ■	31 DL James Wilson
	DL Shane Bonham
	DL Paul Yatkowski
	DL Horace Morris
	LB George Kidd / Scott Galyon
	LB Reggie Ingram
	LB Ben Talley
	DB DeRon Jenkins
	DB Ronald Davis / Shawn Summers
	DB Jason Parker
	DB Victor Brown

RUSHING: Garner 159/1161y, Stewart 86/537y,
Aaron Hayden (TB) 28/217y
PASSING: Shuler 184-285/2354y, 25TD, 64.6%
RECEIVING: Faulkner 40/680y, Fleming 39/596y,
Williams 39/513y
SCORING: John Becksvoort (K) 95pts, Fleming 66pts,
Stewart 54pts

1994 8-4

23 UCLA	25 WR Joey Kent / Nilo Silvan
41 Georgia	23 WR Billy Williams
0 Florida	31 T Jason Layman
21 Mississippi St.	24 G Kevin Mays
10 Washington St.	9 C Bubba Miller (G)
38 Arkansas	21 G Jeff Smith (C)
13 Alabama	17 T Leslie Ratliffe
31 South Carolina	22 TE Scott Pfeifer / David Horn
24 Memphis	13 QB Peyton Manning / Brandon Stewart
52 Kentucky	0 TB James Stewart / Aaron Hayden
65 Vanderbilt	0 FB Mose Phillips
45 Virginia Tech ■	23 DL Steve White
	DL Leland Taylor
	DL Shane Burton / Corey Stone
	DL Ben Talley (LB)
	LB Scott Galyon
	LB Tyrone Hines
	LB George Kidd
	DB Ronald Davis
	DB DeRon Jenkins / Shawn Summers
	DB Jason Parker
	DB Raymond Austin

RUSHING: Stewart 170/1028y, Hayden 157/819y,
Jay Graham (K) 61/275y
PASSING: Manning 89-144/1141y, 11 TD, 61.8%
RECEIVING: Kent 36/470y, Williams 20/217y, Stewart 17/147y
SCORING: Stewart 84pts

1995 11-1

27 East Carolina	7 WR Joey Kent/Peerless Price/Nilo Silvan
30 Georgia	27 WR Marcus Nash / Andy McCullough
37 Florida	62 T Jason Layman
52 Mississippi St.	14 G Jeff Smith
31 Oklahoma State	0 C Bubba Miller / Diron Robinson
49 Arkansas	31 G Trey Peterson
41 Alabama	14 T Robert Poole / Trey Teague
56 South Carolina	21 TE Scott Pfeifer / Dustin Moore
42 Southern Miss.	0 QB Peyton Manning
34 Kentucky	31 TB Jay Graham / Mark Levine
12 Vanderbilt	7 FB Chester Ford
20 Ohio State ■	14 DL Leonard Little / Jonathan Brown
	DL Shane Burton / Mercedes Hamilton
	DL Billy Beron / Ron Green / Bill Duff
	DL Stan White / Jeff Coleman
	LB Scott Galyon
	LB Tyrone Hines
	LB Jesse Sanders / Al Wilson
	DB Terry Fair
	DB DeRon Jenkins
	DB Tori Noel / Cory Gaines
	DB Raymond Austin

RUSHING: Graham 272/1438y, Levine 42/197y,
Jeremaine Copeland (WR) 14/73y
PASSING: Manning 244-380/2954y, 22 TD, 64.2%
RECEIVING: Kent 69/1055y, Nash 43/512y,
Maurice Staley (WR) 25/307y
SCORING: Jeff Hall (K) 95pts

1996 10-2

62 UNLV	3 WR Joey Kent / Jeremaine Copeland
35 UCLA	20 WR Marcus Nash / Andy McCullough
29 Florida	35 T Chad Clifton / Jarvis Reado
41 Mississippi	3 G Spencer Riley
29 Georgia	17 C Trey Teague
20 Alabama	13 G Mercedes Hamilton / Diron Robinson
31 South Carolina	14 T Robert Poole
17 Memphis	21 TE Dustin Moore / Eric Diogu
55 Arkansas	14 QB Peyton Manning
56 Kentucky	10 TB Jay Graham / Mark Levine
14 Vanderbilt	7 FB Chester Ford / Ronnie Pillow
48 Northwestern ■	28 DL Leonard Little / Corey Terry
	DL Bill Duff / Buck Buxton
	DL Ron Green / Billy Ratliff
	DL Jonathan Brown / Jeff Coleman
	LB Craig King
	LB Tyrone Hines / Antron Peebles
	LB Al Wilson
	DB Terry Fair / Gerald Griffin
	DB Dwayne Goodrich / Steve Johnson
	DB Tori Noel
	DB Jason Parker / Cory Gaines

RUSHING: Graham 179/797y, Levine 43/202y, Darden 26/97y
PASSING: Manning 243-380/3287y, 20 TD, 63.9%
RECEIVING: Kent 68/1080y, Nash 53/688y,
Peerless Price (WR) 32/609y
SCORING: Jeff Hall (K) 77pts

1997 11-2

52 Texas Tech	17 WR Peerless Price / Jeremaine Copeland
30 UCLA	24 WR Marcus Nash / Cedrick Wilson
20 Florida	33 T Chad Clifton
31 Mississippi	17 G Spencer Riley
38 Georgia	13 C Trey Teague
38 Alabama	21 G Mercedes Hamilton / Diron Robinson
22 South Carolina	7 T Cosey Coleman
44 Southern Miss.	20 TE Antron Peebles / Eric Diogu
30 Arkansas	22 QB Peyton Manning
59 Kentucky	31 TB Jamal Lewis / Mark Levine
17 Vanderbilt	10 FB Shawn Bryson / Phillip Crosby
30 Auburn □	29 DL Jonathan Brown / Shaun Ellis
17 Nebraska ■	42 DL Bill Duff / Darwin Walker
	DL Ron Green / Billy Ratliff
	DL Corey Terry / Jeff Coleman
	LB Raynoch Thompson
	LB Leonard Little
	LB Al Wilson
	DB Terry Fair / Gerald Griffin
	DB Dwayne Goodrich / Steve Johnson
	DB Cory Gaines / Deon Grant
	DB Tori Noel

RUSHING: Lewis 232/1364y, Levine 28/172y, Bryson 36/146y
PASSING: Manning 287-477/3819y, 36TD, 60.2%
RECEIVING: Nash 76/1170y, Copeland 58/732y, Price 48/698y
SCORING: Jeff Hall (K) 95pts

1998 13-0

34 Syracuse	33 WR Peerless Price / David Martin
20 Florida	17 WR Cedrick Wilson / Jeremaine Copeland
42 Houston	7 T Chad Clifton
17 Auburn	9 G Mercedes Hamilton
22 Georgia	3 C Spencer Riley
35 Alabama	18 G Cosey Coleman
49 South Carolina	14 T Jarvis Reado
37 Ala.-Birm'ham	13 TE John Finlayson
28 Arkansas	24 QB Tee Martin
59 Kentucky	21 TB Travis Henry / Jamal Lewis
41 Vanderbilt	0 FB Shawn Bryson
24 Mississippi St.□	14 DL Shaun Ellis
23 Florida State ■	16 DL Ron Green / Billy Ratliff
	DL Darwin Walker
	DL Corey Terry / Jeff Coleman
	LB Raynoch Thompson
	LB Al Wilson
	LB Eric Westmoreland
	DB Steve Johnson / Andre Lott
	DB Dwayne Goodrich / Gerald Griffin
	DB Deon Grant
	DB Fred White

RUSHING: Henry 176/970y, Lewis 73/497y, Stephens 107/477y
PASSING: Martin 153-267/2164y, 19 TD, 57.3%
RECEIVING: Price 61/920y, Wilson 33/558y, Copeland 29/438y
SCORING: Jeff Hall (K) 104pts

1999 9-3

42 Wyoming	17 WR David Martin / Donte Stallworth
21 Florida	23 WR Cedrick Wilson / Eric Parker
17 Memphis	16 T Chad Clifton / Reggie Coleman
24 Auburn	0 G Fred Weary / Toby Champion
37 Georgia	20 C Spencer Riley
21 Alabama	7 G Cosey Coleman
30 South Carolina	7 T Josh Tucker
38 Notre Dame	14 TE John Finlayson / Neil Johnson
24 Arkansas	28 QB Tee Martin
56 Kentucky	21 TB Jamal Lewis / Travis Henry
38 Vanderbilt	10 FB Phillip Crosby / Will Bartholomew
21 Nebraska ■	31 DL Shaun Ellis / Roger Alexander
	DL John Henderson / Billy Ratliff
	DL Darwin Walker
	DL Will Overstreet
	LB Eric Westmoreland
	LB Dom'n'q'e Stevens'n/Keyon Whites'de
	LB Raynoch Thompson/Anth'ny Sessions
	DB Andre Lott
	DB Dwayne Goodrich
	DB Deon Grant / Mikki Allen
	DB Fred White / Derrick Edmunds

RUSHING: Lewis 182/816y, Henry 125/790y, Martin 81/317y
PASSING: Martin 165-305/2317y, 12 TD, 54.1%
RECEIVING: Wilson 57/827y, Parker 30/411y,
Stallworth 23/407y
SCORING: Alex Walls (K) 59pts

2000 8-4

19 So. Mississippi	16 WR Eric Parker / David Martin
23 Florida	27 WR Cedrick Wilson / Leonard Scott
70 La.-Monroe	3 T Reggie Coleman
31 Louisiana State	38 G Anthony Herrera
10 Georgia	21 C Fred Weary / Scott Wells
20 Alabama	10 G Toby Champion
17 South Carolina	14 T Michael Munoz
19 Memphis	17 TE John Finlayson / Neil Johnson
63 Arkansas	20 QB Casey Clausen / A.J. Suggs
59 Kentucky	20 TB Travis Henry / Travis Stephens
28 Vanderbilt	26 FB Will Bartholomew
21 Kansas State ■	35 DL DeAngelo Lloyd / Bernard Jackson
	DL John Henderson / Rashad Moore
	DL Edward Kendrick /Albert Haynesworth
	DL Will Overstreet / Constantin Ritzmann
	LB Eric Westmoreland
	LB Dominique Stevenson
	LB Anthony Sessions / Eddie Moore
	DB Willie Miles / Jabari Greer
	DB Teddy Gaines
	DB Rashad Baker / Tad Golden
	DB Andre Lott / Steven Marsh

RUSHING: Henry 253/1369y, Stephens 81/359y, Scott 6/70y
PASSING: Clausen 121-194/1473y, 15 TD, 62.4%,
Suggs 81-139/785y, 5 TD, 58.3%
RECEIVING: Wilson 62/681y, Donte Stallworth (WR) 35/519y,
Martin 29/285y, Parker 23/333y
SCORING: Alex Walls (K) 93pts, Wilson 74pts, Henry 66pts

2001 11-2

33 Syracuse	9 WR Kelley Washington / Bobby Graham
13 Arkansas	3 WR Eric Parker / Donte Stallworth
26 LSU	18 T Reggie Coleman / Sean Young
24 Georgia	26 G Fred Weary / Anthony Herrera
35 Alabama	24 C Scott Wells
17 South Carolina	10 G Chavis Smith / Jason Respert
28 Notre Dame	18 T Will Ofenheusle
49 Memphis	28 TE John Finlayson / Jason Witten
38 Kentucky	35 QB Casey Clausen
38 Vanderbilt	0 TB Travis Stephens / Cedric Houston
34 Florida	32 FB Will Bartholomew
20 LSU □	31 DL Bernard Jackson / Omari Hand
45 Michigan ■	17 DL John Henderson
	DL Albert Haynesworth / Rashad Moore
	DL Will Overstreet / Constantin Ritzmann
	LB Eddie Moore
	LB Dominique Stevenson
	LB Keyon Whiteside / Kevin Burnett
	DB Teddy Gaines / Andre Lott
	DB Jabari Greer
	DB Rashad Baker
	DB Julian Battle

RUSHING: Stephens 291/1464y, Houston 18/106y,
Troy Fleming (TB) 24/102y
PASSING: Clausen 227-354/2969y, 22TD, 64.1%
RECEIVING: Washington 64/1010y, Stallworth 41/821y,
Witten 28/293y
SCORING: Alex Walls (K) 84pts, Stallworth 68pts, Stephens 66pts

SCORES, LINEUPS, AND STATISTICS

2002 8-5

47 Wyoming	7 WR Tony Brown / Kelley Washington
26 Middle Tenn.	3 WR Leonard Scott / Jonathan Wade
13 Florida	30 T Michael Munoz
35 Rutgers	14 G Jason Respert / Sean Young
41 Arkansas	38 C Scott Wells
13 Georgia	18 G Anthony Herrera / Rob Smith
14 Alabama	34 T Will Ofenheusle
18 South Carolina	10 TE Jason Witten
3 Miami	26 QB Casey Clausen
35 Mississippi St.	17 TB Cedric Houston / Jabari Davis
24 Vanderbilt	0 FB Troy Fleming
24 Kentucky	0 DL Omari Hand / Parys Haralson
3 Maryland■	30 DL Rashad Moore
	DL Aubrayo Franklin
	DL Demetrin Veal / Mondre Dickerson
	LB Eddie Moore / Steven Marsh
	LB Keyon Whiteside / Robert Peace
	LB Jason Mitchell / Kevin Simon
	DB Willie Miles
	DB Jabari Greer / Julian Battle
	DB Rashad Baker / Mark Jones
	DB Gibral Wilson

RUSHING: Houston 153/779y, Davis 125/569y, Derrick Tinsley (TB) 45/202y
PASSING: Clausen 194-310/2297y, 11TD, 62.6%
RECEIVING: Witten 39/493y, Brown 39/477, Washington 23/443y
SCORING: Davis 60pts, Alex Walls (K) 56pts, Houston 36pts

2003 10-3

24 Fresno State	6 WR Tony Brown / Chris Hannon
34 Marshall	24 WR James Banks / Mark Jones (DB)
24 Florida	10 T Michael Munoz
23 South Carolina	20 G Anthony Herrera
21 Auburn	28 C Scott Wells
14 Georgia	41 G Chavis Smith / Cody Douglas
51 Alabama	43 T Sean Young
23 Duke	6 TE Victor McClure
10 Miami	6 QB Casey Clausen
59 Mississippi St.	21 TB Cedric Houston / Jabari Davis
48 Vanderbilt	0 FB Troy Fleming / William Revill
20 Kentucky	7 DL Parys Haralson
14 Clemson■	27 DL J.T. Mapu
	DL Greg Jones / Mondre Dickerson
	DL Constantin Ritzmann / Jason Hall
	LB Kevin Simon / Omar Gaither
	LB Robert Peace
	LB Kevin Burnett / Jason Mitchell
	DB Jabari Greer / Mark Jones (WR)
	DB Jason Allen / Antwan Stewart
	DB Rashad Baker / Corey Campbell
	DB Gibral Wilson

RUSHING: Houston 149/744y, Davis 124/565y, Gerald Riggs (TB) 46/207y
PASSING: Clausen 233-412/2968y, 27 TD, 56.6%
RECEIVING: Banks 42/621y, Jones 36/556y, Fleming 36/262y
SCORING: James Wilhoit (K) 92pts, Davis 48pts, Banks 44pts

2004 10-3

42 UNLV	17 WR Tony Brown / Derrick Tinsley
30 Florida	28 WR Chris Hannon / Jayson Swain
42 Louisiana Tech	17 T Michael Munoz / Arron Sears
10 Auburn	34 G Rob Smith
19 Georgia	14 C Jason Respert / Chuck Prugh
21 Mississippi	17 G Cody Douglas / Richie Gandy (C)
17 Alabama	13 T Albert Toeaina
43 South Carolina	29 TE Justin Reed /Chris Brown/Vic McClure
13 Notre Dame	17 QB Erik Ainge/Brent Schaeffer/Ri'k Clausen
38 Vanderbilt	33 TB Cedric Houston / Gerald Riggs
37 Kentucky	31 FB Cory Anderson
28 Auburn □	38 DL Parys Haralson / Turk McBride
38 Texas A&M■	7 DL Jesse Mahelona
	DL Justin Harrell
	DL Karlton Neal
	LB Omar Gaither
	LB Jason Mitchell / Kevin Simon
	LB Kevin Burnett
	DB Roshaun Fellows / Jonathan Wade
	DB Jonathan Hefney
	DB Jason Allen / Corey Campbell
	DB Brandon Johnson / Robert Boulware

RUSHING: Riggs 193/1107y, Houston 181/1005y, David Yancey (TB) 24/116y
PASSING: Ainge 109-198/1452y, 17TD, 55.1%, Clausen 81-136/949y, 8TD, 59.6%, Schaeffer 18-37/302y, 2TD, 48.6%
RECEIVING: Brown 31/388y, Swain 29/388y, Robert Meachem (WR) 25/459y
SCORING: James Wilhoit (K) 74pts, Houston 56pts, Riggs & Bret Smith (WR) 36pts

2005 5-6

17 Ala.-Birm'ham	10 WR C.J. Fayton / Robert Meachem
7 Florida	16 WR Chris Hannon / Jayson Swain
30 LSU	27 T Arron Sears
27 Mississippi	10 G Rob Smith / David Ligon (C)
14 Georgia	27 C Richie Gandy / Anthony Parker
3 Alabama	6 G Cody Douglas / Ramon Foster
15 South Carolina	16 T Albert Toeaina / Eric Young
21 Notre Dame	41 TE Chris Brown
20 Memphis	16 QB Rick Clausen / Erik Ainge
24 Vanderbilt	28 TB Gerald Riggs / Arian Foster
27 Kentucky	8 FB Cory Anderson
	DL Jason Hall
	DL Justin Harrell / Turk McBride
	DL Jesse Mahelona / Tony McDaniel
	DL Parys Haralson
	LB Omar Gaither / Jerod Mayo
	LB Kevin Simon / Marvin Mitchell
	LB Jason Mitchell
	DB Inquoris Johnson / Jason Allen
	DB Jonathan Wade / Roshaun Fellows
	DB Jonathan Hefney
	DB Antwan Stewart / Demetrice Morley

RUSHING: Foster 183/879y, Riggs 127/530y
PASSING: Clausen 120-209/1441y, 6TD, 57.4%, Ainge 66-145/737y, 5TD, 45.5%
RECEIVING: Meachem 29/383y, Swain 27/380y, Fayton 24/272y, Hannon 24/268y, Bret Smith (WR) 21/223y
SCORING: James Wilhoit (K) 63pts, Foster 30pts, 3 with 18pts

2006 9-4

35 California	18 WR Robert Meachem
31 Air Force	30 WR Jayson Swain / Bret Smith
20 Florida	21 T Arron Sears
33 Marshall	9 G David Ligon
41 Memphis	7 C Josh McNeil / Michael Frogg
51 Georgia	33 G Anthony Parker / Jacques McClendon
16 Alabama	13 T Eric Young
31 South Carolina	24 TE Chris Brown / Brad Cottam
24 LSU	28 QB Erik Ainge
14 Arkansas	31 TB LaMarcus Coker / Arian Foster
39 Vanderbilt	10 FB Cory Anderson
17 Kentucky	12 DL Xavier Mitchell
10 Penn State■	20 DL Turk McBride / Justin Harrell
	DL Matt McGlothlin / Demonte Bolden
	DL Antonio Reynolds / Robert Ayers
	LB Ryan Karl
	LB Marvin Mitchell
	LB Jerrod Mayo / Rico McCoy
	DB Jonathan Wade
	DB Antwan Stewart / Inquoris Johnson
	DB Jonathan Hefney
	DB Demetrice Morley / Antonio Wardlow

RUSHING: Coker 108/696y, Montario Hardesty (TB) 107/384y, Foster 91/322y
PASSING: Ainge 233-348/2989y, 19TD, 67.0%
RECEIVING: Meachem 71/1298y, Swain 49/688y, Smith 39/453y, Brown 31/239y
SCORING: James Wilhoit (K) 96pts, Meachem 66pts, Coker & Swain 36pts

2007 10-4

31 California	45 WR Lucas Taylor
39 Southern Miss	19 WR Austin Rogers / Casey Woods
20 Florida	59 WR Josh Briscoe / Kenny O'Neal
48 Arkansas State	27 T Chris Scott
35 Georgia	14 G Anthony Parker
33 Mississippi St.	21 C Josh McNeil
17 Alabama	41 G Jacques McClendon
27 South Carolina	24 T Eric Young / Ramon Foster (G)
59 La.-Lafayette	7 TE Chris Brown /Brad Cottam /Jeff Cottam
34 Arkansas	13 QB Erik Ainge
25 Vanderbilt	24 RB Arian Foster / Montario Hardesty
52 Kentucky	50 DL Xavier Mitchell / Wes Brown
14 LSU□	21 DL Dan Williams / J.T. Mapu
21 Wisconsin■	17 DL Demonte Bolden / Walter Fisher
	DL Antonio Reynolds / Robert Ayers
	LB Ryan Karl
	LB Jerod Mayo / Ellix Wilson
	LB Rico McCoy
	DB DeAngelo Willingham / Antonio Gaines
	DB Brent Vinson / Marsalous Johnson
	DB Jonathan Hefney / Jarod Parrish
	DB Eric Berry / Nevin McKenzie

RUSHING: Foster 245/1193y, Hardesty 89/373y, Lennon Creer (RB)
PASSING: Ainge 325-519/3522y, 31TD, 62.6%
RECEIVING: Taylor 13/1000y, Rogers 56/624y, Briscoe 56/557y, C. Brown 41/282y
SCORING: Daniel Lincoln (K) 115pts, Foster 84pts, C. Brown & Briscoe 36pts

2008 5-7

24 UCLA	27 WR Lucas Taylor / Josh Briscoe
35 Ala.-Birm'ham	3 WR Gerald Jones / Austin Rogers
6 Florida	30 T Chris Scott
12 Auburn	14 G Anthony Parker / Vladimir Richard
13 N. Illinois	9 C Josh McNeill
14 Georgia	26 G Jacques McClendon
34 Mississippi St.	3 T Ramon Foster
9 Alabama	29 TE Luke Stocker/Jeff Cottam/Br'n Warren
6 South Carolina	27 QB Jonathan Crompton / Nick Stephens
7 Wyoming	13 TB Arian Foster / Montario Hardesty
20 Vanderbilt	10 FB Kevin Cooper
28 Kentucky	10 DL Wes Brown / Ben Martin
	DL Demonte Bolden
	DL Dan Williams / Walter Fisher
	DL Robert Ayers / Chris Walker
	LB Nevin McKenzie / Adam Myers-White
	LB Ellix Wilson / Nick Reveiz
	LB Rico McCoy / Savion Frazier
	DB DeAngelo Willingham
	DB Dennis Rogan / Marsalous Johnson
	DB Demetrice Morley
	DB Eric Berry

RUSHING: Foster 131/570y, Lennon Creer (TB) 73/388y, Hardesty 76/271y
PASSING: Crompton 86-167/889y, 4 TD, 51.5%, Stephens 63-130/840y, 4TD, 48.5%
RECEIVING: Jones 30/323y, Taylor 26/332y, Foster 19/166y
SCORING: Daniel Lincoln (K) 152pts, Hardesty 36pts, Jones 30pts

2009 7-6

63 W. Kentucky	7 WR Gerald Jones / Marsalis Teague
15 UCLA	19 WR Quintin Hancock / Denarius Moore
13 Florida	23 T Chris Scott
34 Ohio Univ.	23 G Cory Sullins / Vladimir Richard
22 Auburn	26 C Cory Sullins
45 Georgia	19 G Jacques McClendon
10 Alabama	12 T Aaron Douglas / Jarrod Shaw
31 South Carolina	13 TE Luke Stocker / Jeff Cottam
56 Memphis	28 QB Jonathan Crompton
17 Mississippi	42 TB Montario Hardesty / Bryce Brown
31 Mississippi	16 FB Kevin Cooper
30 Kentucky	24 DL Ben Martin / Gerald Williams
14 Virginia Tech■	37 DL Dan Williams
	DL Wes Brown / Montori Hughes
	DL Chris Walker / Willie Bohannon
	LB LaMarcus Thompson / Savion Frazier
	LB Herman Lathers / Nick Reveiz
	LB Rico McCoy
	DB Dennis Rogan / Brent Vinson
	DB Art Evans / Marsalous Johnson
	DB Janzen Jackson / Prentiss Waggner
	DB Eric Berry

RUSHING: Hardesty 282/1345y, Brown 101/460y, David Oku (TB) 23/94y
PASSING: Crompton 224-384/2800y, 27TD, 58.3%
RECEIVING: Jones 46/680y, Moore 40/540y, Stocker 29/389y, Hancock 27/298y
SCORING: Hardesty 84pts, Daniel Lincoln (K) 63pts, Moore 42pts

2010 6-7

50 UT-Martin	0 WR Denarius Moore / Justin Hunter
13 Oregon	48 WR Gerald Jones / Zach Rogers
17 Florida	31 T Dallas Thomas
32 UAB	29 G JerQuari Schofield / Zach Fulton
14 LSU	16 C James Stone (G) / Darin Gooch
14 Georgia	41 G Jarrod Shaw
10 Alabama	41 T Ja'Wuan James
24 South Carolina	38 TE Luke Stocker
50 Memphis	14 QB Matt Simms / Tyler Bray
52 Mississippi	14 TB Tauren Poole
24 Vanderbilt	10 FB Kevin Cooper / Channing Fulgate
24 Kentucky	14 DL Gerald Williams / Corey Miller
27 North Carolina■	30 DL Malik Jackson
	DL Victor Thomas / Montori Hughes
	DL Chris Walker / Jacques Smith
	LB LaMarcus Thompson / Daryl Vereen
	LB Nick Reveiz / Austin Johnson
	LB Herman Lathers / Savion Frazier
	DB Art Evans / Eric Gordon
	DB Marsalis Teague / Brent Brewer
	DB Janzen Jackson / Anthony Anderson
	DB Prentiss Waggner

RUSHING: Poole 204/1034y, Rajion Neal (FB) 46/197y, David Oku (TB) 42/174y
PASSING: Bray 125-224/1849y, 18TD, 55.8%, Simms 113-195/1460y, 8TD, 57.9%
RECEIVING: Jones 55/596y, Moore 47/981y, Stocker 39/417y
SCORING: Poole 72pts, Moore 60pts, Daniel Lincoln (K) 57pts

TEXAS

University of Texas (Founded 1883)
Austin, Texas
Nickname: Longhorns
Colors: Burnt Orange and White
Stadium: Darrell K. Royal-Texas Memorial Stadium (1924) 94,113
Conference Affiliations: Southwest Athletic (Charter Member, 1915-1995), Big Twelve, South (1996-present)

CAREER RUSHING YARDS	Attempts	Yards
Ricky Williams (1995-98)	1011	6279
Cedric Benson (2001-04)	1112	5540
Earl Campbell (1974-77)	765	4443
Jamaal Charles (2005-07)	533	3328
Chris Gilbert (1966-68)	595	3231
Vince Young (2003-05)	457	3127
Roosevelt Leaks (1972-74)	555	2923
A.J. "Jam" Jones (1978-81)	645	2874
Hodges Mitchell (1997-00)	517	2664
Eric Metcalf (1985-88)	586	2661

CAREER PASSING YARDS	Comp.-Att.	Yards
Colt McCoy (2006-09)	1157-1645	13,253
Major Applewhite (1998-01)	611-1,065	8353
James Brown (1994-97)	546-1,003	7638
Peter Gardere (1989-92)	561-1,025	7396
Chris Simms (1999-02)	535-911	7097
Vince Young (2003-05)	444-718	6040
Bret Stafford (1984-87)	378-714	4735
Shea Morenz (1993-94)	307-570	3774
Bobby Layne (1944-47)	210-400	3145
Garrett Gilbert (2009-10)	290-507	3054

CAREER RECEIVING YARDS	Catches	Yards
Roy Williams (2000-03)	241	3866
Jordan Shipley (2006-09)	248	3191
Mike Adams (1992-96)	177	3032
Quan Cosby (2005-08)	212	2598
B.J. Johnson (2000-03)	152	2389
Kwame Cavil (1997-99)	174	2279
Limas Sweed (2003-07)	124	1915
Tony Jones (1986-89)	108	1842
Jordan Shipley (2006-08)	132	1706
Wane McGarity (1995-98)	95	1687

SEASON RUSHING YARDS	Attempts	Yards
Ricky Williams (1998)	361	2124
Ricky Williams (1997)	279	1893
Cedric Benson (2004)	326	1834
Earl Campbell (1977)	267	1744
Jamaal Charles (2007)	258	1619

SEASON PASSING YARDS	Comp.-Att.	Yards
Colt McCoy (2008)	332-433	3859
Colt McCoy (2009)	332-470	3521
Major Applewhite (1999)	271-467	3357
Colt McCoy (2007)	276-424	3303
Chris Simms (2002)	235-396	3207

SEASON RECEIVING YARDS	Catches	Yards
Jordan Shipley (2009)	116	1485
Kwame Cavil (1999)	100	1188
Roy Williams (2002)	64	1142
Quan Cosby (2008)	92	1123
Wane McGarity (1998)	58	1087

GAME RUSHING YARDS	Attempts	Yards
Ricky Williams (1998 vs. Iowa State)	37	350
Roosevelt Leaks (1973 vs. SMU)	37	342
Ricky Williams (1998 vs. Rice)	30	318

GAME PASSING YARDS	Comp.-Att.	Yards
Major Applewhite (2001 vs. Washington)	37-55	473
Colt McCoy (2009 vs. C. Florida)	33-42	470
Chris Simms (2002 vs. Nebraska)	29-47	419

GAME RECEIVING YARDS	Catches	Yards
Jordan Shipley (2009 vs. C. Florida)	11	273
Johnny "Lam" Jones (1979 vs. Baylor)	8	198
B.J. Johnson (2000 vs. Texas A&M)	6	187
B.J. Johnson (2003 vs. Iowa State)	7	187

GREATEST COACH:

The name Darrell Royal has become synonymous with University of Texas football, which is not too bad for a former Oklahoma quarterback and defensive back, who still holds the Sooners career interceptions (caught) record with 18. But that was before he would coach the Longhorns to 167wins in 20 years in Austin. That was before he would win national titles for the 1963 and 1969 seasons, with a share of one in 1970. That was before the 11 Southwest Conference championships and 16 bowl appearances.

After short stops as the head coach at Mississippi State and Washington, Royal was an immediate success as the Texas head coach. The team he inherited had won one game in 1956. In 1957, in year one of the Royal regime, they won 6 and earned a berth in the Sugar Bowl. Texas had found their rightful ball coach. By 1958 they began an eight-game win streak against his alma mater with a 15-14 upset of no. 2 Oklahoma. Then in 1959 they enjoyed a 9-1 regular season and Cotton Bowl berth. All of that was just a set-up to the 1960s, when Texas fielded challengers to the national crown on an annual basis. They won two titles and narrowly missed others in 1961, 1962, and 1964.

Although the Longhorns fell behind rival Oklahoma in the 1970s, they still won the SWC five of the seven years Royal coached them. He retired at the pinnacle of his profession, despite leaving behind enough talent for another near Texas title in 1977.

TEXAS' 55 GREATEST SINCE 1953

OFFENSE

WIDE RECEIVER: Mike Adams, B.J. Johnson, Jordan Shipley, Roy Williams
TIGHT END: Pat Fitzgerald, Pete Lammons
TACKLE: Leonard Davis, Bob Simmons, Jerry Sisemore, Terry Tausch, Bobby Wuensch
GUARD: Doug Dawson, Derrick Dockery, Herb Gray, Dan Neil
CENTER: Gene Chilton, Bill Wyman
QUARTERBACK: Colt McCoy, James Street, Vince Young
RUNNING BACK: Cedric Benson, Earl Campbell, Chris Gilbert, Roosevelt Leaks, Ricky Williams
FULLBACK: Steve Worster

DEFENSE

END: Bill Atessis, Tony Brackens, Carlton Massey, Cory Redding
TACKLE: Scott Appleton, Tony Degrate, Casey Hampton, Steve McMichael, Brad Shearer, Kenneth Sims
LINEBACKER: Britt Hager, Derrick Johnson, Jeff Leiding, Cordy Robertson
CORNERBACK: Mossy Cade, Raymond Clayborn, Quentin Jammer, Bryant Westbrook
SAFETY: Jerry Gray, Michael Huff, Johnnie Johnson, Stanley Richard

SPECIAL TEAMS

RETURN SPECIALIST: Nathan Vashar
PLACE KICKER: Jeff Ward
PUNTER: Russell Erxleben

TWO-WAY PLAYERS

TACKLE-DEFENSIVE TACKLE: Don Talbert
GUARD-END-LINEBACKER: Tommy Nobis, Johnny Treadwell
QUARTERBACK-SAFETY: Bill Bradley

PERFORMANCE FORMULA:
TEXAS' 10 BEST SEASONS

2005	1.9011	1 of 70
2008	1.8017	2 of 71
2009	1.7483	2 of 71
1969	1.7357	2 of 70
1970	1.7175	2 of 70
1963	1.6942	1 of 70
1977	1.6887	3 of 70
1972	1.6871	3 of 70
2004	1.6868	5 of 72
1960	1.6440	3 of 71

TEXAS LONGHORNS

Year	W-L-T	AP Poll	Conference Standing	Toughest Regular Season Opponents	Coach (Record at School)	Bowl Games
1953	7-3	11	1t	Oklahoma 8-1-1, Rice 8-2, Baylor 7-3	Ed Price	
1954	4-5-1		5	Oklahoma 10-0, No. Dame 9-1, Arkansas 8-2, Baylor 7-3, Rice 7-3	Ed Price	
1955	5-5		3	Oklahoma 10-0, TCU 9-1, Texas A&M 7-2-1, Texas Tech 7-2-1	Ed Price	
1956	1-9		7	Oklahoma 10-0, Texas A&M 9-0-1, Baylor 8-2, Southern Cal 8-2	Ed Price (33-27-1)	
1957	6-4-1	11	2	Oklahoma 9-1, Texas A&M 8-2, Rice 7-3, Baylor 6-3-1	Darrell Royal	Sugar 7 Mississippi 38
1958	7-3		4	Oklahoma 9-1, TCU 8-2, SMU 6-4	Darrell Royal	
1959	9-2	4	1t	Arkansas 8-2, TCU 8-2, Oklahoma 7-3	Darrell Royal	
1960	7-3-1		2t	Baylor 8-2, Arkansas 8-2, Rice 7-3	Darrell Royal	Bluebonnet 3 Alabama 3
1961	10-1	3	1t	Arkansas 8-2, Rice 7-3	Darrell Royal	Cotton 12 Mississippi 7
1962	9-1-1	4	1	Arkansas 9-1, Oklahoma 8-2, Oregon 6-3-1	Darrell Royal	Cotton 0 LSU 13
1963	11-0	1	1	Oklahoma 8-2, Baylor 7-3, Rice 6-4	Darrell Royal	Cotton 28 Navy 6
1964	10-1	5	2	Arkansas 10-0, Oklahoma 6-3-1, Texas Tech 6-3-1	Darrell Royal	Orange 21 Alabama 17
1965	6-4		4t	Arkansas 10-0, Texas Tech 8-2, TCU 6-4	Darrell Royal	Bluebonnet 19 Mississippi 0
1966	7-4		2	Arkansas 8-2, SMU 8-2, southern Cal 7-3	Darrell Royal	
1967	6-4		3t	Oklahoma 9-1, Southern Cal 9-1, Texas A&M 6-4, Texas Tech 6-4	Darrell Royal	
1968	9-1-1	3	1t	Arkansas 9-1, Oklahoma 7-3, SMU 7-3, Houston 6-2-2	Darrell Royal	Cotton 36 Tennessee 13
1969	11-0	1	1	Arkansas 9-1, Oklahoma 6-4	Darrell Royal	Cotton 21 Notre Dame 17
1970	10-1	3	1	Arkansas 9-2, Texas Tech 8-3, Oklahoma 7-4	Darrell Royal	Cotton 11 Notre Dame 24
1971	8-3	18	1	Oklahoma 10-1, Arkansas 8-2-1, TCU 6-4-1	Darrell Royal	Cotton 6 Penn State 30
1972	10-1	3	1	Oklahoma 10-1, Texas Tech 8-3, SMU 7-4, Utah State 8-3	Darrell Royal	Cotton 17 Alabama 13
1973	8-3	14	1	Oklahoma 10-01, Texas Tech 10-1	Darrell Royal	Cotton 3 Nebraska 19
1974	8-4	17t	2t	Oklahoma 11-0, Texas A&M 8-3, Baylor 8-3, Boston College 8-3	Darrell Royal	Gator 3 Auburn 27
1975	10-2	6	1t	Oklahoma 10-1, Texas A&M 10-1, Arkansas 9-2	Darrell Royal (167-47-5)	Bluebonnet 38 Colorado 21
1976	5-5-1		5	Texas Tech 10-1, Texas A&M 9-2, Houston 8-2, Oklahoma 8-2-1	Fred Akers	
1977	11-1	4	1	Oklahoma 10-1, Arkansas 9-2, Texas A&M 8-3, Texas Tech 7-4	Fred Akers	Cotton 10 Notre Dame 38
1978	9-3	9	2t	Oklahoma 10-1, Arkansas 9-2, Houston 9-2, Texas A&M 7-4	Fred Akers	Sun 42 Maryland 0
1979	9-3	12	3	Oklahoma 10-1, Arkansas 10-1, Houston 10-1, Baylor 7-4	Fred Akers	Sun 7 Washington 14
1980	7-5		4t	Oklahoma 9-2, Baylor 10-1, SMU 8-3	Fred Akers	Bluebonnet 7 North Carolina 16
1981	10-1-1	2	2	SMU 10-1, Miami 9-2, Arkansas 8-3, Houston 7-3-1	Fred Akers	Cotton 14 Alabama 12
1982	9-3	17	2	SMU 10-0-1, Arkansas 8-2-1, Oklahoma 8-3	Fred Akers	Sun 10 North Carolina 26
1983	11-1	5	1	Auburn 10-1, SMU 10-1, Baylor 7-3-1, Oklahoma 8-4	Fred Akers	Cotton 9 Georgia 10
1984	7-4-1		3t	Oklahoma 9-1-1, SMU 9-2, Arkansas 7-3-1, Auburn 8-4, TCU 8-3	Fred Akers	Freedom 17 Iowa 55
1985	8-4		2t	Oklahoma 10-1, Arkansas 9-2, Texas A&M 9-2, Baylor 8-3	Fred Akers (86-31-2)	Bluebonnet 16 Air Force 24
1986	5-6		5	Oklahoma 10-1, Arkansas 9-2, Texas A&M 9-2, Baylor 8-3	David McWilliams	
1987	7-5		2t	Oklahoma 11-0, Auburn 9-1-1, Texas A&M 9-2, Arkansas 9-3	David McWilliams	Bluebonnet 32 Pittsburgh 27
1988	4-7		4t	Arkansas 10-1, Oklahoma 9-2, Houston 9-2, BYU 9-3	David McWilliams	
1989	5-6		4t	Colorado 11-0, Arkansas 10-1, Houston 9-2, Texas Tech 8-3	David McWilliams	
1990	10-2	12	1	Colorado 10-1-1, Houston 10-1, Penn State 9-2, Oklahoma 8-3	David McWilliams	Cotton 3 Miami 46
1991	5-6		5t	Texas A&M 10-1, Oklahoma 8-3, Baylor 8-3	David McWilliams (31-26)	
1992	6-5		2t	Texas A&M 12-0, Syracuse 9-2	John Mackovic	
1993	5-5-1		2t	Texas A&M 10-1, Colorado 7-3-1, Louisville 8-3	John Mackovic	
1994	8-4	25	1t	Texas A&M 10-0-1, Colorado 10-1, Baylor 7-4, TCU 7-4	John Mackovic	Sun 35 North Carolina 31
1995	10-2-1	14	1	Notre Dame 9-2, Texas A&M 8-3, Texas Tech 8-3, Baylor 7-4	John Mackovic	Sugar 10 Virginia Tech 28
1996	8-5	23	S1	Colorado 9-2, Notre Dame 8-3, Virginia 7-4, Texas Tech 7-4	John Mackovic	Fiesta 15 Penn State 38
1997	4-7		S4t	Texas A&M 9-2, UCLA 9-2, Oklahoma State 8-3, Missouri 7-4	John Mackovic (41-28-2)	
1998	9-3	15	S2	Kansas State 11-0, UCLA 10-1, Texas A&M 10-2, Nebraska 9-3	Mack Brown	Cotton 38 Mississippi State 11
1999	9-5	21	S1	Nebraska 10-1, Kansas State 10-1, Stanford 8-3, Texas A&M 8-3	Mack Brown	Cotton 6 Arkansas 27
2000	9-3	12	S2	Oklahoma 11-0, Texas A&M 7-4, Texas Tech 7-5	Mack Brown	Holiday 30 Oregon 35
2001	11-2	5	S1	Oklahoma 10-2, Colorado 9-2, Texas Tech 7-4, Texas A&M 7-4	Mack Brown	Holiday 47 Washington 43
2002	11-2	6	S2	Oklahoma 10-2, Kansas State 10-2, Texas Tech 8-5	Mack Brown	Cotton 35 LSU 20
2003	10-3	12	S2	Oklahoma 12-0, Kansas St. 10-3, Nebraska 9-3, Oklahoma St. 9-3	Mack Brown	Holiday 20 Washington State 28
2004	11-1	5	S2	Oklahoma 10-1, Texas Tech 7-4, Texas A&M 7-4, Colorado 7-4	Mack Brown	Rose 38 Michigan 37
2005	13-0	1	S1	Ohio State 9-2, Oklahoma 7-4, Texas Tech 9-2	Mack Brown	Rose 41 Southern California 38
2006	10-3	13	S2	Ohio State 12-0, Oklahoma 10-2, Texas A&M 9-3, Nebraska 9-3	Mack Brown	Alamo 26 Iowa 24
2007	10-3	10t	S2	Central Florida 9-3, Oklahoma 10-2, Texas Tech 8-4	Mack Brown	Holiday 52 Arizona State 34
2008	12-1	4	S1t	Oklahoma 12-1, Missouri 9-4, Oklahoma State 9-3, Texas Tech 11-1	Mack Brown	Fiesta 24 Ohio State 21
2009	13-1	2	S1	Texas Tech 8-4, Oklahoma 7-5, Oklahoma State 9-3, Nebraska 9-4	Mack Brown	BCS Title 21 Alabama 37
2010	5-7		S6	Oklahoma 11-2, Nebraska 10-3, Oklahoma State 10-2, Texas A&M 9-3	Mack Brown (133-34)	

TOTAL: 475-188-10 .7132 (6 of 70)

Bowl Games since 1953: 20-20-1 .5000 (35 of 70)

GREATEST TEAM SINCE 1953: The Longhorns have had a number of great teams over the years, but the 2005 has set a new standard of excellence in Austin. While the talented defense employed by the Longhorns certainly was similar to every great Texas team of the past, the x factor was Vince Young, the most dynamic player in school history. By beating Ohio State in Columbus and Southern California in its backyard, the Longhorns proved that they were an all-time great team.

1953 7-3

7 LSU	20 E Gilmer Spring
41 Villanova	12 T Buck Lansford
28 Houston	7 G Kirby Miller / Don McGraw
14 Oklahoma	19 C Johnny Tatum / Leighton Younger
16 Arkansas	19 G Phil Branch
13 Rice	18 T Herb Gray (G) / Cliff Polk
16 SMU	7 E Carlton Massey / Menan Schriewer
21 Baylor	20 QB Charley Brewer / John Andrews
13 TCU	3 HB Delano Womack / Ed Kelley
21 Texas A&M	12 HB Billy Quinn / George Robinson
	FB Doug Cameron / William Long

RUSHING: Cameron 136/518y, Womack 64/296y, Quinn 56/228y
PASSING: Brewer 33-68/533y, 3TD, 48.5%
RECEIVING: Massey 11/165y, Womack 8/143y, Spring 6/129y
SCORING: Womack 42pts, Cameron 36pts,
  Branch (G-K) & Brewer 18pts

1954 4-5-1

20 LSU	6 E Howard Moon / Morton Moriarty
0 Notre Dame	21 T Buck Lansford
40 Washington St.	14 G Kirby Miller
7 Oklahoma	14 C Johnny Tatum
7 Arkansas	20 G Herb Gray
7 Rice	13 T Bob Flinn / Ben Woodson
13 SMU	13 E Menan Schriewer
7 Baylor	13 QB Charley Brewer / Pat Tolar
35 TCU	34 HB Delano Womack / Joe Youngblood
22 Texas A&M	13 HB Billy Quinn (FB) / Chester Simcik
	FB Don Maroney / Bill Long

RUSHING: Quinn 83/442y, Womack 58/267y, Maroney 66/264y
PASSING: Brewer 28-71/473y, 3TD, 39.4%
RECEIVING: Schriewer 17/306y, Womack 5/158y, Moon 5/73y
SCORING: Maroney 24pts, Youngblood (HB-K) 19pts

1955 5-5

14 Texas Tech	20 E Menan Schriewer / Howard Moon
35 Tulane	21 T Garland Kennon
7 Southern Cal	19 G Louis Del Homme / Langford Sneed
0 Oklahoma	20 C Johnny Tatum
20 Arkansas	27 G Herb Gray
32 Rice	14 T Bob Tucker / J.T. Seaholm
19 SMU	18 E Ed Kelley / Pat Tolar
21 Baylor	20 QB Charley Brewer / Joe Clements
20 TCU	47 HB Walter Fondren
21 Texas A&M	6 HB Ed Hawkins / Joe Youngblood
	FB Delano Womack / Don Maroney

RUSHING: Fondren 108/577y, Womack 116/501y,
  Hawkins 33/177y
PASSING: Clements 65-128/818y, 6TD, 50.8%
RECEIVING: Schriewer 21/301y, Fondren 14/158y, Wash 11/182y
SCORING: Fondren 49pts, Womack 24pts, 3 tied w/ 18pts

1956 1-9

20 Southern Cal	44 E Wayne Wash / Joe Losack
7 Tulane	6 T J.T. Seaholm / Wes Wyman
6 West Virginia	7 G Louis Del Homme / Don Wilson
0 Oklahoma	45 C Arlis Parkhurst
14 Arkansas	32 G Don Wilson / Bill Carrico
7 Rice	28 T Garland Kennon / Will Wyman
19 SMU	20 E Bobby Bryant / Mike Trant
7 Baylor	10 QB Joe Clements / Vince Matthews
0 TCU	46 HB Walter Fondren / Mickey Smith
21 Texas A&M	34 HB Carl Wylie / Clair Branch
	FB Jimmy Welch / Don Maroney

RUSHING: Fondren 115/493y, Welch 61/219y, Branch 46/201y
PASSING: Clements 74-151/793y, 7TD, 49%
RECEIVING: Bryant 24/301y, Fondren 22/318y, Losack 11/153y
SCORING: Fondren 47pts, Branch 24pts, Clements 12pts

1957 6-4-1

26 Georgia	7 E Maurice Doke / Larry Stepens
20 Tulane	6 T J.T. Seaholm / Wes Wyman
21 South Carolina	27 G Don Wilson / Henry Anderson
7 Oklahoma	21 C Louis Del Homme / Arlis Parkhurst
17 Arkansas	0 G Robert Lee / Jim Shillingburg
19 Rice	14 T Garland Kennon / Will Wyman
12 SMU	19 E Richard Schulte / Monte Lee
7 Baylor	7 QB Walter Fondren / Bobby Lackey
14 TCU	2 HB Mickey Smith / George Blanch
9 Texas A&M	7 HB Roy Alvis / Rene Ramirez
7 Mississippi■	39 FB Mike Dowdle / Don Allen

RUSHING: Dowdle 99/429y, Blanch 65/284y, Ramirez 53/282y
PASSING: Fondren 33-49/428y, 5TD, 67.3%
RECEIVING: Blanch 11/174y, Ramirez 9/115y, Alvis 9/100y
SCORING: Ramirez 30pts, Lackey 29pts, Dowdle & Blanch 24pts

1958 7-3

13 Georgia	8 E Bobby Bryant / Richard Schulte
21 Tulane	20 T Dick Jones / Tillman O'Brien
12 Texas Tech	7 G H.G. Anderson / Bob Harwerth
15 Oklahoma	14 C Artis Parkhurst / Jerry Muennink
24 Arkansas	6 G John Padgett
7 Rice	34 T Jim Shillingburg / Larry Stephens
10 SMU	26 E Maurice Doke
20 Baylor	15 QB Bobby Lackey
8 TCU	22 HB George Blanch / Bobby Ray Matocha
27 Texas A&M	0 HB Rene Ramirez / Drew Morris
	FB Don Allen / Mike Dowdle

RUSHING: Dowdle 85/345y, Ramirez 72/323y, Blanch 86/316y
PASSING: Lackey 15-46/242y, 2TD, 32.6%
RECEIVING: Bryant 14/233y, Ramirez 7/102y, Morris 7/72y
SCORING: Lackey (QB-K) 41pts, Ramirez 30pts, Dowdle 24pts

1959 9-2

20 Nebraska	0 E Larry Cooper / Richard Schulte
26 Maryland	0 T Larry Stephens / Don Talbert
33 Cal	0 G Maurice Doke
19 Oklahoma	12 C Jerry Muennink
13 Arkansas	12 G Babe Dreymala / Bob Harwerth
28 Rice	6 T Dick Jones / Eddie Padgett
21 SMU	0 E Monte Lee
13 Baylor	12 QB Bobby Lackey / Mike Cotten
9 TCU	14 HB Jack Collins
20 Texas A&M	17 HB Rene Ramirez / Bob Gurwitz
14 Syracuse■	23 FB Clair Branch / Mike Dowdle

RUSHING: Collins 89/450y, Ramirez 62/355y, Dowdle 75/282y
PASSING: Lackey 11-23/142y, 2TD, 47.8%
RECEIVING: Collins 8/134y, Cooper 6/62y, Ramirez 5/41y
SCORING: Lackey (QB-K) 45pts, Collins 42pts, Dowdle 30pts

1960 7-3-1

13 Nebraska	14 E Tommy Lucas / Bob Moses
34 Maryland	0 T Jim Moffett / Don Talbert
17 Texas Tech	0 G Monte Lee / Johnny Treadwell
24 Oklahoma	0 C Bill Laughlin / David Kristynik
23 Arkansas	24 G Marv Kubin / H.G. Anderson
0 Rice	7 T Dick Jones / Eddie Padgett
17 SMU	7 E Larry Cooper / Buddy Fults
12 Baylor	7 QB Mike Cotton / Johnny Genung
3 TCU	2 HB Jack Collins / Dave Russell
21 Texas A&M	14 HB James Saxton / Bob Gurwitz
3 Alabama■	3 FB Ray Poage / Pat Culpepper

RUSHING: Saxton 76/407y, Poage 70/247y, Collins 54/238y
PASSING: Cotton 32-58/539y, 3TD, 55.2%
RECEIVING: Saxton 9/185y, Jerry Cook (HB) 9/99y, Poage 7/119y
SCORING: Cotton 30pts, Collins 26pts, Daniel Petty (K) 25pts

1961 10-1

28 California	3 E Bob Moses
42 Texas Tech	14 T Ed Padgett / Scott Appleton
41 Washington St.	8 G Marv Kubin / David McWilliams
28 Oklahoma	7 C Dave Kristynik / Perry McWilliams
33 Arkansas	7 G Johnny Treadwell / George Brucks
34 Rice	7 T Don Talbert / Ken Ferguson
27 SMU	0 E Tommy Lucas / Buddy Fults
33 Baylor	7 QB Mike Cotton / Duke Carlisle (D)
0 TCU	6 WB Jack Collins / David Russell (D)
25 Texas A&M	0 HB James Saxton / Tom Ford / Jerry Cook
12 Mississippi■	7 FB Ray Poage / Pat Culpepper (D)

RUSHING: Saxton 107/846y, Cook 96/527y, Ford 83/415y
PASSING: Cotton 44-77/500y, 7TD, 57.1%
RECEIVING: Moses 14/177y, Collins 13/152y, Saxton 7/123y
SCORING: Saxton & Cook 56pts, Eldon Moritz (K) 34pts

1962 9-1-1

25 Oregon	13 E Tommy Lucas
34 Texas Tech	0 T Scott Appleton / Staley Faulkner
35 Tulane	8 G Marv Kubin / George Brucks
9 Oklahoma	6 C Perry McWilliams / David McWilliams
7 Arkansas	3 G Johnny Treadwell
14 Rice	14 T Ken Ferguson / Gordon Roberts
6 SMU	0 E Sandy Sands / Charles Talbert
27 Baylor	12 QB Tom Wade/Duke Carlisle/John Genung
14 TCU	0 WB Ernie Koy / Joe Dixon (D)
13 Texas A&M	3 HB Tommy Ford / Jerry Cook
0 LSU■	13 FB Ray Poage / Pat Culpepper

RUSHING: Poage 141/452y, Ford 112/424y, Cook 85/346y
PASSING: Wade 33-78/434y, 3TD, 42.3%
RECEIVING: Sands 12/148y, Lucas 9/157y, Koy 9/103y
SCORING: Cook 42pts, Poage 30pts, Ford 24pts

1963 11-0

21 Tulane	0 E Ben House / Knox Nunnally
49 Texas Tech	7 T Scott Appleton / Clayton Lacy
34 Oklahoma State	7 G George Brucks / Frank Bedrick
28 Oklahoma	7 C David McWilliams / Clarence Bray
17 Arkansas	13 G Tommy Nobis / Olen Underwood
10 Rice	6 T Staley Faulkner / Gordon Roberts
17 SMU	12 E Charles Talbert / Pete Lammons
7 Baylor	0 QB Duke Carlisle / Jim Hudson (D)
17 TCU	0 WB Phil Harris / Joe Dixon (D)
15 Texas A&M	13 TB Tommy Ford
28 Navy■	6 FB Harold Philipp / Tim Doerr (D)

RUSHING: Ford 160/738y, Carlisle 129/415y, Philipp 76/381y
PASSING: Carlisle 33-79/416y, 1TD, 41.8%
RECEIVING: Talbert 14/188y, Lammons 7/97y, Sauer 6/97y
SCORING: Ford 54pts, Hugh Crosby (K) 51pts, Harris 38pts

1964 10-1

31 Tulane	0 E George Sauer / Sandy Sands
23 Texas Tech	0 T Gene Bledsoe
17 Army	6 G Frank Bedrick / Lee Hensley
28 Oklahoma	7 C Olen Underwood / Jack Howe
13 Arkansas	14 G Tommy Nobis
6 Rice	3 T John Elliott
7 SMU	0 TE Pete Lammons
20 Baylor	14 QB Marvin Kristynik
28 TCU	13 WB Phil Harris
26 Texas A&M	7 TB Ernie Koy
21 Alabama■	17 FB Harold Philipp
	DL Dan Maudlin
	DL Clayton Lacy
	DL Howard Goad / Jack Howe
	DL Frank Bedrick
	DL Diron Talbert
	DL Knox Nunnally / Pete Lammons
	LB Tommy Nobis
	LB Fred Edwards
	DB Joe Dixon
	DB Anthony King
	DB Gary Moore

RUSHING: Koy 154/574y, Philipp 123/553y, Kristynik 82/248y
PASSING: Kristynik 41-99/563y, 2TD, 41.4%
RECEIVING: Lammons 13/204y, Sauer 12/166y, Harris 12/156y
SCORING: Koy 48pts, David Conway (K) 45pts, Philipp 30pts

1965 6-4

31 Tulane	0 E Kelly Baker / Ed Small
33 Texas Tech	7 T Gene Bledsoe
27 Indiana	12 G Frank Bedrick
19 Oklahoma	0 C Jack Howe
24 Arkansas	27 G Tommy Nobis / Ronnie Landry
17 Rice	20 T Howard Goad
14 SMU	31 E Pete Lammons
35 Baylor	14 QB Marvin Kristynik
10 TCU	25 WB Les Derrick
21 Texas A&M	17 TB Phil Harris / Jim Helms / Linus Baer
	FB Tom Stockton / Charles Owens
	DL Barney Giles
	DL Frank Bedrick
	DL John Elliott / Joel Brame
	DL Diron Talbert
	DL Bob Stanley / Jack Howe
	DL Pete Lammons / Bill Sullivan
	LB Tommy Nobis
	LB Fred Edwards
	DB Ronnie Ehrig
	DB Phil Harris / Peter Gallaher
	DB Gary Moore

RUSHING: Stockton 127/517y, Harris 84/367y, Owens 37/243y
PASSING: Kristynik 72-148/1005y, 8TD, 48.6%
RECEIVING: Lammons 27/405y, Derrick 20/337y, Harris 14/157y
SCORING: David Conway (K) 45pts, Derrick 30pts,
  Lammons 26pts

SCORES, LINEUPS, AND STATISTICS

1966 7-4

6	Southern Cal	10 E Ed Small
31	Texas Tech	21 T Howard Goad
35	Indiana	0 G Danny Abbott
9	Oklahoma	18 C Loyd Wainscott / Barry Stone (T)
7	Arkansas	12 G Ron Landry
14	Rice	6 T Gene Bledsoe (C)
12	SMU	13 TE Ragan Gennusa / Tom Higgins
26	Baylor	14 QB Bill Bradley
13	TCU	3 WB Jim Helms / Greg Lott
22	Texas A&M	14 TB Chris Gilbert
19	Mississippi■	0 FB Linus Baer
		DL Barney Giles / Mike Perrin
		DL Mike Robuck / D.H. Martin
		DL John Elliott / Jerry Pritchard
		DL Diron Talbert
		DL Bob Stanley
		DL Corby Robertson
		LB Fred Edwards
		LB Joel Brame
		DB Les Derrick
		DB Dick Watt / Denny Aldridge
		DB Pat Harkins

RUSHING: Gilbert 206/1080y, Bradley 124/335y, Baer 47/211y
PASSING: Bradley 36-76/535y, 4TD, 47.4%
RECEIVING: Gennusa 19/243y, Higgins 12/201y, Helms 8/76y
SCORING: David Conway (K) 41pts, Gilbert & Bradley 36pts

1967 6-4

13	Southern Cal	17 E Ragan Gennusa / Tom Higgins
13	Texas Tech	19 T Howard Fest / Tommy Souders
19	Oklahoma State	0 G Danny Abbott
9	Oklahoma	7 C Ken Gidney (G) / Forrest Wiegand
21	Arkansas	12 G Warren Gremmel
28	Rice	6 T Tommy Rohrer
35	SMU	28 TE Deryl Comer / Ed Small
24	Baylor	0 QB Bill Bradley
17	TCU	24 WB Randy Peschel
7	Texas A&M	10 HB Chris Gilbert
		FB Linus Baer
		DL Mike Perrin
		DL Loyd Wainscott
		DL Jim Williamson
		DL D.H. Martin / Leo Brooks
		DL Bob Stanley
		DL Corby Robertson (LB) / Mack McKinney
		LB Joel Brame
		LB Glen Halsell
		DB Dick Watt / Ronnie Ehrig
		DB Denny Aldridge
		DB Pat Harkins

RUSHING: Gilbert 205/1019y, Bradley 172/443y, Koy 103/355y
PASSING: Bradley 72-153/1181y, 4TD, 47.1%
RECEIVING: Gennusa 19/310y, Peschel 19/296y, Higgins 17/316y
SCORING: Gilbert 48pts, Bobby Layne, Jr. (K) 28pts

1968 9-1-1

20	Houston	20 E Cotton Speyrer
22	Texas Tech	31 T Bobby Wuensch
31	Oklahoma State	3 G Danny Abbott / Mike Dean
26	Oklahoma	20 C Forrest Wiegand
39	Arkansas	29 G Ken Gidney
38	Rice	14 T Tommy Souders / Bob McKay
38	SMU	7 TE Deryl Comer
47	Baylor	26 QB Bill Bradley / James Street
47	TCU	21 HB Chris Gilbert
35	Texas A&M	14 HB Ted Koy
36	Tennessee■	13 FB Steve Worster
		DL Leo Brooks / Jim Williamson
		DL Loyd Wainscott
		DL Tom Campbell / Mack McKinney
		DL Bill Atessis
		DL Bill Zapalac
		LB Corby Robertson
		LB Glen Halsell
		LB Greg Ploetz / Scott Henderson
		DB Ronnie Ehrig
		DB Bill Bradley / Denny Aldridge
		DB Freddie Steinmark

RUSHING: Gilbert 184/1132y, Worster 161/806y, Koy 108/601y
PASSING: Street 67-135/1099y, 6TD, 49.6%
RECEIVING: Speyrer 26/449y, Comer 14/223y, Worster 8/64y
SCORING: Gilbert 82pts, Worster 78pts, Happy Feller (K) 54pts

1969 11-0

17	California	0 WR Cotton Speyrer / Ken Ehrig
49	Texas Tech	7 T Bobby Wuensch
56	Navy	17 G Bobby Mitchell / Randy Stout
27	Oklahoma	17 C Forrest Wiegand
31	Rice	0 G Mike Dean
45	SMU	14 T Bob McKay
56	Baylor	14 TE Randy Peschel / Tommy Woodard
69	TCU	7 QB James Street
49	Texas A&M	12 HB Jim Bertelsen / Terry Collins
15	Arkansas	14 HB Ted Koy / Billy Dale
21	Notre Dame■	17 FB Steve Worster / Bobby Callison
		DL David Arledge / Scott Palmer
		DL Leo Brooks / Carl White
		DL Greg Ploetz
		DL Bill Atessis
		LB Mike Campbell
		LB Bill Zapalac
		LB Scott Henderson / David Richardson
		LB Glen Halsell
		DB Danny Lester / Paul Kristynik
		DB Tom Campbell
		DB Freddie Steinmark / Rick Nabors

RUSHING: Bertelsen 104/740y, Worster 136/649y, Koy 84/441y
PASSING: Street 40-81/699y, 3TD, 49.4%
RECEIVING: Speyrer 30/492y, Peschel 14/228y, Ehrig 10/167y
SCORING: Bertelsen 78pts, Happy Feller (K) 61pts, Worster 54pts

1970 10-1

56	California	15 WR Cotton Speyrer / Danny Lester
35	Texas Tech	13 T Bobby Wuensch
20	UCLA	17 G Bobby Mitchell
41	Oklahoma	9 C Jim Achilles
45	Rice	21 G Mike Dean
42	SMU	15 T Jerry Sisemore
21	Baylor	14 TE Deryl Comer
58	TCU	0 QB Eddie Phillips
52	Texas A&M	14 HB Jim Bertelsen
42	Arkansas	7 HB Bill Dale / Terry Collins
11	Notre Dame■	24 FB Steve Worster
		DL Bill Atessis
		DL Scott Palmer
		DL Ray Dowdy
		DL David Arledge
		LB Bill Zapalac
		LB Randy Braband / David Richardson
		LB Scott Henderson
		LB Stan Mauldin
		DB Alan Lowry
		DB Danny Lester / Mike Bayer
		DB Rick Nabors

RUSHING: Worster 160/898y, Bertelsen 148/891y, Phillips 149/666y
PASSING: Phillips 39-96/695y, 4TD, 40.6%
RECEIVING: Lester 17/365y, Speyrer 9/152y, Bertelsen 6/89y
SCORING: Worster 84pts, Bertelsen 78pts, Phillips 72pts

1971 8-3

28	UCLA	10 WR Pat Kelly / Jimmy Moore
28	Texas Tech	0 T Bill Wyman
35	Oregon	7 G Travis Roach
27	Oklahoma	48 C Jeff Zapalac
7	Arkansas	31 G Don Crosslin
39	Rice	10 T Jerry Sisemore
22	SMU	18 TE Rick Davis / Stan Hicks
24	Baylor	0 QB Donnie Wigginton / Eddie Phillips
31	TCU	0 HB Jim Bertelsen
34	Texas A&M	14 HB Don Burrisk / Don Steakley
6	Penn State■	30 FB Bobby Callison / Dennis Ladd
		DL Jay Arnold / Don Ealey
		DL Ray Dowdy
		DL Greg Ploetz
		DL Stan Hicks / Malcolm Minnick
		LB Glen Gaspard / Greg Dahlberg
		LB Randy Braband
		LB Stan Mauldin / Bruce Cannon
		LB Tommy Woodard / Tommy Landry
		DB Mike Rowan / Ronnie Workman
		DB Mike Bayer
		DB Alan Lowry

RUSHING: Bertelsen 160/879y, Wigginton 109/485y, Callison 108/446y
PASSING: Wigginton 35-67/544y, 1TD, 52.2%
RECEIVING: Kelly 17/226y, Davis 9/166y, Bertelsen 5/57y
SCORING: Wigginton 84pts, Bertelsen 42pts, Ladd 30pts

1972 10-1

23	Miami	10 WR Jimmy Moore / Pat Kelly
25	Texas Tech	20 T Steve Oxley
27	Utah State	12 G Don Crosslin / Bruce Hebert
0	Oklahoma	27 C Bill Wyman
35	Arkansas	15 G Travis Roach
45	Rice	9 T Jerry Sisemore
17	SMU	9 TE Julius Whittier / Rick Davis
17	Baylor	3 QB Alan Lowry
27	TCU	0 HB Don Ealey / Lonnie Bennett
38	Texas A&M	3 HB Tommy Landry / Don Burrisk
17	Alabama■	13 FB Roosevelt Leaks
		DL Jay Arnold / Bill Rutherford
		DL Fred Currin
		DL Doug English
		DL Malcolm Minnick
		LB Bruce Cannon
		LB Sherman Lee
		LB Glen Gaspard
		LB Randy Braband
		DB Mike Bayer
		DB Mike Rowan
		DB Tommy Keel

RUSHING: Leaks 230/1099y, Lowry 168/661y, Ealey 44/213y
PASSING: Lowry 46-117/766y, 1TD, 39.3%
RECEIVING: Moore 23/413y, Kelly 6/124y, Bennett 4/66y
SCORING: Lowry 66pts, Billy Schott (K) 52pts, Leaks 50pts

1973 8-3

15	Miami	20 WR Jimmy Moore / Pat Kelly
28	Texas Tech	12 T Will Wilcox
41	Wake Forest	0 G Don Crosslin
13	Oklahoma	52 C Jim Wyman
34	Arkansas	6 G Bruce Hebert
55	Rice	13 T Bob Simmons
42	SMU	14 TE Parker Alford / Tom Ingram
42	Baylor	6 QB Marty Akins / Mike Presley
52	TCU	7 HB Lonnie Bennett / Tommy Landry
42	Texas A&M	13 HB Joe Aboussie
3	Nebraska■	19 FB Roosevelt Leaks
		DL Bill Rutherford
		DL Fred Currin / Rick Thurman
		DL Doug English
		DL Malcolm Minnick
		LB Sherman Lee / Greg Dahlberg
		LB Glen Gaspard
		LB Wade Johnston
		DB Terry Melancon
		DB Jay Arnold
		DB Joe Bob Bizzell / Tommy Keel
		DB Gary Yeoman

RUSHING: Leaks 229/1415y, Akins 118/492y, Aboussie 51/346y
PASSING: Akins 35-70/475y, 4TD, 50%
RECEIVING: Kelly 19/268y, Moore 8/93y, Pat Padgett (WR) 5/96y
SCORING: Leaks 84pts, Billy Schott (K) 58pts, Presley 54pts

1974 8-4

42	Boston College	19 WR Pat Padgett
34	Wyoming	7 T Rick Thurman / George James
3	Texas Tech	26 G Will Wilcox
35	Washington	21 C Bob Tresch
13	Oklahoma	16 G Bruce Hebert
38	Arkansas	7 T Bob Simmons
27	Rice	6 TE Tom Ingram / Joe Samford
35	SMU	15 QB Marty Akins / Mike Presley
24	Baylor	34 HB Gralyn Wyatt / Raymond Clayborn
81	TCU	16 HB Jimmy Walker
32	Texas A&M	3 FB Earl Campbell / Roosevelt Leaks
3	Auburn■	27 DL Lionell Johnson / David McLeod
		DL Brad Shearer / Fred Currin
		DL Doug English
		DL Travis Couch / Rick Burleson
		LB Bill Hamilton
		LB Wade Johnston
		LB Sherman Lee
		DB Sammie Mason / Paul Jette
		DB Alfred Jackson / Mike Hartinger
		DB Fred Sarchet
		DB Terry Melancon

RUSHING: Campbell 162/928y, Akins 132/659y, Wyatt 76/590y
PASSING: Akins 19-47/250y, 1TD, 40.4%
RECEIVING: Padgett 12/141y, Ingram 7/104y, Samford 6/97y
SCORING: Billy Schott (K) 65pts, Akins 60pts, Wyatt 48pts

1975 10-2

46 Colorado State	0 WR Alfred Jackson
28 Washington	10 T George James / David Studdard
42 Texas Tech	18 G Will Wilcox
61 Utah State	7 C Billy Gordon
17 Oklahoma	24 G Charles Wilcox
24 Arkansas	18 T Bob Simmons
41 Rice	9 TE Tom Ingram / Joe Samford
30 SMU	22 QB Marty Akins / Ted Constanzo
37 Baylor	21 HB Gralyn Wyatt / Ivey Suber
27 TCU	11 HB Jimmy Walker
10 Texas A&M	20 FB Earl Campbell
38 Colorado■	21 DL Rick Burleson / Steve Straty
	DL Brad Shearer
	DL Robert Rickman / Ernest Lee
	DL Tim Campbell / Rick Burleson
	LB Lionell Johnson
	LB Bill Hamilton
	LB Rick Fenlaw
	DB Paul Jette
	DB Raymond Clayborn
	DB Steve Collier
	DB Fred Sarchet

RUSHING: Campbell 198/1118y, Akins 149/777y, Wyatt 76/451y
PASSING: Akins 31-56/463y, 2TD, 55.4%
RECEIVING: Jackson 32/596y, Samford 4/45y, Wyatt 3/15y
SCORING: Cambell 78pts, Russell Erxleben (K) 67pts, Wyatt 48pts

1976 5-5-1

13 Boston College	14 WR Alfred Jackson / Mike Lockett
17 North Texas	14 T David Studdard
42 Rice	15 G Charles Wilcox
6 Oklahoma	6 C Billy Gordon
13 SMU	12 G Rick Ingraham
28 Texas Tech	31 T George James / Jim Yarbrough
0 Houston	30 TE Joe Samford / Gil Harris
34 TCU	7 QB Mike Cordaro / Mark McBath
10 Baylor	20 HB Lam Jones / Ivey Suber
3 Texas A&M	27 HB Jimmy Walker / Ham Jones
29 Arkansas	12 FB Earl Campbell / Jimmy Johnson
	DL Tim Campbell / Jim Gresham
	DL Brad Shearer
	DL Ernest Lee
	DL Rick Burleson
	LB Bill Hamilton
	LB Rick Fenlaw
	LB Lionell Johnson / Morgan Copeland
	DB Raymond Clayborn
	DB Paul Jette
	DB Steve Collier / Ricky Churchman
	DB Glenn Blackwood / Johnnie Johnson

RUSHING: Campbell 138/653y, L. Jones 118/624y, Johnson 48/272y
PASSING: Cordaro 22-49/407y, 2TD, 44.9%
RECEIVING: Jackson 19/364y, Lockett 13/197y, Samford 4/53y
SCORING: Russell Erxleben (K) 56pts, L. Jones 30pts, 3 tied w/ 18pts

1977 11-1

44 Boston College	0 WR Lam Jones
68 Virginia	0 WR Alfred Jackson
72 Rice	15 T George James
13 Oklahoma	6 G Rick Ingraham
13 Arkansas	9 C Wes Hubert
30 SMU	14 G Jim Yarbrough
26 Texas Tech	0 T Dave Studdard
35 Houston	21 TE Gil Harris / Steve Hall
44 TCU	14 QB Randy McEachern / Mark McBath
29 Baylor	7 HB Ham Jones
57 Texas A&M	28 HB Earl Campbell
10 Notre Dame■	38 DL Henry Williams / Dwight Jefferson
	DL Brad Shearer
	DL Steve McMichael / Bill Acker
	DL Tim Campbell
	LB Mark Martignoni
	LB Morgan Copeland
	LB Lance Taylor
	DB Derrick Hatchett
	DB Glenn Blackwood
	DB Ricky Churchman
	DB Johnnie Johnson

RUSHING: Campbell 267/1744y, H. Jones 92/489y, McBath 26/213y
PASSING: McEachern 45-89/906y, 8TD, 50.6%
RECEIVING: L. Jones 21/543y, Jackson 19/481y, Harris 8/93y
SCORING: Campbell 114pts, Russell Erxleben (K) 81pts, L. Jones 42pts

1978 9-3

34 Rice	0 WR Lam Jones
17 Wyoming	3 WR Ronnie Miksch / Les Koenning
24 Texas Tech	7 T Craig Rider
10 Oklahoma	31 G Jim Yarbrough / Mike Baab
26 North Texas	16 C Wes Hubert
28 Arkansas	21 G Joe Shearin
22 SMU	3 T Terry Tausch
7 Houston	10 TE Les Studdard / Lawrence Sampleton
41 TCU	0 QB Randy McEachern / Donnie Little
14 Baylor	18 HB Jam Jones
22 Texas A&M	7 FB Ham Jones / LeRoy King
42 Maryland■	0 DL Dwight Jefferson
	DL Steve McMichael
	DL Bill Acker
	DL Henry Williams / Ronnie Bones
	LB Bruce Scholtz
	LB Robin Sendlein
	LB Lance Taylor / Doug Shankle
	DB Derrick Hatchett
	DB Ricky Churchman
	DB Glenn Blackwood
	DB Johnnie Johnson

RUSHING: J. Jones 121/465y, Little 73/410y, H. Jones 111/403y
PASSING: McEachern 40-96/658y, 7TD, 41.7%
RECEIVING: L. Jones 25/446y, Miksch 14/142y, Sampleton 8/196y
SCORING: Russell Erxleben (K) 63pts, L. Jones 42pts, H. Jones 26pts

1979 9-3

17 Iowa State	9 WR Lam Jones
21 Missouri	0 WR Les Koenning
26 Rice	9 T Craig Rider
16 Oklahoma	7 G Joe Shearin
14 Arkansas	17 C Wes Hubert
30 SMU	6 G Terry Tausch
14 Texas Tech	6 T Les Studdard
21 Houston	13 TE Lawrence Sampleton
35 TCU	10 QB Donnie Little
13 Baylor	0 HB Jam Jones
7 Texas A&M	13 FB LeRoy King / Rodney Tate
7 Washington■	14 DL Henry Williams
	DL Steve McMichael
	DL Bill Acker / Kenneth Sims
	DL Ron Bones / Tim Campbell
	LB Chuck Holloway
	LB Robin Sendlein
	LB Doug Shankle
	DB Vance Bedford
	DB Ricky Churchman
	DB Derrick Hatchett
	DB Jonnie Johnson

RUSHING: J. Jones 188/918y, Little 126/410y, King 78/353y
PASSING: Little 56-113/750y, 2TD, 50%
RECEIVING: L. Jones 36/535y, Koenning 18/326y, Sampleton 16/315y
SCORING: John Goodson (K) 72pts, J. Jones 60pts, Little 18pts

1980 7-5

23 Arkansas	17 WR Les Koenning
35 Utah State	17 WR Maurice McCloney / Herkie Walls
35 Oregon State	0 T Terry Tausch
41 Rice	28 G Les Studdard
20 Oklahoma	30 C Mike Baab
6 SMU	20 G Joe Shearin / Alan Williams
20 Texas Tech	24 T John Tobolka / Bryan Millard
15 Houston	13 TE Lawrence Sampleton
51 TCU	26 QB Donnie Little
0 Baylor	16 HB Jam Jones / Rodney Tate
14 Texas A&M	24 FB Darryl Clark / Carl Robinson
7 North Carolina■	16 DL Ken McCune
	DL Kenneth Sims
	DL Steve Massey / Dan Hunter
	DL Dewey Turner / Kiki DeAyala
	LB Doug Shankle
	LB Robin Sendlein
	LB Bruce Scholtz
	DB William Graham
	DB Derrick Hatchett
	DB Bobby Johnson
	DB Levi Mays

RUSHING: Jones 146/657y, Little 122/486y, Clark 82/353y
PASSING: Little 82-155/1098y, 5TD, 52.9%
RECEIVING: Koenning 27/401y, Sampleton 20/381y, Clark 18/130y
SCORING: John Goodson (K) 62pts, Jones 54pts, Little 42pts

1981 10-1-1

31 Rice	3 WR Maurice McCloney / Herkie Walls
23 North Texas	10 WR Donnie Little
14 Miami	7 T John Tobolka / Bryan Millard
34 Oklahoma	14 G Joe Shearin
11 Arkansas	42 C Mike Baab
9 SMU	7 G Doug Dawson
26 Texas Tech	9 T Terry Tausch
14 Houston	14 TE Lawrence Sampleton
31 TCU	15 QB Rick McIvor / Robert Brewer
34 Baylor	12 HB Jam Jones / John Walker
21 Texas A&M	13 FB Darryl Clark / Carl Robinson
14 Alabama■	12 DL Kiki DeAyala
	DL Kenneth Sims / Ralph Darnell
	DL Mark Weber / John Haines
	DL Eric Holle / Mike Buchanan
	LB Bruce Scholtz
	LB Doug Shankle
	LB Jeff Leiding
	DB Vance Bedford
	DB Mike Hatchett
	DB William Graham
	DB Bobby Johnson / Craig Curry

RUSHING: Jones 190/834y, Walker 154/714y, Robinson 50/225y
PASSING: McIvor 56-139/918y, 5TD, 40.3%
RECEIVING: Little 18/338y, Robinson 14/113y, Sampleton 13/179y
SCORING: Raul Allegre (K) 70pts, Walker 38pts, Jones 36pts

1982 9-3

21 Utah	12 WR Herkie Walls
21 Missouri	0 WR Brent Duhon
34 Rice	7 T Casey Smith
22 Arkansas	28 G Doug Dawson
17 SMU	30 C Mike Ruether
27 Texas Tech	0 G Kirk McJunkin / Adam Schreiber
50 Houston	0 T Bryan Millard
38 TCU	21 TE Bobby Micho
31 Baylor	23 QB Robert Brewer
53 Texas A&M	16 HB Darryl Clark / John Walker
33 Arkansas	7 FB Terry Orr / Ervin Davis
10 North Carolina■	26 DL Kiki DeAyala / Ed Williams
	DL John Haines / Ralph Darnell
	DL Tony Degrate
	DL Eric Holle
	LB Larry Ford / June James
	LB Jeff Leiding / Tony Edwards
	LB Mark Lang
	DB Fred Acorn / Jitter Fields
	DB Mossy Cade
	DB Craig Curry
	DB Jerry Gray / Richard Peavy

RUSHING: Clark 198/1049y, Walker 86/381y, Davis 56/278y
PASSING: Brewer 91-193/1415y, 12TD, 47.2%
RECEIVING: Walls 25/702y, Duhon 21/367y, Micho 16/255y
SCORING: Raul Allegre (K) 77pts, Walls 66pts, Davis 48pts

1983 11-1

20 Auburn	7 WR Bill Boy Bryant / Kelvin Epps
26 North Texas	6 WR Brent Duhon
42 Rice	6 T Casey Smith
28 Oklahoma	16 G Doug Dawson / Adam Schreiber
31 Arkansas	3 C Mike Ruether / David Jones
15 SMU	12 G Kirk McJunkin
20 Texas Tech	3 T Gene Chilton
9 Houston	3 TE Mike Chapman
20 TCU	14 QB Rob Moerschell
24 Baylor	21 HB John Walker / Anthony Byerly
45 Texas A&M	13 FB Ronnie Robinson
9 Georgia■	10 DL Eric Holle
	DL Tony Degrate
	DL John Haines
	DL Ed Williams
	LB Mark Lang
	LB Tony Edwards / Jeff Leiding
	LB June James / Ty Allert
	DB Mossy Cade
	DB Fred Acorn / Craig Curry
	DB Jerry Gray
	DB Richard Peavy

RUSHING: Robinson 81/479y, Walker 101/392y, Luck 82/375y
PASSING: Moerschell 44-110/871y, 5TD, 40%
RECEIVING: Duhon 13/344y, Bryant 12/218y, Epps 8/275y
SCORING: Jeff Ward (K) 76pts, Duhon 30pts, Moerschell 26pts

SCORES, LINEUPS, AND STATISTICS

1984 7-4-1

35 Auburn	27 WR Brent Duhon
28 Penn State	3 WR Bill Boy Bryant
38 Rice	13 T John Stuart
15 Oklahoma	15 G Bryan Chester
24 Arkansas	18 C Gene Chilton
13 SMU	7 G Bruce Blackmar / Paul Jetton
13 Texas Tech	10 T Greg Wright
15 Houston	29 TE William Harris
44 TCU	23 QB Todd Dodge
10 Baylor	24 HB Kevin Nelson
12 Texas A&M	37 FB Terry Orr / Jerome Johnson
17 Iowa■	55 DL Blake Brawner
	DL Bill Heathcock / Ralph Darnell
	DL Tony Degrate
	DL James McKinney
	LB Tony Edwards
	LB June James
	LB Ty Allert
	DB Stephen Braggs
	DB Anthony Griffin / Tony Tillmon
	DB James Lott
	DB Jerry Gray

RUSHING: Orr 125/580y, Nelson 104/404y, Johnson 58/218y
PASSING: Dodge 100-210/1599y, 11TD, 47.6%
RECEIVING: Harris 34/637y, Bryant 23/387y, Duhon 18/318y
SCORING: Jeff Ward (K) 63pts, Orr 48pts, Johnson 30pts

1985 8-4

21 Missouri	17 WR Russell Hays / Gabriel Johnson
38 Stanford	34 WR Everett Gay
44 Rice	16 T Steve Eargle / Rick Houston
7 Oklahoma	14 G Paul Jetton / Bruce Blackmar
15 Arkansas	13 C Gene Chilton
14 SMU	44 G Bryan Chester
34 Texas Tech	21 T John Stuart / Billy Ray Todd
34 Houston	24 TE William Harris
20 TCU	0 QB Bret Stafford / Todd Dodge
17 Baylor	10 HB Charles Hunter / Edwin Simmons
10 Texas A&M	42 FB Darron Norris
16 Air Force■	24 DL James McKinney / Thomas Aldridge
	DL Brian Espinosa / Rocky Reid
	DL Terry Steelhammer / Steve Llewellyn
	DL Blake Brawner
	LB Ty Allert
	LB Britt Hager / Mike January
	LB Chris Duliban
	DB Stephen Braggs / Tony Tillmon
	DB Eric Jeffries / Anthony Griffin
	DB Richard Peavy
	DB Gerard Senegal / James Lott

RUSHING: Hunter 154/717y, Norris 69/441y, Simmons 86/369y
PASSING: Stafford 60-108/943y, 3TD, 55.6%
RECEIVING: Gay 22/431y, Harris 15/272y, Johnson 12/190y
SCORING: Jeff Ward (K) 84pts, Norris 30pts, 3 tied w/ 24pts

1986 5-6

20 Stanford	31 WR Gabriel Johnson
27 Missouri	25 WR Everett Gay
17 Rice	14 T Steve Eargle
12 Oklahoma	47 G Paul Jetton
14 Arkansas	21 C Carter Hill / Alan Champagne
27 SMU	24 G Billy Ray Todd
21 Texas Tech	23 T Bruce Blackmar / Rick Houston
30 Houston	10 TE Tim McCray / Stephen Clark
45 TCU	16 QB Bret Stafford
13 Baylor	18 HB Eric Metcalf / Charles Hunter
3 Texas A&M	16 FB Darron Norris
	DL Thomas Aldridge
	DL Brian Espinosa
	DL Terry Steelhammer / Steve Llewellyn
	DL Blake Brawner
	LB Duane Duncum / Britt Hager
	LB Mike January
	LB Bobby Rhodes / Lee Brockman
	DB Anthony Griffin
	DB Stephen Braggs
	DB Eric Jeffries / John Hagy
	DB Gerard Senegal

RUSHING: Norris 130/496y, Metcalf 92/310y, Stafford 89/239y
PASSING: Stafford 176-329/2233y, 12TD, 54%
RECEIVING: Metcalf 42/556y, Johnson 30/526y, Gay 26/341y
SCORING: Jeff Ward (K) 59pts, Metcalf 42pts, Norris 26pts

1987 7-5

3 Auburn	31 WR Tony Jones
17 BYU	22 WR Gabriel Johnson / Jorrick Battle
61 Oregon State	16 T Ed Cunningham
45 Rice	26 G Paul Jetton
9 Oklahoma	44 C Alan Champagne
16 Arkansas	14 G Omar Saleh
41 Texas Tech	27 T Brian Nielsen / Charles Seafous
40 Houston	60 TE Stephen Clark
24 TCU	21 QB Bret Stafford
34 Baylor	16 HB Eric Metcalf
13 Texas A&M	20 FB Darron Norris
32 Pittsburgh■	27 DL Thomas Aldridge
	DL Steve Llewellyn / Roger Fritcher
	DL Ken Hackemack / Rocky Allen
	DL Bobby Duncam
	LB Britt Hager / Lee Beckleman
	LB Lee Brockman
	LB Duane Duncum
	DB John Hagy
	DB Stanley Richard / Fred Stromile
	DB Gerard Senegal
	DB Anthony Griffin / Paul Behrman

RUSHING: Metcalf 223/1161y, Norris 121/635y,
PASSING: Stafford 127-245/1321y, 7TD, 51.8%
RECEIVING: Johnson 40/466y, Metcalf 33/238y, Jones 31/467y
SCORING: Wayne Clements (K)78pts, Metcalf 68pts, 3 tied w/ 24pts

1988 4-7

6 BYU	47 WR Johnny Walker
47 New Mexico	0 WR Tony Jones
27 North Texas	24 T Charles Seafous
20 Rice	14 G Duane Miller
13 Oklahoma	28 C Alan Champagne
24 Arkansas	27 G Omar Saleh
32 Texas Tech	33 T Stan Thomas
15 Houston	66 TE Stephen Clark / Keith Cash
30 TCU	21 QB Mark Murdock / Shannon Kelley
14 Baylor	17 HB Eric Metcalf / Chris Samuels
24 Texas A&M	28 FB Darron Norris
	DL Bobby Duncam / Mark Steed
	DL Steve Llewellyn / Rocky Allen
	DL Ken Hackemack / Roger Fritcher
	DL Oscar Giles / Warren Bolden
	LB Duane Duncum / Bobby Rhodes
	LB Britt Hager
	LB Lee Brockman
	DB Willie Mack Garza
	DB Mark Berry
	DB Stanley Richard
	DB Paul Behrman

RUSHING: Metcalf 218/932y, Norris 137/507y, Samuels 45/202y
PASSING: Murdock 98-202/1189y, 10TD, 48.5%
Kelley 70-134/862y, 3TD, 52.2%
RECEIVING: Jones 42/838y, Metcalf 42/333y, Norris 18/65y
SCORING: Wayne Clements (K) 66pts, Metcalf 60pts,
Ker Cash 28pts

1989 5-6

6 Colorado	27 WR Johnny Walker
45 SMU	13 WR Tony Jones
12 Penn State	16 T Ed Cunningham
31 Rice	30 G Duane Miller
28 Oklahoma	24 C Patrick McFarlin / Todd Smith
24 Arkansas	20 G Jeff Boyd / Kevin Wiley
17 Texas Tech	24 T Stan Thomas
9 Houston	47 TE Kerry Cash
31 TCU	17 QB Peter Gardere / Mark Murdock
7 Baylor	50 HB Adrian Walker / Chris Samuels
10 Texas A&M	21 FB Jason Burleson / Winfred Tubbs
	DL Mark Steed / Shane Dronett
	DL James Patton / Rocky Allen
	DL Ken Hackemack
	DL Oscar Giles
	LB Duane Duncum / Boone Powell
	LB Brian Jones
	LB Anthony Curl
	DB Mark Berry
	DB Stanley Richard / Van Malone
	DB Willie Mack Garza / Grady Cavness
	DB Lance Gunn

RUSHING: A. Walker 193/814y, Samuels 89/410y, Tubbs 51/233y
PASSING: Gardere 107-186/1511y, 5TD, 57.5%
RECEIVING: J. Walker 55/785y, Jones 30/449y, Cash 28/391y
SCORING: Wayne Clements (K) 70pts, A. Walker 36pts,
J. Walker 24pts

1990 10-2

17 Penn State	13 WR Johnny Walker
22 Colorado	29 WR Keith Cash
26 Rice	10 T Chuck Johnson
14 Oklahoma	13 G Duane Miller
49 Arkansas	17 C Todd Smith
52 SMU	3 G Jeff Boyd
41 Texas Tech	22 T Stan Thomas
45 Houston	24 TE Kerry Cash
38 TCU	10 QB Peter Gardere
23 Baylor	13 HB Phil Brown / Chris Samuels
28 Texas A&M	27 FB Butch Hadnot / Adrian Walker
3 Miami■	46 DL Shane Dronett
	DL James Patton
	DL Tommy Jeter
	DL Oscar Giles
	LB Boone Powell / Winfred Tubbs
	LB Brian Jones
	LB Anthony Curl
	DB Mark Berry
	DB Grady Cavness
	DB Lance Gunn
	DB Stanley Richard

RUSHING: Hadnot 99/541y, Brown 113/508y, A. Walker 98/449y
PASSING: Gardere 159-282/2131y, 11TD, 56.4%
RECEIVING: Walker 40/565y, Kth Cash 33/605y, Samuels 26/253y
SCORING: Michael Pollak (K) 99pts, Hadnot 48pts, Kth Cash 38pts

1991 5-6

6 Mississippi State	13 WR Darrick Duke
10 Auburn	14 WR Kenny Neal / Justin McLemore
28 Rice	7 T Alan Luther / Chuck Johnson
10 Oklahoma	7 G Scott Gooch
13 Arkansas	14 C Turk McDonald
34 SMU	0 G Jeff Boyd
23 Texas Tech	14 T Shay Shafie
14 Houston	23 TE Curtis Thrift
32 TCU	0 QB Peter Gardere
11 Baylor	21 HB Phil Brown / Butch Hadnot
14 Texas A&M	31 FB Shane Childers / Adrian Walker
	DL Shane Dronett
	DL James Patton
	DL Tommy Jeter
	DL Bo Robinson
	LB Boone Powell
	LB Anthony Curl
	LB Mical Padgett / Chris Rapp
	DB Grady Cavness
	DB Mark Berry
	DB Lance Gunn
	DB Willie Mack Garza

RUSHING: Hadnot 109/501y, Brown 83/420y, Walker 81/358y
PASSING: Gardere 114-228/1390y, 5TD, 50%
RECEIVING: Duke 35/497y, Neal 25/372y, Thrift 21/236y
SCORING: Jason Ziegler (K) 26pts, Duke 20pts, 3 tied w/ 18pts

1992 6-5

10 Mississippi State	28 WR Kenny Neal / Mike Adams
21 Syracuse	31 WR Justin McLemore / Lovell Pinkney
33 North Texas	15 T Troy Riemer
23 Rice	21 G Alan Luther
34 Oklahoma	24 C Turk McDonald
45 Houston	38 G Jeff Boyd
44 Texas Tech	33 T Blake Brockermeyer
14 TCU	23 TE Jason Burleson / David Bearden
35 SMU	14 QB Peter Gardere
20 Baylor	21 RB Adrian Walker / Curtis Jackson
13 Texas A&M	34 RB Phil Brown
	DL Bo Robinson
	DL Todd Hunt
	DL Dominic Bustamante / Shane Rink
	DL Norman Watkins
	LB/DB Kevin Watler / Van Malone
	LB Winfred Tubbs
	LB Anthony Curl
	DB Joey Ellis
	DB Grady Cavness
	DB Willie Mack Garza
	DB Lance Gunn

RUSHING: Walker 129/852y, Brown 82/404y, Jackson 62/237y
PASSING: Gardere 181-329/2364y, 16TD, 55%
RECEIVING: Brown 31/361y, Neal 29/424y, Pinkney 22/458y
SCORING: Scott Szeredy (K) 80pts, Brown, Walker &
Gardere 30pts

1993 5-5-1

14 Colorado	36 WR Lovell Pinkney
21 Syracuse	21 WR Mike Adams
10 Louisville	41 T Troy Riemer
55 Rice	38 G John Elmore / Duane Whetstone
17 Oklahoma	38 C Dan Neil (G) / Trent Elliott
37 SMU	10 G Joe Phillips
22 Texas Tech	31 T Blake Brockermeyer
34 Houston	16 TE Jimmy Hakes / Steve Bradley
24 TCU	3 QB Shea Morenz
38 Baylor	17 RB Phil Brown / Rodrick Walker
9 Texas A&M	18 RB Curtis Jackson / Anthony Holmes
	DL Norman Watkins
	DL Thomas Baskin
	DL Stonie Clark / James Lane
	DL Tony Brackens / Brian Vasek
	LB Kevin Watler / Jason Reeves
	LB Winfred Tubbs
	LB Robert Reed
	DB Joey Ellis
	DB Bryant Westbrook / Pascal Watty
	DB Chris Carter
	DB Van Malone

RUSHING: Brown 126/770y, Walker 70/345y, Jackson 73/291y
PASSING: Morenz 183-335/2341y, 13TD, 54.6%
RECEIVING: Adams 52/908y, Pinkney 47/686y, Brown 35/281y
SCORING: Scott Szeredy (K) 77pts, Adams 52pts, Brown 42pts

1994 8-4

30 Pittsburgh	28 WR Eric Jackson
30 Louisville	16 WR Lovell Pinkney / Matt Davis
34 TCU	18 T Blake Brockermeyer
31 Colorado	34 G John Elmore
17 Oklahoma	10 C Dan Neil
17 Rice	19 G Corby Brooks / Trent Elliott
42 SMU	20 T Joe Phillips / Dominic Bustamante
9 Texas Tech	33 TE Steve Bradley / Pat Fitzgerald
10 Texas A&M	34 QB Shea Morenz / James Brown
48 Houston	13 RB Juan Kemp / Anthony Holmes
63 Baylor	35 RB Rodrick Walker / Darrell Wilson
35 North Carolina■	31 DL Thomas Baskin / Shane Rink
	DL Chris Akins / Stonie Clark
	DL Tony Brackens
	LB Robert Reed / Dwight Kirkpatrick
	LB Tyson King / Tremaine Brown
	LB Kyle Richardson / Kevin Watler
	LB Norman Watkins
	DB Joey Ellis
	DB Bryant Westbrook / Taje Allen
	DB Chris Carter / Victor Frazier
	DB Tre Thomas

RUSHING: Walker 129/598y, Holmes 120/524y, Wilson 55/226y
PASSING: Morenz 124-235/1368y, 12TD, 52.8%
Brown 80-115/1047y, 12TD, 69.6%
RECEIVING: Jackson 43/762y, Pinkney 30/436y, Jackson 27/401y
SCORING: Phil Dawson (K) 80pts, Jackson 50pts, Pinkney 42pts

1995 10-2-1

38 Hawaii	17 WR Justin McLemore / Matt Davis
38 Pittsburgh	27 WR Mike Adams
27 Notre Dame	55 T John Elmore
35 SMU	10 G Corby Brooks
37 Rice	13 C Ryan Fiebiger
24 Oklahoma	24 G Dan Nell
17 Virginia	16 T Dom Bustamante / Octavious Bishop
48 Texas Tech	7 TE Pat Fitzgerald / Steve Bradley
52 Houston	20 QB James Brown
27 TCU	19 RB Shon Mitchell
21 Baylor	13 RB Ricky Williams
16 Texas A&M	6 DL Shane Rink / Stonie Clark
10 Virginia Tech■	28 DL Chris Akins
	DL Tony Brackens
	LB Jason Reeves
	LB Tyson King
	LB Kyle Richardson
	LB Robert Reed
	DB Taje Allen
	DB Bryan Westbrook
	DB Chris Carter
	DB Tre Thomas / Robert Crenshaw

RUSHING: Mitchell 176/1099y, Williams 166/990y, Brown 66/166y
PASSING: Brown 163-322/2447y, 19TD, 50.6%
RECEIVING: Adams 53/876y, McLemore 30/488y,
Fitzgerald 30/445y
SCORING: Phil Dawson (K) 86pts, Mitchell 60pts, Fitzgerald &
Williams 48pts

1996 8-5

40 Missouri	10 WR Matt Davis / Curtis Jackson
41 New Mexico St.	7 WR Mike Adams / Wane McGarity
24 Notre Dame	27 T Octavious Bishop
13 Virginia	37 G Ben Adams
71 Oklahoma State	14 C Ryan Fiebiger
27 Oklahoma	30 G Dan Neil
24 Colorado	28 T Jay Humphrey
28 Baylor	23 TE Pat Fitzgerald
38 Texas Tech	32 QB James Brown
38 Kansas	17 RB Shon Mitchell / Priest Holmes
51 Texas A&M	15 FB Ricky Williams
37 Nebraska□	27 DL Chris Akins
15 Penn State■	38 DL Casey Hampton / Clarence Martin
	DL Gray Mosier
	LB Dwight Kirkpatrick / Matt Jones
	LB Tyson King
	LB Dusty Renfro / Kyle Richardson
	LB Aaron Humphrey
	DB Bryant Westbrook
	DB Taje Allen
	DB Chris Carter
	DB Tre Thomas

RUSHING: Williams 205/1272y, Mitchell 117/625y,
Holmes 59/324y
PASSING: Brown 170-299/2468y, 17TD, 56.9%
RECEIVING: Adams 56/942y, Fitzgerald 38/545y,
Williams 25/291y
SCORING: Phil Dawson (K) 108pts, Williams & Holmes 84pts

1997 4-7

48 Rutgers	14 WR Bryan White / Cortney Epps / K. Cavil
3 UCLA	66 WR Wane McGarity / Jamel Thompson
38 Rice	31 T Octavious Bishop
16 Oklahoma State	42 G Roger Roesler / Travis Wood
27 Oklahoma	24 C Ryan Fiebiger
29 Missouri	37 G Ben Adams
30 Colorado	47 T Jay Humphrey
21 Baylor	23 TE Steve Bradley / Derek Lewis
10 Texas Tech	24 QB James Brown
45 Kansas	31 RB Ricky Williams
16 Texas A&M	27 RB Ricky Brown / Jeffrey Clayton
	DL Gray Mosier / Chris Smith
	DL Cedric Woodard / Casey Hampton
	DL Chris Akins / Shaun Rogers
	DL Aaron Humphrey (LB) / Michael Boudoin
	LB Brandon Nava
	LB Dusty Renfro
	LB Anthony Hicks / Dwight Kirkpatrick
	DB Quentin Jammer / Joe Walker
	DB Quinton Wallace
	DB Donald McCowen
	DB Aaron Babino / Tony Holmes

RUSHING: Williams 279/1878y, Ricky Brown 31/159y
PASSING: Brown 133-267/1691y, 5TD, 49.8%
RECEIVING: Cavil 23/316y, White 22/272y, Lewis 20/192y
SCORING: Williams 152pts, Phil Dawson (K) 65pts, Lewis 12pts

1998 9-3

66 New Mexico St.	36 WR Wane McGarrity
31 UCLA	49 WR Kwame Cavil
7 Kansas State	48 T Octavious Bishop / Leonard Davis
59 Rice	21 G Roger Roesler
54 Iowa State	33 C Russell Gaskamp
34 Oklahoma	3 G Ben Adams
30 Baylor	20 T Jay Humphrey
20 Nebraska	16 TE Derek Lewis
37 Oklahoma State	34 QB Major Applewhite / Richard Walton
35 Texas Tech	42 RB Ricky Williams
26 Texas A&M	24 FB Ricky Brown
38 Mississippi St.■	11 DL Aaron Humphrey
	DL Casey Hampton
	DL Cedric Woodard / Shaun Rogers
	DL J.J. Kelly / Jermain Anderson
	LB Anthony Hicks / Aaron Babino
	LB Dusty Renfro
	LB De'Andre Lewis
	DB Tony Holmes / Ervis Hill
	DB Joe Walker
	DB Quentin Jammer
	DB Donald McCowen

RUSHING: Williams 361/2124y, Hodges Mitchell (RB) 23/111y
PASSING: Applewhite 159-273/2453y, 18TD, 58.2%
RECEIVING: McGarity 58/1087y, Cavil 51/775y, Williams 24/262y
SCORING: Williams 168pts, Kris Stockton (K) 94pts,
McGarrity 54pts

1999 9-5

20 N. Carolina St.	23 WR Ryan Nunez / Montrell Flowers
69 Stanford	17 WR Kwame Cavil
38 Rutgers	21 T Leonard Davis / Mike Williams
18 Rice	13 G Roger Roesler / Derrick Dockery
62 Baylor	0 C Matt Anderson / Marcel Blanchard
17 Kansas State	35 G Antwan Kirk-Hughes
38 Oklahoma	28 T Cory Quye
24 Nebraska	20 TE Mike Jones
44 Iowa State	41 QB Major Applewhite
34 Oklahoma State	21 RB Hodges Mitchell / Victor Ike
58 Texas Tech	7 RB Ricky Brown / Kenny Hayter
16 Texas A&M	20 DL Aaron Humphrey / Cory Redding
6 Nebraska□	22 DL Casey Hampton
6 Arkansas■	27 DL Shaun Rogers
	DL Cedric Woodard
	LB Aaron Babino / Tyrone Jones
	LB De'Andre Lewis
	LB Everick Rawls
	DB Ahmad Brooks / Rod Babers
	DB Ervis Hill / Joe Walker
	DB Greg Brown
	DB Lee Jackson

RUSHING: Mitchell 256/1343y, Ike 68/274y, Hayter 33/113y
PASSING: Applewhite 271-467/3357y, 21TD, 58%
RECEIVING: Cavil 100/1188y, Nunez 56/600y, Flowers 34/552y
SCORING: Kris Stockton (K) 107pts, Chris Robertson (RB) 66pts,
Mitchell 60pts

2000 9-3

52 La-Lafayette	10 WR Roy Williams / Montrell Flowers
24 Stanford	27 WR B.J. Johnson / Brandon Healy
48 Houston	0 T Leonard Davis
42 Oklahoma State	7 G Derrick Dockery
14 Oklahoma	63 C Matt Anderson
28 Colorado	14 G Antwan Kirk-Hughes / Tillman Holloway
46 Missouri	12 T Mike Williams / Cory Quye
48 Baylor	14 TE Mike Jones / Brock Edwards
29 Texas Tech	17 QB Major Applewhite / Chris Simms
51 Kansas	16 RB Hodges Mitchell / Kenny Hayter
43 Texas A&M	17 RB Matt Trissel / Victor Ike
30 Oregon■	35 DL Kalen Thornton / Cole Pittman
	DL Casey Hampton
	DL Shaun Rogers / Marcus Tubbs
	DL Cory Redding
	LB Tyrone Jones
	LB De'Andre Lewis
	LB Everick Rawls
	DB Quentin Jammer / Ahmad Brooks
	DB Rod Babers
	DB Dakarai Pearson / Lee Jackson
	DB Greg Brown

RUSHING: Mitchell 224/1118y, Hayter 60/220y, Ike 36/156y
PASSING: Applewhite 152-279/2164y, 18TD, 54.5%
RECEIVING: Johnson 41/698y, Williams 40/809y, Mitchell 37/386y
SCORING: Kris Stockton (K) 107pts, Mitchell 70pts, Williams 62pts

2001 11-2

41 New Mexico St.	7 WR Roy Williams
44 North Carolina	14 WR B.J. Johnson
53 Houston	26 T Robbie Doane
42 Texas Tech	7 G Derrick Dockery / Tillman Holloway
3 Oklahoma	14 C Matt Anderson
45 Oklahoma State	17 G Antwan Kirk-Hughes
41 Colorado	7 T Mike Williams
35 Missouri	16 TE Bo Scaife / Brock Edwards
49 Baylor	10 QB Chris Simms
59 Kansas	0 RB Cedric Benson / Ivan Williams
21 Texas A&M	7 RB Matt Trissel / Victor Ike
37 Colorado□	39 DL Kalen Thornton / Jermain Anderson
47 Washington■	43 DL Marcus Tubbs
	DL Maurice Gordon
	DL Cory Redding
	LB Tyrone Jones / Derrick Johnson
	LB D.D. Lewis
	LB Everick Rawls
	DB Quentin Jammer
	DB Rod Babers
	DB Ahmad Brooks
	DB Nathan Vasher / Dakarai Pearson

RUSHING: Benson 223/1053y, I. Williams 101/519y, Ike 41/165y
PASSING: Simms 214-362/2603y, 22TD, 59.1%
RECEIVING: R. Williams 67/836y, Johnson 41/539y,
Scaife 30/396y
SCORING: Dusty Mangum (K) 102pts, Benson 78pts,
R. Williams 42pts

2002 11-2

27 North Texas	0 WR B.J. Johnson
52 North Carolina	21 WR Roy Williams / Sloan Thomas
41 Houston	11 T Robbie Doane
49 Tulane	0 G Tillman Holloway
17 Oklahoma State	15 C Jason Glynn
24 Oklahoma	35 G Derrick Dockery (T) / Beau Baker
17 Kansas State	14 T Jonathan Scott
21 Iowa State	10 TE Brock Edwards / David Thomas
27 Nebraska	24 QB Chris Simms
41 Baylor	0 RB Cedric Benson / Selvin Young
38 Texas Tech	42 FB Ivan Williams / Matt Trissel
50 Texas A&M	20 DL Cory Redding / Kalen Thornton
35 LSU■	20 DL Rodrique Wright / Miguel McKay
	DL Marcus Tubbs / Stevie Lee
	DL Bryan Pickryl / Austin Sendlein
	LB Lee Jackson
	LB Reed Boyd
	LB Derrick Johnson
	DB Rod Babers
	DB Nathan Vasher / Cedric Griffin
	DB Dakarai Pearson
	DB Michael Huff

RUSHING: Benson 305/1293y, Young 85/408y
PASSING: Simms 196/235/3207y, 26TD, 59.3%
RECEIVING: Williams 64/1142y, Johnson 40/603y,
  Thomas 30/383y
SCORING: Dusty Mangum (K) 102pts, Williams 78pts,
  Benson 72pts

2003 10-3

66 New Mexico St.	7 WR Roy Williams
28 Arkansas	38 WR B.J. Johnson
48 Rice	7 WR Sloan Thomas / Tony Jeffery
63 Tulane	18 T Jonathan Scott
24 Kansas State	20 G Tillman Holloway
13 Oklahoma	65 C Jason Glynn
40 Iowa State	19 G Will Allen / Mike Garcia
56 Baylor	0 T Justin Blalock / William Winston
31 Nebraska	7 TE David Thomas / Bo Scaife
55 Oklahoma State	16 QB Vince Young / Chance Mock
43 Texas Tech	40 RB Cedric Benson
46 Texas A&M	15 DL Kalen Thornton / Mike Williams
20 Washington St■	28 DL Marcus Tubbs
	DL Rodrique Wright
	DL Tim Crowder / Austin Sendlein
	LB Reed Boyd
	LB Aaron Harris / Brian Robison
	LB Derrick Johnson
	DB Cedric Griffin
	DB Nathan Vasher
	DB Phillip Geiggar / Dakarai Pearson
	DB Michael Huff / Michael Griffin

RUSHING: Benson 258/1360y, Young 135/998y,
  Brett Robin (RB) 49/251y
PASSING: Mock 100-183/1469y, 16TD, 54.6%
  Young 84-143/1155y, 6TD, 58.7%
RECEIVING: Williams 70/1079y, Johnson 30/549y,
  S. Thomas 20/336y
SCORING: Benson 134pts, Dusty Mangum (K) 71pts, Young 68pts

2004 11-1

65 North Texas	0 WR Tony Jeffrey
22 Arkansas	20 WR Limas Sweed / Nate Jones
35 Rice	13 T Jonathan Scott
44 Baylor	14 G Kasey Studdard
0 Oklahoma	12 C Jason Glynn
28 Missouri	20 G Will Allen / Mike Garcia
51 Texas Tech	21 T Justin Blalock
31 Colorado	7 TE David Thomas / Bo Scaife
56 Oklahoma State	35 QB Vince Young
27 Kansas	23 TB Cedric Benson
26 Texas A&M	13 FB/WR Will Matthews / Brian Carter
38 Michigan■	37 DL Brian Robison
	DL Larry Dibbles
	DL Rodrique Wright / Frank Okam
	DL Tim Crowder
	LB Eric Hall
	LB Aaron Harris
	LB Derrick Johnson
	DB Tarell Brown
	DB Cedric Griffin / Aaron Ross
	DB Phillip Geiggar
	DB Michael Huff / Michael Griffin

RUSHING: Benson 326/1834y, Young 167/1079y,
  Ramonce Taylor (RB) 28/284y
PASSING: Young 148-250/1849y, 12TD, 59.2%
RECEIVING: Jeffrey 33/437y, Scaife 26/348y, Thomas 25/430y
SCORING: Benson 120pts, Young 84pts, Dusty Mangum (K) 83pts

2005 13-0

60 La.-Lafayette	3 WR Limas Sweed
25 Ohio State	22 WR Billy Pittman / Quan Cosby
51 Rice	10 WR/TE Brian Carter / Neale Tweedie
51 Missouri	20 T Jonathan Scott
45 Oklahoma	12 G Kasey Studdard
42 Colorado	17 C Lyle Sendlein
52 Texas Tech	17 G Will Allen
47 Oklahoma State	28 T Justin Blalock
62 Baylor	0 TE David Thomas
66 Kansas	14 QB Vince Young
40 Texas A&M	29 RB S. Young/J. Charles/Rnce. Taylor
70 Colorado□	3 DL Tim Crowder
41 Southern Cal■	38 DL Rodrique Wright / Larry Dibbles
	DL Frank Okam
	DL Brian Robison / Brian Orakpo
	LB Robert Killebrew / Drew Kelson
	LB Aaron Harris
	LB Rashad Bobino
	DB Cedric Griffin
	DB Tarell Brown / Aaron Ross
	DB Michael Griffin / Marcus Griffin
	DB Michael Huff

RUSHING: V. Young 155/1050y, Charles 119/878y,
  Taylor 76/513y
PASSING: Young 212-325/3036y, 26TD, 65.2%
RECEIVING: Thomas 50/613y, Sweed 36/545y,
  Pittman 34/750y
SCORING: David Pino (K) 113y, Taylor 90pts, Charles 78pts

2006 10-3

56 North Texas	7 WR Limas Sweed / Jordan Shipley
7 Ohio State	24 WR Billy Pittman
52 Rice	7 WR/TE Quan Cosby / Jermich Finley
37 Iowa State	14 T Tony Hills
56 Sam Houston St.	3 G Kasey Studdard
28 Oklahoma	10 C Lyle Sendlein
63 Baylor	31 G Cedric Dockery
22 Nebraska	20 T Justin Blalock (G) / Adam Ulatoski
35 Texas Tech	31 TE Neale Tweedle
36 Oklahoma State	10 QB Colt McCoy / Jevan Snead
42 Kansas State	45 RB Selvin Young / Jamaal Charles
7 Texas A&M	12 DL Tim Crowder / Brian Orakpo
26 Iowa■	24 DL Derek Lokey / Roy Miller
	DL Frank Okam
	DL Brian Robison / Aaron Lewis
	LB Robert Killebrew
	LB Rashad Bobino
	LB Scott Derry / Roddrick Muckelroy
	DB Aaron Ross
	DB Tarell Brown
	DB Marcus Griffin / Matt Melton
	DB Michael Griffin

RUSHING: Charles 156/831y, Young 137/591y,
  Henry Melton (RB) 15/193y
PASSING: McCoy 217-318/2570y, 29TD, 68.2%
  Snead 26-49/371y, 53.1%
RECEIVING: Sweed 46/801y, Cosby 45/525y, Pittman 35/456y
SCORING: Sweed 72pts, Greg Johnson (K) 51pts,
  Young & Charles 48pts

2007 10-3

21 Arkansas State	13 WR Nate Jones
34 TCU	13 WR Limas Sweed / Jordan Shipley
35 Central Florida	32 WR Quan Cosby
58 Rice	14 T Tony Hills
21 Kansas State	41 G Chris Hall (C-T) / Charlie Tanner
21 Oklahoma	28 C Dallas Griffin / Buck Burnette
56 Iowa State	3 G Cedric Dockery
31 Baylor	10 T Adam Ulatoski
28 Nebraska	25 TE Jermich Finley
38 Oklahoma State	35 QB Colt McCoy
59 Texas Tech	43 RB Jamaal Charles / Vondrell McGee
30 Texas A&M	38 DL Lamarr Houston
52 Arizona State■	34 DL Derek Lokey
	DL Frank Okam / Roy Miller
	DL Brian Orakpo / Aaron Lewis
	LB Robe Killebrew / Rodd Muckelroy
	LB Rashad Bobino / Jared Norton
	LB Scott Derry / Sergio Kindle
	DB Ryan Palmer
	DB Brandon Foster / Deon Beasley
	DB Marcus Griffin
	DB Erick Johnson / Ishie Oduegwu

RUSHING: Charles 258/1619y, McCoy 114/492y, McGee 75/297y
PASSING: McCoy 276-424/3303y, 22TD, 65.1%
RECEIVING: Jones 70/795y, Cosby 60/680y, Finley 45/575y
SCORING: Ryan Bailey (K) 112pts, Charles 108pts, McGee 48pts

2008 12-1

52 Florida Atlantic	10 WR Quan Cosby
42 Texas-El Paso	13 WR Jordan Shipley / John Chiles
52 Rice	10 WR Malcolm Williams / Brandon Collins
52 Arkansas	10 WR/TE James Kirkendoll / Greg Smith
38 Colorado	14 T Adam Ulatoski
45 Oklahoma	35 G Charlie Tanner / Michael Huey
56 Missouri	31 C Chris Hall / David Snow
28 Oklahoma State	24 G Cedric Dockery
33 Texas Tech	39 T Kyle Hix
45 Baylor	21 QB Colt McCoy
35 Kansas	7 RB Chris Ogbonnoya / Vondrell McGee
49 Texas A&M	9 DL Brian Orakpo
24 Ohio State■	21 DL Roy Miller
	DL Lamarr Houston / Aaron Lewis
	DL Henry Melton
	LB Sergio Kindle
	LB Jared Norton / Rashad Bobino
	LB Rodd Muckelroy
	DB Ryan Palmer / Curtis Brown
	DB Chykie Brown / Dean Beasley
	DB Earl Thomas
	DB Blake Gideon

RUSHING: McCoy 136/561y, McGee 88/376,
  Ogbonnoya 74/373y
PASSING: McCoy 332-433/3859y, 34TD, 76.7%
RECEIVING: Cosby 92/1123y, Shipley 89/1060y,
  Ogbonnoya 46/540y
SCORING: Hunter Lawrence (K) 90pts, Shipley 78pts,
  Johnson 72pts

2009 13-1

59 La.-Monroe	20 WR Jordan Shipley
41 Wyoming	10 WR James Kirkendoll / Marquise Goodwin
34 Texas Tech	24 WR Malcolm Williams / John Chiles
64 Texas-El Paso	7 T Adam Ulatoski
38 Colorado	14 G Charlie Tanner
16 Oklahoma	13 C Chris Hall
41 Missouri	7 G Michael Huey / David Snow
41 Oklahoma State	14 T Kyle Hix
35 C. Florida	3 TE/WR Greg Smith / Dan Buckner
47 Baylor	14 QB Colt McCoy / Garrett Gilbert
51 Kansas	20 RB Tre Newton / Vondrell McGee
49 Texas A&M	39 DL Sergio Kindle (LB)
13 Nebraska□	12 DL Kheest Randall / Ben Alexander
21 Alabama■	37 DL Lamarr Houston
	DL Sam Acho
	LB Keenan Robinson
	LB Rudd Muckelroy / Dustin Earnest
	DB/LB Aaron Williams / Emmanuel Acho
	DB Chykie Brown
	DB Curtis Brown
	DB Earl Thomas
	DB Blake Gideon / Nolan Brewster

RUSHING: Newton 116/552y, McCoy 129/348y,
  Cody Johnson (RB) 87/335y, McGee 56/300y
PASSING: McCoy 332-470/3521y, 27TD, 70.6%
RECEIVING: Shipley 116/1485y, Kirkendoll 48/461y,
  Buckner 45/442y, Williams 39/550y, Chiles 34/319y
SCORING: Hunter Lawrence (K) 133pts, Shipley 90pts,
  Cody Johnson (RB) 72pts

2010 5-7

34 Rice	17 WR Marquise Goodwin / Malcolm Williams
34 Wyoming	7 WR John Chiles / Mike Davis
24 Texas Tech	14 WR James Kirkendoll
12 UCLA	34 T Kyle Nix / Paden Kelly
20 Oklahoma	28 G Michael Huey / Trey Hopkins
20 Nebraska	13 C David Snow
9 Iowa State	28 G Mason Walters
22 Baylor	30 T Britt Mitchell
14 Kansas State	39 TE Barrett Matthews / Greg Smith
16 Oklahoma State	33 QB Garrett Gilbert
51 FIU	17 RB Foswhitt Whittaker / Cody Johnson
17 Texas A&M	24 DL Eddie Jones
	DL Kheeston Randall
	DL Alex Okafor / Tyrell Higgins
	DL Sam Ocho / Jackson Jeffcoat
	LB Keena Robinson / Jordan Hicks
	LB Emmanuel Acho / Dustin Earnest
	LB/DB Dravannti Johnson / Aaron Williams
	DB Chykie Brown / Carrington Byndom
	DB Curtis Brown
	DB Blake Gideon
	DB Kenny Vaccaro / Christian Scott

RUSHING: Johnson 134/592y, Gilbert 100/380y, Whittaker 80/351y
PASSING: Gilbert 260-441/2744y, 10TD, 59%
RECEIVING: Kirkendoll 52/707y, Davis 47/478y, Whittaker 34/217y
  Goodwin 31/324y
SCORING: Justin Tucker (K) 96pts, Johnson 36pts, Gilbert 32pts

TEXAS A&M

Texas Agriculture & Mechanical University (Founded 1876)
College Station, Texas
Nickname: Aggies
Colors: Maroon and White
Stadium: Kyle Field (1929) 83,000
Conference Affiliations: Southwest (1915-95),
 Big Twelve South (1996-present)

CAREER RUSHING YARDS

	Attempts	Yards
Darren Lewis (1987-90)	909	5012
Curtis Dickey (1976-79)	697	3703
Greg Hill (1991-93)	631	3262
Rodney Thomas (1991-94)	604	3014
George Woodard (1975-77, 1979)	625	2911
Bubba Bean (1972-75)	482	2846
Dante Hall (1996-99)	522	2818
Courtney Lewis (2003-06)	517	2711
Johnny Hector (1979-82)	550	2587
Roger Vick (1983-86)	573	2471

CAREER PASSING YARDS

	Comp.-Att.	Yards
Jerrod Johnson (2007-10)	650-1109	8011
Reggie McNeal (2002-05)	478-875	6992
Corey Pullig (1992-95)	560-992	6846
Kevin Murray (1983-86)	544-926	6506
Stephen McGee (2005-08)	485-815	5475
Edd Hargett (1966-68)	400-821	5379
Mark Farris (1999-2002)	435-755	4949
Branndon Stewart (1996-98)	325-623	4325
Randy McCown (1996-99)	277-536	4187
Gary Kubiak (1979-82)	314-595	4078
Dustin Long (2001-03)	240-437	3218

CAREER RECEIVING YARDS

	Catches	Yards
Terrence Murphy (2001-04)	172	2600
Jeff Fuller (2008-10)	163	2264
Bethel Johnson (1999-2002)	117	1740
Tony Harrison (1990-93)	89	1576
Albert Connell (1995-96)	98	1525
Shea Walker (1983-86)	98	1411
Rod Harris (1985-88)	87	1395
Mike Whitwell (1978-81)	61	1372
Bob Long (1966-68)	79	1298
Barney Harris (1967-69)	91	1298

SEASON RUSHING YARDS

	Attempts	Yards
Darren Lewis (1988)	306	1692
Darren Lewis (1990)	291	1691
Greg Hill (1992)	267	1339
Bob Smith (1950)	199	1302
Greg Hill (1991)	240	1216

SEASON PASSING YARDS

	Comp.-Att.	Yards
Jerrod Johnson (2009)	296-497	3579
Reggie McNeal (2004)	200-344	2791
Mark Farris (2000)	208-347	2551
Dustin Long (2002)	177-333	2509
Kevin Murray (1986)	212-349	2463

SEASON RECEIVING YARDS

	Catches	Yards
Jeff Fuller (2010)	72	1066
Robert Ferguson (2000)	58	885
Albert Connell (1996)	57	872
Ryan Tannehill (2008)	55	844
Ken McLean (1965)	60	835

GAME RUSHING YARDS

	Attempts	Yards
Bob Smith (1950 vs. SMU)	29	297
Darren Lewis (1990 vs. Texas Tech)	34	232
Curtis Dickey (1978 vs. Texas Christian)	34	230

GAME PASSING YARDS

	Comp.-Att.	Yards
Ryan Tannehill (2010 vs. Texas Tech)	36-50	449
Jerrod Johnson (2008 vs. Kansas State)	29-41	419
Jerrod Johnson (2010 vs. Oklahoma St.)	40-62	409

GAME RECEIVING YARDS

	Catches	Yards
Ken McLean (1965 vs. Texas)	13	250
Ryan Tannehill (2008 vs. Kansas State)	12	210
Albert Connell (1996 vs. Colorado)	18	208

GREATEST COACH:

Not every Aggies fan liked quiet, low-key R.C. Slocum, who stressed defense and running the football, but when the dust had settled on his 14-year coaching career he had a record of 123-47-2 for a very good .7209 winning percentage. That number was far better than the winning done by far more famous Aggies coaches Bear Bryant, Gene Stallings, and Jackie Sherrill.

Slocom won three straight Southwest Conference titles, was denied a fourth by sanctions, and tied for second three times. He also won two straight South Division championships in the first three years of the Big 12.

TEXAS A&M'S 55 GREATEST SINCE 1953

OFFENSE

WIDE RECEIVER: Albert Connell, Bethel Johnson, Bob Long, Terrence Murphy
TIGHT END: Rod Bernstine, Richard Osborne
TACKLE: Ken Beck, Matt McCall, Cory Risien, Richmond Webb
GUARD: Jerry Fontenot, Dennis Goehring, Mo Moorman
CENTER: Mike Arthur, Matt Darwin, Seth McKinney
QUARTERBACK: Edd Hargett, Kevin Murray, Bucky Richardson
RUNNING BACK: Bubba Bean, Curtis Dickey, Greg Hill, Darren Lewis
FULLBACK: Ja'Mar Toombs, George Woodard, Robert Wilson

DEFENSE

END: Jacob Green, John Roper, John Tracey
TACKLE: Sam Adams, Ray Childress, Charlie Krueger, Brandon Mitchell
LINEBACKER: Marcus Buckley, Quinton Coryatt, Johnny Holland, Robert Jackson, Dat Nguyen, Ed Simonini, Aaron Wallace
CORNERBACK: Aaron Glenn, Ray Mickens, Kevin Smith, Pat Thomas
SAFETY: Kip Corrington, Dave Elmendorf, Brandon Jennings, Tommy Maxwell

SPECIAL TEAMS 7

RETURN SPECIALISTS: Leeland McElroy
PLACE KICKER: Tony Franklin
PUNTER: Shane Lechler

MULTIPLE POSITIONS

QUARTERBACK-FULLBACK-DEFENSIVE BACK: Roddy Osborne
CORNERBACK-TAILBACK: Ross Brupbacher

TWO-WAY PLAYERS

HALFBACK-CORNERBACK: John David Crow
FULLBACK-LINEBACKER: Jack Pardee

PERFORMANCE FORMULA:
TEXAS A&M'S 10 BEST SEASONS

1956	1.6360	4 of 69
1994	1.6066	6 of 71
1991	1.5658	8 of 71
1993	1.5637	8 of 70
1992	1.5580	6 of 70
1976	1.5205	6 of 70
1985	1.5202	10 of 70
1998	1.4971	10 of 70
1987	1.4906	8 of 69
1975	1.4467	10 of 70

TEXAS A&M AGGIES

Year	W-L-T	AP Poll	Conference Standing	Toughest Regular Season Opponents	Coach (Record at School)	Bowl Games			
1953	4-5-1		6t	Kentucky 7-2-1, Texas Tech 10-1, Rice 8-2	Ray George (12-14-4)				
1954	1-9		7	Texas Tech 7-2-1; Baylor 7-3, Arkansas 8-2, Rice 7-3	Paul "Bear" Bryant				
1955	7-2-1	14	2	UCLA 9-1, TCU 9-1	Bear Bryant				
1956	9-0-1	5	1	Houston 7-2-1, TCU 7-3, Baylor 8-2	Bear Bryant				
1957	8-3	9	3	Baylor 6-3-1, Rice 7-3, Texas 6-3-1	Bear Bryant (25-14-2)	Gator	0	Tennessee	3
1958	4-6		5t	TCU 8-2, SMU 6-4, Texas 7-3	Jim Myers				
1959	3-7		7	Michigan State 5-4, TCU 8-2, Arkansas 8-2, Texas 9-1	Jim Myers				
1960	1-6-3		7	Baylor 8-2, Arkansas 8-2, Rice 7-3, Texas 7-3	Jim Myers				
1961	4-5-1		4	LSU 9-1, Arkansas 8-2, Rice 7-3, Texas 9-1	Jim Myers (12-24-4)				
1962	3-7		4t	LSU 8-1-1, Arkansas 9-1, Texas 9-0-1	Hank Foldberg				
1963	2-7-1		8	LSU 7-3, Ohio State 5-3-1, Baylor 7-3, Texas 10-0	Hank Foldberg				
1964	1-9		7	LSU 7-2-1, Southern Calif. 7-3, Arkansas 10-0, Texas 9-1	Hank Foldberg (6-23-1)				
1965	3-7		7t	LSU 7-3, Texas Tech 8-2, Arkansas 10-0, Texas 6-4	Gene Stallings				
1966	4-5-1		4	Georgia Tech 9-1, Arkansas 8-2, SMU 8-2, Texas 6-4	Gene Stallings				
1967	7-4		1	Purdue 8-2, LSU 6-3-1, Florida State 7-2-1, Texas 6-4	Gene Stallings	Cotton	20	Alabama	16
1968	3-7		6t	LSU 7-3, Florida State 8-2, Arkansas 9-1, Texas 8-1-1	Gene Stallings				
1969	3-7		6t	LSU 9-1, Nebraska 8-2, Arkansas 9-1, Texas 10-0	Gene Stallings				
1970	2-9		8	LSU 9-2, Ohio State 9-0, Michigan 9-1, Arkansas 9-2, Texas 10-0	Gene Stallings				
1971	5-6		4	LSU 8-3, Nebraska 12-0, Arkansas 8-2-1, Texas 8-2	Gene Stallings (27-45-1)				
1972	3-8		7t	Nebraska 8-2-1, LSU 9-1-1 Texas Tech 8-3, Texas 9-1	Emory Bellard				
1973	5-6		6	LSU 9-2, Texas Tech 10-1, Texas 8-2	Emory Bellard				
1974	8-3	15	2t	Clemson 7-4, Baylor 8-3, Texas 8-3	Emory Bellard	Liberty	0	Southern California	20
1975	10-2	11	1t	Texas 9-2, Arkansas 9-2	Emory Bellard	Sun	37	Florida	14
1976	10-2	7	3	Houston 9-2, Baylor 7-3-1, Texas 5-5-1	Emory Bellard	Bluebonnet	28	Southern California	47
1977	8-4		3	Texas Tech 7-4, Michigan 10-1, Arkansas 10-1, Texas 11-0	Emory Bellard				
1978	8-4	18	5	Houston 9-2, Arkansas 9-2, Texas 8-3	Emory Bellard (48-27), Tom Wilson [4-2]	Hall of Fame	28	Iowa State	12
1979	6-5		5	BYU 11-0, Houston 10-1, Arkansas 10-1, Texas 9-2	Tom Wilson				
1980	4-7		6	Georgia 11-0, Penn State 9-2, Baylor 10-1, SMU 8-3	Tom Wilson				
1981	7-5		5	SMU 10-1, Arkansas 8-3, Texas 9-1-1	Tom Wilson (21-19)	Independence	33	Oklahoma State	16
1982	5-6		6t	Boston College 8-2-1, SMU 10-0-1, Arkansas 8-2-1, Texas 9-2	Jackie Sherrill				
1983	5-5-1		3t	Baylor 7-3-1, SMU 10-1, Texas 11-0	Jackie Sherrill				
1984	6-5		7	Houston 7-4, SMU 9-2, Arkansas 7-3-1, TCU 8-3, Texas 7-3-1	Jackie Sherrill				
1985	10-2	6	1	Alabama 8-2-1, Baylor 8-3, Arkansas 9-2, Texas 8-3	Jackie Sherrill	Cotton	36	Auburn	16
1986	9-3	12	1	LSU 9-2, Baylor 8-3, Arkansas 9-2	Jackie Sherrill	Cotton	12	Ohio State	28
1987	10-2	9	1	LSU 9-1-1, Washington 6-4-1, Texas Tech 6-4-1, Arkansas 9-3	Jackie Sherrill (52-28-1)	Cotton	35	Notre Dame	10
1988	7-5		2	Nebraska 11-1, Okla. St. 9-2, Arkansas 10-1, Alabama 8-3	R.C. Slocum				
1989	8-4	20	2t	Washington 7-4, Texas Tech 8-3, Houston 9-2, Arkansas 10-1	R.C. Slocum	Hancock	28	Pittsburgh	31
1990	9-3-1	13	2t	Houston 10-1, Texas 10-1	R.C. Slocum	Holiday	65	BYU	14
1991	10-2	12	1	Tulsa 9-2, Baylor 8-3, TCU 7-4	R.C. Slocum	Cotton	2	Florida State	10
1992	12-1	7	1	Stanford 9-3, Rice 6-5, Baylor 6-5, Texas 6-5	R.C. Slocum	Cotton	3	Notre Dame	28
1993	10-2	8	1	Oklahoma 8-3, Texas Tech 6-5, Louisville 8-3	R.C. Slocum	Cotton	21	Notre Dame	24
1994	10-0-1	8	Ineligible	Baylor 7-4, Texas 7-4, TCU 7-4	R.C. Slocum				
1995	9-3	15	2t	Colorado 9-2, Texas Tech 8-3, Texas 10-1-1	R.C. Slocum	Alamo	22	Michigan	20
1996	6-6		S3	BYU 13-1, Colorado 9-2, Kansas State 9-2, Texas 8-4	R.C. Slocum				
1997	9-4	20	S1	Kansas State 10-1, Oklahoma State 8-3	R.C. Slocum	Cotton	23	UCLA	29
1998	11-3	11	S1	Florida State 11-1, Nebraska 9-3, Texas 8-3	R.C. Slocum	Sugar	14	Ohio State	24
1999	8-4	23	S2t	Southern Miss 9-3, Oklahoma 7-4, Nebraska 10-1, Texas 9-3	R.C. Slocum	Alamo	0	Penn State	24
2000	7-5		S3	Notre Dame 9-2, Kansas State 10-2, Oklahoma 11-0, Texas 9-2	R.C. Slocum	Independence	41	Mississippi State	43
2001	8-4		S3	Colorado 9-2, Oklahoma 10-2, Texas 10-1	R.C. Slocum				
2002	6-6		S5	Virginia Tech 9-4, Oklahoma 10-2, Texas 10-2	R.C. Slocum (123-47-2)				
2003	4-8		S5	Utah 9-2, Nebraska 9-3, Okla. St. 9-3, Oklahoma 12-0, Texas 10-2	Dennis Franchione				
2004	7-5		S3t	Utah 11-0, Oklahoma State 7-4, Oklahoma 11-0, Texas 10-1	Dennis Franchione	Cotton	7	Tennessee	38
2005	5-6		S4	Clemson 7-4, Iowa State 7-4, Texas Tech 9-2, Texas 12-0	Dennis Franchione				
2006	9-4		S3	Missouri 8-4, Oklahoma 10-2, Nebraska 9-3, Texas 9-3	Dennis Franchione	Holiday	10	California	45
2007	7-6		S3t	Kansas 11-1, Oklahoma 10-2, Missouri 11-1, Texas 9-3	Dennis Franchione (32-28), Gary Darnell [0-1]	Alamo	17	Penn State	24
2008	4-8		S5t	Oklahoma State 9-3, Texas Tech 11-1, Oklahoma 12-1, Texas 11-1	Mike Sherman				
2009	6-7		S5	Oklahoma State 9-3, Texas Tech 8-4, Oklahoma 7-5, Texas 13-0	Mike Sherman	Independence	20	Georgia	44
2010	9-4		S1t	Okla. St. 10-2, Arkansas 10-2, Mizzou 10-2, Oklahoma 11-2, Nebr. 10-3	Mike Sherman (19-19)	Cotton	24	Louisiana State	41

TOTAL: 369-280-12 .5673 (28 of 70)

Bowl Games since 1953: 8-17 .3200 (67 of 70)

GREATEST TEAM SINCE 1953: Perhaps the brain says the best was the 1994 Wrecking Crew-led Aggies who were denied a Southwest Conference championship and a bowl date, but the heart says the 1956 "Junction Boys," who in two years went from a depleted 1-9 squad to undefeated SWC champions. The names of Bear Bryant, John David Crow, Dennis Goehring, Lloyd Hale, Bobby Drake Keith, Charlie Krueger, Bobby Marks, Roddy Osborne, Jack Pardee, Jack Powell, Gene Stallings, Jim Stanley, Loyd Taylor, John Tracey, Don Watson, and Jimmy Wright are 'nuff said.

1953 4-5-1

7	Kentucky	6 E Bill Schroeder / Eric Miller
14	Houston	14 T Jack Powell
14	Georgia	12 G Ray Barrett / Sidney Theriot
27	Texas Tech	14 C Fred Broussard / Cooper Robbins
20	TCU	7 G Marvin Tate / Bob Gosney
13	Baylor	14 T Lawrence Winkler / Durwood Scott
14	Arkansas	41 E Bennie Sinclair / Johnny Salyer (FB)
0	SMU	23 QB Don Ellis
7	Rice	34 HB Connie Magouirk / Joe Schero
12	Texas	21 HB Billy Pete Huddleston / Joe Boring
		FB Bob Easley / Don Kachtik

RUSHING: Magouirk 52/283y, Easley 73/266y, Kachtik 64/231y
PASSING: Ellis 76-171/950y, 4TD, 44.4%
RECEIVING: Sinclair 19/287y, Schroeder 17/215y,
Schero 14/213y
SCORING: Ellis (QB-K) 37pts, Magouirk 30pts, 3 with 12pts

1954 1-9

9	Texas Tech	41 E Gene Stallings / Paul Kennon
6	Oklahoma State	14 T Darrell Brown / Norb Ohlendorf
6	Georgia	0 G Sidney Theriot / Ray Barrett
7	Houston	10 C Lloyd Hale / Richard Vick
20	TCU	21 G Marv Tate / Dennis Goehring
7	Baylor	20 T Larence Winkler / Henry Clark
7	Arkansas	14 E Bennie Sinclair / Bill Schroeder
3	SMU	6 QB Ellwood Kettler
19	Rice	29 HB Don Watson / Joe Boring
13	Texas	22 HB Don Kachtik / Billy Pete Huddleston
		FB Bob Easley / Jack Pardee

RUSHING: Kettler 149/446y, Kachtik 84/379y, Huddleston 42/190y,
Schero 37/166y, Watson 39/141y
PASSING: Kettler 36-72/471y, 2TD, 50.0%
RECEIVING: Sinclair 22/293y, Schero 7/78y, Stallings 4/77y,
Bobby Drake Keith (HB) 4/41y
SCORING: Kettler (QB-K) 54pts, Kachtik 12pts, 5 with 6pts

1955 7-2-1

0	UCLA	21 E Gene Stallings / Don Robbins
28	LSU	0 T Charlie Krueger / Darrell Brown
21	Houston	3 G Jim Stanley / Murry Trimble
27	Nebraska	0 C Lloyd Hale / Herb Wolf
19	TCU	16 G Dennis Goehring / Dee Powell
19	Baylor	7 T Jack Powell / Henry Clark
7	Arkansas	7 E Bobby Marks / Bobby Drake Keith
13	SMU	2 QB Jimmy Wright / Bobby Joe Conrad
20	Rice	12 HB John David Crow
6	Texas	21 HB Don Watson / Loyd Taylor
		FB Jack Pardee / Roddy Osborne

RUSHING: Pardee 83/452y
PASSING: Wright 24-67/368y, 35.8%
RECEIVING: Marks 7/94y
SCORING: Taylor (HB-K) 31pts

1956 9-0-1

19	Villanova	0 E Bobby Marks / Gene Stallings
9	LSU	6 T Charlie Krueger
40	Texas Tech	7 G Jim Stanley / Carl Luna
14	Houston	14 C Lloyd Hale / Dee Powell
7	TCU	6 G Dennis Goehring
19	Baylor	13 T Jack Powell / Bobby Lockett
27	Arkansas	0 E John Tracey / Bobby Drake Keith
33	SMU	7 QB Roddy Osborne / Jimmy Wright
21	Rice	7 HB John David Crow / Ken Hall
34	Texas	21 HB Loyd Taylor / Don Watson
		FB Jack Pardee / Richard Gay

RUSHING: Osborne 141/568y, Crow 101/561y, Pardee 103/463y
PASSING: Wright 16-31/224y, 5TD, 51.6%,
Osborne 14-23/258y, TD, 60.9%
RECEIVING: Crow 7/125y, Taylor 5/75y, Stallings 4/74y,
Marks 4/70y
SCORING: Crow 60pts, Taylor (HB-K), Pardee, & Osborne 30pts

1957 8-3

21	Maryland	13 E Bobby Marks / Don McClelleand
21	Texas Tech	0 T Charlie Krueger
28	Missouri	0 G Jim Stanley / Carl Luna
28	Houston	6 C John Gilbert / Gale Oliver
7	TCU	0 G Darrell Brown / Tommy Howard
14	Baylor	0 T Ken Beck / A.L. Simmons
7	Arkansas	6 E John Tracey
19	SMU	6 QB Roddy Osborne / Charlie Milstead
6	Rice	7 HB John David Crow / Carlos Esquivel
7	Texas	9 HB Bobby Joe Conrad / Loyd Taylor
0	Tennessee■	3 FB Richard Gay / Gordon LeBoeuf

RUSHING: Crow 129/562y, Osborne 121/496y, Taylor 59/226y
PASSING: Milstead 14-37/185y, TD, 37.8%
Osborne 10-27/166y, 3TD, 37.0%
RECEIVING: Tracey 8/103y, Taylor 6/104y, Smith 6/67y,
Marks 6/63y
SCORING: Osborne 48pts, Crow (HB-K) 37pts, Milstead 24pts

1958 4-6

14	Texas Tech	15 E Don Smith / Ralph Smith
7	Houston	39 T Gale Oliver / Carl Luna
12	Missouri	0 G Allen Goehring / Buddy Payne
14	Maryland	10 C Roy Northrup
8	TCU	24 G Carter Franklin / Bill Godwin
33	Baylor	27 T Ken Beck
8	Arkansas	21 E John Tracey / Teddy Estes
0	SMU	33 BB Richard Gay
28	Rice	21 TB Charlie Milstead / Paul Dudley
0	Texas	27 WB Randy Sims / Powell Berry
		FB Gordon LeBoeuf / Ken Hall (WB)

RUSHING: Hall 70/237y, Milstead 112/197y, LeBoeuf 56/157y
PASSING: Milstead 88-167/1135y, 5TD, 52.7%
RECEIVING: Tracey 37/466y, Sims 22/292y, Hall 13/215y
SCORING: Milstead 36pts, LeBoeuf 30pts, 3 with 12pts

1959 3-7

14	Texas Tech	20 E Ralph Smith
9	Michigan State	7 T Gale Oliver / A.L. Simmons
7	Miss. Southern	3 G Allen Goehring / Harry Labar
28	Houston	6 C Roy Northrup / Larry Broaddus
6	TCU	39 G Buddy Payne / Carter Franklin
0	Baylor	13 T Bill Godwin
7	Arkansas	12 E Bob Phillips / Teddy Estes
11	SMU	14 QB Charlie Milstead
2	Rice	7 HB Jesse McGuire / Powell Berry
17	Texas	20 WB Robert Sanders / Randy Sims
		FB Gordon LeBoeuf

RUSHING: LeBoeuf 113/341y, Sanders 36/150y,
Angermiller 28/88y
PASSING: Milstead 62-117/752y, 4TD, 53.0%
RECEIVING: Hill 19/341y, Sims 16/136y, Estes 13/165y
SCORING: Sims (WB-K) 31pts, Milstead 18pts, LeBoeuf 12pts

1960 1-6-3

0	LSU	9 E Ralph Smith / Don McClelland
14	Texas Tech	14 T Wayland Simmons
14	Trinity	0 G Harry Labar / Walter LaGrone
0	Houston	7 C Roy Northrup / Jerry Hopkins
14	TCU	14 G Jim Phillips
0	Baylor	14 T George Hogan
3	Arkansas	7 E Rob Phillips / Russell Hill / Mike Clark
0	SMU	0 QB Powell Berry / Daryle Keeling
14	Rice	21 HB Ron Ledbetter / Babe Craig
14	Texas	21 WB Bob Caskey / Randy Sims
		FB Lee Roy Caffey / Sam Byer

RUSHING: Byer 105/381y, Caffey 60/247y, Sims 49/230y
PASSING: Keeling 18-50/204y, TD, 36.0%
RECEIVING: Sims 5/66y, Estes 5/21y, Few 4/35y, Smith 4/34y
SCORING: Byer & Sims (WB-K) 18pts, Craig 14pts

1961 4-5-1

7	Houston	7 E Russell Hill / Joel Latham
7	LSU	16 T Wayland Simmons / George Hogan
38	Texas Tech	7 G Walter LaGrone
55	Trinity	0 C Jerry Jenkins / Jerry Hopkins
14	TCU	15 G Jim Phillips
23	Baylor	0 T Jim Craig
8	Arkansas	15 E Daryle Keeling / Bobby Huntington
25	SMU	12 QB John Erickson / Jim Keller
7	Rice	21 HB George Hargett / Travis Reagan
0	Texas	25 HB Jim Linnstaedter / Bob Caskey
		FB Lee Roy Caffey / Sam Byer

RUSHING: Caffey 85/371Y, Byer 74/256Y, Linnstaedter 60/243y
PASSING: Erickson 34-73/468y, 2TD, 46.6%
RECEIVING: Reagan 10/201y, Caskey 9/86y, Huntington 7/65y
SCORING: Reagan 38pts, Byer 18pts, Keeling (E-K) 17pts

1962 3-7

0	LSU	21 E Russell Hill / Joel Latham
3	Houston	6 T Ray Gene Hinze
7	Texas Tech	3 G Ronney Moore
6	Florida	42 C Jerry Hopkins
14	TCU	20 G Jim Phillips
6	Baylor	3 T Jim Craig
7	Arkansas	17 E Bobby Huntington / Mike Clark
12	SMU	7 QB Jim Keller / Jim Willenborg
3	Rice	23 HB Travis Reagan / George Hargett
3	Texas	13 HB Jim Linnstaedter
		FB Lee Roy Caffey / Jerry Rogers

RUSHING: Linnstaedter 36/167y, Caffey 36/143y,
Reagan 26/141y
PASSING: Keller 30-80/343y, 37.5%,
Willenborg 18-49/169y, 36.7%
RECEIVING: Hargett 14/194y, McLean 11/91y, Kipp 6/57y
SCORING: Clark (E-K) 25pts, 6 with 6pts

1963 2-7-1

6	LSU	14 E John Brotherton
0	Ohio State	17 T Ray Gene Hinze
0	Texas Tech	10 G Michael Swan
23	Houston	13 C Ray Kubala
14	TCU	14 G Rodney Moore
7	Baylor	34 T Jim Craig
7	Arkansas	21 E Ronnie Carpenter
7	SMU	9 QB Jim Linnstaedter / Jim Willenborg
13	Rice	6 HB Travis Reagan
13	Texas	15 HB George Hargett
		FB Budgie Ford / Jerry Rogers

RUSHING: Ford 62/234y, Rogers 64/177y, Linnstaedter 49/103y
PASSING: LaGrange 28-73/393y, 0TD, 38.3%,
Keller 15-32/290y, 2TD, 46.9%
RECEIVING: Hargett 12/162y, Reagan 11/189y, Ford 11/154y
SCORING: Rogers, Reagan, & Bobby Lee (K) 18pts

1964 1-9

6	LSU	9 E John Brotherton / Ed Breding (DL)
0	Houston	10 T Jack Pyburn
12	Texas Tech	16 G Don Koehn
7	Southern Cal	31 C Andy Overton
9	TCU	14 G Gary Kovar / Rodney Moore (LB)
16	Baylor	20 T Ray Gene Hinze
0	Arkansas	17 E Billy Uzzell / Marvin Dawkins
23	SMU	0 QB Dan McIhany / Ed McKaughan
8	Rice	19 HB Lloyd Curington/Jim Stabler/J. Nichols
7	Texas	26 HB Dan Westerfield / Mike Pitman (DB)
		FB Budgie Ford / Ken Caffey (LB)

RUSHING: Curington 99/287y, Stabler 79/200y,
McKaughan 71/160y
PASSING: McIlhany 47-111/598y, 2TD, 42.3%,
McKaughan 38-82/443y, 0TD, 46.3%
RECEIVING: Uzzell 22/246y, Brotherton 20/226y,
Westerfield 18/246y
SCORING: Bubber Collins (HB) & Glynn Lindsey (K) 12pts,
6 with 6pts

1965 3-7

0	LSU	10 WR Dude McLean / Joe Weiss
14	Georgia Tech	10 T Robert Barnett
16	Texas Tech	20 G Don Koehn
10	Houston	7 C Jim Singleton
9	TCU	17 G Gary Kovar
0	Baylor	31 T Jack Pyburn
0	Arkansas	31 TE Ed Breding (T) / John Poss
0	SMU	10 QB Harry Ledbetter
14	Rice	13 TB Bill Sallee / Lloyd Curington
17	Texas	21 WB Jim Stabler
		FB Dan Schneider / Bubber Collins
		DL Jerry Kachtik
		DL John Nilson
		DL Tom Murrah
		DL Ken Lamkin (OT) / Richard Paris
		DL Grady Allen / Tuffy Fletcher
		LB Joe Wellborn
		LB Robert Cortez
		DB Jim Kauffman
		DB Eddie McKaughan /Charles LeGrange
		DB Jerry Nichols
		DB Ken Caffey (TB) / Gary Kemph

RUSHING: Sallee 84/263y, Schneider 59/211y, Caffey 28/108y
PASSING: Ledbetter 83-182/940y, 5TD, 45.6%
RECEIVING: McLean 60/835y, Stabler 12/145y, 3 with 5
SCORING: Glynn Lindsey (K) 20pts, Curington,
Stabler & McLean 12pts

1966 4-5-1

3 Georgia Tech	38 WR Larry Lee / Tommy Maxwell
13 Tulane	21 T Jack Pyburn / Ed Breding
35 Texas Tech	14 G Don Koehn
7 LSU	7 C Jim Singleton
35 TCU	7 G Gary Kovar
17 Baylor	13 T Mo Moorman (DL)
0 Arkansas	34 TE Tom Buckman
14 SMU	21 QB Edd Hargett
7 Rice	6 HB Wendell Housley (WB) / Bill Sallee
14 Texas	22 WB Bob Long
	FB Ronnie Lindsey / Joe Weiss
	DL Tuffy Fletcher
	DL Rolf Krueger
	DL Ken Lamkin
	DL Harvey Aschenbeck
	DL Grady Allen
	LB Robert Cortez
	LB Bill Hobbs / Buster Adami
	DB Lawson Howard
	DB Dan Westerfield
	DB Curley Hallman
	DB Harry Ledbetter / Joe Wood

RUSHING: Housley 155/548y
PASSING: Hargett 132-265/1532y, 10TD, 49.8%
RECEIVING: Maxwell 27/445y
SCORING: Maxwell 26pts

1967 7-4

17 SMU	20 WR Tommy Maxwell (DB)
20 Purdue	24 T Dan Schneider / Carl Gough (DL)
6 LSU	17 G Mark Weaver
18 Florida State	19 C Jack Kovar
28 Texas Tech	24 G Mo Moorman / Robert Cortez (LB)
20 TCU	0 T Rolf Krueger (DL)
21 Baylor	3 TE Tom Buckman
33 Arkansas	21 QB Edd Hargett
18 Rice	3 TB Larry Stegent / Wendell Housley
10 Texas	7 WB Bob Long
20 Alabama■	16 FB Bill Sallee
	DL Gary Kitchens / Jim Piper
	DL Buster Adami (LB) / Walter Mohn
	DL Bill Kubecka
	DL Harvey Aschenbeck
	DL Grady Allen / Gaddy Wells
	LB Bill Hobbs
	LB Robert Cortez (G) / Mike Caswell
	DB Tommy Sooy / Ross Brupbacher (TB)
	DB Jack Whitmore / Jimmy Adams (WR)
	DB Curley Hallman
	DB Ivan Jones

RUSHING: Stegent 161/568y, Sallee 56/221y, Housley 56/196y
PASSING: Hargett 99-208/1526y, 16TD, 47.6%
RECEIVING: Stegent 27/365y, Long 24/541y, Maxwell 18/250y
SCORING: Long 48pts, Stegent 42pts, Charlie Riggs (K) 39pts

1968 3-7

12 LSU	13 WR Tommy Maxwell (DB) /Jimmy Adams
35 Tulane	3 T Mike Stinson
14 Florida State	20 G Jim Parker (T) / Gary Gruben
16 Texas Tech	21 C Jack Kovar
27 TCU	7 G Rusty Stallings / Allan Hanson
9 Baylor	10 T Tom Buckman
22 Arkansas	25 TE Barney Harris / Mike Sigman
23 SMU	36 QB Edd Hargett
24 Rice	14 TB Larry Stegent / Jimmy Sheffield
14 Texas	35 WB Bob Long / Dave Elmendorf (FB-DB)
	FB Wendell Housley
	DL Jim Piper
	DL Rolf Krueger
	DL Lynn Odom / Winston Beam
	DL Harvey Aschenbeck / Dale Watts
	DL Mike DeNiro
	LB Bill Hobbs
	LB Buster Adami / Mike Caswell
	DB Curley Hallman
	DB Ross Brupbacher / Jack Whitmore
	DB Tommy Sooy / Billy Seely (WB)
	DB Ivan Jones / Lynn Fister

RUSHING: Stegent 105/492y, Housley 75/255y, Elmendorf 29/177y
PASSING: Hargett 169-348/2321y, 16TD, 48.6%
RECEIVING: Harris 49/745y, Long 32/507y, Stegent 32/317y
SCORING: Long 48pts, Stegent 40pts, Charlie Riggs (K) 34pts

1969 3-7

6 LSU	35 WR Barney Harris / Jimmy Adams
0 Nebraska	14 T Randy Maddox / Joe Shaw
20 Army	13 G Jim Parker
9 Texas Tech	13 C Jack Kovar / Mike Stinson
6 TCU	16 G Rusty Stallings / Allan Hanson
24 Baylor	0 T Mike Fields / Andy Philley
13 Arkansas	35 TE Ross Brupbacher
20 SMU	10 QB Rocky Self / Jimmy Sheffield
6 Rice	7 TB Larry Stegent / Steve Burks
12 Texas	49 WB Billy Seeley
	FB Marc Black / Gary Armbrister
	DL Jim Piper
	DL Billy Bob Barnett / Van Odom
	DL Lynn Odom
	DL Dale Watts
	DL Mike DeNiro
	LB Steve Luebbehusen
	LB Buster Adami / Mike Caswell
	DB Ed Ebrom
	DB Corky Sheffield / Chris Johnson
	DB Dave Elmendorf / Tommy Sooy (WR)
	DB David Hoot

RUSHING: Stegent 197/676y, Self 127/324y, Black 71/255y
PASSING: Self 87-199/1136y, 6TD, 43.7%
RECEIVING: Harris 34/191y, Brupbacher 22/395y, Black 14/105y
SCORING: Brupbacher 36pts, Stegent 24pts, Mike Bellar (K) 20pts

1970 2-9

41 Wichita State	14 WR Hugh McElroy / Joey Herr
20 LSU	18 T Buster Callaway / Benny DeWitt
13 Ohio State	56 G Lenard Millsap
10 Michigan	14 C Mike Park
7 Texas Tech	21 G Leonard Forey
15 TCU	31 T Mike Fields / Andy Philley
24 Baylor	29 TE Homer May
6 Arkansas	45 QB Lex James / Joe Mac King
3 SMU	6 HB Brad Dusek / Johnny Gardner
17 Rice	18 HB Steve Burks / Jimmy Sheffield
14 Texas	52 FB Marc Black / Doug Neill
	DL Todd Christopher
	DL Boice Best / Dale Watts
	DL Van Odom / Winston Beam (G)
	DL Max Bird / Barb Hinnant
	LB Steve Luebbehusen
	LB Mike Lord / Gary McCaffrey
	LB Kent Finley
	DB Ed Ebrom / Chris Johnson
	DB Robert Murski
	DB Dave Elmendorf / Lee Hitt
	DB David Hoot

RUSHING: Neill 107/426y, Burks 113/413y, Dusek 83/267y
PASSING: James 111-225/1662y, 6TD, 49.3%
RECEIVING: May 26/479y, McElroy 21/423y, Herr 21/362y
SCORING: Pat McDermott (K) 34pts, Burks & May 32pts

1971 5-6

41 Wichita State	7 WR Robert Murski / John Gardner
0 LSU	37 T Buster Callaway
7 Nebraska	34 G Todd Christopher
0 Cincinnati	17 C Robert Gerasimowicz
7 Texas Tech	28 G Leonard Forey / Mike Park
3 TCU	14 T Andy Philley / Ralph Sacra
10 Baylor	9 TE Homer May / Mitch Robertson
17 Arkansas	9 QB Joe Mac King / Lex James
27 SMU	10 TB Mark Green
18 Rice	13 WB Joey Herr / Hugh McElroy
14 Texas	34 FB Doug Neill / Marc Black
	DL Max Bird
	DL Boice Best
	DL Van Odom / Bill Wiebold
	DL James Dubcak
	DL Kent Finley
	LB Grady Hoermann / Mike Lord
	LB Steve Luebbehusen
	DB Ed Ebrom
	DB Bland Smith / Lee Hitt
	DB Brad Dusek / Mike Bunger
	DB David Hoot / Larry Ellis

RUSHING: Green 181/593y, Neill 108/437y, Black 54/210y
PASSING: King 36-87/559y, 3TD, 41.4%, James 22-57/286y, 2TD, 38.6%
RECEIVING: Murski 17/212y, May 15/250y, Herr 9/143y
SCORING: Green 42pts, Pat McDermott (K) 35pts, 2 with 12pts

1972 3-8

36 Wichita State	13 WR Carl Roaches
7 Nebraska	37 T Mike Park
17 LSU	42 G Todd Christopher / Ricky Seeker
14 Army	24 C Skip Kuehn
14 Texas Tech	17 G Buster Callaway
10 TCU	13 T Ralph Sacra
13 Baylor	15 TE Richard Osborne / Homer May
10 Arkansas	7 QB Don Dean / Lex James
27 SMU	17 HB Mark Green / Ronnie Hubby
14 Rice	20 HB Alvin "Skip" Walker / Bubba Bean
3 Texas	38 FB Brad Dusek
	DL Max Bird
	DL Boice Best
	DL Bill Wiebold
	DL Don Long
	LB Ed Simonini
	LB Grady Hoermann
	LB Dennis Carruth / Kent Finley (DL)
	DB Corky Sheffield
	DB Robert Murski / Pat Thomas
	DB Al Thurmond / Dwight LaBauve
	DB Larry Ellis

RUSHING: Dusek 124/549y, Green 59/311y, Walker 78/311y
PASSING: Dean 57-113/820y, 3TD, 50.4%, James 29-64/352y, TD, 45.3%
RECEIVING: Osborne 31/440y, May 18/346y, Roaches 11/195y
SCORING: Pat McDermott (K) 33pts, Roaches 24pts, 4 with 18pts

1973 5-6

48 Wichita State	0 WR Carl Roaches
23 LSU	28 T Glenn Bujnoch
24 Boston College	32 G Bruce Welch
30 Clemson	15 C Ricky Seeker
16 Texas Tech	28 G Bud Trammell / Billy Lemons
35 TCU	16 T Dennis Smelser
28 Baylor	22 TE Richard Osborne
10 Arkansas	14 QB David Walker / Mike Jay
45 SMU	10 HB Bubba Bean
20 Rice	24 WB Skip Walker
13 Texas	42 FB Alvin Bowers / Bucky Sams
	DL Don Long
	DL Ted Lamp
	DL Warren Trahan
	DL Blake Schwarz / Paul Hulin
	LB Ed Simonini
	LB Ken Stratton
	LB Garth Ten Napel / Lester Hayes
	DB Pat Thomas
	DB Tim Gray
	DB James Daniels
	DB Larry Ellis / Jackie Williams

RUSHING: Bean 112/711y, Bowers 153/696y, S. Walker 98/618y
PASSING: Jay 36-86/682y, 2 TD, 41.9%, D. Walker 31-69/426y, 0TD, 44.9%
RECEIVING: Osborne 29/405y, Roaches 21/391y
SCORING: Randy Haddox (K) 62pts, S. Walker 48pts, Bowers 42pts

1974 7-4

24 Clemson	0 WR Carl Roaches / Mike Floyd
21 LSU	14 T Glenn Bujnoch / George Burger
28 Washington	15 G Craig Glendenning / Bruce Welch
10 Kansas	28 C Ricky Seeker / Henry Tracy
28 Texas Tech	7 G Billy Lemons
17 TCU	0 T Dennis Smelser / Dennis Swilley
20 Baylor	0 TE Richard Osborne
20 Arkansas	10 QB David Walker
14 SMU	18 HB Bubba Bean
37 Rice	7 HB Skip Walker / Ronnie Hubby
3 Texas	32 FB Bucky Sams / Jerry Honore
	DL Don Long / Tank Marshall
	DL Edgar Fields / Ted Lamp
	DL Warren Trahan / Jimmy Dean
	DL Paul Hulin / Blake Schwarz
	LB Ed Simonini
	LB Ken Stratton / John McCrumbly
	LB Garth Ten Napel / Lester Hayes (DB)
	DB Pat Thomas
	DB Tim Gray / Tony Blankenship
	DB Al Thurmond / James Daniels
	DB Jackie Williams

RUSHING: Bean 158/938y, Sams 129/629y
PASSING: D. Walker 46-102/666y, 3TD, 45.1%
RECEIVING: Osborne 13/145y
SCORING: Walker & Randy Haddox (K) 54pts

1975 10-2

7 Mississippi	0 WR Carl Roaches / Mike Floyd
39 LSU	8 T Frank Myers
43 Illinois	13 G Craig Glendenning
10 Kansas State	0 C Mark Dennard
38 Texas Tech	9 G Dennis Swilley / Billy Lemons
14 TCU	6 T Dennis Smelser
19 Baylor	10 TE Richard Osborne
36 SMU	3 QB David Shipman / Mike Jay
33 Rice	14 HB Bubba Bean
20 Texas	10 HB Skip Walker / Ronnie Hubby
6 Arkansas	31 FB George Woodard / Bucky Sams
0 Southern Cal ■	20 DL Tank Marshall
	DL Edgar Fields
	DL Jimmy Dean
	DL Blake Schwarz
	LB Ed Simonini
	LB Robert Jackson / Grady Wilkerson
	LB Garth Ten Napel / Kevin Monk
	DB Pat Thomas / Tony Blankenship
	DB William Thompson
	DB Lester Hayes / Reggie Williams
	DB Jackie Williams

RUSHING: Bean 144/944y, Woodard 128/604y
PASSING: Shipman 24-60/422y, 2TD, 40.0%,
Jay 10-24/134y, TD, 41.7%
RECEIVING: Osborne 13/191y, Roaches 8/109y, Walker 6/171y
SCORING: Tony Franklin (K) 63pts, Bean 48pts,
Walker & Woodard 30pts

1976 10-2

19 Virginia Tech	0 WR Mike Floyd / Doug Teague
34 Kansas State	14 T Frank Myers
10 Houston	21 G Craig Glendenning
14 Illinois	7 C Mark Dennard / Matt Freeman
16 Texas Tech	27 G Dennis Swilley
24 Baylor	0 T Cody Risien / Billy Lemons
57 Rice	34 TE Gary Haack
36 SMU	0 QB David Walker / David Shipman
31 Arkansas	10 HB Curtis Dickey
59 TCU	10 HB David Brothers / Adgar Armstrong
27 Texas ■	3 FB George Woodard / Eddie Hardin
37 Florida ■	14 DL Tank Marshall / Stacy Breihan
	DL Edgar Fields
	DL Jimmy Dean
	DL Phil Bennett / Eddie Heath
	LB Robert Jackson / Frankie Lemons
	LB Kevin Monk
	LB Jesse Hunnicutt / Grady Wilkerson
	DB Mike Williams / Charles Bell
	DB William Thompson
	DB Carl Grulich / Reggie Williams
	DB Lester Hayes

RUSHING: Woodard 239/1153y, Dickey 142/726y,
Walker 96/277y
PASSING: Walker 51-90/675y, 3TD, 56.7%
RECEIVING: Haack 21/265y, Dickey 13/146y, Teague 12/274y
SCORING: Woodard 102pts, Tony Franklin (K) 81pts,
Dickey 50pts

1977 8-4

28 Kansas	14 WR Doug Teague / Darrell Smith
27 Virginia Tech	6 T Frank Myers / Zach Guthrie
33 Texas Tech	17 G Ed Pustejovsky / Kenny Kirk
3 Michigan	41 C Mark Dennard / Preston Dickson
38 Baylor	31 G Thomas Gregory / Doug Holmes
28 Rice	14 T Cody Risien
38 SMU	21 TE Russell Mikeska / Chuck Carr
20 Arkansas	26 QB David Walker / Mike Mosley
52 TCU	23 HB Curtis Dickey / Adgar Armstrong
28 Texas	57 HB David Brothers
27 Houston	7 FB George Woodard / Eddie Hardin
28 Southern Cal ■	47 DL Jacob Green
	DL Johnnie Donahue / James Zachery
	DL Steve Spitzenberger / Garry Milligan
	DL Phil Bennett / Eddie Heath
	LB Frankie Lemons / Roderick Reed
	LB Kevin Monk / Doug Carr
	LB Floyd Randle
	DB Mike Williams / Elroy Steen
	DB Darrell Smith / Gregory Clark
	DB Carl Grulich
	DB Kenneth Taylor / Jimmy Hamilton

RUSHING: Woodard 245/1107y, Dickey 178/978y,
Walker 128/394y
PASSING: Walker 49-107/750y, 8TD, 45.8%
RECEIVING: Dickey 17/231y, Smith 12/234y, Woodard 9/83y
SCORING: Tony Franklin (K) 86pts, Woodard 78pts,
Dickey 36pts

1978 8-4

37 Kansas	10 WR Doug Teague / Al Nasser
37 Boston College	2 T Curtis Jennings / Zach Guthrie
58 Memphis State	0 G Ed Pustejovsky / Johnnie Svatek
38 Texas Tech	9 C Preston Dickson
0 Houston	33 G Paul Hagerty / Kyle Golson
6 Baylor	24 T Cody Risien
38 Rice	21 TE Chuck Carr / Russell Mikeska
20 SMU	17 QB Mike Mosley / David Beal
7 Arkansas	26 TB Curtis Dickey / Adgar Armstrong
15 TCU	7 WB Gerald Carter
7 Texas	22 FB David Brothers / Raymond Belcher
28 Iowa State ■	12 DL Jacob Green
	DL Eugene Sanders / Johnnie Donahue
	DL Garry Milligan / Gerald Galloway
	DL James Zachery / Stacy Breihan
	LB Mike Little
	LB Doug Carr / Randy Harvey
	LB Cal Peveto / Floyd Randle
	DB Elroy Steen
	DB Darrell Smith / Leandrew Brown
	DB Carl Grulich / Lynn Honeycutt
	DB Kenneth Taylor / Jimmy Hamilton

RUSHING: Dickey 205/1146y, Brothers 129/584y,
Belcher 73/354y
PASSING: Mosley 80-139/1157y, 4TD, 57.6%
RECEIVING: Mikeska 29/429y, Teague 26/342y, Carter 22/372y
SCORING: Tony Franklin (K) 61pts, Dickey 54pts,
Brothers & Mosley 30pts

1979 6-5

17 BYU	18 WR Doug Teague / Mike Whitwell
7 Baylor	17 WR Gerald Carter / David Scott
27 Penn State	14 T Zach Guthrie
17 Memphis State	7 G Ed Pustejovsky / Doug Holmes
20 Texas Tech	21 C Preston Dickson / David Bandy
14 Houston	17 G Thomas Gregory / Kyle Golson
41 Rice	15 T Phillip Simpson
47 SMU	14 TE Chuck Carr / Jimmy Hamilton
10 Arkansas	22 QB Mike Mosley / David Beal
30 TCU	7 TB Curtis Dickey / David Brothers
13 Texas	7 FB David Hill / George Woodard
	DL Jacob Green
	DL Johnnie Svatek
	DL Arlis James
	DL Keith Baldwin
	LB Mike Little / Randy Harvey
	LB Doug Carr / Bobby Strogen
	LB Cal Peveto / Will Wright
	DB Leandrew Brown / Darrell Adams
	DB Dan Davis
	DB Carl Grulich / Van Barnett
	DB John Dawson / Elroy Steen

RUSHING: Dickey 172/853y, Mosley 135/505y,
Johnny Hector (TB) 99/378y
PASSING: Mosley 82-142/938y, 2TD, 57.8%
RECEIVING: Carter 39/528y, Scott 9/118y, Teague 9/117y
SCORING: Dickey 54pts, David Hardy (K) 53pts, Mosley 42pts

1980 4-7

23 Mississippi	20 WR Mike Whitwell
0 Georgia	42 WR Billy Cannon Jr / David Scott
9 Penn State	25 T Zach Guthrie
41 Texas Tech	21 G John Osborn
13 Houston	17 C David Bandy
7 Baylor	46 G Flint Risien
6 Rice	10 T Tim Ward
0 SMU	27 TE Pat Flinn
24 Arkansas	27 QB Mike Mosley / David Beal
13 TCU	10 RB Johnny Hector / Thomas Sanders
24 Texas	14 FB Earnest Jackson / David Hill
	DL Paul Pender / Jon Van Sant
	DL Mack Moore / Keith Guthrie
	DL Arlis James / Fred Caldwell
	DL Keith Baldwin
	LB Mike Little
	LB Doug Carr / Bobby Strogen
	LB Will Wright / Jerry Bullitt
	DB Leandrew Brown
	DB Dan Davis / Greg Williams
	DB Jeff Farrar / Van Barnett
	DB Lynn Honeycutt

RUSHING: Hector 173/928y, Jackson 98/356y, Mosley 51/205y,
Sanders 52/201y
PASSING: Beal 45-94/671y, 4TD, 47.9%,
Mosley 33-75/369y, TD, 44.0%
RECEIVING: Whitwell 30/603y, Jackson 14/194y, Scott 13/208y
SCORING: Hector 30pts, Beal 26pts, David Hardy (K) 21pts

1981 7-5

29 California	28 WR Mike Whitwell
12 Boston College	13 WR Don Jones
43 Louisiana Tech	7 T Bryan Dausin
24 Texas Tech	23 G Flint Risien
7 Houston	6 C David Bandy
17 Baylor	19 G Aubrey Raiford
51 Rice	26 T Matt Darwin / Tommy Robison
7 SMU	27 TE Mark Lewis / Larry Edmondson
7 Arkansas	10 QB Gary Kubiak
37 TCU	7 RB Johnny Hector / Thomas Sanders
13 Texas	21 FB Earnest Jackson
33 Oklahoma St. ■	16 DL Jon Van Sant / Paul Pender
	DL Ray Childress / Keith Guthrie
	DL Fred Caldwell
	DL Keith Baldwin
	LB Mike Little
	LB Bobby Strogen / Greg Berry
	LB Will Wright
	DB Greg Williams
	DB Dan Davis / Darrell Adams
	DB Billy Cannon / Jeff Fuller
	DB Jeff Farrar / Jeff Fuller

RUSHING: Jackson 153/887y, Hector 138/727y,
Sanders 94/344y
PASSING: Kubiak 111-209/1808y, 11TD, 53.1%
RECEIVING: Whitwell 27/731y, Hector 24/214y,
Jackson 18/202y
SCORING: David Hardy (K) 65pts, Hector 42pts, Jones 36pts

1982 5-6

16 Boston College	38 WR Don Jones / Jimmy Teal
61 Texas-Arlington	22 WR Jimmie Williams / John Kellen
38 Louisiana Tech	27 T Bryan Dausin
15 Texas Tech	24 G Flint Risien
20 Houston	24 C Matt Darwin
28 Baylor	23 G Greg Porter / Ken Reeves
49 Rice	7 T Tommy Robison
9 SMU	47 TE Jeff Paine / Mark Lewis
0 Arkansas	35 QB Gary Kubiak
34 TCU	14 RB Johnny Hector / Mike Marshall
16 Texas	53 RB Earnest Jackson / George Smith
	DL Jon Van Sant
	DL Ray Childress
	DL Keith Guthrie / Fred Caldwell
	DL Paul Pender / Thomas Graham
	LB Jerry Bullitt / Will Wright
	LB Bobby Strogen / Greg Berry
	LB Jeff Fuller (DB) / Rusty Nettles
	DB Greg Williams
	DB Billy Brown / Darrell Adams
	DB Domingo Bryant / Wayne Asberry
	DB Billy Cannon Jr.

RUSHING: Hector 140/554y, Smith 48/240y, Jackson 46/161y,
Marshall 47/160y
PASSING: Kubiak 181-324/1948y, 19TD, 55.8%
RECEIVING: Jones 32/461y, Hector 29/218y, Smith 23/120y,
Teal 22/324y
SCORING: David Hardy (K) 80pts, Jones & Hector 30pts

1983 5-5-1

17 California	19 WR Shea Walker / Jeff Nelson
38 Arkansas State	17 WR Jimmie Williams / Don Jones
15 Oklahoma State	34 T Nate Steadman
0 Texas Tech	3 G Randy Dausin
30 Houston	7 C Matt Darwin
13 Baylor	13 G Ken Reeves / Randy Wylie
29 Rice	10 T Tommy Robison
7 SMU	10 TE Rich Siler
36 Arkansas	23 QB Kevin Murray
20 TCU	10 RB Rod Bernstine / Jimmie Hawkins
13 Texas	45 FB Roger Vick / George Smith
	DL Ray Childress
	DL Keith Guthrie / Rod Saddler
	DL Chris Lammers
	LB Billy Cannon, Jr. / Darrell Smith
	LB Greg Berry
	LB Jerry Bullitt / Mike Ashley
	LB Jeff Paine / Jeff Fuller
	DB Ken Ford / Tony Slaton
	DB Bill Brown / Darrell Austin
	DB Wayne Asberry
	DB Domingo Bryant

RUSHING: Vick 91/425y, Bernstine 87/319y, Smith 41/179y,
Woodside 43/179y
PASSING: Murray 132-249/1544y, 14TD, 53.0%
RECEIVING: Siler 40/465y, Bernstine 24/217y, Walker 21/275y
SCORING: Alan Smith (K) 72pts, Siler 24pts,
Murray & Nelson 18pt

1984 6-5

20 Texas-El Paso	17 WR Jimmy Teal / Greg Dillon
38 Iowa State	17 WR Jeff Nelson
22 Arkansas State	21 T Doug Williams
12 Texas Tech	30 G Randy Dausin
7 Houston	9 C Matt Darwin
16 Baylor	20 G Nate Steadman
38 Rice	14 T Ken Reeves
20 So. Methodist	28 TE Mark Lewis / Rod Bernstine
0 Arkansas	28 QB Craig Stump / Kevin Murray
35 Texas Christian	21 RB Roger Vick / Anthony Toney
37 Texas	12 FB Thomas Sanders
	DL Ray Childress
	DL Sammy O'Brient / David Dowell
	DL Rod Saddler / Jay Muller
	LB Steve Bullitt / Darrell Smith
	LB Todd Howard / Scott Polk
	LB Johnny Holland
	LB Ken Ford / Lance Jackson
	DB Darrell Austin / James Flowers
	DB Wayne Asberry / Tony Slaton
	DB Jimmy Hawkins
	DB Domingo Bryant

RUSHING: Sanders 167/738y, Toney 80/393y, Vick 91/322y
PASSING: Stump 94-189/1135y, 10TD, 49.7%,
Murray 43-77/534y, 4TD, 55.8%
RECEIVING: Teal 35/631y, Nelson 20/226y, Lewis 16/226y
SCORING: Alan Smith (K) 51pts, Teal 38pts, Toney 36pts

1985 10-2

10 Alabama	23 WR Shea Walker
31 NE Louisiana	17 WR Jeff Nelson / Rod Harris
45 Tulsa	10 T Doug Williams
28 Texas Tech	27 G Randy Dausin
43 Houston	16 C Matt Wilson
15 Baylor	20 G Randy Wylie
43 Rice	28 T Louis Cheek
19 SMU	17 TE Rod Bernstine / Rich Siler
10 Arkansas	6 QB Kevin Murray
53 TCU	6 RB Roger Vick / Keith Woodside
42 Texas	10 FB Anthony Toney
36 Auburn■	16 DL Jay Muller / Guy Broom
	DL Sammy O'Brient
	DL Rod Saddler
	LB Larry Kelm / Steve Bullitt
	LB Todd Howard / Dana Baptiste
	LB Johnny Holland
	LB John Roper / Lance Jackson
	DB Darrell Austin
	DB James Flowers / Wayne Asberry
	DB Kip Corrington / Alex Morris
	DB Domingo Bryant / Jimmy Hawkins

RUSHING: Toney 191/845y, Vick 171/764y, Woodside 47/351y
PASSING: Murray 147-251/1965y, 13TD, 58.6%
RECEIVING: Nelson 51/651y, Walker 30/489y,
Woodside 27/281y
SCORING: Toney & Eric Franklin (K) 74pts, Vick 60pts

1986 9-3

17 LSU	35 WR Shea Walker
48 No. Texas St.	28 WR Rod Harris / Tony Thompson
16 Southern Miss	7 T Louis Cheek
45 Texas Tech	8 G Trace McGuire
19 Houston	7 C Matt Wilson
31 Baylor	30 G Jerry Fontenot
45 Rice	10 T Marshall Land / Frank Case
39 SMU	35 TE Rod Bernstine / Sylvester Morgan
10 Arkansas	4 QB Kevin Murray
74 TCU	10 RB Keith Woodside / Ira Valentine
16 Texas	3 FB Roger Vick / Melvin Collins
12 Ohio State■	28 DL Jay Muller
	DL Sammy O'Brient
	DL Rod Saddler
	LB Larry Kelm / Steve Bullitt
	LB Todd Howard / Dana Baptiste
	LB Johnny Holland
	LB John Roper
	DB James Flowers
	DB Alex Morris / Rod Anthony
	DB Kip Corrington / Jeff Holley
	DB Terrance Brooks

RUSHING: Vick 220/960y, Woodside 97/569y, Collins 38/247y
PASSING: Murray 212-349/2463y, 17TD,, 60.7%
RECEIVING: Bernstine 65/710y, Woodside 52/603y,
Walker 40/565y
SCORING: Scott Slater (K) 100pts, Vick 60pts, Woodside 42pts

1987 10-2

3 LSU	17 WR Rod Harris / Percy Waddle
29 Washington	12 WR Gary Oliver
27 Southern Miss	14 T Louis Cheek / L.B. Moon
21 Texas Tech	27 G Richmond Webb
22 Houston	17 C Matt Wilson
34 Baylor	10 G Jerry Fontenot / Trace McGuire
34 Rice	21 T Tony Bartley / Darren Grudt
32 Louisiana Tech	3 TE Sylvester Morgan / Brian Ross
14 Arkansas	0 QB Craig Stump / Lance Pavlas
42 TCU	24 RB Darren Lewis / Keith Woodside
20 Texas	13 FB Matt Gurley / Melvin Collins
35 Notre Dame■	10 DL Guy Broom / Leon Cole
	DL Sammy O'Brient
	DL Terry Price
	LB John Roper
	LB Adam Bob / Basil Jackson
	LB Dana Baptiste / Joe Johnson
	LB Aaron Wallace / Tim Landrum
	DB Tony Jones / Mickey Washington
	DB Alex Morris / Gary Jones
	DB Kip Corrington
	DB Terrance Brooks

RUSHING: Lewis 127/668y, Woodside 112/620y,
Bucky Richardson (QB) 62/423y, Gurley 93/379y
PASSING: Stump 41-98/524y, 2TD, 41.8%,
Pavlas 41-83/451y, 2TD, 49.4%,
Bucky Richardson (QB) 16-45/156y, TD, 35.6%
RECEIVING: Woodside 25/237y, Harris 19/281y,
Waddle 12/194y
SCORING: Scott Slater (K) 70pts, Lewis 48pts, Gurley 36pts

1988 7-5

14 Nebraska	23 WR Rod Harris / Percy Waddle
0 LSU	27 WR Gary Oliver / Cornelius Patterson
15 Oklahoma State	52 T Jerry Fontenot
50 Texas Tech	15 G Richmond Webb
30 Houston	16 C Mike Arthur
28 Baylor	14 G L.B. Moon
24 Rice	10 T Matt McCall
56 Louisiana Tech	17 TE Brian Ross / Mike Jones
20 Arkansas	25 QB Bucky Richardson / Chris Osgood
18 TCU	0 RB Darren Lewis / Randy Simmons
28 Texas	24 FB Robert Wilson / Larry Horton
10 Alabama■	30 DL O'Neill Gilbert
	DL Leon Cole / Jeff Huff
	DL Terry Price
	LB John Roper
	LB Adam Bob / Basil Jackson
	LB Dana Batiste / Joe Johnson
	LB Aaron Wallace / Jeroy Robinson
	DB Mickey Washington
	DB Alex Morris / Lafayette Turner
	DB William Thomas / Chris Crooms
	DB Gary Jones / Brent Smith

RUSHING: Lewis 306/1692y, Richardson 108/554y,
Wilson 84/425y
PASSING: Osgood 54-112/656y, 3TD, 48.2%,
Richardson 42-88/544y, TD, 47.7%
RECEIVING: Harris 37/592y, Horton 17/122y, Jones 14194y/
SCORING: Wilson 60pts, Richardson 56pts,
Scott Slater (K) 49pts

1989 8-4

28 LSU	16 WR Percy Waddle / Shane Garrett
6 Washington	19 WR Cornelius Patterson / Gary Oliver
44 TCU	7 T Richmond Webb
31 Southern Miss.	14 G Keith Alex
24 Texas Tech	27 C Mike Arthur
17 Houston	13 G Mike Pappas / Darren Grudt
14 Baylor	11 T Matt McCall
45 Rice	7 TE Mike Jones / Derek Ware
63 SMU	14 QB Lance Pavlas / Chris Osgood
22 Arkansas	23 TB Darren Lewis / Keith McAfee
21 Texas	10 FB Robert Wilson / Doug Carter
28 Pittsburgh■	31 DL Kevin Tucker / Jayson Black
	DL Pat Henry / John Miller
	DL Terry Price
	LB Aaron Wallace
	LB Anthony Williams / John Cooper
	LB Jeroy Robinson / Trent Lewis
	LB William Thomas / James Webb
	DB Kevin Smith
	DB Derrick Frazier / Mickey Washington
	DB Larry Horton / Chris Crooms
	DB Gary Jones / Dion Snow

RUSHING: Lewis 185/961y, Wilson 125/590y, McAfee 79/309y
PASSING: Pavlas 134-227/1681y, 10TD, 59.0%
RECEIVING: Waddle 36/600y, Jones 36/501y, Wilson 17/163y
SCORING: Layne Talbot (K) 71pts, Lewis 66pts, Wilson 44pts

1990 9-3-1

28 Hawaii	13 WR Gary Oliver / Tony Harrison
63 SW Louisiana	14 WR Shane Garrett / Cornelius Patterson
40 North Texas	8 T Matt McCall
8 LSU	17 G John Ellisor
28 Texas Tech	24 C Mike Arthur
31 Houston	36 G Mike Pappas
20 Baylor	20 T Jason Rockhold / Dexter Wesley
41 Rice	15 TE Dennis Ransom / Derek Ware
38 SMU	17 QB Bucky Richardson / Lance Pavlas
20 Arkansas	16 TB Darren Lewis / Keith McAfee
56 TCU	10 FB Robert Wilson / Doug Carter
27 Texas	28 DL Albert Jones / Eric England
65 BYU■	14 DL John Miller / Lance Teichelman
	DL Jayson Black
	LB Marcus Buckley / Tyrone Malone
	LB Quintin Coryatt
	LB Anthony Williams / Jason Atkinson
	LB William Thomas / Otis Nealy
	DB Kevin Smith / Billy Mitchell
	DB Derrick Frazier / Marlin Haynes
	DB Larry Horton
	DB Chris Crooms / Eric Moore

RUSHING: Lewis 291/1691y, Wilson 134/724y,
Richardson 97/670y
PASSING: Richardson 59-116/847y, 4TD, 50.9%,
Pavlas 56-89/871y, 8TD, 62.9%
RECEIVING: Oliver 28/455y, Garrett 24/469y, Ware 11/181y
SCORING: Lewis 114pts, Layne Talbot (K) 80pts,
Richardson 48pts

1991 10-2

45 LSU	7 WR Tony Harrison
34 Tulsa	35 WR Brian Mitchell / Ryan Mathews
34 SW Louisiana	7 T Keith Alex
37 Texas Tech	14 G John Ellisor
34 Baylor	12 C Chris Dausin
27 Houston	18 G Tyler Harrison / Jeff Jones
38 Rice	21 T Dexter Wesley
44 TCU	7 TE Greg Schorp
13 Arkansas	3 QB Bucky Richardson / Jeff Granger
65 SMU	6 TB Greg Hill / Rodney Thomas
31 Texas	14 FB Doug Carter / Clif Groce
2 Florida State■	10 DL Sam Adams
	DL Mark Wheeler / Pat Henry
	DL Eric England / Lance Teichelman
	LB Marcus Buckley / Charles Burrell
	LB Quintin Coryatt
	LB Jason Atkinson / Reggie Graham
	LB Otis Nealy / Steve Solari
	DB Kevin Smith / Marlin Haynes
	DB Derrick Frazier
	DB Patrick Bates / Ramsey Bradberry
	DB Chris Crooms

RUSHING: Hill 240/1216y, Richardson 103/448y,
Keith McAfee 77/372y, carter 71/359y
PASSING: Richardson 79-156/1492y, 8TD, 50.6%
RECEIVING: Harrison 31/577y, Mitchell 19/519y,
Mathews 13/276y
SCORING: Terry Ventoulias (K) 88pts, Hill 72pts,
Richardson 60pts

1992 12-1

10 Stanford	7 WR Tony Harrison
31 LSU	22 WR Brian Mitchell / Ryan Mathews
19 Tulsa	9 T Jason Mathews / Todd Mathison
26 Missouri	13 G John Ellisor
19 Texas Tech	17 C Chris Dausin
35 Rice	9 G Tyler Harrison / Jeff Jones
19 Baylor	13 T Dexter Wesley / James Brooks
41 SMU	7 TE Greg Schorp / James McKeehan
40 Louisville	18 QB Corey Pullig / Jeff Granger
38 Houston	30 TB Greg Hill / Rodney Thomas
37 TCU	10 FB Doug Carter / Clif Groce
34 Texas	13 DL Sam Adams
3 Notre Dame■	28 DL Eric England / Lance Teichelman
	DL Kefa Chatham
	LB Marcus Buckley
	LB Jessie Cox / Larry Jackson
	LB Jason Atkinson / Reggie Graham
	LB Steve Solari / Antonio Shorter
	DB Aaron Glenn
	DB Derrick Frazier / Ray Mickens
	DB Patrick Bates
	DB Michael Hendricks / Chris Colon

RUSHING: Hill 267/1339y, Thomas 154/856y, Groce 30/185y
PASSING: Pullig 63-126/953y, 3TD, 50.0%,
Granger 69-157/844y, 7TD, 43.9%
RECEIVING: Schorp 24/280y, Harrison 22/454y,
Mathews 21/359y
SCORING: Hill 102pts, Terry Venetoulias (K) 87pts,
Thomas 78pts

1993 10-2

24 LSU	0 WR Tony Harrison
14 Oklahoma	44 WR Brian Mitchell
73 Missouri	0 T Jason Mathews
31 Texas Tech	6 G Calvin Collins
34 Houston	10 C Chris Dausin
34 Baylor	17 G Tyler Harrison
38 Rice	10 T Dexter Wesley
37 SMU	13 TE Greg Schorp / James McKeehan
42 Louisville	7 QB Corey Pullig
59 TCU	3 TB Greg Hill / Rodney Thomas
18 Texas	9 FB Clif Groce / Detron Smith
21 Notre Dame■	24 DL Sam Adams
	DL Lance Teichelman
	DL Eric England
	LB Antonio Shorter
	LB Larry Jackson / Reggie Brown
	LB Jason Atkinson
	LB Steve Solari / Chris Colon
	DB Aaron Glenn / Donovan Greer
	DB Ray Mickens / Billy Mitchell
	DB Junior White
	DB Michael Hendricks / Steve Kenney

RUSHING: Thomas 191/996y, Hill 124/707y
PASSING: Pullig 144-243/1732y, 17TD, 59.3%
RECEIVING: Harrison 31/481y, McElroy 19/224y
SCORING: Terry Venetoulias (K) 90pts, McElroy 84pts

1994 10-0-1

18 LSU	13 WR Chris Sanders
36 Oklahoma	14 WR Brian Mitchell
41 Southern Miss	17 T Jeff Jones / Chris Ruhman
23 Texas Tech	17 G Calvin Collins
38 Houston	7 C Brandon Ward
41 Baylor	21 G John Richard / Koby Hackradt
7 Rice	0 T Hunter Goodwin
21 SMU	21 TE James McKeehan / Hayward Clay
34 Texas	10 QB Corey Pullig
26 Louisville	10 TB Rodney Thomas / Leeland McElroy
34 TCU	17 FB Clif Groce / Detron Smith
	DL Brandon Mitchell / David Maxwell
	DL Edward Jasper
	DL Larry Jackson / Steve McKinney
	LB Antonio Armstrong / Phillip Meyers
	LB Larry Walker
	LB Reggie Graham / Trent Driver
	LB Reggie Brown / Keith Mitchell
	DB Donovan Greer
	DB Ray Mickens / Andre Williams
	DB Dennis Allen / Sherrod Wyatt
	DB Michael Hendricks / Typail McMullen

RUSHING: Thomas 199/868y, McElroy 130/707y,
Wilbert Biggens (TB) 43/192y
PASSING: Pullig 161-269/2056y, 13TD, 59.9%
RECEIVING: Mathews 29/395y, Mitchell 27/334y,
Sanders 22/422y
SCORING: Thomas 96pts, Kyle Bryant (K) 82pts, McElroy 60pts

1995 9-3

33 LSU	17 WR Chris Sanders / Donte Hawkins
52 Tulsa	9 WR Albert Connell / Aaron Oliver
21 Colorado	29 T Chris Ruhman / Cameron Spikes
7 Texas Tech	14 G Calvin Collins
20 SMU	17 C Koby Hackradt
24 Baylor	9 G Steve McKinney
31 Houston	7 T Hunter Goodwin / Brandon Houston
17 Rice	10 TE Hayward Clay / Derrick Spiller
56 Middle Tenn. St.	30 QB Corey Pullig / Kevin Colon
38 TCU	6 TB Leeland McElroy / Eric Bernard
6 Texas	16 FB Detron Smith / D'Andre Hardeman
22 Michigan■	20 DL Brandon Mitchell / David Maxwell
	DL Edward Jasper
	DL Pat Williams / Marcus Heard
	LB Keith Mitchell / Warrick Holdman
	LB Dat Nguyen
	LB Larry Walker
	LB Reggie Brown
	DB Donovan Greer / Andre Williams
	DB Ray Mickens
	DB Dennis Allen / Toya Jones
	DB Typail McMullen

RUSHING: McElroy 246/1122y, Hardeman 62/313y,
Sirr Parker (TB) 71/312y
PASSING: Pullig 165-307/2105y, 14TD, 53.7%
RECEIVING: Connell 41/653y, McElroy 25/379y,
Sanders 23/281y
SCORING: McElroy 96pts, Kyle Bryant (K) 52pts

1996 6-6

37 BYU	41 WR Donte Hawkins / Leroy Hodge
22 SW Louisiana	28 WR Albert Connell / Aaron Oliver
55 North Texas	0 T Chris Ruhman
10 Colorado	24 G Semisi Heilmuli
63 Louisiana Tech	13 C Calvin Collins / Koby Hackradt
24 Iowa State	21 G Steve McKinney
20 Kansas State	23 T Cameron Spikes / Brandon Houston
10 Texas Tech	13 TE Derrick Spiller / Dan Campbell
38 Oklahoma State	19 QB Branndon Stewart
24 Baylor	7 TB Sirr Parker / Eric Bernard
33 Oklahoma	16 FB D'Andre Hardeman
15 Texas	51 DL Brandon Mitchell / Zerick Rollins
	DL Edward Jasper / Marcus Heard
	DL Pat Williams / Brad Crowley
	LB Warrick Holdman / Chris Thierry
	LB Dat Nguyen
	LB Trent Driver / Sean Coryatt
	LB Keith Mitchell / Phillip Meyers
	DB Donovan Greer
	DB Shun Horn / Jason Webster
	DB Brandon Jennings / Toya Jones
	DB Rich Coady

RUSHING: Parker 149/704y, Hardeman 109/669y, Hall 92/642y,
Bernard 116/598y
PASSING: Stewart 146-299/1904y, 9TD, 48.8%
RECEIVING: Connell 57/872y, Hawkins 32/409y, Spiller 14/194y
SCORING: Hardeman 108pts, Kyle Bryant (K) 89pts

1997 9-4

59 Sam Houston St.	6 WR Leroy Hodge / Chris Taylor
66 SW Louisiana	0 WR Aaron Oliver / Chris Cole
36 North Texas	10 T Chris Ruhman / Rex Tucker
16 Colorado	10 G Semisi Heilmuli
56 Iowa State	17 C Koby Hackradt / Toby McCarthy
17 Kansas State	36 G Steve McKinney / Brandon Houston
13 Texas Tech	16 T Cameron Spikes / Shea Holder
28 Oklahoma State	25 TE Derrick Spiller / Dan Campbell
38 Baylor	10 QB Branndon Stewart / Randy McCown
51 Oklahoma	7 TB Dante Hall / Sirr Parker
27 Texas	16 FB Marc Broyles / D'Andre Hardeman
15 Nebraska □	54 DL Zerick Rollins / Rocky Bernard
23 UCLA■	29 DL Marcus Heard / Ron Edwards
	DL Brad Crowley / Ronald Flemons
	LB Warrick Holdman / Jason Glenn
	LB Dat Nguyen / Sean Coryatt
	LB Trent Driver / Cornelius Anthony
	LB Phillip Meyers / Roylin Bradley
	DB Sedrick Curry
	DB Jason Webster / Shun Horn
	DB Brandon Jennings
	DB Rich Coady / Michael Jameson

RUSHING: Hall 134/973y, Parker 149/800y, Hardeman 91/508y
PASSING: Stewart 111-196/1429y, 10TD, 56.6%,
McCown 48-84/602y, 2TD, 57.1%
RECEIVING: Spiller 25/436y, Cole 25/333y, Hodge 23/336y
SCORING: Kyle Bryant (K) 102pts, Parker 60pts

1998 11-3

14 Florida State	23 WR Leroy Hodge
28 Louisiana Tech	7 WR Chris Cole / Chris Taylor
24 Southern Miss.	7 T Andy Vincent
28 North Texas	9 G Semisi Heilmuli
24 Kansas	21 C Seth McKinney
28 Nebraska	21 G Cameron Spikes
35 Baylor	14 T Shea Holder / Rex Tucker
17 Texas Tech	10 TE Derrick Spiller / Dan Campbell
17 Oklahoma State	16 QB Randy McCown / Branndon Stewart
29 Oklahoma	0 TB Dante Hall / Sirr Parker
17 Missouri	14 FB Ja'Mar Toombs / Marc Broyles
24 Texas	26 DL Rocky Bernard
36 Kansas State □	33 DL Ron Edwards
14 Ohio State■	24 DL Ronald Flemons
	LB Warrick Holdman / Jason Glenn
	LB Dat Nguyen
	LB Cornelius Anthony / Sean Coryatt
	LB Roylin Bradley / Chris Thierry
	DB Sedrick Curry / Jay Brooks
	DB Jason Webster
	DB Brandon Jennings
	DB Rich Coady

RUSHING: Hall 243/1024y, Toombs 86/422y, Parker 69/226y
PASSING: McCown 66-130/1025y, 6TD, 50.8%,
Stewart 68-128/992y, 7TD, 53.1%
RECEIVING: Cole 38/667y, Spiller 20/269y, Taylor 15/306y,
Hodge 15/214y
SCORING: Russell Bynum (K) 78pts, Hall 48pts

1999 8-4

37 Louisiana Tech	17 WR Chris Taylor/Leroy Hodge / Chris Cole
62 Tulsa	13 WR Bethel Johnson / Matt Bumgardner
23 Southern Miss	6 T Andy Vincent / Tango McCauley
19 Texas Tech	21 G Semisi Heimuli
45 Baylor	13 C Seth McKinney
34 Kansas	17 G Chris Valletta
6 Oklahoma	51 T Shea Holder / Michael Mahan
21 Oklahoma State	3 TE RoDerrick Broughton/Mich'el de la Torre
0 Nebraska	37 QB Randy McCown
51 Missouri	14 TB Dante Hall / Eric Bernard
20 Texas	16 FB Ja'Mar Toombs
0 Penn State■	24 DL Rocky Bernard / Terry Nichols
	DL Ron Edwards / Stephen Young
	DL Ronald Flemons
	LB Jason Glenn / Christian Rodriguez
	LB Brian Gamble
	LB Cornelius Anthony
	LB Roylin Bradley
	DB Sedrick Curry / Jay Brooks
	DB Jason Webster / Sammy Davis
	DB Brandon Jennings
	DB Michael Jameson

RUSHING: Toombs 147/583y, Hall 53/179y
PASSING: McCown 152-295/2374y, 14TD, 51.5%
RECEIVING: Taylor 33/591y, Johnson 27/514y, Hodge 25/314y,
Cole 22/363y
SCORING: Terence Kitchens (K) 75pts, Toombs 54pts

2000 7-5

10 Notre Dame	24 WR Robert Ferguson / Chris Taylor
51 Wyoming	3 WR Bethel Johnson / Greg Porter
45 Texas-El Paso	17 T Tango McCauley
33 Texas Tech	15 G Chris Valletta
19 Colorado	26 C Seth McKinney
24 Baylor	0 G Taylor Whitley
30 Iowa State	7 T Michael Mahan
26 Kansas State	10 TE RoD'r'k Broughton/Michael de la Torre
21 Oklahoma State	16 QB Mark Farris
31 Oklahoma	35 TB Richard Whitaker / Joe Weber
17 Texas	43 FB Ja'Mar Toombs
41 Mississippi St.■	43 DL Ty Warren
	DL Ron Edwards / Stephen Young
	DL Ronald Flemons
	LB Jason Glenn / Christian Rodriguez
	LB Brian Gamble
	LB Cornelius Anthony
	LB Roylin Bradley / Jarrod Penright
	DB Sean Weston / Jay Brooks
	DB Sammy Davis
	DB Michael Jameson
	DB Terrence Kiel

RUSHING: Whitaker 84/455y, Weber 101/444y,
Toombs 117/355y
PASSING: Farris 208-347/2551y, 10TD, 59.9%
RECEIVING: Ferguson 58/885y, Johnson 42/440y,
Taylor 32/390y
SCORING: Toombs 84pts

2001 8-4

38 McNeese State	24 WR Jamaar Taylor / Greg Porter
28 Wyoming	20 WR Terrence Murphy / Dwayne Goynes
21 Oklahoma State	7 T Michael Mahan / Jami Hightower
24 Notre Dame	3 G Billy Yates / John Kirk
16 Baylor	10 C Seth McKinney
21 Colorado	31 G Taylor Whitley
31 Kansas State	24 T Andre Brooks / Alan Reuber
4 Iowa State	21 TE Thomas Carriger / Michael de la Torre
0 Texas Tech	12 QB Mark Farris
10 Oklahoma	31 TB Derek Farmer / Keith Joseph
7 Texas	21 FB Joe Weber
28 TCU■	9 DL Evan Perroni
	DL Ty Warren / Marcus Jasmin
	DL Rocky Bernard / Linnis Smith
	LB Christian Rodriguez / Jesse Hunnicutt
	LB Brian Gamble
	LB Jared Morris
	LB Jarrod Penright
	DB Sean Weston / Byron Jones
	DB Sammy Davis
	DB Jay Brooks
	DB Terrence Kiel

RUSHING: Farmer 110/503y, Joseph 100/371y
Oschlor Flemming (TB) 50/216y
PASSING: Farris 203-347/2094y, 8TD, 58.5%
RECEIVING: Taylor 39/489y, Murphy 36/518y, Goynes 24/250y
SCORING: Cody Scates (K) 50pts, Weber 36pts

2002 6-6

31 La.-Lafayette	7 WR Jamaar Taylor / Terrence Murphy
14 Pittsburgh	12 WR Bethel Johnson
3 Virginia Tech	13 T Jami Hightower
31 Louisiana Tech	3 G Billy Yates
47 Texas Tech	48 C Geoff Hangartner
41 Baylor	0 G Taylor Whitley
47 Kansas	22 T Andre Brooks (G) / Alan Reuber
31 Nebraska	38 TE Greg Porter / Thomas Carriger
23 Oklahoma State	28 QB Dustin Long / Reggie McNeal
30 Oklahoma	26 TB Derek Farmer
27 Missouri	33 FB Joe Weber
20 Texas	50 DL Ty Warren / David Ross
	DL Marcus Jasmin / Johnny Jolly
	DL Linnis Smith
	LB Jesse Hunnicutt
	LB Brian Gamble
	LB Jared Morris / Randall Webb
	LB Jarrod Penright / Everett Smith
	DB Sean Weston / Byron Jones
	DB Sammy Davis
	DB Jaxson Appel
	DB Terrence Kiel / Keelan Jackson

RUSHING: Farmer 172/739y, Weber 83/274y, McNeal 37/137y
PASSING: Long 177-333/2509y, 19TD, 53.2%,
 McNeal 24-45/456y, 6TD, 53.3%,
 Mark Farris (QB) 18-45/251y, 0TD, 40.0%
RECEIVING: Porter 48/669y, Taylor 44/760y, Johnson 40/718y
SCORING: Todd Pegram (K) 68pts, Johnson 48pts,
 Farmer 42pts

2003 4-8

26 Arkansas State	11 WR Jamaar Taylor / Tim Van Zant
28 Utah	26 WR Terrence Murphy
19 Virginia Tech	35 T Alex Kotzur
26 Pittsburgh	37 G John Kirk
28 Texas Tech	59 C Geoff Hangartner / James Milkavich
73 Baylor	10 G Aldo De La Garza
12 Nebraska	48 T Alan Reuber
10 Oklahoma State	38 TE Andy Matakis / Quinlin Germany
45 Kansas	33 QB Reggie McNeal / Dustin Long
0 Oklahoma	77 TB Courtney Lewis / Derek Farmer
22 Missouri	45 FB Keith Joseph / Jason Carter
15 Texas	46 DL David Ross
	DL Johnny Jolly
	DL Marcus Jasmin / Brian Patrick
	DL Linnis Smith / Mike Montgomery
	LB Justin Warren
	LB Scott Stickane / Jared Morris
	LB Everett Smith / Ta Ta Thompson
	DB Sean Weston
	DB Byron Jones
	DB Jaxson Appel / Melvin Bullitt
	DB Ronald Jones

RUSHING: Lewis 186/1024y, McNeal 127/370y, Farmer 82/340y
PASSING: McNeal 113-221/1782y, 8TD, 51.1%,
 Long 63-104/709y, 4TD, 60.6%
RECEIVING: Murphy 44/762y, Van Zant 30/367y, Taylor 25/456y
SCORING: Todd Pegram (K) 82pts, Lewis 72pts

2004 7-5

21 Utah	41 WR DeQawn Mobley / Earvin Taylor
31 Wyoming	0 WR Terrence Murphy / Jason Carter
27 Clemson	6 T Geoff Hangartner / Alex Kotzur
42 Kansas State	30 G Aldo De La Garza
34 Iowa State	3 C Chris Yoder
36 Oklahoma State	20 G Kirk Elder
29 Colorado	26 T Jami Hightower / Corey Clark
34 Baylor	35 TE Boone Stutz / Joey Thomas
35 Oklahoma	42 QB Reggie McNeal
32 Texas Tech	25 TB Courtney Lewis
13 Texas	26 FB Keith Joseph / Chris Alexander
7 Tennessee ■	38 DL Mike Montgomery
	DL Johnny Jolly
	DL Joseph "Red" Bryant
	DL Jason Jack / Jorrie Adams
	LB Lee Foliaki / Keelan Jackson
	LB Justin Warren
	LB Archie McDaniel / Renuel Greene
	DB Byron Jones / Broderick Newton
	DB Jonte Buhl / Eric Mayes
	DB Jaxson Appel
	DB Japhus Brown / Melvin Bullitt

RUSHING: Lewis 175/742y, McNeal 151/718y, Joseph 58/207y
PASSING: McNeal 200-344/2791y, 14TD, 58.1%
RECEIVING: Murphy 56/721y, Carter 36/468y, Taylor 22/285y
SCORING: Todd Pegram (K) 73pts, Lewis 66pts, McNeal 48pts

2005 5-6

24 Clemson	25 WR Jason Carter / Howard Morrow
66 SMU	8 WR DeQawn Mobley / Chad Schroeder
44 Texas State	31 WR Pierre Brown / Earvin Taylor
16 Baylor	13 T Yemi Babalola / Jami Hightower
20 Colorado	41 G Kirk Elder
62 Oklahoma St.	23 C Cody Wallace / Chris Yoder
30 Kansas State	28 G Dominique Steamer/Aldo De La Garza
4 Iowa State	42 T Corey Clark
17 Texas Tech	56 TE Martellus Bennett / Boone Stutz
30 Oklahoma	36 QB Reggie McNeal / Stephen McGee
29 Texas	40 TB Courtney Lewis / Jorvorski Lane
	DL Jason Jack / Michael Bennett
	DL Johnny Jolly / David Ross
	DL Red Bryant / Bryce Reed
	DL Chris Harrington
	LB Lee Foliaki / Devin Gregg
	LB Justin Warren
	LB Archie McDaniel / Renuel Greene
	DB Marquis Carpenter / Ronald Jones
	DB Brock Newton / Danny Gorrer
	DB Jaxson Appel
	DB Melvin Bullitt / Japhus Brown

RUSHING: Lewis 109/723y, McNeal 96/664y, Lane 119/595y
PASSING: McNeal 141-265/1963y, 16TD, 53.2%,
 McGee 24-53/283y, 2TD, 45.3%
RECEIVING: Carter 54/827y, Schroeder 20/335y,
 Mobley 19/252y, Bennett 18/162y
SCORING: Todd Pegram (K) 86pts, Lane 54pts, Lewis 48pts

2006 9-4

35 Citadel	3 WR L'Tydrick Riley
51 La.-Lafayette	7 WR Chad Schroeder
28 Army	24 WR Earvin Taylor / Pierre Brown
45 Louisiana Tech	14 T Travis Schneider / Yemi Babalola
27 Texas Tech	31 G Kirk Elder
21 Kansas	18 C Cody Wallace
25 Missouri	19 G Grant Dickey / Chris Yoder
34 Oklahoma State	33 T Corey Clark
31 Baylor	21 TE Martellus Bennett
16 Oklahoma	17 QB Stephen McGee
27 Nebraska	28 TB Jorvorski Lane / Mike Goodson
12 Texas	7 DL Jason Jack / Michael Bennett
10 California ■	45 DL Marques Thornton / Henry Smith
	DL Red Bryant / Bryce Reed
	DL Chris Harrington / Cyril Obiozor
	LB Mark Dodge / Misi Tupe
	LB Justin Warren / Matt Featherston
	LB Devin Gregg
	DB Arkeith Brown / Marquis Carpenter
	DB Danny Gorrer
	DB Brock Newton / Japhus Brown
	DB Melvin Bullitt

RUSHING: Goodson 127/847y, Lane 166/725y,
 McGee 146/666y, Courtney Lewis (TB) 47/222y
PASSING: McGee 194-313/2295y, 12TD, 62.0%
RECEIVING: Schroeder 39/612y, Bennett 38/497y,
 Riley 23/238y
SCORING: Lane 119pts, Layne Neumann (K) 59pts,
 McGee 26pts

2007 7-6

38 Montana State	7 WR Kerry Franks
47 Fresno State	45 WR Earvin Taylor / Pierre Brown
54 La.-Monroe	14 T Travis Schneider
17 Miami	34 G Kirk Elder
34 Baylor	10 C Cody Wallace
24 Oklahoma State	23 G Chris Yoder / Michael Shumard
7 Texas Tech	35 T Corey Clark
36 Nebraska	14 TE Martellus Bennett / Joey Thomas
11 Kansas	19 QB Stephen McGee
14 Oklahoma	42 TB Jorvorskie Lane / Mike Goodson
26 Missouri	40 FB Chris Alexander
38 Texas	30 DL Chris Harrington / Von Miller
17 Penn State ■	24 DL Henry Smith / Kellen Heard
	DL Red Bryant / Lucas Patterson
	DL Cyril Obiozor / Michael Bennett
	LB Mark Dodge / Matt Featherston
	LB Misi Tupe / Anthony Lewis
	LB Jordan Pugh / Kenny Brown
	DB Arkeith Brown / Jordan Peterson
	DB Marquis Carpenter / Danny Gorrer
	DB Devin Gregg / Stephen Hodge
	DB Alton Dixon

RUSHING: McGee 181/899y, Lane 169/780y, Goodson 153/711y
PASSING: McGee 211-364/2311y, 12TD, 58.0%
RECEIVING: Bennett 49/587y, Goodson 36/361y,
 Franks 27/488y, Taylor 26/266y
SCORING: Lane 104pts, Matt Szymanski (K) 84pts,
 Goodson 48pts

2008 4-8

14 Arkansas St.	18 WR Jeff Fuller / Ryan Tannehill
28 New Mexico	22 WR Terrence McCoy / Howard Morrow
23 Miami	41 T Michael Shumard
21 Army	17 G Evan Elke
28 Oklahoma State	56 C Kevin Matthews
30 Kansas State	44 G Lee Grimes (T) / Vincent Williams
25 Texas Tech	43 T Travis Schneider / Robbie Frost
49 Iowa State	35 TE Jamie McCoy
24 Colorado	17 QB Jerrod Johnson / Stephen McGee
28 Oklahoma	66 TB Mike Goodson / Cyrus Gray
21 Baylor	41 FB Jorvorski Lane
9 Texas	49 DL Cyril Obiozor
	DL Tony Jerod-Eddie / Kellen Heard
	DL Lucas Patterson / Eddie Brown
	DL Michael Bennett
	LB Garrick Williams / Johnathan Haynes
	LB Matt Featherston
	LB Von Miller / Johnathan Batson (DB)
	DB Arkeith Brown / Danny Gorrer
	DB Jordan Pugh / Terrence Frederick
	DB Trent Hunter / Jordan Peterson
	DB Alton Dixon (LB) / Devin Gregg

RUSHING: Goodson 94/406y, Gray 75/363y, Johnson 94/114y
PASSING: Johnson 194-326/2435y, 21TD, 59.5%,
 McGee 56-85/586y, 2TD, 65.9%
RECEIVING: Tannehill 55/844y, Fuller 50/630y,
 J. McCoy 43/500y, Goodson 37/386y
SCORING: Fuller 56pts, Goodson 48pts,
 Randy Bullock (K) 38pts

2009 6-7

41 New Mexico	6 WR Jeff Fuller / Brandal Jackson
38 Utah State	30 WR Howard Morrow / Ryan Swope
56 Ala.-Birmingham	19 WR Uzoma Nwachukwu / Ryan Tannehill
19 Arkansas	47 T Michael Shumard (G) / Stephan Berrera
31 Oklahoma State	36 G Evan Elke
14 Kansas State	62 C Kevin Matthews
52 Texas Tech	30 G Brandon Lewis / Matt Allen
35 Iowa State	10 T Lee Grimes / Danny Baker
34 Colorado	35 TE Jamie McCoy
10 Oklahoma	65 QB Jerrod Johnson
38 Baylor	3 RB Cyrus Gray / Christine Michael
39 Texas	49 DL Matt Moss
20 Georgia ■	44 DL Lucas Patterson
	DL Eddie Brown / Tony Jerod-Eddie
	DL Von Miller / Matt Featherston
	LB Garrick Williams / Sean Porter
	LB Kyle Mangan
	LB Michael Hodges / Jonathan Stewart
	DB Terrence Frederick
	DB Dustin Harris / Justin McQueen
	DB Jordan Pugh / Steven Campbell
	DB Trent Hunter

RUSHING: Michael 166/844y, Gray 159/757y, Johnson 145/506y
PASSING: Johnson 296-497/3579y, 30TD, 59.6%
RECEIVING: Tannehill 46/609y, Nwachukwu 40/708y,
 Morrow 43/449y, Fuller 41/568y
SCORING: Randy Bullock (K) 87pts, Michael 60pts,
 Gray & Johnson 48pts

2010 9-4

48 Stephen F. Austin	7 WR Jeff Fuller / Brandal Jackson
48 Louisiana Tech	16 WR Uzoma Nwachukwu / Terrence McCoy
27 FIU	20 WR Ryan Swope / Kenric McNeal
35 Oklahoma State	38 T Luke Joeckel
17 Arkansas	24 G Brian Thomas (T)
9 Missouri	30 C Matt Allen
45 Kansas	10 G Patrick Lewis
45 Texas Tech	27 T Jake Matthews / Evan Eike
33 Oklahoma	19 TE Nehemiah Hicks / Hutson Prioleau
42 Baylor	30 QB Jerrod Johnson / Ryan Tannehill
9 Nebraska	6 TB Cyrus Gray / Christine Michael
24 Texas	17 DL Lucas Patterson
24 LSU ■	41 DL Johnathan Mathis / Eddie Brown
	DL Tony Jerod-Eddie / Spencer Nealy
	DL Von Miller / Damontre Moore
	LB Michael Hodges
	LB Garrick Williams
	LB Sean Porter
	DB Terrence Frederick
	DB Coryell Judie / Dustin Harris
	DB Trent Hunter
	DB Steven Terrell / Steven Campbell

RUSHING: Gray 200/1133y, Michael 126/631y, Johnson 79/146y
PASSING: Johnson 158-279/1947y, 14TD, 56.6%,
 Tannehill 152-234/163y, 13TD, 65%
RECEIVING: Fuller 72/1066y, Swope 72/825y, Nwachukwu 36/407y
SCORING: Randy Bullock (K) 98pts, Gray 78pts, Fuller 72pts

TEXAS CHRISTIAN

Texas Christian University (Founded 1873)
Fort Worth, Texas
Nickname: Horned Frogs
Colors: Purple and White
Stadium: Amon G. Carter Stadium (1930) 44,008
Conference Affiliations: Southwest Athletic Conference (1923-95),
Western Athletic Conference (1996-00), Conference USA
(2001-04), Mountain West Conference (2005-present)

CAREER RUSHING YARDS	Attempts	Yards
LaDainian Tomlinson (1997-00)	907	5263
Tony Jeffrey (1984-87)	665	3749
Andre Davis (1992-95)	638	3182
Lonta Hobbs (2002-06)	596	3000
Kenneth Davis (1982-85)	493	2994
Basil Mitchell (1994-98)	547	2783
Robert Merrill (2003-05)	567	2771
Curtis Modkins (1989-92)	672	2763
Jim Swink (1954-56)	413	2618
Aaron Brown (2005-08)	487	2596

CAREER PASSING YARDS	Comp.-Att.	Yards
Andy Dalton (2007-10)	812-1317	10,314
Max Knake (1992-95)	622-1115	7370
Steve Stamp (1978-81)	350-674	5123
Casey Printers (1999-01)	324-578	4621
Jeff Ballard (2003-06)	330-540	4204
Leon Clay (1989-92)	326-656	3963
Steve Judy (1969-71)	317-679	3886
Brandon Hassell (2001-04)	259-457	3762
David Rascoe (1985-88)	306-655	3696
Sammy Baugh (1934-36)	270-587	3384

CAREER RECEIVING YARDS	Catches	Yards
Mike Renfro (1974-77)	162	2739
Jimmy Young (2007-10)	147	2316
Stephen Shipley (1989-92)	152	2251
Stanley Washington (1979-82)	125	2209
James Maness (1981-84)	97	2171
Kelly Blackwell (1988-91)	181	2155
Cory Rodgers (2003-05)	150	2111
Reggie Harrell (2001-04)	103	1812
John Washington (1993-96)	135	1685
Richard Woodley (199-93)	134	1620

SEASON RUSHING YARDS	Attempts	Yards
LaDainian Tomlinson (2000)	369	2158
LaDainian Tomlinson (1999)	268	1850
Kenneth Davis (1984)	211	1611
Andre Davis (1994)	260	1494
Tony Jeffrey (1987)	202	1353

SEASON PASSING YARDS	Comp.-Att.	Yards
Andy Dalton (2010)	209-316	2857
Andy Dalton (2009)	199-323	2756
Max Knake (1994)	184-316	2624
Andy Dalton (2007)	222-371	2459
Jeff Ballard (2006)	190-307	2394

SEASON RECEIVING YARDS	Catches	Yards
Reggie Harrell (2003)	58	1012
Jimmy Young (2008)	59	988
James Maness (1984)	40	871
Stanley Washington (1981)	49	854
Cory Rodgers (2004)	61	836

GAME RUSHING YARDS	Attempts	Yards
LaDainian Tomlinson (1999 vs. UTEP)	43	406
Tony Jeffrey (1986 vs. Tulane)	16	343
Andre Davis (1994 vs. New Mexico)	31	325

GAME PASSING YARDS	Comp.-Att.	Yards
Matt Vogler (1990 vs. Houston)	44-79	690
Matt Vogler (1990 vs. Texas Tech)	36-72	419
Steve Stamp (1980 vs. Baylor)	28-53	408

GAME RECEIVING YARDS	Catches	Yards
Jimmy Young (2008 vs. Wyoming)	5	226
Jimmy Oliver (1994 vs. Texas Tech)	7	206
Vernon Wells (1976 vs. Tennessee)	10	204

GREATEST COACH:

Gary Patterson knew losing ways. Having played for Kansas State in the early 1980s, Patterson understood that the culture of losing the Wildcats overcame a few years later was similar to the work required in Fort Worth in recent years with Texas Christian. He fully understood that his own hard work, and that of a crack coaching staff, was the best way to prevent a relapse to the dark days of the past.

Inheriting a rebuilt program from Dennis Franchione, Patterson took the Horned Frogs one step further. In his first six years as the head coach, TCU finished in the Top 25 an astonishing five times. For a program that suffered through a 1-10 season as recently as 1997, the work that first Franchione, and now Patterson, is doing is nothing short of miraculous. Patterson's 73 wins already place him third, just one behind Abe Martin, on the all-time school chart and he will soon challenge the great Dutch Meyer's mark of 109 if he continues to churn out double-digit win totals. His crowning glory was the 2005 season, the team's first in the Mountain West Conference. Picked to finish in the middle of the pack, Patterson's troops not only swept their way to the title, but knocked off Oklahoma in week one. They closed out the season with a victory over another Big 12 school, Iowa State, in the Houston Bowl to finish the season 11-1 and ranked 11th in the country. It was the Horned Frogs' second 11-win season in three years.

Patterson's teams won with defense—his teams twice led the nation in that category--and a balanced, if unspectacular offense.

TEXAS CHRISTIAN'S 55 GREATEST SINCE 1953

OFFENSE

WIDE RECEIVER: James Maness, Mike Renfro, Stephen Shipley, Stanley Washington
TIGHT END: Kelly Blackwell, Bryan Engram
TACKLE: Anthony Alabi, Norm Evans, Barret Robbins, Herb Taylor
GUARD: Steve Garmon, Guy Morriss, Morgan Williams
CENTER: W.C. Nix III, Ryan Tucker, Dale Walker
QUARTERBACK: Jeff Ballard, Andy Dalton, Sonny Gibbs
RUNNING BACK: Kenneth Davis, Tony Jeffrey, Jim Swink, LaDainian Tomlinson
FULLBACK: Tommy Crutcher, Jack Spikes

DEFENSE

END: Tommy Blake, Roosevelt Collins, Jerry Hughes, Chase Ortiz, Aaron Schobel
TACKLE: Mitchell Benson, Don Floyd, Norman Hamilton, Bob Lilly, Shawn Worthen
LINEBACKER: LaMarcus McDonald, Darrell Patterson, Jason Phillips, Joe Phipps, Dede Terveen
CORNERBACK: Lyle Blackwood, Ron Fraley, Jason Goss, Cubby Hudler, Tony Rand
SAFETY: Marvin Godbolt, Frank Horak, Falanda Newton

SPECIAL TEAMS

RETURN SPECIALISTS: LaTarence Dunbar, Cory Rodgers
PLACE KICKER: Nick Browne, Michael Reeder
PUNTER: Chris Becker

TWO-WAY PLAYERS

CENTER-LINEBACKER: Ken Henson, Hugh Pitts

PERFORMANCE FORMULA:
TEXAS CHRISTIAN'S 10 BEST SEASONS

2010	1.7390	2 of 71
2009	1.6917	5 of 71
2008	1.5729	8 of 71
2005	1.5559	7 of 70
1955	1.5459	7 of 69
2000	1.4781	11 of 70
1958	1.4482	12 of 70
2006	1.4353	17 of 72
1959	1.4195	10 of 70
2002	1.4128	15 of 70

TEXAS CHRISTIAN HORNED FROGS

Year	W-L-T	AP Poll	Conference Standing	Toughest Regular Season Opponents	Coach (Record at School)	Bowl Games		
1953	3-7		6t	Michigan State 8-1, Rice 8-2, Texas 7-3	Abe Martin			
1954	4-6		6	Oklahoma 10-0, Arkansas 8-2, Baylor 7-3	Abe Martin			
1955	9-2	6	1	Texas A&M 7-2-1, Miami 6-3, Texas Tech 7-2-1	Abe Martin	Cotton	13 Mississippi	14
1956	8-3		2	Texas A&M 9-0-1, Miami 8-1-1, Baylor 8-2	Abe Martin	Cotton	28 Syracuse	27
1957	5-4-1		5t	Ohio State 8-1, Rice 7-3, Texas A&M 8-2	Abe Martin			
1958	8-2-1	10	1	Iowa 7-1-1, SMU 6-4, Rice 5-5	Abe Martin	Cotton	0 Air Force	0
1959	8-3	7	1t	LSU 9-1, Texas 9-1, Arkansas 8-2	Abe Martin	Bluebonnet	7 Clemson	23
1960	4-4-2		5	Arkansas 8-2, Kansas 7-2-1, Rice 7-3	Abe Martin			
1961	3-5-2		5	Ohio State 8-0-1, Texas 9-1, Arkansas 8-2	Abe Martin			
1962	6-4		3	Texas 9-0-1, Arkansas 9-1, LSU 8-1-1	Abe Martin			
1963	4-5-1		5	Texas 10-0, Baylor 7-3, LSU 7-3	Abe Martin			
1964	4-6		6	Arkansas 10-0, Texas 9-1, Florida State 8-1-1	Abe Martin			
1965	6-5		2t	Arkansas 10-0, Nebraska 10-0, Texas Tech 8-2	Abe Martin	Sun	12 Texas Western	13
1966	2-8		6t	Nebraska 9-1, SMU 8-2, Arkansas 8-2	Abe Martin (74-67-7)			
1967	4-6		3t	Texas A&M 6-4, LSU 6-3-1, Texas Tech 6-4	Fred Taylor			
1968	3-7		6t	Texas 8-1-1, Arkansas 9-1, SMU 7-3	Fred Taylor			
1969	4-6		3t	Texas 10-0, Arkansas 9-1, Ohio State 8-0	Fred Taylor			
1970	4-6-1		4t	Texas 10-0, Arkansas 9-2, Texas Tech 8-4	Fred Taylor (15-25-1)			
1971	6-4-1		3	Penn State 10-1, Arkansas 8-2-1, Texas 8-2	Jim Pittman (3-3-1), Billy Tohill [3-1]			
1972	5-6		7t	Texas 9-1, Notre Dame 8-2, Texas Tech 8-3	Billy Tohill			
1973	3-8		8	Ohio State 9-0-1, Texas 8-2, Texas Tech 9-1	Billy Tohill (11-15)			
1974	1-10		8	Alabama 11-0, Texas 8-3, Baylor 8-3	Jim Shofner			
1975	1-10		7t	Texas A&M 10-1, Alabama 10-1, Arizona State 11-0	Jim Shofner			
1976	0-11		9	Houston 9-2, Texas Tech 10-1, Texas A&M 9-2	Jim Shofner (2-31)			
1977	2-9		8	Texas 11-0, Arkansas 10-1, Texas A&M 8-3	F.A. Dry			
1978	2-9		9	Penn State 11-0, Houston 9-2, Texas 8-3	F.A. Dry			
1979	2-8-1		8	Arkansas 10-1, Houston 10-1, Texas 9-2	F.A. Dry			
1980	1-10		9	Georgia 11-0, Baylor 10-1, Houston 6-5	F.A. Dry			
1981	2-7-2		8	SMU 10-1, Texas 9-1-1, Houston 7-3-1	F.A. Dry			
1982	3-8		8	SMU 10-0-1, Texas 9-2, Arkansas 8-2-1	F.A. Dry (12-51-3)			
1983	1-8-2		8	Texas 11-0, SMU 10-1, Baylor 7-3-1	Jim Wacker			
1984	8-4		3t	SMU 9-2, Houston 7-4, Texas 7-3-1	Jim Wacker	Bluebonnet	14 West Virginia	31
1985	3-8		9	Texas A&M 9-2, Arkansas 9-2, Baylor 8-3	Jim Wacker			
1986	3-8		8	Texas A&M 9-2, Arkansas 9-2, Baylor 8-3	Jim Wacker			
1987	5-6		5t	Texas A&M 9-2, BYU 9-3, Texas 6-5	Jim Wacker			
1988	4-7		4t	Arkansas 10-1, Georgia 8-3, Houston 9-2	Jim Wacker			
1989	4-7		6t	Arkansas 10-1, Houston 9-2, Texas A&M 8-3	Jim Wacker			
1990	5-6		4t	Texas 10-1, Houston 10-1, Texas A&M 8-3-1	Jim Wacker			
1991	7-4		5t	Texas A&M 10-1, Baylor 8-3, Arkansas 6-5	Jim Wacker (40-58-2)			
1992	2-8-1		8	Miami 11-0, Texas A&M 12-0, Baylor 7-4	Pat Sullivan			
1993	4-7		6	Texas A&M 10-1, Oklahoma 8-3, Texas Tech 6-5	Pat Sullivan			
1994	7-5		1t	Texas A&M 10-0-1, Texas 7-4, Baylor 7-4	Pat Sullivan	Independence	10 Virginia	20
1995	6-5		5	Texas 10-1-1, Texas A&M 8-3, Texas Tech 8-3	Pat Sullivan			
1996	4-7		5t	BYU 12-1, Utah 8-3, Rice 7-4	Pat Sullivan			
1997	1-10		7t	North Carolina 10-1, New Mexico 9-3, BYU 6-5	Pat Sullivan (24-42-1)			
1998	7-5		4	Air Force 11-1, Colorado State 8-4, Wyoming 8-3	Dennis Franchione	Sun	28 Southern California	19
1999	8-4		1t	Fresno State 8-4, Hawaii 8-4, Rice 5-6	Dennis Franchione	Mobile	28 East Carolina	14
2000	10-2	21	1t	UTEP 8-3, Fresno State 7-4, San Jose State 7-5	Dennis Franchione (25-11)	Mobile	21 Southern Miss	28
2001	6-6		5t	Nebraska 11-1, Louisville 10-2, East Carolina 6-5	Gary Patterson	Galleryfurniture	9 Texas A&M	28
2002	10-2	23	1t	Cincinnati 7-6, Louisville 7-5, Southern Miss 7-5	Gary Patterson	Liberty	17 Colorado State	3
2003	11-2	25	2	Southern Miss 9-3, Navy 8-4, Louisville 9-3	Gary Patterson	Fort Worth	31 Boise State	34
2004	5-6		6t	Louisville 10-1, Texas Tech 7-4, Northwestern 6-6	Gary Patterson			
2005	11-1	11	1	Oklahoma 7-4, BYU 6-5, Colorado State 6-5	Gary Patterson	Houston	27 Iowa State	24
2006	11-2	22	2	BYU 10-2, Texas Tech 7-5, Utah 7-5	Gary Patterson	Poinsettia	37 Northern Illinois	7
2007	8-5		5	Texas 9-3, Air Force 9-3, BYU 10-2	Gary Patterson	Texas	20 Houston	13
2008	11-2	7	2	Oklahoma 12-1, BYU 9-3, Utah 12-0	Gary Patterson	Poinsettia	17 Boise State	16
2009	12-1	6	1	Clemson 9-5, Air Force 7-5, BYU 10-2, Utah 9-3	Gary Patterson	Fiesta	10 Boise State	17
2010	13-0	2	1	Baylor 7-5, Air Force 8-4, Utah 10-2, San Diego State 8-4	Gary Patterson (98-27)	Rose	21 Wisconsin	19

TOTAL: 304-327-15 .4822 (49 of 70)   **Bowl Games since 1953:**   9-9-1 .5000 (Tied 39 of 70)

GREATEST TEAM SINCE 1953: The 2010 season went perhaps as well as could have been expected for the Horned Frogs. Did they get to play in the BCS Title Game? No, but a spot in the Rose Bowl was a wonderful consolation prize for a squad that sliced through its regular season schedule with nary a hiccup. And by beating Wisconsin in Pasadena, TCU not only finished 13-0 and earned a final no. 2 ranking but proved that they belong among the nation's finest programs. With quarterback Andy Dalton rewriting the school's record book and a defense that continued a decade-long level of dominance, the 2010 TCU Horned Frogs earned our top spot in this category over an excellent group from 1955 that lost two games against tougher competition.

1953 3-7

13 Kansas	0	E Bryan Engram / Guy Thompson
6 Arkansas	13	T R. C. Harris
19 Michigan State	26	G Morgan Williams
7 Texas A&M	20	C Hugh Pitts
21 Penn State	27	G Claude Roach
7 Baylor	25	T Ray Hill
21 Washington St.	7	E Johnny Crouch / Don Sanford
3 Texas	13	QB Ray McKown / Mal Fowler
6 Rice	19	HB Marshall Robinson/ Ronnie Clinkscale
13 SMU	0	HB Ron Fraley / David Finney
		FB Sammy Morrow / Danny Hallmark

RUSHING: Morrow 55/220y
PASSING: McKown 36-91/564y, 2TD, 39.6%
RECEIVING: Fraley 15/209y
SCORING:

1954 4-6

27 Kansas	6	E Johnny Crouch / Bryan Engram
16 Oklahoma	21	T Norman Hamilton / Dick Laswell
13 Arkansas	20	G Bill Alexander / Vern Hallbeck
20 Southern Cal	7	C Hugh Pitts / Malcolm Wallace (G)
21 Texas A&M	7	G Vern Uecker / Bill Yung
20 Penn State	7	T Ray Hill / Don Cooper
7 Baylor	12	E Tom Vaught / Jim Cooper
34 Texas	35	QB Ronnie Clinkscale / Chuck Curtis
0 Rice	6	HB Jim Swink
6 SMU	21	HB Ray Taylor / Ken Wineburg
		FB Buddy Dike / Henry Crowsey

RUSHING: Swink 99/670y, Dike 91/369y, Taylor 56/271y
PASSING: Clinkscale 21-57/341y, 36.8%, 2 TD
  Curtis 19-53/339y, 35.8%, 2 TD
RECEIVING: Taylor 10/219y, Crouch 10/185y, Swink 9/104y
SCORING: Swink 37pts, Clink 30pts, Curtis & Taylor 18pts

1955 9-2

47 Kansas	14	E Bryan Engram / John Nikkel
32 Texas Tech	0	T Norm Hamilton
26 Arkansas	0	G Joe Williams / Bill Alexander
21 Alabama	0	C Hugh Pitts
16 Texas A&M	19	G Vern Uecker / Bill Yung
21 Miami	19	T Don Cooper / John Groom
28 Baylor	6	E O'Day Williams / Jim Cooper
47 Texas	20	QB Chuck Curtis
35 Rice	0	HB Jim Swink / Del Shofner
20 SMU	13	HB Ray Taylor / Ken Wineburg
13 Mississippi■	14	FB Vernon Hallbeck / Harold Pollard

RUSHING: Swink 157/1283y, Taylor 72/368y, Hallbeck 94/367y
PASSING: Curtis 36-68/608y, 8TD, 52.9
RECEIVING: Taylor 13/189y, Williams 9/162y, Engram 8/115y
SCORING: Swink 125pts, Pollard (FB-K) 34pts, 4 tied w/ 24pts

1956 8-3

32 Kansas	0	E John Nikkel / Chico Mendoza
41 Arkansas	6	T Norm Hamilton
23 Alabama	6	G Joe Williams / John Mitchell
6 Texas A&M	7	C Jim Ozee / Dale Walker
0 Miami	14	G Vern Uecker / Jay McCullough
7 Baylor	6	T Don Cooper / John Groom
7 Texas Tech	21	E O'Day Williams / Harold Pollard
46 Texas	0	QB Chuck Curtis / Hunter Enis
20 Rice	17	HB Jim Swink / Billy Vacek
21 SMU	6	HB Ken Wineburg / Jim Shofner
28 Syracuse■	27	FB Buddy Dike / Vern Hallbeck

RUSHING: Swink 157/665y, Dike 118/658y, Wineburg 83/598y
PASSING: Curtis 53-119/867y, 5TD, 44.5%
RECEIVING: Swink 19/390y, Williams 12/189y, Wineburg 11/138y
SCORING: Wineburg 42pts, Swink 39pts, Dike 36pts

1957 5-4-1

13 Kansas	13	E Chico Mendoza / Delzon Elenburg
18 Ohio State	14	T Ken Miller / Don Floyd
7 Arkansas	20	G Jerry Holland / Jerry Salley
28 Alabama	0	C Jim Ozee / Dale Walker
0 Texas A&M	7	G John Mitchell / Ramon Armstrong
26 Marquette	7	T Joe Robb / John Groom (G)
19 Baylor	6	E John Nikkel
2 Texas	14	QB Dick Finney / Hunter Enis
0 Rice	20	HB Jim Shofner / Jack Reding
21 SMU	0	HB Marvin Lasater / Marshall Harris
		FB Buddy Dike / Jack Spikes (HB)

RUSHING: Shofner 131/682y, Lasater 110/488y, Dike 133/464y
PASSING: Finney 14-37/230y, 0TD, 37.8%
RECEIVING: Lasater 6/124y, Nikkel 4/71y, Elenburg 4/44y
SCORING: Shofner 40pts, Finney 25pts, Dike 24pts

1958 8-2-1

42 Kansas	0	E Jimmy Gilmore / Milt Ham
0 Iowa	17	T Don Floyd / William Roach
12 Arkansas	7	G Sherrill Headrick
26 Texas Tech	0	C Dale Walker / Arvie Martin
24 Texas A&M	8	G Ramon Armstrong / Roy Lee Rambo
22 Baylor	0	T Joe Robb / Bob Lilly
36 Marquette	8	E B. Meyer/ PaulPeebles/ JustinRowland
22 Texas	8	QB Hunter Enis / Larry Dawson
21 Rice	10	HB Marvin Lasater / Billy Gault
13 SMU	20	HB Marshall Harris / Carlos Vacek
0 Air Force■	0	FB Jack Spikes / Merlin Priddy

RUSHING: Spikes 124/580y, Priddy 44/303y, Lasater 77/264y
PASSING: Enis 51-103/585y, 9TD, 49.5%
RECEIVING: Harris 19/265y, Gilmore 14/204y, Meyer 9/113y
SCORING: Harris 26pts, Gilmore 24pts, Spikes 20pts

1959 8-3

14 Kansas	7	E Milt Ham / Paul Peebles
0 LSU	10	T Don Floyd
0 Arkansas	3	G Roy Lee Rambo / Sherrill Headrick
14 Texas Tech	14	C Arvie Martin
39 Texas A&M	6	G Ramon Armstrong
13 Pittsburgh	3	T Bob Lilly
14 Baylor	0	E Jimmy Gilmore / Bubba Meyer
14 Texas	9	QB Jack Sledge / Don George
35 Rice	6	HB Marvin Lasater / Harry Moreland
19 SMU	0	HB Marshall Harris / Larry Terrell
7 Clemson■	23	FB Jack Spikes

RUSHING: Spikes 140/660y, Lasater 76/350y, Harris 75/337y
PASSING: George 24-65/315y, 2TD, 38.7%
RECEIVING: Meyer 8/88y, Moreland 7/92y, Ham 6/78y
SCORING: Moreland & Lasater 36pts, Spikes 21pts

1960 4-4-2

7 Kansas	21	E Milt Ham / Aubrey Linne
7 Southern Cal	6	T Bobby Plummer / Ted Crenwelge
0 Arkansas	3	G Dick Holden / Buddy Lucas/B. Phillips
21 Texas Tech	7	C Arvie Martin / Lanny Verner
14 Texas A&M	14	G Ray Pinion / Dugan Miligan
7 Pittsburgh	7	T Bob Lilly
14 Baylor	6	E Buddy Iles
2 Texas	3	QB Don George / Sonny Gibbs
0 Rice	23	HB Larry Dawson /H. Moreland/Bud Priddy
13 SMU	0	HB Larry Terrell / Roy Dent
		FB Max Pierce / R.E. Dodson

RUSHING: Dodson 70/276y, Gibbs 35/233y, Dawson 51/224y
PASSING: Gibbs 47-111/473y, 3TD, 42.3%
RECEIVING: Iles 24/237y, Ham 14/198y, Moreland 12/103y
SCORING: Gibbs 24pts, Moreland 18pts, Dodson (FB-K) 17pts

1961 3-5-2

17 Kansas	16	E Dale Glasscock
7 Ohio State	7	T Don Jackson
3 Arkansas	28	G Bill Phillips
0 Texas Tech	10	C Bobby Biehunko / Don Smith
15 Texas A&M	14	G Ray Pinion
14 Baylor	28	T Bobby Plummer
7 UCLA	28	E Buddy Iles
6 Texas	0	QB Sonny Gibbs
16 Rice	35	HB Donny Smith
28 SMU	28	HB Marvin Chipman
		FB Tommy Crutcher

RUSHING: Crutcher 148/577y, Gibbs 74/199y, Smith 47/171y
PASSING: Gibbs 71-137/999y, 6TD, 51.8%
RECEIVING: Iles 31/479y, Crutcher 10/93y, Glasscock 9/157y
SCORING: Gibbs & Crutcher 18pts, 3 tied w/ 12pts

1962 6-4

6 Kansas	3	E Ben Nix / Lynn Morrison
20 Miami	21	T Joe Owens / Rickey Williams
14 Arkansas	42	G Robert Mangum
35 Texas Tech	13	C Ken Henson
20 Texas A&M	14	G Bernard Bartek
28 Baylor	26	T Rudy Mathews
0 LSU	5	E Tom Magoffin
0 Texas	14	QB Sonny Gibbs
30 Rice	7	HB Donny Smith / Larry Bulaich
14 SMU	9	HB Jim Fauver / Jerry Terrell
		FB Tommy Crutcher

RUSHING: Crutcher 106/533y, Fauver 69/231y, Gibbs 76/179y
PASSING: Gibbs 89-169/1013y, 9TD, 52.7%
RECEIVING: Magoffin 32/430y, Nix 20/272y, Fauver 11/69y
SCORING: Gibbs 42pts, Jim McAteer (K) 21pts, Fauver 20pts

1963 4-5-1

10 Kansas	6	E Lynn Morrison / Larry Perry
13 Florida State	0	T Rick Williams / Norm Evans / Joe Owens
3 Arkansas	18	G Robert Mangum
35 Texas Tech	3	C Ken Henson
14 Texas A&M	14	G Steve Garmon
13 Baylor	32	T Jim Fox
14 LSU	28	T Tom Magoffin
0 Texas	17	QB Gray Mills
22 SMU	15	HB Marv Chipman / Donny Smith
7 Rice	32	HB Jim Fauver
		FB Tommy Crutcher

RUSHING: Crutcher 108/473y, Fauver 85/338y, Chipman 32/234y
PASSING: Mills 45-96/523y, 2TD, 48.4%
RECEIVING: Fauver 11/167y, Magofin 8/115y, Perry 8/85y
SCORING: Jim McAteer (K) 23pts, Chipman 20pts, Fauver 18pts

1964 4-6

3 Kansas	7	E Joe Ball
0 Florida State	10	T Norm Evans
6 Arkansas	29	G Russell Stout
10 Texas Tech	25	C Ken Henson
14 Texas A&M	9	G Steve Garmon
14 Clemson	10	T Bobby Smith
17 Baylor	14	E Sonny Campbell
13 Texas	28	QB Randy Howard / Kent Nix
0 Rice	31	WB Bobby Sanders / David Smith
17 SMU	6	HB Jim Fauver
		FB Larry Bulaich / Earnest Bayer
		DL Darrell Mott / Larry Perry
		DL Ronnie Nixon
		DL Steve Garmon
		DL Gary Cooper / Porter Williams
		DL Norm Evans
		DL Joe Ball
		LB Ken Henson
		LB Harvey Reeves
		DB John Richards
		DB Dan Jones
		DB Frank Horak

RUSHING: Fauver 154/789y, Bulaich 115/133y, Bayer 34/133y
PASSING: Nix 51-117/624y, 4TD, 43.6
RECEIVING: Campbell 35/502y, Smith 8/95y, Ball 7/70y
SCORING: Bruce Alford (K) 22pts, Howard 18pts, Sanders 12pts

1965 6-5

14 Nebraska	34	E Joe Ball
7 Florida State	3	T Adon Sitra
9 Arkansas	28	G Butch Gilliam
24 Texas Tech	28	C Jim Nayfa
17 Texas A&M	9	G Russell Stout
0 Clemson	3	T Bobby Barker
10 Baylor	7	E Sonny Campbell
25 Texas	10	QB Kent Nix / P.D. Shabay
42 Rice	14	WB David Smith
10 SMU	0	HB Steve Landon
12 Texas Western■	13	FB Kenny Post
		DL Doyle Johnson
		DL Danny Cross
		DL Gary Cooper
		DL Porter Williams
		DL Ronny Nixon
		DL Larry Perry
		LB Paul Smith / Bobby Nelson
		LB E.A. Gresham
		DB Dan Jones / Cubby Hudler
		DB John Richards
		DB Frank Horak

RUSHING: Post 150/555y, Landon 121/492y, Shabay 50/72y
PASSING: Nix 50-106/634y, 6TD, 47.2%
RECEIVING: Campbell 32/437y, Ball 22/226y, Landon 11/76y
SCORING: Bruce Alford (K) 41pts, Landon 36pts,
  Campbell & Smith 18pts

1966 2-8

10 Nebraska	14 E Joe Sherrell / Gordon Nees
7 Ohio State	14 T Charles Young / Fred Barber
0 Arkansas	21 G Rick Sheddy / Gene Mayes
6 Texas Tech	3 C Fred Wright / Bob Nelson / Jim Nayfa
7 Texas A&M	35 G Butch Gilliam
6 Auburn	7 T Adon Sitra
6 Baylor	0 E Sonny Campbell
3 Texas	13 QB P.D. Shabay / Rick Bridges
10 Rice	21 HB Steve Landon / Ross Montgomery
0 SMU	21 HB David Smith / Allen Brown
	FB Kenny Post / Norm Bulaich
	DL Doyle Johnson
	DL Danny Cross
	DL Ronnie Nixon
	DL Porter Williams
	DL Mike Bratcher
	DL Ron McMillon / Rodney Marek
	LB E.A. Gresham
	DB John Richards
	DB Cubby Hudler
	DB Frank Horak
	DB Paul Smith

RUSHING: Montgomery 109/467y, Post 87/257y, Bulaich 69/246y
PASSING: Bridges 42-86/520y, 1TD, 48.9%
Shabay 43-99/384y, 1TD, 43.4%
RECEIVING: Campbell33/442y, Brown23/259y,
Montgomery16/189y
SCORING: Bruce Alford (K) 25pts, 5 tied w/ 6pts

1967 4-6

9 Iowa	24 E Bill Ferguson
9 Georgia Tech	24 T Charles Young
0 Arkansas	26 G Dale Johnston
0 Texas A&M	20 C E.A. Gresham
0 Nebraska	29 G James Ray
29 Baylor	7 T Fred Barber / Paul Smith
16 Texas Tech	0 E Steve Jamail
24 Texas	17 QB P.D. Shabay / Dan Carter
14 Rice	10 WB Marty Whelan / Steve Landon
14 SMU	28 HB Ross Montgomery
	FB Kenny Post / Sammy Rabb
	DL Pat Walker
	DL Danny Cross
	DL Larry Adams
	DL Donnie Terveen / Louis Pyle
	DL Terry Shackelford / Mike Bratcher
	DL Jim Vanderslice
	LB Steve Gunn / Lane Ladewig
	DB Cubby Hudler
	DB Mike Hall
	DB Billy Lloyd
	DB Charles Brightwell / Ted Fay

RUSHING: Montgomery 198/700y, Rabb 66/281y, Carter 68/204y
PASSING: Shabay 50-99/689y, 2TD, 50.5%
Carter 46-119/559y, 1TD, 38.7%
RECEIVING: Ferguson 27/419y, Montgomery 18/177y,
Whelan 17/253y
SCORING: Montgomery 54pts, Post 18pts,
Wayne Merritt (K) 17pts

1968 3-7

7 Georgia Tech	17 WR Linzy Cole
28 Iowa	17 WR Jerry Miller / Allen Brown
7 Arkansas	17 T Gerald Kirby / Fred Barber
14 SMU	21 G James Ray
7 Texas A&M	27 C John Ruthstrom
7 LSU	10 G William Riley
14 Baylor	14 T Charles Bales
14 Texas Tech	31 TE Fred Nix / Jerry Miller
21 Texas	47 QB Ted Fay
24 Rice	14 HB Ross Montgomery / Marty Whelan
	FB Norm Bulaich / Sammy Rabb
	DL Clay Mitchell
	DL Larry Adams
	DL Dave Holt
	DL Terry Shackelford
	LB Pat Walker / Andy Durrett / Randy Hale
	LB Steve Gunn / Dave McDaniel
	LB Jim Vanderslice / John Nichols
	DB Greg Webb / Robbie Mayfield
	DB Mike Hall
	DB Billy Lloyd
	DB Charles Brightwell

RUSHING: Montgomery 170/645y, Bulaich 82/503y,
Whelan 69/246y
PASSING: Fay 70-144/978y, 3TD, 48.6%
RECEIVING: Cole 21/368y, Brown 14/268y, Nix 10/117y
SCORING: Montgomery 42pts, Fay 30pts, Wayne Merritt (K) 26pts

1969 4-6

35 Purdue	42 WR Jerry Miller
0 Ohio State	62 T Gerald Kirby
6 Arkansas	24 G Danny Lamb / William Riley
17 SMU	19 C John Ruthstrom
16 Texas A&M	6 G Jim Ray
9 Miami	14 T Jerry Cooper
31 Baylor	14 TE J.R. Eubanks
35 Texas Tech	26 QB Steve Judy
7 Texas	69 HB Linzy Cole
21 Rice	17 HB Sammy Rabb / Norm Bulaich
	FB Marty Whelan
	DL Clay Mitchell / Bob Creech (LB)
	DL Chuck Forney
	DL Donnie Terveen / Craig Fife / Dave Holt
	DL Terry Shackelford
	LB Pat Walker
	LB Andy Durrett
	LB Jim Vanderslice
	DB Greg Webb
	DB Jimmy Tidwell
	DB Ted Fay
	DB Larry Wright

RUSHING: Whelan 153/657y, Judy 105/342y, Bulaich 63/296y
PASSING: Judy 144-283/1677y, 12TD, 50.9%
RECEIVING: Miller 41/569y, Cole 32/471y, Whelan 18/182y
SCORING: Cole 60pts, Wayne Merritt (K) 33pts, Judy 24pts

1970 4-6-1

31 UT-Arlington	7 WR John Hetherly / Lane Bowen
0 Purdue	15 WR Larry Speake
14 Wisconsin	14 T Gerald Kirby
14 Arkansas	49 G Lloyd Draper / Jerry Wauson
20 Oklahoma State	34 C John Ruthstrom
31 Texas A&M	15 G Ronnie Peoples / J.R. Eubanks
24 Baylor	17 T Dean Wilkerson
14 Texas Tech	22 TE Frankie Grimmett
0 Texas	58 QB Steve Judy
15 Rice	17 HB Ray Rhodes / James Hodges
26 SMU	17 FB Larry Harris / Bobby Davis
	DL Gary Martinec
	DL Larry Dibbles
	DL Dave Glass / Roy Topham
	DL Ken Steel
	DL Bob Creech
	LB James Helwig
	LB Doug McKinnon / Tookie Beery
	DB Greg Webb / Dave Dixon/ Ervin Garnett
	DB Danny Colbert
	DB Hodges Mitchell
	DB Rich Wiseman

RUSHING: Rhodes 176/786y, Hodges 121/492y, Davis 69/363y
PASSING: Judy 113-247/1327y, 5TD, 45.7%
RECEIVING: Grimmett 27/286y, Bowen 21/353y, Speake 16/198y
SCORING: Judy 36pts, Rhodes 30pts, Busty Underwood (K) 28pts

1971 6-4-1

42 UT-Arlington	0 WR Larry Speake / Freddie Pouncy
26 Washington	44 WR/HB Lane Bowen / Billy Sadler
15 Arkansas	49 T Sid Bond / Lloyd Draper
14 Oklahoma State	14 G Scott Walker
14 Texas A&M	3 C Rick Garnett
14 Penn State	66 G Guy Morriss
34 Baylor	27 T Jerry Wauson
17 Texas Tech	6 TE Ronnie Peoples / John Hetherly
0 Texas	31 QB Steve Judy
20 Rice	19 HB Larry Harris / Steve Patterson
18 SMU	16 FB Bobby Davis
	DL Gary Martinec
	DL Charles Davis
	DL Craig Fife / Ken Steel
	DL Bob Schobel
	LB Frankie Grimmett
	LB Tookie Beery / Jim McNiel
	LB Doug McKinnon
	DB Lyle Blackwood
	DB David McGinnis
	DB Gary Whitman
	DB Harold Muckleroy / Rich Wiseman

RUSHING: Davis 130/701y, Harris 105/447y, Patterson 78/354y
PASSING: Judy 60-139/882y, 6TD, 43.2%
RECEIVING: Peoples 15/185y, Pouncy 13/228y, Bowen 10/106y
SCORING: Berl Simmons (K) 40pts, Harris 36pts, Pouncy 24pts

1972 5-6

31 Indiana	28 WR Steve Patterson
38 UT-Arlington	14 T Lloyd Draper
13 Arkansas	27 G Ronnie Peoples
35 Tulsa	9 C Leon Bartlett / Scott Walker
13 Texas A&M	10 G Guy Morriss
0 Notre Dame	21 T Jerry Wauson
9 Baylor	42 TE Lane Bowen
31 Texas Tech	7 QB K. Marshall/ TerryDrennan/ Perry Senn
0 Texas	27 HB Mike Luttrell
21 Rice	25 HB Billy Sadler
22 SMU	35 FB Ronnie Webb
	DL Ed Robinson
	DL Charlie Davis
	DL Ken Steel / Tommy Van Wart
	DL Rusty Putt
	LB Gary Whitman
	LB Dede Terveen
	LB Tookie Beery
	DB Lyle Blackwood
	DB Dave McGinnis
	DB Chad Utley
	DB Terry Drennan / Gene Hernandez

RUSHING: Luttrell 178/906y, Webb 115/484y, Sadler 95/281y
PASSING: Drennan 26-47/310y, 3TD, 55.3%
RECEIVING: Patterson 22/255y, Bowen 16/112y, Sadler 10/182y
SCORING: Luttrell 60pts, Berl Simmons (K) 55pts, Sadler 20pts

1973 3-8

49 UT-Arlington	13 WR Dave Duncan
3 Ohio State	37 WR Steve Patterson
5 Arkansas	13 T Sid Bond
30 Idaho	14 G John McWilliams
16 Texas A&M	35 C Leon Bartlett
7 Tennessee	39 G Terry Champagne
34 Baylor	28 T Merle Wang
10 Texas Tech	24 TE John Ott
7 Texas	52 QB Kent Marshall / Lee Cook
9 Rice	14 HB Mike Luttrell
19 SMU	21 FB Tim Pulliam / Bobby Cowan
	DL Rusty Putt
	DL Charlie Davis
	DL Tommy Van Wart
	DL Ed Robinson
	LB Mike Hanna
	LB Dede Terveen
	LB Gene Moser
	DB Gene Hernandez
	DB Allen Hooker
	DB Gary Whitman
	DB Dennis McGehee

RUSHING: Luttrell 208/865y, Pulliam 71/268y, Marshall 105/230y
PASSING: Marshall 47-110/575y, 2TD, 42.7%
RECEIVING: Patterson 19/248y, Ott 16/199y, Luttrell 15/150y
SCORING: Berl Simmons (K) 35pts, Lutt 30pts,
Marshall & Patterson 24pts

1974 1-10

12 UT-Arlington	3 WR Gary Patterson
7 Arizona State	37 WR Dave Duncan / Mike Renfro
7 Minnesota	9 T Scott O'Glee
0 Arkansas	49 G Johnny McWilliams
13 SMU	33 C Jerry Caillier
0 Texas A&M	17 G Terry Champagne
3 Alabama	41 T Merle Wang
7 Baylor	21 TE Ron Parker
0 Texas Tech	28 QB Lee Cook
16 Texas	81 HB Dennis McGehee / Ronnie Littleton
14 Rice	26 FB Mike Luttrell
	DL Keith Judy
	DL J.G. Crouch / Jim McNiel
	DL Tommy Van Wart
	DL Chad Utley
	LB Gene Moser / Joe Segulja
	LB Dede Terveen
	LB Mike Hanna
	DB Gene Hernandez
	DB Allen Hooker
	DB Terry Drennen
	DB Tim Pulliam

RUSHING: Luttrell 161/541y, Littleton 52/221y, McGehee 52/157y
PASSING: Cook 106-237/1191y, 5TD, 44.7%
RECEIVING: Luttrell 35/252y, Renfro 21/362y, Patterson 20/362y
SCORING: Tony Biasatti (K) 19pts, Luttrell & Patterson 18pts

1975 1-10

7 UT-Arlington	24 WR Mike Renfro
10 Arizona State	33 WR Vernon Wells
14 Nebraska	56 T Russell Stewart / Anthony Mican
8 Arkansas	19 G Bryan King
13 SMU	28 C Jerry Cailler
6 Texas A&M	14 G Mark Krug
0 Alabama	45 T Mike McLeod
6 Baylor	24 TE Ron Parker
0 Texas Tech	34 QB Lee Cook
11 Texas	27 HB Ronnie Littleton / Ricky Wright
28 Rice	21 FB Bobby Cowan / Raymond Woodard
	DL Marshall Harris
	DL Alan Teichelman
	DL Lynn Davis
	DL Scott O'Glee / J.G. Crouch
	LB Keith Judy / Mack George
	LB Joe Segulja
	LB Bob Dobryl / Jerry Gaither
	DB Marvin Brown / Dennis McGehee
	DB Allen Hooker
	DB Mike Blackwood / Darryl Lowe
	DB Tim Pulliam

RUSHING: Littleton 88/232y, Wright 69/174y, Woodard 63/151y
PASSING: Cook 105-226/1307y, 5TD, 46.5%
RECEIVING: Renfro 49/810y, Parker 21/289y, Wells 18/350y
SCORING: Cook 20pts, Wells, Cowan & Renfro 12pts

1976 0-11

14 SMU	34 WR Mike Renfro
0 Tennessee	31 WR Vernon Wells
10 Nebraska	64 T Earl Reeves
14 Arkansas	46 G Jim Blackwelder
23 Rice	26 C Jerry Cailler
0 Miami	49 G Mike McLeod (T) / David Cody
21 Houston	49 T Don Davis
10 Texas Tech	14 TE James Wright
7 Texas	34 QB Jimmy Dan Elzner / Steve Bayuk
10 Texas A&M	59 TB Tony Accomando
19 Baylor	24 FB Lorance Wills / Audie Woods
	DL Marshall Harris
	DL Alan Teichelman
	DL Lynn Davis / Tom Warden
	DL Scott O'Glee
	LB Jerry Gaither / Mack George
	LB Joe Segulja
	LB Billy Neel
	DB Perry Colston / Steve Barnes
	DB Ricky Wright
	DB Richard Hein
	DB Darryl Lowe

RUSHING: Accomando 88/283y, Wills 62/195y, Bayuk 69/184y
PASSING: Elzner 100-223/1354y, 5TD, 42.9%
RECEIVING: Renfro 42/773y, Wells 32/556y, Woods 20/120y
SCORING: Ruben Ray (K) 32pts, Accomando 30pts, Renfro & Wells 18pts

1977 2-9

21 SMU	45 WR Mike Renfro
24 Oregon	29 WR Tony Accomando
0 Southern Cal	51 T Don Davis
6 Arkansas	42 G Frank Hartman
35 Rice	15 C Alan Teichelman
21 Miami	17 G Bill Kinder
14 Houston	42 T Mark Krug
17 Texas Tech	49 TE James Wright
14 Texas	44 QB Steve Bayuk
23 Texas A&M	52 TB Jimmy Allen
9 Baylor	48 FB Duncan Still / Ray Williams
	DL Barry Crayton / Bob Cummings
	DL Lynn Davis / Ricky Allen
	DL John Ferguson / Wesley Roberts
	DL James Price
	DL John Wade / Darron Mosley
	LB Jim Bayuk / Billy Neel
	LB Charlie Abel
	DB Perry Colston
	DB Mark Labhart
	DB Steve Barnes
	DB Allen Roberts

RUSHING: Allen 125/445y, Williams 43/170y, Bayuk 134/154y
PASSING: Bayuk 114-250/1474y, 14TD, 45.6%
RECEIVING: Renfro 50/794y, Milton 18/351y, Wright 15/175y
SCORING: Renfro 60pts, Bayuk 24pts, Tony Biasatti (K) 22pts

1978 2-9

14 SMU	45 WR Bobby Stewart
14 Oregon	10 WR Mike Milton
0 Penn State	58 T Bobby Richardson / Don Davis
3 Arkansas	42 G John Ferguson
14 Rice	21 C Eddie Grimes
13 Tulane	7 G Donald Ray Richard
21 Baylor	28 T Mark Krug
6 Houston	63 TE Brad Bowen / James Harris
17 Texas Tech	27 QB Steve Bayuk
0 Texas	41 TB Jimmy Allen
7 Texas A&M	15 FB Duncan Still / Craig Richardson
	DL John Wade / Kelvin Newton
	DL Marshall Harris
	DL David Braxton / James Price
	DL Wesley Roberts
	DL Kevin Moody / Ted Brack
	LB Charlie Abel
	LB Jim Bayuk
	DB Chris Judge
	DB Perry Colston
	DB Al Futrell / Kim DeLoney
	DB Steve Barnes

RUSHING: Allen 151/502y, Richardson 42/117y, Bayuk 140/108y
PASSING: Bayuk 114-241/1118y, 4TD, 47.3%
RECEIVING: C. Richardson 46/360y, Milton 34/592y, Stewart 12/184y
SCORING: Greg Porter (K) 33pts, Milton 20pts, Allen 18pts

1979 2-8-1

7 SMU	27 WR Bobby Stewart
19 Tulane	33 WR Phillips Epps
14 UT-Arlington	21 T Bobby Richardson / Dudley Stephenson
13 Arkansas	16 G Frank Hartman
17 Rice	7 C Eddie Grimes / Mike Hartman
24 Tulsa	17 G Donald Ray Richard
3 Baylor	16 T Steve Wilson
10 Houston	21 TE Brad Bowen / Stan Talley
3 Texas Tech	3 QB Steve Stamp / Kevin Haney
10 Texas	35 TB Craig Richardson
7 Texas A&M	30 FB Jimmy Allen
	DL Wesley Roberts
	DL David Braxton / Garland Short
	DL John McClean
	LB Kevin Moody
	LB Darrell Patterson
	LB Kelvin Newton
	LB Kevin Turner / Mike Dry
	DB Ray Berry
	DB Al Futrell
	DB Chris Judge
	DB Steve Barnes

RUSHING: Allen 147/498y, Haney 134/421y, Richardson 71/336y
PASSING: Stamp 64-137/777y, 2TD, 46.7%
RECEIVING: Stewart 20/274y, Epps 15/206y, Richardson 12/104y
SCORING: Greg Porter (K) 49pts, Haney 24pts, Stamp 12pts

1980 1-10

7 Auburn	10 WR Bobby Stewart
14 SMU	17 WR Stanley Washington
3 Georgia	31 T Bill Butler
7 Arkansas	44 G Don Baker
24 Rice	28 C Mike Hartman
17 Tulsa	23 G Donald Ray Richard
6 Baylor	21 T Steve Wilson
5 Houston	37 TE Daron Mosley / Mike Johnson
24 Texas Tech	17 QB Steve Stamp
26 Texas	51 TB Marcus Gilbert / J.C. Morris
10 Texas A&M	13 FB Kevin Haney / West Brooks
	DL Charles Champine
	DL Garland Short / Lionel Williams
	DL John McClean
	LB Joe Vail
	LB Darrell Patterson
	LB Kelvin Newton
	LB Mike Dry / Jim Bayuk
	DB Thomas Bell
	DB Joe Breedlove / Reginald Cottingham
	DB Ken Bener
	DB Zane Drake / Robert Lyles

RUSHING: Gilbert 90/350y, Morris 64/211y, Haney 88/168y
PASSING: Stamp 127-247/1830y, 14TD, 51.4%
RECEIVING: Stewart 46/688y, Washington 34/501y, Epps 21/420y
SCORING: Washington 48pts, Greg Porter (K) 33pts, Stewart 30pts

1981 2-7-2

16 Auburn	24 WR Stanley Washington
38 UT-Arlington	16 WR Phillips Epps
9 SMU	20 T Keith Hall
28 Arkansas	24 G Donald Baker
28 Rice	41 C Mike Hartman / Steve Cotaya
13 Utah State	13 G Ed Minter
21 Baylor	34 T Steve Wilson
16 Houston	20 TE Bob Fields
39 Texas Tech	39 QB Steve Stamp / Reuben Jones
15 Texas	31 TB Marcus Gilbert
7 Texas A&M	37 FB J.C. Morris / Kevin Haney
	DL Donald Ray Richard / John McClean
	DL Lionel Williams
	DL Greg Townsend / Garland Short
	LB Mike Dry
	LB Joe Hines
	LB Darrell Patterson / Gary Spann
	LB Ron Zell Brewer
	DB Anthony Allen
	DB Reginald Cottingham
	DB John Preston / Lawrence Johnson
	DB Ken Bener

RUSHING: Gilbert 117/498y, Haney 67/206y, Morris 47/170y
PASSING: Stamp 130-235/2013y, 14TD, 55.3%
RECEIVING: Washington 49/854y, Haney 33/381y, Gilbert 27/228y
SCORING: Greg Porter (K) 62pts, Gilbert 38pts, Washington & Epps 36pts

1982 2-8-1

24 Utah State	9 WR Stanley Washington
19 Kansas	30 WR James Maness
13 SMU	16 T Steve Page / David Johnson
0 Arkansas	35 G Don Baker
24 Rice	16 C Steve Cotaya
9 Mississippi	27 G Elton Baptiste
38 Baylor	14 T Keith Hall
27 Houston	31 TE Bob Fields
14 Texas Tech	16 QB Reuben Jones / Eddie Clark
21 Texas	38 RB Marcus Gilbert
14 Texas A&M	34 RB Zane Drake / Kenneth Davis
	DL Kyle Clifton
	DL Mike Taliferro / L.B. Washington
	DL Darron Turner / Lynwood Williams
	DL Greg Townsend
	DL Chris Williams / Ron Zell Brewer
	LB Joe Hines
	LB Darrell Patterson
	DB Sean Thomas
	DB Anthony Allen / Reggie Cottingham
	DB Allanda Smith / Ken Bener
	DB Byron Linwood / Marvin Foster

RUSHING: Gilbert 166/849y, Davis 113/549y, Jones 103/197y
PASSING: Jones 65-136/1036y, 2TD, 47.8%
RECEIVING: Washington 32/617y, Maness 19/554y, Davis 14/68y
SCORING: Ken Ozee (K) 45pts, Gilbert, Davis, Maness & Jones 30pts

1983 1-8-2

16 Kansas	16 WR Greg Arterberry / Dwayne May
3 Kansas State	20 WR James Maness
17 SMU	21 T Steve Page
21 Arkansas	38 G Ike Tyre
34 Rice	3 C Mike Flynn
7 Mississippi	20 G Elton Baptiste / Tommy Shehan
21 Baylor	56 T Bill Harp / James Benson
21 Houston	28 TE Dan Sharpe
10 Texas Tech	10 QB Anthony Sciaraffa / Anthony Gulley
14 Texas	20 RB Kenneth Davis
10 Texas A&M	20 RB Blanford Paul / Egypt Allen
	DL Ron Zell Brewer / Kevin Dean
	DL Mike Taliferro / Bill Tommaney
	DL L.B. Washington / Kent Tramel
	DL David Caldwell
	DL Frank Willis / Robert Lyles
	LB Kyle Clifton
	LB Gary Spann
	DB Sean Thomas / Reginald Cottingham
	DB John Thomas
	DB Allanda Smith
	DB Byron Linwood

RUSHING: Davis 145/682y, Paul 48/224y, Allen 61/217y
PASSING: Sciaraffa 95-183/1423y, 3TD, 51.9%
RECEIVING: Maness 37/690y, Sharp 21/282y, May 17/213y
SCORING: Ken Ozee (K) 48pts, Allen & Sciaraffa 24pts

1984 8-4

62 Utah State	18 WR Gary Ford
42 Kansas State	10 WR James Maness
17 SMU	26 T Steve Page
32 Arkansas	31 G Joe Young
45 Rice	24 C Mike Flynn
34 N. Texas St.	3 G Tommy Shehan
38 Baylor	28 T James Benson
21 Houston	14 TE Dan Sharp
27 Texas Tech	16 QB Anthony Gulley / Anthony Sciaraffa
23 Texas	44 RB Kenneth Davis
21 Texas A&M	35 RB Tony Jeffrey
14 West Virginia■	31 DL Kevin Dean
	DL Bill Tommaney
	DL Kent Tramel
	DL Darron Turner / L.B. Washington
	DL David Caldwell
	LB Gearld Taylor / Andy Pitts
	LB Gary Spann
	DB Sean Thomas
	DB Billy Jones
	DB Byron Linwood
	DB Garland Littles

RUSHING: Davis 211/1611y, Jeffrey 165/840y, Gulley 118/314y
PASSING: Gulley 71-131/1022y, 6TD, 54.2%
RECEIVING: Sharp 42/596y, Maness 40/871y, Davis 13/200y
SCORING: Davis 102pts, Ken Ozee (K) 72pts, Jeffrey 30pts

1985 3-8

30 Tulane	13 WR Ricky Stone
24 Kansas State	22 WR Keith Burnett
21 SMU	56 T Ed Laswell
0 Arkansas	41 G Bernie Henton / Tracy Simien
27 Rice	34 C W.C. Nix
14 N. Texas St.	10 G Tommy Shehan
0 Baylor	45 T Brian Brazil
21 Houston	26 TE Gary Ford / Bill Tommaney
7 Texas Tech	63 QB Scott Ankrom / David Rascoe
0 Texas	20 RB Bobby Davis / Jarrod Delaney
6 Texas A&M	53 RB Tony Jeffrey / Stephan Howland
	DL David Caldwell
	DL Trent Edwards / Frank Hawkins
	DL Kent Tramel
	DL Mitchell Benson / Ron Lewis
	DL Floyd Terrell / David Spradlin
	LB Scott Harris
	LB Kevin Dean
	DB Billy Jones
	DB Ricky Rougely / Joe Johnson
	DB Falanda Newton
	DB Garland Littles

RUSHING: Jeffrey 176/695y, Davis 90/442y, Howland 42/263y
PASSING: Rascoe 71-165/941y, 5TD, 43%
RECEIVING: Stone 22/281y, Jeffrey 17/229y, Delaney 16/200y
SCORING: Ken Ozee (K) 40pts, Jeffrey 32pts, Ankrom 24pts

1986 3-8

48 Tulane	31 WR Reggie Davis
35 Kansas State	22 WR Jarrod Delaney
21 SMU	31 T Jeff Hopkins / Dennis Gooch
17 Arkansas	34 G Mike Bulla
31 Rice	37 C Clint Hailey / Doug Elms / Jeff Daily
20 N. Texas St.	24 G W.C. Nix / Jess Williams
17 Baylor	28 T Brian Brazil
30 Houston	14 TE Gary Ford / Bill Tommaney
14 Texas Tech	36 QB David Rascoe
16 Texas	45 RB Tony Jeffrey / Tony Darthard
10 Texas A&M	74 RB Bobby Davis / Roscoe Tatum
	DL Ron Lewis / Gregg Jones
	DL Frank Hawkins
	DL Tracy Simien
	DL Mitchell Benson
	DL David Caldwell / Greg Moore
	LB Scott Harris / John Dull
	LB Kevin Dean
	DB Tony Brooks
	DB John Booty
	DB Falanda Newton / Billy Jones
	DB Garland Littles / Joe Johnson

RUSHING: Jeffrey 122/861y, Davis 78/386y, Rascoe 125/339y
PASSING: Rascoe 89-180/985y, 6TD, 49.4%
RECEIVING: Delaney 26/382y, R. Davis 21/243y, Jeffrey 11/112y
SCORING: Lee Newman (K) 77pts, Jeffrey 56pts, Rascoe 24pts

1987 5-6

20 Boston College	38 WR Reggie Davis
10 Air Force	21 WR/FB Jarrod Delaney / Scott Bednarski
33 BYU	12 T Jeff Hopkins
10 Arkansas	20 G Robby Adams
30 Rice	16 C Clint Hailey
19 N. Texas St.	10 G Mike Sullivan
24 Baylor	0 T Brian Brazil
35 Houston	7 TE Rick Stone
35 Texas Tech	36 QB David Rascoe
21 Texas	24 RB Tony Jeffrey
24 Texas A&M	42 RB Tony Darthard
	DL Tracy Simien
	DL Mitchell Benson
	DL Kent Tramel / Fred Washington
	DL David Spradlin
	LB Floyd Terrell
	LB Paul Llewellyn
	LB Greg Moore / Gregg Jones
	DB Andre Spencer
	DB Levoil Crump
	DB Falanda Newton
	DB Tommy Sharp

RUSHING: Jeffrey 202/1353y, Darthard 142/878y, Rascoe 130/373y
PASSING: Rascoe 88-173/1110y, 9TD, 50.9%
RECEIVING: Delaney 23/284y, Stone 20/201y, Davis 17/270y, Jeffrey 17/257y
SCORING: Jeffrey 66pts, Lee Newman (K) 63pts, Rascoe 36pts

1988 4-7

10 Georgia	38 WR Reggie Davis
49 Bowling Green	12 WR Jarrod Delaney
31 Boston College	17 T Bill Elliott
10 Arkansas	53 G Rob Adams
21 Rice	10 C Jeff Dailey
18 BYU	31 G Mike Sullivan
24 Baylor	14 T Bret Alexander
12 Houston	40 TE Kelly Blackwell
10 Texas Tech	23 QB David Rascoe
21 Texas	30 RB Tony Darthard
0 Texas A&M	18 RB Cedric Jackson
	DL Tracy Simien
	DL Fred Washington
	DL Mitchell Benson
	DL Darrell Davis / Roosevelt Collins
	LB Richard Booker
	LB Paul Llewellyn / Jordy Reynolds
	LB Scott Harris / Greg Moore
	DB Andre Spencer
	DB Robert McWright / Stanley Petry
	DB Levoil Crump / Romeo Smith
	DB Falanda Newton

RUSHING: Darthard 192/854y, Ankrom 144/639y, Jackson 105/467y
PASSING: Rascoe 58-137/660y, 3TD, 42.3%
RECEIVING: Delaney 30/440y, Blackwell 20/172y, Davis 15/188y
SCORING: Lee Newman (K) 47pts, Ankrom 38pts, Darthard 30pts

1989 4-7

10 Missouri	14 WR Allan Foret / Stephen Shipley
7 Texas A&M	44 WR Todd Holmes
19 So. Mississippi	17 WR Michael Jackson
28 SMU	10 T Bubba Walker
19 Arkansas	41 G Mike Sullivan
30 Rice	16 C Jody Morse (T) / Mike Bulla
27 Air Force	9 G Bill Elliott
9 Baylor	27 T Bret Alexander
10 Houston	55 TE Kelly Blackwell / Mike Noack
7 Texas Tech	37 QB Ron Jiles
17 Texas	31 RB Tommy Palmer / Curtis Modkins
	DL Darrell Davis
	DL Fred Washington
	DL John Marsh / Buddy Wyatt
	DL Roosevelt Collins
	LB Richard Booker
	LB Brad Smith / Ivory Christian
	LB Jason Cauble / Greg Moore
	DB Larry Brown / Ed Galaviz
	DB Robert McWright
	DB Levoil Crump
	DB Stephen Conley / Reggie Campbell

RUSHING: Palmer 118/642y, Modkins 120/522y, Jiles 115/343y
PASSING: Jiles 145-286/1763y, 9TD, 50.9%
RECEIVING: Jackson 42/411y, Blackwell 33/389y, Shipley 23/491y
SCORING: Kevin Cordesman (K) 44pts, Palmer 36pts, Jackson & Shipley 18pts

1990 5-6

3 Washington St.	21 WR Stephen Shipley
20 Missouri	19 WR Kyle McPherson
31 Oklahoma State	21 WR Richard Woodley
42 SMU	21 T Bill Elliott
54 Arkansas	26 G Mike Sullivan
38 Rice	28 C David Breedlove
21 Baylor	27 G John Marsh / Jody Morse
35 Houston	56 T Bret Alexander
28 Texas Tech	40 TE Kelly Blackwell
10 Texas	38 QB Leon Clay / Matt Vogler
10 Texas A&M	56 RB Curtis Modkins / Cedric Jackson
	DL Tunji Bolden
	DL Kenneth Walton / Dan Dougherty
	DL James Prather
	DL Roosevelt Collins
	LB Richard Booker / Reggie Anderson
	LB Brad Smith
	LB Jason Cauble
	DB Larry Brown
	DB Anthony Hickman
	DB Levoil Crump / Greg Evans
	DB Jonathan Rand

RUSHING: Modkins 209/893y, Clay 71/203y
PASSING: Vogler 136-281/1646y, 7TD, 48.4%
Clay 119-223/1565y, 16TD, 53.4%
RECEIVING: Blackwell 64/832y, Shipley 59/796y, Woodley 56/653y
SCORING: Jeff Wilkinson (K) 68pts, Shipley 38pts, 4 tied w/ 30pts

1991 7-4

60 New Mexico	7 WR Stephen Shipley
22 Ball State	16 WR Kyle McPherson / David Lewis
24 Oklahoma State	21 WR Richard Woodley
30 Texas Tech	16 T Keith Wagner
21 Arkansas	22 G Bennie Scott
9 Baylor	28 C Jody Morse
18 SMU	26 G David Breedlove
7 Texas A&M	10 T Mike Black / John Marsh
0 Texas	44 TE Kelly Blackwell
49 Houston	32 QB Tim Schade / Leon Clay
	45 RB Curtis Modkins / Derrick Cullors
	DL Tunji Bolden
	DL Thomas Lewis
	DL Alex Molina / Royal West
	DL Roosevelt Collins
	LB Scott Hines
	LB Brad Smith
	LB Reggie Anderson
	DB Steve Reed / Rico Wesley
	DB Anthony Hickman
	DB Tony Rand
	DB Greg Evans

RUSHING: Modkins 181/659y
PASSING: Schade 101-168/1253y, 5TD, 60.1%
RECEIVING: Blackwell 64/762y, Shipley 34/464y, Woodley 27/301y
SCORING:

1992 2-8-1

7 New Mexico	24 WR Stephen Shipley / Kyle McPherson
17 W. Michigan	17 WR Jimmy Oliver / Richard Woodley
9 SMU	21 T Mike Black
13 Oklahoma State	11 G Boyd Milby
20 Baylor	41 C Jody Morse
10 Miami	45 G David Breedlove
12 Rice	29 T Barret Robbins
46 Houston	49 TE Mike Noack
23 Texas	14 QB Leon Clay / Max Knake
28 Texas Tech	31 TB Curtis Modkins / Derrick Cullors
10 Texas A&M	37 FB John Oglesby
	DL Vincent Pryor
	DL Royal West
	DL Brian Brooks
	DL Tunji Bolden / Chris Piland
	LB Mike Moulton
	LB Sadd Jackson / Brad Smith
	LB Lenoy Jones
	DB Rico Wesley / Steve Reed
	DB Anthony Hickman
	DB David King / Tony Rand
	DB Greg Evans

RUSHING: Modkins 162/689y
PASSING: Clay 143-287/1526y, 8TD, 49.8%
RECEIVING: Shipley 36/500y, Oglseby 26/143y
SCORING:

1993 4-7

3 Oklahoma	35 WR Richard Woodley
35 New Mexico	34 WR John Washington / Jimmy Oliver
15 SMU	21 T Boyd Milby
22 Oklahoma State	27 G Bart Epperson
19 Rice	34 C Kevin Brewer
14 Tulane	7 G Chuck Wills
38 Baylor	13 T Barret Robbins
28 Houston	10 TE Brian Collins
21 Texas Tech	49 QB Max Knake
3 Texas	24 TB Andre Davis
3 Texas A&M	59 FB John Oglesby
	DL Vincent Pryor
	DL Brian Brooks / Aaron Burton
	DL Royal West
	DL Chris Piland
	LB Reggie Anderson
	LB Mike Moulton
	LB Lenoy Jones / Tyrone Roy
	DB Charles McWilliams
	DB Calvin Jones / Rico Wesley
	DB Manvel Hopes
	DB Greg Evans

RUSHING: Davis 189/867y
PASSING: Knake 207-357/2130y, 12TD, 58%
RECEIVING: Oglesby 47/404y, Woodley 34/435y
SCORING: Davis 54pts

1994 7-5

17 North Carolina	27 WR John Washington
44 New Mexico	29 WR Chris Brasfield / Jimmy Oliver
31 Kansas	21 T Ryan Tucker
18 Texas	34 G Boyd Milby
18 Baylor	42 C Barret Robbins
30 Tulane	28 G Bart Epperson / Chuck Wills
31 Houston	10 T Brandon Hickman
27 Rice	25 TE Brian Collins
35 SMU	14 QB Max Knake
17 Texas A&M	34 TB Andre Davis
24 Texas Tech	21 FB Koi Woods
10 Virginia■	20 DL Gaylon Hyder / Aaron Burton
	DL Royal West
	DL Hayes Rydel / Michael Janak
	LB Chris Piland / Vincent Pryor
	LB Mike Moulton
	LB Reggie Anderson
	LB Lenoy Jones / Jay Davern
	DB Mikyha Martin
	DB Chuckie McWilliams
	DB Manvel Hopes
	DB Rick LaFavers / Geoff Stephens

RUSHING: Davis 260/1494y, Woods 78/304y,
Derrick Cullors (TB) 27/149y
PASSING: Knake 184-316/2624y, 24TD, 58.2%
RECEIVING: Davis 47/522y, Collins 32/369y, Washington 25/438y
SCORING: Davis 66pts, Michael Reeder (K) 65pts, Collins 42pts

1995 6-5

27 Iowa State	10 WR John Washington / Jason Tucker
20 Kansas	38 WR Chris Brasfield / Troy Williams
16 Vanderbilt	3 T Clifford Barnes
31 Houston	21 G Fabian Stegall
33 Rice	28 C Ryan Tucker
16 Tulane	11 G Kevin Brewer
24 Baylor	27 T Kevin Holmes / Mark Cortez
19 SMU	16 TE Brian Collins
6 Texas Tech	27 QB Max Knake
19 Texas	27 TB Andre Davis / Matt Moore
6 Texas A&M	38 FB Koi Woods
	DL Hayes Rydel / Chance McCarty
	DL Gaylon Hyder
	DL Bernard Oldham / Michael Janak
	DL Chris Piland
	LB Lenoy Jones
	LB Tyrone Roy
	LB Geoff Stephens
	DB Godfrey White / Cedric Allen
	DB Chuckie McWilliams / Manvel Hopes
	DB Rick LaFavers
	DB Chris Staten / Mikyha Martin

RUSHING: Davis 186/820y, Woods 74/347y, Moore 64/226y
PASSING: Knake 199-369/2237y, 10TD, 53.9%
RECEIVING: Washington 52/699y, Tucker 31/433y, Davis 31/282y
SCORING: Michael Reeder (K) 89pts, Davis & Washington 42pts

1996 4-7

20 Oklahoma	7 WR John Washington
17 Kansas	52 WR Jason Tucker
7 New Mexico	27 T Mark Cortez
7 Tulane	35 G Fabian Stegall
18 UTEP	0 C Ryan Tucker
7 Utah	21 G Clifton Clemons
21 BYU	45 T Greg Davis
42 UNLV	34 TE Travis Wilson / Mike Brown
31 Tulsa	24 QB Jeff Dover
17 Rice	30 TB Basil Mitchell
24 SMU	27 FB Lance Williams / Koi Woods
	DL Matt Harper
	DL Bernard Oldham / Marcus Anderson
	DL Michael Janak
	DL Chance McCarty
	LB Geoff Stephens
	LB Scott Taft
	LB Jay Davern
	DB Godfrey White
	DB Cedric Allen
	DB Chris Staten
	DB Reggie Hunt

RUSHING: Mitchell 221/953y,
PASSING: Dover 129-221/1456y, 9TD, 58.4%
RECEIVING: Mitchell 40/344y, Washington 39/353y
SCORING:

1997 1-10

10 Kansas	17 WR Torrie Simmons
18 Utah	32 WR Tavarus Moore / Patrick Batteaux
16 Vanderbilt	40 T Mark Cortez (G) / Paul Harmon
10 North Carolina	31 G Shane Ladewig
19 UNLV	21 C Doug Loeser
22 Tulsa	33 G Russ Sanders / Robert Wallace
10 BYU	31 T Mike Keathley / David Bobo
10 New Mexico	40 TE Mike Brown
19 Rice	38 QB Jeff Dover / Derek Canine
17 UTEP	24 TB Basil Mitchell / LaDainian Tomlinson
21 SMU	18 FB Lou Porch
	DL Chance McCarty
	DL J.W. Wilson / Marcus Anderson
	DL Matt Harper / Kyle Williams
	DL Aaron Schobel
	LB Marcus Anderson / Marvin Mullins
	LB Scott Taft
	LB Joseph Phipps / Jason Illian
	DB Barry Browning
	DB Corey Masters / Greg Walls
	DB LaVar Veale / Landry Burdine
	DB Chris Staten

RUSHING: Mitchell 159/719y, Tomlinson 126/538y,
PASSING: Dover 97-199/1063y, 5TD, 48.7%
Canine 56-119/685y, 3TD, 47.1%
RECEIVING: Batteaux 27/396y, Simmons 27/314y, Brown 26/292y
SCORING: Michael Reeder (K) 49pts, Tomlinson 36pts,
Mitchell 32pts

1998 7-5

31 Iowa State	21 WR Mike Scarborough
9 Oklahoma	10 WR Michael Crawford / Cedric James
35 Air Force	34 WR Royce Huffman
19 Vanderbilt	16 T Michael Keathley / David Bobo
21 Fresno State	10 G Greg Davis
6 SMU	10 C Jeff Garner / Shane Ladewig
21 Colorado State	42 G Jeff Millican (T) / Robert Wallace
27 Wyoming	34 T Russ Sanders
12 Rice	14 TE Jason Illian
17 Tulsa	7 QB Patrick Batteaux
41 UNLV	18 TB Basil Mitchell / LaDainian Tomlinson
28 Southern Cal■	19 DL Kam Hunt / Raymone Lacey
	DL Shawn Worthen / Kyle Williams
	DL J.W. Wilson
	DL Aaron Schobel / London Dunlap
	LB Joseph Phipps
	LB Shannon Brazzell / Cody Mortensen
	DB Andre Bruce
	DB Greg Walls
	DB Curtis Fuller / LaVar Veale
	DB Reggie Hunt
	DB Russell Gary

RUSHING: Mitchell 166/1111y, Tomlinson 144/717y,
Batteaux 149/479y
PASSING: Batteaux 55-114/519y, 1TD, 48.2%
RECEIVING: Scarborough 19/223y, Crawford 15/206y,
James 13/167y
SCORING: Chris Kaylakie (K) 69pts, Tomlinson 48pts,
Mitchell 36pts

1999 8-4

31 Arizona	35 WR Mike Scarborough
7 Northwestern	17 WR Tim Maiden / LaTarence Dunbar
24 Arkansas State	21 T Michael Keathley
19 Fresno State	26 G Victor Payne
42 San Jose State	0 C Jeff Garner
56 Tulsa	17 G Jeff Millican
21 Rice	42 T David Bobo
34 Hawaii	14 TE B.J. Roberts
34 North Texas	3 QB Casey Printers / Patrick Batteaux
52 UTEP	24 TB LaDainian Tomlinson
21 SMU	0 FB George Layne
28 East Carolina■	14 DL Doug Shanks
	DL Shawn Worthen
	DL J.W. Wilson / Kyle Williams
	DL Aaron Scobel / London Dunlap
	LB Chad Bayer
	LB Shannon Brazzell / Terrance Maiden
	DB Greg Walls
	DB Jason Goss
	DB Reggie Hunt
	DB Curtis Fuller
	DB Russell Gary / Cody Slinkard

RUSHING: Tomlinson 268/1850y, Batteaux 92/333y,
Layne 44/186y
PASSING: Printers 86-150/1213y, 8TD, 57.3%
RECEIVING: Scarborough 35/524y, Dunlap 20/315y,
Maiden 12/134y
SCORING: Tomlinson 108pts, Chris Kaylakie (K) 70pts,
Scarborough 48pts

2000 10-2

41 Nevada	10 WR Tim Maiden
41 Northwestern	14 WR Cedric James
52 Arkansas State	3 T Mike Keathley
24 Navy	0 G Victor Payne
41 Hawaii	21 C Jeff Garner
17 Tulsa	3 G Jeff Millican
37 Rice	0 T David Bobo
24 San Jose State	27 TE B. J. Roberts / Matt Schobel
24 Fresno State	7 QB Casey Printers
47 UTEP	14 TB LaDainian Tomlinson
62 SMU	7 FB G. Layne/Chad Purcel/L Dunbar
21 S. Mississippi■	28 DL Chad McCarty
	DL Shawn Worthen
	DL Stuart Ashley
	DL Aaron Schobel
	LB Chad Bayer
	LB Shannon Brazzell / Terrance Maiden
	DB Greg Walls / Bo Springfield
	DB Jason Goss / Kenneth Hilliard
	DB Charlie Owens
	DB Curtis Fuller
	DB Russell Gary

RUSHING: Tomlinson 369/2158y, Layne 46/279, Printers 84/265y
PASSING: Printers 102-176/1584y, 16TD, 58%
RECEIVING: Maiden 19/348y, James 19/310, Dunbar 17/371y
SCORING: Tomlinson 132pts, Chris Kaylakie (K) 98pts,
Layne 48 pts

2001 6-6

7 Nebraska	21 WR LaTarence Dunbar
19 North Texas	5 WR Adrian Madise
38 SMU	10 WR/FB Terran Williams / Reggie Holts
24 Northwestern St.	27 T John Glud
34 Houston	17 G Victor Payne
22 Tulane	48 C Jamal Powell
38 Army	20 G J.T. Aughinbaugh
30 East Carolina	37 T Brady Barrick
17 UAB	38 TE Matt Schobel / B.J. Roberts
37 Louisville	22 QB Casey Printers / Sean Stilley
14 S. Mississippi	12 TB Ricky Madison / Corey Connally
9 Texas A&M■	28 DL Chad McCarty
	DL John Turntine / Richard Evans
	DL Chad Pugh
	DL Bobby Pollard / Joe Hill
	LB LaMarcus McDonald
	LB Chad Bayer
	DB Jason Goss
	DB Bo Springfield / Tyrone Sanders
	DB Kenneth Hilliard
	DB Charlie Owens
	DB Marvin Godbolt

RUSHING: Madison 174/611y, Connally 98/444y
PASSING: Printers 136-252/1824y, 13TD, 54%
RECEIVING: Madise 50/819y, Dunbar 41/529y, Schobel 19/310y
SCORING: Nick Browne (K) 72pts, Dunbar, Madison &
Schobel 30pts

2002 10-2

29 Cincinnati	36 WR LaTarence Dunbar / Terran Williams
48 Northwestern	24 WR A. Madise /Reggie Harrell/Kevin Brown
17 SMU	6 T Anthony Alabi
16 North Texas	10 G John Glud
34 Houston	17 C'Chase Johnson
46 Army	27 G J.T. Aughinbaugh / Josh Harbuck
45 Louisville	31 T Jamal Powell (C) / Jon Morgan
37 S. Mississippi	3 TE Quint Ellis / Cody McCarty
17 Tulane	10 QB Sean Stilley / Tye Gunn
28 East Carolina	31 TB Ricky Madison / Lonta Hobbs
27 Memphis	20 FB Reggie Holts
17 Colorado State ■	3 DL Robert Pollard / Andrew Calovich
	DL John Turntine / Richard Evans
	DL Chad Pugh / Brandon Johnson
	DL Bo Schobel / Ranorris Ray
	LB LaMarcus McDonald
	LB Martin Patterson / Josh Goolsby
	DB Jason Goss
	DB Tyrone Sanders / Mark Walker
	DB Marvin Godbolt / Jeremy Modkins
	DB Kenneth Hilliard
	DB Jared Smitherman

RUSHING: Hobbs 157/1029y, Madison 155/719y,
  Corey Connally (TB) 54/188y
PASSING: Stilley 114-204/1371y, 6TD, 55.9%
  Gunn 57-91/632y, 6TD, 62.6%
RECEIVING: Madise 32/524y, Dunbar 31/449y, Brown 16/208y
SCORING: Nick Browne (K) 105pts, Hobbs 78pts, Dunbar 36pts

2003 11-2

38 Tulane	35 WR Reggie Harrell
17 Navy	3 WR Bruce Galbert / Cory Rodgers
30 Vanderbilt	14 T Anthony Alabi
13 Arizona	10 G John Glud
27 Army	0 C Chase Johnson / Stephen Culp
13 South Florida	10 G Zach Bray
27 UAB	24 T Herbert Taylor
62 Houston	55 TE Cody McCarty / Stanley Moss
31 Louisville	28 QB Brandon Hassell / Tye Gunn
43 Cincinnati	10 TB Robert Merrill / Lonta Hobbs
28 Southern Miss	40 FB Kenny Hayter
20 SMU	13 DL Bo Schobel
31 Boise State ■	34 DL Chad Pugh / Terence James
	DL Ranorris Ray / Brandon Johnson
	DL Robert Pollard
	LB Josh Goolsby
	LB Martin Patterson
	DB Mark Walker
	DB Tyrone Sanders
	DB Chris Peoples / Marvin Godbolt
	DB Jeremy Modkins
	DB Brandon Williams

RUSHING: Merrill 201/1107y, Hobbs 169/659y, Hassell 120/369y
PASSING: Hassell 136-240/2039y, 10TD, 56.7%
  Gunn 61-102/788y, 2TD, 59.8%
RECEIVING: Harrell 58/1012y, Rodgers 37/590y, Galbert 19/269y
SCORING: Nick Browne (K) 122pts, Hobbs 54pts, Rodgers 48pts

2004 5-6

48 Northwestern	45 WR Cory Rodgers / Quentily Harmon
44 Navy	0 WR Reggie Harrell / Ryan Pearson
35 Texas Tech	70 WR/FB Michael DePriest / Marcus Draper
44 South Florida	45 T Anthony Alabi
21 Army	17 G Shane Sims
25 UAB	41 C Chase Johnson
34 Houston	27 G Zach Bray
10 Cincinnati	21 T Herbert Taylor
28 Louisville	55 TE Cody McCarty / Trey Englert
42 Southern Miss	17 QB Brandon Hassell / Tye Gunn
31 Tulane	35 TB Robert Merrill / Lonta Hobbs
	DL Jamison Newby
	DL Jared Kesler
	DL Terence James / Tommy Blake
	DL Ranorris Roy
	LB Martin Patterson
	LB Andrew Ward / David Hawthorne
	DB Mark Walker / Drew Coleman
	DB Quincy Butler / Jerome Braziel
	DB Jeremy Modkins / Brian Bonner
	DB Marvin Godbolt
	DB Elvis Gallegos / David Roach

RUSHING: Merrill 179/753y, Hobbs 125/647y
PASSING: Hassell 123-217/1724y, 10TD, 56.7%
  Gunn 71-131/1065y, 9TD, 54.2%
RECEIVING: Rodgers 61/836y, Harrell 32/595y, Harmon 20/319y
SCORING: Hobbs 72pts, Peter LoCoco (K) 57pts, Rodgers 54pts

2005 11-1

17 Oklahoma	10 WR Cory Rodgers / Donald Massey
10 SMU	21 WR Matt Grimmett/ Quentily Harmon
23 Utah	20 WR Derek Moore / Walter Bryant
51 BYU	50 T Michael Toudouze
49 New Mexico	28 G Shane Sims / Matty Lindner
28 Wyoming	14 C Stephen Culp
38 Army	17 G Ben Angeley / Giles Montgomery
48 Air Force	10 T Herb Taylor
23 San Diego State	20 TE Chad Andrus / Brent Hecht
33 Colorado State	6 QB Jeff Ballard / Tye Gunn
51 UNLV	3 RB Robert Merrill / Aaron Brown
27 Iowa State ■	24 DL Chase Ortiz
	DL Ranorris Ray
	DL Jared Kesler / Zarnell Fitch
	DL Tommy Blake / Jamison Newby
	LB David Hawthorne/ Robert Henson
	LB Jason Phillips
	DB Quincy Butler
	DB Drew Coleman
	DB Marvin White / David Roach
	DB Jeremy Modkins
	DB Eric Buchanan / Brian Bonner

RUSHING: Merrill 187/911y, Brown 128/758y, Ballard 93/314y
PASSING: Ballard 139-232/1801y, 13TD, 59.9%
  Gunn 64-136/646y, 2TD, 47.1%
RECEIVING: Rodgers 52/685y, Harmon 28/318y, Massey 21/203y
SCORING: Chris Manfredini (K) 79pts, Rodgers 72pts, Merrill 60pts

2006 11-2

17 Baylor	7 WR Michael DePriest/Ervin Dickerson
46 UC Davis	13 WR Quentily Harmon / Derek Moore
12 Texas Tech	3 WR/TE Donald Massey/Shae Reagan
17 BYU	31 T Herb Taylor
7 Utah	20 G Matty Lindner
31 Army	17 C Blake Schlueter
26 Wyoming	3 G Maurice Bouldwin
25 UNLV	10 T Wade Sisk
27 New Mexico	21 TE Chad Andrus / Brent Hecht
52 San Diego State	0 QB Jeff Ballard
45 Colorado State	14 RB Lonta Hobbs (FB) / Aaron Brown
38 Air Force	24 DL Chase Ortiz
37 N. Illinois ■	7 DL James Vess / Cody Moore
	DL Jarrarcea Williams
	DL Tommy Blake
	LB David Hawthorne/ Robert Henson
	LB Jason Phillips
	DB Nick Sanders
	DB Rafael Priest
	DB David Roach / Stephen Coleman
	DB Marvin White / Stephen Hodge
	DB Brian Bonner / Eric Buchanan

RUSHING: Brown 154/801y, Hobbs 145/665y, Ballard 110/423y
PASSING: Ballard 190-307/2394y, 13TD, 61.9%
RECEIVING: Harmon 52/791y, Brown 34/455y, Massey 26/332y
SCORING: Chris Manfredini (K) 72pts, Brown 60pts, Ballard 48pts

2007 8-5

27 Baylor	0 WR Derek Moore/D. Massey/Justin Watts
13 Texas	34 WR Marcus Brock / Walter Bryant
17 Air Force	20 WR Ervin Dickerson / Jimmy Young
21 SMU	7 T Marsh Newhouse
24 Colorado State	12 G Matty Lindner / Preston Phillips
21 Wyoming	24 C Blake Schlueter / Tony Savino
38 Stanford	36 G Gil Montgomery
20 Utah	27 T Nic Richmond / Marcus Cannon
37 New Mexico	0 TE Shae Reagan / Quinton Cunigan
22 BYU	27 QB Andy Dalton / Marcus Jackson
34 UNLV	10 RB Aaron Brown / Joseph Turner
45 San Diego State	33 DL Chase Ortiz / Jerry Hughes
20 Houston ■	13 DL Kelly Griffin / John Fonua
	DL Cody Moore / Cory Grant
	DL Tommy Blake / Matt Panfil
	LB David Hawthorne / Robert Henson
	LB Jason Phillips / Daryl Washington
	DB Nick Sanders
	DB Rafael Priest / Torrey Stewart
	DB David Roach
	DB Steven Coleman / Stephen Hodge
	DB Brian Bonner

RUSHING: Turner 115/597y, Brown 106/490y,
  Ryan Christian (RB) 88/321y
PASSING: Dalton 222-371/2459y, 10TD, 59.8%
  Jackson 35-69/368y, 3TD, 50.7%
RECEIVING: Dickerson 40/514y, Massey 29/364y, Bryant 27/337y
SCORING: Chris Manfredini (K) 103pts, Turner 36pts, Dalton 30pts

2008 11-2

26 New Mexico	3 WR Jimmy Young / Jonathan Jones
67 Stephen F Austin	7 WR Walter Bryant / Antoine Hicks
31 Stanford	14 WR Bart Johnson / Jeremy Kerley
48 SMU	7 Marsh Newhouse
10 Oklahoma	35 G Preston Phillips / Kyle Dooley
41 San Diego State	3 C Blake Schlueter
13 Colorado State	7 G Gil Montgomery
32 BYU	3 T Marcus Cannon / Vic Richmond
54 Wyoming	7 TE Shae Reagan / Evan Frosch
44 UNLV	14 QB Andy Dalton / Marcus Jackson
10 Utah	13 RB J. Turner / A. Brown / Ryan Christian
44 Air Force	10 DL Jerry Hughes
17 Boise State ■	16 DL James Vess
	DL Cody Moore
	DL Matt Panfil
	LB Robert Henson / Daryl Washington
	LB Jason Phillips
	DB Nick Sanders
	DB Rafael Priest
	DB Steven Coleman
	DB Tejay Johnson
	DB Stephen Hodge

RUSHING: Turner 146/577y, Brown 99/547y, Dalton 113/432y
PASSING: Dalton 182-307/2242y, 11TD, 59.3%
  Jackson 35-62/372y, 3TD, 56.5%
RECEIVING: Young 59/988y, Christian 30/321y, Bryant 27/298y
SCORING: Rose Evans (K) 97pts, Turner 66pts, Dalton 48pts

2009 12-1

30 Virginia	14 WR Antoine Hicks
56 Texas State	21 WR Jimmy Young / Ryan Christian
14 Clemson	10 WR Jeremy Kerley / Bart Johnson
39 SMU	14 T Marsh Newhouse
20 Air Force	17 G Kyle Dooley
44 Colorado State	6 C Jake Kirkpatrick
38 BYU	7 G Josh Vernnon / Blaize Foltz
41 UNLV	0 T Marcus Cannon
55 San Diego State	12 TE Evan Frosch / Logan Brock
55 Utah	28 QB Andy Dalton
45 Wyoming	10 TB Joseph Turner / Ed Wesley
51 New Mexico	10 DL Jerry Hughes
10 Boise State ■	17 DL Kelly Griffin
	DL Cory Grant
	DL Wayne Daniels
	LB Daryl Washington
	LB Tank Carder / Tanner Brock
	DB Nick Sanders / Jason Teague
	DB Rafael Priest / Greg McCoy
	DB Tejay Johnson
	DB Alex Ibiloye / Tekerrein Cuba
	DB Tyler Luttrell / Colin Jones

RUSHING: Turner 147/754y, Matthew Tucker (TB) 105/676y,
  Wesley 101/638y, Dalton 116/512y
PASSING: Dalton 199-323/2756y, 23TD, 61.6%
RECEIVING: Kerley 44/532y, Toung 33/517y, Johnson 33/410y
  Christian 24/284y, Hicks 23/478y
SCORING: Ross Evans (K) 106pts, Turner 66pts, Hicks 60pts

2010 13-0

30 Oregon State	21 WR Jeremy Kerley / Skye Dawson
62 Tennessee Tech	7 WR Jimmy Young / Antoine Hicks
45 Baylor	10 WR Josh Boyce / Bart Johnson
41 SMU	24 T Marcus Cannon
27 Colorado State	0 G Kyle Dooley / Spencer Thompson
45 Wyoming	0 C Jake Kirkpatrick
31 BYU	3 G Josh Vernon
38 Air Force	7 T Zach Roth / Jeff Olson
48 UNLV	6 TE Evan Frosch / Logan Brock
47 Utah	7 QB Andy Dalton
40 San Diego State	35 RB Ed Wesley / Matt Tucker
66 New Mexico	17 DL Stansly Maponga / Ross Forrest
21 Wisconsin ■	19 DL Kelly Griffin / D.J. Yendrey
	DL Cory Grant
	DL Wayne Daniels
	LB Tanner Brock
	LB Tank Carder / Kenny Cain
	DB Jason Teague
	DB Greg McCoy / Travaras Battle
	DB Tejay Johnson
	DB Alex Ibiloye / Tekerrein Cuba
	DB Colin Jones / Jurell Thompson

RUSHING: Wesley 166/1078y, Tucker 148/709y,
  Waymon James (RB) 87/513y
PASSING: Dalton 209-316/2857y, 27TD, 66.1%
RECEIVING: Kerley 56/575y, Boyce 34/646y, Young 32/486y
  Johnson 31/419y
SCORING: Ross Evans (K) 101pts, Kerley 72pts, Wesley 66pts

TEXAS TECH

Texas Tech University (Founded 1923)
Lubbock, Texas
Nickname: Red Raiders
Colors: Scarlet and Black
Stadium: Jones Stadium (1947) 53,000
Conference Affiliations: Border (1932-55), Independent (1956-59), Southwest (1960-95), Big Twelve South (1996-present)

CAREER RUSHING YARDS	Attempts	Yards
Byron Hanspard (1994-96)	760	4219
James Gray (1986-89)	742	4066
Ricky Williams (1997-01)	789	3661
Byron Morris (1991-93)	638	3544
Taurean Henderson (2002-05)	577	3241
James Hadnot (1976-79)	532	2794
Larry Isaac (1973-76)	538	2633
Baron Batch (2006, 08-10)	467	2501
Donny Anderson (1963-65)	526	2280
Shannon Woods (2005-08)	401	2249

CAREER PASSING YARDS	Comp.-Att.	Yards
Graham Harrell (2005-08)	1403-2062	15,793
Kliff Kingsbury (1999-02)	1231-1883	12,429
Robert Hall (1990-93)	548-997	7908
Taylor Potts (2007-10)	733-1106	7835
Zebbie Lethridge (1994-97)	519-1070	6789
Billy Joe Tolliver (1985-88)	493-1008	6756
B.J. Symons (2000-03)	554-797	6378
Sonny Cumbie (2001-04)	462-704	5116
Ron Reeves (1978-81)	352-763	4688
Cody Hodges (2002-05)	360-543	4308

CAREER RECEIVING YARDS	Catches	Yards
Michael Crabtree (2007-08)	231	3127
Wes Welker (2000-03)	259	3069
Lloyd Hill (1990-93)	189	3059
Carlos Francis (2000-03)	216	3027
Jarrett Hicks (2003-06)	198	2859
Detron Lewis (2007-10)	238	2729
Nehemiah Glover (2001-04)	223	2725
Joel Filani (2003-06)	175	2667
Mickey Peters (2000-03)	196	2318
Danny Amendola (2004-07)	119	2246

SEASON RUSHING YARDS	Attempts	Yards
Byron Hanspard (1996)	339	2084
Byron Morris (1993)	298	1752
Ricky Williams (1998)	336	1582
James Gray (1989)	263	1509
Byron Hanspard (1995)	248	1374

SEASON PASSING YARDS	Comp.-Att.	Yards
B.J. Symons (2003)	470-719	5833
Graham Harrell (2007)	512-713	5705
Graham Harrell (2008)	442-626	5111
Kliff Kingsbury (2002)	479-712	5017
Sonny Cumbie (2004)	421-642	4742

SEASON RECEIVING YARDS	Catches	Yards
Michael Crabtree (2007)	134	1962
Joel Filani (2006)	91	1300
Lloyd Hill (1992)	76	1261
Danny Amendola (2007)	109	1245
Carlos Francis (2003)	75	1177
Jarrett Hicks (2004)	76	1177

GAME RUSHING YARDS	Attempts	Yards
Byron Hanspard (1996 vs. Baylor)	35	287
James Gray (1989 vs. Duke)	33	280
Byron Hanspard (1996 vs. Oklahoma St.)	32	272

GAME PASSING YARDS	Comp.-Att.	Yards
B.J. Symons (2003 vs. Mississippi)	44-64	661
Graham Harrell (2007 vs. Oklahoma St.)	46-67	646
Cody Hodges (2005 vs. Kansas State)	44-65	643

GAME RECEIVING YARDS	Catches	Yards
Joel Filani (2005 vs. Kansas State)	10	255
Rodney Blackshear (1991 vs. Houston)	5	251
Leonard Harris (1983 vs. Houston)	12	248

GREATEST COACH:

Mike Leach has an unenviable task. Each season he must knock heads with perennial powers Texas and Oklahoma, plus would-be power Texas A&M, to just win the South Division of the Big 12 Conference. Good luck. Despite the reality of underdog status twice each year before the season even begins, Leach has created an atmosphere of winning in Lubbock that could last for a long time. While all of the attention has centered on his pass-happy offense, with good reason, Leach has created a program that is bigger than a collection of passers and pass catchers.

Leach came to Texas Tech from Oklahoma, where in one season he installed his vision of offensive play, as he did previously at Kentucky, featuring an intelligent quarterback reading the defense and then finding any one of a number of receivers open for a short or intermediate pass. They run this dozens of times a game, forcing opponents to cover everyone adequately. Of course with the depth of receiving talent employed by Leach when an assistant or with Texas Tech as head man, he will almost always have a mismatch somewhere.

The results speak for themselves. The Red Raiders have earned a bowl bid in every season since Leach became head coach in 2000. His offense annually challenges for the NCAA passing title, which they have won multiple times, while setting many NCAA, conference and school records. Quarterbacks such as Kliff Kingsbury, B.J. Symons, and Graham Harrell and receivers like Wes Welker, Carlos Francis and two-time Biletnikoff Award-winning wide receiver Michael Crabtree may come and go, but one things is constant: Leach's Red Raiders will win and do so in an exciting fashion.

TEXAS TECH'S 55 GREATEST SINCE 1953

OFFENSE

WIDE RECEIVER: Michael Crabtree, Carlos Francis, Jarrett Hicks, Lloyd Hill, Dave Parks, Wes Welker
TIGHT END: Andre Tillman
TACKLE: Dan Irons, Dan Kaufman, Charles Odiome
GUARD: Don King, Mike Sears, Bill Shaha, Phil Tucker
CENTER: Toby Cecil, Jerry Turner
QUARTERBACK: Joe Barnes, Graham Harrell, Kliff Kingsbury, Billy Joe Tolliver
RUNNING BACK: Donny Anderson, Bobby Cavazos, James Gray, Byron Hanspard, Byron Morris
FULLBACK: Billy Taylor

DEFENSE

END: Bruce Dowdy, Adell Duckett, Aaron Hunt, Montae Reagor
TACKLE: Ecomet Burley, Ronald Byers, Gabriel Rivera, Donald Rives
LINEBACKER: Lawrence Flugence, Brad Hastings, Thomas Howard, Dwayne Jiles, Zach Thomas
CORNERBACK: Carl Carter, Denton Fox, Ken Perkins
SAFETY: Marcus Coleman, Kevin Curtis, Curtis Jordan, Tate Randle, Tracy Saul, Ted Watts

SPECIAL TEAMS

RETURN SPECIALISTS: Tyrone Thurman
PLACE KICKER: Ricky Gann
PUNTER: Maury Buford

MULTIPLE POSITIONS

HALFBACK-WIDE RECEIVER-RETURNMAN: Lawrence Williams
FULLBACK-TIGHT END: James Hadnot

TWO-WAY PLAYERS

TACKLE-DEFENSIVE TACKLE: Jerry Walker
CENTER-LINEBACKER: E.J. Holub

PERFORMANCE FORMULA:
TEXAS TECH'S 10 BEST SEASONS

1953	1.6445	4 of 69
1973	1.6159	9 of 70
2008	1.5466	9 of 71
1976	1.4936	8 of 70
2005	1.3996	18 of 70
1995	1.3817	17 of 70
1954	1.3601	16 of 69
1955	1.3527	18 of 69
1989	1.3318	21 of 70
2009	1.3175	19 of 72

TEXAS TECH RED RAIDERS

Year	W-L-T	AP Poll	Conference Standing	Toughest Regular Season Opponents	Coach (Record at School)	Bowl Games		
1953	11-1	12	1	Oklahoma A&M 7-3, Texas Western 7-2, Miss. St.	DeWitt Weaver	Gator	35 Auburn	13
1954	7-2-1		1	Arizona 7-3, Oklahoma A&M 5-4-1, LSU 5-6	DeWitt Weaver			
1955	7-3-1		1	TCU 9-1, Texas 5-5, Houston 6-4	DeWitt Weaver	Sun	14 Wyoming	21
1956	2-7-1			Texas A&M 9-0-1, Baylor 8-2, TCU 7-3	DeWitt Weaver			
1957	2-8			Texas A&M 8-2, Arkansas 6-4, Oklahoma State 6-3-1	DeWitt Weaver			
1958	3-7			TCU 8-2, Texas 7-3, Tulsa 7-3	DeWitt Weaver			
1959	4-6			TCU 8-2, Arkansas 8-2, SMU 5-4-1	DeWitt Weaver			
1960	3-6-1		6	Arkansas 8-2, Baylor 8-2, Rice 7-3	DeWitt Weaver (49-51-5)			
1961	4-6		6t	Texas 9-1, Arkansas 8-2, Rice 7-3	J.T. King			
1962	1-9		8	Texas 9-0-1, Arkansas 9-1, LSU 8-1-1	J.T. King			
1963	5-5		6t	Texas 10-0, Baylor 7-3, Rice 6-4	J.T. King			
1964	6-4-1		4t	Arkansas 10-0, Texas 9-1, Baylor 5-5	J.T. King	Sun	0 Georgia	7
1965	8-3		2t	Arkansas 10-0, Texas 6-4, TCU 6-4	J.T. King	Gator	21 Georgia Tech	31
1966	4-6		6t	Arkansas 8-2, SMU 8-2, Texas 6-4	J.T. King			
1967	6-4		2	Florida State 7-2-1, Texas 6-4, Texas A&M 6-4	J.T. King			
1968	5-3-2		4	Arkansas 9-1, Texas 8-1-1, SMU 7-3	J.T. King			
1969	5-5		3t	Texas 10-0, Arkansas 9-1, Oklahoma State 5-5	J.T. King (44-45-3)			
1970	8-4		3	Texas 10-0, Arkansas 9-2, Mississippi State 6-5	Jim Carlen	Sun	9 Georgia Tech	17
1971	4-7		7	Texas 8-2, Arkansas 8-2-1, Boston College 9-2	Jim Carlen			
1972	8-4		2t	Texas 9-1, SMU 7-4, TCU 5-6	Jim Carlen	Sun	28 North Carolina	32
1973	11-1	11	2	Texas 8-2, Oklahoma State 5-4-2, Arkansas 5-5-1	Jim Carlen	Gator	28 Tennessee	19
1974	6-4-2		6	Texas 8-3, Texas A&M 8-3, Arizona 9-2	Jim Carlen (37-20-2)	Peach	6 Vanderbilt	6
1975	6-5		4	Texas A&M 10-1, Texas 9-2, Arkansas 9-2	Steve Sloan			
1976	10-2	13	1t	Houston 10-1, Texas A&M 9-2, Colorado 8-3	Steve Sloan	Bluebonnet	24 Nebraska	27
1977	7-5		4t	Texas 11-0, Arkansas 10-1, Texas A&M 8-3	Steve Sloan (23-12)	Tangerine	17 Florida State	40
1978	7-4		4	Southern Cal 10-1, Houston 9-2, Arkansas 9-2	Rex Dockery			
1979	3-6-2		7	Southern Cal 10-0-1, Arkansas 10-1, Houston 10-1	Rex Dockery			
1980	5-6		6t	North Carolina 10-1, Baylor 10-1, SMU 8-3	Rex Dockery (15-16-2)			
1981	1-9-1		9	Texas 9-1-1, SMU 10-1, Washington 9-2	Jerry Moore			
1982	4-7		6t	SMU 10-0-1, Texas 9-2, Washington 9-2	Jerry Moore			
1983	3-7-1		6	Texas 11-0, SMU 10-1, Air Force 9-2	Jerry Moore			
1984	4-7		8	SMU 9-2, Texas 7-3-1, Houston 7-4	Jerry Moore			
1985	4-7		7	Texas A&M 9-2, Arkansas 9-2, Baylor 8-3	Jerry Moore (16-37-2)			
1986	7-5		4	Miami 11-0, Texas A&M 9-2, Arkansas 9-2	David McWilliams (7-4) Spike Dykes [1-0]	Independence	17 Mississippi	20
1987	6-4-1		4	Florida State 10-1, Texas A&M 9-2, Arkansas 8-4	Spike Dykes			
1988	5-6		3	Arkansas 10-1, Oklahoma State 9-2, Texas A&M 7-4	Spike Dykes			
1989	9-3	19	3	Arkansas 10-1, Houston 9-2, Texas A&M 8-3	Spike Dykes	All American	49 Duke	21
1990	4-7		4t	Miami 9-2, Texas 10-1, Houston 10-1	Spike Dykes			
1991	6-5		2t	Texas A&M 10-1, Baylor 8-3, Arkansas 6-5	Spike Dykes			
1992	5-6		2t	Texas A&M 12-0, North Carolina St. 9-2-1, Baylor 6-5	Spike Dykes			
1993	6-6		2t	Nebraska 11-0, Texas A&M 10-1, No. Carolina St. 7-4	Spike Dykes	Sun	10 Oklahoma	41
1994	6-6		1t	Nebraska 12-0, Texas A&M 10-0-1, Texas 7-4	Spike Dykes	Cotton	14 Southern California	55
1995	9-3	23	2t	Penn State 8-3, Texas 9-2-1, Arkansas 8-3	Spike Dykes	Copper	55 Air Force	41
1996	7-5		S2	Nebraska 10-1, Kansas State 9-2, Texas 7-4	Spike Dykes	Alamo	0 Iowa	27
1997	6-5		S2t	Nebraska 11-0, Tennessee 11-0, Kansas State 10-1	Spike Dykes			
1998	7-5		S3	Texas A&M 10-2, Texas 8-3, Missouri 7-4	Spike Dykes	Independence	18 Mississippi	35
1999	6-5		S2t	Texas 9-3, Texas A&M 8-3, Oklahoma 7-4	Spike Dykes (82-67-1)			
2000	7-6		S4	Oklahoma 11-0, Kansas State 10-2, Texas 9-2	Mike Leach	Galleryfurniture	27 East Carolina	40
2001	7-5		S3t	Nebraska 11-1, Texas 10-1, Oklahoma 10-2	Mike Leach	Alamo	16 Iowa	19
2002	9-5		S3t	Ohio State 13-0, Oklahoma 10-2, Texas 10-2	Mike Leach	Tangerine	55 Clemson	15
2003	8-5		S4	Oklahoma 12-0, Texas 10-2, Oklahoma State 9-3	Mike Leach	Houston	38 Navy	14
2004	8-4	18	S3t	Oklahoma 11-0, Texas 10-1, Texas A&M 7-4	Mike Leach	Holiday	45 California	31
2005	9-3	20	S2t	Texas 11-0, Oklahoma 7-4, Colorado 7-4	Mike Leach	Holiday	10 Alabama	13
2006	8-5		S4	Oklahoma 10-2, Texas 9-3, TCU 10-2	Mike Leach	Insight	44 Minnesota	41
2007	9-4	22	S3t	Missouri 11-1, Texas 9-3, Oklahoma 10-2	Mike Leach	Gator	31 Virginia	28
2008	11-2	12	S1t	Nebraska 8-4, Texas 11-1, Oklahoma State 9-3, Oklahoma 12-1	Mike Leach	Cotton	34 Mississippi	47
2009	9-4	21	S3t	Texas 13-0, Houston 10-3, Nebraska 9-4, Oklahoma State 9-3	Mike Leach (84-43) Ruffin McNeill [1-0]	Alamo	41 Michigan State	31
2010	8-5		S4t	Oklahoma State 10-2, Texas A&M 9-3, Oklahoma 11-2	Tommy Tuberville (8-5)	Dallas Classic	45 Northwestern	38

TOTAL: 356-289-14 .5508 (32 of 70) **Bowl Games since 1953:** 11-16-1 .4107 (56 of 70)

GREATEST TEAM SINCE 1953: Although they ended the season on a low note, with a 47-34 loss to Mississippi in the Cotton Bowl, the 2008 edition of the Red Raiders reached loftier heights than previous Texas Tech squads. Led by quarterback Graham Harrell and his favorite target, wide receiver Michael Crabtree, Texas Tech marched through the first half of their schedule with nary a hiccup, reaching the nation's Top Ten by October. But before coach Mike Leach's Red Raiders were to be taken seriously as a contender for the national championship, they would have to negotiate a brutal November stretch that featured consecutive match-ups with the three toughest opponents for them to play: Texas, Oklahoma State and Oklahoma. Top-ranked Texas came to Lubbock with their own sites set on the BCS title game. They left with their first loss after Crabtree's sensational catch-and-run for winning touchdown in game's closing moments. Oklahoma State was then dispatched in a rout and Texas Tech was suddenly and deservedly ranked no. 2 in the country. Alas, the Oklahoma Sooners, playing at home and with far more experience in these types of games, ended the Red Raiders dream in convincing fashion, 65-21.

1953 11-1

40 W. Texas State	14 E Vic Spooner / Dean White
27 Texas Western	6 T Jimmy Williams
27 Oklahoma A&M	13 G Don Gray
14 Texas A&M	27 C Dwayne West
34 Pacific	7 G Arlen Wesley
71 N. Mexico A&M	0 T Jerry Walker
27 Mississippi St.	20 E Paul Erwin / Claude Harland
52 Arizona	27 QB Jack Kirkpatrick / Jerry Johnson
49 Tulsa	7 HB Bobby Cavazos
41 Houston	21 HB Tom Janes / Don Lewis
46 Hardin-Simmons	12 FB James Sides
35 Auburn ■	13

RUSHING: Cavazos 97/747y
PASSING: Kirkpatrick 22-46/343y
RECEIVING: Cavazos 9/116y
SCORING: Cavazos 80pts

1954 7-2-1

41 Texas A&M	9 E Dean White / Don Waygood
33 W. Texas State	7 T Bill Herschman / Minor Nelson
13 Oklahoma A&M	13 G Howard Hurt / Hal Broadfoot
55 Texas Western	28 C Dwayne West / Ralph Martin
13 LSU	20 G Arlen Wesley / Bobby Hunt
7 Pacific	20 T Jerry Walker / Bob Kilcullen
28 Arizona	14 E Claude Harland / Jay Fikes
55 Tulsa	13 QB Jerry Johnson / Jack Kirkpatrick
61 Houston	14 HB Rick Spinks / M.C. Northam
61 Hardin-Simmons	19 HB Ronnie Herr / Walter Bryan
	FB James Sides / Lonnie Graham

RUSHING: Graham 50/457y, Bryan 79/456y, Herr 75/436y
PASSING: Johnson 27-61/569y, 7TD, 44.3%
RECEIVING: White 10/252y, Harland 9/126y, Bryan 6/71y
SCORING: Herr & Bryan 48pts, Spinks (HB-K) 41pts

1955 7-3-1

20 Texas	14 E Don Waygood / Ken Vakey
0 TCU	32 T Bill Hershman / Bob Kilcullen
24 Oklahoma A&M	6 G Hal Broadfoot
27 Texas Western	27 C Dwayne West / Hilton Hayes
0 Houston	7 G Arlen Wesley / Doug Campbell
27 W. Texas State	24 T Minor Nelson / Jerry Walker
27 Arizona	7 E Pat Hartsfield / Jay Fikes
34 Tulsa	7 QB Buddy Hill / Jack Kirkpatrick
13 Pacific	7 HB M.C. Northam / Hugh Fewin
16 Hardin-Simmons	14 HB Don Schmidt / Ronnie Herr
14 Wyoming ■	21 FB James Sides / Lonnie Graham

RUSHING: Schmidt 105/508y, Graham 77/442y, Herr 66/344y
PASSING: Hill 33-60/481y, 2TD, 55%
RECEIVING: Vakey 13/186y, Hartsfield 11/136y, Waygood 6/104y
SCORING: Schmidt 42pts, Herr 30pts, Sides & Northam 24pts

1956 2-7-1

13 Texas Western	17 E Ken Vakey / Dan Law
0 Baylor	27 T Charlie Moore / Cullen Hunt
7 Texas A&M	40 G Hal Broadfoot / Doug Campbell (T)
14 W. Texas State	34 C Jack Henry / Barton Massey
21 Arizona	7 G Ray Howard / Floyd Hood
13 Oklahoma A&M	13 T Phil Williams / Bob Kilcullen
21 TCU	7 E Pat Hartsfield / Bobby Young
7 Tulsa	10 QB Don Williams / Buddy Hill
7 Houston	20 HB Duke Frisbie / Ronnie Herr
14 Hardin-Simmons	41 HB Hugh Fewin / M.C. Northam
	FB Doug Duncan/G. Bentley/Charlie Dixon

RUSHING: Duncan 67/360y, Dixon 45/274y, Bentley 65/267y
PASSING: Hill 24-52/326y, 1TD, 46.2%
RECEIVING: Vakey 14/180y, Young 8/101y, Fewin 8/63y
SCORING: Williams (QB-K) 28pts, Fewin 24pts, Hill 15pts

1957 2-8

0 W. Texas State	19 E Gerald Seeman / Gary Selfridge
0 Texas A&M	21 T Jim Henderson / Bobby Cline
14 LSU	19 G Charlie Moore
14 Texas Western	26 C Jack Henry / Bill Turnbo
12 Baylor	15 G Ed Strickland
28 Arizona	6 T Phil Williams / Jerry Stockton
0 Oklahoma State	13 E Pat Hartsfield / Bob Stafford
0 Tulsa	3 QB Jerry Bell / Floyd Dellinger
26 Hardin-Simmons	21 HB Milton Vaughn / Ronnie Rice
26 Arkansas	47 HB Jimmy Knox
	FB Gene Bentley / Floyd Cole

RUSHING: Rice 67/426y, Knox 78/346y, Bentley 70/249y
PASSING: Bell 37-77/489y, 4TD, 48.1%
RECEIVING: Knox14/201y, Seeman13/162y, Hartsfield 11/150y
SCORING: Bell (QB-K) 31pts, Rice & Knox 24pts

1958 3-7

15 Texas A&M	14 E Bob Witucki
32 W. Texas State	7 T Jim Henderson / Roger Nesbitt
7 Texas	12 G Gerald Seeman (E) / Fred Weaver
0 TCU	26 C E.J. Holub / Bill Turnbo
7 Baylor	26 G Gene Bentley / Jere Don Mohon
0 Tulane	27 T Phil Williams
33 Arizona	6 E Jerry Selfridge / Jim Brock
7 Tulsa	9 QB Jerry Bell / Ken Talkington
8 Arkansas	14 HB Ronnie Rice / Dan Gurley
17 Houston	22 HB Floyd Dellinger / John Roberts
	FB Doug Duncan / Glen Amerson

RUSHING: Rice 67/263y, Dellinger 70/241y, Duncan 60/236y
PASSING: Bell 48-92/435y, 3TD, 52.2%
RECEIVING: Dellinger 20/213y, Witucki 17/223y,Selfridge 12/149y
SCORING: Bell & Dellinger 23pts, Witucki & Seeman 18pts

1959 4-6

20 Texas A&M	14 E Don Waygood / Jim Brock
15 Oregon State	14 T Jerry Selfridge (TE) / Larry Mullins
8 Tulsa	9 G Fred Weaver
8 TCU	14 C E.J. Holub / Bill Turnbo
7 Baylor	14 G Blake Adams / Jere Don Mohon
13 SMU	21 T Bobby Cline / Pat Holmes
7 Tulane	17 E Mike Seay
26 Arizona	30 QB Ken Talkington / Glen Amerson
27 Houston	0 HB Mickie Barron / Ronnie Rice
8 Arkansas	27 SB Dan Gurley / Bake Turner
	FB Dick Stafford / Carl Gatlin

RUSHING: Gatlin 49/211y
PASSING: Talkington 65-116/603y, 6TD, 56%
RECEIVING: Turner 22/444y, Waygood 16/154y, Gurley 13/204y
SCORING: Talkington (QB-K) 45pts, Turner & Gurley 28pts

1960 3-6-1

38 W. Texas State	14 E Don Waygood / Jerry Garrison
14 Texas A&M	14 T Larry Mullins
0 Texas	17 G Charles Edgemon / Ed Strickland
7 TCU	21 C E.J. Holub
7 Baylor	14 G Jere Don Mohon
28 SMU	7 T Tom Pace
6 Rice	30 E Jerry Elbert / Mike Seay
35 Tulane	21 QB Glen Amerson / Johnny Lovelace
7 Wyoming	10 HB Bake Turner / Dan Gurley
6 Arkansas	34 HB Dick Polson
	FB Coolidge Hunt

RUSHING: Hunt 127/527y, Polson 34/187y, Turner 36/150y
PASSING: Amerson 33-80/464y, 5TD, 41.3%
RECEIVING: Polson 13/155y, Waygood 12/129y, Turner 9/173y
SCORING: Amerson (QB-K) & Polson 32pts, Hunt 26pts

1961 4-6

0 Mississippi State	6 E Dave Parks / Jimmy Hacker
14 Texas	42 T Larry Mullins
7 Texas A&M	38 G Kelly Mitchell / Ken Milliken
10 TCU	0 C Jerry Elbert
19 Baylor	17 G Nathan Armstrong
7 SMU	8 T Pat Holmes / Bill Shaha
7 Rice	42 E Bob Witucki / Larry Jones (D)
14 Boston College	6 QB Johnny Lovelace / Doug Cannon
0 Arkansas	28 HB Bill Worley / Bake Turner
16 W. Texas State	14 HB David Rankin / Charles McEntire (D)
	FB Coolidge Hunt / H.L. Daniels

RUSHING: Hunt 128/486y, Lovelace 89/282y, Worley 49/217y
PASSING: Cannon 37-77/442y, TD, 48.1%
RECEIVING: Witucki 26/335y, Parks 16/209y, Hacker 5/60y
SCORING: Daniels (FB-K) 26pts, Hunt 24pts, Rankin 18pts

1962 1-9

27 W. Texas State	30 E Dave Parks / Jerry Don Balch
0 Texas	34 T Nathan Armstrong / Bill Malone
3 Texas A&M	7 G Kelly Mitchell / Richard Willis
13 TCU	35 C C.C. Willis / Jerry Elbert
6 Baylor	28 G Glen Koch / Jimmy Walker
0 SMU	14 T Bill Shaha / Ken Milliken
0 Rice	14 E Charles Gladson / Jerry Garrison
13 Boston College	42 QB Rich Mahan/ J. Lovelace/ L. Jones (D)
21 Colorado	12 HB Bill Worley / Roger Gill
0 Arkansas	34 WB C.W. Williams / David Rankin
	FB Coolidge Hunt / H.L. Daniels

RUSHING: Gill 61/379y, Hunt 80/272y, Worley 48/236y
PASSING: Mahan 26-67/260y, 0TD, 38.8%
RECEIVING: Parks 32/399y, Garrison 11/150y, Balch 6/72y
SCORING: Hunt 24pts, Gill 18pts, Daniels (FB-K) 17pts

1963 5-5

16 Washington St.	7 E Dave Parks / David Rankin
7 Texas	49 T John Porter / Bill McLelland
10 Texas A&M	0 G C.C. Willis / Richard Willis
3 TCU	35 C Reg Scarborough / Butch Thompson
17 Baylor	21 G Bill Shaha / Bill Malone
13 SMU	6 T John Carrell / Jimmy Walker
3 Rice	17 E Tommy Doyle / Jerry Don Balch
51 Kansas State	13 QB Earl Elledge / Jim Ellis / Bill Worley (D)
3 Texas Western	3 HB John Agan / Bill Weise / Roger Gill
20 Arkansas	27 HB Donny Anderson / Bob Yancer (D)
	FB Leo Lowery / Jim Zanios / Ken Gill (D)

RUSHING: Anderson 146/609y, Zanios 53/194y, Weise 38/175y
PASSING: Elledge 39-92/480y, 4TD, 42.4%
RECEIVING: Parks 32/499y, Anderson 15/199y, Doyle 10/113y
SCORING: H.L. Daniels (K) 39pts, Anderson & Parks 24pts

1964 6-4-1

27 Mississippi St.	7 E Jerry Don Balch
0 Texas	23 T John Porter
16 Texas A&M	12 G James Henkel
25 TCU	10 C Reg Scarborough
10 Baylor	28 G James Cecil / Ray Garrett
12 SMU	0 T Chester Howard
6 Rice	6 E Charles Gladson
48 W. Texas State	0 QB Tom Wilson
28 Washington St.	10 HB Johnny Agan
0 Arkansas	10 HB Donny Anderson
0 Georgia ■	7 FB Jim Zanios
	DL Joe Ray Hurley / Tommy Doyle
	DL Marc Bryant
	DL Ronnie Reeger
	DL Samuel Cornelius
	LB John Carrell
	LB James Henkel
	LB C.C. Willis
	LB Butch Thompson
	DB Bob Yancer
	DB Jimmie Don Edwards
	DB Teddy Roberts

RUSHING: Anderson 211/966y, Agan 99/451y, Zanios 94/408y
PASSING: Wilson 65-119/777y, 5TD, 54.6%
RECEIVING: Anderson 32/396y, Agan 12/80y, Balch 11/174y
SCORING: Anderson 42pts, Zanios 30pts, Wilson 24pts

1965 8-3

26 Kansas	7 E Terry Scarborough
7 Texas	33 T John Porter
20 Texas A&M	16 G Phil Tucker / James Cecil
28 TCU	24 C Jerry Turner
17 Oklahoma State	14 G E. Shester Howard
26 SMU	24 T Stan Edwards
27 Rice	0 E Jerry Shipley
28 New Mexico St.	9 QB Tom Wilson
34 Baylor	22 HB Johnny Agan / Mike Leinart
24 Arkansas	42 HB Donny Anderson
21 Georgia Tech ■	31 FB Kenny Baker
	DL Joe Ray Hurley
	DL George Marc Bryant
	DL James Henkel
	DL Mickey Merritt
	DL Pat Knight / Ronnie Pack
	DL Terry McWhorter / Dennis Tucker
	LB Ken Gill / Jim Haney
	LB John Carrell
	DB Bob Yancer
	DB Jimmie Don Edwards
	DB David Lynn Baugh

RUSHING: Anderson 169/705y, Leinart 59/231y, Agan 58/198y
PASSING: Wilson 172-283/2119y, 18TD, 60.8%
RECEIVING: Anderson 60/797y, Shipley 47/563y, Leinart 22/202y
SCORING: Anderson 102pts, Leinart 36pts,Bob Bearden (K) 32pts

1966 4-6

23 Kansas	7 E Larry Gilbert
21 Texas	31 T Stan Edwards
14 Texas A&M	35 G Don King
3 TCU	6 C Jerry Turner
33 Florida State	42 G John Avent / Ronnie Pack
7 SMU	24 T Phil Tucker
35 Rice	19 E Terry Scarborough / Lou Breuer
10 Oklahoma State	7 QB John Scovell
14 Baylor	29 HB Mike Leinart
21 Arkansas	16 HB Roger Freeman / Jerry Lovelace
	FB Kenny Baker
	DL George Cox
	DL Gene Darr
	DL Mickey Merritt / Joe Brown
	DL Doug Young / Jim Moylan
	DL James Henkel
	DL Terry McWhorter / Pat Knight
	LB James Haney / Ed Mooney
	LB Jimmie Don Edwards
	DB Guy Griffis
	DB Hal Hudson / Gary Golden
	DB David Lynn Baugh

RUSHING: Leinart 102/495y, Scovell 112/280y, Freeman 50/220y
PASSING: Scovell 107-232/1323y, 8TD, 46.1%
RECEIVING: Gilbert 52/767y, Leinart 24/165y, Baker 22/277y
SCORING: Scovell 30pts, Kenny Vinyard (K) 27pts, 3 tied w/ 24pts

1967 6-4

52 Iowa State	0 WR Larry Gilbert / Bobby Allen
19 Texas	13 T Stan Edwards
3 Mississippi St.	7 G Phil Tucker
24 Texas A&M	28 C Jerry Turner
12 Florida State	28 G Don King / Ronnie Sowell
21 SMU	7 T Mike Patterson
24 Rice	10 TE Lou Breuer
0 TCU	16 QB John Scovell / Joe Matulich
31 Baylor	29 HB Mike Leinart / Jimmy Bennett
31 Arkansas	27 HB Kenny Baker
	FB Jackie Stewart / Tony Butler
	DL George Cox / Jim Haney /Kevin Oliver
	DL Jim Moylan / Dicky Grigg
	DL Pete Norwood / Joe Brown
	DL Gene Darr / Leon Lovelace
	DL Pat Knight / Floyd Lowery
	LB Ed Mooney
	LB Dennis Lane / Fred Warren
	DB Kevin Ormes / Gary Seat
	DB Ronnie Rhoads
	DB Eddy Windom / Denton Fox
	DB Larry Alford / Gary Golden

RUSHING: Leinart 103/689y, Scovell 107/438y, Baker 84/345y
PASSING: Scovell 44-114/470y, 2TD, 38.6%
RECEIVING: Gilbert 35/491y, Baker 12/99y, Breuer 9/124y
SCORING: Leinart 54pts, Kenny Vinyard (K) 46pts, Scovell 30pts

1968 5-3-2

10 Cincinnati	10 WR Bobby Allen / David May
31 Texas	22 T Mike Holladay
43 Colorado State	13 G Ronnie Sowell / Andy Reed
21 Texas A&M	16 C Jackie Booe
28 Mississippi St.	28 G Don King
18 SMU	39 T Mike Patterson
38 Rice	15 TE Lou Breuer / Charles Evans
31 TCU	14 QB Joe Matulich
28 Baylor	42 HB Jimmy Bennett
7 Arkansas	42 HB Roger Freeman
	FB Tony Butler / Jackie Stewart
	DL Bruce Dowdy
	DL Jim Moylan
	DL Joe Brown
	DL Leon Lovelace
	DL Richard Campbell
	LB Rob Junell / Fred Warren
	LB Dennis Lane
	DB Ronnie Rhoads
	DB Denton Fox
	DB Gary Golden
	DB Kenny Alford

RUSHING: Freeman 129/471y, Stewart 69/321y, Bennett 84/281y
PASSING: Matulich 73-152/864y, 9TD, 48%
RECEIVING: Allen 35/546y, May 19/306y, Freeman 19/149y
SCORING: Freeman 72pts, Kenny Vinyard (K) 48pts, Allen & Evans 24pts

1969 5-5

38 Kansas	22 WR Johnny Odom
7 Texas	49 WR Ken Kattner / David May
10 Oklahoma State	17 T Mike Holladay
13 Texas A&M	9 G David Browning
26 Mississippi St.	30 C Mark Hazelwood
27 SMU	24 G Jesse Richardson
24 Rice	14 T Jerry Ryan / Phil Barney
26 TCU	35 TE Charles Evans
41 Baylor	7 QB Charles Napper / Joe Matulich
0 Arkansas	33 HB Danny Hardaway
	FB Miles Langehennig / Jimmy Bennett
	DL Bruce Dowdy
	DL Wayne McDermand
	DL Pete Norwood
	DL Dickie Grigg
	DL Richard Campbell
	LB Larry Molinare
	LB Dennis Lane
	DB Denton Fox
	DB Jerry Watson
	DB Dale Rebold
	DB John Howard

RUSHING: Hardaway 159/483y, Langehennig 86/336y, Matulich 79/153y
PASSING: Napper 65-153/901y, 5TD, 42.5%
RECEIVING: Odom 23/320y, Evans 20/193y, May 18/340y
SCORING: Jerry Don Sanders (K) 56pts

1970 8-4

21 Tulane	14 WR Johnny Odom
23 Kansas	0 WR Robby Best
13 Texas	35 T David Browning
63 UC S. Barbara	21 G Harold Lyons
21 Texas A&M	7 C Jesse Richardson
16 Mississippi St.	20 G Jerry Ryan
14 SMU	10 T Russell Ingram
3 Rice	0 TE David May
22 TCU	14 QB Charles Napper
7 Baylor	3 HB Larry Hargrave / Miles Langehennig
10 Arkansas	24 FB Doug McCutchen
9 Georgia Tech■	17 DL Bruce Dowdy
	DL Wayne McDermand
	DL Jim Dyer / Donald Rives
	DL Bob Mooney
	DL Harold Hurst / Davis Corley
	LB Larry Molinare
	LB Mike Watkins
	DB Ken Perkins
	DB Marc Dove / Jerry Watson
	DB Bruce Bushong
	DB Dale Rebold

RUSHING: McCutchen 227/1068y, Hargrave 112/553y, Langehennig 90/468y
PASSING: Napper 86-155/979y, 9TD, 55.5%
RECEIVING: Odom 26/331y, Best 24/298y
SCORING: Dickie Ingram (K) 43pts, Langehennig 30pts, Odom & McCutchen 24pts

1971 4-7

9 Tulane	15 WR Johnny Odom / Ronnie Samford
10 New Mexico	13 WR Robby Best / Ronnie Ross
0 Texas	28 T David Browning
13 Arizona	6 G Dennis Allen / Harold Lyons
28 Texas A&M	7 C Russell Ingram / Jon Hill
14 Boston College	6 G Jerry Ryan
17 SMU	18 T Gary Shuler
7 Rice	9 TE Harry Case
6 TCU	17 QB Charles Napper / Jimmy Carmichael
27 Baylor	0 HB James Mosley / Miles Langehennig
0 Arkansas	15 FB Doug McCutchen
	DL Harold Hurst / Andy Lowe
	DL Davis Corley
	DL Donald Rives
	DL Tim Schaffner
	DL Gaines Baty
	LB Larry Molinare
	LB Mike Watkins
	LB Marc Dove
	DB Ken Perkins
	DB Bruce Bushong
	DB Dale Rebold

RUSHING: McCutchen 131/560y, Mosley 101/470y, Langehennig 95/392y
PASSING: Carmichael 38-80/423y, TD, 47.5%
RECEIVING: Odom 20/242y, Samford 13/137y, Ross 11/154y
SCORING: Don Grimes (K) 35pts

1972 8-4

45 Utah	2 WR Calvin Jones
41 New Mexico	16 WR Ronnie Samford
20 Texas	25 T Tom Furguson
35 Tulsa	18 G Dennis Allen
17 Texas A&M	14 C Russell Ingram
35 Arizona	10 G Harold Lyons
17 SMU	3 T Gary Shuler
10 Rice	6 TE Andre Tillman
7 TCU	31 QB Joe Barnes
13 Baylor	7 HB George Smith / Doug McCutchen
14 Arkansas	24 FB James Mosley
28 North Carolina■	32 DL Gaines Baty
	DL Tim Schaffner
	DL Donald Rives
	DL Davis Corley
	DL Aubrey McCain
	LB Quinton Robinson
	LB Tom Ryan
	DB Ken Wallace
	DB Randy Olson
	DB Danny Willis
	DB Greg Waters

RUSHING: Smith 107/740y, McCutchen 138/606y, Barnes 148/510y
PASSING: Barnes 86-168/1142y, 4TD, 51.2%
RECEIVING: Tillman 21/285y, Jones 15/255y, Smith 12/193y
SCORING: Don Grimes (K) 70pts

1973 11-1

29 Utah	22 WR Calvin Jones
41 New Mexico	7 WR Lawrence Williams (HB)
12 Texas	28 T Freddie Chandler
20 Oklahoma State	7 G Dennis Allen
28 Texas A&M	16 C Jim Frasure
31 Arizona	17 G Floyd Keeney
31 SMU	14 T Tom Furguson
19 Rice	6 TE Andre Tillman
24 TCU	10 QB Joe Barnes
55 Baylor	24 HB Larry Isaac / Rufus Myers
24 Arkansas	17 FB James Mosley / John Garner
28 Tennessee■	19 DL Aubrey McCain
	DL Brian Bernwanger
	DL David Knaus
	DL Ecomet Burley
	DL Tommy Cones
	LB Tom Ryan
	LB George Herro
	DB Randy Olson
	DB Kenneth Wallace
	DB Danny Willis
	DB Curtis Jordan

RUSHING: Barnes 135/568y, Isaac 87/526y, Myer 103/374y
PASSING: Barnes 73-125/978y, 58.4%
RECEIVING: Tillman 26/428y
SCORING: Isaac 60pts

1974 6-4-2

24 Iowa State	3 WR Lawrence Williams
21 New Mexico	21 WR Sammy Williams
26 Texas	3 T Floyd Keeney / John Fitzpatrick
14 Oklahoma State	13 G Daylon Byerly
7 Texas A&M	28 C Jim Frasure
17 Arizona	8 G Mike Sears
20 SMU	17 T Tommy Lusk
7 Rice	21 TE Pat Felux
28 TCU	0 QB Tommy Duniven / Don Roberts
10 Baylor	17 HB Larry Isaac
13 Arkansas	21 FB John Garner
6 Vanderbilt■	6 DL Tommy Cones
	DL Kim Bergman / Gary Monroe
	DL David Knaus / Ray Hennig
	DL Ecomet Burley
	DL Thomas Howard
	LB Charlie Beery
	LB Tom Dyer
	DB Tony Green
	DB Selco Ramirez
	DB Randy Olson
	DB Curtis Jordan

RUSHING: Isaac 155/671y, Garner 113/506y, Roberts 93/411y
PASSING: Duniven 43-82/522y, 5TD, 52.4%
RECEIVING: L. Williams 27/477y, Felux 8/83y, S. Williams 7/75y
SCORING: Isaac 48pts, Brian Hall (K) 37pts, L. Williams 36pts

1975 6-5

31 Florida State	20 WR Sammy Williams
24 New Mexico	17 WR Ricky Bates
18 Texas	42 T Dan Irons
16 Oklahoma State	17 G Tommy Lusk
9 Texas A&M	38 C Terry Anderson / David Dudley
28 Arizona	32 G Mike Sears
37 SMU	20 T Greg Davis
28 Rice	24 TE Pat Felux
34 TCU	0 QB Tommy Duniven / Rodney Allison
33 Baylor	10 HB Larry Isaac / Billy Taylor
14 Arkansas	31 FB Jimmy Williams / Rufus Myers
	DL Wesley Schmidt
	DL Ray Hennig
	DL Ecomet Burley
	DL Bill Bothwell
	DL Richard Arledge
	LB Thomas Howard
	LB Harold Buell
	DB Mike Barnes / Eric Felton
	DB Tony Green
	DB Curtis Jordan
	DB Selco Ramirez

RUSHING: Isaac 151/751y, Myers 67/307y, J. Williams 147/622y
PASSING: Duniven 72-125/1038y, 5TD, 57.7%
RECEIVING: S. Williams 34/496y, Isaac 18/191y, Bates 12/256y
SCORING: Brian Hall (K) 48pts, Isaac, Myers & Taylor 30pts

1976 10-2

24 Colorado	7 WR Sammy Williams
20 New Mexico	16 WR Brian Nelson / Godfrey Turner
27 Texas A&M	16 T Greg Davis
37 Rice	13 G Greg Wessels / Kenny Thiel
52 Arizona	27 C Terry Anderson
31 Texas	28 G Mike Sears
14 TCU	10 T Dan Irons
34 SMU	7 TE Sylvester Brown
19 Houston	27 QB Rodney Allison
30 Arkansas	7 HB Larry Isaac
24 Baylor	21 FB Billy Taylor / Jimmy Williams
24 Nebraska■	27 DL Harold Buell
	DL Bill Bothwell
	DL Jim Krahl / Curtis Reed
	DL Richard Arledge
	LB Thomas Howard
	LB Gary McCright
	LB Mike Mock
	DB Eric Felton
	DB Don Roberts
	DB Larry Dupre
	DB Greg Frazier

RUSHING: Isaac 145/685y, Taylor 132/627y, Williams 140/523y
PASSING: Allison 83-139/1458y, 8TD, 59.7%
RECEIVING: S. Williams 32/601y, Isaac 16/165y, Taylor 14/185y
SCORING: Brian Hall (K) 78pts, Allison 60pts, Taylor 50pts

1977 7-5

17 Baylor	7 WR Sammy Williams
29 New Mexico	14 WR Brian Nelson
17 Texas A&M	33 T Ken Walter
10 North Carolina	26 G Greg Wessels
32 Arizona	7 G Joe Walstad / Larry Martin
42 Rice	26 T Dan Irons
0 Texas	17 TE James Hadnot
49 TCU	7 QB Rodney Allison / Tres Adami
45 SMU	45 HB Mark Julian / Mark Johnson
7 Houston	17 FB Billy Taylor
14 Arkansas	40 DL Andrew Thomas / David Hill
17 Florida State■	DL Curtis Reed / Kim Taliaferro
	DL Jim Krahl
	DL Richard Arledge / Olan Tisdale
	LB Gary McCright
	LB Mike Mock
	LB Don Kelly
	DB Larry Dupre
	DB Eric Felton
	DB Larry Flowers / Willie Stephens
	DB Greg Frazier

RUSHING: Taylor 209/931y, Julian 83/337y, Johnson 49/213y
PASSING: Allison 50-83/589y, 5TD, 60.2%
RECEIVING: Taylor 30/186y, Williams 19/318y, Nelson 17/223y
SCORING: Taylor 78pts, Bill Adams (K) 60pts, Johnson 26pts

1978 7-4

9 Southern Cal	17 WR Godfrey Turner
41 Arizona	26 WR Brian Nelson
7 Texas	24 T Ken Walter
9 Texas A&M	38 G Larry Martin
36 New Mexico	23 C Kim Taliaferro
42 Rice	28 G Joe Walsted
27 Baylor	9 T Robert Caughlin
27 TCU	17 TE Mark Harrelson
19 SMU	16 QB Ron Reeves
22 Houston	21 TB Phil Weatherall
7 Arkansas	49 FB James Hadnot
	DL Jim Verden
	DL Curtis Reed / Jamie Giles
	DL David Hill
	LB Roger Jones / Andy Thomas
	LB Jeff McKinney
	LB Don Kelly
	LB Jeff Copeland / Rusty Maroney
	DB Willie Stephens
	DB Alan Swann
	DB Larry Flowers
	DB Johnny Quinney / Ted Watts

RUSHING: Hadnot 251/1369y, Reeves 170/411y, Weatherall 56/313y
PASSING: Reeves 77-161/1195y, 9TD, 47.8%
RECEIVING: Nelson 26/443y, Turner 22/483y, Hadnot 20/152y
SCORING: Bill Adams (K) 74pts, Reeves 48pts, Hadnot 38pts

1979 3-6-2

7 Southern Cal	21 WR Howie Lewis
17 New Mexico	7 WR Edwin Newsome
14 Arizona	14 T Ken Walter
17 Baylor	27 G George Smitherman
21 Texas A&M	20 C Joe Walstad (G) / Denny Harris
6 Arkansas	20 G Larry Martin
30 Rice	7 T Mark Gesch
6 Texas	14 TE L.M. Cummings / Kevin Kolbye
3 TCU	3 QB Ron Reeves / Jim Hart
10 SMU	35 TB Mark Olbert
10 Houston	14 FB James Hadnot
	DL Jim Verden
	DL Gabriel Rivera
	DL David Hill
	LB Jeff McKinney
	LB Lewis Washington / Roger Jones
	LB Jeff Copeland
	LB Johnny Quinney
	DB Larry Flowers
	DB Willie Stephens
	DB Ted Watts
	DB Tate Randle

RUSHING: Hadnot 273/1371y, Reeves 130/363y, Hart 68/151y
PASSING: Reeves 51-120/656y, 6TD, 42.5%
RECEIVING: Lewis 24/317y, Hadnot 10/93y, Cummings 9/79y
SCORING: Bill Adams (K) 61pts, Reeves 24pts, Lewis 18pts

1980 5-6

35 Texas-El Paso	7 WR Jamie Harris
3 North Carolina	9 WR Renie Baker
28 New Mexico	17 T Vic White
3 Baylor	11 G Mark Gesch
21 Texas A&M	41 C Jeff Crombie / Denny Harris
10 Rice	3 G Matt Harlien
24 Texas	20 T Robert Caughlin
17 TCU	24 TE Kevin Kolbye
14 SMU	0 QB Ron Reeves
7 Houston	34 TB Anthony Hutchison / Greg Tyler
16 Arkansas	22 FB Wes Hightower
	DL Jamie Giles
	DL Gabriel Rivera
	DL Dane Kerns / Jim Verden
	LB Jeff McCowan / Lewis Washington
	LB Terry Baer
	LB Jeff McKinney
	LB Stan Williams
	DB Greg Iseral / Ricky Sanders
	DB Jim Hart
	DB Tate Randle
	DB Ted Watts

RUSHING: Hightower 126/515y, Hutchison 84/407y, Tyler 77/323y
PASSING: Reeves 115-228/1461y, 9TD, 50.4%
RECEIVING: Baker 40/625y, Harris 24/368y, Hutchison 11/102y
SCORING: Hightower 36pts, John Greve (K) 27pts, Tyler 24pts

1981 1-9-1

27 Colorado	45 WR Troy Smith
28 New Mexico	21 WR Renie Baker / Bryan Williamson
15 Baylor	28 T Vic White
23 Texas A&M	24 G Blake Feldt
14 Arkansas	26 C Jeff Crombie
23 Rice	30 G George Smitherman
7 Washington	14 T David Joeckel
9 Texas	26 TE Curt Cole
39 TCU	39 QB Ron Reeves
6 SMU	30 TB Anthony Hutchison / Robert Lewis
7 Houston	15 FB Wes Hightower / Freddie Wells
	DL Kenneth Sternes / Van Hughes
	DL Gabe Rivera
	DL Ron Byers / Brad White
	DL C.M. Pier
	LB Stan Williams
	LB Terry Baer
	LB Lewis Washington
	DB Robin Gatewood / Greg Miller
	DB Greg Iseral
	DB Tate Randle
	DB Stan David

RUSHING: Hutchison 100/545y, Lewis 82/319y, Wells 34/199y
PASSING: Reeves 109-254/1376y, 7TD, 42.9%
RECEIVING: Baker 28/453y, Williamson 22/332y, Smith 18/318y
SCORING: Hutchison 36pts, John Greve (K) 35pts, 3 tied w/ 24pts

1982 4-7

0 New Mexico	14 WR Leonard Harris
31 Air Force	30 WR Bryan Williamson
23 Baylor	24 T Matt Harlein
24 Texas A&M	15 G Joe McIntyre
3 Arkansas	21 C David Joeckel
23 Rice	21 G Blake Feldt / Danny Buzzard
3 Washington	10 T Joe Walter / Pat Hrncir
0 Texas	27 TE Buzz Tatom
16 TCU	14 QB Jim Hart
27 SMU	34 TB Anthony Hutchison / Robert Lewis
7 Houston	24 FB Wes Hightower / Gregg Lambert
	DL Jeff McCowan / Wayne Dawson
	DL Gabe Rivera
	DL Ron Byers / Mike Kinsey
	DL Hasson Arbubakrr
	DL Kenneth Sternes
	LB Kerry Tecklenburg
	LB Stan Williams
	DB Greg Iseral
	DB Clay Renfroe / Carl Carter
	DB Stan David
	DB Ricky Sanders / Rusty Roark

RUSHING: Hutchison 204/796y, Lewis 88/369y, Hart 136/215y
PASSING: Hart 107-227/1081y, 7TD, 47.1%
RECEIVING: Harris 30/366y, Tatom 21/247y, Williamson 19/185y
SCORING: Ricky Gann (K) 53pts, Hutchison 30pts, Tatom 24pts

1983 3-7-1

13 Air Force	28 WR Leonard Harris
26 Baylor	11 WR Troy Smith
3 Texas A&M	0 T Joe Walter
10 New Mexico	30 G Danny Buzzard
14 Rice	3 C Jim McIntyre
20 Tulsa	59 G Joe McMeans
3 Texas	20 T Matt Harlien
10 TCU	10 TE Buzz Tatom
7 SMU	33 QB Jim Hart
41 Houston	43 TB Robert Lewis / Timmy Smith
13 Arkansas	16 FB Freddie Wells
	DL Wayne Dawson
	DL Brad White
	DL Ron Byers
	DL David Bowdre
	DL Mike Kinsey / Jeff McCowan
	LB Dwayne Jiles
	LB Kerry Tecklenburg
	DB Carl Carter
	DB Randy Bozeman
	DB Chuck Alexander / Rusty Roark
	DB Stan David

RUSHING: Lewis 175/750y, Smith 94/442y, Hart 103/208y
PASSING: Hart 108-216/1216y, 5TD, 50%
RECEIVING: Harris 35/506y, Tr. Smith 23/243y, Tatom 17/192y
SCORING: Ricky Gann (K) 48pts, Hart 36pts, Harris & Lewis 18pts

1984 4-7

44 UT-Arlington	7 WR Charles Simpson
24 New Mexico	29 WR Troy Smith
9 Baylor	18 T Joe Walter
30 Texas A&M	12 G Aubrey Richburg
0 Arkansas	24 C Jim McIntire / Chris Tanner
30 Rice	10 G Jeff Keith (T) / Joe McMeans
20 Tulsa	17 T Sid Chambers
10 Texas	13 TE Buzz Tatom
16 TCU	27 QB Aaron Keesee
0 SMU	31 TB Timmy Smith / Robert Lewis
17 Houston	24 FB Freddie Wells
	DL Calvin Riggs
	DL Brad White
	DL Ron Byers
	DL Tim Crawford / Larry Mathis
	LB Brad Hastings
	LB Mike Kinsey
	LB Dwayne Jiles
	DB Carl Carter
	DB Roland Mitchell
	DB Merv Scurlark
	DB Leonard Jones

RUSHING: Smith 164/711y, Wells 110/614y, Lewis 74/268y
PASSING: Keesee 70-140/755y, 6TD, 50%
RECEIVING: Tatom 20/312y, Wells 20/111y, Tr. Smith 19/252y
SCORING: Ricky Gann (K) 68pts, Ti. Smith 24pts,
  Lewis & Tr. Smith 18pts

1985 4-7

32 New Mexico	31 WR Wayne Walker
21 Tulsa	17 WR Eddy Anderson
28 N. Texas State	7 T Aubrey Richburg
0 Baylor	31 G Jeff Keith
27 Texas A&M	28 C Chris Tanner
0 Arkansas	31 G Sid Chambers / Mike McBride
27 Rice	29 T Jesse Smith
21 Texas	34 TE Ricky Boysaw
63 TCU	7 QB Billy Joe Tolliver / Aaron Keesee
7 SMU	9 TB Ansel Cole / Ervin Farris
16 Houston	17 FB James McGowen / Isaac Garnett
	DL Tim Crawford
	DL Artis Jackson / Danny Schwertner
	DL Scott Davis
	DL Calvin Riggs / Larry Mathis
	LB Mike Kinsey
	LB Brad Hastings
	LB James Johnson / Michael Johnson
	DB Carl Carter
	DB Roland Mitchell
	DB King Simmons
	DB Leonard Jones

RUSHING: McGowen 107/479y, Garnett 72/272y, Cole 46/223y
PASSING: Tolliver 61-124/863y, 7TD, 49.2%
  Keeser 48-123/720y, 3TD, 39%
RECEIVING: Walker 26/447y, Anderson 12/162y, Farris 12/130y
SCORING: Marc Mallery (K) 43pts, Cole 36pts,
  Farris & Smith 24pts

1986 7-5

41 Kansas State	7 WR Wayne Walker
11 Miami	61 WR Eddy Anderson
14 New Mexico	7 T David Stickels
14 Baylor	45 G Jeff Keith
8 Texas A&M	45 C Chris Tanner
17 Arkansas	7 G Mike McBride
49 Rice	21 T Aubrey Richburg
23 Texas	21 TE Travis Price / Tim Tannehill
36 TCU	14 QB Billy Joe Tolliver
7 SMU	13 IB James Gray / Ervin Fariss
34 Houston	7 FB Isaac Garnett
17 Mississippi■	20 DL Calvin Riggs / Terry Lynch
	DL Desmond Royal / Danny Schwertner
	DL Artis Jackson
	DL Ricky Boysaw / James Mosley
	LB James Johnson / Gary Warren
	LB Michael Johnson
	LB Brad Hastings
	DB Roland Mitchell
	DB Leonard Jones
	DB Merv Scurlark / Boyd Cowan
	DB Eric Everett

RUSHING: Gray 108/613y, Garnett 102/554y, Farris 119/533y
PASSING: Tolliver 145-333/1602y, 4TD, 43.5%
RECEIVING: Walker 38/717y, Anderson 37/402y, Price 21/236y
SCORING: Scott Segrist (K) 64pts, Walker 38pts, Farris 36pts

1987 6-4-1

16 Florida State	40 WR Eddy Anderson
33 Colorado State	24 WR Wayne Walker
43 Lamar	14 T Charles Odiorne / Tommy Webb
22 Baylor	36 G Mike McBride
27 Texas A&M	21 C Bryan Lee
0 Arkansas	31 G Jeff Keith
59 Rice	7 T David Stickels
42 Tulsa	7 TE Phil Young
27 Texas	41 QB Billy Joe Tolliver
36 TCU	35 IB James Gray
10 Houston	10 FB Ervin Farris / Cliff Winston
	DL James Mosley
	DL Desmond Royal / Troy Henington
	DL Artis Jackson
	DL Ricky Boysaw / Terry Lynch
	LB Michael Johnson
	LB Tony Durden
	LB Brian Rollins
	DB Lemuel Stinson
	DB Eric Everett
	DB Boyd Cowan
	DB Donald Harris

RUSHING: Gray 199/1006y, Winston 87/514y, Farris 67/351y
PASSING: Tolliver 97-196/1422y, 7TD, 49.5%
RECEIVING: Walker 32/659y, Anderson 30/449y, Gray 20/171y
SCORING: Gray 78pts, Scott Segrist (K) 73pts,
  Walker & Garnett 30pts

1988 5-6

24 North Texas	29 WR Eddy Anderson / Wayne Walker
19 Arizona	35 WR Tyrone Thurman
36 Baylor	6 T Charles Odiorne
15 Texas A&M	50 G Chris Shafer
10 Arkansas	31 C Len Wright
38 Rice	36 G Nathan Richburg
33 Texas	32 T Tommy Webb / Jessie Hurst
23 TCU	10 TE Charles Lott / Kevin Sprinkles
59 Lamar	28 QB Billy Joe Tolliver
29 Houston	30 IB James Gray / Cliff Winston
42 Oklahoma State	45 FB Ervin Farris
	DL Terry Lynch / John Elliott
	DL Charles Perry
	DL Desmond Royal
	DL Tom Mathiasmeier
	LB Dal Watson / Charles Rowe
	LB Mike Derryberry
	LB James Mosley
	DB Sammy Walker / Dean Marusak
	DB Merv Scurlark
	DB Boyd Cowan
	DB Donald Harris

RUSHING: Gray 172/978y, Winston 71/338y, Farris 52/260y
PASSING: Tolliver 190-354/2869y, 20TD, 53.7%
RECEIVING: Thurman 48/726y, Farris 39/537y, Gray 27/351y
SCORING: Gray 90pts, Scott Segrist (K) 78pts,
  Farris & Thurman 30pts

1989 9-3

24 Arizona	14 WR Travis Price
27 New Mexico	20 WR Anthony Manyweather
31 Oklahoma State	15 T Charles Odiorne
15 Baylor	29 G Nathan Richburg / Jason Duvall
27 Texas A&M	24 C Len Wright
13 Arkansas	45 G Arcadio Saenz
41 Rice	25 T Tommy Webb
24 Texas	17 TE Kevin Sprinkles
37 TCU	7 QB Jamie Gill
48 SMU	24 IB James Gray / Anthony Lynn
24 Houston	40 FB Cliff Winston / Louis Sheffield
49 Duke■	21 DL Marcus Washington
	DL Troy Henington
	DL Charles Perry
	DL Tom Mathiasmeier
	LB Stephon Weatherspoon
	LB Matt Wingo
	LB Charles Rowe
	DB Sammy Walker
	DB Ronald Ferguson
	DB Brian Dubiski
	DB Tracy Saul / David McFarland

RUSHING: Gray 263/1509y, Lynn 124/568y, Winston 50/275y
PASSING: Gill 105-186/1464y, 12TD, 56.5%
RECEIVING: Price 23/389y, Sprinkles 15/249y, Sheffield 13/211y
SCORING: Gray 120pts, Lin Elliott (K) 61pts, Lynn 38pts

1990 4-7

10 Ohio State	17 WR Rodney Blackshear / Anthony Stinnett
35 Houston	51 WR Anthony Manyweather / Lloyd Hill
34 New Mexico	32 T Bill DuBose
15 Baylor	21 G Jason Duvall
24 Texas A&M	28 C Brad Elam / Brent Barton
47 Arkansas	44 G Bingo Mancillas / Peter Allen
21 Rice	42 T Charlie Biggurs
10 Miami	45 TE Jeff Hulme
22 Texas	41 QB Jamie Gill / Robert Hall
40 TCU	28 IB Anthony Lynn / Donald Marshall
62 SMU	7 FB Shane Sears / Louis Sheffield
	DL Marcus Washington
	DL Greg Burden / Fred Petty
	DL Brad Phelps / Jon Wood
	DL Mike Liscio
	LB Charles Rowe
	LB Matt Wingo
	LB Stephon Weatherspoon
	DB Sammy Walker
	DB Ronald Ferguson / Tony Brown
	DB Brian Dubiski
	DB Tracy Saul

RUSHING: Lynn 224/884y, Marshall 45/230y, Sheffield 37/111y
PASSING: Hall 110-217/1581y, 7TD, 50.7%
RECEIVING: Blackshear 44/973y, Manyweather 25/355y,
  Hill 23/363y
SCORING: Lin Elliott (K) 74pts, Blackshear 60pts, Lynn 56pts

1991 6-5

41 Cal St. Fullerton	7 WR Rodney Blackshear / Lloyd Hill
13 Oregon	28 WR Anthony Stinnett
17 Wyoming	22 T Stacey Petrich
16 TCU	30 G Jason Duvall
14 Texas A&M	37 C Scott Fitzgerald / Brad Elam
38 SMU	14 G Stance Labaj / Bingo Mancillas
40 Rice	20 T Charlie Biggurs
15 Texas	23 TE Don Hasley / Jeff Hulme
38 Arkansas	21 QB Robert Hall / Jamie Gill
31 Baylor	24 IB Anthony Lynn / Bam Morris
52 Houston	46 FB Anthony McDowell / Louis Sheffield
	DL Shawn Jackson / Brad Phelps
	DL Fred Petty
	DL Harry Dyas / Kevin Jackson
	LB Ben Kirkpatrick
	LB Steve Carr / Bryan Gerlich
	LB Matt Wingo
	LB Mike Liscio
	DB Donny Brooks
	DB Anthony Wiley / Tony Brown
	DB Tracy Saul
	DB Brian Dubiski

RUSHING: Morris 98/514y, Lynn 133/459y, Hall 91/278y
PASSING: Hall 111-220/1788y, 10TD, 50.5%
RECEIVING: Hill 33/641y, Blackshear 30/649y, Stinnett 26/344y
SCORING: Lin Elliott (K) 85pts, Hall & Blackshear 36pts

1992 5-6

9 Oklahoma	34 WR Lloyd Hill
49 Wyoming	32 WR Derrell Mitchell / Donald Marshall
13 Oregon	16 T Stacey Petrich
36 Baylor	17 G Pete Allen / Scott Fitzgerald
17 Texas A&M	19 C Brad Elam
13 N. Carolina St.	48 G Stance Labaj
39 SMU	25 T Charlie Biggurs
33 Texas	44 TE Scott Aylor / Don Hasley
3 Rice	34 QB Robert Hall / Jason Clemmons
31 TCU	28 IB Bam Morris
44 Houston	35 FB Bruce Hill
	DL Harry Dyas / John Pitts
	DL Steve Hoffman / Stephen Gaines
	DL Shawn Jackson
	LB Mike Liscio
	LB Brady Field / Shawn Banks
	LB Quincy White / Anthony Armour
	LB Ben Kirkpatrick
	DB Anthony Wiley / Chris Kenney
	DB Donny Brooks
	DB Tracy Saul
	DB Bart Thomas / Marcus Coleman

RUSHING: Morris 242/1279y, Hill 60/288y,
  Claskel Freeman (IB) 54/187y
PASSING: Hall 111-219/1645y, 10TD, 50.7%
RECEIVING: Hill 76/1261y, Mitchell 43/624y, Marshall 18/229y
SCORING: Hill 72pts, Jon Davis (K) 69pts, Morris 62pts

1993 6-6

55 Pacific	7 WR Lloyd Hill
27 Nebraska	50 WR Derrel Mitchell
37 Georgia	52 T Stacey Petrich
26 Baylor	28 G Scott Fitzgerald / Bingo Mancillas
6 Texas A&M	31 C Brad Elam
34 N. Carolina St.	36 G Peter Allen
45 Rice	16 T Jeff Wood / Ronnie Seals
31 Texas	22 TE Scott Aylor
49 TCU	21 QB Robert Hall
41 SMU	24 TB Bam Morris
58 Houston	7 FB Bruce Hill
10 Oklahoma■	41 DL Byron Wright
	DL Shawn Jackson
	DL Stephen Gaines
	DL Damon Wickware
	LB Anthony Armour
	LB Zach Thomas
	LB Shawn Banks
	DB Cat Adams / Anthony Wiley
	DB Shawn Hurd / Donny Brooks
	DB Dewayne Bryant
	DB Marcus Coleman

RUSHING: Morris 298/1752y
PASSING: Hall 216-341/2894y, 21TD, 63.3%
RECEIVING: Hill 57/794y, Mitchell 688y
SCORING: Morris 134pts, Jon Davis (K) 84pts

1994 6-6

37 New Mexico	31 WR Sheldon Bass
16 Nebraska	42 WR Stacy Mitchell
11 Oklahoma	17 T Ben Kaufman
35 SMU	7 G Casey Jones
17 Texas A&M	23 C Scott Fitzgerald
21 Rice	24 G Robert Rivera / Ed Hendrix
38 Baylor	7 T Jeff Wood
33 Texas	9 TE Scott Aylor
39 SW Louisiana	7 QB Zebbie Lethridge / Tony Darden
34 Houston	0 TB Byron Hanspard / Alton Crain
21 TCU	24 FB Todd Walker / Rod Hobbs
14 Southern Cal■	55 DL Jabbar Thomas
	DL Damon Wickware
	DL Chris Ori
	DL Byron Wright / Tony Daniels
	LB Robert Johnson
	LB Zach Thomas
	LB Shawn Banks
	DB Cat Adams / Verone McKinley
	DB Shawn Hurd
	DB Bart Thomas
	DB Marcus Coleman

RUSHING: Hanspard 173/761y
PASSING: Lethridge 132-261/1596y, 12TD, 50.6%
RECEIVING: Bass 34/400y
SCORING: Jon Davis (K) 55pts

1995 9-3

23 Penn State	24 WR Stacy Mitchell / Tony Darden
41 Missouri	14 WR Field Scovell
7 Baylor	9 T Ben Kaufman
14 Texas A&M	7 G Casey Jones
63 Arkansas State	25 C Kevin Ward / Jay Pugh
31 Rice	26 G Ed Hendrix
34 New Mexico	7 T Lynn Scherler / Chris Whitney
7 Texas	48 TE Jerrod Fiebiger
27 TCU	6 QB Zebbie Lethridge
45 SMU	14 TB Byron Hanspard
38 Houston	26 FB Rod Hobbs / Todd Walker
55 Air Force■	41 DL Monte Reagor / Sean Johnson
	DL Corey Chandler
	DL Cody McGuire
	DL Anthony Armour / Allen Wallace
	LB Robert Johnson
	LB Zach Thomas
	LB Shawn Banks
	DB Shawn Hurd
	DB Verone McKinley
	DB Dane Johnson
	DB Marcus Coleman

RUSHING: Hanspard 248/1374y
PASSING: Lethridge 136-281/1885y, 13TD, 48.4%
RECEIVING: Hanspard 35/474y,
SCORING: Hanspard 108pts, Tony Rogers (K) 70pts,
　Lethridge 54pts

1996 7-5

14 Kansas State	21 WR Donnie Hart / Malcolm McKenzie
31 Oklahoma State	3 WR Field Scovell
12 Georgia	15 T Ben Kaufman
58 Utah State	20 G Chris Whitney / Corey Jones
45 Baylor	24 C Jay Pugh
30 Kansas	17 G Shane Dunn
10 Nebraska	24 T Lynn Scherler
13 Texas A&M	10 TE Kyle Allamon / Brad Spinks
32 Texas	38 QB Zebbie Lethridge
56 SW Louisiana	21 TB Byron Hanspard
22 Oklahoma	12 FB Ryan Jones / Sammy Morris
0 Iowa■	27 DL Monte Reagor
	DL Cody McGuire
	DL John Abendschan / Corey Chandler
	DL Tony Daniels / Taurus Rucker
	LB Robert Johnson
	LB Eric Butler / Kevin McCullar
	LB Ryan Donahue / Anthony Armour
	DB Tony Darden / Duane Price
	DB Corey Turner
	DB Dane Johnson
	DB Jody Brown

RUSHING: Hanspard 339/2084y, Lethridge 130/342y,
　Adrian Ervin (TB) 35/280y
PASSING: Lethridge 117-267/1686y, 11TD, 43.6%
RECEIVING: Hart 22/494y, McKenzie 21/227y, Hanspard 17/192y
SCORING: Hanspard 84pts, Jaret Greaser (K) 64pts,
　Lethridge 44pts

1997 6-5

17 Tennessee	52 WR Donnie Hart
59 SW Louisiana	14 WR Malcolm McKenzie / Derek Dorris
27 North Texas	30 T Jonathan Gray
35 Baylor	14 G Jayson Hanson / Curtis Lowery
17 Kansas	7 C Jay Pugh
0 Nebraska	29 G Chris Whitney / Erik Carruth
16 Texas A&M	13 T Justin Collingsworth
2 Kansas State	13 TE Tim Winn / Kyle Allamon
24 Texas	10 QB Zebbie Lethridge
27 Oklahoma State	3 TB Ricky Williams
21 Oklahoma	32 FB Jonathan Hawkins
	DL Montae Reagor
	DL Stoney Garland
	DL Cody McGuire
	DL Taurus Rucker / Devin Lemons
	LB Ty Ardoin / Tim Duffie
	LB Eric Butler / Kyle Shipley
	LB Kevin McCullar / Rob Cartwright
	DB Darwin Brown
	DB Tony Darden
	DB Dane Johnson / John Norman
	DB Duane Price / Reagan Bownds

RUSHING: Williams 201/894y, Hawkins 51/208y,
　Lethridge 107/133y
PASSING: Lethridge 134-261/1622y, 6TD, 51.3%
RECEIVING: McKenzie 42/462y, Hart 41/609y, Hawkins 11/97y
SCORING: Lethridge 44pts, Tony Rogers (K) 34pts,
　Jaret Greaser (K) 31pts

1998 7-5

35 Texas-El Paso	3 WR Donnie Hart
30 North Texas	0 WR Derek Dorris
34 Fresno State	28 T Jonathan Gray
3 Iowa State	24 G Curtis Lowery / John DePasquale
31 Baylor	29 C Robert Haddon / Kyle Sanders
24 Oklahoma St.	17 G Erik Carruth
17 Colorado	19 T Steve McFadden / Justin Collingsworth
10 Texas A&M	17 TE Kyle Allaman / Tim Winn
26 Missouri	28 QB Rob Peters / Matt Tittle
42 Texas	35 TB Ricky Williams
17 Oklahoma	20 FB Jonathan Hawkins
18 Mississippi■	35 DL Monte Reagor
	DL Cody Patton / Jason Jones
	DL Kris Kocurek
	DL Taurus Rucker / Devin Lemons.
	LB Ty Ardoin / Dorian Pitts
	LB Kyle Shipley
	LB Kevin McCullar / Tim Duffie
	DB Darwin Brown
	DB Oscar Solis
	DB John Norman / Kevin Curtis
	DB Reagan Bownds / Keith Cockrum

RUSHING: Williams 306/1582y, Rickey Hunter (TB) 59/262y
PASSING: Peters 96-183/1269y, 9TD, 52.5%
RECEIVING: Hart 48/871y, Dorris 28/395y, Hawkins 21/252y
SCORING: Williams 78pts, Chris Birkholz (K) 71pts, Hart 42pts

1999 6-5

13 Arizona State	31 WR Tim Baker / Dee Jackson
38 La-Lafayette	17 WR Derek Dorris / Darrell Jones
14 North Texas	21 T Rex Richards / Matt Heider
21 Texas A&M	19 G Curtis Lowery
21 Oklahoma State	41 C Kyle Sanders
31 Colorado	10 G Jason May / Paul Erickson
35 Baylor	7 T Jonathan Gray
7 Missouri	34 TE Kyle Allaman / Tim Winn
28 Iowa State	16 QB Rob Peters
7 Texas	58 TB Ricky Williams
38 Oklahoma	28 FB Sammy Morris
	DL Devin Lemons / Aaron Hunt
	DL Robert Wyatt / Lamont Anderson
	DL Kris Kocurek
	DL Taurus Rucker
	LB Keith Cockrum / Jonathan Hawkins
	LB Kyle Shipley
	LB Tim Duffie
	LB Reagan Bownds / John Norman
	DB Anthony Malbrough / Antwan Alexander
	DB Oscar Solis
	DB Kevin Curtis / Mark Washington

RUSHING: Williams 112/658y, Morris 140/562y,
　James Easterling (TB) 63/263y
PASSING: Peters 105-211/1437y, 9TD, 49.8%
RECEIVING: Morris 23/386y, Baker 22/370y, Dorris 19/285y
SCORING: Chris Birkholz (K) 51pts, Williams 42pts, Morris 32pts

2000 7-6

24 New Mexico	3 WR Derek Dorris
38 Utah State	16 WR Darrell Jones / Carlos Francis
13 North Texas	7 WR/RB Tim Baker / Shaud Williams
26 La.-Lafayette	0 T Paul Erickson / John DePasquale
15 Texas A&M	33 G Matt Heider / Lance Williams
28 Baylor	0 C Toby Cecil / Kyle Sanders
3 Nebraska	56 G Casey Keck
23 Kansas State	28 T Rex Richards
45 Kansas	39 TE Cole Roberts / Mickey Peters
17 Texas	29 QB Kliff Kingsbury
58 Oklahoma State	0 RB Ricky Williams
27 East Carolina■	27 DL Aaron Hunt
	40 DL Kris Kocurek
	DL Robert Wyatt
	DL Devin Lemons
	LB Dorian Pitts
	LB Lawrence Flugence
	LB John Norman
	DB Antwan Alexander / Paul McClendon
	DB Derrick Briggs
	DB Mark Washington
	DB Kevin Curtis

RUSHING: R. Williams 127/421y, S. Williams 55/223y
PASSING: Kingsbury 362-585/3418y, 21TD, 61.9%
RECEIVING: Baker 69/765y, Dorris 56/574y, R. Williams 52/228y
SCORING: Chris Birkholz (K) 71pts, Dorris 54pts,
　R. Williams 42pts

2001 7-5

42 New Mexico	30 WR Wes Welker
42 North Texas	14 WR Cole Roberts / Mickey Peters
7 Texas	42 WR Anton Paige / Nehemiah Glover
31 Kansas	34 WR/RB Carlos Francis / Preston Hartfield
38 Kansas State	19 T Paul Erickson / Daniel Loper
31 Nebraska	41 G Matt Heider / Dylan Gandy
63 Baylor	9 C Toby Cecil
12 Texas A&M	0 G Rex Richards
49 Oklahoma State	30 T Casey Keck / Jason May
13 Oklahoma	30 QB Kliff Kingsbury
58 Stephen F. Austin	3 RB Ricky Williams
16 Iowa■	19 DL Rodney McKinney
	DL Lamont Anderson
	DL Clayton Harmon / Robert Wyatt
	DL Aaron Hunt
	LB Mike Smith / Toby Shain
	LB Lawrence Flugence
	LB Jonathan Hawkins
	DB Ricky Sailor / C.J. Johnson
	DB Joselio Hanson
	DB Ryan Aycock / Paul McClendon
	DB Kevin Curtis

RUSHING: Williams 142/726y, Welker 15/97y
PASSING: Kingsbury 365-529/3502y, 25TD, 69%
RECEIVING: Williams 92/617y, Peters 51/569y, Francis 50/703y
SCORING: Williams 108pts, Robert Treece (K) 79pts,
　Welker 36pts

2002 9-5
21 Ohio State	45 WR Wes Welker (RB)
24 SMU	14 WR Mickey Peters
42 Mississippi	28 WR Carlos Francis
48 N. Carolina St.	51 WR Nehemiah Glover
49 New Mexico	0 T Daniel Loper
48 Texas A&M	47 G Toby Cecil / Dylan Gandy
17 Iowa State	31 C Casey Keck
52 Missouri	38 G Rex Richards
13 Colorado	37 T E.J. Whitley
62 Baylor	11 QB Kliff Kingsbury
49 Oklahoma State	24 RB Tarean Henderson / Jay Munlin
42 Texas	38 DL Adell Duckett / Rodney McKinney
15 Oklahoma	60 DL Lamont Anderson
55 Clemson■	15 DL Josh Page
	DL Aaron Hunt / Marquis Turner
	LB Mike Smith / Geremy Woods
	LB Lawrence Flugence
	LB John Saldi / Jason Wesley
	DB Ricky Sailor
	DB Joselio Hanson
	DB Raymond Pierce / Vince Meeks
	DB Ryan Aycock

RUSHING: Henderson 153/793y, Munlin 54/254y, Welker 31/244y
PASSING: Kingsbury 479-712/5017y, 45TD, 67.3%
RECEIVING: Henderson 98/613y, Welker 86/1054y, Peters 64/749y
SCORING: Robert Treece (K) 93pts, Henderson 78pts, Welker & Glover 60pts

2003 8-5
58 SMU	10 WR Carlos Francis
42 New Mexico	28 WR Nehemiah Glover / Jarrett Hicks
21 N. Carolina St.	49 WR Wes Welker / Clay McGuire
49 Mississippi	45 T Daniel Looper
59 Texas A&M	28 G Cody Campbell / Dylan Gandy
52 Iowa State	21 C Toby Cecil
49 Oklahoma State	51 G Manuel Ramirez
31 Missouri	62 T E.J. Whitley (G) / Casey Keck
26 Colorado	21 TE Mickey Peters / Joey Hawkins
62 Baylor	14 QB B.J. Symons
40 Texas	43 RB Taurean Henderson / Johnnie Mack
25 Oklahoma	56 DL Adell Duckett / Seth Nitschmann
38 Navy■	14 DL Fred Thrweatt / Pat Majondo-Mwamba
	DL Ken Scott / Chris Hudler
	DL Gathan McGinnis
	LB Mike Smith / Fletcher Session
	LB Brock Stratton
	LB John Saldi
	DB Chad Johnson
	DB Marcus Boyd / Jabari Smith
	DB Vincent Meeks / Byron Johnson
	DB Ryan Aycock

RUSHING: Henderson 124/736y, Mack 42/307y, Welker 27/146y
PASSING: Symons 470-719/5833y, 52TD, 65.4%
RECEIVING: Welker 97/1099y, Peters 78/975y, Henderson 78/611y
SCORING: Henderson 96pts, Keith Toogood (K) 90pts, Welker & Peters 72pts

2004 8-4
27 SMU	13 WR Jarrett Hicks
24 New Mexico	27 WR Cody Fuller
70 TCU	35 WR Trey Haverty / Danny Amendola
31 Kansas	30 WR/RB Nehemiah Glover / Clay McGuire
13 Oklahoma	28 T Dan Loper
70 Nebraska	10 G Cody Campbell
21 Texas	51 C Dylan Gandy
35 Kansas State	25 G Manuel Ramirez
42 Baylor	17 T E.J. Whitley
25 Texas A&M	32 QB Sonny Cumbie
31 Oklahoma State	15 RB Taurean Henderson / Johnnie Mack
45 California■	31 DL Seth Nitschmann
	DL Chris Hudler
	DL Ken Scott / Deke Bake
	DL Adell Duckett / Keyunta Dawson
	LB Mike Smith
	LB Brock Stratton
	LB John Saldi / Fletcher Session
	DB Antonio Huffman
	DB Khalid Naziruddin
	DB Vincent Meeks
	DB Chad Johnson / Josh Rangel

RUSHING: Henderson 162/840y, Mack 57/328y
PASSING: Cumbie 421-642/4742y, 33TD, 65.5%
RECEIVING: Haverty 77/1019y, Hicks 76/1177y, Glover 62/660y
SCORING: Henderson 108pts, Hicks 80pts, Alex Trlica (K) 76pts

2005 9-3
56 Fla. International	3 WR Jarrett Hicks
80 Sam Houston St.	21 WR R. Johnson/Bristol Olomua(TE)
63 Indiana State	7 WR Joel Filani
30 Kansas	17 WR Danny Amendola / L. A. Reed
34 Nebraska	31 T Glenn January
59 Kansas State	20 G E.J. Whitley (T) / Bryan Kegans
17 Texas	52 C Brandon Jones
28 Baylor	0 G Manuel Ramirez
56 Texas A&M	17 T Gabe Hall
17 Oklahoma State	24 QB Cody Hodges
23 Oklahoma	21 RB Taurean Henderson
10 Alabama■	13 DL Randall Cherry/B. Bischofberger
	DL Chris Hudler
	DL Ken Scott / McKinner Dixon
	DL Keyunta Dawson
	LB John Saldi
	LB Fletcher Session
	LB Sylvester Brinkley
	DB Antonio Huffman / Chris Parker
	DB Khalid Naziruddin
	DB Dwayne Slay
	DB Vincent Meeks / Joe Garcia

RUSHING: Henderson 148/872y, Hodges 109/191y, Shannon Woods (RB) 24/168y
PASSING: Hodges 353-531/4238y, 31TD, 66.5%
RECEIVING: Johnson 67/951y, Henderson 67/528y, Filani 65/1048y
SCORING: Henderson 132pts, Alex Trlica (K) 99pts, Hicks 60pts

2006 8-5
35 SMU	3 WR Danny Amendola / L. A. Reed
38 Texas-El Paso	35 WR Joel Filani
3 TCU	12 WR Jarrett Hicks / Todd Walker
62 S.E. Louisiana	0 WR Robert Johnson / Grant Walker
31 Texas A&M	27 T Glenn January
31 Missouri	38 G Louis Vasquez / Ofa Mohetau
6 Colorado	30 C Brandon Jones
42 Iowa State	26 G Manuel Ramirez / Brandon Carter
31 Texas	35 T Gabe Hall
55 Baylor	21 QB Graham Harrell
24 Oklahoma	34 RB Shannon Woods
30 Oklahoma State	24 DL Keyunta Dawson
44 Minnesota■	41 DL Chris Hudler
	DL Dek Bake / Ken Scott
	DL Jake Ratliff / Seth Nitschmann
	LB Kellen Tillman / Brent Slaughter
	LB Brock Stratton
	LB Fletcher Session / Paul Williams
	DB Antonio Huffman
	DB Chris Parker / Marcus Bunton
	DB Darcel McBath
	DB Joe Garcia

RUSHING: Woods 152/926y
PASSING: Harrell 412-617/4555y, 38TD, 66.8%
RECEIVING: Filani 91/1300y, Johnson 89/871y, Woods 75/572y
SCORING: Alex Trlica (K) 96pts, Filani 78pts, Woods 72pts

2007 9-4
49 SMU	9 WR Eric Morris
45 UTEP	31 WR Danny Amendola
59 Rice	24 WR Edward Britton / L.A. Reed
45 Oklahoma State	49 WR Michael Crabtree
75 Northwestern St.	7 T Rylan Reed
42 Iowa State	17 G Louis Vasquez
35 Texas A&M	7 C Shawn Byrnes / Stephen Hamby
10 Missouri	41 G Brandon Carter
26 Colorado	31 T Marlon Winn / Andrew Johnson
38 Baylor	7 QB Graham Harrell
43 Texas	59 RB Shannon Woods / Aaron Crawford
34 Oklahoma	27 DL Jake Ratliff / Richard Jones
31 Virginia■	28 DL Colby Whitlock
	DL Rajon Henley
	DL Brandon Williams / Daniel Howard
	LB Brian Duncan / Kellen Tillman
	LB Paul Williams / Victor Hunter
	LB Marlon Williams
	DB Jamar Wall / Marcus Bunton
	DB Chris Parker
	DB Darcel McBath / Daniel Charbonnet
	DB Joe Garcia

RUSHING: Woods 84/439y, Crawford 46/185y, Kobey Lewis (RB) 42/156y
PASSING: Harrell 468-644/5298y, 45TD, 72.7%
RECEIVING: Crabtree 125/1861y, Amendola 103/1177y, Morris 66/690y
SCORING: Crabtree 126pts, Alex Trlica (K) 99pts, Woods 60pts

2008 11-2
49 E. Washington	24 WR Detron Lewis
35 Nevada	19 WR Michael Crabtree
43 SMU	7 WR Lyle Leong / Edward Britton
56 Massachusetts	14 WR Eric Morris / Tramain Swindall
58 Kansas State	28 T Rylan Reed
37 Nebraska	31 G Louis Vasquez
43 Texas A&M	7 C Stephen Hamby
63 Kansas	21 G Brandon Carter
39 Texas	33 T Marlon Winn
56 Oklahoma State	20 QB Graham Harrell
21 Oklahoma	65 RB Shannon Woods / Baron Batch
35 Baylor	28 DL Brandon Williams
34 Mississippi■	47 DL Richard Jones / Rajon Henley
	DL Colby Whitlock
	DL Jake Ratliff / McKinner Dixon
	LB Bront Bird
	LB Brian Duncan
	LB Marlon Williams
	DB Brent Nickerson / L.A. Reed
	DB Jamar Wall
	DB Darcel McBath / Jordy Rowland
	DB Daniel Charbonnet / Anthony Hines

RUSHING: Batch 111/742y, Woods 135/670y
PASSING: Harrell 406-568/4747y, 41TD, 71.5%
RECEIVING: Crabtree 93/1136y, Lewis 71/869y, Morris 64/682y
SCORING: Crabtree 108pts, Woods 84pts, Morris 66pts

2009 9-4
38 North Dakota	13 WR Alex Torres
55 Rice	10 WR Edward Britton / Lyle Leong
24 Texas	34 WR Detron Lewis / Austin Zouzalik
28 Houston	29 WR/RB Tramain Swindall / Eric Stephens
48 New Mexico	28 T Chris Olson (G) / Terry McDaniel
66 Kansas State	14 G Lonnie Edwards / Mickey Okafor
31 Nebraska	10 C Shawn Byrnes / Justin Keown
30 Texas A&M	52 G Brandon Carter
42 Kansas	21 T Marlon Winn / LaAdrian Waddle
17 Oklahoma State	24 QB Taylor Potts / Steven Sheffield
41 Oklahoma	13 RB Baron Batch
20 Baylor	13 DL Brandon Sharpe / Rajon Henley
41 Michigan State■	31 DL Richard Jones
	DL Colby Whitlock
	DL Daniel Howard
	LB Bront Bird / D.J. Johnson
	LB Brian Duncan
	LB Marlon Williams
	DB Jamar Wall
	DB LaRon Moore / Will Ford
	DB Cody Davis / Julius Howard
	DB Franklin Mitchem / Brett Dewhurst

RUSHING: Batch 168/884y, Stephens 49/254y, Harrison Jeffers 35/217y
PASSING: Potts 309-470/3440y, 22TD, 65.7% Sheffield 101-136/1219y, 14TD, 74.3%
RECEIVING: Torres 67/806y, Lewis 65/844y, Batch 57/395y Swindall 55/694y, Leong 45/571y, Zouzalik 35/469y
SCORING: Matt Williams (K) 93pts, Batch 90pts, Leong 54pts

2010 8-5
35 SMU	27 WR Lyle Leong / Austin Zouzalik
52 New Mexico	17 WR Tramain Swindall / Jacoby Franks
14 Texas	24 WR Detron Lewis / Cornelius Douglas
38 Iowa State	52 WR/RB Alex Torres / Eric Stephens
45 Baylor	38 T LaAdrian Waddle
17 Oklahoma State	34 G Lonnie Edwards
27 Colorado	24 C Justin Keown
27 Texas A&M	45 G Deveric Gallington
24 Missouri	17 T Mickey Okafor / Chris Olson (TE)
7 Oklahoma	45 QB Taylor Potts / Steven Sheffield
64 Weber State	21 RB Baron Batch
35 Houston	20 DL Sam Fehoko (LB) / Scott Smith
45 Northwestern■	38 DL Donald Langley / Kerry Hyder
	DL Colby Whitlock
	DL Brian Duncan / Pearlie Graves
	LB Julius Howard / Tyrone Sonier
	LB Bront Bird / Cqulin Hubert
	DB Jarvis Phillips (LB) / Derrick Mays
	DB D.J. Johnson / Will Ford
	DB Cody Davis / Eugene Neboh
	DB Tre Porter / Frank Mitchem
	DB LaRon Moore / Brett Dewhurst

RUSHING: Batch 177/816y, Stephens 127/668y
PASSING: Potts 369-551/3726y, 35TD, 67% Sheffield 33-58/359y, 3TD, 56.9%
RECEIVING: Lewis 87/852y, Leong 74/926y, Torres 39/481y
SCORING: Leong 114pts, Matt Williams (K) 83pts, Batch & Stephens 48pts

U.C.L.A.

University of California at Los Angeles (Founded 1919)
Los Angeles, California
Nickname: Bruins
Colors: Blue, Powder Blue, and Gold
Stadium: Rose Bowl (1922) 91,136
Conference Affiliations: Pacific Coast (1928-58), AAWU (1959-67),
   Pac-8/10 (1968-present)

CAREER RUSHING YARDS	Attempts	Yards
Gaston Green (1984-87)	708	3731
Freeman McNeil (1977-80)	605	3195
DeShaun Foster (1998-2001)	722	3194
Karim Abdul-Jabbar (1992-95)	608	3182
Wendell Tyler (1973-76)	526	3181
Skip Hicks (1993-94, 96-97)	638	3140
Theotis Brown (1976-78)	526	2914
Chris Markey (2004-07)	579	2733
Kevin Nelson (1980-83)	574	2583
Maurice Drew (2003-05)	481	2503

CAREER PASSING YARDS	Comp.-Att.	Yards
Cade McNown (1995-98)	694-1250	10,708
Drew Olson (2002-05)	664-1148	8532
Cory Paus (1999-2002)	439- 816	6877
Tom Ramsey (1979-82)	441- 751	6168
Tommy Maddox (1990-91)	391- 670	5363
Troy Aikman (1987-88)	406- 627	5298
Wayne Cook (1991-94)	352- 612	4723
Dennis Dummit (1969-70)	289- 552	4356
Gary Beban (1965-67)	243- 465	4087
Matt Stevens (1983-86)	231- 431	2931

CAREER RECEIVING YARDS	Catches	Yards
Danny Farmer (1996-99)	159	3020
Craig Bragg (2001-04)	193	2845
Kevin Jordan (1992-95)	179	2548
J.J. Stokes (1991-94)	154	2469
Freddie Mitchell (1998-2000)	119	2135
Brian Poli-Dixon (1997-2001)	139	2127
Jim McElroy (1994-97)	101	2029
Sean LaChapelle (1989-92)	142	2027
Willie "Flipper" Anderson (1984-87)	105	2023
Mike Sherrard (1982-85)	128	1965

SEASON RUSHING YARDS	Attempts	Yards
Karim Abdul-Jabbar (1995)	296	1571
Gaston Green (1986)	253	1405
Freeman McNeil (1979)	271	1396
Wendell Tyler (1975)	208	1388
Theotis Brown (1978)	211	1283

SEASON PASSING YARDS	Comp.-Att.	Yards
Cade McNown (1998)	207-357	3470
Drew Olson (2005)	242-378	3198
Cade McNown (1997)	189-312	3116
Tom Ramsey (1982)	209-336	2986
Troy Aikman (1988)	228-354	2771

SEASON RECEIVING YARDS	Catches	Yards
Freddie Mitchell (2000)	77	1494
Danny Farmer (1998)	58	1274
Kevin Jordan (1994)	73	1228
J.J. Stokes (1993)	82	1181
Craig Bragg (2003)	73	1065

GAME RUSHING YARDS	Attempts	Yards
Maurice Drew (2004 vs. Washington)	26	322
DeShaun Foster (2001 vs. Washington)	31	301
Theotis Brown (1978 vs. Oregon)	26	274

GAME PASSING YARDS	Comp.-Att.	Yards
Cade McNown (1998 vs. Miami)	26-35	513
Drew Olson (2005 vs. Arizona State)	22-27	510
Tommy Maddox (1990 vs. Southern Calif.)	26-40	409

GAME RECEIVING YARDS	Catches	Yards
J.J. Stokes (1992 vs. Southern Calif.)	6	263
Craig Bragg (2002 vs. Oregon)	9	230
Danny Farmer (1999 vs. Oregon)	7	196

GREATEST COACH:

Picking the greatest coach for almost every school is fairly easy. Usually one man has stood above all others in winning percentage, years on the job, lifting the program to greater heights, or any combination of these three attributes. The UCLA coaching legacy is less pronounced: Red Sanders established a nine-year dominance of the west with a .7732 winning percentage, Tommy Prothro retrieved the Bruins' excellence after seven years under break-even and delivered UCLA's first Rose Bowl victory over no. 1 Michigan State in the 1966 game, and Dick Vermeil didn't stay long but won another Rose Bowl upset and left for the NFL with a .7174 percentage.

The coach who earns the accolades as having done the greatest job in Westwood was Terry Donahue, whose face was the football program for 20 mostly glorious years from 1976 to 1995. Donahue won 151, lost 74, and tied 8 for a .6652 percentage. Donahue won five conference titles and eight bowl games in a row including a trio of Rose Bowls. Since he left for the broadcast booth, the Bruins have slipped below the .6000 mark

UCLA'S 55 GREATEST SINCE 1953

OFFENSE

WIDE RECEIVER: Danny Farmer, Sean LaChapelle, Mike Sherrard, J.J. Stokes
TIGHT END: Marcedes Lewis, Tim Wrightman
TACKLE: Bill Leeka, Jonathan Ogden, Vaughn Parker
GUARD: Jim Brown, Randy Cross, Larry Lee, Jim Salsbury
CENTER: Frank Cornish, Dave Dalby
QUARTERBACK: Troy Aikman, Gary Beban, Cade McNown
RUNNING BACK: Mel Farr, Gaston Green, Skip Hicks, Kermit Johnson, Freeman McNeil
WINGBACK: Jim Decker
FULLBACK: Theotis "Big Foot" Brown, Bob Davenport

DEFENSE

END: Dave Ball, Fred McNeill
TACKLE: Jack Ellena, Manu Tuiasosopo
NOSE GUARD: John Richardson, Terry Tumey
LINEBACKER: Mike Ballou, Spencer Havner, Carnell Lake, Jamir Miller, Ken Norton, Jerry Robinson, Rob Thomas
CORNERBACK: Jimmy Allen, Carlton Gray, Darryl Henley, Ricky Manning, Jr., Bob Stiles
SAFETY: Matt Darby, Kenny Easley, Don Rogers, Shaun Williams

SPECIAL TEAMS

RETURN SPECIALIST: Maurice Drew
PLACE KICKER: John Lee, Justin Medlock
PUNTER: Kirk Wilson

MULTIPLE POSITIONS

TACKLE-DEFENSIVE TACKLE: Irv Eatman

TWO-WAY PLAYERS

TAILBACK-DEFENSIVE BACK-PUNTER: Paul Cameron
END-DEFENSIVE END: Rommie Loudd

PERFORMANCE FORMULA:
UCLA'S 10 BEST SEASONS

1954	1.6954	3 of 69
1955	1.6367	4 of 69
1982	1.5997	4 of 70
1988	1.5863	6 of 69
1987	1.5778	7 of 69
1997	1.5706	9 of 70
1998	1.5669	8 of 71
1965	1.5651	6 of 70
1969	1.5621	6 of 70
1953	1.4981	8 of 69

U.C.L.A. BRUINS

Year	W-L-T	AP Poll	Conference Standing	Toughest Regular Season Opponents	Coach (Record at School)	Bowl Games		
1953	8-2	5	1	Stanford 6-3-1, Wisconsin 6-2-1, Southern Calif. 6-3-1	Henry "Red" Sanders	Rose	20 Michigan State	28
1954	9-0	2	1	Maryland 7-2-1, Southern California 8-3	Red Sanders			
1955	9-2	4	1	Texas A&M 7-2-1, Maryland 10-0, Oregon State 6-3, Stanford 6-3-1	Red Sanders	Rose	14 Michigan State	17
1956	7-3		2t	Michigan 7-2, Oregon State 7-2-1, Southern California 8-2	Red Sanders			
1957	8-2		3	Oregon 7-3, Oregon State 8-2, Stanford 6-4	Red Sanders (66-19-1)			
1958	3-6-1		6	Pittsburgh 5-4-1, Florida 6-3-1, Washington St. 7-3, California 7-3	George Dickerson (1-2), Bill Barnes [2-4-1]			
1959	5-4-1		1t	Purdue 5-2-2, Washington 9-1, Southern Calif. 8-2, Syracuse 10-0	Bill Barnes			
1960	7-2-1		3	Purdue 4-3-3, Washington 9-1, NC State 6-3-1, Duke 7-3	Bill Barnes			
1961	7-4	16	1	Michigan 6-3, Ohio State 8-0-1, Washington 5-4-1	Bill Barnes	Rose	3 Minnesota	21
1962	4-6		5	Ohio State 6-3, Washington 7-1-2, Southern Calif. 10-0-	Bill Barnes			
1963	2-8		3	Pittsburgh 9-1, Penn State 7-3, Syracuse 8-2, Southern Calif. 7-3	Bill Barnes			
1964	4-6		4	Syracuse 7-3, Notre Dame 9-1, Illinois 6-3, Southern Calif. 7-3	Bill Barnes (31-34-2)			
1965	8-2-1	4	1	Mich. St. 10-0, Missouri 7-2-1, So. Calif. 7-2-1, Tennessee 7-1-2	Tommy Prothro	Rose	14 Michigan State	12
1966	9-1	5	2	Syracuse 8-2, Missouri 6-3-1, Southern California 7-3	Tommy Prothro			
1967	7-2-1	11+	2	Tennessee 9-1, Penn State 8-2, Southern Calif. 9-1, Syracuse 8-2	Tommy Prothro			
1968	3-7		5	Penn St. 10-0, California 7-3-1, Tennessee 8-1-1, So. Calif. 9-0-1	Tommy Prothro			
1969	8-1-1	13	2t	Oregon State 6-4, Stanford 7-2-1, Southern California 9-0-1	Tommy Prothro			
1970	6-5		2t	Texas 10-0, Stanford 8-3, Tennessee 10-1	Tommy Prothro (41-18-3)			
1971	2-7-1		8	Texas 8-2, Michigan 11-0, Washington 8-3, Stanford 8-3	Pepper Rodgers			
1972	8-3	15	2	Nebraska 8-2-1, Michigan 10-1, Washington 8-3, So. Calif. 11-0	Pepper Rodgers			
1973	9-2	12	2	Nebraska 8-2-1, Stanford 7-4, Southern California 9-1-1	Pepper Rodgers (19-12-1)			
1974	6-3-2		3	Michigan State 7-3-1, California 7-3-1, Southern California 9-2-1	Dick Vermeil			
1975	9-2-1	5	1t	Tennessee 7-5, Ohio State 11-0, California 8-3, Southern Calif. 7-4	Dick Vermeil (15-5-3)	Rose	23 Ohio State	10
1976	9-2-1	15	2	Ohio State 8-2-1, Southern California 10-1	Terry Donahue	Liberty	6 Alabama	36
1977	7-4		2	Stanford 8-3, California 7-4, Washington 8-3, So. Calif. 7-4	Terry Donahue			
1978	8-3-1	14	2	Washington 7-4, Stanford 7-4, Southern California 11-1	Terry Donahue	Fiesta	10 Arkansas	10
1979	5-6		7	Houston 10-1, Purdue 9-2, Ohio State 11-0, Southern Calif. 10-0-1	Terry Donahue			
1980	9-2	13	2	Purdue 8-3, Ohio State 9-2, Southern California 8-2-1	Terry Donahue			
1981	7-4		4t	Wash. St. 8-2-1, Washington 9-2, Arizona St. 9-2, So. California 9-2	Terry Donahue	Bluebonnet	14 Michigan	33
1982	10-1-1	5	1	Michigan 8-3, Arizona 6-4-1, Washington 9-2, So. California 8-3	Terry Donahue	Rose	24 Michigan	14
1983	7-4-1	17	1	Georgia 9-1-1, Nebraska 12-0, BYU 10-1, Washington 8-3	Terry Donahue	Rose	45 Illinois	9
1984	9-3	9	3	Nebraska 9-2, Southern California 8-3	Terry Donahue	Fiesta	39 Miami	37
1985	9-2-1	7	1	BYU 11-2, Tennessee 8-2-1, Arizona State 8-3, Arizona 8-3	Terry Donahue	Rose	45 Iowa	28
1986	8-3-1	14	2t	Oklahoma 10-1, Arizona State 9-1-1, Washington 8-2-1	Terry Donahue	Freedom	31 BYU	10
1987	10-2	9	1t	Nebraska 10-1, Arizona State 6-4-1, Southern California 8-3	Terry Donahue	Aloha	20 Florida	16
1988	10-2	6	2	Nebraska 11-1, Washington State 8-3, Southern California 10-1	Terry Donahue	Cotton	17 Arkansas	3
1989	3-7-1		9	Tennessee 10-1, Michigan 10-1, Southern California 8-2-1	Terry Donahue			
1990	5-6		6t	Oklahoma 8-3, Michigan 8-3, Washington 9-2, So. California 8-3-1	Terry Donahue			
1991	9-3	19	2t	BYU 8-3-1, Tennessee 9-2, California 9-2, Stanford 8-3	Terry Donahue	John Hancock	6 Illinois	3
1992	6-5		8	BYU 8-4, Stanford 9-3, Washington State 8-3, So. California 6-4-1	Terry Donahue			
1993	8-4	18	1t	California 8-4, Nebraska 11-0, Arizona 9-2	Terry Donahue	Rose	16 Wisconsin	21
1994	5-6		5t	Tennessee 7-4, Nebraska 12-0, Arizona 8-3, So. California 7-3-1	Terry Donahue			
1995	7-5		5t	Miami 8-3, Oregon 9-2, Southern California 8-2-1	Terry Donahue (151-74-8)	Aloha	30 Kansas	51
1996	5-6		4	Tennessee 9-2, Michigan 8-3, Arizona State 11-0, Washington 9-2	Bob Toledo			
1997	10-2	5	1t	Wash. State 10-1, Tennessee 10-1, Washington 7-4	Bob Toledo	Cotton	29 Texas A&M	23
1998	10-2	8	1	Texas 8-3, Arizona 11-1, Oregon 8-3, So. Calif. 8-4, Miami 8-3	Bob Toledo	Rose	31 Wisconsin	38
1999	4-7		9	Boise State 9-3, Stanford 8-3, Oregon 8-3, Washington 7-4	Bob Toledo			
2000	6-6		5t	Michigan 8-3, Oregon 9-2, Oregon State 10-1, Washington 10-1	Bob Toledo	Sun	20 Wisconsin	21
2001	7-4		6	Washington 8-3, Stanford 9-2, Washington St. 9-2, Oregon 10-1	Bob Toledo			
2002	8-5		5t	Colorado 9-3, Southern California 10-2, Washington State 10-2	Bob Toledo (49-32), Ed Kezirian [1-0]	Las Vegas	27 New Mexico	13
2003	6-7		6t	Oklahoma 12-0, Washington St. 9-3, Oregon 8-4, So. Calif. 11-1	Karl Dorrell	Silicon Valley	9 Fresno State	17
2004	6-6		5t	Oklahoma St. 7-4, Southern California 12-0	Karl Dorrell	Las Vegas	21 Wyoming	24
2005	10-2	16	3	Oklahoma 7-4, California 7-4, Southern California 12-0	Karl Dorrell	Sun	50 Northwestern	38
2006	7-6		4	Notre Dame 10-2, California 9-3, Oregon State 9-4, So. Calif. 10-2	Karl Dorrell	Emerald	27 Florida State	44
2007	6-7		4t	BYU 10-2, Arizona State 10-2, Oregon 8-4, Southern California 10-2	Karl Dorrell (35-27), DeWayne Walker [0-1]	Las Vegas	16 BYU	17
2008	4-8		8	BYU 10-2, Oregon 9-3, California 8-4, Southern California 11-1	Rick Neuheisel			
2009	7-6		8	Stanford 8-4, Oregon 10-2, California 8-4, Southern California 8-4	Rick Neuheisel	Eagle Bank	30 Temple	21
2010	4-8		9	Stanford 11-1, Oregon 12-0, Southern Cal 8-5	Rick Neuheisel (15-22)			

TOTAL: 399-236-17 .6250 (19 of 70)   **Bowl Games since 1953:**   14-13-1 .5179 (34 of 70)

GREATEST TEAM SINCE 1953: The 1954 edition of Red Sanders' Bruins were recognized as the UP coaches' national championship as well as being tapped by the Football Writers Association and two smaller rating services, Dunkel and Litkenhous. UCLA was a dynamic scoring machine, averaging 33.67 points per game while permitting only 4.44 points per game. Except for a 12-7 win over defending national champion Maryland and a surprisingly tough 21-20 win over a weak 2-8 Washington team, UCLA was never close to being challenged. The true challenge could have awaited the Bruins in the Rose Bowl in AP's no. 1 team, undefeated Ohio State. But in 1954, the Pacific Coast Conference didn't allow its members to attend the Rose Bowl two years in a row, and UCLA had been to Pasadena the season before.

1953 8-2
41	Oregon State	0	E Bob Heydenfeldt / Rommie Loudd
19	Kansas	7	T Jack Ellena / Warner Benjamin
12	Oregon	0	G Sam Boghosian / Hardiman Cureton
13	Wisconsin	0	C Ira Pauly / Johnny Peterson
20	Stanford	21	G Jim Salsbury
44	Washington St.	7	T Chuck Doud / Joe Ray
20	California	7	E Myron Berliner / Bob Long /John Smith
22	Washington	6	BB Don Foster / Terry Debay
13	Southern Cal	0	TB Paul Cameron
20	Michigan St.■	28	WB Bill Stits / Jim Decker
			FB Bob Davenport / Pete Dailey

RUSHING: Cameron 146/665y, Davenport 113/438y,
　Stits 46/316y
PASSING: Cameron 39-106/478y, 7TD, 36.8%
RECEIVING: Stits 9/208y, Heydenfeldt 8/121y, Long 7/56y
SCORING: Cameron (TB-K) 78pts, Davenport 42pts, Stits 36pts

1954 9-0
67	San Diego Navy	0	E Bob Heyenfeldt / Rommie Loudd
32	Kansas	7	T Jack Ellena / Warner Benjamin
12	Maryland	7	G Sam Boghosian / Hardiman Cureton
21	Washington	20	C Johnny Peterson / Steve Palmer
72	Stanford	0	G Jim Salsbury / Jim Brown
61	Oregon State	0	T Joe Ray / Gil Moreno
27	California	6	E Bob Long / Roger White / John Smith
41	Oregon	0	BB Terry Debay / Bob Bergdahl (FB)
34	Southern Cal	0	TB Primo Villanueva / Doug Bradley
			WB Jim Decker / Johnny Hermann
			FB Bob Davenport / Doug Peters

RUSHING: Decker 47/508y, Villanueva 87/486y,
　Davenport 105/479y, Gerry McDougall (TB) 43/226y
PASSING: Villanueva 23-49/400y, 46.9%,
　Bradley 20-31/229y, 2TD, 64.5%
RECEIVING: Loudd 13/157y, Long 11/157y, Heydenfeldt 6/110y
SCORING: N/A

1955 9-2
21	Texas A&M	0	E John Hermann/John Smith/P. O'Garro
0	Maryland	7	T Roger White / Russ Hampton
55	Washington St.	0	G Hardiman Cureton / Don Birren
38	Oregon State	0	C Steve Palmer / Jim Matheny
21	Stanford	13	G Jim Brown / Esker Harris
33	Iowa	13	T Gil Moreno / Gerald Penner
47	California	0	E Rommie Loudd / Tom Adams
34	Pacific	0	BB Bob Bergdahl/Don Shinnick/B.Ballard
19	Washington	17	TB Sam Brown / Ronnie Knox
17	Southern Cal	7	WB Jim Decker / Chuck Hollaway
14	Michigan St.■	17	FB Bob Davenport / Doug Peters

RUSHING: Brown 144/892y, Davenport 100/415y, Peters 60/267y
PASSING: Knox 36-63/526y, 6 TDs, 57.2%
RECEIVING: Hollaway 10/184y, O'Garro 10/66y, Ballard 8/75y
SCORING: Brown (TB-K) 69pts, Davenport 42pts,
　Peters (FB-K) 37pts

1956 7-3
13	Utah	7	E Dick Wallen / Pete O'Garro
13	Michigan	42	T Jim Dawson / Wilbert Anderson
6	Oregon	0	G Clint Whitfield / Don Birren
28	Washington St.	0	C Jim Matheny / Dan Peterson
34	California	20	G Esker Harris / Bob Dutcher
7	Oregon State	21	T Bill Leeka / Preston Dills
14	Stanford	13	E Tom Adams / Hal Smith
13	Washington	9	BB Bob Bergdahl / Don Shinnick
13	Kansas	0	TB Doug Bradley / Kirk Wilson /Don Long
7	Southern Cal	10	WB Louie Elias / Chuck Holloway
			FB Barry Billington

RUSHING: Billington 106/396y, Long 56/204y, Elias 48/156y
PASSING: Bradley 22-48/293y, 3 TDs, 45.9%
　Long 19-38/243y, 0 TDs, 50.0%, Wilson 15-44/230y, TD, 34.1%
RECEIVING: Wallen 23/308y, Smith 10/135y, O'Garro 8/116y
SCORING: Long (TB-K) & Wilson (TB-K) 19pts, 3 with 18pts

1957 8-2
47	Air Force	0	E Dick Wallen
16	Illinois	6	T Jim Dawson / Bob Dinaberg
0	Oregon	21	G Clint Whitfield / Kurt Lewin
19	Washington	0	C Dan Peterson / Dennis Dressel
26	Oregon State	7	G Rod Cochran / Joe Harper
6	Stanford	20	T Bill Leeka / Jim Wallace
16	California	14	E Jim Steffen
19	Washington St.	13	BB Steve Gertsman / Dave Peterson
21	Pacific	0	TB Don Long / Kirk Wilson /Chuck Kendall
20	Southern Cal	9	WB Phil Parslow / Bill Mason
			FB Barry Billington / Ray Smith

RUSHING: Kendall 98/388y, Long 101/372y, Wilson 68/295y
PASSING: Long 35-56/479y, 4 TDs, 62.5%
　Wilson 18-42/276y, TD, 42.8%,
　Kendall 16-32/254y, 2 TDs, 50.0%
RECEIVING: Wallen 20/303y, Mason 9/160y, Parslow 8/108y
SCORING: Long 48pts, Billington 24pts

1958 3-6-1
6	Pittsburgh	27	E Dick Wallen / John Brown
18	Illinois	14	T Jim Wallace/Jim Dawson/Trusse Norris
0	Oregon State	14	G Bob King / Clint Whitfield /Jack Metcalf
14	Florida	21	C Harry Baldwin / Dick Butler
20	Washington	0	G Joe Harper / Rod Cochran
19	Stanford	21	T Bill Leeka / Paul Oglesby
20	Washington St.	38	E Jim Steffen / John Pierovich
17	California	20	BB Dave Peterson / Art Phillips
7	Oregon	3	TB Don Long / Billy Kilmer / Skip Smith
15	Southern Cal	15	WB Phil Parslow /Marv Luster/John Davis
			FB Ray Smith / Gene Gaines

RUSHING: R.Smith 79/307y, S.Smith 51/197y, Kilmer 50/195y
PASSING: Long 36-64/395y, 4 TDs, 56.3%
RECEIVING: Wallen 19/211y, Brown 16/259y, Steffen 12/151y
SCORING: Wallen 18pts, Steffen 16pts, S. Smith 14pts

1959 5-4-1
0	Purdue	0	E Marv Luster / Don Vena
21	Pittsburgh	25	T Jim Wallace / Steve Bauwens
19	California	12	G Jack Metcalf / Dave Dabov
7	Air Force	20	C Harry Baldwin / Ron Hull
7	Washington	23	G Rod Cochran / Marshall Shirk
55	Stanford	13	T Paul Oglesby / Tony Longo
21	N. Carolina St.	12	E Trusse Norris / Glen Almquist
10	Southern Cal	3	BB Art Phillips / Ivory Jones
21	Utah	6	TB Billy Kilmer / Bobby Smith /Skip Smith
8	Syracuse	36	WB Gene Gaines / Jim Johnson
			FB Ray Smith

RUSHING: R. Smith 122/417y, Kilmer 94/388y,
　S. Smith 43/289y, B. Smith 93/289y
PASSING: Kilmer 41-101/702y, 7 TDs, 40.6%
RECEIVING: Luster 22/366y, Johnson 14/289y, Vena 5/86y
SCORING: R. Smith 36pts, Luster 30pts, Johnson 24pts

1960 7-2-1
8	Pittsburgh	7	E Marv Luster / Don Vena / Jim Stanley
27	Purdue	27	T Steve Bauwens / Foster Anderson
8	Washington	10	G Jack Metcalf / Jack Macari
26	Stanford	8	C Ron Hull / Harry Baldwin
7	N. Carolina St.	0	G Dave Dobov / Dave Stout / Tom Paton
28	California	0	T Marshall Shirk
22	Air Force	6	E Earl Smith /Tom Gutman /Chuck Hicks
6	Southern Cal	17	BB Bob Stevens / Duane Wills / Joe Zeno
16	Utah	9	TB Billy Kilmer / Bobby Smith
27	Duke	6	WB Jim Johnson / Gene Gaines
			FB Skip Smith / Almose Thompson

RUSHING: Kilmer 163/803y, B. Smith 54/281y, S. Smith 51/231y
PASSING: Kilmer 64-129/1086y, 8TD, 49.5%
RECEIVING: Luster 17/250y, Johnson 14/254y, Vena 9/120y
SCORING: Kilmer 52pts, Thompson 30pts, S. Smith 18pts

1961 7-4
19	Air Force	6	E Don Vena / Mel Profit
6	Michigan	29	T Foster Anderson / Steve Bauwens
3	Ohio State	13	G Frank Macari/Dick Allen/Joe Bauwens
28	Vanderbilt	21	C Ron Hull / Andy Von Sonn
20	Pittsburgh	6	G Tom Paton / Dave Stout
20	Stanford	0	T Marshall Shirk / Phil Oram
35	California	15	E Tom Gutman/Chuck Hicks/Dave Gibbs
28	TCU	7	BB Bob Stevens / John Walker
13	Washington	17	TB Bobby Smith / Mike Haffner
10	Southern Cal	7	WB Kermit Alexander / Rob Smith
3	Minnesota■	21	FB Almose Thompson / Joe Zeno

RUSHING: Haffner 107/696y, B.Smith 166/631y,
　Thompson 93/370y
PASSING: B. Smith 16-33/305y, TD, 48.5%,
　Haffner 14-34/231y, TD, 41.2%
RECEIVING: Alexander 11/271y, Vena 9/103y, Gutman 5/79y
SCORING: B. Smith (TB-K) 85pts, Haffner 48pts, Alexander 18pts

1962 4-6
9	Ohio State	7	E Al Geverink / Gary Callies
35	Colorado State	7	T Joe Bauwens / Kent Francisco
6	Pittsburgh	8	G John Walker / Dick Peterson
7	Stanford	17	C Andy Von Sonn
26	California	16	G Dave Stout /Tony Fiorentino /W.Dathe
11	Air Force	17	T Phil Oram / Randy Schwartz
0	Washington	30	E Mel Profit / Dave Gibbs
3	Southern Cal	14	QB Ezell Singleton/Larry Zeno/Carl Jones
14	Utah	11	HB Kermit Alexander
7	Syracuse	12	HB Rob Smith / Dan Ghormley
			FB Mitch Dimkich / Warren Jackson

RUSHING: Alexander 82/472y, Jackson 58/275y, Zeno 72/252y
PASSING: Zeno 25-62/458y, 2TD, 40.3%,
　Jones 25-52/412y, 2TD, 45.5%
RECEIVING: Profit 12/229y, Alexander 12/178y, Callies 9/96y
SCORING: Alexander (HB-K) 45pts, Zeno (QB-K) 27pts

1963 2-8
0	Pittsburgh	20	E Kurt Altenberg / Jim Stanley
14	Penn State	17	T Mitch Johnson / John Pentecost
10	Stanford	9	G John Walker / John LoCurto
7	Syracuse	29	C Prentice O'Leary
12	Notre Dame	27	G Walt Dathe / Russ Balducci
12	Illinois	18	T Kent Francisco
0	California	25	E Mel Profit / Dave Gibbs
21	Air Force	48	QB Larry Zeno / Steve Sindell
14	Washington	0	HB Byron Nelson / Carl Jones
6	Southern Cal	26	HB Mike Haffner / Bob Richardson

RUSHING: Colletto 47/179y, Zeno 104/173y, Nelson 37/114y
PASSING: Zeno 77-154/1036y, 6TD, 50.0%
RECEIVING: Profit 28/393y, Altenberg 24/419y, Nelson 21/291y
SCORING: Nelson 36pts, Zeno 14pts, Profit & Altenberg 8pts

1964 4-6
17	Pittsburgh	12	E Kurt Altenberg / Don Francis
21	Penn State	14	T Mitch Johnson / John Pentecost
27	Stanford	20	G Dick Peterson / John Richardson (DL)
0	Syracuse	39	C Prentice O'Leary
24	Notre Dame	24	G Russ Balducci / Barry Leventhal
7	Illinois	26	T Kent Francisco / Steve Butler
25	California	21	E Dick Witcher / Ted Bashore
15	Air Force	24	QB Larry Zeno / Byron Nelson (DB)
20	Washington	22	HB Mel Farr / Cornell Champion
13	Southern Cal	34	HB Mike Haffner / Ray Armstrong
			FB Jim Colletto / Paul Horgan

RUSHING: Zeno 113/325y, Horgan 75/233y, Champion 62/222y
PASSING: Zeno 97-196/1363y, 13TD, 49.4%
RECEIVING: Haffner 31/515y, Altenberg 31/428y,
　Witcher 15/243y
SCORING: Altenberg 36pts, Zeno 35pts, Witcher 30pts

1965 8-2-1
3	Michigan State	13	WR Kurt Altenberg
24	Penn State	22	T Russ Balducci
24	Syracuse	14	G Rich Deakers
14	Missouri	14	C Mo Freedman / John Esquiaga
56	California	3	G Barry Leventhal
10	Air Force	10	T Larry Slagle
28	Washington	24	E Byron Nelson
30	Stanford	13	QB Gary Beban
20	Southern Cal	16	HB Mel Farr / Steve Durbin
34	Tennessee	37	WB Dick Witcher / Ray Armstrong
14	Michigan St.■	12	FB Paul Horgan / Steve Stanley
			DL Jim Colletto
			DL Terry Donahue
			DL John Richardson
			DL Steve Butler / Dick Donald
			DL Al Claman
			DL Jerry Klein / Wade Pearson
			LB Dallas Grider
			LB Erwin Dutcher / Jim Miller
			DB Bob Stiles
			DB Bob Richardson
			DB Tim McAteer / Sandy Green

RUSHING: Farr 122/821y, Beban 194/590y, Horgan 122/450y
PASSING: Beban 78-152/1483y, 9TD, 51.3%
RECEIVING: Altenberg 32/599y, Witcher 17/396y, Nelson 17/193y
SCORING: Beban 84pts, Farr 48pts, Kurt Zimmerman (K) 45pts

1966 9-1

57 Pittsburgh	14 WR Harold Busby / Dave Nuttall
31 Syracuse	12 T Tom Ware
24 Missouri	15 G Rich Deakers
27 Rice	24 C John Erquiaga / Paul Mayfield
49 Penn State	11 G Dennis Murphy
28 California	15 T Larry Slagle
38 Air Force	13 TE Rich Spindler
3 Washington	16 QB Gary Beban / Norm Dow
10 Stanford	0 TB Mel Farr
14 Southern Cal	7 WB Corn'll Champion/Ray Armstr'ng(WR)
	FB Steve Stanley / Rick Purdy
	DL Vic Lepisto
	DL Terry Donahue / Hal Griffin
	DL John Richardson
	DL Dick Donald / Larry Agajanian
	DL Al Claman / Mike Roof
	DL Erwin Dutcher / Mike McCaffrey
	LB Dallas Grider
	LB Don Manning / Wade Pearson
	DB Mark Gustafson
	DB Andy Herrera
	DB Sandy Green / Tim McAteer

RUSHING: Farr 138/809y, Beban 123/454y, Purdy 62/324y
PASSING: Beban 78-157/1245y, 6TD, 49.7%
RECEIVING: Busby 29/474y, Farr 12/225y, Armstrong 10/123y
SCORING: Beban 64pts, Farr 62pts, Kurt Zimmerman (K) 51pts

1967 7-2-1

20 Tennessee	16 WR Dave Nuttall / Ron Copeland
40 Pittsburgh	8 T Gordon Bosserman
51 Washington St.	23 G Ken Bajema
17 Penn State	15 G John Erquiaga
37 California	14 G Dennis Murphy
21 Stanford	16 T Larry Salgle / Mike Arnold
16 Oregon State	16 TE Rich Spindler
48 Washington	0 QB Gary Beban
20 Southern Cal	21 TB Greg Jones / Paul Derflinger
14 Syracuse	32 WB Harold Busby / Steve Stanley
	FB Rick Purdy / Mike Garratt
	DL Vic Lepisto / Lee McElroy
	DL Hal Griffin / Vince Bischof
	DL Larry Agajanian
	DL Floyd Reese
	DL Al Claman
	DL Kim Griffith / Steve Smalley
	LB Mike Ballou
	LB Dan Manning / Don Widmer
	DB Mark Gustafson / Lynn Hinshaw
	DB Andy Herrera
	DB Sandy Green

RUSHING: Jones 111/662y, Purdy 117/617y, Beban 145/227y
PASSING: Beban 87-156/1359y, 8TD, 55.7%
RECEIVING: Nuttall 37/612y, Busby 16/227y, Spindler 14/149y
SCORING: Beban 66pts, Zenon Andrusyshyn (K) 64pts,
Jones 36pts

1968 3-7

63 Pittsburgh	7 WR Harold Busby / Ron Copeland
31 Washington St.	21 T Gordon Bosserman
7 Syracuse	20 G Dennis Alumbaugh
6 Penn State	21 C Greg McLandrich
15 California	39 G Ron Tretter / Rick Perttula
20 Stanford	17 T Steve Freistas / Scott Steele
18 Tennessee	42 TE Mike Garratt
21 Oregon State	45 QB Bill Bolden (TB) / Jim Nader
0 Washington	6 TB Greg Jones
16 Southern Cal	28 WB George Farmer / Gwen Cooper
	FB Rick Purdy / Mickey Cureton (TB)
	DL Hal Griffin / Vince Bischoff
	DL Larry Agajanisn
	DL Floyd Reese / Bob Geddes
	DL Wes Grant
	LB Kim Griffith / Lee McElroy
	LB Mike Ballou
	LB Don Widmer
	LB Dick Davidson / Doug Huff
	DB Danny Graham
	DB Mark Gustafson
	DB Dennis Spurling

RUSHING: Jones 121/497y, Cureton 86/365y, Purdy 51/189y
PASSING: Nader 72-163/1008y, 7TD, 44.2%,
Bolden 26-57/395y, 3TD, 45.6%
RECEIVING: Copeland 21/372y, Garratt 21/243y, Busby 13/156y
SCORING: Jones 28pts, Zenon Andrusyshn (K) 25pts,
3 with 24pts

1969 8-1-1

37 Oregon State	0 WR Gwen Cooper / Rick Wilkes
42 Pittsburgh	8 T Gordon Bosserman
34 Wisconsin	23 G Ron Tretter
36 Northwestern	0 C Dave Dalby
46 Washington St.	14 G Dennis Alumbaugh
32 California	0 T Steve Preston / Lee McElroy
20 Stanford	20 TE Mike Garratt / Bob Christiansen
57 Washington	14 QB Dennis Dummit / Jim Nader
13 Oregon	10 TB Greg Jones / Bill Bolden
12 Southern Cal	14 WB George Farmer / Brad Lyman
	FB Mickey Cureton / Bob Manning
	DL Bob Geddes
	DL Bruce Jorgensen / Tim Oesterling
	DL Floyd Reese
	DL Wes Grant
	LB Don Widmer / Vince Bischof
	LB Mike Ballou
	LB Jim Ford
	DB Danny Graham
	DB Doug Huff
	DB Ron Carver / Frank Jones
	DB Dennis Spurling / Jerry Jaso

RUSHING: Jones 158/761y, Cureton 114/721y, Manning 61/222y
PASSING: Dummit 114-208/1963y, 15TD, 54.8%
RECEIVING: Cooper 38/734y, Farmer 36/651y, Garratt 17/240y
SCORING: Jones 60pts, Zenon Andrusyshyn (K) 57pts,
Cooper 54pts

1970 6-5

14 Oregon State	9 WR Rick Wilkes / Reggie Echols
24 Pittsburgh	15 T Greg Pearson
12 Northwestern	7 G Bob Bartlett
17 Texas	20 C Dave Dalby
40 Oregon	41 G Brian Goodman
24 California	21 T Bruce Walton / Steve Freitas
7 Stanford	9 TE Bob Christiansen
54 Washington St.	9 QB Dennis Dummit
20 Washington	61 WB Marv Kendricks/Art'r Sims/Randy Tyl'r
45 Southern Cal	20 WB Terry Vernoy / Brad Lyman
17 Tennessee	28 FB Gary Campbell / Bob Manning
	DL Craig Campbell / Bruce Bergey
	DL Tim Oesterling
	DL Jim Berg / Tom Daniels
	LB Phil Hendricks / Paul Moyneur
	LB Bob Pifferini / Max Knupper
	LB Greg Snyder / Vincent Mok
	LB Rob Scribner / Jack Lassner
	DB Allan Ellis / Frank Jones
	DB Reynaud Moore
	DB Ron Carver / Alan Lemmerman
	DB Doug Huff / Jerry Jaso

RUSHING: Kendricks 107/573y, Sims 107/463y, Tyler 80/364y
PASSING: Dummit 175-344/2392y, 14TD, 51.0%
RECEIVING: Wilkes 43/595y, Christiansen 32/496y,
Vernoy 26/420y
SCORING: Tyler & Kendricks 40pts, Dummit & Campbell 32pts

1971 2-7-1

25 Pittsburgh	29 WR Terry Vernoy / Reggie Echols
10 Texas	28 T Greg Pearman / Zeno Veal
0 Michigan	38 G Randy Gaschler
17 Oregon State	34 C Dave Dalby
34 Washington St.	21 G Brian Goodman
28 Arizona	12 T Bruce Walton
24 California	31 TE Bob Christiansen / Mike Clayton
12 Washington	23 QB Scott Henderson / Mike Flores
9 Stanford	20 HB Marv Kendricks / Randy Tyler
7 Southern Cal	7 HB Kermit Johnson
	FB Gary Campbell
	DL Cal Peterson / Max Knupper
	DL Jim Berg
	DL Ed Galigher
	DL Mike Pavich
	DL Craig Campbell
	DL Fred McNeill
	LB Bob Pefferini
	LB Vincent Mok / Greg Snyder
	DB Allan Ellis
	DB Rob Scribner / Alan Lemmerman
	DB Ron Carver /Jim Bright /Paul Moyneur

RUSHING: Kendricks 131/556y, Johnson 80/414y, Tyler 87/354y
PASSING: Flores 51-111/671y,1TD, 45.8%
RECEIVING: Vernoy 21/281y, Christiansen 18/312y,
Echols 8/167y
SCORING: Efren Herrera (K) 46pts, Hendricks 42pts, Tyler 14pts

1972 8-3

20 Nebraska	17 WR Brad Lyman / Terry Vernoy
38 Pittsburgh	28 T Ed Kezirian
9 Michigan	26 G Russ Leal
65 Oregon	20 C Randy Gaschler
42 Arizona	31 G Steve Klosterman
37 Oregon State	7 T Bruce Walton / Al Oliver
49 California	13 TE Jack Lessner / Gene Bleymaier
35 Washington St.	20 QB Mark Harmon / Rob Scribner
28 Stanford	23 HB James McAlister / Russel Charles
21 Washington	30 HB Kermit Johnson
7 Southern Cal	24 FB Randy Tyler / Gary Campbell
	DL Cal Peterson
	DL Gerry Roberts
	DL Rick Baska / Greg Norfleet
	DL Gerald Peeke
	DL Tom Waddell / Art Fry
	DL Fred McNeill / Paul Moyneur
	LB Steve Hookano
	LB Gene Settles / Herschel Ramsey
	DB Allan Ellis
	DB Jimmy Allen
	DB Jim Bright / Mike Fryer

RUSHING: Johns'n 140/952y, McAlist'r 158/778y, Scribn'r 65/498y
PASSING: Harmon 30-70/574y, 42.9%
RECEIVING: Lyman 13/211y, Lassner 6/108y, Vernoy 4/89y
SCORING: Efren Herrera (K) 63pts, McAlister 54pts,
Johnson & Harmon 42pts

1973 9-2

13 Nebraska	40 WR Norm Andersen / Steve Monahan
55 Iowa	18 T Ed Kezarian
34 Michigan State	21 G Myke Horton / Gene Clark
66 Utah	16 C Randy Cross / Art Kuehn
59 Stanford	13 G Steve Klosterman
24 Washington St.	13 T Al Oliver / Bob Reyes
61 California	21 TE Raymond Burks / Eugene Jones
62 Washington	13 QB Mark Harmon / John Sciarra
27 Oregon	7 HB Russel Charles / Eddie Ayers
56 Oregon State	14 HB Kermit Johnson
13 Southern Cal	23 FB James McAlister / Charlie Schuhmann
	DL Cal Peterson
	DL Pat Sweetland / Gerald Peeke
	DL Greg Norfleet / Mike Martinez
	DL Bill Sandifer
	DL Fred McNeill / Dale Curry
	LB Gene Settles / Rick Baska
	LB Fulton Kuykendall / Tom Waddell
	DB John Nanoski / Alton McSween
	DB Jimmy Allen / Matt Fahl
	DB Kent Pearce
	DB Jim Bright / Herschel Ramsey

RUSHING: Johnson 150/1129y, McAlister 123/714y,
Harmon 74/532y
PASSING: Sciarra 27-62/503y, 3TD, 43.5%,
Harmon 13-30/271y, 3TD, 43.3%
RECEIVING: Andersen 19/315y, Burks 9/271y, Monahan 6/92y
SCORING: Johnson 96pts, Efren Herrera (K) 84pts,
McAlister 48pts

1974 6-3-2

17 Tennessee	17 WR Norm Andersen
10 Iowa	21 WR Wally Henry / Steve Monahan
56 Michigan State	14 T Gene Clark / Jack DeMartinis
27 Utah	14 G Randy Cross
13 Stanford	13 C Art Kuehn
17 Washington St.	13 G Myke Horton
28 California	3 T Phil McKinnely / Bob Reyes
9 Washington	31 TE Gene Bleymaier
21 Oregon	0 QB John Sciarra / Jeff Dankworth
33 Oregon State	14 HB Russel Charles / Eddie Ayers
9 Southern Cal	34 HB Wendell Tyler / Carl Zaby
	DL Rick Kukulica / Cliff Frazier
	DL Mike Martinez / Greg Norfleet
	DL Tim Tennigkeit / Bob Crawford
	LB Herschel Ramsey (DB) / Terry Tautolo
	LB Fult'n Kuykendall/Frank Manumaleuna
	LB Gene Settles / Tom Waddell
	LB Dale Curry
	DB John Nanoski / Barry Person
	DB Phil Kimble / Matt Fahl
	DB Kent Pearce
	DB Greg Williams

RUSHING: Charles 132/763y, Tyler 96/544y, Sciarra 91/400y
PASSING: Sciarra 47-92/835y, 51.1%,
Dankworth 20-46/309y, 1TD, 43.5%
RECEIVING: Andersen 27/480y, Bleym'r 13/245y,
Henry 13/206y
SCORING: Brett White (K) 54pts, Sciarra, Zaby,
Charlie Schuhmann (HB) & Dankworth 24pts

1975 9-2-1

37 Iowa State	21 WR Norm Andersen / James Sarpy
34 Tennessee	28 WR Wally Henry / Severn Reese
20 Air Force	20 T Gus Coppens
20 Ohio State	41 G Phil McKinnely
31 Stanford	21 C Milt Kahn
37 Washington St.	23 G Randy Cross
28 California	14 T Jack DeMartinis / Rob Kezirian
13 Washington	17 TE Don Peterson / Rick Walker
50 Oregon	17 QB John Sciarra
31 Oregon State	9 HB Wendell Tyler
25 Southern Cal	22 HB Eddie Ayers / Carl Zaby
23 Ohio State■	10 DL Pete Pele
	DL Cliff Frazier
	DL Tim Tennigkeit / Manu Tuiasosopo
	LB Dale Curry
	LB Terry Tautolo / Jeff Muro
	LB Raymond Bell / Bill Baggott
	LB Raymond Burks / Frank Stephens
	DB Barry Person / Levi Armstrong
	DB Harold Hardin / James Owens
	DB Oscar Edwards / Matt Fahl
	DB Pat Schmidt / Jeff Smith

RUSHING: Tyler 208/1388y, Sciarra 198/787y, Ayers 154/699y
PASSING: Sciarra 74-145/1313y, 8TD, 51.0%
RECEIVING: Henry 17/287y, Andersen 15/256y, Walker 12/268y
SCORING: Sciarra 84pts, Ayers 60pts, Brett White 53pts

1976 9-2-1

28 Arizona State	10 WR Wally Henry / Homer Butler
37 Arizona	9 T Gus Coppens
40 Air Force	7 G Keith Eck
10 Ohio State	10 C Mitch Kahn
38 Stanford	20 G Greg Taylor
62 Washington St.	3 T Rob Kezirian / Bruce Davis
35 California	19 TE Don Peterson
30 Washington	21 TE Rick Walker
46 Oregon	0 QB Jeff Dankworth / Steve Bukich
45 Oregon State	14 HB Wendell Tyler / Jim Brown
14 Southern Cal	24 HB Theotis Brown / James Owens
6 Alabama■	36 DL Manu Tuiasosopo / Tim Tennigkeit
	DL Steve Tetrick
	DL Pete Pele / Dave Morton
	LB Raymond Burks
	LB Jerry Robinson
	LB Raymond Bell / Tom Murphy
	LB Frank Stephens
	DB Levi Armstrong
	DB Harold Hardin / Johnny Lynn
	DB Oscar Edwards
	DB Pat Schmidt / Michael Coulter

RUSHING: T. Brown 200/1092y, Tyler 181/1003y, Dankworth 155/815y
PASSING: Dankworth 66-120/866y, 4TD, 55.0%
RECEIVING: Henry 22/370y, T. Brown 12/92y, Butler 11/166y
SCORING: T. Brown 78pts, Frank Corral (K) 69pts, Dankworth 66pts

1977 7-4

13 Houston	17 WR Kent Brisbin / James Sarpy
17 Kansas	7 WR Homer Butler
13 Minnesota	27 T Max Montoyo
34 Iowa	16 G Bryce Adkins
28 Stanford	32 C Brent Boyd
27 Wash. State (F-L)	16 G Jim Main
21 California	19 T Gus Coppens
20 Washington	12 TE Don Peterson
21 Oregon	3 QB Rick Bashore
48 Oregon State	18 HB James Owens / Ernie Saenz
27 Southern Cal	29 HB Theotis Brown / Glenn Cannon
	DL Billy Don Jackson
	DL Steve Tetrick / Dave Morton
	DL Manu Tuiasosopo
	LB John Fowler
	LB Jerry Robinson
	LB Jeff Muro / Rick Obbema
	LB Frank Stephens
	DB Levi Armstrong
	DB Bobby Hosea / Brian Baggott
	DB Kenny Easley / Michael Coulter
	DB Johnny Lynn / Michael Molina

RUSHING: Owens 176/938y, Brown 115/539y, Bashore 131/317y
PASSING: Bashore 74-149/1015y, 9TD, 49.7%
RECEIVING: Butler 25/584y, Brown 16/135y, Owens 15/146y
SCORING: Frank Corral (K) 54pts, Brown 42pts, Owens 30pts

1978 8-3-1

10 Washington	7 WR Severn Reece / Dokie Williams
13 Tennessee	0 WR Michael Brant
24 Kansas	28 T Max Montoyo
17 Minnesota	3 G Larry Lee
27 Stanford	26 C Scott Reid / Dave Otey
45 Washington St.	31 G Jim Main / Luis Sharpe
45 California	0 T Bruce Davis / Curt Mohl
24 Arizona	14 TE Kent Brisbin / Tim Wrightman
23 Oregon	21 QB Rick Bashore / Steve Bukich
13 Oregon State	15 HB James Owens / Freeman McNeil
10 Southern Cal	17 HB Theotis Brown
10 Arkansas■	10 DL Billy Don Jackson
	DL Manu Tuiasosopo/Raymond Robinson
	DL Don Hopwood / Mark Tuinei
	LB Glenn Wisdom
	LB Jerry Robinson
	LB Jeff Muro / Arthur Akers
	LB Chris Elias / Brad Plemmons
	DB Johnny Lynn
	DB Bobby Hosea / Jimmy Turner
	DB Kenny Easley
	DB Michael Molina / Scott Stauch

RUSHING: Brown 211/1283y, Owens 177/818y, McNeil 81/408y
PASSING: Bashore 62-129/811y, 2TD, 48.4%
RECEIVING: Reece 15/340y, Brown 10/74y, Brant 9/135y
SCORING: Peter Boermeester (K) 75pts, Bashore 48pts, Owens 42pts

1979 5-6

16 Houston	24 WR Jojo Townsell / Michael Brant
31 Purdue	21 WR Willie Curran
37 Wisconsin	12 T Greg Christiansen
13 Ohio State	17 G Larry Lee
24 Stanford	27 C Brent Boyd
14 Washington St.	17 G Jim Main / John Tautolo
28 California	27 T Luis Sharpe / Irv Eatman
14 Washington	34 TE Tim Wrightman
31 Arizona State	28 QB Rick Bashore / Tom Ramsey
35 Oregon	0 TB Freeman McNeil / Anthony Edgar
14 Southern Cal	49 FB Tao Saipale / Dan Lei
	DL Mark Tuinei
	DL Mark Ferguson / Karl Morgan
	DL Joe Gary / Martin Moss
	LB Larry Hall / Chris Elias
	LB Arthur Akers / Avon Riley
	LB Billy Don Jackson
	LB Scott Stauch / Brad Plemmons
	DB Phil Hubbard / Tom Sullivan
	DB Lupe Sanchez
	DB Kenny Easley
	DB Brian Baggott / Dave Gomer

RUSHING: McNeil 271/1396y, Edgar 129/536y, Saipale 71/279y
PASSING: Bashore 60-122/964y, 8TD, 49.2%
RECEIVING: Wrightman 22/321y, Townsell 20/440y, Curran 20/287y
SCORING: Peter Boermeester (K) 69pts, McNeil 38pts, Townsell 36pts

1980 9-2

56 Colorado	14 WR Cormac Carney / Michael Brant
23 Purdue	14 WR Jojo Townsell / Willie Curran
35 Wisconsin	0 T Gregg Charitiansen / Curt Mohl
17 Ohio State	0 G Larry Lee
35 Stanford	21 C Dave Otey / Dan Dufour
32 California	9 G John Tautolo
17 Arizona	23 T Luis Sharpe
14 Oregon	20 TE Tim Wrightman / Ronnie DeBose
23 Arizona State	14 QB Tom Ramsey / Jay Schroeder
20 Southern Cal	17 TB Freeman McNeil / Kevin Nelson
34 Oregon State	3 FB Frank Bruno / Jairo Penaranda
	DL Joe Gary / Mike Barbee
	DL Martin Moss / Karl Morgan
	DL Irv Eatman
	LB Larry Hall
	LB Arthur Akers
	LB Avon Riley / Blanchard Montgomery
	LB Scott Stauch
	DB Lupe Sanchez / Mike Durden
	DB Jimmy Turner
	DB Kenny Easley
	DB Tom Sullivan

RUSHING: McNeil 203/1105y, Nelson 101/481y, Bruno 83/364y
PASSING: Ramsey 82-148/1116y, 9TD, 55.4%, Schroeder 37-65/634y, 4TD, 56.9%
RECEIVING: Carney 33/591y, Wrightman 16/236y, Townsell 13/185y
SCORING: McNeil 66pts, Norm Johnson (K) 62pts, 2 with 24pts

1981 7-4-1

35 Arizona	18 WR Cormac Carney
31 Wisconsin	13 WR Jojo Townsell / Dokie Williams
7 Iowa	20 T Dan Mahlstedt
27 Colorado	7 G Steve Williams / Blake Wingle
23 Stanford	26 C Dave Otey / Dan Dufour
17 Washington St.	17 G Chris Yelich / Duval Love
34 California	6 T Luis Sharpe
28 Oregon	11 TE Tim Wrightman / Harper Howell
31 Washington	0 QB Tom Ramsey
34 Arizona State	24 TB Kevin Nelson / Danny Andrews
21 Southern Cal	22 FB Frank Bruno / Frank Cephous
14 Michigan■	33 DL Joe Gary / Martin Moss
	DL Karl Morgan
	DL Irv Eatman
	LB Ike Gordon / Glenn Windom
	LB Ron Butler / Blanchard Montgomery
	LB Gene Newborn
	LB Brad Plemmons
	DB Jimmy Turner / Lupe Sanchez
	DB Walter Lang
	DB Don Rogers
	DB Tom Sullivan

RUSHING: Nelson 195/883y, Bruno 75/267y, Cephous 39/179y
PASSING: Ramsey 134-230/1793y, 16TD, 58.3%
RECEIVING: Carney 29/539y, Wrightman 28/308y, Townsell 26/430y
SCORING: Norm Johnson (K) 76pts, Wrightman 36pts, 2 with 30pts

1982 10-1-1

41 Long Beach St.	10 WR Cormac Carney
51 Wisconsin	26 WR Jojo Townsell / Dokie Williams
31 Michigan	27 T Irv Eatman (DL) / Steve Gemza
34 Colorado	6 G Blake Wingle
24 Arizona	24 C Dan Dufour / Steve Williams
42 Washington St.	17 G Chris Yelich / Don Mahlstedt
47 California	31 T Duval Love
40 Oregon	12 TE Paul Bergmann / Harper Howell
7 Washington	10 QB Tom Ramsey
38 Stanford	35 TB Kevin Nelson / Danny Andrews
20 Southern Cal	19 FB Frank Bruno / Frank Cephous
24 Michigan■	14 DL David Randle / Mark Walen
	DL Karl Morgan / Mark Ferguson
	DL Mike Barbee
	LB Neal Dellocono
	LB Lee Knowles / Rex Gray
	LB Blanchard Montgomery
	LB Eugene Leoni / Doug West
	DB Lupe Sanchez
	DB Jimmy Turner / Mike Durden
	DB Don Rogers
	DB Tom Sullivan / Walter Lang

RUSHING: Andrews 97/482y, Cephous 91/397y, Nelson 90/321y
PASSING: Ramsey 209-336/2986y, 21TD, 62.2%
RECEIVING: Carney 46/779y, Townsell 41/718y, Bergmann 41/577y
SCORING: John Lee (K) 87pts, Townsell 66pts, Ramsey 42pts

1983 7-4-1

8 Georgia	19 WR Mike Sherrard
26 Arizona State	26 WR Mike Young / Karl Dorrell
10 Nebraska	42 T Scott Gordon / Steve Gemza
35 BYU	37 G Mike Hartmeier / Mark Mannon (C)
39 Stanford	21 C Dave Baran
24 Washington St.	14 G Jim McCullough / Chris Yelich
20 California	16 T Duval Love
27 Washington	24 TE Paul Bergmann / Harper Howell
24 Oregon	13 QB Rick Neuheisel / Steve Bono
24 Arizona	27 TB Kevin Nelson
27 Southern Cal	17 FB Frank Cephous / Danny Andrews
45 Illinois■	9 DL David Randle / Jeff Chaffin
	DL Chris Block
	DL Kenny Page
	LB Neal Dellocono / Tony Phillips
	LB Lee Knowles / Mike Mahan
	LB Tommy Taylor / Gene Mewborn
	LB Doug West
	DB Lupe Sanchez / Chuckie Miller
	DB Ron Pitts
	DB Don Rogers
	DB Joe Gasser / Herb Welch

RUSHING: Nelson 188/898y, Cephous 120/490y, Andrews 111/450y
PASSING: Neuheisel 185-267/2245y, 13TD, 69.3%
RECEIVING: Sherrard 48/709y, Bergmann 44/499y, Dorrell 26/390y
SCORING: John Lee (K) 81pts, Nelson 46pts, Dorrell 36pts

1984 9-3

18 San Diego State	15 WR Mike Sherrard / Paco Craig
23 Long Beach St.	17 WR Mike Young / Al Wilson
3 Nebraska	42 T Mike Hartmeier / Robert Cox
33 Colorado	16 G Mark Mannon
21 Stanford	23 C Dave Baran / Joe Goebel
27 Washington St.	24 G Jim McCullough
17 California	14 T Duval Love
21 Arizona State	13 TE Derek Tennell / Russ Warnick
18 Oregon	20 QB Steve Bono / Matt Stevens
26 Oregon State	17 TB Danny Andrews / Gaston Green
29 Southern Cal	10 FB Bryan Wiley
39 Miami■	37 DL David Randle
	DL Chris Block / Terry Tumey
	DL Mark Walen
	LB Neal Dellocono / Ron Butler
	LB Tommy Taylor
	LB Lee Knowles / Ken Norton, Jr
	LB Tony Phillips / Eric Smith
	DB Herb Welch / Chuckie Miller
	DB Ron Pitts
	DB James Washington
	DB Dennis Price / Craig Rutledge

RUSHING: Andrews 158/605y, Green 91/516y, Wiley 87/402y
PASSING: Bono 136-245/1576y, 9TD, 55.5%
RECEIVING: Sherrard 43/729y, Young 35/488y, Andrews 24/185y
SCORING: John Lee (K) 117pts, Green & Young 30pts

1985 9-2-1

27 BYU	24 WR Mike Sherrard / "Flipper" Anderson
26 Tennessee	26 WR Karl Dorrell / Al Wilson
34 San Diego State	16 T Robert Cox
14 Washington	21 G Mike Hartmeier
40 Arizona State	17 C Joe Goebel
34 Stanford	9 G Jim McCullough
31 Washington St.	30 T Jim Warnick / John Kidder
34 California	7 TE Derek Tunnell
24 Arizona	19 QB David Norrie / Matt Stevens
41 Oregon State	0 TB Gaston Green/James Primus/Eric Ball
13 Southern Cal	17 FB Mel Farr, Jr / Marcus Greenwood
45 Iowa ■	28 DL Frank Batchkoff / Doug Wassel
	DL Terry Tumey / Jim Wahler
	DL Mark Walen / Jeff Glasser
	LB Melvin Jackson / Carnell Lake
	LB Tommy Taylor
	LB Steve Jarecki / Ken Norton, Jr
	LB Eric Smith / Chance Johnson
	DB Chuckie Miller / Marcus Turner
	DB Dennis Price / Darryl Henley
	DB James Washington
	DB Craig Rutledge / Joe Gasser

RUSHING: Green 158/712y, Ball 122/703y, Primus 106/471y
PASSING: Norrie 136-214/1819y, 10TD, 63.6%
RECEIVING: Dorrell 39/565y, Sherrard 35/513y, Tennell 24/252y
SCORING: John Lee (K) 105pts, Ball 66pts, Green 40pts

1986 8-3-1

3 Oklahoma	38 WR Willie "Flipper" Anderson
45 San Diego State	14 WR Karl Dorrell / Paco Craig
41 Long Beach St.	23 T Eric Rogers / Jim Warnick
9 Arizona State	16 G Jim Alexander / Frank Cornish
32 Arizona	25 C Joe Goebel / Tory Pankopf
36 California	10 G Onno Zwaneveld
54 Washington St.	16 T John Kidder
49 Oregon State	0 TE Derek Tunnell
23 Stanford	28 QB Matt Stevens
17 Washington	17 TB Gaston Green/James Primus/Eric Ball
45 Southern Cal	25 FB Mel Farr, Jr / Marcus Greenwood
31 BYU■	10 DL Frank Batchkoff / Doug Wassel
	DL Terry Tumey / Mike Lodish
	DL Jim Wahler / Jeff Glasser
	LB Carnell Lake
	LB Ken Norton, Jr / Brian Jones
	LB Chance Johnson / Greg Bolin
	LB Eric Smith / Billy Ray
	DB Chuckie Miller / Dennis Price
	DB Darryl Henley / Marcus Turner
	DB James Washington
	DB Craig Rutledge / Alan Dial

RUSHING: Green 253/1405y, Primus 98/459y, Greenwood 35/240y
PASSING: Stevens 150-280/1869y, 11TD, 53.6%
RECEIVING: Anderson 36/675y, Dorrell 35/451y, Craig 17/287y
SCORING: Green 102pts, Dave Franey (K) 87pts, Primus 48pts

1987 10-2

47 San Diego State	14 WR Flipper Anderson / Mike Farr
33 Nebraska	42 WR Paco Craig / Corwin Anthony
17 Fresno State	0 T Russ Warnick
34 Arizona	24 G Rick Meyer
49 Stanford	0 C Frank Cornish
41 Oregon	10 G John Kidder
42 California	18 T David Richards
31 Arizona State	23 TE Charles Arbuckle / Joe Pickert
52 Oregon State	17 QB Troy Aikman / Brendan McCracken
47 Washington	14 TB Gaston Green / Eric Ball /Brian Brown
13 Southern Cal	17 FB Mel Farr, Jr. / James Primus
20 Florida■	16 DL Jeff Glasser / Mike Lodish
	DL Terry Tumey
	DL Jim Wahler
	LB Carnell Lake
	LB Ken Norton, Jr.
	LB Chance Johnson
	LB Melvin Jackson / Ben Hummel
	DB Darryl Henley / Randy Beverly
	DB Dennis Price / Marcus Turner
	DB James Washington
	DB Alan Dial

RUSHING: Green 206/1098y, Brown 79/421y, Ball 81/373y
PASSING: Aikman 178-273/2527y, 17TD, 65.2%
RECEIVING: Anderson 48/903y, Craig 29/520y, Mike Farr 24/294y
SCORING: Alfredo Velasco (K) 108pts, Green 76pts, Ball 42pts

1988 10-2

59 San Diego State	6 WR Reggie Moore / Dave Keating
41 Nebraska	28 WR Mike Farr / Scott Miller
56 Long Beach St.	3 T Bobby Menifield (G) / Keith Jacobson
24 Washington	19 G Rick Meyer
38 Oregon State	21 C Frank Cornish
38 California	21 G Lance Zeno
24 Arizona	3 T Bill Paige
30 Washington St.	34 TE Charles Arbuckle / Corwin Anthony
16 Oregon	6 QB Troy Aikman
27 Stanford	17 TB Eric Ball / Shawn Wills / Brian Brown
22 Southern Cal	31 FB Mark Estwick
17 Arkansas■	3 DL Mike Lodish
	DL Jim Wahler / Emmanuel Onwutuebe
	DL Bryan Wilcox / Steve Mehr
	LB Eric Smith / Marvcus Patton
	LB Craig Davis / Stacy Argo
	LB Chance Johnson / Doug Kline
	LB Carnell Lake / Billy Ray
	DB Darryl Henley / Randy Beverly
	DB Marcus Turner / Dion Lambert
	DB Eric Turner
	DB Matt Darby

RUSHING: Ball 166/784y, Wills 94/622y, Brown 91/410y
PASSING: Aikman 228-354/2771y, 24TD, 64.4%
RECEIVING: Farr 66/700y, Moore 38/627y, Keating 23/341y
SCORING: Alfredo Velasco (K) 94pts, Moore & Ball 36pts

1989 3-7-1

6 Tennessee	24 WR Reggie Moore
28 San Diego State	25 WR Mike Farr / Scott Miller
23 Michigan	24 T Keith Jacobson
24 California	6 G Rick Meyer/Mark Wilder/Sc'tt Spalding
33 Arizona State	14 C Frank Cornish
7 Arizona	42 G Lance Zeno
17 Oregon State	18 T Bill Paige
27 Washington	28 TE Charles Arbuckle / Corwin Anthony
14 Stanford	17 QB Bret Johnson / Jim Bonds
20 Oregon	38 TB Brian Brown / Kevin Williams
10 Southern Cal	10 FB Mark Estwick / Shawn Wills (TB)
	DL Mike Lodish / Siitupe Tuala
	DL Brian Kelly / Jon Pryor
	DL Brad Bryson / Bryan Wilcox
	LB Rocen Keeton
	LB Craig Davis / Pat McPherson
	LB Stacy Argo / Meech Shaw
	LB Marvcus Patton
	DB Carlton Gray / Randy Beverly
	DB Dion Lambert / Michael Williams
	DB Eric Turner
	DB Matt Darby / Mark McGill

RUSHING: Brown 130/463y, Wills 118/440y, Williams 85/380y
PASSING: Johnson 145-252/1791y, 12TD, 57.5%
RECEIVING: Arbuckle 33/309y, Farr 30/471y, Miller 23/414y
SCORING: Alfredo Velasco 63pts, Williams 36pts, Miller 30pts

1990 5-6

14 Oklahoma	34 WR Reggie Moore/Sean LaChapelle (TE)
32 Stanford	31 WR Scott Miller / Michael Moore
15 Michigan	38 T Craig Novitsky
30 Washington St.	20 G Scott Spalding
21 Arizona	28 C Lance Zeno / Aron Gideon
45 San Diego State	31 G Vaughn Parker (T)
31 California	38 T Rick Fuller / Derek Stevens
26 Oregon State	17 TE Randy Austin / Rick Daly / C.Anthony
24 Oregon	28 QB Tommy Maddox
25 Washington	22 TB Brian Brown / Kevin Williams
42 Southern Cal	45 FB Kevin Smith / Shawn Wills
	DL Mike Chalenski / Bruce Walker (LB)
	DL Emmanuel Onwutuebe / Siitupe Tuala
	DL Matt Werner / Brian Kelly
	LB Arnold Ale / Scott Lockwood
	LB Meech Shaw
	LB Stacy Argo / James Malone
	LB Roman Phifer / Rocen Keeton
	DB Carlton Gray / Michael Williams
	DB Dion Lambert / Damion Lyons
	DB Eric Turner
	DB Matt Darby / Travis Collier

RUSHING: Williams 191/1141y
PASSING: Maddox 182-327/2682y, 17TD, 55.7%
RECEIVING: LaChapelle 73/1056y
SCORING: Louis Perez (K) 80pts

1991 9-3

27 BYU	23 WR Sean LaChapelle / Bryan Adams
16 Tennessee	30 WR Paul Richardson / Michael Moore
37 San Diego State	12 T Craig Novitsky
24 California	27 G Scott Spalding
54 Arizona	14 C Aron Gideon
44 Oregon State	7 G Mike Linn / Marc Wilder
21 Arizona State	16 T Vaughn Parker / Rick Fuller
44 Washington St.	3 TE Rick Daly
10 Stanford	27 QB Tommy Maddox
16 Oregon	9 TB Ricky Davis / Shawn Wills
24 Southern Cal	21 FB Kevin Williams / Kaleaph Carter
6 Illinois■	3 DL Mike Chelenski
	DL Emmanuel Onwutuebe
	DL Matt Werner / Bruce Walker
	LB Arnold Ale
	LB Stacy Argo / Rod Smalley
	LB James Malone / Jamir Miller
	LB Randy Cole
	DB Carlton Gray / Michael Williams
	DB Carl Greenwood / Dion Lambert
	DB Othello Henderson
	DB Matt Darby / Travis Collier

RUSHING: Williams 168/1141y, Wills 67/419y, Davis 71/329y
PASSING: Maddox 209-343/2681y, 16 TDs, 60.9%
RECEIVING: LaChapelle 73/1056y, Richardson 29/397y, Williams 21/143y
SCORING: Louis Perez (K) 80pts, LaChapelle 66pts, Williams 54pts

1992 6-5

37 Cal-Fullerton	14 WR Sean LaChapelle / J.J. Stokes
17 BYU	10 WR Kevin Jordan / Mike Nguyen
35 San Diego State	7 T Jonathan Ogden
3 Arizona	23 G Craig Novitsky (T) / Ron Nielsen
7 Stanford	19 C Aron Gideon
17 Washington St.	30 G Derek Stevens
0 Arizona State	20 T Vaughn Parker
12 California	48 T Rick Daly / Brian Allen
26 Oregon State	14 QB Rob Walker/J'hn Barnes/Wayne Cook
9 Oregon	6 TB Kevin Williams / Daron Washington
38 Southern Cal	37 FB Kaleaph Carter / James Milliner
	DL Mike Chalenski / London Woodfin
	DL Sale Isaia / Bruce Walker
	DL Matt Werner / Gary Walton
	LB Jamir Miller (DE) / Rod Smalley
	LB Arnold Ale / Carrick O'Quinn
	LB Nkosi Littleton / Brian Tighe
	LB Donnie Edwards / Bradley Craig
	DB Carlton Gray
	DB Carl Greenwood / Rob Gamble
	DB Othello Henderson / Michael Williams
	DB Marvin Goodwin / Donovan Gallatin

RUSHING: Williams 115/582y, Washington 89/415y
PASSING: Walker 84-154/791y, 3TD, 54.6%, Barnes 61-117/957y, 5TD, 52.1%
RECEIVING: Stokes 41/728y, LaChapelle 30/364y, Nguyen 25/316y
SCORING: Louis Perez (K) 63pts, Stokes 42pts, 2 with 30pts

1993 8-4

25 California	27 WR J.J. Stokes
13 Nebraska	14 WR Kevin Jordan / Mike Nguyen
28 Stanford	25 T Jonathan Ogden
52 San Diego State	13 G Craig Novitsky (T) / Karl Schroller
68 BYU	14 C Mike Flanagan / James Christensen
39 Washington	25 G Derek Stevens / Matt Soenksen
20 Oregon State	17 T Vaughn Parker
37 Arizona	17 TE Brian Allen / Brian Richards
40 Washington St.	27 QB Wayne Cook / Rob Walker
3 Arizona State	9 RB Skip Hicks / Ricky Davis
27 Southern Cal	21 RB James Milliner / Sharmon Shah
16 Wisconsin■	21 DL Sale Isaia / Grady Stretz
	DL George Kase / Travis Kirschke
	DL Matt Werner / London Woodfin
	LB Donnie Edwards
	LB Nkosi Littleton
	LB Shane Jasper / Carrick O'Quinn
	LB Jamir Miller / Rod Smalley
	DB Teddy Lawrence / Paul Guidry
	DB Carl Greenwood / Robert Gamble
	DB Travis Collier / Tommy Bennett
	DB Marvin Goodwin / Donovan Goodwin

RUSHING: Hicks 100/563y, Davis 129/541y, Milliner 57/366y
PASSING: Cook 165-297/2067y, 18TD, 55.6%
RECEIVING: Stokes 82/1181y, Jordan 45/612y, Nguyen 26/300y
SCORING: Stokes 102pts, Bjorn Merten (K) 95pts, 2 with 30pts

1994 5-6

25 Tennessee	23 WR J.J. Stokes / Mike Nguyen
17 SMU	10 WR Kevin Jordan / Jim McElroy
21 Nebraska	49 T Jonathan Ogden
0 Washington St.	21 G James Christensen
10 Washington	37 C Mike Flanagan
7 California	26 G Matt Soenksnen
14 Oregon State	23 T Chad Overhauser
24 Arizona	34 TE Brian Richards
31 Stanford	30 QB Wayne Cook / Ryan Fien
59 Arizona State	23 TB Sharmon Shah* / Skip Hicks
31 Southern Cal	19 FB Daron Washington / James Milliner
	DL Sale Isaia / Gary Walton
	DL George Kase
	DL Travis Kirschke
	LB Donnie Edwards
	LB Phillip Ward
	LB Shane Jasper
	LB Rod Smalley / Tommy Bennett
	DB Teddy Lawrence
	DB Carl Greenwood / Javelin Guidry
	DB Paul Guidry / Shaun Williams
	DB Abdul McCullough

RUSHING: Shah 210/1227y, Washington 46/214y,Hicks 40/161y
PASSING: Cook 179-302/2501y, 15TD, 59.3%
RECEIVING: Jordan 73/1228y, Stokes 26/505y, Washington 26/195y
SCORING: Bjorn Merten (K) 60pts
* Sharmon Shah changed his name to Karim Abdul-Jabbar after 1994 season.

1995 7-5

31 Miami	8 WR Eric Scott / Jim McElroy
23 BYU	9 WR Kevin Jordan / Derek Ayers
31 Oregon	38 T Jonathan Ogden
15 Washington St.	24 G Chad Overhauser
45 Fresno State	21 C Mike Flanagan
17 Arizona	10 G James Christensen
42 Stanford	28 T Mike Rohme / Andy Meyers
33 California	16 TE Brian Richards / Mike Grieb
33 Arizona State	37 QB Cade McNown / Ryan Fien
14 Washington	38 TB Karim Abdul-Jabbar*
24 Southern Cal	20 FB Cheyane Caldwell / James Milliner
30 Kansas■	51 DL Danjuan Magee
	DL George Kase
	DL Gary Walton / Phillip Ward
	DL Grady Stretz / Travis Kirschke
	LB Tommy Bennett
	LB Brian Willmer
	LB Abdul McCullough / Ramogi Huma
	DB Teddy Lawrence / Javelin Guidry
	DB Paul Guidry
	DB Shaun Williams
	DB Ted Nwoke / Anthony Cobbs

RUSHING: Abdul-Jabbar 270/1419y, Milliner 74/288y, McNown 60/229y
PASSING: McNown 109-211/1577y, 4TD, 51.7%
RECEIVING: Jordan 41/539y, Ayers 21/290y, McElroy 19/403y
SCORING: Abdul-Jabbar 82pts

1996 5-6

20 Tennessee	35 WR Derek Ayers / Danny Farmer
44 NE Louisiana	0 WR Jim McElroy / Eric Scott
9 Michigan	38 T Kris Farris
41 Oregon	22 G Chad Sauter
34 Arizona State	42 C Shawn Stuart
21 Washington	41 G Andy Meyers / Sean Gully
38 California	29 T Chad Overhauser
20 Stanford	21 TE Jamal Clark / Mike Grieb
38 Washington St.	14 QB Cade McNown
17 Arizona	35 TB Skip Hicks / Keith Brown
48 Southern Cal	41 FB Craig Walendy / Durell Price
	DL Weldon Forte / Darren Cline
	DL Jeff Ruckman
	DL Damon Smith
	DL Travis Kirschke / Brendon Ayanbadejo
	LB Danjuan Magee / Anthony Cobbs
	LB Brian Willmer / Michael Wiley
	LB Phillip Ward
	DB Kusanti Abdul-Salaam / Paul Guidry
	DB Javelin Guidry / Aaron Roques
	DB Shaun Williams
	DB Abdul McCullough / Larry Atkins

RUSHING: Hicks 224/1034y, Price 61/210y, Brown 39/149y
PASSING: McNown 176-336/2424y, 12TD, 52.4%
RECEIVING: Farmer 31/524y, McElroy 26/527y, Hicks 21/283y
SCORING: Hicks 120pts, Bjorn Merten (K) 80pts, Brown, Farmer & McNown 24pts

1997 10-2

34 Washington St.	37 WR Jim McElroy
24 Tennessee	30 WR Danny Farmer / Brad Melsby
66 Texas	3 T Kris Farris
40 Arizona	27 G Chad Sauter
66 Houston	10 C Shawn Stuart
39 Oregon	31 G Andy Meyers
34 Oregon State	10 T Chad Overhauser / Brian Polak (G)
35 California	17 TE Mike Grieb / Ryan Neufeld
27 Stanford	7 QB Cade McNown
52 Washington	28 TB Skip Hicks/Jerm'ne Lewis/Keith Brown
31 Southern Cal	24 FB Craig Walendy / Cheyane Caldwell
29 Texas A&M■	23 DL Weldon Forte / Micah Webb
	DL Pete Holland / Jeff Ruckman
	DL Brendon Ayanbedajo / Trevor Turner
	LB Ali Abdul Azziz / Michael Wiley
	LB Ramogi Huma
	LB Brian Willmer
	LB Danjuan Magee / Wasswa Serwanga
	DB Jason Bell / Ryan Roques
	DB Javelin Guidry
	DB Shaun Williams
	DB Larry Atkins / DuVal Hicks

RUSHING: Hicks 227/1142y, Lewis 55/276y, Brown 67/272y
PASSING: McNown 173-283/2877y, 22TD, 61.1%
RECEIVING: McElroy 42/904y, Farmer 37/609y, Hicks 19/336y
SCORING: Hicks 156pts

1998 10-2

49 Texas	31 WR Brian Poli-Dixon / Jon Dubravac
42 Houston	24 WR Danny Farmer / Brad Melsby
49 Washington St.	17 T Kris Farris
52 Arizona	28 G Oscar Cabrara
41 Oregon	38 C Shawn Stuart / Troy Danoff
28 California	16 G Andy Meyers / Matt Phelan
28 Stanford	24 T Brian Polak / Josh Webb
41 Oregon State	34 TE Mike Grieb / Ryan Neufeld
36 Washington	24 QB Cade McNown
34 Southern Cal	17 TB Jermaine Lewis/Keith Brown/D. Foster
45 Miami	49 FB Durell Price
31 Wisconsin■	38 DL Pete Holland
	DL Micah Webb / Ken Kocher
	DL Kenyon Coleman
	LB Santi Hall
	LB Tony White
	LB Ryan Nece / Robert Thomas
	LB Brendon Ayanbadejo / Ali Abdul Azziz
	DB Marques Anderson
	DB Jason Bell
	DB Larry Atkins / Ryan Roques
	DB Jason Stephens

RUSHING: Foster 116/635y, Lewis 120/503y, Brown 96/420y
PASSING: McNown 188-323/3130y, 58.2%
RECEIVING: Farmer 58/1274y, Poli-Dixon 44/712y, Melsby 16/331y, Grieb 16/274y, Foster 16/163y
SCORING: Chris Sailer (K) 104pts, Lewis 78pts, Foster 72pts

1999 4-7

38 Boise State	7 WR Brian Poli-Dixon
20 Ohio State	42 WR Danny Farmer / Freddie Mitchell
35 Fresno State	21 T Blake Worley
32 Stanford	42 G Oscar Cabrera
27 Arizona State	28 C Troy Danoff
34 Oregon	29 G Mike Saffer
0 California	17 T Brian Polak
7 Oregon State	55 TE Gabe Crecion / Bryan Fletcher
7 Arizona	33 QB Cory Paus / Drew Bennett
23 Washington	20 TB J'rm'ne Lew's/K'th Br'wn/D'Sh'n Fost'r
7 Southern Cal	17 FB Durell Price / Matt Stanley
	DL Kenyon Coleman
	DL Ken Kocher
	DL Pete Holland / Anthony Fletcher
	DL Rusty Williams / Stephen Sua
	LB Ali Abdul Azziz
	LB Robert Taylor / Tony White
	LB Ryan Nece
	DB Marques Anderson
	DB Ricky Manning, Jr / Jason Bell
	DB Lovell Houston / Ryan Roques
	DB Jason Stephens / Eric Whitfield

RUSHING: Brown 98/421y, Foster 111/375y, Lewis 63/216y
PASSING: Paus 95-197/1336y, 7TD, 48.2%
RECEIVING: Mitchell 38/533y, Farmer 29/573y, Melsby 22/279y
SCORING: Chris Griffith (K) 64pts, Foster 38pts, Brown 30pts

2000 6-6

35 Alabama	24 WR Brian Poli-Dixon / Jon Dubravac
24 Fresno State	21 WR Freddie Mitchell
23 Michigan	20 T Bryce Bohlander
10 Oregon	29 G Brian Polak / Blake Worley
38 Arizona State	31 C Troy Danoff
38 California	46 G Oscar Cabrera
38 Oregon State	44 T Mike Saffer
27 Arizona	24 TE Gabe Crecion / Bryan Fletcher
37 Stanford	35 QB Cory Paus / Ryan McCann
28 Washington	35 TB DeShaun Foster / Jermaine Lewis
35 Southern Cal	38 FB Ed Íeremia-Stansbury / Matt Stanley
20 Wisconsin■	21 DL Mat Ball / Sean Phillips
	DL Anthony Fletcher
	DL Rodney Leisle / Ken Kocher
	DL Rusty Williams / Stephen Sua
	LB Tony White / Santi Hall
	LB Robert Thomas
	LB Ryan Nece / Marcus Reese
	DB Ricky Manning, Jr
	DB Jason Bell
	DB Jason Zdenek / Lovell Houston
	DB Marques Anderson / Jason Stephens

RUSHING: Foster 269/1037y, Lewis 56/208y, Akil Harris (TB) 45/201y
PASSING: Paus 134-241/2154y, 17TD, 55.6%, McCann 60-120/688y, 4TD, 50.0%
RECEIVING: Mitchell 77/1494y, Poli-Dixon 53/750y, Foster 16/142y
SCORING: Foster 78pts, Chris Griffith (K) 77pts, Mitchell 54pts

2001 7-4

20 Alabama	17 WR Brian Poli-Dixon / Ryan Smith
41 Kansas	17 WR Tab Perry / Craig Bragg
13 Ohio State	6 T Bryce Bohlander
38 Oregon State	7 G Eyoseph Efseaff
35 Washington	13 C Troy Danoff / John Ream (G)
56 California	17 G Shane Lehmann / Steven Vieira
28 Stanford	38 T Mike Saffer
14 Washington St.	20 TE Bryan Fletcher / Mike Seidman
20 Oregon	21 QB Cory Paus / Ryan McCann
0 Southern Cal	27 TB DeShaun Foster / Akil Harris
52 Arizona State	42 FB Ed Íeremia-Stansbury / Matt Stanley
	DL Kenyon Coleman
	DL Ken Kocher / Anthony Fletcher
	DL Rodney Leisle
	DL Dave Ball
	LB Brandon Chillar / Mat Ball
	LB Robert Thomas
	LB Ryan Nece / Marcus Reese
	DB Ricky Manning, Jr
	DB Matt Ware / Joe Hunter
	DB Marques Anderson / Kevin Brant
	DB Jason Stephens / Ben Emanuel

RUSHING: Foster 216/1109y
PASSING: Paus 101-194/1740y, 8TD, 52.1%
RECEIVING: Bragg 29/408y
SCORING: Foster 78pts

2002 8-5

30 Colorado State	19 WR Craig Bragg
38 Oklahoma State	24 WR Tab Perry
17 Colorado	31 T Bryce Bohlander
43 San Diego State	7 G Eyoseph Efseaff
43 Oregon State	35 C Mike McCloskey
30 Oregon	31 G Steven Vieira
12 California	17 T Mike Saffer
28 Stanford	18 TE Mike Seidman / Keith Carter
34 Washington	24 QB Drew Olson
37 Arizona	7 TB Tyler Ebell / Akil Harris
21 Southern Cal	52 FB Manuel White
27 Washington St.	48 DL Rusty Williams / Mat Ball
27 New Mexico■	13 DL Kyle Morgan
	DL Rodney Leisle / Ryan Boschetti
	DL Dave Ball / Asi Faoa
	LB Brandon Chillar
	LB Marcus Reese
	LB Spencer Havner
	DB Ricky Manning, Jr.
	DB Matt Ware / Joe Hunter
	DB Ben Emanuel
	DB Jarrad Page

RUSHING: Ebell 234/994y, White 85/381y, Harris 80/323y
PASSING: Paus 109-184/1647y, 10TD, 59.2%,
Olson 53-104/702y, 3TD, 51.0%
RECEIVING: Bragg 55/889y, Seidman 41/631y, Perry 35/698y
SCORING: Ebell 60pts, Bragg 54pts, Nate Fiske (K) 53pts

2003 6-7

14 Colorado	16 WR Craig Bragg
6 Illinois	3 WR Ryan Smith / Junior Taylor
24 Oklahoma	59 T Steven Vieira
20 San Diego State	10 G Eyoseph Efseaff
46 Washington	16 C Robert Chai
24 Arizona	21 G Paul Mociler / Kevin Brown
23 California	20 T Ed Blanton
20 Arizona State	13 TE Blane Kerizian / Marcedes Lewis
14 Stanford	21 QB Drew Olson / Matt Moore
13 Washington St.	31 TB Tyler Ebell / Maurice Drew
13 Oregon	31 FB Manuel White / Pat Norton
22 Southern Cal	47 DL Mat Ball
9 Fresno State■	17 DL Rodney Leisle / Asi Faoa
	DL Ryan Boschetti / C.J. Niusulu
	DL Dave Ball
	LB Brandon Chillar
	LB Justin London / Dennis Link
	LB Spencer Havner
	DB Matt Clark
	DB Matt Ware / Keith Short
	DB Ben Emanuel / Nnamdi Ohaeri
	DB Jarrad Page / Kevin Brant

RUSHING: Drew 135/582y, Ebell 116/501y, White 96/379y
PASSING: Olson 173-325/2067y, 10 TDs, 53.2%,
Moore 52-103/555y, 2 TDs, 50.5%
RECEIVING: Bragg 73/1065y, Lewis 30/377y, Smith 28/277y
SCORING: Justin Medlock (K) 68pts, Drew 42pts, Bragg 30pts

2004 6-6

20 Oklahoma State	31 WR Craig Bragg / Tab Perry
35 Illinois	17 WR Junior Taylor
37 Washington	31 T Paul Mociler
33 San Diego St.	10 G Robert Cleary / Shannon Tevaga
37 Arizona	17 C Mike McCloskey / Robert Chai
28 California	45 G Steven Vierra (T)
42 Arizona State	48 T Ed Blanton
21 Stanford	0 TE Marcedes Lewis / Keith Carter
29 Washington St.	31 QB Drew Olson / David Koral
34 Oregon	26 TB Maurice Drew / Manuel White (FB)
24 Southern Cal	29 FB Michael Pitre
21 Wyoming ■	24 DL Kyle Morgan
	DL Kevin Brown
	DL C.J. Niusulu / Eyoseph Efseaff
	DL Justin Hickman / Brigham Harwell
	LB Wesley Walker / Aaron Whittingham
	LB Justin London / Ben Lorier
	LB Spencer Havner
	DB Matt Clark
	DB Marcus Cassel / Trey Brown
	DB Ben Emanuel / Chris Horton
	DB Jarrad Page / Eric McNeal

RUSHING: Drew 160/1007y, White 164/764y,
Chris Markey (TB) 66/350y
PASSING: Olson 196-341/2565y, 20TD, 57.5%
RECEIVING: Bragg 36/483y, Taylor 32/463y, Lewis 32/402y
SCORING: Justin Medlock (K) 87pts, Drew 72pts, White 56pts

2005 10-2

44 San Diego St.	21 WR Marcus Everett
63 Rice	21 WR Joe Cowan / Brandon Breazell
41 Oklahoma	24 T Ed Blanton
21 Washington	17 G Robert Cleary
47 California	40 C Mike McCloskey / Robert Chai
44 Washington St.	41 G Shannon Tevaga
51 Oregon State	28 T Brian Abraham
30 Stanford	27 TE Marcedes Lewis
14 Arizona	52 QB Drew Olson
45 Arizona State	35 TB Maurice Drew/Chris Markey/Kahil Bell
19 Southern Cal	66 FB Michael Pitre
50 Northwestern■	38 DL Justin Hickman / Nikola Dragovic
	DL Brigham Harwell / Kenneth Lombard
	DL Chase Moline / Kevin Brown
	DL Kyle Morgan/Wm. Snead/Bruce Davis
	LB Wesley Walker / John Hale
	LB Justin London / Christian Taylor
	LB Spencer Havner
	DB Trey Brown
	DB Marcus Cassel
	DB Dennis Keyes / Eric McNeal
	DB Jarrad Page / Chris Horton

RUSHING: Drew 186/914y, Markey 110/561y, Bell 52/310y
PASSING: Olson 242-378/3198y, 34TDs, 64.0%
RECEIVING: Lewis 58/741y, Cowan 35/469y, Everett 32/390y,
Drew 31/453y
SCORING: Drew 120pts, Justin Medlock (K) 89pts, Lewis 60pts

2006 7-6

31 Utah	10 WR Marcus Everett / Junior Taylor
26 Rice	16 WR Brandon Breazell / Matt Willis
19 Washington	29 T Noah Sutherland
31 Stanford	0 G Chris Joseph
27 Arizona	7 C Robert Chai
20 Oregon	30 G Shannon Tevaga
20 Notre Dame	20 T Aleksey Lanis
15 Washington St.	37 TE Logan Paulsen
24 California	38 QB Patrick Cowan / Ben Olson
25 Oregon State	7 TB Chris Markey / Kahlil Bell
24 Arizona State	12 FB Michael Pitre / Chane Moline (TB)
13 Southern Cal	9 DL Justin Hickman
27 Florida State■	44 DL Brigham Harwell / Kenneth Lombard
	DL Kevin Brown
	DL Bruce Davis
	LB Aaron Whittington / John Hale
	LB Christian Taylor / Kyle Bosworth
	LB Reggie Carter / Eric McNeal
	DB Trey Brown
	DB Rodney Van / Alterraun Verner
	DB Dennis Keyes
	DB Chris Horton

RUSHING: Markey 227/1107y, Bell 60/239y, Cowan 54/108y,
Moline 33/101y
PASSING: Cowan 145-276/1782y, 11TDs, 52.5%,
Olson 79-124/822y, 5TDs, 63.7%
RECEIVING: Markey 35/261y, Everett 31/450y, Taylor 28/331y,
Paulsen 27/331y
SCORING: Justin Medlock (K) 113pts, Moline & Everett 30pts

2007 6-7

45 Stanford	17 WR Joe Cowan / Dominique Johnson
27 BYU	17 WR Brandon Breazell / Terrence Austin
6 Utah	44 T Micah Kia / Aleksey Lanis
44 Washington	31 G Shannon Tevaga / P.J. Irvin
40 Oregon State	14 C Chris Joseph
6 Notre Dame	20 G Micah Reed / Noah Sutherland
30 California	21 T Brian Abraham
7 Washington St.	27 TE Logan Paulsen / William Snead
27 Arizona	34 QB Ben Olson/Pat Cowan/Osaar Rasshan
20 Arizona State	24 TB Chris Markey / Kahil Bell
16 Oregon	0 FB Trevor Theriot
7 Southern Cal	24 DL Tom Blake / Korey Bosworth
16 BYU■	17 DL Kevin Brown / Brigham Harwell
	DL Brian Price / Jess Ward
	DL Bruce Davis / Nikola Dragovic
	LB Kyle Bosworth / Aaron Whittington
	LB Christian Taylor
	LB Reggie Carter
	DB Trey Brown
	DB Alterraun Verner / Rodney Van
	DB Dennis Keyes / Matt Slater
	DB Chris Horton

RUSHING: Bell 142/795y, Markey 176/715y,
Chane Moline (TB) 55/196y
PASSING: Olson 71-147/1040y, 7TD, 48.3%,
P. Cowan 72-135/696y, 4TD, 53.3%
RECEIVING: Breazell 51/810y, J. Cowan 29/405y,
Johnson 25/322y
SCORING: Kai Forbath (K) 105pts, Bell 30pts,
Breazell & Johnson 24pts

2008 4-8

27 Tennessee	24 WR Taylor Embree / Dominique Johnson
0 BYU	59 WR Terrence Austin / Marcus Everett
10 Arizona	31 T Jeff Baca / Micah Kia (G)
31 Fresno State	36 G Darius Savage / Sonny Tevaga
28 Washington St.	3 C Jake Dean / Micah Reed (G)
24 Oregon	31 G Scott Glicksberg
23 Stanford	20 T Nick Ekbatani (G) / Mike Harris
20 California	41 TE Ryan Moya / Cory Harkey / Jeff Miller
6 Oregon State	34 QB Kevin Craft
27 Washington	12 TB Kahlil Bell / Derrick Coleman
9 Arizona State	34 FB Chane Moline
7 Southern Cal	28 DL Tom Blake / Reginald Stokes
	DL Brian Price
	DL Brigham Harwell
	DL Korey Bosworth
	LB John Hale / Kyle Bosworth
	LB Steve Sloan
	LB Reggie Carter / Akeem Ayers
	DB Michael Norris / Courtney Viney
	DB Alterraun Verner
	DB Rahim Moore / Glenn Love
	DB Bret Lockett / Aaron Ware

RUSHING: Bell 141/397y, Coleman 53/284y, Moline 30/118y
PASSING: Craft 232-417/2341y, 7TDs, 55.6%
RECEIVING: Austin 53/460y, Embree 40/531y, Moya 38/364y,
Johnson 34/373y
SCORING: Kai Forbath (K) 78pts, Bell 48pts, Moya 18pts

2009 7-6

33 San Diego State	14 WR Taylor Embree / Nathan Rosario
19 Tennessee	15 WR Terrence Austin
23 Kansas State	9 T Xavier Su'a-Filo
16 Stanford	24 G Jeff Baca / Jake Dean
10 Oregon	24 C Kai Maiava
26 California	45 G Ryan Taylor / Nick Ekbatani
13 Arizona	27 T Mike Harris
19 Oregon State	26 TE Logan Paulsen / Ryan Moya
24 Washington	23 QB Kevin Prince / Kevin Craft
43 Washington St.	7 TB Johnathan Franklin / Derrick Coleman
23 Arizona State	13 FB Chance Moline / Trevor Theriot
7 Southern Cal	28 DL Datone Jones
30 Temple■	21 DL Brian Price
	DL Jerzy Siewierski / Jess Ward
	DL Korey Bosworth / Damien Holmes
	LB Akeem Ayers
	LB Reggie Carter
	LB Kyle Bosworth / Sean Westgate
	DB Sheldon Price / Courtney Viney
	DB Alterraun Verner / Aaron Hester
	DB Rahim Moore
	DB Tony Dye / Glenn Love

RUSHING: Franklin 126/566y, Coleman 54/244y, Moline 60/207y
PASSING: Prince 173-308/2050y, 8TD, 56.2%
Craft 232-417/2341y, 7TD, 55.6%
RECEIVING: Embree 45/608y, Rosario 42/723y, Austin 37/455y
Paulsen 29/362y, Moline 29/247y
SCORING: Kai Forbath (K) 108pts, Moline 36pts, Franklin 32pts

2010 4-8

22 Kansas State	31 WR Taylor Embree / Randal Carroll
0 BYU	35 WR Nelson Rosario / Ricky Marvray
31 Houston	13 T Sean Sheller / Micah Kia
34 Texas	12 G Darius Savage
42 Washington St.	28 C Ryan Taylor
7 California	35 G Eddie Williams
13 Oregon	60 T Mike Harris
21 Arizona	29 TE Cory Harkey
17 Oregon State	14 QB Richard Brehart / Kevin Prince
7 Washington	24 TB Johnathan Franklin / Derrick Coleman
34 Arizona State	55 FB Morrel Presley / Anthony Barr
14 Southern Cal	28 DL Owamagbe Odighizuwa/Reggie Stokes
	DL Nate Chandler / Cassius Marsh
	DL David Carter / Justin Edison
	DL Keenan Graham / Damien Holmes
	LB Sean Westgate
	LB Pat Larimore / Jordan Zumwalt
	LB Akeem Ayers (DL)
	DB Aaron Hester / Courtney Viney
	DB Sheldon Price / Andrew Abbott
	DB Rahm Moore
	DB Tony Dye

RUSHING: Franklin 214/1127y, Coleman 82/487y,
Malcolm Jones (RB) 55/200y
PASSING: Brehart 119-212/1296y, 6TD, 56.1%
Prince 42-94/384y, 3TD, 44.7%
RECEIVING: Embree 32/409y, Rosario 29/309y, Marvray 20/188y
SCORING: Kai Forbath (K) 66pts, Franklin 48pts, Coleman 30pts

VANDERBILT

Vanderbilt University (Founded 1873)
Nashville, Tennessee
Nickname: Commodores
Colors: Black and Gold
Stadium: Vanderbilt (1981) 39,790
Conference Affiliation: Southeastern (Charter member 1933-present)

CAREER RUSHING YARDS	Attempts	Yards
Frank Mordica (1976-79)	546	2632
Carl Woods (1983-86)	619	2490
Jamie O'Rourke (1971, 73-74)	498	2202
Jermaine Johnson (1993-95)	486	2152
Jared McGrath (1997-2000)	492	2151
Lonnie Sadler (1972-75)	569	2096
Rodney Williams (1998-2001)	452	2021
Everett Crawford (1984-87)	395	1814
Dean Davidson (1947-50)	337	1731
Phil King (1955-57)	342	1717

CAREER PASSING YARDS	Comp.-Att.	Yards
Jay Cutler (2002-05)	710-1242	8697
Greg Zolman (1998-2001)	596-1156	7981
Whit Taylor (1979-82)	555-1016	6307
Kurt Page (1981-84)	531-936	6233
Eric Jones (1986-88)	365-661	5029
Damian Allen (1994-97)	307-699	3704
John Gromos (1985, 87-89)	287-580	3514
Chris Nickson (2005-08)	284-540	3406
Bill Wade (1949-51)	201-437	3397
Mackenzi Adams (2006-09)	257-493	2779

CAREER RECEIVING YARDS	Catches	Yards
Boo Mitchell (1985-88)	188	2964
Dan Stricker (1999-2002)	182	2880
Earl Bennett (2005-07)	236	2852
Martin Cox (1975-78)	132	2275
Chuck Scott (1981-84)	145	2219
Clarence Sevillian (1989-92)	99	1978
Erik Davis (2002-05)	124	1767
Keith Edwards (1980, 82-83)	200	1757
Carl Parker (1983, 85-87)	118	1721
Tavarus Hogans (1996-99)	110	1645

SEASON RUSHING YARDS	Attempts	Yards
Corey Harris (1991)	229	1103
Jermaine Johnson (1995)	267	1072
Frank Mordica (1978)	173	1065
Jamie O'Rourke (1974)	201	933
Jermain Johnson (1994)	167	877

SEASON PASSING YARDS	Comp.-Att.	Yards
Kurt Page (1983)	286-493	3178
Jay Cutler (2005)	273-462	3073
Eric Jones (1988)	195-360	2548
Greg Zolman (2001)	186-357	2512
Whit Taylor (1982)	228-406	2481

SEASON RECEIVING YARDS	Caught	Yards
Boo Mitchell (1988)	78	1213
Earl Bennett (2006)	82	1146
Bob Goodridge (1967)	79	1114
Dan Stricker (2001)	65	1079
Dan Stricker (2000)	61	994

GAME RUSHING YARDS	Attempts	Yards
Frank Mordica (1978 vs. Air Force)	N/A	321
Doug Mathews (1969 vs. Tulane)	N/A	214
Frank Mordica (1979 vs. Citadel)	N/A	187
Jamie O'Rourke (1971 vs. Tulane)	N/A	187

GAME PASSING YARDS	Comp.-Att.	Yards
Whit Taylor (1981 vs. Tennessee)	N/A	464
Whit Taylor (1982 vs. Air Force)	N/A	452
Chris Nickson (2006 vs. Kentucky)	23-37	446

GAME RECEIVING YARDS	Caught	Yards
Earl Bennett (2007 vs. Richmond)	13	223
Clarence Sevillian (1992 vs. Tennessee)	N/A	222
Earl Bennett (2007 vs. Kentucky)	11	220

GREATEST COACH:

The list of coaches at Vanderbilt is awash in losing records. This is because Vanderbilt, as a private school with an excellent academic reputation, truthfully has been in over its head for a very long time against the roster of large, state-supported football powers that make up the rest of the Southeastern Conference.

Like nearly every other Vandy coach, Art Guepe, a 10-year survivor in Nashville, left with a losing record. Vanderbilt has enjoyed only eight winning seasons in 55 years, yet Guepe coached four in a five-year period. But, if his last three receding years could be magically removed, Guepe it turns out enjoyed 33-30-7 record from 1953 to 1959.

The heights of Guepe's reign were reached in 1955 when the Commodores beat Alabama, Kentucky, and Florida to finish the regular season 7-3 and earn a Gator Bowl berth against SEC power Auburn. The Commodores stunningly belted the Tigers 25-13 that Saturday in December 1955.

VANDERBILT'S 55 GREATEST SINCE 1953

OFFENSE

WIDE RECEIVER: Earl Bennett, Preston Brown, Waymon Buggs, Martin Cox, Bob Goodrich, Boo Mitchell, Chuck Scott
TIGHT END: Pat Akos, Allama Matthews, Carl Parker, Jim Popp
TACKLE: Bob Asher, Larry Wagner, Will Woolford
GUARD: Kim Hammond, Gene Moshier
CENTER: Jeff Barnett, Cody Binkley
QUARTERBACK: Jay Cutler, Kurt Page, Whit Taylor
RUNNING BACK: Corey Harris, Charley Horton, Frank Mordica, Tom Moore, Jamie O'Rourke
FULLBACK: Phil King, Carl "Goo Baby" Woods

DEFENSE

END: Steve Beardon, Tommy Harkins, Pat Toomay
TACKLE: Art Demmas, Dennis Harrison, James Manley
NOSE GUARD: Bobby Goodall
LINEBACKER: Gerald Collins, Jamie Duncan, Chris Gaines, Chip Healy, Moses Osemwegie, Shelton Quarles, Ed Smith, Jamie Winborn
CORNERBACK: Corey Chavous, Leonard Coleman
SAFETY: Jeff Brothers, Jay Chesley, Ken Stone

SPECIAL TEAMS

PLACE KICKER: Mark Adams
PUNTER: Jim Arnold, Bill Marinangel

MULTIPLE POSITIONS

TIGHT END-TAILBACK: Barry Burton

TWO-WAY PLAYERS

GUARD-LINEBACKER: George Deiderich
GUARD-LINEBACKER: Billy Grover
FULLBACK-LINEBACKER: Jim Butler

PERFORMANCE FORMULA:
VANDERBILT'S 10 BEST SEASONS

1955	1.3472	20 of 69
1982	1.1929	31 of 70
1958	1.1611	26 of 70
1959	1.1355	27 of 70
2008	1.1062	41 of 71
1956	1.0412	37 of 69
1968	1.0184	41 of 70
1975	.9949	42 of 70
2007	.9488	52 of 70
1991	.9334	47 of 71

VANDERBILT COMMODORES

Year	W-L-T	AP Poll	Conference Standing	Toughest Regular Season Opponents	Coach (Record at School)	Bowl Games		
1953	3-7		10t	Alabama 6-2-3, Mississippi 7-2-1, Ga. Tech 8-2-1, Kentucky 7-2-1	Art Guepe			
1954	2-7		11t	Baylor 7-3, Mississippi 9-1, Rice 7-3, Kentucky 7-3	Art Guepe			
1955	8-3		5	Mississippi 9-1, Kentucky 6-3-1, Tennessee 6-3-1 8-2,	Art Guepe	Gator	25 Auburn	13
1956	5-5		8t	Mississippi 7-3, Florida 6-3-1, Tennessee 10-0	Art Guepe			
1957	5-3-2		6	Mississippi 8-1-1, Penn State 6-3-1, Florida 6-2-1, Tennessee 7-3	Art Guepe			
1958	5-2-3		4	Missouri 5-4-1, Alabama 5-4-1, Clemson 8-2, Florida 6-3-1	Art Guepe			
1959	5-3-2		6	Georgia 9-1, Alabama 7-1-2, Mississippi 9-1	Art Guepe			
1960	3-7		12	Alabama 8-1-1, Mississippi 9-0-1, Florida 8-2, Tennessee 6-2-2	Art Guepe			
1961	2-8		12	Alabama 10-0, Georgia Tech 7-3, Mississippi 9-1	Art Guepe,			
1962	1-9		11	West Va. 8-2, Alabama 9-1, Mississippi 9-0, Boston College 8-2	Art Guepe (39-54-7)			
1963	1-7-2		10	Alabama 8-2, Florida 6-3-1, Mississippi 7-0-2, Boston College 6-3	Jack Green			
1964	3-6-1		10	Georgia Tech 7-3, Georga 6-3-1, Alabama 10-0	Jack Green			
1965	2-7-1		9t	Ga. Tech 6-3-1, Alabama 8-1-1, Va. Tech 7-3, Tennessee 7-1-2	Jack Green			
1966	1-9		10	Georgia Tech 9-1, Florida 8-2, Alabama 10-0, Tennessee 7-3	Jack Green (7-29-4)			
1967	2-7-1		9	Alabama 8-1-1, Florida 6-4, Mississippi 6-3-1, Tennessee 9-1	Bill Pace			
1968	5-4-1		8	Army 7-3, Alabama 8-2, Georgia 8-0-2, Tennessee 8-1-1	Bill Pace			
1969	4-6		7	Michigan 8-2, Alabama 6-4, Florida 8-1-1, Tennessee 9-1	Bill Pace			
1970	4-7		9	No. Carolina 8-3, Mississippi 7-3, Tennessee 10-1	Bill Pace			
1971	4-6-1		7	Alabama 11-0, Georgia 10-1, Tennessee 9-2	Bill Pace			
1972	3-8		10	Alabama 10-1, Georgia 7-4, Tennessee 9-2	Bill Pace (22-38-3)			
1973	5-6		9	Alabama 11-1, Georgia 6-4-1, Tennessee 8-3	Steve Sloan			
1974	7-3-2		7	Alabama 11-0, Florida 8-3, Tennessee 6-3-2	Steve Sloan (12-9-2)	Peach	6 Texas Tech	6
1975	7-4		6	Alabama 10-1, Georgia 9-2, Tennessee 7-5	Fred Pancoast			
1976	2-9		10	Oklahoma 8-2-1, Alabama 8-3, Georgia 10-1	Fred Pancoast			
1977	2-9		9	Oklahoma 10-1, Alabama 10-1, LSU 8-3, Kentucky 10-1	Fred Pancoast			
1978	2-9		10	Arkansas 9-2, Alabama 10-1, Georgia 9-1-1	Fred Pancoast (13-31)			
1979	1-10		9	Alabama 11-0, Tulane 9-2, Auburn 8-3, Tennessee 7-4	George MacIntyre			
1980	2-9		9	Maryland 8-3, Miss. St. 9-2, Alabama 9-2, Georgia 11-0, Miami 8-3	George MacIntyre			
1981	4-7		10	Alabama 9-1-1, Miami 9-2, Georgia 10-1, Tennessee 7-4	George MacIntyre			
1982	8-4		3	North Carolina 8-3, Alabama 7-4, Florida 8-3, Georgia 11-0	George MacIntyre	Hall of Fame	28 Air Force	36
1983	2-9		9	Maryland 8-3, Florida 8-2-1, Georgia 9-1-1, Virginia Tech 9-2	George MacIntyre			
1984	5-6		7	Maryland 8-3, LSU 8-2-1, Kentucky 8-3, Tennessee 7-3-1	George MacIntyre			
1985	3-7-1		7	Alabama 8-2-1, LSU 9-1-1, Georgia 7-3-1, Tennessee 8-1-2	George MacIntyre (25-52-1)			
1986	1-10		9	Alabama 9-3, Auburn 9-2, Georgia 8-3, Virginia Tech 8-2-1	Watson Brown			
1987	4-7		7	Alabama 7-4, Auburn 9-1-1, Georgia 8-3, Tennessee 9-2-1	Watson Brown			
1988	3-8		9	Alabama 8-3, Duke 7-3-1, Georgia 8-3, Army 9-2	Watson Brown			
1989	1-10		10	Alabama 10-1, Florida 7-4, Mississippi 7-4, Tennessee 10-1	Watson Brown			
1990	1-10		9	Alabama 7-4, Auburn 7-3-1, Mississippi 9-2, Tennessee 8-2-2	Watson Brown (10-45)			
1991	5-6		6t	Syracuse 9-2, Alabama 10-1, Georgia 8-3, Tennessee 9-2	Gerry DiNardo			
1992	4-7		E5t	Alabama 12-0, Georgia 9-2, Florida 8-4, Tennessee 8-3	Gerry DiNardo			
1993	4-7		E6	Alabama 8-2-1, Auburn 11-0, Florida 9-2, Tennessee 9-1-1	Gerry DiNardo			
1994	5-6		E5	Alabama 11-0, Florida 9-1-1, Tennessee 7-4	Gerry DiNardo (18-26)			
1995	2-9		E6	Alabama 8-3, Notre Dame 9-2, Florida 11-0, Tennessee 10-1	Rod Dowhower			
1996	2-9		E6	No. Dame 8-3, Alabama 9-3, LSU 9-2, Florida 10-1, Tennessee 9-2	Rod Dowhower (4-18)			
1997	3-8		E6	LSU 8-3, Georgia 9-2, Florida 9-2, Tennessee 10-1	Woody Widenhofer			
1998	2-9		E5	Mississippi State 8-3, Georgia 8-3, Florida 9-2, Tennessee 11-0	Woody Widenhofer			
1999	5-6		E5	Alabama 9-2, Mississippi State 9-2, Florida 9-2, Tennessee 9-2	Woody Widenhofer			
2000	3-8		E5	Auburn 9-2, Florida 9-2, Tennessee 8-3	Woody Widenhofer			
2001	2-9		E6	Georgia 8-3, South Carolina 8-3, Florida 9-2, Tennessee 10-1	Woody Widenhofer (15-40)			
2002	3-9		E6	Auburn 8-4, Georgia 11-1, Alabama 10-3, Florida 8-4	Bobby Johnson			
2003	2-10		E5t	Mississippi 9-3, TCU 11-1, Georgia 10-2, Tennessee 10-2	Bobby Johnson			
2004	2-9		E5t	Navy 9-2, Georgia 9-2, LSU 9-2, Tennessee 9-2	Bobby Johnson			
2005	5-6		E4t	LSU 10-2, Georgia 10-2, Florida 8-3	Bobby Johnson			
2006	4-8		E6	Michigan 11-1, Arkansas 10-2, Florida 11-1, Tennessee 9-3	Bobby Johnson			
2007	5-7		E6	Auburn 8-4, Georgia 10-2, Florida 9-3, Tennessee 9-3	Bobby Johnson			
2008	7-6		E3t	Rice 9-3, Mississippi 8-4, Georgia 9-3, Florida 12-1	Bobby Johnson	Music City	16 Boston College	14
2009	2-10		E6	LSU 9-3, Mississippi 8-4, Georgia Tech 11-2, Florida 12-1	Bobby Johnson (30-65)			
2010	2-10		E6	LSU 10-2, South Carolina 9-4, Arkansas 10-2	Robbie Caldwell (2-10)			

TOTAL: 194-401-17 .3309 (70 of 70)

Bowl Games since 1953: 2-1-1 .6250 (8 of 70)

GREATEST TEAM SINCE 1953: Two Commodore teams deserve mention: Art Guepe's 1955 squad with Art Demmas, Larry Frank, Tommy Harkins, Charley Horton, Phil King, Don Orr, and Joe Stephenson, and the 1982 edition that George MacIntyre coached to third place in the SEC. The 1982 Commodores were led by Whit Taylor's 22 touchdown passes, but the nod goes to the 1955 team. Upsetting an SEC rival like Auburn in the Gator Bowl means everything.

1953 3-7

7	Pennsylvania	13 E Charles Hawkins / Tom McKinnon
12	Alabama	21 T Buck Watson
6	Mississippi	28 G Pete Williams / John Hall
6	Baylor	47 C Larry Stone / Barry Heywood
28	Virginia	13 G Bobby Goodall / Connie Demmas
0	Georgia Tech	43 T Art Demmas / Royalyn Keathley
14	Kentucky	40 E Joe Stephenson / Earl Jalufka
21	Tulane	7 QB Jim Looney / Billy Holmes
31	Middle Tenn.	13 HB Charley Horton / Buddy Stack
6	Tennessee	33 HB Floyd Teas / Bill Krietemeyer (QB)
		FB Dan Byers / Charles Newman

RUSHING: Horton 75/461y, Byers 59/324y, TD, Krietemeyer 89/264y
PASSING: Looney 31-82/362y, TD, 37.8%,
  Holmes 33-66/274y, 3TD, 50.0%
RECEIVING: Hawkins 19/269y, McKinnon 10/96y, Horton 8/51y
SCORING: Byers 30pts, Krietemeyer 24pts, Teas 18pts

1954 2-7

19	Baylor	25 E Tommy Harkins / Terry Fails
14	Alabama	28 T Buck Watson / Tommy Woodruff
7	Mississippi	22 G Larry Frank / Larry Hayes
14	Georgia	16 C Jim Cunningham
13	Rice	34 G Bobby Goodall
7	Kentucky	19 T Pete Williams / Art Demmas
0	Tulane	6 E Joe Stephenson / Earl Jalufka
34	Villanova	19 QB Jim Looney / Don Orr
26	Tennessee	0 HB Charley Horton / Mike Jabaley
		HB Charley Rolfe / Buddy Stack
		FB Don Hunt

RUSHING: Hunt 95/474y, Horton 69/376y, Rolfe 44/146y
PASSING: Looney 54-132/813y, 4TD, 40.9%
RECEIVING: Stephenson 16/352y, Harkins 16/237y, Fails 8/93y
SCORING: Horton 42pts, Hunt 24pts, Goodall (G-K) 17pts

1955 8-3

13	Georgia	14 E Tommy Harkins / Earl Jalufka
21	Alabama	6 T Tommy Woodruff
0	Mississippi	13 G Larry Hayes
12	Chattanooga	0 C Jim Cunningham / Barry Heywood
46	Middle Tenn.	0 G Larry Frank / Lucian Tatum
34	Virginia	7 T Art Demmas / Mario Wodka
34	Kentucky	0 E Joe Stephenson / Bob Taylor
20	Tulane	7 QB Don Orr / Billy Holmes
21	Florida	8 HB Charley Horton
14	Tennessee	20 HB Joe Scales / Charley Rolfe
25	Auburn ■	13 FB Phil King / Steve Pepoy

RUSHING: King 98/628y, Horton 113/621y, Hunt 74/416y
PASSING: Orr 30-80/486y, 2TD, 37.5%
RECEIVING: Stephenson 11/204y, Horton 5/99y, Jalufka 3/50y,
  Scales 3/38y
SCORING: Horton (HB-K) 73pts, King 30pts, Hunt & Scales 24pts

1956 5-5

14	Georgia	0 E Bob Laws / Harold Brown
46	Chattanooga	7 T Pat Swan / Jimmy Linville
32	Alabama	7 G Billy Grover
0	Mississippi	16 C Billy Parker / Doyle Richardson
7	Florida	21 G Lucian Tatum / George Deiderich
23	Middle Tenn.	13 T Art Demmas / Mario Wodka
6	Virginia	2 E Henry Tyler / Bob Taylor
6	Kentucky	7 QB Don Orr / Boyce Smith
6	Tulane	13 HB Phil King / Mike Jabaley
7	Tennessee	27 HB Jack Hudson / Joe Scales
		FB Jimmy Ray / Jim Butler

RUSHING: King 129/651y, Butler 71/258y, Ray 57/234y
PASSING: Smith 27-57/362y, TD, 47.4%,
  Orr 17-40/216y, 2TD, 42.5%
RECEIVING: Taylor 12/187y, King 10/122y, Hudson 7/38y
SCORING: King (HB-K) 47pts, Smith 24pts, Butler 18pts

1957 5-3-2

7	Missouri	7 E Bob Laws / Rayford Hilley
9	Georgia	6 T Pat Swan / Jimmy Linville
6	Alabama	6 G George Deiderich / Monte Willamson
0	Mississippi	28 C Ben Donnell / Doyle Richardson
32	Penn State	20 G Billy Grover
7	LSU	0 T Mario Wodka / Larry Wagner
12	Kentucky	7 E Bob Taylor / Ron Miller
7	Florida	14 QB Boyce Smith
27	Citadel	0 HB Phil King / Jim McKee
6	Tennessee	20 HB Tom Moore / Danny McCall
		FB Jim Butler / Jimmy Ray

RUSHING: King 115/438y, Butler 96/384y, Moore 65/346y
PASSING: Smith 49-98/664y, 8 TD, 50.0%
RECEIVING: King 14/172y, Laws 11/130y, Taylor 10/133y
SCORING: King (HB-K), Moore & Smith 18pts

1958 5-2-3

12	Missouri	8 E Rayford Hilley /Fred Riggs /Dan Boone
21	Georgia	14 T Tom Redmond
0	Alabama	0 G Billy Grover
7	Clemson	12 C Ben Donnell
6	Florida	6 G George Deiderich
39	Virginia	6 T Larry Wagner
28	Miami	15 E Lew "Rooster" Akin / Ron Miller
0	Kentucky	0 QB Boyce Smith
12	Tulane	0 HB John Rolfe / David Ray
6	Tennessee	10 HB Tom Moore
		FB Jim Butler / Pete Thompson

RUSHING: Moore 145/584y, Butler 96/356y, Thompson 47/172y
PASSING: Smith 49-105/638y, 6 TD, 46.7%
RECEIVING: Moore 12/135y, Rolfe 10/160y, Akin 10/147y
SCORING: Moore & Akin 26pts, Ray & Butler 18pts

1959 5-3-2

6	Georgia	21 E Fred Riggs / Rayford Hilley
7	Alabama	7 T Dan Boone / Joe Wildman
0	Mississippi	33 G Dunlap Hurst / John Cropp
13	Florida	6 C Cody Binkley / Bob Simmons
33	Virginia	0 G Joe Bates / Ed Dudley
6	Minnesota	20 T Larry Wagner
11	Kentucky	6 E Rooster Akin / Ron Miller
6	Tulane	6 QB Russ Morris / Jim McKee
42	Florence State	7 HB Dillon Johnston / Thom Garden
14	Tennessee	0 HB Tom Moore / Mack Rolfe
		FB Bobby Nay / Jim Burton

RUSHING: Moore 125/676y, Garden 49/269y, Nay 64/236y
PASSING: Morris 44-92/579y, TD, 47.8%
RECEIVING: Moore 14/170y, Akin 12/193y, Miller 5/90y,
  Riggs 5/59y
SCORING: Moore 60pts, Garden 18pts, Burton & McKee 12pts

1960 3-7

7	Georgia	18 E Fred Riggs
0	Alabama	21 T Joe Wildman / Mickey Cobb
0	Mississippi	26 G John Cropp / George McGugin
0	Florida	12 C Cody Binkley
23	Marquette	6 G Bill Corbin / Don Brothers
22	Clemson	20 T Jerry Murray
0	Kentucky	27 E Wade Butcher
22	William & Mary	8 QB Russ Morris / Hank Lesesne
0	Tulane	20 HB Ed Creagh / Jeff Starling
0	Tennessee	35 HB Charley Funk / Terrell Dye
		FB Bobby Nay / Jim Johnson

RUSHING: Johnson 77/312y, Lesesne 48/149y, Creagh 44/129y
PASSING: Lesesne 54-130/620y, 4 TD, 41.5%,
  Morris 22-61/193y, 0 TD, 36.1%
RECEIVING: Starling 14/127y, Dye 12/151y, 4 with 8
SCORING: Johnson 18pts, Dye 2pts, Morris 10pts

1961 2-8

16	West Virginia	6 E Wade Butcher / Dick Teets
21	Georgia	0 T Bill Corbin / Wayne Hall
6	Alabama	35 G John Cropp / Bill Waldrup
21	UCLA	28 C Cody Binkley
0	Florida	7 G Jule Crocker
0	Mississippi	47 T Sam Sullins / Mike Reese
3	Kentucky	16 E Bruce Hammer / Gary Hudson
7	Tulane	17 QB Hank Lesesne / Jon Cleveland
7	South Carolina	23 HB Ed Creagh / Steve Shaw
7	Tennessee	41 HB Terrell Dye / Jeff Starling
		FB Billy Crawford / Jack Lusk

RUSHING: Lesesne 112/325y, Crawford 54/190y, Yusk 43/178y
PASSING: Lesesne 50-126/607y, 7 TD, 39.7%
RECEIVING: Starling 25/273y, Shaw 7/60y, Hammer 5/49,
  Dye 5/44y
SCORING: Starling 24pts, Grady Wade (K) 15pts, Hammer 12pts

1962 1-9

0	West Virginia	26 E Dick Teets / Gary Hudson
0	Georgia	10 T Joe Graham / Nick Spiak
7	Alabama	17 G Tom Kenny
6	Citadel	21 C Jule Crocker / Bill Juday
7	Florida	42 G Bill Waldrup / Tommy Gaudet
0	Mississippi	35 T Sam Sullins / Mike Reese
22	Boston College	27 E Tommy Martin / Richard Bohner
0	Kentucky	7 QB Hank Lesesne / Jon Cleveland
20	Tulane	0 HB Jeff Starling / Arthur Guepe
0	Tennessee	30 HB Terrell Dye / Bennett Baldwin
		FB Billy Crawford / Charley Funk

RUSHING: Lesesne 105/214y, Guepe 41/176y, Crawford 43/144y
PASSING: Lesesne 65-157/741y, 3 TD, 41.4%
RECEIVING: Starling 34/494y, Teets 16/160y, Guepe 10/96y
SCORING: Starling 14pts, Bohner 12pts, Grady Wade (K) 10pts

1963 1-7-2

13	Furman	14 E Tommy Martin
0	Georgia	20 T Joe Graham / Nick Spiak
6	Alabama	21 G Jimmy Wyatt / Tom Kenny
0	Florida	21 C Sam Sullins
7	Mississippi	27 G Paul Guffee
6	Boston College	19 T Gary Hart
0	Kentucky	0 E Randy Humble / Tom Zimmerman
10	Tulane	10 QB Jon Cleveland / Dave Malone (DB)
31	Geo. Wash'gton	0 HB Toby Wilt / Bennett "Bumpy" Baldwin
0	Tennessee	14 HB Tommy Clark / Phil Brooks
		FB Bill Waldrup/Wayne Anth'ny/C.Trabue

RUSHING: Waldrup 67/244y, Wilt 48/174y, Brooks 41/144y
PASSING: Cleveland 39-94/512y, 2 TD, 41.5%,
  Dave Waller (QB) 22-53/222y, 0 TD, 41.5%
RECEIVING: Baldwin 15/176y, Wilt 14/157y, Martin 9/103y
SCORING: Wilt (HB-K) 19pts, Waldrup 18pts, Waller 12pts

1964 3-6-1

2	Georgia Tech	14 E Bumpy Baldwin / Chuck Ousley
0	Georgia	7 T Joe Graham / Steve Smith
0	Alabama	24 G Jimmy Wyatt / Wilford Fuqua (LB)
9	Wake Forest	6 C Bill Juday / Steve Kiss (LB)
14	Geo Wash'ton	0 G Paul Guffee / Dave Maddux (LB)
7	Mississippi	7 T Gary Hart
21	Kentucky	22 E Steve Skupas / Jim Thomas
2	Tulane	7 QB Dave Waller / Bob Kerr
17	Miami	35 HB Bob Sullins / Dave Malone (DB)
7	Tennessee	0 HB Toby Wilt / Sim Davis (DB)
		FB Charlie Trabue / Phil Brooks

RUSHING: Sullins 133/512y, Trabue 69/217y, Wilt 33/115y
PASSING: Waller 61-141/646y, TD, 43.3%
RECEIVING: Baldwin 20/261y, Ousley 13/155y, Wilt 10/109y
SCORING: Waller 18pts, Bevil & Richard Lemay (K) 12pts

1965 2-7-1

10	Georgia Tech	10 WR Tom Wilson / Chuck Ousley
10	Georgia	24 T John Hammersmith
0	Wake Forest	9 G Frank Curtin
7	Alabama	22 C Chester Parker
21	Virginia Tech	10 G Scott Hall
7	Mississippi	24 T Steve Smith
13	Tulane	0 TE Randy Humble
0	Kentucky	34 QB Bob Kerr / Dave Waller
14	Miami	28 HB Chuck Boyd / Lance Spalding
3	Tennessee	21 WB Toby Wilt / Rusty Cantwell (HB)
		FB Jim Whiteside
		DL Steve Skupas
		DL Richard Lemay / Sid Ransom
		DL Chris Collins
		DL Lane Wolbe
		LB Steve Kiss
		LB Jimmy Wyatt
		LB Dave Maddux
		DB Phil Brooks / Bernie Kemple
		DB Charlie Orth
		DB Cloyce Darnell / Steve Bevil
		DB John Gamble

RUSHING: Whiteside 103/297y, Kerr 98/249y, Boyd 66/195y
PASSING: Kerr 33-82/346y 2 TD, 40.2%,
  Waller 20-43/227y, 2 TD, 46.5%
RECEIVING: Wilt 13/171y, Humble 12/115y, Ousley 11/108y
SCORING: Humble 18pts, Wilt (WB-K) 13pts,
  Whiteside & Boyd 12pts

1966 1-9

24 The Citadel	0 WR Chuck Boyd (TB) / Dave Semlow
0 Georgia Tech	42 T John Hammersmith
0 Florida	13 G Steve Kiss
6 Virginia Tech	21 C Butch Brown
6 Alabama	42 G Frank Curtin (DL)
12 Tulane	13 T George Parker / Dan Cundiff
10 Kentucky	14 TE Steve Skupas / Bob Ivey
14 Navy	30 QB Roger May / Gary Davis
0 Mississippi	34 TB Steve Bevil / Donnie North
0 Tennessee	28 WB Rusty Cantwell
	FB Jim Whiteside
	DL Bob Pegg
	DL Sid Ransom
	DL Dee Thompson
	DL Kelly Meyer
	DL Jim Thomas
	LB Chip Healy
	LB Scott Hall (OG) / Dave Maddox
	DB Charley Orth
	DB Trow Gillespie
	DB Bernie Kemple / Cloyce Darnell
	DB Bob Goodridge

RUSHING: Whiteside 94/267y, May 76/162y, Bevil 30/76y
PASSING: Davis 62-153/777y, 0 TD, 40.5%,
May 20-51/129y, 2 TD, 39.2%
RECEIVING: Cantwell 17/157y, Boyd 16/167y, Skupas 13/139y
SCORING: Davis 18pts, Whiteside 12pts,
Reinhard Klaas (K) 11pts

1967 2-7-1

10 Georgia Tech	17 WR Bob Ivey
14 William & Mary	12 T Bob Asher
21 North Carolina	7 G Bill Long
21 Alabama	35 C Steve Ernst
22 Florida	27 G Dee Thompson / Scott Hall
14 Tulane	27 T Frank Curtin
7 Kentucky	12 TE Bob Goodridge
35 Navy	35 QB Roger May / Gary Davis
7 Mississippi	28 TB Jim Whiteside / John Valput
14 Tennessee	41 WB Lee Noel / Dave Strong
	FB Rex Raines / Dan Lipperman
	DL Bob Pegg / Pat Toomay
	DL Chris Collins
	DL Bill McDonald / Mike Greene
	DL Sid Ransom
	DL Mike Giltner
	LB Mike Patterson / Mike Stahl
	LB Chip Healy / Les Lyle
	DB Mal Wall
	DB Trow Gillespie / Christie Hauck
	DB Bernie Kemple
	DB Neal Smith / Bob Wright

RUSHING: Whiteside 105/244y, Raines 50/214y, Strong 28/178y
PASSING: May 82-149/929y, 9 TD, 55.0%,
Davis 60-108/844y, 5 TD, 55.6%
RECEIVING: Goodridge 79/1114y, Wjiteside 27/211y,
Ivey 20/245y
Goodridge 36pts, Strong 32pts, Whiteside 30pts

1968 5-4-1

25 VMI	12 WR Curt Chesley
17 Army	13 T Bob Pegg
7 North Carolina	8 G Mike Greene (T) / Mike Patterson
7 Alabama	31 C Steve Ernst
6 Georgia	32 G Chuck Springfield
14 Florida	14 T Bob Asher / Chris Hinkle
21 Tulane	7 TE Karl Weiss
6 Kentucky	0 QB John Miller / Chuck Boyd (TB)
53 Davidson	20 TB Alan Spear / Donnie North
7 Tennessee	10 WB Dave Strong
	FB Rex Raines / John Valput
	DL Mike Giltner
	DL John Robinson
	DL Bill McDonald / Terry Reeves
	DL Les Lyle
	DL Pat Toomay
	LB Chip Healy
	LB Steve Fritts
	DB Trow Gillespie
	DB Doug Mathews
	DB Neal Smith
	DB Christie Hauck

RUSHING: Spear 142/438y, Boyd 80/272y, Raines 53/205y
PASSING: Miller 99-201/1164y, 5 TD, 49.3%
RECEIVING: Chesley 48/543y, Spear 16/211y, Weiss 15/178y
SCORING: Strong 42pts, Spear 24pts, Ernest Perez (K) 14pts

1969 4-6

14 Michigan	42 WR Curt Chesley
6 Army	16 T Don "Duck" Johnston
22 North Carolina	38 G Mike Patterson
14 Alabama	10 C Sandy Haury
8 Georgia	40 G Chuck Springfield
20 Florida	41 T Bob Asher / Larry Hayes
26 Tulane	23 TE Karl Weiss
42 Kentucky	6 QB Watson Brown / Denny Painter
63 Davidson	8 TB Doug Mathews
27 Tennessee	40 WB Dave Strong
	FB Dave Lipperman
	DL John Carney
	DL John Robinson
	DL Bill McDonald
	DL Les Lyle
	DL Pat Toomay
	LB Steve Fritts / Joe Wood
	LB Terry Rettig
	DB Greg O'Neal
	DB Doug Mathews
	DB Neal Smith
	DB Christie Hauck / Sam Kiser

RUSHING: Mathews 167/849y, Brown 121/295y,
Lipperman 41/190y
PASSING: Brown 69-111/696y, 6 TD, 62.2%,
Painter 41-90/611y, 5 TD, 45.5%
RECEIVING: Chesley 44/516y, Weiss 24/279y, Strong 22/301y
SCORING: Brown 58pts, Strong 50pts, Mathews 36pts

1970 4-7

39 Tenn-Chatt'ga	6 WR Curt Chesley / Steve Wyrick
52 Citadel	0 T Duck Johnston
6 Mississippi St.	20 G John Drake
7 North Carolina	10 C Sandy Haury
11 Alabama	35 G Jeff Gibson
3 Georgia	37 T Larry Hayes / Gino Marchetti (G)
16 Mississippi	26 TE Karl Weiss
7 Tulane	10 QB Steve Burger / Denny Painter
18 Kentucky	17 TB Mack Brown / William James
36 Tampa	28 WB Allan Spear / Jeff Peeples
6 Tennessee	24 FB Dwight Blair / Bill Young
	DL John Carney / Mike Hammerschmidt
	DL Mike Kirk
	DL David Haun / Terry Reeves
	DL John Robinson
	DL George Abernathy / Buzz Hamilton
	LB Steve Fritts / Joe Wood
	LB Terry Rettig / Barrett Sutton
	DB Greg O'Neal
	DB Ken Stone
	DB George Tomlinson
	DB Sam Kiser / Willie Diehl

RUSHING: Burger 162/552y, Brown 82/364y, James 32/108y
PASSING: Painter 43-106/563y, TD, 40.6%,
Burger 38-68/459y, 5 TD, 55.9%
RECEIVING: Chesley 33/393y, Weiss 20/337y, Peeples
SCORING: Burger 60pts, Robert Bayless (K) 32pts, Brown 24pts

1971 4-6-1

24 Tenn-Chatt'ga	7 WR Gary Chesley / Walter Overton
0 Louisville	0 T Jim Avery
49 Mississippi St.	19 G Linc Fuge / Gino Marchetti
23 Virginia	27 C Wayne Jacobs / John Drake
0 Alabama	42 G L.T. Southall / Sandy Haury
0 Georgia	24 T Larry Hayes
7 Mississippi	28 TE Jim Mahan
13 Tulane	9 QB Steve Burger / Steve Lainhart
7 Kentucky	14 HB Jamie O'Rourke
10 Tampa	7 HB Dennis Mazar / Jeff Peeples
7 Tennessee	19 FB Dwight Blair / Bill Young
	DL John Carney
	DL Mike Kirk
	DL David Haun
	DL Mark Ilgenfritz
	DL George Abernathy
	LB Joe Wood
	LB Joe Cook / Barrett Sutton
	DB Doug Nettles / Greg O'Neal
	DB Tommy Tompkins
	DB Ken Stone / Sam Kiser
	DB Willie Diehl / George Tomlinson

RUSHING: O'Rourke 165/677y, Burger 172/413y, Blair 59/226y
PASSING: Burger 57-134/671y, TD, 42.5%
RECEIVING: Chesley 19/253y, Overton 12/196y,
O'Rourke 7/41y
SCORING: Burger 48pts, O'Rourke 24pts,
Taylor Stokes (K) 18pts

1972 3-8

24 Tenn-Chatt'ga	7 WR Doug Martin / Dan Mahaffey
6 Mississippi St.	10 T Charlie Parrish
21 Alabama	48 G Jim Avery
10 Virginia	7 C Blake Anderson
21 William & Mary	17 G Linc Fuge
3 Georgia	28 T L.T. Southall
7 Mississippi	31 TE Jim Mahan
7 Tulane	21 QB Steve Lainhart / Watson Brown
13 Kentucky	14 TB Steve Burger / Lonnie Sadler
7 Tampa	30 WB Walter Overton / Jeff Peeples
10 Tennessee	30 FB Anthony Joseph
	DL Mark Llewellyn
	DL Mike Kirk
	DL Tom Galbierz
	DL Mark Ilgenfritz
	DL George Abernathy
	LB Barrett Sutton
	LB Joe Cook / Greg Fritz
	DB Doug Nettles
	DB Tommy Tompkins
	DB Ken Stone
	DB George Tomlinson

RUSHING: Sadler 122/423y, Burger 80/343y, Overton 47/277y
PASSING: Lainhart 34-89/524y, 3 TD, 38.2%,
Brown 20-53/291y, TD, 37.7%
RECEIVING: Overton 20/317y, Martin 18/329y,
Mahaffey 15/226y
SCORING: Hawkins Golden (K) 27pts, Overton 24pts,
Burger 18pts

1973 5-6

14 Tenn-Chatt'ga	12 WR Jesse Mathers
21 Mississippi St.	52 WR Doug Martin / Mark Dietrich
0 Alabama	44 T Howard Buck
39 Virginia	22 G Gene Moshier
20 William & Mary	7 C L.T. Southall
18 Georgia	14 G David Alsup / David Harber
14 Mississippi	24 T Linc Fuge
17 Kentucky	27 TE Matt Gossage / Barry Burton
3 Tulane	24 QB Fred Fisher / Steve Lainhart
18 Tampa	16 TB Jamie O'Rourke / Lonnie Sadler
17 Tennessee	20 FB Martin Garcia / Preston Brogdon
	DL Mark Llewellyn / Joe Reynolds
	DL Mark Ilgenfritz
	DL Tom Galbierz / Eldridge
	DL Mickey Jacobs
	DL Tate Rich / Williams or Smith
	LB Damon Regen (OG) / Tom Schaffler
	LB Bo Patton
	DB Ed Oaks / Tommy Tompkins
	DB Doug Nettles / Bubba Byrd
	DB Scott Wingfield
	DB Steve Curnette

RUSHING: O'Rourke 132/592y, Sadler 143/527y, Fisher 130/373y
PASSING: Fisher 128-234/1450y, 11 TD, 54.7%
RECEIVING: Mathers 34/423y, Burton 22/308y, Martin 21/340y
SCORING: Hawkins Golden (K) 47pts, Burton 30pts,
O'Rourke 24pts

1974 7-3-2

28 Tenn-Chatt'ga	6 WR Jesse Mathers
45 VMI	7 WR Doug Martin / Walter Overton
10 Alabama	23 T Howard Buck
24 Florida	10 G David Alsup
31 Georgia	38 C Bill Holby
24 Mississippi	14 G Gene Moshier
38 Army	14 T David Harber / Matt Gossage
12 Kentucky	38 TE Barry Burton
30 Tulane	22 QB David Lee / Fred Fisher
44 Louisville	0 RB Lonnie Sadler / Adolph Groves
21 Tennessee	21 RB Jamie O'Rourke / Martin Garcia
6 Texas Tech■	6 DL Joe Reynolds
	DL Mark Llewellyn
	DL Tom Galbierz / David Hale
	DL Mickey Jacobs
	DL Tom Schaffler
	LB Damon Regen / Kimmie Weaver
	LB Mark Adams / Greg Fritz
	DB Steve Curnette / Bubba Byrd
	DB Ed Oaks
	DB Scott Wingfield / Reggie Calvin
	DB Jay Chesley

RUSHING: O'Rourke 201/933y, Sadler 140/610y, Groves 51/335y
PASSING: Lee 85-159/1173y, 7 TD, 52.4%
RECEIVING: Mathers 23/369y, Burton 22/378y, Martin 19/279y
SCORING: O'Rourke 72pts, Mike Adams (K) 67pts

1975 7-4

17 Tenn-Chatt'ga	7 WR Jesse Mathers
9 Rice	6 WR Martin Cox
7 Alabama	40 T Matt Gossage
6 Tulane	3 G Tom Ballman
0 Florida	35 C Bill Holby
3 Georgia	47 G Frank Smith
3 Mississippi	17 T David Harber
17 Virginia	14 TE Barry Burton (TB)
13 Kentucky	3 QB Fred Fisher
23 Army	14 TB Lonnie Sadler / Ed Parrish / Paul Izjar
17 Tennessee	14 FB David Johnson / Adolph Groves
	DL Joe Reynolds
	DL Dennis Harrison
	DL Tom Galbierz / Tim English
	DL Mickey Jacobs / Mitch Lilly
	DL Tim Riley / Ed Smith
	LB Kimmie Weaver
	LB Damon Regen / Randy Sittason
	DB Steve Curnette / Walter Jordan
	DB Reggie Calvin
	DB Ed Oaks
	DB Jay Chesley

RUSHING: Sadler 175/536y, Groves 64/242y, Burton 23/176y
PASSING: Fisher 51-106/552y, TD, 48.1%
RECEIVING: Burton 31/306y, Mathews 16/214y, Sadler 14/110y
SCORING: Mark Adams (K) 47pts, Sadler 24pts,
Burton & Groves 12pts

1976 2-9

3 Oklahoma	24 WR Martin Cox
27 Wake Forest	24 T Bob McNamara
14 Alabama	42 G Tom Ballman
13 Tulane	24 C Mike Birdsong / Terry Logan
20 LSU	33 G Mike Ralston
0 Georgia	45 T Jerry Roberts
3 Mississippi	20 TE Greg Eveland / Hal Kemp
0 Kentucky	14 QB Mike Wright / Jerry Hampton
34 Air Force	10 TB Adolph Groves / Ed Parrish
7 Cincinnati	33 WB Daryl Mills / Preston Brown
10 Tennessee	13 FB Frank Mordica / David Johnson
	DL Tim Riley
	DL Dennis Harrison
	DL Tim English / David Hale
	DL Mitch Lilly
	DL Ed Smith
	LB Kimmie Weaver
	LB Randy Sittason / John Pointer
	DB Walter Jordan
	DB Reggie Calvin
	DB Brenard Wilson / John O'Neal
	DB Ronnie Myrick / Tim Barrett

RUSHING: Groves 76/347y, Mordica 78/288y, Wright 107/286y
PASSING: Hampton 53-107/805y, 3 TD, 49.5%,
Wright 51-118/788y, 3 TD, 43.2%
RECEIVING: Cox 38/738y, Kemp 18/251y, Groves 15/190y
SCORING: Greg Martin (K) 35pts, Cox, Wright & Brown 12pts

1977 2-9

23 Oklahoma	25 WR Martin Cox / Roger Alsup
3 Wake Forest	0 T Jeff Dungan / Bob McNamara
12 Alabama	24 G Jerry Roberts
7 Tulane	36 C Tom Woodroof / John Wooten
15 LSU	28 G Mike Ralston
13 Georgia	24 T Mike Birdsong
14 Mississippi	26 TE Hal Kemp / Greg Eveland
6 Kentucky	28 QB Mike Wright
28 Air Force	34 TB Frank Mordica / Preston Brown
13 Cincinnati	9 WB Daryl Mills
7 Tennessee	42 FB Ed Parrish
	DL Kimmie Weaver
	DL Dennis Harrison
	DL Mitch Lilly / Loie Hudgins
	DL Mike Gothard
	LB Randy Sittason
	LB Ed Smith / Ernest Cecil
	LB John Pointer
	DB Walter Jordan / Ralph Johnson
	DB Reggie Calvin / Mike Hill
	DB Brenard Wilson
	DB Ronnie Myrick / Tim Barrett

RUSHING: Mordica 133/449y, Parrish 54/203y, Wright 159/188y
PASSING: Wright 106-211/1383y, 5 TD, 50.2%
RECEIVING: Cox 48/783y, Brown 23/146y, Kemp 21/350y
SCORING: Greg Martin (K) 35pts, Cox, Mordica & Brown 18pts

1978 2-9

17 Arkansas	48 WR Martin Cox / Charles Edwards
17 Furman	10 WR Preston Brown / Roger Alsup
28 Alabama	51 T Tom Woodroof
3 Tulane	38 G Loie Hudgins
7 Auburn	49 C John Wooten / Keith Phillips
10 Georgia	31 G Greg Eveland
10 Mississippi	37 T Mike Ralston
14 Memphis State	35 TE Flavious Smith
2 Kentucky	53 QB Van Heflin / Scotti Madison
41 Air Force	27 TB Frank Mordica / Terry Potter
15 Tennessee	41 FB Lester Mack
	DL Norwood Ervin
	DL Rodney Gurley
	DL Kenny Cole
	DL Tim Moore
	DL Robin Giltner
	LB Randy Sittason
	LB Phil Swindoll / John Pointer
	DB Walter Jordan
	DB Roy Williams
	DB Eddie Hood / Jim Sherman
	DB Ronnie Myrick

RUSHING: Mordica 173/1065y, Heflin 155/236y, Mack 33/153y
PASSING: Heflin 76-155/984y, 3TD, 49.0%
RECEIVING: Cox 40/674y, Edwards 8/138y, Mordica 7/16y
SCORING: Mordica 48pts, Mike Woodard (K) 34pts, Potter 20pts

1979 1-10

13 Indiana	44 WR Charles Edwards
14 Citadel	27 WR Preston Brown / Waymon Buggs
3 Alabama	66 T Ronald Hale
14 Tulane	42 G Loie Hudgins
34 Auburn	52 C Keith Phillips
10 Georgia	31 G Ken Hammond
28 Mississippi	63 T Mike Ralston
13 Memphis State	3 TE Flavious Smith
10 Kentucky	29 QB Van Heflin / Whit Taylor
29 Air Force	30 RB Terry Potter
10 Tennessee	31 RB Frank Mordica
	DL Joe Staley
	DL Ricky Dean
	DL Rodney Gurley / Tim Moore
	DL Phil Swindoll
	LB Andy Ervin
	LB Andrew Coleman
	LB John Pointer
	DB Mark Brown
	DB Eddie Hood / Roy Williams
	DB Jim Sherman
	DB Ronnie Myrick / Mark Matthews

RUSHING: Mordica 162/830y, Potter 131/578y, Heflin 99/341y
PASSING: Heflin 64-124/748y, 4TD, 51.6%,
Taylor 46-80/609y, 3TD, 57.5%
RECEIVING: Brown 52/786y, Smith 25/288y, Buggs 17/141y
SCORING: Mike Woodard (K) 39pts, Mordica 36pts, Heflin 24pts

1980 2-9

6 Maryland	31 WR Charles Edwards
14 Mississippi St.	24 WR Waymon Buggs
0 Alabama	41 T Karl Jordan
21 Tulane	43 G Loie Hudgins
0 Georgia	41 C Keith Phillips
14 Mississippi	27 G Joey Hancock
14 Memphis State	10 T Ken Hammond / Loie Hudgins
10 Kentucky	31 TE Flavious Smith
17 Miami	24 QB Whit Taylor
31 Tenn.-Chatt'ga	29 RB Terry Potter / Van Heflin
13 Tennessee	51 RB Marcus Williams / Tom High
	DL Joe Staley
	DL Tim Moore
	DL Rodney Gurley
	DL John Clemens / Steve Bearden
	LB Tim Bryant / Terry Dugan
	LB Andrew Coleman
	LB Phil Swindoll
	DB Leonard Coleman
	DB Mark Brown
	DB Manuel Young
	DB Tom Burson / Mark Matthews

RUSHING: Potter 149/579y, Williams 94/329y, High 70/246y
PASSING: Taylor 72-173/899y, TD, 41.6%
RECEIVING: Buggs 37/448y, Smith 18/266y, Edwards 10/133y
SCORING: Potter 42pts, Mike Woodard (K) 32pts, 3 with 12pts

1981 4-7

23 Maryland	17 WR Waymon Buggs
9 Mississippi St.	29 WR Phil Roach / Butch Bullen
7 Alabama	28 T Ken Hammond / Pat Saindon
16 Miami	48 G Jeff Madden
10 Tulane	14 C Joey Hancock
21 Georgia	53 G Karl Jordan
27 Mississippi	27 T Loie Hudgins
26 Memphis State	0 TE Allama Matthews / Greg Simmons
10 Kentucky	17 QB Whit Taylor
28 Tenn-Chatt'ga	38 TB Van Heflin / Norman Jordan
34 Tennessee	38 FB Ernie Goolsby / Louie Stephenson
	DL John Clemens
	DL Tim Moore / Willie Twyford
	DL Rodney Gurley
	DL Steve Bearden / Glenn Watson
	LB Tim Bryant / Terry Dugan
	LB Andrew Coleman / Steve McCoy
	LB Joe Staley / Mike Matthews
	DB Marcus Williams / Clay Parker
	DB Leonard Coleman
	DB Manuel Young
	DB Tom Moore / Mark Matthews

RUSHING: Heflin 105/374y, Goolsby 75/310y,
Jim Bronner (TB) 28/159y
PASSING: Taylor 209-357/2318y, 15TD, 58.5%
RECEIVING: Buggs 54/778y, Matthews 50/704y, Jordan 49/454y
SCORING: Mike Woodard (K) 47pts, Heflin 42pts, 3 with 24pts

1982 8-4

24 Memphis State	14 WR Phil Roach / Ardell Fuller
10 North Carolina	34 WR Chuck Scott / Clay Parker
21 Alabama	24 T Rob Monaco
24 Tulane	21 G Pat Saindon
31 Florida	29 C Bill Fletcher
13 Georgia	27 G Karl Jordan
19 Mississippi	10 T Ken Sample / David Cathey
23 Kentucky	10 TE Allama Matthews
45 Virginia Tech	0 QB Whit Taylor
27 Tenn-Chatt'ga	16 TB Keith Edwards / Norman Jordan
28 Tennessee	21 FB Ernie Goolsby / Jim Bronner
28 Air Force ■	36 DL Steve Bearden / John Windham
	DL Willie Twyford
	DL Steve Wade
	DL John Clemens / Glenn Watson
	LB Bob O'Connor / Mike Matthews
	LB Jeff McFarran / Steve McCoy
	LB Joe Staley / Jeff Cartwright
	DB Mark Matthews / Kermit Sykes
	DB Leonard Coleman
	DB Manuel Young
	DB Tom Moore / Mark Brown

RUSHING: Edwards 88/340y, Goolsby 43/203y, Taylor 153/198y
PASSING: Taylor 228-406/2481y, 22TD, 56.2%
RECEIVING: Matthews 61/797y, Jordan 56/470y,
Edwards 43/272y
SCORING: Matthews 84pts, Ricky Anderson (K) 73pts,
Edwards & Scott 24pts

1983 2-9

14 Maryland	21 WR Phil Roach / Joe Kelly
29 Iowa State	26 WR Ardell Fuller / Clay Parker
24 Alabama	44 T Rob Monaco
30 Tulane	17 G Will Wolford
10 Florida	29 C Jim Dralle / Bill Fletcher
13 Georgia	20 G Dave Logie / Ken Sample
14 Mississippi	21 T Darrell Denson
7 Memphis State	24 TE Chuck Scott (WR) / Jim Popp
8 Kentucky	17 QB Kurt Page
10 Virginia Tech	21 TB Carl Woods / Keith Edwards
24 Tennessee	34 FB Louie Stephenson / Ted McCullough
	DL Glenn Watson / Steve Bearden
	DL Steve Wade / Willie Twyford
	DL Karl Jordan (LB) / Scott Anderson
	DL John Windham / Chuck DeGroot
	LB Bob O'Connor
	LB Steve McCoy
	LB Bob Sanchez / Jeff Holt
	DB Kermit Sykes
	DB Leonard Coleman
	DB Tom Morre / Rick Risser
	DB Tim Johnson / Mike Matthews

RUSHING: Woods 160/644y, Edwards 59/216y,
Stephenson 24/68y
PASSING: Page 286-493/3178y, 14 TD, 58.0%
RECEIVING: Edwards 97/909y, Scott 70/971y,
Stephenson 29/203y
SCORING: Scott 56pts, Ricky Anderson (K) 49pts,
Woods & Roach 24pts

1984 5-6

26 Kansas State	14 WR Ardell Fuller / Butch Bullen
23 Maryland	14 WR Chuck Scott / Al Rogers
41 Kansas	6 T Will Wilford
30 Alabama	21 G Steve Olinger
23 Tulane	27 C Jim Drale
27 LSU	34 G Dave Logie
35 Georgia	62 T Mark Herrmann / Mike Kraemer
37 Mississippi	20 TE Jim Popp
18 Kentucky	27 QB Kurt Page
3 Virginia Tech	23 TB Everett Crawford / Keith Edwards
13 Tennessee	29 FB Carl Woods / Kenny Weatherspoon
	DL Glenn Watson / Chuck DeGroot
	DL Steve Wade
	DL Karl Jordan
	DL John Windham / Henry Belin
	LB Mac McCarroll / Jeff Cartwright
	LB Steve McCoy / Marvin Thomas
	LB Armando Fitz / Mark Woehler
	DB Thanh Anderson
	DB Kermit Sykes
	DB Manuel Young / Tom Burson
	DB Jeff Holt / Tim Johnson

RUSHING: Woods 192/688y, Crawford 83/434y,
  Weatherspoon 20/79y
PASSING: Page 203-350/2405y, 16TD, 58.0%
RECEIVING: Edwards 60/576y, Scott 54/975y, Popp 29/278y
SCORING: Ricky Anderson (K) 70pts, Scott 52pts, Kelly 44pts

1985 3-7-1

7 Tenn-Chatt'ga	0 WR Boo Mitchell
16 Kansas	42 WR Clay Parker
17 Iowa State	20 T Will Wolford
20 Alabama	40 G Daryl Holt / Steve Olinger
24 Tulane	17 C Shayne Adair / John Short
7 LSU	49 G Dave Logie
13 Georgia	13 T Mark Herrmann / Mike Kraemer
7 Mississippi	35 TE Carl Parker (WR) / Jim Popp
31 Kentucky	24 QB John Gromos / Mark Wracher
24 Virginia Tech	38 TB Everett Crawford
0 Tennessee	30 FB Carl Woods / Kenny Weatherspoon
	DL Marvin Thomas / Henry Belin
	DL Steve Wade
	DL David Wurm
	DL John Windham / Eric Snyder
	LB Armando Fitz / Mac McCarroll
	LB Chris Gaines
	LB Mark Wohler
	DB Thanh Anderson
	DB Kermit Sykes / Andy Baker
	DB Noel Wells / Mike MacIntyre
	DB Jeff Holt

RUSHING: Woods 160/615y, Crawford 108/448y,
  Weatherspoon 40/155y
PASSING: Gromos 124-224/1483y, 6TD, 55.4%
RECEIVING: Crawford 50/533y, Mitchell 45/739y,
  Carl Parker 45/493y
SCORING: Alan Herline (K) 46pts, Crawford 36pts, Woods 30pts

1986 1-10

10 Alabama	42 WR Boo Mitchell
21 Maryland	35 WR Carl Parker / Tony Pearcey
17 Tulane	35 T Mills Fleming
24 Duke	18 G Mike Johnson
9 Auburn	31 C Daryl Holt
16 Georgia	38 G Greg Smith
12 Mississippi	7 T Mike McDonald
Memphis State	22 TE Steve Kosanovich
22 Kentucky	34 QB Mark Wracher / Tim Richardson
21 Virginia Tech	29 TB Everett Crawford / Rodney Barrett
20 Tennessee	35 FB Carl Woods / Kenny Weatherspoon
	DL Marvin Thomas / DeMond Winston
	DL Mac McCarroll
	DL David Wurm
	DL Eric Snyder / Henry Belin
	LB Armando Fitz / Kenny Pulce
	LB Chris Gaines
	LB Mark Woehler / Bob Scanlon
	DB Thanh Anderson / Allan Roman
	DB Andy Baker
	DB Joe Gentry / Noel Wells
	DB Tim Johnson / Torrey Price

RUSHING: Woods 107/543y, Crawford 64/311y,
  Eric Jones (QB) 66/241y
PASSING: Wracher 75-134/827y, 2 TD, 56.0%,
  Richardson 49-114/718y, 4 TD, 43.0%
RECEIVING: Crawford 40/517y, Mitchell 31/463y,
  Parker 31/422y
SCORING: Alan Herline (K) 47pts, Crawford 30pts, Parker 24pts

1987 4-7

27 Memphis State	17 WR Boo Mitchell / Rodney Barrett
31 Duke	35 WR Carl Parker / Tony Pearcey
23 Alabama	30 T Greg Smith
17 Tulane	27 G Mike Johnson
15 Auburn	48 C Daryl Holt
24 Georgia	52 G Charles Pierson
14 Mississippi	42 T Mills Fleming
27 Rutgers	13 TE Steve Kosanovich
38 Maryland	29 QB Eric Jones
34 Maryland	24 TB Everett Crawford / Mark Johnson
36 Tennessee	38 FB Andy McCarroll
	DL Chuck DeGroot
	DL David Wurm
	DL Doug Bradley / Cedric Moore
	DL Eric Snyder
	LB Billy Cunningham / Chris Gaines
	LB DeMond Winston
	LB Bob Scanlon / Renford Reese
	DB Allan Roman
	DB Torrey Price
	DB Joe Gentry / Noel Wells
	DB Andy Baker

RUSHING: Jones 179/665y, Crawford 140/621y,
  McCarroll 146/552y
PASSING: Jones 139-229/1954y, 16TD, 60.7%
RECEIVING: Parker 42/806y, Crawford 35/376y,
  Mitchell 34/549y
SCORING: Parker 72pts, Johnny Clark (K) 70pts, Jones 36pts

1988 3-8

24 Mississippi St.	20 WR Boo Mitchell .
31 Rutgers	30 T Greg Smith
10 Alabama	44 G Charles Pierson / Mike Johnson
15 Duke	17 C John Short / Jim Arnouts
22 Georgia	41 G Bobby Craycraft
24 Florida	9 T Craig Witt / Mills Fleming
28 Mississippi	36 TE Steve Kosanovich / Nabil El Sheshai
13 Kentucky	14 QB Eric Jones
19 Army	24 TB Mark Johnson / Brad Gaines
9 Memphis State	28 WB Kerry Clem / Tony Pearcey
7 Tennessee	14 FB Andy McCarroll / Sean Guerin
	DL Derrick Sartor / Joel Walker
	DL Cedric Moore
	DL Doug Bradley / Tom Wroblewski
	DL Rod Keith / Kenny Pulce
	LB Billy Cunningham / David Summers
	LB DeMond Winston / Bob Scanlon
	LB Scott Brown
	DB Bill Fitzpatrick
	DB Steve Law / Torrey Price
	DB Renford Reese / Tim Richardson
	DB Joe Gentry

RUSHING: Jones 144/305y, M. Johnson 61/295y,
  McCarroll 99/284y
PASSING: Jones 196-360/2548y, 11TD, 54.4%
RECEIVING: Mitchell 78/1213y, Kosanovich 29/296y,
  Gaines 21/248y
SCORING: Johnny Clark (K) 52pts, Jones & Mitchell 30pts

1989 1-10

7 Mississippi St.	42 WR Clarence Sevillian / Derrick Gragg
54 Ohio University	10 WR Corey Harris / Mark Johnson
14 Alabama	20 T Greg Smith
10 Memphis State	13 G Charles Pierson
11 Florida	34 C Kevin Brothen
16 Georgia	35 G Kevin Dowling / Lloyd Griffin
16 Mississippi	24 T Bobby Craycroft / Grant Glewwe
0 Virginia Tech	18 TE Brad Gaines / Nabil El Sheshai
11 Kentucky	15 QB John Gromos / Mike Healey
13 Tulane	37 TB Anthony Carter / Tony Jackson
10 Tennessee	17 FB Carlos Thomas
	DL Derrick Sartor
	DL Cedric Moore / Joel Walker
	DL Doug Bradley
	DL Rod Keith / Kenny Pulce
	LB Andy McCarroll
	LB DeMond Winston
	LB Scott Brown
	DB Renford Reese
	DB Steve Law / Torrey Price
	DB Chris Donnelly
	DB Steve Medes

RUSHING: Thomas 61/254y, Carter 79/249y, Jackson 64/206y
PASSING: Gromos 154-320/1744y, 9TD, 48.1%
RECEIVING: Gaines 67/634y, Harris 45/653y, Sevillian 21/359y
SCORING: Johnny Clark (K) 43pts, Harris 42pts, Gaines 18pts

1990 1-10

7 SMU	44 WR Clarence Sevillian / Eric Weir
24 LSU	21 WR Anthony Carter / Derrick Gragg
28 Alabama	59 T Bobby Craycroft
14 Syracuse	49 G Jim Arnouts / Thor Erikson
6 Auburn	56 C Kevin Brothen
28 Georgia	39 G Mark Mikesell
13 Mississippi	14 T Grant Glewwe
21 Kentucky	28 TE Pat Akos
38 Army	42 QB Marcus Wilson / Mike Healey
28 Wake Forest	56 TB Corey Harris / Mark Johnson
20 Tennessee	49 FB Carlos Thomas
	DL John DeWitt / Derrick Sartor
	DL Mike Gandolfo / Tom Wroblewski
	DL Kenny Pulce / Joel Walker
	DL Rod Keith / Derick Bossier
	LB Shelton Quarles
	LB Gerald Collins / Ashley Stanford
	LB Louis Wooldridge / Gary Rogers
	DB Robert Davis
	DB Robbie Young / Scott Walker
	DB Aaron Smith / Chris Donnelly
	DB Steve Medes / Rico Francis

RUSHING: Thomas 113/680y, Wilson 116/446y,
  Johnson 62/421y, Harris 55/341y
PASSING: Healey 75-130/1041y, 10TD, 57.7%,
  Wilson 38-92/515y, 0TD, 41.3%
RECEIVING: Sevillian 29/536y, Johnson 20/242y, Harris 19/216y
SCORING: Jeff Owen (K) 42pts, Thomas & Wilson 36pts

1991 5-6

10 Syracuse	37 WR Clarence Sevillian
14 SMU	11 T Bobby Craycroft
LSU	16 G Ryan Bell
17 Alabama	48 C Kevin Brothen / Richard Saenz
13 Duke	17 G John Dooling
22 Auburn	24 T Grant Glewwe / Eric Dahlberg
27 Georgia	25 TE Pat Akos / David Neal
30 Mississippi	27 QB Marcus Wilson / Jeff Brothers
41 Army	10 TB Corey Harris / Tony Jackson
17 Kentucky	7 WB Derrick Payne
0 Tennessee	45 FB Carlos Thomas
	DL John DeWitt
	DL Louis Wooldridge / Mike Gandolfo
	DL Alan Young
	LB Gary Rogers / Ricky Melton
	LB Rod Keith
	LB Gerald Collins / Steve Breazeale
	LB Shelton Quarles
	DB Robert Davis
	DB Robbie Young
	DB Aaron Smith
	DB Rico Francis

RUSHING: Harris 229/1103y, Wilson 136/496y, Thomas 63/298y
PASSING: Wilson 32-63/491y, 3TD, 50.8%,
  Brothers 21-45/278y, 0TD, 46.7%,
  Healey 20-39/352y, 2TD, 51.3%
RECEIVING: Harris 23/283y, Sevillian 16/382y, Akos 11/121y
SCORING: Wilson 68pts, Jeff Owen (K) 53pts, Harris 24pts

1992 4-7

8 Alabama	25 WR Clarence Sevillian
42 Duke	37 T Eric Dahlberg
31 Mississippi	9 G Ryan Bell
7 Auburn	31 C Richard Saenz
6 Wake Forest	40 G Mark Mikesell
20 Georgia	30 T Owen Neil
17 South Carolina	7 TE Pat Akos
20 Kentucky	7 QB Marcus Wilson
27 Navy	7 TB Tony Jackson / Cliff Deese
21 Florida	41 WB Derek Wilham
25 Tennessee	29 FB Royce Love
	DL John DeWitt
	DL Gary Rogers / Bill Sullivan
	DL Alan Young / James Manley
	DL Tony Cates
	LB Rico Francis
	LB Brad Brown / Steve Breazeale
	LB Shelton Quarles / Bryan DeGraffenreid
	DB Robert Davis
	DB Robbie Young
	DB Jeff Brothers
	DB Aaron Smith / Nizam Walter

RUSHING: Jackson 114/652y, Deese 103/538y,
  Wilson 181/488y
PASSING: Wilson 75-164/1030y, 5TD, 45.7%
RECEIVING: Sevillian 33/701y, Jackson 18/114y, Akos 9/93y
SCORING: Rob Chura (K) 48pts, Wilson 42pts, Sevillian 32pts

1993 4-7

27 Wake Forest	12 WR Eric Lewis / Gabe Banks
6 Alabama (F-W)	17 T Eric Dahlberg / Bryan Josey
7 Mississippi	49 G Ryan Bell
10 Auburn	14 C Richard Saenz
17 Cincinnati	7 G Mark Mikesell
3 Georgia	41 T Owen Neil
0 South Carolina	22 TE Robert Crouch / Jason Tomichek
12 Kentucky	7 QB Ronnie Gordon
41 Navy	7 TB Tony Jackson / Clifford Deese
0 Florida	52 WB Kenny Simon
14 Tennessee	62 FB Roybe Love
	DL John DeWitt
	DL Brian Boykin / Bill Sulivan
	DL James Manley
	DL Alan Young / Brian DeGraffenreid
	LB Rico Francis / Mark Jefcoat
	LB Gerald Collins / Kirk Williams
	LB Shelton Quarles
	DB Robert Davis
	DB Byron King / DeReal Finklin
	DB Aaron Smith
	DB Eric Vance

RUSHING: Jackson 120/607y, Deese 78/315y, Simon 74/292y
PASSING: Gordon 40-98/400y, 0 TD, 40.8%
RECEIVING: Simon 15/166y, Jackson 9/70y,
Sanford Ware (WR) 7/97y, Tomichek 7/71y
SCORING: Steve Yenner (K) 39pts, Gordon 24pts,
Jackson 18pts

1994 5-6

35 Wake Forest	14 WR Gabe Banks / Sanford Ware
7 Alabama	17 WR Kenny Simon
14 Mississippi	20 T Bryan Josey / Allen DeGraffenreid
6 Arkansas	42 G Will Jacobs
34 Cincinnati	24 C Richard Saenz
43 Georgia	30 G Owen Neil / Mike Jones
16 South Carolina	19 T Robert Crouch
17 N. Illinois	16 TE Jason Tomichek
24 Kentucky	6 QB Ronnie Gordon / Damian Allen
7 Florida	24 TB Jermaine Johnson / Clifford Deese
0 Tennessee	65 FB Eric Lewis
	DL Brian Boykin
	DL Matt Schuckman / Bill Sullivan
	DL James Manley
	DL Jay Stallworth / Brian DeGraffenreid
	LB Mark Jefcoat
	LB Gerald Collins / Jamie Duncan
	LB Kirk Williams / Shawn Stuckey
	DB Corey Chavous / Derrick Atterberry
	DB Anthony Azama / DeReal Finklin
	DB Eric Vance
	DB Matt Anderson

RUSHING: Johnson 167/877y, Gordon 161/577y, Lewis 86/499y
PASSING: Gordon 86-203/991y, 2TD, 42.4%
RECEIVING: Simon 20/271y, Banks 18/217y, Ware 16/126y
SCORING: Gordon 78pts

1995 2-9

25 Alabama	33 WR Sanford Ware / Robert Simmons
0 Notre Dame	41 WR Duane Todd / Kenny Simon
3 TCU	16 T Allen DeGraffenreid / Clay Condrey
7 Arkansas	35 G Chad Wood / Will Jacobs
6 Georgia	17 C Jim Anguiano
14 South Carolina	52 G Mike Jones / Derrick May
10 Mississippi	21 T Robert Crouch / David Coppeans
14 Kentucky	10 TE Jaon Tomichek
29 Louisiana Tech	6 QB Damian Allen / Ronnie Gordon
7 Florida	38 RB Jermaine Johnson / Clifford Deese
7 Tennessee	12 RB Royce Love / Jason Dunnavant
	DL Brian Boykin
	DL Matt Schuckman / Alphonso Harvey
	DL James Manley / Jason Smith
	DL Jay Stallworth
	LB Mark Jefcoat
	LB Jamie Duncan
	LB Carlton Hall / Kirk Williams
	DB Corey Chavous
	DB DeReal Finklin / Fred Vinson
	DB Marcus A. Williams / Rahim Batten
	DB Eric Vance

RUSHING: Johnson 267/1072y, Gordon 57/73y, Deese 26/47y
PASSING: Allen 62-136/728y, 4TD, 45.6%,
Gordon 62-133/584y, 2TD, 46.6%
RECEIVING: Ware 34/402y, Todd 21/289y, Dunnavant 12/112y
SCORING: Steve Yenner (K) 26pts, Johnson 24pts

1996 2-9

7 Notre Dame	14 WR Zach Winkler / Billy Miller
26 Alabama	36 WR Todd Yoder / Tavarus Hogans
9 Mississippi	20 T Allen DeGraffenreid / Clay Condrey
0 LSU	35 G Will Jacobs
19 North Texas	7 C Jim Anguiano / Jeff Barnett
2 Georgia	13 G Michael Saltsman / Shawn Wilson
0 South Carolina	27 T Raminte Byndom
31 Ala.-Birm'ham	15 TE Jason Tomichek / Fred Baker
21 Florida	28 QB Damian Allen
0 Kentucky	25 RB O.J. Fleming / Marcus A. Williams
7 Tennessee	14 RB Jason Dunnavant / Alvin Duke
	DL Brian Boykin
	DL Matt Schuckman / Ian Smith
	DL Jason Hill / Alphonso Harvey
	DL Jay Stallworth / Glenn Young
	LB Mark Jefcoat
	LB Jamie Duncan / Carlton Hall
	LB Antony Jordan
	DB Corey Chavous
	DB DeReal Finklin / Rahim Batten
	DB Eric Vance / Ainsley Battle

RUSHING: Dunnavant 131/374y, Williams 82/268y,
Duke 76/223y
PASSING: Allen 118-279/1472y, 5TD, 42.3%
RECEIVING: Yoder 21/471y, Dunnavant 16/182y,
Fleming 14/156y, Winkler 14/101y
SCORING: Dunnavant & Yoder 18pts

1997 3-8

29 North Texas	12 WR Anthony Azama / Andre Woods
0 Alabama	20 WR Todd Yoder / Tavarus Hogans
40 TCU	16 T Clay Condrey
3 Mississippi	15 G Jim Anguiano / Darren Rothenberg
6 LSU	7 C Jeff Barnett
17 N. Illinois	7 G Michael Saltsman / Shawn Wilson
13 Georgia	34 T Raminte Byndom / Brian Gruber
3 South Carolina	35 TE Elliott Carson / O.J. Fleming
7 Florida	20 QB Damian Allen
10 Kentucky	21 RB Jared McGrath / Jimmy Williams
10 Tennessee	17 FB Paul Morgan
	DL Glenn Young
	DL Ryan Aulds / Jason Smith
	DL Alphonso Harvey / Ian Smith
	DL Jay Stallworth / Russ Nicoll
	LB Carlton Hall / Lamont Turner
	LB Jamie Duncan
	LB Antony Jordan / Chris Cook
	DB Corey Chavous
	DB Fred Vinson / Damien Charley
	DB Rahim Batten / Jamie Watkins
	DB Ainsley Battles

RUSHING: Williams 98/527y, McGrath 127/491y,
Morgan 62/256y
PASSING: Allen 128-283/1544y, 8TD, 45.2%
RECEIVING: Williams 24/183y, Yoder 21/324y, Hogans 20/381y
SCORING: John Markham (K) 48pts, Hogans 18pts

1998 2-9

0 Mississippi St.	42 WR Tavarus Hogans / Todd Yoder
7 Alabama	32 WR Nezih Hasanoglu / Adam Ditto
6 Mississippi	30 T Brian Gruber
16 TCU	19 G Darren Rothenberg
24 W. Michigan	27 C Jeff Barnett
6 Georgia	31 G Michael Saltsman
17 South Carolina	14 T Raminte Byndom
36 Duke	33 TE Elliott Carson
13 Florida	45 QB David Wallace / Greg Zolman
17 Kentucky	55 RB Rodney Williams / Lew Thomas
0 Tennessee	41 FB Jared McGrath
	DL Doyle Crosby
	DL Ryan Aulds
	DL Chuck Losey
	LB Matt Stewart
	LB Jamie Winborn
	LB Lamont Turner
	LB Nate Morrow
	DB Jimmy Williams (WR)
	DB Brian Taylor / Fred Vinson
	DB Harold Lercius
	DB Ainsley Battles

RUSHING: R. Williams 126/608y, McGrath 115/528y,
Thomas 66/286y
PASSING: Wallace 79-174/678y, 4TD, 45.4%,
Zolman 69-145/969y, 4TD, 47.6%
RECEIVING: Hogans 28/366y, Carson 25/190y,
Hasanoglu 19/250y
SCORING: John Markham (K) 38pts,

1999 5-6

17 Alabama	28 WR Tavarus Hogans
34 N. Illinois	31 WR Dan Stricker / Todd Yoder (FB)
37 Mississippi	34 T Brian Gruber
31 Duke	14 G Jim May
14 Mississippi St.	42 C Jeff Barnett
58 Citadel	0 G Michael Saltsman
17 Georgia	27 T Raminte Byndom
11 South Carolina	10 TE Elliott Carson
6 Florida	13 QB Greg Zolman
17 Kentucky	19 RB Rodney Williams / Jared McGrath
10 Tennessee	38 FB Lew Thomas
	DL Doyle Crosby
	DL Ryan Aulds
	DL Russ Nicoll
	LB Matt Stewart / Brandon Walthour
	LB Jamie Winborn
	LB Lamont Turner
	LB Nate Morrow
	DB Jimmy Williams
	DB Rushen Jones / Brian Taylor
	DB Harold Lercius
	DB Ainsley Battles

RUSHING: Williams 148/644y, McGrath 118/575y,
Thomas 19/66y
PASSING: Zolman 154-300/2059y, 10TD, 51.3%
RECEIVING: Hogans 53/837y, Yoder 25/361y, Carson 25/267y
SCORING: John Markham (K) 62pts, Williams 54pts,
Zolman 36pts

2000 3-8

30 Miami (Ohio)	33 WR Dan Stricker
10 Alabama	28 WR Chris Young
7 Mississippi	12 WR Anthony Jones / M.J. Garrett
26 Duke	7 T Brisn Gruber / Jordan Pettit
0 Auburn	33 G Michael Saltsman
17 Wake Forest	10 C Jamie Byrum
19 Georgia	29 G Jim May / Duncan Cave
14 South Carolina	30 T Pat Green
20 Florida	43 TE Elliott Carson / Tom Simone
24 Kentucky	20 QB Greg Zolman
26 Tennessee	28 RB Jared McGrath / Ray Perkins
	DL Doyle Crosby
	DL Brett Beard
	DL Wally Conyers
	LB Matt Stewart / Hunter Hillenmeyer
	LB Jamie Winborn / Mike Adam
	LB Antuian Bradford
	LB Nate Morrow
	DB Jimmy Williams / Brian Taylor
	DB Rushen Jones / Aaron McWhorter
	DB Hariold Lercius
	DB Justin Giboney / Jonathan Shaub

RUSHING: McGrath 133/527y, Perkins 87/425y,
Rodney Williams (RB) 49/141y
PASSING: Zolman 187-354/2441y, 13TD, 52.8%
RECEIVING: Stricker 61/994y, Carson 29/372y, Young 14/119y
SCORING: John Markham (K) 61pts, McGrath & Stricker 30pts

2001 2-9

28 Middle Tenn.	37 WR Dan Stricker
9 Alabama	12 WR M.J. Gasrrett
28 Richmond	22 WR Anthony Jones
21 Auburn	24 T Justin Geisinger / Jordan Pettit
14 Georgia	30 G Jim May
14 South Carolina	46 C Jamie Byrum
42 Duke	28 G Brian Kovolisky
13 Florida	71 T Pat Green / Kenan Arkan
30 Kentucky	56 TE Tom Simone
0 Tennessee	38 QB Greg Zolman
27 Mississippi	38 RB Rodney Williams / Lew Thomas
	DL Doyle Crosby / Trey Holloway
	DL Brett Beard / Robert Dinwiddie
	DL Wally Conyers
	DL Chuck Losey / Ryan Nungasser
	LB Antuian Bradford
	LB Hunter Hillenmeyer / Pat Brunner
	LB Nate Morrow
	DB Aaron McWhorter
	DB Rushen Jones
	DB Justin Giboney / Jonathan Shaub
	DB Harold Lercius

RUSHING: Thomas 105/675y, Williams 131/590y
PASSING: Zolman 186-357/2512y, 14TD, 52.1%
RECEIVING: Stricker 65/1079y, Garrett 27/455y,
Mathenia 22/258y
SCORING: Stricker 48pts, Thomas 30pts

2002 3-9

3 Georgia Tech	45 WR Dan Stricker
49 Furman	18 WR M.J. Garrett
6 Auburn	31 T Justin Geisinger
38 Mississippi	45 G Jim May
14 South Carolina	20 C Jamie Byrum
20 Middle Tenn.	21 G Brian Kovolisky
17 Georgia	48 T Kenan Arkan
28 Connecticut	24 TE Tom Simone / Nick Getter
8 Alabama	30 QB Jay Cutler
17 Florida	21 TB Kwane Doster / Norvaal McKenzie
21 Kentucky	41 FB Matthew Tant
0 Tennessee	24 DL Jovan Haye

DL Matt Clay / Robert Dinwiddie
DL Aaron Carter
DL Chuck Losey
LB Herdley Harrison / Brandon Walthour
LB Hunter Hillenmeyer / Pat Brunner
LB Morgan Osemwegie
DB Dominique Morris / Aaron McWhorter
DB Rushen Jones / Lorenzo Parker
DB Jonathan Shaub
DB Justin Giboney

RUSHING: Doster 160/798y
PASSING: Cutler 103-212/1433y, 9TD, 48.6%
RECEIVING: Stricker 44/620y
SCORING: Stricker 36pts

2003 2-10

21 Mississippi	24 WR Brandon Smith / Marlon White
51 Chattanooga	6 WR Erik Davis / Chris Young
7 Auburn	45 T Justin Geisinger
14 TCU	30 G Brian Kovolisky
17 Georgia Tech	24 C Tom Sorensen / Steven Brent
21 Mississippi St.	30 G Mac Pyle
27 Navy	37 T Brian Stamper / Kenan Arkan
8 Georgia	27 TE Dustin Dunning / Nick Getter
24 South Carolina	35 QB Jay Cutler
17 Florida	35 TB Norval McKenzie / Kwane Doster
28 Kentucky	17 FB Matthew Tant
0 Tennessee	48 DL Jovan Haye

DL Robert Dinwiddie / Aaron Carter
DL Ralph McKenzie / Matt Clay
DL Chris Booker
LB Herdley Harrison
LB Otis Washington / Pat Brunner
LB Moses Osemwegie / Kevin Joyce
DB Dominique Morris
DB Bill Alford / Lorenzo Parker
DB Kelechi Ohanaja
DB Andrew Pace

RUSHING: N. McKenzie 162/639y, Doster 90/386y, Cutler 115/299y
PASSING: Cutler 187-327/2347y, 18TD, 57.2%
RECEIVING: Davis 41/638y, Smith 39/595y, White 21/239y
SCORING: Davis 48pts, Tolga Ertugrul (K) 35pts, N. McKenzie & Tant 30pts

2004 2-9

6 South Carolina	31 WR Brandon Smith / Marlon White
23 Mississippi	26 WR Erik Davis / Chris Young
26 Navy	29 T Justin Geisinger
31 Mississippi St.	13 G Brian Kovolisky
34 Rutgers	37 C Trey Holloway
3 Georgia	33 G Nigel Seaman
19 E. Kentucky	7 T Brian Stamper
7 LSU	24 TE Dustin Dunning / Jonathan Loyte
17 Florida	34 QB Jay Cutler
13 Kentucky	14 TB Norval McKenzie / Kwane Doster
33 Tennessee	38 FB Matthew Tant

DL Jovan Haye
DL Robert Dinwiddie / Ralph McKenzie
DL Ray Brown / Matt Clay
DL Aaron Carter
LB Herdley Harrison
LB Otis Washington / Jonathan Goff
LB Moses Osemwegie / Kevin Joyce
DB Dominique Morris /Cheron Thompson
DB Bill Alford / Lorenzo Parker
DB Kelechi Ohanaja
DB Andrew Pace

RUSHING: McKenzie 102/446y, Doster 89/437y, Cutler 109/349y
PASSING: Cutler 147-241/1844y, 10TD, 61.0%
RECEIVING: Smith 41/553y, Davis 37/510y, White 29/457y
SCORING: Patrick Johnson (K) 39pts, Cutler 36pts, Jennings 30pts

2005 5-6

24 Wake Forest	20 WR Earl Bennett
28 Arkansas	24 WR Marlon White / Erik Davis
31 Mississippi	23 T Ryan King
37 Richmond	13 G Chris Williams
15 Middle Tenn.	17 C Trey Holloway
6 LSU	34 G Josh Eames
17 Georgia	34 T Brian Stamper
28 South Carolina	35 TE Dustin Dunning
42 Florida	49 QB Jay Cutler
43 Kentucky	48 RB Jeff Jennings
28 Tennessee	24 FB Steven Bright

DL Herdley Harrison / Curtis Gatewood
DL Ralph McKenzie
DL Lamar Divens / Theo Horrocks
DL Chris Booker
LB Kevin Joyce / Marcus Buggs
LB Jonathan Goff
LB Moses Osemwegie
DB Andrew Pace
DB Josh Allen / Cheron Thompson
DB Reshard Langford
DB Kelichi Ohanaja / Ben Koger

RUSHING: Cassen Jackson-Garrison (RB) 97/539y, Jennings 123/448y, Cutler 106/215y
PASSING: Cutler 273-462/3073y, 21TD, 59.1%
RECEIVING: Bennett 79/876y, Davis 46/619y, Dunning 35/389y, White 34/350y
SCORING: Bryant Hahnfeldt (K) 68pts, Bennett 54pts, Cassen Jackson-Garrison (RB) 48pts

2006 4-8

7 Michigan	27 WR Earl Bennett / Sean Walker
10 Alabama	13 WR Marlon White / George Smith
19 Arkansas	21 T Chris Williams
38 Tennessee St.	9 G Josh Eames / Ryan Custer
43 Temple	14 C Hamilton Holliday
10 Mississippi	17 G Merritt Kirchoffer (T) / Mac Pyle
24 Georgia	22 T Elliott Hood / Brian Stamper
13 South Carolina	31 TE Brad Allen
45 Duke	28 QB Chris Nickson
19 Florida	25 RB Cassen Jackson-Garrison
26 Kentucky	38 FB Steven Bright
10 Tennessee	39 DL Curtis Gatewood / Steven Stone

DL Ray Brown
DL Theo Horrocks
DL Chris Booker / Broderick Stewart
LB Kevin Joyce
LB Jonathan Goff
LB Marcus Buggs / Brandon Bryant
DB Joel Caldwell / D.J. Moore
DB Josh Allen / Darlron Spead
DB Reshard Langford
DB Ryan Hamilton / Ben Koger

RUSHING: Nickson 146/694y, Jackson-Garrison 152/614y, Jared Hawkins (RB) 43/298y
PASSING: Nickson 160-292/2085y, 15TD, 54.8%
RECEIVING: Bennett 82/1146y, White 25/313y, Smith 21/313y,
SCORING: Nickson 54pts, Bryant Hahnfeldt (K) 51pts, Bennett & Jackson-Garrison 36pts

2007 5-7

41 Richmond	17 WR George Smith
10 Alabama	24 WR Sean Walker / Justin Wheeler
31 Mississippi	17 WR Earl Bennett
30 E. Michigan	7 T Chris Williams
7 Auburn	35 G Josh Eames / Ryan Custer
17 Georgia	20 C Hamilton Holliday
17 South Carolina	6 G Merritt Kirchoffer
24 Miami (Ohio)	13 T Brian Stamper
22 Florida	49 TE Brad Allen / Jake Bradford
20 Kentucky	27 QB Chris Nickson / Mackenzi Adams
24 Tennessee	25 TB Cassen Jackson-Garrison/Jf. Jennings
17 Wake Forest	31 DL Steven Stone / Broderick Stewart

DL Gabe Hall
DL Theo Horrocks
DL Curtis Gatewood
LB Marcus Buggs / John Stokes
LB Jonathan Goff
LB Patrick Benoist / Brandon Bryant
DB D.J. Moore / Josh Allen
DB Myron Lewis / Darlron Spead
DB Ryan Hamilton / Joel Caldwell
DB Reshard Langford

RUSHING: Jackson-Garrison 148/594y, Jeff Jennings (TB) 96/346y, Adams 87/289y
PASSING: Adams 101-182/1043y, 9TD, 55.5%, Nickson 62-119/763y, 6TD, 52.1%
RECEIVING: Bennett 75/830y, Smith 32/397y, Walker 20/270y
SCORING: Bryant Hahnfeldt (K) 67pts, Bennett & Jackson-Garrison 30pts

2008 7-6

34 Miami (Ohio)	13 WR Jamie Graham / George Smith
24 South Carolina	17 WR Sean Walker
38 Rice	21 WR Justin Wheeler / D.J. Moore (DB)
23 Mississippi	17 T Reilly Lauer
14 Auburn	13 G Ryan Custer / Kyle Fischer (T)
14 Mississippi St.	17 C Bradley Vierling
14 Georgia	24 G Eric Hensley / Joey Bailey
7 Duke	10 T Thomas Welch
14 Florida	42 TE Brandon Barden / Jake Bradford
31 Kentucky	24 QB Chris Nickson / Mackenzi Adams
10 Tennessee	20 TB Jared Hawkins / Jeff Jennings
10 Wake Forest	23 DL Steven Stone / Teriall Brannon
16 Boston College ■	14 DL Greg Billinger

DL Adam Smotherman / T.J. Greenstone
DL Broderick Stewart / Theron Kadri
LB John Stokes
LB Chris Marve
LB Patrick Benoist
DB D.J. Moore (WR) / Jared Fagan
DB Myron Lewis
DB Ryan Hamilton
DB Reshard Langford / Joel Caldwell

RUSHING: Hawkins 139/593y, Nickson 128/542y, Adams 62/136y
PASSING: Adams 77-156/882y, 5TD, 49.4%, Nickson 61-127/545y, 4TD, 48.0%
RECEIVING: Walker 36/520y, Barden 28/209y, Graham 17/125y
SCORING: Bryant Hahnfeldt (K) 69pts, Nickson 36pts, Hawkins 30pts

2009 2-10

45 W. Carolina	0 WR Udom Umoh / Jamie Graham (DB)
9 LSU	23 WR John Cole / Turner Wimberly
3 Mississippi St.	15 WR Alex Washington
36 Rice	17 T Thomas Welch
7 Mississippi	23 G Ryan Custer / Kyle Fischer
13 Army	16 C Bradley Vierling
10 Georgia	34 G Eric Hensley
10 South Carolina	14 T Reilly Lauer / James Williams
31 Georgia Tech	56 TE Brandon Barden / Austin Monahan
3 Florida	27 QB Larry Smith / Mackenzie Adams
13 Kentucky	24 TB Warren Norman / Zac Stacy
16 Tennessee	31 DL Steven Stone / Tim Fugger

DL Greg Billinger / T.J. Greenstone
DL Adam Smotherman
DL Broderick Stewart / Theron Kadri
LB Brent Trice / John Stokes
LB Chris Marve
LB Patrick Benoist
DB Casey Hayward / Eddie Foster
DB Myron Lewis / Jamie Graham (WR)
DB Joel Caldwell / Ryan Hamilton
DB Sean Richardson

RUSHING: Norman 145/783y, Stacy 107/478y, Smith 85/213y
PASSING: Smith 106-227/1126y, 4TD, 46.7%, Adams 64-125/630y, 2TD, 51.2%
RECEIVING: Cole 36/382y, Barden 29/357y, Umoh 20/267y, Norman 19/108y
SCORING: Ryan Fowler (K) 68pts, Norman 42pts, Stacy 18pts

2010 2-10

21 Northwestern	23 WR Jonathan Krause / Turner Wimberly
3 LSU	27 WR Udom Umoh / Troy Herndon
28 Mississippi	14 WR John Cole / Jordan Matthews
21 Connecticut	40 T Wesley Johnson
52 E. Michigan	6 G Jabo Burrow
0 Georgia	43 C Logan Stewart / Joey Bailey
7 South Carolina	21 G Kyle Fischer
14 Arkansas	49 T Ryan Seymour / Caleb Welchans (G)
14 Florida	55 TE Brandon Barden / Mason Johnston
20 Kentucky	38 QB Larry Smith / Jared Funk
10 Tennessee	24 TB W. Norman/Zac Stacy/Kennard Reeves
13 Wake Forest	34 DL Tim Fugger / Johnell Thomas

DL Rob Lohr
DL T.J. Greenstone / Colt Nichter
DL Theron Kadri
LB John Stokes / Trey Wilson
LB Chris Marve
LB/DB Nate Campbell / Andre Hal
DB Casey Hayward / Jamie Graham
DB Eddie Foster
DB Kenny Ladler / Jay Fullam
DB Sean Richardson / Eric Samuels

RUSHING: Norman 77/459y, Stacy 66/331y, Reeves 76/306y
PASSING: Smith 117-247/1262y, 6TD, 47.4%, Funk 52-109/651y, 5TD, 47.7%
RECEIVING: Barden 34/425y, Cole 25/317y, Krause 24/243y
SCORING: Ryan Fowler (K) 47pts, Matthews, Norman & Smith 24pts

VIRGINIA

University of Virginia (Founded 1819)
Charlottesville, Virginia
Colors: Orange and Blue
Nicknames: Cavaliers, Wahoos
Stadium: David A. Harrison Field at Scott Stadium (1931) 61,500
Conference Affiliations: Southern (1922-35), Independent (1936-53),
   Atlantic Coast (1954-present)

CAREER RUSHING YARDS	Attempts	Yards
Thomas Jones (1996-99)	809	3998
Tiki Barber (1993-96)	651	3389
Terry Kirby (1989-92)	567	3348
John Papit (1947-50)	537	3238
Wali Lundy (2002-05)	742	3193
Tommy Vigorito (1977-80)	648	2913
Frank Quayle (1966-68)	514	2695
Jim Bakhtiar (1955-57)	555	2434
Alvin Pearman (2001-04)	500	2394
Barry Word (1982-85)	405	2257

CAREER PASSING YARDS	Comp.-Att.	Yards
Matt Schaub (2000-03)	716-1069	7502
Shawn Moore (1987-90)	421-762	6629
Jameel Sewell (2006-07, 2009)	514-903	5366
Scott Gardner (1972-75)	390-816	5218
Aaron Brooks (1995-98)	357-651	5118
Marc Verica (2007-10)	487-813	4992
Marques Hagans (2002-05)	408-655	4877
Mike Groh (1992-95)	339-582	4366
Dan Ellis (1997-2000)	291-507	3974
Don Majkowski (1983-86)	286-579	3901

CAREER RECEIVING YARDS	Catches	Yards
Billy McMullen (1999-2002)	210	2978
Herman Moore (1988-90)	114	2504
John Ford (1984, 1986-88)	128	2399
Tyrone Davis (1991-94)	103	2153
Germane Crowell (1994-97)	122	2142
Patrick Jeffers (1992-95)	108	1785
Heath Miller (2002-04)	144	1703
Dave Sullivan (1970-72)	120	1578
Bruce McGonnigal (1987-90)	103	1556
Terrence Wilkins (1995-98)	97	1495

SEASON RUSHING YARDS	Attempts	Yards
Thomas Jones (1999)	334	1798
Tiki Barber (1995)	265	1397
Tiki Barber (1996)	250	1360
Thomas Jones (1998)	238	1303
Barry Word (1985)	207	1224

SEASON PASSING YARDS	Comp.-Att.	Yards
Matt Schaub (2002)	288-418	2976
Matt Schaub (2003)	281-403	2952
Marc Verica (2010)	233-396	2799
Mike Groh (1995)	182-330	2510
Marques Hagans (2005)	213-343	2492

SEASON RECEIVING YARDS	Catches	Yards
Herman Moore (1990)	54	1190
Billy McMullen (2001)	83	1060
Germane Crowell (1997)	53	969
Billy McMullen (2002)	69	894
John Ford (1987)	48	855

GAME RUSHING YARDS	Attempts	Yards
John Papit (1948 vs. Washington & Lee)	16	224
Alvin Pearman (2004 vs. Duke)	38	223

GAME PASSING YARDS	Comp.-Att.	Yards
Marc Verica (@010 vs. Duke)	24-46	417
Matt Schaub (2003 vs. N.C. State)	41-55	393
Aaron Brooks (1997 vs. Virginia Tech)	23-34	390

GAME RECEIVING YARDS	Catches	Yards
Ken Shelton (1974 vs. William & Mary)	9	241
Dontrelle Inman (2010 vs. Duke)	10	239
Herman Moore (1990 vs. Georgia Tech)	9	234

GREATEST COACH

George Welsh had been the nation's leading passer as a senior quarterback at the Naval Academy in 1955 and became one the the most successful coaches at Navy from 1973 to 1981.

Suddenly, Welsh ventured out for greener pastures that were somewhat barren to begin with. Virginia had enjoyed only two winning seasons since the 1949-1952 teams completed a 31-7 run. But, Welsh turned the Cavaliers into a consistent threat for the Atlantic Coast Conference title. Although Welsh would secure shares of only two ACC crowns, he developed an outstanding program that won 134, lost 86, and tied three in his 19 years at the football helm in Charlottesville.

Welsh was named to the College Hall of Fame in 2004, going in as a coach from Navy and Virginia. Upon completion of Welsh's career, his 189 victories ranked him 24th in Division One (FBS) wins.

VIRGINIA'S 55 GREATEST SINCE 1953

OFFENSE

WIDE RECEIVER: Germane Crowell, Tyrone Davis, Billy McMullen, Herman Moore
TIGHT END: Ed Carrington, Bruce McGonnigal, Heath Miller
TACKLE: Jim Dombrowski, D'Brickashaw Ferguson, Noel LaMantagne, Ray Roberts
GUARD: Elton Brown, Mark Dixon, Tom Glassic, Bob Olderman
CENTER: Dan Ryczek, John St. Clair
QUARTERBACK: Shawn Moore, Matt Schaub
RUNNING BACK: Tiki Barber, Thomas Jones, Terry Kirby, Frank Quayle
FULLBACK: Jim Bakhtiar, Charles Way

DEFENSE

END: Stuart Anderson, Don Parker, Mike Frederick, Patrick Kerney, Chris Long,
   Ray Savage, Chris Slade
TACKLE: Antonio Dingle, Henry Jordan, Andy Selfridge
LINEBACKER: Dick Ambrose, Ahmad Brooks, James Farrior, Jeff Lageman, Wali Rainer,
   Jamie Sharper
CORNERBACK: Ronde Barber, Joe Crocker
SAFETY: Pat Chester, Percy Ellsworth, Keith Lyle, Lester Lyles, Keith McMeans, Anthony Poindexter

SPECIAL TEAMS

RETURN SPECIALIST: Sonny Randle
PLACE KICKER: Connor Hughes, Rafael Garcia
PUNTER: Will Brice

MULTIPLE POSITIONS

END-TACKLE-DEFENSIVE END-DEFENSIVE TACKLE: Dave Graham

TWO-WAY PLAYERS

GUARD-LINEBACKER: John Polzer

PERFORMANCE FORMULA:
VIRGINIA'S 10 BEST SEASONS

1994	1.4046	11 of 71
1998	1.3894	20 of 71
1989	1.3546	17 of 70
2004	1.3536	17 of 72
1984	1.3228	16 of 70
1995	1.3180	19 of 70
1991	1.3090	21 of 70
2002	1.2533	27 of 70
1996	1.2507	26 of 70
1993	1.2302	27 of 70

VIRGINIA CAVALIERS

Year	W-L-T	AP Poll	Conference Standing	Toughest Regular Season Opponents	Coach (Record at School)	Bowl Games		
1953	1-8		-	South Carolina 7-3, George Washington 5-4, Duke 7-2-1	Ned McDonald			
1954	3-6		7	Penn State 7-2, Virginia Tech 8-0-1, Army 7-2, West Virginia 8-1	Ned McDonald			
1955	1-9		8	Clemson 7-3, Virginia Tech 6-3-1, Vanderbilt 7-3, Pittsburgh 7-3	Ned McDonald (5-23)			
1956	3-7		8	South Carolin a7-3, Virginia Tech 7-2-1, Navy 6-1-2, Clemson 7-1-2	Ben Martin			
1957	3-6-1		6	West Virginia 7-2-1, Duke 6-2-2, Clemson 7-3, Army 7-2, VMI 9-0-1	Ben Martin (7-12-1)			
1958	1-9		8	Clemson 8-2, Army 8-0-1, Vanderbilt 5-2-3	Dick Voris			
1959	0-10		8	Clemson 8-2, VMI 8-1-1, Wake Forest 6-4, South Carolina 6-4	Dick Voris			
1960	0-10		6	NC State 6-3-1, Clemson 6-4, Navy 9-1, Maryland 6-4	Dick Voris (1-29)			
1961	4-6		8	Duke 7-3, Navy 7-3, Maryland 7-3	Bill Elias			
1962	5-5		7	Virginia Tech 5-5, Maryland 6-4, Rutgers 5-5	Bill Elias			
1963	2-7-1		8	North Caroplina 8-2, Virginia Tech 8-2, NC State 8-2, Boston Coll. 6-3	Bill Elias (16-23-1)			
1964	5-5		8	Duke 4-5-1, Virginia Tech 6-4, NC State 5-5, North Carolina 5-5	George Blackburn			
1965	5-5		7	Duke 6-4, West Virginia 6-4, Virginia Tech 7-3, Georgia Tech 6-3-1	George Blackburn			
1966	4-6		3t	Clemson 6-4, Virginia Tech 8-1-1, Georgia Tech 9-1	George Blackburn			
1967	5-5		4	Army 8-2, NC State 8-2	George Blackburn			
1968	7-3		3	Purdue 8-2, NC State 6-4	George Blackburn			
1969	3-7		8	Clemson 4-6, North Carolina 5-5	George Blackburn (29-32)			
1970	5-6		8	Duke 6-5, Wake Forest 6-5, North Carolina 8-3	Don Lawrence			
1971	3-8		3t	Michigan 11-0, Army 6-4, North Carolina 9-2	Don Lawrence			
1972	4-7		6t	West Virginia 8-3, NC State 7-3-1, North Carolina 10-1	Don Lawrence (11-22)			
1973	4-7		4	NC State 8-3, Missouri 7-4, Maryland 8-3	Sonny Randle			
1974	4-7		6	NC State 9-2, North Carolina 7-4, Clemson 7-4, Maryland 8-3	Sonny Randle (5-17)			
1975	1-10		7	Virginia Tech 8-3, East Carolina 8-3, Maryland 8-2-1	Dick Bestwick			
1976	2-9		6	South Carolina 6-5, North Carolina 9-2, Maryland 11-0	Dick Bestwick			
1977	1-9-1		6	Texas 11-0, Clemson 8-2-1, North Carolina 8-2-1	Dick Bestwick			
1978	2-9		7	Clemson 10-1, Maryland 9-2, NC State 8-3	Dick Bestwick			
1979	6-5		6	Clemson 8-3, Navy 7-4, North Carolina 7-3-1, Maryland 7-4	Dick Bestwick			
1980	4-7		4t	Navy 8-3, Virginia Tech 8-3, North Carolina 10-1, Maryland 8-3	Dick Bestwick (16-49-1)			
1981	1-10		7	West Virginia 8-3, Clemson 11-0, North Carolina 9-2	George Welsh			
1982	2-9		6	Clemson 9-1-1, North Carolina 7-4, Maryland 8-3, Virginia Tech 7-4	George Welsh			
1983	6-5		4t	Maryland 8-3, Clemson 9-1-1, North Carolina 8-3, Virginia Tech 9-2	George Welsh			
1984	8-2-2	20	2	Clemson 7-4, Virginia Tech 8-3, Maryland 8-3	George Welsh	Peach	27 Purdue	24
1985	6-5		3t	Georgia Tech 8-2-1, West Virginia 7-3-1, Maryland 8-3	George Welsh			
1986	3-8		6t	Virginia Tech 8-2-1, NC State 8-2-1, North Carolina 7-3-1	George Welsh			
1987	8-4		2	Georgia 8-3, Clemson 9-2, South Carolina 8-3, Wake Forest 7-4	George Welsh	All-American	22 Brigham Young	16
1988	7-4		2	Duke 7-3-1, Clemson 9-2, Louisville 8-3, NC State 7-3-1	George Welsh	Citrus	21 Illinois	31
1989	10-3	18	1t	Notre Dame 11-1, Penn State 7-3-1, Duke 8-3, Clemson 9-2	George Welsh	Sugar	22 Tennessee	23
1990	8-4	23	2t	Clemson 9-2, William & Mary 9-2, Georgia Tech 10-0-1	George Welsh	Gator	14 Oklahoma	48
1991	8-3-1		4	Clemson 9-1-1, North Carolina 7-4, NC State 9-2	George Welsh			
1992	7-4		4t	North Carolina 8-3, Florida State 10-1, NC State 9-2-1	George Welsh	Carquest	13 Boston College	31
1993	7-5		3t	Florida St. 11-1, North Carolina 10-2, Clemson 8-3, Virginia Tech 8-3	George Welsh	Independence	20 Texas Christian	10
1994	9-3	15	3t	Florida State 9-1-1, North Carolina 8-3, Duke 8-3, NC State 8-3	George Welsh	Peach	34 Georgia	27
1995	9-4	16	1t	Michigan 9-3, Clemson 8-3, Texas 10-1-1, Florida St. 9-2, Va. Tech 9-2	George Welsh	Carquest	21 Miami	31
1996	7-5		4	Texas 8-4, Florida State 11-0, North Carolina 9-2, Virginia Tech 10-1	George Welsh			
1997	7-4		3t	Auburn 9-2, North Carolina 10-1, Florida State 1-1	George Welsh	Peach	33 Georgia	35
1998	9-3	18	3	Georgia tech 9-2, Florida State 11-1, Virginia Tech 8-3	George Welsh	MicronPC	21 Illinois	63
1999	7-5		2t	BYU 8-3, Virginia Tech 11-0, Florida State 11-0, Georgia Tech 8-3	George Welsh (134-86-3)	Oahu	14 Georgia	37
2000	6-6		4	Clemson 9-2, Florida State 11-1, Georgia Tech 9-2, Virginia Tech 10-1	Al Groh			
2001	5-7		7t	Maryland 10-1, Florida State 7-4, NC State 7-4, Virginia Tech 8-3	Al Groh			
2002	9-5	22	2t	Penn State 9-3, NC State 10-3, Maryland 10-3, Virginia Tech 9-4	Al Groh	Cont'l Tire	48 West Virginia	22
2003	8-5		4t	Clemson 8-4, Florida State 10-2, Maryland 9-3, Virginia Tech 8-4	Al Groh	Cont'l Tire	23 Pittsburgh	16
2004	8-4	23	3t	Florida State 8-3, Miami 8-3, Virginia Tech 10-2	Al Groh	MC Computers	34 Fresno State	37
2005	7-5		Cst5	Boston College 8-3, Virginia Tech 10-2, Miami 9-2	Al Groh	Music City	34 Minnesota	31
2006	5-7		Cst3	Georgia Tech 9-3, Maryland 8-4, Virginia Tech 10-2	Al Groh			
2007	9-4		Cst2	Connecticut 9-4, Wake Forest 9-4, Virginia Tech 11-3	Al Groh	Gator	28 Texas Tech	31
2008	5-7		Cst5	Southern California 11-1, Georgia Tech 9-3, Virginia Tech 9-4	Al Groh			
2009	3-9		Cst6	TCU 12-0, Georgia Tech 11-2, Clemson 8-5, Virginia Tech 9-3	Al Groh (59-53)			
2010	4-8		Cst5t	So. California 8-5, Florida State 9-4, Maryland 8-4, Virginia Tech 11-2	Mike London (4-8)			

TOTAL: 286-355-6 .4467 (56 of 70)   **Bowl Games since 1953:** 7-10 .4118 (55 of 70)

GREATEST TEAM SINCE 1953: Coach George Welsh's 1990 Cavaliers made it all the way to no. 1 in the nation only to lose an early November heartbreaker to Georgia Tech. After that home defeat, Virginia was upset by Maryland and beaten by rival Virginia Tech. An injury-riddled Cavs team was nipped in the Sugar Bowl by Tenneesee. As excellent as the 1990 team was, the 1995 team had the most talent. It was ranked 16th at season's end, just one spot off the previous year's 15th, the highest in Virginia history. Welsh's 1995 squad finished only 9-4 but became one of only four teams ever to lose twice on a game's last play in the same season. Virginia lost one-point heartbreakers at no. 14 Michigan and no. 16 Texas. The Cavs featured All-American safety Percy Ellsworth and 22 players who received All-ACC mention, including tailback Tiki Barber, his twin and cornerback Ronde, quarterback Mike Groh, linebackers James Farrior and Jamie Sharper, offensive tackle Jason Augustino, defensive linemen Duane Ashman, Todd White and Jon Harris, and safety-linebacker Anthony Poindexter.

1953 1-8

6	Virginia Tech	20 E Ray Quillen / Fred Moyer / Jesse Hagy
0	South Carolina	19 T Joe Mehalick
24	Geo. Wash'ton	20 G Bill Stallings / Don Alexander
6	VMI	21 C Jim Pugh / Bob Gut (T)
13	Vanderbilt	28 G John Polzer / Preston Harrison
6	Duke	48 T Paul Phipps (E) / Carlton Schelhorn
0	Pittsburgh	26 E Bob Pogue / Charles Modlin
13	Wash'ton & Lee	27 QB Rives Bailey / Dan Rose
7	North Carolina	33 HB Stanwood Knowles / Joe Niedbala
		HB Hank Strempek (FB) / Peter Potter
		FB Jim Elekes / Herb Hartwell

RUSHING: Strempek 93/315y
PASSING: Bailey 41-88/517y, 3TD, 46.6%
RECEIVING: Moyer 10/174y
SCORING: Strempek 18pts

1954 3-6

27	Lehigh	21 E Bob Pogue / Ray Quillen
14	Geo. Wash'ton	13 T Henry Jordan / Jim Elekes
7	Penn State	34 G Frank Fannon / Jim St. Clair
21	VMI	0 C Owen Meadows / Don Kovach
0	Virginia Tech	6 G John Polzer
20	Army	21 T Carlton Schelhorn
0	South Carolina	27 E Bob Gunderman / Fred Moyer
14	North Carolina	26 QB Rives Bailey / Bill Clarke
10	West Virginia	14 HB Stanwood Knowles / Eddie Knowles
		HB Nick Lawyer / Joe Niedbala
		FB Hank Strempek / Herb Hartwell

RUSHING: Hartwell 93/390y
PASSING: Bailey 23-63/309y, 1TD, 36.5%
RECEIVING: Strempek 6/156y
SCORING: Hartwell 24pts

1955 1-9

7	Clemson	20 E Bob Gunderman / Fred Polzer
0	Geo. Wash'ton	13 T Henry Jordan / Harold Outten
7	Penn State	26 G Jay Corson / Frank Fannon
20	VMI	13 C Jim Keyser / Don Kovach
13	Virginia Tech	17 G John Polzer / Jim St. Clair
7	Vanderbilt	34 T Jim Elekes / John Diehl
7	Pittsburgh	18 E Jesse Hagy / Tucker McLaughlin
7	Wake Forest	13 QB Bill Clarke / Rives Bailey
14	North Carolina	26 HB Herb Hartwell / Wilson Tinsley
14	South Carolina	21 HB Ronnie Jenkins / Ralph Kneeland
		FB Jim Bakhtiar / Steve Hoffer

RUSHING: Bakhtiar 158/73y, Kneeland 58/382y, Hartwell 59/376y
PASSING: Clarke 37-80/372y, 2 TD, 46.3%
RECEIVING: Hagy 12/173y, Bakhtiar 8/55y, 2 with 7
SCORING: Bakhtiar (FB-K) 36pts, Hartwell & Tinsley 12pts

1956 3-7

18	VMI	0 E Fred Polzer / Calvin Fowler
7	Duke	40 T Henry Jordan
7	Wake Forest	6 G Jay Corson / Jim St. Clair
13	South Carolina	27 C Jim Keyser / Don Kovach
24	Lehigh	12 G Harold Outten / Bob Canevari
7	Virginia Tech	14 T Ron Melnik
2	Vanderbilt	6 E Bob Gunderman / Tucker McLaughlin
7	N. Carolina (F-W)	21 QB Nelson Yarbrough / Bill Clarke
7	Navy	34 HB Ulmo "Sonny" Randle / Alvin Cash
0	Clemson	7 HB Ralph Kneeland / Ronnie Jenkins
		FB Jim Bakhtiar

RUSHING: Bakhtiar 203/879y, Cash 46/149y, Kneeland 42/103y
PASSING: Yarbrough 43-91/626y, TD, 47.3 %,
Clarke 31-70/269y, TD, 44.3%
RECEIVING: Polzer 24/221y, Gunderman 15/153y,
McLaughlin 8/74y
SCORING: Bakhtiar (FB-K) 30pts, Yarbrough 18pts, 2 with 12

1957 3-6-1

6	West Virginia	6 E Dave Graham / Pat Whitaker
0	Duke	40 T Jim Keyser (G) / Joe White
28	Wake Forest	20 G Jim McShane / Jim Candler
6	Clemson	20 C Bob Canevari / Scott Teunis
38	Virginia Tech	7 G Frank Call
12	Army	20 T Harold Outten / George Sempeles
7	VMI	20 E Fred Polzer / Mike Riley
0	South Carolina	13 QB Nelson Yarbrough / Reece Whitley
0	Maryland	12 HB Sonny Randle / Carl Moser
20	North Carolina	13 HB Tom Gravins / Alvin Cash
		FB Jim Bakhtiar

RUSHING: Bakhtiar 194/822y, Moser 58/199y, Gravins 48/159y
PASSING: Whitley 42-99/501y, 5TD, 42.4%
RECEIVING: Polzer 25/232y, Randle 14/168y, Moser 9/154y
SCORING: Bakhtiar (FB-K) 43pts, Polzer & Yarbrough 24pts

1958 1-9

15	Clemson	20 E Mike Scott / Maynard Rice
15	Duke	12 T Wayne Whalen / Bob Carlisle
14	N.Carolina St.	26 G Jim McShane
13	Virginia Tech	22 C Bob Canevari / Bob Edwards
6	Army	35 G Frank Call / Frank Hamilton
6	Vanderbilt	35 T Irvin Shendow / John Marlow
0	VMI	39 E Bob Williams / Brerry Jones
0	North Carolina	42 QB Reece Whitley / Arnold Dempsey
14	South Carolina	28 HB Jim Roberson / Tom Gravins
6	Maryland	44 WB Sonny Randle / Alan Reynolds
		FB John Barger

RUSHING: Gravins 56/258y, Barger 73/198y, Roberson 54/180y
PASSING: Dempsey 74-152/697y, 2TD, 48.7%
RECEIVING: Randle 47/642y, Williams 14/166y, Roberson 12/59y
SCORING: Randle 32pts, Barger & Gravins (HB-K) 12pts

1959 0-10

0	William & Mary	37 E Henry Koehler / Ken Sappington
0	Clemson	47 T John Marlow / Bill Kanto
10	Florida	55 G Lou Martig / Emory Thomas
12	VMI	19 C Bob Edwards / Terry Canale
14	Virginia Tech	40 G Frank Hamilton
0	Vanderbilt	33 T Ron Gassert / Roger Zensen
12	Wake Forest	34 E Brerry Jones / Dick Hunton
20	So.Carolina	32 QB Stanford Fischer / Arnold Dempsey
0	North Carolina	41 HB Fred Trainor
12	Maryland	55 HB Tom Gravins / Ted Denby
		FB Fred Shepherd / Harold Rust

RUSHING: Gravins 86/354y, Shepherd 54/172y, Denby 45/131y
PASSING: Fischer 58-119/603y, 13TD, 48.7%
RECEIVING: Jones 20/207y, Denby 14/170y, 2 with 13
SCORING: Gravins (HB-K) 35pts, Shepherd 12pts, 5 with 6pts

1960 0-10

21	William & Mary	41 E Dennis Andrews / Ed Menzer
7	N. Carolina St.	26 T John Marlow / Bill Kanto
7	Clemson	21 G Emory Thomas / Bob Rowley
16	VMI	30 C Bill Lang / Andy Moran
6	Virginia Tech	40 G Turnley Todd / Frank Hamilton
20	Wake Forest	28 T Ron Gassert
6	Navy	41 E Joe Kehoe
12	Maryland	44 QB Gary Cuozzo / Stanford Fischer
8	North Carolina	35 HB Ted Rzempoluch / Bobby Freeman
0	South Carolina	26 HB Carl Kuhn / Tony Ulehla
		FB Fred Shepherd / John Barger

RUSHING: Shepherd 126/529y, Kuhn 53/257y, Ulehla 43/239y
PASSING: Cuozzo 40-103/397y, 4TD, 38.8%
RECEIVING: Kehoe 34/378y, Ulehla 7/86y, Shepherd 7/68y
SCORING: Ulehla 26pts, Shepherd 24pts, Kuhn 16pts

1961 4-6

21	William & Mary	6 E Dennis Andrews / Myron McWilliams
0	Duke	42 T Dave Graham / Bill Kanto
14	N. Carolina St.	21 G Bob Rowley / Duane Bickers
14	VMI	7 C Andy Moran / Bill Lang
0	Virginia Tech	20 G Emory Thomas / Turnley Todd
15	Wake Forest	21 T Ron Gassert / Terry Duffy
28	South Carolina	20 E Joe Kehoe / Park Plank
3	Navy	13 QB Gary Cuozzo / Stanford Fischer
28	Maryland	16 HB Ted Rzempoluch / Bobby Freeman
0	North Carolina	24 HB Carl Kuhn / Tony Ulehla
		FB Doug Thomson / Willis Williams

RUSHING: Thomson 70/294y, Ulehla 54/200y, Freeman 62/187y
PASSING: Cuozzo 42-93/371y, 5TD, 45.2%,
Fischer 27-69/361y, TD, 39.1%
RECEIVING: Ulehla 9/85y, Rzempoluch 7/64y, 3 with 6
SCORING: Rowley (G-K) 21pts, Hepler & Thomson 18pts

1962 5-5

19	William & Mary	7 E Myron McWilliams / Dennis Andrews
15	Virginia Tech	20 T Dave Graham
28	VMI	6 G Bob Rowley / Leonard Hrica
14	Wake Forest	12 C Andy Moran / Bill Lang
34	Davidson	7 G Duane Bickers / Turnley Todd
6	South Carolina	40 T Terry Duffy / Dick Myers
7	North Carolina	11 E Jim Hoffrath
12	N. Carolina St.	24 QB Gary Cuozzo / Carl Kuhn
18	Maryland	40 HB Bobby Freeman
41	Rutgers	0 HB Terry Sieg / John Greene
		FB Ted Rzempoluch

RUSHING: Rzempoluch 77/347y, Kuhn 57/255y,
Freeman 56/212y
PASSING: Cuozzo 98-181/1136y, 5TD, 54.1%
RECEIVING: Sieg 27/281y, Freeman 21/292y, Hoffrath 16/266y
SCORING: Cuozzo 36pts, Freeman 30pts, 2 with 24pts

1963 2-7-1

7	North Carolina	11 E Myron McWilliams
8	Duke	30 T Bob Kowalkowski / Dick Myers
0	Virginia Tech	10 G Duane Bickers
6	VMI	0 C Turnley Todd / Jim Donley
10	South Carolina	10 G Leonard Hrica / Bruce Perry
0	Clemson	35 T Bill Mason / Patrick McFalls
3	N. Carolina St.	15 E Stuart Christhilf / Larry Molinari
9	William & Mary	7 QB Tom Hodges / Bob Dunphey
21	Boston College	30 HB John Hepler / Henry Massie
6	Maryland	21 HB John Pincavage / Terry Sieg
		FB Bob Prusmack / Edwin Barker

RUSHING: Pincavage 61/256y, Prusmack 72/220y,
Dunphey 86/228y
PASSING: Hodges 39-90/540y, 2TD, 43.3%
RECEIVING: Pincavage 15/136y, Molinari 11/147y, Hepler 7/56y
SCORING: Dunphey 28pts, Pincavage 12pts,
Tom Shuman (K) 10pts

1964 5-5

21	Wake Forest	31 E Ken Poates / Larry Molinari (DL)
0	Duke	30 T Patrick McFalls
20	Virginia Tech	17 G Charles Hart / Don Parker (DL)
20	VMI	19 C James Sledd / Jim Donley (LB)
35	Army	14 G Ted Torok / Jim Winget (MG)
15	N. Carolina St.	24 T Bob Kowalkowski / Bruce Robbins (DL)
7	Clemson	29 E Ed Carrington / Patrick Vaughan (DL)
14	William & Mary	13 QB Bob Davis / Tom Hodges
31	North Carolina	27 HB Carroll Jarvis / George Stetter (DB)
0	Maryland	10 HB John Pincavage / Roger Davis
		FB Bob Dunphey /John Depenbrock (DB)

RUSHING: B. Davis 84/436y, Jarvis 84/330y, Dunphey 55/233y
PASSING: B. Davis 81-156/1054y, 2TD, 51.9%
RECEIVING: Pincavage 30/331y, R. Davis 15/230y,
Poates 15/200y
SCORING: B. Davis 62pts, Jarvis 24pts, Tom Shuman (K) 21pts

1965 5-5

7	Duke	21 E Ken Poates
14	Clemson	20 T Paul Lockwood
21	North Carolina	17 G Bob Prusmack
14	VMI	10 C James Sledd
41	West Virginia	0 G Charles Hart
14	Virginia Tech	22 T Jim Copeland
0	N. Carolina St.	13 E Ed Carrington
7	South Carolina	17 QB Tom Hodges / Bob Davis (HB)
19	Georgia Tech	42 HB Roger Davis
33	Maryland	27 HB John Pincavage
		FB Carroll Jarvis (HB) / Bob Dunphey
		DL Don Parker / Al Groh
		DL Randall Harris
		DL Jim Winget / Anthony Popeck
		DL Bob Kowalkowski / John Naponick
		DL Larry Molinari
		LB Leonard Hrica / Mark Probst
		LB Jim Donley
		DB Dennis Borchers
		DB Paul Klingensmith / Tom Krebs
		DB Ralph Corley / Jim Morgan
		DB George Stetter

RUSHING: Jarvis 106/385y, B. Davis 78/289y, Dunphey 49/144y
PASSSING: Hodges 108-198/1299y, 4TD, 54.5%,
B. Davis 47-87/580y, 5TD, 54.0%
RECEIVING: Pincavage 45/584y, Carrington 26/352y,
Poates 22/355y, B. Davis 22/249y
SCORING: B. Davis & Carrington 36pts, Hodges 26pts

SCORES, LINEUPS, AND STATISTICS

1966 4-6

24 Wake Forest	10 WR Ken Poates
35 Clemson	40 WR Jeff Anderson
8 Duke	27 T Jim Copeland
6 Tulane	20 G Bob Buchanan / Greg Shelly
38 VMI	27 C Fred Jones / Dave McWilliams
7 Virginia Tech	24 G Mike Jarvis
21 N. Carolina St.	42 T Paul Lockwood
53 Georgia Tech	14 E Ed Carrington / Bill Lockwood
41 Maryland	17 QB Bob Davis
21 North Carolina	14 HB Frank Quayle
	FB Carroll Jarvis
	DL Don Parker / Rick Brand
	DL Randall Harris
	DL John Naponick
	DL Tony Popeck / Paul Yewisiak
	DL Joe Hoppe / Van Krebs
	LB Chuck Hammer
	LB Mal MacGregor / Steve Bryan
	DB Dennis Borchers
	DB Paul Klingensmith / Steve Schilke
	DB Jim Morgan
	DB George Stetter

RUSHING: Quayle 162/727y, Jarvis 97/421y, Davis 87/227y
PASSING: Davis 107-222/1461y, 10TD, 48.2%
RECEIVING: Carrington 32/411y, Quayle 28/420y, Anderson 18/269y
SCORING: Quayle 66pts, Davis 40pts, Braxton Hill (K) 36pts

1967 5-5

7 Army	26 WR Joe Hoppe / Jeff Calamos
35 Buffalo	12 WR Stan Kemp
14 Wake Forest	12 T Paul Rogers
6 Duke	13 G Bob Buchanan
23 South Carolina	24 C Dave McWilliams
13 VMI	18 G Mike Jarvis
8 N. Carolina St.	30 T Greg Shelly
40 North Carolina	17 TE Scott Montgomery / Danny Fassio
14 Tulane	10 QB Gene Arnette
12 Maryland	7 TB Frank Quayle
	FB Jeff Anderson / Dave Wyncoop
	DL Tom Patton / Laurie Croft
	DL Rick Brand
	DL John Naponick / Steve Bryan
	DL Rick Constantine / Jim Willits
	DL Al Sinesky / Van Krebs
	LB Bob Paczkowski / Boyd Page
	LB Mal MacGregor / Jim Ralston
	DB Dennis Borchers / Steve Schilke
	DB Peter Schmidt / Pete Gray
	DB Paul Reeve / Paul Klingensmith
	DB Bob Rannigan / Bill Lockwood

RUSHING: Anderson 183/774y, Quayle 177/755y, Arnette 112/289y
PASSING: Arnette 73-147/984y, 3 TD, 49.7%
RECEIVING: Quayle 25/299y, Hoppe 21/318y, Kemp 12/134y
SCORING: Quayle 60pts, Arnette 30pts, Braxton Hill (K) 20pts

1968 7-3

6 Purdue	44 WR Rick Moschel / Jim Carrington
47 VMI	0 WR Jeff Calamos / Chuck Mooser
41 Davidson	14 T Paul Rogers / Rick Kotulak
50 Duke	20 G Chuck Hammer
0 N. Carolina St.	19 C Dan Ryczek
24 Navy	0 G Jim Shannon / Tommy Thomas
28 South Carolina	49 T Greg Shelly
41 North Carolina	6 TE Joe Hoppe / Bob Bischoff
63 Tulane	47 QB Gene Arnette / Danny Fassio
28 Maryland	23 TB Frank Quayle / Dave Wyncoop
	FB Jeff Anderson
	DL Tommy Patton / Al Ferrara
	DL Rick Brand
	DL Rick Constantine / Jim Willits
	DL Al Sinesky / Charlie Blandford
	LB Boyd Page / Randy Lestyk
	LB Paul Reid
	LB Bob Paczkoski / Ed Kihm
	DB Andy Minton
	DB Peter Schmidt
	DB Paul Reeve / Bill Lockwood
	DB Bob Rannigan

RUSHING: Quayle 175/1213y, Anderson 170/734y, Arnette 88/292y
PASSING: Arnette 106-206/1463y, 14TD, 51.5%
RECEIVING: Quayle 30/426y, Hoppe 16/277y, Anderson 15/213y, Mooser 15/188y
SCORING: Quayle 84pts, Anderson 62pts, Mooser 38pts

1969 3-7

14 Clemson	21 WR Bob Bischoff / Jim Carrington
10 Duke	0 WR Chuck Mooser
28 William & Mary	15 T Rick Kotulak
28 VMI	10 G Jim Shannon
0 N. Carolina St.	31 C Dan Ryczek / John Blackburn
0 Navy	10 G Tommy Thomas
0 North Carolina	12 T Gary Saft
21 Wake Forest	23 TE Rick Moschel / Joe Smith
0 Tulane	31 QB Danny Fassio / Mike Cubbage
14 Maryland	17 TB Jim Lacey / Dave Wyncoop
	FB Gary Helman
	DL Tom Patton
	DL Randy Lestyk / Mark Christhilf
	DL Andy Selfridge / Jim Willits
	DL Al Sinesky
	LB Page Boyd / Rick McFarland
	LB Paul Reid / Chuck Blandford
	LB Ed Kihm / Dave Turner
	DB Andy Minton
	DB Peter Schmidt / Russ Bauda
	DB Bill Lockwood / Robbie Gustafson
	DB Bob Rannigan / Bob McGrail

RUSHING: Helman 229/851y, Lacey 128/613y, Fassio 111/223y
PASSING: Fassio 68-150/828y, 2TD, 45.3%
RECEIVING: Bischoff 35/498y, Mooser 15/144y, Lacey 12/127y
SCORING: Helman (FB-K) 43pts, Carrington 22pts, Lacey 18pts

1970 5-6

7 Virginia Tech	0 WR Dave Sullivan / Jim Carrington
17 Clemson	27 WR Bob Bischoff / Bill Davis
7 Duke	17 T Abby Sallenger
7 Wake Forest	27 G Jim Shannon
49 VMI	10 C Dan Ryczek / Stormy Costas
21 Army	20 G Tom Kennedy / Bill Farrell
33 William & Mary	6 T Gary Saft / Bob Burkley
15 North Carolina	30 TE Joe Smith
16 N. Carolina St.	21 QB Bill Troup / Larry Albert
54 Colgate	12 TB Jim Lacey / Dave Bratt
14 Maryland	17 FB Gary Helman / Greg Dickerhoof
	DL Billy Williams
	DL Randy Lestyk / Bob bressan
	DL Andy Selfridge
	DL Ed Kihm / Dennis Scott
	LB Charlie Blandford / Kevin Michaels
	LB Paul Reid / Chuck Belic
	LB Dave Turner / Rick McFarland
	DB Andy Minton
	DB Russ Bauda / Chris Brown
	DB Robbie Gustafson
	DB Bob McGrail / Billy League

RUSHING: Helman 172/743y, Lacey 131/609y, Bratt 53/188y
PASSING: Troup 93-184/1289y, 10TD,50.5%
RECEIVING: Sullivan 37/523y, Bischoff 35/499y, Smith 15/291y
SCORING: Helman (FB-K) 54pts, Lacey & Carrington 36pts

1971 3-8

6 Navy	10 WR Bill Davis / Dave Sullivan
0 Michigan	56 T Bill Farrell
0 Duke	28 G Steve Shawley
27 Vanderbilt	23 C Paul Ryczek
14 South Carolina	34 G Tom Kennedy / Greg Godfrey
15 Clemson	32 T Dale Dickerson
9 Army	14 E Joe Smith / Mike McGugan
14 N. Carolina St.	10 QB Harrison Davis / Larry Albert
0 Virginia Tech	6 TB Kent Merritt
20 North Carolina	32 SB Chuck Belic
29 Maryland	27 FB Gary Helman / Greg Dickerhoof
	DL Billy Williams
	DL Bob Bressan / Leroy Still
	DL Andy Selfridge
	DL Stanley Land / Dennis Scott
	LB Kevin Michaels / Craig Critchley
	LB Chuck Belic / Harry Gehr
	LB Rick McFarland
	DB Gerard Mullins
	DB Bob McGrail
	DB Bill Kettunen / Chris Brown
	DB Steve Sroba / Billy League

RUSHING: Merritt 188/839y,Helman 67/238y,Dickerhoof 37/172y
PASSING: H. Davis 63-176/806y, 3TD, 35.8%, Albert 57-112/668y, 4TD, 50.9%
RECEIVING: B. Davis 49/617y, Sullivan 32/393y, McGugan 12/158y
SCORING: Billy Maxwell (K) 36pts, Merritt 24pts, Sullivan 18pts

1972 4-7

24 South Carolina	16 WR Dave Sullivan
24 Virginia Tech	20 T Dale Dickerson
10 West Virginia	48 G Tom Glassic / Greg Godfrey
13 Duke	37 C Paul Ryczek
7 Vanderbilt	10 G Steve Shawley / Tom Kennedy
45 VMI	14 T Bill Farrell / Jon Sims
21 Clemson	37 E Mike McGugan / Ken Shelton
23 Maryland	24 QB Har'n Davis/Geo. Allen/Scott Gardner
14 N. Carolina St.	35 TB Kent Merritt/John Rainey/Ray'd Keys
15 Wake Forest	12 SB Chuck Belic / Billy Lanahan
	FB Mike Lacica / Greg Dickerhoof
	DL Stanley Land
	DL Tom McGraw
	DL John Walker / Leroy Still
	DL Craig Critchley
	LB Dick Ambrose / Terry McGovern
	LB Kevin Michaels
	LB Danny Blakley
	DB Gerard Mullins / Eric Dahlgren
	DB Chris Turner / Carl Mams
	DB Steve Sroba / Chris Brown
	DB Mike Cornachione

RUSHING: Merritt 118/575y, Rainey 67/223y, Keys 42/170y
PASSING: Allen 55-115/650y, 5TD, 47.8%, Davis 48-131/624y, 6TD, 36.6%, Gardner 48-115/640y, 4TD, 41.7%
RECEIVING: Sullivan 51/662y, Belic 39/613y, McGugan 13/167y
SCORING: Billy Maxwell (K) 47pts, Sullivan 44pts, Belic 30pts

1973 4-7

16 VMI	0 WR Harrison Davis / Ken Shelton
23 N. Carolina St.	43 WR Mike Bennett
7 Missouri	31 T Dale Dickerson / Doug Parcells
7 Duke	3 G Tom Glassic
22 Vanderbilt	39 C Paul Ryczek
27 Clemson	32 G Steve Shawley / Dennis Kuczynski
13 Virginia Tech	27 T John Sims / Phil Silas
21 Wake Forest	10 TE Jim Colleran / Mike McGugan
44 North Carolina	40 QB Scott Gardner
0 Maryland	33 TB Billy Copeland / Kent Merritt
17 West Virginia	42 FB Mike Dowe
	DL Butch Powers / Stanley Land
	DL Ron Morley / Leroy Still
	DL Tom McGraw / John Walker
	DL Bob Meade / Craig Critchley
	LB Jim Grobe
	LB Dick Ambrose / Harry Gehr
	LB Billy Dennis / Dan Blakley
	DB Gerard Mullins
	DB Doug Jones / Eric Dahlgren
	DB Steve Sroba
	DB Mike Cornachione / Tony Zmudzin

RUSHING: Copeland 130/700y, Merritt 105/502y, Gardner 108/433y
PASSING: Gardner 99-234/1687y, 10TD, 42.3%
RECEIVING: Davis 44/773y, Colleran 19/336y, Bennett 17/289y
SCORING: Davis & Gardner 30pts, Copeland 24pts

1974 4-7

28 Navy	35 WR Ken Shelton
38 William & Mary	28 WR Tom Fadden
7 Duke	27 T Doug Parcells
24 Georgia Tech	28 G Tom Glassic
21 N. Carolina St.	22 C Rich Switalski
28 Virginia Tech	27 G Dennie Kuczynski
14 Wake Forest	0 T Paul Tamulonis / Hans Baumann
10 North Carolina	24 TE Jim Wicks / Jim Colleran
28 VMI	10 QB Scott Gardner
9 Clemson	28 TB Billy Copeland / Joe Sroba
0 Maryland	10 FB David Sloan / Mike Dowe
	DL Butch Powers
	DL John Walker
	DL Tom McGraw
	DL Bob Meade / Mike Ozdowski
	LB Jim Grobe
	LB Dick Ambrose
	LB Billy Dennis
	LB Tony Zmudzin
	DB Eric Dahlgren
	DB Doug Jones
	DB Jay Morris

RUSHING: Sroba 167/632y
PASSING: Gardner 110-195/1344y, 14TD, 56.4%
RECEIVING: Fadden 34/416y
SCORING: Shelton 54pts

1975 1-10

14 Navy	42 WR Tom Fadden
22 VMI	21 WR Joe Sroba
11 Duke	26 T Doug Parcells
28 North Carolina	31 G Tom Glassic
14 South Carolina	41 C Rich Switalski
17 Virginia Tech	24 G Dennis Kuczynski
21 Wake Forest	66 T Paul Tamulonis
14 Vanderbilt	17 TE Jim Colleran / Jim Wicks
10 East Carolina	61 QB Scott Gardner
0 Syracuse	37 TB Billy Copeland / Raymond Keys
24 Maryland	62 FB David Sloan / Mike Dowe
	DL Butch Powers / Lee Browning
	DL Mike Ozdowski
	DL Chip Ciardy
	DL Bob Meade
	DL John Choma / Dennis Hackworth
	DL Kevin Bowie / Wagner Ramsey
	LB Frank Morris / John Kenney
	LB Sam Pfabe
	DB Derrick Galsper / Ron Walchack
	DB Joe Roseborough
	DB Jay Morris / Tracy Moon

RUSHING: Sloan 176/848y, Copeland 116/602y
PASSING: Gardner 133-272/1547y, 5TD, 48.9%
RECEIVING: Fadden 48/620y, Wicks 24/285y, Sloan 23/179y
SCORING: Sloan 54pts, Copeland & Gardner 24pts

1976 2-9

17 Washington	38 WR Tom Fadden
0 William & Mary	14 WR Andre Grier / Tracy Moon
6 Duke	21 T Mike Wallace
14 Georgia Tech	35 G Ric Zimmerman
7 South Carolina	35 C Kenny Fulp / Jeff Morrow
10 Virginia Tech	14 G Dennis Kuczynski
18 Wake Forest	17 T Hans Baumann
7 VMI	13 TE Jim Wicks / Mike Newhall
21 Lehigh	20 QB Andy Hitt
6 North Carolina	31 TB Raymond Keys / Billy Copeland
0 Maryland	28 FB David Sloan / Skip Browning
	DL Butch Powers / Wagner Ramsey
	DL Grant Hudson / Mike Ozdowski
	DL Sam Pfabe (G) / Jim Linkenauger
	DL Lee Browning
	DL Vince Mattox / Louis Collins
	LB Steve Potter / Bryan Coleman
	LB Joe Turner / Russ Meyer
	DB Derrick Galsper
	DB Mike Brancati
	DB Jay Morris / Bill Bridges
	DB Tony Blount / Bob Bowden

RUSHING: Keys 120/505y, Copeland 81/365y, Sloan 95/312y
PASSING: Hitt 98-220/1222y, 7TD, 44.5%
RECEIVING: Wicks 29/297y, Fadden 17/188y, Sroba 12/169y
SCORING: Joe Jenkins (K) 28pts, Grier & Keys 18pts

1977 1-9-1

0 N. Carolina St.	14 WR Jim Theiling / Teddy Marchibroda
0 Texas	68 WR Greg Taylor / Tom Champlin
7 Duke	31 T John Choma
0 West Virginia	13 G Eddie Smith / Jack Banbury
0 Clemson	31 C Kenny Fulp
14 Virginia Tech	14 G Jeff Morrow
12 Wake Forest	10 T Ric Zimmerman / Hans Baumann
3 Syracuse	6 TE Mike Newhall / Tim Moon
6 VMI	30 QB Chip Mark / Bryan Shumock (DB)
14 North Carolina	35 RB Skip Browning / Billy Harris
0 Maryland	28 RB Tommy Vigorito / Paul Izlar
	DL Steve Potter
	DL Grant Hudson / Caesar Alvarez
	DL Mike Budd
	DL Lee Browning
	DL Kelvin Anderson / Joe Turner
	LB Bryan Coleman / Kenny Newsome
	LB Tony Blount
	DB Drew Schuett
	DB Derrick Glasper
	DB Jerome Morris / Joe Roseborough
	DB Bob Bowden

RUSHING: Harris 119/339y, Vigorito 95/326y, Izlar 74/231y
PASSING: Mark 65-124/720y, 3TD, 52.4%
RECEIVING: Theiling 16/170y, Vogorito 15/65y, Newhall 14/170y
SCORING: Russ Henderson (K) 19pts, Newhall 12pts, 4 with 6pts

1978 2-9

0 Wake Forest	14 WR Jim Theiling / Teddy Marchibroda
0 Navy	32 WR Tom Champlin / Louis Collins
21 Army	17 T Ric Zimmerman
0 VMI	17 G Al Alvarez
13 Duke	20 C Brian Musselman
14 Clemson	30 G Kurt Pierce
17 Virginia Tech	7 T Eddie Smith
17 West Virginia	20 TE Mike Newhall / Gary Gomolak
7 Maryland	17 QB Chip Mark / Mickey Spady
20 North Carolina	38 RB Greg Taylor / Dan Hottowe
21 N. Carolina St.	24 RB Tommy Vigorito
	DL Steve Potter / Kelvin Anderson
	DL Grant Hudson
	DL Stuart Anderson / Kevin Lewis
	DL Lee Browning / Caesar Alvarez
	DL Quentin Murray
	LB Bryan Holoman / Bryan Coleman
	LB Ken Newsome
	DB Mike Brancati / Bobby Call
	DB Derrick Glasper
	DB Bryan Shumock / Joe Roseborough
	DB Tony Blount

RUSHING: Vigorito 168/800y, Taylor 138/551y, Spady 94/177y
PASSING: Mark 37-71/458y, 2TD, 52.1%,
   Spady 26-60/268y, 0TD, 43.3%
RECEIVING: Theiling 16/239y, Vigorito 13/53y, Newhall 12/184y,
   Marchibroda 12/156y
SCORING: Dan Hottowe (K) 27pts, Vigorito 24pts, Taylor 18pts

1979 6-5

31 Richmond	0 WR Teddy Marchibroda / Louis Collins
27 N. Carolina St.	31 WR Tim Moon / Andre Grier
19 VMI	0 T Ron Kort
30 Duke	12 G Kurt Pierce
7 Clemson	17 C Brian Musselman
69 James Madison	9 G Dan McKillican
10 Navy	17 T Mike Sewak / Jeff Morrow
31 Georgia	0 TE Mike Newhall / Gary Gomolak
20 Virginia Tech	18 QB Todd Kirtley
7 North Carolina	13 RB Greg Taylor / Vincent Mattox
7 Maryland	17 RB Tommy Vigorito / Mark Sanford
	DL Steve Potter / Kelvin Anderson
	DL Dave Sullivan
	DL Grant Hudson
	DL Stuart Anderson
	DL Quentin Murray
	LB Bryan Holoman / Bryan Coleman
	LB Ken Newsome / Jim Hyson
	DB Mike Brancati
	DB Bobby Call / Sean McCall
	DB Bryan Shumock / Pat Chester
	DB Tony Blount

RUSHING: Vigorito 184/1044y, Taylor 166/933y, Sanford 22/99y
PASSING: Kirtley 88-178/1159y, 6TD, 49.4%
RECEIVING: Newhall 20/196y, Marchibroda 17/242y,
   Moon 13/158y
SCORING: Taylor 66pts, Wayne Morrison (K) 56pts,
   Vigorito 42pts

1980 4-7

6 Navy	3 WR Cole Egan / Billy Smith
13 N. Carolina St.	27 WR Henry Johnson / Bob Sweeney
20 Duke	17 T Ron Kort / Grant Scott
21 West Virginia	45 G Kurt Pierce / Joe Gulaskey
24 Clemson	27 C Brian Musselman
0 Virginia Tech	30 G Dan McKillican / Jim Harris
24 Wake Forest	21 T Dave Sullivan
16 Tennessee	13 TE Kevin Riccio / Erik Polfelt
17 Rutgers	19 QB Todd Kirtley
3 North Carolina	26 HB Tommy Vigorito / Quentin Walker
0 Maryland	31 FB Mark Sanford / Ken Word
	DL Keith Lee / Ponder Harrison
	DL Stuart Anderson
	DL Ron Booker / Jim Hyson
	DL Mike Budd
	DL Quentin Murray
	LB Mark La Neve / Bert Krupp
	LB Rickey Callinder / Ken Newsome
	DB Bryan Shumock / Darryl Smith
	DB Corwin Word / Sean McCall
	DB Pat Chester
	DB Jon Tenuta / Rich Riccardi

RUSHING: Vigorito 201/742y, Walker 78/343y, Hall 33/150y
PASSING: Kirtley 94-183/1156y, 3TD, 51.4%
RECEIVING: Vigorito 29/239y, Sanford 24/169y, Egan 23/447y
SCORING: Wayne Morrison (K) 48pts, Vigorito 36pts,
   2 with 12pts

1981 1-10

18 West Virginia	32 WR Henry Johnson / Billy Smith
0 Rutgers	3 WR Greg Taylor / Nick Merrick
24 Duke	29 T Steve Sermonet
24 N. Carolina St.	30 G Joe Gulaskey / Brian Tomlin
0 Clemson	27 C Grant Scott
3 South Carolina	21 G Randy Brookshire / Jerry Glover
21 Wake Forest	24 T Dave Sullivan
12 VMI	10 TE Kevin Riccio / Billy Griggs
14 North Carolina	17 QB Gordie Whitehead
7 Maryland	48 TB Derek Jenkins / Darren Goode
3 Virginia Tech	20 FB Eric Fears / Mark Sanford
	DL Ed Reynolds / Bill Gormley
	DL Mike Budd / Ron Mattes
	DL Reggie Woods
	DL Stuart Anderson / Erik Polfelt
	LB Keith Lee
	LB Rickey Callinder / John Lunderman
	LB Bryan Holoman / Bert Krupp
	DB Howard Lewis / William Frazier
	DB Corwin Word / Darryl Reaves
	DB Bob Sweeney / Carlos Lopez
	DB Bart Farinholt

RUSHING: Jenkins 118/412y, Goode 78/276y, Fears 51/244y
PASSING: Whitehead 95-178/1116y, 9TD, 53.4%
RECEIVING: Riccio 32/351y, Johnson 27/427y, Taylor 25/418y
SCORING: Wayne Morrison (K) 33pts, Riccio 30pts, Taylor 18pts

1982 2-9

16 Navy	30 WR Henry Johnson / Billy Smith
17 James Madison	21 WR Nick Merrick / Quentin Walker
17 Duke	51 T Jim Dombrowski
13 N. Carolina St.	16 G Jim Huddleston
0 Clemson	48 C Grant Scott / Jerry Glover
24 Wake Forest	27 G Bob Olderman
37 VMI	6 T Joe Gulaskey / Dave Sullivan
32 Georgia Tech	38 TE Kevin Riccio / Billy Griggs
14 North Carolina	27 QB Wayne Schuchts / Mike Eck
14 Maryland	45 TB Antonio Rice / Barry Word
14 Virginia Tech	21 FB Derek Jenkins / Eric Fears
	DL Steve Morse / Ed Reynolds
	DL Ron Mattes
	DL Jim Hyson / Scott Matheson
	DL Chris McMahon
	LB Rickey Callinder (FB)
	LB Charles McDaniel
	LB Russ Swan
	DB Darryl Smith / Darryl Reaves
	DB Howard Lewis
	DB Pat Chester
	DB Rich Riccardi / Bart Farinholt

RUSHING: Rice 196/764y, Walker 82/449y, B. Word 43/226y
PASSING: Schuchts 72-176/1243y, 6TD, 40.9%
RECEIVING: Johnson 21/377y, Riccio 20/283y, Merrick 19/418y
SCORING: Wayne Morrison (K) 56pts, Rice 36pts, Walker 20pts

1983 6-5

38 Duke	30 WR Billy Smith / Nick Merrick
27 Navy	16 WR Quentin Walker
21 James Madison	14 T Jim Dombrowski
26 N. Carolina St.	14 G Bob Olderman
3 Maryland	23 C Harold Garren
21 Clemson	42 G Jim Huddleston / Steve Karriker
38 VMI	10 T Randy Brookshire
34 Wake Forest	38 TE Billy Griggs / Bryan Hitchcock
27 Georgia Tech	31 QB Wayne Schuchts / Don Majkowski
17 North Carolina	14 RB Howard Petty / Antonio Rice
0 Virginia Tech	48 FB Derek Jenkins
	DL Mark Wiley / Scott Hillman
	DL Ron Mattes
	DL David Bond / Edgar Davis
	DL Tom Kilgannon / Scott Matheson
	DL Rickey Callinder / John Muntz (LB)
	LB Russ Swan / Mark Balezentis
	LB Charles McDaniel / Scott Lageman
	DB Howard Lewis / William Frazier
	DB Ray Daly
	DB Bart Farinholt / Bob Sweeney
	DB Lester Lyles

RUSHING: Petty 169/835y, Jenkins 97/573y, Rice 75/306y
PASSING: Schuchts 129-261/1881y, 11TD, 49.4%
RECEIVING: Smith 42/777y, Griggs 23/300y, Petty 23/116y
SCORING: Kenny Stadlin (K) 64pts, Petty 42pts, Jenkins 30pts

1984 8-2-3

0 Clemson	55 WR Nick Merrick
35 VMI	7 WR John Ford / Jon Muha
21 Navy	9 T Jim Dombrowski
26 Virginia Tech	23 G Bob Olderman
38 Duke	10 C Harold Garren
20 Georgia Tech	20 G Mike Battle
28 Wake Forest	9 T Paul Sierocinski / Scott Chapin
27 West Virginia	7 TE Bryan Hitchcock / Geno Zimmerlink
45 N. Carolina St.	0 QB Don Majkowski
24 North Carolina	24 TB Howard Petty / Barry Word
34 Maryland	45 FB Steve Morse / Antonio Rice
27 Purdue■	24 DL Sean Scott / Mark Wiley
	DL Ron Mattes
	DL David Bond
	DL Tom Kilgannon / Scott Matheson
	DL Scott Hillman / Chris McMahon
	LB Charles McDaniel / John Muntz
	LB Russ Swan / Scott Lageman
	DB William Frazier
	DB Ray Daly
	DB Bob Sweeney / Kevin Gould
	DB Lester Lyles

RUSHING: Petty 170/811y, Word 105/603y, Morse 106/529y
PASSING: Majkowski 83-168/1235y, 8TD, 49.4%
RECEIVING: Zimmerlink 22/350y, Muha 22/283y, Ford 19/545y
SCORING: Kenny Stadlin (K) 64pts, Petty 48pts, Ford 42pts

1985 6-5

40 VMI	15 WR Geno Zimmerlink
24 Georgia Tech	13 WR Jon Muha / Quanah Bullock
13 Navy	17 T Jim Dombrowski
37 Duke	14 G Mike Battle
24 Clemson	27 C Harold Garren
10 Virginia Tech	28 G Jim Huddleston
20 Wake Forest	18 T Paul Sierocinski
27 West Virginia	7 TE Joel Dempsey
22 N. Carolina St.	23 QB Don Majkowski
24 North Carolina	22 TB Barry Word / Howard Petty
21 Maryland	33 FB Kevin Morgan / Antonio Rice
	DL Sean Scott
	DL Billy Keys
	DL Scott Matheson
	DL Scott Urch / Rayotis Perkins
	DL Scott Hillman / Elton Toliver
	LB Charles McDaniel
	LB Russ Swan / Scott Lageman
	DB Chris Warren / Luis Cardenas
	DB Ryan Jackson / Curtis Turner
	DB Kevin Gould
	DB Kevin Ferguson / Eric Clay

RUSHING: Word 207/1224y, Petty 145/525y, Morgan 101/491y
PASSING: Majkowski 95-199/1233y, 7TD, 47.7%
RECEIVING: Muha 24/299y, Zimmerlink 23/408y, Dempsey 11/162y, Word 11/76y
SCORING: Kenny Stadlin (K) 76pts, Majkowski, Word & Petty 36pts

1986 3-8

30 South Carolina	20 WR John Ford / Tim Finkielston
10 Navy	20 WR Keith Mattioli
14 Georgia Tech	28 T Scott Urch
13 Duke	20 G Roy Brown / Chris Minear (T)
30 Wake Forest	28 C Tim Morris
17 Clemson	31 G John Fetsko
10 Virginia Tech	42 T Paul Sierocinsk
37 William & Mary	41 TE Joel Dempsey / Darryl Hammond
20 N. Carolina St.	16 QB Don Majkowski / Scott Secules
7 North Carolina	27 TB Antonio Rice / Chris Warren
10 Maryland	42 FB Durwin Greggs / Kevin Morgan
	DL David Griggs / Don Bryant (DB)
	DL Rayotis Perkins / Craig Murden
	DL Judd Rupp / Tim O'Connor
	DL Billy Keys / Roy Brown
	DL Sean Scott / Preston Hicks
	LB Ray Savage/Delano Tyler/Jim Sanford
	LB Phil Thomas / Jeff Lageman
	DB Kevin Gould
	DB Kevin Cook
	DB Eric Clay / Mike Pettine
	DB Dennis Fields / Ryan Jackson

RUSHING: Greggs 83/404y, Warren 80/380y, Morgan 90/377y, Rice 92/355y
PASSING: Majkowski 104-199/1375y, 7TD, 52.3%, Secules 75-146/956y, 4 TD, 51.4%
RECEIVING: Mattioli 44/717y, Ford 32/555y, Rice 20/146y, Morgan 20/122y
SCORING: Jeff Gaffney (K) 53pts, Ford 30pts, Mattioli & Morgan 18pts

1987 8-4

22 Georgia	30 WR John Ford / Derek Dooley
19 Maryland	21 WR Keith Mattioli / Tim Finkelston
14 Virginia Tech	13 T Chris Minear / Paul Collins
42 Duke	17 G Roy Brown
30 VMI	0 C Tim Morris / Trevor Ryals
21 Clemson	38 G John Fetsko
10 South Carolina	58 T Timothy O'Connor / Paul Siercinski
35 Wake Forest	21 TE Joel Dempsey / Bruce McGonnigal
23 Georgia Tech	14 QB Scott Secules
20 North Carolina	17 TB Marcus Wilson / Kevin Morgan
34 N. Carolina St.	31 FB Durwin Greggs
22 BYU■	16 DL Sean Scott / Preston Hicks
	DL Eric Hairston / Chris Stearns
	DL Ron Carey / Davian Clifton
	DL Elton Toliver / Joe Hall
	DL Ray Savage / Jim Sanford
	LB Jeff Lageman / Matt Woods
	LB Phil Thomas / David Griggs
	DB Keith McMeans
	DB Tony Covington / Ryan Jackson
	DB Kevin Cook / Mike Pettine
	DB Darryl Hammond / Eric Clay

RUSHING: Wilson 172/692y, Morgan 107/489y, Greggs 111/436y
PASSING: Secules 174-296/2311y, 12TD, 58.8%
RECEIVING: Ford 48/855y, Finkelston 31/430y, Mattioli 29/428y
SCORING: Marl Inderlied (K) 70pts, Ford & Wilson 42pts

1988 7-4

31 William & Mary	23 WR John Ford / Derek Dooley
14 Penn State	42 WR Tim Finkelston / Herman Moore
17 Georgia Tech	16 T Paul Collins
34 Duke	38 G Roy Brown
7 Clemson	10 C Tim Morris / Leonard Pritchard
28 Louisville	30 G Trevor Ryals
34 Wake Forest	14 T Timothy O'Connor / Ray Roberts
16 Virginia Tech	10 TE Joel Dempsey / Bruce McGonnigal
19 N. Carolina St.	14 QB Shawn Moore
27 North Carolina	24 TB Marcus Wilson / Nikki Fisher
24 Maryland	23 FB Durwin Greggs / Kevin Morgan
	DL Don Reynolds / Preston Hicks
	DL Chris Stearns / Billy Keys
	DL Ron Carey / Matt Quigley
	DL Joe Hall / Elton Toliver
	DL Ray Savage / Jim Sanford
	LB Jeff Lageman / Phil Thomas
	LB David Griggs / Matt Woods
	DB Jason Wallace
	DB Tony Covington
	DB Keith McMeans / Kevin Cook
	DB Tyron Lewis

RUSHING: Wilson 89/429y, S. Moore 159/368y, Fisher 80/329y
PASSING: S. Moore 141-282/2158y, 15TD, 50.0%
RECEIVING: Ford 29/444y, McGonnigal 26/471y, H. Moore 24/466y
SCORING: Mark Inderlied (K) 69pts, S. Moore 60pts, H. Moore & Finkelston 24pts

1989 10-3

13 Notre Dame	36 WR Herman Moore / Derek Dooley
14 Penn State	6 WR Tim Finkelston / Brian Satola
17 Georgia Tech	10 T Ray Roberts
49 Duke	28 G Roy Brown / Jeff Tomlin
24 William & Mary	12 C Tim Morris
20 Clemson	34 G Trevor Ryals / Tim Samec
50 North Carolina	17 T Tim O'Connor / Paul Collins
47 Wake Forest	28 TE Bruce McGonnigal
16 Louisville	15 QB Shawn Moore
20 N. Carolina St.	9 TB Marcus Wilson / Terry Kirby
32 Virginia Tech	25 FB Durwin Greggs / Gary Steele
48 Maryland	21 DL Chris Slade / Don Reynolds
21 Illinois■	31 DL Billy Keys / Chris Stearns
	DL Ron Carey
	DL Joe Hall
	DL Ray Savage / James Pearson
	LB Elton Tolliver / Matt Woods
	LB Phil Thomas / Mike Williams
	DB Jason Wallace / Kevin Cook
	DB Tony Covington
	DB Tyrone Lewis / David Brown
	DB Keith McMeans

RUSHING: Wilson 223/1098y, S. Moore 139/505y, Kirby 63/311y
PASSING: S. Moore 125-221/2078y, 18TD, 56.6%
RECEIVING: McGonnigal 42/634y, H. Moore 36/848y, Finkelston 20/442y, Wilson 20/161y
SCORING: Jake McInerney (K) 88pts, H. Moore 60pts, S. Moore 54pts

1990 8-4

59 Kansas	10 WR Herman Moore
20 Clemson	7 WR Derek Dooley / Terrence Tomlin
56 Navy	14 T Ray Roberts
59 Duke	0 G Chris Stearns / Mark Dixon
63 William & Mary	35 C Trevor Ryals
31 N. Carolina St.	0 G Jeff Tomlin / Chris Borsari
49 Wake Forest	14 T Paul Collins / Jim Reid
38 Georgia Tech	41 TE Bruce McGonnigal / Aaron Mundy
24 North Carolina	10 QB Shawn Moore / Matt Blundin
30 Maryland	35 TB Terry Kirby / Nikki Fisher
13 Virginia Tech	38 FB David Sweeney / Gary Steele
22 Tennessee■	23 DL Chris Slade / Rickie Peete
	DL Don Reynolds / Ken Miles
	DL Ron Carey / Matt Quigley
	DL Joe Hall / Marcus Washington
	DL Benson Goodwyn / Gene Tolliver
	LB P.J. Killian / Eugene Rodgers
	LB James Pearson / Yusef Jackson
	DB Jason Wallace
	DB Tony Covington / Greg Jeffries
	DB Keith McMeans / Buddy Omohundro
	DB Tyrone Lewis

RUSHING: Kirby 165/1020y, Fisher 121/848y, S. Moore 94/306y
PASSING: S. Moore 144-241/2262y, 21 TD, 59.8%
RECEIVING: H. Moore 54/1190y, Kirby 33/324y, Dooley 27/422y
SCORING: Jake McInerney (K) 94pts, H. Moore 82pts, Kirby 66pts

1991 8-3-1

6 Maryland	17 WR Tyrone Davis / Terrence Tomlin
17 Navy	10 WR Andrew Dausch / Larry Holmes
21 Georgia Tech	24 T Ray Roberts
34 Duke	3 G Mark Dixon / Jeff Tomlin
31 Kansas	19 C Tim Samec
20 Clemson	20 G Jim Reid (T) / Charles Keiningham
14 North Carolina	9 T David Ware
48 Wake Forest	4 TE Aaron Mundy
42 VMI	0 QB Matt Blundin / Bobby Goodman
42 N. Carolina St.	10 TB Terry Kirby / Nikki Fisher
38 Virginia Tech	0 FB Gary Steele / Charles Way
14 Oklahoma	48 DL Chris Slade
	DL Don Reynolds
	DL Matt Quigley / Mark Krichbaum
	DL Mike Frederick / Ryan Kuehl
	LB Gene Toliver / Randy Neal
	LB Eugene Rodgers / Curtis Hicks
	LB P.J. Killian / Yusef Jackson
	DB Greg Jeffries / Carl Smith
	DB Greg McClellan / Daymon Anderson
	DB Keith Lyle
	DB Tyrone Lewis

RUSHING: Kirby 164/887y, Fisher 131/658y, Steele 48/189y
PASSING: Blundin 135-224/1902y, 19TD, 60.3%
RECEIVING: Kirby 37/406y, Mundy 31/409y, Holmes 27/462y
SCORING: Michael Husted (K) 72pts, Kirby 54pts, Holmes 48pts

1992 7-4

28 Maryland	15 WR Tyrone Davis / Patrick Jeffers
53 Navy	0 WR Demetrius "Pete" Allen
55 Georgia Tech	24 T Jim Reid
55 Duke	28 G Mark Dixon
28 Clemson	17 C Tim Samec / Bryan Heath (G)
7 North Carolina	29 G Charles Keiningham
33 William & Mary	27 T David Ware / Chris Harrison
3 Florida State	4 TE Aaron Mundy / Bobby Neely
7 N. Carolina St.	13 QB Bobby Goodman / Mike Groh
41 Virginia Tech	31 TB Terry Kirby / Jerrod Washington
	38 FB Gary Steele / Charles Way
	DL Chris Slade
	DL Ryan Kuehl / Kenneth Miles
	DL Mark Krichbaum
	DL Mike Frederick / Matt Mikeska
	LB Gene Toliver / Tom Burns
	LB Randy Neal / Curtis Hicks
	LB P.J. Killian / Skeet Jones
	DB Greg Jeffries / Joe Crocker
	DB Greg McClellan / Daymon Anderson
	DB Keith Lyle / Carl Smith
	DB Daymon Anderson / Percy Ellsworth

RUSHING: Kirby 175/1130y
PASSING: Goodman 130-232/1707y, 21TD, 56.0%
RECEIVING: Kirby 28/241y
SCORING: Michael Husted (K) 74pts

1993 7-5

43 Maryland	29 WR Tyrone Davis / Patrick Jeffers
38 Navy	0 WR Pete Allen / Larry Holmes
35 Georgia Tech	14 T Jim Reid / Greg Powell
35 Duke	0 G Mark Dixon
41 Ohio University	7 C Bryan Heath
14 Florida State	40 G Peter Collins
17 North Carolina	10 T John Slocum / Jason Augustino
29 N. Carolina St.	34 TE Bobby Neely
21 Wake Forest	9 QB Bobby Goodman / Symmion Willis
14 Clemson	23 TB Jerrod Washington / Kevin Brooks
17 Virginia Tech	20 FB Charles Way
13 Boston Coll.■	31 DL Matt Mikeska / Jon Harris
	DL Ryan Kuehl / Duane Ashman
	DL Mark Krichbaum
	DL Mike Frederick
	LB Tom Burns / James Farrior
	LB Randy Neal
	LB Jamie Sharper / Skeet Jones
	DB Carl Smith / Joe Crocker
	DB Greg McClellan
	DB Keith Lyle / Joe Rowe
	DB Paul London / Percy Ellsworth

RUSHING: Kirby 175/1130y, Washington 124/643y, Brooks 33/242y
PASSING: Goodman 130-232/1707y, 21 TD, 56.0%
RECEIVING: Kirby 28/241y, Mundy 27/411y, Davis 23/548y
SCORING: Michael Husted (K) 74pts, Kirby 48pts, Davis 42pts

1994 9-3

17 Florida State	41 WR Tyrone Davis
47 Navy	10 WR Pete Allen / Patrick Jeffers
9 Clemson	6 T Jason Augustino
37 William & Mary	3 G Jeremy Raley / Tom Locklin
42 Wake Forest	6 C Bryan Heath / Dave Gathman
24 Georgia Tech	7 G John Slocum
34 North Carolina	10 T Chris Harrison
25 Duke	28 TE Bobby Neely
46 Maryland	21 QB Mike Groh / Symmion Willis
42 Virginia Tech	23 TB Kevin Brooks / Tiki Barber
27 N. Carolina St.	30 FB Charles Way
20 TCU■	10 DL Duane Ashman / Jon Harris
	DL Ryan Kuehl
	DL Todd White / Tony Agee
	DL Mike Frederick
	LB James Farrior
	LB Randy Neal
	LB Jamie Sharper / Skeet Jones
	DB Ronde Barber
	DB Joe Crocker
	DB Carl Smith
	DB Percy Ellsworth / Paul London

RUSHING: Brooks 173/741y, T. Barber 120/591y, Way 118/517y
PASSING: Groh 138-216/1711y, 13TD, 63.9%
RECEIVING: Davis 38/691y, Jeffers 33/560y, Neely 19/168y, T. Barber 19/126y
SCORING: Rafael Garcia (K) 85pts, Davis 62pts, Brooks 48pts

1995 9-4

17 Michigan	18 WR Germane Crowell / Patrick Jeffers
40 William & Mary	16 WR Pete Allen / Derick Byrd /Bryan Owen
29 N. Carolina St.	24 T Jason Augustino
41 Georgia Tech	14 G Jeremy Raley
22 Clemson	3 C Tom Locklin / Dave Gathman
35 Wake Forest	17 G John Slocum
17 North Carolina	22 T Chris Harrison
44 Duke	30 TE Bobby Neely / Walt Derey
16 Texas	17 QB Mike Groh
33 Florida State	28 TB Tiki Barber / Kevin Brooks
21 Maryland	18 FB Darrell Medley
29 Virginia Tech	36 DL Jon Harris / Eddie Robertson
34 Georgia■	27 DL Tony Agee / Tony Dingle
	DL Todd White
	DL Duane Ashman
	LB James Farrior
	LB Skeet Jones / Wali Rainer
	LB Jamie Sharper
	DB Ronde Barber / Adrian Burnim
	DB Joe Crocker / Sam McKiver
	DB Paul London/Anthony Poindexter (LB)
	DB Percy Ellsworth / Joe Williams

RUSHING: T. Barber 265/1397y, Brooks 128/561y, Medley 33/135y
PASSING: Groh 182-330/2510y, 15 TD, 55.2%
RECEIVING: Jeffers 34/517y, Allen 33/652y, Crowell 27/371y
SCORING: T. Barber 96pts, Rafael Garcia (K) 91pts, Crowell 30pts

1996 7-5

55 C. Michigan	21 WR Germane Crowell / Derick Byrd
21 Maryland	3 WR Bryan Owen / Terrence Wilkins
42 Wake Forest	7 T Doug Karczewski
37 Texas	13 G Jeremy Raley
7 Georgia Tech	13 C Tom Locklin
62 N. Carolina St.	14 G Trevor Britton
24 Florida State	31 T Julius Williams / Michael Kelly
27 Duke	3 TE Walt Derey / Casey Crawford
16 Clemson	24 QB Tim Sherman / Aaron Brooks
20 North Carolina	17 TB Tiki Barber / Thomas Jones
9 Virginia Tech	26 FB Darrell Medley / Anthony Southern
21 Miami■	31 DL Jon Harris / Patrick Kerney
	DL Tony Dingle / Maurice Anderson
	DL Todd White / Johnny Shivers
	DL Duane Ashman / Travis Griffith
	LB James Farrior
	LB Wali Rainer / Dillon Taylor
	LB Jamie Sharper / Shannon Taylor
	DB Ronde Barber / Antwan Harris
	DB Joe Rowe / Sam McKiver
	DB Anthony Poindexter / Wale Elegbe
	DB Stephen Phelan / Joe Williams

RUSHING: T. Barber 250/1360y, Sherman 69/228y, Jones 36/205y
PASSING: Sherman 102-203/1572y, 4 TD, 50.2%
RECEIVING: Crowell 33/687y, Owen 22/390y, T. Barber 22/258y
SCORING: Rafael Garcia (K) 96pts, T. Barber 90pts, 4 with 18pts

1997 7-4

17 Auburn	28 WR Germane Crowell
26 Richmond	7 WR Bryan Owen / Terrence Wilkins
20 North Carolina	48 T Doug Karczewski
21 Wake Forest	13 G Noel LaMontagne
21 Clemson	7 C Matthew Link / John St. Clair
13 Duke	10 G Fady Chamoun
21 Florida State	47 T Robert Hunt / Julius Williams
45 Maryland	0 TE Billy Baber / Casey Crawford
35 Georgia Tech	31 QB Aaron Brooks
24 N. Carolina St.	31 TB Thomas Jones / Antwoine Womack
34 Virginia Tech	20 FB Charles Kirby / Anthony Southern
	DL Travis Griffith
	DL Johnny Shivers
	DL Tony Dingle / Maurice Anderson
	DL Patrick Kerney / Shannon Taylor
	LB Wale Elegbe / Donny Green
	LB Wali Rainer
	LB Byron Thweatt
	DB Dwayne Stukes
	DB Joe Williams / Antwan Harris
	DB Anthony Poindexter
	DB Stephen Phelan / Adrian Burnim

RUSHING: Jones 201/692y, Brooks 85/255y, Womack 44/208y
PASSING: Brooks 164-270/2282y, 20TD, 60.7%
RECEIVING: Crowell 53/969y, Wilkins 37/506y, Southern 18/207y
SCORING: Crowell & John Allen Roberts (K) 56pts, Brooks & Jones 30pts

1998 9-3

19 Auburn	0 WR Kevin Coffey / Demetrius Dotson
31 Maryland	19 WR Terrence Wilkins / Ahmad Hawkins
20 Clemson	18 T Josh Lawson
24 Duke	0 G Noel LaMontagne / Evan Routzahn
52 San Jose State	14 C John St. Clair
38 Georgia Tech	41 G Fady Charmoun
23 N. Carolina St.	13 T Robert Hunt
38 Wake Forest	17 TE Casey Crawford / Billy Baber
14 Florida State	45 QB Aaron Brooks
30 North Carolina	13 TB Thomas Jones / Antwoine Womack
36 Virginia Tech	32 FB Anthony Southern
33 Georgia■	35 DL Travis Griffith / Darryl Sanders
	DL Antonio Dingle / Maurice Anderson
	DL Monsanto Pope / Kofi Bawuah
	DL Patrick Kerney
	LB Donny Green
	LB Wali Rainer / Yubrenal Isabelle
	LB Byron Thweatt / John Duckett
	DB Tim Spruill
	DB Antwan Harris / Dwayne Stukes
	DB Anthony Poindexter/Wale Elegbe (LB)
	DB Adrian Burnim

RUSHING: Jones 238/1303y, Womack 112/708y, Brooks 84/227y
PASSING: Brooks 156-290/2319y, 12TD, 53.8%
RECEIVING: Wilkins 45/811y, Jones 28/179y, Coffey 23/583y
SCORING: Jones 90pts, Todd Braverman (K) 74pts, Coffey 68pts

1999 7-5

20 North Carolina	17 WR Kevin Coffey / Billy McMullen
14 Clemson	33 WR Ahmad Hawkins / Demetrius Dotson
35 Wake Forest	7 T Josh Lawson
45 BYU	40 G Noel LaMontagne (T) /Jared Woodson
7 Virginia Tech	31 C John St. Clair
17 Duke	24 G Evan Routzahn
47 N. Carolina St.	26 T Brad Barnes
10 Florida State	35 TE Billy Baber / Casey Crawford
45 Georgia Tech	38 QB Dan Ellis
50 Buffalo	21 TB Thomas Jones / Arlen Harris
34 Maryland	30 FB Anthony Southern/Patrick Washington
21 Illinois■	63 DL Travis Griffith / Kofi Bawuah
	DL Maurice Anderson / Monsanto Pope
	DL Johnny Shivers / Colin McWeeny
	DL Ljubomir Stamenich /Merrill Robertson
	LB Shannon Taylor
	LB Yubrenal Isabelle
	LB Byron Thweatt / Angelo Crowell
	DB Dwayne Stukes / Jermaine Lauzon
	DB Antwan Harris / Tim Spruill
	DB Chris Williams / Shernard Newby
	DB Jerton Evans

RUSHING: Jones 334/1798y, Harris 30/112y
PASSING: Ellis 156-258/2050y, 20TD, 60.5%
RECEIVING: McMullen 28/483y, Coffet 28/437y, Jones 22/239y
SCORING: Jones 102pts, Todd Braverman (K) 57pts, Coffey 42pts

2000 6-6

35 BYU	38 WR Kevin Coffey / Demetrius Dotson
34 Richmond	6 WR Billy McMullen / James Johnson
26 Duke	10 T Jermese Jones
10 Clemson	31 G Josh Lawson / Jared Woodson
27 Wake Forest	10 C Dustin Keith
31 Maryland	23 G Evan Routzahn
3 Florida State	37 T Brad Barnes
17 North Carolina	6 TE Billy Baber / Chris Luzar
0 Georgia Tech	35 QB Dan Ellis
24 N. Carolina St.	17 TB Antwoine Womack / Tyree Foreman
21 Virginia Tech	42 FB Patrick Washington / Arlen Harris
14 Georgia■	37 DL Ljubomir Stanenich
	DL George Stanley / Colin McWeeny
	DL Monsanto Pope / Larry Simmons
	DL Darryl Sanders / Merrill Robertson
	LB Byron Thweatt / William Clark
	LB Yubrenal Isabelle
	LB Donny Green / Angelo Crowell
	DB Tim Spruill / Rashad Roberson
	DB Ahmad Hawkins
	DB Shernard Newby
	DB Jerton Evans / Devon Simmons

RUSHING: Womack 210/1028y, Foreman 72/397y, Harris 25/101y
PASSING: Ellis 116-210/1642y, 7TD, 55.2%
RECEIVING: McMullen 30/541y, Dotson 26/378y,Coffey 20/283y
SCORING: David Greene (K) 60pts, Womack 54pts, Foreman 48pts

2001 5-7

17 Wisconsin	26 WR Billy McMullen
17 Richmond	16 WR Michael McGrew / Tavon Mason
26 Clemson	24 T Kevin Bailey (C) / Mike Mullins
31 Duke	10 G Josh Lawson
21 Maryland	41 C Jared Woodson
24 North Carolina	30 G Evan Routzahn / Elton Brown
7 Florida State	43 T Jermese Jones
0 N. Carolina St.	24 TE Chris Luzar / Kase Luzar
30 Wake Forest	34 QB Matt Schaub / Bryson Spinner
39 Georgia Tech	38 TB A. Pearman / A. Womack/ Arlen Harris
17 Virginia Tech	31 FB Tyree Foreman / Jonathan Ward
20 Penn State	14 DL Ljubomir Stamenich / Larry Simmons
	DL Monsanto Pope / George Stanley
	DL Darryl Sanders / Chris Canty
	LB Raymond Mann
	LB Angelo Crowell
	LB Merrill Robertson / Earl Sims
	LB John Duckett / William Clark
	DB Art Thomas / Jamaine Winborne
	DB Almondo Curry / Rashad Roberson
	DB Shernard Newby / Chris Williams
	DB Jerton Evans

RUSHING: Pearman 88/371y, Harris 92/368y, Womack 63/263y
PASSING: Schaub 140-240/1524y, 10TD, 58.3%, Spinner 121-206/1334y, 14TD, 58.7%
RECEIVING: McMullen 83/1060y, C. Luzar 33/380y, McGrew 31/302y, Mason 30/341y
SCORING: McMullen 72pts, David Greene (K) 63pts, 2 with 24pts

2002 9-5

29 Colorado State	35 WR Billy McMullen
19 Florida State	40 WR Michael McGrew / Ottowa Anderson
34 South Carolina	21 T D'Brickashaw Feguson
48 Akron	29 G Brian Barthelmes / Ben Carber
38 Wake Forest	34 C Zac Yarbrough / Kevin Bailey
27 Duke	22 G Elton Brown / Mark Farrington
22 Clemson	17 T Mike Mullins
37 North Carolina	27 TE Heath Miller / Patrick Estes
15 Georgia Tech	23 QB Matt Schaub / Marques Hagans
14 Penn State	35 TB Wali Lundy/Al Pearm'n/Marq's Weeks
14 N. Carolina St.	9 FB Kase Luzar / Jason Snelling
48 Maryland	13 DL Brennan Schmidt
9 Virginia Tech	21 DL Andrew Hoffman
48 West Virginia■	22 DL Chris Canty / Kwakou Robinson
	LB Bryan White / Raymond Mann
	LB Angelo Crowell
	LB Merrill Robertson / Rich Bedesem
	LB Darryl Blackstock / Dennis Haley
	DB Almondo Curry / Art Thomas
	DB Jamaine Winborne
	DB Chris Williams / Willie Davis
	DB Jerton Evans / Shernard Newby

RUSHING: Lundy 196/826y, Pearman 83/343y, Weeks 41/210y
PASSING: Schaub 288-418/2976y, 38TD, 68.9%
RECEIVING: McMullen 69/894y, Lundy 58/435y, Miller 33/327y
SCORING: Lundy 60pts, Miller 54pts, Kurt Smith (K) 43pts

2003 8-5

27 Duke	0 WR Ryan Sawyer / Art Thomas
7 South Carolina	31 WR Ottowa Anderson
59 W. Michigan	16 T D'Brickashaw Ferguson
27 Wake Forest	24 G Ian-Yates Cunningham
38 North Carolina	13 C Zac Yarbrough / Kevin Bailey
27 Clemson	30 G Elton Brown / Brian Barthelmes (T)
14 Florida State	19 T Brad Butler
24 Troy State	0 TE Heath Miller / Patrick Estes
37 N. Carolina St.	51 QB Matt Schaub / Marques Hagans
17 Maryland	27 TB Wali Lundy / Alvin Pearman
29 Georgia Tech	21 FB Kase Luzar
35 Virginia Tech	21 DL Brennan Schmidt / Kwakou Robinson
23 Pittsburgh■	16 DL Andrew Hoffman / Melvin Massey
	DL Chris Canty
	LB Raymond Mann / Dennis Haley
	LB Kai Parham / Rich Bedesem
	LB Ahmad Brooks
	LB Darryl Blackstock
	DB Almondo Curry / Marcus Hamilton
	DB Tony Franklin
	DB Jermaine Hardy / Jay Dorsey
	DB Jamaine Winborne

RUSHING: Lundy 227/929y, Pearman 134/643y, Hagans 16/96y
PASSING: Schaub 281-403/2952y, 18TD, 69.7%
RECEIVING: Miller 70/835y, Pearman 63/518y, Sawyer 39/481y
SCORING: Connor Hughes (K) 109pts, Lundy 84pts, Pearman 48pts

2004 8-4

44 Temple	14 WR Deyon Williams / Imhotep Durham
56 North Carolina	24 WR Michael McGrew / Fontel Mines
51 Akron	0 T D'Brickashaw Ferguson
31 Syracuse	10 G Brian Barthelmes
30 Clemson	10 C Zac Yarbrough
3 Florida State	36 G Elton Brown
37 Duke	16 T Brad Butler
16 Maryland	0 TE Heath Miller / Patrick Estes
21 Miami	31 QB Marques Hagans
30 Georgia Tech	10 TB Alvin Pearman / Wali Lundy
10 Virginia Tech	24 FB Jason Snelling / Tom Santi
34 Fresno State■	37 DL Brennan Schmidt / Chris Johnson
	DL Andrew Hoffman
	DL Chris Canty / Kwakou Robinson
	LB Dennis Haley
	LB Kai Parham / Rich Bedesem
	LB Ahmad Brooks
	LB Darryl Blackstock
	DB Marcus Hamilton / Philip Brown
	DB Tony Franklin
	DB Jermaine Hardy
	DB Marquis Weeks

RUSHING: Pearman 195/1037y, Lundy 175/864y, Hagans 77/394y
PASSING: Hagans 164-261/2024y, 9TD, 62.8%
RECEIVING: Miller 41/541y, McGrew 30/355y, Pearman 29/402y
SCORING: Lundy 102pts, Connor Hughes (K) 93pts, Pearman 72pts

2005 7-5

31 W. Michigan	19 WR Fontel Mines
27 Syracuse	24 WR Deyon Williams
38 Duke	7 T D'Brickashaw Ferguson
33 Maryland	45 G Branden Albert
17 Boston College	28 C Brian Barthelmes / Jordy Lipsey
26 Florida State	21 G Marshal Ausberry
5 North Carolina	7 T Brad Butler / Eddie Pnigis
51 Temple	3 TE Jonathan Stupar
27 Georgia Tech	17 TE Tom Santi / John Phillips
14 Virginia Tech	52 QB Marques Hagans
17 Miami	25 TB Wali Lundy / Jason Snelling
34 Minnesota■	31 DL Chris Long
	DL Kwakou Robinson / Keenan Carter
	DL Brennan Schmidt
	LB Jermaine Dias / Mark Miller
	LB Kia Parham / Antonio Appleby
	LB Bryan White / Ahmad Brooks
	LB Clint Sintim
	DB Marcus Hamilton
	DB Chris Gorham / Mike Brown
	DB Tony Franklin
	DB Byron Glasby / Nate Lyles

RUSHING: Lundy 144/574y, Snelling 58/325y, Hagans 115/310y
PASSING: Hagans 213-343/2492y, 14TD, 62.1%
RECEIVING: Williams 58/767y, Mines 28/345y, Stupar 24/319y
SCORING: Connor Hughes (K) 99pts, Lundy 66pts, Williams 42pts

2006 5-7

13 Pittsburgh	38 WR Fontel Mines
13 Wyoming	12 WR Kevin Ogletree
10 W. Michigan	17 T Zak Stair / Eugene Monroe
7 Georgia Tech	24 G Branden Albert
37 Duke	0 C Jordy Lipsey
21 East Carolina	31 G Ian-Yates Cunningham
26 Maryland	28 T Will Barker
23 North Carolina	0 TE Jonathan Stupar
14 N. Carolina St.	7 TE Tom Santi / John Phillips
0 Florida State	33 QB Jameel Sewell / Christian Olsen
17 Miami	7 TB Jason Snelling / Cedric Peerman
0 Virginia Tech	17 DL Jeffrey Fitzgerald
	DL Allen Billyk / Keenan Carter
	DL Chris Long / Kevin Crawford
	LB Jermaine Dias
	LB Antonio Appleby
	LB Jon Copper / Rashawn Jackson
	LB Clint Sintim
	DB Marcus Hamilton / Mike Brown
	DB Chris Cook / Chris Gorham
	DB Byron Glasby / Tony Franklin
	DB Nate Lyles

RUSHING: Snelling 183/772y, Sewell 95/200y, Peerman 46/153y
PASSING: Sewell 143-247/1342y, 5TD, 57.9%
RECEIVING: Ogletree 52/582y, Snelling 29/282y, Santi 29/253y, Mines 27/256y
SCORING: Chris Gould (K) 51pts, Snelling 42pts, Ogletree & Sewell 24pts

2007 9-4

3 Wyoming	23 WR Staton Jobe / Andrew Pearman
24 Duke	13 WR Maurice Covington / Chris Gorham
22 North Carolina	20 T Eugene Monroe
28 Georgia Tech	23 G Branden Albert (G) / Gordie Sammis
44 Pittsburgh	14 C Jordy Lipsey
23 Middle Tenn.	21 G Ian-Yates Cunningham
17 Connecticut	16 T Will Barker
18 Maryland	17 TE Jonathan Stupar
24 N. Carolina St.	29 TE Tom Santi / John Phillips
17 Wake Forest	16 QB Jameel Sewell
48 Miami	0 TB Cedric Peerman / Mikell Simpson
21 Virginia Tech	33 DL Jeffrey Fitzgerald
28 Texas Tech■	31 DL Allen Billyk / Nate Collins
	DL Chris Long
	LB Jermaine Dias / Denzel Burrell
	LB Antonio Appleby
	LB Jon Copper
	LB Clint Sintim
	DB Vic Hall / Ras-I Dowling
	DB Chris Cook / Mike Parker
	DB Byron Glaspy
	DB Nate Lyles / Jamaal Jackson

RUSHING: Peerman 113/585y, Simpson 113/570y, Sewell 126/279y, Keith Payne (TB) 58/219y
PASSING: Sewell 214-364/2176y, 12TD, 58.8%
RECEIVING: Simpson 43/402y, Stupar 40/359y, Santi 36/418y
SCORING: Chris Gould (K) 83pts, Simpson 60pts, Peerman 30pts

2008 5-7

7 Southern Cal	52 WR Kevin Ogletree
16 Richmond	0 WR Maurice Covington
10 Connecticut	45 WR Cary Koch / Rashawn Jackson (FB)
3 Duke	31 T Eugene Monroe
31 Maryland	0 G Austin Pasztor / Zak Stair
35 East Carolina	20 C Jack Shields
16 North Carolina	13 G B.J. Cabbell
24 Georgia Tech	17 T Will Barker
7 Miami	28 TE John Phillips / Andrew Devlin
17 Wake Forest	28 QB Marc Verica / Peter Lalich
3 Clemson	13 TB Cedric Peerman / Mikell Simpson
14 Virginia Tech	17 DL Alex Field
	DL Nick Jenkins / Nate Collins
	DL Matt Conrath / John-Kevin Dolce
	LB Clint Sintim
	LB Jon Copper
	LB Antonio Appleby / Darren Childs
	LB Denzel Burrell / Aaron Clark
	DB Vic Hall (TB) / Chase Minnifield
	DB Ras-I Dowling / Mike Parker
	DB Byron Glaspy
	DB Corey Mosley / Brandon Woods

RUSHING: Peerman 153/774y, Simpson 87/262y, Hall 16/109y
PASSING: Verica 226-354/2037y, 8TD, 63.8%, Lalich 39-74/359y, 0TD, 52.7%
RECEIVING: Ogletree 58/723y, Phillips 48/385y, Peerman 44/193y, Covington 33/414y
SCORING: Peerman 42pts, Ogletree 36pts, Yannick Reyering (K) 34pts

2009 3-9

14 William & Mary	26 WR Kris Burd / Matt Snyder
14 TCU	30 WR Vic Hall (QB) / Javaris Brown
34 Southern Miss	37 T Landon Bradley
16 North Carolina	3 G Austin Pasztor
47 Indiana	7 C Jack Shields
20 Maryland	9 G B.J. Cabbell
9 Georgia Tech	34 T Will Barker
17 Duke	28 TE Joe Torchia / John Phillips
3 Miami	52 QB Jameel Sewell / Marc Verica
10 Boston College	14 TB Mikell Simpson / Tim Smith (WR)
21 Clemson	34 FB Rashawn Jackson
13 Virginia Tech	42 DL Matt Conrath / Zane Parr
	DL Nick Jenkins / John-Kevin Dolce
	DL Nate Collins
	DL Cam Johnson / Aaron Clark
	LB Darren Childs / Tucker Windle
	LB Steve Greer
	LB Denzel Burell
	DB Chris Cook / Chase Minnifield
	DB Ras-I Dowling
	DB Rodney McLeod
	DB Brandon Woods / Corey Mosley

RUSHING: Jackson 96/461y, Simpson 85/366y, Sewell 136/167y
PASSING: Sewell 157-292/1848y, 7TD, 53.8%
RECEIVING: Burd 31/413y, Simpson 27/236y, Jackson 25/222y, Hall 24/274y
SCORING: Robert Randolph (K) 57pts, Sewell 42pts, Simpson 36pts

2010 4-8

34 Richmond	13 WR Kris Burd
14 Southern Cal	17 WR Dontrelle Inman
48 VMI	7 T Oday Aboushi
14 Florida State	34 G Austin Pasztor
21 Georgia Tech	33 C Anthony Mihota
10 North Carolina	44 G B.J. Cabbell
48 E. Michigan	21 T Morgan Moses / Landon Bradley
24 Miami	19 TE Colter Phillips / Joe Torchia
48 Duke	55 QB Marc Verica
23 Maryland	42 TB Perry Jones / Keith Payn
13 Boston College	17 FB/WR Max Milien / Matt Snyder
7 Virginia Tech	37 DL Zane Parr / Jake Snyder
	DL Matt Conrath / John-Kevin Dolce
	DL Nick Jenkins
	DL Cam Johnson
	LB LaRoy Reynolds / Steve Greer
	LB Aaron Taliaferro / Darnell Carter
	LB Ausar Walcott
	DB Devin Wallace / Mike Parker
	DB Chase Minnifield / Ras-I Dowling
	DB Corey Mosley / Trey Womack
	DB Rodney McLeod / Dom Joseph

RUSHING: Payne 160/749y, Jones 137/646y
PASSING: Verica 233-396/2799y, 14TD, 58.8%
RECEIVING: Burd 58/799y, Inman 51/815y, Jones 31/224y, Snyder 30/393y
SCORING: Payne 96pts, Robert Randolph (K) 73pts, Burd 30pts

VIRGINIA TECH

Virginia Polytechnic Institute and State University (Founded 1872)
Blacksburg, Virginia
Nickname: Hokies, Gobblers
Colors: Maroon and Orange
Stadium: Lane (1964) 66,233
Conference Affiliations: Southern (1921-64), Independent (1965-90),
    Big East (1991-2003), Atlantic Coast (2004-present)

CAREER RUSHING YARDS	Attempts	Yards
Cyrus Lawrence (1979-82)	843	3767
Kevin Jones (2001-03)	616	3475
Roscoe Coles (1974-77)	656	3459
Maurice Williams (1983-86)	550	2981
Branden Ore (2005-07)	617	2776
Lee Suggs (1999-02)	535	2767
Dwayne Thomas (1992-95)	576	2696
Ken Oxendine (1994-97)	526	2645
Eddie Hunter (1983-86)	466	2523
Phil Rogers (1973-75)	528	2461

CAREER PASSING YARDS	Comp.-Att.	Yards
Tyrod Taylor (2007-10)	495-865	7017
Bryan Randall (2001-04)	490-833	6508
Don Strock (1970-72)	440-829	6009
Will Furrer (1988-91)	494-920	5915
Maurice DeShazo (1991-94)	397-745	5720
Sean Glennon (2005-08)	386-656	4867
Jim Druckenmiller (1993-96)	313-582	4383
Steve Casey (1978-81)	342-647	4299
Mark Cox (1981-85)	281-518	3526
Michael Vick (1999-2000)	177-313	3074

CAREER RECEIVING YARDS	Catches	Yards
Ricky Scales (1972-74)	113	2272
Antonio Freeman (1991-94)	121	2207
Jarrett Boykin (2008-10)	123	2123
Ernest Wilford (2000-03)	126	2052
Andre Davis (1998-01)	103	1986
Josh Morgan (2004-07)	122	1817
Eddie Royal (2004-07)	119	1778
Danny Coale (2008-10)	105	1754
Myron Richardson (1986-89)	100	1541
Bryan Still (1992-95)	74	1458

SEASON RUSHING YARDS	Attempts	Yards
Ryan Williams (2009)	293	1655
Kevin Jones (2003)	281	1647
Cyrus Lawrence (1981)	325	1403
Lee Suggs (2002)	257	1325
Darren Evans (2008)	287	1265

SEASON PASSING YARDS	Comp.-Att.	Yards
Don Strock (1972)	228-427	3243
Tyrod Taylor (2010)	188-315	2743
Don Strock (1971)	195-356	2577
Marcus Vick (2005)	177-289	2393
Tyrod Taylor (2009)	136-243	2311

SEASON RECEIVING YARDS	Catches	Yards
Andre Davis (1999)	35	962
Ernest Wilford (2002)	51	925
Ernest Wilford (2003)	55	886
Jarrett Boykin (2010)	53	847
Ricky Scales (1972)	43	826

GAME RUSHING YARDS	Attempts	Yards
Darren Evans (2008 vs. Maryland)	32	253
Kevin Jones (2003 vs. Pittsburgh)	30	241
Kenny Lewis (1978 vs. Virginia Military)	34	223

GAME PASSING YARDS	Comp.-Att.	Yards
Don Strock (1972 vs. Houston)	34-53	527
Bryan Randall (2002 vs. Syracuse)	23-35	504
Bryan Randall (2003 vs. California)	24-34	398

GAME RECEIVING YARDS	Catches	Yards
Ernest Wilford (2002 vs. Syracuse)	8	279
Ricky Scales (1972 vs. Wake Forest)	9	213
Antonio Freeman (1993 vs. Temple)	8	194

GREATEST COACH:

Schools have had mixed results when hiring an ex-player as head coach. For every Knute Rockne or Bear Bryant that succeeds, there are hundreds who fail miserably. In some circumstances a former player can appreciate the unique pluses and minuses of a particular school.

That is certainly true of Frank Beamer, one of several successful coaches in the history of Virginia Tech, and the one who elevated the program to the highest of heights. A three-year starter for the Hokies during the "Liberty Bowl Years", 1966-68, Beamer experienced winning football at the school, while also learning a great deal about the sport from his head coach Jerry Claiborne. With Claiborne playing for, and learning from, Bryant, Beamer can trace his coaching legacy only two generations to the genius of Bryant. That legacy greatly shaped his coaching.

After a successful run as the head coach of Murray State, Beamer was hired by his alma mater. Thanks to his predecessor Bill Dooley, the program was in transition from being a regional power to a national one, using the soon-to-be-formed Big East football conference as the conduit. It was time for new blood.

There was plenty of patience for Beamer, who inherited NCAA sanctions, as he had losing seasons four of his first six years. By 1993, everything was in place for a hugely successful run. The Hokies won nine games that year and have averaged more than nine wins per season since 1993. They have been a dominant team in two major conferences, the Big East and the ACC, and have been a regular member of the weekly rankings.

Although his teams have featured some exciting offensive talent, the Hokies have become so well known for scoring without having the ball, whether it be on defense or with special teams, that a new phrase has entered sports dictionaries: "BeamerBall." The Hokies have scored touchdowns in a host of different ways, from returns of fumbles and interceptions to kick returns and blocked kicks. The very first touchdown scored in the Beamer era, in 1987, came on Jon Jeffries's 92-yard kick return. There would be plenty more just like it.

VIRGINIA TECH'S 55 GREATEST SINCE 1953

OFFENSE

WIDE RECEIVER: Carroll Dale, Antonio Freeman, Ricky Scales, Ernest Wilford
TIGHT END: Ken Barefoot
TACKLE: Duane Brown, Eugene Chung, Dave Kadela, Jimmy Martin
GUARD: Gennaro DiNapoli, Newt Green, Matt Lehr, Chris Malone
CENTER: Bill Conaty, Jake Grove, Jim Pyne
QUARTERBACK: Bryan Randall, Don Strock, Michael Vick
RUNNING BACK: Kevin Jones, Cyrus Lawrence, Ken Oxendine, Lee Suggs
FULLBACK: Sonny Utz

DEFENSE

END: Nathaniel Adibi, Cornell Brown, John Engelberger, George Foussekis, Corey Moore, Darryl Tapp
TACKLE: J.C. Price, David Pugh, Bruce Smith
LINEBACKER: Ken Brown, Vince Hall, Mike Johnson, Rick Razzano, Ben Taylor, Mike Widger
CORNERBACK: Tyronne Drakeford, Victor Harris, Anthony Midget, Ronyell Whitaker, Jimmy Williams
SAFETY: Corey Bird, Frank Loria, Willie Pile, Preston Prioleau

SPECIAL TEAMS

RETURN SPECIALISTS: Andre Davis, DeAngelo Hall
PLACE KICKER: Shayne Graham
PUNTER: Nic Schmitt

MULTIPLE POSITIONS

QUARTERBACK-RUNNING BACK-PUNTER: Bob Schweikert

TWO-WAY PLAYERS

TACKLE-DEFENSIVE TACKLE: Don Oakes, George Preas

PERFORMANCE FORMULA:
VIRGINIA TECH'S 10 BEST SEASONS

Year	Rating	Rank
2000	1.7182	4 of 70
1999	1.6603	4 of 71
2005	1.6490	4 of 70
2009	1.5289	8 of 72
1996	1.5265	11 of 70
2007	1.4980	9 of 70
1995	1.4823	10 of 70
2010	1.4744	13 of 71
1998	1.4545	13 of 71
2004	1.4503	11 of 72

VIRGINIA TECH HOKIES

Year	W-L-T	AP Poll	Conference Standing	Toughest Regular Season Opponents	Coach (Record at School)	Bowl Games
1953	5-5		5t	West Virginia 8-1, Richmond 5-3-1	Frank Moseley	
1954	8-0-1	16	3	Clemson 5-5, Richmond 5-4	Frank Moseley	
1955	6-3-1		2	Clemson 7-3, Wake Forest 5-4-1, George Washington 5-4	Frank Moseley	
1956	7-2-1		2	Clemson 7-1-2, Tulane 6-4, Florida State 5-4-1	Frank Moseley	
1957	4-6		7t	North Carolina State 7-1-2, West Virginia 7-2-1, VMI 9-0-1	Frank Moseley	
1958	5-4-1		2	Florida State 7-3, Mississippi So. 9-0, VMI 6-2-2	Frank Moseley	
1959	6-4		3	Wake Forest 6-4, VMI 8-1-1	Frank Moseley	
1960	6-4		2t	North Carolina State 6-3-1, Clemson 6-4, VMI 7-2-1	Frank Moseley (54-42-4)	
1961	4-5		7	VMI 6-4, Richmond 5-5	Jerry Claiborne	
1962	5-5		6	Army 6-4, West Virginia 8-2, Richmond 6-3	Jerry Claiborne	
1963	8-2		1	North Carolina State 8-2, West Virginia 4-6	Jerry Claiborne	
1964	6-4		2	Syracuse 7-3, Florida State 8-1-1, West Virginia 7-3	Jerry Claiborne	
1965	7-3			West Virginia 6-4, VMI 6-4	Jerry Claiborne	
1966	8-2-1			Florida State 6-4, Tulane 5-4-1	Jerry Claiborne	Liberty 7 Miami 14
1967	7-3			Florida State 7-2-1, Miami 7-3, West Virginia 5-4-1	Jerry Claiborne	
1968	7-4			Alabama 8-2, Florida State 8-2, West Virginia 7-3, Richmond 7-3	Jerry Claiborne	Liberty 17 Mississippi 34
1969	4-5-1			Alabama 6-4, Florida State 6-3-1, South Carolina 7-3	Jerry Claiborne	
1970	5-6			Alabama 6-5, Florida State 7-4, Wake Forest 6-5, Villanova 9-2	Jerry Claiborne (61-39-2)	
1971	4-7			Houston 9-2, Florida St. 8-3, Wake Forest 6-5, So. Mississippi 6-5	Charlie Coffey	
1972	6-4-1			Alabama 10-1, SMU 7-4, Florida State 7-4, Houston 6-4-1	Charlie Coffey	
1973	2-9			Alabama 11-0, Houston 10-1, South Carolina 7-4, SMU 6-4-1	Charlie Coffey (12-20-1)	
1974	4-7			Houston 8-3, SMU 6-4-1, Miami 6-5, Kentucky 6-5	Jimmy Sharpe	
1975	8-3			West Virginia 8-3, Auburn 3-6-2	Jimmy Sharpe	
1976	6-5			Texas A&M 9-2, Kent State 8-4	Jimmy Sharpe	
1977	3-7-1			Kentucky 10-1, Florida State 9-2, Texas A&M 8-3, Clemson 8-2-1	Jimmy Sharpe (21-22-1)	
1978	4-7			Alabama 10-1, Clemson 10-1, Florida State 8-3, Tulsa 9-2	Bill Dooley	
1979	5-6			Alabama 11-0, Florida State 11-0, Clemson 8-3, Wake Forest 8-3	Bill Dooley	
1980	8-4			Florida State 10-1, Clemson 6-5	Bill Dooley	Peach 10 Miami 20
1981	7-4			Miami 9-2, West Virginia 8-3, Duke 6-5, VMI 6-3-1	Bill Dooley	
1982	7-4			West Virginia 9-2, Vanderbilt 8-3, Miami 7-4	Bill Dooley	
1983	9-2			West Virginia 8-3, Virginia 6-5	Bill Dooley	Independence 7 Air Force 23
1984	8-4			West Virginia 7-4, Clemson 7-4, Wake Forest 6-5	Bill Dooley	
1985	6-5			Florida 9-1-1, West Virginia 7-3-1, Syracuse 7-4, Clemson 6-5	Bill Dooley	Peach 25 North Carolina State 24
1986	9-2-1	20		Clemson 7-2-2, Kentucky 5-5-1	Bill Dooley (63-38-1)	
1987	2-9			Miami 11-0, Syracuse 11-0, Clemson 9-2, South Carolina 8-3	Frank Beamer	
1988	3-8			West Virginia 11-0, Florida State 10-1, Clemson 9-2, Syracuse 9-2	Frank Beamer	
1989	6-4-1			Virginia 10-2, West Virginia 8-2-1, Clemson 9-2, Florida State 9-2	Frank Beamer	
1990	6-5			Georgia Tech 10-0-1, Florida State 9-2, Virginia 8-3	Frank Beamer	
1991	5-6			Florida State 10-2, Virginia 8-2-1, North Carolina St. 9-2, Oklahoma 8-3	Frank Beamer	
1992	2-8-1		7	Miami 11-0, Syracuse 9-2, North Carolina State 9-2-1, Virginia 7-4	Frank Beamer	
1993	9-3	22	4	West Virginia 11-0, Miami 9-2, Boston College 8-3, Virginia 7-4	Frank Beamer	Independence 45 Indiana 20
1994	8-4	17	2	Miami 10-1, Virginia 8-3, Syracuse 7-4	Frank Beamer	Gator 23 Tennessee 45
1995	10-2	13	1t	Miami 8-3, Syracuse 8-3, Virginia 8-4	Frank Beamer	Sugar 28 Texas 10
1996	10-2	10	1t	Miami 8-3, Syracuse 8-3, West Virginia 8-3, Virginia 7-4	Frank Beamer	Orange 21 Nebraska 41
1997	7-5		2	Syracuse 8-4, Virginia 7-4, West Virginia 7-4	Frank Beamer	Gator 3 North Carolina 42
1998	9-3	23	2t	Virginia 9-2, Syracuse 8-3, Miami 8-3, West Virginia 8-3	Frank Beamer	Music City 38 Alabama 7
1999	11-1	2	1	Boston College 8-3, Virginia 7-4, Miami 8-4	Frank Beamer	Sugar 29 Florida State 46
2000	11-1	6	2	Miami 10-1, Pittsburgh 7-4	Frank Beamer	Gator 41 Clemson 20
2001	8-4	15	3t	Miami 11-0, Syracuse 9-3	Frank Beamer	Gator 17 Florida State 30
2002	10-4	21	4t	Miami 12-0, West Virginia 9-3, Boston College 8-4, Pitt 8-4, Virginia 8-5	Frank Beamer	San Francisco 20 Air Force 13
2003	8-5		4	Miami 11-2, Pittsburgh 8-4, West Virginia 8-4, Virginia 7-5	Frank Beamer	Insight 49 California 52
2004	10-3	10	1	Southern Cal 12-0, West Virginia 8-3, Virginia 8-3, Miami 83, Pitt 8-3	Frank Beamer	Sugar 13 Auburn 16
2005	11-2	7	Cst1	West Virginia 10-1, Miami 9-2, Boston College 8-3, Georgia Tech 7-4	Frank Beamer	Gator 35 Louisville 24
2006	10-3	19	Cst2	Wake Forest 10-2, Georgia Tech 9-3, Boston College 9-3, Clemson 8-4	Frank Beamer	Peach 24 Georgia 31
2007	11-3	9	Cst1	LSU 10-2, Clemson 9-3, Boston College 10-2, Virginia 9-3	Frank Beamer	Orange 21 Kansas 24
2008	10-4	15	Cst1t	Georgia Tech 9-3, Nebraska 8-4, Boston College 9-4	Frank Beamer	Orange 20 Cincinnati 7
2009	10-3	10	Cst2	Alabama 13-0, Nebraska 9-4, Miami 9-3, Georgia Tech 11-2	Frank Beamer	Chick-fil-A 37 Tennessee 14
2010	11-3	16	Cst1	Boise State 11-1, North Carolina State 8-4, Florida State 9-4	Frank Beamer (198-95-2)	Orange 12 Stanford 40

TOTAL: 402-242-11 .6221 (20 of 70)   **Bowl Games since 1953:** 9-14 .3913 (59 of 70)

GREATEST TEAM SINCE 1953: They had a lead in the BCS Championship Game entering the fourth quarter, but alas, that final period was won easily by the healthier Florida State Seminoles and the 1999 season came to an end for the Hokies with a no. 2 finish. It was a national coming out party for quarterback Michael Vick, while the aggressive defense had the Seminoles worried until they ran out of cornerbacks.

1953 5-5

7 Marshall	0 E Tom Petty / Charlie Herb
20 Virginia	6 T Frank Brown / Tom Richards
13 Rutgers	20 G Billy Kerfoot / Ernie Wolfe
21 Richmond	7 C Jim Randall / Hunter Swink
7 William & Mary	13 G Harold Grizzard / Jim Haren
32 Wash. & Lee	12 T George Preas
22 The Citadel	0 E Bob Luttrell / Bob Allen
7 West Virginia	12 QB Johnny Dean / Jack Williams
0 Miami	26 HB Doug Creger / Bobby Scruggs
13 VMI	16 HB Dickey Beard / Howie Wright
	FB Don Welsh / Leo Burke

RUSHING: Beard 60/349y
PASSING: Dean 26-62/314y, 0TD, 41.9%
RECEIVING: Petty 10/216y
SCORING: Williams 30pts

1954 8-0-1

30 No. Carolina St.	13 E Tom Petty
32 Wake Forest	0 T Bill Jamerson / Tom Richards
18 Clemson	7 G Billy Kerfoot / Jim Haren
19 Richmond	12 C Jack Prater / Charles Cuba
6 Virginia	0 G Jim Locke / Phil Unger
7 William & Mary	7 T George Preas
20 Geo. Wash'ton	13 E Bob Luttrell / Grover Jones
20 Waynesburg	6 QB Johnny Dean / Billy Cranwell
45 VMI	9 HB Howie Wright / Bobby Scruggs
	HB Dickie Beard / Dave Ebert
	FB Leo Burke / Don Divers

RUSHING: Beard 128/647y, Wright 60/365y, Ebert 47/323y
PASSING: Cranwell 18-37/316y, 7TD, 48.6%
RECEIVING: Petty 9/236y, Beard 7/81y, Jones 3/47y
SCORING: Beard (HB-K) 39pts, Petty & Dean 30pts

1955 6-3-1

0 Wake Forest	13 E Roger Simmons / John Herndon
33 Pennsylvania	0 T Bill Jamerson / Tom Richards
14 William & Mary	7 G John Hall / Pat Carpenito
24 Florida State	20 C Jack Prater
7 Richmond	7 G Phil Unger / Bill Daley
17 Virginia	13 T Jim Locke / Bobby Cruickshank
7 Geo. Wash'ton	13 E Grover Jones
16 Clemson	21 QB Leo Burke / Billy Cranwell
34 No. Carolina St.	26 HB Dave Ebert / Bobby Scruggs
39 VMI	13 HB Dickie Beard / Ray England
	FB Don Divers / Hayes Burleson

RUSHING: Beard 92/382y, Divers 77/316y, Burke 73/220y
PASSSING: Cranwell 25-54/458y, 4TD, 46.3%
RECEIVING: Simmons 9/153y, Divers 8/122y, Bobby Wolfenden (HB) 6/123y
SCORING: Divers & Burke 42pts, Beard (HB-K) 29pts

1956 7-2-1

37 East Carolina	2 E Carroll Dale
14 Tulane	21 T Bill Daley / Tom Dalzell
35 No. Carolina St.	6 G Pat Carpenito / Frank Webster (C)
20 Florida State	7 C John Hall
34 William & Mary	7 G Ben Schmidt / Bobby Cruikshank
46 Richmond	14 T Jim Burks / Russell Moon
14 Virginia	7 E Grover Jones / Jim Hedrick
6 Clemson	21 QB Jimmy Lugar
13 Wake Forest	13 HB Bobby Wolfenden / Dave Ebert
45 VMI	0 HB Ray England / Barry Frazee
	FB Bobby Conner / Don Divers

RUSHING: Wolfenden 74/459y, Conner 82/387y, England 70/384y
PASSING: Lugar 32-76/556y, 6TD, 42.1%
RECEIVING: Dale 8/157y, Jones 7/100y, Divers 6/62y
SCORING: Lugar 48pts, England 32pts, Wolfenden & Divers 30pts

1957 4-6

14 Tulane	13 E Carroll Dale / Ed Brinkley
0 West Virginia	14 T Pat Carpenito (G) / Russell Moon
7 William & Mary	13 G Nick Mihales
21 Villanova	14 C Frank Webster / Jim Randall
7 Virginia	38 G Ben Schmidt
7 Florida State	20 T Jim Burks / Doug Royals
42 Richmond	7 E Billy Tilling / Ken Byrd
10 Wake Forest	3 QB Jimmy Lugar / Billy Cranwell
0 No. Carolina St.	12 HB Corbin Bailey / Alger Pugh
6 VMI	14 HB Ray England / Barry Frazee
	FB Bobby Conner

RUSHING: Bailey 89/366y, Conner 78/314y, England 77/302y
PASSING: Cranwell 36-57/391y, 0TD, 63.2%
RECEIVING: Dale 17/171y, Pugh 11/77y, Brinkley 8/124y
SCORING: Frazee (HB-K) 34pts, Conner 24pts, Lugar 18pts

1958 5-4-1

28 West Texas St.	12 E Carroll Dale
6 Wake Forest	13 T Don Oakes
27 William & Mary	15 G Mike Zeno
22 Virginia	13 C Nick Mihales
0 Florida State	28 G Duncan Holsclaw / Tommy O'Brien
20 West Virginia	21 T Jim Burks
14 No. Carolina St.	14 E Ken Byrd / Allen Whittier
27 Richmond	23 QB Billy Holsclaw
0 Southern Miss.	41 HB Jay Whitesell
21 VMI	16 HB Pat Henry / Dickie Snead
	FB Bobby Cranwell / Sam Shaffer

RUSHING: Henry 78/375y, Holsclaw 103/214y, Shaffer 62/202y
PASSING: Holsclaw 70-127/1013y, 9TD, 55.1%
RECEIVING: Dale 25/459y, Byrd 10/168y, Henry 9/95y
SCORING: Henry 44pts, Dale 40pts, Holsclaw 26pts

1959 6-4

13 No. Carolina St.	15 E Carroll Dale
18 Wake Forest	27 T Joe Moss / Bernie Vishneski
20 William & Mary	14 G Mike Zeno
6 Florida State	7 C Chuck Stephens / Charles Hines
40 Virginia	14 G Jim Paine
24 Villanova	14 T Allen Whittier / Don Oakes
51 Richmond	29 E Ken Byrd
26 West Texas	21 QB Frank Eastman / Charlie Speck
12 West Virginia	0 HB Alger Pugh / Ray Massie / Terry Strock
12 VMI	37 HB Pat Henry / Dickie Snead / Buddy Perry
	FB Sam Shaffer / Art Pruett

RUSHING: Pugh 112/615y, Shaffer 50/184y, Perry 54/173y
PASSING: Eastman 32-68/548y, 10TD, 47.1%
RECEIVING: Dale 17/408y, Pugh 14/240y, Strock 9/132y
SCORING: Pugh 66pts, Dale 38pts, Stephens (K) & Strock 18pts

1960 6-4

14 No. Carolina St.	29 E Jim Farr / Charlie Speck
15 West Virginia	0 T Don Oakes / Joe Moss
7 Clemson	13 G Mike Zeno / Ray Barile
22 Wake Forest	13 C Rickey Tolley / Charlie Hines
27 William & Mary	0 G Duncan Holsclaw
40 Virginia	8 T Allen Whittier
20 Richmond	0 E Walt Harris / Leon Tomblin
7 Davidson	9 QB Warren Price
8 Geo. Wash'ton	21 HB Bob Crabtree / Johnny Watkins
13 VMI	12 HB Terry Strock / Buddy Perry
	FB Don Vaught / Art Pruett

RUSHING: Price 98/350y, Strock 94/343y, Vaught 86/330y
PASSING: Price 29-73/386y, 7TD, 39.7%
RECEIVING: Strock 16/236y, Speck 9/111y, Watkins 5/52y
SCORING: Strock 42pts, Price 34pts, Watkins & Vaught 18pts

1961 4-5

20 William & Mary	6 E Leon Tomblin
0 West Virginia	28 T Joe Moss
14 Tulane	27 G Ray Barile / Bloice Davison
20 Virginia	0 C Charlie Hines / Randall Edwards
10 Florida State	7 G Newt Green
0 Richmond	11 T Gene Breen
15 Wake Forest	14 E Dick Goode / Charlie Speck
14 Geo.Wash'ton	3 QB Terry Strock / Warren Price
0 VMI	6 HB Tommy Walker/Ron Hawkins/B. Weihe
	HB Buddy Perry / Warren Maccaroni
	FB Art Pruett / Gerald Bobbitte

RUSHING: Price 93/356y, Bobbitte 62/261y, Strock 52/223y
PASSING: Price 37-93/381y, 5TD, 39.8%
RECEIVING: Strock 10/68y, Weihe 8/85y, Tomblin 5/62y
SCORING: Strock & Price 18pts, Aster Sizemore (K) 13pts

1962 5-5

0 William & Mary	3 E Jake Adams / Tommy Marvin
15 Geo. Wash'ton	14 T Gene Breen
0 West Virginia	14 G Jim Hickam / Mike Hvozdovic
20 Virginia	15 C Dave Gillespie / Burt Rodgers
13 Richmond	7 G Newt Green / Vic Kreiter
12 Army	20 T Lynn Jones / Dave Green
7 Florida State	20 E Kyle Albright
24 Tulane	22 QB Pete Cartwright / Bob Schweickert
37 Wake Forest	8 HB T. Walker / Buddy Wiehe / Mike Cahill
9 VMI	14 HB Tommy Hawkins / Billy Babb
	FB Gerald Bobbitte / Sonny Utz / Phil Cary

RUSHING: Bobbitte 95/312y, Schweickert 51/308y, Cary 76/283y
PASSING: Cartwright 26-60/266y, 3TD, 43.3%
RECEIVING: Marvin 11/137y, Cahill 8/102y, Adams 8/64y
SCORING: Schweickert 30pts, Bobbitte & Cahill 18pts

1963 8-2

14 Kentucky	32 E Tommy Marvin
27 Wake Forest	0 T Gene Breen
10 Virginia	0 G Mike Hvozdovic
22 Geo. Wash'ton	8 C Burt Rodgers
28 William & Mary	13 G Newt Green
31 Florida State	23 T Lynn Jones
14 Richmond	8 E Jake Adams
7 No. Carolina St.	13 QB Bob Schweickert
28 West Virginia	3 HB Mike Cahill / Tommy Walker
35 VMI	20 HB Tommy Hawkins / Darrell Page
	FB Sonny Utz

RUSHING: Schweickert 155/839y, Utz 134/567y, Page 61/195y
PASSING: Schweickert 62-116/687y, 6TD, 53.4%
RECEIVING: Marvin 28/303y, Walker 11/131y, Adams 6/54y
SCORING: Utz 60pts, Schweickert 48pts, Dick Cranwell (K) 34pts

1964 6-4

18 Tampa	14 E Tommy Marvin / Judd Bigelow (LB)
21 Wake Forest	38 T Sands Woody / Erick Johnson
17 Virginia	20 G Mike Hvozdovic / John Sheehy
33 Geo. Wash'ton	0 C Les Hanly / Dave Farmer
10 West Virginia	23 G Mike Saunders / Billy Edwards (LB)
20 Florida State	11 T Joe Bloomer / Andy Bowling (DL)
27 William & Mary	20 E Bob Churchill / John Shipley (DL)
28 No. Carolina St.	19 QB Bob Schweickert / Bobby Owens
15 Syracuse	20 TB Sal Garcia / Tommy Francisco
35 VMI	13 WB Tommy Groom / John Raible (DB)
	FB Sonny Utz

RUSHING: Utz 175/777y, Schweickert 131/576y, Francisco 54/298y
PASSING: Schweickert 52-109/833y, 9TD, 47.7%
RECEIVING: Marvin 21/330y, Francisco 17/303y, Churchill 8/101y
SCORING: Utz 66pts, Schweickert 56pts, Dick Cranwell (K) 30pts

1965 7-3

12 Wake Forest	3 E Gene Fisher / Bill Kegley
25 Richmond	7 T Ron McGuigan / Erick Johnson
9 William & Mary	7 G John Sheehy
17 Geo. Wash'ton	12 C Les Hanly / Milt Miller
10 Vanderbilt	21 G Bob Griffith (DL) / Damon Dedo (T)
22 Virginia	14 T Donnie Bruce
6 Florida State	7 TE Ken Barefoot / John Shipley
22 West Virginia	31 QB Bobby Owens / Tommy Stafford
21 Villanova	19 TB Tommy Francisco/Dickie Longerbeam
44 VMI	13 WB Tommy Groom / Eddie Bulheller
	FB Sal Garcia / Claude Messamore
	DL George Foussekis
	DL Sands Woody / Jeff Haynes
	DL Mike Saunders
	DL Don Thacker
	DL Andy Bowling (LB)
	DL Dan Mooney / John Raible
	LB Clarence Culpepper
	LB Billy Edwards / Pete Wrenn
	DB Wayne Rash / Bill Skinner
	DB Jimmy Richards
	DB Frank Loria

RUSHING: Owens 146/526y, Francisco 109/504y, Longerbeam 66/298y
PASSING: Owens 68-122/891y, 6 TD, 55.7%
RECEIVING: Fisher 30/387y, Barefoot 20/250y, Francisco 7/71y
SCORING: Owens 42pts, John Utin (K) 36pts, Francisco 30pts

1966 8-2-1

0 Tulane	13 WR Gene Fisher
49 Geo. Wash'ton	0 T Donnie Bruce
13 West Virginia	13 G Damon Dedo / Bob Griffith (C)
7 Kentucky	0 C Ken Whitley (LB) / Scott Dawson
21 Vanderbilt	6 G Sands Woody (DL) / Richard Mollo
24 Virginia	7 T Erick Johnson
23 Florida State	21 TE Ken Barefoot
11 Wake Forest	0 QB Tommy Stafford
20 William & Mary	18 TB Tommy Francisco/Dickie Longerbeam
70 VMI	12 WB Eddie Bulheller
7 Miami	14 FB Tommy Groom / Geo. Constantinides
	DL George Foussekis
	DL Jim Harvey
	DL Dave Farmer
	DL Don Thacker
	DL Andy Bowling
	DL Dan Mooney
	LB Clarence Culpepper
	LB Sal Garcia
	DB Ron Davidson
	DB Frank Beamer / Jimmy Richards
	DB Frank Loria

RUSHING: Francisco 203/753y, Stafford 160/583y,
 Constantinides60/248y
PASSING: Stafford 53-113/610y, 5TD, 46.9%
RECEIVING: Barefoot 22/267y, Fisher 13/185y, Francisco 8/46y
SCORING: Francisco 84pts, John Utin (K) 40pts, Barefoot 30pts

1967 7-3

13 Tampa	3 E Gene Fisher / Bobby Slaughter
31 William & Mary	7 T Jerry Green
15 Kansas State	3 G Bob Griffith / Judd Bigelow
3 Villanova	0 C Scott Dawson
24 Kentucky	14 G Damon Dedo / Chet Forrester
45 Richmond	14 T Richard Mollo / Preston Blackburn
20 West Virginia	7 TE Ken Barefoot
7 Miami	14 QB Al Kincaid / Wayne Rash
15 Florida State	38 HB Terry Smoot / George Constantinides
10 VMI	12 WB Dickie Longerbeam / Burt Henderson
	FB Rick Piland / Ken Edwards (WB)
	DL George Foussekis
	DL Jim Harvey
	DL Don Thacker
	DL Larry Creekmore
	DL Jeff Haynes / Pete Dawyot
	DL Dan Mooney
	LB Pete Wrenn
	LB Clarence Culpepper / Mike Widger
	DB Ron Davidson / Randy Treadwell
	DB Frank Beamer
	DB Frank Loria

RUSHING: Smoot 68/356y, Constantinides 84/293y,
 Kincaid 119/230y
PASSING: Kincaid 64-132/556y, 3TD, 48.4%
RECEIVING: Barefoot 26/225y, Fisher 12/126y, Piland 11/96y
SCORING: John Utin (K) 47pts, Constantinides 38pts,
 Smoot 24pts

1968 7-4

7 Alabama	14 WR Danny Cupp / Bobby Slaughter
12 William & Mary	0 T Preston Blackburn / Art Aguilar
19 Kansas State	34 G Butch Hall
7 Wake Forest	6 C David Bailey / Nick Del Viscio (LB)
8 Miami	13 G John Maxwell
27 West Virginia	12 T Jerry Green
40 Florida State	22 TE Rick Piland
31 Richmond	18 QB Al Kincaid
17 South Carolina	6 TB Terry Smoot / Perry Tiberio
55 VMI	6 WB Dickie Longerbeam
17 Mississippi■	34 FB Geo. Constantinides / Ken Edwards
	DL Jud Brownell
	DL Pete Dawyot
	DL Paul Ripley / Steve Bocko
	DL Larry Creekmore
	DL Waddey Harvey
	DL Joe Tucker
	LB Mike Widger (DB)
	LB Nick Del Viscio (C) / Ken Edwards (FB)
	DB Randy Treadwell
	DB Frank Beamer
	DB Ron Davidson / Lenny Smith

RUSHING: Smoot 196/820y, Edwards 67/465y,
 Kincaid 104/208y
PASSING: Kincaid 47-97/537y, 2TD, 48.5%
RECEIVING: Cupp 21/323y, Smoot 12/62y, Piland 8/98y
SCORING: Jack Simcsak (K) 51pts, Smoot 48pts,
 Edwards 36pts

1969 4-5-1

13 Alabama	17 WR Jimmy Quinn
10 Wake Forest	16 T Tom Parks
10 Richmond	17 G Butch Hall
6 Kentucky	7 C Dave Bailey / Nick Del Viscio
16 South Carolina	17 G Preston Blackburn / Rod Cox
21 Buffalo	7 T Jerry Green / Bill House
43 William & Mary	7 TE Bobby Slaughter / Dee Crigger
10 Florida State	10 QB Al Kincaid / Bob German
48 Duke	12 TB Terry Smoot / Perry Tiberio
52 VMI	0 WB Ken Edwards
	FB Vince Russo / Jimmy Quinn
	DL Tom Mikulski / Bruce Runyan
	DL Steve Bocko / Kevin Meehan
	DL Jim Pigninelli / Sammy Bria
	DL Larry Creekmore
	DL Pete Dawyot / Eddie Johns
	DL Joe Tucker
	LB Mike Widger / Larry Smith
	LB Scott Hawkins / John Ivanac
	DB Tom Bosiack
	DB Donnie Cooke / Bruce Glatthorn
	DB Lenny Smith / Ronnie Holsinger

RUSHING: Smoot 246/940y, Tiberio 92/435y, Edwards 67/298y
PASSING: German 51-105/743y, 2TD, 48.6%
RECEIVING: Smoot 18/161y, Quinn 11/215y, Tiberio 11/172y
SCORING: Smoot 72pts, Jack Simcsak (K) 58pts,
 Edwards 30pts

1970 5-6

0 Virginia	7 WR Jimmy Quinn (WB) / Nick Colobro
18 Alabama	51 T Bill House / Buddy DeMarr
20 Memphis State	21 G John Schneider / Rod Cox
7 South Carolina	24 C Wayne Stinnette
9 Wake Forest	28 G Dave Bailey (C) / Jack Abraham
17 Tulsa	14 T Butch Hall
31 Buffalo	14 TE Mike Burnop / Bob Karlsen
34 William & Mary	14 QB Gil Schwabe/Don Strock / Bob German
34 Villanova	7 TB Bruce Denardo/J. Dobbins/R. Matijevich
8 Florida State	34 WB Jim Polito / Larry Kushner
20 VMI	14 FB Perry Tiberio
	DL Bruce Runyan
	DL Eddie Johns
	DL Sammy Bria
	DL Jim Pigninelli
	DL Kevin Meehan / Duke Strager
	DL Tom Mikulski
	LB Nick Del Viscio (DL) / Larry Smith
	LB John Ivanac / Tommy Carpenito
	DB Ronnie Holsinger/Bruce Glatthorn (WR)
	DB Donnie Cooke
	DB Tom Bosiack / Lenny Smith

RUSHING: Tiberio 184/764y, Quinn 71/433y, Dobbins 74/365y
PASSING: Schwabe 61-126/815y, 5TD, 48.4%
RECEIVING: Quinn 30/481y, Tiberio 13/132y, Matijevich 11/69y
SCORING: Tiberio 60pts, Quinn 38pts,
 Dobbins & Matijevich 18pts

1971 4-7

9 Wake Forest	20 WR Donnie Reel / Dick Maksanty
16 Oklahoma State	24 WR Jimmy Quinn / Ed Tennis
3 Florida State	17 T Terry Stewart / Tom Reynolds
39 Tulsa	46 G Barry DeMarr
41 William & Mary	30 C Wayne Stinnette / Rod Sedwick
37 Ohio Univ.	29 G John Schneider
27 Kentucky	33 T Bill House
6 Virginia	0 TE Mike Burnop / Nick Colobro
29 Houston	56 QB Don Strock
8 Southern Miss	17 TB James Barber / Rich Matijevich
34 VMI	0 FB Vince Russo / John Dobbins
	DL Eddie Johns
	DL John Sprenkle / Bill Ellenbogen
	DL Sammy Bria / Dennis Cogan
	DL Kevin Meehan / Bruce Runyan
	LB Larry Smith / Kent Henry
	LB Dennis Dodson
	LB Tommy Carpenito
	DB Bobby Dabbs
	DB Bruce Glatthorn / Randy McCann
	DB Ronnie Holsinger / Jerry Gaines
	DB Tim Bosiack / Jerry Scharnus

RUSHING: Barber 93/501y, Matijevich 75/349y, Russo 57/219y
PASSING: Strock 195-356/2577y, 12TD, 54.7%
RECEIVING: Burnop 46/558y, Reel 37/705y, Quinn 31/566y
SCORING: Barber 54pts, Dan Strock (K) 43pts, Reel 30pts

1972 6-4-1

20 Virginia	24 WR Donnie Reel / Craig Valentine
15 Florida State	27 WR Kit Utz / Ricky Scales
13 SMU	10 T Bruce Lemmert
27 Houston	27 G Steve Maguigan / Pete Horoszko
34 Oklahoma State	32 C Rod Sedwick
53 Ohio Univ.	21 G Chuck Schoenadel / John Schneider
16 William & Mary	17 T Tom Reynolds
27 Southern Miss.	14 TE Mike Burnop
45 South Carolina	20 QB Don Strock
13 Alabama	52 RB James Barber / Paul Adams
44 Wake Forest	9 RB John Dobbins / Rodney Schnurr
	DL Larry Bearekman
	DL John Sprenkle / Charley Martin
	DL Bill Ellenbogen
	DL Rich Eastling / John Heizer
	LB Donnie Sprouse
	LB Tom Shirley / Dennis Dodson
	LB Kent Henry
	DB Bobby Dabbs
	DB John Bell/ Howard Keyes/ Barry Garber
	DB Jerry Scharnus
	DB Randy McCann / Chuck Perdue

RUSHING: Barber 186/624y, Adams 50/187y, Dobbins 33/115y
PASSING: Strock 228-427/3243y, 16TD, 53.4%
RECEIVING: Scales 43/826y, Barber 35/278y, Burnop 34/459y
SCORING: Barber 78pts, Dave Strock (K) 73pts, Scales 42pts

1973 2-9

24 William & Mary	31 WR Billy Hardee / Steve Galloway
26 Kentucky	31 WR Ricky Scales / Jerry Inge
10 West Virginia	24 T Bruce Lemmert
6 SMU	37 G Pete Horoszko
24 South Carolina	54 G Steve Philbrick
27 Houston	15 T Tom Reynolds / Paul Lawrence
27 Virginia	77 TE Skip Creasey / Kevin Dick
6 Alabama	49 QB Rick Popp /Eddie Joyce /Bruce Arians
16 Memphis State	13 TB Phil Rogers / Danny Ludd
36 Florida State	22 FB James Barber
21 VMI	DL Doug Thacker / Keith McCarter
	DL Larry Herndon
	DL T. Beasley/Tom Turner/Brent Bledsoe
	DL Bill Houseright / Jim Heizer
	LB Tom Shirley / Kent Henry
	LB Charley Martin
	LB Dennis Dodson
	DB Morris Blueford / David Halstead
	DB Lynn McCoy / Flash Davis
	DB Jerry Scharnus
	DB John Bell

RUSHING: Rogers 175/1036y, Barber 175/927y, Ludd 13/53y
PASSING: Popp 70-131/784y, 7TD, 53.4%,
 Joyce 47-88/534y, 3TD, 53.4%
RECEIVING: Scales 36/772y, Hardee 29/441y, Rogers 27/97y
SCORING: Wayne Latimer (K) 61pts, Scales & Barber 48pts

1974 4-7

7 Kentucky	38 WR Ricky Scales
25 SMU	28 T Keith Gibson / Skip Creasey
12 Houston	49 G Steve Philbrick
17 VMI	22 C Randy Vey
31 South Carolina	17 G Don Rudzinski / Bill Wallace / Rick Law
27 Virginia	28 T Rondal Davis / Allen Cure
41 Richmond	7 TE Kevin Dick / Luke Marsingill
7 Miami	14 QB Bruce Arians
34 William & Mary	15 HB Phil Rogers
56 Florida State	21 HB George Heath / Roscoe Coles
21 West Virginia	22 FB Paul Adams / Greg Toal
	DL Ken Lambert
	DL Brent Bledsoe
	DL Charley Martin / Bill Houseright
	DL Tom Beasley / Larry Bearekman
	DL Keith McCarter / Stuart Patterson
	LB Rick Razzano
	LB Doug Thacker/ Ricky Bush / Curt Lowery
	DB Henry Bradley / Flash Davis
	DB Billy Hardee
	DB Tom Cooper / Barry Garber
	DB John Bell / Chuck Perdue

RUSHING: Rogers 153/663y, Coles 95/623y, Adams 77/354y
PASSING: Arians 53-118/952y, 3TD, 44.9%
RECEIVING: Scales 34/674y, Dick 10/169y, Rogers 7/62y
SCORING: Arians 68pts, Rogers 42pts, Wayne Latimer (K) 38pts

1975 8-3

8 Kentucky	27 WR Steve Galloway / Jerry Inge
11 Kent State	17 T Keith Gibson / Allen Cure
21 Richmond	9 G Steve Philbrick / Leonard Walker
23 Auburn	16 C Blair Buskirk
13 Florida State	10 G Larry Capps / Barry Miller
24 Virginia	17 T Rondal Davis
7 West Virginia	10 TE Kevin Dick / Dave Dolphin
24 William & Mary	7 QB Phil Rogers
34 Houston	28 HB Roscoe Coles
33 VMI	0 HB George Heath / Morris Bluefield
40 Wake Forest	10 FB Paul Adams
	DL Stuart Patterson
	DL Tom Beasley
	DL Bill Houseright
	DL Mike Faulkner
	DL Keith McCarter
	LB Rick Razzano
	LB Doug Thacker
	DB Flash Davis
	DB Billy Hardee
	DB Henry Bradley / David Lamie
	DB Chuck Perdue

RUSHING: Coles 194/1045y, Adams 176/768y, Rogers 200/762y
PASSING: Rogers 25-53/379y, 3TD, 47.2%
RECEIVING: Galloway 18/378y, Coles 8/79y, Inge 4/83y
SCORING: Coles 60pts, Rogers 56pts, Wayne Latimer (K) 48pts

1976 6-5

23 Wake Forest	6 WR Moses Foster
0 Texas A&M	19 T Keith Gibson
16 Southern Miss	7 G Barry Miller / Mike Roy
15 William & Mary	27 C Blair Buskirk / Mike Heizer
37 VMI	7 G Leonard Walker
14 Virginia	10 T Rondal Davis
42 Kent State	14 TE Mickey Fitzgerald / Dave Dolphin
24 West Virginia	7 QB Mitcheal Barnes / David Lamie
31 Tulsa	35 HB Roscoe Coles
0 Richmond	16 HB George Heath
21 Florida State	28 FB Paul Adams / Chuck Nuttycombe
	DL Stuart Patterson
	DL Tom Beasley / Doug McDougald
	DL Curt Lowery / Bill Houseright
	DL Mike Faulkner
	DL Keith McCarter
	LB Rick Razzano
	LB Mike Stollings / Steve Cannon
	DB Tom Cooper (TE) / Henry Bradley
	DB Gene Bunn
	DB Gary Smith / Dale Babione
	DB Chip Keatley / Eddie Snell

RUSHING: Coles 209/1119y, Adams 167/675y, Heath 116/512y
PASSING: Barnes 39-72/589y, 5TD, 54.2%
RECEIVING: Foster 20/429y, Dolphin 10/147y, Coles 5/31y
SCORING: Coles 56pts, Paul Engle (K) 45pts, Adams 36pts

1977 3-7-1

6 Texas A&M	27 WR Ellis Savage
20 Memphis State	21 T Greg Birtsch
13 Clemson	31 G John Latina
17 William & Mary	8 C Tony Smith / Mike Heizer
14 Virginia	14 G Leonard Walker
14 Richmond	17 T Ed Lewis / Barry Miller
0 Kentucky	32 TE Mickey Fitzgerald (FB) / Jerry Onhaizer
21 Florida State	23 QB David Lamie
14 West Virginia	20 TB Roscoe Coles
28 Wake Forest	10 WB Dennis Scott
27 VMI	7 FB Dickie Holway
	DL Kent Knupp / James Johnson
	DL Bill Houseright
	DL Danny Hill / Chris Albrittain
	DL Doug McDougald
	DL David DeHart
	LB Rick Razzano
	LB Jerry Sheehan
	DB Gary Smith / Eddie Snell
	DB Gene Bunn
	DB Denny Windmuller
	DB Henry Bradley / Nick Rapone

RUSHING: Coles 158/672y
PASSING: Lamie 43-107/752y, 0TD, 40.2%
RECEIVING: Savage 23/416y
SCORING: Lamie 48pts

1978 4-7

33 Tulsa	35 WR Ron Zollicoffer / Ellis Savage
28 Wake Forest	6 T Joe Sansone / Ed Lewis
7 Auburn	18 G Gary Smith / Steve Wirt
22 William & Mary	19 C Roe Waldron / Tory Smith
7 Clemson	38 G Jeff Bailey / John Latinall
16 West Virginia	3 T Leonard Walker
7 Virginia	17 TE Dave Dolphin / Paul Watkins
0 Alabama	35 QB David Lamie / Steve Casey
0 Kentucky	28 TB Kenny Lewis
14 Florida State	24 WB Dennis Scott
28 VMI	2 FB Mickey Fitzgerald
	DL James Johnson
	DL Doug McDougald
	DL Danny Hill / Chris Albrittain
	DL Mike Faulkner
	DL Charles Novell
	LB Lewis Stuart / Jerry Sheehan
	LB Chip Keatley / Nate Parker
	DB Denny Windmuller
	DB Jerome Pannell / Lawrence Young
	DB Gene Bunn
	DB Gary Smith

RUSHING: Lewis 184/1020y, Fitzgerald 107/545y,
Casey 87/241y
PASSING: Casey 61-118/678y, 2TD, 51.7%,
Lamie 34-79/546y, 3TD, 43.0%
RECEIVING: Scott 21/300y, Zollicoffer 16/243y, Savage 16/226y
SCORING: Lewis 60pts, Fitzgerald 18pts, Paul Engle (K) 17pts

1979 5-6

15 Louisville	14 WR R. Zollicoffer/ T. McKee/ M. Giacolone
41 Appalachian St.	32 T Wayne Mutter / Wally Browne
35 William & Mary	14 G Gary Smith / Tom Webb
10 Florida State	17 C Roe Waldron
14 Wake Forest	19 G Jeff Bailey
0 Clemson	21 T Steve Wirt
34 Richmond	0 TE Paul Watkins
7 Alabama	31 QB Steve Casey
23 West Virginia	34 TB Kenny Lewis / Cyrus Lawrence
18 Virginia	20 WB Sidney Snell / Don Larue
27 VMI	20 FB M. Fitzgerald/Tony Blackmon/M.Rogers
	DL Rob Purdham
	DL Doug McDougald / Steve Jacobsen
	DL Danny Hill
	DL Mike Faulkner
	DL Nate Parker
	LB Chris Cosh
	LB Lewis Stuart
	DB Jerome Pannell
	DB Paul Davis / Lawrence Young
	DB Matt Mead
	DB Mike Schamus

RUSHING: Lawrence 177/791y
PASSING: Casey 105-190/1419y, 10TD, 55.3%
RECEIVING: Snell 43/706y
SCORING: Lawrence 54pts

1980 8-4

16 Wake Forest	7 WR Mike Giacolone
35 E. Tenn. St.	7 T Steve Wirt / Wayne Mutter
7 William & Mary	3 G Gary Smith
38 James Madison	6 C Roe Waldron
10 Clemson	13 G George Evans / Lowell Eakin
34 Rhode Island	7 T Wally Browne
30 Virginia	0 TE Rob Purdham
7 Richmond	18 QB Steve Casey / Jeff Bolton
34 West Virginia	11 TB Cyrus Lawrence / Johnnie Edmonds
7 Florida State	31 WB Sidney Snell
21 VMI	6 FB Scott Dovel
10 Miami■	20 DL Rick Miley
	DL Padro Phillips
	DL Mike Borden
	DL Mike Kovac
	DL Robert Brown
	LB Lewis Stuart / Mike Johnson
	LB Ashley Lee / Ron Luraschi
	DB Paul Davis
	DB Lawrence Young
	DB John Scott
	DB Carl McDonald / Jerome Pannell

RUSHING: Lawrence 271/1221y
PASSING: Casey 97-176/1119y, 13TD, 55.1%
RECEIVING: Snell 43/568y
SCORING: Lawrence & Snell 48pts

1981 7-4

28 Richmond	12 WR Tony McKee / Mike Giacolone
47 William & Mary	3 T Wayne Mutter / Gary Smith
30 Wake Forest	14 G George Evans / Tom Mehr
17 Memphis State	13 C Mark Udinski
7 Duke	14 G Jim Smith / Vincent Johnson
6 West Virginia	27 T Wally Browne
34 Appalachian St.	12 TE Rob Pardham
29 Kentucky	3 QB Steve Casey / Jeff Bolton
14 Miami	21 TB Cyrus Lawrence
0 VMI	6 WB Billy Hite
20 Virginia	3 FB Tony Paige
	DL Rick Miley
	DL Padro Phillips
	DL B.J. Zwinak
	DL Steve Jacobsen
	DL Robert Brown
	LB Mike Johnson / Ron Luraschi
	LB Ashley Lee
	DB Gillett Ford
	DB Jack Clarke
	DB Mike Scharnus / John Scott
	DB Jeremiah Thomas / George Yeager

RUSHING: Lawrence 325/1403y
PASSING: Casey 79-163/1083y, 4TD, 48.5%
RECEIVING: Giacolone 28/514y
SCORING: Don Wade (K) 62pts

1982 7-4

20 Richmond	9 WR Mike Giacolone / Tony McKee
8 Miami	14 T Ed Keiffer
47 William & Mary	3 G Jim Smith / Kent Thomas
10 Wake Forest	13 C Mark Udinski
22 Duke	21 G Vincent Johnson / George Evans
6 West Virginia	16 T Wally Browne
34 Appalachian St.	0 TE Mike Shaw
29 Kentucky	3 QB Todd Greenwood / Mark Cox
0 Vanderbilt	45 TB Billy Hite / Cyrus Lawrence
14 VMI	3 WB Steve Scaggs / Clarence Nelson
21 Virginia	14 FB Tony Paige
	DL Rick Miley
	DL Padro Phillips / James Patterson
	DL Thor Kritsky
	DL Bruce Smith
	DL David Marvel
	LB Mike Johnson
	LB James Robinson
	DB Gillett Ford / Derek Carter
	DB Jake Clarke
	DB John Scott / Ray Fitts
	DB Jeremiah Thomas / Bryan Burleigh

RUSHING: Hite 145/622y, Lawrence 70/352y, Paige 64/305y
PASSING: Greenwood 82-148/987y, 6TD, 55.4%
Cox 59-102/673y
RECEIVING: Giacolone 34/405y, Shaw 25/343y, Paige 20/152y
SCORING: Don Wade (K) 41pts, Lawrence 30pts, Shaw 26pts

1983 9-2

6 Wake Forest	13 WR Steve Ellsworth / Scott Rider
17 Memphis State	10 T Ed Keiffer / Tom Hartman
28 VMI	0 G Kent Thomas / Scott Cruise
31 Louisville	0 C Mark Johnson / Jon Ritz
27 Duke	14 G Vincent Johnson / Tom Mehr
0 West Virginia	13 T Billy Leeson / Stuart Plank
38 Richmond	0 TE Mike Shaw / Joe Jones
59 William & Mary	21 QB Mark Cox / Todd Greenwood
26 Tulane	10 TB Otis Copeland / Maurice Williams
21 Vanderbilt	10 WB Clarence Nelson
48 Virginia	0 FB Tony Paige / Nigel Bowe
	DL Jesse Penn
	DL James Patterson
	DL Orlando Williams / Robby Jackson
	DL Bruce Smith
	DL David Marvel / Cornell Urquhart
	LB Mike Johnson
	LB James Robinson / Noland Hazzard
	DB Derek Carter
	DB Jake Clarke / Leon Gordon
	DB Ashley Lee / Ray Fitts
	DB Bryan Burleigh / Bob Thomas

RUSHING: Copeland 158/709y, Williams 68/442y,
Eddie Hunter (TB) 61/395y
PASSING: Cox 86-156/1189y, 9TD, 55.1%
RECEIVING: Shaw 23/357y, Nelson 21/236y, Ellsworth 17/306y
SCORING: Don Wade (K) 61pts, Copeland 42pts,
Hunter & Williams 24pts

1984 8-4

21 Wake Forest	20 WR Donald Wayne Snell / Steve Ellsworth
7 West Virginia	14 T Scott Cruise
21 Richmond	13 G Vincent Johnson / Kent Thomas
23 Virginia	26 C Mark Johnson / Greg Brooks
54 VMI	7 G Tom Mehr
27 Duke	0 T Billy Leeson / Jim Davie
38 William & Mary	14 TE Joe Jones
9 Temple	7 QB Mark Cox / Todd Greenwood
13 Tulane	6 TB Maurice Williams
10 Clemson	17 WB Terrence Howell
23 Vanderbilt	3 FB Nigel Bowe
7 Air Force ■	23 DL Jesse Penn
	DL Morgan Roane
	DL Mark Webb
	DL Bruce Smith
	DL Cornell Urquhart
	LB Paul Nelson / Lawrence White
	LB Vince Daniels
	DB Derek Carter / Ray Fitts
	DB Leon Gordon
	DB Ashley Lee
	DB Bob Thomas / Bryan Burleigh

RUSHING: Williams 149/574y
PASSING: Cox 86-164/983y, 5TD, 52.4%
RECEIVING: Joe Jones 39/452y
SCORING: Don Wade (K) 60pts

1985 6-5

14 Cincinnati	31 WR Donald Wayne Snell / Steve Ellsworth
14 Richmond	24 T Stuart Plank / Ron Singleton
17 Clemson	20 G Kent Thomas / Kevin Keefe
24 Syracuse	14 C Mark Johnson / Bob Frulla
9 West Virginia	24 G Tom Mehr
40 William & Mary	10 T Scott Cruise / Jim Davie
28 Virginia	10 TE Terrence Howell / Greg Brooks
18 Florida	35 QB Mark Cox / Todd Greenwood
31 Memphis State	10 TB Maurice Williams / Eddie Hunter
41 Louisville	17 WB Desmar Becton / Allan Thomas
38 Vanderbilt	24 FB Earnie Jones
	DL Curtis Taliaferro / Noland Hazzard (DB)
	DL Horacio Moronto / Dwight Ausbrooks
	DL Mark Webb
	DL Ranier Coleman / Joe Turner
	DL Morgan Roane / Joe Ledbetter
	LB Paul Nelson / Lawrence White
	LB Jamal Agemy
	DB Ray Fitts
	DB Eric Hayes / Billy Myers
	DB Carter Wiley / Bo Blankenship
	DB Alan Harris

RUSHING: Williams 167/936y
PASSING: Greenwood 85-169/919y, 7TD, 50.3%
RECEIVING: Snell 31/369y
SCORING: Williams 54pts

1986 9-2-1

20 Cincinnati	24 WR Myron Richardson
20 Clemson	14 WR David Everett / Donald Wayne Snell
26 Syracuse	17 T Jim Davie / Todd Grantham
37 E. Tenn. St.	10 G Kevin Keefe
13 West Virginia	7 C John FitzHugh / Chris Henderson
27 South Carolina	27 G Tom Hall / Ernie Davis
13 Temple (F-W)	29 T Ron Singleton / Rodney Good
42 Virginia	10 TE Steve Johnson
17 Kentucky	15 QB Erik Chapman
17 Richmond	10 TB Maurice Williams / Eddie Hunter
29 Vanderbilt	21 FB Earnie Jones/Sean Donnelly/Rich Fox
25 N. Carolina St. ■	24 DL Curtis Taliaferro
	DL Scott Hill
	DL Mark Webb
	DL Horacio Moronto / Al Wiley
	DL Morgan Roane
	LB Lawrence White / Leslie Bailey
	LB Jamel Agemy / Randy Cockrell
	DB Scott Rice
	DB Billy Myers / Bo Blankenship
	DB Mitch Dove
	DB Carter Wiley / Eddie Neel

RUSHING: Williams 166/1029y
PASSING: Chapman 113-222/1627y, 10TD, 50.9%
RECEIVING: Snell 34/661y
SCORING: Chris Kinzer (K) 93pts

1987 2-9

10 Clemson	22 WR Myron Richardson
13 Virginia	14 WR Karl Borden / Nick Cullen
3 Syracuse	35 T Larry Peery
31 Navy	11 G Kevin Keefe / Tom Hall
10 South Carolina	40 C John FitzHugh / Mark Briscoe
23 East Carolina	32 G Glenn Watts / Ernie Davis
38 Tulane	57 T Todd Grantham
7 Kentucky	14 TE Steve Johnson / Brian McCall
16 West Virginia	28 QB Erik Chapman
13 Miami	27 TB Jon Jeffries / Ralph Brown
21 Cincinnati	20 FB Earnie Jones / Rich Fox
	DL Jimmy Whitten / Al Chamblee
	DL Scott Hill / Al Wiley
	DL Bo Cothran / Chris Matheny
	DL Joe Ledbetter / Rich Williams
	LB Randy Cockrell / Don Stokes
	LB Jock Jones
	LB Bobby Martin / Darwin Herdman
	DB Scott Rice
	DB Billy Myers
	DB Roger Brown
	DB Carter Wiley

RUSHING: Jeffries 125/599y
PASSING: Chapman 119-231/1340y, 10TD, 51.5%
RECEIVING: Johnson 38/475y
SCORING: Chris Kinzer (K) 47pts

1988 3-8

7 Clemson	40 WR Myron Richardson
27 East Carolina	16 WR Nick Cullen
13 Southern Miss	35 T Skip Pavlik
0 Syracuse	35 G Larry Peery / Glenn Watts
10 West Virginia	22 C Rob Vaughan
24 South Carolina	26 G William Boatwright / Tom Hall
41 Cincinnati	14 T Todd Grantham
10 Virginia	16 TE Brian McCall / Ken Barefoot, Jr.
3 Louisville	13 QB Will Furrer
14 Florida State	41 TB Ralph Brown / Jon Jeffries
27 James Madison	6 FB Phil Bryant / Rich Fox / Malcom Blacken
	DL Al Chamblee / Anthony Pack
	DL Scott Hill
	DL Horacio Moronta
	DL Jimmy Whitten
	LB Sean Lucas / Darwin Herdman
	LB Don Stokes / Bobby Martin
	LB Randy Cockrell / Leslie Bailey
	LB Jock Jones / Archie Hopkins
	DB John Granby
	DB Roger Brown / Damien Russell
	DB Scott Rice / Will Gowin

RUSHING: Brown 140/514y, Jeffries 98/383y, Blacken 65/247y
PASSING: Furrer 128-279/1384y, 6TD, 45.9%
RECEIVING: Richardson 36/583y, Cullen 24/271y, McCall 16/169y
SCORING: Chris Kinzer (K) 56pts, Brown 24pts, Jeffries 18pts

1989 6-4-1

29 Akron	3 WR Myron Richardson / Bo Campbell
17 South Carolina	17 WR Nick Cullen / Marcus Mickel
7 Clemson	27 T Eugene Chung
23 Temple	0 G Skip Pavlik / John Rehme
12 West Virginia	10 C Rob Vaughan
7 Florida State	41 G William Boatwright / Ernie Davis
10 East Carolina	14 T Jimmy Bryson
30 Tulane	13 TE Brian McCall
18 Vanderbilt	0 QB Will Furrer / Rodd Wooten
25 Virginia	32 TB Vaughn Hebron / Tony Kennedy
25 No. Carolina St.	23 FB Rich Fox / Phil Bryant
	DL Al Chamblee
	DL Scott Hill / Chris Matheny
	DL Bryan Campbell / Stephan Holloway
	DL Jimmy Whitten
	LB Bobby Martin / Darwin Herdman
	LB Randy Cockrell / Don Stokes
	LB Jock Jones / Anthony "Wooster" Pack
	LB Sean Lucas / Archie Hopkins
	DB John Granby / Karl Borden
	DB Roger Brown
	DB Damien Russell

RUSHING: Hebron 134/584y, Kennedy 137/534y
PASSING: Furrer 45-88/589y, 3TD, 51.1%
RECEIVING: Richardson 27/450y, Mickel 26/320y
SCORING: Mickey Thomas (K) 77pts

1990 6-5

13 Maryland	20 WR Nick Cullen / Bo Campbell
21 Bowling Green	7 WR Marcus Mickel
24 East Carolina	23 T Eugene Chung
24 South Carolina	35 G Glenn Watts / Todd Meade
28 Florida State	39 C Jim Pyne
26 West Virginia	21 G William Boatwright / John Rehme
28 Temple	31 T Marc Verniel / Chris Holt
20 Southern Miss.	16 TE Greg Daniels
20 No. Carolina St.	16 QB Will Furrer
3 Georgia Tech	6 TB Vaughn Hebron / Tony Kennedy
38 Virginia	13 FB Phil Bryant
	DL Al Chamblee / David Wimmer
	DL Jerome Preston
	DL Bryan Campbell / Stephan Holloway
	DL Jimmy Whitten / Wooster Pack
	LB Darwin Herdman / P.J. Preston
	LB Melendez Byrd
	LB Rusty Pendleton
	LB Archie Hopkins / Mark Scott
	DB Greg Lassiter / Karl Borden
	DB Tyronne Drakeford / Scott Rice
	DB Damien Russell / John Rivers

RUSHING: Hebron 133/640y, Kennedy 144/517y, Bryant 76/293y
PASSING: Furrer 173-296/2122y, 19TD, 58.4%
RECEIVING: Mickel 38/409y, Cullen 37/568y, Campbell 22/389y
SCORING: Mickey Thomas (K) 59pts, Kennedy & Hebron 42pts

1991 5-6

41 James Madison	12 WR Bo Campbell
0 N. Carolina St.	7 WR Steve Sanders
21 South Carolina	28 T Eugene Chung / Mike Smith
17 Oklahoma	27 G Damien McMahon
20 West Virginia	14 C Jim Pyne
20 Florida State	33 G William Boatwright
56 Cincinnati	9 T Marc Verniel / Chris Holt
41 Louisville	13 TE Greg Daniels / John Burke
42 Akron	24 QB Will Furrer
17 East Carolina	24 TB Tony Kennedy / Vaughn Hebron
0 Virginia	38 FB Phil Bryant / Mark Poindexter
	DL James Hargrove / Bernard Basham
	DL Jerome Preston
	DL Bryan Campbell
	DL Wooster Pack / Billy Swarm
	LB P.J. Preston
	LB Melendez Byrd
	LB Rusty Pendleton
	LB Ken Brown
	DB John Granby / Stacy Henley
	DB Tyronne Drakeford / Greg Lassiter
	DB Damien Russell / Kirk Alexander

RUSHING: Kennedy 143/684y
PASSING: Furrer 148-257/1820y, 15TD, 57.6%
RECEIVING: Campbell 29/494y
SCORING: Kennedy 66pts

1992 2-8-1

49 James Madison	20 WR Antonio Freeman
27 East Carolina	30 WR Steve Sanders
26 Temple	7 T Mike Smith
7 West Virginia	16 G Jared Hamlin
17 Louisville	21 C Jim Pyne
13 No. Carolina St.	13 G Chris Malone
23 Miami	43 T Marc Verniel / Marvin Arrington
49 Rutgers	50 TE John Burke
9 Syracuse	28 QB Maurice DeShazo
12 Southern Miss.	13 TB Vaughn Hebron / Tony Kennedy
38 Virginia	41 FB Mark Poindexter
	DL Bernard Basham
	DL Jerome Preston
	DL Don Davis
	DL Billy Swarm
	LB P.J. Preston
	LB Rusty Pendleton
	LB Melendez Byrd
	LB Ken Brown
	DB Tyronne Drakeford / John Rivers
	DB Stacy Henley
	DB Kirk Alexander

RUSHING: Hebron 105/579y
PASSING: DeShazo 101-215/1504y, 12TD, 47%
RECEIVING: Freeman 32/644y
SCORING: Ryan Williams (K) 64pts

1993 9-3

33 Bowling Green	16 WR Antonio Freeman
63 Pittsburgh	21 WR Steve Sanders / Cornelius White
2 Miami	21 T Chris Barry / Mike Bianchin
55 Maryland	28 G Damien McMahon
13 West Virginia	14 C Jim Pyne
55 Temple	7 G Chris Malone
49 Rutgers	42 T Billy Conaty / Jay Hagood
31 East Carolina	12 TE John Burke / Bryan Jennings
34 Boston College	48 QB Maurice DeShazo
45 Syracuse	24 TB Dwayne Thomas / Tommy Edwards
20 Virginia	17 FB Joe Swarm / Brian Edmonds
45 Indiana■	20 DL Lawrence Lewis
	DL J.C. Price
	DL Waverly Jackson
	DL Cornell Brown
	LB George DelRicco
	LB Ken Brown
	LB DeWayne Knight
	DB Tyronne Drakeford
	DB Scott Jones / William Yarborough
	DB Antonio Banks
	DB Torrian Gray

RUSHING: Thomas 214/1130y, Edwards 78/357y, Swarm 73/345y
PASSING: DeShazo 129-230/2080y, 22TD, 56.1%
RECEIVING: Freeman 32/644y, Sanders 29/552y, Still 15/260y
SCORING: Thomas 72pts, Ryan Williams (K) 66pts, Edwards 60pts

1994 8-4

34 Arkansas State	7 WR Antonio Freeman / Jermaine Holmes
24 Southern Miss.	14 WR Bryan Still / Cornelius White
12 Boston College	7 T Jay Hagood
34 West Virginia	6 G Chris Malone
20 Syracuse	28 C Billy Conaty
41 Temple	13 G Damien McMahon / Jared Hamlin
27 East Carolina	20 T Mike Bianchin / T.J. Washington
45 Pittsburgh	7 TE Kevin Martin / Bryan Jennings
3 Miami	24 QB Maurice DeShazo
41 Rutgers	34 TB D.Thomas/T. Edwards / Ken Oxendine
23 Virginia	42 FB Brian Edmonds
23 Tennessee■	45 DL Hank Coleman / Lawrence Lewis
	DL J.C. Price / Jeff Holland
	DL Waverly Jackson / Jim Baron
	DL Cornell Brown
	LB George DelRicco
	LB Ken Brown / Tony Morrison
	LB Brandon Semones
	DB Larry Green / Stacy Henley
	DB William Yarborough
	DB Antonio Banks
	DB Torrian Gray

RUSHING: Thomas 142/655y, Edwards 115/378y, Edmonds 55/290y
PASSING: DeShazo 164-296/2110y, 13TD, 55.4%
RECEIVING: Freeman 38/586y, Holmes 34/432y, Still 23/500y
SCORING: Ryan Williams (K) 78pts, Freeman 36pts, Thomas 30pts

1995 10-2

14 Boston College	20 WR Jermaine Holmes / Shawn Scales
0 Cincinnati	16 WR Bryan Still / Angelo Harrison
13 Miami	7 T Mike Bianchin / T.J. Washington
26 Pittsburgh	16 G Gennaro DiNapoli
14 Navy	0 C Billy Conaty
77 Akron	27 G Chris Malone / Todd Washington
45 Rutgers	17 T Jay Hagood / Anthony Kapp
27 West Virginia	0 TE Bryan Jennings
31 Syracuse	7 QB Jim Druckenmiller
38 Temple	16 TB Dwayne Thomas / Ken Oxendine
36 Virginia	29 FB Brian Edmonds / Marcus Parker
28 Texas■	10 DL Hank Coleman / Danny Wheel
	DL J.C. Price / Brad Baylor
	DL Jim Baron / Waverly Jackson
	DL Cornell Brown
	LB George DelRicco
	LB Myron Newsome
	LB Brandon Semones
	DB Larry Green
	DB Loren Johnson / Antonio Banks
	DB William Yarborough
	DB Torrian Gray / Korey Irby

RUSHING: Thomas 167/673y, Oxendine 106/593y, Parker 46/267y
PASSING: Druckenmiller 151-294/2103y, 14TD, 51.4%
RECEIVING: Still 32/628y, Holmes 29/468y, White 22/312y
SCORING: Atle Larsen (K) 69pts, Thomas 48pts, Holmes 42pts

1996 10-2

21 Akron	18 WR Shawn Scales / Michael Stuewe
45 Boston College	7 WR Cornelius White / Angelo Harrison
30 Rutgers	14 T T.J. Washington / Derek Smith
21 Syracuse	52 G Gennaro DiNapoli
38 Temple	0 C Billy Conaty
34 Pittsburgh	17 G Todd Washington / Dwight Vick
47 SW Louisiana	16 T Jay Hagood / William Flowers
35 East Carolina	14 TE Bryan Jennings / Pedro Edison
21 Miami	7 QB Jim Druckenmiller / Al Clark
31 West Virginia	14 TB Ken Oxehdine / Shyrone Stith
26 Virginia	9 FB Brian Edmonds / Marcus Parker
21 Nebraska■	41 DL John Engelberger / Chris Cyrus
	DL Kerwin Hairston / Carl Bradley
	DL Waverly Jackson
	DL Cornell Brown / Danny Wheel
	LB Steve Tate / Tyron Edmond
	LB Myron Mewsome / Jamel Smith
	LB Brandon Semones / Korey Irby
	DB Loren Johnson
	DB Antonio Banks / Anthony Midget
	DB Torrian Gray / Keion Carpenter
	DB Pierson Prioleau

RUSHING: Oxendine 150/890y, Stith 89/474y, Parker 82/467y
PASSING: Druckenmiller 142-250/2071y, 17TD, 56.8%
RECEIVING: Scales 30/510y, White 30/449y, Stuewe 25/385y
SCORING: Oxendine 78pts, Shayne Graham (K) 69pts, Edmonds 36pts

1997 7-5

59 Rutgers	19 WR Shawn Scales / Michael Stuewe
31 Syracuse	3 WR Angelo Harrison / Marcus
Gildersleeve	
23 Temple	13 T Derek Smith
50 Arkansas State	0 G Gennaro DiNapoli
17 Miami (Ohio)	24 C Todd Washington
17 Boston College	7 G Dwight Vick / Josh Redding
17 West Virginia	30 T Brad Baylor / Dave Kadela
7 Ala.-Birm'ham	25 QB Al Clark / Nick Sorensen
27 Miami	34 TB Ken Oxendine / Lamont Pegues
23 Pittsburgh	30 FB Marcus Parker / Cullen Hawkins
20 Virginia	42 DL John Engelberger
3 North Carolina■	DL Kerwin Hairston
	DL Nat Williams / Carl Bradley
	DL Danny Wheel / Corey Moore
	LB Steve Tate / Michael Hawkes
	LB Jamel Smith
	LB Cory Bird
	DB Loren Johnson / Ike Charlton
	DB Anthony Midget
	DB Keion Carpenter / Lorenzo Ferguson
	DB Pierson Prioleau

RUSHING: Oxendine 237/904y
PASSING: Clark 110-192/1476y, 10TD, 57.3%
RECEIVING: Parker 20/212y
SCORING: Shayne Graham (K) 92pts

1998 9-3

38 East Carolina	3 WR Ricky Hall / Marcus Gildersleeve
37 Clemson	0 WR Angelo Harrison / Ken Handy
27 Miami	20 T Derek Smith
27 Pittsburgh	7 G Dwight Vick / Matt Lehr
17 Boston College	0 C Tim Schnecker / Keith Short
24 Temple	58 G Joe Marchant / Josh Redding
41 Ala.-Birm'ham	0 T Dave Kadela
27 West Virginia	13 TE Derek Carter
26 Syracuse	28 QB Al Clark / Nick Sorensen
47 Rutgers	7 TB Lamont Pegues / Shyrone Stith
32 Virginia	36 FB Jarrett Ferguson / Cullen Hawkins
38 Alabama■	7 DL John Engelberger / Chris Cyrus
	DL Carl Bradley
	DL Nat Williams
	DL Corey Moore / Ryan Smith
	LB Michael Hawkes
	LB Jamel Smith
	LB Lorenzo Ferguson / Phillip Summers
	DB Loren Johnson / Anthony Midget
	DB Ike Charlton
	DB Keion Carpenter
	DB Pierson Prioleau / Cory Bird

RUSHING: Pegues 178/745y, Stith 133/699y, Ferguson 34/199y
PASSING: Clark 77-148/1050y, 9TD, 48.6%
Sorenson 31-59/306y, 2TD, 52.5%
RECEIVING: Hall 37/650y, Harrison 18/212y, Hawkins 8/82y
SCORING: Shayne Graham (K) 103pts, Hall 60pts, Pegues 42pts

1999 11-1

47 James Madison	0 WR Ricky Hall / Emmett Johnson
31 Ala.-Birm'ham	10 WR Andre Davis / Terrell Parham
31 Clemson	11 T Anthony Lambo
31 Virginia	9 G Matt Lehr
58 Rutgers	20 C Keith Short / Steve DeMasi
62 Syracuse	0 G Josh Redding
30 Pittsburgh	17 T Dave Kadela
22 West Virginia	20 TE Derek Carter / Browning Wynn
43 Miami	10 QB Michael Vick
62 Temple	7 TB Shyrone Stith / Andre Kendrick
38 Boston College	14 FB Jarrett Ferguson / Cullen Hawkins
29 Florida State■	46 DL John Engelberger / Chris Cyrus
	DL Nathaniel Williams / Chad Beasley
	DL Carl Bradley / David Pugh
	DL Corey Moore / Derrius Monroe
	LB Jamel Smith
	LB Michael Hawkes
	LB Ben Taylor / Tee Butler
	DB Anthony Midget / Ronyell Whitaker
	DB Ike Charlton / Larry Austin
	DB Nick Sorensen
	DB Cory Bird / Phillip Summers

RUSHING: Stith 226/1119y, Kendrick 103/645y, Vick 108/585y
PASSING: Vick 90-152/1840y, 12TD, 59.2%
RECEIVING: Davis 35/962y, Hall 25/398y, Johnson 10/147y
SCORING: Shayne Graham (K) 107pts, Stith 78pts, Davis 72pts

2000 11-1

52 Akron	23 WR Emmett Johnson
45 East Carolina	28 WR Andre Davis / Shawn Witten
49 Rutgers	0 T Anthony Lambo
48 Boston College	34 G Matt Lehr
35 Temple	13 C Steve DeMasi / Jake Grove
48 West Virginia	20 G Josh Redding / Luke Owens
22 Syracuse	14 T Dave Kadela
37 Pittsburgh	34 TE Browning Wynn / Bob Slowikowski
21 Miami	41 QB Michael Vick
44 C. Florida	21 TB Lee Suggs / Andre Kendrick
42 Virginia	21 FB Jarrett Ferguson / Cullen Hawkins
41 Clemson■	20 DL Nathaniel Adibi / Jim Davis
	DL Chad Beasley / Channing Reed
	DL David Pugh / Dan Wilkinson
	DL Lamar Cobb / Cols Colas
	LB Ben Taylor
	LB Jake Housewright / Brian Welch
	LB Phillip Summers / Nick Sorensen
	DB Ronyell Whitaker
	DB Larry Austin / Eric Green
	DB Willie Pile / Kevin McCadam
	DB Cory Bird / Billy Hardee

RUSHING: Suggs 222/1207y, Vick 104/617y, Kendrick 107/547y
PASSING: Vick 87-161/1234y, 8TD, 54%
RECEIVING; Johnson 34/574y, Davis 24/318y, Wilford 12/141y
SCORING: Suggs 168pts, Carter Warley (K) 77pts, Vick 48pts

2001 8-4

52 Connecticut	10 WR Emmett Johnson / Ernest Wilford
31 W. Michigan	0 WR Andre Davis / Shawn Witten
50 Rutgers	0 T Anthony Davis
46 C. Florida	14 G Luke Owens
35 West Virginia	0 C Steve DeMasi
34 Boston College	20 G Jake Grove / James Miller
14 Syracuse	22 T Matt Wincek
7 Pittsburgh	38 TE Bob Slowikowski / Browning Wynn
35 Temple	0 QB Grant Noel
31 Virginia	17 TB Kevin Jones / Keith Burnell
24 Miami	26 FB Jarrett Ferguson / Doug Easlick
17 Florida State■	30 DL Nathaniel Adibi
	DL Chad Beasley
	DL David Pugh
	DL Lamar Cobb / Cols Colas
	LB Mike Daniels / Deon Provitt
	LB Jake Houseright / Brian Welch
	LB Ben Taylor / Vegas Robinson
	DB Larry Austin / DeAngelo Hall
	DB Ronyell Whitaker
	DB Willie Pile / Vincent Fuller
	DB Kevin McCadam / Michael Crawford

RUSHING: Jones 195/957y, Burnell 151/708y, Ferguson 38/169y
PASSING: Noel 161-281/2095y, 17TD, 57.3%
RECEIVING: Davis 44/781y, Ferguson 30/288y, Witten 16/161y
SCORING: Carter Warley (K) 82pts, Davis & Burnell 54pts

2002 10-4

63 Arkansas State	7 WR Ernest Wilford
26 LSU	8 WR Shawn Witten / Terrell Parham
47 Marshall	21 T Anthony Davis
13 Texas A&M	3 G Jacob Gibson
30 W. Michigan	0 C Jake Grove
28 Boston College	23 G Luke Owens / James Miller
35 Rutgers	14 T Jimmy Martin
20 Temple	10 TE Keith Willis
21 Pittsburgh	28 QB Bryan Randall
42 Syracuse	50 TB Lee Suggs / Kevin Jones
18 West Virginia	21 FB Doug Easlick
21 Virginia	9 DL Nathaniel Adibi
45 Miami	56 DL Jason Lallis
20 Air Force ■	13 DL Kevin Lewis
	DL Cols Colas / Lamar Cobb
	LB Brandon Manning / Mike Daniels
	LB Mikal Baaqee
	LB Vegas Robinson
	DB DeAngelo Hall / Garnell Wilds
	DB Ronyell Whitaker
	DB Willie Pile
	DB Michael Crawford / Billy Hardee

RUSHING: Suggs 257/1329y, Jones 160/874y, Randall 171/539y
PASSING: Randall 158-248/2134y, 12TD, 63.7%
RECEIVING: Wilford 51/925y, Witten 25/306y, Parham 18/156y
SCORING: Suggs 144pts, Carter Warley (K) 63pts, Jones 54pts

2003 8-5

49 C. Florida	28 WR Ernest Wilford / Chris Shreve
43 James Madison	0 WR Justin Hamilton / Richard Johnson
35 Texas A&M	19 T Jimmy Martin
47 Connecticut	13 G Will Montgomery
48 Rutgers	22 C Jake Grove
51 Syracuse	7 G Jacob Gibson / James Miller
7 West Virginia	28 T Jon Dunn
31 Miami	7 TE Keith Willis / Jeff King
28 Pittsburgh	31 QB Bryan Randall / Marcus Vick
24 Temple	23 TB Kevin Jones / Cedric Humes
27 Boston College	34 FB Doug Easlick
21 Virginia	35 DL Nathaniel Adibi / Darryl Tapp
49 California ■	52 DL Kevin Lewis / Tim Sandridge
	DL Jonathan Lewis
	DL Cols Colas
	LB Brandon Manning / Aaron Rouse
	LB Mikal Baaqee / Jordan Trott
	LB Vegas Robinson
	DB DeAngelo Hall / Vincent Fuller
	DB Garnell Wilds / Eric Green
	DB Jimmy Williams
	DB Michael Crawford

RUSHING: Jones 281/1647y, Randall 82/404y, Humes 65/380y
PASSING: Randall 150-245/1996y, 15TD, 61.2%
RECEIVING: Wilford 55/886y, Hamilton 23/282y,
Easlick 16/132y, Jones 14/161y
SCORING: Jones 126pts, Carter Warley (K) 90pts, Hall 36pts

2004 10-3

13 Southern Cal	24 WR Eddie Royal
63 W. Michigan	0 WR Josh Hyman
41 Duke	17 T Jimmy Martin
16 N. Carolina St.	17 G Jason Murphy / Reggie Butler
19 West Virginia	13 C Will Montgomery
17 Wake Forest	0 G James Miller
62 Florida A&M	28 T Jon Dunn
34 Georgia Tech	20 TE Jeff King
27 North Carolina	24 QB Bryan Randall
55 Maryland	6 TB Mike Imoh / Cedric Humes
24 Virginia	10 FB/TE John Kinzer / Jared Mazzetta
16 Miami	10 DL Jim Davis / Chris Ellis
13 Auburn ■	16 DL Noland Burchette
	DL Jonathan Lewis
	DL Darryl Tapp
	LB James Anderson / Aaron Rouse
	LB Mikal Baaqee / Xavier Adibi
	LB Vince Hall / Blake Warren
	DB Eric Green
	DB Jimmy Williams
	DB Vincent Fuller / Mike Daniels
	DB James Griffin

RUSHING: Imoh 158/720y, Humes 130/605y, Randall 136/511y
PASSING: Randall 170-306/2264y, 21TD, 55.6%
RECEIVING: Royal 28/470y, Hyman 27/491y, King 25/304y
SCORING: Brandon Pace (K) 106pts, Imoh 36pts, Hyman &
Humes 30pts

2005 11-2

20 N. Carolina St.	16 WR Eddie Royal / Josh Morgan
45 Duke	0 WR David Clowney / Josh Hyman
45 Ohio Univ.	0 T Jimmy Martin
51 Georgia Tech	7 G Will Montgomery (C) / Reggie Butler
34 West Virginia	17 C Danny McGrath
41 Marshall	14 G Jason Murphy
28 Maryland	9 T Duane Brown
30 Boston College	10 TE Jeff King
7 Miami	17 TE/FB John Klinzer / Jesse Allen
52 Virginia	14 QB Marcus Vick
30 North Carolina	3 TB Cedric Humes/Mike Imoh/Branden Ore
22 Florida State □	27 DL Darryl Tapp / Orion Martin
35 Louisville ■	24 DL Jonathan Lewis
	DL Tim Sandidge / Carlton Powell
	DL Chris Ellis / Noland Burchette
	LB Vince Hall
	LB Xavier Adibi
	LB James Anderson
	DB Roland Minor / Brandon Flowers
	DB Jimmy Williams
	DB Justin Hamilton / D.J. Parker
	DB Aaron Rouse

RUSHING: Humes 162/752y, Ore 109/647y, Imoh 106/419y
PASSING: Vick 177-289/2393y, 17TD, 61.2%
RECEIVING: Clowney 34/619y, Morgan 28/471y, Royal 27/315y
SCORING: Brandon Pace (K) 108pts, Humes 66pts,
Vick, King & Ore 36pts

2006 10-3

38 Northeastern	0 WR Josh Morgan / Justin Harper
35 North Carolina	10 WR Eddie Royal / David Clowney
36 Duke	0 T Brandon Frye / Brandon Gore
29 Cincinnati	13 G Ryan Shuman / Nick Marshman
27 Georgia Tech	38 C Danny McGrath
3 Boston College	22 G Sergio Render
36 Southern Miss	6 T Duane Brown
24 Clemson	7 TE Greg Boone / Ed Wang
17 Miami	10 QB Sean Glennon
23 Kent State	0 TB Branden Ore / Kenny Lewis
27 Wake Forest	6 FB/TE Jesse Allen / Sam Wheeler
17 Virginia	0 DL Chris Ellis / Orion Martin
24 Georgia ■	31 DL Carlton Powell
	DL Barry Booker
	DL Noland Burchette
	LB Brenden Hill
	LB Vince Hall
	LB Xavier Adibi
	DB Brandon Flowers
	DB Victor Harris
	DB D.J. Parker
	DB Aaron Rouse / Cary Wade

RUSHING: Ore 241/1137y, Lewis 54/215y
PASSING: Glennon 170-302/2191y, 11TD, 56.3%
RECEIVING: Clowney 34/424y, Morgan 33/448y, Royal 31/497y
SCORING: Ore 102pts, Brandon Pace (K) 92pts,
Morgan & Royal 24pts

2007 11-3

17 East Carolina	7 WR Josh Morgan
7 LSU	48 WR Eddie Royal / Josh Hyman
28 Ohio	7 WR/FB Justin Harper/Carlton Weatherford
44 William & Mary	3 T Duane Brown
17 North Carolina	10 G Nick Marshman (T)/Richard Graham
41 Clemson	23 C Ryan Sherman / Beau Warren
43 Duke	14 G Sergio Render
10 Boston College	14 T Ed Wang
27 Georgia Tech	3 TE Sam Wheeler / Greg Boone
40 Florida State	21 QB Sean Glennon / Tyrod Taylor
44 Miami	14 RB Branden Ore / Kenny Lewis
33 Virginia	21 DL Chris Ellis
30 Boston College □	16 DL Carlton Powell / Kory Robertson
21 Kansas ■	24 DL Barry Booker
	DL Orion Martin / Nekos Brown
	LB Cam Martin / Cody Grimm
	LB Vince Hall / Brett Warren
	LB Xavier Adibi
	DB Brandon Flowers
	DB Victor Harris
	DB D.J. Parker
	DB Kam Chancellor

RUSHING: Ore 267/992y, Taylor 102/429y, Lewis 57/205y
PASSING: Glennon 143-235/1796y, 12TD, 60.9%
Taylor 72-134/927y, 5TD, 53.7%
RECEIVING: Morgan 46/552y, Harper 41/635y, Royal 33/496y
SCORING: Jed Dunlevy (K) 108pts, Ore 60pts,
Harper, Royal & Taylor 36pts

2008 10-4

22 East Carolina	27 WR Jarrett Boykin / Dyrell Roberts
24 Furman	7 WR Danny Coale
20 Georgia Tech	17 T Ed Wang
20 North Carolina	17 G Nick Marshman / Jaymes Brooks
35 Nebraska	30 C Ryan Shuman
27 W. Kentucky	13 G Sergio Render
23 Boston College	28 T Blake DeChrostopher/Richard Graham
20 Florida State	30 TE Greg Boone / Chris Drager
23 Maryland	13 QB Tyrod Taylor / Sean Glennon
14 Miami	16 TB Darren Evans / Kenny Lewis, Jr.
14 Duke	3 FB/TE Devin Perez / Andre Smith
17 Virginia	14 DL Jason Worilds / Nekos Brown
30 Boston College □	12 DL John Graves
20 Cincinnati ■	7 DL Cordarrow Thompson
	DL Orion Martin
	LB Brett Warren
	LB Purnell Sturdivant
	LB Cam Martin / Cody Grimm
	DB V. Harris (WR) / Rashad Carmichael
	DB Stephan Virgil
	DB Kam Chancellor
	DB Dorian Porch / Davon Morgan

RUSHING: Evans 287/1265y, Taylor 147/738y, Lewis 64/237y
PASSING: Taylor 99-137/1036y, 2TD, 57.2%
Glennon 65-108/743y, 3TD, 60.2%
RECEIVING: Coale 36/408y, Boykin 30/441y, Boone 22/278y
SCORING: Dustin Keys (K) 101pts, Evans 66pts, Taylor 42pts

2009 10-3

24 Alabama	34 WR Danny Coale
52 Marshall	10 WR Jarrett Boykin / Xavier Boyer
16 Nebraska	15 WR/TE Dyrell Roberts / Andre Smith
31 Miami	7 T Ed Wang
34 Duke	26 G Sergio Render / Greg Nosal
48 Boston College	14 C Beau Warren / Michael Via
23 Georgia Tech	28 G Jaymes Brooks
17 North Carolina	20 T Blake DeChristopher / Andrew Lanier
16 East Carolina	3 TE G. Boone/Sam Wheeler/Ken Jefferson
36 Maryland	9 QB Tyrod Taylor
38 N. Carolina St.	10 TB Ryan Williams
42 Virginia	13 DL Jason Worilds
37 Tennessee ■	14 DL John Graves / Demetrius Taylor
	DL Cordarrow Thompson
	DL Nekos Brown
	LB Jake Johnson / Lyndell Gibson
	LB Barquell Rivers / Alonzo Tweedy
	LB Cody Grimm / Cam Martin
	DB Rashad Carmichael / Cris Hill
	DB Stephan Virgil / Eddie Whitley
	DB Kam Chancellor
	DB Dorian Porch / Davon Morgan

RUSHING: Williams 293/1655y, Taylor 106/370y,
Josh Oglesby (TB) 78/335y
PASSING: Taylor 136-243/2311y, 13TD, 56.0%
RECEIVING: Boykin 40/835y, Coale 30/614y, Roberts 22/390y
SCORING: Williams 132pts, Matt Waldron (K) 108pts, Boykin 36pts

2010 11-3

30 Boise State	33 WR Jarrett Boykin
16 James Madison	21 WR Danny Coale / Marcus Davis
49 East Carolina	27 T Andrew Lanier
19 Boston College	0 G Greg Nosal / David Nang
41 N. Carolina St.	30 C Beau Warren
45 C. Michigan	21 G Jaymes Brooks
52 Wake Forest	21 T Blake DeChristopher
44 Duke	7 TE Andre Smith / Eric Martin
28 Georgia Tech	21 QB Tyrod Taylor
26 North Carolina	10 TB Darren Evans / Ryan Wailams
31 Miami	17 FB/WR Kenny Younger / Dyrel Roberts
37 Virginia	7 DL Steven Friday / J.R. Collins
44 Florida State □	33 DL John Graves
12 Stanford ■	40 DL Antoine Hopkins
	DL Chris Drager / James Gayle
	LB Bruce Taylor / Tariq Edwards
	LB Jack Tyler / Lyndell Gibson
	LB/DB Jeron Gouveia-Winslow / Kyle Fuller
	DB Rashad Carmichael
	DB Jayron Hosley
	DB Eddie Whitley / Antone Exum
	DB Davon Morgan

RUSHING: Evans 151/854y, Taylor 146/659y,
David Wilson (TB) 113/619y, Williams 110/477y
PASSING: Taylor 188-315/2743y, 24TD, 59.7%
RECEIVING: Boykins 53/847y, Coale 39/732y, Roberts 21/303y
SCORING: Chris Hazley (K) 116pts, Evans & Williams 66pts

WAKE FOREST

Wake Forest University (Founded 1834)
Winston-Salem, North Carolina (Wake Forest, N.C., prior to 1956)
Nickname: Demon Deacons
Colors: Old Gold and Black
Stadium: BB&T Field at Groves Stadium (1968) 31,500
Affiliations: Southern Conference (1936-52),
  Atlantic Coast Conference (1953-present)

CAREER RUSHING YARDS	Attempts	Yards
Chris Barclay (2002-05)	840	4036
James McDougald (1976-79)	895	3865
Michael Ramseur (1982-85)	753	3325
Tarance Williams (1999-2002)	575	2581
Morgan Kane (1996-99)	647	2550
Topper Clemons (1982-85)	506	2479
John Leach (1990-93)	474	2246
Larry Hopkins (1970-71)	452	2212
Anthony Williams (1988-91)	511	2203
Larry Russell (1969-71)	639	1923

CAREER PASSING YARDS	Comp.-Att.	Yards
Riley Skinner (2006-09)	903-1349	9762
Brian Kuklick (1994-98)	665-1230	8017
Mike Elkins (1985-88)	609-1109	7304
Gary Schofield (1981-83)	640-1113	7205
Jay Venuto (1979-80)	412-776	5056
Rusty LaRue (1992-95)	472-786	5016
Keith West (1989-92)	365-683	4747
James MacPherson (1999-2002)	349-639	4716
Norman Snead (1958-60)	272-601	4040
Phil Barnhill (1987-90)	310-656	3931

CAREER RECEIVING YARDS	Caught	Yards
Ricky Proehl (1986-89)	188	2949
Desmond Clark (1995-98)	216	2834
Jammie Deese (1996-99)	184	2348
Wayne Baumgardner (1978-81)	135	2303
Todd Dixon (1990-93)	134	2300
James Brim (1983-86)	153	2040
Jason Anderson (2001-04)	115	2066
Red O'Quinn (1946-49)	122	1974
Thabiti Davis (1994-97)	161	1865
Steve Brown (1987-90)	122	1678

SEASON RUSHING YARDS	Attempts	Yards
Larry Hopkins (1971)	249	1228
James McDougald (1979)	260	1177
Morgan Kane (1999)	275	1161
Chris Barclay (2005)	218	1127
John Leach (1993)	215	1089

SEASON PASSING YARDS	Comp.-Att.	Yards
Riley Skinner (2009)	264-400	3160
Rusty LaRue (1995)	264-421	2775
Brian Kuklick (1998)	216-396	2683
Jay Venuto (1980)	214-413	2624
Gary Schofield (1981)	241-404	2572

SEASON RECEIVING YARDS	Catches	Yards
Ricky Proehl (1989)	65	1053
Kenneth Moore (2007)	98	1011
Wayne Baumgardner (1979)	55	1000
Desmond Clark (1997)	72	950
James Brim (1986)	66	930

GAME RUSHING YARDS	Attempts	Yards
John Leach (1993 vs. Maryland)	46	329
James McDougald (1976 vs. Clemson)	45	249
Nub Smith (1949 vs. William & Mary)	N/A	246

GAME PASSING YARDS	Comp.-Att.	Yards
Rusty LaRue (1995 vs. N. Carolina St.)	50-67	545
Gary Schofield (1981 vs. Maryland)	43-62	504
Rusty LaRue (1995 vs. Georgia Tech)	41-65	501

GAME RECEIVING YARDS	Catches	Yards
Wayne Baumgardner (1980 vs. So. Car.)	12	271
John Henry Mills (1990 vs. Duke)	14	230
James Brim (1986 vs. N. Carolina St.)	15	194
Fabian Davis (2000 vs. Navy)	N/A	194

GREATEST COACH

When thinking of schools as graveyards for coaches, one usually does not come up with Wake Forest. Yet, the Demon Deacons have gone through a dozen coaches since 1953.

So, a round of applause is due the current Wake Forest coach Jim Grobe. Grobe has done a magnificent job bringing the Deacons to a competitive level and finally the 2006 Atlantic Coast Conference championship. By the combined virtue of lack of student body size and strong academic requirements that at least approach the levels of ACC rivals Duke, North Carolina, and Virginia, Wake Forest faces an uphill battle every year in trying to stay abreast of league giants like Clemson, Florida State, and Miami.

Grobe owns the only winning record of any Wake Forest coach since D.C. Walker left the school in 1950.

WAKE FOREST'S 55 GREATEST SINCE 1953

\OFFENSE

WIDE RECEIVER: Desmond Clark, Jammie Deese, Todd Dixon, Kenneth Moore, Ricky Proehl
TIGHT END: Phil Denfield, Pete Manning, John Henry Mills, Steve Young
TACKLE: Ben Coleman, Tim Morrison, Steve Vallos
GUARD: Bill Ard, Bill Bobbora, Michael Collins, Paul Kiser
CENTER: Steve Justice, Eddie Moore, Larry Tearry
QUARTERBACK: Brian Kuklick, Riley Skinner, Norman Snead, Jay Venuto
RUNNING BACK: Chris Barclay, Bill Barnes, James McDougald
FULLBACK: Larry Hopkins, Brian Piccolo

DEFENSE

END: Calvin Pace, Gary Baldinger, Mike McCrary, Bill Ruby
TACKLE: Bob Bartholomew, Win Headley, Fred Robbins
NOSE GUARD: James Parker
LINEBACKER: Jon Abbate, Nick Arcaro, Carlos Bradley, Don Cervi, Aaron Curry, John Mazalewski
CORNERBACK: Ronnie Burgess, A.J. Greene, Alphonso Smith, Riley Swanson
SAFETY: Bill Armstrong, Richard Goodpasture, Andy Harper, Digit Laughridge

SPECIAL TEAMS

PLACE KICKER: Ryan Plackemeier, Sam Swank
PUNTER: Harry Newsome, Chuck Ramsey

MULTIPLE POSITIONS

GUARD-FULLBACK-LINEBACKER: Gerald Huth

PERFORMANCE FORMULA:
WAKE FOREST'S 10 BEST SEASONS

2006	1.3355	22 of 72
2007	1.2651	23 of 70
2008	1.2007	34 of 71
1979	1.1806	30 of 70
1992	1.1597	29 of 70
1970	1.1308	30 of 70
1999	1.1036	35 of 71
2002	1.0834	46 of 70
1959	1.0741	41 of 70
1987	1.0721	35 of 69

WAKE FOREST DEMON DEACONS

Year	W-L-T	AP Poll	Conference Standing	Toughest Regular Season Opponents	Coach (Record at School)	Bowl Games		
1953	3-6-1		3t	Duke 7-2-1, Maryland 10-0, West Virginia 8-1	Tom Rogers			
1954	2-7-1		6	Virginia Tech 8-0-1, Maryland 7-2-1, Duke 7-2-1	Tom Rogers			
1955	5-4-1		4	West Virginia 8-2, Maryland 10-0, Clemson 7-3, Duke 7-2-1	Tom Rogers (21-25-4)			
1956	2-5-3		8	Clemson 7-1-2, Virginia Tech 7—2-1, South Carolina 7-3	Paul Amen			
1957	0-10		8	Florida 6-2-1, Duke 6-2-2, NC State 7-1-2, West Virginia 7-2-1	Paul Amen			
1958	3-7		6	Florida State 7-3, Clemson 8-2, Auburn 9-0-1	Paul Amen			
1959	6-4		4t	Virginia Tech 6-4, Clemson 8-2, South Carolina 6-4	Paul Amen (11-26-3)			
1960	2-8		6t	Clemson 6-4, Maryland 6-4, NC State 6—3-1, Duke 7-3, LSU 5-4-1	Bill Hillebrand			
1961	4-6		5t	Duke 7-3, Auburn 6-4, Maryland 7-3	Bill Hillebrand			
1962	0-10		8	Army 6-4, Maryland 6-4, Clemson 6-4, Duke 8-2	Bill Hillebrand			
1963	1-9		7	Virginia Tech 8-2, North Carolina 8-2, Army 7-3, NC State 8-2	Bill Hillebrand (7-33)			
1964	5-5		3t	Virginia Tech 6-4, North Carolina 5-5, Maryland 5-5, NC State 5-5	Bill Tate			
1965	3-7		8	Virginia Tech 7-3, NC State 6-4, Duke 6-4	Bill Tate			
1966	3-7		6	Clemson 6-4, Virginia Tech 8-1-1, Memphis State 7-2, Florida St. 6-4	Bill Tate			
1967	4-6		5	Clemson 6-4, Houston 7-3, NC State 8-2, Tulsa 7-3	Bill Tate			
1968	2-7-1		6	Virginia Tech 7-3, Purdue 8-2, Florida State 8-2	Bill Tate (17-32-1)			
1969	3-7		7	Auburn 8-2, North Carolina 5-5, South Carolina 7-3	Cal Stoll			
1970	6-5		1	Virginia Tech 6-4, No. Carolina 5-5, Maryland 5-5, NC State 5-5	Cal Stoll			
1971	6-5		3t	North Carolina 9-2, Duke 6-5, South Carolina 6-5	Cal Stoll (15-17)			
1972	2-9		7t	SMU 7-4, Tennessee 9-2, NC State 7-3-1, North Carolina 10-1	Tom Harper (2-9)			
1973	1-9-1		8	Texas 8-2, South Carolina 7-4, Maryland 8-3, NC State 8-3	Chuck Mills			
1974	1-10		8	NC State 9-2, Oklahoma 11-0, Penn State 9-2, Maryland 8-3	Chuck Mills			
1975	3-8		4	NC State 7-3-1, Maryland 8-2-1, Virginia Tech 8-3	Chuck Mills			
1976	5-6		3	Michigan 10-1, Maryland 11-0, North Carolina 9-2	Chuck Mills			
1977	1-10		8	NC State 7-4, North Carolina 8-2-1, Maryland 7-4, Clemson 8-2-1	Chuck Mills (11-43-1)			
1978	1-10		6	LSU 8-3, NC State 8-3, Purdue 8-2-1, Maryland 9-2, Clemson 10-1	John Mackovic			
1979	8-4		2t	North Carolina 7-3-1, Auburn 8-3, Clemson 8-3, South Carolina 8-3	John Mackovic	Citrus	10 Louisiana State	34
1980	5-6		4t	Va. Tech 8-3, North Carolina 10-1, Maryland 8-3, South Carolina 8-3	John Mackovic (14-20)			
1981	4-7		6	Virginia Tech 7-4, North Carolina 9-2, Clemson 11-0	Al Groh			
1982	3-8		7	Auburn 8-3, Maryland 8-3, Clemson 9-1-1	Al Groh			
1983	4-7		6t	Virginia Tech 9-2, North Carolina 8-3, Maryland 8-3, Clemson 9-1-1	Al Groh			
1984	6-5		4	Virginia Tech 8-3, Maryland 8-3, Virginia 7-2-2, Clemson 7-4	Al Groh			
1985	4-7		8	Tennessee 8-2-1, Maryland 8-3, Georgia Tech 8-2-1	Al Groh			
1986	5-6		6t	NC State 8-2-1, North Carolina 7-3-1, Clemson 7-2-2	Al Groh (26-40)			
1987	7-4		3t	Virginia 7-4, Clemson 9-2, South Carolina 8-3	Bill Dooley			
1988	6-4-1		4t	NC State 7-3-1, Michigan 8-2-1, Clemson 9-2, Duke 7-3-1	Bill Dooley			
1989	2-8-1		7	Virginia 10-2, Clemson 9-2, Duke 8-3	Bill Dooley			
1990	3-8		8	North Carolina 6-4-1, Virginia 8-3, Clemson 9-2, Georgia Tech 10-0-1	Bill Dooley			
1991	3-8		8	NC State 9-2, Virginia 8-2-1, Clemson 9-1-1	Bill Dooley			
1992	8-4	25	4t	North Carolina 8-3, Florida State 10-1, NC State 9-2-1	Bill Dooley (29-36-2)	Independence	39 Oregon	35
1993	2-9		9	North Carolina 10-2, Clemson 8-3, Florida State 11-1	Jim Caldwell			
1994	3-8		7t	Florida St. 9-1-1, Virginia 8-3, NC State 8-3, Duke 8-3, No. Carolina 8-3	Jim Caldwell			
1995	1-10		9	Appalachian St. 11-0, Clemson 8-3, Virginia 8-4, Florida State 9-2	Jim Caldwell			
1996	3-8		8	Northwestern 9-2, North Carolina 9-2, Florida State 11-0	Jim Caldwell			
1997	5-6		6t	Virginia 7-4, North Carolina 10-1, Clemson 7-4, Florida State 10-1	Jim Caldwell			
1998	3-8		6t	Air Force 10-1, Virginia 9-2, Florida State 11-1, Georgia Tech 9-2	Jim Caldwell			
1999	7-5		5t	Florida State 11-0, Georgia Tech 8-3	Jim Caldwell	Aloha	23 Arizona State	3
2000	2-9		8	Clemson 9-2, Georgia Tech 9-2, Florida State 11-1	Jim Caldwell (26-63)			
2001	6-5		7t	Maryland 10-1, NC State 7-4, North Carolina 7-5, Georgia Tech 7-5	Jim Grobe			
2002	7-6		7	NC State 10-3, Florida State 9-4, Maryland 10-3	Jim Grobe	Seattle	38 Oregon	17
2003	5-7		7	Purude 9-3, Florida State 10-2, Connecticut 9-3, Maryland 9-3	Jim Grobe			
2004	4-7		10t	Boston College 8-3, Virginia Tech 10-2, Florida State 8-3, Miami 8-3	Jim Grobe			
2005	4-7		Atl4t	Florida State 8-4, Boston College 8-3, Miami 9-2	Jim Grobe			
2006	11-3	18	Atl1	Clemson 8-4, Boston College 9-3, Virginai Tech 10-2, Maryland 8-4	Jim Grobe	Orange	13 Louisville	24
2007	9-4		Atl2t	Boston College 10-2, Virginia 9-3, Clemson 9-3	Jim Grobe	Meineke	24 Connecticut	10
2008	8-5		Atl3t	Mississippi 8-4, Florida State 8-4, Boston College 9-4	Jim Grobe	Eagle	29 Navy	19
2009	5-7		Atl4	Stanford 8-4, Clemson 8-5, Miami 9-3, Georgia Tech 11-2	Jim Grobe			
2010	3-9		Atl6	Stanford 11-1, Florida State 9-4, Virginia Tech 11-2	Jim Grobe (62-60)			

TOTAL: 230-396-10 .3695 (67 of 70)

Bowl Games since 1953: 5-2 .7143 (1 of 70)

GREATEST TEAM SINCE 1953: It can be none other than Jim Grobe's stunning conference championship outfit of 2006 that won 11 and lost three. On the preseason ACC media tour, almost no members of the media visited Grobe's booth to talk about the Deacons. Grobe, who had redshirted several fine players to prepare for a push in 2006, expressed surprise, saying, "I thought we might be pretty good." He was right. Only two other Wake Forest squads since 1953 had won as many as eight games.

1953 3-6-1

14	William & Mary	16	E Ed Stowers / David Lee
0	Duke	19	T Bob Bartholomew / Ernie Fitzgibbons
18	Villanova	12	G Gerald Huth / J.C. Turner
13	North Carolina	18	C Joe Dupree
20	N. Carolina St.	7	G Tony Trentini / Mark Viola
13	Richmond	13	T Rocky Littleton
0	Clemson	18	E Bob Ondilla
7	Boston College	20	QB Joe White / Sonny George
10	Furman	21	HB John Parham
19	South Carolina	13	HB Bob Frederick
			FB Bruce Hillenbrand

RUSHING: Parham 96/304y, Frederick 68/272y, Hillenbrand 64/256y
PASSING: White 32-87/486y, 3TD, 36.8%
RECEIVING: Ondilla 21/294y, Stowers 19/235y, Parham 4/45y
SCORING: George 32pts, Frederick, Ondilla & Frederick 18pts

1954 2-7-1

14	Geo. Wash'gton	0	E Ed Stowers /David Lee/Tommy Whims
0	Virginia Tech	32	T Bob Bartholomew
26	N. Carolina St.	0	G Gerald Huth (FB) / Bo Claxton
13	Maryland	13	C Joe Dupree / Mike Soltis
7	North Carolina	14	G Tony Trentini / Mark Viola
20	Clemson	32	T Rocky Littleton / Don Garrison
0	Richmond	13	E Dick Daniels / Jack Ladner
21	Duke	28	QB Nick Consoles / Joe White
9	William & Mary	13	HB John Parham / Bill Barnes
19	South Carolna	20	HB Bob Frederick / Burt Harrison
			FB Nick Maravic / Charles Topping

RUSHING: Maravic 98/430y, Parham 62/238y, Frederick 71/230y
PASSING: Consoles 54-115/ 743y, 6TD, 47.0%
RECEIVING: Stowers 22/277y, Lee 9/99y, Parham 8/100y
SCORING: Maravic 24pts, Daniels, Frederick, & Stowers 18pts

1955 5-4-1

13	Virginia Tech	0	E David Lee
34	South Carolina	19	T Bob Bartholomew
0	West Virginia	46	G Bo Claxton
7	Maryland	28	C Joe Dupree / Eddie Moore
13	N. Carolina St.	13	G Tony Trentini
25	North Carolina	0	T Rocky Littleton / Jim Horn
13	Clemson	19	E Jack Ladner
13	William & Mary	7	QB Nick Consoles
13	Virginia	7	HB Bill Barnes
0	Duke	14	HB John Parham / Dick Daniels
			FB Bruce Hillenbrand

RUSHING: Barnes 116/401y, Parham 67/333y, Hillenbrand 26/136y
PASSING: Consoles 66-123/787y, 6TD, 53.7%
RECEIVING: Barnes 31/349y, Parham 18/376y, Ladner 13/207y
SCORING: Parham 51pts, Barnes 20pts, 2 with 12pts

1956 2-5-3

39	William & Mary	0	E David Lee / Aubrey Currie
0	Maryland	6	T Jim Horn
6	Virginia	7	G Bruce Smathers / Hughie Lewis
0	Clemson	17	C Eddie Moore
14	Florida State	14	G Bo Claxton
6	North Carolina	6	T George Johnson
13	N. Carolina St.	0	E Ralph Brewster / Jack Ladner
13	Virginia Tech	13	QB Charlie Carpenter
0	Duke	26	HB Jim Dalrymple
0	South Carolina	13	HB Dick Daniels
			FB Bill Barnes / Bruce Hillenbrand

RUSHING: Barnes 168/1010y, Daniels 53/204y, Dalrymple 47/192y
PASSING: Carpenter 34-91/495y, 2TD, 37.4%
RECEIVING: Ladner 12/125y, Daniels 11/192y, Dalrymple 8/63y
SCORING: Barnes 44pts, Carpenter 12pts, 5 with 6pts

1957 0-10

0	Florida	27	E Ralph Brewster / Barry Hines
20	Virginia	28	T Frank Thompson
0	Maryland	27	G Hughie Lewis
7	Duke	34	C Eddie Moore / Karl Munn
7	North Carolina	14	G Jim Horn / Bruce Smathers
0	N. Carolina St.	19	T George Johnson
3	Virginia Tech	10	E John Niznik / Aubrey Currie
14	West Virginia	27	QB Jim Dalrymple
6	Clemson	13	HB Larry Brooks
7	South Carolina	26	HB Pete Barham / Bill Pegram
			FB Neil McLean / Pete Manning

RUSHING: MacLean 108/542y, Barham 87/354y, Manning 64/201y
PASSING: Dalrymple 21-61/261y, 0TD, 34.4%
RECEIVING: Currie 9/97y, Brewster 8/92y, Niznik 6/57y
SCORING: MacLean (FB-K) 28pts, Dalrymple 12pts, 4 with 6pts

1958 3-7

34	Maryland	0	E Pete Manning / Dan Herring
13	Virginia Tech	6	T Frank Thompson / Al Conover
24	Florida State	27	G Nick Patella
13	N. Carolina St.	0	C Buck Jolly
7	Villanova	9	G Hughie Lewis / Bruce Smathers
7	North Carolina	26	T Eddie Ladd / Wayne Wolff
12	Clemson	14	E John Niznik / Aubrey Currie
0	Duke	29	QB Norman Snead
7	Auburn	21	HB Jim Dalrymple / Bobby Robinson
7	South Carolina	24	HB Jerry Ball / Buster Ledford
			FB Neil MacLean / Joe Bonecutter

RUSHING: MacLean 139/624y, Dalrymple 50/202y, Bonecutter 37/178y
PASSING: Snead 67-151/1003y, 5TD, 44.4%
RECEIVING: Manning 25/307y, Dalrymple 13/192y, Robinson 11/164y
SCORING: MacLean (FB-K) 38pts, Dalrymple 24pts, 2 with 18pts

1959 6-4

22	Florida State	20	E Pete Manning / Bill Hull
27	Virginia Tech	18	T Al Conover
0	Tulane	6	G Nick Patella / Bob Irwin
10	Maryland	7	C Buck Jolly
17	N. Carolina St.	14	G Paul Martineau / Larry Fleisher
19	North Carolina	21	T Wayne Wolff / Bob McCreary
34	Virginia	12	E Bobby Allen / Bill Ruby
15	Duke	27	QB Norman Snead
31	Clemson	33	HB Bobby Robinson
43	South Carolina	20	HB Jerry Ball / Winston Futch
			FB Neil MacLean / Joe Bonecutter

RUSHING: MacLean 105/373y, Bonecutter 84/372y, Robinson 60/287y
PASSING: Snead 82-191/1361y, 12TD, 42.9%
RECEIVING: Allen 25/462y, Manning 21/363y, Ball 8/68y
SCORING: MacLean (FB-K) 43pts, Allen & Ball 24pts

1960 2-8

7	Clemson	28	E Bill Hull / Henry Newton
6	Florida State	14	T Al Conover
13	Virginia Tech	22	G Jim Pearce
13	North Carolina	12	C Jimmy Lanier
13	Maryland	14	G Paul Martineau
28	Virginia	20	T Wayne Wolff / Bob McCreary
12	N. Carolina St.	14	E Bobby Allen / Bill Ruby
7	Duke	34	QB Norman Snead
0	LSU	16	HB Bobby Robinson / Donnie Frederick
20	South Carolina	41	HB Jerry Ball / Winston Futch
			FB Joe Bonecutter / Bruce McDonnell

RUSHING: Robinson 57/232y, Frederick 43/182y, Ball 38/175y
PASSING: Snead 123-259/1676y, 10TD, 47.5%
RECEIVING: Allen 23/391y, Hull 21/301y, Frederick 13/164y
SCORING: Allen 30pts, Robinson & Frederick 24pts

1961 4-6

0	Baylor	31	E Bill Hull / Henry Newton
7	South Carolina	10	T Paul Martineau / Bruce Nation
3	Duke	23	G Bob Irwin
17	Clemson	13	C Farrell Egge / Larry Coker
0	N. Carolina St.	7	G Bill Shendow / William Faircloth
21	Virginia	15	T Jimmy Williams / Kent Martin
7	Auburn	21	E Bill Ruby / Jim Tejeck
24	Virginia Tech	15	QB Chuck Reiley
7	Maryland	20	HB Donnie Frederick
17	North Carolina	14	HB Alan White / Winston Futch
			FB Bruce McDonnell / Gerald Rudelitsch

RUSHING: White 93/586y, Frederick 74/254y, Rudelitsch 51/150y
PASSING: Reiley 32-88/516y, 4 TD, 36.4%
RECEIVING: Frederick 11/237y, Hull 9/161y, White 5/48y
SCORING: Frederick 32pts, White 24pts, Walker 23pts

1962 0-10

14	Army	40	E Richard Cameron / Wilbert Faircloth
2	Maryland	13	T Tommy Brawley / Tom Lally
7	Clemson	24	G Bob Irwin / Paul Shearer
6	South Carolina	27	C Farrell Egge / Bill Hopkins
12	Virginia	14	G Bill Shendow / William Faircloth
14	North Carolina	23	T Kent Martin / Wesley Cox
0	Tennessee	23	E Henry Newton / Jim Tejeck
8	Virginia Tech	37	QB John Mackovic / Wally Bridwell
0	Duke	50	HB Donnie Frederick / Neal McDuffie
3	N. Carolina St.	27	HB Sam Green / Wayne Welborn
			FB Brian Piccolo / Larry Thomason

RUSHING: Piccolo 77/324y, Frederick 68/212y, Thomason 41/165y
PASSING: Mackovic 57-130/594y, 3 TD, 43.8%
RECEIVING: Newton 19/265y, Tejeck 16/199y, Frederick 13/120y
SCORING: Newton 12pts, Thomason 12pts, Walker 8pts

1963 1-9

10	East Carolina	20	E Richard Cameron / Wilbert Faircloth
0	Virginia Tech	27	T William Faircloth
0	North Carolina	21	G Farrell Egge / Lewis Duncan
0	Florida State	35	C Bill Hopkins
0	Army	47	G Ron Kadon / Paul Shearer
0	Maryland	32	T Jim Mayo / William Salter
0	Clemson	36	E Jim Tejeck
7	Duke	39	QB Karl Sweetan / Ralph Brandewiede
20	South Carolina	19	HB Wayne Welborn
0	N. Carolina St.	42	HB Jimmy Bedgood / Joe Carazo
			FB Brian Piccolo / Joe Berra

RUSHING: Piccolo 84/367y, Bedgood 47/201y, Welborn 49/139y
PASSING: Sweetan 79-218/674y, TD, 36.2%
RECEIVING: Welborn 17/102y, Cameron 16/159y, Piccolo 10/126y
SCORING: Piccolo (FB-K) 23pts, Sweetan 8pts, Tejeck 6pts

1964 5-5

31	Virginia	21	E Richard Cameron (DL) / Joe Sepic
38	Virginia Tech	21	T William Salter / Tommy Brawley
0	North Carolina	23	G Lynn Nesbitt (DL) / Bill Marks (LB)
6	Vanderbilt	9	C Bob Oplinger / Dick Penn (LB)
2	Clemson	21	G Bill Hopkins / Earl Coleman
21	Maryland	17	T Jim Beaudoin / John Snow
14	Memphis State	23	E John Grimes / Ray Slone (DL)
20	Duke	7	QB John Mackovic
13	South Carolina	23	HB Wayne Welborn
27	N. Carolina St.	13	HB Joe Carazo / Andy Harper (DB)
			FB Brian Piccolo / Joe Berra (DB)
			DL Richard Cameron (E)
			DL John Snow / Werner Hauer
			DL Lynn Nesbit
			DL Ray Slone (E)
			LB Don McMurray
			LB Bill Marks (G)
			LB Dick Penn (C)
			DB Doug Golightly
			DB Andy Harper (HB)
			DB Joe Berra (FB)
			DB Don Davis / Sammy Decker

RUSHING: Piccolo 252/1044y, Welborn 77/385y, Mackovic 72/174y
PASSING: Mackovic 89-195/1340y, 3TD, 45.6%
RECEIVING: Cameron 29/410y, Carazo 22/302y, Grimes 10/147y
SCORING: Piccolo (FB-K) 111pts, Welborn & Mackovic 18pts

1965 3-7

3	Virginia Tech	12	E Joe Sepic
11	N. Carolina St.	13	T Tommy Brawley
7	Vanderbilt	0	G Don McMurray
7	Vanderbilt	10	C Bob Oplinger / Dick Penn
7	South Carolina	38	G Earl Coleman / Don Hensley
12	North Carolina	10	T Jim Beaudoin
13	Clemson	26	E Ken Henry
0	Florida State	35	QB Jon Wilson / Ken Hauswald (FB)
7	Duke	40	HB Andy Heck
21	Memphis State	20	HB Joe Carazo / Doug Golightly
			FB Mike Kelly / Eddie McKinney
			DL Ray Slone
			DL John Snow / Bob Grant
			DL Lynn Nesbitt
			DL Tom Stuetzer
			LB Bo Williams
			LB Don Hensley
			LB Jim Hobbs
			DB Butch Baker
			DB Andy Harper
			DB Joe Berra
			DB Don Davis

RUSHING: Heck 151/497y, Carazo 61/216y, Golightly 38/136y
PASSING: Wilson 44-104/513y, 4TD, 42.3%
Hauswald 40-96/445y, 1TD, 41.7%
RECEIVING: Henry 30/367y, Carazo 29/308y, Kelly 7/58y
SCORING: McKinney 18pts, Heck 14pts, Kelly & Henry 12pts

1966 3-7

10	Virginia	24 WR Ken Henry / Bob Brenner
7	Maryland	34 WR Eddie Arrington / Ivey Smith
12	N. Carolina St.	15 T Bill Scheib
6	Auburn	14 G Don McMurray / Howard Stanback
10	South Carolina	6 C Bob Oplinger
3	North Carolina	0 G Don Hensley
21	Clemson	23 T Lynn Nesbitt
0	Virginia Tech	11 TE Rick Decker / Rick White
21	Memphis State	7 QB Ken Erickson
0	Florida State	28 TB Andy Heck / Jimmy Johnson
		FB Ken Hauswald
		DL Ray Slone
		DL Robert Grant
		DL John Snow (OT) / Lloyd Halvorson
		DL John McQueeney / Lynn Nesbitt
		DL Bill Overton
		DL Tom Stuetzer
		LB Jimmy Clack (C) / Mike Blasiole
		LB Bo Williams / Chick George
		DB Digit Laughridge
		DB Butch Baker / Ed Atkinson
		DB Andy Harper

RUSHING: Heck 127/608y, Johnson 99/380y, Hauswald 68/226y
PASSING: Erickson 57-126/787y, 3TD, 45.2%
RECEIVING: Henry 20/279y, Arrington 15/199y, Hauswald 13/244y
SCORING: Chick George (K) 22pts, Hauswald 14pts, 4 with 12pts

1967 4-6

13	Duke	31 WR Ken Henry (DB) / David Stanley
6	Clemson	23 WR Fred Angerman / Tom Gavin
6	Houston	50 T Bill Scheib / Lloyd Halvorson
12	Virginia	14 G Tom Jones / Larry Hambrick
10	Memphis State	42 C Joe Dobner
7	N. Carolina St.	24 G Don Hensley
20	North Carolina	10 T Jimmy Clack / Bill Overton
35	South Carolina	21 TE Rick Decker / Rick White (WR)
31	Tulsa	24 QB Freddie Summers
35	Maryland	17 TB Jack Dolbin / Jimmy Johnson
		FB Ron Jurewicz / David Smith
		DL Robert Grant
		DL Joe Theriault
		DL John McQueeney / Bill Graves
		DL Dan White / Ivey Smith
		LB Chick George
		LB Carlyle Pate / Ken Hemphill
		LB Chuck White / Bob Flynn
		DB Carlton Baker / Tom Deacon
		DB Larry Pons / Don Dever
		DB Digit Laughridge
		DB Gary Williard (LB)

RUSHING: Summers 179/510y, Dolbin 84/490y, Jurewicz 77/346y
PASSING: Summers 77-159/909y, 2TD, 48.4%
RECEIVING: Decker 29/352y, Henry 21/233y, Jurewicz 9/73y
SCORING: Summers 60pts, Buz Leavitt (FB) 24pts, Chick George (K) 22pts

1968 2-7-1

6	N. Carolina St.	10 WR Fred Angerman
20	Clemson	20 WR Rick White / Eddie Arrington
19	Minnesota	24 T Lloyd Halvorson
6	Virginia Tech	7 G Larry Hambrick
27	Purdue	28 C Joe Dobner
48	North Carolina	31 G Howard Stanback / Tom Jones
38	Maryland	14 T Jimmy Clack
21	South Carolina	34 TE Ron Jurewicz / Fred Cooke
3	Duke	18 QB Freddie Summers
24	Florida State	42 TB Jack Dolbin / Lee Clymer
		FB Jimmy Johnson / Buz Leavitt
		DL Roman Wszelaki / Al Beard
		DL Win Headley
		DL John McQueeney / Bill Scheib
		DL Ed George / Gerald McGowan
		LB Carlyle Pate / Dann White
		LB John Mazalewski / Chick George
		LB Ivey Smith / Ken Hemphill
		DB Dick Bozoian / Larry Pons
		DB Gary Williard
		DB Digit Laughridge / Tom Deacon
		DB Terry Kuharchek / Tom Gavin

RUSHING: Summers 159/439y, Clymer 105/389y, Dolbin 76/343y
PASSING: Summers 125-250/1664y, 9TD, 50.0%
RECEIVING: Jurewicz 28/451y, White 28/451y, Angerman 18/244y
SCORING: Summers 42pts, Clymer 36pts, Tom Deacon (K) 36pts

1969 3-7

22	N. Carolina St.	21 WR Fred Angerman / Don Kobos
0	Auburn	57 T Ed George
16	Virginia Tech	10 G Tom Jones
14	Maryland	19 C Joe Dobner / Nick Vrhovac
20	Duke	27 G Bill Bobbora / Tom Martin
14	Clemson	28 T Vince Nedimyer
3	North Carolina	23 TE Gary Winrow / Bob Brenner
23	Virginia	21 QB Larry Russell / Ken Erickson
6	South Carolina	24 HB Buz Leavitt / Tom Gavin
7	Miami	49 HB Jack Dolbin
		FB Ron Jurewicz
		DL Win Headley
		DL Dick Chulada / Roman Wszelaki
		DL Gerald McGowan / Mike Magnot
		DL Jim Schubert / Terry Bennett
		LB Larry Causey / Chuck White
		LB John Mazalewski
		LB Ed Bradley / Ed Stetz
		LB Frank Hawkins
		DB Dick Bozoian / Gary Johnson
		DB Larry Pons
		DB Terry Kuharchek / Pat McHenry

RUSHING: Russell 187/471y, Leavitt 113/461y, Jurewicz 54/180y, Dolbin 44/178y
PASSING: Russell 70-153/794y, TD, 45.8%
RECEIVING: Winrow 27/277y, Kobos 15/196y, Jurewicz 14/175y
SCORING: Tracy Lounsbury (K) 29pts, Leavitt 28pts, Russell 24pts

1970 6-5

12	Nebraska	36 WR Steve Bowden / Bill Gebert
7	South Carolina	43 T Gerald McGowan
14	Florida State	19 G Ted Waite
27	Virginia	7 C Nick Vrhovac / Gary German
28	Virginia Tech	9 G Bill Bobbora / Tom Martin
36	Clemson	20 T Vince Nedimyer / Terry Bennett
14	North Carolina	13 TE Dave Doda
7	Tennessee	41 TE Gary Winrow / Dave Lindsay
28	Duke	14 QB Larry Russell
16	N. Carolina St.	13 RB Ken Garrett / Gary Johnson
2	Houston	26 FB Larry Hopkins
		DL Win Headley
		DL Dick Chulada / Mike Magnot
		DL Joe Theriault / Archie Logan
		DL John Phillips
		LB Ed Bradley / Tony Mangiaracina
		LB Ed Stetz / Carlyle Pate
		LB Larry Causey
		DB Dick Bozoian
		DB Pat McHenry
		DB Terry Kuharchek
		DB Frank Fussell / Junior Moore

RUSHING: Hopkins 203/984y, Russell 196/649y, Garrett 110/452y
PASSING: Russell 55-109/671y, 4TD, 50.5%
RECEIVING: Winrow 20/253y, Bowden 15/219y, Garrett 11/79y
SCORING: Russell 62pts, Tracy Lounsbury (K) 35pts, Hopkins & Garrett 30pts

1971 6-5

27	Davidson	7 WR Mike Capone / Jim McMahen
20	Virginia Tech	9 T Robert Carroll / Bill Holthouser
10	Miami	29 G Ted Waite / Mike Arrthur
18	Maryland	14 C Nick Vrhovac / Gary German
14	N. Carolina St.	21 G Bob Bobbora
51	Tulsa	21 T Bruce Reinert / Terry Bennett
3	North Carolina	7 TE Dave Doda
9	Clemson	10 TE Kevin Byrnes / Ernie jakubovic
36	William & Mary	29 QB Larry Russell
23	Duke	7 RB Ken Garrett / Gary Johnson
7	South Carolina	24 FB Larry Hopkins
		DL John Hardin / Archie Logan
		DL Dick Chulada / Joe Teriault
		DL Steve Komondorea
		DL Randy Cox
		LB Ed Bradley / Tony Margiaracina
		LB Ed Stetz / Nick Arcaro
		LB Larry Causey
		DB Pat McHenry
		DB Steve Bowden
		DB Sammy Rothrock / Rich Sievers
		DB Frank Fussell / Junior Moore

RUSHING: Hopkins 249/1228y, Garrett 129/864y, Russell 256/803y
PASSING: Russell 29-73/290y, 2TD, 39.7%
RECEIVING: Doda 6/31y, Capone 4/99y, Byrnes 4/49, Garrett 4/19y
SCORING: Russell 94pts, Hopkins 32pts, Garrett 32pts

1972 2-9

26	Davidson	20 WR Gary Johnson / Jim McMahen
10	SMU	56 WR Richard Carter / Carl Lowe
6	Tennessee	45 T Randy Halsall / Lew Henderson
0	Maryland	23 G Stuart Hughes
13	N. Carolina St.	42 C Vince Greco / Gary German
0	North Carolina	21 G Ron Lennon / Sid Geible
0	Clemson	31 T Bruce Reinert
3	South Carolina	35 TE Nick Ortega / Kevin Byrnes
9	Duke	7 QB Kit Basler / Andy Carlson
12	Virginia	15 RB Ken Garrett
9	Virginia Tech	44 RB Frank Harsh / Clayton Heath
		DL John Hardin
		DL Steve Komondorea
		DL David Bailey / Lee Allen
		DL Rich Gregory / Neville Davis
		LB Norris Thomas
		LB Nick Arcaro / Tony Mangiaracino
		LB Donnie Brown / David Mebs
		DB Junior Moore
		DB James Hargrove
		DB Sammy Rothrock / Rich Sievers
		DB Felix Glasco

RUSHING: Harsh 157/663y, Garrett 83/357y, Heath 68/216y
PASSING: Carlton 24-70/268y, TD, 34.3%
RECEIVING: Johnson 9/135y, Carter 6/153y, Ortega 6/78y
SCORING: Heath 24pts, Ramsey 24pts, 6 with 6pts

1973 1-9-1

9	Florida State	7 WR Bill Millner
14	William & Mary	15 WR Walter Sims
0	Richmond	41 T Randy Halsall / Turbe Turbeville
0	Texas	41 G Bruce Miller / Tim Tremblay
12	South Carolina	28 C Vince Greco / Tony Barnes
0	Maryland	37 G Mike Arthur
10	Virginia	21 T Lew Henderson / Ron Lennon
8	Clemson	35 TE Dan Stroup / Dean Brendel
7	Duke	7 QB Andy Carlton / Bill Armstrong
0	North Carolina	42 TB Clayton Heath / Terry Karl
13	N. Carolina St.	52 FB Frank Harsh
		DL John Hardin / J.D. Harris
		DL Dave Bartholomew
		DL Keith Carter / John Bryce
		DL David Bailey
		DL Rich Gregory / Doug Benfield
		LB Steve Colavito / Norris Thomas
		LB David Mebs / Randy Carroll
		DB Randy Stits (WR) / Spencer Horne
		DB Tom Lockridge / Ed McDonald
		DB Rich Sievers / Tim Fischer
		DB Felix Glasco / Bob Richards

RUSHING: Heath 178/616y, Harsh 75/312y, Karl 42/110y
PASSING: Carlton 51-141/605y, 2TD, 36.2%
RECEIVING: Sims 12/143y, Millner 11/169y, Stroup 7/72y
SCORING: Chuck Ramsey (K) 23pts, 7 with 6pts

1974 1-10

15	N. Carolina St.	33 WR Bill Millner
6	William & Mary	17 WR Walter Sims
0	North Carolina	31 T Jackie Robinson / Carmen Frangiosa
0	Oklahoma	63 G Randy Woodle
0	Penn State	55 C Larry Tearry
0	Maryland	47 G Rich Geiger
0	Virginia	14 T Lew Henderson / Larry Tearry
9	Clemson	21 TE Tom Fehring / Steve Young
7	Duke	23 QB Mike McGlamry / Solomon Everett
21	South Carolina	34 TB Clark Gaines / John Kronforst
16	Furman	10 FB Frank Harsh / Jim Mach
		DL J.D. Harris / Dave LaCrosse
		DL Dave Bartholomew
		DL Keith Carter / Carmen Frangiosa
		DL David Bailey / John Bryce
		DL Doug Benfield / Lou Tilley
		LB Randy Carroll
		LB David Mebs
		DB Ed McDonald
		DB Tom Lockridge / Gary Hegh
		DB Bill Armstrong
		DB Bob Richards

RUSHING: Gaines 98/329y, Mach 103/301y, Kronforst 47/228y
PASSING: McGlamry 50-115/585y, TD, 43.5%
RECEIVING: Fehring 17/234y, Gaines 12/128y, Sims 11/237y
SCORING: Gaines 20pts, Joe Bunch (K) 16pts, 6 with 6pts

1975 3-8

7 SMU	14 WR Bill Millner / Al Zyskowski
30 N. Carolina St.	22 WR Solomon Everett
17 Appalachian St.	19 T Jackie Robinson
16 Kansas State	17 G Randy Woodle / Carmen Frangiosa
14 Clemson	16 C Larry Tearry
0 Maryland	27 G Tom Parker / Mike Milanovich
66 Virginia	21 T Dan Fulton
21 North Carolina	9 TE Steve Young
14 Duke	42 QB Jerry McManus / Mike McGlamry
26 South Carolina	37 TB Clark Gaines / John Zeglinski
10 Virginia Tech	40 FB Frank Harsh / Jim Mach
	DL Dave LaCrosse
	DL John Bryce
	DL Bruce Hopkins
	DL Doug Benfield / John Sabia
	LB Terry Giblin / Carl Curry
	LB Randy Carroll
	LB Don Cervi / Lou Tilley
	DB Ed McDonald
	DB James Royster
	DB Bill Armstrong
	DB Mike LaVallee

RUSHING: Gaines 238/929y, Zeglinski 137/591y, Harsh 56/225y
PASSING: McManus 77-152/950y, 10TD, 50.7%
RECEIVING: Millner 28/327y, Zeglinski 27/354y, Young 16/221y
SCORING: Zeglinski 60pts, Gaines 26pts, Joe Bunch (K) 20pts

1976 5-6

6 Virginia Tech	23 WR Bill Millner
20 N. Carolina St.	18 WR Solomon Everett
24 Vanderbilt	27 T Jackie Robinson
13 Kansas State	0 G Randy Woodle
0 Michigan	31 C Larry Tearry
20 Clemson	14 G Carmen Frangiosa / Dave Hettinger
15 Maryland	17 T Dan Fulton / Steve Bernardo
17 Virginia	18 TE Steve Young
14 North Carolina	34 QB Mike McGlamry
38 Duke	17 TB James McDougald / John Zeglinski
10 South Carolina	7 FB Stan Rolark / Mark Cregar
	DL Dave LaCrosse
	DL John Bryce / Jim Dumser
	DL Reuben Turner
	DL Steve Check / Bruce Hopkins
	DL John Sabia
	LB Don Cervi
	LB Randy Carroll / Ed Walker
	DB James Royster
	DB Dan Smading
	DB Bill Armstrong
	DB Mike LaVallee / Reggie Tice

RUSHING: McDougald 232/1018y, Zeglinski 82/229y, Cregar 54/222y
PASSING: McGlamry 91-183/1066y, 4TD, 49.7%
RECEIVING: Young 36/414y, Millner 32/486y, Zeglinski 11/86y
SCORING: McDougald 60pts, Bob Hely (K) 46pts, Young 18pts

1977 1-10

24 Furman	13 WR Tom Smith / Solomon Everett
0 Vanderbilt	3 WR John Zeglinski
14 N. Carolina St.	41 T Jackie Robinson / Steve Bernardo
17 Purdue	26 G Bill Ard
3 North Carolina	24 C Steve Truitt
7 Maryland	35 G Tim Davis
10 Virginia	12 T Carmen Frangiosa
0 Clemson	26 TE Steve Young
14 Duke	38 QB Mike McGlamry
14 South Carolina	24 TB James McDougald / Ronchie Johnson
10 Virginia Tech	28 FB Stan Rolark / Mark Cregar
	DL Steve Vance / Mac Haupt
	DL Frank Armstrong / Dwayne Crayton
	DL Reuben Turner / Steve Truitt
	DL Bruce Hopkins
	DL Mike Wisher / C.D. Osborne
	LB Don Cervi
	LB Ed Walker
	DB James Royster
	DB Charlie Viana / Dan Smading
	DB George Ervin / Mark Mattiko
	DB Mark Lancaster

RUSHING: McDougald 242/987y, Johnson 39/133y, Rolark 37/126y
PASSING: McGlamry 133-252/1532y, 5TD, 52.8%
RECEIVING: Young 51/483y, Zeglinski 31/486y, Smith 24/312y
SCORING: McDougald 30pts, Young 18pts, Bob Hely (K) 16pts

1978 1-10

14 Virginia	0 WR Wayne Baumgardner
6 Virginia Tech	28 WR Tom Smith / Eddie Wright
11 LSU	13 T Jackie Robinson
10 N. Carolina St.	34 G Bill Ard
7 Purdue	14 C Steve Truitt
29 North Carolina	34 G Rob Brassell / Tim Davis
0 Maryland	39 T Syd Kitson
7 Auburn	21 TE Mike Mullen
6 Clemson	51 QB David Webber / Ken Daly
0 Duke	3 TB James McDougald / Ronchie Johnson
14 South Carolina	37 FB Albert Kirby / Wayne McMillan
	DL Eddie Yarnell / C.D. Osborne
	DL Dwayne Crayton
	DL James Parker
	DL Bruce Hopkins / Steve Vance
	DL Mike Wisher / Mike Maxwell
	LB Carlos Bradley / Rick Dadouris
	LB Marc Hester / Paul Eberle
	DB James Royster
	DB Larry Ingram
	DB George Ervin / Mark Mattiko
	DB Marc Lancaster

RUSHING: McDougald 146/629y, Kirby 111/416y, McMillan 17/77y
PASSING: Webber 101-182/1070y, 2TD, 55.5%
RECEIVING: Mullen 22/307y, Kirby 21/229y, Baumgardner 20/272y
SCORING: McDougald 24pts, Wright 18pts

1979 8-4

30 Appalachain St.	23 WR Wayne Baumgardner
22 Georgia	21 WR Kenny Duckett
23 East Carolina	20 T Ward Cridland
14 N. Carolina St.	17 G Bill Ard
19 Virginia Tech	14 C Steve Truitt
24 North Carolina	19 G Greg Brown
25 Maryland	17 T Richard Baldinger
42 Auburn	38 TE Mike Mullen
0 Clemson	31 QB Jay Venuto
17 Duke	14 TB James McDougald
14 South Carolina	35 FB Henderson Threatt / Albert Kirby
10 LSU■	34 DL Eddie Yarnell
	DL Dwayne Crayton
	DL Alex Brown
	DL James Parker
	DL Mike Wisher / Mike Maxwell
	LB Carlos Bradley
	LB Joel Triplett
	DB George Ervin / Lewis Owens
	DB Derek Crocker
	DB Larry Ingram / Landon King
	DB Eddie Green / Andy Seay

RUSHING: McDougald 275/1231y, Kirby 76/410y, Threatt 22/83y
PASSING: Venuto 208-386/2597y, 17TD 53.9%
RECEIVING: Baumgardner 61/1128y, Kirby 48/329y, Mullen 33/380y
SCORING: McDougald 78pts, Baumgardner 56pts, Frank Harnisch (K) 42pts

1980 5-6

7 Virginia Tech	16 WR Wayne Baumgardner
24 Citadel	7 WR Kenny Duckett / Derek Crocker
27 N. Carolina St.	7 T Jeff Gjerde
27 William & Mary	7 G Bill Ard
9 North Carolina	27 C Steve Truitt
10 Maryland	11 G Greg Brown / Les Tripp
21 Virginia	24 T Richard Baldinger
33 Clemson	35 TE Mike Mullen / Bill Ruffner
27 Duke	24 QB Jay Venuto
38 South Carolina	39 TB Wayne McMillan / Carlos Cunningham
28 Appalachain St.	16 FB Henderson Threatt
	DL Eddie Yarnell
	DL Terry Vogler
	DL Alex Brown
	DL Ken Tatko / Dwayne Crayton
	DL Mike Hodgson / Mike Wisher
	LB Carlos Bradley / Kent Simon
	LB Joel Triplett / Max Maxwell
	DB Pierre Brown
	DB John Swider / Lewis Owens
	DB Andy Seay / Landon King
	DB Eddie Green

RUSHING: McMillan 152/694y, Threatt 65/240y, Cunningham 64/236y
PASSING: Venuto 214-413/2624y, 21TD, 51.8%
RECEIVING: Duckett 50/656y, Baumgardner 41/764y, Ruffner 24/198y
SCORING: Duckett 72pts, McMillan 48pts, Phil Denfield (K) 40pts

1981 4-7

6 South Carolina	23 WR Wayne Baumgardner
23 N. Carolina St.	28 WR Kenny Duckett
24 Auburn	21 T Richard Baldinger
14 Virginia Tech	30 G Pat Slenski
15 Appalachian St.	14 C Joe Carroll
10 North Carolina	48 G Danny Martin
33 Maryland	45 T John Zalucky / Glen Campbell
24 Virginia	21 TE Phil Denfeld
24 Clemson	82 QB Gary Schofield
10 Duke	31 TB Wayne McMillan / Duane Owens
34 Richmond	22 FB Dan Dougherty / Carlos Cunningham
	DL Eric Metzler / David Phiel
	DL Alex Brown
	DL Mike Hodgson
	LB Joel Triplett
	LB Steve Litaker
	LB Kent Simon
	LB Steve Hammond
	DB Henderson Threatt / Lewis Owens
	DB Eddie Green / Donald Johnson
	DB Ronnie Burgess / Andy Seay
	DB Danny Rocco / Landon King

RUSHING: McMillan 90/407y, Owens 84/303y, Dougherty 52/177y
PASSING: Schofield 241-404/2572y, 18TD, 59.7%
RECEIVING: Denfeld 51/461y, Duckett 37/457y, Dougherty 32/164y
SCORING: Denfield 49pts, Duckett 42pts, McMillan 24pts

1982 3-8

31 W. Carolina	10 WR Tim Ryan / David "Chip" Richmond
10 Auburn	28 WR Tommy Gregg
0 N. Carolina St.	30 T Glen Campbell
31 Appalachian St.	22 G Danny Martin
13 Virginia Tech	10 C Michael Nesselt
7 North Carolina	24 G Ken McAllister
31 Maryland	52 T Bobby Morrison
27 Virginia	34 TE Phil Denfeld / Dexter Hawkins
26 Duke	46 QB Gary Schofield
7 Georgia Tech	45 TB Michael Ramseur / Topper Clemons
17 Clemson	21 FB Dan Dougherty / Carlos Cunningham
	DL Bruce Mark
	DL Tony Coates
	DL Tim Salley
	LB Kent Simon
	LB Steve Litaker / Tony Scott
	LB Malcolm Hairston
	LB Pierre Brown / Jeff Cook
	DB Ronnie Burgess
	DB Donald Johnson / Eddie Green
	DB Andy Seay
	DB Danny Rocco

RUSHING: Ramseur 245/966y, Clemons 73/269y, Dougherty 42/146y
PASSING: Schofield 212-376/2380y, 10TD, 56.4%
RECEIVING: Denfeld 42/424y, Ryan 36/580y, Gregg 34/405y
SCORING: Denfeld 53pts, Ramseur 48pts, Ryan 24pts

1983 4-7

25 Appalachian St.	27 WR Tim Ryan / James Brim
13 Virginia Tech	6 WR Duane Owens / Chip Richmond
21 W. Carolina	0 T Tim Morrison
31 Richmond	6 G Danny Martin
15 N. Carolina St.	38 C Michael Nesselt
10 North Carolina	30 G Ken McAllister
33 Maryland	36 T Bobby Morrison
38 Virginia	34 TE Kevin Wieczorek / Dexter Hawkins
17 Clemson	24 QB Gary Schofield
21 Duke	31 RB Topper Clemons / Dan Dougherty
33 Georgia Tech	49 RB Michael Ramseur / Ira McKeller
	DL Bruce Mark / David Phiel
	DL Gary Baldinger / Randall Singleton
	DL Tim Salley / Mike Hodgson
	LB Danny Rocco / Pierre Brown
	LB Steve Litaker / Tony Scott
	LB Malcolm Hairston / John Piedmonte
	LB Ken Grantham / Todd Landis
	DB Ronnie Burgess
	DB Rory Holt
	DB Reggie McCummings/Cha's Redmon
	DB Donald Johnson

RUSHING: Ramseur 125/629y, Clemons 132/462y, McKeller 61/250y
PASSING: Schofield 184-333/2253y, 16TD, 56.2%
RECEIVING: Owens 46/447y, Ryan 36/483y, Richmond 27/460y
SCORING: Ramseur 48pts, Owens, 42pts, Clemons 36pts

1984 6-5

20 Virginia Tech	21 WR James Brim
17 Appalachian St.	13 WR Duane Owens / Tommy Gregg
24 N. Carolina St.	15 T Tim Morrison / Glen Campbell
17 Maryland	38 G Paul Kiser
29 Richmond	13 C Michael Nesselt
14 North Carolina	3 G Ken McAllister
9 Virginia	28 T Bobby Morrison
34 William & Mary	21 TE Kevin Wieczorek / Mike Matella
14 Clemson	37 QB Foy White
20 Duke	16 RB Topper Clemons / Chip Rives
7 Georgia Tech	24 RB Michale Ramseur / Darryl McGill
	DL Bruce Mark
	DL Tony Coates / Randall Singleton
	DL Gary Baldinger
	LB Tony Garbarczyk / Carl Nesbit
	LB Tony Scott / Jimmie Simmons
	LB Steve Lambert
	LB Malcolm Hairston / Joe Walker
	DB Ronnie Burgess / Marvin Young
	DB Rory Holt
	DB Reggie McCummings
	DB Donald Johnson / Ken Grantham

RUSHING: Ramseur 214/961y, Clemons 137/732y, McGill 39/162y
PASSING: White 143-252/1544y, 12TD, 56.7%
RECEIVING: Owens 30/420y, Brim 26/407y, Ramseur 24/235y
SCORING: Ramseur 66pts, Doug Illing (K) 22pts, Owens 20pts

1985 4-7

30 William & Mary	23 WR James Brim
30 Boston Univ.	0 WR David Chambers
17 N. Carolina St.	20 T Tim Morrison (G) /Gregg Harris
24 Appalachian St.	21 G Paul Kiser
29 Tennessee	31 C Brian Paschal / Frank Carmines
14 North Carolina	34 G Paul Mann / Ken Keesee
3 Maryland	26 T Mike Rice
18 Virginia	20 TE Kevin Wieczorek / Greg Scales
10 Clemson	26 QB Mike Elkins / Foy White
27 Duke	7 RB Michael Ramseur / Darryl McGill
10 Georgia Tech	41 RB Topper Clemons / Chip Rives
	DL Bruce Mark
	DL Randall Singleton
	DL Gary Baldinger
	LB Tony Garbarczyk
	LB Tony Scott / Jimmie Simmons
	LB Steve Lambert / Toby Cole
	LB Joe Walker / Dexter Victor
	DB A.J. Greene
	DB Marvin Young / Tony Mosley
	DB Reggie McCummings
	DB Ken Grantham

RUSHING: Clemons 164/916y, Ramseur 169/769y, McGill 45/250y
PASSING: White 132-210/1322y, 14TD, 62.9%
RECEIVING: Ramseur 54/450y, Brim 51/578y, Chambers 27/340y
SCORING: Clemons 44pts, Illing 38pts, Scales 36pts

1986 5-6

21 Appalachian St.	13 WR James Brim
31 Boston Univ.	0 WR David Chambers / Ricky Proehl
38 N. Carolina St.	42 T Tim Morrison (G)
49 Army	14 G Paul Kiser
28 Virginia	30 C Frank Carmines
30 North Carolina	40 G Paul Mann / Jay Deaver
27 Maryland	21 T Gregg Harris / Mike Rice
20 Clemson	28 TE Greg Scales
36 Duke	38 QB Mike Elkins
21 South Carolina	48 RB Darryl McGiil / Mark Young
24 Georgia Tech	21 RB Chip Rives
	DL Mike Hooten
	DL Ronnie Grinton
	DL Terrence Ryan
	DL Kelly Vaughan / Terry Smith
	LB Steve Lambert / David Whitley
	LB Scott Roberts
	LB Jimmie Simmons / Carl Nesbit
	DB A.J. Greene / Tony Mosley
	DB Rory Holt
	DB Ernie Purnsley
	DB Joe Walker / Dexter Victor

RUSHING: McGill 184/859y, Rives 144/679y, Young 61/305y
PASSING: Elkins 205-380/2541y, 17TD, 53.9%
RECEIVING: Brim 66/930y, Scales 34/475y, Rives 32/246y
SCORING: Rives 72pts, McGill 68pts, Wilson Hoyle (K) 59pts

1987 7-4

24 Richmond	0 WR Steve Brown
21 N. Carolina St.	3 T Rod Ferguson / Rusty Bumgardner
16 Appalachian St.	12 G Jay Deaver / Rob Watson
17 Army	13 C Tony Mayberry
22 North Carolina	14 G Roger Foltz
0 Maryland	14 T Joe Kenn (G) / Steve Fleming
21 Virginia	35 TE James Phillips / Greg Scales
17 Clemson	31 QB Mike Elkins
30 Duke	27 TB Mark Young / Darryl McGill
0 South Carolina	30 WB Rickey Proehl
33 Georgia Tech	6 FB Chip Rives
	DL Mike Hooten / Carl Nesbit
	DL Marvin Mitchell
	DL Terry Smith
	DL Kelly Vaughan
	DL David Braxton
	LB Jimmie Simmons
	LB David Whitley / Warren Belin
	DB A.J. Greene
	DB Tony Mosley
	DB Ernie Purnsley / Kyle White
	DB Joe Walker / Dexter Victor

RUSHING: Young 179/795y, McGill 76/313y, Tony Rogers (TB) 66/265y
PASSING: Elkins 169-317/1915y, 7TD, 53.3%
RECEIVING: Proehl 54/788y, Young 19/206y, Jarvis 19/157y
SCORING: Wilson Hoyle (K) 69pts, Proehl 42pts, Young 24pts

1988 6-4-1

31 Villanova	11 WR Steve Brown
35 Illinois State	0 T Rod Ferguson
6 N. Carolina St.	14 G Jay Deaver
9 Michigan	19 C Tony Mayberry
42 North Carolina	24 G Joe Kenn
27 Maryland	24 T Robbie Lingerfelt
14 Virginia	34 TE David Jarvis / Carl Pennington
21 Clemson	38 QB Mike Elkins
35 Duke	16 TB Mark Young / Tony Rogers
28 Georgia Tech	24 WB Ricky Proehl
34 Appalachain St.	34 FB Brian Johnson / Bob Niedbala
	DL Mike Hooten
	DL Marvin Mitchell
	DL Terry Smith / Mike Smith
	DL Kelly Vaughan
	DL David Braxton / James DuBose
	LB Rodney Hogue
	LB Warren Belin /
	DB A.J. Greene
	DB Tony Mosley
	DB Ernie Purnsley
	DB Brad Benson

RUSHING: Young 165/711y, Rogers 99/448y, Anthony Williams (TB) 72/384y
PASSING: Elkins 165-280/2205y, 14TD, 58.9%
RECEIVING: Proehl 51/845y, Brown 37/509y, Jarvis 29/373y
SCORING: Proehl 66pts, Wilson Hoyle (K) 58pts, Young 44pts

1989 2-8-1

10 Appalachian St.	15 WR Steve Brown / Bobby Jones
17 N. Carolina St.	27 T Rod Ferguson
10 Army	14 G Steven Ainsworth / Scott Swanson
17 Rice	17 C Tony Mayberry
17 North Carolina	16 G Robbie Lingerfelt / Tom Mordica
7 Maryland	27 T Louis Altobelli
28 Virginia	47 TEScott Clinard / Rusty Bumgardner
10 Clemson	44 QB Phil Barnhill
35 Duke	52 TB Tony Rogers / Anthony Williams
29 Tulsa	17 WB Ricky Proehl
14 Georgia Tech	43 FB Bob Niedbala / Brian Johnson
	DL Todd Middleton / Rudy Thompson
	DL Marvin Mitchell / Aubrey Hollifield
	DL Mike Smith
	DL Terry Smith
	DL James DuBose / Maurice Miller
	LB Warren Belin
	LB Levern Belin / Rodney Hogue
	DB George Coghill / Mark Stackhouse
	DB Tony Hollis / Ron Lambert
	DB Lamont Scales
	DB Brad Benson / Maurice Miller

RUSHING: Williams 119/430y, Rogers 106/394y, Barnhill 92/366y
PASSING: Barnhill 182-377/2454y, 17TD, 48.3%
RECEIVING: Proehl 65/1053y, Brown 32/531y, Jones 22/310y
SCORING: Proehl 66pts, Wilson Hoyle (K) 44pts, Barnhill 18pts

1990 3-8

17 Rice	33 WR Steve Brown / Darrell France
23 Appalachian St.	12 T Robbie Lingerfelt
15 N. Carolina St.	20 G Tom Mordica
52 Army	14 C Mark Williams / Mike Siders
24 North Carolina	43 G Steven Ainsworth
13 Maryland	41 T David Lowe / Rusty Bumgardner
14 Virginia	49 TE John Henry Mills / Walter Rasby
6 Clemson	24 QB Phil Barnhill / Keith West
20 Duke	57 TB Anthony Williams / Tony Rogers
7 Georgia Tech	42 WB Gregg Long / Bobby Jones
56 Vanderbilt	28 FB Bob Niedbala / Mitch Kennedy
	DL Mike McCrary
	DL Aubrey Hollifield
	DL Mike Smith
	DL Tryg Brody
	DL Maurice Miller / Rudy Thompson
	LB Warren Belin / Diron Reynolds
	LB Scott Shelhamer / Levern Belin
	DB George Coghill
	DB Mark Stackhouse
	DB Lamont Scales / Ron Lambert
	DB Tony Hollis / Terrence Singletary

RUSHING: Williams 181/866y, Rogers 68/277y, Barnhill 75/121y
PASSING: Barnhill 125-276/1443y, 6TD, 45.3%
RECEIVING: Mills 46/623y, Brown 35/454y, France 18/222y, Jones 18/178y
SCORING: David Behrmann (K) 59pts, Williams 54pts, Dixon & Rogers 24pts

1991 3-8

40 W. Carolina	24 WR Todd Dixon
3 N. Carolina St.	30 T Tom Kleinlein
14 Northwestern	41 G Tom Mordica
3 Appalachian St.	17 C Mike Siders
10 North Carolina	24 G Steven Ainsworth
22 Maryland	23 T David Lowe
7 Virginia	48 TE John Henry Mills / Walter Rasby
10 Clemson	28 QB Keith West
31 Duke	14 TB Anthony Williams / John Leach
3 Georgia Tech	27 WB Bobby Jones / Gregg Long
52 Navy	24 FB Bob Niedbala / Mitch Kennedy
	DL Mike McCrary
	DL Marvin Mitchell / Jay Williams
	DL Aubrey Hollifield
	DL Tryg Brody / Fred Booe
	DL Maurice Miller / Gleen Hart
	LB Mike Neubeiser / Kevin Giles
	LB Scott Shelhamer
	DB George Coghill
	DB Ron Lambert
	DB Lamont Scales / Darrell France
	DB Tony Hollis / Maurice Gravely

RUSHING: Williams 139/523y, Leach 104/503y, Kennedy 26/164y
PASSING: West 153-296/1969y, 9TD, 51.7%
RECEIVING: Mills 51/559y, Dixon 35/695y, Jones 30/433y
SCORING: Mike Green (K) 61pts, Dixon 42pts, Williams 24pts

1992 8-4

17 North Carolina	35 WR Todd Dixon / Marlon Estes
10 Appalachian St.	7 T Ben Coleman
7 Florida State	35 G Tom Mordica (T) / Reggie Avery
17 Virginia	31 C Eddie McKeel / Mike Siders
40 Vanderbilt	6 G Kevin Smith
30 Maryland	23 T Elton Ndoma-Ogar / David Lowe
23 Army	7 TE John Henry Mills / Walter Rasby
18 Clemson	15 QB Keith West
28 Duke	14 TB Ned Moultrie / John Leach
23 Georgia Tech	10 WB Bobby Jones
14 N. Carolina St.	42 FB Wendell Wells / Mitch Kennedy
39 Oregon■	35 DL Mike McCrary
	DL Jay Williams / Arna Bontemps
	DL Dred Booe
	DL Rudy Thompson
	DL Maurice Miller
	LB Kevin Giles / Ted VanHyfte
	LB Scott Shelhamer
	DB George Coghill
	DB Ron Lambert / Brent Morehead
	DB Lamont Scales / Kevin Cole
	DB Richard Goodpasture/Ma'rice Gravely

RUSHING: Moultrie 167/777y, Leach 149/691y, Wells 53/274y
PASSING: West 174-308/2301y, 13TD, 56.5%
RECEIVING: Dixon 56/916y, Mills 38/452y, Leach 29/274y
SCORING: Mike Green (K) 58pts, Dixon 54pts, Leach 46pts

1993 2-9

12 Vanderbilt	27 WR Todd Dixon / Marlon Estes
16 N. Carolina St.	34 WR Travis Johns / Roger Pettus
20 Appalachian St.	3 T Elton Ndoma-Ogar
14 Northwestern	26 G Kevin Smith
35 North Carolina	45 C Eddie McKeel
20 Clemson	16 G Tony Yarnell
13 Duke	21 T David Lowe
0 Florida State	54 TE Walter Rasby
9 Virginia	21 QB Jim Kemp / Rusty LaRue
28 Georgia Tech	38 RB John Leach
32 Maryland	33 FB Ned Moultrie
	DL Harold Gragg
	DL Dred Booe
	DL Jay Williams
	DL Semmajh Taylor / Rick Gardner
	LB Kevin Giles
	LB Tucker Grace / Mike Neubeiser
	LB Jimmy Quander / Diron Reynolds
	DB Brent Morehead / Alexis Sockwell
	DB Tom Stuetzer / Major Griffey
	DB Kevin Cole / Terrence Suber
	DB Richard Goodpasture/Ma'rice Gravely

RUSHING: Leach 215/1089y, Moultrie 93/364y, Kemp 53/76y
PASSING: Kemp 126-217/1488y, 6TD, 58.1%,
LaRue 67-121/854y, TD, 55.4%
RECEIVING: Leach 41/340y, Dixon 33/558y, Rasby 32/347y
SCORING: Leach 66pts, Mike Green (K) 41pts, Dixon 38pts

1994 3-8

14 Vanderbilt	35 WR Dan Ballou / Thabiti Davis
12 Appalachian St.	10 WR Adam Dolder / Darrell Braswell
14 Florida State	56 WR Roger Pettus
7 Maryland	31 T Elton Ndoma-Ogar
33 Army	27 G Bill Leeder
6 Virginia	42 C Eddie McKeel
3 N. Carolina St.	34 G Tony Yarnell
26 Duke	51 T Doug Marsigli
8 Clemson	24 TE Matt McNeel / Rhett Blanchard
0 North Carolina	50 QB Rusty LaRue
20 Georgia Tech	13 RB Jeremiah Williams / Herman Lewis
	DL Jimmy Quander / Harold Gragg
	DL Robert Fatzinger
	DL Steve Vaughan
	DL Rick Gardner / Semmajh Taylor
	LB Kevin Giles / Jon Mannon
	LB Mike Neubeiser
	LB Tucker Grace / LaDwaun Harrison
	DB Brent Morehead
	DB Major Griffey / Alexis Sockwell
	DB Terrence Suber / Tom Stuetzer
	DB Richard Goodpasture

RUSHING: Sherron Gudger (RB) 78/261y
PASSING: LaRue 132-230/1303y, 5TD, 57.4%
RECEIVING: Pettus 30/312y
SCORING: Bill Hollows (K) 35pts

1995 1-10

22 Appalachian St.	24 WR Dan Ballou / Desmond Clark
9 Tulane	35 WR Marlon Estes / Darrell Braswell
14 Clemson	29 WR Thabiti Davis
30 Navy	7 T Elton Ndoma-Ogar
17 Virginia	35 G Chris Gaskell
6 Maryland	9 C Bill Leeder / Greg McCracken / Bo Loy
13 Florida State	72 G Tony Yarnall (T) / Taris Clark
7 North Carolina	31 T Doug Marsigli (G)
26 Duke	42 TE William Clark
23 Georgia Tech	24 QB Rusty LaRue
23 N. Carolina St.	52 RB John Lewis / Herman Lewis
	DL David Zadel
	DL Rob Hyman / Jerome Simkins
	DL Robert Fatzinger / Aljamont Joyner
	DL Rick Gardner
	LB Jeffrey Muyres (DB) / Tom Stuetzer
	LB Kelvin Moses
	LB Tucker Grace
	DB D'Angelo Solomon
	DB Brent Morehead / Major Griffey
	DB Terrence Suber
	DB Alexis Sockwell

RUSHING: J. Lewis 110/304y, H. Lewis 52/120y,
Gardell Chavis (RB) 15/33y
PASSING: LaRue 264-421/2775y, 17TD, 62.7%
RECEIVING: Estes 68/833y, Braswell 51/557y, Davis 36/415y
SCORING: Estes 60pts, J. Lewis 48pts, Bill Hollows (K) 27pts

1996 3-8

19 Appalachian St.	13 WR Desmond Clark
28 Northwestern	27 WR Jammie Deese / Kai Sneed
10 Georgia Tech	30 WR Thabiti Davis
7 Virginia	42 T Jeff Flowe
10 Clemson	21 G Doug Marsigli / Sam Settar
6 North Carolina	45 C Chris Gaskell
0 Maryland	52 G Tony Yarnell / Taris Clark
18 Navy	47 T Brian Wolverton
7 Florida State	44 TE Joe Zelenka
17 Duke	16 QB Brian Kuklick
22 N. Carolina St.	37 RB Morgan Kane
	DL Robert Fatzinger / Clinton Wilburn
	DL Fred Robbins / Da'Vaughn Mellerson
	DL Aljamont Joyner / Kelvin Shackleford
	DL Harold Gragg
	LB David Zadel
	LB Kelvin Moses / Dustin Lyman
	LB Jon Mannon / Abdul Guice
	DB D'Angelo Solomon / Reggie Austin
	DB Major Griffey / Dameon Daniel
	DB Jeffrey Muyres
	DB Tom Stuetzer / David Moore

RUSHING: Kane 135/490y
PASSING: Kuklick 205-396/2526y, 11TD, 51.8%
RECEIVING: Clark 61/782y
SCORING: Clark 36pts, Bill Hollows (K) 30pts

1997 5-6

27 Northwestern	20 WR Jammie Deese / Brandon Perry
24 East Carolina	25 WR Desmond Clark
26 Georgia Tech	28 WR Thabiti Davis / William Merritt
19 N. Carolina St.	18 T Jeff Flowe / Todd Hollowell
13 Virginia	21 G Sam Settar
12 North Carolina	30 C Chris Gaskell / Wil Spires
35 Maryland	17 G Taris Clark
38 Duke	24 T Brian Wolverton
16 Clemson	33 TE Joe Zelenka / James Lik
28 Rutgers	14 QB Brian Kuklick / Ben Sankey
7 Florida State	58 RB Morgan Kane / Herman Lewis
	DL Kelvin Jones /
	DL Aljamont Joyner/Da'Vaughn Mellerson
	DL Kelvin Shackleford
	DL Fred Robbins / Robert Fatzinger
	LB Dustin Lyman / Abdul Guice
	LB Kelvin Moses
	LB David Zadel / Mark Makovec
	DB D'Angelo Solomon / Reggie Austin
	DB Dameon Daniel / Keyshorn Smith
	DB Jeffrey Muyres
	DB DaLawn Parrish / David Moore

RUSHING: Lewis 114/491y, Kane 109/445y,
Kito Gary (RB) 52/274y
PASSING: Kuklick 190-312/2180y, 15TD, 60.9%,
Sankey 54-93/606y, TD, 58.1%
RECEIVING: Clark 72/950y, Deese 54/697y, Davis 49/494y
SCORING: Matthew Burdick (K) 69pts, Clark & Davis 30pts

1998 3-8

0 Air Force	42 WR Jammie Deese
26 Navy	14 WR Desmond Clark
29 Clemson	19 WR Marvin Chalmers
27 Appalachian St.	30 T Marlon Curtis / Jeff Flowe
16 Duke	19 G Brian Wolverton
20 Maryland	10 C Wil Spires
31 North Carolina	38 G Sam Settar
17 Virginia	38 T Michael Collins
27 N. Carolina St.	38 TE Joe Zelenka / James Lik
7 Florida State	24 QB Brian Kuklick / Ben Sankey
35 Georgia Tech	63 RB Morgan Kane / Kito Gary
	DL Brian Ray / Clinton Wilburn
	DL Fred Robbins / Kelvin Shackleford
	DL Da'Vaughn Mellerson
	DL Kelvin Jones / Mat Petz
	LB Ed Kargbookorogie / Dustin Lyman
	LB Kelvin Moses / Jon Mannon
	LB Abdul Guice / Mark Makovec
	DB Reggie Austin
	DB Dameon Daniel / Keyshorn Smith
	DB Jeffrey Muyres
	DB DaLawn Parrish / David Moore

RUSHING: Kane 128/454y, Gary 75/194y, Sankey 14/65y
PASSING: Kuklick 216-396/2683y, 14TD, 54.5%,
Sankey 38-58/468y, 4TD, 65.5%
RECEIVING: Deese 68/826y, Clark 59/866y, Chalmers 31/438y
SCORING: Matthew Burdick (K) 63pts, Clark 48pts

1999 7-5

34 Army	15 WR Jammie Deese / Jimmy Caldwell
7 Virginia	35 WR Marvin Chalmers / Fabian Davis
31 N. Carolina St.	7 T Todd Hollowell
17 Rutgers	10 G Sam Settar / Mike Moosbrugger
14 Maryland	17 C Vince Azzolina
10 Florida State	3 G Brian Wolverton
47 Ala.-Birm'ham	3 T Michael Collins
3 Clemson	12 TE James Lik / Ray Thomas
19 North Carolina	3 QB Ben Sankey
35 Duke	48 RB Morgan Kane / Chris McCoy
26 Georgia Tech	23 FB Ovie Mughelli / Rhamen Love-Lane
23 Arizona State■	3 DL Bryan Ray
	DL Fred Robbins
	DL Kelvin Shackleford / Nate Bolling
	DL Kelvin Jones / Brad Smith
	LB Dustin Lyman / Ed Kargbookorogie
	LB Kelvin Moses / Marquis Hopkins
	LB Mark DeOrio / Nick Bender
	DB Reggie Austin
	DB Keyshorn Smith / Adrian Duncan
	DB DaLawn Parrish
	DB David Moore / Tehran Carpenter

RUSHING: Kane 275/1161y, Sankey 150/405y, McCoy 32/128y
PASSING: Sankey 133-224/1496y 9TD, 59.4%
RECEIVING: Deese 32/444y, Lik 19/211y, Caldwell 19/161y
SCORING: Matthew Burdick (K) 75pts, Kane 72pts,
Sankey 30pts

2000 2-9

16 Appalachian St.	20 WR Ira Williams / Jimmy Caldwell
14 North Carolina	35 WR Fabian Davis / John Stone
7 Clemson	55 T Seth Houk / Tyson Clabo
10 Virginia	27 G Mike Moosbrugger
10 Vanderbilt	17 C Vince Azzolina
20 Georgia Tech	52 G Michael Collins
7 Maryland	37 T Tim Bennett
28 Duke	26 TE Ray Thomas
6 Florida State	35 QB Anthony Young / C.J. Leak
49 Navy	26 RB Tarence Williams
14 N. Carolina St.	32 RB Fred Staton / Jamie Scott
	DL Bryan Ray / Calvin Pace
	DL Montique Sharpe/Da'Vau'hn Mellers'n
	DL Nate Bolling / Masanori Toguchi
	DL Bryan Ray
	LB Nick Bender / Jamaal Argrow
	LB Marquis Hopkins
	LB Ed Kargbookorogie
	DB Adrian Duncan
	DB Quinton Williams / Chris Justice
	DB Walter Simmons / Obi Chukwumah
	DB Michael Clinkscale

RUSHING: T. Williams 80/448y, Young 62/328y, Staton 36/119y
PASSING: James MacPherson (QB) 113-207/1324y, 3TD, 54.6%
Leak 30-70/341y, 0TD, 42.9%
RECEIVING: I. Williams 45/495y, Davis 21/336y,
Thomas 13/137y
SCORING: T. Williams 42pts, Tyler Ashe (K) 37pts

2001 6-5

20 Appalachian St.	10 WR Jason Anderson / Jax Landfried
21 East Carolina	19 WR Fabian Davis / John Stone (RB)
20 Maryland	27 T Mark Moroz
24 Florida State	48 G Mike Moosbrugger / Tyson Clabo
14 N. Carolina St.	17 C Vince Azzolina
42 Duke	35 G Michael Collins / Blake Henry
14 Clemson	21 T Tim Bennett
34 Virginia	30 TE Ray Thomas
32 North Carolina	31 QB James McPherson/Anth'ny Young
33 Georgia Tech	38 RB Tarence Williams / Fred Staton
38 N. Illinois	35 FB Ovie Mughelli / Nick Burney
	DL Calvin Pace
	DL Montique Sharpe
	DL Nate Bolling / Rod Stephon
	LB Kellen Brantley
	LB Marquis Hopkins
	LB Tehran Carpenter / Dion Williams
	DB Eric King
	DB Marcus McGruder
	DB Quinton Williams
	DB Obi Chukwumah / Elliott Ivey
	DB Caron Bracy / Dominic Anderson

RUSHING: Williams 249/1018y, Staton 137/583y,
Stone 58/315y, Young 39/191y
PASSING: MacPherson 113-209/1555y, 5TD, 54.1%
RECEIVING: Anderson 28/472y, Davis 24/306y, Stone 23/294y
SCORING: Tyler Ashe (K) 66pts, Williams 60pts

2002 7-6

41 N. Illinois	42 WR Jax Landfried / Jason Anderson
27 East Carolina	22 WR Fabian Davis / Anthony Young
13 N. Carolina St.	32 T Mark Moroz
24 Purdue	21 G Blake Henry
34 Virginia	38 C Blake Lingruen
24 Georgia Tech	21 G Tyson Clabo
36 Duke	10 T Tim Bennett
23 Clemson	31 TE Ray Thomas
31 North Carolina	0 QB James McPherson/Cory Randolph
21 Florida State	34 RB Tarence Williams / Chris Barclay
30 Navy	27 FB Ovie Mughelli / Nick Burney
14 Maryland	32 DL Calvin Pace
38 Oregon ■	17 DL Montique Sharpe
	DL Rod Stephen / Jamaal Argrow
	LB Jamie Scott
	LB Brad White / Dion Williams
	LB Kellen Brantley
	DB Eric King
	DB Daryl Shaw
	DB Quinton Williams
	DB Warren Braxton
	DB Caron Bracy / Obi Chukwumah

RUSHING: Williams 186/852y, Barclay 144/703y, Davis 52/446y
PASSING: McPherson 123-223/1837y, 8TD, 55.2%
RECEIVING: Landfried 38/533y, Davis 37/575y, Anderson 23/535y
SCORING: Matt Wisnosky (K) 84pts, Mughelli 72pts, Barclay 54pts

2003 5-7

32 Boston College	28 WR Jason Anderson / Nate Morton
38 N. Carolina St.	24 WR Willie Idlette / Anthony Young
10 Purdue	16 T Tyson Clabo (G) / Wesley Bryant
34 East Carolina	16 G Arby Jones
24 Virginia	27 C Blake Lindgruen
7 Georgia Tech	24 G Steve Vallos
42 Duke	13 T Mark Moroz / Greg Adkins
24 Florida State	48 TE Josh Warren
45 Clemson	17 QB Cory Randolph
34 North Carolina	42 RB Chris Barclay / Cornelius Birgs
17 Connecticut	51 FB Nick Burney
28 Maryland	41 DL Jerome Nichols / Arthur Orlebar
	DL Goryal Scales / Cori Stukes
	DL Jyles Tucker / John Finklea
	LB Dion Williams / Jamaal Argrow
	LB Brad White
	LB Kellen Brantley
	DB Eric King
	DB Marcus McGruder /Riley Swanson
	DB Warren Braxton
	DB Quinton Williams / Josh Gattis
	DB Caron Bracy/Obi Chukwumah (LB)

RUSHING: Barclay 235/1192y, Randolph 94/404y, Birgs 103/344y
PASSING: Randolph 144-246/1773y, 8TD, 58.5%
RECEIVNG: Anderson 44/751y, Idlette 32/319y, Davis 19/249y
SCORING: Barclay 72pts, Ryan Plackemeier (K) 31pts, Birgs 30pts

2004 4-7

30 Clemson	37 WR Nate Morton / Jason Anderson
31 East Carolina	17 WR Kevin Marion / Chris Davis
42 N. Carolina A&T	3 T Wesley Bryant
17 Boston College	14 G Arby Jones
21 N. Carolina St.	27 C Blake Lindgruen
10 Virginia Tech	17 G Steve Vallos (T) / Greg Adkins
17 Florida State	20 T Matt Brim
24 Duke	22 TE Zac Selmon / R.D. Montgomery
24 North Carolina	31 QB Cory Randolph / Ben Mauk
7 Miami	52 RB Chris Barclay / Micah Andrews
7 Maryland	13 FB Dan Callahan
	DL Matt Robinson / Bryan Andrews
	DL Jerome Nichols
	DL Goryal Scales
	DL Jyles Tucker / Jeremy Thompson
	LB Caron Bracy
	LB Brad White / Pierre Easley
	LB Jon Abbate
	DB Eric King
	DB Marcus McGruder /Riley Swanson
	DB Josh Gattis / Warren Braxton
	DB Patrick Ghee

RUSHING: Barclay 243/1010y, Mauk 58/295y, Randolph 92/287y
PASSING: Randolph 78-147/972y, 3TD, 53.1%, Mauk 49-94/572y, 2TD, 52.1%
RECEIVING: Morton 26/391y, Barclay 21/118y, Anderson 20/308y
SCORING: Barclay 54pts, Andrews 36pts, Matt Wisnosky (K) 32pts

2005 4-7

20 Vanderbilt	24 WR Nate Morton / Chris Davis
3 Nebraska	31 WR Demir Bolden / Kenneth Moore
44 East Carolina	34 T Wesley Bryant / Greg Adkins
12 Maryland	22 G Arby Jones
31 Clemson	27 C Steve Justice
24 Florida State	41 G Matthew Brim
30 Boston College	35 T Steve Vallos
27 N. Carolina St.	19 TE Zac Selmon / John Tereshinski
44 Duke	6 QB Ben Mauk / Cory Randolph
17 Georgia Tech	30 RB Chris Barclay / Micah Andrews
17 Miami	47 FB Damon McWhite / Richard Belton
	DL Matt Robinson
	DL Zach Stukes / Jyles Tucker
	DL Goryal Scales
	DL Jeremy Thompson / Bryan Andrews
	LB Aaron Curry
	LB Jon Abbate
	LB Stanley Arnoux / Pierre Easley
	DB Riley Swanson / Kevin Patterson
	DB Alphonso Smith
	DB Josh Gattis / Chip Vaughn
	DB Patrick Ghee / Dominic Anderson

RUSHING: Barclay 218/1127y, Andrews 110/621y
PASSING: Mauk 85-158/845y, 1TD, 845y, Randolph 85-131/821y, 5TD, 64.9%
RECEIVING: Morton 39/482y, Barclay 26/159y, Davis 23/220y, Boldin 15/224y, Belton 13/85y
SCORING: Sam Swank (K) 86pts, Barclay 60pts

2006 11-3

20 Syracuse	10 WR Nate Morton / Kevin Marion
14 Duke	13 WR Willie Idlette
24 Connecticut	13 T Steve Vallos
27 Mississippi	3 G Louis Frazier
34 Liberty	14 C Steve Justice
17 Clemson	22 G Chris DeGeare
25 N. Carolina St.	23 T Arby Jones / Jeff Griffin
24 North Carolina	17 TE Zac Selmon / John Tereshinski
21 Boston College	14 QB Riley Skinner
30 Florida State	0 RB Kenneth Moore (WR) / Kevin Harris
6 Virginia Tech	27 FB Richard Belton
38 Maryland	24 DL Jyles Tucker
9 Georgia Tech ☐	6 DL Bryan Andrews
13 Louisville ■	24 DL Jamil Smith
	DL Zach Stukes / Jeremy Thompson
	LB Aaron Curry
	LB Jon Abbate
	LB Stanley Arnoux
	DB Alphonso Smith / Kevin Patterson
	DB Riley Swanson
	DB Josh Gattis
	DB Patrick Ghee

RUSHING: Moore 105/507y, Harris 78/393y, Bryant 84/336y, Micah Andrews (RB) 58/256y, Belton 51/227y, Marion 23/210y
PASSING: Skinner 171-260/2051y, 9TD, 65.8%
RECEIVING: Morton 38/617y, Idlette 37/511y, Moore 32/314y
SCORING: Sam Swank (K) 102pts, Harris 36pts, Morton & Idlette 24pts

2007 9-4

28 Boston College	38 WR Kenneth Moore / Demir Boldin
17 Nebraska	20 WR Chip Brinkman / Kevin Marion
21 Army	10 T Louis Frazier
31 Maryland	24 G Matthew Brim / Barrett McMillin
41 Duke	36 C Steve Justice
24 Florida State	21 G Chris DeGeare
44 Navy	24 T Joe Birdsong / Jeff Griffin
37 North Carolina	10 TE Zac Selmon / John Tereshinski
16 Virginia	17 QB Riley Skinner / Brett Hodges
10 Clemson	44 RB Josh Adams / Micah Andrews
38 N. Carolina St.	18 FB Rich Belton / De'Angelo Bryant
31 Vanderbilt	17 DL Matt Robinson / Anthony Davis
24 Connecticut ■	10 DL Boo Robinson
	DL Zach Stukes / John Russell
	DL Jeremy Thompson
	LB Aaron Curry / Dominique Midgett
	LB Stanley Arnoux
	LB Chantz McClinic / Hunter Haynes
	DB Alphonso Smith / Channing Schofield
	DB Brandon Ghee / Kerry Major
	DB Chip Vaughn / Alex Frye
	DB Kevin Patterson / Aaron Mason

RUSHING: Adams 219/953y, Andrews 116/420y, Moore 44/316y
PASSING: Skinner 236-326/2204y, 12TD, 72.4%
RECEIVING: Moore 98/1011y, Adams 34/123y, Tereshinski 28/355y, Brinkman 27/225y
SCORING: Sam Swank (K) 98pts, Adams 72pts, Moore 54pts

2008 8-5

41 Baylor	13 WR D.J. Boldin
30 Mississippi	28 WR Chip Brinkman
12 Florida State	3 T Joe Birdsong
17 Navy	24 G Joe Looney / Russell Nenon (C)
12 Clemson	7 C Trey Bailey
0 Maryland	26 G Barrett McMillin
10 Miami	16 T Jeff Griffin (G) / Doug Weaver
33 Duke	30 TE Ben Wooster / Andrew Parker
28 Virginia	17 QB Riley Skinner
17 N. Carolina St.	21 TB Brandon Pendergrass / Josh Adams
21 Boston College	24 FB Mike Rinfrette / Kevin Harris
23 Vanderbilt	10 DL Matt Robinson
29 Navy ■	19 DL Boo Robinson / Michael Carter
	DL John Russell
	DL Kyle Wilber / Anthony Davis
	LB Aaron Curry
	LB Stanley Arnoux
	LB Chantz McClinic
	DB Alphonso Smith
	DB Brandon Ghee / Josh Bush
	DB Chip Vaughn / Alex Frye
	DB Kevin Patterson

RUSHING: Pendergrass 150/528y, Adams 122/402y, Harris 33/176y
PASSING: Skinner 232-363/2347y, 13TD, 63.9%
RECEIVING: Bolden 81/848y, Williams 26/309y, Wooster 24/211y, Brinkman 22/251y
SCORING: Sam Swank (K) 51pts, Pendergrass & Popham 30pts

2009 5-7

21 Baylor	24 WR Marshall Williams / Jordan Williams
24 Stanford	17 WR Devon Brown / Chris Givens
35 Elon	7 T Chris DeGeare
24 Boston College	27 G Joe Looney
30 N. Carolina St.	24 C Russell Nenon
42 Maryland	32 G Barrett McMillin
3 Clemson	38 T Jeff Griffin / Joe Birdsong
10 Navy	13 TE Andrew Parker / Cameron Ford
27 Miami	28 QB Riley Skinner
27 Georgia Tech	30 TB Josh Adams / Brandon Pendergrass
28 Florida State	41 FB Mike Rinfrette / Tommy Bohannon
45 Duke	34 DL Tristan Dorty / Will Wright
	DL Boo Robinson / Michael Carter
	DL John Russell
	DL Kyle Wilber / Geno Orange
	LB Jonathan Jones / Joey Ehrmann
	LB Dominique Midgett / Lee Malchow
	LB Matt Woodlief / Hunter Haynes
	DB Brandon Ghee / Dominique Tate
	DB Kenny Okoro / Michael Williams
	DB Josh Bush / Alex Frye
	DB Cyhl Quarles

RUSHING: Adams 113/541y, Pendergrass 83/399y, Harris 36/156y, Brown 36/150y
PASSING: Skinner 264-400/3160y, 26TD, 66%
RECEIVING: Brown 61/671y, M. Williams 60/867y, Givens 45/629y, Adams 28/327y
SCORING: Jimmy Newman (K) 67pts, Givens 48pts, Brown 42pts

2010 3-9

53 Presbyterian	13 WR Devon Brown / Danny Dembry
54 Duke	48 WR Marshall Williams
24 Stanford	68 WR/FB Chris Givens / Tommy Bohanon
0 Florida State	31 T Dennis Godfrey
20 Georgia Tech	24 G Joe Looney / Gabe Irby
27 Navy	28 C Russell Nenon
21 Virginia Tech	52 G Michael Hoag / Garrick Williams
14 Maryland	62 T Doug Weaver
13 Boston College	23 TE Andrew Parker / Cameron Ford
3 N. Carolina St.	38 QB Tanner Price / Ted Stachitas
10 Clemson	30 RB Josh Adams / Josh Harris
34 Vanderbilt	13 DL Tristan Dorty (LB) / Kevin Smith
	DL Frank Souza / Gelo Orange
	DL Nikita Whitlock / Kris Redding
	DL Kyle Wilber (LB) / Zach Thompson
	LB Joey Ehrmann / Kyle Jarrett
	LB Hunter Haynes / Scott Betros
	LB Matt Woodlief / Riley Haynes
	DB Kenny Okoro / Kevin Johnson
	DB Josh Bush / A.J. Marshall
	DB Daniel Mack / Alex Frye
	DB Cyhi Quarles / Duran Lowe

RUSHING: Harris 126/720y, Adams 91/316y, Stachitas 35/171y
PASSING: Price 137-241/1349y, 7TD, 56.8%, Stachitas 12-23/131y, 0TD, 52.2%
RECEIVING: Brown 39/302y, Givens 35/514y, Williams 24/272y
SCORING: Jimmy Newman (K) 67pts, Givens & Harris 42pts

WASHINGTON

University of Washington (1861)
Seattle, Washington
Nickname: Huskies
Colors: Purple and Gold
Stadium: Husky Stadium (1920) 72,500
Conference Affiliations: Pacific Coast (Charter member, 1916-58),
  AAWU (1959-68), Pacific 8/10 (1969-present)

CAREER RUSHING YARDS	Attempts	Yards
Napoleon Kaufman (1991-94)	710	4041
Joe Steele (1976-79)	663	3091
Greg Lewis (1987-90)	529	2678
Vince Weathersby (1985-88)	572	2653
Chris Polk (2008-10)	506	2561
Hugh McElhenny (1949-51)	451	2499
Louis Rankin (2004-07)	488	2480
Rich Alexis (2000-03)	582	2371
Robin Earl (1973-76)	463	2351
Jacque Robinson (1981-84)	503	2300

CAREER PASSING YARDS	Comp.-Att.	Yards
Cody Pickett (1999-03)	792-1373	9916
Jake Locker (2007-10)	619-1148	7639
Brock Huard (1996-98)	422-776	5742
Damon Huard (1992-95)	458-764	5692
Marques Tuiasosopo (1997-00)	418-761	5501
Sonny Sixkiller (1970-72)	385-811	5496
Cary Conklin (1986-89)	401-747	4850
Steve Pelluer (1980-83)	436-755	4603
Don Heinrich (1949-52)	335-610	4392
Chris Chandler (1984-87)	326-587	4161

CAREER RECEIVING YARDS	Catches	Yards
Reggie Williams (2001-03)	238	3536
Jermaine Kearse (2008-10)	133	2172
Mario Bailey (1988-91)	131	2093
Jerome Pathon (1995-97)	125	2063
Anthony Russo (2004-07)	122	1944
Scott Phillips (1973-76)	111	1866
Charles Federick (2001-04)	121	1735
Paul Skansi (1979-82)	138	1723
Brian Slater (1985-88)	87	1648
Sonny Shackelford (2003-06)	119	1648

SEASON RUSHING YARDS	Attempts	Yards
Corey Dillon (1996)	271	1555
Chris Polk (2010)	260	1415
Napoleon Kaufman (1994)	255	1390
Napoleon Kaufman (1993)	226	1299
Louis Rankin (2007)	233	1294

SEASON PASSING YARDS	Comp.-Att.	Yards
Cody Pickett (2002)	365-612	4458
Cody Pickett (2003)	257-454	3043
Cary Conklin (1989)	208-365	2569
Damon Huard (1995)	184-287	2415
Cody Pickett (2001)	169-301	2403

SEASON RECEIVING YARDS	Catches	Yards
Reggie Williams (2002)	94	1454
Jerome Pathon (1997)	69	1245
Reggie Williams (2003)	89	1109
Andre Riley (1989)	53	1039
Mario Bailey (1991)	62	1037

GAME RUSHING YARDS	Attempts	Yards
Hugh McElhenny (1950 vs. Wash. State)	20	296
Chris Polk (2010 vs. Washington State)	29	284
Corey Dillon (1996 vs. Oregon)	32	259

GAME PASSING YARDS	Comp.-Att.	Yards
Cody Pickett (2001 vs. Arizona)	29-49	455
Cody Pickett (2002 vs. Idaho)	32-44	438
Cody Pickett (2002 vs. UCLA)	29-60	429

GAME RECEIVING YARDS	Catches	Yards
Dave Williams (1965 vs. UCLA)	10	257
Andre Riley (1989 vs. Arizona State)	9	223
Charles Frederick (2004 vs. Oregon State)	9	216

GREATEST COACH:

It is never easy replacing a legend. When you are an unknown coach yourself, it is that much more difficult. But Don James not only replaced the popular and successful Jim Owens, he took the Washington program to heights never before reached. Before long he became the face of the program in much the way Owens had been.

James, who came to Seattle after a successful run at Kent State, stayed for 18 seasons, winning 153 games including 10 of 15 bowls games. He brought six Husky squads to the Rose Bowl and won four times. The pinnacle of success occurred near the end of his run when he helped bring to the University of Washington its first-ever national championship, awarded to the 12-0 1991 team.

James retired following the next season under odd circumstances. In August of 1993 the Huskies were put on two-year probation by the Pac 10 and James abruptly quit in protest. That decision and the levied sanctions helped slow down some of the gains the program had made under James but did not diminish his overall legacy.

WASHINGTON'S 55 GREATEST SINCE 1953

OFFENSE

WIDE RECEIVER: Mario Bailey, Spider Gaines, Jerome Pathon, Reggie Williams
TIGHT END: Mark Bruener, Dave Williams
TACKLE: Lincoln Kennedy, Jeff Toews, Mike Zandofsky
GUARD: Chuck Allen, Milt Bohart, Benji Olson, Chad Ward
CENTER: Bern Brostek, Ed Cunningham, Olin Kreutz, Roy McKasson
QUARTERBACK: Steve Pelluer, Marques Tuiasosopo
RUNNING BACK: Napoleon Kaufman, Greg Lewis, Chris Polk, Joe Steele
FULLBACK: Junior Coffey, Robin Earl

DEFENSE

END: Jason Chorak, Tom Greenlee, Daniel Te'o-Nesheim
TACKLE: Steve Emtman, Ron Holmes, Doug Martin, Dave Pear, Reggie Rogers, Larry Tripplett
LINEBACKER: Dave Hoffmann, Michael Jackson, George Jugum, Joe Kelly, Dan Lloyd,
  Mark Stewart
CORNERBACK: Nesby Glasgow, Ray Horton, Vestee Jackson, Calvin Jones, Al Worley
SAFETY: Lawyer Milloy, Tony Parrish, Tim Peoples

SPECIAL TEAMS

RETURN SPECIALIST: Jim Krieg
PLACE KICKER: Chuck Nelson
PUNTER: Skip Boyd

MULTIPLE POSITIONS

NOSEGUARD-LINEBACKER: Mark Jerue

TWO-WAY PLAYERS

TACKLE-DEFENSIVE TACKLE: Kurt Gegner
LINEBACKER-GUARD: Rick Redman
QUARTERBACK-DEFENSIVE BACK: Bob Schloredt

PERFORMANCE FORMULA:
WASHINGTON'S 10 BEST SEASONS

1991	1.8618	1 of 71
1990	1.6369	4 of 70
2000	1.6107	6 of 70
1984	1.6044	3 of 70
1959	1.5985	4 of 70
1960	1.5806	4 of 70
1982	1.4765	10 of 70
1996	1.4740	13 of 70
1992	1.4539	11 of 70
1986	1.4447	11 of 70

WASHINGTON HUSKIES

Year	W-L-T	AP Poll	Conference Standing	Toughest Regular Season Opponents	Coach (Record at School)	Bowl Games		
1953	3-6-1		7	UCLA 8-1, Utah 8-2, Southern California 6-3-1, Stanford 6-3-1	John Cherberg			
1954	2-8		8	UCLA 8-0, Southern California 8-3, Baylor 7-3	John Cherberg			
1955	5-4-1		5	UCLA 9-1, Oregon State 6-3, Stanford 6-3-1, Southern California 6-4	John Cherberg (10-18-2)			
1956	5-5		5	Southern Cal 8-2, Minnesota 6-1-2, Oregon State 7-2-1, UCLA 7-3	Darrell Royal (5-5)			
1957	3-6-1		6	Ohio State 8-1, UCLA 8-2, Oregon State 8-2	Jim Owens			
1958	3-7		8	Ohio State 6-1-2, California 7-3, Washington St. 7-3, Oregon 6-4	Jim Owens			
1959	10-1	8	1	Southern California 8-2, Oregon 8-2, Washington St. 6-4	Jim Owens	Rose	44 Wisconsin	8
1960	10-1	6	1	Navy 9-1, UCLA 7-2-1, Oregon 7-2-1, Oregon State 6-3-1	Jim Owens	Rose	17 Minnesota	7
1961	5-4-1		2t	UCLA 7-3, Purdue 6-3	Jim Owens			
1962	7-1-2		2	Southern California 10-0, Oregon State 8-2, Oregon 6-3-1	Jim Owens			
1963	6-5		1	Pittsburgh 9-1, Oregon 7-3, Southern California 7-3, Air Force 7-3	Jim Owens	Rose	7 Illinois	17
1964	6-4		3	Oregon State 8-2, Oregon 7-2-1, Southern California 7-3	Jim Owens			
1965	5-5		4	Southern Cal 7-2-1, UCLA 7-2-1, Ohio State 7-2, Washington State 7-3	Jim Owens			
1966	6-4		4	UCLA 9-1, Southern California 7-3, Oregon State 7-3	Jim Owens			
1967	5-5		4t	Southern California 9-1, UCLA 7-2-1, Oregon State 7-2-1	Jim Owens			
1968	3-5-2		8	Southern Cal 9-0-1, Oregon State 7-3, California 7-3-1, Stanford 6-3-1	Jim Owens			
1969	1-9		7	So. Cal 9-0-1, Ohio St. 8-1, UCLA 8-1-1, Michigan 8-2, Stanford 7-2-1	Jim Owens			
1970	6-4		2t	Michigan 9-1, Stanford 8-3, Oregon 6-4-1	Jim Owens			
1971	8-3	19	3	Stanford 8-3, Southern California 6-4-1, TCU 6-4, California 6-5	Jim Owens			
1972	8-3		3t	Southern California 11-0, UCLA 8-3, Washington State 7-4	Jim Owens			
1973	2-9		8	Southern California 9-1-1, UCLA 9-2, Stanford 7-4	Jim Owens			
1974	5-6		5t	Southern California 9-1-1, Texas 8-3, Texas A&M 8-3, California 7-3-1	Jim Owens (99-82-6)			
1975	6-5		3t	Arizona State 11-0, Alabama 10-1, Texas 9-2, UCLA 8-2-1, California 8-3	Don James			
1976	5-6		4t	Southern California 10-1, UCLA 9-1-1, Colorado 8-3	Don James			
1977	10-2	10	1	Southern California 7-4, Stanford 8-3, UCLA 7-4, Minnesota 7-4	Don James	Rose	27 Michigan	20
1978	7-4		2t	Alabama 10-1, Southern California 10-1, UCLA 8-3, Arizona State 8-3	Don James			
1979	10-2	11	2	Southern California 10-01, Pittsburgh 9-1, Oregon 6-5	Don James	Sun	14 Texas	7
1980	9-3	16	1	Southern California 8-2-1, Navy 8-3, Oregon 6-3-2, Arizona State 7-4	Don James	Rose	6 Michigan	23
1981	10-2	10	1	Southern California 9-2, Arizona State 9-2, UCLA 7-3-1	Don James	Rose	28 Iowa	0
1982	10-2	7	2	UCLA 9-1-1, Arizona 9-2, Arizona State 9-2, California 7-4	Don James	Aloha	21 Maryland	20
1983	8-4		2	Michigan 9-2, Arizona 7-3-1, Washington St. 7-4, UCLA 6-4-1	Don James	Aloha	10 Penn State	13
1984	11-1	2	2	Southern Cal 8-3, Arizona 7-4, Houston 7-4	Don James	Orange	28 Oklahoma	17
1985	7-5		4t	BYU 11-2, UCLA 8-2-1, Arizona State 8-3, Oklahoma State 8-3	Don James	Freedom	20 Colorado	17
1986	8-3-1	18	2t	Arizona State 9-1-1, UCLA 7-3-1, Ohio State 9-3, Stanford 8-3	Don James	Sun	6 Alabama	28
1987	7-4-1		3	UCLA 9-2, Texas A&M 9-2, Southern California 8-3	Don James	Independence	24 Tulane	12
1988	6-5		6	Southern Cal 10-1-1, Army 9-2, UCLA 9-2, Washington State 8-3	Don James			
1989	8-4	23	2t	Colorado 11-0, Southern California 9-1-1, Texas A&M 8-3, Arizona 7-4	Don James	Freedom	34 Florida	7
1990	10-2	5	1	Colorado 10-1-1, Southern California 8-3-1, Oregon 8-3, Arizona 7-4	Don James	Rose	46 Iowa	34
1991	12-0	2	1	Nebraska 9-1-1, California 9-2, Stanford 8-3	Don James	Rose	34 Michigan	14
1992	9-3	11	1	Nebraska 9-2, Stanford 9-3, Washington State 8-3	Don James (153-57-2)	Rose	31 Michigan	38
1993	7-4		Ineligible	Ohio State 9-1-1, UCLA 8-3, California 8-4	Jim Lambright			
1994	7-4		Ineligible	Miami 10-1, Oregon 9-3, Ohio State 9-3	Jim Lambright			
1995	7-4-1		1t	Ohio State 11-1, Notre Dame 9-2, Oregon 9-2, Southern California 8-2-1	Jim Lambright	Sun	18 Iowa	38
1996	9-3	16	2	Arizona State 11-0, BYU 13-1, Notre Dame 8-3	Jim Lambright	Holiday	21 Colorado	33
1997	8-4	18	4	Nebraska 12-0, Washington State 10-1, UCLA 9-2, Arizona State 8-3	Jim Lambright	Aloha	51 Michigan State	23
1998	6-6		5	Arizona 11-1, UCLA 10-1, Nebraska 9-3, Oregon 8-3	Jim Lambright (44-25-1)	Oahu	25 Air Force	45
1999	7-5		2	Stanford 8-3, Oregon 8-3, BYU 8-3	Rick Neuheisel	Holiday	20 Kansas State	24
2000	11-1	3	1t	Miami 10-1, Oregon State 10-1, Oregon 9-2	Rick Neuheisel	Rose	34 Purdue	24
2001	8-4	19	2t	Miami 11-0, Michigan 8-3, Stanford 9-2, Washington State 9-2	Rick Neuheisel	Holiday	43 Texas	47
2002	7-6		4t	Southern Cal 10-2, Washington State 10-2, Michigan 9-3	Rick Neuheisel (33-16)	Sun	24 Purdue	34
2003	6-6		5t	Southern Cal 11-1, Ohio St. 10-2, Washington State 9-3, Oregon 8-4	Keith Gilbertson			
2004	1-10		10	Southern California 12-0, California 10-1, Oregon State 6-5	Keith Gilbertson (7-16)			
2005	2-9		9t	Southern Cal 12-0, Oregon 10-1, UCLA 9-2, Notre Dame 9-2	Tyrone Willingham			
2006	5-7		9	Southern Cal 10-2, Oklahoma 10-2, California 9-3, Oregon State 9-4	Tyrone Willingham			
2007	4-9		10	Ohio State 11-1, So. California 10-2, Arizona State 10-2, Hawaii 12-0	Tyrone Willingham			
2008	0-12		10	Oregon 9-3, BYU 10-2, Oklahoma 12-1, Southern California 11-1	Tyrone Willingham (11-37)			
2009	5-7		7	LSU 9-3, Stanford 8-4, Oregon 10-2, Oregon State 8-4	Steve Sarkisian			
2010	7-6		3t	Nebraska 10-3, Stanford 11-1, Oregon 12-0	Steve Sarkisian (12-13)	Holiday	19 Nebraska	7

TOTAL: 374-269-11 .5803 (26 of 70) **Bowl Games since 1953:** 15-11 .5769 (23 of 70)

GREATEST TEAM SINCE 1953: Winning all 12 games while capturing a share of the only national title in school history allows the 1991 squad to run away with this category. While the offense did its job, this team won with defense, holding six opponents to less than 10 points with two shutouts. One of history's greatest players, tackle Steve Emtman, ed the Huskies defense.

1953 3-6-1

20 Colorado	21 E George Black / Jim Houston
0 Michigan	50 T Duane Wardlow / Jerry Esser
28 Oregon State	0 G Jim Noe / Earl Monlux
13 Southern Cal	13 C Vern Lindskog / Jacl Lindskog
14 Oregon	6 G Milt Bohart
7 Stanford	13 T Dean Chambers
21 Utah	14 E Jim Warsinski / Doug McClary
25 California	53 QB Sandy Lederman / Dean Rockey
6 UCLA	22 HB Mike Monroe
20 Washington St.	25 HB Stew Crook / Bill Albrecht
	FB Bob McNamee / Jack Nugent

RUSHING: Dunn 52/236y, Crook 60/213y, Nugent 51/203y
PASSING: Lederman 92-189/1157y, 8TD, 48.7 %
RECEIVING: Warsinski 21/255y, Houston 14/190y, Black 13/272y
SCORING: Black 24pts, Kyllingstad 18pts, Niles (K) 15pts

1954 2-8

7 Utah	6 E Corky Lewis / Bud Green
0 Michigan	14 T George Strugar / Ed Sheron
17 Oregon State	7 G Larry Rhodes
20 UCLA	21 C Dell Jensen / Pete Arrivey
7 Baylor	34 G Earl Monlux
7 Stanford	13 T Fred Robinson / Ray Michanczyk
7 Oregon	26 E Doug McClary / Jim Houston
6 California	27 QB Sandy Lederman / Bobby Cox
0 Southern Cal	41 HB Dean Derby / Bill Albrecht
7 Washington St.	26 HB Bobby Dunn / Stew Crook
	FB Bob McNamee

RUSHING: McNamee 78/291y, Crook 62/270y, Dunn 61/194y
PASSING: Cox 66-146/809y, 4TD, 45.2%
RECEIVING: Lewis 21/250y, Houston 14/217y, Dunn 11/134y
SCORING: Dunn (HB-K) 22pts, Lewis 12pts, Derby 8pts

1955 5-4-1

14 Idaho	7 E Corky Lewis
30 Minnesota	0 T George Strugar / Ed Sheron
19 Oregon	7 G Fred Robinson / Gene Pederson
7 Southern Cal	0 C Dell Jensen / Bert Watson
7 Baylor	13 G Earl Monlux
7 Stanford	7 T Dick Day / Don McCumby
7 Oregon State	13 E Bud Green / Jim Houston
6 California	20 QB Steve Roake / Sandy Lederman
17 UCLA	19 HB Mike Monroe / Dean Derby
27 Washington St.	7 HB Jim Jones
	FB Credell Green / Bob McNamee

RUSHING: Green 108/652y, Monroe 95/392y, Jones 72/273y
PASSING: Roake 27-61/410y, 3TD, 44.3%
RECEIVING: Houston 16/149y, Lewis 8/177y, Monroe 6/85y
SCORING: Green 30pts, Derby 20pts, Jones & Houston 18pts

1956 5-5

53 Idaho	21 E Corky Lewis
14 Minnesota	34 T Don McCumby
28 Illinois	13 G Dick Day / Gene Pederson
20 Oregon	7 C Ben Hammond
7 Southern Cal	35 G Whitey Core
7 California	16 T George Strugar / Gene Hallock
20 Oregon State	28 E Bruce Claridge / Chet Harvey
9 UCLA	13 QB Al Ferguson
34 Stanford	13 HB Luther Carr / Mike McCluskey
40 Washington St.	26 HB Dean Derby / Bob Herring
	FB Credell Green / Jim Jones

RUSHING: Carr 75/469y, Green 95/395y, Derby 88/395y
PASSING: Ferguson 20-41/418y, 3TD, 48.8%
RECEIVING: Derby 9/97y, Lewis 6/139y, McCluskey 5/118y
SCORING: Derby 63pts, McCluskey 36pts, Carr 30pts

1957 3-6-1

6 Colorado	6 E Bruce Claridge / Dick McVeigh
7 Minnesota	46 T Don McCumby / Jim McCarter
7 Ohio State	35 G Don Armstrong
0 UCLA	19 C Marv Bergmann / Reese Lindquist
14 Stanford	21 G Whitey Core
19 Oregon State	6 T Dick Day / Jim Heck
12 Southern Cal	19 E Duane Lowell / Carl Morgan
13 Oregon	6 QB Al Ferguson / Bob Dunn
35 California	27 HB Mike McCluskey / Luther Carr
7 Washington St.	27 HB Dick Payseno / Don Millich
	FB Jim Jones

RUSHING: Jones 105/488y, Payseno 89/412y, McCluskey72/351y
PASSING: Dunn 16-55/227y, 2TD, 29.1%
RECEIVING: Claridge 7/92y, Millich 6/97y, Payseno 5/112y
SCORING: Claridge 27pts, Ferguson, Millich & Payseno 18pts

1958 3-7

14 San Jose State	6 E Bruce Claridge / Stan Chapple
24 Minnesota	21 T Kurt Gegner / Bob Echols
7 Ohio State	12 G Don Armstrong / Jim Heck
12 Stanford	22 C George Pitt / Roy McKasson
0 UCLA	20 G Chuck Allen
12 Oregon State	14 T Bill Kinnune / Barr Bullard
0 Oregon	0 E Pat Claridge / Duane Lowell
6 Southern Cal	21 QB Bob Hivner / Bob Schloredt
7 California	12 HB Luther Carr / George Fleming
14 Washington St.	18 HB Mike McCluskey / Carver Gayton
	FB Don McKeta

RUSHING: McCluskey 60/292y, Hivner 91/247y, Schloredt74/240y
PASSING: Hivner 48-115/587y, 3TD, 41.7%
RECEIVING: Carr 14/238y, McCloskey 10/128y,
  B. Claridge 10/104y
SCORING: Hivner 36pts, McCloskey 18pts, Gayton &Fleming12pts

1959 10-1

21 Colorado	12 E Lee Folkins / Pat Claridge
23 Idaho	0 T Kurt Gegner
51 Utah	6 G Chuck Allen / Jack Walters
10 Stanford	0 C Roy McKasson / George Pitt
15 Southern Cal	22 G Bill Kinnune / Jim Skaggs
13 Oregon	12 T Barry Bullard / Ben Davidson
23 UCLA	7 E John Meyers / Stan Chapple
13 Oregon State	9 QB Bob Schloredt / Bob Hivner
20 California	0 HB George Fleming / Don Millich
20 Washington St.	0 HB Don McKeta / Brent Wooten
44 Wisconsin■	8 FB Ray Jackson / Joe Jones

RUSHING: Jackson 95/460y, McKeta 64/287y, Jones 61/284y
PASSING: Schloredt 39-75/733y, 5TD, 52%
RECEIVING: Folkins 12/214y, Fleming 11/199y, Aguirre 8/121y
SCORING: Schloredt 54pts, Fleming (HB-K) 52pts, McKeta 30pts

1960 10-1

55 Pacific	6 E Lee Folkins / Pat Claridge
41 Idaho	12 T Kurt Gegner / Stan Chapple
14 Navy	15 G Chuck Allen / Sam Hurworth
29 Stanford	10 C Roy McKasson / Tim Bullard
10 UCLA	8 G Bill Kinnune / Rod Scheyer
30 Oregon State	29 T Dave Enslow / Ray Mansfield
7 Oregon	6 E Jim Skaggs /J.Meyers/Ben Davidson (T)
34 Southern Cal	0 QB B.Schloredt/B.Hivner/Kermit Jorgensen
27 California	7 HB George Fleming / Charlie Mitchell
8 Washington St.	7 HB Don McKeta / Brent Wooten
17 Minnesota■	7 FB Ray Jackson / Joe Jones

RUSHING: Mitchell 74/467y, Jackson 108/440y, Fleming 68/293y
PASSING: Hivner 31-57/580y, 6TD, 54.4%
RECEIVING: Claridge 13/252y, McKinney 9/214y, Folkins 7/152y
SCORING: Fleming 65pts, Mitchell, Jackson & Jorgensen 30pts

1961 5-4-1

6 Purdue	13 E Lee Bernhardi / Gary Clark
20 Illinois	7 T Rod Scheyer
22 Pittsburgh	17 G Dave Phillips / Norm Dicks
14 California	21 C Ray Mansfield / Tim Bullard
13 Stanford	0 G Jim Skaggs
6 Oregon	7 T John Meyers / Jake Kupp
0 Southern Cal	0 E Duane Locknane / Andy Alkire
0 Oregon State	3 QB Kermit Jorgensen / Pete Ohler
17 UCLA	13 HB Billy Siler/Dave Kopay/Bob Monroe
21 Washington St.	17 HB C. Mitchell /Nat Whitmyer /Martin Wyatt
	FB Jim Stiger / Tony Kopay

RUSHING: Stiger 130/582y, Mitchell 96/457y, Jorgensen 114/331y
PASSING: Ohler 17-59/394y, 3TD, 28.8%
RECEIVING: Bernhardi 5/137y, Mitchell 5/72y, Wyatt 5/49y
SCORING: Whitmyer & Mitchell 20pts, 4 tied w/ 12pts

1962 7-1-2

7 Purdue	7 E Lee Bernhardi / Gary Clark
28 Illinois	7 T Rod Scheyer / Jake Kupp / Jon Knoll
41 Kansas State	0 G Rick Redman / Dave Phillips
14 Oregon State	13 C Ray Mansfield / Glen Kezer
14 Stanford	0 G Rick Sortun / Norm Dicks
21 Oregon	21 T Mike Briggs / Jerry Knoll
0 Southern Cal	14 E Duane Locknane / Bill Diehl
27 California	0 QB Billy Siler /Pete Ohler /Bill Douglas
30 UCLA	0 HB Charlie Mitchell / Nat Whitmyer
26 Washington St.	21 HB Jim Stiger /Martin Wyatt / Dave Kopay
	FB Junior Coffey / Bob Monroe

RUSHING: Coffey 98/581y, Mitchell 102/438y, Monroe 83/348y
PASSING: Ohler 16-38/174y, TD, 42.1%
RECEIVING: Mitchell 9/108y, Bernhardi 8/207y, Clark 6/68y
SCORING: Coffey 48pts, Mitchell 30pts, Jim Norton (T-K) 23pts

1963 6-5

7 Air Force	10 E Ralph Winters / Al Libke
6 Pittsburgh	13 T Jerry Knoll / Jim Norton
7 Iowa	17 G Rick Redman
34 Oregon State	7 C John Stupey
19 Stanford	11 G Rick Sortun / Koll Hagen
26 Oregon	19 T Mike Briggs
22 Southern Cal	7 E Don Safford / Jake Kupp
39 California	26 QB Bill Douglas
0 UCLA	14 HB Dave Kopay / Steve Bramwell
16 Washington St.	0 HB Ron Medved
7 Illinois■	17 FB Junior Coffey / Charlie Browning

RUSHING: Browning 84/421y, Kopay 71/417y, Coffey 90/385y
PASSING: Douglas 62-111/929y, 6TD, 55.9%
RECEIVING: Kopay 12/175y, Libke 10/192y, Medved 10/125y
SCORING: Coffey 36pts, Kopay 24pts, Browning & Bramwell 18pts

1964 6-4

2 Air Force	3 E Dave Williams / Al Libke
35 Baylor	14 T Jon Knoll / Bruce Kramer
18 Iowa	28 G Mike Ryan / Paul Scheyer
7 Oregon State	9 C Bill Barnes / Lyle Norwood
6 Stanford	0 G Roger Dunn
0 Oregon	7 T Dale Stephens / Jerry Knoll
14 Southern Cal	13 E Gary Carr / Omar Parker
21 California	16 QB Bill Douglas/Jim Sartoris/Todd Hullin
22 UCLA	20 HB Steve Bramwell / Ron Medved
14 Washington St.	0 HB Charlie Browning
	FB Junior Coffey / Jeff Jordon
	DL Mike Otis
	DL Fred Forsberg
	DL Jim Norton
	DL Jerry Williams / Jim Lambright
	DL Koll Hagen
	DL Steve Hinds
	LB Rick Redman
	DB Mike Stroud / Tom Greenlee
	DB Mason Mitchell
	DB Ralph Winters / Al Libke
	DB Dick Wetterauer / Jim Sampson

RUSHING: Coffey 147/638y, Browning 96/474y, Jordon 79/378y
PASSING: Douglas 33-64/360y, 0TD, 51.6%
RECEIVING: Carr 14/190y, Browning 13/137y, Medved 10/111y
SCORING: Browning 42pts, Medved (HB-K) 28pts, Jordon 24pts

1965 5-5

14 Idaho	9 E Dave Williams / Gary Carr
14 Baylor	17 T Mac Bledsoe / Jim Kirk
21 Ohio State	23 G Mike Ryan
0 Southern Cal	34 C Bill Barnes / Greg Cass
12 California	16 G Roger Dunn
24 Oregon	20 T Bob Richardson / Gary Brandt
41 Stanford	8 E Bruce Kramer / Omar Parker
24 UCLA	28 QB Todd Hullin
28 Oregon State	21 HB Ron Medved
27 Washington St.	9 HB Don Moore / Steve Bramwell
	FB Jeff Jordon
	DL Tom Greenlee
	DL Fred Forsberg
	DL Jerry Williams
	DL Dick Wetterauer
	DL Steve Thompson
	DL Joe Mancuso
	LB Mike Otis
	LB Steve Hinds
	DB Bill Stifter / Vince Lorrain
	DB Dave Dillon / Al Libke
	DB Ralph Winters

RUSHING: Moore 144/637y, Medved 90/394y, Jordon 76/222y
PASSING: Hullin 90-168/1318y, 13TD, 53.6%
RECEIVING: Williams 38/795y, Medved 15/173y, Kramer 15/158y
SCORING: Williams 60pts, Medved (HB-K) 55pts, Moore 36pts

1966 6-4

19 Idaho	7 E Dave Williams
0 Air Force	10 T Jim Kirk / Mac Bledsoe
38 Ohio State	22 G Gary Brandt / Rick McHale
14 Southern Cal	17 C Bill Barnes / Greg Cass
20 California	24 G Mike Ryan / Larry Jakl
10 Oregon	7 T Bob Richardson / Avery Schwartz
22 Stanford	20 E Jeff Huget / Omar Parker
16 UCLA	3 QB Tom Sparlin
13 Oregon State	24 HB Jim Cope / Don Martin
19 Washington St.	7 HB Bill Parker / Don Moore
	FB Jeff Jordon / Jim McCabe
	DL Dean Halverson
	DL Bill Glennon
	DL Mike Maggart
	DL Jerry Williams / Bob Anderson
	DL Steve Thompson
	DL Tom Greenlee
	LB Cliff Coker / George Jugum
	DB Frank Smith / Dave Dillon
	DB Al Worley / Harrison Wood
	DB Dave DuPree / Vince Lorrain
	DB Bob Pederson

RUSHING: Moore 88/447y, Parker 87/304y, Jordon 65/191y
PASSING: Sparlin 68-165/954y, 4TD, 41.2%
RECEIVING: Cope 25/379y, Williams 21/303y, Parker 6/72y
SCORING: Martin (HB-K) 45pts, Jordon 42pts, Cope 24pts

1967 5-5

7 Nebraska	17 E Harrison Wood
17 Wisconsin	0 T Bob Richardson
30 Air Force	7 G Jim Harris / Dick McHale
13 Oregon State	6 C Ron Hudson / Bob Schoepper
36 Oregon	0 G Dick Zatkovich
6 Southern Cal	23 T Mac Bledsoe
23 California	6 E Jeff Huget
7 Stanford	14 QB Tom Manke / Tom Sparlin
0 UCLA	48 WB Jim Cope / Harvey Blanks
7 Washington St.	9 HB Gerald Wea
	FB Tom Verti / Gary James
	DL Dean Halverson
	DL Bill Glennon
	DL Rick Sharp / Bob Anderson
	DL Mike Maggart
	DL Steve Thompson
	DL Otis Washington
	LB Cliff Coker / George Jugum
	DB Al Worley
	DB Bill Sprinkle/Dave DuPree/Bob Berg
	DB Bob Pederson
	DB Dan Spriesterbach

RUSHING: Manke 139/483y, James 73/314y, Wea 77/289y
PASSING: Manke 32-81/613y, 5TD, 39.5%
RECEIVING: Cope 20/284y, Wood 13/364y, Blanks 6/63y
SCORING: Don Martin (K) 44pts, Wood 24pts, Manke 18pts

1968 3-5-2

35 Rice	35 E Jeff Huget / Harrison Wood
21 Wisconsin	17 T Bob Schoepper Augie Rios
21 Oregon State	35 G Jim Harris / Wayne Sortun
0 Oregon	3 C Bruce Jarvis
7 Southern Cal	14 G Ken Ballenger
37 Idaho	7 T Avery Schwartz
7 California	7 TE Ernie Janet / Ace Bulger
20 Stanford	35 QB Jerry Kaloper
6 UCLA	0 WB Harvey Blanks
0 Washington St.	24 HB Jim Cope
	FB Carl Wojciechowski / Bo Cornell
	DL Otis Washington
	DL Bob Anderson / Lee Brock
	DL Rick Sharp
	DL Mike Maggart
	DL Mark Hannah
	DL Clyde Werner / Ken Lee
	LB George Jogum
	DB Al Worley
	DB Lamar Mills / Bob Berg
	DB Dan Spriesterbach
	DB Tom Verti

RUSHING: Wojciechowski 138/651y, Blanks 99/509y, Cope 70/313y
PASSING: Kaloper 43-115/595y, 0TD, 37.4%
RECEIVING: Wood 17/250y, Wojciechowski 10/138y, Blanks 9/132y
SCORING: Cornell 36pts, Blanks 30pts, Ron Volbrecht (K) 24pts

1969 1-9

11 Michigan State	27 WR Ralph Bayard / Dan Roberson
7 Michigan	45 T Dan Cunningham
14 Ohio State	41 G Ernie Janet (T) / Tom Nelson
13 California	44 C Ken Ballenger (G) / Bruce Jarvis
6 Oregon State	10 G Rick Keely / Wayne Sortun
7 Oregon	22 T Augie Rios
14 UCLA	57 TE Ace Bulger / Dan Gosselin
7 Stanford	21 QB Gene Willis / Steve Hanzlik
7 Southern Cal	16 HB Luther Sligh / Joe Bell
30 Washington St.	21 HB Buddy Kennamer / Ron Preston
	FB Bo Cornell
	DL Lee Brock
	DL Tom Failla / Rob Fink
	DL Rick Sharp
	DL Mark Hannah
	LB Bob Lovelein / Tom Verti
	LB Clyde Werner / Rick Huget
	LB Alan Craig
	DB Mark McMahon
	DB Gary Carr / Ron Volbrecht
	DB Mark Day / Bob Burmeister / Tom Verti
	DB Bob Berg

RUSHING: Cornell 136/613y, Kennamer 76/276y, Bell 42/221y
PASSING: Willis 33-99/568y, 5TD, 33.3%
RECEIVING: Bayard 13/290y, Bulger 13/180y, Roberson 7/167y
SCORING: Cornell 24pts, Volbrecht (DB-K) 15pts, 5 tied w/ 12pts

1970 6-4

42 Michigan State	16 WR Ralph Bayard / Ira Hammon
3 Michigan	17 WR Jim Krieg
56 Navy	7 T Dan Cunningham
28 California	31 G Ernie Janet
25 Southern Cal	28 C Bruce Jarvis
29 Oregon State	20 G Wayne Sortun
29 Oregon	23 T Lane Ronnebaum
22 Stanford	29 TE Ace Bulger / John Brady (RB)
61 UCLA	20 QB Sonny Sixkiller
43 Washington St.	25 TB Darrell Downey / Joe Bell
	FB Bo Cornell
	DL Kurt Matter / Ken Lee
	DL Gordy Guinn / Mark Turner
	DL Tom Failla
	DL Dave Worgan / Al Kravitz
	LB Rick Huget
	LB Ron Shepherd
	LB Jim Katsenes
	DB Cal Jones
	DB Bob Burmeister
	DB Mark McMahon
	DB Bill Cahill

RUSHING: Cornell 97/340y, Downey 85/334y, Brady 15/199y
PASSING: Sixkiller 186-362/2303y, 15TD, 51.4%
RECEIVING: Krieg 54/738y, Cornell 33/327y, Downey 30/288y
SCORING: Cornell 54pts, Steve Wiezbowski (K) 53pts, Downey 32pts

1971 8-3

65 UCSB	7 WR Tom Scott
38 Purdue	35 WR Jim Krieg
44 TCU	26 T Steve Anderson / Rod Stanley
52 Illinois	14 G Steve Wallin / Dale Enders
6 Stanford	17 C Jim Andrilenas / Al Kelso
21 Oregon	23 G Fred Miller
38 Oregon State	14 T Rick Hayes
23 UCLA	12 TE John Brady
30 California	7 QB Sonny Sixkiller
12 Southern Cal	13 TB Luther Sligh/Pete Taggares/Jim Eicher
28 Washington St.	20 FB Jerry Ingalls
	DL Kurt Matter
	DL Gordy Guinn
	DL Ben Albrecht
	DL Al Kravitz / Dave Worgan
	LB Bob Ferguson
	LB Alan Craig / Rich Sweatt
	LB Rick Huget
	DB Cal Jones / Dick Galuska
	DB Charles Buckland / Phil Andre
	DB Larry Worley / Tony Bonwell
	DB Bill Cahill

RUSHING: Taggares 102/410y, Eicher 70/264y, Scott 32/221y
PASSING: Sixkiller 126-297/2068y, 13TD, 42.4%
RECEIVING: Scott 35/820y, Krieg 22/482y, Brady 21/361y
SCORING: Steve Wiezbowski (K) 59pts, Scott 42pts, Ingalls & Taggares 36pts

1972 8-3

13 Pacific	6 WR Tom Scott / Walter Oldes
14 Duke	6 WR Scott Loomis / Don Wesley
22 Purdue	21 T Jim Smith / Rick Hayes
31 Illinois	11 G Pete Elswick / Fred Miller
23 Oregon	17 C Al Kelso
0 Stanford	24 G Steve Wallin / Dave Enders
7 Southern Cal	34 T Steve Schulte
35 California	21 TE John Brady
23 Oregon State	16 QB Sonny Sixkiller / Greg Collins
30 UCLA	21 TB Glenn Bonner / Barry Houlihan
10 Washington St.	27 FB Pete Taggares / Luther Sligh
	DL Kurt Matter
	DL Gordy Guinn
	DL Ben Albrecht / Dave Pear
	DL Dave Worgan / Don Gorman
	LB Bob Ferguson
	LB Ron Shepherd / Jim Kristoff
	LB Brian Doheny / Washington Kennan
	DB Cal Jones / Roberto Jourdan
	DB Phil Andre
	DB Tony Bonwell
	DB Bill Cahill / Hans Woldseth

RUSHING: Taggares 127/450y, Boner 95/351y, Houlihan 47/174y
PASSING: Sixkiller 73-152/1125y, 7TD, 48%
RECEIVING: Brady 30/450y, Taggares 27/335y, Loomis 14/236y
SCORING: Taggares 66pts, Steve Wiezbowski (K) 38pts, Brady 18pts

1973 2-9

7 Hawaii	10 WR Walter Oldes / Ken Conley
21 Duke	23 WR Mark McDonald / Scott Phillips
21 Syracuse	7 T John Whitacre / Rod Stanley
49 California	54 G Lou Quinn / Pete Elswick
7 Oregon State	31 C Ray Pinney / Jim Andrilenas
14 Stanford	23 G Charles Jackson / Bob Graves
0 Oregon	58 T Rick Hayes
13 UCLA	62 TE Nelse Petermann / Reggie Brown
41 Idaho	14 QB Chris Rowland / Dennis Fitzpatrick
19 Southern Cal	42 TB Glenn Bonner / Donald Waters
26 Washington St.	52 FB Pete Taggares
	DL Murphy McFarland / Bob Martin
	DL Dave Pear
	DL Mike Dochow
	DL Joe Tabor / Paul Strohmeier
	LB Washington Kennan / Dean Schlamp
	LB Dan Lloyd
	LB Jim Kristoff / Clifton Marcus
	DB Roberto Jourdan
	DB Bob Bousted / Frank Reed
	DB Steve Lipe / Mark Kreutz
	DB Alvin Burleson

RUSHING: Taggares 93/342y, Bonner 68/270y, Fitzpatrick 54/155y
PASSING: Rowland 97-234/1521y, 15TD, 41.5%
RECEIVING: Oldes 27/450y, McDonald 22/294y, Phillips 18/369y
SCORING: Conley 24pts, 5 tied w/ 18pts

1974 5-6

21 Cincinnati	17 WR Scott Phillips
31 Iowa State	28 WR Mark McDonald
15 Texas A&M	28 T Don Wardlow
21 Texas	35 G Eddie Ray / Lou Quinn
9 Oregon State	23 C Ray Pinney
17 Stanford	34 G Charles Jackson
66 Oregon	0 T Carl Van Valkenburg
31 UCLA	9 TE Paul Bianchini
26 California	52 QB Chris Rowland / Denny Fitzpatrick
11 Southern Cal	42 TB Willie Hendricks
24 Washington St.	17 FB Robin Earl
	DL Bob Martin
	DL Dave Pear
	DL Mike Green
	DL Paul Strohmeier
	LB Jim Kristoff
	LB Cornelius Chenevert
	LB Dan Lloyd
	DB Frank Reed
	DB Pedro Hawkins
	DB Steve Lipe
	DB Al Burleson

RUSHING: Fitzpatrick 137/897y, Earl 108/606y, Hendricks 60/269y
PASSING: Rowland 59-124/848y, 5TD, 47.6%
RECEIVING: Phillips 34/716y, Bianchini 14/180y, Earl 13/198y
SCORING: Earl 60pts, Steve Robbins (K) 50pts, Fitzpatrick 36pts

1975 6-5

12 Arizona State	35 WR Craig Davillier / Leon Garrett
10 Texas	28 WR Scott Phillips
14 Navy	13 T Don Wardlow
27 Oregon	17 G Eddie Ray / Dave Stromswold
0 Alabama	52 C Ray Pinney
21 Stanford	24 G Carl Van Valkenburg (T) / Jeff Toews
35 Oregon State	7 T John Whitacre
17 UCLA	13 TE Nelse Petermann / Gordy Bronson
24 California	27 QB Warren Moon / Chris Rowland
8 Southern Cal	7 TB James Anderson / Greg Martin
28 Washington St.	27 FB Robin Earl
	DL Stan Walderhaug / Mike Green
	DL Charles Jackson
	DL Bob Graves
	LB Paul Strohmeier
	LB Dan Lloyd / Randy Earl
	LB Mike Baldassin / Michael Jackson
	LB Dean Schlamp
	DB Roberto Jourdan
	DB Frank Reed
	DB Al Burleson
	DB Ron Olson

RUSHING: Earl 167/782y, Anderson 124/441y, Martin 93/229y
PASSING: Moon 48-122/587y, 2TD, 39.3%
Rowland 45-117/597y, 4TD, 38.5%
RECEIVING: Phillips 33/433y, Petermann 10/139y, Davillier 9/108y
SCORING: Steve Robbins (K) 42pts, Anderson 30pts, Martin 24pts

1976 5-6

38 Virginia	17 WR Leon Garrett / Spider Gaines
7 Colorado	21 WR Scott Phillips
13 Indiana	20 T Robert Westlund
38 Minnesota	7 G Dave Stromswold / Marshall Cromer
24 Oregon State	12 C Blair Bush
28 Stanford	34 G Jeff Toews / Phil Foreman
14 Oregon	7 T Carl Van Valkenburg / Steve Bauer
21 UCLA	30 TE Don Wardlow / Scott Greenwood
0 California	7 QB Warren Moon
3 Southern Cal	20 TB Robin Earl
51 Washington St.	32 FB Ron Rowland / Joe Steele
	DL Dave Browning
	DL Charles Jackson
	DL Keith Richardson / Doug Martin
	LB Stan Walderhaug / Bret Gagliardi
	LB Rob Gehring / Antowaine Richardson
	LB Mike Baldassin
	LB Michael Jackson
	DB Nesby Glasgow
	DB Wayne Moses / Lance Theoudele
	DB John Edwards
	DB Kyle Heinrich

RUSHING: Rowland 203/1002y, Earl 188/963y, Steele 77/421y
PASSING: Moon 81-175/1106y, 6TD, 46.3%
RECEIVING: Phillips 26/348y, Garrett 15/197y, Gaines 11/245y
SCORING: Earl 44pts, Steele 42pts, Steve Robbins (K) 42pts

1977 10-2

18 Mississippi St.	27 WR Spider Gaines
24 San Jose State	3 WR Gary Briggs / Keith Richardson
20 Syracuse	22 T Roger Westlund
17 Minnesota	19 G Phil Foreman
54 Oregon	0 C Blair Bush
45 Stanford	21 G Marshall Cromer / Steve Bauer
14 Oregon State	6 T Jeff Toews
12 UCLA	20 TE Scott Greenwood
50 California	31 QB Warren Moon
28 Southern Cal	15 TB Joe Steele / Ron Rowland
35 Washington St.	15 FB Ron Gipson
27 Michigan■	20 DL Doug Martin
	DL Cliff Bethea / Scott Long
	DL Dave Browning / Ron Grant
	LB Antowaine Richardson / Bret Gagliardi
	LB Michael Jackson
	LB Bruce Harrell / Willy Gaiola
	LB John Kerley
	DB Nesby Glasgow
	DB Wayne Moses / Lance Theoudele
	DB John Edwards / Greg Grimes
	DB Kyle Heinrich

RUSHING: Steele 198/865y, Gipson 119/575y, Moon 99/266y
PASSING: Moon 113-199/1584y, 11TD, 57.1%
RECEIVING: Gaines 30/660y, Steele 25/210y,
Greenwood 22/403y
SCORING: Steve Robbins (K) 79pts, Steele 78pts, Gaines &
Moon 36pts

1978 7-4

7 UCLA	10 WR Spider Gaines
31 Kansas	2 WR Keith Richardson
7 Indiana	14 T Robert Westlund / Joe Stanford
34 Oregon State	0 G Phil Foreman
17 Alabama	20 C Tom Turnure
34 Stanford	31 G Dan Chavira
20 Oregon	14 T Jeff Toews
41 Arizona State	7 TE/TB Scott Greenwood / Kyle Stevens
31 Arizona	21 QB Tom Porras / Tom Flick
10 Southern Cal	28 TB Joe Steele
38 Washington St.	8 FB Ron Gipson / Toussaint Tyler
	DL Doug Martin
	DL Stafford Mays
	DL Chris Linnin
	LB John Kerley / Bret Gagliardi
	LB Michael Jackson
	LB Bruce Harrell / Willy Galoia
	LB Antowaine Richardson
	DB Mark Lee / Lance Theoudele
	DB Nesby Glasgow
	DB Kyle Heinrich
	DB Greg Grimes

RUSHING: Steele 237/1111y, Tyler 76/421y, Stevens 46/241y
PASSING: Porras 84-176/1151y, 6TD, 47.7%
RECEIVING: Richardson 24/330y, Gaines 23/517y, Steele 16/110y
SCORING: Mike Lansford (K) 72pts, Porras 36pts, Steele &
Gaines 30pts

1979 10-2

38 Wyoming	2 WR Aaron Williams / Ron Blacken
41 Utah	7 WR Paul Skansi/K. Richardson/Gary Briggs
21 Oregon	17 T Joe Sanford
49 Fresno State	14 G Phil Foreman
41 Oregon State	0 C Tom Turnure
7 Arizona State	12 G Dan Chavira
14 Pittsburgh	26 T Randy Van Divier
34 UCLA	14 TE David Bayle
28 California	24 QB Tom Porras / Tom Flick
17 Southern Cal	24 TB Joe Steele / Vince Coby / Kyle Stevens
17 Washington St.	7 FB Toussaint Tyler
14 Texas■	7 DL Doug Martin / Fletcher Jenkins
	DL Chris Linnin / Rusty Olsen
	DL Stafford Mays / Mark Jerue
	LB Jim Pence / Bret Gagliardi
	LB Bruce Harrell / Ken Driscoll
	LB Jerry McLain / Pete Tormey
	LB Antowaine Richardson / Jim Pence
	DB Mark Lee
	DB Lance Theoudele
	DB Derek Harvey
	DB Greg Grimes / Kenny Gardner

RUSHING: Steele 151/694y, Tyler 130/618y, Coby 102/422y
PASSING: Porras 115-190/1571y, 60.2%
Porras 64-127/680y, 3TD, 50.4%
RECEIVING: Skansi 31/378y, Blacken 25/360y, Steele 17/136y
SCORING: Steele 74pts, Mike Lansford (K) 71pts, Coby 36pts

1980 9-3

50 Air Force	7 WR Aaron Williams / Ron Blacken
45 Northwestern	7 WR Paul Skansi / Anthony Allen
10 Oregon	34 T Curt Marsh
24 Oklahoma State	18 G James Carter / Pat Bresolin
41 Oregon State	6 C Mike Reilly
27 Stanford	24 G Mike Curtis
10 Navy	24 T Randy Van Divier
25 Arizona State	0 TE David Bayle
45 Arizona	22 QB Tom Flick
20 Southern Cal	10 TB Kyle Stewart
30 Washington St.	23 FB Toussaint Tyler (TB)/ Willie Rosborough
6 Michigan■	23 DL Fletcher Jenkins
	DL Rusty Olsen / Scott Garnett
	DL Mark Jerue
	LB Bret Gagliardi
	LB Mark Stewart
	LB Ken Driscoll
	LB Jerry McLain / Steve Pope
	DB Ray Horton / William Reed
	DB Bill Stapleton / Dennis Brown
	DB Ken Gardner / Chris O'Connor
	DB Derek Harvey / Ken Gardner

RUSHING: Stevens 148/706y
PASSING: Flick 168-280/2178y, 15TD, 60%
RECEIVING: Bayle 36/315y
SCORING: Chuck Nelson (K) 85pts

1981 10-2

34 Pacific	14 WR Anthony Allen / Aaron Williams
20 Kansas State	3 WR Paul Skansi
17 Oregon	3 T Eric Moran
7 Arizona State	26 G James Carter
27 California	26 C Paul Coty
56 Oregon State	17 G Pat Zakskorn / Pat Bresolin
14 Texas Tech	7 T Don Dow
42 Stanford	31 TE Willie Rosborough / Rick Mallory
0 UCLA	31 QB Steve Pelluer / Tim Cowan
13 Southern Cal	3 TB Ron Jackson / Dennis Brown
23 Washington St.	10 FB Vince Coby / Chris James
28 Iowa■	0 DL Fletcher Jenkins
	DL Ray Cattage
	DL Scott Garnett / Lynn Madsen
	LB Mark Stewart
	LB Tony Caldwell / Stewart Hill
	LB Mark Jerue
	LB Ken Driscoll / Tom Burnham
	DB Ray Horton
	DB Bill Stapleton
	DB Robert Leaphart
	DB Chris O'Connor

RUSHING: Jackson 159/623y
PASSING: Pelluer 110-234/1138y, 9TD, 47%
RECEIVING: Allen 29/389y
SCORING: Chuck Nelson (K) 77pts

1982 10-2

55 Texas-El Paso	0 WR Anthony Allen / Aaron Williams
23 Arizona	13 WR Paul Skansi
37 Oregon	21 T Eric Moran
46 San Diego St.	25 G Rick Mallory
50 California	7 C Paul Coty / Scott Fausset
34 Oregon State	17 G Pat Zakskorn
10 Texas Tech	3 T Don Dow
31 Stanford	43 TE Willie Rosborough / Leroy Lutu
10 UCLA	7 QB Steve Pelluer / Tim Cowan
41 Arizona State	13 TB Jacque Robinson / Sterling Hinds
20 Washington St.	24 FB Chris James
21 Maryland■	20 DL Lynn Madsen / Ron Holmes
	DL Dean Browning / Scott Garnett
	DL Ray Cattage
	LB Mark Stewart
	LB Ken Driscoll
	LB Tim Meamber / Stewart Hill
	LB Tony Caldwell
	DB Ray Horton / Robert Leaphart
	DB Bill Stapleton
	DB Vince Newsome
	DB Chris O'Connor

RUSHING: Robinson 222/926y, James 92/373y, Hinds 78/332y
PASSING: Pelluer 111-198/1229y, 10TD, 56.1%
RECEIVING: Skansi 50/631y, Allen 42/558y, Williams 23/319y
SCORING: Chuck Nelson (K) 109pts, Robinson 42pts, Allen 36pts

1983 8-4

34 Northwestern	0 WR Danny Greene / Mark Pattison
25 Michigan	24 WR Dave Stransky
14 Louisiana State	40 T Dennis Maher / Rob Kuharski
27 Navy	10 G Rick Mallory
34 Oregon State	7 C Dan Eernissee
32 Stanford	15 G Ted Brose
32 Oregon	3 T Lance Dodson / Dennis Maher
24 UCLA	27 TE Tony Wroten / Larry Michael
23 Arizona	22 QB Steve Pelluer
24 Southern Cal	0 TB Sterling Hinds / Jacque Robinson
6 Washington St.	17 FB Walt Hunt
10 Penn State■	13 DL Dean Browning / Scott Garnett
	DL Lynn Madsen
	DL Ron Holmes
	LB Stewart Hill
	LB Tim Meamber
	LB Joe Krakoski / Joe Kelly
	LB Fred Small
	DB Vestee Jackson
	DB J.C. Pearson
	DB Robert Leaphart / Jim Rodgers
	DB Vince Albritton

RUSHING: Hinds 159/826y, Hunt 75/350y, Robinson 48/296y
PASSING: Pelluer 213-317/2212y, 11TD, 67.2%
RECEIVING: Pattison 38/400y, Greene 37/599y, Stransky 37/449y
SCORING: Jeff Jaeger (K) 97pts, Greene 36pts, Hinds 30pts

1984 11-1

26 Northwestern	0 WR Mark Pattison
20 Michigan	11 WR Danny Greene
35 Houston	7 T Dennis Maher
53 Miami-Ohio	7 G Al Robertson
19 Oregon State	7 C Dan Eernissee
37 Stanford	15 G Tim Burham / Doug Crow
17 Oregon	10 T Kevin Gogan / Dennis Soldat
28 Arizona	12 TE Tony Wroten / Rod Jones
44 California	14 QB Hugh Millen / Paul Sicuro
7 Southern Cal	16 TB Jacque Robinson / Ron Jackson
38 Washington St.	29 FB Walt Hunt / Rick Fenney
28 Oklahoma ■	17 DL Tony Lewis
	DL Steve Alford
	DL Ron Holmes
	LB Fred Small
	LB Tim Meamber
	LB Joe Kelly
	LB Reggie Rogers / Ron Hadley
	DB Vestee Jackson
	DB J.C. Pearson
	DB Tim Peoples
	DB Jim Rodgers

RUSHING: Robinson 195/901y, Jackson 102/368y, Fenney 77/305y
PASSING: Millen 89-171/1051y, 5TD, 52%
RECEIVING: Greene 29/395y, Robinson 23/167y, Pattison 21/445y
SCORING: Jeff Jaeger (K) 96pts, Robinson 84pts, Pattison 26pts

1985 7-5

17 Oklahoma State	31 WR Lonzell Hill
3 Brigham Young	31 WR David Trimble / Darryl Franklin
29 Houston	12 T Dennis Soldat
21 UCLA	14 G Garth Thomas / Mike Zandofsky
19 Oregon	13 C Dan Agen
28 California	12 G Tim Burnham
20 Oregon State	21 T Kevin Gogan
34 Stanford	0 TE Rod Jones
7 Arizona State	36 QB Hugh Millen / Chris Chandler
20 Southern Cal	17 TB Vince Weathersby / David Toy
20 Washington St.	21 FB Rick Fenney / Tony Covington
20 Colorado	17 DL Andy Fuimaona / Steve Alvord
	DL Jim Matthews / Brian Habib
	DL Reggie Rogers
	LB Bo Yates
	LB Joe Kelly / Tom Erlandson
	LB David Rill
	LB Ron Hadley
	DB Ron Milus
	DB Vestee Jackson
	DB Tim Peoples / Darryl Hall
	DB Tony Zackery / Allen James

RUSHING: Fenney 104/497y, Weathersby 123/467y, Covington 88/371y
PASSING: Millen 158-264/1565y, 6TD, 59.8%
RECEIVING: Hill 46/696y, Weathersby 46/314y, Jones 33/315y
SCORING: Jeff Jaeger (K) 82pts, Hill 48pts, Fenney 30pts

1986 8-3-1

40 Ohio State	7 WR Lonzell Hill
52 Brigham Young	21 WR Darryl Franklin
10 Southern Cal	20 T Clay Griffith
50 California	18 G Brett Wiese / Garth Thomas
24 Stanford	14 C Bern Brostek
48 Bowling Green	0 G Mike Zandofsky
38 Oregon	3 T Kevin Gogan / Rick McLeod
21 Arizona State	34 TE Rod Jones
28 Oregon State	12 QB Chris Chandler
17 UCLA	17 TB Vince Weathersby
44 Washington St.	23 FB Rick Fenney / Tony Covington
6 Alabama ■	28 DL Reggie Rogers
	DL Steve Alvord
	DL Brian Habib
	LB Bo Yates
	LB David Rill
	LB Tom Erlandson
	LB Steve Roberts
	DB Tony Zackery
	DB Art Malone
	DB Allen James
	DB Tim Peoples

RUSHING: Weathersby 160/880y, Fenney 121/508y, Covington 67/214y
PASSING: Chandler 160-275/1994y, 20TD, 58.2%
RECEIVING: Hill 43/721y, Jones 31/309y, Franklin 26/427y
SCORING: Jeff Jaeger (K) 93pts, Hill 48pts, Fenney 42pts

1987 7-4-1

31 Stanford	21 WR Darryl Franklin
28 Purdue	10 WR Brian Slater
12 Texas A&M	29 T Rick McLeod
31 Pacific	3 G Brett Wiese
22 Oregon	29 C Bern Brostek
27 Arizona State	14 G Mike Zandofsky (T) / Jeff Pahukoa
23 Southern Cal	37 T Kelly John-Lewis
28 Oregon State	12 TE Scott Jones / Bill Ames
21 Arizona	21 QB Chris Chandler
14 UCLA	47 TB Vince Weathersby
34 Washington St.	19 FB Aaron Jenkins / Tony Covington
24 Tulane ■	12 DL Travis Richardson / Bob Willig
	DL Brian Habib
	DL Dennis Brown
	LB Martin Harrison
	LB David Rill
	LB Tom Erlandson / Bruce Beall
	LB Bo Yates
	DB Art Malone / Demouy Williams
	DB Le-Lo Lang / Tony Zackery
	DB Darryl Hall / Eugene Burkhalter
	DB Will Rideout / Ricky Andrews

RUSHING: Weathersby 146/682y, Jenkins 129/668y, Covington 59/232y
PASSING: Chandler 128-249/1739y, 9TD, 51..4%
RECEIVING: Franklin 43/712y, Slater 38/696y, Weathersby 28/233y
SCORING: Brandy Brownlee 63pts, Covington 54pts, Jenkins & Slater 30pts

1988 6-5

20 Purdue	6 WR Scott Fitzgerald / Andre Riley
31 Army	17 WR Brian Slater
35 San Jose State	31 T Scott Jones
17 UCLA	24 G Dean Kirkland / Jeff Pahukoa
10 Arizona State	0 C Bern Brostek
27 Southern Cal	28 G Brett Wiese / Kelly John-Lewis
14 Oregon	17 T Mike Zandofsky
28 Stanford	25 TE Mark Kilpack
13 Arizona	16 QB Cary Conklin
28 California	27 TB Vince Weathersby / Greg Lewis
31 Washington St.	32 FB Aaron Jenkins
	DL Bob Willig / Travis Richardson
	DL Jeff Kohlwes/Dorie Murrey/Art Hunter
	DL Dennis Brown
	LB Martin Harrison / Virgil Jones
	LB Ricky Andrews
	LB Chico Fraley
	LB Brett Collins / Greg Travis
	DB Le-Lo Lang
	DB Tony Zackery / Art Malone
	DB Eugene Burkhalter / Dana Hall
	DB Eric Briscoe / Darryl Hall

RUSHING: Jenkins 138/691y, Weathersby 143/624y, Lewis 39/154y
PASSING: Chandler 153-302/1833y, 11TD, 50.7%
RECEIVING: Slater 38/737y, Weathersby 30/186y, Kilpack 21/175y
SCORING: John McCallum (K) 60pts, Slater 42pts, Weathersby 36pts

1989 8-4

19 Texas A&M	6 WR Andre Riley
38 Purdue	9 WR Orlando McKay
17 Arizona	20 T Jeff Pahukoa / Adam Cooney
28 Colorado	45 G Rick Schulberg / Ed Cunningham
16 Southern Cal	24 C Bern Brostek
20 Oregon	14 G Dean Kirkland
29 California	16 T Siupeli Malamala
28 UCLA	27 TE Bill Ames
32 Arizona State	34 QB Cary Conklin
51 Oregon State	14 TB Greg Lewis
20 Washington St.	9 FB James Compton / Darius Turner
34 Florida ■	7 DL Travis Richardson
	DL John Cook
	DL Dennis Brown / Steve Emtman
	LB Martin Harrison
	LB Dave Hoffmann / Chico Fraley
	LB James Clifford
	LB Greg Travis / Brett Collins
	DB Le-Lo Lang / Dana Hall
	DB Charles Mincy / William Doctor
	DB Eugene Burkhalter
	DB Eric Briscoe / Jaime Fields (LB)

RUSHING: Lewis 239/1100y, Compton 34/162y
PASSING: Conklin 208-365/2569y, 16TD, 57%
RECEIVING: Riley 53/1039y, Lewis 45/350y, Ames 34/276y
SCORING: John McCallum 70pts, Lewis 68pts, Riley 26pts

1990 10-2

20 San Jose State	17 WR Mario Bailey
20 Purdue	14 WR Orlando McKay
31 Southern Cal	0 T Jeff Pahukoa
14 Colorado	20 G Rick Schulberg / Lincoln Kennedy
42 Arizona State	14 C Ed Cunningham
38 Oregon	17 G Dean Kirkland
52 Stanford	16 T Siupeli Malamala
46 California	7 TE Aaron Pierce / Mark Kilpack
54 Arizona	10 QB Mark Brunell
22 UCLA	25 TB Greg Lewis / Beno Bryant
55 Washington St.	10 FB Darius Turner
46 Iowa ■	34 DL Steve Emtman
	DL John Cook
	DL Travis Richardson
	LB Donald Jones
	LB Brett Collins / Jaime Fields
	LB Dave Hoffmann
	LB Chico Fraley
	DB Charles Mincy
	DB Dana Hall
	DB Eric Briscoe
	DB Tommie Smith / Shane Pahukoa

RUSHING: Lewis 229/1279y, Brunell 105/444y, Bryant 73/386y
PASSING: Brunell 118-253/1732y, 14TD, 46.6%
RECEIVING: Bailey 40/667y, Lewis 20/345y, McKay 19/337y
SCORING: Brunell 70pts, Lewis 54pts, Bryant 48pts

1991 12-0

42 Stanford	7 WR Mario Bailey
36 Nebraska	21 WR Orlando McKay
56 Kansas State	3 T Lincoln Kennedy
54 Arizona	0 G Kris Rongen
48 Toledo	0 C Ed Cunningham
24 California	17 G Pete Kaligis / Jim Nevelle
29 Oregon	7 T Siupeli Malamala
44 Arizona State	16 TE Aaron Pierce
14 Southern Cal	3 QB Billy Joe Hobert
58 Oregon State	6 RB Beno Bryant/Jay Barry/N. Kaufman
56 Washington St.	21 FB Matt Jones
34 Michigan ■	14 DL Andy Mason
	DL Steve Emtman
	DL Tyrone Rogers
	LB Donald Jones
	LB Dave Hoffmann
	LB Chico Fraley
	LB Jaime Fields / Brett Collins
	DB Dana Hall
	DB Walter Bailey / William Doctor
	DB Shane Pahukoa
	DB Tommie Smith / Paxton Tailele

RUSHING: Bryant 158/943y, Barry 146/718y, Kaufman 67/307y
PASSING: Hobert 173-285/2271y, 22TD, 60.7%
RECEIVING: Bailey 62/1037y, McKay 47/627y, Pierce 23/280y
SCORING: Bailey 102pts, Barry 68pts, Travis Hanson (K) 64pts

1992 9-3

31 Arizona State	7 WR Damon Mack / Damon Barry
27 Wisconsin	10 WR Joe Kralik / Jason Shelley
29 Nebraska	14 T Lincoln Kennedy
17 Southern Cal	10 G Andrew Peterson
35 California	16 C Jim Nevelle
24 Oregon	3 G Frank Garcia / Pete Kaligis
31 Pacific	7 T Tom Gallagher
41 Stanford	7 TE Mark Bruener
3 Arizona	16 QB Mark Brunell / Billy Joe Hobert
45 Oregon State	16 TB Napoleon Kaufman / Jay Barry
23 Washington St.	42 FB Darius Turner / Matt Jones
31 Michigan ■	38 DL Jamal Fountaine
	DL Mike Lustyk / Steve Hoffmann
	DL D'Marco Farr
	LB Andy Mason
	LB Dave Hoffmann
	LB James Clifford
	LB Jaime Fields
	DB Walter Bailey
	DB Josh Moore
	DB Shane Pahukoa
	DB Tommie Smith / Louis Jones

RUSHING: Kaufman 162/1045y, Turner 46/217y, Brunell 68/197y
PASSING: Brunell 109-189/1304y, 5TD, 57.7%
    Hobert 71-136/716y, 5TD, 52.2%
RECEIVING: Kralik 33/487y, Bruener 21/210y, Shelley 20/382y
SCORING: Travis Hanson (K) 66pts, Brunell 48pts, Kaufman 36pts

1993 7-4

31 Stanford	14 WR Jason Shelley / Theron Hill
12 Ohio State	21 WR Joe Kralick / Dave Janoski
35 East Carolina	0 T Pete Pierson
52 San Jose State	17 G Andrew Peterson
24 California	23 C Jim Nevelle
25 UCLA	39 G Frank Garcia / Pat Kesi
21 Oregon	6 T Tom Gallagher
17 Arizona State	32 TE Mark Bruener / Ernie Conwell
28 Oregon State	21 QB Damon Huard / Eric Bjorson
17 Southern Cal	22 TB Napoleon Kaufman / Beno Bryant
26 Washington St.	3 FB Matt Jones
	DL Jamal Fountaine
	DL D'Marco Farr
	DL Trevor Highfield / Cedric White
	LB Donovan Schmidt / Deke Devers
	LB Steve Springstead
	LB Hillary Butler / Ink Aleaga
	LB Andy Mason / Richie Chambers
	DB Reggie Reser
	DB Russell Hairston
	DB Lamar Lyons / Lawyer Milloy
	DB Louis Jones / David Killpatrick

RUSHING: Kaufman 226/1299y, Bryant 75/331y, Jones 48/147y
PASSING: Huard 116-197/1282y, 9TD, 58.9%
RECEIVING: Bruener 30/414y, Kaufman 23/139y, Hill 21/220y
SCORING: Kaufman 84pts, Travis Hanson (K) 69pts, Bryant 24pts

1994 7-4

17 Southern Cal	24 WR Eric Bjorson
25 Ohio State	16 WR Dave Janoski
38 Miami	20 T Andrew Peterson
37 UCLA	10 G Trevor Highfield
34 San Jose State	20 C Frank Garcia
35 Arizona State	14 G Pat Kesi
20 Oregon	31 T Eric Battle
24 Oregon State	10 TE Mark Bruener
28 Stanford	46 QB Damon Huard
31 California	19 TB Napoleon Kaufman
6 Washington St.	23 FB/TE Richard Thomas / Ernie Conwell
	DL Deke Devers
	DL Steve Hoffman
	DL David Richie / Mike Ewaliko
	LB Donovan Schmidt / Justin Thomas
	LB Ink Aleaga / John Fiala
	LB David Killpatrick
	LB Richie Chambers
	DB Reggie Reser
	DB Russell Hairston
	DB Lawyer Milloy
	DB Lamar Lyons / Tony Parrish

RUSHING: Kaufman 255/1390y, Thomas 73/316y,
 Leon Neal (TB) 51/210y
PASSING: Huard 153-275/1887y, 13TD, 55.6%
RECEIVING: Bjorson 49/770y, Bruener 34/331y,
 Kaufman 24/199y
SCORING: John Wales (K) 79pts, Kaufman 54pts, Bjorson 44pts

1995 7-4-1

23 Arizona State	20 WR Dave Janoski
20 Ohio State	30 WR Fred Coleman
21 Army	13 T Bob Sapp
26 Oregon State	16 G Pat Kesi
21 Notre Dame	29 C Trevor Highfield
38 Stanford	28 G Benji Olson
31 Arizona	17 T Eric Battle
21 USC	21 TE Ernie Conwell
22 Oregon	24 QB Damon Huard
38 UCLA	14 TB Rashaan Shehee / Leon Neal
33 Washington St.	30 FB/TE Richard Thomas / Cam Cleeland
18 Iowa■	38 DL Deke Devers / Darius Jones
	DL David Richie / Mike Ewaliko
	DL Steve Hoffmann / Sekou Wiggs
	LB Jason Chorak
	LB Ink Aleaga
	LB Jerry Jensen / John Fiala
	LB Reggie Davis / Ikaika Malloe (DB)
	DB Reggie Reser
	DB Scott Greenlaw
	DB Lawyer Milloy
	DB Tony Parrish

RUSHING: Shehee 166/957y
PASSING: Huard 184-287/2415y, 11TD, 64.1%
RECEIVING: Janoski 40/657y, Conwell 24/343y
SCORING: Shehee 90pts

1996 9-3

42 Arizona State	45 WR Jerome Pathon / Fred Coleman
29 BYU	17 WR Dave Janoski / Gerald Harris
31 Arizona	17 T Tony Coats
27 Stanford	6 G Bob Sapp / Ben Kadletz
20 Notre Dame	54 C Olin Kreutz
41 UCLA	21 G Benji Olson
33 Oregon	14 T Lynn Johnson / Mostafa Sobhi
21 USC	10 TE Cam Cleeland
42 Oregon State	3 QB Brock Huard / Shane Fortney
53 San Jose State	10 TB Corey Dillon / Rashaan Shehee
31 Washington St.	24 FB/TE Mike Reed / Jeremy Brigham
21 Colorado■	33 DL Chris Campbell
	DL Mac Tuiaea
	DL David Richie
	LB Jason Chorak
	LB Ink Aleaga
	LB John Fiala / Lester Towns
	LB Jerry Jensen
	DB Mel Miller
	DB Jermaine Smith / Kyle Roberts
	DB Tony Parrish
	DB Nigel Burton

RUSHING: Dillon 271/1555y, Shehee 65/242y,
 Terry Hollimon (TB) 26/186y
PASSING: Huard 108-217/168y, 13TD, 49.8%
RECEIVING: Pathon 41/618y, Cleeland 23/354y, Janoski 21/243y
SCORING: Dillon 138pts, John Wales (K) 58pts, Pathon 42pts

1997 8-4

42 BYU	20 WR Jerome Pathon / Andre DeSaussure
36 San Diego State	3 WR Fred Coleman
14 Nebraska	27 WR/FB Ja'Warren Hooker / Mike Reed
26 Arizona State	14 T Tony Coats
30 California	3 G Benji Olson
58 Arizona	28 C Olin Kreutz
45 Oregon State	17 G Chad Ward / Ben Kadletz
27 Southern Cal	0 T Aaron Dalan
28 Oregon	31 TE Cam Cleeland / Jeremy Brigham
28 UCLA	52 QB Brock Huard
35 Washington St.	41 RB Rashaan Shehee / Maurice Shaw
51 Michigan State■	23 DL Jabari Issa / Chris Campbell
	DL Mac Tuiaea
	DL Sekou Wiggs
	LB Jason Chorak
	LB Marques Hairston / Jeremiah Pharms
	LB Lester Towns
	LB Jerry Jensen
	DB Mel Miller
	DB Jermaine Smith
	DB Tony Parrish
	DB Nigel Burton

RUSHING: Shehee 139/862y, Shaw 125/538y,
 Jason Harris (RB) 60/269y
PASSING: Huard 146-244/2140y, 23TD, 59.8%
RECEIVING: Pathon 69/1245y, Coleman 42/723y,
 Cleeland 19/276y
SCORING: Shehee 54pts, Nick Lentz (K) 51pts, Pathon 50pts

1998 6-6

42 Arizona State	38 WR Gerald Harris / Ja'Warren Hooker
20 BYU	10 WR Andre DeSaussure / Dane Looker
7 Nebraska	55 T Elliot Silvers
28 Arizona	31 G Tony Coats
53 Utah State	12 C Brad Hutt / Ben Cadletz
21 California	13 G Chad Ward
35 Oregon State	34 T Aaron Dalan
10 Southern Cal	33 TE Reggie Davis / John Westra
22 Oregon	27 QB Brock Huard / Marques Tuiasosopo
24 UCLA	36 TB Willie Hurst / Jason Harris
16 Washington St.	9 FB/WR Pat Conniff / Chris Juergens
25 Air Force■	45 DL Josh Smith / Ryan Julian
	DL Mac Tuiaea
	DL Jabari Issa
	LB Jeremiah Pharms
	LB Lester Towns / Jeff Johnson
	LB Marques Hairston
	LB Todd Johnson
	DB Toure Butler
	DB Jermaine Smith / Wondame Davis
	DB Brendan Jones / Hakim Akbar
	DB Nigel Burton

RUSHING: Hurst 149/538y
PASSING: Huard 168-315/1924y, 15TD, 53.3%
RECEIVING: Looker 64/662y
SCORING: Joe Jarzynka (K) 49pts

1999 7-5

28 BYU	35 WR Chris Juergens / Todd Elstrom
21 Air Force	31 WR Gerald Harris / Dane Looker
31 Colorado	24 T Elliot Silvers
34 Oregon	20 G Rock Nelson / Dominic Daste
47 Oregon State	21 C Kyle Benn
7 Arizona State	28 G Chad Ward
31 California	27 T Kurth Connell
35 Stanford	30 TE Jerramy Stevens
33 Arizona	25 QB Marques Tuiasosopo
20 UCLA	23 TB Willie Hurst / Maurice Shaw
24 Washington St.	14 FB/TE Pat Conniff / Anthony Mizin
20 Kansas State■	24 DL Mac Tuiaea / Toalei Mulitauaopele
	DL Jabari Issa
	DL Larry Triplett
	LB Jeremiah Pharms
	LB Lester Towns
	LB Derrell Daniels
	LB Jafar Williams / Anthony Kelly
	DB Anthony Vontoure / Omare Lowe
	DB Jermaine Smith / Roderick Green
	DB Curtis Williams
	DB Hakim Akbar

RUSHING: Hurst 126/546y, Tuiasosopo 138/541y, Shaw 110/440y
PASSING: Tuiasosopo 171-295/2221y, 12TD, 58%
RECEIVING: Juergens 42/516y, Harris 37/571y Stevens 21/265y
SCORING: John Anderson (K) 73pts, Tuiasosopo & Shaw 36pts

2000 11-1

44 Idaho	20 WR Justin Robbins / Wilbur Hooks
34 Miami	29 WR Todd Elstrom
17 Colorado	14 T Elliot Silvers
16 Oregon	23 G Matt Frize / Nick Newton
33 Oregon State	30 C Kyle Benn
21 Arizona State	15 G Chad Ward
36 California	24 T Wes Call
31 Stanford	28 TE Jerramy Stevens
35 Arizona	32 QB Marques Tuiasosopo
35 UCLA	28 TB Paul Arnold / Rich Alexis / Willie Hurst
51 Washington St.	3 FB Pat Conniff
34 Purdue■	24 DL Marcus Robertson
	DL Larry Tripplett
	DL Ryan Julian
	LB Jeremiah Pharms
	LB Derrell Daniels / Jamaun Willis
	LB/DB Ben Mahdavi / Derrick Johnson
	LB Jafar Williams / Anthony Kelley
	DB Omare Lowe
	DB Anthony Voutoure / Chris Massey
	DB Curtis Williams / Greg Carothers
	DB Hakim Akbar

RUSHING: Alexis 118/738y, Hurst 66/402y, Tuiasosopo 126/394y
PASSING: Tuiasosopo 170-323/2146y, 14TD, 52.6%
RECEIVING: Elstrom 47/683y, Stevens 43/600y, Robbins 22/267y
SCORING: John Anderson (K) 74pts, Alexis 54pts, Hurst 44pts

2001 8-4

23 Michigan	18 WR Paul Arnold / Todd Elstrom
53 Idaho	3 WR Reggie Williams
31 California	28 T Khalif Barnes
27 Southern Cal	24 G Nick Newton
13 UCLA	35 C Kyle Benn
31 Arizona	28 G Elliot Zajac
33 Arizona State	31 T Todd Bachert
42 Stanford	28 TE Kevin Ware/Joe Collier/J. Stevens
24 Oregon State	49 QB Cody Pickett / Taylor Barton
26 Washington St.	14 TB Willie Hurst / Rich Alexis
7 Miami	65 FB Ken Walker
43 Texas■	47 DL Marcus Robertson
	DL Larry Triplett
	DL Jerome Stevens / Josh Miller
	LB Kai Ellis / Zach Tuiasosopo
	LB Jamaun Willis
	LB Ben Mahdavi
	LB Sam Blanche / Anthony Kelley
	DB Omare Lowe
	DB Chris Massey / Roc Alexander
	DB Wondame Davis / Owen Biddle
	DB Greg Carothers

RUSHING: Hurst 138/607y, Alexis 125/391y
PASSING: Pickett 169-301/2403y, 10TD, 56.1%
RECEIVING: Williams 55/973y, Arnold 43/649y, Elstrom 35/490y
SCORING: John Anderson (K) 76pts, Hurst 48pts, Pickett &
 Alexis 30pts

2002 7-6

29 Michigan	31 WR Paul Arnold / Pat Reddick
34 San Jose State	10 WR Reggie Williams
38 Wyoming	7 T Khalif Barnes
41 Idaho	27 G Aaron Butler
27 California	34 C Todd Bachert
32 Arizona	28 G Elliot Zajac / Dan Dicks
21 Southern Cal	41 T Nick Newton
16 Arizona State	27 TE Kevin Ware
24 UCLA	34 QB Cody Pickett
41 Oregon State	29 TB Rich Alexis / Braxton Cleman
42 Oregon	14 FB/TE Zach Tuiasosopo / Joe Toledo
29 Washington St.	26 DL Manase Hopoi
24 Purdue ■	34 DL Terry Johnson / Jerome Stevens
	DL Josh Miller
	DL Kai Ellis
	LB Jafar Williams
	LB Marquis Cooper / Joe Lobendahn
	LB Ben Mahdavi
	DB Nate Robinson / Roc Alexander
	DB Derrick Johnson / Evan Benjamin
	DB James Sims / Jimmy Newell
	DB Greg Carothers / Owen Biddle

RUSHING: Alexis 202/688y, Cleman 74/228y, Chris Singleton (TB) 64/224y
PASSING: Pickett 365-612/4458y, 28TD, 59.6%
RECEIVING: Williams 94/1454y, Reddick 54/583y, Charles Frederick 45/651y
SCORING: John Anderson (K) 108pts, Williams 66pts, Alexis 60pts

2003 6-6

9 Ohio State	28 WR Reggie Williams
38 Indiana	13 WR Charles Frederick / Jordan Slye
45 Idaho	14 T Khalif Barnes
28 Stanford	17 G Dan Dicks / Brad Vanneman
16 UCLA	46 C Todd Bachert
17 Nevada	28 G Clay Walker / Tusi Sa'au
38 Oregon State	17 T Nick Newton
23 Southern Cal	43 TE Ben Bandel / Joe Toledo / Jon Lyon
42 Oregon	10 QB Cody Pickett
22 Arizona	27 TB R. Alexis/Ken James/Shelton Sampson
7 California	54 FB/WR Zach Tuiasosopo / Isaiah Stanback
27 Washington St.	19 DL Manuse Hopoi
	DL Graham Lasee / Donny Mateaki
	DL Jerome Stevens
	DL Terry Johnson / Ty Eriks
	LB Greg Carothers
	LB Tim Galloway / Joe Lobendahn
	LB Marquis Cooper
	DB Sam Cunningham / Roc Alexander
	DB Derrick Johnson / Chris Massey
	DB Jimmy Newell
	DB Evan Benjamin / Owen Biddle

RUSHING: Alexis 138/566y, James 122/530y, Shelton Sampson (RB) 60/274y
PASSING: Pickett 257-454/3043y, 15TD, 56.6%
RECEIVING: Williams 89/1109y, Frederick 59/831y, Lyon 17/231y
SCORING: Evan Knudson (K) 63pts, Williams & Sampson 48pts

2004 1-10

16 Fresno State	35 WR Sonny Shackelford / Charles Frederick
31 UCLA	37 WR Craig Chambers / Bobby Whithorne
3 Notre Dame	38 T Ryan Brooks / Khalif Barnes
13 Stanford	27 G Clay Walker / Tusi Sa'au
21 San Jose State	6 C Brad Vanneman
14 Oregon State	29 G Stanley Daniels
0 Southern Cal	38 T Robin Meadow
6 Oregon	31 TE Joe Toledo / Jon Lyon
13 Arizona	23 QB Casey Paus / Isaiah Stanback
12 California	42 TB Kenny James / Shelton Sampson
25 Washington St.	28 FB/WR James Sims
	DL Dan Milstein / Mike Mapuolesega
	DL Manase Hopoi
	DL Jordan White-Frisbee
	DL Brandon Ala / Greyson Gunheim
	LB Joe Lobendahn
	LB Scott White / Tim Galloway
	LB Evan Benjamin
	DB Derrick Johnson / Matt Fountaine
	DB Sam Cunningham
	DB Dashon Goldson / Jimmy Newell
	DB C.J. Wallace

RUSHING: James 172/702y, Sims 59/212y, Sampson 51/189y
PASSING: Paus 116-274/1476y, 5TD, 42.3%
RECEIVING: Shackelford 21/298y, Chambers 19/408y, Toledo 19/202y
SCORING: James 30pts, Evan Knudson (K) 24pts, Michael Braunstein (K) 20pts

2005 2-9

17 Air Force	20 WR Sonny Shackelford
17 California	56 WR Anthony Russo
34 Idaho	6 T Robin Meadow / Chad Macklin
17 Notre Dame	36 G Stanley Daniels / Clay Walker
17 UCLA	21 C Brad Vanneman
21 Oregon	45 G Tusi Sa'au
24 Southern Cal	51 T Joe Toledo / Tai Alailefaleula
20 Arizona State	44 TE Robert Lewis / Johnie Kirton
10 Oregon State	18 QB Isaiah Stanback
38 Arizona	14 TB Louis Rankin / James Sims
22 Washington St.	26 FB/WR Mark Palaita / Craig Chambers
	DL Donny Mateaki
	DL Wilson Afoa / Mike Mapuolesega
	DL Manase Hopoi
	DL Grayson Gunheim
	LB Evan Benjamin
	LB Joe Lobendahn / Tahj Bomar
	LB Scott White
	DB Matt Fountaine / Durrell Moss
	DB Roy Lewis / Josh Okoebor
	DB Dashon Goldson
	DB C.J. Wallace / Darin Harris

RUSHING: Sims 112/495y, Rankin 104/485y, Stanback 100/353y
PASSING: Stanback 143-264/2136y, 9TD, 54.2%
RECEIVING: Shackelford 41/592y, Chambers 31/573y, Russo 30/487y
SCORING: Evan Knudson (K) 61pts, Sims & Chambers 36pts

2006 5-7

35 San Jose State	29 WR Sonny Shackelford
20 Oklahoma	37 WR Anthony Russo
21 Fresno State	20 T Robin Meadow / Chad Macklin
29 UCLA	19 G Stanley Daniels / Clay Walker
21 Arizona	10 C Brad Vanneman
20 Southern Cal	26 G Tusi Sa'au
17 Oregon State	27 T Joe Toledo / Alailefalula
24 California	31 TE Robert Lewis / Johnie Kirton
23 Arizona State	26 QB Isaiah Stanback
14 Oregon	34 TB Louis Rankin / James Sims
3 Stanford	20 FB/WR Mark Palaita / Craig Chambers
35 Washington St.	32 DL Daniel Te'o-Nesheim
	DL Wilson Afoa
	DL Donny Mateaki / Jordan Reffett
	DL Grayson Gunheim / Brandon Ala
	LB Dan Howell / Chris Stevens
	LB Tahj Bomar
	LB Scott White
	DB Matt Fountaine / Dashon Goldson
	DB Roy Lewis / Mesphin Forrester
	DB Jason Wells / Chris Hemphill
	DB C.J. Wallace

RUSHING: Rankin 142/666y, James 108/416y, Stanback 100/353y
PASSING: Stanback 101-189/1325y, 10TD, 53.4%
Bonnell 72-164/916y, 7TD, 43.9%
RECEIVING: Shackelford 50/666y, Russo 32/552y, Ellis 18/230y
SCORING: Michael Braunstein (K) 62pts, Shackelford 42pts, James 30pts

2007 4-9

42 Syracuse	12 WR Anthony Russo
24 Boise State	10 WR Marcel Reece / Corey Williams
14 Ohio State	33 T Ben Ossai / Cody Habben
31 UCLA	44 G Ryan Tolar
24 Southern Cal	27 C Juan Garcia
20 Arizona State	44 G Casey Bulyca / Jordan White-Frisbee
34 Oregon	55 T Chad Macklin
41 Arizona	48 TE Michael Gottlieb / Robert Lewis
27 Stanford	9 QB Jake Locker
23 Oregon State	29 RB Louis Rankin
37 California	23 FB Paul Homer
35 Washington St.	42 DL Daniel Te'o-Nesheim
28 Hawaii	35 DL Jordan Reffett
	DL Wilson Afoa
	DL Greyson Gunheim
	LB Dan Howell / Chris Stevens
	LB Trenton Tuiasosopo / Donald Butler
	LB E.J. Savannah / Mason Foster
	DB Roy Lewis / Vonzell McDowell
	DB Byron Davenport / Jason Wells
	DB Darin Harris / Nate Williams
	DB Mesphin Forrester

RUSHING: Rankin 233/1294y, Locker 172/986y, Brandon Johnson (RB) 51/196y
PASSING: Locker 155-328/2062y, 14TD, 47.3%
RECEIVING: Russo 49/766y, Reece 39/761y, Rankin 20/126y
SCORING: Ryan Perkins (K) 90pts, Locker 78pts, Rankin 54pts

2008 0-12

10 Oregon	44 WR D'Andre Goodwin / Devin Aguilar
27 BYU	28 WR Alvin Logan / Jermaine Kearse
14 Oklahoma	55 T Ben Ossai / Skyler Fancher
28 Stanford	35 G Jordan White-Frisbee
14 Arizona	48 C Juan Garcia
13 Oregon State	34 G Casey Bulyca / Ryan Tolar
7 Notre Dame	33 T Cody Habben
0 Southern Cal	56 TE Kavario Middleton / Michael Gottlieb
19 Arizona State	39 QB Ronnie Fouch / Jake Locker
7 UCLA	27 TB Willie Griffin / Terrance Dailey
13 Washington St.	16 FB Paul Homer / Brandon Johnson
7 California	48 DL Daniel Te'o-Nesheim
	DL Cameron Eisara / Alameda Ta'amu
	DL Senio Kelemete
	DL Darrion Jones
	LB Chris Stevens / Joshua Gage
	LB Donald Butler / Trenton Tuiasosopo
	LB Mason Foster
	DB Quinton Richardson
	DB Mesphin Forrester
	DB Nate Williams
	DB John Fogerson / Tripper Johnson

RUSHING: Dailey 75/338y, Griffin 63/219y, Johnson 76/194y
PASSING: Fouch 113-250/1339y, 4TD, 45.2%
Locker 50-93/512y, 1TD, 53.8%
RECEIVING: Goodwin 60/692y, Kearse 20/310y, Aguilar 20/246y
SCORING: Ryan Perkins (K) 38pts, Johnson and Locker 18pts

2009 5-7

23 LSU	31 WR Devin Aguilar / D'Andre Goodman
42 Idaho	23 WR Jermaine Kearse
16 Southern Cal	13 WR/TE James Johnson / Chris Izbicki
14 Stanford	34 T Ben Ossai (G) / Drew Schaefer
30 Notre Dame	37 G Gregory Christine / Nick Wood
36 Arizona	33 C Ryan Tolar (G) / Mykenna Ikehara
17 Arizona State	24 G Senio Kelemete / Morgan Rosborough
19 Oregon	43 T Cody Habben
23 UCLA	24 TE Kavario Middleton
21 Oregon State	48 QB Jake Locker
30 Washington St.	0 TB Chris Polk / Paul Homer (FB)
42 California	10 DL Daniel Te'o-Nesheim
	DL Alameda Ta'amu
	DL Cameron Elisara / Everrette Thompson
	DL Darrion Jones / Talia Crichton
	LB Mason Foster / Joshua Gage
	LB Donald Butler
	LB E.J. Savannah / Cort Dennison
	DB Adam Long / Quinton Richardson
	DB Desmond Trufant / Vonzell McDowell
	DB Nath'n Fellner/Just'n Glenn/Jas'n Wells
	DB Nate Williams / Greg Walker

RUSHING: Polk 226/1113y, Locker 112/388y
PASSING: Locker 230-394/2800y, 21TD, 58.4%
RECEIVING: Kearse 50/866y, Aguilar 42/593y, Johnson 39/422y, Middleton 26/257y, Polk 25/171y
SCORING: Eric Folk (K) 89pts, Kearse 50pts, Locker 42pts

2010 7-6

17 BYU	23 WR D'Andre Goodwin / Devin Aguilar
41 Syracuse	20 WR Jermaine Kearse / Kevin Smith
21 Nebraska	56 T Senio Kelemete
32 Southern Cal	31 G Ryan Tolar / Erik Kohler
14 Arizona State	24 C Drew Schaefer
35 Oregon State	34 G Gregory Christine (C) / Colin Porter
14 Arizona	44 T Cody Habben
0 Stanford	41 TE Dan Kanczugowski / Marlion Barnett
16 Oregon	53 QB Jake Locker / Keith Price
24 UCLA	7 TB Chris Polk
16 California	13 FB Austin Sylvester / Jesse Callier
35 Washington St.	28 DL E. Thompson / De'Shon Matthews
19 Nebraska ■	7 DL Alameda Ta'amu / Sione Potoae
	DL Cam Elisara / Semisi Tokolahi
	DL Hau'oli Jamora / Talia Crichton
	LB Mason Foster
	LB Cort Dennison
	LB Victor Aiyewa
	DB Quinton Richardson
	DB Desmond Trufant
	DB Nathan Fellner
	DB Nate Williams

RUSHING: Polk 260/1415y, Callier 77/433y, Locker 114/385y
PASSING: Locker 184-332/2265y, 17TD, 55.4%
RECEIVING: Kearse 63/1005y, Goodwin 44/530y, Aguilar 28/352y
SCORING: Erik Folk (K) & Kearse 72pts, Polk 54pts

WASHINGTON STATE

Washington State University (Founded 1890)
Pullman, Washington
Nicknames: Cougars
Colors: Crimson and Gray
Stadium: Martin (1972) 35,117
Conference Affiliations: Pacific Coast (1916-58), Independent (1959-61), AAWU (1962-67), Pac-8/10 (1968-present)

CAREER RUSHING YARDS	Attempts	Yards
Rueben Mayes (1982-85)	636	3519
Steve Broussard (1986-89)	610	3054
Shaumbe Wright-Fair (1989-92)	618	2938
Tim Harris (1979-82)	542	2830
Jerome Harrison (2004-05)	482	2800
Kerry Porter (1982-86)	560	2618
Dwight Tardy (2006-09)	528	2241
Michael Black (1996-97)	424	2129
Ken Grandberry (1971-73)	453	2102
Tali Ena (1976-79)	372	1888

CAREER PASSING YARDS	Comp.-Att.	Yards
Alex Brink (2004-07)	848-1451	10,913
Jason Gesser (1999-2002)	611-1118	8830
Jack Thompson (1975-78)	601-1086	7818
Ryan Leaf (1994-97)	473- 880	7433
Drew Bledsoe (1990-92)	532- 979	7373
Tim Rosenbach (1986-88)	474- 789	5995
Mark Rypien (1981-85)	326- 613	4573
Chad Davis (1994-95)	371- 640	4167
Ty Paine (1970-72)	325- 725	4136
Matt Kegel (2000-03)	305- 568	3982
Steve Birnbaum (1996-99)	306- 595	3934

CAREER RECEIVING YARDS	Catches	Yards
Brandon Gibson (2005-08)	182	2756
Jason Hill (2004-06)	148	2704
Hugh Campbell (1960-62)	176	2452
Nian Taylor (1996-99)	140	2447
Tim Stallworth (1986-89)	125	2250
Phillip Bobo (1990-92)	148	2182
C.J. Davis (1988-92)	128	2168
Deron Pointer (1991-93)	112	2098
Mike Levenseller (1975-77)	121	2051
Michael Bumpas (2004-07)	195	2022

SEASON RUSHING YARDS	Attempts	Yards
Jerome Harrison (2005)	308	1900
Rueben Mayes (1984)	258	1637
Shaumbe Wright-Fair (1992)	264	1330
Steve Broussard (1988)	222	1280
Steve Broussard (1989)	260	1237

SEASON PASSING YARDS	Comp.-Att.	Yards
Ryan Leaf (1997)	227-410	3968
Alex Brink (2007)	305-503	3818
Jason Gesser (2002)	236-402	3408
Drew Bledsoe (1992)	241-432	3246
Timm Rosenbach (1988)	218-338	3097

SEASON RECEIVING YARDS	Catches	Yards
Brandon Gibson (2007)	67	1180
Nakoa McElrath (2001)	72	1163
Tim Stallworth (1988)	63	1151
Mike Levenseller (1976)	67	1127
Jason Hill (2005)	62	1097

GAME RUSHING YARDS	Attempts	Yards
Rueben Mayes (1984 vs. Oregon)	39	357
Bernard Jackson (1971 vs. Oregon)	N/A	261
Jerome Harrison (2005 vs. UCLA)	34	260

GAME PASSING YARDS	Comp.-Att.	Yards
Alex Brink (2005 vs. Oregon State)	31-59	531
Drew Bledsoe (1992 vs. Utah)	N/A-N/A	476
Alex Brink (2007 vs. San Diego State)	38-47	469

GAME RECEIVING YARDS	Catches	Yards
Deron Pointer (1993 vs. Arizona State)	10	255
Nian Taylor (1998 vs. Idaho)	N/A	254
Gale Cogdill (1958 vs. Northwestern)	N/A	252

GREATEST COACH

Mike Price was a special coach at Washington State. Remember, the school is located in remote eastern Washington. It suffers a distinct Pacific-10 recruiting disadvantage as compared to the glitter of Los Angeles, the sophistication of the San Francisco Bay area, and fun-in-the-sun of Arizona.

Although Price rode a victory rollercoaster—in the 1990s for example, Washington State had consecutive years with win totals of 4, 9, 5, 8, 3, 5, 10, and 3—he took his Cougars to five bowl games and a share of two conference titles.

Price left after the 2002 season with an 83-78 record, although his departure to Alabama would turn out—due to off-the-field behavior that got him fired—to be one of the worst career decisions ever made by any football coach. Still, Mike Price is well-loved in The Palouse for bringing some of Washington State's best seasons and opening up a dynamic passing attack. Price coached five of the all-time leading Cougar passers: Alex Brink, Jason Gesser, Ryan Leaf, Drew Bledsoe, and Chad Davis.

WASHINGTON STATE'S 55 GREATEST SINCE 1953

OFFENSE

WIDE RECEIVER: Gail Cogdill, C.J. Davis, Tim Stallworth, Nian Taylor
TIGHT END: Pat Beach, Hugh Campbell
TACKLE: Calvin Armstrong, Scott Sanderson
GUARD: Dan Lynch, Steve Ostermann, Josh Parrish, Derrick Roche, Mike Utley
CENTER: Geoff Reece
QUARTERBACK: Drew Blesdoe, Alex Brink, Jason Gesser, Ryan Leaf, Jack Thompson
RUNNING BACK: Michael Black, Steve Broussard, Jerome Harrison, Rueben Mayes, Shaumbe Wright-Fair
FULLBACK: Keith Lincoln

DEFENSE

END: Dorian Boose, Mkristo Bruce, DeWayne Patterson,
TACKLE: Leon Bender, Chad Eaton, Alan Kennedy, Rien Long, Keith Millard
LINEBACKER: James Darling, Will Derting, Steve Gleason, Anthony McClanahan, Mark Fields, Tom Poe
CORNERBACK: Jason David, Bill Gaskins, Ken Greene, Lionel Thomas, Marcus Trufant
SAFETY: Eric Coleman, Paul Sorensen, Lamont Thompson

SPECIAL TEAMS

RETURN SPECIALISTS: Kitrick Taylor, Dee Moronkola
PLACE KICKER: Drew Dunning, Jason Hanson
PUNTER: Gavin Hedrick

MULTIPLE POSITIONS

WIDE RECEIVER-TIGHT END-HALFBACK-DEFENSIVE END-DEFENSIVE BACK: Bill Steiger
GUARD-DEFENSIVE TACKLE: Konrad Pimiskern

PERFORMANCE FORMULA: WASHINGTON STATE'S 10 BEST SEASONS

1997	1.5047	11 of 70
2001	1.4538	13 of 70
2002	1.4242	13 of 70
2003	1.4084	15 of 71
1988	1.4038	15 of 69
1992	1.2904	18 of 70
1994	1.2715	25 of 71
1981	1.2664	23 of 70
1958	1.2539	19 of 70
1972	1.1808	25 of 70

WASHINGTON STATE COUGARS

Year	W-L-T	AP Poll	Conference Standing	Toughest Regular Season Opponents	Coach (Record at School)	Bowl Games		
1953	4-6		5	Southern California 6-3-1, Iowa 5-3-1, UCLA 8-1, Stanford 6-3-1	Al Kircher			
1954	4-6		5	Southern California 8-3, California 5-5, Oregon 6-4	Al Kircher			
1955	1-7-2		8	Southern California 6-4, UCLA 9-1, Oregon State 6-3	Al Kircher (13-25-2)			
1956	3-6-1		7	UCLA 7-3, Oregon State 7-2-1, Southern California 8-2	Jim Sutherland			
1957	6-4		4	Iowa 7-1-1, Oregon 7-3, Oregon State 8-2, UCLA 8-2	Jim Sutherland			
1958	7-3		2	Northwestern 5-4, California 7-3, Oregon State 6-4	Jim Sutherland			
1959	6-4			Oregon 8-2 (played twice), Washington 9-1	Jim Sutherland			
1960	4-5-1			Arizona State 7-3, Oregon 7-2-1, Oregon State 6-3-1, Washington 9-1	Jim Sutherland			
1961	3-7			Missouri 7-2-1, Utah 6-4, Texas 9-1, Washington 5-4-1	Jim Sutherland			
1962	5-4-1		3	Arizona State 7-2-1, Oregon St. 8-2, Oregon 6-3-1, Washington 7-1-2	Jim Sutherland			
1963	3-6-1		4	Army 7-3, Oregon 7-3, Washington 6-4	Jim Sutherland (37-39-4)			
1964	3-6-1		6t	Wyoming 6-2-2; Oregon State 8-2, Oregon 7-2-1	Bert Clark			
1965	7-3		3	Minnesota 5-4-1, Oregon State 5-5, Arizona State 6-4, Washington 5-5	Bert Clark			
1966	3-7		6t	Houston 8-2, Oregon State 7-3, Washington 6-4	Bert Clark			
1967	2-8		7t	So. Calif. 9-1, Oklahoma 9-1, UCLA 7-2-1, Arizona St. 8-2	Bert Clark (15-24-1)			
1968	3-6-1		7	Arizona State 8-2, Stanford 6-3-1, Oregon State 7-3, Arizona 8-2	Jim Sweeney			
1969	1-9		8	UCLA 8-1-1, Stanford 7-2-1, Southern California 9-0-1	Jim Sweeney			
1970	1-10		8	Arizona St. 10-0, Stanford 8-3, Southern Calif. 6-4-1, Washington 6-4	Jim Sweeney			
1971	4-7		7	Stanford 8-3, Southern Calif. 6-4-1, Washington 8-3	Jim Sweeney			
1972	7-4		3t	UCLA 8-3, Southern Calif. 11-0, Washington 8-3	Jim Sweeney			
1973	5-6		4	Arizona State 10-1, Ohio State 9-0-1, Southern Calif. 9-1-1, UCLA 9-2	Jim Sweeney			
1974	2-9		7	Ohio State 10-1, Southern Calif. 9-2-1, UCLA 6-3-2	Jim Sweeney			
1975	3-8		8	Kansas 7-4, California 8-3, Southern California 7-4, UCLA 8-2-1	Jim Sweeney (26-59-1)			
1976	3-8		6	Kansas 6-5, Minnesota 6-5, So. Calif. 10-1, UCLA 9-1-1, Stanford 6-5	Jackie Sherrill (3-8)			
1977	6-5		5t	Nebraska 8-3, Michigan St. 7-3-1, Stanford 8-3, Washington 8-3	Warren Powers (6-5)			
1978	3-7-1		10	Arizona State 8-3, UCLA 8-3, Stanford 7-4, Washington 7-4	Jim Walden			
1979	3-8		9	Ohio State 11-0, Southern Calif. 10-0-1, Washington 8-3	Jim Walden			
1980	4-7		6t	Arizona State 7-4, Oregon 6-3-2, Washington 9-2	Jim Walden			
1981	8-3-1		4t	Arizona State 9-2, UCLA 7-3-1, Southern Calif. 9-2, Washington 9-2	Jim Walden	Holiday	36 Brigham Young	38
1982	3-7-1		8	UCLA 9-1-1, Tennessee 6-4-1, California 7-4, Washington 9-2	Jim Walden			
1983	7-4		3	Michigan 9-2, Arizona 7-3-1, Washington 8-3	Jim Walden			
1984	6-5		5	Tennessee 7-3-1, Ohio State 9-2, UCLA 8-3, Washington 10-1	Jim Walden			
1985	4-7		7	Arizona 8-3, Ohio State 8-3, UCLA 8-2-1, Arizona State 8-3	Jim Walden			
1986	3-7-1		8	Arizona State 9-1-1, Stanford 8-3, Arizona 8-3, Washington 8-2-1	Jim Walden (41-55-4)			
1987	3-7-1		9	Wayoming 10-2, Michigan 7-4, Colorado 7-4, Southern Calif. 8-3	Dennis Erickson			
1988	9-3	15	3t	Illinois 6-4-1, Arizona 7-4, UCLA 9-2	Dennis Erickson (12-10-1)	Aloha	24 Houston	22
1989	6-5		7t	BYU 10-2, So. Calif. 8-2-1, Oregon 7-4, Arizona 7-4, Washington 7-4	Mike Price			
1990	3-8		9	BYU 10-2, Southern Calif. 8-3-1, Washington 9-2	Mike Price			
1991	4-7		6t	Ohio State 8-3, UCLA 8-3, Washington 11-0	Mike Price			
1992	9-3	17	3t	Southern Calif. 6-4-1, Stanford 9-3, Washington 9-2	Mike Price	Copper	31 Utah	28
1993	5-6		7	Michigan 9-4, California 8-4, Arizona 10-3, UCLA 8-3, Washington 7-4	Mike Price			
1994	8-4	19	4	Oregon 9-3, UCLA 8-3, Southern Calif. 7-3-1	Mike Price	Alamo	10 Baylor	3
1995	3-8		8t	UCLA 7-4, Nebraska 11-0, Southern Calif. 8-2-1, Oregon 9-2	Mike Price			
1996	5-6		5t	Colorado 9-2, Washington 9-2	Mike Price			
1997	10-2	9	1t	UCLA 9-2, Arizona State 8-3, Washington 7-4	Mike Price	Rose	16 Michigan	21
1998	3-8		10	UCLA 10-1, Oregon 8-3, Southern Calif. 8-4, Arizona 11-1	Mike Price			
1999	3-9		10	Utah 8-3, Stanford 8-3, Oregon 8-3	Mike Price			
2000	4-7		8t	Boise State 9-2, Oregon State 10-1, Oregon 9-2, Washington 10-1	Mike Price			
2001	10-2	11	2t	Colorado 9-2, Stanford 9-2, Oregon 10-1, Washington 8-3	Mike Price	Sun	33 Purdue	27
2002	10-3	10	1t	Ohio State 13-0, Southern California 10-2, Arizona State 8-5	Mike Price (83-78)	Rose	14 Oklahoma	34
2003	10-3	9	2	Oregon 8-4, Oregon State 7-5, Southern California 11-1	Bill Doda	Holiday	28 Texas	20
2004	5-6		7	Colorado 7-5, Southern California 12-0, Arizona State 8-3	Bill Doda			
2005	4-7		9t	UCLA 9-2, Southern California 12-0, Oregon 10-1	Bill Doda			
2006	6-6		5t	Auburn 10-2, Southern Calif. 10-2, Oregon State 9-4, California 9-3	Bill Doda			
2007	5-7		7t	Wisconsin 9-3, Southern California 10-2, Arizona State 10-2 Oregon 8-4	Bill Doda (30-29)			
2008	2-11		9	Oklahoma State 9-3, California 8-4, Oregon 9-3, Southern California 11-1	Paul Wulff			
2009	1-11		10	Stanford 8-4, Oregon 10-2, Arizona 8-4, Oregon State 8-4	Paul Wulff			
2010	2-10		10	Oklahoma State 10-2, So. California 8-5, Oregon 12-0, Stanford 11-1	Paul Wulff (5-32)			

TOTAL: 262-358-13 .4269 (60 of 70)   Bowl Games since 1953:   5-3 .6250 (7 of 70)

GREATEST TEAM SINCE 1953: Washington State had not attended the Rose Bowl since way back in 1931, so when Leon Bender, Michael Black, Dorian Boose, Steve Gleason, Chris Jackson, Ryan Leaf, and Dee Moronkola led Mike Price's 1997 Cougars to Pasadena, where they gave a good accounting of themselves against no. 1 Michigan, it was one of the truly great years in Wazzu history.

1953 4-6

13 Southern Cal	29 E Russ Quackenbush
26 Pacific	20 T Tom Gunnari / Vic Weitz
12 Iowa	54 G Gottlieb Ribary / Phil Gardner
7 Oregon	0 C Skip Pixley / Herb Carlson
30 Idaho	13 G Jerry Brockey / Mel Thompson
7 UCLA	44 T Milt Schwenk / Joe Polowkski
19 Stanford	48 E Howard McCants / Arnie Pelluer
7 TCU	21 QB Bob Burkhart
0 Oregon State	7 HB Wayne Berry / Jim Hagerty
25 Washington	20 HB Duke Washington (FB) / Mert Purnell
	FB Vaughn Hitchcock / Chuck Beckel

RUSHING: Berry 92/388y, Hitchcock 66/257y, Beckel 94/218y
PASSING: Berry 25-51/359y, 3TD, 49.0%,
Burkhart 14-38/193y, TD, 36.9%
RECEIVING: Quackenbush 12/117y, McCants 8/107y,
Berry 7/93y
SCORING: Beckel 36pts, Berry 30pts,
Hagerty & Washington 18pts

1954 4-6

0 Southern Cal	39 E Russ Quackenbush / Lew Turner
18 Pacific	0 T Tom Gunnari
14 Texas	40 G Vaughn Hitchcock / Doug Liefeste
34 Oregon State	6 C Skip Pixley / Bruce Nevitt
*7 California	17 G Jim Welch
0 Idaho	10 T Jerry Brockey
30 Stanford	26 E Arnie Pelluer / Randy Glazbrook
6 Michigan State	54 QB Bob Iverson / Frank Sarno
14 Oregon	26 HB Bob Miller / Mert Purnell
26 Washington	7 HB Jim Hagerty
	FB Duke Washington / Chuck Beckel

RUSHING: Washington 105/616y
PASSING: Iverson 45-98/496y TD, 45.9%
RECEIVING:
SCORING:

1955 1-7-2

12 Southern Cal	50 E Russ Quackenbush / Lew Turner
0 Kansas	13 T Jim Welch
0 UCLA	55 G Tom Gunnari / Gail Strait
20 California	20 C Skip Pixley / Doug Lefeiste
9 Idaho	0 G Vaughn Hitchcock / Burl Grinols
6 Oregon State	14 T Jerry Brockey / Gene Baker
0 Pacific	30 E Arnie Pelluer / Pete Toomey
0 Oregon	35 QB Bob Iverson / Frank Sarno
13 San Jose State	13 HB Jim Hagerty / Rey Alvarado
7 Washington	27 HB Dewey Keith / Bill Steiger
	FB Bill Kramer / Bob Miller / Dennis Rath

RUSHING: Alvarado 72/286y, Kramer 42/208y, Hagerty 60/172y
PASSING: Iverson 49-95/568y, TD, 51.5%
RECEIVING: Pelluer 17/215y, Toomey 12/149y, Steiger 9/82y
SCORING: Iverson (QB-K) 18pts, Rath 12pts, Sarno (QB-K) 7pts

1956 3-6-1

26 Stanford	40 E Bill Steiger / Lew Turner
33 San Jose State	18 T Al Williamson / Don Nelson
33 Idaho	19 G Gail Strait / Ken Gardner
0 UCLA	28 C Ted Gray / Jack Atwood
0 Oregon State	21 G Gene Baker / Ev Gust
12 Pacific	33 T Burl Grinols / Vel West
12 Southern Cal	28 E Don Ellingsen /Don Gest/Jack Fanning
7 Oregon	7 QB Bobby Newman / Bunny Aldrich
14 California	13 HB Chuck Morrell / Rey Alvarado
26 Washington	40 SB Dick Windham / Ron Hare
	FB Eddie Stevens / Jim Frankson

RUSHING: Morrell 121/528y, Stevens 107/360y, Frankson 32/138y
PASSING: Newman 91-170/1240y, 8TD, 53.5%,
Aldrich 57-101/804y, 5TD, 56.4%
RECEIVING: Steiger 39/607y, Ellingsen 27/455y, Gest 26/299y
SCORING: Steiger 36pts, Morrell & Stevens 18pts

1957 6-4

34 Nebraska	12 E Ted Gray / Gail Cogdill
13 California	7 T Al Williamson / Gene Baker
13 Iowa	20 G George Somnis / Angelo Brovelli
21 Stanford	18 C Gail Strait / Marvin Nelson
13 Oregon	14 G Dick Farrar
13 Southern Cal	12 T Dan Verhey / Ray Blier
25 Oregon State	39 E Don Ellingsen / Jack Fanning
13 UCLA	19 QB Bobby Newman / Bunny Aldrich
21 Idaho	13 HB Chuck Morrell / Carl Ketchie
27 Washington	7 SB Don Ellersick / LaRoy Rath
	FB Eddie Stevens / Dick Windham

RUSHING: Ketchie 84/419y, Stevens 53/265y, Ellersick 41/185y
PASSING: Newman 104-188/1391y, 13TD, 55.3%
RECEIVING: Ellingsen 45/559y, Fanning 24/457y, Cogdill 15/246y
SCORING: Fanning 54pts, Ellingsen (E-K) 25pts,
Newman (QB-K) 23pts

1958 7-3

40 Stanford	6 E Don Ellersick / Don Ellingsen
28 Northwestern	29 T Dan Verhey / Ray Blier
14 California	34 G Dick Farrar
8 Idaho	0 C Marvin Nelson / Ted Gray
6 Oregon	0 G Angelo Brovelli
6 Southern Cal	14 T Merl Hitzel / Al Williamson
38 UCLA	20 E Gail Cogdill / Jack Fanning
7 Oregon State	0 QB Bobby Newman / Dave Wilson
34 Pacific	0 HB Keith Lincoln / Chuck Morrell (FB)
18 Washington	14 SB LaRoy Rath / Bill Steiger
	FB Carl Ketchie/Ted Cano/Eddie Stevens

RUSHING: Morrell 133/571y, Lincoln 68/288y, Cano 52/266y
PASSING: Newman 51-79/541y, 6TD, 64.6%,
Wilson 43-63/641y, 8TD, 68.3%
RECEIVING: Cogdill 21/479y, Rath 17/195y, Ellersick 15/151y
SCORING: Cogdill 40pts, Morrell 30pts, Ellersick & Cano 24pts

1959 6-4

6 California	20 E Gail Cogdill
30 San Jose State	6 T Dick Farrar / Garner Ekstran
6 Oregon	14 G Bill Berry / Pat Crook
20 Pacific	12 C Marv Nelson / Merl Hitzel
36 Stanford	19 G Ron Green / Roger Dupral
27 Idaho	5 T Myke Lindsey / Jim Greig
14 Oregon State	0 E Ed Shaw / Pete Schenck
6 Oregon	7 QB Mel Melin / Mike Agee
0 Washington	20 HB Keith Lincoln / Perry Harper
32 Houston	18 SB Don Ellersick
	FB LaRoy Rath / George Reed

RUSHING: Lincoln 124/670y, Reed 62/224y, Rath 43/213y
PASSING: Melin 41-98/526y, 3TD, 41.8%,
Agee 36-69/429y, 4TD, 52.2%
RECEIVING: Cogdill 28/531y, Ellersick 26/302y, Schenck 18/213y
SCORING: Cogdill 40pts, Lincoln 34pts, Agee 18pts

1960 4-5-1

15 Stanford	14 E Hugh Campbell / Pete Schenck
26 Denver	28 T Garner Ekstran / Dick Copple
21 Arizona State	24 G Roger Duprel
21 California	21 C Tom Erlandson / Pat Crook
12 Oregon	21 G Jim Greig
51 Pacific	12 T Ron Green / Bob Colleran
29 San Jose State	6 E Lee Schroeder / Perry Harper
10 Oregon State	20 QB Mel Melin
18 Idaho	7 HB Keith Lincoln / Harold Haddock
7 Washington	8 SB Jim Boylan
	FB Dave Kerrone / Louis Blakely

RUSHING: Lincoln 94/543y, Kerrone 74/297y, Blakely 38/220y
PASSING: Melin 119-220/1638y, 11TD, 54.1%
RECEIVING: Campbell 66/881y, Boylan 21/340y, Schenck 18/255y
SCORING: Campbell 76pts, Kerrone 26pts, Blakely 18pts

1961 3-7

6 Missouri	21 E Hugh Campbell
14 Utah State	34 T John Wyffels / Jim Jensen
8 Texas	41 G Jerry Conine / Lorin Christean
34 Idaho	0 C Tom Erlandson / Roy Busse
7 Indiana	33 G Pat Crook
19 San Jose State	21 T Bob Colleran / Bob Hoien
6 Oregon State	14 E Harvey West / Ron Langhans
22 Oregon	21 QB Mel Melin / Dave Mathieson
30 Stanford	0 HB John Browne / Dave Kerrone
17 Washington	21 HB Pete Schenck / Jim Boylan
	FB George Reed

RUSHING: Reed 131/489y
PASSING: Melin 66-134/814y, 7TD, 49.3%
RECEIVING: Campbell 53/723y
SCORING: Reed 48pts

1962 5-4-1

49 San Jose State	8 E Hugh Campbell
21 Wyoming	15 T Larry Reisbig / Glenn Baker
24 Arizona State	24 G Chuck Barnes / Ron Langhans (LB)
21 Stanford	6 C Dean Kalahar / Roy Busse (LB)
21 Indiana	15 G Jerry Kirk / Dale Knuth
12 Pacific	13 T Blain Eliot / Lorin Christean
12 Oregon State	18 E Clete Baltes / Mike Abbott
10 Oregon	28 QB Dave Mathieson
22 Idaho	14 HB Ken Graham / John Browne
21 Washington	26 SB Gerry Shaw / Herm McKee (DB)
	FB George Reed / Clancy Williams (HB)

RUSHING: Reed 132/503y, Graham 43/176y, Browne 52/163y
PASSING: Mathieson 104-199/1492y, 12TD, 52.3%
RECEIVING: Campbell 57/848y, Shaw 19/356y,
Graham 15/204y
SCORING: Reed 60pts, Campbell 48pts, Shaw 30pts

1963 3-6-1

7 Texas Tech	16 E Gerry Shaw / Tom Kelley
14 Iowa	14 T Wendell Wardell / Brian Beveridge
7 Arizona	2 G Roy Busse (C) / Bill Cook
8 San Jose State	13 C Dean Kalahar
6 Oregon State	30 G Dale Knuth
0 Army	23 T Jim Paton
14 Idaho	10 TE Clete Baltes
7 Oregon	21 QB Dave Mathieson/Tom Roth/Dale Ford
32 Stanford	15 HB Clancy Williams
0 Washington	16 HB Ken Graham
	FB John Browne / Herm McKee

RUSHING: Williams 105/523y
PASSING: Mathieson 85-175/859y, 4TD, 48.6%
RECEIVING: Shaw 32/309y
SCORING: Williams 14pts

1964 3-6-1

29 Stanford	23 E Tom Kelley / Gerry Shaw
7 Wyoming	28 T Bob Trygstad / Wayne Foster
12 Arizona	28 G Jim Nelson / Bill Kennedy (DL)
50 Pacific	0 C Ron Vrlicak / Dave Thomas
16 San Jose State	14 G Wally Dempsey / Larry Griffith (LB)
13 Idaho	28 T Joe Broeker / Jim Paton
7 Oregon State	24 TE Rich Sheron / Bud Norris
21 Oregon	21 QB Dave Roth
10 Texas Tech	28 HB Clancy Williams
0 Washington	14 HB Willie Gaskins / Mike Cadigan
	FB Larry Eilmes

RUSHING: Williams 147/783y, Eilmes 111/497y,
Petersen 124/276y
PASSING: Petersen 36-77/478y, TD, 46.8%,
Roth 23-53/307y, 0TD, 43.4%
RECEIVING: Williams 17/210y, Kelley 16/218y, Sheron 15/165y
SCORING: Williams 36pts, Eilmes 30pts, Gaskins & Roth 24pts

1965 7-3

7 Iowa	0 WR Doug Flansburg
14 Minnesota	13 T Brian Beveridge / Jim Guinn
13 Idaho	17 G Robin Larson
24 Villanova	14 C Ron Vrlicak
21 Arizona	3 G Dave Middendorf
8 Indiana	7 T Dave Thomas / Greg Elliot
10 Oregon State	8 TE Rich Sheron / Dennis Birney (DL)
27 Oregon	7 QB Tom Roth
6 Arizona State	7 HB Ammon McWashington / Ted Gerela
9 Washington	27 HB Joe Lynn / Bob Simpson
	FB Larry Eilmes
	DL Craig Goodwin
	DL Burgess Bauder
	DL Bob Trygstad / Jerry Anderson
	DL Wayne Foster / Bill Mansfield
	DL Walt Frierson
	LB Dick Baird / Steve Boots
	LB Larry Griffith
	LB Mark Wicks / Ron Orr
	DB Jim Newson
	DB Willie Gaskins
	DB Dave Petersen

RUSHING: Eilmes 180/818y, McWashington 106/434y,
Lynn 41/159y
PASSING: Roth 98-190/1257y, 5TD, 51.6%
RECEIVING: Flansburg 46/578y, Sheron 17/282y,
Eilmes 12/132y
SCORING: Eilmes 36pts, McWashington 20pts,
Gerela (FB-K) 19pts

1966 3-7

6 California	21 E Doug Flansburg
7 Houston	21 T Dave Thomas
14 Baylor	20 G Dave Harris / Robin Larson
24 Arizona State	15 C Ron Vrlicak
15 Utah	26 G Dave Middendorf
14 Idaho	7 T Greg Elliot
13 Oregon State	41 TE Rich Sheron
14 Oregon	13 QB Jerry Henderson
18 Arizona	28 HB Ammon McWashington
7 Washington	19 HB Del Carmichael / Joe Lynn (LB)
	FB Ted Gerela
	DL Craig Goodwin
	DL Bill Mansfield / Bill Kennedy
	DL Bob Trygstad / Jerry Anderson
	DL Burgess Bauder / J.R. Edington
	DL Walt Frierson
	LB Larry Griffith
	LB Steve Bartelle / Dick Baird
	DB Bud Norris / Rick Reed
	DB Bob Simpson / Dave Petersen
	DB Mike Cadigan
	DB Mark Wicks

RUSHING: McWashington 94/298y
PASSING: Henderson 95-174/989y, 2TD, 54.6%
RECEIVING: Flansburg 54/613y
SCORING: Gerela (FB-K) 42pts

1967 2-8

0 Southern Cal	49 E Doug Flansburg
0 Oklahoma	21 T Dave Golinsky
23 UCLA	51 G Dave Middendorf
7 Baylor	10 C Dave Harris
10 Stanford	31 G Bill McCain
20 Arizona State	31 T Steve Van Sinderen
7 Oregon State	35 TE Bob Simpson
13 Oregon	17 QB Jerry Henderson
52 Idaho	14 HB Mark Williams / Glen Shaw
9 Washington	7 HB Johnny Davis
	FB Del Carmichael
	DL Wayne Swayda
	DL Hank Bendix
	DL Jim Gunn
	DL Ernest Thomas
	LB Jim Vest
	LB Steve Boots
	LB Dick Baird
	DB Gregg Field
	DB Rick Reed
	DB Mike Cadigan
	DB Mark Wicks

SCORING: Williams 114/415y
PASSING: Henderson 67-144/836y, 4TD, 46.5%
RECEIVING: Flansburg 39/461y
SCORING: Carmichael 32pts

1968 3-6-1

14 Idaho	7 WR Fred Moore / Ed Armstrong
21 UCLA	31 WR Larry Thatcher / Johnny Davis
14 Utah	7 T Dave Golinsky
14 Arizona State	41 G Bill McCain
21 Stanford	21 C Dave Harris
8 Oregon State	16 G Jim Hellyer
14 Arizona	28 T Steve Van Sinderen
13 Oregon	27 TE Ron Souza
46 San Jose State	0 QB Jerry Henderson
24 Washington	0 TB Glen Shaw / Richard Lee Smith
	FB Del Carmichael
	DL Wayne Swayda
	DL Dave Berger
	DL Don Engler
	DL Gary Branson
	DL Dave Crema
	LB Steve Bartelle
	LB Terry Durst
	DB Rick Reed
	DB Mark Williams
	DB Jim Petersen
	DB Dick Schultz

RUSHING: Smith 105/326y
PASSING: Henderson 137-246/1586y, 4TD, 55.7%
RECEIVING: Souza 33/343y
SCORING: Hank Grenda (K) 28pts

1969 1-9

19 Illinois	18 WR Fred Moore / Ed Armstrong
35 Iowa	61 WR Johnny Davis
24 Oregon	25 T Hank Bendix
14 UCLA	46 G Jim Giesa
0 Stanford	49 C Mike Lynch
0 California	17 G Jim Hellyer
20 Pacific	27 T Buzz Brazeau
7 Southern Cal	28 TE Hugh Klopfenstein
3 Oregon State	38 QB Jack Wigmore
21 Washington	30 TB Richard Lee Smith / Chuck Hawthorne
	FB Bob Ewen
	DL Dave Crema
	DL Dave Berger
	DL Don Engler
	DL Brian Lange
	DL Ernie Thomas
	LB Terry Durst
	LB Joe Richer
	DB Lionel Thomas
	DB Steve Kerby
	DB Eric Dahl
	DB Roger LeClerc

RUSHING: Smith 134/485y
PASSING: Wigmore 65-149/876y, 4TD, 43.6%
RECEIVING: Moore 31/523y
SCORING: Wigmore 24pts

1970 1-10

31 Kansas	48 WR Ed Armstrong / Jim Oggs
44 Idaho	16 WR Tony Lomax / Brock Aynsley
14 Michigan State	28 T Buzz Brazeau
13 Oregon	28 G Jim Giesa
30 Arizona State	37 C John Hook
16 Stanford	63 G Steve Busch
0 California	45 T Wallace Williams / Mike Talbot
9 UCLA	54 TE Hugh Klopfenstein
33 Southern Cal	70 QB Ty Paine
16 Oregon State	28 TB Bernard Jackson
25 Washington	43 FB Bob Ewen
	DL Terry Durst
	DL Marc Pence / Dennis Mitchell
	DL Brian Lange
	DL Pete Lazzarini
	LB Dana Dogterom / Crosby Anderson
	LB Rod Mumma / Martin Ancellotti
	LB Randy Johnson / Pat Messinger
	DB Ron Mims
	DB Lionel Thomas / Steve Kerby
	DB Nile DeCuire
	DB Tim Thompson / Bob Leslie

RUSHING: Ewan 142/667y
PASSING: Paine 123-267/1581y, 3TD, 46.1%
RECEIVING: Armstrong 33/488y
SCORING: Jackson 52pts

1971 4-7

0 Kansas	34 WR Ike Nelson / Brock Aynsley
28 Arizona	39 WR Bobby Redmond / Tony Lomax
31 Minnesota	20 T Buzz Brazeau / Mike Talbot
34 Utah	12 G Jim Giesa
21 UCLA	34 C John Hook / Mike Hill
23 California	24 G Steve Busch / Bill Moos
24 Stanford	23 T Wallace Williams
31 Oregon	21 TE Jim Forrest
20 Southern Cal	30 QB Ty Paine
14 Oregon State	21 TB Bernard Jackson
20 Washington	28 FB Ken Grandberry / Ken Lyday
	DL Mike Johnson
	DL Greg Craighead
	DL Harold Bradford / Tom Wickert
	DL Brian Lange
	LB Bob Leslie / Clyde Warehime
	LB Steve Busch / Tom Poe
	LB Randy Pickering / Crosby Anderson
	DB Ron Mims
	DB Robin Sinclair / Tyrone Daisy
	DB Harry Thompson / Chuck Hawthorne
	DB Eric Johnson / Nile DeCuire

RUSHING: Jackson 177/1189y, Grandberry 103/626y,
Paine 130/482y
PASSING: Paine 91-217/1206y, 5TD, 41.9%
RECEIVING: Nelson 23/349y, Lomax 16/210y, Jackson 14/185y
SCORING: Jackson 84pts, Don Sweet (K) 58pts, Paine 38pts

1972 7-4

18 Kansas	17 WR Brock Aynsley / Fritz Brayton
23 California	37 WR Greg Johnson / Bob Redmond
28 Arizona	6 T Bill Moos
25 Utah	44 G Mike Hill
35 Idaho	14 C Geoff Reese
31 Oregon	14 G Steve Ostermann
37 Oregon State	7 T Tom Wickert
20 UCLA	35 TE Jim Forrest / Bob Engel
3 Southern Cal	44 QB Ty Paine
27 Stanford	13 TB Ken Grandberry / Charles Anderson
27 Washington	10 FB Steve Hamilton / Andrew Jones
	DL Mike Johnson
	DL Greg Craighead
	DL Dennis Mitchell
	DL Jim Robinson / Tom Caraher
	LB Clyde Warehime
	LB Tom Poe / Jerry Burkhalter
	LB Gary Larsen / Steve Roberts
	DB Robin Sinclair / Fran Kachaturian
	DB Tyrone Daisy
	DB Eric Johnson
	DB Mike Carter / Harry Thompson

RUSHING: Grandberry 214/833y, Hamilton 163/717y,
Paine 127/250y
PASSING: Paine 111-241/1349y, 7TD, 46.1%
RECEIVING: Grandberry 28/273y, Aynsley 23/344y,
Redmond 22/324y
SCORING: Grandberry 72pts, Joe Danelo (K) 63pts, Paine 48pts

1973 5-6

8 Kansas	29 WR Fritz Brayton
9 Arizona State	20 WR Greg Johnson / Rick Riegle
51 Idaho	24 T Mike Hill
3 Ohio State	27 G Wilbur McKinney / Bob Drinkwalter
35 Southern Cal	46 C Geoff Reese / Steve Morton
13 UCLA	24 G Steve Ostermann / Bob Aldrich
14 Stanford	45 T Tom Wickert
21 Oregon	14 TE Tim Krause / Bob Engel
13 Oregon State	7 QB Chuck Peck
31 California	28 TB Ken Grandberry / Ron Cheatham
52 Washington	26 FB Andrew Jones / Jim Lewis
	DL Rod Anderson
	DL Greg Craighead
	DL Lee Weatherford
	DL Joe Daniels / Don Olsen
	LB Clyde Warehime
	LB Tom Poe
	LB Gary Larsen / Steve Roberts
	DB Robin Sinclair
	DB Morris Noble / Basil Kimbrew
	DB Eric Johnson / Woodrow Perkins
	DB Mike Carter / Dennis Clancy

RUSHING: Jones 207/1059y
PASSING: Peck 76-145/1023y, 4TD, 52.4%
RECEIVING: Brayton 23/175y
SCORING: Joe Danello (K) 60pts

1974 2-9

7 Kansas	14 WR Ray Kimble / Duke Fergerson
17 Idaho	10 WR Dennis Pearson
19 Illinois	21 T Earl Owens / Dan Smith
7 Ohio State	42 G Jon DesPois / Mark Young
7 Southern Cal	54 C Geoff Reece / Robert Aldrich
13 UCLA	17 G Steve Ostermann
18 Stanford	20 T Robin Ross
21 Oregon	16 TE Carl Barschig / Eason Ramson
3 Oregon State	17 QB Chuck Peck / John Hopkins
33 California	37 TB Ron Cheatham
17 Washington	24 FB Andrew Jones / Vern Chamberlain
	DL Tim Ochs
	DL Dennis Dobberpuhl
	DL Mark Husfloen
	DL Joe Daniels / Lee Weatherford
	LB Don Hover / Dean Pedigo
	LB Scott Mullennix / Steve Roberts
	LB Gary Larsen / Bill Patterson
	DB Robert Crow
	DB Tony Heath / Basil Kimbrew
	DB Mike Mitchell / Rufus Cunningham
	DB Mike Carter / Dennis Clancy

RUSHING: Cheatham 110/616y, Chamberlain 79/364y,
Jones 89/351y
PASSING: Hopkins 45-82/522y, 4TD, 54.9%,
Peck 36-90/478y, 1TD, 40.0%
RECEIVING: Barschig 32/423y, Kimble 16/151y,
Cheatham 10/132y, Fergerson 10/123y
SCORING: Peck 30pts, Joe Danelo (K) 40pts, 2 with 18pts

1975 3-8

18 Kansas	14 WR Mike Levenseller / Ray Kimble
30 Utah	14 WR Brian Kelly / Dennis Pearson
21 California	33 T Dan Smith
21 Illinois	27 G Mark Young
10 Southern Cal	28 C Jon DesPois / Dave Tobin
23 UCLA	37 G Bob Hill
14 Stanford	54 T Robin Ross
14 Oregon	26 TE Carl Barschig / Eason Ramson
0 Oregon State	7 QB John Hopkins / Jack Thompson
84 Idaho	27 TB Dan Doornink / Dexter Tisby
27 Washington	28 FB Vaughn Williams / Vern Chamberlain
	DL Lee Braach
	DL Tim Ochs / Terry Anderson
	DL Dennis Dobberpuhl / George Yarno
	DL Mark Husfloen
	LB Jerry Payne / Dean Pedigo
	LB Scott Mullennix
	LB Bill Patterson / Jeff Jones
	DB Ken Greene / Robert Crow
	DB Tony Heath / Basil Kimbrew
	DB Rufus Cunningham
	DB Mark Patterson / Tony Cook

RUSHING: Williams 134/662y, Doornink 139/607y, Chamberlain 76/359y
PASSING: Hopkins 81-146/1022y, 3TD, 55.5%, Thompson 26-54/351y, 3TD, 48.1%
RECEIVING: Kelly 28/371y, Pearson 21/291y, Barschig 12/170y
SCORING: Chuck Diedrick (K) 52pts, Williams 38pts, Doornink 30pts

1976 3-8

16 Kansas	35 WR Mike Levenseller / Bob Bratkowski
14 Minnesota	28 WR Brian Kelly / Bevan Maxey
26 Wisconsin	35 T Bob Hill / Allan Kennedy
45 Idaho	6 G Tom Larson
14 Southern Cal	23 C Jon DesPois / Larry Finan
3 UCLA	62 G Larry Finan
16 Stanford	22 T Dave Lemke
23 Oregon	22 TE Eason Ramson / Ron Bull
29 Oregon State	24 QB Jack Thompson / John Hopkins
22 California	23 RB Dan Doornink Tali Ena
32 Washington	51 RB Harold Gillum / Mike Washington
	DL Mel Sanders
	DL Tim Ochs
	DL George Yarno
	DL Spud Harris
	DL Tom Thompson / Mark Hicks
	LB Jeff Jones / Don Hover
	LB Dean Pedigo
	DB Ken Greene
	DB Mark Patterson / Bob Gregor
	DB John Troppman
	DB Don Schwartz

RUSHING: Doornink 129/422y, Washington 32/167y, Gillum 35/145y
PASSING: Thompson 208-355/2762y, 20TD, 58.6%
RECEIVING: Levenseller 67/1124y, Doornink 53/469y, Kelly 44/746y
SCORING: Doornink 54pts, Levenseller 50pts, Kelly 44pts

1977 6-5

19 Nebraska	10 WR Mike Levenseller / Bob Bratkowski
23 Michigan State	21 WR Brian Kelly / Bevan Maxey
12 Kansas	14 T Barry Zanck
7 Southern Cal	41 G Tom Larsen / Mike Lemke
17 California	10 C Mark Chandless
16 UCLA (F-W)	27 G Larry Finan
29 Stanford	31 T Dave Lemke
56 Oregon	20 TE Eason Ramson
24 Oregon State	10 QB Jack Thompson
45 Idaho	17 RB Dan Doornink / Tali Ena
15 Washington	35 RB Mike Washington / Harold Gillum
	DL Scott Pelluer / Mark Hicks
	DL Spud Harris
	DL Terry Anderson
	DL George Yarno / Steve Swift
	DL Tom Thompson / Dan Reardon
	LB Don Hover / Don Nevels
	LB Dean Pedigo / Raleigh Fletcher
	DB Mark Patterson / John Troppman
	DB Ken Greene
	DB Bob Gregor / Mike Snow
	DB Don Schwartz

RUSHING: Doornink 144/591y, Washington 89/338y, Ena 82/316y
PASSING: Thompson 192-329/2372y, 13TD, 58.4%
RECEIVING: Kelly 44/675y, Levenseller 43/736y, Doornink 35/358y
SCORING: Paul Watson (K) 59pts, Kelly 48pts, 2 with 24pts

1978 3-7-1

34 UNLV	7 WR Mike Wilson / Bevan Maxey
28 Idaho	0 WR Jim Whatley
51 Arizona State	26 T Allan Kennedy
21 Army	21 G Tom Larsen
31 UCLA	45 C Mark Chandless
27 Stanford	43 G Gene Emerson / Steve Jackson
7 Oregon (F-W)	31 T Mike Lemke
31 Oregon State	32 TE Gus Hobus / Pat Beach
14 California	22 QB Jack Thompson
24 Arizona	31 RB Ray Williams / Mike Washington
8 Washington	38 FB Tali Ena
	DL Greg Porter / Steve Swift
	DL Brian Flones
	DL George Yarno
	LB Melvin Sanders / Scott Pelluer
	LB Sam Busch / Don Nevels
	LB Raleigh Fletcher
	LB Tom Thompson / Mikr Branigan
	DB Randal Simmons
	DB Jeff Files / Don McCall
	DB Bob Gregor / Gary Teague
	DB Mike Snow

RUSHING: Ena 132/728y, Williams 82/412y, Washington 80/363y
PASSING: Thompson 175-348/2333y, 17TD, 50.3%
RECEIVING: Ena 42/409y, Wilson 31/451y, Whatley 27/426y
SCORING: Ena 48pts, Paul Watson (K) 46pts, Washington 38pts

1979 3-8

7 Arizona	22 WR Bevan Maxey / Mike Wilson
34 Montana	14 WR Jim Whatley
29 Ohio State	45 T Steve Johnson / John Little
35 Syracuse	52 G Greg Sykes
21 Southern Cal	51 C Scott Rogers / Gene Emerson
17 UCLA	14 G Steve Jackson
17 Arizona St.(F-W)	28 T Allan Kennedy
26 Oregon (F-W)	37 TE Pat Beach
45 Oregon State	42 QB Steve Grant
13 California	45 RB Ray Williams / Tim Harris
7 Washington	17 RB Tali Ena / Brian Sickler
	DL Mike Walker / Ken Collins
	DL Brian Flones
	DL Matt Elisara / Greg Porter
	LB Scott Pelluer
	LB Ken Emmil / Sam Busch
	LB Don Nevels
	LB Melvin Sanders / Tony Busch
	DB Mike Snow / Gary Teague
	DB Bob Gregor / Hugh Parker
	DB Don McCall
	DB John S. West

RUSHING: Ena 158/844y, Williams 84/421y, Harris 67/414y
PASSING: Grant 120-224/1565y, 9TD, 53.6%
RECEIVING: Whatley 31/513y, Maxey 30/409y, Beach 23/354y
SCORING: Mike DeSanto (K) 47pts, Ena & Grant 38pts

1980 4-7

26 San Jose State	31 WR Mike Wilson / Jeff Keller
23 Tennessee	35 WR Jim Whatley / Paul Escalera
31 Army	18 T Steve Johnson
22 Pacific	24 G Greg Sykes / Greg Porter
21 Arizona State	27 C Gene Emerson
38 Arizona	14 G Gary Patrick / John Dreyer
34 Stanford	48 T Allan Kennedy
10 Oregon	20 TE Pat Beach
28 Oregon State	7 QB Samoa Samoa
31 California	17 RB Tim Harris / Al Bowens
23 Washington	30 RB Mike Washington
	DL Ken Collins / Ken Jacobsen
	DL Brian Flones
	DL Matt Elisara
	LB Scott Pelluer / Dirk Hunter
	LB Ken Emmil / Brent White
	LB Lee Blakeney /
	LB Melvin Sanders / Brian Sickler
	DB Nate Bradley / Joe Taylor
	DB Jeff Files / Gary Teague
	DB Paul Sorensen / Peter Shaw
	DB John S. West

RUSHING: Harris 167/801y, Washington 83/464y, Samoa 137/453y
PASSING: Samoa 105-200/1668y, 9TD, 52.5%
RECEIVING: Beach 20/318y, Whatley 18/433y, Escalera 16/217y, Harris 16/157y
SCORING: Samoa 68pts, Mike DeSanto (K) 65pts, Harris 42pts

1981 8-3-1

33 Montana State	21 WR Jeff Keller / T.J. Jones
14 Colorado	10 WR Paul Escalera / Jeff Poppe
24 Arizona State	21 T Charlie Flager / John Winslow
31 Pacific	0 G Mark McKay
23 Oregon State	0 C Steve Sabahar
17 UCLA	17 G Gary Patrick / Dan Lynch
34 Arizona	19 T Kevin Sloan
17 Southern Cal	41 TE Pat Beach
39 Oregon	7 QB Clete Casper / Ricky Turner
19 California	0 RB Tim Harris / Mike Martin
10 Washington	23 RB Robert Williams / James Matthews
36 BYU■	38 DL Ken Collins
	DL Matt Elisara / Pat Lynch
	DL Mike Walker / Keith Millard
	LB Sonny Elkinton / Junior Tupuola
	LB Brent White / Rico Tipton
	LB Lee Blakeney
	LB Ken Emmil / Mark Pleis
	DB Nate Bradley
	DB Jeff Files / Rod Retherford
	DB Paul Sorensen / Peter Shaw
	DB John S. West / Joe Taylor

RUSHING: Harris 161/931y, Turner 85/456y, Williams 82/445y
PASSING: Casper 84-156/1008y, TD, 53.8%, Turner 51-107/772y, 0TD, 47.7%
RECEIVING: Keller 39/535y, Escalera 20/259y, Beach 17/230y
SCORING: Martin 54pts, Turner 50pts, Kevin Morris (K) 48pts

1982 3-7-1

34 Idaho	14 WR T.J. Jones / Dede Moore
0 Colorado	12 WR Mike Peterson / John Breland
11 Minnesota	41 T John Winslow
3 Tennessee	10 G Gary Patrick
14 Oregon State	14 C Steve Sebahar
17 UCLA	42 G Dan Lynch / Greg Porter
26 Stanford	31 T Kevin Sloan
17 Arizona	34 TE Vince Leighton
10 Oregon	3 QB Clete Casper / Ricky Turner
14 California	34 RB Tim Harris / Rueben Mayes
24 Washington	20 RB James Matthews / Robert Williams
	DL Eric Williams
	DL Pat Lynch
	DL Keith Millard / John Dreyer
	LB Brad Harrington
	LB Ben Carrillo
	LB Junior Tupuola
	LB Mark Pleis / Mike Beasley
	DB Rod Retherford
	DB Mark Blocker / Tracy Adkins
	DB Steve Haub
	DB Jerald Waters / Joe Taylor

RUSHING: Harris 147/684y, Matthews 147/680y, Mayes 89/425y
PASSING: Casper 91-184/1072y, 5TD, 49.5%, Turner 29-76/376y, TD, 38.2%
RECEIVING: Peterson 26/440y, Harris 18/126y, 3 with 11
SCORING: Matthews 42pts, John Traut (K) 38pts, Turner 20pts

1983 7-4

27 Montana State	7 WR John Marshall / Michel James
17 Michigan	20 WR John Breland/Sam Burris/Kit'k Taylor
6 Arizona	45 T Charlie Flager
41 UNLV	28 G Dan Lynch / Mike Dreyer
17 Southern Cal	38 C Curt Ladines / Pili Tutuvanu
14 UCLA	24 G Mike Palumbo / Kirk Samuelson
31 Arizona State	21 T John Winslow
24 Oregon	7 TE Vince Leighton / Jamie Olesen
27 Oregon State	9 QB Ricky Turner
16 California	6 RB Rueben Mayes
17 Washington	6 RB Kerry Porter / Richard Calvin
	DL Eric Williams / Erik Howard
	DL Pat Lynch / Milford Hodge
	DL Keith Millard
	LB Mike Beasley / Sonny Elkinton
	LB Ben Carrillo / Rico Tipton
	LB Lee Blakeney
	LB Jim Krakoski / Brad Harrington
	DB Tracy Adkins
	DB Cedrick Brown / Erwin Chappel
	DB Jerald Waters / Rob Treece
	DB Joe Taylor / Steve Haub

RUSHING: Porter 195/1000y, Turner 151/331y, Mayes 61/221y
PASSING: Turner 100-172/1351y, 8TD, 58.1%
RECEIVING: Marshall 21/328y, Burris 16/225y, Taylor 15/244y, James 15/228y
SCORING: John Traut (K) 73pts, Porter 48pts, Turner 24pts

1984 6-5

27 Tennessee	34 WR John Marshall / Sammy Burris
42 Utah	40 WR Michael James / Rick Chase
0 Ohio State	44 T Jamie White
16 Ball State	14 G Dan Lynch
27 Southern Cal	29 C Curt Ladines
24 UCLA	27 G Kirk Samuelson
49 Stanford	42 T Mike Dreyer
50 Oregon	41 TE Vince Leighton
20 Oregon State	3 QB Mark Rypien
33 California	7 RB Rueben Mayes
29 Washington	38 RB Richard Calvin / Kerry Porter
	DL Erik Howard / Rob Cleveland
	DL Milford Hodge
	DL Brent White
	LB Jeff Loomis / Junior Tupuola
	LB Rico Tipton
	LB Lee Blakeney
	LB Jim Krakoski / Brad Harrington
	DB Ricky Reynolds / Erwin Chappel
	DB Cedrick Brown
	DB Jerald Waters
	DB Jeff Dullum / Ron Collins

RUSHING: Mayes 258/1637y, Calvin 84/403y, Rypien 101/275y
PASSING: Rypien 134-271/1927y, 14TD, 49.4%
RECEIVING: Marshall 34/534y, Burris 22/310y, Chase 21/282y
SCORING: Mayes 72pts, John Traut (K) 71pts, Marshall 38pts

1985 4-7

39 Oregon	42 WR Rick Chase / Michel James
20 California	19 WR Kitrick Taylor / Cotton Sears
7 Arizona	12 T Mike Schuster / Rod Durand
37 Utah	44 G Ian Lindner
32 Ohio State	48 C Curt Ladines / Mitch Dillard
34 Oregon State	0 G Mike Dreyer / Alan Boatman
30 UCLA	31 T Mike Utley
16 Arizona State	21 TE Chris Leighton / Mel Orchard
13 Southern Cal	31 QB Mark Rypien
64 Montana State	14 RB Rueben Mayes
21 Washington	20 RB Kerry Porter / Junior Tautalatasi
	DL Rob Cleveland / Marv Adams
	DL Erik Howard / Nick Volk
	DL Tim Petek / Ivan Cook
	DL Mike Beasley
	LB Dean Turulja
	LB Brian Forde
	LB Maury Metcalf / Jeff Loomis
	DB Ricky Reynolds / Shawn Landrum
	DB Cedrick Brown / Erwin Chappel
	DB Kevin Thomasson / Ron Collins
	DB Artie Holmes / Ron Lee

RUSHING: Mayes 228/1236y, Porter 114/441y, Tautalatasi 53/364y
PASSING: Rypien 159-273/2174y, 14TD, 58.2%
RECEIVING: Chase 37/411y, Taylor 33/489y, Mayes 24/252y
SCORING: Mayes 68pts, John Traut (K) 49pts, Taylor 42pts

1986 3-7-1

34 UNLV	14 WR Rick Chase / Kitrick Taylor
13 San Jose State	20 WR Michel James / Victor Wood
21 California	31 T Ken Kuiper / John Husby
21 Arizona State	21 G Ian Lindner
24 Oregon State	14 C Alan Boatman / Dave Fakkema
34 Southern Cal	14 G Mike Utley
16 UCLA	54 T Chris Dyko
12 Stanford	42 TE Chris Leighton / Mel Orchard
6 Arizona	31 QB Ed Blount / Timm Rosenbach
17 Oregon	27 RB Ed Tingstad / Steve Broussard
23 Washington	44 RB Kerry Porter
	DL Marvin Adams / Chris Hiller
	DL Rob Carpenter / Mark Ledbetter
	DL Tim Downing Tony Savage
	DL Chris Hiller / Ivan Cook
	LB Maury Metcalf / Bob O'Neal
	LB Brian Forde / Tuneau Alipate
	LB Bob Gregory
	LB Ricky Reynolds
	DB Shawn Landrum / James Hasty
	DB Kevin Thomasson / Artie Holmes
	DB Ron Collins / Ron Lee

RUSHING: Porter 205/921y, Broussard 53/283y, Blount 119/184y
PASSING: Blount 117-227/1882y, 11TD, 51.5%
RECEIVING: James 33/481y, Taylor 27/523y, Chase 24/298y
SCORING: Taylor 54pts, Kevin Adams (K) 42pts, Porter 24pts

1987 3-7-1

41 Fresno State	24 WR Tim Stallworth / William Pellum
43 Wyoming	28 WR Victor Wood / Elmer Thomas
18 Michigan	44 T John Husby / Ken Kuiper
17 Colorado	26 G Jim Mitchalczik / Rod Durand
7 Stanford	44 C Paul Wulff / Dave Fakkema
7 Arizona State	38 G Mike Utley / Mike Smith
45 Arizona	28 T Chris Dyko
7 Southern Cal	42 TE Chris Leighton / Doug Wellsandt
17 Oregon	31 QB Timm Rosenbach
19 Washington	34 RB Steve Broussard / Rich Swinton
17 California	17 RB Richard Calvin / Ed Tingstad
	DL Randy Gray
	DL Tim Downing / Jeron Woodley
	DL Tony Savage / Dan Webber
	DL Ivan Cook
	LB Maury Metcalf / Bob O'Neal
	LB Tuineau Aliparte / Keith Rice
	LB Brian Forde / Chad Dezellem
	DB Vernon Todd
	DB Shawn Landrum / Roosevelt Noble
	DB Chris Moton
	DB Artie Holmes / Jay Languein

RUSHING: Calvin 180/822y, Rosenbach 138/297y, Broussard 75/254y
PASSING: Rosenbach 222-390/2446y, 11TD, 56.9%
RECEIVING: Broussard 59/701y, Leighton 38/394y, Calvin 33/246y
SCORING: Kevin Adams (K) 56pts, Broussard 54pts, Rosenbach 30pts

1988 9-3

44 Illinois	7 WR Victor Wood / C.J. Davis
41 Minnesota	9 WR Tim Stallworth / Michael Wimberly
28 Oregon	43 T John Husby
52 Tennessee	24 G Jim Michalczik
44 California	13 C Paul Wulff
28 Arizona	45 G Mike Utley
28 Arizona State	31 T Chris Dyko
34 UCLA	30 TE Doug Wellsandt
24 Stanford	21 QB Tim Rosenbach
36 Oregon State	27 RB Steve Broussard / Rich Swinton
32 Washington	31 RB Ed Tingstad
24 Houston■	22 DL Randy Gray
	DL Tim Downing / Mark Ledbetter
	DL Tony Savage
	DL Ivan Cook / Jeron Woodley
	LB Maury Metcalf / Bob O'Neal
	LB Dan Grayson / Tuineau Alipate
	LB Keith Rice
	DB Vernon Todd
	DB Roosevelt Noble
	DB Chris Moton
	DB Artie Holmes / Jay Languein

RUSHING: Broussard 222/1280y
PASSING: Rosenbach 218-338/3097y, 24TD, 64.5%
RECEIVING: Stallworth 63/1151y
SCORING: Jason Hanson (K) 91pts

1989 6-5

41 Idaho	7 WR Calvin Griggs
46 BYU	41 WR Tim Stallworth / Jody Sears
41 Oregon State	3 WR C.J. Davis / Ron Young
29 Wyoming	23 T John Husby
17 Southern Cal	18 G Mike Smith / Robert Norvell (C)
51 Oregon	38 C Paul Wulff
31 Stanford	13 G Steve Cromer / Andy Tribble
21 Arizona	23 T Bob Garman
39 Arizona State	44 TE Doug Wellsandt
26 California	38 QB Aaron Garcia / Brad Gossen
9 Washington	20 RB Steve Broussard / Rich Swinton
	DL Randy Gray / Kirk Westerfield
	DL Tim Downing / Jeron Woodley
	DL Tony Savage
	DL Marlin Brown
	LB Mark Ledbetter / Rod Plummer
	LB Dan Grayson
	DB Ron Ricard
	DB Roosevelt Noble
	DB Alvin Dunn
	DB Chris Moton / Michael Wright
	DB Lewis Bush / John Diggs

RUSHING: Broussard 260/1237y, Paul Carr (RB) 28/179y, Swinton 25/79y
PASSING: Garcia 115-189/1591y, 11TD, 60.8%, Gossen 88-137/1372y, 9TD, 64.2%
RECEIVING: Broussard 39/326y, Wellsandt 31/409y, Stallworth 30/548y
SCORING: Broussard 104pts, Jason Hanson (K) 99pts, Stallworth 42pts

1990 3-8

21 TCU	3 WR Calvin Griggs
13 Wyoming	34 WR Phillip Bobo
36 BYU	50 WR Ron Young / Augustin Olobia
41 California	31 T Michael Bailey
20 UCLA	30 G Mike Smith
17 Southern Cal	30 C Bob Norvell
55 Oregon State	24 G Steve Cromer
34 Arizona	42 T Bob Garman
13 Stanford	31 TE Clarence Williams
26 Arizona State	51 QB Brad Gossen / Drew Bledsoe
10 Washington	55 RB Shaumbe Wright-Fair / Rich Swinton
	DL Kirk Westerfield
	DL Konrad Pimiskern / Gabriel Oladipo
	DL Jeron Woodley
	DL Dan Webber / Lee Tilleman
	LB Chris Moton / Anthony McClanahan
	LB Rod Plummer
	LB Curt Newton
	DB Ron Ricard
	DB Michael Wright / Anthony Prior
	DB John Diggs
	DB Alvin Dunn

RUSHING: Wright-Fair 162/739y
PASSING: Bledsoe 92-189/1368y, 9TD, 48.7%
RECEIVING: Bobo 51/758y
SCORING: Jason Hanson (K) 80pts

1991 4-7

14 Oregon	40 WR Deron Pointer
30 Fresno State	34 WR C.J. Davis / Albert Kennedy
19 Ohio State	33 WR Phillip Bobo
40 UNLV	13 T Jim Eucker / Michael Bailey
55 Oregon State	7 G Josh Dunning
27 Southern Cal	34 C Steve Wolfe
17 Arizona State	3 G Konrad Pimiskern
3 UCLA	44 T Bob Garman
40 Arizona	27 TE Clarence Williams
14 Stanford	49 QB Drew Bledsoe
21 Washington	56 RB Shaumbe Wright-Fair / Derek Sparks
	DL Lee Tilleman
	DL Kirk Westerfield / Todd Shaw
	DL Chris Frank / Ray Hall
	DL DeWayne Patterson
	LB Kurt Loertscher
	LB Anthony McClanahan
	LB Lewis Bush
	DB Torey Hunter
	DB Michael Wright / Greg Burns
	DB John Rushing
	DB Anthony Prior / Singor Mobley

RUSHING: Wright-Fair 187/843y, Sparks 58/259y, Paul Carr (RB) 51/186y
PASSING: Bledsoe 199-358/2741y, 17TD, 55.6%
RECEIVING: Bobo 54/759y, Davis 34/600y, Williams 31/389y
SCORING: Jason Hanson (K) 58pts, Bobo 38pts, Wright-Fair 36pts

1992 9-3

25 Montana	13 WR Deron Pointer / Keith Reynolds
23 Arizona	20 WR C.J. Davis / Shane DeLaCruz
39 Fresno State	37 WR Phillip Bobo
51 Tempe	10 T Jim Eucker / Michael Bailey
35 Oregon State	10 G Josh Dunning
30 UCLA	17 C Robbie Tobeck
21 Southern Cal	31 G Konrad Pimiskern
17 Oregon	34 T Bob Garman / Clay Reis
20 Arizona State	18 TE Clarence Williams / Brett Carolan
3 Stanford	40 QB Drew Bledsoe
42 Washington	23 RB Shaumbe Wright-Fair / Derek Sparks
31 Utah■	28 DL Lewis Bush / Don Sasa
	DL Brian Ford / Chad Eaton
	DL Ray Hall
	DL DeWayne Patterson
	LB Ron Childs / T.J. Folkers
	LB Anthony McClanahan
	LB Lewis Bush / Kurt Loertscher
	DB Torey Hunter
	DB Greg Burns / Robert Turner
	DB John Rushing
	DB Singor Mobley / Todd Jensen

RUSHING: Wright-Fair 264/1381y, Sparks 69/234y, Delton Johnson (RB) 16/53y
PASSING: Bledsoe 241-432/3246y, 20TD, 55.8%
RECEIVING: Davis 63/1024y, Bobo 43/665y, Pointer 37/623y
SCORING: Wright-Fair 78pts, Aaron Price (K) 70pts, Pointer 36pts

1993 5-6

14 Michigan	41 WR Keith Reynolds / Chad Carpenter
54 Montana State	14 WR Shane DeLaCruz / Jay Dumas
51 Oregon State	6 WR Deron Pointer / Albert Kennedy
3 Southern Cal	34 T Michael Bailey
12 Pacific	0 G Josh Dunning
44 Arizona State	25 C Steve Wolfe
34 California	7 G Marc McCloskey / Ron Lewis
6 Arizona	9 T Clay Reis / Scott Sanderson
23 Oregon	46 TE Brett Carolan / Eric Moore
27 UCLA	40 QB Mike Pattinson / Shawn Deeds
3 Washington	26 RB Kevin Hicks / Delton Johnson
	DL Ray Hall / Don Sasa
	DL Brian Ford
	DL Chad Eaton / Todd Shaw
	DL DeWayne Patterson / Chris Hayes
	LB Ron Childs / James Darling
	LB Anthony McClanahan
	LB T.J. Folkers
	DB Torey Hunter
	DB Greg Burn
	DB John Rushing / Todd Jensen
	DB Singor Mobley / Girmar Johnson

RUSHING: Hicks 128/497y, Johnson (RB) 122/461y,
 Will Haskell (RB) 36/222y
PASSING: Pattinson 110-200/1430y, 10TD, 55.0%
RECEIVING: Carolan 49/591y, Pointer 47/996y,
 Reynolds 46/547y
SCORING: Aaron Price (K) 77pts, Pointer 54pts,
 Hicks & Johnson 30pts

1994 8-4

10 Illinois	9 WR Jay Dumas / Chad Carpenter
24 Fresno State	3 WR Albert Kennedy / Bryant Thomas
21 UCLA	0 T Scott Sanderson
9 Tennessee	10 G Paul Reed / Jason McEndoo
21 Oregon	7 C Marc McCloskey
7 Arizona	10 G Ron Lewis
28 Arizona State	21 T Clay Reis / John Scukanec
26 California	23 TE Eric Moore
10 Southern Cal	23 QB Chad Davis
3 Oregon State	21 RB Frank Madu / Kevin Hicks
23 Washington	6 RB Derek Sparks
10 Baylor■	3 DL Dwyane Sanders
	DL Don Sasa / Leon Bender
	DL Chad Eaton
	DL DeWayne Patterson / Robert Booth
	LB Ron Childs
	LB Mark Fields
	LB Chris Hayes / James Darling
	DB Torey Hunter
	DB Brian Walker
	DB John Rushing / Ray Jackson
	DB Singor Mobley / Derek Henderson

RUSHING: Madu 139/489y, Sparks 111/292y, Hicks 87/273y
PASSING: Davis 170-304/2013y, 10TD, 55.9%
RECEIVING: Dumas 36/376y, Kennedy 28/489y, Moore 28/316y
SCORING: Tony Truant (K) 53pts, Kennedy 24pts

1995 3-8

13 Pittsburgh	17 WR Chad Carpenter
38 Montana	21 WR Jay Dumas / Shawn McWashington
24 UCLA	15 WR Bryant Thomas / Shawn Tims
21 Nebraska	35 T Scott Sanderson
40 Oregon State	14 G Jason McEndoo
14 Southern Cal	26 C Cory Withrow
7 Oregon	7 G Marc McCloskey / Mike Sage
14 Arizona	24 T John Scukanec / Ryan McShane
11 California	27 TE Eric Moore / David Knuff
24 Stanford	36 QB Chad Davis / Ryan Leaf
30 Washington	33 RB Frank Madu / Miguel Meriwether
	DL Dwyane Sanders
	DL Darryl Jones / Delmar Morais
	DL Gary Holmes
	DL Shane Doyle
	LB Johnny Nansen
	LB James Darling
	LB Chris Hayes / Brandon Moore
	DB Shad Hinchen / Dee Moronkola
	DB Brian Walker
	DB Derek Henderson
	DB Duane Stewart

RUSHING: Madu 173/870y, Derek Sparks (RB) 70/234y,
 Meriwether 30/146y
PASSING: Davis 174-301/1868y, 12TD, 57.8%
RECEIVING: Dumas 50/463y, Moore 43/486y,
 Carpenter 32/415y, Thomas 32/333y
SCORING: Tony Truant (K) 50pts, Madu 48pts

1996 5-6

19 Colorado	37 WR Chad Carpenter / Kevin McKenzie
38 Temple	34 WR Shawn McWashington
55 Oregon	44 WR Shawn Tims / Chris Jackson
52 San Jose St.	16 T Scott Sanderson / Rob Rainville
26 Arizona	34 G Jason McEndoo
24 Oregon State	3 C Cory Withrow
21 California	18 G Bryan Chiu / Mike Sage
24 Southern Cal	29 T Ryan McShane
14 UCLA	38 TE David Knuff / Love Jefferson
17 Stanford	33 QB Ryan Leaf
24 Washington	31 RB Michael Black / Miguel Meriwether
	DL Dorian Boose
	DL Leon Bender
	DL Gary Holmes / Takari Blash
	DL Shane Doyle / Jonathan Nance
	LB Johnny Nansen / Kenny Moore
	LB James Darling / Todd Nelson
	LB Brandon Moore / Steve Gleason
	DB Shad Hinchen / LeJuan Gibbons
	DB Derek Henderson / Dee Moronkola
	DB Ray Jackson
	DB Duane Stewart

RUSHING: Black 182/948y, Meriwether 41/177y
PASSING: Leaf 194-373/2811y, 21TD, 52.0%
RECEIVING: Carpenter 47/623y, McKenzie 31/626y,
 Taylor 22/398y
SCORING: Tony Truant (K) 62pts, Black 54pts, Carpenter 48pts

1997 10-2

37 UCLA	34 WR Chris Jackson / Kevin McKenzie
28 Southern Cal	21 WR Shawn McWashington
35 Illinois	22 WR Shawn Tims / Nian Taylor
58 Boise State	0 T Rob Rainville / Ryan Tujague
24 Oregon	13 G Jason McEndoo
63 California	37 C Lee Harrison
35 Arizona	34 G Cory Withrow
31 Arizona State	44 T Ryan McShane
77 SW Louisiana	7 TE Love Jefferson / Brenden Marshall
38 Stanford	28 QB Ryan Leaf
41 Washington	35 RB Michael Black / DeJuan Gilmore
16 Michigan■	21 DL Dorian Boose
	DL Leon Bender / Taeao Salausa
	DL Gary Holmes
	DL Shane Doyle / Delmar Morais
	LB Steve Gleason
	LB Todd Nelson
	LB Brandon Moore
	DB LeJuan Gibbons
	DB Dee Moronkola
	DB Ray Jackson / Lamont Thompson
	DB Duane Stewart

RUSHING: Black 235/1157y, Gilmore 29/275y,
 Jason Clayton (RB) 14/118y
PASSING: Leaf 227-410/3968y, 33TD, 56.0%
RECEIVING: McKenzie 50/833y, Jackson 49/916y, Tims 35/497y
SCORING: Rian Lindell (K) 89pts, Black 72pts, Jackson 66pts

1998 3-8

20 Illinois	13 WR Jerry Roquemore
33 Boise State	21 WR Nian Taylor
24 Idaho	16 WR Leaford Hackett
14 California	24 T Rob Rainville
17 UCLA	49 G Ryan Tujague
29 Oregon	51 C Lincoln Walden-Schulz
14 Southern Cal	42 G Mike Sage / Ryan Raymond
28 Arizona State	38 T Reed Raymond / Joe Criscione
7 Arizona	41 TE Love Jefferson / Corey Scott
28 Stanford	38 QB Steve Birnbaum / Paul Mencke
9 Washington	16 RB Kevin Brown / DeJuan Gilmore
	DL Jonathan Nance
	DL Rob Meier
	DL Austin Matson / Joey Hollenbeck
	DL Jesse Ratcliff / Mark Hedeen
	LB Steve Gleason / Grady Emerson
	LB James Price
	LB Brad Philley / Raonall Smith
	DB Chris Martin
	DB Dee Moronkola / LeJuan Gibbons
	DB Lamont Thompson
	DB Earl Riley / Billy Newman

RUSHING: Brown 215/1046y, Gilmore 65/305y, Mencke 36/124y
PASSING: Birnbaum 114-235/1677y, 6 TD, 48.5%,
 Mencke 71-156/1043y, 10 TD, 45.5%
RECEIVING: Hackett 54/680y, Taylor 45/847y, Jefferson 19/340y
SCORING: Rian Lindell (K) 59pts, Taylor 48pts,
 Brown & Hackett 24pts

1999 3-9

7 Utah	27 WR Farwan Zubedi / Curtis Nettles
17 Stanford	54 WR Nian Taylor / Marcus Williams
17 Idaho	28 WR Leaford Hackett / Collin Henderson
24 Arizona	30 T Ryan Tujague / Phil Locker
31 California	7 G Mike Schwarz / Derrick Roche
44 La.-Lafayette	0 C Lincoln Walden-Schulz
21 Arizona State	33 G Ryan Raymond
13 Oregon State	27 T Reed Raymond
10 Oregon	52 TE Russell Mizin
28 Southern Cal	31 QB Steve Birnbaum / Jason Gesser
14 Washington	24 RB Deon Burnett / Adam Hawkins
22 Hawaii	14 DL Austin Matson / Mark Hedeen
	DL Rob Meier
	DL Tomasi Kongaika
	DL Jesse Ratcliff
	LB Steve Gleason / Fred Shavies
	LB Curtis Holden / Raonall Smith
	LB Grady Emmerson / Serign Marong
	DB Marcus Trufant / LeJuan Gibbons
	DB Chris Martin
	DB Lamont Thompson / Torry Hollimon
	DB Billy Newman / Earl Riley

RUSHING: Burnett 209/974y, Hawkins 60/252y, Gesser 41/145y
PASSING: Birnbaum 174-307/2022y, 11TD, 56.7%,
 Gesser 48-95/445y, 0TD, 50.5%
RECEIVING: Taylor 51/627y, Hackett 44/525y, Zubedi 29/369y
SCORING: Burnett 72pts, Rian Lindell (K) 64pts, Williams 24pts

2000 4-7

10 Stanford	24 WR Farwan Zubedi / Curtis Nettles
38 Utah	21 WR Nakeo McElrath
34 Idaho	38 WR Milton Wynn / Collin Henderson
21 California	17 T Phil Locker / Josh Parrish
42 Boise State	35 G Joey Hollenbeck
47 Arizona	53 C Tyler Hunt
20 Arizona State	23 G Ryan Redmond / Derrick Roche
9 Oregon State	38 T Reed Raymond
24 Oregon	27 TE Russell Mizin / Mark Baldwin
33 Southern Cal	27 QB Jason Gesser
3 Washington	51 RB Dave Minnich / Deon Burnett
	DL Austin Matson / Tupo Tuupo
	DL Tomasi Kongaika / Tai Tupai
	DL Rien Long
	DL Fred Shavies
	LB James Price
	LB Raonell Smith
	LB Melvin Simmons / Al Genatone
	DB Marcus Trufant
	DB Mike Freeman / Jason David
	DB Lamont Thompson
	DB Billy Newman

RUSHING: Minnich 165/754y, Burnett 93/353y,
 Adam Hawkins (RB) 64/123y
PASSING: Gesser 246-461/1967y, 16TD, 52.0%
RECEIVING: Wynn 52/964y, Williams 33/643y, McElrath 14/303y
SCORING: Anousith Wilaikul (K) 40pts, Wynn 36pts,
 Williams & McElrath 30pts

2001 10-2

36 Idaho	7 WR Mike Bush
41 Boise State	20 WR Nakoa McElrath / Trandon Harvey
51 California	20 WR Collin Henderson / Jerome Riley
48 Arizona	21 T Josh Parrish
34 Oregon State	27 G Joey Hollenbeck / Phil Locker
45 Stanford	39 C Tyler Hunt
53 Montana State	28 G Derrick Roche
17 Oregon	24 T Calvin Armstrong / Sam Lightbody
20 UCLA	14 TE Jeremy Thielbahr / Mark Baldwin
28 Arizona State	16 QB Jason Gesser
14 Washington	26 RB Dave Minnich / John Tippins
33 Purdue■	27 DL Tupo Tuupo / D.D. Acholonu
	DL Tai Tupai / Jeremey Williams
	DL Rien Long
	DL Fred Shavies / Isaac Brown
	LB James Price / Ira Davis
	LB Raonall Smith
	LB Alex Nguae / Al Genatone
	DB Marcus Trufant
	DB Jason David / Curtis Nettles
	DB Lamont Thompson / Erik Coleman
	DB Billy Newman

RUSHING: Minnich 192/815y, Tippins 71/268y,
 Allen Thompson (RB) 40/150y
PASSING: Gesser 199-375/3010y, 26TD, 53.1%
RECEIVING: McElrath 72/1163y, Bush 46/959y, Riley 36/630y
SCORING: Drew Dunning 101pts, Bush 60pts, McElrath 54pts

2002 10-3

31 Nevada	7 WR Mike Bush
49 Idaho	14 WR Jerome Riley / Scott Lunde
7 Ohio State	25 WR Devard Darling / Sammy Moore
45 Montana State	28 T Calvin Armstrong
48 California	38 G Josh Parrish
30 Southern Cal	27 C Tyler Hunt
36 Stanford	11 G Billy Knotts
21 Arizona	13 T Sam Lightbody
44 Arizona State	22 TE Troy Bienemann / Adam West
32 Oregon	21 QB Jason Gesser
26 Washington	29 RB Jermaine Green / John Tippins
48 UCLA	27 DL Isaac Brown
14 Oklahoma■	34 DL Jeremey Williams
	DL Rien Long
	DL Fred Shavies / D.D. Acholonu
	LB Will Derting / Ira Davis
	LB Mawuli Davis / Kevin Sperry
	LB Al Genatone / Pat Bennett
	DB Marcus Trufant
	DB Jason David / Karl Paymah
	DB Erik Coleman
	DB Virgil Williams

RUSHING: Green150/829y, Tippins 115/568y,
Jonathan Smith (RB) 72/284y
PASSING: Gesser 236-402/3408y, 28TD, 58.7%
RECEIVING: Riley 57/939y, Darling 54/800y, Bush 49/699y
SCORING: Drew Dunning (K) 113pts, Darling 72pts, Green 60pts

2003 10-3

25 Idaho	0 WR Sammy Moore / Chris Jordan
26 Notre Dame	29 WR Devard Darling / Trandon Harvey
47 Colorado	26 WR Scott Lunde
23 New Mexico	13 T Calvin Armstrong
5 Oregon	16 G Josh Parrish / Riley Fitt-Chappell
30 Arizona	7 C Mike Shelford
24 Stanford	14 G Nick Mihlhauser (C) / Billy Knotts
36 Oregon State	30 T Sam Lightbody
16 Southern Cal	43 TE Troy Bienemann / Cody Boyd
31 UCLA	13 QB Matt Kegel
34 Arizona State	19 RB Jonathan Smith / Jermaine Green
19 Washington	27 DL Isaac Brown
28 Texas■	20 DL Jeremy Williams / Steve Cook
	DL Tai Tupai / Josh Shavies
	DL D.D. Acholonu
	LB Will Derting / Scott Davis
	LB Don Jackson / Aaron Wagner
	LB Al Genatone / Pat Bennett
	DB Karl Paymah
	DB Jason David / Don Turner
	DB Erik Coleman / Hamza Abdullah
	DB Virgil Williams / Jeremy Bohannon

RUSHING: Smith 224/961y, Chris Bruhn (RB) 78/353y,
Green 82/285y
PASSING: Kegel 218-394/2947y, 21TD, 55.3%
RECEIVING: Darling 50/830y, Lunde 42/610y, Smith 33/349y
SCORING: Drew Dunning (K) 116pts, Smith 66pts,
Darling & Moore 42pts

2004 5-6

21 New Mexico	17 WR Jason Hill
12 Colorado	20 WR Michael Bumpus / Marty Martin
49 Idaho	8 WR Chris Jordan / Trandon Harvey
20 Arizona	19 T Calvin Armstrong
38 Oregon	41 G Bobby Byrd
17 Stanford	23 C Nick Mihlhauser
19 Oregon State	38 G Norvell Holmes / Patrick Afif
12 Southern Cal	42 T Sam Lightbody
31 UCLA	29 TE Troy Bienemann / Cody Boyd
28 Arizona State	45 QB Alex Brink / Josh Swogger
28 Washington	25 RB Jerome Harrison / Chris Bruhn
	DL Adam Braidwood
	DL Steve Cook / Odell Howard
	DL Aaron Johnson / Ropati Pitoitua
	DL Mkristo Bruce
	LB Scott Davis
	LB Will Derting
	LB Pat Bennett / Steve Dildine
	DB Karl Paymuh
	DB Alex Teems / Wally Dada
	DB Hamza Abdullah / Husain Abdullah
	DB Jeremy Bohannon / Eric Frampton

RUSHING: Harrison 174/900y, Bruhn 76/291y,
Allen Thompson (RB) 54/271y
PASSING: Brink 97-194/1305y, 7TD, 50.0%,
Swogger 91-193/1283y, 13TD, 47.2%
RECEIVING: Hill 45/1007y, Bumpus 35/318y, Bienemann 26/288y,
Jordan 20/356y

2005 4-7

38 Idaho	26 WR Jason Hill / Greg Prator
55 Nevada	21 WR Michael Bumpus / Brandon Gibson
48 Grambling	7 WR Trandon Harcey / Chris Jordan
33 Oregon State	44 T Bobby Byrd
21 Stanford	24 G Sean O'Connor / Norvell Holmes
41 UCLA	44 C Nick Mihlhauser
38 California	42 G Riley Fitt-Chappell
13 Southern Cal	55 T Charles Harris
24 Arizona State	27 TE Troy Bienemann / Cody Boyd
31 Oregon	34 QB Alex Brink
26 Washington	22 RB Jerome Harrison
	DL Adam Braidwood
	DL Fevaea'l Ahmu
	DL Aaron Johnson / Ropati Pitoitua
	DL Mkristo Bruce
	LB Scott Davis / Cory Evans
	LB Greg Trent / Will Derting
	LB Steve Dildine
	DB Omowale Dada / Don Turner
	DB Alex Teems
	DB Husain Abdullah / Dwayne Patterson
	DB Eric Frampton

RUSHING: Harrison 308/1900y,
DeMaundray Woolridge (RB) 52/312y, Brink 56/106y
PASSING: Brink 205-358/2891y, 24TDs, 57.3%
RECEIVING: Hill 62/1097y, Bumpus 30/357y, Harvey 25/431y,
Bienemann 24/278y, Harrison 24/206y
SCORING: Harrison 102pts, Loren Langley (K) 80pts, Hill 78pts

2006 6-6

14 Auburn	40 WR Jason Hill / Charles Dillon
56 Idaho	10 WR Michael Bumpus
17 Baylor	15 WR Brandon Gibson / Chris Jordan
36 Stanford	10 T Bobby Byrd
22 Southern Cal	28 G Sean O'Connor (T)
13 Oregon State	6 C Kenny Alfred / Josh Duin
3 California	21 G Dan Rowlands / Andy Roof
34 Oregon	23 T Charles Harris
37 UCLA	15 TE Cody Boyd / Jed Collins
17 Arizona	25 QB Alex Brink
14 Arizona State	47 RB Dwight Tardy/DeMaundray Woolridge
32 Washington	35 DL Lance Broadus / Mike Graise
	DL Ropati Pitoitua
	DL Aaron Johnson / Fevaea'l Ahmu
	DL Mkristo Bruce
	LB Scott Davis
	LB Greg Trent / Brian Hall
	LB Steve Dildine / Cory Evans
	DB Don Turner / Brian Williams
	DB Tyron Brackenridge
	DB Husain Abdullah
	DB Eric Frampton

RUSHING: Tardy 145/667y, Derrell Hutsona (RB) 59/379y,
Woolridge 78/330y
PASSING: Brink 241-396/2899y, 19TDs, 60.9%
RECEIVING: Bumpus 60/558y, Gibson 49/731y, Hill 41/600y
SCORING: Loren Langley (K) 44pts, Hill 42pts,
Collins & Tardy 30pts

2007 5-7

21 Wisconsin	42 WR Charles Dillon / Jeshua Anderson
45 San Diego State	17 WR Michael Bumpas
45 Idaho	28 WR Brandon Gibson
14 Southern Cal	47 T Vaughn Lesuma
20 Arizona	48 G Bobby Byrd
20 Arizona State	23 C Kenny Alfred / Andrew Roxas
7 Oregon	53 G Dan Rowlands
27 UCLA	7 T Micah Hannam
17 California	20 TE Jed Collins / Devin Frischknecht
33 Stanford	17 QB Alex Brink
17 Oregon State	52 RB Dwight Tardy / Chris Ivory
42 Washington	35 DL Lance Broadus / Mike Graise
	DL A'l Ahmu
	DL Ropati Pitoitua / Aaron Johnson
	DL Matt Mullennix / Kevin Kooyman
	LB Cory Evans
	LB Greg Trent / Kendrick Dunn
	LB Andy Mattingly
	DB Chima Nwachukwu
	DB Devin Giles
	DB Husain Abdullah / Christian Bass
	DB Alfonso Jackson / Xavier Hicks

RUSHING: Tardy 143/676y, Ivory 60/313y,
Kevin McCall (RB) 78/294y
PASSING: Brink 305-503/3818y, 26TD, 60.6%
RECEIVING: Bumpas 70/789y, Gibson 67/1180y, Collins 52/512y
SCORING: Remeen Abdollmohammadi (K) 76pts, Gibson 54pts,
Tardy 36pts

2008 2-11

13 Oklahoma State	39 WR Jeshua Anderson / Jared Karstetter
3 California	66 WR Brandon Gibson
17 Baylor	45 WR Daniel Blackledge / Kevin Norrell
48 Portland State	9 T Vaughn Lesuma (G) / Joe Eppele
14 Oregon	63 G Andrew Roxas / Steven Ayers
3 UCLA	28 C Kenny Alfred
13 Oregon State	66 G Brian Danaher / B.J. Guerra
0 Southern Cal	69 T Micah Hannam
0 Stanford	58 TE Devin Frischknecht / Ben Woodard
28 Arizona	59 QB Kevin Lopina / Marshall Lobbestael
0 Arizona State	31 RB Dwight Tardy / Logwone Mitz
16 Washington	13 DL Kevin Kooyman
10 Hawaii	24 DL A'l Ahmu / Adam Hineline
	DL Matt Eichelberger / Toby Turpin
	DL Matt Mullennix / Andy Mattingly
	LB Myron Beck / Cory Evans
	LB Greg Trent
	LB Louis Bland / Kendrick Dunn
	DB Romeo Pellum / Devin Giles
	DB Markus Dawes / Tyron Justin
	DB Xavier Hicks / Alfonso Jackson
	DB Chima Nwachukwu / Tyree Toomer

RUSHING: Tardy 133/481y, Mitz 90/441y,
Chantz Staden (RB) 52/141y
PASSING: Lopina 87-153/841y, 0TD, 56.9%,
Lobbestael 53-103/571y, 4TD, 51.5%,
Gary Rogers 34-68/352y, 2TD, 50.0%
RECEIVING: Gibson 57/673y, Anderson 33/305y, Tardy 18/87y
SCORING: Nico Grasu (K) 40pts, Mitz, Tardy & Lopina 18pts

2009 1-11

13 Stanford	39 WR Jeffrey Solomon / Daniel Blackledge
20 Hawaii	38 WR Jeffrey Simone
30 SMU	27 WR Jared Karstetter / Johnny Forzani
6 Southern Cal	27 T Steven Ayers / Alex Reitnouer (G)
6 Oregon	52 G Zack Williams
14 Arizona State	27 C Kenny Alfred
17 California	49 G B.J. Guerra / Joe Eppele
14 Notre Dame	40 T Micah Hannam
7 Arizona	48 TE Tony Thompson / Skylar Stormo
7 UCLA	43 QB Marshall Lobbestael / Jeff Tuel
10 Oregon State	42 RB Dwight Tardy / Logwone Mitz
0 Washington	30 DL Casey Hamlett
	DL Bernard Wolfgramm
	DL Toby Turpin / Dan Spitz
	DL Travis Long
	LB Andy Mattingly / Myron Beck
	LB Alex Hoffman-Ellis / Louis Bland
	LB Jason Stripling / Mike Ledgerwood
	DB Brandon Jones / Aire Justin
	DB Terrance Hayward / Daniel Simmons
	DB Chima Nwachukwu / Jay Matthews
	DB Xavier Hicks

RUSHING: Tardy 107/417y, James Montgomery (RB) 37/167y
Mitz 53/160y, Carl Winston (RB) 36/142y
PASSING: Tuel 71-121/789y, 6TD, 58.7%
Lobbestael 67-144/655y, 3TD, 46.5%
Kevin Lopina (QB) 54-103/596y, 2TD, 52.4%
RECEIVING: Karstetter 38/540y, Simone 36/330y,
Solomon 25/298y, Blackledge 23/212y
SCORING: Karstetter 36pts, Nico Grasu (K) 30pts,
Forzani & Tardy 12pts

2010 2-10

17 Oklahoma State	66 WR Marquess Wilson / Jefferey Solomon
23 Montana State	22 WR Dan Blackledge / Isiah Barton
21 SMU	35 WR Jared Karstetter / Gino Simone
16 Southern Cal	50 T John Fullington / David Gonzales
28 UCLA	42 G Wade Jacobson / Andrew Roxas
23 Oregon	43 C Zack Williams / Darren Mackle
7 Arizona	24 G B.J. Guerra
28 Stanford	38 T Micah Hannam
0 Arizona State	42 TE/RB Skylar Storm / Logwone Mitz
13 California	20 QB Jeff Tuel
31 Oregon State	14 RB James Montgomery/ Marcus Richmond
28 Washington	35 DL Travis Long
	DL Brandon Rankin / Anthony Laurenzi
	DL Bernard Wolfgramm / Justin Clayton
	DL Kevin Kooyman / Casey Hamlett
	LB Myron Beck / Sekope Kaufusi
	LB C.J. Mizell / Mike Ledgerwood
	LB Alex Hoffman-Ellis / Hallston Higgins
	DB Nolan Washington
	DB Aire Justin / Dan Simmons
	DB Tyree Toomer / Casey Locker
	DB Deone Bucannon / Chima Nwachukwu

RUSHING: Montgomery 122/478y, Mitz 74/263y, Tuel 134/255y
PASSING: Tuel 219-366/2780y, 18TD, 59.8%
RECEIVING: Karstetter 62/658y, Wilson 55/1006y,
Blackledge 30/456y
SCORING: Karstetter 42pts, Wilson 36pts, Montgomery 30pts

WEST VIRGINIA

West Virginia University
Morgantown, West Virginia
Nickname: Mountaineers
Colors: Old Gold and Blue
Stadium: Mountaineer Field (1980) 60,000
Conference Affiliations: Southern (1950-67), Independent (1968-1990), Big East Conference (Charter Member, 1991-present)

CAREER RUSHING YARDS	Attempts	Yards
Avon Cobourne (1999-02)	1050	5164
Pat White (2005-08)	684	4480
Noel Devine (2007-10)	729	4317
Amos Zereoue (1996-98)	786	4086
Steve Slaton (2005-07)	664	3923
Arthur Owens (1972-75)	416	2648
Robert Walker (1992-95)	529	2620
Quincy Wilson (1999-03)	474	2608
Robert Alexander (1977-80)	491	2456
Undra Johnson (1985-88)	442	2211

CAREER PASSING YARDS	Comp.-Att.	Yards
Marc Bulger (1996-99)	630-1023	8153
Pat White (2005-08)	507-783	6051
Chad Johnston (1993-96)	428-839	5954
Oliver Luck (1978-81)	466-911	5765
Rasheed Marshall (2001-04)	433-795	5558
Major Harris (1987-89)	324-586	5173
Dan Kendra (1974-77)	348-672	4781
Bernie Galiffa (1970-72)	310-623	4426
Mike Sherwood (1968-70)	329-573	4321
Jeff Hostetler (1983-83)	310-601	4261

CAREER RECEIVING YARDS	Catches	Yards
David Saunders (1995-98)	191	2608
Khori Ivy (1997-00)	160	2402
Shawn Foreman (1995-98)	169	2347
Rahsaan Vanterpool (1993-96)	126	2022
Jock Sanders (2007-10)	206	1980
Rich Hollins (1980-83)	104	1968
Cedric Thomas (1976-80)	110	1930
Antonio Brown (1998-01)	155	1905
Chris Henry (2003-04)	93	1878
Darrell Miller (1978-82)	111	1799

SEASON RUSHING YARDS	Attempts	Yards
Steve Slaton (2006)	248	1744
Avon Cobourne (2002)	335	1710
Amos Zereoue (1997)	281	1589
Noel Devine (2009)	241	1465
Amos Zereoue (1998)	283	1462

SEASON PASSING YARDS	Comp.-Att.	Yards
Marc Bulger (1998)	274-419	3607
Geno Smith (2010)	241-372	2763
Bernie Galiffa (1972)	164-334	2496
Marc Bulger (1997)	192-323	2465
Oliver Luck (1981)	216-394	2448

SEASON RECEIVING YARDS	Catches	Yards
David Saunders (1996)	76	1043
Chris Henry (2003)	41	1006
Shawn Foreman (1998)	63	948
Shawn Foreman (1997)	77	928
David Saunders (1998)	77	883

GAME RUSHING YARDS	Attempts	Yards
Kay-Jay Harris (2004 vs. East Carolina)	25	337
Kerry Marbury (1971 vs. Temple)	22	291
Avon Cobourne (2002 vs. East Carolina)	30	260

GAME PASSING YARDS	Comp.-Att.	Yards
Marc Bulger (1998 vs. Missouri)	34-50	429
Mike Sherwood (1968 vs. Pittsburgh)	27-37	416
Marc Bulger (1998 vs. Pittsburgh)	26-43	409

GAME RECEIVING YARDS	Catches	Yards
Chris Henry (2003 vs. Syracuse)	6	209
Rahsaan Vanterpool (1994 vs. Pitt)	9	205
Pat Greene (1997 vs. Pitt)	12	205

GREATEST COACH:

An old quarterback himself, Don Nehlen knew his signal-callers. From Oliver Luck and Jeff Hostetler at the beginning of his 21-year run in Morgantown, through Major Harris to Marc Bulger, the talent was on hand to lead the Mountaineers into the upper echelon of the college football world. It all paid off to the tune of 149 wins, with 22 coming from two perfect regular seasons. Both of those seasons, 1988 and 1993, ended in post-season defeat. But, the mere fact that they were playing in major bowls with national championship consequences was heady stuff for a program whose rivals included Richmond and VMI only a few years before Nehlen's hire.

With ambitions equaling those of the university and great community support, Nehlen was focused on upgrading Mountaineer football from day one. New modern-looking home and road uniforms complete with a new logo, were ordered. The inroads made into national recruiting by predecessors Bobby Bowden and Frank Cignetti were continued, to great success. Another key element was stability in the coaching staff; for the large part Nehlen and his staff were committed to West Virginia football.

Signature wins were next on the agenda and Luck led a victory over Florida in the Peach Bowl after the 1981 season, and Hostetler led a victory over Oklahoma in 1982. West Virginia also had to establish an ability to play with the area powers and in 1984 they swept Pittsburgh and Penn State, beating the Nittany Lions for the first time since 1955. Nehlen and the Mountaineers were here to stay.

WEST VIRGINIA'S 55 GREATEST SINCE 1953

OFFENSE

WIDE RECEIVER: Danny Buggs, Shawn Foreman, Khori Ivy, David Saunders
TIGHT END: Anthony Becht
TACKLE: Bruce Bosley, Rich Braham, Brian Jozwiak, Rick Phillips
GUARD: Ken Sandor, John Stroia, B.C. Williams
CENTER: Mike Compton, Pete Goimarac, Dan Mozes
QUARTERBACK: Marc Bulger, Major Harris, Pat White
RUNNING BACK: Avon Cobourne, Noel Devine, Artie Owens, Steve Slaton, Amos Zereoue
FULLBACK: Larry Krutko, Pete Wood

DEFENSE

END: Gene Heeter, John Spraggins
TACKLE: Keilen Dykes, Mike Fox, Sam Huff, Jeff Merrow, John Thornton
LINEBACKER: Canute Curtis, Steve Grant, Chris Haering, Gene Lamone, Kevin McLee, Darryl Talley, Grant Wiley
CORNERBACK: Aaron Beasley, Mark Collins, Adam Jones, Steve Newberry
SAFETY: Bo Orlando, Tom Pridemore, Eric Wicks, Darrell Whitmore

SPECIAL TEAMS

RETURN SPECIALISTS: John Mallory, Shawn Terry
PLACE KICKER: Paul Woodside
PUNTER: Todd Sauerbrun

MULTIPLE POSITIONS

FULLBACK-TIGHT END-KICKER: Jim Braxton
MIDDLE GUARD-LINEBACKER: Carl Crennel
LINEBACKER-SAFETY: Barrett Green

TWO-WAY PLAYERS

GUARD-CENTER-LINEBACKER: Chuck Howley

PERFORMANCE FORMULA:
WEST VIRGINIA'S 10 BEST SEASONS

1988	1.6517	4 of 69
2007	1.6378	2 of 70
1993	1.6298	6 of 70
2005	1.5817	6 of 70
2006	1.5558	8 of 72
1969	1.5408	9 of 70
1954	1.4731	11 of 69
1983	1.4588	10 of 70
1955	1.4512	9 of 69
1982	1.4390	13 of 70

WEST VIRGINIA MOUNTAINEERS

Year	W-L-T	AP Poll	Conference Standing	Toughest Regular Season Opponents	Coach (Record at School)	Bowl Games		
1953	8-2	10	1	South Carolina 7-3, Penn State 6-3, Virginia Tech 5-5	Art Lewis	Sugar	19 Georgia Tech	42
1954	8-1	12	1	Penn State 7-2, South Carolina 6-4	Art Lewis			
1955	8-2	19	1	Pitt 7-3, Syracuse 5-3, Penn State 5-4	Art Lewis			
1956	6-4		1t	Miami 8-1-1, Pitt 7-2-1, Penn State 6-2-1	Art Lewis			
1957	7-2-1		1t	Wisconsin 6-3, Penn State 6-3, Syracuse 5-3-1	Art Lewis			
1958	4-5-1		1	Oklahoma 9-1, Syracuse 8-1, Penn State 6-3-1	Art Lewis			
1959	3-7		6	Syracuse 10-0, Southern Cal 8-2, Penn State 8-2	Art Lewis (58-32-2)			
1960	0-8-2		9	Syracuse 7-2, Oregon 7-2-1, Penn State 6-3, Maryland 6-4	Gene Corum			
1961	4-6		3t	Syracuse 7-3, Penn State 7-3, Army 6-4	Gene Corum			
1962	8-2		1t	Penn State 9-1, Oregon State 8-2	Gene Corum			
1963	4-6		2	Navy 9-1, Syracuse 8-2, Penn State 7-3, Oregon 7-3	Gene Corum			
1964	7-4		1	Syracuse 7-3, Penn State 6-4, Virginia Tech 6-4	Gene Corum	Liberty	6 Utah	32
1965	6-4		1	Syracuse 7-3, Kentucky 6-4, Virginia Tech 7-3	Gene Corum (29-30-2)			
1966	3-5-2		1	Syracuse 8-2, Virginia Tech 8-1-1, Penn State 5-5	Jim Carlen			
1967	5-4-1		1	Penn State 8-2, Syracuse 8-2, Virginia Tech 7-3	Jim Carlen			
1968	7-3			Penn State 10-0, Syracuse 6-4, Virginia Tech 7-3	Jim Carlen			
1969	10-1	17		Penn State 10-0, Syracuse 5-5	Jim Carlen (25-13-3)	Peach	14 South Carolina	3
1970	8-3			Penn State 7-3, Syracuse 6-4, Duke 6-5	Bobby Bowden			
1971	7-4			Penn State 10-1, Boston College 9-2, Cal 6-5, Temple 6-2-1	Bobby Bowden			
1972	8-4			Penn State 10-1, Stanford 6-5, Richmond 6-4	Bobby Bowden	Peach	13 N. Carolina State	49
1973	6-5			Maryland 8-3, Pitt 6-4-1, Boston College 7-4	Bobby Bowden			
1974	4-7			Penn State 9-2, Pitt 7-4, Boston College 8-3, Miami 6-5	Bobby Bowden			
1975	9-3	20		Penn State 9-2, Cal 8-3, Virginia Tech 8-3, Pitt 7-4	Bobby Bowden (42-26)	Peach	13 N. Carolina State	10
1976	5-6			Pitt 11-0, Maryland 11-0, Penn State 7-4, Boston College 8-3	Frank Cignetti			
1977	5-6			Penn State 10-1, Kentucky 10-1, Pitt 8-2-1, Maryland 7-4	Frank Cignetti			
1978	2-9			Penn State 11-0, Oklahoma 10-1, Pitt 8-3, N. Carolina St. 8-3	Frank Cignetti			
1979	5-6			Pitt 10-1, Penn State 7-4, N. Carolina St. 7-4, Syracuse 6-5	Frank Cignetti (17-27)			
1980	6-6			Pitt 10-1, Penn State 9-2, Maryland 8-3, Virginia Tech 8-3	Don Nehlen			
1981	9-3	17		Pitt 10-1, Penn State 9-2	Don Nehlen	Peach	26 Florida	6
1982	9-3	19		Penn State 10-1, Pitt 9-2, Oklahoma 8-3, Boston College 8-2-1	Don Nehlen	Gator	12 Florida State	31
1983	9-3	16		Miami 10-1, Boston College 9-2, Pitt 8-2-1, Penn State 7-4-1	Don Nehlen	Hall of Fame	20 Kentucky	16
1984	8-4			Boston College 9-2, Maryland 8-3, Virginia Tech 8-3, Rutgers 7-3	Don Nehlen	Bluebonnet	31 TCU	14
1985	7-3-1			Penn State 11-0, Maryland 8-3, Syracuse 7-4	Don Nehlen			
1986	4-7			Penn State 11-0, Virginia Tech 8-2-1, Boston College 8-3	Don Nehlen			
1987	6-6			Syracuse 11-0, Penn State 8-3, Pitt 8-3	Don Nehlen	Sun	33 Oklahoma State	35
1988	11-1	5		Syracuse 9-2, Pitt 6-5, Rutgers 5-6	Don Nehlen	Fiesta	21 Notre Dame	34
1989	8-3-1	21		Pitt 7-3-1, Penn State 7-3-1, Syracuse 7-4, Virginia Tech 6-4-1	Don Nehlen	Gator	7 Clemson	27
1990	4-7			Penn State 9-2, Louisville 9-1-1, Syracuse 6-4-2	Don Nehlen			
1991	6-5			Miami 11-0, Penn State 10-2, Syracuse 9-2	Don Nehlen			
1992	5-4-2			Miami 11-0, Syracuse 9-2, Boston College 8-2-1, Penn State 7-4	Don Nehlen			
1993	11-1	7	1	Miami 9-2, Virginia Tech 8-3, Boston College 8-3, Louisville 8-3	Don Nehlen	Sugar	7 Florida	41
1994	7-6		3t	Nebraska 12-0, Miami 10-1, Virginia Tech 8-3, Syracuse 7-4	Don Nehlen	Carquest	21 South Carolina	24
1995	5-6		4t	Virginia Tech 9-2, Miami 8-3, Syracuse 8-3	Don Nehlen			
1996	8-4		4	Virginia Tech 10-1, Miami 8-3, Syracuse 8-3	Don Nehlen	Gator	13 North Carolina	20
1997	7-5		3t	Syracuse 9-3, Virginia Tech 7-4, Notre Dame 7-5	Don Nehlen	Carquest	30 Georgia Tech	35
1998	8-4		2t	Ohio State 11-1, Miami 8-3, Virginia Tech 8-3, Syracuse 8-3	Don Nehlen	Insight.com	31 Missouri	34
1999	4-7		4t	Virginia Tech 11-0, Boston College 8-3, Miami 8-4	Don Nehlen			
2000	7-5		5t	Miami 10-1, Virginia Tech 10-1, Notre Dame 9-2, Pitt 7-4	Don Nehlen (149-93-4)	Music City	49 Mississippi	38
2001	3-8		7	Miami 11-0, Maryland 10-1, Virginia Tech 8-3, Syracuse 9-3	Rich Rodriguez			
2002	9-4	25	2	Miami 12-0, Maryland 10-3, Virginia Tech 9-4, Pitt 8-4, BC 8-4	Rich Rodriguez	Continental Tire	22 Virginia	48
2003	8-5		1t	Miami 10-2, Maryland 9-3, Pitt 8-4, Virginia Tech 8-4	Rich Rodriguez	Gator	7 Maryland	41
2004	8-4		1t	Virginia Tech 10-2, Miami 8-3, Pitt 8-3, Boston College 8-3	Rich Rodriguez	Gator	18 Florida State	30
2005	10-1	5	1	Virginia Tech 10-1, Louisville 9-2, Rutgers 7-4	Rich Rodriguez	Sugar	38 Georgia	35
2006	11-2	10	2t	Louisville 11-1, Rutgers 10-2, South Florida 8-4, Maryland 8-4	Rich Rodriguez	Gator	38 Georgia Tech	35
2007	11-2	6	1	South Florida 9-3, Mississippi State 7-5, Connecticut 9-3	Rich Rodriguez (60-26)			
					Bill Stewart [1-0]	Fiesta	48 Oklahoma	28
2008	9-4	23	2t	Rutgers 8-5, Cincinnati 11-2, Pittsburgh 9-3	Bill Stewart	Meineke Care	31 North Carolina	30
2009	9-4	25	2t	Auburn 7-5, Cincinnati 12-0, Pittsburgh 9-3	Bill Stewart	Gator	21 Florida State	33
2010	9-4		1t	LSU 10-2, Connecticut 8-4, Pittsburgh 8-4	Bill Stewart (28-12)	Champs Sports	7 North Carolina State	23

TOTAL: 394-250-11 .6099 (21 of 70) **Bowl Games since 1953:** 10-17 .3846 (62 of 70)

GREATEST TEAM SINCE 1953: The 11-1 squad from 1993 gets the nod here, topping some more-celebrated units thanks to a schedule that was much tougher than those faced by other successful West Virginia teams. Not blessed with an abundance of star players, the 1993 team just knew how to win, in sweeping its regular season schedule en route to a Big East tile and Lambert Trophy win.

1953 8-2
17	Pittsburgh	7 E Joe Papetti / Jim Starkey
47	Waynesburg	19 T Bruce Bosley
40	Wash. & Lee	14 G Gene Lamone / Phil Canton
27	Geo. Wash'gton	6 C Bob Orders / Chick Donaldson
52	VMI	20 G Sam Huff / Frank Federovitch
20	Penn State	19 T Ralph Starkey / Ray Walsh
12	Virginia Tech	7 E Bill Marker / Billy Hillen
14	South Carolina	20 QB Freddie Wyant / Ted Anderson
61	N. Carolina St.	0 HB Jack Stone / Bob Moss
19	Georgia Tech■	42 HB Joe Marconi / Carl Norman
		FB Tommy Allman / Bob Snider

RUSHING: Allman 88/501y
PASSING: Wyant 41-102/642y, 4TD, 40.2%
RECEIVING: Marker 16/301y
SCORING: Stone (HB-K) 49pts

1954 8-1
26	South Carolina	6 E Billy Hillen / Joe Kopnisky
13	Geo. Wash'gton	7 T Bruce Bosley
19	Penn State	14 G Gene Lathey / Bill Underdonk
40	VMI	6 C Chick Donaldson
10	Pittsburgh	13 G Gene Lamone / Jerry Urda
39	Fordham	9 T Sam Huff
20	William & Mary	6 E John Kernic / Max Ludwig
28	N. Carolina St.	3 QB Freddie Wyant
14	Virginia	10 HB Bob Moss / Jack Rabbits
		HB Dick Nicholson / Harry Sweeney
		FB Joe Marconi/Carl Norman/Dan Williams

RUSHING: Nicholson 62/416y, Norman 65/332y, Moss 43/293y
PASSING: Wyatt 40-97/563y, 4TD, 41.2%
RECEIVING: Hillen 9/98y, Williams 6/36y, Kernic 5/95y
SCORING: Wyant 48pts, Donaldson (C-K) 25pts, Marconi 24pts

1955 8-2
33	Richmond	12 E Joe Papetti / Gary Bunn
46	Wake Forest	0 T Bruce Bosley / Bill Trozzo
47	VMI	12 G Chuck Howley
39	William & Mary	19 C Tom Domen / Ronald Klim
21	Penn State	7 G Gene Lathey / Bob Guenther
39	Marquette	0 T Sam Huff (G) / Bill Underdonk
13	Geo. Wash'gton	7 E Joe Kopnisky
7	Pittsburgh	26 QB Freddie Wyant / Mickey Trimarki
13	Syracuse	20 HB Bob Moss / Jack Rabbits
27	N. Carolina St.	7 HB Joe Marconi / Ralph Anastasio
		FB Larry Krutko / Paul Shepherd

RUSHING: Moss 98/807y, Krutko 73/420y, Marconi 66/380y
PASSING: Wyant 38-74/591y, 5TD, 51.4%
RECEIVING: Kopnisky 12/141y, Moss 9/221y, Bunn 8/176y
SCORING: Moss 60pts, Marconi 42pts, Rabbits 24pts

1956 6-4
13	Pittsburgh	14 E Bruce McClung / Roger Chancey
30	Richmond	6 T Jim Pickett / Barry Blake
7	Texas	6 G Joe Nicely / Dick Guesman
20	Syracuse	27 C Chuck Howley / Tom Domen
20	William & Mary	13 G Gene Lathey
6	Penn State	16 T Bill Underdonk / Paul Sharkady
14	Geo. Wash'gton	0 E Joe Kopnisky / John Bowles
13	VMI	6 QB Mickey Trimarki / Alex Szuch
7	Furman	0 HB Bob Snider / Jack Rabbits
0	Miami	18 HB Sammy Sizemore/R. Anastasio
		FB Larry Krutko / Noel Whipky

RUSHING: Krutko 124/584y, Whipkey 70/337y, Rabbits 50/244y
PASSING: Trimarki 33-98/419y, 1TD, 33.7%
RECEIVING: Kopnisky 19/295y, McClung 8/105y, Anastasio 8/109y
SCORING: Krutko & Whipky 24pts, Snider (HB-K) 21pts

1957 7-2-1
6	Virginia	6 E Bruce McClung
14	Virginia Tech	0 T Bill Trozzo / Jim Pickett
13	Wisconsin	45 G Joe Nicely / Dick Guesman
46	Boston Univ.	6 C Tom Domen / Chuck Billak
34	Geo. Wash'gton	14 G Howley / Bob Guenther
19	William & Mary	0 T Paul Sharkady / James Hillen
6	Penn State	27 E Terry Fairbanks / Roger Chancey
7	Pittsburgh	6 QB Mickey Trimarki / Dick Longfellow
27	Wake Forest	14 HB Ray Peterson / Bill McClure
7	Syracuse	9 HB Ralph Anastasio/Mel Reight/Dave Rider
		FB Larry Krutko / Glen Shamblin

RUSHING: Krutko 100/403y, Peterson 60/394y, Anastasio 64/314y
PASSING: Longfellow 32-78/405y, 3TD, 41%
RECEIVING: Anastasio 7/108y, Reight 7/90y, Chancey 7/75y
SCORING: Krutko 30pts, Trimarki 24pts, 3 tied w/ 18pts

1958 4-5-1
66	Richmond	22 E Bruce McClung / Ben McComb
14	Oklahoma	47 T Dick Guesman / Bill Trozzo
12	Indiana	13 G Ed Sommer / J.D. Miller
30	Boston Univ.	36 C Joe Wirth / Chuck Billak
8	Pittsburgh	15 G Carl Dannenberg / Bill Lopasky
21	Virginia Tech	20 T Pete Tolley / James Hillen
35	Geo. Wash'gton	12 E Terry Fairbanks / Phil Messinger
14	Penn State	14 QB Dick Longfellow / Danny Williams
56	William & Mary	6 HB Ray Peterson / John Marra
12	Syracuse	15 HB Mel Reight / Dave Rider
		FB Noel Whipkey / Bob Benke

RUSHING: Peterson 81/333y, Longfellow 86/254y, Reight 77/285y
PASSING: Longfellow 79-156/948y, 6TD, 50.6%
RECEIVING: Reight 31/329y, Fairbanks 16/331y, Peterson 15/169y
SCORING: Reight 58pts, Longfellow 36pts, Williams 32pts

1959 3-7
7	Maryland	27 E Bob Timmerman / Ben McComb
10	Richmond	7 T Carl Dannenberg
10	Geo. Wash'gton	8 G Bill Lopasky / Bill Winter
0	Boston Univ.	7 C Joe Wirth / Vearl Haynes
23	Pittsburgh	15 G Pete Tolley
0	Syracuse	44 T Glenn Bowman
10	Penn State	28 E Dave Hess / Dick Struck
0	Southern Cal	36 QB Danny Williams / Carmen Pomponio
0	Virginia Tech	12 HB Ray Peterson / Richard Herrig
14	Citadel	20 HB Dave Rider / John Marra
		FB Bob Benke / Tom Huston / Curt Harman

RUSHING: Peterson 116/505y, Marra 47/219y, Benke 58/194y
PASSING: Williams 28-99/310y, 1TD, 28.3%
RECEIVING: Marra 16/177y, Peterson 7/61y, Timmerman 6/89y
SCORING: John Thalkston (K) 18pts, Peterson & Pomponio 12pts

1960 0-8-2
8	Maryland	31 E Bob Timmerman / Ken Herock
0	Virginia Tech	15 T Bill Winter
0	Illinois	33 G Keith Melenyzer / Charles Bonar
6	Richmond	6 C Charles Lanasa / Bill Schillings
0	Pittsburgh	42 G Pete Tolley / Robert Fuller
0	Syracuse	45 T Glenn Bowman
13	Penn State	34 E Dick Struck / Gene Heeter
7	Boston Univ.	7 QB Dale Evans/ D. Williams/ C. Pomponio
6	Oregon	20 HB Jim Bargeloh /Don Myers/R. Holdinsky
0	Geo.Wash'gton	26 HB Eli Kosanovich/Gene Lamb/John Marra
		FB Bob Benke / Tom Woodeshick

RUSHING: Benke 50/187y, Bargeloh 47/173y, Myers 35/156y
PASSING: Evans 34-85/466y, 1TD, 40%
RECEIVING: Timmerman 9/99y, Heeter 8/203y, Herock 6/71y
SCORING: Moss 12pts, 4 tied w/ 6pts

1961 4-6
26	Richmond	35 E Ken Herock / Bob Timmerman
6	Vanderbilt	6 T Bill Winter / Ron Haggerty
14	Syracuse	29 G Bob DeLorenzo / Fred Adkins
28	Virginia Tech	0 C Pete Goimarac / John Skinner
20	Pittsburgh	6 G Keith Melenyzer / David Santrock
6	Boston Univ.	12 T Frank Sirianni / Stephen Edwards
7	Army	3 E Dave Struck / Paul Gray
12	Geo.Wash'gton	7 QB Fred Colvard / Dale Evans
6	Penn State	20 HB Jim Moss / R. Holdinsky/ Fred Colvard
9	Indiana	17 HB Tom Woodeshick / Eli Kosanovich
		FB Glenn Holton / Steve Berzansky

RUSHING: Holton 79/372y, Moss 64/342y, Woodeshick 68/337y
PASSING: Colvard 31-71/482y, 3TD, 43.7%
RECEIVING: Berzansky 10/116y, Holton 7/79y, 2 tied w/ 5
SCORING: Colvard 26pts, Holdinsky & Holton 18pts

1962 8-2
26	Vanderbilt	0 E Ken Herock / Raymond Bazzoli
14	Virginia Tech	0 T Bernie Carney
7	Boston Univ.	0 G Bob DeLorenzo / Alan Hoover
15	Pittsburgh	8 C Pete Goimarac
27	Geo.Wash'gton	25 G Keith Melenyzer / Don Young
22	Oregon State	51 T Frank Sirianni / Phil Sizemore
28	William & Mary	13 E Gene Heeter / Milt Clegg
6	Penn State	34 QB Jerry Yost / John Burnison
49	Citadel	0 HB Tom Yeater / Jim Moss
17	Syracuse	6 HB Glenn Holton / Eli Kosanovich
		FB Tom Woodeshick / Ron Colaw

RUSHING: Woodeshick 89/433y, Holton 87/311y, Yost 49/227y
PASSING: Yost 75-152/1134y, 11TD, 49.3%
RECEIVING: Heeter 19/284y, Herock 14/174y, Holton 11/119y
SCORING: Holton 36pts, Heeter 28pts, Yost & Woodeshick 20pts

1963 4-6
7	Navy	51 E Bill Sullivan / Bob Dunlevy
34	Boston Univ.	0 T Bernie Carney / Charles Bursich
0	Oregon	35 G Alan Hoover / Roger Alford
20	William & Mary	16 C Pete Goimarac / Jim Mazzella
10	Pittsburgh	13 G Steve Kush / Don Young
9	Penn State	20 T Joe Pabian / Ken Woodeshick
20	Geo. Wash'gton	16 E Fred Hauff / Milt Clegg
13	Syracuse	15 QB Jerry Yost / Bill Fleming
3	Virginia Tech	28 HB Tom Yeater / Richie Martha
38	Furman	7 HB Homer Criddle /G. Holton /Dick Rader
		FB Dick Leftridge

RUSHING: Leftridge 79/393y, Criddle 48/248y, Yeater 61/242y
PASSING: Yost 62-140/685y, 7TD, 44.3%
RECEIVING: Berzansky 12/125y, Hauff 10/112y, Leftridge 10/89y
SCORING: Leftridge 42pts, Chuck Kinder (K) 32pts, Yost 18pts

1964 7-4
20	Richmond	10 E Bob Dunlevy
7	Citadel	3 T Don Vail / Gene Cicarelli
0	Rice	24 G Roger Alford
0	Pittsburgh	14 C Gary Barnette
23	Virginia Tech	10 G Steve Kush
8	Penn State	37 T Stan Lysick
26	Kentucky	21 E Milt Clegg
20	Geo. Wash'gton	19 QB Allen McClune / Eddie Pastilong
24	William & Mary	14 HB Dick Madison / Homer Criddle
28	Syracuse	27 HB John Piscorik / Tom Yeater
6	Utah■	32 FB Dick Leftridge / Ron Colaw
		DL Fred Hauff / Gordon Lambert
		DL Joe Taffoni
		DL Don Young
		DL Alan Hoover
		DL Charles Bursich
		DL Bill Sullivan
		LB Wayne Vassalotti
		LB Jim Mazzella
		DB George Morris
		DB Richie Martha
		DB Jim Sypult

RUSHING: Leftridge 125/534y, Piscorik 70/259y, Colaw 60/220y
PASSING: McCune 73-127/1034y, 11TD, 57.5%
RECEIVING: Clegg 31/437y, Dunlevy 18/279y, Madison 15/240y
SCORING: Madison 34pts, Leftridge 30pts, Clegg 24pts

1965 6-4
56	Richmond	0 E Bob Dunlevy
34	William & Mary	14 T Dale Stortz
63	Pittsburgh	48 G Roger Alford
25	Citadel	2 C Gary Barnette
0	Virginia	41 G Steve Kush
6	Penn State	44 T Stan Lysick
8	Kentucky	28 E Larry Canterbury / Jim Harris
31	Virginia Tech	22 QB Allen McCune
19	Syracuse	41 HB Dick Rader
37	Geo. Wash'gton	24 HB Garrett Ford
		FB Dick Leftridge
		DL Dick Hardison / Gordon Lambert
		DL Richie Rodes
		DL Joe Taffoni
		DL Don Cookman
		DL Jim Fisher
		DL Bill Sullivan
		LB Ernie Wheeler
		LB Doug Hoover
		DB Richie Martha
		DB Doug Stanley
		DB Jim Sypult / John Mallory

RUSHING: Ford 140/894y, Leftridge 144/774y, Rader 29/164y
PASSING: McCune 91-182/1274y, 15TD, 50%
RECEIVING: Dunlevy 29/480y, Ford 16/179y, Harris 14/182y
SCORING: Ford 58pts, Leftridge 54pts, Chuck Kinder (K) 41pts

1966 3-5-2

15 Duke	34 E Jim Sypult
24 William & Mary	13 T Danny Williamson / Pat Buratti
13 Virginia Tech	13 G Norm Hill / Dan Hodges
14 Pittsburgh	17 C Greg Dragovich
9 Maryland	28 G Wayne Vassalotti / Dale Stortz
6 Penn State	38 T George Begalla
14 Kentucky	14 E Larry Canterbury
35 Citadel	0 QB Tom Digon / Pete Secret
21 Geo. Wash'gton	6 WB Steve Edwards / Larry Sine
7 Syracuse	34 TB Garrett Ford
	FB John Piscorik
	DL Dick Hardison / Gary Young
	DL Richie Rodes
	DL Bob Cummings / Frank Malardie
	DL Don Cookman
	DL Danny Williamson
	LB Ron Yuss / Doug Hoover
	LB Baker Brown
	DB Dick Whitman
	DB John Finnerty
	DB John Mallory
	DB Herb Snyder / Charles Wood

RUSHING: Ford 236/1068y, Edwards 59/293y, Secret 52/232y
PASSING: Digon 28-54/323y, 2TD, 51.9%
RECEIVING: Sine 9/99y, Sypult 6/60y, 2 tied w/ 5
SCORING: Ford 42pts, Chuck Kinder (K) 30pts, Mallory 24pts

1967 5-4-1

40 Villanova	0 E Oscar Patrick / Emo Schupbach
27 Richmond	6 T George Begalla / Dan Hodges
21 VMI	9 G Wayne Brooks
6 Syracuse	23 C Tom Kucer
15 Pittsburgh	0 G Mike Germak
14 Penn State	21 T Norman Hill
7 Virginia Tech	20 TE Jim Smith
7 Kentucky	22 QB Tom Digon
16 William & Mary	16 WB Ron Pobolish / Eddie Silverio
35 Davidson	0 HB Ben Siegfried / Garrett Ford
	FB Gary Thall
	DL Dick Hardison
	DL Richie Rodes
	DL Carl Crennel
	DL George Henshaw
	DL Danny Williamson
	LB Ron Yuss
	LB Baker Brown
	DB Dick Whitman
	DB Terry Snively
	DB Herb Snyder
	DB John Mallory

RUSHING: Siegfried 93/334y, Ford 77/204y, Thall 46/194y
PASSING: Digon 62-108/684y, 4TD, 57.4%
RECEIVING: Patrick 19/326y, Smith 18/194y, Thall 12/88y
SCORING: Ken Juskowich (K) 56pts, Pobolish 30pts, Ford 24pts

1968 7-3

17 Richmond	0 E Oscar Patrick / Emo Schupbach
38 Pittsburgh	15 T Tom Kucer
20 Penn State	31 G Wayne Brooks
14 VMI	7 C Dick Roberts
20 William & Mary	0 G Ron Cecil / Mike Germak
12 Virginia Tech	27 T Mickey Plumley
16 Kentucky	35 TE Jim Smith / Bob Zambo
17 Citadel	0 QB Mike Sherwood
30 Villanova	20 WR Wayne Porter
23 Syracuse	6 HB Eddie Silverio / Bob Gresham
	FB Jim Braxton / Gary Thall
	DL Dale Farley
	DL Charlie Fisher
	DL Carl Crennel
	DL George Henshaw
	DL Bob Starford
	LB Baker Brown
	LB Danny Smith / Marv Six
	DB Thad Kucherawy
	DB Mike Slater / John Finnerty
	DB Terry Snively
	DB Ron Pobolish / John Hale

RUSHING: Silverio 143/559y, Braxton 83/272y, Gresham 71/160y
PASSING: Sherwood 151-264/1998y, 12TD, 57.2%
RECEIVING: Patrick 50/770y, Porter 37/493y, Braxton 18/276y
SCORING: Ken Juskowich (K) 45pts, Silverio 42pts, Patrick 30pts

1969 10-1

57 Cincinnati	11 WR Oscar Patrick
31 Maryland	7 T Wayne Brooks
35 Tulane	17 G Mickey Plumley
32 VMI	0 C Dick Roberts
0 Penn State	20 G Ron Cecil
49 Pittsburgh	18 T Tim Horvath
7 Kentucky	6 TE Jim Smith
31 William & Mary	0 QB Mike Sherwood
33 Richmond	21 WB Wayne Porter / Eddie Williams
13 Syracuse	10 HB Bob Gresham
14 South Carolina ■	3 FB Jim Braxton
	DL John Hale
	DL Charlie Fisher
	DL George Henshaw
	DL Art Holdt / Bob Starford
	LB Dave Benn / Danny Smith
	LB Carl Crennel
	LB Dale Farley
	DB Leon Jenkins
	DB Mike Slater
	DB Ron Pobolish

RUSHING: Gresham 206/1155y, Braxton 199/843y,
  Williams 88/589y
PASSING: Sherwood 61-116/773y, 7TD, 52.6%
RECEIVING: Gresham 15/147y, Porter 12/164y, 3 tied w/ 9
SCORING: Braxton (FB-K) 113pts, Gresham 60pts, Williams 24pts

1970 8-3

43 William & Mary	7 WR Nate Stephens / Chris Potts
49 Richmond	10 WR Wayne Porter
47 VMI	10 T John Houghton
16 Indiana	10 G Bob Zitelli
13 Duke	21 C Dick Roberts
35 Pittsburgh	36 G Tom Horvath
24 Colorado State	21 T B.C. Williams
8 Penn State	42 TE Jim Braxton
28 East Carolina	14 QB Mike Sherwood
28 Syracuse	19 TB Bob Gresham / Eddie Williams
20 Maryland	10 FB Pete Wood
	DL Bob Sims
	DL Charlie Fisher
	DL Danny Wilfong
	DL John Hale
	LB Dave Benn
	LB Dale Farley
	LB Danny Smith
	DB Leon Jenkins
	DB Mike Slater
	DB Algie Labrasca
	DB David Morris

RUSHING: Gresham 140/866y, Wood 131/713y,
  Williams 124/524y
PASSING: Sherwood 117-193/1550y, 15TD, 60.6%
RECEIVING: Potts 31/346y, Braxton 27/565y, Wood 20/135y
SCORING: Braxton (TE-K) 75pts, Gresham 48pts, Wood 42pts

1971 7-4

45 Boston College	14 WR Harry Blake
10 California	20 WR Chris Potts / Bernie Kirchner
16 Richmond	3 T Terry Voithofer
20 Pittsburgh	9 G Adam Guichoski
28 William & Mary	23 C Gerald Schultze
44 East Carolina	21 G B.C. Williams
43 Temple	33 T Bill Samuelson
7 Penn State	35 TE Nate Stephens
15 Duke	31 QB Bernie Galiffa
28 VMI	3 TB Kerry Marbury
24 Syracuse	28 FB Pete Wood / Brian Chiles
	DL Bob Sims
	DL Frank Samsa
	DL Dennis Reid
	DL Tom Tamburino
	LB Tom Zakowski
	LB Billy Joe Mantooth
	LB Terry King
	DB Leon Jenkins
	DB Tom Geishauser
	DB David Morris
	DB John Harcharic

RUSHING: Marbury 145/890y, Wood 145/724y, Chiles 97/486y
PASSING: Galiffa 121-238/1543y, 8TD, 50.8%
RECEIVING: Blake 27/388y, Stephens 24/393y, Kirchner 24/288y
SCORING: Wood 68pts, Frank Nester (K) 41pts, Chiles 38pts

1972 8-4

25 Villanova	6 WR Marshall Mills
28 Richmond	7 WR Danny Buggs
48 Virginia	10 T Walt Bragg
35 Stanford	41 G Dan Larcamp
49 William & Mary	34 C Gerald Schultze
36 Temple	39 G Doug Stevens
31 Tulane	19 T Bill Samuelson
19 Penn State	28 TE Nate Stephens
38 Pittsburgh	20 QB Bernie Galiffa
50 VMI	24 TB Kerry Marbury
43 Syracuse	12 FB Brian Chiles
13 N. Carolina St.■	49 DL Bob Sims
	DL Dennis Reid
	DL Jeff Merrow
	DL Frank Samsa
	LB Tom Zakowski
	LB Billy Joe Mantooth
	LB Bruce Huffman
	DB Rich Weiskircher
	DB Tom Geishauser
	DB David Morris
	DB Doug Chaney

RUSHING: Marbury 150/775y, Chiles 104/402y, Buggs 21/396y
PASSING: Galiffa 164-334/2496y, 17TD, 49.1%
RECEIVING: Mills 39/659y, Stephens 36/577y, Buggs 35/791y
SCORING: Marbury 108pts, Buggs 84pts, Frank Nester (K) 81pts

1973 6-5

20 Maryland	13 WR Marshall Mills
24 Virginia Tech	10 WR Danny Buggs
17 Illinois	10 T Rick Pennypacker / Dan Larcamp
14 Indiana	28 G Walt Bragg
7 Pittsburgh	35 C Al Gluchoski
17 Richmond	38 G Dave Wilcher / Bob Dessimoz
14 Penn State	62 T Dave Van Halanger
20 Miami	14 TE Dave Jagdmann
13 Boston College	25 QB Ade Dillon
42 Virginia	17 TB Dwayne Woods / Artie Owens
24 Syracuse	14 FB Mike Nelson / Mike Hubbard
	DL Andy Peters
	DL John Adams
	DL Jeff Merrow
	DL Ron Brown
	LB Tom Zakowski
	LB Bruce Huffman
	LB John Spraggins
	DB Charlie Miller
	DB Marcus Mauney
	DB John Harcharic
	DB Jack Eastwood

RUSHING: Woods 186/818y, Owens 70/391y, Nelson 51/194y
PASSING: Dillon 46-97/762y, 4TD, 47.4%
RECEIVING: Jagdmann 30/424y, Mills 29/397y, Buggs 27/624y
SCORING: Frank Nester (K) & Buggs 48pts, Owens &
  Woods 30pts

1974 4-7

25 Richmond	29 WR Marshall Mills / Bernie Kirchner
16 Kentucky	6 WR Danny Buggs
14 Tulane	17 T Dave Van Halanger / Charles Kelly
24 Indiana	0 G Steve Earley
14 Pittsburgh	31 C Al Gluchoski
20 Mia mi	21 G Bob Kaminski
12 Penn State	21 T Tom Brandner
3 Boston College	35 TE Randy Swinson / John Coker
39 Syracuse	11 QB Chuck Fiorante / Kirk Lewis
21 Temple	35 TB Artie Owens
22 Virginia Tech	21 FB Heywood Smith / Ron Lee
	DL John Spaggins
	DL John Adams
	DL Jeff Merrow
	DL Rich Lukowski
	LB Steve Dunlap
	LB Ken Culbertson
	LB Bruce Huffman
	DB Mark Burke / Rory Fields
	DB Charlie Miller
	DB Marcus Mauney
	DB Jack Eastwood

RUSHING: Owens 174/1130y, Lee 115/543y, Smith 131/479y
PASSING: Fiorante 43-87/592y, 2TD, 49.4%
RECEIVING: Mills 36/445y, Buggs 24/381y, Swinson 19/278y
SCORING: Owens 42pts, Smith 36pts, Lee 30pts

1975 9-3

50 Temple	7 WR Steve Lewis
28 California	10 WR Scott MacDonald / Tom Bowden
35 Boston College	18 T Rick Pennypacker / Tom Brandner
28 SMU	25 G Steve Earley
0 Penn State	39 C Al Gluchoski / Greg Dorn
14 Tulane	16 G Bob Kaminsky
10 Virginia Tech	7 T Dave Van Halanger
38 Kent State	13 TE Randy Swinson
17 Pittsburgh	14 QB Dan Kendra / Danny Williams
31 Richmond	13 TB Artie Owens / Dwayne Woods
19 Syracuse	20 FB Ron Lee
13 N. Carolina St.■	10 DL Andy Peters
	DL Chuck Smith
	DL Joe Jelich
	DL Rich Lukowski
	DL Gary Lombard
	LB Ken Culbertson / Steve Dunlap
	LB Ray Marshall
	DB Chuck Braswell
	DB Johnny Schell
	DB Tom Pridemore
	DB Mark Burke

RUSHING: Owens 159/1055y, Lee 155/623y, Woods 93/493y
PASSING: Kendra 98-189/1315y, 6TD, 51.9%
RECEIVING: Lewis 21/296y, MacDonald 20/392y, Swinson 19/282y
SCORING: Lee 60pts, Bill McKenzie (K) 47pts, Owens & Woods 36pts

1976 5-6

28 Villanova	7 WR Steve Lewis
3 Maryland	24 WR Tommy Bowden / Cedric Thomas
10 Kentucky	14 T Wayne Gatewood
9 Richmond	6 G Tom Antion
42 Temple	0 C Clay Singletary
3 Boston College	14 G Steve Earley
0 Penn State	33 T Tom Creeden
7 Virginia Tech	24 TE Ben McDay
32 Tulane	28 QB Dan Kendra
16 Pittsburgh	24 TB Dwayne Woods / Dave Riley
34 Syracuse	28 FB Walter Easley / Paul Lumley
	DL Fran Gleason
	DL Chuck Smith
	DL Joe Jelich
	DL Norm Patterson
	DL Ken Braswell
	LB Ken Culbertson
	LB Jeff Macerelli
	DB Harold Woods
	DB Johnny Schell
	DB Tom Pridemore
	DB Kevin Berkey / Paul Jordan

RUSHING: Woods 121/588y, Lumley 116/509y, Easley 124/493y
PASSING: Kendra 123/1476y, 9TD, 48.5%
RECEIVING: Lewis 48/737y, McDay 13/214y, Thomas 12/152y
SCORING: Bill McKenzie (K) 52pts, Lewis 36pts, Easley 30pts

1977 5-6

36 Richmond	0 WR Rich Duggan
24 Maryland	16 WR Steve Lewis / Cedric Thomas
13 Kentucky	28 T Tom Creeden
13 Virginia	0 G Wayne Gatewood / Terry Alessi
38 Temple	16 C Clay Singletary
24 Boston College	28 G Jim Himic / Alan Thomas
28 Penn State	49 T Randy Weppler
36 Villanova	41 TE Randy Swinson
3 Pittsburgh	44 QB Dan Kendra
20 Virginia Tech	14 TB Dave Riley / Robert Alexander
9 Syracuse	28 FB Walt Easley / Paul Lumley
	DL Doc Holiday / Fran Gleason
	DL Robin Meeley
	DL Joe Jelich
	DL Al Pisula / Lester Johnson
	DL Delbert Fowler
	LB Ken Braswell / Bill McLee
	LB Jeff Macerelli
	DB John Lasavage / Fulton Walker
	DB Harold Woods
	DB Kevin Berkey
	DB Tom Pridemore

RUSHING: Riley 125/616y, Easley 117/447y, Alexander 95/426y
PASSING: Kendra 121-226/1674y, 13TD, 53.5%
RECEIVING: Thomas 37/699y, Swinson 25/357y, Riley 20/143y
SCORING: Bill McKenzie (K) & Thomas 48pts, Easley 42pts

1978 2-9

14 Richmond	12 WR Steve Lewis
10 Oklahoma	52 WR Rich Duggan / Darrell Miller
15 N. Carolina St.	29 T Tom Creeden
21 Cal	28 G Jim Himic
15 Syracuse	31 C Jim Gianola / Pat Conochan
3 Virginia Tech	16 G Terry Alessi / Gordon Gordon
27 Temple	28 T Randy Weppler
21 Penn State	49 TE Robin Meeley
20 Virginia	17 QB Dutch Hoffman
7 Pittsburgh	52 TB Robert Alexander / Fulton Walker
14 Colorado State	50 FB Dane Conwell
	DL Ken Braswell
	DL Doc Holiday / Norm Patterson
	DL Joe Jelich
	DL Al Pisula
	DL Delbert Fowler
	LB John Garcia
	LB Jeff Macerelli
	DB John LaSavage
	DB Fulton Walker
	DB Jerry Holmes
	DB John Bendana

RUSHING: Conwell 88/412y, Walker 79/392y, Alexander 74/310y
PASSING: Hoffman 105-238/1479y, 9TD, 44.1%
RECEIVING: Lewis 38/629y, Duggan 23/372y, Miller 13/193y
SCORING: Steve Sinclair (K) 43pts, Lewis 30pts, Conwell 24pts

1979 5-6

16 Temple	38 WR Darrell Miller
14 Syracuse	24 WR Cedric Thomas
14 N. Carolina St.	38 T Alan Thomas
20 Richmond	18 G Jim Himic
10 Kentucky	6 C Pat Conochan
20 Boston College	18 G Gordon Gordon
27 Tulane	17 T Frank Kinczel
6 Penn State	31 TE Rich Duggan / Mark Raugh
34 Virginia Tech	23 QB Oliver Luck
17 Pittsburgh	24 TB Robert Alexander
7 Arizona State	42 FB Eldridge Dixon
	DL Delbert Fowler
	DL Danny Lee
	DL Dave Oblak
	DL John Bendana
	LB Darryl Talley
	LB Mike Dawson
	LB Walter Easley
	DB Everett Pettaway
	DB Fulton Walker
	DB Jerry Holmes
	DB Sedrick King

RUSHING: Alexander 118/656y, Dixon 101/461y, Luck 204/407y
PASSING: Luck 103-231/1292y, 8TD, 44.6%
RECEIVING: Miller 33/507y, Thomas 23/341y, Raugh 11/138y
SCORING: Steve Sinclair (K) 35pts, Luck 30pts, Dixon 24pts

1980 6-6

41 Cincinnati	27 WR Darrell Miller
52 Colorado State	24 WR Cedric Thomas
11 Maryland	14 T Keith Jones
31 Richmond	28 G Gordon Gordon
45 Virginia	21 C Pat Conochan
13 Hawaii	16 G Chuck Gambil
14 Pittsburgh	42 T Alan Thomas
15 Penn State	20 TE Mark Raugh / Dave Johnson
11 Virginia Tech	34 QB Oliver Luck
41 Temple	28 TB Robert Alexander
24 Rutgers	15 FB Walt Easley / Eldridge Dixon
7 Syracuse	20 DL Calvin Turner
	DL Todd Campbell
	DL Bob Crites / John Bendana
	LB Delbert Fowler
	LB Dave Preston
	LB Dennis Fowlkes
	LB Darryl Talley
	DB Steve Newberry
	DB Fulton Walker
	DB Allen Moreland
	DB Lind Murray

RUSHING: Alexander 204/1064y, Easley 189/833y, Dixon 34/171y
PASSING: Luck 135-254/1874y, 19TD, 53.1%
RECEIVING: Alexander 31/629y, Thomas 31/607y, Miller 23/393y
SCORING: Thomas 60pts, Steve Sinclair (K) 58pts, Easley 48pts

1981 9-3

32 Virginia	18 WR Gary Mullen
17 Maryland	13 WR Rich Hollins
49 Colorado State	3 T Frank Kinczel
38 Boston College	10 G Andre Gist
0 Pittsburgh	17 C Bill Legg
27 Virginia Tech	6 G Mike Durrette
7 Penn State	30 T Keith Jones
20 East Carolina	3 TE Mark Raugh
24 Temple	19 QB Oliver Luck
20 Rutgers	3 TB Curlin Beck
24 Syracuse	27 FB Dane Conwell / Mickey Walczak
26 Florida■	6 DL Todd Campbell
	DL Dave Oblak
	DL Calvin Turner
	LB Jeff Seals
	LB Jeff Deem
	LB Dennis Fowlkes
	LB Darryl Talley
	DB Steve Newberry / Reggie Armstead
	DB Tim Agee
	DB Lind Murray
	DB Sedrick King

RUSHING: Beck 123/497y, Conwell 128/439y, Walczak 73/274y
PASSING: Luck 216-394/2448y, 16TD, 54.8%
RECEIVING: Raugh 64/601y, Walczak 49/338y, Hollins 37/754y
SCORING: Walczak 48pts, Murat Turcan (K) 44pts, Hollins 36pts

1982 9-3

41 Oklahoma	27 WR Darrell Miller / Rich Hollins
19 Maryland	18 WR Wayne Brown
43 Richmond	10 T Kurt Kehl
13 Pittsburgh	16 G Andre Gist / Bill Legg
20 Boston College	13 C Dave Johnson
16 Virginia Tech	9 G Scott Barrows
0 Penn State	24 T Ray Hoisington / Jim Rodgers
30 East Carolina	3 TE Mark Raugh
20 Temple	17 QB Jeff Hostetler
44 Rutgers	17 TB Curlin Beck / Tom Gray
26 Syracuse	0 FB Ron Wolfley
12 Florida State■	31 TE Todd Campbell
	DL Dave Oblak
	DL Chuck Harris
	LB Darryl Talley
	LB Dave Preston
	LB Dennis Fowlkes
	LB Steve Hathaway / Ed Hughes
	DB Reggie Armstead
	DB Steve Newberry
	DB Anthony Daniels / Gregg McGowan
	DB Tim Agee

RUSHING: Beck 76/350y, Gray 81/324y, Wolfley 89/323y
PASSING: Hostetler 127-264/1798y, 10TD, 48.1%
RECEIVING: Raugh 32/423y, Miller 29/465y, Gray 19/164y
SCORING: Paul Woodside (K) 110pts, Hollins 30pts, Beck 24pts

1983 9-3

55 Ohio Univ.	3 WR Rich Hollins
48 Pacific	7 WR Wayne Brown / Gary Mullen
31 Maryland	21 T Kurt Kehl
27 Boston College	17 G Dave DeJarnett
24 Pittsburgh	21 C Bill Legg
13 Virginia Tech	0 G Scott Barrows
23 Penn State	41 T Brian Jozwiak
3 Miami	20 TE Rob Bennett
27 Temple	9 QB Jeff Hostetler
35 Rutgers	7 TB Tom Gray / Pat Randolph
16 Syracuse	27 FB Ron Wolfley
20 Kentucky■	16 DL Jim Merritts
	DL Dave Oblak
	DL Rich Walters
	LB Ed Hughes
	LB Dave Preston
	LB Derek Christian
	LB Steve Hathaway
	DB Anthony Daniels
	DB Mike Scott
	DB Tim Agee
	DB Steve Newberry

RUSHING: Gray 110/498y, Wolfley 122/485y, Randolph 119/545y
PASSING: Hostetler 173-309/2345y, 16TD, 56%
RECEIVING: Hollins 50/781y, Bennett 24/343y, Mullen 20/363y
SCORING: Paul Woodside (K) 100pts, Gray 36pts, Hollins 30pts

SCORES, LINEUPS, AND STATISTICS

1984 8-4

38 Ohio Univ.	0 WR Gary Mullen
30 Louisville	6 WR Willie Drewery
14 Virginia Tech	7 T Brian Jozwiak
17 Maryland	20 G Scott Barrows
28 Pittsburgh	10 C Bill Legg
20 Syracuse	10 G Dave DeJarnett
21 Boston College	20 T Chuck Jolliff / Kurt Kehl
17 Penn State	14 TE Rob Bennett / Todd Fisher
7 Virginia	27 QB Kevin White
19 Rutgers	23 TB Tom Gray / Pat Randolph
17 Temple	19 FB Ron Wolfley
31 TCU ■	14 DL Jeff Lucas
	DL Brad Hunt
	DL David Grant
	LB West Turner / Scott Dixon
	LB Derek Christian
	LB Matt Smith / Dave Preston
	LB Fred Smalls / Cam Zopp
	DB Andrew Jones
	DB Stacy Smith
	DB Travis Curtis
	DB Anthony Daniels

RUSHING: Wolfley 127/475y, Gray 101/416y, Randolph 129/416y
PASSING: White 128-232/1727y, 9TD, 55.2%
RECEIVING: Drewery 36/594y, Mullen 31/557y, Fisher 21/205y
SCORING: Paul Woodside (K) 73pts, Gray & Wolfley 30pts

1985 7-3-1

52 Louisville	13 WR Robert White
20 Duke	18 WR Harvey Smith
0 Maryland	28 T Brian Jozwiak
10 Pittsburgh	10 G Gary Pounds
24 Virginia Tech	9 C Dave Griffith
13 Boston College	6 G Rick Phillips / John Barton
0 Penn State	27 T Chuck Jolliff
7 Virginia	27 TE Gary Basil
27 Rutgers	0 QB Mike Timko
23 Temple	10 TB John Holifield / Undra Johnson
13 Syracuse	10 FB Tom Gray
	DL Brad Hunt
	DL David Grant
	DL Jeff Lucas
	LB Fred Smalls
	LB Van Richardson
	LB Derek Christian
	LB Matt Smith
	DB Travis Curtis
	DB Stacy Smith
	DB Larry Holley
	DB Willie Edwards

RUSHING: Holifield 140/595y, Gray 121/376y, Johnson 49/257y
PASSING: Timko 44-84/567y, 4TD, 52.4%
RECEIVING: Gray 26/233y, Holifield 18/170y, White 15/201y
SCORING: Charlie Baumann (K) 63pts, Holifield 42pts, Gray 18pts

1986 4-7

47 N. Illinois	14 WR Harvey Smith / Calvin Phillips
24 East Carolina	21 WR John Talley
3 Maryland	24 T Rick Phillips
16 Pittsburgh	48 G John Stroia
7 Virginia Tech	13 C Kevin Koken
14 Miami	58 G Bob Kovach
10 Boston College	19 T Brian Smider
0 Penn State	19 TE Gary Basil
24 Rutgers	17 QB Mike Timko
42 Louisville	19 TB Undra Johnson / John Holifield
23 Syracuse	34 FB Chris Peccon
	DL Brad Hunt
	DL David Grant
	DL Jeff Lucas
	LB Robert Pickett
	LB Matt Smith
	LB Darren Whitten / Eric Lester
	LB Darnell Warren
	DB Willie Edwards
	DB Preston Waters
	DB Larry Holley
	DB Bo Orlando

RUSHING: Johnson 138/652y, Holifield 156/645y, Pat Randolph (TB) 27/251y
PASSING: Timko 90-189/1191y, 8TD, 47.6%
RECEIVING: Smith 28/456y, Talley 27/353y, C. Phillips 20/289y
SCORING: Johnson 36pts, Charlie Baumann (K) 31pts, Smith 30pts

1987 6-6

23 Ohio Univ.	3 WR Harvey Smith
3 Ohio State	24 WR John Talley
20 Maryland	25 T Rick Phillips
3 Pittsburgh	6 G Bob Kovach
49 East Carolina	0 C Kevin Koken
45 Cincinnati	17 G John Stroia
37 Boston College	16 T Brian Smider
21 Penn State	25 TE Keith Winn
28 Virginia Tech	16 QB Major Harris
37 Rutgers	13 TB A.B. Brown / Undra Johnson
31 Syracuse	32 FB Craig Taylor
	DL Brad Hunt
	DL David Grant
	DL Chris Parker
	LB Dale Jackson
	LB Chris Haering
	LB Robert Pickett
	LB Darnell Warren
	DB Stacy Smith / Terry White
	DB Willie Edwards
	DB Preston Waters
	DB Bo Orlando

RUSHING: Brown 199/975y, Harris 143/615y, Johnson 115/593y
PASSING: Harris 79-155/1200y, 10TD, 51%
RECEIVING: Talley 25/307y, Smith 13/205y, Winn 13/184y
SCORING: Charlie Baumann (K) 78pts, Brown & Harris 36pts

1988 11-1

62 Bowling Green	14 WR Calvin Phillips
45 Cal St. Fullerton	10 WR Grantis Bell / Reggie Rembert
55 Maryland	24 T Rick Phillips
31 Pittsburgh	10 G John Stroia
22 Virginia Tech	10 C Kevin Koken
30 East Carolina	10 G Bob Kovach
59 Boston College	19 T Brian Smider
51 Penn State	30 TE Keith Winn
51 Cincinnati	13 QB Major Harris
35 Rutgers	25 TB A.B. Brown / Undra Johnson
31 Syracuse	9 FB Craig Taylor
21 Notre Dame ■	34 DL Chris Parker
	DL Jim Gray / Scott Summits
	DL Mike Fox
	LB Renaldo Turnbull / Dale Jackson
	LB Chris Haering
	LB Theron Ellis
	LB Robert Pickett
	DB Alvoid Mays
	DB Willie Edwards
	DB Darrell Whitmore
	DB Bo Orlando / Lawrence Drumgoole

RUSHING: Brown 178/962y, Johnson 140/709y, Harris 134/610y
PASSING: Harris 105-186/1915y, 14TD, 56.5%
RECEIVING: Phillips 24/611y, Rembert 23/516y, Winn 16/211y
SCORING: Charlie Baumann (K) 117pts, Johnson 72pts, Rembert 62pts

1989 8-3-1

35 Ball State	10 WR Reggie Rembert
14 Maryland	10 WR Greg Dykes
45 South Carolina	21 T Jack Linn
30 Louisville	21 G Scott Parker
31 Pittsburgh	31 C Jeff Price
10 Virginia Tech	12 G Dale Wolfley
69 Cincinnati	3 T Matt Wracher
44 Boston College	30 TE Adrian Moss
9 Penn State	19 QB Major Harris
21 Rutgers	20 TB Garrett Ford / Eugene Napoleon
24 Syracuse	17 FB Rico Tyler
7 Clemson ■	27 DL Mike Fox
	DL Jim Gray
	DL Scott Summits / Skip Fuller
	LB Lonnie Brockman
	LB Chris Haering
	LB Theron Ellis / Steve Grant
	LB Renaldo Turnbull
	DB Basil Proctor
	DB Darren Fulton
	DB Darrell Whitmore
	DB Preston Waters

RUSHING: Harris 155/936y, Ford 148/733y, Napoleon 102/417y
PASSING: Harris 142-245/2058y, 17TD, 58%
RECEIVING: Rembert 47/850y, Dykes 25/427y, Moss 21/321y
SCORING: Brad Carroll (K) 72pts, Rembert 68pts, Harris & Ford 36pts

1990 4-7

35 Kent State	24 WR Ray Staten
10 Maryland	14 WR James Jett
7 Louisville	9 T Jeff Sniffen /Verne Howard/Rich Braham
38 Pittsburgh	24 G Larry Cook
21 Virginia Tech	26 C Mike Compton
28 Cincinnati	20 G Dale Wolfley (C) / Lorenzo Styles
14 Boston College	27 T John Ray
19 Penn State	31 TE Darrell Mitchell
28 Rutgers	3 QB Greg Jones
7 Syracuse	31 TB Michael Beasley / Jon Jones
10 South Carolina	29 FB Rico Tyler
	DL Jim Gray / Rick Dolly
	DL Steve Redd
	DL Gary Tillis
	LB Tarris Alexander / Boris Graham
	LB Steve Grant
	LB E.J. Wheeler
	LB Theron Ellis
	DB Cecil Doggette / Tim Newsom
	DB Leroy Axem / Sam Wilson
	DB Darrell Whitmore
	DB Mike Collins

RUSHING: Beasley 125/607y, Jones 94/503y, Tyler 93/455y
PASSING: Jones 121-247/1481y, 7TD, 49%
RECEIVING: Jett 31/652y, Mitchell 23/237y, Staten 15/143y
SCORING: Jones 36pts, Brad Carroll (K), Tyler & Ford 24pts

1991 6-5

3 Pittsburgh	34 WR James Jett
24 Bowling Green	17 WR Michael Beasley
21 South Carolina	16 T Rich Braham
37 Maryland	7 G Lorenzo Styles
14 Virginia Tech	20 C Mike Compton
10 Temple	9 G Joe Ayuso
31 Boston College	24 T John Ray
6 Penn State	51 TE Alex Shook
28 Rutgers	3 QB Darren Studstill
3 Miami	27 TB Adrian Murrell
10 Syracuse	16 FB Garrett Ford / Rodney Woodard
	DL Tom Briggs
	DL Rick Dolly
	DL Jim Gray
	DL Boris Graham
	LB Wes Richardson / Darrick Wiley
	LB Steve Grant
	LB James Wright / Tarris Alexander
	DB Cecil Doggette
	DB Leroy Axem
	DB Darrell Whitmore / Tim Newsom
	DB Mike Collins

RUSHING: Murrell 201/904y, Ford 80/335y, Studstill 88/307y
PASSING: Studstill 85-168/1055y, 8TD, 50.6%
RECEIVING: Shook 23/246y, Beasley 17/272y, Woodard 15/153y
SCORING: Murrell 48pts, Mark Johnson (K) 41pts, Beasley & Woodard 18pts

1992 5-4-2

29 Miami (Ohio)	29 WR James Jett / Jay Kearney
44 Pittsburgh	6 WR Ed Hill
34 Maryland	33 T Rich Braham
16 Virginia Tech	7 G Lorenzo Styles
24 Boston College	24 C Mike Compton
10 Syracuse	17 G Dale Williams / Jim LeBlanc
26 Penn State	40 T Calvin Edwards / Robert Nelson
23 Miami	35 TE John Cappa
41 East Carolina	28 QB Darren Studstill / Jake Kelchner
9 Rutgers	13 TB Adrian Murrell / Jon Jones
23 Louisiana Tech	3 FB Rodney Woodard / Jim Freeman
	DL Tom Briggs
	DL Rick Dolly
	DL Barry Hawkins / Scott Gaskins
	DL Boris Graham
	LB Darrick Wiley / Puppy Wright
	LB Matt Taffoni / Wes Richardson
	LB Tim Brown
	DB Kwame Smith
	DB Tommy Orr / Leroy Axem
	DB David Mayfield
	DB Mike Collins

RUSHING: Murrell 222/1145y, Jones 65/429y, Woodard 69/318y
PASSING: Studstill 89-159/1065y, 9TD, 56%
Kelchner 66-119/901y, 6TD, 55.5%
RECEIVING: Hill 43/540y, Kearney 20/282y, Jett 19/382y
SCORING: Mike Vanderjagt (K) 72pts, Murrell 54pts, Hill 36pts

1993 11-1

48 E. Michigan	6 WR Ed Hill / Jay Kearney
42 Maryland	37 WR Mike Baker
35 Missouri	3 T Rich Braham
14 Virginia Tech	13 G Tom Robsock
36 Louisville	34 C Dale Williams (G) / Dan Harless
42 Pittsburgh	21 G Jim LeBlanc
43 Syracuse	0 T Chris Klick / Calvin Edwards
58 Rutgers	22 TE Nate Rine
49 Temple	7 QB Jake Kelchner
17 Miami	14 TB Robert Walker / Jimmy Gary
17 Boston College	14 FB Jim Freeman / Rodney Woodard
7 Florida■	41 DL Scott Gaskins
	DL Barry Hawkins
	DL Steve Perkins
	LB Darrick Wiley
	LB Matt Taffoni
	LB Wes Richardson
	LB Tim Brown
	DB Aaron Beasley / Vann Washington
	DB Tommy Orr
	DB David Mayfield
	DB Mike Collins

RUSHING: Walker 214/1250y, Woodard 72/328y, Freeman 65/294y
PASSING: Kelchner 110-174/1688y, 12TD, 63.2%
RECEIVING: Baker 42/714y, Kearney 29/750y, Hill 25/442y
SCORING: Walker 66pts, Todd Sauerbrun (K) 54pts, Woodard 36pts

1994 7-6

0 Nebraska	31 WR Rashaan Vanterpool
16 Ball State	14 WR Zach Abraham
2 Rutgers	17 T Joe DeLong
13 Maryland	24 G Tom Robsock
6 Virginia Tech	34 C Derrick Bell / Jay Brooks
34 Missouri	10 G Buddy Hager
47 Pittsburgh	41 T Chris Klick
6 Miami	38 TE Lovett Purnell
52 Louisiana Tech	16 QB Chad Johnston / Eric Boykin
55 Temple	17 TB Robert Walker / Jimmy Gary
21 Boston College	20 FB Jim Freeman / Kantroy Barber
13 Syracuse	0 DL Steven Perkins
21 South Carolina■	24 DL Barry Hawkins
	DL John Browning
	LB Canute Curtis
	LB J.T. Thomas
	LB Matt Taffoni
	LB Puppy Wright
	DB Aaron Beasley
	DB Mike Logan / Harold Kidd
	DB Vann Washington
	DB Charles Emanuel / David Mayfield

RUSHING: Walker 179/749y
PASSING: Johnston 124-242/1863y, 16TD, 51.2%
RECEIVING: Vanterpool 50/849y, Purnell 41/547y
SCORING: Bryan Baumann (K) 71pts

1995 5-6

24 Purdue	26 WR Rashaan Vanterpool
24 Temple	13 WR David Saunders
17 Maryland	31 T Bryan Washington
45 Kent State	6 G Ted Daniels / Bill McElroy
20 East Carolina	23 C Derrick Bell
31 Boston College	19 G Buddy Hager / Mike Horn
0 Syracuse	22 T Joe DeLong / Frank Birts
0 Virginia Tech	27 TE Lovett Purnell
59 Rutgers	26 QB Chad Johnston
12 Miami	17 TB Robert Walker / Jimmy Gary
21 Pittsburgh	0 FB Kantroy Barber / Leroy White
	DL John Browning / John Thornton
	DL Henry Slay / Charlton Forbes
	DL Kevin Landolt
	LB Canute Curtis
	LB Elige Longino / Jamie Sweeney
	LB J.T. Thomas
	LB Bernard Russ / Bernardo Amerson
	DB Aaron Beasley
	DB Mike Logan
	DB Vann Washington
	DB Charles Emanuel

RUSHING: Walker 122/508y, Gary 132/504y, Barber 93/362y
PASSING: Johnston 127-248/2019y, 13TD, 51.2%
RECEIVING: Saunders 38/682y, Purnell 37/614y, Vanterpool 34/606y
SCORING: Bryan Baumann (K) 59pts, Gary & Purnell 36pts

1996 8-4

34 Pittsburgh	0 WR Rashaan Vanterpool / Shawn Foreman
34 W. Michigan	9 WR David Saunders
10 East Carolina	9 T Solomon Page
20 Purdue	6 G Mike Horn
13 Maryland	0 C Eric de Groh
34 Boston College	17 G Bryan Pukenas
30 Temple	10 T Sam Austin
7 Miami	10 TE Chad Wable / Anthony Becht
7 Syracuse	30 QB Chad Johnston
55 Rutgers	14 TB Amos Zereoue
14 Virginia Tech	31 FB Mark Plants / Anthony Green
13 North Carolina■	20 DL Henry Slay
	DL John Thornton
	DL Bob Baum
	LB Canute Curtis / Gary Stills
	LB Bernard Russ
	LB Jason Williams / John Hadley
	LB Elige Longino
	DB Perlo Bastien
	DB Mike Logan
	DB Vann Washington
	DB Charles Emanuel

RUSHING: Zereoue 222/1035y, Alvin Swope (TB) 61/297y, Khari Mott (TB) 32/183y
PASSING: Johnston 167-334/1958y, 12TD, 50%
RECEIVING: Saunders 76/1043y, Vanterpool 31/421y, Foreman 25/415y
SCORING: Jay Taylor (K) 77pts, Zereoue 60pts, Saunders 30pts

1997 7-5

42 Marshall	31 WR Shawn Foreman
24 East Carolina	17 WR Pat Greene / Khori Ivy
24 Boston College	31 T Solomon Page
28 Miami	17 G Randy Dunnigan / Steve Ford
48 Rutgers	0 C Eric de Groh
31 Maryland	14 G Bryan Pukenas / Bill McElroy (C)
30 Virginia Tech	17 T Sam Austin
10 Syracuse	40 TE Chad Wable / Anthony Becht
41 Temple	21 QB Marc Bulger
14 Notre Dame	21 TB Amos Zereoue / Curtis Keaton
38 Pittsburgh	41 FB Leroy White
30 Georgia Tech■	35 DL Henry Slay
	DL John Thornton
	DL Bob Baum / Kevin Landolt
	LB Gary Stills / Ryan Brady
	LB Steve Lippe / Damon Cogdell
	LB John Hadley / Jason Williams
	LB Jamie Sweeney / K.C. Schiller
	DB Perlo Bastien / Charles Fisher
	DB Nate Terry
	DB Gary Thompkins / Dave Lightcap
	DB Barrett Green

RUSHING: Zereoue 264/1504y, Keaton 60/268y
PASSING: Bulger 167-283/2112y, 59%, 12 TD
RECEIVING: Foreman 64/796y, Greene 30/462y, Ivy 18/269y
SCORING: Zereoue 96pts, Jay Taylor (K) 82pts, Foreman 32pts

1998 8-4

17 Ohio State	34 WR Shawn Foreman / Khori Ivy
42 Maryland	20 WR David Saunders / Pat Greene
44 Tulsa	21 T Solomon Page
45 Navy	24 G Randy Dunnigan / Mike Enick
37 Temple	7 C Eric de Groh
31 Miami	34 G Bryan Pukenas
13 Virginia Tech	27 T Brock Holland / Tanner Russell
35 Syracuse	28 TE Anthony Becht
28 Rutgers	14 QB Marc Bulger
35 Boston College	10 TB Amos Zereoue
52 Pittsburgh	14 FB Anthony Green
31 Missouri■	34 DL Kevin Landolt / Greg Robinette
	DL John Thornton
	DL Charlton Forbes / Ryan Brady
	LB Gary Stills / Damon Cogdell
	LB Barrett Green
	LB Kyle Kayden
	LB Chris Edmonds
	DB Perlo Bastien
	DB Scooter Davis / Nate Terry
	DB Jerry Porter
	DB Gary Thompkins / Boo Sensibaugh

RUSHING: Zereoue 283/1462y, Alvin Swope (TB) 54/283y
PASSING: Bulger 274-419/3607y, 31TD, 65.4%
RECEIVING: Saunders 77/883y, Foreman 63/948y, Ivy 41/658y
SCORING: Zereoue 84pts, Taylor 78pts, Foreman & Saunders 48pts

1999 4-7

23 East Carolina	30 WR Khori Ivy / Antonio Brown
32 Miami (Ohio)	37 WR Carlos Osegueda / Pat Greene
0 Maryland	33 T Matt Wilson
7 Syracuse	30 G Terry Dixon / Wes Ours
28 Navy	31 C John Conte
62 Rutgers	16 G Rick Gilliam
20 Temple	17 T Tanner Russell
20 Miami	28 TE Anthony Becht
20 Virginia Tech	22 QB Marc Bulger / Brad Lewis
17 Boston College	34 TB Avon Cobourne / Cooper Rego
52 Pittsburgh	21 FB Anthony Green
	DL Ryan Brady
	DL Greg Robinette
	DL Antwan Lake
	LB Mark Thurston / Kevin Freeman
	LB Barrett Green
	LB Kyle Kayden
	LB Chris Edmonds
	DB Perlo Bastien
	DB Nate Terry / Scooter Davis
	DB J. Porter/Rick Sherrod/Boo Sensibaugh
	DB Gary Thompkins

RUSHING: Cobourne 224/1139y, Rego 81/340y, Quincy Wilson (TB) 27/146y
PASSING: Bulger 145-239/1729y, 11TD, 60.7%
RECEIVING: Ivy 53/666y, Brown 50/462y, Becht 35/510y
SCORING: Taylor 72pts, Cobourne 60pts, 3 tied w/30 pts

2000 7-5

34 Boston College	14 WR Khori Ivy / Shawn Terry
30 Maryland	17 WR Antonio Brown
10 Miami	47 T Matt Wilson
29 Temple	24 G Terry Dixon
20 Virginia Tech	48 C Rick Gilliam
28 Idaho	16 G Brad Knell
28 Notre Dame	42 T Tanner Russell
27 Syracuse	31 TE Sean Berton
31 Rutgers	24 QB Brad Lewis
42 East Carolina	34 TB Avon Cobourne / Cooper Rego
28 Pittsburgh	38 FB Wes Ours
49 Mississippi■	38 DL Antwan Lake / William Perry
	DL David Upchurch
	DL Jason Davis
	LB Chris Edmonds
	LB Grant Wiley
	LB Kyle Kayden / Corey McIntyre
	LB David Carter / James Davis
	DB Richard Bryant
	DB Brian King / Lance Frazier
	DB Rick Sherrod
	DB Shawn Hackett

RUSHING: Cobourne 224/1018y, Rego 132/521y, Brown 23/126y
PASSING: Lewis 123-238/1819y, 13TD, 48.4%
RECEIVING: Brown 51/877y, Ivy 47/806y, Braxton 9/237y
SCORING: Rego 54pts, Jon Ohliger (K) 48pts, Ivy 42pts

2001 3-8

10 Boston College	34 WR Phil Braxton / Shawn Terry
20 Ohio Univ.	3 WR Antonio Brown / Michael Page
34 Kent State	14 WR Shawn Terry
20 Maryland	32 T Lance Nimmo
0 Virginia Tech	35 G Ken Sandor / Jeff Berk
24 Notre Dame	34 C Zack Dillow
3 Miami	45 G Brad Knell
80 Rutgers	7 T Tim Brown
13 Syracuse	24 TE/WR Tory Johnson / A.J. Nastasi
14 Temple	17 QB Brad Lewis
17 Pittsburgh	23 RB Avon Cobourne
	DL James Davis
	DL Antwan Lake
	DL David Upchurch
	DL Kevin Freeman / Tim Love
	LB Grant Wiley / Corey McIntyre
	LB Kyle Kayden
	LB Shawn Hackett
	DB Richard Bryant
	DB Lance Frazier/Brian King/Lewis Daniels
	DB Rick Sherrod
	DB Angel Estrada / O'Rondai Cox

RUSHING: Cobourne 267/1298y, Rasheed Marshall (QB) 48/210y
PASSING: Lewis 135-237/1339y, 7TD, 57%
RECEIVING: Nastasi 42/334y, Brown 31/291y, Terry 29/291y
SCORING: Brenden Rauh (K) 64pts, Cobourne 54pts, Marshall & Nastasi 18pts

2002 9-4

56 Tenn.-Chatt'ga	7 WR Phil Braxton
17 Wisconsin	34 WR Miquelle Henderson
35 Cincinnati	32 WR Derrick Smith / Michael Page
37 East Carolina	17 T Lance Nimmo
40 Maryland	48 G Jeff Berk
40 Rutgers	0 C Zack Dillow
34 Syracuse	7 G Ken Sandor / Geoff Lewis
23 Miami	40 T Tim Brown / Ben Timmons
46 Temple	20 TE Josh Bailey / Tory Johnson
24 Boston College	14 QB Rasheed Marshall
21 Virginia Tech	18 TB Avon Cobourne / Quincy Wilson
24 Pittsburgh	17 DL Jason Davis / Kevin Freeman
22 Virginia ■	48 DL Tim Love
	48 DL David Upchurch
	LB Grant Wiley
	LB Ben Collins (DB) / Adam Lehnortt
	LB James Davis
	DB Brian King / Lewis Daniels
	DB Lance Frazier / Adam Jones
	DB Jahmile Addae
	DB Angel Estrada
	DB Jermaine Thaxton / Arthur Harrison

RUSHING: Cobourne 335/1710y, Wilson 140/901y, Marshall 173/666y
PASSING: Marshall 139-259/1616y, 9TD, 53.7%
RECEIVING: Henderson 40/496y, Braxton 20/379y, Smith 17/202y
SCORING: Cobourne 102pts, Todd James (K) 79pts, Marshall 78pts

2003 8-5

17 Wisconsin	24 WR Chris Henry / Miquelle Henderson
48 East Carolina	7 WR Dee Alston / Rayshawn Bolden
13 Cincinnati	15 T Michael Watson
7 Maryland	34 G Dan Mozes / Jeremy Sheffey
20 Miami	22 C Jeremy Hines / Ben Timmons
34 Rutgers	19 G Jeff Berk (T) / Travis Garrett
28 Virginia Tech	7 T Garin Justice / Josh Stewart
36 Central Florida	19 TE Tory Johnson / Ryan Thomas
35 Boston College	28 TE/WR Josh Bailey / Travis Garvin
52 Pittsburgh	31 QB Rasheed Marshall
34 Syracuse	23 TB Quincy Wilson / Kay-Jay Harris
45 Temple	28 DL Ernest Hunter
7 Maryland ■	41 DL Ben Lynch
	DL Fred Blueford / Jason Hardee
	LB Scott Gyorko / Kevin McLee
	LB Adam Lehnortt
	LB Grant Wiley
	DB Lance Frazier
	DB Adam Jones / Anthony Mims
	DB Brian King
	DB Mike Lorello
	DB Leandre Washington/Lawrence Audena

RUSHING: Wilson 282/1380y, Harris 91/524y, Marshall 101/303y
PASSING: Marshall 109-215/1729y, 15TD, 50.7%
RECEIVING: Henry 41/1006y, Henderson 18/209y, Garvin 17/306y
SCORING: Brad Cooper (K) 79pts, Wilson 78pts, Henry 60pts

2004 8-4

56 East Carolina	23 WR Chris Henry / Charles Hales
45 Central Florida	20 WR Miquelle Henderson / John Pennington
19 Maryland	16 WR/RB Eddie Jackson / Pernell Williams
45 James Madison	10 T Garin Justice
13 Virginia Tech	19 G Dan Mozes
31 Connecticut	19 C Tim Brown
27 Syracuse	6 G Jeff Berk / Jeremy Sheffey
35 Rutgers	30 T Mike Watson
42 Temple	21 TE Ryan Thomas / Brad Palmer
17 Boston College	36 QB Rasheed Marshall
13 Pittsburgh	16 RB Kay-Jay Harris / Jason Colson
18 Florida State ■	30 DL Keilen Dykes / Ernest Hunter
	DL Ben Lynch
	DL Jason Hardee
	LB Scott Gyorko / Jay Henry
	LB Adam Lehnortt
	LB Kevin McLee / Jeff Noechel
	DB Adam Jones
	DB Anthony Mims
	DB Jahmile Addae
	DB Mike Lorello
	DB Lawrence Audena

RUSHING: Harris 165/959y, Marshall 169/861y, Colson 142/706y
PASSING: Marshall 144-242/1886y, 19TD, 59.5%
RECEIVING: Henry 52/872y, Harris 20/181y, Jackson 18/246y
SCORING: Harris 78pts, Henry 72pts, Brad Cooper (K) 70pts

2005 11-1

15 Syracuse	7 WR Brandon Myles
35 Wofford	7 WR Dorrell Jalloh/ Rayshawn Bolden
31 Maryland	19 WR Darius Reynaud / Vaughn Rivers
20 East Carolina	15 T Travis Garrett
17 Virginia Tech	34 G Ryan Stanchek / John Bradshaw
27 Rutgers	14 C Dan Mozes (G) / Jeremy Hines
46 Louisville	44 G Jeremy Sheffley
45 Connecticut	13 T Garin Justice
38 Cincinnati	0 TE/FB Josh Bailey / Owen Schmitt
45 Pittsburgh	13 QB Pat White / Adam Bednarik
28 South Florida	13 TB Steve Slaton / Pernell Williams
38 Georgia ■	35 DL Craig Wilson / Warren Young
	DL Ernest Hunter / Pat Liebig
	DL Keilen Dykes
	LB Jeff Noechel /. Bobby Hathaway
	LB Jay Henry / Marc Magro
	LB Kevin McLee / Mortty Ivy
	DB Anthony Mims
	DB Dee McCann / Antonio Lewis
	DB Jahmile Addae
	DB Mike Lorello
	DB Eric Wicks

RUSHING: Slaton 205/1128y, White 131/952y, Schmitt 48/380y
PASSING: White 65-114/828y, 8TD, 57%
Bednarik 55-75/532y, 4TD, 73.3%
RECEIVING: Myles 34/536y, Reynaud 30/297y, Slaton 12/95y
SCORING: Slaton 114pts, Pat McAfee (K) 81pts, White 42pts

2006 11-2

42 Marshall	10 WR Brandon Myles
52 E. Washington	3 WR Rayshawn Bolden /Dorrell Jalloh
45 Maryland	24 WR Darius Reynaud / Tito Gonzalez
27 East Carolina	10 T Travis Garrett
42 Mississippi St.	14 G Ryan Stanchek / John Bradshaw
41 Syracuse	17 C Dan Mozes (G) / Jeremy Hines
37 Connecticut	11 G Jeremy Sheffley
34 Louisville	44 T Garin Justice
42 Cincinnati	24 TE/FB Michael Villagrana/O. Schmitt
45 Pittsburgh	27 QB Pat White / Jarrett Brown
19 South Florida	24 TB Steve Slaton
41 Rutgers	39 DL Johnny Dingle / James Ingram
38 Georgia Tech ■	35 DL Warren Young / Pat Liebig
	DL Keilen Dykes / Craig Wilson
	LB Kevin McLee
	LB Jay Henry / Marc Magro
	LB Bobby Hathaway / Reed Williams
	DB Antonio Lewis / Larry Williams
	DB Vaughn Rivers / Marke Harrison
	DB Quinton Andrews
	DB John Holmes / Ridwan Malik
	DB Eric Wicks / Charles Pugh

RUSHING: Slaton 248/1744y, White 165/1219y, Schmitt 65/351y
PASSING: White 118-179/1655y, 13TD, 65.9%
Brown 28-47/384y, 2TD, 59.6%
RECEIVING: Reynaud 39/520y, Myles 36/522y, Slaton 27/360y
SCORING: Pat McAfee (K) 113pts, Slaton & White 108pts

2007 11-2

62 W. Michigan	24 WR Darius Reynaud/Brandon Hogan
48 Marshall	23 WR Tito Gonzales / Jock Sanders (TB)
31 Maryland	14 WR Dorrell Jalloh
48 East Carolina	7 T Ryan Stanchek
13 South Florida	21 G Greg Isdaner
55 Syracuse	13 C Mike Dent
38 Mississippi St.	13 G Jake Figner (T) / Eric Rodemoyer
31 Rutgers	3 T Selvish Capers
38 Louisville	31 QB Pat White
28 Cincinnati	23 TB Steve Slaton / Noel Devine
66 Connecticut	21 FB Owen Schmidt (TE)
9 Pittsburgh	13 DL Johnny Dingle
48 Oklahoma ■	28 DL Keilan Dykes
	DL Scooter Berry / Chris Neild
	LB Marc Magro
	LB Reed Williams
	LB Mortty Ivy
	DB Antonio Lewis / Johnny Holmes
	DB Larry Williams / Vaughn Rivers
	DB Ryan Mundy
	DB Eric Wicks
	DB Quinton Andrews / Ridwan Malik

RUSHING: White 197/1335y, Slaton 211/1051y, Devine 73/627y
PASSING: White 144-216/1724y, 14TD, 66.7%
RECEIVING: Reynaud 64/733y, Slaton 26/350y, Jalloh 24/272y
SCORING: Slaton 108pts, Pat McAfee (K) 103pts, White 84pts

2008 9-4

48 Villanova	21 WR Alric Arnett
3 East Carolina	24 WR Wes Lyons / Tito Gonzalez
14 Colorado	17 WR/FB Jock Sanders / Will Johnson
27 Marshall	3 WR/TE Dorrell Jalloh / Tyler Urban
24 Rutgers	17 T Ryan Stanchek
17 Syracuse	6 G Greg Isdaner / Don Barclay
34 Auburn	17 C Mike Dent / Eric Jobe
35 Connecticut	13 G Jake Figner
23 Cincinnati	26 T Selvish Capers
35 Louisville	21 QB Pat White
15 Pittsburgh	19 RB Noel Devine
13 South Florida	7 DL Doug Slavonic / Julian Miller
31 North Carolina ■	30 DL Chris Neild / Pat Liebig
	DL Scooter Berry
	LB Mortty Ivy
	LB Anthony Leonard / Pat Lazear
	LB J.T. Thomas
	DB Ellis Lankster
	DB Brandon Hogan / Kent Richardson
	DB Robert Sands / Eain Smith
	DB Quinton Andrews
	DB Sidney Glover / Franchot Allen

RUSHING: Devine 206/1289y, White 191/974y, Sanders 48/250y
PASSING: White 180-274/1842y, 21TD, 65.7%
RECEIVING: Sanders 53/462y, Arnett 35/466y, Devine 35/185y
SCORING: Pat McAfee (K) 87pts, Sanders 54pts, White 50pts

2009 9-4

33 Liberty	20 WR Alric Arnett
35 East Carolina	20 WR Wes Lyons / Tavon Austin
30 Auburn	41 WR Jock Sanders
35 Colorado	24 T Don Barclay
34 Syracuse	13 G Josh Jenkins
24 Marshall	7 C Eric Jobe
28 Connecticut	24 G Joe Madsen
19 South Florida	30 T Selvish Capers
17 Louisville	9 TE/WR Tyler Urban / Brad Starks
21 Cincinnati	24 QB Jarrett Brown
19 Pittsburgh	16 RB Noel Devine / Ryan Clarke
24 Rutgers	21 DL Julian Miller
21 Florida State ■	33 DL Chris Neild
	DL Josh Taylor / Scooter Berry
	LB Pat Lazear
	LB Reed Williams / Anthony Leonard
	LB J.T. Thomas
	DB Brandon Hogan
	DB Keith Tandy
	DB Nate Sowers / Kent Richardson
	DB Robert Sands / Eain Smith
	DB Sidney Glover / Franchot Allen

RUSHING: Devine 241/1465y, Brown 117/466y, Clarke 60/250y
PASSING: Brown 187-296/2144y, 11TD, 63.2%
Geno Smith (QB) 32-49/309y, 1TD, 65.3%
RECEIVING: Sanders 72/688y, Arnett 43/586y, Starks 29/405y
Devine 22/177y, Lyons 20/263y
SCORING: Devine 84pts, Tyler Bitancurt (K) 80pts, Clarke 48pts

2010 9-4

31 Coastal Carolina	0 WR Tavon Austin / Brad Starks
24 Marshall	21 WR Jock Sanders / J.D. Woods
31 Maryland	17 WR Stedman Bailey / J.D. Woods
14 LSU	20 T Don Barclay / Matt Timmerman (TE)
49 UNLV	10 G Josh Jenkins / Cole Bowers
20 South Florida	6 C Joe Madsen
14 Syracuse	19 G Eric Jobe
13 Connecticut	16 T Jeff Braun
37 Cincinnati	10 TE/FB Will Johnson/ T. Urban / Ryan Clarke
17 Louisville	10 QB Geno Smith
35 Pittsburgh	10 RB Noel Devine / Shawne Alston
35 Rutgers	14 DL Scooter Berry / Bruce Irvin
7 N. Carolina St. ■	23 DL Chris Neild
	DL Julian Miller / Jorge Wright
	LB Anthony Leonard
	LB Najee Goode / Pat Lazear
	LB J.T. Thomas
	DB Brandon Hogan / Pat Miller
	DB Keith Tandy / Brodrick Jenkins
	DB Sidney Glover / Eain Smith
	DB Robert Sands
	DB Terrence Garvin

RUSHING: Devine 208/934y, Clarke 80/291y, Alston 56/248y
PASSING: Smith 241-372/2763y, 24TD, 64.8%
RECEIVING: Sanders 69/728y, Austin 58/787y, Devine 34/258y
SCORING: Tyler Bitancurt (K) 71pts, Austin 54pts, Clarke 48pts

WISCONSIN

University of Wisconsin (Founded 1849)
Madison, Wisconsin
Nickname: Badgers
Colors: Cardinal and White
Stadium: Camp Randall Stadium (1917) 80,321
Conference Affiliation: Big Ten (Charter member, 1896-present)

CAREER RUSHING YARDS	Attempts	Yards
Ron Dayne (1996-99)	1220	7125
Anthony Davis (2001-04)	908	4676
P.J. Hill (2006-08)	770	3942
Billy Marek (1972-75)	719	3709
Brent Moss (1991-94)	694	3428
Terrell Fletcher (1991-94)	614	3414
John Clay (2008-10)	629	3413
Alan Ameche (1951-54)	701	3345
Larry Emery (1983-86)	582	2979
Rufus Ferguson (1970-72)	594	2814

CAREER PASSING YARDS	Comp.-Att.	Yards
Darrell Bevell (1992-95)	646-1052	7686
John Stocco (2003-06)	534-934	7217
Brooks Bollinger (1999-02)	414-771	5627
Scott Tolzien (2008-10)	410-602	5271
Randy Wright (1981-83)	377-714	5003
Mike Samuel (1995-98)	390-711	4989
Jim Sorgi (2000-03)	288-519	4498
Tony Lowery (1987-91)	355-648	4006
Neil Graff (1969-71)	273-551	3699
Mike Howard (1983-86)	307-547	3402

CAREER RECEIVING YARDS	Catches	Yards
Lee Evans (1999-03)	175	3468
Brandon Williams (2002-05)	202	2924
Travis Beckum (2006-08)	159	2149
Al Toon (1982-84)	131	2103
Chris Chambers (1997-00)	127	2004
Tony Simmons (1994-97)	99	1991
Lee DeRamus (1991-93)	119	1974
Pat Richter (1960-62)	121	1873
Jonathan Orr (2002-05)	107	1824
Donald Hayes (1995-97)	106	1575

SEASON RUSHING YARDS	Attempts	Yards
Ron Dayne (1996)	325	2109
Ron Dayne (1999)	337	2034
Michael Bennett (1999-00)	310	1681
Brent Moss (1993)	312	1637
Brian Calhoun (2005)	348	1636

SEASON PASSING YARDS	Comp.-Att.	Yards
John Stocco (2005)	197-328	2920
Scott Tolzien (2009)	211-328	2705
Tyler Donovan (2007)	193-333	2607
Scott Tolzien (2010)	194-266	2459
Darrell Bevell (1993)	187-276	2390

SEASON RECEIVING YARDS	Catches	Yards
Lee Evans (2001)	75	1545
Lee Evans (2003)	64	1213
Brandon Williams (2005)	59	1095
Travis Beckum (2007)	75	982
Lee DeRamus (1993)	54	920

GAME RUSHING YARDS	Attempts	Yards
Ron Dayne (1996 vs. Hawaii)	36	339
Billy Marek (1974 vs. Minnesota)	43	304
Anthony Davis (2002 vs. Minnesota)	45	301

GAME PASSING YARDS	Comp.-Att.	Yards
Darrell Blevell (1993 vs. Minnesota)	31-48	423
Tyler Donovan (2007 vs. Ilinois)	27-49	392
Jim Sorgi (2003 vs. Michigan State)	16-24	380

GAME RECEIVING YARDS	Catches	Yards
Lee Evans (2003 vs. Michigan State)	10	258
Al Toon (1983 vs. Purdue)	8	252
Lee Evans (2001 vs. Michigan State)	9	228

GREATEST COACH:

Barry Alvarez did such a good job as head coach of Wisconsin from 1990 through 2005, that it is easy to forget just how low the program had fallen before his arrival. He took three squads to the Rose Bowl, winning all three games. Overall, his won-loss record was 118-73-7 and his bowl mark was an astonishing 8-3.

Before Barry? In the preceding four years the Badgers won nine games. The last time they won as many as eight games was 1962, which happens to be the final Rose Bowl appearance for the school before Barry. Before Barry, Wisconsin was a hockey school.

Alvarez applied lessons learned from his college coach, Nebraska's Bob Devaney, and the two men who hired him for college assistant jobs: Hayden Fry and Lou Holtz. It took time. Year one featured one win, against Ball State. Years two and three were better: 5-6 records for each one. But now the freshmen were seniors and better classes followed.

The next year was a special one for Wisconsin football. After sweeping through a weak September schedule, the Badgers were still below the national radar. They upped their conference record to 3-0 with a two-touchdown win at Purdue and people took notice. But then rival Minnesota booted the Badgers from the Top 20 and unbeaten ranks. With Michigan and Ohio State appearing next on the schedule, lesser Badger teams would have folded. But not this one, loaded with players dripping with character. Michigan fell 13-10 and then, after a sobering week when the school recovered from the shock of an in-stadium stampede that injured dozens, Wisconsin tied no. 3 Ohio State 14-14. A sweep of Illinois and Michigan State coupled with Ohio State's loss to Michigan allowed Wisconsin to clinch a tie for the Big Ten crown and a Rose Bowl berth. Still considered an upstart, Wisconsin proved it belonged with a 21-16 win over UCLA. The school's first-ever New Year's Day win produced its first 10-win season.

That magical season was just a beginning. Ten more bowl teams awaited, headlined by the 1998-99 teams that won 11 and 10 games respectively with Rose Bowl wins each time.

WISCONSIN'S 55 GREATEST SINCE 1953

OFFENSE

WIDE RECEIVER: Chris Chambers, Lee Evans, Al Toon, Brandon Williams
TIGHT END: Travis Beckum, Pat Richter
TACKLE: Jeff Dellenbach, Aaron Gibson, Paul Gruber, Dennis Lick, Chris McIntosh, Joe Thomas
GUARD: Chuck Belin, Bill Ferrario, Joe Rudolph
CENTER: Ken Bowman, Al Johnson, Cory Raymer
QUARTERBACK: Darrell Blevell, John Stocco
RUNNING BACK: Brian Calhoun, Anthony Davis, Ron Dayne, Billy Marek
FULLBACK: Alan Ameche

DEFENSE

END: Tom Burke, Dan Davey, Bill Gregory, Tarek Saleh, Darryl Sims
TACKLE: Wendell Bryant, Anttaj Hawthorne, Tim Krumrie, Dan Lanphear
LINEBACKER: Ken Criter, Dave Crossen, Nick Griesen, Dave Lokanc, Jim Melka, Pete Monty, Jerry Stalcup
CORNERBACK: Jamar Fletcher, Jack Ikegwuonu, Richard Johnson, Nate Odomes, Troy Vincent
SAFETY: Jason Doering, David Greenwood, Jim Leonhard

SPECIAL TEAMS

RETURN SPECIALISTS: Nick Davis, Ira Matthews
PLACE KICKER: Todd Gregoire
PUNTER: Kevin Stemke

MULTIPLE POSITIONS

CENTER-GUARD-TACKLE: Joe Panos

TWO-WAY PLAYERS

QUARTERBACK-DEFENSIVE BACK: Dale Hackbart

PERFORMANCE FORMULA: WISCONSIN'S 10 BEST SEASONS

1998	1.6309	4 of 71
1962	1.5534	5 of 70
2006	1.5368	9 of 72
1993	1.5195	11 of 70
1999	1.4824	10 of 71
1958	1.4799	8 of 70
2010	1.4673	14 of 71
1954	1.4587	10 of 69
1953	1.4273	10 of 69
2009	1.4001	17 of 71

WISCONSIN BADGERS

Year	W-L-T	AP Poll	Conference Standing	Toughest Regular Season Opponents	Coach (Record at School)	Bowl Games		
1953	6-2-1	15	3	UCLA 8-1, Illinois 7-1-1, Ohio State 6-3, Penn State 6-3	Ivy Williamson			
1954	7-2	9	2	Ohio State 9-0, Minnesota 7-2, Rice 7-3, Purdue 5-3-1	Ivy Williamson			
1955	4-5		6	Michigan State 8-1, Ohio State 7-2, Southern Cal 6-4	Ivy Williamson (41-19-4)			
1956	1-5-3		9	Iowa 8-1, Southern Cal 8-2, Minnesota 6-1-2, Michigan State 7-2	Milt Bruhn			
1957	6-3	19	4t	Ohio State 8-1, Michigan State 8-1, Iowa 7-1-1, West Virginia 7-2-1	Milt Bruhn			
1958	7-1-1	7	2	Iowa 7-1-1, Ohio State 6-1-2, Purdue 6-1-2	Milt Bruhn	Rose	8 Washington	44
1959	7-3	6	1	Northwestern 6-3, Purdue 5-2-2, Illinois 5-3-1	Milt Bruhn			
1960	4-5		9	Iowa 8-1, Minnesota 8-1, Ohio State 7-2	Milt Bruhn			
1961	6-3		5	Ohio State 8-0-1, Michigan State 7-2, Utah 6-4	Milt Bruhn	Rose	37 Southern California	42
1962	8-2	2	1	Northwestern 7-2, Minnesota 6-2-1, Ohio State 6-3	Milt Bruhn			
1963	5-4		5	Illinois 7-1-1, Michigan State 6-2-1, Ohio State 5-3-1	Milt Bruhn			
1964	3-6		7t	Notre Dame 9-1, Ohio State 7-2, Purdue 6-3, Illinois 6-3	Milt Bruhn			
1965	2-7-1		7t	Nebraska 10-0, Ohio State 7-2, Southern Cal 7-2-1, Purdue 7-2-1	Milt Bruhn			
1966	3-6-1		7	Nebraska 9-1, Purdue 8-2, Southern Cal 7-3	Milt Bruhn (52-45-6)			
1967	0-9-1		9t	Indiana 9-1, Arizona State 8-2, Minnesota 8-2, Ohio State 6-3	John Coatta			
1968	0-10		10	Ohio State 9-0, Michigan 8-2, Arizona State 8-2	John Coatta			
1969	3-7		5t	Ohio State 8-1, UCLA 8-1-1, Michigan 8-2	John Coatta (3-26-1)			
1970	4-5-1		5t	Ohio State 9-0, Michigan 9-1, Penn State 7-3, Oklahoma 7-4	John Jardine			
1971	4-6-1		6t	Louisiana State 8-3, Northwestern 7-4, Ohio State 6-4	John Jardine			
1972	4-7		9	Ohio State 9-1-1, Louisiana State 9-1-1, Purdue 6-5	John Jardine			
1973	4-7		8	Ohio State 9-0-1, Michigan 10-0-1, Nebraska 8-2-1, Minnesota 7-4	John Jardine			
1974	7-4		4	Ohio State 10-1, Michigan 10-1, Nebraska 8-3	John Jardine			
1975	4-6-1		6	Ohio State 10-1, Michigan 8-1-2, Minnesota 6-5	John Jardine			
1976	5-6		7t	Michigan 10-1, Ohio State 8-2-1, Indiana 5-6	John Jardine			
1977	5-6		8	Michigan 10-1, Ohio State 9-2, Michigan State 7-3-1, Minnesota 7-4	John Jardine (37-47-3)			
1978	5-4-2		6	Michigan 10-1, Michigan State 8-3, Purdue 7-2-1, Ohio State 7-3-1	Dave McClain			
1979	4-7		7t	Ohio State 11-0, Purdue 9-2, Michigan 8-3, Indiana 7-4	Dave McClain			
1980	4-7		6t	Michigan 9-2, Ohio State 9-2, BYU 11-1, UCLA 9-2	Dave McClain	Garden State	21 Tennessee	28
1981	7-5		3t	Iowa 8-3, Michigan 8-3, Ohio State 8-3, UCLA 7-3-1	Dave McClain	Independence	14 Kansas State	3
1982	7-5		4	UCLA 9-1-1, Ohio State 8-3, Michigan 8-3, Iowa 7-4, Indiana 7-4	Dave McClain			
1983	7-4		4	Illinois 10-1, Michigan 9-2, Iowa 9-2, Ohio State 8-3	Dave McClain			
1984	7-4-1		4	Ohio State 9-2, Purdue 7-4, Iowa 7-4-1	Dave McClain (46-42-3)	Hall of Fame	19 Kentucky	20
1985	5-6		8	Iowa 10-1, Michigan 9-1-1, Ohio State 8-3	Jim Hilles (3-9)			
1986	3-9		8t	Michigan 10-1, Ohio State 8-3, Iowa 8-3	Don Morton			
1987	3-8		10	Iowa 9-3, Michigan State 8-2-1, Michigan 7-4	Don Morton			
1988	1-10		9t	Miami 10-1, Michigan 8-2-1, Iowa 6-3-3	Don Morton			
1989	2-9		9	Miami 10-1, Michigan 10-1, Illinois 9-2, Michigan State 7-4	Don Morton (6-27)			
1990	1-10		10	Michigan 8-3, Iowa 8-3, Ohio State 7-3-1, Indiana 8-3	Barry Alvarez			
1991	5-6		8t	Iowa 10-1, Ohio State 8-3, Indiana 6-4-1	Barry Alvarez			
1992	5-6		6t	Washington 9-2, Ohio State 8-2-1	Barry Alvarez			
1993	10-1-1	6	1t	Ohio State 9-1-1, Indiana 8-3, Michigan 7-4	Barry Alvarez	Rose	21 UCLA	16
1994	8-3-1		3	Colorado 10-1, Ohio State 9-3, Michigan 8-3	Barry Alvarez	Hall of Fame	34 Duke	20
1995	4-5-2		7t	Ohio State 11-1, Northwestern 10-1, Colorado 9-2, Penn State 8-3	Barry Alvarez	Copper	38 Utah	10
1996	8-5		7	Penn State 10-2, Ohio State 10-1, Northwestern 9-2, Iowa 8-3	Barry Alvarez	Outback	6 Georgia	33
1997	8-5		5	Michigan 11-0, Penn State 9-2, Syracuse 9-3, Purdue 8-3	Barry Alvarez	Rose	38 UCLA	31
1998	11-1	6	1t	Michigan 9-3, Penn State 8-3, Purdue 8-4	Barry Alvarez	Rose	17 Stanford	9
1999	10-2	4	1	Michigan 9-2, Michigan State 9-2, Minnesota 8-3, Purdue 7-4	Barry Alvarez	Sun	21 UCLA	20
2000	9-4	23	5t	Oregon 9-2, Purdue 8-3, Ohio State 8-3, Northwestern 8-3	Barry Alvarez			
2001	5-7		8t	Illinois 10-1, Oregon 10-1, Michigan 8-3	Barry Alvarez	Alamo	31 Colorado	28
2002	8-6		8t	Ohio State 13-0, Iowa 11-1, Michigan 9-3, West Virginia 9-3	Barry Alvarez	Music City	14 Auburn	28
2003	7-6		7t	Ohio State 10-2, Purdue 9-3, Minnesota 9-3, West Virginia 8-4	Barry Alvarez	Outback	21 Georgia	24
2004	9-3	17	3	Iowa 9-2, Purdue 7-4, Ohio State 7-3	Barry Alvarez (118-73-7)	Capital One	24 Auburn	10
2005	10-3	15	3t	Penn State 10-1, Michigan 7-4, Northwestern 7-4, Minnesota 7-4	Bret Bielema	Capital One	17 Arkansas	14
2006	12-1	7	2t	Michigan 11-1, Penn State 8-4, Purdue 8-5, Iowa 6-6	Bret Bielema	Outback	17 Tennessee	21
2007	9-4	24	4	Ilinois 9-3, Penn State 8-4, Ohio State 11-1, Michigan 8-4	Bret Bielema	Champs Sports	13 Florida State	42
2008	7-6		6t	Ohio State 10-2, Penn State 11-1, Iowa 8-4, Michigan State 9-3	Bret Bielema	Champs Sports	20 Miami	13
2009	10-3	16	4t	Ohio State 10-2, Iowa 10-2, Northwestern 8-4	Bret Bielema (49-16)	Rose	19 TCU	21
2010	11-2	7	1t	Michigan State 11-1, Ohio State 11-1, Iowa 7-5				

TOTAL: 331-294-18 .5288 (38 of 70)

Bowl Games since 1953: 11-10 .5238 (31 of 70)

GREATEST TEAM SINCE 1953: Milt Bruhn's 1962 Badgers won the Big Ten in a dogfight over Minnesota, Northwestern and Ohio State and then produced a thrilling rally in the Rose Bowl before falling to the top-ranked Southern California Trojans. That match-up was the first between the two top-ranked teams since 1946, while Wisconsin also played the no. 1 team earlier in the season in Northwestern, a team they routed 37-6.

1953 6-2-1

20 Penn State	0 E Norb Esser
13 Marquette	11 T Windy Gulseth
0 UCLA	13 G Clarence Stensby / John Dixon
28 Purdue	19 C Gary Messner / Bill McNamara
19 Ohio State	20 G Norm Amudsen / Don Ursin
10 Iowa	7 T Mark Hoegh
34 Northwestern	13 E Ron Locklin / James Temp
34 Illinois	7 QB Jim Miller / Gus Vergetis
21 Minnesota	21 HB Clary Bratt/Rog Dornburg/Harland Carl
	HB Bob Gingrass / Jerry Witt
	FB Alan Ameche

RUSHING: Ameche 165/801y, Carl 32/222y, Witt 25/207y
PASSING: Miller 36-69/683y, 6TD, 52.2%
RECEIVING: Esser 19/238y, Locklin 13/209y, Carl 7/164y
SCORING: Miller 36pts, Ameche & Carl 30pts

1954 7-2

52 Marquette	14 E Jim Temp / Jim Reinke
6 Michigan State	0 T Wells Gray / Jim Grosklaus
13 Rice	7 G Clarence Stensby
20 Purdue	6 C Gary Messner / Bill McNamara
14 Ohio State	31 G Bob Konovsky
7 Iowa	13 T John Dittrich
34 Northwestern	13 E Ron Locklin / Dave Howard
27 Illinois	14 QB Jim Miller / Jim Haluska
27 Minnesota	0 HB Bob Gingrass / Pat Levenhagen
	HB Clary Bratt / Billy Lowe
	FB Alan Ameche

RUSHING: Ameche 146/641y, Miller 74/261y, Bratt 44/226y
PASSING: Miller 46-88/608y, 5TD, 52.3%
RECEIVING: Locklin 22/218y, Temp 13/181y, Howard 11/176y
SCORING: Ameche 54pts, Bratt 30pts, Gingrass 26pts

1955 4-5

28 Marquette	14 E Dick Kolian
37 Iowa	14 T John Dittrich / Bill Hertel
9 Purdue	0 G Wells Gray / Mike Baggot
21 Southern Cal	33 C Bill McNamara / Tom Rabas
16 Ohio State	26 G Paul Shwaiko
0 Michigan State	27 T Bob Konovsky / Martin Booher
41 Northwestern	14 E Jim Reinke / Dave Howard
14 Illinois	17 QB Jim Miller / Jim Haluska
6 Minnesota	21 HB Pat Levenhagen / Danny Lewis
	HB Billy Lowe / John Bridgeman
	FB Charlie Thomas / Glenn Bestor

RUSHING: Thomas 98/477y, Levenhagen 73/349y, Lowe 65/320y
PASSING: Haluska 71-132/1036y, 6TD, 53.8%
RECEIVING: Levenhagen 17/178y, Howard 15/273y,
Kolian 15/205y

SCORING: Thomas 36pts, Paul Shwaiko (K) 23pts, 2 tied w/ 18pts

1956 1-5-3

41 Marquette	0 E Dave Kocourek / Jim Reinke
6 Southern Cal	13 T John Heineke / Jerry Cvengros
7 Iowa	13 G Steve Ambrose
6 Purdue	6 C Art Bloedorn / Dick Teteak
0 Ohio State	21 G Bill Gehler / Martin Morris
0 Michigan State	33 T Martin Booher
7 Northwestern	17 E Dave Howard / Dick Kolian
13 Illinois	13 QB Sid Williams / Ron Carlson
13 Minnesota	13 HB Danny Lewis / Earl Hagberg
	HB Billy Lowe / John Bridgeman
	FB Pat Levenhagen / Glenn Bestor

RUSHING: Lewis 100/554y, Bridgeman 75/337y, Lowe 61/61/216y
PASSING: Williams 10-19/216y, 0TD, 52.5%
RECEIVING: Howard 16/247y, Bridgeman 6/58y, Lewis 3/52y
SCORING: Lewis, Lowe & Melvin 18pts

1957 6-3

60 Marquette	6 E Dave Kocourek / Jim Holmes
45 West Virginia	13 T Dan Lanphear / Lowell Jenkins
23 Purdue	14 G Bill Gehler
7 Iowa	21 C Dick Teteak / Art Bloehorn
13 Ohio State	16 G Jerry Stalcup / Jim Fraser
7 Michigan State	21 T Karl Holzwarth / Jim Heineke
41 Northwestern	12 E Earl Hill / Tom Peters
24 Illinois	13 QB Sid Williams / Dale Hackbart
14 Minnesota	6 HB Danny Lewis / Ron Steiner
	HB Eddie Hart / Bob Altmann
	FB Jon Hobbs

RUSHING: Lewis 95/611y, Hackbart 52/319y, Steiner 34/256y
PASSING: Williams 25-54/457y, 4TD, 46.3%
RECEIVING: Lewis 12/171y, Hill 11/197y
SCORING: Lewis & Hackbart 36pts, Williams 25pts

1958 7-1-1

20 Miami	0 E Dave Kocourek / Jim Holmes
50 Marquette	0 T Dan Lanphear / Lowell Jenkins
31 Purdue	6 G Jim Fraser / Paul Shwaiko
9 Iowa	20 C Dick Teteak
7 Ohio State	7 G Jerry Stalcup
9 Michigan State	7 T Jim Heineke
17 Northwestern	13 E Earl Hill / Henry Derleth
31 Illinois	12 QB Dale Hackbart / Sid Williams
27 Minnesota	12 HB Ron Steiner /Bob Altmann /Bill Hobbs
	HB Bob Zeman / Eddie Hart
	FB Jon Hobbs / Tom Wiesner

RUSHING: Hobbs 117/401y, Hackbart 101/391y, Steiner 42/239y
PASSING: Hackbart 46-99/641y, 4TD, 46.5%
RECEIVING: Steiner 11/171y, Kocourek 9/119y
SCORING: Hackbart 56pts, Hobbs 34pts, Hart 24pts

1959 7-3

16 Stanford	14 E Allan Schoonover / Jim Holmes
44 Marquette	6 T Dan Lanphear
0 Purdue	21 G Ron Perkins / Don Schade
25 Iowa	16 C Bob Nelson
12 Ohio State	3 G Jerry Stalcup
19 Michigan	10 T Jim Heineke / Terry Huxhold
24 Northwestern	19 E Henry Derleth
6 Illinois	9 QB Dale Hackbart / Jim Bakken
11 Minnesota	7 HB Bill Hobbs / Ron Steiner
8 Washington■	44 HB Bob Zeman / Bob Altmann
	FB Tom Wiesner / Eddie Hart

RUSHING: Hackbart 103/387y, Hart 88/318y, Wiesner 89/311y
PASSING: Hackbart 51-108/734y, 2TD, 47.2%
RECEIVING: Derleth 15/217y, Schoonover 10/290y
SCORING: Hackbart 42pts,Karl Holzwarth (K) 31pts,Wiesner 30pts

1960 4-5

24 Stanford	7 E Ron Carlson / Ron Staley
35 Marquette	6 T Terry Huxhold / Dick Grimm
24 Purdue	13 G Don Schade / Dale Mathews
21 Iowa	28 C John Gotta
7 Ohio State	34 G Gerry Kulcinski
16 Michigan	13 T Ron Perkins / Brian Moore
0 Northwestern	21 E Pat Richter / Henry Derleth
14 Illinois	35 QB Ron Miller / Jim Bakken
7 Minnesota	26 HB Merritt Norvell / Elmars Ezerins
	HB Erv Kunesh / Gerry Nena
	FB Tom Weisner / Gary Kroner

RUSHING: Wiesner 87/374y, Norvell 61/241y
PASSING: Miller 97-188/1351y, 8TD, 51.6%
RECEIVING: Richter 25/362y, Wiesner 20/356y, Staley 19/215y
SCORING: Kunesh (HB-K) 22pts, Norvell, Staley & Miller 18pts

1961 6-3

7 Utah	0 E Dave Bichler / Ron Staley
0 Michigan State	20 T Dale Mathews / Roger Pillath
6 Indiana	3 G Don VanderVelden / Dion Kempthorne
23 Oregon State	20 C Dick Baer / Ken Bowman
15 Iowa	47 G Jim Schenk / Don Schade
21 Ohio State	30 T Brian Moore / Jim Jax
29 Northwestern	10 E Pat Richter / Ron Carlson
55 Illinois	7 QB Ron Miller / Jim Bakken
23 Minnesota	21 HB Bill Smith / Lou Holland
	HB Jim Nettles / Merritt Norvell
	FB Jim Purnell / Gary Kroner

RUSHING: Nettles 39/213y, Holland 62/177y, Smith 43/153y
PASSING: Miller 104-198/1487y, 11TD, 52.6%
RECEIVING: Richter 47/817y, Staley 18/234y, Holland 9/119y
SCORING: Richter 48pts, Jim Bakken (QB-K) 34pts, Holland 24pts

1962 8-2

69 New Mexico St.	13 E Ron Carlson / Ron Leafblad
30 Indiana	6 T Roger Pillath / Lee Bernet
17 Notre Dame	8 G Dion Kempthorne / Mike Gross
42 Iowa	14 C Ken Bowman / Joe Heckl
7 Ohio State	14 G Steve Underwood
34 Michigan	12 T Andy Wojdula / Roger Jacobazzi
37 Northwestern	6 E Pat Richter / Larry Howard (DE)
35 Illinois	6 QB Ron Vander Kelen
14 Minnesota	9 HB Lou Holland / Carl Silvestri
37 Southern Cal■	42 HB Bill Smith / Ron Smith /Jim Nettles (DB)
	FB Ralph Kurek / Rick Reichardt (DB)

RUSHING: Kurek 67/367y, Smith 50/277y, Holland 49/273y
PASSING: Vander Kelen 124-216/1582y, 14TD, 57.4%
RECEIVING: Richter 49/694y, Holland 21/219y, Kroner 13/179y
SCORING: Holland 72pts, Kroner (HB-K) 59pts,
Smith & Kurek 42pts

1963 5-4

41 W. Michigan	0 E Bobby Johnson / Jimmy Jones
14 Notre Dame	9 T Roger Pillath / Lee Bernet
38 Purdue	20 G Jon Hohman / Bob Pickens
10 Iowa	7 C Ken Bowman / Joe Heckl
10 Ohio State	13 G Mike Gross / Ray Marcin
13 Michigan State	30 T Roger Jacobazzi / Andy Wojdula
17 Northwestern	14 E Ron Lealblad / Ralph Farmer
7 Illinois	17 QB Hal Brandt / Dave Fronek
0 Minnesota	14 HB Lou Holland / Carl Silvestri
	HB Rick Reichardt / Jim Nettles
	FB Ralph Kurek / Jim Purnell

RUSHING: Holland 88/511y, Silvestri 72/351y, Kurek 84/262y
PASSING: Brandt 86-181/1006y, 6TD, 47.5%
RECEIVING: Reichardt 26/383y, Jones 22/379y, Holland 14/100y
SCORING: Holland 42pts, Dave Fronek (K) 28pts,
Brandt & Jones 18pts

1964 3-6

17 Kansas State	7 E Ron Leafblad
7 Notre Dame	31 T Lee Bernet
7 Purdue	28 G Jon Hohman
31 Iowa	21 C Ernie Von Heimburg
3 Ohio State	28 G Charles Currier
6 Michigan State	22 T Albert Piraino / Mike Sachen
13 Northwestern	17 E Ralph Farmer / Joel Jenson
0 Illinois	29 QB Harold Brandt
14 Minnesota	7 WB Jimmy Jones (E) / Carl Silvestri
	HB Ron Smith / Dave Neubauer
	FB Ralph Kurek
	DL Rodger Alberts / Larry Howard
	DL Mike London
	DL Steve Young / Bob Monk
	DL Roger Jacobazzi
	DL Eric Rice / William Maselter
	LB Bob Richter / Duncan Hoffman
	LB Tom Brigham
	LB Carl Silvestri
	DB James Grudzinski
	DB Gary Pinnow / Ralph Kurek
	DB Dave Fronek

RUSHING: Smith 101/438y, Kurek 103/343y, Silvestri 45/229y
PASSING: Brandt 85-176/1059y, 4TD, 48.3%
RECEIVING: Jones 34/529y, Leafblad 15/139y, Smith 13/114y
SCORING: Jones 24pts, Kurek 18pts, Jesse Kaye (K) 17pts

1965 2-7-1

0 Colorado	0 WR Louis Jung
6 Southern Cal	26 WR Dennis Lager
16 Iowa	13 T Phil Sobocinski
0 Nebraska	37 G John Roedel
21 Northwestern	7 C Tony Loukas
10 Ohio State	20 G Richard LaCroix
14 Michigan	50 T Charles Currier
7 Purdue	45 TE Bill Fritz
0 Illinois	51 QB Chuck Burt
7 Minnesota	42 HB Jesse Kaye / Tom Schinke
	FB Tom Jankowski
	DL Rodger Alberts / Warren Dyer
	DL Tom Domres
	DL Michael London
	DL Bill Maselter
	DL Eric Rice
	LB Bob Richter
	LB Ray Marcin
	DB Bob Grossman
	DB Tom Brigham
	DB Dave Fronek
	DB Dave Berg

RUSHING: Jankowski 86/271y, Schinke 39/112y, Kaye 48/111y
PASSING: Burt 121-235/1143y, 5TD, 51.5%
RECEIVING: Lager 39/396y, Jung 32/326y, Fritz 31/271y
SCORING: Fritz 24pts, Jung & Lager 12pts

1966 3-6-1

20 Iowa State	10 WR Bill Yanakos / Vic Janule
3 Southern Cal	38 WR Bill Fritz
7 Iowa	0 T Tony Loukas
3 Nebraska	31 G Phil Peterson
3 Northwestern	5 C Wally Schoessow
13 Ohio State	24 G Richard LaCroix / John Brockett
17 Michigan	28 T Phil Sobocinski
0 Purdue	23 TE Tom McCauley
14 Illinois	49 QB John Boyajian / John Ryan
7 Minnesota	6 HB Lynn Buss / John K. Wood
	FB Wayne Todd
	DL Warren Dyer
	DL Tom Domres
	DL Bill Grisley / Ed Hoffman
	DL Wayne Kostka
	DL Eric Rice
	LB Bob Richter
	LB Sam Wheeler
	DB Dave Berg
	DB Tom Schinke
	DB Gary Reineck
	DB Mike Cavill

RUSHING: Todd 128/480y, Wood 49/138y, Buss 41/118y
PASSING: Boyajian 64-129/863y, 3TD, 49.6%
  Ryan 43-98/489y, 3TD, 43.9%
RECEIVING: McCauley 46/689y, Fritz 24/290y, Yanakos 14/126y
SCORING: Schinke (DB-K) 31pts, McCauley 18pts, Todd 14pts

1967 0-9-1

0 Washington	17 WR Mel Reddick
16 Arizona State	42 WR Tom McCauley
7 Michigan State	35 T Brandt Jackson
11 Pittsburgh	13 G Don Murphy
21 Iowa	21 C Rex Blake
13 Northwestern	17 G Wally Schoessow
9 Indiana	14 T Ed Hoffman
15 Ohio State	17 TE Bill Fritz
14 Michigan	27 QB John Boyajian / John Ryan
14 Minnesota	21 HB John Smith / Dick Schumitsch
	FB Wayne Todd
	DL Wayne Tietz
	DL Bill Grisley / Don Bliss
	DL Lynn Buss
	DL Tom Domres
	DL Len Fields / Gary Swalve
	LB Ken Criter
	LB Sam Wheeler
	DB Mike Cavill
	DB Walter Ridlon
	DB Mel Walker
	DB Gary Reineck

RUSHING: Smith 96/362y, Todd 55/249y, Schumitsch 54/220y
PASSING: Boyajian 79-152/966y, 3TD, 51.9%
RECEIVING: Reddick 42/524y, McCauley 37/525y, Fritz 27/248y
SCORING: Tom Schinke (K) 26pts, Ryan 24pts, Boyajian 18pts

1968 0-10

7 Arizona State	55 WR Mel Reddick / Bill Yanakos
17 Washington	21 T Brandt Jackson
0 Michigan State	39 G Wally Schoessow
0 Utah State	20 C Karl Rudat
0 Iowa	41 G Don Murphy
10 Northwestern	13 T Ed Hoffman
20 Indiana	21 TE Jim Mearlon
8 Ohio State	43 QB John Ryan
9 Michigan	34 WB Stu Voight
15 Minnesota	23 HB John Smith / Joe Dawkins
	FB Wayne Todd
	DL Lynn Buss
	DL Jim DeLisle
	DL Bill Gregory
	DL Gary Buss
	LB Chuck Winfrey
	LB Ken Criter
	LB Dick Hyland
	LB Ed Albright
	DB Mike Cavill
	DB Tom McCauley
	DB Gary Reineck

RUSHING: Todd 100/364y, Smith 100/339y, Dawkins 59/186y
PASSING: Ryan 84-202/855y, 3TD, 41.6%
RECEIVING: Reddick 34/375y, Voight 18/167y, Yanakos 12/78y
SCORING: Ryan 24pts, Voight 20pts, James Johnson (K) 9pts

1969 3-7

21 Oklahoma	48 WR Ike Isom
23 UCLA	34 WR Mel Reddick
7 Syracuse	43 T Elbert Walker / Roger Jaeger
23 Iowa	17 G Mike Musha
7 Northwestern	27 C Jim Fedenia / Jim Nowak
36 Indiana	34 G Brad Monroe
7 Michigan	35 T Mike McClish
7 Ohio State	62 TE Stu Voight
55 Illinois	14 QB Neil Graff
10 Minnesota	35 HB Joe Dawkins / Dan Crooks
	FB Alan Thompson
	DL Gary Buss
	DL Jim DeLisle
	DL Ed Albright
	DL Bill Gregory
	DL Rudy Schmidt
	LB Chuck Winfrey
	LB Harry Alford
	DB Nathaniel Butler / Lee Wilder
	DB Neovia Greyer
	DB Dick Hyland
	DB Pete Higgins / Bill Yarbrough

RUSHING: Thompson 224/907y, Dawkins 129/612y,
  Crooks 55/229y
PASSING: Graff 93-191/1086y, 7TD, 48.7%
RECEIVING: Voight 39/439y, Reddick 37/421y, Isom 14/178y
SCORING: Thompson 54pts, Roger Jaeger (K) 46pts

1970 4-5-1

7 Oklahoma	21 WR Terry Whittaker
14 TCU	14 WR Albert Hannah
29 Penn State	16 T Elbert Walker
14 Iowa	24 G Dennis Stephenson
14 Northwestern	24 C Jim Fedenia
30 Indiana	12 G Keith Nosbusch
15 Michigan	29 T Roger Jaeger
7 Ohio State	24 TE Larry Mialik
29 Illinois	17 QB Neil Graff
39 Minnesota	14 TB Rufus Ferguson
	FB Alan Thompson
	DL Bill Gregory
	DL Jim DeLisle
	DL Mike Mayer
	DL Ted Jefferson
	LB Dave Lokanc
	LB Gary Buss
	LB Chuck Winfrey
	DB Dan Crooks
	DB Nate Butler
	DB Neovia Greyer
	DB Ron Buss

RUSHING: Ferguson 130/588y, Thompson 124/455y,
  Graff 161/248y
PASSING: Graff 83-174/1313y, 11TD, 47.7%
RECEIVING: Mialik 33/702y, Whittaker 15/242y, Hannah 10/156y
SCORING: Mialik 42pts, Ferguson 36pts, Thompson 32pts

1971 4-6-1

31 N. Illinois	0 WR Terry Whittaker / Tim Klosek
20 Syracuse	20 WR Albert Hannah
28 LSU	38 T Elbert Walker
11 Northwestern	24 G Bob Braun
35 Indiana	29 C Mike Webster
31 Michigan State	28 G Roger Jaeger
6 Ohio State	31 T Keith Nosbusch
16 Iowa	20 TE Tom Lonnberg / Larry Mialik
14 Purdue	10 QB Neil Graff
27 Illinois	35 TB Rufus Ferguson
21 Minnesota	23 FB Alan Thompson
	DL Mike Seifert
	DL Jim Schymanski
	DL Bob Storck
	DL Bill Poindexter
	DL Ed Albright
	LB Dave Lokanc
	LB Todd Nordwig
	DB Chris Davis
	DB Greg Johnson
	DB Neovia Greyer
	DB Ron Buss

RUSHING: Ferguson 249/1222y, Thompson 124/643y,
  Graff 77/186y
PASSING: Graff 97-186/1300y, 5TD, 52.2%
RECEIVING: Hannah 39/608y, Klosek 25/439y, Lonnberg 16/213y
SCORING: Ferguson 80pts, Thompson 50pts,
  Roger Jaeger (K) 36pts

1972 4-7

31 N. Illinois	7 WR Jeff Mack
31 Syracuse	7 WR Mike Haas
7 LSU	27 T Keith Nosbusch / Charles Deerwester
21 Northwestern	14 G Mike Becker
7 Indiana	33 C Mike Webster
0 Michigan State	31 G Dennis Manic
20 Ohio State	28 T Dennis Lick / Duane Johnson
16 Iowa	14 TE Jack Novak
6 Purdue	27 QB Rudy Steiner
7 Illinois	27 TB Rufus Ferguson / Tim Austin
6 Minnesota	14 FB Charles Richardson / Gary Lund
	DL Bob Storck / Angelo Messina
	DL Jim Schymanski
	DL Mike Jenkins / Mark Levenhagen
	DL Mike Seifert
	LB Ed Bosold / Mark Zakula
	LB Dave Lokanc
	LB Rick Jakious
	DB Dan Baron
	DB Chris Davis
	DB Ron Buss
	DB Randy Safranek

RUSHING: Ferguson 215/1004y, Mack 68/286y,
  Richardson 63/266y
PASSING: Steiner 62-150/1080y, 9TD, 41.3%
RECEIVING: Mack 27/528y, Novak 20/352y, Haas 7/146y
SCORING: Ferguson 42pts, Mack 36pts, Richard Barrios (K) 30pts

1973 4-7

13 Purdue	14 WR Jeff Mack
25 Colorado	28 WR Art Sanger / Rod Rhodes
16 Nebraska	20 T Duane Johnson
37 Wyoming	28 G Bob Braun
0 Ohio State	24 C Mike Webster
6 Michigan	35 G Dennis Manic
31 Indiana	7 T Dennis Lick
0 Michigan State	21 TE Jack Novak
35 Iowa	7 QB Gregg Bohlig
36 Northwestern	34 TB Bill Marek
17 Minnesota	19 FB Ken Starch
	DL Mike Vesperman
	DL Jim Schymanski
	DL Mike Jenkins / Brian Harney
	DL Gary Dickert
	DL Mark Zakula
	LB Ed Bosold
	LB Rick Jakious
	DB Al Peabody
	DB Chris Davis
	DB Terry Buss
	DB Mark Cullen

RUSHING: Marek 241/1207y, Starch 117/632y,
  Selvie Washington (RB) 66/269
PASSING: Bohlig 78-172/1711y, 8TD, 45.3%
RECEIVING: Mack 14/227y, Novak 13/282y, Rhodes 13/230y
SCORING: Marek 84pts, Washington 26pts, Mack 24pts

1974 7-4

28 Purdue	14 WR Art Sanger
21 Nebraska	20 WR Jeff Mack
21 Colorado	24 T Dennis Lick / John Reimer
59 Missouri	20 G Rich Kocek
7 Ohio State	52 C Joe Norwick
20 Michigan	24 G Terry Stieve
35 Indiana	25 T Duane Johnson
21 Michigan State	28 TE Jack Novak
28 Iowa	15 QB Gregg Bohlig
52 Northwestern	7 TB Bill Marek / Mike Morgan
49 Minnesota	14 FB Ken Starch
	DL Mike Vesperman / Randy Frokjer
	DL Gary Dickert / Andrew Michuda
	DL Mike Jenkins
	DL John Rasmussen
	DL Mark Zakula
	LB John Zimmerman / Jim Franz
	LB Rick Jakious
	DB Ken Simmons / Greg Lewis
	DB Al Peabody
	DB Steve Wagner
	DB Terry Buss

RUSHING: Marek 205/1215y, Starch 110/637y, Morgan 85/461y
PASSING: Bohlig 79-143/1212y, 8TD, 55.3%
RECEIVING: Sanger 18/236y, Mack 16/353y, Novak 16/331y
SCORING: Marek 114pts, Vince Lamia (K) 49pts, Morgan 48pts

1975 4-6-1

6 Michigan	23 WR Ray Bailey / Randy Rose
48 South Dakota	7 WR Ira Mathews
21 Missouri	28 T Dennis Lick
7 Kansas	41 G Terry Lyons
17 Purdue	14 C Joe Norwick
0 Ohio State	56 G Terry Stieve
17 Northwestern	14 T John Reimer
18 Illinois	9 TE Ron Egloff
28 Iowa	45 QB Mike Carroll
9 Indiana	9 TB Bill Marek
3 Minnesota	24 FB Ken Starch
	DL Pat Collins
	DL Dave Anderson / John Rasmussen
	DL Mike Grice
	DL Andrew Michuda / Bob Czechowicz
	DL Dennis Stejskal
	LB Jim Franz / John Zimmerman
	LB Mike Kelly
	DB Terry Buss
	DB Ken Simmons
	DB Steve Wagner
	DB Greg Lewis

RUSHING: Marek 272/1281y, Starch 94/392y,
Larry Canada (TB) 50/257y
PASSING: Carroll 58-123/708y, 0TD, 47.2%
RECEIVING: Bailey 18/223y, Marek 10/113y, Rose 9/137y
SCORING: Marek 80pts, Vince Lamia (K) 37pts,
Ronnie Pollard (TB) 18pts

1976 5-6

27 Michigan	40 WR David Charles
45 North Dakota	9 T Steve Lick
35 Washington St.	26 G Brad Jackomino / Dave Krall
24 Kansas	34 C Jim Moore
16 Purdue	18 G Terry Lyons
20 Ohio State	30 T Tom Kaltenberg
28 Northwestern	25 TE Ron Egloff
25 Illinois	31 QB Mike Carroll
38 Iowa	21 HB Mike Morgan / Ronnie Pollard
14 Indiana	15 HB Larry Canada
26 Minnesota	17 FB Ira Matthews
	DL Dennis Stejskal
	DL Andrew Michuda
	DL Dan Relich / Steve DiSalvo
	DL John Rasmussen
	DL Pat Collins
	LB Dave Crossen
	LB Tim Halleran
	DB Lawrence Johnson
	DB Dan Schieble
	DB Scott Erdmann
	DB Greg Gordon

RUSHING: Canada 221/993y, Matthews 106/535y,
Morgan 37/231y
PASSING: Carroll 132-262/1627y, 13TD, 50.4%
RECEIVING: Charles 34/449y, Egloff 20/308y, Matthews 19/238y
SCORING: Vince Lamia (K) 72pts, Matthews 60pts, Canada 36pts

1977 5-6

30 Indiana	14 WR David Charles
14 N. Illinois	3 T Steve Lick
22 Oregon	10 G Brad Jackomino
19 Northwestern	7 C Jim Moore
26 Illinois	0 G Dave Krall
0 Michigan	56 T Tom Kaltenberg / Ray Snell
7 Michigan State	9 TE Greg Barber
0 Ohio State	42 QB Anthony Dudley / Charles Green
0 Purdue	22 HB Ira Matthews / Terry Breuscher
8 Iowa	24 HB Mike Morgan
7 Minnesota	13 FB Tim Halleran
	DL Dave Ahrens
	DL Tom Schremp
	DL Dan Relich
	DL Bob Czechowicz
	DL Dennis Stejskal
	LB Dave Crossen
	LB Lee Washington
	DB Scott Erdmann
	DB Lawrence Johnson
	DB Dan Schieble
	DB Greg Gordon

RUSHING: Morgan 124/478y, Matthews 73/351y,
Breuscher 81/347y
PASSING: Dudley 64-127/877y, 2TD, 50.4%
RECEIVING: Charles 29/437y, Breuscher 28/343y,
Matthews 10/147y
SCORING: Steve Veith (K) 39pts, Morgan, Halleran &
Charles 18pts

1978 5-4-2

7 Richmond	6 WR David Charles
28 Northwestern	7 WR Wayne Souza
22 Oregon	19 T Henry Addy
34 Indiana	7 G Brad Jackomino
20 Illinois	20 C Jim Moore
0 Michigan	42 G Dave Krall
2 Michigan State	55 T Ray Snell
14 Ohio State	49 TE Ray Sydnor
24 Purdue	24 QB Mike Kalasmiki /John Josten /C. Green
24 Iowa	38 TB Ira Matthews
48 Minnesota	10 FB Tom Stauss
	DL Dave Ahrens
	DL Tom Schremp
	DL Dan Relich
	DL Armand Cabral
	DL Guy Boliaux / Don Lorenz
	LB Dave Crossen
	LB Kurt Holm / Dennis Christenson
	DB Lawrence Johnson
	DB Greg Gordon
	DB Scott Erdmann / George Welch
	DB Dan Schieble

RUSHING: Matthews 130/654y, Stauss 82/485y, Green 75/247y
PASSING: Kalasmiki 107-231/1378y, 12TD, 46.4%
RECEIVING: Charles 38/573y, Sydnor 27/392y, Souza 24/323y
SCORING: Matthews 42pts, Charles 32pts, Steve Veith (K) 30pts

1979 4-7

20 Purdue	41 WR Tim Stracka
38 Air Force	0 WR Tom Stauss
12 UCLA	37 T Ray Snell
17 San Diego State	24 G Bob Winckler / Leo Joyce
0 Indiana	3 C Joe Rothbauer
38 Michigan State	29 G Jim Martine
0 Ohio State	59 T Jerome Doerger
13 Iowa	24 TE Ray Sydnor
0 Michigan	54 QB Mike Kalasmiki / Steve Parish
28 Northwestern	3 TB Chucky Davis
42 Minnesota	37 FB Dave Mohapp / Gerald Green
	DL Dave Ahrens / Jeff Vine
	DL Tom Schremp
	DL Tim Krumrie
	DL Armand Cabral
	DL Guy Boliaux / Kyle Borland
	LB Dennis Christenson
	LB Larry Spurlin
	DB Ross Anderson
	DB Mike Casey / Dan Messenger
	DB George Welch
	DB Terrence Stroede / David Greenwood

RUSHING: Mohapp 117/603y, Davis 72/407y, Green 66/308y
PASSING: Kalasmiki 72-137/1082y, 5TD, 52.6%
RECEIVING: Stauss 38/660y, Stracka 25/289y, Sydnor 22/318y
SCORING: Steve Veith (K) 31pts, 5 tied w/ 24pts

1980 4-7

6 Purdue	12 WR Tim Stracka
3 BYU	28 WR Marv Neal / Thad McFadden
0 UCLA	35 T Jerome Doerger
35 San Diego State	12 G Bob Winckler
0 Indiana	24 C Joe Rothbauer
17 Michigan State	7 G Leo Joyce
0 Ohio State	21 T Ron Versnik / Carlton Walker
13 Iowa	22 TE Howard Ruetz
0 Michigan	24 QB John Josten / Jess Cole
39 Northwestern	19 TB John Williams / Troy King
25 Minnesota	7 FB Dave Mohapp
	DL Tom Houston / Mark Shumate
	DL Tim Krumrie
	DL Mike Herrington / Darryl Sims
	LB Guy Boliaux
	LB Dave Levenick
	LB Dave Ahrens
	LB Ed Senn / Tom Booker
	DB Ross Anderson
	DB Dan Messenger
	DB Von Mansfield / Vaughn Thomas
	DB David Greenwood

RUSHING: Williams 119/526y, Mohapp 109/506y, King 87/425y
PASSING: Josten 53-138/622y, TD, 38.4%
RECEIVING: Stracka 28/462y, McFadden 10/134y, Neal 10/119y
SCORING: Cole 30pts, Mark Doran (K) 25pts, Mohapp 24pts

1981 7-5

21 Michigan	14 WR Michael Jones / Al Seamonson
13 UCLA	31 WR Thad McFadden / Marvin Neal
21 W. Michigan	10 T Bob Winckler
20 Purdue	14 G Carlton Walker / Mark Subach
24 Ohio State	21 C Ron Versnik
14 Michigan State	33 G Leo Joyce
21 Illinois	23 T Jerome Doerger
52 Northwestern	0 TE Jeff Nault
28 Indiana	7 QB Jess Cole
7 Iowa	17 TB John Williams / Chucky Davis
26 Minnesota	21 FB Dave Mohapp
21 Tennessee■	28 DL Mark Shumate
	DL Tim Krumrie
	DL Darryl Sims
	LB Guy Boliaux
	LB Dave Levenick
	LB Larry Spurlin
	LB Jim Melka / Kyle Borland
	DB Clint Sims / Ron Steverson
	DB Von Mansfield / Brian Marrow
	DB Matt Vanden Boom
	DB David Greenwood

RUSHING: Williams 116/634y, Davis 88/457y, Mohapp 94/421y
PASSING: Cole 85-200/1180y, 12TD, 42.5%
RECEIVING: Jones 23/407y, Davis 21/178y, Nault 13/165y
SCORING: Mark Doran (K) 44pts, Neal 30pts, 3 tied w/ 24pts

1982 7-5

9 Michigan	20 WR Al Toon
26 UCLA	51 WR Tim Stracka / Michael Jones
36 Toledo	27 T Bob Winckler
35 Purdue	31 G Bob Landsee
6 Ohio State	0 C Ron Versnik
24 Michigan State	23 G Kevin Belcher / Mark Subach
28 Illinois	29 T Jeff Dellenbach
54 Northwestern	20 TE Jeff Nault
17 Indiana	20 QB Randy Wright
14 Iowa	28 TB Troy King / Chucky Davis
24 Minnesota	0 FB Gerald Green
14 Kansas State■	3 DL Darryl Sims
	DL Tim Krumrie
	DL Mark Shumate
	LB Kyle Borland
	LB Jim Melka
	LB Jody O'Donnell
	LB Mike Herrington / Brad Grabow
	DB Richard Johnson / Richard Baxter
	DB John Josten / Clint Sims/ Brian Marrow
	DB Matt VandenBoom / Vaughn Thomas
	DB David Greenwood

RUSHING: King 94/674y, Davis 61/351y, Green 74/315y
PASSING: Wright 165-306/2109y, 13TD, 53.9%
RECEIVING: Stracka 34/527y, Toon 32/472y, Nault 25/323y
SCORING: King 42pts, Toon 32pts, Wright 30pts

1983 7-4

37 N. Illinois	9 WR Michael Jones
21 Missouri	20 WR Al Toon
21 Michigan	38 T Jeff Dellenbach
49 Northwestern	0 G Chris Osswald
15 Illinois	27 C Dan Turk
56 Minnesota	17 G Dave Mielke / Bob Landsee
45 Indiana	14 T Kevin Belcher
27 Ohio State	45 TE Bret Pearson
0 Iowa	34 QB Randy Wright
42 Purdue	38 TB Gary Ellerson / Larry Emery
32 Michigan State	0 FB Joe Armentrout
	DL Scott Bergold
	DL Lance Branaman
	DL Jim Kmet
	LB Rick Graf / Michael Reid
	LB Russ Fields
	LB Jim Melka
	LB Mike Herrington
	DB Richard Baxter / Ken Stills
	DB Russ Bellford / Richard Johnson
	DB Averick Walker
	DB Brian Marrow

RUSHING: Ellerson 161/777y, Emery 56/336y,
Armentrout 52/325y
PASSING: Wright 173-323/2329y, 19TD, 53.6%
RECEIVING: Toon 45/881y, Pearson 34/373y, Jones 24/281y
SCORING: Ellerson 66pts, Kevin Rohde (K) 63pts, Toon 54pts

1984 7-4-1

27 N. Illinois	14 WR Michael Jones / Thad McFadden
35 Missouri	34 WR Al Toon
14 Michigan	20 T Jeff Dellenbach
31 Northwestern	16 G Kevin Belcher / Chris Osswald
6 Illinois	22 C Dan Turk
14 Minnesota	17 G Dave Mielke
20 Indiana	16 T Bob Landsee
20 Ohio State	14 TE Bret Pearson
10 Iowa	10 QB Mike Howard
30 Purdue	13 TB Larry Emery / Marck Harrison
20 Michigan State	10 FB Joe Armentrout
19 Kentucky ■	20 DL Darryl Sims
	DL Michael Boykins / Lance Branaman
	DL Scott Bergold
	LB Rick Graf
	LB Michael Reid
	LB Jim Melka
	LB Tim Jordan / Craig Raddatz
	DB Russ Bellford
	DB Richard Johnson
	DB Ken Stills
	DB Craig Raddatz

RUSHING: Harrison 179/848y, Emery 109/675y, Armentrout 89/430y
PASSING: Howard 182-314/2127y, 11TD, 58%
RECEIVING: Toon 54/750y, Pearson 41/415y, McFadden 22/292y
SCORING: Todd Gregoire (K) 84pts, Emery, Toon & Jones 30pts

1985 5-6

38 N. Illinois	17 WR Fred Bobo / Jim Ross
26 UNLV	23 WR Tim Fullington
41 Wyoming	17 T Paul Gruber
6 Michigan	33 G Brian Jansen
13 Iowa	23 C Bill Schick
14 Northwestern	17 G Bob Landsee
25 Illinois	38 T Glenn Derby / Mike Gorman
31 Indiana	20 TE Scott Sharron
18 Minnesota	27 QB Mike Howard / Bud Keyes
12 Ohio State	7 TB Larry Emery
7 Michigan State	41 FB Joe Armentrout / Marvin Artley
	DL Lance Branaman
	DL Michael Boykins
	DL Jim Kmet / Dick Teets
	LB Rick Graf / Joe Marconi
	LB Craig Raddatz
	LB Russ Fields / Charlie Fawley
	LB Tim Jordan
	DB Nate Odomes
	DB Troy Spencer
	DB Robb Johnston
	DB Pete Nowka / Eric Sydnor

RUSHING: Emery 224/1113y, Armentrout 86/553y, Artley 40/196y
PASSING: Keyes 60-147/829y, 8TD, 40.8%
RECEIVING: Sharron 26/236y, Armentrout 22/223y, Fullington 21/403y
SCORING: Todd Gregoire (K) 67pts, Emery 48pts, Fullington & Armentrout 30pts

1986 3-9

17 Hawaii	20 WR Scott Bestor
35 N. Illinois	20 WR Reggie Tompkins
7 UNLV	17 T Keith Peterson / John Hallberg
12 Wyoming	21 G Glenn Derby / Solomon Ashby
17 Michigan	34 C Rod Lossow
6 Iowa	17 G Todd Nelson
35 Northwestern	27 T Paul Gruber
15 Illinois	9 TE Brian Anderson
3 Indiana	21 QB Bud Keyes / Mike Howard
20 Minnesota	27 TB Larry Emery / Marvin Artley
17 Ohio State	30 FB Joe Armentrout
	DL Jim Kmet
	DL Michael Boykins
	DL Dick Teets / Chad VandeZande
	LB Tim Jordan / Tim Knoeck
	LB Rick Graf
	LB Michael Reid
	LB Charlie Fawley / Craig Raddatz
	DB Nate Odomes
	DB Bobby Taylor
	DB Keith Browning / Bob Johnston
	DB Pete Nowka

RUSHING: Emery 193/855y, Artley 77/324y, Armentrout 65/268y
PASSING: Keyes 93-174/1002y, 5TD, 53.4%. Howard 57-113/586y, 5TD, 50.4%
RECEIVING: Tompkins 32/443y, Armentrout 23/205y, Bestor 19/247y
SCORING: Todd Gregoire (K) 61pts, Emery 24pts, Armentrout & Keyes 18pts

1987 3-8

28 Hawaii	7 WR David Burks
28 Utah	31 WR Scott Bestor
30 Ball State	13 T Paul Gruber
0 Michigan	49 G Glenn Derby
10 Iowa	31 C Rod Lossow
14 Illinois	16 G Todd Nelson
24 Northwestern	27 T Steve Rux
14 Purdue	49 TE Brian Anderson
26 Ohio State	24 QB Tony Lowery / Bud Keyes
19 Minnesota	22 TB Steve Vinci / Louis Curtis
9 Michigan State	30 FB Marvin Artley / Fred Owens
	DL Don Davey
	DL Chad VandeZande
	DL John Banaszak / Leon Johnson
	DL Dan Batsch
	LB Dan Kissling
	LB David Wings
	LB Pete Nowka
	LB Malvin Hunter / Vic Fortino
	DB Brad Mayo
	DB LaMarr White / Robert Williams
	DB Gregg Thomas

RUSHING: Artley 148/955y, Vinci 44/290y, Lowery 114/279y
PASSING: Lowery 42-89/572y, 2TD, 47.2%
RECEIVING: Bestor 18/257y, Burks 17/208y, Anderson 13/150y
SCORING: Todd Gregoire (K) 66pts, Artley 54pts, Owens 18pts

1988 1-10

14 W. Michigan	24 WR David Burks / Bill Williams
17 N. Illinois	19 WR Scott Bestor
3 Miami	23 T Brady Pierce
14 Michigan	62 G Todd Nelson
6 Iowa	31 C Matt Joki / Jim Basten
6 Illinois	34 G Joe Magazzeni
14 Northwestern	35 T Keith Peterson / David Rapps
6 Purdue	9 TE Brian Anderson
12 Ohio State	34 QB Tony Lowery / Lionell Crawford
14 Minnesota	7 RB Marvin Artley
0 Michigan State	36 RB Steve Vinci
	DL Chad VandeZande
	DL John Banaszak
	DL Don Davey
	LB Dan Batsch
	LB David Wings
	LB Malvin Hunter
	LB Dan Kissling / Duer Sharp
	DB Eddie Fletcher / Brad Mayo
	DB LaMarr White
	DB Greg Thomas
	DB Pete Newko / Rafael Robinson

RUSHING: Artley 132/516y, Crawford 160/350y, Vinci 63/331y
PASSING: Lowery 67-121/712y, TD, 55.4%
RECEIVING: Bestor 26/327y, Anderson 19/216y, Williams 13/170y
SCORING: Robb Mehring (K) 27pts, Crawford 18pts, Rich Thompson (K) 11pts

1989 2-9

3 Miami	51 WR Tim Ware / Tony Spaeth
23 Toledo	10 WR Aaron Brown
14 California	20 T Brady Pierce
0 Michigan	24 G Chuck Belin
24 Iowa	31 C Rick Godfrey
35 Northwestern	31 G Nick Polczinski
9 Illinois	32 T Jim Basten
22 Minnesota	24 TE Kerry Miller / Craig Hudson
17 Indiana	45 QB Lionell Crawford / Sean Wilson
22 Ohio State	42 RB Robert Williams / Jimmy Henderson
3 Michigan State	31 RB Leon Hunt
	DL Don Davey
	DL John Banaszak
	DL Leon Johnson / Dan Batsch
	LB Dan Kissling / Tim Knoeck
	LB Brendan Lynch
	LB Gary Casper / Malvin Hunter
	LB Duer Sharp
	DB LaMarr White / Troy Vincent
	DB Eddie Fletcher
	DB Rafael Robinson
	DB Greg Thomas

RUSHING: Henderson 102/426y, Hunt 91/406y, Crawford 82/390y
PASSING: Wilson 66-129/667y, 3TD, 51.2%
RECEIVING: Hudson 24/206y, Spaeth 14/152y, Miller 13/390y
SCORING: Rich Thompson (K) 50pts, Hunt & Crawford 24pts

1990 1-10

12 California	28 WR Tim Ware / Bill Williams
24 Ball State	7 WR Tony Spaeth / Lionell Crawford
18 Temple	24 T Brady Pierce
3 Michigan	41 G Jim Basten
10 Iowa	30 C Rick Godfrey
34 Northwestern	44 G Nick Polczinski / Chuck Belin
3 Illinois	21 T David Senczyszyn
3 Minnesota	21 TE Kerry Miller / Dave Czech
3 Indiana	20 QB Tony Lowery
10 Ohio State	35 TB Robert Williams / Rafael Robinson
9 Michigan State	14 FB Mark Montgomery / Rory Lee
	DL Don Davey
	DL Lamark Shackerford / Pat McGettigan
	DL Dan Batsch
	LB Curt Maternowski / Aaron Norvell
	LB Malvin Hunter
	LB Gary Casper
	LB Brendan Lynch
	DB Troy Vincent
	DB Eddie Fletcher
	DB Greg Thomas
	DB Scott Nelson

RUSHING: R. Williams 139/541y, Robinson 73/235y, Montgomery 38/116y
PASSING: Lowery 159-280/1757y, 5TD, 56.8%
RECEIVING: B. Williams 30/342y, Spaeth 29/290y, Crawford 26/288y
SCORING: Rich Thompson (K) 41pts, R. Williams & Lee 18pts

1991 5-6

31 W. Illinois	13 WR Lee DeRamus / Tim Ware
7 Iowa State	6 WR Aaron Brown / Tom Browne
21 E. Michigan	6 T Mike Verstegen / Bill Maksen
16 Ohio State	31 G Chuck Belin
6 Iowa	10 C Cory Raymer / Jeff Rasmussen
7 Purdue	28 G Mike Bryan / Joe Panos (C)
20 Indiana	28 T Tyler Adam
6 Illinois	22 TE Michael Roan / Dave Czech
7 Michigan State	20 QB Tony Lowery / Jay Macias
19 Minnesota	16 TB Terrell Fletcher / Brent Moss
32 Northwestern	14 FB Mark Montgomery / Jason Burns
	DL Mike Thompson
	DL Lee Krueger / Lamark Shackerford
	DL Carlos Fowler / Jerry Huggett
	LB Dwight Reese
	LB Brendan Lynch
	LB Gary Casper
	LB Duer Sharp / Nick Rafko
	DB Troy Vincent
	DB Eddie Fletcher / Rafael Robinson
	DB Scott Nelson / Melvin Tucker
	DB Reggie Holt

RUSHING: Fletcher 109/446y, Montgomery 64/230y, Moss 61/219y
PASSING: Lowery 87-158/965y, 6TD, 55.1%
RECEIVING: DeRamus 23/374y, Brown 27/333y, Roan 19/231y
SCORING: Fletcher 30pts, Rich Thompson (K) 23pts, DeRamus 18pts

1992 5-6

10 Washington	27 WR Lee DeRamus
39 Bowling Green	18 WR Tim Ware / Aaron Brown
18 N. Illinois	17 T Mike Verstegen
20 Ohio State	16 G Chuck Belin
22 Iowa	23 C Cory Raymer
19 Purdue	16 G Mike Bryan / Joe Rudolph
3 Indiana	10 T Joe Panos
12 Illinois	13 TE Michael Roan
10 Michigan State	26 QB Darrell Bevell
34 Minnesota	6 TB Terrell Fletcher / Jason Burns
25 Northwestern	27 FB Brent Moss (TB) / Mark Montgomery
	DL Mike Thorrpton
	DL Lamark Shackerford
	DL Carlos Fowler
	LB Dwight Reese / Curt Maternowski
	LB Gary Casper
	LB Aaron Norvell
	LB Chad Yocum / Nick Rafko
	DB Jeff Messenger
	DB Korey Manley
	DB Scott Nelson
	DB Reggie Holt

RUSHING: Moss 165/739y, Fletcher 96/496y, Burns 85/344y
PASSING: Bevell 125-245/1479y, 8TD, 51%
RECEIVING: DeRamus 42/680y, Ware 18/215y, Roan 18/174y
SCORING: Rich Thompson (K) 82pts, Moss 54pts, DeRamus 36pts

1993 10-1-1

35 Nevada	17 WR Lee DeRamus
24 SMU	16 WR J.C. Dawkins
28 Iowa State	7 T Mike Verstagen
27 Indiana	15 G Joe Rudolph
53 Northwestern	14 C Cory Raymer
42 Purdue	28 G Steve Stark
21 Minnesota	28 T Joe Panos
13 Michigan	10 TE Michael Roan
14 Ohio State	14 QB Darrell Bevell
35 Illinois	10 RB Brent Moss / Terrell Fletcher
41 Michigan State	20 FB Mark Montgomery
21 UCLA■	16 DL Mike Thompson
	DL Lamark Shackerford
	DL Carlos Fowler
	LB Chris Hein
	LB Eric Unverzagt
	LB Yusef Burgess
	LB Bryan Jurewicz
	DB Kenny Gales
	DB Jeff Messenger / Donny Brady
	DB Scott Nelson
	DB Reggie Holt / Jamel Brown

RUSHING: Moss 312/1637y, Fletcher 165/996y, Montgomery 50/230y
PASSING: Bevell 187-276/2390y, 19TD, 67.8%
RECEIVING: DeRamus 54/920y, Dawkins 36/512y, Roan 34/396y
SCORING: Moss 96pts, Fletcher 60pts, DeRamus 36pts

1994 8-3-1

56 E. Michigan	0 WR Haywood Simmons / Kevin Huntley
17 Colorado	55 WR J.C. Dawkins / Reggie Torian
62 Indiana	13 T Mike Verstegen
10 Mich. St. (F-W)	29 G Joe Rudolph
46 Northwestern	14 C Cory Raymer
27 Purdue	27 G Steve Stark / Jamie Vandervelt
14 Minnesota	17 T Jerry Wunsch
31 Michigan	19 TE Michael Roan
3 Ohio State	24 QB Darrell Bevell
38 Cincinnati	17 RB Brent Moss / Terrell Fletcher
19 Illinois	13 FB Ron Johnson
34 Duke■	20 DL Mike Thompson
	DL Jason Maniecki
	DL Bryan Jurewicz / Rod Spiller
	LB Tarek Saleh / Chad Cascadden
	LB Eric Unverzagt
	LB Pete Monty
	LB Chris Hein
	DB Kenny Gales
	DB Donny Brady
	DB Jeff Messenger
	DB Jamel Brown

RUSHING: Fletcher 244/1476y, Moss 156/833y, Royce Roberson (RB) 59/303y
PASSING: Bevell 139-231/1544y, 17TD, 60.2%
RECEIVING: Johnson 33/268y, Dawkins 27/260y, Fletcher 23/180y
SCORING: Fletcher 80pts, Rick Schnetzky (K) 56pts, Simmons & Moss 48pts

1995 4-5-2

7 Colorado	43 WR Tony Simmons / Donald Hayes
24 Stanford	24 WR Michael London
42 SMU	0 T Cayetano Castro
17 Penn State	9 G Jamie Vandervelt
16 Ohio State	27 C Mike Rader
0 Northwestern	35 G Steve Stark / James Darby
45 Michigan State	14 T Jerry Wunsch
27 Purdue	38 TE Matt Nyquist
34 Minnesota	27 QB Darrell Bevell
20 Iowa	33 RB Carl McCullough / Aaron Stecker
3 Illinois	3 FB Cecil Martin
	DL Bryan Jurewicz
	DL Jason Maniecki
	DL Rod Spiller
	DL Tarek Saleh
	LB Eric Unverzagt
	LB Pete Monty
	LB Daryl Carter / Chad Yocum
	DB Jason Suttle
	DB Cyrill Weems
	DB Kevin Huntley
	DB Leonard Taylor

RUSHING: McCullough 276/1038y, Stecker 86/334y
PASSING: Bevell 195-300/2273y, 15TD, 65%
RECEIVING: London 41/587y, Nyquist 37/354y, Simmons 29/504y
SCORING: John Hall (K) 48pts, Simmons 42pts, Stecker 36pts

1996 8-5

24 E. Michigan	3 WR Donald Hayes
52 UNLV	17 WR Tony Simmons / Ahmad Merritt
14 Stanford	0 T Chris McIntosh
20 Penn State	23 G Jamie Vandervelt
14 Ohio State	14 C Derek Engler
30 Northwestern	34 G Cayetano Castro
13 Michigan State	30 T Jerry Wunsch
33 Purdue	25 TE Kevin Lyles
45 Minnesota	28 QB Mike Samuel
0 Iowa	31 RB Ron Dayne / Carl McCullough
35 Illinois	15 FB Cecil Martin / Aaron Gibson
59 Hawaii	10 DL Tarek Saleh
38 Utah■	10 DL Neil Miklusak
	DL Bryan Jurewicz
	DL Rod Spiller / Tom Burke
	LB Daryl Carter
	LB Pete Monty
	LB David Lysek / Brian Flanigan
	DB Cyrill Weems / LaMar Campbell
	DB Jason Suttle
	DB Kevin Huntley / Bobby Myers
	DB Bob Adamov / Giscard Bernard

RUSHING: Dayne 325/2109y, McCullough117/534y, Aaron Stecker (RB) 36/292y
PASSING: Samuel 148-254/1752y, 8TD, 58.3%
RECEIVING: Hayes 44/629y, Simmons 20/346y, Lyles 20/169y
SCORING: Dayne 126pts, John Hall 86pts (K), Samuel 30pts

1997 8-5

0 Syracuse	34 WR Donald Hayes
28 Boise State	24 WR Tony Simmons / Kevin Huntley
56 San Jose State	10 T Chris McIntosh
36 San Diego State	10 G Bill Ferrario
27 Indiana	26 C Casey Rabach
26 Northwestern	25 G Dave Costa
31 Illinois	7 T Aaron Gibson (FB) / Pat Daley
20 Purdue	45 TE Eric Grams / Ryan Sondrup
22 Minnesota	21 QB Mike Samuel
13 Iowa	10 RB Ron Dayne / Carl McCullough
16 Michigan	26 FB Cecil Martin
10 Penn State	35 DL Tom Burke
6 Georgia■	33 DL Ross Kolodziej
	DL Chris Janek / Erik Mahlik
	DL John Favret
	LB David Lysek
	LB Donnel Thompson
	LB Bob Adamov / Donny Eicher
	DB Jason Suttle / Donte King
	DB LaMar Campbell
	DB Bobby Myers / Jason Doering
	DB Leonard Taylor

RUSHING: Dayne 263/1457y, McCullough 85/377y, Eddie Faulkner (TB) 90/353y
PASSING: Samuel 141-254/1896y, 8TD, 55.5%
RECEIVING: Hayes 45/618y, Simmons 28/553y, Martin 16/116y
SCORING: Dayne 90pts, Matt Davenport (K) 73pts, Samuel 48pts

1998 11-1

26 San Diego State	14 WR Chris Chambers
45 Ohio	0 WR Ahmad Merritt / Nick Davis
52 UNLV	7 T Chris McIntosh
38 Northwestern	7 G Bill Ferrario
24 Indiana	20 C Casey Rabach
31 Purdue	24 G Dave Costa
37 Illinois	3 T Aaron Gibson
31 Iowa	0 TE Dague Retzlaff / Eric Grams
26 Minnesota	7 QB Mike Samuel
10 Michigan	27 RB Ron Dayne
24 Penn State	3 FB Cecil Martin
38 UCLA■	31 DL Tom Burke
	DL Ross Kolodziej
	DL Eric Mahlik / Chris Jannek
	DL John Favret
	LB Bob Adamov
	LB Donnel Thompson / Bobby Myers
	LB Chris Ghidorzi / Roger Knight
	DB Mike Echols / Donte King
	DB Jamar Fletcher
	DB Jason Doering
	DB Leonard Taylor

RUSHING: Dayne 295/1525y, Samuel 129/382y, Carlos Daniels (RB) 67/ 279y
PASSING: Samuel 90-172/1175y, 6TD, 52.3 %
RECEIVING: Chambers28/563y, Martin 19/139y, Davis 10/127y
SCORING: Matt Davenport (K) 99pts, Dayne 90pts, Samuel 60pts

1999 10-2

49 Murray State	10 WR Chris Chambers / Ahmad Merritt
50 Ball State	10 WR Nick Davis / Demetrius Brown
12 Cincinnati	17 T Chris McIntosh
16 Michigan	21 G Bill Ferrario
42 Ohio State	17 C Casey Rabach
20 Minnesota	17 G Dave Costa
59 Indiana	0 T Mark Tauscher
40 Michigan State	10 TE Dague Retzlaff / John Sigmund
35 Northwestern	19 QB Brooks Bollinger / Scott Kavanagh
28 Purdue	21 RB Ron Dayne
41 Iowa	3 FB Chad Kuhns
17 Stanford■	9 DL Ross Kolodziej
	DL Eric Mahlik
	DL Wendell Bryant / Jake Sprague
	DL John Favert / Sam Mueller
	LB Roger Knight / Dan Lisowski
	LB Chris Ghidorzi
	LB Donnel Thompson
	DB Mike Echols / Joey Boese
	DB Jamar Fletcher
	DB Jason Doering
	DB Bobby Myers

RUSHING: Dayne 337/2034y, Bollinger 109/454y, Michael Bennett (TB) 57/298y
PASSING: Bollinger 82/140/1133y 8TD, 58.6%
RECEIVING: Chambers 41/576y, Davis 19/346y, Brown 13/150y
SCORING: Dayne 120pts, Vitaly Pisetsky (K) 94pts Bollinger 36pts

2000 9-4

19 W. Michigan	7 WR Chris Chambers / Conroy Whyt
27 Oregon	23 WR Lee Evans / Nick Davis
28 Cincinnati	25 T Ben Johnson / Dave Costa
44 Northwestern	47 G Bill Ferrario
10 Michigan	13 C Al Johnson
7 Ohio State	3 G Casey Rabach
17 Michigan State	10 T Brian Lamont / Josh Jakubowski
24 Purdue	30 TE John Sigmund / Mark Anelli
13 Iowa	7 QB Brooks Bollinger / Jim Sorgi
41 Minnesota	20 TB Michael Bennett / Eddie Faulkner
43 Indiana	22 FB Chad Kuhns
34 Hawaii	18 DL Ross Kolodziej
21 UCLA■	20 DL Eric Mahlik
	DL Wendell Bryant
	DL John Favret / Ben Herbert
	LB Roger Knight
	LB Nick Greisen
	LB Jeff Mack / Bryson Thompson
	DB Jamar Fletcher / Carlease Clark
	DB Mike Echols / B.J.Tucker
	DB Jason Doering / Devery Hughes
	DB Joey Boese

RUSHING: Bennett 310/1681y, Bollinger 157/459y, Faulkner 58/244y
PASSING: Bollinger 110-209/1479y 10TD, 52.6%
RECEIVING: Chambers 52/813y, Evans 33/634y, Davis 21/246y
SCORING: Vitaly Pisetsky (K) 70pts, Bennett 66pts, Bollinger 36pts

2001 5-7

26 Virginia	17 WR Nick Davis / Darrin Charles
28 Oregon	31 WR Lee Evans
20 Fresno State	32 T Ben Johnson
18 Penn State	6 G Dan Buenning
24 W. Kentucky	6 C Al Johnson
32 Indiana	63 G Jonathan Clinkscale / Kalvin Barrett
20 Ohio State	17 T Jason Jowers
35 Illinois	42 TE Mark Anelli / Bob Docherty
28 Michigan State	42 QB Brooks Bollinger / Jim Sorgi
34 Iowa	28 RB Anthony Davis / Jerone Pettus
17 Michigan	20 FB/TE Chad Kuhns / Tony Paciotti
31 Minnesota	42 DL Chuck Smith
	DL Ben Herbert
	DL Wendell Bryant
	DL Delante McGrew / E. James / J. Welsh
	LB Jeff Mack / Jason Schick
	LB Bryson Thompson
	LB Nick Greisen
	DB Mike Echols
	DB Scott Starks / B. J. Tucker
	DB Joey Boese
	DB Michael Broussard

RUSHING: Davis 291/1466y, Bollinger 92/388y, Pettus 60/255y
PASSING: Bollinger 91-177/1257y, 6TD, 51.4%
Sorgi 64-132/1096y, 9TD, 48.5%
RECEIVING: Evans 75/1545y, Anelli 35/357y, N. Davis 30/378y
SCORING: A. Davis 66pts, Evans 54pts, Mark Neuser (K) 51pts

2002 8-6

23 Fresno State	21 WR Jonathan Orr
27 UNLV	7 WR Darrin Charles / Brandon Williams
34 West Virginia	17 T Ben Johnson
24 N. Illinois	21 G Dan Buennig / Kalvin Barrett
31 Arizona	10 C Al Johnson
31 Penn State	34 G Jonathan Clinkscale
29 Indiana	32 T Jason Jowers
14 Ohio State	19 TE Tony Paciotti / Bob Docherty
42 Michigan State	24 QB Brooks Bollinger / Jim Sorgi
3 Iowa	20 RB Anthony Davis / Dwayne Smith
20 Illinois	37 FB Matt Bernstein / Russ Kuhns
14 Michigan	21 DL Jake Sprague
49 Minnesota	31 DL Anttaj Hawthorne
31 Colorado ∎	28 DL Jason Jefferson / Darius Jones
	DL Eramus James / Jonathan Welsh
	LB Alex Lewis / Broderick Williams
	LB Jeff Mack / Kyle McCorison
	LB LaMarr Watkins / Kareem Timbers
	DB Scott Starks
	DB B. J. Tucker
	DB Ryan Aiello / Brett Bell
	DB Jim Leonhard / Robert Brooks

RUSHING: Davis 300/1555y, Smith 110/552y, Bollinger 160/466y
PASSING: Bollinger 131-245/1758y, 14TD, 53.5%
RECEIVING: Williams 52/663y, Orr 47/842y, Charles 25/323y
SCORING: Davis 78pts, Mike Allen (K) 66pts,
   Bollinger & Orr 48pts

2003 7-6

24 West Virginia	17 WR Lee Evans
48 Akron	31 WR Brandon Williams / Jonathan Orr
5 UNLV	23 T Morgan Davis
38 North Carolina	27 G Dan Buenning
38 Illinois	20 C Donovan Raiola
30 Penn State	23 G Jon Clinkscale
17 Ohio State	10 T Mike Lorenz
23 Purdue	26 TE/WR Tony Paciotti / Darrin Charles
7 Northwestern	16 QB Jim Sorgi / Matt Schabert
34 Minnesota	37 RB Dwayne Smith / Anthony Davis
56 Michigan State	21 FB/TE Matt Bernstein / Jason Pociask
21 Iowa	27 DL Darius Jones / Nick Cochart
14 Auburn ∎	28 DL Anttaj Hawthorne
	DL Jason Jefferson
	DL Jonathan Welsh
	LB Jeff Mack
	LB Alex Lewis / Kyle McCorison
	LB Kareem Timbers / Chris Catalano
	DB Scott Starks / Brett Bell
	DB Levonne Rowan / Chuckie Cowans
	DB Jim Leonhard
	DB Ryan Aiello / Robert Brooks

RUSHING: Smith 165/857y, Davis 116/682y,
   Booker Stanley (RB) 133/523y
PASSING: Sorgi 140-248/2251y, 17TD, 56.5%
RECEIVING: Evans 64/1213y, Williams 49/649y, Charles 20/310y
SCORING: Evans 78pts, Mike Allen (K) 59pts, Smith 54pts

2004 9-3

34 Central Florida	6 WR Darrin Charles / Owen Daniels
18 UNLV	3 WR Brandon Williams / Jonathan Orr
9 Arizona	7 T Joe Thomas
16 Penn State	3 G Dan Buenning
24 Illinois	7 C Donovan Raiola
24 Ohio State	13 G Jon Clinkscale
20 Purdue	17 T Morgan Davis / Mike Lorenz
24 Northwestern	12 TE Tony Paciotti / Jason Pociask
38 Minnesota	14 QB John Stocco
14 Michigan State	49 RB Anthony Davis / Booker Stanley
7 Iowa	30 FB Matt Bernstein
21 Georgia ∎	24 DL Erasmus James / Joe Monty
	DL Anttaj Hawthorne
	DL Jason Jefferson
	DL Jonathan Welsh / Jamal Cooper
	LB Mark Zalewski
	LB Reginald Cribbs / Andy Crooks
	LB Dontez Sanders
	DB Scott Starks
	DB Brett Bell
	DB Jim Leonhard
	DB Robert Brooks / Johnny White

RUSHING: Davis 201/973y, Stanley 115/350y, Bernstein 83/300y
PASSING: Stocco 169-321/1989y, 9TD, 52.6%
RECEIVING: Williams 42/517y, Daniels 25/291y, Charles 25/233y
SCORING: Davis 66pts, Mike Allen (K) 63pts, Stocco 24pts

2005 10-3

56 Bowling Green	42 WR Jonathan Orr
65 Temple	0 WR Brandon Williams
14 North Carolina	5 T Joe Thomas
23 Michigan	20 G Matt Lawrence / Marcus Coleman
41 Indiana	24 C Donovan Raiola
48 Northwestern	51 G Jason Palermo
38 Minnesota	34 T Kraig Urbik
31 Purdue	20 TE Jason Pociask / Owen Daniels
41 Illinois	24 QB John Stocco
14 Penn State	35 TB Brian Calhoun
10 Iowa	20 FB Matt Bernstein / Chris Pressley
41 Hawaii	24 DL Joe Monty / Jamal Cooper
24 Auburn ∎	10 DL Jason Chapman / Mike Newkirk
	DL Nick Hayden
	DL Matt Shaughnessy / Kurt Ware
	LB LaMarr Watkins
	LB Mark Zalewski / Andy Crooks
	LB Dontez Sanders
	DB Allen Langford / Jack Ikegwuonu
	DB Brett Bell / Levonne Rowan
	DB Roderick Rogers
	DB Joe Stellmacher / Johnny White

RUSHING: Calhoun 348/1636y, Booker Stanley (RB) 69/340y
PASSING: Stocco 197-328/2920y, 21TD, 60.1%
RECEIVING: Williams 59/1095y, Calhoun 53/571y, Orr 40/688y
SCORING: Calhoun 144pts, Taylor Mehlhaff (K) 98pts,
   Orr & Williams 48pts

2006 12-1

35 Bowling Green	14 WR Luke Swan
34 W. Illinois	10 WR Paul Hubbard
14 San Diego State	0 T Joe Thomas
13 Michigan	27 G Andy Kemp
52 Indiana	17 C Marcus Coleman
41 Northwestern	9 G Kraig Urbik
48 Minnesota	12 T Eric VandenHeuvel
24 Purdue	3 TE Andy Crooks/Travis Beckum (WR)
30 Illinois	24 QB John Stocco / Tyler Donovan
13 Penn State	3 TB P. J. Hill / Dywon Rowan
14 Iowa	21 FB Bill Rentmeester
35 Buffalo	3 DL Joe Monty / Jamal Cooper
17 Arkansas ∎	14 DL Jason Chapman
	DL Nick Hayden / Mike Newkirk
	DL Matt Shaughnessy
	LB DeAndre Levy
	LB Mark Zalewski
	LB Jonathan Casillas
	DB Allen Langford / Ben Strickland
	DB Jack Ikegwuonu
	DB Roderick Rogers / Zach Hampton
	DB Joe Stellmacher

RUSHING: Hill 311/1569y, Lance Smith (RB) 95/345y,
   Rowan 39/184y
PASSING: Stocco 158-268/2185y, 17TD, 59%
   Donovan 37-58/564y, 4TD, 63.8%
RECEIVING: Beckum 61/903y, Hubbard 38/627y, Swan 35/595y
SCORING: Hill 96pts, Taylor Mehlhaff (K) 92pts, 4 tied w/ 30pts

2007 9-4

42 Washington St.	21 WR Paul Hubbard / Luke Swan
20 UNLV	13 WR Kyle Jefferson
45 The Citadel	31 T Gabe Carimi
17 Iowa	13 G Andy Kemp / John Moffitt
37 Michigan State	34 C Marcus Coleman
26 Illinois	31 G Kraig Urbik (T)
7 Penn State	38 T Eric Vanden Heuvel
44 N. Illinois	3 TE Garrett Graham / Travis Beckum (WR)
33 Indiana	3 QB Tyler Donovan
17 Ohio State	38 RB P.J. Hill / Zach Brown
37 Michigan	21 FB/TE Chris Pressley / Andy Crooks
41 Minnesota	34 DL Mike Newkirk / Kirk DeCremer
17 Tennessee ∎	21 DL Jason Chapman
	DL Nick Hayden
	DL Matt Shaughnessy
	LB Deandre Levy
	LB Elijah Hodge / Culme St. Jean
	LB Jonathan Casillas
	DB Allen Langford / Aaron Henry
	DB Jack Ikegwuonu / Ben Strickland
	DB Shane Carter
	DB Aubre Pleasant

RUSHING: Hill 233/1212y, Brown 119/568y, Lance Smith 71/429y
PASSING: Donovan 193-333/2607y, 17TD, 58%
RECEIVING: Beckum 75/982y, Graham 30/328y, Jefferson 26/412y
SCORING: Taylor Melhaff (K) 105pts, Hill 90pts, Beckum 36pts

2008 7-6

38 Akron	17 WR David Gilreath / Nick Toon
51 Marshall	14 WR Isaac Anderson / Kyle Jefferson
13 Fresno State	10 T Gabe Carimi / Josh Oglesby
25 Michigan	27 G Andy Kemp
17 Ohio State	20 C John Moffitt
7 Penn State	48 G Kraig Urbik / Bill Nagy
16 Iowa	38 T Eric VandenHeuvel
27 Illinois	17 TE Garrett Graham / Mickey Turner
24 Michigan State	25 QB Dustin Sherer / Allan Evridge
55 Indiana	20 RB P.J. Hill / John Clay
35 Minnesota	32 FB/TE Chris Pressley / Travis Beckum
36 Cal Poly	35 DL O'Brien Schofield / Dan Moore
13 Florida State ∎	42 DL Jason Chapman
	DL Mike Newkirk
	DL Matt Shaughnessy
	LB DeAndre Levy
	LB Jaevery McFadden / Culmer St. Jean
	LB Jonat Casillas / Blake Sorensen
	DB Niles Brinkley / Mario Goins
	DB Allen Langford
	DB Chris Maragos / Shane Carter
	DB Jay Valai / Aubre Pleasant

RUSHING: Hill 226/1161y, Clay 155/884y, Brown 55/305y
PASSING: Sherer 104-191/1389y, 6TD, 54.5%
   Evridge 71-132/949y, 5TD, 53.8%
RECEIVING: Graham 40/540y, Gilreath 31/520y,
   Beckum 23/264y
SCORING: Philip Welch (K) 99pts, Hill 80pts, Clay 54pts

2009 10-3

28 N. Illinois	20 WR Nick Toon
34 Fresno State	31 WR Isaac Anderson / David Gilreath
44 Wooford	14 T Gabe Carimi
38 Michigan State	30 G John Moffitt (C) / Travis Frederick
31 Minnesota	28 C Peter Konz
13 Ohio State	31 G Kevin Zeitler / Jake Bscherer
10 Iowa	20 T Josh Oglesby
37 Purdue	0 TE Garrett Graham
31 Indiana	28 TE Lance Kendricks / Mickey Turner
45 Michigan	24 QB Scott Tolzien
31 Northwestern	33 RB John Clay / Zach Brown
51 Hawaii	10 DL O'Brien Schofield
20 Miami ∎	14 DL Dan Moore
	DL Jeffrey Stehle / Patrick Butrym
	DL J.J. Watt
	LB Jaevery McFadden
	LB Culmer St. John / Blake Sorensen
	LB Chris Borland / Mike Taylor
	DB Niles Brinkley / Antonio Fenelus
	DB Devin Smith / Aaron Henry
	DB Chris Maragos
	DB Jay Valai

RUSHING: Clay 287/1517y, Montee Ball (RB) 98/391y,
   Brown 66/279y
PASSING: Tolzien 211-328/2705y, 16TD, 64.3%
RECEIVING: Toon 54/805y, Graham 51/624y, Anderson 30/480y,
   Kendricks 29/356y
SCORING: Clay 108pts, Philip Welch (K) 98pts, Graham 42pts

2010 11-2

41 UNLV	21 WR Nick toon / David Gilreath
27 San Jose State	14 WR/TE Isaac Anderson / Jacob Pedersen
20 Arizona State	19 T Gabe Carimi
70 Austin Peay	3 G John Moffitt /
24 Michigan State	34 C Peter Konz / Bill Nagy (G-TE)
41 Minnesota	23 G Kevin Zeitler
31 Ohio State	18 T Ricky Wagner/ Casey Dehn/ J. Oglesby
31 Iowa	30 TE Lance Kendricks
34 Purdue	13 TE/FB Jake Byrne / Brady Ewing
83 Indiana	20 QB Scott Tolzien
48 Michigan	28 RB Montee Ball / John Clay / James White
70 Northwestern	23 DL Louis Nzegwu
19 TCU ∎	21 DL Patrick Butrym / Bryce Gilbert
	DL Jordan Kohout / Ethan Hemer
	DL J.J. Watt
	LB Blake Sorensen / Chris Borland
	LB Culme St. Jean
	LB Mike Taylor / Kevin Claxton
	DB Niles Brinkley / Devin Smith
	DB Antonio Fenelus
	DB Aaron Henry
	DB Jay Valai / Shelton Johnson

RUSHING: White 156/1052y, Clay 187/1012y, Ball 163/996y
PASSING: Tolzien 194-266/2459y, 16TD, 72.9%
RECEIVING: Kendricks 43/663y, Toon 36/459y, Anderson 24/233y
SCORING: Philip Welch (K) 118pts, Ball 108pts, Clay & White 84pts

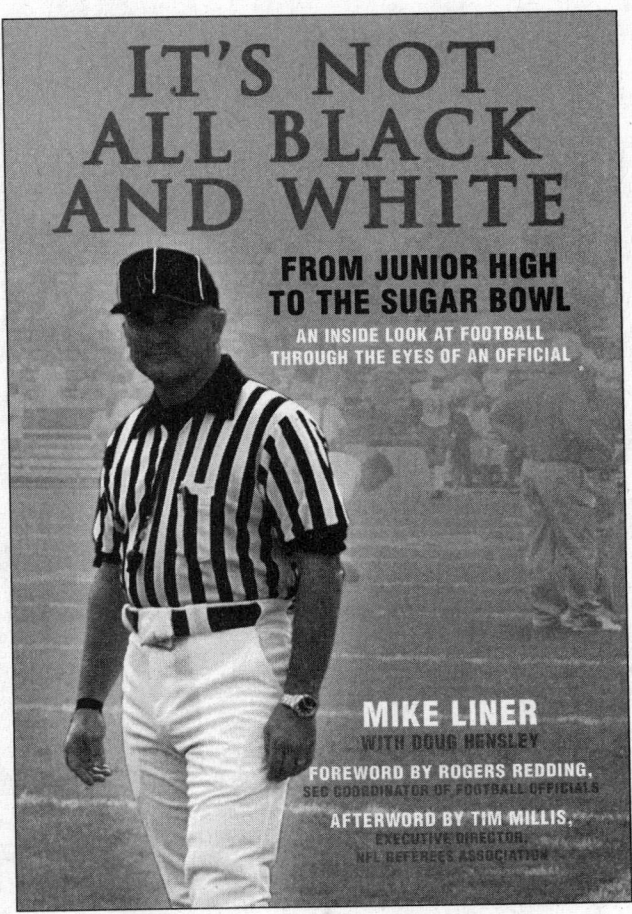

It's Not All Black and White

From Junior High to the Sugar Bowl, an Inside Look at Football through the Eyes of an Official

by Mike Liner with Doug Hensley

From junior high football games to the Sugar Bowl with a national championship up for grabs, Mike Liner has seen it all in football. President and CEO of a bank by day, Liner has been a Texas football official on Fridays and Saturdays for the past thirty-five years. *It's Not All Black and White* offers a view of college football seen through a different set of eyes, the eyes of an official. Liner takes readers through the story of his ascension up the officiating hierarchy and describes the bumps in the road he encountered along the way. In doing so, he puts a human face on an aspect of football that all too often is dehumanized—the officiating of the game.

With a foreword by Rogers Redding, SEC Coordinator of Football Officials, and an afterword by Tim Mills, Executive Director of the NFL Referees Association, *It's Not All Black and White* lifts the curtain on big-time college football, revealing what Liner saw as he observed it and why the game means so much to him. Liner also recounts important lessons he learned through football about life as a business leader, as a family man, and as someone whose faith has grown through the years.

$22.95 Hardcover • 256 pages

Beyond Xs and Os

What I Learned About Friendship and Success from a College Football Legend

by Tom Berthel and Hayden Fry

Foreword by Kirk Ferentz, Head Coach, University of Iowa

Tom Berthel first met Hall of Fame football coach Hayden Fry when, in the mid-1980s, his investment firm, Berthel Fisher & Co., became a corporate sponsor of the University of Iowa Athletic Department. This business partnership not only helped Berthel Fisher establish a winning public image, but it also gave birth to one of the most important and enduring friendships of Tom Berthel's life. Fry became a mentor and father figure to Berthel, and the wisdom Fry bestowed on him through their mutual friendship taught Berthel invaluable lessons in leadership, motivation, and what it takes to be a winner in business and in life.

These are the lessons that form the core of *Beyond Xs and Os*. In the book, Tom Berthel recounts the many lessons he learned from Coach Fry—some but not all related to football—and explains how they helped shape his life and business. In each chapter, Berthel outlines a specific lesson he learned from Coach Fry, explains how he integrated these philosophies into his business and personal life, and offers advice to help readers apply them to their own lives and businesses. Each chapter also features a special "Postgame with Coach Fry" sidebar written by the venerable Coach Fry himself, in which he reflects on the events and lessons depicted in the chapter and offers a deeper perspective on each, enriching the lesson.

$24.95 Hardcover • 288 pages

Beyond Xs and Os

What I Learned About Leadership and Success from a College Football Coach

The Gipper
George Gipp, Knute Rockne, and the Dramatic Rise of Notre Dame Football
by Jack Cavanaugh

"Win one for the Gipper." Has there ever been a better-known and widely-used exhortative phrase in sports? Not likely. But who was the "Gipper," this mythical sports figure whose nickname has aroused, in turn, awe, wonderment, curiosity, and amusement since the second decade of the twentieth century, and why is his story important? Answering those questions is the formidable task taken on here by veteran sportswriter Jack Cavanaugh, whose Pulitzer Prize-nominated biography of boxing legend Gene Tunney was referred to as "impressively researched and richly detailed" by *Sports Illustrated*.

More than eight decades after his death, George Gipp is still regarded by football historians as Notre Dame's best all-around player. And it was Gipp and his legendary coach, Knute Rockne, who were largely responsible for putting the small Midwestern all-male school on the map. Exhaustively researched and meticulously reported, *The Gipper* is the definitive examination of the enigmatic Gipp, his larger-than-life coach, and a bygone golden era in sports and American culture.

$24.95 Hardcover • 320 pages